THE RISK MANAGEMENT ASSOCIATION
Serving the Financial Services Industry

ANNUAL STATEMENT STUDIES

Financial Ratio Benchmarks

2011
2012

TABLE OF CONTENTS

...neral Industries Format means that a valid construction NAICS was assigned to the subject companies contained in the sample; ...ever, the financial statements were prepared using a general or traditional manufacturing or service industries presentation of results ...us using a percentage-of-completion method of accounting. Industries found in the percentage-of-completion presentation follow the ...entation used by RMA in the past.

About RMA

Founded in 1914, The Risk Management Association is a not-for-profit, member-driven professional association whose sole purpose is to advance the use of sound risk principles in the financial services industry. RMA promotes an enterprise approach to risk management that focuses on credit risk, market risk, and operational risk.

Headquartered in Philadelphia, Pennsylvania, RMA has 3,000 institutional members that include banks of all sizes as well as nonbank financial institutions. They are represented in the association by 18,000 risk management professionals who are chapter members in financial centers throughout North America, Europe, and Asia/Pacific. Visit RMA on the Web at www.rmahq.org.

RMA ACKNOWLEDGES AND THANKS THE FOLLOWING INSTITUTIONS, CONTRIBUTORS TO THE 2011 STATEMENT STUDIES DATA SUBMISSION PROGRAM.

ALABAMA

BBVA Compass
Regions Bank

ARKANSAS

Simmons First National Bank

CALIFORNIA

Bank of Agriculture & Commerce
Bank of the West
Citizens Business Bank
Farmers & Merchants Bank
    Central CA
Grand Point Bank
Pacific Enterprise Bank
Security Business Bank of
    San Diego
Sonoma Bank
Tri Counties Bank
Valley Community Bank
Wells Fargo Bank N.A.
Westamerica Bank

COLORADO

Alpine Bank
American National Bank
oBank
Colorado Business Bank
First National Bank of Durango
Sunflower Bank

CONNETICUTT

Chelsea Groton Bank
me Bank
Jewett City Savings Bank
Mutual Savings Bank
Windsor Federal Savings

Florida

Bank of Tampa
Capital City Bank
Seacoast National Bank

GEORGIA

Bank of Atlanta
First American Bank & Trust Co.
Georgia Bank & Trust Company
HeritageBank Of The South
    Brand Banking Company

HAWAII

American Savings Bank
Central Pacific Bank
First Hawaiian Bank
Hawaii National Bank

IOWA

American Trust & Savings Bank
Farmers State Bank
Heartland Financial USA, Inc.
Security National Bank
Wells Fargo Bank Iowa N.A.

IDAHO

Mountain West Bank

ILLINOIS

Albany Bank & Trust Co. N.A.
Alpine Bank & Trust Co.
American National Bank
    DeKalb County
Busey Bank
First Midwest Bank
Glenview State Bank
National Republic Bank Chicago

INDIANA

1st Source Bank
Campbell and Fetter Bank
First Merchants Corporation
Lake City Bank
Old National Bank
STAR Financial Bank

KANSAS

Alliance Bank
Emprise Bank
Fidelity Bank
INTRUST Bank N.A.
Midland National Bank
Silver Lake Bank
Sunflower Bank

KENTUCKY

Central Bank & Trust Co.
Community Trust Bank Inc.

LOUISIANA

Red River Bank
South Louisiana Bank

MASSACHUSETTS

Bank of Canton
BankFive
Bristol County Savings Bank
Charles River Bank
Community Bank
Lowell Five Cent Savings Bank
North Middlesex Savings Bank
Peoples Savings Bank
Rockland Trust Company
United Bank
Westfield Bank

MARYLAND

First United Bank & Trust
Frederick County Bank
National Penn Bank
New Windsor State Bank
OBA Bank
Sandy Spring Bank
Susquehanna Bank
The Bank of Glen Burnie
The Columbia Bank

MAINE

Gorham Savings Bank
Kennebunk Savings
Norway Savings Bank
Skowhegan Savings Bank
The First, N.A.

MICHIGAN

Citizens Bank
Citizens National Bank
Commercial Bank
Huron Community Bank
Mercantile Bank of Michigan
The State Bank
United Bank of Michigan

MINNESOTA

AgriBank, FCB
AgStar Financial Services
American Bank of St. Paul
Anchor Bank, N.A.

Beacon Bank
Citizens Independent Bank
Community Bank Corporation
Fidelity Bank
First Minnetonka City Bank
Infinia Bank
KleinBank
Merchants Bank N.A.
Northeast Bank
Roundbank
StearnsBank N.A.
US Bank National Association
Western Bank

MISSOURI

BanCorp South
Boone County
Cass Commercial Bank
Central Bank of Lake of the Ozarks
Central Trust Bank
City Bank and Trust Company
Commerce Bank N.A.
Empire Bank
First Banks
First Central Bank
First National Bank of
    Audrain County
First National Bank of St. Louis
Hawthorn Bank
Jefferson Bank of Missouri
Metcalf Bank
Pulaski Bank
Royal Banks of Missouri
Sunflower Bank

MISSISSIPPI

BanCorp South
The Peoples Bank
Trustmark National Bank

MONTANA

First Interstate Bancsystem

NORTH CAROLINA

Bank of America
Branch Banking and Trust
First Citizens Bank & Trust Co.
SunTrust Banks, Inc

NORTH DAKOTA

Alerus Financial N.A.
Frandson Bank & Trust
State Bank & Trust

NEBRASKA

First National Bank & Trust
First National Bank North Platte

First National Bank of Omaha
Union Bank & Trust Company

NEW HAMPSHIRE

Connecticut River Bank
Laconia Savings Bank
Mascoma Savings Bank

NEW JERSEY

Harmony Bank
Peapack-Gladstone Bank
Skylands Community Bank
TD Banknorth N.A.
The Bank
Union Center National Bank

NEW YORK

Adirondack Bank
Alliance Bank N.A.
Bank of Castile
Canandaigua National Bank & Trust
Chemung Canal Trust Co.
CIT Group Inc.
Citibank N.A.
Community Bank N.A.
HSBC Bank USA N.A.
M&T Bank NA
National Union Bank of Kinderhook
NBT Bank N.A.
State Bank of Long Island
Steuben Trust Co.
Suffolk County National Bank
The Adirondack Trust Company
The Bank of New York Mellon
Tioga State Bank

OHIO

First Financial Bank, N.A.
FirstMerit Bank N.A.
Huntington National Bank
KeyBank
Liberty Savings Bank FSB
North Side Bank & Trust Co.
Second National Bank, a division of
    The Park National Bank

OKLAHOMA

ONB Bank
Ozark Mountain Bank
Stillwater National Bank
Third National Bank

OREGON

Bank of Astoria
Pacific Continental Bank
People's Bank of Commerce
West Coast Bank

PENNSYLVANIA

AmeriServ Financial Bank
Bryn Mawr Trust Co.
CNB Bank
Community Bank
DNB First, National Association
Dollar Bank, FSB
Fidelity Bank Pa SB
Fidelity Deposit & Discount Bank
First Columbia Bank & Trust Co.
First Commonwealth Bank
First Liberty Bank & Trust
First National Bank of Pennsylvania
Firstrust Bank
FNB Bank
Fulton Bank
Lafayette Ambassador Bank
Luzerne Bank
Mainline National Bank
National Penn Bank
PeoplesBank a Codorus
    Valley Company
PNC Bank
S&T Bank
Somerset Trust Company
Swineford National Bank
The Bank of New York Mellon
Univest National Bank & Trust Co.
VIST Financial Corp.
Washington Financial
Woodlands Bank
York Traditions Bank

RHODE ISLAND

Citizens Financial Group
The Washington Trust Company

SOUTH CAROLINA

Conway National Bank
Harbor National Bank

SOUTH DAKOTA

First Interstate Bancsystem
First National Bank in Sioux Falls
First Premier Bank
Home Federal Bank

TENNESSEE

First Farmers & Merchants Bank
First Tennessee Bank

TEXAS

Amarillo National Bank
American Bank of Texas
Bank of the West
Broadway Bank
Comerica Bank

Extraco Banks, N.A.
First State Bank Central Texas
First Victoria National Bank
Frost National Bank
Southside Bank
Southwest Bank

UTAH

Bank of Utah
Zions Bancorporation

VIRGINIA

Capital One N.A.
First Community Bank
Monarch Bank
StellarOne
TowneBank
United Bank
Virginia Commerce Bank
Virginia National Bank

VERMONT

Community National Bank
Mascoma Savings Bank
Merchants Bank
National Bank of Middlebury
The Bank of Bennington

WASHINGTON

Bank of the Pacific
Banner Bank

Columbia State Bank
Northwest Farm Credit Services
Security State Bank
Skagit State Bank
Sterling Savings Bank
Washington Trust Bank
Whidbey Island Bank

WISCONSIN

Associated Bank Green Bay N.A.
Bank of Sun Prairie
First National Bank Fox Valley
Horicon Bank
Johnson Bank
M&I Marshall & Ilsley Bank
TCF National Bank
The Business Bank

WEST VIRGINIA

United Bank
WesBanco Bank

WYOMING

First Interstate Bancsystem

Introduction to

Annual Statement Studies:
Financial Ratio Benchmarks,
2011-2012
and
General Organization of Content

The notes below will explain the presentation of *Annual Statement Studies: Financial Ratio Benchmarks,* describe how the book is organized, and answer most of your questions.

- **The Quality You Expect from RMA:** RMA is the most respected source of objective, unbiased information on issues of importance to credit risk professionals. For over 92 years, RMA's *Annual Statement Studies®* has been the industry standard for comparison financial data. Material contained in today's *Annual Statement Studies* was first published in the March 1919 issue of the *Federal Reserve Bulletin.* In the days before computers, the *Annual Statement Studies* data was recorded in pencil on yellow ledger paper! Today, it features data for over 762 industries derived <u>directly</u> from more than 250,000 statements of financial institutions' borrowers and prospects.

- **Data That Comes Straight from Original Sources:** The more than 250,000 statements used to produce the composites presented here come directly from RMA member institutions and represent the financials from their commercial customers and prospects. RMA does not know the names of the individual entities. In fact, to ensure confidentiality, company names are removed before the data is even delivered to RMA. The raw data making up each composite is not available to any third party.

- **Data Presented in Common Size:** *Annual Statement Studies: Financial Ratio Benchmarks* contains composite financial data. Balance sheet and income statement information is shown in common size format, with each item a percentage of total assets and sales. RMA computes common size statements for each individual statement in an industry group, then aggregates and averages all the figures. In some cases, because of computer rounding, the figures to the right of the decimal point do not balance exactly with the totals shown. A minus sign beside the value indicates credits and losses.

- **Includes the Most Widely Used Ratios:** Nineteen of the most widely used ratios in the financial services industry accompany the balance sheet information, including various types of liquidity, coverage, leverage, and operating ratios.

- **Organized by the NAICS for Ease of Use:** This edition is organized according to the North American Industry Classification System (NAICS), a product of the U.S. Office of Management and Budget. At the top of each page of data, you will find the NAICS.

- **Twenty Sections Outline Major Types of Businesses:** To provide further delineation, the book is divided into 20 sections outlining major lines of businesses. If you know the NAICS number you are looking for, use the NAICS-page guide provided in the front of this book. In general, the book is arranged in ascending NAICS numerical order. For your convenience, full descriptions of each NAICS are presented in this book. In addition, you will find a text-based index near the end of the book.

- **You Do Not Know the NAICS Code You Are Looking for...** If you do not know the precise industry NAICS you are looking for, contact the Census Bureau at 1-888-75NAICS or naics@census.gov. Describe the activity of the establishment for which you need an industry code and you will receive a reply. Another source to help you assign the correct NAICS industry name and number can be found at www.census.gov/epcd/www/naics.html.

- **Can't Find the Industry You Want?** There are a number of reasons you may not find the industry you are looking for (i.e., you know you need industry xxxxxx but it is not in the product). Many times we have information on an industry, but it is not published because the sample size was too small or there were significant questions concerning the data. (For an industry to be displayed in the *Annual Statement Studies: Financial Ratio Benchmarks,* there must be at least 30 valid statements submitted to RMA.) In other instances, we simply do not have the data. Generally, most of what we receive is published.

- **Composite Data Not Shown?** When there are fewer than 10 financial statements in a particular asset or sales size category, the composite data is not shown because a sample this small is not considered representative and could be misleading. However, all the data for that industry is shown in the All Sizes column. The total number of statements for each size category is shown in bold print at the top of each column. In addition, the number of statements used in a ratio array will differ from the number of statements in a sample because certain elements of data may not be present in all financial statements. In these cases, the number of statements used is shown in parentheses to the left of the array.

- **Presentation of the Data on Each Page-Spread:** For all non-contracting spread statements, the data for a particular industry appears on both the left and right pages. The heading Current Data Sorted by Assets is in the five columns on the left side. The center section of the double-page presentation contains the Comparative Historical Data, with the All Sizes column for the current year shown under the heading 4/1/xx-3/31/xx. Comparable data from past editions of the *Annual Statement Studies: Financial Ratio Benchmarks* also appears in this section. Current Data Sorted by Sales is displayed in the five columns to the far right.

- **Companies with Less than $250 Million in Total Assets:** In our presentation, we used companies having less than $250 million in total assets—except in the case of contractors who use the percentage-of-completion method of accounting. *The section for contractors using the percentage-of-completion method of accounting contains data only sorted by revenue.* There is no upper limit placed on revenue size for any industry. Its information is found on only one page.

- **Page Headers:** The information shown at the top of each page includes the following: 1) the identity of the industry group; 2) its North American Industry Classification System (NAICS); 3) a breakdown by size categories of the types of financial statements reported; 4) the number of statements in each category; 5) the dates of the statements used; and 6) the size categories. For instance, 16 (4/1-9/30/10) means that 16 statements with fiscal dates between April 1 and September 30, 2010 make up part of the sample.

- **Page Footers:** At the bottom of each page, we have included the sum of the sales (or revenues) and total assets for all the financial statements in each size category. This data allows recasting of the common size statements into dollar amounts. To do this, divide the number at the bottom of the page by the number of statements in that size category. Then multiply the result by the percentages in the common size statement.
  Please note: The dollar amounts will be an appoximation because RMA computes the balance sheet and income statement percentages for each individual statement in an industry group, then aggregates and averages all the figures.

- **Our Thanks to CFMA:** RMA appreciates the cooperation of the Construction Financial Management Association permitting us to reproduce excerpts from its *Construction Industry Annual Financial Survey*. This data complements the RMA contractor industry data. For more details on this data, please visit www.cfma.org.

- **Recommended for Use as General Guidelines:** RMA recommends you use *Annual Statement Studies: Financial Ratio Benchmarks* data only as general guidelines and not as absolute industry norms. There are several reasons why the data may not be fully representative of a given industry:

1. **Data Not Random**—The financial statements used in the *Annual Statement Studies: Financial Ratio Benchmarks* are not selected by any random or statistically reliable method. RMA member banks voluntarily submit the data they have available each year with no limitation on company size.

2. **Categorized by Primary Product Only**—Many companies have varied product lines; however, the *Annual Statement Studies: Financial Ratio Benchmarks* categorizes them by their primary product NAICS number only.

3. **Small Samples**—Some of the industry samples are small in relation to the total number of firms for a given industry. A relatively small sample can increase the chances that some composites do not fully represent an industry.

4. **Extreme Statements**—An extreme or outlier statement can occasionally be present in a sample, causing a disproportionate influence on the industry composite. This is particularly true in a relatively small sample.

5. **Operational Differences**—Companies within the same industry may differ in their method of operations, which in turn can directly influence their financial statements. Since they are included in the sample, these statements can significantly affect the composite calculations.

6. **Additional Considerations**—There are other considerations that can result in variations among different companies engaged in the same general line of business. These include different labor markets, geographical location, different accounting methods, quality of products handled, sources and methods of financing, and terms of sale.

For these reasons, RMA does not recommend using the *Annual Statement Studies: Financial Ratio Benchmarks* figures as absolute norms for a given industry. Rather, you should use the figures only as general guidelines and as a supplement to the other methods of financial analysis. RMA makes no claim regarding how representative the figures printed in this book are.

DEFINITION OF RATIOS
INTRODUCTION

On each data page, below the common-size balance sheet and income statement information, you will find a series of ratios computed from the financial statement data.

Here is how these figures are calculated for any given ratio:

1. The ratio is computed for each financial statement in the sample.

2. These values are arrayed (listed) in an order from the strongest to the weakest. In interpreting ratios, the "strongest" or "best" value is not always the largest numerical value, nor is the "weakest" always the lowest numerical value. (For certain ratios, there may be differing opinions as to what constitutes a strong or a weak value. RMA follows general banking guidelines consistent with sound credit practice to resolve this problem.)

3. The array of values is divided into four groups of equal size. The description of each ratio appearing in the *Statement Studies* provides details regarding the arraying of the values.

What Are Quartiles?

Each ratio has three points, or "cut-off values," that divide an array of values into four equal-sized groups called quartiles, as shown below. The quartiles include the upper quartile, upper-middle quartile, lower-middle quartile, and the lower quartile. The upper quartile is the cut-off value where one-quarter of the array of ratios falls between it and the strongest ratio. The median is the midpoint—that is, the middle cut-off value where half of the array falls above it and half below it. The lower quartile is the point where one-quarter of the array falls between it and the weakest ratio. In many cases, the average of two values is used to arrive at the quartile value. You will find the median and quartile values on all *Statement Studies* data pages in the order indicated in the chart below.

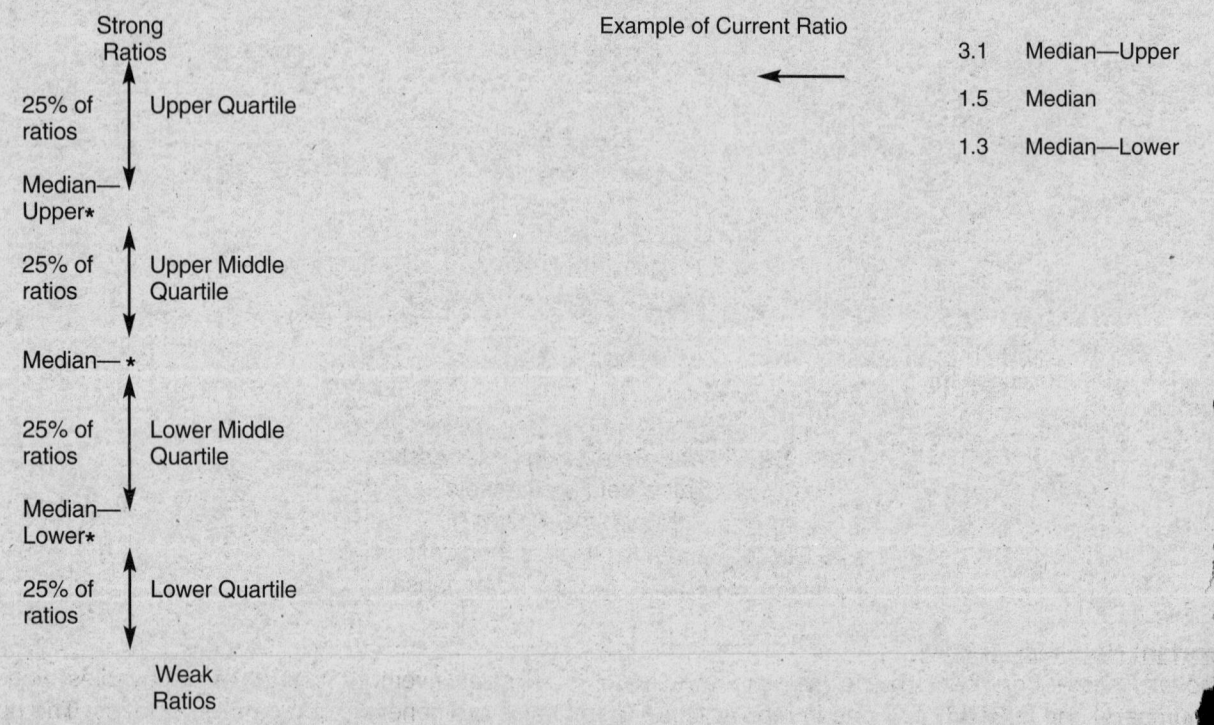

Strong Ratios

25% of ratios	Upper Quartile
Median—Upper*	
25% of ratios	Upper Middle Quartile
Median— *	
25% of ratios	Lower Middle Quartile
Median—Lower*	
25% of ratios	Lower Quartile

Weak Ratios

Example of Current Ratio

3.1	Median—Upper
1.5	Median
1.3	Median—Lower

Why Use Medians/Quartiles Instead of the Average?

There are several reasons medians and quartiles are used instead of an average. Medians and quartiles elim[inate] the influence an "outlier" (an extremely high or low value compared to the rest of the values). They also more a[ccu]rately reflect the ranges of ratio values than a straight averaging method would.

It is important to understand that the spread (range) between the upper and lower quartiles represents the m[iddle] 50% of all the companies in a sample. Therefore, ratio values greater than the upper quartile or less than the [lower] quartile may begin to approach "unusual" values.

Non-Conventional Values:

For some ratio values, you will occasionally see an entry that is other than a conventional number. These entries are defined as follows:

(1) <u>UND</u>—This stands for "undefined," the result of the denominator in a ratio calculation approaching zero.

(2) <u>NM</u>—This may occasionally appear as a quartile or median for the ratios sales/working capital, debt/worth, and fixed/worth. It stands for "no meaning" in cases where the dispersion is so small that any interpretation is meaningless.

(3) <u>999.8</u>—When a ratio value equals 1,000 or more, it also becomes an "unusual" value and is given the "999.8" designation. This is considered to be a close enough approximation to the actual unusually large value.

Linear versus Nonlinear Ratios:

An array that is ordered in ascending sequence or in descending sequence is linear. An array that deviates from true ascending or true descending when its values change from positive to negative (low to high positive, followed by high to low negative) is nonlinear.

A specific example of a nonlinear ratio would be the Sales/Working Capital ratio. In other words, when the Sales/Working Capital ratio is positive, then the top quartile would be represented by the *lowest positive* ratio. However, if the ratio is negative, the top quartile will be represented by the *highest negative* ratio! In a nonlinear array such as this, the median could be either positive or negative because it is whatever the middle value is in the particular array of numbers.

Nonlinear Ratios

Sales/Working Capital
Fixed/Worth
Debt/Worth

Linear Ratios

Current Ratio
Quick Ratio
Sales Receivables
Days' Receivables
Cost of Sales/Inventory
Days' Inventory
Cost of Sales/Payables
Days' Payables
EBIT/Interest
Net Profit + Deprec, Depletion, Amort/Current Maturities Long-Term Debt
% Profits Before Taxes/Tangible Net Worth
% Profits Before Taxes/Total Assets
Sales/Net Fixed Assets
Sales/Total Assets
% Depreciation, Depletion, Amortization/Sales
% Officers', Directors', Owners' Compensation/Sales

portant Notes on Ratios:

nover Ratios—For certain ratios (sales/receivables, cost of sales/inventory, cost of sales/payables) you will see numbers, one in **BOLD** and one in regular type. These ratios are generally called turnover ratios. The number in **LD** represents **the number of days** and the number in regular type is the **number of times**. Please see the definition of sales/receivables on the following pages for a more complete description of the two types of calculations and each means.

tory Presentations—**Inventory presentations** are based on fiscal year-end point-in-time balances, not average. In addition, our data capture does not permit us to know what method of inventory accounting (LIFO or FIFO, stance) was used.

following ratios contained in the *Statement Studies* are grouped into five principal categories: liquidity, coverage, rage, operating, and specific expense items.

LIQUIDITY RATIOS

Liquidity is a measure of the quality and adequacy of current assets to meet current obligations as they come du other words, can a firm quickly convert its assets to cash—without a loss in value—in order to meet its immediate short-term obligations? For firms such as utilities that can readily and accurately predict their cash inflows, liquid not nearly as critical as it is for firms like airlines or manufacturing businesses that can have wide fluctuation demand and revenue streams. These ratios provide a level of comfort to lenders in case of liquidation.

1. Current Ratio

How to Calculate: Divide total current assets by total current liabilities.

$$\frac{\text{Total Current Assets}}{\text{Total Current Liabilities}}$$

How to Interpret: This ratio is a rough indication of a firm's ability to service its current obligations. Generally higher the current ratio, the greater the "cushion" between current obligations and a firm's ability to pay them. Wh stronger ratio shows that the numbers for current assets exceed those for current liabilities, the composition and ity of current assets are critical factors in the analysis of an individual firm's liquidity.

The ratio values are arrayed from the highest positive to the lowest positive.

2. Quick Ratio

How to Calculate: Add cash and equivalents to trade receivables. Then, divide by total current liabilities.

$$\frac{\text{Cash \& Equivalents} + \text{Trade Receivables (net)}}{\text{Total Current Liabilities}}$$

How to Interpret: Also known as the "acid test" ratio, this is a stricter, more conservative measure of liquidity tha current ratio. This ratio reflects the degree to which a company's current liabilities are covered by its most liquid rent assets, the kind of assets that can be converted quickly to cash and at amounts close to book value. Inve and other less liquid current assets are removed from the calculation. Generally, if the ratio produces a value t less than 1 to 1, it implies a "dependency" on inventory or other "less" current assets to liquidate short-term debt.

The ratio values are arrayed from the highest positive to the lowest positive.

3. Sales/Receivables

How to Calculate: Divide net sales by trade receivables.

$$\frac{\text{Net Sales}}{\text{Trade Receivables (net)}}$$

Please note—In the contractor section, both accounts receivable-progress billings and accounts receivable-current r tion are included in the receivables figure used in calculating the revenues/receivables and receivables/payables rati

How to Interpret: This ratio measures the number of times trade receivables turn over during the year. The hi the turnover of receivables, the shorter the time between sale and cash collection.

> For example, a company with sales of $720,000 and receivables of $120,000 would have a sales/receivables ratio of 6.0. This means receivables turn over six times a year. If a company's receivables appear to be turning more slowly than the rest of the industry, further research is needed and the quality of the receivables should be examined closely.

Cautions—A problem with this ratio is that it compares one day's receivables, shown at statement date, to total ar sales and does not take into consideration seasonal fluctuations. An additional problem in interpretation may when there is a large proportion of cash sales to total sales.

When the receivables figure is zero, the quotient will be undefined (UND) and represents the best possible ratio ratio values are therefore arrayed starting with undefined (UND) and then from the numerically highest value t numerically lowest value. The only time a zero will appear in the array is when the sales figure is low and the quo rounds off to zero. By definition, this ratio cannot be negative.

4. Days' Receivables

The sales/receivables ratio will have a figure printed in bold type directly to the left of the array. This figure is the days' receivables.

How to Calculate the Days' Receivables: Divide the sales/receivables ratio into 365 (the number of days in one year).

$$\frac{365}{\text{Sales/Receivable ratio}}$$

How to Interpret the Days' Receivables: This figure expresses the average number of days that receivables are outstanding. Generally, the greater the number of days outstanding, the greater the probability of delinquencies in accounts receivable. A comparison of a company's daily receivables may indicate the extent of a company's control over credit and collections.

Please note—You should take into consideration the terms offered by a company to its customers because these may differ from terms within the industry.

> For example, using the sales/receivable ratio calculated above, 365 ÷ 6 = 61 (i.e., the average receivable is collected in 61 days).

5. Cost of Sales/Inventory

How to Calculate: Divide cost of sales by inventory.

$$\frac{\text{Cost of Sales}}{\text{Inventory}}$$

How to Interpret: This ratio measures the number of times inventory is turned over during the year.

High Inventory Turnover—On the positive side, high inventory turnover can indicate greater liquidity or superior merchandising. Conversely, it can indicate a shortage of needed inventory for sales.

Low Inventory Turnover—Low inventory turnover can indicate poor liquidity, possible overstocking, or obsolescence. On the positive side, it could indicate a planned inventory buildup in the case of material shortages.

Cautions—A problem with this ratio is that it compares one day's inventory to cost of goods sold and does not take seasonal fluctuations into account. When the inventory figure is zero, the quotient will be undefined (UND) and represents the best possible ratio. The ratio values are arrayed starting with undefined (UND) and then from the numerically highest value to the numerically lowest value. The only time a zero will appear in the array is when the figure for cost of sales is very low and the quotient rounds off to zero.

Please note—For service industries, the cost of sales is included in operating expenses. In addition, please note that the data collection process does not differentiate the method of inventory valuation.

6. Days' Inventory

The days' inventory is the figure printed in bold directly to the left of the cost of sales/inventory ratio.

How to Calculate the Days' Inventory: Divide the cost of sales/inventory ratio into 365 (the number of days in one year).

$$\frac{365}{\text{Cost of Sales/Inventory ratio}}$$

How to Interpret: Dividing the inventory turnover ratio into 365 days yields the average length of time units are in inventory.

7. Cost of Sales/Payables

How to Calculate: Divide cost of sales by trade payables.

$$\frac{\text{Cost of Sales}}{\text{Trade Payables}}$$

Please note—In the contractor section, both accounts payable-trade and accounts payable-retention are included in the payables figure used in calculating the cost of revenues/payables and receivables/payables ratios.

How to Interpret: This ratio measures the number of times trade payables turn over during the year. The higher the turnover of payables, the shorter the time between purchase and payment. If a company's payables appear to be turning more slowly than the industry, then the company may be experiencing cash shortages, disputing invoices with suppliers, enjoying extended terms, or deliberately expanding its trade credit. The ratio comparison of company to industry suggests the existence of these or other possible causes. If a firm buys on 30-day terms, it is reasonable to expect this ratio to turn over in approximately 30 days.

Cautions—A problem with this ratio is that it compares one day's payables to cost of goods sold and does not take seasonal fluctuations into account. When the payables figure is zero, the quotient will be undefined (UND) and represents the best possible ratio. The ratio values are arrayed starting with undefined (UND) and then from the numerically highest to the numerically lowest value. The only time a zero will appear in the array is when the figure for cost of sales is very low and the quotient rounds off to zero.

8. Days' Payables

The days' payables is the figure printed in bold type directly to the left of the cost of sales/payables ratio.

How to Calculate the Days' Payables: Divide the cost of sales/payables ratio into 365 (the number of days in one year).

$$\frac{365}{\text{Cost of Sales/Payables ratio}}$$

How to Interpret: Division of the payables turnover ratio into 365 days yields the average length of time trade debt is outstanding.

9. Sales/Working Capital

How to Calculate: Divide net sales by net working capital (current assets less current liabilities equals net working capital).

$$\frac{\text{Net Sales}}{\text{Net Working Capital}}$$

How to Interpret: Because it reflects the ability to finance current operations, working capital is a measure of the margin of protection for current creditors. When you relate the level of sales resulting from operations to the underlying working capital, you can measure how efficiently working capital is being used.

Low ratio (close to zero)—A low ratio may indicate an inefficient use of working capital.

High ratio (high positive or high negative)—A very high ratio often signifies overtrading, which is a vulnerable position for creditors.

Please note—sales/working capital ratio is a nonlinear array. In other words, an array that is NOT ordered from highest positive to highest negative as is the case for linear arrays. The ratio values are arrayed from the lowest positive to the highest positive, to undefined (UND), and then from the highest negative to the lowest negative. If working capital is zero, the quotient is undefined (UND).

If the sales/working capital ratio is positive, then the top quartile would be represented by the *lowest positive* ratio. However, if the ratio is negative, the top quartile will be represented by the *highest negative* ratio! In a nonlinear array such as the sales/working capital ratio, the median could be either positive or negative because it is whatever the middle value is in the particular array of numbers.

Cautions—When analyzing this ratio, you need to focus on working capital, not on the sales figure. Although sales cannot be negative, working capital can be. If you have a large, positive working capital number, the ratio will be small *and* positive—which is good. Because negative working capital is bad, if you have a large, negative working capital number, the sales/working capital ratio will be small *and* negative—which is NOT good. Therefore, the lowest positive ratio is the best and the lowest negative ratio is the worst. If working capital is a small negative number, the ratio will be large, which is the best of the negatives.

COVERAGE RATIOS

Coverage ratios measure a firm's ability to service its debt. In other words, how well does the flow of a company's funds cover its short-term financial obligations? In contrast to liquidity ratios that focus on the possibility of liquidation, coverage ratios seek to provide lenders a comfort level based on the belief the firm will remain a viable enterprise.

1. Earnings Before Interest and Taxes (EBIT)/Interest

How to Calculate: Divide earnings (profit) before annual interest expense and taxes by annual interest expense.

$$\frac{\text{Earnings Before Interest \& Taxes}}{\text{Annual Interest Expense}}$$

How to Interpret: This ratio measures a firm's ability to meet interest payments. A high ratio may indicate that a borrower can easily meet the interest obligations of a loan. This ratio also indicates a firm's capacity to take on additional debt.

Please note—Only statements reporting annual interest expense were used in the calculation of this ratio. The ratio values are arrayed from the highest positive to the lowest positive and then from the lowest negative to the highest negative.

2. Net Profit + Depreciation, Depletion, Amortization/Current Maturities Long-Term Debt

How to Calculate: Add net profit to depreciation, depletion, and amortization expenses. Then, divide by the current portion of long-term debt.

$$\frac{\text{Net Profit + Depreciation, Depletion, Amortization Expenses}}{\text{Current Portion of Long-Term Debt}}$$

How to Interpret: This ratio reflects how well cash flow from operations covers current maturities. Because cash flow is the primary source of debt retirement, the ratio measures a firm's ability to service principal repayment and take on additional debt. Even though it is a mistake to believe all cash flow is available for debt service, this ratio is still a valid measure of the ability to service long-term debt.

Please note—Only data for corporations with the following items was used:

(1) Profit or loss after taxes (positive, negative, or zero).

(2) A positive figure for depreciation/depletion/amortization expenses.

(3) A positive figure for current maturities of long-term debt.

Ratio values are arrayed from the highest to the lowest positive and then from the lowest to the highest negative.

LEVERAGE RATIOS

How much protection do a company's assets provide for the debt held by its creditors? Highly leveraged firms are companies with heavy debt in relation to their net worth. These firms are more vulnerable to business downturns than those with lower debt-to-worth positions. While leverage ratios help measure this vulnerability, keep in mind that these ratios vary greatly depending on the requirements of particular industry groups.

1. Fixed/Worth

How to Calculate: Divide fixed assets (net of accumulated depreciation) by tangible net worth (net worth minus intangibles).

$$\frac{\text{Net Fixed Assets}}{\text{Tangible Net Worth}}$$

How to Interpret: This ratio measures the extent to which owner's equity (capital) has been invested in plant and equipment (fixed assets). A lower ratio indicates a proportionately smaller investment in fixed assets in relation to net worth and a better "cushion" for creditors in case of liquidation. Similarly, a higher ratio would indicate the opposite situation. The presence of a substantial number of fixed assets that are leased—and not appearing on the balance sheet—may result in a deceptively lower ratio.

Fixed assets may be zero, in which case the quotient is zero. If tangible net worth is zero, the quotient is undefined (UND). If tangible net worth is negative, the quotient is negative.

Please note—Like the sales/working capital ratio discussed above, this fixed/worth ratio is a nonlinear array. In other words, it is an array that is NOT ordered from highest positive to highest negative as a linear array would be. The ratio values are arrayed from the lowest positive to the highest positive, to undefined (UND), and then from the highest negative to the lowest negative.

If the Fixed/Worth ratio is positive, then the top quartile would be represented by the *lowest positive* ratio. However, if the ratio is negative, the top quartile will be represented by the *highest negative* ratio! In a nonlinear array such as this, the median could be either positive or negative because it is whatever the middle value is in the particular array of numbers.

2. Debt/Worth

How to Calculate: Divide total liabilities by tangible net worth.

$$\frac{\text{Total Liabilities}}{\text{Tangible Net Worth}}$$

How to Interpret: This ratio expresses the relationship between capital contributed by creditors and that contributed by owners. Basically, it shows how much protection the owners are providing creditors. The higher the ratio, the greater the risk being assumed by creditors. A lower ratio generally indicates greater long-term financial safety. Unlike a highly leveraged firm, a firm with a low debt/worth ratio usually has greater flexibility to borrow in the future.

Tangible net worth may be zero, in which case the ratio is undefined (UND). Tangible net worth may also be negative, which results in the quotient being negative. The ratio values are arrayed from the lowest to highest positive, to undefined, and then from the highest to lowest negative.

Please note—Like the sales/working capital ratio discussed above, this debt/worth ratio is a nonlinear array. In other words, it is an array that is NOT ordered from highest positive to highest negative as a linear array would be. The ratio values are arrayed from the lowest positive to the highest positive, to undefined (UND), and then from the highest negative to the lowest negative.

If the debt/worth ratio is positive, then the top quartile would be represented by the *lowest positive* ratio. However, if the ratio is negative, the top quartile will be represented by the *highest negative* ratio! In a nonlinear array such as this, the median could be either positive or negative because it is whatever the middle value is in the particular array of numbers.

OPERATING RATIOS

Operating ratios are designed to assist in the evaluation of management performance.

1. % Profits Before Taxes/Tangible Net Worth

How to Calculate: Divide profit before taxes by tangible net worth. Then, multiply by 100.

$$\frac{\text{Profit Before Taxes}}{\text{Tangible Net Worth}} \times 100$$

How to Interpret: This ratio expresses the rate of return on tangible capital employed. While it can serve as an indicator of management performance, you should always use it in conjunction with other ratios. Normally associated with effective management, a high return could actually point to an undercapitalized firm. Conversely, a low return that's usually viewed as an indicator of inefficient management performance could actually reflect a highly capitalized, conservatively operated business.

This ratio has been multiplied by 100 because it is shown as a percentage.

Profit before taxes may be zero, in which case the ratio is zero. Profits before taxes may be negative, resulting in negative quotients. Firms with negative tangible net worth have been omitted from the ratio arrays. Negative ratios will therefore only result in the case of negative profit before taxes. If the tangible net worth is zero, the quotient is undefined (UND). If there are fewer than 10 ratios for a particular size class, the result is not shown. The ratio values are arrayed starting with undefined (UND), then from the highest to the lowest positive values, and finally from the lowest to the highest negative values.

2. % Profits Before Taxes/Total Assets

How to Calculate: Divide profit before taxes by total assets and multiply by 100.

$$\frac{\text{Profit Before Taxes}}{\text{Total Assets}} \times 100$$

How to Interpret: This ratio expresses the pre-tax return on total assets and measures the effectiveness of management in employing the resources available to it. If a specific ratio varies considerably from the ranges found in this book, the analyst will need to examine the makeup of the assets and take a closer look at the earnings figure. A heavily depreciated plant and a large amount of intangible assets or unusual income or expense items will cause distortions of this ratio.

This ratio has been multiplied by 100 since it is shown as a percentage. If profit before taxes is zero, the quotient is zero. If profit before taxes is negative, the quotient is negative. These ratio values are arrayed from the highest to the lowest positive and then from the lowest to the highest negative.

3. Sales/Net Fixed Assets

How to Calculate: Divide net sales by net fixed assets (net of accumulated depreciation).

$$\frac{\text{Net Sales}}{\text{Net Fixed Assets}}$$

How to Interpret: This ratio is a measure of the productive use of a firm's fixed assets. Largely depreciated fixed assets or a labor-intensive operation may cause a distortion of this ratio.

If the net fixed figure is zero, the quotient is undefined (UND). The only time a zero will appear in the array will be when the net sales figure is low and the quotient rounds off to zero. These ratio values cannot be negative.

They are arrayed from undefined (UND) and then from the highest to the lowest positive values.

4. Sales/Total Assets

How to Calculate: Divide net sales by total assets.

$$\frac{\text{Net Sales}}{\text{Total Assets}}$$

How to Interpret: This ratio is a general measure of a firm's ability to generate sales in relation to total assets. It should be used only to compare firms within specific industry groups and in conjunction with other operating ratios to determine the effective employment of assets.

The only time a zero will appear in the array will be when the net sales figure is low and the quotient rounds off to zero. The ratio values cannot be negative. They are arrayed from the highest to the lowest positive values.

EXPENSE TO SALES RATIOS

The following two ratios relate specific expense items to net sales and express this relationship as a percentage. Comparisons are convenient because the item, net sales, is used as a constant. Variations in these ratios are most pronounced between capital- and labor-intensive industries.

1. % Depreciation, Depletion, Amortization/Sales

How to Calculate: Divide annual depreciation, amortization, and depletion expenses by net sales and multiply by 100.

$$\frac{\text{Depreciation, Amortization, Depletion Expenses}}{\text{Net Sales}} \times 100$$

2. % Officers', Directors', Owners' Compensation/Sales

How to Calculate: Divide annual officers', directors', owners' compensation by net sales and multiply by 100. Include total salaries, bonuses, commissions, and other monetary remuneration to all officers, directors, and/or owners of the firm during the year covered by the statement. This includes drawings of partners and proprietors.

$$\frac{\text{Officers', Directors', Owners' Compensation}}{\text{Net Sales}} \times 100$$

Only statements showing a positive figure for each of the expense categories shown above were used. The ratios are arrayed from the lowest to highest positive values.

Explanation of Noncontractor Balance Sheet and Income Data

Cash & Equivalents
All cash, marketplace, securities, and other near-cash items. Excludes sinking funds.

Trade Receivables (net)
All accounts from trade, net of allowance for doubtful accounts.

Inventory
Anything constituting inventory for the firm.

All Other Current
Any other current assets. Does not include prepaid items.

Total Current
Total of all current assets listed above.

Fixed Assets (net)
All property, plant, leasehold improvements and equipment, net of accumulated depreciation or depletion.

Intangibles (net)
Intangible assets, including goodwill, trademarks, patents, catalogs, brands, copyrights, formulas, franchises, and mailing lists, net of accumulated amortization.

All Other Non-Current
Prepaid items and any other non-current assets.

Total
Total of all items listed above.

ASSETS
Cash & Equivalents
Trade Receivables (net)
Inventory
All Other Current
Total Current
Fixed Assets (net)
Intangibles (net)
All Other Non-Current
Total

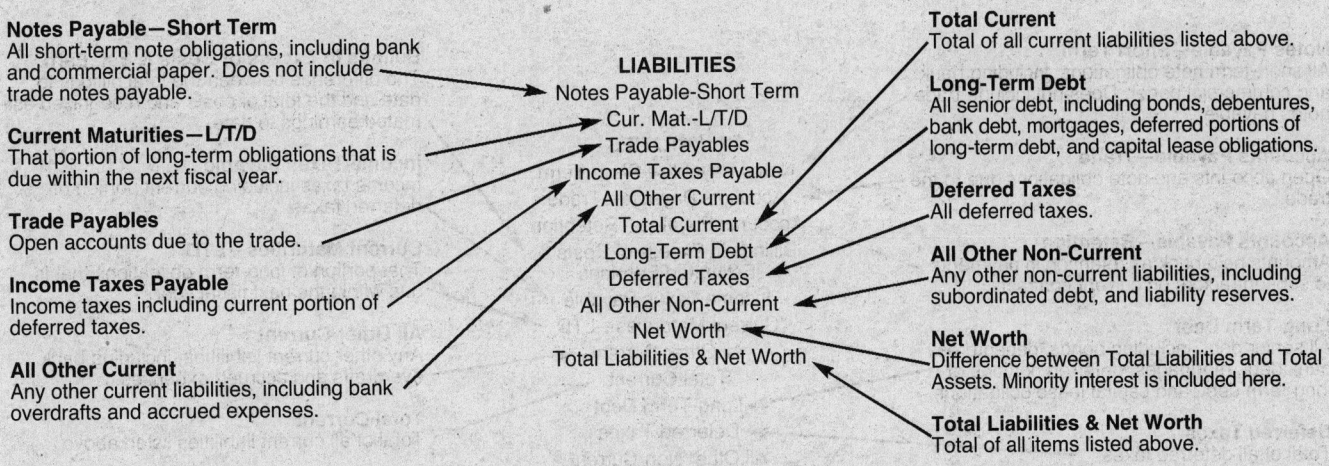

Notes Payable—Short Term
All short-term note obligations, including bank and commercial paper. Does not include trade notes payable.

Current Maturities—L/T/D
That portion of long-term obligations that is due within the next fiscal year.

Trade Payables
Open accounts due to the trade.

Income Taxes Payable
Income taxes including current portion of deferred taxes.

All Other Current
Any other current liabilities, including bank overdrafts and accrued expenses.

Total Current
Total of all current liabilities listed above.

Long-Term Debt
All senior debt, including bonds, debentures, bank debt, mortgages, deferred portions of long-term debt, and capital lease obligations.

Deferred Taxes
All deferred taxes.

All Other Non-Current
Any other non-current liabilities, including subordinated debt, and liability reserves.

Net Worth
Difference between Total Liabilities and Total Assets. Minority interest is included here.

Total Liabilities & Net Worth
Total of all items listed above.

LIABILITIES
Notes Payable-Short Term
Cur. Mat.-L/T/D
Trade Payables
Income Taxes Payable
All Other Current
Total Current
Long-Term Debt
Deferred Taxes
All Other Non-Current
Net Worth
Total Liabilities & Net Worth

Net Sales
Gross sales, net of returns and discounts allowed, if any.

Gross Profit
Net sales minus cost of sales.

Operating Expenses
All selling and general & administrative expenses. Includes depreciation, but not interest expense.

Operating Profit
Gross profit minus operating expenses.

All Other Expenses (net)
Includes miscellaneous other income and expenses (net), such as interest expense, miscellaneous expenses not included in general & administrative expenses, netted against recoveries, interest income, dividends received and miscellaneous income.

Profit Before Taxes
Operating profit minus all other expenses (net).

INCOME DATA
Net Sales
Gross Profit
Operating Expenses
Operating Profit
All Other Expenses (net)
Profit Before Taxes

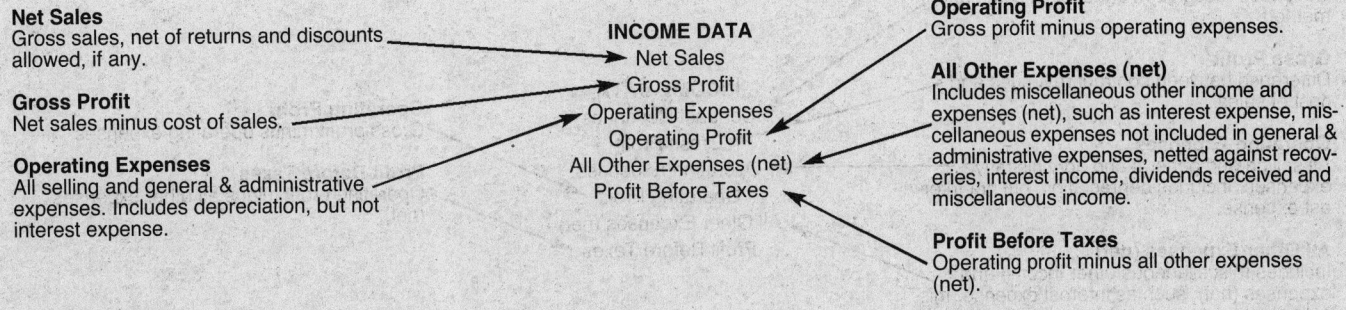

Explanation of Contractor Percentage-of-Completion Basis of Accounting Balance Sheet and Income Data

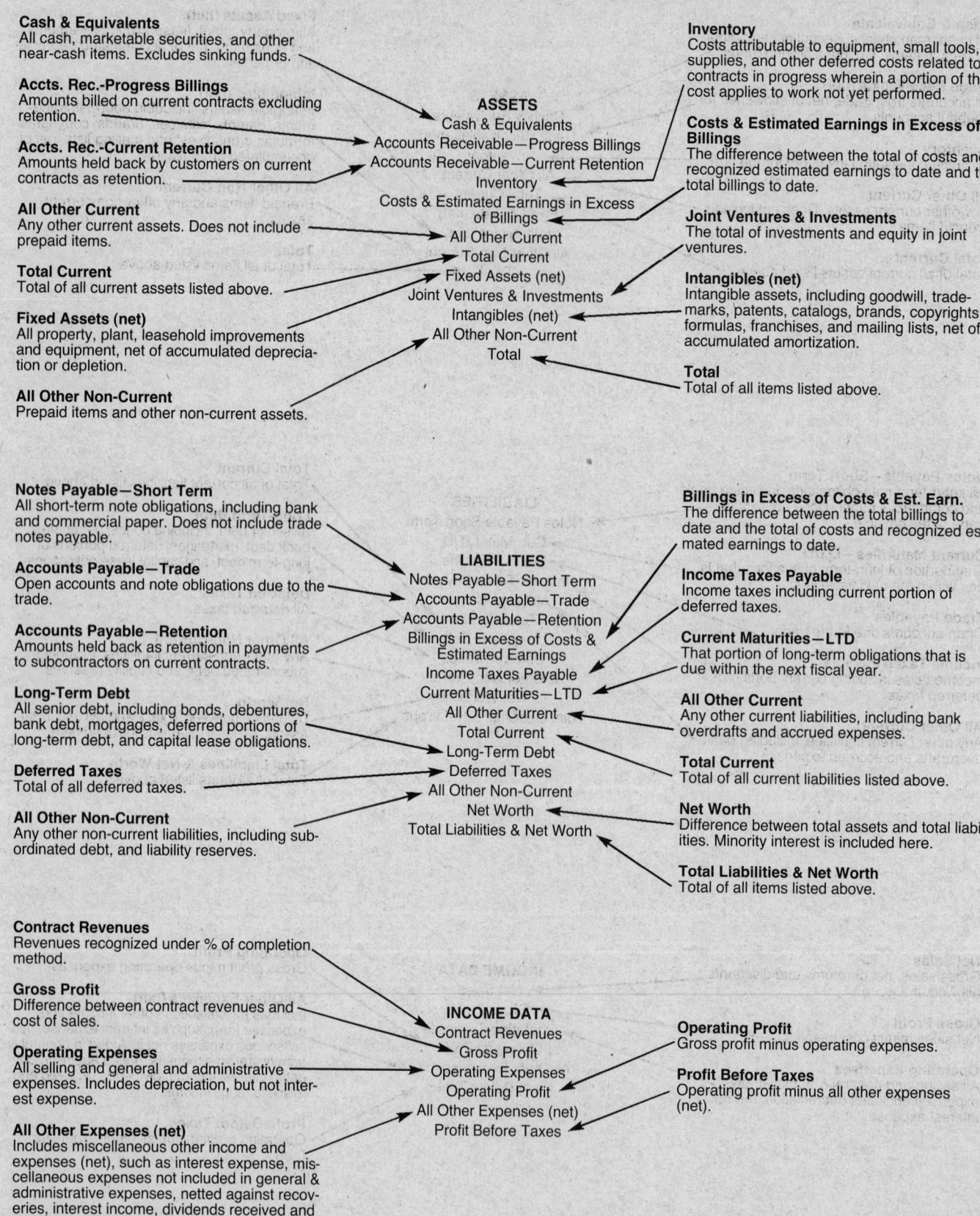

Cash & Equivalents
All cash, marketable securities, and other near-cash items. Excludes sinking funds.

Accts. Rec.-Progress Billings
Amounts billed on current contracts excluding retention.

Accts. Rec.-Current Retention
Amounts held back by customers on current contracts as retention.

All Other Current
Any other current assets. Does not include prepaid items.

Total Current
Total of all current assets listed above.

Fixed Assets (net)
All property, plant, leasehold improvements and equipment, net of accumulated depreciation or depletion.

All Other Non-Current
Prepaid items and other non-current assets.

Inventory
Costs attributable to equipment, small tools, supplies, and other deferred costs related to contracts in progress wherein a portion of the cost applies to work not yet performed.

Costs & Estimated Earnings in Excess of Billings
The difference between the total of costs and recognized estimated earnings to date and the total billings to date.

Joint Ventures & Investments
The total of investments and equity in joint ventures.

Intangibles (net)
Intangible assets, including goodwill, trademarks, patents, catalogs, brands, copyrights, formulas, franchises, and mailing lists, net of accumulated amortization.

Total
Total of all items listed above.

ASSETS
Cash & Equivalents
Accounts Receivable—Progress Billings
Accounts Receivable—Current Retention
Inventory
Costs & Estimated Earnings in Excess of Billings
All Other Current
Total Current
Fixed Assets (net)
Joint Ventures & Investments
Intangibles (net)
All Other Non-Current
Total

Notes Payable—Short Term
All short-term note obligations, including bank and commercial paper. Does not include trade notes payable.

Accounts Payable—Trade
Open accounts and note obligations due to the trade.

Accounts Payable—Retention
Amounts held back as retention in payments to subcontractors on current contracts.

Long-Term Debt
All senior debt, including bonds, debentures, bank debt, mortgages, deferred portions of long-term debt, and capital lease obligations.

Deferred Taxes
Total of all deferred taxes.

All Other Non-Current
Any other non-current liabilities, including subordinated debt, and liability reserves.

Billings in Excess of Costs & Est. Earn.
The difference between the total billings to date and the total of costs and recognized estimated earnings to date.

Income Taxes Payable
Income taxes including current portion of deferred taxes.

Current Maturities—LTD
That portion of long-term obligations that is due within the next fiscal year.

All Other Current
Any other current liabilities, including bank overdrafts and accrued expenses.

Total Current
Total of all current liabilities listed above.

Net Worth
Difference between total assets and total liabilities. Minority interest is included here.

Total Liabilities & Net Worth
Total of all items listed above.

LIABILITIES
Notes Payable—Short Term
Accounts Payable—Trade
Accounts Payable—Retention
Billings in Excess of Costs & Estimated Earnings
Income Taxes Payable
Current Maturities—LTD
All Other Current
Total Current
Long-Term Debt
Deferred Taxes
All Other Non-Current
Net Worth
Total Liabilities & Net Worth

Contract Revenues
Revenues recognized under % of completion method.

Gross Profit
Difference between contract revenues and cost of sales.

Operating Expenses
All selling and general and administrative expenses. Includes depreciation, but not interest expense.

All Other Expenses (net)
Includes miscellaneous other income and expenses (net), such as interest expense, miscellaneous expenses not included in general & administrative expenses, netted against recoveries, interest income, dividends received and miscellaneous income.

INCOME DATA
Contract Revenues
Gross Profit
Operating Expenses
Operating Profit
All Other Expenses (net)
Profit Before Taxes

Operating Profit
Gross profit minus operating expenses.

Profit Before Taxes
Operating profit minus all other expenses (net).

For further analysis, please refer to *Industry Default Probabilities and Cash Flow Measures*

If you think *Financial Ratio Benchmarks* is a valuable resource, wait until you see its companion study. Now in its eleventh year and bigger than ever, *Industry Default Probabilities and Cash Flow Measures* is a major expansion of our *Annual Statement Studies.* It brings together the power of Moody's RiskCalc Plus for private companies and the *Statement Studies* database to provide distribution statistics on one-year and five-year probability of default estimates by industry. The new benchmarks add substantial value to the critical analysis of cash flow for private companies.

The latest edition of *Industry Default Probabilities and Cash Flow Measures* includes many new industries, stronger statements, four years of historical data sorted by assets and sales. In short, it is more like our traditional *Statement Studies.*

Industry Default Probabilities and Cash Flow Measures includes:

- Probability of default estimates on a percentage scale, mapped to a "dot" EDF bond rating scale.
- Cash flow measures on a common-size percentage scale. Ratios include:
  - Cash from Trading
  - Cash after Operations
  - Net Cash after Operations
  - Cash after Debt Amortization
  - Debt Service P&I Coverage
  - Interest Coverage (Operating Cash)
- Change in position, normalized, year over year, for eight financial statement line items. Ratios include:
  - Change in Inventory
  - Total Current Assets (TCA)
  - Total Assets (TA)
  - Retained Earnings (RE)
  - Net Sales (NS)
  - Cost of Goods Sold (CGS)
  - Profit before Interest & Taxes (PBIT)
  - Depreciation/Depletion/Amortization (DDA)
- Trend data available for five years.
- Other ratios.
  - Sustainable Growth Rate
  - Funded Debt/EBITDA
- Data arrayed by asset and sales size.

Please see the next page for a copy of a sample report. For more information regarding the *Industry Default Probabilities and Cash Flow Measures,* please call 1-800-677-7621!

INDUSTRY DEFAULT PROBABILITIES AND CASH FLOW MEASURES SAMPLE REPORT

AGRICULTURE—Wheat Farming NAICS 111140

Current Data Sorted by Assets						Type of Statement	Comparative Historical Data	
2	2	7	11	4	4	Unqualified	2	13
1	3	10	5		1	Reviewed	6	8
5	4	6	1			Compiled	9	14
5	9	1				Tax Returns	11	21
	9	15	12	2	2	Other	12	33
	31 (4/1-9/30/07)		90 (10/1/07-3/31/08)				4/1/03-3/31/04	4/1/04-3/31/05
0-500M	500M-2MM	2-10MM	10-50MM	50-100MM	100-250MM	Assets Size	ALL	ALL
13	27	39	29	6	7	Number of Statements	40	89
%	%	%	%	%	%	EXPECTED DEFAULT FREQUENCY	%	%
.20	.24	.23	.19				.58	.14
.48	.73 (38)	.41	.49			Risk Calc EDF	1.16 (81)	.27
1.03	1.27	1.10	.98			(1 yr)	2.98	.86
Baa1 1.74	Baa1 1.66	Baa1 1.41	Baa1 1.38			Moodys EDF Rating (see note) Risk Calc EDF (5 yr)	Ba1 5.52	A3 1.18
Baa3 4.14	Baa3 4.14	Baa3 3.03	Baa2 2.67				Ba2 7.92	Baa2 2.65
Ba2 5.97	Ba2 6.88	Ba2 5.94	Ba1 5.21				Ba3 12.23	Ba1 5.21
%	%	%	%	%	%	CASH FLOW MEASURES	%	%
						Cash from Trading/Sales		
27.4	20.8	14.1	25.5			Cash after Operations/Sales	12.9	24.6
12.6	10.8	5.9	8.7				4.8	6.6
4.3	3.3	.1	1.0				.3	.6
27.3	19.2	13.6	24.7			Net Cash after Operations/Sales	12.6	23.2
13.0	10.9	6.6	9.3				4.4	6.5
4.4	1.6	.1	1.5				.5	1.1
8.1	12.7	5.0	5.3			Net Cash after Debt Amortization/Sales	6.3	9.3
2.9	2.4	.4	1.5				1.2	2.2
-.3	-4.6	-1.6	-6.8				-4.5	-4.0
9.2	3.2	3.4	5.1			Debt Service P&I Coverage	2.8	4.9
(11) 2.1	(25) 1.3	(34) 1.5	(27) 1.4				(34) 1.3 (81)	2.0
1.4	.0	.1	.5				.0	.2
12.0	5.8	7.2	5.6			Interest Coverage (Operating Cash)	7.0	8.8
(11) 4.1	(25) 1.9	(32) 2.7	(26) 3.1				(33) 2.5 (81)	3.3
2.1	.0	-.2	.4				.2	.4
	41.7	70.2	53.8			Δ Inventory	36.7	16.8
	(16) 2.0	(21) 24.1	(18) 12.4				(24) 3.2 (60)	-1.1
	-7.5	2.8	-1.0				-11.4	-22.5
33.7	40.6	38.7	26.7			Δ Total Current Assets	27.6	21.4
.0	15.9	14.7	3.4				5.2	10.2
-36.0	-7.5	.2	-9.8				-10.4	-11.4
21.9	24.2	28.5	27.9			Δ Total Assets	28.0	30.0
4.9	2.3	11.8	5.0				4.8	7.9
-23.2	-5.1	1.8	-1.7				-3.1	-2.8
148.6	24.3	73.8	33.2			Δ Retained Earnings	25.8	49.2
52.3	(26) 6.3	27.7	8.5				(39) 3.4 (85)	10.3
-47.1	-3.1	8.4	6.4				-14.1	-9.8
45.8	34.0	41.2	27.0			Δ Net Sales	21.6	28.2
9.5	15.3	14.5	8.1				3.2	7.9
-3.0	-2.8	4.9	-3.3				-7.8	.0
						Δ Cost of Goods Sold		
231.5	79.6	189.7	90.0			Δ Profit before Int. & Taxes	150.6	95.7
58.1	(26) 1.2	25.5	9.3				30.8 (88)	11.5
-12.5	-32.4	-26.5	-28.5				-28.0	-26.9
143.8	12.9	38.6	5.9			Δ Depr./Depl./Amort.	31.0	19.8
(10) -4.1	(25) -14.5	(38) 5.1	(27) -4.0				(34) 5.2 (71)	.0
-77.6	-60.0	-18.5	-10.4				-23.0	-12.6
59.0	22.1	62.3	21.4			RATIOS Sustainable Growth Rate	38.2	26.1
-34.8	(26) 8.1	17.4	7.9				8.2 (87)	5.8
-64.5	.5	-3.7	2.3				-.8	-2.6
.3	.3	.6	1.4			Funded Debt/EBITDA	1.3	.7
.6	2.4	1.4	2.7				3.4	3.4
3.7	7.0	3.7	7.3				7.3	6.6
23696M	71595M	494325M	1060928M	676390M	2248216M	Net Sales ($)	593939M	1930153M
2688M	30938M	203770M	681568M	448459M	1210501M	Total Assets ($)	433841M	1644466M

M = $ thousand   MM = $ million

Note: The ratings are Moody's.edf rating (e.g. Ba1.edf) and not Moody's Investor Services Long-Term Bond Ratings. If a number of statements appears for the Risk Calc EDF (1 yr), it also applies to the (5 yr).

AGRICULTURE—Wheat Farming NAICS 111140

Comparative Historical Data			Type of Statement	Current Data Sorted by Sales					
24	21	30	Unqualified	1	6	2	2	5	14
14	20	19	Reviewed		2	1	5	6	5
23	27	12	Compiled	2	2	1	4	3	
24	35	15	Tax Returns	3	6	4	2	2	
52	46	45	Other	10	7	4	6	10	8
4/1/05-3/31/06 ALL	4/1/06-3/31/07 ALL	4/1/07-3/31/08 ALL		31 (4/1-9/30/07)		90 (10/1/07-3/31/08)			
			Sales Size	0-1MM	1-3MM	3-5MM	5-10MM	10-25MM	25MM & OVER
137	149	121	Number of Statements	16	23	12	17	26	27
%	%	%	**EXPECTED DEFAULT FREQUENCY**	%	%	%	%	%	%
.17	.15	.24		.28	.24	.22	.18	.27	.19
(126) .37	(136) .24	(119) .48	Risk Calc EDF	.71	.49	.48	(25) .41	(26) .48	.38
.89	.67	1.11	(1 yr)	1.40	1.03	1.12	1.20	1.16	.89
A3 1.28	A2 .94	Baa1 1.61	Moodys EDF Rating (see note) Risk Calc EDF	Baa2 2.67	Baa2 2.04	Baa1 1.55	A3 1.31	Baa1 1.84	A3 1.29
Baa3 3.13	Baa2 2.10	Baa3 3.15	(5 yr)	Ba1 4.39	Baa2 2.67	Baa3 3.19	Baa3 2.99	Baa3 3.12	Baa2 2.43
Ba1 5.72	Ba1 4.78	Ba2 6.02		Ba2 6.50	Ba1 5.75	Ba2 6.50	Ba2 6.24	Ba2 6.56	Ba1 5.47
%	%	%	**CASH FLOW MEASURES**	%	%	%	%	%	%
			Cash from Trading/Sales						
16.3	19.1	21.2	Cash after Operations/Sales	67.9	24.8	21.2	15.7	14.9	12.1
6.7	8.3	8.9		20.5	15.9	11.6	9.6	4.5	4.9
.6	-.4	2.0		7.9	3.9	-.2	1.6	.0	.8
17.3	20.4	19.3	Net Cash after Operations/Sales	66.7	24.2	17.9	14.6	14.8	12.3
7.0	8.9	9.1		23.6	17.9	8.5	10.4	4.8	5.7
1.0	1.6	1.6		6.7	5.8	-.1	1.6	-.4	.9
8.0	7.9	6.6	Net Cash after Debt Amortization/Sales	21.6	13.9	6.7	11.5	4.6	4.6
1.9	2.3	2.2		6.0	2.5	-1.2	4.6	.2	2.5
-2.0	-5.9	-2.2		.6	-4.7	-4.8	-1.2	-6.4	-.4
7.4	5.9	4.2	Debt Service P&I Coverage	2.1	5.0		23.3	5.1	5.0
(125) 2.1	(137) 2.0	(110) 1.5		(15) 1.4	(21) 1.7		2.5	(22) 1.2	(26) 1.7
.6	.3	.5		1.0	.6		1.1	-.2	.7
12.2	10.4	6.5	Interest Coverage (Operating Cash)	4.0	5.2		30.1	6.9	8.8
(118) 3.9	(132) 4.2	(107) 3.1		(15) 2.1	(21) 2.0	(16)	6.6	(20) 2.4	(26) 4.9
.5	.8	.7		1.3	.9		.4	-1.3	1.5
16.9	30.7	48.7	Δ Inventory				72.6	56.9	48.5
(91) 3.0	(87) 7.3	(69) 10.6				(11)	23.9	(16) 5.3	(24) 13.5
-13.9	-6.5	.0					1.4	-5.1	1.4
34.7	40.2	32.1	Δ Total Current Assets	37.4	18.6	39.1	39.4	62.0	29.7
6.8	12.9	12.5		26.6	10.7	.8	13.2	10.7	10.6
-12.1	-2.4	-6.5		-25.4	-27.2	-28.8	-5.1	-3.3	3.0
26.7	31.9	24.4	Δ Total Assets	14.5	34.3	28.5	42.1	22.7	24.6
6.0	9.3	7.7		2.8	5.1	6.3	7.3	12.2	15.2
-5.8	-.5	-.8		-.7	-1.8	-4.5	-7.1	1.3	.1
42.7	40.2	52.3	Δ Retained Earnings	116.1	52.3	84.4	572.4	45.3	41.4
(131) 16.2	(148) 11.0	(119) 11.1		1.8	9.5	16.9	30.9	(25) 8.6	(26) 18.4
-2.5	-3.3	-.7		-45.1	-1.8	-20.8	-20.8	7.3	.6
25.9	24.9	30.4	Δ Net Sales	20.0	33.8	41.7	25.7	62.1	30.0
7.4	8.5	10.6		3.7	16.5	18.7	9.4	10.7	10.3
-2.4	-.9	1.8		-4.9	-1.6	1.9	-1.4	4.4	3.7
			Δ Cost of Goods Sold						
102.7	94.1	102.0	Δ Profit before Int. & Taxes	68.7	176.0	215.7	126.9	117.7	51.9
16.3	9.9	(120) 10.4		(15) 1.0	11.5	54.2	41.3	26.1	.1
-27.2	-27.1	-24.8		-18.2	-39.8	-46.4	-34.2	-21.4	-14.0
19.7	33.3	17.9	Δ Depr./Depl./Amort.	3.1	17.8	40.8	19.0	25.1	15.5
(119) -3.6	(135) 1.7	(111) -3.0		(14) -20.9	(20) .9	-29.5	(16) -3.7	(24) 5.6	(25) 1.0
-28.4	-14.8	-27.3		-69.5	-14.7	-62.6	-18.0	-32.8	-6.9
35.8	32.1	28.7	**RATIOS** Sustainable Growth Rate	18.5	15.8	32.6	225.5	32.8	23.9
(136) 5.2	(147) 8.7	(120) 7.9		2.5	(22) 3.6	6.2	27.7	9.1	4.4
-10.9	-8.7	-3.7		-46.9	-39.2	.2	-3.3	-5.9	-3.7
.4	.9	.7	Funded Debt/EBITDA	.8	1.3	.0	.8	.1	1.2
2.3	2.3	2.2		2.8	5.9	2.3	1.3	1.3	2.3
6.5	5.7	5.9		5.4	9.0	3.5	6.9	3.5	3.7
4750465M	4122798M	4575150M	Net Sales ($)	6832M	42569M	49530M	125607M	430732M	3919880M
2237648M	2722141M	2577924M	Total Assets ($)	11216M	130824M	44166M	108700M	439722M	1843296M

© RMA 2008   M = $ thousand   MM = $ million

See Pages 00 through 00 for Explanation of Ratios and Data

Note: The ratings are Moody's.edf rating (e.g. Ba1.edf) and not Moody's Investor Services Long-Term Bond Ratings. If a number of statements appears for the Risk Calc EDF (1 yr), it also applies to the (5 yr).

NAICS CODES APPEARING IN THE STATEMENT STUDIES

NAICS CODES APPEARING IN THE STATEMENT STUDIES

NAICS CODES APPEARING IN THE STATEMENT STUDIES

NAICS CODES APPEARING IN THE STATEMENT STUDIES

NAICS Codes	Page	NAICS Codes	Page	NAICS Codes	Page
487210	1084-1085	524114	1196-1197	541712	1308-1309
488119	1086-1087	524126	1198-1199	541720	1310-1311
488190	1088-1089	524127	1200-1201	541810	1312-1313
488320	1090-1091	524128	1202-1203	541820	1314-1315
488330	1092-1093	524210	1204-1205	541840	1316-1317
488390	1094-1095	524292	1206-1207	541850	1318-1319
488410	1096-1097	524298	1208-1209	541860	1320-1321
488490	1098-1099	525910	1210-1211	541870	1322-1323
488510	1100-1101	525990	1212-1213	541890	1324-1325
488991	1102-1103	531110	1216-1217	541910	1326-1327
488999	1104-1105	531120	1218-1219	541921	1328-1329
492110	1106-1107	531130	1220-1221	541922	1330-1331
493110	1108-1109	531190	1222-1223	541940	1332-1333
493120	1110-1111	531210	1224-1225	541990	1334-1335
493130	1112-1113	531311	1226-1227	551111	1338-1339
493190	1114-1115	531312	1228-1229	551112	1340-1341
511110	1118-1119	531320	1230-1231	561110	1344-1345
511120	1120-1121	531390	1232-1233	561210	1346-1347
511130	1122-1123	532111	1234-1235	561311	1348-1349
511140	1124-1125	532112	1236-1237	561320	1350-1351
511199	1126-1127	532120	1238-1239	561330	1352-1353
511210	1128-1129	532210	1240-1241	561422	1354-1355
512110	1130-1131	532291	1242-1243	561439	1356-1357
512131	1132-1133	532299	1244-1245	561440	1358-1359
512191	1134-1135	532310	1246-1247	561499	1360-1361
512199	1136-1137	532411	1248-1249	561510	1362-1363
515112	1138-1139	532412	1250-1251	561520	1364-1365
515120	1140-1141	532420	1252-1253	561599	1366-1367
515210	1142-1143	532490	1254-1255	561612	1368-1369
517110	1144-1145	533110	1256-1257	561621	1370-1371
517210	1146-1147	541110	1260-1261	561710	1372-1373
517911	1148-1149	541191	1262-1263	561720	1374-1375
517919	1150-1151	541199	1264-1265	561730	1376-1377
518210	1152-1153	541211	1266-1267	561740	1378-1379
519130	1154-1155	541214	1268-1269	561790	1380-1381
519190	1156-1157	541219	1270-1271	561910	1382-1383
522220	1160-1161	541310	1272-1273	561920	1384-1385
522291	1162-1163	541320	1274-1275	561990	1386-1387
522292	1164-1165	541330	1276-1277	562111	1388-1389
522294	1166-1167	541370	1278-1279	562119	1390-1391
522298	1168-1169	541380	1280-1281	562211	1392-1393
522310	1170-1171	541410	1282-1283	562212	1394-1395
522320	1172-1173	541430	1284-1285	562219	1396-1397
522390	1174-1175	541511	1286-1287	562910	1398-1399
523110	1176-1177	541512	1288-1289	562920	1400-1401
523120	1178-1179	541513	1290-1291	562998	1402-1403
523130	1180-1181	541519	1292-1293	611110	1406-1407
523140	1182-1183	541611	1294-1295	611210	1408-1409
523910	1184-1185	541612	1296-1297	611310	1410-1411
523920	1186-1187	541613	1298-1299	611430	1412-1413
523930	1188-1189	541614	1300-1301	611519	1414-1415
523991	1190-1191	541618	1302-1303	611610	1416-1417
523999	1192-1193	541620	1304-1305	611620	1418-1419
524113	1194-1195	541690	1306-1307	611699	1420-1421

NAICS CODES APPEARING IN THE STATEMENT STUDIES

DESCRIPTION OF INDUSTRIES INCLUDED IN THE STATEMENT STUDIES

AGRICULTURE, FORESTRY, FISHING AND HUNTING

MINING

MINING

CONSTRUCTION-GENERAL

UTILITIES

CONSTRUCTION—GENERAL

CONSTRUCTION-GENERAL

CONSTRUCTION-GENERAL

MANUFACTURING

MANUFACTURING

MANUFACTURING

MANUFACTURING

MANUFACTURING

MANUFACTURING

MANUFACTURING

MANUFACTURING

MANUFACTURING

MANUFACTURING

MANUFACTURING

MANUFACTURING

MANUFACTURING

MANUFACTURING

MANUFACTURING

MANUFACTURING

MANUFACTURING

MANUFACTURING

WHOLESALE

WHOLESALE

RETAIL

RETAIL TRADE

RETAIL

RETAIL

RETAIL

RETAIL

TRANSPORTATION

TRANSPORTATION AND WAREHOUSING

TRANSPORTATION

INFORMATION

INFORMATION

INFORMATION

FINANCE

FINANCE AND INSURANCE

FINANCE

REAL ESTATE

REAL ESTATE AND RENTAL AND LEASING

REAL ESTATE

PROFESSIONAL SERVICES

PROFESSIONAL, SCIENTIFIC, AND TECHNICAL SERVICES

541110 **Offices of Lawyers.** This industry comprises offices of legal practitioners known as lawyers or attorneys (i.e., counselors-at-law) primarily engaged in the practice of law. Estab-lishments in this industry may provide expertise in a range or in specific areas of law, such as criminal law, corporate law, family and estate law, patent law, real estate law, or tax law. 1260-1261

541191 **Title Abstract and Settlement Offices.** This U.S. industry comprises establishments (except offices of lawyers and attorneys) primarily engaged in one or more of the following activities: (1) researching public land records to gather information relating to real estate titles; (2) preparing documents necessary for the transfer of the title, financing, and settlement; (3) conducting final real estate settlements and closings; and (4) filing legal and other documents relating to the sale of real estate. Real estate settlement offices, title abstract companies, and title search companies are included in this industry. 1262-1263

541199 **All Other Legal Services.** This U.S. industry comprises establishments of legal practitioners (except offices of lawyers and attorneys, settlement offices, and title abstract offices). These establishments are primarily engaged in providing specialized legal or paralegal services. . . 1264-1265

541211 **Offices of Certified Public Accountants.** This U.S. industry comprises establishments of accountants that are certified to audit the accounting records of public and private organizations and to attest to compliance with generally accepted accounting practices. Offices of certified public accountants (CPAs) may provide one or more of the following accounting services: (1) auditing financial statements; (2) designing accounting systems; (3) preparing financial statements; (4) developing budgets; and (5) providing advice on matters related to accounting. These establishments may also provide related services, such as bookkeeping, tax return preparation, and payroll processing. 1266-1267

541214 **Payroll Services.** This U.S. industry comprises establishments (except offices of CPAs) engaged in the following without also providing accounting, bookkeeping, or billing services: (1) collecting information on hours worked, pay rates, deductions, and other payroll- related data from their clients and (2) using that information to generate paychecks, payroll reports, and tax filings. These establishments may use data processing and tabulating techniques as part of providing their services. 1268-1269

541219 **Other Accounting Services.** This U.S. industry comprises establishments (except offices of CPAs) engaged in providing accounting services (except tax return preparation services only or payroll services only). These establishments may also provide tax return preparation or payroll services. Accountant (except CPA) offices, bookkeeper offices, and billing offices are included in this industry. 1270-1271

541310 **Architectural Services.** This industry comprises establishments primarily engaged in planning and designing residential, institutional, leisure, commercial, and industrial buildings and structures by applying knowledge of design, construction procedures, zoning regulations, building codes, and building materials. 1272-1273

541320 **Landscape Architectural Services.** This industry comprises establishments primarily engaged in planning and designing the development of land areas for projects, such as parks and other recreational areas; airports; highways; hospitals; schools; land subdivisions; and commercial, industrial, and residential areas, by applying knowledge of land characteristics, location of buildings and structures, use of land areas, and design of landscape projects. 1274-1275

541330 **Engineering Services.** This industry comprises establishments primarily engaged in applying physical laws and principles of engineering in the design, development, and utilization of machines, materials, instruments, structures, processes, and systems. The assignments undertaken by these establishments may involve any of the following activities: provision of advice, preparation of feasibility studies, preparation of preliminary and final plans and designs, provision of technical services during the construction or installation phase, inspection and evaluation of engineering projects, and related services. 1276-1277

541370 **Surveying and Mapping (except Geophysical) Services.** This industry comprises establishments primarily engaged in performing surveying and mapping services of the surface of the earth, including the sea floor. These services may include surveying and mapping of areas above or below the surface of the earth, such as the creation of view easements or segregating rights in parcels of land by creating underground utility easements. 1278-1279

PROFESSIONAL SERVICES

PROFESSIONAL SERVICES

MANAGEMENT OF COMPANIES AND ENTERPRISES

ADMINISTRATIVE AND SUPPORT AND WASTE MANAGEMENT AND REMEDIATION SERVICES

ADMIN & WASTE MANAGEMENT SERVICES

ADMIN & WASTE MANAGEMENT SERVICES

EDUCATION

EDUCATIONAL SERVICES

HEALTH CARE AND SOCIAL ASSISTANCE

HEALTH CARE

HEALTH CARE

ENTERTAINMENT

ARTS, ENTERTAINMENT, AND RECREATION

RESTAURANT/LODGING

ACCOMMODATION AND FOOD SERVICES

OTHER SERVICES (EXCEPT PUBLIC ADMINISTRATION)

OTHER SERVICES

OTHER SERVICES

PUBLIC ADMINISTRATION

NAICS #

813910 **Business Associations.** This industry comprises establishments primarily engaged in promoting the business interests of their members. These establishments may conduct research on new products and services; develop market statistics; sponsor quality and certification standards; lobby public officials; or publish newsletters, books, or periodicals for distribution to their members.. 1622-1623

813920 **Professional Organizations.** This industry comprises establishments primarily engaged in promoting the professional interests of their members and the profession as a whole. These establishments may conduct research; develop statistics; sponsor quality and certi-fication standards; lobby public officials; or publish newsletters, books, or periodicals for distribution to their members.. 1624-1625

813930 **Labor Unions and Similar Labor Organizations.** This industry comprises establishments primarily engaged in promoting the interests of organized labor and union employees. 1626-1627

813990 **Other Similar Organizations (except Business, Professional, Labor, and Political Organizations).** This industry comprises establishments (except religious organizations, social advocacy organizations, civic and social organizations, business associations, professional organizations, labor unions, and political organizations) primarily engaged in promoting the interest of their members. 1628-1629

814110 **Private Households.** This industry comprises private households primarily engaged in employing workers on or about the premises in activities primarily concerned with the operation of the household. These private households may employ individuals, such as cooks, maids, nannies, and butlers, and outside workers, such as gardeners, caretakers, and other maintenance workers. 1630-1631

PUBLIC ADMINISTRATION

921110 **Executive Offices.** This industry comprises government establishments serving as offices of chief executives and their advisory committees and commissions. This industry includes offices of the president, governors, and mayors, in addition to executive advisory commissions. 1634-1635

921120 **Legislative Bodies.** This industry comprises government establishments serving as legislative bodies and their advisory committees and commissions. Included in this industry are legislative bodies, such as Congress, state legislatures, and advisory and study legislative commissions. 1636-1637

921140 **Executive and Legislative Offices, Combined.** This industry comprises government establishments serving as councils and boards of commissioners or supervisors and such bodies where the chief executive (e.g., county executive or city mayor) is a member of the legislative body (e.g., county or city council) itself. 1638-1639

921150 **American Indian and Alaska Native Tribal Governments.** This industry comprises American Indian and Alaska Native governing bodies. Establishments in this industry perform legislative, judicial, and administrative functions for their American Indian and Alaska Native lands. Included in this industry are American Indian and Alaska Native councils, courts, and law enforcement bodies. 1640-1641

921190 **Other General Government Support.** This industry comprises government establishments primarily engaged in providing general support for government. Such support services include personnel services, election boards, and other general government support establishments that are not classified elsewhere in public administration. 1642-1643

922160 **Fire Protection.** This industry comprises government establishments primarily engaged in fire fighting and other related fire protection activities. Government establishments providing combined fire protection and ambulance or rescue services are classified in this industry. ... 1644-1645

923110 **Administration of Education Programs.** This industry comprises government establishments primarily engaged in the central coordination, planning, supervision and administration of funds, policies, intergovernmental activities, statistical reports and data collection, and centralized programs for educational administration. Government scholarship programs are included in this industry. 1646-1647

CONSTRUCTION—PERCENTAGE OF COMPLETION

CONSTRUCTION-% OF COMPLETION

CONSTRUCTION-% OF COMPLETION

AGRICULTURE, FORESTRY, FISHING AND HUNTING

Current Data Sorted by Assets   Comparative Historical Data

0-500M	500M-2MM 6 (4/1-9/30/10)	2-10MM	10-50MM 54 (10/1/10-3/31/11)	50-100MM	100-250MM	Type of Statement	4/1/06-3/31/07 ALL	4/1/07-3/31/08 ALL
		1	2		2	Unqualified	4	6
		3	3			Reviewed	5	8
1	1	3	1			Compiled	4	2
3	7	4	1			Tax Returns	3	5
5	4	8	8	1	2	Other	4	17
9	12	19	15	1	4	NUMBER OF STATEMENTS	20	38
%	%	%	%	%	%	**ASSETS**	%	%
	2.8	9.3	7.8			Cash & Equivalents	11.7	14.0
	3.8	10.9	24.5			Trade Receivables (net)	26.3	16.2
	9.6	14.6	15.1			Inventory	15.8	18.5
	.6	8.2	4.0			All Other Current	2.0	5.9
	16.8	43.0	51.4			Total Current	55.8	54.6
	61.6	50.5	31.0			Fixed Assets (net)	37.1	36.0
	.1	1.4	12.7			Intangibles (net)	1.3	2.4
	21.4	5.1	4.9			All Other Non-Current	5.8	7.0
	100.0	100.0	100.0			Total	100.0	100.0
						LIABILITIES		
	11.4	9.6	6.7			Notes Payable-Short Term	12.3	12.4
	1.5	9.9	3.2			Cur. Mat.-L.T.D.	3.9	2.7
	10.1	9.3	10.6			Trade Payables	12.1	10.1
	.0	.9	.4			Income Taxes Payable	.0	.0
	.6	10.7	9.6			All Other Current	6.0	9.2
	23.6	40.4	30.5			Total Current	34.4	34.4
	29.1	23.9	22.5			Long-Term Debt	26.3	31.9
	.0	.3	2.3			Deferred Taxes	.2	.0
	3.1	2.0	2.5			All Other Non-Current	9.1	5.7
	44.2	33.4	42.2			Net Worth	30.0	27.9
	100.0	100.0	100.0			Total Liabilities & Net Worth	100.0	100.0
						INCOME DATA		
	100.0	100.0	100.0			Net Sales	100.0	100.0
						Gross Profit		
	77.3	89.3	90.2			Operating Expenses	96.3	91.2
	22.7	10.7	9.8			Operating Profit	3.7	8.8
	6.7	1.6	3.4			All Other Expenses (net)	1.9	8.3
	16.0	9.2	6.5			Profit Before Taxes	1.8	.5
						RATIOS		
	2.1	1.6	2.6			Current	3.0	3.0
	1.2	.8	1.6				1.3	1.4
	.6	.5	1.1				1.1	1.0
	1.7	1.0	1.6			Quick	2.9	1.4
	.3	.3	.7				.9	.9
	.1	.1	.5				.5	.2
	0 UND	0 UND	28 13.1			Sales/Receivables	14 25.3	0 UND
	10 35.6	11 33.0	45 8.2				45 8.1	10 36.9
	37 10.0	34 10.6	75 4.9				59 6.2	42 8.7
						Cost of Sales/Inventory		
						Cost of Sales/Payables		
	9.3	8.4	4.2			Sales/Working Capital	5.0	5.8
	19.5	-37.1	8.5				14.7	17.1
	-8.4	-7.9	79.7				101.8	UND
	7.4	10.0	13.4			EBIT/Interest	8.0	5.7
	(10) 3.1	(16) 4.0	7.5				(14) 2.1	(25) 2.4
	1.2	2.2	1.2				.2	.9
						Net Profit + Depr., Dep., Amort./Cur. Mat. L/T/D		
	.9	.6	.3			Fixed/Worth	.5	.1
	1.7	1.3	.9				1.1	.9
	4.1	2.9	59.2				3.6	15.7
	.4	.8	.7			Debt/Worth	.8	.9
	1.6	2.5	2.0				2.6	2.1
	5.6	3.6	137.4				3.6	20.5
	42.6	62.5	41.2			% Profit Before Taxes/Tangible Net Worth	49.1	48.1
	(11) 6.8	(18) 26.4	(12) 32.3				(16) 14.6	(30) 10.4
	-.2	6.9	6.3				-1.2	-1.2
	10.9	11.0	17.9			% Profit Before Taxes/Total Assets	13.1	16.0
	3.2	6.7	11.7				4.0	3.4
	.0	1.8	1.2				-2.3	-1.0
	5.9	13.2	26.1			Sales/Net Fixed Assets	21.7	83.2
	.8	4.4	13.9				7.6	9.3
	.2	1.0	1.2				1.1	.5
	1.6	2.4	2.5			Sales/Total Assets	2.8	3.0
	.3	1.6	1.7				1.9	1.6
	.2	.5	.4				.8	.3
		1.2	1.3			% Depr., Dep., Amort./Sales	.6	.6
		(16) 2.4	(14) 1.8				(18) 2.0	(25) 1.7
		9.6	8.1				6.1	6.5
						% Officers', Directors' Owners' Comp/Sales		1.9
								(12) 4.6
								6.2
8679M	11061M	160240M	439115M	57623M	814847M	Net Sales ($)	404011M	1065309M
2487M	15013M	100802M	279906M	88829M	608288M	Total Assets ($)	393064M	473036M

M = $ thousand   MM = $ million
See Pages 9 through 22 for Explanation of Ratios and Data

Comparative Historical Data | Current Data Sorted by Sales

	4/1/08-3/31/09 ALL	4/1/09-3/31/10 ALL	4/1/10-3/31/11 ALL	Type of Statement	0-1MM	1-3MM	3-5MM	5-10MM	10-25MM	25MM & OVER
	2	10	5	Unqualified	1			1	2	4
	12	2	6	Reviewed						3
	1	8	6	Compiled	1	2	1	2	1	
	4	22	15	Tax Returns	7	4	2	1	2	
	7	25	28	Other	6	5	2	2		6
					6 (4/1-9/30/10)			54 (10/1/10-3/31/11)		
	26	67	60	NUMBER OF STATEMENTS	15	11	5	6	10	13
	%	%	%	**ASSETS**	%	%	%	%	%	%
	13.6	14.5	9.7	Cash & Equivalents	12.4	8.7			9.9	6.9
	24.5	12.0	12.6	Trade Receivables (net)	.9	8.1			18.7	28.6
	12.4	14.5	16.2	Inventory	7.6	17.9			16.2	30.5
	7.6	3.8	4.5	All Other Current	1.6	1.1			6.1	4.6
	58.0	44.7	43.0	Total Current	22.5	35.8			50.8	70.6
	34.8	41.5	43.0	Fixed Assets (net)	67.8	41.3			24.2	19.5
	2.7	6.5	5.5	Intangibles (net)	1.2	8.3			16.7	4.2
	4.5	7.3	8.5	All Other Non-Current	8.5	14.6			8.3	5.7
	100.0	100.0	100.0	Total	100.0	100.0			100.0	100.0
				LIABILITIES						
	4.4	14.2	10.0	Notes Payable-Short Term	8.5	14.2			10.2	7.9
	3.1	4.1	5.2	Cur. Mat.-L.T.D.	6.4	4.4			3.5	2.3
	13.0	7.2	8.7	Trade Payables	.3	12.0			15.5	15.6
	.1	.1	.4	Income Taxes Payable	.0	.2			.4	.1
	10.3	7.0	7.6	All Other Current	.8	6.9			9.4	9.7
	31.0	32.6	32.0	Total Current	16.0	37.7			38.9	35.5
	18.7	37.7	24.7	Long-Term Debt	26.5	28.0			23.3	17.1
	.4	.4	.8	Deferred Taxes	.0	.0			.6	2.9
	7.0	2.5	3.3	All Other Non-Current	.0	1.8			.6	8.1
	42.9	26.8	39.3	Net Worth	57.5	32.5			36.6	36.5
	100.0	100.0	100.0	Total Liabilities & Net Worth	100.0	100.0			100.0	100.0
				INCOME DATA						
	100.0	100.0	100.0	Net Sales	100.0	100.0			100.0	100.0
				Gross Profit						
	95.1	85.9	86.7	Operating Expenses	73.5	89.5			88.1	95.4
	4.9	14.1	13.3	Operating Profit	26.5	10.5			11.9	4.6
	3.2	6.6	3.6	All Other Expenses (net)	8.0	2.0			3.6	1.0
	1.7	7.6	9.7	Profit Before Taxes	18.5	8.5			8.3	3.6
				RATIOS						
	5.2	2.8	2.4	Current	1.8	5.7			1.9	3.0
	1.6	1.5	1.3		1.1	1.1			1.4	1.8
	1.1	.8	.6		.3	.1			1.0	1.3
	2.1	1.6	1.3	Quick	1.3	.8			1.5	2.0
	.9	.9	.6		.3	.5			.8	.7
	.5	.2	.2		.1	.1			.3	.5
	8 46.7	0 UND	0 UND	Sales/Receivables	0 UND	0 UND			1 377.7	40 9.2
	45 8.0	4 96.2	18 20.5		0 UND	0 UND			30 12.4	49 7.5
	63 5.8	37 9.8	48 7.7		26 14.2	42 8.6			55 6.6	65 5.6
				Cost of Sales/Inventory						
				Cost of Sales/Payables						
	3.8	6.8	5.2	Sales/Working Capital	4.9	6.0			7.9	3.2
	10.5	12.3	17.2		46.3	85.2			15.8	6.3
	94.0	-24.9	-10.6		-4.9	-8.2			NM	15.6
	8.8	8.9	10.5	EBIT/Interest		19.8			8.7	16.6
	(20) 4.2	(47) 3.8	(51) 5.5			(10) 5.1			5.8	5.8
	.6	1.2	1.7			.5			2.9	1.5
			7.8	Net Profit + Depr., Dep., Amort./Cur. Mat. L/T/D						
		(13)	3.9							
			1.9							
	.1	.2	.5	Fixed/Worth	.4	.6			.5	.3
	.8	1.2	1.1		1.3	1.3			1.3	.6
	1.4	9.9	2.9		2.6	6.1			NM	1.5
	.6	.6	.7	Debt/Worth	.3	.2			2.2	1.1
	1.2	2.1	1.9		.6	2.7			3.3	2.0
	3.9	29.7	3.8		1.7	6.1			NM	2.6
	35.0	36.5	43.4	% Profit Before Taxes/Tangible Net Worth	28.1					38.5
	(25) 19.1	(51) 12.0	(53) 20.8		(14) 6.9				(12)	15.8
	-2.0	4.3	2.4		.3					7.7
	13.8	14.9	14.8	% Profit Before Taxes/Total Assets	14.3	44.6			22.2	14.2
	7.0	5.2	6.3		2.8	3.2			9.5	6.1
	-2.4	.3	1.2		.4	-3.6			7.1	1.6
	44.8	31.1	17.7	Sales/Net Fixed Assets	.9	37.3			34.4	27.0
	11.0	5.8	5.5		.3	9.9			12.9	17.0
	1.5	1.0	.9		.2	.9			5.1	6.3
	2.5	3.2	2.4	Sales/Total Assets	.4	7.2			2.9	2.6
	2.0	1.8	1.6		.3	2.4			2.0	2.1
	.9	.5	.4		.2	.5			1.3	1.3
	.7	1.1	1.3	% Depr., Dep., Amort./Sales						.9
	(23) 2.3	(54) 4.2	(47) 2.8						(12)	1.7
	8.9	12.5	8.3							2.7
		2.6		% Officers', Directors' Owners' Comp/Sales						
		(21) 5.1								
		11.4								
	685004M	751059M	1491565M	Net Sales ($)	6169M	18856M	19697M	47851M	156393M	1242599M
	596750M	462939M	1095325M	Total Assets ($)	27848M	35256M	19043M	44529M	107330M	861319M

M = $ thousand   MM = $ million
See Pages 9 through 22 for Explanation of Ratios and Data

Current Data Sorted by Assets   Comparative Historical Data

						Type of Statement		
1	2		3	2	4	Unqualified	26	35
	4	6	6		1	Reviewed	21	24
1	2	3	2			Compiled	30	16
7	7		1			Tax Returns	44	19
	6	13	10	5	1	Other	63	70
	16 (4/1-9/30/10)		**77 (10/1/10-3/31/11)**				**4/1/06-3/31/07 ALL**	**4/1/07-3/31/08 ALL**
0-500M	500M-2MM	2-10MM	10-50MM	50-100MM	100-250MM	NUMBER OF STATEMENTS		
9	21	28	22	7	6		184	164
%	%	%	%	%	%	**ASSETS**	%	%
	12.0	8.3	7.4			Cash & Equivalents	13.4	12.3
	11.2	16.9	22.3			Trade Receivables (net)	18.1	20.5
	6.7	13.3	18.1			Inventory	15.7	15.4
	12.7	1.3	3.3			All Other Current	3.2	4.3
	42.6	39.8	51.1			Total Current	50.3	52.6
	48.2	47.4	43.9			Fixed Assets (net)	39.5	35.9
	.0	5.4	1.5			Intangibles (net)	4.3	4.4
	9.1	7.3	3.5			All Other Non-Current	5.9	7.1
	100.0	100.0	100.0			Total	100.0	100.0
						LIABILITIES		
	12.4	20.0	13.7			Notes Payable-Short Term	13.2	15.6
	4.1	2.7	8.1			Cur. Mat.-L.T.D.	3.8	3.7
	9.2	6.3	15.2			Trade Payables	8.9	10.1
	.0	.3	.8			Income Taxes Payable	.3	.5
	18.6	6.0	7.4			All Other Current	11.4	8.6
	44.3	35.2	45.2			Total Current	37.5	38.5
	21.0	22.3	10.8			Long-Term Debt	23.4	25.0
	.0	.4	2.2			Deferred Taxes	.2	.3
	8.7	1.9	7.0			All Other Non-Current	5.4	7.1
	26.0	40.1	34.8			Net Worth	33.4	29.2
	100.0	100.0	100.0			Total Liabilities & Net Worth	100.0	100.0
						INCOME DATA		
	100.0	100.0	100.0			Net Sales	100.0	100.0
						Gross Profit		
	87.1	88.4	91.6			Operating Expenses	88.8	86.5
	12.9	11.6	8.4			Operating Profit	11.2	13.5
	4.8	7.8	.8			All Other Expenses (net)	3.8	4.6
	8.1	3.7	7.6			Profit Before Taxes	7.4	8.9
						RATIOS		
	2.1	2.5	1.8				2.3	2.4
	1.0	1.3	1.1			Current	1.3	1.4
	.2	.7	.9				.9	1.0
	1.3	1.5	1.3				1.8	1.8
	.4	.6	.7			Quick	.8	1.0
	.0	.1	.3				.3	.4
	0 UND	0 UND	8 44.0				1 496.4	0 999.8
	0 UND	28 12.8	38 9.7			Sales/Receivables	23 16.2	28 13.1
	23 16.2	41 9.0	78 4.7				55 6.6	53 6.9
						Cost of Sales/Inventory		
						Cost of Sales/Payables		
	10.4	4.9	6.4				5.7	4.7
	-65.9	20.0	37.8			Sales/Working Capital	18.5	16.8
	-4.5	-7.7	-25.6				-70.7	-114.5
	26.5	11.0	26.4				8.5	7.6
	(17) 5.4	(24) 2.3	(21) 5.1			EBIT/Interest	(146) 3.4	(133) 3.4
	.9	.9	1.4				1.6	1.5
						Net Profit + Depr., Dep.,	6.8	5.9
						Amort./Cur. Mat. L/T/D	(28) 1.9	(25) 2.5
							1.3	.8
	.4	.6	.7				.3	.3
	1.5	1.1	1.3			Fixed/Worth	1.1	1.2
	NM	753.1	2.4				5.2	4.8
	.7	.5	1.0				.7	.8
	2.1	1.1	2.0			Debt/Worth	2.5	2.5
	NM	937.1	6.9				15.1	11.0
	50.6	34.3	47.9			% Profit Before Taxes/Tangible	64.1	53.1
	(16) 15.1	(22) 6.1	(20) 14.0			Net Worth	(150) 23.7	(134) 20.3
	1.4	-.9	1.6				4.2	6.3
	13.8	16.0	14.9			% Profit Before Taxes/Total	15.1	15.8
	5.5	2.1	4.9			Assets	6.5	6.6
	-.2	-.5	.8				.7	2.0
	33.9	25.8	22.3				28.8	31.0
	4.3	2.3	3.7			Sales/Net Fixed Assets	6.5	7.7
	.6	.5	1.1				1.6	2.5
	3.1	3.5	2.5				3.1	3.3
	1.5	1.0	1.1			Sales/Total Assets	1.7	1.7
	.6	.3	.8				.8	.9
	1.0	1.4	.8				.9	.8
	(16) 3.9	(24) 7.7	3.5			% Depr., Dep., Amort./Sales	(145) 2.7	(126) 2.0
	11.6	16.8	7.6				7.1	5.5
						% Officers', Directors'	1.3	.8
						Owners' Comp/Sales	(57) 2.7	(42) 3.1
							5.7	7.0
8170M	52189M	283312M	1184723M	1005887M	1244812M	Net Sales ($)	4999043M	5938124M
2540M	25829M	140812M	493359M	504699M	940238M	Total Assets ($)	3126190M	3618296M

Comparative Historical Data / Current Data Sorted by Sales

	4/1/08-3/31/09 ALL	4/1/09-3/31/10 ALL	4/1/10-3/31/11 ALL	0-1MM	1-3MM	3-5MM	5-10MM	10-25MM	25MM & OVER
Type of Statement				16 (4/1-9/30/10)			77 (10/1/10-3/31/11)		
Unqualified	24	21	12	2	1				9
Reviewed	21	16	17		1	5	1	4	6
Compiled	15	17	8	2	2	1	1	2	
Tax Returns	26	22	21	12	2	4	1	2	1
Other	53	51	35	4	6	4	3	6	12
NUMBER OF STATEMENTS	139	127	93	20	12	14	7	13	27
ASSETS	%	%	%	%	%	%	%	%	%
Cash & Equivalents	12.3	13.8	9.9	7.5	10.7	14.6		9.0	6.7
Trade Receivables (net)	18.0	14.5	15.2	.5	8.6	11.1		25.3	27.0
Inventory	18.3	10.3	13.8	1.0	17.4	7.1		14.7	24.0
All Other Current	3.5	4.8	5.3	4.4	2.7	11.4		9.1	3.3
Total Current	52.0	43.4	44.2	13.4	39.5	44.2		58.0	60.9
Fixed Assets (net)	35.1	46.4	45.3	78.4	49.0	41.7		31.6	30.1
Intangibles (net)	4.7	3.6	3.9	4.4	.0	4.2		6.8	4.8
All Other Non-Current	8.2	6.6	6.5	3.8	11.6	9.9		3.6	4.1
Total	100.0	100.0	100.0	100.0	100.0	100.0		100.0	100.0
LIABILITIES									
Notes Payable-Short Term	13.9	12.9	14.6	9.0	15.7	17.6		15.9	14.0
Cur. Mat.-L.T.D.	2.9	4.0	5.0	8.2	2.2	3.2		3.0	6.3
Trade Payables	11.7	9.3	9.2	1.8	1.2	14.7		11.8	15.0
Income Taxes Payable	.4	.3	.3	.0	.0	.5		.3	.7
All Other Current	8.6	13.2	11.2	14.4	3.6	13.6		15.2	10.9
Total Current	37.5	39.6	40.2	33.4	22.6	49.5		46.2	46.9
Long-Term Debt	21.2	32.6	21.0	42.3	14.2	17.0		11.0	16.6
Deferred Taxes	.4	.4	.7	.0	.0	.8		2.3	.7
All Other Non-Current	5.9	3.8	5.0	2.6	2.3	8.7		5.4	7.3
Net Worth	35.0	23.7	33.1	21.8	60.9	23.9		35.1	28.4
Total Liabilities & Net Worth	100.0	100.0	100.0	100.0	100.0	100.0		100.0	100.0
INCOME DATA									
Net Sales	100.0	100.0	100.0	100.0	100.0	100.0		100.0	100.0
Gross Profit									
Operating Expenses	88.1	89.6	88.3	73.0	91.4	97.8		92.9	92.9
Operating Profit	11.9	10.4	11.7	27.0	8.6	2.2		7.1	7.1
All Other Expenses (net)	3.6	3.5	4.7	13.7	3.3	1.2		.2	1.3
Profit Before Taxes	8.4	6.9	7.0	13.3	5.3	1.0		6.9	5.7
RATIOS									
Current	2.3	2.6	2.0	1.1	5.9	1.9		2.7	2.0
	1.4	1.3	1.1	.3	2.5	1.0		1.3	1.3
	.9	.7	.6	.1	.8	.5		.8	1.1
Quick	1.7	1.9	1.3	1.0	3.8	1.2		2.5	1.5
	.8	.8	.6	.2	.3	.6		.7	.8
	.4	.2	.2	.1	.0	.1		.3	.3
Sales/Receivables	2 152.3	0 UND	0 UND	0 UND	0 UND	0 UND		29 12.5	19 18.8
	28 13.0	19 19.2	15 23.9	0 UND	0 UND	7 55.1		42 8.7	50 7.3
	47 7.8	44 8.4	53 6.8	2 155.0	56 6.5	34 10.6		63 5.8	66 5.5
Cost of Sales/Inventory									
Cost of Sales/Payables									
Sales/Working Capital	5.4	4.9	6.4	NM	1.8	12.1		4.7	6.9
	16.2	16.5	35.8	-5.1	16.0	NM		21.0	18.8
	-67.8	-16.2	-8.2	-.7	-21.9	-6.9		-28.0	56.2
EBIT/Interest	16.0	9.8	15.2	16.4	3.2	20.8		33.1	10.5
	(111) 4.0	(109) 2.6	(80) 3.7	(11) 2.8	(10) 2.2	2.5	(12) 6.5	4.2	
	1.4	.5	1.2	.9	1.3	-.1		3.0	2.1
Net Profit + Depr., Dep., Amort./Cur. Mat. L/T/D	8.6	2.3	13.4						
	(22) 3.2	(18) 1.5	(11) 1.9						
	1.6	1.0	.8						
Fixed/Worth	.2	.4	.6	1.1	.4	.8		.4	.4
	.8	1.2	1.3	3.5	.7	2.3		1.5	.9
	2.3	5.4	7.3	-75.3	1.4	-3.5		NM	2.8
Debt/Worth	.7	.6	.6	.6	.2	.9		.8	1.1
	1.9	2.0	2.1	3.9	.5	3.2		2.0	3.7
	6.7	15.2	31.6	-8.0	1.4	-19.6		NM	9.0
% Profit Before Taxes/Tangible Net Worth	48.5	32.3	37.8	18.6	22.2	364.4		68.2	51.7
	(118) 16.6	(101) 8.7	(74) 13.3	(13) 8.6	3.8	(10) 19.6	(10) 16.8	(23) 27.5	
	4.1	-1.1	1.0	.2	-.7	-1.1		.8	4.7
% Profit Before Taxes/Total Assets	15.4	12.0	13.6	5.7	4.2	12.2		21.0	19.5
	5.6	2.3	4.2	3.1	1.5	1.9		9.3	5.7
	1.0	-.7	.0	-.4	-.6	-1.4		1.7	1.6
Sales/Net Fixed Assets	48.0	20.8	23.1	1.4	4.3	61.4		68.7	48.6
	7.6	3.7	3.6	.3	1.7	6.7		23.2	11.0
	2.3	.8	.7	.1	.7	.7		1.3	3.6
Sales/Total Assets	3.1	2.7	3.0	1.0	1.4	3.4		4.0	3.7
	2.0	1.4	1.3	.2	1.0	1.9		1.2	2.5
	.8	.5	.5	.1	.5	.6		.9	1.2
% Depr., Dep., Amort./Sales	.8	1.9	1.0	6.0		.5		.6	.5
	(109) 2.5	(99) 5.1	(75) 4.0	(15) 16.9		(12) 3.8	(11) 2.7	(22) 1.3	
	6.3	12.1	13.7	22.2		11.9		6.5	3.6
% Officers', Directors' Owners' Comp/Sales	1.3	1.6	1.1						
	(29) 3.3	(37) 3.9	(25) 3.4						
	5.5	7.1	6.3						
Net Sales ($)	8189597M	3637165M	3779093M	8700M	19959M	56324M	50987M	184655M	3458468M
Total Assets ($)	3930356M	1792627M	2107477M	33682M	32953M	54376M	103055M	164378M	1719033M

M = $ thousand   MM = $ million
See Pages 9 through 22 for Explanation of Ratios and Data

AGRICULTURE—Corn Farming NAICS 111150

Current Data Sorted by Assets							Comparative Historical Data	
	1	1	2	1		Unqualified	7	8
	1	3	2	1		Reviewed	9	7
1		6	2			Compiled	9	6
6	11	11	3			Tax Returns	19	22
	2	12	1	2	1	Other	11	7
	6 (4/1-9/30/10)		64 (10/1/10-3/31/11)				4/1/06-3/31/07	4/1/07-3/31/08
0-500M	500M-2MM	2-10MM	10-50MM	50-100MM	100-250MM	Type of Statement	ALL	ALL
7	15	33	10	4	1	**NUMBER OF STATEMENTS**	55	50
%	%	%	%	%	%	**ASSETS**	%	%
	11.0	6.3	6.4			Cash & Equivalents	5.4	4.9
	2.0	8.7	7.4			Trade Receivables (net)	9.2	7.0
	14.9	21.5	22.4			Inventory	18.6	16.8
	3.3	4.2	8.5			All Other Current	8.1	6.4
	31.3	40.7	44.7			Total Current	41.2	35.1
	57.6	51.9	45.8			Fixed Assets (net)	52.1	54.0
	.0	.7	.0			Intangibles (net)	.1	2.0
	11.2	6.6	9.4			All Other Non-Current	6.5	9.0
	100.0	100.0	100.0			Total	100.0	100.0
						LIABILITIES		
	49.0	18.6	14.1			Notes Payable-Short Term	26.5	17.3
	.6	7.6	3.1			Cur. Mat.-L.T.D.	3.7	6.4
	2.2	3.7	10.8			Trade Payables	5.7	4.7
	.0	.0	.0			Income Taxes Payable	.6	.1
	.5	5.0	4.0			All Other Current	6.3	8.6
	52.2	34.7	32.0			Total Current	42.9	37.1
	30.6	21.6	20.5			Long-Term Debt	28.2	29.0
	.0	.6	1.8			Deferred Taxes	.4	.4
	4.6	1.2	6.4			All Other Non-Current	1.6	2.5
	12.5	41.8	39.3			Net Worth	26.9	31.0
	100.0	100.0	100.0			Total Liabilties & Net Worth	100.0	100.0
						INCOME DATA		
	100.0	100.0	100.0			Net Sales	100.0	100.0
						Gross Profit		
	93.2	89.3	86.0			Operating Expenses	88.5	93.4
	6.8	10.7	14.0			Operating Profit	11.5	6.6
	4.5	3.4	6.4			All Other Expenses (net)	5.8	2.3
	2.2	7.3	7.6			Profit Before Taxes	5.7	4.3
						RATIOS		
	1.6	2.7	2.1			Current	1.8	2.0
	.3	1.7	1.4				1.1	1.1
	.1	.6	.7				.3	.6
	.7	1.3	.7			Quick	.7	.6
	.0	.2	.3				.2	.2
	.0	.1	.0				.1	.1
0 UND	0 UND	0 UND				Sales/Receivables	0 UND	0 UND
0 UND	1 468.3	16 22.9					0 UND	0 UND
0 UND	38 9.7	58 6.3					41 8.9	19 18.7
						Cost of Sales/Inventory		
						Cost of Sales/Payables		
	3.6	1.9	4.1			Sales/Working Capital	4.6	4.6
	-3.7	5.0	14.9				13.2	20.9
	-2.2	-8.3	-5.8				-4.4	-9.3
	13.3	13.1				EBIT/Interest	5.4	4.2
	(14) 2.5	(29) 5.0					(47) 1.9	(46) 2.2
	-.2	1.3					.6	1.1
						Net Profit + Depr., Dep., Amort./Cur. Mat. L/T/D		
	.6	.6	.3			Fixed/Worth	.5	.8
	4.7	1.0	1.1				1.4	1.3
	-5.3	4.9	3.1				5.5	NM
	.9	.3	.6			Debt/Worth	.6	.6
	6.8	1.0	1.5				2.3	1.9
	-6.8	5.2	4.6				15.0	NM
		29.2				% Profit Before Taxes/Tangible Net Worth	30.2	24.2
		(29) 11.5					(43) 8.0	(38) 8.8
		1.4					.2	3.0
	19.6	10.8	11.9			% Profit Before Taxes/Total Assets	8.8	9.9
	4.8	5.5	1.6				1.8	4.4
	-4.8	.6	.1				-1.3	.4
	6.6	3.3	10.1			Sales/Net Fixed Assets	13.3	6.1
	1.2	1.1	2.0				2.0	1.9
	.8	.5	.1				.5	.5
	1.9	1.1	1.8			Sales/Total Assets	1.8	2.3
	.9	.6	.8				.8	.9
	.6	.3	.1				.3	.4
	5.0	2.8	1.3			% Depr., Dep., Amort./Sales	2.8	2.1
	(12) 14.4	(28) 9.7	4.6				(44) 6.4	(47) 5.6
	28.0	17.4	9.7				13.3	11.7
						% Officers', Directors' Owners' Comp/Sales	2.2	1.5
							(11) 3.0	(13) 4.1
							27.8	6.5
7070M	18100M	119304M	211561M	196076M	80950M	Net Sales ($)	325337M	764427M
1650M	16492M	143430M	170019M	274951M	150814M	Total Assets ($)	357582M	657420M

M = $ thousand   MM = $ million
See Pages 9 through 22 for Explanation of Ratios and Data

Comparative Historical Data

Current Data Sorted by Sales

			Type of Statement						
4	4	5	Unqualified	2				1	2
11	7	7	Reviewed		2		2	1	2
11	8	9	Compiled		5	1	2	1	
29	27	31	Tax Returns	13	14	1	2		1
16	15	18	Other	3	7	3		2	3
4/1/08-3/31/09 ALL	4/1/09-3/31/10 ALL	4/1/10-3/31/11 ALL		6 (4/1-9/30/10)			64 (10/1/10-3/31/11)		
				0-1MM	1-3MM	3-5MM	5-10MM	10-25MM	25MM & OVER
71	61	70	NUMBER OF STATEMENTS	18	28	5	6	5	8
%	%	%	ASSETS	%	%	%	%	%	%
7.1	8.9	8.6	Cash & Equivalents	7.5	9.8				
10.7	7.0	5.9	Trade Receivables (net)	1.9	2.9				
16.7	15.8	18.8	Inventory	6.9	13.4				
4.1	5.2	4.9	All Other Current	3.1	3.2				
38.6	37.0	38.2	Total Current	19.3	29.4				
52.3	51.1	51.6	Fixed Assets (net)	72.0	60.5				
1.9	1.2	1.9	Intangibles (net)	.0	1.5				
7.2	10.7	8.2	All Other Non-Current	8.6	8.7				
100.0	100.0	100.0	Total	100.0	100.0				
			LIABILITIES						
21.5	21.7	28.5	Notes Payable-Short Term	13.4	39.3				
7.3	4.3	5.5	Cur. Mat.-L.T.D.	4.1	2.7				
3.8	4.5	3.9	Trade Payables	2.2	.4				
.0	.1	.0	Income Taxes Payable	.0	.0				
9.5	4.4	4.3	All Other Current	3.1	3.2				
42.0	34.9	42.3	Total Current	22.9	45.6				
32.9	26.6	29.3	Long-Term Debt	37.8	35.9				
.2	.6	.6	Deferred Taxes	.0	.0				
3.3	2.7	2.6	All Other Non-Current	3.9	3.8				
21.7	35.2	25.2	Net Worth	35.4	14.8				
100.0	100.0	100.0	Total Liabilties & Net Worth	100.0	100.0				
			INCOME DATA						
100.0	100.0	100.0	Net Sales	100.0	100.0				
			Gross Profit						
85.0	88.7	89.2	Operating Expenses	88.6	88.4				
15.0	11.3	10.8	Operating Profit	11.4	11.6				
3.4	5.0	3.9	All Other Expenses (net)	5.1	4.5				
11.6	6.3	6.9	Profit Before Taxes	6.3	7.1				
			RATIOS						
1.7	1.8	2.2		4.1	2.6				
1.2	1.1	1.3	Current	1.2	1.0				
.3	.4	.4		.1	.3				
1.1	.8	.9		2.4	.6				
.3	.3	.2	Quick	.3	.2				
.1	.0	.0		.0	.0				
0 UND	0 UND	0 UND		0 UND	0 UND				
2 217.9	0 UND	0 UND	Sales/Receivables	0 UND	0 UND				
40 9.1	31 11.9	28 12.8		0 UND	10 36.0				
			Cost of Sales/Inventory						
			Cost of Sales/Payables						
4.2	5.6	3.3		2.6	2.4				
25.7	20.6	8.9	Sales/Working Capital	87.5	NM				
-7.2	-4.0	-3.6		-3.3	-2.4				
7.3	7.0	9.4		8.9	9.2				
(66) 3.1	(54) 2.9	(62) 3.8	EBIT/Interest	(14) 3.5	(25) 2.3				
1.3	1.0	.9		-.2	.6				
			Net Profit + Depr., Dep., Amort./Cur. Mat. L/T/D						
.8	.6	.6		.9	.7				
1.8	1.3	1.2	Fixed/Worth	1.6	1.3				
90.5	3.4	23.6		8.9	-5.6				
1.0	.6	.5		.3	.3				
2.3	1.7	1.9	Debt/Worth	2.8	2.8				
-739.0	5.6	289.4		7.9	-7.6				
50.7	26.8	30.9		38.3	24.1				
(53) 18.7	(52) 11.2	(54) 12.2	% Profit Before Taxes/Tangible Net Worth	(16) 5.3	(18) 6.1				
3.5	.8	1.5		.0	1.5				
15.4	10.8	11.6		7.2	9.9				
5.2	4.1	5.2	% Profit Before Taxes/Total Assets	4.4	1.8				
.6	.1	.1		-1.2	-2.0				
7.1	6.6	8.8		2.1	3.4				
2.1	1.9	1.7	Sales/Net Fixed Assets	.5	1.1				
.5	.4	.6		.2	.5				
2.7	2.2	1.7		.8	1.9				
.9	.8	.7	Sales/Total Assets	.5	.6				
.4	.3	.5		.1	.3				
1.6	2.7	3.6		7.0	6.1				
(58) 6.6	(54) 6.8	(59) 7.7	% Depr., Dep., Amort./Sales	(16) 18.6	(23) 10.6				
15.0	16.4	17.6		26.4	17.6				
2.2	.7	.3			.2				
(20) 3.6	(16) 2.1	(16) 1.5	% Officers', Directors' Owners' Comp/Sales		(10) 1.1				
5.0	3.7	3.7			2.9				
768872M	694681M	633061M	Net Sales ($)	10525M	49887M	21434M	44078M	65591M	441546M
820588M	580585M	757356M	Total Assets ($)	48257M	110962M	22708M	28389M	54100M	492940M

© RMA 2011   M = $ thousand   MM = $ million
See Pages 9 through 22 for Explanation of Ratios and Data

Current Data Sorted by Assets   Comparative Historical Data

Type of Statement	0-500M	500M-2MM	2-10MM	10-50MM	50-100MM	100-250MM		4/1/06-3/31/07 ALL	4/1/07-3/31/08 ALL
Unqualified		1	3	3	1	2		9	10
Reviewed		1	3	4				3	11
Compiled	1	2	11	5				22	12
Tax Returns	7	12	12	5				25	25
Other	1	14	14	6	1	1		25	24
		19 (4/1-9/30/10)		91 (10/1/10-3/31/11)					
NUMBER OF STATEMENTS	9	30	43	23	2	3		84	82
ASSETS	%	%	%	%	%	%		%	%
Cash & Equivalents		8.4	6.6	2.1				6.6	7.6
Trade Receivables (net)		9.7	14.4	8.6				7.3	7.6
Inventory		19.7	21.7	19.7				17.2	17.5
All Other Current		3.4	5.0	5.8				8.6	9.8
Total Current		41.2	47.6	36.2				39.7	42.6
Fixed Assets (net)		49.3	45.6	57.1				48.1	41.6
Intangibles (net)		3.1	.2	1.5				1.1	1.1
All Other Non-Current		6.4	6.6	5.2				11.1	14.7
Total		100.0	100.0	100.0				100.0	100.0
LIABILITIES									
Notes Payable-Short Term		16.9	21.9	14.2				35.4	31.4
Cur. Mat.-L.T.D.		3.7	3.5	2.5				2.1	8.4
Trade Payables		5.5	8.9	6.0				5.9	7.1
Income Taxes Payable		.2	.1	.4				.2	.3
All Other Current		2.0	5.3	4.3				9.0	7.1
Total Current		28.3	39.7	27.3				52.5	54.3
Long-Term Debt		25.3	26.4	27.7				22.1	26.3
Deferred Taxes		.3	.4	.2				.1	.1
All Other Non-Current		5.6	1.5	3.4				3.2	4.1
Net Worth		40.5	32.0	41.3				22.0	15.2
Total Liabilties & Net Worth		100.0	100.0	100.0				100.0	100.0
INCOME DATA									
Net Sales		100.0	100.0	100.0				100.0	100.0
Gross Profit									
Operating Expenses		90.0	88.1	88.8				88.3	86.6
Operating Profit		10.0	11.9	11.2				11.7	13.4
All Other Expenses (net)		3.8	3.2	7.3				3.2	3.8
Profit Before Taxes		6.1	8.7	3.9				8.5	9.6
RATIOS									
Current		2.8	2.2	1.9				1.4	2.1
		1.8	1.2	1.3				1.0	1.1
		1.1	1.0	1.1				.7	.4
Quick		2.4	.8	.6				.7	.9
		.8	.3	.3				.2	.3
		.1	.1	.1				.1	.1
Sales/Receivables	0 UND	0 UND	0 UND				0 UND	0 UND	
	0 UND	8 46.9	12 31.1				0 UND	1 598.5	
	20 18.7	49 7.5	57 6.4				23 16.2	19 18.9	
Cost of Sales/Inventory									
Cost of Sales/Payables									
Sales/Working Capital		3.3	2.1	4.2				9.4	4.0
		15.6	18.3	10.2				-321.1	34.8
		56.8	-105.4	31.7				-5.9	-5.0
EBIT/Interest		16.0	7.1	7.5				5.4	5.4
	(23)	4.8	(41) 3.3	(18) 3.9			(73)	2.3	(71) 2.7
		1.6	1.4	2.1				.4	1.4
Net Profit + Depr., Dep., Amort./Cur. Mat. L/T/D									
Fixed/Worth		.7	.7	.7				.7	.5
		1.0	1.2	1.2				1.3	1.0
		2.3	3.6	2.4				2.6	11.7
Debt/Worth		.4	.9	.5				.7	.8
		1.6	1.5	1.7				2.1	3.0
		6.7	6.9	3.6				13.1	128.6
% Profit Before Taxes/Tangible Net Worth		74.9	37.1	21.2				31.6	37.5
	(25)	24.6	(38) 19.2	(21) 7.0			(70)	10.4	(64) 15.4
		3.3	3.3	3.6				.0	2.4
% Profit Before Taxes/Total Assets		22.2	10.9	4.5				9.1	15.3
		7.0	5.0	2.7				4.3	4.7
		1.8	1.6	.6				-1.1	.8
Sales/Net Fixed Assets		11.4	10.4	4.0				12.1	17.4
		3.5	2.0	1.1				2.5	3.9
		.8	.7	.2				.7	1.0
Sales/Total Assets		2.9	1.6	1.5				2.4	2.6
		1.1	.7	.6				1.1	1.3
		.6	.4	.2				.4	.6
% Depr., Dep., Amort./Sales		3.1	1.3	2.9				1.5	1.6
	(20)	8.4	(36) 6.4	6.9			(64)	6.2	(61) 5.0
		18.2	13.1	11.3				9.8	9.8
% Officers', Directors' Owners' Comp/Sales		1.4	.8					1.6	1.7
	(10)	3.0	(10) 2.9				(17)	4.2	(20) 3.8
		5.3	6.0					8.8	6.1
Net Sales ($)	4906M	60231M	297157M	672885M	204317M	425067M		1001840M	1283224M
Total Assets ($)	2423M	33400M	198198M	515593M	167124M	378404M		595848M	792676M

M = $ thousand   MM = $ million
See Pages 9 through 22 for Explanation of Ratios and Data

Comparative Historical Data   Current Data Sorted by Sales

			Type of Statement						
11	17	10	Unqualified				1	2	7
11	12	8	Reviewed		1	1	2	2	2
21	19	19	Compiled		8	5	2	2	1
36	35	36	Tax Returns	1	15	3	1	2	
19	23	37	Other	15	10	9	3	5	2
4/1/08-3/31/09	4/1/09-3/31/10	4/1/10-3/31/11		8					
ALL	ALL	ALL		19 (4/1-9/30/10)			91 (10/1/10-3/31/11)		
				0-1MM	1-3MM	3-5MM	5-10MM	10-25MM	25MM & OVER
98	106	110	NUMBER OF STATEMENTS	24	34	18	9	13	12
%	%	%	ASSETS	%	%	%	%	%	%
5.7	9.9	7.0	Cash & Equivalents	5.6	8.6	2.4		9.5	8.5
9.9	11.1	11.0	Trade Receivables (net)	5.7	1.8	18.2		23.4	18.7
16.4	19.1	19.7	Inventory	12.1	17.6	27.2		21.8	28.5
8.2	3.8	5.3	All Other Current	2.6	6.5	3.6		5.8	11.5
40.2	43.9	43.0	Total Current	26.0	34.6	51.4		60.5	67.2
47.2	43.8	49.0	Fixed Assets (net)	67.2	56.0	35.4		34.7	30.2
.6	1.2	1.3	Intangibles (net)	.1	1.6	2.8		.5	.3
12.0	11.0	6.8	All Other Non-Current	6.7	7.8	10.4		4.3	2.2
100.0	100.0	100.0	Total	100.0	100.0	100.0		100.0	100.0
			LIABILITIES						
24.2	21.1	18.3	Notes Payable-Short Term	16.7	16.7	32.4		9.6	16.8
11.0	8.6	3.8	Cur. Mat.-L.T.D.	5.9	4.0	2.5		3.4	2.3
5.4	6.7	6.9	Trade Payables	.5	1.5	8.9		19.4	17.8
.2	.2	.2	Income Taxes Payable	.0	.3	.0		.5	.2
8.6	8.0	4.5	All Other Current	.8	1.7	6.4		7.4	12.5
49.4	44.5	33.6	Total Current	23.9	24.2	50.2		40.3	49.6
26.8	24.9	26.0	Long-Term Debt	20.8	36.0	22.9		20.7	16.8
.2	.3	.3	Deferred Taxes	.0	.2	.0		1.2	.6
3.8	1.8	9.5	All Other Non-Current	25.7	9.1	1.6		.1	1.3
19.7	28.5	30.7	Net Worth	29.6	30.5	25.3		37.6	31.8
100.0	100.0	100.0	Total Liabilties & Net Worth	100.0	100.0	100.0		100.0	100.0
			INCOME DATA						
100.0	100.0	100.0	Net Sales	100.0	100.0	100.0		100.0	100.0
			Gross Profit						
88.0	90.7	88.4	Operating Expenses	86.5	85.2	88.7		92.3	95.0
12.0	9.3	11.6	Operating Profit	13.5	14.8	11.3		7.7	5.0
3.2	1.9	4.3	All Other Expenses (net)	8.5	4.7	2.1		1.1	-.1
8.8	7.4	7.3	Profit Before Taxes	5.0	10.1	9.2		6.6	5.1
			RATIOS						
1.6	1.8	2.3		3.9	2.3	1.7		2.2	1.6
1.1	1.2	1.4	Current	1.3	2.0	1.3		1.5	1.3
.3	.8	1.0		.2	1.0	.9		1.1	1.1
.6	1.0	1.0		2.7	1.4	1.0		1.9	.9
(96) .2	.4	.4	Quick	.3	.3	.1		.6	.4
.0	.1	.1		.1	.1	.1		.3	.2
0 UND	0 UND	0 UND		0 UND	0 UND	1 323.6	10 36.1	7 49.4
2 218.7	9 40.2	5 80.6	Sales/Receivables	0 UND	0 UND	26 14.2	26 14.0	14 25.7
27 13.7	35 10.4	36 10.1		15 23.9	0 UND	46 8.0	53 6.9	31 11.8
			Cost of Sales/Inventory						
			Cost of Sales/Payables						
6.6	4.3	3.4		1.2	1.9	6.0		7.9	7.8
62.3	20.4	13.7	Sales/Working Capital	5.7	10.7	20.8		10.2	19.2
-4.2	-28.6	288.1		-4.7	NM	-7.9		75.7	30.8
5.7	7.1	8.6		10.5	11.2	6.7		7.8	13.2
(92) 3.0	(95) 2.8	(93) 4.4	EBIT/Interest	(16) 2.1	(30) 5.5	(17) 3.5	(12) 4.0	(11) 7.0
1.1	1.3	1.6		.4	1.3	2.1		2.7	2.3
	6.3	7.2	Net Profit + Depr., Dep.,						
	(13) 3.9	(15) 3.4	Amort./Cur. Mat. L/T/D						
	2.2	1.9							
.7	.6	.7		.8	.8	.6		.4	.4
1.5	1.1	1.2	Fixed/Worth	1.2	1.2	1.1		.9	1.0
13.1	3.1	2.8		NM	3.9	7.3		2.1	1.7
1.1	.8	.6		.2	.5	.9		.9	1.8
2.9	2.0	1.8	Debt/Worth	1.0	1.4	3.2		2.0	2.5
87.4	7.5	6.2		NM	7.1	204.2		3.9	3.3
58.6	34.2	43.6		6.0	32.3	83.5		29.8	44.1
(78) 22.1	(89) 12.9	(94) 15.9	% Profit Before Taxes/Tangible Net Worth	(18) 1.8	(28) 12.8	(15) 60.8		17.1	32.8
6.1	2.4	3.4		-1.4	2.5	9.1		10.5	14.3
12.0	13.7	11.1		4.2	12.2	19.3		11.2	14.9
5.7	4.6	4.4	% Profit Before Taxes/Total Assets	1.7	5.1	5.0		5.3	10.8
.5	.9	1.4		-1.6	.5	2.2		3.2	3.2
11.7	13.0	9.2		1.5	3.9	9.9		43.8	16.8
3.1	3.1	2.0	Sales/Net Fixed Assets	.7	1.1	3.0		5.5	9.5
.7	.8	.7		.2	.6	1.0		1.9	4.3
2.4	2.7	2.2		.9	1.7	2.2		4.8	4.4
1.2	1.2	.9	Sales/Total Assets	.5	.6	1.0		2.9	2.4
.6	.5	.4		.2	.4	.4		.7	1.2
2.2	1.3	2.4		6.4	7.2	.4		1.0	.4
(83) 6.7	(89) 4.2	(90) 6.9	% Depr., Dep., Amort./Sales	(19) 13.2	(27) 9.9	(12) 4.2	(11) 2.0	1.2
14.4	13.0	13.1		36.6	23.1	10.5		6.8	2.8
1.1	1.4	1.0	% Officers', Directors' Owners' Comp/Sales	.9					
(31) 1.6	(37) 3.7	(27) 2.7		(14) 3.3					
3.1	5.8	4.3		4.7					
4659895M	4342060M	1664563M	Net Sales ($)	10241M	65743M	72140M	62539M	250365M	1203535M
1245167M	2187837M	1295142M	Total Assets ($)	47838M	143760M	92744M	115785M	219424M	675591M

© RMA 2011   M = $ thousand   MM = $ million
See Pages 9 through 22 for Explanation of Ratios and Data

Current Data Sorted by Assets   Comparative Historical Data

0-500M	500M-2MM	2-10MM	10-50MM	50-100MM	100-250MM	Type of Statement	4/1/06-3/31/07 ALL	4/1/07-3/31/08 ALL
		1	4	1	1	Unqualified	8	6
	2	5	9	2	1	Reviewed	7	14
	7	6	11	1	1	Compiled	20	15
4			1			Tax Returns	8	7
1	1	4	5	3	1	Other	23	19
	12 (4/1-9/30/10)		60 (10/1/10-3/31/11)					
5	10	16	30	7	4	**NUMBER OF STATEMENTS**	66	61
%	%	%	%	%	%	**ASSETS**	%	%
	11.1	9.8	2.6			Cash & Equivalents	6.4	9.4
	8.5	21.9	11.5			Trade Receivables (net)	10.5	12.7
	11.8	4.8	21.9			Inventory	15.5	13.2
	.9	10.1	6.6			All Other Current	4.3	4.7
	32.4	46.6	42.6			Total Current	36.7	40.0
	55.4	43.5	48.4			Fixed Assets (net)	47.3	40.0
	5.6	.0	1.6			Intangibles (net)	3.4	3.8
	6.6	9.9	7.5			All Other Non-Current	12.7	16.1
	100.0	100.0	100.0			Total	100.0	100.0
						LIABILITIES		
	40.5	10.2	16.9			Notes Payable-Short Term	18.9	16.2
	4.0	2.1	3.8			Cur. Mat.-L.T.D.	10.5	9.7
	.7	11.9	4.6			Trade Payables	4.3	7.0
	.3	.3	2.2			Income Taxes Payable	1.0	.3
	.7	10.3	4.0			All Other Current	5.9	7.2
	46.1	34.8	31.6			Total Current	40.5	40.4
	32.3	25.3	23.1			Long-Term Debt	36.0	27.8
	1.4	.0	.3			Deferred Taxes	.2	.5
	.3	2.2	1.3			All Other Non-Current	4.7	5.1
	19.8	37.6	43.7			Net Worth	18.7	26.2
	100.0	100.0	100.0			Total Liabilities & Net Worth	100.0	100.0
						INCOME DATA		
	100.0	100.0	100.0			Net Sales	100.0	100.0
						Gross Profit		
	95.7	91.9	87.2			Operating Expenses	87.7	86.1
	4.3	8.1	12.8			Operating Profit	12.3	13.9
	-1.4	.6	2.7			All Other Expenses (net)	2.5	4.3
	5.7	7.4	10.1			Profit Before Taxes	9.8	9.6
						RATIOS		
	6.9	2.5	2.1				1.7	2.9
	1.3	1.2	1.4			Current	1.1	1.2
	.2	.6	.9				.5	.9
	3.7	1.6	.7				.8	1.8
	.8	.5	.3			Quick	.3	.7
	.0	.3	.2				.1	.1
0 UND	0 UND	0 UND	0 UND				0 UND	0 UND
0 UND	0 UND	48 7.6	30 12.1			Sales/Receivables	16 23.0	23 16.1
29 12.8	29 12.8	58 6.3	69 5.3				60 6.1	49 7.4
						Cost of Sales/Inventory		
						Cost of Sales/Payables		
	2.2	4.7	2.8				4.2	4.6
	30.4	24.4	5.7			Sales/Working Capital	61.1	16.1
	-4.1	-17.7	-18.3				-5.9	-12.9
		7.2	8.8				7.9	10.7
	(14)	1.5	(28) 4.7			EBIT/Interest	(55) 3.1	(50) 2.1
		.7	1.6				1.6	1.3
							5.8	2.9
						Net Profit + Depr., Dep., Amort./Cur. Mat. L/T/D	(11) 3.3	(10) 1.5
							1.3	-.4
	.7	.4	.6				.8	.3
	7.2	.8	1.1			Fixed/Worth	1.5	1.2
	NM	2.2	2.0				9.8	5.2
	.3	.9	.9				.9	.4
	9.3	1.7	1.3			Debt/Worth	2.0	1.8
	NM	5.0	2.0				21.2	18.7
		21.4	25.4				36.3	36.8
		4.3	(29) 15.2			% Profit Before Taxes/Tangible Net Worth	(52) 17.0	(52) 10.0
		-1.8	3.6				6.7	5.3
	20.3	10.3	10.7				13.7	9.0
	6.1	.9	6.9			% Profit Before Taxes/Total Assets	5.9	4.5
	1.1	-.8	1.4				1.2	1.4
	12.9	18.5	3.4				5.2	7.9
	3.3	2.6	1.8			Sales/Net Fixed Assets	2.7	2.9
	1.3	1.3	.7				1.2	1.1
	3.1	3.0	1.0				1.8	1.8
	2.0	1.4	.6			Sales/Total Assets	1.1	1.0
	.9	.8	.4				.5	.5
		.5	4.2				3.5	2.7
	(13)	4.6	5.9			% Depr., Dep., Amort./Sales	(53) 5.2	(51) 5.0
		9.3	9.3				7.7	7.9
			.6				1.4	
		(10)	1.5			% Officers', Directors' Owners' Comp/Sales	(16) 3.2	
			3.6				6.4	
7534M	19558M	178383M	937917M	231966M	229625M	Net Sales ($)	1349823M	1487510M
1778M	11620M	98492M	754210M	422564M	631406M	Total Assets ($)	1263850M	1264892M

M = $ thousand   MM = $ million
See Pages 9 through 22 for Explanation of Ratios and Data

Comparative Historical Data | | | Current Data Sorted by Sales

			Type of Statement						
6	8	7	Unqualified			1	1		5
19	13	17	Reviewed			1	3	8	5
23	12	21	Compiled	2	2	1	3	9	4
6	23	12	Tax Returns	2	7		1		
16	15	15	Other	2		2	1	7	3
4/1/08-	4/1/09-	4/1/10-			12 (4/1-9/30/10)		60 (10/1/10-3/31/11)		
3/31/09	3/31/10	3/31/11							
ALL	ALL	ALL		0-1MM	1-3MM	3-5MM	5-10MM	10-25MM	25MM & OVER
70	71	72	NUMBER OF STATEMENTS	6	9	7	9	24	17
%	%	%	ASSETS	%	%	%	%	%	%
5.5	8.1	6.2	Cash & Equivalents					3.7	2.1
11.9	11.3	11.9	Trade Receivables (net)					14.1	18.8
17.8	13.3	15.5	Inventory					16.7	21.7
5.3	5.9	6.4	All Other Current					11.4	6.9
40.5	38.7	40.0	Total Current					45.9	49.6
44.4	48.6	48.3	Fixed Assets (net)					44.4	33.5
3.8	2.1	1.9	Intangibles (net)					1.7	2.1
11.4	10.6	9.8	All Other Non-Current					8.1	14.9
100.0	100.0	100.0	Total					100.0	100.0
			LIABILITIES						
17.4	21.4	20.2	Notes Payable-Short Term					17.2	13.7
6.2	6.5	3.6	Cur. Mat.-L.T.D.					2.4	3.2
4.3	5.8	5.8	Trade Payables					5.1	11.4
.6	.4	1.0	Income Taxes Payable					2.3	.6
8.9	6.1	5.0	All Other Current					5.3	6.5
37.4	40.2	35.6	Total Current					32.2	35.4
26.9	31.6	29.7	Long-Term Debt					20.7	21.3
.5	.3	.5	Deferred Taxes					.1	.9
3.6	3.2	1.6	All Other Non-Current					1.3	2.7
31.7	24.7	32.7	Net Worth					45.7	39.7
100.0	100.0	100.0	Total Liabilities & Net Worth					100.0	100.0
			INCOME DATA						
100.0	100.0	100.0	Net Sales					100.0	100.0
			Gross Profit						
86.1	90.9	90.4	Operating Expenses					92.1	91.2
13.9	9.1	9.6	Operating Profit					7.9	8.8
3.7	2.4	1.3	All Other Expenses (net)					.6	-.7
10.2	6.6	8.3	Profit Before Taxes					7.3	9.5
			RATIOS						
2.4	2.3	2.2						2.1	1.8
1.2	1.2	1.3	Current					1.6	1.3
.6	.7	.8						.9	1.2
1.2	1.5	1.1						.9	.8
.3	.5	.4	Quick					.4	.4
.1	.1	.2						.1	.2
0 UND	0 UND	0 UND					9 42.8	28 13.2	
28 12.9	21 17.6	28 13.0	Sales/Receivables				34 10.7	45 8.2	
56 6.5	58 6.3	58 6.3					67 5.4	61 6.0	
			Cost of Sales/Inventory						
			Cost of Sales/Payables						
2.9	3.5	3.5						3.3	5.3
12.9	14.9	13.2	Sales/Working Capital					5.7	8.4
-9.8	-6.3	-13.6						-17.3	49.7
6.9	9.3	7.2						8.1	9.0
(61) 3.6	(64) 3.3	(65) 2.8	EBIT/Interest				(22) 2.8	(16) 3.7	
1.5	.7	1.1						.9	2.6
4.2	5.8	7.0	Net Profit + Depr., Dep.,						
(17) 2.7	(16) 3.1	(12) 2.7	Amort./Cur. Mat. L/T/D						
1.4	.0	.6							
.7	.7	.7						.6	.5
1.3	1.9	1.3	Fixed/Worth					.9	.9
3.7	4.7	2.7						2.2	1.6
.7	1.1	.9						.6	.9
1.8	2.7	1.5	Debt/Worth					1.1	1.7
20.4	9.3	4.5						3.1	3.3
54.6	40.8	29.3	% Profit Before Taxes/Tangible					26.9	37.1
(59) 18.5	(60) 15.1	(66) 10.8	Net Worth					4.4	18.1
4.5	-2.9	.9						-.4	10.8
13.9	11.4	10.6	% Profit Before Taxes/Total					10.5	9.1
5.6	5.9	4.9	Assets					2.3	7.1
1.4	-1.1	.4						.0	3.9
5.6	4.1	4.3						4.4	11.1
2.2	2.2	2.0	Sales/Net Fixed Assets					2.0	2.9
1.1	1.1	.7						.6	1.3
1.9	1.8	2.0						1.4	2.7
.9	1.0	.7	Sales/Total Assets					.7	.8
.5	.5	.5						.4	.5
3.2	3.1	3.3						4.2	2.6
(63) 5.0	(65) 5.6	(66) 5.9	% Depr., Dep., Amort./Sales				(22) 5.7	(16) 4.9	
7.5	9.3	10.1						8.1	6.5
1.1	1.1	.9	% Officers', Directors'						
(13) 4.5	(19) 2.1	(17) 1.7	Owners' Comp/Sales						
7.5	5.4	4.5							
1762945M	1696471M	1604983M	Net Sales ($)	3441M	16225M	28633M	63995M	378933M	1113756M
1862901M	1509619M	1920070M	Total Assets ($)	9151M	30653M	31723M	107717M	699564M	1041262M

M = $ thousand   MM = $ million
See Pages 9 through 22 for Explanation of Ratios and Data

Current Data Sorted by Assets | Comparative Historical Data

© RMA 2011

0-500M	500M-2MM	2-10MM	10-50MM	50-100MM	100-250MM	Type of Statement	4/1/06-3/31/07 ALL	4/1/07-3/31/08 ALL
		1	5	5	2	Unqualified	7	12
		3	7	3		Reviewed	11	11
	4	9	1			Compiled	15	13
3	4	10	1			Tax Returns	12	12
2	3	18	16	5	2	Other	39	32
	26 (4/1-9/30/10)		78 (10/1/10-3/31/11)					
5	11	41	30	13	4	NUMBER OF STATEMENTS	84	80
%	%	%	%	%	%	ASSETS	%	%
	9.0	11.1	8.8	5.3		Cash & Equivalents	7.0	8.8
	12.1	22.9	17.4	14.1		Trade Receivables (net)	17.5	17.4
	8.3	9.0	15.8	18.1		Inventory	15.4	14.5
	4.3	5.3	7.8	5.0		All Other Current	6.6	5.8
	33.7	48.2	49.9	42.5		Total Current	46.5	46.4
	57.5	35.6	38.7	32.3		Fixed Assets (net)	40.7	39.3
	.2	1.2	.4	7.7		Intangibles (net)	1.7	1.8
	8.6	14.9	10.9	17.5		All Other Non-Current	11.1	12.5
	100.0	100.0	100.0	100.0		Total	100.0	100.0
						LIABILITIES		
	6.9	19.6	8.8	7.3		Notes Payable-Short Term	17.1	17.7
	6.0	3.6	3.3	4.0		Cur. Mat.-L.T.D.	2.5	3.1
	13.4	14.7	7.0	7.9		Trade Payables	9.8	11.7
	.2	.2	.7	.0		Income Taxes Payable	.4	.4
	29.5	7.9	8.1	5.0		All Other Current	6.5	9.8
	55.9	46.1	27.9	24.2		Total Current	36.3	42.7
	29.7	24.7	13.7	15.9		Long-Term Debt	19.5	16.9
	.0	.5	1.3	1.4		Deferred Taxes	.6	.7
	41.4	6.5	4.5	7.1		All Other Non-Current	3.7	5.4
	-26.9	22.3	52.6	51.5		Net Worth	39.9	34.3
	100.0	100.0	100.0	100.0		Total Liabilties & Net Worth	100.0	100.0
						INCOME DATA		
	100.0	100.0	100.0	100.0		Net Sales	100.0	100.0
						Gross Profit		
	86.8	96.9	92.7	95.7		Operating Expenses	93.0	94.2
	13.2	3.1	7.3	4.3		Operating Profit	7.0	5.8
	.8	.1	.4	.5		All Other Expenses (net)	1.3	1.5
	12.4	3.0	6.9	3.8		Profit Before Taxes	5.6	4.4
						RATIOS		
	13.3	1.8	3.1	2.6			2.7	2.3
	1.6	1.3	1.9	1.8		Current	1.2	1.3
	.0	.6	1.1	1.6			.9	.8
	4.1	1.6	2.0	1.2			1.2	1.4
	1.3	.9	.8	.9		Quick	.5	.6
	.0	.3	.4	.5			.2	.2
0	UND	3 135.2	18 20.8	30 12.0			0 999.8	0 999.8
2	217.3	29 12.8	39 9.4	36 10.2		Sales/Receivables	27 13.5	24 15.5
26	14.2	53 6.9	56 6.5	53 6.9			47 7.8	46 7.9
						Cost of Sales/Inventory		
						Cost of Sales/Payables		
	6.4	8.7	3.1	4.1			6.2	5.7
	21.0	20.8	7.0	5.4		Sales/Working Capital	21.5	19.7
	-1.9	-23.7	33.3	10.7			-51.8	-38.1
		15.6	9.8	10.4			11.8	15.5
		(40) 5.5	(27) 4.7	(12) 3.3		EBIT/Interest	(72) 3.0	(70) 5.0
		.9	1.2	.0			.4	1.2
		11.1					7.7	19.0
		(10) 2.6				Net Profit + Depr., Dep.,	(14) 2.9	(13) 4.4
		1.0				Amort./Cur. Mat. L/T/D	1.7	1.2
	.3	.4	.3	.4			.5	.4
	.9	1.2	.8	.7		Fixed/Worth	.9	.8
	-.9	6.7	1.4	2.4			1.9	2.6
	.1	.8	.4	.5			.5	.6
	.7	2.7	1.0	1.1		Debt/Worth	1.4	1.2
	-2.1	11.9	2.4	4.5			4.6	3.7
		41.6	26.9	16.4		% Profit Before Taxes/Tangible	50.0	30.7
		(33) 16.5	9.0	(11) 2.2		Net Worth	(75) 15.1	(69) 15.2
		2.4	1.4	-9.4			-.2	2.2
	25.8	13.2	13.1	13.1		% Profit Before Taxes/Total	21.6	14.7
	12.7	5.5	5.5	8.2		Assets	4.2	5.4
	3.6	-.1	.9	-2.1			-1.9	-.5
	18.8	18.7	13.3	7.3			11.1	12.7
	4.7	6.2	4.1	5.4		Sales/Net Fixed Assets	5.1	4.8
	3.1	3.8	1.9	1.7			2.5	2.3
	4.6	3.8	2.4	1.5			3.3	2.9
	3.3	2.1	1.5	1.1		Sales/Total Assets	2.0	1.8
	2.4	1.4	1.0	.7			1.2	1.1
		1.1	1.1	2.3			1.8	1.4
		(35) 2.8	(26) 2.9	3.1		% Depr., Dep., Amort./Sales	(69) 3.0	(64) 2.9
		4.1	5.0	5.2			4.7	4.9
		1.1					1.1	1.2
		(11) 1.3				% Officers', Directors'	(23) 3.0	(20) 2.1
		4.8				Owners' Comp/Sales	5.0	4.6
3907M	49732M	574117M	1080337M	1104989M	522197M	Net Sales ($)	2138147M	2953240M
1143M	14824M	182022M	641468M	943961M	450497M	Total Assets ($)	1437164M	1924935M

M = $ thousand   MM = $ million
See Pages 9 through 22 for Explanation of Ratios and Data

Comparative Historical Data				Current Data Sorted by Sales					
			Type of Statement						
13	18	13	Unqualified				2	2	11
24	19	13	Reviewed				2	3	8
20	21	14	Compiled		2	2	6	3	1
15	19	18	Tax Returns	4	2	2	4	4	2
31	41	46	Other	2	3	5	8	11	17
4/1/08-3/31/09 ALL	4/1/09-3/31/10 ALL	4/1/10-3/31/11 ALL		26 (4/1-9/30/10)			78 (10/1/10-3/31/11)		
				0-1MM	1-3MM	3-5MM	5-10MM	10-25MM	25MM & OVER
103	118	104	NUMBER OF STATEMENTS	6	7	9	20	23	39
%	%	%	ASSETS	%	%	%	%	%	%
7.8	9.7	9.8	Cash & Equivalents				9.3	13.7	7.6
16.9	17.0	17.7	Trade Receivables (net)				17.0	21.1	20.3
16.2	13.2	12.6	Inventory				9.2	6.9	16.9
6.1	5.8	5.6	All Other Current				3.9	7.8	6.2
47.0	45.6	45.8	Total Current				39.4	49.4	51.0
38.5	40.5	38.1	Fixed Assets (net)				49.4	32.0	35.2
3.1	1.4	1.6	Intangibles (net)				.0	1.2	3.5
11.5	12.5	14.5	All Other Non-Current				11.2	17.4	10.4
100.0	100.0	100.0	Total				100.0	100.0	100.0
			LIABILITIES						
15.7	13.8	14.3	Notes Payable-Short Term				10.6	13.9	10.5
4.2	3.0	3.9	Cur. Mat.-L.T.D.				4.1	2.7	4.1
11.6	10.3	10.8	Trade Payables				6.2	14.0	11.1
.5	.3	.5	Income Taxes Payable				.1	1.2	.3
12.7	16.4	9.3	All Other Current				9.6	8.2	8.3
44.6	43.7	38.7	Total Current				30.6	39.9	34.3
20.8	26.4	21.6	Long-Term Debt				27.9	19.0	15.6
.8	1.0	.8	Deferred Taxes				1.8	1.2	.6
5.2	8.6	10.4	All Other Non-Current				5.4	13.5	2.6
28.6	20.3	28.4	Net Worth				34.4	26.4	46.8
100.0	100.0	100.0	Total Liabilities & Net Worth				100.0	100.0	100.0
			INCOME DATA						
100.0	100.0	100.0	Net Sales				100.0	100.0	100.0
			Gross Profit						
95.0	93.8	93.9	Operating Expenses				94.8	96.8	94.7
5.0	6.2	6.1	Operating Profit				5.2	3.2	5.3
1.8	1.7	.5	All Other Expenses (net)				-1.0	1.8	.2
3.2	4.5	5.6	Profit Before Taxes				6.1	1.4	5.1
			RATIOS						
2.4	2.6	2.5					3.1	3.0	2.4
1.2	1.5	1.6	Current				1.8	1.2	1.8
.8	.8	.8					1.3	.5	1.1
1.2	1.6	1.5					2.4	1.9	1.3
.5	.7	.9	Quick				1.4	.8	.9
.3	.3	.4					.5	.3	.6
1 254.7	1 426.3	4 99.4					7 54.6	18 20.1	22 16.6
29 12.4	28 13.1	30 12.2	Sales/Receivables				30 12.0	31 11.8	36 10.2
51 7.1	49 7.4	51 7.1					54 6.7	57 6.5	48 7.6
			Cost of Sales/Inventory						
			Cost of Sales/Payables						
6.0	5.0	5.5					7.4	5.4	4.8
18.9	13.6	12.5	Sales/Working Capital				10.4	15.7	8.7
-26.4	-25.2	-43.0					136.4	-37.0	44.5
7.6	9.6	10.2					18.0	11.3	11.6
(90) 3.3	(102) 3.6	(97) 5.1	EBIT/Interest	(19) 3.4		(22) 6.5			(36) 5.2
.6	.5	.9					1.1	-1.1	1.2
3.9	11.6	11.1							16.6
(23) 2.1	(27) 3.6	(26) 2.8	Net Profit + Depr., Dep., Amort./Cur. Mat. L/T/D					(13) 7.2	
1.3	1.5	.8							.9
.4	.5	.4					.7	.3	.5
1.0	1.1	.9	Fixed/Worth				1.1	1.0	.7
2.6	NM	2.4					NM	2.0	1.4
.6	.6	.5					.4	.4	.5
1.5	1.9	1.5	Debt/Worth				1.4	2.4	1.1
10.4	NM	6.1					NM	5.6	2.5
37.3	33.2	36.6					41.8	47.9	24.0
(81) 10.6	(89) 12.9	(88) 16.0	% Profit Before Taxes/Tangible Net Worth	(15) 16.2		(20) 15.1			(36) 15.0
.1	2.3	2.4					5.6	4.1	.8
13.1	15.3	13.4					12.7	17.0	13.1
3.9	4.7	7.5	% Profit Before Taxes/Total Assets				7.7	4.0	8.2
-.2	-.4	.1					.7	-3.6	.7
13.5	14.4	13.6					6.9	20.4	11.4
7.2	4.9	5.6	Sales/Net Fixed Assets				4.9	8.4	6.4
3.1	2.4	2.4					1.3	3.2	2.5
3.3	3.3	3.3					3.0	3.7	3.3
1.9	1.7	1.7	Sales/Total Assets				2.1	1.8	1.6
1.1	1.1	1.1					1.0	1.1	1.2
1.4	1.2	1.5					2.0	1.2	1.5
(94) 2.6	(104) 2.4	(89) 3.1	% Depr., Dep., Amort./Sales	(18) 4.3		(18) 1.7			(37) 2.8
4.3	5.2	4.7					6.5	3.7	4.3
1.0	1.5	1.0							.6
(32) 2.4	(38) 1.9	(24) 1.5	% Officers', Directors' Owners' Comp/Sales					(11) 1.6	
6.3	3.8	4.3							3.0
4110465M	4996250M	3335279M	Net Sales ($)	2848M	14883M	38554M	139860M	341928M	2797206M
2490137M	3235705M	2233915M	Total Assets ($)	3578M	18848M	29833M	138855M	299228M	1743573M

M = $ thousand   MM = $ million
See Pages 9 through 22 for Explanation of Ratios and Data

Current Data Sorted by Assets   Comparative Historical Data

	0-500M	500M-2MM	2-10MM	10-50MM	50-100MM	100-250MM	Type of Statement	4/1/06-3/31/07 ALL	4/1/07-3/31/08 ALL
				2	3	8	Unqualified	5	9
	1	1	1	2		1	Reviewed	2	6
		6	7	6	2		Compiled	13	10
	5	8	15	1			Tax Returns	7	10
		2	3	4			Other	6	6
		27 (4/1-9/30/10)		51 (10/1/10-3/31/11)					
NUMBER OF STATEMENTS	6	17	26	15	5	9		33	41
	%	%	%	%	%	%	**ASSETS**	%	%
		12.8	7.3	10.3			Cash & Equivalents	14.9	18.9
		11.0	5.8	7.2			Trade Receivables (net)	6.1	4.3
		3.3	3.2	7.8			Inventory	5.6	9.1
		6.2	3.2	1.3			All Other Current	4.3	1.3
		33.4	19.5	26.7			Total Current	31.0	33.6
		46.8	60.8	48.9			Fixed Assets (net)	51.3	50.1
		.2	1.7	1.2			Intangibles (net)	.6	1.2
		19.6	18.0	23.1			All Other Non-Current	17.1	15.2
		100.0	100.0	100.0			Total	100.0	100.0
							LIABILITIES		
		13.5	12.3	13.7			Notes Payable-Short Term	11.2	5.9
		7.5	5.8	1.8			Cur. Mat.-L.T.D.	3.1	2.8
		4.5	2.7	4.5			Trade Payables	3.3	4.7
		.0	.0	.2			Income Taxes Payable	.1	.3
		13.5	12.3	8.2			All Other Current	8.0	10.9
		39.1	33.1	28.4			Total Current	25.8	24.6
		29.8	46.7	21.5			Long-Term Debt	52.8	29.8
		.0	.1	1.9			Deferred Taxes	.0	1.1
		11.3	5.6	1.0			All Other Non-Current	5.2	4.9
		19.8	14.5	47.3			Net Worth	16.2	39.6
		100.0	100.0	100.0			Total Liabilities & Net Worth	100.0	100.0
							INCOME DATA		
		100.0	100.0	100.0			Net Sales	100.0	100.0
							Gross Profit		
		102.0	86.1	90.8			Operating Expenses	86.9	80.4
		-2.0	13.9	9.2			Operating Profit	13.1	19.6
		3.7	6.0	.0			All Other Expenses (net)	1.9	3.4
		-5.7	7.9	9.2			Profit Before Taxes	11.2	16.2
							RATIOS		
		1.2	2.6	2.1				3.3	3.4
		.9	.4	1.4			Current	1.2	1.8
		.1	.1	.4				.6	1.0
		1.1	2.3	1.7				2.2	2.4
		.5	.2	.8			Quick	.6	1.1
		.0	.0	.3				.2	.4
	0	UND	0 UND	0 UND				0 UND	0 UND
	0	UND	0 UND	22 16.8			Sales/Receivables	7 55.0	0 UND
	6	58.1	27 13.3	80 4.5				69 5.3	18 19.7
							Cost of Sales/Inventory		
							Cost of Sales/Payables		
		14.9	14.4	2.9				3.6	3.4
		-31.0	-6.6	25.5			Sales/Working Capital	99.4	12.4
		-3.5	-2.4	-8.5				-6.1	-512.6
		2.6	7.3	36.3				6.7	20.7
	(14)	.8	(23) 2.7	(14) 4.0			EBIT/Interest	(28) 2.8	(35) 5.6
		-3.3	.0	-1.5				1.3	2.1
							Net Profit + Depr., Dep., Amort./Cur. Mat. L/T/D		
		1.2	.7	.6				.8	.6
		3.4	1.8	.7			Fixed/Worth	1.8	1.1
		-38.4	73.5	1.2				UND	5.9
		.6	.7	.2				.8	.3
		14.7	2.6	.4			Debt/Worth	2.3	1.2
		-195.6	NM	1.6				UND	8.2
		7.7	50.1	34.4				58.4	33.8
	(11)	-3.3	(20) 6.1	(13) 9.9			% Profit Before Taxes/Tangible Net Worth	(25) 29.6	(34) 17.5
		-27.6	-1.9	1.6				4.6	5.2
		4.3	7.9	11.4				15.1	16.4
		-1.4	3.6	4.0			% Profit Before Taxes/Total Assets	5.4	9.1
		-8.5	-1.7	-1.5				1.1	2.2
		18.0	2.5	2.7				5.6	6.4
		1.4	.9	.9			Sales/Net Fixed Assets	1.2	1.5
		.7	.4	.4				.5	.6
		2.2	1.1	1.2				1.6	1.5
		.7	.6	.5			Sales/Total Assets	.5	.6
		.5	.2	.3				.3	.4
		1.8	2.0	3.8				5.3	1.6
	(16)	6.0	(24) 4.8	(14) 7.2			% Depr., Dep., Amort./Sales	(26) 7.5	(37) 5.7
		12.1	10.0	11.9				11.8	9.3
							% Officers', Directors' Owners' Comp/Sales		
	4716M	35384M	131034M	198824M	261105M	1126662M	Net Sales ($)	359568M	947315M
	1529M	21421M	129286M	261674M	347065M	1484580M	Total Assets ($)	756157M	1375214M

M = $ thousand   MM = $ million
See Pages 9 through 22 for Explanation of Ratios and Data

Comparative Historical Data | Current Data Sorted by Sales

Type of Statement									
	4/1/08-3/31/09 ALL	**4/1/09-3/31/10 ALL**	**4/1/10-3/31/11 ALL**	**0-1MM**	**1-3MM**	**3-5MM**	**5-10MM**	**10-25MM**	**25MM & OVER**
					27 (4/1-9/30/10)		51 (10/1/10-3/31/11)		
Unqualified	14	13	14				2		12
Reviewed	5	6	5	1			2	1	1
Compiled	11	13	21	6	2	2	5	4	2
Tax Returns	11	16	29	13	10	5	1		
Other	7	19	9	3	2	1	1	2	
NUMBER OF STATEMENTS	48	67	78	23	14	8	11	7	15
ASSETS	%	%	%	%	%	%	%	%	%
Cash & Equivalents	12.8	13.8	9.2	5.2	16.6		14.9		7.9
Trade Receivables (net)	7.3	9.3	7.0	.5	3.3		16.8		9.9
Inventory	8.5	7.9	6.7	3.0	2.9		5.0		21.6
All Other Current	1.6	6.9	3.7	3.3	8.8		2.3		1.6
Total Current	30.1	37.9	26.6	12.0	31.6		38.9		41.0
Fixed Assets (net)	53.6	46.2	53.1	57.4	48.0		44.4		49.5
Intangibles (net)	.9	1.1	1.4	1.8	.2		.3		1.2
All Other Non-Current	15.3	14.7	18.9	28.9	20.2		16.4		8.3
Total	100.0	100.0	100.0	100.0	100.0		100.0		100.0
LIABILITIES									
Notes Payable-Short Term	7.3	11.9	13.0	9.4	12.3		25.2		11.7
Cur. Mat.-L.T.D.	2.9	4.1	4.8	3.8	10.7		2.2		3.3
Trade Payables	6.1	8.0	3.7	.7	.3		10.3		6.5
Income Taxes Payable	.5	.0	.0	.0	.1		.1		.1
All Other Current	4.9	8.1	10.2	13.0	9.3		10.5		5.1
Total Current	21.8	32.0	31.7	26.9	32.7		48.4		26.7
Long-Term Debt	30.4	29.8	34.9	36.8	26.3		40.7		24.1
Deferred Taxes	1.6	.8	.8	.9	.0		.2		2.1
All Other Non-Current	4.1	3.6	6.2	15.4	1.1		1.0		4.2
Net Worth	42.2	33.7	26.4	20.1	39.8		9.8		42.9
Total Liabilities & Net Worth	100.0	100.0	100.0	100.0	100.0		100.0		100.0
INCOME DATA									
Net Sales	100.0	100.0	100.0	100.0	100.0		100.0		100.0
Gross Profit									
Operating Expenses	88.1	91.1	91.1	89.6	88.3		98.5		91.7
Operating Profit	11.9	8.9	8.9	10.4	11.7		1.5		8.3
All Other Expenses (net)	4.3	4.7	5.2	10.3	3.2		.8		3.2
Profit Before Taxes	7.6	4.2	3.7	.0	8.5		.7		5.1
RATIOS									
Current	3.2	2.6	1.9	1.5	1.6		4.3		2.0
	1.2	1.2	1.0	.4	1.0		.8		1.8
	.6	.6	.2	.0	.1		.6		1.1
Quick	2.2	1.7	1.3	.7	1.6		3.7		1.4
	.7	.7	.5	.3	.2		.8		.5
	.3	.2	.1	.0	.0		.4		.3
Sales/Receivables	0 UND	0 UND	0 UND	0 UND	0 UND		17 21.6		22 16.8
	4 90.3	2 151.2	0 UND	0 UND	0 UND		28 13.0		27 13.7
	36 10.3	41 9.0	33 11.2	0 UND	0 UND		39 9.3		41 8.9
Cost of Sales/Inventory									
Cost of Sales/Payables									
Sales/Working Capital	2.5	2.6	6.0	9.1	8.4		5.5		3.5
	18.1	19.4	NM	-5.5	NM		-16.7		11.2
	-11.9	-13.9	-3.9	-1.7	-4.7		-10.2		27.2
EBIT/Interest	10.5	10.9	8.0	3.1	27.4		10.4		8.1
	(38) 2.6	(59) 2.6	(68) 2.1	(17) .8	(12) 4.2		(10) -1.2		2.9
	1.1	.5	.0	-2.6	.3		-3.9		1.2
Net Profit + Depr., Dep., Amort./Cur. Mat. L/T/D	17.3		12.1						
	(11) 8.4		(14) 3.0						
	1.6		1.5						
Fixed/Worth	.7	.4	.7	.7	.6		.6		.7
	1.2	1.1	1.4	1.7	1.3		.8		1.2
	4.6	4.4	17.2	-1.7	12.1		-82.6		1.8
Debt/Worth	.4	.4	.5	.7	.6		.2		.7
	1.2	1.5	1.5	2.4	1.2		.4		1.5
	5.3	11.6	34.6	-3.8	19.4		-388.0		2.3
% Profit Before Taxes/Tangible Net Worth	22.2	40.6	36.2	7.7	50.6				41.6
	(43) 5.8	(52) 5.9	(61) 6.4	(15) -.6	(12) 6.8				9.9
	.6	-1.8	-2.5	-12.9	-4.5				.6
% Profit Before Taxes/Total Assets	12.1	10.8	7.2	4.0	12.8		5.9		12.8
	2.9	3.2	2.6	-.7	4.4		-.3		3.6
	.0	-1.5	-2.7	-6.5	-1.8		-17.0		.4
Sales/Net Fixed Assets	3.7	14.6	3.2	1.3	9.8		14.2		3.5
	1.3	1.8	1.2	.7	1.5		1.8		1.4
	.5	.8	.6	.4	.4		.9		.8
Sales/Total Assets	1.3	1.6	1.3	.6	1.1		3.0		1.6
	.7	.8	.6	.3	.7		1.0		.9
	.3	.4	.3	.2	.4		.5		.4
% Depr., Dep., Amort./Sales	2.4	1.9	3.0	5.6	2.0		1.4		2.8
	(44) 6.1	(53) 5.0	(73) 5.6	(22) 8.9	(12) 5.4		3.1	(14)	4.3
	12.3	9.5	10.3	22.0	12.8		8.2		7.5
% Officers', Directors' Owners' Comp/Sales			1.2						
		(10)	2.3						
			7.5						
Net Sales ($)	1503199M	1632191M	1757725M	13224M	26942M	30843M	74966M	110845M	1500905M
Total Assets ($)	2113556M	2443328M	2245555M	76270M	52138M	47331M	102551M	172320M	1794945M

M = $ thousand   MM = $ million
See Pages 9 through 22 for Explanation of Ratios and Data

Current Data Sorted by Assets   **Comparative Historical Data**

0-500M	500M-2MM	2-10MM	10-50MM	50-100MM	100-250MM	Type of Statement	4/1/06-3/31/07 ALL	4/1/07-3/31/08 ALL
						Unqualified	4	3
						Reviewed	7	8
						Compiled	12	11
1 3	1 4 1	2 4 3	3 3 4 3	1 2 1	1 1 1	Tax Returns	10	1
			11 (4/1-9/30/10)			Other	6	7
			29 (10/1/10-3/31/11)					
4	6	9	13	5	3	**NUMBER OF STATEMENTS**	39	30
%	%	%	%	%	%	**ASSETS**	%	%
			7.6			Cash & Equivalents	7.5	6.4
			9.5			Trade Receivables (net)	9.2	9.8
			23.2			Inventory	19.3	20.4
			5.0			All Other Current	5.0	2.6
			45.3			Total Current	41.0	39.3
			49.0			Fixed Assets (net)	47.1	54.8
			.3			Intangibles (net)	.2	.2
			5.4			All Other Non-Current	11.6	5.6
			100.0			Total	100.0	100.0
						LIABILITIES		
			17.4			Notes Payable-Short Term	12.6	17.1
			6.3			Cur. Mat.-L.T.D.	6.5	4.5
			4.2			Trade Payables	5.0	4.8
			.1			Income Taxes Payable	.0	.1
			3.4			All Other Current	12.9	2.7
			31.4			Total Current	37.0	29.2
			24.3			Long-Term Debt	37.6	26.0
			2.5			Deferred Taxes	.2	.3
			1.2			All Other Non-Current	3.5	1.2
			40.6			Net Worth	21.6	43.3
			100.0			Total Liabilties & Net Worth	100.0	100.0
						INCOME DATA		
			100.0			Net Sales	100.0	100.0
						Gross Profit		
			82.0			Operating Expenses	84.3	88.0
			18.0			Operating Profit	15.7	12.0
			2.5			All Other Expenses (net)	3.4	2.5
			15.5			Profit Before Taxes	12.3	9.5
						RATIOS		
			1.9			Current	2.5	2.1
			1.5				1.3	1.4
			1.0				.9	1.0
			.9			Quick	1.3	1.2
			.4				(38) .6	.4
			.3				.1	.0
		1	505.5			Sales/Receivables	0 UND	0 UND
		40	9.1				11 34.0	14 26.3
		84	4.3				45 8.2	45 8.2
						Cost of Sales/Inventory		
						Cost of Sales/Payables		
			2.8			Sales/Working Capital	3.5	3.7
			4.9				25.2	12.5
			-62.5				-21.5	NM
			9.1			EBIT/Interest	9.0	6.1
			4.1				(35) 4.3	(29) 3.9
			2.1				1.6	1.1
						Net Profit + Depr., Dep., Amort./Cur. Mat. L/T/D		
			.6			Fixed/Worth	.8	1.1
			1.3				1.4	1.3
			2.3				4.2	2.2
			.7			Debt/Worth	.6	.4
			1.5				1.9	1.8
			2.9				8.2	3.2
			32.9			% Profit Before Taxes/Tangible Net Worth	44.5	35.9
			23.6				(31) 31.8	22.1
			13.4				13.9	.7
			15.7			% Profit Before Taxes/Total Assets	21.7	16.7
			9.7				14.3	8.5
			3.6				3.9	.6
			3.1			Sales/Net Fixed Assets	6.0	2.5
			1.3				1.9	1.6
			.8				1.1	1.1
			1.0			Sales/Total Assets	1.9	1.5
			.7				1.0	.9
			.5				.6	.7
			3.3			% Depr., Dep., Amort./Sales	3.2	3.2
		(12)	6.0				(34) 5.0	(25) 5.1
			8.2				6.6	8.5
						% Officers', Directors' Owners' Comp/Sales		
2229M	23825M	42832M	301651M	160329M	421075M	Net Sales ($)	556097M	741511M
854M	6477M	36400M	385389M	332703M	591737M	Total Assets ($)	516871M	830751M

M = $ thousand   MM = $ million
See Pages 9 through 22 for Explanation of Ratios and Data

Comparative Historical Data   Current Data Sorted by Sales

Type of Statement	4/1/08-3/31/09 ALL	4/1/09-3/31/10 ALL	4/1/10-3/31/11 ALL		0-1MM	1-3MM	3-5MM	5-10MM	10-25MM	25MM & OVER
Unqualified	7	2	4							4
Reviewed	5	3	8			1		1	3	3
Compiled	15	9	12		2		2	2	3	3
Tax Returns	3	7	7		4	1	2	2		
Other	5	6	9		1	1		2		3
					11 (4/1-9/30/10)			29 (10/1/10-3/31/11)		
NUMBER OF STATEMENTS	35	27	40		7	3	4	7	6	13
	%	%	%		%	%	%	%	%	%
ASSETS										
Cash & Equivalents	6.8	7.7	8.3							5.3
Trade Receivables (net)	11.8	10.4	9.5							11.9
Inventory	28.1	18.0	15.6							26.1
All Other Current	2.8	2.8	3.8							4.4
Total Current	49.5	38.9	37.2							47.7
Fixed Assets (net)	46.6	55.1	52.6							42.7
Intangibles (net)	.7	.9	.8							1.7
All Other Non-Current	3.2	5.2	9.4							7.8
Total	100.0	100.0	100.0							100.0
LIABILITIES										
Notes Payable-Short Term	18.9	19.9	11.3							12.5
Cur. Mat.-L.T.D.	2.7	2.9	5.5							3.0
Trade Payables	6.1	4.4	5.1							4.3
Income Taxes Payable	.0	.0	.1							.0
All Other Current	6.1	5.4	3.9							5.6
Total Current	33.8	32.7	25.8							25.4
Long-Term Debt	25.4	29.1	32.6							19.9
Deferred Taxes	.3	.8	1.2							.8
All Other Non-Current	.7	9.6	7.2							1.3
Net Worth	39.8	27.8	33.2							52.6
Total Liabilities & Net Worth	100.0	100.0	100.0							100.0
INCOME DATA										
Net Sales	100.0	100.0	100.0							100.0
Gross Profit										
Operating Expenses	86.4	95.4	87.1							83.1
Operating Profit	13.6	4.6	12.9							16.9
All Other Expenses (net)	2.5	2.0	4.3							1.9
Profit Before Taxes	11.1	2.7	8.6							15.0
RATIOS										
Current	3.3	1.6	2.1							3.2
	1.5	1.2	1.2							1.9
	1.1	.7	.9							1.4
Quick	1.1	1.1	.9							.9
	.6	.5	.7							.8
	.0	.2	.3							.3
Sales/Receivables	0 UND	0 999.8	0 UND							36 10.2
	16 23.1	27 13.6	32 11.3							54 6.7
	59 6.2	52 7.1	64 5.7							97 3.8
Cost of Sales/Inventory										
Cost of Sales/Payables										
Sales/Working Capital	3.0	5.0	3.5							2.1
	6.4	25.5	17.8							3.4
	38.5	-12.3	-87.4							7.9
EBIT/Interest	9.4	5.6	6.9							8.6
	(32) 3.4	(25) 2.3	(37) 2.7							5.6
	1.6	.6	1.2							2.6
Net Profit + Depr., Dep., Amort./Cur. Mat. L/T/D										
Fixed/Worth	.9	.8	.8							.6
	1.2	1.6	1.7							.8
	3.0	4.2	2.7							1.1
Debt/Worth	.8	.8	.7							.6
	1.7	2.2	2.0							.9
	4.1	4.8	5.3							1.3
% Profit Before Taxes/Tangible Net Worth	51.0	28.0	26.9							25.0
	(34) 19.2	(22) 12.8	(38) 16.9							17.2
	1.6	.8	-.8							10.8
% Profit Before Taxes/Total Assets	16.4	12.6	11.8							15.4
	8.1	3.2	5.0							9.4
	1.5	-1.7	-.3							3.7
Sales/Net Fixed Assets	4.1	3.8	4.5							3.1
	1.8	2.0	1.5							1.3
	1.2	1.2	.8							1.1
Sales/Total Assets	1.3	2.1	1.7							1.0
	.8	.9	.7							.7
	.6	.7	.5							.6
% Depr., Dep., Amort./Sales	3.6	4.1	2.9							3.2
	(29) 4.6	(25) 5.8	(33) 6.1							(11) 7.5
	6.4	7.6	8.9							8.8
% Officers', Directors' Owners' Comp/Sales										
Net Sales ($)	726160M	446648M	951941M		4186M	6210M	13872M	52262M	97098M	778313M
Total Assets ($)	725391M	461559M	1353560M		10352M	3737M	23743M	45347M	159671M	1110710M

© RMA 2011

M = $ thousand   MM = $ million
See Pages 9 through 22 for Explanation of Ratios and Data

Current Data Sorted by Assets

Comparative Historical Data

						Type of Statement		
	2	2	2	1	1	Unqualified	10	5
	7	7	3	3		Reviewed	13	4
	4	8	1			Compiled	11	15
4	9	7	1	1		Tax Returns	19	21
2	7	15	16	2	3	Other	26	33
	6 (4/1-9/30/10)		95 (10/1/10-3/31/11)				4/1/06-3/31/07	4/1/07-3/31/08
0-500M	500M-2MM	2-10MM	10-50MM	50-100MM	100-250MM		ALL	ALL
6	22	39	23	7	4	NUMBER OF STATEMENTS	79	78
%	%	%	%	%	%	ASSETS	%	%
	11.9	8.2	4.4			Cash & Equivalents	7.5	6.8
	8.5	12.0	12.3			Trade Receivables (net)	11.1	9.4
	6.2	8.8	8.1			Inventory	10.5	9.9
	4.3	3.0	7.9			All Other Current	4.8	4.2
	30.9	32.1	32.8			Total Current	34.0	30.3
	59.9	61.3	56.8			Fixed Assets (net)	55.2	55.9
	.9	.5	2.7			Intangibles (net)	1.9	2.5
	8.4	6.2	7.8			All Other Non-Current	8.9	11.4
	100.0	100.0	100.0			Total	100.0	100.0
						LIABILITIES		
	18.3	9.1	9.4			Notes Payable-Short Term	13.1	14.1
	2.0	8.8	1.9			Cur. Mat.-L.T.D.	2.8	2.7
	4.7	2.4	4.4			Trade Payables	3.8	3.5
	.6	.0	.0			Income Taxes Payable	.0	.1
	1.9	3.7	4.1			All Other Current	3.9	9.0
	27.5	24.0	19.8			Total Current	23.5	29.4
	64.0	42.7	41.8			Long-Term Debt	39.0	41.7
	.0	.0	.2			Deferred Taxes	.2	.2
	10.3	1.5	18.1			All Other Non-Current	4.7	7.8
	-1.7	31.7	20.1			Net Worth	32.7	20.9
	100.0	100.0	100.0			Total Liabilties & Net Worth	100.0	100.0
						INCOME DATA		
	100.0	100.0	100.0			Net Sales	100.0	100.0
						Gross Profit		
	83.2	77.6	86.2			Operating Expenses	90.4	90.4
	16.8	22.4	13.8			Operating Profit	9.6	9.6
	8.9	8.7	9.5			All Other Expenses (net)	5.8	5.2
	7.9	13.8	4.3			Profit Before Taxes	3.8	4.4
						RATIOS		
	7.5	5.6	3.7				4.1	3.3
	1.5	1.8	1.8			Current	2.0	1.6
	.1	.6	1.0				.8	.4
	4.5	3.7	2.6				2.3	1.8
	.8	.8	.9			Quick	.9	.6
	.1	.3	.5				.2	.1
0	UND	0 UND	10 35.2				0 UND	0 UND
0	UND	18 20.7	81 4.5			Sales/Receivables	32 11.3	11 32.6
42	8.7	105 3.5	117 3.1				120 3.0	76 4.8
						Cost of Sales/Inventory		
						Cost of Sales/Payables		
	2.3	1.6	1.6				1.9	2.6
	52.4	10.8	4.5			Sales/Working Capital	5.7	10.1
	-2.7	-15.7	-36.9				-17.0	-6.0
	5.0	9.9	6.9				4.7	3.7
(19)	3.3	(33) 3.5	(17) 3.2			EBIT/Interest	(62) 1.9	(61) 1.4
	1.3	1.2	.4				.5	.3
						Net Profit + Depr., Dep., Amort./Cur. Mat. L/T/D	5.1	
							(15) 1.8	
							.5	
	1.0	.6	.6				.6	.8
	3.2	1.6	2.8			Fixed/Worth	1.2	1.7
	-2.0	8.8	-3.3				10.0	-14.2
	1.1	.6	.5				.5	.5
	9.0	1.5	2.1			Debt/Worth	1.7	1.9
	-3.8	10.3	-6.9				13.4	-19.2
	38.9	26.5	15.7			% Profit Before Taxes/Tangible Net Worth	20.4	17.3
(12)	19.0	(33) 13.7	(15) 6.1				(62) 6.5	(55) 6.5
	6.4	.7	-.1				-7.8	-10.3
	15.7	12.1	7.4			% Profit Before Taxes/Total Assets	12.2	9.9
	5.5	5.6	1.5				1.8	2.5
	.9	-.2	-2.5				-3.5	-2.7
	3.6	1.9	1.4				4.8	3.4
	1.3	.7	.7			Sales/Net Fixed Assets	.9	1.2
	.6	.4	.3				.6	.7
	1.2	.9	.6				1.0	1.1
	.6	.5	.3			Sales/Total Assets	.6	.6
	.4	.3	.2				.4	.4
	6.8	4.0	4.6				3.6	3.8
(17)	8.6	(34) 9.6	8.5			% Depr., Dep., Amort./Sales	(68) 7.2	(68) 6.9
	16.6	14.0	18.1				13.9	13.4
						% Officers', Directors' Owners' Comp/Sales	3.2	1.8
							(19) 7.5	(14) 2.9
							9.8	7.4
6077M	23669M	124958M	210691M	341504M	469110M	Net Sales ($)	1046827M	1155100M
1826M	25531M	170382M	455202M	528785M	588172M	Total Assets ($)	1375487M	1346911M

M = $ thousand   MM = $ million
See Pages 9 through 22 for Explanation of Ratios and Data

Comparative Historical Data | | | | Current Data Sorted by Sales

			Type of Statement						
3	3	6	Unqualified				2	3	1
17	15	15	Reviewed		6	1	3	3	2
11	18	13	Compiled	3	8		2		
30	29	22	Tax Returns	13	5	1	2		1
32	48	45	Other	11	13	9	3	5	4
4/1/08-3/31/09 ALL	4/1/09-3/31/10 ALL	4/1/10-3/31/11 ALL		0-1MM	6 (4/1-9/30/10) 1-3MM	3-5MM	5-10MM	95 (10/1/10-3/31/11) 10-25MM	25MM & OVER
93	113	101	NUMBER OF STATEMENTS	27	32	11	12	11	8
%	%	%	ASSETS	%	%	%	%	%	%
7.9	8.7	8.8	Cash & Equivalents	9.5	9.2	10.2	6.5	8.4	
8.8	7.7	10.7	Trade Receivables (net)	3.5	9.5	19.8	14.9	9.5	
9.8	9.3	8.7	Inventory	3.9	7.2	10.9	7.5	15.4	
7.4	6.3	4.6	All Other Current	2.7	3.2	4.1	9.8	7.7	
33.8	32.1	32.8	Total Current	19.5	29.0	45.0	38.7	41.0	
53.5	57.7	58.5	Fixed Assets (net)	71.7	62.4	52.0	51.6	47.3	
1.2	1.6	1.3	Intangibles (net)	.4	.7	.5	5.1	.3	
11.4	8.7	7.3	All Other Non-Current	8.4	7.9	2.5	4.6	11.5	
100.0	100.0	100.0	Total	100.0	100.0	100.0	100.0	100.0	
			LIABILITIES						
13.0	13.8	16.1	Notes Payable-Short Term	13.6	27.5	9.7	10.6	6.1	
2.7	2.9	4.8	Cur. Mat.-L.T.D.	12.2	2.6	1.0	3.0	1.5	
3.4	3.0	3.7	Trade Payables	.9	1.7	7.7	3.8	4.4	
.0	.1	.1	Income Taxes Payable	.0	.4	.0	.0	.0	
6.4	4.0	3.4	All Other Current	2.7	2.6	1.7	3.7	9.5	
25.6	23.8	28.2	Total Current	29.4	34.8	20.1	21.1	21.5	
42.3	44.7	47.5	Long-Term Debt	59.5	55.7	55.3	31.2	23.7	
.6	.3	.1	Deferred Taxes	.2	.0	.0	.3	.2	
8.6	6.7	7.1	All Other Non-Current	9.5	2.7	4.4	11.6	7.9	
22.9	24.5	17.1	Net Worth	1.4	6.7	20.2	35.8	46.7	
100.0	100.0	100.0	Total Liabilities & Net Worth	100.0	100.0	100.0	100.0	100.0	
			INCOME DATA						
100.0	100.0	100.0	Net Sales	100.0	100.0	100.0	100.0	100.0	
			Gross Profit						
90.8	83.5	82.4	Operating Expenses	74.6	81.1	84.9	89.1	89.4	
9.2	16.5	17.6	Operating Profit	25.4	18.9	15.1	10.9	10.6	
7.2	8.0	8.1	All Other Expenses (net)	16.1	5.6	8.2	3.5	5.3	
2.0	8.6	9.5	Profit Before Taxes	9.2	13.2	6.9	7.4	5.4	
			RATIOS						
4.3	5.2	5.3	Current	4.5	5.5	16.4	5.8	4.9	
1.5	1.9	1.8		.4	1.8	3.3	2.9	2.3	
.6	.8	.7		.1	.6	1.1	1.1	1.1	
2.2	2.7	3.4	Quick	1.7	4.0	16.1	3.1	2.5	
(92) .7	.7	.8		.2	.8	2.7	1.9	.8	
.1	.1	.2		.0	.3	.7	.6	.5	
0 UND	0 UND	0 UND	Sales/Receivables	0 UND	0 UND	0 UND	14 25.8	29 12.4	
10 36.2	9 42.5	20 18.3		0 UND	21 17.3	50 7.3	28 13.1	42 8.8	
72 5.1	73 5.0	95 3.8		2 161.6	109 3.3	178 2.0	100 3.7	117 3.1	
			Cost of Sales/Inventory						
			Cost of Sales/Payables						
2.4	1.9	1.6	Sales/Working Capital	1.7	2.0	1.5	1.6	.9	
14.2	5.8	6.8		-16.8	17.6	2.1	6.3	4.1	
-7.5	-11.6	-13.6		-1.4	-7.6	57.7	38.3	19.2	
4.4	9.5	8.5	EBIT/Interest	5.7	8.1		10.8	24.0	
(68) 1.5	(89) 3.3	(85) 3.5		(19) 3.3	(27) 3.5		5.3	(10) 2.8	
-.3	1.0	1.3		1.3	1.5		1.1	.2	
4.3	9.7	4.6	Net Profit + Depr., Dep., Amort./Cur. Mat. L/T/D						
(16) 2.1	(17) 3.4	(13) 3.4							
-.1	1.8	1.6							
.9	.7	.7	Fixed/Worth	1.2	.7	.5	.5	.3	
1.5	1.5	1.7		4.8	1.7	1.1	3.9	.9	
-8.5	41.7	-17.5		-9.3	-11.4	40.8	-3.1	11.7	
.6	.5	.6	Debt/Worth	1.1	.3	.7	.3	.1	
2.5	1.7	1.9		6.1	2.0	1.6	3.4	.9	
-12.9	NM	-21.3		-14.0	-13.8	43.9	-6.9	19.1	
24.7	30.0	25.6	% Profit Before Taxes/Tangible Net Worth	29.0	32.7				
(64) 4.0	(85) 9.6	(73) 11.0		(18) 16.1	(23) 11.0				
-7.5	-.2	1.7		7.7	-4.2				
7.1	11.1	11.5	% Profit Before Taxes/Total Assets	8.1	19.9	20.5	10.7	7.5	
.5	3.6	5.2		4.1	7.6	3.4	7.7	2.3	
-4.8	-.5	-.2		-.1	-.2	-2.5	.2	-2.2	
6.4	2.6	2.3	Sales/Net Fixed Assets	1.2	1.8	7.6	5.5	2.2	
1.2	.9	.9		.6	1.0	.8	1.2	.6	
.5	.4	.4		.3	.4	.3	.9	.4	
1.1	1.1	.9	Sales/Total Assets	.7	1.0	1.2	1.1	.9	
.6	.6	.6		.4	.6	.5	.7	.3	
.3	.3	.3		.2	.3	.3	.5	.3	
3.5	3.5	3.9	% Depr., Dep., Amort./Sales	4.4	7.5		3.5	3.2	
(79) 8.6	(93) 6.7	(90) 8.3		(23) 8.6	(27) 9.8		4.3	8.5	
14.7	11.6	15.6		18.3	15.9		8.8	16.4	
1.3	1.7	1.5	% Officers', Directors' Owners' Comp/Sales						
(20) 4.0	(23) 4.9	(16) 3.5							
6.4	8.7	8.8							
1028417M	1223504M	1176009M	Net Sales ($)	14949M	59108M	39733M	94689M	177330M	790200M
1190133M	1634792M	1769898M	Total Assets ($)	52368M	155534M	91265M	139436M	554611M	776684M

M = $ thousand   MM = $ million
See Pages 9 through 22 for Explanation of Ratios and Data

Current Data Sorted by Assets | Comparative Historical Data

0-500M	500M-2MM	2-10MM	10-50MM	50-100MM	100-250MM	Type of Statement	4/1/06-3/31/07 ALL	4/1/07-3/31/08 ALL
		5	2	1	1	Unqualified	2	2
	1	5	7	1	1	Reviewed	1	2
1	1	4	1	1		Compiled	5	6
3	4	8	3		1	Tax Returns	3	3
2	5					Other	5	5
	5 (4/1-9/30/10)		53 (10/1/10-3/31/11)					
6	11	22	13	3	3	**NUMBER OF STATEMENTS**	16	18
%	%	%	%	%	%	**ASSETS**	%	%
	7.8	5.2	6.4			Cash & Equivalents	12.7	5.8
	7.2	16.5	27.3			Trade Receivables (net)	9.9	9.8
	16.8	6.5	16.8			Inventory	14.7	19.4
	2.0	6.1	4.4			All Other Current	4.3	6.5
	33.8	34.3	54.9			Total Current	41.6	41.4
	52.7	60.6	36.7			Fixed Assets (net)	52.9	47.6
	.8	1.0	.1			Intangibles (net)	.1	.2
	12.7	4.1	8.3			All Other Non-Current	5.4	10.8
	100.0	100.0	100.0			Total	100.0	100.0
						LIABILITIES		
	10.8	31.3	7.3			Notes Payable-Short Term	18.4	26.6
	17.3	2.4	1.2			Cur. Mat.-L.T.D.	2.2	3.0
	1.3	2.8	17.0			Trade Payables	2.7	5.4
	.0	.1	.2			Income Taxes Payable	.6	.6
	7.6	4.5	16.8			All Other Current	4.9	11.8
	37.0	41.1	42.7			Total Current	28.8	47.5
	44.6	38.1	25.2			Long-Term Debt	31.4	21.4
	.0	.0	2.3			Deferred Taxes	1.4	.7
	6.1	4.3	5.5			All Other Non-Current	3.6	5.0
	12.3	16.6	24.4			Net Worth	34.9	25.4
	100.0	100.0	100.0			Total Liabilities & Net Worth	100.0	100.0
						INCOME DATA		
	100.0	100.0	100.0			Net Sales	100.0	100.0
						Gross Profit		
	85.8	81.2	90.7			Operating Expenses	83.1	91.1
	14.2	18.8	9.3			Operating Profit	16.9	8.9
	2.1	4.4	3.4			All Other Expenses (net)	4.1	6.1
	12.1	14.3	5.9			Profit Before Taxes	12.8	2.7
						RATIOS		
	9.4	2.7	2.4				5.6	4.2
	1.0	1.1	1.2			Current	2.1	1.2
	.4	.4	1.0				1.1	.4
	3.6	1.8	1.3				5.2	3.7
	.5	.7	.8			Quick	.7	.3
	.0	.2	.4				.3	.1
0 UND	0 UND	44 8.3					0 UND	0 UND
0 UND	35 10.3	93 3.9				Sales/Receivables	35 10.4	9 42.7
11 34.2	262 1.4	268 1.4					74 4.9	38 9.6
						Cost of Sales/Inventory		
						Cost of Sales/Payables		
	2.7	1.9	1.3				1.8	4.6
	-278.1	210.0	7.1			Sales/Working Capital	8.4	25.8
	-5.4	-4.4	NM				27.3	-1.3
	7.5	7.8	4.9				23.5	2.0
	3.4	(20) 3.3	1.8			EBIT/Interest	(15) 4.6	(15) 1.2
	1.7	1.1	.9				1.4	-.5
						Net Profit + Depr., Dep., Amort./Cur. Mat. L/T/D		
	.5	.9	.7				.5	.5
	1.5	1.7	1.3			Fixed/Worth	1.0	1.6
	3.4	NM	4.9				1.9	-6.3
	.9	.9	1.5				.9	.9
	2.3	1.9	3.6			Debt/Worth	1.3	3.6
	6.0	NM	10.0				3.4	-10.2
		28.9	42.0				55.4	23.5
	(17) 9.1	(12) 16.2				% Profit Before Taxes/Tangible Net Worth	(14) 23.9	(13) 5.5
	3.9	3.8					8.0	-5.1
	25.7	22.6	8.9				29.6	3.6
	5.0	4.5	1.9			% Profit Before Taxes/Total Assets	6.8	2.2
	1.9	.4	-1.0				1.7	-2.9
	12.6	2.2	6.7				5.1	9.7
	4.7	1.1	1.8			Sales/Net Fixed Assets	2.1	2.3
	.8	.7	.8				.8	.8
	2.3	1.3	1.3				1.3	2.5
	1.5	.6	.7			Sales/Total Assets	.9	1.1
	.8	.4	.3				.6	.5
		5.3	1.7				2.0	1.5
	(15) 8.0	(11) 2.9				% Depr., Dep., Amort./Sales	4.7	(17) 3.1
	13.8	9.2					9.8	6.7
						% Officers', Directors' Owners' Comp/Sales		
6235M	28945M	133831M	298621M	268400M	296867M	Net Sales ($)	251230M	571060M
883M	14514M	109282M	253789M	202174M	409397M	Total Assets ($)	300571M	353557M

M = $ thousand   MM = $ million
See Pages 9 through 22 for Explanation of Ratios and Data

Comparative Historical Data   ## Current Data Sorted by Sales

			Type of Statement						
11	4	4	Unqualified				2		2
11	7	14	Reviewed	1	3	3	1	4	2
10	10	9	Compiled	2	3	2		2	
8	10	11	Tax Returns	2	5	1	2	1	
21	24	20	Other	2	8	5	1		4
4/1/08-3/31/09	4/1/09-3/31/10	4/1/10-3/31/11			5 (4/1-9/30/10)		53 (10/1/10-3/31/11)		
ALL	ALL	ALL		0-1MM	1-3MM	3-5MM	5-10MM	10-25MM	25MM & OVER
61	55	58	NUMBER OF STATEMENTS	7	19	11	6	7	8
%	%	%	ASSETS	%	%	%	%	%	%
7.6	7.3	9.2	Cash & Equivalents		9.2	7.8			
16.3	15.9	15.1	Trade Receivables (net)		12.1	16.0			
9.8	11.8	11.5	Inventory		7.8	4.0			
5.1	5.3	5.4	All Other Current		6.3	2.6			
38.8	40.3	41.1	Total Current		35.4	30.4			
47.7	48.7	49.0	Fixed Assets (net)		57.5	48.6			
.3	.7	.7	Intangibles (net)		1.1	.0			
13.1	10.2	9.3	All Other Non-Current		6.1	21.0			
100.0	100.0	100.0	Total		100.0	100.0			
			LIABILITIES						
23.6	18.3	18.1	Notes Payable-Short Term		13.9	22.5			
1.3	3.5	5.7	Cur. Mat.-L.T.D.		11.5	1.5			
4.3	6.3	6.6	Trade Payables		2.4	2.0			
.7	.2	.1	Income Taxes Payable		.0	.0			
2.9	6.4	7.5	All Other Current		.8	1.9			
32.7	34.7	38.0	Total Current		28.7	27.9			
25.3	33.4	30.0	Long-Term Debt		43.3	30.2			
2.2	.3	.5	Deferred Taxes		.0	.0			
1.8	5.7	4.7	All Other Non-Current		6.2	.0			
38.0	25.9	26.7	Net Worth		21.8	41.9			
100.0	100.0	100.0	Total Liabilties & Net Worth		100.0	100.0			
			INCOME DATA						
100.0	100.0	100.0	Net Sales		100.0	100.0			
			Gross Profit						
84.6	88.7	83.7	Operating Expenses		80.4	82.2			
15.4	11.3	16.3	Operating Profit		19.6	17.8			
3.4	3.9	2.9	All Other Expenses (net)		2.3	4.6			
12.1	7.4	13.4	Profit Before Taxes		17.2	13.1			
			RATIOS						
3.2	2.6	4.7	Current		7.5	7.2			
1.6	1.3	1.2			1.2	2.0			
1.0	.7	.6			.5	.6			
2.9	1.8	2.4	Quick		6.4	6.4			
1.0	.7	.6			.5	1.3			
.3	.2	.2			.3	.4			
0 UND	0 UND	0 UND	Sales/Receivables	0 UND	0 UND				
36 10.2	29 12.6	24 15.4		11 34.2	71 5.1				
203 1.8	95 3.8	162 2.3		170 2.2	252 1.4				
			Cost of Sales/Inventory						
			Cost of Sales/Payables						
2.2	3.6	2.0	Sales/Working Capital		1.9	1.3			
6.1	8.9	14.4			16.0	49.9			
369.1	-21.8	-10.3			-5.6	-3.3			
15.9	5.9	10.8	EBIT/Interest		9.9				
(56) 2.9	(50) 2.6	(54) 3.9		(18) 3.1					
.0	.8	1.3			1.5				
12.1	3.9	23.2	Net Profit + Depr., Dep., Amort./Cur. Mat. L/T/D						
(12) 5.1	(15) 2.9	(12) 2.4							
3.5	1.5	1.4							
.6	1.0	.6	Fixed/Worth		.6	.5			
1.0	1.2	1.3			1.9	.9			
2.7	3.6	3.3			72.5	1.9			
.4	1.2	.7	Debt/Worth		.9	.1			
1.2	2.3	2.0			2.0	1.7			
7.1	9.0	8.3			72.3	2.3			
30.7	35.0	42.3	% Profit Before Taxes/Tangible Net Worth		40.0	43.7			
(51) 11.6	(46) 7.4	(50) 16.2		(15) 26.6	(10) 6.1				
-2.3	.3	4.6			3.7	4.1			
19.9	11.5	18.3	% Profit Before Taxes/Total Assets		25.7	16.9			
5.3	3.8	5.0			5.2	3.2			
-3.0	-.5	1.1			1.7	1.4			
5.2	5.3	7.1	Sales/Net Fixed Assets		4.9	12.6			
1.6	2.0	1.7			1.2	1.9			
.7	.7	.8			.7	.9			
1.8	2.0	2.0	Sales/Total Assets		1.5	1.9			
.7	.7	.8			.8	.6			
.4	.4	.4			.5	.3			
2.5	2.6	2.6	% Depr., Dep., Amort./Sales		7.1				
(49) 5.2	(44) 9.2	(40) 6.6		(10) 14.5					
10.7	13.7	12.2			18.4				
1.7		2.2	% Officers', Directors' Owners' Comp/Sales						
(10) 5.1		(12) 5.2							
10.2		9.1							
982100M	789742M	1032899M	Net Sales ($)	2480M	36893M	41306M	38418M	115257M	798545M
1146874M	712848M	990039M	Total Assets ($)	10313M	57696M	131462M	103285M	129626M	557657M

© RMA 2011

M = $ thousand   MM = $ million
See Pages 9 through 22 for Explanation of Ratios and Data

AGRICULTURE—Mushroom Production   NAICS 111411

Current Data Sorted by Assets · **Comparative Historical Data**

Type of Statement	0-500M	500M-2MM	2-10MM	10-50MM	50-100MM	100-250MM		4/1/06-3/31/07 ALL	4/1/07-3/31/08 ALL
Unqualified			1	1	1	1		2	3
Reviewed		6	6	5				6	6
Compiled			6	6				12	13
Tax Returns	2	2	2					7	9
Other	1	2	4	4	2			12	8
		9 (4/1-9/30/10)		43 (10/1/10-3/31/11)					
NUMBER OF STATEMENTS	3	10	19	16	3	1		39	39
	%	%	%	%	%	%		%	%
ASSETS									
Cash & Equivalents		6.8	3.4	2.0				2.1	5.7
Trade Receivables (net)		16.4	24.9	16.0				25.9	23.9
Inventory		26.8	16.0	11.5				13.7	14.3
All Other Current		1.1	1.5	1.9				3.0	.6
Total Current		51.0	45.8	31.5				44.7	44.5
Fixed Assets (net)		44.8	40.1	62.8				44.6	43.1
Intangibles (net)		.1	.8	.7				3.0	2.2
All Other Non-Current		4.1	13.3	4.9				7.7	10.2
Total		100.0	100.0	100.0				100.0	100.0
LIABILITIES									
Notes Payable-Short Term		9.6	11.4	7.6				8.1	13.6
Cur. Mat.-L.T.D.		2.5	3.6	6.5				10.8	8.2
Trade Payables		38.3	16.5	15.2				18.6	20.8
Income Taxes Payable		.0	.0	.0				.2	.2
All Other Current		6.8	2.7	3.1				6.9	6.6
Total Current		57.2	34.1	32.3				44.6	49.4
Long-Term Debt		29.3	31.4	48.1				28.9	37.3
Deferred Taxes		.0	.2	.3				.7	.4
All Other Non-Current		.0	2.7	2.1				5.6	1.5
Net Worth		13.5	31.6	17.2				20.1	11.4
Total Liabilities & Net Worth		100.0	100.0	100.0				100.0	100.0
INCOME DATA									
Net Sales		100.0	100.0	100.0				100.0	100.0
Gross Profit									
Operating Expenses		97.2	96.7	89.2				95.8	98.2
Operating Profit		2.8	3.3	10.8				4.2	1.8
All Other Expenses (net)		1.9	-.2	7.7				.5	1.6
Profit Before Taxes		.9	3.5	3.1				3.6	.2

RATIOS

Ratio	0-500M	500M-2MM	2-10MM	10-50MM	50-100MM	100-250MM		4/1/06-3/31/07	4/1/07-3/31/08
Current		2.5	1.8	1.8				1.5	1.6
		1.2	1.4	.9				1.1	1.1
		.4	1.0	.5				.8	.5
Quick		1.4	1.3	1.1				.9	1.0
		.7	.7	.5				.7	.5
		.1	.6	.2				.2	.3
Sales/Receivables		0 UND	16 23.4	0 UND				13 27.3	2 148.4
		18 20.4	29 12.6	29 12.7				35 10.3	29 12.4
		20 18.5	36 10.2	36 10.2				46 7.9	37 9.8
Cost of Sales/Inventory									
Cost of Sales/Payables									
Sales/Working Capital		10.6	11.3	11.7				11.3	21.4
		45.1	22.4	-55.8				57.5	170.0
		-6.2	-225.3	-14.5				-27.7	-22.2
EBIT/Interest		4.3	11.2	2.8				3.2	6.9
		1.3	(17) 4.5	(13) 2.1				(34) 1.1	(36) 1.2
		-.3	1.4	.9				.2	-.1
Net Profit + Depr., Dep., Amort./Cur. Mat. L/T/D									
Fixed/Worth		.5	.5	1.5				.9	.8
		1.4	1.1	5.1				1.6	1.7
		NM	6.0	17.3				11.0	16.6
Debt/Worth		.7	.9	2.9				1.8	1.4
		1.2	1.5	5.7				4.2	4.8
		NM	8.8	31.9				21.4	247.6
% Profit Before Taxes/Tangible Net Worth			46.5	38.7				31.0	47.0
			(16) 24.5	(13) 21.9				(31) 2.5	(30) 7.0
			.6	9.5				-17.3	-9.7
% Profit Before Taxes/Total Assets		8.9	17.6	6.7				7.9	12.1
		.0	8.3	3.7				.4	.5
		-3.6	.0	.2				-3.1	-3.4
Sales/Net Fixed Assets		18.6	16.4	5.5				13.7	21.0
		13.0	6.1	2.1				7.5	9.0
		3.1	3.4	1.4				2.9	4.2
Sales/Total Assets		5.2	3.8	2.8				6.2	6.3
		3.9	2.8	1.2				2.9	3.7
		2.1	1.7	.9				1.2	2.1
% Depr., Dep., Amort./Sales			1.2	2.1				1.3	.6
			(15) 2.4	(15) 3.4				(35) 2.5	(35) 1.8
			4.1	7.0				4.9	4.0
% Officers', Directors' Owners' Comp/Sales			1.1					.9	.7
			(10) 1.5					(14) 1.6	(14) 1.5
			3.2					1.8	2.9
Net Sales ($)	1232M	35041M	274340M	558224M	291179M	111013M		787452M	615247M
Total Assets ($)	649M	10398M	95405M	287829M	201728M	118774M		382728M	245030M

M = $ thousand   MM = $ million
See Pages 9 through 22 for Explanation of Ratios and Data

Comparative Historical Data | Current Data Sorted by Sales

Type of Statement

Type of Statement	4/1/08-3/31/09 ALL	4/1/09-3/31/10 ALL	4/1/10-3/31/11 ALL	0-1MM	1-3MM	3-5MM	5-10MM	10-25MM	25MM & OVER
Unqualified	1	2	4				1		3
Reviewed	3	7	11		2	1		6	2
Compiled	12	25	18		2	3	4	5	4
Tax Returns	2	4	6	3	1	1	1		
Other	3	13	13	1	1	2	1	2	6
				3 (4/1-9/30/10)	9			43 (10/1/10-3/31/11)	
NUMBER OF STATEMENTS	21	51	52	4	6	7	7	13	15

4/1/08-3/31/09 ALL	4/1/09-3/31/10 ALL	4/1/10-3/31/11 ALL		0-1MM	1-3MM	3-5MM	5-10MM	10-25MM	25MM & OVER
%	%	%	**ASSETS**	%	%	%	%	%	%
1.8	3.9	5.4	Cash & Equivalents					2.9	4.0
22.5	18.3	18.4	Trade Receivables (net)					14.7	27.0
15.0	16.3	17.2	Inventory					13.7	13.8
1.0	1.2	1.9	All Other Current					1.9	3.6
40.3	39.7	42.9	Total Current					33.2	48.4
51.0	50.5	48.1	Fixed Assets (net)					53.0	41.6
2.2	1.5	.8	Intangibles (net)					.9	1.2
6.5	8.4	8.2	All Other Non-Current					12.9	8.7
100.0	100.0	100.0	Total					100.0	100.0
			LIABILITIES						
11.0	14.3	8.9	Notes Payable-Short Term					11.4	8.7
8.9	4.8	4.0	Cur. Mat.-L.T.D.					4.7	5.8
15.7	14.3	19.4	Trade Payables					11.7	22.6
.3	.4	.0	Income Taxes Payable					.0	.0
2.4	6.1	4.9	All Other Current					2.5	8.2
38.3	39.9	37.2	Total Current					30.3	45.3
37.5	43.2	35.6	Long-Term Debt					40.8	28.1
.4	.9	.2	Deferred Taxes					.5	.4
.1	1.6	2.2	All Other Non-Current					5.0	2.3
23.6	14.4	24.7	Net Worth					23.3	23.9
100.0	100.0	100.0	Total Liabilities & Net Worth					100.0	100.0
			INCOME DATA						
100.0	100.0	100.0	Net Sales					100.0	100.0
			Gross Profit						
97.8	93.9	94.1	Operating Expenses					95.6	97.6
2.2	6.1	5.9	Operating Profit					4.4	2.4
1.7	4.0	3.1	All Other Expenses (net)					1.1	2.0
.5	2.1	2.8	Profit Before Taxes					3.3	.4
			RATIOS						
2.1	1.9	2.0	Current					1.5	1.9
1.1	.9	1.2						1.1	1.0
.6	.5	.7						.9	.7
1.0	1.0	1.2	Quick					1.0	1.4
.7	.5	.6						.6	.7
.3	.2	.3						.5	.4
20 17.8	0 UND	6 60.1	Sales/Receivables					10 35.6	26 14.0
33 10.9	25 14.8	25 14.8						25 14.6	34 10.8
37 9.9	42 8.8	34 10.8						31 11.6	36 10.1
			Cost of Sales/Inventory						
			Cost of Sales/Payables						
14.0	11.4	11.0	Sales/Working Capital					15.4	12.9
65.0	-247.5	46.8						249.0	-999.8
-12.7	-14.9	-18.1						-60.1	-15.7
8.6	7.3	6.3	EBIT/Interest					9.3	11.8
1.0 (48)	2.2 (45)	2.8						2.8 (12)	4.3
-.6	.4	.8						1.2	1.7
			Net Profit + Depr., Dep., Amort./Cur. Mat. L/T/D						
.6	1.0	.6	Fixed/Worth					.8	.7
1.8	3.2	1.6						2.7	1.2
-43.6	-6.0	7.1						20.3	5.6
1.1	1.7	1.0	Debt/Worth					1.4	1.3
4.0	4.6	2.6						3.7	2.5
-59.6	-26.9	8.7						53.8	13.2
26.8	33.3	42.3	% Profit Before Taxes/Tangible Net Worth					42.3	39.2
(15) 17.2	(35) 16.1	(43) 21.5						(11) 25.5	(13) 29.6
-11.2	-6.2	2.5						.2	17.2
9.1	10.7	10.2	% Profit Before Taxes/Total Assets					13.7	10.7
.2	3.3	5.0						5.8	6.7
-8.3	-2.1	-1.1						.5	-2.6
8.6	14.4	14.1	Sales/Net Fixed Assets					8.0	13.7
4.4	3.8	5.4						5.7	5.6
2.1	1.9	2.3						1.7	4.6
3.1	4.1	3.7	Sales/Total Assets					3.7	3.7
2.3	2.2	2.2						2.0	2.9
1.4	1.0	1.2						1.2	1.5
1.2	1.7	1.8	% Depr., Dep., Amort./Sales					1.9	.9
(19) 1.7	(50) 2.9	(45) 2.6						(11) 2.4	(14) 2.0
6.1	6.7	6.2						6.1	2.9
	1.0	1.1	% Officers', Directors' Owners' Comp/Sales						
(19)	1.3	(22) 1.5							
	2.4	2.7							
429662M	997478M	1271029M	Net Sales ($)	1498M	13288M	28254M	57086M	210588M	960315M
215262M	602912M	714783M	Total Assets ($)	1933M	32520M	14843M	39318M	115891M	510278M

M = $ thousand   MM = $ million
See Pages 9 through 22 for Explanation of Ratios and Data

Current Data Sorted by Assets

Comparative Historical Data

Type of Statement	0-500M	500M-2MM	2-10MM	10-50MM	50-100MM	100-250MM	4/1/06-3/31/07 ALL	4/1/07-3/31/08 ALL
Unqualified			1	9	5	4	17	18
Reviewed		2	11	15			25	27
Compiled	6	8	12	6			33	28
Tax Returns	11	11	5				25	27
Other	8	14	23	18	3	5	56	58
		54 (4/1-9/30/10)		123 (10/1/10-3/31/11)				
NUMBER OF STATEMENTS	25	35	52	48	8	9	156	158
ASSETS	%	%	%	%	%	%	%	%
Cash & Equivalents	18.7	6.3	5.4	2.1			8.2	6.8
Trade Receivables (net)	11.8	11.7	18.1	8.8			12.7	12.2
Inventory	24.9	21.3	31.8	37.2			26.1	30.9
All Other Current	8.2	3.0	2.4	3.1			2.5	2.3
Total Current	63.6	42.4	57.7	51.2			49.5	52.2
Fixed Assets (net)	27.1	41.0	35.6	39.6			41.4	39.2
Intangibles (net)	6.1	4.5	2.3	1.5			2.0	1.6
All Other Non-Current	3.2	12.2	4.3	7.8			7.0	7.0
Total	100.0	100.0	100.0	100.0			100.0	100.0
LIABILITIES								
Notes Payable-Short Term	26.0	19.3	16.0	14.0			16.4	16.3
Cur. Mat.-L.T.D.	6.2	3.4	2.3	4.6			3.3	3.7
Trade Payables	8.5	8.4	13.5	8.7			8.5	11.4
Income Taxes Payable	.0	.2	.9	2.2			1.2	1.2
All Other Current	5.6	7.5	4.9	6.1			10.0	8.9
Total Current	46.3	38.9	37.5	35.5			39.3	41.5
Long-Term Debt	38.5	23.0	20.6	22.1			23.7	28.7
Deferred Taxes	.0	.4	1.4	1.6			.9	.9
All Other Non-Current	11.4	4.4	3.5	6.5			7.5	7.7
Net Worth	3.8	33.3	37.0	34.3			28.7	21.2
Total Liabilities & Net Worth	100.0	100.0	100.0	100.0			100.0	100.0
INCOME DATA								
Net Sales	100.0	100.0	100.0	100.0			100.0	100.0
Gross Profit	50.1	50.0	36.8	37.2			42.9	38.2
Operating Expenses	46.2	46.5	33.7	34.3			37.2	34.2
Operating Profit	3.9	3.5	3.1	3.0			5.7	4.0
All Other Expenses (net)	1.7	1.6	1.6	2.1			2.0	2.3
Profit Before Taxes	2.1	1.9	1.5	.9			3.7	1.7
RATIOS								
Current	6.3	2.8	3.6	2.3			3.2	2.9
	1.7	1.4	1.7	1.3			1.5	1.5
	.8	.4	1.2	1.0			.9	1.0
Quick	1.7	1.2	1.4	.5			1.5	1.0
	.7	.3	.7	.3			.5	.4
	.1	.1	.3	.1			.2	.2
Sales/Receivables	0 UND	0 UND	14 25.4	9 42.6			2 156.7	2 218.0
	4 86.2	10 37.9	32 11.4	21 17.5			17 21.3	19 18.9
	19 18.9	40 9.1	52 7.1	45 8.0			47 7.8	47 7.8
Cost of Sales/Inventory	0 UND	0 UND	10 35.0	68 5.4			0 748.1	10 36.5
	18 20.4	28 13.3	84 4.3	154 2.4			59 6.1	85 4.3
	79 4.6	166 2.2	277 1.3	355 1.0			196 1.9	234 1.6
Cost of Sales/Payables	0 UND	0 UND	13 27.8	18 20.4			0 UND	0 999.8
	5 78.2	7 53.7	23 16.0	32 11.6			18 19.9	25 14.6
	23 16.2	42 8.6	63 5.8	59 6.2			48 7.6	55 6.6
Sales/Working Capital	7.0	5.2	3.2	3.4			3.9	4.2
	12.9	23.6	7.7	11.1			11.1	11.0
	-101.5	-11.2	46.6	-141.8			-112.9	-82.7
EBIT/Interest	12.9	8.4	4.8	3.7			6.8	4.0
	(22) 2.2	(32) 2.7	(47) 1.5	(47) 1.6			(145) 2.5	(150) 1.8
	-.4	1.0	-.1	.2			.7	.4
Net Profit + Depr., Dep., Amort./Cur. Mat. L/T/D				2.9			3.7	3.7
				(18) 1.8			(29) 2.1	(41) 1.8
				.7			1.1	.7
Fixed/Worth	.2	.5	.3	.6			.6	.5
	.4	1.1	.8	1.3			1.1	1.2
	-.7	-1.8	2.2	2.8			4.7	4.9
Debt/Worth	.8	.4	.7	1.1			.6	1.0
	1.7	1.3	2.0	2.2			1.6	2.7
	-2.0	-8.7	4.4	4.1			8.8	9.8
% Profit Before Taxes/Tangible Net Worth	53.2	31.9	19.5	30.2			35.5	26.4
	(17) 28.9	(24) 7.2	(48) 7.6	(45) 5.9			(131) 15.8	(129) 11.6
	-9.7	-2.1	-10.7	-2.3			1.3	.3
% Profit Before Taxes/Total Assets	20.1	16.5	6.8	5.5			11.6	8.8
	7.0	5.0	2.1	1.9			5.1	3.8
	-3.9	.0	-2.5	-1.6			-1.3	-2.1
Sales/Net Fixed Assets	62.2	21.3	11.4	7.8			10.0	10.3
	15.5	6.0	5.6	3.3			4.8	4.6
	6.8	2.5	2.4	1.4			2.7	2.5
Sales/Total Assets	5.2	3.5	2.4	1.9			2.9	2.7
	3.4	2.2	1.4	1.0			1.8	1.6
	2.6	1.2	.9	.6			.9	.9
% Depr., Dep., Amort./Sales	1.1	1.5	1.7	2.2			1.6	1.9
	(19) 2.1	(29) 3.4	(44) 3.1	(46) 3.8			(141) 3.1	(143) 2.9
	3.7	5.4	5.1	5.4			4.8	4.7
% Officers', Directors' Owners' Comp/Sales	3.0	2.4	1.9				1.9	1.9
	(15) 5.9	(23) 4.3	(17) 3.6				(63) 2.8	(59) 2.8
	9.5	8.4	5.4				7.9	7.9
Net Sales ($)	26662M	79538M	447989M	1262297M	515477M	1275843M	3904061M	3254239M
Total Assets ($)	7195M	35982M	244026M	1007902M	561553M	1489959M	2340671M	3128917M

M = $ thousand   MM = $ million
See Pages 9 through 22 for Explanation of Ratios and Data

Comparative Historical Data | | | | Current Data Sorted by Sales

			Type of Statement						
22	27	19	Unqualified				2	5	12
33	33	28	Reviewed	1	5	6	10	6	
37	44	32	Compiled	4	9	5	10	4	
23	23	27	Tax Returns	7	13	4	3		
80	65	71	Other	13	12	9	11	6	20
4/1/08-3/31/09	4/1/09-3/31/10	4/1/10-3/31/11			54 (4/1-9/30/10)		123 (10/1/10-3/31/11)		
ALL	ALL	ALL		0-1MM	1-3MM	3-5MM	5-10MM	10-25MM	25MM & OVER
195	192	177	**NUMBER OF STATEMENTS**	24	35	23	32	25	38
%	%	%	**ASSETS**	%	%	%	%	%	%
5.7	5.2	6.3	Cash & Equivalents	11.5	9.6	4.1	5.9	3.3	3.7
13.1	11.2	12.7	Trade Receivables (net)	10.2	11.9	10.6	15.4	12.5	14.3
33.6	33.3	30.5	Inventory	25.4	26.2	24.6	34.7	39.5	31.7
3.2	2.8	3.4	All Other Current	6.2	3.9	1.7	4.1	2.5	2.3
55.6	52.5	53.0	Total Current	53.3	51.6	41.1	60.1	57.8	52.0
34.3	37.4	36.7	Fixed Assets (net)	34.8	37.7	42.0	33.9	34.2	37.8
2.1	3.1	3.4	Intangibles (net)	8.3	1.4	4.4	.7	3.8	3.5
7.9	7.0	7.0	All Other Non-Current	3.6	9.4	12.6	5.3	4.1	6.7
100.0	100.0	100.0	Total	100.0	100.0	100.0	100.0	100.0	100.0
			LIABILITIES						
20.9	19.1	17.3	Notes Payable-Short Term	25.2	15.3	19.1	16.3	21.1	11.3
4.0	3.8	3.9	Cur. Mat.-L.T.D.	6.2	2.9	2.7	3.2	2.6	5.4
10.3	10.2	9.9	Trade Payables	4.0	9.2	8.9	9.5	10.8	14.6
.8	1.1	1.1	Income Taxes Payable	.0	.2	.9	1.8	.0	2.9
8.9	7.7	5.8	All Other Current	6.1	6.3	7.1	3.6	5.5	6.6
45.0	41.9	38.0	Total Current	41.6	33.9	38.7	34.4	40.0	40.8
22.9	27.6	24.0	Long-Term Debt	40.9	25.2	16.5	20.0	22.5	21.2
.9	.9	1.0	Deferred Taxes	.0	.9	.1	2.0	1.3	1.2
7.0	5.9	5.6	All Other Non-Current	10.1	6.2	2.9	3.1	4.9	6.2
24.2	23.8	31.4	Net Worth	7.4	33.7	41.8	40.5	31.2	30.5
100.0	100.0	100.0	Total Liabilties & Net Worth	100.0	100.0	100.0	100.0	100.0	100.0
			INCOME DATA						
100.0	100.0	100.0	Net Sales	100.0	100.0	100.0	100.0	100.0	100.0
39.7	40.0	41.1	Gross Profit	58.2	46.5	43.4	37.2	34.6	31.3
37.5	37.7	38.1	Operating Expenses	53.6	42.8	41.1	34.6	29.3	30.8
2.2	2.4	3.0	Operating Profit	4.5	3.7	2.3	2.6	5.3	.5
2.4	3.2	2.0	All Other Expenses (net)	3.1	2.0	2.1	1.2	1.9	1.8
-.2	-.8	1.0	Profit Before Taxes	1.4	1.7	.1	1.4	3.4	-1.3
			RATIOS						
3.0	2.4	2.8		6.2	4.9	2.8	2.9	3.1	1.7
1.4	1.4	1.5	Current	1.8	2.4	.8	1.6	1.4	1.4
.8	.8	1.0		.5	.9	.5	1.2	1.1	1.0
1.0	.8	.9		1.6	1.7	.5	1.1	.6	.8
(193) .4	.4	.5	Quick	.6	.5	.3	.6	.3	.5
.2	.1	.1		.1	.1	.1	.3	.1	.2
13 29.2	8 47.5	6 61.7		0 UND	0 UND	7 50.6	17 21.4	8 44.2	8 47.8
27 13.5	21 17.7	22 16.4	Sales/Receivables	12 31.7	11 33.7	18 20.2	30 12.4	22 16.4	29 12.4
49 7.4	47 7.7	46 7.9		45 8.1	42 8.7	30 12.0	46 8.0	45 8.1	50 7.4
28 13.2	28 13.1	14 25.7		0 UND	0 UND	11 32.4	54 6.8	53 6.8	37 9.8
112 3.3	107 3.4	82 4.5	Cost of Sales/Inventory	36 10.0	32 11.5	42 8.7	128 2.9	157 2.3	87 4.2
358 1.0	297 1.2	252 1.4		188 1.9	169 2.2	156 2.3	314 1.2	383 1.0	166 2.2
7 53.2	4 86.9	6 61.8		0 UND	0 UND	8 45.5	4 85.0	18 19.8	23 15.6
29 12.5	28 13.0	24 15.1	Cost of Sales/Payables	4 87.1	9 39.3	29 12.6	17 21.6	34 10.6	31 11.9
64 5.7	68 5.4	55 6.7		27 13.6	40 9.2	58 6.3	65 5.6	64 5.7	60 6.1
2.8	3.3	4.1		2.4	4.5	7.7	3.3	3.1	7.2
9.6	10.7	10.9	Sales/Working Capital	18.0	8.2	-44.5	7.5	9.6	12.9
-27.3	-22.4	-149.8		-5.0	-200.0	-11.2	15.9	53.9	132.6
4.3	5.3	5.2		7.1	5.3	5.1	5.1	3.8	6.0
(183) 1.7	(176) 1.6	(164) 1.9	EBIT/Interest	(20) 1.8	(32) 1.5	2.5	(30) 1.4	(22) 2.2	(37) 1.9
-.6	-.8	-.1		-.1	.0	-1.8	-.5	1.0	-2.6
2.7	4.4	4.3							3.2
(42) 1.4	(54) 2.4	(35) 1.7	Net Profit + Depr., Dep., Amort./Cur. Mat. L/T/D					(17) 1.9	
-.7	1.4	.5							.7
.4	.4	.4		.2	.3	.5	.3	.4	.6
1.0	1.3	1.0	Fixed/Worth	2.6	.6	1.1	.8	1.1	1.2
3.8	5.2	3.0		-.8	5.4	4.3	1.9	2.7	2.0
.8	.9	.7		.5	.4	.4	.5	1.1	1.2
2.1	2.3	1.8	Debt/Worth	4.6	1.2	2.5	1.5	2.1	2.0
10.3	8.9	5.5		-2.4	5.4	5.6	3.5	4.7	6.2
22.3	29.9	27.5		45.8	19.6	17.1	15.8	27.4	30.6
(162) 7.6	(159) 7.0	(150) 7.5	% Profit Before Taxes/Tangible Net Worth	(16) 10.5	(28) 5.9	(19) 5.5	(30) .9	(23) 11.2	(34) 12.9
-4.9	-7.9	-5.1		-16.2	-9.4	-4.3	-8.2	1.5	-7.8
7.4	8.7	8.9		16.5	11.8	11.5	5.8	6.6	9.0
1.9	1.9	2.9	% Profit Before Taxes/Total Assets	5.8	2.8	5.0	.6	3.7	3.1
-3.9	-3.9	-2.0		-3.2	-3.1	-1.7	-2.4	.4	-5.9
10.9	10.0	13.4		47.3	21.3	19.0	10.9	13.8	7.2
4.6	4.4	5.3	Sales/Net Fixed Assets	6.8	5.8	5.8	6.5	3.9	3.9
2.4	2.1	2.2		1.4	2.4	1.5	2.4	1.5	2.2
2.3	2.6	2.8		3.2	3.5	3.6	2.2	2.1	2.3
1.3	1.2	1.4	Sales/Total Assets	1.5	1.9	1.5	1.3	1.0	1.5
.7	.8	.8		.6	.8	.3	.8	.6	1.0
1.7	1.9	1.8		2.0	1.5	2.7	1.7	2.4	1.6
(168) 3.2	(173) 3.5	(150) 3.4	% Depr., Dep., Amort./Sales	(17) 3.6	(30) 3.3	(19) 3.9	(30) 2.7	(22) 4.1	(32) 3.0
5.0	5.5	5.1		7.1	5.3	6.5	4.4	5.5	4.5
2.0	2.1	2.2		5.5	2.4	3.3			
(60) 3.5	(56) 3.1	(62) 4.2	% Officers', Directors' Owners' Comp/Sales	(10) 9.5	(22) 3.9	(13) 4.9			
9.3	8.4	8.4		13.4	6.9	7.5			
4651251M	4705062M	3607806M	Net Sales ($)	14005M	60580M	88839M	229442M	412014M	2802926M
4790815M	4689088M	3346617M	Total Assets ($)	15295M	53830M	130923M	221292M	640671M	2284606M

M = $ thousand   MM = $ million
See Pages 9 through 22 for Explanation of Ratios and Data

Current Data Sorted by Assets   Comparative Historical Data

	0-500M	500M-2MM	2-10MM	10-50MM	50-100MM	100-250MM		4/1/06-3/31/07 ALL	4/1/07-3/31/08 ALL
							Type of Statement		
Unqualified								5	2
Reviewed			5					4	7
Compiled	4	7	6					16	10
Tax Returns	6	10	4	3		2		10	14
Other	1	4	6					10	13
	3 (4/1-9/30/10)			55 (10/1/10-3/31/11)					
NUMBER OF STATEMENTS	11	21	21	3		2		45	46
	%	%	%	%	%	%	**ASSETS**	%	%
	18.2	10.2	8.4				Cash & Equivalents	11.6	12.3
	.0	6.9	8.4				Trade Receivables (net)	11.3	12.9
	.0	5.4	5.0				Inventory	10.4	7.4
	10.2	6.2	2.9				All Other Current	7.9	5.6
	28.4	28.7	24.8				Total Current	41.2	38.2
	50.7	51.8	67.1				Fixed Assets (net)	50.0	53.0
	.0	.1	.1				Intangibles (net)	1.0	1.0
	20.8	19.4	8.0				All Other Non-Current	7.8	7.8
	100.0	100.0	100.0				Total	100.0	100.0
							LIABILITIES		
	67.2	40.6	14.3				Notes Payable-Short Term	40.9	36.1
	22.2	6.8	8.0				Cur. Mat.-L.T.D.	10.0	19.0
	.0	.5	.4				Trade Payables	3.1	5.3
	.0	.0	.0				Income Taxes Payable	.4	.0
	5.3	8.9	1.8				All Other Current	8.0	5.4
	94.8	56.9	24.6				Total Current	62.5	65.8
	39.6	31.5	41.4				Long-Term Debt	24.8	30.7
	.0	.0	.0				Deferred Taxes	.2	.1
	11.7	.5	2.1				All Other Non-Current	.7	2.1
	-46.0	11.2	31.9				Net Worth	11.8	1.3
	100.0	100.0	100.0				Total Liabilities & Net Worth	100.0	100.0
							INCOME DATA		
	100.0	100.0	100.0				Net Sales	100.0	100.0
							Gross Profit		
	93.6	89.7	90.5				Operating Expenses	90.3	93.5
	6.4	10.3	9.5				Operating Profit	9.7	6.5
	.0	4.4	6.9				All Other Expenses (net)	4.3	3.2
	6.4	5.9	2.6				Profit Before Taxes	5.4	3.3
							RATIOS		
	1.2	1.1	3.0					1.4	1.6
	.3	.5	1.1				Current	1.0	1.0
	.0	.2	.3					.5	.4
	.5	.7	2.3					1.0	1.1
	.2	.3	.8				Quick	.6	.5
	.0	.0	.1					.1	.2
	0 UND	0 UND	0 UND					0 UND	0 UND
	0 UND	0 UND	1 576.2				Sales/Receivables	0 UND	8 43.9
	0 UND	0 UND	54 6.8					58 6.3	95 3.8
							Cost of Sales/Inventory		
							Cost of Sales/Payables		
	685.0	55.2	2.6					10.2	9.3
	-11.0	-4.8	111.6				Sales/Working Capital	194.5	681.5
	-2.8	-3.1	-2.9					-2.8	-3.2
	10.8	11.2	8.1					4.5	4.7
	(10) 2.5	(18) 2.2	(19) 2.5				EBIT/Interest	(41) 1.8	(40) 1.0
	1.2	-.9	-1.1					-.5	-2.1
							Net Profit + Depr., Dep., Amort./Cur. Mat. L/T/D		
	.1	.8	1.1					.7	.7
	2.2	1.8	1.8				Fixed/Worth	1.3	1.6
	-1.7	NM	5.7					3.6	-14.2
	2.0	.6	.5					.6	.8
	-8.0	2.6	1.8				Debt/Worth	1.7	3.1
	-1.7	NM	6.4					11.9	-9.7
		56.2	36.8					31.7	22.5
	(16) 7.6	(17) 7.5					% Profit Before Taxes/Tangible Net Worth	(36) 8.4	(32) 3.5
	.0	-5.5						-7.1	-6.2
	105.2	16.7	14.0					11.8	12.6
	4.8	3.5	.4				% Profit Before Taxes/Total Assets	2.4	.0
	.9	-5.4	-5.0					-2.7	-4.8
	483.7	17.3	1.7					7.7	5.2
	9.2	1.5	1.0				Sales/Net Fixed Assets	2.2	1.9
	3.7	.8	.4					1.0	.9
	10.3	1.8	1.0					2.1	1.8
	3.2	.9	.8				Sales/Total Assets	1.2	1.1
	.9	.6	.3					.5	.5
		1.5	3.7					2.7	2.8
	(20) 6.9	8.3					% Depr., Dep., Amort./Sales	(38) 6.1	(35) 6.2
		12.1	13.6					11.0	9.7
							% Officers', Directors' Owners' Comp/Sales		
	11780M	39505M	57324M	31694M		439370M	Net Sales ($)	664656M	496764M
	2125M	24276M	84811M	43905M		311746M	Total Assets ($)	445090M	358832M

© RMA 2011

M = $ thousand   MM = $ million
See Pages 9 through 22 for Explanation of Ratios and Data

Comparative Historical Data				Current Data Sorted by Sales					
			Type of Statement						
2	3	2	Unqualified						2
15	9	8	Reviewed		3	1	3	1	
16	15	17	Compiled	10	4	3			1
17	20	20	Tax Returns	8	8	2	1	1	
12	10	11	Other	1	7	1	2		
4/1/08-3/31/09 ALL	4/1/09-3/31/10 ALL	4/1/10-3/31/11 ALL		0-1MM	3 (4/1-9/30/10) 1-3MM	3-5MM	55 (10/1/10-3/31/11) 5-10MM	10-25MM	25MM & OVER
62	57	58	**NUMBER OF STATEMENTS**	19	22	7	6	2	2
%	%	%	**ASSETS**	%	%	%	%	%	%
12.4	11.8	10.9	Cash & Equivalents	9.4	13.6				
12.6	7.0	6.9	Trade Receivables (net)	3.0	8.9				
12.0	9.1	6.6	Inventory	4.4	3.9				
4.0	3.7	6.0	All Other Current	5.9	2.3				
41.0	31.5	30.5	Total Current	22.7	28.7				
50.0	53.5	55.2	Fixed Assets (net)	59.5	60.5				
.6	1.8	.2	Intangibles (net)	.1	.1				
8.4	13.2	14.2	All Other Non-Current	17.7	10.6				
100.0	100.0	100.0	Total	100.0	100.0				
			LIABILITIES						
28.2	21.7	34.9	Notes Payable-Short Term	45.8	20.6				
11.8	6.9	10.0	Cur. Mat.-L.T.D.	4.8	14.3				
2.0	1.3	.7	Trade Payables	.6	.2				
.0	.1	.0	Income Taxes Payable	.0	.0				
5.1	20.4	6.0	All Other Current	4.3	2.4				
47.1	50.4	51.7	Total Current	55.5	37.6				
28.5	26.6	35.3	Long-Term Debt	21.7	45.7				
.0	.0	.1	Deferred Taxes	.0	.0				
3.5	4.0	3.3	All Other Non-Current	.3	7.7				
20.9	19.0	9.6	Net Worth	22.5	9.1				
100.0	100.0	100.0	Total Liabilities & Net Worth	100.0	100.0				
			INCOME DATA						
100.0	100.0	100.0	Net Sales	100.0	100.0				
			Gross Profit						
89.4	85.9	90.4	Operating Expenses	86.3	94.7				
10.6	14.1	9.6	Operating Profit	13.7	5.3				
2.2	4.3	4.2	All Other Expenses (net)	7.4	4.1				
8.4	9.8	5.4	Profit Before Taxes	6.3	1.2				
			RATIOS						
3.2	2.1	1.7	Current	2.1	1.7				
1.6	1.1	.7		.4	.5				
.7	.3	.2		.1	.2				
2.5	1.3	1.1	Quick	.8	1.2				
.8	.6	.3		.3	.4				
.2	.1	.0		.0	.0				
0 UND	0 UND	0 UND	Sales/Receivables	0 UND	0 UND				
2 222.4	0 UND	0 UND		0 UND	0 UND				
87 4.2	43 8.5	30 12.2		0 UND	1 308.3				
			Cost of Sales/Inventory						
			Cost of Sales/Payables						
3.4	5.2	4.4	Sales/Working Capital	7.8	4.3				
11.1	150.5	-21.0		-4.8	-13.8				
-6.7	-5.5	-3.2		-1.8	-3.2				
7.0	7.8	9.7	EBIT/Interest	4.8	4.1				
(60) 3.0	(46) 2.2	(52) 2.6		(16) 1.4	(19) 1.2				
1.1	.8	.5		-.2	-1.1				
			Net Profit + Depr., Dep., Amort./Cur. Mat. L/T/D						
.7	.8	.8	Fixed/Worth	.9	1.0				
1.3	1.3	1.7		1.5	2.5				
7.9	-11.8	NM		4.6	-3.5				
.7	.6	.6	Debt/Worth	.4	.8				
2.1	1.6	2.3		1.0	3.1				
UND	-11.8	-13.9		7.9	-5.2				
34.7	38.5	43.0	% Profit Before Taxes/Tangible Net Worth	7.6	55.1				
(48) 15.8	(41) 12.0	(43) 7.7		(16) 1.5	(14) 7.1				
2.1	1.8	-2.4		-18.2	-4.5				
15.8	16.8	18.6	% Profit Before Taxes/Total Assets	6.8	12.7				
4.3	5.8	2.4		.9	.7				
.2	-.5	-4.0		-5.7	-4.9				
13.6	9.2	10.3	Sales/Net Fixed Assets	6.5	10.4				
2.1	2.1	1.6		.7	1.8				
.9	.9	.7		.3	.8				
1.9	1.8	1.5	Sales/Total Assets	1.1	2.1				
1.1	1.1	.9		.5	.9				
.5	.5	.5		.2	.6				
3.6	3.1	2.5	% Depr., Dep., Amort./Sales	2.8	2.5				
(50) 5.9	(45) 7.4	(51) 7.3		(17) 7.4	(20) 8.6				
14.1	14.9	12.3		25.2	12.3				
3.5		2.7	% Officers', Directors' Owners' Comp/Sales						
(11) 7.2		(11) 4.1							
10.8		10.5							
637995M	155569M	579673M	Net Sales ($)	10216M	38882M	25320M	37935M	27950M	439370M
630295M	226656M	466863M	Total Assets ($)	27677M	46497M	18387M	47800M	14756M	311746M

M = $ thousand   MM = $ million
See Pages 9 through 22 for Explanation of Ratios and Data

Current Data Sorted by Assets   **Comparative Historical Data**

Type of Statement	0-500M	500M-2MM	2-10MM	10-50MM	50-100MM	100-250MM	4/1/06-3/31/07 ALL	4/1/07-3/31/08 ALL
Unqualified			4	12	1	2	13	18
Reviewed	1	3	13	15	6	1	30	35
Compiled	5	13	25	19	2	1	58	65
Tax Returns	19	31	29	3	1		88	82
Other	13	19	38	15	4	1	83	76
	51 (4/1-9/30/10)		244 (10/1/10-3/31/11)					
NUMBER OF STATEMENTS	38	66	109	64	13	5	272	276
	%	%	%	%	%	%	%	%
ASSETS								
Cash & Equivalents	19.1	14.8	7.0	6.8	3.5		8.1	8.0
Trade Receivables (net)	5.6	3.9	8.8	15.0	11.1		11.3	9.2
Inventory	11.0	6.1	15.8	20.5	15.7		11.4	13.1
All Other Current	7.2	6.6	4.0	6.0	4.1		5.2	6.4
Total Current	43.0	31.4	35.6	48.4	34.4		36.0	36.8
Fixed Assets (net)	45.3	50.8	54.2	41.8	50.6		52.8	52.1
Intangibles (net)	.5	2.4	1.2	2.3	5.4		1.2	2.5
All Other Non-Current	11.2	15.4	9.0	7.5	9.7		10.0	8.6
Total	100.0	100.0	100.0	100.0	100.0		100.0	100.0
LIABILITIES								
Notes Payable-Short Term	43.2	39.1	13.9	16.4	7.6		22.8	24.4
Cur. Mat.-L.T.D.	14.2	8.9	3.6	3.0	2.6		4.7	6.3
Trade Payables	3.4	3.0	3.6	8.1	4.7		4.8	5.5
Income Taxes Payable	.0	.1	.3	1.0	.2		.4	.5
All Other Current	14.4	5.0	4.1	5.0	3.1		8.2	8.7
Total Current	75.1	56.1	25.5	33.5	18.1		40.9	45.3
Long-Term Debt	41.6	47.9	29.6	18.7	29.5		27.4	30.8
Deferred Taxes	.0	.2	.6	1.3	1.1		.4	.5
All Other Non-Current	6.2	5.9	7.8	7.2	5.5		5.2	4.3
Net Worth	-22.9	-10.1	36.5	39.4	45.8		26.1	19.1
Total Liabilties & Net Worth	100.0	100.0	100.0	100.0	100.0		100.0	100.0
INCOME DATA								
Net Sales	100.0	100.0	100.0	100.0	100.0		100.0	100.0
Gross Profit								
Operating Expenses	93.7	93.4	88.7	86.9	84.7		90.7	88.9
Operating Profit	6.3	6.6	11.3	13.1	15.3		9.3	11.1
All Other Expenses (net)	1.7	3.1	3.1	3.3	.5		3.2	3.2
Profit Before Taxes	4.7	3.6	8.2	9.8	14.8		6.1	7.9
RATIOS								
Current	3.1	2.2	3.2	2.4	3.0		1.9	1.9
	1.3	.9	1.6	1.3	2.4		1.1	1.1
	.2	.1	.7	1.0	1.4		.4	.3
Quick	2.2	1.0	1.3	1.1	1.9		1.1	1.0
	.6	.2	(108) .5	.5	1.1		(271) .4	.3
	.1	.1	.1	.2	.2		.1	.1
Sales/Receivables	0 UND	0 UND	0 UND	2 161.6	5 69.5		0 UND	0 UND
	0 UND	0 UND	11 31.8	45 8.1	30 12.0		4 87.4	5 75.0
	1 522.3	0 798.2	48 7.6	88 4.1	122 3.0		48 7.6	35 10.4
Cost of Sales/Inventory								
Cost of Sales/Payables								
Sales/Working Capital	8.4	10.5	3.4	2.7	2.2		7.2	4.5
	550.6	-65.1	9.7	6.5	3.0		54.0	51.5
	-6.2	-4.1	-13.3	119.8	6.2		-5.8	-5.4
EBIT/Interest	13.2	7.5	9.3	9.1	9.7		5.0	6.1
	(31) 3.3	(62) 2.5	(102) 3.6	(58) 3.6	5.2		(245) 2.4	(249) 2.8
	.9	.5	1.0	2.0	2.6		.7	1.1
Net Profit + Depr., Dep., Amort./Cur. Mat. L/T/D			5.0	5.9			4.3	5.2
			(21) 1.7	(15) 3.6			(38) 2.1	(39) 2.3
			.6	1.0			.9	1.4
Fixed/Worth	.3	.8	.7	.5	.5		.7	.7
	1.2	2.0	1.3	1.0	1.4		1.4	1.5
	-2.6	-2.3	3.5	1.9	2.3		6.5	17.6
Debt/Worth	.5	.8	.4	.5	.9		.6	.7
	2.0	4.2	1.6	1.5	1.5		1.7	2.2
	-2.8	-3.6	4.8	3.5	2.0		16.3	34.1
% Profit Before Taxes/Tangible Net Worth	101.0	53.7	26.8	32.5	30.1		28.5	41.0
	(23) 39.9	(44) 18.9	(92) 8.2	(63) 12.8	(12) 20.3		(217) 12.9	(221) 17.4
	.8	3.8	1.1	2.9	5.1		.5	4.3
% Profit Before Taxes/Total Assets	45.6	21.2	11.9	8.8	13.1		11.0	15.0
	22.0	4.9	3.7	3.9	8.0		4.0	5.8
	-.8	-1.2	.1	1.3	3.3		-.6	.4
Sales/Net Fixed Assets	124.0	10.0	7.6	8.6	6.0		7.1	7.1
	7.1	3.8	1.7	2.2	.9		2.3	2.6
	1.9	1.4	.7	.6	.5		.9	1.0
Sales/Total Assets	6.4	3.3	1.7	1.6	1.0		2.2	2.2
	2.8	1.7	.8	.7	.5		1.1	1.3
	1.2	.9	.5	.4	.3		.5	.5
% Depr., Dep., Amort./Sales	2.9	2.9	2.3	2.6	4.1		2.8	2.5
	(21) 9.4	(50) 7.4	(89) 6.3	(59) 4.8	6.5		(225) 6.0	(241) 5.7
	19.9	14.8	11.9	9.1	9.8		10.0	11.1
% Officers', Directors' Owners' Comp/Sales	4.9	2.5	1.3				1.3	1.6
	(11) 8.6	(23) 4.0	(28) 2.8				(84) 3.3	(58) 3.3
	15.2	7.2	9.1				5.4	7.2
Net Sales ($)	52179M	139914M	707677M	1460791M	692941M	792964M	3520128M	3275098M
Total Assets ($)	10753M	65233M	508822M	1374406M	880081M	773656M	2996729M	3026334M

© RMA 2011

M = $ thousand   MM = $ million
See Pages 9 through 22 for Explanation of Ratios and Data

Comparative Historical Data / Current Data Sorted by Sales

			Type of Statement	0-1MM	1-3MM	3-5MM	5-10MM	10-25MM	25MM & OVER
26	21	19	Unqualified			2	2	3	12
46	41	39	Reviewed	3	6	2	7	10	11
68	65	65	Compiled	5	23	7	15	8	7
91	107	82	Tax Returns	27	27	13	8	6	1
81	76	90	Other	22	26	12	12	10	8
4/1/08-3/31/09 ALL	4/1/09-3/31/10 ALL	4/1/10-3/31/11 ALL		51 (4/1-9/30/10)			244 (10/1/10-3/31/11)		
312	310	295	NUMBER OF STATEMENTS	57	82	36	44	37	39
%	%	%	**ASSETS**	%	%	%	%	%	%
8.3	9.8	10.1	Cash & Equivalents	9.4	12.6	8.1	9.9	10.4	7.6
8.9	8.8	8.8	Trade Receivables (net)	4.7	4.9	7.3	9.0	14.7	18.7
13.3	12.1	14.3	Inventory	10.6	9.2	17.4	15.3	15.3	25.2
6.7	5.0	5.8	All Other Current	3.3	5.9	5.0	7.1	6.4	7.5
37.2	35.7	38.9	Total Current	28.0	32.6	37.9	41.3	46.6	59.0
50.9	52.9	48.9	Fixed Assets (net)	61.3	52.5	48.4	50.6	37.4	32.8
1.0	1.5	1.8	Intangibles (net)	1.6	1.2	.4	.2	5.0	3.6
11.0	10.0	10.3	All Other Non-Current	9.2	13.6	13.3	7.9	10.9	4.6
100.0	100.0	100.0	Total	100.0	100.0	100.0	100.0	100.0	100.0
			LIABILITIES						
22.6	21.3	23.6	Notes Payable-Short Term	14.4	40.6	20.8	20.3	13.1	17.6
5.5	4.7	5.9	Cur. Mat.-L.T.D.	4.8	8.6	10.3	4.3	3.0	2.7
5.0	4.0	4.6	Trade Payables	2.6	2.3	2.7	3.3	8.9	11.4
.4	.5	.4	Income Taxes Payable	.0	.3	.1	.4	1.4	.3
6.9	8.1	6.2	All Other Current	8.9	6.2	4.8	2.9	4.8	8.5
40.4	38.6	40.6	Total Current	30.6	57.9	38.7	31.1	31.1	40.4
28.8	30.8	32.6	Long-Term Debt	37.3	42.5	37.3	32.1	16.8	16.1
.5	.5	.6	Deferred Taxes	.0	.6	.2	1.0	.4	1.4
4.6	6.4	6.9	All Other Non-Current	9.4	4.0	6.3	7.1	4.7	11.7
25.7	23.7	19.3	Net Worth	22.7	-5.0	17.5	28.7	47.0	30.4
100.0	100.0	100.0	Total Liabilities & Net Worth	100.0	100.0	100.0	100.0	100.0	100.0
			INCOME DATA						
100.0	100.0	100.0	Net Sales	100.0	100.0	100.0	100.0	100.0	100.0
			Gross Profit						
90.4	88.9	90.0	Operating Expenses	84.6	91.3	85.6	91.6	94.0	93.3
9.6	11.1	10.0	Operating Profit	15.4	8.7	14.4	8.4	6.0	6.7
3.1	3.3	2.8	All Other Expenses (net)	7.7	2.4	2.9	1.2	-.1	.9
6.5	7.8	7.2	Profit Before Taxes	7.7	6.2	11.5	7.2	6.0	5.8
			RATIOS						
2.1	2.3	2.7	Current	4.0	3.0	2.3	2.9	2.8	2.4
1.1	1.1	1.3		1.3	1.0	1.3	1.5	1.9	1.5
.4	.4	.6		.3	.2	.4	.7	1.1	1.1
1.0	1.3	1.3	Quick	1.6	1.3	.9	1.4	1.6	1.2
.4 (309)	.4 (294)	.5		.5 (81)	.3	.4	.6	.8	.5
.1	.1	.1		.1	.1	.1	.1	.3	.3
0 UND	0 UND	0 UND	Sales/Receivables	0 UND	0 UND	0 UND	0 UND	3 146.0	20 17.9
8 44.7	3 132.0	2 176.6		0 UND	0 UND	0 UND	1 656.5	50 7.3	31 11.9
42 8.7	40 9.2	46 7.9		11 34.6	26 13.9	65 5.6	45 8.2	84 4.3	53 6.8
			Cost of Sales/Inventory						
			Cost of Sales/Payables						
4.4	4.7	4.0	Sales/Working Capital	3.4	4.0	3.4	3.0	2.8	4.3
27.0	32.7	16.1		14.8	-108.1	24.5	11.2	7.9	9.7
-6.9	-8.8	-11.4		-6.5	-4.4	-8.2	-25.7	42.3	65.8
7.1	9.4	9.0	EBIT/Interest	4.8	8.0	8.7	11.3	13.2	10.5
(281) 2.6	(273) 3.1	(270) 3.3		(47) 2.2	(79) 3.2	(32) 5.2	(40) 3.3	(35) 3.7	(37) 4.7
.9	.9	1.2		.4	.8	2.1	1.0	1.8	2.2
5.5	6.0	5.9	Net Profit + Depr., Dep., Amort./Cur. Mat. L/T/D		3.9			5.8	13.7
(56) 2.9	(55) 2.3	(50) 2.7			(10) 1.2			(11) 2.0	(16) 5.0
1.3	.9	1.2			.1			.5	2.4
.7	.7	.6	Fixed/Worth	.7	.7	.3	.5	.5	.4
1.3	1.3	1.3		1.4	1.9	1.3	1.3	1.0	1.0
4.5	4.3	4.4		6.6	-7.3	3.8	3.9	2.1	1.5
.7	.6	.6	Debt/Worth	.5	.7	.9	.4	.4	.9
1.7	1.7	1.7		1.6	2.4	1.8	1.6	1.4	1.9
7.3	6.8	8.1		22.3	-7.4	5.6	4.9	2.9	4.2
34.3	33.8	33.0	% Profit Before Taxes/Tangible Net Worth	30.1	65.7	33.6	32.7	46.9	32.4
(259) 12.1	(257) 13.5	(238) 12.5		(45) 5.6	(55) 14.1	(29) 15.6	(38) 5.8	(35) 18.7	(36) 20.8
1.0	.6	2.7		-2.8	2.2	5.9	1.2	5.0	5.8
12.1	14.2	14.1	% Profit Before Taxes/Total Assets	7.7	22.3	21.6	15.5	13.8	13.6
4.2	4.9	4.9		2.4	5.0	7.1	3.7	6.7	6.0
-.3	-.4	.5		-2.2	-.6	1.5	.0	2.4	2.3
6.9	7.7	9.0	Sales/Net Fixed Assets	3.2	6.4	13.6	9.7	14.6	14.8
2.2	2.1	2.7		.9	2.9	2.3	2.0	3.9	7.6
.9	.9	.9		.4	1.1	.8	.9	1.5	3.3
2.1	2.2	2.3	Sales/Total Assets	1.3	2.6	2.4	2.2	2.1	3.5
1.0	1.1	1.0		.6	1.2	1.0	1.0	1.0	2.1
.5	.5	.5		.3	.6	.5	.5	.5	.9
3.1	2.8	2.7	% Depr., Dep., Amort./Sales	6.0	4.4	3.1	2.8	2.5	1.0
(269) 6.2	(243) 6.6	(237) 6.3		(45) 11.1	(59) 8.2	(25) 7.6	(36) 6.9	(34) 4.1	(38) 2.0
11.2	10.7	11.7		22.9	12.9	13.6	10.8	5.6	5.7
2.0	1.5	1.8	% Officers', Directors' Owners' Comp/Sales	3.9	2.6				
(83) 3.3	(87) 3.1	(67) 4.2		(18) 8.1	(21) 4.6				
6.4	6.3	8.5		13.9	10.6				
3863180M	4030350M	3846466M	Net Sales ($)	27460M	158924M	142589M	304477M	590598M	2622418M
3928484M	3238317M	3612951M	Total Assets ($)	114746M	208319M	189912M	441036M	834566M	1824372M

© RMA 2011   M = $ thousand   MM = $ million
See Pages 9 through 22 for Explanation of Ratios and Data

Current Data Sorted by Assets   Comparative Historical Data

Type of Statement	0-500M	500M-2MM	2-10MM	10-50MM	50-100MM	100-250MM		4/1/06-3/31/07 ALL	4/1/07-3/31/08 ALL
Unqualified			1	2	1	2		10	7
Reviewed		1	9	12	1			20	15
Compiled	3	5	7	9				30	32
Tax Returns	17	18	19	3	1			39	36
Other	2	14	19	13	1			31	39
		15 (4/1-9/30/10)		145 (10/1/10-3/31/11)					
NUMBER OF STATEMENTS	22	38	55	39	4	2		130	129
ASSETS	%	%	%	%	%	%		%	%
Cash & Equivalents	16.0	5.8	4.9	2.6				8.4	10.1
Trade Receivables (net)	1.5	4.1	6.4	2.7				6.5	5.7
Inventory	16.2	19.0	31.7	31.0				29.7	25.1
All Other Current	8.4	3.2	3.4	4.8				4.9	4.5
Total Current	42.2	32.1	46.4	41.1				49.6	45.4
Fixed Assets (net)	51.1	60.5	44.6	46.1				41.7	46.7
Intangibles (net)	1.8	.1	.1	.7				.3	.8
All Other Non-Current	4.9	7.3	8.9	12.1				8.4	7.0
Total	100.0	100.0	100.0	100.0				100.0	100.0
LIABILITIES									
Notes Payable-Short Term	74.7	28.4	31.1	26.0				29.4	28.7
Cur. Mat.-L.T.D.	4.0	2.5	2.2	1.9				3.1	4.0
Trade Payables	.6	.9	3.1	1.8				2.9	4.1
Income Taxes Payable	.1	.0	.4	.4				.3	.3
All Other Current	29.5	3.8	5.7	3.4				7.6	4.5
Total Current	109.0	35.7	42.5	33.4				43.3	41.8
Long-Term Debt	22.8	32.5	14.8	20.8				22.7	20.2
Deferred Taxes	.0	.0	.3	.3				.4	.2
All Other Non-Current	8.8	8.6	5.0	1.2				4.2	4.4
Net Worth	-40.6	23.3	37.5	44.3				29.4	33.5
Total Liabilties & Net Worth	100.0	100.0	100.0	100.0				100.0	100.0
INCOME DATA									
Net Sales	100.0	100.0	100.0	100.0				100.0	100.0
Gross Profit									
Operating Expenses	74.7	92.8	94.2	92.5				92.2	91.0
Operating Profit	25.3	7.2	5.8	7.5				7.8	9.0
All Other Expenses (net)	1.4	4.9	-.2	3.2				3.8	4.0
Profit Before Taxes	23.9	2.3	6.0	4.3				4.0	5.0
RATIOS									
Current	2.2	1.8	2.3	1.9				2.4	2.3
	.7	.9	1.2	1.3				1.2	1.2
	.1	.3	.8	1.0				.6	.7
Quick	1.0	.7	.5	.3				.7	.8
	.1	.2	(53) .2	.1				(128) .2	(128) .2
	.0	.0	.0	.0				.1	.0
Sales/Receivables	0 UND	0 UND	0 UND	0 UND				0 UND	0 UND
	0 UND	0 UND	0 UND	4 90.8				0 UND	0 UND
	0 UND	1 292.6	17 21.2	21 17.0				15 23.7	15 24.3
Cost of Sales/Inventory									
Cost of Sales/Payables									
Sales/Working Capital	4.5	7.0	3.6	2.4				3.5	4.0
	-18.3	-42.9	7.8	5.9				62.0	21.9
	-3.5	-3.5	-7.3	-68.0				-6.8	-12.2
EBIT/Interest	6.5	4.2	7.1	8.0				3.6	4.6
	(15) 3.5	(35) 1.7	(52) 2.6	(32) 2.5				(110) 1.7	(112) 1.8
	1.3	-.2	1.3	1.3				.1	.9
Net Profit + Depr., Dep., Amort./Cur. Mat. L/T/D								10.0	6.6
								(14) 4.6	(11) 3.6
								1.8	1.0
Fixed/Worth	.3	.7	.5	.6				.3	.5
	1.9	2.0	.9	1.1				1.1	1.3
	-.9	-4.7	2.0	1.8				3.4	4.2
Debt/Worth	.4	.4	.5	.7				.8	.6
	2.1	2.6	1.7	1.2				2.0	1.5
	-2.2	-9.0	4.4	2.8				9.2	9.1
% Profit Before Taxes/Tangible Net Worth	57.3	33.9	21.5	23.5				24.7	20.7
	(14) 19.9	(26) 7.1	(48) 7.0	5.8				(109) 6.5	(107) 7.4
	9.3	-4.4	2.1	.6				-1.1	1.0
% Profit Before Taxes/Total Assets	30.6	10.6	8.4	7.9				8.1	7.3
	11.7	1.6	2.9	2.4				2.4	2.6
	1.8	-4.3	.6	.3				-1.5	-.3
Sales/Net Fixed Assets	267.6	4.1	9.3	4.6				23.1	14.2
	4.4	1.2	1.7	1.0				3.1	2.1
	.6	.6	.7	.5				.7	.7
Sales/Total Assets	3.5	1.4	1.6	.9				1.8	1.9
	1.1	.7	.7	.6				1.1	1.0
	.4	.4	.4	.2				.5	.5
% Depr., Dep., Amort./Sales	.6	2.2	1.4	1.7				.8	1.0
	(14) 7.7	(32) 9.2	(46) 5.0	(35) 5.1				(103) 3.9	(104) 3.7
	21.5	20.4	9.0	12.8				10.5	10.6
% Officers', Directors' Owners' Comp/Sales			.6					.5	.9
		(11) 1.4						(29) 1.5	(32) 1.9
		3.8						5.6	6.4
Net Sales ($)	22216M	93382M	462687M	589638M	674752M	576687M		3335504M	2505764M
Total Assets ($)	5177M	38572M	260896M	938140M	310285M	315617M		1635775M	1790535M

M = $ thousand   MM = $ million
See Pages 9 through 22 for Explanation of Ratios and Data

Comparative Historical Data | Current Data Sorted by Sales

6	6	6	Type of Statement / Unqualified		1		2		3
17	13	23	Reviewed	1	3	3	6	4	6
33	28	24	Compiled	8	1	3	4	4	4
44	56	58	Tax Returns	27	18	4	2	4	3
47	31	49	Other	17	13	2	9	7	1
4/1/08-3/31/09 ALL	4/1/09-3/31/10 ALL	4/1/10-3/31/11 ALL		15 (4/1-9/30/10)			145 (10/1/10-3/31/11)		
				0-1MM	1-3MM	3-5MM	5-10MM	10-25MM	25MM & OVER
147	134	160	**NUMBER OF STATEMENTS**	53	36	12	23	19	17
%	%	%	**ASSETS**	%	%	%	%	%	%
7.0	8.3	6.4	Cash & Equivalents	9.8	3.5	4.6	4.1	6.7	6.3
7.1	5.6	4.3	Trade Receivables (net)	1.6	4.3	6.7	3.0	6.1	10.8
27.0	26.7	25.6	Inventory	15.6	21.0	28.8	41.5	33.8	33.4
6.4	5.6	4.3	All Other Current	4.4	2.8	1.7	6.3	1.5	9.2
47.5	46.1	40.6	Total Current	31.4	31.7	41.8	54.9	48.1	59.8
44.9	42.3	50.1	Fixed Assets (net)	61.1	56.7	46.8	36.8	41.6	31.8
.1	1.7	.5	Intangibles (net)	.6	.3	.3	.3	.0	1.8
7.5	9.9	8.7	All Other Non-Current	7.0	11.3	11.1	8.0	10.2	6.7
100.0	100.0	100.0	Total	100.0	100.0	100.0	100.0	100.0	100.0
			LIABILITIES						
25.8	41.7	34.5	Notes Payable-Short Term	42.8	28.1	27.1	41.0	26.5	27.2
4.9	4.0	2.4	Cur. Mat.-L.T.D.	2.8	3.2	2.2	1.8	1.8	1.5
2.5	2.2	3.4	Trade Payables	.7	.9	2.7	1.8	2.2	21.4
.7	.1	.3	Income Taxes Payable	.0	.0	1.3	.8	.3	.0
7.2	5.7	7.9	All Other Current	14.7	1.8	2.1	7.7	6.0	5.9
41.1	53.6	48.4	Total Current	61.0	34.0	35.3	53.0	36.7	55.9
21.0	19.5	21.7	Long-Term Debt	25.9	23.7	24.1	15.3	15.4	18.8
.4	.5	.2	Deferred Taxes	.0	.2	.5	.2	.5	.1
5.4	4.5	5.3	All Other Non-Current	4.7	13.1	2.8	.9	2.3	2.1
32.1	21.7	24.3	Net Worth	8.3	29.1	37.3	30.7	45.1	23.1
100.0	100.0	100.0	Total Liabilities & Net Worth	100.0	100.0	100.0	100.0	100.0	100.0
			INCOME DATA						
100.0	100.0	100.0	Net Sales	100.0	100.0	100.0	100.0	100.0	100.0
			Gross Profit						
94.4	95.4	90.3	Operating Expenses	84.4	91.5	94.4	98.8	85.9	96.5
5.6	4.6	9.7	Operating Profit	15.6	8.5	5.6	1.2	14.1	3.5
2.9	2.2	2.0	All Other Expenses (net)	4.3	1.3	.2	.9	1.2	.2
2.8	2.4	7.7	Profit Before Taxes	11.3	7.1	5.3	.3	13.0	3.3
			RATIOS						
2.2	1.8	2.0	Current	3.5	2.3	1.9	1.3	2.7	1.7
1.1	1.1	1.2		.8	1.2	1.2	1.2	1.9	1.2
.7	.7	.6		.2	.5	.6	.8	1.1	1.1
.7	.7	.5	Quick	.9	.5	.4	.2	1.4	.6
.2 (132)	.2 (158)	.2		.2 (35)	.0 (11)	.0	.1	.3	.2
.0	.0	.0		.1	.0	.0	.0	.1	.1
0 UND	0 UND	0 UND	Sales/Receivables	0 UND	0 UND	0 UND	0 UND	0 UND	1 663.1
0 UND	0 UND	0 UND		0 UND	0 UND	0 UND	1 399.5	11 31.8	3 126.7
18 20.2	19 19.3	11 33.5		0 UND	1 659.6	8 44.6	56 6.5	19 19.3	20 18.3
			Cost of Sales/Inventory						
			Cost of Sales/Payables						
4.1	4.3	3.5	Sales/Working Capital	1.9	2.1	4.0	3.8	4.0	7.4
27.1	40.3	16.1		-31.8	19.2	7.5	11.7	5.2	37.0
-6.2	-8.3	-7.1		-2.2	-5.8	-3.7	-9.1	92.6	NM
3.2	4.5	5.9	EBIT/Interest	5.4	4.4	7.2	4.4	12.2	6.9
(124) 1.7	(122) 1.1	(140) 2.5		(40) 2.4	(33) 2.2	2.5	(21) 2.7	(17) 5.2	2.5
.0	-1.2	1.1		-.6	1.1	1.8	1.2	1.4	1.4
5.2	8.0	6.7	Net Profit + Depr., Dep., Amort./Cur. Mat. L/T/D						
(16) 1.0	(15) 2.3	(14) 2.5							
-2.6	.8	.9							
.5	.4	.5	Fixed/Worth	.7	.6	.5	.3	.4	.2
1.1	1.1	1.2		1.7	1.2	1.2	1.1	.6	1.5
2.9	3.4	4.0		-20.5	NM	4.9	1.6	1.2	4.3
.6	.7	.6	Debt/Worth	.3	.4	.7	1.2	.6	1.1
1.7	1.7	1.6		1.7	1.9	1.5	1.6	1.1	2.5
6.4	8.9	5.9		-26.4	-11.0	7.5	3.8	2.0	7.0
16.4	18.3	25.4	% Profit Before Taxes/Tangible Net Worth	24.7	13.0	16.8	23.6	34.7	54.2
(121) 3.8	(105) 2.7	(132) 7.5		(39) 6.4	(26) 5.8	(11) 7.2	(22) 6.5	(18) 20.6	(16) 10.8
-3.5	-6.4	1.0		-2.3	1.3	4.6	-.8	3.2	4.3
5.9	5.9	10.2	% Profit Before Taxes/Total Assets	11.9	8.2	4.7	5.9	16.5	9.4
1.5	.7	3.0		2.5	2.2	3.2	2.0	8.9	4.0
-3.0	-5.1	.1		-3.1	.1	1.1	.3	1.3	1.5
12.5	16.4	6.3	Sales/Net Fixed Assets	2.8	2.7	3.2	11.1	11.0	41.6
2.7	2.6	1.5		.8	1.1	1.5	3.8	2.2	9.3
.7	.8	.6		.3	.6	.7	.9	.8	4.1
1.9	1.9	1.5	Sales/Total Assets	.9	1.7	1.3	1.6	2.0	5.5
.8	1.0	.7		.4	.6	.8	.8	1.0	1.6
.4	.4	.4		.3	.4	.4	.4	.6	.9
1.0	1.0	1.6	% Depr., Dep., Amort./Sales	3.6	4.0	1.8	.6	1.2	.2
(122) 4.7	(113) 4.5	(129) 5.4		(37) 11.1	(33) 8.1	(10) 5.1	(20) 4.0	(15) 4.6	(14) .6
11.1	13.0	12.7		24.9	13.8	10.6	10.7	7.7	1.3
.7	.8	1.6	% Officers', Directors' Owners' Comp/Sales						
(39) 2.1	(42) 2.0	(31) 3.1							
5.5	4.6	7.5							
1588660M	1211848M	2419362M	Net Sales ($)	21905M	65993M	45539M	165122M	282140M	1838663M
1307862M	1243164M	1868687M	Total Assets ($)	102948M	195080M	76258M	328886M	335405M	830110M

M = $ thousand   MM = $ million
See Pages 9 through 22 for Explanation of Ratios and Data

Current Data Sorted by Assets | Comparative Historical Data

0-500M	500M-2MM	2-10MM	10-50MM	50-100MM	100-250MM	Type of Statement	4/1/06-3/31/07 ALL	4/1/07-3/31/08 ALL
		5	17	11	7	Unqualified	39	34
	4	17	22	7	2	Reviewed	41	49
	8	17	7		1	Compiled	36	27
2	11	8	2			Tax Returns	22	15
1	7	19	29	10	4	Other	63	72
	49 (4/1-9/30/10)		169 (10/1/10-3/31/11)					
3	30	66	77	28	14	**NUMBER OF STATEMENTS**	201	197
%	%	%	%	%	%	**ASSETS**	%	%
	3.1	3.1	4.8	4.1	2.3	Cash & Equivalents	4.2	4.3
	14.6	17.6	13.9	13.8	7.2	Trade Receivables (net)	15.8	16.5
	42.2	40.1	39.1	49.9	66.1	Inventory	42.3	43.6
	1.0	6.7	11.5	5.9	4.7	All Other Current	7.6	6.5
	60.9	67.5	69.4	73.8	80.3	Total Current	69.8	70.9
	28.6	25.3	22.5	21.5	15.9	Fixed Assets (net)	21.0	21.0
	.0	1.6	.3	.2	.1	Intangibles (net)	.3	.3
	10.5	5.6	7.9	4.5	3.8	All Other Non-Current	8.9	7.8
	100.0	100.0	100.0	100.0	100.0	Total	100.0	100.0
						LIABILITIES		
	58.6	32.2	32.0	37.8	42.5	Notes Payable-Short Term	35.6	39.8
	7.7	2.1	1.4	1.3	1.2	Cur. Mat.-L.T.D.	1.8	1.4
	9.5	7.6	7.6	5.0	3.7	Trade Payables	5.5	5.8
	.0	.1	.4	.1	.1	Income Taxes Payable	.4	.3
	6.3	7.3	8.0	5.4	7.7	All Other Current	7.2	6.8
	82.2	49.2	49.5	49.6	55.1	Total Current	50.5	54.0
	43.7	13.9	13.2	9.6	8.7	Long-Term Debt	12.3	12.1
	.1	.2	.5	.3	.3	Deferred Taxes	.3	.5
	9.1	4.4	3.5	3.9	.9	All Other Non-Current	3.3	4.2
	-35.0	32.3	33.3	36.6	34.9	Net Worth	33.6	29.4
	100.0	100.0	100.0	100.0	100.0	Total Liabilities & Net Worth	100.0	100.0
						INCOME DATA		
	100.0	100.0	100.0	100.0	100.0	Net Sales	100.0	100.0
						Gross Profit		
	91.0	93.1	92.9	94.7	91.4	Operating Expenses	94.5	94.8
	9.0	6.9	7.1	5.3	8.6	Operating Profit	5.5	5.2
	2.9	1.3	2.6	.3	2.3	All Other Expenses (net)	2.3	3.3
	6.1	5.5	4.4	5.0	6.3	Profit Before Taxes	3.2	2.0
						RATIOS		
	1.8	2.4	1.8	1.9	1.5		1.8	1.9
	1.1	1.3	1.3	1.4	1.4	Current	1.3	1.3
	.6	1.0	1.1	1.2	1.2		1.1	1.1
	.8	1.0	.7	.6	.3		.6	.7
	.1	(65) .3	.3	.4	.1	Quick	(200) .3	.3
	.0	.1	.1	.1	.0		.1	.1
	0 UND	0 UND	3 115.1	6 64.7	6 64.3		1 281.3	2 188.8
	7 53.0	13 27.9	24 15.3	34 10.7	9 41.0	Sales/Receivables	17 21.4	19 18.8
	35 10.5	63 5.8	45 8.2	65 5.7	28 12.9		54 6.7	50 7.3
						Cost of Sales/Inventory		
						Cost of Sales/Payables		
	8.5	3.3	3.2	3.3	4.0		4.6	4.2
	72.4	9.9	9.4	6.1	5.7	Sales/Working Capital	9.0	10.1
	-7.3	-226.5	27.1	16.0	6.9		36.0	43.2
	8.4	5.9	8.2	6.6	9.5		4.3	3.7
	(26) 2.0	(62) 2.9	(71) 3.5	(27) 4.8	5.7	EBIT/Interest	(186) 1.8	(185) 1.6
	.3	1.2	1.4	3.1	3.2		.7	.6
			11.4			Net Profit + Depr., Dep.,	5.7	11.3
		(12) 6.9				Amort./Cur. Mat. L/T/D	(29) 2.2	(30) 2.4
			4.1				1.3	.8
	.2	.1	.2	.2	.1		.2	.2
	.6	.5	.5	.5	.3	Fixed/Worth	.5	.5
	-2.6	2.2	1.2	1.0	.7		1.3	1.4
	1.0	.9	.9	.8	1.8		1.0	1.0
	3.5	2.6	2.6	2.3	2.1	Debt/Worth	2.3	2.6
	-5.4	5.9	6.5	4.3	2.9		4.6	5.5
	24.6	24.5	29.4	28.7	31.7	% Profit Before Taxes/Tangible	21.2	20.0
	(19) 9.8	(58) 12.5	(71) 14.5	(27) 17.7	24.8	Net Worth	(190) 8.5	(178) 7.9
	.0	.7	5.3	10.7	16.1		-1.0	-3.2
	13.0	9.3	8.8	7.5	9.9	% Profit Before Taxes/Total	7.8	6.3
	4.0	3.9	4.2	6.1	7.9	Assets	2.3	2.3
	-3.1	.0	1.0	3.5	5.5		-.5	-1.3
	80.6	106.5	30.0	21.8	35.5		29.1	29.6
	14.2	10.3	10.2	10.3	15.4	Sales/Net Fixed Assets	9.5	9.9
	3.8	2.1	4.0	5.0	3.9		5.1	5.2
	3.9	2.4	1.9	1.6	1.8		2.0	2.2
	2.3	1.7	1.2	1.2	1.3	Sales/Total Assets	1.5	1.5
	1.1	.8	.8	.9	.8		1.0	1.0
	.8	.6	.8	.7	.5		.8	.7
	(20) 2.1	(51) 1.9	(67) 1.3	(23) 1.4	(12) .9	% Depr., Dep., Amort./Sales	(170) 1.5	(164) 1.4
	4.8	3.9	3.2	2.3	2.0		2.6	2.5
		.4	.3			% Officers', Directors'	.4	.4
		(12) 1.1	(12) 1.2			Owners' Comp/Sales	(49) 1.5	(45) 1.3
		6.4	3.1				3.8	3.7
1766M	90667M	955938M	2275152M	2678804M	2605591M	Net Sales ($)	9238645M	8389083M
904M	30227M	373714M	1649049M	2070121M	2103442M	Total Assets ($)	6043572M	5536584M

M = $ thousand   MM = $ million
See Pages 9 through 22 for Explanation of Ratios and Data

Comparative Historical Data | | | | Current Data Sorted by Sales

			Type of Statement						
38	40	40	Unqualified				1	8	31
47	51	52	Reviewed	2	3	2	11	14	20
39	32	33	Compiled	1	3	5	8	9	7
16	18	23	Tax Returns	4	11	2	5	1	
80	57	70	Other	7	8	3	6	19	27
4/1/08-3/31/09 ALL	4/1/09-3/31/10 ALL	4/1/10-3/31/11 ALL		49 (4/1-9/30/10)			169 (10/1/10-3/31/11)		
				0-1MM	1-3MM	3-5MM	5-10MM	10-25MM	25MM & OVER
220	198	218	**NUMBER OF STATEMENTS**	14	25	12	31	51	85
%	%	%	**ASSETS**	%	%	%	%	%	%
5.4	4.8	4.4	Cash & Equivalents	14.3	2.5	2.2	3.5	4.3	4.1
16.6	15.7	14.5	Trade Receivables (net)	3.2	15.8	9.0	14.1	19.6	13.9
41.3	40.5	42.5	Inventory	26.0	36.0	31.6	43.1	39.0	50.5
6.6	6.0	7.4	All Other Current	2.3	2.4	2.5	5.6	11.8	8.3
69.9	67.0	68.8	Total Current	45.9	56.6	45.3	66.3	74.8	76.8
21.8	24.2	23.8	Fixed Assets (net)	42.5	36.1	45.8	26.1	16.6	17.5
.3	.2	.6	Intangibles (net)	1.1	1.2	.1	.6	.8	.4
8.0	8.6	6.8	All Other Non-Current	10.5	6.1	8.8	7.0	7.8	5.3
100.0	100.0	100.0	Total	100.0	100.0	100.0	100.0	100.0	100.0
			LIABILITIES						
36.2	38.8	36.7	Notes Payable-Short Term	10.8	42.3	70.1	36.0	34.6	36.2
1.4	2.0	2.5	Cur. Mat.-L.T.D.	1.8	6.5	7.7	2.8	1.2	1.2
5.8	6.3	7.2	Trade Payables	3.3	5.0	11.1	8.7	6.3	7.9
.2	.2	.2	Income Taxes Payable	.0	.0	.2	.1	.1	.3
6.4	6.9	7.1	All Other Current	.9	4.3	7.2	6.2	9.6	7.8
50.0	54.1	53.7	Total Current	16.8	58.0	96.4	53.9	51.8	53.5
13.5	14.9	17.8	Long-Term Debt	41.4	57.6	18.4	12.1	8.9	9.4
.4	.4	.3	Deferred Taxes	.0	.0	.4	.3	.1	.5
3.1	4.4	4.4	All Other Non-Current	.0	4.2	23.3	4.4	1.9	3.9
33.0	26.1	23.9	Net Worth	41.8	-19.9	-38.6	29.3	37.3	32.7
100.0	100.0	100.0	Total Liabilities & Net Worth	100.0	100.0	100.0	100.0	100.0	100.0
			INCOME DATA						
100.0	100.0	100.0	Net Sales	100.0	100.0	100.0	100.0	100.0	100.0
			Gross Profit						
95.7	97.1	92.5	Operating Expenses	72.7	86.9	93.3	93.7	95.3	95.2
4.3	2.9	7.5	Operating Profit	27.3	13.1	6.7	6.3	4.7	4.8
2.4	1.6	1.9	All Other Expenses (net)	8.4	3.3	3.2	3.1	.7	.6
1.9	1.3	5.5	Profit Before Taxes	19.0	9.8	3.5	3.2	4.0	4.2
			RATIOS						
2.0	1.7	2.0		12.4	1.9	3.0	2.1	2.2	1.7
1.3	1.2	1.3	Current	3.3	1.2	1.1	1.2	1.4	1.4
1.1	1.0	1.1		1.1	.7	.6	.9	1.1	1.2
.8	.7	.7		7.7	1.1	.8	.6	.9	.6
(216) .3	(196) .2	(217) .3	Quick	.8	.1	.2	.2	(50) .3	.3
.1	.1	.1		.1	.0	.0	.0	.1	.1
1 282.6	4 102.4	1 359.2		0 UND	0 UND	0 UND	0 UND	3 110.2	4 84.6
16 22.7	17 21.0	16 22.8	Sales/Receivables	0 UND	0 UND	0 UND	21 17.7	22 16.5	24 15.3
53 6.9	45 8.2	45 8.1		33 11.0	71 5.1	27 13.5	51 7.2	61 5.9	49 7.5
			Cost of Sales/Inventory						
			Cost of Sales/Payables						
4.0	5.2	3.4		1.0	2.5	8.1	3.2	3.4	4.1
10.5	11.3	9.1	Sales/Working Capital	5.0	9.2	NM	24.5	8.2	8.1
27.7	156.8	52.4		45.5	-8.1	-2.8	-64.4	29.9	20.9
4.5	5.5	7.5			12.2	2.6	4.6	9.4	7.5
(205) 1.5	(190) 1.6	(201) 3.5	EBIT/Interest	(21) 2.4	.9	(29) 1.8	(50) 4.3	(81) 4.6	
-.1	-.5	1.4		1.0	-13.9	1.3	1.3	2.2	
11.7	6.5	10.0							10.7
(20) 3.3	(19) 1.8	(27) 6.8	Net Profit + Depr., Dep., Amort./Cur. Mat. L/T/D					(19) 7.4	
-.5	.2	1.7							3.9
.1	.2	.2		.0	.3	.5	.3	.0	.2
.6	.6	.5	Fixed/Worth	.4	1.1	1.2	.9	.4	.4
1.3	1.4	1.3		NM	-2.3	9.0	3.4	1.0	.8
.8	1.0	.9		.1	1.4	.8	1.0	.8	1.3
2.3	2.5	2.5	Debt/Worth	.7	4.4	2.1	2.9	1.7	2.4
5.8	5.4	6.3		NM	-4.4	9.6	10.0	5.6	4.4
25.9	22.4	29.1		29.5	40.3	16.3	18.9	26.0	30.5
(197) 5.8	(176) 5.8	(191) 15.9	% Profit Before Taxes/Tangible Net Worth	(11) 9.6	(16) 7.8	(10) 5.2	(26) 8.5	(47) 17.7	(81) 19.6
-5.4	-7.0	5.2		.5	.6	-4.7	2.9	4.8	9.6
9.1	6.8	8.9		14.7	12.6	4.5	7.0	10.0	9.1
1.7	1.5	4.9	% Profit Before Taxes/Total Assets	4.9	3.5	-.8	2.1	5.0	5.9
-3.3	-3.2	.7		-.2	.1	-3.9	.8	.3	3.2
36.3	29.0	38.9		UND	25.1	14.2	19.4	134.0	40.8
10.7	10.5	10.9	Sales/Net Fixed Assets	3.0	3.3	2.8	4.9	17.0	11.7
4.8	3.8	3.9		.7	1.0	.8	2.3	6.9	5.6
2.3	2.3	2.1		1.2	2.2	3.3	2.4	2.3	2.1
1.6	1.6	1.4	Sales/Total Assets	.7	.8	1.3	1.4	1.6	1.5
1.0	.9	.8		.2	.4	.3	.8	.9	1.0
.7	.7	.8			1.1	1.5	.6	.7	.7
(175) 1.4	(167) 1.5	(174) 1.4	% Depr., Dep., Amort./Sales	(19) 4.0	(10) 5.1	(27) 1.7	(38) 1.1	(73) 1.1	
2.4	3.1	3.3			13.9	9.5	3.7	2.6	1.8
.3	.4	.4							.2
(46) .8	(44) 1.0	(39) 1.2	% Officers', Directors' Owners' Comp/Sales					(17) .4	
2.2	3.7	3.6							3.2
10754155M	9641184M	8607918M	Net Sales ($)	8640M	47307M	45826M	228272M	789277M	7488596M
6575425M	5784216M	6227457M	Total Assets ($)	28914M	103675M	82587M	257931M	594806M	5159544M

M = $ thousand   MM = $ million
See Pages 9 through 22 for Explanation of Ratios and Data

Current Data Sorted by Assets

Comparative Historical Data

						Type of Statement		
2	12	2 138	4 262	1 25	6 9	Unqualified	9 256	6 257
	9	59	32	1	1	Reviewed	64	80
6	18	17	1		1	Compiled	31	51
	10	30	31	5	4	Tax Returns	50	52
	37 (4/1-9/30/10)		648 (10/1/10-3/31/11)			Other	4/1/06-3/31/07	4/1/07-3/31/08
0-500M	500M-2MM	2-10MM	10-50MM	50-100MM	100-250MM		ALL	ALL
8	49	246	330	32	20	NUMBER OF STATEMENTS	410	446
%	%	%	%	%	%	ASSETS	%	%
	5.1	1.2	1.0	1.0	3.2	Cash & Equivalents	1.9	1.9
	5.6	5.7	6.1	5.2	8.2	Trade Receivables (net)	6.6	8.6
	10.1	12.0	11.6	10.4	9.5	Inventory	13.4	14.1
	3.6	3.2	2.5	1.6	1.6	All Other Current	2.5	4.0
	24.5	22.2	21.2	18.2	22.5	Total Current	24.4	28.6
	59.5	65.8	67.6	68.6	62.3	Fixed Assets (net)	64.8	60.3
	2.5	1.4	.7	.7	3.2	Intangibles (net)	1.2	1.5
	13.5	10.6	10.6	12.4	12.0	All Other Non-Current	9.7	9.6
	100.0	100.0	100.0	100.0	100.0	Total	100.0	100.0
						LIABILITIES		
	15.4	14.0	13.4	11.5	12.1	Notes Payable-Short Term	15.9	14.5
	7.4	7.9	5.8	5.0	6.6	Cur. Mat.-L.T.D.	5.3	4.9
	5.0	5.3	3.9	3.7	3.7	Trade Payables	4.3	3.5
	.0	.1	.0	.0	.0	Income Taxes Payable	.0	.1
	10.9	3.0	2.5	1.4	6.2	All Other Current	2.9	3.4
	38.7	30.3	25.6	21.6	28.5	Total Current	28.4	26.4
	69.1	45.4	41.7	49.1	35.4	Long-Term Debt	44.0	40.6
	.0	.2	.1	.2	.2	Deferred Taxes	.2	.2
	17.6	5.6	4.5	1.0	3.6	All Other Non-Current	3.4	5.2
	-25.4	18.5	28.2	28.0	32.3	Net Worth	24.0	27.7
	100.0	100.0	100.0	100.0	100.0	Total Liabilities & Net Worth	100.0	100.0
						INCOME DATA		
	100.0	100.0	100.0	100.0	100.0	Net Sales	100.0	100.0
						Gross Profit		
	94.4	89.1	87.7	88.7	86.3	Operating Expenses	97.8	81.8
	5.6	10.9	12.3	11.3	13.7	Operating Profit	2.2	18.2
	4.6	6.3	5.7	5.0	7.9	All Other Expenses (net)	7.1	6.6
	1.0	4.6	6.6	6.3	5.9	Profit Before Taxes	-4.9	11.5
						RATIOS		
	1.9	1.1	1.3	1.2	1.4		1.3	1.7
	.8	.8	.9	.9	1.1	Current	.8	1.1
	.2	.4	.6	.7	.5		.6	.8
	.8	.4	.4	.6	.7		.5	.7
	.3	.2	.3	.3	.3	Quick	.2 (444)	.3
	.1	.1	.1	.1	.2		.1	.2
0 UND	14 25.3	18 20.8	21 17.5	19 19.2			16 23.3	17 21.2
0 UND	20 18.7	27 13.3	31 11.8	28 13.3		Sales/Receivables	23 15.9	30 12.3
26 13.9	30 12.0	35 10.6	41 8.8	58 6.2			36 10.1	47 7.7
						Cost of Sales/Inventory		
						Cost of Sales/Payables		
	27.3	38.7	12.7	16.0	10.3		15.3	6.9
	-67.5	-15.6	-17.7	-36.8	NM	Sales/Working Capital	-17.6	49.9
	-3.6	-4.9	-6.0	-7.8	-3.4		-6.6	-13.5
	4.1	4.1	4.5	3.8	7.1		1.4	5.3
(41)	1.4 (232)	2.1 (319)	2.6	2.2 (18)	2.7	EBIT/Interest	(395) .3 (426)	3.4
	-1.0	1.0	1.4	1.2	1.1		-.9	1.8
		3.2					3.9	3.9
	(11)	1.2				Net Profit + Depr., Dep., Amort./Cur. Mat. L/T/D	(24) 1.6 (17)	2.1
		.8					.4	.4
	1.1	1.7	1.4	1.6	1.6		1.4	1.2
	-9.5	2.8	2.5	2.5	2.3	Fixed/Worth	2.6	2.1
	-1.2	21.9	4.8	6.0	3.8		6.3	4.8
	1.8	1.4	1.3	1.3	1.2		1.4	1.2
	-18.5	3.3	2.7	2.7	2.2	Debt/Worth	2.8	2.3
	-2.8	27.4	5.4	6.3	7.6		7.4	5.8
	27.6	31.4	26.3	17.5	19.8		6.7	51.2
(23)	8.5 (193)	13.1 (296)	14.1 (28)	11.4 (18)	11.2	% Profit Before Taxes/Tangible Net Worth	(356) -6.6 (400)	30.7
	-5.8	3.0	4.7	7.3	2.2		-26.3	12.8
	9.1	7.8	7.8	5.7	8.1		1.8	15.3
	1.9	3.1	4.0	3.3	3.6	% Profit Before Taxes/Total Assets	-2.6	9.0
	-7.2	-.2	1.2	.3	-.7		-8.1	2.4
	5.4	1.7	1.3	.9	1.8		1.5	2.1
	2.8	1.2	.9	.7	.7	Sales/Net Fixed Assets	1.0	1.2
	1.7	.8	.7	.5	.6		.7	.9
	2.5	1.0	.8	.6	1.0		.9	1.0
	1.6	.8	.6	.5	.5	Sales/Total Assets	.6	.8
	1.0	.6	.5	.4	.4		.5	.6
	4.5	6.6	7.4	6.0	2.6		8.2	5.9
(44)	9.0 (237)	10.0 (314)	10.1 (30)	9.8 (13)	9.6	% Depr., Dep., Amort./Sales	(390) 11.3 (422)	8.5
	12.3	12.8	13.1	13.9	12.5		14.6	11.6
	1.0	.8	.5				.8	.5
(14)	2.7 (63)	1.4 (63)	.8			% Officers', Directors' Owners' Comp/Sales	(126) 1.7 (113)	1.0
	6.4	3.4	1.6				3.5	2.5
11564M	101973M	1314429M	4394880M	1214819M	2906073M	Net Sales ($)	4840161M	5023836M
1999M	59249M	1526084M	6842769M	2221295M	2960079M	Total Assets ($)	6144693M	7351873M

M = $ thousand   MM = $ million
See Pages 9 through 22 for Explanation of Ratios and Data

Comparative Historical Data

Current Data Sorted by Sales

					Type of Statement						
13		17		13	Unqualified		2			3	8
365		354		448	Reviewed	6	32	53	159	151	47
106		103		102	Compiled	6	18	27	34	15	2
47		44		42	Tax Returns	8	21	9	2	2	
61		68		80	Other	7	8	12	21	21	11
4/1/08- 3/31/09 ALL		4/1/09- 3/31/10 ALL		4/1/10- 3/31/11 ALL			37 (4/1-9/30/10)		648 (10/1/10-3/31/11)		
						0-1MM	1-3MM	3-5MM	5-10MM	10-25MM	25MM & OVER
592		586		685	**NUMBER OF STATEMENTS**	27	81	101	216	192	68
%		%		%	**ASSETS**	%	%	%	%	%	%
1.4		1.6		1.5	Cash & Equivalents	2.6	3.4	1.7	.7	1.2	2.3
7.0		5.5		6.2	Trade Receivables (net)	3.2	5.0	5.6	6.3	6.9	7.1
15.4		11.1		11.4	Inventory	1.4	9.9	9.9	13.0	11.8	13.0
3.0		2.6		2.8	All Other Current	7.7	2.0	3.4	2.6	2.9	1.3
26.9		20.8		21.9	Total Current	14.8	20.3	20.7	22.6	22.9	23.8
61.1		67.0		65.9	Fixed Assets (net)	70.5	66.3	67.2	65.1	64.9	67.3
.6		1.0		1.2	Intangibles (net)	.6	2.5	1.6	1.1	.5	1.1
11.5		11.2		11.0	All Other Non-Current	14.1	10.9	10.5	11.2	11.7	7.8
100.0		100.0		100.0	Total	100.0	100.0	100.0	100.0	100.0	100.0
					LIABILITIES						
15.8		14.8		13.8	Notes Payable-Short Term	10.9	11.6	12.1	15.3	14.6	13.4
5.0		6.1		7.0	Cur. Mat.-L.T.D.	13.2	7.2	7.9	6.1	7.1	5.4
4.4		4.4		4.4	Trade Payables	1.2	3.2	5.5	5.0	4.1	4.9
.0		.0		.0	Income Taxes Payable	.0	.0	.0	.1	.0	.0
3.1		3.1		3.6	All Other Current	7.1	2.9	5.4	3.0	3.2	3.8
28.4		28.5		28.9	Total Current	32.4	24.9	30.9	29.6	28.9	27.4
38.8		48.7		45.2	Long-Term Debt	64.5	58.2	48.9	40.9	41.5	40.9
.2		.2		.1	Deferred Taxes	.0	.1	.2	.1	.1	.1
3.9		4.4		5.6	All Other Non-Current	13.3	9.7	7.1	4.0	4.8	2.7
28.8		18.2		20.1	Net Worth	-10.2	7.0	12.9	25.4	24.7	28.8
100.0		100.0		100.0	Total Liabilties & Net Worth	100.0	100.0	100.0	100.0	100.0	100.0
					INCOME DATA						
100.0		100.0		100.0	Net Sales	100.0	100.0	100.0	100.0	100.0	100.0
					Gross Profit						
92.1		110.1		88.7	Operating Expenses	70.8	91.4	91.7	89.2	87.8	89.1
7.9		-10.1		11.3	Operating Profit	29.2	8.6	8.3	10.8	12.2	10.9
5.1		7.3		5.8	All Other Expenses (net)	22.3	6.0	4.9	5.8	4.3	4.8
2.8		-17.4		5.4	Profit Before Taxes	6.9	2.5	3.4	4.9	7.9	6.0
					RATIOS						
1.5		1.2		1.2		.8	1.7	1.1	1.2	1.3	1.3
1.0		.8		.8	Current	.2	.9	.8	.8	.9	1.0
.7		.5		.5		.0	.4	.4	.6	.6	.6
.5		.4		.4		.4	.6	.4	.4	.5	.5
(588) .2		.2		.2	Quick	.1	.3	.2	.2	.3	.3
.1		.1		.1		.0	.1	.1	.1	.1	.1
13 27.2	18	20.1	16	23.0		0 UND	0 UND	15 23.8	17 21.6	18 20.7	18 20.5
22 16.4	24	14.9	23	16.0	Sales/Receivables	0 UND	15 25.0	19 19.2	24 15.0	28 12.9	26 14.2
37 10.0	40	9.1	33	11.2		0 UND	30 12.2	31 11.8	32 11.4	36 10.2	37 10.0
					Cost of Sales/Inventory						
					Cost of Sales/Payables						
7.8		19.4		20.0		-333.5	12.7	86.9	20.4	13.1	14.5
-210.0		-11.4		-19.5	Sales/Working Capital	-3.1	-72.3	-14.8	-14.3	-25.6	-165.4
-8.4		-4.1		-5.6		-1.2	-5.7	-4.3	-5.8	-7.2	-6.6
3.5		-.4		4.4		6.1	4.0	3.4	4.2	5.0	5.5
(573) 1.6	(555)	-2.5	(648)	2.3	EBIT/Interest	(11) 1.6	(70) 1.8	(100) 1.7	(211) 2.2	(189) 3.1	(67) 2.4
.2		-5.8		1.2		.2	.4	.7	1.1	1.6	1.5
3.0		2.6		3.2					2.0		
(29) 1.3	(26)	.2	(28)	1.9	Net Profit + Depr., Dep., Amort./Cur. Mat. L/T/D				(11) 1.2		
.6		-1.0		.9					.8		
1.2		1.5		1.5		1.6	1.5	1.9	1.4	1.5	1.6
2.0		2.9		2.7	Fixed/Worth	3.9	3.4	3.2	2.6	2.5	2.3
3.9		9.8		7.6		-3.2	-5.1	-82.5	5.9	4.4	4.4
1.2		1.5		1.3		2.3	1.3	1.7	1.2	1.3	1.4
2.2		3.3		2.9	Debt/Worth	5.3	3.2	4.9	3.0	2.6	2.5
5.0		13.5		11.1		-4.4	-6.8	-106.8	9.2	5.2	4.5
17.2		-6.0		27.6		19.6	25.9	31.9	27.0	30.2	23.9
(536) 6.9	(474)	-29.1	(561)	13.3	% Profit Before Taxes/Tangible Net Worth	(18) 3.8	(52) 8.9	(74) 12.9	(188) 13.2	(169) 17.4	(60) 13.0
-5.0		-71.1		3.7		1.6	1.5	2.9	2.4	6.7	8.5
6.2		-3.1		7.8		3.5	7.8	5.7	8.1	8.6	7.3
1.8		-10.0		3.5	% Profit Before Taxes/Total Assets	1.0	2.1	2.6	3.3	4.9	3.7
-2.1		-16.4		.4		-1.5	-3.0	-.9	.2	1.8	1.0
1.9		1.3		1.6		2.2	3.0	1.6	1.5	1.5	1.6
1.2		.8		1.0	Sales/Net Fixed Assets	.3	1.3	1.1	1.0	1.0	1.0
.8		.6		.7		.1	.5	.8	.7	.8	.7
1.0		.7		.9		1.0	1.6	1.0	.9	.9	1.0
.7		.5		.7	Sales/Total Assets	.2	.8	.7	.7	.7	.7
.5		.4		.5		.1	.4	.6	.5	.5	.5
6.5		9.0		6.9		7.6	6.6	6.8	7.2	6.8	4.3
(559) 8.9	(555)	12.5	(644)	10.1	% Depr., Dep., Amort./Sales	(22) 19.5	(76) 10.8	(98) 10.5	(209) 9.9	(181) 9.7	(58) 8.6
12.2		16.4		12.9		26.6	13.3	13.7	12.4	12.6	12.8
.6		.7		.6			2.0		.9	.4	
(153) 1.2	(137)	1.5	(146)	1.3	% Officers', Directors' Owners' Comp/Sales	(21) 3.4	(27) 1.5	(49) 1.3	(39) .6		
2.6		2.9		2.3			7.3	3.4	1.9	1.1	
10964876M		8143166M		9943738M	Net Sales ($)	14020M	163192M	403697M	1597402M	2938783M	4826644M
11314558M		11505553M		13611475M	Total Assets ($)	77616M	304862M	600656M	2648498M	4579106M	5400737M

© RMA 2011

M = $ thousand   MM = $ million
See Pages 9 through 22 for Explanation of Ratios and Data

Current Data Sorted by Assets / Comparative Historical Data

0-500M	500M-2MM	2-10MM	10-50MM	50-100MM	100-250MM	Type of Statement	4/1/06-3/31/07 ALL	4/1/07-3/31/08 ALL
		1	4	4	1	Unqualified	21	9
		3	5	1		Reviewed	8	9
	3	2	4			Compiled	12	11
4	10	4				Tax Returns	14	20
	6	8	8	2	1	Other	33	36
	7 (4/1-9/30/10)		64 (10/1/10-3/31/11)					
4	19	18	21	7	2	**NUMBER OF STATEMENTS**	88	85
%	%	%	%	%	%	**ASSETS**	%	%
	4.4	2.1	2.8			Cash & Equivalents	3.2	2.8
	6.8	4.1	6.7			Trade Receivables (net)	8.7	9.1
	18.3	43.9	34.7			Inventory	33.6	29.3
	6.8	1.6	1.2			All Other Current	5.0	3.7
	36.3	51.7	45.3			Total Current	50.5	44.8
	60.7	37.6	47.3			Fixed Assets (net)	43.3	44.2
	.4	.1	3.0			Intangibles (net)	.3	.4
	2.6	10.6	4.4			All Other Non-Current	5.9	10.5
	100.0	100.0	100.0			Total	100.0	100.0
						LIABILITIES		
	26.1	32.3	17.8			Notes Payable-Short Term	18.3	17.6
	5.6	4.8	3.0			Cur. Mat.-L.T.D.	3.4	5.0
	3.4	9.4	4.2			Trade Payables	7.6	5.8
	.0	.0	.2			Income Taxes Payable	.1	.1
	8.3	3.4	2.4			All Other Current	7.1	4.6
	43.5	49.9	27.5			Total Current	36.5	33.2
	41.9	41.2	24.5			Long-Term Debt	28.3	35.6
	.0	.0	.7			Deferred Taxes	.5	.4
	6.3	6.9	2.3			All Other Non-Current	5.1	4.5
	8.4	2.0	44.9			Net Worth	29.6	26.2
	100.0	100.0	100.0			Total Liabilities & Net Worth	100.0	100.0
						INCOME DATA		
	100.0	100.0	100.0			Net Sales	100.0	100.0
						Gross Profit		
	96.6	89.9	88.9			Operating Expenses	94.4	97.2
	3.4	10.1	11.1			Operating Profit	5.6	2.8
	3.7	1.2	.5			All Other Expenses (net)	1.8	2.1
	-.3	8.9	10.6			Profit Before Taxes	3.8	.7
						RATIOS		
	2.1	2.0	2.6			Current	2.4	2.3
	.9	1.3	1.6				1.6	1.3
	.3	.7	1.2				1.0	.8
	.9	.2	.5			Quick	(87) .6	(83) .6
	.2	.1	.1				.3	.2
	.0	.1	.0				.1	.1
0 UND	0 UND	0 UND	2 204.5			Sales/Receivables	0 UND	0 UND
0 UND	0 UND	5 69.6	6 62.7				7 54.2	7 49.0
17 21.9	17 21.9	8 45.7	33 11.1				26 14.1	26 13.9
						Cost of Sales/Inventory		
						Cost of Sales/Payables		
	6.6	7.8	3.9			Sales/Working Capital	4.3	4.6
	-35.8	14.5	6.0				9.2	15.8
	-5.5	-7.5	14.6				72.0	-19.2
	4.2	7.3	13.9			EBIT/Interest	9.5	5.6
	(15) 1.0	3.2	3.9				(84) 3.3	(80) 1.3
	-3.9	.9	2.7				.8	-1.2
						Net Profit + Depr., Dep., Amort./Cur. Mat. L/T/D		
	1.2	.3	.8			Fixed/Worth	.3	.5
	5.8	3.5	1.3				1.1	1.1
	-2.7	-1.4	2.3				3.0	3.3
	.8	2.1	.6			Debt/Worth	.7	.9
	108.8	9.7	1.2				1.9	1.7
	-4.1	-3.3	4.5				5.9	6.6
	106.8	35.8	37.8			% Profit Before Taxes/Tangible Net Worth	29.7	21.1
	(10) 7.7	(10) 28.8	(19) 18.4				(78) 16.4	(76) 6.6
	-4.1	.7	8.3				2.8	-15.5
	11.8	18.1	10.8			% Profit Before Taxes/Total Assets	13.5	8.6
	.1	6.9	8.7				6.4	1.0
	-9.0	-1.0	4.6				-.4	-6.6
	6.4	256.3	5.1			Sales/Net Fixed Assets	12.3	13.0
	2.4	3.5	2.0				3.2	3.1
	.6	1.0	1.0				1.4	1.6
	2.6	2.4	1.6			Sales/Total Assets	1.9	2.0
	1.2	1.5	1.0				1.2	1.2
	.6	.8	.6				.7	.8
	3.6	2.5	2.5			% Depr., Dep., Amort./Sales	2.1	1.8
	(17) 7.8	(13) 5.6	(18) 5.2				(72) 4.3	(62) 4.1
	27.0	6.5	8.6				8.9	11.2
						% Officers', Directors' Owners' Comp/Sales	.6	.5
							(18) 1.7	(17) 1.3
							5.0	4.5
3434M	35374M	153269M	512761M	878434M	197369M	Net Sales ($)	2607019M	2739630M
1404M	22562M	87028M	445948M	524503M	391946M	Total Assets ($)	2057350M	1961762M

© RMA 2011

M = $ thousand　　MM = $ million
See Pages 9 through 22 for Explanation of Ratios and Data

Comparative Historical Data

Current Data Sorted by Sales

Type of Statement

			Type of Statement						
13	9	10	Unqualified			2			8
12	8	9	Reviewed		1	1		3	4
4	13	9	Compiled		1	4		2	
23	18	18	Tax Returns	9	6	2			
28	23	25	Other		7	2	2	7	7
4/1/08-3/31/09 ALL	4/1/09-3/31/10 ALL	4/1/10-3/31/11 ALL		7 (4/1-9/30/10)			64 (10/1/10-3/31/11)		
				0-1MM	1-3MM	3-5MM	5-10MM	10-25MM	25MM & OVER

| 2029348M | 2009538M | 1780641M | NUMBER OF STATEMENTS | 4569M | 28763M | 18451M | 84286M | 184979M | 1459593M |

ALL=80	71	71	NUMBER OF STATEMENTS	9	15	5	11	12	19
%	%	%	**ASSETS**	%	%	%	%	%	%
4.9	3.8	3.7	Cash & Equivalents		5.4		3.8	2.0	3.6
3.2	6.1	5.3	Trade Receivables (net)		6.7		3.1	2.8	8.6
27.4	30.3	32.1	Inventory		25.8		23.1	65.8	38.9
3.3	2.5	3.7	All Other Current		3.4		7.6	2.2	5.3
38.8	42.8	44.9	Total Current		41.4		37.6	72.8	56.3
49.5	48.8	47.2	Fixed Assets (net)		47.7		57.9	23.5	30.8
.3	2.1	1.1	Intangibles (net)		.5		.0	1.4	2.8
11.5	6.3	6.9	All Other Non-Current		10.4		4.4	2.3	10.1
100.0	100.0	100.0	Total		100.0		100.0	100.0	100.0
			LIABILITIES						
16.9	28.4	25.7	Notes Payable-Short Term		32.7		35.1	37.2	25.1
4.0	5.2	5.1	Cur. Mat.-L.T.D.		3.8		2.8	4.4	3.3
3.8	8.0	5.1	Trade Payables		2.8		6.9	9.1	5.5
.1	.2	.1	Income Taxes Payable		.0		.0	.3	.0
6.6	4.3	4.1	All Other Current		9.8		.6	4.3	3.1
31.3	46.2	40.1	Total Current		49.0		45.5	55.2	37.1
40.0	40.8	34.9	Long-Term Debt		27.2		26.9	24.9	20.3
.1	.4	.2	Deferred Taxes		.0		1.0	.4	.1
4.2	4.7	4.6	All Other Non-Current		7.9		.3	13.3	2.4
24.4	8.0	20.2	Net Worth		15.9		26.3	6.1	40.2
100.0	100.0	100.0	Total Liabilities & Net Worth		100.0		100.0	100.0	100.0
			INCOME DATA						
100.0	100.0	100.0	Net Sales		100.0		100.0	100.0	100.0
			Gross Profit						
97.0	102.9	91.4	Operating Expenses		92.7		91.4	92.3	91.6
3.0	-2.9	8.6	Operating Profit		7.3		8.6	7.7	8.4
3.4	2.4	1.6	All Other Expenses (net)		.6		.2	.2	.1
-.4	-5.3	7.0	Profit Before Taxes		6.7		8.4	7.5	8.3
			RATIOS						
2.1	1.6	2.1			2.0		2.6	1.7	2.4
1.3	1.2	1.3	Current		1.0		1.6	1.4	1.5
.8	.6	.8			.4		.7	1.2	1.1
.6	.5	.4			.5		.3	.1	.8
(79) .2	.2	.1	Quick		.2		.1	.1	.2
.1	.1	.0			.0		.0	.0	.1
0 UND	0 UND	0 UND		0 UND		0 UND	2 221.8	3 116.5	
4 100.2	7 53.8	4 92.8	Sales/Receivables	0 UND		5 77.3	5 69.6	11 34.1	
18 20.5	19 19.4	18 20.5		17 21.9		32 11.4	6 62.3	31 11.7	
			Cost of Sales/Inventory						
			Cost of Sales/Payables						
4.8	7.6	5.5			6.6		5.0	4.9	4.6
15.5	27.8	13.8	Sales/Working Capital		394.8		6.0	9.9	11.2
-21.6	-13.6	-16.7			-3.7		-7.6	12.8	22.7
3.6	1.9	8.2			13.0		12.5	6.2	8.6
(72) .4	(63) -.1	(67) 3.5	EBIT/Interest	(13) 2.7		3.3	3.8	3.9	
-3.6	-6.4	1.2			-.8		.9	2.2	2.5
			Net Profit + Depr., Dep., Amort./Cur. Mat. L/T/D						
.8	.9	.7			.2		1.0	.0	.5
1.4	1.8	1.3	Fixed/Worth		1.6		1.5	1.5	.9
5.0	-7.1	-7.4			-2.7		-1.5	NM	1.3
.8	1.3	1.0			1.1		.5	2.3	1.0
2.2	3.6	2.3	Debt/Worth		9.8		1.2	5.1	1.2
12.4	-18.3	-10.7			-5.2		-25.9	-8.5	3.4
15.2	16.1	39.4							45.4
(68) .0	(51) -1.0	(50) 18.7	% Profit Before Taxes/Tangible Net Worth					(17)	28.0
-35.8	-55.9	5.6							9.8
5.6	3.0	14.5			32.7		10.2	12.1	18.7
-.6	-1.5	7.1	% Profit Before Taxes/Total Assets		4.5		5.4	7.8	8.4
-12.4	-20.5	.1			-9.0		-1.1	5.4	4.1
6.5	8.6	7.3			6.4		3.3	UND	9.8
2.3	3.1	2.9	Sales/Net Fixed Assets		3.1		1.0	8.3	4.7
1.1	1.2	1.0			1.9		.9	1.9	2.8
1.7	2.1	2.0			2.8		2.0	3.0	1.9
1.2	1.3	1.2	Sales/Total Assets		1.6		.7	1.9	1.6
.8	.7	.7			.9		.6	.8	1.0
2.6	2.2	2.6			6.2		1.8		1.7
(64) 6.0	(59) 5.0	(60) 5.2	% Depr., Dep., Amort./Sales	(12) 7.5		(10) 4.3		(17)	2.6
18.8	11.9	8.7			13.7		9.3		4.2
.7	.6	.5							
(14) 1.7	(15) 1.5	(15) 2.1	% Officers', Directors' Owners' Comp/Sales						
5.0	5.5	4.3							
2029348M	2009538M	1780641M	Net Sales ($)	4569M	28763M	18451M	84286M	184979M	1459593M
1808970M	1549897M	1473391M	Total Assets ($)	9467M	22547M	14194M	114061M	158643M	1154479M

Current Data Sorted by Assets / Comparative Historical Data

	0-500M	500M-2MM	2-10MM	10-50MM	50-100MM	100-250MM	Type of Statement	4/1/06-3/31/07 ALL	4/1/07-3/31/08 ALL
			1	3	8	2	Unqualified	18	10
			1	4	1		Reviewed	7	4
		1	5				Compiled	6	5
	1	5	3				Tax Returns	6	7
	4	2	5	3	4	2	Other	12	15
	10 (4/1-9/30/10)			**45 (10/1/10-3/31/11)**					
NUMBER OF STATEMENTS	5	8	15	10	13	4		49	41

	%	%	%	%	%	%		%	%
							ASSETS		
Cash & Equivalents			14.8	14.7	7.9			8.3	12.6
Trade Receivables (net)			21.0	14.4	9.9			11.6	17.2
Inventory			9.7	17.2	21.0			15.9	17.3
All Other Current			.7	3.1	1.2			3.4	3.3
Total Current			46.2	49.4	39.9			39.2	50.3
Fixed Assets (net)			48.3	37.5	48.9			52.7	42.6
Intangibles (net)			2.8	.8	3.3			1.8	2.6
All Other Non-Current			2.8	12.3	7.9			6.4	4.5
Total			100.0	100.0	100.0			100.0	100.0
							LIABILITIES		
Notes Payable-Short Term			9.9	5.2	5.1			10.8	8.2
Cur. Mat.-L.T.D.			4.3	4.3	2.6			5.2	4.3
Trade Payables			13.8	6.6	6.4			9.9	11.2
Income Taxes Payable			.0	.5	2.6			.2	.8
All Other Current			5.7	3.5	6.0			3.9	10.9
Total Current			33.7	20.1	22.7			30.0	35.5
Long-Term Debt			23.9	15.8	20.7			30.4	21.6
Deferred Taxes			.0	.8	2.2			1.0	.4
All Other Non-Current			2.6	.1	2.9			4.1	1.4
Net Worth			39.7	63.2	51.6			34.5	41.1
Total Liabilities & Net Worth			100.0	100.0	100.0			100.0	100.0
							INCOME DATA		
Net Sales			100.0	100.0	100.0			100.0	100.0
Gross Profit									
Operating Expenses			90.6	92.2	93.3			98.9	88.0
Operating Profit			9.4	7.8	6.7			1.1	12.0
All Other Expenses (net)			3.2	.2	.7			3.2	1.8
Profit Before Taxes			6.2	7.6	6.0			-2.1	10.2

RATIOS

	0-500M	500M-2MM	2-10MM	10-50MM	50-100MM	100-250MM	Ratio	ALL	ALL
			5.0	4.4	2.3		Current	2.3	3.3
			1.0	2.9	1.9			1.4	1.3
			.8	1.9	1.2			.8	.8
			3.5	2.7	1.2		Quick	1.5	1.9
			.9	1.4	.8			.6	.7
			.2	1.1	.3			.3	.4
			0 UND	25 14.8	19 19.2		Sales/Receivables	15 23.7	22 16.8
			16 22.7	32 11.4	31 11.8			28 13.2	30 12.4
			23 15.5	51 7.2	35 10.5			40 9.1	36 10.1
							Cost of Sales/Inventory		
							Cost of Sales/Payables		
			14.0	3.4	5.9		Sales/Working Capital	6.5	5.4
			-164.0	6.1	6.8			15.1	14.2
			-27.1	10.7	23.6			-17.5	-23.2
			20.5				EBIT/Interest	2.5	14.1
			(11) 11.0					(40) .9	(33) 5.7
			.7					-1.3	2.4
							Net Profit + Depr., Dep., Amort./Cur. Mat. L/T/D	2.6	
								(13) 1.2	
								.1	
			.4	.5	.6		Fixed/Worth	1.0	.5
			1.2	.7	.9			1.6	.9
			3.7	.8	2.0			4.1	3.5
			.1	.2	.5		Debt/Worth	1.0	.7
			1.9	.7	1.1			2.2	2.4
			46.9	1.2	2.2			5.2	5.0
			109.5	30.9	26.2		% Profit Before Taxes/Tangible Net Worth	15.9	69.6
			(13) 36.1	21.7	16.9			(43) 2.1	(38) 45.2
			2.9	5.6	5.9			-24.4	16.6
			46.4	24.3	13.0		% Profit Before Taxes/Total Assets	6.0	31.5
			5.4	9.8	9.6			-.2	12.3
			-.3	3.0	1.9			-6.0	4.5
			16.5	6.2	4.6		Sales/Net Fixed Assets	5.0	13.3
			7.8	3.8	2.9			2.4	4.6
			4.5	2.7	1.7			1.5	2.7
			4.8	2.2	1.7		Sales/Total Assets	2.1	2.5
			3.5	1.6	1.2			1.3	1.8
			1.8	.9	1.0			.8	1.4
			1.8		2.1		% Depr., Dep., Amort./Sales	2.4	1.5
			(13) 3.6	(10) 4.5				(43) 5.8	(35) 2.7
			7.2		5.8			11.6	6.1
							% Officers', Directors' Owners' Comp/Sales		
Net Sales ($)	1279M	26824M	266795M	529036M	1458756M	976141M		1965652M	2306692M
Total Assets ($)	1161M	12358M	84722M	302048M	1020301M	572183M		1672456M	1330454M

M = $ thousand   MM = $ million
See Pages 9 through 22 for Explanation of Ratios and Data

Comparative Historical Data | Current Data Sorted by Sales

4/1/08-3/31/09 ALL	4/1/09-3/31/10 ALL	4/1/10-3/31/11 ALL	Type of Statement	0-1MM	1-3MM	3-5MM	5-10MM	10-25MM	25MM & OVER
							10 (4/1-9/30/10)	45 (10/1/10-3/31/11)	
14	14	14	Unqualified					4	10
6	7	6	Reviewed				1	1	4
5	5	7	Compiled			2		2	1
11	12	12	Tax Returns	1		1	1	3	
8	15	16	Other	7	1	1	1	5	9
44	53	55	NUMBER OF STATEMENTS	8	1	4	3	15	24
%	%	%	**ASSETS**	%	%	%	%	%	%
17.5	9.8	10.6	Cash & Equivalents					16.9	10.3
14.0	14.1	14.5	Trade Receivables (net)					14.2	17.4
16.7	16.9	15.8	Inventory					10.6	20.9
2.7	1.9	1.2	All Other Current					1.7	1.5
51.0	42.6	42.1	Total Current					43.5	50.1
43.0	48.8	51.0	Fixed Assets (net)					49.9	40.7
1.3	1.5	1.8	Intangibles (net)					.7	2.0
4.8	7.1	5.1	All Other Non-Current					6.0	7.1
100.0	100.0	100.0	Total					100.0	100.0
			LIABILITIES						
6.9	5.1	6.0	Notes Payable-Short Term					10.6	4.7
5.6	3.9	3.6	Cur. Mat.-L.T.D.					2.3	3.1
10.5	10.3	8.1	Trade Payables					5.6	11.8
.7	.6	.7	Income Taxes Payable					.0	1.6
10.2	5.3	7.3	All Other Current					3.7	6.2
33.9	25.1	25.8	Total Current					22.1	27.5
23.7	25.0	25.1	Long-Term Debt					25.3	14.7
1.0	1.3	.7	Deferred Taxes					.0	1.5
2.0	7.8	3.1	All Other Non-Current					1.7	1.8
39.5	40.8	45.4	Net Worth					51.0	54.5
100.0	100.0	100.0	Total Liabilities & Net Worth					100.0	100.0
			INCOME DATA						
100.0	100.0	100.0	Net Sales					100.0	100.0
			Gross Profit						
86.8	93.0	92.4	Operating Expenses					92.3	94.0
13.2	7.0	7.6	Operating Profit					7.7	6.0
2.5	1.5	2.0	All Other Expenses (net)					.9	-.1
10.7	5.5	5.6	Profit Before Taxes					6.8	6.0
			RATIOS						
3.8 / 1.8 / 1.1	3.0 / 2.0 / .9	4.2 / 1.9 / .9	Current					5.0 / 1.5 / .9	3.5 / 2.1 / 1.2
2.0 / 1.0 / .5	1.5 / .9 / .4	2.2 / .9 / .4	Quick					4.3 / 1.3 / .3	1.8 / 1.0 / .6
0 UND / 21 17.6 / 26 13.8	0 UND / 23 15.9 / 31 11.9	1 297.1 / 22 16.8 / 36 10.1	Sales/Receivables					11 34.3 / 23 15.5 / 58 6.3	19 19.5 / 26 13.9 / 34 10.8
			Cost of Sales/Inventory						
			Cost of Sales/Payables						
5.0 / 10.1 / 168.2	5.6 / 9.1 / -120.6	6.0 / 10.4 / -42.8	Sales/Working Capital					6.2 / 19.6 / -70.3	5.3 / 6.4 / 23.4
(35) 32.7 / 10.2 / 1.9	(41) 29.0 / 4.2 / 1.8	(43) 12.6 / 5.6 / 1.1	EBIT/Interest					(13) 17.8 / 8.8 / 1.6	(17) 17.8 / 8.6 / 3.8
	(10) 5.0 / 1.9 / 1.1		Net Profit + Depr., Dep., Amort./Cur. Mat. L/T/D						
.4 / .8 / 2.0	.5 / 1.0 / 2.5	.6 / 1.0 / 2.9	Fixed/Worth					.5 / 1.0 / 1.4	.5 / .7 / 1.7
.3 / 1.1 / 4.5	.3 / 1.2 / 2.9	.3 / 1.2 / 3.1	Debt/Worth					.1 / 1.2 / 1.9	.3 / .9 / 2.0
(40) 65.0 / 41.0 / 10.5	(48) 24.3 / 13.3 / 5.5	(49) 34.6 / 16.9 / 4.6	% Profit Before Taxes/Tangible Net Worth					(14) 55.4 / 18.2 / 6.1	26.6 / 17.0 / 8.8
41.4 / 14.7 / 1.8	13.9 / 6.5 / 1.3	15.3 / 8.1 / 1.4	% Profit Before Taxes/Total Assets					46.4 / 8.1 / 2.1	13.8 / 11.1 / 2.9
14.5 / 5.0 / 2.3	10.4 / 3.5 / 1.6	7.6 / 3.8 / 1.9	Sales/Net Fixed Assets					9.6 / 5.0 / 2.3	6.0 / 3.9 / 2.3
2.9 / 1.8 / 1.2	3.1 / 1.6 / 1.0	3.0 / 1.6 / 1.0	Sales/Total Assets					4.2 / 1.8 / .9	2.3 / 1.6 / 1.1
(34) 1.5 / 3.6 / 8.8	(44) 1.9 / 4.5 / 10.1	(43) 2.2 / 4.5 / 8.6	% Depr., Dep., Amort./Sales					(13) 1.8 / 3.7 / 8.0	(17) 2.0 / 4.3 / 5.8
	(10) .8 / 1.5 / 2.5		% Officers', Directors' Owners' Comp/Sales						
3274193M	2978291M	3258831M	Net Sales ($)	3327M	1270M	16810M	20417M	268054M	2948953M
1773839M	1784788M	1992773M	Total Assets ($)	5297M	8813M	7012M	8899M	217875M	1744877M

© RMA 2011

M = $ thousand   MM = $ million
See Pages 9 through 22 for Explanation of Ratios and Data

Current Data Sorted by Assets   Comparative Historical Data

						Type of Statement		
						Unqualified		
						Reviewed	2	1
						Compiled		1
1	1	1				Tax Returns	1	4
6		2				Other	10	10
4	4	1		1			9	5
	1	2		3	2		4/1/06-	4/1/07-
	1 (4/1-9/30/10)			28 (10/1/10-3/31/11)			3/31/07	3/31/08
							ALL	ALL
0-500M	500M-2MM	2-10MM	10-50MM	50-100MM	100-250MM	NUMBER OF STATEMENTS	22	21
11	6	6	4	2				
%	%	%	%	%	%	ASSETS	%	%
24.8						Cash & Equivalents	20.1	18.5
2.6					D	Trade Receivables (net)	11.6	15.5
8.7					A	Inventory	8.0	7.1
9.0					T	All Other Current	5.0	2.1
45.1					A	Total Current	44.6	43.1
41.7						Fixed Assets (net)	38.5	41.0
.9					N	Intangibles (net)	1.1	3.3
12.3					O	All Other Non-Current	15.9	12.7
100.0					T	Total	100.0	100.0
					A	LIABILITIES		
32.5					V	Notes Payable-Short Term	31.9	9.2
3.4					A	Cur. Mat.-L.T.D.	3.5	13.0
2.5					I	Trade Payables	16.6	7.7
.1					L	Income Taxes Payable	.0	.0
5.0					A	All Other Current	17.2	20.5
43.5					B	Total Current	69.3	50.4
25.8					L	Long-Term Debt	29.2	34.7
.0					E	Deferred Taxes	.0	.0
14.1						All Other Non-Current	13.0	15.0
16.6						Net Worth	-11.5	-.1
100.0						Total Liabilties & Net Worth	100.0	100.0
						INCOME DATA		
100.0						Net Sales	100.0	100.0
						Gross Profit		
81.1						Operating Expenses	95.4	91.0
18.9						Operating Profit	4.6	9.0
1.9						All Other Expenses (net)	6.0	3.6
17.0						Profit Before Taxes	-1.4	5.4
						RATIOS		
2.2							2.0	5.4
.5						Current	.8	1.2
.4							.3	.3
1.2							1.9	5.4
.4						Quick	.7	.5
.2							.1	.1
0 UND							0 UND	0 UND
0 UND						Sales/Receivables	15 24.1	17 20.9
0 UND							62 5.9	67 5.5
						Cost of Sales/Inventory		
						Cost of Sales/Payables		
13.4							2.8	5.6
-88.1						Sales/Working Capital	-509.1	45.0
-23.3							-1.7	-3.5
							16.9	11.3
						EBIT/Interest	(18) 1.9	(15) 1.6
							-1.0	.9
						Net Profit + Depr., Dep., Amort./Cur. Mat. L/T/D		
.1							.1	.1
1.0						Fixed/Worth	2.2	1.8
-1.1							-.7	-1.2
.3							1.1	.2
3.3						Debt/Worth	2.8	2.6
-2.6							-2.4	-6.0
						% Profit Before Taxes/Tangible Net Worth	60.5 (13) 14.4 -9.9	45.6 (15) 3.2 -1.0
73.6							14.5	14.7
16.6						% Profit Before Taxes/Total Assets	-.7	1.7
.0							-11.3	-1.4
166.0							48.0	42.0
34.3						Sales/Net Fixed Assets	6.6	4.0
1.9							2.0	1.5
5.7							2.6	2.4
3.1						Sales/Total Assets	1.3	1.2
1.6							.7	.6
						% Depr., Dep., Amort./Sales	.9 (16) 2.5 7.7	1.1 (15) 4.8 21.4
						% Officers', Directors' Owners' Comp/Sales		
8214M	9395M	55575M	76924M	33030M		Net Sales ($)	113989M	110004M
2607M	5375M	32183M	122337M	146820M		Total Assets ($)	140808M	132623M

M = $ thousand   MM = $ million
See Pages 9 through 22 for Explanation of Ratios and Data

Comparative Historical Data / Current Data Sorted by Sales

Type of Statement	4/1/08-3/31/09 ALL	4/1/09-3/31/10 ALL	4/1/10-3/31/11 ALL		0-1MM	1-3MM	3-5MM	5-10MM	10-25MM	25MM & OVER
					1 (4/1-9/30/10)			28 (10/1/10-3/31/11)		
Unqualified		1								1
Reviewed	1	2	3		1	2				
Compiled	3	5	2		7	1				
Tax Returns	8	7	12		3	3	1	3	2	1
Other	11	12	12			2			2	
NUMBER OF STATEMENTS	23	27	29		11	8	1	3	4	2
	%	%	%		%	%	%	%	%	%
ASSETS										
Cash & Equivalents	12.9	16.3	17.7		22.7					
Trade Receivables (net)	17.8	7.3	6.8		2.6					
Inventory	2.0	5.2	5.2		1.0					
All Other Current	2.0	5.4	7.8		9.0					
Total Current	34.7	34.2	37.4		35.2					
Fixed Assets (net)	49.2	48.7	50.1		58.3					
Intangibles (net)	.1	2.3	.4		.2					
All Other Non-Current	16.1	14.8	12.0		6.3					
Total	100.0	100.0	100.0		100.0					
LIABILITIES										
Notes Payable-Short Term	30.3	16.4	18.4		30.4					
Cur. Mat.-L.T.D.	4.4	7.1	3.4		1.3					
Trade Payables	21.5	8.0	9.7		2.5					
Income Taxes Payable	.1	.0	.0		.0					
All Other Current	35.4	15.5	21.2		7.3					
Total Current	91.7	47.0	52.7		41.5					
Long-Term Debt	25.7	43.7	38.8		27.8					
Deferred Taxes	.2	.0	.0		.0					
All Other Non-Current	12.8	4.9	11.7		16.1					
Net Worth	-30.4	4.5	-3.1		14.7					
Total Liabilities & Net Worth	100.0	100.0	100.0		100.0					
INCOME DATA										
Net Sales	100.0	100.0	100.0		100.0					
Gross Profit										
Operating Expenses	103.2	93.0	93.0		74.9					
Operating Profit	-3.2	7.0	7.0		25.1					
All Other Expenses (net)	3.4	2.2	3.5		5.9					
Profit Before Taxes	-6.7	4.8	3.5		19.1					
RATIOS										
Current	1.2 / .4 / .1	3.0 / .7 / .2	2.1 / .5 / .2		2.0 / .9 / .4					
Quick	1.1 / .3 / .1	1.6 / .5 / .2	1.2 / .4 / .2		2.0 / .9 / .1					
Sales/Receivables	0 UND / 23 16.1 / 89 4.1	0 UND / 1 725.0 / 43 8.4	0 UND / 3 109.6 / 47 7.7		0 UND / 0 UND / 0 UND					
Cost of Sales/Inventory										
Cost of Sales/Payables										
Sales/Working Capital	13.2 / -15.4 / -1.9	4.4 / -73.8 / -1.6	15.9 / -29.0 / -4.5		17.7 / -29.0 / -4.9					
EBIT/Interest	(21) 3.1 / 1.0 / -6.2	(25) 4.8 / 1.3 / -4.0	(20) 16.9 / 2.7 / -1.7							
Net Profit + Depr., Dep., Amort./Cur. Mat. L/T/D										
Fixed/Worth	.6 / 2.8 / -.5	.5 / 4.0 / -1.7	.4 / 1.4 / -1.1		.1 / 1.1 / -1.1					
Debt/Worth	1.1 / 3.5 / -2.3	.8 / 16.3 / -4.1	.4 / 3.3 / -3.4		.2 / 2.8 / -2.3					
% Profit Before Taxes/Tangible Net Worth	(14) 18.0 / -.8 / -30.7	(16) 71.8 / 3.0 / -29.7	(19) 159.0 / 12.5 / -4.2							
% Profit Before Taxes/Total Assets	8.5 / .2 / -11.9	17.6 / 1.6 / -10.7	22.8 / 5.3 / -4.0		27.4 / 6.8 / -3.1					
Sales/Net Fixed Assets	14.4 / 4.8 / 1.3	36.2 / 2.1 / .7	38.6 / 3.1 / .8		166.0 / 1.9 / .4					
Sales/Total Assets	3.0 / 1.4 / .5	2.5 / 1.0 / .5	3.8 / 1.1 / .5		3.1 / 1.6 / .3					
% Depr., Dep., Amort./Sales	(15) 3.7 / 5.8 / 24.2	(15) 3.0 / 7.1 / 22.8	(17) 2.1 / 6.6 / 27.3							
% Officers', Directors' Owners' Comp/Sales		(12) 1.7 / 5.4 / 10.6	(14) .8 / 3.5 / 8.3							
Net Sales ($)	134532M	130833M	183138M		4843M	16364M	3086M	20848M	63049M	74948M
Total Assets ($)	169222M	148793M	309322M		7725M	7633M	4231M	92760M	149043M	47930M

© RMA 2011
M = $ thousand   MM = $ million
See Pages 9 through 22 for Explanation of Ratios and Data

Current Data Sorted by Assets   Comparative Historical Data

Type of Statement

Type of Statement	0-500M	500M-2MM	2-10MM	10-50MM	50-100MM	100-250MM	4/1/06-3/31/07 ALL	4/1/07-3/31/08 ALL
Unqualified			1	7	2	4	17	15
Reviewed		1	4	11	1	1	11	11
Compiled	2	7	9	3	1		16	12
Tax Returns	6	5	4		1		15	18
Other	1	9	15	12	3	3	42	27

Period labels: 17 (4/1-9/30/10) ; 95 (10/1/10-3/31/11)

	0-500M	500M-2MM	2-10MM	10-50MM	50-100MM	100-250MM		4/1/06-3/31/07 ALL	4/1/07-3/31/08 ALL
NUMBER OF STATEMENTS	9	22	33	33	7	8		101	83
ASSETS	%	%	%	%	%	%		%	%
Cash & Equivalents		18.0	6.7	3.4				9.7	6.4
Trade Receivables (net)		12.8	12.4	7.0				10.2	8.8
Inventory		11.5	19.0	10.8				15.2	18.4
All Other Current		4.0	5.8	4.3				4.7	4.4
Total Current		46.4	43.9	25.5				39.9	37.9
Fixed Assets (net)		33.1	38.1	56.1				44.3	46.8
Intangibles (net)		4.3	.2	.3				.4	1.2
All Other Non-Current		16.1	17.9	18.1				15.4	14.1
Total		100.0	100.0	100.0				100.0	100.0
LIABILITIES									
Notes Payable-Short Term		14.7	15.1	9.1				14.8	16.4
Cur. Mat.-L.T.D.		4.0	10.5	5.4				7.3	6.8
Trade Payables		6.8	4.9	3.0				7.2	5.3
Income Taxes Payable		.0	.0	.6				.1	.3
All Other Current		9.4	10.8	4.4				8.5	5.6
Total Current		34.9	41.4	22.4				37.9	34.4
Long-Term Debt		22.5	15.5	31.5				32.0	30.0
Deferred Taxes		.0	.2	1.2				.3	.6
All Other Non-Current		7.6	5.1	3.7				3.6	7.3
Net Worth		35.0	37.8	41.1				26.2	27.7
Total Liabilities & Net Worth		100.0	100.0	100.0				100.0	100.0
INCOME DATA									
Net Sales		100.0	100.0	100.0				100.0	100.0
Gross Profit									
Operating Expenses		95.8	90.6	87.1				84.9	88.4
Operating Profit		4.2	9.4	12.9				15.1	11.6
All Other Expenses (net)		.1	1.2	2.7				5.7	4.0
Profit Before Taxes		4.1	8.2	10.2				9.4	7.7
RATIOS									
Current		3.1	2.5	1.6				2.7	2.9
		1.4	1.1	1.2				1.1	1.1
		.8	.5	.6				.5	.6
Quick		1.7	1.3	.9				1.3	1.3
		1.0	.3	.4				.5	.4
		.2	.1	.1				.2	.1
Sales/Receivables	0 UND		4 95.7	5 75.1				0 UND	0 UND
	4 100.2		10 34.9	14 26.1				9 39.6	10 37.3
	22 16.7		24 15.3	28 13.2				23 16.2	22 16.7
Cost of Sales/Inventory									
Cost of Sales/Payables									
Sales/Working Capital		11.2	8.6	9.2				5.6	6.5
		21.4	247.8	25.5				46.2	52.7
		-36.6	-8.0	-23.2				-11.2	-11.5
EBIT/Interest		14.1	6.1	7.5				6.9	4.3
		(16) 3.6	(28) 3.2	(30) 3.3				(85) 2.1	(69) 2.0
		1.0	1.1	1.2				.8	1.0
Net Profit + Depr., Dep., Amort./Cur. Mat. L/T/D								21.5	4.7
								(11) 6.8	(16) 1.3
								.9	.4
Fixed/Worth		.3	.3	.8				.3	.6
		.8	.8	1.6				1.1	1.4
		NM	4.8	2.8				3.7	3.9
Debt/Worth		.2	.4	.8				.8	1.0
		2.0	2.1	1.5				2.0	2.2
		NM	9.8	4.2				8.3	10.5
% Profit Before Taxes/Tangible Net Worth		53.5	45.4	28.5				46.6	35.5
		(17) 7.2	(30) 14.6	6.9				(88) 12.6	(74) 13.2
		.9	3.1	1.1				-.9	.5
% Profit Before Taxes/Total Assets		13.5	10.4	8.4				13.9	6.7
		2.2	2.4	4.2				5.3	3.4
		-1.5	.8	.4				-.4	.0
Sales/Net Fixed Assets		146.2	41.9	3.9				18.5	23.3
		14.0	7.4	1.1				4.6	3.0
		5.0	2.9	.5				1.1	.7
Sales/Total Assets		4.8	4.4	1.2				3.4	3.5
		3.4	2.3	.7				1.2	1.0
		1.5	1.1	.3				.4	.3
% Depr., Dep., Amort./Sales		.2	.4	1.4				1.3	1.2
		(13) 1.6	(27) 1.7	(30) 5.2				(79) 3.6	(74) 4.4
		14.1	5.1	9.4				10.2	10.4
% Officers', Directors' Owners' Comp/Sales			.6					1.0	1.2
		(10) 1.1						(28) 2.8	(18) 2.0
		2.1						6.1	5.2
Net Sales ($)	11041M	94794M	391930M	816096M	267100M	741295M		1909258M	1527490M
Total Assets ($)	2432M	26922M	162016M	784017M	475528M	1273272M		1945321M	1957947M

M = $ thousand   MM = $ million
See Pages 9 through 22 for Explanation of Ratios and Data

Comparative Historical Data			Type of Statement	Current Data Sorted by Sales					
			Unqualified	1		1	2	2	8
			Reviewed		2	3	2	6	5
			Compiled	2	4	3	5	7	1
			Tax Returns	7	1	2	3	2	
			Other	2	7	6	5	16	7
				17 (4/1-9/30/10)		**95 (10/1/10-3/31/11)**			
4/1/08-3/31/09 ALL	4/1/09-3/31/10 ALL	4/1/10-3/31/11 ALL		0-1MM	1-3MM	3-5MM	5-10MM	10-25MM	25MM & OVER
105	114	112	**NUMBER OF STATEMENTS**	12	14	15	17	33	21
%	%	%	**ASSETS**	%	%	%	%	%	%
8.3	6.7	8.1	Cash & Equivalents	6.0	13.2	6.2	14.0	6.5	5.2
7.5	9.5	10.3	Trade Receivables (net)	.6	7.9	14.6	9.8	11.7	12.4
17.0	18.0	12.7	Inventory	2.1	.3	6.0	21.3	19.0	15.3
3.8	3.5	4.3	All Other Current	13.5	4.0	4.9	.8	1.9	5.1
36.5	37.7	35.4	Total Current	22.2	25.4	31.7	45.9	39.0	38.0
45.5	45.0	45.3	Fixed Assets (net)	47.4	48.3	51.9	41.7	41.9	45.6
1.1	1.6	1.2	Intangibles (net)	1.2	3.5	3.4	.1	.2	.5
16.9	15.6	18.1	All Other Non-Current	28.8	22.8	13.0	12.3	18.9	15.9
100.0	100.0	100.0	Total	100.0	100.0	100.0	100.0	100.0	100.0
			LIABILITIES						
20.5	15.7	14.3	Notes Payable-Short Term	32.7	17.5	5.6	14.9	12.1	10.9
4.8	7.5	6.8	Cur. Mat.-L.T.D.	14.9	4.3	5.6	8.1	6.1	4.7
4.3	3.9	4.2	Trade Payables	3.5	1.9	2.5	7.8	4.3	4.0
.0	.1	.2	Income Taxes Payable	.0	.0	.3	.0	.3	.3
8.3	8.5	8.5	All Other Current	8.9	5.6	17.7	7.8	8.2	4.8
38.0	35.7	34.0	Total Current	60.1	29.3	31.7	38.6	31.0	24.8
33.3	31.6	26.2	Long-Term Debt	27.0	23.8	33.6	11.4	23.5	38.3
.4	.6	.4	Deferred Taxes	.0	.0	.0	1.8	.3	.5
3.7	5.7	5.7	All Other Non-Current	11.1	7.9	6.2	7.7	3.9	2.0
24.7	26.5	33.7	Net Worth	1.8	39.1	28.5	40.4	41.4	34.5
100.0	100.0	100.0	Total Liabilities & Net Worth	100.0	100.0	100.0	100.0	100.0	100.0
			INCOME DATA						
100.0	100.0	100.0	Net Sales	100.0	100.0	100.0	100.0	100.0	100.0
			Gross Profit						
89.6	94.1	90.5	Operating Expenses	84.2	82.3	90.5	91.1	93.1	95.1
10.4	5.9	9.5	Operating Profit	15.8	17.7	9.5	8.9	6.9	4.9
6.0	3.0	2.8	All Other Expenses (net)	2.7	4.6	4.3	3.7	1.1	2.4
4.5	2.9	6.7	Profit Before Taxes	13.1	13.1	5.2	5.2	5.8	2.4
			RATIOS						
2.9	2.8	2.0		2.8	1.5	6.3	2.3	2.4	1.9
1.2	1.1	1.2	Current	.3	1.1	1.4	1.0	1.2	1.6
.5	.5	.6		.1	.5	.4	.4	.6	.8
1.5	1.3	1.1		.6	1.4	1.8	1.2	.9	1.0
.4	.4	.5	Quick	.1	.8	.7	.5	.5	.7
.1	.2	.2		.0	.3	.1	.2	.2	.3
1 384.6	0 UND	2 194.7		0 UND	0 UND	2 213.1	4 104.2	4 85.0	10 36.1
9 41.3	11 33.4	11 34.1	Sales/Receivables	0 UND	0 UND	14 26.6	9 39.3	18 20.5	17 21.9
22 16.9	24 15.2	26 14.3		0 UND	36 10.3	39 9.3	13 27.9	28 13.2	35 10.4
			Cost of Sales/Inventory						
			Cost of Sales/Payables						
4.7	5.8	9.7		16.9	16.4	8.3	10.8	8.2	8.1
63.8	35.0	37.5	Sales/Working Capital	-5.2	67.8	18.5	-183.0	20.8	18.0
-11.5	-8.3	-13.2		-.5	-13.2	-9.4	-4.0	-18.6	-38.2
3.3	4.5	7.7				6.9	8.4	7.9	3.7
(86) 1.2	(99) 1.3	(92) 3.1	EBIT/Interest		(12) 1.5	(14) 3.1	(32) 3.4	(19) 2.8	
-.6	-.9	1.1				1.1	.7	1.1	1.3
6.1	4.7	6.5							
(16) 1.2	(15) 1.2	(16) 1.7	Net Profit + Depr., Dep., Amort./Cur. Mat. L/T/D						
.4	-.7	.5							
.4	.5	.5		.6	.5	.8	.4	.3	.6
1.4	1.7	1.3	Fixed/Worth	3.5	1.2	1.9	.7	1.0	1.5
4.8	5.3	3.7		-.8	NM	10.4	7.4	2.7	2.0
.9	1.0	.6		1.6	.4	.8	.2	.5	1.0
2.2	2.3	1.8	Debt/Worth	2.9	1.3	1.8	2.1	1.4	2.1
11.0	8.4	6.6		-5.8	NM	15.0	14.1	5.5	4.2
25.6	26.5	34.4			19.0	14.2	29.2	48.4	30.9
(88) 5.5	(98) 2.6	(99) 9.6	% Profit Before Taxes/Tangible Net Worth	(11) 9.6	(12) 6.8	(16) 6.1	(32) 10.1	(20) 14.6	
-4.5	-8.4	1.6			2.8	2.2	.5	.3	3.6
7.0	7.3	9.6		14.6	9.9	9.4	18.1	10.4	9.2
1.1	.6	2.4	% Profit Before Taxes/Total Assets	1.7	3.4	1.8	1.6	2.3	5.3
-3.5	-3.0	-.4		-7.3	-1.8	-1.0	-.9	-.2	.4
18.2	15.6	15.7		172.8	27.4	14.2	67.7	16.5	11.4
3.3	3.6	4.2	Sales/Net Fixed Assets	5.2	2.8	2.4	5.9	4.3	3.6
.4	.8	.9		.3	.3	.4	.7	1.3	1.0
3.6	3.2	3.6		2.2	2.6	3.5	4.5	4.0	3.3
1.0	1.2	1.4	Sales/Total Assets	1.0	1.1	1.5	2.5	1.4	1.3
.3	.4	.5		.1	.2	.3	.4	.8	.7
.8	1.0	.7			1.4	1.2	.2	.8	.4
(93) 3.5	(93) 4.3	(90) 3.6	% Depr., Dep., Amort./Sales	(12) 7.8	(10) 9.4	(14) 1.3	(29) 4.4	(17) 3.9	
10.1	11.4	9.4			10.2	13.7	3.8	7.3	9.0
1.0	1.2	1.1							
(24) 1.7	(23) 1.7	(22) 2.0	% Officers', Directors' Owners' Comp/Sales						
2.9	4.3	5.0							
2148210M	1822116M	2322256M	Net Sales ($)	5369M	27468M	55943M	116149M	541981M	1575346M
2586946M	2183243M	2724187M	Total Assets ($)	23363M	92858M	169794M	198210M	650827M	1589135M

M = $ thousand   MM = $ million
See Pages 9 through 22 for Explanation of Ratios and Data

Current Data Sorted by Assets   Comparative Historical Data

Type of Statement

0-500M	500M-2MM	2-10MM	10-50MM	50-100MM	100-250MM	Type of Statement	4/1/06-3/31/07 ALL	4/1/07-3/31/08 ALL
			1		2	Unqualified	13	7
	2	9	3			Reviewed	21	19
2	12	10	3	1		Compiled	34	32
6	20	8				Tax Returns	40	37
3	4	13	2	1		Other	27	32
23 (4/1-9/30/10)			79 (10/1/10-3/31/11)					
11	38	40	9	2	2	NUMBER OF STATEMENTS	135	127

0-500M	500M-2MM	2-10MM	10-50MM	50-100MM	100-250MM		4/1/06-3/31/07	4/1/07-3/31/08
%	%	%	%	%	%	**ASSETS**	%	%
20.8	16.0	4.4				Cash & Equivalents	10.3	9.7
7.4	10.2	13.7				Trade Receivables (net)	9.9	8.3
5.4	8.0	18.4				Inventory	16.6	14.3
5.2	1.7	4.3				All Other Current	3.6	3.9
38.8	35.9	40.8				Total Current	40.4	36.1
45.8	55.2	47.0				Fixed Assets (net)	50.1	53.1
3.8	1.9	2.4				Intangibles (net)	1.7	1.6
11.7	6.9	9.8				All Other Non-Current	7.8	9.1
100.0	100.0	100.0				Total	100.0	100.0
						LIABILITIES		
11.9	11.3	15.8				Notes Payable-Short Term	18.5	12.9
9.6	12.0	8.9				Cur. Mat.-L.T.D.	8.6	11.5
4.8	5.9	8.2				Trade Payables	6.2	6.7
.0	.2	.3				Income Taxes Payable	.3	.2
9.5	3.2	8.0				All Other Current	4.7	3.8
35.8	32.6	41.1				Total Current	38.4	35.1
38.5	37.3	25.9				Long-Term Debt	32.7	38.3
.0	.6	1.7				Deferred Taxes	.8	.6
50.5	2.7	3.1				All Other Non-Current	4.2	3.6
-24.8	26.8	28.1				Net Worth	24.0	22.4
100.0	100.0	100.0				Total Liabilities & Net Worth	100.0	100.0
						INCOME DATA		
100.0	100.0	100.0				Net Sales	100.0	100.0
72.1	45.7	32.7				Gross Profit	35.9	37.0
66.7	43.2	31.8				Operating Expenses	32.2	34.5
5.4	2.5	.9				Operating Profit	3.6	2.5
.3	.1	.2				All Other Expenses (net)	1.1	1.0
5.1	2.4	.7				Profit Before Taxes	2.5	1.5
						RATIOS		
6.9	2.4	1.4					1.9	2.1
.9	1.2	1.0				Current	1.1	1.0
.6	.6	.6					.4	.4
3.3	1.8	.8					1.4	1.3
.9	.7	(39) .4				Quick	(134) .5	(126) .5
.2	.2	.1					.2	.2
0 UND	0 UND	5 77.6					0 UND	0 UND
0 UND	7 51.6	21 17.1				Sales/Receivables	10 36.6	8 48.0
2 146.9	20 18.2	31 11.9					22 16.2	20 18.1
0 UND	0 UND	0 UND					0 UND	0 UND
0 UND	0 999.8	9 42.6				Cost of Sales/Inventory	15 24.5	8 43.4
0 UND	48 7.6	70 5.2					62 5.9	58 6.3
0 UND	0 UND	4 96.1					0 UND	0 849.0
0 UND	11 33.0	16 22.5				Cost of Sales/Payables	8 45.5	8 47.9
0 UND	33 11.0	37 9.8					24 15.1	26 14.1
8.8	10.4	16.2					9.9	12.9
-188.8	79.6	201.9				Sales/Working Capital	113.2	295.8
-30.0	-13.0	-18.5					-13.4	-13.9
16.3	7.8	4.3					5.4	4.2
3.0	(37) 2.8	(36) 1.3				EBIT/Interest	(129) 1.8	(119) 1.7
1.4	-.3	-.5					.9	-.2
						Net Profit + Depr., Dep.,	4.3	3.2
						Amort./Cur. Mat. L/T/D	(21) 2.0 (23) 1.7	
							1.2	.8
3.3	.7	.9					.7	.8
-1.6	1.6	1.5				Fixed/Worth	1.8	3.0
-.7	56.6	NM					8.5	21.0
3.2	.7	1.1					.8	1.1
-9.1	1.4	2.4				Debt/Worth	3.4	3.9
-4.1	169.7	NM					20.6	39.3
	40.1	19.0					41.4	33.3
	(30) 16.0	(30) 3.3				% Profit Before Taxes/Tangible	(113) 9.7	(98) 12.8
	-.9	-12.2				Net Worth	.6	.6
22.3	18.9	9.5					13.1	10.0
17.2	6.2	1.2				% Profit Before Taxes/Total	3.6	3.7
1.6	-2.7	-3.9				Assets	-.2	-5.7
28.0	10.5	10.1					11.4	10.8
8.6	4.7	4.4				Sales/Net Fixed Assets	4.5	4.4
5.9	2.3	2.3					2.2	2.4
8.1	3.7	3.3					3.5	3.3
5.6	2.4	1.9				Sales/Total Assets	2.1	2.3
2.1	1.7	1.2					1.4	1.6
	3.6	2.4					2.8	2.7
	(34) 7.2	(35) 5.7				% Depr., Dep., Amort./Sales	(114) 6.9	(112) 8.3
	13.1	9.7					11.7	11.8
	1.8	1.3					1.8	1.8
	(23) 2.9	(21) 2.9				% Officers', Directors'	(56) 3.3	(63) 3.5
	6.5	5.1				Owners' Comp/Sales	5.5	5.4
14845M	124868M	424826M	327299M	265132M	428676M	Net Sales ($)	1805721M	1687253M
3072M	42911M	180372M	182697M	103913M	353597M	Total Assets ($)	1255678M	865255M

M = $ thousand   MM = $ million
See Pages 9 through 22 for Explanation of Ratios and Data

Comparative Historical Data | Current Data Sorted by Sales

4/1/08-3/31/09 ALL	4/1/09-3/31/10 ALL	4/1/10-3/31/11 ALL	Type of Statement	0-1MM	1-3MM	3-5MM	5-10MM	10-25MM	25MM & OVER
5	2	3	Unqualified						
16	19	14	Reviewed		3	1	1	7	3
17	37	28	Compiled		8	7	6	5	2
36	39	34	Tax Returns	6	13	6	6	3	2
28	25	23	Other	1	6	4	4	5	3
					23 (4/1-9/30/10)		79 (10/1/10-3/31/11)		
102	122	102	**NUMBER OF STATEMENTS**	7	30	18	17	20	10
%	%	%	**ASSETS**	%	%	%	%	%	%
10.5	14.3	10.8	Cash & Equivalents		16.2	13.8	6.3	4.0	8.1
9.7	9.8	11.4	Trade Receivables (net)		10.8	11.6	13.4	10.7	18.8
13.4	12.6	12.1	Inventory		6.4	12.7	15.1	16.4	16.6
3.3	4.7	3.4	All Other Current		1.9	3.2	4.4	3.6	2.8
36.9	41.4	37.7	Total Current		35.3	41.3	39.2	34.7	46.2
51.7	48.1	50.0	Fixed Assets (net)		56.2	49.2	49.5	50.7	35.6
3.2	1.9	2.1	Intangibles (net)		2.9	2.0	.3	2.1	.5
8.1	8.5	10.2	All Other Non-Current		5.6	7.5	10.9	12.4	17.7
100.0	100.0	100.0	Total		100.0	100.0	100.0	100.0	100.0
			LIABILITIES						
14.1	11.4	12.2	Notes Payable-Short Term		8.7	20.5	8.6	11.8	12.0
10.3	8.7	10.6	Cur. Mat.-L.T.D.		11.0	5.5	15.6	8.9	18.2
5.1	5.5	6.5	Trade Payables		6.1	5.8	7.0	9.3	6.2
.0	.1	.2	Income Taxes Payable		.1	.6	.3	.0	.0
7.6	7.7	5.8	All Other Current		4.9	8.2	5.1	6.0	6.7
37.2	33.4	35.3	Total Current		30.9	40.6	36.7	36.1	43.2
32.9	34.5	30.8	Long-Term Debt		42.5	22.9	29.3	27.7	12.9
.5	.7	.9	Deferred Taxes		.7	.8	1.3	1.7	.3
4.6	4.2	8.1	All Other Non-Current		10.0	4.9	1.4	4.9	.5
24.8	27.2	25.0	Net Worth		15.9	30.9	31.4	29.6	43.2
100.0	100.0	100.0	Total Liabilities & Net Worth		100.0	100.0	100.0	100.0	100.0
			INCOME DATA						
100.0	100.0	100.0	Net Sales		100.0	100.0	100.0	100.0	100.0
36.0	39.2	40.6	Gross Profit		57.7	36.7	32.1	29.9	12.2
34.5	36.8	38.0	Operating Expenses		56.5	33.8	30.4	26.0	10.4
1.5	2.5	2.6	Operating Profit		1.2	2.9	1.6	3.8	1.7
.7	.5	.1	All Other Expenses (net)		.1	.1	-1.0	.4	.3
.7	2.0	2.5	Profit Before Taxes		1.1	2.8	2.6	3.4	1.4
			RATIOS						
2.5	2.5	2.0			2.4	2.1	2.0	1.7	2.1
1.1	1.3	1.1	Current		1.1	1.2	1.1	.9	1.2
.5	.5	.6			.6	.4	.6	.6	.6
1.5	1.8	1.4			2.2	.9	1.0	.7	1.3
(100) .5	(121) .6	(101) .6	Quick		.7	.6	(16) .7	.4	.8
.2	.2	.2			.2	.3	.2	.2	.1
0 UND	0 UND	0 UND			0 UND	5 72.2	0 UND	6 60.9	6 63.0
6 56.3	9 39.3	10 36.3	Sales/Receivables		8 47.0	20 18.2	14 26.1	12 31.4	10 35.7
15 23.9	25 14.9	28 13.2			29 12.5	26 14.1	32 11.4	29 12.4	31 11.9
0 UND	0 UND	0 UND			0 UND	0 UND	0 UND	1 431.2	2 178.5
5 76.1	6 57.3	2 162.5	Cost of Sales/Inventory		0 UND	0 UND	0 UND	8 44.7	21 17.5
43 8.5	43 8.6	48 7.6			75 4.9	54 6.7	40 9.2	58 6.3	45 8.0
0 940.2	0 UND	0 UND			0 UND	3 114.6	1 567.5	4 92.6	2 155.8
6 56.4	7 55.2	9 41.7	Cost of Sales/Payables		8 45.9	14 25.7	15 23.7	9 41.0	8 44.3
19 19.6	23 15.8	33 11.0			65 5.6	27 13.7	41 9.0	34 10.8	10 35.3
10.8	7.0	9.6			10.2	6.4	9.9	17.6	6.0
83.4	41.6	55.7	Sales/Working Capital		82.3	40.2	136.8	-102.4	195.6
-13.0	-14.4	-18.1			-11.0	-9.0	-19.9	-22.7	-16.1
5.4	4.3	6.4			5.0	7.1	6.4	9.4	
(96) 1.9	(111) 1.7	(95) 2.7	EBIT/Interest		1.4	(15) 2.8	(15) 2.5	(19) 3.4	
-.9	.1	.3			-1.1	-.4	1.3	1.0	
4.2	2.9	1.1	Net Profit + Depr., Dep.,						
(13) 1.9	(17) 1.7	(15) .7	Amort./Cur. Mat. L/T/D						
.9	.7	.4							
.7	.6	.8			1.4	.6	.7	.8	.2
1.7	1.9	1.6	Fixed/Worth		2.2	1.3	1.6	1.4	1.1
NM	13.5	101.4			-2.4	40.6	13.4	NM	1.6
.7	.6	.9			.9	.6	.7	.9	.9
2.1	2.7	1.8	Debt/Worth		2.5	1.3	1.6	2.0	1.5
NM	22.2	170.1			-8.5	100.3	53.5	NM	2.5
32.0	29.8	32.9	% Profit Before Taxes/Tangible		24.5	33.3	33.0	38.7	14.3
(77) 10.8	(98) 9.6	(78) 11.5	Net Worth		(21) 7.7	(15) 3.8	(14) 14.3	(15) 12.8	8.5
-3.7	-2.3	-.7			-8.8	-9.1	3.3	1.0	-1.7
11.4	11.5	12.5	% Profit Before Taxes/Total		11.8	14.6	15.5	9.9	6.9
3.6	2.7	4.7	Assets		1.4	3.7	7.9	7.5	3.5
-7.4	-1.8	-2.9			-6.4	-3.6	1.1	.2	-.6
8.9	17.6	11.3			6.3	7.5	10.8	15.0	43.7
5.1	4.9	4.7	Sales/Net Fixed Assets		4.0	4.7	4.8	4.4	8.8
2.6	2.7	2.3			2.1	2.3	2.5	1.9	4.8
3.5	3.1	3.7			2.8	2.9	4.1	3.6	5.0
2.4	2.2	2.1	Sales/Total Assets		2.0	2.1	2.0	2.4	3.7
1.6	1.6	1.3			1.2	1.2	1.6	1.1	1.3
2.4	2.1	2.4			5.7	3.9	2.4	1.1	
(82) 7.1	(108) 5.8	(87) 6.3	% Depr., Dep., Amort./Sales		(25) 9.7	(16) 6.2	(15) 6.3	(19) 4.3	
12.7	11.3	10.4			13.1	10.5	10.4	8.9	
1.5	1.7	1.9	% Officers', Directors'		2.5	1.9			
(51) 2.1	(57) 3.2	(54) 2.9	Owners' Comp/Sales		(20) 3.6	(10) 3.4			
4.0	6.4	6.6			7.1	6.6			
1119120M	1110257M	1585646M	Net Sales ($)	4591M	62527M	69963M	111381M	272186M	1064998M
564898M	711237M	866562M	Total Assets ($)	2185M	44528M	43294M	58102M	178634M	539819M

© RMA 2011

M = $ thousand   MM = $ million
See Pages 9 through 22 for Explanation of Ratios and Data

AGRICULTURE—Finfish Fishing NAICS 114111

Current Data Sorted by Assets						Type of Statement	Comparative Historical Data	
		1	5	1	1	Unqualified	9	9
	1	1	1			Reviewed	2	6
	1	2	1			Compiled	3	4
4	6					Tax Returns	7	5
3	3	7	4	1	2	Other	21	21
	5 (4/1-9/30/10)		40 (10/1/10-3/31/11)				4/1/06-3/31/07	4/1/07-3/31/08
0-500M	500M-2MM	2-10MM	10-50MM	50-100MM	100-250MM		ALL	ALL
7	11	11	11	2	3	NUMBER OF STATEMENTS	42	45
%	%	%	%	%	%	**ASSETS**	%	%
	19.1	17.5	10.4			Cash & Equivalents	11.1	14.7
	9.5	6.4	4.9			Trade Receivables (net)	7.8	10.7
	4.9	12.8	13.6			Inventory	10.4	10.8
	.1	6.0	2.4			All Other Current	4.2	3.4
	33.7	42.8	31.3			Total Current	33.4	39.5
	27.9	32.5	40.5			Fixed Assets (net)	42.3	34.5
	20.7	17.6	19.3			Intangibles (net)	12.3	12.9
	17.6	7.2	9.0			All Other Non-Current	12.0	13.1
	100.0	100.0	100.0			Total	100.0	100.0
						LIABILITIES		
	42.3	8.6	3.8			Notes Payable-Short Term	7.4	6.0
	9.6	5.7	4.4			Cur. Mat.-L.T.D.	4.3	4.2
	7.8	9.8	4.9			Trade Payables	8.2	4.7
	.0	.0	.0			Income Taxes Payable	.3	.2
	2.6	4.8	8.1			All Other Current	5.3	4.8
	62.2	28.8	21.2			Total Current	25.5	19.9
	48.4	34.4	36.5			Long-Term Debt	41.1	34.5
	.0	1.1	.8			Deferred Taxes	.3	.4
	14.4	2.9	1.8			All Other Non-Current	5.2	5.3
	-25.1	32.8	39.7			Net Worth	27.8	39.9
	100.0	100.0	100.0			Total Liabilities & Net Worth	100.0	100.0
						INCOME DATA		
	100.0	100.0	100.0			Net Sales	100.0	100.0
						Gross Profit		
	84.2	85.5	92.6			Operating Expenses	83.9	85.9
	15.8	14.5	7.4			Operating Profit	16.1	14.1
	3.3	3.2	4.3			All Other Expenses (net)	1.9	2.2
	12.5	11.3	3.1			Profit Before Taxes	14.2	11.9
						RATIOS		
	1.4	2.0	2.1				2.6	4.8
	.6	1.3	1.6			Current	1.5	1.9
	.0	1.0	.9				.7	1.1
	1.4	1.2	1.5				1.7	2.4
	.5	1.0	.9			Quick	.8	1.3
	.0	.3	.2				.5	.7
0 UND	0 UND	1 387.1					0 UND	0 UND
0 UND	1 491.0	15 25.0				Sales/Receivables	8 44.3	14 27.0
0 UND	22 16.3	34 10.6					28 13.2	37 9.8
						Cost of Sales/Inventory		
						Cost of Sales/Payables		
	12.5	6.8	4.7				5.3	4.7
	-27.0	24.7	9.1			Sales/Working Capital	14.1	9.1
	-.8	462.1	-64.9				-27.0	30.9
	50.2	55.7	8.6				14.6	11.3
(10)	4.0 (10)	8.4 (10)	1.5			EBIT/Interest	4.6	(43) 4.2
	.5	3.1	-.7				2.2	2.3
						Net Profit + Depr., Dep., Amort./Cur. Mat. L/T/D		
	.0	.3	1.1				.7	.5
	-.7	1.0	1.8			Fixed/Worth	1.8	1.4
	-.3	-3.7	-5.0				-3.9	3.7
	17.4	.8	1.1				.9	.7
	-2.5	2.1	3.9			Debt/Worth	2.8	2.2
	-1.6	-6.1	-6.1				-16.2	21.6
							77.5	80.6
						% Profit Before Taxes/Tangible Net Worth	(30) 36.3	(36) 40.2
							8.8	15.2
	20.5	44.4	11.3				27.5	26.4
	12.5	21.4	1.5			% Profit Before Taxes/Total Assets	10.7	9.3
	-3.5	3.3	-4.7				2.8	2.8
	UND	21.9	4.0				8.8	10.0
	9.5	11.2	3.4			Sales/Net Fixed Assets	4.8	4.3
	3.4	3.5	1.2				2.2	2.0
	2.9	3.7	1.5				2.9	2.3
	1.3	2.4	.8			Sales/Total Assets	1.5	1.2
	.7	1.1	.4				.8	.8
		1.8	4.0				2.0	2.8
	(10)	3.4	6.9			% Depr., Dep., Amort./Sales	(36) 3.8	(37) 4.3
		5.9	19.5				8.7	9.0
							.5	1.3
						% Officers', Directors' Owners' Comp/Sales	(13) 1.5	(16) 2.6
							6.0	5.7
16455M	31742M	166501M	319947M	77067M	772048M	Net Sales ($)	1199565M	1236803M
1550M	11228M	68408M	291078M	146048M	546128M	Total Assets ($)	971806M	978190M

M = $ thousand   MM = $ million
See Pages 9 through 22 for Explanation of Ratios and Data

Comparative Historical Data / Current Data Sorted by Sales

Type of Statement

					0-1MM	1-3MM	3-5MM	5-10MM	10-25MM	25MM & OVER
6	9	8		Unqualified				1	2	5
2	4	3		Reviewed				1	1	1
6	8	4		Compiled	1	1	2			
10	14	10		Tax Returns	6	3			1	
33	24	20		Other	1	3	2	3	4	7
4/1/08-3/31/09	4/1/09-3/31/10	4/1/10-3/31/11					5 (4/1-9/30/10)		40 (10/1/10-3/31/11)	
ALL	ALL	ALL			0-1MM	1-3MM	3-5MM	5-10MM	10-25MM	25MM & OVER
57	59	45		**NUMBER OF STATEMENTS**	8	7	4	5	8	13

%	%	%			%	%	%	%	%	%
				ASSETS						
14.8	13.6	17.6		Cash & Equivalents						11.7
8.7	4.5	6.8		Trade Receivables (net)						10.8
8.8	7.6	9.1		Inventory						17.6
5.8	1.9	2.8		All Other Current						3.0
38.0	27.6	36.2		Total Current						43.1
35.7	36.0	32.9		Fixed Assets (net)						31.1
15.4	20.2	20.3		Intangibles (net)						15.5
10.9	16.2	10.6		All Other Non-Current						10.3
100.0	100.0	100.0		Total						100.0
				LIABILITIES						
10.4	27.7	43.3		Notes Payable-Short Term						4.9
13.5	6.6	5.9		Cur. Mat.-L.T.D.						4.1
5.9	3.5	6.1		Trade Payables						8.9
.2	.1	.0		Income Taxes Payable						.0
14.5	6.7	8.4		All Other Current						9.5
44.5	44.5	63.7		Total Current						27.5
46.1	42.5	33.3		Long-Term Debt						26.1
.5	.4	.5		Deferred Taxes						.7
2.2	2.7	6.2		All Other Non-Current						5.4
6.7	9.7	-3.8		Net Worth						40.3
100.0	100.0	100.0		Total Liabilities & Net Worth						100.0
				INCOME DATA						
100.0	100.0	100.0		Net Sales						100.0
				Gross Profit						
86.4	86.4	88.6		Operating Expenses						90.1
13.6	13.6	11.4		Operating Profit						9.9
3.6	3.9	3.0		All Other Expenses (net)						1.5
10.0	9.6	8.3		Profit Before Taxes						8.4
				RATIOS						
3.3	2.3	1.9		Current						3.3
1.7	1.3	1.3								1.4
1.0	.3	.4								1.1
2.4	1.8	1.4		Quick						1.8
1.1	.5	.8								.9
.3	.2	.2								.3
0 UND	0 UND	0 UND		Sales/Receivables						11 34.0
13 28.2	0 UND	1 387.1								25 14.7
39 9.5	20 18.0	25 14.9								38 9.7
				Cost of Sales/Inventory						
				Cost of Sales/Payables						
4.2	5.9	8.0		Sales/Working Capital						4.6
10.5	20.9	45.1								16.7
-650.6	-4.9	-10.6								62.2
10.8	11.7	12.7		EBIT/Interest						14.7
(51) 5.6	(54) 4.0	(40) 4.0								7.4
2.0	.7	.6								2.5
				Net Profit + Depr., Dep., Amort./Cur. Mat. L/T/D						
.5	.5	.4		Fixed/Worth						.6
1.5	1.7	1.8								1.1
-1.5	-1.2	-1.1								1.9
.7	.8	2.0		Debt/Worth						1.0
2.1	9.2	7.0								3.1
-5.9	-2.4	-2.7								5.0
60.9	55.6	109.5		% Profit Before Taxes/Tangible Net Worth						79.6
(39) 31.1	(33) 26.9	(26) 37.1							(11)	45.1
8.0	1.7	4.9								9.8
28.7	18.5	21.0		% Profit Before Taxes/Total Assets						11.3
9.2	5.9	6.2								9.0
1.6	-.9	-4.1								3.4
10.7	19.6	22.7		Sales/Net Fixed Assets						10.0
4.4	3.8	6.7								3.9
2.1	1.6	2.9								2.7
2.6	2.2	3.4		Sales/Total Assets						3.8
1.2	1.1	1.3								1.2
.7	.7	.7								.6
1.8	2.4	2.9		% Depr., Dep., Amort./Sales						1.7
(47) 4.6	(44) 5.6	(34) 6.0							(10)	3.8
7.5	11.7	12.8								6.4
2.0				% Officers', Directors' Owners' Comp/Sales						
(11) 4.4										
7.7										
1439570M	1439716M	1383760M		Net Sales ($)	3880M	12162M	16394M	35417M	132027M	1183880M
1213677M	1121023M	1064440M		Total Assets ($)	5019M	6139M	45858M	32231M	101540M	873653M

© RMA 2011

M = $ thousand   MM = $ million

See Pages 9 through 22 for Explanation of Ratios and Data

Current Data Sorted by Assets   Comparative Historical Data

						Type of Statement		
	1		1	1		Unqualified		1
	5	3	3	1		Reviewed	7	4
4	9	1	2			Compiled	7	12
1	9	5				Tax Returns	11	20
1			4			Other	12	11
	14 (4/1-9/30/10)		36 (10/1/10-3/31/11)				12 4/1/06-3/31/07	11 4/1/07-3/31/08
0-500M	500M-2MM	2-10MM	10-50MM	50-100MM	100-250MM		ALL	ALL
5	24	9	10	2		NUMBER OF STATEMENTS	37	48
%	%	%	%	%	%	ASSETS	%	%
	13.0		6.4			Cash & Equivalents	22.1	14.7
	8.8		3.5		D	Trade Receivables (net)	14.1	7.2
	4.1		4.4		A	Inventory	6.4	5.4
	3.5		5.0		T	All Other Current	3.1	4.5
	29.4		19.3		A	Total Current	45.7	31.8
	31.3		32.3			Fixed Assets (net)	42.5	42.5
	29.6		23.9		N	Intangibles (net)	4.0	15.2
	9.7		24.5		O	All Other Non-Current	7.8	10.5
	100.0		100.0		T	Total	100.0	100.0
					A	LIABILITIES		
	8.3		2.8		V	Notes Payable-Short Term	9.0	7.4
	4.2		3.9		A	Cur. Mat.-L.T.D.	3.1	17.2
	7.3		3.3		I	Trade Payables	8.3	5.1
	2.0		.7		L	Income Taxes Payable	.2	.0
	11.5		1.0		A	All Other Current	19.9	21.8
	33.3		11.7		B	Total Current	40.5	51.5
	34.0		30.0		L	Long-Term Debt	20.3	36.4
	.0		.6		E	Deferred Taxes	.4	2.0
	11.3		2.8			All Other Non-Current	4.2	10.9
	21.4		54.9			Net Worth	34.6	-.8
	100.0		100.0			Total Liabilities & Net Worth	100.0	100.0
						INCOME DATA		
	100.0		100.0			Net Sales	100.0	100.0
						Gross Profit		
	86.9		76.6			Operating Expenses	92.5	86.2
	13.1		23.4			Operating Profit	7.5	13.8
	5.0		7.8			All Other Expenses (net)	3.8	3.4
	8.1		15.5			Profit Before Taxes	3.7	10.4
						RATIOS		
	4.9		4.6				3.3	3.6
	.8		1.1			Current	1.7	1.4
	.1		.5				.9	.2
	4.0		1.6				2.9	2.2
	.5		.5			Quick	1.2	1.1
	.1		.3				.5	.1
0	UND		0 UND				0 UND	0 UND
0	UND		7 55.1			Sales/Receivables	0 UND	0 UND
33	11.2		32 11.3				25 14.8	20 18.0
						Cost of Sales/Inventory		
						Cost of Sales/Payables		
	4.2		3.3				6.1	8.4
	-55.7		41.0			Sales/Working Capital	21.3	24.1
	-2.6		-17.1				-61.1	-25.6
	15.9						7.9	8.5
(18)	6.6					EBIT/Interest	(32) 4.0	(43) 3.0
	1.4						1.6	.7
						Net Profit + Depr., Dep., Amort./Cur. Mat. L/T/D		
	.5		.1				.5	.7
	1.7		.5			Fixed/Worth	.9	1.5
	-.4		2.6				2.2	49.7
	.6		.2				.8	1.0
	7.5		.6			Debt/Worth	1.6	4.2
	-1.6		NM				4.4	-2.8
	58.6						78.4	95.7
(14)	29.2					% Profit Before Taxes/Tangible Net Worth	(33) 33.8	(31) 38.0
	-2.5						6.7	8.4
	27.5		15.9				25.5	25.8
	14.0		5.5			% Profit Before Taxes/Total Assets	9.4	7.3
	-1.5		-.7				2.3	.8
	30.2		UND				35.8	26.6
	6.6		3.1			Sales/Net Fixed Assets	8.0	7.2
	2.0		1.6				1.7	2.3
	2.1		1.2				5.0	3.6
	1.2		.8			Sales/Total Assets	2.1	1.8
	.8		.5				.8	.9
	2.3						.7	.9
(16)	7.5					% Depr., Dep., Amort./Sales	(30) 3.9	(39) 4.9
	12.9						8.0	8.4
							.7	.5
(17)						% Officers', Directors' Owners' Comp/Sales	1.7	(12) 1.9
							6.7	8.4
4568M	44996M	31416M	191767M	186855M		Net Sales ($)	264969M	401652M
1557M	26514M	40230M	222088M	143944M		Total Assets ($)	144898M	148873M

M = $ thousand   MM = $ million
See Pages 9 through 22 for Explanation of Ratios and Data

Comparative Historical Data | Current Data Sorted by Sales

1	1	2	Type of Statement						
6	5	5	Unqualified				1		1
5	8	10	Reviewed				1	2	2
21	20	14	Compiled	4	2	2	1		1
10	10	19	Tax Returns	4	10		1	2	1
4/1/08-	4/1/09-	4/1/10-	Other	4	7	2	3	2	1
3/31/09	3/31/10	3/31/11			14 (4/1-9/30/10)		36 (10/1/10-3/31/11)		
ALL	ALL	ALL		0-1MM	1-3MM	3-5MM	5-10MM	10-25MM	25MM & OVER
43	44	50	**NUMBER OF STATEMENTS**	12	19	4	6	4	5
%	%	%	**ASSETS**	%	%	%	%	%	%
13.6	14.2	10.5	Cash & Equivalents	7.3	10.1				
5.3	7.6	6.3	Trade Receivables (net)	1.3	4.3				
6.4	4.8	5.4	Inventory	.0	3.7				
1.4	1.8	3.3	All Other Current	1.2	3.3				
26.8	28.4	25.4	Total Current	9.8	21.5				
44.7	32.8	34.7	Fixed Assets (net)	38.5	30.3				
18.7	23.4	24.8	Intangibles (net)	41.1	30.0				
9.8	15.5	15.0	All Other Non-Current	10.6	18.2				
100.0	100.0	100.0	Total	100.0	100.0				
			LIABILITIES						
8.4	9.8	9.7	Notes Payable-Short Term	10.6	14.9				
4.2	4.6	3.5	Cur. Mat.-L.T.D.	5.8	2.5				
4.3	5.9	7.2	Trade Payables	4.4	6.9				
.3	.0	1.4	Income Taxes Payable	2.2	1.7				
6.6	6.0	7.9	All Other Current	10.3	10.2				
23.8	26.4	29.7	Total Current	33.2	36.2				
38.8	50.4	37.1	Long-Term Debt	36.6	49.2				
.3	.4	.3	Deferred Taxes	.0	.0				
11.3	8.6	7.0	All Other Non-Current	4.5	13.5				
25.8	14.2	26.0	Net Worth	25.7	1.1				
100.0	100.0	100.0	Total Liabilities & Net Worth	100.0	100.0				
			INCOME DATA						
100.0	100.0	100.0	Net Sales	100.0	100.0				
			Gross Profit						
91.2	84.7	86.7	Operating Expenses	87.1	84.6				
8.8	15.3	13.3	Operating Profit	12.9	15.4				
2.3	4.7	5.1	All Other Expenses (net)	13.6	4.4				
6.5	10.7	8.2	Profit Before Taxes	-.7	11.0				
			RATIOS						
2.4	2.2	2.6		1.5	1.2				
1.1	1.2	.9	Current	.1	.7				
.2	.3	.1		.0	.1				
1.4	1.9	1.6		1.2	1.0				
.6	.7	.5	Quick	.1	.3				
.1	.3	.1		.0	.1				
0 UND	0 UND	0 UND		0 UND	0 UND				
0 UND	0 UND	0 UND	Sales/Receivables	0 UND	0 UND				
25 14.5	18 20.6	31 11.8		0 UND	33 11.0				
			Cost of Sales/Inventory						
			Cost of Sales/Payables						
7.9	9.0	6.7		NM	22.6				
172.8	46.4	-538.7	Sales/Working Capital	-3.5	-39.3				
-11.2	-10.4	-4.1		-1.4	-3.6				
7.2	12.1	16.5			9.1				
(38) 2.6	(38) 3.6	(41) 4.0	EBIT/Interest	(18) 4.0					
.5	.9	.5			.5				
			Net Profit + Depr., Dep., Amort./Cur. Mat. L/T/D						
.9	.3	.4		.2	.6				
1.7	1.0	.9	Fixed/Worth	2.1	8.9				
-5.6	-2.8	-6.4		10.9	-.2				
.5	.7	.5		2.4	1.8				
3.9	4.0	3.5	Debt/Worth	10.0	-12.1				
-2.7	-2.2	-2.0		-1.3	-1.6				
49.4	77.0	47.1	% Profit Before Taxes/Tangible Net Worth						
(29) 11.1	(26) 29.9	(33) 20.3							
-5.4	7.2	-1.5							
18.9	32.6	23.6	% Profit Before Taxes/Total Assets	11.5	27.5				
4.7	8.0	7.0		.3	17.8				
-1.4	.9	-2.3		-7.1	-2.2				
9.5	50.6	19.1		UND	40.4				
2.9	8.7	4.9	Sales/Net Fixed Assets	3.6	6.2				
1.5	1.9	1.9		1.2	2.1				
2.3	2.7	1.9		1.2	2.1				
1.1	1.1	1.1	Sales/Total Assets	.8	1.2				
.7	.6	.7		.3	.7				
4.4	2.0	2.7			2.0				
(33) 8.0	(32) 4.3	(37) 7.2	% Depr., Dep., Amort./Sales	(14) 6.8					
12.9	10.6	12.6			13.8				
2.9	1.6	1.9	% Officers', Directors' Owners' Comp/Sales						
(16) 4.6	(17) 3.6	(15) 3.7							
10.5	8.6	10.1							
203517M	280397M	459602M	Net Sales ($)	7470M	30679M	16813M	43899M	55210M	305531M
188036M	276781M	434333M	Total Assets ($)	20656M	33188M	7444M	49955M	62632M	260458M

M = $ thousand   MM = $ million
See Pages 9 through 22 for Explanation of Ratios and Data

Current Data Sorted by Assets

Comparative Historical Data

Type of Statement

	0-500M	500M-2MM	2-10MM	10-50MM	50-100MM	100-250MM		4/1/06-3/31/07 ALL	4/1/07-3/31/08 ALL
Unqualified	1	3	15	2	1	1		25	22
Reviewed		2	8	3				10	7
Compiled	1	2	8	2				4	7
Tax Returns	7	9	5					6	7
Other	5	1	3	5				3	2
		36 (4/1-9/30/10)		48 (10/1/10-3/31/11)					
NUMBER OF STATEMENTS	14	17	39	12	1	1		48	45
	%	%	%	%	%	%		%	%
ASSETS									
Cash & Equivalents	28.2	14.2	9.7	5.4				10.5	8.9
Trade Receivables (net)	8.7	8.3	20.7	7.1				15.1	14.6
Inventory	6.0	14.1	11.1	38.9				12.4	11.4
All Other Current	5.7	7.2	3.3	2.3				5.8	4.9
Total Current	48.6	43.8	44.7	53.7				43.8	39.8
Fixed Assets (net)	38.5	45.8	43.1	34.1				45.9	50.0
Intangibles (net)	.0	1.1	1.7	1.0				.4	.3
All Other Non-Current	12.8	9.2	10.4	11.1				9.9	9.9
Total	100.0	100.0	100.0	100.0				100.0	100.0
LIABILITIES									
Notes Payable-Short Term	21.4	6.4	6.5	21.5				8.8	10.5
Cur. Mat.-L.T.D.	10.7	6.2	5.9	1.9				4.0	5.2
Trade Payables	3.4	7.7	10.6	5.2				6.0	5.0
Income Taxes Payable	.0	.2	.3	.5				.3	.2
All Other Current	11.3	11.8	10.3	12.1				10.1	9.2
Total Current	46.7	32.3	33.7	41.1				29.3	30.2
Long-Term Debt	34.5	36.0	16.6	21.5				17.8	22.9
Deferred Taxes	.0	.7	.1	.4				.2	.2
All Other Non-Current	14.3	3.5	1.6	3.8				1.1	1.3
Net Worth	4.5	27.5	48.0	33.1				51.6	45.4
Total Liabilties & Net Worth	100.0	100.0	100.0	100.0				100.0	100.0
INCOME DATA									
Net Sales	100.0	100.0	100.0	100.0				100.0	100.0
Gross Profit									
Operating Expenses	92.6	90.5	91.2	85.6				88.5	86.2
Operating Profit	7.4	9.5	8.8	14.4				11.5	13.8
All Other Expenses (net)	-.2	.4	.2	.8				.0	.7
Profit Before Taxes	7.6	9.1	8.6	13.6				11.5	13.0
RATIOS									
Current	10.7	3.0	2.5	1.7				2.8	2.4
	.9	1.7	1.3	1.4				1.5	1.2
	.2	.4	1.0	1.0				1.1	1.0
Quick	10.0	1.8	1.2	1.2				1.3	1.7
	.7	.9	.8	.3				.9	1.0
	.1	.1	.6	.1				.5	.3
Sales/Receivables	0 UND	0 UND	13 27.2	3 114.2				8 43.3	7 52.5
	0 999.8	8 47.9	64 5.7	8 46.8				23 15.9	21 17.4
	8 45.5	18 20.8	105 3.5	33 11.2				50 7.3	56 6.5
Cost of Sales/Inventory									
Cost of Sales/Payables									
Sales/Working Capital	11.0	4.2	4.8	8.2				4.4	4.3
	-126.3	13.1	12.5	15.8				10.1	12.0
	-11.0	-5.6	107.0	71.0				60.8	-179.6
EBIT/Interest	(11) 30.0	(13) 26.6	(32) 41.8	40.0				(46) 24.3	(39) 29.4
	1.2	5.6	6.7	9.3				5.2	3.5
	.8	1.8	1.0	3.1				1.9	1.4
Net Profit + Depr., Dep., Amort./Cur. Mat. L/T/D								(14) 10.5	(13) 12.4
								3.3	3.6
								2.1	1.7
Fixed/Worth	.0	.3	.4	.5				.5	.5
	1.5	1.1	.8	.8				.8	1.0
	-6.1	NM	1.5	1.5				1.3	1.4
Debt/Worth	.3	.3	.3	1.1				.4	.4
	6.0	1.7	.9	3.4				.8	1.0
	-7.8	NM	2.8	4.7				1.8	2.0
% Profit Before Taxes/Tangible Net Worth	(10) 81.6	(13) 43.2	(34) 34.0	39.6				(46) 50.3	(42) 56.9
	22.4	13.9	14.6	28.6				18.6	15.6
	-2.3	9.1	2.1	12.2				4.8	2.8
% Profit Before Taxes/Total Assets	30.9	19.3	15.0	16.0				24.9	25.1
	1.4	4.7	6.7	8.3				6.8	6.1
	-2.4	.6	-.1	3.4				2.4	1.4
Sales/Net Fixed Assets	UND	12.5	5.6	22.1				7.4	8.6
	10.9	4.8	2.4	5.7				3.1	2.0
	2.9	2.2	.9	1.9				1.6	1.4
Sales/Total Assets	9.1	3.3	1.8	1.8				2.2	1.9
	4.2	2.3	1.0	1.2				1.3	1.1
	1.8	1.0	.6	.8				.8	.7
% Depr., Dep., Amort./Sales	2.0		2.2	.7				2.7	2.3
		(16) 6.6	(36) 5.4	(11) 2.0				(44) 4.7	5.3
		11.3	10.5	3.3				9.5	10.1
% Officers', Directors' Owners' Comp/Sales			(10) 2.5						
			5.5						
			8.6						
Net Sales ($)	20374M	39101M	269202M	307209M	4132M	1003747M		281880M	230058M
Total Assets ($)	3749M	19470M	181705M	241420M	81265M	186873M		209436M	299748M

M = $ thousand   MM = $ million
See Pages 9 through 22 for Explanation of Ratios and Data

Comparative Historical Data / Current Data Sorted by Sales

Current Data columns grouped: **36 (4/1-9/30/10)** covers 0-1MM, 1-3MM, 3-5MM; **48 (10/1/10-3/31/11)** covers 5-10MM, 10-25MM, 25MM & OVER.

4/1/08-3/31/09 ALL	4/1/09-3/31/10 ALL	4/1/10-3/31/11 ALL		0-1MM	1-3MM	3-5MM	5-10MM	10-25MM	25MM & OVER
			Type of Statement						
20	25	23	Unqualified		6	6	6	2	3
8	15	13	Reviewed		4	3	2	4	
7	7	13	Compiled	3	6	1		1	2
7	15	21	Tax Returns	5	7	6	2	1	2
4	18	14	Other	4	4		1	3	2
46	80	84	**NUMBER OF STATEMENTS**	12	27	16	11	11	7
%	%	%		%	%	%	%	%	%
			ASSETS						
11.3	12.7	12.9	Cash & Equivalents	11.0	16.6	18.5	12.5	2.7	
16.1	14.5	15.2	Trade Receivables (net)	10.0	9.6	22.9	12.0	20.1	
12.7	12.6	15.0	Inventory	2.8	9.7	9.8	10.3	40.0	
3.8	2.5	4.3	All Other Current	5.3	7.0	2.4	2.5	2.0	
43.9	42.3	47.4	Total Current	29.0	42.9	53.6	37.2	64.8	
44.1	45.9	40.9	Fixed Assets (net)	54.8	47.7	38.2	45.3	22.6	
.1	.7	1.2	Intangibles (net)	.0		.3	7.3	1.1	
11.9	11.0	10.5	All Other Non-Current	16.1	9.4	7.9	10.2	11.5	
100.0	100.0	100.0	Total	100.0	100.0	100.0	100.0	100.0	
			LIABILITIES						
9.9	9.0	12.0	Notes Payable-Short Term	20.3	8.9	8.9	.4	22.8	
6.0	6.3	6.0	Cur. Mat.-L.T.D.	6.9	4.8	9.8	10.5	1.8	
8.5	7.3	7.9	Trade Payables	1.9	6.0	8.6	6.6	12.3	
.1	.1	.2	Income Taxes Payable	.0	.0	.2	1.0	.5	
9.8	15.9	10.9	All Other Current	5.0	8.2	13.1	24.3	3.0	
34.4	38.5	37.1	Total Current	34.2	27.9	40.5	42.7	40.5	
19.1	21.0	23.8	Long-Term Debt	35.9	27.2	26.6	18.6	14.1	
.1	.1	.3	Deferred Taxes	.0	.5	.0	.4	.5	
2.1	5.3	4.5	All Other Non-Current	2.8	3.0	11.7	2.0	3.9	
44.3	35.2	34.3	Net Worth	27.1	41.3	21.3	36.3	41.0	
100.0	100.0	100.0	Total Liabilities & Net Worth	100.0	100.0	100.0	100.0	100.0	
			INCOME DATA						
100.0	100.0	100.0	Net Sales	100.0	100.0	100.0	100.0	100.0	
			Gross Profit						
87.8	89.0	90.3	Operating Expenses	91.0	88.4	92.8	85.1	92.8	
12.2	11.0	9.7	Operating Profit	9.0	11.6	7.2	14.9	7.2	
-.6	1.5	.2	All Other Expenses (net)	2.5	-.8	-.5	1.1	-.5	
12.8	9.4	9.5	Profit Before Taxes	6.5	12.3	7.7	13.8	7.7	
			RATIOS						
2.3	2.5	2.7		2.2	14.0	2.6	2.3	1.7	
1.3	1.3	1.4	Current	.5	2.1	1.5	1.4	1.6	
1.0	.7	.9		.1	.9	.7	1.0	1.2	
1.5	1.9	1.5		1.8	4.4	1.8	1.2	1.2	
.9	.8	.8	Quick	.4	.8	1.2	1.0	.2	
.6	.2	.3		.0	.5	.3	.4	.1	
2 208.6	1 249.4	3 114.2		0 UND	0 999.8	1 312.0	12 29.3	3 110.3	
23 15.9	20 18.5	18 20.8	Sales/Receivables	0 UND	12 31.3	23 16.1	24 15.5	23 15.7	
69 5.3	44 8.3	65 5.6		37 10.0	83 4.4	92 4.0	69 5.3	54 6.8	
			Cost of Sales/Inventory						
			Cost of Sales/Payables						
4.8	5.2	5.2		13.5	3.6	7.4	6.0	6.6	
13.9	13.2	14.7	Sales/Working Capital	-9.9	8.1	11.6	15.4	10.6	
-412.2	-23.4	-39.1		-3.1	-60.2	-39.1	107.0	23.4	
22.7	16.6	30.1			30.0	25.4		13.7	
(38) 4.6	(61) 3.0	(69) 5.8	EBIT/Interest		(19) 7.8	(14) 6.9		5.1	
-.6	.5	1.2			1.0	1.6		2.2	
	4.7	3.7	Net Profit + Depr., Dep.,						
(10) 1.8	(10) 3.1		Amort./Cur. Mat. L/T/D						
	.4	1.8							
.4	.5	.4		1.1	.4	.3	.5	.3	
.9	.9	.8	Fixed/Worth	2.9	1.1	.6	1.2	.5	
1.3	2.3	2.7		NM	1.7	NM	3.7	.8	
.4	.4	.5		.8	.2	.3	.5	.6	
.9	1.1	1.8	Debt/Worth	2.7	.9	1.2	2.1	2.1	
3.2	5.1	5.0		NM	5.0	NM	5.8	3.9	
49.3	38.5	40.4	% Profit Before Taxes/Tangible		36.6	32.9		37.2	
(43) 14.4	(69) 15.8	(71) 16.3	Net Worth		(23) 16.2	(12) 10.4		19.4	
1.1	-.8	4.4			.6	8.5		4.4	
29.2	16.8	15.6	% Profit Before Taxes/Total	16.0	19.7	9.1	28.2	21.4	
6.2	6.7	5.4	Assets	.1	4.7	5.4	8.8	4.2	
-4.5	-1.9	.3		-.7	-.9	2.4	2.6	1.1	
7.7	8.7	15.9		8.7	4.4	156.9	6.5	25.9	
2.8	3.0	3.9	Sales/Net Fixed Assets	2.4	1.8	8.2	4.3	8.7	
1.2	1.2	1.7		.6	.9	2.7	1.8	6.0	
1.9	2.8	2.7		2.1	1.3	7.1	2.3	2.6	
1.1	1.3	1.2	Sales/Total Assets	1.1	.9	2.9	1.1	2.0	
.7	.6	.7		.4	.4	1.0	.9	1.1	
2.2	2.4	1.5			4.3	.5	2.8	.9	
(45) 4.2	(67) 5.0	(72) 4.9	% Depr., Dep., Amort./Sales		(25) 7.1	(14) 2.7	(10) 5.5	1.5	
9.2	10.0	8.7			12.3	5.7	8.8	3.3	
	.8	2.3	% Officers', Directors'						
(13) 2.3	(23) 5.0		Owners' Comp/Sales						
7.8	10.3								
337202M	1589947M	1643765M	Net Sales ($)	5125M	54162M	58030M	75981M	180092M	1270375M
301384M	614038M	714482M	Total Assets ($)	9479M	89721M	110134M	60758M	129431M	314959M

© RMA 2011

M = $ thousand   MM = $ million
See Pages 9 through 22 for Explanation of Ratios and Data

Current Data Sorted by Assets   Comparative Historical Data

Type of Statement	0-500M	500M-2MM	2-10MM	10-50MM	50-100MM	100-250MM		4/1/06-3/31/07 ALL	4/1/07-3/31/08 ALL
	17 (4/1-9/30/10)		60 (10/1/10-3/31/11)						
Unqualified		1	3	4				8	7
Reviewed		3	6	1	1			7	7
Compiled	3	4	5	1	1			17	21
Tax Returns	8	9	2					28	22
Other	2	7	12	1	2	1		6	14
NUMBER OF STATEMENTS	13	24	28	7	4	1		66	71
	%	%	%	%	%	%		%	%
ASSETS									
Cash & Equivalents	10.2	11.6	10.0					13.3	12.3
Trade Receivables (net)	8.4	17.0	20.7					16.2	14.9
Inventory	7.2	14.0	18.6					14.0	12.7
All Other Current	10.0	2.7	4.9					5.3	4.0
Total Current	35.7	45.3	54.3					48.8	43.8
Fixed Assets (net)	53.8	38.9	36.4					39.0	46.3
Intangibles (net)	1.8	3.8	1.8					2.9	2.8
All Other Non-Current	8.7	11.9	7.5					9.4	7.1
Total	100.0	100.0	100.0					100.0	100.0
LIABILITIES									
Notes Payable-Short Term	36.5	13.8	8.7					16.8	17.8
Cur. Mat.-L.T.D.	8.0	5.4	6.3					5.7	6.9
Trade Payables	6.6	10.5	9.3					10.8	9.1
Income Taxes Payable	.2	.1	.2					.2	.2
All Other Current	5.7	16.7	6.7					8.0	8.4
Total Current	56.8	46.5	31.2					41.6	42.5
Long-Term Debt	21.5	42.7	15.8					23.8	29.0
Deferred Taxes	.2	.3	.7					.3	.1
All Other Non-Current	6.2	6.5	6.6					7.2	3.8
Net Worth	15.3	4.0	45.7					27.1	24.6
Total Liabilties & Net Worth	100.0	100.0	100.0					100.0	100.0
INCOME DATA									
Net Sales	100.0	100.0	100.0					100.0	100.0
Gross Profit									
Operating Expenses	86.2	95.6	92.6					95.5	95.0
Operating Profit	13.8	4.4	7.4					4.5	5.0
All Other Expenses (net)	3.7	1.6	.6					1.1	.9
Profit Before Taxes	10.2	2.7	6.8					3.4	4.0
RATIOS									
Current	4.2	2.7	4.7					3.6	2.2
	1.0	1.3	1.5					1.1	1.2
	.2	.5	1.0					.7	.6
Quick	3.5	1.7	2.3					2.0	1.7
	.6	.9	.9					.7	.6
	.0	.3	.5					.3	.3
Sales/Receivables	0 UND	0 UND	7 51.7					1 439.6	0 732.8
	0 UND	23 15.7	27 13.3					17 21.4	19 19.2
	8 44.2	57 6.4	49 7.5					46 7.9	45 8.1
Cost of Sales/Inventory									
Cost of Sales/Payables									
Sales/Working Capital	4.5	5.8	4.6					6.8	8.3
	244.0	17.5	11.8					38.8	37.8
	-4.8	-10.1	113.8					-15.5	-17.9
EBIT/Interest	16.2	7.8	53.0					8.9	9.0
	(11) 6.0	(21) 4.2	(24) 3.6					(60) 3.0	(66) 2.7
	.8	1.6	2.0					1.2	.7
Net Profit + Depr., Dep., Amort./Cur. Mat. L/T/D								15.2	11.0
								(10) 5.1	(15) 2.0
								2.3	.8
Fixed/Worth	.6	.3	.3					.4	.6
	1.0	1.8	.9					2.1	1.8
	NM	19.3	2.3					11.5	90.0
Debt/Worth	.8	1.3	.3					.8	.6
	1.0	4.2	1.7					4.0	4.4
	NM	27.7	4.5					32.4	140.5
% Profit Before Taxes/Tangible Net Worth	68.1	96.5	40.5					71.5	69.8
	(10) 34.6	(19) 19.5	(27) 16.8					(54) 28.7	(55) 16.8
	-5.2	8.7	7.6					6.8	1.3
% Profit Before Taxes/Total Assets	44.0	16.1	21.9					17.4	13.0
	10.5	3.8	7.0					7.5	5.0
	-3.1	1.8	3.6					.9	-1.3
Sales/Net Fixed Assets	9.8	11.9	15.4					19.3	13.2
	4.9	6.2	5.4					7.6	4.9
	1.6	2.4	2.1					3.7	2.4
Sales/Total Assets	3.4	2.3	2.9					3.2	3.6
	1.7	1.6	1.6					2.2	1.9
	.9	1.3	1.2					1.5	1.2
% Depr., Dep., Amort./Sales		3.0	1.9					1.7	1.8
		(17) 6.9	(23) 5.5					(57) 3.9	(68) 4.9
		11.8	11.8					7.2	11.1
% Officers', Directors' Owners' Comp/Sales	1.2							2.5	1.6
	(15) 3.1							(29) 5.0	(27) 4.9
	6.5							8.8	9.4
Net Sales ($)	9406M	54999M	239701M	329897M	305358M	53204M		1011066M	684447M
Total Assets ($)	3220M	25082M	124967M	201679M	250143M	130015M		582563M	395444M

M = $ thousand   MM = $ million
See Pages 9 through 22 for Explanation of Ratios and Data

Comparative Historical Data				Current Data Sorted by Sales					
			Type of Statement		**1**		**4**	**4**	**3**
7	7	8	Unqualified						1
7	10	11	Reviewed		2	1	2	3	
16	18	14	Compiled	3	6	1	2	2	
12	18	19	Tax Returns	9	6	2	1	1	
10	16	25	Other	3	6	1	9	3	3
4/1/08-3/31/09 ALL	4/1/09-3/31/10 ALL	4/1/10-3/31/11 ALL		17 (4/1-9/30/10) 0-1MM	1-3MM	3-5MM	60 (10/1/10-3/31/11) 5-10MM	10-25MM	25MM & OVER
52	69	77	**NUMBER OF STATEMENTS**	15	21	5	16	13	7
%	%	%		%	%	%	%	%	%
			ASSETS						
13.6	16.1	9.5	Cash & Equivalents	8.3	9.9		7.7	11.9	
18.8	11.3	16.3	Trade Receivables (net)	7.8	14.1		22.7	23.9	
18.5	13.7	15.6	Inventory	6.4	11.0		23.5	15.8	
4.7	3.3	4.7	All Other Current	3.7	5.8		7.0	3.1	
55.7	44.4	46.1	Total Current	26.2	40.9		60.9	54.7	
35.3	39.8	40.4	Fixed Assets (net)	55.7	46.6		31.2	35.6	
1.1	2.1	3.3	Intangibles (net)	6.7	.9		2.8	.3	
7.9	13.7	10.2	All Other Non-Current	11.4	11.6		5.0	9.4	
100.0	100.0	100.0	Total	100.0	100.0		100.0	100.0	
			LIABILITIES						
12.2	15.5	16.0	Notes Payable-Short Term	14.3	25.5		6.8	15.1	
5.2	5.3	5.8	Cur. Mat.-L.T.D.	6.3	6.2		8.8	2.1	
9.9	4.5	9.0	Trade Payables	5.5	10.1		11.5	5.8	
.2	.4	.3	Income Taxes Payable	.2	.0		.0	1.0	
10.2	8.5	9.7	All Other Current	2.1	19.8		7.5	8.3	
37.7	34.1	40.7	Total Current	28.4	61.7		34.5	32.4	
24.9	28.8	26.1	Long-Term Debt	35.6	41.9		12.8	9.9	
.5	.2	.4	Deferred Taxes	.2	.3		1.1	.0	
2.1	2.2	5.8	All Other Non-Current	7.5	2.2		7.5	3.3	
34.8	34.7	27.0	Net Worth	28.4	-6.0		44.0	54.4	
100.0	100.0	100.0	Total Liabilities & Net Worth	100.0	100.0		100.0	100.0	
			INCOME DATA						
100.0	100.0	100.0	Net Sales	100.0	100.0		100.0	100.0	
			Gross Profit						
92.8	90.2	91.8	Operating Expenses	80.2	98.4		94.6	92.9	
7.2	9.8	8.2	Operating Profit	19.8	1.6		5.4	7.1	
-.1	2.0	1.3	All Other Expenses (net)	6.2	1.1		-.1	-.8	
7.4	7.7	6.8	Profit Before Taxes	13.7	.5		5.4	7.9	
			RATIOS						
3.0	2.6	2.7		1.9	2.4		6.4	4.6	
1.6	1.4	1.3	Current	1.0	1.2		1.5	1.2	
1.0	.6	.8		.3	.4		1.0	.8	
1.6	2.2	1.8		1.7	1.2		2.2	2.7	
.8	.7	.6	Quick	.6	.6		.8	.8	
.3	.2	.3		.1	.2		.5	.3	
4 89.8	0 UND	1 384.7		0 UND	0 UND		20 17.9	1 326.5	
27 13.5	15 23.9	24 15.4	Sales/Receivables	0 UND	24 15.0		45 8.1	24 15.1	
62 5.9	41 8.9	49 7.5		10 38.4	50 7.2		63 5.8	42 8.7	
			Cost of Sales/Inventory						
			Cost of Sales/Payables						
4.7	4.8	5.6		2.7	10.0		3.7	5.6	
13.1	15.6	19.0	Sales/Working Capital	280.5	41.4		9.3	52.6	
426.9	-38.7	-24.8		-5.7	-4.8		113.8	-25.2	
11.0	21.4	12.7		13.4	5.4		54.5	33.9	
(47) 4.5	(62) 4.6	(68) 4.3	EBIT/Interest	(13) 6.8	(18) 2.9		(13) 3.2	(12) 4.8	
2.0	1.7	1.9		1.2	.6		2.2	2.0	
	6.6	17.5	Net Profit + Depr., Dep.,						
	(16) 3.3	(13) 3.5	Amort./Cur. Mat. L/T/D						
	1.7	.6							
.4	.3	.4		.6	.6		.2	.2	
.8	.7	1.1	Fixed/Worth	1.7	2.3		.9	.7	
2.2	2.7	3.2		11.0	NM		1.7	1.5	
.7	.4	.7		.9	1.2		.4	.3	
2.0	1.6	2.0	Debt/Worth	1.3	3.2		1.8	.8	
5.2	3.8	5.7		10.5	NM		3.0	2.2	
62.3	42.5	50.2	% Profit Before Taxes/Tangible	86.7	45.6		31.5	47.5	
(49) 29.9	(62) 21.1	(67) 20.1	Net Worth	(12) 45.3	(16) 14.3		(15) 15.7	25.3	
10.5	6.4	8.7		12.1	-5.9		6.7	12.9	
22.7	16.8	19.7	% Profit Before Taxes/Total	21.0	11.5		21.6	26.7	
8.8	8.1	6.7	Assets	10.3	4.3		6.2	8.9	
2.5	1.7	2.0		1.8	-5.0		3.3	4.2	
18.4	14.4	11.8		5.1	7.0		20.7	17.8	
6.8	8.6	5.1	Sales/Net Fixed Assets	3.2	4.2		5.7	8.8	
3.5	2.6	2.3		.9	2.2		3.8	2.2	
3.1	2.8	2.5		1.7	2.1		2.9	4.2	
1.9	1.7	1.5	Sales/Total Assets	1.2	1.5		1.8	1.9	
1.4	1.1	1.1		.7	1.3		1.2	1.2	
1.5	1.6	2.4		5.2	3.9		2.6	1.7	
(44) 3.6	(54) 4.8	(61) 5.2	% Depr., Dep., Amort./Sales	(11) 8.9	(17) 6.9		(11) 6.2	(12) 2.7	
10.2	10.4	10.1		18.7	13.8		9.9	3.8	
.9	1.3	1.8	% Officers', Directors'						
(21) 1.7	(22) 4.6	(28) 3.4	Owners' Comp/Sales						
6.8	10.5	6.5							
1384893M	1600354M	992565M	Net Sales ($)	6797M	35264M	18170M	106357M	225530M	447M
771715M	1071308M	735106M	Total Assets ($)	9280M	26626M	9236M	60527M	157615M	471822M

© RMA 2011

M = $ thousand   MM = $ million
See Pages 9 through 22 for Explanation of Ratios and Data

Current Data Sorted by Assets   Comparative Historical Data

Type of Statement

0-500M	500M-2MM	2-10MM	10-50MM	50-100MM	100-250MM	Type of Statement	4/1/06-3/31/07 ALL	4/1/07-3/31/08 ALL
1	4	6	27	9	4	Unqualified	61	47
	7	23	26	6		Reviewed	53	55
7	10	17	10	1		Compiled	41	49
2	11	5	2		4	Tax Returns	19	11
		24	13	6		Other	55	58
101 (4/1-9/30/10)			124 (10/1/10-3/31/11)					
10	32	75	78	22	8	NUMBER OF STATEMENTS	229	220

0-500M %	500M-2MM %	2-10MM %	10-50MM %	50-100MM %	100-250MM %		%	%
						ASSETS		
13.8	16.3	9.8	8.4	5.4		Cash & Equivalents	7.4	8.8
8.3	17.6	24.8	20.6	13.5		Trade Receivables (net)	21.5	19.0
3.2	9.6	16.2	20.4	22.6		Inventory	21.4	20.5
2.1	4.0	4.6	5.6	8.6		All Other Current	6.2	6.1
27.3	47.5	55.3	55.0	50.1		Total Current	56.4	54.3
48.5	43.9	34.4	38.3	36.1		Fixed Assets (net)	34.4	36.7
1.7	1.4	1.7	1.3	3.5		Intangibles (net)	1.2	1.1
22.5	7.2	8.5	5.4	10.2		All Other Non-Current	8.1	7.8
100.0	100.0	100.0	100.0	100.0		Total	100.0	100.0
						LIABILITIES		
14.5	14.5	8.7	11.7	10.6		Notes Payable-Short Term	15.3	14.5
6.4	6.3	3.2	2.9	2.4		Cur. Mat.-L.T.D.	3.2	3.6
7.2	9.1	17.8	13.6	12.6		Trade Payables	17.0	13.4
.1	.0	.1	.5	.2		Income Taxes Payable	.1	.2
4.4	11.4	10.9	12.3	15.0		All Other Current	10.3	11.3
32.6	41.3	40.8	41.0	40.7		Total Current	45.9	43.0
26.2	25.7	17.5	16.1	16.7		Long-Term Debt	19.5	18.9
.0	.3	.4	1.2	.9		Deferred Taxes	.7	.7
2.0	9.0	2.2	3.1	1.0		All Other Non-Current	3.8	2.8
39.2	23.7	39.1	38.7	40.7		Net Worth	30.1	34.6
100.0	100.0	100.0	100.0	100.0		Total Liabilities & Net Worth	100.0	100.0
						INCOME DATA		
100.0	100.0	100.0	100.0	100.0		Net Sales	100.0	100.0
						Gross Profit		
83.6	92.6	88.2	89.7	94.0		Operating Expenses	93.2	92.6
16.4	7.4	11.8	10.3	6.0		Operating Profit	6.8	7.4
5.5	4.0	1.7	1.0	1.0		All Other Expenses (net)	1.1	1.8
10.8	3.4	10.1	9.3	5.0		Profit Before Taxes	5.6	5.6
						RATIOS		
1.5	2.5	1.7	1.9	1.6			1.8	1.8
.8	1.6	1.3	1.4	1.3		Current	1.2	1.2
.3	.5	.9	1.0	1.1			1.0	1.0
1.1	2.2	1.3	1.3	1.0			1.0	1.1
.7	.6	(74) .8	.8	.5		Quick	.6	.6
.3	.2	.4	.4	.3			.4	.3
0 UND	0 UND	7 48.8	26 14.3	20 18.2			14 26.1	12 31.5
0 UND	5 69.6	30 12.2	41 9.0	37 10.0		Sales/Receivables	32 11.5	30 12.2
23 15.5	34 10.8	70 5.2	81 4.5	59 6.2			54 6.7	52 7.1
						Cost of Sales/Inventory		
						Cost of Sales/Payables		
24.7	8.6	7.5	4.9	7.7			6.6	6.4
-136.3	16.7	20.6	11.2	14.0		Sales/Working Capital	17.3	19.1
-11.0	-5.7	-56.1	91.7	27.4			NM	-499.5
	11.1	30.4	14.9	7.8			7.5	7.0
	(25) 4.2	(71) 6.2	(76) 6.4	4.3		EBIT/Interest	(215) 2.9	(209) 3.1
	.8	2.2	2.8	.9			1.3	1.3
		5.8	7.3				9.1	7.8
		(18) 2.5	(30) 3.4			Net Profit + Depr., Dep., Amort./Cur. Mat. L/T/D	(71) 3.2	(75) 3.7
		1.4	2.1				1.3	1.1
.3	.4	.3	.6	.6			.5	.5
1.2	1.0	.9	.9	.9		Fixed/Worth	.9	1.0
1.6	NM	1.8	1.7	1.3			1.7	2.0
.8	.6	.8	.9	1.0			1.1	.9
1.0	1.7	1.9	1.6	1.7		Debt/Worth	2.0	2.0
1.3	NM	4.0	3.3	4.3			4.7	4.8
	61.9	42.8	39.7	28.0			32.8	36.4
	(24) 32.0	(71) 21.9	(74) 20.9	(21) 17.9		% Profit Before Taxes/Tangible Net Worth	(212) 17.6	(201) 18.5
	2.6	4.8	9.0	.7			4.8	5.3
13.3	20.4	14.8	12.5	9.3			12.4	11.9
6.9	8.6	8.5	6.2	4.8		% Profit Before Taxes/Total Assets	5.3	5.5
-21.0	-1.4	1.6	3.8	-.1			.8	1.0
31.6	20.0	21.0	9.2	13.2			14.5	14.5
4.0	8.3	7.6	4.8	4.9		Sales/Net Fixed Assets	7.0	6.5
1.5	2.0	2.1	1.8	1.2			3.0	2.3
5.4	4.3	3.1	2.3	1.8			3.0	2.9
2.0	2.0	1.7	1.3	1.5		Sales/Total Assets	1.8	1.7
.4	1.0	.9	.8	.6			1.0	1.0
	1.5	.9	1.2	1.0			1.0	1.1
	(26) 4.1	(66) 2.9	(74) 2.6	(21) 2.0		% Depr., Dep., Amort./Sales	(209) 1.9	(200) 2.1
	11.6	6.3	6.8	5.7			4.2	4.7
	1.8	.9	.5				1.1	.8
	(12) 3.5	(22) 1.6	(17) 1.3			% Officers', Directors' Owners' Comp/Sales	(53) 2.1	(41) 1.2
	8.1	5.7	3.7				4.3	3.0
64.-M	118606M	767220M	3072513M	2168116M	2267566M	Net Sales ($)	10279836M	8374995M
2621M	40494M	392244M	1879559M	1535488M	1346422M	Total Assets ($)	5184469M	5006363M

© RMA 2011

M = $ thousand   MM = $ million
See Pages 9 through 22 for Explanation of Ratios and Data

Comparative Historical Data

Current Data Sorted by Sales

Comparative Historical Data				Current Data Sorted by Sales					
			Type of Statement						
48	55	46	Unqualified		1	1	4	10	30
55	51	60	Reviewed		5	3	10	18	24
42	33	35	Compiled		5	5	11	9	4
18	19	24	Tax Returns	1	7	4	2	1	1
73	72	60	Other	9	9	10	7	10	20
4/1/08-	4/1/09-	4/1/10-		4	101 (4/1-9/30/10)		124 (10/1/10-3/31/11)		
3/31/09	3/31/10	3/31/11		0-1MM	1-3MM	3-5MM	5-10MM	10-25MM	25MM & OVER
ALL	ALL	ALL							
236	230	225	**NUMBER OF STATEMENTS**	14	27	23	34	48	79
%	%	%	**ASSETS**	%	%	%	%	%	%
8.6	9.3	10.0	Cash & Equivalents	9.9	8.5	17.3	9.4	9.3	9.0
20.3	19.2	20.1	Trade Receivables (net)	14.1	10.6	11.1	27.5	26.4	20.0
19.8	18.9	17.4	Inventory	.0	5.8	13.6	17.5	19.0	24.7
5.8	5.5	5.2	All Other Current	3.0	5.1	5.1	5.5	4.5	6.0
54.5	52.8	52.7	Total Current	27.0	30.0	47.0	60.0	59.1	59.7
36.7	38.1	37.6	Fixed Assets (net)	58.4	52.6	45.6	32.5	32.0	32.2
1.3	1.6	1.7	Intangibles (net)	1.7	.2	2.0	.8	2.7	1.8
7.4	7.5	8.0	All Other Non-Current	12.9	17.2	5.4	6.7	6.2	6.4
100.0	100.0	100.0	Total	100.0	100.0	100.0	100.0	100.0	100.0
			LIABILITIES						
12.4	11.5	11.3	Notes Payable-Short Term	16.5	11.0	4.1	13.0	10.5	12.3
4.3	4.1	3.6	Cur. Mat.-L.T.D.	5.5	5.7	8.8	1.6	2.4	2.5
14.5	14.1	13.8	Trade Payables	3.4	7.0	7.8	18.3	16.5	16.3
.3	.2	.3	Income Taxes Payable	.0	.3	.0	.4	.5	.2
10.6	10.0	11.6	All Other Current	4.4	14.2	10.1	9.7	12.9	12.6
42.0	39.8	40.6	Total Current	29.7	38.3	30.8	43.0	42.8	43.8
17.7	20.3	18.3	Long-Term Debt	47.7	29.1	24.5	12.1	11.1	14.7
.6	.6	.7	Deferred Taxes	.0	.6	.3	.6	1.0	.9
3.6	3.0	3.4	All Other Non-Current	2.4	6.1	1.7	5.7	2.2	2.9
36.0	36.3	37.0	Net Worth	20.3	26.0	42.7	38.6	42.9	37.6
100.0	100.0	100.0	Total Liabilties & Net Worth	100.0	100.0	100.0	100.0	100.0	100.0
			INCOME DATA						
100.0	100.0	100.0	Net Sales	100.0	100.0	100.0	100.0	100.0	100.0
			Gross Profit						
91.0	91.8	89.9	Operating Expenses	71.5	86.0	91.7	88.0	93.0	92.8
9.0	8.2	10.1	Operating Profit	28.5	14.0	8.3	12.0	7.0	7.2
1.4	1.6	1.9	All Other Expenses (net)	16.0	2.3	1.0	1.1	.6	.6
7.6	6.6	8.2	Profit Before Taxes	12.5	11.7	7.3	10.9	6.4	6.6
			RATIOS						
1.8	1.8	1.8	Current	1.7	1.7	4.2	2.4	2.0	1.8
1.3	1.3	1.3		.7	.8	1.5	1.4	1.3	1.4
1.0	1.0	1.0		.3	.3	.9	1.0	1.0	1.1
1.1	1.2	1.3	Quick	1.1	1.4	2.2	1.6	1.3	1.1
(235) .6	(229) .6	(224) .7		.6	.5	.7	.8	(47) .9	.7
.3	.3	.3		.1	.2	.4	.5	.4	.3
12 31.4	11 32.4	9 39.4	Sales/Receivables	0 UND	0 UND	1 688.4	26 14.2	16 23.1	23 15.9
30 12.0	32 11.3	34 10.7		0 UND	4 93.1	6 64.8	51 7.2	36 10.0	35 10.3
60 6.1	50 7.2	63 5.8		57 6.4	57 6.4	39 9.4	110 3.3	72 5.1	50 7.3
			Cost of Sales/Inventory						
			Cost of Sales/Payables						
6.7	5.9	6.9	Sales/Working Capital	4.7	9.8	4.9	3.1	10.7	6.5
19.1	15.7	13.6		-75.0	-14.0	10.4	11.4	13.6	13.2
-228.5	-174.6	-114.1		-2.0	-3.9	-50.8	-854.8	81.2	43.3
12.5	11.4	14.1	EBIT/Interest	27.7	6.5	10.1	39.4	21.2	14.4
(225) 3.5	(219) 4.1	(210) 5.7		(10) 3.9	(23) 3.0	(21) 2.9	(33) 6.6	(46) 6.5	(77) 6.2
1.7	1.4	2.1		.1	.9	1.1	2.2	3.6	2.5
8.8	9.5	7.3	Net Profit + Depr., Dep.,					6.4	7.4
(82) 3.6	(73) 3.4	(65) 3.7	Amort./Cur. Mat. L/T/D				(15) 4.8	(31) 3.7	
1.3	1.4	2.0						2.0	2.3
.5	.5	.4	Fixed/Worth	.4	.4	.7	.3	.4	.5
.9	1.0	.9		1.7	1.5	1.0	.9	.8	.9
1.8	2.0	1.7		-12.5	4.6	1.8	1.5	1.3	1.3
.9	.9	.8	Debt/Worth	.6	1.0	.3	.6	.8	1.0
1.8	1.7	1.7		1.2	1.7	1.6	1.8	1.7	1.7
4.6	3.6	3.8		-13.5	4.0	4.0	4.6	2.9	3.5
40.8	35.6	39.5	% Profit Before Taxes/Tangible	44.0	35.8	59.4	50.6	43.1	32.6
(215) 20.1	(208) 16.7	(207) 20.5	Net Worth	(10) 19.5	(24) 23.2	(22) 12.3	(31) 19.9	(46) 26.5	(74) 20.7
7.9	4.6	7.3		-38.5	2.6	.4	7.3	12.6	9.0
13.4	12.2	12.9	% Profit Before Taxes/Total	20.7	12.6	16.0	18.4	13.0	11.6
6.3	5.8	7.0	Assets	5.2	5.0	7.0	8.0	9.3	6.4
1.4	.9	1.8		-6.1	-.1	.5	1.9	5.2	3.0
17.3	14.2	14.8	Sales/Net Fixed Assets	9.0	4.6	11.6	19.3	27.2	12.9
6.3	6.1	6.0		1.7	2.0	4.2	6.8	10.1	7.4
2.2	1.9	1.9		.2	.9	1.1	2.3	1.9	3.8
3.0	2.7	2.7	Sales/Total Assets	1.2	1.8	2.8	2.1	3.5	2.7
1.7	1.6	1.6		.7	.9	1.3	1.5	1.9	1.8
.9	.9	.8		.2	.4	.8	.7	.9	1.3
.9	1.2	1.2	% Depr., Dep., Amort./Sales	11.9	3.1	2.0	1.4	.7	1.0
(208) 2.0	(204) 2.3	(203) 2.7		(11) 21.4	(26) 6.4	(19) 6.6	(31) 3.2	(42) 1.7	(74) 1.7
6.1	5.8	6.8		56.1	13.4	10.0	5.3	5.9	3.2
1.0	.9	.8	% Officers', Directors'				1.4	.7	.2
(43) 1.3	(44) 1.5	(57) 1.8	Owners' Comp/Sales			(13) 2.3	(11) 1.3	(13) .8	
3.1	4.1	5.2					6.1	11.8	2.5
11506260M	11802094M	8400474M	Net Sales ($)	5277M	49822M	98266M	240411M	825934M	7180764M
5797190M	6712774M	5196828M	Total Assets ($)	10887M	84631M	99812M	238737M	653579M	4109182M

M = $ thousand   MM = $ million
See Pages 9 through 22 for Explanation of Ratios and Data

Current Data Sorted by Assets

Comparative Historical Data

0-500M	500M-2MM	2-10MM	10-50MM	50-100MM	100-250MM	Type of Statement	4/1/06-3/31/07 ALL	4/1/07-3/31/08 ALL
	1	1	1	1	1	Unqualified	2	3
	1	2	2			Reviewed		2
	4	2	2			Compiled	1	4
2	3		2			Tax Returns	1	2
1		1	4			Other	6	3
	8 (4/1-9/30/10)		23 (10/1/10-3/31/11)					
3	9	6	11	1	1	**NUMBER OF STATEMENTS**	10	14
%	%	%	%	%	%		%	%
						ASSETS		
			16.2			Cash & Equivalents	15.6	21.3
			13.0			Trade Receivables (net)	20.0	5.9
			9.0			Inventory	3.3	10.1
			1.0			All Other Current	4.2	3.3
			39.2			Total Current	43.2	40.5
			35.0			Fixed Assets (net)	31.8	42.4
			.9			Intangibles (net)	1.2	.4
			24.9			All Other Non-Current	23.8	16.7
			100.0			Total	100.0	100.0
						LIABILITIES		
			10.3			Notes Payable-Short Term	3.7	6.0
			3.5			Cur. Mat.-L.T.D.	3.1	5.1
			6.7			Trade Payables	11.4	9.7
			.0			Income Taxes Payable	.2	.0
			6.7			All Other Current	8.7	6.2
			27.3			Total Current	27.1	27.0
			22.9			Long-Term Debt	27.5	25.9
			.0			Deferred Taxes	.0	.0
			3.5			All Other Non-Current	1.5	5.9
			46.3			Net Worth	43.9	41.2
			100.0			Total Liabilties & Net Worth	100.0	100.0
						INCOME DATA		
			100.0			Net Sales	100.0	100.0
						Gross Profit		
			86.5			Operating Expenses	92.8	92.5
			13.5			Operating Profit	7.2	7.5
			1.5			All Other Expenses (net)	.0	1.3
			12.0			Profit Before Taxes	7.2	6.2
						RATIOS		
			5.2			Current	4.1	3.3
			1.5				2.1	1.5
			.4				.9	.5
			4.9			Quick	2.6	2.5
			1.3				1.2	.8
			.1				.1	.0
			0 UND			Sales/Receivables	0 UND	0 UND
			21 17.8				46 7.9	0 UND
			55 6.6				69 5.3	10 36.1
						Cost of Sales/Inventory		
						Cost of Sales/Payables		
			4.3			Sales/Working Capital	2.2	5.0
			10.0				3.1	24.4
			-10.2				NM	-21.3
						EBIT/Interest		25.1
							(12)	11.6
								1.7
						Net Profit + Depr., Dep., Amort./Cur. Mat. L/T/D		
			.2			Fixed/Worth	.4	.2
			.8				.7	.6
			1.9				1.3	1.7
			.5			Debt/Worth	.3	.5
			1.1				1.6	1.2
			2.3				4.1	2.3
			52.9			% Profit Before Taxes/Tangible Net Worth	42.2	68.5
			31.5				20.1 (12)	24.7
			7.0				8.7	2.6
			21.3			% Profit Before Taxes/Total Assets	16.2	32.8
			11.6				6.0	6.6
			1.7				1.8	1.2
			22.6			Sales/Net Fixed Assets	17.0	24.6
			2.6				4.3	6.8
			.6				2.2	3.1
			1.7			Sales/Total Assets	2.4	3.6
			1.4				1.0	1.8
			.3				.5	.3
						% Depr., Dep., Amort./Sales		1.3
							(11)	2.2
								7.1
						% Officers', Directors' Owners' Comp/Sales		
3792M	30157M	53654M	227653M	240039M	39464M	Net Sales ($)	167732M	113190M
874M	8463M	25482M	216158M	78661M	114763M	Total Assets ($)	279947M	170610M

© RMA 2011

M = $ thousand   MM = $ million
See Pages 9 through 22 for Explanation of Ratios and Data

Comparative Historical Data   Current Data Sorted by Sales

			Type of Statement	0-1MM	1-3MM	3-5MM	5-10MM	10-25MM	25MM & OVER
3	3	5	Unqualified		1		1	1	3
5	5	5	Reviewed		1	2	1	1	
6	6	8	Compiled		4		1	1	2
1	3	7	Tax Returns	1	2	2		2	2
5	2	6	Other	1	1				2
4/1/08-3/31/09 ALL	4/1/09-3/31/10 ALL	4/1/10-3/31/11 ALL			8 (4/1-9/30/10)			23 (10/1/10-3/31/11)	
20	**19**	**31**	**NUMBER OF STATEMENTS**	**2**	**9**	**4**	**3**	**6**	**7**
%	%	%		%	%	%	%	%	%
			ASSETS						
24.4	24.7	21.1	Cash & Equivalents						
7.9	7.3	13.8	Trade Receivables (net)						
4.4	3.5	8.1	Inventory						
9.7	6.6	6.6	All Other Current						
46.4	42.1	49.6	Total Current						
40.7	45.1	35.4	Fixed Assets (net)						
5.9	.3	1.1	Intangibles (net)						
7.0	12.6	13.9	All Other Non-Current						
100.0	100.0	100.0	Total						
			LIABILITIES						
10.8	6.0	11.2	Notes Payable-Short Term						
5.3	6.1	3.3	Cur. Mat.-L.T.D.						
9.7	7.8	9.2	Trade Payables						
.0	.0	.3	Income Taxes Payable						
12.1	9.3	10.0	All Other Current						
37.8	29.2	34.0	Total Current						
18.6	20.9	17.7	Long-Term Debt						
.0	1.0	.1	Deferred Taxes						
6.0	.2	2.9	All Other Non-Current						
37.7	48.9	45.3	Net Worth						
100.0	100.0	100.0	Total Liabilities & Net Worth						
			INCOME DATA						
100.0	100.0	100.0	Net Sales						
			Gross Profit						
93.4	87.1	90.7	Operating Expenses						
6.6	12.9	9.3	Operating Profit						
1.3	1.7	-.1	All Other Expenses (net)						
5.3	11.2	9.4	Profit Before Taxes						
			RATIOS						
2.4	3.3	4.8	Current						
1.1	1.3	1.5							
.6	.4	.8							
1.8	2.9	4.4	Quick						
.9	.7	1.3							
.1	.0	.4							
0 UND	0 UND	0 UND	Sales/Receivables						
0 UND	0 UND	15 24.6							
31 11.8	23 15.7	34 10.7							
			Cost of Sales/Inventory						
			Cost of Sales/Payables						
4.4	4.3	5.2	Sales/Working Capital						
24.7	39.8	13.0							
-12.3	-4.5	-16.9							
17.0	14.0	18.6	EBIT/Interest						
(15) 2.9	(15) 6.6	(22) 4.7							
-.3	4.1	2.6							
			Net Profit + Depr., Dep., Amort./Cur. Mat. L/T/D						
.3	.3	.2	Fixed/Worth						
1.1	1.1	.6							
3.2	1.6	1.9							
.6	.4	.5	Debt/Worth						
2.0	.9	1.2							
7.8	3.8	3.0							
24.8	52.7	50.7	% Profit Before Taxes/Tangible Net Worth						
(17) 8.5	(18) 28.4	(30) 28.4							
-5.7	12.4	8.5							
10.8	21.8	19.2	% Profit Before Taxes/Total Assets						
1.0	11.6	8.0							
-2.4	3.3	2.1							
20.3	17.2	28.0	Sales/Net Fixed Assets						
4.7	3.9	6.1							
2.7	1.6	2.3							
2.5	3.0	3.2	Sales/Total Assets						
1.7	1.7	1.8							
.8	.6	1.2							
1.7	2.1	1.9	% Depr., Dep., Amort./Sales						
(18) 4.1	(17) 5.5	(21) 4.7							
8.2	9.2	9.0							
		.5	% Officers', Directors' Owners' Comp/Sales						
	(10)	3.6							
		6.3							
226803M	150428M	594759M	Net Sales ($)	1585M	16594M	15110M	22169M	85971M	453330M
341424M	220297M	444401M	Total Assets ($)	4073M	41936M	18456M	13465M	87207M	279264M

© RMA 2011

M = $ thousand   MM = $ million
See Pages 9 through 22 for Explanation of Ratios and Data

Current Data Sorted by Assets

Comparative Historical Data

	0-500M	500M-2MM	2-10MM	10-50MM	50-100MM	100-250MM	Type of Statement		4/1/06-3/31/07 ALL	4/1/07-3/31/08 ALL
		2	3 5 6	7 3	4	1	Unqualified		14	14
	2	3					Reviewed		7	9
	15	12	8				Compiled		15	13
	3	10	7	2	1	1	Tax Returns		28	22
		15 (4/1-9/30/10)		80 (10/1/10-3/31/11)			Other		11	22
NUMBER OF STATEMENTS	20	27	29	12	5	2			75	80
	%	%	%	%	%	%	**ASSETS**		%	%
	22.7	10.5	8.4	11.9			Cash & Equivalents		11.0	11.8
	3.8	13.2	18.9	15.2			Trade Receivables (net)		19.5	19.6
	15.1	19.4	14.5	20.2			Inventory		16.4	14.7
	1.5	3.8	4.8	5.8			All Other Current		2.9	3.5
	43.1	46.9	46.7	53.1			Total Current		49.8	49.6
	44.3	43.2	41.9	35.4			Fixed Assets (net)		36.3	37.6
	3.8	2.8	4.5	4.8			Intangibles (net)		3.4	3.1
	8.8	7.1	7.0	6.7			All Other Non-Current		10.4	9.6
	100.0	100.0	100.0	100.0			Total		100.0	100.0
							LIABILITIES			
	25.0	8.8	13.2	8.3			Notes Payable-Short Term		13.3	11.4
	2.8	4.7	5.0	1.6			Cur. Mat.-L.T.D.		3.6	2.2
	4.3	9.6	12.1	11.5			Trade Payables		10.9	13.1
	.1	.0	.3	.6			Income Taxes Payable		.2	.2
	14.2	11.0	6.9	6.1			All Other Current		13.9	11.3
	46.4	34.0	37.4	28.1			Total Current		42.0	38.1
	36.4	31.1	22.0	12.8			Long-Term Debt		24.5	21.6
	.0	.0	.3	.5			Deferred Taxes		.2	.4
	29.0	9.8	3.2	1.2			All Other Non-Current		4.1	4.3
	-12.0	25.1	37.1	57.4			Net Worth		29.1	35.6
	100.0	100.0	100.0	100.0			Total Liabilities & Net Worth		100.0	100.0
							INCOME DATA			
	100.0	100.0	100.0	100.0			Net Sales		100.0	100.0
							Gross Profit			
	94.5	95.8	92.7	92.8			Operating Expenses		92.6	89.7
	5.5	4.2	7.3	7.2			Operating Profit		7.4	10.3
	1.7	3.5	3.1	2.4			All Other Expenses (net)		2.0	2.2
	3.7	.8	4.1	4.8			Profit Before Taxes		5.4	8.1
							RATIOS			
	3.3	2.2	1.6	3.2					2.8	2.8
	1.2	1.4	1.2	1.6			Current		1.3	1.5
	.3	.6	.4	1.0					.6	1.0
	1.9	1.2	1.2	1.8					1.6	1.6
	.4 (26)	.5	.6	.8			Quick		.8	.9
	.1	.3	.2	.4					.3	.4
	0 UND	0 UND	9 39.4	22 16.3					2 200.1	7 53.5
	0 UND	5 71.0	24 15.5	27 13.7			Sales/Receivables		23 16.1	26 13.9
	2 176.3	28 13.1	38 9.5	46 7.9					50 7.3	47 7.7
							Cost of Sales/Inventory			
							Cost of Sales/Payables			
	23.5	9.1	7.5	4.3					5.4	4.7
	257.1	26.2	42.5	12.5			Sales/Working Capital		26.1	15.2
	-24.5	-112.6	-8.1	-159.8					-13.4	-160.1
	16.8	6.6	16.4						8.0	12.1
(14)	3.4	(24) 2.1	(26) 3.3				EBIT/Interest	(60)	3.1	(62) 3.6
	1.4	.0	1.7						1.6	1.3
							Net Profit + Depr., Dep., Amort./Cur. Mat. L/T/D			
	.4	.5	.2	.1					.3	.3
	1.6	1.8	1.1	.6			Fixed/Worth		.8	.8
	-.8	-29.7	3.1	1.3					3.5	2.0
	.4	1.2	.8	.3					.5	.5
	1.7	3.2	1.8	.7			Debt/Worth		2.4	1.4
	-2.2	-130.7	4.9	2.0					10.2	4.4
	98.9	48.2	36.3	33.1			% Profit Before Taxes/Tangible Net Worth		49.9	35.3
(12)	43.5	(20) 13.5	(26) 15.5	11.3				(63)	18.6	(71) 14.8
	5.5	-1.6	4.6	9.2					4.5	4.8
	42.6	13.3	20.1	14.8			% Profit Before Taxes/Total Assets		11.6	14.7
	21.3	3.0	3.5	8.0					6.3	5.7
	4.4	-4.0	1.4	4.4					1.4	1.0
	35.9	24.3	26.7	17.0			Sales/Net Fixed Assets		27.4	16.4
	10.9	8.3	5.5	6.9					6.6	5.4
	4.7	1.6	.9	4.3					2.5	2.5
	7.0	4.0	3.8	2.8			Sales/Total Assets		3.1	2.7
	3.6	2.9	1.6	1.6					2.1	1.7
	2.5	1.3	.8	1.1					.9	.7
	1.4	.5	1.5	2.0			% Depr., Dep., Amort./Sales		1.1	1.4
(10)	3.7	(21) 1.8	(23) 2.8	(10) 3.1				(63)	2.7	(63) 2.9
	9.8	6.1	11.0	11.7					5.5	6.2
	2.5	2.1	.9				% Officers', Directors' Owners' Comp/Sales		1.7	1.0
(10)	6.2	(11) 2.2	(14) 1.7					(35)	3.8	(27) 3.6
	9.5	13.1	4.8						12.4	13.4
	15758M	86199M	359155M	600581M	728053M	461525M	Net Sales ($)		1892459M	2130115M
	3550M	29237M	132893M	278685M	333597M	323561M	Total Assets ($)		954633M	1580938M

M = $ thousand   MM = $ million
See Pages 9 through 22 for Explanation of Ratios and Data

Comparative Historical Data				Current Data Sorted by Sales					
13	12	15	**Type of Statement** Unqualified					4	11
9	8	10	Reviewed	1	1		2	3	3
11	23	11	Compiled	3	2	2	2	2	
24	31	35	Tax Returns	13	14	4	2		2
28	32	24	Other	7	6	3	2	3	3
4/1/08- 3/31/09 ALL	4/1/09- 3/31/10 ALL	4/1/10- 3/31/11 ALL		15 (4/1-9/30/10)			80 (10/1/10-3/31/11)		
				0-1MM	1-3MM	3-5MM	5-10MM	10-25MM	25MM & OVER
85	106	95	**NUMBER OF STATEMENTS**	24	23	9	8	12	19
%	%	%	**ASSETS**	%	%	%	%	%	%
9.5	10.6	12.0	Cash & Equivalents	17.6	6.8			11.0	7.0
16.0	18.9	13.5	Trade Receivables (net)	3.0	8.8			17.2	26.0
17.8	17.0	17.7	Inventory	6.7	18.2			25.9	21.8
3.3	2.8	3.8	All Other Current	1.2	3.7			4.3	6.7
46.7	49.3	47.0	Total Current	28.4	37.4			58.4	61.5
39.3	34.9	40.7	Fixed Assets (net)	57.0	51.5			31.5	20.5
5.9	5.9	4.9	Intangibles (net)	6.2	4.3			3.3	8.3
8.1	9.9	7.4	All Other Non-Current	8.3	6.9			6.8	9.7
100.0	100.0	100.0	Total	100.0	100.0			100.0	100.0
			LIABILITIES						
12.5	19.9	13.3	Notes Payable-Short Term	18.0	10.8			19.5	10.2
3.9	4.8	3.7	Cur. Mat.-L.T.D.	3.8	4.7			2.1	1.0
11.0	13.5	9.6	Trade Payables	1.5	6.8			8.9	16.8
.2	.2	.2	Income Taxes Payable	.1	.1			.6	.4
11.7	9.7	9.5	All Other Current	10.4	9.8			9.5	8.0
39.2	48.0	36.3	Total Current	33.8	32.1			40.6	36.5
28.3	28.1	26.0	Long-Term Debt	35.8	47.0			10.9	7.3
.4	.4	.3	Deferred Taxes	.0	.0			1.0	1.0
3.8	3.4	10.3	All Other Non-Current	27.1	10.1			2.1	2.0
28.2	20.1	27.0	Net Worth	3.2	10.8			45.4	53.2
100.0	100.0	100.0	Total Liabilties & Net Worth	100.0	100.0			100.0	100.0
			INCOME DATA						
100.0	100.0	100.0	Net Sales	100.0	100.0			100.0	100.0
			Gross Profit						
90.7	94.2	93.8	Operating Expenses	92.0	93.9			97.0	95.0
9.3	5.8	6.2	Operating Profit	8.0	6.1			3.0	5.0
3.7	.8	2.6	All Other Expenses (net)	5.1	5.3			-.2	-.5
5.6	5.0	3.6	Profit Before Taxes	2.9	.8			3.2	5.5
			RATIOS						
2.2	2.0	2.3	Current	1.8	2.4			2.2	2.6
1.3	1.4	1.4		.9	.9			1.3	1.7
.7	.4	.7		.1	.4			1.1	1.1
1.3	1.4	1.3	Quick	1.3	1.0			1.3	1.7
.7	.7	(94) .6		.3	.4			.7	.7
.3	.2	.3		.1	.2			.4	.4
1 275.2	3 120.9	0 UND	Sales/Receivables	0 UND	0 UND			12 30.9	16 23.5
21 17.4	19 19.0	17 21.9		0 UND	9 41.7			32 11.4	26 14.1
41 8.9	40 9.2	33 11.1		2 156.1	23 15.8			44 8.4	40 9.1
			Cost of Sales/Inventory						
			Cost of Sales/Payables						
5.9	7.2	7.7	Sales/Working Capital	12.2	26.2			9.0	5.7
27.5	34.2	30.9		NM	-143.4			14.5	11.7
-18.8	-17.5	-49.5		-7.8	-10.4			190.9	88.3
16.8	12.5	12.2	EBIT/Interest	5.6	9.1			9.9	55.1
(69) 3.1	(88) 3.3	(80) 3.6		(17) 2.1	(20) 2.2		(11) 4.9	(17) 12.4	
.9	.8	1.5		.4	.0			2.2	4.3
10.7		15.9	Net Profit + Depr., Dep., Amort./Cur. Mat. L/T/D						
(10) 4.8		(12) 4.7							
.8		2.3							
.3	.3	.3	Fixed/Worth	.8	.5			.4	.1
.9	.7	1.1		2.4	2.2			1.0	.5
6.4	3.5	3.6		-1.4	-2.5			1.4	1.0
.7	.7	.7	Debt/Worth	.4	1.4			.6	.5
1.9	2.1	2.0		2.8	3.5			1.9	1.2
12.0	11.7	5.7		-3.0	-7.9			2.8	3.2
49.2	48.5	44.9	% Profit Before Taxes/Tangible Net Worth	43.5	50.3			18.0	49.9
(70) 13.1	(84) 10.7	(76) 15.5		(16) 12.2	(15) 5.9			11.4	(18) 21.0
.5	.4	5.1		1.7	-18.6			6.9	13.6
18.7	17.8	22.0	% Profit Before Taxes/Total Assets	29.5	25.3			8.6	20.3
4.3	4.4	7.7		4.5	3.0			4.0	11.2
-.3	-.4	1.4		-1.6	-7.6			2.7	5.7
21.5	44.1	22.3	Sales/Net Fixed Assets	11.1	14.3			18.0	114.7
6.0	10.3	8.3		3.7	5.4			9.3	10.1
1.7	4.2	2.3		.5	1.0			5.5	5.3
3.2	4.7	3.9	Sales/Total Assets	3.6	2.9			3.4	5.5
1.7	2.5	2.4		2.1	1.7			2.2	2.9
.6	1.4	1.1		.4	.8			1.6	1.5
1.4	.7	1.4	% Depr., Dep., Amort./Sales	3.2	1.8			1.6	.5
(71) 3.0	(78) 1.9	(71) 2.9		(16) 7.0	(17) 6.4		(10) 2.1	(15) 1.7	
6.3	4.5	6.7		23.8	10.9			2.9	3.9
1.5	1.8	1.2	% Officers', Directors' Owners' Comp/Sales		2.2				
(31) 3.1	(47) 4.8	(35) 2.5			(10) 5.5				
8.0	9.1	7.8			13.6				
2571115M	2585266M	2251271M	Net Sales ($)	12479M	45764M	36951M	53824M	187076M	1915177M
1344095M	1339829M	1101523M	Total Assets ($)	19709M	55854M	15605M	25861M	84281M	900213M

M = $ thousand   MM = $ million
See Pages 9 through 22 for Explanation of Ratios and Data

Current Data Sorted by Assets   Comparative Historical Data

0-500M	500M-2MM	2-10MM	10-50MM	50-100MM	100-250MM	Type of Statement	4/1/06-3/31/07 ALL	4/1/07-3/31/08 ALL
		7	22	8	33	Unqualified	65	57
1	1	4	7	1		Reviewed	11	7
1	5	9	3			Compiled	19	14
3	9	10			1	Tax Returns	12	14
1	15	26	27	10	20	Other	122	105
	19 (4/1-9/30/10)		205 (10/1/10-3/31/11)					
6	30	56	59	19	54	**NUMBER OF STATEMENTS**	229	197
%	%	%	%	%	%	**ASSETS**	%	%
	11.4	13.5	7.4	13.0	5.8	Cash & Equivalents	11.3	10.2
	23.7	22.0	13.0	5.6	6.1	Trade Receivables (net)	12.3	15.4
	3.0	3.5	3.9	1.4	1.6	Inventory	1.5	1.8
	7.8	3.9	5.0	2.1	2.5	All Other Current	4.8	4.0
	45.9	42.9	29.4	22.1	16.1	Total Current	29.9	31.3
	38.2	41.1	57.8	66.4	73.7	Fixed Assets (net)	58.6	56.2
	7.2	2.0	4.0	.6	2.9	Intangibles (net)	1.1	2.0
	8.7	14.1	8.9	10.9	7.3	All Other Non-Current	10.4	10.5
	100.0	100.0	100.0	100.0	100.0	Total	100.0	100.0
						LIABILITIES		
	11.0	7.1	4.5	.2	.6	Notes Payable-Short Term	6.7	6.8
	3.0	2.7	4.9	7.0	3.7	Cur. Mat.-L.T.D.	2.6	3.2
	7.7	10.7	8.3	5.0	4.9	Trade Payables	11.0	10.7
	.0	.1	.3	.1	.1	Income Taxes Payable	.1	.4
	9.4	9.2	5.4	4.3	6.1	All Other Current	7.1	7.4
	31.1	29.8	23.3	16.5	15.4	Total Current	27.5	28.4
	26.6	13.8	18.2	17.6	25.7	Long-Term Debt	21.7	25.0
	.0	.1	.9	1.5	1.5	Deferred Taxes	1.6	.9
	5.5	4.5	7.4	5.5	5.3	All Other Non-Current	4.5	7.6
	36.8	51.9	50.2	58.9	52.1	Net Worth	44.8	38.1
	100.0	100.0	100.0	100.0	100.0	Total Liabilities & Net Worth	100.0	100.0
						INCOME DATA		
	100.0	100.0	100.0	100.0	100.0	Net Sales	100.0	100.0
	50.8	45.0	57.3	59.2	64.2	Gross Profit	59.4	57.0
	40.4	28.9	36.3	36.4	46.3	Operating Expenses	32.4	33.4
	10.4	16.1	21.0	22.8	18.0	Operating Profit	27.0	23.6
	.8	1.8	5.0	1.5	5.4	All Other Expenses (net)	2.0	4.4
	9.6	14.3	15.9	21.4	12.6	Profit Before Taxes	25.0	19.2
						RATIOS		
	4.4	4.4	3.6	5.0	2.2	Current	2.2	2.7
	1.5	1.4	1.5	2.2	1.2		1.2	1.2
	.9	.8	.8	.8	.7		.6	.7
	3.7	3.8	2.0	4.2	1.4	Quick	1.9	1.9
	1.1	1.3	1.0	1.7	.9		.9	1.0
	.4	.7	.5	.6	.5		.4	.5
2 215.7	14 25.8	10 37.8	17 21.6	41 8.9		Sales/Receivables	8 47.0	13 27.5
32 11.5	45 8.2	41 9.0	36 10.1	60 6.1			37 9.8	42 8.8
78 4.7	95 3.8	65 5.6	65 5.6	83 4.4			62 5.9	76 4.8
0 UND	0 UND	0 UND	0 UND	0 UND		Cost of Sales/Inventory	0 UND	0 UND
0 UND	0 UND	0 UND	1 263.9	3 110.3			0 UND	0 UND
0 UND	9 39.8	18 19.8	22 16.5	24 14.9			2 203.5	3 146.0
0 UND	8 45.9	15 25.1	11 33.6	42 8.7		Cost of Sales/Payables	15 24.4	12 30.5
19 19.2	25 14.5	49 7.4	38 9.6	117 3.1			72 5.1	56 6.5
64 5.7	92 4.0	140 2.6	275 1.3	231 1.6			197 1.9	184 2.0
	3.9	3.8	4.3	1.7	4.5	Sales/Working Capital	6.4	6.6
	12.3	15.5	16.6	5.1	20.9		30.6	22.1
	-450.2	-75.5	-9.6	-27.5	-8.2		-10.6	-9.6
	24.3	37.2	51.2	7.5	7.3	EBIT/Interest	44.8	21.3
(24) 8.5	(43) 7.5	(52) 9.0	(15) 5.1	(44) 3.3			(183) 9.1	(161) 4.8
	.9	1.1	1.2	3.2	1.0		2.9	1.5
						Net Profit + Depr., Dep., Amort./Cur. Mat. L/T/D	373.2	82.2
							(28) 35.8	(21) 8.3
							2.7	3.0
	.4	.3	.7	.8	1.1	Fixed/Worth	.7	.7
	.9	.9	1.1	1.1	1.5		1.3	1.2
	NM	1.8	1.9	1.7	2.3		2.8	3.3
	.4	.2	.3	.2	.4	Debt/Worth	.4	.4
	1.0	.9	.9	.7	1.0		1.1	1.3
	NM	3.6	2.0	1.3	2.0		3.8	5.3
	55.4	34.8	49.1	34.4	26.3	% Profit Before Taxes/Tangible Net Worth	58.9	55.6
(23) 29.8	(50) 19.2	(53) 20.6	(18) 15.8	(51) 11.9			(208) 33.1	(172) 22.9
	2.3	3.1	2.8	8.0	-.5		16.8	8.1
	23.5	20.3	21.9	15.1	10.9	% Profit Before Taxes/Total Assets	29.0	22.1
	9.1	7.9	9.4	7.8	3.7		14.4	8.1
	-2.1	1.1	.5	3.7	-.4		5.1	1.9
	21.2	19.3	3.0	1.5	.9	Sales/Net Fixed Assets	3.4	4.3
	6.2	3.0	1.1	.7	.4		1.1	1.3
	2.0	1.0	.5	.3	.2		.5	.4
	3.1	2.2	1.2	.9	.5	Sales/Total Assets	1.4	1.5
	1.5	1.0	.6	.4	.3		.7	.6
	.9	.4	.3	.3	.2		.3	.3
	3.5	.8	6.7	7.4	5.9	% Depr., Dep., Amort./Sales	4.2	2.6
(16) 7.5	(41) 7.0	(54) 11.6	(13) 11.9	(27) 17.6			(163) 8.6	(135) 8.9
	15.4	14.9	23.3	26.9	25.4		17.9	19.8
		1.4				% Officers', Directors', Owners' Comp/Sales	.7	1.4
		(11) 2.7					(19) 3.0	(23) 4.4
		5.5					5.1	7.5
3050M	76247M	768299M	1860202M	711701M	3970445M	Net Sales ($)	9850729M	12816137M
1265M	33959M	296600M	1626114M	1266834M	8682070M	Total Assets ($)	10591730M	10808083M

M = $ thousand   MM = $ million
See Pages 9 through 22 for Explanation of Ratios and Data

Comparative Historical Data   **Current Data Sorted by Sales**

Type of Statement									
	59	61	70	Unqualified	1		4	11	13	42
	12	9	14	Reviewed	2	1	3	7
	16	15	18	Compiled	3	7	2	3	2	1
	16	16	23	Tax Returns	3	10	1	4	3	2
	112	107	99	Other	12	15	8	13	21	30

Label	4/1/08-3/31/09 ALL	4/1/09-3/31/10 ALL	4/1/10-3/31/11 ALL	0-1MM	1-3MM	3-5MM	5-10MM	10-25MM	25MM & OVER
				19 (4/1-9/30/10)		205 (10/1/10-3/31/11)			
NUMBER OF STATEMENTS	215	208	224	19	32	17	32	42	82
ASSETS	%	%	%	%	%	%	%	%	%
Cash & Equivalents	10.3	10.5	9.5	9.2	8.3	10.4	9.5	10.9	9.3
Trade Receivables (net)	12.3	11.2	14.7	14.5	22.3	13.7	17.0	10.7	13.1
Inventory	2.2	2.6	3.0	2.3	2.8	1.0	2.0	3.6	3.7
All Other Current	5.5	6.0	4.1	11.1	1.7	3.0	7.8	2.9	2.9
Total Current	30.3	30.2	31.4	37.0	35.2	28.0	36.3	28.0	29.0
Fixed Assets (net)	59.1	56.3	55.5	51.9	45.3	53.9	55.7	58.9	58.9
Intangibles (net)	1.8	2.4	3.3	3.7	5.4	4.1	1.3	2.9	3.1
All Other Non-Current	8.8	11.1	9.9	7.4	14.1	14.0	6.7	10.2	9.0
Total	100.0	100.0	100.0	100.0	100.0	100.0	100.0	100.0	100.0
LIABILITIES									
Notes Payable-Short Term	6.3	5.0	5.1	19.7	8.2	7.6	3.1	3.0	1.8
Cur. Mat.-L.T.D.	3.4	3.5	4.0	3.0	2.5	1.1	6.4	3.4	4.7
Trade Payables	10.0	7.6	7.8	2.8	8.3	5.6	8.5	7.1	9.3
Income Taxes Payable	.1	.1	.1	.0	.0	.1	.2	.1	.2
All Other Current	6.9	7.4	7.1	9.7	9.3	5.1	5.5	6.3	7.1
Total Current	26.8	23.6	24.1	35.3	28.4	19.5	23.8	19.9	23.0
Long-Term Debt	23.6	29.8	20.1	22.7	25.1	19.2	14.9	18.8	20.4
Deferred Taxes	.9	.8	.8	.0	.0	.2	.6	.6	1.5
All Other Non-Current	4.9	6.6	5.6	1.4	6.5	7.1	9.6	5.1	4.5
Net Worth	43.8	39.2	49.5	40.6	40.1	53.9	51.2	55.6	50.6
Total Liabilties & Net Worth	100.0	100.0	100.0	100.0	100.0	100.0	100.0	100.0	100.0
INCOME DATA									
Net Sales	100.0	100.0	100.0	100.0	100.0	100.0	100.0	100.0	100.0
Gross Profit	59.7	54.8	55.1	69.1	51.7	51.2	52.6	59.2	52.9
Operating Expenses	35.1	43.5	37.8	52.9	35.4	31.7	35.7	40.0	36.2
Operating Profit	24.7	11.3	17.3	16.2	16.2	19.5	16.8	19.1	16.7
All Other Expenses (net)	4.6	4.8	3.3	4.5	1.9	2.2	5.1	2.6	3.5
Profit Before Taxes	20.1	6.5	14.0	11.7	14.3	17.3	11.8	16.5	13.2
RATIOS									
Current	3.0	3.0	3.4	3.7	3.0	5.3	4.5	7.0	2.6
	1.4	1.3	1.5	1.4	1.3	1.8	1.9	1.5	1.4
	.6	.8	.8	.2	.8	.8	.8	.7	.8
Quick	2.2	2.1	2.3	1.4	3.0	5.2	3.4	3.1	1.8
	.9	.9	1.1	.8	1.2	1.3	.8	1.0	1.0
	.4	.4	.6	.1	.7	.6	.7	.6	.6
Sales/Receivables	7 50.6	11 32.7	18 20.5	2 208.7	25 14.9	15 24.1	11 33.7	11 34.3	25 14.5
	23 15.7	40 9.2	45 8.2	38 9.7	51 7.2	32 11.3	58 6.3	45 8.0	45 8.2
	47 7.8	63 5.8	73 5.0	95 3.8	103 3.6	57 6.4	113 3.2	71 5.2	66 5.6
Cost of Sales/Inventory	0 UND	0 UND	0 UND	0 UND	0 UND	0 UND	0 UND	0 UND	0 UND
	0 UND	0 UND	0 UND	0 UND	0 UND	0 UND	0 UND	0 UND	3 113.2
	2 241.5	18 20.2	19 19.7	0 UND	0 UND	8 46.7	17 21.8	13 28.6	23 16.0
Cost of Sales/Payables	9 39.0	7 53.9	11 34.5	0 UND	2 193.0	6 61.9	21 17.3	10 38.0	15 23.9
	46 8.0	36 10.1	47 7.8	12 29.3	28 13.2	34 10.9	42 8.7	59 6.2	56 6.5
	211 1.7	100 3.7	136 2.7	107 3.4	131 2.8	69 5.3	103 3.5	169 2.2	156 2.3
Sales/Working Capital	5.8	4.5	4.0	2.0	4.8	4.8	2.6	2.7	5.9
	22.7	14.7	14.3	10.7	14.4	17.1	8.0	15.8	20.9
	-15.7	-15.2	-20.9	-2.2	-46.4	NM	-21.7	-15.8	-27.4
EBIT/Interest	29.7	9.7	25.6	11.1	36.9	39.0	40.7	38.2	17.0
	(174) 7.7	(174) 2.5	(182) 5.3	(15) 4.0	(26) 13.3	(14) 7.8	(26) 6.5	(33) 6.4	(68) 4.3
	1.8	-.6	1.2	1.7	.7	4.4	.2	.1	1.6
Net Profit + Depr., Dep., Amort./Cur. Mat. L/T/D	107.4	37.0	35.7						96.6
	(12) 11.5	(20) 2.0	(18) 4.2						(11) 4.4
	3.5	.3	2.2						2.6
Fixed/Worth	.7	.6	.7	.7	.6	.5	.4	.8	.7
	1.4	1.4	1.2	1.2	1.0	.9	1.1	1.1	1.4
	3.0	2.6	2.0	3.4	4.8	4.1	1.8	1.6	2.3
Debt/Worth	.4	.4	.3	.4	.3	.3	.3	.2	.4
	1.1	1.2	.9	1.5	.9	.9	.9	.7	1.0
	4.7	3.6	2.5	5.0	10.6	3.7	1.4	1.4	2.3
% Profit Before Taxes/Tangible Net Worth	58.0	22.9	39.2	44.0	30.7	47.3	36.2	33.3	46.1
	(189) 23.2	(188) 6.2	(200) 17.0	(16) 19.2	(26) 17.0	(16) 20.4	(29) 11.0	(37) 13.0	(76) 18.5
	6.5	-4.0	2.0	-3.5	-1.3	3.6	.5	1.7	4.7
% Profit Before Taxes/Total Assets	25.1	12.0	18.0	14.0	20.8	18.5	17.8	15.7	17.6
	10.3	2.8	6.8	5.5	8.7	6.0	5.3	6.2	7.3
	2.4	-2.4	.5	-4.2	-1.2	2.1	.2	-.7	1.4
Sales/Net Fixed Assets	6.5	5.9	4.0	6.2	7.9	12.6	3.3	3.2	3.9
	1.3	1.1	1.3	2.0	2.5	2.3	1.2	.9	1.2
	.4	.4	.4	.7	.7	.3	.4	.3	.4
Sales/Total Assets	1.8	1.4	1.5	1.3	1.7	1.7	1.3	1.2	1.2
	.7	.5	.6	.5	.7	1.3	.6	.5	.6
	.3	.3	.3	.3	.4	.3	.2	.3	.3
% Depr., Dep., Amort./Sales	3.1	4.8	4.2	1.3	6.1	1.6	7.9	6.3	2.2
	(142) 9.9	(135) 14.1	(155) 11.1	(11) 11.8	(19) 9.8	(13) 11.2	(28) 12.9	(33) 11.5	(51) 6.7
	20.6	27.5	19.8	16.1	23.1	18.5	24.8	30.4	17.0
% Officers', Directors' Owners' Comp/Sales	1.1	2.5	2.0						
	(32) 4.3	(24) 5.9	(23) 4.1						
	8.9	12.2	8.5						
Net Sales ($)	9792082M	7145647M	7389944M	10906M	64790M	68127M	254573M	719696M	6271852M
Total Assets ($)	11145386M	11651379M	11906842M	25211M	105582M	144238M	776826M	2105387M	8749598M

M = $ thousand   MM = $ million
See Pages 9 through 22 for Explanation of Ratios and Data

Current Data Sorted by Assets

Comparative Historical Data

						Type of Statement		
		2	10	10	7	Unqualified	18	20
		4	3			Reviewed	8	5
	3	2	1	1	1	Compiled	16	11
	3	2	1			Tax Returns	5	4
		8	10	7	12	Other	27	28
	15 (4/1-9/30/10)		72 (10/1/10-3/31/11)				4/1/06-3/31/07	4/1/07-3/31/08
0-500M	500M-2MM	2-10MM	10-50MM	50-100MM	100-250MM		ALL	ALL
6		18	25	18	20	NUMBER OF STATEMENTS	74	68
%	%	%	%	%	%	ASSETS	%	%
		10.1	9.4	16.1	2.9	Cash & Equivalents	10.0	10.9
		16.8	14.2	10.5	10.7	Trade Receivables (net)	14.5	16.7
		14.8	7.7	7.5	5.2	Inventory	6.1	3.9
		5.6	3.5	2.1	2.3	All Other Current	5.0	4.5
		47.2	34.8	36.2	21.2	Total Current	35.5	36.0
		44.3	43.5	43.2	59.7	Fixed Assets (net)	47.4	44.3
		1.6	.8	2.9	5.4	Intangibles (net)	3.6	3.9
		6.8	20.9	17.7	13.7	All Other Non-Current	13.6	15.9
		100.0	100.0	100.0	100.0	Total	100.0	100.0
						LIABILITIES		
		8.2	2.4	.9	.3	Notes Payable-Short Term	7.7	5.3
		8.6	6.2	4.7	6.5	Cur. Mat.-L.T.D.	6.7	6.0
		15.4	11.9	6.6	7.2	Trade Payables	11.3	14.3
		.0	.1	.2	.5	Income Taxes Payable	.1	.1
		15.6	5.5	8.0	10.0	All Other Current	13.7	12.7
		47.8	26.0	20.4	24.6	Total Current	39.4	38.4
		13.1	18.1	15.3	20.8	Long-Term Debt	29.5	26.5
		.0	.4	1.3	2.8	Deferred Taxes	.7	.6
		6.9	12.2	17.4	16.4	All Other Non-Current	7.9	7.8
		32.2	43.3	45.6	35.5	Net Worth	22.5	26.7
		100.0	100.0	100.0	100.0	Total Liabilities & Net Worth	100.0	100.0
						INCOME DATA		
		100.0	100.0	100.0	100.0	Net Sales	100.0	100.0
		33.9	30.8	27.5	23.7	Gross Profit	26.4	24.3
		26.4	21.1	15.4	11.2	Operating Expenses	20.1	19.3
		7.5	9.7	12.1	12.5	Operating Profit	6.3	5.0
		.5	-.5	-.1	1.7	All Other Expenses (net)	1.8	1.1
		7.0	10.2	12.2	10.7	Profit Before Taxes	4.5	3.9
						RATIOS		
		1.8	2.9	2.4	1.2		1.8	1.8
		1.2	1.6	1.6	.9	Current	1.1	1.0
		.5	.7	1.2	.7		.6	.6
		1.2	2.1	2.1	.8		1.3	1.4
		.6	1.3	1.0	.5	Quick	.7	.8
		.1	.3	.4	.4		.3	.3

	0	UND	24	15.4	17	21.3	20	18.7	Sales/Receivables	13	29.0	10	37.1
	25	14.8	30	12.0	31	12.0	28	13.0		23	15.8	22	16.8
	51	7.2	38	9.7	43	8.5	38	9.5		39	9.3	37	9.8
	0	UND	1	496.0	11	32.1	6	57.1	Cost of Sales/Inventory	0	UND	0	UND
	3	128.6	11	32.8	20	18.1	13	28.4		5	75.6	3	117.7
	154	2.4	53	6.9	48	7.7	31	11.6		27	13.4	20	18.4
	12	31.5	18	20.0	18	19.9	18	20.3	Cost of Sales/Payables	13	27.8	15	25.1
	21	17.7	30	12.3	27	13.7	27	13.3		22	16.7	26	14.2
	62	5.9	47	7.7	37	9.9	33	10.9		39	9.3	43	8.4

			2-10MM	10-50MM	50-100MM	100-250MM		ALL	ALL
			9.1	4.5	3.7	48.7	Sales/Working Capital	13.1	9.6
			45.9	17.3	11.0	-47.3		75.1	195.3
			-13.1	-17.4	50.4	-19.1		-9.9	-21.9
			23.0	31.9	32.3	16.6	EBIT/Interest	11.6	13.3
(16)			8.8 (24)	9.8 (17)	12.2 (19)	6.7		(68) 3.9	(60) 2.2
			.2	1.8	4.2	1.7		.7	.3
							Net Profit + Depr., Dep., Amort./Cur. Mat. L/T/D	6.6	2.9
								(14) 1.3	(12) 1.6
								.9	.9
			.8	.5	.6	.9	Fixed/Worth	.7	.6
			1.6	.7	1.3	1.7		1.8	1.8
			2.7	2.2	2.0	4.9		20.5	8.0
			.8	.6	.7	.8	Debt/Worth	.8	.6
			2.4	1.3	1.4	1.9		2.6	2.5
			17.7	2.8	2.5	7.1		81.3	91.5
			111.7	55.0	36.4	54.9	% Profit Before Taxes/Tangible Net Worth	105.7	66.6
(15)			39.4 (23)	24.7 (17)	26.4 (18)	29.1		(61) 28.1	(55) 20.5
			.5	8.9	20.2	24.8		6.6	-7.2
			24.8	30.9	20.8	11.6	% Profit Before Taxes/Total Assets	24.0	14.9
			16.7	9.3	12.2	7.9		7.6	3.6
			-2.1	2.5	6.6	4.1		.0	-3.2
			19.8	5.9	5.6	3.5	Sales/Net Fixed Assets	9.2	9.6
			6.3	3.8	3.2	1.4		3.1	3.4
			2.9	2.6	1.7	.9		1.8	1.9
			4.7	2.2	1.4	1.4	Sales/Total Assets	2.7	3.2
			2.1	1.7	1.1	.9		1.5	1.6
			1.6	1.0	.8	.7		1.0	.9
			1.5	3.2	3.8		% Depr., Dep., Amort./Sales	2.8	2.0
(16)			4.0 (24)	5.1 (15)	5.7			(56) 4.9	(52) 4.8
			13.7	8.0	6.4			9.8	7.8
							% Officers', Directors' Owners' Comp/Sales	1.3	
								(11) 4.1	
								7.6	

							Net Sales ($)		
44818M	248340M	954525M	1705378M	4364965M		Net Sales ($)	4038302M	4657346M
7550M	86678M	539785M	1369500M	3452791M		Total Assets ($)	2788313M	3161034M

See Pages 9 through 22 for Explanation of Ratios and Data

Comparative Historical Data

Current Data Sorted by Sales

				Type of Statement	0-1MM	1-3MM	3-5MM	5-10MM	10-25MM	25MM & OVER
28		30	29	Unqualified				1	7	21
9		4	7	Reviewed		1		3	1	2
4		5	8	Compiled	1			1	2	4
11		7	6	Tax Returns		2	2	1	1	
43		41	37	Other				3	5	29
4/1/08-3/31/09 ALL		4/1/09-3/31/10 ALL	4/1/10-3/31/11 ALL			15 (4/1-9/30/10)			72 (10/1/10-3/31/11)	
95		87	87	NUMBER OF STATEMENTS	1	2	3	9	16	56
%		%	%	ASSETS	%	%	%	%	%	%
11.6		12.8	10.6	Cash & Equivalents					14.6	9.3
19.8		14.1	13.2	Trade Receivables (net)					11.5	12.6
6.4		6.5	8.6	Inventory					8.9	6.6
2.3		2.5	3.4	All Other Current					4.4	2.6
40.1		35.9	35.7	Total Current					39.5	31.0
45.1		46.9	45.5	Fixed Assets (net)					48.2	49.0
3.4		3.5	2.5	Intangibles (net)					.8	3.0
11.4		13.7	16.3	All Other Non-Current					11.6	16.9
100.0		100.0	100.0	Total					100.0	100.0
				LIABILITIES						
4.3		4.3	2.9	Notes Payable-Short Term					5.3	1.2
6.1		6.1	6.1	Cur. Mat.-L.T.D.					2.9	5.5
15.8		9.9	11.5	Trade Payables					12.3	10.0
.1		.3	.2	Income Taxes Payable					.1	.3
16.1		9.8	9.8	All Other Current					6.9	10.0
42.4		30.4	30.5	Total Current					27.5	26.8
22.6		20.8	17.1	Long-Term Debt					12.7	17.2
.4		.7	1.0	Deferred Taxes					.6	1.4
7.8		14.4	17.3	All Other Non-Current					7.3	15.5
26.7		33.8	34.1	Net Worth					51.9	39.1
100.0		100.0	100.0	Total Liabilities & Net Worth					100.0	100.0
				INCOME DATA						
100.0		100.0	100.0	Net Sales					100.0	100.0
25.7		26.4	30.4	Gross Profit					31.6	26.7
18.7		14.2	19.8	Operating Expenses					22.8	15.7
7.0		12.2	10.5	Operating Profit					8.8	11.0
.7		2.1	.5	All Other Expenses (net)					-.1	.2
6.4		10.2	10.0	Profit Before Taxes					9.0	10.9
				RATIOS						
1.7		2.0	2.0						3.6	1.9
1.2		1.1	1.2	Current					2.0	1.1
.6		.8	.7						.8	.7
1.5		1.5	1.6						2.4	1.2
.8		.8	.7	Quick					1.6	.6
.4		.4	.3						.6	.3
14 25.7	16	22.8	15 23.9						0 756.8	17 21.6
27 13.4	26	13.9	29 12.5	Sales/Receivables					30 12.2	27 13.4
40 9.0	40	9.2	38 9.7						38 9.7	37 9.8
0 UND	2	187.6	2 176.6						0 UND	6 64.7
6 56.2	14	26.1	12 31.0	Cost of Sales/Inventory					12 30.4	13 27.1
23 15.8	35	10.5	51 7.1						68 5.3	38 9.6
14 26.3	16	22.4	17 21.9						18 20.0	17 21.6
26 14.2	23	16.2	26 13.9	Cost of Sales/Payables					26 14.1	27 13.6
48 7.6	38	9.5	37 9.8						34 10.6	37 9.8
8.7		7.9	6.9						3.4	9.3
40.1		47.0	35.1	Sales/Working Capital					9.0	58.4
-12.5		-25.4	-20.6						NM	-21.2
13.6		30.2	25.4						28.7	28.6
(83) 5.2	(81)	10.6	(81) 9.0	EBIT/Interest					(14) 14.3	(52) 10.2
1.0		1.8	2.3						1.5	3.1
8.6		8.7		Net Profit + Depr., Dep.,						
(17) 2.3	(15)	2.3		Amort./Cur. Mat. L/T/D						
.8		.8								
.7		.7	.6						.5	.7
1.6		1.5	1.2	Fixed/Worth					1.0	1.4
6.3		4.3	2.4						1.7	2.4
.9		.9	.7						.4	.8
2.4		2.3	1.5	Debt/Worth					.8	1.4
12.2		10.9	4.4						2.4	3.3
64.1		79.4	53.4	% Profit Before Taxes/Tangible					107.0	52.9
(77) 32.5	(73)	33.5	(78) 28.8	Net Worth					(15) 24.7	(51) 28.6
3.3		12.6	18.4						4.0	20.8
25.9		23.5	22.0	% Profit Before Taxes/Total					26.8	21.7
8.7		13.9	10.6	Assets					16.7	10.8
.1		1.5	3.2						-.2	4.8
11.0		5.5	6.7						6.2	5.8
3.7		3.0	3.6	Sales/Net Fixed Assets					3.2	3.4
1.9		1.6	1.9						2.3	1.2
2.8		2.1	2.3						3.1	2.1
1.6		1.3	1.4	Sales/Total Assets					1.6	1.2
1.0		.9	.9						.9	.9
1.6		2.7	2.5						2.7	3.0
(75) 4.6	(62)	5.7	(65) 5.2	% Depr., Dep., Amort./Sales					7.3	(38) 4.8
7.5		8.4	8.8						11.7	6.3
.6				% Officers', Directors'						
(11) 1.5				Owners' Comp/Sales						
5.9										
8426836M		7820633M	7318026M	Net Sales ($)	745M	2711M	11507M	63206M	284534M	6955323M
5129130M		5922641M	5456304M	Total Assets ($)	578M	1813M	6884M	48204M	193347M	5205478M

M = $ thousand   MM = $ million
See Pages 9 through 22 for Explanation of Ratios and Data

Current Data Sorted by Assets | Comparative Historical Data

Period annotations for current data: **7 (4/1–9/30/10)** covers 0-500M · 500M-2MM · 2-10MM; **57 (10/1/10–3/31/11)** covers 10-50MM · 50-100MM · 100-250MM.

	0-500M	500M-2MM	2-10MM	10-50MM	50-100MM	100-250MM	Type of Statement	4/1/06-3/31/07 ALL	4/1/07-3/31/08 ALL
		1	3	7	2	6	Unqualified	22	23
		1	5	2			Reviewed	11	10
		2	1	1			Compiled	8	7
							Tax Returns	4	9
	1	2	8	15	3	4	Other	26	29
	1	6	17	25	5	10	**NUMBER OF STATEMENTS**	71	78
	%	%	%	%	%	%		%	%
							ASSETS		
			10.5	9.3		6.6	Cash & Equivalents	9.9	9.0
			15.1	9.2		13.7	Trade Receivables (net)	16.4	12.9
			13.8	18.5		7.0	Inventory	11.1	13.8
			3.5	6.8		6.9	All Other Current	2.4	2.2
			42.9	43.9		34.2	Total Current	39.9	37.9
			51.2	45.4		47.4	Fixed Assets (net)	49.0	52.4
			.5	5.4		9.0	Intangibles (net)	4.6	3.6
			5.3	5.3		9.5	All Other Non-Current	6.5	6.1
			100.0	100.0		100.0	Total	100.0	100.0
							LIABILITIES		
			5.9	4.3		1.8	Notes Payable-Short Term	3.5	5.0
			5.6	5.5		7.2	Cur. Mat.-L.T.D.	4.0	4.4
			5.7	6.6		9.1	Trade Payables	8.0	7.8
			.5	.1		.0	Income Taxes Payable	.2	.2
			5.3	3.3		7.3	All Other Current	8.3	5.1
			23.0	19.8		25.4	Total Current	24.0	22.6
			16.1	25.0		20.1	Long-Term Debt	26.5	25.5
			1.1	.6		2.7	Deferred Taxes	1.0	1.4
			1.4	2.4		7.5	All Other Non-Current	4.1	4.8
			58.4	52.2		44.3	Net Worth	44.4	45.7
			100.0	100.0		100.0	Total Liabilities & Net Worth	100.0	100.0
							INCOME DATA		
			100.0	100.0		100.0	Net Sales	100.0	100.0
			33.5	26.8		31.2	Gross Profit	29.9	34.2
			27.7	18.8		18.7	Operating Expenses	16.7	23.8
			5.8	8.0		12.5	Operating Profit	13.2	10.4
			.3	1.6		5.0	All Other Expenses (net)	2.1	2.9
			5.5	6.4		7.4	Profit Before Taxes	11.1	7.5
							RATIOS		
			6.8	5.3		2.7		3.3	3.4
			1.8	2.9		1.6	Current	1.7	2.1
			1.0	1.5		1.3		1.2	1.2
			2.3	2.9		1.8		2.2	2.1
			.9	1.4		.8	Quick	1.1	1.0
			.7	.3		.4		.7	.5
			25 14.9	23 16.1		35 10.3		29 12.7	24 15.4
			34 10.8	34 10.9		42 8.8	Sales/Receivables	41 8.9	35 10.4
			48 7.5	49 7.5		61 6.0		52 7.0	44 8.2
			0 UND	42 8.7		15 24.4		18 20.8	22 16.9
			20 18.5	101 3.6		33 11.2	Cost of Sales/Inventory	40 9.2	50 7.3
			76 4.8	152 2.4		100 3.7		72 5.1	96 3.8
			8 48.6	19 19.2		22 16.4		17 21.4	17 22.0
			17 21.3	25 14.9		32 11.4	Cost of Sales/Payables	26 13.9	26 13.8
			37 9.9	46 8.0		63 5.8		38 9.7	43 8.4
			3.2	2.0		2.8		3.6	4.0
			9.8	4.7		8.3	Sales/Working Capital	10.4	6.9
			-186.0	10.4		NM		32.7	72.5
			11.2	17.9				21.9	9.5
			(15) 3.4	(23) 3.1			EBIT/Interest	(59) 6.4	(68) 4.0
			1.2	.6				2.7	1.8
								7.4	6.8
							Net Profit + Depr., Dep., Amort./Cur. Mat. L/T/D	(12) 2.7	(15) 3.7
								1.5	1.5
			.4	.7		.9		.7	.8
			1.0	1.0		1.3	Fixed/Worth	1.1	1.3
			1.6	1.5		3.6		2.3	2.2
			.5	.2		.7		.4	.5
			.7	1.0		2.9	Debt/Worth	1.3	1.3
			1.1	1.8		4.4		3.8	3.3
			27.2	14.9		21.1		53.3	38.9
			9.1	(22) 10.1		10.2	% Profit Before Taxes/Tangible Net Worth	(64) 22.5	(71) 17.0
			1.3	3.9		-4.4		13.1	8.7
			13.6	6.6		9.5		17.9	13.1
			5.6	4.2		5.2	% Profit Before Taxes/Total Assets	8.8	7.7
			.8	-.2		-.7		4.9	2.7
			4.4	3.1		4.5		3.9	3.7
			2.6	1.8		1.9	Sales/Net Fixed Assets	2.1	2.1
			1.4	1.0		1.0		1.4	1.3
			2.3	1.1		1.4		1.6	1.6
			1.1	.8		.8	Sales/Total Assets	1.0	1.1
			.8	.5		.5		.8	.8
			5.2	4.8				3.5	3.9
			(15) 7.9	9.5			% Depr., Dep., Amort./Sales	(62) 5.8	(68) 6.5
			10.6	12.6				9.3	10.7
								1.7	1.1
							% Officers', Directors' Owners' Comp/Sales	(11) 3.0	(16) 1.5
								15.5	7.3
	106M	9942M	127574M	506056M	319265M	1451574M	Net Sales ($)	2086664M	3066362M
	369M	7413M	88850M	565774M	348189M	1354344M	Total Assets ($)	2367110M	3134426M

M = $ thousand   MM = $ million
See Pages 9 through 22 for Explanation of Ratios and Data

Comparative Historical Data | Current Data Sorted by Sales

14 / 7 / 11 / 9 / 26	15 / 13 / 8 / 9 / 32	15 / 6 / 7 / 3 / 33	**Type of Statement**	0-1MM	1-3MM	3-5MM	5-10MM	10-25MM	25MM & OVER
			Unqualified				1	5	9
			Reviewed	1	2		1	2	
			Compiled		2	1	1	3	
			Tax Returns		3				
			Other	2	2	5	5	9	10
4/1/08-3/31/09 ALL	4/1/09-3/31/10 ALL	4/1/10-3/31/11 ALL			7 (4/1-9/30/10)			57 (10/1/10-3/31/11)	
67	77	64	**NUMBER OF STATEMENTS**	3	9	6	8	19	19
%	%	%	**ASSETS**	%	%	%	%	%	%
10.7	8.2	9.1	Cash & Equivalents					9.7	5.6
14.8	12.1	12.5	Trade Receivables (net)					12.8	14.6
14.9	15.2	13.7	Inventory					16.4	10.5
2.2	1.8	5.7	All Other Current					3.6	5.2
42.5	37.3	41.1	Total Current					42.6	36.0
48.4	52.6	47.2	Fixed Assets (net)					49.9	43.6
3.1	3.3	5.2	Intangibles (net)					2.8	12.0
6.0	6.8	6.5	All Other Non-Current					4.6	8.5
100.0	100.0	100.0	Total					100.0	100.0
			LIABILITIES						
6.3	12.7	4.7	Notes Payable-Short Term					6.6	3.9
5.8	4.4	6.0	Cur. Mat.-L.T.D.					3.9	5.0
6.5	6.7	8.1	Trade Payables					8.7	8.3
.0	.1	.2	Income Taxes Payable					.5	.1
7.5	4.1	4.8	All Other Current					5.9	5.7
26.2	28.0	23.8	Total Current					25.5	23.1
28.2	24.4	22.5	Long-Term Debt					24.2	21.8
.9	1.0	1.1	Deferred Taxes					1.7	1.7
3.4	5.2	4.8	All Other Non-Current					2.2	7.4
41.4	41.3	47.8	Net Worth					46.4	45.9
100.0	100.0	100.0	Total Liabilities & Net Worth					100.0	100.0
			INCOME DATA						
100.0	100.0	100.0	Net Sales					100.0	100.0
29.6	33.0	30.9	Gross Profit					25.9	22.8
23.8	23.7	22.8	Operating Expenses					15.5	14.2
5.9	9.3	8.1	Operating Profit					10.3	8.7
1.0	2.1	1.6	All Other Expenses (net)					3.9	1.2
4.8	7.2	6.5	Profit Before Taxes					6.4	7.5
			RATIOS						
3.6 / 1.9 / 1.1	4.3 / 2.2 / 1.1	3.9 / 2.2 / 1.1	Current					3.3 / 1.8 / 1.0	2.9 / 2.3 / 1.1
2.4 / 1.0 / .5	2.1 / 1.1 / .4	2.3 / 1.0 / .4	Quick					1.8 / .9 / .5	2.0 / .9 / .4
21 17.7 / 30 12.2 / 44 8.3	27 13.7 / 38 9.5 / 46 7.9	26 13.8 / 39 9.5 / 50 7.3	Sales/Receivables					23 15.7 / 39 9.4 / 61 6.0	33 11.1 / 38 9.5 / 48 7.6
7 50.7 / 40 9.0 / 82 4.4	16 22.7 / 61 6.0 / 118 3.1	11 32.9 / 42 8.7 / 123 3.0	Cost of Sales/Inventory					6 60.0 / 82 4.4 / 128 2.8	17 21.3 / 40 9.1 / 80 4.6
14 26.4 / 21 17.4 / 33 11.2	14 25.3 / 27 13.4 / 46 7.9	16 22.5 / 25 14.8 / 47 7.8	Cost of Sales/Payables					20 18.7 / 26 13.8 / 47 7.8	17 21.5 / 22 16.6 / 47 7.8
4.1 / 9.5 / 51.9	3.2 / 6.7 / 54.5	2.6 / 6.8 / 31.9	Sales/Working Capital					2.3 / 6.5 / -269.5	4.3 / 6.9 / 22.4
8.8 / (60) 2.8 / .9	11.1 / (70) 3.6 / 1.7	8.0 / (57) 3.2 / 1.5	EBIT/Interest					12.6 / (17) 3.9 / 2.3	14.2 / (18) 5.3 / 1.7
15.2 / (16) 4.1 / 2.1	11.4 / (14) 3.3 / 1.4	3.2 / (12) 1.4 / .1	Net Profit + Depr., Dep., Amort./Cur. Mat. L/T/D						
.7 / 1.1 / 2.8	.7 / 1.1 / 2.0	.7 / 1.0 / 1.6	Fixed/Worth					.8 / 1.1 / 1.6	.8 / 1.1 / 3.6
.6 / 1.5 / 3.8	.4 / 1.1 / 2.7	.5 / 1.0 / 3.4	Debt/Worth					.7 / 1.0 / 2.3	.5 / 2.0 / 6.8
34.8 / (59) 13.1 / 2.0	30.7 / (71) 13.3 / 3.9	19.7 / (57) 10.3 / 2.7	% Profit Before Taxes/Tangible Net Worth					24.8 / (18) 12.4 / 5.9	22.6 / (17) 9.9 / 4.2
14.4 / 6.1 / .4	10.8 / 5.2 / 1.9	9.3 / 4.9 / 1.2	% Profit Before Taxes/Total Assets					14.1 / 6.0 / 2.1	11.5 / 5.6 / 1.5
5.2 / 2.7 / 1.5	3.1 / 1.8 / 1.0	3.7 / 2.2 / 1.2	Sales/Net Fixed Assets					3.7 / 1.8 / 1.1	4.1 / 2.3 / 1.6
2.0 / 1.2 / .8	1.4 / .9 / .6	1.3 / .9 / .7	Sales/Total Assets					1.6 / .9 / .6	1.3 / 1.1 / .7
4.0 / (60) 6.2 / 9.6	4.5 / (68) 8.0 / 11.8	5.1 / (57) 8.8 / 11.4	% Depr., Dep., Amort./Sales					4.9 / (18) 8.0 / 10.3	3.4 / (15) 6.3 / 12.3
1.6 / (22) 3.1 / 8.7	2.2 / (21) 4.7 / 9.4	1.9 / (15) 5.0 / 7.1	% Officers', Directors' Owners' Comp/Sales						
1738397M	1953770M	2414517M	Net Sales ($)	1685M	19705M	24551M	61820M	342545M	1964211M
1667753M	2214606M	2364939M	Total Assets ($)	2752M	42560M	34960M	75800M	486104M	1722763M

© RMA 2011

M = $ thousand   MM = $ million

See Pages 9 through 22 for Explanation of Ratios and Data

Current Data Sorted by Assets   Comparative Historical Data

Type of Statement	0-500M	500M-2MM	2-10MM	10-50MM	50-100MM	100-250MM		4/1/06-3/31/07 ALL	4/1/07-3/31/08 ALL
Unqualified		1	1	7	3	2		9	10
Reviewed		1	2	5				9	13
Compiled		2	3	2				5	8
Tax Returns	1	2	2					4	4
Other	2	6	9	7	1			27	28
		7 (4/1-9/30/10)		52 (10/1/10-3/31/11)					
NUMBER OF STATEMENTS	3	12	17	21	4	2		54	63
	%	%	%	%	%	%		%	%
ASSETS									
Cash & Equivalents		6.2	8.0	9.1				8.2	6.8
Trade Receivables (net)		9.9	11.5	12.9				13.8	13.4
Inventory		14.8	22.0	11.4				16.1	9.9
All Other Current		2.8	4.6	3.4				4.4	5.2
Total Current		33.6	46.1	36.8				42.4	35.3
Fixed Assets (net)		52.4	42.3	48.1				48.5	48.8
Intangibles (net)		2.8	7.3	4.8				2.6	6.7
All Other Non-Current		11.1	4.3	10.4				6.5	9.2
Total		100.0	100.0	100.0				100.0	100.0
LIABILITIES									
Notes Payable-Short Term		6.4	5.7	3.3				6.1	5.3
Cur. Mat.-L.T.D.		9.3	5.9	3.9				5.4	7.2
Trade Payables		5.5	8.0	6.8				8.4	8.2
Income Taxes Payable		.0	.1	.0				.2	.3
All Other Current		5.1	10.5	3.0				4.4	5.4
Total Current		26.4	30.2	17.1				24.5	26.4
Long-Term Debt		48.4	16.8	16.1				27.5	30.8
Deferred Taxes		.4	.1	2.4				.7	.8
All Other Non-Current		20.5	8.1	8.4				6.5	5.5
Net Worth		4.3	44.8	56.0				40.9	36.4
Total Liabilities & Net Worth		100.0	100.0	100.0				100.0	100.0
INCOME DATA									
Net Sales		100.0	100.0	100.0				100.0	100.0
Gross Profit		55.4	30.5	30.1				31.9	29.4
Operating Expenses		50.3	21.1	18.3				21.5	18.1
Operating Profit		5.1	9.3	11.8				10.4	11.3
All Other Expenses (net)		10.5	.9	1.8				1.8	3.3
Profit Before Taxes		-5.4	8.4	10.0				8.6	8.1
RATIOS									
Current		5.2	4.1	7.6				2.7	3.1
		2.6	1.7	2.6				1.7	1.5
		.5	.8	1.0				1.3	.8
Quick		1.6	1.4	4.1				1.6	1.6
		1.1	.6	1.7				1.0	.9
		.4	.3	.8				.5	.4
Sales/Receivables	0 UND	7 53.7	28 13.0					14 25.2	22 16.7
	33 11.0	32 11.6	49 7.5					35 10.5	38 9.5
	54 6.8	49 7.4	72 5.1					52 7.0	51 7.2
Cost of Sales/Inventory	11 32.6	25 14.5	11 32.5					16 22.5	13 28.0
	84 4.3	82 4.4	66 5.5					43 8.4	47 7.8
	350 1.0	141 2.6	141 2.6					85 4.3	75 4.8
Cost of Sales/Payables	0 UND	7 54.9	12 30.6					14 26.5	14 26.5
	37 9.9	20 18.5	26 14.3					22 16.3	22 16.8
	211 1.7	63 5.8	52 7.0					42 8.6	40 9.0
Sales/Working Capital		4.4	3.7	2.1				4.6	5.1
		15.5	7.4	3.3				9.4	8.5
		-4.8	-11.4	-151.8				19.6	-14.2
EBIT/Interest		2.9	7.0	27.0				13.6	7.2
	(11) 1.2	(14) 3.2	(20) 5.3					(51) 4.6	(57) 3.1
		-.1	.9	1.3				1.8	1.0
Net Profit + Depr., Dep., Amort./Cur. Mat. L/T/D								17.2	9.0
								(10) 4.5	(21) 3.1
								3.0	1.3
Fixed/Worth		.6	.5	.5				.7	.7
		NM	.8	.8				1.1	1.5
		-3.2	6.5	2.1				2.5	8.8
Debt/Worth		1.1	.5	.2				.5	.5
		NM	1.1	.6				1.2	1.9
		-5.6	7.7	4.0				3.3	21.6
% Profit Before Taxes/Tangible Net Worth			22.5	26.0				62.8	37.2
		(14) 6.9	(19) 12.4					(47) 25.8	(51) 22.0
			3.6	2.6				10.0	12.3
% Profit Before Taxes/Total Assets		5.5	8.9	14.7				20.2	11.5
		1.3	3.6	5.0				9.5	7.8
		-13.0	.1	.3				2.3	.3
Sales/Net Fixed Assets		5.3	8.5	3.2				5.8	3.9
		2.2	3.5	2.1				3.3	2.2
		1.3	1.2	.8				1.9	1.3
Sales/Total Assets		1.9	1.9	1.2				2.2	1.6
		1.1	1.2	.8				1.4	1.0
		.8	.6	.5				.9	.7
% Depr., Dep., Amort./Sales		10.6	1.9	4.7				2.4	4.1
	(10) 15.9	(16) 6.2	(19) 8.1					(44) 5.4	(59) 6.8
		19.0	11.7	10.4				8.3	10.9
% Officers', Directors' Owners' Comp/Sales									1.3
								(10)	2.0
									3.4
Net Sales ($)	1426M	22418M	99036M	473558M	201167M	157438M		1757024M	1595412M
Total Assets ($)	843M	16555M	74542M	514456M	275856M	218845M		1370223M	1707801M

© RMA 2011

M = $ thousand   MM = $ million
See Pages 9 through 22 for Explanation of Ratios and Data

Comparative Historical Data   ## Current Data Sorted by Sales

4/1/08- 3/31/09 ALL	4/1/09- 3/31/10 ALL	4/1/10- 3/31/11 ALL	Type of Statement	0-1MM	1-3MM	3-5MM	5-10MM	10-25MM	25MM & OVER
					7 (4/1-9/30/10)			52 (10/1/10-3/31/11)	
12	11	14	Unqualified	1	1		2	2	8
10	10	8	Reviewed		1		3	1	2
10	9	7	Compiled	1	2	1	3		
2	4	5	Tax Returns	3	1	1		1	
30	23	25	Other	3	8	2	4	4	4
64	**57**	**59**	**NUMBER OF STATEMENTS**	**8**	**13**	**4**	**12**	**8**	**14**
%	%	%	**ASSETS**	%	%	%	%	%	%
7.2	8.5	7.7	Cash & Equivalents		5.3		12.0		7.8
14.5	15.3	11.1	Trade Receivables (net)		9.9		8.1		17.0
13.9	14.2	16.2	Inventory		11.7		22.8		17.1
1.2	2.4	3.9	All Other Current		3.7		.9		6.5
36.9	40.4	38.9	Total Current		30.6		43.8		48.5
48.6	48.4	47.9	Fixed Assets (net)		54.9		47.5		41.2
6.7	4.8	4.6	Intangibles (net)		8.6		1.1		2.7
7.8	6.4	8.6	All Other Non-Current		6.0		7.6		7.6
100.0	100.0	100.0	Total		100.0		100.0		100.0
			LIABILITIES						
5.5	4.9	5.8	Notes Payable-Short Term		5.2		5.1		8.4
5.2	5.1	5.6	Cur. Mat.-L.T.D.		8.1		7.3		3.0
7.4	9.8	6.5	Trade Payables		4.5		8.5		8.8
.2	.1	.0	Income Taxes Payable		.0		.2		.0
4.7	5.4	6.3	All Other Current		12.0		4.8		4.8
22.9	25.3	24.2	Total Current		29.8		26.0		25.1
28.1	28.2	24.7	Long-Term Debt		43.7		16.0		15.0
.7	.9	1.0	Deferred Taxes		.4		.6		3.1
7.7	8.1	10.1	All Other Non-Current		19.3		2.4		2.4
40.6	37.5	40.0	Net Worth		6.9		55.1		54.4
100.0	100.0	100.0	Total Liabilties & Net Worth		100.0		100.0		100.0
			INCOME DATA						
100.0	100.0	100.0	Net Sales		100.0		100.0		100.0
25.6	31.9	37.6	Gross Profit		39.9		35.5		24.0
18.8	24.6	29.1	Operating Expenses		34.9		26.1		20.4
6.8	7.3	8.4	Operating Profit		5.0		9.4		3.6
2.1	2.3	3.4	All Other Expenses (net)		5.8		.4		.1
4.7	5.0	5.0	Profit Before Taxes		-.8		9.0		3.5
			RATIOS						
4.1	4.4	4.6	Current		3.4		3.0		6.8
1.7	2.1	1.8			.9		1.8		2.3
.9	1.0	1.0			.4		1.2		1.0
1.8	2.0	1.8	Quick		1.4		2.3		3.9
.9	.9	.9			.5		.9		1.0
.4	.6	.4			.3		.4		.8
21 17.0	26 13.9	22 16.7	Sales/Receivables		14 25.6		23 16.1		45 8.1
37 9.9	39 9.4	37 9.8			36 10.2		33 10.9		60 6.1
51 7.2	52 7.1	57 6.4			58 6.3		43 8.5		82 4.5
14 25.4	20 18.6	23 15.8	Cost of Sales/Inventory		14 25.6		2 201.0		12 30.7
51 7.2	71 5.2	87 4.2			97 3.7		119 3.1		84 4.4
89 4.1	115 3.2	167 2.2			163 2.2		166 2.2		171 2.1
10 36.8	14 26.8	10 38.2	Cost of Sales/Payables		7 55.9		12 31.4		13 28.2
19 19.3	23 15.9	24 15.3			24 15.3		23 15.9		33 11.2
33 11.2	47 7.7	65 5.6			77 4.8		64 5.7		66 5.5
4.4	2.9	2.9	Sales/Working Capital		4.3		2.4		2.1
10.0	6.7	6.1			-34.6		4.4		4.0
-73.7	NM	-54.5			-5.1		218.3		NM
6.6	11.5	7.2	EBIT/Interest		2.5		15.3		12.1
(55) 2.7	(51) 2.1	(53) 3.1			(12) .8		(11) 3.9		3.6
-.6	-.3	.8			.0		1.1		1.1
8.6	15.1	11.1	Net Profit + Depr., Dep., Amort./Cur. Mat. L/T/D						
(12) 2.4	(16) 4.7	(12) 2.0							
.7	1.4	1.0							
.7	.6	.5	Fixed/Worth		1.7		.5		.5
1.3	1.1	1.2			-19.8		.6		.8
4.8	4.0	15.0			-2.8		1.3		1.6
.4	.3	.3	Debt/Worth		2.0		.4		.3
1.5	1.0	1.1			-30.0		.7		.8
6.5	12.2	41.8			-5.3		1.5		2.8
30.7	23.5	20.8	% Profit Before Taxes/Tangible Net Worth				14.9		14.7
(55) 16.3	(47) 12.3	(47) 7.2					(11) 7.2		6.2
-6.0	1.6	.3					2.6		-.1
14.2	14.7	12.0	% Profit Before Taxes/Total Assets		4.3		12.4		6.8
6.6	3.2	3.3			-.6		4.9		2.9
-3.8	-2.5	-.4			-6.6		.8		.1
4.1	3.8	5.1	Sales/Net Fixed Assets		5.0		8.8		3.4
2.5	2.4	2.3			2.2		1.3		2.5
1.5	1.2	1.2			1.3		.7		1.8
1.6	1.4	1.4	Sales/Total Assets		1.9		1.4		1.4
1.2	1.0	.9			1.0		.6		.9
.7	.7	.5			.6		.5		.7
3.7	4.0	4.9	% Depr., Dep., Amort./Sales		8.0		4.7		4.7
(56) 7.4	(48) 7.7	(53) 8.6			12.9		(11) 8.1		(12) 5.3
10.8	12.2	12.9			18.0		14.4		8.4
1.5		2.0	% Officers', Directors' Owners' Comp/Sales						
(10) 2.1		(11) 4.1							
4.2		5.9							
1937836M	1582390M	955043M	Net Sales ($)	4275M	27780M	13992M	90570M	129999M	688427M
1668728M	1581474M	1101097M	Total Assets ($)	11630M	35678M	10243M	130052M	139630M	773864M

M = $ thousand   MM = $ million
See Pages 9 through 22 for Explanation of Ratios and Data

Current Data Sorted by Assets   Comparative Historical Data

0-500M	500M-2MM	2-10MM	10-50MM	50-100MM	100-250MM	Type of Statement	4/1/06-3/31/07 ALL	4/1/07-3/31/08 ALL
		2	17	7	5	Unqualified	34	33
2	3	16	8	1		Reviewed	40	47
2	13	9	4			Compiled	38	28
6	8	7	1			Tax Returns	21	26
3	17	26	13	5	4	Other	47	69
	23 (4/1-9/30/10)		156 (10/1/10-3/31/11)					
13	41	60	43	13	9	NUMBER OF STATEMENTS	180	203
%	%	%	%	%	%	**ASSETS**	%	%
14.5	12.1	10.3	10.2	8.0		Cash & Equivalents	11.3	10.7
6.0	18.5	15.3	15.0	15.4		Trade Receivables (net)	18.5	16.2
5.0	12.9	9.8	7.3	8.0		Inventory	9.2	8.5
14.9	1.5	2.0	1.5	2.0		All Other Current	2.4	3.0
40.4	45.0	37.4	34.1	33.4		Total Current	41.4	38.4
45.9	44.0	50.3	55.6	42.2		Fixed Assets (net)	49.4	50.6
.6	3.5	2.6	2.0	6.0		Intangibles (net)	2.7	2.6
13.2	7.5	9.7	8.4	18.5		All Other Non-Current	6.4	8.5
100.0	100.0	100.0	100.0	100.0		Total	100.0	100.0
						LIABILITIES		
22.0	7.6	6.1	3.8	2.2		Notes Payable-Short Term	5.9	5.8
9.1	7.8	8.5	5.6	4.6		Cur. Mat.-L.T.D.	5.6	7.0
5.5	12.9	8.7	7.0	5.8		Trade Payables	8.1	6.6
.0	.0	.4	.1	.0		Income Taxes Payable	.3	.6
20.6	10.9	3.4	4.0	3.8		All Other Current	6.1	6.3
57.2	39.1	27.1	20.5	16.5		Total Current	26.0	26.3
58.1	43.7	29.0	21.5	25.8		Long-Term Debt	26.8	25.7
.0	.2	.2	1.0	1.9		Deferred Taxes	.8	1.0
1.9	4.0	5.7	5.0	7.7		All Other Non-Current	7.1	5.4
-17.4	13.0	38.0	52.1	48.1		Net Worth	39.3	41.6
100.0	100.0	100.0	100.0	100.0		Total Liabilities & Net Worth	100.0	100.0
						INCOME DATA		
100.0	100.0	100.0	100.0	100.0		Net Sales	100.0	100.0
43.3	51.7	31.2	24.6	27.8		Gross Profit	33.6	34.3
38.2	47.5	29.3	19.3	18.6		Operating Expenses	22.8	24.9
5.1	4.2	1.9	5.3	9.2		Operating Profit	10.8	9.4
2.1	1.6	2.0	.6	3.7		All Other Expenses (net)	1.3	2.2
3.0	2.6	.0	4.8	5.5		Profit Before Taxes	9.5	7.3
						RATIOS		
1.2	4.4	2.7	3.9	5.6		Current	3.0	2.9
.6	1.5	1.5	1.6	2.2			1.7	1.7
.3	.6	.8	.9	.9			1.1	.9
.8	1.9	1.6	2.7	3.4		Quick	2.1	2.1
.5	1.0	1.0	1.2	.8			(179) 1.2	1.0
.1	.4	.5	.6	.5			.6	.5
0 UND	15 24.8	23 16.0	28 12.8	45 8.0		Sales/Receivables	28 12.9	25 14.5
2 167.0	34 10.7	42 8.6	47 7.8	74 5.0			42 8.8	40 9.2
22 16.5	62 5.9	62 5.9	68 5.4	84 4.3			55 6.6	55 6.7
0 UND	0 UND	0 UND	4 91.1	40 9.0		Cost of Sales/Inventory	0 999.8	0 UND
0 UND	26 13.8	26 13.8	23 15.6	46 8.0			20 18.7	20 18.1
34 10.8	114 3.2	85 4.3	47 7.7	101 3.6			62 5.8	60 6.1
0 UND	9 40.5	10 35.4	11 33.7	19 18.9		Cost of Sales/Payables	13 28.0	12 31.6
1 511.0	35 10.6	34 10.7	19 19.3	26 14.0			25 14.8	20 18.2
18 20.4	89 4.1	75 4.9	32 11.3	61 6.0			41 9.0	37 9.9
16.1	3.7	5.6	3.1	1.4		Sales/Working Capital	4.4	4.6
-106.3	14.5	9.7	11.3	8.2			10.1	11.1
-3.5	-8.7	-25.7	-56.8	-22.6			84.4	-75.3
18.5	5.7	3.9	12.6	5.4		EBIT/Interest	15.2	11.2
(11) 1.0	(32) 1.4	(53) 1.7	(42) 3.8	(11) 3.8			(163) 4.6	(177) 3.0
-5.8	-.2	-.6	1.5	.9			1.5	1.2
		5.0	5.5			Net Profit + Depr., Dep., Amort./Cur. Mat. L/T/D	4.7	3.4
		(14) 1.6	(15) 4.4				(42) 1.9	(36) 2.0
		1.1	2.1				1.2	1.0
.4	.9	.6	.6	.8		Fixed/Worth	.7	.7
1.0	3.9	1.4	1.1	1.0			1.2	1.2
-3.7	-2.7	4.6	1.6	1.3			3.0	2.8
.4	1.6	.7	.3	.4		Debt/Worth	.5	.5
1.9	7.7	1.6	.7	1.1			1.4	1.1
-2.5	-8.8	5.6	1.8	4.1			4.4	4.3
	57.2	19.3	19.4	27.3		% Profit Before Taxes/Tangible Net Worth	48.1	37.8
	(26) 15.4	(50) 1.5	(40) 8.0	(12) 6.7			(153) 24.3	(175) 16.7
	-9.2	-20.3	2.5	-.6			6.7	3.4
18.7	13.1	9.0	8.6	7.5		% Profit Before Taxes/Total Assets	22.3	16.5
2.8	3.9	.7	4.3	3.5			9.4	6.4
-19.8	-3.1	-4.7	.8	-.3			1.9	.3
52.9	8.7	3.8	3.0	3.0		Sales/Net Fixed Assets	5.1	4.7
5.2	2.8	2.3	1.6	1.9			2.7	2.7
1.7	1.8	1.4	.9	.7			1.7	1.4
2.8	2.2	1.6	1.5	1.2		Sales/Total Assets	1.9	1.9
1.1	1.5	1.1	.9	.6			1.4	1.2
.9	.8	.7	.6	.3			.8	.8
	2.9	5.5	5.5	4.9		% Depr., Dep., Amort./Sales	4.5	4.3
	(33) 5.7	(52) 9.4	(41) 9.2	(12) 7.5			(159) 6.8	(181) 7.4
	14.5	16.3	15.4	11.7			11.5	12.6
	1.5	1.5	1.4			% Officers', Directors' Owners' Comp/Sales	1.8	1.9
	(21) 4.1	(20) 2.3	(10) 2.3				(59) 2.7	(62) 3.4
	8.3	4.4	3.1				6.4	6.7
5488M	81301M	357790M	975886M	668106M	1099144M	Net Sales ($)	4415077M	4411726M
3303M	47774M	313683M	910837M	853620M	1315005M	Total Assets ($)	3437926M	3710540M

Comparative Historical Data   Current Data Sorted by Sales

4/1/08-3/31/09 ALL	4/1/09-3/31/10 ALL	4/1/10-3/31/11 ALL	Type of Statement	0-1MM	1-3MM	3-5MM	5-10MM	10-25MM	25MM & OVER
29	30	31	Unqualified		1		6	9	15
41	30	30	Reviewed	3	5	3	10	6	3
27	28	28	Compiled	4	10	7	4	3	
28	31	22	Tax Returns	9	5	4	3	1	
61	57	68	Other	8	15	14	9	10	12
				23 (4/1-9/30/10)			156 (10/1/10-3/31/11)		
186	176	179	**NUMBER OF STATEMENTS**	24	36	28	32	29	30
%	%	%	**ASSETS**	%	%	%	%	%	%
9.2	11.7	10.6	Cash & Equivalents	10.0	12.2	9.1	11.3	9.3	11.3
16.4	13.7	15.2	Trade Receivables (net)	8.0	11.5	17.9	19.0	14.5	19.6
9.3	9.5	9.5	Inventory	10.5	14.8	9.9	5.0	5.5	10.4
2.4	3.4	2.8	All Other Current	9.6	.7	.6	3.2	1.3	2.6
37.3	38.3	38.1	Total Current	38.1	39.3	37.4	38.5	30.5	44.0
50.6	48.1	48.8	Fixed Assets (net)	45.5	51.1	51.5	50.6	51.6	41.8
3.4	4.0	3.0	Intangibles (net)	2.1	3.3	3.1	.8	6.1	2.3
8.6	9.5	10.2	All Other Non-Current	14.3	6.3	7.9	10.1	11.8	11.9
100.0	100.0	100.0	Total	100.0	100.0	100.0	100.0	100.0	100.0
			LIABILITIES						
6.3	5.1	6.6	Notes Payable-Short Term	17.6	6.4	4.4	4.2	5.6	3.7
7.4	6.9	7.1	Cur. Mat.-L.T.D.	7.8	7.4	11.3	8.0	4.3	4.3
7.5	6.7	8.6	Trade Payables	4.9	11.7	12.2	6.7	6.1	9.1
.3	.2	.2	Income Taxes Payable	.0	.0	.2	.4	.4	.1
7.7	6.8	6.6	All Other Current	10.5	11.5	4.6	4.0	2.8	6.1
29.3	25.7	29.2	Total Current	40.8	36.9	32.7	23.3	19.2	23.4
31.0	27.4	32.2	Long-Term Debt	63.3	35.2	38.5	21.0	21.2	20.5
.5	.5	.6	Deferred Taxes	.0	.4	.5	.0	1.0	1.6
5.3	5.7	5.1	All Other Non-Current	5.6	2.2	4.3	5.7	8.3	4.9
33.9	40.7	32.9	Net Worth	-9.8	25.3	24.0	50.0	50.3	49.7
100.0	100.0	100.0	Total Liabilties & Net Worth	100.0	100.0	100.0	100.0	100.0	100.0
			INCOME DATA						
100.0	100.0	100.0	Net Sales	100.0	100.0	100.0	100.0	100.0	100.0
30.7	34.2	34.3	Gross Profit	51.0	39.9	38.4	36.0	21.6	21.0
27.0	30.8	30.3	Operating Expenses	44.6	40.7	32.0	31.7	18.7	14.2
3.8	3.4	4.0	Operating Profit	6.3	-.8	6.4	4.3	2.9	6.7
2.3	2.1	1.7	All Other Expenses (net)	3.8	1.8	1.3	2.3	.4	.9
1.5	1.3	2.3	Profit Before Taxes	2.6	-2.6	5.1	2.0	2.5	5.8
			RATIOS						
2.6	3.6	2.9	Current	3.5	3.9	2.7	2.7	3.9	3.9
1.4	1.7	1.5		1.1	1.3	1.6	1.6	1.6	1.9
.8	.9	.8		.4	.6	.8	.9	.8	1.2
1.8	2.1	1.8	Quick	1.1	2.0	2.0	1.6	3.5	2.4
(185) 1.0	1.0	1.0		.5	.9	1.1	1.3	1.1	1.1
.5	.5	.5		.2	.3	.5	.6	.6	.7
25 14.8	26 13.8	23 15.8	Sales/Receivables	0 UND	16 23.0	23 16.0	30 12.0	34 10.7	39 9.4
40 9.1	41 8.9	40 9.1		20 18.3	34 10.9	36 10.0	52 7.0	42 8.8	58 6.2
60 6.1	59 6.1	67 5.5		45 8.1	59 6.2	79 4.6	70 5.2	67 5.4	75 4.9
0 UND	0 UND	3 145.2	Cost of Sales/Inventory	0 UND	0 UND	0 UND	0 UND	6 63.8	21 17.3
19 18.9	31 11.9	26 13.8		18 20.4	49 7.5	28 12.9	13 28.4	16 22.2	43 8.5
67 5.5	89 4.1	80 4.6		182 2.0	145 2.5	116 3.1	41 8.9	39 9.2	68 5.4
9 40.4	11 34.2	11 34.4	Cost of Sales/Payables	0 UND	7 49.2	8 44.3	12 29.9	10 35.3	18 20.7
19 18.8	24 15.5	24 15.3		16 23.1	42 8.6	27 13.7	24 15.3	17 21.1	24 15.0
43 8.5	51 7.1	55 6.6		50 7.4	92 4.0	99 3.7	42 8.6	33 11.0	43 8.5
4.8	3.1	3.8	Sales/Working Capital	2.1	4.3	5.8	3.4	4.0	3.0
13.1	8.5	11.3		NM	13.6	10.2	8.4	15.3	6.6
-19.6	-39.8	-20.2		-4.5	-6.8	-25.7	-50.1	-27.7	18.2
6.2	9.9	5.5	EBIT/Interest	3.0	3.6	6.4	4.5	11.5	16.3
(169) 2.0	(152) 1.9	(158) 2.1		(21) 1.1	(27) .8	(26) 3.2	(28) 2.1	(28) 2.5	(28) 4.2
.1	-.3	.0		-1.1	-1.9	.6	-3.0	1.4	1.7
3.0	3.9	4.8	Net Profit + Depr., Dep., Amort./Cur. Mat. L/T/D					12.6	4.5
(28) 1.9	(33) 1.9	(36) 1.8						(12) 4.3	(10) 2.1
.4	1.0	1.1						1.7	.6
.8	.6	.7	Fixed/Worth	.6	.9	1.0	.6	.6	.5
1.5	1.2	1.3		3.5	2.2	2.1	1.1	1.1	.8
4.9	3.0	5.3		-6.6	-3.1	-21.8	1.5	3.1	1.4
.7	.5	.6	Debt/Worth	1.2	.6	1.1	.5	.4	.3
1.7	1.3	1.6		9.1	2.6	4.3	1.0	.7	1.1
8.8	4.3	11.8		-8.1	-12.6	-29.3	1.8	3.0	2.2
29.0	20.6	23.1	% Profit Before Taxes/Tangible Net Worth	70.8	16.5	28.0	19.2	18.3	21.5
(152) 9.6	(149) 3.8	(144) 7.0		(15) 24.0	(25) -.1	(20) 3.3	(31) 4.9	(25) 6.4	(28) 11.7
-2.2	-7.8	-5.6		-7.5	-17.5	-20.2	-13.8	.4	3.4
11.8	9.7	9.6	% Profit Before Taxes/Total Assets	11.1	8.0	13.1	9.3	8.5	8.9
2.9	1.9	2.8		1.5	-.3	5.7	2.3	3.7	4.9
-2.4	-3.4	-2.5		-6.7	-5.8	-1.0	-5.2	.8	1.2
5.2	4.5	4.1	Sales/Net Fixed Assets	6.8	5.0	5.6	4.0	3.6	4.0
2.6	2.3	2.2		2.0	2.5	2.2	2.2	2.2	2.8
1.2	1.0	1.2		1.0	1.0	1.5	1.0	1.2	1.7
1.9	1.6	1.6	Sales/Total Assets	1.2	1.6	1.8	1.7	1.7	1.6
1.3	1.0	1.0		.9	1.0	1.3	.9	1.0	1.1
.7	.6	.6		.5	.6	.8	.6	.7	.6
4.0	4.5	4.7	% Depr., Dep., Amort./Sales	5.4	3.4	7.6	5.2	4.6	4.7
(167) 7.7	(155) 8.4	(152) 8.7		(16) 15.7	(28) 6.7	(24) 11.0	(30) 9.7	8.0	(25) 5.5
13.1	16.4	14.5		24.0	16.7	14.6	15.4	11.7	8.7
1.4	1.5	1.5	% Officers', Directors' Owners' Comp/Sales	2.5	2.8	1.5	1.5		
(57) 3.5	(45) 3.2	(56) 2.7		(10) 7.4	(13) 7.5	(11) 2.3	(11) 2.1		
6.6	8.2	7.4		8.8	18.4	3.0	3.1		
3706324M	3433877M	3187715M	Net Sales ($)	10800M	63521M	112977M	243375M	491587M	2265455M
3312624M	3224234M	3444222M	Total Assets ($)	14637M	82768M	113910M	319396M	636377M	2277134M

M = $ thousand   MM = $ million
See Pages 9 through 22 for Explanation of Ratios and Data

Current Data Sorted by Assets   Comparative Historical Data

						Type of Statement		
		1	2	5	7	Unqualified	9	19
	2	5	5	1		Reviewed	11	12
1	4	6	3			Compiled	10	18
7	11	11	2			Tax Returns	10	7
2	12	14	24	10	5	Other	38	51
	14 (4/1-9/30/10)		121 (10/1/10-3/31/11)				4/1/06-3/31/07 ALL	4/1/07-3/31/08 ALL
0-500M	500M-2MM	2-10MM	10-50MM	50-100MM	100-250MM			
10	29	32	36	16	12	NUMBER OF STATEMENTS	78	107
%	%	%	%	%	%	**ASSETS**	%	%
23.3	11.3	16.1	9.7	6.3	7.3	Cash & Equivalents	13.1	12.0
16.9	23.5	19.5	23.6	14.4	9.9	Trade Receivables (net)	20.9	17.7
3.7	5.3	5.8	4.8	6.2	4.5	Inventory	4.3	3.7
.6	2.6	8.4	4.5	3.1	4.9	All Other Current	3.3	3.5
44.4	42.7	49.7	42.6	30.0	26.5	Total Current	41.6	36.9
39.1	48.1	39.9	47.7	63.4	70.7	Fixed Assets (net)	47.6	52.0
9.4	.7	1.7	5.1	3.8	1.4	Intangibles (net)	1.6	4.9
7.1	8.5	8.7	4.5	2.9	1.4	All Other Non-Current	9.2	6.2
100.0	100.0	100.0	100.0	100.0	100.0	Total	100.0	100.0
						LIABILITIES		
15.7	5.8	7.0	3.2	7.0	.8	Notes Payable-Short Term	5.5	6.5
23.4	7.6	7.4	8.4	5.3	4.0	Cur. Mat.-L.T.D.	4.0	5.7
13.9	6.7	9.7	14.4	8.4	6.5	Trade Payables	8.9	7.9
.0	.0	.1	.5	.0	.2	Income Taxes Payable	.4	.3
4.8	8.2	8.7	7.5	9.5	8.4	All Other Current	11.1	8.8
57.8	28.3	32.9	34.0	30.3	19.9	Total Current	29.9	29.2
60.7	39.1	23.7	15.4	44.1	22.6	Long-Term Debt	23.0	22.5
.0	.2	.7	.4	4.6	1.6	Deferred Taxes	.3	.9
4.1	6.3	3.9	2.6	6.5	4.0	All Other Non-Current	9.9	5.9
-22.7	26.2	38.8	47.6	14.6	52.0	Net Worth	36.8	41.6
100.0	100.0	100.0	100.0	100.0	100.0	Total Liabilties & Net Worth	100.0	100.0
						INCOME DATA		
100.0	100.0	100.0	100.0	100.0	100.0	Net Sales	100.0	100.0
						Gross Profit		
94.5	84.8	83.6	91.7	94.9	89.7	Operating Expenses	80.5	84.9
5.5	15.2	16.4	8.3	5.1	10.3	Operating Profit	19.5	15.1
1.8	2.3	2.1	1.6	5.5	4.0	All Other Expenses (net)	1.8	1.9
3.6	12.9	14.3	6.7	-.4	6.3	Profit Before Taxes	17.7	13.2
						RATIOS		
3.0	4.2	2.6	2.0	2.3	1.7		2.6	2.2
1.2	1.8	1.9	1.3	1.0	1.2	Current	1.6	1.3
.3	.5	.9	.8	.6	.9		.8	.7
2.1	2.9	2.1	1.6	1.6	1.5		2.3	1.9
1.2	1.1	1.3	1.0	.6	.8	Quick	1.2	1.1
.2	.3	.6	.5	.3	.5		.7	.6
0 UND	0 UND	22 16.7	31 11.7	50 7.3	53 6.8		23 16.2	19 19.3
3 131.4	25 14.4	40 9.1	59 6.2	65 5.6	65 5.6	Sales/Receivables	46 8.0	49 7.4
31 11.8	62 5.9	72 5.1	89 4.1	83 4.4	75 4.8		67 5.4	71 5.1
						Cost of Sales/Inventory		
						Cost of Sales/Payables		
13.4	6.3	3.4	4.7	4.7	3.6		7.2	5.6
NM	17.3	7.9	17.6	NM	15.4	Sales/Working Capital	12.5	17.7
-4.4	-8.9	-31.5	-25.2	-5.3	-39.4		-25.4	-11.5
25.6	12.1	21.7	13.1	7.2	12.6		28.9	17.3
3.7	(23) 5.6	(28) 9.0	(33) 4.3	(13) 1.7	1.7	EBIT/Interest	(69) 10.1	(93) 6.8
-2.8	.7	1.6	-2.1	-.6	-.7		4.0	2.2
						Net Profit + Depr., Dep.,	11.2	18.6
						Amort./Cur. Mat. L/T/D	(12) 6.5	(19) 9.3
							4.8	2.1
1.5	.8	.2	.6	.9	1.0		.4	.8
NM	1.7	1.2	1.1	1.9	1.5	Fixed/Worth	1.1	1.3
-.3	17.4	3.0	2.5	2.7	2.1		3.1	3.4
4.6	1.0	.7	.8	.6	.5		.4	.6
NM	1.6	1.7	1.0	1.6	.9	Debt/Worth	1.2	1.7
-2.2	36.4	10.3	2.8	2.7	2.2		4.6	6.7
	144.3	67.6	45.3	18.8	19.0	% Profit Before Taxes/Tangible	86.8	77.8
(24) 42.7		(29) 33.1	(34) 9.8	(15) 6.2	3.0	Net Worth	(72) 49.5	(90) 42.0
4.9		8.4	-5.5	-8.5	-5.3		23.6	18.5
70.7	40.0	29.5	18.5	8.0	9.2	% Profit Before Taxes/Total	31.5	25.6
17.3	10.7	11.3	4.5	2.2	1.3	Assets	14.5	12.5
-18.6	1.6	2.0	-1.5	-3.0	-3.1		7.4	3.9
23.7	15.2	18.5	8.4	2.2	1.2		8.6	5.4
8.7	4.7	4.3	2.3	.9	.7	Sales/Net Fixed Assets	3.7	2.4
6.0	2.2	1.8	1.2	.6	.4		1.5	1.2
6.5	3.4	2.0	1.6	1.1	.7		2.4	2.0
3.5	2.0	1.4	1.2	.7	.5	Sales/Total Assets	1.6	1.3
2.7	1.3	1.0	.6	.5	.4		1.0	.6
	3.1	3.5	5.0	8.0		% Depr., Dep., Amort./Sales	2.5	3.0
(16)	5.5	(24) 7.5	(34) 8.1	(13) 13.0			(58) 5.7	(86) 7.0
	12.0	13.8	16.2	23.3			9.6	11.8
	3.9					% Officers', Directors'	.7	1.4
(13)	6.3					Owners' Comp/Sales	(22) 2.7	(25) 2.8
	8.6						6.1	5.9
11236M	83048M	270014M	1445229M	890889M	996857M	Net Sales ($)	2274329M	3104123M
2490M	32812M	165229M	787679M	1100779M	1904860M	Total Assets ($)	1606205M	3036347M

Comparative Historical Data / Current Data Sorted by Sales

Hist 1	Hist 2	Hist 3	Type of Statement	0-1MM	1-3MM	3-5MM	5-10MM	10-25MM	25MM & OVER
18	18	15	Unqualified				2	1	12
13	13	13	Reviewed		1	4	1	3	4
8	11	14	Compiled		5	4	3	1	1
16	19	26	Tax Returns	3	9	7	1	4	2
72	64	67	Other	8	7	4	10	13	25
4/1/08-3/31/09 ALL	4/1/09-3/31/10 ALL	4/1/10-3/31/11 ALL		14 (4/1-9/30/10)		121 (10/1/10-3/31/11)			
127	125	135	NUMBER OF STATEMENTS	11	22	19	17	22	44
%	%	%	ASSETS	%	%	%	%	%	%
9.8	10.5	12.0	Cash & Equivalents	9.2	22.9	11.5	17.5	8.6	6.9
17.5	18.5	19.8	Trade Receivables (net)	7.8	18.8	22.7	20.3	24.5	19.5
4.3	7.6	5.2	Inventory	.7	1.9	7.6	6.7	3.1	7.4
3.1	3.7	4.6	All Other Current	.0	3.3	5.6	6.6	7.8	3.5
34.6	40.3	41.5	Total Current	17.7	46.9	47.4	51.1	44.1	37.3
53.0	48.2	49.2	Fixed Assets (net)	61.9	42.2	46.4	43.0	44.5	55.5
4.0	5.0	3.2	Intangibles (net)	9.6	1.0	.1	2.4	3.7	4.0
8.4	6.5	6.1	All Other Non-Current	10.8	9.9	6.1	3.5	7.7	3.1
100.0	100.0	100.0	Total	100.0	100.0	100.0	100.0	100.0	100.0
			LIABILITIES						
7.5	5.2	5.8	Notes Payable-Short Term	11.9	4.5	4.9	4.9	9.0	4.1
6.1	8.2	8.3	Cur. Mat.-L.T.D.	12.1	11.2	10.6	5.4	7.6	6.5
9.7	8.7	10.2	Trade Payables	12.5	5.4	7.8	7.9	12.3	12.8
.2	.1	.2	Income Taxes Payable	.0	.0	.0	.1	.3	.4
8.3	7.6	8.0	All Other Current	6.6	11.5	5.1	10.8	5.4	8.2
31.8	29.8	32.6	Total Current	43.2	32.6	28.4	29.2	34.6	32.0
25.5	26.7	29.8	Long-Term Debt	48.5	41.0	33.6	27.1	12.3	27.8
.7	1.1	1.0	Deferred Taxes	.0	.3	1.1	.2	.3	2.2
4.2	8.1	4.4	All Other Non-Current	7.6	4.8	4.7	5.1	2.1	4.1
37.8	34.4	32.2	Net Worth	.7	21.3	32.2	38.4	50.6	33.8
100.0	100.0	100.0	Total Liabilties & Net Worth	100.0	100.0	100.0	100.0	100.0	100.0
			INCOME DATA						
100.0	100.0	100.0	Net Sales	100.0	100.0	100.0	100.0	100.0	100.0
			Gross Profit						
85.1	92.5	88.7	Operating Expenses	66.3	87.1	92.4	90.0	89.0	92.8
14.9	7.5	11.3	Operating Profit	33.7	12.9	7.6	10.0	11.0	7.2
3.2	2.2	2.6	All Other Expenses (net)	11.2	-.2	2.3	1.9	.6	3.1
11.8	5.3	8.7	Profit Before Taxes	22.5	13.0	5.3	8.1	10.4	4.1
			RATIOS						
2.0	2.8	2.5	Current	.7	4.2	2.8	3.0	2.0	1.7
1.1	1.3	1.4		.3	2.2	2.0	1.9	1.5	1.2
.6	.8	.7		.1	.9	1.0	.8	.6	.8
1.7	2.1	1.9	Quick	.7	3.2	2.3	2.0	1.6	1.6
.8	.9	1.0		.3	1.8	1.4	1.2	1.2	.7
.5	.5	.4		.1	.5	.9	.4	.5	.4
12 31.1	25 14.8	22 16.6	Sales/Receivables	0 UND	0 UND	21 17.0	32 11.4	28 13.2	45 8.1
38 9.7	44 8.3	48 7.6		15 23.9	17 20.9	47 7.7	44 8.3	56 6.5	63 5.8
63 5.8	70 5.2	70 5.2		29 12.5	52 7.0	74 5.0	99 3.7	83 4.4	76 4.8
			Cost of Sales/Inventory						
			Cost of Sales/Payables						
6.1	5.1	5.0	Sales/Working Capital	-8.3	6.2	3.0	3.0	5.5	4.9
86.8	15.5	16.1		-2.8	13.1	9.0	5.9	12.2	20.6
-8.7	-18.6	-9.5		-2.5	-86.0	-331.2	-37.4	-9.0	-13.2
19.0	9.6	13.0	EBIT/Interest		22.5	10.2	11.9	38.2	11.1
(113) 5.2	(106) 2.1	(119) 4.3			(15) 5.6	(17) 2.2	1.5	10.8	(39) 3.8
1.7	-.5	.6			-1.6	.0	-3.6	1.9	.8
6.1	4.6	4.8	Net Profit + Depr., Dep., Amort./Cur. Mat. L/T/D						
(22) 2.6	(21) 2.4	(21) 1.8							
2.0	1.4	.9							
.7	.6	.8	Fixed/Worth	1.7	.7	.7	.3	.4	.9
1.4	1.4	1.4		11.1	1.8	1.7	1.0	.9	1.5
4.0	3.4	2.9		-1.9	10.8	7.4	2.1	2.4	2.7
.6	.6	.7	Debt/Worth	4.2	.5	.8	.6	.7	.7
1.4	1.4	1.5		11.0	2.2	1.6	1.2	1.2	1.5
4.8	5.8	6.4		-4.3	32.8	11.5	9.9	2.1	2.7
65.8	47.8	58.0	% Profit Before Taxes/Tangible Net Worth		220.7	85.3	34.0	63.1	32.2
(109) 30.5	(107) 10.7	(119) 18.1		(18) 59.4	(16) 8.2	(15) 6.9	(21) 37.1	(42) 10.6	
6.4	-5.1	-1.2			6.5	-1.9	-10.7	4.6	-2.6
25.0	14.6	22.0	% Profit Before Taxes/Total Assets	13.7	42.8	22.0	41.2	26.9	9.0
10.4	5.4	6.7		5.7	17.6	4.4	2.4	12.4	4.3
.6	-4.4	-1.1		3.8	3.9	-2.0	-1.4	2.2	-1.2
6.8	8.1	9.5	Sales/Net Fixed Assets	5.7	16.5	14.1	10.0	15.0	3.5
2.7	2.7	2.7		.9	6.4	4.4	2.6	3.3	1.8
1.2	1.1	1.1		.3	3.3	1.4	1.1	1.5	.7
2.1	2.2	2.1	Sales/Total Assets	2.6	3.8	2.7	1.6	2.2	1.6
1.4	1.1	1.3		.8	2.4	1.6	1.0	1.5	.9
.7	.6	.6		.3	1.7	.9	.5	.8	.5
3.9	3.7	4.2	% Depr., Dep., Amort./Sales		2.7	2.7	4.4	4.9	4.2
(103) 8.0	(89) 9.1	(98) 7.9		(14) 5.5	(14) 5.8	(14) 8.7	(19) 8.2	(31) 9.3	
14.3	13.6	14.7			11.9	12.3	28.2	15.9	14.9
1.4	1.1	1.1	% Officers', Directors' Owners' Comp/Sales						
(30) 4.3	(30) 4.6	(33) 4.1							
8.7	10.6	8.6							
3264442M	3106694M	3697273M	Net Sales ($)	5787M	42335M	77518M	130204M	343582M	3097847M
3181116M	3491082M	3993849M	Total Assets ($)	11646M	27606M	63950M	228313M	285225M	3377109M

M = $ thousand   MM = $ million
See Pages 9 through 22 for Explanation of Ratios and Data

Current Data Sorted by Assets   **Comparative Historical Data**

0-500M	500M-2MM	2-10MM	10-50MM	50-100MM	100-250MM	Type of Statement	4/1/06-3/31/07 ALL	4/1/07-3/31/08 ALL
	1	4	39	18	23	Unqualified	59	79
	4	18	18	3	1	Reviewed	24	27
2	10	18	5	2	1	Compiled	41	40
8	18	12	4			Tax Returns	21	27
10	33	91	89	41	28	Other	145	177
	76 (4/1-9/30/10)		425 (10/1/10-3/31/11)					
20	66	143	155	64	53	**NUMBER OF STATEMENTS**	290	350
%	%	%	%	%	%	**ASSETS**	%	%
31.0	17.1	10.1	9.1	7.6	6.3	Cash & Equivalents	10.0	10.1
13.9	24.0	30.1	29.6	17.5	20.5	Trade Receivables (net)	28.4	28.1
5.3	8.6	7.3	6.7	11.0	9.8	Inventory	6.6	7.2
4.3	2.8	3.4	4.8	3.1	3.9	All Other Current	5.6	5.5
54.5	52.4	51.0	50.1	39.3	40.5	Total Current	50.6	50.9
36.0	37.8	39.1	38.2	40.9	41.6	Fixed Assets (net)	39.7	39.2
3.6	2.6	4.1	5.8	14.1	14.4	Intangibles (net)	4.0	4.7
6.0	7.1	5.8	5.9	5.7	3.5	All Other Non-Current	5.6	5.2
100.0	100.0	100.0	100.0	100.0	100.0	Total	100.0	100.0
						LIABILITIES		
19.4	9.4	7.9	5.8	5.2	4.1	Notes Payable-Short Term	8.9	8.2
10.8	6.1	5.5	5.1	5.3	3.8	Cur. Mat.-L.T.D.	3.4	4.8
14.1	7.7	12.7	11.9	8.4	10.5	Trade Payables	11.2	10.7
.0	.0	.5	.4	.4	.8	Income Taxes Payable	.7	.7
8.2	11.5	10.1	9.0	6.1	5.6	All Other Current	9.9	10.0
52.4	34.9	36.7	32.1	25.5	24.8	Total Current	34.0	34.3
9.8	23.3	16.0	16.8	22.3	16.0	Long-Term Debt	17.8	20.6
.0	.0	.7	1.0	2.1	2.7	Deferred Taxes	.9	1.0
13.2	4.9	6.5	4.7	5.4	5.8	All Other Non-Current	3.6	4.5
24.7	36.9	40.2	45.4	44.7	50.7	Net Worth	43.7	39.6
100.0	100.0	100.0	100.0	100.0	100.0	Total Liabilities & Net Worth	100.0	100.0
						INCOME DATA		
100.0	100.0	100.0	100.0	100.0	100.0	Net Sales	100.0	100.0
						Gross Profit		
91.1	90.5	90.4	89.4	91.3	87.7	Operating Expenses	83.8	86.7
8.9	9.5	9.6	10.6	8.7	12.3	Operating Profit	16.2	13.3
.8	.5	2.5	2.4	5.0	4.1	All Other Expenses (net)	2.1	1.7
8.1	9.0	7.1	8.2	3.8	8.2	Profit Before Taxes	14.1	11.6
						RATIOS		
6.7	5.0	2.4	2.8	2.6	2.6	Current	2.7	2.7
1.6	2.3	1.5	1.5	1.5	1.6		1.6	1.5
.5	1.0	.8	1.0	.9	1.2		1.0	1.0
6.2	4.1	2.0	2.1	1.6	1.9	Quick	2.0	2.1
1.6	1.8	1.1	1.2	.9	1.0		1.2	1.1
.3	.8	.6	.7	.7	.7		.7	.6
0 UND	0 UND	32 11.5	42 8.6	42 8.6	51 7.1	Sales/Receivables	35 10.4	34 10.7
0 UND	20 17.9	58 6.3	62 5.9	60 6.1	68 5.4		58 6.2	56 6.6
33 11.0	51 7.1	79 4.6	85 4.3	76 4.8	91 4.0		83 4.4	72 5.1
						Cost of Sales/Inventory		
						Cost of Sales/Payables		
6.2	5.2	5.8	4.1	3.5	4.0	Sales/Working Capital	5.3	5.2
269.9	11.8	12.6	9.7	10.7	6.8		10.8	13.5
-9.5	NM	-37.0	-181.7	-48.2	23.8		222.5	-272.5
129.2	54.1	18.9	23.7	5.4	12.2	EBIT/Interest	30.7	24.6
(11) 31.2	(50) 5.5	(126) 5.3	(140) 6.8	(52) 2.4	(48) 5.2		(241) 9.6	(313) 8.1
2.3	1.4	.4	2.3	.0	2.5		3.1	2.9
		7.4	5.7	3.2	4.2	Net Profit + Depr., Dep., Amort./Cur. Mat. L/T/D	10.1	13.2
		(17) 2.3	(43) 2.1	(16) 1.3	(14) 2.2		(66) 3.4	(77) 4.2
		1.4	1.0	.4	.7		1.3	1.4
.1	.1	.4	.3	.6	.7	Fixed/Worth	.4	.4
1.0	.8	.9	.9	1.4	1.1		.9	1.1
4.0	4.5	2.5	2.3	3.6	2.6		2.0	2.3
.2	.4	.5	.6	.6	.5	Debt/Worth	.6	.7
2.0	1.5	1.4	1.6	1.6	2.1		1.5	1.6
NM	6.2	5.6	-3.3	6.3	3.9		3.5	4.3
291.9	91.1	60.1	53.1	34.3	39.8	% Profit Before Taxes/Tangible Net Worth	69.8	78.7
(15) 68.9	(54) 23.6	(122) 26.6	(146) 26.3	(54) 15.2	(48) 26.4		(268) 43.8	(311) 44.7
-73.8	2.7	6.6	8.7	-1.7	7.5		17.4	22.4
181.4	37.5	28.5	21.1	11.6	13.5	% Profit Before Taxes/Total Assets	30.0	28.6
33.0	12.7	10.0	8.3	4.9	7.0		15.4	15.5
-53.4	1.4	-.6	2.0	-3.7	2.6		4.9	5.2
178.8	41.0	21.9	14.1	7.7	4.8	Sales/Net Fixed Assets	14.9	17.3
28.9	7.3	5.4	3.9	2.2	2.5		4.8	5.1
9.0	3.3	1.8	2.0	1.4	1.0		2.1	2.1
13.4	4.0	2.7	2.0	1.3	1.2	Sales/Total Assets	2.7	2.7
5.2	2.5	1.8	1.4	.9	.8		1.7	1.7
2.1	1.5	1.0	.9	.6	.6		.9	1.0
	1.7	1.1	2.0	4.3	.4	% Depr., Dep., Amort./Sales	1.5	1.1
	(37) 5.6	(103) 4.8	(140) 5.1	(48) 8.1	(29) 4.0		(227) 3.7	(276) 3.4
	13.0	12.9	10.2	11.7	9.4		6.4	7.3
1.8	2.4	1.2	.5			% Officers', Directors' Owners' Comp/Sales	1.3	1.0
(11) 4.1	(26) 5.0	(49) 2.8	(12) 1.9				(62) 3.1	(77) 2.4
6.7	8.0	5.0	5.7				11.5	6.5
42776M	262958M	1624613M	6560076M	4971682M	11131441M	Net Sales ($)	12171108M	19467672M
5070M	85268M	775006M	3639197M	4589890M	8532847M	Total Assets ($)	9428953M	11894206M

M = $ thousand   MM = $ million
See Pages 9 through 22 for Explanation of Ratios and Data

Comparative Historical Data | | | | **Current Data Sorted by Sales** | | | | | |

Hist 1	Hist 2	Hist 3	Type of Statement						
86	80	85	Unqualified	1		1	4	12	67
34	36	44	Reviewed	1	2	5	7	14	15
45	36	38	Compiled	3	7	5	11	5	7
19	32	42	Tax Returns	3	10	6	17	3	3
195	226	292	Other	14	26	21	40	68	123
4/1/08-3/31/09 ALL	4/1/09-3/31/10 ALL	4/1/10-3/31/11 ALL		76 (4/1-9/30/10)			425 (10/1/10-3/31/11)		
				0-1MM	1-3MM	3-5MM	5-10MM	10-25MM	25MM & OVER
379	410	501	NUMBER OF STATEMENTS	22	45	38	79	102	215
%	%	%	**ASSETS**	%	%	%	%	%	%
8.6	10.8	10.8	Cash & Equivalents	12.7	15.9	18.4	12.2	10.4	7.9
27.3	20.7	25.9	Trade Receivables (net)	13.8	22.7	21.2	25.6	26.9	28.2
7.7	6.7	8.0	Inventory	2.0	5.8	8.1	8.7	7.3	9.0
5.1	3.5	3.8	All Other Current	6.0	4.8	1.5	3.1	3.7	4.1
48.7	41.7	48.4	Total Current	34.6	49.2	49.2	49.6	48.3	49.2
40.0	43.7	39.0	Fixed Assets (net)	57.3	40.8	40.6	41.3	36.2	36.9
5.2	7.5	6.8	Intangibles (net)	1.9	3.8	4.0	2.1	8.7	9.2
6.1	7.1	5.8	All Other Non-Current	6.3	6.1	6.2	6.9	6.7	4.7
100.0	100.0	100.0	Total	100.0	100.0	100.0	100.0	100.0	100.0
			LIABILITIES						
7.6	7.1	7.2	Notes Payable-Short Term	8.3	10.4	8.3	9.5	4.7	6.5
4.8	5.2	5.5	Cur. Mat.-L.T.D.	3.3	9.5	5.1	6.8	4.7	4.7
11.4	9.6	11.1	Trade Payables	7.2	9.7	7.3	10.7	10.6	12.9
.6	.3	.4	Income Taxes Payable	.0	.2	.1	.2	.5	.5
8.5	8.9	8.9	All Other Current	7.1	16.3	10.1	6.2	10.9	7.3
32.9	31.1	33.0	Total Current	26.0	46.1	30.9	33.5	31.4	31.9
20.0	21.5	17.8	Long-Term Debt	24.5	22.1	19.3	19.2	16.5	16.0
1.0	1.2	1.1	Deferred Taxes	.0	.0	.5	1.0	.8	1.7
4.2	6.7	5.8	All Other Non-Current	12.7	7.6	5.0	6.1	4.4	5.3
41.9	39.5	42.4	Net Worth	36.9	24.2	44.3	40.3	46.9	45.2
100.0	100.0	100.0	Total Liabilities & Net Worth	100.0	100.0	100.0	100.0	100.0	100.0
			INCOME DATA						
100.0	100.0	100.0	Net Sales	100.0	100.0	100.0	100.0	100.0	100.0
			Gross Profit						
87.4	92.0	90.0	Operating Expenses	85.9	86.9	91.2	92.9	88.9	90.2
12.6	8.0	10.0	Operating Profit	14.1	13.1	8.8	7.1	11.1	9.8
1.8	2.8	2.6	All Other Expenses (net)	3.9	1.9	1.8	1.7	3.7	2.6
10.8	5.2	7.4	Profit Before Taxes	10.2	11.2	7.0	5.4	7.4	7.2
			RATIOS						
2.6	2.6	3.0		8.6	4.0	3.3	2.8	3.2	2.5
1.6	1.4	1.6	Current	2.4	1.3	1.6	1.5	1.7	1.5
1.0	.8	1.0		.4	.6	.8	.9	1.1	1.1
1.9	2.0	2.3		5.7	3.8	3.1	2.5	2.5	1.9
(378) 1.1	1.1	1.1	Quick	1.6	1.0	1.3	1.0	1.3	1.1
.7	.5	.7		.1	.4	.6	.6	.7	.7
31 11.8	28 13.2	33 11.0		0 UND	0 UND	11 32.1	28 13.0	38 9.5	43 8.5
54 6.8	49 7.4	57 6.4	Sales/Receivables	0 UND	28 12.9	59 6.2	48 7.5	59 6.2	61 6.0
79 4.6	69 5.3	78 4.7		46 8.0	103 3.6	75 4.8	80 4.6	81 4.5	78 4.7
			Cost of Sales/Inventory						
			Cost of Sales/Payables						
5.1	5.3	4.4		2.9	3.8	4.1	6.3	4.1	4.5
11.3	13.8	10.7	Sales/Working Capital	6.6	24.1	9.2	12.4	10.0	10.1
-363.3	-18.7	-166.3		-3.6	-15.3	-11.4	-51.4	77.6	76.2
23.9	12.7	20.4		31.8	18.2	53.2	15.2	24.3	18.3
(332) 7.7	(354) 3.3	(427) 5.2	EBIT/Interest	(10) 1.7	(38) 5.7	(32) 5.8	(66) 3.7	(90) 5.2	(191) 5.2
2.5	.1	1.4		-2.6	.6	.7	-.8	1.4	2.1
10.2	4.9	5.1						5.9	4.9
(88) 3.4	(84) 2.3	(92) 2.0	Net Profit + Depr., Dep., Amort./Cur. Mat. L/T/D					(22) 2.1	(58) 2.0
1.6	1.2	1.0						1.1	1.0
.4	.5	.4		.5	.4	.2	.3	.3	.5
1.1	1.4	1.0	Fixed/Worth	2.0	1.3	.7	1.1	.9	1.1
2.9	4.0	2.6		6.8	-5.7	2.2	2.4	2.4	2.3
.7	.7	.5		.2	.4	.4	.5	.5	.6
1.7	1.8	1.6	Debt/Worth	1.9	2.2	1.2	1.6	1.3	1.7
4.2	6.1	4.1		8.1	-13.2	3.4	3.9	3.3	3.8
69.8	45.5	55.5		32.4	106.4	72.6	62.8	56.8	51.1
(341) 36.2	(346) 15.8	(439) 25.5	% Profit Before Taxes/Tangible Net Worth	(19) 8.7	(31) 32.6	(34) 24.5	(71) 17.7	(90) 22.8	(194) 26.8
12.8	-2.3	6.7		-10.4	2.9	4.6	-5.6	9.3	7.7
26.7	16.4	22.9		25.8	35.4	28.0	26.6	24.1	18.8
12.4	4.7	8.3	% Profit Before Taxes/Total Assets	2.9	11.0	8.9	8.8	9.8	8.3
3.5	-1.9	1.2		-10.9	-.3	1.2	-1.4	1.1	2.0
16.7	12.6	18.1		9.0	28.9	30.9	20.1	19.6	15.7
4.2	3.0	4.4	Sales/Net Fixed Assets	1.7	4.9	5.2	6.2	4.4	3.9
1.8	1.4	1.8		.4	1.9	1.5	1.7	2.0	1.9
2.6	2.3	2.5		2.0	2.4	2.6	3.3	2.1	2.2
1.6	1.3	1.5	Sales/Total Assets	.7	1.5	1.4	2.0	1.5	1.4
.9	.7	.8		.2	1.0	.8	1.0	.9	.8
1.1	2.0	1.8		5.7	4.9	1.1	2.6	1.7	1.2
(297) 3.9	(303) 5.7	(366) 5.3	% Depr., Dep., Amort./Sales	(16) 15.2	(24) 11.9	(26) 5.0	(52) 6.1	(85) 6.2	(163) 4.0
8.0	12.5	10.8		26.4	21.8	18.0	12.0	10.7	7.8
1.6	1.3	1.2			3.2	2.7	1.9	.8	.5
(66) 3.1	(88) 3.4	(109) 2.9	% Officers', Directors' Owners' Comp/Sales		(15) 5.6	(18) 4.3	(30) 3.0	(18) 1.9	(23) .8
7.0	8.5	5.8			9.5	6.5	5.7	4.0	2.0
22856599M	17491067M	24593546M	Net Sales ($)	11397M	90931M	150096M	575738M	1748142M	22017242M
14725459M	17354542M	17627278M	Total Assets ($)	25675M	101251M	142628M	497030M	1657802M	15202892M

M = $ thousand   MM = $ million
See Pages 9 through 22 for Explanation of Ratios and Data

UTILITIES

Current Data Sorted by Assets   Comparative Historical Data

0-500M	500M-2MM	2-10MM	10-50MM	50-100MM	100-250MM	Type of Statement	4/1/06-3/31/07 ALL	4/1/07-3/31/08 ALL
1		18	55	40	37	Unqualified	343	308
	3	9	1	1		Reviewed	19	12
	2	1	1		1	Compiled	7	9
3	3	5		1	1	Tax Returns	5	4
5	4	14	20	16	13	Other	39	58
	52 (4/1-9/30/10)		202 (10/1/10-3/31/11)					
9	12	47	77	57	52	**NUMBER OF STATEMENTS**	413	391
%	%	%	%	%	%	**ASSETS**	%	%
	28.9	11.6	10.0	5.2	6.6	Cash & Equivalents	7.8	6.9
	17.1	16.8	11.4	6.8	11.1	Trade Receivables (net)	10.0	9.7
	2.9	6.7	4.1	3.4	1.9	Inventory	2.3	2.6
	2.7	3.6	2.6	1.8	3.0	All Other Current	2.7	2.2
	51.6	38.7	28.0	17.2	22.7	Total Current	22.8	21.3
	36.6	45.2	57.4	66.1	61.3	Fixed Assets (net)	63.3	64.7
	2.0	4.1	4.4	1.3	1.8	Intangibles (net)	2.0	2.2
	9.7	12.0	10.2	15.4	14.2	All Other Non-Current	11.9	11.8
	100.0	100.0	100.0	100.0	100.0	Total	100.0	100.0
						LIABILITIES		
	9.2	4.6	2.4	3.6	2.5	Notes Payable-Short Term	2.7	2.5
	3.8	3.4	1.9	2.4	1.7	Cur. Mat.-L.T.D.	2.2	2.9
	7.5	12.8	6.7	5.3	6.5	Trade Payables	6.5	6.6
	.0	.2	.4	.1	.2	Income Taxes Payable	.4	.4
	7.8	14.5	7.8	3.9	8.9	All Other Current	5.4	5.2
	28.3	35.4	19.2	15.4	19.9	Total Current	17.3	17.6
	45.8	23.2	29.2	34.3	33.7	Long-Term Debt	36.3	37.1
	.0	2.1	1.3	.9	1.7	Deferred Taxes	.9	.7
	8.4	9.0	5.9	9.4	5.6	All Other Non-Current	5.2	5.2
	17.6	30.4	44.5	40.1	39.2	Net Worth	40.3	39.4
	100.0	100.0	100.0	100.0	100.0	Total Liabilities & Net Worth	100.0	100.0
						INCOME DATA		
	100.0	100.0	100.0	100.0	100.0	Net Sales	100.0	100.0
						Gross Profit		
	86.5	86.1	88.4	91.8	88.0	Operating Expenses	90.2	89.1
	13.5	13.9	11.6	8.2	12.0	Operating Profit	9.8	10.9
	6.4	3.8	2.3	1.4	3.8	All Other Expenses (net)	2.9	2.8
	7.1	10.1	9.3	6.8	8.2	Profit Before Taxes	7.0	8.1
						RATIOS		
	2.4	1.8	2.2	1.8	1.5		1.8	1.7
	2.0	1.3	1.7	1.1	1.1	Current	1.2	1.1
	.4	.8	1.0	.8	.7		.8	.8
	2.2	1.5	1.7	1.2	1.4		1.4	1.3
	1.8	.9	1.0	.8	.9	Quick	.9	.8
	.3	.4	.6	.6	.5		.5	.5
0 UND		13 29.1	28 13.2	25 14.7	26 14.0		26 13.8	26 14.3
33 11.1		39 9.3	40 9.2	34 10.7	37 9.8	Sales/Receivables	36 10.2	36 10.2
53 6.9		58 6.3	53 6.9	41 8.9	52 7.1		47 7.8	46 7.9
						Cost of Sales/Inventory		
						Cost of Sales/Payables		
	3.3	6.7	4.3	7.2	11.2		7.4	8.9
	9.1	16.6	9.2	54.3	37.0	Sales/Working Capital	33.7	46.0
	-12.4	-30.5	-98.2	-18.3	-12.5		-20.5	-18.4
		15.0	7.8	4.2	6.3		3.8	4.0
	(39) 4.3	(70) 3.7	(56) 2.8	(50) 3.2		EBIT/Interest	(384) 2.4	(358) 2.4
		.9	2.2	2.0	2.2		1.6	1.7
		53.5	20.3	12.7			6.8	7.0
		(11) 2.7	(17) 3.6	(10) 3.2		Net Profit + Depr., Dep., Amort./Cur. Mat. L/T/D	(57) 3.3	(52) 3.7
		1.2	1.5	1.2			2.2	1.5
	.0	1.0	1.0	1.2	1.1		1.2	1.1
	.6	2.2	1.4	1.6	1.7	Fixed/Worth	1.8	1.8
	4.6	4.7	2.4	2.1	2.3		2.5	2.5
	.4	.7	.6	.8	1.2		.9	.9
	1.3	2.4	1.3	1.4	1.6	Debt/Worth	1.6	1.6
	14.4	9.9	2.9	1.9	2.6		2.4	2.4
	32.9	35.5	21.4	12.0	15.7		13.2	13.0
(10) 11.1	(38) 16.1	(70) 9.7	(53) 8.0	(50) 9.3		% Profit Before Taxes/Tangible Net Worth	(399) 7.5	(372) 8.3
	-15.8	1.1	5.8	5.5	6.7		4.7	5.1
	18.4	14.5	7.6	5.1	5.9		4.9	5.1
	6.4	4.7	4.4	3.5	3.3	% Profit Before Taxes/Total Assets	3.1	3.4
	-5.0	-.9	2.2	2.1	2.2		1.7	1.8
	81.9	17.2	2.6	1.4	1.2		1.2	1.1
	6.6	2.8	.8	.7	.8	Sales/Net Fixed Assets	.7	.7
	.6	.5	.5	.5	.5		.5	.5
	3.3	2.5	1.3	.8	.8		.8	.8
	1.2	.9	.5	.5	.6	Sales/Total Assets	.5	.5
	.5	.4	.4	.4	.4		.4	.4
		1.1	4.2	4.6	3.1		4.6	4.7
	(42) 5.3	(72) 6.8	(55) 6.6	(48) 5.5		% Depr., Dep., Amort./Sales	(386) 6.3	(372) 6.4
		8.8	10.7	8.5	7.6		8.6	8.3
							2.0	2.6
						% Officers', Directors' Owners' Comp/Sales	(19) 3.2	(20) 4.2
							5.6	5.4
9521M	19366M	508258M	1655402M	3075301M	6676020M	Net Sales ($)	18744209M	18663848M
2385M	11513M	283854M	2079113M	4162706M	8163836M	Total Assets ($)	28033672M	28108211M

M = $ thousand   MM = $ million
See Pages 9 through 22 for Explanation of Ratios and Data

Comparative Historical Data

Current Data Sorted by Sales

			Type of Statement						
158	461	151	Unqualified	4	6	10	14	37	80
11	11	14	Reviewed	2	2		3	5	2
5	6	5	Compiled	1	1	1			2
4	4	12	Tax Returns	6	4	1			1
54	73	72	Other	5	4	4	6	21	32
4/1/08-3/31/09 ALL	4/1/09-3/31/10 ALL	4/1/10-3/31/11 ALL		52 (4/1-9/30/10) 0-1MM	1-3MM	3-5MM	202 (10/1/10-3/31/11) 5-10MM	10-25MM	25MM & OVER
232	555	254	**NUMBER OF STATEMENTS**	18	17	16	23	63	117
%	%	%	**ASSETS**	%	%	%	%	%	%
9.0	6.5	9.6	Cash & Equivalents	12.7	10.2	15.2	13.0	8.3	8.4
13.5	8.7	12.0	Trade Receivables (net)	10.1	11.2	11.3	9.0	12.2	13.0
3.0	2.5	4.0	Inventory	3.9	2.7	2.4	4.0	4.0	4.4
4.0	2.5	2.6	All Other Current	2.6	2.1	2.2	3.2	2.7	2.7
29.5	20.1	28.3	Total Current	29.4	26.1	31.1	29.3	27.3	28.4
55.7	65.1	55.5	Fixed Assets (net)	54.0	56.7	49.3	55.2	58.7	54.8
2.1	2.3	3.1	Intangibles (net)	3.8	9.4	3.1	2.7	3.1	2.1
12.6	12.5	13.1	All Other Non-Current	12.9	7.8	16.5	12.8	10.9	14.6
100.0	100.0	100.0	Total	100.0	100.0	100.0	100.0	100.0	100.0
			LIABILITIES						
3.1	3.2	4.3	Notes Payable-Short Term	15.6	.5	5.4	1.9	4.7	3.3
4.1	3.0	2.4	Cur. Mat.-L.T.D.	5.3	3.1	1.1	4.4	1.8	2.0
8.3	5.5	8.4	Trade Payables	13.3	8.4	4.9	6.3	6.7	9.4
.4	.3	.2	Income Taxes Payable	.0	.1	.1	.5	.2	.2
6.8	5.0	9.8	All Other Current	17.2	18.3	18.0	7.0	6.6	8.5
22.6	17.1	25.1	Total Current	51.3	30.3	29.6	20.1	20.1	23.4
33.4	38.3	32.7	Long-Term Debt	63.0	55.9	15.3	34.3	28.4	29.0
1.3	.4	1.3	Deferred Taxes	.0	3.7	3.5	1.7	.7	1.1
7.4	4.5	7.8	All Other Non-Current	10.9	12.4	6.0	7.7	6.9	7.4
35.4	39.7	33.1	Net Worth	-25.3	-2.3	45.7	36.2	43.9	39.0
100.0	100.0	100.0	Total Liabilities & Net Worth	100.0	100.0	100.0	100.0	100.0	100.0
			INCOME DATA						
100.0	100.0	100.0	Net Sales	100.0	100.0	100.0	100.0	100.0	100.0
			Gross Profit						
89.2	90.9	88.4	Operating Expenses	74.1	79.2	88.4	91.1	89.3	91.0
10.8	9.1	11.6	Operating Profit	25.9	20.8	11.6	8.9	10.7	9.0
3.2	2.4	3.2	All Other Expenses (net)	10.5	12.6	1.3	2.6	1.7	1.8
7.6	6.7	8.4	Profit Before Taxes	15.4	8.2	10.3	6.3	8.9	7.2
			RATIOS						
1.9	1.7	2.0		2.0	2.3	4.1	2.3	2.0	1.8
1.3	1.2	1.2	Current	.6	1.6	1.6	1.7	1.2	1.1
.9	.8	.8		.2	.9	1.1	.8	.8	.8
1.5	1.3	1.5		1.6	2.1	3.1	1.7	1.6	1.3
.9	.8	.9	Quick	.3	1.0	1.1	1.2	.8	.9
.6	.5	.5		.1	.5	.5	.4	.5	.5
26 14.0	26 14.3	25 14.9		0 UND	19 19.2	25 14.3	26 14.0	28 13.1	24 15.0
36 10.2	35 10.3	37 9.9	Sales/Receivables	18 19.9	46 7.9	36 10.2	40 9.2	41 8.8	35 10.3
53 6.9	47 7.8	50 7.2		54 6.8	66 5.6	43 8.5	57 6.4	53 6.8	46 8.0
			Cost of Sales/Inventory						
			Cost of Sales/Payables						
7.6	8.7	6.1		4.3	3.2	4.2	3.3	5.7	9.0
20.1	37.1	24.5	Sales/Working Capital	-8.7	9.0	6.8	6.7	17.2	41.7
-31.4	-20.0	-17.2		-4.7	NM	46.8	-11.7	-16.0	-25.8
5.4	3.5	6.0		16.8	3.6	19.6	5.6	5.4	6.5
(205) 3.0	(523) 2.3	(228) 3.1	EBIT/Interest	(13) 1.2	(13) 1.7	(12) 4.7	(20) 2.9	(59) 3.0	(111) 3.3
1.9	1.8	2.0		-.8	.2	.5	1.0	1.9	2.3
7.3	5.8	16.3						6.3	15.8
(47) 2.7	(62) 2.9	(48) 3.7	Net Profit + Depr., Dep., Amort./Cur. Mat. L/T/D				(11) 3.6	(19) 4.8	
1.4	1.6	1.7						2.5	3.0
.8	1.2	1.0		.8	1.8	.5	1.1	1.0	1.1
1.5	1.8	1.6	Fixed/Worth	2.5	2.5	1.5	2.1	1.4	1.5
2.5	2.5	2.6		NM	-.7	2.4	4.4	2.3	2.1
.7	1.0	.8		.7	1.3	.3	.6	.7	.9
1.6	1.5	1.4	Debt/Worth	2.7	2.4	1.3	2.6	1.4	1.4
3.1	2.4	3.0		-3.0	-3.1	4.9	14.0	2.8	2.3
23.2	12.0	16.7		17.4	17.6	18.5	18.7	14.8	16.2
(213) 8.8	(531) 7.7	(223) 9.2	% Profit Before Taxes/Tangible Net Worth	(13) 14.7	(12) 7.9	(13) 13.7	(20) 12.7	(59) 8.3	(106) 9.3
4.4	5.0	5.8		-8.8	-3.0	5.8	3.5	5.1	6.6
7.2	4.6	7.4		14.2	5.2	14.1	5.2	9.4	6.8
3.5	3.1	3.9	% Profit Before Taxes/Total Assets	5.2	3.0	4.8	3.3	3.7	3.9
1.3	1.9	1.9		-2.4	-.7	-.2	-.4	2.0	2.4
4.4	1.1	4.0		18.1	3.9	85.8	1.8	3.5	3.9
1.0	.7	.8	Sales/Net Fixed Assets	.8	.5	.7	.7	.7	1.0
.6	.5	.5		.3	.4	.5	.4	.5	.7
1.3	.7	1.3		1.8	.8	3.2	.9	1.6	1.4
.7	.5	.6	Sales/Total Assets	.4	.4	.5	.4	.5	.7
.4	.4	.4		.3	.2	.4	.3	.4	.5
3.0	5.1	3.6		1.3	3.9	6.6	5.3	4.3	2.9
(212) 5.8	(531) 6.7	(229) 6.1	% Depr., Dep., Amort./Sales	(13) 5.8	(15) 8.2	(11) 10.7	(21) 9.2	(60) 7.1	(109) 4.8
8.3	8.7	9.1		13.0	16.9	13.8	14.3	10.4	6.8
3.6	1.7	1.0							
(20) 5.1	(17) 4.4	(25) 4.0	% Officers', Directors' Owners' Comp/Sales						
9.1	6.8	6.5							
14267877M	24178816M	11943868M	Net Sales ($)	10597M	29876M	60041M	163820M	1088897M	10590637M
15783151M	40692192M	14703407M	Total Assets ($)	21948M	129715M	176888M	409400M	2216184M	11749272M

© RMA 2011

M = $ thousand   MM = $ million
See Pages 9 through 22 for Explanation of Ratios and Data

Current Data Sorted by Assets   Comparative Historical Data

Type of Statement	0-500M	500M-2MM	2-10MM	10-50MM	50-100MM	100-250MM	4/1/06-3/31/07 ALL	4/1/07-3/31/08 ALL
Unqualified		2	6	22	7	17	75	62
Reviewed	1		11	6	1	1	18	16
Compiled	4		6	3			21	17
Tax Returns	2	3	3	1			15	6
Other	2	5	14	13	6	9	49	50
		43 (4/1-9/30/10)		102 (10/1/10-3/31/11)				
NUMBER OF STATEMENTS	9	10	40	45	14	27	178	151
	%	%	%	%	%	%	%	%
ASSETS								
Cash & Equivalents		11.5	14.4	13.1	14.5	6.7	10.1	10.9
Trade Receivables (net)		21.7	26.9	18.0	24.8	10.2	21.1	22.5
Inventory		3.5	8.3	3.9	7.5	6.3	10.3	7.9
All Other Current		2.1	2.2	4.2	1.7	4.6	3.1	3.8
Total Current		38.8	51.8	39.3	48.6	27.8	44.6	45.0
Fixed Assets (net)		50.6	36.6	46.3	38.8	62.4	42.4	44.3
Intangibles (net)		3.4	2.4	5.7	2.5	2.7	5.1	4.3
All Other Non-Current		7.3	9.2	8.8	10.1	7.1	7.9	6.3
Total		100.0	100.0	100.0	100.0	100.0	100.0	100.0
LIABILITIES								
Notes Payable-Short Term		.7	8.1	6.4	6.8	4.3	7.1	8.0
Cur. Mat.-L.T.D.		3.0	3.8	1.6	.8	1.9	3.4	1.9
Trade Payables		15.2	21.3	14.2	20.6	9.5	17.3	16.2
Income Taxes Payable		.4	.2	.3	.0	.5	.3	.3
All Other Current		7.4	4.6	8.8	5.7	6.0	9.9	7.5
Total Current		26.8	37.9	31.2	34.0	22.1	37.9	34.0
Long-Term Debt		32.0	13.8	16.2	17.8	21.8	24.1	23.4
Deferred Taxes		1.2	1.3	3.5	1.2	4.5	2.1	1.7
All Other Non-Current		3.9	3.6	3.2	4.3	7.0	4.6	4.1
Net Worth		36.0	43.3	45.9	42.7	44.5	31.3	36.8
Total Liabilities & Net Worth		100.0	100.0	100.0	100.0	100.0	100.0	100.0
INCOME DATA								
Net Sales		100.0	100.0	100.0	100.0	100.0	100.0	100.0
Gross Profit								
Operating Expenses		85.3	91.8	93.6	82.4	86.2	92.6	89.4
Operating Profit		14.7	8.2	6.4	17.6	13.8	7.4	10.6
All Other Expenses (net)		4.9	1.9	1.4	2.5	3.5	2.0	3.0
Profit Before Taxes		9.8	6.3	5.0	15.0	10.3	5.3	7.6
RATIOS								
Current		2.3	1.8	1.9	2.2	1.8	1.8	2.0
		1.7	1.4	1.3	1.3	1.1	1.2	1.3
		1.0	1.0	.8	.9	.8	.9	1.0
Quick		2.3	1.5	1.5	1.6	1.3	1.2	1.5
		1.4	1.0	1.1	1.1	.6	.8 (150)	1.0
		.6	.6	.6	.5	.4	.5	.6
Sales/Receivables		8 44.1	13 28.1	13 27.6	23 15.5	22 16.9	15 24.3	15 23.9
		24 15.1	27 13.7	24 15.4	49 7.5	33 10.9	28 13.0	31 11.9
		51 7.1	39 9.4	51 7.1	69 5.3	46 7.9	46 8.0	50 7.3
Cost of Sales/Inventory								
Cost of Sales/Payables								
Sales/Working Capital		6.2	11.2	6.9	5.8	7.3	10.8	7.3
		19.6	32.5	31.5	22.6	38.0	53.1	23.5
		NM	NM	-23.4	-40.8	-16.5	-33.8	999.8
EBIT/Interest			11.8	20.0	28.4	6.4	7.4	7.0
		(34)	4.3	(38) 7.4	(12) 6.2	(26) 4.8	(151) 3.2	(129) 4.0
			1.9	2.7	3.1	2.3	1.6	1.9
Net Profit + Depr., Dep., Amort./Cur. Mat. L/T/D			11.5	7.4		10.9	6.2	9.5
		(10)	5.8	(16) 3.1		(10) 7.8	(37) 2.9	(43) 3.5
			3.3	2.1		1.1	1.8	1.6
Fixed/Worth		1.0	.2	.6	.1	.9	.5	.7
		1.5	1.0	1.1	1.0	1.6	1.5	1.3
		3.1	1.5	2.5	2.5	2.2	3.8	2.8
Debt/Worth		.7	.9	.8	.7	.8	.9	.9
		2.5	1.8	1.5	1.6	1.8	2.5	2.3
		4.8	2.5	2.8	3.3	2.2	7.4	5.3
% Profit Before Taxes/Tangible Net Worth			31.7	22.2	51.5	22.5	43.9	39.4
		(39)	16.8	(43) 14.8	27.9	14.5	(152) 15.4	(137) 16.0
			5.0	6.2	13.8	5.4	6.5	7.4
% Profit Before Taxes/Total Assets		29.6	11.1	9.7	14.4	6.9	10.2	11.9
		8.4	6.7	5.4	8.4	5.8	4.9	5.2
		3.6	2.2	1.7	4.4	2.4	1.0	2.1
Sales/Net Fixed Assets		31.0	208.1	29.0	202.9	1.0	39.3	32.6
		3.4	17.0	2.0	2.5	.8	3.8	2.9
		.6	1.5	.8	.6	.6	1.3	1.0
Sales/Total Assets		7.0	7.7	3.0	3.7	.7	3.8	4.2
		1.9	3.1	.9	.9	.5	1.6	1.5
		.4	1.0	.5	.3	.4	.8	.6
% Depr., Dep., Amort./Sales			.5	.9	.1	4.4	1.2	.9
		(35)	3.0	(43) 4.4	(12) 5.7	(22) 5.8	(151) 3.6	(129) 3.7
			6.3	6.9	14.8	12.3	5.4	6.4
% Officers', Directors' Owners' Comp/Sales			.7				.6	.6
		(10)	1.0				(26) 1.0	(20) 1.5
			3.7				1.7	2.5
Net Sales ($)	28630M	37795M	1232157M	1974378M	2330544M	6917621M	20540237M	20177920M
Total Assets ($)	2998M	11001M	237634M	1040928M	1022734M	4381762M	7960914M	6681617M

© RMA 2011

M = $ thousand   MM = $ million
See Pages 9 through 22 for Explanation of Ratios and Data

Comparative Historical Data / Current Data Sorted by Sales

					Type of Statement						
	50		47	54	Unqualified	1	4	1	4	13	31
	17		15	20	Reviewed	1	2		4	4	9
	10		14	13	Compiled	1	2	3	1	3	3
	7		6	9	Tax Returns	1	1		5	2	
	58		57	49	Other	5	2	1	3	11	27
	4/1/08-3/31/09 ALL		4/1/09-3/31/10 ALL	4/1/10-3/31/11 ALL			43 (4/1-9/30/10)			102 (10/1/10-3/31/11)	
						0-1MM	1-3MM	3-5MM	5-10MM	10-25MM	25MM & OVER
	142		139	145	NUMBER OF STATEMENTS	9	11	5	17	33	70
	%		%	%	ASSETS	%	%	%	%	%	%
	9.7		13.0	12.1	Cash & Equivalents		20.1		10.8	13.5	11.8
	22.4		19.6	19.9	Trade Receivables (net)		5.3		13.5	16.1	26.4
	7.9		6.6	6.5	Inventory		2.7		8.7	5.1	7.4
	3.8		3.1	3.2	All Other Current		1.4		1.8	1.5	5.0
	43.8		42.4	41.7	Total Current		29.5		34.8	36.2	50.6
	43.5		46.2	46.0	Fixed Assets (net)		64.2		51.8	51.0	36.8
	4.0		4.3	3.8	Intangibles (net)		3.5		6.3	4.5	2.9
	8.7		7.1	8.5	All Other Non-Current		2.8		7.0	8.3	9.8
	100.0		100.0	100.0	Total		100.0		100.0	100.0	100.0
					LIABILITIES						
	7.4		5.8	5.8	Notes Payable-Short Term		.4		3.0	5.3	8.3
	3.5		2.8	2.5	Cur. Mat.-L.T.D.		3.4		4.3	1.2	1.8
	17.7		16.6	16.7	Trade Payables		4.1		18.1	11.7	21.9
	.4		.4	.3	Income Taxes Payable		.4		.4	.0	.4
	8.3		8.8	7.8	All Other Current		4.3		9.5	6.1	7.8
	37.3		34.4	33.1	Total Current		12.6		35.3	24.3	40.1
	19.2		17.8	19.4	Long-Term Debt		42.0		16.7	17.0	13.9
	1.8		2.2	2.5	Deferred Taxes		2.6		2.3	3.1	2.7
	4.0		4.8	4.0	All Other Non-Current		2.2		6.1	4.1	4.2
	37.8		40.8	41.0	Net Worth		40.5		39.6	51.6	39.0
	100.0		100.0	100.0	Total Liabilties & Net Worth		100.0		100.0	100.0	100.0
					INCOME DATA						
	100.0		100.0	100.0	Net Sales		100.0		100.0	100.0	100.0
					Gross Profit						
	89.9		89.4	90.2	Operating Expenses		71.8		95.2	91.8	91.4
	10.1		10.6	9.8	Operating Profit		28.2		4.8	8.2	8.6
	2.1		2.6	2.2	All Other Expenses (net)		10.6		1.4	1.9	.9
	8.0		7.9	7.6	Profit Before Taxes		17.7		3.4	6.3	7.7
					RATIOS						
	1.7		1.8	1.9			4.7		1.7	2.0	1.9
	1.2		1.2	1.3	Current		2.2		1.2	1.3	1.3
	.9		.8	.8			1.4		.8	.8	.9
	1.2		1.3	1.5			4.5		1.2	1.6	1.4
	.9		.9	1.0	Quick		1.5		.9	1.0	.9
	.5		.5	.5			.6		.5	.4	.5
14	25.2	13	28.4	14 25.7		0 UND		15 24.7	19 19.1	15 24.3
29	12.8	26	13.9	28 12.9	Sales/Receivables	5 69.1		38 9.6	35 10.4	26 13.9
47	7.8	45	8.1	45 8.1		34 10.7		54 6.7	60 6.0	43 8.4
					Cost of Sales/Inventory						
					Cost of Sales/Payables						
	13.1		8.8	8.2			1.5		8.2	7.0	10.5
	43.9		44.3	32.3	Sales/Working Capital		5.7		34.1	30.6	35.7
	-48.7		-40.0	-45.3			14.1		-33.5	-13.6	-94.6
	7.0		12.0	13.0					13.3	15.3	12.2
(119)	4.2	(112)	5.3	(123) 4.9	EBIT/Interest			(12) 2.9	(30) 4.8	(63) 5.7
	2.3		2.0	2.4					1.0	2.2	3.2
	8.6		8.3	11.0	Net Profit + Depr., Dep.,					8.5	11.8
(28)	3.1	(27)	3.4	(39) 4.3	Amort./Cur. Mat. L/T/D				(10) 3.3	(20) 7.8
	1.9		1.6	2.3						2.3	2.6
	.7		.5	.5			.9		1.0	.6	.2
	1.2		1.1	1.1	Fixed/Worth		1.5		1.6	1.1	1.0
	2.6		2.3	2.2			3.3		NM	2.3	2.0
	1.0		.7	.7			.4		.4	.6	1.1
	2.0		1.7	1.8	Debt/Worth		2.4		1.7	1.1	1.9
	4.0		3.4	2.8			3.4		NM	2.2	3.1
	35.5		37.8	31.6	% Profit Before Taxes/Tangible		36.9		15.9	22.5	39.4
(132)	17.7	(129)	17.8	(136) 15.5	Net Worth	(10) 12.6		(13) 4.8	10.4	(69) 21.3
	8.1		5.8	6.3			6.3		-2.0	6.2	12.6
	8.9		12.2	10.0	% Profit Before Taxes/Total		9.3		7.3	7.9	11.7
	5.2		6.4	5.6	Assets		5.0		2.6	5.2	6.8
	2.8		1.8	2.1			1.1		-1.0	3.3	2.9
	40.4		52.7	43.5			3.6		10.5	16.5	217.3
	3.4		2.9	2.4	Sales/Net Fixed Assets		.5		1.4	1.3	17.0
	1.0		.8	.8			.2		.9	.6	.9
	4.6		3.7	4.3			2.2		2.3	2.6	7.0
	1.6		1.6	1.3	Sales/Total Assets		.4		.9	.8	3.0
	.7		.5	.5			.2		.5	.4	.6
	.7		.6	.5			1.5		2.8	1.9	.1
(123)	3.0	(114)	4.2	(128) 4.5	% Depr., Dep., Amort./Sales			(16) 5.5	(32) 5.5	(57) 1.2
	5.2		7.1	7.9			20.4		10.0	9.3	5.5
	.4		.9	.8							.5
(26)	1.4	(24)	2.1	(23) 2.1	% Officers', Directors' Owners' Comp/Sales					(12) .9
	3.5		2.9	3.7							2.5
	19888544M		11249834M	12521125M	Net Sales ($)	4177M	24360M	18921M	130346M	529931M	11813390M
	6714545M		6835692M	6697057M	Total Assets ($)	7184M	63720M	8045M	175907M	1018781M	5423420M

M = $ thousand   MM = $ million
See Pages 9 through 22 for Explanation of Ratios and Data

Current Data Sorted by Assets

Comparative Historical Data

Type of Statement								
Unqualified	1	7	31	43	14	15	114	99
Reviewed	1	1	11	2			18	11
Compiled	3	6	10	3			16	11
Tax Returns	11	11	7	2		1	15	21
Other	7	11	20	15	2	3	58	55

	0-500M	500M-2MM	2-10MM	10-50MM	50-100MM	100-250MM	4/1/06-3/31/07 ALL	4/1/07-3/31/08 ALL
	61 (4/1-9/30/10)			177 (10/1/10-3/31/11)				
NUMBER OF STATEMENTS	23	36	79	65	16	19	221	197
ASSETS	%	%	%	%	%	%	%	%
Cash & Equivalents	20.8	13.2	12.9	6.7	7.5	5.3	9.2	9.6
Trade Receivables (net)	16.1	16.8	12.8	5.8	1.9	2.2	7.8	10.7
Inventory	3.3	7.3	6.2	3.4	.3	.4	4.2	5.0
All Other Current	3.5	4.5	2.4	1.8	.7	1.6	2.2	3.2
Total Current	43.7	41.8	34.2	17.7	10.4	9.5	23.4	28.5
Fixed Assets (net)	42.9	47.3	53.3	69.5	83.5	77.7	68.6	62.6
Intangibles (net)	4.8	2.1	4.2	3.7	1.6	2.0	1.8	2.3
All Other Non-Current	8.7	8.8	8.3	9.0	4.5	10.8	6.2	6.5
Total	100.0	100.0	100.0	100.0	100.0	100.0	100.0	100.0
LIABILITIES								
Notes Payable-Short Term	11.0	10.1	4.6	4.6	.1	1.4	4.1	3.8
Cur. Mat.-L.T.D.	6.6	3.9	2.4	3.4	1.9	.8	2.7	3.4
Trade Payables	9.5	10.7	8.2	2.2	.7	1.3	4.3	5.9
Income Taxes Payable	.0	.0	.1	.1	.0	.2	.2	.1
All Other Current	47.3	12.5	11.0	4.6	2.8	2.4	4.3	6.7
Total Current	74.3	37.2	26.2	14.9	5.5	6.2	15.6	19.9
Long-Term Debt	39.8	24.4	19.0	30.3	35.0	30.1	32.0	34.2
Deferred Taxes	.1	.3	.2	.4	1.5	3.2	.9	.6
All Other Non-Current	12.9	8.0	9.2	9.0	2.8	11.9	9.7	8.6
Net Worth	-27.0	30.1	45.4	45.4	55.2	48.6	41.8	36.6
Total Liabilities & Net Worth	100.0	100.0	100.0	100.0	100.0	100.0	100.0	100.0
INCOME DATA								
Net Sales	100.0	100.0	100.0	100.0	100.0	100.0	100.0	100.0
Gross Profit								
Operating Expenses	91.3	89.3	89.5	83.5	81.0	84.0	80.7	86.0
Operating Profit	8.7	10.7	10.5	16.5	19.0	16.0	19.3	14.0
All Other Expenses (net)	.9	3.9	5.3	7.2	5.7	7.4	6.0	4.7
Profit Before Taxes	7.8	6.9	5.2	9.3	13.3	8.7	13.3	9.3
RATIOS								
Current	2.5	2.2	5.2	3.5	3.8	2.6	3.4	2.9
	1.0	1.2	1.7	1.6	1.6	1.3	1.6	1.5
	.4	.8	1.0	.8	1.1	1.0	.9	.9
Quick	2.0	1.7	3.0	2.9	3.5	1.7	2.9	2.3
	.8	.9	1.4	1.1	1.4	.9	1.3	1.1
	.4	.4	.6	.5	.5	.6	.5	.6
Sales/Receivables	0 UND	5 75.6	19 19.3	25 14.9	26 14.0	22 16.9	20 17.9	23 15.7
	0 UND	34 10.6	35 10.4	38 9.5	35 10.6	35 10.5	34 10.7	34 10.6
	27 13.7	56 6.6	50 7.3	50 7.2	43 8.4	57 6.4	49 7.4	52 7.1
Cost of Sales/Inventory								
Cost of Sales/Payables								
Sales/Working Capital	7.5	5.4	3.3	2.6	1.8	3.1	2.4	2.8
	UND	28.3	8.2	7.0	4.7	7.6	8.9	9.6
	-8.7	-20.1	-393.3	-17.6	48.7	-66.4	-52.0	-51.9
EBIT/Interest	7.8	7.5	5.9	6.6	6.6	4.5	5.7	5.0
	(15) 3.1	(30) 3.7	(61) 2.2	(53) 2.8	(14) 3.2	(17) 2.8	(186) 3.0	(159) 2.5
	1.0	.8	.3	1.5	.9	1.8	1.5	1.2
Net Profit + Depr., Dep., Amort./Cur. Mat. L/T/D				7.8			10.5	5.7
				(13) 2.6			(44) 4.0	(29) 3.1
				1.1			2.1	1.2
Fixed/Worth	.9	.6	.7	1.0	1.1	1.3	1.0	1.0
	-4.0	1.4	1.1	1.6	1.4	1.5	1.6	1.7
	-.3	13.6	2.4	4.1	2.3	3.0	3.3	4.6
Debt/Worth	.7	.9	.3	.6	.3	.4	.5	.6
	-10.7	2.8	.8	1.1	.6	1.6	1.3	1.9
	-1.9	17.2	5.8	4.8	1.5	2.5	3.6	5.8
% Profit Before Taxes/Tangible Net Worth	43.1	41.7	13.4	17.0	6.8	11.3	16.6	17.4
	(10) 14.3	(30) 7.4	(67) 3.5	(61) 4.9	(15) 4.2	(18) 5.3	(203) 8.3	(171) 6.7
	-3.2	-.5	-.7	.5	.8	1.8	2.4	.6
% Profit Before Taxes/Total Assets	23.5	14.0	6.0	5.2	4.5	4.3	6.7	6.2
	8.9	3.1	1.6	2.1	1.8	1.8	3.0	2.5
	.0	.2	-1.6	.1	.1	.8	1.1	.2
Sales/Net Fixed Assets	29.0	27.1	6.7	.7	.2	.4	.9	4.1
	6.2	3.9	.8	.3	.2	.2	.3	.4
	1.4	.4	.3	.2	.1	.2	.2	.2
Sales/Total Assets	5.4	2.7	1.9	.4	.2	.2	.6	1.5
	1.9	1.2	.4	.2	.2	.2	.2	.3
	.7	.3	.2	.1	.1	.1	.2	.2
% Depr., Dep., Amort./Sales	3.1	2.7	2.1	8.1	11.8	11.8	7.7	4.1
	(13) 6.6	(28) 5.9	(67) 10.9	(62) 15.6	14.8	(18) 14.3	(209) 12.5	(181) 12.4
	10.6	15.8	18.3	26.2	21.8	23.0	18.9	18.6
% Officers', Directors' Owners' Comp/Sales			(12) 1.4				1.9	1.2
			3.7				(31) 3.7	(32) 2.6
			7.7				5.7	6.1
Net Sales ($)	13980M	63262M	422236M	742579M	192293M	1222982M	1708226M	2487855M
Total Assets ($)	4720M	42447M	388321M	1459423M	1167945M	3255311M	6334368M	5937739M

M = $ thousand   MM = $ million
See Pages 9 through 22 for Explanation of Ratios and Data

Comparative Historical Data / Current Data Sorted by Sales

	4/1/08-3/31/09 ALL	4/1/09-3/31/10 ALL	4/1/10-3/31/11 ALL	0-1MM	1-3MM	3-5MM	5-10MM	10-25MM	25MM & OVER
				61 (4/1-9/30/10)			177 (10/1/10-3/31/11)		
Type of Statement									
Unqualified	92	113	111	18	28	14	19	22	10
Reviewed	17	14	15	2	2	1	4	5	1
Compiled	17	12	22	6	5	2	2	5	2
Tax Returns	30	24	32	15	10	3		3	1
Other	57	55	58	14	17	4	11	6	6
NUMBER OF STATEMENTS	213	218	238	55	62	24	36	41	20
	%	%	%	%	%	%	%	%	%
ASSETS									
Cash & Equivalents	8.3	9.3	11.1	15.6	7.9	13.3	9.3	12.1	6.8
Trade Receivables (net)	10.0	8.5	10.2	3.1	10.9	9.1	12.2	16.5	12.8
Inventory	4.5	3.5	4.4	1.4	3.0	3.8	6.5	7.9	7.3
All Other Current	2.2	1.6	2.5	2.9	1.7	4.9	1.4	2.5	2.7
Total Current	25.0	22.9	28.2	23.0	23.4	31.2	29.3	38.9	29.7
Fixed Assets (net)	63.3	66.7	59.8	62.8	67.7	55.5	57.0	53.3	50.4
Intangibles (net)	2.2	2.6	3.5	3.9	2.3	5.7	4.9	1.2	5.3
All Other Non-Current	9.6	7.8	8.5	10.3	6.5	7.7	8.7	6.6	14.7
Total	100.0	100.0	100.0	100.0	100.0	100.0	100.0	100.0	100.0
LIABILITIES									
Notes Payable-Short Term	4.0	3.5	5.5	6.8	5.5	2.4	8.6	2.8	5.4
Cur. Mat.-L.T.D.	3.8	3.2	3.2	4.3	3.3	2.0	3.5	2.7	1.5
Trade Payables	5.7	4.6	6.0	1.0	6.3	4.8	7.0	11.8	6.6
Income Taxes Payable	.3	.1	.1	.0	.0	.1	.1	.1	.3
All Other Current	8.3	7.8	11.7	23.2	9.6	12.7	5.6	7.5	5.5
Total Current	22.1	19.2	26.4	35.3	24.7	22.0	24.7	24.8	19.2
Long-Term Debt	29.7	29.4	26.8	36.0	25.4	30.6	19.2	23.8	21.7
Deferred Taxes	.8	.6	.6	.3	.0	.9	.0	1.1	2.9
All Other Non-Current	7.3	7.0	9.1	11.3	6.3	10.4	11.6	6.6	11.1
Net Worth	40.1	43.8	37.0	17.2	43.6	36.1	44.5	43.7	45.1
Total Liabilties & Net Worth	100.0	100.0	100.0	100.0	100.0	100.0	100.0	100.0	100.0
INCOME DATA									
Net Sales	100.0	100.0	100.0	100.0	100.0	100.0	100.0	100.0	100.0
Gross Profit									
Operating Expenses	85.6	87.4	87.0	84.7	87.3	79.7	91.2	90.4	86.6
Operating Profit	14.4	12.6	13.0	15.3	12.7	20.3	8.8	9.6	13.4
All Other Expenses (net)	6.2	5.0	5.4	6.5	5.7	9.0	3.5	2.6	6.1
Profit Before Taxes	8.2	7.6	7.6	8.8	7.1	11.3	5.3	7.1	7.3
RATIOS									
Current	3.0	3.5	3.2	3.2	4.1	2.2	2.7	3.0	2.4
	1.3	1.5	1.5	1.4	1.8	1.8	1.5	1.6	1.3
	.7	.7	.9	.6	.8	.8	1.0	1.1	.7
Quick	2.4	2.7	2.8	2.7	3.5	2.2	2.0	2.8	1.0
	1.1	1.1	1.2	1.3	1.6	1.5	1.2	1.2	.8
	.4	.5	.5	.4	.5	.4	.5	.6	.4
Sales/Receivables	17 21.1	16 22.6	17 22.1	0 UND	18 20.7	2 152.7	26 14.0	28 13.0	18 19.9
	32 11.2	31 12.0	34 10.8	15 24.9	32 11.6	33 11.2	39 9.5	39 9.4	33 10.9
	48 7.6	44 8.4	49 7.4	38 9.7	45 8.2	59 6.2	47 7.8	59 6.1	50 7.3
Cost of Sales/Inventory									
Cost of Sales/Payables									
Sales/Working Capital	3.8	3.0	3.2	2.3	2.9	3.3	4.0	2.9	5.4
	12.1	10.5	9.3	13.1	15.1	7.8	11.9	6.8	17.5
	-11.2	-19.0	-40.5	-4.4	-20.6	-20.8	-70.1	218.2	-20.1
EBIT/Interest	6.9	5.7	6.3	6.9	5.3	5.1	7.0	7.4	10.6
	(175) 2.8	(188) 2.4	(190) 2.5	(39) 2.3	(49) 2.3	(19) 2.0	(31) 2.7	(35) 2.7	(17) 4.5
	1.5	1.0	1.0	1.0	.5	1.1	.2	.9	2.2
Net Profit + Depr., Dep., Amort./Cur. Mat. L/T/D	8.8	8.4	10.1					8.4	
	(35) 4.5	(38) 2.8	(32) 3.6					(11) 2.0	
	1.8	1.3	1.0					.2	
Fixed/Worth	.9	1.0	.9	1.1	1.0	1.0	.8	.5	.3
	1.4	1.4	1.4	2.2	1.5	1.9	1.0	1.2	1.4
	3.1	3.0	4.7	-29.5	2.5	NM	5.4	2.2	2.8
Debt/Worth	.5	.5	.5	.5	.4	.8	.4	.5	.5
	1.2	1.1	1.2	2.1	.9	1.8	.8	1.5	1.4
	3.9	3.1	6.4	-36.5	3.6	NM	6.0	3.1	3.1
% Profit Before Taxes/Tangible Net Worth	17.5	13.4	15.5	14.9	8.5	14.3	21.0	16.2	48.6
	(185) 5.4	(197) 4.4	(201) 4.7	(40) 3.4	(54) 4.6	(18) 6.1	(32) 3.9	(38) 4.8	(19) 12.3
	.8	.0	.2	.0	.3	.0	-.1	-.3	4.4
% Profit Before Taxes/Total Assets	6.7	6.0	6.6	11.1	5.7	7.9	5.6	5.6	17.4
	2.2	2.1	2.1	2.3	1.9	2.4	1.8	1.6	4.0
	.3	.0	.0	.0	-.5	.2	-.6	-1.5	1.1
Sales/Net Fixed Assets	4.2	3.1	5.6	1.4	3.7	5.3	11.7	10.1	15.2
	.4	.3	.5	.4	.3	.8	.6	.7	1.1
	.2	.2	.2	.2	.2	.2	.2	.2	.3
Sales/Total Assets	1.6	1.0	1.7	.7	1.4	1.2	2.0	2.1	1.9
	.3	.3	.3	.3	.3	.3	.4	.5	.7
	.2	.2	.2	.2	.2	.2	.2	.2	.2
% Depr., Dep., Amort./Sales	5.1	8.2	5.3	7.7	10.4	3.1	2.8	4.7	1.3
	(199) 12.6	(197) 14.1	(204) 12.3	(43) 15.9	(51) 15.8	(23) 8.3	(33) 9.7	(35) 11.8	(19) 10.5
	19.5	21.4	20.2	26.8	24.3	18.3	17.4	20.2	14.0
% Officers', Directors' Owners' Comp/Sales	1.6	2.7	1.7	.7					
	(39) 3.3	(28) 7.5	(29) 6.7		(11) 6.7				
	5.7	10.1	12.0		11.1				
Net Sales ($)	4606446M	2132768M	2657332M	26645M	113787M	90145M	265171M	604833M	1556751M
Total Assets ($)	6585724M	6318440M	6318167M	145105M	483529M	315021M	997067M	1902898M	2474547M

M = $ thousand   MM = $ million
See Pages 9 through 22 for Explanation of Ratios and Data

CONSTRUCTION—GENERAL INDUSTRIES FORMAT*

Current Data Sorted by Assets   **Comparative Historical Data**

Type of Statement	0-500M	500M-2MM	2-10MM	10-50MM	50-100MM	100-250MM	4/1/06-3/31/07 ALL	4/1/07-3/31/08 ALL
Unqualified		3	12	30	13	9	154	108
Reviewed	2	26	81	31	8	1	311	196
Compiled	27	57	68	25	2		493	352
Tax Returns	178	270	207	36	3	4	1520	1050
Other	88	176	280	139	22	12	1215	1061

151 (4/1-9/30/10)   1,659 (10/1/10-3/31/11)

	0-500M	500M-2MM	2-10MM	10-50MM	50-100MM	100-250MM	4/1/06-3/31/07 ALL	4/1/07-3/31/08 ALL
NUMBER OF STATEMENTS	295	532	648	261	48	26	3693	2767
	%	%	%	%	%	%	%	%
ASSETS								
Cash & Equivalents	20.8	10.1	9.0	7.1	7.8	8.8	9.5	9.1
Trade Receivables (net)	11.5	11.2	8.8	5.4	7.1	8.6	7.0	6.6
Inventory	23.9	45.7	56.0	62.8	54.3	49.1	58.3	58.3
All Other Current	4.6	4.8	5.5	2.5	4.8	2.5	5.5	5.9
Total Current	60.8	71.8	79.3	77.8	74.1	69.0	80.4	80.0
Fixed Assets (net)	22.6	17.6	12.5	10.9	12.9	16.1	12.3	12.2
Intangibles (net)	1.5	.7	.6	.8	1.7	.4	.8	.8
All Other Non-Current	15.1	9.9	7.6	10.4	11.2	14.6	6.6	7.1
Total	100.0	100.0	100.0	100.0	100.0	100.0	100.0	100.0
LIABILITIES								
Notes Payable-Short Term	31.7	28.7	34.0	36.1	27.1	32.6	41.3	40.0
Cur. Mat.-L.T.D.	4.3	3.9	2.6	2.4	4.6	2.7	4.2	5.6
Trade Payables	11.0	9.7	7.5	6.9	8.6	8.4	8.0	7.6
Income Taxes Payable	.2	.1	.1	.0	.1	.1	.1	.2
All Other Current	26.2	13.2	13.7	12.2	20.3	6.5	11.8	12.3
Total Current	73.5	55.6	58.0	57.6	60.6	50.1	65.5	65.6
Long-Term Debt	17.2	16.6	12.9	13.5	15.0	13.6	13.7	13.9
Deferred Taxes	.0	.1	.0	.4	.0	.0	.0	.0
All Other Non-Current	8.7	4.0	4.2	3.8	4.3	3.5	3.6	3.6
Net Worth	.6	23.7	24.9	24.8	19.7	32.8	17.2	16.8
Total Liabilties & Net Worth	100.0	100.0	100.0	100.0	100.0	100.0	100.0	100.0
INCOME DATA								
Net Sales	100.0	100.0	100.0	100.0	100.0	100.0	100.0	100.0
Gross Profit	26.6	18.8	17.0	15.2	18.9	21.2	18.6	17.7
Operating Expenses	23.0	16.0	13.4	13.0	15.1	20.2	12.8	13.8
Operating Profit	3.7	2.8	3.6	2.2	3.8	1.0	5.8	3.9
All Other Expenses (net)	.7	1.5	2.1	2.2	2.1	3.3	1.1	1.7
Profit Before Taxes	2.9	1.3	1.4	.0	1.6	-2.4	4.7	2.2
RATIOS								
Current	2.5	2.4	2.1	2.0	2.0	3.4	1.7	1.7
	1.1	1.2	1.3	1.3	1.3	1.5	1.2	1.2
	.4	.9	1.0	1.1	.9	.7	1.0	1.0
Quick	1.4	1.1	.6	.4	.2	.8	.5	.5
	(294) .4	(527) .2	(647) .1	.1	.1	.2	(3673) .1	(2750) .1
	.1	.0	.0	.0	.0	.1	.0	.0
Sales/Receivables	0 UND	0 UND	0 UND	0 UND	0 UND	0 UND	0 UND	0 UND
	0 UND	0 UND	0 999.8	1 690.1	0 988.2	2 192.1	0 UND	0 UND
	7 53.5	20 18.5	21 17.0	9 40.5	9 40.6	18 19.8	6 64.4	5 69.6
Cost of Sales/Inventory	0 UND	0 UND	44 8.3	144 2.5	48 7.6	0 UND	6 60.0	3 117.1
	0 UND	93 3.9	218 1.7	290 1.3	273 1.3	224 1.6	189 1.9	211 1.7
	51 7.2	261 1.4	481 .8	594 .6	405 .9	560 .7	376 1.0	426 .9
Cost of Sales/Payables	0 UND	0 UND	6 63.2	9 40.7	17 21.8		0 UND	0 UND
	0 UND	6 61.5	12 31.2	15 25.0	14 25.5	25 14.4	9 42.7	8 46.2
	10 34.9	27 13.7	31 11.9	30 12.1	26 14.2	44 8.3	26 14.1	24 15.2
Sales/Working Capital	11.7	4.8	2.5	2.2	2.4	1.7	5.0	4.2
	278.0	14.3	7.9	6.3	7.1	4.0	14.5	12.7
	-13.4	-39.0	589.8	35.8	-75.9	-62.2	705.0	-563.9
EBIT/Interest	13.2	10.1	9.4	7.3	10.1	2.3	17.4	9.7
	(201) 3.3	(373) 2.8	(476) 2.2	(212) 1.9	(40) 2.6	(22) 1.5	(2730) 4.5	(2020) 2.4
	-1.2	-.3	-.3	.0	.6	-1.5	1.4	.6
Net Profit + Depr., Dep., Amort./Cur. Mat. L/T/D		6.4	13.2	23.3			6.7	5.3
		(18) 1.8	(28) 1.5	(13) 1.9			(133) 2.6	(111) 1.7
		.0	.3	1.0			.5	.0
Fixed/Worth	.0	.0	.0	.0	.0	.1	.0	.0
	.7	.3	.2	.1	.1	.2	.2	.2
	-10.0	3.5	1.4	1.0	1.2	.8	1.6	1.6
Debt/Worth	1.1	1.1	1.4	1.4	1.1	.6	2.4	2.3
	5.4	3.7	4.0	3.6	3.4	1.8	6.7	6.1
	-4.9	41.1	13.9	9.6	9.6	7.2	30.2	29.0
% Profit Before Taxes/Tangible Net Worth	139.9	58.3	34.2	25.0	30.0	22.9	88.3	59.7
	(192) 41.7	(421) 16.1	(560) 9.7	(236) 7.5	(41) 8.0	(23) 2.4	(3136) 40.8	(2324) 21.2
	1.1	.8	-3.6	-4.8	-.9	-5.0	11.8	.9
% Profit Before Taxes/Total Assets	34.8	11.5	7.8	5.8	8.3	3.5	13.0	9.3
	9.2	3.7	1.8	1.3	1.3	.6	4.9	2.8
	-4.4	-1.6	-1.6	-1.6	-1.9	-3.3	.8	-.8
Sales/Net Fixed Assets	UND	444.9	419.5	294.0	144.2	148.8	541.4	515.9
	63.5	42.5	59.1	59.4	56.7	26.4	82.2	72.2
	16.1	8.1	8.5	5.7	9.0	8.9	17.9	16.7
Sales/Total Assets	9.6	3.2	1.9	1.6	1.6	2.0	2.6	2.4
	4.7	1.9	1.1	.9	1.1	1.0	1.5	1.3
	2.4	.9	.6	.5	.6	.5	.8	.7
% Depr., Dep., Amort./Sales	.4	.3	.2	.2	.2	.2	.2	.2
	(137) 1.1	(292) .7	(344) .5	(134) .5	(31) .3	(18) .6	(2013) .4	(1498) .5
	2.9	1.9	1.4	1.4	1.0	1.2	1.0	1.1
% Officers', Directors' Owners' Comp/Sales	2.5	1.8	1.1	.5			1.3	1.3
	(159) 5.1	(242) 3.0	(244) 2.2	(68) 1.5			(1666) 2.5	(1210) 2.7
	8.8	6.4	3.9	3.0			5.1	5.2
Net Sales ($)	410547M	1385747M	4121830M	6725096M	5569608M	7334336M	64147870M	54946332M
Total Assets ($)	72341M	614243M	3036624M	5642020M	3328039M	4054251M	45232760M	38704255M

Comparative Historical Data				Current Data Sorted by Sales					
			Type of Statement						
101	78	67	Unqualified		2	4	6	5	50
179	192	149	Reviewed	1	21	22	41	41	23
279	233	179	Compiled	31	35	35	42	31	5
969	904	698	Tax Returns	218	233	111	84	36	16
897	734	717	Other	119	193	113	109	103	80
4/1/08-3/31/09 ALL	4/1/09-3/31/10 ALL	4/1/10-3/31/11 ALL		151 (4/1-9/30/10) 0-1MM	1-3MM	3-5MM	1,659 (10/1/10-3/31/11) 5-10MM	10-25MM	25MM & OVER
2425	2141	1810	**NUMBER OF STATEMENTS**	369	484	285	282	216	174
%	%	%	**ASSETS**	%	%	%	%	%	%
9.0	10.4	10.9	Cash & Equivalents	10.6	11.8	9.7	11.1	11.9	10.1
7.7	9.5	9.4	Trade Receivables (net)	5.4	7.1	10.3	14.6	11.0	12.4
55.6	50.4	48.6	Inventory	42.4	50.0	51.5	46.4	51.7	52.6
4.3	4.3	4.7	All Other Current	4.8	4.2	4.2	5.6	5.1	4.2
76.6	74.6	73.6	Total Current	63.2	73.1	75.7	77.7	79.8	79.3
14.0	15.6	15.5	Fixed Assets (net)	23.8	16.3	13.1	12.2	10.7	10.6
.7	.8	.8	Intangibles (net)	.7	.8	.9	1.0	.6	1.0
8.7	9.0	10.1	All Other Non-Current	12.3	9.7	10.3	9.2	8.9	9.0
100.0	100.0	100.0	Total	100.0	100.0	100.0	100.0	100.0	100.0
			LIABILITIES						
37.3	34.5	32.2	Notes Payable-Short Term	34.0	32.5	31.0	30.9	32.4	31.1
5.4	4.8	3.3	Cur. Mat.-L.T.D.	4.2	4.5	3.1	1.9	1.9	2.5
7.4	8.1	8.7	Trade Payables	5.2	7.3	8.9	11.0	10.6	13.4
.1	.1	.1	Income Taxes Payable	.1	.2	.2	.1	.2	.1
12.7	14.1	15.4	All Other Current	19.0	15.0	15.7	15.7	12.3	12.2
63.0	61.6	59.7	Total Current	62.4	59.4	58.9	59.5	57.5	59.4
15.7	15.1	14.8	Long-Term Debt	23.7	14.9	12.4	11.8	10.3	10.3
.0	.1	.1	Deferred Taxes	.0	.0	.1	.1	.4	.1
3.3	5.3	4.8	All Other Non-Current	6.0	5.8	3.9	3.7	3.8	4.1
18.0	18.0	20.5	Net Worth	7.8	19.9	24.7	24.9	28.0	26.1
100.0	100.0	100.0	Total Liabilties & Net Worth	100.0	100.0	100.0	100.0	100.0	100.0
			INCOME DATA						
100.0	100.0	100.0	Net Sales	100.0	100.0	100.0	100.0	100.0	100.0
17.9	18.1	18.9	Gross Profit	28.5	18.0	15.8	15.7	14.9	16.7
15.9	17.5	15.8	Operating Expenses	24.2	15.3	12.8	13.0	12.0	13.3
2.0	.6	3.1	Operating Profit	4.3	2.7	3.0	2.7	2.9	3.4
2.0	2.0	1.8	All Other Expenses (net)	4.5	1.2	.7	.8	1.0	1.5
.0	-1.4	1.4	Profit Before Taxes	-.2	1.5	2.2	1.8	1.8	1.9
			RATIOS						
1.8	2.1	2.2		2.5	2.4	2.3	1.9	2.0	2.0
1.2	1.2	1.3	Current	1.1	1.3	1.3	1.2	1.3	1.4
1.0	1.0	.9		.6	.9	1.0	1.0	1.0	1.1
.6	.8	.8		.6	.7	.9	.9	.8	.9
(2414) .1	(2138) .1	(1803) .2	Quick	(368) .1	(481) .1	(283) .2	.2	(215) .2	.2
.0	.0	.0		.0	.0	.0	.0	.1	.1
0 UND	0 UND	0 UND		0 UND	0 UND	0 UND	0 UND	0 UND	0 UND
0 UND	0 999.8	0 UND	Sales/Receivables	0 UND	0 UND	0 999.8	1 268.2	2 223.0	2 166.8
9 40.2	17 21.7	15 23.6		1 274.0	9 42.1	18 20.6	34 10.6	19 19.6	22 16.8
3 145.5	0 UND	0 UND		0 UND	0 UND	6 58.7	0 UND	0 891.0	0 UND
206 1.8	165 2.2	140 2.6	Cost of Sales/Inventory	143 2.6	155 2.3	111 3.3	119 3.1	163 2.2	161 2.3
488 .7	441 .8	368 1.0		735 .5	424 .9	310 1.2	277 1.3	306 1.2	305 1.2
0 UND	0 UND	0 UND		0 UND	0 UND	0 UND	3 133.8	8 48.6	9 40.0
7 50.9	9 40.5	9 39.2	Cost of Sales/Payables	0 UND	5 74.5	7 49.7	13 27.7	15 24.2	19 19.3
24 15.2	27 13.3	27 13.7		17 21.6	25 14.7	25 14.4	31 11.9	28 13.0	35 10.3
3.6	3.2	3.5		1.9	2.7	4.3	4.9	4.1	3.5
12.0	11.5	11.4	Sales/Working Capital	22.7	11.2	12.6	12.2	9.7	8.0
-54.1	-45.5	-55.0		-5.4	-28.9	-999.3	-547.3	88.4	37.6
7.5	6.5	9.9		6.0	7.0	11.7	16.5	13.2	16.6
(1791) 1.8	(1602) 1.5	(1324) 2.3	EBIT/Interest	(239) 1.3	(327) 1.6	(217) 2.7	(226) 3.2	(171) 2.5	(144) 3.0
-.5	-1.7	-.2		-2.3	-1.0	-.4	.3	.7	.7
8.4	5.2	8.7			3.0	12.3	10.2	13.9	36.1
(126) 2.0	(76) 1.1	(68) 1.8	Net Profit + Depr., Dep., Amort./Cur. Mat. L/T/D		(11) .7	(13) 3.7	(17) 2.2	(12) 1.6	(11) 2.9
.0	-.1	.3			.2	.4	.6	.4	.6
.0	.0	.0		.0	.0	.0	.0	.0	.0
.2	.2	.2	Fixed/Worth	.6	.3	.2	.2	.1	.1
2.3	3.0	2.3		23.6	3.3	1.2	1.2	1.1	.5
1.9	1.5	1.3		1.6	1.2	1.1	1.3	1.2	1.1
5.3	4.5	3.9	Debt/Worth	7.1	4.3	3.4	3.7	3.3	2.5
33.0	42.3	24.4		-23.5	41.1	14.1	12.7	9.3	5.8
41.5	34.1	46.6		59.7	43.1	55.8	44.4	48.3	32.1
(1962) 10.1	(1698) 7.5	(1473) 13.7	% Profit Before Taxes/Tangible Net Worth	(257) 6.8	(383) 11.3	(240) 17.5	(245) 16.1	(193) 14.3	(155) 15.3
-7.7	-10.0	-1.9		-9.2	-1.1	.3	-1.1	1.4	.5
7.5	7.5	10.4		9.0	10.0	13.7	10.9	11.5	11.1
1.2	1.0	2.6	% Profit Before Taxes/Total Assets	.3	2.2	4.2	3.8	2.9	3.6
-2.8	-4.2	-1.9		-4.1	-2.4	-1.2	-.5	-.5	-.5
412.6	316.6	407.2		UND	851.4	543.8	249.9	322.9	266.1
56.7	49.0	54.8	Sales/Net Fixed Assets	22.8	52.2	65.3	59.5	84.7	82.2
10.5	7.6	9.0		2.7	7.2	14.2	12.2	13.4	18.0
2.3	2.7	2.9		2.0	2.9	3.7	2.9	2.8	2.5
1.2	1.3	1.5	Sales/Total Assets	.8	1.4	1.9	1.9	1.6	1.6
.6	.6	.7		.3	.6	1.0	1.0	.9	1.1
.3	.3	.2		.8	.2	.2	.3	.1	.2
(1364) .6	(1229) .7	(956) .6	% Depr., Dep., Amort./Sales	(176) 2.3	(236) .6	(141) .6	(167) .6	(130) .4	(106) .3
1.3	1.7	1.7		4.8	1.5	1.2	1.2	.8	.8
1.3	1.4	1.4		3.9	1.8	1.4	1.0	.7	.4
(1021) 2.8	(914) 2.8	(726) 2.9	% Officers', Directors' Owners' Comp/Sales	(136) 7.1	(205) 3.2	(138) 2.5	(134) 1.7	(84) 1.4	(29) 1.7
5.4	5.3	5.8		11.8	6.5	4.8	3.2	2.8	2.5
32153669M	27531598M	25547164M	Net Sales ($)	192146M	914199M	1108335M	2007205M	3318131M	18007148M
26028273M	20723665M	16747518M	Total Assets ($)	448569M	1192217M	977736M	1580291M	2954651M	9594054M

M = $ thousand   MM = $ million
See Pages 9 through 22 for Explanation of Ratios and Data

Current Data Sorted by Assets | | | | | | | **Comparative Historical Data**

0-500M	500M-2MM	2-10MM	10-50MM	50-100MM	100-250MM	Type of Statement	4/1/06-3/31/07 ALL	4/1/07-3/31/08 ALL
		9	12	3	3	Unqualified	48	28
1	5	10	4		1	Reviewed	59	45
1		7	1			Compiled	31	30
5	11	7	2			Tax Returns	97	64
4	10	18	9	3		Other	87	90
	14 (4/1-9/30/10)		112 (10/1/10-3/31/11)					
11	26	51	28	6	4	**NUMBER OF STATEMENTS**	322	257
%	%	%	%	%	%	**ASSETS**	%	%
23.5	17.4	10.8	16.1			Cash & Equivalents	10.3	13.8
23.6	23.3	25.8	36.3			Trade Receivables (net)	20.7	22.5
13.3	28.6	24.8	10.2			Inventory	34.4	28.0
14.4	7.6	10.2	9.3			All Other Current	8.9	7.9
74.8	76.8	71.7	71.9			Total Current	74.3	72.1
12.5	15.7	16.9	10.8			Fixed Assets (net)	16.2	17.2
.4	.9	3.7	4.5			Intangibles (net)	1.5	1.3
12.3	6.6	7.7	12.7			All Other Non-Current	8.0	9.5
100.0	100.0	100.0	100.0			Total	100.0	100.0
						LIABILITIES		
30.6	16.0	15.7	10.1			Notes Payable-Short Term	27.0	20.2
.3	2.3	1.0	1.0			Cur. Mat.-L.T.D.	3.7	6.8
13.7	13.2	17.5	29.0			Trade Payables	15.9	16.7
.0	.0	.1	.0			Income Taxes Payable	.3	.6
15.0	20.1	15.9	12.9			All Other Current	15.3	13.4
59.6	51.6	50.2	53.1			Total Current	62.2	57.6
1.6	10.7	15.0	7.9			Long-Term Debt	11.6	14.8
.0	.0	.1	.1			Deferred Taxes	.1	.1
6.1	1.4	2.7	2.7			All Other Non-Current	3.3	2.6
32.7	36.2	32.1	36.2			Net Worth	22.8	24.9
100.0	100.0	100.0	100.0			Total Liabilties & Net Worth	100.0	100.0
						INCOME DATA		
100.0	100.0	100.0	100.0			Net Sales	100.0	100.0
40.7	13.5	14.7	13.2			Gross Profit	19.5	18.9
31.2	13.3	15.4	11.4			Operating Expenses	12.6	14.6
9.5	.2	-.7	1.8			Operating Profit	7.0	4.3
.2	.1	3.6	.6			All Other Expenses (net)	1.0	.5
9.3	.2	-4.2	1.2			Profit Before Taxes	6.0	3.8
						RATIOS		
2.5	2.9	2.6	1.6			Current	1.7	2.0
1.1	1.3	1.6	1.3				1.2	1.3
.4	1.0	1.1	1.2				1.0	1.0
1.4	1.5	1.6	1.3			Quick	1.2	1.3
.7	.8	1.0	1.0				.4	.8
.1	.2	.1	.8				.0	.1
0 UND	0 UND	0 UND	40 9.2			Sales/Receivables	0 UND	0 UND
0 UND	14 26.3	30 12.3	61 6.0				6 57.2	16 23.5
31 11.6	51 7.1	60 6.1	73 5.0				44 8.2	55 6.6
0 UND	0 UND	0 UND	0 UND			Cost of Sales/Inventory	0 UND	0 UND
0 UND	0 999.8	0 UND	0 UND				17 22.0	0 999.8
5 77.2	263 1.4	527 .7	7 50.8				258 1.4	228 1.6
0 UND	0 UND	7 53.9	30 12.0			Cost of Sales/Payables	2 166.2	2 185.6
16 23.5	13 27.8	23 16.1	47 7.7				16 22.8	17 21.9
67 5.4	26 13.9	48 7.7	79 4.6				42 8.7	40 9.2
7.8	4.7	3.4	9.1			Sales/Working Capital	6.4	5.7
104.4	15.1	9.1	16.1				19.1	18.9
-434.2	-332.6	20.5	22.5				-273.5	-144.9
	29.4	52.1	48.2			EBIT/Interest	25.3	15.2
	(16) 4.3	(33) 2.0	(22) 10.2				(225) 6.9	(184) 3.4
	.6	-4.0	1.2				1.6	.8
						Net Profit + Depr., Dep., Amort./Cur. Mat. L/T/D	5.1	22.1
							(33) 2.7	(20) 4.1
							1.0	.7
.0	.0	.0	.1			Fixed/Worth	.0	.1
.6	.1	.1	.1				.2	.3
UND	2.4	.6	.3				1.8	2.0
.2	.8	1.0	1.0			Debt/Worth	1.6	1.2
4.3	1.6	3.0	2.2				4.3	3.4
UND	22.1	4.4	3.3				16.4	14.4
	82.2	32.4	42.2			% Profit Before Taxes/Tangible Net Worth	75.4	68.0
	(22) 27.6	(45) 4.5	(26) 11.3				(276) 35.4	(220) 26.5
	-8.5	-17.0	2.3				9.5	1.7
63.6	25.4	8.5	11.4			% Profit Before Taxes/Total Assets	18.5	16.9
9.2	6.0	.3	3.0				7.0	5.1
.0	-3.5	-5.9	.3				1.1	-.1
UND	397.2	577.8	149.7			Sales/Net Fixed Assets	318.4	258.3
138.5	64.8	84.0	49.5				58.7	52.6
38.0	12.3	8.2	9.2				12.5	8.2
8.1	3.7	3.4	3.3			Sales/Total Assets	3.5	3.7
6.3	2.6	1.4	2.5				1.9	2.0
2.9	.6	.3	.9				.9	.9
	.3	.2	.2			% Depr., Dep., Amort./Sales	.2	.2
	(12) 1.4	(29) .5	(24) .4				(201) .5	(164) .5
	3.5	1.6	1.1				1.4	1.2
	2.0					% Officers', Directors' Owners' Comp/Sales	1.0	1.3
	(12) 2.6						(123) 2.3	(92) 2.5
	4.8						4.8	4.8
26845M	80953M	548451M	1498289M	803983M	186769M	Net Sales ($)	7553592M	6650354M
2967M	30220M	269074M	650530M	440345M	510656M	Total Assets ($)	4548691M	3995736M

© RMA 2011

M = $ thousand   MM = $ million
See Pages 9 through 22 for Explanation of Ratios and Data

Comparative Historical Data | Current Data Sorted by Sales

4/1/08-3/31/09 ALL	4/1/09-3/31/10 ALL	4/1/10-3/31/11 ALL	Type of Statement	0-1MM	1-3MM	3-5MM	5-10MM	10-25MM	25MM & OVER
19	33	27	Unqualified					9	18
30	33	21	Reviewed	1	2		6	8	4
17	13	9	Compiled	1	3	2	1	1	1
47	45	25	Tax Returns	12	8	3	1	1	
78	64	44	Other	6	8	7	5		9
				14 (4/1-9/30/10)			112 (10/1/10-3/31/11)		
191	188	126	**NUMBER OF STATEMENTS**	20	21	12	17	24	32
%	%	%	**ASSETS**	%	%	%	%	%	%
14.3	17.8	15.6	Cash & Equivalents	15.5	11.2	6.8	13.8	18.1	20.8
22.4	25.5	26.9	Trade Receivables (net)	4.9	7.8	14.2	39.7	41.7	39.9
26.4	22.6	19.7	Inventory	33.9	45.5	35.4	4.6	7.7	4.9
7.2	9.0	9.4	All Other Current	14.4	6.2	7.3	6.2	10.2	10.2
70.3	75.0	71.5	Total Current	68.6	70.8	63.8	64.3	77.7	75.9
18.3	13.3	16.8	Fixed Assets (net)	20.2	19.3	27.1	22.1	7.8	12.9
1.8	1.1	2.8	Intangibles (net)	2.9	.0	1.8	.1	6.0	4.0
9.6	10.6	8.9	All Other Non-Current	8.4	9.9	7.3	13.5	8.4	7.2
100.0	100.0	100.0	Total	100.0	100.0	100.0	100.0	100.0	100.0
			LIABILITIES						
20.0	17.6	14.7	Notes Payable-Short Term	23.2	25.9	34.1	8.0	5.8	4.9
2.5	2.6	1.2	Cur. Mat.-L.T.D.	3.8	.4	.7	.6	.8	.8
18.4	20.1	18.9	Trade Payables	3.8	6.2	6.4	21.4	27.3	33.7
.2	.3	.1	Income Taxes Payable	.0	.0	.0	.0	.2	.1
14.7	14.1	15.7	All Other Current	14.0	19.1	11.6	13.3	13.5	19.1
55.8	54.8	50.6	Total Current	44.9	51.7	52.9	43.3	47.6	58.6
16.8	11.0	12.4	Long-Term Debt	20.4	20.2	13.3	11.5	4.1	8.8
.1	.2	.0	Deferred Taxes	.0	.0	.0	.0	.2	.0
3.4	3.8	2.5	All Other Non-Current	3.4	3.0	.6	4.0	1.5	2.4
23.9	30.3	34.4	Net Worth	31.3	25.2	33.2	41.2	46.7	30.1
100.0	100.0	100.0	Total Liabilities & Net Worth	100.0	100.0	100.0	100.0	100.0	100.0
			INCOME DATA						
100.0	100.0	100.0	Net Sales	100.0	100.0	100.0	100.0	100.0	100.0
20.6	19.6	17.9	Gross Profit	29.9	15.2	19.1	16.3	12.7	16.5
17.2	15.9	16.3	Operating Expenses	27.8	19.4	17.5	13.8	11.7	11.4
3.4	3.7	1.6	Operating Profit	2.1	-4.2	1.7	2.5	1.1	5.1
1.3	1.1	2.0	All Other Expenses (net)	7.9	2.8	1.0	.9	-.7	.8
2.1	2.6	-.4	Profit Before Taxes	-5.7	-7.1	.6	1.6	1.8	4.2
			RATIOS						
1.9	2.2	2.1		5.9	3.3	1.4	2.5	2.2	1.5
1.3	1.4	1.3	Current	1.8	1.2	1.2	1.5	1.7	1.3
1.0	1.1	1.1		.8	.9	.8	1.0	1.3	1.2
1.2	1.4	1.5		1.1	1.5	1.0	2.4	1.8	1.4
.7	(186) 1.0	1.0	Quick	.1	.2	.3	1.4	1.3	1.2
.1	.2	.2		.0	.0	.1	1.0	.9	1.0
0 UND	0 930.5	0 UND		0 UND	0 UND	0 UND	17 21.4	32 11.4	39 9.5
19 18.9	33 11.1	33 11.0	Sales/Receivables	0 UND	0 UND	0 UND	52 7.1	50 7.3	59 6.2
49 7.5	62 5.9	63 5.8		8 43.2	22 16.8	31 11.9	68 5.3	71 5.2	69 5.3
0 UND	0 UND	0 UND		0 UND	0 UND	0 UND	0 UND	0 UND	0 UND
0 UND	0 UND	0 UND	Cost of Sales/Inventory	56 6.5	165 2.2	22 16.7	0 UND	0 UND	0 UND
308 1.2	161 2.3	53 6.8		1006 .4	1002 .4	460 .8	1 516.9	0 UND	0 UND
2 154.7	8 45.3	7 50.6		0 UND	1 616.5	0 UND	7 49.2	22 16.6	35 10.5
24 15.0	31 11.8	25 14.4	Cost of Sales/Payables	7 50.5	16 22.7	8 43.6	15 24.8	35 10.4	49 7.5
48 7.6	58 6.3	57 6.5		61 6.0	48 7.7	22 16.8	66 5.5	54 6.8	72 5.1
5.6	5.0	5.0		.7	2.2	4.8	5.7	7.3	9.7
16.0	12.1	12.1	Sales/Working Capital	1.4	10.4	18.5	18.1	9.3	15.7
-999.8	71.1	50.1		UND	NM	-144.3	NM	13.1	21.7
31.1	27.6	36.1				2.8	29.2	49.4	64.5
(134) 5.6	(135) 3.9	(86) 4.0	EBIT/Interest		(15) 1.2	(11) 2.4	(11) 20.5	(19) 10.2	(24) 10.9
.0	.2	-.8				-1.9	-5.0	-4.4	-3.7 ... 1.6
14.8	32.6	28.5							
(16) 5.0	(21) 5.7	(14) .9	Net Profit + Depr., Dep., Amort./Cur. Mat. L/T/D						
.6	2.4	-2.3							
.0	.0	.0		.0	.0	.0	.1	.1	.0
.2	.1	.1	Fixed/Worth	.1	.2	.3	.4	.1	.1
1.1	.8	1.1		15.0	4.4	1.0	1.6	.3	1.0
1.4	1.0	1.0		.4	1.0	1.1	.7	.8	1.5
3.4	2.1	2.3	Debt/Worth	5.2	3.8	3.5	1.5	1.2	2.7
11.5	9.4	4.4		UND	10.2	4.2	3.6	2.6	3.7
51.7	38.8	46.8		52.3	13.7	59.8	55.6	33.8	61.8
(171) 22.7	(162) 14.8	(112) 10.0	% Profit Before Taxes/Tangible Net Worth	(16) -.9	(17) 4.5	(11) 3.9	(16) 12.9	(23) 6.2	(29) 29.7
-2.3	1.8	-6.0		-21.6	-11.8	-82.6	-6.2	-9.7	9.1
12.8	10.2	11.8		9.8	3.1	25.5	17.6	11.0	18.3
4.0	3.8	2.0	% Profit Before Taxes/Total Assets	-1.6	.3	4.7	4.6	2.2	6.2
-1.7	-.4	-3.6		-7.4	-4.6	-6.5	-7.2	-4.9	1.7
395.1	305.9	289.8		UND	523.3	999.8	125.2	150.0	321.5
52.5	60.2	64.8	Sales/Net Fixed Assets	34.2	67.2	77.2	25.0	76.1	96.7
5.5	13.4	9.0		1.1	3.7	5.4	4.1	17.0	33.8
3.7	3.4	3.7		.7	2.2	3.9	4.4	3.9	3.7
1.8	2.0	2.3	Sales/Total Assets	.3	.4	1.9	3.1	3.3	2.7
.6	.9	.4		.2	.3	.5	1.4	1.7	2.1
.2	.2	.3					.4	.2	.2
(117) .6	(111) .6	(77) .5	% Depr., Dep., Amort./Sales				(14) .9	(17) .5	(29) .3
1.7	1.4	1.8					1.9	.7	.1
1.1	1.3	1.1							
(64) 2.5	(60) 2.7	(30) 2.0	% Officers', Directors' Owners' Comp/Sales						
7.6	6.0	5.8							
4877904M	6868698M	3145290M	Net Sales ($)	8061M	38614M	44608M	115660M	421081M	2517266M
2899208M	2499353M	1903792M	Total Assets ($)	31317M	86096M	48358M	114743M	297783M	1325495M

M = $ thousand   MM = $ million
See Pages 9 through 22 for Explanation of Ratios and Data

Current Data Sorted by Assets   Comparative Historical Data

							Type of Statement		
1		3	10	7	4		Unqualified	32	29
	6	9	12	2			Reviewed	54	36
1	2	12	2				Compiled	64	49
17	26	24	5				Tax Returns	110	126
7	17	32	30	5	3		Other	153	144
	16 (4/1-9/30/10)		221 (10/1/10-3/31/11)					4/1/06- 3/31/07	4/1/07- 3/31/08
0-500M	500M-2MM	2-10MM	10-50MM	50-100MM	100-250MM			ALL	ALL
26	51	80	59	14	7		**NUMBER OF STATEMENTS**	413	384
%	%	%	%	%	%		**ASSETS**	%	%
22.0	8.5	7.2	12.5	18.2			Cash & Equivalents	8.5	6.9
5.7	9.9	6.6	6.1	9.7			Trade Receivables (net)	8.2	7.3
23.2	42.7	56.2	55.7	38.1			Inventory	56.6	61.3
7.5	6.7	4.2	3.9	3.6			All Other Current	6.7	4.6
58.5	67.7	74.2	78.3	69.6			Total Current	80.0	80.2
32.2	18.7	18.2	11.5	14.8			Fixed Assets (net)	12.6	12.2
.0	.4	.7	.5	.3			Intangibles (net)	.8	.6
8.9	13.1	6.9	9.7	15.3			All Other Non-Current	6.5	7.0
100.0	100.0	100.0	100.0	100.0			Total	100.0	100.0
							LIABILITIES		
39.3	26.8	27.6	22.4	15.0			Notes Payable-Short Term	38.7	42.4
1.1	2.7	1.3	2.5	1.2			Cur. Mat.-L.T.D.	3.2	3.6
6.7	8.0	7.0	5.6	9.6			Trade Payables	8.6	6.8
.0	.1	.2	.2	.4			Income Taxes Payable	.2	.1
16.2	15.8	13.1	12.4	10.0			All Other Current	12.6	9.8
63.3	53.3	49.1	43.0	36.2			Total Current	63.4	62.8
26.4	16.8	16.4	18.0	12.8			Long-Term Debt	12.2	12.6
.0	.3	.0	.0	.3			Deferred Taxes	.2	.0
4.4	2.2	8.6	7.7	6.5			All Other Non-Current	4.3	4.3
5.9	27.5	26.0	31.3	44.1			Net Worth	19.9	20.2
100.0	100.0	100.0	100.0	100.0			Total Liabilities & Net Worth	100.0	100.0
							INCOME DATA		
100.0	100.0	100.0	100.0	100.0			Net Sales	100.0	100.0
18.3	23.3	17.7	19.0	17.5			Gross Profit	19.9	18.9
16.7	20.5	15.2	16.9	14.1			Operating Expenses	13.2	13.4
1.6	2.8	2.5	2.2	3.4			Operating Profit	6.7	5.5
.4	1.2	3.6	2.6	4.8			All Other Expenses (net)	.9	1.7
1.2	1.6	-1.0	-.5	-1.3			Profit Before Taxes	5.8	3.7
							RATIOS		
2.0	2.5	2.4	3.3	6.2				1.7	1.7
1.1	1.3	1.3	1.5	1.6			Current	1.2	1.2
.3	.9	1.0	1.2	1.3				1.0	1.0
1.3	.8	.8	.9	2.2				.5	.4
.2 (50)	.3 (79)	.1	.2	1.0			Quick (411)	.1	.1
.0	.0	.0	.0	.1				.0	.0
0 UND	0 UND	0 UND	0 UND	0 UND				0 UND	0 UND
0 UND	0 UND	1 318.6	1 646.2	25 14.7			Sales/Receivables	0 999.8	0 999.8
1 446.3	24 15.3	14 26.3	12 29.6	72 5.1				9 39.6	10 36.2
0 UND	0 UND	42 8.7	76 4.8	2 165.2				8 46.2	33 11.1
0 UND	155 2.4	245 1.5	272 1.3	213 1.7			Cost of Sales/Inventory	212 1.7	235 1.6
36 10.0	305 1.2	664 .5	483 .8	671 .5				392 .9	466 .8
0 UND	0 UND	2 164.0	8 44.2	10 37.2				0 973.5	0 996.0
0 UND	4 96.8	12 31.6	15 23.8	31 11.7			Cost of Sales/Payables	11 33.5	10 37.4
4 102.9	27 13.6	38 9.7	32 11.4	59 6.2				29 12.8	27 13.5
13.6	2.3	2.0	1.8	1.2				4.5	3.6
537.9	11.3	6.7	3.1	2.0			Sales/Working Capital	12.4	9.7
-13.4	-37.3	87.5	7.8	11.1				82.2	71.1
10.4	10.6	8.2	7.6	84.0				21.0	11.2
(18) 4.2	(43) 1.9	(55) 1.7	(49) 2.0	(10) 21.1			EBIT/Interest (319)	5.2 (287)	2.8
.5	-1.0	-.2	-.4	4.9				1.5	.7
								10.4	17.9
							Net Profit + Depr., Dep., Amort./Cur. Mat. L/T/D (18)	4.6 (22)	3.1
								1.4	.0
.0	.0	.0	.0	.0				.0	.0
.4	.2	.1	.1	.1			Fixed/Worth	.1	.1
NM	6.4	2.4	.4	.5				1.2	1.2
.9	.8	1.3	1.1	.6				2.3	2.3
2.9	2.0	3.7	1.9	1.2			Debt/Worth	5.4	5.6
-4.4	17.5	11.1	8.0	3.3				18.8	18.2
177.0	34.9	27.1	19.7	14.4				84.6	52.4
(18) 61.1	(42) 6.1	(71) 7.4	(52) 7.9	6.9			% Profit Before Taxes/Tangible Net Worth (367)	43.3 (332)	20.6
-24.8	-5.0	-9.2	-2.4	-.2				13.3	2.4
36.2	9.3	6.6	6.5	7.4				14.5	8.7
9.6	2.7	1.5	2.4	3.2			% Profit Before Taxes/Total Assets	6.0	2.9
-16.0	-1.5	-3.0	-2.3	.0				1.0	-.4
UND	643.8	980.2	383.1	88.0				263.0	289.2
79.6	29.7	63.9	57.6	34.3			Sales/Net Fixed Assets	73.1	77.3
10.2	6.1	3.4	8.5	2.3				17.0	14.8
9.3	2.5	2.0	1.7	1.4				2.5	2.1
4.9	1.3	1.1	.9	.8			Sales/Total Assets	1.4	1.2
2.4	.6	.3	.5	.4				.8	.7
.8	.3	.1	.2					.2	.2
(10) 1.3	(33) .6	(37) .4	(31) .5				% Depr., Dep., Amort./Sales (246)	.4 (221)	.5
2.2	2.1	1.5	2.2					1.0	1.1
	1.8	.8	.6					1.3	1.1
(28)	3.2 (28)	1.8 (10)	1.6				% Officers', Directors' Owners' Comp/Sales (163)	2.4 (162)	2.1
	6.1	3.5	3.4					6.3	4.3
29469M	102609M	483833M	1585111M	1074262M	1731763M		Net Sales ($)	11295282M	8061190M
5893M	59008M	384446M	1342270M	1087904M	1146178M		Total Assets ($)	8729070M	6884569M

© RMA 2011

M = $ thousand   MM = $ million
See Pages 9 through 22 for Explanation of Ratios and Data

Comparative Historical Data | Current Data Sorted by Sales

Type of Statement									
Unqualified	25	26	25	1			2	4	18
Reviewed	38	30	29		1	6	8	9	5
Compiled	26	29	17	1	5	2	6	2	1
Tax Returns	97	96	72	25	31	3	8	5	1
Other	133	108	94	19	20	9	16	15	15
	4/1/08-3/31/09 ALL	4/1/09-3/31/10 ALL	4/1/10-3/31/11 ALL	16 (4/1-9/30/10) 0-1MM	1-3MM	3-5MM	221 (10/1/10-3/31/11) 5-10MM	10-25MM	25MM & OVER
NUMBER OF STATEMENTS	319	289	237	46	57	20	40	35	39
ASSETS	%	%	%	%	%	%	%	%	%
Cash & Equivalents	9.5	8.4	11.2	10.9	7.6	10.2	8.2	12.9	18.9
Trade Receivables (net)	6.3	7.5	7.3	4.6	4.4	9.7	8.9	7.2	12.1
Inventory	57.4	52.4	48.4	42.0	51.6	47.0	45.6	60.5	44.2
All Other Current	3.7	4.3	5.0	3.6	3.9	13.1	4.6	5.4	4.4
Total Current	76.9	72.7	72.0	61.0	67.4	80.1	67.4	86.0	79.6
Fixed Assets (net)	14.6	15.8	17.9	24.8	27.1	9.4	20.4	6.4	8.7
Intangibles (net)	.3	1.0	.5	.3	.3	.6	1.1	.1	.6
All Other Non-Current	8.2	10.4	9.6	13.8	5.2	9.9	11.1	7.5	11.2
Total	100.0	100.0	100.0	100.0	100.0	100.0	100.0	100.0	100.0
LIABILITIES									
Notes Payable-Short Term	39.3	33.2	26.5	30.0	32.7	30.3	23.0	27.6	13.9
Cur. Mat.-L.T.D.	4.1	3.8	1.9	2.5	1.8	.8	2.7	2.2	.5
Trade Payables	6.4	7.8	7.1	5.3	3.8	8.2	9.7	5.2	12.7
Income Taxes Payable	.0	.1	.1	.1	.0	.1	.1	.0	.4
All Other Current	10.8	13.0	13.4	17.6	16.3	8.6	9.2	11.7	12.8
Total Current	60.7	57.9	49.0	55.5	54.7	48.1	44.7	46.7	40.3
Long-Term Debt	13.2	16.6	17.7	27.5	20.4	21.4	15.1	9.6	10.5
Deferred Taxes	.1	.1	.1	.0	.0	.7	.0	.0	.1
All Other Non-Current	4.9	6.1	6.3	3.3	5.9	3.0	9.6	10.0	5.1
Net Worth	21.1	19.3	26.9	13.7	18.9	26.9	30.6	33.7	44.0
Total Liabilties & Net Worth	100.0	100.0	100.0	100.0	100.0	100.0	100.0	100.0	100.0
INCOME DATA									
Net Sales	100.0	100.0	100.0	100.0	100.0	100.0	100.0	100.0	100.0
Gross Profit	16.8	15.6	19.4	26.4	20.2	17.8	16.8	14.7	17.4
Operating Expenses	15.3	15.8	17.1	22.9	20.5	18.5	13.8	12.4	12.2
Operating Profit	1.4	-.2	2.2	3.5	-.3	-.8	3.0	2.3	5.2
All Other Expenses (net)	2.3	2.3	2.5	3.6	2.8	3.2	3.2	1.0	.7
Profit Before Taxes	-.8	-2.5	-.2	-.2	-3.2	-3.9	-.2	1.3	4.5
RATIOS									
Current	1.9 / 1.2 / 1.0	2.0 / 1.3 / .9	2.7 / 1.4 / 1.0	1.9 / 1.3 / .6	3.1 / 1.2 / .9	2.6 / 1.7 / 1.1	2.1 / 1.3 / 1.0	2.7 / 1.8 / 1.3	4.7 / 1.7 / 1.3
Quick	.5 / (316) .1 / .0	.7 / (286) .1 / .0	.9 / (235) .2 / .0	.6 / (45) .1 / .0	.5 / .1 / .0	1.1 / .1 / .0	.9 / (39) .1 / .0	1.1 / .2 / .0	1.3 / .7 / .2
Sales/Receivables	0 UND / 0 999.8 / 8 47.5	0 UND / 0 999.8 / 12 30.5	0 UND / 0 920.7 / 17 20.9	0 UND / 0 UND / 9 40.6	0 UND / 0 UND / 13 27.2	0 UND / 1 718.3 / 24 15.3	0 UND / 2 179.4 / 20 18.5	0 UND / 1 311.9 / 7 55.8	0 UND / 1 396.8 / 47 7.8
Cost of Sales/Inventory	2 176.5 / 245 1.5 / 525 .7	4 99.2 / 209 1.7 / 494 .7	1 407.2 / 200 1.8 / 453 .8	0 UND / 353 1.0 / 1373 .3	32 11.6 / 219 1.7 / 483 .8	0 UND / 185 2.0 / 1123 .3	0 UND / 152 2.4 / 347 1.1	120 3.0 / 263 1.4 / 379 1.0	1 403.0 / 175 2.1 / 276 1.3
Cost of Sales/Payables	1 350.2 / 9 39.7 / 26 14.0	0 999.8 / 10 37.3 / 29 12.7	0 UND / 11 32.6 / 33 10.9	0 UND / 1 569.0 / 51 7.2	0 UND / 4 100.3 / 23 16.1	0 UND / 11 33.4 / 40 9.2	3 113.5 / 10 35.6 / 40 9.1	7 53.9 / 14 25.9 / 20 17.8	11 32.6 / 23 15.7 / 36 10.0
Sales/Working Capital	2.5 / 8.8 / 440.2	2.3 / 9.4 / -40.9	2.1 / 5.9 / NM	.9 / 17.1 / -3.4	1.9 / 25.6 / -15.9	2.6 / 5.5 / 13.9	2.5 / 7.4 / 87.5	2.0 / 3.4 / 5.6	2.2 / 4.1 / 12.7
EBIT/Interest	5.1 / (235) 1.5 / -1.0	5.1 / (221) .8 / -1.8	9.3 / (181) 2.4 / -.2	3.8 / (28) 1.2 / -1.1	9.8 / (41) 1.7 / -.6	11.6 / (17) 1.1 / -.8	6.8 / (33) 2.2 / -.5	8.5 / (29) 3.0 / -1.1	37.1 / (33) 7.3 / 2.8
Net Profit + Depr., Dep., Amort./Cur. Mat. L/T/D	22.5 / (12) 4.5 / .4	5.6 / (16) 1.2 / -.1	7.1 / (10) 1.9 / .0						
Fixed/Worth	.0 / .2 / 1.9	.0 / .2 / 2.8	.0 / .1 / 1.6	.0 / .4 / 7.6	.0 / 1.0 / 8.0	.0 / .1 / .3	.0 / .2 / 2.3	.0 / .1 / .4	.0 / .1 / .3
Debt/Worth	1.6 / 4.3 / 15.8	1.4 / 3.9 / 83.4	1.0 / 2.4 / 11.0	1.5 / 3.1 / NM	1.2 / 7.1 / 195.0	.9 / 2.5 / 15.6	1.1 / 2.1 / 8.7	1.0 / 2.1 / 7.6	.7 / 1.3 / 3.0
% Profit Before Taxes/Tangible Net Worth	30.0 / (269) 7.6 / -6.5	28.0 / (226) 5.3 / -12.5	31.7 / (204) 8.4 / -5.1	24.4 / (35) 3.1 / -9.2	33.3 / (44) 5.2 / -21.7	33.2 / (17) 1.8 / -15.9	40.9 / (37) 12.2 / -14.7	34.1 / (32) 9.8 / .3	31.5 / 11.4 / 3.5
% Profit Before Taxes/Total Assets	5.7 / 1.0 / -3.1	5.4 / .3 / -5.0	8.6 / 2.3 / -2.3	6.6 / .4 / -1.6	5.3 / .8 / -5.3	9.4 / .3 / -3.8	10.6 / 2.6 / -3.5	6.5 / 2.8 / -.8	10.5 / 5.1 / 1.7
Sales/Net Fixed Assets	314.8 / 58.8 / 9.6	220.3 / 47.3 / 6.2	625.0 / 45.1 / 6.7	UND / 11.4 / .7	956.7 / 36.7 / 3.8	800.2 / 46.7 / 13.8	481.8 / 35.2 / 9.6	599.5 / 84.3 / 15.1	223.0 / 63.0 / 17.3
Sales/Total Assets	2.0 / 1.1 / .6	2.2 / 1.0 / .5	2.2 / 1.2 / .5	1.4 / .5 / .2	2.7 / 1.2 / .5	3.0 / 1.7 / .4	2.6 / 1.3 / .8	2.0 / 1.2 / .8	2.3 / 1.5 / .9
% Depr., Dep., Amort./Sales	.2 / (172) .5 / 1.6	.3 / (167) .7 / 1.5	.2 / (124) .6 / 1.9	.9 / (18) 1.7 / 3.2	.3 / (29) .8 / 2.0	.2 / (13) .8 / 2.6	.1 / (22) .6 / 1.7	.1 / (20) .4 / 1.3	.1 / (22) .2 / .6
% Officers', Directors', Owners' Comp/Sales	1.1 / (103) 2.2 / 3.9	.9 / (92) 2.4 / 5.1	1.3 / (75) 2.3 / 5.0		1.9 / (24) 3.3 / 5.8	1.0 / (14) 3.2 / 4.8	.5 / (14) 1.8 / 2.1	(10) .7 / 2.8	
Net Sales ($)	5965667M	6700173M	5007047M	24006M	98056M	81174M	314668M	583596M	3905547M
Total Assets ($)	5457664M	5848096M	4025699M	79823M	298560M	136428M	370930M	533063M	2606895M

M = $ thousand   MM = $ million
See Pages 9 through 22 for Explanation of Ratios and Data

Current Data Sorted by Assets — Comparative Historical Data

0-500M	500M-2MM	2-10MM	10-50MM	50-100MM	100-250MM	Type of Statement	4/1/06-3/31/07 ALL	4/1/07-3/31/08 ALL
1		2	2		1	Unqualified	1	
	2	5	1			Reviewed	11	10
3	9	6	1			Compiled	9	9
28	15	4		1		Tax Returns	37	39
22	15	7	2	1	2	Other	25	28
		15 (4/1-9/30/10)	115 (10/1/10-3/31/11)					
54	41	24	6	2	3	NUMBER OF STATEMENTS	83	86
%	%	%	%	%	%	ASSETS	%	%
20.6	14.0	16.0				Cash & Equivalents	16.1	15.7
17.6	39.3	35.0				Trade Receivables (net)	19.0	26.5
6.8	7.8	10.0				Inventory	21.3	14.6
6.7	6.0	5.8				All Other Current	7.5	10.1
51.6	67.2	66.9				Total Current	64.0	66.8
32.0	18.5	20.2				Fixed Assets (net)	23.2	21.6
5.9	7.8	7.0				Intangibles (net)	2.8	3.4
10.2	6.5	5.9				All Other Non-Current	10.0	8.3
100.0	100.0	100.0				Total	100.0	100.0
						LIABILITIES		
37.9	14.0	5.7				Notes Payable-Short Term	17.7	17.4
9.9	5.0	4.9				Cur. Mat.-L.T.D.	8.2	6.1
27.3	15.0	21.0				Trade Payables	21.3	16.1
.0	.0	.4				Income Taxes Payable	.2	.4
13.5	15.9	13.7				All Other Current	13.6	16.4
88.6	50.0	45.7				Total Current	60.9	56.4
46.9	11.2	12.4				Long-Term Debt	14.0	18.7
.1	.0	.6				Deferred Taxes	.1	.1
10.3	11.9	5.8				All Other Non-Current	6.6	7.0
-46.1	27.0	35.5				Net Worth	18.5	17.9
100.0	100.0	100.0				Total Liabilities & Net Worth	100.0	100.0
						INCOME DATA		
100.0	100.0	100.0				Net Sales	100.0	100.0
36.7	35.2	29.2				Gross Profit	29.3	28.8
31.7	30.9	24.4				Operating Expenses	26.0	23.7
5.0	4.2	4.7				Operating Profit	3.2	5.0
1.0	1.0	.2				All Other Expenses (net)	.4	1.1
4.1	3.2	4.5				Profit Before Taxes	2.8	3.9

RATIOS

0-500M	500M-2MM	2-10MM	10-50MM	50-100MM	100-250MM	Ratio	4/1/06-3/31/07 ALL	4/1/07-3/31/08 ALL
2.0 .8 .3	2.4 1.4 .8	2.2 1.2 1.0				Current	2.4 1.2 .8	2.2 1.3 .9
1.4 .5 .1	1.9 1.2 .3	1.7 1.0 .7				Quick	1.7 .7 .1	1.6 .9 .4
0 UND 2 168.4 18 19.8	7 53.5 38 9.7 68 5.4	21 17.2 42 8.8 59 6.1				Sales/Receivables	0 UND 8 47.4 31 11.6	0 UND 17 21.4 46 7.9
0 UND 0 UND 2 206.5	0 UND 0 UND 4 102.7	0 UND 0 UND 1 673.0				Cost of Sales/Inventory	0 UND 0 UND 59 6.2	0 UND 0 UND 18 20.7
0 UND 8 44.1 23 15.8	5 78.9 17 21.1 33 11.0	14 26.3 25 14.7 40 9.2				Cost of Sales/Payables	1 483.0 14 27.0 30 12.1	0 UND 16 23.0 36 10.2
24.8 -70.6 -9.5	6.5 19.3 -52.4	6.8 19.7 -999.8				Sales/Working Capital	9.1 49.7 -25.2	8.3 27.1 -47.5
17.8 (46) 3.2 1.1	24.4 (35) 3.3 -1.3	21.5 (22) 7.7 2.7				EBIT/Interest	12.2 (59) 4.5 1.1	18.5 (69) 5.9 1.1
						Net Profit + Depr., Dep., Amort./Cur. Mat. L/T/D		8.6 (10) 2.7 .2
.2 2.6 -.3	.2 .4 -5.5	.2 .4 2.4				Fixed/Worth	.2 .7 6.0	.2 .5 12.8
1.1 6.7 -1.9	1.1 1.9 -15.7	1.3 2.3 7.2				Debt/Worth	.9 3.6 22.5	.9 3.8 60.7
141.8 (31) 35.4 .9	72.0 (30) 28.0 -.4	68.2 (20) 45.2 9.1				% Profit Before Taxes/Tangible Net Worth	100.0 (67) 34.6 8.7	86.8 (67) 31.6 8.8
38.9 18.8 .2	22.1 5.5 -2.2	19.4 12.7 3.2				% Profit Before Taxes/Total Assets	19.2 7.6 .0	26.6 7.5 1.3
139.1 38.9 10.7	131.6 22.9 10.4	65.4 24.3 10.2				Sales/Net Fixed Assets	79.5 28.9 14.4	124.4 32.1 10.9
9.7 6.7 3.5	5.6 3.2 1.8	4.1 3.1 1.9				Sales/Total Assets	5.1 3.2 1.3	5.5 3.5 1.5
.6 (27) 1.4 2.4	.3 (29) .9 2.1	.5 (17) 1.2 2.8				% Depr., Dep., Amort./Sales	.3 (56) .8 1.5	.5 (58) 1.1 2.0
3.1 (35) 6.3 9.6	1.8 (21) 3.0 4.7					% Officers', Directors' Owners' Comp/Sales	2.6 (49) 4.0 7.2	2.3 (52) 3.5 9.0
86448M 12113M	195269M 48594M	281152M 91089M	282799M 132102M	1034110M 149931M	1124650M 663280M	Net Sales ($) Total Assets ($)	1141863M 411056M	871204M 426249M

© RMA 2011

M = $ thousand   MM = $ million
See Pages 9 through 22 for Explanation of Ratios and Data

Comparative Historical Data / Current Data Sorted by Sales

Type of Statement

	4/1/08-3/31/09 ALL	4/1/09-3/31/10 ALL	4/1/10-3/31/11 ALL	0-1MM	1-3MM	3-5MM	5-10MM	10-25MM	25MM & OVER
Unqualified	2	7	6		1			2	3
Reviewed	18	13	8		1	3		2	2
Compiled	17	15	19	3	3	6		2	1
Tax Returns	48	34	48	15	16	7	6	3	1
Other	32	37	49	11	14	8	4	6	6
				15 (4/1-9/30/10)			115 (10/1/10-3/31/11)		
NUMBER OF STATEMENTS	117	106	130	30	34	19	19	15	13

Assets

	%	%	%	%	%	%	%	%	%
Cash & Equivalents	14.9	16.5	16.6	16.2	14.8	19.9	15.3	25.6	8.4
Trade Receivables (net)	28.5	28.5	28.6	10.4	24.3	39.4	46.7	34.2	32.9
Inventory	10.7	9.5	8.4	17.3	6.5	5.5	3.4	.0	14.6
All Other Current	6.8	10.4	6.7	7.2	5.5	4.4	7.2	7.7	9.7
Total Current	60.9	65.0	60.3	51.1	51.2	69.2	72.6	67.5	65.6
Fixed Assets (net)	26.4	21.4	23.4	28.2	31.6	21.4	17.6	19.7	6.8
Intangibles (net)	2.6	6.1	8.2	8.0	9.3	5.1	2.3	7.4	19.3
All Other Non-Current	10.1	7.5	8.1	12.3	7.9	4.3	7.4	5.4	8.3
Total	100.0	100.0	100.0	100.0	100.0	100.0	100.0	100.0	100.0

Liabilities

Notes Payable-Short Term	19.5	17.3	21.5	43.5	24.7	15.5	11.2	6.7	2.6
Cur. Mat.-L.T.D.	4.4	4.2	7.0	10.9	6.1	11.2	2.8	3.5	4.8
Trade Payables	24.8	14.6	21.0	11.5	30.2	15.7	23.6	26.5	15.9
Income Taxes Payable	.3	.2	.2	.0	.0	.4	.2	.0	.7
All Other Current	20.3	21.4	15.2	13.1	12.8	14.1	23.3	9.5	22.4
Total Current	69.3	57.7	64.8	79.0	73.9	56.9	61.2	46.2	46.4
Long-Term Debt	23.7	20.0	28.3	31.9	33.8	47.3	11.3	2.6	32.0
Deferred Taxes	.1	.1	.2	.0	.1	.1	.8	.0	.9
All Other Non-Current	7.2	11.5	9.1	10.3	11.2	2.2	14.2	12.1	.1
Net Worth	-.2	10.7	-2.5	-21.5	-18.9	-6.5	12.5	39.1	20.6
Total Liabilities & Net Worth	100.0	100.0	100.0	100.0	100.0	100.0	100.0	100.0	100.0

Income Data

Net Sales	100.0	100.0	100.0	100.0	100.0	100.0	100.0	100.0	100.0
Gross Profit	29.5	32.1	34.4	37.4	39.1	38.2	28.1	24.2	30.9
Operating Expenses	25.5	29.4	29.7	32.6	33.9	31.7	25.8	19.9	25.9
Operating Profit	4.0	2.7	4.8	4.8	5.2	6.5	2.4	4.4	5.0
All Other Expenses (net)	1.2	.6	1.2	1.1	.8	2.1	.0	.2	4.1
Profit Before Taxes	2.8	2.1	3.6	3.7	4.5	4.4	2.4	4.2	.9

Ratios

Current	2.0	2.6	2.2	1.7	2.9	2.3	1.9	2.3	2.3
	1.2	1.4	1.1	.7	1.0	1.3	1.1	1.3	1.2
	.8	.8	.6	.1	.6	.4	.7	.9	1.0
Quick	1.8	1.8	1.6	.8	1.9	2.2	1.8	2.3	1.2
	.9	.9	.9	.2	.8	1.2	1.0	1.1	.9
	.3	.4	.3	.0	.2	.3	.6	.8	.6
Sales/Receivables	0 UND	0 UND	0 UND	0 UND	0 UND	0 UND	13 28.1	11 32.1	27 13.5
	19 19.4	25 14.7	22 16.4	0 UND	9 39.6	35 10.6	44 8.3	28 13.1	43 8.5
	47 7.7	51 7.1	45 8.0	34 10.8	34 10.7	58 6.3	64 5.7	44 8.3	72 5.0
Cost of Sales/Inventory	0 UND	0 UND	0 UND	0 UND	0 UND	0 UND	0 UND	0 UND	0 UND
	0 UND	0 UND	0 UND	0 UND	0 UND	0 UND	0 UND	0 UND	3 118.2
	9 38.6	9 40.8	3 116.1	74 4.9	2 228.2	1 381.5	1 326.9	0 UND	40 9.1
Cost of Sales/Payables	1 365.8	1 546.5	1 308.6	0 UND	0 UND	0 UND	13 28.8	15 24.4	17 21.9
	15 25.0	14 25.5	16 22.6	2 170.5	8 42.9	11 33.2	23 15.7	18 19.8	28 13.0
	35 10.4	32 11.2	33 11.1	25 14.9	28 12.8	23 15.9	47 7.7	36 10.1	48 7.7
Sales/Working Capital	9.4	7.8	9.7	6.3	9.5	9.9	8.3	12.4	6.6
	30.4	20.4	59.3	-17.3	341.0	19.3	119.7	45.8	25.2
	-40.4	-41.0	-19.7	-8.4	-27.3	-12.1	-41.0	-84.7	NM
EBIT/Interest	13.0	10.9	17.8	8.3	42.0	6.7	44.8	22.8	
	(97) 4.4	(81) 2.9	(110) 4.2	(25) 1.4	(30) 4.0	(16) 3.7	(17) 8.7	(13) 12.5	
	1.4	-1.2	.7	-.7	1.1	1.1	-1.7	5.8	
Net Profit + Depr., Dep., Amort./Cur. Mat. L/T/D	16.2								
	(16) 2.7								
	.6								
Fixed/Worth	.1	.2	.2	.2	.2	.1	.2	.1	.2
	.8	.8	1.0	5.8	1.0	.4	.7	.3	1.6
	UND	-2.4	-1.1	-.8	-.6	-1.1	-2.4	1.2	-.2
Debt/Worth	1.2	.8	1.1	2.5	1.0	.8	1.2	.6	1.7
	3.4	3.4	3.9	UND	2.8	3.4	4.8	1.9	6.3
	-37.9	-7.7	-4.4	-2.3	-4.3	-4.0	-7.8	3.8	-3.1
% Profit Before Taxes/Tangible Net Worth	68.0	81.9	95.6	130.1	122.6	132.9	79.7	95.2	
	(85) 29.5	(69) 34.6	(87) 35.4	(16) 33.7	(24) 22.0	(12) 29.0	(13) 17.4	(14) 52.9	
	4.7	4.3	5.5	-3.4	.2	2.7	-16.1	12.5	
% Profit Before Taxes/Total Assets	22.6	22.6	28.3	28.9	37.1	28.9	19.1	25.8	21.4
	7.2	6.7	12.4	6.8	16.8	12.7	7.0	15.4	6.5
	.8	-2.5	-.4	-2.7	-.1	.1	-3.8	4.7	2.0
Sales/Net Fixed Assets	98.2	81.1	117.6	180.9	91.9	191.7	194.9	201.0	115.7
	25.7	28.3	32.6	16.6	27.7	32.9	52.6	51.8	69.4
	8.0	12.0	10.7	4.9	10.7	13.0	16.6	10.8	25.5
Sales/Total Assets	6.9	5.6	7.2	6.0	9.3	8.1	7.2	6.9	3.6
	3.3	3.5	3.7	2.4	5.2	4.2	4.3	4.7	2.2
	2.0	2.1	2.1	1.1	2.7	2.0	3.2	2.9	1.3
% Depr., Dep., Amort./Sales	.5	.6	.3	1.0	.5	1.1	.2		
	(86) 1.1	(73) 1.2	(79) 1.1	(15) 2.1	(22) 1.2	(11) 1.8	(15) .9		
	2.3	2.1	2.3	3.5	2.7	4.3	1.7		
% Officers', Directors' Owners' Comp/Sales	2.3	3.0	2.0	3.2	3.3	1.4	1.6		
	(69) 3.9	(53) 5.5	(69) 3.8	(12) 5.5	(22) 5.1	(14) 3.6	(11) 2.0		
	6.2	8.5	7.3	15.1	9.1	9.2	2.5		
Net Sales ($)	1885023M	3148923M	3004428M	14313M	62494M	75095M	130553M	223717M	2498256M
Total Assets ($)	488971M	853858M	1097109M	13859M	15658M	24276M	32291M	54915M	956110M

M = $ thousand   MM = $ million
See Pages 9 through 22 for Explanation of Ratios and Data

Current Data Sorted by Assets

Comparative Historical Data

						Type of Statement		
7	7	45	71	23	10	Unqualified	218	172
7	56	126	24	4	1	Reviewed	224	170
6	8	9	4			Compiled	34	24
30	28	26	4		2	Tax Returns	99	84
22	32	69	24	9	7	Other	154	147
	119 (4/1-9/30/10)		535 (10/1/10-3/31/11)				4/1/06-3/31/07	4/1/07-3/31/08
0-500M	500M-2MM	2-10MM	10-50MM	50-100MM	100-250MM		ALL	ALL
65	131	275	127	36	20	NUMBER OF STATEMENTS	729	597
%	%	%	%	%	%	ASSETS	%	%
20.5	20.2	20.3	25.9	25.9	19.8	Cash & Equivalents	19.0	18.7
31.8	39.3	42.3	42.2	37.3	33.9	Trade Receivables (net)	45.0	40.3
.6	3.8	4.3	3.2	.4	3.0	Inventory	4.1	6.7
3.9	7.9	8.0	7.6	9.6	6.5	All Other Current	9.6	9.6
56.8	71.2	75.0	79.0	73.3	63.2	Total Current	77.7	75.3
28.9	18.2	15.4	13.0	14.7	26.1	Fixed Assets (net)	14.6	16.9
4.0	1.6	1.8	1.6	3.7	3.3	Intangibles (net)	1.0	1.1
10.3	9.0	7.9	6.5	8.3	7.4	All Other Non-Current	6.8	6.7
100.0	100.0	100.0	100.0	100.0	100.0	Total	100.0	100.0
						LIABILITIES		
23.3	10.4	5.9	4.0	1.2	8.0	Notes Payable-Short Term	7.3	7.2
3.5	3.0	2.5	1.1	.9	3.9	Cur. Mat.-L.T.D.	3.0	3.1
21.1	22.0	26.6	30.4	23.5	21.8	Trade Payables	31.1	27.4
.4	.6	.5	.2	.3	.8	Income Taxes Payable	.4	.5
17.7	13.6	13.4	16.5	25.6	15.6	All Other Current	18.3	17.9
66.0	49.6	49.0	52.2	51.5	50.1	Total Current	60.0	56.2
16.9	9.0	7.0	4.7	6.2	13.8	Long-Term Debt	8.0	8.7
.1	.3	.3	.2	.1	.1	Deferred Taxes	.3	.4
11.3	2.8	1.2	1.4	3.6	15.2	All Other Non-Current	2.1	3.1
5.7	38.2	42.5	41.5	38.5	20.7	Net Worth	29.5	31.6
100.0	100.0	100.0	100.0	100.0	100.0	Total Liabilities & Net Worth	100.0	100.0
						INCOME DATA		
100.0	100.0	100.0	100.0	100.0	100.0	Net Sales	100.0	100.0
37.3	21.7	16.8	13.9	13.4	22.9	Gross Profit	16.5	17.6
34.8	20.3	15.2	11.0	9.3	16.7	Operating Expenses	12.6	13.5
2.5	1.4	1.6	3.0	4.1	6.3	Operating Profit	4.0	4.2
.2	.5	.2	.4	-.1	2.5	All Other Expenses (net)	.0	.0
2.3	.9	1.4	2.6	4.2	3.8	Profit Before Taxes	4.0	4.2
						RATIOS		
2.0	2.5	2.2	2.1	1.7	2.1		1.7	1.9
1.0	1.6	1.5	1.4	1.4	1.3	Current	1.3	1.3
.5	1.1	1.2	1.2	1.2	1.1		1.1	1.1
1.9	2.1	1.8	1.8	1.5	1.8		1.4	1.5
.9	1.3	1.3	1.3	1.3	1.2	Quick	1.1 (596)	1.1
.4	.9	1.0	1.1	1.0	.9		.9	.8

												Sales/Receivables				
1	265.5	24	15.2	37	9.8	48	7.6	46	7.9	41	8.9		35	10.3	28	13.0
22	16.5	44	8.3	59	6.2	61	6.0	64	5.7	48	7.6		54	6.8	50	7.2
56	6.5	70	5.2	84	4.4	82	4.5	81	4.5	69	5.3		72	5.1	72	5.1
0	UND	0	UND	0	UND	0	UND	0	UND	0	UND	Cost of Sales/Inventory	0	UND	0	UND
0	UND	0	UND	0	UND	0	UND	0	UND	0	809.5		0	UND	0	UND
0	UND	1	365.4	2	185.8	2	167.3	0	UND	8	46.2		0	972.9	1	357.3
0	UND	11	32.8	25	14.8	23	16.0	29	12.6	17	21.6	Cost of Sales/Payables	20	18.6	16	22.6
13	28.1	27	13.7	39	9.3	47	7.8	43	8.5	45	8.1		39	9.4	37	9.9
50	7.3	50	7.2	64	5.7	68	5.4	58	6.3	65	5.6		58	6.3	59	6.2

15.1		5.8		5.6		5.1		5.7		8.0		Sales/Working Capital		8.7		7.5
999.8		13.1		10.5		10.6		10.3		13.3				17.7		16.2
-7.8		52.8		34.5		19.5		20.3		92.5				42.3		48.2

	19.6		13.7		28.9		95.2		98.1		28.0	EBIT/Interest		39.8		49.8
(48)	3.7	(98)	3.0	(205)	5.6	(99)	15.8	(32)	16.5	(18)	6.8		(587)	9.7	(476)	11.5
	-2.1		-5.1		.7		2.5		1.9		1.7			3.1		3.2

			6.2		10.0		15.8					Net Profit + Depr., Dep., Amort./Cur. Mat. L/T/D		14.8		14.4
		(16)	2.4	(53)	3.6	(27)	3.7						(156)	4.8	(125)	5.2
			-1.2		.5		1.1							1.9		2.1

.3		.1		.1		.1		.1		.3		Fixed/Worth		.1		.1
.9		.3		.2		.2		.3		.6				.3		.3
-1.0		1.1		.6		.5		.7		1.0				.8		.8

.7		.7		.7		.8		.9		1.7		Debt/Worth		1.3		1.1
12.3		1.6		1.5		2.0		2.2		2.8				2.5		2.3
-3.5		3.3		3.0		3.0		3.9		3.8				5.4		4.9

	88.0		30.7		27.3		28.4		39.6		42.8	% Profit Before Taxes/Tangible Net Worth		62.2		60.5
(38)	25.5	(115)	7.2	(268)	9.8	(123)	13.6		10.9	(16)	16.9		(670)	32.7	(558)	32.3
	-22.1		-14.3		-3.7		1.4		4.1		7.8			11.0		12.9

29.9		10.2		10.7		10.0		10.3		8.4		% Profit Before Taxes/Total Assets		17.4		18.9
9.3		3.3		3.7		4.1		3.7		4.2				8.1		9.7
-8.9		-7.3		-1.1		.3		1.7		2.0				2.3		3.0

102.6		67.7		77.6		127.0		73.3		46.6		Sales/Net Fixed Assets		123.5		94.4
24.7		28.4		29.2		35.8		38.8		10.8				41.7		35.1
7.5		14.2		11.4		12.4		9.7		3.2				14.9		12.2

7.0		4.2		3.4		3.2		2.9		3.4		Sales/Total Assets		4.1		4.0
3.7		3.1		2.5		2.4		1.9		2.1				3.0		3.0
2.6		2.1		1.8		1.8		1.2		1.1				2.2		2.1

	.5		.5		.4		.2		.3		.4	% Depr., Dep., Amort./Sales		.2		.3
(38)	1.3	(103)	1.0	(232)	.8	(120)	.6	(34)	.6	(14)	.9		(621)	.6	(496)	.7
	2.9		2.2		1.9		1.6		1.9		2.3			1.5		1.7

	3.7		1.9		1.5		.6					% Officers', Directors' Owners' Comp/Sales		1.0		1.0
(35)	7.5	(57)	3.0	(108)	2.5	(28)	.9						(275)	2.2	(221)	2.1
	9.6		5.1		4.3		2.1							4.3		4.0

85128M	493206M	3453021M	6773284M	4983400M	8575760M	Net Sales ($)	31762449M	30603987M
18968M	154180M	1364158M	2837883M	2466015M	3256888M	Total Assets ($)	10745251M	10619952M

M = $ thousand   MM = $ million
See Pages 9 through 22 for Explanation of Ratios and Data

Comparative Historical Data			Type of Statement	Current Data Sorted by Sales					
129	188	156	Unqualified	1	3	1	13	30	108
175	238	218	Reviewed	4	26	30	60	63	35
39	51	27	Compiled	5	6	6	5	3	2
98	131	90	Tax Returns	19	29	13	16	7	6
139	196	163	Other	10	32	19	34	27	41
4/1/08-3/31/09 ALL	4/1/09-3/31/10 ALL	4/1/10-3/31/11 ALL		119 (4/1-9/30/10)			535 (10/1/10-3/31/11)		
				0-1MM	1-3MM	3-5MM	5-10MM	10-25MM	25MM & OVER
580	804	654	NUMBER OF STATEMENTS	39	96	69	128	130	192
%	%	%	ASSETS	%	%	%	%	%	%
19.9	22.8	21.7	Cash & Equivalents	15.3	18.1	23.3	19.2	22.8	25.1
39.0	36.1	40.1	Trade Receivables (net)	20.4	32.7	35.8	43.5	44.2	44.4
5.5	5.3	3.4	Inventory	9.0	5.3	4.3	3.6	2.3	1.5
8.0	7.1	7.5	All Other Current	2.3	6.5	6.5	8.3	8.8	8.1
72.4	71.3	72.7	Total Current	47.1	62.6	69.8	74.6	78.2	79.1
18.8	18.5	17.1	Fixed Assets (net)	36.5	22.0	20.9	15.6	14.1	12.4
1.0	1.2	2.1	Intangibles (net)	5.5	2.7	.6	1.5	2.4	1.7
7.8	9.0	8.1	All Other Non-Current	11.0	12.7	8.7	8.3	5.3	6.7
100.0	100.0	100.0	Total	100.0	100.0	100.0	100.0	100.0	100.0
			LIABILITIES						
7.3	8.9	8.0	Notes Payable-Short Term	28.1	13.6	11.3	6.1	5.6	2.7
3.3	2.9	2.4	Cur. Mat.-L.T.D.	4.9	3.7	2.5	2.6	2.0	1.3
26.6	24.1	25.6	Trade Payables	13.1	18.5	22.1	22.3	30.5	31.7
.5	.4	.5	Income Taxes Payable	.0	.7	.5	.4	.7	.3
18.1	16.4	15.2	All Other Current	20.4	14.3	10.6	14.9	12.5	18.2
55.8	52.8	51.6	Total Current	66.6	50.8	47.1	46.3	51.3	54.3
11.0	10.2	8.1	Long-Term Debt	22.9	13.7	10.8	6.2	4.7	5.0
.2	.3	.3	Deferred Taxes	.2	.3	.3	.2	.3	.2
2.0	3.2	3.1	All Other Non-Current	14.7	2.7	4.7	1.4	1.3	2.8
31.0	33.5	36.9	Net Worth	-4.5	32.5	37.1	45.9	42.4	37.7
100.0	100.0	100.0	Total Liabilties & Net Worth	100.0	100.0	100.0	100.0	100.0	100.0
			INCOME DATA						
100.0	100.0	100.0	Net Sales	100.0	100.0	100.0	100.0	100.0	100.0
18.7	19.6	19.3	Gross Profit	43.3	27.4	22.8	18.6	14.6	12.7
15.1	17.3	17.1	Operating Expenses	36.0	25.8	22.5	17.9	12.3	9.6
3.6	2.2	2.2	Operating Profit	7.4	1.6	.2	.8	2.2	3.0
.5	.4	.3	All Other Expenses (net)	5.2	.1	.1	-.3	.0	.2
3.1	1.8	1.8	Profit Before Taxes	2.2	1.5	.1	1.0	2.2	2.8
			RATIOS						
1.9	2.1	2.1		2.7	2.5	2.5	2.8	2.0	1.9
1.3	1.4	1.5	Current	.9	1.4	1.6	1.6	1.5	1.4
1.1	1.1	1.1		.3	.8	1.0	1.1	1.2	1.2
1.6	1.7	1.8		1.6	2.0	2.3	2.3	1.7	1.6
1.1	1.2	1.3	Quick	.4	1.2	1.3	1.4	1.3	1.3
.8	.8	.9		.1	.5	.9	1.0	1.0	1.1
27 13.5	25 14.6	33 10.9		0 UND	17 21.7	18 20.5	35 10.3	37 9.8	45 8.2
48 7.7	45 8.1	56 6.6	Sales/Receivables	19 19.7	42 8.7	44 8.3	60 6.0	58 6.3	59 6.2
71 5.2	68 5.4	78 4.7		70 5.3	73 5.0	69 5.3	87 4.2	80 4.6	79 4.6
0 UND	0 UND	0 UND		0 UND	0 UND	0 UND	0 UND	0 UND	0 UND
0 UND	0 UND	0 UND	Cost of Sales/Inventory	0 UND	0 UND	0 UND	0 UND	0 UND	0 UND
1 305.2	1 484.9	1 333.1		182 2.0	3 117.4	0 UND	2 170.7	1 340.0	1 338.2
17 21.7	16 23.1	19 19.7		0 UND	8 43.6	15 23.7	18 20.7	25 14.4	27 13.4
34 10.8	32 11.4	37 9.9	Cost of Sales/Payables	13 28.1	26 13.8	29 12.4	33 11.2	43 8.4	44 8.3
55 6.7	56 6.5	62 5.9		75 4.8	58 6.3	57 6.4	56 6.5	69 5.3	66 5.5
7.9	7.0	6.0		7.1	5.4	5.0	5.3	6.1	6.5
17.0	13.6	12.2	Sales/Working Capital	-150.5	14.3	16.3	9.5	10.7	11.4
75.3	52.2	38.9		-3.0	-17.8	-225.9	35.7	21.4	20.9
35.4	38.3	29.0		11.3	14.0	15.0	28.7	28.6	76.0
(463) 8.0	(612) 6.3	(500) 6.2	EBIT/Interest	(22) 2.8	(71) 2.9	(53) 3.4	(104) 4.8	(95) 7.3	(155) 14.0
1.6	.6	.4		-.1	-2.2	-6.0	-3.3	1.9	2.5
13.5	10.8	10.6					11.6	9.0	15.1
(114) 4.3	(152) 3.1	(111) 3.6	Net Profit + Depr., Dep., Amort./Cur. Mat. L/T/D			(26) 3.0	(28) 4.3	(42) 4.4	
1.4	.8	1.0					.1	1.6	1.0
.1	.1	.1		.4	.1	.1	.1	.1	.1
.4	.3	.3	Fixed/Worth	14.0	.4	.3	.2	.2	.2
.9	.9	.8		-1.8	1.8	1.5	.6	.6	.5
1.1	.9	.7		1.3	.5	.7	.6	.8	1.0
2.4	1.8	1.7	Debt/Worth	94.0	1.6	1.4	1.3	1.6	2.0
5.4	4.2	3.6		-4.1	12.6	7.8	2.5	3.0	3.1
52.8	39.5	30.2		78.0	42.0	30.6	24.4	27.4	33.4
(525) 23.0	(723) 14.3	(596) 10.7	% Profit Before Taxes/Tangible Net Worth	(21) 4.7	(78) 11.1	(58) 5.6	(123) 9.4	9.5	(186) 14.7
6.2	.3	-1.7		-8.6	-11.6	-17.0	-13.8	2.1	2.6
17.4	13.3	11.0		12.9	13.3	11.3	10.5	10.8	10.0
6.8	4.4	3.8	% Profit Before Taxes/Total Assets	3.3	4.6	2.8	3.9	3.4	4.3
.9	-.7	-1.8		-2.8	-6.8	-6.1	-5.4	.8	.8
105.9	92.8	80.7		31.7	67.5	68.3	69.6	91.3	118.3
35.6	30.6	29.2	Sales/Net Fixed Assets	6.0	17.7	28.7	25.5	31.4	47.6
9.5	9.6	10.5		1.1	7.6	9.4	13.6	12.5	13.7
3.9	3.9	3.6		2.6	4.1	4.2	3.6	3.4	3.6
2.9	2.7	2.7	Sales/Total Assets	1.4	2.8	2.9	2.7	2.7	2.7
1.9	1.8	1.8		.4	1.4	1.8	1.9	2.1	2.0
.3	.4	.3		1.3	.7	.4	.4	.4	.2
(473) .7	(650) .8	(541) .8	% Depr., Dep., Amort./Sales	(22) 3.3	(65) 1.5	(52) .9	(107) .8	(121) .8	(174) .5
2.0	2.3	1.9		5.5	2.9	2.2	1.9	1.5	1.3
1.0	1.5	1.3		3.1	3.0	2.2	1.5	1.3	.6
(211) 2.7	(315) 3.1	(241) 2.7	% Officers', Directors' Owners' Comp/Sales	(13) 7.5	(43) 5.9	(27) 3.3	(61) 2.9	(49) 2.1	(48) .9
4.5	5.5	5.1		16.7	8.3	5.0	4.4	3.8	2.3
23063911M	31546146M	24363799M	Net Sales ($)	17849M	182562M	273233M	924325M	2089286M	20876544M
8899647M	12009036M	10098092M	Total Assets ($)	34773M	137144M	152030M	415685M	962718M	8395742M

Current Data Sorted by Assets

Comparative Historical Data

	0-500M	500M-2MM	2-10MM	10-50MM	50-100MM	100-250MM	Type of Statement	4/1/06-3/31/07 ALL	4/1/07-3/31/08 ALL
	4	16	136	183	47	38	Unqualified	462	419
	13	155	341	69	1		Reviewed	504	527
	12	31	31	5	1	3	Compiled	94	81
	48	63	31	3	1		Tax Returns	157	142
	23	92	173	52	13	14	Other	322	339
		297 (4/1-9/30/10)		1,302 (10/1/10-3/31/11)					
NUMBER OF STATEMENTS	100	357	712	312	63	55		1539	1508

ASSETS

	%	%	%	%	%	%		%	%
Cash & Equivalents	25.8	21.0	23.7	28.7	32.2	28.1		19.2	20.9
Trade Receivables (net)	28.7	38.9	44.0	42.7	36.6	41.0		46.6	45.8
Inventory	3.2	4.1	1.9	1.7	1.8	1.0		4.0	3.9
All Other Current	7.6	9.9	10.4	8.8	9.0	8.8		9.3	9.0
Total Current	65.3	73.9	80.0	82.0	79.7	78.9		79.1	79.6
Fixed Assets (net)	21.4	15.3	12.3	11.3	11.9	13.8		14.1	13.8
Intangibles (net)	4.4	1.5	1.1	1.6	2.2	1.1		1.1	1.1
All Other Non-Current	8.8	9.3	6.6	5.2	6.2	6.2		5.7	5.5
Total	100.0	100.0	100.0	100.0	100.0	100.0		100.0	100.0

LIABILITIES

Notes Payable-Short Term	28.3	8.8	4.8	2.3	2.3	1.1		6.6	6.0
Cur. Mat.-L.T.D.	3.3	2.0	1.3	3.2	.7	.7		2.2	2.1
Trade Payables	19.7	25.9	32.4	35.2	35.7	35.3		33.6	32.2
Income Taxes Payable	.2	.6	.5	.2	.1	.1		.5	.6
All Other Current	21.9	11.8	13.9	17.9	21.7	25.0		17.9	18.6
Total Current	73.4	49.2	52.9	58.8	60.4	62.1		60.9	59.5
Long-Term Debt	16.1	8.5	4.8	5.1	4.1	10.2		7.9	7.2
Deferred Taxes	.0	.4	.4	.3	.3	.2		.3	.3
All Other Non-Current	10.2	3.2	1.7	2.4	1.4	2.5		2.8	2.2
Net Worth	.2	38.8	40.2	33.4	33.7	24.9		28.2	30.8
Total Liabilties & Net Worth	100.0	100.0	100.0	100.0	100.0	100.0		100.0	100.0

INCOME DATA

Net Sales	100.0	100.0	100.0	100.0	100.0	100.0		100.0	100.0
Gross Profit	28.4	21.2	14.9	12.4	11.6	9.7		16.7	16.2
Operating Expenses	28.0	19.9	12.7	10.1	8.5	6.5		12.6	12.2
Operating Profit	.4	1.3	2.2	2.4	3.0	3.2		4.1	4.0
All Other Expenses (net)	.9	.3	.2	.1	.5	.6		.3	.2
Profit Before Taxes	-.6	1.1	2.0	2.3	2.6	2.6		3.9	3.8

RATIOS

Current	2.6	2.8	2.1	1.7	1.5	1.4		1.6	1.7
	1.1	1.6	1.5	1.4	1.3	1.3		1.3	1.3
	.5	1.1	1.2	1.2	1.2	1.2		1.1	1.1
Quick	2.5	2.2	1.7	1.5	1.3	1.3		1.4	1.5
	.9 (356)	1.3	1.3	1.3	1.2	1.1		(1538) 1.1	(1506) 1.2
	.3	.9	1.0	1.0	1.0	.9		.9	.9
Sales/Receivables	0 UND	24 15.2	37 10.0	46 7.9	40 9.1	45 8.2		34 10.7	35 10.5
	21 17.3	43 8.4	55 6.6	61 5.9	54 6.8	61 6.0		54 6.7	53 6.9
	43 8.5	67 5.5	79 4.6	82 4.4	78 4.7	72 5.1		75 4.9	72 5.0
Cost of Sales/Inventory	0 UND	0 UND	0 UND	0 UND	0 UND	0 UND		0 UND	0 UND
	0 UND	0 UND	0 UND	0 UND	0 UND	0 UND		0 UND	0 UND
	0 UND	0 UND	0 UND	0 UND	0 999.8	0 999.8		0 999.8	0 999.8
Cost of Sales/Payables	0 UND	16 23.4	28 13.2	37 9.9	38 9.7	41 8.9		22 16.8	22 16.8
	10 35.0	33 11.0	45 8.1	57 6.4	58 6.3	55 6.6		42 8.7	42 8.8
	36 10.1	54 6.8	67 5.4	78 4.7	77 4.7	72 5.1		62 5.9	62 5.9
Sales/Working Capital	9.6	5.4	6.1	6.5	8.2	9.1		9.3	9.0
	63.5	12.4	11.2	11.2	12.4	14.8		18.3	17.2
	-19.2	45.4	27.0	20.0	23.7	25.1		41.1	36.8
EBIT/Interest	9.5	23.3	33.2	71.3	81.0	58.6		45.1	58.4
	(68) 1.0	(266) 3.8	(538) 5.5	(223) 11.6	(43) 36.0	(43) 21.7		(1190) 11.3	(1169) 13.9
	-3.4	-3.8	-2.3	1.3	6.4	3.7		3.3	3.4
Net Profit + Depr., Dep., Amort./Cur. Mat. L/T/D		5.3	13.2	19.5	19.7	19.9		13.9	18.1
	(46) 1.3	(164) 3.6	(73) 4.7	(13) 5.4	(18) 5.4			(320) 5.2	(319) 5.5
	-3.2	.8	1.8	2.0	2.4			1.8	2.2
Fixed/Worth	.1	.1	.1	.1	.1	.1		.1	.1
	1.0	.3	.2	.2	.2	.2		.3	.3
	-.8	.9	.5	.5	.4	.5		.7	.7
Debt/Worth	.7	.6	.8	1.2	1.5	2.1		1.3	1.3
	3.4	1.3	1.6	1.9	2.1	3.0		2.7	2.6
	-3.1	3.7	3.3	3.9	4.1	4.3		5.3	5.3
% Profit Before Taxes/Tangible Net Worth	77.5	35.6	30.7	29.1	38.0	37.2		58.9	61.6
	(64) 10.1	(315) 8.9	(687) 10.9	(302) 13.9	(61) 16.1	(53) 19.4		(1426) 31.9	(1415) 33.0
	-2.8	-7.8	-1.4	2.2	4.7	10.0		11.6	12.1
% Profit Before Taxes/Total Assets	17.1	13.7	10.7	9.9	11.7	9.9		18.0	17.3
	1.2	3.9	4.0	3.7	4.3	5.1		8.4	8.8
	-15.9	-4.9	-1.3	.6	1.6	2.0		2.7	2.6
Sales/Net Fixed Assets	402.8	116.5	120.4	146.8	149.0	89.9		139.3	131.4
	37.8	31.8	45.8	54.7	53.5	39.6		49.3	49.4
	12.2	13.2	16.6	18.0	21.6	17.2		18.1	18.7
Sales/Total Assets	7.6	4.3	3.6	3.2	3.0	3.1		4.2	4.1
	4.3	3.0	2.8	2.6	2.5	2.8		3.2	3.2
	2.1	2.1	2.0	1.8	2.0	2.1		2.3	2.4
% Depr., Dep., Amort./Sales	.5	.4	.3	.2	.2	.3		.2	.2
	(59) 1.6	(265) .9	(603) .6	(278) .4	(56) .4	(47) .4		(1292) .5	(1295) .4
	2.9	2.1	1.3	1.1	1.3	1.0		1.2	1.0
% Officers', Directors' Owners' Comp/Sales	2.2	2.0	1.2	.8	.4			1.0	1.1
	(60) 4.6	(174) 3.3	(292) 1.9	(74) 1.2	(10) .7			(588) 2.1	(570) 2.1
	8.1	5.8	3.2	1.9	1.2			3.8	3.8
Net Sales ($)	150796M	1411646M	10121947M	17603794M	11378788M	22133457M		73775968M	92185632M
Total Assets ($)	27104M	427350M	3522985M	6762384M	4485269M	8122429M		24703208M	26275257M

M = $ thousand   MM = $ million
See Pages 9 through 22 for Explanation of Ratios and Data

Comparative Historical Data | | | Current Data Sorted by Sales

				Type of Statement						
510		437	424	Unqualified	4	4	11	37	95	273
682		617	579	Reviewed	14	67	78	141	192	87
83		86	83	Compiled	10	19	17	20	9	8
215		154	146	Tax Returns	31	49	21	19	20	6
436		390	367	Other	22	58	41	69	93	84
4/1/08-3/31/09 ALL		4/1/09-3/31/10 ALL	4/1/10-3/31/11 ALL		297 (4/1-9/30/10)			1,302 (10/1/10-3/31/11)		
					0-1MM	1-3MM	3-5MM	5-10MM	10-25MM	25MM & OVER
1926		1684	1599	NUMBER OF STATEMENTS	81	197	168	286	409	458
%		%	%	ASSETS	%	%	%	%	%	%
23.4		25.9	24.7	Cash & Equivalents	20.1	20.8	21.4	23.1	25.6	28.6
43.9		40.2	41.3	Trade Receivables (net)	19.7	32.5	39.3	42.1	44.8	45.9
3.3		2.7	2.4	Inventory	8.8	5.3	3.8	2.3	1.0	.9
9.0		8.5	9.7	All Other Current	7.7	9.4	10.2	9.5	10.3	9.6
79.6		77.2	78.1	Total Current	56.4	68.0	74.6	76.9	81.8	84.9
13.1		14.7	13.4	Fixed Assets (net)	27.7	18.7	15.8	14.4	11.1	9.0
.8		1.5	1.5	Intangibles (net)	2.6	2.6	1.8	1.2	1.2	1.2
6.4		6.6	7.1	All Other Non-Current	13.3	10.7	7.8	7.5	5.9	4.9
100.0		100.0	100.0	Total	100.0	100.0	100.0	100.0	100.0	100.0
				LIABILITIES						
6.0		6.2	6.5	Notes Payable-Short Term	24.2	12.7	9.3	7.0	3.3	2.1
2.0		2.0	1.9	Cur. Mat.-L.T.D.	2.6	2.7	2.4	1.7	1.1	2.1
32.3		29.7	30.9	Trade Payables	14.9	19.4	23.4	29.2	34.6	39.3
.5		.5	.4	Income Taxes Payable	.5	.7	.5	.7	.4	.1
17.7		15.1	15.4	All Other Current	22.6	11.9	12.4	11.7	15.2	19.3
58.5		53.5	55.1	Total Current	64.8	47.3	48.0	50.2	54.6	62.9
6.6		6.9	6.5	Long-Term Debt	17.1	12.7	9.2	5.7	4.3	3.5
.3		.3	.3	Deferred Taxes	.1	.3	.4	.6	.4	.2
2.9		2.2	2.7	All Other Non-Current	6.2	6.6	3.3	2.1	1.2	2.0
31.7		37.0	35.3	Net Worth	11.9	33.0	39.0	41.3	39.6	31.4
100.0		100.0	100.0	Total Liabilties & Net Worth	100.0	100.0	100.0	100.0	100.0	100.0
				INCOME DATA						
100.0		100.0	100.0	Net Sales	100.0	100.0	100.0	100.0	100.0	100.0
16.5		16.8	16.4	Gross Profit	39.0	23.4	23.0	16.1	13.4	9.8
13.0		14.6	14.4	Operating Expenses	36.2	22.3	20.6	14.6	11.0	7.6
3.5		2.2	2.0	Operating Profit	2.8	1.0	2.4	1.4	2.4	2.1
.3		.3	.3	All Other Expenses (net)	3.9	.4	.1	.1	.0	-.1
3.2		1.9	1.7	Profit Before Taxes	-1.1	.6	2.2	1.3	2.4	2.3
				RATIOS						
1.8		2.1	2.0		2.5	3.3	2.7	2.3	1.9	1.6
1.3		1.5	1.4	Current	1.2	1.7	1.7	1.6	1.5	1.4
1.1		1.2	1.2		.3	.9	1.1	1.2	1.2	1.2
1.6		1.8	1.8		2.3	2.8	2.2	1.9	1.7	1.4
1.2		1.3 (1598)	1.3	Quick	.7	1.3	1.3 (285)	1.3	1.3	1.2
.9		1.0	.9		.2	.6	.9	1.0	1.0	1.0
32 11.4	29 12.5	34 10.8			0 UND	17 21.6	29 12.4	30 12.0	38 9.6	43 8.5
50 7.2	48 7.6	53 6.9		Sales/Receivables	28 13.1	44 8.3	49 7.4	51 7.2	54 6.7	58 6.3
70 5.2	68 5.4	75 4.9			74 4.9	75 4.9	79 4.6	76 4.8	76 4.8	74 4.9
0 UND	0 UND	0 UND			0 UND	0 UND	0 UND	0 UND	0 UND	0 UND
0 UND	0 UND	0 UND		Cost of Sales/Inventory	0 UND	0 UND	0 UND	0 UND	0 UND	0 UND
0 UND	0 UND	0 UND			9 41.4	0 UND	0 967.1	0 UND	0 UND	0 UND
21 17.3	21 17.6	24 15.1			0 UND	10 35.4	15 23.6	23 15.9	30 12.2	37 9.8
41 9.0	39 9.3	44 8.3		Cost of Sales/Payables	24 15.2	29 12.7	35 10.3	38 9.5	47 7.7	54 6.7
61 6.0	59 6.2	67 5.4			77 4.7	55 6.6	59 6.2	65 5.6	67 5.4	72 5.1
8.5		6.7	6.4		2.9	4.1	5.2	5.8	6.5	8.6
17.1		13.2	11.9	Sales/Working Capital	18.0	9.4	10.5	11.5	11.6	13.2
41.3		32.2	29.7		-3.9	-49.5	34.7	27.4	27.2	22.6
61.0		39.6	36.0		5.0	11.9	30.4	16.4	40.6	72.6
(1449) 12.3	(1235) 7.8	(1181) 5.8	EBIT/Interest	(50) .3	(145) 1.7	(130) 3.9	(223) 4.0	(298) 7.6	(335) 16.9
2.2		.5	-1.1		-3.4	-4.3	-2.9	-4.3	-1.0	2.8
17.8		12.6	13.5			5.7	3.4	8.9	20.3	16.2
(380) 6.3	(333) 4.4	(316) 3.7	Net Profit + Depr., Dep., Amort./Cur. Mat. L/T/D	(18) 2.3	(27) .8	(72) 2.2	(93) 6.4	(104) 4.9
2.0		.9	.9			-1.5	-2.1	-.3	1.3	2.1
.1		.1	.1		.1	.1	.1	.1	.1	.1
.2		.2	.2	Fixed/Worth	.7	.3	.3	.2	.2	.2
.6		.6	.6		84.2	1.6	.9	.6	.4	.4
1.1		.8	.8		.5	.5	.6	.7	.8	1.4
2.3		1.8	1.8	Debt/Worth	2.3	1.3	1.2	1.4	1.7	2.2
4.8		3.8	3.8		NM	6.7	4.3	2.8	3.3	3.9
53.1		38.3	33.2	% Profit Before Taxes/Tangible Net Worth	28.1	27.9	38.9	32.8	34.3	34.7
(1801) 26.4	(1573) 14.3	(1482) 11.7		(61) 2.3	(162) 5.7	(147) 11.3	(270) 11.0	(397) 11.2	(445) 16.7
7.0		1.2	.0		-9.4	-10.4	-1.8	-8.9	-.8	3.7
16.4		12.9	11.2		7.3	10.4	16.0	12.4	11.1	10.5
7.2		4.6	3.9	% Profit Before Taxes/Total Assets	.0	2.4	4.4	3.7	4.0	4.5
1.8		1.4	-1.0		-11.9	-6.7	-2.9	-3.7	-.6	1.0
138.1		116.5	125.1		41.5	88.0	87.4	110.0	138.7	149.7
55.7		44.2	43.7	Sales/Net Fixed Assets	11.8	23.9	28.9	41.2	52.4	65.8
19.2		15.4	15.8		2.8	8.6	11.5	14.4	20.6	26.5
4.3		4.1	3.7		2.4	3.7	3.8	3.9	3.8	3.6
3.3		3.0	2.8	Sales/Total Assets	1.4	2.3	2.6	2.8	2.9	2.9
2.3		2.1	2.0		.6	1.5	1.8	1.9	2.2	2.3
.2		.3	.3		1.2	.5	.6	.3	.3	.2
(1610) .5	(1423) .6	(1308) .6	% Depr., Dep., Amort./Sales	(49) 3.0	(136) 1.4	(126) 1.3	(240) .8	(354) .5	(403) .4
1.1		1.4	1.1		5.3	2.9	2.4	1.4	1.1	.7
1.0		1.2	1.2		1.7	2.3	1.8	1.3	1.1	.7
(722) 2.2	(629) 2.5	(617) 2.2	% Officers', Directors' Owners' Comp/Sales	(35) 6.1	(102) 3.8	(84) 3.0	(140) 2.2	(156) 1.6	(100) 1.1
4.1		4.7	4.3		11.5	6.6	6.3	3.8	1.9	1.8
102254767M	80513771M	62800428M	Net Sales ($)	45191M	396597M	684372M	2084580M	6533304M	53056384M
33527574M	25080585M	23347521M	Total Assets ($)	62113M	252188M	338529M	1004097M	2762256M	18928338M

M = $ thousand   MM = $ million
See Pages 9 through 22 for Explanation of Ratios and Data

Current Data Sorted by Assets | Comparative Historical Data

Type of Statement	0-500M	500M-2MM	2-10MM	10-50MM	50-100MM	100-250MM		4/1/06-3/31/07 ALL	4/1/07-3/31/08 ALL
Unqualified		5	38	51	7	11		123	117
Reviewed	3	27	88	22		1		147	151
Compiled	3	10	7	1				32	22
Tax Returns	14	14	12	2				33	36
Other	6	21	45	36	4	2		89	110
		82 (4/1-9/30/10)		348 (10/1/10-3/31/11)					
NUMBER OF STATEMENTS	26	77	190	112	11	14		424	436
ASSETS	%	%	%	%	%	%		%	%
Cash & Equivalents	16.1	14.2	15.6	17.3	18.7	23.7		14.4	13.4
Trade Receivables (net)	19.5	32.3	33.4	35.3	27.4	26.2		36.4	35.6
Inventory	5.3	4.2	3.6	2.5	3.1	2.7		2.6	3.0
All Other Current	4.6	6.3	9.2	8.9	8.5	9.8		7.4	8.5
Total Current	45.5	57.0	61.9	64.0	57.7	62.5		60.8	60.6
Fixed Assets (net)	42.7	33.2	30.4	27.2	19.8	21.8		32.8	31.7
Intangibles (net)	.1	2.5	1.2	2.0	6.0	11.8		1.5	1.7
All Other Non-Current	11.7	7.4	6.5	6.8	16.4	3.9		4.8	6.0
Total	100.0	100.0	100.0	100.0	100.0	100.0		100.0	100.0
LIABILITIES									
Notes Payable-Short Term	27.6	9.0	6.4	2.8	7.4	.2		6.0	6.7
Cur. Mat.-L.T.D.	8.1	4.8	5.0	3.6	2.0	3.7		5.8	5.8
Trade Payables	19.8	20.0	17.2	19.2	11.7	16.1		17.2	16.4
Income Taxes Payable	.6	.7	.5	.3	.3	.4		.9	1.0
All Other Current	5.8	5.7	7.9	11.0	15.1	14.2		11.4	12.4
Total Current	61.9	40.2	36.9	37.0	36.6	34.7		41.4	42.3
Long-Term Debt	45.3	17.2	10.8	11.4	8.4	16.0		15.4	15.6
Deferred Taxes	.0	1.0	1.3	.4	.5	.4		.8	.8
All Other Non-Current	25.5	3.3	2.4	2.4	.9	2.6		2.4	2.9
Net Worth	-32.7	38.3	48.6	48.8	53.6	46.4		39.9	38.5
Total Liabilties & Net Worth	100.0	100.0	100.0	100.0	100.0	100.0		100.0	100.0
INCOME DATA									
Net Sales	100.0	100.0	100.0	100.0	100.0	100.0		100.0	100.0
Gross Profit	51.3	30.6	18.7	16.5	21.3	19.3		23.8	24.1
Operating Expenses	48.8	28.2	16.5	13.5	15.1	14.8		18.2	18.9
Operating Profit	2.5	2.5	2.3	3.0	6.1	4.5		5.6	5.2
All Other Expenses (net)	.6	.5	-.2	.3	.3	.0		.3	.3
Profit Before Taxes	1.9	2.0	2.4	2.7	5.8	4.5		5.3	4.8
RATIOS									
Current	2.6	2.9	2.6	2.6	2.2	2.4		2.1	2.0
	.6	1.8	1.7	1.7	1.8	1.5		1.4	1.5
	.4	1.0	1.2	1.3	1.4	1.4		1.2	1.1
Quick	1.6	2.3	2.1	2.1	1.7	1.9		1.8	1.7
	.5	1.4	1.3	1.4	1.5	1.2		1.2	1.2
	.2	.7	.9	1.0	.8	.9		.9	.9
Sales/Receivables	0 UND	21 17.7	41 9.0	51 7.2	42 8.6	45 8.2		40 9.2	41 8.9
	15 23.7	40 9.2	58 6.2	66 5.5	67 5.4	59 6.2		58 6.3	58 6.3
	29 12.4	68 5.4	76 4.8	83 4.4	79 4.6	77 4.7		78 4.7	80 4.6
Cost of Sales/Inventory	0 UND	0 UND	0 UND	0 UND	0 UND	0 UND		0 UND	0 UND
	0 UND	0 UND	0 UND	0 UND	0 UND	4 83.0		0 UND	0 UND
	6 59.7	8 47.5	4 83.4	4 86.7	4 84.1	17 21.5		3 116.0	4 95.3
Cost of Sales/Payables	0 UND	14 26.3	19 18.9	26 14.0	13 27.1	25 14.5		18 20.7	18 19.8
	10 36.9	38 9.7	33 11.2	38 9.6	19 19.7	42 8.6		31 11.9	33 11.2
	55 6.6	54 6.7	50 7.3	59 6.2	59 6.2	65 5.7		48 7.6	51 7.2
Sales/Working Capital	11.5	6.1	5.1	4.3	4.5	3.5		6.8	6.5
	-25.1	11.9	9.6	7.1	8.4	6.9		12.8	11.6
	-7.7	-798.1	22.8	16.3	11.5	9.7		33.4	36.0
EBIT/Interest	7.0	7.6	19.4	46.1	126.3	168.0		21.4	19.4
	(23) 2.0	(63) 1.9	(172) 3.6	(97) 7.4	(10) 8.8	(12) 3.5		(394) 6.9	(396) 6.2
	.0	-3.5	-.9	1.4	4.3	1.7		2.6	1.6
Net Profit + Depr., Dep., Amort./Cur. Mat. L/T/D		4.9	3.9	13.7				5.3	4.9
		(12) -1.7	(59) 1.9	(35) 3.4				(135) 2.6	(144) 2.5
		-2.5	1.0	1.8				1.6	1.2
Fixed/Worth	.4	.3	.3	.2	.2	.2		.4	.4
	2.1	.8	.6	.6	.3	.4		.7	.7
	-.9	2.3	1.2	1.1	.8	NM		1.4	1.5
Debt/Worth	1.1	.6	.5	.6	.5	.6		.8	.8
	7.6	1.3	1.1	1.2	.7	1.6		1.6	1.4
	-2.3	5.3	2.1	2.1	2.4	NM		2.7	2.8
% Profit Before Taxes/Tangible Net Worth	130.5	33.7	25.9	26.0	37.8	37.0		49.4	45.0
	(17) 31.0	(65) 7.2	(184) 6.9	(109) 12.0	(10) 13.7	(11) 19.5		(406) 26.1	(410) 21.2
	-3.7	-21.0	-6.9	1.2	6.8	10.2		9.2	6.2
% Profit Before Taxes/Total Assets	22.1	15.5	12.0	11.4	15.8	13.0		19.0	16.9
	13.5	2.8	3.5	4.2	7.1	6.3		9.3	8.6
	-5.7	-9.5	-3.5	.5	4.2	2.6		3.1	2.1
Sales/Net Fixed Assets	25.0	27.5	16.9	16.7	15.3	14.8		15.2	15.2
	10.3	7.4	7.8	7.8	6.9	8.2		7.9	7.7
	6.2	4.4	3.8	4.3	5.5	4.7		4.7	4.6
Sales/Total Assets	5.2	3.8	2.7	2.4	2.3	2.0		2.9	2.7
	3.9	2.6	2.0	1.9	1.5	1.6		2.2	2.2
	2.5	1.7	1.4	1.5	.9	1.1		1.7	1.6
% Depr., Dep., Amort./Sales	1.6	1.0	1.9	1.5	1.5	.9		1.8	1.8
	(20) 4.7	(59) 3.1	(175) 3.5	(109) 3.1	2.4	(11) 3.0		(386) 3.1	(382) 3.3
	9.8	6.6	5.8	4.7	4.2	5.7		5.3	5.1
% Officers', Directors' Owners' Comp/Sales	3.1	2.4	1.6	.8				1.3	1.5
	(19) 6.0	(39) 6.1	(88) 3.0	(27) 1.5				(202) 2.9	(188) 3.2
	12.4	7.1	4.9	2.3				5.8	5.9
Net Sales ($)	29064M	262661M	2067689M	4524208M	1260185M	3162030M		11220441M	13900791M
Total Assets ($)	6496M	94835M	964618M	2459085M	815203M	2071768M		5140310M	6839536M

M = $ thousand   MM = $ million
See Pages 9 through 22 for Explanation of Ratios and Data

	Comparative Historical Data		Type of Statement	Current Data Sorted by Sales					
115	119	112	Unqualified		5	6	10	32	59
168	162	141	Reviewed	3	14	23	37	48	16
34	22	21	Compiled	2	8	2	5	3	1
37	42	42	Tax Returns	12	11	4	5	9	1
111	133	114	Other	9	11	15	22	24	33
4/1/08-3/31/09 ALL	4/1/09-3/31/10 ALL	4/1/10-3/31/11 ALL		82 (4/1-9/30/10)			348 (10/1/10-3/31/11)		
				0-1MM	1-3MM	3-5MM	5-10MM	10-25MM	25MM & OVER
465	478	430	**NUMBER OF STATEMENTS**	26	49	50	79	116	110
%	%	%	**ASSETS**	%	%	%	%	%	%
15.3	17.1	16.2	Cash & Equivalents	16.0	12.3	16.1	14.1	17.6	18.0
32.8	31.2	32.5	Trade Receivables (net)	17.9	22.3	32.0	31.3	37.2	36.6
3.9	3.9	3.5	Inventory	5.6	7.0	4.4	2.5	2.9	2.3
7.6	7.3	8.3	All Other Current	6.1	3.9	7.4	8.5	9.2	10.2
59.6	59.6	60.5	Total Current	45.6	45.4	59.9	56.4	66.9	67.2
32.3	31.0	30.2	Fixed Assets (net)	45.5	38.0	32.2	33.6	27.0	23.3
1.7	1.9	2.0	Intangibles (net)	.1	3.2	.5	1.8	1.3	3.6
6.4	7.6	7.2	All Other Non-Current	8.8	13.5	7.4	8.1	4.8	5.9
100.0	100.0	100.0	Total	100.0	100.0	100.0	100.0	100.0	100.0
			LIABILITIES						
5.3	5.7	7.0	Notes Payable-Short Term	20.6	10.6	10.3	6.3	4.9	3.4
5.5	5.8	4.7	Cur. Mat.-L.T.D.	5.4	5.7	4.0	7.0	4.3	3.1
15.6	15.9	18.2	Trade Payables	15.5	18.1	15.2	19.1	17.6	20.3
.8	.6	.5	Income Taxes Payable	1.9	.2	.6	.6	.4	.3
10.7	9.8	8.6	All Other Current	3.5	3.6	6.2	7.8	9.5	12.8
38.0	37.7	39.0	Total Current	46.8	38.1	36.2	40.9	36.7	39.9
14.9	15.9	14.3	Long-Term Debt	48.2	20.8	12.5	11.8	10.2	10.3
.9	.9	.9	Deferred Taxes	.0	.8	1.6	1.3	.9	.5
3.0	2.8	3.9	All Other Non-Current	25.8	3.6	4.4	1.9	1.8	2.4
43.3	42.8	41.9	Net Worth	-21.0	36.7	45.3	44.3	50.5	47.0
100.0	100.0	100.0	Total Liabilities & Net Worth	100.0	100.0	100.0	100.0	100.0	100.0
			INCOME DATA						
100.0	100.0	100.0	Net Sales	100.0	100.0	100.0	100.0	100.0	100.0
24.0	24.3	22.3	Gross Profit	50.9	36.4	23.1	19.6	18.6	15.0
20.5	21.6	19.7	Operating Expenses	46.3	34.7	21.5	18.1	15.6	11.2
3.5	2.8	2.7	Operating Profit	4.6	1.6	1.5	1.5	3.0	3.7
.4	.2	.1	All Other Expenses (net)	1.7	.1	.6	-.3	.2	-.1
3.1	2.6	2.5	Profit Before Taxes	2.9	1.6	1.0	1.8	2.8	3.8
			RATIOS						
2.4	2.5	2.6		4.1	2.6	2.9	2.5	2.7	2.2
1.6	1.6	1.7	Current	1.2	1.5	2.0	1.4	1.8	1.6
1.2	1.1	1.2		.5	.7	1.0	.9	1.4	1.3
2.0	2.1	2.1		3.8	2.1	2.6	2.2	2.1	2.0
1.3	1.3	1.3	Quick	.7	1.1	1.7	1.2	1.5	1.3
.9	.8	.8		.3	.5	.7	.6	1.1	1.0
36 10.0	35 10.5	36 10.1		0 UND	9 39.0	36 10.1	33 11.2	43 8.4	47 7.8
54 6.8	55 6.7	56 6.5	Sales/Receivables	25 14.8	30 12.0	64 5.7	58 6.3	56 6.5	66 5.6
75 4.9	74 4.9	76 4.8		46 8.0	76 4.8	87 4.2	72 5.1	76 4.8	78 4.6
0 UND	0 UND	0 UND		0 UND	0 UND	0 UND	0 UND	0 UND	0 UND
0 UND	0 UND	0 UND	Cost of Sales/Inventory	0 UND	0 UND	0 UND	0 UND	0 UND	0 UND
6 64.9	6 59.6	5 66.5		27 13.3	14 25.6	1 595.2	7 54.4	4 86.2	5 75.9
16 22.2	16 22.8	19 19.3		0 UND	11 34.3	10 37.2	22 16.2	20 18.4	23 16.0
27 13.5	31 11.8	35 10.4	Cost of Sales/Payables	16 22.2	40 9.1	31 11.8	37 9.8	32 11.3	38 9.5
47 7.7	51 7.2	54 6.7		77 4.8	58 6.2	53 6.9	58 6.3	46 8.0	59 6.2
5.9	5.6	5.1		6.3	5.9	3.9	5.6	5.0	4.7
11.0	10.0	9.0	Sales/Working Capital	273.8	15.5	7.0	14.3	8.7	8.3
28.5	37.6	36.3		-8.0	-25.1	84.6	-48.6	16.7	16.5
23.5	18.3	21.5		6.4	6.2	12.2	14.5	36.8	41.1
(428) 4.8	(428) 4.4	(377) 4.3	EBIT/Interest	(22) 3.1	(43) 1.7	(44) 4.2	(68) 1.3	(102) 5.3	(98) 7.6
.5	.4	-.2		-1.6	-3.1	-2.0	-3.7	1.3	2.1
5.7	6.7	7.2			5.6		5.1	3.6	13.8
(153) 2.5	(137) 2.2	(118) 2.5	Net Profit + Depr., Dep., Amort./Cur. Mat. L/T/D		(10) .4		(21) 1.6	(36) 1.9	(42) 4.6
1.2	1.2	1.1			-2.1		.6	1.1	1.9
.3	.3	.3		.3	.4	.3	.4	.2	.2
.7	.7	.6	Fixed/Worth	2.2	1.0	.7	.8	.5	.5
1.4	1.4	1.4		15.3	3.0	1.5	1.9	1.0	1.1
.7	.6	.6		.5	.6	.6	.5	.5	.6
1.3	1.2	1.2	Debt/Worth	4.5	1.3	.9	1.1	.9	1.4
2.4	2.7	2.7		-3.4	3.9	2.6	2.6	1.7	2.4
36.9	30.7	30.5		99.0	36.1	25.6	27.8	26.5	31.7
(440) 14.8	(441) 11.8	(396) 9.5	% Profit Before Taxes/Tangible Net Worth	(19) 21.6	(41) 6.7	(45) 6.8	(73) 2.2	(113) 9.5	(105) 15.4
-1.2	.1	-2.0		-13.1	-18.6	-15.5	-19.5	1.0	3.4
15.8	13.8	13.3		17.5	14.7	9.5	14.6	13.7	12.4
6.2	4.7	4.0	% Profit Before Taxes/Total Assets	6.1	1.4	2.7	.8	3.7	6.0
-.9	-.6	-1.9		-9.8	-9.6	-6.0	-7.6	.4	1.5
15.7	17.0	17.9		18.3	15.4	19.3	13.3	21.0	18.2
7.4	7.9	8.0	Sales/Net Fixed Assets	5.7	6.3	6.6	5.6	9.4	9.6
3.9	4.2	4.4		2.1	3.3	3.6	3.6	4.8	6.2
2.8	2.8	2.8		4.0	3.8	2.7	2.6	2.9	2.6
2.1	2.0	2.1	Sales/Total Assets	2.4	1.9	1.9	1.9	2.3	2.1
1.5	1.5	1.5		1.3	1.2	1.4	1.3	1.7	1.6
1.9	1.8	1.6		1.6	2.3	2.3	2.4	1.6	1.2
(423) 3.6	(414) 3.6	(385) 3.3	% Depr., Dep., Amort./Sales	(19) 4.8	(39) 5.0	(42) 5.9	(71) 4.1	(109) 2.8	(105) 2.7
5.7	5.9	5.7		11.3	7.2	8.5	6.6	4.4	3.9
1.3	1.4	1.8		4.6	3.0	2.8	1.9	1.2	.5
(195) 2.9	(212) 2.9	(174) 3.1	% Officers', Directors' Owners' Comp/Sales	(19) 7.6	(25) 6.2	(24) 5.0	(33) 2.9	(51) 2.3	(22) 1.4
5.6	6.1	6.1		12.7	7.3	6.8	3.9	4.0	2.4
13785628M	11964460M	11305837M	Net Sales ($)	17151M	103291M	193247M	562926M	1805237M	8623985M
6528201M	6530784M	6412005M	Total Assets ($)	11720M	68183M	147138M	366775M	913187M	4905002M

© RMA 2011   M = $ thousand   MM = $ million
See Pages 9 through 22 for Explanation of Ratios and Data

Current Data Sorted by Assets							Comparative Historical Data	
						Type of Statement		
		3	7	5	3	Unqualified	22	32
	2	6	4	1		Reviewed	10	15
	5	4	1			Compiled	12	9
	1	6	1			Tax Returns	3	6
	4	8	17	3	6	Other	21	37
	21 (4/1-9/30/10)		66 (10/1/10-3/31/11)				4/1/06-3/31/07 ALL	4/1/07-3/31/08 ALL
0-500M	**500M-2MM**	**2-10MM**	**10-50MM**	**50-100MM**	**100-250MM**			
	12	27	30	9	9	**NUMBER OF STATEMENTS**	68	99
%	%	%	%	%	%	**ASSETS**	%	%
DATA NOT AVAILABLE	9.7	17.2	12.5			Cash & Equivalents	11.8	12.3
	33.7	28.2	28.5			Trade Receivables (net)	36.6	32.5
	3.5	2.7	5.8			Inventory	4.6	5.3
	2.9	4.3	3.4			All Other Current	8.0	6.6
	49.8	52.4	50.2			Total Current	61.0	56.7
	42.9	39.7	36.6			Fixed Assets (net)	30.3	34.5
	.0	4.6	7.8			Intangibles (net)	4.1	3.6
	7.4	3.3	5.4			All Other Non-Current	4.5	5.2
	100.0	100.0	100.0			Total	100.0	100.0
						LIABILITIES		
	1.0	13.0	9.7			Notes Payable-Short Term	10.5	8.2
	6.0	4.7	6.5			Cur. Mat.-L.T.D.	5.0	6.3
	9.3	10.2	11.0			Trade Payables	16.9	11.4
	1.3	.1	.5			Income Taxes Payable	1.2	.5
	5.9	10.7	8.5			All Other Current	14.2	11.0
	23.5	38.6	36.3			Total Current	47.7	37.5
	18.8	13.2	16.6			Long-Term Debt	19.2	18.4
	1.7	1.6	1.4			Deferred Taxes	1.0	1.2
	6.1	2.1	3.2			All Other Non-Current	3.9	2.2
	49.9	44.5	42.6			Net Worth	28.2	40.8
	100.0	100.0	100.0			Total Liabilties & Net Worth	100.0	100.0
						INCOME DATA		
	100.0	100.0	100.0			Net Sales	100.0	100.0
						Gross Profit		
	74.4	92.3	88.7			Operating Expenses	93.2	87.4
	25.6	7.7	11.3			Operating Profit	6.8	12.6
	7.0	.7	2.8			All Other Expenses (net)	.7	1.6
	18.5	7.0	8.5			Profit Before Taxes	6.0	11.0
						RATIOS		
	5.5	2.6	2.9				2.0	2.6
	1.8	1.3	1.7			Current	1.5	1.5
	1.1	.8	.9				1.1	1.1
	4.9	1.5	2.7				1.7	2.3
	1.5	1.1	1.3			Quick	1.1	1.2
	1.0	.8	.6				.8	.8
	25 14.4	17 21.1	43 8.6				35 10.5	34 10.8
	55 6.7	41 8.9	55 6.6			Sales/Receivables	59 6.2	52 7.0
	98 3.7	66 5.5	79 4.6				79 4.6	68 5.3
						Cost of Sales/Inventory		
						Cost of Sales/Payables		
	3.9	9.8	4.1				7.0	6.4
	12.3	22.6	10.2			Sales/Working Capital	12.6	10.4
	60.2	-27.6	-72.4				54.6	47.4
		35.0	23.3				24.9	32.4
		(26) 8.6	(25) 4.1			EBIT/Interest	(58) 8.7	(89) 9.7
		1.6	1.4				1.9	3.4
			9.7				7.8	4.5
			(10) 1.3			Net Profit + Depr., Dep., Amort./Cur. Mat. L/T/D	(22) 3.7	(26) 2.4
			.1				1.9	1.3
	.5	.4	.5				.4	.4
	.7	1.2	1.5			Fixed/Worth	.8	.8
	1.3	1.9	3.0				1.7	2.1
	.5	.5	.3				.8	.6
	.9	1.4	1.6			Debt/Worth	2.1	1.5
	1.8	4.0	6.4				3.7	3.7
	100.4	91.7	45.9				76.3	76.4
	(11) 34.2	(24) 20.9	(25) 25.7			% Profit Before Taxes/Tangible Net Worth	(60) 47.7	(87) 41.7
	13.4	4.5	6.4				17.7	18.1
	40.5	20.3	17.5				33.1	31.5
	18.1	7.2	9.1			% Profit Before Taxes/Total Assets	14.6	13.7
	4.8	1.7	2.0				4.1	5.8
	13.3	16.6	8.5				30.2	21.3
	7.3	6.9	5.1			Sales/Net Fixed Assets	9.6	7.7
	1.1	3.3	3.4				4.5	3.8
	3.8	3.5	2.3				3.4	2.9
	2.4	2.2	1.6			Sales/Total Assets	2.2	2.3
	.4	1.3	1.2				1.6	1.4
		1.6	2.3				.7	.7
		(23) 2.9	(27) 4.5			% Depr., Dep., Amort./Sales	(57) 2.0	(86) 1.7
		5.7	6.5				3.8	4.3
							.8	.9
						% Officers', Directors' Owners' Comp/Sales	(21) 1.4	(29) 2.3
							3.9	4.9
	33432M	317910M	1414452M	730894M	2512352M	Net Sales ($)	3413120M	7356188M
	14121M	130811M	793107M	634787M	1553039M	Total Assets ($)	1653302M	3572069M

M = $ thousand MM = $ million

See Pages 9 through 22 for Explanation of Ratios and Data

Comparative Historical Data / Current Data Sorted by Sales

				Type of Statement						
21	25	18		Unqualified		2		2	3	13
12	14	13		Reviewed		2		1	5	5
10	12	10		Compiled	1	2	2	3	2	
8	4	8		Tax Returns	1		1	1	3	2
32	39	38		Other	1	4	1	4	6	22
4/1/08- 3/31/09 ALL	4/1/09- 3/31/10 ALL	4/1/10- 3/31/11 ALL			0-1MM	1-3MM 21 (4/1-9/30/10)	3-5MM	5-10MM	10-25MM 66 (10/1/10-3/31/11)	25MM & OVER
83	94	87		NUMBER OF STATEMENTS	3	8	4	11	19	42
%	%	%		ASSETS	%	%	%	%	%	%
15.5	15.0	14.6		Cash & Equivalents				18.3	16.7	14.4
30.8	24.5	28.3		Trade Receivables (net)				27.5	31.5	28.0
3.6	4.5	3.4		Inventory				1.4	6.6	2.8
5.9	5.9	4.5		All Other Current				4.1	5.0	4.9
55.8	49.9	50.8		Total Current				51.3	59.8	50.1
35.5	35.9	36.8		Fixed Assets (net)				24.9	34.4	35.0
3.4	7.3	7.6		Intangibles (net)				17.9	1.1	10.5
5.3	6.8	4.8		All Other Non-Current				5.9	4.8	4.4
100.0	100.0	100.0		Total				100.0	100.0	100.0
				LIABILITIES						
6.6	6.0	8.2		Notes Payable-Short Term				6.4	14.7	7.3
5.4	4.3	5.4		Cur. Mat.-L.T.D.				7.2	4.3	5.4
12.0	11.8	10.3		Trade Payables				12.2	13.2	9.8
.7	.8	.4		Income Taxes Payable				.9	.5	.3
12.1	10.1	8.9		All Other Current				19.0	7.4	8.5
36.7	33.1	33.1		Total Current				45.7	40.2	31.3
18.6	19.4	14.7		Long-Term Debt				19.1	13.3	12.7
1.0	2.0	2.4		Deferred Taxes				1.8	1.0	3.4
3.6	3.4	3.5		All Other Non-Current				4.7	2.3	3.9
40.1	42.1	46.2		Net Worth				28.8	43.2	48.6
100.0	100.0	100.0		Total Liabilties & Net Worth				100.0	100.0	100.0
				INCOME DATA						
100.0	100.0	100.0		Net Sales				100.0	100.0	100.0
				Gross Profit						
90.5	93.5	88.9		Operating Expenses				90.0	94.6	90.8
9.5	6.5	11.1		Operating Profit				10.0	5.4	9.2
1.3	2.9	2.5		All Other Expenses (net)				1.9	.3	2.5
8.2	3.6	8.5		Profit Before Taxes				8.0	5.1	6.6
				RATIOS						
2.4	2.5	2.8						1.6	2.8	3.0
1.5	1.5	1.5		Current				1.2	1.6	1.7
.9	1.0	1.0						.8	1.1	1.0
2.1	2.1	2.4						1.3	1.6	2.8
1.3	1.1	1.3		Quick				1.1	1.4	1.4
.8	.7	.8						.7	.9	.8
26 14.1	28 13.2	34 10.6						15 24.8	32 11.4	38 9.5
47 7.8	42 8.6	55 6.7		Sales/Receivables				43 8.4	43 8.5	58 6.3
66 5.5	57 6.4	76 4.8						68 5.4	58 6.2	81 4.5
				Cost of Sales/Inventory						
				Cost of Sales/Payables						
6.8	5.4	4.8						15.0	7.0	4.4
12.5	13.1	12.3		Sales/Working Capital				64.2	14.8	9.4
-47.6	NM	-160.0						-40.0	73.2	NM
41.1	22.5	26.9						20.0	23.8	41.1
(78) 10.3	(86) 5.5	(76) 9.0		EBIT/Interest	(10) 7.9	(18) 5.0	(36) 6.8
2.3	.6	2.0						3.0	1.3	1.8
7.0	9.1	7.9								2.2
(23) 3.2	(29) 2.8	(21) 2.2		Net Profit + Depr., Dep., Amort./Cur. Mat. L/T/D					(10) 1.3
1.7	1.1	.6								-.1
.2	.4	.5						1.0	.2	.5
.9	1.0	1.1		Fixed/Worth				4.8	.8	1.1
2.0	2.7	1.9						-.4	1.6	2.0
.6	.6	.5						1.4	.5	.4
1.5	1.9	1.3		Debt/Worth				14.6	1.1	1.3
3.1	4.5	4.0						-2.7	2.7	3.3
79.9	44.7	65.5							29.5	53.6
(74) 40.7	(81) 15.7	(75) 25.6		% Profit Before Taxes/Tangible Net Worth	(18) 20.6	(36) 28.2
13.1	.2	7.5							1.5	10.0
33.7	18.9	19.5						20.3	11.7	17.5
14.1	5.5	9.7		% Profit Before Taxes/Total Assets				10.1	5.7	9.3
4.2	-1.3	3.8						6.4	.8	3.9
28.4	13.5	13.2						26.3	16.6	8.4
7.7	6.6	5.9		Sales/Net Fixed Assets				12.0	10.3	5.4
3.5	3.0	3.4						6.4	4.1	3.4
3.3	3.1	2.5						4.6	3.5	2.3
2.5	1.7	1.7		Sales/Total Assets				1.7	2.2	1.6
1.6	1.1	1.2						1.3	1.6	1.2
.7	1.1	2.2							1.7	2.6
(65) 2.5	(78) 3.5	(67) 4.2		% Depr., Dep., Amort./Sales	(17) 2.5	(33) 4.5
6.7	6.1	7.4							4.5	7.7
1.1	.7	1.3								
(23) 2.2	(23) 1.9	(17) 2.1		% Officers', Directors' Owners' Comp/Sales						
5.5	10.8	5.6								
4550801M	6162375M	5009040M		Net Sales ($)	431M	18568M	14637M	78544M	335130M	4561730M
2306040M	4165268M	3125865M		Total Assets ($)	3657M	16540M	9244M	76233M	159119M	2861072M

M = $ thousand   MM = $ million
See Pages 9 through 22 for Explanation of Ratios and Data

Current Data Sorted by Assets | Comparative Historical Data

0-500M	500M-2MM	2-10MM	10-50MM	50-100MM	100-250MM	Type of Statement	4/1/06-3/31/07 ALL	4/1/07-3/31/08 ALL
	2	11	11	2	3	Unqualified	15	16
	8	21	7	1		Reviewed	16	19
	6	3	1			Compiled	2	3
8	3	5	1			Tax Returns	3	6
4	7	10	9	2	1	Other	20	27
	14 (4/1-9/30/10)		112 (10/1/10-3/31/11)					
12	26	50	29	5	4	**NUMBER OF STATEMENTS**	56	71
%	%	%	%	%	%	**ASSETS**	%	%
21.6	8.7	14.4	12.5			Cash & Equivalents	15.7	9.7
18.4	38.9	40.6	35.8			Trade Receivables (net)	36.9	40.5
10.3	5.8	4.8	8.4			Inventory	3.5	3.3
15.6	5.3	9.3	10.0			All Other Current	9.4	9.6
66.0	58.7	69.1	66.7			Total Current	65.5	63.2
29.6	33.5	23.3	22.3			Fixed Assets (net)	28.6	28.8
.0	.3	.6	5.9			Intangibles (net)	1.2	1.2
4.6	7.5	7.1	5.1			All Other Non-Current	4.7	6.8
100.0	100.0	100.0	100.0			Total	100.0	100.0
						LIABILITIES		
22.9	14.5	7.9	5.6			Notes Payable-Short Term	10.1	11.0
20.4	8.8	4.4	4.2			Cur. Mat.-L.T.D.	5.6	4.0
7.5	14.9	17.9	22.4			Trade Payables	18.2	15.7
.0	.1	.3	.6			Income Taxes Payable	.3	.5
36.2	6.6	9.9	14.9			All Other Current	12.3	12.5
87.1	45.0	40.4	47.8			Total Current	46.5	43.6
40.2	12.6	9.6	7.7			Long-Term Debt	12.6	11.5
.0	.1	.4	.9			Deferred Taxes	.3	.5
19.6	5.0	2.5	1.4			All Other Non-Current	2.2	5.6
-46.8	37.3	47.1	42.2			Net Worth	38.4	38.8
100.0	100.0	100.0	100.0			Total Liabilities & Net Worth	100.0	100.0
						INCOME DATA		
100.0	100.0	100.0	100.0			Net Sales	100.0	100.0
50.5	30.6	25.9	18.5			Gross Profit	23.6	25.1
51.9	25.6	22.0	14.7			Operating Expenses	18.4	19.2
-1.4	5.0	3.9	3.8			Operating Profit	5.2	5.9
.6	1.1	.3	-.1			All Other Expenses (net)	.2	.7
-2.0	3.9	3.5	3.8			Profit Before Taxes	5.0	5.1
						RATIOS		
2.5	2.3	2.4	1.9			Current	2.3	2.3
.9	1.3	1.8	1.4				1.5	1.5
.4	1.0	1.3	1.1				1.1	1.2
1.5	2.0	2.3	1.4			Quick	2.0	1.9
.5	1.1	1.3	1.0				1.1	1.2
.2	.7	1.0	.8				.8	.8
0 UND	28 13.2	41 8.8	42 8.7			Sales/Receivables	40 9.0	45 8.1
1 269.0	52 7.0	59 6.2	55 6.7				54 6.8	62 5.9
30 12.0	72 5.0	87 4.2	80 4.6				67 5.5	83 4.4
0 UND	0 UND	0 UND	0 UND			Cost of Sales/Inventory	0 UND	0 UND
0 UND	0 999.8	0 UND	2 180.1				0 UND	0 913.5
0 UND	16 23.3	12 29.5	41 9.0				6 57.9	7 54.7
0 UND	5 69.6	16 23.2	23 15.6			Cost of Sales/Payables	17 21.2	15 23.6
0 UND	19 19.1	27 13.7	36 10.2				29 12.5	31 11.6
22 16.8	50 7.3	58 6.3	57 6.4				42 8.7	43 8.5
8.7	8.1	5.5	5.3			Sales/Working Capital	6.7	6.1
-142.5	24.6	7.3	15.2				13.1	12.4
-8.7	NM	17.6	33.5				55.8	36.9
14.2	17.1	38.0	74.4			EBIT/Interest	15.8	9.6
(11) 10.3	4.1	(46) 7.6	(26) 8.9				(49) 5.1	(61) 5.1
-7.2	1.6	3.7	.8				1.3	2.0
		4.7				Net Profit + Depr., Dep., Amort./Cur. Mat. L/T/D	13.1	5.4
	(16) 2.7						(15) 5.2	(16) 2.9
		1.1					1.8	1.5
.2	.5	.2	.1			Fixed/Worth	.4	.4
-36.1	.9	.5	.5				.7	.7
-.1	1.9	1.0	1.0				1.5	1.1
1.8	.6	.6	.7			Debt/Worth	.8	.8
-59.4	1.9	1.2	1.8				1.8	1.5
-1.6	5.9	2.6	4.1				4.2	4.3
	42.3	51.9	54.3			% Profit Before Taxes/Tangible Net Worth	74.6	48.2
	(23) 19.3	25.7	(28) 28.3				(52) 38.3	(68) 27.5
	3.5	5.8	-1.6				6.1	10.0
35.4	17.6	16.2	16.9			% Profit Before Taxes/Total Assets	25.0	16.5
24.4	8.1	8.4	7.7				11.9	11.8
-41.3	1.2	1.7	-.7				1.0	2.7
167.2	24.6	27.8	110.2			Sales/Net Fixed Assets	20.7	19.6
57.9	9.1	13.1	14.0				8.5	8.4
5.2	4.5	5.5	4.6				5.2	5.1
7.3	3.4	3.1	2.8			Sales/Total Assets	3.5	2.9
3.8	2.5	2.3	2.1				2.5	2.2
2.8	2.1	1.8	1.2				1.8	1.7
	1.3	1.5	.8			% Depr., Dep., Amort./Sales	1.2	1.2
	(21) 3.5	(46) 2.7	(24) 1.8				(47) 2.7	(61) 2.2
	8.9	4.6	6.3				5.0	3.9
	1.1	1.3				% Officers', Directors' Owners' Comp/Sales	1.8	1.5
	(11) 7.0	(20) 2.8					(19) 5.6	(23) 3.0
	12.7	5.0					8.3	6.1
18118M	99332M	590712M	1231409M	621653M	956080M	Net Sales ($)	1625071M	1967284M
2239M	35798M	238195M	635672M	380891M	618665M	Total Assets ($)	691458M	1113720M

Comparative Historical Data   Current Data Sorted by Sales

Comparative			Type of Statement	0-1MM	1-3MM	3-5MM	5-10MM	10-25MM	25MM & OVER
18	26	29	Unqualified		1	1	5	5	17
20	31	37	Reviewed		3	6	12	8	8
4	17	10	Compiled		4	2	3		1
12	8	17	Tax Returns	4	5	1	3	3	1
32	37	33	Other	3	4	4	7	5	10
4/1/08-3/31/09 ALL	4/1/09-3/31/10 ALL	4/1/10-3/31/11 ALL			14 (4/1-9/30/10)		112 (10/1/10-3/31/11)		
86	119	126	**NUMBER OF STATEMENTS**	7	17	14	30	21	37
%	%	%	**ASSETS**	%	%	%	%	%	%
12.0	12.8	13.3	Cash & Equivalents		8.9	11.1	14.0	14.6	12.2
40.9	37.3	35.7	Trade Receivables (net)		35.1	26.2	45.9	34.7	36.7
2.6	4.0	6.5	Inventory		7.1	8.5	5.3	6.0	5.9
8.8	8.4	9.6	All Other Current		6.1	12.5	6.5	10.1	12.5
64.3	62.5	65.1	Total Current		57.2	58.4	71.7	65.4	67.2
26.0	30.3	26.1	Fixed Assets (net)		32.2	32.2	23.0	23.2	22.1
3.2	2.7	2.1	Intangibles (net)		.2	.2	.7	2.7	5.0
6.5	4.5	6.7	All Other Non-Current		10.4	9.1	4.6	8.7	5.8
100.0	100.0	100.0	Total		100.0	100.0	100.0	100.0	100.0
			LIABILITIES						
7.9	9.2	9.7	Notes Payable-Short Term		11.6	10.1	13.0	4.5	4.1
7.4	5.6	6.8	Cur. Mat.-L.T.D.		10.4	4.3	10.4	6.1	4.2
17.3	15.6	17.1	Trade Payables		11.3	13.6	18.6	20.2	20.4
.3	.5	.3	Income Taxes Payable		.7	.1	.1	.1	.5
10.0	11.3	13.2	All Other Current		18.0	9.0	7.6	11.7	16.1
42.9	42.1	47.1	Total Current		52.0	37.1	49.8	42.6	45.3
14.1	14.0	13.5	Long-Term Debt		14.2	36.9	8.8	8.2	10.5
.6	.5	.4	Deferred Taxes		.1	.1	.4	.2	1.0
5.3	7.3	4.4	All Other Non-Current		4.1	3.5	3.6	1.4	1.8
37.2	36.1	34.5	Net Worth		29.7	22.4	37.3	47.5	41.4
100.0	100.0	100.0	Total Liabilities & Net Worth		100.0	100.0	100.0	100.0	100.0
			INCOME DATA						
100.0	100.0	100.0	Net Sales		100.0	100.0	100.0	100.0	100.0
26.8	27.5	26.8	Gross Profit		35.8	32.2	28.3	23.5	16.7
20.4	23.1	23.1	Operating Expenses		30.9	29.4	25.2	20.0	11.6
6.4	4.3	3.7	Operating Profit		4.8	2.8	3.1	3.5	5.1
.6	.8	.6	All Other Expenses (net)		.5	.5	.5	.6	.7
5.8	3.5	3.1	Profit Before Taxes		4.3	2.2	2.6	2.9	4.4
			RATIOS						
2.5	2.2	2.3	Current		3.7	2.3	2.6	2.2	1.9
1.5	1.6	1.5			1.2	1.8	1.8	1.7	1.5
1.2	1.1	1.1			.6	1.3	1.1	1.2	1.2
2.0	2.0	1.7	Quick		2.9	1.8	2.4	1.7	1.5
1.3	1.2	1.1			1.0	1.1	1.4	1.2	1.1
.9	.8	.8			.5	.7	.9	.9	.8
37 9.9	38 9.6	34 10.9	Sales/Receivables		26 14.0	6 64.0	43 8.5	40 9.2	42 8.7
55 6.7	58 6.3	54 6.8			47 7.8	49 7.4	57 6.4	49 7.5	59 6.2
73 5.0	72 5.1	74 4.9			76 4.8	75 4.9	82 4.4	85 4.3	73 5.0
0 UND	0 UND	0 UND	Cost of Sales/Inventory		0 UND	0 UND	0 UND	0 UND	0 UND
0 UND	0 UND	1 481.7			0 UND	2 178.4	1 683.1	1 596.9	2 218.8
5 76.8	9 39.4	17 21.8			23 15.5	33 11.0	13 27.5	16 23.4	22 16.5
12 30.6	12 31.1	15 25.1	Cost of Sales/Payables		12 29.6	5 69.6	15 24.7	16 23.2	18 20.3
22 16.4	27 13.6	27 13.4			24 15.2	40 9.0	27 13.4	21 17.2	34 10.9
52 7.1	47 7.7	54 6.7			36 10.3	61 6.0	54 6.7	65 5.6	49 7.5
7.5	5.6	6.0	Sales/Working Capital		8.3	6.3	5.8	5.7	5.3
12.8	12.0	11.5			33.0	8.1	14.3	7.5	9.9
24.8	62.2	52.5			-21.7	37.4	57.0	24.3	29.1
31.3	20.4	22.3	EBIT/Interest		17.5	10.9	21.8	45.7	74.4
(75) 7.8	(108) 6.5	(117) 7.2			(16) 4.7	(13) 3.3	(28) 9.0	(20) 5.5	(34) 11.9
2.9	1.1	1.9			-.8	1.1	4.4	1.7	2.0
15.4	7.3	7.3	Net Profit + Depr., Dep., Amort./Cur. Mat. L/T/D					4.7	
(27) 3.1	(25) 2.6	(31) 2.4						(11) 3.4	
2.0	1.4	.6						1.0	
.3	.3	.2	Fixed/Worth		.2	.2	.3	.2	.2
.6	.7	.6			1.0	.9	.6	.5	.5
1.6	1.7	1.3			3.9	1.5	1.1	1.0	1.0
.8	.8	.7	Debt/Worth		.5	.7	.6	.7	.7
1.4	1.6	1.7			2.1	1.7	1.4	1.0	1.8
3.2	5.1	4.0			6.0	3.7	3.9	3.7	3.3
78.1	59.0	50.7	% Profit Before Taxes/Tangible Net Worth		54.4	32.1	48.6	51.8	56.6
(78) 42.4	(104) 23.9	(114) 24.4			(15) 40.0	(12) 8.6	(28) 24.4	15.1	(35) 23.7
14.7	.8	3.5			8.7	1.1	7.0	1.4	3.6
26.7	22.5	18.0	% Profit Before Taxes/Total Assets		26.8	17.4	16.3	13.5	18.2
13.5	9.3	7.7			7.4	5.4	11.3	7.1	8.6
4.4	-.4	1.1			-5.9	.4	4.6	.6	1.1
33.1	26.0	36.8	Sales/Net Fixed Assets		21.1	40.0	27.8	80.5	54.1
15.5	9.5	10.5			6.8	8.0	14.4	14.5	10.9
5.6	4.4	5.1			3.1	4.1	6.7	4.5	5.8
3.6	3.3	3.2	Sales/Total Assets		3.2	2.9	3.9	2.9	2.9
2.5	2.3	2.4			2.1	2.2	3.0	2.3	2.2
2.0	1.6	1.6			1.5	1.7	2.0	1.8	1.3
.9	1.4	1.4	% Depr., Dep., Amort./Sales		2.7	1.0	1.5	1.4	.8
(72) 1.9	(96) 2.6	(100) 2.7			(13) 5.6	(10) 4.8	(27) 2.6	(19) 2.7	(29) 1.7
3.9	5.3	6.3			11.6	11.0	4.2	4.5	4.2
2.6	1.1	1.4	% Officers', Directors' Owners' Comp/Sales			1.3			
(27) 5.4	(27) 2.5	(42) 3.4				(15) 3.1			
9.5	4.3	7.8				6.9			
2883814M	4043366M	3517304M	Net Sales ($)	3306M	36649M	56906M	224470M	356598M	2839375M
1314575M	2168586M	1911460M	Total Assets ($)	1169M	22094M	25663M	90308M	203927M	1568299M

M = $ thousand   MM = $ million
See Pages 9 through 22 for Explanation of Ratios and Data

Current Data Sorted by Assets   Comparative Historical Data

Type of Statement

Type of Statement	0-500M	500M-2MM	2-10MM	10-50MM	50-100MM	100-250MM		4/1/06-3/31/07 ALL	4/1/07-3/31/08 ALL
Unqualified		3	5	10	2	11		91	76
Reviewed			7	11	14	3	1	88	51
Compiled	3	12	32	9	1	1		132	105
Tax Returns	21	60	71	16	1	1		404	352
Other	21	60	133	74	13	10		399	384

Period splits (current): 45 (4/1-9/30/10); 561 (10/1/10-3/31/11)

	0-500M	500M-2MM	2-10MM	10-50MM	50-100MM	100-250MM		Hist 4/1/06-3/31/07 ALL	Hist 4/1/07-3/31/08 ALL
NUMBER OF STATEMENTS	45	142	252	123	20	24		1114	968
ASSETS (%)	%	%	%	%	%	%		%	%
Cash & Equivalents	13.9	7.9	6.2	5.7	2.4	11.6		7.8	6.7
Trade Receivables (net)	5.3	4.4	2.5	2.9	1.9	6.7		4.9	4.5
Inventory	27.9	40.2	35.4	32.6	21.6	11.9		40.0	38.7
All Other Current	5.8	4.5	3.8	3.8	6.6	3.2		4.9	5.1
Total Current	52.9	57.1	47.9	45.0	32.6	33.4		57.6	55.0
Fixed Assets (net)	37.5	33.5	41.5	37.6	52.5	41.3		28.4	30.2
Intangibles (net)	.4	1.5	1.8	2.1	1.0	1.4		1.1	1.1
All Other Non-Current	9.2	7.9	8.8	15.3	13.9	23.9		12.9	13.6
Total	100.0	100.0	100.0	100.0	100.0	100.0		100.0	100.0
LIABILITIES									
Notes Payable-Short Term	27.3	18.7	15.5	15.6	2.6	8.6		21.3	19.8
Cur. Mat.-L.T.D.	21.4	2.9	3.0	2.6	8.2	6.8		3.3	4.7
Trade Payables	4.0	2.2	2.2	2.4	1.9	5.7		4.3	3.5
Income Taxes Payable	.0	.0	.0	.1	.0	.2		.1	.1
All Other Current	25.2	10.5	11.9	8.2	12.3	12.4		10.5	10.3
Total Current	77.8	34.3	32.6	28.9	25.0	33.7		39.4	38.4
Long-Term Debt	34.8	33.5	38.4	27.6	38.8	26.6		29.3	31.4
Deferred Taxes	.0	.0	.0	.1	.1	.2		.1	.1
All Other Non-Current	7.7	4.0	4.4	5.1	7.1	2.8		4.6	4.4
Net Worth	-20.4	28.2	24.6	38.4	28.9	36.7		26.7	25.8
Total Liabilities & Net Worth	100.0	100.0	100.0	100.0	100.0	100.0		100.0	100.0
INCOME DATA									
Net Sales	100.0	100.0	100.0	100.0	100.0	100.0		100.0	100.0
Gross Profit									
Operating Expenses	83.1	83.0	78.7	83.8	83.1	89.0		79.4	82.4
Operating Profit	16.9	17.0	21.3	16.2	16.9	11.0		20.6	17.6
All Other Expenses (net)	9.5	12.1	11.9	11.0	10.7	5.1		6.7	8.3
Profit Before Taxes	7.4	4.9	9.3	5.2	6.2	5.8		13.9	9.3

RATIOS

Ratio	0-500M	500M-2MM	2-10MM	10-50MM	50-100MM	100-250MM		Hist 4/1/06-3/31/07	Hist 4/1/07-3/31/08
Current	2.5	4.1	4.1	4.2	4.4	2.2		3.4	4.0
	.8	1.6	1.4	1.5	1.2	1.3		1.3	1.3
	.2	.7	.5	.7	.3	.1		.8	.7
Quick	.6	1.3	1.1	1.6	.6	1.3		.9	1.0
	.1	.2	(251) .2	.2	.2	.4		(1111) .2	(963) .2
	.0	.0	.0	.0	.0	.1		.0	.0
Sales/Receivables	0 UND	0 UND	0 UND	0 UND	0 UND	2 240.9		0 UND	0 UND
	0 UND	0 UND	0 UND	0 778.0	5 67.5	13 28.9		0 UND	0 UND
	4 102.8	0 UND	6 59.4	15 24.7	30 12.2	34 10.9		9 38.9	10 37.2
Cost of Sales/Inventory									
Cost of Sales/Payables									
Sales/Working Capital	1.2	.6	.9	.6	.8	1.9		1.5	1.3
	-30.3	4.1	7.0	4.0	21.7	5.0		7.6	7.2
	-1.8	-14.0	-5.1	-5.3	-.9	-1.2		-14.7	-8.1
EBIT/Interest	4.2	5.6	5.9	4.2	3.0	5.8		15.9	8.2
	(23) 1.3	(69) 1.0	(126) 2.1	(73) 1.8	(12) .7	(18) 2.9		(658) 4.0	(565) 2.5
	.1	-1.5	.5	-.3	-2.8	1.0		1.4	.6
Net Profit + Depr., Dep., Amort./Cur. Mat. L/T/D				2.6				5.2	3.8
				(10) 1.5				(34) 1.8	(25) 1.0
				.8				.4	-.1
Fixed/Worth	.0	.0	.0	.0	1.1	.5		.0	.0
	1.0	.1	1.0	.7	4.2	1.1		.2	.4
	-12.4	4.7	7.3	2.9	NM	2.1		3.0	3.6
Debt/Worth	1.1	.7	.9	.6	.8	.8		1.1	1.1
	13.2	2.5	3.2	2.2	4.3	1.7		3.6	3.8
	-4.5	243.0	43.6	6.3	NM	4.0		17.4	19.7
% Profit Before Taxes/Tangible Net Worth	28.6	30.5	36.5	14.2	22.4	18.4		64.0	43.9
	(27) 4.3	(110) 2.6	(202) 7.7	(112) 3.5	(15) 2.2	(22) 3.6		(946) 26.1	(806) 11.8
	-3.6	-4.5	-1.0	-2.2	-.3	.9		5.1	-.2
% Profit Before Taxes/Total Assets	13.9	7.8	6.4	3.4	2.3	5.1		14.2	8.8
	1.9	.3	1.8	1.0	.5	1.6		5.1	2.2
	-3.4	-2.7	-.7	-1.0	-1.4	-.8		.6	-.9
Sales/Net Fixed Assets	UND	UND	508.1	48.5	9.6	4.3		UND	999.8
	64.3	64.1	2.1	2.1	.4	1.0		19.1	10.0
	.7	.3	.2	.2	.1	.3		1.1	.6
Sales/Total Assets	2.1	.9	.6	.4	.3	.8		1.2	1.0
	.7	.3	.2	.2	.1	.3		.5	.4
	.3	.1	.1	.1	.1	.1		.2	.2
% Depr., Dep., Amort./Sales	1.5	.7	1.6	1.8	2.7	.9		.3	.5
	(17) 7.8	(52) 9.5	(125) 7.0	(72) 8.1	(12) 10.3	(17) 5.2		(567) 1.4	(503) 2.4
	21.6	23.9	19.1	23.8	16.0	11.2		9.3	11.9
% Officers', Directors' Owners' Comp/Sales		1.5		1.2	3.4			1.3	1.5
		(16) 3.0		(16) 3.7	(10) 5.2			(207) 2.8	(164) 4.1
		6.7		6.2	13.5			6.0	9.0
Net Sales ($)	28204M	116864M	585917M	994948M	375427M	2183289M		14772444M	10960909M
Total Assets ($)	12316M	174556M	1180972M	2748119M	1410042M	3779331M		22010397M	18481255M

M = $ thousand   MM = $ million
See Pages 9 through 22 for Explanation of Ratios and Data

Comparative Historical Data | **Current Data Sorted by Sales**

		Comparative Historical Data		Type of Statement	0-1MM	1-3MM	3-5MM	5-10MM	10-25MM	25MM & OVER
	60	49	31	Unqualified	8	3	4	1	8	7
	60	51	36	Reviewed	10	5	5	6	4	6
	94	69	58	Compiled	24	18	6	7	2	1
	293	263	170	Tax Returns	104	43	9	11	2	1
	398	313	311	Other	131	78	36	31	18	17
	4/1/08-3/31/09 ALL	4/1/09-3/31/10 ALL	4/1/10-3/31/11 ALL		45 (4/1-9/30/10)			561 (10/1/10-3/31/11)		
	905	745	606	NUMBER OF STATEMENTS	277	147	60	56	34	32
	%	%	%	**ASSETS**	%	%	%	%	%	%
	6.9	7.5	7.2	Cash & Equivalents	5.3	9.1	7.9	8.8	6.9	11.0
	4.5	4.5	3.4	Trade Receivables (net)	1.6	2.0	7.1	5.1	6.9	11.1
	36.9	31.5	34.0	Inventory	31.8	41.4	33.8	35.2	30.9	20.7
	3.7	4.3	4.2	All Other Current	4.6	2.6	3.8	4.6	5.0	7.2
	52.1	47.8	48.7	Total Current	43.3	55.1	52.6	53.8	49.8	50.1
	34.1	36.4	38.9	Fixed Assets (net)	47.8	32.3	36.1	25.3	33.8	27.2
	1.2	1.8	1.6	Intangibles (net)	1.1	1.1	1.4	5.1	1.3	3.6
	12.6	14.0	10.7	All Other Non-Current	7.9	11.5	9.8	15.9	15.2	19.1
	100.0	100.0	100.0	Total	100.0	100.0	100.0	100.0	100.0	100.0
				LIABILITIES						
	18.0	18.0	16.4	Notes Payable-Short Term	14.9	17.7	22.9	13.7	21.9	10.7
	3.4	4.4	4.6	Cur. Mat.-L.T.D.	6.5	2.6	2.1	3.3	3.0	5.6
	4.6	3.5	2.5	Trade Payables	.8	1.4	4.6	3.5	10.0	8.6
	.1	.1	.0	Income Taxes Payable	.0	.0	.0	.1	.0	.2
	11.8	12.1	11.8	All Other Current	9.7	11.8	15.6	12.5	20.1	12.9
	37.8	38.1	35.4	Total Current	32.0	33.6	45.3	33.2	55.0	38.0
	35.1	34.3	34.3	Long-Term Debt	40.5	30.9	33.7	25.2	25.9	22.8
	.1	.0	.0	Deferred Taxes	.0	.0	.1	.1	.1	.1
	3.5	3.8	4.7	All Other Non-Current	5.9	3.1	4.7	5.1	2.2	3.3
	23.5	23.8	25.5	Net Worth	21.6	32.3	16.2	36.4	16.7	35.9
	100.0	100.0	100.0	Total Liabilties & Net Worth	100.0	100.0	100.0	100.0	100.0	100.0
				INCOME DATA						
	100.0	100.0	100.0	Net Sales	100.0	100.0	100.0	100.0	100.0	100.0
				Gross Profit						
	83.9	82.4	81.6	Operating Expenses	75.3	84.9	86.7	84.9	89.1	98.0
	16.1	17.6	18.4	Operating Profit	24.7	15.1	13.3	15.1	10.9	2.0
	10.3	11.8	11.3	All Other Expenses (net)	16.9	8.9	6.5	4.7	5.7	.2
	5.8	5.8	7.1	Profit Before Taxes	7.8	6.2	6.8	10.4	5.2	1.8
				RATIOS						
	3.6	3.0	3.9	Current	4.1	5.2	3.2	3.5	3.6	2.3
	1.3	1.3	1.4		1.5	1.6	1.1	1.4	1.1	1.4
	.6	.5	.6		.3	.8	.5	.7	.5	1.0
	.9	1.1	1.2	Quick	.9	1.2	1.1	1.4	1.2	1.3
	(904) .2	(744) .2	(605) .2		.2	.2	(59) .2	.4	.2	.5
	.0	.0	.0		.0	.0	.0	.1	.0	.1
	0 UND	0 UND	0 UND	Sales/Receivables	0 UND	0 UND	0 UND	0 UND	0 UND	1 422.6
	0 UND	0 UND	0 UND		0 UND	0 UND	1 341.8	2 153.2	6 56.9	9 41.0
	12 31.4	13 27.6	8 45.9		0 UND	4 100.1	24 15.5	21 17.5	24 15.1	42 8.7
				Cost of Sales/Inventory						
				Cost of Sales/Payables						
	.9	1.0	.8	Sales/Working Capital	.5	.9	1.9	1.0	2.5	3.1
	8.5	8.5	6.0		6.1	4.1	8.4	6.5	29.0	6.5
	-5.6	-3.6	-4.9		-2.7	-7.4	-4.7	-14.1	-6.6	209.1
	6.2	5.2	5.4	EBIT/Interest	4.0	6.2	7.6	19.0	5.7	3.5
	(480) 2.1	(401) 1.7	(321) 1.8		(111) 1.2	(84) 1.8	(38) 2.5	(36) 2.6	(24) 2.6	(28) 2.0
	-.1	-.9	-.3		-.3	-.6	-1.0	.4	1.1	.5
	4.3	8.7	6.5	Net Profit + Depr., Dep., Amort./Cur. Mat. L/T/D						
	(22) 1.2	(24) 1.8	(26) 2.1							
	.2	.7	1.0							
	.0	.0	.0	Fixed/Worth	.0	.0	.1	.0	.2	.0
	.7	.9	.8		1.6	.3	1.2	.5	.7	.9
	4.9	6.3	4.9		24.0	2.4	16.5	1.9	3.8	2.3
	1.2	1.2	.8	Debt/Worth	.9	.7	.8	.5	1.1	.8
	3.7	3.4	2.7		3.4	2.1	2.8	2.2	3.3	2.4
	30.2	35.2	32.0		-990.3	7.8	NM	5.7	36.1	5.0
	25.1	22.3	23.8	% Profit Before Taxes/Tangible Net Worth	14.9	26.9	36.3	47.4	26.1	23.6
	(733) 5.6	(594) 3.7	(488) 5.0		(207) 1.9	(128) 6.5	(45) 9.3	(49) 12.5	(28) 11.2	(31) 8.9
	-4.6	-5.4	-2.5		-3.4	-5.5	-.2	2.2	2.3	.9
	5.4	4.5	5.5	% Profit Before Taxes/Total Assets	3.4	7.6	10.8	24.0	5.2	6.3
	1.0	.8	1.1		.6	1.6	1.8	3.4	2.5	2.3
	-1.6	-2.1	-1.5		-1.8	-1.9	-2.7	.2	-.7	.1
	999.8	265.7	UND	Sales/Net Fixed Assets	UND	UND	96.7	148.8	130.3	110.3
	6.6	2.9	2.8		.5	8.9	2.9	5.4	3.2	4.8
	.4	.2	.2		.1	.3	.5	1.6	.4	1.3
	.8	.6	.7	Sales/Total Assets	.3	.7	1.5	1.3	1.3	1.7
	.3	.2	.2		.2	.4	.5	.7	.5	.9
	.1	.1	.1		.1	.1	.2	.2	.2	.4
	.7	1.2	1.7	% Depr., Dep., Amort./Sales	5.1	1.4	1.0	.8	1.2	.5
	(446) 4.6	(404) 5.7	(295) 7.9		(114) 17.4	(70) 8.3	(30) 5.5	(37) 4.0	(21) 6.3	(23) 2.2
	15.6	16.4	19.8		26.7	19.3	14.9	5.5	14.5	6.2
	1.6	1.4	1.8	% Officers', Directors' Owners' Comp/Sales	1.8	2.8				
	(152) 3.8	(91) 3.0	(52) 3.7		(15) 5.6	(18) 3.9				
	8.2	6.8	6.3		11.2	6.2				
	10713760M	5060144M	4284649M	Net Sales ($)	106994M	257454M	230034M	407642M	555889M	2726636M
	14235730M	10918647M	9305336M	Total Assets ($)	840658M	1312706M	864006M	1301550M	1629671M	3356745M

© RMA 2011   M = $ thousand   MM = $ million
See Pages 9 through 22 for Explanation of Ratios and Data

Current Data Sorted by Assets — **Comparative Historical Data**

0-500M	500M-2MM	2-10MM	10-50MM	50-100MM	100-250MM	Type of Statement	405	380
2	8	102	187	54	34	Unqualified	405	380
5	47	120	42	1		Reviewed	224	207
6	19	16	3			Compiled	44	35
12	15	12	4			Tax Returns	44	43
5	34	79	72	18	15	Other	171	197
	157 (4/1-9/30/10)			755 (10/1/10-3/31/11)			4/1/06-3/31/07 ALL	4/1/07-3/31/08 ALL
30	123	329	308	73	49	**NUMBER OF STATEMENTS**	888	862
%	%	%	%	%	%	**ASSETS**	%	%
24.4	16.5	15.8	20.3	25.3	18.1	Cash & Equivalents	16.3	17.9
14.7	33.3	31.6	27.9	23.2	20.2	Trade Receivables (net)	32.3	30.5
1.5	3.4	3.6	4.4	3.7	5.1	Inventory	3.5	3.5
6.5	5.5	6.3	7.0	8.2	6.8	All Other Current	6.8	6.7
47.2	58.7	57.3	59.5	60.4	50.2	Total Current	59.0	58.7
37.7	33.5	35.1	32.3	27.8	34.1	Fixed Assets (net)	33.9	34.3
2.0	1.2	1.4	1.6	3.1	6.3	Intangibles (net)	1.2	.9
13.2	6.6	6.2	6.6	8.7	9.3	All Other Non-Current	5.9	6.1
100.0	100.0	100.0	100.0	100.0	100.0	Total	100.0	100.0
						LIABILITIES		
19.8	7.3	5.7	3.2	1.8	2.2	Notes Payable-Short Term	5.1	4.3
15.0	5.8	5.5	4.3	2.9	2.9	Cur. Mat.-L.T.D.	5.4	5.4
14.6	15.2	15.8	16.2	15.9	12.7	Trade Payables	15.8	15.2
2.5	.3	.4	.3	.5	.2	Income Taxes Payable	.7	.6
11.5	6.9	9.4	11.1	14.8	14.0	All Other Current	11.0	12.0
63.4	35.5	36.6	35.1	35.8	32.0	Total Current	38.0	37.5
41.2	17.1	14.6	12.9	9.4	13.7	Long-Term Debt	15.3	16.0
.3	1.3	1.2	1.2	1.6	.8	Deferred Taxes	1.2	1.1
10.0	5.8	1.9	2.4	2.4	3.2	All Other Non-Current	3.0	2.3
-14.6	40.3	45.7	48.4	50.8	50.3	Net Worth	42.5	43.1
100.0	100.0	100.0	100.0	100.0	100.0	Total Liabilities & Net Worth	100.0	100.0
						INCOME DATA		
100.0	100.0	100.0	100.0	100.0	100.0	Net Sales	100.0	100.0
39.0	28.2	18.5	13.9	12.5	13.7	Gross Profit	20.1	20.5
36.8	25.7	16.6	10.8	8.2	9.5	Operating Expenses	14.3	14.1
2.2	2.6	2.0	3.1	4.3	4.2	Operating Profit	5.8	6.4
1.0	.4	.1	.1	-.2	.3	All Other Expenses (net)	.1	.3
1.3	2.1	1.9	3.1	4.5	3.9	Profit Before Taxes	5.7	6.1
						RATIOS		
3.7	3.2	2.6	2.3	2.3	2.1		2.2	2.2
1.0	1.8	1.7	1.6	1.8	1.6	Current	1.5	1.6
.3	1.1	1.1	1.3	1.4	1.2		1.2	1.2
2.6	2.7	2.1	1.8	1.9	1.5		1.8	1.8
.8	1.5	1.4	1.3	1.4	1.2	Quick	1.3	1.3
.3	.9	.9	1.0	1.0	.8		.9	.9
0 UND	22 16.6	31 11.9	32 11.4	33 11.1	37 9.8		31 11.6	32 11.3
4 99.0	44 8.3	48 7.5	48 7.6	45 8.1	50 7.2	Sales/Receivables	52 7.1	49 7.5
34 10.6	65 5.6	70 5.2	71 5.2	65 5.6	66 5.5		71 5.1	70 5.2
0 UND	0 UND	0 UND	0 UND	0 UND	4 89.2		0 UND	0 UND
0 UND	0 UND	0 999.8	2 165.1	2 203.4	13 29.0	Cost of Sales/Inventory	0 883.1	0 784.4
0 UND	2 147.0	10 38.2	13 28.2	12 29.4	22 16.5		8 43.2	8 47.2
0 UND	6 60.2	12 31.2	19 19.5	21 17.7	23 16.1		15 23.6	15 23.6
4 89.4	20 18.5	26 13.9	32 11.5	33 11.2	33 10.9	Cost of Sales/Payables	28 13.0	29 12.7
16 23.0	44 8.3	44 8.2	48 7.6	48 7.6	45 8.1		44 8.3	43 8.5
10.9	5.3	5.7	5.8	4.2	4.9		6.4	6.1
NM	11.1	10.7	8.9	7.7	8.4	Sales/Working Capital	11.3	10.7
-11.0	75.2	45.6	17.0	12.8	30.3		27.5	24.3
7.5	13.4	15.1	19.2	87.3	29.1		22.1	21.2
(24) 3.7	(108) 3.8	(301) 4.2	(273) 5.3	(68) 10.4	(48) 7.5	EBIT/Interest	(826) 6.9	(780) 7.2
-1.7	.3	-.3	1.5	3.5	2.1		2.6	2.9
2.7	4.5	4.5	7.8	8.8			5.7	6.0
(24) 1.3	(108) 2.3	(104) 2.1	(36) 3.4	(13) 2.9		Net Profit + Depr., Dep., Amort./Cur. Mat. L/T/D	(299) 2.7	(288) 2.6
-.8	.8	1.2	1.7	1.5			1.6	1.6
.5	.3	.4	.4	.3	.4		.4	.4
2.2	.7	.7	.7	.5	.7	Fixed/Worth	.8	.8
-.5	1.5	1.4	1.1	.9	1.4		1.4	1.3
.4	.5	.6	.6	.6	.8		.8	.7
16.6	1.0	1.2	1.2	.9	1.4	Debt/Worth	1.4	1.3
-2.0	3.4	2.3	2.0	1.8	1.9		2.5	2.5
73.5	42.7	27.7	25.2	32.5	23.2		46.0	46.1
(16) 12.0	(105) 13.2	(312) 11.7	(303) 11.2	(71) 13.6	(48) 11.0	% Profit Before Taxes/Tangible Net Worth	(856) 24.4	(840) 26.3
-20.6	-.4	-1.5	1.5	3.7	3.3		10.0	11.3
37.7	21.6	13.2	11.7	12.1	9.7		19.1	19.1
11.9	5.1	5.0	4.9	6.2	4.8	% Profit Before Taxes/Total Assets	9.6	10.1
-12.3	-2.1	-1.8	.6	1.8	1.2		3.7	4.3
50.5	19.9	13.5	12.3	11.8	7.6		13.0	12.0
10.7	9.5	7.2	5.9	6.5	5.3	Sales/Net Fixed Assets	7.5	6.9
5.9	5.1	3.8	3.6	4.1	3.2		4.5	4.1
6.1	3.5	3.0	2.4	2.0	1.9		2.9	2.8
4.0	2.7	2.2	1.9	1.8	1.5	Sales/Total Assets	2.2	2.1
2.4	1.7	1.6	1.5	1.4	1.2		1.7	1.6
2.3	1.8	2.1	2.2	1.9	2.0		1.8	1.9
(21) 4.9	(90) 3.3	(311) 3.3	(289) 3.4	(69) 3.5	(31) 3.1	% Depr., Dep., Amort./Sales	(802) 2.9	(774) 3.2
8.5	6.3	5.8	5.2	4.6	6.1		4.5	4.8
3.7	2.3	1.6		.4			1.2	1.3
(10) 6.9	(65) 3.6	(124) 2.6	(79) 1.6	(13) .9		% Officers', Directors' Owners' Comp/Sales	(302) 2.4	(254) 2.6
8.2	7.6	4.8	3.5	2.2			4.8	5.0
33627M	431323M	3910244M	14393437M	8958464M	11910142M	Net Sales ($)	40273744M	42180404M
7177M	159976M	1686758M	7368061M	4994513M	7722065M	Total Assets ($)	20003568M	22228306M

M = $ thousand   MM = $ million
See Pages 9 through 22 for Explanation of Ratios and Data

Comparative Historical Data			Type of Statement	Current Data Sorted by Sales					
418	408	387	Unqualified	4	3	9	35	72	264
223	237	215	Reviewed	3	23	34	61	63	31
40	45	44	Compiled	8	11	7	10	4	4
41	46	43	Tax Returns	5	9	9	11	7	2
241	272	223	Other	8	24	20	28	51	92
4/1/08-3/31/09 ALL	4/1/09-3/31/10 ALL	4/1/10-3/31/11 ALL		157 (4/1-9/30/10)		755 (10/1/10-3/31/11)			
				0-1MM	1-3MM	3-5MM	5-10MM	10-25MM	25MM & OVER
963	1008	912	**NUMBER OF STATEMENTS**	28	70	79	145	197	393
%	%	%	**ASSETS**	%	%	%	%	%	%
18.6	20.1	18.6	Cash & Equivalents	21.7	14.4	16.7	16.8	17.9	20.4
30.0	27.3	28.7	Trade Receivables (net)	16.5	23.0	30.3	32.9	30.4	27.9
3.9	3.9	3.9	Inventory	5.6	3.0	2.2	3.4	3.7	4.4
7.6	7.2	6.6	All Other Current	5.4	4.7	6.7	5.7	6.8	7.3
60.0	58.4	57.8	Total Current	49.2	45.1	56.0	58.8	58.8	60.1
33.1	33.5	33.4	Fixed Assets (net)	42.8	41.8	34.1	34.0	33.0	31.0
1.2	1.3	1.9	Intangibles (net)	.9	1.6	1.3	2.3	1.3	2.2
5.6	6.7	7.0	All Other Non-Current	7.2	11.5	8.7	4.9	6.9	6.6
100.0	100.0	100.0	Total	100.0	100.0	100.0	100.0	100.0	100.0
			LIABILITIES						
4.7	4.9	5.0	Notes Payable-Short Term	19.5	5.6	7.5	6.7	4.9	2.8
5.0	5.1	5.1	Cur. Mat.-L.T.D.	14.6	6.1	6.7	5.6	4.9	3.8
15.7	14.9	15.6	Trade Payables	5.7	14.2	13.2	16.5	15.5	16.8
.4	.5	.4	Income Taxes Payable	2.8	.4	.1	.3	.5	.3
11.3	10.8	10.4	All Other Current	12.2	7.2	7.9	8.0	9.3	12.7
36.9	36.1	36.5	Total Current	54.9	33.5	35.4	37.1	35.2	36.4
14.9	14.7	14.8	Long-Term Debt	33.8	20.7	17.0	16.7	12.9	12.1
1.1	1.2	1.2	Deferred Taxes	1.0	1.3	.7	1.2	1.5	1.2
2.6	2.7	3.0	All Other Non-Current	12.1	7.4	2.9	1.9	2.0	2.4
44.4	45.4	44.5	Net Worth	-1.5	37.0	44.0	43.0	48.5	47.9
100.0	100.0	100.0	Total Liabilities & Net Worth	100.0	100.0	100.0	100.0	100.0	100.0
			INCOME DATA						
100.0	100.0	100.0	Net Sales	100.0	100.0	100.0	100.0	100.0	100.0
18.0	18.8	18.2	Gross Profit	36.1	33.2	23.6	20.9	16.8	12.9
13.6	15.1	15.5	Operating Expenses	34.2	31.2	21.1	20.1	13.5	9.5
4.4	3.8	2.7	Operating Profit	1.9	2.0	2.5	.9	3.4	3.4
.3	.3	.1	All Other Expenses (net)	1.3	.5	.3	.0	.0	.1
4.1	3.5	2.6	Profit Before Taxes	.7	1.5	2.3	.8	3.4	3.3
			RATIOS						
2.4	2.5	2.5	Current	2.8	2.7	3.8	2.7	2.6	2.2
1.6	1.7	1.6		.9	1.6	1.9	1.7	1.7	1.6
1.2	1.2	1.2		.3	.9	.9	1.1	1.2	1.3
2.0	2.1	2.1	Quick	2.1	2.3	3.5	2.4	2.2	1.7
1.3	1.3	1.3		.7	1.4	1.5	1.5	1.3	1.3
.9	.9	.9		.3	.7	.8	.9	.9	1.0
28 13.0	28 13.1	30 12.3	Sales/Receivables	0 UND	17 21.0	20 18.3	35 10.3	31 11.8	31 11.7
47 7.8	46 8.0	47 7.7		31 11.8	39 9.4	50 7.3	53 6.9	48 7.6	47 7.8
68 5.4	67 5.5	68 5.4		84 4.4	65 5.6	69 5.3	76 4.8	68 5.4	66 5.5
0 UND	0 UND	0 UND	Cost of Sales/Inventory	0 UND	0 UND	0 UND	0 UND	0 UND	0 UND
1 661.9	0 755.6	1 673.4		0 UND	0 UND	0 UND	0 UND	1 577.3	3 109.9
9 41.3	10 38.0	11 34.5		0 UND	0 UND	6 59.4	5 68.4	11 32.2	13 27.6
14 25.3	14 25.3	14 25.9	Cost of Sales/Payables	0 UND	4 100.4	6 64.2	14 25.7	13 29.1	20 18.1
28 13.1	28 13.2	28 12.9		13 28.3	19 19.2	15 24.5	31 11.8	26 14.1	32 11.5
44 8.3	44 8.3	45 8.1		24 15.4	51 7.2	42 8.7	50 7.3	47 7.8	44 8.3
5.8	5.3	5.6	Sales/Working Capital	3.2	5.1	4.9	5.4	5.6	5.8
10.1	9.5	9.6		-64.7	13.9	8.5	10.9	9.8	9.0
23.3	24.5	26.3		-5.8	-56.8	-172.4	36.6	26.4	18.0
22.5	22.6	17.1	EBIT/Interest	7.7	10.1	14.7	10.7	15.1	30.6
(881) 6.1	(907) 5.8	(822) 5.0		(23) 1.9	(59) 2.6	(69) 3.4	(133) 3.2	(172) 5.6	(366) 6.8
1.8	1.4	1.1		-2.3	-.6	-1.2	-1.7	1.4	1.7
5.5	5.9	4.8	Net Profit + Depr., Dep., Amort./Cur. Mat. L/T/D		2.3	2.6	2.9	5.0	6.1
(316) 2.4	(339) 2.5	(285) 2.3			(12) .9	(13) 1.0	(40) 1.5	(72) 2.5	(145) 2.7
1.4	1.2	1.1			-.8	-.3	-.5	1.5	1.4
.4	.4	.4	Fixed/Worth	.2	.5	.3	.4	.3	.4
.7	.7	.7		1.7	1.0	.7	.7	.7	.7
1.3	1.2	1.2		-6.4	3.1	1.4	1.5	1.1	1.1
.6	.6	.6	Debt/Worth	.7	.5	.4	.6	.5	.6
1.3	1.1	1.2		2.7	1.4	.9	1.3	1.1	1.2
2.4	2.2	2.3		-3.1	4.6	3.0	2.7	1.8	2.0
36.4	30.1	27.7	% Profit Before Taxes/Tangible Net Worth	27.3	37.0	31.4	30.0	26.2	26.2
(926) 17.2	(963) 14.8	(855) 11.6		(17) 8.9	(59) 6.2	(68) 14.5	(134) 10.1	(192) 13.4	(385) 11.9
5.1	2.4	1.2		-21.2	-12.8	-7.1	-8.7	2.5	3.0
15.4	14.3	13.3	% Profit Before Taxes/Total Assets	19.4	19.2	17.1	13.2	13.2	12.4
7.2	6.2	5.1		1.9	2.4	7.6	3.4	6.3	5.4
1.7	.9	.2		-11.2	-5.7	-5.0	-5.2	.5	.9
14.4	12.9	13.3	Sales/Net Fixed Assets	12.0	16.5	12.7	14.2	13.9	12.9
7.5	6.8	6.8		6.4	5.1	6.4	6.9	7.7	6.8
4.1	3.9	3.9		1.7	1.8	4.1	3.9	3.8	4.2
2.9	2.7	2.7	Sales/Total Assets	3.9	3.1	3.2	3.1	2.9	2.5
2.2	2.0	2.0		1.5	1.8	2.2	2.3	2.1	2.0
1.7	1.5	1.5		.9	1.1	1.5	1.5	1.6	1.5
1.8	1.9	2.1	% Depr., Dep., Amort./Sales	3.2	2.5	2.4	1.9	2.0	2.0
(870) 3.0	(889) 3.4	(811) 3.4		(23) 8.0	(53) 5.3	(63) 4.0	(129) 3.5	(186) 3.1	(357) 3.3
4.8	5.2	5.3		16.7	12.7	7.1	5.9	4.6	4.7
1.0	1.3	1.2	% Officers', Directors' Owners' Comp/Sales		2.5	2.6	1.7	1.1	.6
(306) 2.1	(332) 2.5	(296) 2.6		(28) 5.8	(42) 3.6	(66) 2.9	(67) 2.2	(87) 1.3	
4.2	5.1	4.5		10.4	5.7	4.2	4.2	2.8	
51292388M	46904068M	39637237M	Net Sales ($)	15407M	137245M	311085M	1036940M	3172411M	34964149M
25842125M	26038659M	21938550M	Total Assets ($)	16680M	115762M	173801M	571280M	1727179M	19333848M

M = $ thousand   MM = $ million
See Pages 9 through 22 for Explanation of Ratios and Data

	Current Data Sorted by Assets						Type of Statement	Comparative Historical Data	
	2	4	34	40	15	12	Unqualified	93	87
	4	17	59	24	3	1	Reviewed	102	119
	3	8	11	2			Compiled	24	22
	17	17	15	1			Tax Returns	47	27
	3	20	29	26	2	3	Other	71	91
		75 (4/1-9/30/10)			297 (10/1/10-3/31/11)			4/1/06-3/31/07	4/1/07-3/31/08
	0-500M	500M-2MM	2-10MM	10-50MM	50-100MM	100-250MM		ALL	ALL
	29	66	148	93	20	16	NUMBER OF STATEMENTS	337	346
	%	%	%	%	%	%	ASSETS	%	%
	18.4	11.2	19.0	17.1	19.6	17.7	Cash & Equivalents	13.7	14.6
	25.4	34.2	30.8	29.9	27.7	30.3	Trade Receivables (net)	35.9	33.6
	3.8	7.1	3.1	2.8	5.8	6.1	Inventory	4.8	4.2
	2.2	4.7	7.5	7.6	9.5	7.3	All Other Current	7.1	7.2
	49.7	57.3	60.3	57.4	62.5	61.4	Total Current	61.5	59.6
	44.9	34.8	31.0	33.3	31.4	22.6	Fixed Assets (net)	31.6	34.1
	.1	1.0	2.4	2.2	.9	3.6	Intangibles (net)	1.1	1.3
	5.2	6.9	6.3	7.1	5.1	12.4	All Other Non-Current	5.8	5.1
	100.0	100.0	100.0	100.0	100.0	100.0	Total	100.0	100.0
							LIABILITIES		
	15.1	8.5	5.3	4.2	2.9	1.4	Notes Payable-Short Term	8.9	6.6
	6.3	6.2	5.7	5.2	2.7	2.0	Cur. Mat.-L.T.D.	5.0	5.4
	9.6	17.2	14.4	16.1	13.9	17.4	Trade Payables	17.1	16.1
	.2	.2	.3	.2	.9	.3	Income Taxes Payable	1.0	1.1
	8.7	17.5	9.6	13.3	18.0	18.3	All Other Current	14.1	12.7
	39.8	49.6	35.3	39.1	38.3	39.4	Total Current	46.1	41.8
	43.1	19.3	12.0	12.8	11.3	12.7	Long-Term Debt	17.3	17.3
	.2	.7	1.1	1.6	1.5	1.1	Deferred Taxes	.9	.8
	21.7	6.4	2.6	3.4	3.3	2.6	All Other Non-Current	1.7	2.1
	-4.9	24.0	49.0	43.1	45.7	44.2	Net Worth	33.9	38.0
	100.0	100.0	100.0	100.0	100.0	100.0	Total Liabilities & Net Worth	100.0	100.0
							INCOME DATA		
	100.0	100.0	100.0	100.0	100.0	100.0	Net Sales	100.0	100.0
	42.1	27.5	24.1	20.8	15.6	14.2	Gross Profit	25.4	26.8
	39.9	26.8	20.2	15.6	10.9	9.6	Operating Expenses	19.4	20.8
	2.2	.7	3.9	5.2	4.7	4.7	Operating Profit	6.0	6.0
	1.1	.8	.5	.4	.9	.0	All Other Expenses (net)	.6	.7
	1.1	-.1	3.3	4.8	3.9	4.6	Profit Before Taxes	5.4	5.4
							RATIOS		
	4.8	2.3	2.6	1.9	2.2	1.8		2.0	2.0
	1.3	1.5	1.7	1.5	1.6	1.4	Current	1.4	1.4
	.5	1.0	1.2	1.1	1.3	1.2		1.1	1.1
	4.1	1.9	2.2	1.7	1.7	1.4		1.8	1.7
(28)	1.4	1.1	1.4	1.2	1.4	1.1	Quick	(336) 1.2	1.2
	.6	.6	.9	.7	.9	.8		.7	.8
0	UND	16 23.2	34 10.6	44 8.3	35 10.5	47 7.8		37 9.9	37 9.9
14	25.3	44 8.3	54 6.7	61 6.7	53 6.9	65 5.6	Sales/Receivables	56 6.5	60 6.1
54	6.8	70 5.2	80 4.5	80 4.6	67 5.4	88 4.2		79 4.6	82 4.5
0	UND	0 UND	0 UND	0 UND	0 UND	0 UND		0 UND	0 UND
0	UND	0 UND	0 UND	0 UND	6 60.2	5 80.9	Cost of Sales/Inventory	0 UND	0 UND
0	UND	23 15.9	5 70.9	8 44.7	17 21.3	21 17.0		4 86.5	5 75.0
0	UND	10 38.3	14 25.6	20 18.6	18 20.3	34 10.8		14 25.6	16 23.4
6	60.3	23 15.5	28 12.9	33 11.0	27 13.7	47 7.7	Cost of Sales/Payables	32 11.5	33 11.0
29	12.4	50 7.3	49 7.4	55 6.6	42 8.6	58 6.3		51 7.1	54 6.8
	11.7	7.2	4.7	5.8	5.7	4.2		7.0	6.5
	65.9	16.6	8.8	10.4	8.8	10.0	Sales/Working Capital	12.8	12.1
	-19.1	-132.9	21.9	79.2	13.5	16.8		99.9	52.2
	11.9	10.1	20.4	27.2	36.5	23.1		19.5	20.6
(22)	1.5	(57) 2.4	(135) 4.3	(89) 4.9	(19) 3.3	(15) 7.6	EBIT/Interest	(308) 5.5	(321) 5.7
	-1.8	-2.8	.5	.8	.4	1.5		2.5	2.1
		2.8	6.3	11.6	6.0		Net Profit + Depr., Dep.,	6.2	5.7
		(10) .4	(45) 2.6	(38) 2.3	(11) 2.8		Amort./Cur. Mat. L/T/D	(110) 2.6	(115) 2.6
		-2.7	1.3	.9	1.3			1.3	1.2
	.6	.3	.3	.3	.4	.3		.3	.4
	4.6	.8	.6	.7	.5	.5	Fixed/Worth	.7	.7
	-1.2	2.7	1.3	1.6	1.1	.9		1.6	1.7
	.6	1.0	.5	.6	.7	.9		.9	.9
	7.8	2.0	1.1	1.6	1.5	1.5	Debt/Worth	1.8	1.7
	-3.3	NM	2.0	3.0	2.1	2.8		3.4	3.4
	99.1	49.3	27.7	33.2	23.0	30.3	% Profit Before Taxes/Tangible	54.2	51.7
(20)	58.3	(50) 10.6	(144) 12.0	(88) 13.7	8.1	15.6	Net Worth	(312) 27.9	(330) 26.7
	-9.6	-3.1	-.3	.5	.0	3.3		11.2	8.2
	44.0	14.9	14.7	13.6	7.9	15.5	% Profit Before Taxes/Total	19.3	17.8
	4.0	2.7	5.0	5.2	3.2	5.6	Assets	9.7	9.2
	-17.7	-10.8	-.5	-.1	.0	1.4		3.3	2.4
	44.8	30.2	15.8	15.1	21.6	12.4		27.0	18.5
	16.0	10.3	7.1	7.5	7.0	6.6	Sales/Net Fixed Assets	9.5	7.3
	4.1	4.9	3.5	3.1	3.8	5.5		4.3	3.5
	9.4	4.3	2.5	2.3	2.5	1.9		3.1	2.8
	4.2	2.7	2.0	1.7	1.7	1.7	Sales/Total Assets	2.3	2.0
	2.6	1.8	1.4	1.2	1.3	1.4		1.6	1.4
	2.5	1.2	1.8	1.5	1.6	1.4		1.0	1.3
(20)	5.1	(53) 3.4	(127) 3.9	(89) 3.2	(14) 2.5	2.1	% Depr., Dep., Amort./Sales	(292) 2.6	(314) 2.9
	11.7	7.1	6.5	6.9	5.1	3.0		5.4	5.5
	5.8	1.5	1.5	.7			% Officers', Directors'	1.3	1.2
(18)	9.1	(32) 3.7	(56) 3.2	(21) 1.2			Owners' Comp/Sales	(126) 3.2	(118) 2.5
	10.3	6.2	5.5	3.7				5.6	5.1
	33705M	232406M	1510598M	3764856M	2863166M	4095776M	Net Sales ($)	13828851M	12918545M
	6664M	75060M	746875M	2137346M	1488197M	2491168M	Total Assets ($)	6619354M	6687852M

© RMA 2011

M = $ thousand   MM = $ million
See Pages 9 through 22 for Explanation of Ratios and Data

Comparative Historical Data | Current Data Sorted by Sales

4/1/08-3/31/09	4/1/09-3/31/10	4/1/10-3/31/11	Type of Statement	0-1MM	1-3MM	3-5MM	5-10MM	10-25MM	25MM & OVER
90	100	107	Unqualified	1	2	2	16	32	54
115	122	108	Reviewed	1	16	15	28	32	16
25	24	24	Compiled	2	8	2	6	5	1
44	41	50	Tax Returns	15	12	8	8	6	1
114	100	83	Other	7	14	6	14	17	25
4/1/08-3/31/09 ALL	4/1/09-3/31/10 ALL	4/1/10-3/31/11 ALL		75 (4/1-9/30/10)			297 (10/1/10-3/31/11)		
388	387	372	NUMBER OF STATEMENTS	26	52	33	72	92	97
%	%	%	**ASSETS**	%	%	%	%	%	%
15.8	17.9	17.1	Cash & Equivalents	12.6	12.2	13.9	17.8	20.1	18.5
33.2	30.2	30.5	Trade Receivables (net)	21.6	29.9	27.3	32.9	29.6	33.5
4.0	3.9	4.1	Inventory	6.3	7.0	4.5	3.8	1.7	4.1
7.1	7.2	6.7	All Other Current	1.9	2.2	5.7	8.0	7.6	9.0
60.0	59.2	58.4	Total Current	42.4	51.3	51.4	62.4	59.1	65.2
32.0	32.3	33.0	Fixed Assets (net)	48.2	39.0	38.4	29.6	33.9	25.5
1.6	1.9	1.9	Intangibles (net)	.1	2.0	4.2	2.3	1.1	2.2
6.4	6.6	6.7	All Other Non-Current	9.2	7.7	6.0	5.8	6.0	7.2
100.0	100.0	100.0	Total	100.0	100.0	100.0	100.0	100.0	100.0
			LIABILITIES						
6.4	6.8	6.1	Notes Payable-Short Term	16.0	10.8	7.0	4.9	3.5	3.8
6.6	5.2	5.4	Cur. Mat.-L.T.D.	5.0	5.5	8.8	6.0	6.3	3.0
16.0	15.3	15.1	Trade Payables	10.6	12.5	15.0	15.0	14.4	18.3
.6	.5	.3	Income Taxes Payable	.0	.2	.1	.5	.2	.4
12.6	12.8	12.7	All Other Current	15.5	6.9	6.5	14.4	11.0	17.4
42.2	40.6	39.5	Total Current	47.1	35.9	37.3	40.9	35.4	42.9
16.3	14.9	15.9	Long-Term Debt	49.9	22.3	14.6	12.3	12.1	10.0
.8	.9	1.1	Deferred Taxes	.0	.9	.9	.9	2.0	.9
2.2	3.8	5.0	All Other Non-Current	20.2	7.1	7.1	2.4	2.5	3.5
38.6	39.8	38.5	Net Worth	-17.3	33.8	40.1	43.5	48.0	42.7
100.0	100.0	100.0	Total Liabilities & Net Worth	100.0	100.0	100.0	100.0	100.0	100.0
			INCOME DATA						
100.0	100.0	100.0	Net Sales	100.0	100.0	100.0	100.0	100.0	100.0
24.6	23.0	24.4	Gross Profit	50.0	29.9	26.0	22.4	22.3	17.4
20.1	20.7	20.8	Operating Expenses	47.4	29.9	23.2	19.3	17.2	12.4
4.4	2.3	3.6	Operating Profit	2.5	.0	2.8	3.1	5.1	5.1
.6	.5	.6	All Other Expenses (net)	3.1	.9	.6	.5	.3	.2
3.8	1.8	3.0	Profit Before Taxes	-.6	-.9	2.3	2.6	4.8	4.9
			RATIOS						
2.0	2.2	2.3	Current	2.3	2.9	2.2	2.5	2.4	1.9
1.5	1.5	1.6		1.1	1.5	1.4	1.8	1.5	1.5
1.1	1.1	1.1		.4	.8	1.0	1.2	1.2	1.2
1.8	1.9	1.9	Quick	1.8	2.6	2.0	2.1	2.2	1.6
1.2 (386)	1.2 (371)	1.3		.9	1.1 (32)	1.2	1.4	1.3	1.3
.8	.7	.8		.2	.5	.7	.9	.8	.8
37 9.9	35 10.5	30 12.3	Sales/Receivables	0 UND	13 28.1	28 13.2	33 10.9	37 10.0	42 8.6
54 6.8	54 6.8	54 6.8		30 12.2	41 8.9	48 7.6	58 6.3	54 6.8	56 6.5
73 5.0	75 4.9	79 4.6		86 4.2	73 5.0	84 4.3	81 4.5	77 4.8	78 4.7
0 UND	0 UND	0 UND	Cost of Sales/Inventory	0 UND	0 UND	0 UND	0 UND	0 UND	0 UND
0 UND	0 UND	0 UND		0 UND	0 UND	0 UND	0 UND	0 UND	0 764.7
6 60.8	8 45.4	8 43.7		12 30.5	14 25.3	16 23.1	9 41.6	4 92.3	11 32.0
14 26.2	14 25.6	15 24.0	Cost of Sales/Payables	0 UND	6 56.7	11 33.1	11 31.8	17 21.1	20 17.8
30 12.3	27 13.3	29 12.6		32 11.5	18 20.5	31 11.6	23 15.6	29 12.6	33 11.0
48 7.5	47 7.8	50 7.3		75 4.8	43 8.5	63 5.8	50 7.4	47 7.7	52 7.1
6.5	5.2	5.8	Sales/Working Capital	8.1	6.4	5.9	4.2	5.7	6.4
12.1	10.5	10.6		95.1	14.6	11.1	7.4	10.3	10.1
71.5	51.9	64.6		-8.9	-44.3	-578.1	-24.8	36.0	33.0
18.3	20.6	18.6	EBIT/Interest	5.5	5.7	12.4	12.7	22.4	36.8
(347) 4.8	(358) 4.0	(337) 3.9		(23) .6	(44) 1.4	(29) 3.7	(63) 3.8	(84) 4.5	(94) 9.0
1.4	.6	.4		-2.5	-5.2	-.8	.5	1.1	1.5
5.9	8.4	6.4	Net Profit + Depr., Dep., Amort./Cur. Mat. L/T/D				5.2	4.5	15.2
(120) 2.3	(123) 2.4	(113) 2.6					(22) 2.4	(34) 1.4	(44) 5.7
1.1	1.1	.9					.9	.7	2.1
.4	.3	.3	Fixed/Worth	.6	.4	.5	.3	.3	.3
.8	.7	.7		3.7	1.0	1.0	.6	.5	.5
1.7	1.6	1.6		-1.4	4.0	2.4	1.2	1.5	1.1
.8	.7	.6	Debt/Worth	1.3	.7	.5	.5	.5	.8
1.7	1.5	1.4		13.0	1.6	1.2	1.0	1.2	1.6
3.5	2.9	3.0		-3.0	5.5	7.9	2.3	2.3	2.8
43.7	34.4	34.1	% Profit Before Taxes/Tangible Net Worth	66.6	49.5	32.9	32.1	31.4	38.0
(360) 23.9	(353) 13.4	(338) 12.7		(17) 8.1	(42) 6.7	(27) 9.3	(68) 12.6	(91) 13.4	(93) 13.3
2.4	.2	.2		-7.8	-14.7	-11.5	1.3	.6	4.3
17.7	13.4	14.6	% Profit Before Taxes/Total Assets	13.4	11.9	14.0	15.6	15.6	14.5
7.8	4.8	4.5		-1.4	2.1	4.9	4.2	5.4	5.7
.7	-1.5	-1.2		-21.9	-14.3	-7.0	-.5	.2	.7
19.9	18.2	18.0	Sales/Net Fixed Assets	30.4	25.0	17.7	17.9	15.7	18.8
7.8	7.4	8.0		7.6	7.6	5.3	7.8	7.6	8.9
3.9	3.8	3.8		2.5	3.0	2.7	5.0	3.4	5.0
2.9	2.6	2.9	Sales/Total Assets	3.5	3.5	2.7	2.9	2.5	2.7
2.1	2.0	2.0		2.1	2.4	1.8	2.0	2.1	2.0
1.5	1.4	1.4		.9	1.4	1.1	1.4	1.4	1.5
1.2	1.3	1.7	% Depr., Dep., Amort./Sales	5.1	1.8	2.6	1.8	1.7	1.3
(331) 2.9	(342) 3.2	(323) 3.6		(15) 10.8	(44) 4.4	(30) 6.1	(62) 3.7	(81) 3.6	(91) 2.2
6.3	6.3	6.6		14.4	7.4	7.9	6.9	6.8	4.3
1.3	1.6	1.4	% Officers', Directors' Owners' Comp/Sales	5.8	3.0	1.8	1.4	1.0	.5
(126) 3.0	(141) 3.6	(129) 3.6		(14) 8.2	(25) 5.0	(19) 4.0	(25) 2.9	(34) 2.0	(12) 1.0
6.0	6.7	6.2		9.9	8.2	6.1	4.8	4.1	3.9
16171289M	15655505M	12500507M	Net Sales ($)	13643M	107804M	128591M	510988M	1492365M	10247116M
8089219M	8215238M	6945310M	Total Assets ($)	21310M	59709M	81180M	338363M	970328M	5474420M

© RMA 2011   M = $ thousand   MM = $ million
See Pages 9 through 22 for Explanation of Ratios and Data

Current Data Sorted by Assets   Comparative Historical Data

	0-500M	500M-2MM	2-10MM	10-50MM	50-100MM	100-250MM	Type of Statement	4/1/06-3/31/07 ALL	4/1/07-3/31/08 ALL
	1	2	19	15	2	1	Unqualified	63	57
	7	26	58	17	1		Reviewed	126	112
	47	18	11	1	1	3	Compiled	56	45
	20	29	10	3	1	2	Tax Returns	77	75
		42	51	16			Other	137	132
		61 (4/1-9/30/10)		344 (10/1/10-3/31/11)					
NUMBER OF STATEMENTS	75	117	149	52	6	6		459	421
	%	%	%	%	%	%	**ASSETS**	%	%
	18.9	14.9	12.7	16.2			Cash & Equivalents	11.4	12.3
	20.8	42.9	40.6	37.2			Trade Receivables (net)	39.1	39.6
	3.0	5.0	3.5	3.3			Inventory	3.1	2.6
	4.7	4.6	6.9	8.8			All Other Current	5.5	5.2
	47.4	67.4	63.6	65.5			Total Current	59.1	59.7
	37.0	23.7	28.5	26.3			Fixed Assets (net)	33.0	32.8
	2.5	2.4	2.2	1.2			Intangibles (net)	1.7	2.0
	13.0	6.5	5.6	7.0			All Other Non-Current	6.3	5.5
	100.0	100.0	100.0	100.0			Total	100.0	100.0
							LIABILITIES		
	36.3	10.5	7.0	5.9			Notes Payable-Short Term	8.0	7.4
	7.5	3.4	4.0	3.5			Cur. Mat.-L.T.D.	5.1	5.5
	12.0	19.2	21.3	18.6			Trade Payables	17.8	17.0
	.0	.3	.3	.4			Income Taxes Payable	.4	.4
	11.5	15.8	8.4	12.9			All Other Current	9.9	10.0
	67.3	49.3	40.9	41.2			Total Current	41.3	40.4
	41.8	14.1	12.6	12.1			Long-Term Debt	19.7	19.6
	.3	.1	.7	1.5			Deferred Taxes	.6	.6
	11.9	5.3	5.4	3.6			All Other Non-Current	4.1	3.0
	-21.2	31.2	40.3	41.7			Net Worth	34.2	36.5
	100.0	100.0	100.0	100.0			Total Liabilities & Net Worth	100.0	100.0
							INCOME DATA		
	100.0	100.0	100.0	100.0			Net Sales	100.0	100.0
	40.8	25.8	22.5	16.3			Gross Profit	29.2	27.1
	41.0	24.6	23.7	17.0			Operating Expenses	23.4	21.6
	-.2	1.2	-1.2	-.7			Operating Profit	5.7	5.5
	.9	.2	.3	.1			All Other Expenses (net)	.5	.5
	-1.1	1.0	-1.5	-.8			Profit Before Taxes	5.2	5.0
							RATIOS		
	1.6	3.0	2.7	2.7			Current	2.3	2.5
	.9	1.5	1.6	1.5				1.5	1.5
	.4	1.0	1.1	1.1				1.0	1.0
	1.3	2.5	2.2	2.1			Quick	1.9	2.2
	.7	1.3	1.3	1.3				1.3 (420)	1.3
	.3	.8	.8	.8				.8	.8
	0 UND	28 13.2	42 8.7	46 7.9			Sales/Receivables	29 12.5	34 10.9
	5 80.9	56 6.6	59 6.2	66 5.5				50 7.3	53 6.9
	42 8.7	83 4.4	86 4.3	96 3.8				76 4.8	75 4.9
	0 UND	0 UND	0 UND	0 UND			Cost of Sales/Inventory	0 UND	0 UND
	0 UND	0 UND	0 UND	1 455.5				0 UND	0 UND
	0 UND	3 132.1	7 50.5	11 33.2				5 76.4	3 119.6
	0 UND	9 40.5	22 16.9	21 17.4			Cost of Sales/Payables	10 35.8	11 33.8
	1 450.0	22 16.3	36 10.1	38 9.6				28 13.3	25 14.8
	23 16.1	48 7.6	59 6.2	54 6.7				46 8.0	44 8.2
	20.7	5.1	4.8	4.4			Sales/Working Capital	7.6	6.9
	-93.9	10.4	10.2	9.1				17.0	13.9
	-14.3	124.0	97.7	42.9				386.0	230.4
	7.1	16.8	7.5	11.3			EBIT/Interest	20.8	20.2
	(66) 2.3	(100) 3.1	(131) 2.3	(44) 2.2				(418) 6.8	(366) 5.4
	-2.4	-1.8	-3.4	-2.7				2.0	1.4
		4.5	4.0	9.9			Net Profit + Depr., Dep., Amort./Cur. Mat. L/T/D	4.4	5.3
		(11) 2.0	(41) 1.8	(19) 3.5				(101) 2.2	(91) 2.5
		-2.0	-1.4	1.3				1.3	1.2
	.4	.2	.3	.2			Fixed/Worth	.3	.3
	3.0	.6	.5	.5				.8	.7
	-1.3	2.2	1.6	1.3				2.3	2.0
	1.0	.6	.7	.8			Debt/Worth	.7	.7
	29.6	1.6	1.3	1.6				1.8	1.7
	-3.6	7.5	3.4	3.4				4.0	4.0
	100.0	43.4	18.4	22.1			% Profit Before Taxes/Tangible Net Worth	64.8	61.3
	(43) 30.6	(95) 12.2	(131) 4.6	(50) 6.6				(409) 35.6	(379) 31.8
	-3.1	-4.7	-12.0	-15.8				12.9	8.8
	33.3	13.2	7.6	10.1			% Profit Before Taxes/Total Assets	25.5	24.2
	4.0	3.2	1.9	2.4				11.5	10.8
	-14.5	-7.0	-7.7	-7.2				3.4	2.3
	68.7	42.3	22.4	26.7			Sales/Net Fixed Assets	27.9	27.2
	18.1	15.1	10.0	10.8				11.2	11.2
	6.9	6.9	5.0	3.7				5.4	5.3
	10.0	3.9	3.0	2.6			Sales/Total Assets	3.9	3.8
	4.8	2.7	2.2	1.9				2.8	2.7
	2.9	1.8	1.6	1.3				2.1	2.0
	1.0	.9	1.2	1.1			% Depr., Dep., Amort./Sales	1.2	1.0
	(48) 3.2	(81) 2.5	(129) 2.6	(49) 2.2				(384) 2.4	(352) 2.3
	7.0	3.9	4.9	4.6				4.8	4.8
	5.3	3.1	1.5	.8			% Officers', Directors' Owners' Comp/Sales	1.6	1.5
	(53) 8.0	(52) 4.7	(67) 2.7	(19) 1.8				(201) 3.1	(189) 3.0
	13.2	6.8	3.8	2.3				6.4	5.4
	98075M	417807M	1388567M	1691621M	1231954M	3761197M	Net Sales ($)	12541854M	9276272M
	17392M	139687M	621532M	894406M	424614M	1051122M	Total Assets ($)	4247805M	3922963M

M = $ thousand   MM = $ million
See Pages 9 through 22 for Explanation of Ratios and Data

Comparative Historical Data				Type of Statement	Current Data Sorted by Sales					
69		42	39	Unqualified		2	2	5	15	15
122		111	103	Reviewed	2	13	16	33	28	11
53		53	38	Compiled	6	12	11	6	1	2
90		88	93	Tax Returns	30	26	14	12	7	4
157		152	132	Other	11	30	23	32	27	9
4/1/08-3/31/09 ALL		4/1/09-3/31/10 ALL	4/1/10-3/31/11 ALL		61 (4/1-9/30/10)			344 (10/1/10-3/31/11)		
					0-1MM	1-3MM	3-5MM	5-10MM	10-25MM	25MM & OVER
491		446	405	NUMBER OF STATEMENTS	49	83	66	88	78	41
%		%	%	ASSETS	%	%	%	%	%	%
12.6		15.6	14.9	Cash & Equivalents	19.7	15.0	14.2	13.5	14.8	13.0
37.4		34.9	36.5	Trade Receivables (net)	17.6	33.1	40.7	40.2	43.0	39.0
3.0		3.8	3.8	Inventory	5.2	3.3	5.5	3.1	2.8	3.5
6.3		6.5	6.0	All Other Current	4.0	5.0	4.3	5.7	8.8	8.1
59.3		60.8	61.1	Total Current	46.5	56.3	64.7	62.5	69.3	63.6
32.1		29.5	29.1	Fixed Assets (net)	42.6	30.8	24.4	29.0	24.0	26.8
2.4		2.5	2.3	Intangibles (net)	2.2	1.9	1.4	4.3	.9	3.3
6.2		7.2	7.5	All Other Non-Current	8.7	11.0	9.5	4.2	5.8	6.4
100.0		100.0	100.0	Total	100.0	100.0	100.0	100.0	100.0	100.0
				LIABILITIES						
8.9		13.0	13.2	Notes Payable-Short Term	42.7	14.6	11.0	6.2	6.8	5.6
5.2		5.2	4.4	Cur. Mat.-L.T.D.	6.1	3.8	5.8	4.5	3.5	2.8
17.2		16.0	18.3	Trade Payables	12.5	13.3	18.2	18.7	25.5	20.5
.5		.4	.3	Income Taxes Payable	.1	.1	.5	.3	.4	.2
11.4		11.3	11.7	All Other Current	7.9	16.9	14.9	7.8	8.9	13.9
43.2		46.0	47.8	Total Current	69.3	48.8	50.5	37.5	45.0	43.0
20.8		18.4	19.4	Long-Term Debt	50.3	19.8	12.8	16.0	9.7	17.7
.7		.5	.6	Deferred Taxes	.0	.2	.8	.9	.6	1.0
5.2		4.9	6.9	All Other Non-Current	14.2	6.4	4.5	5.5	5.1	9.6
30.0		30.2	25.4	Net Worth	-33.7	24.8	31.4	40.2	39.6	28.7
100.0		100.0	100.0	Total Liabilities & Net Worth	100.0	100.0	100.0	100.0	100.0	100.0
				INCOME DATA						
100.0		100.0	100.0	Net Sales	100.0	100.0	100.0	100.0	100.0	100.0
25.4		26.4	26.2	Gross Profit	43.8	32.4	26.3	22.8	17.1	16.6
22.6		25.9	26.3	Operating Expenses	44.8	33.0	25.9	23.9	16.7	14.9
2.8		.5	-.2	Operating Profit	-.9	-.6	.4	-1.1	.4	1.7
.7		.7	.4	All Other Expenses (net)	1.0	.6	.3	.4	-.1	.7
2.1		-.2	-.6	Profit Before Taxes	-2.0	-1.1	.1	-1.5	.5	1.0
				RATIOS						
2.5		2.4	2.6		2.2	2.9	2.9	2.7	2.6	2.1
1.5		1.4	1.4	Current	1.1	1.5	1.4	1.8	1.5	1.4
1.0		.9	.9		.3	.7	.9	1.0	1.1	1.1
2.2		2.1	2.2		1.4	2.6	2.5	2.3	2.1	1.5
1.3		1.2	1.2	Quick	.8	1.2	1.3	1.5	1.3	1.2
.7		.7	.7		.3	.5	.8	.8	.8	.8
29	12.4	30 12.1	28 13.2		0 UND	20 18.3	27 13.7	41 9.0	37 9.7	37 9.8
50	7.3	52 7.0	51 7.1	Sales/Receivables	5 74.5	52 7.0	62 5.9	53 6.9	53 7.0	55 6.6
73	5.0	73 5.0	81 4.5		50 7.3	87 4.2	84 4.3	79 4.6	85 4.3	82 4.4
0	UND	0 UND	0 UND		0 UND	0 UND	0 UND	0 UND	0 UND	0 UND
0	UND	0 UND	0 UND	Cost of Sales/Inventory	0 UND	0 UND	0 UND	0 UND	0 UND	1 713.1
5	70.4	5 71.6	5 69.1		0 UND	3 138.4	5 69.4	7 54.6	8 45.3	9 42.3
12	31.2	10 36.4	11 31.7		0 UND	1 281.7	12 31.6	15 23.7	25 14.5	18 19.8
25	14.8	25 14.5	29 12.7	Cost of Sales/Payables	8 48.0	17 21.9	29 12.5	29 12.6	38 9.6	32 11.5
47	7.8	45 8.1	50 7.2		47 7.8	48 7.6	50 7.3	51 7.1	54 6.8	54 6.8
7.0		6.3	5.5		9.7	5.9	5.4	5.4	4.5	6.7
14.7		13.3	14.0	Sales/Working Capital	270.5	14.4	15.2	10.5	11.0	13.6
-188.6		-68.2	-83.1		-11.9	-22.8	-83.2	NM	79.5	31.9
13.1		9.7	9.6		6.1	8.2	12.1	12.0	8.6	6.7
(437)	3.3	(386) 1.6	(351) 2.3	EBIT/Interest	(40) 2.1	(71) 1.7	(61) 2.4	(78) 2.4	(67) 2.3	(34) 3.0
-.5		-2.9	-2.7		-1.7	-2.9	-1.7	-3.4	-2.7	-.2
5.3		6.7	5.2				3.7	4.2	9.7	6.6
(107)	1.9	(76) 2.1	(79) 2.1	Net Profit + Depr., Dep., Amort./Cur. Mat. L/T/D		(16) 2.2	(22) 1.4	(20) 2.4	(18) 3.3
1.0		.7	-.1				-.8	-4.9	-.7	1.9
.3		.2	.3		.5	.3	.2	.3	.2	.2
.8		.7	.6	Fixed/Worth	2.5	.6	.5	.5	.5	.6
3.0		2.5	3.1		-1.4	17.1	1.8	4.1	1.2	1.6
.8		.7	.7		1.1	.6	.6	.6	.7	.9
1.9		1.6	1.7	Debt/Worth	29.6	1.7	1.8	1.2	1.3	2.3
6.2		8.7	8.8		-3.0	137.7	13.7	6.3	3.1	4.9
46.4		34.9	27.4		65.2	46.5	30.5	36.6	20.2	20.2
(415)	17.5	(370) 10.2	(327) 8.6	% Profit Before Taxes/Tangible Net Worth	(28) 13.6	(63) 4.8	(53) 13.6	(76) 5.2	(70) 6.4	(37) 8.9
.1		-11.6	-7.5		-2.2	-7.5	-8.1	-17.6	-10.8	1.1
17.1		12.2	11.3		28.9	11.8	13.2	11.1	7.7	8.6
5.1		1.6	2.4	% Profit Before Taxes/Total Assets	4.0	.9	3.3	1.7	2.2	3.6
-2.5		-9.1	-7.2		-24.2	-13.8	-5.0	-10.6	-3.6	.3
27.0		33.8	31.1		32.5	24.8	43.3	28.7	30.9	31.1
12.0		11.4	12.5	Sales/Net Fixed Assets	7.3	11.0	15.7	11.9	14.5	15.8
4.9		5.1	5.7		2.8	5.6	7.0	5.5	5.8	6.5
3.9		3.6	3.8		7.1	3.9	4.3	3.2	3.5	3.3
2.6		2.5	2.5	Sales/Total Assets	2.7	2.7	2.6	2.5	2.4	2.5
1.8		1.7	1.7		1.0	1.6	1.9	1.7	1.7	1.7
1.1		1.1	1.1		3.1	1.3	.9	1.3	1.0	1.3
(409)	2.5	(354) 2.4	(313) 2.6	% Depr., Dep., Amort./Sales	(34) 5.4	(55) 2.9	(49) 2.1	(76) 2.6	(67) 2.0	(32) 2.2
4.6		4.9	5.0		14.4	6.6	3.7	5.0	3.5	3.8
1.5		2.2	2.0		6.1	3.3	4.0	1.5	1.1	.6
(212)	3.3	(201) 4.1	(194) 4.1	% Officers', Directors' Owners' Comp/Sales	(27) 12.8	(49) 5.6	(31) 5.2	(35) 2.3	(38) 2.3	(14) 1.2
5.7		7.2	7.6		15.6	8.4	8.4	4.4	3.4	1.8
1133060 1M		8409892M	8589221M	Net Sales ($)	25934M	166360M	258521M	623848M	1199414M	6315144M
4635720M		3447673M	3148753M	Total Assets ($)	22613M	86228M	115577M	321827M	584860M	2017648M

M = $ thousand   MM = $ million
See Pages 9 through 22 for Explanation of Ratios and Data

Current Data Sorted by Assets   Comparative Historical Data

							Type of Statement		
		1	8	12	3	4	Unqualified	53	35
	3	7	44	7			Reviewed	58	50
	6	12	6	2			Compiled	25	15
	9	13	7				Tax Returns	35	18
	7	16	23	15		1	Other	46	43
		33 (4/1-9/30/10)		173 (10/1/10-3/31/11)				4/1/06-3/31/07	4/1/07-3/31/08
	0-500M	500M-2MM	2-10MM	10-50MM	50-100MM	100-250MM		ALL	ALL
	25	49	88	36	3	5	NUMBER OF STATEMENTS	217	161
	%	%	%	%	%	%	ASSETS	%	%
	12.3	13.4	11.8	15.6			Cash & Equivalents	11.6	11.0
	29.7	43.3	44.1	31.4			Trade Receivables (net)	47.9	49.9
	13.2	4.4	4.8	7.0			Inventory	5.1	6.2
	5.1	7.7	9.2	12.2			All Other Current	8.3	8.8
	60.3	68.8	70.0	66.1			Total Current	72.8	75.9
	35.6	20.3	21.4	26.9			Fixed Assets (net)	20.2	18.9
	1.5	2.7	.7	1.2			Intangibles (net)	1.2	1.2
	2.6	8.2	8.0	5.8			All Other Non-Current	5.8	4.0
	100.0	100.0	100.0	100.0			Total	100.0	100.0
							LIABILITIES		
	24.3	16.0	10.8	8.3			Notes Payable-Short Term	10.5	8.0
	8.2	2.7	2.8	2.9			Cur. Mat.-L.T.D.	3.2	2.5
	11.9	17.5	17.4	11.1			Trade Payables	15.7	18.6
	.0	.2	.7	.1			Income Taxes Payable	.6	.7
	17.9	12.8	10.9	10.6			All Other Current	16.8	18.0
	62.4	49.3	42.7	33.0			Total Current	46.9	47.8
	26.6	11.6	9.2	12.1			Long-Term Debt	14.3	9.9
	.6	.2	.7	.9			Deferred Taxes	.5	.4
	14.4	6.8	3.3	3.1			All Other Non-Current	2.7	2.5
	-3.9	32.2	44.1	50.8			Net Worth	35.6	39.4
	100.0	100.0	100.0	100.0			Total Liabilties & Net Worth	100.0	100.0
							INCOME DATA		
	100.0	100.0	100.0	100.0			Net Sales	100.0	100.0
	39.0	33.4	20.4	21.6			Gross Profit	24.4	23.6
	37.5	35.5	21.8	18.2			Operating Expenses	18.4	16.9
	1.5	-2.1	-1.4	3.4			Operating Profit	6.0	6.7
	.9	.3	.3	.3			All Other Expenses (net)	.7	.5
	.6	-2.4	-1.7	3.1			Profit Before Taxes	5.3	6.2
							RATIOS		
	3.3	2.5	2.8	3.5				2.5	2.5
	.9	1.5	1.7	2.0			Current	1.5	1.6
	.6	1.0	1.2	1.3				1.2	1.2
	1.6	2.2	2.1	2.8				2.0	1.9
	.6	1.1	1.3	1.4			Quick	1.3 (160)	1.3
	.4	.7	.9	.8				.9	1.0
3	133.4	33 11.0	51 7.2	59 6.2				47 7.8	46 7.9
31	11.7	57 6.4	79 4.6	79 4.6			Sales/Receivables	68 5.4	69 5.3
64	5.7	80 4.5	114 3.2	99 3.7				91 4.0	88 4.1
0	UND	0 UND	0 UND	0 UND				0 UND	0 UND
0	UND	0 UND	1 257.2	9 40.6			Cost of Sales/Inventory	0 UND	1 367.5
37	10.0	9 42.2	17 21.5	42 8.6				12 29.7	15 24.9
2	221.3	4 81.9	21 17.2	18 20.6				11 32.8	14 26.0
13	27.3	28 13.0	36 10.1	33 11.2			Cost of Sales/Payables	25 14.6	27 13.5
48	7.6	56 6.5	50 7.2	46 7.9				44 8.2	45 8.2
	7.2	5.7	4.1	2.8				5.8	5.3
	-97.9	16.2	6.9	5.1			Sales/Working Capital	10.5	10.0
	-8.5	113.8	24.4	11.5				21.7	25.4
	5.7	6.7	6.4	17.5				27.3	28.6
(22)	3.0	(36) 2.0	(81) 1.4	(34) 3.1			EBIT/Interest	(188) 6.2	(149) 8.3
	-.6	-19.0	-8.9	-.5				2.4	3.3
			2.3	5.6				9.0	12.6
			(31) 1.0	(12) 1.3			Net Profit + Depr., Dep., Amort./Cur. Mat. L/T/D	(59) 4.2	(42) 5.4
			-5.6	.0				2.2	2.8
	.7	.3	.2	.2				.2	.2
	6.6	.6	.4	.5			Fixed/Worth	.4	.4
	-1.0	3.6	.8	1.4				1.1	.8
	.8	.5	.5	.3				.8	.7
	11.6	2.0	1.2	1.1			Debt/Worth	1.8	1.7
	-6.2	22.8	3.0	2.1				3.9	3.5
	71.5	63.2	10.2	21.3				63.9	64.1
(16)	10.1	(41) 9.7	(81) 1.0	(35) 6.3			% Profit Before Taxes/Tangible Net Worth	(199) 35.7	(153) 33.2
	.0	-20.9	-13.4	-.3				12.7	16.8
	16.3	11.3	4.5	12.3				21.7	25.6
	8.7	2.3	.3	3.8			% Profit Before Taxes/Total Assets	11.8	12.2
	-4.3	-19.8	-10.1	-.2				3.3	5.1
	29.3	48.8	32.5	14.2				44.4	44.0
	13.2	19.5	12.1	7.0			Sales/Net Fixed Assets	19.7	22.8
	6.6	10.1	5.2	3.3				7.6	9.8
	5.2	3.7	2.4	1.8				3.3	3.5
	3.3	2.6	1.9	1.6			Sales/Total Assets	2.6	2.7
	2.2	2.0	1.3	1.2				2.0	2.1
	1.0	.9	.8	1.5				.7	.5
(19)	2.1	(33) 2.0	(78) 1.5	(35) 2.3			% Depr., Dep., Amort./Sales	(187) 1.1	(140) 1.0
	4.6	3.7	3.2	3.7				2.6	2.0
	2.6	3.4	1.6					1.8	1.5
(15)	8.4	(25) 5.0	(44) 2.7				% Officers', Directors' Owners' Comp/Sales	(87) 3.3	(63) 2.9
	11.9	7.8	4.5					5.9	6.1
	30639M	163659M	850506M	1206534M	208039M	1644499M	Net Sales ($)	6538115M	5766299M
	7751M	57952M	419892M	794346M	211843M	865511M	Total Assets ($)	2829812M	2259480M

M = $ thousand   MM = $ million
See Pages 9 through 22 for Explanation of Ratios and Data

Comparative Historical Data | Current Data Sorted by Sales

			Type of Statement						
39	32	28	Unqualified	1		1	3	8	16
57	63	61	Reviewed			10	24	16	3
16	23	26	Compiled		7				
24	33	29	Tax Returns	4	8	5	7	2	
42	56	62	Other	6	11	6	3	3	
				4	12	11	8	15	12

4/1/08-3/31/09	4/1/09-3/31/10	4/1/10-3/31/11		33 (4/1-9/30/10)		173 (10/1/10-3/31/11)			
ALL	ALL	ALL		0-1MM	1-3MM	3-5MM	5-10MM	10-25MM	25MM & OVER
178	207	206	NUMBER OF STATEMENTS	15	38	33	45	44	31
%	%	%	ASSETS	%	%	%	%	%	%
12.6	16.0	13.1	Cash & Equivalents	12.5	12.2	13.5	11.1	16.2	12.9
43.9	37.0	39.4	Trade Receivables (net)	24.3	42.3	41.8	40.5	42.6	34.7
7.2	5.9	6.1	Inventory	11.5	7.8	3.8	6.0	4.9	6.1
8.5	8.7	8.7	All Other Current	6.3	6.9	6.1	11.5	8.4	11.4
72.3	67.6	67.4	Total Current	54.6	69.1	65.1	69.0	72.0	65.1
21.5	24.0	24.0	Fixed Assets (net)	33.5	21.4	27.3	22.8	20.2	26.1
1.3	2.2	1.7	Intangibles (net)	1.9	2.8	1.0	.4	1.4	3.0
4.9	6.2	6.9	All Other Non-Current	10.0	6.7	6.5	7.7	6.4	5.8
100.0	100.0	100.0	Total	100.0	100.0	100.0	100.0	100.0	100.0
			LIABILITIES						
11.3	11.4	13.3	Notes Payable-Short Term	26.0	18.8	12.1	11.7	10.0	8.6
2.9	3.5	3.4	Cur. Mat.-L.T.D.	12.6	1.7	4.2	3.3	1.9	2.7
15.3	15.3	15.5	Trade Payables	11.2	16.9	17.3	14.4	15.5	15.3
.6	.5	.4	Income Taxes Payable	.0	.0	.9	.8	.1	.1
14.6	16.7	12.4	All Other Current	11.0	15.9	12.8	10.3	10.6	14.3
44.6	47.4	45.0	Total Current	60.8	53.4	47.3	40.5	38.1	41.0
10.4	12.0	12.8	Long-Term Debt	35.1	12.9	14.1	8.3	8.7	13.2
.7	.6	.6	Deferred Taxes	.0	.6	.7	.6	.6	.6
5.3	6.1	5.3	All Other Non-Current	11.9	9.0	4.3	5.8	1.5	3.6
39.0	33.9	36.3	Net Worth	-7.8	24.1	33.6	44.9	51.1	41.6
100.0	100.0	100.0	Total Liabilities & Net Worth	100.0	100.0	100.0	100.0	100.0	100.0
			INCOME DATA						
100.0	100.0	100.0	Net Sales	100.0	100.0	100.0	100.0	100.0	100.0
23.4	26.5	26.0	Gross Profit	47.6	32.4	25.2	25.6	19.5	18.6
17.6	24.7	26.4	Operating Expenses	47.3	34.6	28.9	25.3	17.5	17.7
5.9	1.8	-.3	Operating Profit	.4	-2.1	-3.7	.3	2.0	.9
.4	.3	.4	All Other Expenses (net)	1.0	.7	-.1	.3	.3	.7
5.4	1.5	-.8	Profit Before Taxes	-.7	-2.8	-3.6	.0	1.6	.2
			RATIOS						
2.5	2.5	2.8		2.5	2.6	2.9	2.6	3.6	2.6
1.6	1.7	1.6	Current	.8	1.2	1.4	1.8	2.1	1.6
1.3	1.2	1.1		.5	1.0	1.0	1.2	1.2	1.4
2.0	2.1	2.2		.9	1.9	2.6	1.9	3.2	2.0
1.4	1.3	1.2	Quick	.6	1.0	1.1	1.4	1.7	1.3
1.0	.8	.8		.4	.6	.7	.9	1.0	1.3
43 8.5	38 9.6	42 8.6		2 219.0	33 10.9	41 9.0	43 8.5	63 5.8	44 8.3
66 5.5	62 5.9	67 5.4	Sales/Receivables	42 8.8	61 6.0	77 4.7	65 5.6	81 4.5	67 5.4
87 4.2	84 4.3	101 3.6		67 5.5	85 4.3	111 3.3	106 3.5	101 3.6	99 3.7
0 UND	0 UND	0 UND		0 UND	0 UND	0 UND	0 UND	0 UND	1 276.7
0 999.8	1 365.4	1 268.1	Cost of Sales/Inventory	0 UND	0 UND	0 UND	0 UND	2 176.8	6 48.3
14 25.7	19 19.6	20 18.1		94 3.9	23 15.5	11 33.2	28 13.2	17 21.1	18 20.1
9 39.4	10 36.4	14 26.7		1 269.0	6 57.3	17 22.0	11 33.4	17 21.3	15 24.9
23 16.2	23 15.6	33 11.1	Cost of Sales/Payables	21 17.2	31 11.9	36 10.1	33 11.1	27 13.4	36 10.1
40 9.2	44 8.3	50 7.4		63 5.8	58 5.4	56 6.5	49 7.4	44 8.2	45 8.1
5.4	4.8	4.2		4.8	5.7	4.6	4.2	3.1	4.1
8.6	8.8	8.2	Sales/Working Capital	-22.0	25.5	10.4	6.9	5.9	7.6
19.5	33.5	56.8		-6.0	-793.0	113.8	19.8	17.1	12.4
36.5	18.4	7.0		4.9	3.5	8.2	12.1	14.0	11.5
(162) 9.4	(185) 4.0	(181) 2.0	EBIT/Interest	(13) 2.0	(29) 2.3	(28) 1.3	(41) 1.7	(39) 1.9	2.9
2.3	-.3	-4.1		-2.2	-13.1	-10.5	-4.5	-2.9	-3.5
11.9	9.0	2.9	Net Profit + Depr., Dep.,				2.4	4.6	5.7
(50) 4.7	(59) 4.1	(46) 1.1	Amort./Cur. Mat. L/T/D			(13) .0	(14) 1.2	(11) 1.5	
1.8	1.1	-1.1				-6.1	.0	-.1	
.1	.2	.2		.9	.1	.3	.2	.2	.3
.4	.5	.6	Fixed/Worth	19.6	.7	.8	.4	.3	.6
1.0	1.2	1.4		-.5	10.8	1.7	.9	.8	1.2
.6	.6	.5		.9	.5	.5	.5	.4	.6
1.4	1.3	1.4	Debt/Worth	51.9	3.4	1.2	1.4	.7	1.2
3.0	4.2	4.6		-5.5	28.1	9.8	2.9	2.1	2.4
61.1	39.2	22.7	% Profit Before Taxes/Tangible		48.0	22.7	26.4	15.6	17.7
(165) 30.1	(182) 13.1	(179) 3.6	Net Worth	(31) 6.5	(28) 1.6	(42) 3.2	(42) 2.8	(28) 5.1	
10.7	.1	-10.3			-85.4	-20.5	-6.2	-6.1	-10.4
22.6	13.6	9.3	% Profit Before Taxes/Total	13.1	9.6	8.4	8.4	9.7	6.1
11.3	5.1	1.6	Assets	5.3	2.8	.4	1.2	1.4	2.0
2.9	-2.7	-8.8		-11.3	-19.2	-13.2	-3.5	-4.2	-6.9
43.3	35.9	29.9		20.3	53.6	33.9	35.1	26.7	18.2
20.4	14.5	12.6	Sales/Net Fixed Assets	6.7	19.2	10.2	13.9	11.2	8.9
7.6	5.8	5.3		2.7	10.3	4.7	6.6	5.6	4.3
3.4	3.2	2.8		3.3	3.6	2.8	2.8	2.3	2.3
2.6	2.2	2.0	Sales/Total Assets	2.2	2.5	2.0	2.1	1.8	1.7
1.9	1.6	1.5		1.2	1.6	1.5	1.4	1.3	1.4
.6	.8	1.0		1.6	.4	1.0	.9	1.1	.9
(154) 1.1	(179) 1.8	(172) 2.0	% Depr., Dep., Amort./Sales	(10) 3.4	(28) 1.8	(27) 2.9	(40) 1.5	(37) 2.0	(30) 2.3
2.4	3.7	3.7		5.3	3.8	5.4	3.2	3.3	3.5
1.3	2.3	2.3			2.7	1.6	3.1	.8	
(73) 2.4	(81) 4.0	(93) 4.2	% Officers', Directors' Owners' Comp/Sales	(26) 5.1	(16) 2.8	(21) 4.3	(17) 2.1		
5.0	8.0	7.3			8.6	4.7	4.8	5.1	
6655704M	6258262M	4103876M	Net Sales ($)	8899M	73394M	131841M	310477M	708765M	2870500M
3051311M	2487838M	2357295M	Total Assets ($)	4959M	35395M	68471M	166299M	442085M	1640086M

M = $ thousand   MM = $ million
See Pages 9 through 22 for Explanation of Ratios and Data

CONSTRUCTION-GENERAL—Framing Contractors NAICS 238130

Current Data Sorted by Assets **Comparative Historical Data**

0-500M	500M-2MM	2-10MM	10-50MM	50-100MM	100-250MM	Type of Statement	4/1/06-3/31/07 ALL	4/1/07-3/31/08 ALL
						Unqualified		
	4	10	1			Reviewed	3	4
2	5	3				Compiled	11	11
8	2	4				Tax Returns	11	6
4	6	7	1			Other	17	18
	10 (4/1-9/30/10)		47 (10/1/10-3/31/11)				28	31
14	17	24	2			NUMBER OF STATEMENTS	70	70
%	%	%	%	%	%	**ASSETS**	%	%
26.2	8.3	15.5				Cash & Equivalents	17.8	12.2
10.3	46.0	46.5				Trade Receivables (net)	32.5	38.7
11.6	9.7	6.2				Inventory	9.7	13.1
2.0	4.9	9.3				All Other Current	7.8	8.6
50.1	68.9	77.5				Total Current	67.9	72.6
29.8	17.8	12.8				Fixed Assets (net)	20.7	18.4
1.8	1.8	3.7				Intangibles (net)	4.5	4.2
18.2	11.4	6.0				All Other Non-Current	6.8	4.7
100.0	100.0	100.0				Total	100.0	100.0
						LIABILITIES		
24.9	14.2	9.9				Notes Payable-Short Term	14.5	11.7
5.1	2.7	1.9				Cur. Mat.-L.T.D.	4.5	3.9
5.9	22.5	17.0				Trade Payables	15.5	21.1
.0	.0	.3				Income Taxes Payable	.2	.2
18.3	8.4	14.1				All Other Current	17.5	14.8
54.1	47.8	43.1				Total Current	52.2	51.7
37.5	19.0	5.5				Long-Term Debt	13.7	14.4
.0	.3	.4				Deferred Taxes	.1	.1
16.1	5.1	2.2				All Other Non-Current	6.3	5.8
-7.8	27.8	48.8				Net Worth	27.6	28.0
100.0	100.0	100.0				Total Liabilities & Net Worth	100.0	100.0
						INCOME DATA		
100.0	100.0	100.0				Net Sales	100.0	100.0
48.9	26.1	19.5				Gross Profit	33.8	29.7
44.6	25.7	18.1				Operating Expenses	30.5	25.1
4.2	.5	1.3				Operating Profit	3.2	4.5
.4	-.1	.0				All Other Expenses (net)	.4	.9
3.9	.5	1.4				Profit Before Taxes	2.8	3.7
						RATIOS		
2.0	3.4	2.4					2.7	2.3
1.0	1.9	2.0				Current	1.6	1.6
.5	.8	1.4					.9	1.1
1.2	1.9	1.8					2.1	1.8
.6	1.3	1.3				Quick	1.1	1.1
.3	.7	1.2					.6	.6
0 UND	30 12.2	50 7.3					12 31.2	21 17.5
0 UND	61 6.0	64 5.7				Sales/Receivables	31 11.9	47 7.7
18 19.8	97 3.8	83 4.4					50 7.4	66 5.6
0 UND	0 UND	0 UND					0 UND	0 UND
0 UND	3 145.1	0 UND				Cost of Sales/Inventory	1 658.2	0 780.5
22 16.9	27 13.3	14 26.3					31 11.8	28 13.0
0 UND	11 33.2	13 28.6					6 62.5	13 28.6
0 UND	25 14.6	22 16.7				Cost of Sales/Payables	18 20.6	29 12.4
13 28.2	62 5.9	44 8.3					36 10.2	54 6.8
22.3	5.7	5.0					8.2	7.3
NM	7.0	7.2				Sales/Working Capital	15.4	11.4
-20.9	-27.4	12.6					-76.7	53.5
5.3	4.2	8.7					25.8	12.6
(11) 3.0	(14) 1.7	(21) 3.5				EBIT/Interest	(61) 6.6	(67) 4.5
.2	-3.4	-2.3					2.1	1.4
								22.6
						Net Profit + Depr., Dep., Amort./Cur. Mat. L/T/D		(12) 2.4
								.3
.1	.2	.1					.1	.1
13.0	1.0	.2				Fixed/Worth	.4	.4
-.7	NM	.5					6.2	UND
.7	.4	.7					.6	.8
39.4	6.0	1.0				Debt/Worth	1.4	2.1
-2.2	NM	1.7					25.6	-264.1
	50.2	20.3					76.1	57.0
	(13) 20.6	(23) 12.4				% Profit Before Taxes/Tangible Net Worth	(54) 38.6	(52) 24.8
	-5.5	-1.7					16.2	9.2
44.3	10.6	7.9					30.2	21.2
11.6	3.9	2.5				% Profit Before Taxes/Total Assets	10.5	9.2
-7.8	-5.8	-3.4					3.6	2.4
115.8	68.0	81.2					74.7	70.1
35.4	34.2	22.1				Sales/Net Fixed Assets	33.8	30.8
8.3	9.7	11.8					13.3	12.2
14.0	3.5	3.2					5.6	4.4
5.7	2.3	2.6				Sales/Total Assets	3.5	3.2
3.3	2.0	1.7					2.5	2.1
	.5	.4					.4	.4
(15)	.8	(19) .8				% Depr., Dep., Amort./Sales	(52) .8	(49) .8
	1.9	2.1					1.6	1.6
		1.1					1.8	1.8
		(14) 1.9				% Officers', Directors' Owners' Comp/Sales	(39) 3.1	(35) 3.5
		3.2					7.6	5.9
21269M	58010M	301778M	39504M			Net Sales ($)	3360458M	2117209M
2828M	21150M	118079M	25064M			Total Assets ($)	1021317M	684479M

Columns 50-100MM and 100-250MM: DATA NOT AVAILABLE

M = $ thousand   MM = $ million
See Pages 9 through 22 for Explanation of Ratios and Data

Comparative Historical Data | Current Data Sorted by Sales

4/1/08-3/31/09 ALL	4/1/09-3/31/10 ALL	4/1/10-3/31/11 ALL	Type of Statement	0-1MM	1-3MM	3-5MM	5-10MM	10-25MM	25MM & OVER
			Unqualified						
2			Reviewed		1	2	5	7	
24	22	15	Compiled	1	3	1	3	1	1
19	11	10	Tax Returns	4	7		3		
26	21	14	Other	1	4	5	2	6	
27	18	18							

Current data period groupings: 10 (4/1-9/30/10) and 47 (10/1/10-3/31/11)

4/1/08-3/31/09 ALL	4/1/09-3/31/10 ALL	4/1/10-3/31/11 ALL		0-1MM	1-3MM	3-5MM	5-10MM	10-25MM	25MM & OVER
98	72	57	NUMBER OF STATEMENTS	6	15	8	13	14	1
%	%	%	**ASSETS**	%	%	%	%	%	%
16.3	19.2	16.2	Cash & Equivalents		14.3		19.3	11.6	
37.2	38.7	37.4	Trade Receivables (net)		30.5		50.3	45.8	
9.6	6.5	8.6	Inventory		10.2		4.9	9.1	
7.7	7.6	6.3	All Other Current		2.7		8.1	11.0	
70.8	72.0	68.5	Total Current		57.7		82.7	77.5	
18.3	15.7	18.4	Fixed Assets (net)		19.9		12.4	13.7	
2.9	4.3	2.5	Intangibles (net)		3.4		1.6	4.2	
8.1	8.0	10.6	All Other Non-Current		18.9		3.4	4.6	
100.0	100.0	100.0	Total		100.0		100.0	100.0	
			LIABILITIES						
10.6	15.4	14.8	Notes Payable-Short Term		25.8		6.8	11.1	
3.0	4.5	2.9	Cur. Mat.-L.T.D.		5.6		2.0	1.4	
22.0	20.4	16.2	Trade Payables		15.1		19.8	16.2	
.2	.3	.1	Income Taxes Payable		.0		.1	.4	
21.2	17.9	13.1	All Other Current		11.3		15.2	11.6	
57.0	58.5	47.1	Total Current		57.7		43.9	40.6	
15.0	14.6	17.3	Long-Term Debt		15.0		10.2	5.1	
.2	.3	.3	Deferred Taxes		.0		1.2	.0	
4.3	5.3	6.4	All Other Non-Current		3.8		2.8	1.2	
23.5	21.3	28.9	Net Worth		23.4		41.9	53.0	
100.0	100.0	100.0	Total Liabilities & Net Worth		100.0		100.0	100.0	
			INCOME DATA						
100.0	100.0	100.0	Net Sales		100.0		100.0	100.0	
28.0	27.8	28.1	Gross Profit		35.0		18.5	18.1	
25.9	25.8	27.1	Operating Expenses		34.4		17.3	19.5	
2.1	2.0	1.0	Operating Profit		.5		1.2	-1.4	
.0	.3	.0	All Other Expenses (net)		-.4		.2	-.4	
2.0	1.7	1.1	Profit Before Taxes		1.0		1.0	-.9	
			RATIOS						
2.5	3.0	2.4	Current		1.9		3.1	2.4	
1.6	1.4	1.9			1.2		2.1	1.9	
.9	.9	1.2			.5		1.4	1.6	
2.0	2.3	1.9	Quick		1.4		3.0	1.8	
1.2	1.1	1.2			.8		1.6	1.3	
.5	.7	.8			.5		1.3	1.1	
16 23.0	16 22.8	17 21.5	Sales/Receivables		0 UND		53 6.8	45 8.1	
33 11.2	47 7.8	52 7.1			41 8.9		70 5.2	64 5.7	
64 5.7	62 5.8	74 4.9			85 4.3		90 4.0	88 4.2	
0 UND	0 UND	0 UND	Cost of Sales/Inventory		0 UND		0 UND	0 UND	
0 UND	0 UND	3 145.1			1 344.3		0 UND	6 62.7	
15 23.8	19 19.1	21 17.0			21 17.0		7 50.1	28 13.1	
9 39.6	5 77.8	8 44.6	Cost of Sales/Payables		0 UND		17 21.0	12 29.2	
19 19.1	20 18.1	18 20.6			14 25.4		35 10.5	21 17.1	
38 9.7	34 10.8	44 8.3			53 6.9		53 6.9	44 8.3	
7.1	5.1	5.7	Sales/Working Capital		6.7		3.0	5.1	
13.5	15.6	8.2			27.4		6.4	7.4	
-57.7	-43.5	202.2			-12.0		9.3	13.5	
18.7	7.8	6.1	EBIT/Interest		6.9		9.1	8.1	
(85) 5.6	(58) 1.4	(48) 2.7			(14) 2.4		(11) .0	(13) 4.9	
.7	-3.6	-2.6			-.7		-5.3	-25.0	
			Net Profit + Depr., Dep., Amort./Cur. Mat. L/T/D						
.1	.1	.1	Fixed/Worth		.1		.1	.1	
.3	.4	.4			.6		.2	.3	
6.5	4.4	4.1			-15.0		.9	.4	
.7	.7	.6	Debt/Worth		.6		.6	.6	
1.5	2.0	1.2			6.0		1.2	1.0	
NM	25.0	21.2			-63.0		6.2	1.2	
58.6	45.0	29.3	% Profit Before Taxes/Tangible Net Worth		22.4		35.3	19.7	
(74) 19.9	(56) 10.7	(46) 12.7			(11) 10.1		(11) 1.8	12.7	
1.6	-10.8	-6.5			-6.0		-10.5	-3.3	
21.4	22.6	11.6	% Profit Before Taxes/Total Assets		11.7		5.4	8.6	
7.1	3.8	4.6			4.6		-1.0	5.4	
-2.0	-7.6	-5.0			-4.5		-7.6	-2.0	
90.0	76.5	76.8	Sales/Net Fixed Assets		105.7		53.3	77.4	
31.5	33.6	31.6			34.2		32.0	20.0	
14.7	15.8	10.2			8.5		11.8	14.6	
5.4	4.9	3.8	Sales/Total Assets		6.5		3.3	3.2	
3.4	3.2	2.7			2.3		2.3	2.9	
2.2	2.3	2.0			1.9		1.3	2.3	
.7	.5	.5	% Depr., Dep., Amort./Sales		.9		.2	.8	
(73) 1.1	(54) 1.0	(45) 1.0			(11) 1.4		(11) .5	(11) 1.0	
1.9	2.0	2.1			2.9		2.1	5.3	
2.2	2.0	1.8	% Officers', Directors', Owners' Comp/Sales				1.3		
(50) 4.7	(42) 5.0	(30) 3.9					(11) 1.9		
6.7	8.7	7.6					4.2		
984730M	502281M	420561M	Net Sales ($)	2981M	27046M	31203M	94190M	231359M	33782M
373768M	184743M	167121M	Total Assets ($)	764M	12221M	8266M	51056M	90676M	4138M

© RMA 2011

M = $ thousand   MM = $ million

See Pages 9 through 22 for Explanation of Ratios and Data

Current Data Sorted by Assets
Comparative Historical Data

Type of Statement	0-500M	500M-2MM	2-10MM	10-50MM	50-100MM	100-250MM		4/1/06-3/31/07 ALL	4/1/07-3/31/08 ALL
Unqualified		1	5	4	1			27	31
Reviewed	1	21	43					107	85
Compiled	3	12	7					39	32
Tax Returns	19	10	5					45	38
Other	8	14	14	7				60	72
		24 (4/1-9/30/10)		151 (10/1/10-3/31/11)					
NUMBER OF STATEMENTS	31	58	74	11	1			278	258
	%	%	%	%	%	%		%	%
ASSETS									
Cash & Equivalents	19.2	18.4	16.5	7.9				14.2	14.2
Trade Receivables (net)	17.0	35.7	45.7	45.9				44.2	47.0
Inventory	7.3	5.8	3.1	7.8				4.7	4.3
All Other Current	10.4	5.5	10.1	10.6				7.2	7.1
Total Current	53.8	65.4	75.4	72.3	D			70.2	72.7
Fixed Assets (net)	24.3	22.9	16.4	18.9	A			21.8	18.6
Intangibles (net)	1.7	2.9	1.8	3.1	T			1.5	.9
All Other Non-Current	20.2	8.9	6.4	5.8	A			6.5	7.9
Total	100.0	100.0	100.0	100.0				100.0	100.0
LIABILITIES					N				
Notes Payable-Short Term	21.5	11.7	8.8	10.0	O			10.0	10.0
Cur. Mat.-L.T.D.	4.7	3.0	2.2	3.8	T			3.1	3.0
Trade Payables	15.1	12.2	16.5	14.0				14.8	16.6
Income Taxes Payable	.1	.7	.8	.3	A			.9	1.1
All Other Current	13.4	10.8	13.4	21.1	V			14.7	15.2
Total Current	54.8	38.4	41.7	49.2	A			43.4	45.8
Long-Term Debt	18.8	16.2	6.4	7.0	I			14.4	11.3
Deferred Taxes	.0	.3	.4	2.1	L			.4	.4
All Other Non-Current	7.9	3.4	2.6	6.5	A			4.0	4.4
Net Worth	18.4	41.7	48.9	35.2	B			37.8	38.2
Total Liabilities & Net Worth	100.0	100.0	100.0	100.0	L			100.0	100.0
INCOME DATA					E				
Net Sales	100.0	100.0	100.0	100.0				100.0	100.0
Gross Profit	46.1	27.7	17.7	23.4				26.7	26.3
Operating Expenses	42.9	29.3	17.9	23.3				20.4	20.5
Operating Profit	3.3	-1.6	-.2	.1				6.3	5.8
All Other Expenses (net)	.5	.2	-.1	3.2				.7	.4
Profit Before Taxes	2.8	-1.8	-.1	-3.1				5.6	5.4
RATIOS									
Current	2.4	3.3	2.9	1.8				2.9	2.6
	1.0	1.8	1.9	1.5				1.7	1.6
	.3	1.1	1.2	1.2				1.2	1.2
Quick	1.7	3.2	2.5	1.6				2.6	2.3
	.4	1.6	1.5	1.1				1.4	(257) 1.4
	.1	.8	1.0	.4				1.0	1.0
Sales/Receivables	0 UND	29 12.5	47 7.8	74 4.9				32 11.3	40 9.1
	8 43.7	57 6.4	74 5.0	89 4.1				61 6.0	64 5.7
	44 8.3	81 4.5	99 3.7	111 3.3				81 4.5	88 4.2
Cost of Sales/Inventory	0 UND	0 UND	0 UND	0 UND				0 UND	0 UND
	0 UND	0 UND	0 UND	1 272.2				0 UND	0 UND
	0 UND	6 58.8	3 119.8	8 43.6				3 133.2	4 95.3
Cost of Sales/Payables	0 UND	8 47.4	15 24.7	23 16.2				9 40.4	11 32.4
	2 211.0	18 19.8	25 14.7	33 11.0				20 18.1	20 18.5
	51 7.2	37 10.0	48 7.6	65 5.6				36 10.2	39 9.3
Sales/Working Capital	12.3	4.5	3.8	4.0				5.3	5.6
	-184.0	9.5	7.0	8.6				10.1	10.8
	-11.6	148.1	20.1	14.4				35.2	33.7
EBIT/Interest	16.7	9.2	8.9	2.5				28.9	30.9
	(24) 5.4	(52) 1.5	(62) 1.9	(10) -1.7				(245) 8.6	(219) 6.4
	1.0	-3.8	-2.9	-20.2				2.2	1.9
Net Profit + Depr., Dep., Amort./Cur. Mat. L/T/D			4.9					11.3	8.9
		(17) 2.2	2.2					(62) 4.6	(50) 3.8
			.7					2.1	1.7
Fixed/Worth	.3	.1	.1	.2				.2	.2
	.8	.4	.3	.3				.4	.3
	-1.4	2.0	.5	1.6				.9	1.0
Debt/Worth	.4	.4	.5	1.1				.6	.6
	7.6	1.0	.9	1.7				1.3	1.4
	-7.5	6.7	2.2	3.5				3.7	4.0
% Profit Before Taxes/Tangible Net Worth	104.0	34.1	12.8					64.2	64.5
	(20) 24.5	(48) 5.3	(70) 3.2					(254) 29.4	(238) 29.4
	-91.4	-20.6	-8.8					11.0	10.0
% Profit Before Taxes/Total Assets	45.1	13.1	6.9	3.5				30.1	23.6
	12.3	.7	1.2	-.2				11.8	10.5
	.8	-12.1	-4.6	-24.3				2.9	2.6
Sales/Net Fixed Assets	82.4	33.8	41.0	35.4				43.4	45.0
	35.9	9.2	17.4	21.2				21.7	20.9
	9.2	6.3	10.4	16.0				10.8	11.1
Sales/Total Assets	7.4	3.1	2.9	2.4				3.8	3.6
	4.7	2.3	2.3	2.0				2.9	2.7
	2.1	1.7	1.5	1.3				2.2	2.2
% Depr., Dep., Amort./Sales	.7	1.4	.8	1.4				.7	.7
	(17) 2.2	(46) 2.6	(65) 1.5	(10) 2.0				(235) 1.3	(212) 1.3
	4.5	4.6	3.0	4.6				2.5	2.3
% Officers', Directors', Owners' Comp/Sales	5.3	3.7	1.0					1.5	1.8
	(23) 9.2	(27) 5.3	(34) 2.7					(153) 3.8	(138) 3.6
	13.2	10.1	5.0					6.4	6.7
Net Sales ($)	34886M	158336M	776382M	349846M	166527M			4801454M	4099025M
Total Assets ($)	7568M	64399M	345461M	194782M	56153M			1910177M	1664492M

© RMA 2011

M = $ thousand   MM = $ million
See Pages 9 through 22 for Explanation of Ratios and Data

Comparative Historical Data | Current Data Sorted by Sales

			Type of Statement						
27	19	11	Unqualified		1	1	1	3	5
88	73	65	Reviewed	1	14	14	18	16	2
21	20	22	Compiled	3	8	2	6	3	
35	44	34	Tax Returns	11	15	4	3	1	
67	50	43	Other	9	10	4	4	13	3
4/1/08- 3/31/09 ALL	4/1/09- 3/31/10 ALL	4/1/10- 3/31/11 ALL		24 (4/1-9/30/10)			151 (10/1/10-3/31/11)		
				0-1MM	1-3MM	3-5MM	5-10MM	10-25MM	25MM & OVER
238	206	175	NUMBER OF STATEMENTS	24	48	25	32	36	10
%	%	%	ASSETS	%	%	%	%	%	%
13.7	16.8	17.1	Cash & Equivalents	16.1	19.3	21.6	16.2	15.5	6.8
46.2	40.2	37.4	Trade Receivables (net)	15.7	30.8	38.0	42.1	51.9	53.0
4.9	4.7	5.0	Inventory	9.3	4.0	4.9	6.2	3.5	1.8
7.5	8.0	8.6	All Other Current	10.2	7.0	8.1	7.2	9.8	14.2
72.4	69.7	68.2	Total Current	51.2	61.1	72.6	71.6	80.7	75.8
18.3	19.7	20.0	Fixed Assets (net)	25.2	27.6	17.9	16.2	13.0	14.4
1.8	2.5	2.2	Intangibles (net)	1.8	1.2	3.6	4.5	.3	4.0
7.5	8.0	9.6	All Other Non-Current	21.8	10.1	6.0	7.7	6.0	5.8
100.0	100.0	100.0	Total	100.0	100.0	100.0	100.0	100.0	100.0
			LIABILITIES						
11.0	11.6	12.0	Notes Payable-Short Term	12.9	18.8	8.8	10.2	7.0	9.1
3.0	3.1	3.0	Cur. Mat.-L.T.D.	4.9	3.0	2.6	2.4	2.0	4.9
16.3	12.3	14.8	Trade Payables	12.2	8.9	17.6	18.6	17.5	21.0
.7	.7	.6	Income Taxes Payable	.1	.6	.8	1.0	.5	.7
15.8	11.8	13.1	All Other Current	11.1	10.8	12.2	12.8	16.9	18.1
46.9	39.6	43.6	Total Current	41.2	42.2	42.0	45.0	43.9	53.9
11.7	12.1	11.9	Long-Term Debt	26.3	15.9	7.3	7.5	5.6	5.9
.3	.4	.4	Deferred Taxes	.0	.3	.8	.3	.3	1.3
4.9	4.8	4.1	All Other Non-Current	10.8	2.4	2.1	4.8	1.8	6.8
36.3	43.1	40.1	Net Worth	21.6	39.2	47.8	42.3	48.4	32.1
100.0	100.0	100.0	Total Liabilities & Net Worth	100.0	100.0	100.0	100.0	100.0	100.0
			INCOME DATA						
100.0	100.0	100.0	Net Sales	100.0	100.0	100.0	100.0	100.0	100.0
23.4	26.9	26.4	Gross Profit	47.6	32.2	19.3	22.3	17.0	12.2
20.4	25.3	26.4	Operating Expenses	48.2	30.6	24.8	20.3	16.4	13.0
3.0	1.6	.0	Operating Profit	-.6	1.6	-5.6	2.0	.6	-.9
.6	.3	.3	All Other Expenses (net)	1.0	.5	-.3	-.1	-.1	2.6
2.4	1.3	-.3	Profit Before Taxes	-1.5	1.1	-5.3	2.1	.8	-3.5
			RATIOS						
2.7	3.6	2.7		2.9	3.2	2.6	3.4	2.7	1.7
1.7	1.8	1.6	Current	1.0	1.6	1.9	1.7	1.9	1.4
1.2	1.2	1.1		.5	1.0	1.2	1.1	1.3	1.2
2.3	3.1	2.4		2.1	3.1	2.3	2.7	2.5	1.6
1.3	1.6	1.3	Quick	.6	1.2	1.7	1.4	1.8	1.2
1.0	1.0	.8		.3	.7	.9	.8	1.1	.7
41 9.0	33 10.9	33 11.1		0 UND	23 15.8	33 11.1	45 8.0	48 7.5	60 6.1
64 5.7	61 5.9	60 6.1	Sales/Receivables	31 11.7	55 6.6	60 6.1	62 5.9	74 5.0	85 4.3
92 4.0	84 4.3	89 4.1		59 6.2	81 4.5	95 3.9	88 4.1	93 3.9	96 3.8
0 UND	0 UND	0 UND		0 UND	0 UND	0 UND	0 UND	0 UND	0 UND
0 UND	0 UND	0 UND	Cost of Sales/Inventory	0 UND	0 UND	0 UND	0 UND	0 UND	1 464.8
3 138.3	3 111.2	4 86.5		0 UND	5 74.9	6 66.0	19 19.4	1 592.3	8 48.6
9 42.2	7 49.2	9 40.5		0 UND	3 115.4	13 28.3	16 23.4	13 28.0	22 16.5
22 17.0	17 22.0	23 16.0	Cost of Sales/Payables	11 32.0	14 25.5	24 15.3	31 11.6	23 16.0	35 10.4
37 9.8	33 11.1	45 8.0		43 8.4	44 8.3	44 8.2	52 7.0	44 8.4	49 7.5
5.1	4.9	4.9		9.7	4.2	4.3	4.1	5.1	8.6
10.2	8.5	10.5	Sales/Working Capital	UND	10.6	6.9	9.0	7.0	11.6
25.8	31.1	108.0		-11.5	NM	23.8	55.7	11.5	17.5
21.7	17.8	9.4		5.6	10.8	13.3	6.3	13.3	8.7
(211) 5.1	(176) 4.5	(149) 1.9	EBIT/Interest	(16) .9	(45) 1.9	(22) -1.0	(25) 2.6	(31) 2.8	1.3
-.2	-1.4	-2.9		-2.7	-.2	-20.7	-.1	-3.2	-18.0
7.8	8.1	4.2							
(39) 4.0	(42) 3.8	(31) 1.4	Net Profit + Depr., Dep., Amort./Cur. Mat. L/T/D						
1.3	1.4	-1.7							
.2	.2	.1		.2	.2	.1	.1	.1	.2
.3	.3	.3	Fixed/Worth	.8	.6	.2	.3	.3	.3
.9	1.0	1.1		-3.6	3.9	1.0	1.1	.5	NM
.6	.4	.5		.4	.3	.5	.6	.5	1.3
1.4	1.1	1.2	Debt/Worth	7.3	1.0	.8	1.5	1.0	2.0
4.1	3.0	4.9		-10.1	12.7	3.3	3.2	2.3	NM
51.5	38.9	21.8		70.6	32.3	8.0	35.4	15.7	
(211) 15.2	(180) 11.0	(148) 3.9	% Profit Before Taxes/Tangible Net Worth	(17) .8	(39) 5.0	(20) -2.9	(29) 9.0	(35) 6.0	
.4	-2.9	-10.7		-164.1	-3.8	-47.4	-2.0	-3.0	
19.0	14.6	12.1		26.3	15.1	4.8	15.8	8.8	5.4
6.9	4.3	1.6	% Profit Before Taxes/Total Assets	.8	2.3	-6.1	2.7	2.2	.4
-1.6	-3.8	-5.4		-14.8	-2.3	-22.9	-3.4	-2.1	-18.9
41.9	37.4	42.8		43.3	38.2	30.1	54.4	52.2	37.0
21.7	20.3	17.4	Sales/Net Fixed Assets	14.7	10.5	19.2	19.8	19.9	21.7
12.3	9.9	8.1		3.8	5.8	8.6	8.2	12.3	17.1
3.7	3.5	3.3		4.8	3.2	3.2	3.2	3.3	3.0
2.7	2.5	2.4	Sales/Total Assets	2.3	2.1	2.1	2.4	2.7	2.4
2.1	1.9	1.6		1.3	1.3	1.7	1.5	2.1	1.9
.6	.6	1.0		2.0	1.3	1.2	.6	.8	.8
(192) 1.3	(174) 1.5	(139) 2.0	% Depr., Dep., Amort./Sales	(11) 3.8	(39) 3.1	(20) 2.0	(28) 1.3	(31) 1.4	1.5
2.1	2.9	3.7		10.4	4.9	4.2	2.8	2.8	2.9
2.0	3.2	2.6		5.3	4.1	3.4	2.1	.8	
(120) 3.9	(121) 5.8	(89) 4.5	% Officers', Directors' Owners' Comp/Sales	(14) 11.5	(28) 7.9	(13) 3.9	(14) 3.2	(17) 1.4	
6.3	10.3	9.4		17.5	10.2	6.1	4.6	4.2	
4830181M	2709288M	1485977M	Net Sales ($)	14706M	90013M	96709M	224042M	545904M	514603M
1964403M	1113575M	668363M	Total Assets ($)	8660M	58963M	45000M	111276M	219166M	225298M

Current Data Sorted by Assets | Comparative Historical Data

0-500M	500M-2MM	2-10MM	10-50MM	50-100MM	100-250MM	Type of Statement	4/1/06-3/31/07 ALL	4/1/07-3/31/08 ALL
1		1	4	2	1	Unqualified	6	7
2	12	32	5			Reviewed	41	48
2	5	11				Compiled	23	13
10	9	5	1			Tax Returns	18	24
3	9	9	4		1	Other	32	34
18	**35**	**58**	**14**	**3**	**1**	**NUMBER OF STATEMENTS**	**120**	**126**
						ASSETS		
7.9	13.0	16.1	24.3			Cash & Equivalents	10.8	12.2
33.6	44.2	45.6	32.6			Trade Receivables (net)	48.9	50.3
23.8	9.3	9.1	9.8			Inventory	11.4	11.0
.7	7.1	9.0	9.4			All Other Current	6.2	5.9
65.9	73.6	79.9	76.2			Total Current	77.2	79.4
20.0	16.4	14.0	20.0			Fixed Assets (net)	14.2	15.2
8.0	3.3	2.1	2.3			Intangibles (net)	1.6	1.5
6.1	6.7	4.0	1.6			All Other Non-Current	7.0	3.9
100.0	100.0	100.0	100.0			Total	100.0	100.0
						LIABILITIES		
24.3	7.8	10.9	9.9			Notes Payable-Short Term	11.4	9.7
4.3	5.7	2.8	1.4			Cur. Mat.-L.T.D.	3.0	2.7
22.9	19.7	18.2	11.5			Trade Payables	21.3	19.7
.3	.1	.4	1.0			Income Taxes Payable	.7	.9
5.9	14.4	12.5	19.7			All Other Current	16.0	18.2
57.8	47.6	44.8	43.4			Total Current	52.4	51.2
24.0	8.4	7.0	6.3			Long-Term Debt	7.0	10.7
.0	.2	.3	.0			Deferred Taxes	.2	.2
7.9	5.6	3.6	.2			All Other Non-Current	4.8	4.3
10.3	38.2	44.4	50.1			Net Worth	35.5	33.7
100.0	100.0	100.0	100.0			Total Liabilities & Net Worth	100.0	100.0
						INCOME DATA		
100.0	100.0	100.0	100.0			Net Sales	100.0	100.0
38.9	31.6	26.9	25.0			Gross Profit	30.1	29.9
38.1	34.6	26.2	21.6			Operating Expenses	25.1	24.5
.8	-3.1	.7	3.3			Operating Profit	5.0	5.4
.5	-.2	.0	.4			All Other Expenses (net)	.6	.6
.2	-2.9	.7	3.0			Profit Before Taxes	4.4	4.8
						RATIOS		
2.9	2.4	2.6	2.3			Current	2.2	2.3
1.6	1.7	1.7	2.0				1.5	1.6
.8	1.2	1.3	1.4				1.2	1.2
1.8	1.9	2.3	1.9			Quick	1.7	2.0
.7	1.2	1.3	1.3				1.2	1.3
.4	.9	.9	1.1				.8	.8
0 UND	37 9.9	57 6.5	57 6.5			Sales/Receivables	39 9.4	39 9.5
29 12.7	64 5.7	79 4.6	68 5.4				63 5.8	64 5.7
41 8.8	87 4.2	96 3.8	96 3.8				84 4.4	89 4.1
8 48.0	0 UND	0 UND	0 UND			Cost of Sales/Inventory	1 482.3	0 999.8
16 23.3	10 35.4	6 65.3	13 27.3				13 27.2	8 44.4
53 6.9	25 14.4	28 12.8	57 6.4				33 11.0	31 11.8
0 908.5	17 21.9	25 14.7	17 21.0			Cost of Sales/Payables	18 20.4	18 20.4
26 14.0	36 10.1	37 10.0	21 17.6				36 10.2	33 11.0
51 7.2	52 7.0	51 7.1	35 10.4				53 6.9	47 7.8
6.8	5.2	3.2	3.1			Sales/Working Capital	6.3	6.1
30.4	9.4	7.6	5.3				10.0	9.4
-22.7	77.0	12.0	9.6				27.2	25.4
6.3	5.8	10.7	67.0			EBIT/Interest	15.9	24.9
(14) .9	(29) .0	(53) 1.7	(12) 9.6				(106) 5.9	(114) 7.3
-9.7	-14.0	-6.1	7.8				2.4	3.1
		(14) 4.5				Net Profit + Depr., Dep., Amort./Cur. Mat. L/T/D	11.7	19.9
		-.4					(36) 3.7	(35) 6.0
		-6.5					1.7	2.5
.2	.1	.1	.2			Fixed/Worth	.1	.1
.4	.4	.3	.2				.3	.3
-.6	2.4	.8	.9				.7	.8
.6	.6	.5	.7			Debt/Worth	.9	.9
2.0	1.4	1.6	1.0				2.0	2.0
-4.9	9.5	3.6	1.6				4.6	4.3
23.4	12.7	16.4	25.2			% Profit Before Taxes/Tangible Net Worth	73.6	61.2
(11) .0	(29) -2.4	(57) 3.2	12.8				(117) 34.6	(115) 33.5
-40.3	-30.5	-13.7	5.3				11.3	14.2
15.4	5.4	5.7	12.4			% Profit Before Taxes/Total Assets	22.3	20.1
1.5	-2.2	1.3	7.3				9.5	9.1
-16.8	-15.1	-4.8	3.1				3.0	4.2
61.4	43.9	45.6	28.2			Sales/Net Fixed Assets	72.8	63.7
30.6	23.7	24.1	9.5				35.0	31.8
11.6	13.1	10.8	4.8				18.2	14.4
5.9	3.5	2.9	2.4			Sales/Total Assets	3.9	3.7
4.2	2.8	2.0	1.5				3.0	2.8
3.0	1.8	1.5	1.3				2.3	2.2
.5	.4	.6	.7			% Depr., Dep., Amort./Sales	.4	.4
(15) .9	(27) 2.0	(55) 1.2	1.0				(104) .8	(102) .7
1.4	2.8	2.1	1.4				1.4	1.3
4.2	2.7	2.6				% Officers', Directors', Owners' Comp/Sales	2.3	2.2
(14) 6.8	(22) 4.1	(32) 5.2					(63) 3.6	(72) 3.6
11.2	8.6	8.2					6.6	6.2
22395M	111068M	520215M	443514M	377472M	208523M	Net Sales ($)	2064617M	4162631M
5034M	38168M	239622M	244982M	194883M	194107M	Total Assets ($)	748620M	1359390M

M = $ thousand   MM = $ million
See Pages 9 through 22 for Explanation of Ratios and Data

Comparative Historical Data | Current Data Sorted by Sales

Comparative Historical periods: 4/1/08-3/31/09 ALL · 4/1/09-3/31/10 ALL · 4/1/10-3/31/11 ALL
Current Data time splits: 28 (4/1-9/30/10) · 101 (10/1/10-3/31/11)

	4/1/08-3/31/09 ALL	4/1/09-3/31/10 ALL	4/1/10-3/31/11 ALL	0-1MM	1-3MM	3-5MM	5-10MM	10-25MM	25MM & OVER
Type of Statement									
Unqualified	12	10	9	1				2	6
Reviewed	69	64	51		6	9	23	10	3
Compiled	14	20	18	2	6	3	3	4	
Tax Returns	23	19	25	4	12	2	6	1	
Other	44	27	26	2	9	2	4	5	4
NUMBER OF STATEMENTS	162	140	129	9	33	16	36	22	13
	%	%	%	%	%	%	%	%	%
ASSETS									
Cash & Equivalents	15.0	17.5	14.9		13.8	7.5	15.6	21.3	18.9
Trade Receivables (net)	47.9	43.1	41.9		34.0	49.5	50.1	43.5	34.5
Inventory	7.8	8.6	11.0		14.6	11.6	5.3	10.2	8.0
All Other Current	7.3	7.4	7.9		4.3	9.1	8.7	7.6	14.4
Total Current	78.1	76.6	75.7		66.7	77.8	79.7	82.7	75.8
Fixed Assets (net)	15.9	16.0	16.1		19.4	17.6	13.8	12.5	16.8
Intangibles (net)	2.5	2.2	3.3		5.2	.7	2.8	1.2	3.1
All Other Non-Current	3.6	5.3	4.9		8.8	3.9	3.6	3.6	4.4
Total	100.0	100.0	100.0		100.0	100.0	100.0	100.0	100.0
LIABILITIES									
Notes Payable-Short Term	11.4	13.7	11.7		16.5	12.1	10.6	6.2	10.4
Cur. Mat.-L.T.D.	3.8	2.4	3.6		4.4	5.3	4.3	1.8	1.3
Trade Payables	18.5	16.6	18.6		19.0	23.9	21.0	12.6	18.1
Income Taxes Payable	1.0	.4	.4		.2	.9	.3	.6	.1
All Other Current	18.6	16.5	13.6		7.8	8.7	15.2	14.0	27.3
Total Current	53.3	49.6	47.8		47.8	50.9	51.3	35.2	57.3
Long-Term Debt	8.9	9.2	9.6		14.1	8.6	6.5	4.9	5.8
Deferred Taxes	.3	.3	.2		.0	.9	.2	.1	.0
All Other Non-Current	4.8	6.3	4.3		10.3	1.3	2.1	4.1	.4
Net Worth	32.7	34.5	38.1		27.9	38.3	40.0	55.7	36.6
Total Liabilties & Net Worth	100.0	100.0	100.0		100.0	100.0	100.0	100.0	100.0
INCOME DATA									
Net Sales	100.0	100.0	100.0		100.0	100.0	100.0	100.0	100.0
Gross Profit	31.0	30.6	29.4		35.9	27.8	27.1	25.3	20.9
Operating Expenses	24.7	26.5	29.2		38.3	31.0	26.2	21.9	18.3
Operating Profit	6.2	4.1	.2		-2.4	-3.2	.9	3.4	2.7
All Other Expenses (net)	.5	.5	.1		-.2	.2	.1	.1	.3
Profit Before Taxes	5.7	3.7	.1		-2.2	-3.4	.8	3.3	2.4
RATIOS									
Current	2.4	2.6	2.5		2.9	2.2	2.3	3.9	2.0
	1.5	1.6	1.7		1.7	1.4	1.5	2.3	1.4
	1.2	1.3	1.3		1.1	1.3	1.2	1.7	1.0
Quick	2.1	2.1	2.0		2.4	1.7	2.1	3.1	1.3
	1.3	1.3	1.3		1.2	.9	1.3	1.9	.9
	.9	.9	.9		.6	.8	.9	1.3	.8
Sales/Receivables	42 8.7	36 10.2	43 8.4		26 14.0	54 6.8	58 6.2	57 6.4	42 8.7
	64 5.7	54 6.7	68 5.4		43 8.5	82 4.4	78 4.7	77 4.7	68 5.4
	86 4.2	78 4.7	94 3.9		66 5.5	95 3.9	97 3.7	96 3.8	88 4.2
Cost of Sales/Inventory	0 UND	0 UND	0 UND		2 195.3	0 UND	0 UND	0 UND	0 UND
	3 110.8	3 104.7	8 43.9		13 28.9	7 50.8	3 122.7	15 24.5	8 45.6
	16 23.3	18 20.1	29 12.4		40 9.2	25 14.5	12 29.3	51 7.1	18 20.4
Cost of Sales/Payables	16 23.0	12 29.4	20 18.0		15 25.2	28 13.0	24 14.9	15 24.2	20 17.9
	29 12.6	24 15.0	33 10.9		34 10.8	49 7.5	37 9.9	27 13.7	41 8.9
	44 8.4	44 8.3	50 7.3		51 7.2	65 5.6	52 7.0	33 10.9	48 7.7
Sales/Working Capital	5.4	5.5	4.2		4.7	4.3	4.4	2.8	5.3
	10.6	10.0	8.3		9.4	9.2	11.7	5.0	10.4
	20.5	21.6	18.4		128.3	13.8	18.7	9.4	NM
EBIT/Interest	41.9	32.3	10.3		5.0	9.9	9.4	19.1	55.5
	(146) 12.9	(123) 6.5	(111) 1.8		(27) .7	(14) .1	(33) 1.8	(20) 6.3	(11) 11.4
	2.1	1.4	-5.5		-5.0	-16.3	-6.1	-9.4	-3.7
Net Profit + Depr., Dep., Amort./Cur. Mat. L/T/D	18.4	-13.8	8.2						
	(45) 6.9	(30) 3.6	(31) 1.4						
	2.1	1.6	-5.5						
Fixed/Worth	.1	.1	.1		.1	.1	.1	.1	.2
	.3	.3	.3		.5	.5	.4	.2	.2
	.8	.7	1.0		-16.6	.8	1.2	.4	1.0
Debt/Worth	.7	.7	.6		.5	1.0	.5	.4	1.0
	1.8	1.6	1.5		1.9	1.6	2.2	.7	2.2
	3.7	3.7	4.0		-61.7	3.3	5.8	1.4	5.9
% Profit Before Taxes/Tangible Net Worth	77.6	44.8	17.7		13.4	8.6	17.3	19.5	40.3
	(146) 35.6	(121) 17.3	(115) 4.1		(24) -1.3	(15) -1.9	(34) 3.2	8.7	19.0
	12.1	4.0	-22.2		-24.2	-37.9	-33.6	-5.4	-24.7
% Profit Before Taxes/Total Assets	28.3	19.2	7.5		6.4	3.5	5.1	12.8	17.3
	12.8	7.2	1.5		-.8	-.8	1.4	4.0	7.7
	2.5	1.3	-6.1		-6.2	-19.0	-8.5	-1.5	-2.2
Sales/Net Fixed Assets	67.0	62.8	44.6		52.6	37.8	68.2	43.1	55.9
	32.4	32.8	22.9		18.1	22.1	24.1	23.9	18.0
	16.2	15.8	10.3		9.1	7.1	12.5	10.9	7.6
Sales/Total Assets	4.0	3.9	3.3		4.2	2.8	3.4	2.9	2.5
	2.9	2.9	2.4		2.8	2.0	2.5	2.2	2.1
	2.2	2.2	1.5		1.5	1.6	1.7	1.5	1.6
% Depr., Dep., Amort./Sales	.4	.5	.6		.5	.8	.5	.6	.5
	(139) .7	(124) 1.0	(115) 1.1		(27) 2.2	(14) 1.3	(34) 1.0	1.0	.9
	1.2	1.6	2.1		2.9	2.0	2.1	1.5	1.5
% Officers', Directors' Owners' Comp/Sales	1.7	2.5	2.7		3.7	4.1	2.5	1.8	
	(87) 2.9	(80) 3.8	(73) 5.4		(23) 5.9	(11) 6.7	(21) 4.0	(13) 4.8	
	5.0	7.8	7.8		10.5	9.0	7.7	5.8	
Net Sales ($)	3571529M	1752771M	1683187M	4880M	61171M	64385M	260684M	325803M	966264M
Total Assets ($)	1308931M	708745M	916796M	2609M	32543M	32151M	115494M	166917M	567082M

M = $ thousand   MM = $ million
See Pages 9 through 22 for Explanation of Ratios and Data

Current Data Sorted by Assets   Comparative Historical Data

0-500M	500M-2MM	2-10MM	10-50MM	50-100MM	100-250MM	Type of Statement	4/1/06-3/31/07 ALL	4/1/07-3/31/08 ALL
	1	15	12	2	1	Unqualified	31	30
3	41	86	11	1		Reviewed	180	140
7	20	10	1			Compiled	49	33
26	24	15			2	Tax Returns	48	51
19	33	33	12			Other	92	90
	50 (4/1-9/30/10)		325 (10/1/10-3/31/11)					
55	119	159	36	3	3	**NUMBER OF STATEMENTS**	400	344
%	%	%	%	%	%	**ASSETS**	%	%
20.9	17.5	15.7	6.9			Cash & Equivalents	12.3	13.9
23.7	39.8	47.2	49.2			Trade Receivables (net)	44.1	44.8
8.1	8.2	4.7	8.0			Inventory	7.3	7.0
4.4	8.0	8.7	13.1			All Other Current	8.0	8.9
57.0	73.4	76.3	77.2			Total Current	71.8	74.6
28.7	16.8	14.7	12.1			Fixed Assets (net)	17.9	16.1
4.2	3.1	2.1	3.1			Intangibles (net)	2.7	2.1
10.1	6.7	6.8	7.6			All Other Non-Current	7.6	7.2
100.0	100.0	100.0	100.0			Total	100.0	100.0
						LIABILITIES		
26.8	11.4	7.0	11.3			Notes Payable-Short Term	11.0	9.8
5.3	2.9	1.8	1.7			Cur. Mat.-L.T.D.	3.7	3.1
19.0	22.2	19.3	23.1			Trade Payables	19.5	19.4
.8	.4	.3	.4			Income Taxes Payable	.8	.5
15.4	10.0	12.7	16.4			All Other Current	14.3	15.6
67.4	46.9	41.1	52.8			Total Current	49.3	48.3
25.0	10.3	6.8	3.6			Long-Term Debt	12.6	11.7
.0	.3	.3	.2			Deferred Taxes	.4	.4
8.6	4.1	2.4	2.5			All Other Non-Current	4.7	4.7
-1.1	38.4	49.3	40.9			Net Worth	32.8	34.9
100.0	100.0	100.0	100.0			Total Liabilties & Net Worth	100.0	100.0
						INCOME DATA		
100.0	100.0	100.0	100.0			Net Sales	100.0	100.0
39.2	28.0	23.3	20.8			Gross Profit	28.7	28.3
34.1	25.5	20.9	20.3			Operating Expenses	23.6	23.5
5.1	2.5	2.4	.5			Operating Profit	5.1	4.8
.1	.0	.1	-.2			All Other Expenses (net)	.4	.4
5.0	2.5	2.3	.8			Profit Before Taxes	4.7	4.4
						RATIOS		
1.9	3.4	2.8	2.0				2.2	2.4
1.0	1.7	1.9	1.5			Current	1.5	1.6
.4	1.1	1.3	1.2				1.2	1.2
1.5	2.5	2.4	1.6				1.9	1.9
.7	1.3	1.6	1.1			Quick	1.2	1.3
.2	.8	1.2	.8				.8	.9
0 UND	24 15.0	45 8.1	53 6.9				31 11.7	31 11.7
7 50.3	38 9.6	62 5.9	75 4.9			Sales/Receivables	52 7.0	52 7.1
31 11.9	60 6.1	83 4.4	93 3.9				74 4.9	73 5.0
0 UND	0 UND	0 UND	1 250.1				0 UND	0 UND
0 UND	4 89.0	4 91.1	6 64.1			Cost of Sales/Inventory	5 72.6	5 81.0
4 84.5	15 23.8	12 29.9	18 20.1				16 23.2	14 25.7
0 UND	11 32.8	17 21.1	27 13.5				13 27.1	13 28.7
11 33.3	28 13.1	30 12.4	35 10.4			Cost of Sales/Payables	25 14.8	25 14.6
34 10.8	48 7.7	47 7.8	52 7.0				42 8.7	40 9.1
21.9	6.8	5.0	5.9				7.1	6.9
999.8	12.2	7.8	11.2			Sales/Working Capital	12.8	12.2
-17.9	55.5	15.1	19.3				39.3	30.7
16.9	13.1	21.0	29.0				21.7	28.8
(44) 6.3	(99) 4.5	(136) 6.2	(34) 4.3			EBIT/Interest	(358) 5.0	(317) 7.0
-1.5	-1.0	1.1	.7				1.8	2.2
	6.4	8.9	7.4				8.2	6.7
	(22) 2.4	(45) 2.7	(18) 3.0			Net Profit + Depr., Dep., Amort./Cur. Mat. L/T/D	(103) 3.2	(75) 3.0
	-.9	.7	1.1				1.3	1.7
.4	.2	.1	.1				.2	.2
6.3	.4	.2	.3			Fixed/Worth	.4	.4
-.8	1.7	.5	.6				1.2	1.0
1.5	.5	.5	.8				.8	.8
32.8	1.4	1.0	1.6			Debt/Worth	1.7	1.6
-4.9	5.6	2.2	2.6				4.5	4.0
269.5	46.9	35.8	22.1				64.3	58.3
(30) 71.0	(97) 9.0	(153) 14.0	(35) 7.6			% Profit Before Taxes/Tangible Net Worth	(354) 24.5	(307) 30.4
12.6	-7.9	.6	-2.2				8.8	9.3
45.3	15.0	15.3	9.3				22.0	24.0
23.1	4.2	6.4	2.2			% Profit Before Taxes/Total Assets	9.3	10.7
-3.8	-2.7	.1	-1.4				2.5	2.6
98.5	53.0	46.6	42.3				48.1	53.6
33.7	25.4	26.3	29.0			Sales/Net Fixed Assets	25.1	27.7
14.0	14.8	13.8	12.2				14.3	15.1
10.1	5.0	3.5	3.2				4.3	4.2
6.4	3.4	2.6	2.6			Sales/Total Assets	3.1	3.2
3.3	2.6	2.1	2.0				2.4	2.4
.5	.6	.6	.8				.7	.6
(32) 1.1	(98) 1.2	(143) 1.1	(33) 1.1			% Depr., Dep., Amort./Sales	(337) 1.2	(281) 1.1
2.1	2.1	1.7	1.5				1.9	1.7
2.9	2.0	1.9	.6				2.0	2.0
(35) 4.0	(68) 3.6	(81) 3.2	(12) 2.6			% Officers', Directors' Owners' Comp/Sales	(201) 3.5	(173) 3.3
7.2	5.4	5.7	6.9				6.5	6.9
94262M	483059M	1884850M	1821892M	575983M	2237014M	Net Sales ($)	7253522M	4524187M
12869M	128965M	682117M	699561M	235265M	626006M	Total Assets ($)	2058356M	1686472M

© RMA 2011

M = $ thousand   MM = $ million
See Pages 9 through 22 for Explanation of Ratios and Data

Comparative Historical Data				Current Data Sorted by Sales					
			Type of Statement						
34	28	31	Unqualified		1	1	2	13	14
141	142	142	Reviewed	1	16	17	54	42	12
46	37	38	Compiled	3	12	8	10	3	2
52	62	67	Tax Returns	12	19	12	11	10	3
116	102	97	Other	5	30	12	17	19	14
4/1/08-3/31/09 ALL	4/1/09-3/31/10 ALL	4/1/10-3/31/11 ALL		50 (4/1-9/30/10) 0-1MM	1-3MM	325 (10/1/10-3/31/11) 3-5MM	5-10MM	10-25MM	25MM & OVER
389	371	375	**NUMBER OF STATEMENTS**	21	78	50	94	87	45
%	%	%	**ASSETS**	%	%	%	%	%	%
13.5	16.1	16.4	Cash & Equivalents	22.1	21.6	14.6	19.0	11.3	10.8
43.9	39.8	41.4	Trade Receivables (net)	12.8	32.5	37.0	43.9	51.5	50.3
7.0	7.6	6.7	Inventory	12.0	7.3	6.8	5.2	6.1	7.2
8.4	7.8	8.4	All Other Current	2.6	6.7	10.6	8.6	7.8	12.3
72.7	71.3	72.8	Total Current	49.5	68.1	69.0	76.7	76.7	80.5
17.8	18.2	17.1	Fixed Assets (net)	35.0	20.9	14.9	14.5	16.0	12.1
2.4	2.4	2.9	Intangibles (net)	4.1	3.7	3.7	2.8	1.3	3.2
7.1	8.0	7.2	All Other Non-Current	11.3	7.4	12.4	6.0	6.1	4.2
100.0	100.0	100.0	Total	100.0	100.0	100.0	100.0	100.0	100.0
			LIABILITIES						
10.1	11.3	12.0	Notes Payable-Short Term	24.7	15.6	17.8	9.3	4.9	13.3
4.1	3.8	2.6	Cur. Mat.-L.T.D.	8.3	2.5	1.7	2.6	2.5	1.4
19.5	18.8	20.4	Trade Payables	20.9	18.6	20.7	20.3	20.6	22.6
.5	.4	.4	Income Taxes Payable	.0	.7	.5	.3	.3	.2
16.7	14.0	12.7	All Other Current	15.0	10.5	11.6	10.7	15.3	16.1
50.9	48.2	48.1	Total Current	68.9	47.8	52.3	43.3	43.4	53.6
11.1	11.2	10.3	Long-Term Debt	32.1	13.6	12.8	5.9	9.0	3.7
.3	.4	.3	Deferred Taxes	.0	.2	.4	.3	.3	.3
5.3	3.5	3.9	All Other Non-Current	11.7	6.1	3.7	1.7	3.2	2.3
32.4	36.7	37.4	Net Worth	-12.7	32.2	30.8	48.7	44.1	40.1
100.0	100.0	100.0	Total Liabilities & Net Worth	100.0	100.0	100.0	100.0	100.0	100.0
			INCOME DATA						
100.0	100.0	100.0	Net Sales	100.0	100.0	100.0	100.0	100.0	100.0
26.9	27.9	27.0	Gross Profit	37.5	35.6	24.4	25.4	22.6	22.4
22.9	25.8	24.4	Operating Expenses	30.3	32.4	23.6	22.8	20.2	19.9
4.0	2.1	2.7	Operating Profit	7.2	3.2	.9	2.6	2.4	2.4
.4	.2	.0	All Other Expenses (net)	-.1	-.2	.1	.0	.2	.1
3.6	1.9	2.6	Profit Before Taxes	7.4	3.4	.8	2.6	2.1	2.3
			RATIOS						
2.2	2.7	2.6	Current	1.9	3.8	2.5	3.2	2.5	2.1
1.5	1.6	1.7		1.0	1.5	1.6	2.0	1.8	1.5
1.1	1.2	1.1		.2	.9	.9	1.3	1.3	1.3
1.8	1.9	2.1	Quick	1.6	2.9	2.1	2.5	2.3	1.5
1.2	1.3	1.3		.3	1.2	1.1	1.7	1.6	1.2
.8	.8	.8		.1	.7	.6	1.1	1.1	.9
30 12.2	25 14.6	27 13.4	Sales/Receivables	0 UND	17 20.9	14 25.6	35 10.5	41 8.9	39 9.5
51 7.1	49 7.4	50 7.3		3 108.0	34 10.8	42 8.7	52 7.0	65 5.6	68 5.3
73 5.0	71 5.1	76 4.8		24 15.2	61 6.0	70 5.2	74 4.9	82 4.4	84 4.3
0 UND	0 UND	0 UND	Cost of Sales/Inventory	0 UND	0 UND	0 UND	0 UND	0 UND	1 624.7
4 82.2	5 67.9	4 98.8		0 UND	5 77.7	3 128.1	3 141.1	5 75.0	5 73.5
14 26.0	17 22.0	13 27.5		10 37.5	16 23.5	15 24.0	11 32.4	13 27.5	13 27.8
14 27.0	14 26.6	14 26.3	Cost of Sales/Payables	0 UND	5 67.1	11 34.3	14 25.9	17 21.1	21 17.1
26 14.2	26 14.1	28 12.9		16 23.1	25 13.8	28 12.9	29 12.7	28 12.9	34 10.9
40 9.1	42 8.8	45 8.2		47 7.7	58 6.3	41 9.0	49 7.4	40 9.2	44 8.3
7.3	6.0	6.1	Sales/Working Capital	12.9	7.0	6.0	5.4	5.8	7.5
12.9	11.9	11.2		-184.0	15.0	15.4	8.5	9.2	11.4
42.1	48.2	44.1		-7.7	-76.6	-66.4	23.2	16.1	20.8
22.6	21.4	19.8	EBIT/Interest	10.4	20.6	8.8	19.9	28.0	35.9
(354) 7.0	(330) 3.7	(318) 5.0		(15) 4.0	(62) 6.1	(44) 3.5	(77) 6.2	(77) 6.6	(43) 5.0
2.1	-1.3	.1		-8.1	.8	-1.3	-.2	.4	1.5
8.4	6.3	6.7	Net Profit + Depr., Dep., Amort./Cur. Mat. L/T/D		5.4	5.5	7.8	13.5	5.7
(77) 3.2	(85) 2.3	(90) 2.7			(11) 2.7	(11) 1.8	(24) 3.9	(25) 2.7	(19) 2.9
1.4	-.4	.6			-.9	.6	-.4	.8	.9
.2	.2	.1	Fixed/Worth	.3	.3	.1	.1	.1	.2
.4	.4	.3		-11.0	.5	.4	.2	.3	.3
1.1	.9	1.0		-.4	4.8	NM	.5	.6	.6
.7	.6	.6	Debt/Worth	1.5	.5	.6	.4	.6	.9
1.6	1.4	1.3		-14.4	2.1	1.5	4.9	1.1	1.4
3.8	3.4	4.4		-2.7	58.5	NM	2.3	2.5	2.6
50.2	48.6	40.4	% Profit Before Taxes/Tangible Net Worth	282.9	67.8	33.6	30.7	40.5	29.8
(337) 21.3	(324) 13.6	(320) 14.3		(10) 29.9	(61) 20.1	(38) 10.6	(86) 10.2	(82) 17.5	(43) 14.5
6.3	-.5	-.6		-6.9	-1.9	-10.5	-.9	-.2	2.3
21.0	19.8	18.6	% Profit Before Taxes/Total Assets	49.4	34.8	13.9	14.9	17.6	12.9
7.9	4.5	5.6		16.8	6.9	3.7	4.8	8.8	4.0
1.8	-2.3	-.7		-7.6	-1.2	-5.8	-.8	-.1	-.1
56.8	45.5	53.0	Sales/Net Fixed Assets	66.2	38.9	87.4	65.3	53.8	49.4
26.1	23.9	26.7		14.1	23.6	27.4	29.3	27.2	30.0
14.6	12.9	14.3		6.5	12.4	16.1	16.3	14.5	16.7
4.1	4.2	4.5	Sales/Total Assets	6.0	5.0	6.4	4.1	4.2	3.6
3.2	3.0	3.1		3.7	3.2	3.3	2.9	3.0	3.0
2.4	2.3	2.3		1.9	2.2	2.4	2.2	2.3	2.2
.6	.7	.7	% Depr., Dep., Amort./Sales	1.1	.7	.6	.5	.6	.8
(326) 1.1	(319) 1.4	(310) 1.1		(12) 1.5	(61) 1.5	(41) 1.6	(77) 1.0	(78) 1.2	(41) 1.0
1.7	2.0	1.9		2.7	2.5	2.2	1.7	1.6	1.4
2.0	2.2	1.9	% Officers', Directors' Owners' Comp/Sales	1.4	2.4	2.6	2.1	1.6	.6
(190) 3.3	(194) 4.0	(198) 3.5		(12) 3.6	(43) 4.7	(31) 4.0	(53) 3.6	(44) 2.4	(15) 2.3
6.0	7.0	5.7		8.9	6.3	7.3	5.1	5.0	5.4
5839019M	5311728M	7097060M	Net Sales ($)	12740M	157749M	194859M	672039M	1277833M	4781840M
2250632M	2099059M	2384783M	Total Assets ($)	4501M	60191M	70826M	238704M	452437M	1558124M

M = $ thousand   MM = $ million
See Pages 9 through 22 for Explanation of Ratios and Data

Current Data Sorted by Assets   Comparative Historical Data

1	2	3	4	1	1	Type of Statement		6	6
	7	15	6			Unqualified			
2	5	2				Reviewed		6	11
8	9	5				Compiled		5	8
9	6	11	4		3	Tax Returns		7	15
						Other		9	13
	10 (4/1-9/30/10)		94 (10/1/10-3/31/11)					4/1/06-3/31/07	4/1/07-3/31/08
0-500M	500M-2MM	2-10MM	10-50MM	50-100MM	100-250MM			ALL	ALL
20	29	36	14	1	4	NUMBER OF STATEMENTS		33	53
%	%	%	%	%	%	ASSETS		%	%
11.1	15.2	13.0	17.1			Cash & Equivalents		9.8	11.3
31.4	41.5	38.2	36.4			Trade Receivables (net)		37.2	39.0
15.0	9.8	8.2	8.3			Inventory		10.1	8.9
6.2	4.8	7.5	4.4			All Other Current		3.5	4.3
63.6	71.3	66.9	66.1			Total Current		60.5	63.5
29.3	18.3	19.8	21.6			Fixed Assets (net)		24.7	24.0
1.1	.3	2.0	.8			Intangibles (net)		5.4	3.6
6.0	10.1	11.2	11.5			All Other Non-Current		9.4	8.8
100.0	100.0	100.0	100.0			Total		100.0	100.0
						LIABILITIES			
24.7	11.0	7.7	3.2			Notes Payable-Short Term		8.4	7.3
5.2	2.7	4.6	3.0			Cur. Mat.-L.T.D.		2.9	4.3
25.1	22.0	18.6	19.2			Trade Payables		17.0	15.2
.0	.5	.1	.1			Income Taxes Payable		.7	.7
10.9	10.3	9.5	9.4			All Other Current		14.9	18.8
65.9	46.4	40.5	34.9			Total Current		43.9	46.4
26.9	7.8	11.9	12.1			Long-Term Debt		20.0	17.8
.0	.2	.6	.2			Deferred Taxes		.4	.2
5.8	6.4	3.4	6.1			All Other Non-Current		6.5	5.9
1.3	39.1	43.5	46.7			Net Worth		29.2	29.8
100.0	100.0	100.0	100.0			Total Liabilities & Net Worth		100.0	100.0
						INCOME DATA			
100.0	100.0	100.0	100.0			Net Sales		100.0	100.0
47.8	28.9	26.6	21.1			Gross Profit		35.0	35.4
43.3	27.2	24.5	18.4			Operating Expenses		29.8	30.2
4.6	1.6	2.1	2.7			Operating Profit		5.1	5.2
.9	.0	.4	-.2			All Other Expenses (net)		1.1	.4
3.7	1.6	1.8	2.9			Profit Before Taxes		4.0	4.8
						RATIOS			
1.7	2.1	2.3	2.7					2.3	2.3
1.3	1.6	1.6	1.7			Current		1.6	1.3
.6	1.1	1.2	1.2					1.1	1.0
1.4	1.9	2.2	2.6					2.0	1.6
.6	1.2	1.2	1.5			Quick		1.2	1.1
.2	.9	.7	1.0					.7	.7

0	UND	24	14.9	35	10.4	51	7.2			Sales/Receivables		22	16.8	28	13.1
17	21.5	39	9.3	47	7.8	62	5.9					39	9.5	51	7.2
56	6.6	53	6.9	75	4.9	87	4.2					76	4.8	80	4.5
0	UND	0	UND	0	UND	0	UND			Cost of Sales/Inventory		0	UND	0	UND
0	UND	0	UND	1	407.2	3	125.3					3	126.0	1	461.0
34	10.6	27	13.3	25	14.5	33	11.0					17	21.1	28	13.2
0	UND	14	25.5	16	22.7	25	14.7			Cost of Sales/Payables		9	40.9	10	36.7
8	44.5	26	14.1	27	13.4	37	9.8					24	15.3	26	14.1
56	6.5	47	7.7	52	7.0	62	5.9					39	9.3	52	7.1

13.5	8.1	6.1	3.8			Sales/Working Capital		8.1	5.9
43.4	15.0	10.2	7.4					12.0	18.9
-22.6	47.5	35.4	21.3					44.7	121.0

	16.0		17.4		15.6		15.1		14.6	39.7
(15)	5.2	(24)	4.4	(30)	3.2	(12)	9.2	EBIT/Interest	(28) 3.9	(47) 7.0
	2.9		.2		.9		4.4		1.4	1.5

					9.1			5.5
				(10)	3.1		Net Profit + Depr., Dep., Amort./Cur. Mat. L/T/D	(11) 1.9
					1.4			1.8

.5	.1	.1	.2			Fixed/Worth		.3	.3
1.5	.3	.3	.4					.8	.9
-1.1	.7	1.3	1.1					2.7	6.0
1.6	.6	.6	.7			Debt/Worth		1.0	1.1
3.0	1.9	1.5	.9					2.7	2.3
-3.8	3.1	3.2	3.3					9.0	10.0

	152.2		43.4		35.7		18.2	% Profit Before Taxes/Tangible Net Worth		74.4	72.4
(14)	74.9	(27)	24.7		15.6	(13)	9.0		(28) 38.7	(44) 41.6
	27.6		-1.2		.4		3.0			17.5	20.9

51.8	20.3	18.1	9.4			% Profit Before Taxes/Total Assets		24.4	26.0
16.4	5.4	4.5	2.9					9.8	14.1
1.4	-.9	.2	1.5					.7	1.6
61.7	88.4	45.7	19.6			Sales/Net Fixed Assets		35.9	48.3
29.4	24.3	16.7	9.9					13.3	13.9
12.5	14.6	9.1	4.4					7.0	8.5
7.7	5.0	3.2	2.5			Sales/Total Assets		4.4	3.7
5.2	3.7	2.7	1.8					2.8	2.8
3.2	2.2	1.6	1.0					2.2	1.9

	1.3		.6		.7		.5	% Depr., Dep., Amort./Sales		1.1	.8
(13)	1.9	(20)	1.1	(34)	1.8	(13)	1.5		(25) 2.2	(45) 1.9
	2.6		4.3		3.3		6.9			3.8	3.3

	3.5		2.4		1.0			% Officers', Directors' Owners' Comp/Sales		2.7	4.5
(14)	8.1	(16)	3.1	(15)	1.7				(17) 4.9	(23) 4.5
	14.2		4.7		4.9					8.4	11.9

24641M	126905M	463415M	634062M	31406M	1361316M	Net Sales ($)		634528M	1050839M
4260M	35340M	163214M	326314M	56331M	628379M	Total Assets ($)		211349M	626142M

M = $ thousand   MM = $ million
See Pages 9 through 22 for Explanation of Ratios and Data

Comparative Historical Data | Current Data Sorted by Sales

Type of Statement									
Unqualified	10	9	11	1	1			2	7
Reviewed	14	21	29		4	3	6	12	4
Compiled	12	12	9	1	2		5	1	
Tax Returns	23	20	22	6	5	6	6		
Other	14	23	33	5	5	6	6	6	5
	4/1/08-3/31/09 ALL	4/1/09-3/31/10 ALL	4/1/10-3/31/11 ALL	\<- 10 (4/1-9/30/10) -> 0-1MM	1-3MM	3-5MM 94 (10/1/10-3/31/11)	5-10MM	10-25MM	25MM & OVER
NUMBER OF STATEMENTS	73	85	104	12	17	16	22	21	16
ASSETS	%	%	%	%	%	%	%	%	%
Cash & Equivalents	15.0	13.6	13.4	15.5	9.3	12.4	12.0	16.7	14.7
Trade Receivables (net)	37.7	34.4	36.2	31.8	32.6	36.3	46.7	32.0	34.1
Inventory	7.0	4.3	10.1	10.1	7.0	21.7	10.4	3.7	9.6
All Other Current	7.6	7.6	5.9	6.9	6.1	2.7	5.6	8.5	5.4
Total Current	67.4	59.9	65.6	64.3	55.0	73.2	74.7	61.0	63.8
Fixed Assets (net)	22.9	29.2	22.5	26.5	33.0	15.3	14.8	23.6	24.8
Intangibles (net)	3.5	2.0	2.3	1.8	.1	.4	.7	3.2	8.1
All Other Non-Current	6.2	8.9	9.6	7.4	11.9	11.1	9.8	12.3	3.3
Total	100.0	100.0	100.0	100.0	100.0	100.0	100.0	100.0	100.0
LIABILITIES									
Notes Payable-Short Term	9.6	12.0	11.5	14.6	16.2	19.1	9.0	6.3	7.0
Cur. Mat.-L.T.D.	8.0	6.7	4.0	4.6	3.6	5.6	4.6	2.4	4.0
Trade Payables	18.3	16.0	20.5	35.3	11.9	15.9	27.0	14.0	22.3
Income Taxes Payable	.5	.1	.2	.0	.0	.2	.5	.1	.2
All Other Current	12.9	15.1	9.8	12.9	6.6	12.8	8.9	10.2	8.2
Total Current	49.2	50.0	46.0	67.4	38.4	53.5	50.1	33.1	41.6
Long-Term Debt	17.5	21.4	14.2	30.0	21.1	3.3	12.5	10.8	12.9
Deferred Taxes	.3	.5	.6	.0	.0	.3	.3	1.0	2.1
All Other Non-Current	8.1	13.0	5.1	7.8	5.6	9.5	2.3	1.3	6.8
Net Worth	24.9	15.1	34.1	-5.2	34.9	33.3	34.9	53.9	36.7
Total Liabilities & Net Worth	100.0	100.0	100.0	100.0	100.0	100.0	100.0	100.0	100.0
INCOME DATA									
Net Sales	100.0	100.0	100.0	100.0	100.0	100.0	100.0	100.0	100.0
Gross Profit	31.9	31.8	30.9	56.1	36.6	25.9	26.3	25.9	23.7
Operating Expenses	27.7	28.6	28.1	51.9	35.9	24.5	23.8	22.8	18.6
Operating Profit	4.2	3.2	2.8	4.2	.7	1.4	2.5	3.1	5.1
All Other Expenses (net)	.3	.6	.5	1.1	.5	.2	.0	.2	1.1
Profit Before Taxes	3.9	2.6	2.3	3.1	.2	1.3	2.5	2.9	4.0
RATIOS									
Current	2.1	2.1	2.3	2.4	1.8	2.7	1.9	2.4	2.6
	1.4	1.4	1.5	1.3	1.6	1.4	1.5	1.7	1.7
	1.0	.9	1.1	.6	1.0	1.2	1.1	1.1	1.2
Quick	1.7	2.0	1.8	1.5	1.7	1.7	1.8	2.2	2.3
	1.2	1.1	1.1	.7	1.2	1.1	1.1	1.6	1.3
	.7	.6	.7	.3	.2	.8	.7	.8	.9
Sales/Receivables	23 16.0	17 21.8	27 13.6	0 UND	1 245.2	28 12.9	35 10.4	32 11.3	42 8.7
	44 8.3	46 7.9	46 7.9	17 21.5	38 9.7	52 7.0	40 9.2	43 8.5	59 6.2
	72 5.1	67 5.5	65 5.6	62 5.9	58 6.3	82 4.4	63 5.8	60 6.0	83 4.4
Cost of Sales/Inventory	0 UND	0 UND	0 UND	0 UND	0 UND	0 UND	0 UND	0 UND	0 UND
	0 UND	1 435.0	1 434.1	0 UND	0 UND	15 24.4	2 243.3	0 UND	3 125.3
	13 27.6	10 35.6	29 12.8	34 10.6	12 31.6	54 6.8	29 12.7	11 31.7	36 10.1
Cost of Sales/Payables	8 47.6	5 70.6	15 25.0	0 UND	4 92.4	18 20.2	16 23.4	15 24.8	20 18.6
	19 18.8	19 18.8	27 13.6	0 UND	18 20.0	27 13.8	30 12.2	27 13.6	35 10.4
	48 7.6	41 8.8	51 7.2	130 2.8	47 7.7	38 9.6	58 6.3	44 8.2	59 6.2
Sales/Working Capital	7.4	5.8	6.2	8.3	7.7	5.3	9.7	3.6	4.8
	18.5	20.8	13.5	49.3	13.6	13.2	14.0	10.0	8.5
	173.8	-90.9	49.4	-27.7	NM	39.2	49.1	42.4	42.3
EBIT/Interest	11.5	11.1	16.0		14.0	47.5	13.4	32.8	18.2
	(63) 5.9	(75) 2.7	(86) 4.5		(16) 4.7	(14) 3.0	(19) 3.2	(16) 5.7	(14) 8.8
	1.6	-.9	1.1		1.0	-1.2	-2.4	1.2	3.4
Net Profit + Depr., Dep., Amort./Cur. Mat. L/T/D	6.4	7.2	6.1						
	(17) 3.8	(18) 3.1	(22) 2.9						
	1.7	1.1	1.6						
Fixed/Worth	.2	.3	.2	.9	.2	.1	.1	.2	.3
	.6	.8	.5	1.8	.6	.3	.3	.3	.6
	1.6	25.3	1.5	-.5	2.1	1.1	1.2	1.2	NM
Debt/Worth	1.0	1.1	.7	1.8	1.1	.5	1.0	.5	.8
	2.2	2.6	1.8	6.0	2.7	2.1	2.0	.8	1.7
	10.1	78.0	3.5	-3.1	3.1	3.1	4.7	1.8	NM
% Profit Before Taxes/Tangible Net Worth	79.8	48.1	43.2		86.3	33.2	45.2	32.2	30.8
	(61) 30.5	(65) 12.1	(92) 17.3		(16) 29.4	(14) 14.6	(21) 26.2	12.4	(12) 8.1
	5.7	.3	1.8		-2.8	-5.7	7.1	.8	3.8
% Profit Before Taxes/Total Assets	20.7	15.9	19.9	33.1	33.5	17.3	14.8	22.1	12.2
	9.4	3.7	5.9	14.9	8.1	4.0	6.8	3.8	4.5
	1.3	-3.0	.4	-3.1	-.8	-1.0	-.9	.4	2.2
Sales/Net Fixed Assets	38.6	27.0	46.6	36.9	30.7	65.9	87.3	36.8	25.5
	20.3	12.8	18.6	29.4	13.5	30.5	31.0	10.9	10.3
	9.2	6.6	8.5	13.2	3.3	16.7	14.9	5.9	5.4
Sales/Total Assets	4.7	4.0	4.3	6.6	5.3	4.0	5.0	3.4	3.2
	3.1	2.8	2.9	4.1	3.4	2.6	3.3	2.1	2.2
	2.1	1.9	1.7	2.4	1.4	1.5	2.7	1.6	.9
% Depr., Dep., Amort./Sales	.7	.9	.7		1.8	.4	.7	.6	.5
	(56) 1.9	(67) 2.4	(83) 1.8		(12) 4.7	(11) 1.1	(18) 1.1	(19) 2.6	(14) 1.7
	3.1	4.0	3.6		7.0	4.0	2.3	3.8	5.5
% Officers', Directors' Owners' Comp/Sales	2.0	2.2	1.5		1.0	1.2	1.1		
	(40) 3.3	(36) 5.7	(50) 3.1		(11) 2.9	(10) 3.2	(10) 2.3		
	6.3	9.6	7.2		10.2	4.9	3.4		
Net Sales ($)	1352128M	1518228M	2641745M	7927M	29620M	59835M	165520M	306073M	2072770M
Total Assets ($)	637650M	537577M	1213838M	2038M	14777M	23999M	54356M	177353M	941315M

M = $ thousand   MM = $ million
See Pages 9 through 22 for Explanation of Ratios and Data

Current Data Sorted by Assets   Comparative Historical Data

						Type of Statement		
2	6	54	80	14	8	Unqualified	194	166
5	121	267	52	2		Reviewed	451	391
31	58	29	2			Compiled	133	105
114	96	28	3	1	1	Tax Returns	186	175
46	93	104	53	11	6	Other	299	283
	263 (4/1-9/30/10)			1,024 (10/1/10-3/31/11)			4/1/06-3/31/07	4/1/07-3/31/08
0-500M	500M-2MM	2-10MM	10-50MM	50-100MM	100-250MM		ALL	ALL
198	374	482	190	28	15	NUMBER OF STATEMENTS	1263	1120
%	%	%	%	%	%	ASSETS	%	%
23.7	13.6	15.7	18.1	17.5	16.1	Cash & Equivalents	12.4	13.9
28.4	46.7	50.5	50.0	44.1	43.5	Trade Receivables (net)	51.2	50.9
7.5	7.4	4.6	2.8	5.2	9.2	Inventory	5.6	5.4
4.6	6.2	10.0	10.9	9.9	9.4	All Other Current	8.6	8.1
64.2	73.9	80.8	81.9	76.7	78.1	Total Current	77.9	78.4
23.9	15.9	12.4	11.6	10.4	10.3	Fixed Assets (net)	15.1	14.8
4.2	2.5	1.6	2.2	6.9	4.4	Intangibles (net)	1.6	1.6
7.7	7.7	5.2	4.3	6.0	7.1	All Other Non-Current	5.4	5.1
100.0	100.0	100.0	100.0	100.0	100.0	Total	100.0	100.0
						LIABILITIES		
26.4	14.1	8.0	5.6	3.6	4.9	Notes Payable-Short Term	11.7	10.6
7.3	2.8	2.0	1.8	2.5	.9	Cur. Mat.-L.T.D.	3.1	3.0
16.6	18.7	20.4	18.9	13.1	17.0	Trade Payables	19.7	19.1
.1	.5	.5	.2	.4	.3	Income Taxes Payable	.8	.7
15.6	11.3	14.6	21.6	21.9	29.3	All Other Current	17.0	17.7
66.1	47.4	45.5	48.1	41.4	52.4	Total Current	52.4	51.1
26.2	10.0	6.1	5.5	15.0	7.1	Long-Term Debt	10.3	10.1
.1	.4	.6	.4	.1	.1	Deferred Taxes	.4	.4
15.4	4.0	2.8	3.0	2.0	2.6	All Other Non-Current	4.3	3.9
-7.8	38.2	44.9	43.0	41.4	37.7	Net Worth	32.6	34.5
100.0	100.0	100.0	100.0	100.0	100.0	Total Liabilties & Net Worth	100.0	100.0
						INCOME DATA		
100.0	100.0	100.0	100.0	100.0	100.0	Net Sales	100.0	100.0
41.4	29.9	21.9	18.2	21.7	18.9	Gross Profit	25.7	26.7
38.8	28.9	19.3	14.6	15.6	14.9	Operating Expenses	21.2	21.8
2.6	1.0	2.5	3.6	6.1	4.0	Operating Profit	4.5	4.9
.7	.4	.2	.3	1.1	1.1	All Other Expenses (net)	.5	.4
1.9	.7	2.4	3.2	5.0	2.9	Profit Before Taxes	4.0	4.5
						RATIOS		
2.8	2.8	2.7	2.2	3.1	2.0	Current	2.3	2.3
1.2	1.7	1.7	1.7	1.8	1.7		1.6	1.6
.6	1.1	1.3	1.4	1.3	1.2		1.2	1.2
2.7	2.3	2.3	1.8	2.4	1.9	Quick	1.9	2.0
.9	(373) 1.4	1.4	1.4	1.5	1.4		1.3	1.3
.4	.8	1.0	1.1	1.1	.9		1.0	1.0
0 UND	41 9.0	52 7.1	61 6.0	54 6.8	60 6.1	Sales/Receivables	43 8.6	44 8.4
20 18.3	57 6.4	70 5.2	74 4.9	80 4.6	70 5.2		64 5.7	64 5.7
55 6.7	76 4.8	90 4.0	96 3.8	95 3.8	83 4.4		85 4.3	82 4.4
0 UND	0 UND	0 UND	0 UND	0 UND	0 UND	Cost of Sales/Inventory	0 UND	0 UND
0 UND	3 130.7	2 206.3	1 487.6	1 391.3	4 95.3		1 245.1	2 229.7
15 23.6	19 18.8	9 41.2	4 81.4	11 33.3	27 13.4		10 35.8	10 35.1
0 UND	15 24.5	17 22.1	22 16.7	19 19.5	17 21.6	Cost of Sales/Payables	16 22.9	15 23.9
12 31.0	28 13.0	33 11.1	31 11.7	24 15.2	30 12.4		28 13.1	27 13.5
48 7.7	47 7.7	49 7.4	47 7.8	40 9.2	44 8.2		43 8.5	41 8.9
11.4	5.5	4.7	4.9	4.3	5.5	Sales/Working Capital	6.5	6.4
82.3	10.6	8.3	7.0	8.2	7.9		11.1	10.7
-17.6	49.3	14.7	12.3	18.2	19.0		25.0	21.8
13.9	12.0	24.3	61.2	236.1	203.7	EBIT/Interest	22.5	27.3
(161) 3.1	(332) 2.3	(398) 4.5	(158) 7.5	(24) 28.6	(14) 33.4		(1136) 7.1	(979) 8.1
-.8	-2.5	-.5	1.9	.7	4.5		2.1	2.5
	4.4	7.2	8.9			Net Profit + Depr., Dep., Amort./Cur. Mat. L/T/D	12.5	13.2
	(49) 1.7	(120) 2.5	(49) 3.1				(303) 4.4	(269) 4.6
	-1.3	.3	1.2				1.8	1.9
.2	.1	.1	.1	.1	.2	Fixed/Worth	.1	.1
1.2	.3	.2	.2	.2	.2		.3	.3
-.7	1.3	.5	.4	.5	.5		.8	.8
.9	.5	.5	.8	.6	1.2	Debt/Worth	.8	.9
7.7	1.4	1.3	1.3	1.6	1.3		1.8	1.7
-3.2	5.7	2.8	2.2	3.3	5.1		3.6	3.7
205.2	35.3	28.6	26.3	54.8	63.6	% Profit Before Taxes/Tangible Net Worth	53.3	60.3
(123) 57.1	(316) 8.2	(457) 10.3	(185) 13.6	(24) 23.1	(14) 17.2		(1122) 26.3	(1005) 29.9
3.1	-14.4	.1	4.0	10.3	13.8		8.6	11.4
35.4	13.2	12.7	12.1	17.3	8.8	% Profit Before Taxes/Total Assets	20.3	22.4
8.1	2.6	3.6	5.1	8.9	7.4		9.3	10.4
-7.8	-8.4	-.5	1.2	.0	4.4		2.4	3.5
105.6	56.8	61.9	63.4	81.0	77.7	Sales/Net Fixed Assets	64.7	67.2
34.1	26.0	34.5	32.5	27.1	29.3		31.7	32.8
14.6	13.5	16.4	15.2	15.2	16.7		16.3	16.0
8.3	3.8	3.3	2.9	2.7	2.8	Sales/Total Assets	3.8	3.9
4.4	2.9	2.6	2.5	2.2	2.3		3.0	3.0
2.8	2.2	2.0	1.9	1.4	1.9		2.4	2.4
.5	.7	.5	.4	.4	.2	% Depr., Dep., Amort./Sales	.5	.5
(124) 1.5	(282) 1.3	(428) .9	(178) .7	(26) .6	(12) .4		(1066) .9	(920) .8
3.2	2.2	1.5	1.3	1.3	1.1		1.6	1.6
4.5	2.8	1.6	.9			% Officers', Directors' Owners' Comp/Sales	1.9	1.9
(131) 7.5	(215) 4.5	(222) 2.8	(53) 2.8				(644) 3.6	(548) 3.5
12.7	7.4	4.6	4.7				6.8	6.9
250627M	1365512M	5818295M	9947376M	4003603M	4873089M	Net Sales ($)	31577882M	27003138M
46236M	437679M	2218258M	3940706M	1811701M	2148893M	Total Assets ($)	9614893M	9919711M

M = $ thousand   MM = $ million
See Pages 9 through 22 for Explanation of Ratios and Data

Comparative Historical Data — Current Data Sorted by Sales

Hist 4/1/08-3/31/09 ALL	Hist 4/1/09-3/31/10 ALL	Hist 4/1/10-3/31/11 ALL	Type of Statement	0-1MM	1-3MM	3-5MM	5-10MM	10-25MM	25MM & OVER
193	194	164	Unqualified		2	6	14	40	102
462	467	447	Reviewed	4	53	71	115	151	53
109	115	120	Compiled	22	40	27	19	10	2
191	210	243	Tax Returns	65	78	48	37	10	5
337	352	313	Other	34	53	43	58	57	68
				263 (4/1-9/30/10)			1,024 (10/1/10-3/31/11)		
1292	**1338**	**1287**	**NUMBER OF STATEMENTS**	125	226	195	243	268	230
%	%	%	**ASSETS**	%	%	%	%	%	%
15.3	18.2	16.7	Cash & Equivalents	20.5	16.7	16.4	16.7	14.8	17.3
49.2	44.2	45.7	Trade Receivables (net)	25.3	41.0	45.3	47.5	53.3	51.1
5.4	5.8	5.7	Inventory	7.4	8.0	7.6	5.4	3.8	3.2
7.8	7.8	8.2	All Other Current	5.8	4.9	6.4	8.4	10.8	10.9
77.7	76.1	76.3	Total Current	59.0	70.6	75.6	77.9	82.7	82.5
15.1	16.1	15.0	Fixed Assets (net)	24.5	18.6	15.5	13.7	12.2	10.6
1.9	2.3	2.5	Intangibles (net)	6.3	2.6	2.0	1.8	1.7	2.3
5.3	5.5	6.2	All Other Non-Current	10.2	8.1	6.9	6.5	3.4	4.7
100.0	100.0	100.0	Total	100.0	100.0	100.0	100.0	100.0	100.0
			LIABILITIES						
10.2	10.5	12.1	Notes Payable-Short Term	28.6	16.6	11.7	11.1	7.8	5.4
3.3	3.5	3.0	Cur. Mat.-L.T.D.	6.3	5.2	2.4	2.5	1.8	1.7
18.0	16.9	18.9	Trade Payables	15.0	18.2	18.0	18.5	21.7	19.7
.6	.5	.4	Income Taxes Payable	.1	.5	.4	.5	.4	.2
18.0	17.0	15.2	All Other Current	13.2	11.6	11.6	14.8	16.0	22.3
50.1	48.5	49.6	Total Current	63.1	52.1	44.1	47.4	47.6	49.3
9.7	9.3	10.4	Long-Term Debt	28.5	13.4	7.6	8.6	7.2	5.9
.4	.5	.4	Deferred Taxes	.0	.3	.6	.7	.4	.4
3.7	3.9	5.1	All Other Non-Current	16.1	7.4	3.0	3.5	3.0	2.8
36.1	37.9	34.4	Net Worth	-7.8	26.8	44.8	39.8	41.9	41.6
100.0	100.0	100.0	Total Liabilities & Net Worth	100.0	100.0	100.0	100.0	100.0	100.0
			INCOME DATA						
100.0	100.0	100.0	Net Sales	100.0	100.0	100.0	100.0	100.0	100.0
26.6	27.6	26.6	Gross Profit	45.1	34.4	27.9	24.1	20.3	17.9
22.2	24.5	24.3	Operating Expenses	43.4	33.2	26.7	20.7	17.6	14.6
4.3	3.1	2.4	Operating Profit	1.7	1.2	1.1	3.4	2.7	3.3
.5	.4	.4	All Other Expenses (net)	1.0	.6	.2	.2	.2	.4
3.8	2.7	2.0	Profit Before Taxes	.7	.6	1.0	3.2	2.5	3.0
			RATIOS						
2.4	2.9	2.6	Current	2.8	2.8	3.0	3.1	2.5	2.1
1.6	1.7	1.7		1.0	1.5	1.8	1.8	1.7	1.7
1.2	1.2	1.2		.5	1.0	1.3	1.2	1.4	1.3
2.0	2.4	2.2	Quick	2.4	2.5	2.5	2.6	2.1	1.8
(1291) 1.4	1.4	(1286) 1.4		(124) .8	1.2	1.4	1.5	1.4	1.4
1.0	1.0	.9		.4	.7	.9	.9	1.1	1.1
41 8.8	37 9.8	42 8.6	Sales/Receivables	0 UND	34 10.6	39 9.4	42 8.6	53 6.9	57 6.4
61 6.0	59 6.2	63 5.8		26 13.9	54 6.8	57 6.4	64 5.7	69 5.3	72 5.1
81 4.5	79 4.6	84 4.3		62 5.9	78 4.7	76 4.8	88 4.2	92 4.0	89 4.1
0 UND	0 UND	0 UND	Cost of Sales/Inventory	0 UND	0 UND	0 UND	0 UND	0 UND	0 UND
1 322.8	1 248.9	1 293.0		0 UND	2 200.3	3 129.4	2 194.2	1 249.7	1 471.2
8 43.0	10 35.5	12 31.2		26 14.0	25 14.4	16 23.2	11 32.5	7 51.2	5 78.6
13 27.4	12 29.5	14 25.3	Cost of Sales/Payables	0 UND	10 37.7	13 27.4	13 28.8	18 20.8	21 17.7
24 15.0	24 15.5	29 12.7		15 24.3	30 12.1	27 13.4	27 13.6	33 11.1	30 12.0
40 9.1	40 9.2	48 7.7		62 5.9	52 7.0	45 8.0	46 8.0	47 7.7	45 8.1
6.5	5.4	5.2	Sales/Working Capital	6.8	5.3	5.3	4.8	5.2	5.4
10.6	9.5	9.4		246.0	12.6	9.3	9.0	8.7	8.1
22.1	24.3	25.2		-11.9	-346.3	22.6	26.0	14.2	14.4
32.0	30.1	21.9	EBIT/Interest	9.0	9.5	13.9	24.9	27.1	65.8
(1123) 7.8	(1107) 6.1	(1087) 3.9		(97) 2.7	(199) 1.9	(163) 2.7	(204) 4.3	(229) 5.3	(195) 9.6
2.0	.3	-.8		-1.6	-3.8	-2.6	.1	1.0	1.9
11.4	8.5	7.5	Net Profit + Depr., Dep., Amort./Cur. Mat. L/T/D		4.1	3.9	10.5	7.8	10.5
(317) 4.2	(310) 2.8	(232) 2.5		(19) .4	(33) .9	(44) 1.7	(67) 2.8	(69) 3.7	
1.4	.9	.1		-2.7	-2.2	-2.3	1.6	1.0	
.1	.1	.1	Fixed/Worth	.1	.2	.1	.1	.1	.1
.3	.3	.3		2.2	.4	.3	.2	.2	.2
.7	.8	.9		-.7	3.0	.7	.7	.5	.4
.8	.6	.7	Debt/Worth	.9	.5	.5	.5	.7	.9
1.6	1.3	1.4		11.1	1.8	1.1	1.1	1.4	1.3
3.7	3.4	4.0		-2.9	14.5	3.6	3.6	2.9	2.3
55.2	43.4	35.4	% Profit Before Taxes/Tangible Net Worth	152.8	47.4	35.1	39.6	27.8	30.4
(1154) 26.0	(1197) 16.6	(1119) 12.1		(73) 31.6	(179) 11.6	(178) 7.1	(214) 11.1	(253) 11.5	(222) 16.0
8.6	2.1	-.4		.0	-18.2	-11.1	.5	1.1	4.4
21.0	18.4	14.3	% Profit Before Taxes/Total Assets	23.3	17.3	12.4	16.3	12.3	12.6
9.5	5.6	4.0		4.7	2.7	2.5	3.6	4.2	6.2
2.1	-.7	-2.6		-13.0	-10.3	-6.7	.1	.2	1.3
67.3	63.4	65.4	Sales/Net Fixed Assets	87.6	52.5	53.0	75.2	63.0	71.0
32.1	29.0	32.1		24.3	22.3	25.1	35.7	36.3	37.3
16.1	14.2	14.7		9.3	12.7	13.7	16.8	18.9	18.0
3.9	3.7	3.6	Sales/Total Assets	5.6	4.1	3.8	3.7	3.4	3.2
3.1	2.9	2.7		2.9	2.8	2.8	2.8	2.7	2.6
2.4	2.2	2.1		1.7	2.0	2.1	2.2	2.2	2.2
.5	.5	.5	% Depr., Dep., Amort./Sales	1.0	.7	.6	.5	.5	.3
(1059) .9	(1087) 1.0	(1050) 1.0		(80) 2.0	(165) 1.5	(148) 1.2	(193) 1.0	(252) .9	(212) .6
1.7	1.8	1.8		3.9	2.4	2.0	1.8	1.4	1.1
2.1	2.4	2.2	% Officers', Directors' Owners' Comp/Sales	6.3	4.0	2.0		1.2	1.0
(629) 4.0	(631) 4.5	(627) 4.1		(73) 10.2	(135) 5.8	(114) 4.1	(135) 3.1	(113) 2.2	(57) 1.8
7.2	7.9	7.2		16.4	8.7	6.1	4.9	4.1	4.2
30381016M	29257198M	26258502M	Net Sales ($)	74195M	442330M	774912M	1742631M	4157269M	19067165M
11552286M	11313277M	10603473M	Total Assets ($)	37201M	177006M	311034M	716897M	1674727M	7686608M

M = $ thousand   MM = $ million
See Pages 9 through 22 for Explanation of Ratios and Data

Current Data Sorted by Assets   Comparative Historical Data

Type of Statement	0-500M	500M-2MM	2-10MM	10-50MM	50-100MM	100-250MM	4/1/06-3/31/07 ALL	4/1/07-3/31/08 ALL
Unqualified	3	3	34	60	11	6	148	139
Reviewed	9	84	239	53	1		375	344
Compiled	23	71	40	1			150	109
Tax Returns	116	91	38	5	1		225	235
Other	60	122	106	35	5	5	243	275
	232 (4/1-9/30/10)			990 (10/1/10-3/31/11)				
NUMBER OF STATEMENTS	211	371	457	154	18	11	1141	1102
	%	%	%	%	%	%	%	%
ASSETS								
Cash & Equivalents	19.5	14.4	14.8	19.8	14.2	22.4	14.1	14.6
Trade Receivables (net)	28.4	41.0	48.9	46.1	45.0	29.6	46.6	45.5
Inventory	11.6	10.5	5.9	4.2	5.8	9.2	7.6	7.3
All Other Current	3.7	5.3	8.5	9.6	6.8	13.8	7.2	6.8
Total Current	63.2	71.2	78.1	79.8	71.9	75.0	75.4	74.2
Fixed Assets (net)	26.2	18.1	14.4	12.6	16.4	8.5	16.4	18.0
Intangibles (net)	2.5	3.5	2.3	3.0	4.4	7.6	2.7	2.2
All Other Non-Current	8.1	7.2	5.2	4.5	7.3	8.9	5.5	5.6
Total	100.0	100.0	100.0	100.0	100.0	100.0	100.0	100.0
LIABILITIES								
Notes Payable-Short Term	27.3	12.4	7.8	4.5	3.3	4.0	8.9	9.3
Cur. Mat.-L.T.D.	6.0	3.1	2.2	1.7	4.2	.7	2.8	3.4
Trade Payables	21.8	20.7	22.7	20.9	18.3	17.4	21.8	21.0
Income Taxes Payable	.2	.3	.5	.4	.3	.0	.7	.7
All Other Current	15.9	11.3	14.5	20.4	24.3	16.6	17.8	17.6
Total Current	71.2	47.8	47.8	48.0	50.3	38.7	52.0	52.0
Long-Term Debt	25.8	13.2	6.8	7.0	19.7	19.4	12.4	14.0
Deferred Taxes	.0	.3	.4	.3	.0	.0	.3	.3
All Other Non-Current	16.1	6.1	3.7	2.4	3.6	3.3	3.6	4.3
Net Worth	-13.2	32.6	41.3	42.3	26.4	38.7	31.8	29.3
Total Liabilties & Net Worth	100.0	100.0	100.0	100.0	100.0	100.0	100.0	100.0
INCOME DATA								
Net Sales	100.0	100.0	100.0	100.0	100.0	100.0	100.0	100.0
Gross Profit	43.3	32.5	23.0	20.0	22.9	32.7	28.3	29.1
Operating Expenses	40.4	30.9	21.1	17.2	19.3	27.7	23.5	24.8
Operating Profit	3.0	1.5	1.9	2.8	3.6	5.1	4.8	4.3
All Other Expenses (net)	.6	.4	.1	-.1	.5	.4	.4	.4
Profit Before Taxes	2.4	1.1	1.8	2.9	3.0	4.6	4.4	4.0
RATIOS								
Current	2.9	2.8	2.3	2.2	2.2	9.5	2.1	2.1
	1.4	1.5	1.6	1.6	1.3	2.5	1.5	1.5
	.6	1.0	1.2	1.4	1.2	1.4	1.2	1.2
Quick	2.1	2.2	2.0	1.9	1.6	2.4	1.8	1.8
	.9	1.2	1.3	1.4	1.2	1.4	(1139) 1.2	(1101) 1.2
	.3	.7	1.0	1.0	1.0	1.0	.9	.9
Sales/Receivables	0 UND	27 13.6	47 7.8	55 6.6	53 6.9	0 UND	31 11.7	30 12.0
	18 20.3	47 7.8	66 5.5	72 5.1	64 5.7	59 6.2	56 6.5	54 6.8
	41 8.9	67 5.5	86 4.3	92 4.0	83 4.4	78 4.7	79 4.6	77 4.7
Cost of Sales/Inventory	0 UND	0 UND	0 UND	0 UND	1 565.4	0 UND	0 UND	0 UND
	5 72.7	8 43.4	5 78.4	2 163.8	6 61.8	1 606.5	4 93.7	4 102.8
	24 15.3	27 13.5	15 24.7	10 36.2	12 31.3	18 20.2	15 24.3	16 22.7
Cost of Sales/Payables	0 UND	15 24.3	23 16.0	23 15.6	21 17.2	17 22.1	17 21.7	16 22.6
	19 18.9	29 12.7	34 10.7	33 11.0	32 11.4	38 9.5	29 12.5	29 12.6
	38 9.5	47 7.7	50 7.3	49 7.4	43 8.4	53 6.8	47 7.8	46 7.9
Sales/Working Capital	10.7	6.1	5.5	4.6	6.2	3.7	7.6	7.3
	43.4	13.3	10.5	8.4	14.9	6.3	13.2	13.1
	-24.5	238.1	20.5	15.1	21.4	17.1	36.5	37.2
EBIT/Interest	10.0	15.9	18.6	44.9	37.0	30.4	22.7	26.6
	(171) 3.0	(322) 3.6	(382) 4.7	(134) 12.7	(15) 8.4	(10) 6.4	(993) 7.7	(971) 7.7
	-.7	-1.0	1.1	2.1	.6	2.5	2.4	2.1
Net Profit + Depr., Dep., Amort./Cur. Mat. L/T/D		6.2	10.0	20.9			11.1	8.6
	(51) 1.5	(118) 2.3	(49) 4.9				(245) 3.9	(228) 4.3
	-1.3	.8	1.7				1.8	2.1
Fixed/Worth	.2	.2	.1	.1	.2	.1	.1	.2
	1.5	.5	.3	.2	.5	.3	.4	.4
	-.6	2.7	.7	.5	1.0	.6	1.1	1.2
Debt/Worth	.9	.7	.8	.9	.9	.7	.9	.9
	6.4	2.2	1.5	1.5	2.3	1.5	2.1	2.1
	-3.0	12.0	3.0	2.6	5.1	3.7	5.0	5.3
% Profit Before Taxes/Tangible Net Worth	100.0	48.8	31.1	35.0	43.7	58.4	64.2	62.0
	(125) 35.9	(298) 13.8	(436) 11.3	(148) 14.9	(16) 19.6	(10) 23.2	(1005) 32.9	(950) 30.2
	3.7	-3.6	.9	3.5	7.7	1.7	11.5	12.0
% Profit Before Taxes/Total Assets	28.8	15.9	12.7	13.2	13.5	15.6	22.0	21.3
	9.1	4.7	3.8	5.8	4.8	7.0	9.9	9.7
	-3.4	-4.0	.2	1.2	.8	.6	3.2	3.0
Sales/Net Fixed Assets	73.1	52.1	50.9	57.0	49.5	69.0	63.3	56.9
	30.1	24.5	28.2	29.3	22.0	36.5	31.4	28.5
	13.1	12.3	16.4	16.2	11.6	19.0	16.6	15.3
Sales/Total Assets	8.6	4.3	3.4	3.0	3.6	2.5	4.3	4.3
	4.8	3.2	2.8	2.4	2.6	2.1	3.2	3.2
	3.3	2.3	2.1	1.9	1.7	1.3	2.5	2.5
% Depr., Dep., Amort./Sales	.7	.6	.5	.5	.5		.5	.4
	(133) 1.3	(283) 1.3	(406) .9	(145) .9	(16) .8		(950) .9	(905) 1.0
	2.2	2.1	1.5	1.4	2.5		1.6	1.7
% Officers', Directors' Owners' Comp/Sales	4.2	2.7	1.5	.9			1.9	2.1
	(140) 7.4	(219) 4.7	(234) 2.9	(59) 1.6			(595) 4.0	(569) 4.1
	11.7	7.3	5.0	3.6			6.5	7.2
Net Sales ($)	271238M	1462076M	5828337M	7833820M	3562479M	4491956M	35204942M	30744019M
Total Assets ($)	51542M	423408M	2095848M	2938574M	1232993M	1622946M	9600015M	8777716M

M = $ thousand   MM = $ million
See Pages 9 through 22 for Explanation of Ratios and Data

Comparative Historical Data / Current Data Sorted by Sales

4/1/08-3/31/09 ALL	4/1/09-3/31/10 ALL	4/1/10-3/31/11 ALL	Type of Statement	0-1MM	1-3MM	3-5MM	5-10MM	10-25MM	25MM & OVER
143	121	117	Unqualified	2	2	2	9	31	71
407	407	386	Reviewed	8	33	48	102	140	55
121	121	135	Compiled	11	40	32	32	17	3
277	251	251	Tax Returns	58	93	40	28	25	7
296	350	333	Other	30	88	47	57	65	46
				232 (4/1-9/30/10)			990 (10/1/10-3/31/11)		
1244	1250	1222	**NUMBER OF STATEMENTS**	109	256	169	228	278	182
%	%	%	**ASSETS**	%	%	%	%	%	%
15.6	17.7	16.2	Cash & Equivalents	17.2	16.4	14.2	15.4	16.5	17.6
44.7	41.4	42.4	Trade Receivables (net)	27.3	34.7	41.6	45.7	49.6	47.8
7.0	7.2	8.1	Inventory	9.6	12.8	8.7	6.9	5.8	5.3
6.9	6.7	6.9	All Other Current	4.6	4.4	6.5	7.4	7.9	9.7
74.2	73.1	73.5	Total Current	58.7	68.2	70.9	75.4	79.8	80.3
16.6	17.6	17.3	Fixed Assets (net)	28.6	20.8	18.5	16.0	13.5	12.3
2.7	3.0	2.9	Intangibles (net)	3.7	3.2	2.7	2.9	3.0	2.0
6.5	6.3	6.3	All Other Non-Current	9.0	7.8	7.9	5.7	3.8	5.4
100.0	100.0	100.0	Total	100.0	100.0	100.0	100.0	100.0	100.0
			LIABILITIES						
10.0	10.2	12.0	Notes Payable-Short Term	26.7	19.0	12.5	8.5	7.3	4.8
3.4	3.3	3.1	Cur. Mat.-L.T.D.	4.0	4.4	4.0	2.7	2.1	1.9
21.0	19.8	21.6	Trade Payables	20.2	17.8	21.5	22.3	24.9	22.2
.6	.4	.4	Income Taxes Payable	.3	.3	.3	.5	.4	.4
17.1	17.0	14.7	All Other Current	16.5	12.1	12.7	12.1	15.3	21.4
52.1	50.7	51.8	Total Current	67.7	53.5	51.1	46.1	49.9	50.7
12.7	12.5	12.4	Long-Term Debt	25.6	18.4	12.7	8.8	6.8	8.6
.3	.3	.3	Deferred Taxes	.0	.3	.2	.3	.6	.1
4.6	5.9	6.4	All Other Non-Current	16.7	9.2	6.0	4.6	3.8	3.0
30.3	30.7	29.1	Net Worth	-10.0	18.6	30.0	40.3	39.0	37.6
100.0	100.0	100.0	Total Liabilities & Net Worth	100.0	100.0	100.0	100.0	100.0	100.0
			INCOME DATA						
100.0	100.0	100.0	Net Sales	100.0	100.0	100.0	100.0	100.0	100.0
28.0	28.9	29.1	Gross Profit	45.1	37.0	30.3	25.8	22.5	21.6
24.1	25.9	27.0	Operating Expenses	42.7	35.3	29.1	24.1	19.7	18.5
3.9	3.1	2.2	Operating Profit	2.4	1.7	1.2	1.7	2.8	3.0
.4	.4	.3	All Other Expenses (net)	.7	.4	.3	.2	.2	-.1
3.6	2.7	1.9	Profit Before Taxes	1.7	1.2	.9	1.5	2.7	3.1
			RATIOS						
2.2	2.4	2.5	Current	2.3	3.3	2.5	2.7	2.3	2.1
1.5	1.6	1.6		1.2	1.7	1.5	1.7	1.6	1.5
1.2	1.2	1.1		.6	1.0	1.0	1.2	1.3	1.3
1.8	2.0	2.0	Quick	2.1	2.4	1.9	2.1	1.9	1.7
1.2	1.3	1.2		.8	1.3	1.2	1.3	1.3	1.3
.9	.9	.8		.6	.6	.9	1.0	1.0	1.0
30 / 12.1	30 / 12.1	30 / 12.0	Sales/Receivables	0 / UND	14 / 26.7	28 / 13.1	35 / 10.5	45 / 8.2	49 / 7.5
53 / 6.9	50 / 7.3	56 / 6.6		25 / 14.5	40 / 9.1	50 / 7.3	60 / 6.1	64 / 5.7	65 / 5.6
76 / 4.8	72 / 5.1	78 / 4.7		56 / 6.6	64 / 5.7	75 / 4.9	78 / 4.7	88 / 4.1	82 / 4.4
0 / UND	0 / UND	0 / UND	Cost of Sales/Inventory	0 / UND	0 / UND	0 / UND	0 / UND	0 / UND	0 / 999.8
3 / 108.6	4 / 88.7	5 / 73.0		3 / 134.0	12 / 30.5	5 / 69.8	5 / 69.7	4 / 82.9	2 / 151.0
14 / 25.5	16 / 22.8	18 / 20.2		24 / 14.9	33 / 11.2	19 / 19.3	13 / 27.6	11 / 33.7	
14 / 25.3	15 / 25.1	17 / 21.1	Cost of Sales/Payables	0 / UND	11 / 34.1	16 / 23.2	19 / 19.3	24 / 15.5	23 / 16.0
28 / 13.0	27 / 13.7	31 / 11.8		21 / 17.1	25 / 14.5	30 / 12.3	31 / 11.6	35 / 10.5	33 / 11.1
45 / 8.1	43 / 8.4	48 / 7.6		58 / 6.3	46 / 8.0	49 / 7.4	48 / 7.7	50 / 7.3	45 / 8.1
7.2	6.1	6.0	Sales/Working Capital	9.4	5.4	6.1	5.9	5.6	6.3
13.1	11.9	11.8		55.2	13.9	13.6	10.8	10.9	10.1
42.0	34.3	41.4		-17.7	227.3	-149.0	29.1	20.0	18.7
27.7	24.4	18.2	EBIT/Interest	5.9	12.3	11.3	18.0	25.4	36.6
(1102) 6.4	(1057) 5.3	(1034) 4.4		(81) 1.9	(221) 2.9	(148) 3.6	(194) 4.6	(230) 6.0	(160) 9.8
1.6	.8	.3		-6.2	-1.9	-.7	1.1	1.5	1.9
9.6	10.6	9.9	Net Profit + Depr., Dep., Amort./Cur. Mat. L/T/D		5.4	5.9	7.1	10.4	20.6
(265) 3.5	(258) 3.7	(230) 2.7			(20) 1.3	(26) 1.4	(46) 1.3	(79) 2.8	(55) 7.4
1.2	1.0	.8			.1	-1.1	-.6	1.3	2.5
.2	.1	.1	Fixed/Worth	.2	.2	.2	.1	.1	.1
.4	.4	.4		1.1	.5	.6	.4	.3	.3
1.2	1.2	1.3		-.6	-199.3	2.9	1.1	.7	.6
.9	.8	.8	Debt/Worth	.9	.6	.8	.6	.9	.9
1.9	1.7	1.8		5.2	2.1	2.5	1.5	1.6	1.7
5.0	4.7	5.7		-3.0	-843.5	11.6	4.2	3.3	3.0
56.2	47.2	41.4	% Profit Before Taxes/Tangible Net Worth	75.0	58.7	40.1	32.2	40.4	36.9
(1069) 27.3	(1048) 19.0	(1033) 13.5		(63) 21.0	(191) 14.6	(136) 12.7	(205) 12.0	(263) 13.2	(175) 16.7
7.5	2.7	1.1		-3.4	-7.0	-3.0	.8	2.9	4.0
21.0	18.1	15.5	% Profit Before Taxes/Total Assets	23.7	19.7	14.2	13.7	14.6	13.8
8.7	6.4	4.7		5.1	4.5	4.1	4.5	4.5	6.4
1.6	.0	-.7		-10.1	-5.3	-2.4	.1	.9	1.4
58.9	57.8	56.2	Sales/Net Fixed Assets	53.8	53.1	58.6	51.9	56.2	61.4
30.6	28.7	27.2		23.1	23.2	22.1	26.7	31.0	31.7
16.7	14.2	14.2		7.1	11.7	11.6	15.4	19.3	18.2
4.3	4.1	4.0	Sales/Total Assets	5.7	4.8	4.2	3.8	3.6	3.5
3.1	3.1	3.0		3.5	3.2	3.1	3.0	2.9	2.8
2.5	2.3	2.2		2.0	2.1	2.3	2.2	2.2	2.2
.5	.5	.6	% Depr., Dep., Amort./Sales	.8	.7	.6	.5	.5	.5
(1041) .9	(1016) 1.1	(990) 1.0		(68) 1.6	(181) 1.4	(135) 1.2	(188) 1.1	(251) .8	(167) .8
1.7	1.8	1.8		3.1	2.2	2.1	2.0	1.4	1.2
2.0	2.0	2.1	% Officers', Directors' Owners' Comp/Sales	4.6	4.0	2.5	1.7	1.3	.9
(685) 3.8	(645) 3.9	(657) 4.2		(64) 9.2	(163) 6.1	(98) 4.2	(125) 3.0	(145) 2.8	(62) 2.3
6.7	7.4	7.4		15.9	8.8	7.9	5.0	5.0	5.5
28993465M	29011800M	23449906M	Net Sales ($)	64905M	508166M	673480M	1669621M	4270096M	16263638M
10095051M	9908455M	8365311M	Total Assets ($)	28130M	186796M	250670M	622377M	1660235M	5617103M

Current Data Sorted by Assets   Comparative Historical Data

						Type of Statement		
	1	2	10	1	2	Unqualified	25	23
3	15	40	12			Reviewed	59	51
3	16	3	1			Compiled	31	34
21	30	10				Tax Returns	37	36
22	27	22	7	1	2	Other	47	55
	38 (4/1-9/30/10)		213 (10/1/10-3/31/11)				4/1/06-3/31/07 ALL	4/1/07-3/31/08 ALL
0-500M	500M-2MM	2-10MM	10-50MM	50-100MM	100-250MM			
49	89	77	30	2	4	NUMBER OF STATEMENTS	199	199
%	%	%	%	%	%	ASSETS	%	%
17.4	14.3	15.2	16.1			Cash & Equivalents	12.9	13.2
32.7	41.9	39.8	36.8			Trade Receivables (net)	41.1	39.9
12.1	10.4	7.2	7.4			Inventory	10.7	10.5
2.2	4.7	7.1	6.1			All Other Current	6.5	5.1
64.4	71.2	69.4	66.5			Total Current	71.3	68.7
20.9	18.6	20.5	25.2			Fixed Assets (net)	19.8	21.3
4.8	1.7	4.2	1.4			Intangibles (net)	2.5	3.0
9.8	8.4	5.9	7.0			All Other Non-Current	6.4	7.1
100.0	100.0	100.0	100.0			Total	100.0	100.0
						LIABILITIES		
26.6	9.4	8.4	4.9			Notes Payable-Short Term	12.4	11.4
3.2	3.5	4.4	6.4			Cur. Mat.-L.T.D.	3.4	3.4
21.3	18.1	14.9	14.3			Trade Payables	16.6	15.5
.1	.4	.5	.6			Income Taxes Payable	.3	.7
13.9	10.3	13.9	16.7			All Other Current	15.6	12.8
65.0	41.7	42.1	42.9			Total Current	48.4	43.9
28.9	15.0	12.8	7.3			Long-Term Debt	13.2	15.8
.0	.2	.4	1.0			Deferred Taxes	.5	.7
8.7	7.7	3.4	7.8			All Other Non-Current	7.0	5.7
-2.6	35.4	41.2	41.1			Net Worth	31.0	34.0
100.0	100.0	100.0	100.0			Total Liabilities & Net Worth	100.0	100.0
						INCOME DATA		
100.0	100.0	100.0	100.0			Net Sales	100.0	100.0
39.0	35.5	27.8	23.0			Gross Profit	29.8	31.4
38.3	33.4	25.1	18.5			Operating Expenses	24.9	26.2
.7	2.1	2.7	4.5			Operating Profit	4.9	5.2
.2	.4	.6	.4			All Other Expenses (net)	.4	.8
.5	1.7	2.2	4.1			Profit Before Taxes	4.5	4.4
						RATIOS		
3.6	3.2	2.5	2.6				2.6	2.5
1.4	1.7	1.6	1.8			Current	1.5	1.6
.7	1.2	1.2	1.1				1.1	1.2
3.1	2.5	2.4	2.5				2.2	2.0
1.2	1.2	1.3	1.4			Quick	1.3 (198)	1.3
.5	1.0	.9	.9				.7	.9
3 113.8	33 11.0	36 10.2	45 8.2				30 12.0	32 11.4
31 11.8	58 6.3	56 6.6	59 6.2			Sales/Receivables	54 6.8	53 7.0
56 6.5	82 4.5	79 4.6	78 4.7				77 4.7	69 5.3
0 UND	0 UND	0 UND	0 UND				0 UND	0 UND
0 999.8	2 172.1	0 999.8	2 153.4			Cost of Sales/Inventory	4 88.4	5 67.0
31 12.0	34 10.8	20 18.4	25 14.9				22 16.5	26 14.0
4 92.4	11 31.8	12 29.4	12 30.1				10 36.0	11 33.8
19 19.5	27 13.3	22 16.4	23 15.7			Cost of Sales/Payables	21 17.6	21 17.6
43 8.5	51 7.2	37 9.9	43 8.5				36 10.1	35 10.4
9.1	5.0	5.3	5.0				6.2	5.7
26.1	10.4	10.4	7.5			Sales/Working Capital	12.0	11.2
-27.7	26.6	23.3	34.4				94.9	39.9
8.1	12.2	19.7	81.4				21.4	15.2
(31) 2.0	(77) 3.6	(67) 3.6	(28) 18.7			EBIT/Interest	(166) 5.2	(166) 4.9
-13.7	1.0	-1.5	1.4				2.0	1.9
			3.8				6.3	8.7
		(15)	.9			Net Profit + Depr., Dep., Amort./Cur. Mat. L/T/D	(35) 2.6	(42) 4.1
			-1.6				1.7	1.8
.1	.1	.1	.1				.2	.2
.7	.3	.4	.4			Fixed/Worth	.4	.4
-.6	1.3	1.8	1.2				1.4	1.4
.5	.8	.8	.5				.7	.9
4.9	1.5	1.8	1.1			Debt/Worth	1.7	1.9
-2.7	5.5	3.4	2.5				5.8	4.9
79.1	48.2	36.5	33.8				53.8	55.9
(31) 37.7	(76) 13.1	(70) 8.8	(28) 10.9			% Profit Before Taxes/Tangible Net Worth	(171) 29.9	(179) 23.6
3.0	-4.4	-6.9	3.4				11.6	11.9
34.9	19.6	15.4	18.0				20.2	19.8
6.9	3.6	4.2	5.3			% Profit Before Taxes/Total Assets	10.2	8.2
-21.9	-.9	-3.1	.5				2.5	2.9
-97.1	68.7	51.3	31.9				46.0	58.0
32.2	28.2	17.1	13.2			Sales/Net Fixed Assets	23.9	21.8
15.7	10.6	8.2	4.2				10.8	8.0
6.4	3.5	3.1	3.2				3.8	4.1
3.9	2.7	2.5	2.4			Sales/Total Assets	2.9	2.9
2.5	1.8	1.7	1.6				2.1	2.0
.8	.6	.5	1.1				.6	.6
(26) 1.9	(60) 1.5	(67) 1.2	(28) 1.8			% Depr., Dep., Amort./Sales	(166) 1.1	(163) 1.4
4.3	2.2	2.8	3.0				2.5	2.7
3.3	2.6	1.9					2.0	2.5
(23) 8.0	(49) 4.5	(32) 5.2				% Officers', Directors' Owners' Comp/Sales	(98) 4.1	(95) 4.5
9.1	7.9	7.2					7.5	7.7
66911M	273376M	827177M	1385244M	240531M	818206M	Net Sales ($)	3101099M	4440884M
13970M	98990M	323672M	602785M	135291M	730959M	Total Assets ($)	1334880M	1637261M

M = $ thousand   MM = $ million
See Pages 9 through 22 for Explanation of Ratios and Data

Comparative Historical Data | Current Data Sorted by Sales

Type of Statement	4/1/08-3/31/09 ALL	4/1/09-3/31/10 ALL	4/1/10-3/31/11 ALL	0-1MM	1-3MM	3-5MM	5-10MM	10-25MM	25MM & OVER
								38 (4/1-9/30/10)	213 (10/1/10-3/31/11)
Unqualified	21	31	16	3	6	11	26	16	13
Reviewed	61	69	70			1		2	8
Compiled	23	27	23	1	13	3	4	1	1
Tax Returns	34	46	61	14	29	8	6	3	1
Other	58	57	81	12	20	13	15	11	10
NUMBER OF STATEMENTS	197	230	251	30	68	36	51	33	33
ASSETS	%	%	%	%	%	%	%	%	%
Cash & Equivalents	12.2	14.2	15.4	15.1	16.6	14.2	12.7	16.8	17.5
Trade Receivables (net)	41.8	36.6	38.4	28.0	38.0	40.4	42.4	41.9	37.2
Inventory	10.3	10.3	9.4	14.2	9.0	11.6	8.2	6.4	8.8
All Other Current	6.5	5.2	5.2	1.0	3.6	7.4	5.9	6.6	7.1
Total Current	70.9	66.4	68.5	58.3	67.2	73.5	69.1	71.7	70.6
Fixed Assets (net)	19.3	22.8	20.9	20.9	22.9	17.1	21.2	18.5	22.6
Intangibles (net)	2.9	3.7	3.1	6.5	1.8	2.6	3.4	4.2	1.4
All Other Non-Current	6.9	7.1	7.6	14.3	8.0	6.8	6.3	5.6	5.3
Total	100.0	100.0	100.0	100.0	100.0	100.0	100.0	100.0	100.0
LIABILITIES									
Notes Payable-Short Term	13.1	13.8	11.9	14.1	18.6	12.6	8.7	7.0	4.8
Cur. Mat.-L.T.D.	3.1	6.1	4.0	4.0	2.7	5.2	6.6	2.6	3.0
Trade Payables	17.9	16.8	17.1	13.4	19.6	19.4	15.5	17.9	14.4
Income Taxes Payable	.3	.4	.4	.2	.4	.1	.8	.6	.1
All Other Current	16.6	14.1	12.8	15.8	10.1	11.8	10.3	17.1	16.7
Total Current	51.0	51.2	46.2	47.4	51.4	49.0	41.9	45.3	38.9
Long-Term Debt	12.6	15.1	16.1	23.1	19.6	22.9	12.6	9.7	6.9
Deferred Taxes	.5	.4	.3	.0	.2	.2	.6	.3	.9
All Other Non-Current	5.4	5.4	6.5	12.2	8.3	3.1	4.6	3.1	7.8
Net Worth	30.5	27.9	30.8	17.4	20.5	24.8	40.4	41.6	45.5
Total Liabilities & Net Worth	100.0	100.0	100.0	100.0	100.0	100.0	100.0	100.0	100.0
INCOME DATA									
Net Sales	100.0	100.0	100.0	100.0	100.0	100.0	100.0	100.0	100.0
Gross Profit	31.9	32.0	32.2	42.2	38.0	30.8	29.4	25.9	23.1
Operating Expenses	26.9	29.8	29.7	43.4	36.1	28.3	26.9	22.1	17.6
Operating Profit	5.0	2.2	2.5	-1.2	1.8	2.5	2.6	3.8	5.5
All Other Expenses (net)	.5	.5	.4	.3	.3	.5	1.0	-.1	.3
Profit Before Taxes	4.5	1.7	2.1	-1.4	1.5	2.0	1.6	4.0	5.2

RATIOS

Ratio	08-09 ALL	09-10 ALL	10-11 ALL	0-1MM	1-3MM	3-5MM	5-10MM	10-25MM	25MM & OVER
Current	2.4	2.7	2.9	7.6	3.1	2.4	2.8	2.1	2.9
	1.6	1.7	1.7	1.6	1.8	1.7	1.7	1.5	2.0
	1.2	1.1	1.2	.8	1.0	1.2	1.2	1.2	1.4
Quick	1.9	2.2	2.5	6.7	2.7	2.2	2.6	1.9	2.6
	1.2	1.2	1.3	1.2	1.2	1.2	1.4	1.2	1.5
	.8	.7	.8	.5	.7	.9	.8	1.0	1.0
Sales/Receivables	31 11.8	30 12.1	31 11.8	13 29.0	26 14.2	16 23.5	41 8.9	34 10.7	42 8.8
	52 7.1	51 7.1	53 6.9	45 8.1	46 8.0	60 6.1	55 6.7	51 7.2	58 6.3
	74 5.0	70 5.2	75 4.8	66 5.6	75 4.9	87 4.2	75 4.9	82 4.5	75 4.9
Cost of Sales/Inventory	0 UND	0 UND	0 UND	0 UND	0 UND	0 UND	0 UND	0 UND	0 UND
	3 109.8	6 65.2	2 232.9	0 UND	0 UND	3 115.6	3 126.1	0 999.8	4 95.4
	31 11.8	33 11.2	25 14.6	70 5.2	25 14.5	22 16.7	25 14.6	14 25.9	26 14.0
Cost of Sales/Payables	11 32.0	10 37.2	12 31.7	3 116.1	12 31.2	8 45.3	12 29.5	13 28.9	13 29.1
	25 14.7	24 15.3	24 15.1	14 25.2	29 12.8	23 15.6	22 16.5	24 15.0	22 16.4
	44 8.4	41 8.8	43 8.5	41 8.9	49 7.4	53 6.9	40 9.1	37 9.9	39 9.4
Sales/Working Capital	6.1	5.4	5.3	2.8	5.3	4.4	6.1	6.5	4.1
	10.2	10.6	10.8	18.5	10.6	14.5	10.9	14.1	6.7
	44.8	332.1	34.7	-20.1	838.2	29.9	25.8	23.3	27.0
EBIT/Interest	23.7	17.9	18.4	5.8	10.7	9.1	11.1	67.3	91.1
	(172) 6.0	(200) 3.7	(208) 3.8	(19) 1.6	(54) 2.7	(33) 4.6	(46) 2.5	(26) 8.6	(30) 19.1
	1.8	-.4	-.1	-13.7	-3.1	1.4	-1.2	.5	2.6
Net Profit + Depr., Dep., Amort./Cur. Mat. L/T/D	17.7	9.8	7.0					8.5	
	(37) 4.4	(34) 3.0	(33) 2.7					(10) 1.6	
	1.7	1.3	.5					-.6	
Fixed/Worth	.1	.2	.1	.1	.1	.1	.1	.1	.1
	.4	.4	.4	2.0	.6	.3	.4	.4	.4
	1.5	2.1	2.4	-.8	6.5	6.1	1.6	1.2	1.0
Debt/Worth	.9	.6	.7	.4	.7	.8	.8	.8	.5
	1.7	1.6	1.6	3.9	1.7	1.7	1.6	1.8	1.1
	5.0	5.9	5.5	-5.1	22.8	32.6	3.7	3.1	2.2
% Profit Before Taxes/Tangible Net Worth	53.6	35.7	45.6	58.0	47.9	53.0	40.1	61.1	36.6
	(172) 26.9	(188) 12.0	(211) 13.1	(20) 22.5	(53) 11.9	(29) 12.8	(47) 8.8	(30) 23.4	(32) 13.5
	11.1	-3.3	-1.8	4.3	-25.6	-2.0	-16.0	3.1	5.6
% Profit Before Taxes/Total Assets	20.3	14.7	19.1	15.8	22.6	15.7	15.0	19.0	19.4
	9.3	4.8	4.6	3.6	4.8	3.6	3.8	8.8	7.6
	2.7	-3.2	-2.1	-13.1	-9.1	.8	-3.2	.8	1.9
Sales/Net Fixed Assets	64.3	46.6	59.9	78.0	79.7	73.2	51.9	60.1	50.2
	28.1	19.9	22.9	21.5	19.4	37.4	25.7	21.0	17.3
	10.4	8.5	8.9	8.9	10.0	13.3	9.5	10.1	4.9
Sales/Total Assets	3.9	3.7	3.6	3.4	3.7	4.6	3.2	3.9	3.2
	3.0	2.8	2.6	2.2	2.8	2.6	2.8	2.9	2.4
	2.2	1.9	1.8	1.2	1.8	1.9	2.1	2.0	1.6
% Depr., Dep., Amort./Sales	.5	.7	.6	1.8	.6	.6	.8	.4	.5
	(158) 1.1	(189) 1.5	(183) 1.5	(15) 2.4	(43) 1.5	(27) 1.2	(39) 1.5	(32) .9	(27) 1.5
	2.3	2.9	2.7	5.0	2.5	2.9	2.2	2.5	2.7
% Officers', Directors', Owners' Comp/Sales	2.0	2.2	2.6	2.9	2.9	1.6	2.0	1.2	
	(92) 4.0	(105) 4.7	(111) 5.3	(12) 6.1	(38) 6.6	(18) 4.0	(21) 5.1	(16) 3.8	
	7.2	7.7	8.2	9.1	8.5	6.2	6.7	7.6	
Net Sales ($)	3546219M	3862510M	3611445M	19012M	131438M	138577M	351473M	537173M	2433772M
Total Assets ($)	1571294M	2061419M	1905667M	11018M	53992M	58866M	161007M	209172M	1411612M

Current Data Sorted by Assets   Comparative Historical Data

0-500M	500M-2MM	2-10MM	10-50MM	50-100MM	100-250MM	Type of Statement	4/1/06-3/31/07 ALL	4/1/07-3/31/08 ALL
2	2	13	19	5	2	Unqualified	42	38
5	24	62	13			Reviewed	110	90
9	24	8	3		3	Compiled	66	45
34	21	8	2			Tax Returns	60	47
26	33	32	13			Other	75	87
	69 (4/1-9/30/10)		294 (10/1/10-3/31/11)					
76	104	123	50	8	2	NUMBER OF STATEMENTS	353	307
%	%	%	%	%	%	ASSETS	%	%
16.5	12.9	15.5	14.9			Cash & Equivalents	9.8	13.0
35.9	51.4	47.8	47.4			Trade Receivables (net)	54.6	54.2
6.4	5.3	4.2	3.3			Inventory	6.2	5.1
4.4	5.6	9.6	12.3			All Other Current	7.9	7.7
63.2	75.2	77.2	77.9			Total Current	78.4	80.1
25.3	16.3	11.2	11.0			Fixed Assets (net)	14.2	12.5
3.8	2.5	2.7	1.2			Intangibles (net)	1.4	1.4
7.7	6.0	8.9	9.9			All Other Non-Current	6.0	6.0
100.0	100.0	100.0	100.0			Total	100.0	100.0
						LIABILITIES		
38.7	15.1	9.3	8.2			Notes Payable-Short Term	14.0	12.3
3.8	2.2	1.6	1.4			Cur. Mat.-L.T.D.	2.9	2.5
16.4	16.5	15.3	14.9			Trade Payables	17.8	14.1
.2	.9	.3	.3			Income Taxes Payable	.8	.6
22.6	10.1	14.5	16.0			All Other Current	17.5	18.2
81.7	44.9	41.0	40.7			Total Current	53.0	47.8
19.7	7.7	7.9	6.0			Long-Term Debt	9.2	7.8
.1	.4	.3	.3			Deferred Taxes	.3	.3
17.9	4.1	3.7	5.7			All Other Non-Current	4.4	4.3
-19.5	42.9	47.1	47.3			Net Worth	33.0	39.8
100.0	100.0	100.0	100.0			Total Liabilities & Net Worth	100.0	100.0
						INCOME DATA		
100.0	100.0	100.0	100.0			Net Sales	100.0	100.0
38.3	25.4	21.7	14.2			Gross Profit	24.9	25.7
37.2	26.6	19.3	13.6			Operating Expenses	19.9	19.9
1.1	-1.3	2.4	.6			Operating Profit	5.0	5.8
.9	.5	.2	.2			All Other Expenses (net)	.3	.2
.2	-1.8	2.2	.3			Profit Before Taxes	4.6	5.6
						RATIOS		
1.9	3.2	3.3	3.2			Current	2.3	2.8
1.0	1.9	2.1	2.0				1.6	1.8
.5	1.2	1.4	1.4				1.1	1.3
1.7	2.8	2.7	2.4			Quick	1.9	2.3
.7	1.5	1.7	1.6				1.3	1.5
.4	.9	1.1	1.1				.8	1.0
0 UND	43 8.6	43 8.4	66 5.6			Sales/Receivables	39 9.4	43 8.5
27 13.5	62 5.9	64 5.7	76 4.8				65 5.6	66 5.5
61 6.0	81 4.5	85 4.3	91 4.0				85 4.3	84 4.3
0 UND	0 UND	0 UND	0 UND			Cost of Sales/Inventory	0 UND	0 UND
0 UND	1 295.8	1 249.6	2 152.1				2 224.9	1 298.2
6 64.1	11 33.5	9 38.5	6 58.6				10 34.9	9 40.0
0 UND	10 37.8	10 35.2	15 24.8			Cost of Sales/Payables	10 35.2	9 41.9
12 29.3	19 19.4	21 17.1	24 15.2				20 18.7	18 20.7
31 11.6	39 9.4	33 11.1	38 9.6				34 10.7	29 12.8
16.3	5.1	4.1	3.7			Sales/Working Capital	7.1	5.8
462.3	8.3	6.6	6.0				11.6	9.1
-14.7	79.1	15.2	11.1				41.7	19.5
8.6	9.5	17.0	18.6			EBIT/Interest	29.6	27.8
(64) 1.5	(91) 1.8	(105) 4.7	(42) 2.2				(320) 6.5	(267) 8.4
-7.9	-17.4	1.0	-6.3				2.1	2.0
	5.4	11.6	10.8			Net Profit + Depr., Dep., Amort./Cur. Mat. L/T/D	12.0	17.6
	(14) .5	(27) 4.9	(18) 2.4				(78) 4.4	(69) 5.4
	-12.7	1.1	-.5				1.8	1.2
.3	.1	.1	.1			Fixed/Worth	.1	.1
1.9	.3	.2	.2				.3	.2
-.3	.9	.4	.5				1.0	.6
1.1	.4	.4	.6			Debt/Worth	.9	.6
14.8	1.1	1.0	1.1				1.8	1.4
-2.8	2.9	2.4	1.8				4.5	3.1
100.0	23.3	29.4	17.4			% Profit Before Taxes/Tangible Net Worth	65.3	63.9
(43) 47.6	(88) 3.6	(113) 9.3	(49) 3.1				(314) 31.6	(287) 33.0
-32.6	-23.5	1.5	-8.7				12.9	9.8
42.7	9.2	12.5	9.4			% Profit Before Taxes/Total Assets	24.3	27.2
4.9	1.2	3.9	1.4				10.7	13.2
-25.7	-15.3	.1	-4.0				2.6	3.8
76.0	64.5	75.5	71.2			Sales/Net Fixed Assets	97.2	99.5
38.4	26.1	36.0	27.8				41.4	46.4
16.7	15.4	18.0	14.6				21.7	21.7
7.5	3.7	3.3	2.7			Sales/Total Assets	4.4	4.0
4.8	2.9	2.6	2.3				3.4	3.2
3.1	2.3	1.9	1.8				2.6	2.5
.6	.4	.4	.3			% Depr., Dep., Amort./Sales	.3	.3
(51) 1.2	(82) .9	(110) .9	(46) .6				(287) .7	(241) .6
1.9	1.8	1.4	1.1				1.1	1.1
3.3	2.9	1.7	1.0			% Officers', Directors' Owners' Comp/Sales	1.8	1.9
(50) 7.2	(72) 5.2	(62) 3.0	(21) 2.3				(177) 3.3	(157) 3.2
11.4	8.1	5.1	3.3				6.8	7.0
95907M	379924M	1523286M	2055216M	2050613M	465393M	Net Sales ($)	7937407M	5783832M
17696M	117794M	581529M	934092M	650503M	233313M	Total Assets ($)	2349514M	2048015M

© RMA 2011

M = $ thousand   MM = $ million
See Pages 9 through 22 for Explanation of Ratios and Data

Comparative Historical Data				Current Data Sorted by Sales					

Type of Statement

				Type of Statement						
41	48	43		Unqualified	1	1	2	1	15	23
123	131	104		Reviewed	2	9	18	34	31	10
41	33	44		Compiled	4	15	10	6	5	4
67	62	68		Tax Returns	21	24	8	5	5	5
101	91	104		Other	12	31	11	24	16	10
4/1/08-3/31/09 ALL	4/1/09-3/31/10 ALL	4/1/10-3/31/11 ALL			69 (4/1-9/30/10)			294 (10/1/10-3/31/11)		
					0-1MM	1-3MM	3-5MM	5-10MM	10-25MM	25MM & OVER
373	365	363		NUMBER OF STATEMENTS	40	80	49	70	72	52
%	%	%		ASSETS	%	%	%	%	%	%
14.1	16.4	15.2		Cash & Equivalents	16.0	14.6	15.1	17.9	11.4	17.3
51.5	45.6	45.7		Trade Receivables (net)	40.3	39.7	48.4	48.4	49.5	47.4
6.0	5.4	4.9		Inventory	6.1	6.4	5.0	4.0	4.8	2.9
6.8	8.1	7.7		All Other Current	4.6	4.1	6.9	9.7	10.3	9.8
78.4	75.4	73.4		Total Current	67.1	64.8	75.3	80.0	76.1	77.5
12.7	14.4	16.0		Fixed Assets (net)	23.9	21.4	17.0	10.3	12.4	13.5
1.4	3.1	2.7		Intangibles (net)	2.2	4.9	3.4	1.2	2.1	2.0
7.5	7.0	7.8		All Other Non-Current	6.7	8.9	4.3	8.5	9.4	7.0
100.0	100.0	100.0		Total	100.0	100.0	100.0	100.0	100.0	100.0
				LIABILITIES						
14.2	17.4	17.1		Notes Payable-Short Term	44.3	20.5	19.3	10.3	9.9	7.8
3.0	2.2	2.2		Cur. Mat.-L.T.D.	3.0	3.3	2.3	2.0	1.3	1.6
14.9	14.1	15.7		Trade Payables	17.9	15.8	14.4	15.7	16.3	14.1
.5	.4	.4		Income Taxes Payable	.3	.5	1.0	.3	.2	.2
18.5	16.3	15.5		All Other Current	26.1	12.2	12.3	12.5	14.7	20.2
51.1	50.4	50.8		Total Current	91.6	52.4	49.4	40.8	42.3	43.8
7.7	11.1	10.4		Long-Term Debt	13.6	17.3	8.3	7.2	6.6	8.7
.2	.4	.3		Deferred Taxes	.2	.4	.3	.3	.2	.2
4.2	4.3	7.1		All Other Non-Current	25.4	7.0	4.1	4.1	2.8	5.7
36.8	33.8	31.4		Net Worth	-31.0	22.9	37.9	47.7	48.0	41.5
100.0	100.0	100.0		Total Liabilities & Net Worth	100.0	100.0	100.0	100.0	100.0	100.0
				INCOME DATA						
100.0	100.0	100.0		Net Sales	100.0	100.0	100.0	100.0	100.0	100.0
26.1	25.5	25.3		Gross Profit	41.6	33.8	21.2	22.3	18.8	16.8
22.4	23.7	24.7		Operating Expenses	39.7	34.8	20.2	21.7	17.1	16.2
3.7	1.8	.7		Operating Profit	1.9	-1.0	.9	.6	1.7	.6
.4	.6	.4		All Other Expenses (net)	1.8	.7	.2	.0	.1	.4
3.3	1.2	.2		Profit Before Taxes	.2	-1.7	.8	.6	1.6	.3
				RATIOS						
2.5	3.1	3.0			1.6	3.0	3.9	3.5	3.1	2.8
1.7	1.8	1.8		Current	.9	1.6	1.8	2.2	2.0	1.9
1.2	1.2	1.1			.6	.9	1.0	1.5	1.2	1.4
2.3	2.5	2.7			1.4	2.8	3.6	3.1	2.3	2.2
1.4	1.5	1.4		Quick	.8	1.3	1.4	1.9	1.5	1.6
.9	.9	.9			.3	.6	.9	1.1	1.0	1.1

41	8.9	39	9.3	40	9.0	Sales/Receivables	3	109.5	19	19.5	41	9.0	45	8.1	44	8.3	59	6.2
62	5.9	60	6.1	62	5.9		46	7.9	50	7.4	59	6.2	64	5.7	66	5.5	75	4.8
82	4.4	78	4.7	83	4.4		73	5.0	73	5.0	93	3.9	84	4.4	84	4.3	89	4.1
0	UND	0	UND	0	UND	Cost of Sales/Inventory	0	UND	0	UND	0	UND	0	UND	0	UND	0	UND
1	398.5	1	345.3	1	333.5		0	UND	1	280.1	1	330.6	0	791.8	4	96.3	2	232.8
10	38.2	9	39.1	9	38.5		8	47.6	14	26.7	10	35.2	7	56.1	13	28.4	4	83.1
9	41.9	9	40.9	10	38.1	Cost of Sales/Payables	0	UND	6	62.3	9	41.3	12	30.6	11	33.3	13	29.0
18	20.6	17	21.3	19	19.2		18	20.3	18	20.4	18	20.0	21	17.2	21	17.2	22	16.5
32	11.5	32	11.5	33	10.9		51	7.2	38	9.6	29	12.8	34	10.8	33	11.1	36	10.2

6.1	5.3	5.0		Sales/Working Capital	13.4	6.0	4.5	4.1	5.2	4.7
9.7	8.7	8.8			-53.2	15.4	8.4	6.5	7.9	6.6
32.3	29.0	88.9			-13.2	-83.9	NM	17.1	19.8	11.1

	25.5		20.9		12.9	EBIT/Interest		4.9		7.5		10.3		17.0		14.6		46.8
(324)	6.7	(317)	5.1	(312)	3.1		(30)	.7	(68)	2.9	(44)	2.7	(60)	4.4	(65)	4.3	(45)	4.8
	1.3		-.4		-5.0			-7.2		-10.3		-11.6		-5.5		.8		-4.8
	17.8		15.4		8.6	Net Profit + Depr., Dep., Amort./Cur. Mat. L/T/D								11.1		11.6		8.7
(72)	4.4	(66)	3.0	(66)	3.1								(12)	3.3	(24)	4.1	(14)	2.1
	.9		.5		-.7									-1.9		1.1		-.5
	.1		.1		.1	Fixed/Worth		.2		.2		.2		.1		.1		.1
	.2		.2		.3			2.9		.6		.2		.1		.2		.2
	.6		.9		.9			-.3		-3.0		2.4		.4		.5		.5
	.7		.6		.6	Debt/Worth		1.3		.6		.3		.4		.4		.6
	1.5		1.3		1.3			19.5		1.9		1.1		.9		1.0		1.3
	3.8		5.5		4.4			-3.0		-16.1		70.7		1.9		2.4		2.0
	51.3		38.5		34.5	% Profit Before Taxes/Tangible Net Worth		100.0		41.1		29.6		35.3		22.4		33.3
(334)	23.7	(310)	13.4	(300)	7.2		(23)	45.5	(58)	8.3	(38)	7.5	(64)	7.0	(69)	5.6	(48)	8.0
	4.8		.1		-5.6			-66.7		-19.1		-8.8		-6.2		1.4		-8.1
	19.7		17.7		12.7	% Profit Before Taxes/Total Assets		39.8		10.5		13.2		12.9		8.9		12.4
	8.6		4.8		2.6			3.4		1.8		1.9		3.8		3.1		2.7
	.7		-2.8		-7.4			-24.9		-22.9		-10.7		-9.4		.2		-5.4
	109.8		77.8		75.2	Sales/Net Fixed Assets		90.2		66.0		47.9		75.9		94.2		83.9
	40.8		37.2		31.0			30.8		22.7		27.6		37.6		34.5		32.3
	19.4		17.2		16.8			9.3		13.2		17.0		21.4		18.2		20.1
	4.2		3.8		3.8	Sales/Total Assets		5.2		5.2		3.8		3.5		3.5		2.9
	3.1		2.9		2.8			3.7		3.1		2.8		2.6		2.9		2.6
	2.4		2.2		2.1			2.1		2.3		2.1		1.9		2.1		2.1
	.3		.4		.4	% Depr., Dep., Amort./Sales		.9		.7		.5		.4		.3		.3
(297)	.7	(300)	.8	(294)	.9		(27)	1.6	(55)	1.2	(42)	.9	(58)	.8	(69)	.8	(43)	.5
	1.4		1.4		1.5			4.3		2.1		1.6		1.3		1.3		1.0
	2.1		2.2		2.0	% Officers', Directors' Owners' Comp/Sales		2.7		4.0		2.6		2.5		1.3		.9
(203)	4.1	(184)	4.4	(208)	4.1		(27)	9.9	(54)	6.8	(33)	4.2	(35)	3.8	(37)	1.9	(22)	1.8
	7.3		8.0		7.9			16.2		9.0		6.4		6.2		3.7		4.1

7181181M	6602220M	6570339M		Net Sales ($)	22309M	154140M	189850M	494764M	1232586M	4476690M
2891712M	3060904M	2534927M		Total Assets ($)	7131M	55199M	74863M	208627M	503798M	1685309M

M = $ thousand   MM = $ million
See Pages 9 through 22 for Explanation of Ratios and Data

Current Data Sorted by Assets / Comparative Historical Data

0-500M	500M-2MM	2-10MM	10-50MM	50-100MM	100-250MM	Type of Statement	4/1/06-3/31/07 ALL	4/1/07-3/31/08 ALL
	2	13	1			Unqualified	23	21
2	25	32	1			Reviewed	70	37
6	11	5	2			Compiled	31	27
26	16	3				Tax Returns	40	34
21	16	11	2			Other	30	47
33 (4/1-9/30/10)			162 (10/1/10-3/31/11)				194	166
55	70	64	6			NUMBER OF STATEMENTS		
%	%	%	%	%	%	**ASSETS**	%	%
22.7	12.7	19.4				Cash & Equivalents	14.2	12.5
30.7	44.3	47.0				Trade Receivables (net)	45.1	44.8
2.6	2.9	2.2				Inventory	2.5	2.3
8.1	8.3	11.9				All Other Current	9.6	9.3
64.1	68.2	80.6	D A T A	D A T A		Total Current	71.4	68.9
24.0	18.9	15.1				Fixed Assets (net)	20.2	22.6
4.1	2.7	1.5	N O T	N O T		Intangibles (net)	1.7	2.2
7.8	10.2	2.9				All Other Non-Current	6.7	6.3
100.0	100.0	100.0	A V A I L A B L E	A V A I L A B L E		Total	100.0	100.0
						LIABILITIES		
35.8	15.1	7.5				Notes Payable-Short Term	11.9	17.2
3.5	2.6	1.4				Cur. Mat.-L.T.D.	2.9	4.0
13.5	12.4	13.8				Trade Payables	14.0	13.9
1.0	.7	.7				Income Taxes Payable	.6	.6
25.1	9.2	15.6				All Other Current	14.1	12.4
79.0	40.0	39.0				Total Current	43.6	48.2
22.2	9.2	4.5				Long-Term Debt	13.8	16.1
.0	.6	.2				Deferred Taxes	.3	.5
14.0	6.4	2.0				All Other Non-Current	1.5	7.7
-15.2	43.8	54.3				Net Worth	40.8	27.5
100.0	100.0	100.0				Total Liabilities & Net Worth	100.0	100.0
						INCOME DATA		
100.0	100.0	100.0				Net Sales	100.0	100.0
48.7	29.4	22.7				Gross Profit	32.7	31.3
44.1	27.8	18.7				Operating Expenses	27.0	26.0
4.6	1.5	4.0				Operating Profit	5.7	5.4
.8	.4	-.3				All Other Expenses (net)	.5	.4
3.8	1.2	4.3				Profit Before Taxes	5.2	4.9
						RATIOS		
4.1	3.6	3.8					3.2	2.7
1.1	1.8	2.3				Current	1.7	1.8
.5	1.2	1.5					1.2	1.1
3.3	3.4	3.0					2.6	2.2
1.0	1.5	1.8				Quick	(193) 1.6	1.5
.3	.9	1.1					.9	.9
0 UND	38 9.7	51 7.1					29 12.5	25 14.4
18 19.8	54 6.8	78 4.7				Sales/Receivables	58 6.3	58 6.3
45 8.1	81 4.5	98 3.7					86 4.2	77 4.7
0 UND	0 UND	0 UND					0 UND	0 UND
0 UND	0 UND	0 UND				Cost of Sales/Inventory	0 UND	0 UND
0 UND	6 65.5	2 242.1					3 137.2	3 133.4
0 UND	6 60.2	10 34.8					7 49.8	6 57.7
12 30.6	16 22.4	16 22.2				Cost of Sales/Payables	20 18.4	19 19.7
27 13.4	32 11.3	34 10.6					36 10.1	35 10.4
8.9	6.1	3.5					5.6	6.0
57.0	11.3	6.0				Sales/Working Capital	9.1	10.6
-13.3	24.5	8.8					31.6	51.3
18.0	18.0	24.1					22.9	26.4
(45) 2.8	(62) 3.6	(48) 7.9				EBIT/Interest	(169) 8.0	(149) 7.8
.0	-.3	1.0					2.3	2.3
	5.4	26.8					12.2	8.6
	(15) 2.3	(15) 5.2				Net Profit + Depr., Dep., Amort./Cur. Mat. L/T/D	(32) 5.2	(28) 5.0
	-.2	3.0					2.2	1.1
.2	.2	.1					.1	.1
1.1	.4	.2				Fixed/Worth	.4	.4
-.6	.8	.4					.8	1.1
.5	.4	.4					.5	.6
2.7	.8	.8				Debt/Worth	1.3	1.4
-3.4	4.3	1.7					3.8	4.0
224.2	31.8	32.6					55.7	58.7
(36) 57.6	(61) 10.0	(62) 10.6				% Profit Before Taxes/Tangible Net Worth	(171) 24.7	(141) 26.3
9.9	-1.5	1.8					9.6	10.0
45.3	15.7	18.9					25.7	31.1
16.5	4.4	5.5				% Profit Before Taxes/Total Assets	11.2	12.2
-6.3	-2.5	1.0					3.1	3.7
98.0	53.3	50.5					69.5	64.1
33.8	21.4	22.5				Sales/Net Fixed Assets	24.2	23.9
16.1	8.5	11.2					11.3	11.8
10.6	3.6	2.9					4.0	4.2
5.2	3.0	2.2				Sales/Total Assets	3.0	3.3
3.1	2.1	1.6					2.2	2.4
.8	.8	.5					.5	.6
(29) 1.2	(57) 1.7	(57) 1.3				% Depr., Dep., Amort./Sales	(159) 1.2	(140) 1.0
2.4	2.5	2.0					2.1	1.9
4.0	3.8	1.4					2.3	2.6
(30) 8.6	(45) 4.6	(31) 2.8				% Officers', Directors' Owners' Comp/Sales	(107) 4.6	(99) 4.8
17.0	7.2	5.2					8.8	8.5
59921M	259772M	652907M	149115M			Net Sales ($)	1929034M	1615756M
10899M	80708M	282830M	86468M			Total Assets ($)	808167M	548628M

© RMA 2011

M = $ thousand   MM = $ million
See Pages 9 through 22 for Explanation of Ratios and Data

Comparative Historical Data | Current Data Sorted by Sales

Type of Statement									
22	19	16	Unqualified		3	1	3	7	2
73	65	60	Reviewed	1	15	10	18	16	
31	31	24	Compiled	2	11	3	5	3	
42	33	45	Tax Returns	12	21	7	4	1	
43	52	50	Other	14	17	5	6	7	1
4/1/08-3/31/09 ALL	4/1/09-3/31/10 ALL	4/1/10-3/31/11 ALL		33 (4/1-9/30/10)		162 (10/1/10-3/31/11)			
				0-1MM	1-3MM	3-5MM	5-10MM	10-25MM	25MM & OVER
211	200	195	NUMBER OF STATEMENTS	29	67	26	36	34	3
%	%	%		%	%	%	%	%	%
			ASSETS						
14.1	16.5	17.9	Cash & Equivalents	24.6	17.9	13.9	17.3	16.9	
45.7	44.0	41.2	Trade Receivables (net)	26.8	36.2	44.2	49.5	52.6	
3.1	2.6	2.6	Inventory	3.1	3.3	2.3	2.7	.6	
10.0	8.4	9.5	All Other Current	10.1	7.0	8.7	10.0	12.9	
73.0	71.5	71.1	Total Current	64.6	64.4	69.0	79.6	83.0	
18.6	19.7	19.1	Fixed Assets (net)	22.8	23.0	18.5	15.7	11.3	
2.0	1.8	2.8	Intangibles (net)	5.4	1.5	7.6	.4	2.1	
6.4	7.1	7.0	All Other Non-Current	7.2	11.2	4.9	4.4	3.6	
100.0	100.0	100.0	Total	100.0	100.0	100.0	100.0	100.0	
			LIABILITIES						
13.7	16.3	18.3	Notes Payable-Short Term	23.7	27.2	10.2	13.4	7.8	
4.8	3.5	2.5	Cur. Mat.-L.T.D.	5.1	2.0	3.1	2.2	1.4	
13.1	12.4	12.9	Trade Payables	12.1	11.8	11.4	11.9	18.8	
.7	.6	.8	Income Taxes Payable	1.9	.2	.5	1.0	.7	
16.8	14.7	15.6	All Other Current	16.6	16.7	15.4	14.4	14.6	
49.2	47.4	50.2	Total Current	59.5	58.0	40.6	43.0	43.3	
11.2	9.4	11.4	Long-Term Debt	11.3	20.6	7.4	4.9	2.6	
.4	.5	.3	Deferred Taxes	.0	.4	1.0	.1	.1	
5.3	7.5	7.1	All Other Non-Current	15.8	6.5	13.3	2.1	1.6	
33.9	35.2	31.1	Net Worth	13.4	14.5	37.8	49.9	52.4	
100.0	100.0	100.0	Total Liabilties & Net Worth	100.0	100.0	100.0	100.0	100.0	
			INCOME DATA						
100.0	100.0	100.0	Net Sales	100.0	100.0	100.0	100.0	100.0	
31.9	32.2	32.4	Gross Profit	52.6	35.7	27.0	26.4	20.2	
26.8	29.5	29.0	Operating Expenses	47.7	34.3	23.5	21.3	16.1	
5.1	2.7	3.4	Operating Profit	4.8	1.5	3.4	5.1	4.1	
.6	.4	.3	All Other Expenses (net)	1.1	.2	.2	-.2	.4	
4.5	2.2	3.1	Profit Before Taxes	3.8	1.3	3.2	5.3	3.8	
			RATIOS						
2.9	3.6	3.9	Current	7.1	4.1	3.3	5.2	3.2	
1.8	1.9	1.9		1.1	1.7	1.9	2.0	2.2	
1.2	1.2	1.1		.5	1.0	1.2	1.3	1.4	
2.6	3.1	3.3	Quick	6.7	3.8	3.0	5.0	2.7	
1.4	1.5	1.5		1.1	1.4	1.7	1.7	1.8	
.9	.9	.8		.3	.7	1.0	1.0	1.0	
32 11.4	28 12.9	27 13.8	Sales/Receivables	0 UND	22 17.0	40 9.2	46 8.0	47 7.8	
57 6.4	55 6.6	53 6.8		14 25.7	45 8.1	69 5.3	77 4.8	68 5.4	
80 4.6	81 4.5	84 4.4		43 8.4	72 5.1	85 4.3	92 4.0	97 3.7	
0 UND	0 UND	0 UND	Cost of Sales/Inventory	0 UND	0 UND	0 UND	0 UND	0 UND	
0 UND	0 UND	0 UND		0 UND	0 UND	0 UND	0 UND	0 UND	
1 336.0	1 248.5	2 199.9		0 UND	7 49.7	2 197.2	1 339.7	1 355.5	
7 51.4	6 61.1	6 64.6	Cost of Sales/Payables	0 UND	3 122.3	4 83.5	7 55.4	12 29.9	
15 24.9	14 25.3	16 23.3		17 22.0	15 24.6	18 20.3	14 25.4	18 20.5	
30 12.1	28 13.1	32 11.4		27 13.6	30 12.2	36 10.2	29 12.5	34 10.9	
5.6	5.0	4.6	Sales/Working Capital	5.5	5.4	4.0	3.9	4.0	
10.3	9.0	9.0		47.1	14.2	8.8	7.5	6.0	
34.3	39.9	44.5		-10.3	999.8	24.0	16.8	10.6	
25.5	23.7	19.5	EBIT/Interest	19.8	11.6	16.5	24.7	44.0	
(184) 8.0	(168) 4.4	(161) 4.1		(23) 3.0	(57) 2.8	(22) 3.9	(27) 8.2	(30) 9.5	
2.0	-1.8	.0		-.1	-2.1	.0	1.2	1.8	
8.3	13.4	9.9	Net Profit + Depr., Dep., Amort./Cur. Mat. L/T/D					25.8	
(44) 3.5	(37) 2.9	(34) 3.4						(12) 6.7	
1.7	.6	.4						.4	
.1	.1	.1	Fixed/Worth	.1	.1	.1	.1	.1	
.4	.3	.4		1.0	.5	.4	.3	.2	
1.0	1.0	1.1		-1.3	2.7	1.2	.8	.3	
.6	.4	.4	Debt/Worth	.3	.4	.4	.2	.4	
1.4	1.0	1.1		2.7	1.2	.8	.9	.8	
4.2	3.1	4.0		-5.0	19.7	5.5	2.6	1.8	
60.0	35.7	45.8	% Profit Before Taxes/Tangible Net Worth	205.0	44.4	29.8	49.8	31.7	
(188) 25.0	(172) 14.1	(165) 15.1		(21) 54.8	(52) 10.2	(21) 4.3	(35) 16.2	(33) 15.2	
9.0	-2.5	1.4		10.3	-7.8	-.9	1.7	2.8	
27.7	19.8	21.7	% Profit Before Taxes/Total Assets	44.1	22.5	21.9	25.7	15.4	
9.0	5.4	6.1		9.6	4.9	3.4	7.7	6.9	
2.8	-4.7	-.9		-12.1	-7.1	-1.0	.8	1.5	
79.2	58.2	66.3	Sales/Net Fixed Assets	123.5	48.1	122.4	90.8	61.4	
27.6	24.0	24.8		32.8	21.2	17.6	26.9	36.2	
13.3	12.2	11.8		13.3	8.6	9.2	14.9	16.9	
4.4	4.4	4.4	Sales/Total Assets	7.4	5.1	3.5	3.3	3.1	
3.3	3.0	2.9		3.6	3.1	3.0	2.7	2.7	
2.4	2.1	2.1		2.3	2.0	2.0	1.8	2.1	
.5	.8	.7	% Depr., Dep., Amort./Sales	1.1	.8	.9	.4	.4	
(167) .9	(166) 1.3	(149) 1.3		(14) 1.7	(50) 1.6	(19) 1.8	(31) 1.5	(32) .7	
1.7	2.3	2.3		2.6	2.9	2.4	2.3	1.4	
2.3	3.1	2.9	% Officers', Directors' Owners' Comp/Sales	8.8	3.4	3.9	1.7	1.2	
(105) 4.6	(113) 5.8	(108) 4.5		(12) 14.9	(46) 5.0	(12) 5.7	(22) 3.3	(16) 2.6	
8.8	10.7	8.4		21.4	8.0	8.1	4.6	4.0	
2593286M	3022234M	1121715M	Net Sales ($)	14405M	133913M	102691M	243636M	516950M	110120M
724646M	888566M	460905M	Total Assets ($)	4274M	51755M	42861M	107971M	205050M	48994M

M = $ thousand   MM = $ million
See Pages 9 through 22 for Explanation of Ratios and Data

Current Data Sorted by Assets | ## Comparative Historical Data

	0-500M	500M-2MM	2-10MM	10-50MM	50-100MM	100-250MM	Type of Statement	4/1/06-3/31/07 ALL	4/1/07-3/31/08 ALL
		1	4	3			Unqualified	8	11
		13	27	5			Reviewed	57	50
	4	14	6				Compiled	27	25
	13	10	7				Tax Returns	20	30
	14	32	22	5			Other	56	64
		25 (4/1-9/30/10)		155 (10/1/10-3/31/11)					
NUMBER OF STATEMENTS	31	70	66	13				168	180
	%	%	%	%	%	%	**ASSETS**	%	%
	11.8	13.2	7.0	8.9	D	D	Cash & Equivalents	9.0	10.3
	33.8	43.8	53.0	49.7	A	A	Trade Receivables (net)	49.3	49.5
	20.8	12.0	13.9	14.3	T	T	Inventory	15.9	12.8
	1.4	4.4	6.7	9.3	A	A	All Other Current	5.1	6.9
	67.8	73.4	80.5	82.3			Total Current	79.3	79.4
	18.3	13.0	12.8	8.3	N	N	Fixed Assets (net)	15.3	14.1
	1.1	3.1	2.1	5.3	O	O	Intangibles (net)	1.2	1.9
	12.7	10.5	4.5	4.1	T	T	All Other Non-Current	4.2	4.5
	100.0	100.0	100.0	100.0			Total	100.0	100.0
					A	A	**LIABILITIES**		
	27.0	16.1	16.6	24.4	V	V	Notes Payable-Short Term	16.9	18.4
	3.4	2.0	2.3	2.0	A	A	Cur. Mat.-L.T.D.	2.8	3.4
	27.9	14.1	19.9	14.0	I	I	Trade Payables	17.4	18.2
	.2	.5	.4	.1	L	L	Income Taxes Payable	.4	.3
	29.0	10.7	11.4	12.9	A	A	All Other Current	13.9	13.9
	87.5	43.4	50.5	53.4	B	B	Total Current	51.6	54.3
	22.4	9.7	9.4	5.7	L	L	Long-Term Debt	11.3	10.5
	.0	.3	.1	.1	E	E	Deferred Taxes		.2
	9.1	4.5	8.8	4.2			All Other Non-Current	3.2	3.8
	-18.9	42.1	31.1	36.7			Net Worth	33.8	31.1
	100.0	100.0	100.0	100.0			Total Liabilities & Net Worth	100.0	100.0
							INCOME DATA		
	100.0	100.0	100.0	100.0			Net Sales	100.0	100.0
	37.3	28.9	24.2	25.3			Gross Profit	27.5	27.3
	32.8	25.7	22.9	22.5			Operating Expenses	23.5	22.8
	4.5	3.2	1.3	2.7			Operating Profit	3.9	4.5
	.2	.4	.5	.4			All Other Expenses (net)	.5	.6
	4.3	2.8	.7	2.3			Profit Before Taxes	3.5	3.9
							RATIOS		
	1.7	3.8	2.6	3.3				2.4	2.2
	1.1	1.7	1.7	1.3			Current	1.6	1.6
	.4	1.2	1.3	1.0				1.2	1.2
	1.6	3.0	2.0	2.5				1.8	1.9
	.4	1.4	1.3	.9			Quick	1.2	1.2
	.1	.8	.9	.7				.8	.8
	0 UND	26 14.0	45 8.1	49 7.4				30 12.1	30 12.2
	20 18.5	54 6.8	66 5.5	73 5.0			Sales/Receivables	49 7.4	55 6.6
	42 8.6	76 4.8	84 4.3	91 4.0				74 4.9	81 4.5
	0 UND	0 999.8	2 184.4	1 356.5				2 178.4	0 UND
	9 40.7	9 40.7	16 23.5	20 18.3			Cost of Sales/Inventory	13 28.9	7 52.2
	36 10.2	30 12.2	35 10.4	40 9.1				27 13.5	24 15.2
	4 102.3	7 51.8	15 24.0	19 19.1				10 35.1	12 30.8
	14 26.6	18 20.6	27 13.6	22 16.3			Cost of Sales/Payables	21 17.4	22 16.8
	31 11.9	34 10.6	43 8.5	29 12.8				34 10.7	35 10.5
	15.6	4.6	6.3	4.9				7.1	7.6
	120.1	11.7	8.8	15.3			Sales/Working Capital	12.2	13.8
	-13.8	39.7	15.4	65.0				34.0	34.6
	14.5	18.5	7.3	26.8				17.1	15.1
	(26) 2.3	(57) 3.9	(62) 2.8	(12) 3.5			EBIT/Interest	(151) 4.2	(160) 4.5
	-2.3	1.1	.8	1.4				1.7	2.2
			3.1				Net Profit + Depr., Dep.,	13.0	21.6
		(17) .8					Amort./Cur. Mat. L/T/D	(35) 4.0	(29) 6.1
			.5					1.2	2.6
	.1	.1	.1	.1				.1	.1
	2.9	.3	.2	.2			Fixed/Worth	.3	.3
	-.3	.7	.7	1.3				.9	.8
	1.4	.4	.8	.6				.8	.9
	UND	1.5	2.1	3.4			Debt/Worth	1.7	1.8
	-2.4	5.4	4.9	8.0				3.9	4.7
	230.3	51.5	20.5	30.5			% Profit Before Taxes/Tangible	62.0	66.4
	(16) 27.7	(63) 21.8	(57) 7.5	(11) 6.4			Net Worth	(152) 28.0	(160) 33.6
	-6.0	-.2	.4	3.4				11.5	12.6
	70.7	23.3	7.8	18.6			% Profit Before Taxes/Total	24.1	21.1
	12.5	6.9	1.9	2.3			Assets	9.4	10.2
	-4.5	-.1	-1.0	1.4				2.0	3.9
	183.7	98.7	87.6	164.2				91.9	100.7
	64.8	39.7	46.0	53.5			Sales/Net Fixed Assets	42.4	43.5
	21.9	17.3	19.1	22.4				18.5	18.4
	11.0	3.8	3.7	3.0				4.9	4.9
	6.4	3.2	3.0	2.8			Sales/Total Assets	3.6	3.4
	4.1	2.4	2.3	2.3				2.7	2.7
	.2	.3	.3	.4				.3	.3
	(19) .8	(51) .8	(60) .6	(10) .7			% Depr., Dep., Amort./Sales	(127) .5	(135) .6
	1.8	1.9	1.2	.9				1.0	1.3
	3.6	2.6	1.8					1.7	2.2
	(12) 6.0	(36) 4.4	(35) 2.9				% Officers', Directors' Owners' Comp/Sales	(79) 3.2	(87) 3.9
	14.0	8.0	4.5					5.2	6.1
	47140M	283888M	856490M	542158M			Net Sales ($)	3329597M	4147738M
	7441M	84416M	256810M	201538M			Total Assets ($)	871630M	1007376M

M = $ thousand   MM = $ million
See Pages 9 through 22 for Explanation of Ratios and Data

Comparative Historical Data

Current Data Sorted by Sales

			Type of Statement						
7	3	8	Unqualified			1		4	3
59	60	45	Reviewed	2	2	6	19	9	7
26	27	24	Compiled	2	5	9	7	1	
40	42	30	Tax Returns	7	9	6	6	2	
52	60	73	Other	4	23	13	15	12	6
4/1/08-3/31/09 ALL	4/1/09-3/31/10 ALL	4/1/10-3/31/11 ALL			25 (4/1-9/30/10)			155 (10/1/10-3/31/11)	
				0-1MM	1-3MM	3-5MM	5-10MM	10-25MM	25MM & OVER
184	192	180	NUMBER OF STATEMENTS	15	39	35	47	28	16
%	%	%	ASSETS	%	%	%	%	%	%
10.7	11.5	10.4	Cash & Equivalents	19.9	11.7	11.2	6.4	10.1	8.8
48.7	46.2	45.9	Trade Receivables (net)	17.3	39.6	45.7	55.9	50.1	51.5
13.3	13.1	14.4	Inventory	9.2	19.0	13.1	13.1	15.5	12.7
6.6	7.1	5.1	All Other Current	5.8	3.2	1.9	5.5	8.0	9.6
79.3	77.9	75.7	Total Current	52.2	73.4	71.8	80.8	83.6	82.6
14.1	14.3	13.5	Fixed Assets (net)	32.2	13.3	13.0	11.4	10.5	9.2
3.2	2.6	2.5	Intangibles (net)	.0	2.6	4.1	2.3	1.4	4.1
3.4	5.2	8.2	All Other Non-Current	15.4	10.6	11.1	5.5	4.5	4.1
100.0	100.0	100.0	Total	100.0	100.0	100.0	100.0	100.0	100.0
			LIABILITIES						
19.5	20.7	18.8	Notes Payable-Short Term	9.2	23.7	17.4	19.5	17.2	19.0
2.4	2.4	2.3	Cur. Mat.-L.T.D.	4.9	3.0	1.6	1.7	2.3	2.0
18.1	18.4	18.6	Trade Payables	31.4	17.0	13.5	17.2	23.8	16.6
.3	.3	.4	Income Taxes Payable	.0	.2	.8	.4	.0	.6
13.1	16.8	14.3	All Other Current	27.5	19.6	11.5	7.5	14.6	14.5
53.4	58.7	54.3	Total Current	73.0	63.6	44.8	46.3	57.9	52.8
11.4	11.5	11.5	Long-Term Debt	25.5	19.3	10.0	6.5	6.8	5.5
.4	.1	.2	Deferred Taxes	.0	.0	.1	.5	.1	.0
4.1	6.1	6.8	All Other Non-Current	8.6	5.6	6.4	8.4	8.0	2.6
30.7	23.6	27.2	Net Worth	-7.1	11.6	38.6	38.4	27.2	39.1
100.0	100.0	100.0	Total Liabilities & Net Worth	100.0	100.0	100.0	100.0	100.0	100.0
			INCOME DATA						
100.0	100.0	100.0	Net Sales	100.0	100.0	100.0	100.0	100.0	100.0
26.3	29.1	28.4	Gross Profit	44.3	33.8	25.0	24.9	24.9	24.0
24.2	27.7	25.7	Operating Expenses	43.2	28.3	22.2	23.2	23.5	21.5
2.1	1.4	2.7	Operating Profit	1.1	5.5	2.7	1.7	1.3	2.5
.6	.1	.4	All Other Expenses (net)	.9	.7	.0	.1	1.0	.2
1.5	1.3	2.3	Profit Before Taxes	.2	4.8	2.7	1.6	.3	2.3
			RATIOS						
2.4	2.8	2.8	Current	2.2	3.6	3.4	2.6	2.3	3.2
1.6	1.6	1.5		1.2	1.3	1.5	1.7	1.6	1.4
1.1	1.1	1.1		.1	1.0	1.1	1.4	1.3	1.1
1.8	2.1	2.1	Quick	1.4	2.7	2.8	2.1	1.8	2.2
(183) 1.1	1.3	1.2		.3	1.0	1.1	1.4	1.2	1.0
.8	.8	.7		.1	.4	.7	1.1	.8	.8
33 10.9	31 11.8	28 12.8	Sales/Receivables	0 UND	15 23.9	28 12.9	53 6.9	32 11.6	44 8.3
52 7.0	54 6.8	54 6.8		6 61.3	35 10.4	52 7.0	66 5.5	52 7.0	59 6.1
76 4.8	78 4.7	76 4.8		58 6.3	66 5.5	79 4.6	84 4.4	76 4.8	88 4.2
1 658.2	0 999.8	1 463.1	Cost of Sales/Inventory	0 UND	0 UND	0 999.8	2 218.9	5 77.9	1 598.3
10 35.9	10 37.5	11 32.1		6 61.8	16 22.7	9 40.7	14 25.2	11 34.4	12 29.4
28 13.3	28 13.1	34 10.8		44 8.2	54 6.8	27 13.8	38 9.6	30 12.1	31 11.7
12 30.2	9 39.6	11 34.0	Cost of Sales/Payables	10 35.3	3 111.6	7 54.0	14 25.8	14 26.3	17 22.0
21 17.6	21 18.3	21 17.3		26 13.9	13 27.5	16 22.5	25 14.8	27 13.5	20 17.9
33 11.2	34 10.8	37 9.9		111 3.3	34 10.7	30 12.1	35 10.3	43 8.4	27 13.7
7.1	5.8	6.2	Sales/Working Capital	4.4	5.6	6.1	6.3	6.9	5.2
11.2	11.5	12.3		33.3	16.7	18.6	8.5	11.1	20.7
33.8	55.5	51.9		-9.6	-57.9	76.2	13.4	38.1	65.0
12.8	12.0	12.2	EBIT/Interest	25.0	21.0	14.9	10.0	6.1	32.5
(166) 2.9	(166) 2.4	(157) 2.9		(10) 1.4	(33) 2.9	(31) 2.2	(43) 3.4	(26) 2.4	(14) 6.2
.4	-.8	.9		-13.0	.7	-.8	1.4	.4	1.6
9.3	11.7	3.9	Net Profit + Depr., Dep., Amort./Cur. Mat. L/T/D						
(25) 3.8	(28) 2.3	(29) 1.3							
1.3	.4	.6							
.1	.1	.1	Fixed/Worth	.3	.1	.1	.1	.1	.1
.3	.3	.3		.9	.4	.2	.2	.3	.2
1.0	.8	1.0		-1.1	-.3	.6	.5	.7	.6
.9	.6	.7	Debt/Worth	1.4	.6	.5	.6	.7	.7
2.0	1.7	2.2		3.7	3.5	2.6	1.3	1.9	2.7
5.8	5.9	7.9		-2.9	-3.4	5.3	3.8	22.8	5.7
47.2	40.2	41.9	% Profit Before Taxes/Tangible Net Worth	63.4	56.6	72.1	24.5	38.6	46.5
(156) 19.4	(166) 13.3	(147) 13.4		(10) 15.3	(25) 23.5	(33) 8.7	(42) 11.2	(22) 10.0	(15) 14.2
.8	-.3	.3		-15.6	2.4	-3.5	.6	1.3	3.8
15.1	16.7	19.9	% Profit Before Taxes/Total Assets	70.7	35.2	23.0	11.5	13.8	20.9
4.7	3.6	4.3		5.2	6.8	1.8	3.5	2.6	4.6
-1.3	-3.5	-.7		-5.2	-1.1	-1.6	.2	-.7	1.7
151.9	113.6	100.3	Sales/Net Fixed Assets	30.9	91.0	156.0	99.0	86.3	166.9
44.2	44.1	46.0		19.6	37.8	57.5	41.8	51.5	80.3
19.2	17.9	19.6		10.2	19.0	18.1	23.8	28.4	25.7
4.7	4.3	4.2	Sales/Total Assets	8.4	5.9	3.9	3.6	4.5	3.5
3.4	3.2	3.1		2.1	3.5	3.2	3.0	3.6	2.9
2.7	2.5	2.4		1.1	2.4	2.4	2.4	2.9	2.7
.3	.3	.3	% Depr., Dep., Amort./Sales	1.6	.2	.3	.3	.3	.2
(147) .6	(144) .7	(140) .7		(13) 1.9	(22) .8	(25) .5	(42) .6	(25) .6	(13) .4
1.3	1.6	1.3		4.0	1.3	1.8	1.3	.9	.8
1.9	2.0	2.1	% Officers', Directors', Owners' Comp/Sales		2.9	2.8	1.7		
(90) 3.1	(96) 4.6	(87) 3.5		(18) 4.0	(20) 5.8	(28) 3.0			
5.7	7.6	7.3			8.3	8.2	4.2		
2238505M	2941922M	1729676M	Net Sales ($)	9742M	69727M	138588M	344155M	463183M	704281M
729133M	689913M	550205M	Total Assets ($)	5929M	23614M	46052M	123432M	138997M	212181M

M = $ thousand MM = $ million
See Pages 9 through 22 for Explanation of Ratios and Data

Current Data Sorted by Assets

Comparative Historical Data

	0-500M	500M-2MM	2-10MM	10-50MM	50-100MM	100-250MM	Type of Statement	4/1/06-3/31/07 ALL	4/1/07-3/31/08 ALL
	1	5	3				Unqualified	3	2
	1	6	15				Reviewed	20	27
	8	9	2	5			Compiled	7	7
	7	10	2				Tax Returns	22	25
	15 (4/1-9/30/10)		9	70 (10/1/10-3/31/11)	1	1	Other	30	28
NUMBER OF STATEMENTS	17	30	31	6	1			82	89

	0-500M %	500M-2MM %	2-10MM %	10-50MM %	50-100MM %	100-250MM %		4/1/06-3/31/07 %	4/1/07-3/31/08 %
ASSETS									
Cash & Equivalents	11.8	13.1	11.5					12.4	9.5
Trade Receivables (net)	12.8	29.9	40.8					38.7	40.3
Inventory	6.7	17.9	13.2					11.3	15.0
All Other Current	4.3	5.2	6.7					7.8	6.4
Total Current	35.6	66.1	72.3					70.2	71.3
Fixed Assets (net)	39.2	22.5	19.6	D				21.9	21.2
Intangibles (net)	.1	3.0	.2	A				1.4	.7
All Other Non-Current	25.1	8.4	7.9	T				6.6	6.9
Total	100.0	100.0	100.0	A				100.0	100.0
LIABILITIES				N					
Notes Payable-Short Term	26.2	17.8	10.0	O				11.8	18.4
Cur. Mat.-L.T.D.	6.9	2.6	4.4	T				2.5	2.7
Trade Payables	25.7	22.7	15.4					15.6	19.9
Income Taxes Payable	.1	.3	.5	A				.8	.2
All Other Current	9.8	10.7	8.6	V				16.1	10.4
Total Current	68.6	54.0	38.9	A				46.8	51.6
Long-Term Debt	46.1	13.7	14.1	I				17.7	16.8
Deferred Taxes	.0	.1	.0	L				.1	.1
All Other Non-Current	8.7	4.6	2.0	A				4.0	7.5
Net Worth	-23.5	27.6	44.9	B				31.4	24.0
Total Liabilities & Net Worth	100.0	100.0	100.0	L				100.0	100.0
INCOME DATA				E					
Net Sales	100.0	100.0	100.0					100.0	100.0
Gross Profit	52.1	34.3	23.8					33.7	32.4
Operating Expenses	47.2	33.9	22.0					28.4	27.9
Operating Profit	4.9	.5	1.7					5.3	4.5
All Other Expenses (net)	2.0	.7	.5					.8	.5
Profit Before Taxes	2.9	-.2	1.3					4.4	4.0
RATIOS									
	2.4	2.6	3.4					2.3	2.5
Current	.6	1.4	1.8					1.5	1.5
	.2	.9	1.3					1.1	1.1
	1.9	2.0	2.3					1.9	2.1
Quick	.4	.9	1.4					1.1	1.0
	.0	.3	.8					.7	.5
	0 UND	24 15.1	50 7.3					21 17.1	20 18.2
Sales/Receivables	6 60.3	41 9.0	74 4.9					39 9.4	49 7.4
	16 22.3	67 5.5	105 3.5					79 4.6	74 5.0
	0 UND	0 UND	2 225.9					0 UND	0 UND
Cost of Sales/Inventory	0 UND	16 22.4	10 36.2					5 73.9	8 47.8
	24 15.3	73 5.0	60 6.1					27 13.7	44 8.3
	0 UND	21 17.7	18 20.8					6 58.4	10 35.6
Cost of Sales/Payables	17 21.9	52 7.1	34 10.7					23 16.2	26 14.0
	144 2.5	74 5.0	49 7.5					43 8.5	55 6.6
	36.2	6.6	3.5					6.6	5.6
Sales/Working Capital	-33.8	14.7	6.4					13.7	12.8
	-7.2	-38.5	10.6					34.9	64.4
	10.5	3.7	4.6					19.1	20.0
EBIT/Interest	(11) 1.8	(24) .0	(28) 1.9					(71) 5.8	(78) 4.0
	-4.3	-8.8	-2.6					2.2	1.5
Net Profit + Depr., Dep., Amort./Cur. Mat. L/T/D									
	.9	.3	.1					.1	.1
Fixed/Worth	5.5	.6	.3					.4	.6
	-.5	4.7	.9					1.8	2.1
	1.5	.7	.6					.8	.7
Debt/Worth	15.2	2.8	1.0					1.9	2.2
	-3.6	32.2	2.3					6.6	7.2
	541.7	29.1	8.8					85.8	54.1
% Profit Before Taxes/Tangible Net Worth	(10) 27.3	(24) 6.1	(29) 4.1					(70) 40.2	(74) 25.6
	5.1	-20.7	-8.3					17.5	8.0
	36.3	10.0	6.2					28.7	21.6
% Profit Before Taxes/Total Assets	7.2	-.5	1.7					14.3	7.4
	-13.8	-11.6	-6.4					3.2	.8
	43.5	41.8	40.0					66.1	53.6
Sales/Net Fixed Assets	12.8	24.3	16.6					27.9	22.1
	6.1	6.6	5.5					12.8	8.6
	6.8	3.4	2.6					4.9	3.9
Sales/Total Assets	3.8	2.3	2.1					3.1	2.8
	2.9	1.6	1.4					2.2	2.1
	.9	.7	.5					.4	.6
% Depr., Dep., Amort./Sales	(11) 1.5	(24) 1.0	(27) .8					(60) .8	(67) 1.1
	7.6	2.3	1.9					1.6	2.3
	1.8	4.1	2.0					2.1	1.6
% Officers', Directors' Owners' Comp/Sales	(12) 4.5	(18) 6.7	(15) 3.6					(34) 3.3	(45) 3.0
	10.4	9.9	5.6					6.0	5.8
Net Sales ($)	15540M	87356M	223700M	188150M	164668M			1359761M	695582M
Total Assets ($)	3512M	34530M	118865M	99318M	82523M			411351M	268752M

© RMA 2011

M = $ thousand   MM = $ million
See Pages 9 through 22 for Explanation of Ratios and Data

Comparative Historical Data | Current Data Sorted by Sales

4/1/08-3/31/09 ALL	4/1/09-3/31/10 ALL	4/1/10-3/31/11 ALL	Type of Statement	0-1MM	1-3MM	3-5MM	5-10MM	10-25MM	25MM & OVER
2	5	3	Unqualified		1		1	1	
26	16	26	Reviewed		2	7	10	4	3
13	8	9	Compiled	2	4	1	1	1	
21	25	19	Tax Returns	7	8	1	2	1	
22	32	28	Other	5	10	5	5	1	2
				15 (4/1-9/30/10)		70 (10/1/10-3/31/11)			
84	86	85	**NUMBER OF STATEMENTS**	14	25	14	19	8	5
%	%	%	**ASSETS**	%	%	%	%	%	%
13.0	13.4	12.6	Cash & Equivalents	5.3	15.5	5.1	17.3		
42.9	29.5	30.1	Trade Receivables (net)	8.3	26.5	34.5	40.5		
14.6	15.6	14.3	Inventory	12.3	13.0	21.8	11.0		
5.0	4.8	5.5	All Other Current	2.4	6.9	4.5	6.2		
75.5	63.3	62.4	Total Current	28.2	61.8	65.9	75.1		
18.4	23.7	24.3	Fixed Assets (net)	42.1	26.3	26.1	16.5		
.3	1.6	1.2	Intangibles (net)	2.2	2.5	.4	.0		
5.8	11.3	12.1	All Other Non-Current	27.5	9.4	7.7	8.4		
100.0	100.0	100.0	Total	100.0	100.0	100.0	100.0		
			LIABILITIES						
19.0	16.1	16.1	Notes Payable-Short Term	17.2	24.4	7.6	12.5		
4.2	2.9	4.4	Cur. Mat.-L.T.D.	7.3	3.0	7.9	2.8		
16.2	17.7	19.6	Trade Payables	29.6	19.2	18.9	18.4		
.9	.3	.3	Income Taxes Payable	.0	.8	.2	.1		
12.4	13.2	10.0	All Other Current	18.5	6.1	7.0	8.5		
52.7	50.2	50.4	Total Current	72.6	53.5	41.5	42.2		
15.8	18.7	20.1	Long-Term Debt	56.2	17.4	18.7	8.7		
.1	.1	.1	Deferred Taxes	.0	.0	.2	.1		
4.7	5.4	4.2	All Other Non-Current	12.1	3.1	.2	4.0		
26.7	25.6	25.2	Net Worth	-40.9	25.8	39.4	44.9		
100.0	100.0	100.0	Total Liabilities & Net Worth	100.0	100.0	100.0	100.0		
			INCOME DATA						
100.0	100.0	100.0	Net Sales	100.0	100.0	100.0	100.0		
33.3	34.2	34.4	Gross Profit	53.7	37.2	32.1	21.1		
30.8	32.3	32.3	Operating Expenses	47.2	37.0	30.0	22.3		
2.5	1.8	2.1	Operating Profit	6.5	.2	2.1	-1.2		
.7	.8	.8	All Other Expenses (net)	2.4	1.0	.6	-.2		
1.8	1.0	1.3	Profit Before Taxes	4.1	-.8	1.4	-1.1		
			RATIOS						
2.4	2.9	3.1	Current	1.1	3.3	2.8	3.2		
1.7	1.5	1.6		.5	1.4	1.9	1.8		
1.1	.7	.8		.2	.7	1.2	1.2		
1.9	2.3	2.1	Quick	.5	3.0	1.5	2.3		
1.2	1.0	1.0		.2	.8	1.1	1.3		
.7	.4	.4		.0	.4	.7	.8		
28 12.9	10 37.0	18 20.4	Sales/Receivables	0 UND	18 20.4	40 9.2	40 9.2		
51 7.2	42 8.8	46 8.0		7 48.9	41 8.8	65 5.7	60 6.1		
80 4.6	69 5.3	79 4.6		34 10.8	63 5.8	87 4.2	96 6.1		
0 UND	0 UND	0 UND	Cost of Sales/Inventory	0 UND	0 UND	0 UND	5 71.8		
9 42.4	9 39.7	9 38.7		0 UND	2 181.8	24 15.0	10 36.2		
51 7.1	46 7.9	57 6.4		78 4.7	56 6.5	142 2.6	20 18.4		
9 38.5	14 27.0	15 24.9	Cost of Sales/Payables	0 UND	1 660.3	27 13.6	17 21.3		
27 13.4	27 13.4	34 10.6		43 8.5	39 9.2	52 7.1	30 12.2		
45 8.2	54 6.7	61 6.0		203 1.8	90 4.1	78 4.7	42 8.7		
5.9	5.4	4.7	Sales/Working Capital	134.8	4.0	4.5	3.5		
10.9	12.7	9.5		-8.1	15.3	6.6	9.2		
93.9	-24.3	-34.0		-3.6	-18.8	NM	23.8		
14.2	8.0	5.1	EBIT/Interest	7.1	3.7	3.7	3.9		
(73) 3.4	(71) 1.9	(69) 1.4		(10) 2.0	(19) -.4	(12) 1.7	(17) -1.2		
-.3	-4.3	-3.7		.1	-17.2	-3.0	-7.5		
4.5	6.9	5.2	Net Profit + Depr., Dep., Amort./Cur. Mat. L/T/D						
(15) 2.4	(11) 3.2	(12) 1.6							
1.0	.5	.1							
.1	.2	.2	Fixed/Worth	1.0	.3	.3	.1		
.3	.5	.6		-8.8	.8	.4	.4		
1.3	4.4	3.3		-.4	3.8	2.9	.9		
.6	.5	.6	Debt/Worth	7.6	.5	.7	.4		
1.3	1.7	1.8		-15.4	2.7	1.0	1.3		
10.1	12.6	11.2		-3.6	15.2	7.0	2.7		
40.6	32.8	26.1	% Profit Before Taxes/Tangible Net Worth		30.6	20.9	7.1		
(69) 22.4	(70) 10.6	(70) 5.6			(20) 8.8	(12) 4.3	-10.7		
4.3	-9.1	-11.0			-19.0	-1.0	-21.9		
23.9	12.6	11.9	% Profit Before Taxes/Total Assets	29.2	9.4	8.6	3.1		
7.3	1.8	2.0		11.7	-1.3	1.8	-4.5		
-2.5	-7.0	-6.5		-.3	-16.0	-8.5	-9.3		
51.5	47.5	40.1	Sales/Net Fixed Assets	25.5	50.0	28.3	41.8		
28.9	15.9	16.6		9.6	21.4	11.6	26.1		
11.6	7.2	6.3		3.2	5.6	3.6	7.9		
4.1	3.8	3.4	Sales/Total Assets	4.8	3.7	2.4	3.6		
3.0	2.6	2.3		2.9	2.4	1.9	2.5		
2.4	1.8	1.5		1.2	1.5	1.5	1.6		
.5	.8	.5	% Depr., Dep., Amort./Sales		.6	.8	.4		
(70) 1.0	(68) 1.7	(69) 1.2		(18) 1.1	(12) 1.7	(17) .5			
1.7	2.9	2.3		1.7	2.7	2.1			
2.4	2.3	2.4	% Officers', Directors' Owners' Comp/Sales		3.6		1.8		
(38) 4.3	(45) 6.0	(46) 4.6		(15) 7.8	(11) 3.6				
7.2	8.8	8.7		10.9	4.8				
1219897M	1195107M	679414M	Net Sales ($)	7842M	47255M	57629M	135345M	98514M	332829M
310646M	440539M	338748M	Total Assets ($)	4570M	22273M	39904M	62890M	56345M	152766M

M = $ thousand   MM = $ million
See Pages 9 through 22 for Explanation of Ratios and Data

Current Data Sorted by Assets   **Comparative Historical Data**

Type of Statement		5	8
Unqualified		5	8
Reviewed		40	39
Compiled		22	14
Tax Returns		35	26
Other		41	32

0-500M	500M-2MM	2-10MM	10-50MM	50-100MM	100-250MM		4/1/06-3/31/07 ALL	4/1/07-3/31/08 ALL
29	45	33	4	2		**NUMBER OF STATEMENTS**	143	119
%	%	%	%	%	%	**ASSETS**	%	%
21.6	14.3	14.4				Cash & Equivalents	11.4	15.0
22.1	33.0	41.8				Trade Receivables (net)	37.1	35.5
11.8	8.9	10.3				Inventory	13.9	11.6
5.2	6.5	7.9				All Other Current	5.8	6.1
60.6	62.7	74.4				Total Current	68.2	68.2
23.5	24.3	19.1				Fixed Assets (net)	22.0	21.1
4.4	3.4	2.9				Intangibles (net)	1.7	3.2
11.5	9.5	3.6				All Other Non-Current	8.1	7.5
100.0	100.0	100.0				Total	100.0	100.0
						LIABILITIES		
35.8	16.4	9.8				Notes Payable-Short Term	10.6	12.2
5.4	2.3	3.0				Cur. Mat.-L.T.D.	3.8	4.3
21.6	16.8	14.8				Trade Payables	17.1	16.7
.0	.5	.2				Income Taxes Payable	.2	.2
16.9	13.7	17.8				All Other Current	15.8	15.4
79.6	49.8	45.7				Total Current	47.6	48.8
24.6	20.1	9.7				Long-Term Debt	17.5	18.3
.0	.2	.7				Deferred Taxes	.2	.1
6.4	4.8	4.7				All Other Non-Current	3.5	6.3
-10.6	25.2	39.3				Net Worth	31.3	26.4
100.0	100.0	100.0				Total Liabilities & Net Worth	100.0	100.0
						INCOME DATA		
100.0	100.0	100.0				Net Sales	100.0	100.0
46.3	30.8	23.7				Gross Profit	31.6	32.9
43.8	32.1	21.0				Operating Expenses	26.4	28.5
2.5	-1.3	2.7				Operating Profit	5.2	4.4
.7	.8	.5				All Other Expenses (net)	.7	1.0
1.9	-2.1	2.2				Profit Before Taxes	4.5	3.4
						RATIOS		
3.9	2.9	3.5					2.9	2.5
1.1	1.8	2.2				Current	1.4	1.5
.3	1.0	1.0					1.1	1.0
1.5	2.4	3.1					1.9	1.8
.4	.8	1.5				Quick	1.0	1.1
.3	.5	.6					.6	.7
0 UND	16 22.2	37 9.9					16 23.3	22 16.5
12 30.4	35 10.6	55 6.6				Sales/Receivables	38 9.7	44 8.3
25 14.6	66 5.5	86 4.2					64 5.7	61 6.0
0 UND	0 UND	0 UND					0 UND	0 UND
1 516.0	1 487.0	7 50.1				Cost of Sales/Inventory	9 41.6	8 44.3
21 17.7	36 10.3	28 13.0					39 9.3	41 9.0
0 UND	8 48.2	11 33.8					6 65.5	8 48.5
13 28.4	20 18.4	19 19.1				Cost of Sales/Payables	21 17.2	23 16.0
45 8.2	38 9.6	43 8.5					42 8.7	48 7.6
9.7	5.7	3.9					6.8	7.7
86.9	17.5	6.8				Sales/Working Capital	17.2	16.0
-12.6	-148.4	NM					195.9	320.7
14.5	17.5	8.5					22.9	17.8
(23) 3.7	(39) 1.0	(29) 2.9				EBIT/Interest	(122) 6.0	(109) 4.1
.9	-6.5	-1.6					1.5	1.3
		13.2					5.7	9.7
	(10) 2.7					Net Profit + Depr., Dep., Amort./Cur. Mat. L/T/D	(22) 3.2	(22) 1.8
		.3					1.9	.7
.2	.1	.1					.2	.2
1.9	.6	.4				Fixed/Worth	.6	.6
-.4	9.8	3.6					2.0	5.1
1.2	.5	.5					.7	.9
5.6	1.9	1.5				Debt/Worth	2.7	2.2
-2.2	22.7	9.2					9.2	94.4
109.4	41.5	26.6					88.8	78.7
(16) 51.0	(35) 11.8	(27) 5.5				% Profit Before Taxes/Tangible Net Worth	(122) 36.2	(95) 24.9
2.7	-30.0	-1.8					14.6	8.0
39.5	13.8	9.8					29.3	20.3
8.5	.2	4.0				% Profit Before Taxes/Total Assets	12.4	7.0
-1.0	-25.3	-.2					1.6	.6
100.4	75.9	48.5					77.2	63.1
34.8	22.1	20.5				Sales/Net Fixed Assets	22.1	19.9
16.5	5.2	9.5					9.8	8.9
9.0	4.6	3.2					4.5	4.8
5.4	2.7	2.6				Sales/Total Assets	3.2	3.1
3.6	1.8	1.9					2.4	2.2
.7	.6	.7					.5	.6
(16) 1.1	(29) 2.2	(31) 1.0				% Depr., Dep., Amort./Sales	(110) 1.0	(92) 1.2
.9	4.4	1.7					2.2	2.4
.8	2.3	1.5					2.0	2.4
(19) .6	(23) 3.2	(15) 3.2				% Officers', Directors' Owners' Comp/Sales	(73) 4.5	(56) 4.1
10	7.5	5.5					8.4	6.4
3842M	155535M	379101M	219299M	796173M		Net Sales ($)	1973594M	2053904M
7322M	48378M	145134M	117203M	150283M		Total Assets ($)	729575M	891497M

Note: Columns 10-50MM, 50-100MM, and 100-250MM are marked "DATA NOT AVAILABLE" for the Assets, Liabilities, Income Data, and Ratios sections.

M = $ thousand   MM = $ million
See Pages 9 through 22 for Explanation of Ratios and Data

Comparative Historical Data

Current Data Sorted by Sales

			Type of Statement	0-1MM	1-3MM	3-5MM	5-10MM	10-25MM	25MM & OVER
8	6	5	Unqualified		2	5	1	1	3
17	34	30	Reviewed				9	12	2
13	15	9	Compiled	1	6	1	1		
27	22	29	Tax Returns	9	14	1	4		1
29	25	40	Other	2	19	10	5	2	2
4/1/08-3/31/09	4/1/09-3/31/10	4/1/10-3/31/11		17 (4/1-9/30/10)			96 (10/1/10-3/31/11)		
ALL	ALL	ALL							
94	102	113	**NUMBER OF STATEMENTS**	12	41	17	20	15	8
%	%	%	**ASSETS**	%	%	%	%	%	%
16.1	17.0	15.8	Cash & Equivalents	19.8	15.2	12.2	21.4	13.6	
38.1	35.7	32.7	Trade Receivables (net)	16.0	26.2	41.4	39.8	44.2	
8.7	9.3	10.1	Inventory	13.4	10.6	7.8	7.6	11.6	
5.4	6.2	7.0	All Other Current	9.9	4.8	3.0	7.3	11.3	
68.3	68.3	65.7	Total Current	59.0	56.9	64.4	75.9	80.7	
24.2	23.3	22.4	Fixed Assets (net)	32.6	27.3	23.3	13.8	13.7	
3.1	3.9	3.5	Intangibles (net)	1.7	3.2	7.1	3.2	2.1	
4.4	4.6	8.4	All Other Non-Current	6.7	12.6	5.3	7.1	3.5	
100.0	100.0	100.0	Total	100.0	100.0	100.0	100.0	100.0	
			LIABILITIES						
16.8	16.1	21.1	Notes Payable-Short Term	25.7	30.4	7.4	12.0	9.9	
3.9	2.9	3.3	Cur. Mat.-L.T.D.	2.8	5.1	1.6	1.6	3.8	
17.8	17.2	17.1	Trade Payables	26.6	13.4	18.9	18.4	18.5	
.1	.2	.3	Income Taxes Payable	.0	.1	.9	.2	.3	
20.0	13.3	16.2	All Other Current	21.5	11.0	22.2	13.8	18.6	
58.8	49.6	58.0	Total Current	76.7	60.0	51.0	46.1	51.1	
16.6	15.1	17.6	Long-Term Debt	19.5	27.1	18.4	11.7	2.7	
.0	.2	.3	Deferred Taxes	.0	.1	1.3	.2	.1	
12.3	10.3	5.1	All Other Non-Current	10.2	5.8	5.9	2.8	2.6	
12.3	24.8	18.9	Net Worth	-6.3	7.1	23.5	39.2	43.4	
100.0	100.0	100.0	Total Liabilities & Net Worth	100.0	100.0	100.0	100.0	100.0	
			INCOME DATA						
100.0	100.0	100.0	Net Sales	100.0	100.0	100.0	100.0	100.0	
32.1	32.5	32.4	Gross Profit	48.7	38.9	28.6	24.0	21.9	
29.7	30.2	31.2	Operating Expenses	53.0	37.3	26.4	22.6	19.9	
2.5	2.4	1.2	Operating Profit	-4.3	1.6	2.2	1.4	2.0	
.7	.5	.7	All Other Expenses (net)	1.2	.8	.5	.6	.2	
1.8	1.9	.5	Profit Before Taxes	-5.5	.8	1.7	.7	1.8	
			RATIOS						
2.1	3.4	3.1		3.1	2.8	5.4	7.1	2.9	
1.3	1.6	1.6	Current	.4	1.3	2.4	1.8	2.1	
.9	.8	.9		.3	.7	1.6	1.0	1.1	
1.7	2.6	2.3		.9	2.1	4.7	5.4	2.4	
1.1	1.1	.8	Quick	.4	.8	1.6	1.4	1.2	
.6	.6	.4		.2	.4	.6	.7	.6	
22 16.8	20 18.5	16 22.4		0 UND	2 153.9	25 14.7	34 10.9	26 14.1	
43 8.5	45 8.1	35 10.6	Sales/Receivables	8 48.6	24 15.0	38 9.5	50 7.4	48 7.6	
72 5.1	75 4.9	61 6.0		26 13.9	61 6.0	79 4.6	64 5.7	86 4.2	
0 UND	0 UND	0 UND		0 UND	0 UND	0 UND	0 UND	0 UND	
1 297.5	7 55.7	4 81.3	Cost of Sales/Inventory	0 UND	4 81.3	0 UND	4 100.4	8 43.8	
21 17.1	28 13.0	29 12.5		22 16.7	38 9.6	35 10.4	17 20.9	25 14.7	
8 47.9	6 56.5	8 48.3		0 UND	4 89.2	9 42.9	10 36.3	12 30.1	
24 15.0	24 15.0	18 19.8	Cost of Sales/Payables	24 15.4	17 21.7	17 21.7	18 20.0	22 16.2	
43 8.5	44 8.3	38 9.6		93 3.9	38 9.5	30 12.0	39 9.5	42 8.6	
7.6	5.3	5.5		5.6	6.2	4.7	3.5	5.4	
23.5	9.9	15.2	Sales/Working Capital	-49.1	39.1	10.1	8.2	8.7	
-30.5	-40.0	-50.8		-6.2	-21.4	19.5	-194.9	98.1	
23.7	12.6	11.8			7.3	79.8	7.6	14.9	
(84) 5.4	(86) 2.2	(97) 2.5	EBIT/Interest		(37) 2.0	(15) 8.9	(16) 1.7	(13) 3.1	
.1	-2.3	-4.4			-4.3	.6	-7.3	.6	
34.9	5.9	30.4							
(12) 4.5	(22) 2.2	(14) 2.7	Net Profit + Depr., Dep., Amort./Cur. Mat. L/T/D						
1.7	-.1	.3							
.3	.2	.1		.1	.3	.1	.1	.1	
.7	.6	.6	Fixed/Worth	NM	1.7	.2	.4	.2	
UND	8.4	-5.3		-.5	-.7	8.8	4.6	.8	
1.1	.8	.6		1.1	1.2	.4	.3	.5	
3.9	2.0	2.0	Debt/Worth	NM	3.3	1.0	1.7	.9	
UND	165.8	-18.5		-2.7	-5.5	19.8	18.2	3.1	
83.2	50.7	43.4			61.0	58.8	18.5	24.4	
(71) 24.6	(78) 10.1	(83) 13.9	% Profit Before Taxes/Tangible Net Worth		(27) 23.7	(14) 28.9	(16) 2.4	(13) 14.0	
1.7	-5.8	-10.4			-9.3	-.7	-59.9	-.8	
19.5	12.4	16.4		25.4	19.4	30.6	10.6	10.2	
7.2	1.2	4.5	% Profit Before Taxes/Total Assets	2.5	3.4	5.2	2.1	3.4	
-1.9	-4.9	-7.2		-43.1	-9.4	-8.3	-11.3	.2	
65.4	52.2	74.5		34.3	62.6	98.2	78.0	53.6	
20.7	19.5	25.0	Sales/Net Fixed Assets	21.3	21.6	65.9	39.1	35.1	
9.5	7.7	9.5		12.6	5.8	3.9	14.9	14.2	
4.7	4.2	4.6		8.6	5.1	4.8	4.2	3.9	
3.0	2.7	3.0	Sales/Total Assets	5.0	2.8	3.1	3.0	3.2	
2.5	1.9	2.0		2.1	1.9	1.8	2.1	2.5	
.6	.7	.7			.8	.4	.5	.7	
(76) 1.1	(84) 1.2	(81) 1.2	% Depr., Dep., Amort./Sales		(23) 2.9	(13) 1.4	(17) .9	(14) 1.0	
2.3	2.5	2.5			4.8	2.4	1.7	1.4	
2.7	2.4	2.3			2.7				
(48) 4.3	(54) 5.0	(59) 4.8	% Officers', Directors' Owners' Comp/Sales		(25) 5.2				
6.7	8.5	7.7			8.7				
1427638M	1270319M	1588537M	Net Sales ($)	7813M	77041M	61397M	138262M	232027M	1071997M
475566M	695967M	468320M	Total Assets ($)	2369M	28980M	25843M	51752M	76435M	282941M

M = $ thousand   MM = $ million
See Pages 9 through 22 for Explanation of Ratios and Data

Current Data Sorted by Assets   Comparative Historical Data

			5	3	2	1	Type of Statement		7	4
	9		20	3			Unqualified		24	16
3	4		4			1	Reviewed		4	10
14	10		4				Compiled		8	12
6	13		9	1	2		Tax Returns		15	17
	22 (4/1-9/30/10)			92 (10/1/10-3/31/11)			Other		4/1/06-3/31/07	4/1/07-3/31/08
0-500M	500M-2MM	2-10MM	10-50MM	50-100MM	100-250MM			ALL	ALL
23	36	42	7	4	2	NUMBER OF STATEMENTS		58	59
%	%	%	%	%	%	ASSETS		%	%
20.7	11.5	14.5				Cash & Equivalents		10.1	9.0
25.7	44.6	46.9				Trade Receivables (net)		42.1	40.5
6.2	11.8	9.8				Inventory		9.7	9.9
1.8	5.2	7.6				All Other Current		5.5	9.7
54.4	73.1	78.8				Total Current		67.4	69.0
34.6	18.5	13.9				Fixed Assets (net)		24.2	20.8
1.9	4.0	3.2				Intangibles (net)		2.8	2.6
9.2	4.4	4.1				All Other Non-Current		5.6	7.5
100.0	100.0	100.0				Total		100.0	100.0
						LIABILITIES			
24.2	14.0	7.0				Notes Payable-Short Term		14.6	13.9
4.0	1.9	2.3				Cur. Mat.-L.T.D.		3.6	3.4
15.7	20.9	21.3				Trade Payables		18.3	23.3
.0	.3	.4				Income Taxes Payable		.9	.3
13.2	18.1	14.7				All Other Current		11.8	14.0
57.1	55.2	45.6				Total Current		49.2	55.0
22.9	11.7	9.8				Long-Term Debt		16.9	26.0
.0	.1	.3				Deferred Taxes		.9	.1
11.3	15.2	4.6				All Other Non-Current		4.0	1.7
8.7	17.9	39.6				Net Worth		29.0	17.2
100.0	100.0	100.0				Total Liabilties & Net Worth		100.0	100.0
						INCOME DATA			
100.0	100.0	100.0				Net Sales		100.0	100.0
44.8	34.8	25.7				Gross Profit		32.9	28.7
41.1	34.1	22.2				Operating Expenses		28.4	25.1
3.6	.7	3.5				Operating Profit		4.5	3.5
.7	.4	.8				All Other Expenses (net)		.6	.7
3.0	.3	2.8				Profit Before Taxes		4.0	2.9
						RATIOS			
2.7	2.4	2.4						2.0	1.9
1.0	1.3	1.8				Current		1.5	1.4
.5	1.0	1.4						1.1	1.1
2.1	2.2	2.0						1.7	1.5
.8	1.1	1.6				Quick		1.2	1.1
.3	.5	1.0						.7	.6

												Sales/Receivables					
0	UND	19	19.2	32	11.5							Sales/Receivables	29	12.4	23	16.1
10	37.4	49	7.4	62	5.9								62	5.9	48	7.7
35	10.5	81	4.5	86	4.3								92	4.0	81	4.5
0	UND	0	UND	0	UND							Cost of Sales/Inventory	0	UND	0	UND
0	UND	8	45.3	3	134.0								7	52.1	3	120.3
11	34.7	23	16.1	20	18.4								27	13.7	27	13.4
0	UND	10	35.5	19	19.0							Cost of Sales/Payables	16	22.8	14	25.5
8	45.2	29	12.7	31	11.7								32	11.5	31	11.9
40	9.0	54	6.8	58	6.3								56	6.6	54	6.7

8.8		8.0		5.7			Sales/Working Capital		6.1	8.1
-417.6		17.7		7.5					10.5	14.3
-20.0		-130.8		16.6					56.8	57.6
11.4		11.2		18.3			EBIT/Interest	12.9		11.8
(17) 7.7	(28)	2.0	(40)	5.2				(53) 3.8	(56)	3.6
-1.9		-4.1		2.2				2.0		.6
				8.9			Net Profit + Depr., Dep.,	7.7		
		(14)		3.9			Amort./Cur. Mat. L/T/D	(18) 4.1		
				.1				1.6		
.6		.2		.1			Fixed/Worth	.2		.2
2.0		.7		.3				.6		.6
-1.3		26.4		.6				1.7		2.7
.6		1.1		.8			Debt/Worth	1.1		1.2
29.2		3.3		1.5				2.5		2.6
-3.5		NM		2.9				7.8		13.9
112.5		54.3		40.9			% Profit Before Taxes/Tangible	64.8		48.7
(13) 55.2	(27)	15.7	(39)	17.7			Net Worth	(50) 17.5	(50)	24.4
18.4		-11.9		2.9				8.7		11.4
47.2		17.3		13.0			% Profit Before Taxes/Total	17.2		18.6
16.1		4.0		5.7			Assets	6.0		6.8
-12.8		-8.1		1.2				2.4		-.3
64.7		92.4		89.9			Sales/Net Fixed Assets	40.0		52.4
19.7		20.7		26.5				17.2		20.8
7.3		12.7		13.3				7.6		8.9
9.1		4.5		3.5			Sales/Total Assets	3.4		4.4
5.4		3.4		2.8				2.5		2.8
2.9		2.1		1.9				1.8		2.2
.9		.4		.4			% Depr., Dep., Amort./Sales	.6		.7
(16) 1.7	(23)	1.3	(37)	1.1				(47) 1.3	(43)	1.1
4.1		2.2		1.7				1.9		2.6
3.2		1.8		1.9			% Officers', Directors'	2.9		2.1
(14) 4.6	(17)	3.2	(19)	3.4			Owners' Comp/Sales	(31) 5.1	(35)	3.1
8.8		6.5		5.5				7.9		6.0

30362M	141507M	492336M	228457M	563197M	690673M	Net Sales ($)		529811M	858498M
4545M	39628M	174352M	101882M	267763M	235840M	Total Assets ($)		239956M	272958M

M = $ thousand   MM = $ million
See Pages 9 through 22 for Explanation of Ratios and Data

Comparative Historical Data | Current Data Sorted by Sales

			Type of Statement	0-1MM	1-3MM	3-5MM	5-10MM	10-25MM	25MM & OVER
5	4	11	Unqualified			1	5	5	
23	31	32	Reviewed		3	5	12	10	2
11	8	12	Compiled		6	2	3	3	1
25	16	28	Tax Returns	8	14		3	3	3
25	24	31	Other	3	5	6	9	3	5
4/1/08-3/31/09 ALL	4/1/09-3/31/10 ALL	4/1/10-3/31/11 ALL		22 (4/1-9/30/10)			92 (10/1/10-3/31/11)		
89	83	114	**NUMBER OF STATEMENTS**	11	28	13	28	21	13
%	%	%	**ASSETS**	%	%	%	%	%	%
10.5	14.0	15.6	Cash & Equivalents	19.4	16.3	11.9	14.0	17.5	14.8
44.8	39.9	41.4	Trade Receivables (net)	19.6	39.3	42.2	44.5	46.3	49.1
8.7	7.7	10.0	Inventory	5.5	9.2	17.5	7.4	9.5	14.6
9.3	5.7	5.7	All Other Current	1.1	3.7	5.0	9.1	7.7	4.2
73.4	67.3	72.7	Total Current	45.5	68.5	76.6	75.0	81.0	82.7
17.6	18.9	19.2	Fixed Assets (net)	44.7	24.3	14.0	15.4	11.4	12.7
4.2	5.6	2.9	Intangibles (net)	.0	2.1	2.8	5.3	3.8	.2
4.8	8.3	5.2	All Other Non-Current	9.9	5.0	6.6	4.3	3.9	4.5
100.0	100.0	100.0	Total	100.0	100.0	100.0	100.0	100.0	100.0
			LIABILITIES						
13.9	10.8	12.4	Notes Payable-Short Term	27.0	18.6	16.1	8.5	4.2	4.6
3.6	4.4	2.3	Cur. Mat.-L.T.D.	2.8	3.7	1.4	2.3	1.8	.8
21.8	16.8	20.3	Trade Payables	12.1	13.8	27.9	21.1	25.4	23.2
.5	.4	.3	Income Taxes Payable	.0	.3	.0	.5	.1	.9
13.6	13.0	15.1	All Other Current	3.1	22.3	17.7	13.7	14.5	11.2
53.4	45.3	50.4	Total Current	45.0	58.8	63.1	46.1	45.9	40.7
14.9	15.1	13.3	Long-Term Debt	16.6	18.3	10.3	14.0	6.0	12.8
.1	.4	.2	Deferred Taxes	.0	.1	.0	.5	.0	.0
5.1	12.0	8.9	All Other Non-Current	6.3	18.6	16.1	3.9	4.1	1.9
26.4	27.2	27.2	Net Worth	31.9	4.2	10.5	35.5	44.0	44.6
100.0	100.0	100.0	Total Liabilities & Net Worth	100.0	100.0	100.0	100.0	100.0	100.0
			INCOME DATA						
100.0	100.0	100.0	Net Sales	100.0	100.0	100.0	100.0	100.0	100.0
30.5	31.2	31.8	Gross Profit	52.4	38.1	29.1	27.2	28.9	17.8
27.2	26.9	29.0	Operating Expenses	44.1	37.8	29.4	24.4	24.0	14.7
3.3	4.3	2.8	Operating Profit	8.3	.4	-.3	2.8	5.0	3.2
.9	.5	.5	All Other Expenses (net)	.7	.6	.2	.7	.6	-.2
2.4	3.8	2.3	Profit Before Taxes	7.6	-.2	-.6	2.1	4.4	3.4
			RATIOS						
2.1	2.2	2.6	Current	2.7	2.6	3.0	2.4	2.6	3.6
1.5	1.6	1.6		1.2	1.1	1.4	1.8	1.8	2.4
1.1	1.1	1.0		.5	.8	1.0	1.3	1.4	1.4
1.7	1.8	2.1	Quick	2.1	2.2	1.9	2.2	2.1	2.2
(88) 1.1	1.2	1.3		1.0	.9	1.0	1.3	1.6	1.6
.7	.8	.7		.3	.4	.5	.8	1.0	1.0
19 19.1	27 13.5	21 17.5	Sales/Receivables	0 UND	0 UND	25 14.6	28 13.0	34 10.8	40 9.2
52 7.0	50 7.3	47 7.8		18 19.8	37 10.0	41 9.0	58 6.3	52 7.0	70 5.2
95 3.9	74 5.0	79 4.6		42 8.7	87 4.2	72 5.1	87 4.2	73 5.0	89 4.1
0 UND	0 UND	0 UND	Cost of Sales/Inventory	0 UND	0 UND	1 456.7	0 UND	0 UND	0 UND
2 206.3	4 101.9	3 134.0		0 UND	1 625.9	14 26.1	3 141.3	1 284.7	7 48.7
16 22.6	16 22.6	20 17.9		27 13.5	19 19.1	34 10.8	14 25.6	35 10.5	51 7.1
12 29.3	7 54.4	10 37.9	Cost of Sales/Payables	0 UND	0 UND	15 23.8	19 19.2	20 18.1	11 32.2
33 11.0	24 14.9	28 12.9		9 42.3	12 29.9	32 11.4	38 9.6	33 10.9	35 10.3
55 6.6	42 8.7	56 6.5		62 5.9	34 10.6	63 5.8	59 6.2	76 4.8	56 6.6
6.2	6.0	6.1	Sales/Working Capital	8.6	8.1	6.5	6.3	5.0	4.0
10.7	10.6	10.8		26.1	164.9	16.6	8.0	8.7	7.1
59.7	156.8	517.7		-8.3	-47.5	-436.5	19.8	16.1	18.6
19.2	17.4	13.8	EBIT/Interest		4.2	19.4	11.9	24.3	17.5
(73) 4.8	(73) 6.5	(98) 5.1		(21) 1.7	(11) 3.0	(26) 5.5	(19) 7.8		7.5
1.7	.6	1.6		-3.3	-6.9	1.8	2.6		4.9
17.2	32.7	8.4	Net Profit + Depr., Dep., Amort./Cur. Mat. L/T/D						
(15) 10.9	(16) 2.4	(24) 3.9							
4.0	.9	.1							
.1	.2	.2	Fixed/Worth	.4	.3	.3	.2	.1	.2
.4	.4	.4		1.4	1.5	.5	.4	.4	.3
2.1	2.8	1.7		UND	-.7	NM	.8	.5	.4
1.2	1.0	1.0	Debt/Worth	.2	1.2	1.0	1.0	.8	.6
2.8	2.6	2.0		1.5	18.3	4.6	2.1	1.4	1.3
8.4	10.8	16.8		UND	-4.2	-36.2	3.2	2.5	2.7
52.6	65.2	44.3	% Profit Before Taxes/Tangible Net Worth		54.8		30.1	43.8	36.9
(72) 29.1	(66) 24.8	(92) 21.1		(17) 26.4		(24) 16.7	(20) 18.9	21.9	
3.9	4.8	3.5		-9.7		3.0	3.2	8.0	
19.7	20.2	18.3	% Profit Before Taxes/Total Assets	47.2	17.1	24.0	15.4	17.8	21.1
7.3	8.7	6.6		16.1	4.0	3.4	4.7	6.9	6.7
.7	-1.7	.4		6.7	-21.1	-12.1	1.0	1.9	1.3
100.2	53.8	73.5	Sales/Net Fixed Assets	19.7	106.7	65.9	74.2	99.6	63.8
32.4	18.8	22.4		7.3	28.2	17.3	23.6	40.0	22.2
13.0	10.3	12.3		3.1	11.3	13.2	14.6	16.5	20.2
4.3	4.2	4.4	Sales/Total Assets	4.4	8.3	4.6	4.2	3.7	3.8
3.0	2.9	3.2		3.2	3.3	3.7	2.8	3.3	2.6
2.0	1.9	2.0		1.6	2.2	2.3	1.9	2.2	1.7
.4	.7	.4	% Depr., Dep., Amort./Sales		.4		.9	.2	.3
(67) 1.0	(62) 1.2	(87) 1.1		(20) 1.7		(19) 1.3	(19) .6	(12) .6	
2.3	2.4	2.1		3.2		2.5	1.2	1.2	
2.1	2.8	1.9	% Officers', Directors' Owners' Comp/Sales		3.2		1.9		
(51) 3.4	(38) 4.2	(53) 3.4		(18) 5.7		(13) 3.2			
7.7	7.2	6.2		10.0		5.2			
1852524M	1183660M	2146532M	Net Sales ($)	5481M	58029M	48430M	209099M	308207M	1517286M
695198M	514719M	824010M	Total Assets ($)	1880M	16656M	15127M	84623M	112890M	592834M

M = $ thousand   MM = $ million
See Pages 9 through 22 for Explanation of Ratios and Data

Current Data Sorted by Assets   **Comparative Historical Data**

Type of Statement	0-500M	500M-2MM	2-10MM	10-50MM	50-100MM	100-250MM		4/1/06-3/31/07 ALL	4/1/07-3/31/08 ALL
Unqualified		7	42	65	7	5		138	140
Reviewed	12	72	175	53	1	1		258	281
Compiled	19	43	20	3	1			76	79
Tax Returns	97	79	24	3				124	114
Other	39	85	109	42	8	5		165	209
		141 (4/1-9/30/10)		875 (10/1/10-3/31/11)					
NUMBER OF STATEMENTS	167	286	370	166	17	10		761	823
	%	%	%	%	%	%		%	%
ASSETS									
Cash & Equivalents	18.4	12.1	11.4	12.9	11.4	13.8		10.5	11.8
Trade Receivables (net)	20.0	31.6	35.0	33.7	22.4	18.2		31.7	30.1
Inventory	5.1	5.0	3.5	4.0	8.4	7.8		3.4	3.5
All Other Current	4.3	4.2	7.4	7.9	7.6	11.8		6.2	6.4
Total Current	47.8	53.0	57.3	58.6	49.8	51.5		51.8	51.9
Fixed Assets (net)	39.9	36.2	34.7	32.9	39.5	29.7		41.6	41.6
Intangibles (net)	3.1	2.4	1.3	1.4	1.6	11.1		1.0	1.0
All Other Non-Current	9.2	8.4	6.6	7.1	9.1	7.7		5.6	5.6
Total	100.0	100.0	100.0	100.0	100.0	100.0		100.0	100.0
LIABILITIES									
Notes Payable-Short Term	20.9	11.4	7.7	6.2	11.8	3.2		8.1	7.5
Cur. Mat.-L.T.D.	9.3	6.0	5.7	5.2	6.3	2.8		7.6	7.2
Trade Payables	15.8	15.1	16.1	16.3	8.5	17.2		14.7	15.0
Income Taxes Payable	.2	.3	.4	.4	.0	1.1		.5	.6
All Other Current	19.0	8.0	9.7	10.5	13.0	11.2		10.6	9.9
Total Current	65.2	40.7	39.7	38.7	39.5	35.5		41.6	40.2
Long-Term Debt	40.2	23.1	15.5	14.7	15.7	24.3		24.0	24.0
Deferred Taxes	.1	.5	1.0	1.1	.5	3.7		1.0	1.0
All Other Non-Current	13.0	4.5	2.3	2.0	2.3	2.9		2.5	2.4
Net Worth	-18.6	31.1	41.6	43.5	42.0	33.6		30.9	32.3
Total Liabilities & Net Worth	100.0	100.0	100.0	100.0	100.0	100.0		100.0	100.0
INCOME DATA									
Net Sales	100.0	100.0	100.0	100.0	100.0	100.0		100.0	100.0
Gross Profit	50.2	35.5	23.4	17.7	23.6	24.0		29.8	28.6
Operating Expenses	45.8	33.7	21.0	14.8	16.9	19.1		23.4	23.2
Operating Profit	4.4	1.8	2.3	2.9	6.7	4.8		6.4	5.4
All Other Expenses (net)	1.0	.4	.3	.5	1.8	.9		.9	.9
Profit Before Taxes	3.3	1.4	2.1	2.4	4.9	3.9		5.5	4.5
RATIOS									
Current	2.1	2.5	2.4	2.2	1.8	2.2		2.0	2.0
	.9	1.4	1.5	1.4	1.3	1.4		1.3	1.3
	.4	.8	1.1	1.1	.9	1.0		1.0	1.0
Quick	1.8	2.2	2.0	1.8	1.6	1.5		1.7	1.7
	.7	1.1	1.2	1.2	1.0	.7		1.1 (821)	1.1
	.2	.6	.8	.9	.3	.5		.7	.7
Sales/Receivables	0 UND	18 20.1	42 8.6	52 7.1	52 7.0	38 9.6		34 10.6	30 12.0
	9 39.3	47 7.7	63 5.8	71 5.2	76 4.8	50 7.2		55 6.6	53 6.9
	35 10.5	69 5.3	85 4.3	91 4.0	84 4.3	77 4.7		76 4.8	78 4.7
Cost of Sales/Inventory	0 UND	0 UND	0 UND	0 UND	0 UND	0 UND		0 UND	0 UND
	0 UND	0 UND	0 UND	1 546.8	1 430.3	14 25.9		0 UND	0 UND
	3 131.0	8 43.5	9 42.9	7 55.1	27 13.7	35 10.5		2 156.2	3 120.0
Cost of Sales/Payables	0 UND	8 47.3	16 22.7	24 15.1	21 17.8	25 14.6		11 32.1	12 31.1
	7 50.1	24 15.5	31 11.6	38 9.5	24 15.3	60 6.1		28 12.9	29 12.6
	42 8.6	47 7.8	54 6.8	58 6.3	45 8.1	120 3.0		50 7.4	51 7.2
Sales/Working Capital	19.6	7.1	5.6	4.8	4.1	5.3		7.9	7.5
	-161.0	17.0	10.4	10.4	7.0	7.4		18.9	19.0
	-10.8	-26.0	68.6	30.4	NM	NM		-193.3	-135.8
EBIT/Interest	11.4	10.8	10.9	11.4	16.7	7.9		13.5	11.7
	(134) 3.9	(250) 2.8	(352) 3.3	(150) 3.6	(16) 3.1	2.7		(704) 4.6	(747) 4.1
	-1.4	-.5	-.4	.3	1.0	.3		1.7	1.3
Net Profit + Depr., Dep., Amort./Cur. Mat. L/T/D		6.6	4.6	6.6				3.9	4.4
	(34) 2.1	(103) 1.9	(62) 2.5					(189) 2.0	(211) 2.2
	.5	.8	1.3					1.2	1.2
Fixed/Worth	.6	.4	.4	.4	.5	.3		.6	.6
	6.9	1.0	.8	.8	.9	1.1		1.2	1.2
	-1.2	4.7	1.5	1.3	1.7	3.6		2.5	2.4
Debt/Worth	1.6	.6	.6	.7	.9	1.3		.9	.9
	39.3	1.9	1.2	1.5	1.2	2.6		2.0	1.9
	-3.3	14.9	2.5	2.6	4.0	5.3		4.7	4.1
% Profit Before Taxes/Tangible Net Worth	236.4	42.5	27.3	24.7	23.6			59.8	48.9
	(95) 50.0	(229) 15.8	(342) 9.2	(163) 10.4	9.9			(679) 29.0	(738) 23.4
	-1.5	-6.9	-3.6	-1.4	.9			10.1	7.5
% Profit Before Taxes/Total Assets	41.7	15.8	11.8	10.4	8.2	11.5		20.7	17.1
	13.4	5.0	4.1	3.7	5.0	4.2		9.2	7.9
	-10.8	-4.2	-2.5	-.5	.2	-.7		2.2	1.5
Sales/Net Fixed Assets	53.9	20.7	12.2	9.3	8.1	9.0		11.2	10.5
	15.3	7.3	5.9	5.7	4.4	4.3		5.6	5.0
	5.1	3.4	3.4	2.9	1.1	3.5		3.3	2.9
Sales/Total Assets	7.1	3.3	2.6	2.2	1.7	1.7		2.8	2.6
	3.8	2.4	1.9	1.6	1.2	1.1		2.1	1.9
	2.3	1.5	1.4	1.1	.7	.7		1.5	1.5
% Depr., Dep., Amort./Sales	1.1	1.9	2.1	2.4	4.4			2.1	2.4
	(107) 3.3	(213) 5.1	(342) 4.4	(148) 4.0	(14) 6.0			(668) 4.3	(724) 4.9
	7.3	9.0	7.7	6.9	11.8			7.4	8.4
% Officers', Directors' Owners' Comp/Sales	3.6	2.4	1.5	.4				1.6	1.5
	(96) 6.6	(144) 4.0	(147) 2.9	(34) 1.4				(341) 3.5	(317) 3.1
	9.8	6.6	5.0	4.1				6.1	6.1
Net Sales ($)	167560M	867264M	3518664M	5697529M	1557019M	1886802M		18046954M	16860067M
Total Assets ($)	37916M	340237M	1791055M	3508027M	1171138M	1717487M		9076734M	9149097M

M = $ thousand   MM = $ million
See Pages 9 through 22 for Explanation of Ratios and Data

Comparative Historical Data / Current Data Sorted by Sales

	4/1/08-3/31/09 ALL	4/1/09-3/31/10 ALL	4/1/10-3/31/11 ALL		141 (4/1-9/30/10) 0-1MM	1-3MM	3-5MM	875 (10/1/10-3/31/11) 5-10MM	10-25MM	25MM & OVER
Type of Statement										
Unqualified	153	158	126			1	10	23	29	63
Reviewed	281	333	313		13	45	46	93	90	26
Compiled	72	96	86		18	28	15	17	7	1
Tax Returns	175	229	203		68	74	29	23	6	3
Other	268	298	288		38	65	34	47	60	44
NUMBER OF STATEMENTS	949	1114	1016		137	213	134	203	192	137
	%	%	%		%	%	%	%	%	%
ASSETS										
Cash & Equivalents	13.1	13.0	13.0		16.1	12.9	13.3	12.8	11.7	12.1
Trade Receivables (net)	30.4	29.6	31.0		17.1	26.4	31.9	34.7	36.8	37.5
Inventory	4.1	5.0	4.4		6.0	4.3	5.9	3.2	3.9	4.1
All Other Current	5.2	6.1	6.1		4.3	4.3	5.2	6.8	7.6	8.7
Total Current	52.9	53.7	54.6		43.4	47.9	56.3	57.5	60.1	62.4
Fixed Assets (net)	39.5	36.2	35.7		42.9	40.6	35.5	33.4	32.2	29.4
Intangibles (net)	1.5	2.2	2.0		3.9	2.2	1.1	1.9	1.4	1.4
All Other Non-Current	6.1	7.9	7.7		9.6	9.2	7.1	7.3	6.3	6.3
Total	100.0	100.0	100.0		100.0	100.0	100.0	100.0	100.0	100.0
LIABILITIES										
Notes Payable-Short Term	8.5	10.3	10.7		17.9	13.6	11.7	7.9	8.1	5.7
Cur. Mat.-L.T.D.	6.9	7.1	6.3		6.9	7.9	6.4	5.9	5.6	4.7
Trade Payables	13.5	14.7	15.7		12.2	14.2	14.7	17.6	17.0	17.7
Income Taxes Payable	.5	.3	.3		.0	.3	.5	.3	.4	.4
All Other Current	10.0	12.7	10.9		18.8	8.8	8.5	9.4	9.4	13.2
Total Current	39.4	45.2	44.0		55.9	44.9	41.8	41.1	40.5	41.7
Long-Term Debt	22.2	19.8	21.6		39.3	28.0	17.6	15.9	17.4	12.5
Deferred Taxes	.7	.7	.8		.2	.5	.7	1.0	1.0	1.0
All Other Non-Current	3.1	4.2	4.6		15.3	4.7	1.8	3.0	1.9	2.8
Net Worth	34.6	30.0	29.0		-10.9	21.8	38.1	39.0	39.3	42.0
Total Liabilities & Net Worth	100.0	100.0	100.0		100.0	100.0	100.0	100.0	100.0	100.0
INCOME DATA										
Net Sales	100.0	100.0	100.0		100.0	100.0	100.0	100.0	100.0	100.0
Gross Profit	28.2	29.0	30.3		51.5	39.4	30.7	24.3	20.4	17.1
Operating Expenses	24.8	27.2	27.6		48.2	36.5	28.6	22.4	17.7	13.4
Operating Profit	3.3	1.8	2.7		3.3	2.8	2.1	1.9	2.7	3.8
All Other Expenses (net)	.8	.8	.5		1.4	.6	.2	.1	.4	.4
Profit Before Taxes	2.5	1.0	2.2		2.0	2.2	1.9	1.8	2.3	3.3
RATIOS										
Current	2.3	2.2	2.3		2.5	2.2	2.5	2.4	2.2	2.2
	1.4	1.4	1.4		1.0	1.2	1.5	1.5	1.5	1.4
	1.0	.9	.9		.4	.7	.9	1.1	1.1	1.2
Quick	2.0	1.8	2.0		1.9	2.0	2.4	2.1	1.8	1.8
	(948) 1.2	(1111) 1.1	1.1		.7	.9	1.3	1.3	1.2	1.2
	.7	.6	.7		.4	.5	.7	.9	.9	.9
Sales/Receivables	27 13.3	28 12.9	26 14.2		0 UND	10 37.7	28 12.9	34 10.7	44 8.3	54 6.7
	52 7.1	53 7.0	54 6.8		14 25.8	41 8.9	57 6.5	55 6.6	63 5.8	72 5.1
	76 4.8	77 4.7	79 4.6		41 8.8	75 4.9	78 4.7	80 4.5	82 4.5	89 4.1
Cost of Sales/Inventory	0 UND	0 UND	0 UND		0 UND	0 UND	0 UND	0 UND	0 UND	0 UND
	0 UND	0 UND	0 UND		0 UND	0 UND	0 UND	0 UND	0 UND	2 242.1
	5 78.1	11 33.9	8 47.4		6 64.3	6 64.4	12 31.2	6 57.9	9 41.8	10 36.2
Cost of Sales/Payables	9 39.5	12 31.2	11 32.5		0 UND	3 114.2	11 32.6	15 23.6	20 18.4	22 16.8
	25 14.6	25 14.4	28 12.8		11 32.5	20 18.7	29 12.5	31 11.7	33 11.0	35 10.4
	45 8.1	49 7.4	51 7.2		48 7.6	53 6.9	48 7.6	53 6.9	50 7.2	52 7.0
Sales/Working Capital	6.6	6.1	6.1		9.5	7.8	6.0	6.0	5.3	5.1
	15.2	16.2	15.2		385.0	45.2	12.4	11.5	11.4	10.2
	-376.3	-37.3	-51.8		-8.5	-22.1	-114.9	115.1	54.7	26.6
EBIT/Interest	11.1	8.5	11.0		7.5	9.2	11.8	10.7	11.8	17.9
	(854) 3.1	(981) 2.2	(912) 3.2		(112) 1.5	(181) 2.7	(125) 3.8	(184) 3.3	(184) 3.6	(126) 4.3
	-.1	-1.0	-.4		-2.8	-.3	-1.2	-.8	.6	.9
Net Profit + Depr., Dep., Amort./Cur. Mat. L/T/D	3.6	3.6	6.3			5.9	3.8	4.1	6.2	8.6
	(232) 1.8	(248) 1.7	(214) 2.2			(21) 2.0	(26) 1.8	(50) 1.8	(62) 2.6	(50) 2.4
	.8	.7	1.0			.7	.8	.7	1.0	1.4
Fixed/Worth	.5	.4	.4		.7	.5	.4	.4	.3	.4
	1.0	1.0	.9		3.6	1.5	.8	.8	.8	.7
	2.3	2.4	2.9		-1.9	-14.7	1.8	1.9	1.5	1.2
Debt/Worth	.7	.7	.7		1.0	.7	.6	.7	.7	.7
	1.6	1.7	1.6		8.8	2.5	1.2	1.4	1.4	1.5
	3.9	5.2	6.7		-3.8	-30.2	3.8	3.6	2.5	2.8
% Profit Before Taxes/Tangible Net Worth	37.7	29.6	35.6		83.9	56.1	37.1	34.3	28.2	25.9
	(841) 15.2	(943) 8.9	(855) 12.5		(86) 16.5	(153) 14.8	(122) 16.1	(178) 9.4	(182) 11.1	(134) 13.2
	.3	-4.2	-3.3		-24.0	-7.6	-6.2	-4.5	-.5	.8
% Profit Before Taxes/Total Assets	14.7	11.5	15.0		21.8	20.6	16.5	14.3	11.1	10.9
	5.0	3.1	4.7		2.0	5.2	5.3	4.4	4.1	5.5
	-2.4	-4.3	-3.0		-15.5	-5.5	-3.1	-2.3	-.4	.2
Sales/Net Fixed Assets	14.0	18.4	17.3		27.4	19.8	16.6	15.8	16.6	11.8
	5.7	6.0	6.6		6.1	5.8	6.6	6.9	6.4	7.0
	3.0	3.1	3.4		2.5	3.2	3.4	3.9	3.6	3.8
Sales/Total Assets	2.9	2.9	3.0		4.2	3.5	3.0	3.2	2.6	2.4
	2.1	2.0	2.0		2.2	2.1	2.1	2.1	2.0	1.8
	1.4	1.3	1.4		1.2	1.4	1.5	1.5	1.5	1.3
% Depr., Dep., Amort./Sales	2.2	1.9	2.0		2.1	2.3	2.4	1.8	1.6	2.1
	(808) 4.5	(933) 4.7	(828) 4.5		(91) 5.8	(159) 5.6	(105) 4.8	(181) 4.2	(177) 3.9	(115) 3.3
	8.3	8.5	7.9		11.3	9.5	8.4	7.5	6.5	5.8
% Officers', Directors' Owners' Comp/Sales	1.8	2.0	1.8		5.5	3.0	2.3	1.5	1.1	.4
	(394) 3.6	(472) 3.5	(425) 3.7		(69) 8.2	(109) 4.8	(63) 3.9	(91) 2.8	(65) 1.6	(28) 1.6
	6.6	7.1	6.9		11.4	7.2	5.6	4.6	3.3	3.6
Net Sales ($)	18204788M	17516180M	13694838M		77525M	410363M	524916M	1407043M	2943098M	8331893M
Total Assets ($)	10069535M	9656220M	8565860M		43632M	279521M	289894M	776293M	1740281M	5436239M

© RMA 2011

M = $ thousand   MM = $ million
See Pages 9 through 22 for Explanation of Ratios and Data

Current Data Sorted by Assets   Comparative Historical Data

						Type of Statement		
1	5	34	44	14	5	Unqualified	122	103
7	92	171	31	1	1	Reviewed	276	255
21	57	30	2	1	1	Compiled	149	135
136	94	37	5		2	Tax Returns	254	225
61	123	124	41	7	6	Other	294	303
	153 (4/1-9/30/10)		1,000 (10/1/10-3/31/11)				4/1/06-3/31/07	4/1/07-3/31/08
0-500M	500M-2MM	2-10MM	10-50MM	50-100MM	100-250MM		ALL	ALL
226	371	396	123	22	15	NUMBER OF STATEMENTS	1095	1021
%	%	%	%	%	%	ASSETS	%	%
19.8	13.3	12.9	14.4	18.3	16.8	Cash & Equivalents	13.2	12.4
25.4	37.4	42.0	34.4	30.7	20.6	Trade Receivables (net)	36.0	35.6
7.5	9.0	6.7	7.4	3.1	2.6	Inventory	8.5	8.3
4.2	4.6	7.6	7.1	6.9	6.4	All Other Current	5.9	6.4
56.9	64.4	69.2	63.3	59.0	46.4	Total Current	63.6	62.7
28.8	24.3	21.9	24.1	35.4	32.0	Fixed Assets (net)	27.1	26.9
4.0	2.8	1.5	6.1	1.0	9.7	Intangibles (net)	2.5	2.8
10.3	8.5	7.3	6.5	4.7	11.9	All Other Non-Current	6.8	7.6
100.0	100.0	100.0	100.0	100.0	100.0	Total	100.0	100.0
						LIABILITIES		
25.2	12.4	8.6	6.1	23.7	5.8	Notes Payable-Short Term	11.8	11.6
6.7	5.2	3.5	3.7	2.7	7.2	Cur. Mat.-L.T.D.	4.3	5.0
17.1	17.6	19.2	15.0	13.2	10.1	Trade Payables	16.4	15.6
.2		.5	.4	.1	.3	Income Taxes Payable	.6	.6
17.7	10.6	11.6	13.7	13.9	15.6	All Other Current	13.3	13.6
66.8	46.2	43.3	38.9	53.5	39.0	Total Current	46.4	46.5
28.4	14.8	10.9	12.4	18.3	29.1	Long-Term Debt	17.4	17.9
.1	.4	.6	.6	1.0	1.9	Deferred Taxes	.5	.3
15.4	5.4	2.5	4.5	2.3	5.8	All Other Non-Current	4.0	4.5
-10.7	33.2	42.7	43.5	24.9	24.1	Net Worth	31.6	30.8
100.0	100.0	100.0	100.0	100.0	100.0	Total Liabilities & Net Worth	100.0	100.0
						INCOME DATA		
100.0	100.0	100.0	100.0	100.0	100.0	Net Sales	100.0	100.0
44.1	36.7	26.4	22.2	21.3	33.7	Gross Profit	33.0	33.4
40.6	33.3	22.9	18.9	19.0	28.1	Operating Expenses	27.8	27.6
3.5	3.4	3.6	3.3	2.3	5.6	Operating Profit	5.1	5.8
.7	.4	.2	.4	1.7	4.9	All Other Expenses (net)	.8	.8
2.8	3.0	3.4	2.9	.7	.7	Profit Before Taxes	4.4	5.0
						RATIOS		
2.6	2.8	2.5	2.6	2.2	2.1		2.4	2.4
1.1	1.5	1.6	1.7	1.5	1.4	Current	1.5	1.5
.5	1.0	1.2	1.2	1.0	1.1		1.1	1.0
2.5	2.3	2.1	2.0	1.8	1.7		1.9	1.9
.8	1.1	1.2	1.4	1.2	1.2	Quick	1.2 (1020)	1.2
.3	.7	.9	.9	.9	.8		.7	.7
0 UND	23 16.1	42 8.6	42 8.7	45 8.0	46 7.9		19 19.5	20 18.1
11 32.4	45 8.1	61 5.9	63 5.8	60 6.1	61 6.0	Sales/Receivables	44 8.2	47 7.8
38 9.6	72 5.1	89 4.1	85 4.3	76 4.8	80 4.6		71 5.2	72 5.1
0 UND	0 UND	0 UND	0 UND	0 UND	0 UND		0 UND	0 UND
0 UND	2 159.9	2 197.2	2 212.0	1 295.8	5 80.2	Cost of Sales/Inventory	1 632.0	0 999.8
10 37.5	22 16.4	20 18.3	24 15.0	12 30.1	22 16.3		18 20.7	17 21.1
0 UND	11 33.2	15 23.9	15 23.7	17 22.0	12 31.7		7 49.9	8 44.7
8 47.6	26 13.9	31 11.9	29 12.8	24 15.1	25 14.5	Cost of Sales/Payables	23 15.6	23 16.1
36 10.0	51 7.2	55 6.6	47 7.7	53 6.8	54 6.8		44 8.3	43 8.6
11.2	6.6	5.1	4.2	5.2	7.7		7.5	8.0
160.1	14.3	9.8	7.8	8.5	13.8	Sales/Working Capital	15.2	14.2
-17.3	-563.5	26.5	23.5	NM	111.9		118.3	750.2
10.3	14.8	21.0	14.1	57.7	139.2		19.3	19.6
(171) 2.6	(319) 4.2	(340) 4.5	(104) 4.9	(15) 7.7	(12) 8.4	EBIT/Interest	(976) 5.7	(902) 5.2
.3	.8	.2	1.1	1.4	2.0		1.7	1.6
	4.1	10.5	5.1			Net Profit + Depr., Dep.,	6.4	12.2
	(36) 1.7	(88) 2.2	(34) 2.0			Amort./Cur. Mat. L/T/D	(205) 2.7	(189) 3.5
	.5	.4	1.2				1.2	1.4
.1	.2	.2	.2	.1	.1		.2	.2
1.6	.6	.4	.5	.7	.6	Fixed/Worth	.7	.6
-1.6	3.0	1.1	1.7	2.4	8.6		2.1	2.2
.7	.6	.6	.7	.8	1.3		.8	.8
6.5	1.8	1.4	1.5	1.6	1.5	Debt/Worth	1.8	1.8
-3.6	9.9	2.9	4.5	2.6	10.0		6.1	6.0
143.8	58.2	41.5	40.3	30.9	45.7	% Profit Before Taxes/Tangible	71.9	70.2
(133) 36.8	(304) 21.5	(376) 15.4	(114) 14.4	(20) 9.5	(13) 21.1	Net Worth	(942) 32.5	(870) 34.5
.0	.9	.5	1.2	-6.0	4.3		10.0	10.3
35.3	18.5	16.7	12.1	10.6	18.2	% Profit Before Taxes/Total	24.0	26.0
9.3	6.7	5.7	5.1	3.7	6.7	Assets	10.4	10.3
-3.8	-.6	-.4	.1	-3.6	2.3		1.9	2.1
159.4	42.2	36.1	33.4	32.4	25.7		42.4	41.5
33.6	16.7	15.4	10.3	5.8	21.8	Sales/Net Fixed Assets	16.8	16.8
10.7	7.1	6.6	3.9	1.5	1.0		7.1	6.6
8.3	4.0	3.0	2.3	2.4	2.7		4.3	4.2
4.9	2.9	2.3	1.8	2.0	1.7	Sales/Total Assets	3.0	2.8
3.0	2.0	1.7	1.3	.8	.5		2.1	1.9
.7	.8	.8	.6	1.2	.6		.7	.7
(127) 1.4	(274) 1.7	(329) 1.6	(112) 2.2	(17) 3.3	(11) 1.7	% Depr., Dep., Amort./Sales	(899) 1.7	(816) 1.7
4.6	3.6	3.4	4.8	9.7	16.3		3.6	3.7
3.4	2.6	1.4	.5			% Officers', Directors'	2.2	2.0
(138) 6.1	(218) 4.6	(177) 3.0	(33) 1.3			Owners' Comp/Sales	(548) 4.4	(496) 4.0
9.8	7.5	4.4	3.0				7.0	7.1
319854M	1286172M	4274122M	4760315M	2681786M	7396577M	Net Sales ($)	24332386M	15704369M
54588M	411647M	1781511M	2540342M	1570668M	2334480M	Total Assets ($)	7998529M	6451664M

© RMA 2011   M = $ thousand   MM = $ million
See Pages 9 through 22 for Explanation of Ratios and Data

Comparative Historical Data | Current Data Sorted by Sales

Type of Statement	Hist 1	Hist 2	Hist 3							
Unqualified	113	112	103	1	6	6	11	32	47	
Reviewed	275	264	303	3	47	51	95	79	28	
Compiled	132	118	111	8	43	28	19	10	3	
Tax Returns	241	283	274	90	76	49	39	13	7	
Other	320	332	362	42	87	53	76	57	47	

	4/1/08-3/31/09 ALL	4/1/09-3/31/10 ALL	4/1/10-3/31/11 ALL	153 (4/1-9/30/10)			1,000 (10/1/10-3/31/11)		
				0-1MM	1-3MM	3-5MM	5-10MM	10-25MM	25MM & OVER
NUMBER OF STATEMENTS	1081	1109	1153	144	259	187	240	191	132
ASSETS	%	%	%	%	%	%	%	%	%
Cash & Equivalents	13.9	15.2	14.7	18.1	15.2	13.2	14.5	12.6	15.6
Trade Receivables (net)	34.2	33.0	36.0	22.4	32.0	38.6	40.2	42.8	37.6
Inventory	8.4	7.6	7.5	6.3	9.3	8.5	7.0	7.1	5.8
All Other Current	6.4	6.1	5.9	4.0	4.4	6.0	7.3	6.5	7.7
Total Current	62.9	61.9	64.1	50.7	60.8	66.2	69.0	69.0	66.7
Fixed Assets (net)	26.9	27.6	24.7	33.3	26.3	23.6	21.7	22.6	21.8
Intangibles (net)	2.8	3.1	3.0	4.3	4.0	2.0	1.6	1.8	5.4
All Other Non-Current	7.4	7.5	8.2	11.6	9.0	8.2	7.7	6.5	6.1
Total	100.0	100.0	100.0	100.0	100.0	100.0	100.0	100.0	100.0
LIABILITIES									
Notes Payable-Short Term	12.0	11.6	13.1	26.8	15.9	12.7	8.0	8.7	8.5
Cur. Mat.-L.T.D.	4.6	5.2	4.7	5.4	5.5	5.5	4.2	3.8	3.5
Trade Payables	15.5	16.4	17.6	13.4	16.4	18.0	18.4	19.8	19.2
Income Taxes Payable	.6	.3	.4	.1	.3	.6	.4	.4	.4
All Other Current	13.5	13.3	12.8	21.6	9.3	10.4	11.7	12.8	15.1
Total Current	46.1	46.8	48.5	67.3	47.5	47.3	42.8	45.4	46.7
Long-Term Debt	17.3	17.5	16.1	30.6	18.4	13.6	12.2	12.5	11.9
Deferred Taxes	.4	.5	.5	.0	.4	.5	.7	.5	.6
All Other Non-Current	3.9	4.2	6.2	17.8	5.3	8.1	3.1	2.1	4.5
Net Worth	32.2	31.0	28.7	-15.7	28.5	30.4	41.3	39.6	36.4
Total Liabilties & Net Worth	100.0	100.0	100.0	100.0	100.0	100.0	100.0	100.0	100.0
INCOME DATA									
Net Sales	100.0	100.0	100.0	100.0	100.0	100.0	100.0	100.0	100.0
Gross Profit	33.1	32.6	32.7	49.3	40.4	30.7	27.7	25.1	22.7
Operating Expenses	28.4	29.2	29.3	45.6	37.0	28.3	24.1	21.4	18.5
Operating Profit	4.7	3.4	3.5	3.7	3.4	2.4	3.6	3.7	4.2
All Other Expenses (net)	.6	.8	.5	1.2	.4	.4	.0	.6	.5
Profit Before Taxes	4.1	2.7	3.0	2.5	3.0	2.0	3.6	3.1	3.8

RATIOS

Ratio	Hist 1	Hist 2	Hist 3	0-1MM	1-3MM	3-5MM	5-10MM	10-25MM	25MM & OVER
Current	2.5	2.6	2.6	2.6	3.2	2.9	2.8	2.5	2.1
	1.5	1.5	1.5	1.0	1.5	1.5	1.6	1.4	1.6
	1.0	1.0	1.0	.4	.8	1.0	1.2	1.1	1.1
Quick	2.0	2.1	2.2	2.4	2.5	2.2	2.3	2.0	1.8
	(1080) 1.2	1.2	1.2	.7	1.1	1.1	1.2	1.2	1.3
	.7	.6	.7	.2	.5	.7	.8	.8	.9
Sales/Receivables	19 18.9	21 17.6	23 15.8	0 UND	14 26.8	28 12.9	32 11.4	41 9.0	40 9.1
	43 8.4	44 8.3	50 7.4	15 25.0	37 9.7	47 7.8	58 6.3	61 6.0	58 6.3
	71 5.2	70 5.2	77 4.7	59 6.2	66 5.5	73 5.0	82 4.4	86 4.2	79 4.6
Cost of Sales/Inventory	0 UND	0 UND	0 UND	0 UND	0 UND	0 UND	0 UND	0 UND	0 UND
	1 325.3	0 844.0	1 479.3	0 UND	1 522.3	2 157.4	2 224.1	2 214.4	2 187.4
	21 17.1	17 21.2	19 18.8	14 25.4	27 13.7	20 18.2	18 20.2	17 21.0	20 18.6
Cost of Sales/Payables	8 44.1	9 39.8	10 35.9	0 UND	7 53.4	9 38.4	12 29.6	16 23.3	17 21.9
	22 16.5	23 15.7	26 14.2	12 29.6	24 15.3	24 15.0	25 14.5	30 12.2	32 11.3
	40 9.1	44 8.3	50 7.3	46 8.0	51 7.1	53 6.9	48 7.6	50 7.2	51 7.2
Sales/Working Capital	6.6	6.5	6.0	8.1	6.1	6.4	5.2	5.7	5.7
	14.1	14.1	13.4	190.8	17.5	14.0	9.8	11.2	10.8
	158.7	-148.5	999.8	-8.5	-58.7	-999.8	28.7	30.7	28.3
EBIT/Interest	18.5	14.8	16.4	7.3	10.2	13.7	20.7	26.4	51.1
	(936) 5.0	(961) 3.7	(961) 4.0	(99) 2.0	(221) 3.5	(162) 2.9	(201) 4.8	(166) 6.6	(112) 5.7
	1.1	.0	.6	-1.5	.6	-.6	1.1	1.2	1.5
Net Profit + Depr., Dep., Amort./Cur. Mat. L/T/D	9.2	4.9	6.1		6.1	2.2	13.1	6.5	12.6
	(222) 3.1	(217) 1.9	(177) 2.1	(21) 3.7	(27) .8	(44) 2.6	(45) 1.8	(36) 3.5	
	1.4	.7	.7	1.0	-.3	1.1	.3	1.5	
Fixed/Worth	.2	.2	.2	.1	.2	.2	.2	.2	.1
	.6	.6	.5	1.8	.7	.6	.4	.4	.5
	2.0	2.3	2.1	-3.4	-83.0	1.6	1.2	1.1	1.2
Debt/Worth	.7	.7	.7	.9	.5	.7	.5	.7	.8
	1.7	1.7	1.7	7.9	1.9	1.9	1.4	1.5	1.6
	5.7	6.7	6.5	-4.5	-147.0	6.8	2.8	3.4	4.5
% Profit Before Taxes/Tangible Net Worth	58.7	49.0	51.1	129.9	57.4	48.2	39.8	46.1	47.8
	(915) 27.0	(936) 16.1	(960) 18.2	(86) 37.9	(194) 15.6	(157) 19.6	(221) 15.6	(181) 18.4	(121) 18.6
	6.5	-.1	.7	-2.2	-1.6	-2.9	1.8	1.0	3.9
% Profit Before Taxes/Total Assets	23.0	19.3	18.2	26.5	18.3	18.4	19.7	17.6	14.7
	8.5	5.3	6.3	7.8	6.5	5.5	6.3	6.8	5.7
	.7	-1.6	-.8	-9.3	-1.8	-2.9	.3	-.1	1.1
Sales/Net Fixed Assets	44.8	38.7	45.8	96.6	43.5	46.4	42.2	40.2	52.9
	17.0	15.0	16.9	12.9	16.0	17.4	16.5	18.5	19.4
	6.1	5.8	6.7	4.5	6.4	7.7	7.8	6.8	6.1
Sales/Total Assets	4.1	3.8	3.9	5.2	4.4	4.8	3.7	3.2	3.0
	2.8	2.6	2.6	2.6	2.9	2.9	2.5	2.5	2.3
	1.9	1.8	1.8	1.4	1.8	2.0	2.0	1.7	1.7
% Depr., Dep., Amort./Sales	.7	.8	.7	1.4	.8	.7	.9	.7	.5
	(869) 1.8	(907) 2.0	(870) 1.7	(76) 3.3	(183) 1.8	(143) 1.5	(194) 1.6	(165) 1.5	(109) 1.4
	3.9	4.2	4.0	8.4	4.3	3.2	3.6	3.6	3.7
% Officers', Directors' Owners' Comp/Sales	2.1	2.2	2.1	4.6	3.0	2.4	2.1	1.1	.6
	(524) 4.1	(567) 4.1	(575) 4.0	(82) 7.3	(156) 5.4	(94) 4.2	(124) 3.4	(80) 1.9	(39) 1.4
	6.9	7.5	7.0	12.3	8.8	5.4	5.7	3.6	3.3
Net Sales ($)	17198724M	17112415M	20718826M	81083M	507320M	732154M	1734402M	3033944M	14629923M
Total Assets ($)	7943967M	8864694M	8693236M	48410M	227676M	318954M	778952M	1749441M	5569803M

© RMA 2011

M = $ thousand   MM = $ million
See Pages 9 through 22 for Explanation of Ratios and Data

Current Data Sorted by Assets   Comparative Historical Data

	0-500M	500M-2MM	2-10MM	10-50MM	50-100MM	100-250MM		4/1/06-3/31/07 ALL	4/1/07-3/31/08 ALL
		46 (4/1-9/30/10)		96 (10/1/10-3/31/11)			**Type of Statement**		
		2	8	23	8	4	Unqualified	52	47
		6	11	10	1		Reviewed	16	18
		4	6	2			Compiled	16	19
		5	8	1			Tax Returns	10	11
	2	4	16	11	2	8	Other	39	42
	2	21	49	47	11	12	**NUMBER OF STATEMENTS**	133	137
	%	%	%	%	%	%	**ASSETS**	%	%
		6.7	7.3	7.9	6.5	7.1	Cash & Equivalents	6.6	7.7
		29.2	25.5	22.0	21.2	21.8	Trade Receivables (net)	25.3	25.9
		29.0	21.9	27.1	14.8	20.2	Inventory	23.4	23.8
		2.8	5.3	2.5	2.1	4.2	All Other Current	2.9	2.8
		67.8	60.0	59.4	44.7	53.4	Total Current	58.2	60.2
		22.4	28.6	29.0	34.4	30.4	Fixed Assets (net)	31.8	30.9
		4.4	3.3	5.3	15.4	8.8	Intangibles (net)	2.5	2.2
		5.4	8.1	6.3	5.5	7.4	All Other Non-Current	7.5	6.7
		100.0	100.0	100.0	100.0	100.0	Total	100.0	100.0
							LIABILITIES		
		9.9	13.6	11.7	5.6	11.3	Notes Payable-Short Term	13.0	11.9
		5.1	3.1	2.1	3.5	1.5	Cur. Mat.-L.T.D.	3.1	2.6
		17.8	14.3	14.4	9.2	13.9	Trade Payables	15.9	17.4
		.0	.0	.6	.1	.1	Income Taxes Payable	.2	.2
		8.4	13.0	8.2	6.9	10.8	All Other Current	8.3	9.5
		41.2	44.0	37.0	25.3	37.6	Total Current	40.6	41.6
		18.6	15.1	11.4	16.4	10.6	Long-Term Debt	15.5	16.0
		.1	.1	.4	.7	2.1	Deferred Taxes	.6	.6
		.9	2.6	5.1	4.9	4.4	All Other Non-Current	3.8	5.7
		39.1	38.1	46.2	52.8	45.3	Net Worth	39.5	36.1
		100.0	100.0	100.0	100.0	100.0	Total Liabilities & Net Worth	100.0	100.0
							INCOME DATA		
		100.0	100.0	100.0	100.0	100.0	Net Sales	100.0	100.0
		28.9	22.7	21.1	29.3	15.1	Gross Profit	23.8	21.1
		24.0	19.0	13.6	20.1	9.4	Operating Expenses	19.3	16.9
		4.9	3.7	7.5	9.2	5.8	Operating Profit	4.5	4.2
		.5	.6	.9	.7	-.1	All Other Expenses (net)	1.1	.4
		4.4	3.1	6.7	8.5	5.9	Profit Before Taxes	3.4	3.8
							RATIOS		
		2.8	2.5	2.9	2.6	1.6	Current	2.2	2.1
		1.4	1.5	1.4	1.7	1.3		1.4	1.4
		1.1	.9	1.1	1.1	1.2		1.1	1.1
		1.1	1.2	1.3	1.8	.9	Quick	1.3	1.1
		.7	.8	.7	.9	.7		.7	.7
		.6	.5	.5	.7	.5		.5	.5
		19 19.0	16 23.1	19 19.0	26 14.1	18 20.2	Sales/Receivables	19 19.7	21 17.8
		28 13.1	30 12.2	29 12.6	31 11.9	25 14.6		29 12.6	26 14.1
		41 8.9	42 8.6	40 9.0	46 7.9	42 8.7		41 8.8	39 9.3
		20 18.6	12 31.5	24 15.2	20 18.2	16 23.5	Cost of Sales/Inventory	18 20.3	16 22.4
		44 8.3	30 12.0	41 8.8	42 8.7	37 9.9		35 10.6	35 10.4
		64 5.7	59 6.1	61 5.9	56 6.6	49 7.5		62 5.9	59 6.2
		7 49.4	10 35.8	13 28.0	13 27.7	16 23.2	Cost of Sales/Payables	13 27.8	13 27.6
		21 17.5	18 20.5	22 16.7	19 18.9	20 18.2		23 15.8	23 15.8
		34 10.7	40 9.2	29 12.5	25 14.3	24 15.4		36 10.3	34 10.8
		10.1	7.9	7.3	5.4	10.9	Sales/Working Capital	9.5	9.5
		18.1	17.5	16.2	11.0	19.1		17.0	19.0
		69.8	-49.7	40.4	77.1	35.6		109.2	63.4
		18.7	18.3	27.2	47.2	23.1	EBIT/Interest	10.8	12.0
		1.7	(47) 7.8	(42) 7.3	14.7	(10) 8.0		(123) 4.4	(128) 3.2
		1.0	2.4	2.1	2.8	4.3		1.8	1.1
				11.2			Net Profit + Depr., Dep., Amort./Cur. Mat. L/T/D	12.3	13.1
				(12) 4.4				(34) 3.5	(35) 2.6
				2.5				1.5	1.3
		.2	.3	.5	.4	.5	Fixed/Worth	.5	.4
		.7	.6	.8	1.0	.8		.8	.8
		1.8	2.0	1.2	4.5	.9		1.8	1.5
		.6	.7	.6	.5	.7	Debt/Worth	.6	.6
		2.7	1.4	1.6	1.1	1.4		1.4	1.6
		6.8	7.8	3.3	6.8	2.4		3.7	3.8
		93.8	46.7	36.8	111.7	45.6	% Profit Before Taxes/Tangible Net Worth	35.0	35.3
		(19) 23.1	(44) 21.1	(46) 24.7	(10) 37.7	(11) 26.9		(119) 20.2	(127) 17.6
		4.0	10.2	9.7	24.4	14.9		7.5	4.4
		26.1	14.3	16.9	29.3	19.4	% Profit Before Taxes/Total Assets	14.4	15.6
		2.8	7.2	11.2	15.2	10.8		7.2	6.6
		-.3	3.4	3.3	4.0	6.5		2.6	.7
		68.3	53.7	19.5	11.2	19.8	Sales/Net Fixed Assets	25.7	29.2
		21.7	13.4	11.5	6.6	8.5		9.7	11.4
		9.6	6.7	5.1	3.9	5.6		5.2	5.1
		4.9	3.9	3.4	3.2	3.5	Sales/Total Assets	3.8	3.9
		4.1	2.8	2.7	2.6	2.7		2.8	2.9
		2.6	1.9	1.9	1.3	2.2		1.9	2.0
		.9	.5	.6	1.2		% Depr., Dep., Amort./Sales	1.1	.7
		(15) 1.1	(43) 1.4	1.3	(10) 2.3			(119) 1.6	(127) 1.5
		1.7	2.7	2.6	4.7			2.6	2.3
			.6				% Officers', Directors' Owners' Comp/Sales	.6	.6
			(13) 1.6	(11) 1.7				(32) 2.1	(31) 1.4
			3.6	3.1				3.8	2.8
	2851M	99593M	765887M	3113080M	1951470M	5394772M	Net Sales ($)	10276492M	8678475M
	734M	25946M	246240M	1093663M	790101M	2030694M	Total Assets ($)	3770994M	3583113M

Comparative Historical Data   Current Data Sorted by Sales

			Type of Statement						
45	41	45	Unqualified				4	4	37
19	22	28	Reviewed		3	1	7	6	11
19	13	12	Compiled	1	1	2	2	4	2
11	16	14	Tax Returns		2	2	4	3	3
61	47	43	Other	2	1	5	8	7	20
4/1/08-3/31/09 ALL	4/1/09-3/31/10 ALL	4/1/10-3/31/11 ALL		0-1MM	46 (4/1-9/30/10) 1-3MM	3-5MM	96 (10/1/10-3/31/11) 5-10MM	10-25MM	25MM & OVER
155	139	142	NUMBER OF STATEMENTS	3	7	10	25	24	73
%	%	%	ASSETS	%	%	%	%	%	%
7.2	7.7	7.2	Cash & Equivalents			6.6	8.0	7.3	7.7
26.1	26.4	24.5	Trade Receivables (net)			26.5	23.4	31.8	22.8
25.1	23.3	23.9	Inventory			23.5	24.1	21.3	25.0
3.4	3.8	3.6	All Other Current			5.8	1.9	7.0	3.1
61.8	61.2	59.3	Total Current			62.5	57.3	67.4	58.6
28.0	29.0	28.2	Fixed Assets (net)			24.6	32.6	23.0	28.4
2.8	2.9	5.6	Intangibles (net)			5.5	1.9	4.9	7.1
7.4	6.8	7.0	All Other Non-Current			7.5	8.2	4.7	5.8
100.0	100.0	100.0	Total			100.0	100.0	100.0	100.0
			LIABILITIES						
13.7	12.0	11.4	Notes Payable-Short Term			12.5	9.5	19.6	9.9
3.5	3.1	2.9	Cur. Mat.-L.T.D.			.4	2.5	4.0	2.2
18.3	16.3	14.4	Trade Payables			14.5	16.7	14.3	14.6
.2	.1	.2	Income Taxes Payable			.0	.1	.0	.4
9.4	10.0	10.4	All Other Current			21.7	11.0	9.3	8.8
45.0	41.5	39.3	Total Current			49.0	39.8	47.2	36.0
13.9	16.6	13.9	Long-Term Debt			24.5	18.4	12.6	11.1
	.2	.4	Deferred Taxes			.0	.1	.1	.7
4.1	3.8	3.5	All Other Non-Current			.6	4.9	.2	4.8
36.5	37.9	42.8	Net Worth			25.9	36.8	39.9	47.4
100.0	100.0	100.0	Total Liabilties & Net Worth			100.0	100.0	100.0	100.0
			INCOME DATA						
100.0	100.0	100.0	Net Sales			100.0	100.0	100.0	100.0
18.7	21.7	23.5	Gross Profit			33.9	22.6	26.0	19.4
15.2	16.3	17.7	Operating Expenses			26.8	19.2	17.6	14.3
3.5	5.4	5.8	Operating Profit			7.0	3.4	8.5	5.2
.3	.5	.6	All Other Expenses (net)			2.0	.1	.2	.3
3.2	5.0	5.2	Profit Before Taxes			5.0	3.3	8.3	4.9
			RATIOS						
2.0	2.5	2.5				3.6	2.6	2.5	2.5
1.4	1.4	1.4	Current			1.2	1.4	1.5	1.5
1.1	1.1	1.1				.8	1.1	1.0	1.2
1.1	1.3	1.2				1.5	1.2	1.6	1.3
.7	.7	.8	Quick			.8	.8	.9	.8
.4	.5	.5				.4	.4	.6	.6
17 21.9	19 19.6	19 19.6		24 14.9	15 24.8	26 14.3	18 20.4		
26 14.1	30 12.1	29 12.6	Sales/Receivables	43 8.6	28 13.1	36 10.1	29 12.7		
35 10.5	41 8.9	42 8.7		50 7.3	39 9.3	49 7.5	40 9.2		
13 28.2	14 26.8	19 19.7		25 14.6	15 24.6	14 25.7	21 17.8		
30 12.1	32 11.5	39 9.4	Cost of Sales/Inventory	61 6.0	30 12.0	25 14.5	39 9.4		
50 7.3	61 6.0	59 6.1		129 2.8	63 5.8	50 7.3	55 6.6		
12 29.6	13 28.6	13 28.4		18 19.8	12 29.3	8 47.1	14 26.3		
20 18.1	22 16.9	20 18.5	Cost of Sales/Payables	30 12.1	23 15.9	18 20.7	19 19.0		
33 11.2	34 10.8	30 12.2		54 6.7	47 7.8	40 9.0	26 14.2		
11.3	7.9	8.2		9.1	8.8	7.2	8.3		
23.7	19.6	17.8	Sales/Working Capital	50.8	20.3	11.8	16.2		
134.2	83.1	60.5		-14.5	87.4	138.0	37.4		
13.8	18.7	22.1		118.0	9.3	24.6	23.5		
(147) 4.8	(126) 5.5	(131) 6.8	EBIT/Interest	3.3	4.3	(23) 8.5	(65) 9.4		
2.3	1.8	2.2		1.3	.8	2.3	3.6		
9.2	8.3	12.9	Net Profit + Depr., Dep.,				14.1		
(39) 3.2	(30) 2.9	(27) 5.2	Amort./Cur. Mat. L/T/D			(22) 5.7			
1.2	.6	2.5				2.9			
.3	.4	.4		.2	.3	.4	.4		
.8	.8	.7	Fixed/Worth	1.5	.8	.7	.7		
1.5	1.9	1.4		NM	5.3	1.8	1.1		
.9	.6	.6		1.7	.6	.8	.6		
1.9	2.0	1.5	Debt/Worth	6.2	2.2	1.7	1.3		
5.6	5.4	4.2		NM	7.2	6.0	2.6		
52.7	59.2	47.4	% Profit Before Taxes/Tangible		31.2	139.1	38.3		
(145) 25.1	(128) 25.9	(132) 24.3	Net Worth	(22) 14.5	34.2	(69) 27.1			
8.4	9.3	9.2			.0	10.9	14.4		
14.9	20.7	16.6		36.3	13.5	19.3	16.8		
8.8	10.0	8.7	% Profit Before Taxes/Total Assets	5.1	5.8	7.8	10.5		
3.6	2.2	2.6		1.4	-.5	4.2	5.7		
33.7	28.4	23.8		91.0	43.5	47.2	21.6		
15.5	12.9	11.6	Sales/Net Fixed Assets	21.9	11.1	11.5	11.7		
6.9	6.2	5.6		4.6	5.4	6.7	6.2		
4.7	4.1	3.8		3.2	4.7	3.5	3.7		
3.2	2.9	2.8	Sales/Total Assets	2.5	2.9	2.8	2.9		
2.4	2.1	2.1		.9	1.8	2.1	2.3		
.6	.8	.7			.7	.8	.7		
(139) 1.2	(116) 1.2	(124) 1.3	% Depr., Dep., Amort./Sales	(22) 1.2	(21) 1.5	(68) 1.2			
2.1	2.6	2.6			4.1	2.6	2.3		
.4	.7	.8	% Officers', Directors'		.7		.5		
(36) 1.1	(28) 1.7	(32) 1.7	Owners' Comp/Sales	(10) 1.2	(11) 1.9				
2.5	4.5	3.1			1.9	3.1			
15008980M	9605336M	11327653M	Net Sales ($)	1766M	16961M	36526M	179338M	421158M	10671904M
4158198M	3672779M	4187378M	Total Assets ($)	7858M	15143M	26804M	78575M	176060M	3882938M

M = $ thousand   MM = $ million
See Pages 9 through 22 for Explanation of Ratios and Data

Current Data Sorted by Assets   Comparative Historical Data

Type of Statement	0-500M	500M-2MM	2-10MM	10-50MM	50-100MM	100-250MM		4/1/06-3/31/07 ALL	4/1/07-3/31/08 ALL
Unqualified			1	8	6	6		28	19
Reviewed		2		1				3	5
Compiled		1	4	1				3	4
Tax Returns		3						3	3
Other	1	2	1	2	1			8	15
		23 (4/1-9/30/10)		18 (10/1/10-3/31/11)					
NUMBER OF STATEMENTS	1	6	8	11	8	7		45	46
	%	%	%	%	%	%		%	%
ASSETS									
Cash & Equivalents				8.6				5.1	5.8
Trade Receivables (net)				15.1				17.9	19.5
Inventory				30.7				23.5	25.8
All Other Current				8.7				4.3	4.4
Total Current				63.1				50.8	55.5
Fixed Assets (net)				31.9				39.8	37.7
Intangibles (net)				.8				3.8	2.1
All Other Non-Current				4.2				5.6	4.7
Total				100.0				100.0	100.0
LIABILITIES									
Notes Payable-Short Term				16.1				12.3	13.7
Cur. Mat.-L.T.D.				2.0				3.9	3.0
Trade Payables				10.6				10.3	12.8
Income Taxes Payable				.4				.3	.2
All Other Current				8.5				7.3	6.0
Total Current				37.6				34.1	35.8
Long-Term Debt				13.1				21.9	18.8
Deferred Taxes				.9				1.7	1.6
All Other Non-Current				1.7				2.8	3.8
Net Worth				46.7				39.5	40.1
Total Liabilties & Net Worth				100.0				100.0	100.0
INCOME DATA									
Net Sales				100.0				100.0	100.0
Gross Profit				22.2				22.1	20.0
Operating Expenses				12.6				18.3	14.6
Operating Profit				9.6				3.8	5.4
All Other Expenses (net)				.8				1.0	1.2
Profit Before Taxes				8.8				2.8	4.2
RATIOS									
Current				3.1				2.1	2.1
				1.7				1.8	1.5
				1.2				1.1	1.2
Quick				1.3				1.0	1.1
				.9				.7	.7
				.2				.4	.4
Sales/Receivables			16	22.9				21 17.5	26 14.2
			25	14.5				32 11.3	35 10.4
			28	13.1				41 9.0	44 8.3
Cost of Sales/Inventory			36	10.0				32 11.5	36 10.2
			58	6.3				57 6.4	57 6.4
			81	4.5				72 5.1	77 4.7
Cost of Sales/Payables			5	75.9				13 28.4	11 34.6
			16	23.4				21 17.8	22 16.5
			29	12.4				36 10.1	38 9.6
Sales/Working Capital				5.9				6.0	7.0
				8.7				9.5	12.2
				22.6				34.2	23.4
EBIT/Interest				41.6				6.3	11.4
				18.0				(44) 3.0	3.7
				4.8				1.3	1.8
Net Profit + Depr., Dep., Amort./Cur. Mat. L/T/D								6.5	7.6
								(12) 3.0	(12) 2.5
								2.5	1.6
Fixed/Worth				.3				.6	.5
				.5				1.2	1.1
				1.1				2.2	1.8
Debt/Worth				.7				.9	.9
				1.1				1.5	1.6
				1.7				4.1	3.6
% Profit Before Taxes/Tangible Net Worth				49.3				25.0	29.1
				38.1				(41) 13.7	18.7
				31.3				5.9	8.2
% Profit Before Taxes/Total Assets				24.7				8.4	12.3
				17.2				4.9	6.3
				7.8				1.5	2.5
Sales/Net Fixed Assets				18.0				10.2	11.5
				5.4				5.2	6.8
				3.9				2.6	3.0
Sales/Total Assets				2.7				2.7	2.9
				2.1				1.9	1.8
				1.8				1.4	1.5
% Depr., Dep., Amort./Sales				1.1				1.6	1.0
			(10)	1.8				(42) 2.8	(41) 2.2
				2.9				3.8	3.3
% Officers', Directors' Owners' Comp/Sales									
Net Sales ($)	100M	33265M	72927M	532655M	1116773M	2120563M		3523782M	5007981M
Total Assets ($)	263M	8317M	34642M	252951M	576934M	1037100M		1959454M	2784036M

M = $ thousand   MM = $ million
See Pages 9 through 22 for Explanation of Ratios and Data

Comparative Historical Data / Current Data Sorted by Sales

			Type of Statement	0-1MM	1-3MM	3-5MM	5-10MM	10-25MM	25MM & OVER
22	18	21	Unqualified				1		20
6	5	3	Reviewed					2	1
5	6	6	Compiled		2		2	1	1
4	4	3	Tax Returns					1	
20	16	8	Other	1	1	1	1		4
4/1/08-3/31/09 ALL	4/1/09-3/31/10 ALL	4/1/10-3/31/11 ALL			23 (4/1-9/30/10)			18 (10/1/10-3/31/11)	
57	49	41	NUMBER OF STATEMENTS	1	2	4	4	4	26
%	%	%	**ASSETS**	%	%	%	%	%	%
4.9	7.5	6.1	Cash & Equivalents						5.3
20.7	20.1	20.9	Trade Receivables (net)						18.5
29.9	26.9	26.1	Inventory						26.2
3.3	3.1	4.9	All Other Current						5.6
58.8	57.6	58.0	Total Current						55.8
32.2	33.2	32.4	Fixed Assets (net)						36.6
3.2	2.6	1.9	Intangibles (net)						2.2
5.9	6.7	7.7	All Other Non-Current						5.4
100.0	100.0	100.0	Total						100.0
			LIABILITIES						
15.6	13.3	11.5	Notes Payable-Short Term						10.9
3.5	3.5	2.6	Cur. Mat.-L.T.D.						1.8
14.1	11.1	11.5	Trade Payables						10.3
.3	.3	.4	Income Taxes Payable						.3
7.4	7.0	6.9	All Other Current						8.0
40.8	35.2	32.9	Total Current						31.2
19.1	17.5	17.2	Long-Term Debt						15.6
1.3	1.2	.8	Deferred Taxes						1.3
4.4	3.9	6.6	All Other Non-Current						3.8
34.4	42.2	42.5	Net Worth						48.0
100.0	100.0	100.0	Total Liabilities & Net Worth						100.0
			INCOME DATA						
100.0	100.0	100.0	Net Sales						100.0
20.0	22.3	20.8	Gross Profit						18.1
15.6	15.9	14.9	Operating Expenses						9.7
4.5	6.4	5.9	Operating Profit						8.4
1.0	1.6	1.2	All Other Expenses (net)						.7
3.4	4.8	4.7	Profit Before Taxes						7.7
			RATIOS						
1.8	2.5	3.3	Current						3.2
1.4	1.6	1.9							1.8
1.2	1.2	1.3							1.4
.9	1.4	1.4	Quick						1.2
.6	.7	.9							.9
.4	.5	.5							.5
25 14.9	22 16.5	22 16.6	Sales/Receivables						25 14.6
31 11.7	28 12.9	30 12.1							30 12.1
38 9.7	36 10.2	47 7.7							42 8.8
34 10.8	33 11.2	33 11.1	Cost of Sales/Inventory						34 10.9
52 7.0	47 7.8	52 7.0							53 6.9
88 4.1	65 5.6	78 4.7							72 5.1
9 41.9	9 39.1	10 36.2	Cost of Sales/Payables						7 52.3
23 16.1	16 23.0	21 17.6							18 20.1
34 10.8	32 11.5	30 12.1							30 12.2
9.1	7.3	6.2	Sales/Working Capital						6.1
13.1	12.1	8.5							8.5
36.7	19.0	18.3							15.1
7.4	25.6	25.9	EBIT/Interest						30.9
(56) 3.7	5.6	(37) 6.8							13.3
1.1	1.7	2.1							3.3
10.9	8.4	17.0	Net Profit + Depr., Dep., Amort./Cur. Mat. L/T/D						17.9
(21) 4.2	(19) 4.7	(12) 6.0						(11)	6.1
1.9	1.9	1.9							2.1
.5	.3	.3	Fixed/Worth						.4
1.0	.9	.7							.8
1.8	1.6	1.4							1.4
1.1	.8	.7	Debt/Worth						.7
2.2	1.7	1.5							1.1
4.0	3.1	3.2							1.8
39.2	45.0	40.7	% Profit Before Taxes/Tangible Net Worth						42.9
(53) 22.7	(48) 30.0	(39) 32.3							34.2
6.2	13.5	15.3							20.4
13.7	22.4	20.1	% Profit Before Taxes/Total Assets						24.5
8.6	11.8	12.1							12.9
.8	2.6	3.3							6.0
15.3	13.0	19.7	Sales/Net Fixed Assets						11.7
8.3	8.7	8.6							5.0
3.9	4.5	3.8							3.7
2.9	3.1	2.7	Sales/Total Assets						2.6
2.2	2.4	2.1							1.9
1.7	1.9	1.6							1.7
1.2	1.1	1.3	% Depr., Dep., Amort./Sales						1.4
(53) 2.0	(43) 1.8	(34) 1.9						(25)	1.9
2.8	2.6	3.2							3.0
			% Officers', Directors' Owners' Comp/Sales						
7591347M	6269175M	3876283M	Net Sales ($)	100M	3978M	16099M	29949M	56166M	3769991M
3724441M	2653058M	1910207M	Total Assets ($)	263M	5240M	9157M	9849M	18713M	1866985M

M = $ thousand   MM = $ million
See Pages 9 through 22 for Explanation of Ratios and Data

Current Data Sorted by Assets   Comparative Historical Data

						Type of Statement		
1		2	7	1	1	Unqualified	15	16
1	1	10	4			Reviewed	12	13
2	3	4				Compiled	12	12
3	3	1				Tax Returns	1	7
3	8	6	7	2	1	Other	27	28
	29 (4/1-9/30/10)		42 (10/1/10-3/31/11)				4/1/06-3/31/07	4/1/07-3/31/08
0-500M	500M-2MM	2-10MM	10-50MM	50-100MM	100-250MM		ALL	ALL
10	15	23	18	3	2	NUMBER OF STATEMENTS	67	76
%	%	%	%	%	%	ASSETS	%	%
8.3	11.6	15.5	5.9			Cash & Equivalents	8.3	9.5
16.6	13.6	15.5	20.1			Trade Receivables (net)	16.1	15.0
40.0	26.4	28.3	26.7			Inventory	33.3	31.8
11.0	4.8	2.7	2.1			All Other Current	2.2	2.6
76.0	56.5	62.0	54.7			Total Current	59.8	58.9
17.5	29.6	32.6	34.6			Fixed Assets (net)	30.7	29.0
4.1	5.0	1.6	6.5			Intangibles (net)	4.4	5.9
2.3	8.9	3.8	4.2			All Other Non-Current	5.0	6.2
100.0	100.0	100.0	100.0			Total	100.0	100.0
						LIABILITIES		
41.0	13.4	6.6	8.9			Notes Payable-Short Term	13.3	15.3
5.5	2.2	3.4	2.9			Cur. Mat.-L.T.D.	2.9	3.5
21.3	15.2	13.2	12.1			Trade Payables	12.7	11.0
.1	.0	.3	.1			Income Taxes Payable	.5	.3
18.5	4.3	10.4	6.3			All Other Current	8.3	7.4
86.4	35.1	33.8	30.3			Total Current	37.6	37.5
23.6	40.4	12.0	13.1			Long-Term Debt	14.9	18.2
.0	.3	1.0	1.1			Deferred Taxes	1.0	.6
19.3	4.2	10.8	7.5			All Other Non-Current	7.3	6.1
-29.3	20.0	42.4	48.0			Net Worth	39.1	37.6
100.0	100.0	100.0	100.0			Total Liabilities & Net Worth	100.0	100.0
						INCOME DATA		
100.0	100.0	100.0	100.0			Net Sales	100.0	100.0
37.4	45.4	38.1	23.6			Gross Profit	31.6	34.8
35.5	41.5	34.3	18.9			Operating Expenses	27.3	30.1
1.9	4.0	3.8	4.7			Operating Profit	4.3	4.7
.7	.9	1.0	1.0			All Other Expenses (net)	1.3	2.3
1.2	3.0	2.8	3.7			Profit Before Taxes	3.0	2.4
						RATIOS		
2.3	6.0	3.3	3.6				2.9	3.3
1.0	1.3	2.0	1.8			Current	1.7	1.7
.7	1.0	1.3	1.4				1.1	1.2
.6	2.3	2.2	2.1				1.4	1.4
.4 (14)	.7	.8	.8			Quick	.6	.7
.2	.4	.6	.5				.4	.4
0 UND	0 957.2	7 51.5	22 16.9				10 34.9	10 35.3
8 47.3	19 19.4	24 15.1	28 12.9			Sales/Receivables	23 15.7	21 17.2
37 9.7	29 12.7	33 11.1	48 7.6				42 8.8	
0 UND	15 24.0	49 7.4	48 7.6				50 7.3	44 8.3
66 5.5	57 6.4	65 5.6	67 5.5			Cost of Sales/Inventory	72 5.0	65 5.6
124 2.9	153 2.4	97 3.7	88 4.2				111 3.3	108 3.4
0 UND	8 44.4	12 29.9	12 30.5				13 27.7	13 28.3
16 23.5	33 10.9	27 13.6	25 14.9			Cost of Sales/Payables	21 17.3	24 15.2
34 10.8	65 5.6	43 8.5	33 11.1				44 8.4	39 9.4
15.8	6.1	5.8	4.4				6.0	5.7
NM	29.2	9.3	8.1			Sales/Working Capital	10.8	10.7
-9.8	349.6	17.2	18.8				85.5	21.9
	4.8	17.2	17.6				10.0	9.3
(13)	3.8 (20)	3.3 (17)	7.1			EBIT/Interest	(62) 3.2	(70) 2.4
	1.5	.2	.9				1.3	.7
			11.1			Net Profit + Depr., Dep.,	10.3	11.6
		(11)	3.5			Amort./Cur. Mat. L/T/D	(20) 5.0	(20) 3.4
			.5				1.3	1.3
.4	.5	.3	.5				.4	.4
1.6	2.2	.7	.5			Fixed/Worth	.8	.8
-.4	-.8	2.6	3.2				1.6	1.9
2.9	.6	.4	.5				.6	.7
NM	2.7	.9	1.3			Debt/Worth	1.7	1.7
-3.5	-2.8	4.3	5.2				4.9	11.4
	36.9	24.6	32.5			% Profit Before Taxes/Tangible	37.6	46.5
(10)	18.9 (20)	12.8 (15)	14.9			Net Worth	(60) 18.2	(63) 16.0
	13.3	1.1	3.5				4.8	2.6
10.3	13.8	14.8	16.0			% Profit Before Taxes/Total	13.3	13.1
1.6	8.2	7.7	6.0			Assets	6.6	5.5
-11.9	2.9	.1	.4				1.3	-1.4
UND	13.7	12.9	10.9				14.0	15.5
28.1	11.1	8.9	5.1			Sales/Net Fixed Assets	8.5	8.2
14.3	7.8	5.5	3.4				5.2	4.5
8.1	3.4	3.0	2.6				3.0	2.8
3.6	2.7	2.6	1.8			Sales/Total Assets	2.4	2.0
2.9	2.1	1.8	1.3				1.7	1.5
	1.2	1.6	1.9				1.4	1.6
(14)	1.8 (21)	2.7	3.0			% Depr., Dep., Amort./Sales	(58) 2.3	(67) 2.2
	2.3	4.1	4.2				3.3	3.4
		1.7				% Officers', Directors'	1.8	3.0
	(10)	2.5				Owners' Comp/Sales	(17) 2.6	(19) 6.4
		5.9					6.4	8.8
11030M	48296M	332612M	920833M	227302M	638881M	Net Sales ($)	3132833M	2237951M
2672M	17389M	132091M	425988M	283785M	245668M	Total Assets ($)	1492357M	1365568M

© RMA 2011

M = $ thousand   MM = $ million
See Pages 9 through 22 for Explanation of Ratios and Data

Comparative Historical Data | Current Data Sorted by Sales

					Type of Statement						
	14		17	12	Unqualified	1				2	9
	17		14	16	Reviewed		1	1	1	9	4
	11		9	9	Compiled	2	1	2	2	2	
	6		9	7	Tax Returns	1	3	2	1		
	31		19	27	Other	1	6	4	1	6	9
	4/1/08-3/31/09 ALL		4/1/09-3/31/10 ALL	4/1/10-3/31/11 ALL			29 (4/1-9/30/10)			42 (10/1/10-3/31/11)	
						0-1MM	1-3MM	3-5MM	5-10MM	10-25MM	25MM & OVER
	79		68	71	NUMBER OF STATEMENTS	5	11	9	5	19	22
	%		%	%	ASSETS	%	%	%	%	%	%
	10.2		9.3	10.2	Cash & Equivalents		8.4			10.1	6.3
	14.7		15.5	16.4	Trade Receivables (net)		10.2			13.0	20.7
	30.7		29.2	28.4	Inventory		42.4			26.7	25.4
	2.3		2.4	4.2	All Other Current		6.1			3.1	2.4
	57.9		56.5	59.2	Total Current		67.1			52.9	54.8
	31.7		33.0	30.0	Fixed Assets (net)		23.3			36.3	32.5
	5.4		5.0	6.0	Intangibles (net)		5.4			6.9	8.1
	5.0		5.5	4.8	All Other Non-Current		4.2			3.9	4.6
	100.0		100.0	100.0	Total		100.0			100.0	100.0
					LIABILITIES						
	9.6		12.1	13.5	Notes Payable-Short Term		40.0			6.7	7.8
	3.0		4.5	3.2	Cur. Mat.-L.T.D.		3.9			4.5	2.4
	11.8		11.1	14.1	Trade Payables		8.0			12.6	11.5
	.2		.3	.2	Income Taxes Payable		.1			.3	.2
	8.5		8.1	9.1	All Other Current		10.9			7.7	9.5
	33.3		36.1	40.1	Total Current		63.0			31.9	31.3
	18.2		18.5	20.4	Long-Term Debt		37.6			17.8	10.2
	.5		.7	.9	Deferred Taxes		.0			1.6	1.2
	4.7		8.4	9.5	All Other Non-Current		4.1			15.5	4.3
	43.3		36.3	29.1	Net Worth		-4.6			33.2	52.9
	100.0		100.0	100.0	Total Liabilities & Net Worth		100.0			100.0	100.0
					INCOME DATA						
	100.0		100.0	100.0	Net Sales		100.0			100.0	100.0
	36.1		35.8	35.5	Gross Profit		43.7			33.2	27.6
	33.4		33.9	31.3	Operating Expenses		41.5			29.3	21.2
	2.7		2.0	4.2	Operating Profit		2.2			3.9	6.4
	1.9		1.0	1.0	All Other Expenses (net)		1.4			1.8	.8
	.9		1.0	3.2	Profit Before Taxes		.8			2.1	5.6
					RATIOS						
	3.3		2.6	3.3			2.7			3.3	3.4
	1.8		1.6	1.6	Current		1.2			1.5	1.8
	1.2		1.1	1.0			.8			1.2	1.2
	1.7		1.4	1.4			.9			1.6	1.5
	.8		.7 (70)	.7	Quick	(10)	.4			.7	.8
	.3		.3	.4			.2			.3	.6
11	33.3	12	30.9	12	29.4		0	UND		12	29.4	22	16.4
24	15.0	20	18.5	24	15.1	Sales/Receivables	5	76.1		24	15.3	29	12.4
32	11.5	32	11.4	36	10.1		20	18.5		33	11.1	49	7.5
47	7.8	39	9.3	35	10.6		63	5.8		52	7.1	33	10.9
69	5.3	63	5.8	66	5.5	Cost of Sales/Inventory	123	3.0		67	5.5	61	6.0
102	3.6	109	3.4	99	3.7		153	2.4		97	3.7	81	4.5
11	34.5	13	27.7	11	31.9		0	UND		12	29.9	11	33.1
26	14.3	24	15.1	26	13.9	Cost of Sales/Payables	13	27.6		31	11.6	25	14.9
40	9.0	39	9.3	40	9.2		44	8.3		46	7.9	32	11.3
	5.1		6.6	6.1			10.6			7.9	4.4
	9.0		12.2	12.9	Sales/Working Capital		40.3			11.4	9.0
	26.5		29.1	180.4			-13.9			18.2	41.5
	6.7		12.6	10.6			2.8			9.1	24.1
(72)	1.6	(64)	1.8	(63)	3.8	EBIT/Interest		1.4	(18)	2.1	(20)	8.4
	-.6		.0	1.1			.4			-.5	2.8
	3.9		7.1	5.3							9.7
(20)	1.5	(20)	2.8	(23)	3.5	Net Profit + Depr., Dep., Amort./Cur. Mat. L/T/D				(13)	3.5
	.5		1.1	2.2							1.8
	.4		.4	.4			.5			.5	.4
	.8		1.1	1.0	Fixed/Worth		-2.3			1.9	.5
	3.3		4.8	9.7			-.6			-30.0	1.7
	.4		.5	.5			.7			.6	.4
	1.6		1.9	2.2	Debt/Worth		-12.0			3.0	.9
	7.6		UND	-107.0			-2.8			-43.7	3.1
	25.8		27.7	28.4						26.7	37.1
(68)	9.0	(52)	11.7	(53)	15.5	% Profit Before Taxes/Tangible Net Worth				(14)	9.1	(20)	16.9
	-4.1		-5.3	4.0						-30.7	3.8
	9.9		12.1	13.6			8.2			10.5	17.0
	2.9		2.6	7.4	% Profit Before Taxes/Total Assets		1.6			3.8	11.9
	-4.4		-3.6	.2			-4.0			-6.0	2.8
	12.9		12.4	15.2			35.8			9.3	13.3
	7.5		7.4	9.4	Sales/Net Fixed Assets		15.2			5.7	6.6
	4.6		4.1	5.1			9.9			3.7	4.0
	3.0		3.0	3.2			4.5			2.8	3.4
	2.1		2.1	2.6	Sales/Total Assets		2.8			2.0	2.2
	1.5		1.6	1.7			2.1			1.7	1.3
	1.2		1.8	1.4						2.0	1.8
(71)	2.3	(58)	2.7	(65)	2.2	% Depr., Dep., Amort./Sales				(17)	3.1	2.4
	3.6		4.3	3.4						5.0	4.1
	2.0		2.1	1.8							
(24)	4.1	(21)	4.4	(24)	3.8	% Officers', Directors' Owners' Comp/Sales					
	7.2		7.2	7.2							
	2285137M		1894995M	2178954M	Net Sales ($)	3693M	18502M	36071M	35625M	287750M	1797313M
	1230427M		1025902M	1107593M	Total Assets ($)	1466M	6797M	12968M	14575M	158317M	913470M

M = $ thousand   MM = $ million
See Pages 9 through 22 for Explanation of Ratios and Data

Current Data Sorted by Assets   **Comparative Historical Data**

0-500M	500M-2MM	2-10MM	10-50MM	50-100MM	100-250MM	Type of Statement	4/1/06-3/31/07 ALL	4/1/07-3/31/08 ALL
1		1	7	4	6	Unqualified	24	24
1		4	8	3	1	Reviewed	10	10
	1	1		1		Compiled	4	2
3	4	1				Tax Returns	7	1
3		4	13	1	6	Other	15	17
____	____	____	____	____	____			
24 (4/1-9/30/10)			48 (10/1/10-3/31/11)					
5	8	10	28	9	12	NUMBER OF STATEMENTS	60	54
%	%	%	%	%	%	**ASSETS**	%	%
		4.3	4.0		5.5	Cash & Equivalents	3.2	4.3
		29.7	18.3		12.3	Trade Receivables (net)	19.6	18.1
		33.3	42.1		40.5	Inventory	34.7	38.8
		2.5	1.5		1.4	All Other Current	2.6	3.4
		69.7	65.9		59.7	Total Current	60.1	64.6
		26.2	23.1		32.1	Fixed Assets (net)	31.8	30.4
		.4	6.1		4.9	Intangibles (net)	5.1	1.8
		3.7	5.0		3.3	All Other Non-Current	3.0	3.2
		100.0	100.0		100.0	Total	100.0	100.0
						LIABILITIES		
		18.3	14.6		11.3	Notes Payable-Short Term	14.8	19.2
		3.0	3.5		2.5	Cur. Mat.-L.T.D.	3.5	2.6
		18.5	16.0		8.7	Trade Payables	13.3	13.0
		.0	.2		.2	Income Taxes Payable	.3	.3
		9.1	7.2		12.4	All Other Current	11.4	9.3
		48.9	41.4		35.1	Total Current	43.3	44.3
		10.7	17.1		13.5	Long-Term Debt	17.0	15.5
		.6	.7		2.1	Deferred Taxes	.6	1.1
		9.4	5.1		4.0	All Other Non-Current	6.0	4.7
		30.4	35.6		45.3	Net Worth	33.1	34.3
		100.0	100.0		100.0	Total Liabilties & Net Worth	100.0	100.0
						INCOME DATA		
		100.0	100.0		100.0	Net Sales	100.0	100.0
		16.1	15.0		15.8	Gross Profit	19.0	18.7
		13.5	11.9		10.1	Operating Expenses	14.7	12.5
		2.6	3.1		5.7	Operating Profit	4.2	6.2
		.6	.9		1.0	All Other Expenses (net)	2.0	1.7
		2.0	2.3		4.7	Profit Before Taxes	2.2	4.5
						RATIOS		
		2.4	2.7		2.0	Current	1.8	2.1
		1.5	1.5		1.8		1.4	1.4
		.9	1.2		1.3		1.1	1.1
		1.0	.9		.8	Quick	.8	.8
		.8	.5		.5		.5	.4
		.5	.3		.3		.3	.3
		17 21.3	27 13.7		24 15.0	Sales/Receivables	28 13.2	25 14.9
		28 13.2	37 9.7		31 11.9		36 10.1	32 11.4
		33 11.1	53 6.9		37 9.7		47 7.7	51 7.2
		15 24.8	64 5.7		86 4.3	Cost of Sales/Inventory	54 6.7	64 5.7
		45 8.1	103 3.6		141 2.6		100 3.7	99 3.7
		53 6.9	180 2.0		187 2.0		153 2.4	154 2.4
		11 32.6	24 15.3		17 21.7	Cost of Sales/Payables	17 21.2	20 18.3
		21 17.8	36 10.1		28 13.2		27 13.5	27 13.5
		27 13.4	48 7.7		42 8.6		50 7.3	47 7.7
		7.5	3.7		3.9	Sales/Working Capital	4.8	5.5
		28.1	8.9		5.4		10.7	10.3
		-80.2	21.3		12.9		71.2	21.5
		27.4	11.1		9.4	EBIT/Interest	4.8	8.2
		3.0	3.0		4.3		(56) 2.4	(53) 2.5
		-5.1	.9		2.4		1.2	1.3
						Net Profit + Depr., Dep., Amort./Cur. Mat. L/T/D	7.7	9.1
							(13) 3.9	(19) 5.0
							2.3	1.5
		.2	.3		.5	Fixed/Worth	.5	.5
		1.5	.7		.6		1.2	1.0
		3.7	2.4		1.4		2.2	1.8
		.9	1.2		.6	Debt/Worth	1.1	1.0
		2.6	2.3		1.4		2.4	2.2
		11.0	7.4		2.4		7.0	5.1
			31.9		26.6	% Profit Before Taxes/Tangible Net Worth	40.1	41.2
			(25) 9.7		(11) 15.9		(53) 15.8	(50) 24.4
			1.8		4.3		4.2	9.6
		14.2	8.8		12.3	% Profit Before Taxes/Total Assets	9.6	15.3
		2.1	3.3		5.5		3.8	4.8
		-7.5	-.4		1.7		.8	1.2
		44.2	12.8		7.8	Sales/Net Fixed Assets	10.2	12.1
		16.7	6.7		5.0		4.9	5.1
		9.1	4.4		2.2		3.3	3.6
		5.1	2.2		1.8	Sales/Total Assets	2.2	2.2
		3.7	1.5		1.4		1.5	1.7
		3.0	1.1		.9		1.2	1.3
			1.3		1.6	% Depr., Dep., Amort./Sales	1.4	1.2
			(25) 2.4		3.0		(56) 2.5	(50) 2.3
			3.7		4.4		4.0	3.1
						% Officers', Directors' Owners' Comp/Sales	1.7	
							(10) 3.3	
							9.8	
2763M	34581M	226651M	1292804M	939023M	2679916M	Net Sales ($)	3989410M	5443186M
797M	10317M	56714M	734095M	684026M	1989196M	Total Assets ($)	2937348M	3190763M

M = $ thousand   MM = $ million
See Pages 9 through 22 for Explanation of Ratios and Data

Comparative Historical Data | Current Data Sorted by Sales

4/1/08-3/31/09 ALL	4/1/09-3/31/10 ALL	4/1/10-3/31/11 ALL	Type of Statement	0-1MM	1-3MM	3-5MM	5-10MM	10-25MM	25MM & OVER
31	23	19	Unqualified	1				2	16
16	17	12	Reviewed	1				1	10
2	3	6	Compiled	1				3	2
4	8	8	Tax Returns	1				1	
14	16	27	Other	1	4	2	1	7	17
				0-1MM	24 (4/1-9/30/10) 1-3MM	3-5MM	48 (10/1/10-3/31/11) 5-10MM	10-25MM	25MM & OVER
67	67	72	**NUMBER OF STATEMENTS**	4	4	2	3	14	45
%	%	%	**ASSETS**	%	%	%	%	%	%
3.3	4.8	6.0	Cash & Equivalents					4.3	3.8
16.5	17.5	18.3	Trade Receivables (net)					19.2	18.0
39.2	35.9	34.3	Inventory					42.7	37.2
3.6	2.7	1.8	All Other Current					2.1	1.9
62.5	61.0	60.4	Total Current					68.2	60.9
29.6	30.8	29.5	Fixed Assets (net)					19.9	30.3
4.2	3.1	4.6	Intangibles (net)					5.7	4.8
3.7	5.1	5.5	All Other Non-Current					6.2	4.0
100.0	100.0	100.0	Total					100.0	100.0
			LIABILITIES						
19.4	16.0	14.0	Notes Payable-Short Term					16.8	15.1
2.7	4.9	3.1	Cur. Mat.-L.T.D.					3.5	2.9
15.9	14.2	15.1	Trade Payables					10.3	15.9
.2	.3	.1	Income Taxes Payable					.0	.2
8.8	7.1	10.1	All Other Current					12.7	7.0
47.0	42.6	42.4	Total Current					43.3	41.1
15.8	18.2	16.6	Long-Term Debt					17.0	15.7
.6	.7	.9	Deferred Taxes					.8	1.1
7.6	7.8	9.8	All Other Non-Current					5.4	5.9
29.0	30.7	30.3	Net Worth					33.5	36.1
100.0	100.0	100.0	Total Liabilties & Net Worth					100.0	100.0
			INCOME DATA						
100.0	100.0	100.0	Net Sales					100.0	100.0
20.7	20.1	19.2	Gross Profit					17.8	14.6
14.7	14.9	16.9	Operating Expenses					14.5	11.4
6.1	5.2	2.4	Operating Profit					3.3	3.2
1.9	1.4	1.0	All Other Expenses (net)					.6	1.2
4.2	3.9	1.3	Profit Before Taxes					2.7	1.9
			RATIOS						
1.7	2.0	2.0	Current					2.9	1.9
1.3	1.4	1.5						1.5	1.5
1.1	1.1	1.1						1.0	1.2
.6	1.0	1.0	Quick					1.0	.8
.4	.5	.5						.6	.5
.2	.3	.3						.3	.3
(26) 13.8	(23) 16.1	(23) 15.6	Sales/Receivables					(17) 21.3	(26) 14.0
(34) 10.7	(32) 11.4	(32) 11.4						(30) 12.1	(34) 10.9
(43) 8.4	(42) 8.6	(43) 8.5						(44) 8.3	(44) 8.2
(50) 7.3	(37) 9.8	(33) 11.0	Cost of Sales/Inventory					(47) 7.7	(44) 8.4
(107) 3.4	(89) 4.1	(79) 4.6						(60) 6.0	(99) 3.7
(167) 2.2	(164) 2.2	(165) 2.2						(175) 2.1	(174) 2.1
(20) 18.2	(15) 25.1	(18) 20.5	Cost of Sales/Payables					(16) 22.4	(24) 15.1
(38) 9.7	(31) 11.7	(29) 12.5						(20) 18.1	(34) 10.6
(56) 6.6	(47) 7.8	(48) 7.7						(28) 13.1	(52) 7.1
5.2	5.7	5.2	Sales/Working Capital					4.5	5.1
12.2	10.6	13.2						10.7	12.0
61.3	47.3	88.1						-80.2	22.9
8.0	10.6	9.8	EBIT/Interest					27.4	8.6
(65) 2.4	(66) 3.2	(69) 3.2						5.0	3.0
1.3	1.5	.1						.6	-.2
4.6	3.6	7.4	Net Profit + Depr., Dep., Amort./Cur. Mat. L/T/D						6.6
(18) 2.1	(21) 1.6	(27) 2.5							(22) 2.7
1.4	1.2	.5							.6
.6	.5	.5	Fixed/Worth					.1	.5
1.1	1.0	1.0						1.4	.8
2.3	2.0	3.0						3.7	2.3
1.4	1.0	1.0	Debt/Worth					1.0	1.1
2.7	2.4	2.2						2.9	2.0
5.3	9.7	7.9						20.4	5.7
41.6	55.7	36.1	% Profit Before Taxes/Tangible Net Worth					69.1	26.5
(57) 16.2	(58) 16.6	(60) 12.3						(12) 10.5	(40) 10.3
5.9	6.6	-.8						.1	-.8
11.2	13.8	9.8	% Profit Before Taxes/Total Assets					8.8	9.0
4.6	5.3	3.9						4.1	3.4
.8	1.5	-2.3						-1.3	-2.0
9.8	10.7	13.2	Sales/Net Fixed Assets					28.8	8.9
5.4	6.3	6.8						14.0	5.8
3.3	2.8	3.9						5.9	3.5
2.1	2.9	3.0	Sales/Total Assets					3.4	2.2
1.5	1.5	1.7						1.8	1.3
1.1	1.1	1.1						1.3	1.1
1.6	1.6	1.4	% Depr., Dep., Amort./Sales					.7	1.7
(62) 2.4	(59) 2.5	(64) 2.5						(11) 1.4	(43) 2.7
3.6	3.8	4.1						3.3	4.3
			% Officers', Directors' Owners' Comp/Sales						
4954708M	5433830M	5175738M	Net Sales ($)	710M	6057M	8328M	22249M	222155M	4916239M
3360152M	3349830M	3475145M	Total Assets ($)	895M	2751M	2874M	4594M	118348M	3345683M

M = $ thousand   MM = $ million
See Pages 9 through 22 for Explanation of Ratios and Data

Current Data Sorted by Assets   Comparative Historical Data

0-500M	500M-2MM	2-10MM	10-50MM	50-100MM	100-250MM		4/1/06-3/31/07 ALL	4/1/07-3/31/08 ALL
						Type of Statement		
		3	8	5	3	Unqualified	16	20
	1	1	6	2		Reviewed	11	11
1	1	4	1			Compiled	5	4
	5	1				Tax Returns	6	4
		6	16	3	1	Other	29	27
	16 (4/1-9/30/10)		52 (10/1/10-3/31/11)					
1	7	15	31	10	4	**NUMBER OF STATEMENTS**	67	66
%	%	%	%	%	%	**ASSETS**	%	%
		6.9	8.0	2.3		Cash & Equivalents	5.7	6.2
		24.4	19.9	17.7		Trade Receivables (net)	22.6	17.6
		25.0	13.9	19.7		Inventory	20.3	20.5
		.9	2.2	4.4		All Other Current	2.2	2.6
		57.3	44.1	44.0		Total Current	50.9	46.9
		33.2	37.4	41.2		Fixed Assets (net)	36.7	40.9
		8.1	13.0	8.0		Intangibles (net)	5.9	8.0
		1.5	5.5	6.8		All Other Non-Current	6.5	4.1
		100.0	100.0	100.0		Total	100.0	100.0
						LIABILITIES		
		7.3	3.6	6.6		Notes Payable-Short Term	11.0	10.3
		1.5	3.4	2.5		Cur. Mat.-L.T.D.	4.0	3.7
		25.7	12.3	11.6		Trade Payables	16.5	16.0
		.7	.3	.2		Income Taxes Payable	.2	.2
		5.6	7.4	10.0		All Other Current	9.3	8.9
		40.8	27.0	30.8		Total Current	41.0	39.1
		13.4	24.2	23.8		Long-Term Debt	18.5	23.7
		.0	1.8	.5		Deferred Taxes	.7	.8
		6.4	4.6	7.4		All Other Non-Current	7.9	9.2
		39.3	42.3	37.4		Net Worth	31.9	27.3
		100.0	100.0	100.0		Total Liabilities & Net Worth	100.0	100.0
						INCOME DATA		
		100.0	100.0	100.0		Net Sales	100.0	100.0
		26.0	24.9	17.3		Gross Profit	28.2	26.8
		21.7	17.6	13.7		Operating Expenses	24.1	23.2
		4.2	7.3	3.6		Operating Profit	4.1	3.6
		.8	1.3	.7		All Other Expenses (net)	1.5	1.5
		3.4	6.0	2.9		Profit Before Taxes	2.7	2.1
						RATIOS		
		2.0	2.6	2.1			1.8	2.1
		1.6	1.7	1.4		Current	1.2	1.2
		1.3	1.2	1.0			.9	.8
		1.0	1.5	1.2			1.0	1.2
		.8	1.0	.6		Quick	.7	.5
		.6	.6	.4			.4	.4
		21 17.7	22 16.8	24 15.0			20 18.0	19 19.3
		31 11.7	26 14.1	26 13.8		Sales/Receivables	29 12.4	24 15.5
		36 10.0	32 11.5	38 9.5			35 10.4	32 11.3
		26 13.9	20 18.2	25 14.5			26 14.1	23 15.9
		43 8.5	25 14.8	49 7.4		Cost of Sales/Inventory	38 9.7	37 9.9
		57 6.4	40 9.1	60 6.1			59 6.2	63 5.8
		25 14.7	13 28.0	18 20.8			19 19.2	18 19.8
		31 11.6	20 17.9	22 16.6		Cost of Sales/Payables	28 13.1	28 12.9
		42 8.7	29 12.8	41 8.8			39 9.3	41 8.9
		8.6	8.0	8.8			11.5	9.4
		18.5	12.1	17.6		Sales/Working Capital	30.3	33.3
		29.0	57.1	NM			-43.9	-29.4
		30.2	16.1	15.5			10.1	7.5
		(14) 5.3	(30) 6.9	4.8		EBIT/Interest	(62) 4.8	(63) 2.9
		1.2	1.0	.5			1.4	1.0
			6.4			Net Profit + Depr., Dep.,	5.5	9.0
			(13) 3.0			Amort./Cur. Mat. L/T/D	(21) 2.5	(20) 4.0
			1.6				1.9	1.3
		.4	.6	.8			.6	.7
		.8	1.0	1.1		Fixed/Worth	1.1	2.0
		3.9	1.8	NM			2.4	279.6
		.5	.5	.8			1.0	.9
		3.4	1.0	1.6		Debt/Worth	1.9	3.2
		8.8	5.2	NM			6.5	296.8
		61.4	47.5			% Profit Before Taxes/Tangible	46.9	40.4
		(13) 21.6	(24) 18.6			Net Worth	(56) 24.2	(51) 18.0
		4.0	8.2				11.7	5.3
		16.9	19.9	19.6		% Profit Before Taxes/Total	14.0	10.7
		12.1	6.5	6.8		Assets	8.5	5.7
		.7	1.4	-.3			1.7	.1
		31.0	8.8	6.2			17.9	11.8
		7.4	5.7	4.9		Sales/Net Fixed Assets	7.3	6.2
		4.3	3.7	3.8			3.8	3.4
		3.8	2.8	2.7			3.6	3.1
		2.7	2.1	2.1		Sales/Total Assets	2.5	2.5
		2.3	1.3	1.5			1.9	1.7
		.8	1.7	2.2			1.2	1.4
		(14) 1.6	(30) 2.8	3.1		% Depr., Dep., Amort./Sales	(54) 2.0	(56) 2.4
		2.9	4.4	4.4			3.0	3.4
						% Officers', Directors'		.9
						Owners' Comp/Sales	(14) 2.5	
								5.0
1525M	22223M	284750M	1619237M	1386653M	852709M	Net Sales ($)	3242060M	3971702M
181M	8054M	93187M	750795M	698949M	477558M	Total Assets ($)	1470407M	1792125M

M = $ thousand   MM = $ million
See Pages 9 through 22 for Explanation of Ratios and Data

Comparative Historical Data | **Current Data Sorted by Sales**

21	20	19	Type of Statement	0-1MM	1-3MM	3-5MM	5-10MM	10-25MM	25MM & OVER
21	20	19	Unqualified					3	16
14	15	10	Reviewed			1		1	8
6	6	7	Compiled	1	2			3	1
3	5	6	Tax Returns				1		
33	34	26	Other	3	2		2	7	17
4/1/08-3/31/09 ALL	4/1/09-3/31/10 ALL	4/1/10-3/31/11 ALL			16 (4/1-9/30/10)			52 (10/1/10-3/31/11)	
77	80	68	**NUMBER OF STATEMENTS**	4	4	4	4	14	42
%	%	%	**ASSETS**	%	%	%	%	%	%
6.4	7.1	5.8	Cash & Equivalents					8.0	6.2
18.7	19.4	21.0	Trade Receivables (net)					23.1	18.3
18.8	19.8	18.4	Inventory					22.6	17.3
1.8	1.6	2.1	All Other Current					.9	2.7
45.7	47.9	47.4	Total Current					54.7	44.5
40.8	37.2	36.7	Fixed Assets (net)					31.6	38.1
9.0	10.1	11.2	Intangibles (net)					9.9	12.3
4.5	4.9	4.7	All Other Non-Current					3.9	5.1
100.0	100.0	100.0	Total					100.0	100.0
			LIABILITIES						
10.8	7.6	5.5	Notes Payable-Short Term					6.6	4.7
4.9	3.5	2.8	Cur. Mat.-L.T.D.					1.4	3.3
14.7	14.1	14.7	Trade Payables					23.3	11.0
.2	.2	.3	Income Taxes Payable					.9	.2
7.9	11.6	8.1	All Other Current					5.4	8.3
38.5	37.1	31.5	Total Current					37.7	27.5
21.0	22.1	22.1	Long-Term Debt					9.3	25.8
.8	.8	.1	Deferred Taxes					.7	1.5
8.9	3.8	11.9	All Other Non-Current					3.1	6.5
30.9	36.2	33.4	Net Worth					49.2	38.6
100.0	100.0	100.0	Total Liabilities & Net Worth					100.0	100.0
			INCOME DATA						
100.0	100.0	100.0	Net Sales					100.0	100.0
24.9	25.4	27.1	Gross Profit					27.6	22.4
21.8	20.2	21.4	Operating Expenses					21.3	16.0
3.1	5.2	5.7	Operating Profit					6.3	6.4
1.2	1.2	1.0	All Other Expenses (net)					.7	1.1
1.9	4.0	4.8	Profit Before Taxes					5.6	5.3
			RATIOS						
2.0	2.2	2.4	Current					2.3	2.4
1.1	1.5	1.6						1.6	1.5
.8	.9	1.2						1.3	1.2
1.0	1.2	1.3	Quick					1.4	1.4
.6	.7	.8						.9	.7
.4	.5	.6						.6	.6
21 17.4	19 19.6	22 16.5	Sales/Receivables					21 17.8	22 16.3
25 14.6	25 14.8	27 13.7						30 12.3	25 14.3
32 11.3	34 10.7	34 10.7						38 9.5	32 11.5
22 16.8	24 15.0	23 15.9	Cost of Sales/Inventory					26 14.0	21 17.7
35 10.5	35 10.3	32 11.5						41 8.8	29 12.5
45 8.1	54 6.7	57 6.4						57 6.4	53 6.9
17 21.9	16 23.3	15 23.8	Cost of Sales/Payables					23 16.1	14 26.9
24 15.0	23 16.1	22 16.6						29 12.7	19 19.5
37 10.0	33 11.1	35 10.4						44 8.3	27 13.5
10.6	8.7	8.3	Sales/Working Capital					6.8	8.2
46.8	16.7	15.5						13.9	13.0
-37.5	-69.6	54.8						24.1	59.9
6.1	15.3	14.5	EBIT/Interest					40.2	12.8
(71) 3.0	(75) 5.0	(66) 6.6						(13) 13.1	(41) 7.1
1.0	1.7	1.2						2.1	1.3
5.2	5.4	6.5	Net Profit + Depr., Dep., Amort./Cur. Mat. L/T/D						6.2
(23) 3.2	(23) 2.4	(27) 3.6							(22) 2.9
1.4	1.7	2.0							2.0
.8	.6	.6	Fixed/Worth					.4	.7
1.8	1.2	1.1						.7	1.1
3.6	2.8	3.9						2.0	NM
.9	.9	.6	Debt/Worth					.4	.6
2.7	2.0	1.6						.7	1.6
8.5	7.7	8.5						4.2	NM
36.4	57.9	55.1	% Profit Before Taxes/Tangible Net Worth					54.8	52.6
(62) 22.2	(67) 32.9	(54) 25.1						(13) 21.6	(32) 26.9
6.7	12.4	8.0						10.3	8.2
9.6	17.8	18.2	% Profit Before Taxes/Total Assets					21.8	19.6
4.6	8.1	8.1						14.3	8.7
.3	2.5	1.4						3.1	3.0
12.7	14.2	11.7	Sales/Net Fixed Assets					27.5	8.7
6.4	7.1	6.1						7.2	5.6
3.3	3.8	4.0						4.3	3.9
3.3	3.3	3.1	Sales/Total Assets					3.4	2.9
2.3	2.5	2.3						2.6	2.1
1.7	1.6	1.7						1.9	1.7
1.4	1.4	1.7	% Depr., Dep., Amort./Sales					1.1	1.9
(65) 2.3	(63) 2.3	(65) 2.5						(13) 1.7	(41) 2.9
3.5	4.0	4.0						4.5	4.0
	1.7	1.6	% Officers', Directors' Owners' Comp/Sales						
	(16) 3.2	(15) 3.2							
	3.8	9.2							
5300375M	5440240M	4167097M	Net Sales ($)		7884M	13817M	30110M	286457M	3828829M
2403785M	2472449M	2028724M	Total Assets ($)		2550M	6376M	21238M	126842M	1871718M

M = $ thousand   MM = $ million
See Pages 9 through 22 for Explanation of Ratios and Data

| Current Data Sorted by Assets | | | | | | | Comparative Historical Data | |

0-500M	500M-2MM	2-10MM	10-50MM	50-100MM	100-250MM	Type of Statement	4/1/06-3/31/07 ALL	4/1/07-3/31/08 ALL
			18	7	6	Unqualified	29	30
		3	7	1		Reviewed	17	14
	1	6	2			Compiled	4	6
1	3	3				Tax Returns	6	8
1	4	7	13	6	7	Other	29	22
2	8	19	40	14	13	**NUMBER OF STATEMENTS**	85	80
%	%	%	%	%	%	**ASSETS**	%	%
		7.0	3.6	3.9	5.0	Cash & Equivalents	4.1	4.8
		17.4	16.7	12.8	13.0	Trade Receivables (net)	17.1	18.4
		32.0	34.7	36.1	31.1	Inventory	35.9	38.1
		1.8	3.3	5.5	2.5	All Other Current	2.7	2.9
		58.1	58.4	58.3	51.6	Total Current	59.9	64.2
		30.2	34.2	25.6	35.8	Fixed Assets (net)	30.6	30.3
		6.2	3.9	8.3	9.4	Intangibles (net)	4.1	2.1
		5.4	3.5	7.8	3.2	All Other Non-Current	5.3	3.4
		100.0	100.0	100.0	100.0	Total	100.0	100.0
						LIABILITIES		
		15.8	13.6	15.1	10.5	Notes Payable-Short Term	14.7	16.9
		3.9	2.7	2.8	1.7	Cur. Mat.-L.T.D.	3.0	3.6
		16.3	12.6	13.1	9.5	Trade Payables	16.4	15.9
		.4	.4	.2	.0	Income Taxes Payable	.1	.1
		3.1	7.0	5.3	12.3	All Other Current	7.7	6.4
		39.6	36.3	36.5	34.0	Total Current	42.0	42.9
		22.8	14.1	12.9	19.2	Long-Term Debt	16.9	17.2
		.2	.6	1.3	.3	Deferred Taxes	.4	.4
		3.1	6.2	3.3	6.5	All Other Non-Current	6.7	11.4
		34.4	42.7	45.9	39.9	Net Worth	34.1	28.1
		100.0	100.0	100.0	100.0	Total Liabilities & Net Worth	100.0	100.0
						INCOME DATA		
		100.0	100.0	100.0	100.0	Net Sales	100.0	100.0
		24.6	23.1	23.2	20.6	Gross Profit	20.9	22.8
		20.1	16.9	15.8	13.8	Operating Expenses	17.2	17.3
		4.5	6.3	7.4	6.9	Operating Profit	3.7	5.5
		1.7	1.2	.6	1.5	All Other Expenses (net)	1.5	1.5
		2.8	5.1	6.8	5.4	Profit Before Taxes	2.2	4.1
						RATIOS		
		2.8	2.0	2.1	2.4	Current	2.2	2.1
		1.7	1.5	1.5	1.8		1.5	1.5
		1.3	1.3	1.1	1.0		1.1	1.1
		.8	.8	.7	.9	Quick	.7	.9
		.6	.5	.4	.6		.5	.5
		.3	.3	.2	.4		.3	.3
		12 29.9	23 16.2	22 16.4	21 17.1	Sales/Receivables	21 17.0	22 16.3
		26 14.3	33 11.0	27 13.6	27 13.3		27 13.4	28 12.9
		30 12.2	39 9.3	30 12.2	34 10.8		37 9.9	38 9.7
		35 10.4	46 7.9	47 7.7	32 11.4	Cost of Sales/Inventory	44 8.3	43 8.6
		54 6.7	78 4.7	112 3.3	62 5.9		83 4.4	84 4.4
		72 5.1	160 2.3	156 2.3	138 2.6		138 2.6	144 2.5
		16 23.0	19 18.8	21 17.2	12 30.6	Cost of Sales/Payables	14 26.5	18 20.5
		21 17.2	23 15.8	37 9.9	24 15.3		27 13.5	30 12.1
		37 9.7	47 7.8	50 7.4	33 10.9		42 8.7	45 8.2
		8.4	5.1	5.2	4.3	Sales/Working Capital	5.4	5.6
		11.4	9.1	11.2	6.9		12.3	11.3
		36.4	21.9	43.7	NM		60.0	42.1
		35.9	17.7	17.5	30.4	EBIT/Interest	7.7	8.9
		(17) 2.9	(38) 6.6	7.0	(12) 5.1		(79) 2.1	(76) 2.9
		1.7	1.6	3.4	1.9		.8	1.4
		7.4				Net Profit + Depr., Dep.,	8.3	9.8
		(20) 4.6				Amort./Cur. Mat. L/T/D	(35) 3.3	(36) 3.5
		1.9					1.4	1.3
		.4	.5	.3	.6	Fixed/Worth	.5	.4
		1.0	.9	.6	1.0		1.0	.9
		5.5	1.5	7.3	23.2		2.0	1.6
		.8	.6	.7	.7	Debt/Worth	.9	1.1
		3.2	1.8	1.1	1.3		2.0	2.1
		9.3	3.0	15.2	45.2		4.9	3.6
		34.1	43.1	42.1	40.6	% Profit Before Taxes/Tangible	29.9	33.4
		(15) 25.0	(37) 20.0	(12) 27.2	(11) 28.0	Net Worth	(72) 12.7	(68) 20.1
		7.7	7.3	6.4	13.7		2.6	8.7
		12.7	14.8	16.5	18.9	% Profit Before Taxes/Total	12.7	13.2
		6.4	7.5	8.9	7.6	Assets	3.8	5.9
		1.8	2.0	4.3	3.6		-1.5	1.5
		25.6	10.2	10.2	7.0	Sales/Net Fixed Assets	14.0	14.4
		9.1	4.7	7.1	5.1		6.6	7.4
		4.9	3.0	5.5	3.3		4.1	4.6
		4.0	2.5	2.1	2.4	Sales/Total Assets	2.8	3.2
		2.6	1.7	1.7	1.6		2.0	2.1
		1.8	1.2	1.3	1.2		1.5	1.5
		1.0	1.6	1.4	2.1	% Depr., Dep., Amort./Sales	1.1	.9
		(18) 1.8	(39) 2.6	1.8	(11) 2.7		(74) 2.2	(72) 1.9
		2.4	3.6	2.7	3.5		3.3	3.2
						% Officers', Directors'	.6	.8
						Owners' Comp/Sales	(17) 1.5	(16) 2.2
							3.9	3.9
414M	28679M	245574M	1934246M	1833295M	3365631M	Net Sales ($)	5945920M	6516618M
366M	8073M	85996M	1028476M	1096324M	1930226M	Total Assets ($)	3453768M	3646516M

Comparative Historical Data / Current Data Sorted by Sales

Hist 4/1/08-3/31/09 ALL	Hist 4/1/09-3/31/10 ALL	Hist 4/1/10-3/31/11 ALL	Type of Statement	0-1MM	1-3MM	3-5MM	5-10MM	10-25MM	25MM & OVER
40	26	31	Unqualified				1	1	29
15	13	11	Reviewed			1		4	6
6	5	9	Compiled	1	1	1		4	2
6	6	7	Tax Returns	1				3	
39	35	38	Other	1	3	2	7	4	23
					32 (4/1-9/30/10)			64 (10/1/10-3/31/11)	
106	85	96	**NUMBER OF STATEMENTS**	3	4	4	9	16	60
%	%	%	**ASSETS**	%	%	%	%	%	%
5.0	5.5	5.2	Cash & Equivalents					7.0	3.1
16.4	17.2	15.6	Trade Receivables (net)					15.2	16.3
36.2	36.4	34.3	Inventory					32.3	35.1
3.0	2.7	3.1	All Other Current					2.5	3.7
60.6	61.8	58.2	Total Current					57.0	58.3
31.5	30.7	31.3	Fixed Assets (net)					31.8	32.1
3.6	3.1	5.6	Intangibles (net)					9.3	4.8
4.4	4.4	4.9	All Other Non-Current					1.9	4.7
100.0	100.0	100.0	Total					100.0	100.0
			LIABILITIES						
14.2	13.3	14.2	Notes Payable-Short Term					7.3	14.5
3.2	2.3	2.6	Cur. Mat.-L.T.D.					4.2	2.5
14.4	13.3	12.8	Trade Payables					14.2	13.0
.1	.3	.3	Income Taxes Payable					.5	.3
6.8	8.3	6.9	All Other Current					2.6	8.2
38.6	37.6	36.7	Total Current					28.8	38.6
16.3	16.7	16.6	Long-Term Debt					17.1	15.3
.7	.6	.5	Deferred Taxes					.6	.6
6.9	5.4	5.6	All Other Non-Current					7.3	4.8
37.5	39.6	40.5	Net Worth					46.2	40.8
100.0	100.0	100.0	Total Liabilities & Net Worth					100.0	100.0
			INCOME DATA						
100.0	100.0	100.0	Net Sales					100.0	100.0
23.4	22.6	25.1	Gross Profit					25.5	20.9
18.1	15.2	18.3	Operating Expenses					18.7	14.6
5.3	7.4	6.7	Operating Profit					6.8	6.3
1.4	1.2	1.3	All Other Expenses (net)					1.2	1.1
3.9	6.2	5.5	Profit Before Taxes					5.5	5.2
			RATIOS						
2.4	2.4	2.3	Current					2.9	2.0
1.6	1.7	1.6						1.9	1.5
1.1	1.2	1.2						1.5	1.2
.8	.9	.9	Quick					1.8	.8
.5	.5	.5						.7	.5
.4	.4	.3						.5	.3
20 18.3	22 16.3	20 17.9	Sales/Receivables					20 18.1	22 16.5
28 13.0	28 12.9	29 12.8						29 12.6	29 12.5
34 10.7	37 9.7	35 10.6						36 10.1	36 10.2
47 7.7	51 7.2	45 8.2	Cost of Sales/Inventory					37 9.8	45 8.2
84 4.4	82 4.4	68 5.3						61 5.9	75 4.9
122 3.0	156 2.3	138 2.6						120 3.0	144 2.5
15 23.9	16 22.4	16 23.4	Cost of Sales/Payables					18 20.7	18 20.1
28 12.8	24 15.5	24 15.4						35 10.6	24 15.4
40 9.0	38 9.6	42 8.7						44 8.3	40 9.2
5.6	5.1	5.5	Sales/Working Capital					5.0	6.2
10.6	8.2	9.5						8.3	11.2
40.0	27.5	25.6						19.9	30.9
9.7	15.9	18.3	EBIT/Interest					46.0	16.7
(100) 3.3	(80) 4.8	(88) 5.6						10.2	(57) 6.2
1.7	2.5	2.4						2.1	2.5
8.5	9.7	8.0	Net Profit + Depr., Dep., Amort./Cur. Mat. L/T/D						8.0
(43) 4.2	(32) 4.6	(42) 4.9							(30) 5.3
1.1	2.6	2.4							2.9
.4	.5	.5	Fixed/Worth					.4	.5
.9	.8	.9						1.1	.9
1.9	1.5	2.2						2.2	1.5
.8	.8	.7	Debt/Worth					.6	.7
1.7	1.3	1.8						1.3	1.7
5.1	3.0	4.3						4.0	3.6
35.6	37.6	42.6	% Profit Before Taxes/Tangible Net Worth					30.4	42.7
(93) 22.1	(76) 24.2	(83) 25.0					(14)	22.4 (54)	21.0
10.6	15.4	9.4						10.8	9.1
13.6	17.3	17.7	% Profit Before Taxes/Total Assets					15.6	15.4
7.3	9.9	7.8						7.7	8.2
1.7	3.7	2.6						2.3	3.2
14.0	13.2	11.9	Sales/Net Fixed Assets					21.0	10.4
7.4	5.8	6.0						5.3	6.4
4.1	3.6	3.6						3.0	4.0
2.7	2.8	2.6	Sales/Total Assets					2.6	2.5
1.9	1.9	1.9						2.0	1.9
1.5	1.4	1.3						1.4	1.3
1.1	1.1	1.5	% Depr., Dep., Amort./Sales					.9	1.6
(91) 2.0	(73) 2.0	(88) 2.2						2.0 (57)	2.2
3.2	3.1	3.3						4.3	3.3
1.2	.7	1.4	% Officers', Directors' Owners' Comp/Sales						
(25) 2.1	(20) 2.0	(16) 3.0							
5.0	3.8	5.5							
10249819M	7247976M	7407839M	Net Sales ($)	1005M	7132M	16894M	71635M	269731M	7041442M
5234612M	3918140M	4149461M	Total Assets ($)	1145M	2912M	9254M	45755M	176095M	3914300M

M = $ thousand   MM = $ million
See Pages 9 through 22 for Explanation of Ratios and Data

Current Data Sorted by Assets   Comparative Historical Data

Type of Statement

	0-500M	500M-2MM	2-10MM	10-50MM	50-100MM	100-250MM		4/1/06-3/31/07 ALL	4/1/07-3/31/08 ALL
Unqualified			2	4	5	4		10	13
Reviewed			3	2	1	1		9	4
Compiled		2		1	1	1		5	6
Tax Returns			1					3	1
Other		3	5	5	1	1		11	17
		16 (4/1-9/30/10)		24 (10/1/10-3/31/11)					
NUMBER OF STATEMENTS		5	11	11	8	5		38	41

Columns 0-500M and 500M-2MM (and other low-count columns) shown as "DATA NOT AVAILABLE." Full percentage data reported only for the 2-10MM and 10-50MM columns.

	2-10MM %	10-50MM %		4/1/06-3/31/07 ALL %	4/1/07-3/31/08 ALL %
ASSETS					
Cash & Equivalents	4.9	5.5		5.8	6.3
Trade Receivables (net)	22.1	16.0		20.2	20.7
Inventory	42.7	33.2		35.0	36.4
All Other Current	2.7	5.2		2.3	3.1
Total Current	72.4	59.9		63.3	66.5
Fixed Assets (net)	17.7	30.9		25.7	23.0
Intangibles (net)	5.4	.6		4.2	4.0
All Other Non-Current	4.5	8.6		6.7	6.5
Total	100.0	100.0		100.0	100.0
LIABILITIES					
Notes Payable-Short Term	20.5	21.0		12.1	17.5
Cur. Mat.-L.T.D.	2.1	3.5		2.4	2.9
Trade Payables	19.2	8.0		20.0	17.6
Income Taxes Payable	.9	1.2		.4	.2
All Other Current	5.0	10.4		7.2	7.4
Total Current	47.6	44.2		42.0	45.6
Long-Term Debt	8.9	11.5		17.1	12.6
Deferred Taxes	1.6	.1		.5	.5
All Other Non-Current	13.1	3.5		6.0	6.6
Net Worth	28.7	40.7		34.4	34.7
Total Liabilities & Net Worth	100.0	100.0		100.0	100.0
INCOME DATA					
Net Sales	100.0	100.0		100.0	100.0
Gross Profit	27.4	23.5		32.1	28.8
Operating Expenses	18.2	18.2		23.9	21.9
Operating Profit	9.2	5.4		8.2	6.9
All Other Expenses (net)	.7	1.2		2.6	1.5
Profit Before Taxes	8.5	4.1		5.6	5.3

RATIOS

	2-10MM	10-50MM		4/1/06-3/31/07	4/1/07-3/31/08
Current	2.1	3.1		2.1	2.3
	1.4	1.3		1.8	1.5
	1.1	1.0		1.2	1.2
Quick	.8	1.3		1.1	1.0
	.6	.4		.6	.5
	.3	.2		.4	.3
Sales/Receivables	16 22.4	36 10.3		23 16.2	22 16.9
	36 10.2	46 8.0		37 10.0	36 10.1
	43 8.5	55 6.6		48 7.6	47 7.8
Cost of Sales/Inventory	40 9.0	14 25.5		51 7.1	54 6.7
	98 3.7	104 3.5		77 4.7	90 4.1
	132 2.8	322 1.1		119 3.1	209 1.7
Cost of Sales/Payables	19 18.8	9 40.7		18 19.9	20 18.5
	34 10.8	22 16.4		31 11.7	29 12.7
	43 8.4	44 8.4		80 4.5	62 5.9
Sales/Working Capital	6.5	2.9		5.6	5.0
	15.6	7.3		9.3	7.4
	50.4	273.4		18.8	18.5
EBIT/Interest	42.0	22.6		7.3	10.8
	8.6	3.1		(37) 4.4	(39) 3.3
	2.6	-.9		2.1	1.2
Net Profit + Depr., Dep., Amort./Cur. Mat. L/T/D				13.2	16.3
				(10) 3.2	(12) 3.9
				1.4	1.7
Fixed/Worth	.2	.3		.5	.4
	.7	.8		1.0	.7
	1.7	1.3		1.9	1.4
Debt/Worth	.9	.5		1.0	1.1
	3.8	2.3		2.3	2.4
	52.9	3.2		10.6	4.1
% Profit Before Taxes/Tangible Net Worth		63.5		31.7	53.2
		14.7		(34) 17.3	(37) 20.8
		-9.0		7.8	1.3
% Profit Before Taxes/Total Assets	31.6	17.0		15.0	15.0
	17.2	5.5		6.3	7.2
	3.1	-3.6		2.3	.5
Sales/Net Fixed Assets	79.3	6.3		23.6	23.8
	20.0	4.3		9.7	8.7
	9.2	2.6		4.9	5.9
Sales/Total Assets	3.4	1.8		2.7	2.7
	2.5	1.2		2.0	1.7
	2.0	.9		1.4	1.4
% Depr., Dep., Amort./Sales		1.5		.9	1.0
		2.4		(35) 1.7	(35) 1.6
		3.3		2.5	2.2
% Officers', Directors' Owners' Comp/Sales					

	500M-2MM	2-10MM	10-50MM	50-100MM	100-250MM		4/1/06-3/31/07	4/1/07-3/31/08
Net Sales ($)	18522M	172053M	295071M	794216M	1267635M		1674071M	2885947M
Total Assets ($)	5147M	67229M	241337M	559490M	915812M		968178M	1703587M

M = $ thousand   MM = $ million
See Pages 9 through 22 for Explanation of Ratios and Data

Comparative Historical Data / Current Data Sorted by Sales

4/1/08-3/31/09 ALL	4/1/09-3/31/10 ALL	4/1/10-3/31/11 ALL		0-1MM	1-3MM	3-5MM	5-10MM	10-25MM	25MM & OVER
			Type of Statement						
14	14	15	Unqualified					4	11
7	8	6	Reviewed				1	3	2
4	3	3	Compiled		2				1
2	3	1	Tax Returns					1	
19	16	15	Other		1		3	5	6
				16 (4/1-9/30/10)			24 (10/1/10-3/31/11)		
46	44	40	**NUMBER OF STATEMENTS**		3		4	13	20
%	%	%	**ASSETS**	%	%	%	%	%	%
4.4	5.3	6.0	Cash & Equivalents	DATA NOT AVAILABLE		DATA NOT AVAILABLE		4.5	5.8
20.2	19.3	17.9	Trade Receivables (net)					16.8	18.3
34.8	41.7	33.2	Inventory					44.5	29.9
3.0	2.0	3.3	All Other Current					5.1	2.5
62.4	68.2	60.4	Total Current					70.8	56.4
23.5	21.2	27.1	Fixed Assets (net)					20.9	29.1
5.7	3.1	4.8	Intangibles (net)					5.0	3.3
8.3	7.5	7.7	All Other Non-Current					3.3	11.1
100.0	100.0	100.0	Total					100.0	100.0
			LIABILITIES						
16.3	15.3	17.5	Notes Payable-Short Term					24.8	16.7
2.8	2.6	2.2	Cur. Mat.-L.T.D.					1.9	2.5
14.3	16.6	14.7	Trade Payables					16.0	14.8
.4	.5	.6	Income Taxes Payable					.8	.4
5.7	6.0	5.9	All Other Current					5.3	7.0
39.5	41.0	40.9	Total Current					48.8	41.5
14.6	14.2	10.6	Long-Term Debt					11.7	12.0
.4	.4	.5	Deferred Taxes					.3	.0
4.8	4.6	8.0	All Other Non-Current					9.5	6.7
40.8	39.8	40.0	Net Worth					29.6	39.7
100.0	100.0	100.0	Total Liabilties & Net Worth					100.0	100.0
			INCOME DATA						
100.0	100.0	100.0	Net Sales					100.0	100.0
28.3	26.4	27.4	Gross Profit					29.6	21.9
20.6	20.7	20.5	Operating Expenses					22.5	16.3
7.7	5.8	6.9	Operating Profit					7.1	5.6
.3	1.3	.7	All Other Expenses (net)					1.5	.2
7.4	4.5	6.2	Profit Before Taxes					5.6	5.5
			RATIOS						
2.8	2.3	2.3	Current					2.1	2.2
1.5	1.5	1.4						1.4	1.3
1.2	1.2	1.2						1.1	1.2
1.1	1.0	1.1	Quick					.7	1.1
.6	.5	.6						.5	.6
.4	.3	.3						.2	.3
24 15.4	**28** 12.9	**19** 19.1	Sales/Receivables					**18** 19.9	**34** 10.8
34 10.6	**36** 10.0	**38** 9.6						**38** 9.7	**44** 8.2
44 8.3	**42** 8.7	**48** 7.6						**46** 7.9	**49** 7.4
46 7.9	**58** 6.3	**40** 9.1	Cost of Sales/Inventory					**45** 8.1	**42** 8.7
86 4.2	**129** 2.8	**97** 3.7						**108** 3.4	**91** 4.0
123 3.0	**177** 2.1	**131** 2.8						**266** 1.4	**123** 3.0
15 25.0	**17** 21.9	**16** 22.3	Cost of Sales/Payables					**9** 38.5	**17** 20.9
22 16.3	**28** 13.0	**30** 12.2						**23** 15.9	**39** 9.4
51 7.2	**83** 4.4	**51** 7.2						**44** 8.3	**71** 5.2
5.1	4.5	5.0	Sales/Working Capital					3.9	5.4
8.9	8.8	9.7						9.9	7.6
34.4	16.9	30.1						144.8	28.8
14.0	33.1	35.6	EBIT/Interest					38.6	35.8
(43) 6.4	(43) 5.5	5.5						4.8	8.2
3.0	1.7	1.3						.2	1.1
30.2	10.6	5.3	Net Profit + Depr., Dep., Amort./Cur. Mat. L/T/D						
(14) 6.6	(15) 3.2	(13) 2.2							
3.1	1.8	-.4							
.3	.2	.4	Fixed/Worth					.3	.4
.7	.5	.8						.8	.7
1.2	1.0	1.7						1.9	1.5
.7	.8	.8	Debt/Worth					1.6	.7
1.9	2.1	2.3						3.0	2.3
3.4	2.9	4.3						4.2	4.8
46.0	51.3	72.4	% Profit Before Taxes/Tangible Net Worth					136.9	55.9
(42) 28.7	(42) 17.8	(37) 22.1						(11) 49.9	21.9
14.3	5.1	5.2						3.8	-1.5
20.6	27.5	17.2	% Profit Before Taxes/Total Assets					32.8	14.2
9.4	8.2	9.2						5.5	9.2
5.3	1.4	1.3						-2.3	.1
26.0	28.3	18.6	Sales/Net Fixed Assets					47.8	9.4
8.7	10.9	6.9						9.3	5.5
5.5	4.1	3.8						3.8	3.7
2.9	2.3	2.4	Sales/Total Assets					2.5	1.8
1.9	1.9	1.7						2.0	1.5
1.4	1.2	1.2						1.2	1.1
.9	.8	.7	% Depr., Dep., Amort./Sales					.5	.8
(41) 1.6	(38) 1.6	(34) 2.2						(11) 2.4	(17) 2.1
2.5	2.9	2.9						3.3	2.7
.9			% Officers', Directors' Owners' Comp/Sales						
(10) 2.9									
7.8									
3898603M	**3003602M**	**2547497M**	Net Sales ($)		**6686M**		**30042M**	**209922M**	**2300847M**
1997420M	**1808109M**	**1789015M**	Total Assets ($)		**2857M**		**10624M**	**146075M**	**1629459M**

M = $ thousand MM = $ million

See Pages 9 through 22 for Explanation of Ratios and Data

Current Data Sorted by Assets   Comparative Historical Data

0-500M	500M-2MM	2-10MM	10-50MM	50-100MM	100-250MM	Type of Statement	4/1/06-3/31/07 ALL	4/1/07-3/31/08 ALL
		1	8	5	7	Unqualified	30	26
		4	1			Reviewed	8	5
	1	2				Compiled	4	6
						Tax Returns	3	2
1		2	11	4	5	Other	19	21
1	1	9	20	9	12	**NUMBER OF STATEMENTS**	64	60
%	%	%	%	%	%		%	%
			8.5		5.2	**ASSETS** Cash & Equivalents	7.1	4.9
			32.3		26.2	Trade Receivables (net)	26.2	30.4
			12.0		9.3	Inventory	13.1	13.1
			2.2		.7	All Other Current	3.0	3.4
			55.1		41.5	Total Current	49.4	51.8
			38.4		37.9	Fixed Assets (net)	39.3	39.3
			2.6		12.1	Intangibles (net)	3.0	1.9
			3.9		8.5	All Other Non-Current	8.3	7.0
			100.0		100.0	Total	100.0	100.0
			5.8		4.4	**LIABILITIES** Notes Payable-Short Term	7.2	7.9
			2.7		5.3	Cur. Mat.-L.T.D.	3.5	3.4
			27.0		18.2	Trade Payables	20.8	24.9
			.0		.4	Income Taxes Payable	.3	.1
			5.9		14.4	All Other Current	10.2	10.6
			41.4		42.7	Total Current	42.0	46.9
			12.3		13.3	Long-Term Debt	18.1	16.1
			1.4		1.2	Deferred Taxes	.7	.6
			4.2		4.2	All Other Non-Current	3.9	3.0
			40.6		38.6	Net Worth	35.3	33.5
			100.0		100.0	Total Liabilties & Net Worth	100.0	100.0
			100.0		100.0	**INCOME DATA** Net Sales	100.0	100.0
			20.3		20.1	Gross Profit	22.3	20.6
			18.8		15.8	Operating Expenses	19.4	19.0
			1.5		4.2	Operating Profit	2.9	1.5
			.3		1.8	All Other Expenses (net)	1.0	.8
			1.2		2.4	Profit Before Taxes	1.9	.7
			1.7		1.5	**RATIOS** Current	1.6	1.6
			1.4		1.0	Current	1.1	1.1
			1.0		.8	Current	.9	1.0
			1.3		1.0	Quick	1.1	1.1
			.9		.7	Quick	.7	.8
			.6		.6	Quick	.5	.6
			(23) 15.9		(20) 18.2	Sales/Receivables	(22) 16.6	(22) 16.4
			(29) 12.8		(23) 16.0	Sales/Receivables	(27) 13.5	(28) 13.2
			(32) 11.5		(25) 14.3	Sales/Receivables	(34) 10.6	(35) 10.3
			(9) 39.7		(5) 80.2	Cost of Sales/Inventory	(9) 39.1	(10) 37.7
			(14) 26.6		(15) 24.1	Cost of Sales/Inventory	(14) 25.7	(13) 28.6
			(19) 19.6		(23) 16.1	Cost of Sales/Inventory	(28) 13.2	(22) 16.6
			(22) 16.5		(11) 32.4	Cost of Sales/Payables	(19) 19.4	(21) 17.2
			(25) 14.5		(19) 18.8	Cost of Sales/Payables	(26) 14.2	(26) 14.2
			(38) 9.7		(42) 8.6	Cost of Sales/Payables	(33) 11.1	(35) 10.5
			13.5		27.0	Sales/Working Capital	19.4	23.5
			26.3		NM	Sales/Working Capital	42.5	50.4
			NM		-38.9	Sales/Working Capital	-148.2	-220.0
			16.8		36.6	EBIT/Interest	9.2	7.7
			(16) 5.6		7.0	EBIT/Interest	(55) 3.3	(55) 1.6
			.3		2.1	EBIT/Interest	1.3	-.2
						Net Profit + Depr., Dep., Amort./Cur. Mat. L/T/D	5.0	5.3
						Net Profit + Depr., Dep., Amort./Cur. Mat. L/T/D	(20) 2.0	(17) 1.8
						Net Profit + Depr., Dep., Amort./Cur. Mat. L/T/D	1.3	1.2
			.6		.8	Fixed/Worth	.7	.6
			.9		1.3	Fixed/Worth	1.2	1.2
			2.2		2.7	Fixed/Worth	2.3	2.7
			.8		.9	Debt/Worth	1.1	1.1
			1.3		2.4	Debt/Worth	1.8	1.8
			3.7		7.8	Debt/Worth	4.4	5.7
			15.1		71.6	% Profit Before Taxes/Tangible Net Worth	36.3	32.0
			9.4		(11) 29.8	% Profit Before Taxes/Tangible Net Worth	(59) 13.2	(56) 8.7
			-7.8		16.3	% Profit Before Taxes/Tangible Net Worth	4.1	-6.7
			9.1		14.7	% Profit Before Taxes/Total Assets	13.1	8.2
			4.2		10.5	% Profit Before Taxes/Total Assets	4.4	1.8
			-1.8		1.7	% Profit Before Taxes/Total Assets	1.6	-2.2
			21.0		28.7	Sales/Net Fixed Assets	13.7	21.5
			8.7		7.2	Sales/Net Fixed Assets	7.9	8.0
			5.6		2.9	Sales/Net Fixed Assets	5.0	5.2
			4.9		7.7	Sales/Total Assets	4.5	4.9
			3.7		2.6	Sales/Total Assets	3.1	3.6
			3.3		1.3	Sales/Total Assets	2.2	2.6
			.7			% Depr., Dep., Amort./Sales	1.3	.9
			(19) 2.0			% Depr., Dep., Amort./Sales	(58) 1.8	(57) 1.7
			2.6			% Depr., Dep., Amort./Sales	3.1	2.7
						% Officers', Directors' Owners' Comp/Sales		
361M	12712M	207215M	2321625M	2513188M	7347065M	Net Sales ($)	9533880M	10208956M
269M	760M	47221M	568475M	661428M	1791658M	Total Assets ($)	3100664M	2956734M

© RMA 2011

M = $ thousand   MM = $ million
See Pages 9 through 22 for Explanation of Ratios and Data

Comparative Historical Data   Current Data Sorted by Sales

4/1/08–3/31/09 ALL	4/1/09–3/31/10 ALL	4/1/10–3/31/11 ALL	Type of Statement	0-1MM	1-3MM	3-5MM	5-10MM	10-25MM	25MM & OVER
19	22	21	Unqualified						21
4	9	5	Reviewed					1	2
4	3	3	Compiled					3	
1	6		Tax Returns						
29	28	23	Other	1			1	1	20
				16 (4/1-9/30/10)			36 (10/1/10-3/31/11)		
57	68	52	**NUMBER OF STATEMENTS**	1			2	6	43
%	%	%	**ASSETS**	%	%	%	%	%	%
7.3	8.6	7.9	Cash & Equivalents						7.5
27.6	24.5	30.0	Trade Receivables (net)						30.3
12.7	13.5	13.1	Inventory						12.7
2.9	2.7	1.8	All Other Current						2.2
50.5	49.2	52.8	Total Current						52.6
42.1	38.7	34.8	Fixed Assets (net)						36.4
1.8	3.3	7.9	Intangibles (net)						6.5
5.6	8.8	4.5	All Other Non-Current						4.5
100.0	100.0	100.0	Total						100.0
			LIABILITIES						
7.4	5.5	5.4	Notes Payable-Short Term						5.8
3.0	3.0	3.1	Cur. Mat.-L.T.D.						3.1
20.1	20.4	22.5	Trade Payables						22.3
.1	.1	.1	Income Taxes Payable						.1
9.3	7.8	10.2	All Other Current						10.9
39.9	36.8	41.4	Total Current						42.3
15.7	18.1	13.1	Long-Term Debt						10.8
.8	1.0	1.1	Deferred Taxes						1.3
4.7	3.6	3.8	All Other Non-Current						4.2
39.0	40.4	40.6	Net Worth						41.5
100.0	100.0	100.0	Total Liabilities & Net Worth						100.0
			INCOME DATA						
100.0	100.0	100.0	Net Sales						100.0
23.5	26.0	20.7	Gross Profit						18.4
20.4	23.5	18.0	Operating Expenses						16.3
3.1	2.4	2.7	Operating Profit						2.0
.5	.2	.6	All Other Expenses (net)						.5
2.7	2.3	2.1	Profit Before Taxes						1.5
			RATIOS						
1.9	1.8	1.8	Current						1.7
1.2	1.3	1.3							1.3
1.0	1.0	.9							.9
1.3	1.2	1.3	Quick						1.2
.9	.9	.9							.9
.6	.6	.6							.6
18 19.8	21 17.5	20 17.9	Sales/Receivables						20 18.0
24 15.5	26 14.2	24 15.0							24 14.9
29 12.4	32 11.3	31 11.8							30 12.0
8 47.3	9 39.1	9 39.7	Cost of Sales/Inventory						9 39.9
12 30.1	15 25.1	16 22.7							14 26.0
21 17.6	30 12.1	23 15.8							21 17.2
13 27.3	18 20.6	18 20.4	Cost of Sales/Payables						17 22.1
21 17.3	27 13.7	23 15.6							23 15.9
27 13.4	38 9.6	34 10.6							36 10.1
14.0	11.8	14.0	Sales/Working Capital						17.0
57.5	28.7	52.2							61.9
NM	501.6	-90.0							-85.9
15.0	21.1	19.8	EBIT/Interest						22.3
(53) 7.3	(63) 5.5	(47) 5.4							(38) 6.6
1.7	2.0	1.2							1.0
10.8	9.8	8.9	Net Profit + Depr., Dep., Amort./Cur. Mat. L/T/D						8.8
(18) 2.8	(26) 3.8	(20) 3.2							(17) 3.5
1.6	2.6	1.9							1.9
.6	.6	.6	Fixed/Worth						.6
.8	.9	.9							.9
2.2	1.7	2.0							2.0
.8	.7	.8	Debt/Worth						.9
1.5	1.3	1.3							1.3
5.3	3.9	4.8							3.6
37.1	34.3	29.3	% Profit Before Taxes/Tangible Net Worth						29.8
(55) 17.1	(64) 19.9	(48) 14.7							(41) 14.5
5.8	6.9	-1.4							-.9
12.5	14.1	12.1	% Profit Before Taxes/Total Assets						11.7
7.3	7.2	5.3							5.6
1.5	2.3	-.5							-.8
18.7	16.7	29.0	Sales/Net Fixed Assets						27.9
8.3	6.7	10.0							10.0
5.0	5.2	5.6							6.1
5.0	4.3	5.3	Sales/Total Assets						5.3
3.4	3.1	3.6							3.7
2.6	2.4	2.7							2.8
.9	1.1	.7	% Depr., Dep., Amort./Sales						.7
(49) 1.5	(61) 1.9	(47) 1.5							(40) 1.4
2.5	3.0	2.6							2.5
	.6		% Officers', Directors' Owners' Comp/Sales						
	(14) 1.6								
	2.8								
11186658M	9894416M	12402166M	Net Sales ($)	361M			15712M	97278M	12288815M
2969915M	2957395M	3069811M	Total Assets ($)	269M			19974M	24575M	3024993M

Note: Columns 0-1MM and 1-3MM are marked "DATA NOT AVAILABLE."

M = $ thousand   MM = $ million
See Pages 9 through 22 for Explanation of Ratios and Data

Current Data Sorted by Assets | | | | | | Comparative Historical Data

						Type of Statement		
		4	10	2	5	Unqualified	29	33
		7	7		1	Reviewed	15	11
		2	2			Compiled	5	4
		4				Tax Returns	4	4
		10	11	2	5	Other	22	23
1	2	10	57	2	5		4/1/06-	4/1/07-
	18 (4/1-9/30/10)		(10/1/10-3/31/11)				3/31/07	3/31/08
0-500M	500M-2MM	2-10MM	10-50MM	50-100MM	100-250MM		ALL	ALL
1	2	27	30	5	10	NUMBER OF STATEMENTS	75	75
%	%	%	%	%	%	**ASSETS**	%	%
		6.3	7.9		7.8	Cash & Equivalents	6.6	5.7
		26.4	21.7		17.9	Trade Receivables (net)	21.5	23.5
		21.9	25.9		26.8	Inventory	23.6	25.6
		5.9	.9		2.9	All Other Current	1.8	1.7
		60.5	56.4		55.3	Total Current	53.6	56.5
		33.1	36.9		37.6	Fixed Assets (net)	39.2	37.0
		.6	3.8		4.8	Intangibles (net)	2.9	2.4
		5.7	2.9		2.4	All Other Non-Current	4.2	4.1
		100.0	100.0		100.0	Total	100.0	100.0
						LIABILITIES		
		11.3	15.1		3.8	Notes Payable-Short Term	9.8	13.1
		2.4	2.7		2.0	Cur. Mat.-L.T.D.	3.5	2.9
		22.7	15.8		13.7	Trade Payables	15.8	18.1
		.0	.1		.0	Income Taxes Payable	.1	.2
		5.2	5.7		9.0	All Other Current	6.4	9.4
		41.6	39.5		28.5	Total Current	35.6	43.6
		18.4	13.2		21.5	Long-Term Debt	21.3	18.4
		.8	.6		3.2	Deferred Taxes	.8	.8
		3.8	5.0		3.0	All Other Non-Current	3.0	3.7
		35.4	41.7		43.8	Net Worth	39.2	33.6
		100.0	100.0		100.0	Total Liabilities & Net Worth	100.0	100.0
						INCOME DATA		
		100.0	100.0		100.0	Net Sales	100.0	100.0
		17.3	16.1		13.5	Gross Profit	16.5	14.5
		13.4	10.8		8.2	Operating Expenses	12.7	11.9
		3.9	5.3		5.3	Operating Profit	3.8	2.6
		1.5	.5		.7	All Other Expenses (net)	.9	.6
		2.4	4.8		4.6	Profit Before Taxes	2.9	2.0
						RATIOS		
		2.6	2.5		2.6		2.2	2.1
		1.6	1.3		1.7	Current	1.6	1.4
		1.0	1.0		1.5		1.1	1.0
		1.5	1.1		1.7		1.2	1.2
		.8	.7		.8	Quick	.8	.7
		.5	.4		.6		.5	.4
	24	15.3	21 17.1	23	15.8		22 16.8	20 18.0
	29	12.5	27 13.6	27	13.6	Sales/Receivables	28 13.2	26 13.9
	38	9.5	33 10.9	29	12.4		34 10.7	35 10.5
	9	38.6	18 20.6	27	13.3		17 21.3	18 20.5
	18	20.8	27 13.4	38	9.6	Cost of Sales/Inventory	31 11.7	30 12.1
	53	6.9	66 5.5	88	4.1		58 6.3	59 6.1
	20	18.4	16 23.4	13	27.4		16 22.9	19 19.4
	26	14.0	22 16.7	23	15.7	Cost of Sales/Payables	24 15.0	24 15.0
	41	9.0	32 11.2	28	13.0		31 11.7	31 11.6
		8.8	8.0		7.1		9.0	9.6
		19.6	26.4		10.5	Sales/Working Capital	20.7	19.8
		999.8	-375.5		15.5		82.1	653.8
		16.3	38.6				9.4	7.2
	(26)	6.7	(29) 10.0			EBIT/Interest	(71) 3.2	(70) 3.0
		.5	3.5				1.3	1.5
			85.6				7.5	9.4
			(10) 7.6			Net Profit + Depr., Dep., Amort./Cur. Mat. L/T/D	(25) 2.2	(25) 3.7
			3.6				1.6	1.4
		.5	.6		.6		.7	.7
		1.1	.9		.7	Fixed/Worth	1.1	1.0
		2.2	1.7		2.7		2.2	1.9
		.6	.7		.4		.7	.9
		1.6	1.8		1.1	Debt/Worth	1.5	1.9
		5.7	3.2		8.2		4.0	3.5
		43.5	53.5				30.1	32.6
	(23)	20.2	(28) 26.4			% Profit Before Taxes/Tangible Net Worth	(68) 13.7	(68) 19.3
		-.4	12.7				4.4	4.1
		18.7	14.6		15.9		12.7	9.0
		8.0	10.5		8.8	% Profit Before Taxes/Total Assets	5.5	4.9
		-.4	5.9		6.5		1.4	1.0
		18.5	13.0		10.4		13.6	13.9
		8.8	7.6		6.2	Sales/Net Fixed Assets	7.0	8.9
		4.8	4.7		4.5		4.0	4.3
		4.2	3.8		2.7		3.8	3.9
		3.4	2.9		2.3	Sales/Total Assets	2.7	3.0
		2.3	2.0		2.1		2.1	2.0
		1.3	1.2				1.3	1.2
	(24)	1.7	(29) 1.9			% Depr., Dep., Amort./Sales	(67) 1.7	(65) 1.5
		2.5	3.1				2.4	2.5
							.8	.6
						% Officers', Directors' Owners' Comp/Sales	(22) 2.0	(23) 1.7
							4.0	3.0
113M	12748M	527539M	1869049M	766788M	3489305M	Net Sales ($)	8285815M	9494272M
44M	3599M	158902M	673460M	353132M	1480345M	Total Assets ($)	3065936M	3437821M

M = $ thousand   MM = $ million
See Pages 9 through 22 for Explanation of Ratios and Data

Comparative Historical Data   Current Data Sorted by Sales

	4/1/08-3/31/09 ALL	4/1/09-3/31/10 ALL	4/1/10-3/31/11 ALL	Type of Statement	0-1MM	1-3MM	3-5MM	5-10MM	10-25MM	25MM & OVER
	26	26	21	Unqualified					2	19
	10	11	15	Reviewed					7	8
	5	7	4	Compiled		1			1	2
	7	5	4	Tax Returns				2	1	1
	39	32	31	Other	1		1	4	6	19
					1	18 (4/1-9/30/10)			57 (10/1/10-3/31/11)	
NUMBER OF STATEMENTS	87	81	75		1	1	1	6	17	49
	%	%	%	**ASSETS**	%	%	%	%	%	%
	7.7	7.7	6.8	Cash & Equivalents					7.2	7.3
	21.7	20.0	22.5	Trade Receivables (net)					22.8	23.4
	23.6	24.7	24.7	Inventory					20.3	24.0
	1.7	2.3	3.0	All Other Current					7.6	1.3
	54.7	54.8	57.0	Total Current					57.9	56.0
	36.6	35.1	36.8	Fixed Assets (net)					36.2	37.3
	3.3	3.0	2.4	Intangibles (net)					.3	3.6
	5.4	7.1	3.8	All Other Non-Current					5.6	3.1
	100.0	100.0	100.0	Total					100.0	100.0
				LIABILITIES						
	9.3	10.3	11.8	Notes Payable-Short Term					12.2	10.9
	2.9	3.2	2.3	Cur. Mat.-L.T.D.					2.0	2.5
	18.1	16.5	17.6	Trade Payables					18.4	17.6
	.2	.2	.1	Income Taxes Payable					.0	.1
	5.9	7.9	5.9	All Other Current					6.3	6.3
	36.4	38.0	37.7	Total Current					38.9	37.5
	19.5	18.6	17.3	Long-Term Debt					14.2	17.3
	.8	.9	1.1	Deferred Taxes					1.7	.9
	3.8	4.8	4.1	All Other Non-Current					2.3	4.3
	39.5	37.7	39.8	Net Worth					42.8	40.1
	100.0	100.0	100.0	Total Liabilities & Net Worth					100.0	100.0
				INCOME DATA						
	100.0	100.0	100.0	Net Sales					100.0	100.0
	17.5	18.9	16.5	Gross Profit					14.0	15.1
	12.9	13.3	11.9	Operating Expenses					10.9	10.6
	4.6	5.6	4.5	Operating Profit					3.0	4.5
	1.0	1.0	.9	All Other Expenses (net)					1.1	.5
	3.6	4.7	3.6	Profit Before Taxes					1.9	4.0
				RATIOS						
	2.3	2.4	2.4						2.7	2.4
	1.6	1.6	1.5	Current					1.6	1.5
	1.1	1.1	1.1						1.3	1.0
	1.4	1.3	1.5						1.7	1.5
	.7	.7	.7	Quick					.8	.7
	.4	.4	.5						.3	.6
	19 19.6	21 17.3	22 16.5						24 15.1	22 16.6
	25 14.4	27 13.4	27 13.4	Sales/Receivables					29 12.4	27 13.5
	33 10.9	31 11.7	33 10.9						38 9.6	32 11.3
	15 23.7	16 23.5	16 22.6						8 45.9	17 21.3
	27 13.3	36 10.2	28 13.0	Cost of Sales/Inventory					17 22.1	23 15.6
	62 5.9	64 5.7	62 5.9						59 6.2	55 6.6
	15 24.4	17 21.6	17 21.9						16 22.8	17 21.6
	21 17.6	26 14.0	25 14.7	Cost of Sales/Payables					24 15.5	24 15.4
	33 11.2	37 9.9	34 10.8						36 10.2	30 12.3
	9.1	7.1	8.8						7.2	9.1
	17.5	15.6	15.2	Sales/Working Capital					13.8	18.7
	74.9	100.4	57.3						27.2	NM
	15.3	22.9	21.1						20.9	26.9
	(80) 5.0	(78) 6.6	(71) 7.4	EBIT/Interest					(16) 2.8	(46) 9.7
	1.8	2.3	2.5						-1.0	3.6
	8.7	8.9	8.0	Net Profit + Depr., Dep.,						23.6
	(31) 2.7	(24) 3.6	(23) 3.9	Amort./Cur. Mat. L/T/D						(16) 5.1
	1.4	1.5	2.8							2.9
	.6	.4	.6						.6	.6
	1.0	.9	1.0	Fixed/Worth					.8	1.0
	2.0	1.9	2.0						2.2	1.9
	.7	.7	.6						.4	.7
	1.7	1.6	1.4	Debt/Worth					1.3	1.4
	3.2	3.6	3.1						4.8	2.8
	45.7	47.4	37.7	% Profit Before Taxes/Tangible					28.7	38.0
	(82) 20.4	(74) 27.5	(68) 23.1	Net Worth					(15) 11.8	(45) 24.4
	9.1	11.3	11.9						-9.2	16.0
	15.9	19.5	16.9	% Profit Before Taxes/Total					12.8	16.2
	7.6	10.9	8.8	Assets					3.5	9.2
	1.9	3.5	3.8						-2.7	6.2
	14.5	14.8	13.7						14.2	13.8
	7.8	6.5	7.1	Sales/Net Fixed Assets					8.8	7.1
	4.6	4.3	4.7						4.4	4.8
	4.0	3.7	3.8						4.0	3.8
	2.9	2.6	2.8	Sales/Total Assets					2.8	2.9
	2.0	1.8	2.1						2.0	2.1
	1.0	1.2	1.3						1.2	1.3
	(77) 1.5	(72) 1.8	(69) 1.8	% Depr., Dep., Amort./Sales					(16) 1.6	(45) 1.9
	2.6	2.6	2.6						2.7	2.5
	.4	.7	.7	% Officers', Directors'						.7
	(23) 1.4	(21) 1.4	(23) 1.4	Owners' Comp/Sales					(12) 1.3	
	2.6	2.2	2.7							3.6
	10976140M	7379129M	6665542M	Net Sales ($)	113M	2573M	4724M	47013M	307161M	6303958M
	3767444M	3040483M	2669482M	Total Assets ($)	44M	3905M	1699M	22449M	126862M	2514523M

M = $ thousand   MM = $ million
See Pages 9 through 22 for Explanation of Ratios and Data

Current Data Sorted by Assets | Comparative Historical Data

Type of Statement	0-500M	500M-2MM	2-10MM	10-50MM	50-100MM	100-250MM		4/1/06-3/31/07	4/1/07-3/31/08
Unqualified				4	1	1		5	8
Reviewed			5	2				3	2
Compiled	1		1					1	3
Tax Returns	3	2						8	3
Other	2	1	4	4	1			15	13
		6 (4/1-9/30/10)		26 (10/1/10-3/31/11)				ALL	ALL
NUMBER OF STATEMENTS	6	3	10	10	2	1		32	29
	%	%	%	%	%	%	**ASSETS**	%	%
			4.8	8.6			Cash & Equivalents	4.6	5.9
			20.6	11.9			Trade Receivables (net)	12.5	11.4
			32.9	18.5			Inventory	17.2	21.1
			1.7	2.0			All Other Current	2.1	3.5
			60.0	40.9			Total Current	36.5	41.9
			31.0	43.9			Fixed Assets (net)	46.3	38.4
			3.8	9.7			Intangibles (net)	11.1	13.8
			5.1	5.4			All Other Non-Current	6.1	5.9
			100.0	100.0			Total	100.0	100.0
							LIABILITIES		
			12.7	13.2			Notes Payable-Short Term	10.1	18.5
			3.1	6.4			Cur. Mat.-L.T.D.	5.5	3.7
			18.2	9.2			Trade Payables	13.0	13.7
			.0	.0			Income Taxes Payable	.0	.0
			4.6	4.8			All Other Current	15.3	3.5
			38.6	33.7			Total Current	43.9	39.4
			17.6	26.8			Long-Term Debt	28.3	22.4
			.3	1.2			Deferred Taxes	.9	1.0
			2.5	5.9			All Other Non-Current	7.2	7.2
			41.0	32.4			Net Worth	19.7	30.0
			100.0	100.0			Total Liabilities & Net Worth	100.0	100.0
							INCOME DATA		
			100.0	100.0			Net Sales	100.0	100.0
			29.8	38.8			Gross Profit	34.0	36.7
			27.4	33.9			Operating Expenses	32.2	35.4
			2.5	4.8			Operating Profit	1.7	1.4
			.9	2.0			All Other Expenses (net)	1.9	2.5
			1.5	2.8			Profit Before Taxes	-.2	-1.2
							RATIOS		
			2.2	3.0				1.8	1.9
			1.6	1.1			Current	1.0	1.4
			.9	.8				.7	.6
			1.2	1.9				.8	.8
			.6	.4			Quick	.6	.4
			.3	.3				.2	.2
			10 38.4	15 23.8				8 44.8	10 36.7
			22 16.6	20 18.0			Sales/Receivables	19 19.0	20 17.9
			29 12.4	31 11.8				31 11.9	27 13.5
			29 12.4	43 8.5				14 25.5	30 12.2
			46 7.9	54 6.7			Cost of Sales/Inventory	33 11.2	50 7.3
			74 5.0	88 4.1				66 5.5	77 4.8
			18 20.2	16 22.9				17 21.6	18 20.5
			24 15.2	27 13.5			Cost of Sales/Payables	25 14.5	29 12.7
			36 10.2	37 9.9				41 8.9	43 8.4
			12.2	4.4				11.5	11.0
			16.4	69.6			Sales/Working Capital	342.0	18.0
			-117.7	-21.1				-15.9	-11.3
			15.3	8.5				5.8	3.1
			6.0	1.6			EBIT/Interest	(28) 1.5	(28) .4
			.3	.5				-.4	-1.4
							Net Profit + Depr., Dep.,	6.5	2.7
							Amort./Cur. Mat. L/T/D	(10) 2.9	(11) .8
								.4	-1.7
			.2	1.0				1.2	.7
			.6	2.1			Fixed/Worth	3.5	2.1
			3.1	-408.3				-5.2	-1.4
			.8	1.2				1.8	1.4
			1.4	2.7			Debt/Worth	4.5	2.3
			4.8	-598.0				-16.4	-6.9
							% Profit Before Taxes/Tangible	42.8	30.1
							Net Worth	(23) 7.9	(19) 9.6
								-22.8	-15.5
			18.7	8.2			% Profit Before Taxes/Total	8.3	6.3
			5.5	1.9			Assets	1.9	-2.8
			-1.3	-1.3				-6.2	-9.0
			29.7	13.5				9.8	15.2
			15.5	4.4			Sales/Net Fixed Assets	6.0	9.4
			6.8	1.5				3.0	3.0
			4.8	2.9				3.1	3.0
			3.7	1.6			Sales/Total Assets	2.1	1.9
			2.2	.9				1.3	1.4
			.8	1.8				1.3	1.2
			1.3	2.3			% Depr., Dep., Amort./Sales	(29) 3.1	(24) 2.0
			3.5	8.3				4.8	4.8
							% Officers', Directors'		2.4
							Owners' Comp/Sales	(11) 3.3	
									4.4
	3206M	9397M	205313M	381104M	208354M	138117M	Net Sales ($)	1414717M	1131306M
	1800M	2488M	58508M	224619M	145740M	130962M	Total Assets ($)	686431M	738061M

Comparative Historical Data / Current Data Sorted by Sales

4/1/08-3/31/09 ALL	4/1/09-3/31/10 ALL	4/1/10-3/31/11 ALL		0-1MM	1-3MM	3-5MM	5-10MM	10-25MM	25MM & OVER
			Type of Statement						
8	5	6	Unqualified					1	5
3	3	7	Reviewed				1	4	2
5	1	2	Compiled		1		1		
2	3	5	Tax Returns	3	1		1		
11	12	12	Other	2	1		1	4	4
				6 (4/1-9/30/10)			26 (10/1/10-3/31/11)		
29	24	32	**NUMBER OF STATEMENTS**	5	3		4	9	11
%	%	%	**ASSETS**	%	%	%	%	%	%
7.1	9.4	7.0	Cash & Equivalents			DATA NOT AVAILABLE			6.1
11.6	12.1	13.3	Trade Receivables (net)						18.8
23.2	21.5	23.6	Inventory						29.5
1.5	2.6	1.4	All Other Current						2.2
43.4	45.7	45.3	Total Current						56.6
37.9	32.2	38.7	Fixed Assets (net)						22.7
11.9	15.6	12.2	Intangibles (net)						16.8
6.8	6.6	3.8	All Other Non-Current						3.9
100.0	100.0	100.0	Total						100.0
			LIABILITIES						
14.9	8.4	13.3	Notes Payable-Short Term						16.2
3.5	2.9	4.9	Cur. Mat.-L.T.D.						3.5
10.7	12.0	12.1	Trade Payables						15.3
.1	.0	.0	Income Taxes Payable						.0
20.4	7.1	4.5	All Other Current						5.0
49.6	30.3	34.9	Total Current						40.0
22.2	28.4	37.0	Long-Term Debt						18.9
.8	.6	1.2	Deferred Taxes						3.3
7.0	7.4	5.2	All Other Non-Current						3.5
20.4	33.3	21.7	Net Worth						34.3
100.0	100.0	100.0	Total Liabilties & Net Worth						100.0
			INCOME DATA						
100.0	100.0	100.0	Net Sales						100.0
38.6	42.4	39.5	Gross Profit						25.7
36.2	36.3	34.7	Operating Expenses						21.4
2.4	6.1	4.9	Operating Profit						4.3
1.5	3.0	1.9	All Other Expenses (net)						1.3
.9	3.1	2.9	Profit Before Taxes						3.0
			RATIOS						
2.2	2.7	2.1							1.7
1.2	1.4	1.2	Current						1.5
.8	.8	.8							1.0
1.1	1.3	.9							1.0
.5	.6	.5	Quick						.5
.3	.4	.3							.3
14 25.9	**13** 28.3	**12** 29.6							**18** 19.8
20 18.7	**19** 19.4	**19** 19.6	Sales/Receivables						**23** 15.7
30 12.3	**29** 12.7	**26** 13.9							**27** 13.6
37 9.8	**36** 10.2	**29** 12.5							**44** 8.3
65 5.6	**57** 6.4	**50** 7.2	Cost of Sales/Inventory						**55** 6.6
90 4.1	**90** 4.0	**87** 4.2							**63** 5.8
17 21.9	**16** 22.3	**15** 25.0							**18** 20.5
25 14.5	**24** 15.2	**24** 15.2	Cost of Sales/Payables						**25** 14.8
35 10.5	**37** 9.8	**36** 10.0							**36** 10.1
8.4	5.0	9.5							13.3
28.9	17.8	27.9	Sales/Working Capital						15.9
-17.8	-50.7	-16.7							-687.8
12.8	8.9	7.4							12.5
(27) 1.5	(23) 3.2	(31) 2.1	EBIT/Interest						2.3
-.4	.7	1.0							.3
7.6		11.0							
(10) 1.8		(10) 4.5	Net Profit + Depr., Dep., Amort./Cur. Mat. L/T/D						
-.5		1.5							
.6	.5	.9							.4
1.5	1.3	2.7	Fixed/Worth						1.1
NM	-5.4	-4.3							-1.7
.8	.7	1.3							1.2
1.6	1.6	4.7	Debt/Worth						1.7
NM	-15.8	-16.0							-4.4
44.9	47.0	42.5							
(22) 12.8	(17) 27.4	(20) 22.7	% Profit Before Taxes/Tangible Net Worth						
-4.9	2.6	.6							
15.8	22.1	15.9							16.6
2.1	4.5	3.6	% Profit Before Taxes/Total Assets						5.4
-5.0	-1.3	.2							-1.9
10.2	19.5	18.1							29.3
6.5	11.1	8.9	Sales/Net Fixed Assets						12.5
3.5	4.9	2.6							5.8
3.0	3.2	3.4							4.3
2.0	2.0	2.3	Sales/Total Assets						2.8
1.2	1.1	1.3							1.6
1.5	1.2	1.4							1.2
(24) 2.0	(20) 2.0	(29) 2.2	% Depr., Dep., Amort./Sales						(10) 1.9
3.6	5.3	5.2							2.5
			% Officers', Directors' Owners' Comp/Sales						
1168840M	915194M	945491M	Net Sales ($)	1831M	3741M		33148M	166897M	739874M
663460M	495742M	564117M	Total Assets ($)	1343M	1505M		38658M	107099M	415512M

M = $ thousand MM = $ million

See Pages 9 through 22 for Explanation of Ratios and Data

Current Data Sorted by Assets   Comparative Historical Data

Type of Statement

Type of Statement	0-500M	500M-2MM	2-10MM	10-50MM	50-100MM	100-250MM	4/1/06-3/31/07 ALL	4/1/07-3/31/08 ALL
Unqualified			3	5	6	2	36	23
Reviewed		1	4	7			16	12
Compiled	2	3	2	3			14	11
Tax Returns	3	7	4	1			2	7
Other		2	7	8	4	1	36	35
		15 (4/1-9/30/10)		60 (10/1/10-3/31/11)				
NUMBER OF STATEMENTS	5	13	20	24	10	3	104	88

Financial Data

	0-500M %	500M-2MM %	2-10MM %	10-50MM %	50-100MM %	100-250MM %	4/1/06-3/31/07 ALL %	4/1/07-3/31/08 ALL %
ASSETS								
Cash & Equivalents		9.4	8.4	14.1	3.8		7.3	7.3
Trade Receivables (net)		28.9	28.0	22.1	25.8		24.2	22.9
Inventory		19.1	23.1	21.1	16.3		22.3	23.1
All Other Current		2.4	1.3	1.3	1.5		2.3	2.2
Total Current		59.9	60.7	58.6	47.5		56.1	55.5
Fixed Assets (net)		34.6	30.7	31.9	36.8		33.3	33.0
Intangibles (net)		.5	.8	2.3	10.3		3.1	4.2
All Other Non-Current		5.1	7.8	7.2	5.5		7.6	7.3
Total		100.0	100.0	100.0	100.0		100.0	100.0
LIABILITIES								
Notes Payable-Short Term		7.0	6.9	7.0	8.2		11.9	12.7
Cur. Mat.-L.T.D.		4.9	2.3	2.9	2.9		2.4	3.0
Trade Payables		21.3	22.5	11.6	9.5		12.1	12.3
Income Taxes Payable		.0	.0	.0	1.9		.2	.2
All Other Current		6.2	10.3	7.0	7.9		7.2	7.2
Total Current		39.5	42.1	28.6	30.3		34.0	35.3
Long-Term Debt		19.6	20.0	17.3	17.9		17.2	20.3
Deferred Taxes		.1	.8	.4	.0		.6	.4
All Other Non-Current		7.6	4.2	3.4	2.7		8.1	7.7
Net Worth		33.3	32.9	50.3	49.0		40.1	36.3
Total Liabilities & Net Worth		100.0	100.0	100.0	100.0		100.0	100.0
INCOME DATA								
Net Sales		100.0	100.0	100.0	100.0		100.0	100.0
Gross Profit		17.4	16.2	18.3	13.0		16.8	19.1
Operating Expenses		16.0	15.9	14.2	8.1		14.0	16.6
Operating Profit		1.4	.3	4.0	4.9		2.7	2.5
All Other Expenses (net)		.0	.6	.2	.6		.5	.8
Profit Before Taxes		1.3	-.3	3.8	4.4		2.3	1.7

RATIOS

	0-500M	500M-2MM	2-10MM	10-50MM	50-100MM	100-250MM	4/1/06-3/31/07	4/1/07-3/31/08
Current		2.9	2.9	3.7	2.0		2.6	2.4
		1.5	1.5	2.0	1.7		1.7	1.6
		.9	1.3	1.2	1.2		1.2	1.1
Quick		2.1	1.6	2.3	1.4		1.5	1.5
		.8	1.0	1.2	1.0		.8	.8
		.5	.5	.7	.8		.6	.5
Sales/Receivables		9 41.3	15 23.6	16 22.5	17 21.2		14 25.2	15 24.5
		18 20.5	19 18.7	20 18.3	27 13.6		21 17.7	19 18.9
		28 12.8	35 10.3	30 12.0	30 12.2		27 13.4	26 14.2
Cost of Sales/Inventory		10 36.1	9 41.2	15 24.1	11 32.6		13 29.0	13 27.9
		16 22.8	20 18.7	24 15.5	14 25.4		21 17.1	25 14.7
		21 17.1	53 6.9	35 10.5	32 11.4		37 9.8	40 9.1
Cost of Sales/Payables		6 66.3	8 44.7	6 59.7	6 63.4		5 66.4	6 65.6
		18 20.8	16 22.7	11 34.3	12 29.7		11 32.8	11 33.1
		32 11.4	29 12.5	24 15.5	14 25.4		19 19.7	19 19.7
Sales/Working Capital		14.5	13.7	7.4	16.9		10.6	11.0
		20.6	19.5	14.4	28.3		20.9	23.1
		-151.4	34.7	41.2	37.9		57.5	66.5
EBIT/Interest		8.7	10.1	14.3	25.7		8.5	6.2
		(12) 2.8	(19) 2.8	(23) 4.2	9.0		(91) 3.3	(79) 2.7
		1.0	-.1	1.1	2.6		1.0	1.0
Net Profit + Depr., Dep., Amort./Cur. Mat. L/T/D							5.6	4.0
							(21) 2.7	(15) 2.9
							1.7	1.6
Fixed/Worth		.2	.2	.4	.6		.4	.3
		.7	.8	.8	1.0		.9	1.0
		2.8	2.1	1.4	1.5		2.3	6.4
Debt/Worth		.8	.7	.4	.6		.8	.8
		2.0	2.3	.9	1.5		1.6	1.8
		7.9	4.6	3.1	3.0		4.4	11.6
% Profit Before Taxes/Tangible Net Worth		30.3	22.2	45.8			42.3	45.1
		(12) 4.7	(19) 9.9	13.4			(95) 16.7	(74) 18.8
		-9.2	2.1	.7			1.6	4.4
% Profit Before Taxes/Total Assets		7.4	11.4	14.8	21.3		14.6	11.5
		2.4	2.9	8.4	13.9		6.1	5.8
		-1.6	-2.5	.3	8.2		.5	.5
Sales/Net Fixed Assets		106.9	38.9	32.8	15.9		31.5	43.4
		8.8	13.7	10.5	12.7		12.8	12.8
		5.2	5.8	4.9	8.2		5.6	5.8
Sales/Total Assets		7.0	6.1	5.1	4.3		6.0	5.7
		4.1	3.8	4.0	3.7		3.8	3.7
		2.9	1.5	1.8	2.7		2.4	2.3
% Depr., Dep., Amort./Sales		.3	.5	.5	.8		.4	.4
		.5	(18) 1.0	(23) 1.0	1.6		(89) 1.3	(76) 1.2
		1.9	2.3	2.3	1.9		2.0	2.2
% Officers', Directors' Owners' Comp/Sales			1.5				.5	1.0
			(11) 3.1				(29) 1.6	(26) 1.9
			5.1				3.8	3.6
Net Sales ($)	6289M	87059M	433505M	2230468M	2430611M	1884512M	10990937M	8975077M
Total Assets ($)	1222M	16253M	107983M	624015M	678882M	504943M	3417256M	2708863M

M = $ thousand   MM = $ million
See Pages 9 through 22 for Explanation of Ratios and Data

Comparative Historical Data / Current Data Sorted by Sales

24	19	16	Type of Statement						
24	19	16	Unqualified					4	12
16	18	12	Reviewed				1	2	9
9	15	10	Compiled					2	3
4	5	15	Tax Returns	1	2	1	1	2	2
30	29	22	Other	1	3	4	4	1	16
4/1/08-3/31/09 ALL	4/1/09-3/31/10 ALL	4/1/10-3/31/11 ALL		0-1MM	1-3MM (15 (4/1-9/30/10))	3-5MM	5-10MM	10-25MM (60 (10/1/10-3/31/11))	25MM & OVER
83	86	75	NUMBER OF STATEMENTS	2	6	7	7	11	42
%	%	%	ASSETS	%	%	%	%	%	%
6.7	10.1	9.9	Cash & Equivalents					4.7	8.3
26.2	23.4	24.8	Trade Receivables (net)					29.5	26.7
23.6	19.1	20.4	Inventory					30.0	19.7
2.1	2.7	1.7	All Other Current					1.7	1.7
58.5	55.3	56.8	Total Current					65.9	56.4
33.7	36.8	34.6	Fixed Assets (net)					25.7	34.2
3.5	3.3	2.6	Intangibles (net)					1.6	3.9
4.2	4.5	6.1	All Other Non-Current					6.9	5.5
100.0	100.0	100.0	Total					100.0	100.0
			LIABILITIES						
10.3	10.7	8.2	Notes Payable-Short Term					6.8	8.0
4.0	3.0	3.1	Cur. Mat.-L.T.D.					1.3	2.8
13.3	10.4	15.5	Trade Payables					25.7	13.2
.2	.1	.3	Income Taxes Payable					.1	.5
8.4	7.8	7.7	All Other Current					15.7	7.7
36.4	32.0	34.8	Total Current					49.5	32.1
19.2	19.5	20.4	Long-Term Debt					16.1	16.4
.3	.3	.4	Deferred Taxes					1.1	.5
8.4	6.3	5.8	All Other Non-Current					2.5	4.2
35.7	41.9	38.5	Net Worth					30.8	46.8
100.0	100.0	100.0	Total Liabilities & Net Worth					100.0	100.0
			INCOME DATA						
100.0	100.0	100.0	Net Sales					100.0	100.0
16.1	22.5	18.4	Gross Profit					11.5	13.7
14.0	20.3	15.9	Operating Expenses					11.6	10.5
2.2	2.2	2.4	Operating Profit					-.1	3.2
.5	.1	.4	All Other Expenses (net)					.2	.2
1.7	2.1	2.0	Profit Before Taxes					-.2	2.9
			RATIOS						
2.3 / 1.7 / 1.1	3.3 / 1.7 / 1.1	3.0 / 1.7 / 1.2	Current					2.6 / 2.2 / 1.3	3.1 / 1.7 / 1.2
1.5 / .9 / .6	2.0 / 1.0 / .5	1.7 / 1.0 / .6	Quick					2.0 / 1.0 / .3	1.7 / 1.0 / .7
(15) 24.2 / (20) 18.2 / (25) 14.3	(14) 25.8 / (21) 17.8 / (29) 12.7	(15) 24.5 / (19) 18.9 / (29) 12.6	Sales/Receivables					(12) 29.4 / (19) 18.9 / (30) 12.1	(16) 23.4 / (20) 18.3 / (28) 12.9
(12) 29.6 / (22) 16.8 / (40) 9.1	(10) 36.6 / (19) 19.1 / (38) 9.5	(11) 32.2 / (20) 18.4 / (36) 10.2	Cost of Sales/Inventory					(11) 33.9 / (23) 16.2 / (73) 5.0	(10) 35.0 / (19) 19.6 / (29) 12.6
(6) 62.5 / (10) 35.6 / (17) 21.7	(5) 76.5 / (10) 37.7 / (20) 18.1	(6) 62.4 / (12) 29.8 / (23) 15.7	Cost of Sales/Payables					(5) 74.7 / (8) 44.3 / (25) 14.8	(6) 60.1 / (12) 31.2 / (17) 21.6
11.6 / 24.2 / 93.9	9.1 / 23.6 / 113.6	10.4 / 20.4 / 54.6	Sales/Working Capital					14.4 / 18.7 / 21.9	10.0 / 24.2 / 39.7
12.1 / (77) 4.4 / 1.0	13.0 / (79) 3.4 / .0	13.3 / (72) 3.7 / 1.0	EBIT/Interest					8.6 / (41) 4.5 / 1.0	27.8 / 8.9 / 1.8
8.5 / (18) 2.0 / .6	4.9 / (17) 2.4 / 1.7	6.7 / (22) 3.9 / 1.1	Net Profit + Depr., Dep., Amort./Cur. Mat. L/T/D						6.7 / (14) 3.9 / 1.1
.4 / .9 / 2.1	.4 / .9 / 2.9	.4 / .9 / 2.1	Fixed/Worth					.2 / .7 / 2.0	.5 / .9 / 1.5
.6 / 1.4 / 4.5	.5 / 1.7 / 4.9	.6 / 1.5 / 4.2	Debt/Worth					1.0 / 1.1 / 2.8	.6 / 1.4 / 3.4
44.3 / (73) 15.4 / 3.4	32.6 / (76) 14.3 / 1.7	38.5 / (70) 13.4 / .5	% Profit Before Taxes/Tangible Net Worth					29.4 / (10) 9.1 / .5	45.1 / (41) 26.6 / 4.7
16.4 / 5.9 / .5	13.7 / 5.4 / -1.1	13.4 / 4.7 / .1	% Profit Before Taxes/Total Assets					16.1 / 3.7 / .1	20.7 / 11.2 / 2.1
35.5 / 12.1 / 6.3	28.2 / 10.4 / 4.4	32.8 / 12.0 / 5.3	Sales/Net Fixed Assets					77.4 / 21.9 / 4.6	22.9 / 12.9 / 7.9
5.8 / 3.8 / 2.6	5.7 / 3.4 / 2.0	5.6 / 3.9 / 2.4	Sales/Total Assets					9.3 / 3.8 / 1.9	5.4 / 4.2 / 3.0
.5 / (77) 1.1 / 1.9	.5 / (78) 1.5 / 2.6	.5 / (71) 1.1 / 2.2	% Depr., Dep., Amort./Sales					.4 / (39) .8 / 3.2	.7 / 1.0 / 1.8
.9 / (26) 1.7 / 4.2	1.0 / (29) 1.9 / 4.8	.8 / (33) 2.0 / 4.0	% Officers', Directors' Owners' Comp/Sales					(12)	.5 / 1.0 / 2.9
8487439M	6551663M	7072444M	Net Sales ($)	909M	11741M	26838M	49182M	191391M	6792383M
2324899M	1720329M	1933298M	Total Assets ($)	203M	4598M	26936M	22945M	63318M	1815298M

© RMA 2011

M = $ thousand   MM = $ million
See Pages 9 through 22 for Explanation of Ratios and Data

Current Data Sorted by Assets   Comparative Historical Data

0-500M	500M-2MM	2-10MM	10-50MM	50-100MM	100-250MM	Type of Statement	4/1/06-3/31/07 ALL	4/1/07-3/31/08 ALL
		3	15	7	4	Unqualified	36	36
	1	25	16	1		Reviewed	30	25
1	3	12	3			Compiled	27	17
5	8	6				Tax Returns	4	10
1	5	14	23	9	5	Other	54	65
	31 (4/1-9/30/10)		136 (10/1/10-3/31/11)					
7	17	60	57	17	9	NUMBER OF STATEMENTS	151	153
%	%	%	%	%	%	ASSETS	%	%
	9.5	9.8	6.3	4.2		Cash & Equivalents	7.4	8.1
	28.1	28.7	22.2	16.1		Trade Receivables (net)	24.6	24.2
	20.7	22.2	22.9	28.6		Inventory	21.5	22.2
	.6	2.2	3.8	1.1		All Other Current	2.4	3.3
	59.0	62.9	55.2	50.0		Total Current	55.9	57.8
	34.5	29.3	35.8	35.1		Fixed Assets (net)	34.7	33.9
	4.8	3.1	1.7	12.7		Intangibles (net)	3.7	3.4
	1.7	4.7	7.3	2.2		All Other Non-Current	5.6	5.0
	100.0	100.0	100.0	100.0		Total	100.0	100.0
						LIABILITIES		
	14.2	9.1	9.0	10.1		Notes Payable-Short Term	11.0	10.9
	2.0	2.2	2.9	3.0		Cur. Mat.-L.T.D.	2.9	3.1
	10.7	16.2	12.5	9.0		Trade Payables	13.8	13.8
	.0	.1	.2	.0		Income Taxes Payable	.1	.1
	8.6	11.2	6.5	4.9		All Other Current	8.6	8.3
	35.5	38.8	31.2	26.9		Total Current	36.3	36.3
	19.2	9.9	21.0	25.6		Long-Term Debt	19.6	17.8
	.1	.1	.9	1.3		Deferred Taxes	.5	.4
	4.5	6.1	9.8	10.5		All Other Non-Current	6.0	6.9
	40.8	45.0	37.1	35.7		Net Worth	37.6	38.6
	100.0	100.0	100.0	100.0		Total Liabilties & Net Worth	100.0	100.0
						INCOME DATA		
	100.0	100.0	100.0	100.0		Net Sales	100.0	100.0
	25.1	20.5	17.9	14.7		Gross Profit	19.6	19.4
	21.6	18.0	15.4	12.5		Operating Expenses	15.7	16.6
	3.5	2.4	2.5	2.2		Operating Profit	4.0	2.7
	1.1	.4	.6	1.6		All Other Expenses (net)	.8	.7
	2.4	2.1	1.9	.6		Profit Before Taxes	3.2	2.1
						RATIOS		
	3.8	3.2	3.3	2.3			2.6	2.9
	2.0	1.9	1.7	1.7		Current	1.5	1.6
	.8	1.2	1.2	1.3			1.1	1.1
	2.8	1.8	1.7	1.0			1.7	1.6
	1.2	1.0	.9	.7		Quick	.8	.9
	.4	.7	.5	.7			.5	.5
	11 33.6	14 25.5	19 19.2	14 25.3			15 23.9	15 24.6
	19 19.0	21 17.6	22 16.8	24 15.5		Sales/Receivables	21 17.0	19 19.0
	26 14.0	26 14.2	28 13.2	32 11.3			27 13.6	27 13.4
	3 131.2	17 21.9	18 19.8	21 17.1			14 26.1	12 29.4
	20 18.5	22 16.4	28 13.2	42 8.8		Cost of Sales/Inventory	24 15.4	20 17.9
	37 9.8	33 10.9	47 7.7	76 4.8			39 9.4	41 8.9
	3 145.9	8 45.0	8 45.6	9 41.4			8 47.9	8 47.3
	11 34.4	13 28.2	12 30.9	13 27.4		Cost of Sales/Payables	13 27.9	13 28.3
	16 23.3	20 18.5	25 14.3	24 15.5			20 18.1	21 17.7
	7.6	9.5	7.1	10.1			10.3	10.4
	20.6	17.5	15.4	15.3		Sales/Working Capital	23.9	20.6
	-88.9	49.2	57.7	23.3			131.4	63.6
	8.9	12.2	10.9	6.5			9.9	7.6
	(16) 5.1	(53) 3.6	(56) 4.8	2.7		EBIT/Interest	(144) 3.9	(139) 3.5
	1.5	1.0	.9	.3			1.6	1.3
		9.4	10.2			Net Profit + Depr., Dep.,	8.6	6.6
		(14) 4.3	(19) 3.6			Amort./Cur. Mat. L/T/D	(44) 2.8	(37) 3.5
		1.4	1.9				1.1	1.7
	.3	.3	.5	1.0			.5	.4
	.8	.5	.9	1.3		Fixed/Worth	1.0	.9
	6.6	1.2	2.1	NM			2.0	2.2
	.5	.4	.8	1.3			.9	.8
	1.3	1.3	1.4	2.6		Debt/Worth	2.0	1.7
	13.4	3.1	5.0	NM			4.6	4.8
	54.0	37.8	46.6	27.8			39.6	35.0
	(15) 16.3	(57) 17.3	(51) 20.2	(13) 16.4		% Profit Before Taxes/Tangible Net Worth	(138) 20.3	(142) 14.4
	5.2	.4	3.4	9.2			7.1	5.5
	10.6	17.5	11.2	9.3			14.5	11.5
	7.6	5.8	6.0	6.7		% Profit Before Taxes/Total Assets	7.0	5.3
	2.6	.1	-.3	-3.4			1.8	1.6
	55.1	51.9	14.4	12.4			28.6	31.9
	15.7	13.5	9.3	7.4		Sales/Net Fixed Assets	11.3	11.5
	4.6	7.5	5.4	4.9			5.1	4.9
	7.6	6.2	4.1	4.1			6.1	5.7
	4.9	4.0	3.0	2.3		Sales/Total Assets	3.6	3.4
	1.6	2.6	1.9	1.7			2.2	2.2
	.8	.9	.9	1.2			.6	.6
	(14) 1.8	(52) 1.5	(55) 1.6	2.1		% Depr., Dep., Amort./Sales	(137) 1.4	(139) 1.3
	3.3	2.2	2.6	3.3			2.8	2.5
	.9	.9	.8				.7	.6
	(13) 2.2	(29) 2.5	(17) 1.7			% Officers', Directors' Owners' Comp/Sales	(53) 1.4	(53) 1.8
	6.3	3.5	4.4				4.2	4.2
9072M	150898M	1520027M	4536582M	3221779M	5094182M	Net Sales ($)	12860938M	16838085M
2199M	21988M	312631M	1364583M	1182535M	1485593M	Total Assets ($)	3896543M	4771745M

M = $ thousand   MM = $ million
See Pages 9 through 22 for Explanation of Ratios and Data

Comparative Historical Data | Current Data Sorted by Sales

				Type of Statement						
30	33	29		Unqualified					2	27
30	29	43		Reviewed				6	10	27
27	25	19		Compiled		1	1	2	9	6
9	10	19		Tax Returns	3	5	2	4	4	1
57	53	57		Other	1	2		4	8	42
4/1/08-3/31/09	4/1/09-3/31/10	4/1/10-3/31/11				31 (4/1-9/30/10)		136 (10/1/10-3/31/11)		
ALL	ALL	ALL			0-1MM	1-3MM	3-5MM	5-10MM	10-25MM	25MM & OVER
153	150	167		**NUMBER OF STATEMENTS**	4	8	3	16	33	103
%	%	%		**ASSETS**	%	%	%	%	%	%
8.5	9.7	8.8		Cash & Equivalents				16.2	9.5	5.8
22.4	20.5	23.3		Trade Receivables (net)				18.6	25.3	24.9
24.4	23.7	22.7		Inventory				20.7	19.6	25.3
2.6	2.7	2.3		All Other Current				6.3	2.1	2.1
57.9	56.6	57.2		Total Current				61.7	56.7	58.1
33.3	33.7	33.7		Fixed Assets (net)				28.9	32.9	32.9
3.6	4.0	4.0		Intangibles (net)				6.4	4.1	3.8
5.2	5.7	5.2		All Other Non-Current				3.0	6.4	5.2
100.0	100.0	100.0		Total				100.0	100.0	100.0
				LIABILITIES						
10.7	10.2	9.3		Notes Payable-Short Term				8.9	7.9	10.4
3.9	3.4	3.1		Cur. Mat.-L.T.D.				1.4	2.3	2.7
12.3	13.2	13.2		Trade Payables				10.1	13.2	14.4
.1	.1	.1		Income Taxes Payable				.0	.1	.2
7.4	8.3	9.0		All Other Current				8.8	5.9	7.0
34.3	35.2	34.8		Total Current				29.1	29.2	34.6
18.3	18.1	20.2		Long-Term Debt				14.6	13.7	19.2
.3	.6	.5		Deferred Taxes				.3	.1	.7
6.2	6.3	7.4		All Other Non-Current				5.8	7.4	8.5
40.8	39.8	37.1		Net Worth				50.2	49.6	36.9
100.0	100.0	100.0		Total Liabilities & Net Worth				100.0	100.0	100.0
				INCOME DATA						
100.0	100.0	100.0		Net Sales				100.0	100.0	100.0
21.4	22.6	20.4		Gross Profit				29.3	22.2	15.2
18.1	18.8	17.6		Operating Expenses				25.0	19.9	12.9
3.3	3.9	2.8		Operating Profit				4.3	2.3	2.3
.7	.7	.7		All Other Expenses (net)				.6	.4	.6
2.6	3.2	2.1		Profit Before Taxes				3.7	1.9	1.6
				RATIOS						
2.9	2.8	2.9						6.9	2.9	2.7
1.8	1.6	1.8		Current				3.4	2.1	1.7
1.2	1.2	1.2						1.0	1.5	1.2
1.6	1.6	1.7						5.2	1.7	1.5
1.0	.9	.9		Quick				1.4	1.1	.9
.6	.5	.6						.5	.8	.6
14 25.3	15 23.9	16 23.5						14 25.8	14 26.8	17 21.0
20 18.5	20 18.1	21 17.4		Sales/Receivables				20 18.1	20 17.9	21 17.0
26 14.0	26 14.1	26 13.8						26 14.2	29 12.8	27 13.4
15 23.9	16 22.7	17 20.9						13 27.7	19 19.5	16 22.2
29 12.8	29 12.5	25 14.8		Cost of Sales/Inventory				22 16.5	26 14.2	25 14.8
51 7.2	50 7.3	43 8.4						60 6.1	33 11.2	45 8.1
7 52.8	8 44.2	8 45.9						5 69.5	8 44.7	9 42.5
12 31.5	14 26.2	13 27.9		Cost of Sales/Payables				12 31.3	14 26.1	13 27.9
21 17.8	27 13.6	21 17.3						22 16.4	25 14.8	21 17.5
7.9	8.1	8.8						4.4	9.0	10.2
16.7	18.6	17.6		Sales/Working Capital				7.0	15.8	19.1
52.0	58.0	49.9						NM	23.0	51.9
9.8	13.7	10.7						13.9	10.1	11.3
(146) 3.4	(139) 5.3	(158) 4.0		EBIT/Interest		(14) 4.1	(30) 3.6			(99) 5.0
.8	1.9	1.2						1.5	.9	1.1
6.6	6.0	9.8								10.1
(38) 2.4	(41) 2.9	(43) 3.6		Net Profit + Depr., Dep., Amort./Cur. Mat. L/T/D					(32) 3.5	
1.0	1.8	1.8								1.9
.5	.4	.4						.3	.3	.5
.8	.9	.9		Fixed/Worth				.5	.7	.9
2.0	2.1	1.9						1.7	1.1	2.1
.8	.6	.7						.2	.7	.8
1.7	1.7	1.6		Debt/Worth				.6	1.3	1.7
4.2	4.7	3.8						18.2	2.5	5.4
37.7	42.2	39.5						42.1	37.3	38.4
(140) 14.3	(136) 22.5	(148) 19.4		% Profit Before Taxes/Tangible Net Worth		(15) 18.7			14.3	(89) 20.1
1.2	9.8	4.0						12.2	-.3	4.0
13.2	17.4	12.3						18.9	14.9	11.7
5.3	9.1	6.4		% Profit Before Taxes/Total Assets				8.6	5.9	6.7
-.2	2.6	.3						2.3	-.3	.0
23.3	22.5	20.8						22.0	24.4	20.3
10.6	10.0	10.4		Sales/Net Fixed Assets				10.5	10.9	10.4
5.6	5.8	5.6						7.1	5.2	6.1
5.2	4.6	5.1						4.8	5.2	5.4
3.3	3.1	3.5		Sales/Total Assets				3.4	3.4	3.7
2.2	2.2	2.2						2.1	2.4	2.3
.8	.8	.9						1.4	1.0	.8
(137) 1.5	(135) 1.5	(149) 1.6		% Depr., Dep., Amort./Sales		(14) 1.7			(31) 1.6	(90) 1.5
2.2	2.4	2.6						2.8	2.2	2.5
1.0	.9	.9						.9	1.2	.6
(44) 2.1	(50) 2.3	(66) 2.0		% Officers', Directors' Owners' Comp/Sales		(11) 3.4			(19) 1.9	(27) 1.2
4.8	3.7	4.4						5.5	2.9	3.3
14382364M	16301591M	14532540M		Net Sales ($)	1933M	14329M	10860M	124010M	528768M	13852640M
4237719M	4947888M	4369529M		Total Assets ($)	1472M	6519M	4249M	52673M	175363M	4129253M

© RMA 2011   M = $ thousand   MM = $ million
See Pages 9 through 22 for Explanation of Ratios and Data

Current Data Sorted by Assets | Comparative Historical Data

Type of Statement

Type of Statement	0-500M	500M-2MM	2-10MM	10-50MM	50-100MM	100-250MM		4/1/06-3/31/07 ALL	4/1/07-3/31/08 ALL
Unqualified			2	1		5		5	7
Reviewed		1	3					3	1
Compiled			1	2	1			2	5
Tax Returns			1	2	1			1	3
Other								5	13
		3 (4/1-9/30/10)		17 (10/1/10-3/31/11)					
	0-500M	500M-2MM	2-10MM	10-50MM	50-100MM	100-250MM		16	29
NUMBER OF STATEMENTS		1	4	8	2	5		16	29

Current data percentage columns (0-500M through 100-250MM) marked: DATA NOT AVAILABLE

ASSETS

	%	%
Cash & Equivalents	7.3	12.0
Trade Receivables (net)	16.0	20.2
Inventory	20.7	13.2
All Other Current	3.2	2.4
Total Current	47.3	47.9
Fixed Assets (net)	48.3	43.4
Intangibles (net)	.4	3.3
All Other Non-Current	4.1	5.5
Total	100.0	100.0

LIABILITIES

Notes Payable-Short Term	13.7	6.7
Cur. Mat.-L.T.D.	4.7	2.9
Trade Payables	6.4	5.8
Income Taxes Payable	.3	.4
All Other Current	8.1	7.9
Total Current	33.2	23.7
Long-Term Debt	25.4	15.8
Deferred Taxes	.1	1.0
All Other Non-Current	2.2	7.5
Net Worth	39.1	52.0
Total Liabilties & Net Worth	100.0	100.0

INCOME DATA

Net Sales	100.0	100.0
Gross Profit	29.1	31.0
Operating Expenses	20.6	22.1
Operating Profit	8.5	8.9
All Other Expenses (net)	2.2	.9
Profit Before Taxes	6.3	8.0

RATIOS

Current	2.6	3.2
	1.7	2.0
	1.1	1.5
Quick	1.0	1.7
	.6	1.4
	.4	1.0
Sales/Receivables	15 23.9	19 19.1
	25 14.5	31 11.7
	30 12.2	38 9.5
Cost of Sales/Inventory	16 23.0	13 28.2
	28 13.2	20 18.3
	78 4.7	47 7.8
Cost of Sales/Payables	6 60.5	5 69.5
	11 33.0	10 36.7
	21 17.2	18 20.8
Sales/Working Capital	8.4	7.9
	14.1	11.4
	116.6	15.1
EBIT/Interest	15.9	19.4
	4.3 (26)	6.2
	3.5	2.7
Net Profit + Depr., Dep., Amort./Cur. Mat. L/T/D		17.6
	(10)	7.9
		1.2
Fixed/Worth	.7	.6
	1.2	.9
	2.2	1.5
Debt/Worth	.6	.5
	1.0	1.0
	2.9	1.6
% Profit Before Taxes/Tangible Net Worth	65.6	47.2
	(15) 28.8	(28) 29.4
	5.9	11.8
% Profit Before Taxes/Total Assets	31.3	22.9
	8.6	11.8
	3.1	5.0
Sales/Net Fixed Assets	10.8	15.8
	4.9	5.5
	2.7	2.7
Sales/Total Assets	3.3	3.3
	2.7	2.7
	1.7	1.4
% Depr., Dep., Amort./Sales	.9	1.1
	(11) 2.6	(25) 1.9
	3.8	4.4
% Officers', Directors' Owners' Comp/Sales		

Net Sales ($) / Total Assets ($)

	500M-2MM	2-10MM	10-50MM	50-100MM	100-250MM		4/1/06-3/31/07	4/1/07-3/31/08
Net Sales ($)	3337M	99462M	400708M	367159M	1611696M		1335437M	2972362M
Total Assets ($)	934M	27548M	160382M	141056M	773715M		677410M	1597521M

M = $ thousand   MM = $ million
See Pages 9 through 22 for Explanation of Ratios and Data

Comparative Historical Data				Current Data Sorted by Sales					

Type of Statement

7	8	8							8
1	4	4	Unqualified						4
2	4	4	Reviewed			1			3
3	2		Compiled						
10	9	4	Tax Returns				1		3
			Other						
4/1/08-	4/1/09-	4/1/10-			3 (4/1-9/30/10)			17 (10/1/10-3/31/11)	
3/31/09	3/31/10	3/31/11		0-1MM	1-3MM	3-5MM	5-10MM	10-25MM	25MM & OVER
ALL	ALL	ALL				1	1		
23	23	20	**NUMBER OF STATEMENTS**						18

%	%	%	**ASSETS**	%	%	%	%	%	%
9.7	11.7	10.5	Cash & Equivalents						10.4
21.0	18.7	19.8	Trade Receivables (net)						19.9
16.2	13.6	14.2	Inventory	D	D			D	14.4
1.8	3.1	2.7	All Other Current	A	A			A	2.6
48.6	47.1	47.3	Total Current	T	T			T	47.3
43.4	47.2	45.9	Fixed Assets (net)	A	A			A	45.2
2.4	2.5	1.8	Intangibles (net)						2.0
5.5	3.2	5.0	All Other Non-Current	N	N			N	5.6
100.0	100.0	100.0	Total	O	O			O	100.0
			LIABILITIES	T	T			T	
8.5	3.9	3.6	Notes Payable-Short Term						4.0
2.1	3.0	1.8	Cur. Mat.-L.T.D.	A	A			A	1.7
8.3	10.6	9.8	Trade Payables	V	V			V	10.4
.0	.0	.0	Income Taxes Payable	A	A			A	.0
9.8	9.8	7.0	All Other Current	I	I			I	7.5
28.7	27.4	22.2	Total Current	L	L			L	23.7
16.5	17.0	17.2	Long-Term Debt	A	A			A	16.9
.1	.5	.6	Deferred Taxes	B	B			B	.7
4.9	8.2	10.7	All Other Non-Current	L	L			L	9.5
49.8	46.8	49.3	Net Worth	E	E			E	49.2
100.0	100.0	100.0	Total Liabilities & Net Worth						100.0
			INCOME DATA						
100.0	100.0	100.0	Net Sales						100.0
24.5	28.3	20.6	Gross Profit						20.8
16.1	21.0	14.9	Operating Expenses						14.6
8.4	7.3	5.7	Operating Profit						6.3
.5	1.0	1.0	All Other Expenses (net)						1.0
7.8	6.3	4.7	Profit Before Taxes						5.2
			RATIOS						
4.0	3.4	3.3							3.3
2.0	2.1	2.1	Current						2.0
1.1	1.2	1.5							1.4
3.2	2.2	2.5							2.0
1.5	1.3	1.5	Quick						1.4
.5	.6	.8							.8

16	23.5	17	20.9	19	19.3							19	19.5
24	15.4	24	15.1	27	13.5	Sales/Receivables						26	14.2
29	12.6	36	10.1	35	10.3							35	10.4
12	30.0	11	34.1	12	30.3							11	32.2
22	16.6	27	13.3	22	16.9	Cost of Sales/Inventory						22	16.9
33	11.2	37	9.9	34	10.8							31	11.9
6	56.9	11	34.7	7	52.2							9	41.3
13	29.1	16	22.5	13	27.6	Cost of Sales/Payables						13	27.6
15	23.8	24	15.0	26	14.1							25	14.6

6.8	5.7	5.5	Sales/Working Capital						5.5
14.2	10.5	9.9							10.5
60.6	55.7	26.8							32.6

	61.0		22.4		16.4								18.4
(22)	19.0	(20)	9.3	(18)	6.8	EBIT/Interest					(16)		10.2
	2.6		1.9		2.7								3.6

			Net Profit + Depr., Dep., Amort./Cur. Mat. L/T/D						
.6	.6	.6							.6
1.0	1.2	1.0	Fixed/Worth						1.0
1.5	1.4	1.5							1.6
.6	.6	.6							.7
1.1	1.0	1.0	Debt/Worth						1.0
2.1	1.7	1.8							1.8

	62.0		44.6		39.4								40.2
	37.1	(22)	29.7		18.9	% Profit Before Taxes/Tangible Net Worth							19.7
	14.6		8.6		9.8								13.0

34.2	27.3	15.6	% Profit Before Taxes/Total Assets						16.5
16.7	11.1	7.2							7.9
2.3	2.0	3.3							4.8
12.6	13.5	11.6	Sales/Net Fixed Assets						12.2
6.5	6.3	6.5							6.5
3.6	2.2	2.6							2.7
3.7	3.8	4.1	Sales/Total Assets						4.2
2.9	2.6	2.8							2.8
2.0	1.5	1.2							1.2

	1.4		1.4		1.6								1.4
(17)	1.8	(18)	2.3	(16)	2.7	% Depr., Dep., Amort./Sales					(14)		2.7
	3.5		4.2		5.3								5.3

			% Officers', Directors' Owners' Comp/Sales						

3970055M	3320555M	2482362M	Net Sales ($)				3337M	7063M	2471962M
1614437M	1560225M	1103635M	Total Assets ($)				934M	9076M	1093625M

M = $ thousand   MM = $ million
See Pages 9 through 22 for Explanation of Ratios and Data

Current Data Sorted by Assets   Comparative Historical Data

0-500M	500M-2MM	2-10MM	10-50MM	50-100MM	100-250MM	Type of Statement	4/1/06-3/31/07 ALL	4/1/07-3/31/08 ALL
1			5	9	8	Unqualified	32	20
		2	5	1	1	Reviewed	13	6
		1		1	1	Compiled	1	1
1		1			1	Tax Returns	1	1
1		9	5	6	2	Other	22	32
	18 (4/1-9/30/10)		42 (10/1/10-3/31/11)					
3	1	13	15	17	11	NUMBER OF STATEMENTS	69	60
%	%	%	%	%	%	**ASSETS**	%	%
		9.4	5.6	1.9	10.8	Cash & Equivalents	4.6	5.1
		23.6	21.2	14.2	13.9	Trade Receivables (net)	16.5	15.6
		22.8	17.2	24.6	22.7	Inventory	22.8	24.0
		2.7	.7	3.5	3.1	All Other Current	1.9	1.4
		58.4	44.8	44.2	50.5	Total Current	45.8	46.0
		30.6	46.3	46.2	42.8	Fixed Assets (net)	45.9	46.2
		2.5	1.7	1.6	4.1	Intangibles (net)	2.3	3.0
		8.4	7.3	8.0	2.6	All Other Non-Current	6.0	4.8
		100.0	100.0	100.0	100.0	Total	100.0	100.0
						LIABILITIES		
		12.8	9.9	3.3	2.7	Notes Payable-Short Term	7.9	11.8
		1.8	3.3	3.0	8.1	Cur. Mat.-L.T.D.	4.4	3.1
		21.8	12.7	8.9	9.4	Trade Payables	11.5	10.5
		.0	.6	.7	1.6	Income Taxes Payable	.2	.3
		4.4	5.8	7.1	10.7	All Other Current	10.0	9.3
		40.7	32.3	23.0	32.5	Total Current	34.0	34.9
		9.5	20.1	17.1	14.4	Long-Term Debt	25.1	23.9
		.3	.8	2.7	1.3	Deferred Taxes	1.2	1.0
		5.0	2.0	3.6	3.9	All Other Non-Current	2.3	3.8
		44.4	44.9	53.6	47.9	Net Worth	37.4	36.3
		100.0	100.0	100.0	100.0	Total Liabilities & Net Worth	100.0	100.0
						INCOME DATA		
		100.0	100.0	100.0	100.0	Net Sales	100.0	100.0
		19.7	20.8	15.8	14.3	Gross Profit	20.1	19.4
		17.3	16.5	11.3	8.2	Operating Expenses	18.2	15.7
		2.4	4.2	4.6	6.1	Operating Profit	1.9	3.7
		.1	.2	.9	.7	All Other Expenses (net)	.7	.9
		2.3	4.1	3.7	5.4	Profit Before Taxes	1.2	2.8
						RATIOS		
		2.3	1.8	2.4	3.6		2.4	2.1
		1.8	1.5	1.9	2.5	Current	1.4	1.5
		1.2	1.0	1.5	.8		1.0	1.0
		1.3	1.3	.9	1.9		1.0	.9
		.9	.9	.6	.7	Quick	.6	.6
		.7	.6	.4	.4		.4	.4
		11 33.9	14 26.2	17 22.1	14 25.6		18 20.3	16 22.4
		15 24.4	18 19.8	25 14.5	18 20.2	Sales/Receivables	20 17.9	20 18.4
		31 11.9	23 15.6	30 12.3	24 15.3		27 13.8	28 12.9
		5 69.0	8 47.1	35 10.6	29 12.7		23 16.1	24 15.4
		20 18.6	26 13.9	40 9.1	40 9.0	Cost of Sales/Inventory	35 10.4	36 10.1
		34 10.6	38 9.5	71 5.2	52 7.0		67 5.5	59 6.2
		8 48.6	10 37.9	12 30.1	12 31.4		12 31.5	14 26.8
		13 29.1	16 23.3	16 23.4	15 23.9	Cost of Sales/Payables	18 20.7	17 21.0
		40 9.1	27 13.3	21 17.3	19 18.9		24 15.5	21 17.2
		12.7	18.4	6.3	5.7		8.7	9.7
		19.3	26.9	11.6	7.0	Sales/Working Capital	21.8	19.9
		65.2	-160.9	18.4	-24.8		-378.0	NM
		10.4	37.0	12.5	42.9		7.7	10.3
		(12) 3.7	17.2	5.4	18.7	EBIT/Interest	(64) 1.7	(57) 2.8
		1.5	1.7	3.5	2.4		-.6	.5
							2.9	3.1
						Net Profit + Depr., Dep., Amort./Cur. Mat. L/T/D	(23) 1.5	(16) 2.0
							.3	1.5
		.2	.9	.5	.5		.8	.8
		.6	1.2	.7	1.1	Fixed/Worth	1.2	1.4
		.9	2.0	1.8	2.5		3.7	2.5
		.7	.7	.4	.3		.8	.8
		1.5	1.8	1.0	1.6	Debt/Worth	1.7	1.9
		3.3	3.0	1.9	3.1		4.6	3.8
		28.8	39.8	22.9	39.7		33.9	34.7
		13.0	33.9	11.9	21.1	% Profit Before Taxes/Tangible Net Worth	(64) 6.0	(55) 15.4
		2.8	9.6	10.3	15.8		-11.0	-1.3
		13.7	29.0	11.4	17.6		11.3	12.0
		2.3	11.2	6.9	11.1	% Profit Before Taxes/Total Assets	2.2	5.4
		.8	2.4	3.8	4.6		-3.3	-.9
		89.4	11.9	8.7	8.5		10.0	8.4
		15.4	7.7	5.6	6.1	Sales/Net Fixed Assets	5.5	5.7
		7.7	4.9	2.6	4.5		3.6	4.1
		6.2	4.4	3.0	3.3		3.3	3.1
		4.2	3.4	2.2	2.3	Sales/Total Assets	2.3	2.5
		3.3	2.5	1.4	2.0		1.7	2.0
		.4	1.3	1.7			1.5	1.3
		(10) 1.2	(14) 1.7	(16) 2.7		% Depr., Dep., Amort./Sales	(56) 2.7	(52) 2.4
		2.1	2.6	3.8			3.6	3.9
						% Officers', Directors' Owners' Comp/Sales		
2135M	4962M	235672M	1230898M	3004028M	4567886M	Net Sales ($)	9623771M	11038751M
674M	616M	58453M	328362M	1319550M	1780420M	Total Assets ($)	4174988M	4302317M

M = $ thousand   MM = $ million
See Pages 9 through 22 for Explanation of Ratios and Data

Comparative Historical Data | | | Current Data Sorted by Sales

			Type of Statement	0-1MM	1-3MM	3-5MM	5-10MM	10-25MM	25MM & OVER
20	27	23	Unqualified	1					22
13	13	8	Reviewed						8
1	1	3	Compiled						3
2	3	2	Tax Returns	1					
24	13	24	Other		1	1	3	6	13
4/1/08-3/31/09	4/1/09-3/31/10	4/1/10-3/31/11			18 (4/1-9/30/10)			42 (10/1/10-3/31/11)	
ALL	ALL	ALL							
60	57	60	**NUMBER OF STATEMENTS**	2	1	1	3	7	46
%	%	%		%	%	%	%	%	%
			ASSETS						
6.7	5.2	6.9	Cash & Equivalents						6.4
17.1	19.1	19.0	Trade Receivables (net)						17.1
23.7	22.5	21.3	Inventory						22.1
1.8	2.1	2.4	All Other Current						2.3
49.4	48.9	49.7	Total Current						47.9
42.6	42.4	41.5	Fixed Assets (net)						43.9
2.3	2.5	2.2	Intangibles (net)						2.1
5.6	6.2	6.7	All Other Non-Current						6.0
100.0	100.0	100.0	Total						100.0
			LIABILITIES						
7.4	10.7	6.8	Notes Payable-Short Term						7.0
6.6	4.4	3.6	Cur. Mat.-L.T.D.						4.3
12.2	13.1	13.0	Trade Payables						10.5
.4	.5	.6	Income Taxes Payable						.8
7.3	8.1	6.7	All Other Current						7.3
33.9	36.8	30.7	Total Current						29.8
22.0	17.8	15.3	Long-Term Debt						16.5
1.3	1.0	1.3	Deferred Taxes						1.7
2.8	3.5	4.4	All Other Non-Current						3.1
40.0	40.9	48.3	Net Worth						48.9
100.0	100.0	100.0	Total Liabilities & Net Worth						100.0
			INCOME DATA						
100.0	100.0	100.0	Net Sales						100.0
16.2	16.0	18.7	Gross Profit						17.0
13.8	11.2	14.5	Operating Expenses						12.4
2.4	4.8	4.2	Operating Profit						4.6
.8	.5	.4	All Other Expenses (net)						.5
1.6	4.3	3.7	Profit Before Taxes						4.0
			RATIOS						
2.3	2.1	2.5							2.5
1.6	1.4	1.8	Current						1.8
1.1	1.0	1.4							1.4
1.0	1.1	1.3							1.0
.7	.7	.8	Quick						.8
.5	.4	.6							.5
15 24.9	15 24.0	14 26.0						14	25.7
19 19.2	19 18.9	19 18.9	Sales/Receivables					20	18.3
24 14.9	28 13.3	28 13.2						28	13.2
20 18.4	15 24.0	20 18.6						25	14.3
36 10.1	30 12.0	33 11.1	Cost of Sales/Inventory					36	10.2
50 7.3	55 6.7	47 7.8						52	7.0
9 39.0	10 36.8	11 33.9						11	33.0
16 23.1	17 22.0	16 23.4	Cost of Sales/Payables					16	23.4
20 17.8	25 14.7	23 16.1						21	17.5
9.4	10.9	8.7							7.1
19.7	24.5	16.2	Sales/Working Capital						18.1
130.6	847.5	29.4							29.0
7.9	13.2	20.2							20.2
(57) 2.3	(53) 4.0	(58) 5.3	EBIT/Interest						5.9
-3.4	1.8	2.4							3.2
5.4	19.2	8.9							8.9
(21) 2.4	(14) 2.8	(17) 4.4	Net Profit + Depr., Dep., Amort./Cur. Mat. L/T/D					(17)	4.4
.7	2.3	2.4							2.4
.8	.7	.5							.5
1.4	1.3	.9	Fixed/Worth						1.0
2.5	2.0	1.9							1.9
.7	.6	.5							.5
1.5	1.5	1.4	Debt/Worth						1.4
4.4	3.4	2.5							2.5
40.4	46.9	36.7							36.6
(56) 12.2	(54) 18.3	18.7	% Profit Before Taxes/Tangible Net Worth						19.9
-13.1	6.2	10.3							10.4
15.2	16.8	17.4							17.1
3.1	8.0	7.1	% Profit Before Taxes/Total Assets						7.8
-8.2	2.5	2.5							4.0
10.4	10.7	12.6							9.9
6.1	6.7	7.4	Sales/Net Fixed Assets						6.4
4.4	4.6	4.6							4.5
3.6	4.6	4.1							3.6
2.6	2.7	2.9	Sales/Total Assets						2.7
2.1	2.1	2.1							2.0
1.3	1.2	1.3							1.4
(48) 2.2	(48) 2.1	(51) 1.9	% Depr., Dep., Amort./Sales					(40)	1.9
3.1	2.9	3.1							3.1
			% Officers', Directors' Owners' Comp/Sales						
12315398M	9997169M	9045581M	Net Sales ($)	689M	1446M	4962M	24753M	117160M	8896571M
4581310M	3568712M	3488075M	Total Assets ($)	319M	355M	616M	14309M	26101M	3446375M

M = $ thousand   MM = $ million
See Pages 9 through 22 for Explanation of Ratios and Data

Current Data Sorted by Assets | Comparative Historical Data

Type of Statement	16 (4/1-9/30/10)		61 (10/1/10-3/31/11)					4/1/06-3/31/07	4/1/07-3/31/08
Unqualified		2	2	5	4	2		20	20
Reviewed			6	8	1			7	13
Compiled			3					3	6
Tax Returns	1	6	5					6	3
Other		2	13	14	2	1		31	39
	0-500M	500M-2MM	2-10MM	10-50MM	50-100MM	100-250MM		ALL	ALL
NUMBER OF STATEMENTS	1	10	29	27	7	3		67	81

	0-500M %	500M-2MM %	2-10MM %	10-50MM %	50-100MM %	100-250MM %		ALL %	ALL %
ASSETS									
Cash & Equivalents		17.9	8.0	5.8				6.3	7.6
Trade Receivables (net)		21.1	26.4	16.9				24.2	22.0
Inventory		23.5	34.1	26.3				31.4	27.4
All Other Current		7.0	3.0	1.8				5.3	4.1
Total Current		69.4	71.5	50.8				67.1	61.1
Fixed Assets (net)		25.0	23.5	38.0				25.6	29.3
Intangibles (net)		.6	2.7	4.4				2.1	2.6
All Other Non-Current		5.0	2.3	6.8				5.1	7.0
Total		100.0	100.0	100.0				100.0	100.0
LIABILITIES									
Notes Payable-Short Term		12.1	16.7	13.5				16.6	18.6
Cur. Mat.-L.T.D.		1.6	3.1	1.8				3.1	3.9
Trade Payables		20.4	18.5	11.9				14.7	13.1
Income Taxes Payable		.0	.3	.1				.5	.1
All Other Current		9.7	10.1	8.7				6.8	7.5
Total Current		43.8	48.8	36.0				41.8	43.3
Long-Term Debt		11.1	9.2	18.6				12.3	13.6
Deferred Taxes		.0	.3	1.5				.2	.2
All Other Non-Current		23.7	6.9	7.5				7.1	4.8
Net Worth		21.5	34.7	36.4				38.6	38.1
Total Liabilties & Net Worth		100.0	100.0	100.0				100.0	100.0
INCOME DATA									
Net Sales		100.0	100.0	100.0				100.0	100.0
Gross Profit		23.7	18.3	19.2				20.1	22.4
Operating Expenses		20.5	15.2	12.9				14.9	17.6
Operating Profit		3.1	3.1	6.3				5.2	4.8
All Other Expenses (net)		.4	-.1	.9				.3	.2
Profit Before Taxes		2.7	3.2	5.4				4.8	4.6
RATIOS									
Current		2.8	2.5	1.7				2.3	2.1
		1.6	1.4	1.3				1.5	1.4
		1.1	1.0	1.1				1.2	1.1
Quick		1.5	1.1	1.0				1.1	1.1
		.9	.7	.7				.7	.6
		.4	.4	.4				.5	.4
Sales/Receivables		4 89.3	19 19.1	19 19.3				25 14.7	17 21.9
		28 12.9	29 12.5	34 10.8				34 10.7	29 12.5
		35 10.4	38 9.6	47 7.8				41 8.8	36 10.3
Cost of Sales/Inventory		0 UND	23 15.7	19 19.1				37 10.0	21 17.7
		21 17.7	45 8.2	54 6.8				55 6.6	46 8.0
		113 3.2	82 4.4	87 4.2				87 4.2	80 4.6
Cost of Sales/Payables		0 UND	7 55.3	11 34.0				12 30.2	10 37.7
		27 13.7	20 18.4	16 22.6				21 17.3	18 20.6
		46 8.0	36 10.1	34 10.8				33 11.0	30 12.3
Sales/Working Capital		7.0	6.9	7.7				5.9	7.9
		16.5	21.1	15.3				12.8	15.3
		255.9	NM	47.8				28.0	68.9
EBIT/Interest			10.8	10.3				9.3	6.4
			(26) 3.7	3.9				(79) 3.3	3.0
			1.9	2.3				1.7	1.8
Net Profit + Depr., Dep., Amort./Cur. Mat. L/T/D				6.3				16.3	12.4
			(12)	2.7				(21) 9.4	(20) 4.2
				1.4				2.9	1.8
Fixed/Worth		.2	.2	.3				.4	.3
		.7	.5	.9				.7	.7
		2.1	1.6	2.8				1.3	1.5
Debt/Worth		1.0	.8	1.0				.9	.9
		1.9	2.1	2.3				1.7	1.7
		95.7	4.1	3.2				3.6	4.8
% Profit Before Taxes/Tangible Net Worth			51.6	32.9				42.9	35.7
			(26) 28.3	(25) 26.5				(63) 21.5	(76) 19.2
			7.6	10.0				8.9	6.6
% Profit Before Taxes/Total Assets		21.3	17.6	11.6				14.5	11.4
		5.8	5.9	6.9				6.6	6.2
		-.3	1.7	3.5				2.1	2.2
Sales/Net Fixed Assets		UND	39.2	16.0				41.9	44.2
		22.3	18.8	7.1				11.9	9.0
		4.2	9.5	1.6				4.4	4.6
Sales/Total Assets		4.3	4.6	2.6				3.4	3.7
		3.0	3.4	2.0				2.3	2.5
		2.0	2.3	1.4				1.6	1.8
% Depr., Dep., Amort./Sales			.3	.8				.6	.7
			(27) 1.3	(26) 1.8				(58) 1.1	(70) 1.3
			2.0	5.1				2.2	2.3
% Officers', Directors' Owners' Comp/Sales			.7					.5	.5
			(14) 1.8					(16) 1.8	(21) 1.8
			2.9					4.6	3.1
Net Sales ($)	2447M	45973M	545478M	1182616M	1042642M	825784M		5116742M	6270274M
Total Assets ($)	53M	11727M	156241M	631786M	496863M	550940M		2488669M	3038572M

© RMA 2011

M = $ thousand   MM = $ million
See Pages 9 through 22 for Explanation of Ratios and Data

Comparative Historical Data — Current Data Sorted by Sales

M = $ thousand   MM = $ million

Current Data date ranges: 16 (4/1–9/30/10) · 61 (10/1/10–3/31/11)

	4/1/08–3/31/09 ALL	4/1/09–3/31/10 ALL	4/1/10–3/31/11 ALL	0-1MM	1-3MM	3-5MM	5-10MM	10-25MM	25MM & OVER
Type of Statement									
Unqualified	22	22	13					1	11
Reviewed	15	19	17			1	1	3	12
Compiled	5	5	3					3	
Tax Returns	7	9	12		5	1	1	4	
Other	31	35	32		2	1	5	9	17
Number of Statements	80	90	77	7	3	7	20	40	
	%	%	%					%	%
ASSETS									
Cash & Equivalents	7.3	7.8	9.4					8.8	7.2
Trade Receivables (net)	23.1	21.0	21.0					29.8	18.7
Inventory	35.4	28.8	29.1					27.6	30.8
All Other Current	2.2	3.7	3.2					3.1	2.5
Total Current	67.9	61.1	62.7					69.4	59.2
Fixed Assets (net)	25.7	30.0	29.7					24.8	33.0
Intangibles (net)	1.1	3.5	3.1					1.8	3.4
All Other Non-Current	5.3	5.3	4.5					4.0	4.4
Total	100.0	100.0	100.0					100.0	100.0
LIABILITIES									
Notes Payable-Short Term	23.1	16.5	16.4					13.6	18.1
Cur. Mat.-L.T.D.	2.9	4.4	2.3					3.5	2.0
Trade Payables	16.5	13.4	14.7					19.5	12.5
Income Taxes Payable	.2	.2	.2					.5	.0
All Other Current	8.8	7.9	9.5					10.2	10.1
Total Current	51.5	42.4	43.1					47.2	42.8
Long-Term Debt	11.1	12.9	12.6					12.8	14.1
Deferred Taxes	.4	.9	1.0					.6	1.5
All Other Non-Current	4.5	5.5	8.7					4.5	7.0
Net Worth	32.6	38.2	34.6					35.0	34.7
Total Liabilties & Net Worth	100.0	100.0	100.0					100.0	100.0
INCOME DATA									
Net Sales	100.0	100.0	100.0					100.0	100.0
Gross Profit	18.7	18.9	18.7					17.2	16.4
Operating Expenses	15.3	16.6	14.1					14.4	11.3
Operating Profit	3.4	2.3	4.6					2.8	5.0
All Other Expenses (net)	.9	.1	.2					-.4	.9
Profit Before Taxes	2.5	2.2	4.4					3.2	4.1
RATIOS									
Current	1.9	2.3	2.1					2.8	1.7
	1.3	1.5	1.4					1.4	1.3
	1.0	1.1	1.1					1.0	1.1
Quick	1.0	1.0	1.1					1.9	.8
	.5	.7	.7					.9	.6
	.3	.4	.4					.4	.4
Sales/Receivables	18 20.7	20 17.8	19 19.3					20 17.9	19 19.2
	30 12.4	30 12.3	31 11.9					28 13.0	31 11.6
	37 9.8	37 9.9	39 9.4					38 9.7	42 8.7
Cost of Sales/Inventory	28 13.0	20 18.6	19 19.7					15 24.7	24 15.2
	58 6.3	46 7.9	47 7.7					31 11.6	54 6.8
	95 3.8	92 4.0	83 4.4					63 5.8	86 4.2
Cost of Sales/Payables	10 37.4	9 42.5	8 47.2					6 60.3	11 34.1
	20 18.5	17 21.4	17 22.0					19 19.4	16 22.8
	33 11.2	31 11.7	35 10.5					35 10.5	32 11.6
Sales/Working Capital	8.7	6.5	7.3					7.5	8.1
	19.6	14.2	16.8					20.1	17.7
	256.3	69.7	74.4					NM	61.0
EBIT/Interest	5.8	8.0	11.6					12.5	11.4
	(76) 2.5	(88) 3.0	(74) 4.9					6.8	(39) 3.7
	1.1	1.1	2.1					2.2	2.1
Net Profit + Depr., Dep., Amort./Cur. Mat. L/T/D	9.1	17.0	22.4						12.5
	(24) 4.8	(27) 4.4	(24) 3.4						(18) 2.5
	2.5	1.3	2.0						1.3
Fixed/Worth	.2	.4	.3					.2	.3
	.7	.8	.7					.7	.8
	1.8	2.1	1.4					1.7	1.4
Debt/Worth	.9	.8	1.0					.7	1.2
	2.1	1.6	2.0					2.1	2.2
	6.4	4.4	3.7					5.2	3.0
% Profit Before Taxes/Tangible Net Worth	36.3	38.9	43.8					52.6	32.9
	(70) 20.2	(79) 16.9	(70) 26.5					(18) 23.6	(37) 26.6
	4.0	1.0	9.3					9.1	11.2
% Profit Before Taxes/Total Assets	11.0	10.4	16.6					17.8	12.8
	4.4	4.2	6.4					5.4	7.3
	.6	.3	2.7					2.9	2.8
Sales/Net Fixed Assets	69.8	44.3	27.9					33.9	26.1
	14.7	10.6	11.1					19.3	8.1
	5.5	3.8	4.2					10.9	3.9
Sales/Total Assets	3.8	3.5	3.6					4.9	3.3
	2.8	2.4	2.4					3.6	2.1
	2.0	1.5	1.7					2.5	1.6
% Depr., Dep., Amort./Sales	.4	.7	.6					.4	.6
	(69) 1.1	(80) 1.5	(68) 1.4					(18) 1.2	(37) 1.4
	2.0	2.7	2.6					2.1	2.6
% Officers', Directors' Owners' Comp/Sales	1.0	.8	.8					.8	
	(21) 2.9	(25) 2.0	(26) 1.8					(11) 2.3	
	4.0	3.5	2.8					3.0	
Net Sales ($)	6301777M	6699831M	3644940M		14787M	12224M	50629M	338783M	3228517M
Total Assets ($)	2882641M	3475089M	1847610M		5768M	5444M	49946M	120918M	1665534M

(Columns 0-1MM, 1-3MM, 3-5MM and 5-10MM: DATA NOT AVAILABLE)

M = $ thousand   MM = $ million
See Pages 9 through 22 for Explanation of Ratios and Data

Current Data Sorted by Assets   Comparative Historical Data

	0-500M	500M-2MM	2-10MM	10-50MM	50-100MM	100-250MM	Type of Statement	4/1/06-3/31/07 ALL	4/1/07-3/31/08 ALL
		2					Unqualified	4	7
			3	1		1	Reviewed	6	15
	1	9	22	3			Compiled	71	118
	16	9	7	4	1		Tax Returns	53	41
	5	9	9	7		2	Other	54	45
	__16 (4/1-9/30/10)__			__95 (10/1/10-3/31/11)__					
	22	**29**	**41**	**15**	**1**	**3**	**NUMBER OF STATEMENTS**	**188**	**226**
	%	%	%	%	%	%	**ASSETS**	%	%
	13.2	16.5	9.0	8.3			Cash & Equivalents	9.9	9.0
	9.3	9.3	7.6	7.1			Trade Receivables (net)	5.5	3.6
	6.3	6.1	4.4	8.9			Inventory	4.2	2.7
	3.0	2.8	.8	2.3			All Other Current	2.0	2.2
	31.8	34.7	21.8	26.5			Total Current	21.5	17.4
	45.9	48.6	44.5	48.4			Fixed Assets (net)	46.6	45.5
	9.1	6.5	21.8	19.2			Intangibles (net)	19.7	24.3
	13.1	10.3	12.0	5.9			All Other Non-Current	12.2	12.7
	100.0	100.0	100.0	100.0			Total	100.0	100.0
							LIABILITIES		
	3.1	8.8	5.0	3.0			Notes Payable-Short Term	2.8	1.8
	3.6	5.4	6.8	5.4			Cur. Mat.-L.T.D.	5.7	6.7
	16.0	8.7	6.4	12.8			Trade Payables	5.3	5.0
	.3	.2	.3	.0			Income Taxes Payable	.1	.1
	7.0	10.5	6.0	7.5			All Other Current	15.7	12.6
	30.1	33.5	24.5	28.8			Total Current	29.6	26.2
	35.8	32.0	33.2	28.5			Long-Term Debt	39.2	46.1
	.0	.0	.2	.8			Deferred Taxes	.1	.1
	11.6	11.9	8.8	12.5			All Other Non-Current	10.5	14.5
	22.5	22.6	33.4	29.4			Net Worth	20.7	13.1
	100.0	100.0	100.0	100.0			Total Liabilities & Net Worth	100.0	100.0
							INCOME DATA		
	100.0	100.0	100.0	100.0			Net Sales	100.0	100.0
	54.6	47.6	42.7	39.0			Gross Profit	45.3	40.1
	51.8	43.8	37.2	32.0			Operating Expenses	38.2	35.1
	2.8	3.7	5.5	7.0			Operating Profit	7.2	5.0
	.7	.4	.9	2.6			All Other Expenses (net)	1.4	1.9
	2.1	3.3	4.6	4.4			Profit Before Taxes	5.8	3.0
							RATIOS		
	2.8	2.6	1.6	1.1				1.5	1.5
	1.2	1.0	1.0	.9			Current	.8	.6
	.3	.5	.4	.5				.3	.3
	2.0	2.4	1.2	.9				1.2	1.2
(21)	.7	.7	.7	.5			Quick (187)	.6 (225)	.4
	.2	.2	.3	.3				.2	.1
0	UND	0 UND	0 999.8	1 700.9			0 UND	0 UND	
0	UND	2 173.0	2 172.3	2 224.9			Sales/Receivables 1 373.1	1 521.4	
8	45.7	15 25.1	26 14.3	28 13.2			8 47.6	5 77.9	
2	164.4	2 150.4	3 116.3	4 86.5			2 151.0	2 171.9	
8	43.2	4 81.6	6 61.4	10 38.0			Cost of Sales/Inventory 4 89.3	3 104.6	
12	29.7	33 10.9	16 23.1	29 12.7			10 37.2	6 62.1	
0	UND	3 115.6	5 67.0	8 44.1			0 822.0	1 260.7	
13	29.0	10 37.6	11 32.0	19 19.1			Cost of Sales/Payables 5 77.2	6 58.3	
46	7.9	30 12.3	27 13.5	40 9.0			18 20.0	18 20.1	
	15.2	12.9	23.9	55.8				37.2	42.0
	243.7	571.4	773.2	-43.2			Sales/Working Capital	-64.5	-34.1
	-13.4	-18.2	-13.7	-14.7				-14.0	-10.0
	27.9	16.8	13.4	9.5				12.0	7.0
(16)	5.2 (26)	6.7	4.5	5.6			EBIT/Interest (165)	4.9 (205)	2.6
	-1.1	1.2	1.7	-.5				1.7	.7
							Net Profit + Depr., Dep.,		4.3
							Amort./Cur. Mat. L/T/D (12)		1.2
									.8
	.3	.8	1.2	1.7				1.1	1.8
	1.8	1.7	2.7	3.2			Fixed/Worth	4.1	-11.1
	-3.8	15.9	-2.0	-1.3				-1.8	-.8
	.5	1.1	1.1	1.5				1.3	2.1
	2.1	2.5	8.3	4.9			Debt/Worth	7.8	-17.0
	-5.5	24.5	-4.9	-2.8				-3.4	-2.3
	93.8	88.1	150.3	81.2			% Profit Before Taxes/Tangible	149.7	102.4
(16)	53.3 (24)	59.5 (26)	33.3 (10)	27.1			Net Worth (108)	62.0 (101)	54.8
	-4.1	18.1	9.8	4.9				29.5	16.9
	41.7	32.8	17.1	21.8			% Profit Before Taxes/Total	29.9	19.8
	9.0	17.8	8.1	8.5			Assets	15.9	6.5
	-6.2	-3.4	1.7	-1.4				3.3	-1.5
	44.9	11.4	10.0	7.7				9.7	8.8
	12.7	7.0	5.4	5.3			Sales/Net Fixed Assets	6.4	5.4
	3.4	4.8	3.5	3.0				3.5	3.0
	6.3	4.2	2.9	2.8				3.8	3.3
	3.7	3.2	2.3	1.9			Sales/Total Assets	2.6	2.1
	2.5	2.5	1.6	1.6				1.6	1.4
	.7	1.6	2.4	2.3				2.1	2.3
(17)	2.8 (23)	2.2 (38)	3.7	3.4			% Depr., Dep., Amort./Sales (173)	3.3 (212)	3.9
	6.3	3.3	5.2	5.1				5.1	5.7
	2.4	2.8	.8					1.6	1.8
(12)	4.3 (11)	3.9 (20)	3.3				% Officers', Directors' (104)	3.1 (112)	3.5
	8.9	5.3	5.0				Owners' Comp/Sales	5.1	6.7
	22912M	118011M	382869M	567947M	131069M	1458780M	Net Sales ($)	2002374M	2565633M
	5326M	33726M	167875M	257224M	68311M	484002M	Total Assets ($)	946085M	1535478M

Comparative Historical Data | | | Current Data Sorted by Sales

			Type of Statement						
5	8	4	Unqualified				1		2
8	9	6	Reviewed			1	1	2	2
101	69	36	Compiled	2	2	3	19	7	3
43	35	33	Tax Returns	11	8	8	3	1	2
31	41	32	Other	6	1	4	9	4	8
4/1/08-3/31/09	4/1/09-3/31/10	4/1/10-3/31/11			16 (4/1-9/30/10)			95 (10/1/10-3/31/11)	
ALL	ALL	ALL		0-1MM	1-3MM	3-5MM	5-10MM	10-25MM	25MM & OVER
188	162	111	**NUMBER OF STATEMENTS**	19	13	16	32	14	17
%	%	%	**ASSETS**	%	%	%	%	%	%
9.8	12.8	11.8	Cash & Equivalents	12.6	14.6	7.9	13.6	11.7	9.0
5.3	6.6	8.6	Trade Receivables (net)	8.0	10.6	5.3	8.9	7.2	11.5
4.3	5.3	6.0	Inventory	5.7	7.6	6.3	3.5	4.4	10.7
2.3	2.2	1.9	All Other Current	.3	7.9	.4	1.5	1.5	1.9
21.6	26.9	28.3	Total Current	26.6	40.7	19.9	27.5	24.8	33.0
45.0	43.9	46.5	Fixed Assets (net)	49.7	48.3	46.3	46.7	40.2	46.4
21.3	18.7	14.2	Intangibles (net)	16.0	1.7	16.7	14.3	20.9	14.0
12.1	10.5	11.0	All Other Non-Current	7.7	9.4	17.1	11.5	14.2	6.6
100.0	100.0	100.0	Total	100.0	100.0	100.0	100.0	100.0	100.0
			LIABILITIES						
3.1	4.2	5.5	Notes Payable-Short Term	1.5	11.7	5.1	5.7	6.1	4.5
6.1	7.3	6.0	Cur. Mat.-L.T.D.	4.2	5.3	5.5	6.7	5.8	8.1
6.5	7.3	10.0	Trade Payables	15.9	9.4	5.7	6.7	9.0	15.1
.1	.1	.2	Income Taxes Payable	.3	.0	.2	.1	.0	.5
18.7	19.7	8.1	All Other Current	6.5	7.1	8.2	8.2	6.9	11.1
34.5	38.6	29.8	Total Current	28.4	33.5	24.6	27.4	27.7	39.3
35.8	35.2	32.6	Long-Term Debt	47.4	29.0	26.3	35.0	27.7	24.3
.0	.0	.2	Deferred Taxes	.0	.0	.0	.0	.8	.5
14.4	11.4	10.5	All Other Non-Current	16.0	3.7	15.7	6.7	7.7	14.2
15.2	14.7	26.9	Net Worth	8.1	33.7	33.4	30.9	36.1	21.7
100.0	100.0	100.0	Total Liabilties & Net Worth	100.0	100.0	100.0	100.0	100.0	100.0
			INCOME DATA						
100.0	100.0	100.0	Net Sales	100.0	100.0	100.0	100.0	100.0	100.0
43.9	45.3	45.7	Gross Profit	57.1	49.1	45.6	45.6	38.8	36.3
39.6	38.7	41.1	Operating Expenses	54.4	45.6	42.3	40.5	30.6	31.5
4.4	6.6	4.6	Operating Profit	2.7	3.5	3.3	5.1	8.1	4.8
1.5	1.5	1.0	All Other Expenses (net)	1.2	.6	.7	.6	1.0	2.0
2.9	5.1	3.6	Profit Before Taxes	1.5	2.8	2.6	4.5	7.1	2.9
			RATIOS						
1.6	1.6	1.8		5.8	8.2	1.5	2.1	1.1	1.3
.6	.8	1.0	Current	1.0	1.4	1.1	1.1	.9	.9
.2	.3	.4		.2	.4	.4	.4	.7	.6
1.3	1.1	1.4		7.6	3.4	1.2	1.6	1.0	1.0
(187) .4	.5 (110)	.7	Quick	(18) .7	1.0	.6	.8	.7	.5
.1	.1	.2		.2	.3	.1	.3	.4	.2
0 UND	0 UND	0 999.8		0 UND	0 UND	0 UND	0 999.8	0 UND	2 238.4
1 675.0	1 468.9	2 172.3	Sales/Receivables	1 446.5	4 89.5	1 608.5	2 164.1	1 264.8	16 23.5
8 47.6	13 27.2	17 21.0		7 50.8	16 23.3	12 30.1	16 22.3	25 14.8	30 12.1
2 160.8	2 154.4	3 114.4		5 79.5	1 397.3	2 156.2	2 146.1	3 116.0	5 79.0
4 89.2	4 81.5	4 47.1	Cost of Sales/Inventory	10 35.1	13 28.2	11 34.8	4 100.6	6 63.4	15 25.1
10 36.8	12 31.4	20 18.3		18 20.4	40 9.1	34 10.8	8 43.4	9 40.9	31 11.9
1 571.6	1 258.9	5 74.3		0 UND	0 UND	5 74.0	1 497.5	4 101.6	10 37.0
7 54.2	9 42.4	13 28.4	Cost of Sales/Payables	14 26.2	9 38.9	13 28.0	11 34.4	11 31.8	34 10.9
16 23.1	23 15.8	35 10.5		46 7.9	20 18.3	33 11.0	27 13.4	19 19.0	52 7.0
40.2	22.5	21.2		11.0	10.1	21.5	20.4	65.0	25.8
-36.8	-38.1	999.8	Sales/Working Capital	UND	41.7	404.7	NM	NM	-78.6
-9.2	-11.3	-14.7		-7.6	-11.3	-19.4	-14.2	-17.7	-13.3
7.3	11.9	13.2		7.0	40.4	13.0	13.9	22.3	10.5
(168) 2.6	(153) 4.4	(102) 5.4	EBIT/Interest	(15) 3.0	(10) 9.2	(15) 2.5	(31) 5.3	7.2	4.7
.5	1.7	1.4		-.8	-.2	.2	1.7	5.5	-.4
	6.0	3.5	Net Profit + Depr., Dep.,						
	(23) 2.5	(13) 1.5	Amort./Cur. Mat. L/T/D						
	1.4	.1							
1.2	1.1	1.0		.3	.4	1.2	.9	1.6	1.5
7.4	7.6	2.3	Fixed/Worth	40.2	1.6	2.3	1.8	2.3	3.2
-1.4	-1.4	-4.1		-2.6	2.6	-2.0	NM	-4.1	-1.6
1.7	1.4	1.0		.9	.5	.9	1.2	1.6	1.8
17.9	19.7	3.1	Debt/Worth	41.2	1.2	2.9	3.2	4.2	5.9
-2.9	-3.4	-7.1		-4.0	2.5	-5.8	NM	-8.3	-4.0
91.6	122.3	89.7	% Profit Before Taxes/Tangible	102.6	90.4	68.2	142.1	154.9	79.5
(103) 43.8	(92) 54.3	(78) 43.8	Net Worth	(12) 53.3	(11) 70.0	(11) 10.8	(24) 43.3	(10) 65.3	(10) 22.3
10.0	20.7	8.4		9.9	8.1	-21.2	11.2	29.7	3.2
18.8	25.3	23.1	% Profit Before Taxes/Total	15.4	45.2	28.6	20.7	26.9	22.5
6.8	11.4	9.9	Assets	8.0	21.3	1.9	9.3	15.6	8.5
-2.6	2.5	.5		-10.6	-1.0	-4.5	2.0	7.4	-4.6
10.5	13.5	11.7		31.1	44.2	18.1	9.5	12.5	7.8
6.1	6.8	6.2	Sales/Net Fixed Assets	5.0	8.0	6.4	5.7	7.5	6.3
3.3	3.7	3.5		2.9	3.2	3.3	4.1	3.7	3.3
3.5	4.0	3.6		4.3	5.6	3.5	3.4	4.0	3.0
2.4	2.6	2.6	Sales/Total Assets	2.5	3.2	2.2	2.8	2.3	2.4
1.6	1.7	1.8		1.7	2.4	1.6	2.3	1.7	1.6
2.0	2.2	1.8		.8	1.6	1.4	1.9	2.0	2.5
(164) 3.7	(142) 3.6	(95) 3.1	% Depr., Dep., Amort./Sales	(14) 4.0	(11) 2.5	(13) 2.2	(28) 3.0	3.5	(15) 3.6
5.6	4.6	5.0		8.0	3.3	4.8	5.0	4.5	5.1
1.7	1.7	1.3						1.6	
(106) 3.4	(65) 3.5	(49) 3.9	% Officers', Directors' Owners' Comp/Sales				(16) 4.2		
5.5	5.7	6.5						5.2	
2097482M	1839260M	2681588M	Net Sales ($)	13402M	24759M	62285M	210668M	235500M	2134974M
936112M	803097M	1016464M	Total Assets ($)	6064M	9377M	36738M	80774M	102968M	780543M

M = $ thousand   MM = $ million
See Pages 9 through 22 for Explanation of Ratios and Data

Current Data Sorted by Assets   **Comparative Historical Data**

Type of Statement	0-500M	500M-2MM	2-10MM	10-50MM	50-100MM	100-250MM			4/1/06-3/31/07 ALL	4/1/07-3/31/08 ALL
Unqualified			5	15	8	4			40	42
Reviewed		3	20	19					32	34
Compiled	2	5	14	2					30	23
Tax Returns	7	2	8						23	27
Other	3	10	20	23	9	8			71	67
		31 (4/1-9/30/10)		156 (10/1/10-3/31/11)						
NUMBER OF STATEMENTS	12	20	67	59	17	12			196	193

	0-500M %	500M-2MM %	2-10MM %	10-50MM %	50-100MM %	100-250MM %			%	%
ASSETS										
Cash & Equivalents	5.5	11.8	8.2	9.7	8.0	7.4			10.2	9.8
Trade Receivables (net)	25.6	24.3	20.4	16.0	13.8	13.1			17.6	17.0
Inventory	16.1	15.5	12.7	9.4	9.0	7.8			10.1	10.2
All Other Current	1.7	2.6	1.8	2.3	3.9	7.2			2.1	2.2
Total Current	48.9	54.2	43.1	37.4	34.7	35.5			39.9	39.3
Fixed Assets (net)	41.8	27.8	46.4	47.4	42.3	46.8			49.2	48.4
Intangibles (net)	4.8	6.9	4.5	6.7	12.0	6.8			4.5	4.3
All Other Non-Current	4.5	11.0	6.0	8.4	11.0	10.9			6.3	8.0
Total	100.0	100.0	100.0	100.0	100.0	100.0			100.0	100.0
LIABILITIES										
Notes Payable-Short Term	8.7	7.5	6.8	4.5	3.3	1.8			5.1	5.1
Cur. Mat.-L.T.D.	7.1	2.3	4.7	4.3	3.1	8.1			5.7	5.7
Trade Payables	18.7	17.1	17.1	11.9	9.6	8.7			14.1	14.8
Income Taxes Payable	.1	.1	.3	.5	.2	.0			.2	.2
All Other Current	35.2	8.1	8.0	7.6	9.5	11.6			9.1	8.6
Total Current	69.8	35.1	36.9	28.7	25.7	30.2			34.2	34.4
Long-Term Debt	35.2	13.8	23.7	22.6	17.3	19.8			26.1	28.0
Deferred Taxes	.0	.0	.4	.8	1.2	.6			.6	.7
All Other Non-Current	10.4	8.8	7.7	5.9	4.9	9.3			10.2	10.2
Net Worth	-15.4	42.3	31.2	42.0	51.0	40.1			28.9	26.7
Total Liabilities & Net Worth	100.0	100.0	100.0	100.0	100.0	100.0			100.0	100.0
INCOME DATA										
Net Sales	100.0	100.0	100.0	100.0	100.0	100.0			100.0	100.0
Gross Profit	44.8	42.5	34.2	30.1	39.8	27.4			33.2	36.5
Operating Expenses	39.4	37.7	30.2	24.2	32.3	23.8			29.0	32.1
Operating Profit	5.4	4.8	4.0	5.8	7.5	3.6			4.2	4.5
All Other Expenses (net)	.2	.8	.8	.8	1.2	1.3			1.4	1.2
Profit Before Taxes	5.3	4.0	3.2	5.0	6.3	2.3			2.9	3.3
RATIOS										
Current	6.9	2.7	1.8	1.9	1.7	2.6			1.9	2.0
	1.2	1.4	1.3	1.2	1.1	1.3			1.3	1.2
	.3	1.0	.8	.8	.9	.9			.8	.9
Quick	4.2	2.3	1.2	1.2	1.3	1.4			1.3	1.3
	.8	1.1	.9	.8	.7	.8			.8	.8
	.1	.6	.4	.5	.6	.4			.5	.5
Sales/Receivables	0 UND	10 36.1	16 23.2	19 18.8	20 17.9	25 14.9			18 20.5	16 22.7
	21 17.0	24 15.4	23 15.5	26 14.1	23 15.8	32 11.5			25 14.6	25 14.9
	28 13.0	40 9.2	35 10.6	33 11.1	28 13.2	44 8.2			34 10.7	34 10.6
Cost of Sales/Inventory	0 UND	8 44.4	8 45.9	12 29.9	14 26.8	18 20.2			9 40.3	10 37.7
	6 64.1	19 19.7	20 18.2	20 18.2	19 19.3	26 14.1			19 19.7	19 19.7
	35 10.5	25 14.8	32 11.6	29 12.6	32 11.5	45 8.0			28 13.1	31 11.6
Cost of Sales/Payables	0 UND	5 78.0	17 21.0	18 19.9	15 24.6	16 23.1			16 22.4	16 23.2
	6 65.1	20 17.9	29 12.5	26 13.9	23 15.7	27 13.6			27 13.5	27 13.3
	31 11.8	45 8.2	39 9.5	35 10.4	41 8.9	42 8.7			43 8.5	43 8.4
Sales/Working Capital	25.0	8.4	15.4	10.2	10.9	6.3			13.0	12.0
	110.3	22.2	31.7	40.8	103.6	24.1			32.1	38.4
	-11.5	666.9	-65.7	-30.9	-131.6	-26.5			-28.5	-49.6
EBIT/Interest		10.5	10.8	20.4	15.4	43.9			10.3	8.7
	(17) 5.3	(65) 3.0	(53) 6.7	(15) 7.9	(11) 3.3				(181) 3.1	(177) 2.9
	1.7	.8	2.5	3.4	1.9				.8	.9
Net Profit + Depr., Dep., Amort./Cur. Mat. L/T/D			4.9	5.1	8.5				4.6	5.6
		(20) 2.4	(22) 3.0	(10) 4.0					(52) 2.7	(53) 2.4
		1.4	1.5	3.2					1.4	1.2
Fixed/Worth	.3	.3	.9	.6	.7	.9			.8	.8
	4.4	.7	1.3	1.6	1.2	1.4			1.7	1.7
	-1.3	5.4	5.6	3.5	2.0	NM			4.9	6.6
Debt/Worth	2.0	.6	.9	.7	.8	1.0			.9	1.1
	10.0	1.2	1.8	1.7	1.1	1.9			2.0	2.1
	-4.0	8.6	8.0	4.2	2.5	NM			6.5	12.4
% Profit Before Taxes/Tangible Net Worth		92.3	42.4	51.2	39.3				48.4	43.5
	(18) 24.8	(58) 17.2	(50) 28.6	(15) 22.7					(157) 20.3	(155) 20.1
	2.1	1.0	9.9	8.3					3.8	3.7
% Profit Before Taxes/Total Assets	50.8	22.0	16.0	19.1	15.0	9.2			15.4	14.2
	11.8	9.2	5.3	11.4	12.4	4.9			6.4	5.4
	-7.5	2.3	.0	4.1	4.1	-.4			-.3	.2
Sales/Net Fixed Assets	51.2	45.2	10.9	7.8	7.5	4.7			9.3	10.4
	18.9	15.8	7.1	4.5	4.5	3.2			5.1	5.3
	8.1	5.9	3.5	3.0	3.8	2.2			2.9	2.9
Sales/Total Assets	7.4	4.7	4.0	2.8	2.4	1.7			3.4	3.6
	5.6	2.9	2.9	2.1	1.9	1.3			2.3	2.5
	3.8	2.4	2.2	1.5	1.5	1.0			1.7	1.6
% Depr., Dep., Amort./Sales		.6	1.6	2.2	2.5				2.0	1.9
		(15) 1.1	(64) 2.7	(16) 3.2	2.9				(179) 2.9	(170) 2.7
		2.5	4.3	4.6	3.6				4.2	4.8
% Officers', Directors' Owners' Comp/Sales		2.7	1.8	1.8					2.3	1.4
		(11) 3.8	(31) 3.5	(14) 3.0					(64) 3.9	(63) 3.5
		6.4	5.0	5.3					6.2	5.7
Net Sales ($)	19323M	94082M	966753M	2999773M	2546759M	2546772M			7706075M	7751334M
Total Assets ($)	3687M	25363M	318784M	1363080M	1290765M	1835937M			3842862M	3794262M

M = $ thousand   MM = $ million
See Pages 9 through 22 for Explanation of Ratios and Data

Comparative Historical Data | Current Data Sorted by Sales

				Type of Statement						
49		41	32	Unqualified				1	4	27
35		51	42	Reviewed			3	7	15	17
25		22	23	Compiled	1	5	2	8	6	1
23		24	17	Tax Returns	1	7		7	2	
70		62	73	Other	1	5	5	8	16	38
4/1/08-3/31/09		4/1/09-3/31/10	4/1/10-3/31/11			31 (4/1-9/30/10)			156 (10/1/10-3/31/11)	
ALL		ALL	ALL		0-1MM	1-3MM	3-5MM	5-10MM	10-25MM	25MM & OVER
202		200	187	NUMBER OF STATEMENTS	3	17	10	31	43	83
%		%	%	ASSETS	%	%	%	%	%	%
7.5		10.8	8.8	Cash & Equivalents		4.4	10.1	8.6	11.5	8.5
18.3		17.8	18.7	Trade Receivables (net)		26.1	10.6	19.2	20.2	17.4
11.6		10.7	11.5	Inventory		19.8	7.1	14.0	10.4	10.5
2.5		3.0	2.6	All Other Current		1.3	2.8	2.4	2.9	2.7
39.8		42.4	41.6	Total Current		51.7	30.6	44.2	45.0	39.1
48.2		44.6	44.1	Fixed Assets (net)		32.0	45.5	43.6	43.2	45.8
4.6		6.1	6.3	Intangibles (net)		10.4	14.2	4.5	4.3	6.5
7.4		7.0	8.0	All Other Non-Current		6.0	9.7	7.8	7.5	8.6
100.0		100.0	100.0	Total		100.0	100.0	100.0	100.0	100.0
				LIABILITIES						
8.3		6.2	5.6	Notes Payable-Short Term		12.8	4.8	4.6	5.5	4.4
4.2		5.1	4.5	Cur. Mat.-L.T.D.		6.8	2.3	4.9	4.3	4.5
14.5		13.0	14.3	Trade Payables		16.8	8.1	15.8	17.8	12.3
.1		.2	.3	Income Taxes Payable		.1	.1	.0	.6	.2
8.7		7.5	10.0	All Other Current		22.7	3.1	8.7	6.4	10.4
35.8		31.9	34.8	Total Current		59.2	18.5	34.0	34.7	32.0
27.6		25.6	22.2	Long-Term Debt		26.2	29.8	23.3	18.3	20.6
.6		.6	.6	Deferred Taxes		.0	.0	.3	.3	1.0
8.6		7.4	7.3	All Other Non-Current		13.8	3.5	9.0	5.2	7.1
27.4		34.4	35.2	Net Worth		.8	48.1	33.4	41.5	39.4
100.0		100.0	100.0	Total Liabilities & Net Worth		100.0	100.0	100.0	100.0	100.0
				INCOME DATA						
100.0		100.0	100.0	Net Sales		100.0	100.0	100.0	100.0	100.0
31.8		36.8	34.5	Gross Profit		40.6	47.6	38.7	32.1	31.1
28.7		30.7	29.5	Operating Expenses		37.8	43.0	35.9	25.6	25.6
3.0		6.1	5.1	Operating Profit		2.8	4.6	2.8	6.5	5.4
1.1		.9	.8	All Other Expenses (net)		.4	1.3	.6	.7	.9
1.9		5.3	4.2	Profit Before Taxes		2.3	3.3	2.1	5.8	4.6
				RATIOS						
1.9		2.3	1.9			6.2	2.2	2.5	1.9	1.7
1.2		1.4	1.3	Current		1.4	1.5	1.3	1.3	1.2
.7		1.0	.9			.5	1.3	1.0	.8	.9
1.2		1.5	1.3			4.0	1.3	1.3	1.2	1.3
.7		.9	.8	Quick		.8	1.0	.8	.9	.7
.4		.5	.5			.3	.7	.3	.5	.5

												Sales/Receivables, etc.											

						Sales/Receivables										
16	22.2	16	22.1	18	20.4		5	68.5	5	72.8	13	28.6	16	23.2	20	17.9
24	15.3	23	15.7	25	14.5		29	12.5	18	20.1	21	17.0	26	14.0	26	14.2
31	11.9	32	11.5	34	10.6		54	6.8	33	11.0	36	10.2	39	9.4	31	11.8

						Cost of Sales/Inventory										
9	42.0	10	36.9	11	33.7		4	94.7	8	46.9	10	37.4	8	46.8	14	26.0
18	19.8	19	19.6	20	18.2		26	14.1	24	15.3	18	19.8	18	19.9	21	17.7
30	12.2	30	12.4	30	12.0		58	6.3	33	11.1	31	11.8	30	12.0	29	12.7

						Cost of Sales/Payables										
14	25.5	15	24.2	15	24.0		2	163.3	0	UND	13	27.3	22	16.6	16	22.4
25	14.7	25	14.7	27	13.5		17	21.0	24	24.2	30	12.4	30	12.1	25	14.3
38	9.6	34	10.7	38	9.5		34	10.7	40	9.2	44	8.3	42	8.7	34	10.8

					Sales/Working Capital						
14.0		10.9	11.8			6.3	9.2	16.4	11.8	11.8
60.3		30.8	34.8			30.4	18.6	34.8	30.1	42.4
-24.2		-164.8	-65.7			-10.0	106.4	999.8	-65.7	-69.3

						EBIT/Interest								
	6.9		13.6		13.6			16.5				10.1		16.4		20.0
(190)	2.4	(183)	4.9	(170)	4.4		(13)	3.3			(30)	2.1	(39)	5.1	(76)	4.7
	.3		2.1		1.6			-1.1				-1.1		2.4		2.1

						Net Profit + Depr., Dep., Amort./Cur. Mat. L/T/D								
	3.5		4.9		4.9									4.3		5.8
(58)	2.2	(61)	2.9	(59)	2.8								(13)	2.5	(34)	3.3
	.7		2.0		1.3									1.3		1.7

					Fixed/Worth						
.9		.7	.7			.4	.4	.3	.6	.8
1.8		1.6	1.4			1.7	.9	1.3	1.1	1.4
16.3		4.6	5.2			-3.3	5.5	5.7	2.9	2.6

					Debt/Worth						
1.1		.9	.9			2.0	.6	.8	.7	.9
2.3		1.9	1.8			13.2	1.3	2.2	1.5	1.7
24.7		7.6	7.7			-7.3	6.1	8.9	3.7	3.7

						% Profit Before Taxes/Tangible Net Worth								
	43.0		66.5		48.8			344.2				40.1		52.8		46.5
(159)	15.7	(170)	31.3	(158)	24.5		(10)	51.4		11.3	(27)	8.9	(41)	25.6	(68)	26.2
	4.4		10.1		7.0			6.9		.9		-9.3		10.1		8.7

					% Profit Before Taxes/Total Assets						
11.8		20.5	17.9			44.2	23.0	16.0	17.9	17.9
4.6		9.1	7.4			7.4	2.9	2.4	10.1	8.6
-1.9		3.1	1.6			-7.0	1.1	-2.2	4.9	2.7

					Sales/Net Fixed Assets						
10.5		11.4	10.8			47.5	15.2	17.0	11.4	7.8
5.2		5.4	5.8			15.1	5.7	5.6	6.7	5.1
3.2		3.4	3.5			6.7	2.1	3.5	3.6	3.3

					Sales/Total Assets						
3.9		3.6	3.6			6.4	2.6	3.8	4.0	3.2
2.6		2.5	2.5			3.9	2.5	2.8	2.5	2.3
1.8		1.7	1.6			1.7	1.5	2.3	1.6	1.6

						% Depr., Dep., Amort./Sales								
	1.6		1.7		1.8			1.2				1.9		1.2		2.2
(179)	2.9	(177)	2.9	(169)	2.9		(10)	2.3			(28)	2.7	(41)	2.7	(79)	3.0
	4.4		4.3		4.3			5.0				4.5		4.3		3.7

						% Officers', Directors' Owners' Comp/Sales								
	1.1		1.2		2.0			2.3				3.0		1.6		1.1
(67)	2.8	(74)	3.2	(67)	3.5		(12)	5.5			(15)	3.7	(13)	2.0	(19)	2.9
	5.0		5.5		6.6			7.4				6.6		4.1		4.2

					Net Sales ($)						
9704262M		9790312M	9173462M	Net Sales ($)	1567M	32412M	37696M	210589M	736007M	8155191M
4459660M		4669417M	4837616M	Total Assets ($)	1330M	13136M	21166M	87974M	360814M	4353196M

M = $ thousand   MM = $ million
See Pages 9 through 22 for Explanation of Ratios and Data

Current Data Sorted by Assets   ## Comparative Historical Data

Type of Statement

Type of Statement	0-500M	500M-2MM	2-10MM	10-50MM	50-100MM	100-250MM		4/1/06-3/31/07 ALL	4/1/07-3/31/08 ALL
Unqualified				6	1			5	5
Reviewed		1		1	1			6	4
Compiled			4	1				6	3
Tax Returns		2		1				2	
Other	2	1	4	6		1		8	9
	2	4 (4/1-9/30/10)		28 (10/1/10-3/31/11)		1			
NUMBER OF STATEMENTS	2	4	9	15	2			27	21

Financial Data

(Current-data columns 0-500M, 500M-2MM, 2-10MM, 50-100MM and 100-250MM: DATA NOT AVAILABLE for Assets/Liabilities/Income)

	10-50MM %		4/1/06-3/31/07 ALL %	4/1/07-3/31/08 ALL %
ASSETS				
Cash & Equivalents	10.1		7.1	6.6
Trade Receivables (net)	14.2		18.7	19.8
Inventory	14.4		14.2	17.3
All Other Current	.7		1.9	1.1
Total Current	39.4		41.9	44.8
Fixed Assets (net)	52.9		38.9	38.4
Intangibles (net)	1.8		11.6	12.3
All Other Non-Current	5.8		7.5	4.5
Total	100.0		100.0	100.0
LIABILITIES				
Notes Payable-Short Term	5.1		13.2	10.8
Cur. Mat.-L.T.D.	4.1		4.3	2.8
Trade Payables	11.4		12.7	13.7
Income Taxes Payable	.2		.1	.1
All Other Current	4.4		7.8	7.9
Total Current	25.1		38.0	35.4
Long-Term Debt	26.0		24.8	18.9
Deferred Taxes	1.5		.6	.8
All Other Non-Current	3.8		5.5	10.7
Net Worth	43.6		31.0	34.2
Total Liabilties & Net Worth	100.0		100.0	100.0
INCOME DATA				
Net Sales	100.0		100.0	100.0
Gross Profit	29.3		32.7	28.6
Operating Expenses	24.0		27.8	22.3
Operating Profit	5.3		5.0	6.2
All Other Expenses (net)	1.1		1.6	.9
Profit Before Taxes	4.1		3.4	5.4

RATIOS

	10-50MM		4/1/06-3/31/07 ALL	4/1/07-3/31/08 ALL
Current	1.5 / 1.2 / 1.1		1.9 / 1.3 / .7	1.8 / 1.3 / .9
Quick	1.2 / .7 / .2		1.2 / .8 / .4	1.2 / .7 / .4
Sales/Receivables	18 20.1 / 27 13.3 / 38 9.5		22 16.7 / 28 13.0 / 41 9.0	24 14.9 / 29 12.4 / 38 9.6
Cost of Sales/Inventory	25 14.4 / 44 8.3 / 69 5.3		19 18.8 / 36 10.2 / 51 7.2	23 16.2 / 42 8.6 / 55 6.6
Cost of Sales/Payables	18 20.7 / 30 12.0 / 64 5.7		22 16.9 / 28 12.9 / 43 8.5	17 21.8 / 30 12.3 / 38 9.5
Sales/Working Capital	10.5 / 49.0 / 72.3		8.8 / 22.9 / -17.6	8.7 / 23.4 / -39.0
EBIT/Interest	(14) 9.5 / 7.1 / -1.5		(23) 6.2 / 1.4 / .5	(20) 14.3 / 4.0 / 1.4
Net Profit + Depr., Dep., Amort./Cur. Mat. L/T/D				
Fixed/Worth	.3 / 1.7 / 2.0		.7 / 1.2 / 4.1	.5 / 1.1 / 2.0
Debt/Worth	.7 / 1.4 / 1.9		.8 / 2.3 / 327.3	.8 / 1.4 / NM
% Profit Before Taxes/Tangible Net Worth	54.4 / 28.5 / -5.8		(21) 49.8 / 10.4 / -2.1	(16) 47.2 / 25.5 / 7.0
% Profit Before Taxes/Total Assets	20.3 / 11.8 / -2.4		16.3 / 2.8 / -1.3	15.8 / 9.5 / 2.0
Sales/Net Fixed Assets	10.0 / 2.5 / 1.5		12.2 / 5.6 / 3.4	12.3 / 6.7 / 3.0
Sales/Total Assets	2.5 / 1.2 / 1.1		3.0 / 2.1 / 1.5	3.0 / 2.4 / 1.4
% Depr., Dep., Amort./Sales	1.6 / 3.1 / 7.7		(24) 1.6 / 2.7 / 3.5	(19) 1.5 / 2.6 / 4.3
% Officers', Directors' Owners' Comp/Sales				

	0-500M	500M-2MM	2-10MM	10-50MM	50-100MM	100-250MM		4/1/06-3/31/07 ALL	4/1/07-3/31/08 ALL
Net Sales ($)	1037M	22862M	61985M	484602M	204273M			1433029M	1517108M
Total Assets ($)	358M	6604M	36059M	324503M	115471M			757365M	681787M

Comparative Historical Data | Current Data Sorted by Sales

					Type of Statement						
	8		3		7	Unqualified					2	5
	1		2		3	Reviewed			2		1	1
	6		4		5	Compiled				3	1	1
	3		3		3	Tax Returns					1	1
	12		14		14	Other	2	1		5		6
	4/1/08-3/31/09		**4/1/09-3/31/10**		**4/1/10-3/31/11**			**4 (4/1-9/30/10)**		**28 (10/1/10-3/31/11)**		
	ALL		**ALL**		**ALL**		**0-1MM**	**1-3MM**	**3-5MM**	**5-10MM**	**10-25MM**	**25MM & OVER**
	30		26		32	NUMBER OF STATEMENTS	2	2	2	8	5	13
	%		%		%	ASSETS	%	%	%	%	%	%
	13.6		10.7		12.5	Cash & Equivalents						13.1
	18.5		18.0		19.0	Trade Receivables (net)						14.5
	18.9		16.5		16.4	Inventory						14.1
	3.5		.8		1.6	All Other Current						.9
	54.6		45.9		49.5	Total Current						42.6
	36.5		40.7		40.6	Fixed Assets (net)						48.0
	4.2		9.9		4.3	Intangibles (net)						4.9
	4.6		3.5		5.6	All Other Non-Current						4.5
	100.0		100.0		100.0	Total						100.0
						LIABILITIES						
	3.7		4.2		7.3	Notes Payable-Short Term						3.1
	5.6		3.5		3.5	Cur. Mat.-L.T.D.						3.9
	16.3		13.6		12.5	Trade Payables						10.3
	.0		.0		.1	Income Taxes Payable						.2
	10.7		7.7		6.5	All Other Current						4.6
	36.3		29.0		29.9	Total Current						22.1
	22.0		19.4		22.6	Long-Term Debt						20.0
	.8		.3		.9	Deferred Taxes						2.1
	4.1		3.5		2.6	All Other Non-Current						4.3
	37.0		47.8		44.0	Net Worth						51.5
	100.0		100.0		100.0	Total Liabilities & Net Worth						100.0
						INCOME DATA						
	100.0		100.0		100.0	Net Sales						100.0
	33.5		34.2		34.5	Gross Profit						27.1
	27.1		25.8		31.1	Operating Expenses						16.2
	6.5		8.4		3.4	Operating Profit						11.0
	1.0		.3		.7	All Other Expenses (net)						.4
	5.5		8.1		2.7	Profit Before Taxes						10.5
						RATIOS						
	3.8		2.2		3.0							2.8
	1.9		1.6		1.6	Current						1.4
	.9		1.2		1.1							1.1
	2.1		1.6		2.0							2.2
	1.2		1.0		1.1	Quick						.8
	.4		.6		.4							.3
18	20.4	18	20.0	19	19.2						18	20.1
25	14.6	26	14.0	29	12.7	Sales/Receivables					27	13.3
33	11.2	31	11.7	45	8.1						37	9.9
18	20.0	20	18.6	29	12.7						25	14.6
30	12.0	34	10.8	42	8.6	Cost of Sales/Inventory					33	11.2
59	6.2	52	7.0	61	6.0						54	6.7
17	22.0	20	17.9	16	22.6						17	22.0
22	16.7	26	14.0	28	12.9	Cost of Sales/Payables					27	13.7
37	9.8	34	10.7	44	8.4						37	10.0
	7.1		8.4		5.4							6.3
	13.8		19.3		15.0	Sales/Working Capital						17.2
	-182.5		36.3		62.3							62.0
	17.3		17.7		14.4							20.0
(23)	4.4	(24)	7.8	(28)	5.1	EBIT/Interest					(12)	7.4
	2.0		1.7		-.5							4.5
						Net Profit + Depr., Dep., Amort./Cur. Mat. L/T/D						
	.4		.6		.3							.3
	.7		1.1		1.3	Fixed/Worth						1.6
	3.7		2.7		2.0							1.8
	.5		.8		.7							.7
	1.1		1.4		1.4	Debt/Worth						1.4
	5.0		4.0		2.7							1.5
	62.0		77.1		47.4							54.2
(24)	29.1	(23)	24.4	(28)	21.8	% Profit Before Taxes/Tangible Net Worth						38.0
	8.6		2.6		3.0							21.2
	27.0		28.0		17.8							29.0
	14.8		11.3		9.7	% Profit Before Taxes/Total Assets						15.5
	1.7		1.3		.1							9.7
	23.8		12.3		16.2							13.8
	7.5		6.7		5.5	Sales/Net Fixed Assets						3.5
	3.9		4.2		1.8							1.6
	4.0		3.6		2.9							2.7
	2.8		2.5		1.9	Sales/Total Assets						1.7
	1.8		1.6		1.1							1.1
	1.0		1.9		1.1							1.6
(26)	2.1	(22)	2.4	(31)	2.9	% Depr., Dep., Amort./Sales						3.1
	3.5		4.6		5.9							7.4
					2.2	% Officers', Directors' Owners' Comp/Sales						
		(12)	3.5									
					14.9							
	1311106M		1593332M		774759M	Net Sales ($)	1037M	5288M	8352M	53259M	74067M	632756M
	443329M		627932M		482995M	Total Assets ($)	358M	4933M	4722M	34711M	46607M	391664M

M = $ thousand   MM = $ million
See Pages 9 through 22 for Explanation of Ratios and Data

Current Data Sorted by Assets   **Comparative Historical Data**

0-500M	500M-2MM	2-10MM	10-50MM	50-100MM	100-250MM	Type of Statement	4/1/06-3/31/07 ALL	4/1/07-3/31/08 ALL
		1	7	1	1	Unqualified	7	4
	1	3	3	2		Reviewed	4	6
1	1					Compiled	2	4
1	1	1				Tax Returns	2	
1	2	2	5	3		Other	3	4
8 (4/1-9/30/10)			**29 (10/1/10-3/31/11)**					
3	5	7	15	6	1	NUMBER OF STATEMENTS	18	18
%	%	%	%	%	%		%	%
						ASSETS		
			4.7			Cash & Equivalents	5.5	6.6
			22.4			Trade Receivables (net)	23.2	24.2
			32.1			Inventory	35.4	34.9
			3.3			All Other Current	4.9	4.2
			62.5			Total Current	69.0	69.8
			27.1			Fixed Assets (net)	24.2	21.6
			8.0			Intangibles (net)	1.6	1.0
			2.5			All Other Non-Current	5.3	7.5
			100.0			Total	100.0	100.0
						LIABILITIES		
			11.0			Notes Payable-Short Term	12.8	14.6
			3.6			Cur. Mat.-L.T.D.	1.2	1.1
			22.7			Trade Payables	21.7	22.0
			.3			Income Taxes Payable	.0	.0
			10.4			All Other Current	9.1	10.1
			47.9			Total Current	44.8	47.8
			23.4			Long-Term Debt	13.4	7.4
			.0			Deferred Taxes	.5	.1
			8.0			All Other Non-Current	7.0	3.6
			20.7			Net Worth	34.3	41.1
			100.0			Total Liabilities & Net Worth	100.0	100.0
						INCOME DATA		
			100.0			Net Sales	100.0	100.0
			21.2			Gross Profit	18.6	23.0
			17.1			Operating Expenses	15.7	15.1
			4.1			Operating Profit	3.0	7.9
			1.1			All Other Expenses (net)	.6	.9
			3.0			Profit Before Taxes	2.4	7.0
						RATIOS		
			1.5				2.4	2.1
			1.2			Current	1.6	1.4
			1.1				1.2	1.2
			.7				1.0	.7
			.5			Quick	.5	.6
			.4				.4	.5
			26 14.1				23 16.1	24 15.4
			32 11.5			Sales/Receivables	33 11.0	35 10.4
			46 7.9				43 8.5	41 8.8
			37 10.0				29 12.4	32 11.4
			54 6.7			Cost of Sales/Inventory	61 6.0	58 6.3
			83 4.4				92 3.9	117 3.1
			20 18.6				16 22.9	16 22.2
			42 8.7			Cost of Sales/Payables	28 13.2	30 12.2
			73 5.0				46 7.9	58 6.2
			13.1				7.1	5.5
			35.4			Sales/Working Capital	9.6	12.1
			53.0				18.3	36.9
			7.9				8.1	11.1
			4.0			EBIT/Interest	(17) 3.8	5.9
			2.9				1.2	2.3
						Net Profit + Depr., Dep., Amort./Cur. Mat. L/T/D		
			.6				.3	.3
			1.6			Fixed/Worth	.8	.5
			8.2				1.5	.9
			2.8				1.1	.9
			4.0			Debt/Worth	2.1	1.4
			18.1				5.3	2.8
			49.2				50.1	64.3
			(12) 44.0			% Profit Before Taxes/Tangible Net Worth	(16) 26.9	19.8
			27.1				8.8	3.9
			11.6				10.9	14.6
			8.7			% Profit Before Taxes/Total Assets	7.1	5.3
			4.3				-.8	2.2
			18.2				23.6	23.8
			11.4			Sales/Net Fixed Assets	13.8	18.0
			7.3				6.6	8.0
			3.5				3.4	3.8
			2.3			Sales/Total Assets	2.9	2.6
			1.6				1.8	1.8
			1.1				.8	.9
			(13) 1.4			% Depr., Dep., Amort./Sales	(17) 1.0	(15) 1.2
			2.3				1.7	1.8
						% Officers', Directors' Owners' Comp/Sales		
5162M	24346M	116496M	866424M	507746M	274951M	Net Sales ($)	840280M	1745480M
850M	7657M	40767M	382259M	386795M	129102M	Total Assets ($)	387151M	837947M

M = $ thousand   MM = $ million
See Pages 9 through 22 for Explanation of Ratios and Data

Comparative Historical Data

Current Data Sorted by Sales

			Type of Statement	0-1MM	1-3MM	3-5MM	5-10MM	10-25MM	25MM & OVER
5	7	10	Unqualified				1	1	9
5	7	9	Reviewed				2	2	5
3	7	2	Compiled			1	1		
1	1	3	Tax Returns	1		1	1	1	
10	14	13	Other	2			1	1	7
4/1/08-3/31/09 ALL	4/1/09-3/31/10 ALL	4/1/10-3/31/11 ALL			**8 (4/1-9/30/10)**			**29 (10/1/10-3/31/11)**	
24	36	37	NUMBER OF STATEMENTS	3		2	6	5	21
%	%	%	ASSETS	%		%	%	%	%
5.0	6.4	9.6	Cash & Equivalents						4.0
30.6	23.4	22.4	Trade Receivables (net)						23.6
33.4	27.6	29.9	Inventory						38.2
1.4	5.3	1.8	All Other Current						2.6
70.5	62.7	63.7	Total Current						68.4
18.4	27.7	25.6	Fixed Assets (net)			DATA			22.2
3.9	4.8	4.7	Intangibles (net)			NOT			6.7
7.2	4.8	5.9	All Other Non-Current			AVAILABLE			2.7
100.0	100.0	100.0	Total						100.0
			LIABILITIES						
19.8	17.6	15.1	Notes Payable-Short Term						14.2
1.8	1.8	2.4	Cur. Mat.-L.T.D.						3.1
21.4	17.2	17.9	Trade Payables						22.3
.2	.6	.2	Income Taxes Payable						.2
9.4	9.5	9.4	All Other Current						11.4
52.7	46.7	45.0	Total Current						51.2
8.1	14.1	20.2	Long-Term Debt						19.1
.1	.4	.2	Deferred Taxes						.1
3.5	5.6	5.8	All Other Non-Current						7.7
35.7	33.2	28.8	Net Worth						21.9
100.0	100.0	100.0	Total Liabilities & Net Worth						100.0
			INCOME DATA						
100.0	100.0	100.0	Net Sales						100.0
25.0	28.3	25.1	Gross Profit						18.9
17.0	20.6	20.3	Operating Expenses						14.4
8.0	7.7	4.8	Operating Profit						4.6
.9	.6	.8	All Other Expenses (net)						.9
7.1	7.1	4.0	Profit Before Taxes						3.6
			RATIOS						
1.8	2.1	2.2							1.5
1.5	1.4	1.3	Current						1.2
1.0	1.1	1.0							1.1
1.3	1.1	1.1							.7
.6	.6	.7	Quick						.5
.5	.5	.4							.4
27 13.7	22 16.8	25 14.4							27 13.7
37 9.8	35 10.4	31 11.7	Sales/Receivables						33 11.0
53 6.9	50 7.2	46 8.0							50 7.4
27 13.5	24 15.1	29 12.4							41 9.0
47 7.8	52 7.0	54 6.7	Cost of Sales/Inventory						71 5.1
85 4.3	83 4.4	87 4.2							112 3.3
15 24.7	17 22.0	16 22.7							19 19.3
28 13.1	28 13.1	26 14.1	Cost of Sales/Payables						27 13.6
60 6.1	43 8.5	49 7.5							63 5.8
6.6	8.3	7.2							10.4
10.9	16.4	20.4	Sales/Working Capital						20.4
183.2	57.1	246.1							49.6
38.1	10.1	7.9							7.7
(23) 5.7	(31) 5.3	(35) 4.5	EBIT/Interest						5.4
2.1	3.6	2.9							3.4
		5.5	Net Profit + Depr., Dep.,						
	(10) 2.5	Amort./Cur. Mat. L/T/D							
		.3							
.3	.4	.4							.6
.5	.7	1.1	Fixed/Worth						1.2
1.2	3.2	4.5							4.0
1.1	1.2	2.1							2.6
1.8	2.5	3.7	Debt/Worth						3.8
8.5	8.6	10.9							14.8
61.9	62.7	48.4							52.8
(20) 39.8	(31) 36.3	(31) 33.1	% Profit Before Taxes/Tangible Net Worth						(18) 44.0
12.4	16.6	17.7							26.1
25.6	20.0	11.6							10.9
7.4	8.2	7.9	% Profit Before Taxes/Total Assets						7.9
1.7	4.7	2.7							4.2
36.5	23.6	25.7							22.0
20.2	13.0	11.4	Sales/Net Fixed Assets						12.0
10.2	4.2	5.1							6.4
4.2	3.4	3.4							3.4
3.0	2.5	2.2	Sales/Total Assets						2.2
1.8	1.6	1.5							1.6
1.1	1.0	1.1							1.1
(20) 1.4	(31) 1.4	(32) 1.6	% Depr., Dep., Amort./Sales						(18) 1.5
1.9	2.3	2.5							2.3
.5									
(11) 1.4			% Officers', Directors' Owners' Comp/Sales						
3.4									
1142073M	1623723M	1795125M	Net Sales ($)	2064M		8532M	39707M	77922M	1666900M
545620M	821941M	947430M	Total Assets ($)	1106M		1995M	23272M	86139M	834918M

M = $ thousand   MM = $ million
See Pages 9 through 22 for Explanation of Ratios and Data

Current Data Sorted by Assets   Comparative Historical Data

0-500M	500M-2MM	2-10MM	10-50MM	50-100MM	100-250MM	Type of Statement	4/1/06-3/31/07 ALL	4/1/07-3/31/08 ALL
	1	2	7	5	3	Unqualified	12	14
	1	8	4			Reviewed	8	10
1	4	3	1			Compiled	8	5
4	6	7				Tax Returns	6	4
1	6	10	10	3	3	Other	27	23
	26 (4/1-9/30/10)		64 (10/1/10-3/31/11)					
6	18	30	22	8	6	**NUMBER OF STATEMENTS**	61	56
%	%	%	%	%	%	**ASSETS**	%	%
	13.6	8.8	6.2			Cash & Equivalents	5.5	4.3
	18.5	24.5	21.5			Trade Receivables (net)	20.1	20.1
	20.3	21.7	23.5			Inventory	19.8	18.4
	2.0	2.0	2.9			All Other Current	1.2	1.9
	54.4	57.0	54.2			Total Current	46.6	44.7
	33.2	34.7	33.6			Fixed Assets (net)	37.8	40.1
	4.2	4.0	7.4			Intangibles (net)	7.3	6.4
	8.2	4.3	4.8			All Other Non-Current	8.3	8.8
	100.0	100.0	100.0			Total	100.0	100.0
						LIABILITIES		
	10.8	5.8	8.6			Notes Payable-Short Term	8.4	10.9
	5.6	5.1	1.6			Cur. Mat.-L.T.D.	4.5	5.7
	12.3	17.8	15.8			Trade Payables	14.3	16.1
	.1	.2	.0			Income Taxes Payable	.3	.2
	8.0	10.6	8.3			All Other Current	10.0	6.2
	36.7	39.3	34.3			Total Current	37.5	39.1
	41.7	22.4	12.3			Long-Term Debt	24.8	27.3
	.4	1.0	1.0			Deferred Taxes	.9	1.1
	12.0	5.4	9.8			All Other Non-Current	12.1	7.1
	9.2	31.9	42.6			Net Worth	24.6	25.4
	100.0	100.0	100.0			Total Liabilities & Net Worth	100.0	100.0
						INCOME DATA		
	100.0	100.0	100.0			Net Sales	100.0	100.0
	38.0	30.0	27.2			Gross Profit	28.8	31.9
	37.9	27.3	22.1			Operating Expenses	25.3	29.1
	.1	2.7	5.1			Operating Profit	3.5	2.8
	.9	.9	1.1			All Other Expenses (net)	1.3	1.9
	-.8	1.8	4.0			Profit Before Taxes	2.2	.9
						RATIOS		
	3.0	2.0	2.3				2.1	1.7
	1.8	1.4	1.6			Current	1.2	1.1
	1.0	.9	1.1				.9	.9
	1.9	1.2	1.4				1.1	1.1
	1.1	.8	.9			Quick	.6	.6
	.4	.5	.6				.5	.4
	12 30.3	19 19.3	20 18.7				23 15.9	25 14.7
	28 13.2	29 12.5	27 13.7			Sales/Receivables	31 11.8	32 11.3
	38 9.7	38 9.6	35 10.5				37 9.9	39 9.4
	19 19.1	19 18.8	27 13.5				22 16.4	23 16.1
	51 7.2	41 9.0	40 9.0			Cost of Sales/Inventory	35 10.3	36 10.1
	91 4.0	68 5.4	59 6.2				56 6.5	59 6.1
	17 21.3	17 21.2	16 22.2				17 21.9	22 16.6
	23 16.0	28 12.9	24 15.2			Cost of Sales/Payables	27 13.6	35 10.5
	51 7.2	40 9.1	39 9.4				38 9.7	50 7.3
	4.4	7.8	7.9				10.2	9.5
	14.8	22.2	11.0			Sales/Working Capital	44.0	51.2
	NM	-78.7	65.4				-34.6	-34.1
	9.0	21.6	19.4				6.9	4.4
	(14) 1.6	(28) 3.0	(17) 5.2			EBIT/Interest	(57) 2.2	(52) 1.9
	-.4	1.3	1.3				.5	.4
						Net Profit + Depr., Dep.,	4.5	5.1
						Amort./Cur. Mat. L/T/D	(24) 2.0 (24) 2.4	
							1.2	1.1
	.6	.5	.5				.7	.7
	1.1	1.3	1.0			Fixed/Worth	1.6	2.1
	-1.4	NM	2.3				NM	-231.6
	.6	1.0	.6				.8	1.2
	2.0	1.9	1.0			Debt/Worth	3.0	3.0
	-5.3	NM	29.5				NM	-262.1
	47.5	38.1	34.8			% Profit Before Taxes/Tangible	47.4	37.3
	(12) 21.7	(23) 14.8	(18) 19.5			Net Worth	(46) 14.5	(41) 15.6
	-13.5	5.0	9.2				-.2	.5
	22.6	9.4	16.5			% Profit Before Taxes/Total	10.3	9.3
	3.8	5.2	7.3			Assets	3.9	3.3
	-15.1	1.3	1.7				-1.9	-2.1
	19.6	21.7	30.0				11.2	10.3
	8.9	7.3	8.3			Sales/Net Fixed Assets	6.1	5.1
	4.9	5.5	5.7				3.8	3.3
	3.7	3.5	3.1				3.1	2.8
	2.3	2.6	2.7			Sales/Total Assets	2.3	2.2
	1.7	2.1	1.7				1.7	1.6
	1.2	1.0	.7				1.2	1.5
	(15) 2.5	(28) 1.6	(19) 1.5			% Depr., Dep., Amort./Sales	(52) 2.4	(52) 2.6
	4.9	2.5	3.2				3.8	4.1
		1.6					1.4	1.8
		(11) 2.8				% Officers', Directors'	(21) 3.0	(16) 3.3
		4.5				Owners' Comp/Sales	6.0	7.3
14414M	58972M	448696M	1605745M	1066804M	1401608M	Net Sales ($)	2627276M	2677418M
1934M	21901M	141465M	637119M	551866M	861532M	Total Assets ($)	1296723M	1343476M

M = $ thousand   MM = $ million
See Pages 9 through 22 for Explanation of Ratios and Data

Comparative Historical Data   Current Data Sorted by Sales

4/1/08-3/31/09 ALL	4/1/09-3/31/10 ALL	4/1/10-3/31/11 ALL		0-1MM	1-3MM	3-5MM	5-10MM	10-25MM	25MM & OVER
			Type of Statement						
13	20	18	Unqualified				1	2	15
14	15	13	Reviewed				2	4	7
5	12	9	Compiled		3	2		3	1
10	9	17	Tax Returns	1	3	5	6	2	
39	31	33	Other	1	5	3	3	5	16
4/1/08-3/31/09 ALL	4/1/09-3/31/10 ALL	4/1/10-3/31/11 ALL		0-1MM	26 (4/1-9/30/10) 1-3MM	3-5MM	64 (10/1/10-3/31/11) 5-10MM	10-25MM	25MM & OVER
81	87	90	**NUMBER OF STATEMENTS**	2	11	10	12	16	39
%	%	%	**ASSETS**	%	%	%	%	%	%
6.2	7.6	9.6	Cash & Equivalents		14.9	16.3	9.2	10.2	5.9
21.4	20.3	20.6	Trade Receivables (net)		18.3	16.0	23.9	25.2	20.4
21.6	20.2	20.4	Inventory		14.4	20.1	19.1	24.2	20.9
3.0	1.8	2.0	All Other Current		1.9	.9	2.3	1.7	2.4
52.1	49.9	52.6	Total Current		49.6	53.2	54.5	61.3	49.6
36.5	36.2	35.7	Fixed Assets (net)		37.6	37.1	36.8	26.3	37.5
6.1	7.4	6.4	Intangibles (net)		1.1	5.9	5.4	7.2	8.2
5.3	6.5	5.2	All Other Non-Current		11.8	3.8	3.2	5.3	4.7
100.0	100.0	100.0	Total		100.0	100.0	100.0	100.0	100.0
			LIABILITIES						
10.0	9.3	7.7	Notes Payable-Short Term		6.8	11.2	4.3	6.7	7.7
4.8	3.6	3.8	Cur. Mat.-L.T.D.		6.1	3.9	5.7	1.6	3.3
18.2	14.8	16.4	Trade Payables		24.8	14.3	17.2	18.6	13.9
.1	.6	.1	Income Taxes Payable		.0	.1	.2	.1	.1
10.2	8.8	11.8	All Other Current		33.7	2.3	11.3	8.2	10.2
43.3	37.1	39.8	Total Current		71.4	31.8	38.7	35.2	35.2
20.4	25.1	23.9	Long-Term Debt		37.0	44.3	22.0	16.5	16.1
.7	1.1	.9	Deferred Taxes		.7	.0	.0	1.6	1.3
8.3	10.6	7.4	All Other Non-Current		8.7	11.8	8.6	4.9	7.0
27.3	26.1	27.9	Net Worth		-17.8	12.1	30.7	41.9	40.4
100.0	100.0	100.0	Total Liabilities & Net Worth		100.0	100.0	100.0	100.0	100.0
			INCOME DATA						
100.0	100.0	100.0	Net Sales		100.0	100.0	100.0	100.0	100.0
27.4	29.8	30.9	Gross Profit		45.0	31.1	33.9	30.9	25.5
24.7	24.6	27.7	Operating Expenses		44.6	26.2	29.8	27.7	21.0
2.7	5.2	3.2	Operating Profit		.5	5.0	4.1	3.2	4.6
1.1	1.2	1.1	All Other Expenses (net)		1.1	1.6	1.2	.7	1.3
1.6	4.0	2.1	Profit Before Taxes		-.6	3.4	2.9	2.5	3.3
			RATIOS						
2.1	2.4	2.3	Current		3.4	3.3	2.2	2.5	2.2
1.3	1.3	1.4			1.5	1.7	1.4	1.7	1.3
.9	1.0	1.0			.7	.7	.8	1.4	1.0
1.1	1.4	1.4	Quick		2.6	2.8	1.5	1.6	1.1
.7	.7	.8			.5	.9	.9	.9	.7
.4	.5	.5			.4	.4	.5	.7	.5
21 17.1	22 16.3	18 20.0	Sales/Receivables		0 999.8	8 48.5	22 16.8	21 17.3	20 18.2
31 11.9	30 12.3	27 13.3			22 16.8	20 18.5	33 11.0	31 11.8	28 13.2
37 10.0	37 9.8	36 10.1			36 10.2	42 8.6	39 9.4	38 9.6	34 10.8
19 18.8	25 14.3	20 18.4	Cost of Sales/Inventory		12 31.7	12 30.1	17 21.4	24 15.3	23 15.6
34 10.9	37 9.9	40 9.2			40 9.2	21 17.7	39 9.4	43 8.5	40 9.2
48 7.6	58 6.3	64 5.7			82 4.5	75 4.9	69 5.3	68 5.3	57 6.4
16 22.7	15 24.2	17 22.0	Cost of Sales/Payables		10 36.5	1 370.0	19 19.5	22 16.4	17 22.1
29 12.4	25 14.6	24 14.9			20 17.8	18 19.8	31 11.7	32 11.5	22 16.6
39 9.4	39 9.3	36 10.2			56 6.5	29 12.5	51 7.2	39 9.3	33 10.9
10.4	8.0	8.9	Sales/Working Capital		13.1	7.2	10.7	7.3	9.6
36.8	26.7	19.0			23.6	35.3	24.6	11.1	22.2
-40.9	-207.4	-825.6			-40.0	-12.3	-38.4	-23.9	314.6
6.2	11.6	19.0	EBIT/Interest				29.7	24.7	11.2
(71) 2.6	(79) 3.8	(78) 3.0					3.7	(14) 5.4	(34) 3.1
.5	1.5	1.1					1.2	1.9	1.5
6.6	11.0	13.2	Net Profit + Depr., Dep., Amort./Cur. Mat. L/T/D						13.2
(31) 3.2	(35) 4.5	(27) 3.6							(17) 3.6
.9	1.9	1.3							1.2
.7	.6	.5	Fixed/Worth		.3	.5	.7	.5	.6
1.3	1.3	1.1			1.7	1.1	2.3	.8	1.2
-17.8	-60.9	NM			-1.1	-6.1	NM	3.3	2.9
1.0	1.1	.8	Debt/Worth		.2	1.4	.7	.7	.8
2.4	2.3	1.7			1.4	61.1	4.4	1.6	1.6
-24.6	-56.1	NM			-3.1	-10.9	NM	52.1	3.7
51.9	50.0	37.1	% Profit Before Taxes/Tangible Net Worth					36.1	33.1
(59) 20.1	(63) 25.8	(68) 18.1						(13) 12.0	(32) 20.4
3.3	11.7	3.2						4.0	10.1
12.3	19.7	12.6	% Profit Before Taxes/Total Assets		54.0	22.6	22.8	12.0	12.5
4.3	7.9	5.6			.0	7.8	4.7	5.6	6.4
-1.0	1.7	.1			-14.1	-1.5	1.1	3.1	2.3
16.6	13.5	18.4	Sales/Net Fixed Assets		21.3	352.0	12.1	29.4	14.7
7.5	6.3	7.4			11.8	10.0	7.5	14.4	6.9
3.9	4.0	4.4			3.2	3.6	4.3	6.8	4.2
3.6	3.2	3.5	Sales/Total Assets		6.1	4.4	3.2	3.8	3.1
2.6	2.3	2.5			1.9	2.6	2.4	2.9	2.4
1.8	1.6	1.8			1.7	1.7	2.0	2.3	1.6
1.4	1.3	1.2	% Depr., Dep., Amort./Sales				.9	.9	1.2
(69) 2.3	(75) 2.2	(77) 1.9					(11) 1.8	(15) 1.6	(34) 1.9
3.4	3.0	3.4					4.2	1.9	3.2
1.6	1.9	1.5	% Officers', Directors', Owners' Comp/Sales						
(19) 3.5	(21) 3.1	(27) 2.6							
4.6	5.2	5.3							
4561088M	5084536M	4596239M	Net Sales ($)	1521M	23143M	36580M	81444M	257802M	4195749M
2017545M	2580963M	2215817M	Total Assets ($)	873M	8526M	15959M	34608M	92669M	2063182M

M = $ thousand   MM = $ million
See Pages 9 through 22 for Explanation of Ratios and Data

Current Data Sorted by Assets

Comparative Historical Data

0-500M	500M-2MM	2-10MM	10-50MM	50-100MM	100-250MM	Type of Statement	4/1/06-3/31/07 ALL	4/1/07-3/31/08 ALL
		3	4	3	2	Unqualified	7	9
	1	8	2			Reviewed	11	3
1	2	2				Compiled	4	7
2	7	3				Tax Returns	4	6
5	4	6	1	3	2	Other	25	15
	11 (4/1-9/30/10)		50 (10/1/10-3/31/11)					
8	14	22	7	6	4	NUMBER OF STATEMENTS	51	40
%	%	%	%	%	%	ASSETS	%	%
	5.3	5.5				Cash & Equivalents	6.1	7.3
	22.9	21.5				Trade Receivables (net)	21.5	21.7
	29.4	24.7				Inventory	23.9	22.3
	2.2	2.3				All Other Current	1.7	2.4
	59.7	54.0				Total Current	53.2	53.7
	28.8	34.7				Fixed Assets (net)	32.9	30.3
	6.0	4.3				Intangibles (net)	5.9	6.3
	5.6	7.0				All Other Non-Current	8.0	9.7
	100.0	100.0				Total	100.0	100.0
						LIABILITIES		
	9.8	10.9				Notes Payable-Short Term	15.4	17.3
	2.8	6.6				Cur. Mat.-L.T.D.	5.1	5.4
	18.7	18.2				Trade Payables	15.5	19.1
	.0	.2				Income Taxes Payable	.2	.1
	12.7	7.5				All Other Current	15.5	7.5
	44.0	43.4				Total Current	51.7	49.5
	21.7	15.0				Long-Term Debt	19.7	20.1
	.0	.6				Deferred Taxes	1.0	.5
	11.6	3.0				All Other Non-Current	4.3	3.5
	22.8	38.0				Net Worth	23.2	26.4
	100.0	100.0				Total Liabilities & Net Worth	100.0	100.0
						INCOME DATA		
	100.0	100.0				Net Sales	100.0	100.0
	37.8	40.2				Gross Profit	42.4	39.9
	34.0	35.8				Operating Expenses	38.0	36.0
	3.7	4.5				Operating Profit	4.4	3.9
	1.3	.7				All Other Expenses (net)	2.3	1.2
	2.4	3.8				Profit Before Taxes	2.1	2.7
						RATIOS		
	2.1	2.1				Current	1.8	2.0
	1.4	1.3					1.3	1.2
	1.0	1.0					1.0	.8
	.9	.9				Quick	1.0	1.1
	.7	.7					.6	.6
	.4	.5					.4	.4
12	30.2	21 17.5				Sales/Receivables	22 16.5	23 15.9
31	12.0	32 11.6					31 11.6	29 12.4
44	8.3	41 8.9					40 9.2	37 9.8
27	13.3	43 8.5				Cost of Sales/Inventory	35 10.3	31 11.9
45	8.1	52 7.0					58 6.3	50 7.3
105	3.5	77 4.8					82 4.5	90 4.1
4	87.7	25 14.6				Cost of Sales/Payables	18 20.1	23 15.7
25	14.8	49 7.5					38 9.7	36 10.0
48	7.6	69 5.3					59 6.2	64 5.7
	10.2	9.3				Sales/Working Capital	10.3	8.3
	23.5	23.5					19.5	22.1
	NM	NM					183.4	-21.9
	15.6	13.5				EBIT/Interest	5.0	6.0
(13)	6.7	(21) 4.2					2.8	(34) 2.8
	1.2	1.4					.9	.1
						Net Profit + Depr., Dep., Amort./Cur. Mat. L/T/D	6.8	
							(15) 1.9	
							1.4	
	.2	.6				Fixed/Worth	.6	.3
	1.2	.9					1.1	1.3
	-11.6	1.7					3.8	NM
	.5	.8				Debt/Worth	1.2	1.0
	2.9	2.0					2.1	3.2
	-23.6	4.1					5.4	NM
	151.2	31.2				% Profit Before Taxes/Tangible Net Worth	33.4	43.7
(10)	24.0	(20) 17.2					(43) 13.5	(30) 21.9
	12.2	5.9					.9	7.9
	36.6	17.2				% Profit Before Taxes/Total Assets	12.8	13.6
	11.6	6.4					4.9	6.0
	.3	1.2					-.2	-3.9
	36.1	14.4				Sales/Net Fixed Assets	16.9	24.9
	20.4	8.8					8.7	10.3
	4.8	4.4					5.0	5.5
	4.2	2.9				Sales/Total Assets	3.1	3.3
	3.5	2.7					2.4	2.5
	2.2	2.1					1.8	1.7
	1.3	1.3				% Depr., Dep., Amort./Sales	1.4	1.4
(11)	1.8	(19) 2.1					(44) 2.8	(27) 2.6
	4.0	3.6					4.7	4.4
		2.1				% Officers', Directors' Owners' Comp/Sales	2.3	2.6
	(11)	4.9					(16) 4.3	(16) 3.4
		5.7					6.5	11.9
5760M	52152M	302692M	483433M	782347M	1207495M	Net Sales ($)	1583095M	1756113M
1848M	15347M	116335M	251430M	443695M	608571M	Total Assets ($)	660508M	874716M

M = $ thousand   MM = $ million
See Pages 9 through 22 for Explanation of Ratios and Data

Comparative Historical Data | Current Data Sorted by Sales

Type of Statement

Type of Statement	4/1/08-3/31/09 ALL	4/1/09-3/31/10 ALL	4/1/10-3/31/11 ALL	0-1MM	1-3MM	3-5MM	5-10MM	10-25MM	25MM & OVER
Unqualified	6	10	12				2	3	9
Reviewed	6	8	11			1		6	2
Compiled	10	8	5		2		2	1	
Tax Returns	7	9	12		6	4	2		
Other	19	24	21	6			4	5	6
	ALL	**ALL**	**ALL**	11 (4/1-9/30/10)			50 (10/1/10-3/31/11)		
NUMBER OF STATEMENTS	48	59	61	6	8	5	10	15	17

Assets, Liabilities, Income Data, Ratios

	4/1/08-3/31/09	4/1/09-3/31/10	4/1/10-3/31/11	0-1MM	1-3MM	3-5MM	5-10MM	10-25MM	25MM & OVER
	%	%	%	%	%	%	%	%	%
ASSETS									
Cash & Equivalents	5.5	7.7	6.3				4.6	4.5	8.2
Trade Receivables (net)	20.4	21.1	21.6				20.6	20.1	19.9
Inventory	24.9	25.2	27.5				25.2	21.1	25.1
All Other Current	3.7	2.3	2.5				2.1	2.5	3.1
Total Current	54.5	56.3	57.8				52.5	48.3	56.3
Fixed Assets (net)	30.8	30.6	30.2				28.2	33.1	31.8
Intangibles (net)	7.5	8.1	5.0				7.9	5.3	6.1
All Other Non-Current	7.2	4.9	7.0				11.4	13.3	5.7
Total	100.0	100.0	100.0				100.0	100.0	100.0
LIABILITIES									
Notes Payable-Short Term	10.0	7.0	12.4				8.8	9.4	12.7
Cur. Mat.-L.T.D.	3.9	5.1	3.8				3.7	7.8	2.5
Trade Payables	18.2	15.0	17.9				15.8	19.2	11.8
Income Taxes Payable	.1	.1	.1				.0	.3	.2
All Other Current	6.1	10.4	8.0				9.4	5.1	9.3
Total Current	38.4	37.6	42.2				37.6	41.8	36.6
Long-Term Debt	25.7	21.2	16.7				22.4	10.6	12.8
Deferred Taxes	.6	.4	.5				.3	.7	1.0
All Other Non-Current	5.5	6.4	7.8				2.9	8.8	6.2
Net Worth	29.8	34.4	32.9				36.8	38.1	43.5
Total Liabilities & Net Worth	100.0	100.0	100.0				100.0	100.0	100.0
INCOME DATA									
Net Sales	100.0	100.0	100.0				100.0	100.0	100.0
Gross Profit	39.6	39.0	37.5				43.5	36.7	33.5
Operating Expenses	38.3	35.7	33.9				37.4	34.3	28.4
Operating Profit	1.3	3.3	3.6				6.2	2.4	5.0
All Other Expenses (net)	.8	.7	.7				.5	.3	.4
Profit Before Taxes	.4	2.6	2.9				5.7	2.1	4.6
RATIOS									
Current	2.2	2.9	2.1				2.0	2.2	3.1
	1.4	2.1	1.4				1.4	1.2	1.8
	.9	1.1	1.0				1.1	.8	1.1
Quick	1.0	1.5	.9				1.0	.8	1.6
	.6	1.0	.7				.6	.7	.7
	.4	.5	.4				.5	.3	.4
Sales/Receivables	19 18.7	22 16.5	20 18.1				13 27.5	21 17.8	23 16.0
	28 13.2	27 13.6	32 11.5				27 13.8	33 11.2	31 11.8
	34 10.9	36 10.2	41 8.9				38 9.7	41 8.9	37 9.8
Cost of Sales/Inventory	33 11.2	37 10.0	40 9.0				25 14.5	42 8.6	43 8.4
	51 7.2	53 6.9	56 6.5				60 6.1	49 7.4	57 6.4
	72 5.1	79 4.6	82 4.4				80 4.6	65 5.7	81 4.5
Cost of Sales/Payables	21 17.8	20 18.5	20 18.3				0 UND	27 13.5	19 19.0
	32 11.6	31 11.6	32 11.3				36 10.1	50 7.3	25 14.8
	56 6.5	48 7.6	58 6.3				53 6.9	68 5.4	33 11.1
Sales/Working Capital	7.5	5.6	7.0				10.7	9.8	5.7
	14.8	11.7	17.7				21.6	27.1	8.9
	-49.2	83.9	556.0				287.5	-20.0	69.3
EBIT/Interest	5.9	15.6	13.0				14.2	14.5	13.6
	(44) 2.1	(50) 4.6	(53) 4.2				9.4	(14) 3.1	(14) 10.1
	.1	1.8	1.4				3.9	1.5	1.9
Net Profit + Depr., Dep., Amort./Cur. Mat. L/T/D	8.0	7.4	15.0						
	(11) 1.9	(10) 4.1	(17) 5.8						
	1.3	2.7	1.7						
Fixed/Worth	.4	.3	.3				.3	.5	.4
	1.2	1.0	.9				.8	1.0	.9
	3.9	6.4	4.3				NM	2.2	3.7
Debt/Worth	1.2	.7	.8				.5	.7	.6
	2.6	1.2	2.4				2.6	2.0	1.4
	9.9	17.9	8.3				NM	2.7	6.9
% Profit Before Taxes/Tangible Net Worth	25.1	47.2	33.3					35.5	25.2
	(41) 15.3	(46) 25.1	(50) 17.2					(13) 16.1	(15) 16.2
	-6.6	13.1	10.2					5.0	15.5
% Profit Before Taxes/Total Assets	10.3	14.4	16.7				41.4	16.9	13.0
	4.2	8.4	6.5				13.3	4.3	7.6
	-1.2	3.1	1.2				6.3	1.0	3.1
Sales/Net Fixed Assets	25.9	24.2	25.6				33.3	13.8	12.2
	9.0	8.5	9.1				15.2	8.5	6.1
	5.1	5.0	4.8				4.6	4.5	4.7
Sales/Total Assets	3.4	3.6	3.1				4.2	2.9	2.6
	2.6	2.4	2.4				2.9	2.6	2.1
	2.1	1.6	1.9				2.2	1.9	1.8
% Depr., Dep., Amort./Sales	1.1	1.3	1.4					1.4	1.5
	(36) 2.5	(46) 2.5	(44) 1.9					(13) 2.3	(13) 1.9
	3.3	3.7	3.6					4.9	3.4
% Officers', Directors' Owners' Comp/Sales	1.8	2.4	2.6						
	(17) 5.0	(19) 3.6	(26) 4.6						
	9.6	6.4	7.1						
Net Sales ($)	2481365M	3179131M	2833879M	2464M	15524M	18175M	68460M	236748M	2492508M
Total Assets ($)	1053172M	1675040M	1437226M	1505M	5152M	7997M	24582M	140051M	1257939M

M = $ thousand   MM = $ million
See Pages 9 through 22 for Explanation of Ratios and Data

Current Data Sorted by Assets   Comparative Historical Data

0-500M	500M-2MM	2-10MM	10-50MM	50-100MM	100-250MM	Type of Statement	4/1/06-3/31/07 ALL	4/1/07-3/31/08 ALL
		1	3	4		Unqualified	5	7
		4	4			Reviewed	10	9
	1	3	2			Compiled	6	7
		1				Tax Returns	1	1
	1	4	7	1	1	Other	9	20
	5 (4/1-9/30/10)		32 (10/1/10-3/31/11)					
2	2	13	16	5	1	**NUMBER OF STATEMENTS**	31	44
%	%	%	%	%	%		%	%
						ASSETS		
		5.7	12.8			Cash & Equivalents	6.7	6.6
		22.1	22.4			Trade Receivables (net)	25.8	18.6
		33.3	24.0			Inventory	27.2	24.9
		3.4	1.8			All Other Current	2.5	3.7
		64.5	61.1			Total Current	62.2	53.9
		27.3	31.3			Fixed Assets (net)	26.8	31.2
		6.6	4.5			Intangibles (net)	6.7	8.5
		1.6	3.1			All Other Non-Current	4.3	6.4
		100.0	100.0			Total	100.0	100.0
						LIABILITIES		
		9.3	3.7			Notes Payable-Short Term	8.5	8.9
		2.7	3.5			Cur. Mat.-L.T.D.	2.4	3.6
		18.4	11.6			Trade Payables	17.3	15.0
		.5	.6			Income Taxes Payable	.9	.3
		3.8	6.9			All Other Current	8.2	6.7
		34.7	26.2			Total Current	37.3	34.5
		13.5	12.6			Long-Term Debt	12.0	17.7
		.3	1.0			Deferred Taxes	1.0	1.3
		1.9	2.8			All Other Non-Current	6.3	5.9
		49.5	57.3			Net Worth	43.4	40.6
		100.0	100.0			Total Liabilities & Net Worth	100.0	100.0
						INCOME DATA		
		100.0	100.0			Net Sales	100.0	100.0
		35.9	38.7			Gross Profit	31.4	34.5
		29.6	26.8			Operating Expenses	23.7	28.0
		6.3	11.9			Operating Profit	7.7	6.6
		.0	.8			All Other Expenses (net)	1.3	1.3
		6.3	11.1			Profit Before Taxes	6.4	5.3
						RATIOS		
		3.7	3.8			Current	2.7	2.9
		2.5	2.4				1.6	1.4
		1.2	1.6				1.2	1.1
		1.9	2.1			Quick	1.4	1.3
		.9	1.3				.9	.7
		.4	.9				.6	.4
		23 15.7	28 13.2			Sales/Receivables	28 13.2	25 14.8
		30 12.3	39 9.3				37 10.0	33 11.1
		37 10.0	45 8.1				46 7.9	44 8.3
		54 6.7	46 8.0			Cost of Sales/Inventory	37 9.8	43 8.6
		74 4.9	68 5.4				59 6.2	61 5.9
		104 3.5	106 3.4				83 4.4	100 3.6
		13 27.4	13 27.7			Cost of Sales/Payables	26 14.2	24 15.0
		30 12.0	29 12.4				35 10.5	40 9.0
		44 8.2	52 7.0				48 7.6	54 6.8
		5.1	3.7			Sales/Working Capital	6.4	4.7
		9.8	6.2				13.8	16.4
		28.0	11.8				23.3	61.1
		55.5	89.3			EBIT/Interest	18.0	12.4
		20.1	(15) 12.0				(29) 5.0	(41) 3.6
		1.8	8.3				2.2	1.8
						Net Profit + Depr., Dep., Amort./Cur. Mat. L/T/D	6.0	5.8
							(14) 3.1	(19) 2.7
							1.7	1.3
		.4	.3			Fixed/Worth	.2	.4
		.7	.6				.8	.7
		1.1	1.1				1.4	2.7
		.4	.4			Debt/Worth	.7	.8
		.8	.7				1.7	1.6
		5.4	1.5				3.0	4.9
		40.6	63.5			% Profit Before Taxes/Tangible Net Worth	60.6	56.2
		(12) 31.3	(15) 30.9				(30) 36.4	(40) 21.0
		5.2	25.5				15.7	7.3
		25.1	25.2			% Profit Before Taxes/Total Assets	22.3	17.8
		10.1	17.6				11.3	8.2
		1.7	8.9				4.4	3.2
		25.4	11.2			Sales/Net Fixed Assets	22.6	14.6
		7.9	7.5				11.3	6.6
		5.6	5.2				5.4	4.0
		2.9	2.6			Sales/Total Assets	3.4	2.9
		2.3	1.9				2.4	1.8
		1.9	1.4				1.7	1.4
		.7	1.3			% Depr., Dep., Amort./Sales	1.0	1.2
		(11) 1.4	1.9				(28) 1.6	(41) 1.9
		3.0	3.3				2.4	3.5
						% Officers', Directors' Owners' Comp/Sales		
13286M	148570M	692863M	535550M	395635M		Net Sales ($)	846261M	1621104M
2735M	59338M	334214M	385811M	129489M		Total Assets ($)	444037M	1015134M

M = $ thousand   MM = $ million
See Pages 9 through 22 for Explanation of Ratios and Data

Comparative Historical Data   **Current Data Sorted by Sales**

Type of Statement period headers — Historical columns: 12 (4/1/08–3/31/09) ALL | 15 (4/1/09–3/31/10) ALL | 14 (4/1/10–3/31/11) ALL. Current Data columns: 5 (4/1–9/30/10) and 32 (10/1/10–3/31/11).

Hist 4/1/08-3/31/09 ALL	Hist 4/1/09-3/31/10 ALL	Hist 4/1/10-3/31/11 ALL	Type of Statement	0-1MM	1-3MM	3-5MM	5-10MM	10-25MM	25MM & OVER
7	9	8	Unqualified				1	1	7
11	8	8	Reviewed					4	3
5	6	6	Compiled				3	2	1
	1	1	Tax Returns					1	
12	15	14	Other		1		1	5	6
35	39	37	**NUMBER OF STATEMENTS**	1	1		5	13	17
%	%	%	**ASSETS**	%	%	%	%	%	%
8.1	12.1	9.9	Cash & Equivalents					6.9	12.8
20.7	22.2	22.6	Trade Receivables (net)					24.2	22.8
27.8	26.8	28.9	Inventory					33.6	26.5
2.6	3.6	2.7	All Other Current					2.6	2.7
59.2	64.8	64.1	Total Current					67.3	64.7
29.5	26.9	28.2	Fixed Assets (net)					20.3	29.5
5.0	4.5	5.3	Intangibles (net)					11.0	2.3
6.2	3.8	2.4	All Other Non-Current					1.4	3.4
100.0	100.0	100.0	Total					100.0	100.0
			LIABILITIES	(DATA NOT AVAILABLE)					
10.9	7.0	7.9	Notes Payable-Short Term					8.4	7.2
3.2	3.2	2.7	Cur. Mat.-L.T.D.					3.7	2.0
15.4	11.7	13.6	Trade Payables					19.5	11.0
.4	.5	.4	Income Taxes Payable					.4	.6
6.5	7.4	5.7	All Other Current					3.7	8.0
36.4	29.7	30.4	Total Current					35.7	28.8
11.1	8.4	13.6	Long-Term Debt					17.9	8.4
.9	.5	.7	Deferred Taxes					.0	1.3
3.6	3.1	3.3	All Other Non-Current					3.5	4.3
48.1	58.3	52.1	Net Worth					42.9	57.2
100.0	100.0	100.0	Total Liabilties & Net Worth					100.0	100.0
			INCOME DATA						
100.0	100.0	100.0	Net Sales					100.0	100.0
31.4	35.5	36.1	Gross Profit					41.9	31.6
24.3	26.1	26.8	Operating Expenses					31.8	20.0
7.2	9.4	9.3	Operating Profit					10.1	11.6
.9	.5	.5	All Other Expenses (net)					.7	.6
6.3	8.9	8.8	Profit Before Taxes					9.3	11.0
			RATIOS						
2.7	3.1	3.9	Current					3.7	3.9
1.6	2.4	2.5						2.6	2.3
1.3	1.7	1.6						1.1	1.6
1.7	1.9	2.2	Quick					1.7	2.6
.9	1.3	1.2						1.1	1.3
.5	.7	.7						.6	.8
26 14.3	28 12.8	27 13.5	Sales/Receivables					30 12.4	27 13.5
36 10.1	38 9.6	33 11.2						34 10.8	38 9.7
48 7.6	44 8.3	44 8.3						48 7.6	45 8.2
39 9.3	43 8.4	48 7.6	Cost of Sales/Inventory					65 5.6	46 7.9
70 5.2	66 5.6	73 5.0						103 3.6	72 5.1
107 3.4	116 3.2	104 3.5						126 2.9	88 4.2
20 17.9	21 17.3	16 23.2	Cost of Sales/Payables					28 12.9	13 27.2
31 11.8	28 12.9	26 13.8						40 9.1	23 16.0
47 7.8	36 10.2	44 8.2						69 5.3	31 11.8
5.4	4.0	3.9	Sales/Working Capital					4.3	3.3
10.3	6.5	6.9						9.4	5.4
24.6	10.6	12.6						29.9	12.1
14.6	43.5	67.6	EBIT/Interest					31.2	143.7
(32) 6.2	(35) 13.1	(36) 12.0						12.0	(16) 28.5
2.8	7.4	5.8						7.3	8.9
8.2	11.9	16.3	Net Profit + Depr., Dep., Amort./Cur. Mat. L/T/D						
(12) 4.2	(16) 4.9	(14) 4.2							
2.7	2.6	2.3							
.3	.3	.3	Fixed/Worth					.3	.3
.7	.5	.6						.4	.5
1.3	.8	1.0						1.9	.7
.6	.4	.5	Debt/Worth					.6	.4
1.3	.7	.9						1.8	.7
2.6	1.3	1.9						9.0	1.5
54.3	38.7	44.7	% Profit Before Taxes/Tangible Net Worth					69.9	54.1
27.3	(37) 24.0	(35) 29.4					(11)	36.0	29.4
13.8	15.6	11.1						25.5	20.2
18.1	24.6	24.0	% Profit Before Taxes/Total Assets					25.1	32.0
10.2	14.4	15.4						15.5	18.8
6.6	8.5	5.7						7.2	6.6
21.5	14.3	19.0	Sales/Net Fixed Assets					47.9	15.5
8.7	8.7	7.9						13.1	7.9
4.3	5.8	5.1						7.0	4.0
2.8	3.0	2.8	Sales/Total Assets					3.0	2.8
2.1	2.0	2.1						2.1	1.8
1.6	1.4	1.5						1.6	1.3
1.3	1.3	1.0	% Depr., Dep., Amort./Sales					.7	1.1
(31) 1.7	(36) 1.9	(35) 1.9					(12)	1.1	1.9
3.3	3.3	3.0						2.9	2.7
		1.1	% Officers', Directors' Owners' Comp/Sales						
(10)	(10) 2.0	(10) 2.8							
	3.9	13.7							
1139553M	1620797M	1785904M	Net Sales ($)	2768M	4727M		38648M	205223M	1534538M
655016M	1075065M	911587M	Total Assets ($)	1124M	2582M		16258M	108309M	783314M

© RMA 2011

M = $ thousand   MM = $ million
See Pages 9 through 22 for Explanation of Ratios and Data

Current Data Sorted by Assets | Comparative Historical Data

0-500M	500M-2MM	2-10MM	10-50MM	50-100MM	100-250MM	Type of Statement	4/1/06-3/31/07 ALL	4/1/07-3/31/08 ALL
		7	3	1	2	Unqualified	6	4
1		2	3			Reviewed	7	9
1		1	2			Compiled	5	2
	1					Tax Returns	3	2
	2	6	4	2	1	Other	10	10
		13 (4/1-9/30/10)	26 (10/1/10-3/31/11)					
2	3	16	12	3	3	NUMBER OF STATEMENTS	31	27
%	%	%	%	%	%	**ASSETS**	%	%
		12.5	6.9			Cash & Equivalents	3.8	8.6
		20.5	21.3			Trade Receivables (net)	18.3	16.8
		27.4	21.4			Inventory	26.2	23.8
		1.5	1.6			All Other Current	1.6	2.1
		61.9	51.2			Total Current	49.9	51.4
		33.4	40.7			Fixed Assets (net)	40.0	36.2
		2.4	5.7			Intangibles (net)	7.0	5.9
		2.3	2.4			All Other Non-Current	3.2	6.6
		100.0	100.0			Total	100.0	100.0
						LIABILITIES		
		10.2	10.8			Notes Payable-Short Term	13.1	12.3
		4.9	4.3			Cur. Mat.-L.T.D.	3.2	3.7
		20.9	12.0			Trade Payables	12.2	12.5
		.4	.3			Income Taxes Payable	.2	.9
		9.1	6.2			All Other Current	7.6	5.9
		45.5	33.6			Total Current	36.4	35.2
		15.5	23.3			Long-Term Debt	22.7	19.4
		.1	.4			Deferred Taxes	1.3	.5
		5.3	5.0			All Other Non-Current	8.6	3.9
		33.7	37.6			Net Worth	31.0	41.0
		100.0	100.0			Total Liabilities & Net Worth	100.0	100.0
						INCOME DATA		
		100.0	100.0			Net Sales	100.0	100.0
		26.0	21.0			Gross Profit	29.2	25.6
		20.2	16.4			Operating Expenses	24.8	20.0
		5.8	4.6			Operating Profit	4.4	5.6
		1.1	1.5			All Other Expenses (net)	2.1	1.2
		4.8	3.1			Profit Before Taxes	2.3	4.4
						RATIOS		
		3.0	2.3			Current	2.5	2.1
		1.5	1.3				1.4	1.5
		.8	1.2				1.1	1.1
		1.9	1.4			Quick	1.3	1.1
		.8	.6				.7	.7
		.4	.5				.4	.4
		21 17.5	30 12.3			Sales/Receivables	25 14.9	23 15.8
		24 15.3	34 10.7				32 11.4	30 12.1
		34 10.8	41 8.8				43 8.5	36 10.2
		32 11.3	36 10.1			Cost of Sales/Inventory	40 9.2	33 11.1
		51 7.1	41 8.9				65 5.7	49 7.5
		75 4.9	48 7.6				98 3.7	90 4.0
		18 20.1	17 21.1			Cost of Sales/Payables	13 27.2	18 19.9
		26 13.8	21 17.6				27 13.5	25 14.6
		48 7.6	31 11.6				39 9.4	32 11.3
		5.5	9.1			Sales/Working Capital	7.1	6.8
		14.9	16.7				16.4	14.5
		NM	31.8				56.6	50.2
		29.1	8.9			EBIT/Interest	(29) 6.2	6.0
		(14) 5.8	4.0				2.1	3.6
		2.2	2.6				1.3	1.6
						Net Profit + Depr., Dep., Amort./Cur. Mat. L/T/D	2.4	4.7
							(11) 1.9	(14) 2.3
							.6	1.1
		.3	.8			Fixed/Worth	1.0	.6
		1.0	1.5				1.5	1.2
		3.2	2.3				4.5	3.4
		.7	1.2			Debt/Worth	1.2	.8
		1.8	2.5				2.0	1.5
		6.5	3.9				8.2	5.7
		34.6	32.4			% Profit Before Taxes/Tangible Net Worth	26.2	41.3
		(15) 21.2	20.4				(25) 11.3	(24) 14.8
		4.8	8.0				2.4	2.6
		14.8	8.8			% Profit Before Taxes/Total Assets	9.2	8.6
		9.3	5.3				3.7	5.5
		.8	3.2				.7	2.7
		19.5	8.6			Sales/Net Fixed Assets	11.4	9.8
		8.8	6.4				6.3	6.8
		4.6	2.6				2.0	3.3
		3.7	2.9			Sales/Total Assets	3.0	2.8
		2.9	1.9				1.9	2.1
		2.1	1.4				1.0	1.2
		1.0	1.2			% Depr., Dep., Amort./Sales	1.2	1.9
		1.7	2.2				(30) 2.3	(25) 3.1
		4.0	3.9				4.2	4.3
						% Officers', Directors' Owners' Comp/Sales		
181M	16756M	219952M	742862M	420040M	582119M	Net Sales ($)	1347150M	1694387M
69M	3527M	83925M	334154M	175929M	434100M	Total Assets ($)	746142M	918695M

M = $ thousand   MM = $ million
See Pages 9 through 22 for Explanation of Ratios and Data

Comparative Historical Data

Current Data Sorted by Sales

			Type of Statement						
8	7	6	Unqualified					1	5
10	6	11	Reviewed	1		1	1	5	3
5	6	4	Compiled					3	1
2	4	3	Tax Returns	1			2		
11	11	15	Other	1	1	1	3	4	6
4/1/08-3/31/09 ALL	4/1/09-3/31/10 ALL	4/1/10-3/31/11 ALL		0-1MM	13 (4/1-9/30/10) 1-3MM	3-5MM	5-10MM	26 (10/1/10-3/31/11) 10-25MM	25MM & OVER
36	34	39	NUMBER OF STATEMENTS	2	1	2	6	13	15
%	%	%	ASSETS	%	%	%	%	%	%
6.8	10.3	10.9	Cash & Equivalents					12.9	6.0
21.3	20.0	20.6	Trade Receivables (net)					20.3	19.9
22.6	29.3	24.3	Inventory					25.8	23.9
1.0	1.2	1.5	All Other Current					1.7	1.9
51.8	60.7	57.3	Total Current					60.7	51.7
36.8	28.8	35.5	Fixed Assets (net)					33.9	38.0
4.3	6.2	4.1	Intangibles (net)					3.1	5.7
7.1	4.3	3.0	All Other Non-Current					2.2	4.6
100.0	100.0	100.0	Total					100.0	100.0
			LIABILITIES						
13.7	10.6	9.2	Notes Payable-Short Term					7.2	10.2
4.2	2.6	4.2	Cur. Mat.-L.T.D.					3.0	3.7
15.0	16.2	16.5	Trade Payables					20.9	12.1
.5	.7	.3	Income Taxes Payable					.6	.2
8.2	19.5	7.6	All Other Current					5.5	7.7
41.5	49.6	37.7	Total Current					37.2	33.8
19.0	15.0	16.8	Long-Term Debt					15.5	14.1
.4	.3	.2	Deferred Taxes					.2	.2
10.4	6.1	4.9	All Other Non-Current					5.4	7.1
28.7	29.0	40.3	Net Worth					41.8	44.8
100.0	100.0	100.0	Total Liabilties & Net Worth					100.0	100.0
			INCOME DATA						
100.0	100.0	100.0	Net Sales					100.0	100.0
27.5	30.2	26.4	Gross Profit					25.4	22.0
23.0	25.9	21.2	Operating Expenses					21.3	16.9
4.5	4.3	5.3	Operating Profit					4.1	5.0
1.3	.5	1.0	All Other Expenses (net)					.5	1.1
3.2	3.8	4.3	Profit Before Taxes					3.6	4.0
			RATIOS						
1.9	2.6	2.8						4.0	1.9
1.3	1.7	1.5	Current					1.3	1.5
1.0	1.0	1.1						1.0	1.2
1.1	1.7	1.7						2.1	1.4
.6	.8	.7	Quick					.6	.7
.4	.4	.5						.4	.5
24 15.3	21 17.8	23 15.9						22 16.7	29 12.6
30 12.4	28 13.0	32 11.5	Sales/Receivables					29 12.7	33 11.0
38 9.5	35 10.4	36 10.0						34 10.8	38 9.6
31 12.0	30 12.0	35 10.5						33 11.0	37 9.9
43 8.6	47 7.7	44 8.4	Cost of Sales/Inventory					44 8.4	44 8.3
61 6.0	76 4.8	64 5.7						56 6.5	66 5.6
16 23.0	16 23.0	17 20.9						18 20.0	17 20.9
29 12.5	24 15.2	25 14.7	Cost of Sales/Payables					36 10.2	22 16.5
35 10.4	41 8.9	42 8.7						53 6.9	33 11.2
9.2	7.5	6.7						5.9	7.8
26.8	13.0	12.1	Sales/Working Capital					17.5	12.1
282.0	-761.3	49.6						197.2	30.9
5.9	24.4	13.5						62.5	12.3
(35) 3.1	(33) 10.2	(35) 6.1	EBIT/Interest				(12) 7.2		9.8
1.8	4.1	2.6						2.0	3.2
5.5	9.5	9.1							6.5
(13) 1.6	(14) 3.5	(21) 2.7	Net Profit + Depr., Dep., Amort./Cur. Mat. L/T/D					(11) 2.6	2.6
1.2	2.2	1.5							1.7
.8	.5	.6						.4	.7
1.3	1.0	1.1	Fixed/Worth					1.1	1.1
5.4	2.2	2.4						3.2	1.8
1.1	.6	.7						.4	.7
2.2	2.1	1.4	Debt/Worth					2.5	1.3
12.5	3.8	3.8						5.7	3.8
66.9	70.6	32.8	% Profit Before Taxes/Tangible Net Worth					32.2	34.1
(30) 18.0	(30) 27.2	(37) 18.5						21.2	18.5
6.6	13.4	8.8						4.6	9.3
11.6	20.9	13.4	% Profit Before Taxes/Total Assets					15.6	10.4
5.4	9.7	6.3						12.1	5.9
2.7	4.3	3.4						1.2	4.7
11.4	25.5	12.4	Sales/Net Fixed Assets					17.1	8.6
7.7	8.9	7.5						9.4	6.3
3.4	5.1	3.1						4.6	3.0
3.5	3.7	3.2	Sales/Total Assets					3.7	2.8
2.5	2.7	2.4						3.1	2.4
1.6	1.6	1.5						1.8	1.5
1.1	.8	1.2	% Depr., Dep., Amort./Sales					1.1	1.2
(33) 2.7	(29) 1.5	(37) 2.2						1.8	2.2
3.6	3.3	3.9						3.0	2.8
		1.5	% Officers', Directors' Owners' Comp/Sales						
	(10) 2.7								
		4.9							
1963688M	1828367M	1981910M	Net Sales ($)	181M	2810M	8527M	46445M	238207M	1685740M
867253M	844840M	1031704M	Total Assets ($)	69M	3354M	4575M	20184M	102448M	901074M

M = $ thousand   MM = $ million
See Pages 9 through 22 for Explanation of Ratios and Data

Current Data Sorted by Assets   Comparative Historical Data

0-500M	500M-2MM	2-10MM	10-50MM	50-100MM	100-250MM	Type of Statement	4/1/06-3/31/07 ALL	4/1/07-3/31/08 ALL
		1	4			Unqualified	9	7
		2	2			Reviewed	4	5
	1	2	2			Compiled	5	5
	1	2	2			Tax Returns	2	
1	1	3	3	2	1	Other	17	14
1	2	10	11	2	1	**NUMBER OF STATEMENTS**	37	31
%	%	%	%	%	%	**ASSETS**	%	%
		7.8	6.8			Cash & Equivalents	6.8	6.1
		23.9	19.8			Trade Receivables (net)	22.3	18.9
		29.5	34.0			Inventory	28.7	26.0
		1.3	1.2			All Other Current	3.6	4.8
		62.4	61.8			Total Current	61.4	55.9
		30.8	34.5			Fixed Assets (net)	27.9	37.1
		3.8	.9			Intangibles (net)	2.9	3.0
		3.0	2.9			All Other Non-Current	7.9	4.0
		100.0	100.0			Total	100.0	100.0
						LIABILITIES		
		13.2	4.7			Notes Payable-Short Term	10.0	8.1
		2.1	3.2			Cur. Mat.-L.T.D.	1.7	4.6
		18.3	10.8			Trade Payables	10.9	12.2
		.4	1.3			Income Taxes Payable	.1	.1
		7.1	5.2			All Other Current	10.1	9.6
		41.1	25.2			Total Current	32.8	34.6
		9.6	12.2			Long-Term Debt	20.1	18.5
		.3	.3			Deferred Taxes	.3	.4
		10.3	.9			All Other Non-Current	8.3	4.8
		38.6	61.4			Net Worth	38.5	41.8
		100.0	100.0			Total Liabilties & Net Worth	100.0	100.0
						INCOME DATA		
		100.0	100.0			Net Sales	100.0	100.0
		35.8	32.2			Gross Profit	32.6	30.8
		31.0	22.1			Operating Expenses	25.2	23.1
		4.8	10.1			Operating Profit	7.4	7.6
		2.0	.8			All Other Expenses (net)	.6	1.3
		2.9	9.3			Profit Before Taxes	6.8	6.3
						RATIOS		
		2.4	5.2			Current	3.3	2.4
		1.7	3.4				2.0	1.5
		.8	1.7				1.2	1.2
		1.4	1.7			Quick	1.5	1.1
		.9	1.3				.7	.8
		.3	1.0				.5	.5
		25 14.6	26 14.0			Sales/Receivables	27 13.3	23 15.7
		31 11.7	30 12.0				39 9.4	33 10.9
		48 7.6	32 11.4				50 7.3	44 8.3
		54 6.8	55 6.6			Cost of Sales/Inventory	47 7.8	36 10.2
		66 5.5	70 5.2				63 5.8	55 6.6
		77 4.8	143 2.6				110 3.3	93 3.9
		25 14.6	17 22.0			Cost of Sales/Payables	18 20.5	18 20.0
		33 11.0	31 11.7				30 12.2	28 12.9
		58 6.3	49 7.5				44 8.3	52 7.0
		7.4	3.0			Sales/Working Capital	4.8	5.4
		10.5	4.9				8.3	11.5
		-256.8	8.0				29.2	23.4
		50.7	116.5			EBIT/Interest	16.0	8.8
		6.5	52.0				(35) 5.1	3.6
		1.4	9.9				1.1	1.5
						Net Profit + Depr., Dep., Amort./Cur. Mat. L/T/D	8.8	
							(10) 4.9	
							1.9	
		.3	.3			Fixed/Worth	.1	.3
		.6	.5				.6	.9
		1.9	.9				1.2	2.2
		1.0	.3			Debt/Worth	.5	.7
		1.6	.3				1.1	1.2
		5.4	1.5				3.8	2.9
		51.9	55.5			% Profit Before Taxes/Tangible Net Worth	61.1	50.2
		16.8	32.4				(33) 17.0	(28) 21.8
		3.7	14.2				5.5	3.3
		29.0	29.5			% Profit Before Taxes/Total Assets	20.0	16.7
		6.8	16.3				7.4	7.6
		.6	9.3				.7	1.2
		26.2	15.9			Sales/Net Fixed Assets	33.1	13.7
		15.2	5.7				12.3	3.6
		5.4	2.6				3.2	2.5
		3.5	2.6			Sales/Total Assets	2.9	2.7
		2.3	2.4				1.8	1.7
		1.6	1.2				1.4	1.3
		1.1	.9			% Depr., Dep., Amort./Sales	1.1	1.0
		1.8	(10) 1.4				(31) 2.1	(27) 3.0
		4.0	3.6				3.4	3.8
						% Officers', Directors' Owners' Comp/Sales	2.1	
							(10) 2.5	
							7.9	
655M	14487M	106856M	369379M	241738M	372310M	Net Sales ($)	1113986M	1121823M
354M	3777M	52272M	213034M	129923M	119227M	Total Assets ($)	797527M	820683M

M = $ thousand   MM = $ million
See Pages 9 through 22 for Explanation of Ratios and Data

Comparative Historical Data | **Current Data Sorted by Sales**

4/1/08-3/31/09 ALL	4/1/09-3/31/10 ALL	4/1/10-3/31/11 ALL	Type of Statement	0-1MM	1-3MM	3-5MM	5-10MM	10-25MM	25MM & OVER
6	5	5	Unqualified					2	3
3	4	4	Reviewed				1	3	
3	3	5	Compiled			1	1	2	1
3	3	2	Tax Returns					2	
11	13	11	Other	1			3	2	5
					3 (4/1-9/30/10)		24 (10/1/10-3/31/11)		
26	28	27	NUMBER OF STATEMENTS	1		1	5	11	9
%	%	%	**ASSETS**	%	%	%	%	%	%
6.6	8.6	7.4	Cash & Equivalents		DATA NOT AVAILABLE			10.3	
17.6	19.4	21.7	Trade Receivables (net)					24.9	
32.9	33.8	31.8	Inventory					28.8	
1.5	2.5	1.5	All Other Current					.8	
58.6	64.4	62.5	Total Current					64.8	
33.0	28.4	30.6	Fixed Assets (net)					27.4	
3.2	2.5	2.2	Intangibles (net)					4.0	
5.2	4.7	4.7	All Other Non-Current					3.7	
100.0	100.0	100.0	Total					100.0	
			LIABILITIES						
11.3	9.7	8.2	Notes Payable-Short Term					6.0	
1.5	4.3	4.8	Cur. Mat.-L.T.D.					3.9	
15.0	12.6	16.1	Trade Payables					15.4	
.4	1.0	.7	Income Taxes Payable					1.2	
7.8	6.3	7.0	All Other Current					6.5	
36.0	33.9	36.7	Total Current					33.1	
15.6	13.7	11.7	Long-Term Debt					10.5	
.6	.4	.3	Deferred Taxes					.3	
13.9	7.8	4.6	All Other Non-Current					.5	
33.9	44.3	46.7	Net Worth					55.6	
100.0	100.0	100.0	Total Liabilties & Net Worth					100.0	
			INCOME DATA						
100.0	100.0	100.0	Net Sales					100.0	
26.7	30.3	32.2	Gross Profit					36.7	
23.4	25.1	24.7	Operating Expenses					26.1	
3.3	5.2	7.5	Operating Profit					10.6	
1.6	.6	1.5	All Other Expenses (net)					.7	
1.7	4.6	6.0	Profit Before Taxes					9.9	
			RATIOS						
2.8	3.7	3.3						3.3	
1.5	2.2	1.9	Current					1.9	
1.2	1.5	1.1						1.4	
1.1	1.7	1.6						1.7	
.7	.9	1.0	Quick					1.3	
.5	.5	.5						.9	
22 16.7	21 17.5	26 14.0						26 14.2	
33 11.0	29 12.4	30 12.0	Sales/Receivables					31 11.9	
39 9.3	42 8.6	37 9.9						63 5.8	
53 6.9	55 6.7	54 6.8						55 6.7	
79 4.6	85 4.3	70 5.2	Cost of Sales/Inventory					74 4.9	
100 3.7	106 3.5	115 3.2						148 2.5	
25 14.6	21 17.1	20 18.1						26 13.8	
35 10.3	29 12.5	32 11.4	Cost of Sales/Payables					31 11.7	
44 8.3	37 9.7	49 7.5						48 7.6	
5.0	4.2	3.6						3.0	
8.6	6.9	8.7	Sales/Working Capital					8.7	
19.7	13.8	44.6						16.9	
10.1	20.4	88.7						188.0	
(25) 2.2	7.0	(26) 12.6	EBIT/Interest					26.7	
.5	2.2	3.1						9.9	
			Net Profit + Depr., Dep., Amort./Cur. Mat. L/T/D						
.4	.4	.3						.3	
.8	.6	.5	Fixed/Worth					.4	
1.6	1.0	1.0						1.0	
.9	.6	.4						.3	
1.6	1.3	1.3	Debt/Worth					1.0	
3.4	3.8	4.0						1.7	
46.8	44.9	54.4						70.8	
(22) 12.0	(26) 18.5	28.9	% Profit Before Taxes/Tangible Net Worth					42.6	
-2.2	10.1	9.4						7.0	
9.5	23.1	28.0						33.2	
3.0	9.5	12.3	% Profit Before Taxes/Total Assets					20.5	
-1.0	2.9	3.3						4.1	
11.5	17.3	20.4						36.5	
6.1	10.1	9.7	Sales/Net Fixed Assets					14.1	
3.4	5.2	4.0						2.6	
2.5	2.8	2.8						3.5	
1.6	2.1	2.1	Sales/Total Assets					2.0	
1.3	1.3	1.6						1.2	
1.3	1.2	.9						1.0	
(24) 2.2	(23) 2.0	(24) 1.5	% Depr., Dep., Amort./Sales					(10) 1.7	
3.5	3.1	2.4						3.6	
			% Officers', Directors' Owners' Comp/Sales						
929724M	1211136M	1105425M	Net Sales ($)	655M		3094M	35298M	175231M	891147M
689274M	647382M	518587M	Total Assets ($)	354M		1810M	25906M	138463M	352054M

M = $ thousand MM = $ million

See Pages 9 through 22 for Explanation of Ratios and Data

Current Data Sorted by Assets   Comparative Historical Data

Type of Statement

	0-500M	500M-2MM	2-10MM	10-50MM	50-100MM	100-250MM		6 4/1/06- 3/31/07 ALL	10 4/1/07- 3/31/08 ALL
Unqualified			5	3	3	3		5	5
Reviewed		2	2	1				3	3
Compiled		1	1	1				3	2
Tax Returns		1	1						
Other	2	1	4	2	2	3			
	9 (4/1-9/30/10)			27 (10/1/10-3/31/11)					
NUMBER OF STATEMENTS	2	4	12	7	5	6		17	20

	0-500M %	500M-2MM %	2-10MM %	10-50MM %	50-100MM %	100-250MM %		4/1/06-3/31/07 ALL %	4/1/07-3/31/08 ALL %
ASSETS									
Cash & Equivalents			12.4					5.5	11.0
Trade Receivables (net)			22.4					24.0	17.4
Inventory			22.4					15.9	14.0
All Other Current			.9					4.3	3.2
Total Current			58.1					49.7	45.7
Fixed Assets (net)			26.4					37.6	35.5
Intangibles (net)			12.9					9.2	14.5
All Other Non-Current			2.6					3.5	4.3
Total			100.0					100.0	100.0
LIABILITIES									
Notes Payable-Short Term			7.3					7.6	5.4
Cur. Mat.-L.T.D.			1.7					4.1	3.1
Trade Payables			21.9					18.3	19.4
Income Taxes Payable			.0					.0	.0
All Other Current			4.7					11.7	15.8
Total Current			35.6					41.8	43.8
Long-Term Debt			13.8					17.4	23.0
Deferred Taxes			.0					.5	.1
All Other Non-Current			8.4					6.5	2.9
Net Worth			42.2					33.9	30.1
Total Liabilties & Net Worth			100.0					100.0	100.0
INCOME DATA									
Net Sales			100.0					100.0	100.0
Gross Profit			27.2					26.1	25.7
Operating Expenses			23.7					22.7	24.4
Operating Profit			3.5					3.4	1.3
All Other Expenses (net)			-.1					1.0	1.3
Profit Before Taxes			3.6					2.4	.1

RATIOS

Ratio	2-10MM	4/1/06-3/31/07 ALL	4/1/07-3/31/08 ALL
Current	2.9 / 1.8 / 1.1	1.9 / 1.2 / .9	2.1 / 1.0 / .7
Quick	1.8 / 1.0 / .5	1.1 / .8 / .5	1.3 / .6 / .4
Sales/Receivables	(16) 23.3 / (20) 18.0 / (29) 12.7	(21) 17.4 / (32) 11.5 / (45) 8.0	(20) 18.1 / (24) 15.0 / (31) 11.7
Cost of Sales/Inventory	(13) 27.1 / (23) 15.8 / (53) 6.9	(12) 30.8 / (28) 13.1 / (46) 7.9	(17) 21.8 / (24) 15.2 / (43) 8.4
Cost of Sales/Payables	(16) 22.9 / (30) 12.2 / (36) 10.0	(21) 17.3 / (29) 12.6 / (43) 8.6	(23) 15.8 / (30) 12.3 / (43) 8.5
Sales/Working Capital	10.0 / 17.4 / 67.0	9.1 / 52.4 / -61.0	14.0 / NM / -17.6
EBIT/Interest	74.7 / 6.2 / 2.9	(16) 7.3 / 3.5 / 1.3	(16) 5.0 / 1.4 / -.8
Net Profit + Depr., Dep., Amort./Cur. Mat. L/T/D			
Fixed/Worth	.4 / .9 / 1.4	.7 / 1.6 / 3.0	1.0 / 1.9 / NM
Debt/Worth	.7 / 2.0 / 3.6	.9 / 1.9 / 11.0	1.3 / 3.3 / NM
% Profit Before Taxes/Tangible Net Worth	49.9 / (10) 27.5 / 11.5	(15) 61.0 / 27.6 / 4.0	(15) 58.0 / 7.0 / -10.1
% Profit Before Taxes/Total Assets	23.4 / 6.0 / 2.9	10.6 / 6.3 / 1.3	5.5 / 2.7 / -13.6
Sales/Net Fixed Assets	59.0 / 12.9 / 5.5	14.6 / 6.7 / 4.3	13.1 / 6.5 / 4.4
Sales/Total Assets	7.1 / 2.9 / 2.2	3.7 / 2.5 / 1.9	3.2 / 2.3 / 2.1
% Depr., Dep., Amort./Sales	1.1 / (11) 1.4 / 1.9	(15) 1.1 / 2.1 / 3.1	(15) 1.4 / 2.5 / 3.8
% Officers', Directors' Owners' Comp/Sales			

	0-500M	500M-2MM	2-10MM	10-50MM	50-100MM	100-250MM		4/1/06-3/31/07	4/1/07-3/31/08
Net Sales ($)	5774M	11898M	232393M	342080M	1112056M	3047232M		2232583M	2767852M
Total Assets ($)	684M	5788M	64467M	164864M	436577M	1179451M		740718M	1050667M

Comparative Historical Data | Current Data Sorted by Sales

			Type of Statement	0-1MM	1-3MM	3-5MM	5-10MM	10-25MM	25MM & OVER
7	9	9	Unqualified						9
5	2	6	Reviewed				1	4	1
4	6	5	Compiled		1		1	2	1
2	3	4	Tax Returns	1	1	1		1	
9	13	12	Other		1	1		2	8
4/1/08-3/31/09 ALL	4/1/09-3/31/10 ALL	4/1/10-3/31/11 ALL		9 (4/1-9/30/10)			27 (10/1/10-3/31/11)		
27	33	36	NUMBER OF STATEMENTS	1	3	2	2	9	19
%	%	%	**ASSETS**	%	%	%	%	%	%
6.2	10.6	12.1	Cash & Equivalents						10.1
18.4	18.9	17.1	Trade Receivables (net)						17.9
17.5	15.0	18.3	Inventory						17.0
1.5	1.4	1.3	All Other Current						1.7
43.6	45.8	48.8	Total Current						46.7
40.8	40.0	37.8	Fixed Assets (net)						38.1
9.9	8.8	9.2	Intangibles (net)						8.8
5.7	5.4	4.2	All Other Non-Current						6.4
100.0	100.0	100.0	Total						100.0
			LIABILITIES						
8.0	6.6	7.4	Notes Payable-Short Term						3.7
3.6	3.1	2.6	Cur. Mat.-L.T.D.						3.2
20.6	20.0	19.7	Trade Payables						20.9
.1	.2	.1	Income Taxes Payable						.1
9.7	9.0	9.2	All Other Current						9.2
42.0	39.0	38.8	Total Current						37.1
29.4	23.7	24.4	Long-Term Debt						26.0
.9	.6	.1	Deferred Taxes						.2
3.1	9.4	10.1	All Other Non-Current						9.3
24.6	27.4	26.6	Net Worth						27.4
100.0	100.0	100.0	Total Liabilities & Net Worth						100.0
			INCOME DATA						
100.0	100.0	100.0	Net Sales						100.0
27.9	26.0	26.1	Gross Profit						20.7
26.9	22.9	22.2	Operating Expenses						17.3
1.0	3.1	3.9	Operating Profit						3.3
1.3	1.4	.9	All Other Expenses (net)						1.0
-.4	1.7	3.1	Profit Before Taxes						2.3
			RATIOS						
2.4	2.5	2.6	Current						2.7
.9	1.1	1.2							1.1
.8	.8	.9							.8
1.0	1.6	1.7	Quick						1.6
.6	.6	.7							.7
.4	.4	.5							.4
19 19.4	19 19.3	16 22.1	Sales/Receivables						18 20.4
23 15.8	25 14.6	22 16.8							22 16.8
29 12.4	31 11.8	29 12.6							30 12.2
15 24.8	10 35.9	12 29.7	Cost of Sales/Inventory						13 27.5
31 11.9	17 21.0	23 15.7							20 18.1
57 6.4	42 8.7	49 7.5							35 10.5
20 18.1	20 18.7	16 22.7	Cost of Sales/Payables						14 26.2
32 11.5	30 12.1	30 12.2							32 11.3
45 8.2	49 7.5	43 8.5							48 7.6
11.4	11.9	10.0	Sales/Working Capital						9.7
-46.2	93.5	42.1							45.9
-23.4	-32.4	-47.2							-36.4
5.2	13.2	24.2	EBIT/Interest						10.4
2.4	(30) 4.7	(33) 3.0						(16)	2.6
.6	1.3	1.4							.9
8.2	12.1		Net Profit + Depr., Dep., Amort./Cur. Mat. L/T/D						
(13) 4.1	(10) 6.2								
1.5	1.2								
1.3	.7	.6	Fixed/Worth						.6
2.9	1.7	1.4							1.5
-4.6	-9.0	-4.6							-4.6
1.4	1.2	.9	Debt/Worth						.9
5.3	3.2	2.7							2.8
-20.6	-20.7	-13.0							-11.5
31.7	74.4	49.6	% Profit Before Taxes/Tangible Net Worth						49.6
(18) 15.7	(23) 52.8	(25) 35.0						(13)	36.2
2.6	11.0	11.4							24.2
8.7	14.3	17.0	% Profit Before Taxes/Total Assets						15.2
4.4	9.5	6.7							8.8
-2.0	2.6	2.4							3.9
10.6	10.3	12.8	Sales/Net Fixed Assets						9.8
6.1	6.9	7.1							7.0
4.0	4.4	3.9							5.1
3.5	3.6	3.8	Sales/Total Assets						3.8
2.3	2.6	2.5							2.5
1.9	2.1	1.8							2.1
1.3	1.2	1.2	% Depr., Dep., Amort./Sales						1.6
(23) 2.7	(27) 2.6	(30) 2.1						(14)	2.6
4.4	3.4	3.2							3.4
		1.8	% Officers', Directors' Owners' Comp/Sales						
	(12)	4.9							
		6.0							
3218909M	4059778M	4751433M	Net Sales ($)	853M	6700M	9136M	13509M	137735M	4583500M
1256857M	1448473M	1851831M	Total Assets ($)	232M	3982M	7205M	5393M	51249M	1783770M

M = $ thousand   MM = $ million
See Pages 9 through 22 for Explanation of Ratios and Data

Current Data Sorted by Assets   **Comparative Historical Data**

0-500M	500M-2MM	2-10MM	10-50MM	50-100MM	100-250MM	Type of Statement		
	1	4	24	7	5	Unqualified	55	42
		18	18	1		Reviewed	41	42
2	4	13				Compiled	27	16
5	12	15	1			Tax Returns	14	21
4	11	30	31	6	8	Other	77	86
	52 (4/1-9/30/10)		168 (10/1/10-3/31/11)				4/1/06-3/31/07 ALL	4/1/07-3/31/08 ALL
0-500M	500M-2MM	2-10MM	10-50MM	50-100MM	100-250MM			
11	28	80	74	14	13	NUMBER OF STATEMENTS	214	207
%	%	%	%	%	%	ASSETS	%	%
25.5	11.0	8.4	5.5	4.5	8.3	Cash & Equivalents	8.0	7.8
20.0	29.5	24.0	21.6	18.2	14.3	Trade Receivables (net)	22.2	21.9
18.1	15.2	29.0	25.6	28.8	22.0	Inventory	24.3	24.5
1.0	1.7	2.6	2.1	4.1	2.8	All Other Current	1.9	3.0
64.6	57.4	64.1	54.8	55.6	47.4	Total Current	56.4	57.2
19.5	33.8	27.7	36.0	36.6	30.5	Fixed Assets (net)	32.1	31.0
9.8	4.8	3.9	5.5	4.6	16.6	Intangibles (net)	4.0	5.6
6.2	4.0	4.2	3.8	3.2	5.4	All Other Non-Current	7.5	6.2
100.0	100.0	100.0	100.0	100.0	100.0	Total	100.0	100.0
						LIABILITIES		
32.1	5.5	8.8	14.7	10.6	4.2	Notes Payable-Short Term	11.5	10.4
5.4	4.9	3.1	3.5	4.8	1.7	Cur. Mat.-L.T.D.	4.7	4.7
17.1	29.6	17.7	13.6	17.7	10.3	Trade Payables	17.5	18.2
.0	.0	.6	.2	.4	.1	Income Taxes Payable	.4	.3
13.1	7.2	9.6	6.7	6.3	12.4	All Other Current	7.9	8.3
67.7	47.1	39.8	38.7	39.9	28.7	Total Current	41.8	41.9
6.4	15.2	14.9	17.1	26.0	12.1	Long-Term Debt	19.4	24.1
.0	.1	.7	.4	.9	2.1	Deferred Taxes	.5	.5
23.9	8.0	10.2	4.1	4.1	3.0	All Other Non-Current	7.5	7.6
2.0	29.6	34.5	39.8	29.1	54.1	Net Worth	30.7	25.9
100.0	100.0	100.0	100.0	100.0	100.0	Total Liabilities & Net Worth	100.0	100.0
						INCOME DATA		
100.0	100.0	100.0	100.0	100.0	100.0	Net Sales	100.0	100.0
49.8	36.3	32.2	23.9	25.6	26.5	Gross Profit	31.0	28.5
41.2	33.1	27.3	17.7	17.3	19.7	Operating Expenses	26.5	24.1
8.6	3.1	4.9	6.2	8.2	6.8	Operating Profit	4.4	4.4
.6	.0	.9	1.2	1.1	2.3	All Other Expenses (net)	1.3	1.6
8.1	3.1	4.0	5.0	7.1	4.5	Profit Before Taxes	3.1	2.8
						RATIOS		
2.9	2.2	2.4	2.3	2.1	2.3	Current	2.2	2.1
1.6	1.3	1.5	1.4	1.3	1.6		1.4	1.4
.5	.8	1.2	1.1	1.1	1.1		1.0	1.0
2.4	1.7	1.4	1.1	.8	1.3	Quick	1.2	1.1
1.0	.8	.8	.6	.5	.9		.6	.7
.3	.4	.5	.4	.4	.4		.5	.5
0 UND	19 18.9	23 15.8	22 16.8	25 14.4	19 19.2	Sales/Receivables	20 18.0	21 17.0
13 29.2	34 10.6	33 11.0	31 11.9	31 11.8	28 13.0		29 12.6	29 12.4
29 12.4	47 7.8	43 8.5	46 7.9	37 10.0	40 9.1		38 9.5	37 9.8
0 UND	2 156.2	23 16.0	29 12.7	37 9.8	32 11.4	Cost of Sales/Inventory	21 17.5	23 15.8
16 22.8	18 19.9	45 8.1	52 7.0	76 4.8	47 7.8		44 8.3	45 8.1
43 8.5	55 6.6	89 4.1	77 4.8	89 4.1	91 4.0		82 4.5	82 4.4
0 UND	20 18.3	15 25.0	18 20.5	24 15.5	13 27.8	Cost of Sales/Payables	19 19.7	17 21.1
28 12.9	41 8.9	26 14.3	27 13.6	29 12.6	31 11.7		30 12.0	32 11.5
41 8.9	79 4.6	49 7.4	37 10.0	54 6.8	41 8.9		45 8.1	51 7.2
9.4	8.0	5.8	6.6	7.4	6.3	Sales/Working Capital	8.5	8.4
19.6	37.3	15.0	17.0	15.8	10.2		19.6	17.9
-34.5	-27.0	39.4	99.6	47.9	NM		-175.0	227.0
	12.7	18.1	14.4	89.5	49.2	EBIT/Interest	8.7	8.6
	(22) 4.6	(71) 6.2	(71) 5.6	6.0	(12) 8.5		(194) 3.1	(189) 2.8
	2.1	1.8	2.0	2.3	6.0		1.3	1.1
		3.3	8.6			Net Profit + Depr., Dep., Amort./Cur. Mat. L/T/D	11.2	8.8
		(11) 1.5	(31) 3.3				(68) 3.3	(63) 4.4
		.8	2.0				1.4	1.5
.0	.3	.2	.7	.6	.4	Fixed/Worth	.4	.5
.2	1.1	.6	1.1	1.9	.9		1.2	1.2
8.0	4.9	2.0	1.8	NM	3.9		3.3	3.3
.5	.9	.7	1.0	1.0	.5	Debt/Worth	.9	1.0
7.8	2.1	1.4	1.8	3.2	1.5		2.3	2.8
-5.3	17.2	7.1	3.6	NM	8.4		9.4	9.7
	119.0	61.6	50.9	41.1	45.8	% Profit Before Taxes/Tangible Net Worth	45.0	51.3
	(23) 23.4	(67) 28.9	(69) 27.9	(11) 25.2	(12) 24.1		(180) 21.9	(166) 29.4
	4.9	7.2	11.7	11.3	13.4		8.0	7.9
120.0	16.9	23.2	16.5	23.2	16.4	% Profit Before Taxes/Total Assets	16.1	16.4
40.8	8.2	8.8	8.8	9.7	10.8		6.6	7.1
9.6	2.9	2.0	3.1	2.3	6.3		1.0	.2
433.5	38.1	46.4	13.3	12.3	11.8	Sales/Net Fixed Assets	22.6	19.8
32.8	10.0	12.9	6.9	6.7	6.9		7.8	9.3
18.1	5.5	4.9	3.7	3.2	3.3		4.7	4.8
9.2	4.2	3.8	3.2	2.6	3.0	Sales/Total Assets	3.7	3.4
4.9	2.6	2.6	2.2	2.0	2.1		2.4	2.5
2.9	1.9	1.7	1.5	1.7	1.1		1.7	1.7
	1.2	.9	1.0	1.1	.8	% Depr., Dep., Amort./Sales	1.0	.9
	(19) 3.0	(65) 2.0	(73) 2.0	1.8	(11) 2.1		(182) 1.9	(171) 1.8
	4.0	4.1	3.4	3.5	5.9		3.2	3.3
	1.8	1.5	.5			% Officers', Directors', Owners' Comp/Sales	1.6	1.6
	(16) 2.8	(30) 3.3	(12) 1.0				(57) 2.7	(57) 2.6
	6.5	6.0	5.7				5.6	5.9
14398M	95517M	1109744M	4447401M	2186906M	4711140M	Net Sales ($)	9402031M	10977839M
2476M	34137M	374914M	1805252M	972366M	2091194M	Total Assets ($)	3858784M	4560094M

M = $ thousand   MM = $ million
See Pages 9 through 22 for Explanation of Ratios and Data

Comparative Historical Data / Current Data Sorted by Sales

Current Data grouping: 52 (4/1-9/30/10) covers 0-1MM / 1-3MM columns; 168 (10/1/10-3/31/11) covers 3-5MM through 25MM & OVER columns.

4/1/08-3/31/09 ALL	4/1/09-3/31/10 ALL	4/1/10-3/31/11 ALL		0-1MM	1-3MM	3-5MM	5-10MM	10-25MM	25MM & OVER
			Type of Statement						
56	56	40	Unqualified					6	34
44	37	38	Reviewed		1	4		16	17
29	20	19	Compiled		4	5	4	5	1
23	34	33	Tax Returns	4	6	12	6	5	
93	97	90	Other	4	11	5	7	18	45
245	244	220	**NUMBER OF STATEMENTS**	8	21	23	21	50	97
%	%	%	**ASSETS**	%	%	%	%	%	%
7.6	7.2	8.4	Cash & Equivalents		11.3	11.3	12.4	5.5	6.7
22.3	21.3	22.7	Trade Receivables (net)		18.6	24.8	23.1	24.8	22.1
24.6	26.6	25.2	Inventory		17.7	16.7	21.8	30.9	27.1
2.5	2.5	2.3	All Other Current		.6	2.2	3.2	3.0	2.3
57.0	57.7	58.6	Total Current		48.3	55.0	60.4	64.2	58.3
31.9	30.8	31.6	Fixed Assets (net)		31.0	38.5	31.2	29.3	32.3
4.7	5.4	5.7	Intangibles (net)		15.5	1.2	1.5	4.3	5.6
6.4	6.1	4.2	All Other Non-Current		5.2	5.2	6.8	2.2	3.9
100.0	100.0	100.0	Total		100.0	100.0	100.0	100.0	100.0
			LIABILITIES						
12.1	10.2	11.4	Notes Payable-Short Term		10.2	8.1	6.6	13.4	11.7
4.0	4.3	3.6	Cur. Mat.-L.T.D.		5.5	2.9	3.9	3.0	3.3
17.6	15.9	17.3	Trade Payables		21.8	18.8	19.4	17.1	15.8
.3	.4	.3	Income Taxes Payable		.5	.2	.3	.6	.2
7.9	9.5	8.4	All Other Current		7.8	7.7	6.3	11.0	7.6
41.9	40.4	41.1	Total Current		45.9	37.7	36.5	45.2	38.6
19.5	19.8	15.8	Long-Term Debt		19.4	19.8	12.8	15.0	15.2
.4	.6	.6	Deferred Taxes		.6	.5	.4	.7	.6
8.7	8.0	7.7	All Other Non-Current		20.0	3.3	13.4	5.0	4.6
29.5	31.3	34.8	Net Worth		14.2	38.7	36.9	34.1	41.0
100.0	100.0	100.0	Total Liabilities & Net Worth		100.0	100.0	100.0	100.0	100.0
			INCOME DATA						
100.0	100.0	100.0	Net Sales		100.0	100.0	100.0	100.0	100.0
28.5	30.7	30.0	Gross Profit		44.8	38.7	36.3	26.7	23.4
23.7	24.5	24.4	Operating Expenses		43.2	32.3	32.7	21.6	16.7
4.8	6.1	5.6	Operating Profit		1.6	6.4	3.6	5.1	6.7
1.2	.8	1.0	All Other Expenses (net)		1.5	.6	.8	.9	1.1
3.6	5.3	4.6	Profit Before Taxes		.1	5.9	2.8	4.2	5.6
			RATIOS						
2.1	2.2	2.2	Current		2.5	3.0	3.9	1.9	2.2
1.4	1.5	1.4			1.0	1.2	1.5	1.4	1.5
1.1	1.1	1.1			.6	.6	1.0	1.1	1.1
1.3	1.2	1.3	Quick		1.5	1.5	2.6	1.2	1.1
.7	.7	.7			.6	1.0	.8	.7	.7
.4	.4	.4			.3	.4	.5	.3	.5
20 18.3	20 18.1	22 16.9	Sales/Receivables		15 23.9	17 21.6	21 17.6	24 15.5	22 16.8
28 12.9	27 13.4	31 11.9			30 12.4	35 10.5	35 10.4	33 11.1	30 12.1
37 9.8	38 9.7	42 8.6			53 6.9	50 7.2	43 8.5	45 8.1	39 9.4
23 16.0	26 13.9	23 16.2	Cost of Sales/Inventory		15 24.9	2 164.1	4 95.8	27 13.6	29 12.8
42 8.6	46 8.0	47 7.8			44 8.2	17 21.0	50 7.3	54 6.8	49 7.4
78 4.7	78 4.7	80 4.5			82 4.5	58 6.3	85 4.3	89 4.1	73 5.0
15 24.1	15 24.2	15 23.6	Cost of Sales/Payables		20 18.5	15 25.0	14 26.0	14 25.8	17 21.3
27 13.6	27 13.5	28 12.9			49 7.5	27 13.7	32 11.4	24 15.5	27 13.6
40 9.2	43 8.5	48 7.6			81 4.5	77 4.7	80 4.6	43 8.6	36 10.2
8.3	7.0	6.7	Sales/Working Capital		8.1	4.6	4.1	8.2	7.2
18.2	18.0	15.8			496.8	25.3	7.0	15.1	15.7
127.1	116.0	103.0			-11.6	-33.5	NM	36.9	45.9
9.8	14.7	15.0	EBIT/Interest		10.9	39.4	25.8	12.6	17.5
(224) 3.6	(224) 5.1	(198) 6.0			(17) 3.6	(21) 9.5	(18) 3.9	(48) 5.0	(89) 6.9
1.1	2.2	2.2			-1.0	2.5	.5	1.7	3.1
8.1	10.9	8.4	Net Profit + Depr., Dep., Amort./Cur. Mat. L/T/D					3.2	8.9
(71) 3.0	(80) 4.5	(59) 3.1						(10) 1.9	(42) 3.5
1.3	2.2	1.9						1.2	2.3
.5	.4	.4	Fixed/Worth		.5	.1	.2	.4	.5
1.1	.9	.9			2.0	1.0	.5	.9	.9
3.2	3.2	2.2			-1.7	3.6	1.7	2.5	1.8
.9	.9	.8	Debt/Worth		1.2	.5	.4	1.0	.8
2.3	2.1	1.8			11.3	1.0	.9	1.9	1.6
7.6	7.6	6.1			-5.9	5.9	6.3	6.0	3.5
53.6	60.0	57.7	% Profit Before Taxes/Tangible Net Worth		135.7	125.4	22.5	64.6	50.4
(208) 22.7	(207) 29.5	(190) 28.8			(13) 25.5	(21) 29.7	(17) 10.3	(45) 40.7	(89) 28.6
7.1	11.5	10.2			-24.0	10.3	-5.7	7.8	15.1
15.6	18.4	20.4	% Profit Before Taxes/Total Assets		18.1	23.5	11.7	23.8	20.1
6.4	9.8	9.2			7.9	9.6	4.2	8.7	10.5
.7	3.4	2.9			-7.8	4.8	-1.5	1.8	4.6
24.9	25.5	21.8	Sales/Net Fixed Assets		29.9	33.5	27.7	28.3	15.0
10.2	10.2	9.1			8.3	9.4	8.2	11.6	8.7
4.6	4.9	4.7			5.3	4.0	4.2	4.5	4.8
3.8	3.9	3.6	Sales/Total Assets		3.9	4.3	3.2	3.8	3.5
2.6	2.6	2.4			2.0	2.3	2.3	2.5	2.4
1.8	1.7	1.7			1.2	1.5	1.5	1.6	1.8
.8	.9	1.0	% Depr., Dep., Amort./Sales		2.1	1.2	1.3	1.2	.9
(204) 1.7	(206) 1.5	(186) 2.0			(14) 3.4	(20) 2.4	(17) 2.7	(42) 2.0	(92) 1.7
2.9	2.8	3.8			4.5	5.8	4.4	4.1	3.0
1.2	1.4	1.3	% Officers', Directors' Owners' Comp/Sales		1.6	3.0			1.3	.4
(61) 2.3	(77) 2.7	(64) 2.8			(15)	(11) 5.8		(14) 2.9	(13) 1.9
4.6	5.8	6.6			6.7	7.9		5.5	1.9
16767927M	15563089M	12565106M	Net Sales ($)	5527M	43916M	95740M	151589M	818936M	11449398M
7383356M	6499468M	5280339M	Total Assets ($)	5920M	29663M	43401M	80138M	400375M	4720842M

M = $ thousand   MM = $ million
See Pages 9 through 22 for Explanation of Ratios and Data

Current Data Sorted by Assets

Comparative Historical Data

	0-500M	500M-2MM	2-10MM	10-50MM	50-100MM	100-250MM	Type of Statement	4/1/06-3/31/07 ALL	4/1/07-3/31/08 ALL
				1	9	14	Unqualified	40	25
		1	1	4			Reviewed	11	8
		1	3	2			Compiled	2	1
		2	3	1			Tax Returns	5	
	1	2	4	15	6	6	Other	35	42
		15 (4/1-9/30/10)		74 (10/1/10-3/31/11)					
NUMBER OF STATEMENTS	1	6	12	35	15	20		93	76
	%	%	%	%	%	%	**ASSETS**	%	%
			8.6	11.9	7.9	6.3	Cash & Equivalents	6.8	7.8
			16.4	18.1	11.0	14.1	Trade Receivables (net)	18.8	18.4
			13.4	14.8	7.3	12.9	Inventory	16.3	15.2
			4.3	2.0	4.1	5.0	All Other Current	2.3	2.8
			42.7	46.8	30.4	38.3	Total Current	44.2	44.3
			36.4	34.3	33.2	30.9	Fixed Assets (net)	35.1	32.1
			9.7	11.5	24.9	21.5	Intangibles (net)	10.8	14.4
			11.3	7.4	11.5	9.3	All Other Non-Current	9.9	9.3
			100.0	100.0	100.0	100.0	Total	100.0	100.0
							LIABILITIES		
			3.1	1.2	3.8	1.2	Notes Payable-Short Term	7.9	5.7
			4.3	4.2	2.5	1.9	Cur. Mat.-L.T.D.	2.6	2.3
			14.6	16.1	6.2	9.6	Trade Payables	16.8	13.7
			.2	.0	.0	.5	Income Taxes Payable	.1	.1
			13.5	8.2	15.1	10.3	All Other Current	8.3	6.6
			35.8	29.8	27.5	23.5	Total Current	35.7	28.4
			21.3	16.1	14.5	20.4	Long-Term Debt	24.8	22.2
			.0	1.2	1.5	1.8	Deferred Taxes	.9	1.3
			4.1	3.9	4.7	4.5	All Other Non-Current	5.8	5.9
			38.9	49.1	51.8	49.7	Net Worth	32.8	42.3
			100.0	100.0	100.0	100.0	Total Liabilities & Net Worth	100.0	100.0
							INCOME DATA		
			100.0	100.0	100.0	100.0	Net Sales	100.0	100.0
			39.1	25.5	39.7	34.1	Gross Profit	32.5	35.4
			33.5	22.8	30.9	22.7	Operating Expenses	29.6	29.3
			5.6	2.6	8.8	11.4	Operating Profit	3.0	6.1
			.7	.6	3.5	.2	All Other Expenses (net)	1.0	1.2
			4.8	2.1	5.3	11.2	Profit Before Taxes	2.0	4.9
							RATIOS		
			1.6	3.2	2.8	2.0		2.2	2.6
			1.3	1.9	1.8	1.4	Current	1.3	1.5
			.7	1.2	.7	1.1		.9	1.1
			.9	1.9	2.0	1.4		1.4	1.5
			.7	1.2	1.0	.7	Quick	.8	1.0
			.4	.5	.5	.3		.4	.6
		19 18.7	20 18.6	20 18.6	16 22.5		Sales/Receivables	24 15.4	23 15.8
		31 11.8	26 14.0	27 13.8	26 13.9			28 13.2	28 13.1
		40 9.0	36 10.1	30 12.2	33 11.1			37 9.8	35 10.6
		18 20.3	18 20.1	17 22.0	20 18.6		Cost of Sales/Inventory	18 20.0	19 19.2
		39 9.4	28 12.8	21 17.4	27 13.8			30 12.1	28 13.2
		60 6.1	46 8.0	39 9.3	65 5.6			48 7.6	46 7.9
		20 17.9	19 19.7	14 26.5	13 27.5		Cost of Sales/Payables	16 23.2	15 25.0
		31 11.9	26 14.1	23 15.9	23 15.6			27 13.7	30 12.1
		56 6.5	38 9.7	44 8.4	43 8.4			49 7.4	50 7.3
		6.6	5.6	4.5	7.6		Sales/Working Capital	11.1	6.7
		28.9	11.2	16.0	17.5			24.3	15.1
		-17.5	65.3	-25.2	59.9			-104.4	63.7
		19.1	15.2	15.5	81.9		EBIT/Interest	10.8	14.8
		(10) 3.3	(30) 3.8	(14) 3.7	(19) 10.7			(87) 3.1	(70) 4.5
		1.6	1.3	1.7	4.8			.8	1.4
			6.5				Net Profit + Depr., Dep., Amort./Cur. Mat. L/T/D	12.6	13.5
			(11) 3.5					(20) 4.6	(17) 2.1
			.3					1.7	1.2
		.7	.4	.9	.7	Fixed/Worth	.6	.4
		1.0	.8	1.2	.9		1.4	1.0
		NM	3.0	1.7	NM		-33.1	6.7
		.7	.4	.7	.8	Debt/Worth	.6	.6
		1.1	.9	1.8	1.2		2.4	1.5
		NM	5.1	3.5	NM		-44.5	21.0
			19.6	28.7	69.6	% Profit Before Taxes/Tangible Net Worth	33.9	48.4
			(29) 6.1	(12) 17.2	(15) 23.8		(66) 19.1	(59) 27.2
			.4	2.7	11.1		2.9	8.1
		14.4	10.4	11.8	19.3	% Profit Before Taxes/Total Assets	13.7	13.3
		4.5	4.4	5.0	8.9		6.2	7.3
		2.2	.4	2.9	3.9		-.4	1.0
		7.7	12.4	19.2	9.6	Sales/Net Fixed Assets	14.8	14.7
		5.7	5.9	6.5	6.7		7.3	8.1
		3.6	4.5	3.0	4.6		4.0	4.7
		2.4	3.7	1.9	2.7	Sales/Total Assets	3.2	3.0
		1.8	2.1	1.5	1.9		2.2	2.0
		1.3	1.4	.5	1.1		1.5	1.4
		2.0	1.8	2.2	1.6	% Depr., Dep., Amort./Sales	1.6	1.5
		(11) 2.9	(32) 3.1	(13) 2.8	(16) 2.3		(73) 3.0	(60) 2.7
		6.5	4.3	5.3	3.2		4.5	4.6
						% Officers', Directors' Owners' Comp/Sales	1.0	
							(12) 2.0	
							5.0	
Net Sales ($)	406M	26427M	109950M	2026339M	1583751M	5812074M		8531733M	8855232M
Total Assets ($)	104M	8331M	60655M	807256M	1062203M	2989352M		4001980M	4300349M

Comparative Historical Data   Current Data Sorted by Sales

			Type of Statement	0-1MM	1-3MM	3-5MM	5-10MM	10-25MM	25MM & OVER
41	36	37	Unqualified					1	36
8	8	6	Reviewed				2	1	3
4	8	6	Compiled				2	2	2
6	5	6	Tax Returns				2		1
35	41	34	Other	1	3		2	9	21
4/1/08-3/31/09	4/1/09-3/31/10	4/1/10-3/31/11			15 (4/1-9/30/10)			74 (10/1/10-3/31/11)	
ALL	ALL	ALL							
94	98	89	**NUMBER OF STATEMENTS**	1	4		9	12	63
%	%	%	**ASSETS**	%	%	%	%	%	%
7.3	8.8	9.6	Cash & Equivalents					13.1	9.0
16.1	16.4	16.1	Trade Receivables (net)					15.1	16.0
15.8	15.4	13.4	Inventory					12.3	12.8
3.3	2.7	3.8	All Other Current					.9	3.6
42.5	43.2	42.8	Total Current					41.4	41.3
33.4	31.8	32.7	Fixed Assets (net)					44.4	31.7
13.1	14.0	15.3	Intangibles (net)					7.0	18.1
10.9	10.9	9.2	All Other Non-Current					7.3	8.8
100.0	100.0	100.0	Total					100.0	100.0
			LIABILITIES						
6.2	4.6	2.3	Notes Payable-Short Term					3.7	1.5
3.5	4.4	3.7	Cur. Mat.-L.T.D.					2.8	3.2
13.2	14.2	12.7	Trade Payables					10.0	12.7
.3	.2	.2	Income Taxes Payable					.0	.2
10.0	9.6	10.3	All Other Current					13.7	9.7
33.1	33.0	29.2	Total Current					30.1	27.4
21.1	18.1	16.9	Long-Term Debt					18.3	17.1
1.0	1.1	1.1	Deferred Taxes					.2	1.5
6.9	6.0	4.0	All Other Non-Current					1.5	4.7
38.0	41.8	48.8	Net Worth					49.9	49.3
100.0	100.0	100.0	Total Liabilties & Net Worth					100.0	100.0
			INCOME DATA						
100.0	100.0	100.0	Net Sales					100.0	100.0
33.3	29.4	32.5	Gross Profit					31.5	30.9
29.1	24.3	26.4	Operating Expenses					33.8	22.9
4.2	5.1	6.1	Operating Profit					-2.3	8.0
.8	.8	.8	All Other Expenses (net)					1.5	1.0
3.4	4.4	5.3	Profit Before Taxes					-3.8	7.0

(Columns 0-1MM through 5-10MM in the Assets/Liabilities/Income sections are marked **DATA NOT AVAILABLE**.)

RATIOS

			Ratio	10-25MM	25MM & OVER
2.4	2.7	2.8		3.5	2.7
1.4	1.5	1.6	Current	1.7	1.6
.9	.9	1.1		1.2	1.1
1.4	1.8	1.7		2.6	1.6
.8	(97) 1.0	.9	Quick	1.4	1.0
.4	.4	.5		.7	.5
20 18.0 / **19** 19.5 / **19** 19.5				**24** 15.0	**17** 22.1
26 14.0 / **25** 14.3 / **27** 13.6			Sales/Receivables	**35** 10.4	**26** 14.2
32 11.3 / **30** 12.0 / **34** 10.9				**44** 8.3	**31** 11.7
20 18.2 / **18** 20.8 / **19** 19.6				**18** 20.3	**18** 20.1
28 12.9 / **26** 14.0 / **27** 13.3			Cost of Sales/Inventory	**60** 6.1	**26** 13.8
50 7.4 / **44** 8.3 / **46** 8.0				**65** 5.6	**39** 9.3
14 25.5 / **13** 27.8 / **17** 21.5				**20** 17.9	**17** 21.7
23 15.9 / **24** 15.2 / **26** 14.1			Cost of Sales/Payables	**26** 13.9	**25** 14.4
42 8.7 / **37** 9.9 / **41** 8.9				**34** 10.9	**40** 9.2
7.7	7.9	5.7		3.1	6.7
22.8	17.6	16.0	Sales/Working Capital	12.4	16.0
-38.8	-122.0	93.8		59.4	65.3
17.4	22.9	18.6		3.9	21.8
(83) 3.6	(87) 5.1	(77) 5.8	EBIT/Interest	(10) .8	(58) 6.7
1.0	1.4	2.0		-2.5	2.5
9.0	10.8	9.7			11.3
(28) 2.9	(28) 3.8	(24) 3.3	Net Profit + Depr., Dep., Amort./Cur. Mat. L/T/D		(20) 3.7
1.3	1.6	.8			1.9
.4	.5	.5		.7	.5
1.3	1.0	.9	Fixed/Worth	.9	.9
11.2	16.3	2.2		1.5	3.0
.7	.5	.6		.5	.6
2.2	1.3	1.0	Debt/Worth	.7	1.1
18.5	91.0	4.6		2.2	5.1
45.6	41.8	36.9		5.4	40.6
(72) 17.3	(75) 19.5	(72) 16.0	% Profit Before Taxes/Tangible Net Worth	(10) .3	(50) 17.3
1.1	4.7	3.2		-19.1	6.2
14.6	14.0	11.9		3.3	12.0
5.5	6.7	5.0	% Profit Before Taxes/Total Assets	.2	6.0
-.1	1.1	2.0		-6.3	3.1
12.4	13.5	12.3		5.7	12.2
7.5	7.8	6.6	Sales/Net Fixed Assets	4.3	6.8
4.7	5.2	4.5		1.3	4.9
3.0	3.0	2.9		2.4	2.8
2.2	2.2	1.9	Sales/Total Assets	1.6	1.9
1.4	1.6	1.3		.7	1.4
1.7	1.8	1.9		2.7	1.7
(82) 2.8	(82) 2.9	(77) 2.7	% Depr., Dep., Amort./Sales	(10) 3.9	(56) 2.7
4.3	4.1	3.9		9.2	3.8
1.1	.8	.8			.8
(13) 2.4	(15) .9	(14) 2.1	% Officers', Directors' Owners' Comp/Sales		(10) 1.1
8.1	2.2	5.7			11.0

				0-1MM	1-3MM	3-5MM	5-10MM	10-25MM	25MM & OVER
8086978M	9022397M	9558947M	Net Sales ($)	406M	9166M		67437M	173994M	9307944M
4004243M	4448167M	4927901M	Total Assets ($)	104M	6281M		37614M	183803M	4700099M

M = $ thousand   MM = $ million
See Pages 9 through 22 for Explanation of Ratios and Data

Current Data Sorted by Assets   Comparative Historical Data

0-500M	500M-2MM	2-10MM	10-50MM	50-100MM	100-250MM	Type of Statement	4/1/06-3/31/07 ALL	4/1/07-3/31/08 ALL
		4	3	1	3	Unqualified	9	9
	1	4	2			Reviewed	10	9
1	1	4	2		1	Compiled	6	4
1	2	2				Tax Returns	2	3
1	2	7		1	2	Other	20	13
							3 (4/1-9/30/10)	36 (10/1/10-3/31/11)
3	6	17	6	2	5	**NUMBER OF STATEMENTS**	47	38
%	%	%	%	%	%	**ASSETS**	%	%
		4.1				Cash & Equivalents	3.9	7.4
		15.2				Trade Receivables (net)	17.6	16.9
		13.1				Inventory	15.8	18.3
		2.3				All Other Current	2.8	3.1
		34.6				Total Current	40.1	45.8
		51.1				Fixed Assets (net)	45.1	44.1
		7.2				Intangibles (net)	9.8	5.3
		7.1				All Other Non-Current	5.0	4.8
		100.0				Total	100.0	100.0
						LIABILITIES		
		12.0				Notes Payable-Short Term	9.9	8.9
		3.6				Cur. Mat.-L.T.D.	6.5	8.8
		12.1				Trade Payables	11.0	12.8
		.0				Income Taxes Payable	.2	.7
		7.4				All Other Current	10.2	9.1
		35.0				Total Current	37.8	40.2
		24.1				Long-Term Debt	33.8	27.9
		1.3				Deferred Taxes	.4	.5
		30.9				All Other Non-Current	8.2	7.4
		8.6				Net Worth	19.9	24.1
		100.0				Total Liabilties & Net Worth	100.0	100.0
						INCOME DATA		
		100.0				Net Sales	100.0	100.0
		41.0				Gross Profit	39.0	38.5
		39.5				Operating Expenses	33.8	31.4
		1.5				Operating Profit	5.1	7.1
		1.3				All Other Expenses (net)	2.5	2.1
		.1				Profit Before Taxes	2.6	5.0
						RATIOS		
		1.7				Current	1.8	2.5
		1.1					1.2	1.1
		.6					.9	.6
		.9				Quick	1.0	1.1
		.6					.7	.6
		.3					.4	.4
		23 16.2				Sales/Receivables	21 17.7	20 18.1
		27 13.6					32 11.5	29 12.4
		35 10.5					40 9.1	35 10.4
		21 17.1				Cost of Sales/Inventory	16 22.2	25 14.9
		31 11.9					32 11.5	44 8.3
		49 7.4					61 5.9	58 6.3
		18 19.8				Cost of Sales/Payables	14 26.4	14 25.8
		31 11.7					26 14.0	30 12.2
		60 6.1					43 8.5	50 7.3
		12.3				Sales/Working Capital	9.9	9.7
		91.6					32.0	46.0
		-11.3					-26.0	-16.1
		19.6				EBIT/Interest	5.7	4.4
		2.6					(43) 1.9	(34) 1.7
		-.4					1.0	.4
						Net Profit + Depr., Dep., Amort./Cur. Mat. L/T/D	2.7	2.4
							(10) 1.2	(10) 1.4
							.3	.7
		.9				Fixed/Worth	1.1	.6
		2.3					2.7	1.8
		NM					-3.3	-4.9
		1.2				Debt/Worth	1.4	.6
		2.2					5.3	2.2
		NM					-9.0	-8.2
		34.4				% Profit Before Taxes/Tangible Net Worth	62.2	31.0
	(13)	10.4					(30) 25.1	(27) 16.0
		-44.4					8.7	7.6
		10.0				% Profit Before Taxes/Total Assets	13.5	11.6
		4.4					3.9	3.5
		-6.4					.2	-2.4
		5.0				Sales/Net Fixed Assets	10.1	9.4
		2.9					3.9	4.8
		2.1					2.2	2.6
		2.2				Sales/Total Assets	2.7	3.3
		1.6					1.9	2.2
		1.2					1.0	1.0
		3.3				% Depr., Dep., Amort./Sales	1.9	1.7
	(15)	5.3					(41) 4.8	(32) 5.1
		7.9					7.6	7.2
						% Officers', Directors' Owners' Comp/Sales	.6	
							(10) 2.2	
							3.6	
1560M	17647M	185231M	297920M	86852M	966359M	Net Sales ($)	1717103M	1458772M
1165M	5640M	100475M	178748M	118064M	805774M	Total Assets ($)	1093823M	945395M

M = $ thousand   MM = $ million
See Pages 9 through 22 for Explanation of Ratios and Data

Comparative Historical Data | Current Data Sorted by Sales

Type of Statement

4/1/08-3/31/09 ALL	4/1/09-3/31/10 ALL	4/1/10-3/31/11 ALL	Type of Statement	0-1MM	1-3MM	3-5MM	5-10MM	10-25MM	25MM & OVER
9	14	7	Unqualified					2	5
7	4	7	Reviewed			1	3	1	2
8	5	7	Compiled	1	1		2	2	1
7	9	5	Tax Returns	1	1		1	1	1
14	14	13	Other	1	2	1	3	3	3
				3 (4/1-9/30/10)			36 (10/1/10-3/31/11)		
45	46	39	NUMBER OF STATEMENTS	3	4	2	9	10	11

%	%	%	ASSETS	%	%	%	%	%	%
5.9	6.4	5.4	Cash & Equivalents					6.1	7.7
15.9	17.5	14.2	Trade Receivables (net)					14.8	17.1
14.9	15.0	15.0	Inventory					12.7	12.1
1.3	2.4	2.5	All Other Current					1.9	2.3
38.0	41.3	37.2	Total Current					35.5	39.2
49.0	44.7	50.5	Fixed Assets (net)					46.6	45.2
7.6	10.6	7.9	Intangibles (net)					6.6	13.5
5.4	3.4	4.5	All Other Non-Current					11.3	2.2
100.0	100.0	100.0	Total					100.0	100.0
			LIABILITIES						
6.8	7.5	6.0	Notes Payable-Short Term					9.0	3.3
6.8	5.5	4.3	Cur. Mat.-L.T.D.					3.8	4.1
10.0	10.5	10.0	Trade Payables					11.9	8.8
.1	.1	.0	Income Taxes Payable					.0	.0
15.9	14.3	7.1	All Other Current					5.9	10.4
39.6	37.8	27.4	Total Current					30.6	26.6
32.4	27.5	21.9	Long-Term Debt					20.1	18.8
.4	.6	1.2	Deferred Taxes					.3	1.5
11.1	14.6	19.9	All Other Non-Current					18.3	43.2
16.5	19.6	29.6	Net Worth					30.7	9.8
100.0	100.0	100.0	Total Liabilities & Net Worth					100.0	100.0
			INCOME DATA						
100.0	100.0	100.0	Net Sales					100.0	100.0
40.9	40.9	42.0	Gross Profit					37.5	30.2
36.1	34.8	38.2	Operating Expenses					35.4	22.5
4.9	6.1	3.8	Operating Profit					2.1	7.8
2.4	2.9	2.5	All Other Expenses (net)					3.3	1.8
2.5	3.2	1.3	Profit Before Taxes					-1.2	6.0

RATIOS

4/1/08-3/31/09	4/1/09-3/31/10	4/1/10-3/31/11	Ratio	0-1MM	1-3MM	3-5MM	5-10MM	10-25MM	25MM & OVER
2.1	2.2	2.5	Current					2.6	2.4
1.2	1.4	1.4						1.2	1.7
.6	.6	.9						.7	1.1
1.1	1.2	1.3	Quick					1.1	1.7
.6	.8	.9						.7	.9
.4	.4	.4						.5	.4
23 16.2	23 15.6	21 17.4	Sales/Receivables					23 15.8	27 13.3
27 13.7	29 12.6	27 13.3						27 13.8	36 10.2
39 9.3	39 9.4	39 9.3						37 9.9	46 7.9
21 17.7	23 15.6	26 13.8	Cost of Sales/Inventory					19 19.1	27 13.5
40 9.2	38 9.5	36 10.1						34 10.7	31 11.8
55 6.6	57 6.4	66 5.6						58 6.3	69 5.3
14 26.7	12 30.3	11 34.8	Cost of Sales/Payables					21 17.5	13 28.4
31 11.6	28 13.1	25 14.8						28 12.9	27 13.1
43 8.6	43 8.5	48 7.6						54 6.8	42 8.7
9.7	7.4	7.2	Sales/Working Capital					5.9	7.2
30.1	17.1	21.4						53.4	8.8
-11.4	-10.7	-30.4						-13.6	25.2
3.9	7.6	4.7	EBIT/Interest					35.0	
(43) 2.2	(42) 2.7	(35) 2.0						2.0	
-.2	1.4	-.9						-1.8	
	2.3		Net Profit + Depr., Dep., Amort./Cur. Mat. L/T/D						
	(10) 2.0								
	1.8								
1.1	1.0	.9	Fixed/Worth					.7	1.0
3.9	2.8	1.6						1.7	1.6
-9.5	-4.9	4.6						NM	-5.7
1.8	1.4	1.0	Debt/Worth					.5	1.0
4.3	3.3	1.9						2.3	1.5
-23.1	-9.6	4.8						NM	-14.0
39.3	52.8	28.8	% Profit Before Taxes/Tangible Net Worth						
(32) 15.3	(31) 29.5	(32) 8.6							
-11.7	5.8	-8.6							
8.2	10.2	9.0	% Profit Before Taxes/Total Assets					11.3	31.6
3.2	5.6	3.4						2.5	2.2
-4.4	-.1	-5.7						-8.6	1.3
7.6	7.6	6.0	Sales/Net Fixed Assets					10.3	7.4
3.1	3.6	2.9						3.6	4.2
1.3	1.9	1.9						1.9	1.2
2.4	2.4	2.3	Sales/Total Assets					2.6	2.8
1.4	1.5	1.6						1.4	1.5
.9	1.1	1.1						1.1	.7
3.3	3.0	3.1	% Depr., Dep., Amort./Sales						
(40) 5.7	(37) 6.2	(32) 5.5							
9.3	8.9	8.5							
			% Officers', Directors' Owners' Comp/Sales						
1596643M	1769423M	1555569M	Net Sales ($)	1560M	6774M	6576M	61875M	155388M	1323396M
1119287M	1369300M	1209866M	Total Assets ($)	1165M	6934M	3135M	39561M	147299M	1011772M

M = $ thousand   MM = $ million
See Pages 9 through 22 for Explanation of Ratios and Data

Current Data Sorted by Assets   Comparative Historical Data

0-500M	500M-2MM	2-10MM	10-50MM	50-100MM	100-250MM	Type of Statement	4/1/06-3/31/07 ALL	4/1/07-3/31/08 ALL
	1	3	6	1	1	Unqualified	11	12
1	3	4	3			Reviewed	6	4
9	6	3	1			Compiled	5	4
1	7	3	1			Tax Returns	2	7
		6	10	4	7	Other	23	19
	7 (4/1-9/30/10)		74 (10/1/10-3/31/11)					
11	**17**	**19**	**21**	**5**	**8**	**NUMBER OF STATEMENTS**	**47**	**46**
%	%	%	%	%	%	**ASSETS**	%	%
9.2	13.8	11.6	8.3			Cash & Equivalents	7.8	9.5
8.1	8.7	9.9	7.6			Trade Receivables (net)	8.3	9.6
27.8	17.5	18.5	11.7			Inventory	13.9	14.2
.2	.9	2.3	2.2			All Other Current	5.6	4.1
45.3	41.0	42.3	29.8			Total Current	35.6	37.4
49.1	52.7	47.3	64.8			Fixed Assets (net)	50.0	51.6
2.0	4.1	6.9	1.6			Intangibles (net)	8.3	6.2
3.7	2.2	3.5	3.8			All Other Non-Current	6.1	4.7
100.0	100.0	100.0	100.0			Total	100.0	100.0
						LIABILITIES		
22.4	6.3	2.5	1.2			Notes Payable-Short Term	4.4	5.0
1.5	2.0	3.6	3.4			Cur. Mat.-L.T.D.	3.2	5.0
9.0	12.5	10.9	7.1			Trade Payables	10.9	12.2
.0	.0	.0	.0			Income Taxes Payable	.1	.2
10.5	4.0	6.7	6.0			All Other Current	9.5	13.5
43.4	24.8	23.8	17.6			Total Current	28.0	35.9
64.4	47.1	32.1	29.8			Long-Term Debt	31.1	32.8
.0	.0	1.7	1.6			Deferred Taxes	1.7	1.0
18.3	8.4	2.2	4.0			All Other Non-Current	3.0	3.1
-26.1	19.7	40.1	47.0			Net Worth	36.3	27.2
100.0	100.0	100.0	100.0			Total Liabilities & Net Worth	100.0	100.0
						INCOME DATA		
100.0	100.0	100.0	100.0			Net Sales	100.0	100.0
57.3	55.6	46.9	37.7			Gross Profit	41.0	39.9
56.0	52.5	31.7	23.0			Operating Expenses	33.7	31.2
1.3	3.2	15.2	14.6			Operating Profit	7.3	8.6
-.6	-.7	1.4	1.6			All Other Expenses (net)	1.5	1.5
2.0	3.9	13.8	13.1			Profit Before Taxes	5.8	7.1
						RATIOS		
2.3	2.3	2.3	2.2				2.0	1.7
1.0	1.8	2.1	1.7			Current	1.1	1.1
.6	1.0	1.1	1.1				.9	.8
1.3	1.8	1.5	1.4				1.0	1.0
.3	1.1	1.0	.7			Quick	.6	.7
.1	.3	.4	.4				.3	.3
0 UND	0 UND	7 50.2	9 40.1				3 117.8	5 72.0
0 UND	10 37.5	23 16.0	19 19.3			Sales/Receivables	22 16.6	21 17.6
9 42.1	18 19.8	31 11.7	24 15.2				35 10.5	29 12.6
18 19.8	29 12.5	52 7.1	39 9.5				29 12.4	25 14.7
65 5.6	60 6.1	64 5.7	48 7.6			Cost of Sales/Inventory	47 7.8	48 7.6
175 2.1	110 3.3	105 3.5	58 6.3				79 4.6	71 5.2
0 UND	20 17.9	33 11.2	15 24.9				11 33.1	16 23.2
0 UND	46 7.9	45 8.1	24 15.3			Cost of Sales/Payables	35 10.3	34 10.6
26 13.8	68 5.4	52 7.0	34 10.6				61 6.0	53 6.8
11.0	5.5	6.2	6.5				8.5	10.9
UND	15.6	7.0	19.7			Sales/Working Capital	65.7	57.9
-11.0	NM	49.4	101.8				-159.8	-23.1
	8.6	18.7	37.9				8.8	15.2
	2.8	14.8	(20) 6.9			EBIT/Interest	(43) 3.8	(41) 5.8
	.9	4.4	4.3				1.6	1.3
						Net Profit + Depr., Dep.,	4.1	7.3
						Amort./Cur. Mat. L/T/D	(15) 3.1	(11) 3.1
							2.0	2.0
2.0	.8	.9	.9				.7	1.0
20.0	2.2	1.2	1.3			Fixed/Worth	1.6	1.7
-.3	3.9	3.6	2.7				3.3	5.0
2.0	1.1	.8	.7				.9	.9
24.0	1.9	1.3	1.1			Debt/Worth	1.5	2.4
-1.9	4.5	4.4	2.1				4.7	6.6
	77.3	105.4	62.2			% Profit Before Taxes/Tangible	51.1	66.2
	(15) 12.5	(16) 65.5	32.5			Net Worth	(41) 18.0	(36) 36.3
	-2.3	27.7	15.4				7.3	11.5
43.8	29.0	43.1	24.1			% Profit Before Taxes/Total	14.7	22.5
6.1	6.7	25.4	11.8			Assets	7.4	11.2
-11.2	-.4	5.5	5.7				1.1	2.5
28.8	11.0	7.8	2.8				8.6	9.7
10.6	3.7	4.2	1.6			Sales/Net Fixed Assets	2.7	3.5
3.7	1.8	2.3	1.3				1.7	1.6
5.9	3.0	2.6	1.6				2.5	2.3
3.3	1.8	1.9	1.2			Sales/Total Assets	1.5	1.4
2.0	1.3	1.2	.9				.9	1.0
	1.4	2.5	2.9				2.6	2.7
	(11) 3.8	(18) 3.8	(19) 4.8			% Depr., Dep., Amort./Sales	(42) 4.0	(39) 4.1
	10.9	6.7	6.9				5.2	5.8
								.4
						% Officers', Directors'		(10) 2.3
						Owners' Comp/Sales		5.6
9343M	37956M	144189M	795554M	659958M	1771090M	Net Sales ($)	1794047M	1789978M
2303M	17718M	82627M	520098M	350652M	1415434M	Total Assets ($)	1447007M	1266627M

M = $ thousand   MM = $ million
See Pages 9 through 22 for Explanation of Ratios and Data

Comparative Historical Data / Current Data Sorted by Sales

4/1/08-3/31/09 ALL	4/1/09-3/31/10 ALL	4/1/10-3/31/11 ALL	Type of Statement	0-1MM	1-3MM	3-5MM	5-10MM	10-25MM	25MM & OVER
13	16	12	Unqualified			2	1	3	6
6	9	7	Reviewed			1	3	1	2
6	6	8	Compiled		4	1	2	1	
12	7	19	Tax Returns	8	5	2	1	3	
31	36	35	Other	3	4	2	6	3	17
4/1/08-3/31/09	4/1/09-3/31/10	4/1/10-3/31/11		7 (4/1-9/30/10)			74 (10/1/10-3/31/11)		
68	74	81	**NUMBER OF STATEMENTS**	11	13	8	13	11	25
%	%	%	**ASSETS**	%	%	%	%	%	%
6.7	8.7	9.2	Cash & Equivalents	10.8	10.8		10.9	9.8	5.0
12.5	10.6	8.6	Trade Receivables (net)	4.8	10.3		9.9	9.5	8.0
16.2	16.0	16.8	Inventory	21.3	22.7		19.5	11.4	12.7
4.2	4.0	1.6	All Other Current	.7	.3		2.6	3.1	1.8
39.6	39.3	36.2	Total Current	37.5	44.1		43.0	33.9	27.6
50.9	49.1	51.6	Fixed Assets (net)	58.8	49.8		49.4	59.6	48.6
5.9	8.2	8.9	Intangibles (net)	2.8	2.0		5.6	1.5	19.8
3.5	3.4	3.3	All Other Non-Current	.9	4.1		2.1	5.0	4.0
100.0	100.0	100.0	Total	100.0	100.0		100.0	100.0	100.0
			LIABILITIES						
5.6	3.8	5.4	Notes Payable-Short Term	23.9	5.2		2.0	2.1	1.0
3.8	5.6	2.9	Cur. Mat.-L.T.D.	1.7	2.0		3.7	3.4	3.6
11.3	9.7	9.6	Trade Payables	2.2	18.0		11.5	8.9	7.8
.1	.2	.0	Income Taxes Payable	.0	.0		.0	.0	.0
12.5	10.3	6.8	All Other Current	5.1	8.4		6.5	6.9	7.8
33.2	29.5	24.7	Total Current	32.8	33.6		23.7	21.3	20.2
29.8	33.3	39.1	Long-Term Debt	70.8	56.1		31.5	30.3	31.4
1.1	.8	1.2	Deferred Taxes	.0	.0		2.0	2.7	1.5
6.4	6.3	6.8	All Other Non-Current	13.0	10.0		2.1	4.4	4.7
29.5	30.0	28.2	Net Worth	-16.6	.3		40.7	41.3	42.2
100.0	100.0	100.0	Total Liabilities & Net Worth	100.0	100.0		100.0	100.0	100.0
			INCOME DATA						
100.0	100.0	100.0	Net Sales	100.0	100.0		100.0	100.0	100.0
39.6	39.3	44.8	Gross Profit	54.5	54.4		43.9	45.9	31.5
33.4	30.3	35.3	Operating Expenses	57.3	50.6		29.2	29.7	20.6
6.2	9.0	9.5	Operating Profit	-2.8	3.9		14.7	16.2	10.9
1.5	1.3	.7	All Other Expenses (net)	.9	-1.3		1.4	1.3	1.4
4.7	7.8	8.7	Profit Before Taxes	-3.7	5.1		13.3	14.9	9.5
			RATIOS						
2.1	1.9	2.3	Current	2.3	2.1		2.4	2.3	1.9
1.1	1.4	1.5		1.1	1.0		2.1	1.7	1.0
.8	.9	.9		.7	.7		1.4	1.0	.8
1.1	1.1	1.3	Quick	1.3	1.6		1.5	1.6	.8
.5	.5	.6		.3	.5		.9	1.0	.5
.3	.3	.3		.2	.2		.6	.4	.4
9 39.7	4 82.6	7 55.7	Sales/Receivables	0 UND	0 UND		8 48.2	17 21.7	9 40.1
23 15.7	21 17.3	17 21.7		0 UND	9 42.1		24 15.5	21 17.1	20 18.2
35 10.4	30 12.2	28 13.2		10 37.5	17 21.9		30 12.2	27 13.6	29 12.7
32 11.3	24 15.3	35 10.5	Cost of Sales/Inventory	49 7.4	14 25.8		52 7.0	36 10.0	17 21.4
51 7.1	47 7.7	53 6.9		81 4.5	53 6.9		64 5.7	42 8.7	36 10.3
84 4.3	67 5.5	79 4.6		110 3.3	178 2.0		101 3.6	56 6.5	54 6.7
18 20.1	15 23.8	16 23.4	Cost of Sales/Payables	0 UND	18 20.1		31 11.8	31 11.9	15 23.7
34 10.7	25 14.6	34 10.8		0 UND	46 7.9		40 9.1	34 10.7	22 16.7
51 7.1	44 8.3	49 7.4		26 13.8	94 3.9		51 7.1	45 8.1	37 9.9
8.5	9.0	6.7	Sales/Working Capital	5.9	6.8		6.2	5.5	9.9
41.7	19.7	27.7		44.0	999.8		6.8	14.4	425.3
-27.9	-51.5	-65.3		-12.2	-24.7		30.9	139.8	-28.5
11.3	13.1	17.9	EBIT/Interest		11.0		17.1	128.4	18.5
(61) 3.0	(69) 5.5	(78) 6.6			5.4		14.5	(10) 7.9	5.4
1.3	2.4	2.1			.8		7.2	4.1	2.6
6.7	5.8	6.1	Net Profit + Depr., Dep., Amort./Cur. Mat. L/T/D						
(18) 3.5	(19) 3.2	(15) 3.4							
1.5	1.8	1.7							
.9	.9	1.0	Fixed/Worth	2.5	.6		.8	1.0	1.2
1.9	1.8	1.6		20.0	2.0		1.2	1.2	1.6
4.4	3.2	7.4		-.8	NM		3.1	4.7	-2.0
1.0	1.0	.9	Debt/Worth	2.1	1.1		1.0	.4	.9
2.1	1.7	1.6		24.0	1.9		1.4	1.0	1.3
5.4	3.6	9.7		-2.0	NM		3.6	4.9	-4.7
44.0	70.3	88.1	% Profit Before Taxes/Tangible Net Worth		143.6		91.6	84.4	60.6
(55) 18.1	(59) 37.0	(64) 36.9			(10) 43.4		(12) 56.9	(10) 35.7	(18) 24.0
3.2	11.1	10.8			-3.2		26.4	19.0	12.0
15.3	22.2	27.7	% Profit Before Taxes/Total Assets	6.1	36.9		39.9	43.1	24.1
5.4	12.8	12.8		-.2	15.7		25.4	15.6	9.8
.7	4.2	2.2		-14.4	-.5		5.8	5.4	3.0
7.3	9.0	8.2	Sales/Net Fixed Assets	6.0	22.8		6.8	5.4	7.2
3.2	3.8	3.4		3.7	8.5		4.2	2.6	2.3
1.7	2.1	1.7		.9	1.8		2.4	1.6	1.5
2.6	2.7	2.8	Sales/Total Assets	3.3	3.7		2.4	2.8	1.9
1.7	1.8	1.5		1.5	2.4		1.8	1.6	1.2
1.2	1.3	1.1		.7	1.3		1.3	1.2	.9
2.4	2.0	2.2	% Depr., Dep., Amort./Sales				3.2	1.8	2.1
(61) 4.3	(65) 3.7	(65) 4.3					(12) 4.4	2.9	(19) 5.3
6.2	7.0	7.0					6.8	5.3	6.9
1.7	.8	2.2	% Officers', Directors' Owners' Comp/Sales						
(16) 2.6	(16) 2.8	(21) 3.5							
3.6	5.2	5.6							
2628678M	4000064M	3418090M	Net Sales ($)	5631M	24793M	30547M	91281M	208426M	3057412M
1894533M	2189696M	2388832M	Total Assets ($)	4222M	16116M	20425M	57376M	146199M	2144494M

© RMA 2011

M = $ thousand   MM = $ million
See Pages 9 through 22 for Explanation of Ratios and Data

Current Data Sorted by Assets   Comparative Historical Data

Type of Statement	0-500M	500M-2MM	2-10MM	10-50MM	50-100MM	100-250MM		4/1/06-3/31/07 ALL	4/1/07-3/31/08 ALL
Unqualified	1		5	9	12	7		27	23
Reviewed		1	13	26	4	2		21	28
Compiled		2	11	4				5	4
Tax Returns	4	8	7	1		1		12	17
Other	4	16	35	28	8	9		52	63
	31 (4/1-9/30/10)			187 (10/1/10-3/31/11)					
NUMBER OF STATEMENTS	9	27	71	68	24	19		117	135
	%	%	%	%	%	%		%	%
ASSETS									
Cash & Equivalents		6.7	3.7	2.7	2.4	2.0		5.0	3.5
Trade Receivables (net)		12.1	9.1	8.3	8.6	10.2		9.0	7.4
Inventory		52.6	48.8	40.1	36.9	37.3		41.7	39.9
All Other Current		.6	1.9	2.2	2.3	2.6		2.4	2.9
Total Current		72.1	63.5	53.3	50.1	52.1		58.1	53.7
Fixed Assets (net)		21.7	32.1	38.4	43.6	33.1		35.0	38.1
Intangibles (net)		3.4	1.8	3.2	4.6	11.4		2.4	3.9
All Other Non-Current		2.8	2.6	5.1	1.7	3.4		4.5	4.3
Total		100.0	100.0	100.0	100.0	100.0		100.0	100.0
LIABILITIES									
Notes Payable-Short Term		15.3	13.3	15.5	11.0	10.0		12.1	13.4
Cur. Mat.-L.T.D.		2.9	1.6	2.0	4.8	1.5		2.4	2.6
Trade Payables		10.4	8.2	5.8	7.0	5.4		7.8	7.0
Income Taxes Payable		.1	.1	.5	.2	.1		.2	.2
All Other Current		5.0	6.0	6.4	7.0	5.3		7.1	6.6
Total Current		33.6	29.3	30.1	30.1	22.3		29.7	29.9
Long-Term Debt		25.6	23.0	22.9	16.5	21.9		19.6	23.3
Deferred Taxes		.1	.3	.7	1.3	1.2		.6	.5
All Other Non-Current		19.1	8.1	6.1	3.8	3.0		6.7	4.1
Net Worth		21.6	39.3	40.1	48.2	51.5		43.4	42.2
Total Liabilities & Net Worth		100.0	100.0	100.0	100.0	100.0		100.0	100.0
INCOME DATA									
Net Sales		100.0	100.0	100.0	100.0	100.0		100.0	100.0
Gross Profit		56.0	48.7	44.6	36.2	38.7		48.6	50.4
Operating Expenses		46.8	40.3	35.2	22.9	25.5		35.7	36.6
Operating Profit		9.2	8.4	9.4	13.3	13.2		12.9	13.8
All Other Expenses (net)		5.3	4.7	4.5	3.2	7.8		3.6	3.6
Profit Before Taxes		4.0	3.7	4.9	10.1	5.5		9.3	10.1
RATIOS									
Current		5.4	4.1	3.3	3.3	5.1		4.1	3.6
		2.6	2.3	2.1	1.7	2.9		2.2	1.9
		1.3	1.7	1.2	1.1	1.6		1.4	1.4
Quick		1.3	.8	.7	.8	.9		.9	.7
		.4	.3	.4	.4	.5		.4	.3
		.2	.2	.2	.2	.4		.2	.2
Sales/Receivables		6 / 59.3	12 / 30.6	29 / 12.5	31 / 11.9	28 / 12.9		13 / 27.9	16 / 22.9
		33 / 11.0	32 / 11.5	41 / 8.9	40 / 9.0	47 / 7.7		31 / 11.7	32 / 11.5
		63 / 5.8	46 / 8.0	62 / 5.9	48 / 7.7	67 / 5.4		51 / 7.2	49 / 7.5
Cost of Sales/Inventory		208 / 1.8	268 / 1.4	264 / 1.4	252 / 1.5	223 / 1.6		218 / 1.7	254 / 1.4
		572 / .6	491 / .7	455 / .8	366 / 1.0	403 / .9		401 / .9	384 / 1.0
		1039 / .4	855 / .4	758 / .5	524 / .7	622 / .6		697 / .5	693 / .5
Cost of Sales/Payables		1 / 460.0	15 / 24.5	21 / 17.1	18 / 19.9	21 / 17.1		15 / 24.3	16 / 23.3
		41 / 8.9	43 / 8.4	50 / 7.3	36 / 10.1	35 / 10.3		45 / 8.1	40 / 9.2
		117 / 3.1	112 / 3.3	78 / 4.7	81 / 4.5	58 / 6.3		101 / 3.6	94 / 3.9
Sales/Working Capital		1.5	1.4	1.5	1.8	1.1		1.7	1.7
		3.0	2.3	2.3	3.6	1.9		2.8	3.2
		10.1	4.6	5.5	169.6	5.4		6.2	6.9
EBIT/Interest		6.6	4.1	7.8	22.5	13.7		7.3	8.7
		(23) 2.6	(64) 1.7	(61) 2.1	5.5	(16) 3.3		(101) 3.2	(125) 3.7
		.8	.4	.6	1.5	1.7		1.3	1.4
Net Profit + Depr., Dep., Amort./Cur. Mat. L/T/D			5.8	5.2		42.7		9.5	11.7
			(16) 1.3	(17) 2.7		(10) 10.4		(40) 5.0	(43) 6.2
			.4	.8		2.9		1.7	1.8
Fixed/Worth		.2	.3	.5	.7	.4		.3	.5
		.3	.8	.9	1.1	.9		.8	.9
		3.0	1.9	2.1	1.6	2.6		1.7	2.1
Debt/Worth		.7	.8	.6	.7	.4		.5	.7
		2.2	1.5	1.8	1.2	1.0		1.3	1.3
		6.3	3.3	4.0	2.0	4.9		2.8	3.9
% Profit Before Taxes/Tangible Net Worth		24.8	26.3	24.0	35.7	26.0		30.5	34.6
		(22) 12.3	(64) 8.2	(63) 5.9	(23) 22.0	(17) 7.4		(106) 18.8	(122) 19.4
		3.5	-2.1	-1.8	2.3	3.3		5.7	5.3
% Profit Before Taxes/Total Assets		7.7	11.6	7.9	13.2	9.3		12.7	14.8
		4.2	2.0	3.0	7.2	4.6		6.4	7.1
		-2.9	-1.5	-.7	.8	1.0		1.1	1.1
Sales/Net Fixed Assets		20.9	11.1	3.5	3.5	4.0		6.1	4.9
		7.0	2.7	1.5	1.8	1.6		2.7	2.1
		2.8	1.3	.6	.8	1.2		1.3	1.0
Sales/Total Assets		1.8	1.0	.9	.8	1.0		1.2	1.1
		.8	.6	.5	.7	.7		.8	.7
		.6	.5	.3	.4	.4		.5	.5
% Depr., Dep., Amort./Sales		1.4	1.3	4.0	2.0	3.1		2.9	3.1
		(20) 2.8	(64) 3.9	(60) 8.0	(23) 5.0	(17) 6.6		(102) 5.2	(113) 5.3
		7.2	7.3	11.5	9.4	8.0		7.9	7.4
% Officers', Directors' Owners' Comp/Sales		3.5						2.9	3.8
		(12) 5.7						(20) 10.6	(24) 7.4
		10.3						16.7	11.8
Net Sales ($)	5033M	35004M	343681M	1162529M	1431160M	2324242M		2976115M	3566142M
Total Assets ($)	2263M	28843M	373395M	1861061M	1786218M	3006081M		3533833M	4160761M

© RMA 2011

M = $ thousand   MM = $ million
See Pages 9 through 22 for Explanation of Ratios and Data

Comparative Historical Data / Current Data Sorted by Sales

Type of Statement									
	22	24	34	Unqualified		1	5	6	7	20

Type of Statement (full)

	4/1/08-3/31/09 ALL	4/1/09-3/31/10 ALL	4/1/10-3/31/11 ALL		0-1MM	1-3MM	3-5MM	5-10MM	10-25MM	25MM & OVER
Unqualified	22	24	34			1	5	6	7	20
Reviewed	51	43	46			5		13	13	10
Compiled	14	16	17		4	4	5	3	1	
Tax Returns	23	22	21		9	6	3		2	1
Other	90	91	100		12	20	18	13	14	23
					31 (4/1-9/30/10)			187 (10/1/10-3/31/11)		
NUMBER OF STATEMENTS	200	196	218		25	36	31	35	37	54
ASSETS	%	%	%		%	%	%	%	%	%
Cash & Equivalents	2.8	3.6	3.9		6.4	5.4	4.8	3.0	3.5	2.2
Trade Receivables (net)	8.4	8.4	9.5		5.6	7.6	11.7	9.5	8.2	12.0
Inventory	45.2	46.8	43.9		52.3	45.4	47.9	43.2	37.0	41.9
All Other Current	2.4	2.1	2.3		4.4	1.1	3.1	1.4	2.1	2.6
Total Current	58.8	60.9	59.6		68.6	59.6	67.4	57.1	50.8	58.7
Fixed Assets (net)	34.1	33.4	33.4		26.9	34.8	28.1	34.2	39.0	34.2
Intangibles (net)	2.9	2.5	3.5		.5	2.7	3.0	3.1	5.7	4.6
All Other Non-Current	4.3	3.1	3.4		4.0	2.9	1.5	5.6	4.5	2.6
Total	100.0	100.0	100.0		100.0	100.0	100.0	100.0	100.0	100.0
LIABILITIES										
Notes Payable-Short Term	15.4	16.1	14.2		19.5	14.3	11.6	17.0	11.4	13.3
Cur. Mat.-L.T.D.	2.5	1.8	2.4		3.5	1.6	3.2	1.4	1.6	3.3
Trade Payables	8.7	8.6	7.9		10.5	7.6	8.5	8.2	5.5	8.2
Income Taxes Payable	.1	.1	.2		.1	.0	.0	.4	.1	.5
All Other Current	7.2	6.2	6.3		8.2	5.4	5.6	5.3	6.5	7.1
Total Current	33.9	32.8	31.1		41.8	28.9	28.9	32.3	25.1	32.3
Long-Term Debt	22.3	21.9	22.3		28.4	28.6	19.6	19.5	23.8	17.4
Deferred Taxes	.3	.4	.6		.1	.0	.1	1.3	.9	.7
All Other Non-Current	6.7	8.5	8.5		25.2	10.3	5.9	8.5	3.3	4.4
Net Worth	36.8	36.4	37.6		4.6	32.2	45.4	38.3	46.9	45.1
Total Liabilties & Net Worth	100.0	100.0	100.0		100.0	100.0	100.0	100.0	100.0	100.0
INCOME DATA										
Net Sales	100.0	100.0	100.0		100.0	100.0	100.0	100.0	100.0	100.0
Gross Profit	51.1	46.4	46.3		58.9	54.2	47.8	43.8	44.9	36.8
Operating Expenses	38.6	38.0	36.6		48.5	45.0	40.6	34.9	35.2	25.1
Operating Profit	12.5	8.4	9.7		10.4	9.2	7.3	8.9	9.7	11.6
All Other Expenses (net)	4.6	5.0	4.8		6.7	7.1	2.7	4.4	5.4	3.2
Profit Before Taxes	8.0	3.4	4.9		3.7	2.1	4.5	4.4	4.3	8.4

RATIOS

Ratio	4/1/08-3/31/09	4/1/09-3/31/10	4/1/10-3/31/11	0-1MM	1-3MM	3-5MM	5-10MM	10-25MM	25MM & OVER
Current	3.2	3.6	3.8	6.6	4.0	6.2	3.1	4.9	3.0
	1.9	2.0	2.1	1.9	2.4	2.8	2.1	2.3	2.0
	1.3	1.3	1.4	1.3	1.6	1.4	1.5	1.2	1.4
Quick	.7	.7	.8	1.0	.5	1.0	.7	1.1	.8
	.3	.3	.4	.2	.3	.6	.4	.5	.4
	.1	.1	.2	.1	.2	.2	.2	.2	.2
Sales/Receivables	12 29.9	15 25.0	19 19.3	0 UND	12 30.3	15 24.1	22 16.7	29 12.5	29 12.5
	33 11.1	34 10.8	36 10.0	14 26.4	28 13.2	32 11.5	39 9.4	40 9.0	43 8.5
	51 7.1	52 7.0	55 6.7	55 6.7	60 6.1	55 6.6	58 6.3	53 6.8	53 6.9
Cost of Sales/Inventory	272 1.3	292 1.3	260 1.4	341 1.1	382 1.0	172 2.1	276 1.3	253 1.4	188 1.9
	490 .7	510 .7	446 .8	684 .5	668 .5	465 .8	419 .9	450 .8	328 1.1
	830 .4	894 .4	741 .5	1404 .3	1149 .3	709 .5	721 .5	796 .5	509 .7
Cost of Sales/Payables	19 19.3	18 20.6	18 20.3	0 UND	13 27.7	21 17.3	22 16.7	15 24.2	21 17.1
	55 6.6	54 6.7	43 8.4	32 11.4	62 5.9	43 8.4	50 7.2	32 11.5	37 9.9
	97 3.8	111 3.3	86 4.2	137 2.7	119 3.1	86 4.2	98 3.7	66 5.5	74 4.9
Sales/Working Capital	1.6	1.4	1.6	1.2	1.1	1.6	1.4	1.5	1.6
	2.9	2.5	2.5	3.0	1.8	2.8	2.4	2.1	3.8
	7.3	6.0	5.6	13.4	3.6	4.5	5.4	6.8	10.1
EBIT/Interest	8.9	7.6	7.8	5.8	2.6	7.8	4.0	9.4	18.7
	(182) 3.0	(174) 2.4	(195) 2.1	(21) 1.3	(30) 1.4	(30) 1.8	(30) 1.2	(32) 1.6	(52) 5.5
	1.2	.5	.8	.5	-.5	1.0	.5	.4	2.4
Net Profit + Depr., Dep., Amort./Cur. Mat. L/T/D	13.6	10.0	9.6					9.6	22.2
	(56) 4.5	(41) 2.5	(53) 3.1					(11) 3.8	(20) 6.4
	1.7	.6	.9					1.1	2.8
Fixed/Worth	.3	.3	.3	.2	.4	.1	.4	.6	.3
	.9	.9	.9	1.4	1.0	.6	.8	.9	1.0
	2.0	2.3	2.0	NM	3.7	1.3	1.9	3.3	1.6
Debt/Worth	.7	.7	.7	1.0	1.3	.5	.6	.6	.8
	1.7	1.8	1.5	3.4	1.9	1.2	1.4	1.5	1.2
	4.3	3.9	4.4	NM	6.0	3.3	4.3	4.4	3.1
% Profit Before Taxes/Tangible Net Worth	34.4	21.8	27.1	32.6	23.0	28.2	18.5	18.2	34.2
	(178) 14.6	(175) 8.9	(195) 9.1	(19) 10.2	(31) 9.3	(28) 6.4	(32) 4.9	(34) 3.9	(51) 24.0
	2.6	-3.1	-.2	-.4	-3.5	.0	-2.6	-2.9	6.0
% Profit Before Taxes/Total Assets	13.2	8.5	9.8	12.5	5.3	11.7	6.3	7.8	13.0
	3.9	2.8	3.3	2.0	1.6	1.9	1.2	1.3	6.5
	.3	-1.5	-.4	-4.3	-3.8	.1	-.9	-.9	2.9
Sales/Net Fixed Assets	8.7	7.8	7.4	17.6	5.2	24.4	5.6	3.4	5.6
	2.1	2.5	2.4	4.9	2.5	4.1	1.6	1.4	2.4
	1.1	.9	1.0	1.8	.6	1.4	.7	.6	1.3
Sales/Total Assets	1.0	1.1	1.0	1.3	.8	1.6	1.0	.8	1.1
	.7	.6	.7	.8	.6	.9	.6	.5	.8
	.4	.4	.4	.5	.3	.5	.4	.3	.6
% Depr., Dep., Amort./Sales	2.3	2.1	2.0	1.0	2.0	1.2	3.0	4.2	1.9
	(158) 4.4	(156) 5.3	(190) 5.0	(20) 4.4	(28) 6.4	(28) 3.6	(31) 6.0	(33) 8.6	(50) 4.0
	8.1	10.4	9.3	11.8	12.0	6.9	10.6	12.0	7.1
% Officers', Directors' Owners' Comp/Sales	2.2	2.2	2.1		2.5				
	(32) 7.7	(26) 5.3	(32) 4.9		(10) 5.2				
	10.2	11.0	8.4		8.2				
Net Sales ($)	4015482M	3921819M	5301649M	13131M	68504M	117865M	253820M	570745M	4277584M
Total Assets ($)	5212880M	5229794M	7057861M	22412M	148557M	171277M	509265M	1314788M	4891562M

M = $ thousand   MM = $ million
See Pages 9 through 22 for Explanation of Ratios and Data

| Current Data Sorted by Assets | | | | | | | Comparative Historical Data | |

Type of Statement

0-500M	500M-2MM	2-10MM	10-50MM	50-100MM	100-250MM	Type of Statement	4/1/06-3/31/07 ALL	4/1/07-3/31/08 ALL
	1		6		3	Unqualified	14	9
	1	4	4	1		Reviewed	6	6
	2		1			Compiled	1	1
	1					Tax Returns	2	2
	1	2	7	1	2	Other	15	13
	7 (4/1-9/30/10)		29 (10/1/10-3/31/11)					
5	7	18	1	5		**NUMBER OF STATEMENTS**	38	31

Data (%)

0-500M	10-50MM		4/1/06-3/31/07 ALL	4/1/07-3/31/08 ALL
%	%	**ASSETS**	%	%
	6.1	Cash & Equivalents	5.9	6.7
	31.2	Trade Receivables (net)	20.7	27.9
D A T A	28.4	Inventory	29.7	30.8
	2.1	All Other Current	4.2	2.9
N O T	67.8	Total Current	60.5	68.2
	27.5	Fixed Assets (net)	29.3	23.7
A V A I L A B L E	.4	Intangibles (net)	3.3	2.3
	4.3	All Other Non-Current	7.0	5.7
	100.0	Total	100.0	100.0
		LIABILITIES		
	6.7	Notes Payable-Short Term	8.9	8.6
	3.6	Cur. Mat.-L.T.D.	3.7	2.6
	15.6	Trade Payables	14.5	14.4
	.3	Income Taxes Payable	.1	.2
	10.3	All Other Current	5.8	5.6
	36.5	Total Current	33.0	31.4
	11.9	Long-Term Debt	18.8	12.4
	.9	Deferred Taxes	.8	.8
	4.8	All Other Non-Current	4.5	6.8
	45.9	Net Worth	42.9	48.6
	100.0	Total Liabilities & Net Worth	100.0	100.0
		INCOME DATA		
	100.0	Net Sales	100.0	100.0
	17.5	Gross Profit	17.8	17.6
	12.3	Operating Expenses	14.1	14.8
	5.2	Operating Profit	3.7	2.8
	.3	All Other Expenses (net)	1.2	-.1
	4.9	Profit Before Taxes	2.5	2.9

Ratios

0-500M	10-50MM	Ratio	4/1/06-3/31/07 ALL	4/1/07-3/31/08 ALL
	3.5		3.7	4.1
	1.8	Current	1.7	2.1
	1.3		1.1	1.5
	1.9		1.3	1.8
	1.1	Quick	.8	1.3
	.5		.4	.7
	36 10.1		21 17.3	36 10.2
	53 6.9	Sales/Receivables	39 9.3	50 7.3
	68 5.4		51 7.1	67 5.5
	40 9.2		35 10.3	38 9.7
	49 7.4	Cost of Sales/Inventory	59 6.2	57 6.3
	79 4.6		86 4.2	96 3.8
	16 23.1		14 25.9	17 21.5
	24 15.4	Cost of Sales/Payables	22 16.8	26 14.1
	48 7.7		45 8.0	38 9.5
	4.6		4.3	3.7
	6.7	Sales/Working Capital	7.8	6.6
	18.6		25.0	10.4
	23.5		3.9	9.0
	(16) 7.6	EBIT/Interest	(34) 2.0	(28) 2.8
	2.9		1.1	1.0
		Net Profit + Depr., Dep.,	4.0	5.4
		Amort./Cur. Mat. L/T/D	(10) 2.4	(10) 3.0
			.9	1.1
	.3		.3	.2
	.5	Fixed/Worth	.6	.5
	1.0		1.4	.9
	.6		.5	.4
	.9	Debt/Worth	1.5	.9
	3.5		4.5	3.8
	53.9	% Profit Before Taxes/Tangible	14.9	29.0
	21.6	Net Worth	(34) 5.3	(28) 8.0
	6.8		1.3	.0
	15.1	% Profit Before Taxes/Total	8.2	12.2
	6.0	Assets	2.6	6.2
	3.7		.3	.0
	25.7		25.1	24.8
	9.0	Sales/Net Fixed Assets	7.9	10.6
	3.5		3.5	4.7
	2.5		2.7	2.7
	2.1	Sales/Total Assets	2.0	2.1
	1.6		1.6	1.7
	.7		.8	.7
	(17) 1.8	% Depr., Dep., Amort./Sales	(33) 2.2	(26) 1.4
	3.4		3.6	2.8
		% Officers', Directors'	2.2	
		Owners' Comp/Sales	(12) 3.3	
			5.7	

Net Sales / Total Assets ($)

	500M-2MM	2-10MM	10-50MM	50-100MM	100-250MM		4/1/06-3/31/07	4/1/07-3/31/08
Net Sales ($)	17270M	88976M	935616M	64966M	1722109M		2675853M	2565520M
Total Assets ($)	5471M	34607M	431594M	53444M	735430M		1386452M	1269797M

M = $ thousand   MM = $ million
See Pages 9 through 22 for Explanation of Ratios and Data

Comparative Historical Data

Current Data Sorted by Sales

4/1/08-3/31/09 ALL	4/1/09-3/31/10 ALL	4/1/10-3/31/11 ALL	Type of Statement	0-1MM	1-3MM	3-5MM	5-10MM	10-25MM	25MM & OVER
13	11	10	Unqualified		1	1	1	4	10
9	11	9	Reviewed			2			2
6	4	3	Compiled			1			1
2	3	1	Tax Returns						
15	13	13	Other		1		2	2	8
					7 (4/1-9/30/10)			29 (10/1/10-3/31/11)	
45	42	36	**NUMBER OF STATEMENTS**		2	4	3	6	21
%	%	%	**ASSETS**	%	%	%	%	%	%
5.3	7.3	6.5	Cash & Equivalents						5.1
23.1	24.2	28.3	Trade Receivables (net)	D					31.1
31.7	29.4	31.2	Inventory	A					27.3
1.9	2.6	3.8	All Other Current	T					5.0
61.9	63.5	69.8	Total Current	A					68.5
28.0	25.3	22.3	Fixed Assets (net)						25.2
.8	3.2	1.0	Intangibles (net)	N					.7
9.4	8.0	6.9	All Other Non-Current	O					5.6
100.0	100.0	100.0	Total	T					100.0
			LIABILITIES	A					
8.2	6.9	7.8	Notes Payable-Short Term	V					4.7
4.6	1.8	2.8	Cur. Mat.-L.T.D.	A					3.6
10.9	12.9	16.2	Trade Payables	I					15.5
.1	.3	.3	Income Taxes Payable	L					.5
12.6	9.1	8.2	All Other Current	A					8.6
36.4	31.1	35.2	Total Current	B					32.9
14.7	13.9	14.3	Long-Term Debt	L					15.5
1.4	1.2	1.0	Deferred Taxes	E					1.6
5.4	4.8	5.3	All Other Non-Current						6.3
42.0	49.0	44.3	Net Worth						43.7
100.0	100.0	100.0	Total Liabilities & Net Worth						100.0
			INCOME DATA						
100.0	100.0	100.0	Net Sales						100.0
16.7	17.3	19.9	Gross Profit						16.9
16.0	15.0	14.4	Operating Expenses						9.7
.7	2.2	5.5	Operating Profit						7.2
.2	1.0	.1	All Other Expenses (net)						.5
.6	1.2	5.4	Profit Before Taxes						6.7
			RATIOS						
3.3	3.7	3.8	Current						3.5
2.1	2.4	2.1							2.2
1.4	1.5	1.4							1.5
1.6	1.8	1.9	Quick						1.7
1.0	1.1	1.1							1.1
.5	.6	.6							.6
32 11.2	32 11.3	32 11.5	Sales/Receivables						34 10.8
41 8.9	46 7.9	41 8.9							52 7.1
55 6.7	57 6.4	59 6.2							59 6.1
38 9.5	39 9.5	40 9.1	Cost of Sales/Inventory						38 9.7
66 5.5	64 5.7	57 6.4							46 7.9
102 3.6	95 3.8	83 4.4							75 4.9
14 25.7	14 25.2	14 25.6	Cost of Sales/Payables						14 25.6
21 17.8	28 13.2	23 16.1							23 15.8
30 12.0	36 10.2	40 9.2							39 9.3
4.2	3.5	4.1	Sales/Working Capital						4.6
6.9	5.5	6.7							6.5
20.8	11.2	15.3							14.2
5.2	6.9	19.8	EBIT/Interest						20.8
(41) 2.3	(36) 1.8	(31) 6.6						(20)	8.5
.5	.6	2.9							3.2
6.9	7.5	27.3	Net Profit + Depr., Dep., Amort./Cur. Mat. L/T/D						31.2
(16) 2.0	(12) 3.4	(12) 8.4						(11)	10.2
.5	.9	2.9							3.9
.3	.2	.2	Fixed/Worth						.2
.5	.4	.4							.5
1.5	1.0	1.0							1.1
.5	.4	.6	Debt/Worth						.7
1.2	.9	.9							1.0
3.3	2.0	3.3							3.1
22.3	11.5	55.8	% Profit Before Taxes/Tangible Net Worth						67.5
(41) 3.7	(38) 2.9	(33) 25.1							25.8
-2.0	-2.4	7.9							9.4
7.5	5.8	17.2	% Profit Before Taxes/Total Assets						27.2
2.1	1.2	7.7							12.8
-3.2	-.8	3.6							3.8
19.6	22.3	47.1	Sales/Net Fixed Assets						43.1
6.8	8.2	16.0							11.7
4.1	3.9	5.9							5.6
2.6	2.4	3.0	Sales/Total Assets						3.0
1.9	1.8	2.3							2.3
1.3	1.3	1.8							1.9
1.0	1.0	.6	% Depr., Dep., Amort./Sales						.4
(41) 2.3	(36) 2.4	(32) 1.2						(19)	1.3
4.1	4.1	2.9							3.1
1.7	1.8		% Officers', Directors' Owners' Comp/Sales						
(13) 4.0	(14) 3.6								
7.9	6.0								
3595307M	2258640M	2828937M	Net Sales ($)		4541M	15555M	22934M	105858M	2680049M
1738984M	1246892M	1260546M	Total Assets ($)		3297M	4830M	13476M	61257M	1177686M

© RMA 2011

M = $ thousand   MM = $ million

See Pages 9 through 22 for Explanation of Ratios and Data

Current Data Sorted by Assets

Comparative Historical Data

0-500M	500M-2MM	2-10MM	10-50MM	50-100MM	100-250MM	Type of Statement		
		4	17	1	3	Unqualified	20	16
	1	5	6			Reviewed	18	17
1	5	5				Compiled	3	5
1	1	2				Tax Returns	7	11
2	3	10	13	1	2	Other	25	26
	19 (4/1-9/30/10)		65 (10/1/10-3/31/11)				4/1/06-3/31/07 ALL	4/1/07-3/31/08 ALL
4	10	26	37	2	5	NUMBER OF STATEMENTS	73	75
%	%	%	%	%	%	ASSETS	%	%
	8.2	7.1	6.1			Cash & Equivalents	5.9	7.5
	39.4	23.3	20.5			Trade Receivables (net)	25.4	26.7
	26.0	38.3	28.0			Inventory	30.1	29.7
	4.0	2.0	3.2			All Other Current	3.0	2.6
	77.5	70.7	57.9			Total Current	64.4	66.5
	21.0	18.5	27.8			Fixed Assets (net)	26.2	22.5
	.0	4.2	6.2			Intangibles (net)	2.9	4.6
	1.5	6.6	8.1			All Other Non-Current	6.5	6.5
	100.0	100.0	100.0			Total	100.0	100.0
						LIABILITIES		
	6.1	12.1	9.8			Notes Payable-Short Term	18.0	11.3
	2.8	2.3	3.9			Cur. Mat.-L.T.D.	3.5	4.4
	23.5	15.5	13.5			Trade Payables	14.3	17.3
	.1	.2	.1			Income Taxes Payable	.3	.2
	13.3	9.8	7.8			All Other Current	7.2	9.1
	45.8	39.9	35.1			Total Current	43.3	42.3
	61.0	15.5	21.2			Long-Term Debt	14.2	16.7
	.0	.2	.8			Deferred Taxes	.4	.7
	14.7	11.2	4.6			All Other Non-Current	8.6	9.2
	-21.5	33.3	38.3			Net Worth	33.4	31.2
	100.0	100.0	100.0			Total Liabilities & Net Worth	100.0	100.0
						INCOME DATA		
	100.0	100.0	100.0			Net Sales	100.0	100.0
	40.1	24.5	21.3			Gross Profit	23.9	24.2
	39.7	21.0	19.4			Operating Expenses	21.8	20.5
	.4	3.6	2.0			Operating Profit	2.2	3.7
	.9	1.0	1.7			All Other Expenses (net)	1.4	1.0
	-.5	2.5	.2			Profit Before Taxes	.8	2.7
						RATIOS		
	2.9	2.9	3.0				2.3	3.4
	2.3	1.9	1.9			Current	1.7	1.8
	1.7	1.3	1.0				1.3	1.3
	2.2	1.2	1.5				1.3	1.8
	1.3	.9	.9			Quick	.8	1.0
	.3	.4	.4				.5	.5
	19 18.8	24 15.3	30 12.2				31 11.8	31 11.9
	38 9.6	41 8.8	43 8.5			Sales/Receivables	45 8.1	44 8.3
	57 6.4	56 6.5	61 5.9				61 6.0	57 6.4
	0 UND	58 6.3	43 8.5				41 8.9	42 8.7
	45 8.1	90 4.1	72 5.1			Cost of Sales/Inventory	66 5.5	65 5.6
	104 3.5	114 3.2	98 3.7				115 3.2	99 3.7
	26 14.3	21 17.5	20 18.5				17 21.0	19 19.2
	31 11.6	37 9.9	33 11.1			Cost of Sales/Payables	29 12.4	29 12.5
	58 6.3	45 8.1	49 7.5				42 8.8	43 8.4
	6.2	3.9	3.9				5.6	4.8
	7.3	7.6	5.9			Sales/Working Capital	7.9	7.5
	NM	17.1	-433.2				19.7	18.2
		16.9	16.0				6.0	11.4
		(25) 4.8	(34) 3.9			EBIT/Interest	(65) 2.5	(66) 2.3
		2.1	-.6				.2	.8
			3.7				3.7	5.6
		(11) 1.2				Net Profit + Depr., Dep., Amort./Cur. Mat. L/T/D	(19) 1.8	(19) 1.5
			-.5				1.4	.8
	.1	.2	.3				.3	.3
	.2	.3	.6			Fixed/Worth	.7	.5
	-.4	2.2	1.3				1.4	1.6
	.6	.7	.4				.8	.7
	.9	1.5	1.1			Debt/Worth	1.5	1.7
	-13.4	9.5	2.2				6.3	7.9
		29.8	29.0				29.4	42.8
		(21) 15.5	(33) 10.2			% Profit Before Taxes/Tangible Net Worth	(64) 8.2	(61) 12.9
		3.7	-6.3				-5.4	-.9
	31.6	10.0	10.3				11.9	15.1
	15.0	5.7	5.7			% Profit Before Taxes/Total Assets	3.4	4.6
	-14.4	1.5	-4.9				-2.8	-.7
	127.5	36.2	11.9				28.7	32.7
	44.9	19.1	8.1			Sales/Net Fixed Assets	9.4	12.0
	5.7	8.3	4.5				4.5	5.0
	4.3	2.7	2.5				2.7	2.7
	3.6	2.2	1.8			Sales/Total Assets	2.1	2.1
	2.3	1.5	1.2				1.4	1.6
		.9	2.1				.8	.9
		(24) 1.7	(33) 3.4			% Depr., Dep., Amort./Sales	(58) 1.8	(64) 2.1
		3.0	4.5				3.2	3.0
							1.9	1.6
						% Officers', Directors' Owners' Comp/Sales	(22) 3.2	(20) 3.6
							7.8	6.6
5994M	34449M	299234M	1657497M	239168M	2006245M	Net Sales ($)	4784154M	3944848M
1124M	10509M	135513M	924404M	145676M	870804M	Total Assets ($)	2249117M	1957269M

© RMA 2011

M = $ thousand   MM = $ million
See Pages 9 through 22 for Explanation of Ratios and Data

Comparative Historical Data   Current Data Sorted by Sales

Current data groupings: **19 (4/1–9/30/10)** covers 0-1MM · 1-3MM · 3-5MM; **65 (10/1/10–3/31/11)** covers 5-10MM · 10-25MM · 25MM & OVER.

4/1/08–3/31/09 ALL	4/1/09–3/31/10 ALL	4/1/10–3/31/11 ALL		0-1MM	1-3MM	3-5MM	5-10MM	10-25MM	25MM & OVER
			Type of Statement						
21	15	25	Unqualified					4	21
18	13	12	Reviewed		1		2	6	3
8	15	11	Compiled		1	6	2	1	1
9	10	5	Tax Returns	1	1	1	2		
28	27	31	Other	1	2	1	2	11	11
84	80	84	**NUMBER OF STATEMENTS**	2	5	8	11	22	36
%	%	%	**ASSETS**	%	%	%	%	%	%
6.9	9.9	7.3	Cash & Equivalents				5.9	5.9	6.6
23.9	25.1	23.9	Trade Receivables (net)				27.0	21.1	22.7
31.1	29.5	30.0	Inventory				28.1	37.7	28.8
1.8	1.9	2.5	All Other Current				5.1	2.1	1.7
63.7	66.4	63.7	Total Current				66.1	66.8	59.9
22.8	22.2	23.4	Fixed Assets (net)				20.5	20.5	26.8
5.3	5.6	6.2	Intangibles (net)				4.2	4.4	6.8
8.2	5.8	6.8	All Other Non-Current				9.3	8.2	6.4
100.0	100.0	100.0	Total				100.0	100.0	100.0
			LIABILITIES						
11.5	8.2	10.2	Notes Payable-Short Term				10.4	8.0	9.8
5.2	5.2	3.5	Cur. Mat.-L.T.D.				3.0	2.5	3.5
14.2	15.0	14.9	Trade Payables				11.9	15.9	14.5
.3	1.4	.2	Income Taxes Payable				.1	.2	.2
9.9	7.3	10.0	All Other Current				11.1	7.1	9.5
41.1	37.0	38.7	Total Current				36.4	33.8	37.5
14.0	17.0	22.2	Long-Term Debt				16.7	12.5	19.4
.5	.6	.4	Deferred Taxes				.4	.7	.4
6.6	7.1	8.2	All Other Non-Current				8.0	11.5	4.6
37.9	38.3	30.5	Net Worth				38.4	41.6	38.1
100.0	100.0	100.0	Total Liabilities & Net Worth				100.0	100.0	100.0
			INCOME DATA						
100.0	100.0	100.0	Net Sales				100.0	100.0	100.0
22.8	24.5	25.3	Gross Profit				32.5	26.2	17.9
21.3	21.6	22.4	Operating Expenses				31.1	24.4	13.3
1.5	3.0	2.9	Operating Profit				1.5	1.7	4.6
1.3	1.2	1.3	All Other Expenses (net)				1.4	1.3	1.7
.3	1.8	1.6	Profit Before Taxes				.1	.5	2.9
			RATIOS						
3.0	3.7	2.9	Current				3.5	3.0	2.8
1.7	2.0	2.0					2.0	2.2	1.9
1.2	1.3	1.2					1.2	1.3	1.0
1.6	2.0	1.5	Quick				1.4	1.4	1.3
.8	1.0	.9					.8	.9	.8
.5	.5	.4					.5	.4	.5
26 · 13.9	29 · 12.8	24 · 14.9	Sales/Receivables				35 · 10.3	22 · 16.9	30 · 12.2
42 · 8.7	45 · 8.2	43 · 8.5					44 · 8.3	44 · 8.3	44 · 8.4
58 · 6.3	56 · 6.5	57 · 6.4					77 · 4.8	57 · 6.4	58 · 6.3
40 · 9.1	32 · 11.3	41 · 9.0	Cost of Sales/Inventory				50 · 7.3	60 · 6.1	40 · 9.0
61 · 6.0	65 · 5.6	73 · 5.0					114 · 3.2	81 · 4.5	61 · 6.0
96 · 3.8	114 · 3.2	106 · 3.4					135 · 2.7	102 · 3.6	89 · 4.1
16 · 23.3	18 · 20.0	19 · 18.8	Cost of Sales/Payables				30 · 12.0	22 · 16.7	17 · 21.5
24 · 15.4	31 · 11.8	33 · 11.1					38 · 9.5	38 · 9.7	33 · 11.1
38 · 9.6	42 · 8.6	49 · 7.5					43 · 8.5	52 · 7.1	49 · 7.5
5.3	4.2	4.5	Sales/Working Capital				3.0	3.9	4.7
8.4	7.2	6.9					8.5	5.8	7.2
23.4	15.2	25.1					18.5	15.3	NM
11.2	12.3	16.4	EBIT/Interest				8.1	24.2	20.1
(79) 2.4	(73) 3.5	(77) 5.2					(10) 2.3	3.9	(33) 8.8
.0	.5	1.0					-8.2	.8	1.6
5.2	5.1	4.9	Net Profit + Depr., Dep., Amort./Cur. Mat. L/T/D						
(24) 1.1	(19) 2.6	(19) 3.3							
-.2	.4	.6							
.2	.2	.2	Fixed/Worth				.2	.1	.3
.5	.5	.5					.7	.3	.5
1.4	1.5	1.7					2.3	1.0	1.4
.8	.6	.6	Debt/Worth				.5	.7	.6
1.5	1.3	1.1					2.6	1.0	1.1
3.9	4.3	3.2					16.1	2.4	2.2
32.1	32.3	29.3	% Profit Before Taxes/Tangible Net Worth					21.4	29.8
(74) 9.4	(66) 10.3	(69) 15.4						(19) 12.7	(32) 15.6
-9.1	-.5	2.6						.4	7.0
10.0	12.7	13.0	% Profit Before Taxes/Total Assets				12.7	10.0	12.5
3.6	4.3	6.5					4.6	5.9	7.0
-4.0	-1.5	.2					-5.6	-.4	.2
26.1	32.5	29.4	Sales/Net Fixed Assets				52.9	36.2	18.1
12.0	11.7	11.5					10.6	16.7	10.4
5.5	5.4	5.4					4.3	3.9	5.9
2.8	2.7	3.0	Sales/Total Assets				2.5	2.7	2.8
2.0	2.0	2.0					1.7	2.0	1.9
1.4	1.4	1.4					1.1	1.1	1.5
.7	.8	1.1	% Depr., Dep., Amort./Sales				1.0	.8	1.6
(72) 1.7	(64) 2.3	(72) 2.5					(10) 3.6	(21) 2.3	(31) 2.5
3.3	4.3	3.8					4.5	4.5	3.4
1.4	1.6	.7	% Officers', Directors' Owners' Comp/Sales						
(21) 3.9	(19) 4.2	(14) 2.5							
6.9	7.0	6.9							
3431212M	3718881M	4242587M	Net Sales ($)	1463M	9157M	30425M	79733M	330277M	3791532M
1962002M	1975096M	2088030M	Total Assets ($)	497M	4376M	12056M	56270M	235041M	1779790M

M = $ thousand   MM = $ million
See Pages 9 through 22 for Explanation of Ratios and Data

Current Data Sorted by Assets

Comparative Historical Data

						Type of Statement		
		1	2			Unqualified	7	1
		6	1			Reviewed	3	7
	1	4	2			Compiled	8	6
1	2					Tax Returns		1
		4	1	1	2	Other	11	11
	11 (4/1-9/30/10)		17 (10/1/10-3/31/11)				4/1/06-3/31/07	4/1/07-3/31/08
0-500M	500M-2MM	2-10MM	10-50MM	50-100MM	100-250MM		ALL	ALL
1	3	15	6	1	2	NUMBER OF STATEMENTS	29	26
%	%	%	%	%	%	ASSETS	%	%
		6.1				Cash & Equivalents	7.7	6.9
		31.2				Trade Receivables (net)	26.0	27.9
		36.5				Inventory	29.7	23.2
		1.8				All Other Current	1.6	1.7
		75.5				Total Current	65.0	59.7
		17.2				Fixed Assets (net)	21.0	24.4
		.0				Intangibles (net)	4.1	3.1
		7.3				All Other Non-Current	10.0	12.7
		100.0				Total	100.0	100.0
						LIABILITIES		
		11.0				Notes Payable-Short Term	12.9	11.1
		1.7				Cur. Mat.-L.T.D.	2.4	1.6
		19.9				Trade Payables	13.2	14.5
		.2				Income Taxes Payable	.6	.7
		6.1				All Other Current	8.4	6.5
		38.8				Total Current	37.5	34.4
		4.8				Long-Term Debt	6.3	8.4
		.6				Deferred Taxes	.2	.4
		8.1				All Other Non-Current	5.7	2.3
		47.7				Net Worth	50.3	54.5
		100.0				Total Liabilities & Net Worth	100.0	100.0
						INCOME DATA		
		100.0				Net Sales	100.0	100.0
		20.5				Gross Profit	25.0	21.6
		18.8				Operating Expenses	21.2	18.7
		1.7				Operating Profit	3.8	2.9
		-.4				All Other Expenses (net)	.6	.5
		2.0				Profit Before Taxes	3.2	2.4
						RATIOS		
		2.9					3.9	4.2
		2.3				Current	2.0	2.5
		1.4					1.1	.9
		1.3					2.0	2.8
		1.0				Quick	1.0	1.5
		.6					.5	.6
		35 10.5					29 12.5	37 9.9
		43 8.5				Sales/Receivables	42 8.6	44 8.2
		58 6.3					50 7.3	52 7.0
		51 7.1					41 9.0	31 11.7
		77 4.7				Cost of Sales/Inventory	68 5.3	59 6.2
		118 3.1					95 3.9	76 4.8
		15 24.1					20 18.1	14 26.6
		34 10.7				Cost of Sales/Payables	24 15.1	26 14.0
		51 7.2					41 9.0	39 9.4
		4.8					4.5	4.1
		5.8				Sales/Working Capital	8.6	7.0
		13.0					42.4	-30.9
		20.6					18.3	21.8
		6.9				EBIT/Interest	(23) 2.8	(25) 2.6
		.4					.6	-.7
						Net Profit + Depr., Dep.,	42.8	9.7
						Amort./Cur. Mat. L/T/D	(10) 4.6	(10) 1.3
							1.0	-2.2
		.1					.1	.2
		.4				Fixed/Worth	.5	.4
		.6					1.0	1.2
		.4					.3	.2
		1.0				Debt/Worth	.9	1.0
		3.1					3.2	4.7
		31.4				% Profit Before Taxes/Tangible	28.4	31.0
	(14)	16.1				Net Worth	(27) 7.4	7.3
		-2.2					-8.3	-7.2
		14.9				% Profit Before Taxes/Total	15.4	15.0
		4.1				Assets	4.6	5.7
		-1.3					-2.7	-3.4
		25.6					37.6	34.7
		17.3				Sales/Net Fixed Assets	10.0	7.7
		8.6					6.4	4.6
		2.9					2.9	2.5
		2.2				Sales/Total Assets	2.1	2.0
		1.6					1.7	1.5
		.5					.9	1.1
		1.1				% Depr., Dep., Amort./Sales	(26) 2.5	(24) 2.2
		1.8					3.8	4.0
						% Officers', Directors' Owners' Comp/Sales		
1119M	10545M	160157M	201961M	227316M	366076M	Net Sales ($)	802247M	657898M
300M	2730M	70569M	117876M	79800M	298872M	Total Assets ($)	423434M	377159M

M = $ thousand   MM = $ million
See Pages 9 through 22 for Explanation of Ratios and Data

Comparative Historical Data ‖ Current Data Sorted by Sales

© RMA 2011
M = $ thousand   MM = $ million
See Pages 9 through 22 for Explanation of Ratios and Data

						Type of Statement		11 (4/1-9/30/10)			17 (10/1/10-3/31/11)		
	2		2		3	Unqualified					1	1	2
	7		9		7	Reviewed					1	5	1
	5		5		7	Compiled			2		1	3	
	1		1		3	Tax Returns		1	2		2		
	8		7		8	Other		1			2	2	4
	7		7		8								
	4/1/08-3/31/09		4/1/09-3/31/10		4/1/10-3/31/11								
	ALL		ALL		ALL		0-1MM	1-3MM	3-5MM	5-10MM	10-25MM	25MM & OVER	
	23		24		28	NUMBER OF STATEMENTS	2	4	4	11		7	
	%		%		%	ASSETS	%	%	%	%	%	%	
	6.0		9.8		9.0	Cash & Equivalents	D				9.8		
	25.0		21.8		26.3	Trade Receivables (net)	A				35.5		
	30.9		37.7		32.8	Inventory	T				37.8		
	2.6		1.8		2.1	All Other Current	A				3.2		
	64.6		71.0		70.3	Total Current					86.3		
	25.2		19.9		23.7	Fixed Assets (net)	N				10.8		
	1.3		.3		.0	Intangibles (net)	O				.0		
	9.0		8.8		6.0	All Other Non-Current	T				2.9		
	100.0		100.0		100.0	Total					100.0		
						LIABILITIES	A						
	9.6		13.3		12.7	Notes Payable-Short Term	V				6.0		
	1.9		1.1		3.5	Cur. Mat.-L.T.D.	A				1.8		
	19.1		15.7		18.1	Trade Payables	I				20.1		
	.2		.2		.2	Income Taxes Payable	L				.2		
	3.6		5.2		5.9	All Other Current	A				4.0		
	34.4		35.4		40.4	Total Current	B				32.1		
	8.7		5.5		9.2	Long-Term Debt	L				4.6		
	.5		.6		.8	Deferred Taxes	E				.0		
	4.7		9.4		4.9	All Other Non-Current					4.6		
	51.6		49.0		44.7	Net Worth					58.7		
	100.0		100.0		100.0	Total Liabilities & Net Worth					100.0		
						INCOME DATA							
	100.0		100.0		100.0	Net Sales					100.0		
	21.9		26.0		24.9	Gross Profit					27.9		
	20.1		25.4		22.9	Operating Expenses					25.8		
	1.9		.6		2.1	Operating Profit					2.1		
	.1		.0		-.2	All Other Expenses (net)					-1.4		
	1.7		.6		2.3	Profit Before Taxes					3.5		
						RATIOS							
	4.6		3.8		3.0						11.8		
	2.5		2.0		2.2	Current					2.5		
	1.2		1.3		1.3						1.8		
	2.2		2.0		1.9						4.1		
	.9		.7		1.0	Quick					1.3		
	.6		.5		.6						1.0		
34	10.8	32	11.3	31	11.7						43	8.5	
40	9.1	44	8.3	40	9.2	Sales/Receivables					57	6.4	
51	7.2	51	7.2	54	6.7						64	5.7	
46	8.0	60	6.1	41	8.9						51	7.1	
58	6.3	85	4.3	70	5.2	Cost of Sales/Inventory					77	4.7	
118	3.1	141	2.6	114	3.2						163	2.2	
12	30.2	15	24.4	13	27.1						10	35.4	
25	14.4	23	16.0	33	11.1	Cost of Sales/Payables					34	10.7	
50	7.3	66	5.5	51	7.1						51	7.2	
	3.7		3.7		4.5						2.4		
	5.6		5.5		6.1	Sales/Working Capital					5.1		
	18.5		12.4		14.8						5.9		
	25.2		9.3		28.8						45.9		
(21)	4.2	(22)	3.2	(26)	7.6	EBIT/Interest				(10)	10.7		
	.2		.2		-1.4						2.9		
						Net Profit + Depr., Dep., Amort./Cur. Mat. L/T/D							
	.2		.1		.1						.1		
	.5		.4		.4	Fixed/Worth					.1		
	.9		.9		2.5						.4		
	.3		.4		.4						.2		
	.8		.8		.9	Debt/Worth					.6		
	3.6		2.8		5.8						2.6		
	26.1		10.4		29.4						34.9		
(21)	10.8	(22)	2.7	(25)	12.9	% Profit Before Taxes/Tangible Net Worth					24.5		
	.0		-1.3		-2.4						-1.6		
	9.8		5.4		13.8						18.4		
	6.7		1.2		4.6	% Profit Before Taxes/Total Assets					7.3		
	-.6		-.9		-1.4						-1.3		
	30.9		36.9		31.3						39.1		
	10.9		12.1		10.2	Sales/Net Fixed Assets					25.5		
	5.2		5.1		5.0						9.5		
	3.0		2.5		2.9						2.9		
	2.1		1.8		2.2	Sales/Total Assets					2.2		
	1.2		1.2		1.4						1.6		
	.9		.9		.6						.1		
(20)	1.7	(22)	1.7	(24)	1.3	% Depr., Dep., Amort./Sales				(10)	.6		
	3.1		3.1		2.2						1.6		
			1.8		2.0								
		(10)	2.3	(15)	5.3	% Officers', Directors' Owners' Comp/Sales							
			5.8		8.0								
	683832M		714475M		967174M	Net Sales ($)	2591M	18055M	23325M	151989M		771214M	
	422299M		421678M		570147M	Total Assets ($)	943M	10867M	10638M	78565M		469134M	

Current Data Sorted by Assets   Comparative Historical Data

0-500M	500M-2MM	2-10MM	10-50MM	50-100MM	100-250MM		4/1/06-3/31/07 ALL	4/1/07-3/31/08 ALL
		13 (4/1-9/30/10)	33 (10/1/10-3/31/11)			**Type of Statement**		
		1	3	3	1	Unqualified	13	12
		8	5			Reviewed	13	14
	3	2				Compiled	10	10
1	2	2				Tax Returns	5	4
1	2	5	6	1		Other	16	11
2	7	18	14	4	1	**NUMBER OF STATEMENTS**	57	51
%	%	%	%	%	%	**ASSETS**	%	%
		5.3	3.5			Cash & Equivalents	8.3	5.8
		31.7	33.2			Trade Receivables (net)	27.1	24.5
		32.3	39.8			Inventory	30.0	36.3
		1.3	3.2			All Other Current	1.4	2.8
		70.5	79.7			Total Current	66.9	69.3
		20.1	12.7			Fixed Assets (net)	23.6	22.4
		4.2	1.3			Intangibles (net)	3.0	1.1
		5.3	6.3			All Other Non-Current	6.4	7.3
		100.0	100.0			Total	100.0	100.0
						LIABILITIES		
		12.8	21.3			Notes Payable-Short Term	16.1	26.1
		1.9	.9			Cur. Mat.-L.T.D.	2.1	4.7
		22.9	19.7			Trade Payables	17.1	18.4
		.2	.2			Income Taxes Payable	.4	.3
		8.1	10.5			All Other Current	9.1	12.4
		45.8	52.7			Total Current	44.8	61.9
		9.0	4.9			Long-Term Debt	15.0	8.0
		.0	.3			Deferred Taxes	.1	.6
		6.1	1.8			All Other Non-Current	5.4	9.6
		39.0	40.4			Net Worth	34.7	19.9
		100.0	100.0			Total Liabilties & Net Worth	100.0	100.0
						INCOME DATA		
		100.0	100.0			Net Sales	100.0	100.0
		27.6	17.3			Gross Profit	28.8	25.9
		23.0	14.3			Operating Expenses	25.9	24.1
		4.6	3.0			Operating Profit	2.9	1.8
		1.1	.9			All Other Expenses (net)	1.4	1.8
		3.5	2.1			Profit Before Taxes	1.5	.0
						RATIOS		
		3.1	2.0			Current	2.6	2.6
		1.4	1.7				1.7	1.4
		1.1	1.2				1.2	1.1
		2.2	1.3			Quick	1.4	1.2
		.6	.6				1.0	.6
		.5	.5				.5	.3
	30	12.3	49 7.5			Sales/Receivables	29 12.5	24 15.0
	41	8.9	54 6.8				39 9.2	40 9.2
	56	6.5	68 5.3				56 6.6	58 6.3
	21	17.2	54 6.8			Cost of Sales/Inventory	31 11.6	45 8.1
	78	4.7	84 4.3				67 5.5	77 4.7
	103	3.5	112 3.3				94 3.9	113 3.2
	18	20.8	28 13.2			Cost of Sales/Payables	19 19.4	16 22.9
	34	10.6	37 9.8				31 11.9	31 11.6
	59	6.2	47 7.8				48 7.6	43 8.5
		8.5	6.6			Sales/Working Capital	4.8	5.2
		12.4	8.4				9.0	10.5
		25.2	14.6				22.4	35.0
		77.5	12.8			EBIT/Interest	9.3	4.8
	(16)	4.8	(13) 4.2				(54) 2.1	(50) 1.6
		2.3	2.4				.1	-.9
						Net Profit + Depr., Dep., Amort./Cur. Mat. L/T/D	3.6	1.9
							(15) 1.8	(12) .9
							.0	-10.6
		.1	.1			Fixed/Worth	.2	.2
		.4	.3				.6	.5
		1.0	.5				1.4	1.5
		.5	.8			Debt/Worth	.7	.7
		2.1	1.4				1.6	2.1
		3.7	3.6				4.3	6.5
		44.0	20.2			% Profit Before Taxes/Tangible Net Worth	45.3	25.4
	(17)	30.1	10.5				(50) 7.3	(42) 6.4
		9.0	9.1				-.9	-2.3
		19.1	7.2			% Profit Before Taxes/Total Assets	16.8	9.3
		7.6	4.2				2.8	2.0
		2.9	2.0				-2.5	-4.7
		109.7	117.4			Sales/Net Fixed Assets	40.9	52.3
		23.4	26.1				12.9	16.2
		5.5	13.1				6.6	7.8
		2.9	2.9			Sales/Total Assets	3.1	3.1
		2.6	2.1				2.0	2.3
		2.1	1.5				1.7	1.7
		.5	.3			% Depr., Dep., Amort./Sales	.5	.4
	(12)	1.1	(12) 1.1				(49) 1.4	(43) 1.0
		2.3	2.1				3.1	2.1
						% Officers', Directors' Owners' Comp/Sales	1.9	1.3
							(20) 3.8	(21) 2.8
							5.8	7.6
1033M	23822M	232673M	735345M	590195M	250575M	Net Sales ($)	2498430M	2069198M
307M	9053M	90955M	335572M	313940M	143242M	Total Assets ($)	1131078M	1002626M

M = $ thousand   MM = $ million
See Pages 9 through 22 for Explanation of Ratios and Data

Comparative Historical Data | Current Data Sorted by Sales

Type of Statement

4/1/08-3/31/09	4/1/09-3/31/10	4/1/10-3/31/11	Type of Statement	0-1MM	1-3MM	3-5MM	5-10MM	10-25MM	25MM & OVER
8	9	8	Unqualified					1	7
10	10	13	Reviewed				2	8	3
7	5	5	Compiled			1	2	2	
4	2	5	Tax Returns		1	2	1	1	
15	16	15	Other	1	2	2	2	3	7
ALL 44	ALL 42	ALL 46	**NUMBER OF STATEMENTS**	2	3	4	5	15	17

Current data period columns: 13 (4/1-9/30/10) covers 0-1MM / 1-3MM / 3-5MM; 33 (10/1/10-3/31/11) covers 5-10MM / 10-25MM / 25MM & OVER.

ASSETS (%)

4/1/08-3/31/09	4/1/09-3/31/10	4/1/10-3/31/11		0-1MM	1-3MM	3-5MM	5-10MM	10-25MM	25MM & OVER
7.2	6.8	5.2	Cash & Equivalents					6.3	5.3
24.6	25.7	30.7	Trade Receivables (net)					28.5	31.8
33.2	33.1	34.3	Inventory					30.8	37.4
2.2	.7	1.8	All Other Current					1.6	3.1
67.2	66.3	72.0	Total Current					67.3	77.7
22.3	21.8	19.5	Fixed Assets (net)					23.0	14.8
4.0	3.0	2.9	Intangibles (net)					2.1	1.3
6.6	8.9	5.5	All Other Non-Current					7.7	6.2
100.0	100.0	100.0	Total					100.0	100.0

LIABILITIES

4/1/08-3/31/09	4/1/09-3/31/10	4/1/10-3/31/11		0-1MM	1-3MM	3-5MM	5-10MM	10-25MM	25MM & OVER
20.0	11.9	14.3	Notes Payable-Short Term					12.8	17.7
5.9	4.6	1.5	Cur. Mat.-L.T.D.					2.0	.8
16.6	17.2	21.0	Trade Payables					19.2	18.9
.4	.3	.2	Income Taxes Payable					.0	.4
7.5	9.9	10.6	All Other Current					7.9	10.1
50.4	43.9	47.6	Total Current					41.8	47.9
9.6	8.6	9.9	Long-Term Debt					12.3	5.6
.1	.2	.1	Deferred Taxes					.0	.3
3.5	2.7	5.5	All Other Non-Current					1.3	5.7
36.5	44.6	36.9	Net Worth					44.6	40.5
100.0	100.0	100.0	Total Liabilities & Net Worth					100.0	100.0

INCOME DATA

4/1/08-3/31/09	4/1/09-3/31/10	4/1/10-3/31/11		0-1MM	1-3MM	3-5MM	5-10MM	10-25MM	25MM & OVER
100.0	100.0	100.0	Net Sales					100.0	100.0
24.6	25.7	24.9	Gross Profit					25.7	18.2
22.5	22.7	21.6	Operating Expenses					20.0	14.8
2.2	3.0	3.3	Operating Profit					5.7	3.4
1.3	1.0	.9	All Other Expenses (net)					1.3	.7
.9	2.0	2.5	Profit Before Taxes					4.4	2.7

RATIOS

4/1/08-3/31/09	4/1/09-3/31/10	4/1/10-3/31/11		0-1MM	1-3MM	3-5MM	5-10MM	10-25MM	25MM & OVER
2.4	2.5	2.3	Current					3.0	2.2
1.5	1.6	1.6						1.4	1.7
1.1	1.2	1.2						1.1	1.2
1.2	1.5	1.4	Quick					2.2	1.3
.7	.6	.6						.6	.7
.3	.4	.5						.5	.6
25 14.6	26 14.2	36 10.3	Sales/Receivables					30 12.1	48 7.6
36 10.1	45 8.1	47 7.7						42 8.8	53 6.9
56 6.5	57 6.5	59 6.2						54 6.8	66 5.5
27 13.5	43 8.6	46 8.0	Cost of Sales/Inventory					21 17.2	52 7.0
63 5.8	69 5.3	76 4.8						53 6.9	74 4.9
117 3.1	125 2.9	103 3.5						101 3.6	104 3.5
18 19.9	16 22.5	19 18.8	Cost of Sales/Payables					18 20.3	22 16.8
29 12.6	33 11.0	37 9.8						35 10.4	36 10.1
50 7.3	50 7.4	58 6.2						45 8.1	50 7.3
5.5	5.8	7.3	Sales/Working Capital					8.6	4.5
9.9	11.4	10.4						12.3	7.6
48.8	25.6	25.0						26.0	14.2
7.7	10.3	11.0	EBIT/Interest					11.6	15.0
(42) 1.8	(38) 3.3	(40) 3.7						(13) 5.2	(15) 4.2
.9	1.2	1.6						2.5	1.2
7.5	14.7		Net Profit + Depr., Dep., Amort./Cur. Mat. L/T/D						
(11) 1.0	(10) 2.6								
-.3	-.3								
.1	.1	.1	Fixed/Worth					.1	.1
.5	.5	.4						.5	.3
1.4	.9	1.4						1.0	.8
.9	.6	.8	Debt/Worth					.6	.8
1.8	1.6	1.8						1.6	1.5
4.0	3.0	4.3						3.0	3.7
20.8	23.2	33.8	% Profit Before Taxes/Tangible Net Worth					36.5	20.8
(41) 5.1	(41) 8.2	(42) 15.9						24.3	9.8
-4.8	1.4	7.7						7.8	6.7
8.0	9.5	10.6	% Profit Before Taxes/Total Assets					23.6	8.3
1.7	3.9	4.7						7.2	4.2
-.5	.9	1.3						3.2	1.3
270.5	54.1	74.6	Sales/Net Fixed Assets					44.6	85.6
19.6	16.8	20.1						21.9	17.2
5.9	4.9	5.9						4.1	7.4
3.5	3.1	3.1	Sales/Total Assets					3.2	2.8
2.0	1.9	2.5						2.6	2.1
1.6	1.6	1.7						1.8	1.6
.3	.5	.5	% Depr., Dep., Amort./Sales					.5	.3
(33) 1.2	(35) 1.2	(34) 1.2						(12) 1.9	(13) 1.1
3.0	2.8	2.3						2.8	2.3
1.3	1.2	1.0	% Officers', Directors' Owners' Comp/Sales						
(18) 3.4	(14) 2.6	(11) 1.9							
5.4	4.6	5.9							
1458822M	1570781M	1833643M	Net Sales ($)	1033M	7062M	16760M	37258M	240677M	1530853M
755675M	763000M	893069M	Total Assets ($)	307M	3842M	5211M	17353M	101599M	764757M

Current Data Sorted by Assets | Comparative Historical Data

0-500M	500M-2MM	2-10MM	10-50MM	50-100MM	100-250MM	Type of Statement	4/1/06-3/31/07 ALL	4/1/07-3/31/08 ALL
		1	2	4		Unqualified	10	12
	1	6	1			Reviewed	8	6
		1				Compiled	4	3
	1					Tax Returns	1	
1	1	7	5	2		Other	20	14
	4 (4/1-9/30/10)		29 (10/1/10-3/31/11)					
1	3	15	8	6		**NUMBER OF STATEMENTS**	43	35
%	%	%	%	%	%	**ASSETS**	%	%
		7.9			D	Cash & Equivalents	5.6	4.6
		24.6			A	Trade Receivables (net)	25.9	25.4
		31.4			T	Inventory	30.5	31.4
		1.3			A	All Other Current	1.3	2.8
		65.1				Total Current	63.2	64.2
		25.8			N	Fixed Assets (net)	26.7	23.9
		4.4			O	Intangibles (net)	4.1	6.6
		4.7			T	All Other Non-Current	6.0	5.3
		100.0				Total	100.0	100.0
					A	**LIABILITIES**		
		6.8			V	Notes Payable-Short Term	10.9	8.8
		2.5			A	Cur. Mat.-L.T.D.	3.1	4.1
		14.2			I	Trade Payables	13.7	17.7
		.0			L	Income Taxes Payable	.2	.3
		6.6			A	All Other Current	7.8	6.8
		30.1			B	Total Current	35.7	37.7
		16.1			L	Long-Term Debt	9.7	13.6
		.9			E	Deferred Taxes	.7	1.0
		1.5				All Other Non-Current	9.3	3.8
		51.5				Net Worth	44.5	43.9
		100.0				Total Liabilities & Net Worth	100.0	100.0
						INCOME DATA		
		100.0				Net Sales	100.0	100.0
		24.3				Gross Profit	27.4	22.8
		20.5				Operating Expenses	21.0	17.9
		3.8				Operating Profit	6.4	4.9
		-.8				All Other Expenses (net)	1.1	1.4
		4.6				Profit Before Taxes	5.3	3.5
						RATIOS		
		3.2					2.8	2.8
		2.3				Current	1.7	1.7
		1.7					1.2	1.2
		1.6					1.3	1.5
		1.3				Quick	.8	.7
		.7					.6	.5
	25	14.7					37 9.9	35 10.5
	37	9.9				Sales/Receivables	44 8.4	48 7.6
	49	7.4					57 6.4	55 6.7
	21	17.0					46 7.9	48 7.5
	66	5.6				Cost of Sales/Inventory	70 5.2	71 5.1
	92	4.0					102 3.6	107 3.4
	13	27.5					16 22.5	21 17.7
	25	14.6				Cost of Sales/Payables	32 11.6	35 10.4
	36	10.2					40 9.1	48 7.6
		5.1					5.0	4.3
		6.2				Sales/Working Capital	8.0	7.1
		14.7					20.7	20.3
		43.8					16.5	11.8
	(14)	9.1				EBIT/Interest	(41) 3.8	(32) 3.4
		2.2					1.4	1.6
							14.8	13.2
	(17)					Net Profit + Depr., Dep., Amort./Cur. Mat. L/T/D	3.7	(13) 2.8
							.8	1.3
		.2					.2	.2
		.4				Fixed/Worth	.6	.6
		.9					1.2	2.2
		.4					.6	.6
		1.0				Debt/Worth	1.5	1.5
		1.5					3.1	5.0
		38.1					48.5	27.6
	(14)	16.5				% Profit Before Taxes/Tangible Net Worth	(41) 18.3	(32) 14.8
		1.5					3.9	6.9
		27.6					18.7	12.6
		9.0				% Profit Before Taxes/Total Assets	7.0	6.3
		2.5					.7	1.8
		33.0					26.4	17.0
		8.6				Sales/Net Fixed Assets	6.3	9.2
		5.1					4.5	5.2
		3.1					2.7	2.6
		2.2				Sales/Total Assets	2.0	2.0
		1.9					1.4	1.5
		1.0					1.0	.9
	(13)	2.8				% Depr., Dep., Amort./Sales	(39) 2.2	(31) 1.6
		3.7					3.8	3.2
							1.4	1.3
						% Officers', Directors' Owners' Comp/Sales	(12) 2.1	(11) 1.8
							6.2	4.7
796M	9259M	168098M	374563M	799186M		Net Sales ($)	1826173M	1649704M
405M	3944M	69472M	218424M	459222M		Total Assets ($)	884897M	833553M

M = $ thousand   MM = $ million
See Pages 9 through 22 for Explanation of Ratios and Data

Comparative Historical Data / Current Data Sorted by Sales

	Hist 1		Hist 2		Hist 3	Type of Statement	0-1MM	1-3MM	3-5MM	5-10MM	10-25MM		25MM & OVER
	13		9		7	Unqualified							6
	7		12		8	Reviewed		1	1	3	3		
	1		2		1	Compiled		1	1				
					3	Tax Returns							
	13		15		14	Other	1	1	1	1	4		7
	4/1/08-3/31/09 ALL		4/1/09-3/31/10 ALL		4/1/10-3/31/11 ALL			4 (4/1-9/30/10)			29 (10/1/10-3/31/11)		
	34		38		33	**NUMBER OF STATEMENTS**	1	3	3	4	9		13
	%		%		%	**ASSETS**	%	%	%	%	%		%
	7.4		10.1		7.7	Cash & Equivalents							9.8
	21.9		25.5		23.2	Trade Receivables (net)							24.0
	28.2		24.2		30.1	Inventory							25.6
	2.4		2.4		1.5	All Other Current							2.1
	60.0		62.2		62.5	Total Current							61.5
	24.5		28.2		26.4	Fixed Assets (net)							26.4
	8.0		4.4		5.9	Intangibles (net)							9.5
	7.5		5.1		5.2	All Other Non-Current							2.6
	100.0		100.0		100.0	Total							100.0
						LIABILITIES							
	14.1		9.6		8.9	Notes Payable-Short Term							8.5
	4.2		5.5		3.1	Cur. Mat.-L.T.D.							3.2
	15.1		13.6		14.2	Trade Payables							12.7
	.2		.2		.1	Income Taxes Payable							.1
	5.8		9.0		7.6	All Other Current							8.3
	39.4		37.9		33.8	Total Current							32.8
	12.5		16.3		17.4	Long-Term Debt							17.3
	1.0		.6		.5	Deferred Taxes							.3
	6.7		4.7		8.4	All Other Non-Current							15.4
	40.3		40.5		39.9	Net Worth							34.1
	100.0		100.0		100.0	Total Liabilities & Net Worth							100.0
						INCOME DATA							
	100.0		100.0		100.0	Net Sales							100.0
	22.4		28.1		24.7	Gross Profit							25.7
	18.8		24.1		20.2	Operating Expenses							17.7
	3.6		4.0		4.5	Operating Profit							8.0
	1.3		1.0		.1	All Other Expenses (net)							1.1
	2.3		3.0		4.4	Profit Before Taxes							7.0
						RATIOS							
	2.5		2.7		3.2	Current							3.1
	1.6		1.8		2.5								2.5
	1.0		1.1		1.3								1.2
	1.2		1.8		1.6	Quick							2.0
	.7		.9		1.2								1.1
	.5		.6		.6								.7
31	11.6	29	12.5	28	13.1	Sales/Receivables						40	9.1
41	9.0	47	7.7	45	8.1							50	7.3
49	7.4	55	6.6	52	7.0							55	6.7
41	8.9	36	10.2	41	8.9	Cost of Sales/Inventory						44	8.3
62	5.8	53	6.9	63	5.8							56	6.5
89	4.1	85	4.3	104	3.5							103	3.5
17	21.6	13	27.7	23	15.8	Cost of Sales/Payables						24	15.0
30	12.1	32	11.5	31	11.6							31	11.6
41	8.9	45	8.1	37	10.0							41	8.9
	5.4		4.6		4.7	Sales/Working Capital							4.3
	10.2		8.7		6.2								5.0
	NM		43.7		17.2								23.0
	9.3		12.3		33.0	EBIT/Interest							33.3
(30)	3.5	(36)	5.4	(30)	7.8								8.4
	1.1		2.3		2.5								4.2
	8.4		3.5			Net Profit + Depr., Dep., Amort./Cur. Mat. L/T/D							
(12)	2.7	(11)	2.6										
	1.7		2.0										
	.4		.3		.4	Fixed/Worth							.6
	.8		.7		.7								1.0
	2.7		2.2		1.8								3.4
	.7		.6		.6	Debt/Worth							.9
	1.6		1.1		1.3								2.4
	7.0		5.4		4.7								13.3
	22.4		45.4		42.1	% Profit Before Taxes/Tangible Net Worth							53.8
(29)	11.5	(33)	23.7	(28)	25.6							(11)	40.7
	2.6		9.8		7.5								27.2
	10.4		16.9		19.3	% Profit Before Taxes/Total Assets							17.6
	3.1		8.2		9.0								12.1
	-1.6		3.3		2.7								7.3
	13.7		18.6		13.0	Sales/Net Fixed Assets							11.1
	7.3		7.3		7.6								7.1
	4.7		4.2		5.1								4.9
	2.5		2.8		2.5	Sales/Total Assets							2.1
	2.0		1.9		2.0								1.9
	1.5		1.5		1.7								1.5
	1.4		.9		1.4	% Depr., Dep., Amort./Sales							2.2
(28)	2.5	(30)	2.3	(28)	2.5							(11)	2.5
	3.9		4.0		3.7								3.7
			1.2			% Officers', Directors' Owners' Comp/Sales							
		(12)	4.6										
			13.8										
	1868814M		1391270M		1351902M	Net Sales ($)	796M	7657M	11429M	33643M	133075M		1165302M
	937999M		824858M		751467M	Total Assets ($)	405M	5254M	5575M	32687M	52501M		655045M

M = $ thousand   MM = $ million
See Pages 9 through 22 for Explanation of Ratios and Data

Current Data Sorted by Assets | Comparative Historical Data

Type of Statement	0-500M	500M-2MM	2-10MM	10-50MM	50-100MM	100-250MM		4/1/06-3/31/07 ALL	4/1/07-3/31/08 ALL
Unqualified				6	3	2		16	13
Reviewed		5	5	3	1	1		7	10
Compiled	2	3	2	1	1			10	10
Tax Returns			1	1				6	5
Other			8	8	2			18	17
	10 (4/1-9/30/10)			43 (10/1/10-3/31/11)					
NUMBER OF STATEMENTS	2	8	16	19	5	3		57	55

ASSETS	0-500M %	500M-2MM %	2-10MM %	10-50MM %	50-100MM %	100-250MM %		%	%
Cash & Equivalents			11.8	12.3				7.6	3.6
Trade Receivables (net)			22.4	21.2				29.7	24.2
Inventory			37.3	37.0				31.6	33.4
All Other Current			.8	4.4				2.1	1.8
Total Current			72.2	74.9				71.0	62.9
Fixed Assets (net)			22.9	19.5				22.6	27.0
Intangibles (net)			.3	1.1				2.0	3.8
All Other Non-Current			4.5	4.5				4.5	6.3
Total			100.0	100.0				100.0	100.0

LIABILITIES									
Notes Payable-Short Term			5.9	10.2				14.1	11.6
Cur. Mat.-L.T.D.			2.6	3.9				3.0	3.4
Trade Payables			20.3	16.9				24.5	25.1
Income Taxes Payable			.1	.0				.5	.0
All Other Current			12.2	11.6				17.0	11.8
Total Current			41.0	42.6				59.2	51.9
Long-Term Debt			9.0	4.6				17.9	19.9
Deferred Taxes			.3	.3				.4	.5
All Other Non-Current			.2	1.0				1.6	1.0
Net Worth			49.5	51.4				20.9	26.6
Total Liabilities & Net Worth			100.0	100.0				100.0	100.0

INCOME DATA									
Net Sales			100.0	100.0				100.0	100.0
Gross Profit			28.4	25.7				28.0	28.9
Operating Expenses			25.6	21.1				23.6	25.3
Operating Profit			2.8	4.6				4.4	3.5
All Other Expenses (net)			.2	.4				1.4	1.4
Profit Before Taxes			2.6	4.2				3.0	2.2

RATIOS			2-10MM	10-50MM				4/1/06-3/31/07	4/1/07-3/31/08
Current			3.1	2.9				2.6	1.9
			1.7	1.9				1.6	1.4
			1.3	1.3				1.0	1.0
Quick			1.6	1.5				1.3	.9
			1.0	.8				.7	.6
			.5	.4				.4	.3
Sales/Receivables			25 14.9	26 13.9				25 14.6	20 18.6
			34 10.9	38 9.7				38 9.6	35 10.4
			44 8.3	52 7.0				58 6.3	49 7.5
Cost of Sales/Inventory			46 7.9	63 5.8				25 14.9	29 12.7
			72 5.1	108 3.4				74 5.0	77 4.7
			112 3.3	120 3.0				98 3.7	130 2.8
Cost of Sales/Payables			21 17.4	29 12.8				24 15.0	26 14.0
			28 13.0	41 9.0				41 8.9	43 8.6
			56 6.5	58 6.3				58 6.3	61 6.0
Sales/Working Capital			5.3	3.4				5.8	7.8
			6.0	6.2				9.5	12.1
			20.3	9.1				112.8	304.2
EBIT/Interest			21.1	235.2				8.1	4.7
			(12) 5.9	(18) 7.3				(53) 3.1	(53) 2.5
			-2.8	-1.1				.7	1.1
Net Profit + Depr., Dep., Amort./Cur. Mat. L/T/D								6.9	3.5
								(12) 2.4	(11) 2.7
								.6	.9
Fixed/Worth			.1	.1				.2	.4
			.3	.3				.6	.8
			1.2	.7				2.1	2.1
Debt/Worth			.5	.4				.9	1.0
			1.0	.9				2.0	2.6
			2.2	2.1				8.0	6.4
% Profit Before Taxes/Tangible Net Worth			30.6	35.5				45.7	34.6
			6.7	12.5				(47) 15.7	(45) 11.7
			-14.9	-2.3				4.7	1.5
% Profit Before Taxes/Total Assets			14.3	12.6				16.8	9.1
			4.3	8.6				5.5	4.5
			-6.5	-1.0				-1.0	.2
Sales/Net Fixed Assets			106.4	46.1				27.7	19.9
			18.5	16.7				12.9	8.8
			3.7	3.9				5.4	4.6
Sales/Total Assets			2.9	2.6				3.4	3.3
			2.1	1.6				2.2	2.2
			1.3	1.4				1.6	1.6
% Depr., Dep., Amort./Sales			.7	1.0				.9	.8
			(13) 1.6	(16) 2.0				(45) 1.8	(50) 1.7
			4.6	4.3				2.7	3.3
% Officers', Directors' Owners' Comp/Sales								1.6	.3
								(16) 4.2	(15) 2.2
								7.2	3.4

	0-500M	500M-2MM	2-10MM	10-50MM	50-100MM	100-250MM			
Net Sales ($)	1635M	52677M	200622M	774297M	497256M	383267M		2232697M	1760213M
Total Assets ($)	584M	12916M	82809M	427143M	319553M	410401M		1241633M	969152M

M = $ thousand   MM = $ million
See Pages 9 through 22 for Explanation of Ratios and Data

Comparative Historical Data   Current Data Sorted by Sales

			Type of Statement						
11	15	11	Unqualified					1	10
12	11	9	Reviewed			2	1	3	3
5	10	10	Compiled	1	2	1	2	2	2
6	4	5	Tax Returns		1	1		2	1
25	22	18	Other		2	2	3	2	11
4/1/08-3/31/09 ALL	4/1/09-3/31/10 ALL	4/1/10-3/31/11 ALL		0-1MM	1-3MM	3-5MM	5-10MM	10-25MM	25MM & OVER
					10 (4/1-9/30/10)			43 (10/1/10-3/31/11)	
59	62	53	NUMBER OF STATEMENTS	1	3	6	6	10	27
%	%	%	**ASSETS**	%	%	%	%	%	%
4.8	8.7	9.9	Cash & Equivalents					14.5	9.2
23.2	19.7	21.4	Trade Receivables (net)					18.9	20.9
34.6	33.2	35.7	Inventory					43.0	35.5
2.6	2.8	3.9	All Other Current					1.2	4.2
65.2	64.5	70.9	Total Current					77.6	69.7
24.9	24.8	22.1	Fixed Assets (net)					16.7	22.7
3.5	2.5	1.5	Intangibles (net)					.3	2.6
6.5	8.1	5.5	All Other Non-Current					5.4	5.0
100.0	100.0	100.0	Total					100.0	100.0
			LIABILITIES						
11.4	7.1	7.5	Notes Payable-Short Term					8.6	8.0
4.0	2.5	3.3	Cur. Mat.-L.T.D.					3.7	3.3
24.4	19.2	21.2	Trade Payables					34.7	15.3
.1	.2	.0	Income Taxes Payable					.0	.1
11.9	11.0	12.5	All Other Current					13.3	9.5
51.8	40.1	44.6	Total Current					60.3	36.3
19.2	19.4	18.3	Long-Term Debt					43.6	7.9
.2	.4	.4	Deferred Taxes					.1	.6
4.3	4.9	1.0	All Other Non-Current					.3	1.7
24.5	35.2	35.8	Net Worth					-4.3	53.6
100.0	100.0	100.0	Total Liabilties & Net Worth					100.0	100.0
			INCOME DATA						
100.0	100.0	100.0	Net Sales					100.0	100.0
28.1	30.4	29.7	Gross Profit					32.5	25.8
25.2	26.4	26.8	Operating Expenses					30.3	20.7
3.0	4.0	2.9	Operating Profit					2.2	5.1
1.9	.7	.6	All Other Expenses (net)					.2	.5
1.1	3.3	2.3	Profit Before Taxes					2.0	4.6
			RATIOS						
2.3	2.5	3.0	Current					2.6	3.0
1.7	1.8	1.7						1.5	2.4
1.2	1.3	1.2						1.0	1.5
1.2	1.3	1.6	Quick					1.7	1.4
.6	.7	.8						.7	.8
.3	.4	.4						.2	.5
23 15.9	21 17.4	25 14.8	Sales/Receivables					10 36.1	28 13.2
34 10.6	37 9.9	35 10.4						26 14.2	40 9.1
48 7.6	48 7.7	49 7.4						35 10.4	56 6.5
42 8.7	41 8.9	51 7.2	Cost of Sales/Inventory					39 9.3	63 5.8
92 4.0	83 4.4	92 4.0						69 5.3	111 3.3
135 2.7	137 2.7	122 3.0						92 4.0	122 3.0
21 17.5	23 15.8	24 14.9	Cost of Sales/Payables					21 17.7	25 14.6
33 11.1	37 9.7	41 9.0						33 11.0	39 9.3
68 5.4	56 6.5	60 6.1						66 5.5	55 6.6
5.9	4.3	4.2	Sales/Working Capital					5.3	3.3
8.4	6.6	6.1						15.1	5.1
21.3	13.6	21.8						NM	9.0
7.7	15.6	19.5	EBIT/Interest						51.9
(56) 2.0	(56) 4.0	(45) 4.7							(26) 8.9
-.4	.8	-1.1							2.4
15.5	7.3		Net Profit + Depr., Dep., Amort./Cur. Mat. L/T/D						
(11) 5.7	(12) 2.7								
2.2	.6								
.2	.2	.1	Fixed/Worth					.1	.1
.7	.5	.4						.4	.3
1.8	1.2	1.0						1.9	.8
.8	.6	.4	Debt/Worth					.6	.4
1.8	1.3	1.0						.9	.9
5.9	2.7	2.6						38.1	1.9
26.6	25.8	30.6	% Profit Before Taxes/Tangible Net Worth						33.4
(50) 11.7	(56) 12.6	(48) 12.0							12.5
3.3	2.0	-1.5							3.0
9.4	13.9	10.6	% Profit Before Taxes/Total Assets					25.2	12.5
3.0	5.9	4.9						.4	6.2
-1.9	.1	-2.5						-12.1	1.2
34.7	27.5	60.1	Sales/Net Fixed Assets					126.3	41.3
10.8	8.9	18.1						26.2	7.7
4.3	4.1	3.9						15.9	3.9
3.1	2.8	2.7	Sales/Total Assets					6.2	2.6
1.9	1.9	1.8						2.8	1.6
1.5	1.3	1.3						2.1	1.3
1.1	1.1	1.0	% Depr., Dep., Amort./Sales						1.2
(53) 2.4	(49) 2.4	(41) 1.8							(23) 2.0
3.8	3.5	4.4							3.0
1.0	2.1	2.0	% Officers', Directors' Owners' Comp/Sales						
(16) 2.1	(13) 3.0	(17) 2.7							
2.6	4.4	6.0							
2469296M	3120075M	1909754M	Net Sales ($)	104M	5246M	23361M	42327M	165821M	1672895M
1421178M	1799781M	1253406M	Total Assets ($)	233M	3386M	15197M	23978M	60513M	1150099M

© RMA 2011   M = $ thousand   MM = $ million
See Pages 9 through 22 for Explanation of Ratios and Data

Current Data Sorted by Assets — Comparative Historical Data

0-500M	500M-2MM	2-10MM	10-50MM	50-100MM	100-250MM		4/1/06-3/31/07 ALL	4/1/07-3/31/08 ALL
		2	7	1	2	Type of Statement / Unqualified	10	11
	5	6	2	1		Reviewed	12	17
	1	1	1			Compiled	5	2
	4	2				Tax Returns	5	5
2	3	3	6	2	3	Other	15	13
	13 (4/1-9/30/10)		41 (10/1/10-3/31/11)					
2	13	14	16	4	5	**NUMBER OF STATEMENTS**	47	48
%	%	%	%	%	%	**ASSETS**	%	%
	8.3	15.5	2.1			Cash & Equivalents	7.7	8.3
	30.1	25.3	34.1			Trade Receivables (net)	21.1	25.2
	31.9	31.9	43.8			Inventory	40.1	42.1
	3.0	3.2	1.9			All Other Current	2.7	1.7
	73.4	75.9	81.9			Total Current	71.7	77.2
	14.9	13.1	7.3			Fixed Assets (net)	16.7	15.7
	.6	2.4	4.2			Intangibles (net)	5.6	2.2
	11.1	8.6	6.5			All Other Non-Current	6.0	4.9
	100.0	100.0	100.0			Total	100.0	100.0
						LIABILITIES		
	10.8	2.6	16.0			Notes Payable-Short Term	12.6	16.4
	2.6	1.3	2.4			Cur. Mat.-L.T.D.	2.8	2.5
	26.5	10.4	15.8			Trade Payables	20.2	16.2
	.1	.6	1.5			Income Taxes Payable	.2	.2
	4.4	8.4	11.8			All Other Current	10.6	10.0
	44.4	23.3	47.5			Total Current	46.4	45.4
	10.8	5.2	8.0			Long-Term Debt	8.1	7.9
	.0	.0	.0			Deferred Taxes	.7	.4
	5.7	1.4	3.1			All Other Non-Current	5.7	3.6
	39.1	70.0	41.3			Net Worth	39.1	42.7
	100.0	100.0	100.0			Total Liabilities & Net Worth	100.0	100.0
						INCOME DATA		
	100.0	100.0	100.0			Net Sales	100.0	100.0
	32.0	35.1	27.7			Gross Profit	32.7	31.2
	36.1	28.9	21.6			Operating Expenses	28.2	28.6
	-4.1	6.2	6.0			Operating Profit	4.5	2.6
	.3	-.2	1.1			All Other Expenses (net)	1.1	.6
	-4.4	6.4	4.9			Profit Before Taxes	3.4	2.0
						RATIOS		
	2.8	11.4	2.4			Current	2.4	2.9
	1.8	3.5	1.9				1.5	1.6
	1.1	2.1	1.3				1.1	1.2
	1.2	6.8	1.3			Quick	1.1	1.3
	.8	2.3	.9				.6	.7
	.6	.8	.4				.4	.5
	5 75.5	22 16.6	46 7.9			Sales/Receivables	19 19.0	31 11.7
	34 10.6	38 9.7	59 6.2				36 10.2	42 8.7
	54 6.7	44 8.2	86 4.2				49 7.4	49 7.5
	19 18.8	51 7.2	69 5.3			Cost of Sales/Inventory	52 7.0	56 6.5
	53 6.9	59 6.2	109 3.4				82 4.5	94 3.9
	111 3.3	111 3.3	138 2.7				136 2.7	136 2.7
	16 23.5	11 32.9	17 21.4			Cost of Sales/Payables	24 15.2	15 24.3
	38 9.5	19 19.1	33 11.0				41 8.9	31 11.6
	66 5.5	34 10.7	58 6.3				52 7.0	53 6.9
	4.6	2.6	4.1			Sales/Working Capital	4.6	4.7
	13.9	5.5	6.7				8.1	7.3
	NM	8.8	13.4				36.7	15.7
	12.4		11.2			EBIT/Interest	13.8	7.2
	(12) 3.0		(15) 3.5				(39) 3.5	(43) 2.7
	-4.1		2.5				.9	1.1
						Net Profit + Depr., Dep., Amort./Cur. Mat. L/T/D	8.4	
							(13) 2.6	
							1.7	
	.1	.0	.1			Fixed/Worth	.1	.1
	.1	.1	.2				.4	.3
	1.3	.3	.5				.9	.8
	.5	.1	.5			Debt/Worth	.7	.5
	2.4	.5	1.5				1.9	1.8
	8.4	.9	4.0				7.5	4.1
	68.4	23.6	37.4			% Profit Before Taxes/Tangible Net Worth	56.9	37.3
	(11) 16.1	8.4	(14) 22.0				(40) 18.8	(46) 11.0
	-10.4	4.0	10.0				4.8	.2
	12.2	14.0	16.1			% Profit Before Taxes/Total Assets	16.3	12.3
	1.5	5.7	5.0				6.6	4.2
	-17.1	2.2	3.0				1.5	.3
	121.6	66.6	201.9			Sales/Net Fixed Assets	50.5	82.9
	57.1	37.8	38.5				18.8	15.2
	15.2	10.9	23.6				8.9	7.4
	5.3	3.2	2.6			Sales/Total Assets	3.1	2.8
	2.9	2.2	2.1				2.1	2.0
	2.1	1.7	1.7				1.7	1.6
	.1	.4	.3			% Depr., Dep., Amort./Sales	.7	.4
	(10) .3	(11) 1.0	(12) .7				(39) 1.4	(40) 1.0
	2.1	2.1	2.6				2.4	2.0
		2.5				% Officers', Directors' Owners' Comp/Sales	1.6	1.4
		(10) 4.1					(12) 4.1	(19) 2.6
		7.1					10.2	4.4
2525M	59419M	148731M	780252M	559338M	1617919M	Net Sales ($)	2289091M	2308432M
530M	15001M	57595M	353153M	290407M	848827M	Total Assets ($)	1269172M	1216139M

© RMA 2011

M = $ thousand   MM = $ million
See Pages 9 through 22 for Explanation of Ratios and Data

Comparative Historical Data / Current Data Sorted by Sales

Type of Statement

Type of Statement	4/1/08-3/31/09 ALL	4/1/09-3/31/10 ALL	4/1/10-3/31/11 ALL	0-1MM	1-3MM	3-5MM	5-10MM	10-25MM	25MM & OVER
Unqualified	9	6	12					3	9
Reviewed	10	13	14		3		4	5	2
Compiled	3	4	3				2	1	
Tax Returns	6	3	6		3	1	2		
Other	13	21	19	1		4	2	1	11
	13 (4/1/08-3/31/09)	21 (4/1/09-3/31/10)	19 (4/1/10-3/31/11)	|← 13 (4/1-9/30/10) →|			|← 41 (10/1/10-3/31/11) →|		
NUMBER OF STATEMENTS	41	47	54	1	6	5	10	10	22

Main Data (values in % unless noted)

	4/1/08-3/31/09 ALL	4/1/09-3/31/10 ALL	4/1/10-3/31/11 ALL	0-1MM	1-3MM	3-5MM	5-10MM	10-25MM	25MM & OVER
ASSETS %	%	%	%	%	%	%	%	%	%
Cash & Equivalents	9.2	9.6	8.1				15.9	4.7	4.6
Trade Receivables (net)	20.2	28.8	29.3				23.9	33.6	31.4
Inventory	35.6	31.3	34.7				33.2	34.0	40.0
All Other Current	1.9	2.3	4.0				3.7	1.9	1.9
Total Current	66.9	72.0	76.2				76.7	74.2	77.9
Fixed Assets (net)	22.1	16.2	11.4				8.7	16.9	8.3
Intangibles (net)	3.9	5.7	4.6				2.1	1.8	9.2
All Other Non-Current	7.1	6.1	7.8				12.5	7.1	4.6
Total	100.0	100.0	100.0				100.0	100.0	100.0
LIABILITIES									
Notes Payable-Short Term	14.6	12.7	11.7				7.6	7.5	13.6
Cur. Mat.-L.T.D.	7.6	2.5	3.1				1.9	2.7	2.4
Trade Payables	17.1	16.2	18.0				17.5	20.7	18.5
Income Taxes Payable	.8	.1	.7				.9	.0	1.3
All Other Current	10.1	13.1	8.3				4.3	11.4	10.6
Total Current	50.2	44.6	41.8				32.0	42.3	46.4
Long-Term Debt	11.7	12.2	10.0				5.5	3.0	14.5
Deferred Taxes	.3	.1	.0				.1	.0	.1
All Other Non-Current	4.8	8.4	4.9				1.2	2.0	4.2
Net Worth	33.1	34.7	43.2				61.2	52.7	34.8
Total Liabilties & Net Worth	100.0	100.0	100.0				100.0	100.0	100.0
INCOME DATA									
Net Sales	100.0	100.0	100.0				100.0	100.0	100.0
Gross Profit	33.8	32.3	30.3				37.0	31.2	24.2
Operating Expenses	33.2	30.6	27.0				31.6	23.7	19.5
Operating Profit	.6	1.7	3.3				5.3	7.5	4.7
All Other Expenses (net)	1.4	.6	.6				-.2	.4	1.3
Profit Before Taxes	-.8	1.1	2.7				5.6	7.1	3.4
RATIOS									
Current	2.9	2.5	3.3				7.8	2.8	2.4
	1.4	1.5	2.1				2.8	1.8	1.7
	1.0	1.2	1.2				1.3	1.1	1.3
Quick	1.2	1.4	1.6				5.0	1.5	1.3
	.6	.8	.9				1.1	.8	.9
	.3	.5	.5				.6	.5	.5
Sales/Receivables	16 22.4	28 12.8	25 14.6				7 54.5	31 11.7	46 8.0
	31 11.7	41 8.8	44 8.4				28 13.0	39 9.3	51 7.2
	47 7.8	66 5.5	62 5.9				45 8.0	57 6.4	69 5.3
Cost of Sales/Inventory	37 10.0	43 8.4	48 7.6				47 7.7	37 10.0	67 5.4
	80 4.5	69 5.3	68 5.3				56 6.5	57 6.4	88 4.1
	152 2.4	112 3.3	117 3.1				111 3.3	104 3.5	124 2.9
Cost of Sales/Payables	16 23.4	16 23.5	16 22.8				7 50.8	18 20.5	18 20.3
	28 13.0	25 14.4	33 11.2				16 22.4	26 14.2	42 8.8
	49 7.4	59 6.2	49 7.4				69 5.3	41 8.9	63 5.8
Sales/Working Capital	4.6	5.0	4.2				3.5	5.5	4.2
	10.8	8.7	6.8				7.4	10.4	7.4
	NM	14.9	19.2				20.0	42.6	12.0
EBIT/Interest	8.3	8.2	11.5						9.3
	(40) 1.6	(37) 3.1	(45) 4.4					(20) 3.6	
	-1.1	.8	.7						1.3
Net Profit + Depr., Dep., Amort./Cur. Mat. L/T/D		4.6	5.5						
		(13) 2.6	(17) 3.1						
		.2	.7						
Fixed/Worth	.1	.1	.1				.1	.1	.1
	.6	.3	.2				.1	.3	.3
	1.7	1.5	.8				.2	.8	NM
Debt/Worth	.6	1.0	.5				.2	.5	.8
	1.6	1.7	1.3				.5	.8	2.2
	3.6	14.6	6.1				1.8	2.3	NM
% Profit Before Taxes/Tangible Net Worth	35.3	28.7	38.2				65.7	38.2	46.9
	(35) 11.5	(38) 9.4	(45) 11.8				10.8	16.5	(17) 22.0
	-5.3	.7	3.7				4.4	2.0	8.9
% Profit Before Taxes/Total Assets	9.9	8.1	11.5				20.6	17.9	10.8
	1.5	3.8	4.5				6.1	5.0	5.0
	-9.9	-1.0	-.2				2.8	1.1	1.2
Sales/Net Fixed Assets	71.9	110.9	88.0				104.8	75.6	130.9
	16.2	30.8	38.5				65.6	33.7	38.5
	5.7	7.2	11.2				14.3	5.6	15.9
Sales/Total Assets	2.8	2.9	3.0				5.2	3.9	2.5
	2.1	2.1	2.2				2.6	2.8	2.1
	1.7	1.6	1.8				1.8	1.7	1.8
% Depr., Dep., Amort./Sales	.7	.5	.3						.5
	(29) 1.5	(31) 1.2	(39) 1.0					(16) 1.1	
	3.1	2.9	1.9						1.6
% Officers', Directors' Owners' Comp/Sales	1.6	2.3	2.0						
	(17) 3.9	(16) 4.0	(21) 3.9						
	8.5	8.2	7.5						
Net Sales ($)	1606865M	1464156M	3168184M	695M	10354M	20089M	65661M	157898M	2913487M
Total Assets ($)	751359M	748485M	1565513M	712M	3765M	9933M	25069M	66223M	1459811M

Current Data Sorted by Assets   **Comparative Historical Data**

Type of Statement	0-500M	500M-2MM	2-10MM	10-50MM	50-100MM	100-250MM		4/1/06-3/31/07 ALL	4/1/07-3/31/08 ALL
Unqualified	1	1	6	4	1	1		6	9
Reviewed	1	2	3	6				12	10
Compiled	1	5	3	2				10	13
Tax Returns	2	5	7	4				9	8
Other								17	10
		10 (4/1-9/30/10)		45 (10/1/10-3/31/11)					
NUMBER OF STATEMENTS	5	13	19	16	1	1		54	50
	%	%	%	%	%	%		%	%
ASSETS									
Cash & Equivalents		7.2	8.8	9.2				8.0	6.2
Trade Receivables (net)		18.5	25.1	26.4				26.2	24.2
Inventory		42.2	33.4	30.5				31.8	30.9
All Other Current		2.0	2.2	3.5				2.1	4.4
Total Current		69.9	69.5	69.6				68.1	65.8
Fixed Assets (net)		24.1	18.9	18.5				22.1	21.4
Intangibles (net)		3.5	4.6	5.4				2.5	5.0
All Other Non-Current		2.5	6.9	6.5				7.2	7.8
Total		100.0	100.0	100.0				100.0	100.0
LIABILITIES									
Notes Payable-Short Term		16.0	8.5	11.9				12.1	11.4
Cur. Mat.-L.T.D.		5.9	1.4	3.4				2.9	2.3
Trade Payables		11.6	14.6	11.9				14.4	14.0
Income Taxes Payable		.0	.8	.1				.1	.1
All Other Current		6.1	7.4	13.0				10.2	10.5
Total Current		39.7	32.7	40.3				39.7	38.3
Long-Term Debt		13.7	10.7	10.5				13.6	12.8
Deferred Taxes		.0	.3	1.7				.1	.1
All Other Non-Current		4.2	8.4	2.4				5.0	12.4
Net Worth		42.3	47.9	45.0				41.6	36.3
Total Liabilities & Net Worth		100.0	100.0	100.0				100.0	100.0
INCOME DATA									
Net Sales		100.0	100.0	100.0				100.0	100.0
Gross Profit		42.8	32.9	24.5				32.0	32.9
Operating Expenses		41.1	29.3	19.0				27.6	29.3
Operating Profit		1.7	3.6	5.5				4.4	3.7
All Other Expenses (net)		.6	.3	.8				.7	.9
Profit Before Taxes		1.1	3.3	4.7				3.7	2.8
RATIOS									
Current		4.3	4.5	3.0				3.5	3.7
		1.7	2.1	2.0				1.8	1.7
		1.1	1.5	1.0				1.3	1.3
Quick		.9	1.9	1.8				1.5	1.5
		.7	1.1	.9				.8	.7
		.5	.5	.4				.6	.5
Sales/Receivables		13 28.9	31 11.9	37 9.8				27 13.3	26 13.8
		27 13.7	39 9.3	64 5.7				39 9.5	34 10.6
		42 8.6	46 8.0	72 5.1				47 7.8	41 8.9
Cost of Sales/Inventory		93 3.9	54 6.8	55 6.7				38 9.6	40 9.1
		140 2.6	73 5.0	79 4.6				58 6.3	63 5.8
		182 2.0	111 3.3	149 2.4				124 2.9	110 3.3
Cost of Sales/Payables		16 22.6	15 24.7	15 24.1				17 22.1	14 25.3
		28 12.9	23 15.9	27 13.4				25 14.9	23 15.6
		50 7.3	50 7.3	46 7.9				38 9.5	34 10.6
Sales/Working Capital		3.2	4.0	3.1				4.7	5.2
		8.0	7.1	5.6				8.7	10.7
		93.8	10.9	NM				19.4	24.3
EBIT/Interest		11.1	14.8	37.2				10.0	8.2
		(14) 1.8	4.7	7.6				(48) 3.5	(46) 2.5
		-6.8	1.0	2.4				1.4	1.3
Net Profit + Depr., Dep., Amort./Cur. Mat. L/T/D								5.3	5.1
								(12) 2.7	(10) 2.2
								1.3	1.1
Fixed/Worth		.2	.1	.1				.2	.2
		.7	.3	.3				.5	.6
		1.1	1.1	1.8				1.2	1.5
Debt/Worth		.5	.3	.5				.5	.6
		1.3	1.3	1.0				1.4	1.8
		4.7	2.0	5.0				3.7	6.1
% Profit Before Taxes/Tangible Net Worth		16.6	43.4	35.7				41.3	46.3
	(11) 4.5	(17) 14.8	(14) 14.4					(49) 18.1	(44) 10.1
		-10.9	3.2	5.4				3.9	-2.6
% Profit Before Taxes/Total Assets		9.4	15.9	12.9				16.2	12.8
		2.6	6.1	5.6				8.4	4.7
		-11.4	.6	2.4				1.3	.2
Sales/Net Fixed Assets		20.7	44.7	20.9				41.5	34.1
		13.1	18.9	11.5				13.1	13.4
		9.4	7.6	6.1				7.9	8.4
Sales/Total Assets		2.9	2.7	2.1				3.2	3.3
		2.4	2.2	1.7				2.4	2.4
		1.6	1.8	1.3				1.9	1.9
% Depr., Dep., Amort./Sales		.4	.5	1.0				.8	.7
	(11) .7	(16) 1.2	(12) 1.8					(46) 1.5	(43) 1.4
		3.4	2.2	2.7				2.4	2.4
% Officers', Directors' Owners' Comp/Sales								2.4	2.8
								(24) 3.1	(23) 3.9
								8.0	9.1
Net Sales ($)	4462M	28202M	196006M	447785M	63913M	145472M		918564M	797005M
Total Assets ($)	1049M	12338M	90532M	281602M	56187M	103807M		454840M	423914M

M = $ thousand   MM = $ million
See Pages 9 through 22 for Explanation of Ratios and Data

Comparative Historical Data | Current Data Sorted by Sales

Type of Statement

			Type of Statement	0-1MM	1-3MM	3-5MM	5-10MM	10-25MM	25MM & OVER
5	5	6	Unqualified			2	2	2	4
9	11	14	Reviewed	1				8	1
11	7	8	Compiled	1	2		1	3	1
12	8	9	Tax Returns		4	2	2	1	
12	16	18	Other	2	4	2	3	4	3
4/1/08-3/31/09 ALL	4/1/09-3/31/10 ALL	4/1/10-3/31/11 ALL			10 (4/1-9/30/10)			45 (10/1/10-3/31/11)	
49	47	55	NUMBER OF STATEMENTS	4	10	6	8	18	9

Assets (%)

Hist 08-09	Hist 09-10	Hist 10-11	ASSETS	1-3MM	10-25MM
7.8	8.2	9.6	Cash & Equivalents	14.3	7.0
22.6	21.7	22.9	Trade Receivables (net)	17.9	26.4
32.3	31.3	33.0	Inventory	41.6	30.0
3.3	3.0	2.5	All Other Current	2.4	1.8
66.1	64.1	68.0	Total Current	76.2	65.2
21.3	23.6	22.1	Fixed Assets (net)	20.0	21.0
2.4	2.2	4.3	Intangibles (net)	.2	7.7
10.2	10.0	5.4	All Other Non-Current	3.6	6.2
100.0	100.0	100.0	Total	100.0	100.0

Liabilities

Hist 08-09	Hist 09-10	Hist 10-11	LIABILITIES	1-3MM	10-25MM
11.9	11.2	11.9	Notes Payable-Short Term	25.7	10.5
2.6	2.2	3.4	Cur. Mat.-L.T.D.	5.5	1.7
12.2	12.0	12.3	Trade Payables	8.9	12.6
.3	.1	.5	Income Taxes Payable	.0	.9
9.9	10.3	10.4	All Other Current	4.8	11.1
36.9	35.8	38.5	Total Current	44.9	36.7
14.6	10.6	11.9	Long-Term Debt	16.9	10.1
.2	.1	.6	Deferred Taxes	.0	1.5
8.8	7.7	7.9	All Other Non-Current	4.2	4.5
39.4	46.0	41.3	Net Worth	34.0	47.2
100.0	100.0	100.0	Total Liabilties & Net Worth	100.0	100.0

Income Data

Hist 08-09	Hist 09-10	Hist 10-11	INCOME DATA	1-3MM	10-25MM
100.0	100.0	100.0	Net Sales	100.0	100.0
36.1	34.6	34.3	Gross Profit	42.4	27.0
31.3	31.8	29.8	Operating Expenses	40.9	22.9
4.8	2.8	4.5	Operating Profit	1.5	4.1
1.3	1.1	.6	All Other Expenses (net)	.5	.9
3.5	1.7	3.9	Profit Before Taxes	1.0	3.3

Ratios

Hist 08-09	Hist 09-10	Hist 10-11	RATIOS	1-3MM	10-25MM
3.7	2.9	3.3	Current	5.3	3.1
2.0	1.8	2.0		2.3	2.0
1.2	1.3	1.1		1.0	1.0
1.6	1.7	1.5	Quick	3.5	1.7
.9	.9	.8		.6	1.0
.5	.5	.5		.3	.5
19 19.5	27 13.6	25 14.7	Sales/Receivables	8 46.4	33 11.1
32 11.3	34 10.7	37 9.9		21 17.7	50 7.3
49 7.5	50 7.3	58 6.3		57 6.4	69 5.3
49 7.5	48 7.6	54 6.7	Cost of Sales/Inventory	79 4.6	54 6.8
79 4.6	82 4.4	80 4.5		111 3.3	75 4.8
115 3.2	140 2.6	140 2.6		164 2.2	112 3.3
12 31.6	12 29.3	16 22.4	Cost of Sales/Payables	8 44.6	19 19.0
20 18.1	24 15.2	25 14.6		17 21.8	27 13.4
41 8.9	39 9.4	46 8.0		33 10.9	42 8.7
4.6	4.8	4.0	Sales/Working Capital	2.6	4.3
9.6	7.6	7.6		10.9	6.7
21.1	18.4	80.5		NM	NM
11.7	12.9	15.6	EBIT/Interest		18.0
(46) 3.6	(40) 2.7	(47) 4.0			(16) 4.0
1.3	-1.8	1.3			1.1
7.2		1.9	Net Profit + Depr., Dep., Amort./Cur. Mat. L/T/D		
(11) 3.4		(10) 1.1			
1.1		.2			
.1	.1	.1	Fixed/Worth	.2	.1
.4	.3	.4		.8	.4
1.0	1.2	1.5		NM	1.7
.5	.5	.5	Debt/Worth	.4	.4
1.5	.9	1.3		1.4	1.3
3.8	2.3	4.3		NM	4.8
42.0	27.7	37.6	% Profit Before Taxes/Tangible Net Worth		43.8
(45) 13.5	(45) 12.9	(47) 11.4			(16) 16.1
2.3	-3.8	1.8			6.2
13.5	11.2	14.6	% Profit Before Taxes/Total Assets	33.3	16.0
7.8	5.2	5.0		1.7	5.6
.5	-2.9	.6		-15.8	.5
38.0	31.3	29.2	Sales/Net Fixed Assets	23.1	26.6
15.0	12.7	13.1		13.8	11.5
8.5	5.4	5.7		9.9	4.9
3.2	2.7	2.6	Sales/Total Assets	4.0	2.2
2.4	2.1	2.1		2.4	1.9
1.8	1.7	1.5		1.7	1.4
.8	.9	.5	% Depr., Dep., Amort./Sales		.9
(37) 1.3	(39) 1.8	(45) 1.4			(13) 1.9
2.8	3.6	2.8			2.8
2.0	1.7	3.3	% Officers', Directors' Owners' Comp/Sales		
(28) 4.4	(20) 3.0	(23) 4.4			
6.1	5.6	5.7			

Dollar Figures

Hist 08-09	Hist 09-10	Hist 10-11		0-1MM	1-3MM	3-5MM	5-10MM	10-25MM	25MM & OVER
898968M	648107M	885840M	Net Sales ($)	1577M	18784M	21468M	61278M	295254M	487479M
488411M	407080M	545515M	Total Assets ($)	1135M	8160M	8771M	29947M	174649M	322853M

M = $ thousand   MM = $ million
See Pages 9 through 22 for Explanation of Ratios and Data

Current Data Sorted by Assets							Comparative Historical Data	

Type of Statement

0-500M	500M-2MM	2-10MM	10-50MM	50-100MM	100-250MM		4/1/06-3/31/07 ALL	4/1/07-3/31/08 ALL
		3	13	2	2	Unqualified	31	26
	4	24	8			Reviewed	24	23
4	4	11	1			Compiled	33	20
3	7	8				Tax Returns	14	12
4	7	16	9		2	Other	45	57
21 (4/1-9/30/10)		111 (10/1/10-3/31/11)						
11	22	62	31	2	4	**NUMBER OF STATEMENTS**	147	138
%	%	%	%	%	%	**ASSETS**	%	%
11.7	12.8	11.9	9.1			Cash & Equivalents	7.1	6.2
30.3	24.1	24.2	25.6			Trade Receivables (net)	25.6	24.6
30.8	32.5	34.0	31.0			Inventory	30.2	32.8
9.7	4.7	3.0	2.2			All Other Current	2.4	2.0
82.6	74.1	73.1	67.9			Total Current	65.2	65.6
10.6	14.0	19.5	19.8			Fixed Assets (net)	23.8	22.6
1.2	4.4	1.6	5.1			Intangibles (net)	4.0	4.8
5.6	7.5	5.7	7.2			All Other Non-Current	7.0	7.1
100.0	100.0	100.0	100.0			Total	100.0	100.0
						LIABILITIES		
18.4	16.5	10.0	6.6			Notes Payable-Short Term	14.2	13.7
3.0	11.7	2.4	1.9			Cur. Mat.-L.T.D.	4.2	3.6
30.4	12.8	19.7	15.6			Trade Payables	15.5	14.5
.1	.1	.1	.3			Income Taxes Payable	.4	.3
14.8	6.6	7.5	12.2			All Other Current	11.0	11.6
66.8	47.6	39.6	36.6			Total Current	45.2	43.7
33.1	27.9	11.9	6.7			Long-Term Debt	17.6	14.6
.0	.2	.0	.8			Deferred Taxes	.5	.3
.0	15.7	8.0	6.2			All Other Non-Current	9.7	6.7
.1	8.6	40.4	49.7			Net Worth	27.0	34.7
100.0	100.0	100.0	100.0			Total Liabilities & Net Worth	100.0	100.0
						INCOME DATA		
100.0	100.0	100.0	100.0			Net Sales	100.0	100.0
44.7	37.8	29.7	23.8			Gross Profit	32.0	30.5
42.8	34.8	23.6	17.2			Operating Expenses	26.9	25.2
1.9	2.9	6.1	6.7			Operating Profit	5.1	5.4
-.3	1.0	1.2	.3			All Other Expenses (net)	1.2	1.5
2.2	1.9	4.8	6.3			Profit Before Taxes	3.9	3.8
						RATIOS		
3.4	4.2	3.6	3.4			Current	2.6	2.5
1.9	1.8	1.9	2.0				1.7	1.7
1.1	1.0	1.3	1.4				1.1	1.3
1.3	2.5	1.9	1.6			Quick	1.4	1.2
1.2	.8	.9	.9				(146) .8	.9
.3	.4	.6	.6				.5	.5
7 50.7	15 24.4	22 16.6	32 11.3			Sales/Receivables	30 12.3	30 12.1
19 18.7	33 11.1	39 9.4	49 7.5				41 9.0	40 9.1
35 10.5	47 7.8	52 7.0	58 6.3				53 6.9	57 6.4
1 277.6	36 10.2	44 8.3	46 7.9			Cost of Sales/Inventory	38 9.5	46 7.9
49 7.4	86 4.2	66 5.5	74 4.9				69 5.3	77 4.8
98 3.7	144 2.5	122 3.0	105 3.5				105 3.5	120 3.0
11 33.0	13 27.1	21 17.1	14 26.6			Cost of Sales/Payables	19 19.5	17 22.0
32 11.6	29 12.8	35 10.5	27 13.6				29 12.7	32 11.5
58 6.3	38 9.5	50 7.4	41 8.9				46 7.9	47 7.8
5.0	4.8	4.1	3.7			Sales/Working Capital	5.5	4.8
16.8	8.8	7.0	5.9				9.3	8.3
122.5	NM	16.3	11.2				41.5	17.1
	4.7	14.4	33.2			EBIT/Interest	7.5	8.0
	(20) 2.4	(60) 4.4	(28) 11.5				(136) 2.9	(123) 2.7
	-.3	1.9	3.1				1.2	1.3
		6.1	65.7			Net Profit + Depr., Dep., Amort./Cur. Mat. L/T/D	10.0	10.7
		(12) 2.3	(11) 4.2				(38) 2.4	(31) 2.4
		.8	3.3				1.1	1.1
.0	.1	.1	.2			Fixed/Worth	.3	.2
.3	1.0	.4	.3				.6	.6
-1.2	-3.6	1.1	.9				1.6	1.7
.5	.8	.7	.6			Debt/Worth	.7	.7
1.3	4.9	1.7	.9				1.8	1.8
-5.2	-56.9	3.6	2.2				5.9	5.6
	51.7	50.7	35.3			% Profit Before Taxes/Tangible Net Worth	40.6	45.9
	(16) 14.5	(58) 20.8	(28) 25.1				(124) 18.5	(117) 18.1
	3.6	6.5	12.0				3.7	5.6
17.3	10.9	15.4	18.1			% Profit Before Taxes/Total Assets	14.4	15.5
7.2	3.5	6.4	9.4				6.6	6.2
2.5	-3.1	2.1	4.7				.6	.8
620.0	106.6	50.3	31.6			Sales/Net Fixed Assets	27.6	29.4
93.9	33.9	22.3	11.3				12.2	12.7
27.1	10.0	6.4	7.3				5.8	6.1
7.0	3.2	3.1	2.4			Sales/Total Assets	3.0	2.8
5.6	2.5	2.3	2.0				2.2	2.1
3.8	1.6	1.6	1.4				1.6	1.5
	.6	.5	1.0			% Depr., Dep., Amort./Sales	.9	.8
	(13) .9	(53) 1.3	(29) 1.6				(128) 1.7	(122) 1.6
	1.6	2.8	2.9				2.9	2.7
	2.0	1.6				% Officers', Directors' Owners' Comp/Sales	2.1	2.7
	(11) 2.9	(25) 2.4					(52) 4.4	(39) 3.7
	7.9	3.5					8.6	6.1
17000M	65055M	710736M	1432342M	281368M	942107M	Net Sales ($)	5415430M	5854754M
2825M	24468M	307536M	727298M	133897M	579071M	Total Assets ($)	3030487M	3175787M

© RMA 2011

M = $ thousand   MM = $ million
See Pages 9 through 22 for Explanation of Ratios and Data

Comparative Historical Data | Current Data Sorted by Sales

Type of Statement	4/1/08-3/31/09 ALL	4/1/09-3/31/10 ALL	4/1/10-3/31/11 ALL		0-1MM	1-3MM	3-5MM	5-10MM	10-25MM	25MM & OVER
Unqualified	23	21	20				1	1	2	16
Reviewed	26	19	36			3	2	7	17	7
Compiled	15	17	20		2	5	2	6	5	
Tax Returns	14	16	18		1	6	3	3	5	
Other	47	52	38		6	3	6	3	9	11
						21 (4/1-9/30/10)		111 (10/1/10-3/31/11)		
NUMBER OF STATEMENTS	125	125	132		9	17	14	20	38	34
ASSETS	%	%	%		%	%	%	%	%	%
Cash & Equivalents	7.3	7.1	11.0			8.3	11.2	15.3	9.7	10.7
Trade Receivables (net)	22.7	24.3	24.7			21.5	26.0	24.4	25.3	24.6
Inventory	33.7	33.0	32.2			36.6	26.3	32.1	36.5	29.0
All Other Current	2.3	2.3	3.8			4.4	7.5	3.1	2.9	2.8
Total Current	66.0	66.6	71.7			70.8	70.9	75.0	74.3	67.1
Fixed Assets (net)	23.4	23.1	17.9			20.8	21.2	16.4	16.3	18.8
Intangibles (net)	5.3	4.6	4.0			.7	4.8	1.0	3.0	7.7
All Other Non-Current	5.2	5.6	6.4			7.7	3.1	7.6	6.5	6.3
Total	100.0	100.0	100.0			100.0	100.0	100.0	100.0	100.0
LIABILITIES										
Notes Payable-Short Term	12.9	13.3	10.6			15.7	8.6	18.0	6.8	5.6
Cur. Mat.-L.T.D.	3.7	4.4	3.9			2.9	14.5	2.4	3.3	1.9
Trade Payables	14.7	17.9	18.2			12.4	18.3	20.1	19.5	16.7
Income Taxes Payable	.2	.3	.2			.1	.1	.2	.0	.4
All Other Current	9.5	8.2	9.5			7.3	7.7	8.0	7.2	13.8
Total Current	41.0	44.1	42.4			38.3	49.2	48.7	36.8	38.3
Long-Term Debt	14.8	16.5	15.6			30.3	25.2	8.9	12.3	9.1
Deferred Taxes	.5	.6	.4			.0	.0	.0	.1	1.3
All Other Non-Current	7.8	8.3	8.2			12.8	9.4	10.1	6.8	6.5
Net Worth	35.9	30.5	33.4			18.6	16.2	32.3	44.0	44.7
Total Liabilties & Net Worth	100.0	100.0	100.0			100.0	100.0	100.0	100.0	100.0
INCOME DATA										
Net Sales	100.0	100.0	100.0			100.0	100.0	100.0	100.0	100.0
Gross Profit	28.5	28.4	30.9			37.4	39.7	28.0	28.7	24.0
Operating Expenses	25.1	25.3	25.4			33.4	33.7	23.5	23.6	16.5
Operating Profit	3.3	3.0	5.4			4.0	6.0	4.5	5.1	7.4
All Other Expenses (net)	1.6	1.0	1.0			1.3	.7	2.6	.8	.8
Profit Before Taxes	1.7	2.1	4.5			2.7	5.4	1.9	4.4	6.6
RATIOS										
Current	2.7	2.7	3.4			5.7	2.9	3.0	3.5	3.0
	1.7	1.6	1.9			2.2	2.0	1.5	2.1	1.8
	1.2	1.1	1.3			1.1	1.3	1.1	1.4	1.3
Quick	1.2	1.3	1.6			2.7	1.4	1.8	1.6	1.6
	.7	.7	.9			1.2	.8	.8	.9	.9
	.5	.5	.5			.3	.5	.6	.5	.6
Sales/Receivables	26 13.9	24 15.2	23 16.0		16 22.5	15 24.4	30 12.1	15 23.7	31 11.9	
	37 9.9	39 9.4	37 9.8		29 12.4	37 9.8	45 8.2	35 10.3	45 8.2	
	50 7.3	54 6.7	50 7.3		47 7.8	53 6.8	57 6.4	46 7.9	52 7.0	
Cost of Sales/Inventory	46 7.9	36 10.2	41 8.9		41 9.0	16 22.3	48 7.6	34 10.7	45 8.0	
	86 4.3	67 5.4	66 5.5		81 4.5	63 5.8	78 4.7	65 5.7	60 6.1	
	131 2.8	120 3.0	114 3.2		148 2.5	152 2.4	118 3.1	122 3.0	89 4.1	
Cost of Sales/Payables	16 23.1	17 21.4	18 20.0		11 34.5	14 25.3	14 26.6	23 15.9	14 26.3	
	32 11.5	30 12.3	32 11.5		23 15.8	31 11.6	37 9.8	32 11.6	30 12.1	
	47 7.8	49 7.5	45 8.0		37 9.9	57 6.4	53 6.9	46 8.0	45 8.1	
Sales/Working Capital	4.6	4.7	4.1		3.7	3.5	4.1	4.2	4.1	
	7.2	7.8	7.2		14.1	6.7	8.2	7.4	7.1	
	34.9	86.6	23.2		61.9	51.4	41.0	15.2	20.5	
EBIT/Interest	7.2	8.3	13.4		5.8	26.9	8.2	14.9	19.5	
	(114) 2.3	(116) 3.0	(123) 4.3		(16) 2.8	(11) 2.8	(19) 3.1	6.0	(31) 11.8	
	.7	-.2	1.8		.6	1.2	1.4	2.1	2.9	
Net Profit + Depr., Dep., Amort./Cur. Mat. L/T/D	4.5	5.2	8.4							39.8
	(31) 1.5	(32) 2.1	(30) 2.6						(14)	3.8
	.3	.0	1.3							2.6
Fixed/Worth	.2	.2	.1		.2	.1	.1	.1	.2	
	.7	.6	.4		1.7	.5	.3	.3	.4	
	1.4	1.8	1.8		-4.2	NM	2.7	.8	1.8	
Debt/Worth	.7	.7	.7		.8	.4	.8	.7	.6	
	1.6	1.8	1.8		8.9	1.5	2.6	1.5	1.0	
	4.8	7.2	6.6		-18.7	NM	6.5	3.0	5.0	
% Profit Before Taxes/Tangible Net Worth	27.5	39.6	45.8		111.0	33.8	29.2	57.0	43.9	
	(108) 9.1	(105) 14.8	(112) 22.0		(12) 19.6	(11) 21.7	(17) 11.3	(37) 24.0	(28) 28.1	
	.1	1.0	7.0		4.4	5.9	5.7	8.0	13.2	
% Profit Before Taxes/Total Assets	10.3	13.0	14.9		11.6	13.6	7.5	18.6	22.7	
	3.9	3.9	6.3		4.9	3.7	3.8	8.0	11.0	
	-.9	-1.6	2.2		-.5	1.0	1.2	4.1	4.9	
Sales/Net Fixed Assets	29.2	37.5	56.1		88.5	431.2	96.1	44.6	27.3	
	12.2	13.1	21.3		20.6	46.3	21.2	22.8	11.4	
	5.1	7.0	9.2		7.9	2.5	8.2	10.8	8.0	
Sales/Total Assets	2.8	3.1	3.2		4.0	3.0	2.6	3.6	2.6	
	2.1	2.2	2.3		2.4	2.2	1.9	2.4	2.0	
	1.5	1.6	1.6		1.5	1.0	1.6	2.1	1.6	
% Depr., Dep., Amort./Sales	1.0	.7	.6		.8	.5	.3	.6	.9	
	(103) 1.7	(104) 1.5	(108) 1.3		(11) .9	(10) 1.6	(16) 1.0	(36) 1.3	(31) 1.7	
	2.7	2.8	2.7		2.0	3.2	2.9	2.3	3.0	
% Officers', Directors' Owners' Comp/Sales	1.5	1.5	1.5						1.6	
	(34) 3.3	(44) 3.6	(50) 2.5						(15) 2.4	
	5.7	5.6	5.5						2.9	
Net Sales ($)	4273886M	4049995M	3448608M		7227M	34883M	56565M	160506M	578927M	2610500M
Total Assets ($)	2389455M	2281048M	1775095M		8804M	20098M	32009M	87068M	260146M	1366970M

© RMA 2011   M = $ thousand   MM = $ million
See Pages 9 through 22 for Explanation of Ratios and Data

Current Data Sorted by Assets   Comparative Historical Data

0-500M	500M-2MM	2-10MM	10-50MM	50-100MM	100-250MM	Type of Statement	4/1/06-3/31/07 ALL	4/1/07-3/31/08 ALL
		1	3	1	3	Unqualified	16	17
	3	7	6			Reviewed	15	14
	1	1	2			Compiled	5	6
3	5					Tax Returns	7	2
1	2	6	11	2	1	Other	9	16
	8 (4/1-9/30/10)		51 (10/1/10-3/31/11)					
4	11	15	22	3	4	NUMBER OF STATEMENTS	52	55
%	%	%	%	%	%	ASSETS	%	%
	12.6	3.5	7.7			Cash & Equivalents	8.6	10.5
	23.0	40.2	26.0			Trade Receivables (net)	29.6	25.9
	39.9	38.0	42.2			Inventory	40.2	35.9
	6.8	.5	1.7			All Other Current	2.5	4.9
	82.3	82.2	77.7			Total Current	80.9	77.2
	4.8	10.6	9.5			Fixed Assets (net)	10.6	12.7
	1.4	.6	5.8			Intangibles (net)	3.0	4.3
	11.6	6.6	6.9			All Other Non-Current	5.5	5.9
	100.0	100.0	100.0			Total	100.0	100.0
						LIABILITIES		
	19.5	23.4	13.5			Notes Payable-Short Term	17.2	13.8
	6.0	.9	3.8			Cur. Mat.-L.T.D.	1.5	2.8
	10.8	14.7	15.8			Trade Payables	15.1	14.5
	.0	.0	.0			Income Taxes Payable	.5	.6
	11.2	12.2	8.5			All Other Current	8.2	8.3
	47.5	51.2	41.7			Total Current	42.5	39.9
	7.6	1.3	5.9			Long-Term Debt	7.6	11.1
	.0	.0	.0			Deferred Taxes	.0	.2
	15.7	5.3	1.3			All Other Non-Current	5.4	3.5
	29.2	42.2	51.0			Net Worth	44.4	45.3
	100.0	100.0	100.0			Total Liabilities & Net Worth	100.0	100.0
						INCOME DATA		
	100.0	100.0	100.0			Net Sales	100.0	100.0
	38.4	35.2	30.1			Gross Profit	28.6	31.8
	34.9	27.7	21.0			Operating Expenses	25.8	29.2
	3.5	7.5	9.1			Operating Profit	2.8	2.5
	4.0	1.2	.0			All Other Expenses (net)	.6	.4
	-.5	6.3	9.0			Profit Before Taxes	2.2	2.1
						RATIOS		
	2.7	2.2	3.2				4.1	4.6
	2.2	1.6	1.7			Current	1.8	1.9
	1.2	1.2	1.4				1.3	1.5
	1.2	1.6	1.7				2.2	1.9
	.8	.7	.8			Quick	.7	1.0
	.3	.5	.5				.5	.5
22 16.4	44 8.3	28 13.0					26 14.0	19 19.0
36 10.1	54 6.8	45 8.2				Sales/Receivables	43 8.6	38 9.6
58 6.3	76 4.8	76 4.8					64 5.7	54 6.7
29 12.5	44 8.4	57 6.5					52 7.0	40 9.2
107 3.4	68 5.3	97 3.8				Cost of Sales/Inventory	107 3.4	89 4.1
183 2.0	165 2.2	121 3.0					136 2.7	188 1.9
8 46.4	7 54.5	9 41.6					21 17.8	16 23.2
26 14.1	21 17.6	32 11.5				Cost of Sales/Payables	30 12.0	25 14.7
37 9.8	45 8.1	57 6.4					47 7.7	42 8.6
	3.7	5.1	4.0				3.5	3.2
	9.8	7.7	5.9			Sales/Working Capital	7.6	4.8
	15.6	31.5	14.1				16.0	15.4
		21.5	38.9				6.8	9.0
	(13)	5.5	(21) 17.8			EBIT/Interest	(47) 2.4	(47) 2.7
		1.5	3.9				.7	-.2
						Net Profit + Depr., Dep., Amort./Cur. Mat. L/T/D		
	.0	.1	.0				.0	.1
	.0	.2	.1			Fixed/Worth	.2	.2
	2.1	.4	.5				.5	.7
	.7	.6	.6				.3	.4
	4.4	1.3	1.1			Debt/Worth	1.3	1.4
	8.5	2.7	2.0				3.7	3.7
		33.0	62.2				29.2	34.9
	(14)	15.6	(21) 23.0			% Profit Before Taxes/Tangible Net Worth	(48) 9.4	(49) 10.8
		6.7	7.7				-6.1	-8.5
	18.5	19.2	28.9				12.1	16.3
	6.1	7.9	13.7			% Profit Before Taxes/Total Assets	3.9	5.2
	-1.9	1.7	4.4				-3.0	-2.4
	999.8	121.0	280.2				105.2	101.6
	158.0	25.1	40.4			Sales/Net Fixed Assets	35.1	26.2
	19.9	13.8	11.3				17.1	14.1
	2.9	3.0	2.5				3.0	3.0
	2.4	2.6	2.0			Sales/Total Assets	2.3	2.2
	1.8	2.1	1.4				1.6	1.5
		.4	.4				.3	.4
	(12)	.9	(15) .9			% Depr., Dep., Amort./Sales	(45) .7	(41) .9
		1.8	1.4				1.3	1.7
							.7	2.0
						% Officers', Directors' Owners' Comp/Sales	(25) 2.3	(20) 5.0
							5.5	11.3
4421M	30684M	224786M	1154395M	253994M	770767M	Net Sales ($)	1794083M	2223090M
859M	11939M	82776M	516266M	225657M	661711M	Total Assets ($)	865337M	1086770M

M = $ thousand   MM = $ million
See Pages 9 through 22 for Explanation of Ratios and Data

Comparative Historical Data | Current Data Sorted by Sales

			Type of Statement						
18	14	8	Unqualified					2	6
16	16	16	Reviewed		2	2	1	5	6
2	7	4	Compiled		1			1	2
1	7	8	Tax Returns		4	1			
17	17	23	Other	3	2	2	2	5	12
4/1/08-3/31/09 ALL	4/1/09-3/31/10 ALL	4/1/10-3/31/11 ALL		0-1MM	8 (4/1-9/30/10) 1-3MM	3-5MM	51 (10/1/10-3/31/11) 5-10MM	10-25MM	25MM & OVER
54	61	59	NUMBER OF STATEMENTS	3	9	5	3	13	26
%	%	%	ASSETS	%	%	%	%	%	%
9.8	13.0	7.8	Cash & Equivalents					3.0	8.2
32.6	31.3	27.8	Trade Receivables (net)					40.5	24.3
34.7	33.3	37.8	Inventory					34.1	40.3
3.8	2.0	3.4	All Other Current					.8	1.7
80.9	79.6	76.8	Total Current					78.4	74.5
10.7	10.5	9.0	Fixed Assets (net)					14.0	9.6
1.9	1.9	5.2	Intangibles (net)					.5	10.9
6.5	8.1	9.0	All Other Non-Current					7.1	4.9
100.0	100.0	100.0	Total					100.0	100.0
			LIABILITIES						
15.8	12.2	15.5	Notes Payable-Short Term					15.1	11.1
4.1	3.8	4.1	Cur. Mat.-L.T.D.					1.4	3.0
16.4	17.6	13.4	Trade Payables					17.9	13.6
.2	.1	.2	Income Taxes Payable					.0	.3
9.5	9.3	12.8	All Other Current					15.8	7.2
46.0	43.1	46.1	Total Current					50.2	35.2
6.7	6.3	6.0	Long-Term Debt					2.6	8.0
.1	.2	.3	Deferred Taxes					.0	.7
5.1	3.9	5.5	All Other Non-Current					.9	1.9
41.9	46.6	42.1	Net Worth					46.3	54.2
100.0	100.0	100.0	Total Liabilties & Net Worth					100.0	100.0
			INCOME DATA						
100.0	100.0	100.0	Net Sales					100.0	100.0
32.5	32.8	33.5	Gross Profit					38.0	28.1
28.0	28.3	26.5	Operating Expenses					26.3	20.2
4.5	4.5	7.0	Operating Profit					11.7	7.8
.4	.7	1.4	All Other Expenses (net)					.5	.8
4.1	3.8	5.7	Profit Before Taxes					11.2	7.0
			RATIOS						
2.6	4.2	3.0						2.5	3.4
1.9	2.0	1.7	Current					1.6	2.3
1.4	1.3	1.3						1.2	1.6
1.5	2.6	1.6						1.6	1.8
.9	1.0	.8	Quick					.7	1.0
.5	.6	.5						.6	.6
28 13.2	29 12.6	26 13.9					44 8.3	28 13.0
48 7.6	46 8.0	46 8.0	Sales/Receivables					54 6.8	44 8.4
74 5.0	67 5.5	63 5.8						78 4.7	62 5.9
49 7.4	43 8.4	50 7.3					47 7.8	57 6.5
89 4.1	84 4.3	89 4.1	Cost of Sales/Inventory					68 5.3	97 3.8
133 2.8	132 2.8	165 2.2						113 3.2	184 2.0
18 20.7	12 31.4	9 42.0					8 47.1	8 43.3
29 12.4	33 11.0	31 11.9	Cost of Sales/Payables					31 11.7	31 11.8
52 7.0	66 5.5	45 8.1						57 6.4	43 8.5
3.9	3.2	4.0						5.1	2.9
6.1	5.5	6.9	Sales/Working Capital					7.3	5.4
11.5	12.9	15.6						31.6	11.7
12.5	24.3	31.2						25.6	43.5
(48) 3.5	(52) 5.0	(52) 6.8	EBIT/Interest				(11) 14.0	(24) 17.9
1.3	1.3	1.5						1.8	1.9
14.8									
(14) 3.9			Net Profit + Depr., Dep., Amort./Cur. Mat. L/T/D						
.7									
.0	.0	.0						.1	.0
.1	.1	.2	Fixed/Worth					.2	.2
.5	.4	.6						.5	.6
.6	.4	.6						.6	.5
1.4	1.0	1.3	Debt/Worth					1.0	1.1
3.4	2.3	3.0						2.0	2.3
36.5	35.9	42.4	% Profit Before Taxes/Tangible					54.0	55.0
(51) 16.8	(56) 16.2	(51) 22.1	Net Worth				(12) 25.2	(23) 22.2
3.7	.9	3.3						8.5	5.7
16.4	15.0	18.7	% Profit Before Taxes/Total					20.0	19.2
5.8	6.6	9.0	Assets					9.0	13.1
1.3	.1	1.7						2.9	3.7
183.1	257.3	159.3						110.6	97.1
39.1	35.8	34.6	Sales/Net Fixed Assets					22.3	26.5
14.2	12.8	13.7						10.3	10.9
2.9	3.1	2.8						2.9	2.5
2.2	2.3	2.2	Sales/Total Assets					2.6	2.0
1.7	1.6	1.6						2.1	1.3
.3	.3	.4						.7	.4
(46) .7	(51) .7	(43) .8	% Depr., Dep., Amort./Sales				(10) 1.5	(21) .8
1.0	1.3	1.4						2.0	1.3
2.5	2.6	2.3							
(18) 4.0	(23) 4.6	(19) 3.4	% Officers', Directors' Owners' Comp/Sales						
5.9	7.2	6.1							
3108503M	2366539M	2439047M	Net Sales ($)	1778M	19053M	20042M	23904M	227945M	2146325M
1452377M	1198601M	1499208M	Total Assets ($)	564M	8221M	22055M	11112M	96464M	1360792M

M = $ thousand   MM = $ million
See Pages 9 through 22 for Explanation of Ratios and Data

Current Data Sorted by Assets   **Comparative Historical Data**

	0-500M	500M-2MM	2-10MM	10-50MM	50-100MM	100-250MM		4/1/06-3/31/07 ALL	4/1/07-3/31/08 ALL
Type of Statement									
Unqualified			1	6	3	4		14	14
Reviewed		2	5	4		1		9	2
Compiled			1					1	1
Tax Returns	2		4					3	1
Other	1	2		7	5			5	11
	5 (4/1-9/30/10)			43 (10/1/10-3/31/11)					
NUMBER OF STATEMENTS	3	4	11	17	8	5		32	29
ASSETS	%	%	%	%	%	%		%	%
Cash & Equivalents			10.4	12.3				13.6	11.1
Trade Receivables (net)			32.0	38.7				28.3	29.5
Inventory			29.3	32.6				32.8	34.8
All Other Current			4.2	3.7				7.3	4.5
Total Current			76.0	87.3				82.0	79.9
Fixed Assets (net)			9.1	5.4				8.3	9.7
Intangibles (net)			4.3	3.5				4.0	5.9
All Other Non-Current			10.5	3.8				5.8	4.5
Total			100.0	100.0				100.0	100.0
LIABILITIES									
Notes Payable-Short Term			23.6	18.6				22.3	13.1
Cur. Mat.-L.T.D.			1.1	2.8				5.2	5.7
Trade Payables			10.9	25.2				14.6	12.3
Income Taxes Payable			.0	.6				.3	.6
All Other Current			6.6	11.7				9.3	10.7
Total Current			42.2	58.9				51.6	42.4
Long-Term Debt			7.3	2.7				15.3	9.5
Deferred Taxes			.0	.0				.2	.3
All Other Non-Current			41.0	24.7				8.1	13.7
Net Worth			9.5	13.7				24.6	34.1
Total Liabilties & Net Worth			100.0	100.0				100.0	100.0
INCOME DATA									
Net Sales			100.0	100.0				100.0	100.0
Gross Profit			34.8	33.6				34.6	36.8
Operating Expenses			32.7	29.3				29.9	30.2
Operating Profit			2.1	4.3				4.6	6.6
All Other Expenses (net)			.7	1.2				.8	1.2
Profit Before Taxes			1.4	3.2				3.8	5.4
RATIOS									
Current			3.2	2.6				3.6	3.4
			1.7	1.4				2.1	2.1
			1.2	1.1				1.4	1.4
Quick			1.6	1.4				1.9	1.8
			.8	.8				.9	1.0
			.6	.6				.5	.5
Sales/Receivables			11 33.3	23 15.9				23 16.1	21 17.2
			43 8.5	42 8.6				43 8.5	47 7.8
			65 5.6	74 5.0				54 6.8	65 5.6
Cost of Sales/Inventory			11 34.4	39 9.3				35 10.3	52 7.0
			44 8.3	58 6.3				66 5.6	66 5.5
			101 3.6	81 4.5				113 3.2	133 2.7
Cost of Sales/Payables			8 45.6	20 18.5				19 19.0	16 22.9
			19 18.7	31 11.7				25 14.4	27 13.6
			29 12.7	75 4.8				37 10.0	37 9.8
Sales/Working Capital			4.3	5.6				3.8	3.8
			8.2	13.0				6.4	6.3
			27.7	40.7				11.2	15.6
EBIT/Interest			4.8	29.0				7.7	7.5
			(10) 2.6	3.8				(26) 3.2	(27) 4.3
			.2	-.4				1.0	1.9
Net Profit + Depr., Dep., Amort./Cur. Mat. L/T/D									
Fixed/Worth			.0	.0				.0	.1
			.2	.2				.1	.1
			.6	NM				1.4	NM
Debt/Worth			1.1	.8				.5	.5
			2.0	3.2				1.0	1.7
			5.8	NM				4.7	NM
% Profit Before Taxes/Tangible Net Worth			31.0	83.1				52.5	54.3
			(10) 3.9	(13) 21.5				(25) 14.9	(22) 30.3
			-18.4	8.5				7.6	6.4
% Profit Before Taxes/Total Assets			11.6	18.9				20.9	21.7
			3.6	6.3				9.5	11.6
			-3.9	-3.7				1.4	3.6
Sales/Net Fixed Assets			171.7	272.2				118.8	152.5
			56.0	101.8				49.7	38.9
			29.6	58.2				18.5	12.1
Sales/Total Assets			4.1	3.8				3.5	3.0
			2.9	2.9				2.7	2.4
			2.3	2.4				1.5	2.0
% Depr., Dep., Amort./Sales				.1				.3	.3
			(15)	.3				(27) .4	(23) .5
				.7				1.0	.9
% Officers', Directors' Owners' Comp/Sales								1.5	
								(14) 3.0	
								5.7	
Net Sales ($)	3286M	13404M	208413M	1406549M	1502385M	1380700M		3186908M	4323863M
Total Assets ($)	1204M	2611M	57913M	477835M	587414M	801606M		1444254M	2081015M

M = $ thousand   MM = $ million
See Pages 9 through 22 for Explanation of Ratios and Data

Comparative Historical Data / Current Data Sorted by Sales

				Type of Statement						
18		18	14	Unqualified						14
6		6	12	Reviewed		2		2	2	6
1		1	2	Compiled				1		
2		3	3	Tax Returns		2		2	1	
11		12	19	Other	1	1		2	1	14
4/1/08-3/31/09		4/1/09-3/31/10	4/1/10-3/31/11			5 (4/1-9/30/10)		43 (10/1/10-3/31/11)		
ALL		ALL	ALL		0-1MM	1-3MM	3-5MM	5-10MM	10-25MM	25MM & OVER
38		41	48	NUMBER OF STATEMENTS	1	5		5	3	34
%		%	%	ASSETS	%	%	%	%	%	%
10.2		15.3	10.6	Cash & Equivalents						11.4
27.7		29.9	32.0	Trade Receivables (net)			D			31.3
36.5		28.7	32.5	Inventory			A			30.9
5.4		3.3	3.5	All Other Current			T			3.1
79.8		77.1	78.5	Total Current			A			76.6
9.4		11.0	9.6	Fixed Assets (net)						10.6
5.0		6.9	6.4	Intangibles (net)			N			8.1
5.7		5.0	5.4	All Other Non-Current			O			4.6
100.0		100.0	100.0	Total			T			100.0
				LIABILITIES			A			
15.5		18.1	17.2	Notes Payable-Short Term			V			16.5
1.9		2.5	3.2	Cur. Mat.-L.T.D.			A			2.5
19.0		17.7	17.4	Trade Payables			I			18.5
.4		.1	.2	Income Taxes Payable			L			.3
12.9		20.6	9.1	All Other Current			A			10.6
49.7		59.1	47.2	Total Current			B			48.5
5.8		4.8	8.6	Long-Term Debt			L			6.3
.2		.2	.0	Deferred Taxes			E			.0
16.6		16.9	22.4	All Other Non-Current						26.1
27.6		18.9	21.9	Net Worth						19.1
100.0		100.0	100.0	Total Liabilties & Net Worth						100.0
				INCOME DATA						
100.0		100.0	100.0	Net Sales						100.0
34.9		32.8	36.5	Gross Profit						34.6
30.8		28.8	31.3	Operating Expenses						29.0
4.1		4.0	5.2	Operating Profit						5.7
1.2		1.7	.6	All Other Expenses (net)						.7
2.9		2.3	4.6	Profit Before Taxes						5.0
				RATIOS						
3.9		2.8	3.1							3.0
1.9		1.8	1.8	Current						1.6
1.2		1.1	1.2							1.1
1.6		1.7	1.5							1.4
.8		1.0	.8	Quick						.8
.3		.5	.6							.6

						Ratios						
7	50.8	22	16.6	18	19.7	Sales/Receivables					16	23.1
36	10.1	41	8.9	41	8.8						43	8.5
53	6.8	64	5.7	64	5.7						62	5.9
43	8.5	29	12.5	34	10.8	Cost of Sales/Inventory					33	11.1
58	6.3	43	8.4	62	5.9						62	5.9
120	3.0	88	4.1	99	3.7						85	4.3
15	24.3	17	21.4	17	21.2	Cost of Sales/Payables					18	20.6
22	16.8	28	13.3	28	13.2						28	12.9
42	8.8	47	7.8	46	7.9						41	8.9
	4.1		4.6		5.0	Sales/Working Capital						6.0
	9.9		9.5		10.4							11.3
	36.7		38.0		27.3							31.1
	7.7		10.4		14.2	EBIT/Interest						22.0
(33)	3.5	(37)	2.1	(44)	4.5						(32)	4.3
	.8		1.0		1.0							.4
			47.9			Net Profit + Depr., Dep., Amort./Cur. Mat. L/T/D						
		(10)	2.5									
			-24.6									
	.1		.1		.1	Fixed/Worth						.1
	.1		.2		.2							.4
	-7.5		NM		2.1							NM
	.5		.7		1.0	Debt/Worth						.9
	1.8		2.1		2.5							2.6
	-8.4		-20.5		11.4							NM
	53.8		70.0		74.5	% Profit Before Taxes/Tangible Net Worth						93.8
(27)	31.3	(30)	32.0	(38)	26.9						(26)	42.0
	14.0		6.8		6.5							6.8
	21.6		12.6		20.6	% Profit Before Taxes/Total Assets						20.8
	9.0		5.8		10.8							11.6
	-.7		.3		.7							-2.1
	176.5		149.3		169.6	Sales/Net Fixed Assets						148.3
	53.5		51.6		61.8							63.3
	19.6		13.7		17.6							16.2
	4.2		3.6		3.6	Sales/Total Assets						3.6
	2.8		2.7		2.6							2.7
	2.1		2.0		2.1							2.0
	.2		.2		.2	% Depr., Dep., Amort./Sales						.1
(31)	.7	(32)	.5	(37)	.5						(30)	.5
	1.0		1.5		1.4							1.6
	1.8		.9		1.5	% Officers', Directors' Owners' Comp/Sales						1.0
(12)	3.8	(15)	2.7	(22)	3.7						(12)	3.6
	6.2		5.0		6.2							5.5

			Net Sales ($)						
4350563M	3469632M	4514737M	Net Sales ($)	653M	8868M		33485M	55819M	4415912M
1839155M	1682373M	1928583M	Total Assets ($)	339M	2814M		15064M	19729M	1890637M

© RMA 2011

M = $ thousand   MM = $ million
See Pages 9 through 22 for Explanation of Ratios and Data

		Current Data Sorted by Assets					Comparative Historical Data	
					4		**Type of Statement**	
	2	3					Unqualified	10	11
			1				Reviewed	6	6
1		2					Compiled	1	2
		2	2	1	4		Tax Returns	6	2
	8 (4/1-9/30/10)		14 (10/1/10-3/31/11)				Other	6	5
								4/1/06- 3/31/07	4/1/07- 3/31/08
0-500M	500M-2MM	2-10MM	10-50MM	50-100MM	100-250MM			ALL	ALL
1	2	7	3	1	8		**NUMBER OF STATEMENTS**	29	26
%	%	%	%	%	%		**ASSETS**	%	%
							Cash & Equivalents	5.0	8.2
							Trade Receivables (net)	32.3	28.1
							Inventory	34.4	40.0
							All Other Current	5.1	4.6
							Total Current	76.8	80.9
							Fixed Assets (net)	13.2	8.4
							Intangibles (net)	3.0	3.8
							All Other Non-Current	7.0	6.9
							Total	100.0	100.0
							LIABILITIES		
							Notes Payable-Short Term	12.6	11.0
							Cur. Mat.-L.T.D.	4.6	4.1
							Trade Payables	17.2	14.4
							Income Taxes Payable	.2	.2
							All Other Current	8.1	12.5
							Total Current	42.7	42.2
							Long-Term Debt	12.7	7.1
							Deferred Taxes	.4	.4
							All Other Non-Current	2.1	1.4
							Net Worth	42.1	48.9
							Total Liabilties & Net Worth	100.0	100.0
							INCOME DATA		
							Net Sales	100.0	100.0
							Gross Profit	37.8	33.9
							Operating Expenses	30.7	29.2
							Operating Profit	7.1	4.7
							All Other Expenses (net)	1.7	.9
							Profit Before Taxes	5.4	3.8
							RATIOS		
							Current	2.8	2.8
								1.8	2.2
								1.3	1.3
							Quick	1.6	1.3
								.8	1.0
								.5	.4
							Sales/Receivables	16 22.3	21 17.1
								53 6.8	38 9.5
								68 5.3	49 7.5
							Cost of Sales/Inventory	43 8.4	54 6.7
								73 5.0	75 4.8
								124 3.0	117 3.1
							Cost of Sales/Payables	16 22.5	14 26.8
								36 10.1	26 13.8
								55 6.7	43 8.5
							Sales/Working Capital	4.2	4.7
								7.1	6.6
								13.4	11.8
							EBIT/Interest	6.1	16.9
								(26) 3.1	(23) 2.6
								1.6	1.3
							Net Profit + Depr., Dep., Amort./Cur. Mat. L/T/D	30.0	
								(12) 6.2	
								2.0	
							Fixed/Worth	.1	.1
								.2	.2
								.3	.3
							Debt/Worth	.8	.5
								1.4	1.0
								3.0	2.6
							% Profit Before Taxes/Tangible Net Worth	30.6	29.0
								(27) 17.0	(25) 15.9
								5.8	4.0
							% Profit Before Taxes/Total Assets	12.8	15.5
								6.1	6.6
								2.3	1.8
							Sales/Net Fixed Assets	67.0	100.9
								30.1	35.4
								15.8	19.1
							Sales/Total Assets	3.2	3.4
								2.4	2.6
								1.8	2.0
							% Depr., Dep., Amort./Sales	.3	.2
								(23) 1.0	(24) .8
								1.3	1.3
							% Officers', Directors' Owners' Comp/Sales	1.6	
								(16) 3.0	
								7.2	
1617M	10347M	81710M	68852M	126770M	2226056M		Net Sales ($)	2882887M	2945119M
464M	2283M	31390M	37032M	56653M	1135473M		Total Assets ($)	1346708M	1463784M

Comparative Historical Data / Current Data Sorted by Sales

4/1/08-3/31/09 ALL	4/1/09-3/31/10 ALL	4/1/10-3/31/11 ALL	Type of Statement	0-1MM	1-3MM	3-5MM	5-10MM	10-25MM	25MM & OVER
9	5	4	Unqualified						4
4	2	5	Reviewed			1	2	1	1
1	1	1	Compiled					1	
2	2	3	Tax Returns		1		1	1	
6	11	9	Other		1		1	1	6
				8 (4/1-9/30/10)			14 (10/1/10-3/31/11)		
22	21	22	NUMBER OF STATEMENTS		2	1	4	4	11
%	%	%	**ASSETS**	%	%	%	%	%	%
4.7	5.5	4.7	Cash & Equivalents	DATA NOT AVAILABLE					4.5
25.9	26.8	25.7	Trade Receivables (net)						31.2
44.7	38.1	36.4	Inventory						30.3
2.8	3.1	5.8	All Other Current						3.1
78.2	73.6	72.5	Total Current						69.1
10.3	9.1	10.1	Fixed Assets (net)						13.8
3.9	5.7	4.2	Intangibles (net)						5.4
7.6	11.6	13.2	All Other Non-Current						11.6
100.0	100.0	100.0	Total						100.0
			LIABILITIES						
15.2	15.6	15.1	Notes Payable-Short Term						16.3
2.7	11.0	3.2	Cur. Mat.-L.T.D.						1.3
14.8	15.4	16.4	Trade Payables						10.1
.3	.8	.6	Income Taxes Payable						1.0
9.3	13.6	10.7	All Other Current						9.6
42.3	56.4	46.0	Total Current						38.4
13.4	10.7	10.3	Long-Term Debt						14.1
.5	.1	1.0	Deferred Taxes						1.9
1.5	3.4	8.9	All Other Non-Current						4.8
42.3	29.4	33.9	Net Worth						40.7
100.0	100.0	100.0	Total Liabilties & Net Worth						100.0
			INCOME DATA						
100.0	100.0	100.0	Net Sales						100.0
34.0	31.7	30.8	Gross Profit						27.9
29.7	27.6	28.9	Operating Expenses						27.5
4.2	4.1	1.9	Operating Profit						.4
1.3	1.9	.7	All Other Expenses (net)						.6
3.0	2.2	1.1	Profit Before Taxes						-.2
			RATIOS						
2.6	2.7	2.6							2.6
1.9	1.7	1.7	Current						1.6
1.3	.8	1.2							1.2
1.1	1.4	1.3							1.7
.7	1.0	.9	Quick						.8
.5	.3	.2							.4
18 19.9	**12** 31.6	**17** 21.3							**30** 12.0
39 9.4	**36** 10.2	**45** 8.1	Sales/Receivables						**52** 7.0
67 5.5	**84** 4.4	**63** 5.8							**69** 5.3
76 4.8	**43** 8.6	**46** 7.9							**53** 6.9
106 3.4	**92** 4.0	**77** 4.7	Cost of Sales/Inventory						**75** 4.9
147 2.5	**144** 2.5	**142** 2.6							**109** 3.4
14 26.7	**19** 18.7	**14** 25.9							**17** 21.1
30 12.0	**24** 15.1	**27** 13.5	Cost of Sales/Payables						**25** 14.9
61 5.9	**57** 6.4	**56** 6.6							**33** 11.2
4.6	4.6	4.5							4.8
6.6	6.5	6.4	Sales/Working Capital						9.4
15.8	-30.7	23.7							22.4
7.3	6.1	6.7							6.2
(20) 2.0	(19) 3.4	(21) 3.8	EBIT/Interest						4.2
1.2	.9	1.9							2.2
			Net Profit + Depr., Dep., Amort./Cur. Mat. L/T/D						
.1	.0	.0							.1
.2	.1	.1	Fixed/Worth						.2
.3	1.7	1.4							2.4
.9	.8	.7							.6
1.5	1.6	1.6	Debt/Worth						1.6
2.2	165.3	7.6							7.5
32.5	29.3	30.8							34.2
(20) 10.3	(17) 18.5	(19) 14.0	% Profit Before Taxes/Tangible Net Worth						(10) 16.6
3.5	3.3	1.6							-50.6
12.1	10.8	12.0							11.6
2.7	3.3	6.5	% Profit Before Taxes/Total Assets						7.1
.9	-1.1	2.1							3.2
62.5	156.7	130.6							50.8
33.7	34.5	46.8	Sales/Net Fixed Assets						33.4
19.4	12.0	11.8							6.1
3.1	3.0	3.1							2.8
2.6	2.3	2.5	Sales/Total Assets						2.3
1.8	2.0	1.3							1.3
.6	.2	.2							
(19) 1.0	(16) .8	(14) .6	% Depr., Dep., Amort./Sales						
1.1	1.3	1.1							
			% Officers', Directors' Owners' Comp/Sales						
2913883M	2202590M	2515352M	Net Sales ($)		3888M	3264M	33594M	61606M	2413000M
1250094M	960675M	1263295M	Total Assets ($)		2972M	1231M	15901M	32570M	1210621M

M = $ thousand MM = $ million

See Pages 9 through 22 for Explanation of Ratios and Data

Current Data Sorted by Assets   **Comparative Historical Data**

0-500M	500M-2MM	2-10MM	10-50MM	50-100MM	100-250MM		4/1/06-3/31/07 ALL	4/1/07-3/31/08 ALL
						Type of Statement		
		2	3	2		Unqualified	14	10
	1	7	4			Reviewed	11	9
		2				Compiled	2	3
		1				Tax Returns	2	2
1	4	5	1		1	Other	10	13
	2 (4/1-9/30/10)		32 (10/1/10-3/31/11)					
1	5	17	8	2	1	**NUMBER OF STATEMENTS**	39	37
%	%	%	%	%	%		%	%
						ASSETS		
		3.5				Cash & Equivalents	4.1	5.0
		22.7				Trade Receivables (net)	28.2	26.3
		45.0				Inventory	41.1	44.6
		10.2				All Other Current	5.0	4.3
		81.4				Total Current	78.4	80.2
		5.9				Fixed Assets (net)	10.4	9.3
		3.3				Intangibles (net)	3.7	6.3
		9.5				All Other Non-Current	7.5	4.3
		100.0				Total	100.0	100.0
						LIABILITIES		
		26.0				Notes Payable-Short Term	20.2	21.5
		.6				Cur. Mat.-L.T.D.	2.0	2.0
		24.5				Trade Payables	13.3	12.8
		.1				Income Taxes Payable	.4	.6
		6.8				All Other Current	9.0	7.1
		57.9				Total Current	44.9	43.9
		4.8				Long-Term Debt	9.3	10.3
		.0				Deferred Taxes	.2	.4
		5.0				All Other Non-Current	16.3	8.8
		32.3				Net Worth	29.3	36.6
		100.0				Total Liabilities & Net Worth	100.0	100.0
						INCOME DATA		
		100.0				Net Sales	100.0	100.0
		30.2				Gross Profit	33.7	30.8
		28.6				Operating Expenses	30.3	28.4
		1.6				Operating Profit	3.4	2.4
		.8				All Other Expenses (net)	2.5	2.1
		.8				Profit Before Taxes	.9	.4
						RATIOS		
		2.2				Current	2.6	2.8
		1.4					1.9	2.1
		.9					1.3	1.4
		1.3				Quick	1.4	1.1
		.4					.8	.8
		.1					.3	.4
	11	32.7				Sales/Receivables	29 12.7	31 11.7
	27	13.6					49 7.4	49 7.5
	52	7.1					69 5.3	70 5.2
	66	5.5				Cost of Sales/Inventory	71 5.2	85 4.3
	113	3.2					127 2.9	138 2.6
	146	2.5					151 2.4	164 2.2
	8	47.9				Cost of Sales/Payables	16 22.9	17 21.6
	31	11.9					29 12.7	29 12.4
	100	3.7					39 9.5	42 8.7
		4.5				Sales/Working Capital	3.9	3.5
		17.3					5.8	4.7
		-45.7					10.8	7.8
		6.5				EBIT/Interest	4.9	5.4
		2.2					(37) 1.6	(34) 2.4
		.5					.8	-.3
						Net Profit + Depr., Dep.,	3.2	
						Amort./Cur. Mat. L/T/D	(11) 1.5	
							.3	
		.0				Fixed/Worth	.1	.1
		.1					.2	.2
		1.1					.7	.6
		1.3				Debt/Worth	1.1	.6
		1.9					1.9	1.4
		6.7					5.5	3.4
		41.2				% Profit Before Taxes/Tangible	41.6	30.3
	(14)	13.4				Net Worth	(33) 10.0	(32) 5.4
		-.8					-.6	-4.9
		11.6				% Profit Before Taxes/Total	17.3	7.0
		2.1				Assets	2.7	3.1
		-2.0					-.3	-3.8
		207.9				Sales/Net Fixed Assets	77.0	84.9
		74.0					23.3	25.9
		27.8					12.3	13.3
		2.9				Sales/Total Assets	2.7	2.4
		2.1					1.9	1.9
		1.7					1.5	1.4
		.2				% Depr., Dep., Amort./Sales	.4	.4
	(12)	.5					(34) 1.1	(34) .8
		1.3					2.2	1.9
						% Officers', Directors'	1.6	1.7
						Owners' Comp/Sales	(17) 3.0	(12) 3.4
							7.6	5.2
604M	18594M	237255M	501919M	251014M	87705M	Net Sales ($)	1665392M	2141627M
199M	7713M	91461M	191305M	136351M	131067M	Total Assets ($)	951365M	1425075M

Comparative Historical Data | Current Data Sorted by Sales

				Type of Statement	0-1MM	1-3MM	3-5MM	5-10MM	10-25MM	25MM & OVER
9		9	7	Unqualified					3	4
11		7	12	Reviewed		1	1	3	2	5
2		1	2	Compiled				3	1	
1		2	2	Tax Returns				1	1	
15		9	11	Other	1	1	1	2	2	2
4/1/08-3/31/09 ALL		4/1/09-3/31/10 ALL	4/1/10-3/31/11 ALL			2 (4/1-9/30/10)			32 (10/1/10-3/31/11)	
38		28	34	**NUMBER OF STATEMENTS**	1	2	2	9	9	11
%		%	%	**ASSETS**	%	%	%	%	%	%
4.6		4.2	4.1	Cash & Equivalents						5.1
26.1		24.5	20.8	Trade Receivables (net)						27.3
43.4		44.0	49.6	Inventory						41.4
3.9		3.5	6.5	All Other Current						4.9
78.0		76.2	81.1	Total Current						78.8
10.6		10.2	6.6	Fixed Assets (net)						9.4
5.7		8.3	5.6	Intangibles (net)						9.2
5.7		5.3	6.7	All Other Non-Current						2.6
100.0		100.0	100.0	Total						100.0
				LIABILITIES						
24.6		15.6	24.4	Notes Payable-Short Term						13.6
.6		1.7	1.9	Cur. Mat.-L.T.D.						.6
11.2		17.9	20.1	Trade Payables						29.3
.1		.7	.1	Income Taxes Payable						.0
8.9		8.2	6.2	All Other Current						5.6
45.4		44.1	52.7	Total Current						49.1
10.7		17.1	5.7	Long-Term Debt						5.5
.4		.5	.5	Deferred Taxes						1.3
5.4		8.4	3.8	All Other Non-Current						3.7
38.1		29.9	37.3	Net Worth						40.5
100.0		100.0	100.0	Total Liabilities & Net Worth						100.0
				INCOME DATA						
100.0		100.0	100.0	Net Sales						100.0
31.8		32.3	33.5	Gross Profit						30.9
31.0		30.4	30.5	Operating Expenses						25.9
.8		2.0	3.1	Operating Profit						5.0
2.4		2.7	.9	All Other Expenses (net)						1.0
-1.6		-.8	2.2	Profit Before Taxes						4.0
				RATIOS						
3.0		3.1	2.8							2.6
1.7		2.1	1.5	Current						1.8
1.3		1.4	1.2							1.2
1.1		1.4	1.3							1.8
.8		.8	.4	Quick						.5
.4		.3	.2							.2
30 12.2		16 23.1	9 40.2							8 47.3
39 9.3		42 8.8	28 12.9	Sales/Receivables						27 13.6
67 5.4		54 6.7	57 6.4							57 6.4
81 4.5		62 5.9	73 5.0							25 14.7
124 3.0		115 3.2	131 2.8	Cost of Sales/Inventory						62 5.9
191 1.9		193 1.9	188 1.9							142 2.6
15 24.8		19 18.9	13 28.8							18 20.4
26 14.1		32 11.3	31 11.6	Cost of Sales/Payables						31 11.9
41 9.0		44 8.4	65 5.6							63 5.8
3.6		4.5	5.0							5.2
5.0		5.8	8.1	Sales/Working Capital						7.6
12.0		11.7	24.8							24.7
4.7		7.5	9.2							22.0
(36) 1.5		1.3	(33) 3.1	EBIT/Interest					(10)	7.0
-1.7		-2.0	.8							1.0
				Net Profit + Depr., Dep., Amort./Cur. Mat. L/T/D						
.1		.1	.0							.1
.3		.3	.1	Fixed/Worth						.3
.7		1.8	1.1							1.2
.9		.9	1.0							.7
2.2		2.1	1.9	Debt/Worth						2.5
4.4		13.4	6.6							5.0
24.1		36.5	63.5							
(34) 3.7		(23) 4.8	(29) 16.5	% Profit Before Taxes/Tangible Net Worth						
-34.6		-18.2	2.7							
7.5		13.5	16.0							19.6
1.0		1.4	4.9	% Profit Before Taxes/Total Assets						16.2
-9.1		-8.6	-.4							.8
51.8		87.2	178.2							196.2
24.3		29.9	59.5	Sales/Net Fixed Assets						52.2
14.0		11.8	24.2							11.9
2.3		3.0	3.0							4.1
1.9		2.0	2.2	Sales/Total Assets						3.1
1.3		1.6	1.5							1.9
.5		.4	.3							.1
(31) .7		(21) 1.0	(24) .6	% Depr., Dep., Amort./Sales					(10)	.5
1.7		2.0	1.4							1.7
2.1										
(15) 5.7				% Officers', Directors' Owners' Comp/Sales						
7.0										
1726394M		2143362M	1097091M	Net Sales ($)	604M	4756M	7898M	60007M	148322M	875504M
1073779M		1075084M	558096M	Total Assets ($)	199M	2644M	4490M	30887M	101374M	418502M

© RMA 2011   M = $ thousand   MM = $ million
See Pages 9 through 22 for Explanation of Ratios and Data

Current Data Sorted by Assets | Comparative Historical Data

Type of Statement	0-500M	500M-2MM	2-10MM	10-50MM	50-100MM	100-250MM	4/1/06-3/31/07 ALL	4/1/07-3/31/08 ALL
Unqualified			1	8	1		6	4
Reviewed	1	7	14	6			15	9
Compiled			1				1	
Tax Returns	3	2					2	1
Other	1	3	3	6		1	8	11
		6 (4/1-9/30/10)		53 (10/1/10-3/31/11)				
NUMBER OF STATEMENTS	5	12	19	20	2	1	32	25
ASSETS	%	%	%	%	%	%	%	%
Cash & Equivalents		11.8	14.3	8.7			5.8	6.0
Trade Receivables (net)		22.3	21.5	29.3			34.7	28.6
Inventory		47.7	38.0	35.3			34.6	35.3
All Other Current		2.2	9.3	6.6			3.0	2.6
Total Current		84.0	83.1	79.9			78.2	72.5
Fixed Assets (net)		4.3	10.1	9.5			12.5	15.2
Intangibles (net)		1.7	.3	7.1			3.0	4.8
All Other Non-Current		10.1	6.5	3.5			6.3	7.5
Total		100.0	100.0	100.0			100.0	100.0
LIABILITIES								
Notes Payable-Short Term		7.9	8.8	14.1			18.3	27.2
Cur. Mat.-L.T.D.		.7	3.6	.8			.9	3.3
Trade Payables		41.8	28.7	22.4			27.1	16.4
Income Taxes Payable		.0	.0	.3			.2	.4
All Other Current		12.1	15.6	15.2			15.1	9.6
Total Current		62.4	56.7	52.8			61.6	56.9
Long-Term Debt		.2	1.2	7.5			4.3	4.8
Deferred Taxes		.0	.0	.0			.2	.0
All Other Non-Current		6.0	3.6	5.1			4.2	3.9
Net Worth		31.4	38.4	34.6			29.8	34.3
Total Liabilities & Net Worth		100.0	100.0	100.0			100.0	100.0
INCOME DATA								
Net Sales		100.0	100.0	100.0			100.0	100.0
Gross Profit		34.3	35.1	34.2			41.3	40.2
Operating Expenses		32.9	31.3	26.6			38.3	35.8
Operating Profit		1.4	3.8	7.6			3.0	4.4
All Other Expenses (net)		.4	.7	1.0			.7	1.1
Profit Before Taxes		1.0	3.1	6.6			2.3	3.3
RATIOS								
Current		1.9	1.8	2.8			1.8	1.9
		1.6	1.4	1.4			1.5	1.4
		1.0	1.2	1.2			1.2	1.2
Quick		.9	.9	1.1			1.1	1.1
		.6	.6	.6			.8	.7
		.2	.3	.3			.5	.2
Sales/Receivables		2 224.4	4 96.9	9 40.9			24 15.2	20 18.5
		16 22.5	22 16.8	41 8.9			42 8.8	35 10.4
		25 14.9	32 11.3	52 7.0			58 6.3	55 6.6
Cost of Sales/Inventory		24 15.5	22 16.3	45 8.0			44 8.2	48 7.6
		51 7.1	47 7.8	66 5.6			62 5.9	75 4.9
		94 3.9	79 4.6	84 4.3			111 3.3	116 3.2
Cost of Sales/Payables		30 12.2	20 18.2	19 19.2			24 15.0	23 16.0
		37 9.9	38 9.6	38 9.6			39 9.3	30 12.1
		61 6.0	63 5.8	54 6.7			82 4.4	40 9.1
Sales/Working Capital		7.4	10.6	7.6			8.7	8.0
		19.8	22.1	16.8			12.8	12.5
		NM	50.2	40.0			27.3	24.6
EBIT/Interest		14.1	4.8	26.6			6.7	7.4
		4.2	(15) 2.4	8.3			(28) 4.2	(23) 2.2
		.1	1.4	3.3			2.0	1.3
Net Profit + Depr., Dep., Amort./Cur. Mat. L/T/D								
Fixed/Worth		.1	.0	.0			.1	.1
		.2	.2	.2			.2	.3
		NM	.6	.6			1.1	1.1
Debt/Worth		1.0	1.1	1.0			1.0	.8
		1.9	1.8	2.6			2.2	1.8
		NM	4.4	7.4			5.3	6.0
% Profit Before Taxes/Tangible Net Worth			74.3	261.4			43.1	38.8
			12.6	(19) 67.3			(28) 26.5	(22) 28.6
			.9	23.9			13.0	8.0
% Profit Before Taxes/Total Assets		20.0	24.6	29.4			14.5	16.6
		4.9	5.9	20.5			6.0	7.3
		-1.2	.6	12.1			3.2	2.0
Sales/Net Fixed Assets		183.7	454.2	257.3			163.5	77.8
		136.9	81.3	60.5			38.9	29.7
		71.4	29.1	21.5			21.3	12.8
Sales/Total Assets		7.2	6.3	4.5			4.4	3.7
		4.5	4.7	3.2			3.3	2.9
		3.0	2.1	2.4			2.4	2.1
% Depr., Dep., Amort./Sales			.1	.1			.2	.2
			(15) .2	(18) .3			(23) .7	(22) .6
			1.4	1.0			1.1	1.4
% Officers', Directors' Owners' Comp/Sales			1.9				1.5	
			(10) 3.9				(16) 2.8	
			5.6				6.3	
Net Sales ($)	5112M	91164M	458342M	1400586M	82687M	258402M	1371162M	1774475M
Total Assets ($)	1560M	17218M	91822M	404963M	114857M	101740M	500709M	658449M

M = $ thousand   MM = $ million
See Pages 9 through 22 for Explanation of Ratios and Data

Comparative Historical Data

Current Data Sorted by Sales

			Type of Statement	0-1MM	1-3MM	3-5MM	5-10MM	10-25MM	25MM & OVER
2	4	10	Unqualified				1	1	8
9	7	29	Reviewed		1	1	9	7	11
	2	1	Compiled					1	
1	1	5	Tax Returns	3		1	1	1	
12	6	14	Other	1	2	1		1	7
4/1/08-3/31/09 ALL	4/1/09-3/31/10 ALL	4/1/10-3/31/11 ALL			6 (4/1-9/30/10)			53 (10/1/10-3/31/11)	
24	20	59	NUMBER OF STATEMENTS	4	3	3	10	13	26
%	%	%	ASSETS	%	%	%	%	%	%
11.7	14.7	12.3	Cash & Equivalents				13.3	16.8	9.1
22.7	30.8	23.6	Trade Receivables (net)				18.6	23.3	28.8
37.2	32.8	38.4	Inventory				45.0	37.2	33.8
4.6	2.9	5.9	All Other Current				7.1	6.1	7.3
76.2	81.3	80.3	Total Current				84.0	83.4	79.0
16.1	11.4	8.5	Fixed Assets (net)				7.5	8.6	9.1
2.7	3.2	5.2	Intangibles (net)				1.6	5.9	7.0
5.0	4.1	6.2	All Other Non-Current				6.8	2.1	4.9
100.0	100.0	100.0	Total				100.0	100.0	100.0
			LIABILITIES						
16.5	14.5	10.2	Notes Payable-Short Term				15.0	3.4	10.3
3.2	1.7	2.2	Cur. Mat.-L.T.D.				1.2	4.9	2.0
21.1	20.4	26.6	Trade Payables				27.6	36.7	25.0
.6	.2	.2	Income Taxes Payable				.0	.0	.4
12.3	10.8	13.3	All Other Current				8.5	14.5	15.8
53.7	47.6	52.5	Total Current				52.4	59.6	53.4
8.8	12.4	3.5	Long-Term Debt				1.1	1.2	6.4
.0	.0	.0	Deferred Taxes				.0	.0	.0
9.1	8.4	5.2	All Other Non-Current				11.5	3.5	3.1
28.4	31.5	38.8	Net Worth				35.0	35.7	37.1
100.0	100.0	100.0	Total Liabilities & Net Worth				100.0	100.0	100.0
			INCOME DATA						
100.0	100.0	100.0	Net Sales				100.0	100.0	100.0
39.4	36.4	35.4	Gross Profit				35.6	34.6	34.0
36.2	31.8	30.4	Operating Expenses				36.4	29.1	27.2
3.2	4.7	5.0	Operating Profit				-.8	5.5	6.8
1.2	.8	.8	All Other Expenses (net)				.6	.8	.7
2.0	3.8	4.3	Profit Before Taxes				-1.4	4.6	6.0
			RATIOS						
2.0	3.1	2.6	Current				2.3	2.2	2.2
1.5	1.5	1.5					1.7	1.2	1.4
1.2	1.3	1.2					1.1	1.2	1.2
1.0	2.1	1.0	Quick				.9	1.0	1.0
.7	.9	.6					.6	.7	.6
.2	.6	.3					.4	.4	.3
6 63.9	15 24.4	5 74.8	Sales/Receivables				12 30.9	4 94.2	7 55.3
25 14.3	38 9.6	22 16.8					17 21.8	22 16.8	25 14.4
35 10.3	64 5.7	41 8.8					24 15.0	35 10.6	44 8.3
35 10.4	37 9.8	27 13.4	Cost of Sales/Inventory				35 10.3	23 16.1	24 15.5
74 5.0	74 4.9	62 5.9					63 5.8	62 5.9	53 6.9
93 3.9	117 3.1	100 3.6					136 2.7	87 4.2	80 4.5
13 28.6	21 17.5	21 17.4	Cost of Sales/Payables				26 14.1	28 13.1	20 18.6
35 10.6	29 12.5	35 10.3					36 10.2	40 9.2	31 11.8
59 6.2	55 6.6	50 7.3					63 5.8	55 6.6	41 9.0
7.8	4.7	6.8	Sales/Working Capital				6.0	9.4	8.4
13.0	8.5	17.1					11.9	27.3	20.4
37.8	19.0	45.4					NM	50.3	61.2
11.4	16.9	13.2	EBIT/Interest					13.6	19.9
(22) 2.9	(16) 3.1	(53) 4.8					(11) 4.8	(25) 6.8	
.3	1.4	1.7						1.6	2.5
		17.2	Net Profit + Depr., Dep., Amort./Cur. Mat. L/T/D						
	(12)	1.9							
		.3							
.1	.0	.0	Fixed/Worth				.0	.1	.0
.4	.2	.2					.2	.3	.2
2.0	1.8	.6					11.4	.6	.6
1.0	.6	1.0	Debt/Worth				1.1	1.0	1.0
2.8	2.8	1.8					2.2	2.7	2.0
7.1	6.9	5.3					90.2	5.9	7.1
58.8	50.8	99.5	% Profit Before Taxes/Tangible Net Worth					105.0	210.6
(20) 24.1	(16) 20.5	(54) 33.5					(12) 37.8	(24) 60.0	
4.0	6.0	6.1						11.8	11.0
12.6	17.1	24.6	% Profit Before Taxes/Total Assets				15.2	38.3	27.9
8.2	9.0	12.1					2.4	7.3	18.0
-5.5	2.5	1.5					-13.9	1.2	6.2
169.9	284.5	239.4	Sales/Net Fixed Assets				450.7	302.8	265.8
21.9	27.7	75.2					90.7	135.8	73.1
12.6	13.1	25.9					60.7	27.0	25.5
4.5	3.8	5.9	Sales/Total Assets				4.7	6.8	6.2
3.0	2.7	3.3					3.8	4.7	3.7
2.5	1.8	2.4					2.1	2.7	2.6
.2	.2	.1	% Depr., Dep., Amort./Sales					.2	.1
(21) .7	(16) .8	(45) .3					(10) .3	(23) .2	
1.9	1.6	.8						1.4	.8
		1.7	% Officers', Directors' Owners' Comp/Sales						
	(20)	2.9							
		5.3							
1095148M	1636232M	2296293M	Net Sales ($)	2180M	7915M	12332M	70395M	212390M	1991081M
417247M	648515M	732160M	Total Assets ($)	1129M	2078M	13164M	24117M	73811M	617861M

M = $ thousand   MM = $ million
See Pages 9 through 22 for Explanation of Ratios and Data

Current Data Sorted by Assets   Comparative Historical Data

	0-500M	500M-2MM	2-10MM	10-50MM	50-100MM	100-250MM	Type of Statement	4/1/06-3/31/07 ALL	4/1/07-3/31/08 ALL
		2	3	7	10	1	Unqualified	12	9
		8	18	6			Reviewed	12	9
		2	1				Compiled	2	3
		2	2				Tax Returns	2	1
		5	2	7	1	2	Other	10	11
		11 (4/1-9/30/10)		68 (10/1/10-3/31/11)					
		19	26	20	11	3	NUMBER OF STATEMENTS	38	33
	%	%	%	%	%	%	ASSETS	%	%
D		11.3	10.8	9.8	7.0		Cash & Equivalents	9.5	11.5
A		22.6	23.3	25.1	16.6		Trade Receivables (net)	29.4	30.3
T		44.1	39.8	41.1	30.1		Inventory	37.5	37.1
A		7.2	10.9	2.4	12.4		All Other Current	2.9	4.1
		85.1	84.8	78.4	66.1		Total Current	79.2	83.0
N		9.7	4.5	8.5	7.2		Fixed Assets (net)	10.2	10.7
O		1.0	5.6	5.3	20.2		Intangibles (net)	5.0	1.6
T		4.1	5.2	7.8	6.5		All Other Non-Current	5.5	4.7
		100.0	100.0	100.0	100.0		Total	100.0	100.0
A							LIABILITIES		
V		8.1	16.3	10.6	21.1		Notes Payable-Short Term	15.6	18.9
A		.2	2.8	1.6	3.0		Cur. Mat.-L.T.D.	3.6	1.9
I		31.6	36.0	22.3	11.8		Trade Payables	12.3	10.6
L		.1	.2	.7	2.3		Income Taxes Payable	.3	.1
A		13.4	12.9	12.2	10.4		All Other Current	10.6	11.1
B		53.5	68.2	47.4	48.6		Total Current	42.3	42.6
L		.9	2.1	8.3	4.4		Long-Term Debt	10.5	7.3
E		.1	.0	.0	2.1		Deferred Taxes	.3	.2
		13.6	18.6	5.3	1.0		All Other Non-Current	6.6	7.8
		31.9	11.1	39.1	43.8		Net Worth	40.3	42.1
		100.0	100.0	100.0	100.0		Total Liabilities & Net Worth	100.0	100.0
							INCOME DATA		
		100.0	100.0	100.0	100.0		Net Sales	100.0	100.0
		34.8	27.8	32.8	38.7		Gross Profit	34.1	38.7
		36.3	25.1	25.4	35.9		Operating Expenses	30.6	35.8
		-1.4	2.7	7.4	2.9		Operating Profit	3.4	2.8
		.5	1.4	1.3	.4		All Other Expenses (net)	2.1	.9
		-1.9	1.3	6.1	2.5		Profit Before Taxes	1.4	1.9
							RATIOS		
		4.4	2.1	2.5	1.7			2.7	2.7
		1.5	1.3	1.6	1.7		Current	1.8	1.7
		1.0	1.0	1.4	1.2			1.4	1.5
		1.3	1.0	1.4	1.0			1.4	1.4
		.5	.6	.7	.6		Quick	.9	.9
		.2	.3	.3	.4			.5	.5
		8 45.0	2 241.8	9 41.8	2 160.9			24 15.5	14 26.6
		13 28.3	17 21.7	29 12.6	25 14.8		Sales/Receivables	36 10.1	36 10.1
		29 12.5	46 7.9	56 6.5	60 6.1			62 5.9	65 5.6
		23 16.0	27 13.6	43 8.6	72 5.1			46 8.0	41 8.8
		55 6.7	46 7.9	69 5.3	87 4.2		Cost of Sales/Inventory	76 4.8	77 4.7
		78 4.7	76 4.8	132 2.8	107 3.4			123 3.0	146 2.5
		12 29.7	20 18.6	14 26.3	26 13.8			14 26.1	13 27.9
		38 9.6	30 12.1	31 11.8	30 12.2		Cost of Sales/Payables	23 15.8	23 15.6
		66 5.6	57 6.4	66 5.5	37 9.9			36 10.0	43 8.5
		5.7	6.1	5.1	5.0			4.5	4.3
		23.7	11.6	9.7	7.6		Sales/Working Capital	7.1	6.5
		-288.4	NM	19.9	18.3			12.7	12.2
		3.4	6.6	18.7	13.0			7.0	10.0
		(12) 1.4	(22) 2.2	(19) 9.9	2.8		EBIT/Interest	(36) 2.4	(29) 2.3
		-2.1	1.5	2.1	.9			1.3	1.1
							Net Profit + Depr., Dep., Amort./Cur. Mat. L/T/D		
		.0	.0	.0	.1			.1	.1
		.1	.1	.2	.3		Fixed/Worth	.1	.2
		1.5	NM	1.7	1.2			.6	.6
		.5	1.0	.6	1.1			.6	.6
		2.1	3.5	2.0	1.3		Debt/Worth	1.5	1.4
		11.9	NM	4.8	28.6			5.7	3.1
		11.8	45.3	118.9				24.7	40.6
		(15) 4.8	(20) 15.3	(16) 45.7			% Profit Before Taxes/Tangible Net Worth	(31) 13.3	(30) 9.2
		.9	6.4	25.0				2.7	.8
		5.0	12.1	30.8	17.2			14.0	17.2
		1.4	3.1	19.2	2.2		% Profit Before Taxes/Total Assets	5.7	3.5
		-9.0	1.3	5.6	-.2			.6	.2
		999.8	538.8	183.0	53.9			121.0	67.5
		124.2	178.4	71.8	46.6		Sales/Net Fixed Assets	54.8	32.8
		36.4	65.8	21.6	17.2			18.6	16.7
		6.8	5.0	3.6	2.8			3.6	3.3
		5.4	3.6	3.1	1.8		Sales/Total Assets	2.6	2.7
		2.6	2.6	2.2	1.1			1.8	1.8
		.1	.1	.3	.3			.3	.3
		(13) .2	(16) .3	(17) .5	(10) .5		% Depr., Dep., Amort./Sales	(30) .5	(29) .6
		.5	.4	.7	1.3			1.4	1.4
		3.0	1.4					.8	.9
		(11) 4.1	(12) 1.9				% Officers', Directors' Owners' Comp/Sales	(13) 1.6	(14) 2.2
		6.5	4.3					6.1	7.1
		101090M	549933M	1545337M	1632261M	483080M	Net Sales ($)	1991533M	1852577M
		21495M	121597M	521142M	836604M	527987M	Total Assets ($)	1124043M	797386M

Comparative Historical Data / Current Data Sorted by Sales

Right-side columns 0-1MM and 1-3MM: DATA NOT AVAILABLE (for ratios/percentages).

	4/1/08-3/31/09 ALL	4/1/09-3/31/10 ALL	4/1/10-3/31/11 ALL	0-1MM	1-3MM	3-5MM	5-10MM	10-25MM	25MM & OVER
Type of Statement				11 (4/1-9/30/10)		68 (10/1/10-3/31/11)			
Unqualified	13	16	23	1		1	1	2	18
Reviewed	9	14	32			5	6	10	11
Compiled	1	1	3	1		1	1		
Tax Returns	6	1	4	1		2	1		
Other	12	19	17			2	3	1	11
NUMBER OF STATEMENTS	41	51	79	3		11	12	13	40
ASSETS	%	%	%	%		%	%	%	%
Cash & Equivalents	9.3	16.0	9.8			13.6	12.8	10.3	7.4
Trade Receivables (net)	29.9	28.2	22.1			29.4	15.5	22.3	21.7
Inventory	38.4	30.4	38.6			42.6	41.7	37.4	38.4
All Other Current	4.9	5.0	7.7			5.3	18.6	8.4	5.4
Total Current	82.5	79.6	78.2			90.8	88.6	78.3	72.9
Fixed Assets (net)	8.0	7.2	7.1			5.7	4.3	6.7	6.8
Intangibles (net)	5.4	6.9	9.0			1.1	2.2	8.1	14.1
All Other Non-Current	4.1	6.2	5.8			2.3	4.8	6.9	6.2
Total	100.0	100.0	100.0			100.0	100.0	100.0	100.0
LIABILITIES									
Notes Payable-Short Term	21.7	12.0	12.9			7.3	13.2	20.7	12.6
Cur. Mat.-L.T.D.	2.3	3.4	1.9			.4	.4	1.4	3.0
Trade Payables	12.0	19.7	26.9			25.1	33.7	28.8	25.0
Income Taxes Payable	.0	.7	.6			.1	.4	.0	1.0
All Other Current	8.3	10.5	12.1			16.7	13.9	15.9	9.9
Total Current	44.4	46.2	54.4			49.8	61.6	66.9	51.5
Long-Term Debt	10.6	7.6	4.7			1.3	1.8	4.7	6.9
Deferred Taxes	.0	.1	.4			.2	.0	.0	.8
All Other Non-Current	6.2	11.2	10.9			5.4	14.9	28.6	4.6
Net Worth	38.8	35.0	29.5			43.4	21.7	-.2	36.2
Total Liabilities & Net Worth	100.0	100.0	100.0			100.0	100.0	100.0	100.0
INCOME DATA									
Net Sales	100.0	100.0	100.0			100.0	100.0	100.0	100.0
Gross Profit	37.7	35.4	33.1			35.2	29.9	34.5	33.6
Operating Expenses	32.7	30.3	29.6			33.9	32.0	30.5	27.6
Operating Profit	5.0	5.1	3.5			1.3	-2.1	3.9	6.0
All Other Expenses (net)	2.0	1.3	1.1			.3	.6	2.6	1.0
Profit Before Taxes	3.0	3.8	2.4			1.0	-2.6	1.3	5.0
RATIOS									
Current	2.7	2.8	2.4			4.7	3.3	2.1	2.3
	2.0	1.9	1.6			1.9	1.3	1.4	1.6
	1.5	1.5	1.2			1.3	.9	1.0	1.2
Quick	1.9	1.6	1.2			1.5	1.8	.9	1.3
	.7	.9	.6			1.0	.3	.5	.7
	.3	.7	.3			.4	.3	.3	.3
Sales/Receivables	11 34.3	17 21.1	6 57.0			4 81.5	2 194.7	8 43.7	5 71.9
	37 9.8	41 9.0	23 16.0			23 16.1	10 35.3	33 11.1	24 15.0
	69 5.3	61 6.0	49 7.5			65 5.6	13 27.2	43 8.5	51 7.1
Cost of Sales/Inventory	48 7.6	33 11.0	32 11.3			34 10.6	21 17.6	33 11.2	38 9.6
	74 4.9	55 6.6	60 6.1			67 5.5	40 9.0	67 5.4	66 5.6
	153 2.4	87 4.2	88 4.1			124 2.9	67 5.4	85 4.3	97 3.7
Cost of Sales/Payables	9 41.2	17 21.2	18 20.6			11 32.3	13 27.5	19 19.1	19 19.3
	26 13.8	32 11.5	32 11.5			38 9.6	37 9.9	26 13.9	31 11.7
	49 7.5	48 7.6	54 6.8			73 5.0	78 4.7	52 7.1	50 7.3
Sales/Working Capital	4.4	4.0	5.4			4.4	8.0	7.4	5.4
	6.3	7.7	10.0			7.3	15.2	10.1	10.0
	12.1	14.7	34.3			26.7	NM	NM	33.6
EBIT/Interest	15.6	12.4	10.0				3.9	4.4	16.9
	(37) 2.8	(42) 3.0	(67) 2.8				(10) 1.8	(10) 2.4	(39) 5.8
	1.3	1.5	1.3				-5.8	1.2	1.9
Net Profit + Depr., Dep., Amort./Cur. Mat. L/T/D		291.3	60.4						73.2
		(11) 12.2	(13) 3.6						(11) 3.6
		.4	1.2						1.3
Fixed/Worth	.0	.0	.0			.0	.0	.0	.1
	.1	.1	.2			.0	.0	.5	.2
	1.0	.6	1.5			.4	NM	-2.1	-4.1
Debt/Worth	.7	.7	1.0			.3	.8	1.5	1.1
	1.3	1.5	2.2			2.0	3.7	3.2	2.0
	11.0	6.3	13.5			5.0	NM	-48.9	-35.5
% Profit Before Taxes/Tangible Net Worth	36.9	53.1	60.6			15.3			100.3
	(34) 13.9	(44) 21.8	(61) 21.5			4.8			(29) 35.3
	4.2	1.5	5.4			.9			23.2
% Profit Before Taxes/Total Assets	16.3	18.4	17.2			4.2	6.2	15.3	20.6
	5.5	6.4	4.2			1.7	1.5	2.4	11.6
	.7	1.2	1.1			.2	-18.7	1.2	2.4
Sales/Net Fixed Assets	283.9	209.7	238.9			733.2	UND	296.7	163.1
	52.7	63.4	84.1			113.4	272.1	47.6	63.0
	22.5	27.4	36.4			36.4	90.1	25.9	39.4
Sales/Total Assets	3.4	3.7	4.7			6.3	6.0	4.6	3.9
	2.6	2.6	3.3			3.6	4.0	3.5	3.1
	2.0	1.8	2.3			2.2	2.9	2.4	1.8
% Depr., Dep., Amort./Sales	.2	.2	.1			.0			.2
	(29) .5	(34) .4	(57) .4			(10) .2			(31) .4
	1.3	.7	.7			.3			.7
% Officers', Directors' Owners' Comp/Sales	1.1	.8	1.2						.7
	(20) 1.9	(21) 2.4	(34) 2.0						(16) 1.4
	5.3	4.1	4.2						2.1
Net Sales ($)	2178863M	2874165M	4311701M	6219M		43700M	93021M	205372M	3963389M
Total Assets ($)	952776M	1401373M	2028825M	2423M		13836M	23354M	78276M	1910936M

M = $ thousand   MM = $ million
See Pages 9 through 22 for Explanation of Ratios and Data

Current Data Sorted by Assets   Comparative Historical Data

0-500M	500M-2MM	2-10MM	10-50MM	50-100MM	100-250MM	Type of Statement	4/1/06-3/31/07 ALL	4/1/07-3/31/08 ALL
	2	2	8		1	Unqualified	14	10
	2	6	4	1		Reviewed	9	11
1	2					Compiled	8	5
5	6	4	1			Tax Returns	2	5
1	2	9	3	1	2	Other	12	15
	9 (4/1-9/30/10)		54 (10/1/10-3/31/11)					
7	14	21	16	2	3	NUMBER OF STATEMENTS	45	46
%	%	%	%	%	%	**ASSETS**	%	%
	10.0	6.0	6.7			Cash & Equivalents	10.1	6.9
	23.0	21.7	21.5			Trade Receivables (net)	23.7	22.4
	39.5	46.2	44.4			Inventory	38.8	40.2
	2.7	5.2	5.2			All Other Current	4.5	4.3
	75.2	79.2	77.8			Total Current	77.1	73.9
	15.7	8.6	12.9			Fixed Assets (net)	12.6	13.7
	6.1	3.0	2.8			Intangibles (net)	5.8	7.0
	3.1	9.1	6.6			All Other Non-Current	4.4	5.4
	100.0	100.0	100.0			Total	100.0	100.0
						LIABILITIES		
	14.8	12.1	12.5			Notes Payable-Short Term	16.3	16.9
	2.4	2.3	4.9			Cur. Mat.-L.T.D.	1.6	1.5
	15.3	18.6	16.2			Trade Payables	15.4	15.9
	.0	.0	.1			Income Taxes Payable	.1	.2
	10.4	11.5	8.9			All Other Current	9.1	6.7
	42.9	44.5	42.6			Total Current	42.6	41.2
	12.5	10.7	7.0			Long-Term Debt	11.1	11.6
	.0	.3	.1			Deferred Taxes	.3	.3
	6.3	12.0	2.1			All Other Non-Current	2.3	4.2
	38.2	32.6	48.2			Net Worth	43.8	42.7
	100.0	100.0	100.0			Total Liabilities & Net Worth	100.0	100.0
						INCOME DATA		
	100.0	100.0	100.0			Net Sales	100.0	100.0
	32.8	31.1	35.5			Gross Profit	34.1	31.4
	31.5	27.6	27.2			Operating Expenses	28.9	26.9
	1.4	3.6	8.3			Operating Profit	5.2	4.5
	1.2	.5	.6			All Other Expenses (net)	1.2	1.4
	.2	3.1	7.7			Profit Before Taxes	4.0	3.1
						RATIOS		
	2.9	3.4	2.9				4.1	4.3
	1.8	1.5	1.8			Current	1.8	1.8
	1.3	1.3	1.4				1.3	1.3
	1.1	.9	1.8				1.8	1.4
	.7	.6	.5			Quick	.9	.6
	.5	.4	.2				.4	.4
	22 16.3	23 15.7	9 39.8				24 14.9	23 15.6
	38 9.7	34 10.8	41 8.9			Sales/Receivables	36 10.1	40 9.2
	45 8.1	49 7.4	53 6.8				56 6.6	56 6.5
	43 8.4	62 5.9	61 6.0				48 7.6	58 6.3
	84 4.4	103 3.5	139 2.6			Cost of Sales/Inventory	124 2.9	109 3.4
	137 2.7	155 2.4	169 2.2				178 2.0	176 2.1
	7 49.8	17 21.5	24 15.4				17 22.1	18 20.8
	34 10.7	33 11.1	44 8.2			Cost of Sales/Payables	31 11.8	25 14.4
	48 7.6	76 4.8	61 6.0				48 7.7	48 7.7
	4.3	3.1	4.6				3.3	3.4
	7.5	5.9	6.4			Sales/Working Capital	6.5	6.3
	21.2	22.1	8.8				17.9	17.0
	8.4	27.0	24.1				9.3	7.1
	(13) 2.7	(19) 4.2	10.8			EBIT/Interest	(44) 4.0	(43) 2.5
	-1.7	2.2	2.9				1.2	1.1
						Net Profit + Depr., Dep.,	17.1	11.5
						Amort./Cur. Mat. L/T/D	(13) 3.4	(10) 5.2
							.1	1.3
	.1	.0	.1				.1	.1
	.5	.2	.2			Fixed/Worth	.2	.2
	NM	.6	.5				.8	.7
	1.0	.6	.5				.5	.4
	1.7	1.9	1.1			Debt/Worth	1.1	1.5
	NM	4.3	1.8				5.4	4.6
	28.9	35.9	44.2			% Profit Before Taxes/Tangible	40.0	35.4
	(11) 10.2	(19) 18.4	(15) 34.1			Net Worth	(39) 14.3	(38) 7.6
	-32.8	10.1	8.7				1.2	.2
	9.0	11.1	24.5			% Profit Before Taxes/Total	17.3	11.6
	3.2	7.6	13.4			Assets	4.2	4.7
	-4.5	3.1	3.3				.7	.1
	53.9	222.1	68.2				50.5	63.9
	21.1	38.3	24.2			Sales/Net Fixed Assets	23.2	18.8
	8.5	13.3	11.7				9.7	9.0
	2.8	2.7	3.0				2.9	3.0
	2.3	2.2	2.3			Sales/Total Assets	2.1	2.1
	1.9	1.4	1.6				1.5	1.5
	.4	.1	.4				.4	.4
	(11) .8	(15) .5	(15) .7			% Depr., Dep., Amort./Sales	(39) .7	(36) 1.2
	1.9	1.3	1.5				1.9	1.8
	1.9	2.2				% Officers', Directors'	1.4	1.2
	(10) 2.9	(10) 2.9				Owners' Comp/Sales	(15) 3.3	(14) 2.6
	4.1	5.9					5.4	4.7
8548M	46016M	235089M	830066M	406211M	639286M	Net Sales ($)	1936880M	2824384M
1986M	19672M	100184M	384998M	155190M	424427M	Total Assets ($)	1183287M	1669346M

M = $ thousand   MM = $ million
See Pages 9 through 22 for Explanation of Ratios and Data

Comparative Historical Data

Current Data Sorted by Sales

				Type of Statement						
13		18	13	Unqualified		1	1	2		9
17		12	13	Reviewed			2	3	3	5
5		7	3	Compiled			2	1		
11		8	16	Tax Returns		3	6	1	1	
18		13	18	Other	5	2	1	1	7	6
					1					
4/1/08-3/31/09 ALL		4/1/09-3/31/10 ALL	4/1/10-3/31/11 ALL		0-1MM	1-3MM 9 (4/1-9/30/10)	3-5MM	5-10MM	10-25MM 54 (10/1/10-3/31/11)	25MM & OVER
64		58	63	NUMBER OF STATEMENTS	6	6	12	8	11	20
%		%	%	ASSETS	%	%	%	%	%	%
9.3		10.4	8.4	Cash & Equivalents			4.5		6.2	7.4
24.6		25.2	22.0	Trade Receivables (net)			23.2		30.4	22.9
38.7		38.0	41.2	Inventory			42.2		41.6	42.0
5.4		2.6	4.1	All Other Current			3.1		1.3	5.2
78.0		76.2	75.7	Total Current			73.0		79.5	77.6
13.6		11.9	13.2	Fixed Assets (net)			13.3		10.6	11.5
2.4		4.7	5.0	Intangibles (net)			10.7		3.9	5.5
6.1		7.2	6.1	All Other Non-Current			3.0		6.0	5.5
100.0		100.0	100.0	Total			100.0		100.0	100.0
				LIABILITIES						
13.6		14.7	16.2	Notes Payable-Short Term			20.9		18.1	12.4
3.0		2.1	4.4	Cur. Mat.-L.T.D.			2.6		5.6	3.6
17.6		16.3	15.2	Trade Payables			12.4		22.6	16.4
.3		.1	.1	Income Taxes Payable			.0		.0	.3
9.2		10.4	9.1	All Other Current			7.2		10.3	9.9
43.6		43.6	44.9	Total Current			43.1		56.6	42.7
11.2		8.0	12.2	Long-Term Debt			10.9		6.3	10.7
.1		.5	.1	Deferred Taxes			.0		.1	.1
5.8		5.8	9.5	All Other Non-Current			1.9		4.9	9.2
39.2		42.1	33.2	Net Worth			44.1		32.2	37.3
100.0		100.0	100.0	Total Liabilties & Net Worth			100.0		100.0	100.0
				INCOME DATA						
100.0		100.0	100.0	Net Sales			100.0		100.0	100.0
34.6		34.1	36.3	Gross Profit			31.3		31.0	35.1
28.9		28.4	32.0	Operating Expenses			30.7		25.9	27.3
5.7		5.6	4.3	Operating Profit			.7		5.1	7.8
.8		.8	.5	All Other Expenses (net)			1.1		.8	.6
4.9		4.8	3.8	Profit Before Taxes			-.4		4.3	7.2
				RATIOS						
4.6		3.9	3.5				3.1		1.9	3.7
1.7		1.8	1.8	Current			1.8		1.3	1.8
1.2		1.3	1.3				1.4		1.2	1.4
2.1		1.7	1.2				1.1		.9	2.1
.6		1.0	.6	Quick			.9		.7	.8
.4		.4	.4				.6		.5	.3

							Sales/Receivables						
13	27.4	20	17.8	22	16.2			31	11.7		30	12.1	9	40.8
35	10.5	37	9.8	37	9.8	Sales/Receivables		40	9.2		41	8.9	43	8.6
51	7.1	49	7.4	52	7.0			51	7.1		52	7.0	58	6.3
51	7.2	49	7.4	56	6.5			47	7.8		61	6.0	53	6.9
83	4.4	88	4.1	106	3.4	Cost of Sales/Inventory		83	4.4		88	4.2	108	3.4
155	2.3	133	2.8	165	2.2			174	2.1		131	2.8	166	2.2
12	31.0	16	22.2	11	32.9			4	99.6		23	15.7	23	16.0
23	16.0	28	12.9	31	11.8	Cost of Sales/Payables		32	11.4		38	9.6	36	10.0
36	10.1	40	9.2	50	7.3			47	7.8		84	4.3	61	6.0

			Sales/Working Capital						
3.6	3.4	3.7				3.2		5.7	3.9
7.1	6.4	6.5	Sales/Working Capital			7.5		9.4	6.4
15.0	16.0	17.7				16.1		29.0	8.8

					EBIT/Interest						
	15.6		21.9		16.5			28.6		11.8	24.1
(53)	3.8	(51)	5.5	(59)	5.8	EBIT/Interest		5.3	(10) 4.7		8.2
	.1		1.7		2.3			-2.5		2.4	2.9

				Net Profit + Depr., Dep., Amort./Cur. Mat. L/T/D						
	22.0			30.5						
(10)	4.5		(14) 5.0		Net Profit + Depr., Dep., Amort./Cur. Mat. L/T/D					
	1.1		1.4							

			Fixed/Worth						
.1	.1	.1				.0		.1	.1
.2	.2	.2	Fixed/Worth			.3		.2	.2
1.0	.5	.9				.6		.9	2.8

			Debt/Worth						
.3	.4	.7				.9		1.9	.5
1.4	1.3	1.8	Debt/Worth			1.7		2.2	1.2
5.4	2.9	5.6				2.9		5.6	5.8

				% Profit Before Taxes/Tangible Net Worth						
	66.2		38.1	42.0			33.2		70.5	43.7
(55)	18.4	(49)	24.1	(51) 18.9	% Profit Before Taxes/Tangible Net Worth	(11) 10.2		(10) 30.5	(16) 32.1
	2.9		5.3	7.7			-55.8		13.0	7.7

			% Profit Before Taxes/Total Assets						
22.9	20.6	15.4				12.9		9.2	24.5
7.2	9.9	8.8	% Profit Before Taxes/Total Assets			7.8		6.7	12.2
-2.3	.7	2.2				-10.8		5.0	3.8

			Sales/Net Fixed Assets						
99.3	101.9	65.8				220.7		51.5	68.2
23.0	34.9	26.4	Sales/Net Fixed Assets			37.6		25.0	32.2
9.5	11.7	11.6				13.4		11.5	13.5

			Sales/Total Assets						
3.1	3.4	2.8				2.6		2.7	3.0
2.3	2.2	2.3	Sales/Total Assets			2.2		2.4	2.4
1.7	1.6	1.8				1.8		1.9	1.6

				% Depr., Dep., Amort./Sales						
	.3		.3	.4						.4
(47)	.7	(42)	.9	(47) .7	% Depr., Dep., Amort./Sales				(17) .7
	1.9		1.6	1.5						1.4

				% Officers', Directors' Owners' Comp/Sales						
	1.5		1.7	1.7						
(27)	4.0	(27)	3.8	(34) 2.9	% Officers', Directors' Owners' Comp/Sales					
	6.0		5.3	5.9						

			Net Sales ($)						
3564311M	2277633M	2165216M	Net Sales ($)	4278M	13300M	46036M	57971M	183821M	1859810M
1840882M	1388805M	1086457M	Total Assets ($)	1749M	6853M	21001M	32046M	93966M	930842M

M = $ thousand   MM = $ million
See Pages 9 through 22 for Explanation of Ratios and Data

Current Data Sorted by Assets   Comparative Historical Data

						Type of Statement		
			7	18	11	3 Unqualified	31	27
	7	27	7			Reviewed	27	37
1	5	7	2			Compiled	19	12
7	16	11	1			Tax Returns	23	23
7	15	24	17	1	6	Other	41	50
	33 (4/1-9/30/10)		167 (10/1/10-3/31/11)				4/1/06-3/31/07	4/1/07-3/31/08
0-500M	500M-2MM	2-10MM	10-50MM	50-100MM	100-250MM		ALL	ALL
15	43	76	45	12	9	NUMBER OF STATEMENTS	141	149
%	%	%	%	%	%	ASSETS	%	%
20.8	10.7	7.5	10.0	5.5		Cash & Equivalents	9.0	8.2
21.7	25.5	23.7	26.9	27.7		Trade Receivables (net)	29.4	27.8
24.7	36.6	45.9	38.8	40.7		Inventory	34.1	35.4
.5	3.5	2.3	5.3	3.2		All Other Current	2.3	3.6
67.5	76.4	79.4	81.0	77.0		Total Current	74.8	74.9
23.1	11.5	10.2	9.7	10.5		Fixed Assets (net)	14.5	12.9
2.7	3.5	2.6	3.3	7.4		Intangibles (net)	5.1	5.1
6.6	8.6	7.8	6.0	5.1		All Other Non-Current	5.6	7.0
100.0	100.0	100.0	100.0	100.0		Total	100.0	100.0
						LIABILITIES		
36.7	15.4	16.0	17.6	13.3		Notes Payable-Short Term	16.4	17.2
6.7	4.0	1.9	2.2	.5		Cur. Mat.-L.T.D.	3.2	3.1
27.8	22.3	23.0	15.7	16.7		Trade Payables	15.8	17.8
.2	.0	.1	.2	.5		Income Taxes Payable	.3	.4
33.2	8.9	6.6	6.8	9.4		All Other Current	11.1	8.0
104.6	50.7	47.5	42.4	40.5		Total Current	46.7	46.4
7.3	10.8	7.2	4.6	6.8		Long-Term Debt	12.7	11.0
.0	.0	.0	.1	.9		Deferred Taxes	.2	.2
15.2	13.0	5.2	6.0	5.2		All Other Non-Current	8.2	7.4
-27.2	25.6	40.1	46.9	46.6		Net Worth	32.2	35.0
100.0	100.0	100.0	100.0	100.0		Total Liabilities & Net Worth	100.0	100.0
						INCOME DATA		
100.0	100.0	100.0	100.0	100.0		Net Sales	100.0	100.0
45.5	40.4	32.3	36.9	30.0		Gross Profit	34.8	37.5
42.0	36.6	28.3	29.7	24.2		Operating Expenses	29.2	32.0
3.6	3.8	4.0	7.2	5.8		Operating Profit	5.6	5.5
1.2	.6	.7	.4	.8		All Other Expenses (net)	1.4	1.5
2.4	3.3	3.3	6.8	5.0		Profit Before Taxes	4.2	4.0
						RATIOS		
1.8	3.7	2.8	3.2	3.5			2.6	2.7
1.2	1.5	1.7	2.0	2.2	Current	1.6	1.6
.4	1.1	1.2	1.4	1.3		1.2	1.2
1.1	1.4	1.6	1.5	1.6			1.5	1.4
.6	.9	.7	.8	.8	Quick	.9	.8
.2	.4	.3	.5	.5		.5	.4
0 UND	16 22.2	19 18.7	23 16.1	43 8.6			29 12.7	28 13.0
16 22.7	28 13.0	34 10.7	45 8.1	50 7.2		Sales/Receivables	42 8.7	41 8.9
30 12.1	60 6.1	51 7.1	64 5.7	58 6.3			54 6.8	60 6.1
0 UND	40 9.1	55 6.6	56 6.5	62 5.9			25 14.7	43 8.5
34 10.8	80 4.6	94 3.9	111 3.3	123 3.0		Cost of Sales/Inventory	78 4.7	92 4.0
60 6.1	119 3.1	169 2.2	150 2.4	133 2.8			142 2.6	157 2.3
17 21.5	15 24.5	19 19.3	16 22.9	22 16.9			15 24.5	15 23.6
46 8.0	30 12.0	31 11.8	34 10.8	43 8.5		Cost of Sales/Payables	28 13.2	30 12.2
97 3.8	74 4.9	56 6.5	60 6.1	58 6.3			50 7.4	57 6.4
18.2	3.6	3.7	3.5	3.4			5.2	4.3
46.3	10.2	9.0	6.0	4.9	Sales/Working Capital	9.6	7.8
-3.5	77.8	23.7	12.5	14.1		19.8	21.8
17.0	6.3	19.8	22.0	210.9			9.2	15.4
(11) 1.1	(33) 2.3	(68) 4.9	(41) 7.9	(11) 4.5		EBIT/Interest	(126) 3.2	(137) 3.8
-3.9	.5	1.4	2.0	.6			1.2	1.4
						Net Profit + Depr., Dep.,	39.4	54.7
						Amort./Cur. Mat. L/T/D	(25) 5.3 (25) 6.7
							1.2	1.8
.1	.1	.1	.1	.1			.1	.1
.9	.3	.2	.1	.3	Fixed/Worth	.3	.3
-.2	-10.1	.7	.4	.5		1.8	1.5
1.2	.8	.5	.4	.6			.8	.6
4.8	2.7	1.3	1.0	1.0	Debt/Worth	2.0	1.7
-2.6	-23.3	3.7	3.3	4.5		7.8	6.6
	43.6	39.0	47.7	51.9		% Profit Before Taxes/Tangible	53.5	63.5
	(29) 12.5	(66) 20.4	(43) 22.1	19.5		Net Worth	(118) 25.6	(128) 21.1
	-.7	5.7	7.9	-3.4			6.8	6.4
41.8	17.2	19.4	24.7	26.9		% Profit Before Taxes/Total	18.9	20.5
6.3	5.6	6.8	11.9	6.7		Assets	7.6	6.7
-19.6	-.6	1.2	3.6	-1.7			1.0	1.8
453.6	124.7	129.1	105.4	52.4			57.9	66.1
69.6	40.6	45.4	41.0	22.7	Sales/Net Fixed Assets	22.8	25.9
14.2	23.9	16.8	14.6	12.4		10.5	11.4
6.7	3.5	3.6	2.8	2.3			3.6	3.0
5.5	2.6	2.4	2.2	2.1	Sales/Total Assets	2.6	2.2
3.5	2.0	1.8	1.5	1.8		1.6	1.5
	.4	.3	.4	.1			.5	.5
	(25) .8	(53) .6	(37) .6	(11) .7		% Depr., Dep., Amort./Sales	(115) 1.2	(114) 1.1
	1.6	1.5	1.2	2.0			1.9	2.1
	2.4	2.2					2.4	1.6
	(22) 4.0	(31) 3.1				% Officers', Directors' Owners' Comp/Sales	(52) 4.3	(54) 3.2
	6.3	5.4					6.9	5.9
21861M	149367M	1030392M	2313065M	1645397M	2064336M	Net Sales ($)	6210307M	6692843M
4436M	49813M	374829M	1004301M	840665M	1267018M	Total Assets ($)	3104416M	3389562M

M = $ thousand   MM = $ million
See Pages 9 through 22 for Explanation of Ratios and Data

Comparative Historical Data / Current Data Sorted by Sales

Type of Statement

Type of Statement	4/1/08-3/31/09 ALL	4/1/09-3/31/10 ALL	4/1/10-3/31/11 ALL	0-1MM	1-3MM	3-5MM	5-10MM	10-25MM	25MM & OVER
Unqualified	45	41	39		1		1	9	28
Reviewed	31	23	41		3	3	7	14	14
Compiled	19	18	15		4	2	6	1	2
Tax Returns	22	28	35	3	12	9	5	5	1
Other	56	59	70	4	14	5	12	14	21

33 (4/1-9/30/10) — 167 (10/1/10-3/31/11)

	4/1/08-3/31/09 ALL	4/1/09-3/31/10 ALL	4/1/10-3/31/11 ALL	0-1MM	1-3MM	3-5MM	5-10MM	10-25MM	25MM & OVER
NUMBER OF STATEMENTS	173	169	200	7	34	19	31	43	66
	%	%	%	%	%	%	%	%	%
ASSETS									
Cash & Equivalents	7.7	10.5	9.8		12.9	8.2	6.5	11.2	8.3
Trade Receivables (net)	26.6	25.6	24.9		24.9	23.4	27.2	23.6	26.5
Inventory	36.5	36.0	40.0		34.7	43.4	46.7	39.2	41.5
All Other Current	3.6	2.6	3.2		1.1	5.2	1.4	4.2	4.1
Total Current	74.4	74.7	78.0		73.5	80.2	81.8	78.1	80.4
Fixed Assets (net)	14.5	12.6	11.3		11.0	6.6	10.6	11.4	9.5
Intangibles (net)	4.5	6.0	3.5		4.5	4.0	1.4	3.0	4.4
All Other Non-Current	6.6	6.7	7.2		11.0	9.2	6.2	7.5	5.7
Total	100.0	100.0	100.0		100.0	100.0	100.0	100.0	100.0
LIABILITIES									
Notes Payable-Short Term	19.7	19.5	17.3		12.9	9.9	28.8	15.1	14.4
Cur. Mat.-L.T.D.	1.9	2.6	3.8		5.3	5.8	.7	1.8	5.3
Trade Payables	16.1	16.3	20.6		23.3	26.6	17.1	20.4	19.9
Income Taxes Payable	.2	.3	.3		.1	.0	.1	.0	.7
All Other Current	8.3	9.0	9.4		13.7	8.7	5.5	7.6	7.7
Total Current	46.2	47.7	51.4		55.3	51.0	52.2	44.9	48.0
Long-Term Debt	11.6	13.2	7.1		11.8	3.8	7.7	7.4	4.1
Deferred Taxes	.2	.3	.2		.0	.0	.0	.0	.6
All Other Non-Current	11.4	7.7	8.0		16.1	10.9	3.7	5.7	5.8
Net Worth	30.6	31.1	33.3		16.8	34.3	36.4	41.9	41.5
Total Liabilties & Net Worth	100.0	100.0	100.0		100.0	100.0	100.0	100.0	100.0
INCOME DATA									
Net Sales	100.0	100.0	100.0		100.0	100.0	100.0	100.0	100.0
Gross Profit	36.5	38.1	36.1		42.1	41.0	34.6	31.1	33.5
Operating Expenses	32.1	33.7	31.0		38.0	38.5	31.0	26.2	26.5
Operating Profit	4.4	4.5	5.1		4.2	2.5	3.6	5.0	7.1
All Other Expenses (net)	1.1	1.2	.7		1.0	.7	.8	.4	.6
Profit Before Taxes	3.3	3.2	4.4		3.2	1.8	2.8	4.5	6.4
RATIOS									
Current	2.7	3.4	3.4		4.0	4.2	2.7	3.4	3.0
	1.6	1.7	1.7		1.6	1.9	1.9	1.6	1.8
	1.2	1.2	1.2		1.1	1.0	1.2	1.3	1.3
Quick	1.3	1.8	1.5		1.5	1.8	1.3	2.1	1.5
	.7	.8	.8		.9	.8	.7	.8	.8
	.4	.4	.4		.4	.3	.3	.3	.4
Sales/Receivables	23 · 15.8	25 · 14.9	19 · 19.1		9 · 42.2	20 · 18.6	29 · 12.8	13 · 27.7	23 · 15.6
	38 · 9.6	39 · 9.4	34 · 10.6		29 · 12.4	28 · 13.0	37 · 9.9	34 · 10.6	42 · 8.6
	54 · 6.7	56 · 6.5	55 · 6.7		56 · 6.5	62 · 5.9	58 · 6.3	46 · 7.9	59 · 6.2
Cost of Sales/Inventory	42 · 8.6	46 · 7.9	49 · 7.4		48 · 7.6	44 · 8.4	57 · 6.4	49 · 7.5	58 · 6.3
	92 · 4.0	96 · 3.8	95 · 3.8		86 · 4.2	119 · 3.1	93 · 3.9	80 · 4.6	112 · 3.2
	141 · 2.6	150 · 2.4	137 · 2.7		124 · 3.0	211 · 1.7	177 · 2.1	123 · 3.0	137 · 2.7
Cost of Sales/Payables	16 · 22.6	18 · 20.1	17 · 21.2		23 · 16.0	14 · 26.1	17 · 21.4	13 · 28.1	21 · 17.4
	29 · 12.5	31 · 11.8	34 · 10.9		38 · 9.6	36 · 10.1	28 · 13.2	25 · 14.7	39 · 9.4
	48 · 7.6	49 · 7.4	59 · 6.2		76 · 4.8	85 · 4.3	51 · 7.2	49 · 7.5	60 · 6.1
Sales/Working Capital	4.8	4.2	3.7		4.1	3.0	4.2	3.5	3.8
	8.7	7.2	8.5		12.9	7.6	6.2	8.1	8.3
	23.5	24.0	26.3		63.1	UND	17.9	22.5	17.1
EBIT/Interest	10.8	16.2	17.8		6.0	32.3	10.5	22.6	24.2
	(161) 2.5	(152) 3.4	(171) 4.4		(27) 3.6	(15) 2.4	(28) 4.0	(39) 5.8	(58) 6.9
	1.0	.8	1.3		.4	-2.7	1.3	1.2	2.3
Net Profit + Depr., Dep., Amort./Cur. Mat. L/T/D	10.1	12.0	30.1						33.4
	(39) 3.2	(32) 4.9	(24) 7.1						(17) 7.0
	.1	.8	3.5						3.3
Fixed/Worth	.1	.1	.1		.1	.1	.1	.1	.1
	.4	.3	.2		.4	.1	.2	.2	.2
	1.4	2.5	1.0		-4.6	-2.2	.7	.7	.5
Debt/Worth	.9	.6	.5		.8	.4	.6	.3	.6
	2.0	2.0	1.4		4.6	1.5	1.1	1.3	1.1
	5.7	13.9	5.6		-15.0	-13.4	3.9	2.8	4.2
% Profit Before Taxes/Tangible Net Worth	44.6	46.6	49.3		59.1	36.4	32.7	36.0	53.5
	(146) 16.2	(136) 20.9	(164) 21.8		(22) 19.1	(13) 16.7	(26) 12.6	(37) 19.2	(62) 28.3
	2.5	3.9	4.4		1.7	3.4	3.2	4.2	9.2
% Profit Before Taxes/Total Assets	16.5	18.5	20.1		19.0	18.0	15.3	23.3	24.5
	4.5	4.9	7.8		7.0	7.3	3.4	6.6	12.2
	.3	.0	1.1		-.7	1.4	.5	.3	5.2
Sales/Net Fixed Assets	60.9	80.7	109.9		150.5	282.6	95.5	129.2	109.3
	24.1	29.8	39.6		44.2	51.0	34.7	32.6	40.9
	10.3	13.1	16.5		17.3	27.6	20.3	14.0	16.1
Sales/Total Assets	3.5	3.1	3.5		3.6	4.1	3.1	4.0	3.1
	2.2	2.2	2.4		2.6	2.3	2.3	2.4	2.3
	1.7	1.5	1.8		1.7	1.3	1.8	1.8	1.9
% Depr., Dep., Amort./Sales	.4	.4	.4		.7	.3	.3	.5	.3
	(141) 1.0	(125) 1.0	(139) .7		(17) 1.1	(12) .6	(24) .7	(29) .7	(55) .6
	2.1	2.1	1.6		2.2	1.2	1.4	1.7	1.4
% Officers', Directors' Owners' Comp/Sales	1.8	2.2	2.0		3.3	1.8	2.5	2.0	.8
	(63) 3.0	(64) 3.3	(68) 3.2		(15) 4.2	(11) 2.7	(15) 3.5	(12) 2.7	(13) 1.4
	5.4	6.1	5.5		7.8	6.5	5.7	4.0	4.2
Net Sales ($)	8733115M	6522008M	7224418M	5130M	65506M	77481M	219441M	686701M	6170159M
Total Assets ($)	4283343M	3547952M	3541062M	2667M	31822M	41167M	102291M	303343M	3059772M

M = $ thousand   MM = $ million
See Pages 9 through 22 for Explanation of Ratios and Data

Current Data Sorted by Assets   Comparative Historical Data

0-500M	500M-2MM	2-10MM	10-50MM	50-100MM	100-250MM		4/1/06-3/31/07 ALL	4/1/07-3/31/08 ALL
						Type of Statement		
	1	3	5	1	1	Unqualified	6	6
	1	3	3			Reviewed	8	7
	1	3				Compiled	5	4
	4					Tax Returns	1	4
	4	3	2	2	1	Other	20	12
0-500M	5 (4/1-9/30/10)		32 (10/1/10-3/31/11)					
	10	12	10	3	2	**NUMBER OF STATEMENTS**	40	33
%	%	%	%	%	%	**ASSETS**	%	%
	10.4	13.2	4.5			Cash & Equivalents	6.9	9.5
	24.9	20.8	24.2			Trade Receivables (net)	28.0	30.6
	32.9	37.1	49.1			Inventory	31.7	31.0
	4.0	4.1	3.5			All Other Current	4.4	2.7
	72.3	75.1	81.4			Total Current	71.0	73.8
	16.0	8.4	6.4			Fixed Assets (net)	17.6	13.7
	5.4	13.8	10.2			Intangibles (net)	6.9	9.9
	6.3	2.6	2.0			All Other Non-Current	4.4	2.6
	100.0	100.0	100.0			Total	100.0	100.0
						LIABILITIES		
	12.0	20.6	19.3			Notes Payable-Short Term	14.1	11.7
	12.2	1.6	2.2			Cur. Mat.-L.T.D.	2.5	2.2
	18.6	18.0	24.7			Trade Payables	16.6	16.8
	.8	.2	.0			Income Taxes Payable	.2	.2
	5.0	3.7	5.9			All Other Current	10.5	5.4
	48.5	44.1	52.1			Total Current	44.0	36.4
	9.0	4.7	3.3			Long-Term Debt	12.3	12.3
	.2	.8	.0			Deferred Taxes	.2	.6
	1.4	4.3	3.9			All Other Non-Current	8.0	8.1
	40.9	46.1	40.7			Net Worth	35.5	42.6
	100.0	100.0	100.0			Total Liabilities & Net Worth	100.0	100.0
						INCOME DATA		
	100.0	100.0	100.0			Net Sales	100.0	100.0
	33.7	24.3	25.3			Gross Profit	25.4	25.3
	27.7	20.1	22.6			Operating Expenses	20.3	19.5
	5.9	4.3	2.7			Operating Profit	5.0	5.8
	.8	3.4	1.3			All Other Expenses (net)	1.6	1.4
	5.2	.9	1.4			Profit Before Taxes	3.4	4.4
						RATIOS		
	2.2	4.1	2.6				2.3	3.0
	1.4	1.3	1.7			Current	1.7	2.0
	1.1	1.3	1.2				1.2	1.4
	1.4	1.6	.9				1.2	1.5
	.7	.7	.7			Quick	.8	1.1
	.4	.4	.2				.4	.7
	12 31.6	23 15.9	13 28.4				25 14.8	26 14.1
	26 13.9	41 8.9	34 10.8			Sales/Receivables	38 9.6	40 9.2
	35 10.4	50 7.3	41 8.9				54 6.7	53 6.9
	28 13.1	49 7.4	31 11.6				34 10.6	27 13.4
	57 6.4	80 4.6	100 3.7			Cost of Sales/Inventory	64 5.7	63 5.8
	88 4.1	122 3.0	183 2.0				106 3.4	89 4.1
	18 20.8	15 24.5	15 23.8				12 30.5	11 34.0
	28 12.9	35 10.4	46 7.9			Cost of Sales/Payables	28 13.1	23 16.0
	42 8.6	58 6.3	73 5.0				50 7.3	40 9.2
	8.9	4.6	5.3				4.8	4.9
	12.0	10.4	10.1			Sales/Working Capital	9.6	8.0
	329.7	22.9	31.5				30.8	13.3
		3.9	9.4				11.2	12.0
		(10) 1.8	3.5			EBIT/Interest	(37) 2.9	(29) 3.1
		.5	.3				1.1	1.0
						Net Profit + Depr., Dep., Amort./Cur. Mat. L/T/D	5.8	
							(11) 1.8	
							.7	
	.1	.1	.1				.1	.1
	.3	.3	.2			Fixed/Worth	.4	.4
	2.5	2.4	.5				1.8	1.2
	.7	.7	.9				1.0	.6
	1.9	2.8	2.8			Debt/Worth	1.9	1.8
	8.0	13.4	5.2				7.2	5.7
		46.0	37.5				60.5	53.6
		(10) 21.7	16.4			% Profit Before Taxes/Tangible Net Worth	(33) 16.4	(27) 21.8
		4.9	-2.1				3.4	-.4
	25.2	9.8	10.0				16.6	23.1
	7.0	4.4	5.7			% Profit Before Taxes/Total Assets	7.3	6.4
	-2.8	.9	-.8				.1	.9
	69.8	76.3	201.3				83.4	68.4
	32.7	35.9	53.2			Sales/Net Fixed Assets	14.0	18.4
	8.9	11.1	17.7				8.9	10.8
	3.6	2.5	3.7				3.2	3.5
	2.7	2.2	3.0			Sales/Total Assets	2.3	2.6
	2.4	1.4	1.7				1.3	1.6
							.5	.4
						% Depr., Dep., Amort./Sales	(36) 1.1	(29) 1.4
							2.7	2.3
							1.4	2.0
						% Officers', Directors' Owners' Comp/Sales	(13) 2.9	(11) 3.2
							6.1	12.4
	36655M	136730M	670686M	318556M	667412M	Net Sales ($)	1660296M	1564717M
	11765M	69771M	230750M	248191M	363483M	Total Assets ($)	795609M	711329M

© RMA 2011

M = $ thousand   MM = $ million
See Pages 9 through 22 for Explanation of Ratios and Data

Comparative Historical Data

Current Data Sorted by Sales

Comparative Historical Data				Type of Statement		Current Data Sorted by Sales					
					0-1MM	1-3MM	3-5MM	5-10MM	10-25MM	25MM & OVER
8		11	10	Unqualified				1	3	6
7		5	7	Reviewed		1			3	3
3		5	4	Compiled			1	1	2	
6		5	4	Tax Returns		1	3			
13		11	12	Other		3		3	2	4
4/1/08-3/31/09 ALL		4/1/09-3/31/10 ALL	4/1/10-3/31/11 ALL			5 (4/1-9/30/10)			32 (10/1/10-3/31/11)		
37		37	37	NUMBER OF STATEMENTS		5	4	5	10	13
%		%	%	ASSETS	%	%	%	%	%	%
8.5		10.3	10.7	Cash & Equivalents		D			14.5	9.0
21.4		29.4	23.6	Trade Receivables (net)		A			19.9	25.2
37.1		33.2	37.3	Inventory		T			46.7	38.0
2.5		2.3	3.7	All Other Current		A			3.7	3.7
69.4		75.2	75.3	Total Current					84.9	75.8
15.8		12.7	11.1	Fixed Assets (net)		N			8.4	9.9
9.4		6.3	9.2	Intangibles (net)		O			5.7	9.4
5.4		5.8	4.3	All Other Non-Current		T			1.0	4.9
100.0		100.0	100.0	Total					100.0	100.0
				LIABILITIES		A				
20.7		23.4	16.1	Notes Payable-Short Term		V			22.2	13.6
4.2		5.5	6.3	Cur. Mat.-L.T.D.		A			3.1	5.8
16.5		14.9	18.5	Trade Payables		I			20.8	18.5
.0		.3	.3	Income Taxes Payable		L			.2	.0
8.6		7.8	5.0	All Other Current		A			6.2	5.4
50.1		51.9	46.2	Total Current		B			52.5	43.3
14.4		12.2	5.8	Long-Term Debt		L			2.5	4.7
.9		.3	.5	Deferred Taxes		E			.4	.4
6.6		4.5	4.0	All Other Non-Current					1.5	6.4
28.0		31.0	43.5	Net Worth					43.1	45.2
100.0		100.0	100.0	Total Liabilties & Net Worth					100.0	100.0
				INCOME DATA						
100.0		100.0	100.0	Net Sales					100.0	100.0
29.4		31.3	28.9	Gross Profit					28.2	27.2
28.2		29.4	24.1	Operating Expenses					25.3	21.6
1.2		1.8	4.8	Operating Profit					2.8	5.6
1.0		.9	1.8	All Other Expenses (net)					1.0	1.2
.3		.9	3.0	Profit Before Taxes					1.8	4.3
				RATIOS						
2.3		2.3	2.6						5.7	3.9
1.5		1.5	1.5	Current					1.4	2.0
1.2		1.1	1.2						1.1	1.3
1.5		1.3	1.5						4.0	1.8
.7		.9	.7	Quick					.4	.9
.3		.5	.4						.3	.2
24 15.4	31 11.7	22 16.7						13 28.4	29 12.8
33 11.0	40 9.1	37 9.8	Sales/Receivables					44 8.4	36 10.2
50 7.3	62 5.9	51 7.1						52 7.0	57 6.4
69 5.3	41 8.9	44 8.3						56 6.5	38 9.5
103 3.5	68 5.3	68 5.3	Cost of Sales/Inventory					114 3.2	68 5.3
124 3.0	114 3.2	123 3.0						179 2.0	125 2.9
17 21.7	13 27.4	16 22.5						11 31.9	16 22.6
31 12.0	30 12.2	31 11.6	Cost of Sales/Payables					39 9.3	31 11.8
56 6.5	52 7.0	59 6.2						77 4.7	63 5.8
4.5		4.8	4.5						3.3	3.6
10.4		11.3	10.1	Sales/Working Capital					14.0	6.7
17.2		33.5	26.6						40.1	22.5
6.3		5.6	6.5							18.1
(34) 1.5	(34) 2.5	(34) 2.8	EBIT/Interest						5.4
.0		.7	.8							1.8
				Net Profit + Depr., Dep., Amort./Cur. Mat. L/T/D						
.1		.1	.1						.1	.1
.6		.3	.3	Fixed/Worth					.2	.1
NM		2.5	.8						.8	.3
.7		.8	.8						.7	.7
3.9		2.5	2.5	Debt/Worth					2.4	2.5
NM		13.8	5.5						6.7	4.1
28.5		48.6	45.0						46.0	39.1
(28) 6.6	(33) 17.8	(34) 19.8	% Profit Before Taxes/Tangible Net Worth					21.7	22.4
-.5		3.9	2.3						-10.1	4.7
7.7		7.8	13.5						12.2	13.9
2.7		3.4	6.4	% Profit Before Taxes/Total Assets					6.4	7.4
-1.6		-1.9	-.3						-3.5	2.4
61.1		106.3	73.7						89.9	166.3
20.2		26.4	27.0	Sales/Net Fixed Assets					35.9	39.1
8.7		10.9	11.3						14.6	14.0
2.9		3.4	3.2						2.8	3.5
2.1		2.3	2.4	Sales/Total Assets					2.2	2.7
1.4		1.8	1.7						1.7	1.3
.5		.5	.4							
(33) 1.0	(27) 1.2	(26) 1.3	% Depr., Dep., Amort./Sales						
2.0		2.0	1.8							
1.6		3.0	1.2							
(12) 4.7	(14) 4.7	(11) 3.7	% Officers', Directors' Owners' Comp/Sales						
6.6		12.3	7.2							
1250868M		1736961M	1830039M	Net Sales ($)		11376M	15811M	41077M	145496M	1616279M
792987M		965221M	923960M	Total Assets ($)		4955M	5023M	25140M	71067M	817775M

M = $ thousand   MM = $ million
See Pages 9 through 22 for Explanation of Ratios and Data

Current Data Sorted by Assets   Comparative Historical Data

	0-500M	500M-2MM	2-10MM	10-50MM	50-100MM	100-250MM		4/1/06-3/31/07 ALL	4/1/07-3/31/08 ALL
Type of Statement									
Unqualified	1	2	5	18	7	3		64	46
Reviewed		15	19	13	3	2		56	46
Compiled			9	2				43	35
Tax Returns	6	8	7	1				26	23
Other	4	10	29	26	5	5		90	88
	39 (4/1-9/30/10)			161 (10/1/10-3/31/11)					
NUMBER OF STATEMENTS	11	35	69	60	15	10		279	238
ASSETS	%	%	%	%	%	%		%	%
Cash & Equivalents	5.3	5.6	6.9	2.8	5.5	10.7		3.8	6.2
Trade Receivables (net)	10.0	12.2	10.8	10.1	7.8	4.4		12.8	11.1
Inventory	23.0	31.8	28.3	29.6	24.4	12.5		27.8	27.0
All Other Current	3.0	.9	3.0	2.1	4.5	2.4		3.8	3.6
Total Current	41.3	50.6	48.9	44.7	42.2	30.0		48.3	47.9
Fixed Assets (net)	47.0	40.0	41.8	45.4	36.0	48.3		41.5	41.9
Intangibles (net)	2.1	2.1	1.2	1.5	.9	3.1		1.3	1.5
All Other Non-Current	9.7	7.4	8.1	8.4	21.0	18.7		8.9	8.8
Total	100.0	100.0	100.0	100.0	100.0	100.0		100.0	100.0
LIABILITIES									
Notes Payable-Short Term	31.5	16.2	13.8	13.6	14.4	3.2		13.2	14.0
Cur. Mat.-L.T.D.	5.5	8.9	4.7	5.5	2.7	7.1		5.6	4.6
Trade Payables	10.6	5.3	5.6	5.5	4.5	3.4		7.0	6.5
Income Taxes Payable	.0	.1	.1	.1	.1	.1		.2	.1
All Other Current	4.5	4.1	4.6	5.5	3.9	3.7		7.6	5.2
Total Current	52.1	34.6	28.7	30.2	25.6	17.5		33.6	30.3
Long-Term Debt	46.3	23.6	22.1	21.6	19.7	29.5		24.4	22.5
Deferred Taxes	.0	.0	.6	.7	.2	1.8		.6	.7
All Other Non-Current	28.8	16.8	6.3	4.1	5.4	8.0		5.8	6.1
Net Worth	-28.0	25.0	42.2	43.4	49.1	43.1		35.5	40.4
Total Liabilities & Net Worth	100.0	100.0	100.0	100.0	100.0	100.0		100.0	100.0
INCOME DATA									
Net Sales	100.0	100.0	100.0	100.0	100.0	100.0		100.0	100.0
Gross Profit	42.6	34.0	26.8	17.0	17.2	16.6		18.2	17.6
Operating Expenses	40.6	31.1	22.6	14.4	12.4	9.1		15.9	16.2
Operating Profit	2.0	2.9	4.2	2.6	4.8	7.4		2.4	1.4
All Other Expenses (net)	.1	1.7	2.1	1.2	1.2	3.9		1.1	1.3
Profit Before Taxes	1.9	1.2	2.1	1.4	3.7	3.6		1.2	.1
RATIOS									
Current	7.0	2.7	2.9	2.4	3.8	5.6		2.6	3.2
	.8	1.6	1.6	1.7	1.7	1.7		1.5	1.7
	.4	.8	1.1	1.1	1.2	.7		1.0	1.1
Quick	1.3	1.2	.9	.8	.9	2.5		.9	1.1
	.3	(34) .3	.5	.4	.5	.8		(277) .5	.5
	.1	.2	.3	.2	.3	.4		.3	.2
Sales/Receivables	0 UND	5 72.0	14 27.0	13 27.7	13 28.5	14 26.3		12 30.4	10 34.8
	4 103.7	14 25.6	20 18.0	18 20.6	22 16.9	18 19.9		18 20.0	17 21.5
	24 15.4	25 14.8	33 11.2	26 14.1	33 11.0	22 16.3		28 12.9	27 13.3
Cost of Sales/Inventory	18 20.5	31 11.9	32 11.4	38 9.5	48 7.6	21 17.0		30 12.3	34 10.7
	24 15.0	70 5.2	69 5.3	75 4.9	90 4.0	53 6.9		54 6.8	58 6.3
	66 5.5	137 2.7	131 2.8	141 2.6	126 2.9	79 4.6		93 3.9	93 3.9
Cost of Sales/Payables	0 UND	2 161.8	6 61.5	7 49.7	5 75.7	7 50.7		6 66.2	5 72.1
	8 45.0	7 49.2	11 32.4	12 30.5	15 25.0	14 26.8		10 35.3	11 33.0
	54 6.7	19 19.6	18 19.8	22 16.9	23 16.1	24 15.0		17 20.9	19 19.0
Sales/Working Capital	13.2	4.6	4.4	4.4	3.4	3.2		5.9	5.0
	-18.0	13.0	9.0	11.0	9.7	18.4		12.8	9.5
	-9.8	-22.4	77.9	134.0	20.5	-15.2		148.2	66.0
EBIT/Interest		13.3	8.1	7.6	8.7			4.9	2.9
		(34) 2.3	(63) 1.8	(57) 2.4	4.5			(268) 1.8	(224) 1.0
		1.4	.4	-.1	2.1			.4	-.8
Net Profit + Depr., Dep., Amort./Cur. Mat. L/T/D			2.9	4.8				4.1	4.0
			(17) 1.5	(22) 2.0				(78) 2.3	(61) 1.6
			.6	1.0				.7	.6
Fixed/Worth	1.3	.4	.4	.6	.3	.3		.5	.5
	-4.9	2.0	.8	1.0	1.1	1.0		1.0	1.0
	-.4	-6.8	1.8	2.0	1.4	7.0		2.1	2.0
Debt/Worth	1.0	.4	.6	.6	.4	.6		.7	.6
	-9.5	3.9	1.3	1.2	1.3	1.3		1.5	1.5
	-1.9	-16.5	2.8	3.1	2.1	7.8		3.4	3.3
% Profit Before Taxes/Tangible Net Worth		49.7	22.0	18.4	24.9	29.2		20.8	14.5
		(23) 27.5	(61) 5.5	(56) 8.6	13.6	8.7		(250) 10.2	(219) 1.3
		5.7	-.1	-4.1	3.3	.8		-2.1	-14.5
% Profit Before Taxes/Total Assets	16.7	19.1	10.1	7.9	11.8	4.8		9.9	5.9
	2.3	7.3	2.3	2.6	5.9	2.8		3.0	.1
	-24.4	1.6	-1.6	-2.3	2.3	.8		-1.8	-5.2
Sales/Net Fixed Assets	19.2	11.5	7.7	6.6	6.8	4.7		8.2	8.2
	8.2	6.9	4.9	3.8	3.4	1.9		5.4	4.6
	4.5	3.6	2.6	1.9	2.3	1.1		2.9	2.5
Sales/Total Assets	6.7	3.4	2.4	2.1	1.7	1.1		2.6	2.5
	3.6	2.3	1.8	1.3	1.3	.8		2.0	1.6
	1.6	1.2	1.0	1.1	.9	.6		1.3	1.1
% Depr., Dep., Amort./Sales		1.5	2.2	2.5	2.3			1.8	1.7
		(29) 2.6	(62) 3.4	(57) 4.1	(13) 5.4			(260) 2.9	(218) 3.7
		6.0	6.4	6.8	7.1			4.9	5.9
% Officers', Directors' Owners' Comp/Sales		1.4	.9					1.3	1.3
		(14) 2.7	(27) 1.3					(76) 2.3	(67) 2.3
		6.4	2.6					3.9	4.1
Net Sales ($)	9852M	111985M	565584M	2242251M	1369698M	1233552M		11441195M	9010451M
Total Assets ($)	2682M	42452M	339537M	1250080M	1060474M	1526051M		7067325M	6407328M

© RMA 2011

Comparative Historical Data / Current Data Sorted by Sales

			Type of Statement						
33	36	33	Unqualified		1	1	2	8	21
39	34	40	Reviewed	1	2	2	11	14	10
27	23	26	Compiled	1	12	5	2	5	1
25	28	22	Tax Returns	4	5	5	6	2	
77	65	79	Other	5	9	11	9	15	30
4/1/08-3/31/09 ALL	4/1/09-3/31/10 ALL	4/1/10-3/31/11 ALL			39 (4/1-9/30/10)			161 (10/1/10-3/31/11)	
				0-1MM	1-3MM	3-5MM	5-10MM	10-25MM	25MM & OVER
201	186	200	**NUMBER OF STATEMENTS**	11	29	24	30	44	62
%	%	%	**ASSETS**	%	%	%	%	%	%
5.5	6.2	5.4	Cash & Equivalents	3.4	2.9	8.9	5.1	6.7	5.0
9.2	11.6	10.2	Trade Receivables (net)	8.8	7.0	11.1	11.8	12.2	9.6
25.9	24.5	27.9	Inventory	18.3	27.2	29.6	34.3	28.9	25.6
2.5	3.0	2.4	All Other Current	.6	1.2	6.2	1.6	2.1	2.5
43.1	45.4	46.1	Total Current	31.1	38.2	55.7	52.8	49.9	42.7
45.4	42.1	42.7	Fixed Assets (net)	57.0	54.1	31.7	38.1	40.1	43.3
1.3	1.4	1.6	Intangibles (net)	2.1	1.5	3.6	.3	1.7	1.3
10.2	11.2	9.6	All Other Non-Current	9.9	6.2	8.9	8.8	8.4	12.8
100.0	100.0	100.0	Total	100.0	100.0	100.0	100.0	100.0	100.0
			LIABILITIES						
13.5	14.3	14.6	Notes Payable-Short Term	29.2	14.2	9.3	21.2	13.8	11.7
6.1	6.6	5.7	Cur. Mat.-L.T.D.	3.4	5.8	10.3	7.2	4.6	4.4
5.7	5.8	5.6	Trade Payables	9.0	4.3	5.5	5.6	5.8	5.5
.1	.1	.1	Income Taxes Payable	.0	.0	.1	.1	.0	.1
7.9	5.4	4.7	All Other Current	4.1	3.4	5.8	2.1	6.6	4.9
33.2	32.2	30.7	Total Current	45.6	27.7	31.0	36.2	30.8	26.6
26.1	27.4	23.7	Long-Term Debt	44.7	37.9	17.7	16.8	22.7	19.8
.6	.5	.5	Deferred Taxes	.0	.0	.3	.3	.9	.7
4.8	6.0	8.7	All Other Non-Current	40.0	15.6	6.7	6.5	3.1	5.9
35.4	33.8	36.3	Net Worth	-31.1	18.8	44.3	40.1	42.6	47.0
100.0	100.0	100.0	Total Liabilities & Net Worth	100.0	100.0	100.0	100.0	100.0	100.0
			INCOME DATA						
100.0	100.0	100.0	Net Sales	100.0	100.0	100.0	100.0	100.0	100.0
19.7	17.6	24.8	Gross Profit	58.5	35.4	29.3	25.1	18.7	16.2
19.2	20.3	21.2	Operating Expenses	58.0	31.4	24.2	20.6	16.0	12.7
.5	-2.8	3.6	Operating Profit	.5	4.0	5.1	4.6	2.7	3.5
1.4	1.3	1.7	All Other Expenses (net)	6.0	3.1	1.0	.7	.9	1.5
-.9	-4.1	1.9	Profit Before Taxes	-5.5	1.0	4.1	3.9	1.8	2.0
			RATIOS						
3.3	3.0	2.7		2.3	2.8	5.4	2.7	2.5	2.9
1.4	1.6	1.6	Current	.8	1.6	2.0	1.4	1.8	1.7
.8	.9	1.0		.3	.5	1.3	.9	1.2	1.1
1.1	1.3	1.0		.4	.8	1.8	.8	1.0	1.0
.4	.6 (199)	.5	Quick	.3	.3 (23)	.7	.4	.5	.5
.2	.2	.2		.1	.1	.3	.3	.3	.3
10 35.5	12 31.5	12 31.7		0 UND	5 70.1	4 84.2	12 29.4	14 25.6	13 28.5
16 23.3	20 17.9	18 20.1	Sales/Receivables	16 22.5	14 25.2	21 17.4	20 18.7	19 19.1	17 21.3
25 14.7	31 11.9	30 12.2		30 12.0	26 14.1	33 11.0	33 11.1	30 12.3	26 13.9
31 11.7	33 11.2	32 11.3		0 UND	18 20.2	19 18.9	40 9.2	40 9.1	31 11.7
60 6.1	60 6.1	66 5.5	Cost of Sales/Inventory	32 11.3	70 5.2	69 5.3	88 4.2	68 5.3	62 5.9
100 3.6	107 3.4	126 2.9		100 3.7	201 1.8	131 2.8	158 2.3	129 2.8	97 3.8
4 97.0	5 75.2	5 72.8		0 UND	1 342.5	2 149.5	6 60.6	7 50.4	6 59.9
9 41.1	10 36.9	11 32.5	Cost of Sales/Payables	13 27.6	9 42.2	8 47.8	12 31.2	11 33.2	12 30.5
19 19.6	19 19.3	21 17.6		96 3.8	26 14.2	30 12.2	20 18.0	18 20.5	20 18.1
6.2	4.7	4.5		12.0	4.3	4.4	5.1	4.4	4.5
16.4	10.8	11.2	Sales/Working Capital	-18.0	10.7	8.2	9.2	9.2	13.2
-31.1	-39.5	-247.8		-2.8	-11.8	22.0	-29.5	53.2	103.4
2.8	2.5	7.7			5.3	24.3	7.5	6.7	7.9
(187) .8	(174) .0	(187) 2.3	EBIT/Interest		1.5	(21) 4.1	(28) 2.3	(41) 2.3	(60) 3.2
-1.7	-3.0	.6			-.4	1.8	1.3	.1	.4
2.3	2.5	4.7						4.3	5.3
(56) 1.0	(42) 1.4	(46) 1.7	Net Profit + Depr., Dep., Amort./Cur. Mat. L/T/D					(17) 1.7	(17) 1.8
.1	.5	1.0						1.1	.9
.6	.5	.5		1.3	.9	.3	.4	.5	.5
1.3	1.3	1.1	Fixed/Worth	-6.8	4.6	.6	.7	.8	1.0
3.7	3.3	3.0		-.4	-5.2	3.0	1.9	2.0	1.5
.7	.6	.6		1.0	1.4	.2	.9	.6	.6
1.7	1.7	1.4	Debt/Worth	-12.9	5.9	.8	1.7	1.1	1.2
5.8	5.5	4.6		-1.9	-15.6	4.0	2.9	3.0	2.3
14.7	12.6	26.0			63.5	33.7	21.3	26.3	24.7
(174) .3	(160) -4.5	(170) 9.9	% Profit Before Taxes/Tangible Net Worth		(18) 5.9	(20) 13.8	(28) 8.7	(39) 8.1	(61) 11.5
-11.8	-18.5	.6			-2.9	3.9	2.5	-2.7	-2.5
4.3	3.8	9.3		9.3	8.1	18.9	10.2	8.2	8.4
-.9	-3.1	2.9	% Profit Before Taxes/Total Assets	-.4	1.6	8.6	3.0	3.1	3.7
-5.9	-11.4	-1.2		-24.4	-3.5	2.1	1.1	-2.3	-1.2
8.6	6.9	8.3		9.6	6.4	15.2	8.9	7.5	7.9
4.0	4.0	4.7	Sales/Net Fixed Assets	4.8	4.0	6.6	5.3	4.8	3.8
2.3	1.9	2.3		.5	1.2	4.5	2.4	2.4	2.4
2.6	2.2	2.5		4.0	2.2	3.1	2.5	2.3	2.2
1.7	1.4	1.6	Sales/Total Assets	1.6	1.1	2.2	1.9	1.6	1.4
1.1	.9	1.0		.4	.7	1.1	1.0	1.1	1.0
2.3	2.6	2.2		2.2	1.5	1.8	2.4	2.5	2.2
(182) 4.0	(172) 4.6	(176) 3.8	% Depr., Dep., Amort./Sales	(10) 9.7	(25) 3.6	(19) 2.9	(27) 3.4	(41) 3.3	(54) 4.3
6.2	7.7	6.8		16.5	7.8	5.8	5.7	5.9	6.5
1.4	1.7	1.1			1.5	.9	1.0	1.0	
(57) 2.6	(57) 2.4	(50) 1.6	% Officers', Directors' Owners' Comp/Sales		(11) 2.8	(12) 1.6	(10) 1.6	(12) 1.5	
4.3	3.9	3.1			6.3	3.7	2.9	2.8	
6149687M	5024584M	5532922M	Net Sales ($)	4967M	55798M	91250M	210179M	697280M	4473448M
4779369M	4710500M	4221276M	Total Assets ($)	7825M	69982M	53237M	142673M	490225M	3457334M

M = $ thousand   MM = $ million
See Pages 9 through 22 for Explanation of Ratios and Data

Current Data Sorted by Assets

Comparative Historical Data

	0-500M	500M-2MM	2-10MM	10-50MM	50-100MM	100-250MM	Type of Statement	4/1/06-3/31/07 ALL	4/1/07-3/31/08 ALL
	1		3	6		1	Unqualified	15	22
			7	3			Reviewed	15	11
	1	2	1	1			Compiled	3	1
			1	2			Tax Returns		2
		3	7	3	2	3	Other	11	15
		9 (4/1-9/30/10)		37 (10/1/10-3/31/11)					
	2	6	20	12	2	4	NUMBER OF STATEMENTS	44	51
	%	%	%	%	%	%	ASSETS	%	%
			6.1	8.5			Cash & Equivalents	6.0	5.2
			20.3	15.1			Trade Receivables (net)	18.7	19.4
			34.5	34.6			Inventory	39.5	38.2
			1.7	2.6			All Other Current	2.1	2.0
			62.6	60.9			Total Current	66.4	64.8
			23.0	32.6			Fixed Assets (net)	26.2	28.1
			1.1	.5			Intangibles (net)	1.0	.9
			13.3	6.0			All Other Non-Current	6.5	6.2
			100.0	100.0			Total	100.0	100.0
							LIABILITIES		
			12.0	9.7			Notes Payable-Short Term	17.8	17.3
			2.3	1.9			Cur. Mat.-L.T.D.	3.8	4.1
			11.4	6.1			Trade Payables	9.5	8.2
			.1	.0			Income Taxes Payable	.2	.3
			6.3	6.1			All Other Current	7.2	6.3
			32.1	23.8			Total Current	38.6	36.2
			16.2	16.0			Long-Term Debt	11.5	17.4
			.0	.9			Deferred Taxes	.7	.5
			1.8	.4			All Other Non-Current	1.2	1.3
			50.0	59.0			Net Worth	48.0	44.6
			100.0	100.0			Total Liabilities & Net Worth	100.0	100.0
							INCOME DATA		
			100.0	100.0			Net Sales	100.0	100.0
			21.9	18.6			Gross Profit	17.1	17.4
			18.9	13.7			Operating Expenses	11.1	12.2
			3.0	5.0			Operating Profit	6.0	5.1
			-.6	.7			All Other Expenses (net)	1.4	.9
			3.6	4.2			Profit Before Taxes	4.6	4.2
							RATIOS		
			3.6	4.7				2.6	3.4
			2.1	2.5			Current	1.7	1.7
			1.3	1.6				1.3	1.4
			1.4	1.3				.9	1.4
			.7	.8			Quick	.6	.6
			.4	.5				.4	.4
			14 25.9	11 31.8				16 23.0	17 21.4
			18 20.1	27 13.7			Sales/Receivables	20 17.8	25 14.4
			29 12.6	36 10.0				33 10.9	33 11.0
			24 15.1	36 10.1				31 11.9	40 9.2
			60 6.0	65 5.6			Cost of Sales/Inventory	58 6.3	64 5.7
			87 4.2	86 4.2				70 5.2	83 4.4
			9 39.6	7 50.2				5 66.9	6 62.5
			11 32.7	10 34.9			Cost of Sales/Payables	10 36.7	11 33.2
			31 11.9	15 24.0				21 17.7	18 20.0
			4.9	4.9				6.5	5.1
			7.5	6.4			Sales/Working Capital	11.1	10.4
			27.8	9.2				26.3	15.9
			22.1	45.7				10.4	9.5
			(19) 8.9	14.2			EBIT/Interest	(41) 4.8	(49) 5.1
			2.7	2.1				2.0	1.4
							Net Profit + Depr., Dep., Amort./Cur. Mat. L/T/D	11.7	6.9
								(16) 2.8 (14) 3.9	
								1.3	1.4
			.2	.2				.4	.4
			.4	.6			Fixed/Worth	.5	.6
			1.0	1.2				.9	.8
			.3	.2				.7	.8
			.8	.6			Debt/Worth	1.3	1.2
			3.0	1.7				2.3	2.1
			36.1	24.7				45.9	40.9
			(18) 11.9	15.4			% Profit Before Taxes/Tangible Net Worth	24.1	(48) 24.4
			5.5	4.2				12.1	4.3
			9.7	15.9				19.0	17.9
			6.4	10.6			% Profit Before Taxes/Total Assets	10.7	9.3
			3.8	1.3				3.8	1.6
			21.4	17.3				22.9	19.8
			12.0	6.5			Sales/Net Fixed Assets	13.9	11.8
			6.6	4.0				8.2	7.3
			3.0	2.7				3.9	3.4
			2.5	2.4			Sales/Total Assets	3.3	2.7
			1.9	1.6				2.0	1.8
			1.0	1.0				.7	.8
			1.4	(11) 1.9			% Depr., Dep., Amort./Sales	(41) 1.2	(47) 1.4
			2.2	2.7				2.2	2.2
							% Officers', Directors' Owners' Comp/Sales		
	1239M	24213M	309517M	629617M	238428M	1281689M	Net Sales ($)	3020973M	3564301M
	172M	8522M	108393M	277449M	111244M	752339M	Total Assets ($)	1280276M	1750364M

© RMA 2011

M = $ thousand   MM = $ million
See Pages 9 through 22 for Explanation of Ratios and Data

Comparative Historical Data   Current Data Sorted by Sales

			Type of Statement	9 (4/1-9/30/10)			37 (10/1/10-3/31/11)		
				0-1MM	1-3MM	3-5MM	5-10MM	10-25MM	25MM & OVER
14	14	11	Unqualified	1		1		3	6
10	7	10	Reviewed				3	5	2
4	6	4	Compiled	1		1	2		
2	3	3	Tax Returns		1	1	1		1
15	22	18	Other		3		3	5	7
4/1/08-3/31/09 ALL	4/1/09-3/31/10 ALL	4/1/10-3/31/11 ALL							
45	52	46	NUMBER OF STATEMENTS	2	3	3	9	13	16
%	%	%	ASSETS	%	%	%	%	%	%
7.1	9.2	7.4	Cash & Equivalents					6.7	8.3
17.2	15.7	21.8	Trade Receivables (net)					14.4	18.6
37.0	32.2	31.4	Inventory					38.6	34.1
2.6	3.1	2.0	All Other Current					1.6	2.3
63.9	60.2	62.6	Total Current					61.4	63.3
26.3	29.5	27.6	Fixed Assets (net)					27.5	27.7
3.5	3.3	.7	Intangibles (net)					1.3	.7
6.3	7.0	9.1	All Other Non-Current					9.8	8.3
100.0	100.0	100.0	Total					100.0	100.0
			LIABILITIES						
15.8	10.5	16.3	Notes Payable-Short Term					16.6	8.5
2.8	2.5	2.3	Cur. Mat.-L.T.D.					1.8	2.3
8.0	7.6	9.5	Trade Payables					8.0	8.6
.1	.2	.0	Income Taxes Payable					.0	.1
6.0	7.5	12.8	All Other Current					4.4	5.9
32.7	28.2	41.0	Total Current					30.8	25.3
15.5	17.1	15.5	Long-Term Debt					13.4	13.1
.4	.1	.4	Deferred Taxes					.5	.8
.7	1.8	1.9	All Other Non-Current					1.4	1.2
50.6	52.7	41.2	Net Worth					54.0	59.7
100.0	100.0	100.0	Total Liabilities & Net Worth					100.0	100.0
			INCOME DATA						
100.0	100.0	100.0	Net Sales					100.0	100.0
17.8	16.1	22.4	Gross Profit					25.3	14.6
13.5	12.7	18.1	Operating Expenses					21.2	10.0
4.3	3.3	4.4	Operating Profit					4.1	4.6
1.0	.2	.1	All Other Expenses (net)					.2	.3
3.3	3.1	4.3	Profit Before Taxes					3.9	4.3
			RATIOS						
3.6	4.5	3.8	Current					3.6	4.0
1.8	2.2	2.0						2.1	2.5
1.4	1.5	1.6						1.3	1.7
1.3	1.6	1.6	Quick					1.4	1.7
.7	.9	.8						.5	1.0
.4	.5	.4						.4	.5
12 31.0	16 22.2	14 25.4	Sales/Receivables					16 23.0	13 28.9
24 14.9	24 15.4	27 13.7						22 16.8	27 13.7
32 11.3	35 10.5	34 10.9						33 11.1	36 10.2
37 9.8	39 9.3	32 11.3	Cost of Sales/Inventory					56 6.5	35 10.3
66 5.5	57 6.4	60 6.1						75 4.9	62 5.9
88 4.1	89 4.1	88 4.2						97 3.8	89 4.1
6 66.1	8 47.9	8 45.3	Cost of Sales/Payables					10 36.8	9 42.6
10 36.1	11 32.0	13 28.2						10 35.0	13 27.6
19 18.9	20 18.7	19 19.2						27 13.7	17 21.0
6.2	4.1	4.8	Sales/Working Capital					4.9	4.8
8.0	6.1	6.9						6.1	6.4
19.1	15.1	14.4						15.4	9.2
12.2	15.7	32.9	EBIT/Interest					30.4	45.7
(42) 3.2	(46) 5.0	(44) 8.9						13.3	9.0
1.0	1.2	2.4						3.8	7.5
13.5	13.3	9.1	Net Profit + Depr., Dep., Amort./Cur. Mat. L/T/D						
(15) 2.1	(15) 6.1	(15) 5.5							
.2	4.2	2.0							
.3	.3	.3	Fixed/Worth					.2	.2
.5	.5	.5						.4	.5
1.0	1.0	1.0						1.2	.7
.6	.4	.3	Debt/Worth					.3	.2
1.0	.9	.9						.6	.6
2.5	1.7	1.8						2.4	1.4
31.0	23.9	28.9	% Profit Before Taxes/Tangible Net Worth					28.7	24.1
16.9	(50) 10.7	(43) 14.0					(12)	9.8	17.1
-.2	4.1	5.7						5.4	8.5
16.1	11.8	14.8	% Profit Before Taxes/Total Assets					14.2	14.3
5.7	7.0	6.9						6.0	10.6
-.1	.5	3.3						3.2	5.5
26.4	17.6	19.4	Sales/Net Fixed Assets					21.3	17.3
10.0	7.3	10.7						11.5	6.8
5.9	5.0	5.3						4.8	5.7
3.4	2.7	3.1	Sales/Total Assets					2.9	2.7
2.2	2.1	2.4						2.4	2.3
1.9	1.5	1.8						2.0	1.8
1.1	.9	.9	% Depr., Dep., Amort./Sales					1.2	.9
(39) 1.7	(44) 1.7	(44) 1.5						1.4	(15) 1.4
2.7	2.4	2.7						2.7	2.1
	.4	.7	% Officers', Directors' Owners' Comp/Sales						
	(13) .8	(14) 1.1							
	2.7	2.9							
3269146M	3645415M	2484703M	Net Sales ($)	1239M	6972M	11233M	69754M	240609M	2154896M
1710228M	2049125M	1258119M	Total Assets ($)	172M	4794M	6845M	30194M	126023M	1090091M

© RMA 2011   M = $ thousand   MM = $ million
See Pages 9 through 22 for Explanation of Ratios and Data

Current Data Sorted by Assets

Comparative Historical Data

Type of Statement										
	1		1	8	5	2	Unqualified		18	10
	1		7	3	1		Reviewed		17	12
	3		1	2			Compiled		8	3
	3						Tax Returns		16	9
	3		11	8	3	3	Other		36	37
	10 (4/1-9/30/10)			56 (10/1/10-3/31/11)					4/1/06-3/31/07	4/1/07-3/31/08
0-500M	500M-2MM		2-10MM	10-50MM	50-100MM	100-250MM			ALL	ALL
	11		20	21	9	5	NUMBER OF STATEMENTS		95	71
%	%		%	%	%	%	ASSETS		%	%
	5.6		4.9	3.5			Cash & Equivalents		5.0	5.7
	28.1		27.3	17.6			Trade Receivables (net)		21.6	24.2
	29.7		29.0	40.4			Inventory		31.0	32.0
	2.1		2.3	3.4			All Other Current		2.1	2.6
	65.5		63.5	64.8			Total Current		59.6	64.5
	28.3		31.0	31.9			Fixed Assets (net)		30.4	27.7
	1.3		2.0	.1			Intangibles (net)		3.0	2.0
	4.9		3.5	3.2			All Other Non-Current		7.0	5.8
	100.0		100.0	100.0			Total		100.0	100.0
							LIABILITIES			
	18.1		12.2	10.3			Notes Payable-Short Term		15.2	14.2
	1.2		5.8	3.8			Cur. Mat.-L.T.D.		3.9	2.8
	16.8		9.2	9.3			Trade Payables		11.0	11.0
	.0		.1	.1			Income Taxes Payable		.2	.2
	6.4		8.1	3.7			All Other Current		6.5	5.6
	42.6		35.4	27.3			Total Current		36.7	33.8
	22.7		13.7	17.6			Long-Term Debt		19.7	16.9
	.1		.1	1.0			Deferred Taxes		.6	.6
	11.2		5.7	1.6			All Other Non-Current		4.6	6.0
	23.4		45.1	52.5			Net Worth		38.4	42.7
	100.0		100.0	100.0			Total Liabilities & Net Worth		100.0	100.0
							INCOME DATA			
	100.0		100.0	100.0			Net Sales		100.0	100.0
	26.8		25.0	21.8			Gross Profit		22.3	20.6
	23.7		21.1	19.0			Operating Expenses		17.5	17.5
	3.1		3.9	2.8			Operating Profit		4.8	3.0
	1.5		.6	.2			All Other Expenses (net)		1.0	.9
	1.6		3.2	2.6			Profit Before Taxes		3.7	2.2
							RATIOS			
	4.6		5.0	4.0					2.9	3.8
	2.0		2.0	2.6			Current		1.5	1.8
	1.0		1.1	1.8					1.2	1.4
	2.6		1.8	1.1					1.4	1.8
	.9		.7	.7			Quick		.7	.9
	.5		.5	.5					.4	.5
20	18.6	23	16.1	29	12.7			Sales/Receivables	23	16.2	24	15.2
31	12.0	33	11.0	36	10.1				32	11.3	35	10.3
50	7.3	50	7.3	44	8.3				48	7.6	46	8.0
36	10.1	13	29.2	86	4.3			Cost of Sales/Inventory	34	10.6	34	10.7
52	7.1	58	6.3	124	2.9				63	5.8	67	5.4
75	4.9	99	3.7	172	2.1				106	3.4	105	3.5
6	58.0	9	40.7	8	47.1			Cost of Sales/Payables	10	36.9	10	36.9
20	18.6	16	23.2	12	30.1				18	20.0	17	21.4
58	6.3	29	12.4	31	11.9				32	11.3	29	12.7
	4.7		4.0	2.5			Sales/Working Capital		5.9	4.2
	12.2		7.6	4.0					11.4	8.2
	76.1		207.3	8.3					37.1	15.8
			15.6	8.0			EBIT/Interest		6.9	8.5
	(16)		2.3	(19)	3.6			(90)	3.1	(68)	3.0
			-4.1	.6					.9	.0
							Net Profit + Depr., Dep., Amort./Cur. Mat. L/T/D		6.1	4.8
								(28)	3.1	(21)	1.7
									1.5	.1
	.3		.3	.4			Fixed/Worth		.4	.3
	.7		.6	.7					.8	.6
	-2.8		1.3	1.0					2.1	1.1
	.6		.5	.5			Debt/Worth		.7	.6
	2.5		1.2	1.0					2.0	1.3
	-4.6		3.7	1.6					5.2	3.9
			31.4	18.3			% Profit Before Taxes/Tangible Net Worth		37.5	29.7
	(17)		14.2	6.5			(84)	14.7	(68)	11.1
			2.8	-1.4					1.2	-10.6
	15.7		20.8	9.4			% Profit Before Taxes/Total Assets		14.1	12.1
	3.4		5.0	3.8					6.1	3.6
	-4.1		.2	-1.1					.1	-3.8
	23.1		23.0	10.4			Sales/Net Fixed Assets		20.5	17.0
	14.3		9.0	5.6					6.7	8.6
	4.4		3.4	2.9					3.8	4.0
	4.7		3.2	2.0			Sales/Total Assets		2.7	2.9
	2.2		2.2	1.4					1.9	2.2
	1.4		1.5	1.0					1.5	1.4
			.8	.9			% Depr., Dep., Amort./Sales		1.2	1.1
	(18)		1.7	(19)	2.3			(87)	2.0	(64)	2.2
			3.9	3.4					3.6	3.8
							% Officers', Directors' Owners' Comp/Sales		1.4	.8
								(28)	2.5	(21)	2.5
									3.8	4.8
	28529M		320940M	804368M	1127647M	1493952M	Net Sales ($)		3288004M	3591248M
	9412M		105129M	459303M	601647M	743919M	Total Assets ($)		1681705M	1844858M

© RMA 2011

M = $ thousand   MM = $ million

See Pages 9 through 22 for Explanation of Ratios and Data

Comparative Historical Data | Current Data Sorted by Sales

4/1/08-3/31/09 ALL	4/1/09-3/31/10 ALL	4/1/10-3/31/11 ALL	Type of Statement	0-1MM	1-3MM	3-5MM	5-10MM	10-25MM	25MM & OVER
12	12	17	Unqualified		1			4	12
9	6	12	Reviewed		1	1	1	5	4
13	8	6	Compiled	1	1		3		1
10	13	3	Tax Returns	1	2				
31	36	28	Other		2	2	2	10	12
					10 (4/1-9/30/10)			56 (10/1/10-3/31/11)	
75	75	66	NUMBER OF STATEMENTS	2	7	3	6	19	29
%	%	%	**ASSETS**	%	%	%	%	%	%
5.7	7.4	5.9	Cash & Equivalents					3.2	8.2
20.9	19.0	21.3	Trade Receivables (net)					27.5	15.8
35.2	32.3	31.5	Inventory					38.5	30.0
2.8	4.0	3.1	All Other Current					1.5	4.7
64.5	62.7	61.8	Total Current					70.7	58.7
27.0	27.2	31.0	Fixed Assets (net)					24.9	31.5
1.5	2.3	1.9	Intangibles (net)					1.7	2.7
7.1	7.8	5.3	All Other Non-Current					2.7	7.1
100.0	100.0	100.0	Total					100.0	100.0
			LIABILITIES						
19.6	17.3	11.3	Notes Payable-Short Term					11.9	8.8
4.4	4.5	4.7	Cur. Mat.-L.T.D.					6.7	4.7
11.5	10.0	10.4	Trade Payables					11.9	8.1
.0	.1	.1	Income Taxes Payable					.1	.1
4.8	5.9	6.5	All Other Current					3.0	8.0
40.4	37.8	32.9	Total Current					33.6	29.6
16.1	16.1	15.0	Long-Term Debt					10.9	12.0
.3	.4	.5	Deferred Taxes					.2	.9
4.4	6.7	5.1	All Other Non-Current					2.3	4.0
38.7	39.0	46.6	Net Worth					53.0	53.5
100.0	100.0	100.0	Total Liabilities & Net Worth					100.0	100.0
			INCOME DATA						
100.0	100.0	100.0	Net Sales					100.0	100.0
22.5	20.4	22.0	Gross Profit					20.7	19.7
21.1	23.0	18.7	Operating Expenses					19.8	15.4
1.5	-2.6	3.3	Operating Profit					.9	4.3
1.3	1.1	.6	All Other Expenses (net)					-.1	.7
.2	-3.7	2.7	Profit Before Taxes					1.0	3.6
			RATIOS						
3.4	3.4	4.3	Current					5.6	4.0
1.7	1.8	2.2						3.1	2.4
1.1	1.2	1.3						1.1	1.5
1.3	1.4	1.5	Quick					2.3	1.3
.6	.6	.8						.8	.8
.3	.4	.5						.5	.5
21 17.7	25 14.6	22 16.9	Sales/Receivables					31 12.0	17 22.0
32 11.5	37 9.9	32 11.3						41 8.8	26 13.9
46 8.0	52 7.1	45 8.1						55 6.6	42 8.6
38 9.6	48 7.7	41 8.8	Cost of Sales/Inventory					46 8.0	42 8.7
69 5.3	80 4.6	65 5.6						138 2.6	59 6.1
135 2.7	155 2.4	125 2.9						177 2.1	109 3.3
6 57.6	9 40.9	8 44.8	Cost of Sales/Payables					7 49.6	8 44.5
17 22.1	14 25.5	15 24.3						13 27.0	14 26.3
32 11.5	33 11.1	31 11.7						50 7.3	27 13.7
3.9	3.1	3.6	Sales/Working Capital					2.7	3.6
9.1	6.7	7.3						4.0	7.3
22.2	13.9	15.3						22.8	11.1
6.0	2.9	10.6	EBIT/Interest					5.3	12.2
(68) 1.7	(69) .6	(57) 2.2						(14) 1.6	(27) 3.8
-1.3	-3.8	.2						-1.8	.2
2.6	3.1	7.6	Net Profit + Depr., Dep., Amort./Cur. Mat. L/T/D						
(17) 2.0	(10) 1.7	(14) 2.6							
-2.2	1.0	.5							
.3	.3	.3	Fixed/Worth					.2	.4
.7	.7	.7						.4	.7
1.6	1.5	1.1						.9	1.0
.5	.5	.5	Debt/Worth					.4	.4
1.7	1.5	1.0						.7	1.0
5.0	6.0	2.6						1.8	2.1
20.0	6.3	23.2	% Profit Before Taxes/Tangible Net Worth					14.3	18.5
(69) 5.3	(63) -2.4	(59) 9.8						(17) 5.9	12.3
-13.8	-14.0	-2.2						-1.2	-2.9
11.1	3.5	10.7	% Profit Before Taxes/Total Assets					5.6	10.7
1.8	-2.1	3.7						1.3	7.6
-9.7	-9.8	-1.5						-1.5	-1.8
19.6	13.7	14.4	Sales/Net Fixed Assets					24.5	11.2
8.7	6.1	7.0						7.0	7.0
4.2	3.8	4.0						3.6	5.2
3.0	2.4	2.7	Sales/Total Assets					2.7	2.8
2.1	1.8	1.9						1.5	2.0
1.2	1.1	1.3						1.2	1.5
.9	1.2	1.0	% Depr., Dep., Amort./Sales					.8	1.2
(68) 2.3	(64) 2.2	(56) 2.2						(16) 1.8	(24) 1.7
4.1	3.8	3.6						3.4	3.7
1.8	1.9	1.0	% Officers', Directors' Owners' Comp/Sales						
(18) 3.3	(15) 4.9	(14) 3.3							
4.7	8.3	5.5							
2228767M	2370256M	3775436M	Net Sales ($)	1494M	13890M	12455M	43559M	266563M	3437475M
1392535M	1578691M	1919410M	Total Assets ($)	1435M	5637M	9711M	23251M	177128M	1702248M

© RMA 2011

M = $ thousand   MM = $ million

See Pages 9 through 22 for Explanation of Ratios and Data

Current Data Sorted by Assets   Comparative Historical Data

0-500M	500M-2MM	2-10MM	10-50MM	50-100MM	100-250MM	Type of Statement	4/1/06-3/31/07 ALL	4/1/07-3/31/08 ALL
	1	1	1			Unqualified	8	9
1	2	11	1			Reviewed	21	22
1	1	8	1			Compiled	26	23
5	7	1				Tax Returns	13	13
1	9	4	3	2	1	Other	34	24
	4 (4/1-9/30/10)		57 (10/1/10-3/31/11)					
7	20	25	6	2	1	**NUMBER OF STATEMENTS**	102	91
%	%	%	%	%	%	**ASSETS**	%	%
	11.1	8.8				Cash & Equivalents	10.6	8.7
	24.3	22.0				Trade Receivables (net)	24.3	22.0
	23.0	22.7				Inventory	23.0	23.2
	5.3	4.2				All Other Current	2.1	4.5
	63.7	57.8				Total Current	60.0	58.4
	31.7	34.1				Fixed Assets (net)	30.3	31.2
	.8	1.0				Intangibles (net)	3.5	4.8
	3.9	7.1				All Other Non-Current	6.3	5.6
	100.0	100.0				Total	100.0	100.0
						LIABILITIES		
	11.8	13.0				Notes Payable-Short Term	12.0	11.0
	3.2	3.0				Cur. Mat.-L.T.D.	4.2	4.8
	13.4	6.3				Trade Payables	10.0	7.8
	.0	.0				Income Taxes Payable	.2	.1
	13.1	8.6				All Other Current	9.5	9.5
	41.5	31.0				Total Current	36.0	33.2
	19.2	11.9				Long-Term Debt	17.0	20.1
	.2	.1				Deferred Taxes	.3	.2
	13.8	15.4				All Other Non-Current	4.8	7.4
	25.2	41.6				Net Worth	41.8	39.1
	100.0	100.0				Total Liabilties & Net Worth	100.0	100.0
						INCOME DATA		
	100.0	100.0				Net Sales	100.0	100.0
	32.4	25.7				Gross Profit	30.3	27.9
	36.0	26.1				Operating Expenses	25.5	28.9
	-3.6	-.4				Operating Profit	4.8	-1.0
	.6	.7				All Other Expenses (net)	.5	1.1
	-4.1	-1.2				Profit Before Taxes	4.3	-2.1
						RATIOS		
	5.9	7.5					3.6	5.0
	1.7	2.9				Current	1.7	2.1
	1.1	1.1					1.2	1.2
	2.0	2.5					2.1	2.5
	1.0	1.4				Quick	1.1	1.0
	.5	.5					.6	.6
	20 17.8	26 14.0					19 19.7	18 20.5
	36 10.3	35 10.3				Sales/Receivables	27 13.4	28 12.9
	51 7.2	51 7.1					39 9.3	40 9.1
	28 13.2	29 12.6					25 14.8	31 11.9
	70 5.2	58 6.3				Cost of Sales/Inventory	38 9.6	39 9.3
	98 3.7	82 4.4					58 6.3	62 5.9
	2 152.2	6 58.5					5 78.7	5 73.3
	14 26.3	13 28.2				Cost of Sales/Payables	9 38.9	9 39.1
	58 6.3	22 16.5					20 18.3	16 22.2
	3.6	4.2					6.1	5.1
	8.7	5.8				Sales/Working Capital	10.6	9.6
	757.8	65.8					39.7	35.6
	.2	7.5					11.9	5.2
	(13) -1.7	(24) .9				EBIT/Interest	(95) 4.3	(85) 1.1
	-3.7	-2.6					1.4	-3.6
						Net Profit + Depr., Dep.,	3.5	3.9
						Amort./Cur. Mat. L/T/D	(14) 2.3 (14) 1.4	
							1.8	-.9
	.4	.4					.4	.4
	1.0	.8				Fixed/Worth	.7	.8
	NM	1.2					1.5	1.5
	.4	.5					.5	.4
	2.1	.9				Debt/Worth	1.4	1.5
	NM	2.5					3.6	3.2
	20.0	10.5					52.8	25.4
	(15) -8.3	(23) .4				% Profit Before Taxes/Tangible Net Worth	(90) 27.4	(76) 4.7
	-32.1	-3.3					9.8	-21.4
	3.8	6.6					22.6	9.7
	-8.0	-.1				% Profit Before Taxes/Total Assets	8.3	-.2
	-20.4	-6.2					2.1	-15.7
	28.2	12.2					25.1	15.2
	6.9	5.8				Sales/Net Fixed Assets	11.4	9.1
	5.5	3.3					5.6	5.6
	3.0	3.1					3.9	3.4
	2.2	2.1				Sales/Total Assets	2.8	2.6
	1.8	1.4					2.1	2.0
	1.9	2.1					1.1	1.5
	(16) 3.4	3.1				% Depr., Dep., Amort./Sales	(91) 2.0	(84) 2.6
	5.5	4.4					3.5	4.1
	.6	.9					1.5	1.6
	(11) 4.3	(11) 2.2				% Officers', Directors' Owners' Comp/Sales	(33) 2.8	(33) 2.7
	11.6	5.6					5.9	4.9
6478M	52395M	239494M	155453M	229946M	116937M	Net Sales ($)	1802993M	1277536M
2291M	22182M	113126M	105021M	116612M	102837M	Total Assets ($)	640692M	574349M

M = $ thousand   MM = $ million
See Pages 9 through 22 for Explanation of Ratios and Data

Comparative Historical Data | Current Data Sorted by Sales

			Type of Statement						
5	4	3	Unqualified		1			1	1
15	16	15	Reviewed		2	3	4	6	1
20	6	10	Compiled		1	1	4	3	1
12	7	13	Tax Returns	5	6	1	1		
19	27	20	Other	2	5	5		4	4
4/1/08- 3/31/09 ALL	4/1/09- 3/31/10 ALL	4/1/10- 3/31/11 ALL		0-1MM	4 (4/1-9/30/10) 1-3MM	3-5MM	57 (10/1/10-3/31/11) 5-10MM	10-25MM	25MM & OVER
71	60	61	**NUMBER OF STATEMENTS**	7	15	10	9	14	6
%	%	%	**ASSETS**	%	%	%	%	%	%
10.4	9.7	9.8	Cash & Equivalents		7.3	15.3		5.8	
20.3	19.8	21.2	Trade Receivables (net)		20.0	18.0		27.8	
21.0	22.4	23.7	Inventory		29.2	20.5		21.4	
5.0	3.5	3.9	All Other Current		4.7	5.9		3.6	
56.7	55.4	58.6	Total Current		61.2	59.6		58.7	
31.9	35.2	33.0	Fixed Assets (net)		33.8	27.1		31.6	
4.0	3.2	1.9	Intangibles (net)		1.2	.0		1.6	
7.4	6.2	6.4	All Other Non-Current		3.8	13.2		8.0	
100.0	100.0	100.0	Total		100.0	100.0		100.0	
			LIABILITIES						
11.1	12.7	15.0	Notes Payable-Short Term		15.7	8.4		16.0	
6.3	5.1	3.6	Cur. Mat.-L.T.D.		2.7	5.9		3.2	
7.9	8.3	8.6	Trade Payables		12.3	10.3		8.6	
.0	.1	.0	Income Taxes Payable		.0	.0		.1	
9.3	8.4	11.3	All Other Current		16.7	13.7		7.6	
34.6	34.6	38.5	Total Current		47.4	38.3		35.6	
17.3	20.0	17.7	Long-Term Debt		18.3	21.2		13.9	
.3	.4	.1	Deferred Taxes		.2	.2		.0	
11.5	14.3	16.5	All Other Non-Current		18.6	16.2		23.1	
36.4	30.7	27.3	Net Worth		15.6	24.2		27.4	
100.0	100.0	100.0	Total Liabilities & Net Worth		100.0	100.0		100.0	
			INCOME DATA						
100.0	100.0	100.0	Net Sales		100.0	100.0		100.0	
26.1	30.5	28.6	Gross Profit		32.5	34.7		20.0	
31.6	35.0	30.8	Operating Expenses		34.1	36.9		21.9	
-5.5	-4.5	-2.2	Operating Profit		-1.6	-2.1		-2.0	
.9	1.4	.7	All Other Expenses (net)		.9	.6		.6	
-6.4	-5.9	-2.8	Profit Before Taxes		-2.5	-2.7		-2.6	
			RATIOS						
5.0	5.1	5.4	Current		4.6	8.8		3.8	
2.2	1.7	2.0			2.2	1.3		2.5	
1.1	1.1	1.1			1.0	.9		1.1	
2.5	2.9	2.4	Quick		1.4	2.8		2.3	
1.1	.9	1.1			1.1	1.0		1.2	
.6	.5	.5			.4	.5		.6	
17 21.5	23 15.6	21 17.0	Sales/Receivables	13 27.2	22 16.7			33 11.1	
28 13.1	32 11.6	34 10.8		22 16.6	33 10.9			36 10.2	
40 9.0	44 8.2	49 7.4		51 7.2	40 9.2			51 7.2	
28 12.9	34 10.7	35 10.3	Cost of Sales/Inventory	42 8.7	23 15.6			26 13.9	
41 8.8	53 6.9	55 6.7		76 4.8	51 7.2			40 9.1	
60 6.1	77 4.8	91 4.0		98 3.7	141 2.6			61 6.0	
5 80.5	8 47.6	6 64.8	Cost of Sales/Payables	2 177.2	6 63.9			7 49.1	
10 37.9	14 26.3	13 29.0		15 24.3	22 16.9			10 35.2	
18 20.3	24 15.4	24 15.0		64 5.7	28 12.9			19 18.7	
4.5	4.7	4.0	Sales/Working Capital		3.9	3.0		4.6	
8.0	9.0	8.3			8.3	39.0		9.6	
123.1	93.8	56.9			-39.3	NM		NM	
2.7	3.3	3.1	EBIT/Interest		2.2			12.1	
(66) -1.4	(55) -1.2	(51) -.3			(12) -1.6			(13) 1.4	
-6.7	-9.6	-3.1			-7.5			-3.3	
			Net Profit + Depr., Dep., Amort./Cur. Mat. L/T/D						
.4	.5	.4	Fixed/Worth		.6	.2		.5	
.8	1.1	.9			1.1	1.1		.9	
1.5	4.5	3.2			-1.8	NM		2.9	
.4	.6	.4	Debt/Worth		.5	.2		.7	
1.2	1.5	1.1			3.0	1.2		1.8	
3.7	12.2	6.9			-5.9	NM		5.8	
5.4	4.7	14.2	% Profit Before Taxes/Tangible Net Worth		61.8			41.1	
(62) -13.5	(48) -6.5	(49) -.2			(10) -3.4			(12) 5.8	
-39.7	-41.2	-18.3			-45.1			-36.8	
1.4	2.2	4.9	% Profit Before Taxes/Total Assets		4.9	3.2		10.5	
-7.8	-7.9	-2.0			-8.7	-2.5		.6	
-25.5	-28.4	-11.6			-23.0	-12.9		-15.1	
14.7	12.3	13.4	Sales/Net Fixed Assets		8.3	24.0		10.4	
8.2	6.2	6.9			6.8	6.8		8.1	
5.0	3.9	4.3			5.3	4.9		5.7	
3.1	2.9	3.0	Sales/Total Assets		3.0	2.9		3.6	
2.2	2.1	2.2			2.2	2.1		2.4	
1.8	1.4	1.5			1.8	1.3		1.7	
2.0	1.6	2.2	% Depr., Dep., Amort./Sales		1.6			2.1	
(65) 2.8	(54) 3.7	(53) 3.1			(13) 3.5			(13) 2.8	
4.4	5.7	4.5			5.5			3.3	
1.1	2.0	1.9	% Officers', Directors' Owners' Comp/Sales						
(27) 3.4	(22) 3.3	(27) 3.6							
6.7	6.4	7.1							
1034004M	585655M	800703M	Net Sales ($)	5667M	24224M	39446M	64241M	221214M	445911M
519959M	308461M	462069M	Total Assets ($)	5190M	13648M	24287M	32072M	100315M	286557M

M = $ thousand   MM = $ million
See Pages 9 through 22 for Explanation of Ratios and Data

Current Data Sorted by Assets   Comparative Historical Data

	0-500M	500M-2MM	2-10MM	10-50MM	50-100MM	100-250MM	Type of Statement	4/1/06-3/31/07 ALL	4/1/07-3/31/08 ALL
			1	5	2	2	Unqualified	23	19
	2	5	18	7	2		Reviewed	44	54
	4	10	7	1			Compiled	40	29
	8	24	10	14		3	Tax Returns	28	23
	11	23	16				Other	79	70
		21 (4/1-9/30/10)		154 (10/1/10-3/31/11)					
NUMBER OF STATEMENTS	25	62	52	27	4	5		214	195

	%	%	%	%	%	%	ASSETS	%	%
	18.8	12.8	7.2	8.1			Cash & Equivalents	6.2	8.3
	23.9	26.1	27.3	15.1			Trade Receivables (net)	28.1	25.9
	24.6	25.5	25.9	26.1			Inventory	26.3	26.1
	1.4	3.4	2.0	2.3			All Other Current	2.7	2.8
	68.6	67.7	62.4	51.6			Total Current	63.3	63.0
	26.5	25.0	30.0	35.3			Fixed Assets (net)	28.5	28.2
	.0	1.5	2.3	8.4			Intangibles (net)	3.5	2.8
	4.9	5.8	5.3	4.7			All Other Non-Current	4.7	5.9
	100.0	100.0	100.0	100.0			Total	100.0	100.0
							LIABILITIES		
	26.2	19.8	12.4	10.4			Notes Payable-Short Term	13.3	12.1
	3.3	4.0	4.9	2.3			Cur. Mat.-L.T.D.	3.7	3.5
	28.5	12.8	12.3	8.0			Trade Payables	13.0	12.7
	.1	.1	.3	.3			Income Taxes Payable	.3	.2
	11.6	14.8	9.5	8.3			All Other Current	10.3	11.8
	69.6	51.4	39.5	29.3			Total Current	40.5	40.2
	20.1	15.3	21.9	17.3			Long-Term Debt	18.2	16.1
	.0	.1	.4	.2			Deferred Taxes	.5	.3
	15.9	5.8	9.7	4.8			All Other Non-Current	9.9	8.8
	-5.4	27.4	28.5	48.4			Net Worth	30.9	34.6
	100.0	100.0	100.0	100.0			Total Liabilities & Net Worth	100.0	100.0
							INCOME DATA		
	100.0	100.0	100.0	100.0			Net Sales	100.0	100.0
	37.4	34.5	25.0	23.3			Gross Profit	27.6	27.9
	36.1	34.3	25.0	20.8			Operating Expenses	23.2	24.4
	1.3	.2	.0	2.5			Operating Profit	4.4	3.5
	.6	.6	.6	1.6			All Other Expenses (net)	1.4	1.2
	.7	-.4	-.6	.9			Profit Before Taxes	2.9	2.3
							RATIOS		
	5.0	3.6	2.7	3.0				2.5	3.1
	1.5	1.6	1.6	2.0			Current	1.6	1.6
	.5	.9	1.1	1.2				1.1	1.1
	2.2	2.3	1.4	1.6				1.4	1.6
	1.1	.9	.9	.8			Quick	.9	.8
	.3	.4	.5	.4				.5	.5
	3 132.2	18 19.9	34 10.8	21 17.0				22 16.9	21 17.2
	18 20.4	35 10.5	41 8.9	35 10.5			Sales/Receivables	35 10.3	32 11.5
	37 9.8	54 6.7	60 6.1	45 8.0				52 7.0	45 8.1
	7 51.4	19 19.1	29 12.6	37 9.9				22 16.7	27 13.6
	27 13.5	39 9.3	55 6.7	63 5.8			Cost of Sales/Inventory	46 8.0	50 7.3
	54 6.7	92 4.0	93 3.9	129 2.8				73 5.0	73 5.0
	8 43.4	9 40.4	14 25.5	12 30.0				9 38.9	10 37.4
	18 20.6	20 17.9	24 15.4	17 22.0			Cost of Sales/Payables	18 20.7	18 20.8
	41 8.9	36 10.1	30 12.2	28 13.0				32 11.5	33 11.2
	7.3	5.3	5.5	5.4				6.4	5.9
	14.1	12.4	9.3	9.5			Sales/Working Capital	11.6	10.9
	-18.4	-32.2	36.7	27.8				58.5	97.9
	8.4	8.7	3.6	5.3				8.0	7.7
	(21) 2.7	(52) 2.4	(48) 1.4	(26) 2.0			EBIT/Interest	(197) 3.1	(180) 2.6
	-6.4	-2.9	-1.9	.3				1.1	.6
							Net Profit + Depr., Dep.,	7.5	3.6
							Amort./Cur. Mat. L/T/D	(43) 3.1 (40) 2.2	
								1.4	.6
	.3	.3	.5	.4				.3	.3
	.8	.7	1.1	1.0			Fixed/Worth	.9	.8
	-.7	-11.9	4.1	1.7				3.5	2.6
	.9	.7	.8	.5				.9	.6
	6.5	1.7	3.1	1.2			Debt/Worth	2.0	2.0
	-3.8	-31.7	14.1	2.7				7.7	6.2
	94.5	30.7	27.8	13.3			% Profit Before Taxes/Tangible	52.2	44.7
	(16) 19.2	(46) 15.0	(44) 4.8	(25) 5.2			Net Worth	(179) 19.8 (164) 15.7	
	-10.4	-.8	-17.6	-2.1				5.4	3.5
	26.4	-10.4	5.4	5.5			% Profit Before Taxes/Total	15.9	13.1
	10.9	4.4	1.3	1.5			Assets	6.9	5.3
	-19.1	-4.6	-9.6	-.8				.7	-1.3
	44.6	31.9	18.9	9.4				26.2	24.0
	18.4	13.3	9.9	5.5			Sales/Net Fixed Assets	10.9	10.6
	8.9	7.2	4.2	3.1				5.4	5.5
	5.9	3.9	2.8	2.2				3.7	3.6
	3.6	2.7	2.4	1.5			Sales/Total Assets	2.7	2.6
	2.9	1.9	1.7	1.2				2.0	1.8
	.8	.8	1.4	1.9				1.0	1.0
	(19) 1.8	(47) 2.2	(47) 2.3	(24) 2.7			% Depr., Dep., Amort./Sales	(194) 1.7 (170) 1.8	
	3.6	3.7	3.5	4.0				3.0	2.9
	3.0	2.5	1.7				% Officers', Directors'	1.2	2.2
	(11) 5.4	(34) 4.4	(24) 3.5				Owners' Comp/Sales	(79) 2.8 (75) 4.8	
	11.7	9.4	5.7					6.3	7.0
	24473M	219478M	561829M	1046864M	622396M	985359M	Net Sales ($)	6498583M	6246532M
	6739M	73320M	248840M	574810M	269565M	726256M	Total Assets ($)	2760365M	2922596M

M = $ thousand   MM = $ million
See Pages 9 through 22 for Explanation of Ratios and Data

Comparative Historical Data | Current Data Sorted by Sales

Type of Statement	4/1/08-3/31/09 ALL	4/1/09-3/31/10 ALL	4/1/10-3/31/11 ALL	0-1MM	1-3MM	3-5MM	5-10MM	10-25MM	25MM & OVER
Unqualified	17	12	10					1	9
Reviewed	46	35	34		4	2	11	14	3
Compiled	34	25	21	4	3	6	5	3	
Tax Returns	27	46	43	6	19	5	10	2	1
Other	59	57	67	4	22	10	6	14	11
				21 (4/1-9/30/10)			154 (10/1/10-3/31/11)		
NUMBER OF STATEMENTS	183	175	175	14	48	23	32	34	24
ASSETS	%	%	%	%	%	%	%	%	%
Cash & Equivalents	8.5	8.2	11.0	20.3	12.9	8.2	9.1	9.5	9.3
Trade Receivables (net)	24.6	24.9	24.0	18.7	22.5	33.7	25.1	25.6	16.9
Inventory	24.7	24.5	25.5	30.4	24.7	23.0	24.4	25.4	28.6
All Other Current	3.0	2.9	2.5	.8	2.0	1.7	4.1	2.6	3.3
Total Current	60.8	60.4	63.1	70.3	62.1	66.5	62.7	63.0	58.1
Fixed Assets (net)	29.7	30.1	28.8	27.0	28.9	28.1	31.5	26.7	29.5
Intangibles (net)	3.8	3.0	2.6	.0	1.6	2.4	1.3	4.5	5.3
All Other Non-Current	5.7	6.5	5.5	2.8	7.3	3.0	4.5	5.7	7.1
Total	100.0	100.0	100.0	100.0	100.0	100.0	100.0	100.0	100.0
LIABILITIES									
Notes Payable-Short Term	15.3	14.9	16.2	38.3	20.5	17.4	12.7	10.0	6.9
Cur. Mat.-L.T.D.	3.7	5.0	3.8	2.1	5.0	2.1	4.1	4.8	2.3
Trade Payables	12.6	14.0	13.9	28.4	13.3	16.9	14.3	9.7	8.8
Income Taxes Payable	.1	.2	.2	.1	.0	.2	.4	.1	.3
All Other Current	9.7	11.3	11.8	16.8	8.4	15.1	14.4	10.1	11.3
Total Current	41.3	45.3	45.8	85.7	47.2	51.7	45.9	34.6	29.6
Long-Term Debt	19.5	21.8	18.2	17.7	21.4	21.6	19.9	14.3	12.1
Deferred Taxes	.3	.4	.3	.0	.2	.1	.2	.3	1.1
All Other Non-Current	9.5	9.0	8.6	18.6	7.4	6.7	4.5	11.7	8.3
Net Worth	29.4	23.5	27.1	-21.8	23.8	19.8	29.5	39.1	48.8
Total Liabilities & Net Worth	100.0	100.0	100.0	100.0	100.0	100.0	100.0	100.0	100.0
INCOME DATA									
Net Sales	100.0	100.0	100.0	100.0	100.0	100.0	100.0	100.0	100.0
Gross Profit	27.1	26.0	29.5	35.5	38.0	32.3	23.7	24.5	21.2
Operating Expenses	26.5	27.7	29.0	35.8	38.7	31.2	22.7	22.9	20.9
Operating Profit	.6	-1.6	.5	-.3	-.6	1.1	1.0	1.6	.4
All Other Expenses (net)	1.2	1.0	.8	.7	1.0	1.0	.4	.7	.9
Profit Before Taxes	-.6	-2.7	-.3	-1.1	-1.6	.1	.6	.9	-.5
RATIOS									
Current	3.0	2.6	3.0	6.3	3.4	2.8	1.9	3.5	2.8
	1.6	1.5	1.6	1.2	1.6	1.7	1.4	1.8	2.2
	1.0	1.0	1.0	.4	.9	1.0	.9	1.2	1.5
Quick	1.7	1.5	1.6	3.8	2.2	1.8	1.1	1.7	1.4
	.9	(174) .8	.9	.6	.9	.9	.7	1.0	.9
	.4	.4	.4	.1	.4	.5	.4	.6	.6
Sales/Receivables	19 18.9	21 17.4	21 17.1	0 UND	18 20.0	35 10.4	14 25.2	27 13.5	23 15.7
	33 11.1	33 10.9	35 10.4	5 71.2	31 11.8	43 8.6	40 9.2	37 10.0	32 11.3
	49 7.5	51 7.1	50 7.3	43 8.4	51 7.2	67 5.4	55 6.7	48 7.6	40 9.1
Cost of Sales/Inventory	19 18.7	20 18.2	24 15.2	13 28.9	23 15.9	16 22.7	14 25.3	30 12.1	44 8.2
	47 7.7	51 7.2	48 7.6	36 10.1	54 6.7	35 10.5	30 12.2	56 6.6	57 6.4
	81 4.5	84 4.3	93 3.9	83 4.4	124 2.9	113 3.2	73 5.0	89 4.1	103 3.6
Cost of Sales/Payables	8 47.2	10 36.0	12 30.3	0 UND	11 31.8	16 23.0	14 25.5	10 37.9	13 28.3
	17 21.8	18 19.9	19 19.2	20 18.7	19 19.4	28 13.2	21 17.8	16 23.3	15 24.3
	34 10.8	37 9.9	33 10.9	43 8.5	39 9.3	42 8.7	33 10.9	27 13.5	25 14.6
Sales/Working Capital	5.7	5.6	5.5	4.8	4.6	5.9	8.1	5.3	5.6
	12.8	11.7	10.4	12.9	9.7	11.5	17.8	11.2	7.2
	108.3	-136.6	181.7	-3.8	-30.3	181.7	-35.3	20.6	14.1
EBIT/Interest	6.8	3.9	6.2	7.2	6.4	3.1	8.9	8.8	6.2
	(173) 1.7	(163) .6	(155) 1.9	(12) 1.1	(40) 2.1	(20) 1.4	(31) 1.4	(30) 2.5	(22) 2.7
	-1.4	-4.4	-1.8	-9.3	-3.0	-2.5	-2.1	-.1	-1.2
Net Profit + Depr., Dep., Amort./Cur. Mat. L/T/D	3.6	3.7	5.2						
	(33) 2.2	(23) 2.1	(22) 2.2						
	-1.6	.3	.0						
Fixed/Worth	.4	.3	.4	.3	.3	.4	.5	.4	.4
	1.0	1.0	.9	.6	1.1	1.3	1.1	.9	.6
	4.5	-27.7	4.7	-1.6	-10.5	-.7	2.4	2.0	1.6
Debt/Worth	.8	.8	.8	1.0	1.0	.8	1.2	.7	.5
	2.1	2.1	2.0	5.6	2.8	3.0	2.3	1.7	1.0
	9.8	-59.8	12.1	-2.0	-27.1	-7.1	7.8	4.2	2.5
% Profit Before Taxes/Tangible Net Worth	39.7	18.7	26.3		31.3	31.3	44.8	25.1	9.5
	(149) 8.6	(131) .8	(140) 6.7	(35) 11.2	(17) 11.4	(28) 5.5	(30) 7.8	(22) 4.5	
	-10.3	-21.0	-6.4	-4.0	.2	-12.5	-2.6	-11.8	
% Profit Before Taxes/Total Assets	11.4	5.0	8.2	28.6	11.3	8.2	7.2	6.0	5.3
	2.2	-1.0	2.2	-1.7	2.9	3.8	1.3	3.8	1.6
	-9.0	-11.1	-5.7	-35.1	-11.6	-4.4	-5.6	-2.9	-6.8
Sales/Net Fixed Assets	19.6	18.1	23.0	34.0	28.3	23.0	22.9	21.4	11.3
	10.2	9.4	10.2	22.6	10.6	9.9	11.6	10.5	6.3
	5.1	4.4	4.8	4.8	4.2	4.8	4.8	4.3	4.9
Sales/Total Assets	3.5	3.2	3.4	5.6	3.7	3.5	3.9	3.0	2.4
	2.5	2.2	2.4	2.9	2.1	2.6	2.6	2.4	1.9
	1.6	1.6	1.6	1.4	1.6	1.6	2.1	1.4	1.4
% Depr., Dep., Amort./Sales	1.1	1.2	1.4	1.4	.8	1.2	1.5	1.4	1.4
	(158) 1.9	(143) 2.3	(144) 2.3	(11) 2.0	(40) 2.6	(19) 1.9	(24) 2.3	(30) 2.2	(20) 2.7
	3.0	3.7	3.7	6.9	4.0	3.0	4.0	2.9	3.9
% Officers', Directors' Owners' Comp/Sales	1.9	2.1	2.2		2.5	2.6	1.4	1.5	
	(70) 4.9	(63) 4.2	(74) 4.2		(25) 5.4	(10) 4.8	(20) 4.1	(11) 2.8	
	8.0	8.3	7.6		9.2	9.9	5.7	5.0	
Net Sales ($)	4702492M	3612346M	3460399M	7958M	89745M	92711M	230507M	570836M	2468642M
Total Assets ($)	2414806M	2082688M	1899530M	3341M	46487M	56301M	99961M	287634M	1405806M

Current Data Sorted by Assets   Comparative Historical Data

0-500M	500M-2MM	2-10MM	10-50MM	50-100MM	100-250MM	Type of Statement	4/1/06-3/31/07 ALL	4/1/07-3/31/08 ALL
		2	6	2		Unqualified	14	16
		9	2			Reviewed	11	14
	2	6		1		Compiled	21	18
	2	4				Tax Returns	10	7
2	5	4	2	2		Other	19	24
		13 (4/1-9/30/10)	38 (10/1/10-3/31/11)					
2	9	25	10	5		NUMBER OF STATEMENTS	75	79
%	%	%	%	%	%	**ASSETS**	%	%
		6.7	4.0			Cash & Equivalents	5.6	5.9
		13.3	9.8			Trade Receivables (net)	19.9	13.6
		32.4	37.2			Inventory	34.2	35.0
		.8	1.7			All Other Current	1.3	2.1
		53.2	52.7			Total Current	61.0	56.6
		40.6	35.1			Fixed Assets (net)	31.7	34.8
		.2	2.5			Intangibles (net)	1.7	2.1
		6.0	9.7			All Other Non-Current	5.7	6.5
		100.0	100.0			Total	100.0	100.0
						LIABILITIES		
		16.2	21.9			Notes Payable-Short Term	20.7	17.3
		4.6	4.7			Cur. Mat.-L.T.D.	3.6	4.0
		8.8	5.6			Trade Payables	10.6	8.6
		.0	.1			Income Taxes Payable	.0	.1
		5.0	6.1			All Other Current	7.7	6.8
		34.6	38.4			Total Current	42.7	36.7
		22.3	10.7			Long-Term Debt	16.7	21.0
		.6	.1			Deferred Taxes	.1	.2
		3.6	4.3			All Other Non-Current	2.5	3.2
		38.9	46.5			Net Worth	38.0	38.8
		100.0	100.0			Total Liabilities & Net Worth	100.0	100.0
						INCOME DATA		
		100.0	100.0			Net Sales	100.0	100.0
		23.4	14.0			Gross Profit	20.6	20.7
		19.0	13.0			Operating Expenses	16.6	17.9
		4.3	1.1			Operating Profit	4.0	2.8
		2.8	.9			All Other Expenses (net)	1.6	1.9
		1.5	.1			Profit Before Taxes	2.4	.9
						RATIOS		
		2.9	1.9				2.5	2.3
		1.5	1.4			Current	1.5	1.4
		.9	1.0				1.1	1.0
		1.1	.6				1.2	.8
		.6	.3			Quick	.5 (78)	.4
		.3	.2				.3	.2
		9 42.8	6 60.4				12 30.2	10 35.7
		21 17.7	20 18.4			Sales/Receivables	21 17.1	17 21.8
		36 10.1	33 10.9				34 10.6	28 13.0
		31 11.9	58 6.3				31 11.7	33 11.1
		81 4.5	76 4.8			Cost of Sales/Inventory	55 6.7	60 6.1
		105 3.5	150 2.4				90 4.0	122 3.0
		5 72.4	5 78.5				5 68.7	7 54.0
		13 27.9	18 20.0			Cost of Sales/Payables	12 31.7	12 29.3
		25 14.4	20 18.0				26 14.0	26 14.1
		4.2	6.2				6.0	6.1
		10.9	16.8			Sales/Working Capital	17.1	11.6
		-513.1	NM				67.3	95.7
		8.4	3.5				6.6	7.1
		(21) 1.7	2.5			EBIT/Interest	(71) 2.8	(76) 2.7
		.1	.6				1.2	.3
						Net Profit + Depr., Dep.,		2.4
						Amort./Cur. Mat. L/T/D	(16) 1.9	
								1.1
		.4	.5				.3	.3
		1.0	.7			Fixed/Worth	.8	.8
		3.7	1.5				1.7	2.0
		.6	.7				.9	.6
		1.8	1.2			Debt/Worth	2.1	1.7
		7.8	3.6				3.7	5.2
		30.2	13.9			% Profit Before Taxes/Tangible	36.9	28.8
		(22) 13.1	7.6			Net Worth	(72) 16.6	(71) 9.6
		.8	-.9				3.2	-1.7
		12.7	3.9			% Profit Before Taxes/Total	13.3	9.0
		2.2	2.6			Assets	5.4	3.4
		-.5	-.3				1.0	-3.7
		12.1	15.0				24.5	22.1
		7.1	6.4			Sales/Net Fixed Assets	8.0	6.9
		2.7	2.4				4.3	3.0
		2.7	2.7				3.8	3.0
		1.9	1.6			Sales/Total Assets	2.3	2.2
		1.6	1.0				1.6	1.4
		1.4	1.3				.9	.9
		(22) 2.8	2.9			% Depr., Dep., Amort./Sales	(63) 1.8	(72) 2.2
		4.4	6.5				4.1	3.8
		1.6					1.2	.7
		(10) 3.1				% Officers', Directors'	(29) 2.5	(25) 2.3
		4.9				Owners' Comp/Sales	4.3	5.8
2764M	30405M	262240M	390879M	815228M		Net Sales ($)	3955106M	4158455M
804M	11675M	126632M	213395M	407456M		Total Assets ($)	1188995M	1528780M

(100-250MM column: DATA NOT AVAILABLE)

M = $ thousand   MM = $ million
See Pages 9 through 22 for Explanation of Ratios and Data

Comparative Historical Data | Current Data Sorted by Sales

					Type of Statement						
6		9		10	Unqualified	1				1	8
7		12		11	Reviewed			1	5	3	2
18		13		9	Compiled		1		6	1	1
5		4		8	Tax Returns	1	3	2	1	1	
17		23		13	Other	1	2	1	2	4	3
4/1/08-3/31/09 ALL		4/1/09-3/31/10 ALL		4/1/10-3/31/11 ALL		13 (4/1-9/30/10)			38 (10/1/10-3/31/11)		
						0-1MM	1-3MM	3-5MM	5-10MM	10-25MM	25MM & OVER
53		61		51	NUMBER OF STATEMENTS	3	6	4	14	10	14
%		%		%	ASSETS	%	%	%	%	%	%
9.1		6.6		5.8	Cash & Equivalents				7.6	5.9	4.3
14.5		12.1		15.2	Trade Receivables (net)				19.9	13.5	13.3
35.2		34.6		33.9	Inventory				33.6	48.8	35.6
1.7		2.2		1.1	All Other Current				.7	1.2	2.1
60.5		55.6		55.9	Total Current				61.7	69.4	55.3
30.6		34.7		36.7	Fixed Assets (net)				31.3	26.5	32.2
1.1		1.7		.7	Intangibles (net)				.4	1.3	1.3
7.8		8.1		6.6	All Other Non-Current				6.6	2.8	11.2
100.0		100.0		100.0	Total				100.0	100.0	100.0
					LIABILITIES						
18.8		16.9		19.6	Notes Payable-Short Term				21.3	19.4	17.8
4.7		6.3		4.1	Cur. Mat.-L.T.D.				2.3	2.6	5.5
8.8		8.3		12.4	Trade Payables				8.9	13.4	7.9
.1		.1		.0	Income Taxes Payable				.0	.0	.1
6.7		6.8		6.0	All Other Current				6.2	3.9	6.4
39.1		38.4		42.1	Total Current				38.7	39.3	37.7
24.4		19.2		17.7	Long-Term Debt				15.2	11.6	12.9
.1		.6		.4	Deferred Taxes				.0	.1	.4
7.7		5.0		4.3	All Other Non-Current				6.3	.7	6.5
28.7		36.8		35.4	Net Worth				39.7	48.4	42.5
100.0		100.0		100.0	Total Liabilties & Net Worth				100.0	100.0	100.0
					INCOME DATA						
100.0		100.0		100.0	Net Sales				100.0	100.0	100.0
21.2		17.2		20.5	Gross Profit				22.1	14.5	13.5
19.0		18.8		18.3	Operating Expenses				17.9	12.7	10.9
2.2		-1.6		2.2	Operating Profit				4.2	1.8	2.6
2.5		1.0		2.0	All Other Expenses (net)				1.4	.6	1.0
-.3		-2.6		.2	Profit Before Taxes				2.8	1.2	1.6
					RATIOS						
2.7		2.1		2.2					3.5	6.9	1.8
1.5		1.7		1.5	Current				1.6	1.8	1.5
1.1		1.1		1.1					1.1	1.1	1.1
1.1		.8		1.0					1.3	1.1	.8
.5		.4		.5	Quick				.6	.5	.5
.2		.3		.3					.3	.4	.3
10	37.6	12	30.4	13	27.6			17	21.1	10	38.2	6	60.4
20	18.5	23	15.9	21	17.4	Sales/Receivables	25	14.9	19	18.8	20	18.3
34	10.6	30	12.2	36	10.0		42	8.7	29	12.7	33	10.9
32	11.5	43	8.6	50	7.3		57	6.4	85	4.3	53	6.9
63	5.8	79	4.6	70	5.2	Cost of Sales/Inventory	74	5.0	100	3.7	65	5.6
123	3.0	130	2.8	104	3.5		91	4.0	115	3.2	104	3.5
4	82.9	7	49.4	6	58.1		9	40.4	5	69.0	5	78.5
12	31.6	13	28.6	17	21.7	Cost of Sales/Payables	18	20.6	15	24.2	15	24.6
26	14.0	30	12.0	29	12.7		27	13.6	29	12.8	24	15.4
	4.8		4.7		6.2			4.5		4.0		7.2
	8.9		8.9		11.3	Sales/Working Capital		11.1		7.4		13.6
	36.9		37.9		161.1			NM		NM		31.5
	4.3		2.6		4.1			4.9				4.1
(50)	1.5	(59)	.0	(46)	1.6	EBIT/Interest	(13)	1.5				3.2
	-1.4		-2.9		-.2			.3				1.4
			4.5			Net Profit + Depr., Dep.,						
		(18)	1.3			Amort./Cur. Mat. L/T/D						
			.5									
	.3		.4		.4			.3		.2		.4
	.9		.8		.8	Fixed/Worth		.9		.5		.6
	4.7		2.6		2.1			2.3		NM		1.7
	.9		.6		.6			.7		.2		.9
	2.2		1.5		1.6	Debt/Worth		1.7		1.5		1.6
	24.7		5.8		5.0			5.2		NM		3.1
	13.6		12.3		21.3			15.6				20.8
(41)	5.5	(52)	-1.8	(46)	7.6	% Profit Before Taxes/Tangible Net Worth		3.6				11.0
	-6.3		-17.4		-2.0			-4.5				2.8
	6.3		4.0		7.8			6.6		16.7		7.9
	1.3		-1.1		1.8	% Profit Before Taxes/Total Assets		.9		4.2		3.6
	-5.5		-7.8		-1.5			-1.2		-3.7		.7
	32.5		16.5		19.2			24.6		26.5		18.6
	7.2		5.0		7.1	Sales/Net Fixed Assets		8.2		10.7		6.7
	3.1		3.1		3.0			2.9		4.7		3.9
	2.9		2.7		2.9			2.9		2.9		3.2
	1.9		1.7		1.9	Sales/Total Assets		1.9		2.3		2.1
	1.3		1.0		1.4			1.5		1.8		1.3
	1.0		1.9		1.1			1.1				1.2
(43)	2.1	(55)	3.8	(48)	2.8	% Depr., Dep., Amort./Sales	(13)	2.6				2.9
	4.4		5.0		4.5			4.6				4.4
	1.3		1.5		1.8							
(28)	4.5	(19)	4.2	(17)	3.4	% Officers', Directors' Owners' Comp/Sales						
	7.0		8.5		5.8							
1084026M		1310147M		1501516M	Net Sales ($)	1961M	11623M	15278M	100844M	165782M	1206028M
554769M		920769M		759962M	Total Assets ($)	7515M	11289M	7186M	59672M	71811M	602489M

M = $ thousand   MM = $ million
See Pages 9 through 22 for Explanation of Ratios and Data

Current Data Sorted by Assets   Comparative Historical Data

Type of Statement	0-500M	500M-2MM	2-10MM	10-50MM	50-100MM	100-250MM		4/1/06-3/31/07 ALL	4/1/07-3/31/08 ALL
Unqualified				4	2			15	10
Reviewed	1	3	11	2				26	22
Compiled	4	7	8					22	20
Tax Returns	6	8	1					16	19
Other	7	13	11					28	41
	21 (4/1-9/30/10)			72 (10/1/10-3/31/11)					
NUMBER OF STATEMENTS	18	31	31	10	3			107	112

	%	%	%	%	%	%		%	%
ASSETS									
Cash & Equivalents	12.2	9.2	5.9	2.5			D	6.6	5.7
Trade Receivables (net)	29.4	31.2	23.1	14.2			A	25.3	27.9
Inventory	14.6	20.6	30.1	39.2			T	26.1	22.7
All Other Current	2.5	2.1	4.1	.8			A	2.8	2.9
Total Current	58.7	63.1	63.1	56.7				60.9	59.2
Fixed Assets (net)	27.5	26.7	25.2	30.9			N	30.3	31.3
Intangibles (net)	1.5	4.3	.8	5.3			O	3.0	3.2
All Other Non-Current	12.4	5.9	10.8	7.1			T	5.9	6.3
Total	100.0	100.0	100.0	100.0				100.0	100.0
LIABILITIES							A		
Notes Payable-Short Term	33.9	24.2	16.7	16.6			V	12.9	13.2
Cur. Mat.-L.T.D.	13.5	7.8	3.5	9.7			A	5.2	6.1
Trade Payables	16.9	18.2	13.3	12.7			I	11.5	11.7
Income Taxes Payable	.0	.5	.0	.0			L	.4	.2
All Other Current	6.3	12.6	5.0	6.5			A	9.5	11.9
Total Current	70.5	63.3	38.5	45.6			B	39.5	43.2
Long-Term Debt	39.8	25.7	13.4	6.7			L	22.1	23.6
Deferred Taxes	.0	.0	.1	.6			E	.3	.3
All Other Non-Current	36.3	16.0	7.2	6.9				6.2	6.5
Net Worth	-46.7	-5.0	40.7	40.3				31.9	26.4
Total Liabilities & Net Worth	100.0	100.0	100.0	100.0				100.0	100.0
INCOME DATA									
Net Sales	100.0	100.0	100.0	100.0				100.0	100.0
Gross Profit	36.1	34.6	20.9	17.1				27.5	27.3
Operating Expenses	38.7	35.5	21.1	15.0				22.3	23.8
Operating Profit	-2.6	-.8	-.2	2.2				5.2	3.5
All Other Expenses (net)	1.1	2.0	.5	1.0				1.3	2.0
Profit Before Taxes	-3.7	-2.9	-.7	1.1				4.0	1.6
RATIOS									
Current	1.8	1.7	3.4	2.3				2.5	2.2
	1.1	1.1	1.7	1.3				1.4	1.4
	.3	.8	1.1	.9				1.2	1.1
Quick	1.6	1.1	2.1	.7				1.1	1.3
	.8	.7	.9	.5				.9 (111)	.8
	.2	.4	.4	.2				.4	.5
Sales/Receivables	1 297.5	21 17.5	25 14.7	19 19.6				17 21.1	23 16.0
	20 17.8	43 8.6	40 9.2	28 12.9				29 12.7	37 9.8
	37 9.8	80 4.5	48 7.7	37 9.8				52 7.0	56 6.5
Cost of Sales/Inventory	0 UND	11 32.5	25 14.7	60 6.1				24 15.2	17 21.2
	9 39.0	43 8.4	60 6.1	91 4.0				40 9.1	46 7.9
	43 8.5	86 4.2	99 3.7	150 2.4				81 4.5	92 4.0
Cost of Sales/Payables	0 UND	13 27.6	10 35.7	11 33.9				8 43.8	10 37.7
	17 21.5	27 13.5	26 14.1	15 24.8				19 19.6	19 18.9
	47 7.8	57 6.4	47 7.8	21 17.8				32 11.3	35 10.5
Sales/Working Capital	15.3	9.8	4.4	6.0				6.2	7.3
	77.1	61.0	11.2	13.0				14.4	13.9
	-9.6	-9.3	40.8	-64.7				37.3	224.8
EBIT/Interest	3.8	3.0	10.6					8.0	5.5
	(13) -.4	(28) 1.1	(27) 1.6					(100) 2.6	(105) 2.3
	-5.5	-2.8	-1.8					.9	.2
Net Profit + Depr., Dep., Amort./Cur. Mat. L/T/D								2.7	2.4
								(18) 1.6	(16) 1.8
								.4	.9
Fixed/Worth	.5	.7	.2	.5				.4	.5
	-3.9	3.4	.5	.6				.9	1.1
	-.2	-1.4	1.7	2.0				2.8	3.6
Debt/Worth	1.7	2.3	.4	.4				.8	1.1
	-7.8	8.7	1.3	1.5				2.4	2.8
	-2.1	-3.9	4.2	4.7				7.3	10.8
% Profit Before Taxes/Tangible Net Worth		37.4	29.6					43.3	55.1
	(18) 4.4	(28) 4.0						(90) 19.3	(93) 13.9
		-35.4	-9.8					1.0	.0
% Profit Before Taxes/Total Assets	10.1	7.2	14.8	7.7				15.4	11.8
	-9.2	.7	2.1	-.2				6.5	4.0
	-47.0	-12.3	-7.7	-9.6				-.3	-3.9
Sales/Net Fixed Assets	110.9	21.2	19.9	9.8				18.9	16.1
	24.2	9.2	10.2	6.5				10.3	8.6
	11.0	5.3	4.9	3.5				4.3	4.0
Sales/Total Assets	12.1	2.8	3.0	1.8				3.3	3.2
	4.1	2.2	2.1	1.6				2.4	2.2
	3.2	1.8	1.4	1.4				1.8	1.7
% Depr., Dep., Amort./Sales	.6	1.8	1.3	1.5				1.2	1.4
	(13) 1.2	(24) 2.4	(26) 2.2	3.0				(92) 1.8	(86) 2.1
	2.9	4.4	3.7	4.7				3.0	3.3
% Officers', Directors' Owners' Comp/Sales	3.8	1.2	.8					1.6	1.5
	(12) 7.3	(16) 4.9	(10) 1.6					(45) 2.8	(41) 3.2
	9.6	7.8	3.5					6.5	5.2
Net Sales ($)	19545M	82313M	320451M	352800M	319979M			2816654M	2561267M
Total Assets ($)	3560M	35306M	147482M	204698M	204090M			1289901M	1512582M

M = $ thousand   MM = $ million
See Pages 9 through 22 for Explanation of Ratios and Data

Comparative Historical Data				Current Data Sorted by Sales					
			Type of Statement						
7	7	6	Unqualified						6
25	21	17	Reviewed		1	5	3	8	
18	19	19	Compiled	3	4	5	4	2	1
29	24	15	Tax Returns	5	6	2	1	1	
48	32	36	Other	6	13	2	7	4	4
4/1/08-3/31/09 ALL	4/1/09-3/31/10 ALL	4/1/10-3/31/11 ALL		21 (4/1-9/30/10)			72 (10/1/10-3/31/11)		
				0-1MM	1-3MM	3-5MM	5-10MM	10-25MM	25MM & OVER
127	103	93	**NUMBER OF STATEMENTS**	14	24	14	15	15	11
%	%	%	**ASSETS**	%	%	%	%	%	%
6.7	7.5	7.8	Cash & Equivalents	8.4	12.1	7.8	4.9	5.2	4.7
26.0	23.2	25.7	Trade Receivables (net)	26.8	30.6	33.9	22.0	20.6	15.0
25.9	26.2	25.1	Inventory	21.1	14.2	20.0	36.4	33.7	33.0
2.5	3.3	2.7	All Other Current	3.0	2.0	2.0	5.3	2.8	.7
61.2	60.3	61.2	Total Current	59.3	59.0	63.7	68.5	62.3	53.4
28.7	27.9	26.9	Fixed Assets (net)	21.2	32.2	23.7	21.2	30.0	30.4
3.6	4.2	3.1	Intangibles (net)	5.6	1.4	3.6	.6	.9	9.3
6.5	7.7	8.8	All Other Non-Current	14.0	7.4	9.0	9.6	6.7	6.9
100.0	100.0	100.0	Total	100.0	100.0	100.0	100.0	100.0	100.0
			LIABILITIES						
17.5	15.5	22.2	Notes Payable-Short Term	27.6	28.7	20.8	21.4	17.1	10.9
5.6	5.9	7.5	Cur. Mat.-L.T.D.	18.7	6.6	3.8	3.0	5.1	9.3
14.0	14.1	15.2	Trade Payables	15.3	20.4	11.0	20.1	12.3	6.6
.2	.1	.2	Income Taxes Payable	.0	.0	1.0	.0	.0	.1
8.7	8.2	8.0	All Other Current	10.7	8.8	10.8	4.2	5.6	7.3
46.1	43.8	53.0	Total Current	72.3	64.5	47.5	48.7	40.1	34.2
18.4	24.1	22.6	Long-Term Debt	42.8	29.5	15.9	16.7	10.2	15.2
.4	.2	.1	Deferred Taxes	.0	.0	.4	.0	.0	.6
6.6	10.7	15.7	All Other Non-Current	43.2	8.9	21.4	14.6	2.8	7.1
28.5	21.2	8.6	Net Worth	-58.3	-2.9	14.9	19.9	46.9	43.0
100.0	100.0	100.0	Total Liabilities & Net Worth	100.0	100.0	100.0	100.0	100.0	100.0
			INCOME DATA						
100.0	100.0	100.0	Net Sales	100.0	100.0	100.0	100.0	100.0	100.0
26.1	27.8	28.0	Gross Profit	40.0	35.1	25.6	21.2	20.1	20.4
25.5	28.5	28.5	Operating Expenses	45.8	35.6	26.0	22.5	17.8	16.7
.7	-.7	-.4	Operating Profit	-5.8	-.5	-.4	-1.2	2.3	3.7
1.1	1.6	1.3	All Other Expenses (net)	1.4	2.4	.6	.9	.0	1.5
-.5	-2.3	-1.7	Profit Before Taxes	-7.3	-2.9	-.9	-2.2	2.3	2.3
			RATIOS						
2.3	3.0	2.3	Current	1.6	1.7	2.7	3.0	2.8	3.4
1.5	1.6	1.3		1.1	1.1	1.3	1.3	1.7	1.7
1.0	1.0	.8		.5	.7	.8	.9	1.2	.9
1.4	1.6	1.3	Quick	1.2	1.3	1.7	2.5	1.4	.9
.7	.8	.7		.6	.8	1.0	.5	.7	.6
.4	.4	.4		.2	.4	.6	.2	.4	.4
18 20.3	21 17.2	21 17.5	Sales/Receivables	14 25.3	16 22.8	27 13.5	22 17.0	21 17.6	21 17.1
29 12.8	36 10.2	36 10.2		32 11.3	37 9.8	41 8.8	38 9.6	33 11.1	25 14.7
49 7.5	53 6.9	49 7.4		58 6.3	65 5.6	74 5.0	48 7.7	40 9.1	38 9.5
14 26.1	15 24.3	12 29.2	Cost of Sales/Inventory	4 81.2	3 130.0	11 34.7	33 10.9	25 14.7	42 8.8
45 8.1	50 7.2	49 7.5		41 8.9	16 22.3	32 11.4	77 4.7	75 4.9	93 3.9
87 4.2	115 3.2	93 3.9		77 4.7	79 4.6	63 5.8	137 2.7	99 3.7	120 3.0
9 40.6	10 36.5	10 37.1	Cost of Sales/Payables	0 UND	11 34.0	5 76.9	8 43.0	11 32.9	10 37.4
20 18.2	20 18.0	20 18.3		23 16.0	29 12.7	16 22.8	41 8.8	19 19.7	12 31.2
31 11.9	42 8.8	47 7.7		50 7.3	62 5.9	39 9.3	51 7.1	29 12.6	17 21.9
7.0	4.5	6.3	Sales/Working Capital	8.2	15.3	5.7	2.8	5.4	4.5
13.3	11.2	17.7		UND	77.1	14.2	1.0	9.8	7.0
-196.0	119.2	-30.3		-4.1	-15.5	-28.7	-81.1	30.9	-83.2
5.5	3.9	3.9	EBIT/Interest	1.2	2.6	4.5	12.3	7.0	10.8
(116) 1.4	(92) 1.1	(80) 1.0		(11) -1.1	(19) .4	(12) 2.4	1.0	(13) 2.1	(10) 3.1
-1.2	-3.9	-2.8		-6.4	-2.8	-7.7	-3.2	.9	-1.0
1.9	3.3	6.0	Net Profit + Depr., Dep., Amort./Cur. Mat. L/T/D						
(20) .6	(19) 1.0	(15) 3.0							
-.1	-.3	.1							
.4	.4	.4	Fixed/Worth	.6	.4	.3	.2	.4	.4
.9	.9	1.0		-4.3	3.3	.8	.7	.5	1.3
2.6	-15.0	-3.0		-.2	-1.6	-1.3	-2.4	.7	5.3
1.0	.7	1.0	Debt/Worth	2.0	2.1	.9	.3	.5	.4
2.3	2.5	3.2		-26.4	7.8	2.5	3.2	1.2	1.0
8.8	-30.0	-7.9		-2.0	-4.1	-4.6	-9.5	2.9	9.8
35.0	24.4	32.9	% Profit Before Taxes/Tangible Net Worth		45.3	24.7	27.9	40.2	42.1
(108) 7.0	(74) 1.3	(65) 4.2			(14) -2.3	(10) -6.3	(11) .7	8.1	(10) 11.6
-20.2	-30.6	-19.3			-35.4	-29.1	-11.0	2.0	-28.1
10.0	7.6	9.0	% Profit Before Taxes/Total Assets	1.8	7.8	7.8	14.8	20.8	9.8
1.4	.3	.7		-17.5	-2.7	4.1	.1	3.3	5.2
-7.4	-10.8	-11.4		-47.7	-15.3	-10.3	-7.9	1.1	-9.6
21.4	19.0	22.3	Sales/Net Fixed Assets	82.5	26.3	22.3	19.9	39.8	11.3
10.3	8.4	10.7		21.3	11.8	10.1	12.1	9.4	5.6
6.0	5.3	5.6		9.8	5.3	7.4	7.1	3.6	3.3
3.5	3.4	3.4	Sales/Total Assets	4.4	4.0	3.3	3.0	3.5	2.3
2.6	2.2	2.2		3.1	2.2	2.4	1.9	2.4	1.6
1.9	1.4	1.6		2.1	1.9	1.9	1.2	1.7	1.4
1.0	1.6	1.4	% Depr., Dep., Amort./Sales	.6	1.2	1.3	1.5	.9	2.4
(111) 1.9	(90) 2.5	(76) 2.3		(10) 1.8	(17) 2.1	(12) 2.4	(14) 2.2	(13) 1.9	(10) 3.4
3.5	4.0	3.7		5.2	3.6	4.3	4.2	3.6	4.7
1.6	2.0	1.1	% Officers', Directors' Owners' Comp/Sales	2.3	3.8				
(54) 3.3	(51) 3.7	(39) 3.8		(12) 7.4	(11) 6.3				
5.5	6.1	7.6		9.6	8.4				
2302769M	1358415M	1095088M	Net Sales ($)	8991M	48165M	54865M	114425M	224868M	643774M
1072040M	836125M	595136M	Total Assets ($)	3780M	21966M	25690M	68927M	98160M	376613M

Current Data Sorted by Assets   Comparative Historical Data

						Type of Statement	12	10
		1	1	2	1	Unqualified	12	10
	1	21	3			Reviewed	53	42
2	11	11	1			Compiled	45	28
8	20	11				Tax Returns	29	33
3	17	21	6	3	2	Other	64	63
	24 (4/1-9/30/10)		122 (10/1/10-3/31/11)				4/1/06-3/31/07 ALL	4/1/07-3/31/08 ALL
0-500M	500M-2MM	2-10MM	10-50MM	50-100MM	100-250MM	NUMBER OF STATEMENTS		
13	49	65	11	5	3		203	176

0-500M %	500M-2MM %	2-10MM %	10-50MM %	50-100MM %	100-250MM %		%	%
						ASSETS		
13.7	9.9	7.3	3.2			Cash & Equivalents	6.7	6.8
29.4	28.8	28.5	20.4			Trade Receivables (net)	30.2	27.2
21.3	24.1	22.6	19.4			Inventory	23.7	23.5
.8	2.3	1.4	4.0			All Other Current	2.7	2.7
65.1	65.0	59.8	47.0			Total Current	63.3	60.2
26.0	25.9	27.3	35.9			Fixed Assets (net)	29.6	31.3
.8	3.6	5.4	8.3			Intangibles (net)	2.7	3.0
8.1	5.5	7.5	8.7			All Other Non-Current	4.3	5.5
100.0	100.0	100.0	100.0			Total	100.0	100.0
						LIABILITIES		
18.2	15.9	12.9	11.4			Notes Payable-Short Term	12.4	14.2
2.5	4.9	4.3	3.8			Cur. Mat.-L.T.D.	4.5	4.3
18.3	11.8	14.8	8.1			Trade Payables	13.4	13.1
.0	.0	.1	.0			Income Taxes Payable	.2	.3
22.6	4.9	6.8	4.1			All Other Current	7.1	8.0
61.5	37.5	38.9	27.4			Total Current	37.6	39.8
31.6	14.1	14.8	18.2			Long-Term Debt	18.5	19.9
.0	.0	.0	.8			Deferred Taxes	.2	.3
9.1	6.3	3.8	3.9			All Other Non-Current	5.5	4.1
-2.3	42.1	42.4	49.7			Net Worth	38.2	35.9
100.0	100.0	100.0	100.0			Total Liabilities & Net Worth	100.0	100.0
						INCOME DATA		
100.0	100.0	100.0	100.0			Net Sales	100.0	100.0
36.7	30.8	22.1	16.7			Gross Profit	25.4	25.7
36.2	28.1	19.6	13.2			Operating Expenses	20.6	22.2
.5	2.7	2.5	3.5			Operating Profit	4.8	3.5
.6	.9	.5	.0			All Other Expenses (net)	.7	.9
-.2	1.8	2.1	3.4			Profit Before Taxes	4.2	2.6
						RATIOS		
3.4	3.5	2.9	2.1			Current	2.8	2.8
1.7	2.0	1.7	2.0				1.6	1.7
.7	1.3	1.1	1.2				1.2	1.1
3.2	2.5	1.9	1.4			Quick	1.5	1.8
1.0	1.3	1.0	1.0				.9	.9
.5	.7	.6	.3				.6	.5
5 71.6	21 17.6	24 14.9	33 10.9			Sales/Receivables	25 14.7	23 15.9
30 12.0	30 12.0	34 10.8	37 9.7				33 11.1	32 11.5
42 8.7	41 8.9	45 8.1	45 8.1				43 8.6	40 9.2
8 46.0	16 22.4	22 16.7	20 18.5			Cost of Sales/Inventory	16 22.3	18 20.4
23 15.9	33 10.9	36 10.1	39 9.3				32 11.4	37 9.9
49 7.5	57 6.4	49 7.4	95 3.8				54 6.7	55 6.6
10 36.9	5 70.3	11 33.1	9 39.4			Cost of Sales/Payables	10 37.2	9 41.7
21 17.3	14 27.0	20 18.2	16 23.2				17 21.8	17 21.9
40 9.1	27 13.4	32 11.4	22 16.6				28 13.2	31 11.9
8.5	6.2	7.7	7.3			Sales/Working Capital	7.8	7.1
14.7	10.1	12.6	9.8				15.5	13.2
-38.2	29.3	102.2	16.3				49.6	59.4
9.5	17.3	16.2	10.6			EBIT/Interest	9.8	8.4
(12) -.2	(46) 2.9	(63) 5.0	4.5				(193) 3.7	(164) 2.7
-4.4	.9	.5	1.5				2.1	1.1
		6.2				Net Profit + Depr., Dep., Amort./Cur. Mat. L/T/D	3.7	9.1
	(10)	2.7					(45) 2.3	(38) 2.5
		.6					1.5	1.6
.3	.2	.3	.5			Fixed/Worth	.4	.4
5.4	.6	.7	1.2				.8	.9
-.7	1.7	1.7	1.6				1.5	1.9
.7	.6	.5	.9			Debt/Worth	.8	.7
5.8	1.3	1.7	1.3				1.8	2.0
-6.3	3.8	3.5	2.1				3.7	3.9
	42.7	34.2	28.0			% Profit Before Taxes/Tangible Net Worth	46.4	42.5
	(45) 17.2	(57) 18.9	15.6				(183) 23.8	(156) 18.8
	1.1	3.0	4.1				9.2	3.4
29.0	17.8	16.5	13.0			% Profit Before Taxes/Total Assets	18.5	18.1
5.4	4.9	6.9	6.9				8.9	5.4
-13.4	-.3	-1.1	1.3				2.9	.5
74.1	30.8	27.5	15.4			Sales/Net Fixed Assets	27.0	25.2
20.3	16.8	11.6	4.2				12.3	11.5
9.6	7.0	6.6	2.8				6.6	5.9
6.9	4.0	3.9	3.0			Sales/Total Assets	4.1	4.0
4.6	3.4	2.7	1.8				3.2	3.0
3.1	2.2	1.7	1.3				2.2	2.0
.2	1.2	.9	1.6			% Depr., Dep., Amort./Sales	.9	1.1
(10) 1.6	(38) 2.0	(60) 1.9	3.3				(185) 1.7	(154) 2.0
3.1	3.1	3.4	4.4				2.8	3.2
	2.0	.9				% Officers', Directors' Owners' Comp/Sales	1.6	1.5
	(28) 3.6	(27) 2.4					(86) 2.6	(73) 2.5
	5.2	4.4					4.9	4.5
24951M	189974M	814348M	499324M	569571M	407286M	Net Sales ($)	5325076M	3673773M
4662M	57866M	293795M	231816M	398639M	445307M	Total Assets ($)	2064807M	1866817M

M = $ thousand   MM = $ million
See Pages 9 through 22 for Explanation of Ratios and Data

Comparative Historical Data | Current Data Sorted by Sales

4/1/08-3/31/09 ALL	4/1/09-3/31/10 ALL	4/1/10-3/31/11 ALL	Type of Statement	0-1MM	1-3MM	3-5MM	5-10MM	10-25MM	25MM & OVER
7	7	5	Unqualified					1	4
28	30	25	Reviewed			2	9	8	6
28	28	25	Compiled		3	4	11	6	
38	35	39	Tax Returns	1	12	8	12	4	
54	44	52	Other	3	15	3	10	15	9
				24 (4/1-9/30/10)			122 (10/1/10-3/31/11)		
155	**144**	**146**	**NUMBER OF STATEMENTS**	4	30	17	42	34	19
%	%	%	**ASSETS**	%	%	%	%	%	%
8.6	8.5	8.1	Cash & Equivalents		10.3	9.9	9.3	6.3	2.6
24.9	26.1	27.1	Trade Receivables (net)		26.2	20.5	26.7	30.6	28.1
25.3	22.7	22.9	Inventory		23.3	21.9	22.2	26.0	20.5
1.3	2.1	1.9	All Other Current		1.3	2.1	1.8	1.4	3.8
60.1	59.4	60.1	Total Current		61.1	54.4	60.0	64.3	55.0
30.0	29.3	28.5	Fixed Assets (net)		29.2	31.6	26.5	26.0	33.6
3.0	4.6	4.7	Intangibles (net)		3.4	7.1	4.2	4.8	5.6
6.9	6.7	6.7	All Other Non-Current		6.3	6.9	9.3	5.0	5.8
100.0	100.0	100.0	Total		100.0	100.0	100.0	100.0	100.0
			LIABILITIES						
15.9	15.7	14.2	Notes Payable-Short Term		21.0	14.6	15.0	10.6	10.5
4.6	4.5	4.2	Cur. Mat.-L.T.D.		4.9	4.4	5.7	2.8	2.6
12.7	12.4	13.1	Trade Payables		12.9	7.9	12.5	16.5	10.5
.1	.2	.1	Income Taxes Payable		.0	.0	.0	.2	.0
5.3	6.2	7.4	All Other Current		4.1	4.6	5.5	6.5	7.8
38.6	39.0	38.9	Total Current		42.9	31.5	38.7	36.6	31.5
19.0	19.2	16.2	Long-Term Debt		22.0	17.9	17.0	12.6	12.6
.2	.1	.2	Deferred Taxes		.0	.0	.0	.2	.9
7.9	5.6	5.3	All Other Non-Current		5.2	6.1	4.0	6.4	4.2
34.4	36.0	39.5	Net Worth		29.9	44.5	40.4	44.2	50.8
100.0	100.0	100.0	Total Liabilities & Net Worth		100.0	100.0	100.0	100.0	100.0
			INCOME DATA						
100.0	100.0	100.0	Net Sales		100.0	100.0	100.0	100.0	100.0
24.1	28.3	26.0	Gross Profit		36.8	27.6	24.1	21.1	20.1
21.1	25.1	23.3	Operating Expenses		34.3	25.2	21.7	18.0	14.9
3.1	3.2	2.7	Operating Profit		2.5	2.5	2.3	3.1	5.2
.6	.8	.7	All Other Expenses (net)		1.4	.4	.5	.3	.8
2.5	2.4	2.1	Profit Before Taxes		1.2	2.1	1.8	2.7	4.4
			RATIOS						
2.9	3.0	2.9	Current		3.4	2.8	3.1	3.4	2.1
1.7	1.6	1.8			1.8	2.0	1.8	1.7	2.0
1.1	1.1	1.2			.9	1.3	1.0	1.2	1.6
1.7	2.0	2.0	Quick		2.5	2.2	2.4	1.6	1.4
.9	.8	1.0			1.3	.7	1.0	1.0	.9
.5	.5	.6			.5	.6	.6	.6	.6
19 18.8	25 14.5	24 15.2	Sales/Receivables		26 14.0	19 19.1	19 18.9	25 14.4	30 12.2
29 12.4	34 10.8	33 10.9			35 10.3	29 12.4	29 12.4	37 9.9	37 9.7
39 9.3	44 8.3	43 8.5			44 8.3	39 9.3	41 8.9	45 8.1	43 8.4
19 18.9	24 15.4	20 18.3	Cost of Sales/Inventory		16 22.2	20 17.9	19 19.1	24 15.5	12 29.2
34 10.6	43 8.5	37 10.0			41 8.9	40 9.2	34 10.9	40 9.2	39 9.3
57 6.4	74 4.9	58 6.3			67 5.5	67 5.4	52 7.0	57 6.3	110 3.3
6 58.0	9 39.3	10 38.3	Cost of Sales/Payables		9 41.3	5 67.2	10 38.0	11 33.5	11 32.6
15 25.0	19 19.5	17 21.7			17 22.0	12 30.8	14 26.0	22 16.9	16 23.2
28 12.9	37 9.9	31 11.7			38 9.5	25 14.4	28 12.8	41 8.9	29 12.4
8.0	6.3	6.9	Sales/Working Capital		5.7	7.8	7.6	8.5	6.5
13.8	12.3	12.0			10.3	10.8	13.5	12.4	9.8
52.8	130.8	39.4			-764.7	24.1	168.3	33.0	16.9
8.8	6.4	14.5	EBIT/Interest		4.7	9.6	12.7	23.0	15.8
(143) 3.0	(137) 2.3	(140) 4.2		(27) 1.8		(16) 3.6	(41) 3.0	(33) 7.7	6.7
1.1	.9	.5			-1.7	1.4	-.3	1.6	2.0
3.1	5.6	6.1	Net Profit + Depr., Dep., Amort./Cur. Mat. L/T/D						
(26) 2.0	(19) 2.6	(21) 2.5							
.7	1.5	1.0							
.3	.3	.3	Fixed/Worth		.3	.3	.2	.3	.5
.8	.8	.7			.9	.9	.7	.7	.7
2.0	3.0	1.8			4.2	2.2	2.4	1.2	1.2
.7	.7	.6	Debt/Worth		.7	.5	.6	.5	.6
1.7	1.9	1.5			1.9	1.4	1.9	1.5	.9
4.1	7.4	3.8			6.3	4.0	4.4	2.3	1.5
35.4	35.8	37.8	% Profit Before Taxes/Tangible Net Worth		75.8	32.3	39.9	33.0	33.9
(135) 14.1	(120) 13.2	(128) 16.4		(24) 36.0		12.3	(35) 10.6	(32) 19.7	(18) 22.3
2.6	.4	2.4			-2.4	2.9	1.3	5.0	6.5
13.4	10.6	16.0	% Profit Before Taxes/Total Assets		16.1	13.4	21.3	16.4	14.1
5.4	3.8	6.2			4.1	4.0	4.1	7.8	8.2
.3	-.1	-1.0			-9.4	1.7	-3.9	1.3	2.3
26.9	26.5	27.1	Sales/Net Fixed Assets		31.2	27.6	24.7	29.4	31.7
13.3	11.5	11.6			12.7	11.3	12.0	14.5	4.2
5.1	4.9	5.6			5.0	5.4	7.0	7.6	2.8
4.4	3.6	4.0	Sales/Total Assets		4.0	3.9	3.9	4.3	3.9
3.0	2.6	2.8			2.7	2.8	3.2	3.6	1.9
2.1	1.7	1.8			1.9	1.6	1.6	2.0	1.1
.9	1.4	1.2	% Depr., Dep., Amort./Sales		1.3	1.0	1.6	.8	1.4
(139) 1.9	(129) 2.4	(127) 2.1		(22) 2.1		(15) 1.9	(38) 2.4	(30) 1.7	2.8
3.2	4.3	3.7			3.4	2.9	4.0	3.3	4.4
1.5	1.7	1.6	% Officers', Directors' Owners' Comp/Sales		3.6		1.8		.8
(77) 2.8	(62) 3.0	(65) 3.5		(17) 5.1		(23) 3.2	(10) 1.9		
4.9	5.9	5.2			7.6		5.0	4.4	
2721399M	2288525M	2505454M	Net Sales ($)	2991M	63636M	67067M	289181M	530529M	1552050M
1248999M	1274339M	1432085M	Total Assets ($)	1237M	26275M	27437M	127252M	201661M	1048223M

M = $ thousand   MM = $ million
See Pages 9 through 22 for Explanation of Ratios and Data

Current Data Sorted by Assets

Comparative Historical Data

	0-500M	500M-2MM	2-10MM	10-50MM	50-100MM	100-250MM		Type of Statement	4/1/06-3/31/07 ALL	4/1/07-3/31/08 ALL
			1	3	1	3		Unqualified	11	13
			4	2				Reviewed	3	3
		2	1	1				Compiled	7	9
			1	1				Tax Returns	4	2
	1		2	2	2	1		Other	17	9
	1	5 (4/1-9/30/10)		22 (10/1/10-3/31/11)						
	1	2	8	9	3	4		NUMBER OF STATEMENTS	42	36
	%	%	%	%	%	%			%	%
								ASSETS		
								Cash & Equivalents	17.1	19.0
								Trade Receivables (net)	12.4	15.7
								Inventory	25.6	26.5
								All Other Current	3.0	1.7
								Total Current	58.0	62.9
								Fixed Assets (net)	29.9	25.1
								Intangibles (net)	5.7	6.2
								All Other Non-Current	6.4	5.7
								Total	100.0	100.0
								LIABILITIES		
								Notes Payable-Short Term	17.6	12.6
								Cur. Mat.-L.T.D.	1.2	1.4
								Trade Payables	10.0	7.6
								Income Taxes Payable	.2	.3
								All Other Current	17.6	17.5
								Total Current	46.5	39.4
								Long-Term Debt	7.8	12.3
								Deferred Taxes	1.0	.6
								All Other Non-Current	3.9	1.9
								Net Worth	40.7	45.8
								Total Liabilities & Net Worth	100.0	100.0
								INCOME DATA		
								Net Sales	100.0	100.0
								Gross Profit	26.2	23.6
								Operating Expenses	18.6	19.1
								Operating Profit	7.5	4.5
								All Other Expenses (net)	1.3	.5
								Profit Before Taxes	6.2	4.0
								RATIOS		
								Current	2.1 / 1.4 / .7	2.4 / 1.6 / 1.3
								Quick	1.2 / .6 / .2	1.5 / .8 / .3
								Sales/Receivables	4 85.0 / 11 33.7 / 21 17.2	9 39.3 / 21 17.7 / 32 11.5
								Cost of Sales/Inventory	17 21.2 / 34 10.6 / 49 7.5	21 17.3 / 36 10.2 / 64 5.7
								Cost of Sales/Payables	7 56.0 / 10 37.9 / 15 24.5	6 65.2 / 11 33.7 / 17 21.7
								Sales/Working Capital	8.3 / 14.5 / -36.4	6.3 / 10.9 / 30.8
								EBIT/Interest	25.8 / (34) 3.8 / -1.2	17.1 / (30) 4.1 / -.3
								Net Profit + Depr., Dep., Amort./Cur. Mat. L/T/D		
								Fixed/Worth	.2 / .6 / 2.7	.1 / .5 / 2.1
								Debt/Worth	.6 / 1.4 / 5.5	.5 / 1.2 / 4.9
								% Profit Before Taxes/Tangible Net Worth	69.5 / (36) 27.0 / 5.2	57.9 / (31) 14.1 / -1.8
								% Profit Before Taxes/Total Assets	21.9 / 8.2 / 1.3	25.2 / 9.9 / -1.6
								Sales/Net Fixed Assets	28.7 / 12.8 / 5.7	38.2 / 10.7 / 5.6
								Sales/Total Assets	3.7 / 2.5 / 1.2	3.1 / 2.6 / 1.3
								% Depr., Dep., Amort./Sales	.4 / (39) 1.0 / 2.0	.4 / (29) .9 / 1.6
								% Officers', Directors' Owners' Comp/Sales	.6 / (11) 1.7 / 3.5	
	3548M	3766M	98470M	371367M	247065M	935151M		Net Sales ($)	2476962M	1890802M
	207M	2386M	37317M	217110M	227983M	744043M		Total Assets ($)	1373299M	1029272M

M = $ thousand   MM = $ million
See Pages 9 through 22 for Explanation of Ratios and Data

Comparative Historical Data · **Current Data Sorted by Sales**

			Type of Statement	0-1MM	1-3MM	3-5MM	5-10MM	10-25MM	25MM & OVER
13	10	8	Unqualified					1	7
11	11	6	Reviewed			1	3	1	1
7	8	3	Compiled		2			1	
2		2	Tax Returns			1		1	
11	11	8	Other			1	1	1	6
4/1/08-3/31/09 ALL	4/1/09-3/31/10 ALL	4/1/10-3/31/11 ALL			5 (4/1-9/30/10)		22 (10/1/10-3/31/11)		
44	40	27	NUMBER OF STATEMENTS		2	2	5	4	14
%	%	%	ASSETS	%	%	%	%	%	%
13.8	16.8	14.5	Cash & Equivalents						11.5
14.8	13.3	18.5	Trade Receivables (net)						14.8
25.6	25.1	24.4	Inventory						25.8
4.0	3.7	2.4	All Other Current						3.6
58.2	58.9	59.7	Total Current						55.8
29.5	29.2	29.6	Fixed Assets (net)						34.1
3.6	3.3	3.0	Intangibles (net)						2.3
8.7	8.6	7.7	All Other Non-Current						7.8
100.0	100.0	100.0	Total						100.0
			LIABILITIES						
12.9	9.4	7.1	Notes Payable-Short Term						4.8
2.2	3.0	4.6	Cur. Mat.-L.T.D.						3.6
7.4	9.2	15.6	Trade Payables						6.7
.3	.1	.0	Income Taxes Payable						.0
14.2	13.3	15.2	All Other Current						13.6
37.0	35.0	42.5	Total Current						28.7
19.4	26.6	29.1	Long-Term Debt						32.3
.2	.4	.2	Deferred Taxes						.4
2.5	6.3	7.6	All Other Non-Current						7.4
40.8	31.7	20.5	Net Worth						31.2
100.0	100.0	100.0	Total Liabilities & Net Worth						100.0
			INCOME DATA						
100.0	100.0	100.0	Net Sales						100.0
24.9	17.5	21.8	Gross Profit						21.2
22.5	22.1	20.5	Operating Expenses						17.0
2.5	-4.6	1.4	Operating Profit						4.3
1.3	1.0	2.6	All Other Expenses (net)						5.3
1.1	-5.6	-1.2	Profit Before Taxes						-1.1
			RATIOS						
2.8	3.5	2.4							3.0
1.6	1.8	1.6	Current						1.8
1.1	1.1	1.2							1.2
1.9	2.4	1.5							1.6
.7	.8	.8	Quick						.9
.3	.4	.5							.4
9 39.5	11 32.1	14 26.1							14 26.2
22 16.8	25 14.3	38 9.5	Sales/Receivables						32 11.5
34 10.7	33 11.0	50 7.3							51 7.2
30 12.0	24 15.3	19 19.1							22 16.9
44 8.4	53 6.8	56 6.5	Cost of Sales/Inventory						70 5.2
74 4.9	104 3.5	85 4.3							112 3.3
5 69.6	5 74.7	9 41.9							6 65.0
11 34.4	10 35.9	15 25.0	Cost of Sales/Payables						13 28.5
27 13.6	24 15.2	41 8.9							26 14.1
4.4	3.4	5.0							4.7
10.9	6.7	8.1	Sales/Working Capital						7.4
49.1	33.4	37.6							28.3
7.5	4.8	15.9							39.1
(36) 2.1	(36) 1.1	(22) 1.7	EBIT/Interest					(11)	5.1
-1.0	-9.9	-.4							.9
			Net Profit + Depr., Dep., Amort./Cur. Mat. L/T/D						
.2	.3	.2							.3
.5	.6	.8	Fixed/Worth						.7
3.0	4.6	1.9							13.4
.5	.7	.9							.8
1.6	1.0	1.5	Debt/Worth						1.5
4.8	7.2	5.1							63.5
27.2	11.7	29.7							31.9
(37) 6.3	(32) 1.3	(23) 3.3	% Profit Before Taxes/Tangible Net Worth					(12)	3.0
-3.9	-16.6	-17.6							-8.2
8.9	5.9	13.9							12.6
3.0	-.3	1.8	% Profit Before Taxes/Total Assets						.9
-4.6	-15.4	-5.3							-3.9
37.3	15.2	28.0							21.0
8.2	6.6	8.4	Sales/Net Fixed Assets						7.7
4.5	3.2	4.4							2.4
2.9	2.5	2.3							1.9
2.0	1.6	1.7	Sales/Total Assets						1.7
1.2	1.1	1.3							1.0
.4	.9	.6							
(40) 1.1	(32) 1.8	(18) 1.7	% Depr., Dep., Amort./Sales						
1.9	2.7	4.2							
			% Officers', Directors' Owners' Comp/Sales						
2324096M	1144337M	1659367M	Net Sales ($)		3766M	7990M	42930M	63762M	1540919M
1699091M	1043870M	1229046M	Total Assets ($)		2386M	3598M	15985M	51149M	1155928M

Note: The columns 0-1MM through 10-25MM in the ASSETS, LIABILITIES, and INCOME DATA sections are marked "DATA NOT AVAILABLE."

© RMA 2011

M = $ thousand   MM = $ million
See Pages 9 through 22 for Explanation of Ratios and Data

Current Data Sorted by Assets							Comparative Historical Data	
						Type of Statement		
		4	4			Unqualified	16	23
	3	8	3			Reviewed	20	16
	3					Compiled	10	13
	2	3				Tax Returns	9	6
2	6	6	4		2	Other	23	29
	6 (4/1-9/30/10)		44 (10/1/10-3/31/11)				4/1/06-3/31/07 ALL	4/1/07-3/31/08 ALL
0-500M	**500M-2MM**	**2-10MM**	**10-50MM**	**50-100MM**	**100-250MM**			
2	14	21	11		2	**NUMBER OF STATEMENTS**	78	87
%	%	%	%	%	%	**ASSETS**	%	%
	6.1	6.8	10.9	DATA NOT AVAILABLE		Cash & Equivalents	9.0	11.2
	19.3	24.7	15.6			Trade Receivables (net)	18.4	16.1
	38.3	19.8	24.5			Inventory	27.5	26.3
	5.2	1.9	6.7			All Other Current	3.5	3.7
	69.0	53.3	57.7			Total Current	58.4	57.3
	17.6	32.7	36.7			Fixed Assets (net)	30.8	29.5
	9.1	4.3	2.0			Intangibles (net)	3.9	5.3
	4.3	9.8	3.6			All Other Non-Current	6.9	7.9
	100.0	100.0	100.0			Total	100.0	100.0
						LIABILITIES		
	22.4	19.2	9.5			Notes Payable-Short Term	11.5	11.0
	1.0	2.5	1.7			Cur. Mat.-L.T.D.	4.2	4.4
	10.6	12.7	10.3			Trade Payables	10.2	9.5
	.0	.0	.1			Income Taxes Payable	.1	.0
	15.0	14.7	13.2			All Other Current	18.1	18.7
	48.9	49.3	34.8			Total Current	44.1	43.6
	3.2	19.3	18.4			Long-Term Debt	16.5	17.8
	.0	.3	.6			Deferred Taxes	.3	.4
	13.0	4.0	3.4			All Other Non-Current	5.1	4.4
	34.9	27.0	42.8			Net Worth	34.0	33.8
	100.0	100.0	100.0			Total Liabilties & Net Worth	100.0	100.0
						INCOME DATA		
	100.0	100.0	100.0			Net Sales	100.0	100.0
	37.4	21.4	22.2			Gross Profit	28.8	27.5
	38.2	22.1	21.8			Operating Expenses	24.6	24.4
	-.8	-.6	.4			Operating Profit	4.1	3.1
	.7	1.8	1.6			All Other Expenses (net)	.7	1.0
	-1.4	-2.4	-1.1			Profit Before Taxes	3.4	2.1
						RATIOS		
	1.8	1.6	3.3				2.0	2.0
	1.4	1.1	1.7			Current	1.4	1.4
	.9	.6	.9				1.0	1.0
	.8	.9	3.0				1.2	1.0
	.4	.6	.6			Quick	.7	.6
	.2	.2	.4				.3	.3
	6 62.7	11 32.1	8 46.0				7 53.1	9 38.4
	16 23.4	33 11.1	53 6.9			Sales/Receivables	18 19.8	21 17.2
	33 11.2	53 6.9	60 6.0				36 10.1	36 10.1
	35 10.3	21 17.4	16 22.2				24 15.0	27 13.4
	70 5.2	55 6.7	35 10.5			Cost of Sales/Inventory	43 8.4	52 7.0
	123 3.0	75 4.8	97 3.8				81 4.5	91 4.0
	2 169.6	10 37.5	6 58.7				9 39.2	9 41.6
	9 41.4	28 13.2	25 14.6			Cost of Sales/Payables	15 24.6	15 24.7
	37 9.8	47 7.8	38 9.5				30 12.3	27 13.4
	6.8	10.6	4.0				8.2	7.4
	14.7	27.5	8.0			Sales/Working Capital	20.4	14.7
	NM	-8.7	-25.5				83.0	695.5
	10.4	5.0	6.6				8.1	6.5
	(13) 4.0	.7	-1.0			EBIT/Interest	(75) 3.5	(78) 2.7
	-1.4	-1.4	-17.8				1.4	-1.1
							8.3	3.8
						Net Profit + Depr., Dep., Amort./Cur. Mat. L/T/D	(20) 3.5	(22) .9
							1.2	-.2
	.1	.4	.4				.4	.4
	.6	.9	1.0			Fixed/Worth	.9	1.1
	1.4	3.2	2.7				2.4	3.6
	1.1	1.4	.6				.8	.8
	4.1	3.4	1.9			Debt/Worth	2.1	2.3
	18.7	7.6	3.3				5.3	8.7
	68.8	34.0	31.1				53.4	41.2
	(13) 25.8	(17) 2.5	(10) -3.5			% Profit Before Taxes/Tangible Net Worth	(65) 32.4	(73) 12.5
	-12.2	-6.9	-17.5				8.0	-7.0
	18.4	4.4	15.3				17.3	10.0
	3.8	-.3	-3.5			% Profit Before Taxes/Total Assets	6.7	3.4
	-.7	-6.0	-11.2				1.2	-5.8
	387.6	23.8	30.6				17.8	16.0
	19.4	7.0	5.6			Sales/Net Fixed Assets	9.5	8.5
	6.9	2.5	1.9				5.1	5.2
	4.3	2.5	2.8				3.5	3.2
	3.0	1.9	1.8			Sales/Total Assets	2.6	2.4
	1.9	1.2	1.1				2.0	1.6
		1.3	1.6				1.0	1.1
		(20) 1.7	2.0			% Depr., Dep., Amort./Sales	(72) 1.8	(77) 1.7
		3.4	4.3				2.7	2.7
							2.0	1.6
						% Officers', Directors' Owners' Comp/Sales	(22) 3.7	(13) 2.2
							5.6	3.1
991M	47285M	234648M	427207M		446128M	Net Sales ($)	2134652M	2635592M
724M	15606M	128697M	220131M		288741M	Total Assets ($)	864966M	1348181M

M = $ thousand MM = $ million

See Pages 9 through 22 for Explanation of Ratios and Data

Comparative Historical Data | Current Data Sorted by Sales

Type of Statement	4/1/08-3/31/09 ALL	4/1/09-3/31/10 ALL	4/1/10-3/31/11 ALL	0-1MM	1-3MM	3-5MM	5-10MM	10-25MM	25MM & OVER
Unqualified	5	7	8			1		4	3
Reviewed	15	15	14		2	2	2	6	2
Compiled	11	3	3			2	1		
Tax Returns	5	6	5		1	1	3		
Other	34	14	20	3	3	3	3	4	4
				6 (4/1-9/30/10)			44 (10/1/10-3/31/11)		
NUMBER OF STATEMENTS	70	45	50	3	6	9	9	14	9
ASSETS	%	%	%	%	%	%	%	%	%
Cash & Equivalents	12.5	8.4	9.1					7.3	
Trade Receivables (net)	19.3	17.2	21.2					24.7	
Inventory	27.1	24.5	26.0					17.2	
All Other Current	4.1	2.5	4.0					3.3	
Total Current	63.1	52.6	60.3					52.5	
Fixed Assets (net)	27.8	32.9	28.1					37.4	
Intangibles (net)	3.2	6.1	5.1					1.0	
All Other Non-Current	5.9	8.4	6.5					9.1	
Total	100.0	100.0	100.0					100.0	
LIABILITIES									
Notes Payable-Short Term	13.2	16.2	17.3					16.7	
Cur. Mat.-L.T.D.	4.3	3.1	3.7					2.4	
Trade Payables	9.5	10.0	10.8					14.9	
Income Taxes Payable	.0	.1	.0					.1	
All Other Current	17.8	19.5	14.3					14.4	
Total Current	44.9	48.9	46.0					48.3	
Long-Term Debt	15.1	18.1	13.1					16.1	
Deferred Taxes	.2	.6	.3					.3	
All Other Non-Current	3.0	5.0	7.3					1.1	
Net Worth	36.8	27.4	33.3					34.1	
Total Liabilities & Net Worth	100.0	100.0	100.0					100.0	
INCOME DATA									
Net Sales	100.0	100.0	100.0					100.0	
Gross Profit	26.4	28.1	26.5					21.3	
Operating Expenses	25.8	31.9	26.6					23.0	
Operating Profit	.6	-3.9	-.1					-1.7	
All Other Expenses (net)	1.0	1.8	1.3					1.1	
Profit Before Taxes	-.4	-5.6	-1.4					-2.9	
RATIOS									
Current	2.2 / 1.3 / 1.0	1.9 / 1.2 / .8	2.2 / 1.3 / .9					1.6 / 1.0 / .8	
Quick	1.3 / .7 / .3	1.0 / .5 / .2	1.0 / .6 / .3					.7 / .6 / .4	
Sales/Receivables	(6) 64.3 / (22) 16.7 / (46) 8.0	(9) 38.5 / (29) 12.6 / (55) 6.6	(10) 38.2 / (28) 12.8 / (53) 6.9					(21) 17.7 / (53) 6.9 / (61) 6.0	
Cost of Sales/Inventory	(31) 11.9 / (46) 7.9 / (85) 4.3	(27) 13.5 / (74) 4.9 / (114) 3.2	(22) 16.8 / (52) 7.0 / (97) 3.8					(18) 20.3 / (32) 11.5 / (70) 5.2	
Cost of Sales/Payables	(5) 67.3 / (13) 27.8 / (28) 13.2	(9) 40.1 / (25) 14.5 / (38) 9.6	(6) 57.8 / (18) 19.9 / (40) 9.2					(19) 19.4 / (31) 11.8 / (50) 7.3	
Sales/Working Capital	6.9 / 14.7 / 254.0	6.8 / 18.9 / -15.6	6.8 / 16.8 / -24.4					13.3 / NM / -14.4	
EBIT/Interest	17.8 / (63) 1.4 / -2.8	6.7 / (41) .7 / -3.8	6.5 / (48) 1.2 / -1.8					2.1 / -.8 / -7.8	
Net Profit + Depr., Dep., Amort./Cur. Mat. L/T/D		4.5 / (12) 2.2 / -3.2							
Fixed/Worth	.3 / .9 / 2.5	.4 / .9 / 3.7	.4 / .8 / 2.1					.7 / 1.2 / 1.9	
Debt/Worth	.8 / 2.2 / 7.9	1.0 / 2.1 / 14.4	1.1 / 2.4 / 6.0					1.1 / 2.5 / 4.4	
% Profit Before Taxes/Tangible Net Worth	34.6 / (64) 5.9 / -38.8	22.4 / (37) 1.4 / -28.2	40.2 / (43) 5.4 / -11.8					7.1 / (13) -11.8 / -22.4	
% Profit Before Taxes/Total Assets	10.4 / 1.5 / -8.4	5.2 / -.6 / -13.7	8.5 / .7 / -6.0					2.8 / -3.5 / -7.5	
Sales/Net Fixed Assets	28.9 / 9.7 / 4.4	13.2 / 5.8 / 2.7	27.2 / 10.1 / 3.1					10.1 / 4.6 / 2.5	
Sales/Total Assets	3.0 / 2.3 / 1.6	2.6 / 1.6 / .9	3.0 / 2.0 / 1.2					2.2 / 1.6 / 1.2	
% Depr., Dep., Amort./Sales	1.0 / (53) 1.5 / 3.1	1.7 / (37) 2.8 / 4.3	1.5 / (41) 1.9 / 3.9					1.6 / 2.2 / 3.8	
% Officers', Directors', Owners' Comp/Sales	1.8 / (17) 2.6 / 4.7		1.5 / (10) 2.6 / 8.4						
Net Sales ($)	1769760M	793099M	1156259M	1375M	13199M	38809M	58410M	215855M	828611M
Total Assets ($)	817904M	424912M	653899M	1283M	6551M	20342M	41871M	128739M	455113M

M = $ thousand   MM = $ million
See Pages 9 through 22 for Explanation of Ratios and Data

Current Data Sorted by Assets   Comparative Historical Data

0-500M	500M-2MM	2-10MM	10-50MM	50-100MM	100-250MM	Type of Statement	4/1/06-3/31/07 ALL	4/1/07-3/31/08 ALL
1	1	5	13	6		Unqualified	28	26
	4	22	9			Reviewed	48	47
1	12	10			1	Compiled	30	23
11	16	9	1			Tax Returns	31	40
9	16	18	13	1	1	Other	67	65
	35 (4/1-9/30/10)		144 (10/1/10-3/31/11)					
21	49	64	36	7	2	NUMBER OF STATEMENTS	204	201
%	%	%	%	%	%	**ASSETS**	%	%
13.6	5.1	6.5	6.2			Cash & Equivalents	6.6	7.7
18.0	21.3	18.5	15.2			Trade Receivables (net)	24.5	22.2
22.9	33.7	32.6	35.4			Inventory	30.1	29.8
4.1	3.1	2.8	2.0			All Other Current	1.9	2.2
58.6	63.1	60.4	58.7			Total Current	63.0	61.9
30.6	29.2	32.0	27.6			Fixed Assets (net)	27.8	28.7
8.8	4.0	3.0	4.4			Intangibles (net)	3.2	3.1
1.9	3.6	4.7	9.3			All Other Non-Current	5.9	6.2
100.0	100.0	100.0	100.0			Total	100.0	100.0
						LIABILITIES		
18.3	18.4	14.6	11.8			Notes Payable-Short Term	14.4	16.6
7.1	4.2	4.3	2.9			Cur. Mat.-L.T.D.	4.4	3.5
13.3	15.1	11.1	7.5			Trade Payables	12.5	11.1
.0	.1	.3	.1			Income Taxes Payable	.3	.2
22.7	8.4	6.3	4.8			All Other Current	9.2	9.6
61.4	46.2	36.6	27.0			Total Current	40.8	41.0
24.2	21.9	16.6	16.8			Long-Term Debt	18.6	19.7
.0	.3	.1	.8			Deferred Taxes	.3	.3
14.8	8.3	7.2	6.4			All Other Non-Current	6.5	5.9
-.4	23.3	39.5	49.0			Net Worth	33.8	33.1
100.0	100.0	100.0	100.0			Total Liabilities & Net Worth	100.0	100.0
						INCOME DATA		
100.0	100.0	100.0	100.0			Net Sales	100.0	100.0
43.2	35.8	24.5	22.9			Gross Profit	29.1	29.3
38.3	32.6	23.2	18.9			Operating Expenses	23.5	25.1
4.9	3.2	1.2	4.0			Operating Profit	5.6	4.2
2.6	.5	.7	.8			All Other Expenses (net)	1.4	1.5
2.4	2.6	.5	3.1			Profit Before Taxes	4.3	2.7
						RATIOS		
2.8	2.8	2.8	3.7				2.9	2.8
1.2	1.9	1.6	2.3			Current	1.6	1.6
.7	.9	1.2	1.4				1.1	1.2
1.4	1.3	1.1	1.8				1.6	1.6
.6	.7	.6	.8			Quick	.8	.7
.3	.2	.3	.3				.4	.4
0 UND	19 19.7	15 24.0	23 16.2				19 19.4	16 22.4
13 27.3	29 12.7	29 12.5	33 11.2			Sales/Receivables	32 11.5	29 12.6
39 9.3	46 8.0	49 7.5	44 8.2				45 8.0	48 7.6
0 UND	26 14.0	37 10.0	68 5.4				28 12.9	24 15.0
27 13.5	71 5.1	76 4.8	108 3.4			Cost of Sales/Inventory	56 6.5	55 6.6
62 5.9	169 2.2	114 3.2	164 2.2				105 3.5	113 3.2
0 UND	9 42.1	9 38.7	11 32.3				10 36.7	9 42.8
4 81.3	25 14.7	21 17.3	21 17.8			Cost of Sales/Payables	22 16.7	20 17.8
29 12.5	46 7.9	34 10.7	30 12.2				38 9.7	35 10.5
12.9	4.8	5.3	3.6				5.9	6.0
41.9	10.3	9.3	4.8			Sales/Working Capital	10.1	9.7
-28.6	-40.7	27.0	8.9				36.4	26.0
10.8	10.1	6.3	7.7				7.7	7.8
(18) 2.6	(45) 4.3	(61) 2.4	(32) 2.6			EBIT/Interest	(185) 3.6	(186) 2.3
.1	1.2	-1.6	1.1				1.6	.7
		6.4	4.5				4.0	5.4
		(12) 1.8	(13) 2.4			Net Profit + Depr., Dep., Amort./Cur. Mat. L/T/D	(48) 2.6	(44) 2.8
		1.0	1.8				1.4	.8
.3	.5	.4	.3				.3	.4
1.3	1.2	.7	.5			Fixed/Worth	.7	.7
-.8	27.7	1.5	1.4				1.6	2.3
.6	1.0	.7	.7				.9	.8
11.1	2.9	1.6	1.1			Debt/Worth	2.0	1.9
-3.0	58.0	3.1	2.0				4.4	5.7
42.6	59.6	21.8	21.6				49.8	39.2
(12) 16.0	(38) 25.7	(59) 8.2	(35) 11.2			% Profit Before Taxes/Tangible Net Worth	(180) 27.8	(170) 16.4
-71.3	8.1	-7.3	.1				10.7	2.2
29.9	14.6	11.0	11.7				17.1	16.7
9.8	6.6	2.7	4.1			% Profit Before Taxes/Total Assets	8.6	4.8
-11.3	.0	-4.8	-.2				2.3	-.3
102.8	19.7	17.5	11.4				26.0	24.2
21.5	9.0	7.1	5.9			Sales/Net Fixed Assets	10.9	9.2
5.3	3.9	3.8	2.8				5.0	4.9
6.2	3.1	2.4	1.9				3.3	3.2
3.9	2.2	1.9	1.5			Sales/Total Assets	2.4	2.2
2.0	1.5	1.4	.9				1.7	1.6
.4	1.0	1.2	1.2				.9	1.1
(12) 2.4	(42) 2.0	(59) 2.6	(33) 2.3			% Depr., Dep., Amort./Sales	(174) 1.8	(160) 2.2
5.4	4.4	4.4	5.7				3.1	3.5
3.9	2.6	1.2					2.0	2.0
(13) 5.9	(24) 6.0	(29) 3.0				% Officers', Directors' Owners' Comp/Sales	(75) 3.6	(77) 4.2
10.3	9.2	4.4					6.6	6.6
21223M	139132M	662737M	1013222M	656483M	332935M	Net Sales ($)	5661468M	4635025M
5569M	57312M	334496M	661603M	471708M	364847M	Total Assets ($)	2614028M	2689599M

M = $ thousand   MM = $ million
See Pages 9 through 22 for Explanation of Ratios and Data

Comparative Historical Data | | Current Data Sorted by Sales

			Type of Statement						
24	20	25	Unqualified		2		3	8	12
42	44	35	Reviewed		1	2	13	14	5
34	24	24	Compiled	3	7	6	3	5	
37	47	37	Tax Returns	8	17	4	8		
59	72	58	Other	5	17	2	8	18	8
4/1/08-3/31/09	4/1/09-3/31/10	4/1/10-3/31/11			35 (4/1-9/30/10)		144 (10/1/10-3/31/11)		
ALL	ALL	ALL		0-1MM	1-3MM	3-5MM	5-10MM	10-25MM	25MM & OVER
196	207	179	NUMBER OF STATEMENTS	16	44	14	35	45	25
%	%	%	ASSETS	%	%	%	%	%	%
7.2	9.1	6.8	Cash & Equivalents	6.1	7.5	6.7	6.8	6.9	6.0
21.0	18.6	18.2	Trade Receivables (net)	13.2	18.6	19.1	22.0	15.0	20.9
30.3	29.8	31.6	Inventory	27.9	29.3	34.9	34.2	30.7	34.4
2.5	2.3	2.8	All Other Current	3.4	3.4	2.3	2.3	2.5	2.7
61.0	59.8	59.5	Total Current	50.6	58.8	63.0	65.3	55.2	63.9
31.4	30.0	30.9	Fixed Assets (net)	38.1	32.9	27.9	28.1	31.3	27.7
2.6	3.5	4.4	Intangibles (net)	8.7	5.1	1.1	4.0	3.8	3.6
5.0	6.6	5.2	All Other Non-Current	2.5	3.2	7.9	2.6	9.6	4.8
100.0	100.0	100.0	Total	100.0	100.0	100.0	100.0	100.0	100.0
			LIABILITIES						
15.3	16.5	15.0	Notes Payable-Short Term	14.6	18.7	19.2	15.1	14.2	7.6
4.2	5.2	4.4	Cur. Mat.-L.T.D.	5.2	6.1	2.6	4.4	3.4	3.5
10.8	11.5	11.5	Trade Payables	6.6	13.8	13.3	15.3	8.8	9.4
.3	.2	.2	Income Taxes Payable	.0	.0	.1	.4	.1	.3
7.8	7.7	8.4	All Other Current	32.3	6.7	4.5	5.4	6.3	6.6
38.5	41.0	39.5	Total Current	58.8	45.3	39.6	40.5	32.8	27.4
18.5	19.2	19.0	Long-Term Debt	22.9	28.0	8.3	16.2	15.6	16.8
.4	.2	.5	Deferred Taxes	.0	.2	.5	.1	.9	1.3
7.1	8.1	8.3	All Other Non-Current	18.1	9.8	10.1	7.7	4.5	5.8
35.5	31.4	32.8	Net Worth	.2	16.8	41.6	35.6	46.1	48.6
100.0	100.0	100.0	Total Liabilties & Net Worth	100.0	100.0	100.0	100.0	100.0	100.0
			INCOME DATA						
100.0	100.0	100.0	Net Sales	100.0	100.0	100.0	100.0	100.0	100.0
27.9	28.4	29.4	Gross Profit	46.0	36.3	30.2	24.4	25.2	20.7
24.8	25.9	26.4	Operating Expenses	41.8	34.6	29.1	20.9	22.3	15.7
3.0	2.5	3.0	Operating Profit	4.2	1.7	1.1	3.5	2.9	5.1
1.4	1.2	.9	All Other Expenses (net)	2.7	1.4	.9	.0	.7	.6
1.6	1.3	2.1	Profit Before Taxes	1.5	.3	.2	3.5	2.2	4.4
			RATIOS						
2.8	3.1	3.2		3.6	2.5	2.5	3.8	2.8	3.7
1.6	1.6	1.7	Current	1.7	1.5	1.6	1.7	1.6	2.3
1.1	1.0	1.1		.6	.9	1.0	1.1	1.2	1.8
1.3	1.4	1.4		1.5	1.2	1.3	1.2	1.2	1.9
.7	.6	.7	Quick	.5	.5	.8	.6	.6	1.0
.3	.3	.3		.1	.2	.2	.3	.3	.6
16 23.1	15 24.0	17 22.1		9 40.3	11 34.1	15 24.1	17 22.1	20 18.0	18 20.0
27 13.4	27 13.5	30 12.2	Sales/Receivables	26 14.3	33 11.1	23 16.0	29 12.7	32 11.4	30 12.2
41 8.8	44 8.3	45 8.1		42 8.8	43 8.5	47 7.7	45 8.1	50 7.3	44 8.2
28 13.0	29 12.6	35 10.5		12 31.0	22 16.6	35 10.5	27 13.3	61 6.0	40 9.0
62 5.9	63 5.8	77 4.8	Cost of Sales/Inventory	51 7.1	57 6.4	76 4.8	55 6.6	94 3.9	65 5.6
110 3.3	133 2.7	131 2.8		192 1.9	148 2.5	120 3.1	118 3.1	138 2.7	102 3.6
8 45.9	10 34.9	9 41.3		0 UND	6 61.8	0 UND	9 42.5	14 26.8	12 30.7
19 19.1	21 17.3	21 17.6	Cost of Sales/Payables	9 38.5	22 17.0	13 27.8	18 20.6	23 16.1	21 17.7
34 10.6	37 9.9	35 10.6		33 11.2	44 8.2	52 7.1	36 10.2	34 10.8	26 14.0
5.6	4.9	4.5		4.1	5.1	5.6	4.5	4.2	4.3
10.6	10.0	8.5	Sales/Working Capital	26.7	12.7	12.0	7.3	8.4	5.5
41.4	186.8	40.5		-11.4	-35.3	-86.1	40.5	18.0	12.7
6.1	6.4	8.1		5.8	9.0	10.1	7.2	7.3	9.1
(181) 2.4	(187) 2.3	(165) 2.9	EBIT/Interest	(14) 1.2	(40) 3.8	5.2	(30) 3.4	(44) 2.4	(23) 4.8
-.1	-.3	.3		-3.2	.4	-2.0	1.1	-1.0	1.8
4.1	3.3	4.8						5.9	4.4
(45) 1.9	(45) 1.3	(34) 2.6	Net Profit + Depr., Dep., Amort./Cur. Mat. L/T/D				(12) 2.8	(11) 2.8
.5	.5	1.1						1.0	1.8
.3	.3	.4		.5	.5	.5	.3	.4	.2
.7	.7	.8	Fixed/Worth	1.7	1.7	.7	.8	.6	.5
1.5	2.5	2.3		-1.1	-2.0	1.3	1.9	1.5	1.3
.8	.8	.7		.4	1.4	.7	.8	.7	.6
1.6	1.9	1.7	Debt/Worth	4.0	3.8	1.2	1.8	1.3	1.3
3.9	8.3	5.8		-4.6	-12.2	9.0	4.5	2.5	2.4
29.9	33.1	32.4		51.3	38.6	24.2	44.3	17.6	31.3
(175) 11.2	(176) 9.2	(152) 11.8	% Profit Before Taxes/Tangible Net Worth	(10) 7.7	(30) 19.3	9.9	(32) 15.7	(42) 7.7	(24) 13.6
-2.3	-5.4	-2.5		-49.1	-6.6	-35.9	1.6	-6.0	6.0
10.8	10.3	12.9		24.2	12.8	15.5	13.9	9.1	13.1
3.1	2.9	4.3	% Profit Before Taxes/Total Assets	4.3	4.3	5.8	5.7	2.2	6.0
-2.7	-4.5	-2.3		-5.3	-4.5	-8.6	.4	-4.4	2.2
20.2	23.8	20.4		31.1	20.9	25.5	22.8	13.5	25.9
8.9	7.7	8.2	Sales/Net Fixed Assets	4.3	9.1	9.2	8.5	6.3	10.5
4.0	3.9	3.7		2.0	3.8	4.2	4.9	2.4	4.5
3.0	3.0	2.8		5.3	3.0	3.3	3.5	2.1	2.9
2.2	1.9	1.9	Sales/Total Assets	1.5	2.2	2.3	2.1	1.5	1.9
1.5	1.3	1.3		1.1	1.5	1.7	1.6	1.1	1.6
1.1	1.1	1.2		3.6	.5	.8	1.2	1.4	.9
(170) 2.5	(175) 2.5	(153) 2.1	% Depr., Dep., Amort./Sales	(12) 6.4	(35) 2.1	(13) 1.5	(29) 1.7	(43) 3.1	(21) 1.6
4.3	4.9	5.3		13.6	4.2	4.8	3.5	5.4	3.0
1.8	2.6	2.2		3.4	4.3		2.1	.8	
(73) 3.1	(77) 4.5	(76) 3.7	% Officers', Directors' Owners' Comp/Sales	(10) 6.5	(19) 6.3		(19) 2.5	(15) 1.1	
5.9	6.9	7.1		10.5	9.9		4.8	3.5	
3670976M	3301153M	2825732M	Net Sales ($)	8354M	86009M	56176M	253769M	670163M	1751261M
2289005M	2233438M	1895535M	Total Assets ($)	7147M	58991M	30075M	151744M	644428M	1003150M

M = $ thousand   MM = $ million
See Pages 9 through 22 for Explanation of Ratios and Data

Current Data Sorted by Assets　　　　　Comparative Historical Data

Type of Statement	0-500M	500M-2MM	2-10MM	10-50MM	50-100MM	100-250MM		4/1/06-3/31/07 ALL	4/1/07-3/31/08 ALL
Unqualified		1	1	12	5	8		19	18
Reviewed		2	6	2		1		12	8
Compiled			4	1				6	2
Tax Returns			1					5	3
Other	1	4	8	17	5	4		28	32
	12 (4/1-9/30/10)		71 (10/1/10-3/31/11)						

	0-500M	500M-2MM	2-10MM	10-50MM	50-100MM	100-250MM		ALL	ALL
NUMBER OF STATEMENTS	1	7	20	32	10	13		70	63
	%	%	%	%	%	%		%	%
ASSETS									
Cash & Equivalents			8.1	4.5	4.5	2.8		5.9	5.0
Trade Receivables (net)			33.9	25.8	15.3	19.1		26.1	22.3
Inventory			22.5	19.6	23.2	19.3		21.6	24.1
All Other Current			3.4	1.4	9.7	3.2		1.3	3.0
Total Current			67.8	51.3	52.7	44.3		54.9	54.4
Fixed Assets (net)			24.2	37.6	38.5	37.1		36.9	36.6
Intangibles (net)			.7	3.3	2.0	11.7		2.6	2.6
All Other Non-Current			7.3	7.7	6.8	6.9		5.6	6.3
Total			100.0	100.0	100.0	100.0		100.0	100.0
LIABILITIES									
Notes Payable-Short Term			11.9	7.2	3.0	.9		11.0	10.2
Cur. Mat.-L.T.D.			4.2	7.6	5.6	2.9		4.9	3.8
Trade Payables			21.3	17.3	13.1	16.5		15.9	18.1
Income Taxes Payable			.1	.7	.7	.2		.1	.1
All Other Current			5.8	6.8	7.1	5.7		5.8	6.5
Total Current			43.2	39.5	29.6	26.1		37.7	38.7
Long-Term Debt			11.4	16.8	23.9	20.4		18.8	23.9
Deferred Taxes			.7	1.0	2.7	2.9		1.2	.8
All Other Non-Current			5.1	9.7	6.1	8.2		4.6	6.5
Net Worth			39.6	32.9	37.7	42.4		37.7	30.1
Total Liabilities & Net Worth			100.0	100.0	100.0	100.0		100.0	100.0
INCOME DATA									
Net Sales			100.0	100.0	100.0	100.0		100.0	100.0
Gross Profit			24.5	17.4	22.2	19.8		20.6	21.3
Operating Expenses			19.8	12.0	18.1	14.4		15.3	18.4
Operating Profit			4.7	5.4	4.1	5.4		5.3	2.9
All Other Expenses (net)			.6	1.6	4.5	1.4		1.0	1.4
Profit Before Taxes			4.1	3.8	-.4	4.0		4.3	1.5
RATIOS									
Current			2.8	1.9	3.2	2.3		2.3	2.4
			1.5	1.4	1.8	1.9		1.5	1.4
			1.1	.9	1.4	1.0		.9	1.1
Quick			2.0	1.3	1.2	1.2		1.3	1.2
			1.0	.8	.9	.8		.8	.6
			.6	.5	.5	.5		.5	.4
Sales/Receivables			25 14.3	25 14.5	29 12.4	26 13.9		31 11.7	28 13.0
			41 8.8	38 9.6	34 10.8	32 11.5		40 9.2	34 10.7
			47 7.7	46 7.9	46 7.9	46 8.0		52 7.0	43 8.5
Cost of Sales/Inventory			16 22.9	22 16.7	37 9.9	29 12.5		25 14.4	30 12.2
			29 12.8	35 10.5	62 5.9	63 5.8		44 8.3	45 8.2
			57 6.4	51 7.1	97 3.8	79 4.6		65 5.6	68 5.4
Cost of Sales/Payables			18 20.0	19 19.3	19 19.2	26 14.1		20 18.6	20 18.4
			29 12.6	22 16.3	26 13.9	35 10.3		33 11.1	30 12.1
			36 10.1	36 10.1	37 10.0	39 9.4		43 8.5	47 7.8
Sales/Working Capital			7.3	8.5	3.4	5.1		7.0	6.3
			16.0	23.9	10.4	6.9		12.1	13.5
			54.6	-32.5	22.7	102.8		-76.9	76.4
EBIT/Interest			21.7	16.2		6.7		9.4	4.8
			(19) 6.8	5.9		(12) 2.4		(62) 3.6	(59) 2.0
			3.1	1.8		1.2		1.4	.8
Net Profit + Depr., Dep., Amort./Cur. Mat. L/T/D				15.7				3.8	2.8
				(10) 4.1				(16) 3.1	(19) 1.5
				2.9				1.7	.4
Fixed/Worth			.1	.7	.5	.7		.4	.8
			.5	1.4	.7	1.2		1.0	1.2
			1.0	3.8	1.6	NM		2.5	3.6
Debt/Worth			.5	1.2	.9	1.0		.8	1.4
			1.9	2.1	1.8	2.2		1.6	2.8
			3.3	7.9	2.4	NM		4.5	4.4
% Profit Before Taxes/Tangible Net Worth			54.5	52.4		26.1		47.5	32.8
			(18) 19.4	(28) 30.4		(10) 12.1		(62) 24.2	(54) 13.0
			7.7	12.4		-.7		5.3	-.2
% Profit Before Taxes/Total Assets			13.6	16.6	13.1	8.9		16.9	10.0
			10.3	12.7	5.7	5.4		7.1	4.5
			2.1	1.5	-8.4	1.2		1.7	-.9
Sales/Net Fixed Assets			39.3	11.3	11.2	7.2		15.8	12.8
			16.7	7.4	5.1	5.8		6.8	7.6
			7.4	4.2	2.5	2.1		2.8	3.3
Sales/Total Assets			4.4	3.5	2.2	2.0		2.9	3.3
			3.5	2.2	1.5	1.3		2.2	2.2
			2.1	1.8	1.2	1.0		1.4	1.4
% Depr., Dep., Amort./Sales			.7	1.3		2.0		1.1	1.3
			(18) 1.3	(30) 2.0		(11) 2.7		(61) 2.3	(53) 2.1
			1.9	4.0		5.0		4.2	3.6
% Officers', Directors' Owners' Comp/Sales								1.3	1.5
								(15) 1.9	(13) 2.5
								3.8	4.4
Net Sales ($)	135M	20386M	300816M	2104329M	1702623M	4180801M		4387691M	4586589M
Total Assets ($)	457M	9686M	91572M	831102M	809894M	1976612M		2491360M	2588737M

M = $ thousand　　MM = $ million
See Pages 9 through 22 for Explanation of Ratios and Data

Comparative Historical Data				Current Data Sorted by Sales					
22	23	27	Type of Statement					1	25
10	13	11	Unqualified	1				5	2
6	3	5	Reviewed		2	2	1	1	3
6	3	1	Compiled			1		1	
29	43	39	Tax Returns						
			Other	1	1	4	4	4	25
4/1/08-3/31/09 ALL	4/1/09-3/31/10 ALL	4/1/10-3/31/11 ALL		0-1MM	12 (4/1-9/30/10) 1-3MM	3-5MM	71 (10/1/10-3/31/11) 5-10MM	10-25MM	25MM & OVER
73	85	83	NUMBER OF STATEMENTS	2	1	6	7	12	55
%	%	%	ASSETS	%	%	%	%	%	%
5.0	4.7	5.8	Cash & Equivalents					4.7	4.6
23.4	24.8	24.7	Trade Receivables (net)					32.4	24.2
24.4	23.5	20.9	Inventory					24.1	20.3
2.3	2.5	3.2	All Other Current					4.1	3.3
55.0	55.5	54.5	Total Current					65.3	52.5
36.3	35.2	34.7	Fixed Assets (net)					26.0	35.9
3.0	2.4	3.9	Intangibles (net)					1.6	4.7
5.6	6.9	7.0	All Other Non-Current					7.1	7.0
100.0	100.0	100.0	Total					100.0	100.0
			LIABILITIES						
11.3	10.3	7.2	Notes Payable-Short Term					12.1	5.5
4.3	4.0	5.3	Cur. Mat.-L.T.D.					3.0	5.9
17.4	17.6	16.9	Trade Payables					20.5	17.6
.2	.4	.4	Income Taxes Payable					.2	.6
5.1	12.5	6.1	All Other Current					6.3	6.5
38.2	44.9	35.9	Total Current					42.0	36.1
26.0	20.8	17.4	Long-Term Debt					14.6	17.7
.9	1.1	1.4	Deferred Taxes					1.7	1.7
7.1	5.3	7.7	All Other Non-Current					2.8	9.0
27.6	27.8	37.6	Net Worth					39.0	35.6
100.0	100.0	100.0	Total Liabilities & Net Worth					100.0	100.0
			INCOME DATA						
100.0	100.0	100.0	Net Sales					100.0	100.0
20.5	21.7	21.3	Gross Profit					20.6	18.0
16.7	15.8	15.5	Operating Expenses					17.6	12.9
3.8	6.0	5.8	Operating Profit					3.0	5.1
1.6	.9	1.5	All Other Expenses (net)					.7	2.0
2.2	5.1	4.3	Profit Before Taxes					2.2	3.1
			RATIOS						
2.3	2.2	2.3						2.8	2.2
1.4	1.4	1.5	Current					1.6	1.6
1.0	1.0	1.1						1.2	1.0
1.2	1.2	1.4						1.9	1.3
.7	.7	.8	Quick					1.0	.8
.4	.5	.5						.6	.5
23 16.0	27 13.8	26 13.9						33 11.1	26 13.9
30 12.3	35 10.3	38 9.7	Sales/Receivables					43 8.5	34 10.6
39 9.4	45 8.2	46 7.9						47 7.7	45 8.2
26 14.3	27 13.6	22 16.8						21 17.1	24 15.1
39 9.3	43 8.5	36 10.2	Cost of Sales/Inventory					32 11.3	38 9.5
58 6.3	65 5.6	65 5.7						39 9.4	65 5.7
20 18.6	21 17.2	20 18.2						11 34.4	20 18.0
26 14.0	29 12.4	28 13.2	Cost of Sales/Payables					25 14.4	28 13.1
38 9.6	40 9.1	37 9.9						37 10.0	37 9.7
8.0	6.9	6.5						7.3	6.3
25.5	17.7	13.9	Sales/Working Capital					14.9	16.1
265.3	NM	75.0						37.3	130.7
6.9	8.0	10.7						22.9	10.8
(66) 2.6	(80) 3.9	(78) 4.5	EBIT/Interest					3.8	(52) 4.3
1.0	.7	1.7						1.1	1.8
3.5	4.8	12.1							11.0
(21) 1.6	(23) 2.5	(32) 3.2	Net Profit + Depr., Dep., Amort./Cur. Mat. L/T/D					(20)	2.5
.7	1.3	1.9							1.5
.4	.5	.5						.1	.5
1.4	1.2	1.0	Fixed/Worth					.8	1.2
10.9	3.3	2.2						1.1	2.3
.8	.8	1.1						1.1	1.2
3.1	2.4	2.0	Debt/Worth					1.9	2.1
19.3	9.3	3.7						3.2	4.4
33.2	48.4	48.1						18.3	49.1
(59) 18.0	(70) 24.2	(73) 21.0	% Profit Before Taxes/Tangible Net Worth				(11)	8.9	(47) 22.1
2.7	4.6	7.0						3.6	11.9
9.9	14.1	14.8						12.3	16.2
4.9	7.2	8.9	% Profit Before Taxes/Total Assets					2.3	8.9
-.2	.5	1.2						.4	1.7
16.5	19.4	13.3						104.7	11.4
7.0	6.4	7.4	Sales/Net Fixed Assets					12.4	7.1
3.8	3.0	3.8						5.9	3.8
3.6	3.2	3.5						4.4	3.4
2.2	2.2	2.2	Sales/Total Assets					3.3	2.1
1.5	1.5	1.6						2.1	1.5
1.1	1.1	1.2						1.0	1.2
(64) 2.1	(75) 2.2	(76) 2.1	% Depr., Dep., Amort./Sales				(10)	1.8	(50) 2.1
3.5	4.4	4.1						2.5	3.5
.7		1.4							
(15) 1.5		(13) 2.3	% Officers', Directors' Owners' Comp/Sales						
3.2		2.9							
5866224M	7062022M	8309090M	Net Sales ($)	876M	2948M	20114M	55553M	207036M	8022563M
2808766M	3517311M	3719323M	Total Assets ($)	1307M	930M	10129M	25808M	78873M	3602276M

© RMA 2011

M = $ thousand   MM = $ million
See Pages 9 through 22 for Explanation of Ratios and Data

Current Data Sorted by Assets   Comparative Historical Data

						Type of Statement		
2		6	16	3	7	Unqualified	45	39
	5	41	21	2		Reviewed	67	64
1	4	21	5			Compiled	24	22
6	6	8			1	Tax Returns	22	13
6	9	35	32	8	1	Other	60	80
	42 (4/1-9/30/10)		204 (10/1/10-3/31/11)				4/1/06-3/31/07	4/1/07-3/31/08
0-500M	500M-2MM	2-10MM	10-50MM	50-100MM	100-250MM		ALL	ALL
15	24	111	74	13	9	NUMBER OF STATEMENTS	218	218
%	%	%	%	%	%	ASSETS	%	%
12.5	8.1	7.4	5.5	5.7		Cash & Equivalents	6.2	6.0
31.6	43.0	29.9	26.8	17.8		Trade Receivables (net)	29.4	28.7
29.0	20.3	16.0	18.0	14.8		Inventory	15.8	16.6
2.5	.6	1.6	2.7	1.2		All Other Current	1.9	1.9
75.6	72.1	54.8	53.0	39.5		Total Current	53.2	53.3
14.0	14.8	34.1	38.3	42.1		Fixed Assets (net)	35.3	33.8
4.9	4.4	4.1	2.1	14.8		Intangibles (net)	4.0	5.7
5.5	8.8	7.0	6.6	3.6		All Other Non-Current	7.4	7.2
100.0	100.0	100.0	100.0	100.0		Total	100.0	100.0
						LIABILITIES		
13.3	9.7	8.2	11.9	2.0		Notes Payable-Short Term	9.4	9.9
3.9	2.6	4.3	5.0	4.2		Cur. Mat.-L.T.D.	5.1	4.5
40.6	30.2	18.1	18.5	9.4		Trade Payables	16.9	17.7
.0	.0	.2	.2	.0		Income Taxes Payable	.2	.2
7.9	12.6	7.3	8.1	6.4		All Other Current	7.8	7.2
65.7	55.1	38.0	43.7	22.0		Total Current	39.4	39.5
25.8	12.0	18.5	19.4	24.2		Long-Term Debt	18.7	20.9
.0	.2	.7	1.0	1.0		Deferred Taxes	.9	1.1
23.8	5.0	4.0	5.1	5.1		All Other Non-Current	6.8	6.0
-15.3	27.7	38.8	30.8	47.7		Net Worth	34.2	32.5
100.0	100.0	100.0	100.0	100.0		Total Liabilities & Net Worth	100.0	100.0
						INCOME DATA		
100.0	100.0	100.0	100.0	100.0		Net Sales	100.0	100.0
36.8	31.8	27.4	22.8	25.1		Gross Profit	26.0	25.4
32.5	28.9	23.0	18.2	17.3		Operating Expenses	21.7	21.1
4.3	2.9	4.4	4.6	7.7		Operating Profit	4.4	4.3
.8	.4	.2	.5	1.3		All Other Expenses (net)	.8	1.2
3.5	2.6	4.2	4.1	6.4		Profit Before Taxes	3.6	3.0
						RATIOS		
2.9	2.3	2.8	1.7	2.3			2.1	2.2
1.5	1.4	1.4	1.2	1.7	Current	1.4	1.4
.8	1.0	1.0	.9	1.4		1.0	1.0
1.3	1.5	1.9	1.1	1.4			1.4	1.4
1.0	1.0	1.0	.7	1.2	Quick	.9	.9
.4	.6	.7	.5	.8		.6	.6

25	14.8	31	11.7	32	11.5	31	11.6	35	10.6			33	11.1	33	11.1
35	10.6	35	10.3	40	9.1	42	8.7	40	9.2	Sales/Receivables	40	9.1	39	9.5
49	7.4	46	7.9	47	7.7	51	7.2	46	8.0		48	7.7	45	8.1
29	12.5	17	22.1	15	24.3	23	15.7	16	22.7		18	20.3	17	21.3
49	7.5	28	13.2	26	14.1	35	10.4	38	9.6	Cost of Sales/Inventory	29	12.6	27	13.7
61	6.0	42	8.8	42	8.8	52	7.1	51	7.1		41	8.9	40	9.0
20	17.9	20	18.5	16	23.2	23	16.0	21	17.2		16	23.2	18	20.8
45	8.0	38	9.7	26	13.9	35	10.6	26	13.9	Cost of Sales/Payables	27	13.6	28	13.2
69	5.3	56	6.5	43	8.5	49	7.5	51	7.2		46	8.0	44	8.3

8.0	10.8	7.4	8.7	7.8			9.5		9.1
17.3	23.4	18.7	29.5	10.7	Sales/Working Capital	18.8		18.9
-31.0	-304.8	520.5	-37.1	13.9		991.1		NM
	17.4	18.6	12.8	17.1	20.3			7.4		7.1
(11)	1.4	(23) 5.4	(105) 5.0	(67) 4.7	6.9	EBIT/Interest	(206) 3.6	(209)	3.5
	-1.2	2.1	2.9	2.1	3.1			1.8		1.6
			6.3	4.6				4.9		5.5
		(30) 2.3	(35) 2.4		Net Profit + Depr., Dep., Amort./Cur. Mat. L/T/D	(79) 2.4	(80)	2.5
			.7	1.7				1.6		1.3
.1	.1	.5	.6	.9			.6		.6
1.7	.4	1.0	1.3	1.2	Fixed/Worth	1.1		1.2
-.1	83.5	2.5	3.1	2.1		2.7		2.8
2.2	1.2	.8	1.1	1.0			.8		.9
-172.0	2.2	1.8	2.1	1.6	Debt/Worth	2.1		2.1
-2.0	109.8	4.8	6.1	2.4		6.0		7.0
	86.7	46.8	46.3	65.3		% Profit Before Taxes/Tangible	37.7		34.2
	(19) 16.6	(101) 24.1	(66) 24.9	(12) 30.4	Net Worth	(193) 21.9	(183)	19.0
	8.2	11.3	12.3	10.5			9.6		6.9
26.6	18.1	16.0	16.7	18.7		% Profit Before Taxes/Total	12.1		12.9
10.8	4.9	8.5	7.7	11.2	Assets	6.9		6.5
-4.1	2.3	3.8	3.0	3.9		2.4		2.1
999.8	156.8	17.0	11.6	6.2			15.0		17.1
72.3	59.9	8.7	6.0	4.4	Sales/Net Fixed Assets	7.0		8.0
15.2	15.4	4.5	4.2	2.5		4.2		4.3
6.1	5.2	3.5	3.0	2.2			3.2		3.4
3.2	3.7	2.5	2.4	1.9	Sales/Total Assets	2.5		2.5
2.2	3.1	1.9	1.9	1.1		1.9		2.0
	.3	1.3	1.6	1.8			1.6		1.3
	(19) .8	(105) 2.0	(71) 2.4	3.0	% Depr., Dep., Amort./Sales	(202) 2.6	(200)	2.3
	2.0	3.2	3.9	6.0			3.8		3.2
	2.2	1.3	.9				1.8		1.4
	(11) 4.6	(43) 2.8	(16) 2.1		% Officers', Directors' Owners' Comp/Sales	(74) 3.0	(77)	2.7
	6.2	5.4	4.4				6.0		6.5

18541M	120789M	1529183M	3944053M	1388773M	2777667M	Net Sales ($)	7066993M	7785557M
3939M	30738M	583827M	1668670M	876353M	1377965M	Total Assets ($)	3425928M	4055056M

M = $ thousand   MM = $ million
See Pages 9 through 22 for Explanation of Ratios and Data

Comparative Historical Data   Current Data Sorted by Sales

Hist 1	Hist 2	Hist 3	Type of Statement	0-1MM	1-3MM	3-5MM	5-10MM	10-25MM	25MM & OVER
26	32	34	Unqualified	2			2	2	28
77	73	69	Reviewed			6	11	32	20
22	25	31	Compiled		2	7	8	8	6
15	14	21	Tax Returns	1	4	3	8	4	1
87	72	91	Other	3	5	6	11	21	45
4/1/08-3/31/09 ALL	4/1/09-3/31/10 ALL	4/1/10-3/31/11 ALL			42 (4/1-9/30/10)		204 (10/1/10-3/31/11)		
227	216	246	NUMBER OF STATEMENTS	6	11	22	40	67	100
%	%	%	**ASSETS**	%	%	%	%	%	%
6.5	6.9	7.0	Cash & Equivalents		6.2	7.6	9.5	6.8	5.5
26.1	28.0	29.6	Trade Receivables (net)		30.5	32.1	31.5	29.8	28.0
16.4	15.9	17.7	Inventory		34.7	16.0	14.5	17.5	17.8
1.7	1.8	1.9	All Other Current		2.6	1.1	.8	1.8	2.5
50.7	52.5	56.2	Total Current		74.0	56.8	56.4	55.9	53.7
36.3	36.0	32.5	Fixed Assets (net)		16.4	28.1	31.0	34.0	35.7
4.8	4.3	4.5	Intangibles (net)		7.7	5.1	3.8	3.5	4.9
8.2	7.3	6.7	All Other Non-Current		1.8	9.9	8.8	6.5	5.6
100.0	100.0	100.0	Total		100.0	100.0	100.0	100.0	100.0
			LIABILITIES						
11.6	9.0	9.4	Notes Payable-Short Term		13.3	10.3	5.1	9.7	10.1
5.0	5.2	4.2	Cur. Mat.-L.T.D.		4.7	4.9	3.5	4.6	4.2
17.4	18.0	20.2	Trade Payables		35.0	17.3	21.4	17.8	18.7
.1	.2	.1	Income Taxes Payable		.0	.0	.1	.2	.1
5.9	5.8	8.1	All Other Current		5.1	12.8	7.2	7.6	7.9
40.0	38.3	42.1	Total Current		58.1	45.3	37.2	39.8	41.0
21.6	19.9	18.7	Long-Term Debt		42.2	19.2	17.8	16.6	18.7
.9	.9	.8	Deferred Taxes		.0	1.0	.4	.7	1.1
4.8	7.3	5.7	All Other Non-Current		29.2	3.0	4.7	3.9	4.8
32.7	33.6	32.8	Net Worth		-29.5	31.5	39.9	39.0	34.4
100.0	100.0	100.0	Total Liabilities & Net Worth		100.0	100.0	100.0	100.0	100.0
			INCOME DATA						
100.0	100.0	100.0	Net Sales		100.0	100.0	100.0	100.0	100.0
22.8	24.0	26.9	Gross Profit		34.8	37.3	29.5	25.3	23.2
20.1	21.8	22.3	Operating Expenses		30.2	32.1	26.9	20.7	18.2
2.7	2.2	4.5	Operating Profit		4.6	5.2	2.6	4.6	5.0
.7	.6	.4	All Other Expenses (net)		.9	.7	.0	.3	.6
2.0	1.6	4.1	Profit Before Taxes		3.7	4.4	2.6	4.4	4.4
			RATIOS						
2.1	2.3	2.2	Current		2.1	3.5	2.7	2.4	1.9
1.3	1.3	1.4			1.3	1.5	1.4	1.5	1.4
1.0	1.0	1.0			.8	.9	1.0	1.0	1.0
1.3	1.5	1.5	Quick		1.1	2.4	1.8	1.8	1.4
.8	.9	.9			.6	1.2	1.1	.9	.8
.6	.6	.6			.4	.4	.8	.8	.8
27 13.6	32 11.3	32 11.5	Sales/Receivables		25 14.8	34 10.8	34 10.7	31 11.9	34 10.9
35 10.4	39 9.3	41 9.0			31 11.9	37 9.9	42 8.7	40 9.2	42 8.7
42 8.7	47 7.8	48 7.6			37 9.8	54 6.7	48 7.7	46 8.0	50 7.3
17 21.2	18 20.1	18 20.0	Cost of Sales/Inventory		29 12.5	14 26.1	15 23.6	16 22.4	20 18.2
26 14.0	28 12.9	30 12.1			49 7.5	40 9.2	25 14.4	29 12.6	33 11.2
39 9.4	42 8.6	47 7.8			89 4.1	69 5.3	36 10.3	42 8.8	47 7.8
15 24.4	16 22.6	19 19.1	Cost of Sales/Payables		36 10.3	14 25.6	16 22.8	16 23.2	22 16.3
25 14.8	30 12.3	31 11.7			45 8.0	25 14.6	24 15.0	27 13.4	33 11.2
39 9.4	46 8.0	49 7.5			69 5.3	54 6.8	56 6.5	40 9.2	49 7.5
9.8	7.4	8.2	Sales/Working Capital		7.8	5.3	6.7	8.4	8.7
25.6	20.7	19.5			25.7	21.6	21.0	18.7	19.5
-428.0	-302.6	-986.1			-31.0	-35.5	209.4	999.8	527.4
6.4	7.6	16.4	EBIT/Interest			8.7	13.4	14.7	18.8
(218) 2.7	(206) 2.8	(228) 5.0				5.1	(36) 4.7	(63) 4.6	(94) 6.3
1.0	1.0	2.8				2.3	2.0	2.8	2.8
3.4	4.5	6.1	Net Profit + Depr., Dep., Amort./Cur. Mat. L/T/D					14.3	7.2
(85) 1.8	(71) 2.3	(83) 2.9						(18) 1.3	(49) 3.0
.9	1.3	1.4						.2	2.0
.6	.6	.5	Fixed/Worth		.8	.3	.3	.4	.6
1.4	1.1	1.1			-.2	.9	.7	1.0	1.2
3.9	2.8	2.7			.0	NM	2.4	2.6	2.5
1.0	.9	.9	Debt/Worth		3.0	.6	.7	.8	1.0
2.1	1.9	2.0			-3.0	1.9	1.7	1.7	2.1
7.0	5.9	5.7			-1.9	NM	3.5	4.3	5.0
30.0	31.1	47.7	% Profit Before Taxes/Tangible Net Worth			40.5	29.3	46.8	52.9
(185) 11.5	(185) 12.2	(212) 23.9			(17) 16.3	(36) 17.0	(61) 26.6	(90) 28.4	
2.0	2.6	11.3				4.4	9.2	11.4	12.7
8.4	9.3	16.8	% Profit Before Taxes/Total Assets		19.6	17.8	11.6	16.0	17.4
3.8	3.8	8.2			10.8	7.0	5.6	9.2	8.8
.0	-.5	3.4			-4.1	3.4	2.0	3.5	3.8
15.5	15.0	20.9	Sales/Net Fixed Assets		852.0	66.9	38.7	19.3	13.6
7.7	7.3	8.4			94.3	12.2	9.3	9.1	6.1
4.4	4.0	4.6			15.2	3.2	4.6	5.4	4.4
3.4	3.1	3.5	Sales/Total Assets		6.1	3.9	3.4	3.6	3.1
2.5	2.4	2.5			4.1	2.3	2.7	2.6	2.4
2.0	1.8	1.9			2.2	1.3	1.8	2.1	1.9
1.4	1.6	1.3	% Depr., Dep., Amort./Sales			.7	1.4	1.0	1.6
(209) 2.3	(199) 2.5	(223) 2.2			(19) 1.9	(35) 2.4	(65) 1.9	(95) 2.3	
3.4	3.7	3.2				2.7	3.8	3.2	3.3
1.1	1.6	1.3	% Officers', Directors' Owners' Comp/Sales		1.6	1.4	1.5	.9	
(70) 2.9	(69) 3.2	(78) 3.3			(11) 4.6	(18) 4.9	(25) 3.1	(19) 1.3	
5.8	6.3	5.6			6.2	6.9	4.0	3.6	
8162256M	7401077M	9779006M	Net Sales ($)	2318M	20892M	90600M	280649M	1084307M	8300240M
3789712M	3754560M	4541492M	Total Assets ($)	1078M	8203M	47972M	129029M	448404M	3906806M

M = $ thousand   MM = $ million
See Pages 9 through 22 for Explanation of Ratios and Data

Current Data Sorted by Assets | Comparative Historical Data

0-500M	500M-2MM	2-10MM	10-50MM	50-100MM	100-250MM	Type of Statement	4/1/06-3/31/07 ALL	4/1/07-3/31/08 ALL
		3	8	3	1	Unqualified	15	14
1	2	10	7			Reviewed	17	11
1	3	1		1		Compiled	4	7
	1	3				Tax Returns	3	3
1		6	14	2		Other	18	26
	19 (4/1-9/30/10)		49 (10/1/10-3/31/11)					
2	7	23	29	6	1	NUMBER OF STATEMENTS	57	61
%	%	%	%	%	%	**ASSETS**	%	%
		6.7	3.9			Cash & Equivalents	5.8	6.3
		25.8	20.9			Trade Receivables (net)	24.9	23.8
		22.3	18.9			Inventory	19.5	21.7
		1.3	3.7			All Other Current	1.9	1.1
		56.0	47.4			Total Current	52.2	53.0
		35.8	45.7			Fixed Assets (net)	39.0	40.2
		1.6	1.6			Intangibles (net)	3.9	3.4
		6.6	5.3			All Other Non-Current	5.0	3.4
		100.0	100.0			Total	100.0	100.0
						LIABILITIES		
		8.6	10.5			Notes Payable-Short Term	8.9	8.0
		4.8	5.4			Cur. Mat.-L.T.D.	4.9	5.8
		10.0	12.7			Trade Payables	13.9	12.9
		.4	.0			Income Taxes Payable	.1	.0
		8.0	10.7			All Other Current	7.3	6.2
		31.9	39.2			Total Current	35.1	32.8
		18.7	19.7			Long-Term Debt	18.6	22.5
		.9	2.2			Deferred Taxes	.7	.8
		1.6	4.2			All Other Non-Current	5.3	5.6
		47.0	34.5			Net Worth	40.4	38.1
		100.0	100.0			Total Liabilities & Net Worth	100.0	100.0
						INCOME DATA		
		100.0	100.0			Net Sales	100.0	100.0
		24.4	24.9			Gross Profit	21.5	22.2
		18.4	17.8			Operating Expenses	17.2	18.0
		6.1	7.1			Operating Profit	4.4	4.2
		.6	1.7			All Other Expenses (net)	1.2	1.8
		5.5	5.4			Profit Before Taxes	3.2	2.4
						RATIOS		
		3.2	2.0				2.3	2.4
		1.6	1.2			Current	1.5	1.6
		1.1	.9				1.1	1.1
		1.6	1.1				1.4	1.3
		1.0	.6			Quick	.8	.8
		.6	.5				.5	.5
		33 11.0	32 11.4				33 11.1	29 12.6
		43 8.4	41 8.9			Sales/Receivables	39 9.3	36 10.1
		48 7.6	49 7.4				51 7.2	46 8.0
		34 10.9	36 10.1				27 13.3	31 11.7
		47 7.8	50 7.3			Cost of Sales/Inventory	43 8.5	49 7.5
		81 4.5	72 5.1				65 5.6	71 5.2
		13 28.5	21 17.2				13 28.2	14 25.7
		19 18.7	32 11.4			Cost of Sales/Payables	23 16.0	23 15.8
		31 11.6	43 8.5				35 10.5	35 10.3
		5.3	6.8				7.2	5.8
		9.6	27.7			Sales/Working Capital	12.7	17.3
		47.8	-28.9				73.9	65.8
		33.3	15.8				6.0	6.9
		(22) 9.2	(27) 5.7			EBIT/Interest	(52) 3.1	(57) 2.8
		2.7	2.8				1.6	1.4
			3.4			Net Profit + Depr., Dep.,	3.7	4.4
			(16) 2.5			Amort./Cur. Mat. L/T/D	(18) 1.9	(27) 2.2
			1.2				1.5	1.1
		.4	.9				.7	.7
		.7	1.5			Fixed/Worth	1.2	1.2
		2.1	2.7				2.0	2.6
		.3	1.1				.9	.9
		1.6	2.0			Debt/Worth	1.5	1.9
		2.9	4.4				5.0	4.8
		54.8	42.4				33.9	37.4
		(22) 24.0	(25) 30.0			% Profit Before Taxes/Tangible Net Worth	(53) 18.6	(55) 17.1
		10.3	15.6				6.0	6.0
		17.4	14.8				12.3	11.4
		10.8	9.6			% Profit Before Taxes/Total Assets	6.0	4.8
		5.7	3.4				2.1	1.6
		10.7	5.4				9.4	8.1
		6.7	3.8			Sales/Net Fixed Assets	4.9	5.0
		3.5	2.9				3.2	3.2
		2.5	2.3				2.4	2.6
		2.2	1.7			Sales/Total Assets	2.1	2.0
		1.7	1.3				1.5	1.6
		2.0	2.4				2.1	2.3
		(20) 3.3	(28) 3.0			% Depr., Dep., Amort./Sales	(46) 3.6	(55) 3.5
		4.6	4.6				4.9	5.4
							1.8	.9
						% Officers', Directors' Owners' Comp/Sales	(16) 2.5	(13) 2.3
							3.4	3.2
618M	23397M	313378M	1406683M	791083M	58294M	Net Sales ($)	1625428M	1913250M
462M	7852M	147836M	768236M	386490M	226427M	Total Assets ($)	905079M	1014068M

Comparative Historical Data / Current Data Sorted by Sales

Type of Statement	4/1/08-3/31/09 ALL	4/1/09-3/31/10 ALL	4/1/10-3/31/11 ALL	0-1MM	1-3MM	3-5MM	5-10MM	10-25MM	25MM & OVER
Unqualified	14	12	15					6	9
Reviewed	14	18	20	1	1		3	11	4
Compiled	4	4	6	1	2				1
Tax Returns	4	4	4			1	1	2	1
Other	27	28	23				1	5	16
					19 (4/1-9/30/10)			49 (10/1/10-3/31/11)	
NUMBER OF STATEMENTS	63	66	68	2	4	2	6	24	30

	%	%	%	%	%	%	%	%	%
ASSETS									
Cash & Equivalents	5.1	4.9	6.8					7.1	5.6
Trade Receivables (net)	21.0	21.4	22.7					22.7	22.0
Inventory	21.4	21.9	20.4					22.3	17.9
All Other Current	1.1	2.9	2.6					1.4	3.9
Total Current	48.5	51.1	52.5					53.5	49.3
Fixed Assets (net)	42.1	41.1	38.7					37.9	43.8
Intangibles (net)	4.3	2.9	2.9					1.8	2.0
All Other Non-Current	5.1	4.9	5.9					6.8	4.8
Total	100.0	100.0	100.0					100.0	100.0
LIABILITIES									
Notes Payable-Short Term	9.3	10.5	8.5					7.5	9.0
Cur. Mat.-L.T.D.	5.6	5.5	4.9					5.3	5.0
Trade Payables	11.9	13.1	11.1					9.8	12.8
Income Taxes Payable	.0	.1	.1					.4	.0
All Other Current	5.4	5.8	8.8					8.2	10.1
Total Current	32.1	35.1	33.5					31.1	37.0
Long-Term Debt	24.6	25.6	20.2					17.9	19.2
Deferred Taxes	.7	.8	1.3					1.1	1.7
All Other Non-Current	3.6	5.4	3.2					3.5	3.6
Net Worth	38.9	33.0	41.9					46.3	38.4
Total Liabilities & Net Worth	100.0	100.0	100.0					100.0	100.0
INCOME DATA									
Net Sales	100.0	100.0	100.0					100.0	100.0
Gross Profit	23.2	24.1	25.8					24.6	23.7
Operating Expenses	18.3	20.0	19.1					17.2	17.1
Operating Profit	4.9	4.1	6.7					7.4	6.6
All Other Expenses (net)	1.5	1.2	.9					.8	1.2
Profit Before Taxes	3.4	2.9	5.8					6.6	5.4
RATIOS									
Current	3.0	2.4	3.2					3.2	1.9
	1.5	1.4	1.5					1.9	1.3
	1.1	1.1	1.1					1.2	1.0
Quick	1.4	1.2	1.6					1.6	1.5
	.8	.7	.8					1.1	.7
	.5	.5	.6					.6	.5
Sales/Receivables	28 12.8	29 12.5	32 11.5					33 11.1	30 12.1
	35 10.3	38 9.7	39 9.3					37 9.7	41 8.9
	43 8.5	47 7.8	48 7.6					47 7.8	49 7.5
Cost of Sales/Inventory	28 13.0	38 9.7	36 10.1					36 10.2	33 10.9
	54 6.7	52 7.0	50 7.3					48 7.6	50 7.3
	70 5.2	68 5.3	68 5.3					75 4.8	65 5.6
Cost of Sales/Payables	15 24.6	16 23.3	14 25.5					12 31.5	20 18.0
	24 14.9	29 12.6	25 14.7					21 17.7	29 12.4
	33 11.0	44 8.3	38 9.6					32 11.5	43 8.4
Sales/Working Capital	5.1	6.2	5.7					4.8	7.3
	12.9	16.4	12.1					8.7	14.8
	65.4	39.7	66.4					41.0	-759.4
EBIT/Interest	8.5	6.7	21.7					37.6	20.3
	(60) 2.7	(64) 3.2	(63) 7.1					8.6	(28) 8.1
	.9	1.3	2.8					3.2	2.9
Net Profit + Depr., Dep., Amort./Cur. Mat. L/T/D	5.9	3.8	5.8					14.7	3.9
	(26) 2.1	(27) 2.4	(29) 2.7					(11) 3.9	(17) 2.6
	.9	1.2	1.6					1.6	1.6
Fixed/Worth	.7	.7	.5					.4	.9
	1.3	1.3	1.0					.7	1.5
	3.9	2.8	2.3					1.5	2.5
Debt/Worth	.7	.8	.6					.3	1.0
	2.0	2.0	1.8					1.2	2.0
	6.3	5.0	3.9					2.9	4.2
% Profit Before Taxes/Tangible Net Worth	28.5	34.4	46.3					44.3	47.8
	(56) 15.7	(57) 18.3	(61) 28.8					(22) 27.6	(27) 30.0
	-1.4	1.1	13.1					12.8	14.6
% Profit Before Taxes/Total Assets	12.6	11.4	17.0					16.8	17.9
	5.6	6.1	11.4					11.5	9.5
	-.3	2.0	4.5					6.6	3.4
Sales/Net Fixed Assets	7.5	7.3	8.7					8.9	6.1
	4.9	4.5	4.9					5.3	4.0
	3.2	3.2	3.3					3.1	3.4
Sales/Total Assets	2.5	2.5	2.4					2.5	2.3
	1.9	1.9	1.9					2.1	1.9
	1.5	1.6	1.6					1.7	1.5
% Depr., Dep., Amort./Sales	1.9	2.2	2.1					2.0	2.3
	(58) 3.3	(60) 3.3	(62) 2.9					(22) 3.3	(29) 2.9
	4.7	4.5	4.2					4.8	3.9
% Officers', Directors' Owners' Comp/Sales	.8	.8	1.3						
	(13) 1.3	(11) 3.5	(14) 2.2						
	2.4	6.3	4.6						
Net Sales ($)	2022448M	2476104M	2593453M	618M	8768M	8310M	41451M	387876M	2146430M
Total Assets ($)	1113274M	1485675M	1537303M	462M	4307M	2290M	26263M	211342M	1292639M

© RMA 2011   M = $ thousand   MM = $ million
See Pages 9 through 22 for Explanation of Ratios and Data

Current Data Sorted by Assets							Comparative Historical Data	
						Type of Statement		
		1	4			Unqualified	19	14
		4	8			Reviewed	19	23
	1	3				Compiled	3	1
	1	1				Tax Returns	3	1
		5	6	1	1	Other	12	15
	6 (4/1-9/30/10)		30 (10/1/10-3/31/11)				4/1/06-3/31/07	4/1/07-3/31/08
0-500M	500M-2MM	2-10MM	10-50MM	50-100MM	100-250MM		ALL	ALL
	2	14	18	1	1	**NUMBER OF STATEMENTS**	56	54
%	%	%	%	%	%	**ASSETS**	%	%
DATA NOT AVAILABLE		7.2	6.8			Cash & Equivalents	6.4	5.7
		24.3	23.7			Trade Receivables (net)	25.7	24.0
		21.4	18.2			Inventory	18.4	19.2
		1.8	2.2			All Other Current	1.3	1.4
		54.7	50.8			Total Current	51.8	50.3
		37.4	42.6			Fixed Assets (net)	36.9	39.5
		1.3	1.7			Intangibles (net)	4.9	4.0
		6.6	4.9			All Other Non-Current	6.3	6.3
		100.0	100.0			Total	100.0	100.0
						LIABILITIES		
		10.5	6.5			Notes Payable-Short Term	7.0	7.9
		4.0	3.3			Cur. Mat.-L.T.D.	8.0	5.6
		11.7	13.3			Trade Payables	14.8	12.9
		.0	.0			Income Taxes Payable	.2	.7
		10.2	4.3			All Other Current	6.8	5.4
		36.4	27.3			Total Current	36.9	32.5
		16.7	22.5			Long-Term Debt	21.1	22.5
		1.0	.9			Deferred Taxes	1.1	1.2
		6.8	4.4			All Other Non-Current	5.4	2.5
		39.1	44.9			Net Worth	35.5	41.3
		100.0	100.0			Total Liabilties & Net Worth	100.0	100.0
						INCOME DATA		
		100.0	100.0			Net Sales	100.0	100.0
		26.6	22.0			Gross Profit	23.4	24.1
		21.1	17.8			Operating Expenses	17.9	17.2
		5.5	4.2			Operating Profit	5.5	6.9
		.7	-.1			All Other Expenses (net)	1.6	1.5
		4.8	4.2			Profit Before Taxes	3.8	5.4
						RATIOS		
		3.0	3.2				2.6	2.4
		1.5	2.2			Current	1.3	1.6
		1.1	1.1				1.0	1.1
		2.1	2.1				1.7	1.5
		.7	1.4			Quick	.8	.9
		.5	.7				.5	.5
		29 12.5	**33** 11.2				**30** 12.4	**28** 12.9
		39 9.3	**36** 10.1			Sales/Receivables	**38** 9.6	**37** 9.9
		49 7.4	**49** 7.5				**48** 7.6	**47** 7.8
		24 15.0	**20** 17.9				**19** 18.9	**22** 16.7
		39 9.3	**29** 12.6			Cost of Sales/Inventory	**32** 11.5	**31** 11.7
		67 5.5	**41** 8.8				**53** 6.9	**57** 6.4
		8 47.7	**18** 20.8				**15** 24.3	**14** 25.5
		19 19.3	**27** 13.6			Cost of Sales/Payables	**25** 14.9	**23** 15.9
		34 10.7	**34** 10.7				**40** 9.0	**40** 9.2
		7.2	5.5				6.9	6.7
		14.1	7.9			Sales/Working Capital	21.2	14.0
		36.8	NM				NM	43.6
		19.9	18.4				6.8	11.3
		6.3	(17) 5.0			EBIT/Interest	(53) 3.1	(52) 4.2
		3.1	2.3				1.9	1.8
							4.6	6.1
						Net Profit + Depr., Dep., Amort./Cur. Mat. L/T/D	(20) 1.7	(27) 1.9
							1.2	.9
		.4	.4				.6	.6
		1.0	1.0			Fixed/Worth	1.3	1.1
		1.4	1.7				3.5	2.0
		.9	.7				.9	.7
		1.3	1.5			Debt/Worth	2.0	1.7
		3.2	2.3				6.3	3.3
		34.3	43.9				44.0	39.4
		(13) 21.7	(17) 22.6			% Profit Before Taxes/Tangible Net Worth	(49) 17.8	(49) 23.8
		9.5	13.1				8.7	7.6
		17.1	15.6				13.1	15.5
		12.6	8.0			% Profit Before Taxes/Total Assets	5.9	7.4
		5.0	3.7				2.5	2.2
		12.3	10.1				13.1	8.8
		6.7	4.6			Sales/Net Fixed Assets	6.1	5.4
		4.4	3.9				3.8	3.6
		2.7	2.6				3.0	2.8
		2.6	2.2			Sales/Total Assets	2.4	2.1
		2.1	1.9				1.6	1.7
		1.7	2.2				1.8	1.8
		(13) 2.3	(17) 2.8			% Depr., Dep., Amort./Sales	(51) 2.9	(52) 2.7
		2.9	4.2				4.3	3.8
							1.5	1.0
						% Officers', Directors' Owners' Comp/Sales	(19) 2.5	(19) 2.1
							5.7	2.7
	12797M	181477M	919900M	81454M	218560M	Net Sales ($)	1784381M	1992769M
	2982M	74525M	412458M	53010M	104126M	Total Assets ($)	897916M	983798M

M = $ thousand MM = $ million

See Pages 9 through 22 for Explanation of Ratios and Data

Comparative Historical Data   ## Current Data Sorted by Sales

4/1/08-3/31/09 ALL	4/1/09-3/31/10 ALL	4/1/10-3/31/11 ALL	Type of Statement	0-1MM	1-3MM	3-5MM	5-10MM	10-25MM	25MM & OVER
10	3	5	Unqualified				1	1	4
16	10	12	Reviewed		1		2	3	8
3	3	4	Compiled			1		1	
2	2	2	Tax Returns		1				
16	18	13	Other		1			5	8
				6 (4/1-9/30/10)			30 (10/1/10-3/31/11)		
47	36	36	NUMBER OF STATEMENTS		2		4	10	20
%	%	%	ASSETS	%	%	%	%	%	%
5.6	6.8	6.9	Cash & Equivalents	D		D		7.3	7.1
26.5	26.8	24.6	Trade Receivables (net)	A		A		27.8	23.7
20.3	20.0	20.4	Inventory	T		T		23.9	17.8
1.9	3.5	1.9	All Other Current	A		A		1.0	2.1
54.4	57.1	53.9	Total Current					60.1	50.7
36.2	37.4	39.3	Fixed Assets (net)	N		N		29.2	42.5
4.1	1.7	1.4	Intangibles (net)	O		O		1.7	1.5
5.3	3.8	5.5	All Other Non-Current	T		T		9.1	5.2
100.0	100.0	100.0	Total					100.0	100.0
			LIABILITIES	A		A			
8.8	8.5	7.8	Notes Payable-Short Term	V		V		9.7	6.1
6.6	5.0	3.5	Cur. Mat.-L.T.D.	A		A		3.3	3.2
17.1	13.5	13.3	Trade Payables	I		I		17.2	12.5
.0	.1	.0	Income Taxes Payable	L		L		.0	.1
8.7	5.9	6.8	All Other Current	A		A		9.8	4.6
41.2	33.1	31.3	Total Current	B		B		40.0	26.6
20.6	23.1	18.9	Long-Term Debt	L		L		18.3	21.0
1.1	.7	1.2	Deferred Taxes	E		E		.9	1.4
5.2	2.0	6.9	All Other Non-Current					3.0	4.2
31.8	41.0	41.7	Net Worth					37.8	46.9
100.0	100.0	100.0	Total Liabilities & Net Worth					100.0	100.0
			INCOME DATA						
100.0	100.0	100.0	Net Sales					100.0	100.0
20.6	23.7	24.1	Gross Profit					26.7	21.9
17.6	19.9	19.2	Operating Expenses					21.7	17.1
3.0	3.8	4.9	Operating Profit					4.9	4.7
1.7	1.1	.2	All Other Expenses (net)					.4	-.1
1.3	2.7	4.6	Profit Before Taxes					4.5	4.8
			RATIOS						
2.4	2.7	3.4						2.4	3.4
1.6	1.7	1.8	Current					1.5	2.2
.9	1.3	1.2						1.1	1.2
1.5	1.8	2.1						1.7	2.1
.9	1.1	1.3	Quick					.7	1.4
.5	.6	.7						.7	.7
28 13.1	31 11.6	31 11.9					26 14.0		32 11.4
36 10.1	39 9.4	38 9.7	Sales/Receivables				35 10.5		36 10.1
47 7.8	47 7.8	51 7.1					49 7.4		57 6.5
22 16.3	22 16.4	22 16.7					25 14.8		21 17.4
31 11.8	34 10.8	30 12.0	Cost of Sales/Inventory				32 11.3		29 12.6
48 7.7	52 7.1	57 6.4					55 6.6		43 8.6
14 26.6	14 26.1	16 22.8					5 69.7		17 21.0
25 14.3	22 16.4	22 16.5	Cost of Sales/Payables				26 14.2		25 14.6
39 9.3	30 12.1	33 11.1					41 8.8		33 11.2
6.9	5.6	5.3						8.9	5.3
15.3	11.9	9.8	Sales/Working Capital					14.1	7.9
-85.4	28.9	36.1						36.8	31.1
8.3	7.5	21.3						20.3	23.7
(46) 3.9	(33) 4.2	(34) 6.5	EBIT/Interest					8.2 (19)	5.8
1.0	1.0	3.0						3.6	2.9
2.8	4.0	8.4							
(17) 1.5	(12) 2.9	(11) 5.8	Net Profit + Depr., Dep., Amort./Cur. Mat. L/T/D						
.3	1.4	2.9							
.7	.5	.5						.4	.5
1.3	1.0	1.0	Fixed/Worth					1.0	1.0
1.7	1.6	1.6						1.4	1.6
.8	.8	.7						1.1	.5
2.2	1.6	1.3	Debt/Worth					1.4	1.1
4.0	2.3	3.0						4.0	2.3
39.7	34.2	34.3							43.8
(43) 14.8	(33) 15.9	(33) 22.6	% Profit Before Taxes/Tangible Net Worth					(19)	26.6
6.6	4.5	11.8							14.2
12.4	12.9	16.1						17.7	15.9
6.0	5.8	10.3	% Profit Before Taxes/Total Assets					14.8	9.7
-1.5	1.0	4.6						3.3	4.8
13.6	11.6	11.6						21.6	9.0
6.1	5.9	5.0	Sales/Net Fixed Assets					10.0	4.6
3.8	4.0	4.1						5.8	4.0
3.0	2.8	2.6						2.8	2.6
2.5	2.2	2.3	Sales/Total Assets					2.6	2.2
1.8	2.0	2.1						2.3	1.7
1.5	1.4	2.0							2.3
(42) 2.8	(33) 2.5	(34) 2.5	% Depr., Dep., Amort./Sales					(19)	2.8
3.7	4.0	3.7							4.2
1.6	.8	.8							
(17) 2.4	(17) 1.9	(17) 1.9	% Officers', Directors' Owners' Comp/Sales						
6.5	3.0	3.0							
1678317M	1104727M	1414188M	Net Sales ($)		4155M		26769M	163350M	1219914M
812598M	528042M	647101M	Total Assets ($)		3687M		11113M	62707M	569594M

M = $ thousand   MM = $ million
See Pages 9 through 22 for Explanation of Ratios and Data

Current Data Sorted by Assets   **Comparative Historical Data**

0-500M	500M-2MM	2-10MM	10-50MM	50-100MM	100-250MM	Type of Statement	4/1/06-3/31/07 ALL	4/1/07-3/31/08 ALL
		1	10	5	4	Unqualified	24	19
	4	12	10		1	Reviewed	19	13
1	2	4	1			Compiled	13	5
1	3	1				Tax Returns	8	10
		8	10	4	4	Other	37	38
	15 (4/1-9/30/10)		71 (10/1/10-3/31/11)					
2	9	26	31	9	9	NUMBER OF STATEMENTS	101	85
%	%	%	%	%	%	**ASSETS**	%	%
		6.9	6.5			Cash & Equivalents	5.7	5.9
		30.3	20.6			Trade Receivables (net)	26.0	27.2
		26.7	25.8			Inventory	25.0	23.5
		.8	2.6			All Other Current	1.9	1.3
		64.8	55.4			Total Current	58.6	57.9
		28.0	37.1			Fixed Assets (net)	32.7	34.5
		4.4	4.2			Intangibles (net)	3.7	4.1
		2.8	3.3			All Other Non-Current	5.1	3.6
		100.0	100.0			Total	100.0	100.0
						LIABILITIES		
		12.6	15.6			Notes Payable-Short Term	11.5	13.2
		4.0	4.9			Cur. Mat.-L.T.D.	3.4	5.0
		14.9	18.1			Trade Payables	18.7	18.9
		.2	.1			Income Taxes Payable	.3	.2
		5.0	5.3			All Other Current	7.0	6.1
		36.8	44.1			Total Current	41.0	43.4
		16.6	16.9			Long-Term Debt	18.0	22.9
		.5	.3			Deferred Taxes	.7	.5
		8.6	3.5			All Other Non-Current	6.3	6.3
		37.5	35.1			Net Worth	34.0	27.0
		100.0	100.0			Total Liabilities & Net Worth	100.0	100.0
						INCOME DATA		
		100.0	100.0			Net Sales	100.0	100.0
		27.0	21.0			Gross Profit	24.4	25.3
		22.8	16.2			Operating Expenses	19.0	20.7
		4.2	4.8			Operating Profit	5.4	4.6
		.8	.5			All Other Expenses (net)	1.3	1.5
		3.4	4.3			Profit Before Taxes	4.1	3.0
						RATIOS		
		3.2	1.8				2.4	2.2
		1.8	1.3			Current	1.6	1.4
		1.2	1.0				1.1	1.0
		2.0	1.0				1.2	1.2
		1.0	.6			Quick	.8	.7
		.7	.3				.6	.5
		29 12.6	22 16.3				32 11.5	31 11.7
		37 9.9	33 10.9			Sales/Receivables	38 9.5	40 9.0
		54 6.7	40 9.1				47 7.8	47 7.7
		23 15.6	39 9.4				33 11.2	33 10.9
		46 8.0	56 6.5			Cost of Sales/Inventory	47 7.7	48 7.6
		68 5.3	74 4.9				66 5.5	67 5.4
		14 25.9	21 17.6				18 19.9	21 17.6
		23 15.6	33 11.1			Cost of Sales/Payables	32 11.4	29 12.4
		36 10.0	50 7.4				47 7.8	45 8.2
		5.4	7.0				6.5	7.0
		9.7	18.2			Sales/Working Capital	10.9	15.0
		27.2	-978.7				70.3	999.8
		8.8	13.5				7.4	6.3
		(24) 6.2	(30) 4.5			EBIT/Interest	(93) 3.4	(82) 3.6
		1.6	1.0				1.4	1.6
			6.2				5.9	5.6
			(14) 2.5			Net Profit + Depr., Dep., Amort./Cur. Mat. L/T/D	(29) 3.4	(26) 3.7
			.8				1.5	1.8
		.2	.7				.5	.6
		.7	1.1			Fixed/Worth	.8	1.1
		1.7	2.1				2.6	2.9
		.7	.9				.8	1.3
		1.5	2.2			Debt/Worth	2.0	2.4
		3.7	6.0				5.2	6.9
		46.3	41.6				47.1	51.3
		(22) 28.4	(26) 22.2			% Profit Before Taxes/Tangible Net Worth	(87) 20.3	(72) 25.7
		8.2	2.2				7.5	11.7
		18.0	19.0				13.3	13.5
		11.4	5.1			% Profit Before Taxes/Total Assets	7.9	7.7
		.7	.5				1.7	3.0
		21.2	10.6				14.1	14.4
		8.9	5.6			Sales/Net Fixed Assets	7.4	7.0
		6.4	3.7				4.4	4.0
		3.3	2.9				3.0	3.2
		2.7	2.1			Sales/Total Assets	2.3	2.4
		2.4	1.6				1.7	1.7
		1.0	1.5				1.5	1.5
		(20) 2.0	(30) 2.7			% Depr., Dep., Amort./Sales	(89) 2.3	(75) 2.6
		3.3	4.3				3.6	3.8
		3.1					2.7	2.7
		(13) 4.1				% Officers', Directors' Owners' Comp/Sales	(27) 4.1	(25) 4.0
		7.5					6.9	9.7
3168M	54330M	424491M	1362528M	1201938M	1801443M	Net Sales ($)	4283533M	4068703M
678M	13017M	148113M	649724M	615908M	1384212M	Total Assets ($)	2144179M	2116773M

M = $ thousand   MM = $ million
See Pages 9 through 22 for Explanation of Ratios and Data

Comparative Historical Data | Current Data Sorted by Sales

			Type of Statement	0-1MM	1-3MM	3-5MM	5-10MM	10-25MM	25MM & OVER
24	25	20	Unqualified				1	1	18
14	17	27	Reviewed			1	4	12	9
6	10	8	Compiled		1	2	3	1	1
6	9	5	Tax Returns		1	1		2	
54	35	26	Other		2	1		8	18
4/1/08-3/31/09 ALL	4/1/09-3/31/10 ALL	4/1/10-3/31/11 ALL			15 (4/1-9/30/10)			71 (10/1/10-3/31/11)	
104	96	86	**NUMBER OF STATEMENTS**		4	4	8	24	46
%	%	%	**ASSETS**	%	%	%	%	%	%
6.2	7.1	7.1	Cash & Equivalents					8.9	4.9
24.0	21.8	23.0	Trade Receivables (net)					26.9	19.9
23.8	22.4	26.0	Inventory		D A T A N O T A V A I L A B L E			25.3	24.7
2.0	2.5	2.1	All Other Current					.9	2.1
56.0	53.9	58.2	Total Current					62.0	51.7
32.8	32.6	32.0	Fixed Assets (net)					28.4	36.0
6.8	8.6	6.9	Intangibles (net)					7.1	8.9
4.4	5.0	2.8	All Other Non-Current					2.5	3.3
100.0	100.0	100.0	Total					100.0	100.0
			LIABILITIES						
11.6	10.6	12.6	Notes Payable-Short Term					16.9	9.9
4.3	4.6	4.3	Cur. Mat.-L.T.D.					4.6	3.8
15.7	13.1	15.2	Trade Payables					13.9	15.2
.2	.2	.2	Income Taxes Payable					.0	.3
5.2	5.5	5.4	All Other Current					5.2	6.0
37.0	34.0	37.6	Total Current					40.6	35.1
19.7	21.1	19.7	Long-Term Debt					14.6	20.4
.5	.8	.9	Deferred Taxes					.0	1.5
5.7	7.0	7.3	All Other Non-Current					5.3	6.5
37.0	37.0	34.5	Net Worth					39.5	36.4
100.0	100.0	100.0	Total Liabilities & Net Worth					100.0	100.0
			INCOME DATA						
100.0	100.0	100.0	Net Sales					100.0	100.0
24.9	25.4	23.5	Gross Profit					26.4	19.5
20.2	20.1	18.5	Operating Expenses					22.2	14.4
4.8	5.3	5.0	Operating Profit					4.2	5.1
1.3	1.9	1.0	All Other Expenses (net)					.8	1.1
3.5	3.4	4.0	Profit Before Taxes					3.4	4.0
			RATIOS						
2.5	3.1	2.8						3.4	2.4
1.6	1.6	1.7	Current					1.9	1.4
1.1	1.1	1.2						1.1	1.1
1.5	1.7	1.6						2.2	1.2
.8	.8	.8	Quick					1.0	.7
.5	.5	.5						.6	.5
27 13.4	28 13.2	28 13.2						34 10.8	27 13.7
36 10.0	39 9.3	36 10.1	Sales/Receivables					40 9.0	31 11.7
46 8.0	46 8.0	44 8.2						52 7.0	41 8.9
31 11.9	33 11.0	37 9.9						27 13.5	40 9.1
50 7.3	49 7.4	55 6.6	Cost of Sales/Inventory					52 7.0	54 6.8
67 5.4	72 5.0	75 4.9						83 4.4	73 5.0
14 25.9	16 23.4	18 19.9						16 22.4	18 19.8
24 14.9	26 14.0	27 13.5	Cost of Sales/Payables					27 13.4	26 14.0
43 8.5	39 9.4	39 9.3						37 9.8	40 9.1
6.4	6.7	6.0						5.2	6.8
12.0	10.9	11.8	Sales/Working Capital					11.3	13.6
88.7	33.7	34.9						55.4	61.6
8.2	10.5	10.0						10.9	8.1
(95) 3.7	(86) 3.8	(81) 4.7	EBIT/Interest					(23) 5.4	(42) 4.1
1.4	1.5	1.7						1.5	1.0
5.8	4.3	4.7	Net Profit + Depr., Dep.,						3.7
(25) 2.4	(19) 2.4	(26) 2.7	Amort./Cur. Mat. L/T/D					(20)	2.5
1.9	.8	1.4							.6
.5	.4	.5						.3	.8
1.0	1.1	1.1	Fixed/Worth					.9	1.4
2.5	3.2	2.7						2.0	6.5
.9	.8	.9						.6	1.1
2.0	2.2	2.3	Debt/Worth					1.9	2.5
6.0	9.0	5.5						4.3	11.6
40.1	43.4	47.1	% Profit Before Taxes/Tangible					37.4	61.8
(87) 16.6	(77) 20.7	(69) 26.2	Net Worth					(20) 24.6	(37) 24.9
6.1	3.4	8.5						2.3	6.8
14.7	14.9	18.0	% Profit Before Taxes/Total					17.6	13.8
7.2	6.7	7.5	Assets					6.8	6.8
1.5	1.4	1.3						-1.1	.5
13.3	12.7	16.2						24.0	10.9
7.6	6.6	7.5	Sales/Net Fixed Assets					8.2	5.5
3.8	3.4	4.1						5.6	3.4
3.1	3.0	3.0						3.2	2.8
2.2	1.9	2.4	Sales/Total Assets					2.5	2.0
1.6	1.4	1.6						1.7	1.4
1.6	1.6	1.2						1.2	1.5
(93) 2.7	(79) 2.9	(75) 2.7	% Depr., Dep., Amort./Sales					(19) 2.4	(44) 3.2
3.4	4.2	3.7						3.9	4.1
1.0	1.2	2.1	% Officers', Directors'					3.1	
(27) 2.3	(23) 3.5	(27) 3.6	Owners' Comp/Sales					(13) 4.1	
4.1	7.0	6.1						7.8	
6506244M	4887744M	4847898M	Net Sales ($)		7789M	17242M	62204M	408953M	4351710M
3378912M	3040989M	2811652M	Total Assets ($)		2856M	6302M	23685M	184103M	2594706M

M = $ thousand   MM = $ million
See Pages 9 through 22 for Explanation of Ratios and Data

Current Data Sorted by Assets   **Comparative Historical Data**

Type of Statement

0-500M	500M-2MM	2-10MM	10-50MM	50-100MM	100-250MM	Type of Statement	4/1/06-3/31/07 ALL	4/1/07-3/31/08 ALL
		1	13	2	2	Unqualified	19	11
	1	17	3			Reviewed	24	19
1	2	3		1	1	Compiled	9	11
1	7	5				Tax Returns	4	9
2	4	8	11	3	3	Other	28	26
	21 (4/1-9/30/10)		70 (10/1/10-3/31/11)					
4	14	34	27	6	6	NUMBER OF STATEMENTS	84	76

Financial Data

0-500M %	500M-2MM %	2-10MM %	10-50MM %	50-100MM %	100-250MM %		4/1/06-3/31/07 ALL %	4/1/07-3/31/08 ALL %
						ASSETS		
	9.4	8.1	8.8			Cash & Equivalents	6.0	5.0
	38.0	30.7	24.0			Trade Receivables (net)	26.8	28.3
	19.5	22.0	28.2			Inventory	26.2	25.4
	2.3	1.0	2.4			All Other Current	1.9	2.4
	69.1	61.8	63.4			Total Current	60.9	61.1
	15.6	27.9	26.7			Fixed Assets (net)	29.4	27.7
	8.3	6.4	3.6			Intangibles (net)	4.5	5.0
	7.0	3.9	6.3			All Other Non-Current	5.2	6.2
	100.0	100.0	100.0			Total	100.0	100.0
						LIABILITIES		
	13.0	14.0	10.9			Notes Payable-Short Term	12.2	10.5
	3.1	3.9	3.2			Cur. Mat.-L.T.D.	3.5	6.3
	25.4	23.0	10.6			Trade Payables	14.9	19.5
	.0	.1	.1			Income Taxes Payable	.3	.3
	3.6	5.5	10.5			All Other Current	10.6	9.8
	45.1	46.6	35.2			Total Current	41.5	46.3
	10.9	10.8	12.5			Long-Term Debt	15.7	21.3
	.0	.2	1.6			Deferred Taxes	.6	.5
	5.7	7.5	5.3			All Other Non-Current	9.2	6.9
	38.4	35.0	45.4			Net Worth	33.0	25.0
	100.0	100.0	100.0			Total Liabilities & Net Worth	100.0	100.0
						INCOME DATA		
	100.0	100.0	100.0			Net Sales	100.0	100.0
	39.1	28.5	22.5			Gross Profit	28.2	28.9
	32.6	23.7	18.0			Operating Expenses	24.5	24.5
	6.5	4.8	4.4			Operating Profit	3.7	4.4
	.5	.5	1.2			All Other Expenses (net)	1.5	1.7
	5.9	4.3	3.2			Profit Before Taxes	2.2	2.7
						RATIOS		
	2.8	2.2	3.8				2.4	2.3
	1.8	1.4	2.1			Current	1.5	1.4
	1.1	1.0	1.1				1.1	1.0
	2.0	1.5	2.4				1.4	1.4
	.9	.9	1.0			Quick	.8	.7
	.7	.6	.6				.5	.5
	30 12.3	36 10.1	38 9.7				32 11.4	32 11.2
	36 10.2	44 8.2	42 8.7			Sales/Receivables	40 9.2	41 9.0
	46 7.9	53 6.9	56 6.5				49 7.5	51 7.1
	16 23.5	28 12.9	54 6.7				30 12.1	28 13.1
	24 15.1	40 9.2	65 5.6			Cost of Sales/Inventory	52 7.1	48 7.6
	43 8.5	56 6.5	95 3.8				82 4.5	76 4.8
	17 20.9	27 13.5	17 22.0				14 26.4	23 15.5
	43 8.4	36 10.2	27 13.3			Cost of Sales/Payables	32 11.3	36 10.2
	68 5.4	45 8.1	36 10.0				49 7.5	55 6.6
	6.8	6.3	3.6				5.8	6.7
	10.7	17.8	6.8			Sales/Working Capital	11.2	14.8
	NM	-548.7	15.7				38.3	-291.0
	18.5	16.6	55.0				7.4	7.3
	(11) 4.9	5.5	(23) 5.2			EBIT/Interest	(74) 3.0	(68) 2.8
	2.0	2.6	.4				1.3	.8
						Net Profit + Depr., Dep.,	5.3	5.3
						Amort./Cur. Mat. L/T/D	(23) 2.6	(30) 2.7
							1.5	.9
	.2	.4	.3				.4	.4
	.4	1.0	.6			Fixed/Worth	.8	.9
	NM	3.5	1.4				3.5	30.8
	.7	.9	.4				.7	.9
	1.4	2.0	1.3			Debt/Worth	1.6	2.3
	NM	13.8	4.8				10.4	81.7
	70.7	65.4	30.4			% Profit Before Taxes/Tangible	45.1	30.5
	(11) 40.1	(29) 27.0	(25) 11.7			Net Worth	(69) 15.6	(59) 15.4
	1.6	9.7	-5.6				5.4	4.4
	30.5	16.8	12.7			% Profit Before Taxes/Total	15.4	11.8
	22.1	6.3	6.6			Assets	5.5	5.3
	1.5	2.2	-1.8				1.4	.0
	81.2	18.7	13.6				17.8	18.6
	22.2	10.6	6.7			Sales/Net Fixed Assets	8.8	10.5
	11.9	5.4	4.9				4.8	5.3
	4.5	3.0	2.2				3.1	3.2
	3.2	2.4	1.8			Sales/Total Assets	2.3	2.5
	2.3	1.9	1.2				1.6	1.7
	.5	1.0	1.2				1.3	1.1
	(12) 1.7	(29) 2.0	(26) 2.3			% Depr., Dep., Amort./Sales	(75) 2.1	(71) 1.8
	3.0	4.0	3.7				3.3	3.3
	2.0	2.0				% Officers', Directors'	1.8	1.8
	(11) 2.5	(17) 3.0				Owners' Comp/Sales	(23) 2.6	(23) 4.2
	4.8	4.1					5.3	7.3
3757M	66345M	445077M	1164766M	668057M	1278435M	Net Sales ($)	3517265M	2461810M
1410M	17366M	182152M	636434M	366817M	960408M	Total Assets ($)	1954458M	1403135M

Comparative Historical Data / Current Data Sorted by Sales

Type of Statement

4/1/08-3/31/09 ALL	4/1/09-3/31/10 ALL	4/1/10-3/31/11 ALL	Type of Statement	0-1MM	1-3MM	3-5MM	5-10MM	10-25MM	25MM & OVER
16	21	18	Unqualified			1	7	4	14
15	21	21	Reviewed					11	2
8	9	8	Compiled	1	1	2	1	2	2
3	6	13	Tax Returns	1		3	5	1	
28	31	31	Other	1	3	3	3	7	16
				21 (4/1-9/30/10)			70 (10/1/10-3/31/11)		
70	88	91	NUMBER OF STATEMENTS	3	4	9	16	25	34

Main Data

09 ALL %	10 ALL %	11 ALL %		0-1MM %	1-3MM %	3-5MM %	5-10MM %	10-25MM %	25MM & OVER %
			ASSETS						
4.7	5.3	7.8	Cash & Equivalents				14.0	7.2	5.9
26.2	25.1	27.8	Trade Receivables (net)				32.8	30.0	24.4
26.0	24.2	24.5	Inventory				18.2	25.0	27.9
2.0	2.8	1.6	All Other Current				1.2	1.5	1.7
58.9	57.5	61.8	Total Current				66.2	63.7	59.9
29.7	29.5	25.9	Fixed Assets (net)				23.0	28.3	26.6
4.8	7.9	7.2	Intangibles (net)				9.7	2.2	8.6
6.5	5.1	5.1	All Other Non-Current				1.1	5.9	4.9
100.0	100.0	100.0	Total				100.0	100.0	100.0
			LIABILITIES						
12.5	11.2	12.5	Notes Payable-Short Term				13.2	13.5	11.0
3.0	4.3	3.3	Cur. Mat.-L.T.D.				3.7	2.8	3.2
15.1	15.3	17.6	Trade Payables				19.2	24.0	12.2
.2	.1	.1	Income Taxes Payable				.2	.1	.1
7.1	9.8	6.8	All Other Current				5.5	4.8	10.8
37.8	40.7	40.3	Total Current				41.8	45.2	37.3
16.4	15.1	11.6	Long-Term Debt				9.9	8.9	12.0
.4	.7	.8	Deferred Taxes				.0	.5	1.7
5.3	7.1	6.0	All Other Non-Current				4.2	9.2	4.6
40.0	36.4	41.2	Net Worth				44.2	36.2	44.3
100.0	100.0	100.0	Total Liabilities & Net Worth				100.0	100.0	100.0
			INCOME DATA						
100.0	100.0	100.0	Net Sales				100.0	100.0	100.0
25.0	25.3	28.0	Gross Profit				33.9	24.6	21.5
21.5	23.7	22.6	Operating Expenses				28.0	21.1	14.7
3.5	1.5	5.4	Operating Profit				5.9	3.5	6.8
1.2	1.0	.7	All Other Expenses (net)				.1	1.0	1.0
2.3	.5	4.7	Profit Before Taxes				5.8	2.5	5.7
			RATIOS						
2.5	2.2	2.6	Current				2.9	3.1	2.4
1.7	1.5	1.6					1.4	1.2	1.9
1.0	1.0	1.1					1.1	1.0	1.1
1.5	1.3	1.6	Quick				2.4	1.9	1.4
.8	.7	.9					.9	.9	.7
.5	.4	.6					.6	.5	.5
30 12.0	32 11.4	35 10.5	Sales/Receivables				33 11.2	36 10.2	35 10.5
38 9.7	41 9.0	41 8.9					41 8.9	45 8.0	38 9.6
44 8.3	50 7.4	53 6.9					54 6.8	52 7.0	57 6.4
32 11.3	34 10.8	29 12.4	Cost of Sales/Inventory				26 13.8	32 11.5	49 7.4
44 8.3	48 7.6	50 7.4					34 10.7	46 7.9	63 5.8
72 5.1	72 5.1	77 4.7					40 9.1	78 4.7	88 4.1
16 23.1	18 19.8	19 18.8	Cost of Sales/Payables				21 17.2	22 16.8	18 20.2
28 13.0	31 11.6	32 11.4					38 9.6	32 11.5	29 12.4
41 8.8	53 6.8	44 8.3					44 8.3	46 7.9	37 10.0
6.6	6.0	5.3	Sales/Working Capital				7.1	4.1	5.0
10.5	13.0	10.9					17.8	13.7	8.3
365.7	NM	102.5					90.4	-132.8	32.0
7.9	5.3	25.1	EBIT/Interest				22.4	21.9	59.3
(65) 2.1	(82) 1.8	(82) 5.2					(15) 5.6	(24) 5.2	(30) 10.9
.6	-1.1	1.8					2.0	2.2	1.8
4.3	3.8	6.1	Net Profit + Depr., Dep., Amort./Cur. Mat. L/T/D						
(20) 1.6	(27) 1.8	(19) 2.3							
1.1	-.1	1.4							
.4	.5	.3	Fixed/Worth				.2	.3	.3
.8	1.2	.7					.8	1.0	.6
2.2	5.3	2.3					3.0	2.3	2.3
.6	.8	.6	Debt/Worth				.5	.7	.5
1.6	2.5	1.6					1.6	1.9	1.6
6.4	12.3	7.2					18.6	6.4	5.8
30.5	34.1	49.9	% Profit Before Taxes/Tangible Net Worth				130.5	31.7	51.8
(63) 9.2	(70) 6.8	(78) 24.0					(13) 35.4	(23) 17.6	(29) 26.1
-3.9	-7.5	5.2					7.0	5.0	9.1
12.1	7.3	18.6	% Profit Before Taxes/Total Assets				26.9	12.7	20.1
3.1	1.9	6.6					14.6	5.1	7.6
-.8	-4.8	1.8					.9	2.0	3.8
14.2	13.2	19.8	Sales/Net Fixed Assets				46.7	16.0	13.7
8.4	7.3	9.9					16.0	7.6	6.7
5.1	4.7	5.1					7.2	4.8	5.1
3.2	2.6	2.9	Sales/Total Assets				4.4	2.8	2.4
2.5	2.0	2.2					2.7	2.4	1.9
1.6	1.6	1.6					2.0	1.4	1.3
1.1	1.2	1.1	% Depr., Dep., Amort./Sales				.6	.9	1.3
(65) 1.7	(79) 2.7	(80) 2.1					(11) 1.7	(22) 2.1	(33) 2.3
3.5	3.9	3.7					2.5	3.9	3.4
2.2	1.5	1.9	% Officers', Directors' Owners' Comp/Sales				2.4		
(17) 4.4	(22) 2.4	(35) 2.7					(10) 3.9		
7.6	5.8	4.8					5.2		
2569110M	4071201M	3626437M	Net Sales ($)	1716M	6379M	37407M	120233M	416044M	3044658M
1298922M	2473815M	2164587M	Total Assets ($)	1148M	2443M	17369M	52374M	217134M	1874119M

M = $ thousand   MM = $ million
See Pages 9 through 22 for Explanation of Ratios and Data

Current Data Sorted by Assets   **Comparative Historical Data**

						Type of Statement		
		1	6	2	3	Unqualified	12	15
		10	5			Reviewed	18	14
		3	1			Compiled	6	5
	1	1	1			Tax Returns	4	2
	4	7	6		2	Other	22	16
	9 (4/1-9/30/10)		43 (10/1/10-3/31/11)				4/1/06-3/31/07 ALL	4/1/07-3/31/08 ALL
0-500M	500M-2MM	2-10MM	10-50MM	50-100MM	100-250MM			
	5	22	18	2	5	NUMBER OF STATEMENTS	62	52
%	%	%	%	%	%	ASSETS	%	%
		7.0	3.2			Cash & Equivalents	5.6	6.0
		26.1	29.2			Trade Receivables (net)	27.2	28.2
		25.9	21.3			Inventory	26.5	26.8
		1.6	5.2			All Other Current	1.8	1.3
		60.6	58.9			Total Current	61.1	62.3
		32.9	26.8			Fixed Assets (net)	29.1	28.9
		3.2	11.1			Intangibles (net)	3.3	2.6
		3.4	3.1			All Other Non-Current	6.5	6.2
		100.0	100.0			Total	100.0	100.0
						LIABILITIES		
		11.4	13.4			Notes Payable-Short Term	13.4	15.6
		5.0	4.1			Cur. Mat.-L.T.D.	3.7	4.0
		18.1	20.9			Trade Payables	20.6	20.8
		.0	.0			Income Taxes Payable	.3	.4
		8.0	7.8			All Other Current	6.6	7.0
		42.5	46.3			Total Current	44.6	47.9
		21.5	17.3			Long-Term Debt	16.5	26.0
		.8	2.0			Deferred Taxes	1.1	1.0
		6.2	3.8			All Other Non-Current	3.2	4.3
		29.0	30.6			Net Worth	34.6	20.9
		100.0	100.0			Total Liabilities & Net Worth	100.0	100.0
						INCOME DATA		
		100.0	100.0			Net Sales	100.0	100.0
		27.5	22.0			Gross Profit	22.3	23.8
		19.9	16.1			Operating Expenses	18.0	20.0
		7.7	5.9			Operating Profit	4.3	3.8
		.9	1.2			All Other Expenses (net)	1.3	1.5
		6.8	4.6			Profit Before Taxes	3.0	2.3
						RATIOS		
		2.3	1.7				2.5	1.9
		1.4	1.2			Current	1.4	1.3
		1.1	.9				1.0	1.0
		1.5	1.0				1.2	1.0
		.7	.7			Quick	.7	.6
		.5	.5				.5	.5
		30 12.1	36 10.3				30 12.0	34 10.7
		38 9.5	46 7.9			Sales/Receivables	39 9.5	41 8.9
		46 7.9	57 6.4				47 7.7	51 7.1
		33 11.0	29 12.5				33 11.0	41 8.9
		50 7.3	41 8.9			Cost of Sales/Inventory	48 7.6	55 6.6
		77 4.8	66 5.6				70 5.2	73 5.0
		22 16.4	27 13.5				21 17.0	16 22.8
		29 12.6	32 11.3			Cost of Sales/Payables	39 9.4	34 10.7
		45 8.1	56 6.5				43 8.5	56 6.5
		7.1	8.1				7.1	6.4
		17.1	22.5			Sales/Working Capital	13.5	13.7
		38.9	-38.5				-290.8	-187.1
		11.9	9.4				9.4	6.3
		(21) 5.2	5.4			EBIT/Interest	(61) 3.2	(48) 2.5
		1.9	1.5				1.5	1.5
		6.9	8.8			Net Profit + Depr., Dep.,	5.4	4.7
		(10) 3.5	(11) 4.3			Amort./Cur. Mat. L/T/D	(26) 1.9	(21) 2.5
		2.0	1.0				1.3	1.8
		.4	.6				.4	.4
		1.4	1.6			Fixed/Worth	.9	1.2
		NM	4.4				2.8	3.2
		.9	1.4				1.3	1.4
		2.9	5.2			Debt/Worth	1.9	3.2
		NM	12.8				4.8	8.3
		48.3	108.3			% Profit Before Taxes/Tangible	48.4	32.5
		(17) 28.3	(16) 18.4			Net Worth	(55) 18.1	(44) 21.1
		14.9	5.1				6.0	5.9
		18.8	18.9			% Profit Before Taxes/Total	12.5	9.5
		8.4	6.0			Assets	5.5	4.7
		2.2	-.1				1.3	1.4
		17.4	23.1				16.9	20.8
		7.6	8.0			Sales/Net Fixed Assets	7.8	8.6
		4.6	5.0				5.1	4.9
		3.2	2.7				3.1	3.0
		2.2	2.1			Sales/Total Assets	2.4	2.3
		1.7	1.8				1.8	1.8
		1.5	1.2				1.1	1.0
		2.7	(17) 2.6			% Depr., Dep., Amort./Sales	(56) 2.0	(47) 1.7
		4.1	3.4				3.2	2.9
							1.7	1.4
						% Officers', Directors'	(20) 2.4	(13) 2.3
						Owners' Comp/Sales	5.0	5.1
	21928M	336147M	820378M	215645M	994049M	Net Sales ($)	2628684M	2704115M
	6130M	140005M	373257M	152424M	601028M	Total Assets ($)	1327811M	1319824M

(First two current-data columns, 0-500M and 500M-2MM: DATA NOT AVAILABLE)

M = $ thousand   MM = $ million
See Pages 9 through 22 for Explanation of Ratios and Data

Comparative Historical Data | Current Data Sorted by Sales

			Type of Statement	0-1MM	1-3MM	3-5MM	5-10MM	10-25MM	25MM & OVER
20	14	12	Unqualified					1	11
15	12	15	Reviewed				3	10	2
7	8	4	Compiled				1	3	
2	7	2	Tax Returns					1	
19	16	19	Other		2	2	3	5	8
4/1/08-3/31/09 ALL	4/1/09-3/31/10 ALL	4/1/10-3/31/11 ALL			9 (4/1-9/30/10)			43 (10/1/10-3/31/11)	
63	57	52	**NUMBER OF STATEMENTS**		2	2	7	20	21
%	%	%	**ASSETS**	%	%	%	%	%	%
4.7	5.2	5.2	Cash & Equivalents					4.7	3.4
24.9	27.8	26.1	Trade Receivables (net)					26.3	29.2
25.2	23.3	23.5	Inventory					28.2	21.8
4.5	1.6	2.6	All Other Current					3.9	2.2
59.3	57.7	57.3	Total Current					63.0	56.6
31.9	30.3	31.3	Fixed Assets (net)					29.8	29.6
3.9	5.4	6.1	Intangibles (net)					3.6	9.1
4.8	6.6	5.2	All Other Non-Current					3.6	4.7
100.0	100.0	100.0	Total					100.0	100.0
			LIABILITIES						
15.1	13.2	10.2	Notes Payable-Short Term					12.8	11.9
7.1	5.7	4.5	Cur. Mat.-L.T.D.					5.4	3.5
16.8	19.4	19.2	Trade Payables					20.0	20.0
.4	.7	.1	Income Taxes Payable					.1	.2
9.0	8.2	7.3	All Other Current					8.6	8.3
48.3	47.2	41.4	Total Current					46.8	44.1
15.4	18.7	20.1	Long-Term Debt					20.2	12.9
1.0	1.0	1.7	Deferred Taxes					.9	3.3
5.2	7.4	4.1	All Other Non-Current					4.4	4.0
30.1	25.8	32.8	Net Worth					27.6	35.8
100.0	100.0	100.0	Total Liabilities & Net Worth					100.0	100.0
			INCOME DATA						
100.0	100.0	100.0	Net Sales					100.0	100.0
20.4	26.1	25.1	Gross Profit					24.1	20.3
17.2	22.1	18.2	Operating Expenses					15.8	15.4
3.2	3.9	6.9	Operating Profit					8.4	4.9
1.3	1.0	1.2	All Other Expenses (net)					.7	1.8
2.0	3.0	5.7	Profit Before Taxes					7.7	3.1
			RATIOS						
1.7	1.9	2.1						1.9	1.8
1.3	1.3	1.4	Current					1.2	1.2
.9	.9	1.1						1.1	1.1
.9	1.1	1.2						.8	1.1
.6	.7	.8	Quick					.6	.8
.4	.5	.5						.5	.5
30 12.0	32 11.3	31 11.9						35 10.5	31 11.9
37 9.9	41 8.8	40 9.1	Sales/Receivables					40 9.1	40 9.1
46 8.0	52 7.0	52 7.0						49 7.4	57 6.4
31 11.8	28 12.9	31 11.8						40 9.1	34 10.6
53 6.9	48 7.6	45 8.1	Cost of Sales/Inventory					59 6.1	44 8.4
69 5.3	73 5.0	67 5.4						78 4.7	59 6.2
20 18.5	19 19.2	24 15.1						23 16.0	27 13.4
31 11.6	32 11.5	30 12.1	Cost of Sales/Payables					31 11.7	31 11.7
37 9.8	58 6.3	48 7.6						55 6.6	46 7.9
8.3	7.9	8.0						8.1	8.2
25.1	19.1	16.9	Sales/Working Capital					19.9	18.8
-47.1	-91.8	52.0						52.7	80.2
5.3	12.4	12.9						13.1	9.0
(62) 3.0	(53) 5.0	(51) 5.2	EBIT/Interest					(19) 8.3	4.7
.9	1.8	1.8						2.2	1.3
3.9	5.2	6.6						6.9	4.2
(32) 2.1	(24) 2.6	(26) 3.2	Net Profit + Depr., Dep., Amort./Cur. Mat. L/T/D					(11) 4.4	(12) 2.5
1.2	1.2	1.9						2.3	1.5
.4	.3	.5						.5	.6
1.3	1.1	1.3	Fixed/Worth					1.3	1.4
3.9	5.1	3.7						5.6	1.9
1.1	1.0	1.0						1.2	1.3
3.0	2.5	2.9	Debt/Worth					3.0	2.2
10.7	14.9	7.9						9.9	9.2
29.4	37.5	43.8						54.2	34.0
(52) 16.8	(44) 16.0	(44) 23.2	% Profit Before Taxes/Tangible Net Worth					(16) 32.5	(19) 13.9
2.8	6.5	9.3						15.7	6.0
9.1	12.9	18.0						24.1	9.1
4.6	7.5	7.2	% Profit Before Taxes/Total Assets					9.4	5.9
-.3	2.5	2.1						2.6	.3
13.5	19.4	17.2						18.7	17.3
8.7	8.6	7.6	Sales/Net Fixed Assets					7.6	8.2
5.3	4.0	4.4						4.4	4.1
2.9	3.0	2.8						2.7	2.8
2.3	2.1	2.1	Sales/Total Assets					2.1	2.2
1.9	1.5	1.7						1.8	1.7
1.3	1.3	1.3						1.6	1.3
(59) 2.1	(50) 2.9	(49) 2.5	% Depr., Dep., Amort./Sales					(18) 2.8	2.3
3.7	4.8	3.6						4.2	3.1
1.9	1.6	.9							
(20) 2.3	(17) 2.3	(16) 2.0	% Officers', Directors' Owners' Comp/Sales						
3.4	5.7	4.5							
3594568M	2683410M	2388147M	Net Sales ($)		5268M	7596M	52392M	337310M	1985581M
1693785M	1400840M	1272844M	Total Assets ($)		2785M	7453M	28134M	153035M	1081437M

(In the Current Data Sorted by Sales section, the 0-1MM through 5-10MM columns for the ASSETS, LIABILITIES and INCOME DATA sections are marked "DATA NOT AVAILABLE.")

© RMA 2011

M = $ thousand   MM = $ million

See Pages 9 through 22 for Explanation of Ratios and Data

Current Data Sorted by Assets							Comparative Historical Data	
			1	5	2	1	**Type of Statement**	
		1	5	5			Unqualified	9	11
	1	1	1				Reviewed	9	8
1	1						Compiled	5	3
							Tax Returns	2	1
		1	5		3		Other	13	11
	9 (4/1-9/30/10)		24 (10/1/10-3/31/11)					4/1/06-3/31/07	4/1/07-3/31/08
0-500M	500M-2MM	2-10MM	10-50MM	50-100MM	100-250MM			ALL	ALL
1	3	8	15	2	4	**NUMBER OF STATEMENTS**	38	34
%	%	%	%	%	%	**ASSETS**	%	%
			4.9			Cash & Equivalents	6.0	7.4
			30.4			Trade Receivables (net)	30.2	28.4
			20.7			Inventory	15.1	16.9
			.8			All Other Current	2.4	1.0
			56.8			Total Current	53.7	53.7
			37.5			Fixed Assets (net)	39.9	39.4
			2.5			Intangibles (net)	1.6	2.2
			3.2			All Other Non-Current	4.8	4.6
			100.0			Total	100.0	100.0
						LIABILITIES		
			11.0			Notes Payable-Short Term	11.2	7.8
			6.7			Cur. Mat.-L.T.D.	5.2	5.9
			11.2			Trade Payables	13.4	15.0
			.1			Income Taxes Payable	.2	.0
			6.7			All Other Current	7.9	8.1
			35.6			Total Current	37.9	36.9
			27.3			Long-Term Debt	25.1	32.1
			1.8			Deferred Taxes	.8	.5
			8.1			All Other Non-Current	4.4	6.0
			27.1			Net Worth	31.9	24.5
			100.0			Total Liabilties & Net Worth	100.0	100.0
						INCOME DATA		
			100.0			Net Sales	100.0	100.0
			20.4			Gross Profit	26.2	24.6
			16.6			Operating Expenses	21.2	19.6
			3.8			Operating Profit	5.0	4.9
			1.2			All Other Expenses (net)	.6	1.2
			2.5			Profit Before Taxes	4.3	3.7
						RATIOS		
			2.4				2.8	1.9
			1.4			Current	1.3	1.3
			1.2				1.0	1.0
			1.6				1.8	1.2
			.9			Quick	1.0	.9
			.7				.6	.7
		38	9.6				42	8.8	36	10.2
		47	7.7			Sales/Receivables	48	7.5	42	8.6
		64	5.7				52	7.0	51	7.1
		28	13.0				17	21.3	21	17.6
		38	9.7			Cost of Sales/Inventory	29	12.4	32	11.5
		78	4.7				43	8.5	51	7.2
		18	20.0				14	26.6	19	19.2
		23	16.1			Cost of Sales/Payables	26	14.2	26	14.1
		28	13.0				37	10.0	39	9.3
			4.6				6.4	7.6
			13.0			Sales/Working Capital	19.5	19.5
			31.2				NM	975.7
			7.8				7.4	5.9
			3.5			EBIT/Interest	(34) 2.8	(33) 3.1
			2.0				1.1	1.1
						Net Profit + Depr., Dep.,	4.0	4.6
						Amort./Cur. Mat. L/T/D	(10) 2.2	(10) 2.6
							1.2	1.7
			.7				.8	.7
			1.5			Fixed/Worth	1.2	1.2
			4.0				3.8	-236.7
			1.4				.9	1.2
			2.2			Debt/Worth	1.9	2.7
			11.1				7.1	-475.7
			51.3			% Profit Before Taxes/Tangible	32.2	41.8
		(13)	22.9			Net Worth	(32) 16.2	(25) 24.6
			3.2				5.2	14.7
			8.6				13.1	13.0
			5.3			% Profit Before Taxes/Total	6.3	5.5
			.3			Assets	.7	.6
			10.1				9.1	10.8
			6.7			Sales/Net Fixed Assets	5.1	6.0
			3.4				3.5	3.7
			2.7				2.7	2.8
			2.0			Sales/Total Assets	2.1	2.2
			1.7				1.8	1.8
			2.3				2.2	2.1
		(13)	3.1			% Depr., Dep., Amort./Sales	(37) 2.9	(32) 2.8
			5.3				3.6	4.3
						% Officers', Directors'	2.7	
						Owners' Comp/Sales	(10) 6.4	
							7.3	
1167M	11666M	140296M	679102M	359897M	2148647M	Net Sales ($)	1201691M	1206123M
445M	3616M	53188M	337381M	139557M	897902M	Total Assets ($)	606659M	554736M

M = $ thousand   MM = $ million
See Pages 9 through 22 for Explanation of Ratios and Data

Comparative Historical Data | Current Data Sorted by Sales

			Type of Statement	0-1MM	1-3MM	3-5MM	5-10MM	10-25MM	25MM & OVER
9	8	9	Unqualified					1	8
7	13	11	Reviewed				2	7	2
5	2	2	Compiled			1		1	
8	5	2	Tax Returns						
10	12	9	Other	2			1	1	7
4/1/08-3/31/09 ALL	4/1/09-3/31/10 ALL	4/1/10-3/31/11 ALL			9 (4/1-9/30/10)		24 (10/1/10-3/31/11)		
39	40	33	**NUMBER OF STATEMENTS**	2		1	3	10	17
%	%	%	**ASSETS**	%	%	%	%	%	%
5.0	6.5	7.1	Cash & Equivalents					10.9	3.6
35.6	33.8	33.3	Trade Receivables (net)					26.5	35.5
17.0	18.3	19.7	Inventory					15.0	23.2
2.4	1.8	1.7	All Other Current					1.3	2.1
60.0	60.4	61.7	Total Current					53.7	64.4
33.0	34.2	31.1	Fixed Assets (net)					39.8	28.2
2.2	2.3	3.5	Intangibles (net)					4.1	3.9
4.8	3.1	3.8	All Other Non-Current					2.4	3.5
100.0	100.0	100.0	Total					100.0	100.0
			LIABILITIES						
15.2	16.7	11.2	Notes Payable-Short Term					9.6	15.5
6.4	4.7	6.9	Cur. Mat.-L.T.D.					5.0	5.2
21.9	24.0	14.5	Trade Payables					8.1	16.9
.0	.0	.5	Income Taxes Payable					.3	.0
9.4	10.4	7.4	All Other Current					6.5	8.3
53.0	55.8	40.5	Total Current					29.4	45.9
26.2	28.1	24.7	Long-Term Debt					19.3	23.1
.5	.9	1.2	Deferred Taxes					2.7	.7
9.9	7.0	8.1	All Other Non-Current					1.8	10.2
10.3	8.2	25.5	Net Worth					46.8	20.0
100.0	100.0	100.0	Total Liabilities & Net Worth					100.0	100.0
			INCOME DATA						
100.0	100.0	100.0	Net Sales					100.0	100.0
23.1	22.4	25.6	Gross Profit					29.7	19.0
21.6	21.1	22.9	Operating Expenses					23.4	17.9
1.5	1.3	2.6	Operating Profit					6.3	1.1
1.5	.8	.7	All Other Expenses (net)					.9	1.4
.0	.5	1.9	Profit Before Taxes					5.4	-.3
			RATIOS						
2.1	2.1	2.5						3.5	2.1
1.3	1.3	1.4	Current					2.2	1.4
.9	.9	1.1						1.1	1.1
1.4	1.5	1.7						2.5	1.2
.8	.8	.9	Quick					1.7	.9
.6	.6	.7						.7	.7
36 10.2	40 9.0	38 9.5						36 10.2	41 8.8
45 8.2	49 7.4	48 7.6	Sales/Receivables					41 9.0	48 7.6
50 7.3	58 6.3	58 6.3						55 6.7	59 6.2
17 22.0	16 22.5	29 12.6						19 19.2	31 11.7
23 15.7	33 10.9	38 9.7	Cost of Sales/Inventory					35 10.4	40 9.2
44 8.3	53 6.9	49 7.4						45 8.2	57 6.4
18 20.6	19 19.2	18 20.5						11 31.8	19 19.7
26 14.3	28 12.9	23 15.8	Cost of Sales/Payables					18 20.5	23 15.8
36 10.0	51 7.2	35 10.4						26 14.2	32 11.5
8.7	8.2	5.1						5.8	5.7
18.1	23.0	13.0	Sales/Working Capital					7.5	14.2
-92.6	-54.4	50.7						87.5	44.6
1.8	3.1	9.2						34.5	8.4
(33) 1.3	(37) 1.6	(31) 4.0	EBIT/Interest					6.6	(16) 3.8
.2	-1.3	2.0						2.8	.0
3.1		3.4							
(10) 1.3		(16) 2.2	Net Profit + Depr., Dep., Amort./Cur. Mat. L/T/D						
1.0		1.3							
.7	.6	.6						.5	.7
1.8	1.6	1.4	Fixed/Worth					.9	1.7
6.0	NM	4.9						2.9	4.9
1.3	1.3	1.2						.4	1.9
3.8	2.7	3.3	Debt/Worth					1.1	5.1
19.2	NM	12.5						6.3	16.8
16.2	22.2	40.6							46.0
(31) 3.4	(30) 5.8	(27) 20.2	% Profit Before Taxes/Tangible Net Worth						(14) 24.3
-13.7	-12.5	.8							-9.1
3.5	6.4	9.4						14.6	8.6
1.1	1.7	5.1	% Profit Before Taxes/Total Assets					4.8	5.3
-2.8	-4.4	-1.2						4.2	-6.6
16.1	14.1	12.6						12.2	12.6
9.6	8.6	8.8	Sales/Net Fixed Assets					4.8	9.8
4.1	4.6	4.5						3.3	6.9
3.5	2.9	2.9						2.9	2.9
2.9	2.5	2.5	Sales/Total Assets					2.0	2.6
2.2	1.9	1.9						1.6	2.0
1.5	1.7	1.7						1.8	1.7
(34) 2.3	(33) 2.3	(26) 2.4	% Depr., Dep., Amort./Sales					3.0	(13) 2.2
3.8	3.4	3.8						4.3	3.3
2.6	1.9								
(13) 5.1	(12) 4.2		% Officers', Directors' Owners' Comp/Sales						
7.1	7.9								
1250840M	1796028M	3340775M	Net Sales ($)	2610M		4088M	19391M	175840M	3138846M
517883M	704963M	1432089M	Total Assets ($)	1521M		1594M	44724M	86170M	1298080M

M = $ thousand   MM = $ million
See Pages 9 through 22 for Explanation of Ratios and Data

Current Data Sorted by Assets   **Comparative Historical Data**

0-500M	500M-2MM	2-10MM	10-50MM	50-100MM	100-250MM	Type of Statement	4/1/06-3/31/07 ALL	4/1/07-3/31/08 ALL
	1	1	1	3	2	Unqualified	13	15
	4		2			Reviewed	3	4
2	2	1	3			Compiled	3	4
	2	1	2			Tax Returns	2	
	5 (4/1-9/30/10)	7	40 (10/1/10-3/31/11)	5	6	Other	7	9
2	**5**	**9**	**13**	**8**	**8**	**NUMBER OF STATEMENTS**	**28**	**32**
%	%	%	%	%	%	**ASSETS**	%	%
			6.8			Cash & Equivalents	8.4	7.9
			16.0			Trade Receivables (net)	23.1	23.4
			21.6			Inventory	20.6	21.7
			1.6			All Other Current	1.6	5.7
			45.9			Total Current	53.8	58.7
			49.2			Fixed Assets (net)	35.4	31.6
			.3			Intangibles (net)	6.9	2.5
			4.5			All Other Non-Current	3.9	7.3
			100.0			Total	100.0	100.0
						LIABILITIES		
			6.3			Notes Payable-Short Term	8.1	8.6
			5.1			Cur. Mat.-L.T.D.	2.2	3.2
			16.4			Trade Payables	17.6	14.7
			.0			Income Taxes Payable	.2	.1
			3.6			All Other Current	6.9	7.9
			31.5			Total Current	34.9	34.5
			29.0			Long-Term Debt	21.9	23.2
			.1			Deferred Taxes	1.5	1.2
			2.6			All Other Non-Current	1.8	2.0
			36.8			Net Worth	39.9	39.2
			100.0			Total Liabilities & Net Worth	100.0	100.0
						INCOME DATA		
			100.0			Net Sales	100.0	100.0
			22.6			Gross Profit	22.2	25.1
			13.6			Operating Expenses	14.4	18.5
			9.0			Operating Profit	7.8	6.5
			1.9			All Other Expenses (net)	1.4	.9
			7.1			Profit Before Taxes	6.4	5.7
						RATIOS		
			1.9				2.4	3.2
			1.4			Current	1.7	1.9
			1.0				1.1	1.2
			1.2				1.5	1.7
			.8			Quick	.8	.8
			.4				.5	.4
			15 24.6				**29** 12.6	**30** 12.3
			28 13.3			Sales/Receivables	**34** 10.6	**33** 10.9
			33 11.0				**45** 8.1	**45** 8.2
			25 14.8				**26** 13.9	**26** 14.1
			42 8.7			Cost of Sales/Inventory	**49** 7.5	**49** 7.5
			69 5.3				**66** 5.5	**62** 5.9
			22 16.6				**24** 14.9	**26** 13.9
			34 10.9			Cost of Sales/Payables	**37** 9.9	**33** 11.1
			49 7.5				**48** 7.6	**48** 7.5
			8.4				6.8	4.4
			22.8			Sales/Working Capital	9.7	9.0
			NM				64.3	20.6
			14.7				9.7	9.3
			6.0			EBIT/Interest	(24) 4.6	(30) 4.6
			3.0				2.4	2.5
						Net Profit + Depr., Dep., Amort./Cur. Mat. L/T/D		
			.6				.4	.2
			1.6			Fixed/Worth	1.1	.8
			3.3				2.5	2.0
			.8				.9	.8
			2.3			Debt/Worth	2.0	2.0
			3.0				3.6	3.4
			56.7				53.3	44.5
			31.6			% Profit Before Taxes/Tangible Net Worth	(24) 36.4	(30) 34.6
			20.6				11.6	10.0
			19.2				17.3	14.1
			9.8			% Profit Before Taxes/Total Assets	9.0	8.6
			6.9				4.0	4.9
			11.4				40.3	21.0
			5.0			Sales/Net Fixed Assets	4.5	7.1
			1.2				3.0	4.3
			2.7				2.7	2.3
			2.2			Sales/Total Assets	2.0	2.1
			1.0				1.5	1.4
			2.3				.5	1.0
			2.5			% Depr., Dep., Amort./Sales	(21) 2.1	(24) 1.7
			5.3				3.7	3.5
						% Officers', Directors' Owners' Comp/Sales		
1027M	14696M	110376M	629178M	928746M	2063850M	Net Sales ($)	2604322M	3392173M
411M	7333M	46427M	336258M	552496M	1365617M	Total Assets ($)	1633511M	1792171M

M = $ thousand   MM = $ million
See Pages 9 through 22 for Explanation of Ratios and Data

Comparative Historical Data / Current Data Sorted by Sales

			Type of Statement	0-1MM	1-3MM	3-5MM	5-10MM	10-25MM	25MM & OVER
12	14	8	Unqualified			1	1	2	5
6	4	6	Reviewed		1			2	2
5	6	8	Compiled	2	2	1	1	2	2
2		1	Tax Returns			1		1	
7	10	22	Other					1	18
4/1/08-3/31/09 ALL	4/1/09-3/31/10 ALL	4/1/10-3/31/11 ALL				5 (4/1-9/30/10)		40 (10/1/10-3/31/11)	
32	34	45	NUMBER OF STATEMENTS	2	3	3	2	8	27
%	%	%	**ASSETS**	%	%	%	%	%	%
7.7	5.2	6.1	Cash & Equivalents						4.9
24.8	20.9	20.9	Trade Receivables (net)						16.9
23.4	19.9	22.0	Inventory						21.0
5.7	4.3	2.1	All Other Current						2.7
61.6	50.4	51.1	Total Current						45.4
34.4	39.5	40.9	Fixed Assets (net)						45.4
.9	6.1	3.9	Intangibles (net)						5.9
3.1	4.1	4.1	All Other Non-Current						3.3
100.0	100.0	100.0	Total						100.0
			LIABILITIES						
9.1	6.4	7.3	Notes Payable-Short Term						5.4
3.2	4.0	4.4	Cur. Mat.-L.T.D.						4.8
16.4	14.4	16.3	Trade Payables						14.4
.1	.1	.0	Income Taxes Payable						.0
7.4	7.1	7.4	All Other Current						6.1
36.2	32.0	35.4	Total Current						30.8
20.2	22.5	23.0	Long-Term Debt						27.7
1.1	1.2	1.9	Deferred Taxes						2.9
1.9	2.3	3.6	All Other Non-Current						3.7
40.7	42.0	36.0	Net Worth						35.0
100.0	100.0	100.0	Total Liabilities & Net Worth						100.0
			INCOME DATA						
100.0	100.0	100.0	Net Sales						100.0
23.5	25.0	21.8	Gross Profit						18.9
17.6	14.0	15.3	Operating Expenses						13.1
6.0	11.0	6.5	Operating Profit						5.7
1.1	1.4	1.6	All Other Expenses (net)						1.9
4.9	9.6	4.8	Profit Before Taxes						3.9
			RATIOS						
2.4	2.2	2.1							2.1
1.5	1.7	1.4	Current						1.5
1.2	1.1	.9							1.1
1.4	1.3	1.1							1.1
.8	.8	.8	Quick						.8
.5	.5	.5							.3
27 13.5	26 14.0	23 16.2							21 17.3
33 11.0	32 11.3	30 12.0	Sales/Receivables						28 13.3
42 8.8	45 8.2	41 8.9							34 10.8
28 13.3	29 12.5	37 9.7							36 10.1
53 6.9	48 7.6	50 7.4	Cost of Sales/Inventory						50 7.4
84 4.3	75 4.8	72 5.1							66 5.5
20 18.2	19 19.1	20 18.7							24 14.9
31 11.7	35 10.4	34 10.9	Cost of Sales/Payables						30 12.3
54 6.7	46 8.0	47 7.8							44 8.4
6.1	6.7	7.5							7.8
11.5	12.5	15.0	Sales/Working Capital						15.0
22.0	36.1	-43.6							38.7
10.3	18.0	11.5							7.3
(27) 6.6	(31) 10.5	(43) 4.7	EBIT/Interest						3.2
2.0	4.0	1.8							1.4
		11.1							16.6
	(13) 3.1		Net Profit + Depr., Dep., Amort./Cur. Mat. L/T/D					(10) 2.4	
		1.3							1.2
.2	.6	.5							.6
.9	1.0	1.5	Fixed/Worth						1.6
1.7	2.4	3.0							3.5
.7	.8	1.0							.8
1.8	1.7	2.3	Debt/Worth						2.3
3.9	3.2	4.4							4.8
68.8	60.8	35.4							27.8
28.5	(32) 46.6	(42) 16.2	% Profit Before Taxes/Tangible Net Worth					(24) 14.8	
9.5	26.2	6.1							1.0
20.5	21.1	13.2							12.8
10.7	12.5	5.6	% Profit Before Taxes/Total Assets						4.3
3.7	7.7	2.3							2.2
43.1	15.4	14.7							8.2
7.1	5.7	5.0	Sales/Net Fixed Assets						4.2
3.4	2.7	3.0							3.0
2.8	3.0	2.6							2.3
2.2	2.1	2.1	Sales/Total Assets						1.9
1.4	1.0	1.3							1.3
.9	1.3	1.9							2.2
(22) 2.0	(29) 2.5	(39) 2.7	% Depr., Dep., Amort./Sales					(23) 2.7	
3.8	4.2	5.6							5.1
			% Officers', Directors' Owners' Comp/Sales						
2601282M	3400060M	3747873M	Net Sales ($)	1027M	6106M	12125M	14918M	121322M	3592375M
1475813M	2108431M	2308542M	Total Assets ($)	411M	4039M	7886M	5272M	70040M	2220894M

M = $ thousand   MM = $ million
See Pages 9 through 22 for Explanation of Ratios and Data

Current Data Sorted by Assets | Comparative Historical Data

						Type of Statement		
		2	14	7	7	Unqualified	31	30
		21	4			Reviewed	23	24
1	3	8	1			Compiled	12	10
2	6	2				Tax Returns	5	4
	3	13	10	3	2	Other	35	36
	20 (4/1-9/30/10)		89 (10/1/10-3/31/11)				4/1/06-3/31/07	4/1/07-3/31/08
0-500M	500M-2MM	2-10MM	10-50MM	50-100MM	100-250MM		ALL	ALL
3	12	46	29	10	9	NUMBER OF STATEMENTS	106	104
%	%	%	%	%	%	ASSETS	%	%
	13.3	9.8	5.8	3.6		Cash & Equivalents	4.7	5.3
	29.1	24.4	21.9	16.6		Trade Receivables (net)	25.4	23.7
	18.9	26.2	27.0	29.1		Inventory	26.0	23.5
	5.8	1.6	1.8	1.1		All Other Current	1.7	1.6
	67.1	62.0	56.5	50.3		Total Current	57.8	54.0
	26.9	28.2	31.0	35.9		Fixed Assets (net)	33.1	35.4
	1.8	3.9	6.4	9.4		Intangibles (net)	3.2	4.5
	4.2	5.9	6.1	4.5		All Other Non-Current	5.9	6.1
	100.0	100.0	100.0	100.0		Total	100.0	100.0
						LIABILITIES		
	8.9	9.6	10.4	10.6		Notes Payable-Short Term	12.2	11.0
	1.4	3.5	4.1	4.0		Cur. Mat.-L.T.D.	4.4	4.4
	9.9	16.6	17.2	10.2		Trade Payables	15.9	13.5
	.7	.0	.0	.2		Income Taxes Payable	.2	.1
	7.2	7.8	6.0	6.5		All Other Current	8.8	7.7
	28.2	37.5	37.7	31.6		Total Current	41.5	36.7
	14.6	14.4	20.4	16.2		Long-Term Debt	17.6	20.3
	.1	.3	1.6	.1		Deferred Taxes	.5	.4
	8.8	5.5	4.3	1.6		All Other Non-Current	6.7	3.1
	48.3	42.3	36.0	50.6		Net Worth	33.6	39.5
	100.0	100.0	100.0	100.0		Total Liabilties & Net Worth	100.0	100.0
						INCOME DATA		
	100.0	100.0	100.0	100.0		Net Sales	100.0	100.0
	30.7	26.4	20.5	19.3		Gross Profit	23.1	24.9
	25.8	20.1	14.5	12.9		Operating Expenses	19.0	19.7
	4.9	6.3	5.9	6.4		Operating Profit	4.2	5.2
	-1.1	.5	1.7	.5		All Other Expenses (net)	1.3	1.4
	6.0	5.8	4.3	5.9		Profit Before Taxes	2.9	3.8
						RATIOS		
	4.3	2.9	2.1	2.2			2.1	2.3
	2.5	1.6	1.5	1.6		Current	1.3	1.4
	1.6	1.1	1.1	1.2			1.0	1.0
	2.6	1.6	1.2	1.2			1.1	1.2
	1.4	.9	.8	.8		Quick	.7	.8
	1.1	.5	.5	.2			.5	.5

												Sales/Receivables				
		22	16.8	27	13.6	32	11.4	27	13.3			Sales/Receivables	30	12.4	30	12.0
		35	10.4	38	9.6	39	9.3	35	10.4				38	9.6	38	9.7
		48	7.6	49	7.5	51	7.2	44	8.3				47	7.7	48	7.6
		8	44.8	24	15.3	30	12.1	40	9.0			Cost of Sales/Inventory	29	12.7	31	11.7
		23	15.9	49	7.4	46	7.9	66	5.5				48	7.6	49	7.4
		53	6.9	79	4.6	78	4.7	95	3.8				77	4.8	69	5.3
		3	115.0	20	17.9	19	19.5	16	22.2			Cost of Sales/Payables	17	21.3	16	22.7
		10	35.3	30	12.2	30	12.2	29	12.7				28	12.9	25	14.4
		25	14.8	41	8.9	55	6.6	36	10.2				43	8.4	41	9.0

								Sales/Working Capital		
	5.6	4.8	7.0	6.7		Sales/Working Capital	7.4	6.9
	6.3	11.8	13.3	8.9			16.6	13.7
	15.9	80.2	91.0	NM			-418.6	NM

									EBIT/Interest				
		37.3		15.7		23.3		26.3			6.0		8.6
	(11)	4.8	(43)	7.0	(26)	5.1		8.9	EBIT/Interest	(100)	2.7	(96)	3.6
		2.2		3.9		2.5		2.4			1.4		1.6

									Net Profit + Depr., Dep., Amort./Cur. Mat. L/T/D				
											2.8		6.0
									Net Profit + Depr., Dep., Amort./Cur. Mat. L/T/D	(35)	2.1	(27)	2.4
											.8		1.2

								Fixed/Worth		
	.1	.3	.5	.3		Fixed/Worth	.4	.6
	.4	.6	1.1	.6			.9	.9
	1.3	2.6	3.3	1.4			3.3	2.9
	.3	.6	.8	.7		Debt/Worth	.7	.7
	1.1	1.5	2.4	1.5			1.9	1.6
	3.4	5.2	6.8	2.1			5.5	5.3

									% Profit Before Taxes/Tangible Net Worth				
		68.1		46.0		52.7		59.1			33.4		49.1
	(11)	28.2	(40)	24.3	(26)	31.9		20.0	% Profit Before Taxes/Tangible Net Worth	(91)	16.4	(92)	20.1
		12.4		10.9		11.4		9.5			6.0		9.5

								% Profit Before Taxes/Total Assets		
	27.2	19.4	15.8	20.3		% Profit Before Taxes/Total Assets	12.0	16.0
	11.2	10.2	8.5	9.0			5.3	6.6
	2.0	5.6	2.9	4.7			1.4	2.7
	61.0	20.2	15.1	12.8		Sales/Net Fixed Assets	15.1	13.2
	14.2	11.6	9.2	9.5			9.4	7.0
	6.1	4.3	5.5	2.1			4.2	3.7
	3.8	3.0	3.0	2.1		Sales/Total Assets	3.3	3.0
	3.0	2.3	2.3	1.8			2.2	2.1
	2.2	1.6	1.4	1.3			1.6	1.6

									% Depr., Dep., Amort./Sales				
		.9		.9		1.0					1.3		1.2
	(11)	1.5	(42)	2.2	(28)	1.9			% Depr., Dep., Amort./Sales	(102)	2.1	(92)	2.4
		4.3		3.8		4.0					3.6		3.4

									% Officers', Directors' Owners' Comp/Sales				
											.9		1.2
									% Officers', Directors' Owners' Comp/Sales	(26)	1.5	(22)	1.7
											4.2		4.2

3583M	41256M	607688M	1416694M	1141825M	2949618M	Net Sales ($)	4500073M	4915119M
583M	12853M	235236M	600166M	667781M	1531220M	Total Assets ($)	2207989M	2567214M

M = $ thousand   MM = $ million
See Pages 9 through 22 for Explanation of Ratios and Data

Comparative Historical Data | Current Data Sorted by Sales

Type of Statement	4/1/08-3/31/09	4/1/09-3/31/10	4/1/10-3/31/11	0-1MM	1-3MM	3-5MM	5-10MM	10-25MM	25MM & OVER
Unqualified	31	30	30				8	4	26
Reviewed	17	17	25		2	2	8	10	3
Compiled	11	9	13	1	2	2	4	4	
Tax Returns	6	9	10	1	5	1	1	2	
Other	52	48	31	1		3	5	7	15
	ALL	ALL	ALL	20 (4/1-9/30/10)			89 (10/1/10-3/31/11)		
NUMBER OF STATEMENTS	117	113	109	3	9	8	18	27	44

ASSETS	%	%	%	%	%	%	%	%	%
Cash & Equivalents	4.4	7.5	8.9				8.1	7.8	6.8
Trade Receivables (net)	23.7	27.0	23.3				22.6	25.8	21.7
Inventory	28.4	24.6	24.7				24.5	25.6	26.1
All Other Current	2.1	1.8	2.0				1.6	2.0	1.5
Total Current	58.6	60.8	58.8				56.8	61.2	56.2
Fixed Assets (net)	30.9	29.0	29.6				32.9	28.4	29.9
Intangibles (net)	5.1	5.8	6.2				4.9	5.5	8.5
All Other Non-Current	5.4	4.4	5.4				5.3	5.0	5.4
Total	100.0	100.0	100.0				100.0	100.0	100.0

LIABILITIES									
Notes Payable-Short Term	14.5	10.5	10.6				9.7	10.0	11.9
Cur. Mat.-L.T.D.	4.6	4.3	3.6				4.5	2.5	3.6
Trade Payables	15.6	17.1	16.2				13.4	18.3	18.0
Income Taxes Payable	.0	.1	.1				.0	.0	.1
All Other Current	8.8	7.8	6.9				6.7	6.4	6.6
Total Current	43.5	39.8	37.5				34.2	37.3	40.2
Long-Term Debt	17.2	17.3	17.9				20.1	10.9	19.5
Deferred Taxes	.5	.5	.7				.3	.3	1.4
All Other Non-Current	5.0	5.9	5.9				13.1	1.0	4.7
Net Worth	33.7	36.5	37.9				32.4	50.4	34.1
Total Liabilties & Net Worth	100.0	100.0	100.0				100.0	100.0	100.0

INCOME DATA									
Net Sales	100.0	100.0	100.0				100.0	100.0	100.0
Gross Profit	23.3	23.7	24.4				26.9	24.3	19.5
Operating Expenses	20.4	19.2	18.7				21.8	18.4	14.5
Operating Profit	2.9	4.5	5.7				5.1	5.9	4.9
All Other Expenses (net)	1.0	1.4	.8				1.4	.4	1.0
Profit Before Taxes	1.9	3.1	4.9				3.7	5.5	3.9

RATIOS									
Current	2.2	2.5	2.4				2.5	2.6	2.1
	1.4	1.7	1.6				1.6	1.4	1.6
	1.1	1.1	1.1				1.1	1.2	1.0
Quick	1.0	1.4	1.4				1.6	1.5	1.2
	.7	.8	.9				1.0	.9	.8
	.4	.5	.5				.5	.5	.5
Sales/Receivables	30 12.3	30 12.0	27 13.5				23 15.6	28 12.8	24 14.9
	37 9.8	40 9.1	37 9.9				40 9.1	39 9.3	35 10.3
	51 7.1	48 7.5	48 7.7				54 6.7	48 7.5	43 8.4
Cost of Sales/Inventory	33 11.0	27 13.7	28 13.0				31 11.9	24 15.5	33 11.1
	55 6.7	44 8.2	46 7.9				47 7.8	39 9.3	48 7.6
	82 4.4	76 4.8	78 4.7				84 4.3	77 4.8	78 4.7
Cost of Sales/Payables	16 22.9	19 18.9	17 21.0				15 25.2	15 24.8	22 16.9
	29 12.8	29 12.7	29 12.8				29 12.4	30 12.2	29 12.6
	46 7.9	44 8.3	44 8.2				36 10.0	45 8.1	45 8.0
Sales/Working Capital	7.0	6.2	6.1				4.8	7.8	6.9
	15.3	10.1	10.8				9.5	13.3	10.1
	134.1	54.4	73.1				91.3	24.7	282.5
EBIT/Interest	5.1	9.3	21.0				7.5	42.6	16.5
	(108) 1.9	(102) 3.9	(100) 6.1				4.9	(24) 10.1	(41) 7.0
	.3	1.8	2.7				3.7	3.5	2.7
Net Profit + Depr., Dep., Amort./Cur. Mat. L/T/D	5.3	6.3	7.9						
	(28) 1.7	(24) 3.3	(16) 3.4						
	.3	1.7	1.3						
Fixed/Worth	.4	.3	.3				.3	.3	.4
	1.0	.8	.8				1.4	.6	.9
	3.0	2.5	2.7				NM	1.6	2.9
Debt/Worth	.8	.7	.7				1.0	.6	.7
	2.3	2.1	1.7				2.4	1.3	2.0
	6.5	5.5	6.1				NM	2.9	6.3
% Profit Before Taxes/Tangible Net Worth	39.3	47.6	51.6				51.6	43.3	52.7
	(98) 14.3	(100) 24.9	(94) 26.1				(14) 17.3	(26) 25.4	(37) 28.4
	1.1	8.7	10.8				10.5	8.9	12.8
% Profit Before Taxes/Total Assets	10.1	15.5	16.8				13.7	21.2	15.6
	3.2	7.2	8.6				8.5	8.9	8.4
	-2.0	2.7	3.7				4.2	3.6	4.0
Sales/Net Fixed Assets	16.3	30.6	18.2				18.2	29.2	16.0
	8.6	10.5	10.0				11.7	10.4	10.1
	4.0	4.1	4.0				3.9	4.8	4.4
Sales/Total Assets	3.1	3.0	3.0				2.6	3.0	3.1
	2.1	2.2	2.2				2.0	2.4	2.2
	1.5	1.5	1.5				1.5	1.7	1.4
% Depr., Dep., Amort./Sales	1.0	1.1	1.0				1.3	.9	1.1
	(104) 1.7	(94) 2.2	(97) 2.0				(17) 2.5	(23) 1.9	(40) 1.9
	3.4	4.8	3.9				6.0	4.0	3.1
% Officers', Directors' Owners' Comp/Sales	1.2	1.9	2.3						
	(21) 2.3	(26) 2.9	(22) 3.3						
	4.4	6.0	6.2						
Net Sales ($)	6509702M	5583491M	6160664M	1910M	21180M	30692M	127232M	464607M	5515043M
Total Assets ($)	3468812M	2820257M	3047839M	949M	12741M	26322M	81432M	211213M	2715182M

M = $ thousand   MM = $ million
See Pages 9 through 22 for Explanation of Ratios and Data

Current Data Sorted by Assets   Comparative Historical Data

						Type of Statement		
	4	22	45	3	3	Unqualified	92	85
	16	85	34			Reviewed	179	158
12	43	48	2			Compiled	103	94
31	57	20	4			Tax Returns	85	75
21	54	87	49	11	6	Other	240	253
	129 (4/1-9/30/10)		528 (10/1/10-3/31/11)				4/1/06-3/31/07	4/1/07-3/31/08
0-500M	500M-2MM	2-10MM	10-50MM	50-100MM	100-250MM		ALL	ALL
64	174	262	134	14	9	NUMBER OF STATEMENTS	699	665
%	%	%	%	%	%	ASSETS	%	%
16.9	11.6	8.4	9.5	3.9		Cash & Equivalents	7.7	8.6
29.3	27.4	28.9	24.3	26.8		Trade Receivables (net)	29.9	28.5
9.4	10.7	10.4	11.5	10.6		Inventory	10.2	9.9
1.6	1.9	2.4	1.9	3.1		All Other Current	1.9	2.3
57.2	51.5	50.1	47.2	44.3		Total Current	49.8	49.2
26.7	37.2	41.2	43.1	44.7		Fixed Assets (net)	40.9	41.1
8.4	4.7	3.9	4.6	7.8		Intangibles (net)	3.9	4.4
7.7	6.6	4.8	5.0	3.2		All Other Non-Current	5.4	5.3
100.0	100.0	100.0	100.0	100.0		Total	100.0	100.0
						LIABILITIES		
18.5	10.5	8.4	6.4	6.1		Notes Payable-Short Term	9.2	8.8
7.2	7.1	8.5	6.1	9.1		Cur. Mat.-L.T.D.	7.3	7.4
16.8	17.6	15.3	11.4	10.1		Trade Payables	15.4	14.7
.7	.1	.1	.3	.1		Income Taxes Payable	.1	.2
22.7	9.1	8.0	7.7	8.3		All Other Current	8.1	8.2
65.8	44.4	40.3	31.8	33.8		Total Current	40.0	39.2
47.5	34.7	26.3	23.5	20.3		Long-Term Debt	28.2	28.6
.0	.6	.9	1.3	3.9		Deferred Taxes	.8	.6
18.9	9.6	5.4	6.0	9.6		All Other Non-Current	5.2	4.0
-32.3	10.6	27.1	37.4	32.3		Net Worth	25.7	27.6
100.0	100.0	100.0	100.0	100.0		Total Liabilities & Net Worth	100.0	100.0
						INCOME DATA		
100.0	100.0	100.0	100.0	100.0		Net Sales	100.0	100.0
56.1	43.2	32.0	27.6	26.9		Gross Profit	34.5	35.5
53.7	40.8	29.3	23.2	19.2		Operating Expenses	30.3	31.1
2.4	2.4	2.7	4.4	7.7		Operating Profit	4.2	4.3
1.1	1.2	1.3	1.2	1.8		All Other Expenses (net)	1.4	1.4
1.3	1.2	1.4	3.1	5.9		Profit Before Taxes	2.8	2.9
						RATIOS		
3.0	2.3	2.1	2.5	2.0			1.9	2.0
1.1	1.3	1.3	1.4	1.4	Current	1.3	1.4
.6	.8	.9	1.0	.8		.9	.9
2.3	1.7	1.6	1.8	1.6			1.5	1.6
.8	1.0	1.0	.9	.8	Quick	1.0	1.0
.4	.6	.7	.7	.5		.7	.7

12	29.2	26	14.0	35	10.4	39	9.3	42	8.6	Sales/Receivables	37	9.7	36	10.2
28	13.2	36	10.0	46	7.9	50	7.2	54	6.8		48	7.7	45	8.1
39	9.3	50	7.3	59	6.1	64	5.7	67	5.4		58	6.3	58	6.3
0	UND	4	104.2	12	29.5	17	21.2	23	15.6	Cost of Sales/Inventory	10	35.5	10	35.1
10	35.5	15	23.9	22	16.3	28	13.1	29	12.5		19	19.0	20	18.5
28	13.1	43	8.5	36	10.2	44	8.4	39	9.3		34	10.8	34	10.8
6	61.9	17	21.8	21	17.7	20	18.4	18	20.9	Cost of Sales/Payables	19	18.9	19	18.9
26	14.1	34	10.7	31	11.8	27	13.4	31	11.7		31	11.9	31	11.9
51	7.2	67	5.4	49	7.4	47	7.8	40	9.1		49	7.4	49	7.4

10.1	9.0	8.0	5.9	8.7		Sales/Working Capital	9.5	7.9
100.8	29.4	18.5	13.8	13.9			24.1	19.1
-14.6	-28.4	-77.5	-770.9	-22.2			-97.4	-74.7

	8.8		5.3		4.9		6.0		8.5			5.7		5.8
(56)	1.2	(165)	1.5	(252)	1.9	(128)	2.8		2.9	EBIT/Interest	(655)	2.6	(627)	2.4
	-1.0		-.2		.5		.9		1.3			1.3		1.0

			4.4		2.7		3.9				3.1		2.9
		(25)	1.8	(68)	1.5	(48)	1.9			Net Profit + Depr., Dep., Amort./Cur. Mat. L/T/D	(209)	1.7	(198)	1.8
			.4		.8		1.3				1.0		1.0

.3	.6	.8	.7	1.2		Fixed/Worth	.8	.8
-2.5	2.0	1.4	1.4	2.0			1.7	1.6
-.4	-2.5	4.7	3.1	NM			5.8	5.6
2.1	1.2	1.1	.8	1.5		Debt/Worth	1.2	1.2
-4.6	5.5	2.6	1.7	1.9			3.0	2.5
-2.0	-6.7	9.7	5.1	NM			11.0	10.5

	96.1		66.7		30.8		30.7		72.1			45.5		41.4
(26)	32.4	(115)	13.0	(216)	11.5	(117)	14.6	(11)	18.9	% Profit Before Taxes/Tangible Net Worth	(565)	19.2	(544)	18.0
	8.3		-4.1		-2.6		.3		13.9			6.6		2.8

18.3	12.6	9.8	10.3	14.4		% Profit Before Taxes/Total Assets	12.3	12.6
5.7	1.9	2.7	5.2	4.9			5.2	5.0
-6.8	-4.3	-1.7	-.3	1.7			1.2	.2
44.4	17.3	8.6	6.2	6.6		Sales/Net Fixed Assets	10.2	9.9
16.9	8.0	5.0	3.8	3.5			5.5	5.3
9.2	4.2	3.3	2.7	2.9			3.4	3.2
5.1	3.6	2.6	2.2	2.0		Sales/Total Assets	2.9	2.8
3.4	2.6	2.1	1.6	1.6			2.2	2.1
2.5	1.9	1.6	1.3	1.3			1.7	1.6

	.9		1.9		3.1		3.6		3.1			2.6		2.7
(47)	2.1	(144)	3.7	(247)	4.3	(125)	4.9		5.3	% Depr., Dep., Amort./Sales	(647)	4.2	(609)	4.2
	4.4		6.1		6.6		7.0		7.0			5.9		5.9
	4.8		2.9		2.1		1.1					2.3		2.3
(37)	10.0	(106)	4.8	(102)	3.3	(28)	2.4			% Officers', Directors' Owners' Comp/Sales	(294)	4.0	(290)	4.2
	15.1		8.5		5.1		5.1					7.2		7.8

65094M	576602M	2661865M	4711229M	1501916M	1276323M	Net Sales ($)	12671043M	12928855M
17130M	214394M	1263769M	2764880M	891715M	1389013M	Total Assets ($)	6914461M	7176700M

M = $ thousand   MM = $ million
See Pages 9 through 22 for Explanation of Ratios and Data

Comparative Historical Data   Current Data Sorted by Sales

Type of Statement									
	73	72	77	Unqualified		4	1	7	24	41

	73	72	77	Unqualified		4	1	7	24	41
	142	136	135	Reviewed		6	17	33	62	17
	102	80	105	Compiled	7	32	25	23	17	1
	107	123	112	Tax Returns	21	31	38	16	6	
	232	247	228	Other	15	34	36	38	51	54
	4/1/08-3/31/09 ALL	4/1/09-3/31/10 ALL	4/1/10-3/31/11 ALL		0-1MM	1-3MM	3-5MM	5-10MM	10-25MM	25MM & OVER
					129 (4/1-9/30/10)		528 (10/1/10-3/31/11)			
NUMBER OF STATEMENTS	656	658	657		43	107	117	117	160	113
	%	%	%	**ASSETS**	%	%	%	%	%	%
Cash & Equivalents	8.3	9.0	10.1		19.4	10.8	9.9	9.1	9.7	7.9
Trade Receivables (net)	27.6	26.9	27.4		21.5	25.6	28.7	27.5	30.8	25.1
Inventory	10.3	9.8	10.6		6.8	11.6	9.6	9.8	11.0	12.6
All Other Current	1.8	2.2	2.1		2.4	2.4	1.4	3.0	1.5	2.3
Total Current	47.9	48.0	50.3		50.0	50.4	49.6	49.3	53.0	47.9
Fixed Assets (net)	41.7	40.6	39.1		30.7	37.0	39.7	41.6	39.3	40.8
Intangibles (net)	4.1	5.5	5.0		9.8	7.0	4.2	2.7	4.1	6.0
All Other Non-Current	6.2	6.0	5.6		9.5	5.5	6.5	6.5	3.6	5.3
Total	100.0	100.0	100.0		100.0	100.0	100.0	100.0	100.0	100.0
				LIABILITIES						
Notes Payable-Short Term	8.8	9.7	9.4		14.7	11.9	11.1	8.8	8.3	5.5
Cur. Mat.-L.T.D.	7.1	7.8	7.5		5.0	8.5	6.9	8.4	8.2	6.5
Trade Payables	14.5	15.1	15.0		10.2	16.3	17.9	15.4	15.2	12.1
Income Taxes Payable	.2	.2	.2		.1	.5	.1	.1	.3	.4
All Other Current	7.8	9.2	9.7		17.0	15.0	6.8	7.9	8.4	8.6
Total Current	38.4	42.0	41.9		47.0	52.1	42.8	40.6	40.3	33.1
Long-Term Debt	31.0	31.0	29.9		43.6	42.2	35.2	25.5	23.0	22.1
Deferred Taxes	.9	.8	.9		.0	.3	.8	.7	1.2	1.7
All Other Non-Current	4.7	5.1	8.0		15.2	13.5	9.3	3.1	5.5	7.6
Net Worth	25.1	21.2	19.2		-5.8	-8.1	11.9	30.1	30.1	35.5
Total Liabilties & Net Worth	100.0	100.0	100.0		100.0	100.0	100.0	100.0	100.0	100.0
				INCOME DATA						
Net Sales	100.0	100.0	100.0		100.0	100.0	100.0	100.0	100.0	100.0
Gross Profit	34.5	35.2	36.1		57.8	47.0	39.1	35.6	28.0	26.8
Operating Expenses	31.8	34.0	33.1		55.2	45.2	37.0	32.7	24.3	21.8
Operating Profit	2.7	1.2	3.1		2.6	1.8	2.1	2.8	3.7	4.9
All Other Expenses (net)	1.4	1.6	1.3		1.2	1.6	1.2	1.1	1.1	1.5
Profit Before Taxes	1.3	-.5	1.8		1.4	.2	.9	1.7	2.6	3.4
				RATIOS						
Current	2.1	2.2	2.3		3.3	2.3	2.3	2.3	2.0	2.3
	1.3	1.2	1.3		1.1	1.1	1.4	1.3	1.4	1.4
	.9	.8	.9		.7	.6	.9	.9	.9	1.0
Quick	1.6	1.7	1.7		2.9	1.7	1.8	1.7	1.6	1.6
	.9	.9	1.0		1.0	.8	1.0	1.0	1.0	.9
	.6	.6	.6		.5	.4	.6	.7	.7	.6
Sales/Receivables	33 11.2	32 11.5	32 11.6		14 26.4	25 14.6	30 12.2	33 11.0	37 9.8	40 9.2
	42 8.7	43 8.5	43 8.4		28 13.2	34 10.9	41 8.9	42 8.7	51 7.2	49 7.4
	54 6.7	56 6.6	59 6.2		52 7.1	43 8.5	51 7.2	54 6.7	63 5.7	63 5.8
Cost of Sales/Inventory	10 37.3	9 40.3	10 35.6		0 UND	6 61.6	4 91.1	11 34.7	14 26.4	20 18.3
	18 19.9	19 18.8	22 16.5		11 33.4	21 17.3	14 26.6	22 16.3	22 16.4	30 12.2
	35 10.6	36 10.0	38 9.5		41 8.9	50 7.3	37 9.9	36 10.1	34 10.7	44 8.4
Cost of Sales/Payables	18 19.9	19 19.4	18 20.4		0 UND	17 21.0	17 21.6	22 16.6	19 19.1	19 19.4
	29 12.4	32 11.3	31 11.8		24 14.9	37 9.9	32 11.5	32 11.4	27 13.5	29 12.5
	46 8.0	52 7.0	51 7.1		70 5.2	71 5.2	55 6.7	48 7.6	46 7.9	44 8.3
Sales/Working Capital	8.6	7.9	8.1		5.8	10.0	8.5	7.9	7.7	6.9
	24.5	28.9	21.4		54.7	57.1	27.5	18.4	17.5	13.8
	-60.1	-24.7	-42.1		-30.7	-11.6	-67.4	-68.5	-81.4	263.7
EBIT/Interest	4.4	3.7	5.4		9.8	3.3	5.6	6.1	6.1	6.1
	(629) 1.8	(619) 1.2	(624) 1.9		(35) 1.4	(103) .8	(112) 1.6	(112) 2.0	(156) 2.3	(106) 2.9
	-.1	-1.4	.4		-.7	-.5	-.1	.5	.9	1.1
Net Profit + Depr., Dep., Amort./Cur. Mat. L/T/D	2.7	2.1	3.4			3.1	4.0	2.6	2.8	4.0
	(193) 1.4	(164) 1.3	(157) 1.8			(14) 1.5	(21) 1.3	(25) 1.2	(54) 1.8	(41) 2.3
	.7	.3	1.0			.3	.2	.5	1.1	1.3
Fixed/Worth	.8	.8	.8		.2	.8	.9	.8	.7	.7
	1.8	1.9	1.6		10.8	9.5	2.5	1.4	1.3	1.4
	8.2	27.4	-111.6		-.6	-.6	-3.2	3.9	3.3	3.4
Debt/Worth	1.2	1.1	1.1		.6	2.1	1.2	.9	1.0	.9
	2.7	2.9	2.8		35.9	23.4	6.4	2.1	2.3	1.8
	17.2	UND	-111.9		-2.0	-2.6	-7.5	6.4	6.4	5.9
% Profit Before Taxes/Tangible Net Worth	32.6	24.9	36.6		51.0	71.9	66.1	32.8	32.8	35.6
	(517) 11.3	(496) 4.6	(490) 14.1		(23) 14.0	(59) 6.6	(79) 19.3	(99) 10.8	(136) 16.5	(94) 16.0
	-3.8	-14.3	-.8		-7.7	-13.3	-1.4	-6.5	.4	5.5
% Profit Before Taxes/Total Assets	9.9	7.4	11.1		21.5	11.3	11.1	9.4	11.5	9.8
	3.0	.6	3.1		6.3	-1.1	2.3	3.1	3.9	5.0
	-2.9	-7.2	-2.3		-5.6	-5.8	-3.6	-2.4	-.1	.1
Sales/Net Fixed Assets	10.8	11.1	12.1		41.8	19.1	14.6	9.8	9.4	6.9
	5.2	4.9	5.9		12.3	7.7	6.9	5.9	5.0	4.2
	3.1	2.9	3.3		6.2	3.3	3.9	3.4	3.1	3.1
Sales/Total Assets	2.9	2.8	2.9		3.4	3.6	3.4	2.9	2.6	2.2
	2.2	2.0	2.2		2.5	2.3	2.5	2.3	2.1	1.7
	1.5	1.4	1.5		1.4	1.5	1.8	1.6	1.5	1.3
% Depr., Dep., Amort./Sales	2.6	2.7	2.6		1.6	1.5	2.3	2.8	3.2	3.3
	(587) 4.2	(579) 4.7	(581) 4.2		(26) 3.3	(94) 4.0	(100) 4.0	(109) 4.4	(151) 4.2	(101) 4.6
	6.5	7.3	6.4		7.2	7.4	6.6	6.6	6.2	5.9
% Officers', Directors' Owners' Comp/Sales	2.4	2.7	2.5		5.6	3.0	2.8	2.4	1.7	.8
	(261) 4.3	(296) 4.7	(274) 4.2		(20) 12.2	(61) 5.8	(73) 4.4	(50) 3.3	(53) 3.3	(17) 1.7
	7.9	8.3	7.5		18.2	10.0	7.5	4.7	5.9	3.3
Net Sales ($)	11811712M	10498479M	10793029M		23601M	207494M	473885M	856228M	2543531M	6688290M
Total Assets ($)	6414191M	6333220M	6540901M		15033M	128381M	216225M	419554M	1385177M	4376531M

M = $ thousand   MM = $ million
See Pages 9 through 22 for Explanation of Ratios and Data

Current Data Sorted by Assets   **Comparative Historical Data**

0-500M	500M-2MM	2-10MM	10-50MM	50-100MM	100-250MM	Type of Statement	4/1/06-3/31/07 ALL	4/1/07-3/31/08 ALL
		1	5	2		Unqualified	11	8
	3	14	8			Reviewed	19	19
	8	4		1		Compiled	15	14
4	11	4				Tax Returns	10	10
3	9	10	8	1		Other	35	24
	13 (4/1-9/30/10)		83 (10/1/10-3/31/11)					
7	31	33	21	4		**NUMBER OF STATEMENTS**	90	75
%	%	%	%	%	%	**ASSETS**	%	%
	12.7	9.9	13.7			Cash & Equivalents	8.8	6.8
	29.6	26.4	22.9			Trade Receivables (net)	27.3	27.0
	10.7	14.3	17.5			Inventory	13.0	12.8
	.4	2.1	2.1			All Other Current	1.8	1.3
	53.5	52.7	56.2			Total Current	50.8	47.9
	33.5	38.3	34.1			Fixed Assets (net)	37.9	40.5
	5.4	5.2	7.4			Intangibles (net)	6.6	8.0
	7.6	3.8	2.3			All Other Non-Current	4.7	3.5
	100.0	100.0	100.0			Total	100.0	100.0
						LIABILITIES		
	10.8	6.3	5.9			Notes Payable-Short Term	10.2	10.8
	3.8	4.6	4.0			Cur. Mat.-L.T.D.	5.7	6.0
	12.1	14.9	9.2			Trade Payables	15.2	12.1
	.1	.0	.0			Income Taxes Payable	.1	.1
	7.2	5.9	13.2			All Other Current	8.3	11.1
	33.9	31.8	32.4			Total Current	39.5	40.0
	17.3	23.3	16.4			Long-Term Debt	24.5	24.6
	.5	.4	.7			Deferred Taxes	.7	.4
	8.4	7.8	9.9			All Other Non-Current	5.1	7.0
	39.9	36.7	40.6			Net Worth	30.2	28.0
	100.0	100.0	100.0			Total Liabilities & Net Worth	100.0	100.0
						INCOME DATA		
	100.0	100.0	100.0			Net Sales	100.0	100.0
	44.1	33.2	29.2			Gross Profit	35.8	37.7
	39.4	29.1	23.6			Operating Expenses	30.8	33.1
	4.7	4.1	5.6			Operating Profit	5.0	4.7
	.5	.6	1.0			All Other Expenses (net)	1.3	2.1
	4.1	3.5	4.6			Profit Before Taxes	3.7	2.6
						RATIOS		
	3.1	2.3	2.8				2.0	2.3
	1.6	1.6	2.2			Current	1.3	1.4
	1.0	1.5	1.1				1.0	.9
	2.4	1.7	2.2				1.5	1.5
	1.1	1.3	1.3			Quick	1.0	.9
	.8	.8	.6				.6	.6
	24 15.5	39 9.4	27 13.3				32 11.3	32 11.5
	34 10.6	44 8.2	37 9.9			Sales/Receivables	41 8.8	40 9.1
	44 8.2	52 7.0	53 6.9				52 7.0	53 6.9
	6 64.6	19 19.0	20 18.7				11 34.3	12 31.6
	15 24.3	34 10.8	40 9.2			Cost of Sales/Inventory	29 12.6	30 12.0
	33 11.0	46 8.0	60 6.1				46 8.0	50 7.3
	11 33.0	22 16.2	14 25.8				19 19.3	17 21.1
	24 15.0	33 10.9	23 16.1			Cost of Sales/Payables	30 12.3	25 14.4
	38 9.6	47 7.7	30 12.2				45 8.1	40 9.1
	8.7	7.5	5.1				9.2	8.0
	17.6	10.8	10.3			Sales/Working Capital	20.1	18.3
	-354.1	19.1	50.8				458.8	-47.3
	12.7	10.9	49.7				7.3	4.2
	(26) 5.8	(32) 2.9	(20) 6.3			EBIT/Interest	(86) 3.3	(74) 2.3
	.7	.6	2.6				1.3	.7
		4.0				Net Profit + Depr., Dep.,	7.5	4.5
		(10) 2.1				Amort./Cur. Mat. L/T/D	(26) 2.1	(17) 2.3
		.7					1.3	1.0
	.4	.5	.5				.8	.8
	1.4	1.3	.8			Fixed/Worth	1.3	1.7
	3.8	2.9	2.7				5.0	8.5
	.3	1.0	.4				1.0	1.0
	2.0	1.7	1.5			Debt/Worth	2.3	2.3
	15.5	6.4	4.0				10.9	19.2
	102.9	42.0	42.2				42.4	30.8
	(27) 24.8	(27) 15.4	(19) 21.7			% Profit Before Taxes/Tangible Net Worth	(74) 21.0	(60) 17.3
	1.3	-.4	15.2				5.9	1.3
	24.9	14.3	16.9				13.3	9.6
	8.1	4.0	9.8			% Profit Before Taxes/Total Assets	6.7	3.9
	-.1	-.3	4.2				1.1	-1.3
	22.8	8.7	14.1				14.6	11.6
	9.3	5.4	5.6			Sales/Net Fixed Assets	6.7	5.0
	5.8	3.2	3.0				3.4	3.2
	3.8	2.6	2.5				3.0	2.8
	2.9	2.2	2.0			Sales/Total Assets	2.2	2.0
	2.2	1.6	1.7				1.7	1.5
	1.8	3.2	3.5				2.3	2.6
	(24) 4.1	(29) 4.4	(20) 4.1			% Depr., Dep., Amort./Sales	(82) 3.5	(67) 3.8
	6.5	5.4	5.0				5.1	5.3
	4.1	1.4					1.4	2.0
	(20) 5.7	(13) 3.9				% Officers', Directors' Owners' Comp/Sales	(37) 3.1	(34) 5.1
	7.6	6.5					7.9	8.3
10504M	109074M	336818M	892558M	343841M		Net Sales ($)	2080788M	1272915M
1749M	38317M	161588M	442632M	313881M		Total Assets ($)	1151547M	856460M

(The 50-100MM and 100-250MM columns show "DATA NOT AVAILABLE.")

M = $ thousand   MM = $ million
See Pages 9 through 22 for Explanation of Ratios and Data

Comparative Historical Data | | | Current Data Sorted by Sales

4/1/08-3/31/09 ALL	4/1/09-3/31/10 ALL	4/1/10-3/31/11 ALL	Type of Statement	0-1MM	1-3MM	3-5MM	5-10MM	10-25MM	25MM & OVER
11	11	8	Unqualified					1	7
18	19	25	Reviewed		1	2	6	10	6
6	5	13	Compiled		2	7	1	2	1
7	10	19	Tax Returns	2	5	7	5		
38	22	31	Other	1	7	5	4	6	8
				__13 (4/1-9/30/10)__		__83 (10/1/10-3/31/11)__			
80	67	96	NUMBER OF STATEMENTS	3	15	21	16	19	22
%	%	%	ASSETS	%	%	%	%	%	%
7.9	11.6	11.2	Cash & Equivalents		11.4	10.2	15.5	7.3	12.3
25.3	24.4	26.7	Trade Receivables (net)		27.6	28.5	30.9	25.4	22.9
15.4	11.7	12.8	Inventory		6.6	10.4	14.2	16.2	16.7
2.8	1.0	1.4	All Other Current		.2	.4	.6	3.6	2.0
51.4	48.6	52.1	Total Current		45.9	49.5	61.3	52.4	53.9
39.6	33.3	34.7	Fixed Assets (net)		30.5	40.8	32.6	37.0	31.4
4.9	10.1	7.8	Intangibles (net)		14.9	2.7	2.9	5.5	12.0
4.1	8.0	5.5	All Other Non-Current		8.7	7.0	3.3	5.1	2.7
100.0	100.0	100.0	Total		100.0	100.0	100.0	100.0	100.0
			LIABILITIES						
13.6	9.6	8.3	Notes Payable-Short Term		13.6	8.9	7.4	8.3	4.3
5.5	5.0	3.8	Cur. Mat.-L.T.D.		2.5	3.6	4.6	4.8	4.0
14.1	10.6	12.8	Trade Payables		11.0	10.8	19.8	12.5	9.6
.0	.0	.0	Income Taxes Payable		.0	.0	.2	.0	.1
6.4	7.3	8.5	All Other Current		3.5	13.3	5.0	6.0	12.8
39.6	32.5	33.4	Total Current		30.5	36.5	37.0	31.6	30.8
21.1	21.8	22.8	Long-Term Debt		37.2	21.3	22.5	15.3	21.3
.5	.4	.8	Deferred Taxes		.0	.6	.5	1.3	1.3
13.8	13.3	11.7	All Other Non-Current		9.5	8.5	6.7	6.4	10.0
25.0	31.9	31.3	Net Worth		22.7	33.1	33.3	45.5	36.7
100.0	100.0	100.0	Total Liabilties & Net Worth		100.0	100.0	100.0	100.0	100.0
			INCOME DATA						
100.0	100.0	100.0	Net Sales		100.0	100.0	100.0	100.0	100.0
32.8	38.8	38.0	Gross Profit		49.5	43.8	36.5	30.3	29.3
30.2	35.2	33.2	Operating Expenses		46.3	38.2	32.2	24.5	24.4
2.6	3.6	4.8	Operating Profit		3.2	5.5	4.3	5.8	4.9
1.8	2.3	.8	All Other Expenses (net)		.7	.5	.2	1.3	1.3
.8	1.3	4.0	Profit Before Taxes		2.6	5.0	4.1	4.5	3.6
			RATIOS						
2.5	2.7	2.6			5.2	2.5	2.6	2.2	2.7
1.4	1.4	1.6	Current		1.6	1.4	1.7	1.6	2.0
1.0	.9	1.1			.7	1.1	1.4	1.4	1.1
1.5	2.0	1.9			4.7	1.9	1.8	1.5	2.2
.8	1.0	1.2	Quick		1.4	1.1	1.2	1.2	1.0
.6	.6	.8			.4	.8	.8	.8	.6
29 12.6	34 10.6	30 12.3			24 15.5	30 12.2	35 10.5	32 11.5	30 12.1
39 9.3	41 9.0	40 9.2	Sales/Receivables		37 9.9	34 10.6	39 9.4	44 8.2	41 8.9
51 7.2	51 7.2	49 7.4			49 7.4	48 7.6	61 6.0	49 7.4	52 7.0
20 18.3	12 29.4	11 33.8			0 UND	10 37.1	14 25.4	27 13.4	20 18.2
37 9.9	26 14.1	28 13.2	Cost of Sales/Inventory		3 106.3	20 18.7	26 14.1	36 10.2	39 9.3
54 6.7	46 7.9	46 7.9			45 8.2	33 11.0	47 7.8	47 7.8	64 5.7
18 20.1	14 25.9	16 22.2			15 24.8	8 46.4	22 16.5	20 18.1	15 24.3
26 13.9	26 14.0	26 13.8	Cost of Sales/Payables		25 14.3	24 15.0	27 13.7	27 13.4	26 14.3
40 9.1	39 9.3	42 8.7			49 7.5	38 9.6	60 6.1	41 9.0	40 9.2
7.9	6.7	7.5			8.7	8.6	7.6	8.4	5.1
20.1	17.1	12.3	Sales/Working Capital		21.3	22.0	10.2	12.0	9.3
424.1	-86.6	48.6			-22.6	50.7	16.6	19.2	35.6
4.5	6.8	12.9			10.2	12.7	13.2	12.2	38.7
(74) 2.3	(60) 2.4	(89) 3.8	EBIT/Interest		(14) 2.6	(18) 5.8	(15) 4.1	(18) 4.4	(21) 3.7
-.2	-1.1	1.3			-1.2	2.0	1.0	.2	1.8
7.5	2.1	7.2	Net Profit + Depr., Dep.,						
(23) 1.7	(16) 1.3	(26) 2.6	Amort./Cur. Mat. L/T/D						
1.1	-.2	1.0							
.8	.5	.6			.4	.7	.6	.4	.6
1.6	1.4	1.4	Fixed/Worth		24.2	1.4	1.4	1.1	1.2
4.6	-10.8	10.1			-.5	2.9	3.6	2.3	NM
.9	.5	.9			.3	1.3	1.2	.6	.4
2.3	2.3	2.2	Debt/Worth		25.8	2.6	2.2	1.4	2.3
9.6	-46.2	19.9			-2.2	6.8	13.2	3.0	NM
26.8	40.9	50.5	% Profit Before Taxes/Tangible			111.2	76.6	51.8	31.0
(66) 11.3	(48) 22.8	(76) 21.7	Net Worth			(18) 26.8	(14) 19.2	(18) 20.4	(17) 19.8
-5.4	3.6	3.6				7.2	3.1	-2.8	13.6
9.9	12.5	19.8	% Profit Before Taxes/Total			20.3	26.8	29.8	19.6	12.2
4.1	5.2	7.2	Assets		4.8	9.1	4.6	5.1	7.1
-5.8	-1.1	1.0			-4.6	2.2	.2	-.5	2.9
11.9	18.2	17.0			22.7	19.3	21.8	8.3	13.9
5.6	5.6	7.0	Sales/Net Fixed Assets		7.6	7.2	7.7	6.0	5.6
3.7	4.1	4.2			5.8	3.3	4.7	3.1	3.9
2.9	3.0	3.1			3.4	3.6	3.8	2.5	2.5
2.1	2.1	2.4	Sales/Total Assets		2.9	2.5	2.6	2.2	1.9
1.7	1.4	1.8			1.8	2.0	1.9	1.7	1.4
2.1	2.6	2.4			1.4	1.7	1.9	3.4	3.5
(72) 3.8	(58) 4.0	(82) 4.4	% Depr., Dep., Amort./Sales		(12) 4.3	(18) 4.0	(14) 4.4	(16) 4.4	(21) 4.1
5.0	6.1	5.5			6.3	6.2	5.3	5.9	5.0
2.8	2.8	3.2				4.3	3.7		
(29) 5.1	(30) 5.7	(40) 4.7	% Officers', Directors' Owners' Comp/Sales			(14) 6.0	(11) 4.1		
6.3	8.4	6.4				8.2	4.8		
1631019M	928541M	1692795M	Net Sales ($)	1946M	32209M	80767M	116817M	286097M	1174959M
869119M	566227M	958167M	Total Assets ($)	619M	15598M	32961M	48138M	144282M	716569M

M = $ thousand   MM = $ million
See Pages 9 through 22 for Explanation of Ratios and Data

Current Data Sorted by Assets   Comparative Historical Data

			2	1	1	2	Type of Statement		
	5		14	4	2		Unqualified	10	6
1	13		5				Reviewed	23	24
9	11		4				Compiled	17	15
3	13		10				Tax Returns	10	15
	16 (4/1-9/30/10)		92 (10/1/10-3/31/11)				Other	31	36
								4/1/06- 3/31/07	4/1/07- 3/31/08
0-500M	500M-2MM	2-10MM	10-50MM	50-100MM	100-250MM			ALL	ALL
13	42	35	10	3	5		NUMBER OF STATEMENTS	91	96
%	%	%	%	%	%		ASSETS	%	%
12.2	11.2	5.3	13.7			Cash & Equivalents	7.5	8.2
31.3	33.9	25.1	26.7			Trade Receivables (net)	30.2	29.8
9.5	14.5	28.5	22.0			Inventory	17.9	18.8
.3	1.4	1.8	4.8			All Other Current	3.1	3.5
53.3	61.1	60.7	67.2			Total Current	58.7	60.3
40.7	26.9	28.3	21.6			Fixed Assets (net)	29.9	31.3
1.3	7.7	6.4	7.0			Intangibles (net)	5.7	3.2
4.8	4.3	4.6	4.2			All Other Non-Current	5.7	5.3
100.0	100.0	100.0	100.0			Total	100.0	100.0
						LIABILITIES		
6.3	8.9	12.7	10.0			Notes Payable-Short Term	15.6	13.9
3.7	5.5	6.4	2.6			Cur. Mat.-L.T.D.	4.5	4.5
33.5	13.8	15.3	13.9			Trade Payables	15.0	14.9
.0	.0	.1	.0			Income Taxes Payable	.2	.5
9.8	7.9	7.6	9.2			All Other Current	12.5	9.1
53.3	36.1	42.1	35.8			Total Current	47.8	42.9
67.4	16.3	22.2	7.1			Long-Term Debt	19.7	20.9
.0	.0	.2	.1			Deferred Taxes	.2	.2
.0	6.1	4.9	4.8			All Other Non-Current	4.0	3.2
-20.8	41.5	30.5	52.2			Net Worth	28.3	32.9
100.0	100.0	100.0	100.0			Total Liabilities & Net Worth	100.0	100.0
						INCOME DATA		
100.0	100.0	100.0	100.0			Net Sales	100.0	100.0
52.9	42.1	34.8	24.7			Gross Profit	39.3	37.7
49.3	38.0	30.8	21.5			Operating Expenses	32.4	33.1
3.6	4.1	3.9	3.3			Operating Profit	6.9	4.6
1.4	1.0	1.2	.1			All Other Expenses (net)	1.4	1.2
2.2	3.1	2.7	3.1			Profit Before Taxes	5.5	3.4
						RATIOS		
2.6	2.9	2.3	2.4				2.1	2.8
1.2	1.7	1.7	2.0			Current	1.4	1.5
.6	1.0	1.2	1.4				1.0	1.0
2.2	2.4	1.3	1.7				1.5	1.8
1.1	1.2	.7	1.4			Quick	.8	.9
.4	.6	.5	.8				.6	.6
13 28.8	28 13.1	24 15.3	29 12.5				31 12.0	28 13.1
29 12.7	37 9.8	37 9.8	42 8.8			Sales/Receivables	46 8.0	40 9.1
33 11.2	59 6.2	56 6.5	60 6.1				58 6.3	53 6.9
7 50.6	6 60.8	35 10.5	9 41.3				17 22.1	13 27.9
16 22.5	23 16.1	62 5.9	48 7.6			Cost of Sales/Inventory	39 9.3	29 12.4
34 10.8	53 6.9	89 4.1	79 4.6				68 5.4	68 5.4
16 22.4	10 36.0	15 24.9	16 23.3				17 22.0	16 23.1
33 10.9	25 14.4	30 12.3	22 16.9			Cost of Sales/Payables	32 11.2	26 14.0
78 4.7	51 7.2	58 6.3	38 9.6				47 7.8	43 8.5
12.6	7.9	5.8	6.1				6.5	6.1
49.2	11.5	10.4	7.4			Sales/Working Capital	16.9	12.1
-27.4	NM	34.8	21.7				999.8	999.8
2.4	22.4	7.7					10.0	7.2
(10) .9	(38) 2.4	(34) 3.7				EBIT/Interest	(86) 3.9	(85) 3.0
-1.0	-1.5	1.2					1.1	1.2
							3.5	8.6
	(23) 1.8					Net Profit + Depr., Dep., Amort./Cur. Mat. L/T/D		(21) 3.8
	1.2						1.2	1.0
.8	.2	.3	.3				.6	.4
34.0	.7	1.2	.6			Fixed/Worth	1.0	.9
-1.0	2.0	1.6	.8				5.9	2.2
5.3	.4	1.3	.7				.9	.6
-24.9	1.3	2.2	1.1			Debt/Worth	2.1	1.9
-2.2	6.7	7.4	2.1				15.0	9.0
	45.5	40.7	22.2			% Profit Before Taxes/Tangible	53.2	40.7
(35) 14.4	(29) 16.8	10.5				Net Worth	(73) 23.8	(83) 19.1
	2.9	1.8	5.9				3.6	7.3
21.1	17.0	11.8	11.3			% Profit Before Taxes/Total	18.4	15.5
3.9	4.4	6.7	5.0			Assets	8.0	6.5
-6.7	-1.4	.3	.6				.2	1.2
25.7	30.4	31.8	27.0				18.7	19.6
12.8	12.5	16.6	20.3			Sales/Net Fixed Assets	8.9	9.2
7.9	6.2	4.1	7.7				5.0	5.3
5.5	3.9	3.0	3.7				3.2	3.4
4.3	2.8	2.2	2.3			Sales/Total Assets	2.3	2.4
3.8	2.0	1.9	1.6				1.7	1.8
2.0	.9	.7					1.3	1.5
(11) 2.8	(35) 2.2	(34) 1.8				% Depr., Dep., Amort./Sales	(73) 2.2	(85) 2.5
4.7	4.8	4.1					3.8	4.4
	3.1	1.8					3.3	2.6
(24) 6.7	(17) 3.8					% Officers', Directors' Owners' Comp/Sales	(36) 5.9	(49) 5.7
	12.4	4.7					10.1	11.1
17277M	143334M	320799M	551850M	392422M	822795M	Net Sales ($)	2028397M	1987536M
3672M	46969M	136514M	210725M	163633M	738882M	Total Assets ($)	980974M	946612M

M = $ thousand   MM = $ million
See Pages 9 through 22 for Explanation of Ratios and Data

Comparative Historical Data / Current Data Sorted by Sales

4/1/08-3/31/09 ALL	4/1/09-3/31/10 ALL	4/1/10-3/31/11 ALL	Type of Statement	0-1MM	1-3MM	3-5MM	5-10MM	10-25MM	25MM & OVER
12	10	6	Unqualified				1	1	4
25	29	25	Reviewed		2	2	10	5	6
19	17	19	Compiled	1	6	8	4		
23	13	24	Tax Returns	4	10	6	3	1	
36	40	34	Other	3	8	4	5	7	7
					16 (4/1-9/30/10)		92 (10/1/10-3/31/11)		
115	109	108	NUMBER OF STATEMENTS	8	26	20	23	14	17
%	%	%	**ASSETS**	%	%	%	%	%	%
7.5	9.8	9.4	Cash & Equivalents		8.9	6.9	10.5	6.3	10.9
29.2	28.3	29.1	Trade Receivables (net)		35.1	30.6	26.3	31.4	23.5
18.4	18.4	19.8	Inventory		9.8	23.4	25.4	28.4	23.2
1.9	3.0	1.7	All Other Current		.6	1.9	.6	3.9	3.6
57.0	59.5	59.9	Total Current		54.5	62.9	62.8	69.9	61.2
32.3	28.9	28.4	Fixed Assets (net)		34.5	28.0	29.5	17.8	23.6
5.3	6.2	7.2	Intangibles (net)		6.6	6.4	3.5	8.1	10.9
5.3	5.5	4.4	All Other Non-Current		4.4	2.7	4.3	4.2	4.3
100.0	100.0	100.0	Total		100.0	100.0	100.0	100.0	100.0
			LIABILITIES						
16.8	9.4	10.0	Notes Payable-Short Term		8.4	10.4	11.1	10.4	10.8
5.1	5.3	5.1	Cur. Mat.-L.T.D.		5.0	9.9	5.6	1.8	2.5
16.6	14.7	16.4	Trade Payables		23.6	17.8	11.9	19.3	11.8
.1	.1	.1	Income Taxes Payable		.0	.0	.1	.2	.1
9.6	10.0	8.1	All Other Current		7.0	7.0	10.4	6.6	8.6
48.2	39.6	39.6	Total Current		44.0	45.0	39.0	38.3	33.8
20.1	21.7	24.6	Long-Term Debt		35.1	19.8	17.6	14.2	18.2
.3	.3	.1	Deferred Taxes		.0	.0	.2	.4	.3
6.3	6.5	5.0	All Other Non-Current		7.4	.9	1.9	10.6	6.5
25.2	31.9	30.6	Net Worth		13.5	34.3	41.3	36.6	41.3
100.0	100.0	100.0	Total Liabilities & Net Worth		100.0	100.0	100.0	100.0	100.0
			INCOME DATA						
100.0	100.0	100.0	Net Sales		100.0	100.0	100.0	100.0	100.0
38.4	38.7	38.7	Gross Profit		47.4	36.2	37.9	30.9	28.2
36.5	37.0	34.6	Operating Expenses		44.8	33.7	32.2	27.8	23.5
1.9	1.7	4.1	Operating Profit		2.6	2.5	5.8	3.1	4.6
1.4	1.2	1.1	All Other Expenses (net)		1.2	1.5	.9	.1	1.4
.5	.5	3.0	Profit Before Taxes		1.3	1.0	4.9	3.0	3.2
			RATIOS						
1.9	2.6	2.4			2.8	2.3	2.4	4.3	2.5
1.3	1.5	1.7	Current		1.5	1.6	2.1	1.8	1.7
.8	1.1	1.1			1.0	.9	1.4	1.2	1.2
1.4	1.9	1.7			2.7	1.5	1.6	2.6	1.8
.8	1.0	1.0	Quick		1.3	.9	1.0	1.0	1.0
.5	.5	.6			.6	.5	.6	.6	.5
27 13.7	28 13.0	25 14.6		29 12.7	29 12.7	17 21.7	30 12.1	29 12.8	
39 9.3	41 8.9	36 10.0	Sales/Receivables	34 10.7	39 9.4	29 12.5	55 6.6	43 8.5	
56 6.5	57 6.4	53 6.8		52 7.0	45 8.1	41 9.0	61 6.6	61 6.0	
11 34.0	10 38.2	14 26.0		2 164.9	21 17.1	23 16.0	23 15.8	40 9.2	
33 11.2	41 8.9	42 8.7	Cost of Sales/Inventory	18 20.0	36 10.2	61 6.0	57 6.4	55 6.7	
66 5.5	77 4.7	69 5.3		40 9.2	61 6.0	102 3.6	81 4.5	101 3.6	
16 22.5	17 21.1	14 25.3		16 23.5	13 28.8	11 33.3	17 21.7	18 20.3	
31 11.7	32 11.5	27 13.6	Cost of Sales/Payables	34 10.9	31 11.9	20 18.3	47 7.8	22 16.3	
55 6.7	43 8.5	51 7.2		62 5.9	60 6.1	39 9.5	60 6.1	35 10.4	
8.5	5.9	7.1			8.9	7.3	6.3	5.0	4.1
19.9	12.1	11.8	Sales/Working Capital		22.1	13.5	9.2	10.3	10.7
-30.3	99.3	77.2			-97.7	-66.9	21.9	23.4	20.0
5.0	5.5	9.4			5.0	28.3	11.6	6.0	13.4
(105) 1.6	(97) 1.5	(98) 2.9	EBIT/Interest		(22) 1.7	(19) 1.7	(22) 5.8	(13) 4.0	(15) 8.0
.1	-2.2	.9			-1.6	-1.5	2.2	-.7	1.3
3.2	5.4	5.2	Net Profit + Depr., Dep.,						
(22) 1.5	(21) 1.6	(20) 1.9	Amort./Cur. Mat. L/T/D						
.8	.5	.8							
.5	.3	.3			.6	.2	.3	.3	.2
1.5	1.0	1.0	Fixed/Worth		1.5	.7	1.0	.5	.8
11.3	4.0	2.3			-3.3	58.3	1.5	1.3	1.5
1.3	.8	.7			.9	.5	.7	1.2	.7
3.4	2.0	1.9	Debt/Worth		4.6	2.3	1.5	2.3	1.6
27.5	18.6	10.5			-4.0	73.5	2.4	6.2	4.9
33.4	36.8	41.9	% Profit Before Taxes/Tangible		57.5	61.5	40.7	57.3	32.2
(89) 11.5	(86) 6.5	(86) 14.8	Net Worth		(17) 10.1	(16) 11.5	(21) 19.1	(13) 20.2	(15) 11.2
-4.2	-8.5	2.1			4.0	-11.6	7.2	-6.1	1.7
11.0	11.0	14.2	% Profit Before Taxes/Total		14.8	14.3	21.6	14.1	11.3
2.9	1.7	5.2	Assets		3.8	1.9	9.5	6.5	5.4
-2.8	-6.5	-.2			-6.5	-2.6	4.7	-1.4	.6
18.1	27.1	28.9			28.3	32.7	34.3	31.3	27.4
8.7	11.5	12.3	Sales/Net Fixed Assets		10.8	14.0	11.0	22.1	11.1
4.4	4.4	5.3			6.2	7.1	4.8	14.8	3.6
3.3	3.4	3.7			4.3	3.8	3.5	3.3	3.6
2.5	2.1	2.6	Sales/Total Assets		3.0	2.5	2.9	2.7	1.8
1.8	1.6	1.9			2.0	2.1	1.9	1.9	1.2
1.6	1.3	.9			1.8	.9	.7	.8	.9
(105) 2.9	(92) 2.6	(96) 2.1	% Depr., Dep., Amort./Sales		(20) 2.9	2.0	1.8	(13) 1.2	(15) 1.3
4.4	4.5	4.1			6.7	3.3	4.0	2.2	3.7
3.2	3.3	2.7			4.6	2.3	2.0		
(65) 5.1	(46) 5.7	(55) 4.5	% Officers', Directors'		(19) 9.9	(11) 3.7	(12) 3.5		
9.8	9.5	10.0	Owners' Comp/Sales		14.4	4.7	4.4		
2245588M	1683417M	2248477M	Net Sales ($)	4758M	45319M	80640M	165961M	206060M	1745739M
999021M	872355M	1300395M	Total Assets ($)	4607M	16783M	31403M	64752M	81786M	1101064M

© RMA 2011

M = $ thousand   MM = $ million
See Pages 9 through 22 for Explanation of Ratios and Data

Current Data Sorted by Assets							Comparative Historical Data	
						Type of Statement		
		1	1			Unqualified	8	8
2	5	7	5			Reviewed	19	20
2	4	7				Compiled	13	16
5	8	2				Tax Returns	24	26
8	6	8	6			Other	26	29
	15 (4/1-9/30/10)		62 (10/1/10-3/31/11)				4/1/06-3/31/07	4/1/07-3/31/08
0-500M	**500M-2MM**	**2-10MM**	**10-50MM**	**50-100MM**	**100-250MM**		**ALL**	**ALL**
17	23	25	12			**NUMBER OF STATEMENTS**	90	99
%	%	%	%	%	%	**ASSETS**	%	%
9.2	5.8	5.7	4.5	DATA NOT AVAILABLE	DATA NOT AVAILABLE	Cash & Equivalents	7.6	7.6
30.4	29.5	30.1	29.1			Trade Receivables (net)	27.3	28.2
6.3	9.9	9.0	13.5			Inventory	10.4	9.6
3.0	3.3	1.1	2.6			All Other Current	1.1	.8
48.9	48.6	45.9	49.6			Total Current	46.4	46.3
34.1	39.0	41.0	42.1			Fixed Assets (net)	38.9	40.4
11.4	4.5	5.8	5.3			Intangibles (net)	5.8	6.3
5.5	8.0	7.3	2.9			All Other Non-Current	8.9	7.0
100.0	100.0	100.0	100.0			Total	100.0	100.0
						LIABILITIES		
17.5	7.4	10.5	7.7			Notes Payable-Short Term	9.4	11.6
7.3	7.0	7.7	8.0			Cur. Mat.-L.T.D.	8.2	7.7
19.2	14.2	13.5	9.0			Trade Payables	13.4	14.3
.0	.1	.0	.0			Income Taxes Payable	.0	.1
18.8	9.4	12.6	6.4			All Other Current	7.3	7.6
62.8	38.1	44.3	31.1			Total Current	38.4	41.2
34.6	45.2	25.5	17.9			Long-Term Debt	32.1	33.9
.8	.1	.5	1.0			Deferred Taxes	.5	.3
30.2	6.3	4.6	19.0			All Other Non-Current	4.7	6.0
-28.4	10.3	25.0	31.1			Net Worth	24.4	18.6
100.0	100.0	100.0	100.0			Total Liabilties & Net Worth	100.0	100.0
						INCOME DATA		
100.0	100.0	100.0	100.0			Net Sales	100.0	100.0
						Gross Profit		
94.3	91.1	93.7	94.9			Operating Expenses	93.9	96.2
5.7	8.9	6.3	5.1			Operating Profit	6.1	3.8
1.6	3.3	1.5	1.7			All Other Expenses (net)	1.4	1.6
4.1	5.6	4.8	3.4			Profit Before Taxes	4.7	2.2
						RATIOS		
2.0	2.1	1.4	1.8				2.0	2.2
.8	1.1	1.0	1.6			Current	1.2	1.2
.5	.8	.7	1.1				.8	.8
1.7	1.3	1.1	1.5				1.5	1.8
.6	.9	.8	1.2			Quick	.9	1.0
.3	.6	.5	.8				.6	.6
16 23.1	**22** 16.6	**34** 10.8	**43** 8.6				**27** 13.5	**27** 13.3
23 15.7	**33** 11.0	**49** 7.5	**64** 5.7			Sales/Receivables	**42** 8.7	**40** 9.1
31 11.9	**46** 7.9	**61** 6.0	**66** 5.6				**51** 7.1	**52** 7.1
						Cost of Sales/Inventory		
						Cost of Sales/Payables		
20.9	11.3	14.7	5.6				9.4	9.6
-55.2	68.7	143.4	14.0			Sales/Working Capital	37.2	42.1
-15.0	-29.8	-13.6	38.6				-31.6	-25.4
9.5	5.5	5.2	8.6				6.2	4.2
(12) 3.4	(22) 2.4	(24) 1.4	3.8			EBIT/Interest	(83) 2.4	(93) 1.9
-.2	.0	-.5	.6				1.0	.4
							3.6	2.4
						Net Profit + Depr., Dep., Amort./Cur. Mat. L/T/D	(22) 1.6	(14) 1.6
							1.0	.8
1.1	.7	.7	.7				.7	.8
-1.5	3.7	1.9	1.1			Fixed/Worth	1.7	1.9
-.3	-2.1	-14.4	2.0				NM	-4.3
2.6	1.2	1.3	.9				1.2	1.7
-4.4	6.8	3.2	1.8			Debt/Worth	2.5	3.8
-1.8	-4.0	-23.8	2.7				NM	-9.4
	54.6	22.1	28.2				44.0	42.5
	(13) 16.2	(18) 8.8	(11) 10.5			% Profit Before Taxes/Tangible Net Worth	(68) 22.5	(68) 17.8
	-1.8	-13.9	3.1				1.0	1.4
36.9	10.2	8.4	14.0				15.7	13.7
12.8	5.6	1.7	2.6			% Profit Before Taxes/Total Assets	5.0	3.4
-7.5	-5.3	-5.7	-.2				.0	-1.0
106.8	17.8	11.5	11.4				13.3	15.5
15.4	6.9	4.6	4.7			Sales/Net Fixed Assets	6.1	6.6
7.9	3.7	2.9	2.1				3.8	3.7
7.4	3.8	2.7	2.2				3.4	3.4
4.0	2.5	2.0	1.8			Sales/Total Assets	2.4	2.4
2.9	1.4	1.4	1.2				1.8	1.7
	2.2	2.4	2.6				2.8	2.4
	(20) 6.1	(22) 5.4	(10) 3.6			% Depr., Dep., Amort./Sales	(80) 4.0	(84) 3.8
	9.0	7.5	6.1				5.6	6.4
	1.8	1.6					2.5	3.0
	(15) 3.6	(10) 2.6				% Officers', Directors' Owners' Comp/Sales	(46) 4.5	(50) 5.3
	7.3	11.5					8.8	8.2
17727M	61806M	225785M	385874M			Net Sales ($)	963014M	1228207M
3585M	25974M	112675M	216222M			Total Assets ($)	490946M	629616M

M = $ thousand MM = $ million

See Pages 9 through 22 for Explanation of Ratios and Data

Comparative Historical Data

	Type of Statement	4/1/08-3/31/09 ALL	4/1/09-3/31/10 ALL	4/1/10-3/31/11 ALL
	Unqualified	3	4	2
	Reviewed	18	16	19
	Compiled	15	15	13
	Tax Returns	23	15	15
	Other	30	31	28
	NUMBER OF STATEMENTS	89	81	77
	ASSETS	%	%	%
	Cash & Equivalents	6.6	7.1	6.3
	Trade Receivables (net)	27.6	28.1	29.8
	Inventory	8.4	9.3	9.4
	All Other Current	2.0	.6	2.4
	Total Current	44.7	45.2	47.9
	Fixed Assets (net)	43.0	38.6	39.1
	Intangibles (net)	5.7	8.2	6.6
	All Other Non-Current	6.7	7.9	6.4
	Total	100.0	100.0	100.0
	LIABILITIES			
	Notes Payable-Short Term	10.8	10.4	10.7
	Cur. Mat.-L.T.D.	7.8	8.6	7.4
	Trade Payables	14.2	15.1	14.3
	Income Taxes Payable	.0	.0	.0
	All Other Current	8.7	8.8	12.0
	Total Current	41.4	42.9	44.5
	Long-Term Debt	36.2	32.7	32.2
	Deferred Taxes	.5	.6	.6
	All Other Non-Current	5.9	5.1	13.0
	Net Worth	16.0	18.8	9.8
	Total Liabilities & Net Worth	100.0	100.0	100.0
	INCOME DATA			
	Net Sales	100.0	100.0	100.0
	Gross Profit			
	Operating Expenses	95.5	97.8	93.3
	Operating Profit	4.5	2.2	6.7
	All Other Expenses (net)	2.6	2.1	2.1
	Profit Before Taxes	1.9	.1	4.6
	RATIOS			
	Current	1.7 / 1.1 / .8	1.6 / 1.1 / .7	1.7 / 1.1 / .8
	Quick	1.4 / .9 / .6	1.3 / .9 / .6	1.3 / .9 / .5
	Sales/Receivables	24 15.5 / 36 10.1 / 51 7.2	29 12.4 / 40 9.2 / 54 6.8	23 15.8 / 37 9.8 / 59 6.2
	Cost of Sales/Inventory			
	Cost of Sales/Payables			
	Sales/Working Capital	13.0 / 43.6 / -24.1	13.0 / 67.2 / -18.6	12.2 / 56.9 / -23.4
	EBIT/Interest	4.5 / (84) 1.8 / -1.0	3.0 / (75) .6 / -2.1	6.2 / (70) 2.1 / .1
	Net Profit + Depr., Dep., Amort./Cur. Mat. L/T/D	2.5 / (20) 1.6 / 1.0	1.5 / (15) .9 / .1	2.6 / (14) 1.8 / .3
	Fixed/Worth	1.0 / 2.5 / -9.7	.8 / 3.4 / -4.0	.8 / 1.9 / -2.1
	Debt/Worth	1.3 / 4.2 / -38.6	1.3 / 5.0 / -10.8	1.2 / 3.6 / -5.0
	% Profit Before Taxes/Tangible Net Worth	41.4 / (64) 14.0 / -5.5	18.5 / (55) .4 / -25.9	35.5 / (49) 14.4 / -1.1
	% Profit Before Taxes/Total Assets	10.7 / 3.0 / -6.8	6.1 / -1.5 / -8.5	12.9 / 4.7 / -4.0
	Sales/Net Fixed Assets	12.8 / 6.4 / 3.4	13.8 / 5.4 / 3.2	16.7 / 6.6 / 3.7
	Sales/Total Assets	3.6 / 2.4 / 1.6	3.1 / 2.2 / 1.5	3.6 / 2.3 / 1.6
	% Depr., Dep., Amort./Sales	2.9 / (77) 4.3 / 6.5	2.9 / (71) 4.8 / 7.0	2.1 / (61) 4.9 / 6.9
	% Officers', Directors', Owners' Comp/Sales	2.6 / (50) 4.2 / 8.3	2.2 / (39) 4.0 / 9.4	1.7 / (38) 3.2 / 8.3
	Net Sales ($)	951117M	838932M	691192M
	Total Assets ($)	510663M	480228M	358456M

Current Data Sorted by Sales

15 (4/1-9/30/10) 62 (10/1/10-3/31/11)

Type of Statement	0-1MM	1-3MM	3-5MM	5-10MM	10-25MM	25MM & OVER
Unqualified	1	3	3	2	8	2
Reviewed						2
Compiled	2	3	6	1	1	
Tax Returns	6	6	3			
Other	6	5	3	5	6	3
NUMBER OF STATEMENTS	15	17	15	8	15	7
ASSETS	%	%	%	%	%	%
Cash & Equivalents	5.4	10.5	6.3		3.3	
Trade Receivables (net)	21.0	26.6	31.7		37.6	
Inventory	4.3	9.0	9.6		11.8	
All Other Current	6.8	.7	1.1		1.2	
Total Current	37.5	46.8	48.7		54.0	
Fixed Assets (net)	44.2	36.5	37.0		40.3	
Intangibles (net)	14.2	5.0	7.2		1.7	
All Other Non-Current	3.9	11.6	7.1		4.1	
Total	100.0	100.0	100.0		100.0	
LIABILITIES						
Notes Payable-Short Term	17.0	7.5	9.4		12.1	
Cur. Mat.-L.T.D.	8.8	7.8	5.3		8.5	
Trade Payables	14.6	12.2	18.0		12.5	
Income Taxes Payable	.0	.0	.0		.0	
All Other Current	9.7	13.7	12.7		13.5	
Total Current	50.2	41.2	45.3		46.5	
Long-Term Debt	53.7	35.5	29.8		19.2	
Deferred Taxes	1.0	.5	.0		.5	
All Other Non-Current	29.9	3.2	11.7		16.4	
Net Worth	-34.6	19.6	13.1		17.4	
Total Liabilities & Net Worth	100.0	100.0	100.0		100.0	
INCOME DATA						
Net Sales	100.0	100.0	100.0		100.0	
Gross Profit						
Operating Expenses	84.7	92.6	94.5		97.8	
Operating Profit	15.3	7.4	5.5		2.2	
All Other Expenses (net)	5.4	1.6	1.0		1.6	
Profit Before Taxes	9.9	5.8	4.5		.7	
RATIOS						
Current	2.0 / .8 / .4	2.9 / 1.2 / .7	1.4 / 1.0 / .8		1.7 / 1.4 / 1.1	
Quick	1.3 / .5 / .1	2.7 / .9 / .5	1.2 / .8 / .6		1.3 / 1.1 / .7	
Sales/Receivables	0 UND / 22 16.6 / 27 13.5	18 20.2 / 29 12.5 / 38 9.6	31 11.7 / 36 10.3 / 46 7.9		45 8.1 / 65 5.6 / 68 5.3	
Cost of Sales/Inventory						
Cost of Sales/Payables						
Sales/Working Capital	15.5 / -55.2 / -6.4	12.2 / 56.9 / -18.1	16.1 / -300.1 / -29.8		10.5 / 15.6 / 74.0	
EBIT/Interest	4.1 / (10) 1.8 / -.2	10.8 / (16) 3.8 / .0	5.5 / (14) 2.3 / -.1		5.1 / 1.4 / .4	
Net Profit + Depr., Dep., Amort./Cur. Mat. L/T/D						
Fixed/Worth	1.6 / -1.5 / -.3	.4 / 1.2 / NM	.7 / -15.4 / -2.1		.6 / 1.1 / 2.6	
Debt/Worth	2.8 / -3.9 / -1.7	1.0 / 2.4 / NM	1.4 / -29.0 / -5.5		1.4 / 2.9 / 7.7	
% Profit Before Taxes/Tangible Net Worth		80.3 / (13) 33.0 / -13.0			16.2 / (12) 9.6 / -.1	
% Profit Before Taxes/Total Assets	28.9 / 5.6 / -11.1	18.0 / 11.7 / -4.1	10.2 / 4.7 / -4.3		5.9 / 1.0 / -.8	
Sales/Net Fixed Assets	103.2 / 7.0 / 2.3	24.4 / 11.0 / 4.5	17.8 / 9.3 / 4.4		30.3 / 4.1 / 3.2	
Sales/Total Assets	4.0 / 2.6 / .8	4.2 / 3.1 / 1.3	4.0 / 2.5 / 2.0		2.7 / 2.1 / 1.7	
% Depr., Dep., Amort./Sales	1.6 / (10) 8.2 / 11.9	1.7 / (13) 4.1 / 7.2	2.1 / (12) 2.8 / 7.8		1.0 / (11) 5.3 / 6.3	
% Officers', Directors', Owners' Comp/Sales		2.2 / (11) 5.8 / 11.4				
Net Sales ($)	7743M	32056M	59815M	58864M	227557M	305157M
Total Assets ($)	6453M	24290M	26124M	28532M	121673M	151384M

M = $ thousand   MM = $ million
See Pages 9 through 22 for Explanation of Ratios and Data

Current Data Sorted by Assets   Comparative Historical Data

0-500M	500M-2MM	2-10MM	10-50MM	50-100MM	100-250MM	Type of Statement	4/1/06-3/31/07 ALL	4/1/07-3/31/08 ALL
		1	2			Unqualified	5	4
	3	6	2			Reviewed	5	5
	2	5				Compiled	4	4
1	3	1				Tax Returns	1	4
2	1	2		5		Other	9	12
3	9	15	9			**NUMBER OF STATEMENTS**	24	29
%	%	%	%	%	%	**ASSETS**	%	%
		7.4	D	D		Cash & Equivalents	9.2	7.3
		25.1	A	A		Trade Receivables (net)	33.5	27.6
		7.9	T	T		Inventory	6.5	10.2
		2.2	A	A		All Other Current	3.0	1.0
		42.5				Total Current	52.2	46.1
		44.6	N	N		Fixed Assets (net)	35.3	42.5
		3.6	O	O		Intangibles (net)	8.2	6.6
		9.2	T	T		All Other Non-Current	4.3	4.8
		100.0				Total	100.0	100.0
			A	A		**LIABILITIES**		
		11.0	V	V		Notes Payable-Short Term	10.6	8.5
		10.9	A	A		Cur. Mat.-L.T.D.	5.2	7.1
		12.1	I	I		Trade Payables	16.8	15.8
		.0	L	L		Income Taxes Payable	.3	.5
		8.8	A	A		All Other Current	12.4	8.9
		42.8	B	B		Total Current	45.3	40.9
		27.3	L	L		Long-Term Debt	28.2	28.9
		.5	E	E		Deferred Taxes	.8	1.4
		5.2				All Other Non-Current	3.6	4.0
		24.2				Net Worth	22.2	24.9
		100.0				Total Liabilities & Net Worth	100.0	100.0
						INCOME DATA		
		100.0				Net Sales	100.0	100.0
		38.0				Gross Profit	42.3	41.4
		36.4				Operating Expenses	38.7	38.8
		1.6				Operating Profit	3.6	2.6
		1.5				All Other Expenses (net)	1.0	2.0
		.1				Profit Before Taxes	2.6	.6
						RATIOS		
		1.8					2.3	1.9
		1.4				Current	1.4	1.3
		.8					.8	.8
		1.4					1.8	1.6
		1.0				Quick	1.1	.9
		.5					.6	.8
		34 10.7					36 10.2	34 10.6
		51 7.1				Sales/Receivables	53 6.8	44 8.4
		58 6.3					58 6.3	58 6.3
		12 29.9					2 146.8	12 31.1
		22 17.0				Cost of Sales/Inventory	14 27.0	24 15.4
		33 11.2					40 9.2	44 8.4
		17 21.2					24 15.2	25 14.4
		30 12.0				Cost of Sales/Payables	53 6.9	38 9.6
		56 6.5					69 5.3	72 5.1
		10.5					5.7	9.3
		18.8				Sales/Working Capital	16.6	22.6
		-17.3					-22.5	-33.6
		3.5					7.5	6.0
		2.4				EBIT/Interest	(22) 2.0	(28) 2.0
		.1					1.0	.3
						Net Profit + Depr., Dep.,		3.7
						Amort./Cur. Mat. L/T/D		(10) 2.2
								1.1
		.8					.7	1.0
		1.8				Fixed/Worth	1.4	2.6
		-6.8					8.7	6.5
		1.5					1.4	1.3
		2.4				Debt/Worth	2.5	3.4
		-41.0					10.8	8.7
		30.9				% Profit Before Taxes/Tangible	45.6	37.0
		(11) 15.6				Net Worth	(21) 22.7	(23) 13.2
		5.6					3.4	1.5
		8.6				% Profit Before Taxes/Total	13.7	11.2
		2.9				Assets	3.7	4.2
		-3.5					.1	-1.8
		7.7					11.5	10.4
		4.5				Sales/Net Fixed Assets	8.0	5.3
		3.3					4.8	3.2
		2.5					2.8	3.0
		2.0				Sales/Total Assets	2.2	2.1
		1.4					1.6	1.4
		4.0					2.6	2.5
		(13) 5.6				% Depr., Dep., Amort./Sales	(21) 3.5	(26) 3.8
		9.5					4.7	5.1
						% Officers', Directors',		3.1
						Owners' Comp/Sales		(12) 5.4
								9.0
16585M	28461M	119048M	251969M			Net Sales ($)	408738M	736054M
1259M	12607M	57891M	193718M			Total Assets ($)	221164M	517471M

M = $ thousand   MM = $ million
See Pages 9 through 22 for Explanation of Ratios and Data

Comparative Historical Data | Current Data Sorted by Sales

4/1/08-3/31/09 ALL	4/1/09-3/31/10 ALL	4/1/10-3/31/11 ALL	Type of Statement	0-1MM	1-3MM	3-5MM	5-10MM	10-25MM	25MM & OVER
4	5	3	Unqualified				1	2	
5	1	11	Reviewed		1	3	3	3	1
6	4	7	Compiled			5	2		
4	5	5	Tax Returns		3	2			
9	12	10	Other		2		1	4	3
4/1/08-3/31/09 ALL	4/1/09-3/31/10 ALL	4/1/10-3/31/11 ALL			8 (4/1-9/30/10)		28 (10/1/10-3/31/11)		
28	27	36	NUMBER OF STATEMENTS		6	10	7	9	4
%	%	%	ASSETS	%	%	%	%	%	%
7.0	12.4	11.7	Cash & Equivalents		D	12.2			
25.6	21.9	22.8	Trade Receivables (net)		A	19.0			
7.4	6.3	6.5	Inventory		T	5.3			
1.4	2.1	2.7	All Other Current		A	.1			
41.5	42.8	43.7	Total Current			36.5			
45.6	43.4	39.3	Fixed Assets (net)		N	52.9			
9.2	8.8	7.0	Intangibles (net)		O	5.9			
3.6	5.0	10.0	All Other Non-Current		T	4.6			
100.0	100.0	100.0	Total			100.0			
			LIABILITIES		A				
13.6	7.7	15.0	Notes Payable-Short Term		V	17.7			
11.2	6.0	8.0	Cur. Mat.-L.T.D.		A	12.8			
13.2	10.8	11.7	Trade Payables		I	10.5			
.1	.0	.0	Income Taxes Payable		L	.0			
8.1	7.5	9.1	All Other Current		A	7.1			
46.1	32.0	43.9	Total Current		B	48.2			
28.6	26.0	24.8	Long-Term Debt		L	40.2			
1.0	.4	.7	Deferred Taxes		E	.2			
6.3	6.7	10.8	All Other Non-Current			.3			
17.9	34.9	19.8	Net Worth			11.1			
100.0	100.0	100.0	Total Liabilties & Net Worth			100.0			
			INCOME DATA						
100.0	100.0	100.0	Net Sales			100.0			
45.1	42.8	38.8	Gross Profit			42.9			
41.2	39.7	36.5	Operating Expenses			42.9			
3.9	3.1	2.3	Operating Profit			-.1			
2.2	2.0	1.7	All Other Expenses (net)			2.3			
1.7	1.1	.6	Profit Before Taxes			-2.3			
			RATIOS						
1.5	2.9	1.8	Current			2.0			
1.0	1.6	1.3				1.0			
.6	.8	.7				.4			
1.1	2.2	1.4	Quick			1.9			
.7	1.1	.9				.7			
.5	.6	.5				.3			
29 12.6	16 22.5	29 12.6	Sales/Receivables			23 15.6			
43 8.5	41 9.0	42 8.7				44 8.2			
55 6.7	61 6.0	54 6.8				52 7.1			
5 73.7	3 106.3	8 47.7	Cost of Sales/Inventory			0 UND			
14 26.1	10 35.5	20 18.4				15 23.6			
40 9.1	24 15.4	27 13.4				31 11.8			
17 21.0	16 22.3	17 22.0	Cost of Sales/Payables			0 UND			
28 13.1	30 12.3	30 12.2				45 8.1			
57 6.4	45 8.1	53 6.9				61 6.0			
13.5	7.1	9.3	Sales/Working Capital			7.9			
UND	21.9	19.7				NM			
-13.2	-42.5	-15.9				-3.9			
4.4	6.9	5.1	EBIT/Interest			2.3			
(26) 1.9	(25) 2.2	(34) 1.7				.0			
1.0	-2.0	-.9				-1.9			
		1.5	Net Profit + Depr., Dep., Amort./Cur. Mat. L/T/D						
	(10)	.4							
		-.2							
1.1	.6	.9	Fixed/Worth			1.2			
2.6	1.5	1.8				NM			
-1.9	-9.2	-4.3				-1.2			
1.6	.6	1.5	Debt/Worth			1.5			
3.3	2.2	2.6				NM			
-5.3	-16.1	-8.3				-6.2			
37.2	33.3	51.7	% Profit Before Taxes/Tangible Net Worth						
(18) 22.3	(20) 9.1	(24) 13.4							
1.7	-30.4	.9							
13.2	10.6	19.2	% Profit Before Taxes/Total Assets			6.7			
4.8	2.4	3.0				-3.2			
.4	-18.1	-4.7				-12.4			
10.2	20.5	12.1	Sales/Net Fixed Assets			5.8			
5.3	4.6	5.1				3.9			
2.8	2.9	3.0				2.3			
3.3	2.7	2.6	Sales/Total Assets			2.3			
2.0	2.3	2.1				2.0			
1.4	1.3	1.4				1.4			
2.6	4.2	3.9	% Depr., Dep., Amort./Sales			4.4			
(25) 4.5	(19) 6.5	(29) 6.3				7.1			
7.2	8.5	9.5				10.7			
1.8		2.5	% Officers', Directors' Owners' Comp/Sales						
(10) 5.0		(14) 4.3							
14.7		9.7							
784331M	612104M	416063M	Net Sales ($)		15681M	37744M	50584M	152525M	159529M
522103M	358072M	265475M	Total Assets ($)		5856M	21712M	21730M	113253M	102924M

M = $ thousand   MM = $ million
See Pages 9 through 22 for Explanation of Ratios and Data

Current Data Sorted by Assets   Comparative Historical Data

0-500M	500M-2MM	2-10MM	10-50MM	50-100MM	100-250MM		4/1/06-3/31/07 ALL	4/1/07-3/31/08 ALL
						Type of Statement		
		2	6			Unqualified	6	8
	3	2	1			Reviewed	14	13
	3	1				Compiled	5	4
1		3				Tax Returns	8	2
1	3	4	5			Other	15	11
	9 (4/1-9/30/10)		26 (10/1/10-3/31/11)					
2	9	12	12			**NUMBER OF STATEMENTS**	48	38
%	%	%	%	%	%		%	%
						ASSETS		
		7.0	16.1	D	D	Cash & Equivalents	7.5	12.4
		30.9	28.4	A	A	Trade Receivables (net)	34.3	33.3
		13.4	11.3	T	T	Inventory	15.8	12.2
		4.8	2.5	A	A	All Other Current	1.1	2.9
		56.1	58.2			Total Current	58.8	60.8
		32.0	17.9	N	N	Fixed Assets (net)	25.1	25.7
		5.9	14.7	O	O	Intangibles (net)	9.4	7.0
		6.0	9.2	T	T	All Other Non-Current	6.7	6.4
		100.0	100.0			Total	100.0	100.0
				A	A	**LIABILITIES**		
		6.3	2.0	V	V	Notes Payable-Short Term	11.9	9.6
		5.9	3.2	A	A	Cur. Mat.-L.T.D.	4.1	4.9
		16.5	11.3	I	I	Trade Payables	18.8	13.8
		.8	.0	L	L	Income Taxes Payable	.2	.0
		8.5	16.8	A	A	All Other Current	10.3	10.8
		38.1	33.3	B	B	Total Current	45.3	39.2
		16.7	8.0	L	L	Long-Term Debt	14.0	13.0
		1.2	.9	E	E	Deferred Taxes	.6	.6
		6.3	12.2			All Other Non-Current	4.0	5.7
		37.7	45.6			Net Worth	36.1	41.6
		100.0	100.0			Total Liabilities & Net Worth	100.0	100.0
						INCOME DATA		
		100.0	100.0			Net Sales	100.0	100.0
		32.1	32.1			Gross Profit	34.9	36.8
		31.9	26.7			Operating Expenses	30.7	31.5
		.2	5.4			Operating Profit	4.2	5.3
		.2	1.0			All Other Expenses (net)	.7	.7
		.0	4.4			Profit Before Taxes	3.5	4.6
						RATIOS		
		2.4	2.4				2.2	2.5
		1.2	1.7			Current	1.6	1.8
		1.0	1.2				1.0	1.1
		1.6	2.1				1.6	1.8
		.8	1.1			Quick	1.0	1.1
		.7	.8				.6	.7
		42 8.7	34 10.8				32 11.5	33 11.2
		48 7.6	39 9.3			Sales/Receivables	42 8.8	39 9.4
		54 6.8	56 6.5				56 6.6	53 6.8
		13 29.2	16 23.2				12 30.8	13 28.8
		31 11.7	24 15.2			Cost of Sales/Inventory	23 15.7	21 17.4
		39 9.3	41 9.0				45 8.2	35 10.5
		22 16.6	13 27.9				18 20.5	14 25.8
		29 12.4	21 17.2			Cost of Sales/Payables	31 11.7	22 16.7
		45 8.1	35 10.5				52 7.1	41 8.9
		6.5	5.3				7.6	6.6
		30.6	9.8			Sales/Working Capital	12.2	11.4
		NM	29.5				451.4	NM
		9.6	40.3				8.3	11.9
		3.2 (10)	2.5			EBIT/Interest	(40) 3.2	(34) 6.0
		-.4	1.2				1.2	1.6
							10.5	
						Net Profit + Depr., Dep., Amort./Cur. Mat. L/T/D	(11) 4.0	
							.5	
		.4	.2				.3	.3
		.9	.4			Fixed/Worth	.7	.7
		1.6	5.6				6.7	1.9
		.7	.6				.6	.6
		1.6	1.0			Debt/Worth	2.1	1.8
		9.4	12.7				12.5	3.7
		35.4	45.0				28.7	46.0
	(10) 10.2		(10) 10.2			% Profit Before Taxes/Tangible Net Worth	(37) 13.6	(33) 23.4
		-12.4	1.0				5.0	11.8
		13.8	16.0				13.1	18.6
		6.4	3.0			% Profit Before Taxes/Total Assets	6.0	10.6
		-2.7	-.4				.5	4.1
		31.6	48.2				27.1	21.8
		6.7	14.6			Sales/Net Fixed Assets	11.6	11.3
		5.1	6.4				6.3	6.6
		3.2	2.7				3.4	3.4
		2.6	2.3			Sales/Total Assets	2.6	2.5
		2.2	1.7				2.0	2.2
		1.5	1.6				1.5	1.0
	(11) 4.2		(11) 2.1			% Depr., Dep., Amort./Sales	(40) 2.5	(33) 2.5
		6.2	3.5				3.4	3.7
							1.9	2.0
						% Officers', Directors' Owners' Comp/Sales	(14) 3.4	(12) 5.5
							7.5	10.6
1982M	24970M	145668M	541290M			Net Sales ($)	1218487M	1018476M
460M	10110M	54608M	225357M			Total Assets ($)	722521M	601975M

M = $ thousand   MM = $ million
See Pages 9 through 22 for Explanation of Ratios and Data

Comparative Historical Data   Current Data Sorted by Sales

			Type of Statement	0-1MM	1-3MM	3-5MM	5-10MM	10-25MM	25MM & OVER
6	4	8	Unqualified					2	6
13	11	6	Reviewed		2	1		3	
3	3	4	Compiled		2	1		1	
3	2	4	Tax Returns		1	1			
11	11	13	Other	1	2	1	1	3	4
4/1/08-3/31/09 ALL	4/1/09-3/31/10 ALL	4/1/10-3/31/11 ALL		_____9 (4/1-9/30/10)_____			_____26 (10/1/10-3/31/11)_____		
36	31	35	NUMBER OF STATEMENTS	1	7	4	3	10	10
%	%	%	ASSETS	%	%	%	%	%	%
13.0	8.7	11.9	Cash & Equivalents					9.4	14.1
30.6	30.4	29.9	Trade Receivables (net)					30.8	29.5
16.3	13.1	13.2	Inventory					13.3	12.0
2.1	1.8	3.9	All Other Current					4.3	2.4
61.9	54.0	58.9	Total Current					57.8	58.1
25.4	29.3	24.4	Fixed Assets (net)					28.5	16.9
7.2	10.8	10.1	Intangibles (net)					10.2	14.4
5.5	5.9	6.6	All Other Non-Current					3.6	10.5
100.0	100.0	100.0	Total					100.0	100.0
			LIABILITIES						
6.6	8.6	4.8	Notes Payable-Short Term					6.3	2.4
3.6	5.1	4.2	Cur. Mat.-L.T.D.					3.4	3.7
14.0	15.3	14.2	Trade Payables					18.6	10.6
.0	.1	.4	Income Taxes Payable					.0	.0
11.6	10.2	13.5	All Other Current					9.5	19.7
35.8	39.4	37.1	Total Current					37.7	36.3
17.1	21.1	13.8	Long-Term Debt					17.5	7.3
.6	.5	.8	Deferred Taxes					.7	1.0
5.7	5.6	10.5	All Other Non-Current					7.2	14.7
40.7	33.4	37.7	Net Worth					36.9	40.7
100.0	100.0	100.0	Total Liabilities & Net Worth					100.0	100.0
			INCOME DATA						
100.0	100.0	100.0	Net Sales					100.0	100.0
32.0	32.4	32.2	Gross Profit					30.8	31.1
30.0	30.7	29.7	Operating Expenses					26.1	26.8
2.0	1.7	2.5	Operating Profit					4.7	4.3
1.2	.6	.7	All Other Expenses (net)					.4	1.2
.8	1.2	1.8	Profit Before Taxes					4.2	3.2
			RATIOS						
2.4	1.8	2.4						2.5	2.0
1.8	1.4	1.4	Current					1.4	1.4
1.1	1.0	1.1						1.1	1.1
1.9	1.4	1.7						1.9	1.8
1.1	1.1	1.0	Quick					.8	1.0
.7	.6	.7						.7	.8
29 12.7	31 11.8	30 12.1						33 10.9	33 11.0
36 10.1	40 9.2	41 8.9	Sales/Receivables					47 7.7	37 10.0
51 7.2	53 6.9	53 6.8						54 6.8	47 7.7
12 30.1	13 28.3	12 29.5						10 37.4	14 26.7
25 14.4	21 17.5	30 12.2	Cost of Sales/Inventory					18 19.8	24 15.1
51 7.1	41 8.9	41 8.9						36 10.0	45 8.1
11 34.3	16 23.3	15 25.0						21 17.6	10 35.5
20 17.8	24 15.4	22 16.6	Cost of Sales/Payables					35 10.4	18 20.4
53 6.9	42 8.7	37 9.8						50 7.2	25 14.4
7.1	7.1	5.3						5.6	5.7
12.6	24.1	16.3	Sales/Working Capital					19.9	13.1
65.7	-763.9	57.2						NM	153.9
7.4	7.1	8.8							
(29) 2.1	(29) 1.6	(33) 2.5	EBIT/Interest						
.1	-1.3	.4							
		3.2	Net Profit + Depr., Dep.,						
	(11) 1.5		Amort./Cur. Mat. L/T/D						
		.6							
.2	.3	.2						.3	.1
.6	1.3	.8	Fixed/Worth					.9	.4
2.1	UND	2.3						NM	NM
.5	.9	.7						.7	.7
1.6	1.9	1.9	Debt/Worth					2.3	1.2
10.6	UND	15.8						NM	NM
35.6	30.4	31.9	% Profit Before Taxes/Tangible						
(30) 14.9	(24) 8.0	(27) 6.1	Net Worth						
1.9	-6.8	-3.2							
15.0	11.3	11.3	% Profit Before Taxes/Total					15.8	16.1
4.2	2.9	3.2	Assets					7.8	2.5
-.5	-4.0	-1.8						1.8	-.9
36.0	30.2	42.4						38.9	50.1
13.5	8.8	13.0	Sales/Net Fixed Assets					6.9	20.4
6.5	4.8	5.3						6.0	6.9
3.8	4.2	3.7						3.4	3.2
2.9	2.4	2.5	Sales/Total Assets					2.6	2.5
2.1	1.7	2.0						2.2	1.8
.9	1.4	1.1							
(30) 1.6	(28) 3.2	(29) 2.6	% Depr., Dep., Amort./Sales						
3.3	4.4	3.9							
1.7		2.6	% Officers', Directors'						
(10) 3.7		(13) 6.5	Owners' Comp/Sales						
10.6		12.0							
1039612M	743851M	713910M	Net Sales ($)	628M	15089M	14482M	21745M	165868M	496098M
556896M	365959M	290535M	Total Assets ($)	258M	6246M	6952M	11005M	79159M	186915M

© RMA 2011

M = $ thousand   MM = $ million
See Pages 9 through 22 for Explanation of Ratios and Data

Current Data Sorted by Assets   Comparative Historical Data

0-500M	500M-2MM	2-10MM	10-50MM	50-100MM	100-250MM	Type of Statement		
	1	1	6	2	1	Unqualified	8	5
		2	5			Reviewed	10	10
		1	1			Compiled	2	1
1	3	1				Tax Returns	3	4
1		4	2		1	Other	13	12
	7 (4/1-9/30/10)		26 (10/1/10-3/31/11)				4/1/06-3/31/07 ALL	4/1/07-3/31/08 ALL
0-500M	500M-2MM	2-10MM	10-50MM	50-100MM	100-250MM			
1	5	9	14	2	2	NUMBER OF STATEMENTS	36	32
%	%	%	%	%	%	ASSETS	%	%
			10.5			Cash & Equivalents	8.5	8.5
			25.9			Trade Receivables (net)	29.5	31.6
			16.6			Inventory	12.6	10.4
			3.5			All Other Current	1.1	1.0
			56.5			Total Current	51.8	51.5
			28.8			Fixed Assets (net)	38.1	36.6
			3.5			Intangibles (net)	4.4	4.4
			11.2			All Other Non-Current	5.7	7.5
			100.0			Total	100.0	100.0
						LIABILITIES		
			3.4			Notes Payable-Short Term	7.4	7.8
			6.5			Cur. Mat.-L.T.D.	4.1	5.6
			9.8			Trade Payables	14.0	14.4
			.1			Income Taxes Payable	.2	.1
			12.7			All Other Current	9.6	6.8
			32.5			Total Current	35.4	34.7
			8.4			Long-Term Debt	18.0	21.4
			1.9			Deferred Taxes	1.1	.9
			7.3			All Other Non-Current	3.4	9.4
			49.8			Net Worth	42.2	33.6
			100.0			Total Liabilities & Net Worth	100.0	100.0
						INCOME DATA		
			100.0			Net Sales	100.0	100.0
			24.8			Gross Profit	29.8	29.2
			22.7			Operating Expenses	23.0	25.2
			2.1			Operating Profit	6.8	4.0
			.4			All Other Expenses (net)	.9	.8
			1.7			Profit Before Taxes	5.9	3.2
						RATIOS		
			4.0				2.3	2.9
			2.0			Current	1.7	1.8
			1.3				1.2	1.0
			3.0				1.8	2.1
			1.0			Quick	1.2	1.1
			.6				.8	.8
		37	9.9				40 9.1	41 8.9
		56	6.5			Sales/Receivables	52 7.0	52 7.0
		59	6.2				67 5.4	66 5.5
		17	21.4				12 30.6	7 49.2
		29	12.7			Cost of Sales/Inventory	26 13.8	16 23.2
		65	5.6				42 8.8	36 10.1
		16	23.1				19 18.8	19 19.0
		22	16.9			Cost of Sales/Payables	25 14.4	23 15.6
		31	11.9				47 7.7	35 10.5
			3.7				5.7	5.6
			6.9			Sales/Working Capital	9.9	15.2
			21.0				44.7	NM
			8.3				8.5	9.8
		(13)	4.4			EBIT/Interest	(31) 2.9	(29) 1.9
			.8				1.4	.5
						Net Profit + Depr., Dep., Amort./Cur. Mat. L/T/D		
			.3				.6	.5
			.6			Fixed/Worth	1.0	.9
			1.2				3.8	2.8
			.4				.6	.5
			1.0			Debt/Worth	1.3	1.4
			6.8				8.2	5.3
			25.7				36.4	29.2
			6.4			% Profit Before Taxes/Tangible Net Worth	(33) 17.1	(26) 7.6
			-.1				4.8	.0
			8.9				14.9	8.7
			2.4			% Profit Before Taxes/Total Assets	6.3	3.0
			-.1				2.1	-2.8
			19.7				11.6	14.0
			6.4			Sales/Net Fixed Assets	3.9	5.1
			3.4				3.0	3.0
			1.9				2.7	2.5
			1.7			Sales/Total Assets	1.7	1.9
			1.5				1.4	1.5
			2.0				2.2	2.6
		(13)	4.1			% Depr., Dep., Amort./Sales	(29) 4.3	(29) 3.9
			6.3				5.6	5.3
						% Officers', Directors' Owners' Comp/Sales		
928M	10039M	113597M	544969M	192224M	516111M	Net Sales ($)	1256727M	1088548M
211M	3867M	48564M	298086M	102885M	443746M	Total Assets ($)	807596M	620387M

© RMA 2011

M = $ thousand   MM = $ million
See Pages 9 through 22 for Explanation of Ratios and Data

Comparative Historical Data   Current Data Sorted by Sales

	Hist 1		Hist 2		Hist 3	Type of Statement	0-1MM	1-3MM	3-5MM	5-10MM	10-25MM	25MM & OVER
	6		6		11	Unqualified	1			1	1	8
	7		7		7	Reviewed				1	4	2
			1		2	Compiled					1	1
	5		1		5	Tax Returns						1
	15		12		8	Other	1	3	1	1	3	3
	4/1/08-3/31/09 ALL		4/1/09-3/31/10 ALL		4/1/10-3/31/11 ALL			7 (4/1-9/30/10)		26 (10/1/10-3/31/11)		
	33		27		33	**NUMBER OF STATEMENTS**	2	3	1	4	9	14
	%		%		%	**ASSETS**	%	%	%	%	%	%
	5.8		8.7		10.3	Cash & Equivalents						10.6
	31.8		24.3		29.1	Trade Receivables (net)						25.5
	10.7		11.7		15.2	Inventory						12.7
	1.7		2.3		3.3	All Other Current						4.1
	50.0		47.0		57.9	Total Current						53.0
	35.3		41.0		30.1	Fixed Assets (net)						36.5
	6.5		4.5		4.2	Intangibles (net)						2.8
	8.2		7.5		7.8	All Other Non-Current						7.7
	100.0		100.0		100.0	Total						100.0
						LIABILITIES						
	5.7		4.3		5.1	Notes Payable-Short Term						2.1
	5.2		6.6		5.9	Cur. Mat.-L.T.D.						6.4
	12.3		9.1		13.0	Trade Payables						11.1
	.0		.1		.1	Income Taxes Payable						.1
	8.2		7.7		11.3	All Other Current						14.5
	31.4		27.8		35.4	Total Current						34.3
	20.0		20.9		11.9	Long-Term Debt						10.0
	1.2		1.4		.9	Deferred Taxes						.6
	5.2		11.5		9.0	All Other Non-Current						6.9
	42.2		38.5		42.8	Net Worth						48.3
	100.0		100.0		100.0	Total Liabilities & Net Worth						100.0
						INCOME DATA						
	100.0		100.0		100.0	Net Sales						100.0
	29.1		30.8		28.0	Gross Profit						22.0
	26.2		26.6		25.4	Operating Expenses						18.9
	2.9		4.2		2.6	Operating Profit						3.1
	.5		1.1		-.1	All Other Expenses (net)						.7
	2.4		3.2		2.7	Profit Before Taxes						2.4
						RATIOS						
	2.9		2.8		3.7							3.3
	1.8		2.2		1.7	Current						2.0
	1.1		1.0		1.0							1.2
	1.9		2.3		2.5							2.6
	1.1		1.3		1.1	Quick						1.1
	.9		.7		.6							.6
44	8.4	36	10.2	36	10.0	Sales/Receivables					45	8.1
55	6.7	44	8.3	53	6.9						56	6.5
67	5.5	58	6.2	59	6.2						59	6.2
6	63.6	10	37.5	9	41.2	Cost of Sales/Inventory					17	21.8
21	17.3	19	19.4	28	13.1						28	13.1
39	9.5	44	8.3	55	6.6						63	5.8
14	25.4	19	19.5	17	21.5	Cost of Sales/Payables					16	23.1
21	17.6	22	16.6	25	14.7						24	14.9
36	10.0	31	11.6	43	8.5						40	9.1
	5.6		5.0		4.0	Sales/Working Capital						4.3
	8.8		6.5		6.8							6.9
	64.2		232.0		NM							NM
	6.0		6.1		11.0	EBIT/Interest						7.2
(29)	1.5	(22)	1.5	(29)	2.9						(12)	2.3
	.1		-3.0		.8							.7
						Net Profit + Depr., Dep., Amort./Cur. Mat. L/T/D						
	.5		.6		.3	Fixed/Worth						.5
	.8		.7		.7							.8
	1.5		2.5		1.9							1.7
	.9		.3		.4	Debt/Worth						.4
	1.2		1.0		1.1							.6
	4.1		5.1		10.4							8.4
	22.9		37.7		35.5	% Profit Before Taxes/Tangible Net Worth						24.7
(31)	7.4	(24)	10.9	(31)	9.1							8.7
	-3.3		-3.7		-.2							.1
	9.5		7.9		12.5	% Profit Before Taxes/Total Assets						6.4
	1.4		4.7		2.7							2.2
	-2.0		-1.6		.0							.1
	11.6		7.6		15.7	Sales/Net Fixed Assets						11.4
	5.3		4.0		7.5							3.7
	2.9		3.1		3.8							3.0
	2.5		2.3		2.4	Sales/Total Assets						1.8
	1.8		1.8		1.9							1.6
	1.3		1.4		1.5							1.4
	2.6		3.6		2.5	% Depr., Dep., Amort./Sales						2.7
(28)	4.5	(22)	4.8	(27)	4.1						(12)	4.0
	5.5		6.1		5.7							5.7
						% Officers', Directors' Owners' Comp/Sales						
	1175119M		1248912M		1377868M	Net Sales ($)	1472M	5245M	4250M	29263M	168202M	1169436M
	781849M		856195M		897359M	Total Assets ($)	812M	2570M	696M	11881M	85682M	795718M

M = $ thousand   MM = $ million
See Pages 9 through 22 for Explanation of Ratios and Data

Current Data Sorted by Assets   Comparative Historical Data

0-500M	500M-2MM	2-10MM	10-50MM	50-100MM	100-250MM	Type of Statement	4/1/06-3/31/07 ALL	4/1/07-3/31/08 ALL
	1	14	22	4	3	Unqualified	59	48
1	10	37	17		1	Reviewed	88	74
12	22	9	3	1		Compiled	62	52
25	20	16				Tax Returns	63	45
10	24	50	32	12	2	Other	123	140
	67 (4/1-9/30/10)		280 (10/1/10-3/31/11)					
48	77	126	74	17	5	NUMBER OF STATEMENTS	395	359
%	%	%	%	%	%	**ASSETS**	%	%
13.8	8.3	9.8	7.4	11.3		Cash & Equivalents	9.2	8.0
29.1	32.0	27.4	25.4	13.7		Trade Receivables (net)	28.4	28.3
8.6	11.5	12.1	13.9	6.7		Inventory	11.8	11.8
2.7	1.4	2.4	2.7	3.7		All Other Current	1.8	1.9
54.1	53.3	51.7	49.4	35.4		Total Current	51.2	49.9
32.0	34.3	36.8	40.3	29.5		Fixed Assets (net)	37.1	38.0
5.0	5.1	5.1	4.7	23.9		Intangibles (net)	4.5	5.3
8.9	7.3	6.3	5.5	11.2		All Other Non-Current	7.1	6.8
100.0	100.0	100.0	100.0	100.0		Total	100.0	100.0
						LIABILITIES		
16.8	9.2	8.1	7.2	3.0		Notes Payable-Short Term	9.7	9.6
5.6	9.1	5.9	5.3	12.2		Cur. Mat.-L.T.D.	6.6	6.6
28.0	17.7	15.0	13.1	8.8		Trade Payables	15.2	16.0
.1	.0	.2	.5	.1		Income Taxes Payable	.2	.1
25.0	7.5	9.5	9.1	7.1		All Other Current	9.5	8.5
75.4	43.5	38.7	35.2	31.3		Total Current	41.1	40.8
39.4	27.7	23.1	21.9	17.0		Long-Term Debt	26.7	26.7
.0	.3	.6	1.2	3.0		Deferred Taxes	.8	.7
17.2	8.9	6.4	6.4	11.2		All Other Non-Current	5.2	5.5
-32.0	19.6	31.1	35.3	37.6		Net Worth	26.2	26.2
100.0	100.0	100.0	100.0	100.0		Total Liabilities & Net Worth	100.0	100.0
						INCOME DATA		
100.0	100.0	100.0	100.0	100.0		Net Sales	100.0	100.0
51.0	44.3	36.9	28.0	30.1		Gross Profit	37.4	35.2
49.9	40.6	32.1	23.8	23.2		Operating Expenses	32.3	31.0
1.0	3.7	4.8	4.2	6.9		Operating Profit	5.1	4.2
.9	1.6	1.4	1.8	2.8		All Other Expenses (net)	1.6	1.3
.1	2.2	3.4	2.4	4.1		Profit Before Taxes	3.5	2.9
						RATIOS		
1.8	2.1	2.4	1.9	1.9			2.0	2.0
1.0	1.2	1.3	1.4	1.0		Current	1.3	1.3
.5	.8	.9	1.0	.7			.9	.9
1.4	1.6	1.8	1.3	1.3			1.6	1.4
.8	1.0	1.0	.9	.8		Quick	.9	.9
.5	.5	.6	.6	.4			.6	.6
20 18.5	30 12.3	32 11.5	41 8.9	29 12.5			32 11.3	34 10.8
34 10.6	38 9.6	44 8.3	55 6.7	39 9.4		Sales/Receivables	44 8.3	45 8.2
41 8.9	51 7.1	59 6.2	66 5.6	57 6.5			57 6.4	58 6.3
4 102.1	4 84.4	11 33.9	18 20.3	5 70.5			9 38.9	11 34.7
11 33.5	14 26.4	25 14.6	33 11.1	23 15.9		Cost of Sales/Inventory	24 15.1	24 15.1
30 12.3	33 11.0	41 8.8	61 6.0	37 9.9			43 8.4	43 8.6
17 21.0	19 19.4	19 18.8	21 17.3	17 21.8			18 20.1	20 18.2
37 9.7	37 9.8	30 12.1	36 10.1	30 12.1		Cost of Sales/Payables	32 11.3	32 11.4
65 5.6	56 6.5	49 7.5	50 7.3	50 7.3			52 7.0	54 6.7
14.3	9.0	7.5	7.7	7.4			8.9	8.4
-323.1	26.6	17.5	13.4	104.1		Sales/Working Capital	21.8	20.3
-11.3	-22.6	-59.9	272.8	-13.1			-52.6	-37.6
3.9	5.1	6.9	7.5	5.7			7.0	5.6
(41) 1.4	(72) 2.4	(115) 3.1	(70) 2.8	(16) 1.6		EBIT/Interest	(362) 2.6	(332) 2.4
-.5	-.1	1.1	1.0	.3			1.0	.8
		5.4	2.9	4.5		Net Profit + Depr., Dep.,	3.4	3.5
	(25) 1.6	(29) 2.1	(10) 1.1			Amort./Cur. Mat. L/T/D	(106) 1.7	(103) 1.9
	1.0	1.4	.3				1.1	1.1
.8	.6	.7	.6	.5			.6	.7
-4.3	1.9	1.3	1.4	1.9		Fixed/Worth	1.5	1.5
-.4	-7.2	4.6	3.5	-1.7			6.0	7.4
1.5	1.4	1.0	.9	1.3			1.0	1.2
-10.9	4.5	2.4	2.1	4.3		Debt/Worth	2.6	2.5
-2.7	-12.3	10.7	5.5	-3.4			16.3	13.2
63.0	47.8	54.8	31.2	33.6		% Profit Before Taxes/Tangible	55.5	43.1
(21) 8.8	(55) 18.8	(105) 18.9	(63) 12.1	(11) 25.9		Net Worth	(316) 22.5	(279) 18.5
-6.5	-2.8	2.9	1.1	-.4			5.1	2.9
15.1	11.8	13.2	8.4	11.3		% Profit Before Taxes/Total	14.6	12.1
1.9	4.4	5.5	4.2	2.7		Assets	5.9	4.9
-9.0	-3.3	.4	.1	-1.6			.0	-.8
32.8	23.7	11.5	7.4	9.7			15.2	12.3
12.0	9.8	6.0	4.1	5.2		Sales/Net Fixed Assets	6.4	5.6
6.6	4.3	3.8	2.9	3.2			3.7	3.2
4.4	3.9	2.8	2.1	1.8			3.1	2.8
3.5	2.7	2.2	1.7	1.4		Sales/Total Assets	2.2	2.1
2.7	2.1	1.7	1.4	.9			1.7	1.5
1.5	2.4	2.0	3.4	3.0			1.9	2.4
(35) 2.8	(60) 3.5	(117) 4.0	(71) 4.7	(15) 6.5		% Depr., Dep., Amort./Sales	(352) 3.5	(314) 3.9
5.1	6.8	6.1	6.1	7.5			5.5	5.9
2.6	3.2	2.5	.6			% Officers', Directors'	2.7	2.6
(33) 7.1	(45) 4.8	(51) 4.2	(17) 1.4			Owners' Comp/Sales	(180) 5.1	(132) 4.7
13.4	7.9	6.1	2.5				8.6	7.1
49722M	271096M	1464576M	2747316M	1654279M	969842M	Net Sales ($)	8541113M	9631928M
13683M	90661M	635407M	1592755M	1159438M	881451M	Total Assets ($)	4604592M	5410876M

© RMA 2011

M = $ thousand   MM = $ million

See Pages 9 through 22 for Explanation of Ratios and Data

Comparative Historical Data | Current Data Sorted by Sales

4/1/08-3/31/09 ALL	4/1/09-3/31/10 ALL	4/1/10-3/31/11 ALL		0-1MM	1-3MM	3-5MM	5-10MM	10-25MM	25MM & OVER
			Type of Statement						
43	47	44	Unqualified		1	1	4	13	25
75	68	65	Reviewed	1	5	6	18	23	12
45	51	47	Compiled	9	17	7	4	8	2
52	45	61	Tax Returns	16	22	11	9	3	
133	130	130	Other	3	20	12	23	34	38
					67 (4/1-9/30/10)		280 (10/1/10-3/31/11)		
348	341	347	**NUMBER OF STATEMENTS**	29	65	37	58	81	77
%	%	%	**ASSETS**	%	%	%	%	%	%
7.9	10.3	9.5	Cash & Equivalents	15.5	8.4	9.4	10.7	8.5	8.4
26.6	26.4	27.4	Trade Receivables (net)	26.0	24.8	33.4	27.9	29.4	24.9
12.5	12.1	11.6	Inventory	6.7	10.3	10.3	11.1	14.3	12.6
1.9	3.3	2.3	All Other Current	3.2	1.2	3.5	2.2	2.1	2.7
48.8	52.2	50.9	Total Current	51.4	44.7	56.7	51.9	54.3	48.7
37.8	37.1	35.9	Fixed Assets (net)	34.2	38.4	31.1	38.4	37.4	33.4
6.2	5.5	6.2	Intangibles (net)	5.4	8.3	4.1	2.2	4.2	11.0
7.2	5.2	7.0	All Other Non-Current	8.9	8.6	8.1	7.5	4.1	7.0
100.0	100.0	100.0	Total	100.0	100.0	100.0	100.0	100.0	100.0
			LIABILITIES						
11.4	11.3	9.0	Notes Payable-Short Term	13.8	11.8	11.3	7.5	8.8	5.2
6.8	7.0	6.9	Cur. Mat.-L.T.D.	4.8	8.1	7.3	8.1	5.7	6.9
14.6	16.0	16.6	Trade Payables	21.9	19.6	19.0	15.4	15.8	12.7
.1	.2	.2	Income Taxes Payable	.0	.1	.1	.1	.2	.5
9.5	11.5	11.0	All Other Current	7.3	19.4	11.1	6.8	9.3	10.1
42.5	46.0	43.7	Total Current	47.7	59.0	48.8	37.8	39.8	35.3
27.4	25.2	25.9	Long-Term Debt	43.1	35.6	21.3	25.6	22.4	17.2
.6	.7	.7	Deferred Taxes	.2	.3	.0	.8	.9	1.5
6.4	7.6	8.6	All Other Non-Current	25.1	8.8	8.9	4.7	5.1	8.7
23.1	20.5	21.1	Net Worth	-16.2	-3.8	21.0	31.1	31.8	37.3
100.0	100.0	100.0	Total Liabilities & Net Worth	100.0	100.0	100.0	100.0	100.0	100.0
			INCOME DATA						
100.0	100.0	100.0	Net Sales	100.0	100.0	100.0	100.0	100.0	100.0
36.9	35.6	38.1	Gross Profit	52.9	48.8	44.4	38.9	30.4	27.9
34.2	34.1	34.1	Operating Expenses	49.5	46.3	39.9	34.3	26.8	22.8
2.8	1.5	4.0	Operating Profit	3.5	2.5	4.5	4.6	3.7	5.1
1.4	1.4	1.6	All Other Expenses (net)	1.1	1.6	1.4	1.8	1.0	2.2
1.3	.2	2.4	Profit Before Taxes	2.4	.9	3.1	2.8	2.6	2.9
			RATIOS						
1.9	1.9	2.0	Current	2.1	1.9	2.1	2.8	2.2	2.0
1.2	1.2	1.3		1.3	.9	1.2	1.5	1.2	1.4
.9	.8	.9		.6	.6	.7	.9	1.0	1.0
1.3	1.3	1.5	Quick	1.6	1.4	1.6	1.7	1.7	1.4
.9	.8	.9		1.0	.7	1.0	1.1	.9	.9
.6	.5	.6		.5	.4	.5	.7	.6	.7
30 · 12.1	29 · 12.7	31 · 11.6	Sales/Receivables	22 · 16.4	28 · 13.2	32 · 11.5	30 · 12.2	38 · 9.7	35 · 10.3
42 · 8.8	42 · 8.8	42 · 8.7		32 · 11.4	36 · 10.1	40 · 9.1	44 · 8.4	53 · 6.9	50 · 7.4
53 · 6.9	56 · 6.5	57 · 6.4		46 · 7.9	46 · 8.0	59 · 6.1	55 · 6.6	64 · 5.7	59 · 6.2
11 · 33.3	8 · 44.0	9 · 39.0	Cost of Sales/Inventory	0 · UND	5 · 71.8	4 · 92.7	11 · 34.0	16 · 22.2	15 · 23.8
23 · 16.2	21 · 17.5	23 · 15.9		7 · 49.6	14 · 26.5	13 · 27.2	21 · 17.0	29 · 12.7	31 · 11.6
45 · 8.1	44 · 8.3	41 · 8.8		34 · 11.0	33 · 11.0	38 · 9.7	36 · 10.0	54 · 6.8	47 · 7.7
19 · 18.9	17 · 21.4	21 · 17.6	Cost of Sales/Payables	8 · 45.1	25 · 14.5	17 · 21.6	19 · 19.3	21 · 17.3	19 · 19.4
31 · 11.6	31 · 11.9	33 · 11.1		37 · 9.8	40 · 9.0	31 · 11.7	28 · 13.1	35 · 10.3	30 · 12.1
52 · 7.0	53 · 6.9	54 · 6.8		67 · 5.4	65 · 5.6	51 · 7.2	46 · 7.9	57 · 6.4	44 · 8.3
9.4	9.1	8.3	Sales/Working Capital	8.5	11.1	8.5	7.5	7.7	7.8
26.2	28.3	21.9		39.5	-69.7	35.3	15.0	18.3	12.4
-33.5	-21.2	-35.2		-13.5	-12.9	-19.8	-55.4	NM	NM
5.4	4.3	5.8	EBIT/Interest	5.5	3.4	6.4	6.5	7.6	7.0
(319) 1.6	(312) 1.4	(319) 2.4		(23) 1.8	(61) 1.6	(36) 3.3	(50) 2.0	(78) 3.0	(71) 3.0
-.2	-.9	.5		.2	-.9	1.3	.3	1.1	.4
2.8	2.5	3.2	Net Profit + Depr., Dep., Amort./Cur. Mat. L/T/D					5.3	3.5
(99) 1.5	(84) 1.4	(75) 1.9						(21) 2.1	(34) 2.1
.8	.3	.9						1.4	.5
.6	.7	.7	Fixed/Worth	.7	1.0	.6	.5	.7	.5
1.6	1.6	1.8		4.2	10.0	1.5	1.3	1.3	1.4
UND	-24.7	46.9		-.5	-.8	6.0	4.0	3.7	3.7
1.1	1.1	1.1	Debt/Worth	1.0	1.9	1.3	1.0	1.0	.9
2.9	3.0	3.0		12.8	76.8	3.2	2.3	2.5	2.1
UND	-36.2	-135.9		-2.8	-3.5	27.0	12.1	7.5	10.8
33.2	34.6	41.7	% Profit Before Taxes/Tangible Net Worth	66.1	38.0	50.9	54.2	32.8	41.8
(261) 10.3	(247) 7.2	(258) 18.3		(16) 21.6	(34) 8.4	(31) 26.6	(47) 18.9	(69) 15.4	(61) 18.8
-3.5	-11.5	.7		-5.1	-15.9	3.6	.3	5.2	.8
9.9	8.2	11.8	% Profit Before Taxes/Total Assets	15.2	8.7	15.0	15.9	10.4	11.8
2.3	1.2	4.4		4.7	3.0	4.9	4.2	4.6	5.3
-4.1	-6.6	-1.0		-6.0	-7.0	.6	-.9	.5	-1.6
13.9	15.5	14.5	Sales/Net Fixed Assets	25.9	16.3	26.4	13.5	9.2	10.8
5.9	5.9	6.5		10.1	6.6	11.7	6.8	6.1	5.2
3.5	3.2	3.6		5.7	3.3	3.8	3.9	3.7	3.2
2.9	3.0	3.0	Sales/Total Assets	3.7	3.5	3.9	3.2	2.7	2.3
2.1	2.1	2.2		2.9	2.5	2.6	2.4	2.0	1.7
1.5	1.5	1.6		2.3	1.8	2.0	1.7	1.6	1.3
2.1	2.4	2.4	% Depr., Dep., Amort./Sales	1.6	2.4	1.7	2.8	2.2	2.4
(299) 4.0	(288) 4.2	(299) 4.0		(22) 3.5	(53) 4.8	(27) 3.3	(54) 4.1	(77) 3.8	(66) 4.6
5.9	6.6	6.3		5.8	7.3	6.3	6.4	5.4	6.8
2.7	2.6	2.2	% Officers', Directors', Owners' Comp/Sales	2.5	3.8	3.5	2.0	1.5	.6
(128) 4.8	(132) 4.8	(148) 4.6		(19) 9.0	(40) 5.2	(20) 4.9	(33) 4.0	(23) 2.8	(13) 1.4
7.3	8.7	8.0		12.9	9.7	7.0	7.9	4.7	3.3
7610589M	5744794M	7156831M	Net Sales ($)	18245M	124317M	156463M	420646M	1336914M	5100246M
4485526M	3235691M	4373395M	Total Assets ($)	7260M	65836M	65978M	205298M	710160M	3318863M

© RMA 2011

M = $ thousand   MM = $ million
See Pages 9 through 22 for Explanation of Ratios and Data

Current Data Sorted by Assets

Comparative Historical Data

Type of Statement	0-500M	500M-2MM	2-10MM	10-50MM	50-100MM	100-250MM		4/1/06-3/31/07 ALL	4/1/07-3/31/08 ALL
Unqualified			3	1					
Reviewed			8	3				3	1
Compiled	1	3	5					19	15
Tax Returns	1	1						12	12
Other	1	3	6	4				5	4
								8	14
	4 (4/1-9/30/10)			35 (10/1/10-3/31/11)					
NUMBER OF STATEMENTS	2	7	22	8				47	46

(50-100MM and 100-250MM columns: DATA NOT AVAILABLE)

	0-500M %	500M-2MM %	2-10MM %	10-50MM %	50-100MM %	100-250MM %		4/1/06-3/31/07 ALL %	4/1/07-3/31/08 ALL %
ASSETS									
Cash & Equivalents			9.9					7.2	10.9
Trade Receivables (net)			28.3					26.5	24.9
Inventory			9.1					12.3	7.8
All Other Current			.7					1.3	1.3
Total Current			48.0					47.2	45.0
Fixed Assets (net)			46.2					41.0	43.5
Intangibles (net)			2.0					5.4	5.0
All Other Non-Current			3.7					6.4	6.5
Total			100.0					100.0	100.0
LIABILITIES									
Notes Payable-Short Term			7.5					8.5	7.7
Cur. Mat.-L.T.D.			10.3					6.4	8.1
Trade Payables			9.3					9.3	7.5
Income Taxes Payable			.0					.4	.2
All Other Current			7.1					9.6	7.6
Total Current			34.2					34.2	31.1
Long-Term Debt			28.7					26.6	27.5
Deferred Taxes			.3					2.1	1.0
All Other Non-Current			21.6					11.0	14.2
Net Worth			15.3					26.1	26.3
Total Liabilities & Net Worth			100.0					100.0	100.0
INCOME DATA									
Net Sales			100.0					100.0	100.0
Gross Profit			31.5					34.1	36.3
Operating Expenses			27.1					30.0	30.3
Operating Profit			4.3					4.1	6.0
All Other Expenses (net)			1.1					1.8	1.3
Profit Before Taxes			3.2					2.3	4.7

RATIOS

	0-500M	500M-2MM	2-10MM	10-50MM	50-100MM	100-250MM		4/1/06-3/31/07 ALL	4/1/07-3/31/08 ALL
Current			2.1					2.5	2.2
			1.4					1.4	1.4
			1.0					1.0	1.0
Quick			1.7					2.1	2.1
			1.1					1.1	1.2
			.7					.7	.7
Sales/Receivables		38	9.6					39 9.4	36 10.1
		45	8.1					46 7.9	46 8.0
		65	5.7					61 6.0	64 5.7
Cost of Sales/Inventory		3	108.4					0 UND	0 UND
		14	25.3					9 41.8	6 59.1
		36	10.0					38 9.7	31 11.6
Cost of Sales/Payables		12	30.6					11 33.0	8 47.6
		18	20.2					20 18.4	16 23.2
		30	12.2					35 10.5	25 14.7
Sales/Working Capital			7.7					6.7	6.9
			19.4					19.5	14.6
			-112.9					788.8	-195.5
EBIT/Interest			6.0					5.5	4.9
			2.7					(46) 1.9	(45) 3.0
			1.0					.8	1.3
Net Profit + Depr., Dep., Amort./Cur. Mat. L/T/D								4.4	3.0
								(11) 2.0	(15) 2.1
								1.6	1.1
Fixed/Worth			1.0					.8	.8
			1.6					1.7	1.3
			2.9					4.5	4.9
Debt/Worth			1.4					1.3	.9
			2.1					2.4	2.3
			4.8					7.5	7.5
% Profit Before Taxes/Tangible Net Worth			53.1					33.0	37.2
		(21)	19.1					(38) 14.6	(40) 22.3
			4.4					.6	6.0
% Profit Before Taxes/Total Assets			14.3					14.4	11.9
			5.3					3.8	6.7
			.0					-.6	1.7
Sales/Net Fixed Assets			6.4					11.0	8.0
			4.4					5.7	4.3
			3.3					2.8	2.8
Sales/Total Assets			2.7					2.8	2.5
			1.9					2.2	1.9
			1.5					1.3	1.2
% Depr., Dep., Amort./Sales			3.0					1.9	2.7
		(19)	6.1					(46) 3.5	(45) 4.6
			7.9					7.2	6.7
% Officers', Directors', Owners' Comp/Sales								2.8	3.3
								(23) 5.5	(28) 5.8
								7.6	10.9
Net Sales ($)	4675M	13216M	189842M	151815M				462804M	339577M
Total Assets ($)	687M	6877M	94221M	126277M				257348M	204720M

M = $ thousand   MM = $ million
See Pages 9 through 22 for Explanation of Ratios and Data

Comparative Historical Data | | | Current Data Sorted by Sales

					Type of Statement							
1		3		4	Unqualified					3	1	
17		10		11	Reviewed			1		4	6	
7		5		9	Compiled	1	2	3		2	1	
7		5		2	Tax Returns	1		1				
13		11		13	Other	1	1	4		3	2	2
4/1/08-3/31/09		4/1/09-3/31/10		4/1/10-3/31/11			4 (4/1-9/30/10)			35 (10/1/10-3/31/11)		
ALL		ALL		ALL		0-1MM	1-3MM	3-5MM		5-10MM	10-25MM	25MM & OVER
41		34		39	**NUMBER OF STATEMENTS**	3	3	9		12	10	2
%		%		%	**ASSETS**	%	%	%		%	%	%
6.6		8.4		9.3	Cash & Equivalents					7.9	8.5	
24.9		28.2		27.5	Trade Receivables (net)					25.7	24.4	
6.7		9.2		7.7	Inventory					10.4	9.0	
1.2		1.0		.7	All Other Current					.3	.5	
39.3		46.8		45.2	Total Current					44.4	42.4	
44.7		39.9		40.6	Fixed Assets (net)					47.3	54.7	
9.1		7.0		6.1	Intangibles (net)					4.7	1.5	
6.9		6.3		8.0	All Other Non-Current					3.6	1.4	
100.0		100.0		100.0	Total					100.0	100.0	
					LIABILITIES							
11.6		12.0		9.5	Notes Payable-Short Term					6.4	4.4	
6.5		7.0		7.3	Cur. Mat.-L.T.D.					11.0	5.6	
9.6		9.3		10.5	Trade Payables					9.6	7.3	
.3		.2		.1	Income Taxes Payable					.0	.2	
9.7		10.0		8.2	All Other Current					10.4	5.2	
37.7		38.5		35.5	Total Current					37.4	22.7	
29.1		30.3		32.6	Long-Term Debt					34.7	25.5	
.6		.2		.3	Deferred Taxes					.0	.4	
19.7		20.6		21.1	All Other Non-Current					32.8	5.9	
12.9		10.4		10.5	Net Worth					-4.9	45.5	
100.0		100.0		100.0	Total Liabilties & Net Worth					100.0	100.0	
					INCOME DATA							
100.0		100.0		100.0	Net Sales					100.0	100.0	
32.0		36.2		34.1	Gross Profit					28.2	29.2	
29.2		34.0		30.9	Operating Expenses					23.2	26.8	
2.8		2.2		3.2	Operating Profit					5.0	2.4	
.8		2.0		.9	All Other Expenses (net)					2.3	.8	
2.0		.2		2.3	Profit Before Taxes					2.7	1.6	
					RATIOS							
2.1		2.5		2.6						1.6	4.1	
1.3		1.3		1.3	Current					1.2	2.2	
.8		.8		.8						.9	1.3	
1.8		2.0		2.0						1.4	3.2	
1.0		1.0		1.1	Quick					.9	1.8	
.6		.7		.6						.6	1.1	
35 10.5	34 10.8	38 9.5			Sales/Receivables				31 11.8	45 8.2	
40 9.1	52 7.0	48 7.6							41 9.0	61 6.0	
54 6.7	68 5.4	66 5.5							59 6.1	74 4.9	
0 UND	0 UND	0 UND			Cost of Sales/Inventory				3 111.1	0 UND	
9 41.3	10 37.2	5 68.5							13 29.1	16 22.3	
25 14.7	30 12.4	31 11.8							38 9.7	42 8.7	
10 37.1	8 46.6	10 35.5			Cost of Sales/Payables				13 27.7	6 57.8	
16 23.5	17 21.0	20 18.6							23 16.1	20 18.2	
24 15.2	31 12.0	32 11.4							30 12.3	33 11.1	
8.0		6.3		5.5	Sales/Working Capital					10.9	3.9	
26.3		22.2		17.0						43.6	6.0	
-22.2		-24.6		-38.5						-111.4	NM	
5.0		4.3		5.3	EBIT/Interest					6.4	3.5	
1.8		1.7		(38) 2.2						4.0	2.2	
1.0		-.6		.7						-.6	1.5	
2.0					Net Profit + Depr., Dep., Amort./Cur. Mat. L/T/D							
(11) 1.5												
.6												
1.0		.9		1.0	Fixed/Worth					1.5	.9	
2.1		1.7		1.6						2.0	1.5	
NM		-2.8		9.6						13.5	2.0	
1.1		1.3		1.2	Debt/Worth					1.4	.6	
3.4		2.8		2.2						2.7	1.2	
NM		-6.8		14.3						26.1	2.8	
27.2		22.1		54.3	% Profit Before Taxes/Tangible Net Worth					121.4	22.0	
(31) 14.4	(24) 1.6	(31) 9.5							(10) 36.5	8.0	
3.2		-18.3		.7						-4.3	1.5	
10.0		9.1		13.4	% Profit Before Taxes/Total Assets					16.8	5.4	
2.9		2.1		4.0						8.7	4.5	
.0		-5.4		-.7						-7.7	1.0	
8.4		18.4		9.5	Sales/Net Fixed Assets					6.1	6.4	
6.0		6.1		4.5						4.6	2.7	
2.5		2.6		3.1						3.2	1.6	
2.8		2.8		2.7	Sales/Total Assets					2.9	2.0	
1.8		1.8		1.9						2.5	1.6	
1.5		1.3		1.3						1.5	1.0	
2.5		1.6		3.0	% Depr., Dep., Amort./Sales					2.7	2.6	
(38) 4.5	(29) 4.1	(31) 5.2							(10) 5.0	7.4	
6.4		9.1		8.8						8.8	11.5	
2.6		2.6		2.8	% Officers', Directors' Owners' Comp/Sales							
(20) 4.7	(18) 3.9	(14) 4.7										
8.9		9.9		6.1									
427670M		328119M		359548M	Net Sales ($)	2190M	4342M	35197M		94960M	163363M	59496M
257344M		208265M		228062M	Total Assets ($)	1640M	2887M	18707M		51746M	121402M	31680M

M = $ thousand   MM = $ million
See Pages 9 through 22 for Explanation of Ratios and Data

Current Data Sorted by Assets   Comparative Historical Data

0-500M	500M-2MM	2-10MM	10-50MM	50-100MM	100-250MM	Type of Statement	6/9/06–3/31/07	4/1/07–3/31/08
		3	2	1		Unqualified	6	5
		9	1			Reviewed	9	10
	2					Compiled	6	1
1	2					Tax Returns	2	1
1	3	4	1			Other	8	15
	10 (4/1-9/30/10)		21 (10/1/10-3/31/11)				4/1/06-3/31/07 ALL	4/1/07-3/31/08 ALL
2	8	16	4	1		NUMBER OF STATEMENTS	31	32
%	%	%	%	%	%	**ASSETS**	%	%
		9.5				Cash & Equivalents	11.1	12.6
		30.3				Trade Receivables (net)	32.5	31.2
		14.2				Inventory	9.2	8.6
		3.9				All Other Current	1.4	1.1
		57.9				Total Current	54.2	53.4
		32.0				Fixed Assets (net)	38.0	32.7
		.6				Intangibles (net)	3.6	4.8
		9.5				All Other Non-Current	4.3	9.1
		100.0				Total	100.0	100.0
						LIABILITIES		
		5.0				Notes Payable-Short Term	6.5	3.7
		3.9				Cur. Mat.-L.T.D.	5.7	6.0
		12.6				Trade Payables	9.9	12.3
		.0				Income Taxes Payable	.1	.0
		9.1				All Other Current	7.9	11.0
		30.5				Total Current	30.2	33.0
		15.2				Long-Term Debt	22.1	14.0
		.5				Deferred Taxes	.5	.4
		3.7				All Other Non-Current	2.1	5.3
		50.0				Net Worth	45.2	47.4
		100.0				Total Liabilities & Net Worth	100.0	100.0
						INCOME DATA		
		100.0				Net Sales	100.0	100.0
		33.1				Gross Profit	37.7	38.8
		26.9				Operating Expenses	32.7	35.4
		6.2				Operating Profit	5.0	3.4
		.1				All Other Expenses (net)	1.2	1.4
		6.1				Profit Before Taxes	3.8	2.1
						RATIOS		
		3.8					3.6	3.8
		2.0				Current	1.8	1.6
		1.0					1.0	1.0
		3.1					2.9	3.3
		1.3				Quick	1.7	1.2
		.7					.8	.9
	41	8.9					43 8.5	37 9.8
	47	7.8				Sales/Receivables	59 6.2	45 8.1
	57	6.4					82 4.4	75 4.8
	18	20.8					12 30.4	14 26.9
	31	11.8				Cost of Sales/Inventory	23 16.0	20 18.0
	47	7.8					40 9.2	33 11.0
	9	38.8					10 35.6	15 23.6
	26	14.3				Cost of Sales/Payables	23 15.8	26 14.0
	49	7.4					44 8.4	49 7.5
		4.6					3.6	2.8
		9.9				Sales/Working Capital	9.1	14.6
		NM					-292.9	NM
		56.4					16.9	9.2
	(15)	9.9				EBIT/Interest	(28) 3.6	(28) 2.5
		2.2					.4	.6
						Net Profit + Depr., Dep., Amort./Cur. Mat. L/T/D		
		.3					.3	.3
		.5				Fixed/Worth	.9	.8
		1.5					3.1	1.7
		.5					.3	.3
		.9				Debt/Worth	1.1	1.2
		2.4					5.1	7.1
		62.6					40.2	34.9
		22.0				% Profit Before Taxes/Tangible Net Worth	(28) 19.3	(27) 5.9
		5.5					-3.7	-.6
		23.3					17.1	15.2
		8.6				% Profit Before Taxes/Total Assets	6.2	5.7
		2.3					-1.9	-.7
		16.0					10.5	11.1
		9.6				Sales/Net Fixed Assets	5.5	6.9
		3.1					3.1	4.3
		2.7					2.2	2.6
		2.4				Sales/Total Assets	1.8	2.2
		1.5					1.2	1.2
		1.3					2.9	2.7
	(15)	2.6				% Depr., Dep., Amort./Sales	(29) 4.6	(29) 4.0
		5.1					6.1	5.9
							4.4	2.0
						% Officers', Directors' Owners' Comp/Sales	(14) 6.7	(13) 4.6
							12.2	11.7
1314M	14608M	203035M	205100M	45808M		Net Sales ($)	312783M	436726M
505M	8234M	90895M	117838M	53720M		Total Assets ($)	186002M	223032M

(Columns 0-500M, 500M-2MM, 10-50MM, 50-100MM, and 100-250MM marked "DATA NOT AVAILABLE" in the balance sheet and income sections.)

M = $ thousand   MM = $ million
See Pages 9 through 22 for Explanation of Ratios and Data

Comparative Historical Data

Current Data Sorted by Sales

							Type of Statement							
	3		2		6		Unqualified			1		1		4
	11		12		11		Reviewed		1		4		4	2
	6		3		2		Compiled		2					
	2		3		3		Tax Returns	1	2					
	13		9		9		Other	1	3		2		2	1
	4/1/08- 3/31/09 ALL		4/1/09- 3/31/10 ALL		4/1/10- 3/31/11 ALL				10 (4/1-9/30/10)			21 (10/1/10-3/31/11)		
								0-1MM	1-3MM	3-5MM	5-10MM	10-25MM	25MM & OVER
	35		29		31		NUMBER OF STATEMENTS	2	8	1	6	7	7
	%		%		%		ASSETS	%	%	%	%	%	%
	9.3		11.3		8.3		Cash & Equivalents						
	31.2		32.8		30.6		Trade Receivables (net)						
	8.6		12.1		13.7		Inventory						
	1.5		4.6		3.3		All Other Current						
	50.5		60.8		56.0		Total Current						
	34.5		30.9		31.2		Fixed Assets (net)						
	6.1		1.3		3.0		Intangibles (net)						
	8.9		7.0		9.8		All Other Non-Current						
	100.0		100.0		100.0		Total						
							LIABILITIES						
	6.6		13.1		11.0		Notes Payable-Short Term						
	11.8		8.7		4.1		Cur. Mat.-L.T.D.						
	13.9		15.2		12.3		Trade Payables						
	.0		.2		.1		Income Taxes Payable						
	8.1		7.3		8.6		All Other Current						
	40.5		44.5		36.0		Total Current						
	24.3		21.6		21.9		Long-Term Debt						
	.4		.4		.8		Deferred Taxes						
	4.8		2.9		4.3		All Other Non-Current						
	30.1		30.5		37.0		Net Worth						
	100.0		100.0		100.0		Total Liabilities & Net Worth						
							INCOME DATA						
	100.0		100.0		100.0		Net Sales						
	33.3		35.6		32.5		Gross Profit						
	31.3		31.5		28.8		Operating Expenses						
	2.0		4.2		3.6		Operating Profit						
	1.3		.9		.6		All Other Expenses (net)						
	.7		3.3		3.1		Profit Before Taxes						
							RATIOS						
	2.9		3.3		3.4								
	1.4		1.5		2.1		Current						
	.8		.9		1.0								
	2.2		2.6		2.4								
	.9		1.0		1.2		Quick						
	.6		.6		.7								
38	9.5	36	10.1	42	8.6								
47	7.8	48	7.6	52	7.1		Sales/Receivables						
60	6.1	62	5.9	60	6.1								
9	39.1	15	24.9	18	20.3								
20	18.5	28	13.1	27	13.7		Cost of Sales/Inventory						
28	13.0	39	9.4	44	8.4								
13	28.7	12	30.0	20	18.3								
26	13.8	27	13.6	25	14.5		Cost of Sales/Payables						
45	8.1	52	7.1	50	7.3								
	5.5		5.3		4.6								
	15.8		12.7		9.0		Sales/Working Capital						
	-35.9		NM		765.7								
	5.4		8.6		14.3								
(33)	1.6	(26)	2.3	(30)	4.8		EBIT/Interest						
	-.1		-.9		.9								
					8.6		Net Profit + Depr., Dep.,						
				(10)	2.4		Amort./Cur. Mat. L/T/D						
					1.4								
	.4		.3		.3								
	1.5		1.3		.7		Fixed/Worth						
	3.2		13.2		1.7								
	.8		.5		.5								
	2.7		2.2		1.8		Debt/Worth						
	20.3		26.7		2.9								
	52.2		29.7		60.1		% Profit Before Taxes/Tangible						
(29)	6.1	(23)	18.3	(28)	15.0		Net Worth						
	-10.6		-10.8		.6								
	8.5		13.6		15.0		% Profit Before Taxes/Total						
	1.2		4.8		5.1		Assets						
	-4.1		-6.0		.1								
	13.4		20.7		13.2								
	7.2		9.2		9.5		Sales/Net Fixed Assets						
	3.8		3.9		3.8								
	2.8		2.9		2.6								
	2.1		2.4		2.2		Sales/Total Assets						
	1.8		1.8		1.4								
	2.5		2.6		1.5								
(29)	4.3	(24)	4.5	(28)	2.6		% Depr., Dep., Amort./Sales						
	6.0		6.1		5.1								
	2.1				1.6								
(14)	4.3			(16)	4.4		% Officers', Directors' Owners' Comp/Sales						
	8.1				12.7								
	497009M		381447M		469865M		Net Sales ($)	1314M	14608M	4182M	42256M	105088M	302417M
	236523M		178924M		271192M		Total Assets ($)	505M	8234M	3450M	23191M	48784M	187028M

M = $ thousand   MM = $ million
See Pages 9 through 22 for Explanation of Ratios and Data

Current Data Sorted by Assets   Comparative Historical Data

0-500M	500M-2MM	2-10MM	10-50MM	50-100MM	100-250MM	Type of Statement	4/1/06-3/31/07 ALL	4/1/07-3/31/08 ALL
		3	1		4	Unqualified	10	8
	2	1	1		2	Reviewed	4	8
	2				1	Compiled	5	3
1	1	2	4	1	7	Tax Returns	1	3
						Other	24	22
		10 (4/1-9/30/10)		23 (10/1/10-3/31/11)				
1	1	7	8	3	13	**NUMBER OF STATEMENTS**	44	44
%	%	%	%	%	%	**ASSETS**	%	%
					10.9	Cash & Equivalents	10.9	15.9
					24.2	Trade Receivables (net)	27.5	24.3
					18.9	Inventory	15.4	21.7
					3.0	All Other Current	3.1	2.2
					57.1	Total Current	56.9	64.1
					36.8	Fixed Assets (net)	35.5	29.7
					.5	Intangibles (net)	2.5	1.0
					5.7	All Other Non-Current	5.1	5.3
					100.0	Total	100.0	100.0
						LIABILITIES		
					6.7	Notes Payable-Short Term	4.0	3.5
					2.5	Cur. Mat.-L.T.D.	3.6	2.5
					21.6	Trade Payables	20.6	24.6
					.5	Income Taxes Payable	.4	.7
					8.5	All Other Current	7.6	9.2
					39.8	Total Current	36.2	40.5
					18.8	Long-Term Debt	18.8	9.5
					.7	Deferred Taxes	1.1	.5
					3.1	All Other Non-Current	5.7	4.4
					37.6	Net Worth	38.3	45.1
					100.0	Total Liabilties & Net Worth	100.0	100.0
						INCOME DATA		
					100.0	Net Sales	100.0	100.0
					18.1	Gross Profit	19.4	19.8
					11.9	Operating Expenses	11.6	14.1
					6.2	Operating Profit	7.8	5.7
					1.2	All Other Expenses (net)	1.1	.9
					5.0	Profit Before Taxes	6.7	4.8
						RATIOS		
					2.4		2.4	2.4
					1.3	Current	1.6	1.8
					1.1		1.2	1.3
					1.4		1.5	1.6
					.7	Quick	1.1	1.1
					.6		.6	.7
				21	17.8		15 25.0	16 23.4
				28	13.2	Sales/Receivables	22 16.5	22 16.3
				55	6.6		30 12.0	35 10.3
				16	22.8		5 69.5	10 37.1
				29	12.5	Cost of Sales/Inventory	15 24.9	24 15.3
				87	4.2		27 13.3	47 7.8
				17	20.9		11 34.5	14 26.5
				33	11.2	Cost of Sales/Payables	19 18.9	25 14.8
				40	9.0		29 12.4	38 9.7
					5.2		9.7	7.4
					13.9	Sales/Working Capital	16.0	14.9
					547.1		62.2	38.3
					57.1		33.6	49.1
					(11) 8.1	EBIT/Interest	(38) 7.1	(38) 12.4
					3.4		2.2	1.9
							80.7	14.5
						Net Profit + Depr., Dep., Amort./Cur. Mat. L/T/D	(11) 8.5	(11) 8.1
							1.1	2.0
					.2		.4	.2
					.9	Fixed/Worth	.9	.6
					1.4		2.3	1.1
					.8		.7	.6
					1.3	Debt/Worth	1.6	1.0
					3.8		3.4	2.1
					33.1		71.2	64.4
					(12) 22.2	% Profit Before Taxes/Tangible Net Worth	(38) 40.7	(42) 27.2
					3.2		14.1	10.5
					20.3		24.8	30.4
					6.9	% Profit Before Taxes/Total Assets	14.0	14.4
					3.3		2.8	3.3
					26.4		47.3	40.0
					5.1	Sales/Net Fixed Assets	18.6	20.9
					2.5		3.4	7.3
					4.2		5.4	4.8
					2.5	Sales/Total Assets	4.0	3.7
					.8		1.6	2.0
							.5	.5
						% Depr., Dep., Amort./Sales	(40) .8	(40) .8
							3.2	1.7
						% Officers', Directors' Owners' Comp/Sales		
4650M	6355M	93591M	902363M	455275M	6627832M	Net Sales ($)	9398206M	9702187M
109M	1623M	25968M	192182M	207849M	1894630M	Total Assets ($)	2098657M	2355480M

© RMA 2011

M = $ thousand   MM = $ million
See Pages 9 through 22 for Explanation of Ratios and Data

Comparative Historical Data

Current Data Sorted by Sales

			Type of Statement	0-1MM	1-3MM	3-5MM	5-10MM	10-25MM	25MM & OVER
15	12	8	Unqualified						8
8	7	4	Reviewed				1		3
5	3	4	Compiled				1	1	2
3		2	Tax Returns			1		1	
15	21	15	Other			1	2	1	11
4/1/08-3/31/09 ALL	4/1/09-3/31/10 ALL	4/1/10-3/31/11 ALL				10 (4/1-9/30/10)		23 (10/1/10-3/31/11)	
46	43	33	NUMBER OF STATEMENTS			2	4	3	24
%	%	%	ASSETS	%	%	%	%	%	%
13.2	13.0	13.9	Cash & Equivalents	D	D				11.6
24.5	23.4	22.6	Trade Receivables (net)	A	A				24.0
17.4	17.8	18.1	Inventory	T	T				19.1
6.0	3.0	4.5	All Other Current	A	A				3.4
61.0	57.1	59.1	Total Current						58.1
30.3	32.2	31.1	Fixed Assets (net)	N	N				33.0
2.8	2.0	2.0	Intangibles (net)	O	O				.7
5.9	8.7	7.8	All Other Non-Current	T	T				8.2
100.0	100.0	100.0	Total						100.0
			LIABILITIES	A	A				
5.7	5.4	4.6	Notes Payable-Short Term	V	V				6.4
2.5	2.7	2.0	Cur. Mat.-L.T.D.	A	A				2.1
19.3	20.9	20.6	Trade Payables	I	I				21.0
.8	.5	.2	Income Taxes Payable	L	L				.3
14.2	14.7	8.1	All Other Current	A	A				7.9
42.5	44.1	35.5	Total Current	B	B				37.7
14.5	8.5	13.3	Long-Term Debt	L	L				14.5
1.4	1.2	.5	Deferred Taxes	E	E				.6
6.0	4.5	3.7	All Other Non-Current						3.1
35.7	41.6	46.9	Net Worth						44.2
100.0	100.0	100.0	Total Liabilties & Net Worth						100.0
			INCOME DATA						
100.0	100.0	100.0	Net Sales						100.0
14.8	17.2	18.1	Gross Profit						16.5
10.1	13.5	13.2	Operating Expenses						12.0
4.7	3.7	4.9	Operating Profit						4.6
-.1	-.3	.0	All Other Expenses (net)						.7
4.8	4.1	4.9	Profit Before Taxes						3.9
			RATIOS						
2.7	2.4	2.6							2.3
1.6	1.3	1.7	Current						1.5
1.1	1.0	1.2							1.2
2.1	1.8	1.8							1.6
.9	1.0	1.0	Quick						.8
.5	.5	.6							.6
9 40.7	14 26.2	16 23.5							19 18.7
17 21.1	23 16.2	26 14.1	Sales/Receivables						27 13.6
31 11.7	40 9.1	50 7.4							50 7.3
3 126.2	5 71.4	7 56.1							8 45.5
10 36.5	15 24.8	17 21.1	Cost of Sales/Inventory						24 15.2
32 11.5	36 10.2	51 7.1							73 5.0
8 44.0	13 28.4	14 25.4							17 21.7
13 27.5	21 17.3	28 13.1	Cost of Sales/Payables						32 11.4
25 14.6	32 11.3	39 9.3							40 9.2
7.5	6.2	5.8							5.6
19.6	31.5	15.7	Sales/Working Capital						22.1
121.3	999.8	60.5							64.7
22.1	39.2	45.2							43.9
(38) 7.0	(35) 7.5	(29) 12.9	EBIT/Interest						(22) 18.6
2.9	1.5	3.4							3.9
21.6			Net Profit + Depr., Dep.,						
(14) 4.2			Amort./Cur. Mat. L/T/D						
1.2									
.3	.3	.2							.3
.9	.8	.5	Fixed/Worth						.6
1.6	1.8	1.2							1.1
.7	.4	.5							.6
1.4	1.0	.9	Debt/Worth						1.1
5.2	6.4	2.5							2.4
51.6	38.1	36.1	% Profit Before Taxes/Tangible						36.1
(41) 34.8	(39) 17.9	(31) 22.3	Net Worth						(23) 22.1
15.7	2.5	3.9							3.9
25.1	14.7	17.2	% Profit Before Taxes/Total						15.7
11.6	8.1	8.3	Assets						7.6
3.6	.8	2.5							2.8
34.1	24.7	38.1							33.2
13.9	10.9	14.8	Sales/Net Fixed Assets						11.5
7.4	5.5	3.1							3.1
6.2	5.4	4.9							5.5
3.8	3.3	2.5	Sales/Total Assets						2.7
2.3	1.5	1.2							1.0
.5	.6	.4							.7
(40) .9	(36) 1.1	(27) 1.1	% Depr., Dep., Amort./Sales						(19) 1.1
2.0	2.4	2.3							2.9
			% Officers', Directors' Owners' Comp/Sales						
15063251M	8695400M	8090066M	Net Sales ($)			8450M	30585M	46438M	8004593M
2542304M	2205486M	2322361M	Total Assets ($)			3368M	12442M	22049M	2284502M

M = $ thousand   MM = $ million
See Pages 9 through 22 for Explanation of Ratios and Data

Current Data Sorted by Assets   **Comparative Historical Data**

0-500M	500M-2MM	2-10MM	10-50MM	50-100MM	100-250MM	Type of Statement	4/1/06-3/31/07 ALL	4/1/07-3/31/08 ALL
		6	16	4	8	Unqualified	31	34
	3	13	7		1	Reviewed	14	23
2		6				Compiled	15	7
2	4	4				Tax Returns	8	6
4	5	12	11	4	2	Other	23	31
	22 (4/1-9/30/10)		92 (10/1/10-3/31/11)					
8	12	41	34	9	10	NUMBER OF STATEMENTS	91	101
%	%	%	%	%	%	**ASSETS**	%	%
	12.7	11.9	14.7		13.4	Cash & Equivalents	12.8	12.2
	27.7	28.2	24.0		17.5	Trade Receivables (net)	26.9	26.4
	6.1	10.6	14.6		17.3	Inventory	10.0	9.2
	3.6	3.3	3.3		3.2	All Other Current	4.8	3.9
	50.1	54.0	56.6		51.3	Total Current	54.6	51.7
	38.8	35.6	35.1		29.7	Fixed Assets (net)	34.6	36.8
	2.7	3.1	3.3		14.5	Intangibles (net)	3.0	2.7
	8.4	7.3	5.0		4.5	All Other Non-Current	7.8	8.9
	100.0	100.0	100.0		100.0	Total	100.0	100.0
						LIABILITIES		
	1.4	6.4	7.5		7.4	Notes Payable-Short Term	5.3	7.6
	1.7	4.0	3.8		1.2	Cur. Mat.-L.T.D.	4.7	5.7
	11.7	16.2	13.3		7.7	Trade Payables	15.3	13.9
	.4	.7	.1		1.2	Income Taxes Payable	.2	.3
	3.9	6.7	4.6		4.0	All Other Current	8.6	6.9
	19.1	34.0	29.4		21.5	Total Current	34.1	34.5
	13.4	16.9	18.4		11.3	Long-Term Debt	16.2	18.4
	.2	.3	1.0		1.7	Deferred Taxes	.5	.7
	11.2	5.0	1.4		6.4	All Other Non-Current	5.7	4.9
	56.0	43.8	49.8		59.1	Net Worth	43.5	41.6
	100.0	100.0	100.0		100.0	Total Liabilties & Net Worth	100.0	100.0
						INCOME DATA		
	100.0	100.0	100.0		100.0	Net Sales	100.0	100.0
	43.7	23.4	19.0		16.9	Gross Profit	20.5	21.1
	33.0	17.9	13.6		9.2	Operating Expenses	15.4	14.7
	10.8	5.5	5.4		7.7	Operating Profit	5.1	6.4
	-.1	-.4	.7		-1.3	All Other Expenses (net)	.7	.4
	10.9	5.9	4.8		9.0	Profit Before Taxes	4.4	5.9
						RATIOS		
	6.1	3.3	2.8		4.1		3.1	2.9
	2.3	1.5	1.6		2.6	Current	1.7	1.8
	1.3	1.0	1.3		1.5		1.1	1.2
	5.6	2.2	2.5		2.1		2.6	2.1
	2.0	1.2	1.0		1.7	Quick	(90) 1.2	(100) 1.4
	.9	.7	.7		.9		.7	.8
13 28.2	26 14.1	25 14.5			15 25.0		20 18.6	26 14.3
30 12.2	49 7.5	36 10.0			41 8.9	Sales/Receivables	37 9.8	39 9.3
79 4.6	60 6.1	60 6.1			64 5.7		54 6.8	57 6.4
0 UND	6 64.7	8 46.6			30 12.3		2 166.9	2 191.2
8 45.7	21 17.7	16 22.7			50 7.3	Cost of Sales/Inventory	14 26.2	13 27.7
20 18.1	32 11.5	43 8.4			63 5.8		33 11.1	28 13.0
5 75.4	15 24.4	11 32.8			16 22.8		11 33.1	14 25.6
22 16.4	31 11.8	25 14.5			22 16.3	Cost of Sales/Payables	23 16.1	22 16.7
30 12.1	47 7.7	46 8.0			32 11.3		41 9.0	40 9.2
	3.4	5.0	4.0		2.8		5.9	6.5
	5.1	12.1	10.6		5.7	Sales/Working Capital	13.5	10.7
	33.3	180.4	31.9		11.8		97.4	34.9
		25.3	7.6		100.4		17.8	21.6
		(38) 7.0	(30) 4.8		17.8	EBIT/Interest	(85) 4.9	(95) 6.6
		2.8	2.2		9.7		2.0	2.3
			7.2				14.4	8.6
		(14)	2.8			Net Profit + Depr., Dep., Amort./Cur. Mat. L/T/D	(24) 3.2	(40) 4.0
			1.8				1.5	1.9
	.3	.4	.5		.3		.4	.4
	.9	1.2	.8		.7	Fixed/Worth	.9	.8
	1.3	2.0	1.5		.9		2.3	1.6
	.3	.5	.5		.3		.4	.4
	.7	1.7	1.2		.7	Debt/Worth	1.3	1.2
	2.1	3.3	2.3		1.9		3.8	2.8
	59.5	45.6	33.7				51.3	66.7
(11)	14.4	(38) 28.6	(33) 16.3			% Profit Before Taxes/Tangible Net Worth	(81) 28.3	(90) 26.9
	6.0	9.4	8.2				12.3	13.1
	35.2	23.5	11.8		16.6		21.3	24.7
	10.6	9.1	7.3		13.3	% Profit Before Taxes/Total Assets	10.8	11.7
	2.6	2.4	2.7		6.2		3.5	4.5
	19.0	16.2	10.5		7.8		14.7	12.5
	6.3	6.9	6.2		6.1	Sales/Net Fixed Assets	6.4	6.7
	3.2	3.7	3.5		3.4		3.6	3.6
	2.6	3.3	3.3		1.7		3.1	3.0
	2.1	2.2	2.2		1.6	Sales/Total Assets	2.2	2.2
	1.1	1.6	1.3		1.1		1.8	1.6
		1.5	1.7				1.9	1.8
		(40) 2.4	(33) 3.2			% Depr., Dep., Amort./Sales	(81) 2.8	(93) 2.9
		3.9	4.6				4.6	4.8
			1.8				1.0	1.2
		(11) 2.7				% Officers', Directors' Owners' Comp/Sales	(27) 3.2	(27) 2.8
			6.8				4.8	5.6
14039M	33892M	520238M	1988721M	1008544M	2148346M	Net Sales ($)	3591215M	3989466M
2708M	15525M	220674M	756544M	660316M	1583653M	Total Assets ($)	1804075M	1913896M

M = $ thousand   MM = $ million
See Pages 9 through 22 for Explanation of Ratios and Data

Comparative Historical Data / Current Data Sorted by Sales

Historical columns are dated **4/1/08-3/31/09 ALL**, **4/1/09-3/31/10 ALL**, **4/1/10-3/31/11 ALL**. Current data groups: **22 (4/1-9/30/10)** covers 0-1MM, 1-3MM, 3-5MM; **92 (10/1/10-3/31/11)** covers 5-10MM, 10-25MM, 25MM & OVER.

Item	4/1/08-3/31/09 ALL	4/1/09-3/31/10 ALL	4/1/10-3/31/11 ALL	0-1MM	1-3MM	3-5MM	5-10MM	10-25MM	25MM & OVER
Type of Statement									
Unqualified	27	32	34		1		3	6	24
Reviewed	28	27	24		3		4	12	4
Compiled	10	9	8	1		1	3	3	
Tax Returns	11	13	10		3	3	2	2	
Other	37	42	38	2	4	4	4	6	19
NUMBER OF STATEMENTS	113	123	114	3	11	8	16	29	47
	%	%	%	%	%	%	%	%	%
ASSETS									
Cash & Equivalents	11.3	14.9	13.7		20.1		15.1	14.3	12.3
Trade Receivables (net)	25.6	25.5	24.1		22.3		23.5	27.8	22.0
Inventory	11.3	11.5	12.3		5.6		10.1	9.9	17.9
All Other Current	4.4	4.4	3.1		.1		.9	4.2	3.7
Total Current	52.6	56.3	53.3		48.2		49.5	56.3	55.9
Fixed Assets (net)	38.8	33.7	35.2		33.7		38.0	35.0	33.3
Intangibles (net)	3.3	2.0	4.8		4.0		4.4	3.2	6.4
All Other Non-Current	5.3	8.0	6.8		14.2		8.1	5.6	4.4
Total	100.0	100.0	100.0		100.0		100.0	100.0	100.0
LIABILITIES									
Notes Payable-Short Term	6.3	5.9	6.2		5.2		8.1	4.8	7.7
Cur. Mat.-L.T.D.	6.1	3.5	3.4		.6		4.4	3.2	3.3
Trade Payables	14.0	14.0	13.3		11.2		13.1	17.7	12.0
Income Taxes Payable	.1	.3	.4		.4		1.4	.1	.3
All Other Current	6.1	8.2	4.9		2.0		5.6	5.6	4.9
Total Current	32.6	32.0	28.1		19.5		32.6	31.5	28.2
Long-Term Debt	20.1	14.0	17.2		13.7		23.2	14.6	15.8
Deferred Taxes	.6	.7	.7		.1		.1	.8	1.1
All Other Non-Current	4.3	4.3	4.6		8.6		3.4	4.7	3.7
Net Worth	42.5	48.9	49.3		58.2		40.6	48.4	51.3
Total Liabilities & Net Worth	100.0	100.0	100.0		100.0		100.0	100.0	100.0
INCOME DATA									
Net Sales	100.0	100.0	100.0		100.0		100.0	100.0	100.0
Gross Profit	19.0	23.9	24.3		44.8		23.6	21.6	17.7
Operating Expenses	15.7	17.9	17.6		37.3		15.3	15.6	12.1
Operating Profit	3.4	6.0	6.7		7.5		8.3	6.0	5.6
All Other Expenses (net)	1.0	.5	.0		-.7		.0	.3	.3
Profit Before Taxes	2.3	5.5	6.7		8.2		8.3	5.7	5.3
RATIOS									
Current	2.5	4.0	3.4		9.3		2.1	4.2	2.9
	1.6	2.0	1.7		3.5		1.4	2.2	1.7
	1.2	1.2	1.3		1.4		1.0	1.2	1.4
Quick	2.1	2.9	2.5		9.3		2.1	2.8	1.9
	1.2	1.4	1.3		1.7		1.2	1.5	1.1
	.6	.8	.7		.9		.7	.9	.6
Sales/Receivables	22 16.5	26 14.0	20 18.4		16 23.5		23 15.8	27 13.4	15 24.5
	35 10.3	38 9.5	38 9.5		38 9.6		39 9.3	47 7.7	34 10.8
	52 7.0	60 6.0	59 6.2		63 5.8		70 5.2	62 5.9	57 6.4
Cost of Sales/Inventory	3 124.2	4 81.3	5 70.2		0 UND		0 UND	5 74.3	11 32.4
	16 22.5	22 16.9	19 19.3		8 43.4		16 22.8	19 18.8	33 11.0
	33 10.9	44 8.3	46 7.9		37 9.9		26 14.2	30 12.0	60 6.1
Cost of Sales/Payables	11 32.8	12 30.3	14 26.2		4 84.0		15 23.6	17 21.9	14 26.0
	21 17.0	24 15.4	25 14.7		21 17.4		26 14.1	41 9.0	23 15.7
	43 8.5	44 8.3	42 8.6		31 11.6		46 7.9	51 7.1	35 10.5
Sales/Working Capital	7.0	4.1	4.0		2.6		4.1	4.3	3.9
	16.0	8.8	9.6		5.4		15.8	9.5	8.1
	45.2	31.7	30.5		34.3		199.2	28.2	24.3
EBIT/Interest	13.0	26.2	21.4				22.2	30.4	20.7
	(104) 4.1	(107) 7.4	(99) 6.0		(14) 7.2		(28) 5.9	(43) 6.6	
	.7	2.8	2.6		3.4		3.5	2.5	
Net Profit + Depr., Dep., Amort./Cur. Mat. L/T/D	6.2	8.8	8.4					18.2	9.3
	(35) 2.8	(32) 4.2	(32) 3.0				(11) 2.6	(15) 3.0	
	1.2	2.6	1.9				1.9	1.7	
Fixed/Worth	.5	.3	.4		.2		.3	.5	.4
	.9	.7	.9		.7		1.4	.8	.8
	2.0	1.4	1.8		1.3		2.9	1.7	1.4
Debt/Worth	.6	.3	.4		.2		.7	.4	.5
	1.4	.9	1.1		1.0		1.7	.9	1.2
	3.3	2.6	2.5		2.6		7.3	3.3	2.2
% Profit Before Taxes/Tangible Net Worth	40.6	44.0	40.7		91.0		68.4	38.3	34.8
	(99) 17.7	(115) 20.2	(106) 19.6		19.6		(15) 35.8	(26) 23.7	(45) 17.1
	2.7	6.1	8.5		3.0		6.0	10.2	7.3
% Profit Before Taxes/Total Assets	15.7	20.0	20.5		37.5		23.9	20.6	14.9
	8.0	9.8	9.7		9.8		11.4	9.1	9.3
	-.2	2.0	3.5		2.3		4.0	3.3	2.6
Sales/Net Fixed Assets	13.0	13.4	13.7		27.0		13.4	16.9	10.0
	6.6	7.1	6.3		9.3		4.9	6.2	6.6
	3.4	3.6	3.4		1.4		2.9	3.5	3.6
Sales/Total Assets	3.2	2.9	3.2		3.6		2.4	3.3	3.1
	2.3	2.2	2.1		1.7		1.8	2.5	2.0
	1.5	1.4	1.3		.9		1.0	1.5	1.4
% Depr., Dep., Amort./Sales	1.6	1.7	1.6				1.8	1.5	1.7
	(108) 2.9	(109) 2.8	(98) 2.5				2.5	2.4	(41) 2.5
	4.3	4.5	4.8				6.4	3.9	4.5
% Officers', Directors' Owners' Comp/Sales	1.3	2.2	1.1						.6
	(29) 2.7	(33) 3.4	(30) 2.7						(11) 1.2
	4.5	5.3	4.8						2.8
Net Sales ($)	4876816M	5781325M	5713780M	1963M	16014M	32341M	108546M	451702M	5103214M
Total Assets ($)	2209285M	2813036M	3239420M	1614M	17191M	10882M	78889M	227209M	2903635M

M = $ thousand   MM = $ million
See Pages 9 through 22 for Explanation of Ratios and Data

Current Data Sorted by Assets   Comparative Historical Data

Type of Statement								
						Unqualified	10	11
		1	5	5	2	Reviewed	11	8
	3	4	4			Compiled	4	4
	1	4				Tax Returns	3	3
1	2					Other	20	22
		6	7		2		4/1/06-3/31/07	4/1/07-3/31/08
	9 (4/1-9/30/10)		38 (10/1/10-3/31/11)				ALL	ALL
0-500M	500M-2MM	2-10MM	10-50MM	50-100MM	100-250MM	NUMBER OF STATEMENTS		
1	6	15	16	5	4		48	48
%	%	%	%	%	%	ASSETS	%	%
		10.7	14.7			Cash & Equivalents	8.0	8.1
		29.5	26.6			Trade Receivables (net)	30.3	29.0
		25.8	30.0			Inventory	28.3	27.9
		1.8	2.2			All Other Current	1.9	3.6
		67.8	73.5			Total Current	68.5	68.6
		23.5	18.5			Fixed Assets (net)	21.2	23.2
		5.5	1.9			Intangibles (net)	5.8	4.1
		3.3	6.0			All Other Non-Current	4.4	4.1
		100.0	100.0			Total	100.0	100.0
						LIABILITIES		
		7.6	8.9			Notes Payable-Short Term	8.9	10.4
		7.0	1.7			Cur. Mat.-L.T.D.	3.5	3.6
		15.6	13.6			Trade Payables	19.7	20.8
		.8	.4			Income Taxes Payable	.4	.9
		6.2	5.3			All Other Current	9.6	6.5
		37.3	29.9			Total Current	42.1	42.2
		8.8	9.0			Long-Term Debt	12.7	12.8
		.7	.9			Deferred Taxes	.7	.9
		1.7	5.3			All Other Non-Current	7.2	3.5
		51.5	54.8			Net Worth	37.4	40.6
		100.0	100.0			Total Liabilities & Net Worth	100.0	100.0
						INCOME DATA		
		100.0	100.0			Net Sales	100.0	100.0
		31.1	34.0			Gross Profit	32.9	29.6
		25.3	27.3			Operating Expenses	27.6	23.9
		5.8	6.7			Operating Profit	5.3	5.7
		.8	-.4			All Other Expenses (net)	1.0	.6
		5.1	7.2			Profit Before Taxes	4.3	5.1
						RATIOS		
		4.9	5.1				2.9	2.5
		1.9	3.3			Current	1.9	1.7
		1.5	1.3				1.1	1.2
		2.8	3.5				1.4	1.4
		1.1	1.9			Quick	1.0	1.0
		.7	.6				.6	.6
		33 11.0	37 9.9				36 10.2	27 13.3
		48 7.5	44 8.2			Sales/Receivables	47 7.8	41 9.0
		54 6.8	52 7.0				55 6.7	51 7.2
		30 12.3	62 5.9				42 8.8	35 10.4
		56 6.5	76 4.8			Cost of Sales/Inventory	66 5.6	61 6.0
		85 4.3	93 3.9				93 3.9	84 4.3
		21 17.3	17 21.8				21 17.3	20 18.3
		35 10.5	30 12.1			Cost of Sales/Payables	37 9.9	32 11.4
		46 8.0	44 8.3				47 7.8	50 7.4
		3.9	2.9				4.2	5.6
		7.9	4.0			Sales/Working Capital	9.4	10.7
		17.3	15.8				53.2	25.9
		48.8	85.8				13.2	11.8
		(14) 6.2	(14) 20.2			EBIT/Interest	(43) 4.0	(44) 4.0
		1.6	2.9				2.0	1.6
						Net Profit + Depr., Dep., Amort./Cur. Mat. L/T/D	9.4	11.1
							(18) 4.9	(19) 3.4
							1.6	.9
		.2	.2				.3	.3
		.3	.2			Fixed/Worth	.5	.5
		1.7	.6				1.9	1.2
		.3	.3				.8	.7
		.9	.6			Debt/Worth	1.7	2.0
		2.0	2.0				4.3	3.3
		62.2	48.4			% Profit Before Taxes/Tangible Net Worth	51.4	61.4
		(13) 30.2	(15) 23.7				(42) 23.2	(45) 27.4
		4.0	3.4				13.0	9.1
		28.8	24.8			% Profit Before Taxes/Total Assets	17.1	19.1
		7.9	11.4				7.1	9.2
		.3	3.8				2.6	2.1
		31.3	26.0			Sales/Net Fixed Assets	32.1	20.7
		11.9	15.3				14.7	11.5
		8.2	9.1				6.4	6.6
		3.3	2.9			Sales/Total Assets	3.4	3.4
		2.3	2.1				2.2	2.5
		1.8	1.6				1.6	1.9
		.8	.7			% Depr., Dep., Amort./Sales	.5	.7
		(14) 1.2	(15) 1.2				(44) 1.3	(38) 1.3
		1.9	2.7				2.4	2.1
						% Officers', Directors' Owners' Comp/Sales	1.6	1.6
							(15) 3.9	(14) 3.1
							9.0	5.0
1482M	27173M	245312M	1002685M	1491171M	1052404M	Net Sales ($)	2662930M	2758432M
316M	8066M	91685M	435665M	346066M	526611M	Total Assets ($)	1241700M	1147234M

M = $ thousand   MM = $ million
See Pages 9 through 22 for Explanation of Ratios and Data

Comparative Historical Data   ## Current Data Sorted by Sales

08-09	09-10	10-11	Type of Statement	0-1MM	1-3MM	3-5MM	5-10MM	10-25MM	25MM & OVER
10	11	13	Unqualified					2	11
13	7	11	Reviewed		1		5	1	4
3	7	5	Compiled				1	2	2
3		3	Tax Returns			2		1	
23	28	15	Other		1	1	1	5	8
4/1/08-3/31/09 ALL	4/1/09-3/31/10 ALL	4/1/10-3/31/11 ALL			9 (4/1-9/30/10)			38 (10/1/10-3/31/11)	
52	53	47	NUMBER OF STATEMENTS		2	3	7	10	25
%	%	%	**ASSETS**	%	%	%	%	%	%
6.7	11.0	10.2	Cash & Equivalents					11.3	11.0
25.6	27.6	29.0	Trade Receivables (net)					31.9	28.4
34.0	28.8	28.3	Inventory					27.1	28.8
2.7	4.2	1.8	All Other Current					1.7	2.0
69.0	71.7	69.2	Total Current					71.9	70.2
22.1	22.3	23.1	Fixed Assets (net)					20.4	22.5
3.5	2.5	3.9	Intangibles (net)					.9	3.8
5.3	3.5	3.8	All Other Non-Current					6.8	3.5
100.0	100.0	100.0	Total					100.0	100.0
			LIABILITIES						
12.9	14.9	10.7	Notes Payable-Short Term					5.8	10.9
3.5	2.5	3.5	Cur. Mat.-L.T.D.					1.5	1.9
15.9	15.6	16.9	Trade Payables					15.1	14.9
.4	.2	.5	Income Taxes Payable					1.4	.3
7.6	7.5	6.1	All Other Current					7.2	5.0
40.3	40.6	37.6	Total Current					30.8	33.1
14.0	8.3	8.7	Long-Term Debt					5.0	8.9
.7	.6	.7	Deferred Taxes					.7	.9
7.6	5.8	4.1	All Other Non-Current					1.6	5.9
37.3	44.6	48.8	Net Worth					61.8	51.2
100.0	100.0	100.0	Total Liabilities & Net Worth					100.0	100.0
			INCOME DATA						
100.0	100.0	100.0	Net Sales					100.0	100.0
30.1	31.8	30.8	Gross Profit					31.9	29.7
24.8	27.0	24.7	Operating Expenses					26.9	22.6
5.3	4.8	6.1	Operating Profit					4.9	7.1
.9	.6	.4	All Other Expenses (net)					.3	.0
4.5	4.2	5.7	Profit Before Taxes					4.6	7.1

(ASSETS through INCOME DATA: "DATA NOT AVAILABLE" in columns 0-1MM, 1-3MM, 3-5MM, 5-10MM)

08-09	09-10	10-11	RATIOS	10-25MM	25MM & OVER
3.1	3.5	4.5	Current	5.2	4.8
1.7	2.0	1.9		2.5	2.3
1.2	1.3	1.4		1.6	1.4
1.4	2.5	2.7	Quick	2.8	3.1
.9	1.0	1.1		1.7	1.2
.5	.6	.6		1.1	.6
22 16.4	29 12.7	31 11.9	Sales/Receivables	36 10.1	32 11.4
34 10.6	42 8.7	43 8.4		52 7.1	42 8.7
49 7.5	52 7.0	50 7.3		56 6.6	46 8.0
38 9.5	34 10.7	41 8.9	Cost of Sales/Inventory	37 9.8	52 7.1
61 6.0	57 6.4	65 5.6		60 6.1	66 5.5
103 3.5	89 4.1	88 4.1		93 3.9	89 4.1
13 27.6	17 21.4	21 17.3	Cost of Sales/Payables	16 22.2	19 19.4
26 14.1	27 13.5	32 11.5		35 10.3	28 13.0
37 9.9	39 9.3	44 8.2		53 6.9	36 10.1
5.3	3.6	3.9	Sales/Working Capital	3.7	3.7
10.6	7.0	7.6		4.9	7.0
31.8	19.8	17.3		15.2	17.2
11.5	21.4	38.8	EBIT/Interest		87.1
(49) 2.7	(50) 8.6	(44) 7.3		(23)	18.7
1.2	3.1	2.1			4.6
9.2	13.0	24.8	Net Profit + Depr., Dep., Amort./Cur. Mat. L/T/D		25.8
(20) 4.0	(17) 5.5	(16) 8.2		(11)	11.8
1.1	2.4	2.9			4.1
.3	.2	.2	Fixed/Worth	.2	.2
.6	.4	.4		.3	.4
1.3	1.2	1.0		.7	.8
.7	.4	.4	Debt/Worth	.2	.4
1.8	1.1	1.0		.5	1.2
3.3	2.4	2.0		1.0	1.9
38.4	47.4	51.3	% Profit Before Taxes/Tangible Net Worth		50.5
(45) 11.5	(50) 25.1	(43) 23.7		(24)	28.2
3.0	6.0	7.5			11.1
14.6	22.1	18.6	% Profit Before Taxes/Total Assets	21.2	31.4
4.5	9.5	9.3		5.0	13.5
1.1	2.6	1.6		.3	6.7
27.3	25.5	26.6	Sales/Net Fixed Assets	13.6	28.9
13.2	14.3	11.9		11.8	13.1
7.6	7.8	8.2		10.7	6.7
3.4	3.1	3.1	Sales/Total Assets	3.0	3.0
2.8	2.5	2.5		2.4	2.4
1.9	1.8	1.7		2.1	1.6
.6	.6	.8	% Depr., Dep., Amort./Sales		.7
(46) 1.3	(49) 1.3	(42) 1.1		(22)	1.0
2.7	1.9	1.8			2.4
2.7	1.4		% Officers', Directors' Owners' Comp/Sales		
(13) 3.2	(12) 2.6				
6.4	14.2				

08-09	09-10	10-11		0-1MM	1-3MM	3-5MM	5-10MM	10-25MM	25MM & OVER
3622616M	3144010M	3820227M	Net Sales ($)		3623M	12603M	51341M	173464M	3579196M
1434220M	1427310M	1408409M	Total Assets ($)		1045M	5250M	26567M	73868M	1301679M

© RMA 2011

M = $ thousand   MM = $ million

See Pages 9 through 22 for Explanation of Ratios and Data

Current Data Sorted by Assets   Comparative Historical Data

	0-500M	500M-2MM	2-10MM	10-50MM	50-100MM	100-250MM		4/1/06-3/31/07 ALL	4/1/07-3/31/08 ALL
							Type of Statement		
			1	6	2	1	Unqualified	8	8
			1	1			Reviewed	3	1
		2	1	1			Compiled	3	8
		2	2		1		Tax Returns	3	5
	1	1	7	1	1	2	Other	14	11
		8 (4/1-9/30/10)	23 (10/1/10-3/31/11)						
		5	11	9	3	3	**NUMBER OF STATEMENTS**	31	33
	%	%	%	%	%	%	**ASSETS**	%	%
D			8.1				Cash & Equivalents	12.8	12.1
A			31.6				Trade Receivables (net)	28.7	24.3
T			31.0				Inventory	18.3	16.3
A			1.2				All Other Current	4.3	6.6
			72.0				Total Current	64.1	59.2
N			16.4				Fixed Assets (net)	29.0	27.6
O			8.4				Intangibles (net)	1.6	4.5
T			3.3				All Other Non-Current	5.2	8.6
			100.0				Total	100.0	100.0
A							**LIABILITIES**		
V			4.9				Notes Payable-Short Term	9.7	16.6
A			5.1				Cur. Mat.-L.T.D.	2.2	2.8
I			17.9				Trade Payables	20.6	20.5
L			.0				Income Taxes Payable	.3	.2
A			9.9				All Other Current	7.1	7.0
B			37.7				Total Current	39.9	47.0
L			17.2				Long-Term Debt	20.3	16.2
E			.1				Deferred Taxes	.4	.2
			1.1				All Other Non-Current	2.6	3.0
			43.8				Net Worth	36.9	33.6
			100.0				Total Liabilities & Net Worth	100.0	100.0
							INCOME DATA		
			100.0				Net Sales	100.0	100.0
			22.2				Gross Profit	25.0	28.1
			13.9				Operating Expenses	15.4	20.9
			8.2				Operating Profit	9.6	7.2
			1.2				All Other Expenses (net)	.8	.7
			7.1				Profit Before Taxes	8.8	6.6
							RATIOS		
			3.7					3.5	2.8
			1.7				Current	1.6	1.3
			1.3					1.1	1.0
			2.4					2.7	1.4
			.7				Quick	1.0	.8
			.7					.5	.4
			14 27.0					22 16.4	11 34.2
			50 7.3				Sales/Receivables	35 10.4	29 12.7
			65 5.6					59 6.2	42 8.7
			15 23.8					4 86.5	1 639.7
			37 9.9				Cost of Sales/Inventory	29 12.8	15 24.5
			112 3.3					53 6.9	50 7.4
			13 28.2					7 54.0	12 29.3
			24 15.1				Cost of Sales/Payables	21 17.0	26 13.9
			38 9.6					39 9.3	40 9.1
			5.0					5.2	6.9
			6.0				Sales/Working Capital	15.4	53.8
			54.6					343.2	-931.8
								23.6	13.6
							EBIT/Interest	(26) 8.1	(30) 2.2
								2.8	1.0
							Net Profit + Depr., Dep., Amort./Cur. Mat. L/T/D		
			.1					.4	.2
			.2				Fixed/Worth	.5	.8
			.9					2.4	12.1
			.8					1.0	.5
			1.4				Debt/Worth	1.8	2.2
			12.5					5.7	26.9
			131.6					68.9	70.4
			(10) 38.2				% Profit Before Taxes/Tangible Net Worth	(28) 47.3	(27) 25.8
			8.8					19.4	7.5
			32.7					21.7	25.8
			5.6				% Profit Before Taxes/Total Assets	10.5	6.5
			2.9					3.1	.3
			108.9					25.1	54.4
			27.7				Sales/Net Fixed Assets	9.4	16.4
			7.7					4.3	5.8
			5.4					4.0	5.2
			2.1				Sales/Total Assets	2.8	3.2
			1.7					1.7	1.8
								.7	.4
							% Depr., Dep., Amort./Sales	(25) 1.2	(25) 1.3
								2.9	2.0
									.9
							% Officers', Directors' Owners' Comp/Sales		(10) 5.6
									12.1
	23121M	208761M	647285M	245385M	935634M		Net Sales ($)	2242903M	3135675M
	6868M	57973M	236160M	214898M	449651M		Total Assets ($)	582144M	934268M

Comparative Historical Data   Current Data Sorted by Sales

					Type of Statement							
	8		14		10	Unqualified				1		9
	5		1		1	Reviewed						1
	4		5		4	Compiled		2		1		1
	2		3		4	Tax Returns			1	1		1
	12		12		12	Other	1	2	2	3		5
	4/1/08-3/31/09 ALL		4/1/09-3/31/10 ALL		4/1/10-3/31/11 ALL			8 (4/1-9/30/10)			23 (10/1/10-3/31/11)	
							0-1MM	1-3MM	3-5MM	5-10MM	10-25MM	25MM & OVER
	31		35		31	NUMBER OF STATEMENTS	1	4	3	6		17
	%		%		%	ASSETS	%	%	%	%	%	%
	14.0		12.6		10.1	Cash & Equivalents						8.5
	24.8		20.8		24.1	Trade Receivables (net)						25.4
	12.4		17.2		20.6	Inventory						13.8
	3.2		1.6		1.7	All Other Current						2.1
	54.4		52.1		56.4	Total Current						49.7
	36.1		35.5		34.2	Fixed Assets (net)						45.4
	3.0		6.4		3.3	Intangibles (net)						2.3
	6.5		5.9		6.1	All Other Non-Current						2.6
	100.0		100.0		100.0	Total						100.0
						LIABILITIES						
	10.0		11.4		5.1	Notes Payable-Short Term						5.9
	5.4		2.8		4.1	Cur. Mat.-L.T.D.						3.9
	16.3		11.6		15.1	Trade Payables						21.1
	.1		.2		.1	Income Taxes Payable						.1
	7.6		7.4		9.3	All Other Current						5.6
	39.4		33.4		33.6	Total Current						36.7
	16.5		22.9		18.5	Long-Term Debt						28.3
	.3		.4		.1	Deferred Taxes						.1
	4.3		2.7		3.3	All Other Non-Current						1.5
	39.5		40.6		44.5	Net Worth						33.5
	100.0		100.0		100.0	Total Liabilities & Net Worth						100.0
						INCOME DATA						
	100.0		100.0		100.0	Net Sales						100.0
	25.6		29.3		24.6	Gross Profit						20.1
	20.1		24.3		18.2	Operating Expenses						14.2
	5.6		5.0		6.4	Operating Profit						6.0
	.3		1.5		1.7	All Other Expenses (net)						2.1
	5.2		3.5		4.7	Profit Before Taxes						3.8
						RATIOS						
	3.5		3.5		4.1							1.9
	1.5		1.6		1.7	Current						1.3
	.8		1.0		1.1							1.1
	2.3		2.4		2.5							1.2
	1.1		1.1	(30)	.9	Quick						.9
	.5		.6		.7							.6
10	35.1	16	22.2	15	23.7						16	23.2
28	12.9	38	9.5	36	10.1	Sales/Receivables					27	13.3
44	8.3	60	6.1	53	6.8						50	7.3
1	253.1	19	18.9	8	44.4						2	154.3
9	39.1	37	10.0	30	12.2	Cost of Sales/Inventory					15	23.8
44	8.2	65	5.6	79	4.6						30	12.2
6	61.1	10	36.8	12	30.3						15	24.4
15	24.2	27	13.7	20	18.0	Cost of Sales/Payables					24	15.1
40	9.1	34	10.8	38	9.6						41	8.9
	5.9		4.8		5.1							8.3
	56.0		7.4		9.6	Sales/Working Capital						36.2
	-119.0		168.5		59.7							118.2
	10.7		9.2		14.5							10.6
(29)	3.9	(32)	3.0	(27)	3.8	EBIT/Interest					(16)	3.8
	1.1		.1		1.4							1.0
						Net Profit + Depr., Dep., Amort./Cur. Mat. L/T/D						
	.4		.5		.2							.5
	.9		1.0		.7	Fixed/Worth						1.3
	3.2		4.2		1.6							2.5
	.7		.5		.6							.9
	1.7		2.1		1.4	Debt/Worth						2.1
	5.8		8.5		4.1							8.6
	59.1		57.3		57.6							50.9
(28)	24.2	(28)	19.4	(30)	21.6	% Profit Before Taxes/Tangible Net Worth					(16)	23.9
	2.1		-1.9		2.2							4.7
	18.0		14.8		11.8							12.3
	10.9		4.6		5.6	% Profit Before Taxes/Total Assets						6.4
	.4		-1.3		1.2							.0
	47.9		18.2		35.2							30.6
	10.8		7.2		10.3	Sales/Net Fixed Assets						3.8
	4.3		2.2		3.2							1.7
	8.2		2.5		4.0							5.8
	2.9		1.9		1.8	Sales/Total Assets						1.7
	1.9		1.1		1.4							1.2
	.5		1.3		.7							1.1
(26)	1.1	(29)	2.5	(25)	1.9	% Depr., Dep., Amort./Sales					(14)	2.6
	2.3		4.9		4.5							6.9
					.5							
		(10)	2.6			% Officers', Directors' Owners' Comp/Sales						
			10.0									
	3905331M		1352138M		2060186M	Net Sales ($)		1894M	13811M	22441M	93229M	1928811M
	1363269M		1020180M		965550M	Total Assets ($)		1049M	6773M	13521M	40380M	903827M

M = $ thousand   MM = $ million

© RMA 2011
See Pages 9 through 22 for Explanation of Ratios and Data

Current Data Sorted by Assets   Comparative Historical Data

0-500M	500M-2MM	2-10MM	10-50MM	50-100MM	100-250MM	Type of Statement	4/1/06-3/31/07 ALL	4/1/07-3/31/08 ALL
1		1	12	5	1	Unqualified	34	22
		17	7	1	1	Reviewed	27	23
1		3				Compiled	9	3
1	2	1	1			Tax Returns	7	4
		17	24	8	6	Other	31	38
	22 (4/1-9/30/10)		88 (10/1/10-3/31/11)					
3	2	39	44	14	8	NUMBER OF STATEMENTS	108	90
%	%	%	%	%	%	ASSETS	%	%
		8.8	10.8	8.8		Cash & Equivalents	7.0	6.7
		25.2	23.5	19.0		Trade Receivables (net)	25.3	25.2
		22.3	21.3	14.6		Inventory	21.0	24.1
		2.2	2.0	3.5		All Other Current	2.7	2.7
		58.6	57.6	45.8		Total Current	56.0	58.7
		31.4	32.1	40.1		Fixed Assets (net)	35.0	31.6
		3.2	5.3	8.5		Intangibles (net)	4.0	5.0
		6.8	5.0	5.7		All Other Non-Current	5.0	4.7
		100.0	100.0	100.0		Total	100.0	100.0
						LIABILITIES		
		11.4	5.0	6.3		Notes Payable-Short Term	7.2	8.3
		3.2	3.6	3.4		Cur. Mat.-L.T.D.	3.8	3.4
		16.7	14.6	8.1		Trade Payables	15.1	15.0
		.3	.4	.5		Income Taxes Payable	.4	.4
		8.3	6.2	5.1		All Other Current	9.6	10.3
		39.9	29.8	23.5		Total Current	36.0	37.3
		16.2	17.3	17.9		Long-Term Debt	21.8	19.3
		.5	1.2	2.4		Deferred Taxes	1.0	.9
		3.7	4.3	7.5		All Other Non-Current	6.5	3.9
		39.7	47.3	48.7		Net Worth	34.7	38.5
		100.0	100.0	100.0		Total Liabilities & Net Worth	100.0	100.0
						INCOME DATA		
		100.0	100.0	100.0		Net Sales	100.0	100.0
		36.5	30.7	29.0		Gross Profit	32.8	30.0
		28.9	20.3	17.1		Operating Expenses	24.8	21.0
		7.6	10.3	11.9		Operating Profit	8.0	9.0
		.7	1.1	.6		All Other Expenses (net)	2.1	1.5
		6.8	9.2	11.3		Profit Before Taxes	5.9	7.6
						RATIOS		
		2.2	3.0	3.5			2.5	2.5
		1.5	2.0	2.0		Current	1.7	1.6
		1.1	1.5	1.4			1.2	1.2
		1.1	1.8	2.3			1.5	1.5
		.7	1.3	1.4		Quick	.9	1.0
		.6	.9	.7			.6	.6
		28 13.3	33 11.1	38 9.7			32 11.4	35 10.5
		37 9.8	43 8.4	46 7.9		Sales/Receivables	41 8.8	46 7.9
		49 7.5	60 6.1	52 7.1			57 6.4	59 6.2
		23 15.7	35 10.3	25 14.4			28 12.8	30 12.3
		54 6.8	54 6.8	49 7.5		Cost of Sales/Inventory	52 7.1	50 7.3
		89 4.1	76 4.8	71 5.1			73 5.0	89 4.1
		25 14.9	25 14.7	20 18.5			19 19.4	22 16.7
		34 10.9	29 12.4	25 14.4		Cost of Sales/Payables	33 11.0	33 11.0
		50 7.4	45 8.1	38 9.5			55 6.6	51 7.1
		7.6	4.4	3.8			6.1	5.4
		13.5	7.7	7.4		Sales/Working Capital	10.2	9.8
		57.2	13.6	16.0			31.5	26.4
		15.2	40.4	51.7			15.8	14.7
		(33) 5.1	(41) 8.5	(13) 12.3		EBIT/Interest	(104) 5.5	(81) 4.8
		2.0	3.6	6.0			1.7	1.4
			9.3				7.7	5.8
			(15) 3.3			Net Profit + Depr., Dep., Amort./Cur. Mat. L/T/D	(31) 4.7	(30) 3.0
			2.2				2.2	1.4
		.4	.4	.6			.4	.4
		.8	.8	1.4		Fixed/Worth	1.0	.9
		2.0	1.5	2.5			3.3	3.0
		.7	.5	.5			.8	.7
		1.5	1.2	1.8		Debt/Worth	1.9	1.6
		4.3	4.0	3.6			6.5	7.0
		68.3	51.4	58.8			55.3	62.5
		(37) 26.0	(42) 30.8	(13) 37.9		% Profit Before Taxes/Tangible Net Worth	(92) 24.2	(82) 26.7
		10.0	11.4	16.2			10.3	10.7
		17.1	23.9	22.1			19.3	19.0
		9.2	12.3	12.5		% Profit Before Taxes/Total Assets	9.5	10.4
		3.5	4.7	10.2			1.8	2.0
		26.1	13.5	6.4			16.8	19.2
		9.4	5.6	4.1		Sales/Net Fixed Assets	5.7	5.2
		4.3	3.4	2.9			2.9	3.7
		3.0	2.4	1.9			2.8	2.7
		2.3	1.7	1.6		Sales/Total Assets	1.9	1.7
		1.7	1.3	1.1			1.3	1.4
		.9	1.0	2.1			1.2	1.2
		(33) 1.4	(43) 2.3	(13) 3.4		% Depr., Dep., Amort./Sales	(87) 2.8	(77) 2.4
		2.7	4.5	5.5			4.7	4.6
		1.2					1.5	1.8
		(17) 3.0				% Officers', Directors' Owners' Comp/Sales	(19) 2.7	(22) 3.3
		5.7					6.5	6.4
440M	5608M	524733M	1804296M	1405903M	1288722M	Net Sales ($)	6652495M	4773369M
641M	1821M	210395M	930715M	906783M	1291910M	Total Assets ($)	4542220M	3290871M

Comparative Historical Data   Current Data Sorted by Sales

			Type of Statement	0-1MM	1-3MM	3-5MM	5-10MM	10-25MM	25MM & OVER
21	31	20	Unqualified	1				4	15
26	20	26	Reviewed		1		7	11	7
8	8	4	Compiled	1		1		2	
2	8	5	Tax Returns	1	2				2
55	47	55	Other	1	1		5	14	34
4/1/08-3/31/09 ALL	4/1/09-3/31/10 ALL	4/1/10-3/31/11 ALL		22 (4/1-9/30/10)			88 (10/1/10-3/31/11)		
112	114	110	**NUMBER OF STATEMENTS**	4	3	2	12	31	58
%	%	%	**ASSETS**	%	%	%	%	%	%
6.4	9.9	9.2	Cash & Equivalents				7.4	8.2	10.8
24.3	24.0	23.4	Trade Receivables (net)				19.8	25.2	23.2
24.4	22.4	20.9	Inventory				20.2	22.6	20.8
1.7	2.0	2.4	All Other Current				.9	2.7	2.8
56.8	58.3	55.9	Total Current				48.2	58.8	57.5
31.2	28.7	33.2	Fixed Assets (net)				33.4	32.9	31.8
6.1	5.0	5.2	Intangibles (net)				7.5	2.5	5.7
5.9	7.9	5.7	All Other Non-Current				11.0	5.8	4.9
100.0	100.0	100.0	Total				100.0	100.0	100.0
			LIABILITIES						
9.2	9.1	7.9	Notes Payable-Short Term				8.7	11.9	4.6
4.2	3.7	3.2	Cur. Mat.-L.T.D.				5.1	2.7	3.2
15.0	15.9	14.0	Trade Payables				12.1	14.0	15.3
.3	.4	.4	Income Taxes Payable				.0	.6	.4
7.5	9.8	6.8	All Other Current				8.0	7.1	6.2
36.2	38.8	32.2	Total Current				33.8	36.2	29.7
19.7	14.8	16.7	Long-Term Debt				26.0	12.7	15.0
1.4	.9	1.3	Deferred Taxes				.0	1.0	1.6
3.1	7.7	4.5	All Other Non-Current				5.0	3.4	5.5
39.5	37.7	45.2	Net Worth				35.1	46.7	48.2
100.0	100.0	100.0	Total Liabilities & Net Worth				100.0	100.0	100.0
			INCOME DATA						
100.0	100.0	100.0	Net Sales				100.0	100.0	100.0
28.5	32.8	33.5	Gross Profit				38.7	34.7	29.3
22.5	24.4	24.0	Operating Expenses				33.9	26.2	18.5
6.1	8.4	9.5	Operating Profit				4.9	8.5	10.8
1.1	1.0	.9	All Other Expenses (net)				1.8	.5	.8
4.9	7.4	8.5	Profit Before Taxes				3.1	7.9	10.1
			RATIOS						
2.3	2.5	2.9	Current				2.9	2.9	3.1
1.7	1.7	1.8					1.5	1.5	2.2
1.1	1.2	1.3					1.1	1.1	1.7
1.4	1.6	1.7	Quick				1.0	1.6	1.7
.9	1.0	1.0					.7	.9	1.3
.6	.6	.7					.6	.6	.9
30 12.2	35 10.4	33 11.1	Sales/Receivables			27 13.6	34 10.8	34 10.7	
40 9.0	44 8.3	43 8.4				35 10.4	43 8.4	45 8.1	
49 7.4	53 6.9	54 6.8				45 8.1	57 6.4	54 6.7	
28 12.8	39 9.4	31 11.8	Cost of Sales/Inventory			5 74.5	40 9.2	34 10.7	
59 6.2	62 5.8	54 6.8				60 6.1	57 6.4	51 7.2	
100 3.7	113 3.2	86 4.2				105 3.5	78 4.7	75 4.8	
23 16.2	22 16.3	24 15.3	Cost of Sales/Payables			16 22.7	25 14.9	24 15.3	
31 11.6	34 10.7	30 12.3				30 12.3	32 11.3	30 12.0	
46 7.9	52 7.1	47 7.7				47 7.8	48 7.7	44 8.4	
5.7	4.6	4.3	Sales/Working Capital				6.7	4.4	3.9
11.0	10.4	8.6					12.4	12.1	7.2
27.2	27.1	21.7					67.1	49.9	13.1
14.9	14.2	28.2	EBIT/Interest				6.7	15.8	48.4
(107) 5.1	(104) 6.7	(98) 8.4				(10) 2.1	(28) 9.8	(54) 12.2	
1.6	2.4	3.2					.4	3.0	4.2
7.7	9.3	11.6	Net Profit + Depr., Dep., Amort./Cur. Mat. L/T/D				7.1	38.3	
(37) 3.5	(36) 3.0	(35) 4.4					(11) 3.3	(20) 5.0	
1.9	1.8	2.5					1.9	2.7	
.3	.3	.4	Fixed/Worth				.7	.5	.4
1.0	.8	.8					1.4	.8	.7
2.0	1.6	1.7					3.3	1.4	1.5
.8	.6	.5	Debt/Worth				.7	.5	.5
1.7	1.6	1.4					2.5	1.3	1.2
4.9	4.1	3.7					16.5	3.5	3.3
54.2	52.3	54.0	% Profit Before Taxes/Tangible Net Worth				56.3	68.2	55.2
(100) 26.0	(102) 28.3	(104) 29.9				(10) 19.9	30.2	(55) 35.9	
7.4	8.1	11.2					6.6	12.0	16.0
16.2	18.9	20.8	% Profit Before Taxes/Total Assets				15.9	20.4	24.5
8.1	9.9	12.0					7.3	9.2	13.0
1.4	2.4	4.6					.9	3.6	7.1
18.1	18.9	12.9	Sales/Net Fixed Assets				10.1	18.0	14.1
6.5	6.6	5.7					8.8	5.8	5.2
3.1	3.3	3.4					3.9	3.4	3.5
3.2	2.6	2.8	Sales/Total Assets				2.9	2.8	2.5
1.9	1.8	1.8					2.1	2.0	1.7
1.2	1.1	1.3					1.4	1.5	1.2
1.1	.8	1.1	% Depr., Dep., Amort./Sales					1.2	.9
(102) 2.2	(99) 2.5	(101) 2.3					(28) 1.9	(56) 2.6	
4.3	5.0	4.5					4.8	4.4	
1.2	.9	1.0	% Officers', Directors' Owners' Comp/Sales						
(25) 3.8	(24) 2.1	(25) 1.7							
6.3	8.4	6.4							
6643890M	4391231M	5029702M	Net Sales ($)	614M	8543M	8284M	89825M	517929M	4404507M
4166481M	2995224M	3342265M	Total Assets ($)	2702M	6260M	7943M	50066M	301000M	2974294M

M = $ thousand   MM = $ million
See Pages 9 through 22 for Explanation of Ratios and Data

Current Data Sorted by Assets							Comparative Historical Data	
						Type of Statement		
		1	3	17	19	Unqualified	16	16
		1				Reviewed		
			1			Compiled		1
						Tax Returns		
		1		7	5	Other	3	6
	12 (4/1-9/30/10)		43 (10/1/10-3/31/11)				4/1/06-3/31/07	4/1/07-3/31/08
0-500M	500M-2MM	2-10MM	10-50MM	50-100MM	100-250MM		ALL	ALL
		3	4	24	24	**NUMBER OF STATEMENTS**	19	23
%	%	%	%	%	%	**ASSETS**	%	%
DATA NOT AVAILABLE	DATA NOT AVAILABLE			11.5	5.3	Cash & Equivalents	16.5	7.4
				6.0	9.0	Trade Receivables (net)	8.0	6.4
				6.9	11.0	Inventory	7.8	7.3
				1.9	4.8	All Other Current	3.9	3.6
				26.3	30.2	Total Current	36.2	24.6
				71.0	65.9	Fixed Assets (net)	53.2	71.0
				.9	.5	Intangibles (net)	1.2	.5
				1.7	3.4	All Other Non-Current	9.4	3.9
				100.0	100.0	Total	100.0	100.0
						LIABILITIES		
				.0	3.4	Notes Payable-Short Term	1.1	1.6
				6.2	5.4	Cur. Mat.-L.T.D.	4.0	4.3
				4.9	6.3	Trade Payables	6.5	5.3
				.0	.0	Income Taxes Payable	.0	.0
				3.0	8.5	All Other Current	4.6	3.7
				14.2	23.7	Total Current	16.1	14.8
				28.1	31.1	Long-Term Debt	16.8	32.8
				.1	.0	Deferred Taxes	.2	.1
				2.1	2.9	All Other Non-Current	2.1	.7
				55.5	42.3	Net Worth	64.7	51.7
				100.0	100.0	Total Liabilties & Net Worth	100.0	100.0
						INCOME DATA		
				100.0	100.0	Net Sales	100.0	100.0
				21.1	16.0	Gross Profit	36.6	21.5
				11.7	9.4	Operating Expenses	9.6	13.5
				9.4	6.5	Operating Profit	27.1	7.9
				1.5	2.1	All Other Expenses (net)	.4	.4
				7.8	4.4	Profit Before Taxes	26.7	7.5
						RATIOS		
				3.2	2.2		3.5	2.6
				2.1	1.6	Current	2.8	1.5
				1.1	1.1		1.7	1.0
				2.0	1.1		2.5	1.6
				1.1	.6	Quick	1.9	.8
				.7	.3		1.3	.5
				10 35.3	**9** 42.7		**14** 26.0	**17** 21.5
				15 24.3	**14** 26.6	Sales/Receivables	**19** 19.0	**25** 14.8
				20 18.0	**22** 16.6		**30** 12.4	**51** 7.1
				14 25.2	**16** 22.8		**13** 27.5	**17** 22.1
				19 19.5	**21** 17.3	Cost of Sales/Inventory	**21** 17.6	**31** 11.7
				31 11.7	**35** 10.6		**36** 10.2	**52** 7.0
				7 53.9	**5** 66.9		**12** 29.7	**13** 27.3
				11 32.3	**8** 47.7	Cost of Sales/Payables	**19** 19.0	**26** 14.0
				22 16.7	**12** 29.2		**36** 10.0	**36** 10.1
				7.9	10.7		5.7	6.0
				12.2	18.9	Sales/Working Capital	7.8	9.7
				92.9	181.8		9.5	82.2
				6.0	5.9		29.8	13.2
				(22) 4.5	3.9	EBIT/Interest	18.9	6.9
				3.0	2.5		9.4	2.0
						Net Profit + Depr., Dep., Amort./Cur. Mat. L/T/D		
				1.1	1.1		.6	1.1
				1.4	1.6	Fixed/Worth	.7	1.5
				1.7	2.1		1.1	2.0
				.5	.9		.3	.6
				.9	1.4	Debt/Worth	.5	.9
				1.5	2.2		1.0	1.5
				27.8	26.6		77.8	36.0
				17.6	15.0	% Profit Before Taxes/Tangible Net Worth	51.7	17.5
				12.2	8.9		28.6	6.6
				14.8	11.5		47.6	20.9
				10.7	7.2	% Profit Before Taxes/Total Assets	40.5	6.2
				6.9	2.8		21.3	2.4
				2.6	2.6		2.8	2.1
				1.9	1.9	Sales/Net Fixed Assets	2.2	1.2
				1.5	1.6		1.8	.6
				1.6	1.6		1.4	1.3
				1.3	1.4	Sales/Total Assets	1.2	.9
				1.2	1.1		.8	.5
				4.0	2.8		2.2	2.4
				(23) 4.7	(20) 3.5	% Depr., Dep., Amort./Sales	(17) 3.4	(19) 3.8
				5.3	4.6		5.2	5.7
						% Officers', Directors' Owners' Comp/Sales		
		51998M	250308M	2540104M	7940764M	Net Sales ($)	1552293M	1726104M
		10890M	158235M	1897063M	3593024M	Total Assets ($)	1250435M	2093096M

M = $ thousand MM = $ million

See Pages 9 through 22 for Explanation of Ratios and Data

Comparative Historical Data

Current Data Sorted by Sales

			Type of Statement						
25	32	40	Unqualified			1			40
		1	Reviewed						
	1	1	Compiled						1
			Tax Returns						
11	10	13	Other			1	1		11
4/1/08-3/31/09 ALL	4/1/09-3/31/10 ALL	4/1/10-3/31/11 ALL		0-1MM	12 (4/1-9/30/10) 1-3MM	3-5MM	43 (10/1/10-3/31/11) 5-10MM	10-25MM	25MM & OVER
36	43	55	**NUMBER OF STATEMENTS**			1	1	1	52
%	%	%	**ASSETS**	%	%	%	%	%	%
7.8	7.7	7.8	Cash & Equivalents	D	D				7.2
5.5	6.2	8.7	Trade Receivables (net)	A	A				8.3
6.8	8.1	10.6	Inventory	T	T				10.5
2.0	1.2	3.2	All Other Current	A	A				3.3
22.1	23.1	30.3	Total Current						29.4
72.6	71.1	64.9	Fixed Assets (net)	N	N				65.6
.6	.6	.7	Intangibles (net)	O	O				.7
4.6	5.3	4.2	All Other Non-Current	T	T				4.3
100.0	100.0	100.0	Total						100.0
			LIABILITIES	A	A				
2.5	2.6	4.3	Notes Payable-Short Term	V	V				4.1
7.9	5.9	5.4	Cur. Mat.-L.T.D.	A	A				5.6
6.2	5.0	5.7	Trade Payables	I	I				5.9
.0	.0	.0	Income Taxes Payable	L	L				.0
3.4	4.1	5.3	All Other Current	A	A				5.5
20.0	17.5	20.7	Total Current	B	B				21.1
34.1	33.5	27.6	Long-Term Debt	L	L				28.3
.0	.0	.0	Deferred Taxes	E	E				.0
1.0	1.6	2.3	All Other Non-Current						2.4
44.9	47.4	49.4	Net Worth						48.2
100.0	100.0	100.0	Total Liabilities & Net Worth						100.0
			INCOME DATA						
100.0	100.0	100.0	Net Sales						100.0
9.7	14.4	18.8	Gross Profit						17.9
10.3	13.2	11.2	Operating Expenses						10.8
-.6	1.2	7.6	Operating Profit						7.1
2.6	1.8	1.2	All Other Expenses (net)						1.2
-3.1	-.6	6.4	Profit Before Taxes						5.8
			RATIOS						
2.4	2.0	2.7							2.4
1.2	1.5	1.7	Current						1.6
1.0	1.1	1.1							1.1
1.1	1.3	1.6							1.5
.8	.9	.8	Quick						.8
.3	.5	.5							.5
8 45.5	11 33.7	10 35.3							10 35.3
12 29.4	15 24.8	15 24.6	Sales/Receivables						14 25.7
21 17.6	19 19.0	22 16.4							20 18.0
13 28.7	13 27.2	15 23.7							15 23.6
20 18.7	22 16.6	23 15.7	Cost of Sales/Inventory						22 16.9
30 12.2	41 9.0	39 9.4							35 10.4
8 48.0	5 73.2	6 57.3							6 56.8
12 30.9	11 33.6	10 37.5	Cost of Sales/Payables						10 38.4
21 17.5	26 14.0	21 17.7							19 19.3
11.7	10.4	9.2							9.3
29.9	20.9	13.1	Sales/Working Capital						13.7
757.8	149.2	92.2							100.4
2.2	4.5	7.9							6.3
(35) .6	(42) 1.8	(53) 4.4	EBIT/Interest					(50) 4.2
-2.3	-.5	2.9							2.9
			Net Profit + Depr., Dep., Amort./Cur. Mat. L/T/D						
1.1	1.1	1.0							1.1
1.9	1.8	1.4	Fixed/Worth						1.5
2.8	2.1	1.8							1.9
.8	.7	.5							.6
1.5	1.4	1.0	Debt/Worth						1.0
2.3	2.0	1.6							1.7
9.4	17.6	26.8	% Profit Before Taxes/Tangible Net Worth						26.6
-2.4	2.1	(54) 17.6							(51) 17.7
-20.4	-13.5	9.4							11.9
3.7	7.4	13.8	% Profit Before Taxes/Total Assets						13.8
-.9	1.1	9.4							9.5
-6.5	-4.2	3.4							4.0
2.4	2.0	2.7							2.7
1.8	1.6	2.0	Sales/Net Fixed Assets						2.0
1.1	1.3	1.5							1.5
1.7	1.5	1.6							1.6
1.4	1.2	1.3	Sales/Total Assets						1.4
.9	1.0	1.2							1.2
2.6	3.6	3.2							3.2
(33) 3.7	(36) 4.8	(49) 4.5	% Depr., Dep., Amort./Sales					(47) 4.5
4.5	6.1	5.1							5.1
			% Officers', Directors' Owners' Comp/Sales						
7730578M	5965772M	10783174M	Net Sales ($)		4351M	5984M	12948M	10759891M
3984549M	4515816M	5659212M	Total Assets ($)		3562M	2514M	62437M	5590699M

M = $ thousand   MM = $ million
See Pages 9 through 22 for Explanation of Ratios and Data

Current Data Sorted by Assets   Comparative Historical Data

0-500M	500M-2MM	2-10MM	10-50MM	50-100MM	100-250MM	Type of Statement	4/1/06-3/31/07 ALL	4/1/07-3/31/08 ALL
1	1	2	16	30	20	Unqualified	54	67
1	1	10	5			Reviewed	19	15
		6	1	1		Compiled	9	4
1	2	4	1			Tax Returns	2	3
3	2	12	21	5	6	Other	36	37
	35 (4/1-9/30/10)		116 (10/1/10-3/31/11)					
5	6	34	44	36	26	NUMBER OF STATEMENTS	120	126
%	%	%	%	%	%	**ASSETS**	%	%
		10.2	8.9	6.3	6.5	Cash & Equivalents	9.9	6.9
		28.8	23.3	11.5	8.7	Trade Receivables (net)	23.0	17.8
		22.0	21.5	11.1	12.0	Inventory	18.2	16.9
		1.6	3.8	4.9	4.0	All Other Current	3.7	3.7
		62.7	57.5	33.8	31.3	Total Current	54.8	45.4
		22.7	30.0	57.6	60.4	Fixed Assets (net)	35.4	42.0
		7.8	6.7	3.0	4.2	Intangibles (net)	4.3	6.7
		6.8	5.8	5.6	4.1	All Other Non-Current	5.4	5.9
		100.0	100.0	100.0	100.0	Total	100.0	100.0
						LIABILITIES		
		10.5	5.0	3.5	3.1	Notes Payable-Short Term	8.2	7.2
		2.7	3.8	4.1	5.9	Cur. Mat.-L.T.D.	2.9	3.6
		19.5	13.0	6.2	5.8	Trade Payables	12.7	11.7
		.1	.3	.1	.3	Income Taxes Payable	.4	.2
		4.8	9.4	5.8	6.9	All Other Current	7.5	7.2
		37.4	31.4	19.7	22.0	Total Current	31.7	30.0
		10.2	15.1	19.5	27.6	Long-Term Debt	17.3	20.3
		.8	.9	.9	.8	Deferred Taxes	.9	.7
		6.5	8.1	2.8	2.1	All Other Non-Current	6.1	4.7
		45.1	44.5	57.1	47.6	Net Worth	44.0	44.3
		100.0	100.0	100.0	100.0	Total Liabilities & Net Worth	100.0	100.0
						INCOME DATA		
		100.0	100.0	100.0	100.0	Net Sales	100.0	100.0
		34.4	28.2	15.7	14.2	Gross Profit	34.0	27.9
		25.9	19.7	9.4	7.5	Operating Expenses	20.5	18.4
		8.5	8.5	6.3	6.8	Operating Profit	13.4	9.5
		.8	1.2	.7	1.4	All Other Expenses (net)	.6	1.6
		7.7	7.3	5.6	5.3	Profit Before Taxes	12.8	7.9
						RATIOS		
		3.3	3.3	3.0	2.2		2.9	2.5
		1.9	2.1	2.3	1.6	Current	1.9	1.6
		1.3	1.3	1.2	1.0		1.2	1.1
		1.8	1.7	1.6	1.1		1.8	1.3
		1.2	1.0	.8	.7	Quick	1.1	.8
		.7	.7	.6	.2		.7	.5
	32 11.3	42 8.7	14 25.2	9 40.4		Sales/Receivables	24 15.1	22 17.0
	42 8.7	49 7.4	22 16.3	18 20.3			43 8.6	37 9.8
	54 6.7	58 6.3	43 8.5	33 11.0			58 6.3	51 7.2
	34 10.7	33 11.1	16 22.2	19 19.4		Cost of Sales/Inventory	28 12.9	28 12.9
	53 6.9	61 6.0	32 11.5	28 13.1			46 7.9	45 8.1
	79 4.6	89 4.1	40 9.1	51 7.2			68 5.4	66 5.5
	20 18.0	25 14.6	5 67.3	8 47.3		Cost of Sales/Payables	17 21.1	16 22.3
	36 10.1	30 12.1	12 30.2	17 21.3			30 12.1	31 11.9
	56 6.6	49 7.4	29 12.7	28 13.3			47 7.8	47 7.7
		4.7	3.9	5.8	9.1	Sales/Working Capital	4.6	5.4
		8.8	6.8	8.4	13.8		8.0	10.2
		16.9	16.6	26.0	140.0		26.5	39.9
		55.0	24.5	12.6	14.9		27.1	18.1
		12.4 (37)	10.9 (35)	4.4	5.2	EBIT/Interest	(117) 8.9	(117) 5.4
		4.6	3.4	1.8	1.8		2.3	2.3
			23.8				17.2	23.8
			(15) 4.5			Net Profit + Depr., Dep., Amort./Cur. Mat. L/T/D	(38) 4.7	(37) 3.6
			2.2				1.9	1.6
		.3	.2	.7	1.0		.4	.5
		.5	.7	1.0	1.5	Fixed/Worth	.9	1.1
		.9	1.4	1.4	1.9		1.7	2.0
		.5	.5	.4	.7		.5	.6
		1.9	1.2	.7	1.0	Debt/Worth	1.5	1.1
		3.8	2.7	1.3	2.6		3.7	2.8
		89.1	43.8	28.0	25.3		63.7	44.4
	(31) 35.1	(39) 26.0	(35) 12.7	(25) 14.7		% Profit Before Taxes/Tangible Net Worth	(107) 36.0	(106) 27.6
		17.1	10.2	2.8	4.3		17.3	14.0
		30.2	20.5	11.4	12.4		31.7	19.5
		16.4	11.4	7.5	8.6	% Profit Before Taxes/Total Assets	12.9	10.6
		5.1	4.7	1.2	1.0		4.8	3.7
		33.7	23.7	2.8	3.6		16.9	11.7
		9.7	8.2	2.4	2.1	Sales/Net Fixed Assets	6.5	4.4
		5.7	3.0	1.8	1.6		2.4	2.1
		2.8	2.4	1.6	1.6		2.4	2.1
		2.0	1.7	1.4	1.3	Sales/Total Assets	1.6	1.5
		1.6	1.0	1.2	1.1		1.2	1.0
		.5	1.1	3.5	3.2		1.1	1.2
	(32) 1.2	(37) 2.7	(35) 4.5	(18) 3.6		% Depr., Dep., Amort./Sales	(106) 2.3	(110) 2.8
		3.3	6.6	5.5	4.3		4.1	4.4
		1.0					1.8	1.5
	(11) 4.5					% Officers', Directors' Owners' Comp/Sales	(25) 2.8	(22) 2.8
		7.1					4.5	5.6
6431M	15582M	402419M	2013419M	3727824M	5343780M	Net Sales ($)	6914720M	8975523M
1424M	7512M	174157M	1147903M	2557792M	3950756M	Total Assets ($)	5062886M	7164486M

M = $ thousand   MM = $ million
See Pages 9 through 22 for Explanation of Ratios and Data

Comparative Historical Data | Current Data Sorted by Sales

4/1/08-3/31/09 ALL	4/1/09-3/31/10 ALL	4/1/10-3/31/11 ALL	Type of Statement	0-1MM	1-3MM	3-5MM	5-10MM	10-25MM	25MM & OVER
64	72	69	Unqualified		1			6	62
18	23	17	Reviewed		2		6	4	5
8	12	8	Compiled			1	4	1	2
2	6	8	Tax Returns	1	2		3	1	1
47	50	49	Other	2	2	2	5	12	26
						35 (4/1-9/30/10)		116 (10/1/10-3/31/11)	
139	163	151	**NUMBER OF STATEMENTS**	3	7	3	18	24	96
%	%	%	**ASSETS**	%	%	%	%	%	%
6.7	8.8	9.2	Cash & Equivalents				12.9	8.1	7.7
18.8	18.0	19.0	Trade Receivables (net)				25.5	22.9	16.7
17.4	17.2	17.1	Inventory				20.5	20.2	16.3
2.6	2.6	3.7	All Other Current				1.4	4.7	3.8
45.5	46.6	48.9	Total Current				60.2	55.9	44.6
41.4	42.8	39.7	Fixed Assets (net)				21.8	27.2	47.0
7.6	4.9	5.7	Intangibles (net)				13.0	8.8	3.4
5.5	5.7	5.7	All Other Non-Current				4.9	8.0	4.9
100.0	100.0	100.0	Total				100.0	100.0	100.0
			LIABILITIES						
7.6	5.9	6.8	Notes Payable-Short Term				6.5	7.2	4.2
3.8	4.1	3.8	Cur. Mat.-L.T.D.				3.4	1.9	4.5
12.0	12.2	12.3	Trade Payables				12.2	14.5	9.5
.2	.2	.2	Income Taxes Payable				.1	.3	.1
7.9	6.6	8.0	All Other Current				6.0	4.6	7.9
31.5	28.8	31.0	Total Current				28.2	28.6	26.3
18.1	19.4	17.2	Long-Term Debt				11.0	15.5	18.7
.5	.6	.8	Deferred Taxes				1.3	.7	.8
5.3	5.3	6.4	All Other Non-Current				8.8	10.4	3.7
44.6	45.9	44.4	Net Worth				50.7	44.8	50.4
100.0	100.0	100.0	Total Liabilities & Net Worth				100.0	100.0	100.0
			INCOME DATA						
100.0	100.0	100.0	Net Sales				100.0	100.0	100.0
19.9	22.3	25.1	Gross Profit				39.4	33.3	19.2
16.1	18.3	18.3	Operating Expenses				28.8	25.1	11.9
3.9	4.0	6.8	Operating Profit				10.6	8.2	7.3
1.5	1.3	.9	All Other Expenses (net)				.7	1.6	.9
2.4	2.8	5.8	Profit Before Taxes				9.9	6.6	6.4
			RATIOS						
2.3	2.5	2.8					4.0	3.3	2.8
1.7	1.7	1.9	Current				1.9	1.9	2.0
1.1	1.2	1.2					1.4	1.4	1.2
1.4	1.4	1.6					2.6	1.6	1.6
.9	.9	1.0	Quick				1.4	1.1	.9
.5	.6	.6					.7	.7	.5
18 20.7	19 19.3	17 21.1					35 10.3	33 11.0	15 24.4
34 10.6	37 9.8	40 9.2	Sales/Receivables				46 7.9	44 8.3	31 11.6
51 7.1	51 7.1	53 6.9					75 4.9	62 5.9	50 7.3
19 19.2	24 15.1	24 15.1					41 9.0	31 11.9	23 16.1
38 9.6	43 8.5	40 9.1	Cost of Sales/Inventory				61 6.0	53 6.9	35 10.5
63 5.8	70 5.2	69 5.3					82 4.4	99 3.7	64 5.7
12 30.9	15 25.1	12 30.0					19 19.5	24 15.0	9 39.1
23 15.6	28 13.0	27 13.7	Cost of Sales/Payables				40 9.1	30 12.1	24 15.4
45 8.1	47 7.8	41 8.8					56 6.6	59 6.2	34 10.8
5.7	4.9	5.2					3.9	4.2	5.4
13.9	9.9	9.1	Sales/Working Capital				7.4	8.0	9.3
77.1	30.4	22.3					15.1	11.6	20.7
13.6	10.8	18.8					51.2	36.0	17.0
(131) 3.3	(153) 4.7	(139) 7.8	EBIT/Interest			(17) 13.5		(23) 9.6	(90) 6.7
-.4	.7	2.7					3.9	1.4	3.3
11.5	9.7	14.8	Net Profit + Depr., Dep.,						28.5
(39) 3.3	(42) 3.7	(38) 4.1	Amort./Cur. Mat. L/T/D					(26)	5.0
.4	1.6	2.0							2.3
.4	.4	.4					.2	.1	.6
1.2	1.0	.9	Fixed/Worth				.4	.6	1.0
2.1	2.2	1.6					1.0	1.6	1.5
.6	.5	.5					.3	.6	.5
1.3	1.1	1.0	Debt/Worth				1.9	1.7	.9
3.3	3.4	2.7					4.5	3.0	1.9
31.1	29.1	38.0	% Profit Before Taxes/Tangible				89.7	74.7	31.6
(121) 11.7	(149) 13.1	(137) 19.3	Net Worth			(16) 33.0		(21) 27.5	(92) 15.9
-5.1	-1.0	8.4					17.7	9.0	7.7
14.4	11.3	18.9	% Profit Before Taxes/Total				25.8	25.7	14.9
5.0	6.2	8.8	Assets				12.5	12.0	8.7
-3.0	-.8	3.4					5.1	1.2	3.5
13.7	13.9	14.2					70.7	32.9	8.4
4.8	3.5	4.4	Sales/Net Fixed Assets				8.4	11.6	2.8
2.3	1.8	2.1					5.7	2.8	2.0
2.4	2.1	2.1					2.2	2.7	2.0
1.6	1.4	1.5	Sales/Total Assets				1.7	1.8	1.5
1.3	1.1	1.2					1.5	.8	1.2
1.0	1.4	1.3					.6	.9	2.0
(119) 2.5	(139) 3.6	(129) 3.5	% Depr., Dep., Amort./Sales			(14) 2.1		1.3	(81) 3.6
4.0	5.7	5.0					3.7	7.1	5.0
1.2	1.0	.9							
(19) 2.9	(34) 2.4	(24) 3.4	% Officers', Directors' Owners' Comp/Sales						
4.6	5.2	5.3							
12180578M	10966745M	11509455M	Net Sales ($)	1190M	13973M	11994M	136152M	393898M	10952248M
7724999M	8233160M	7839544M	Total Assets ($)	550M	6519M	10010M	84783M	349815M	7387867M

© RMA 2011

M = $ thousand   MM = $ million
See Pages 9 through 22 for Explanation of Ratios and Data

Current Data Sorted by Assets   Comparative Historical Data

0-500M	500M-2MM	2-10MM	10-50MM	50-100MM	100-250MM	Type of Statement	4/1/06-3/31/07 ALL	4/1/07-3/31/08 ALL
	1	6	23	9	13	Unqualified	54	48
	3	26	15		1	Reviewed	40	38
1	7	6	1	1		Compiled	21	16
4	5	3	2			Tax Returns	10	14
	3	34	37	6	6	Other	93	95
	36 (4/1-9/30/10)			176 (10/1/10-3/31/11)				
5	19	75	78	15	20	**NUMBER OF STATEMENTS**	218	211
%	%	%	%	%	%	**ASSETS**	%	%
	16.6	8.2	3.9	6.6	7.0	Cash & Equivalents	6.5	6.5
	40.7	27.7	26.8	22.1	22.3	Trade Receivables (net)	27.2	28.4
	22.9	26.3	28.5	19.7	17.7	Inventory	23.2	23.0
	1.9	2.7	3.0	2.0	1.5	All Other Current	2.5	3.1
	82.0	64.9	62.2	50.4	48.5	Total Current	59.5	61.0
	14.2	28.3	26.3	29.9	37.1	Fixed Assets (net)	31.1	29.7
	.8	2.3	7.1	15.3	11.6	Intangibles (net)	5.0	5.1
	3.1	4.5	4.4	4.4	2.9	All Other Non-Current	4.4	4.2
	100.0	100.0	100.0	100.0	100.0	Total	100.0	100.0
						LIABILITIES		
	10.7	11.4	11.5	8.2	3.3	Notes Payable-Short Term	11.6	11.9
	1.7	3.8	2.6	2.5	1.7	Cur. Mat.-L.T.D.	3.5	3.4
	25.5	16.7	17.2	15.7	13.9	Trade Payables	17.2	18.8
	.1	.2	.1	.1	.3	Income Taxes Payable	.2	.4
	8.5	6.5	13.2	6.0	5.2	All Other Current	8.0	6.4
	46.5	38.5	44.6	32.4	24.4	Total Current	40.6	41.0
	6.4	14.0	11.7	14.6	29.6	Long-Term Debt	19.6	18.1
	.2	.3	.5	1.6	2.7	Deferred Taxes	.7	.4
	7.4	7.8	5.5	6.6	9.2	All Other Non-Current	7.2	4.8
	39.5	39.4	37.8	44.8	34.1	Net Worth	32.0	35.8
	100.0	100.0	100.0	100.0	100.0	Total Liabilities & Net Worth	100.0	100.0
						INCOME DATA		
	100.0	100.0	100.0	100.0	100.0	Net Sales	100.0	100.0
	38.0	28.5	20.4	23.6	21.8	Gross Profit	25.2	24.2
	31.9	22.6	15.2	18.1	13.2	Operating Expenses	19.2	18.9
	6.1	6.0	5.2	5.5	8.6	Operating Profit	6.0	5.3
	.1	1.1	.8	1.1	2.7	All Other Expenses (net)	1.6	1.3
	6.0	4.9	4.4	4.4	5.9	Profit Before Taxes	4.4	4.1
						RATIOS		
	4.7	3.0	2.2	2.5	2.5		2.2	2.4
	1.7	1.8	1.5	1.6	2.0	Current	1.5	1.5
	1.1	1.1	1.1	1.1	1.7		1.1	1.1
	3.0	1.9	1.1	1.7	1.5		1.4	1.3
	1.5	1.0	.7	.9	1.3	Quick	.9	.9
	.7	.5	.5	.6	.8		.5	.6
	31 11.9	36 10.2	39 9.3	40 9.1	41 8.8		33 10.9	36 10.2
	55 6.6	44 8.3	47 7.7	49 7.4	51 7.1	Sales/Receivables	44 8.3	45 8.1
	71 5.1	54 6.7	54 6.7	58 6.3	62 5.9		54 6.7	59 6.2
	31 11.9	34 10.8	45 8.2	31 11.6	30 12.0		27 13.7	32 11.6
	50 7.2	60 6.0	66 5.5	57 6.4	49 7.5	Cost of Sales/Inventory	48 7.6	51 7.2
	97 3.8	83 4.4	89 4.1	85 4.3	80 4.6		73 5.0	70 5.2
	37 9.9	19 19.0	25 14.4	34 10.8	31 11.8		20 17.8	23 15.8
	56 6.6	31 11.9	35 10.5	40 9.2	35 10.3	Cost of Sales/Payables	33 11.1	37 9.9
	65 5.6	54 6.8	44 8.3	57 6.4	51 7.2		46 7.9	51 7.2
	3.3	5.2	6.4	4.0	5.0		6.6	5.5
	8.1	9.2	11.5	8.6	6.9	Sales/Working Capital	11.7	10.8
	33.2	32.3	33.1	46.7	8.2		57.0	48.3
	13.5	18.4	12.9	18.2	24.6		10.5	10.1
	(13) 7.3	(70) 5.5	(71) 5.6	(12) 5.4	7.0	EBIT/Interest	(197) 3.8	(199) 3.4
	1.3	1.8	2.5	-8.7	2.0		1.5	1.4
		10.7	13.3				8.4	9.0
		(16) 5.9	(26) 3.6			Net Profit + Depr., Dep., Amort./Cur. Mat. L/T/D	(57) 3.5	(57) 4.0
		3.1	1.5				1.9	1.4
	.1	.3	.4	.7	.8		.5	.3
	.3	.7	.8	1.0	2.2	Fixed/Worth	1.1	.8
	.9	1.9	2.3	4.9	-7.9		3.5	2.3
	.6	.6	.8	.6	.9		.9	.9
	1.3	1.6	2.1	1.5	5.4	Debt/Worth	2.3	2.0
	4.7	3.4	7.7	14.1	-22.6		8.2	6.7
	49.7	47.9	63.9	42.0	60.4		48.6	44.6
	(17) 41.2	(66) 23.9	(70) 25.1	(12) 13.9	(13) 23.0	% Profit Before Taxes/Tangible Net Worth	(187) 25.7	(182) 23.7
	3.6	11.6	9.5	-6.1	21.1		11.7	7.3
	37.8	21.6	14.6	9.1	15.0		16.1	15.4
	8.3	7.8	8.0	5.5	8.5	% Profit Before Taxes/Total Assets	8.5	6.2
	.4	2.3	2.6	-.2	2.4		2.1	1.3
	77.2	19.2	14.1	7.1	5.4		16.2	15.9
	31.8	7.3	6.8	6.1	4.5	Sales/Net Fixed Assets	7.6	7.1
	13.1	5.0	4.5	3.8	2.6		4.0	4.2
	3.3	2.8	2.7	1.9	2.1		2.9	2.8
	2.4	2.3	2.0	1.5	1.4	Sales/Total Assets	2.1	2.2
	2.1	1.7	1.5	1.1	1.0		1.6	1.5
	.5	1.3	1.3	1.7	1.5		1.0	1.1
	(14) 1.4	(66) 2.2	(70) 2.7	2.8	(10) 2.4	% Depr., Dep., Amort./Sales	(193) 2.1	(183) 2.2
	2.8	4.7	4.1	3.4	3.5		3.7	3.7
	2.7	1.5	.4				1.3	1.4
	(11) 4.5	(28) 3.3	(16) 1.2			% Officers', Directors', Owners' Comp/Sales	(65) 3.5	(50) 4.1
	13.1	6.3	5.0				5.9	8.5
4905M	70724M	934767M	3452106M	1863577M	5663009M	Net Sales ($)	10495362M	11212450M
917M	25819M	403076M	1633633M	1118507M	3525014M	Total Assets ($)	5145470M	6311043M

M = $ thousand   MM = $ million
See Pages 9 through 22 for Explanation of Ratios and Data

Comparative Historical Data | Current Data Sorted by Sales

			Type of Statement	0-1MM	1-3MM	3-5MM	5-10MM	10-25MM	25MM & OVER
50	52	52	Unqualified			1	1	8	42
45	42	45	Reviewed		1	1	11	20	12
18	17	15	Compiled		4	4	4	1	2
12	16	14	Tax Returns	5	3	1	3	1	1
104	87	86	Other			7	15	27	37
4/1/08-3/31/09 ALL	4/1/09-3/31/10 ALL	4/1/10-3/31/11 ALL			36 (4/1-9/30/10)		176 (10/1/10-3/31/11)		
229	214	212	**NUMBER OF STATEMENTS**	5	8	14	34	57	94
%	%	%	**ASSETS**	%	%	%	%	%	%
7.0	7.4	7.2	Cash & Equivalents			19.8	5.7	7.2	4.6
26.0	25.8	27.6	Trade Receivables (net)			30.6	28.2	24.3	29.0
23.7	24.6	25.9	Inventory			20.3	26.7	24.7	26.2
2.8	2.9	2.5	All Other Current			1.7	1.8	4.2	2.2
59.4	60.7	63.2	Total Current			72.3	62.5	60.4	62.0
29.8	29.3	27.1	Fixed Assets (net)			21.1	28.6	30.1	26.5
5.7	5.0	5.7	Intangibles (net)			1.0	3.2	6.1	7.7
5.1	5.0	4.1	All Other Non-Current			5.5	5.7	3.5	3.8
100.0	100.0	100.0	Total			100.0	100.0	100.0	100.0
			LIABILITIES						
11.3	13.4	10.3	Notes Payable-Short Term			8.8	10.0	9.8	10.9
4.2	3.8	2.8	Cur. Mat.-L.T.D.			6.0	3.5	2.8	2.8
16.8	16.8	17.3	Trade Payables			17.3	16.4	14.1	19.4
.6	.3	.1	Income Taxes Payable			.0	.1	.3	.1
8.5	6.7	9.2	All Other Current			4.8	7.8	13.3	7.4
41.3	41.0	39.7	Total Current			36.9	37.7	40.3	40.1
16.5	14.8	13.8	Long-Term Debt			8.1	17.9	11.9	14.8
.7	.7	.7	Deferred Taxes			.3	.3	.4	1.1
8.8	7.5	7.0	All Other Non-Current			11.5	10.4	3.9	6.3
32.8	36.0	38.8	Net Worth			43.1	33.7	43.4	37.7
100.0	100.0	100.0	Total Liabilties & Net Worth			100.0	100.0	100.0	100.0
			INCOME DATA						
100.0	100.0	100.0	Net Sales			100.0	100.0	100.0	100.0
21.8	25.3	25.9	Gross Profit			37.3	29.2	26.8	19.7
18.3	21.1	19.9	Operating Expenses			28.9	22.9	21.7	13.7
3.5	4.2	6.0	Operating Profit			8.4	6.3	5.1	6.0
1.8	1.0	1.0	All Other Expenses (net)			.7	1.1	.9	1.0
1.7	3.1	4.9	Profit Before Taxes			7.7	5.2	4.3	5.0
			RATIOS						
2.6	2.5	2.5	Current			4.9	2.9	2.8	2.4
1.4	1.6	1.7				2.3	1.7	1.7	1.6
1.0	1.1	1.1				1.1	1.1	1.1	1.2
1.4	1.5	1.6	Quick			2.9	1.7	1.8	1.3
.8	.8	.9				1.7	.9	.9	.8
.5	.5	.5				.7	.4	.5	.6
30 12.1	36 10.1	38 9.6	Sales/Receivables			40 9.0	35 10.5	33 11.1	39 9.3
38 9.7	47 7.8	47 7.8				68 5.4	48 7.5	43 8.4	49 7.4
51 7.2	57 6.5	56 6.5				74 4.9	57 6.4	49 7.5	58 6.3
29 12.4	36 10.0	38 9.6	Cost of Sales/Inventory			33 11.0	38 9.7	36 10.1	39 9.4
52 7.1	55 6.6	58 6.2				77 4.7	69 5.3	59 6.2	55 6.7
73 5.0	83 4.4	84 4.4				102 3.6	104 3.5	86 4.2	75 4.9
16 22.6	22 16.3	24 15.5	Cost of Sales/Payables			33 11.0	19 19.7	19 19.0	30 12.3
28 12.9	36 10.0	36 10.2				54 6.8	28 12.8	28 13.2	36 10.1
45 8.1	49 7.4	51 7.1				70 5.2	52 7.0	51 7.2	47 7.8
5.9	5.4	5.5	Sales/Working Capital			2.8	5.2	5.3	5.9
13.0	11.8	9.4				5.8	9.8	10.0	9.5
87.6	77.2	29.8				60.0	44.1	27.3	28.4
8.6	11.1	17.1	EBIT/Interest			13.8	15.4	24.3	18.4
(209) 2.7	(196) 4.0	(189) 6.0			(11) 7.3	(31) 4.6	(49) 5.6	(89) 7.0	
.5	1.0	2.0				1.1	1.6	1.8	2.7
7.6	5.3	11.6	Net Profit + Depr., Dep., Amort./Cur. Mat. L/T/D					16.0	13.3
(62) 2.6	(48) 2.4	(60) 5.3						(13) 5.4	(38) 4.4
1.0	.8	2.1						.1	2.2
.3	.3	.3	Fixed/Worth			.1	.3	.4	.4
.8	.7	.7				.2	.8	.7	.8
2.7	2.1	2.3				1.4	2.7	2.6	2.6
.9	.6	.7	Debt/Worth			.5	.9	.4	.9
2.4	1.9	1.7				1.4	1.9	1.3	2.1
6.6	5.8	7.1				2.9	9.1	5.1	10.1
36.7	40.0	54.8	% Profit Before Taxes/Tangible Net Worth			47.5	49.7	50.2	60.5
(195) 13.3	(187) 18.4	(182) 24.7			(13) 44.3	(29) 17.9	(48) 22.3	(82) 25.3	
.0	5.3	8.7				30.2	7.8	6.2	12.9
10.8	12.6	16.9	% Profit Before Taxes/Total Assets			38.8	13.8	17.2	15.1
4.5	5.5	7.9				16.2	7.2	8.2	8.1
-1.1	.0	2.4				4.4	1.5	2.4	3.1
21.4	18.7	19.4	Sales/Net Fixed Assets			60.8	20.2	12.9	14.9
7.4	6.5	7.0				13.0	6.6	6.5	6.6
4.1	4.2	4.5				3.3	3.8	4.3	4.6
2.9	2.7	2.7	Sales/Total Assets			2.4	2.5	2.6	2.8
2.1	1.9	2.1				1.8	2.0	2.0	2.1
1.5	1.4	1.5				1.1	1.6	1.5	1.5
1.2	1.1	1.3	% Depr., Dep., Amort./Sales				1.7	1.5	1.2
(193) 2.2	(181) 2.5	(178) 2.3				(30) 3.6	(54) 2.4	(75) 1.9	
4.0	4.5	3.9					5.5	4.7	3.0
1.8	1.7	1.3	% Officers', Directors' Owners' Comp/Sales				3.2	1.2	.6
(53) 3.4	(57) 3.7	(59) 3.4				(16) 4.1	(14) 1.9	(15) 1.1	
6.0	8.0	7.0					9.0	5.9	3.4
15610292M	11283485M	11989088M	Net Sales ($)	3132M	18156M	54218M	249192M	983785M	10680605M
7691781M	6707986M	6706966M	Total Assets ($)	4980M	6099M	40338M	130497M	543846M	5981206M

M = $ thousand   MM = $ million

See Pages 9 through 22 for Explanation of Ratios and Data

Current Data Sorted by Assets   Comparative Historical Data

						Type of Statement		
	1	5	5	3	1	Unqualified	15	13
	3	6	6			Reviewed	6	9
	5	2				Compiled	6	4
	1	3				Tax Returns	6	6
1	3	4	6	1	1	Other	16	11
	18 (4/1-9/30/10)		39 (10/1/10-3/31/11)				4/1/06-3/31/07	4/1/07-3/31/08
0-500M	500M-2MM	2-10MM	10-50MM	50-100MM	100-250MM		ALL	ALL
1	13	20	17	4	2	NUMBER OF STATEMENTS	49	43
%	%	%	%	%	%	**ASSETS**	%	%
	11.4	10.8	5.6			Cash & Equivalents	6.2	6.9
	20.0	21.0	20.0			Trade Receivables (net)	23.9	24.8
	30.4	31.5	21.7			Inventory	31.1	31.3
	3.1	2.2	2.4			All Other Current	1.7	4.8
	64.8	65.5	49.7			Total Current	62.9	67.8
	26.3	27.9	40.5			Fixed Assets (net)	27.8	26.7
	2.9	1.9	3.5			Intangibles (net)	3.8	1.8
	6.0	4.7	6.3			All Other Non-Current	5.5	3.8
	100.0	100.0	100.0			Total	100.0	100.0
						LIABILITIES		
	7.7	14.9	11.1			Notes Payable-Short Term	16.0	15.8
	6.5	3.8	3.8			Cur. Mat.-L.T.D.	3.1	4.2
	10.8	12.7	11.9			Trade Payables	22.1	19.2
	.2	.7	.4			Income Taxes Payable	.2	.5
	13.0	5.8	5.3			All Other Current	10.2	9.1
	38.1	37.9	32.5			Total Current	51.6	48.8
	21.5	16.8	23.3			Long-Term Debt	17.5	22.0
	.7	.3	1.0			Deferred Taxes	.7	.8
	3.1	3.1	4.9			All Other Non-Current	5.5	5.4
	36.6	41.9	38.2			Net Worth	24.8	23.0
	100.0	100.0	100.0			Total Liabilities & Net Worth	100.0	100.0
						INCOME DATA		
	100.0	100.0	100.0			Net Sales	100.0	100.0
	35.6	32.7	33.5			Gross Profit	27.9	27.5
	30.1	23.4	26.9			Operating Expenses	24.2	23.1
	5.5	9.4	6.6			Operating Profit	3.7	4.4
	.5	1.3	1.7			All Other Expenses (net)	3.1	2.4
	5.0	8.1	4.8			Profit Before Taxes	.6	1.9
						RATIOS		
	4.8	2.4	2.8				1.8	2.1
	1.7	1.8	1.7			Current	1.2	1.3
	1.5	1.2	1.1				.9	1.1
	1.9	1.2	1.4				.8	1.1
	.8	.8	.8			Quick	.5	.7
	.5	.5	.6				.4	.4
	16 / 23.0	20 / 18.3	26 / 13.9				26 / 14.2	27 / 13.7
	25 / 14.6	30 / 12.0	38 / 9.5			Sales/Receivables	34 / 10.6	36 / 10.2
	44 / 8.3	63 / 5.8	56 / 6.5				47 / 7.7	54 / 6.7
	42 / 8.8	48 / 7.5	37 / 9.8				42 / 8.8	42 / 8.6
	77 / 4.8	86 / 4.2	55 / 6.6			Cost of Sales/Inventory	69 / 5.3	66 / 5.5
	172 / 2.1	104 / 3.5	86 / 4.2				123 / 3.0	103 / 3.5
	5 / 76.3	23 / 16.0	23 / 15.8				27 / 13.5	20 / 18.6
	18 / 20.7	28 / 13.1	33 / 11.1			Cost of Sales/Payables	42 / 8.7	42 / 8.7
	45 / 8.1	42 / 8.6	43 / 8.5				76 / 4.8	67 / 5.4
	5.3	5.6	5.3				7.8	7.0
	8.4	9.3	10.5			Sales/Working Capital	18.5	10.5
	15.9	17.5	277.0				-62.1	48.4
	9.5	29.4	15.1				3.8	6.6
	(11) 3.8	(18) 5.6	(15) 3.7			EBIT/Interest	(45) 1.5	(38) 1.9
	1.0	1.8	1.6				.9	.8
						Net Profit + Depr., Dep.,	8.6	8.1
						Amort./Cur. Mat. L/T/D	(11) 2.9	(10) 2.1
							1.0	1.2
	.3	.3	.5				.6	.6
	.6	.8	.9			Fixed/Worth	1.0	1.1
	3.7	1.6	4.3				5.8	3.7
	.5	.6	.7				1.3	1.2
	1.0	1.8	1.6			Debt/Worth	3.7	4.1
	11.1	2.9	4.6				22.4	15.8
	31.7	52.9	35.1			% Profit Before Taxes/Tangible	36.4	52.1
	(11) 27.0	(18) 21.5	(15) 21.4			Net Worth	(39) 7.7	(36) 20.6
	7.9	6.7	18.1				.9	4.5
	17.2	18.2	13.1			% Profit Before Taxes/Total	8.4	11.5
	9.7	11.3	6.9			Assets	2.5	2.9
	.6	2.7	3.2				-.2	-.6
	21.3	13.4	9.4				25.9	23.2
	11.3	8.9	6.6			Sales/Net Fixed Assets	9.9	12.3
	4.1	5.1	1.6				3.2	6.0
	2.7	2.9	2.9				3.4	3.1
	2.4	2.1	1.7			Sales/Total Assets	1.9	2.2
	1.1	1.6	1.1				1.4	1.7
	1.2	1.0	2.2				.7	.6
	(10) 1.9	(19) 1.6	(16) 2.6			% Depr., Dep., Amort./Sales	(43) 1.7	(37) 1.7
	3.4	3.2	7.1				3.3	3.0
						% Officers', Directors'	3.4	3.4
						Owners' Comp/Sales	(11) 5.3	(12) 4.6
							10.2	6.6
648M	39797M	222737M	726076M	518105M	385525M	Net Sales ($)	1507598M	2075756M
249M	17469M	102341M	378737M	269626M	226498M	Total Assets ($)	531778M	833880M

M = $ thousand   MM = $ million
See Pages 9 through 22 for Explanation of Ratios and Data

Comparative Historical Data / Current Data Sorted by Sales

	4/1/08-3/31/09 ALL	4/1/09-3/31/10 ALL	4/1/10-3/31/11 ALL	0-1MM	1-3MM	3-5MM	5-10MM	10-25MM	25MM & OVER
					18 (4/1-9/30/10)			39 (10/1/10-3/31/11)	
Type of Statement									
Unqualified	15	17	15	1	1	1		2	10
Reviewed	8	13	15			2	4	7	2
Compiled	3	4	7		2	2	1	2	
Tax Returns	6	3	4		1		3		
Other	19	10	16	3		2	2	3	6
NUMBER OF STATEMENTS	51	47	57	4	4	7	10	14	18
	%	%	%	%	%	%	%	%	%
ASSETS									
Cash & Equivalents	6.7	8.5	8.6				10.2	6.3	5.8
Trade Receivables (net)	23.4	25.4	21.5				20.9	18.2	28.3
Inventory	32.9	31.4	27.0				29.8	26.0	25.2
All Other Current	2.8	1.6	3.4				4.6	2.3	3.8
Total Current	65.8	66.9	60.4				65.5	52.8	63.1
Fixed Assets (net)	26.6	25.4	31.6				29.2	40.7	28.0
Intangibles (net)	3.0	2.8	2.7				.6	1.9	3.0
All Other Non-Current	4.5	5.0	5.3				4.8	4.6	5.9
Total	100.0	100.0	100.0				100.0	100.0	100.0
LIABILITIES									
Notes Payable-Short Term	20.2	16.0	11.2				16.9	14.2	8.0
Cur. Mat.-L.T.D.	5.1	3.5	4.2				1.7	3.9	3.4
Trade Payables	20.7	18.5	12.7				11.1	11.7	17.1
Income Taxes Payable	.6	.5	.6				.0	1.1	.8
All Other Current	6.2	7.9	7.6				7.0	4.6	8.7
Total Current	52.7	46.4	36.2				36.6	35.6	38.1
Long-Term Debt	18.6	13.5	19.9				14.7	27.3	15.4
Deferred Taxes	.4	.9	.6				.3	.8	.7
All Other Non-Current	5.8	2.5	3.8				4.8	1.9	5.1
Net Worth	22.5	36.7	39.4				43.6	34.4	40.7
Total Liabilties & Net Worth	100.0	100.0	100.0				100.0	100.0	100.0
INCOME DATA									
Net Sales	100.0	100.0	100.0				100.0	100.0	100.0
Gross Profit	29.2	30.8	33.8				32.8	36.4	24.8
Operating Expenses	23.2	23.9	25.9				27.0	29.1	19.2
Operating Profit	6.0	6.9	7.9				5.9	7.2	5.6
All Other Expenses (net)	1.9	1.6	1.1				.7	1.6	.6
Profit Before Taxes	4.1	5.3	6.8				5.2	5.6	5.0
RATIOS									
Current	2.2	2.4	2.5				3.4	2.4	2.2
	1.3	1.7	1.7				1.6	1.9	1.6
	1.1	1.2	1.2				1.2	1.1	1.3
Quick	.9	1.3	1.5				1.5	1.3	1.5
	.7	.7	.8				.7	.9	.8
	.3	.5	.5				.5	.5	.6
Sales/Receivables	26 14.0	18 20.0	19 19.0				22 16.8	16 22.9	24 15.4
	38 9.5	30 12.3	31 11.7				27 13.6	32 11.5	43 8.4
	48 7.6	62 5.9	58 6.3				58 6.3	58 6.3	69 5.3
Cost of Sales/Inventory	44 8.4	44 8.3	42 8.8				49 7.5	34 10.6	40 9.2
	77 4.8	84 4.3	61 6.0				74 4.9	55 6.6	52 7.0
	105 3.5	123 3.0	102 3.6				93 3.9	126 2.9	71 5.1
Cost of Sales/Payables	19 19.3	21 17.3	20 18.2				15 24.5	27 13.5	21 17.1
	35 10.5	36 10.1	29 12.6				25 14.4	32 11.5	34 10.8
	52 7.1	71 5.2	46 7.9				42 8.7	42 8.7	66 5.5
Sales/Working Capital	7.8	6.0	5.4				5.3	5.1	5.5
	15.0	8.8	9.5				9.0	9.2	10.3
	59.0	22.4	17.5				17.3	NM	19.4
EBIT/Interest	8.0	10.7	15.4					35.8	15.3
	(46) 3.9	(44) 4.3	(51) 4.1					(13) 5.8	(17) 3.7
	1.5	1.7	1.9					2.0	2.6
Net Profit + Depr., Dep., Amort./Cur. Mat. L/T/D	24.6	5.6	49.1						
	(11) 11.0	(14) 2.1	(14) 3.0						
	2.1	1.2	1.6						
Fixed/Worth	.5	.4	.4				.4	.5	.5
	.8	.6	.8				.7	1.1	.7
	4.8	1.2	1.6				1.3	4.2	1.0
Debt/Worth	1.3	.6	.6				.5	.6	1.0
	2.7	1.4	1.4				1.9	2.0	1.5
	34.3	3.8	3.2				2.6	7.7	2.8
% Profit Before Taxes/Tangible Net Worth	48.7	37.2	40.7					33.6	40.7
	(41) 28.0	(40) 20.3	(51) 22.3					(12) 21.8	(17) 21.3
	9.4	8.5	13.0					9.0	15.5
% Profit Before Taxes/Total Assets	16.2	15.6	15.6				19.3	14.4	15.1
	6.9	6.7	8.0				10.6	7.4	7.0
	2.9	2.5	2.7				2.0	2.2	3.4
Sales/Net Fixed Assets	17.4	17.3	12.5				11.9	13.4	11.8
	10.6	9.5	8.2				9.2	4.4	9.4
	6.5	5.9	4.3				5.5	1.4	6.5
Sales/Total Assets	3.1	2.8	2.7				2.7	2.9	3.2
	2.1	2.1	2.0				2.4	1.6	2.2
	1.7	1.6	1.4				1.7	1.1	1.7
% Depr., Dep., Amort./Sales	.9	.9	1.2				1.2	1.0	1.2
	(42) 1.8	(39) 1.4	(50) 2.2				2.2	2.6	(16) 2.1
	2.9	2.7	3.4				3.4	7.2	2.3
% Officers', Directors' Owners' Comp/Sales	1.4	3.2	1.9						
	(14) 3.8	(15) 4.5	(17) 4.6						
	6.1	6.8	9.6						
Net Sales ($)	2268082M	2604101M	1892888M	2529M	7356M	26576M	73652M	233630M	1549145M
Total Assets ($)	990805M	1109116M	994920M	4674M	5083M	13754M	33751M	171318M	766340M

M = $ thousand   MM = $ million
See Pages 9 through 22 for Explanation of Ratios and Data

Current Data Sorted by Assets / Comparative Historical Data

0-500M	500M-2MM	2-10MM	10-50MM	50-100MM	100-250MM		4/1/06-3/31/07 ALL	4/1/07-3/31/08 ALL
						Type of Statement		
	1	2	6	3		Unqualified	6	5
	1	3	3			Reviewed	4	3
	1	3				Compiled	1	6
1	1	1	1			Tax Returns	2	4
1	3	3	3			Other	14	12
	7 (4/1-9/30/10)		30 (10/1/10-3/31/11)					
2	7	12	13	3		**NUMBER OF STATEMENTS**	27	30
%	%	%	%	%	%	**ASSETS**	%	%
		5.2	8.7		DATA NOT AVAILABLE	Cash & Equivalents	6.6	7.7
		25.1	25.4			Trade Receivables (net)	21.1	24.0
		28.1	28.2			Inventory	25.0	26.8
		1.0	3.6			All Other Current	2.5	1.8
		59.4	65.9			Total Current	55.2	60.3
		36.0	29.2			Fixed Assets (net)	37.8	33.5
		2.7	.1			Intangibles (net)	.7	1.3
		2.0	4.7			All Other Non-Current	6.3	4.9
		100.0	100.0			Total	100.0	100.0
						LIABILITIES		
		12.4	14.1			Notes Payable-Short Term	9.4	15.6
		3.7	2.4			Cur. Mat.-L.T.D.	5.3	3.1
		12.6	15.8			Trade Payables	20.7	16.9
		.0	.0			Income Taxes Payable	.2	.3
		11.3	13.4			All Other Current	12.0	10.7
		40.0	45.7			Total Current	47.6	46.7
		17.5	19.4			Long-Term Debt	21.1	16.4
		2.1	.3			Deferred Taxes	.9	.6
		6.0	3.6			All Other Non-Current	1.6	4.1
		34.4	31.0			Net Worth	28.8	32.2
		100.0	100.0			Total Liabilties & Net Worth	100.0	100.0
						INCOME DATA		
		100.0	100.0			Net Sales	100.0	100.0
		34.7	20.3			Gross Profit	28.2	27.5
		28.3	14.6			Operating Expenses	25.0	22.4
		6.4	5.7			Operating Profit	3.1	5.0
		-.3	.0			All Other Expenses (net)	1.7	.6
		6.7	5.7			Profit Before Taxes	1.4	4.5
						RATIOS		
		4.2	1.8				1.6	1.7
		1.4	1.5			Current	1.3	1.2
		.9	1.2				1.0	.9
		3.0	1.1				.8	1.1
		.5	.8			Quick	.6	.6
		.4	.5				.3	.4
		33 10.9	**25** 14.7				**18** 20.6	**19** 19.3
		45 8.1	**34** 10.7			Sales/Receivables	**32** 11.3	**32** 11.3
		68 5.3	**44** 8.3				**57** 6.4	**58** 6.3
		42 8.7	**32** 11.6				**36** 10.0	**40** 9.2
		76 4.8	**50** 7.3			Cost of Sales/Inventory	**72** 5.1	**60** 6.1
		135 2.7	**86** 4.3				**111** 3.3	**92** 4.0
		19 18.8	**23** 16.1				**24** 15.2	**19** 18.9
		33 11.1	**26** 13.9			Cost of Sales/Payables	**38** 9.6	**35** 10.6
		44 8.3	**37** 9.9				**62** 5.9	**52** 7.1
		4.4	7.3				11.6	8.3
		12.0	12.0			Sales/Working Capital	16.2	23.4
		-17.2	24.0				-265.9	-44.9
		14.5	21.8				3.8	8.1
		5.8	(12) 5.1			EBIT/Interest	(26) 1.9	3.4
		2.5	2.7				1.3	1.8
						Net Profit + Depr., Dep., Amort./Cur. Mat. L/T/D		
		.6	.5				.6	.6
		1.0	.9			Fixed/Worth	1.0	.9
		2.0	3.2				2.3	2.6
		.9	1.3				1.3	1.2
		2.4	2.6			Debt/Worth	2.6	3.4
		4.4	6.8				11.5	7.2
		45.9	107.6				39.3	67.1
		(11) 30.1	41.1			% Profit Before Taxes/Tangible Net Worth	(24) 17.3	(27) 28.3
		9.5	12.9				3.0	20.4
		17.6	21.3				10.0	19.7
		9.1	7.9			% Profit Before Taxes/Total Assets	3.6	9.1
		3.0	5.2				.9	2.5
		13.6	18.8				12.7	14.6
		6.2	12.0			Sales/Net Fixed Assets	4.9	6.9
		2.6	6.1				2.5	4.2
		2.7	3.9				3.2	2.9
		1.9	2.2			Sales/Total Assets	1.7	1.8
		1.2	1.7				1.2	1.6
		1.8	.7				1.5	1.1
		(11) 2.4	1.5			% Depr., Dep., Amort./Sales	(25) 2.6	(29) 2.0
		3.8	2.1				6.3	2.9
						% Officers', Directors' Owners' Comp/Sales		
1508M	**54384M**	**117338M**	**1033480M**	**465411M**		Net Sales ($)	**1786856M**	**1207091M**
406M	**10180M**	**61085M**	**380148M**	**263487M**		Total Assets ($)	**681148M**	**501770M**

M = $ thousand MM = $ million

See Pages 9 through 22 for Explanation of Ratios and Data

Comparative Historical Data | Current Data Sorted by Sales

			Type of Statement						
7	13	12	Unqualified				1	1	10
2	2	7	Reviewed				3	2	2
6	6	4	Compiled			1	2		
2	8	4	Tax Returns				1	1	1
11	7	10	Other	2	2		2		3
4/1/08-3/31/09 ALL	4/1/09-3/31/10 ALL	4/1/10-3/31/11 ALL			7 (4/1-9/30/10)			30 (10/1/10-3/31/11)	
				0-1MM	1-3MM	3-5MM	5-10MM	10-25MM	25MM & OVER
28	36	37	NUMBER OF STATEMENTS	2	4	1	9	5	16
%	%	%	ASSETS	%	%	%	%	%	%
6.3	8.4	9.5	Cash & Equivalents						11.7
23.3	21.7	24.9	Trade Receivables (net)						29.1
28.8	24.1	26.0	Inventory						26.3
2.4	3.2	2.4	All Other Current						3.8
60.9	57.3	62.7	Total Current						71.0
31.8	34.5	31.1	Fixed Assets (net)						20.9
.9	3.8	1.4	Intangibles (net)						1.0
6.4	4.4	4.8	All Other Non-Current						7.2
100.0	100.0	100.0	Total						100.0
			LIABILITIES						
17.8	13.0	12.0	Notes Payable-Short Term						12.6
3.2	5.2	3.0	Cur. Mat.-L.T.D.						2.2
20.1	12.9	16.0	Trade Payables						18.7
.2	.2	.1	Income Taxes Payable						.1
10.0	11.6	11.1	All Other Current						15.2
51.2	42.9	42.2	Total Current						48.9
21.8	19.4	20.9	Long-Term Debt						12.5
.7	.8	.9	Deferred Taxes						.1
4.1	5.6	5.5	All Other Non-Current						5.2
22.2	31.3	30.5	Net Worth						33.4
100.0	100.0	100.0	Total Liabilities & Net Worth						100.0
			INCOME DATA						
100.0	100.0	100.0	Net Sales						100.0
27.9	30.8	29.0	Gross Profit						21.4
21.9	27.3	22.0	Operating Expenses						14.9
6.0	3.6	7.0	Operating Profit						6.4
1.5	.1	.0	All Other Expenses (net)						.0
4.5	3.5	7.0	Profit Before Taxes						6.5
			RATIOS						
1.4	2.1	2.0							2.0
1.2	1.3	1.5	Current						1.4
1.0	1.0	1.1							1.2
.8	1.1	1.3							1.3
.6	.7	.8	Quick						.8
.3	.4	.5							.5
20 / 18.6	17 / 21.4	27 / 13.8						23 / 15.7
33 / 11.1	30 / 12.0	37 / 9.8	Sales/Receivables					40 / 9.0
59 / 6.2	49 / 7.5	47 / 7.7						45 / 8.2
37 / 9.9	21 / 17.6	31 / 11.7						27 / 13.4
76 / 4.8	55 / 6.6	61 / 6.0	Cost of Sales/Inventory					55 / 6.7
97 / 3.8	92 / 4.0	109 / 3.3						97 / 3.8
24 / 15.0	14 / 25.7	18 / 20.1						18 / 20.1
40 / 9.2	22 / 16.3	27 / 13.3	Cost of Sales/Payables					25 / 14.5
60 / 6.1	49 / 7.5	42 / 8.7						39 / 9.4
14.5	7.6	6.8							6.7
23.7	18.2	12.2	Sales/Working Capital						12.2
-194.8	-241.8	76.6							30.3
9.1	9.5	16.4							24.5
(27) 5.6	(35) 3.7	(35) 6.0	EBIT/Interest					(14) 9.3
1.4	1.0	2.4							2.9
		15.5							
		(10) 4.5	Net Profit + Depr., Dep., Amort./Cur. Mat. L/T/D						
		1.4							
.4	.6	.5							.3
1.2	1.3	.9	Fixed/Worth						.7
2.8	3.7	2.0							1.4
1.6	1.2	.9							.7
4.0	3.9	2.7	Debt/Worth						2.6
7.1	12.8	5.4							7.7
64.7	61.1	55.3	% Profit Before Taxes/Tangible Net Worth					58.4
(25) 48.4	(33) 29.9	(34) 33.5						36.5
16.1	3.1	8.7							9.3
16.0	14.8	18.0	% Profit Before Taxes/Total Assets					22.8
7.4	8.4	7.7							9.1
1.0	.5	3.5							5.0
15.1	18.1	15.3	Sales/Net Fixed Assets						20.5
8.3	6.7	11.0							13.8
3.4	3.3	4.8							7.0
2.9	3.3	2.9	Sales/Total Assets						4.4
1.7	2.0	2.1							2.2
1.5	1.5	1.5							1.7
.9	.8	.9	% Depr., Dep., Amort./Sales						.9
(25) 2.0	(34) 2.1	(34) 1.9						(15) 1.5
5.7	3.9	3.3							2.0
		1.6	% Officers', Directors' Owners' Comp/Sales						
		(13) 3.9							
		5.1							
2959133M	2192171M	1672121M	Net Sales ($)	909M	7963M	4203M	65633M	82687M	1510726M
1109573M	1052433M	715306M	Total Assets ($)	1306M	5304M	1800M	39089M	42251M	625556M

M = $ thousand   MM = $ million
See Pages 9 through 22 for Explanation of Ratios and Data

Current Data Sorted by Assets   Comparative Historical Data

						Type of Statement		
		3	5	5	2	Unqualified	21	13
		3	4		1	Reviewed	4	5
	3	1				Compiled	3	3
	1	3	1			Tax Returns	1	3
1	5	5	8	1	2	Other	14	9
	16 (4/1-9/30/10)		33 (10/1/10-3/31/11)				4/1/06-3/31/07 ALL	4/1/07-3/31/08 ALL
0-500M	500M-2MM	2-10MM	10-50MM	50-100MM	100-250MM	NUMBER OF STATEMENTS	43	33
1	4	15	18	6	5			
%	%	%	%	%	%	ASSETS	%	%
		9.0	14.3			Cash & Equivalents	9.6	9.7
		30.8	21.5			Trade Receivables (net)	24.5	23.9
		23.2	32.8			Inventory	27.1	35.6
		1.8	3.8			All Other Current	4.4	2.7
		64.9	72.3			Total Current	65.6	71.8
		16.5	16.2			Fixed Assets (net)	20.8	15.9
		13.1	7.0			Intangibles (net)	8.1	8.3
		5.6	4.4			All Other Non-Current	5.5	4.0
		100.0	100.0			Total	100.0	100.0
						LIABILITIES		
		9.0	6.5			Notes Payable-Short Term	14.9	12.9
		4.5	2.3			Cur. Mat.-L.T.D.	1.6	4.6
		16.4	12.9			Trade Payables	10.8	17.1
		.1	.6			Income Taxes Payable	.5	.8
		7.9	14.6			All Other Current	12.1	9.1
		38.1	37.0			Total Current	39.9	44.4
		23.1	7.1			Long-Term Debt	11.0	13.4
		.0	.9			Deferred Taxes	.7	.4
		7.1	10.8			All Other Non-Current	5.1	4.1
		31.8	44.3			Net Worth	43.3	37.7
		100.0	100.0			Total Liabilities & Net Worth	100.0	100.0
						INCOME DATA		
		100.0	100.0			Net Sales	100.0	100.0
		43.0	32.9			Gross Profit	36.7	32.3
		32.0	26.1			Operating Expenses	29.1	23.7
		11.0	6.8			Operating Profit	7.6	8.5
		1.0	.3			All Other Expenses (net)	1.4	1.7
		10.0	6.5			Profit Before Taxes	6.2	6.9
						RATIOS		
		3.0	3.3				2.7	2.3
		1.7	2.2			Current	1.5	1.8
		1.2	1.3				1.3	1.2
		1.6	1.9				1.4	1.3
		1.0	.9			Quick	.8	.7
		.6	.5				.5	.4
		25 14.4	27 13.4				36 10.3	28 12.9
		58 6.2	41 8.9			Sales/Receivables	51 7.1	44 8.2
		92 4.0	61 5.9				70 5.2	71 5.2
		59 6.2	70 5.2				56 6.5	74 5.0
		91 4.0	101 3.6			Cost of Sales/Inventory	86 4.2	115 3.2
		132 2.8	135 2.7				138 2.6	162 2.3
		22 16.6	22 16.4				17 21.6	23 15.9
		40 9.1	30 12.2			Cost of Sales/Payables	34 10.7	44 8.4
		92 4.0	56 6.6				58 6.2	56 6.5
		3.2	3.3				3.6	4.7
		5.2	4.8			Sales/Working Capital	6.3	7.0
		13.7	9.9				18.2	14.3
		11.7	171.8				13.2	19.4
		(14) 4.0	(16) 10.9			EBIT/Interest	(40) 4.6	(29) 6.3
		2.3	2.7				1.6	1.9
							16.6	
						Net Profit + Depr., Dep., Amort./Cur. Mat. L/T/D	(15) 6.0	
							2.0	
		.2	.1				.2	.1
		.6	.3			Fixed/Worth	.7	.4
		4.0	3.0				1.4	1.6
		.9	.3				.6	.8
		2.9	1.4			Debt/Worth	2.0	1.8
		16.4	11.8				4.0	10.6
		62.3	47.7				43.6	51.2
		(12) 42.9	(15) 27.4			% Profit Before Taxes/Tangible Net Worth	(42) 18.4	(29) 26.9
		12.8	23.1				7.7	13.8
		16.6	20.5				13.1	14.8
		8.5	12.8			% Profit Before Taxes/Total Assets	7.7	10.6
		5.6	6.2				2.0	3.1
		34.3	26.9				27.3	44.9
		8.8	18.0			Sales/Net Fixed Assets	9.7	12.9
		6.1	7.7				5.0	6.2
		2.1	2.1				2.3	2.4
		1.7	1.8			Sales/Total Assets	1.7	1.5
		1.0	1.5				1.1	1.3
		1.2	1.3				1.1	.8
		(12) 2.0	(17) 2.3			% Depr., Dep., Amort./Sales	(36) 2.2	(27) 1.8
		3.4	2.9				2.9	2.8
						% Officers', Directors' Owners' Comp/Sales		
5443M	20818M	139940M	702349M	552036M	1784455M	Net Sales ($)	1310681M	1646637M
496M	5675M	82614M	378867M	489432M	732289M	Total Assets ($)	841984M	1072428M

M = $ thousand   MM = $ million
See Pages 9 through 22 for Explanation of Ratios and Data

Comparative Historical Data | Current Data Sorted by Sales

Type of Statement	4/1/08-3/31/09 ALL	4/1/09-3/31/10 ALL	4/1/10-3/31/11 ALL	0-1MM	1-3MM	3-5MM	5-10MM	10-25MM	25MM & OVER
Unqualified	17	21	15				1	5	9
Reviewed	10	8	8				1	2	5
Compiled	4	5	4			1	3		
Tax Returns	5	1	5			1	1	3	
Other	13	13	17			1	5	2	9
					16 (4/1-9/30/10)		33 (10/1/10-3/31/11)		
NUMBER OF STATEMENTS	49	48	49		3		11	12	23
	%	%	%	%	%	%	%	%	%
ASSETS									
Cash & Equivalents	13.4	15.4	14.1				15.2	16.2	14.3
Trade Receivables (net)	22.1	21.2	24.8				37.4	17.4	22.2
Inventory	36.3	29.4	26.4				18.1	26.3	30.0
All Other Current	3.5	4.5	2.8				.6	4.2	3.2
Total Current	75.3	70.5	68.1				71.3	64.1	69.6
Fixed Assets (net)	18.2	19.9	17.0				7.4	19.0	20.6
Intangibles (net)	3.2	6.6	8.9				10.4	10.5	5.9
All Other Non-Current	3.3	3.0	6.0				10.8	6.4	4.0
Total	100.0	100.0	100.0				100.0	100.0	100.0
LIABILITIES									
Notes Payable-Short Term	17.6	8.4	6.6				4.6	6.7	5.3
Cur. Mat.-L.T.D.	3.9	2.4	2.8				2.8	5.0	1.6
Trade Payables	15.5	15.7	15.3				21.1	14.1	14.1
Income Taxes Payable	.3	.7	.4				.2	.9	.3
All Other Current	10.7	12.5	11.6				8.8	12.3	13.7
Total Current	48.1	39.7	36.6				37.4	38.9	34.9
Long-Term Debt	14.8	14.4	14.2				24.8	9.3	10.1
Deferred Taxes	.4	.4	.8				.0	.1	1.5
All Other Non-Current	3.0	9.1	6.4				8.3	5.0	6.6
Net Worth	33.7	36.4	41.9				29.5	46.7	46.9
Total Liabilities & Net Worth	100.0	100.0	100.0				100.0	100.0	100.0
INCOME DATA									
Net Sales	100.0	100.0	100.0				100.0	100.0	100.0
Gross Profit	30.9	35.0	34.8				43.0	36.3	27.3
Operating Expenses	26.2	27.6	26.2				32.3	26.6	20.9
Operating Profit	4.8	7.4	8.6				10.6	9.7	6.4
All Other Expenses (net)	1.4	.8	.6				.2	.7	.3
Profit Before Taxes	3.3	6.5	8.0				10.4	9.0	6.1
RATIOS									
Current	2.6	3.2	3.2				3.2	3.8	3.2
	1.4	1.8	2.2				2.4	1.7	2.5
	1.2	1.2	1.3				1.3	1.1	1.5
Quick	1.7	2.1	1.9				2.0	1.7	2.2
	(48) .6	1.0	1.2				1.6	.8	1.2
	.3	.4	.6				1.0	.4	.6
Sales/Receivables	21 17.1	21 17.6	26 14.2				18 20.2	17 21.7	29 12.8
	34 10.8	36 10.3	44 8.3				52 7.0	35 10.3	40 9.2
	49 7.5	46 7.9	61 6.0				92 4.0	55 6.7	59 6.2
Cost of Sales/Inventory	61 5.9	54 6.8	48 7.5				17 21.7	44 8.3	49 7.5
	99 3.7	80 4.6	91 4.0				83 4.4	86 4.2	91 4.0
	140 2.6	129 2.8	133 2.7				100 3.7	144 2.5	121 3.0
Cost of Sales/Payables	22 16.3	14 25.6	22 16.4				20 17.9	21 17.3	26 14.2
	34 10.8	42 8.7	34 10.7				39 9.2	26 14.3	31 11.9
	52 7.0	65 5.7	56 6.5				62 5.9	41 8.9	42 8.8
Sales/Working Capital	4.1	4.1	3.3				4.6	3.9	3.3
	10.8	7.5	5.2				5.2	9.1	4.4
	27.0	21.8	10.5				12.5	34.1	9.1
EBIT/Interest	17.1	19.8	60.8					129.5	79.2
	(45) 5.8	(42) 7.5	(45) 7.3					(11) 4.6	(22) 20.0
	1.6	3.3	2.8					1.9	3.0
Net Profit + Depr., Dep., Amort./Cur. Mat. L/T/D	13.4	14.0	31.6						
	(12) 6.0	(13) 8.4	(14) 5.2						
	1.9	3.0	3.0						
Fixed/Worth	.1	.2	.1				.0	.1	.1
	.4	.5	.3				.2	.7	.3
	1.5	2.3	2.0				-1.2	1.5	1.9
Debt/Worth	.9	.5	.5				.7	.3	.3
	2.4	2.0	1.8				2.2	1.8	1.9
	6.3	10.9	9.9				-99.2	15.1	2.9
% Profit Before Taxes/Tangible Net Worth	46.2	58.0	47.9					53.7	44.6
	(43) 26.1	(40) 35.3	(41) 26.1					(10) 22.6	(21) 25.4
	9.7	19.9	15.9					14.8	16.5
% Profit Before Taxes/Total Assets	14.9	27.5	18.0				46.3	19.7	18.7
	8.6	12.1	10.9				12.4	9.7	11.5
	2.2	5.2	5.4				5.6	4.1	5.3
Sales/Net Fixed Assets	34.6	34.0	29.8				UND	23.8	19.3
	13.7	12.5	13.2				39.6	12.8	9.3
	5.8	5.6	6.7				13.2	5.9	5.9
Sales/Total Assets	3.0	2.8	2.3				4.9	2.0	2.2
	1.9	1.8	1.7				2.1	1.6	1.6
	1.5	1.5	1.3				1.7	1.5	1.2
% Depr., Dep., Amort./Sales	.8	.9	1.2					.9	1.5
	(43) 1.5	(41) 1.7	(41) 2.2					(11) 1.8	(21) 2.2
	2.7	3.1	3.0					3.0	2.9
% Officers', Directors' Owners' Comp/Sales	1.2	1.0	1.0						
	(14) 3.7	(11) 1.9	(11) 1.9						
	6.4	7.2	5.9						
Net Sales ($)	2910263M	2677307M	3205041M			6237M	77109M	209112M	2912583M
Total Assets ($)	1376819M	1476161M	1689373M			6713M	40255M	122188M	1520217M

Note: For 0-1MM, 1-3MM and 3-5MM size ranges the statement detail reads "DATA NOT AVAILABLE."

M = $ thousand   MM = $ million
See Pages 9 through 22 for Explanation of Ratios and Data

Current Data Sorted by Assets   Comparative Historical Data

0-500M	500M-2MM	2-10MM	10-50MM	50-100MM	100-250MM		4/1/06-3/31/07 ALL	4/1/07-3/31/08 ALL
						Type of Statement		
			10	5	9	Unqualified	23	17
	1	7	7			Reviewed	4	4
	2	4	1			Compiled	7	6
						Tax Returns	3	6
1	1	13	15	13	10	Other	28	33
	19 (4/1-9/30/10)		80 (10/1/10-3/31/11)					
1	4	24	33	18	19	**NUMBER OF STATEMENTS**	65	66
%	%	%	%	%	%	**ASSETS**	%	%
		11.2	10.8	13.3	14.3	Cash & Equivalents	12.9	10.3
		23.1	17.6	13.7	13.7	Trade Receivables (net)	22.8	18.8
		32.5	26.0	22.8	16.1	Inventory	25.9	25.6
		2.9	3.0	2.8	3.4	All Other Current	3.0	3.7
		69.7	57.5	52.5	47.5	Total Current	64.6	58.4
		19.0	26.6	24.6	20.6	Fixed Assets (net)	25.0	27.2
		2.9	12.3	17.4	25.4	Intangibles (net)	6.9	8.4
		8.3	3.6	5.5	6.5	All Other Non-Current	3.5	6.0
		100.0	100.0	100.0	100.0	Total	100.0	100.0
						LIABILITIES		
		13.6	6.8	8.6	1.4	Notes Payable-Short Term	8.9	7.9
		1.8	4.4	3.1	3.2	Cur. Mat.-L.T.D.	5.4	2.4
		25.6	14.8	7.2	8.3	Trade Payables	14.7	13.6
		.6	.2	.7	.4	Income Taxes Payable	.8	.5
		7.5	9.8	14.2	9.4	All Other Current	10.5	12.1
		49.0	36.0	33.9	22.8	Total Current	40.3	36.4
		6.7	15.7	19.4	13.0	Long-Term Debt	11.8	14.5
		.3	.5	.9	3.4	Deferred Taxes	.9	.4
		5.2	6.4	12.9	7.4	All Other Non-Current	8.0	11.9
		38.7	41.3	32.9	53.5	Net Worth	39.1	36.8
		100.0	100.0	100.0	100.0	Total Liabilties & Net Worth	100.0	100.0
						INCOME DATA		
		100.0	100.0	100.0	100.0	Net Sales	100.0	100.0
		38.0	42.5	53.0	48.1	Gross Profit	45.0	45.6
		33.8	34.5	43.6	35.4	Operating Expenses	38.0	37.7
		4.2	8.0	9.5	12.7	Operating Profit	6.9	7.9
		.2	1.7	2.6	2.3	All Other Expenses (net)	1.6	1.5
		4.0	6.3	6.8	10.4	Profit Before Taxes	5.4	6.4
						RATIOS		
		3.9	2.5	2.4	4.0	Current	2.7	2.8
		2.1	1.8	1.5	2.1		1.6	1.8
		1.1	1.1	1.1	1.6		1.3	1.1
		1.3	1.3	1.1	2.0	Quick	1.3	1.5
		1.0	.7	.7	1.1		.8	.8
		.5	.5	.4	.9		.5	.5
		25 14.9	29 12.8	6 60.1	27 13.6	Sales/Receivables	28 13.1	20 18.4
		34 10.6	36 10.1	41 8.9	35 10.4		39 9.3	35 10.3
		48 7.6	50 7.3	58 6.3	46 7.9		58 6.3	49 7.5
		53 6.8	56 6.5	71 5.2	50 7.3	Cost of Sales/Inventory	59 6.2	68 5.4
		96 3.8	100 3.6	103 3.5	112 3.3		90 4.0	89 4.1
		125 2.9	147 2.5	140 2.6	157 2.3		143 2.5	142 2.6
		20 18.2	27 13.4	20 18.3	26 14.2	Cost of Sales/Payables	30 12.1	23 15.7
		39 9.4	50 7.3	40 9.0	36 10.1		42 8.7	40 9.0
		88 4.2	66 5.6	64 5.7	51 7.1		61 5.9	57 6.4
		3.9	4.8	5.0	3.0	Sales/Working Capital	4.6	4.6
		7.8	7.4	9.4	4.4		8.5	8.7
		64.7	23.2	NM	8.5		16.2	44.9
		78.8	22.1	33.5	74.9	EBIT/Interest	(59) 18.1	(57) 17.7
	(17)	9.1	(30) 6.8	(16) 3.7	(15) 7.1		2.8	5.0
		3.7	2.5	-.1	2.5		1.0	1.8
			7.3			Net Profit + Depr., Dep., Amort./Cur. Mat. L/T/D	(17) 5.9	(17) 17.1
		(13)	1.8				2.4	5.7
			1.3				1.4	2.1
		.1	.5	.4	.4	Fixed/Worth	.3	.4
		.4	.8	2.4	.6		.7	.8
		1.1	2.6	-2.5	-2.7		1.5	2.2
		.3	.7	1.2	.5	Debt/Worth	.7	.8
		1.0	1.7	4.4	1.2		1.6	1.8
		11.8	6.6	-6.6	-12.5		6.5	12.1
		54.2	47.6	99.3	59.8	% Profit Before Taxes/Tangible Net Worth	(58) 57.2	(53) 68.0
	(21)	29.8	(27) 33.1	(12) 31.3	(14) 29.0		25.2	26.2
		13.6	11.5	7.3	22.0		.3	15.0
		26.9	17.4	25.9	22.0	% Profit Before Taxes/Total Assets	19.2	20.5
		12.4	9.0	7.0	13.1		7.7	8.5
		2.9	4.1	-5.0	4.0		.1	3.6
		54.7	19.2	17.0	12.8	Sales/Net Fixed Assets	21.6	21.2
		19.6	8.6	6.5	7.1		12.3	9.1
		8.3	4.2	3.2	3.0		3.6	3.7
		3.0	2.3	2.5	1.6	Sales/Total Assets	2.7	2.7
		2.3	1.7	1.2	1.2		2.0	1.9
		1.9	1.3	.8	.9		1.1	1.3
		.8	1.7	1.4	1.4	% Depr., Dep., Amort./Sales	(58) 1.2	(55) 1.0
	(22)	1.6	(27) 2.3	(16) 2.7	(14) 2.6		2.0	2.0
		2.7	3.8	5.9	4.1		3.5	3.2
						% Officers', Directors' Owners' Comp/Sales	(15) 2.3	(17) 1.3
							3.4	4.0
							5.1	7.6
692M	8177M	354728M	1337779M	1869911M	4102887M	Net Sales ($)	3075447M	4156857M
277M	3944M	134193M	748272M	1189191M	2939086M	Total Assets ($)	1687579M	2284541M

M = $ thousand   MM = $ million
See Pages 9 through 22 for Explanation of Ratios and Data

Comparative Historical Data

Current Data Sorted by Sales

26	27	24	Type of Statement					2	22
11	11	15	Unqualified		1	2		7	5
4	5	7	Reviewed	2	1	2		1	1
3		10	Compiled						
35	33	53	Tax Returns	1	3	1		14	34
4/1/08-3/31/09 ALL	4/1/09-3/31/10 ALL	4/1/10-3/31/11 ALL	Other	19 (4/1-9/30/10)			80 (10/1/10-3/31/11)		
				0-1MM	1-3MM	3-5MM	5-10MM	10-25MM	25MM & OVER
79	86	99	NUMBER OF STATEMENTS	3	5	5		24	62
%	%	%	**ASSETS**	%	%	%	%	%	%
10.8	12.5	12.5	Cash & Equivalents					8.6	13.1
18.4	17.8	18.1	Trade Receivables (net)					18.5	16.6
27.7	25.7	24.8	Inventory					29.3	23.1
4.3	2.8	2.9	All Other Current					3.5	3.1
61.3	58.8	58.3	Total Current					59.9	56.0
23.4	23.7	23.1	Fixed Assets (net)					25.1	24.3
9.8	11.3	12.9	Intangibles (net)					10.5	14.6
5.6	6.2	5.6	All Other Non-Current					4.5	5.1
100.0	100.0	100.0	Total					100.0	100.0
			LIABILITIES						
8.6	6.4	8.8	Notes Payable-Short Term					12.2	6.6
5.0	2.6	3.2	Cur. Mat.-L.T.D.					4.3	3.0
13.6	14.6	14.6	Trade Payables					14.7	13.4
.4	.5	.5	Income Taxes Payable					.2	.5
11.9	10.9	9.6	All Other Current					8.0	11.0
39.4	35.0	36.8	Total Current					39.4	34.6
11.4	16.1	13.9	Long-Term Debt					14.2	14.4
.7	.8	1.1	Deferred Taxes					.3	1.5
4.0	10.3	7.4	All Other Non-Current					13.7	6.0
44.5	37.9	40.9	Net Worth					32.4	43.5
100.0	100.0	100.0	Total Liabilities & Net Worth					100.0	100.0
			INCOME DATA						
100.0	100.0	100.0	Net Sales					100.0	100.0
49.0	48.5	45.3	Gross Profit					47.7	43.7
43.6	39.4	37.0	Operating Expenses					40.4	34.4
5.4	9.0	8.3	Operating Profit					7.4	9.3
1.5	1.5	1.7	All Other Expenses (net)					2.4	1.2
3.9	7.5	6.6	Profit Before Taxes					5.0	8.1
			RATIOS						
3.2	2.6	2.9						4.4	2.8
1.7	1.7	1.8	Current					2.2	1.7
1.2	1.3	1.2						1.3	1.2
1.4	1.4	1.4						1.8	1.3
.8	.7	.9	Quick					.9	.8
.5	.4	.5						.5	.5
23 15.7	19 18.7	26 13.9						31 11.8	25 14.5
37 9.8	34 10.7	38 9.5	Sales/Receivables					34 10.6	38 9.7
48 7.6	48 7.5	50 7.3						50 7.3	47 7.7
72 5.1	59 6.2	63 5.8						69 5.3	60 6.1
98 3.7	102 3.6	104 3.5	Cost of Sales/Inventory					113 3.2	97 3.8
147 2.5	149 2.4	143 2.6						193 1.9	138 2.6
21 17.6	28 13.1	26 14.2						27 13.8	25 14.6
44 8.4	43 8.4	40 9.0	Cost of Sales/Payables					43 8.5	38 9.5
66 5.5	65 5.6	63 5.8						79 4.6	55 6.6
4.6	4.5	4.3						3.3	4.4
7.6	8.2	7.3	Sales/Working Capital					5.9	7.4
21.6	22.0	27.0						24.9	21.2
25.8	38.7	28.8						13.6	29.3
(70) 7.7	(76) 8.9	(83) 6.9	EBIT/Interest				(20)	5.4	(53) 7.0
2.1	2.6	2.0						-.6	2.2
17.9	18.2	7.4							6.6
(28) 6.1	(26) 4.8	(32) 2.4	Net Profit + Depr., Dep., Amort./Cur. Mat. L/T/D					(22)	2.1
2.3	1.5	1.2							.8
.3	.3	.4						.4	.5
.6	.8	.8	Fixed/Worth					1.0	.7
1.5	2.5	6.3						-2.1	2.6
.5	.7	.7						.4	.7
1.3	1.9	1.6	Debt/Worth					1.6	1.6
4.4	5.7	36.5						-13.8	14.3
46.0	90.8	56.2						44.9	57.8
(69) 22.2	(72) 42.9	(78) 29.8	% Profit Before Taxes/Tangible Net Worth				(17)	26.8	(50) 35.9
5.1	16.0	13.4						5.2	16.7
17.5	24.1	22.0						19.7	22.4
6.4	10.0	9.6	% Profit Before Taxes/Total Assets					9.9	10.2
1.3	2.9	2.9						-5.5	3.7
24.5	26.4	22.1						20.5	16.8
11.0	9.6	9.8	Sales/Net Fixed Assets					11.4	7.5
4.7	4.0	4.2						4.1	3.5
2.7	2.7	2.5						2.4	2.5
1.9	1.8	1.7	Sales/Total Assets					1.8	1.6
1.3	1.2	1.1						1.2	1.1
1.2	1.3	1.3						1.2	1.4
(67) 2.2	(71) 2.2	(81) 2.3	% Depr., Dep., Amort./Sales				(23)	2.3	(51) 2.3
3.0	3.7	3.7						3.1	4.3
1.3	1.4	1.1							
(15) 2.3	(19) 2.9	(15) 2.1	% Officers', Directors' Owners' Comp/Sales						
3.9	4.6	3.5							
5790794M	5303972M	7674174M	Net Sales ($)	1634M		19870M	35096M	406016M	7211558M
3128958M	3205736M	5014963M	Total Assets ($)	1591M		10248M	33654M	300366M	4669104M

(Right-hand columns 0-1MM through 5-10MM for ASSETS, LIABILITIES and most RATIOS: DATA NOT AVAILABLE)

M = $ thousand   MM = $ million
See Pages 9 through 22 for Explanation of Ratios and Data

Current Data Sorted by Assets   Comparative Historical Data

Type of Statement	0-500M	500M-2MM	2-10MM	10-50MM	50-100MM	100-250MM		4/1/06-3/31/07 ALL	4/1/07-3/31/08 ALL
Unqualified			5	23	6	16		51	43
Reviewed		2	10	10	2			15	22
Compiled		4	9	6		1		11	10
Tax Returns	3	1	8					7	7
Other	4	6	26	29	12	13		65	76
		31 (4/1-9/30/10)		165 (10/1/10-3/31/11)					
NUMBER OF STATEMENTS	7	13	58	68	20	30		149	158
ASSETS	%	%	%	%	%	%		%	%
Cash & Equivalents		11.0	13.0	16.8	17.4	14.7		11.3	13.1
Trade Receivables (net)		35.9	26.7	18.7	19.0	17.3		22.8	22.4
Inventory		26.1	20.1	21.4	15.1	14.9		20.4	21.7
All Other Current		2.3	3.6	3.2	3.8	4.0		3.2	2.8
Total Current		75.2	63.4	60.2	55.3	50.9		57.7	60.0
Fixed Assets (net)		16.7	25.3	26.7	23.6	24.9		24.0	24.1
Intangibles (net)		2.4	3.3	9.3	15.2	19.6		9.4	8.7
All Other Non-Current		5.6	8.0	3.8	6.0	4.7		9.0	7.2
Total		100.0	100.0	100.0	100.0	100.0		100.0	100.0
LIABILITIES									
Notes Payable-Short Term		12.1	7.5	3.9	2.2	3.7		8.5	8.0
Cur. Mat.-L.T.D.		4.3	3.2	2.9	2.7	2.0		2.5	3.0
Trade Payables		18.3	16.4	10.9	9.5	6.2		13.6	12.5
Income Taxes Payable		.3	.4	.4	.2	.3		.4	.4
All Other Current		6.8	9.8	9.1	11.1	12.7		12.0	11.4
Total Current		41.9	37.4	27.1	25.7	24.9		37.0	35.2
Long-Term Debt		6.7	11.7	10.1	15.3	15.0		17.0	18.4
Deferred Taxes		.0	.5	.6	.9	.9		.8	.8
All Other Non-Current		3.3	5.2	7.3	5.9	9.2		7.8	6.2
Net Worth		48.1	45.2	54.9	52.2	50.0		37.4	39.3
Total Liabilities & Net Worth		100.0	100.0	100.0	100.0	100.0		100.0	100.0
INCOME DATA									
Net Sales		100.0	100.0	100.0	100.0	100.0		100.0	100.0
Gross Profit		37.7	45.2	42.1	51.2	45.9		46.3	43.5
Operating Expenses		31.5	37.9	33.0	44.0	31.4		39.5	36.1
Operating Profit		6.2	7.3	9.0	7.2	14.6		6.8	7.4
All Other Expenses (net)		1.8	.1	1.0	1.4	2.2		1.2	1.0
Profit Before Taxes		4.4	7.1	8.0	5.9	12.4		5.6	6.5
RATIOS									
Current		2.7	3.7	4.0	3.7	3.0		2.8	3.0
		1.6	1.9	2.3	2.0	2.1		1.8	1.8
		1.2	1.1	1.4	1.5	1.4		1.2	1.2
Quick		2.1	2.0	2.4	2.3	1.9		1.7	1.7
		1.0	1.0	1.3	1.4	1.0		.9	1.0
		.6	.7	.7	.6	.8		.6	.6
Sales/Receivables		17 21.0	27 13.7	33 10.9	25 14.7	36 10.1		33 11.1	32 11.3
		33 11.2	39 9.5	44 8.4	54 6.7	46 7.9		47 7.7	45 8.2
		43 8.5	52 7.1	58 6.3	94 3.9	76 4.8		71 5.1	58 6.3
Cost of Sales/Inventory		8 46.1	15 23.6	49 7.5	70 5.2	75 4.9		55 6.7	44 8.2
		41 8.8	75 4.9	84 4.3	113 3.2	121 3.0		96 3.8	87 4.2
		90 4.0	120 3.1	127 2.9	194 1.9	145 2.5		133 2.7	124 3.0
Cost of Sales/Payables		9 42.7	18 19.9	22 16.6	44 8.3	16 22.9		25 14.9	23 15.9
		17 21.1	33 11.2	33 11.1	61 5.9	37 9.9		43 8.4	38 9.7
		34 10.9	59 6.2	54 6.7	109 3.3	49 7.4		82 4.5	62 5.9
Sales/Working Capital		6.5	4.5	3.2	1.8	2.6		3.7	3.6
		16.1	7.8	4.7	4.3	4.1		6.3	6.9
		27.0	38.2	11.3	9.2	9.3		29.9	22.1
EBIT/Interest		20.9	31.4	32.2	25.9	43.8		21.2	14.9
		(11) 12.8	(48) 14.1	(61) 12.1	(14) 2.5	(28) 10.2		(139) 5.5	(135) 4.2
		3.0	2.8	2.9	-3.4	2.3		1.5	1.2
Net Profit + Depr., Dep., Amort./Cur. Mat. L/T/D			11.7	14.7		39.5		12.4	13.3
			(12) 4.4	(31) 3.6		(15) 4.9		(45) 3.9	(46) 2.5
			1.9	1.8		2.2		1.7	1.0
Fixed/Worth		.1	.2	.2	.2	.4		.3	.3
		.3	.6	.6	.8	.7		.7	.7
		.6	1.6	1.0	2.4	NM		2.9	2.4
Debt/Worth		.7	.4	.4	.5	.5		.5	.6
		1.2	1.5	.8	1.3	1.4		1.5	1.5
		3.1	4.7	1.9	4.6	NM		12.8	5.2
% Profit Before Taxes/Tangible Net Worth		66.9	66.0	45.6	38.5	41.1		53.8	59.4
		28.1	(54) 31.1	(64) 24.8	(17) 13.1	(23) 29.3		(117) 24.7	(131) 17.0
		14.4	8.4	10.0	.6	14.4		8.7	1.8
% Profit Before Taxes/Total Assets		34.2	28.8	21.0	17.0	21.1		17.3	20.7
		12.2	13.1	11.6	2.9	7.9		7.8	7.7
		7.4	4.9	4.7	-3.1	4.1		1.3	-.4
Sales/Net Fixed Assets		251.1	37.8	23.2	36.9	10.2		19.7	26.7
		33.4	11.7	8.5	7.3	4.9		7.0	9.2
		12.1	4.3	2.6	2.4	2.0		3.6	3.5
Sales/Total Assets		6.2	3.2	2.1	1.5	1.5		2.2	2.6
		3.8	2.1	1.4	.9	.9		1.5	1.7
		3.0	1.5	1.0	.7	.7		.9	1.1
% Depr., Dep., Amort./Sales			.6	1.4	1.6	2.0		1.0	1.0
			(52) 1.6	(63) 2.6	(15) 2.4	(27) 3.4		(132) 2.3	(131) 2.2
			3.1	4.6	4.1	5.2		4.4	4.3
% Officers', Directors' Owners' Comp/Sales			2.5	.6				2.3	1.6
			(20) 3.4	(14) 2.2				(31) 4.0	(40) 4.0
			7.3	3.1				7.3	9.6
Net Sales ($)	6746M	85441M	749267M	2691956M	1695283M	5144229M		7545077M	8356015M
Total Assets ($)	1803M	18189M	326741M	1693478M	1381718M	4623342M		6625316M	5951400M

M = $ thousand   MM = $ million
See Pages 9 through 22 for Explanation of Ratios and Data

Comparative Historical Data | Current Data Sorted by Sales

4/1/08-3/31/09 ALL	4/1/09-3/31/10 ALL	4/1/10-3/31/11 ALL	Type of Statement	0-1MM	1-3MM	3-5MM	5-10MM	10-25MM	25MM & OVER
49	46	50	Unqualified			1	2	11	36
27	27	24	Reviewed		1	1	2	11	9
11	13	20	Compiled		1	3	5	4	7
18	17	12	Tax Returns	2	3	2	2	2	1
78	100	90	Other	3	6	10	24		47
				31 (4/1-9/30/10)		165 (10/1/10-3/31/11)			
NUMBER OF STATEMENTS									
183	203	196		5	5	13	21	52	100
%	%	%	**ASSETS**	%	%	%	%	%	%
13.2	14.0	15.4	Cash & Equivalents			24.5	11.5	12.8	15.9
21.6	22.0	21.6	Trade Receivables (net)			9.7	28.0	24.2	21.1
19.8	19.8	20.1	Inventory			19.1	18.8	23.8	18.2
3.2	3.2	3.6	All Other Current			4.6	3.1	2.7	3.8
57.8	59.0	60.8	Total Current			57.9	61.4	63.5	59.0
23.6	24.9	24.5	Fixed Assets (net)			26.6	23.6	27.3	23.3
11.4	11.0	8.9	Intangibles (net)			1.8	6.9	5.1	13.0
7.2	5.1	5.8	All Other Non-Current			13.7	8.0	4.0	4.7
100.0	100.0	100.0	Total			100.0	100.0	100.0	100.0
			LIABILITIES						
6.4	6.2	5.5	Notes Payable-Short Term			7.2	7.9	6.3	4.2
3.3	3.6	2.9	Cur. Mat.-L.T.D.			5.1	5.9	1.7	2.6
12.9	12.1	12.6	Trade Payables			12.9	16.0	15.7	10.4
.3	.3	.3	Income Taxes Payable			.6	.5	.2	.3
12.3	12.4	10.4	All Other Current			3.7	9.3	8.5	12.0
35.2	34.7	31.7	Total Current			29.5	39.7	32.4	29.4
16.4	15.5	11.8	Long-Term Debt			10.8	13.3	9.9	12.0
.9	.7	.6	Deferred Taxes			.0	.3	.9	.6
6.6	5.7	6.5	All Other Non-Current			5.2	5.4	5.5	7.6
40.9	43.4	49.5	Net Worth			54.5	41.2	51.3	50.4
100.0	100.0	100.0	Total Liabilities & Net Worth			100.0	100.0	100.0	100.0
			INCOME DATA						
100.0	100.0	100.0	Net Sales			100.0	100.0	100.0	100.0
45.6	42.1	44.7	Gross Profit			47.5	42.9	43.0	44.4
38.2	35.2	35.8	Operating Expenses			45.2	35.1	34.3	34.3
7.4	6.9	8.9	Operating Profit			2.3	7.8	8.7	10.1
1.4	1.7	.9	All Other Expenses (net)			.1	.9	.4	1.3
6.0	5.2	8.0	Profit Before Taxes			2.3	6.9	8.3	8.7
			RATIOS						
3.1	3.1	3.5	Current			9.2	2.4	4.6	3.2
1.8	1.8	2.0				1.8	1.3	2.2	2.1
1.3	1.2	1.3				.8	1.2	1.2	1.4
1.8	1.9	2.1	Quick			7.3	1.3	2.6	2.1
1.0	1.0	1.2				.7	.9	1.3	1.2
.6	.6	.7				.2	.7	.7	.8
31 11.8	30 12.2	30 12.1	Sales/Receivables			11 32.4	26 13.8	33 10.9	34 10.8
42 8.6	43 8.5	41 8.9				18 20.2	40 9.0	40 9.2	44 8.3
57 6.4	59 6.2	58 6.3				35 10.5	53 6.9	57 6.4	65 5.7
43 8.6	40 9.0	39 9.3	Cost of Sales/Inventory			16 22.9	13 27.4	38 9.5	49 7.4
86 4.2	74 4.9	87 4.2				102 3.6	57 6.4	99 3.7	96 3.8
135 2.7	119 3.1	131 2.8				140 2.6	102 3.6	126 2.9	136 2.7
21 17.6	20 18.6	20 17.9	Cost of Sales/Payables			17 21.2	16 22.6	20 18.3	27 13.5
34 10.7	36 10.1	36 10.3				24 15.2	34 10.6	33 11.2	39 9.5
68 5.4	57 6.4	56 6.6				48 7.5	71 5.2	49 7.4	58 6.3
3.6	3.5	3.4	Sales/Working Capital			2.5	7.6	3.9	3.1
7.4	7.2	6.0				5.3	16.1	6.0	4.5
24.9	22.7	18.8				-107.3	27.0	20.6	10.9
14.1	17.1	32.1	EBIT/Interest			23.4	22.0	32.6	40.6
(155) 4.7	(168) 4.2	(166) 10.2				(11) 3.4	(18) 4.9	(45) 7.5	(85) 12.0
.8	1.6	2.6				-2.2	2.0	2.8	3.1
10.1	6.1	13.4	Net Profit + Depr., Dep., Amort./Cur. Mat. L/T/D					19.8	12.9
(59) 3.3	(57) 1.9	(66) 3.3						(19) 9.8	(40) 2.9
.9	.7	1.6						2.7	1.6
.3	.2	.2	Fixed/Worth			.2	.1	.2	.2
.7	.7	.6				.3	.8	.7	.6
1.8	2.4	1.5				1.1	1.8	1.3	1.6
.5	.6	.4	Debt/Worth			.2	.8	.3	.5
1.7	1.6	1.1				.7	2.0	1.0	1.1
7.1	6.8	3.2				3.0	6.3	3.9	3.0
57.5	52.7	52.5	% Profit Before Taxes/Tangible Net Worth			26.6	110.9	56.2	43.9
(151) 18.3	(173) 23.1	(176) 28.2				(12) 15.7	(19) 20.5	(50) 32.1	(86) 28.6
.9	6.2	9.1				-6.1	4.4	8.4	10.7
21.2	16.3	22.9	% Profit Before Taxes/Total Assets			20.7	21.1	26.7	20.7
6.8	7.6	10.1				7.6	9.5	11.8	9.9
-.5	2.1	3.8				-9.0	1.9	3.6	4.2
27.9	30.0	28.4	Sales/Net Fixed Assets			35.2	86.1	27.4	26.4
8.0	8.3	9.5				5.8	11.9	8.3	8.8
3.5	3.2	3.0				2.5	5.4	3.1	2.7
2.5	2.6	2.5	Sales/Total Assets			2.6	3.6	2.7	2.0
1.5	1.5	1.5				1.5	2.2	1.8	1.3
1.1	.9	1.0				.9	1.3	1.2	.9
1.4	1.1	1.2	% Depr., Dep., Amort./Sales			.7	.4	1.1	1.4
(157) 2.6	(161) 2.6	(170) 2.3				(10) 4.0	(18) 1.5	(47) 2.3	(87) 2.4
4.3	4.7	4.3				9.6	3.8	4.2	4.1
1.9	1.6	1.9	% Officers', Directors' Owners' Comp/Sales					1.1	.8
(45) 4.0	(36) 3.0	(43) 2.9						(13) 2.5	(16) 2.5
8.8	5.6	5.8						5.7	3.5
10435939M	11077764M	10372922M	Net Sales ($)	2299M	11462M	53753M	157146M	883268M	9264994M
7667393M	9093741M	8045271M	Total Assets ($)	1178M	6046M	47620M	88893M	616646M	7284888M

M = $ thousand   MM = $ million
See Pages 9 through 22 for Explanation of Ratios and Data

Current Data Sorted by Assets   Comparative Historical Data

0-500M	500M-2MM	2-10MM	10-50MM	50-100MM	100-250MM	Type of Statement	4/1/06-3/31/07 ALL	4/1/07-3/31/08 ALL
		1	8	3	2	Unqualified	23	22
	4	14	8	2		Reviewed	33	27
	4	13	2			Compiled	17	21
2	3	4				Tax Returns	11	12
2	11	21	13	4	4	Other	34	45
		17 (4/1-9/30/10)	108 (10/1/10-3/31/11)					
4	22	53	31	9	6	**NUMBER OF STATEMENTS**	118	127
%	%	%	%	%	%	**ASSETS**	%	%
	6.1	7.2	8.5			Cash & Equivalents	8.5	8.6
	25.2	24.1	23.6			Trade Receivables (net)	26.7	27.5
	30.7	32.1	27.7			Inventory	26.1	25.7
	1.4	1.9	3.2			All Other Current	2.6	2.1
	63.4	65.4	63.0			Total Current	63.8	63.9
	22.3	20.6	22.2			Fixed Assets (net)	21.5	19.5
	6.5	4.6	8.7			Intangibles (net)	7.9	7.5
	7.8	9.5	6.1			All Other Non-Current	6.8	9.1
	100.0	100.0	100.0			Total	100.0	100.0
						LIABILITIES		
	18.4	10.3	8.2			Notes Payable-Short Term	9.4	11.3
	2.5	4.9	2.7			Cur. Mat.-L.T.D.	3.7	3.3
	20.1	14.3	10.9			Trade Payables	14.4	17.3
	.1	.1	.2			Income Taxes Payable	.3	.3
	6.7	7.2	10.9			All Other Current	10.0	7.6
	47.8	36.8	33.0			Total Current	37.8	39.7
	17.0	13.0	12.5			Long-Term Debt	18.4	15.2
	.0	.5	.5			Deferred Taxes	.4	.4
	15.3	4.7	3.8			All Other Non-Current	6.8	6.4
	20.0	45.0	50.3			Net Worth	36.7	38.2
	100.0	100.0	100.0			Total Liabilities & Net Worth	100.0	100.0
						INCOME DATA		
	100.0	100.0	100.0			Net Sales	100.0	100.0
	36.1	34.0	33.9			Gross Profit	34.0	35.4
	31.6	28.5	26.2			Operating Expenses	28.3	29.7
	4.5	5.5	7.7			Operating Profit	5.6	5.7
	.8	.9	1.1			All Other Expenses (net)	1.4	1.1
	3.6	4.7	6.6			Profit Before Taxes	4.2	4.6
						RATIOS		
	3.5	3.7	3.0				3.2	3.4
	1.5	1.9	2.2			Current	1.9	2.0
	.9	1.2	1.4				1.2	1.2
	2.2	2.0	1.5				1.8	1.7
	.7	.8	1.2			Quick	1.0	1.0
	.3	.5	.7				.7	.6
25 14.7		31 11.8	33 10.9				32 11.5	30 12.1
36 10.2		39 9.3	45 8.1			Sales/Receivables	41 8.8	43 8.5
45 8.1		50 7.3	53 6.9				53 6.9	55 6.7
37 10.0		50 7.3	58 6.3				40 9.0	39 9.3
61 6.0		80 4.6	72 5.1			Cost of Sales/Inventory	67 5.4	65 5.6
111 3.3		107 3.4	104 3.5				94 3.9	90 4.1
19 19.6		21 17.2	16 22.8				20 18.4	20 18.3
28 13.0		38 9.7	30 12.0			Cost of Sales/Payables	31 11.7	36 10.2
60 6.0		47 7.7	47 7.8				45 8.1	53 6.8
	6.4	4.5	4.6				4.7	4.8
	10.1	6.5	6.1			Sales/Working Capital	8.8	8.3
	-116.0	20.1	11.7				23.2	30.7
	36.6	11.4	26.6				14.5	13.4
	(20) 4.0	(45) 4.6	(28) 9.2			EBIT/Interest	(111) 5.5	(117) 4.4
	.9	1.8	2.6				1.8	1.7
		8.5	4.6				16.8	6.0
		(11) 2.9	(15) 2.7			Net Profit + Depr., Dep., Amort./Cur. Mat. L/T/D	(34) 4.2	(35) 2.9
		1.1	1.0				1.2	1.6
	.1	.2	.3				.3	.2
	.5	.5	.4			Fixed/Worth	.6	.5
	-29.7	1.4	1.4				2.9	1.6
	.5	.5	.4				.6	.5
	2.0	1.3	1.2			Debt/Worth	1.7	1.8
	-32.9	4.1	3.1				5.8	6.7
	50.4	41.4	61.6				52.3	48.5
	(16) 23.4	(47) 16.7	(30) 28.6			% Profit Before Taxes/Tangible Net Worth	(101) 22.0	(104) 20.6
	10.3	6.6	10.0				11.1	8.4
	17.6	12.8	20.7				16.6	16.7
	6.3	7.8	9.6			% Profit Before Taxes/Total Assets	7.9	7.9
	-.1	2.7	5.2				3.0	1.8
	76.3	29.0	17.8				23.9	31.8
	31.8	13.9	9.7			Sales/Net Fixed Assets	11.5	12.2
	9.0	6.4	7.8				6.6	7.3
	3.5	2.9	2.3				3.0	3.0
	2.4	2.2	2.1			Sales/Total Assets	2.3	2.3
	1.8	1.5	1.6				1.6	1.5
	.2	.7	1.0				1.0	.8
	(17) .6	(47) 1.3	1.4			% Depr., Dep., Amort./Sales	(101) 1.7	(116) 1.5
	2.3	2.3	2.0				2.6	2.3
	2.6	2.1					1.1	1.7
	(14) 3.8	(17) 3.4				% Officers', Directors' Owners' Comp/Sales	(32) 3.1	(39) 4.1
	7.3	9.1					6.4	7.2
6424M	72533M	510545M	1348072M	912781M	918051M	Net Sales ($)	3708307M	3603763M
1497M	27000M	242118M	704547M	665682M	888929M	Total Assets ($)	1858871M	2159134M

M = $ thousand   MM = $ million
See Pages 9 through 22 for Explanation of Ratios and Data

Comparative Historical Data | Current Data Sorted by Sales

4/1/08-3/31/09 ALL	4/1/09-3/31/10 ALL	4/1/10-3/31/11 ALL	Type of Statement	0-1MM	1-3MM	3-5MM	5-10MM	10-25MM	25MM & OVER
17	15	14	Unqualified		1	4	4	4	10
26	33	28	Reviewed	1	1	4	4	12	6
18	16	19	Compiled		2	1	11	3	2
12	18	9	Tax Returns		3	1	4	1	
74	58	55	Other	1	9	6	10	9	20
				17 (4/1-9/30/10)			108 (10/1/10-3/31/11)		
147	140	125	**NUMBER OF STATEMENTS**	2	15	12	29	29	38
%	%	%	**ASSETS**	%	%	%	%	%	%
7.0	9.4	7.8	Cash & Equivalents		7.7	12.2	5.5	7.1	8.2
24.8	24.4	23.4	Trade Receivables (net)		19.5	24.5	25.2	26.5	22.0
26.7	25.0	28.2	Inventory		30.3	27.7	30.4	30.7	24.4
2.6	3.0	2.6	All Other Current		.9	.9	2.3	1.4	4.8
61.1	61.8	62.1	Total Current		58.4	65.4	63.2	65.6	59.4
22.2	24.2	21.8	Fixed Assets (net)		31.1	21.1	22.5	18.8	21.1
8.2	7.1	8.3	Intangibles (net)		7.7	5.2	4.1	7.6	13.5
8.6	6.9	7.9	All Other Non-Current		2.7	8.3	10.1	8.0	6.0
100.0	100.0	100.0	Total		100.0	100.0	100.0	100.0	100.0
			LIABILITIES						
12.1	9.5	10.2	Notes Payable-Short Term		22.3	10.0	6.9	13.4	6.1
3.3	4.5	3.5	Cur. Mat.-L.T.D.		7.0	1.6	4.2	4.0	2.1
15.4	13.9	14.1	Trade Payables		18.0	21.4	13.5	16.2	9.9
.1	.2	.1	Income Taxes Payable		.2	.0	.1	.1	.2
8.0	7.9	8.3	All Other Current		6.0	11.0	6.6	8.0	10.4
38.9	35.9	36.3	Total Current		53.5	44.0	31.3	41.7	28.6
14.3	13.0	15.3	Long-Term Debt		17.5	11.9	17.6	13.0	16.4
.4	.5	.6	Deferred Taxes		.0	.0	.4	.7	.9
10.9	9.5	7.3	All Other Non-Current		9.3	29.2	4.4	4.0	4.8
35.5	41.0	40.5	Net Worth		19.8	14.9	46.2	40.6	49.2
100.0	100.0	100.0	Total Liabilities & Net Worth		100.0	100.0	100.0	100.0	100.0
			INCOME DATA						
100.0	100.0	100.0	Net Sales		100.0	100.0	100.0	100.0	100.0
32.7	35.6	35.1	Gross Profit		45.1	36.0	35.0	30.8	34.4
27.3	31.7	28.8	Operating Expenses		41.3	30.7	29.0	25.1	26.7
5.3	3.9	6.3	Operating Profit		3.8	5.2	6.0	5.7	7.7
1.4	1.0	1.2	All Other Expenses (net)		1.8	.8	.7	.8	1.7
3.9	3.0	5.1	Profit Before Taxes		1.9	4.4	5.4	4.9	6.1
			RATIOS						
2.9	3.3	3.5			2.5	3.8	3.9	2.6	3.6
1.8	1.8	2.1	Current		1.2	1.6	2.6	1.6	2.4
1.1	1.2	1.2			.9	.8	1.5	1.1	1.5
1.6	1.9	2.0			1.0	1.9	2.3	1.5	1.8
.9	.9	.9	Quick		.6	.8	1.3	.8	1.2
.5	.6	.6			.2	.4	.5	.5	.8
28 13.1	31 12.0	31 11.8		30 12.0	27 13.7	29 12.4	33 11.1	34 10.8	
40 9.1	41 8.9	42 8.7	Sales/Receivables	39 9.5	33 11.1	39 9.3	42 8.7	46 8.0	
52 7.1	51 7.1	51 7.2		56 6.5	54 6.8	50 7.3	49 7.5	53 6.9	
37 9.8	43 8.4	50 7.3		37 9.8	37 9.9	45 8.1	52 7.0	64 5.7	
63 5.8	68 5.4	72 5.1	Cost of Sales/Inventory	74 4.9	61 6.0	82 4.5	66 5.5	76 4.8	
90 4.0	99 3.7	104 3.5		228 1.6	102 3.6	106 3.4	92 4.0	97 3.8	
17 21.2	18 20.2	21 17.7		15 24.4	23 16.1	20 18.1	24 15.3	16 22.3	
29 12.6	30 12.2	32 11.5	Cost of Sales/Payables	74 4.9	42 8.6	25 14.3	36 10.1	28 13.0	
47 7.8	47 7.8	48 7.7		134 2.7	63 5.8	45 8.1	46 7.9	45 8.1	
5.0	4.3	4.5			4.7	3.9	4.4	5.9	3.7
8.6	7.3	6.9	Sales/Working Capital		12.3	10.1	6.2	7.9	5.9
43.5	19.2	18.5			-71.2	-22.3	13.7	44.8	9.8
9.8	11.3	15.7			15.8	8.6	31.7	11.3	26.6
(129) 2.7	(127) 3.6	(111) 5.6	EBIT/Interest	(14) 1.7	(10) 4.0	(26) 9.0	(25) 5.3	(35) 7.7	
.9	-.1	1.9		.1	.0	1.8	3.0	2.4	
6.7	8.7	6.6							8.6
(36) 2.1	(42) 3.2	(36) 2.9	Net Profit + Depr., Dep., Amort./Cur. Mat. L/T/D					(20) 3.0	
1.1	1.2	1.1							1.1
.2	.2	.2			.7	.2	.2	.3	.3
.7	.5	.5	Fixed/Worth		1.1	.4	.4	.5	.5
2.7	2.3	2.0			-.3	3.0	1.6	1.9	1.6
.7	.5	.5			.5	.9	.5	.7	.4
2.0	1.2	1.3	Debt/Worth		2.1	2.6	1.0	2.5	1.0
8.9	5.1	4.2			-5.8	3.5	3.3	5.0	4.1
43.6	28.8	45.8				74.1	52.1	52.2	45.3
(120) 17.4	(118) 11.3	(105) 21.1	% Profit Before Taxes/Tangible Net Worth			(11) 14.4	(25) 14.5	(25) 30.9	(33) 19.6
1.3	1.6	8.7				3.8	6.5	11.3	8.9
12.8	12.4	13.7			13.7	12.7	24.0	13.6	12.5
5.5	4.4	7.3	% Profit Before Taxes/Total Assets		6.6	5.0	7.4	10.1	7.2
-.1	-.2	3.2			-.5	-.3	1.8	4.4	5.1
28.3	24.8	27.7			127.2	52.8	37.5	24.8	15.6
11.7	10.9	12.9	Sales/Net Fixed Assets		7.6	18.1	14.3	13.5	9.2
5.7	4.9	5.6			1.4	8.0	5.0	8.5	4.9
3.1	2.9	2.7			2.4	3.5	3.1	2.9	2.3
2.3	2.0	2.1	Sales/Total Assets		1.9	2.4	2.2	2.3	1.8
1.6	1.4	1.5			.9	1.5	1.5	1.9	1.2
1.0	.9	.8			.2	.5	.5	.8	1.3
(125) 1.7	(126) 1.6	(110) 1.4	% Depr., Dep., Amort./Sales	(10) 2.7	(11) .9	(25) 1.5	(28) 1.2	(36) 1.7	
2.5	2.7	2.3			7.8	2.6	2.8	1.7	2.4
2.5	2.0	2.0				1.5			
(41) 4.2	(52) 4.9	(39) 3.4	% Officers', Directors' Owners' Comp/Sales			(12) 3.1			
7.0	7.9	7.2				6.3			
4529226M	4122661M	3768406M	Net Sales ($)	1541M	28194M	47433M	209598M	448609M	3033031M
2686336M	2569791M	2529773M	Total Assets ($)	907M	19761M	32195M	106733M	210216M	2159961M

M = $ thousand   MM = $ million
See Pages 9 through 22 for Explanation of Ratios and Data

Current Data Sorted by Assets **Comparative Historical Data**

						Type of Statement		
		1	9	1	2	Unqualified	24	17
	4	10	4	1		Reviewed	19	15
	1	3	1			Compiled	8	9
2	3	4				Tax Returns	6	7
3	3	6	9	2	1	Other	39	35
	11 (4/1-9/30/10)		56 (10/1/10-3/31/11)				4/1/06-3/31/07	4/1/07-3/31/08
0-500M	500M-2MM	2-10MM	10-50MM	50-100MM	100-250MM		ALL	ALL
2	11	24	23	4	3	NUMBER OF STATEMENTS	96	83
%	%	%	%	%	%	**ASSETS**	%	%
	15.7	7.8	4.8			Cash & Equivalents	6.2	9.2
	29.3	28.1	25.4			Trade Receivables (net)	29.1	27.7
	24.2	33.0	30.1			Inventory	25.1	26.8
	.6	2.2	2.4			All Other Current	2.4	2.0
	69.8	71.0	62.8			Total Current	62.9	65.8
	21.2	14.9	21.2			Fixed Assets (net)	25.2	20.6
	3.9	4.1	9.4			Intangibles (net)	5.4	6.2
	5.2	10.0	6.7			All Other Non-Current	6.5	7.4
	100.0	100.0	100.0			Total	100.0	100.0
						LIABILITIES		
	12.0	9.0	8.0			Notes Payable-Short Term	11.3	10.2
	3.5	2.6	8.1			Cur. Mat.-L.T.D.	3.2	3.4
	17.4	18.1	12.8			Trade Payables	15.8	15.4
	.0	.1	.1			Income Taxes Payable	.2	.2
	11.2	6.8	9.2			All Other Current	11.2	8.5
	44.1	36.6	38.2			Total Current	41.8	37.7
	21.6	7.3	11.7			Long-Term Debt	14.0	10.7
	.0	.1	1.2			Deferred Taxes	.8	.5
	4.1	7.0	7.2			All Other Non-Current	8.9	11.6
	30.2	48.9	41.7			Net Worth	34.5	39.5
	100.0	100.0	100.0			Total Liabilities & Net Worth	100.0	100.0
						INCOME DATA		
	100.0	100.0	100.0			Net Sales	100.0	100.0
	35.8	37.1	27.8			Gross Profit	31.4	33.8
	31.3	32.6	21.6			Operating Expenses	26.8	28.3
	4.5	4.5	6.2			Operating Profit	4.6	5.5
	.6	-.3	.9			All Other Expenses (net)	1.5	1.3
	3.9	4.9	5.3			Profit Before Taxes	3.2	4.2
						RATIOS		
	2.6	2.7	2.6			Current	2.6	3.1
	1.3	2.1	1.6				1.6	1.8
	1.3	1.3	1.2				1.1	1.1
	1.6	1.4	1.3			Quick	1.6	1.8
	.8	1.0	.7				.9	1.0
	.6	.7	.6				.5	.5
26 13.9		38 9.6	36 10.2			Sales/Receivables	35 10.3	33 11.2
33 10.9		43 8.5	45 8.1				42 8.6	43 8.5
44 8.3		51 7.2	57 6.4				55 6.7	53 6.9
14 25.5		61 6.0	55 6.7			Cost of Sales/Inventory	39 9.5	44 8.3
60 6.1		77 4.7	71 5.1				49 7.4	60 6.1
109 3.3		114 3.2	101 3.6				79 4.6	83 4.4
2 197.6		25 14.5	23 16.2			Cost of Sales/Payables	21 17.2	22 16.7
18 20.1		42 8.6	31 11.8				35 10.6	33 10.9
58 6.3		66 5.5	44 8.2				50 7.3	48 7.6
	5.2	4.7	4.9			Sales/Working Capital	6.4	5.1
	14.4	7.1	7.4				10.5	8.5
	23.1	15.8	34.8				45.5	30.0
		27.5	31.7			EBIT/Interest	11.0	9.4
		(20) 8.7	(22) 5.3				(87) 4.9	(71) 4.2
		4.0	2.7				2.0	1.7
			8.2			Net Profit + Depr., Dep.,	13.9	5.0
			(10) 3.7			Amort./Cur. Mat. L/T/D	(38) 4.6	(29) 2.8
			2.3				1.3	1.0
	.1	.1	.2			Fixed/Worth	.3	.2
	.3	.2	.6				.8	.4
	3.0	.5	1.3				2.1	1.7
	.6	.5	.9			Debt/Worth	.9	.8
	2.1	1.3	2.1				1.7	1.9
	4.1	2.3	4.2				4.5	4.7
		42.9	47.9			% Profit Before Taxes/Tangible	46.6	60.0
		19.9	(22) 31.4			Net Worth	(82) 26.8	(75) 21.5
		9.3	12.3				9.1	8.2
	14.6	14.8	20.4			% Profit Before Taxes/Total	16.9	15.0
	4.8	8.3	8.3			Assets	9.7	7.7
	2.1	3.9	4.3				2.1	2.1
	105.2	127.9	17.4			Sales/Net Fixed Assets	19.4	42.6
	41.0	31.6	11.9				11.3	14.3
	4.7	10.7	7.6				6.0	6.7
	3.6	3.2	2.4			Sales/Total Assets	3.1	3.1
	2.7	2.3	2.1				2.4	2.3
	1.9	1.7	1.8				1.8	1.7
		.4	1.1			% Depr., Dep., Amort./Sales	.9	.4
		(19) 1.2	(21) 1.4				(85) 1.6	(72) 1.1
		1.7	2.0				2.6	2.0
		2.8				% Officers', Directors'	1.9	2.8
		(16) 3.7				Owners' Comp/Sales	(25) 3.3	(21) 9.0
		7.6					7.5	14.4
934M	41836M	227452M	1102407M	469703M	446885M	Net Sales ($)	3903138M	2969444M
566M	14241M	101122M	536894M	281899M	340996M	Total Assets ($)	2075274M	1560080M

M = $ thousand   MM = $ million
See Pages 9 through 22 for Explanation of Ratios and Data

Comparative Historical Data | Current Data Sorted by Sales

			Type of Statement	0-1MM	1-3MM	3-5MM	5-10MM	10-25MM	25MM & OVER
15	16	13	Unqualified				6	2	11
21	18	19	Reviewed		1	5		3	4
9	4	5	Compiled		1		3	1	
7	5	9	Tax Returns	2	1		5	1	
29	32	21	Other		3		1	6	11
4/1/08-3/31/09 ALL	4/1/09-3/31/10 ALL	4/1/10-3/31/11 ALL			11 (4/1-9/30/10)		56 (10/1/10-3/31/11)		
81	75	67	NUMBER OF STATEMENTS	2	6	5	15	13	26
%	%	%	**ASSETS**	%	%	%	%	%	%
9.9	6.2	9.0	Cash & Equivalents				7.3	10.0	5.1
25.1	25.9	26.8	Trade Receivables (net)				34.3	27.5	25.0
27.9	26.3	29.1	Inventory				36.2	32.3	26.2
1.8	3.0	1.9	All Other Current				1.2	3.3	2.4
64.7	61.3	66.8	Total Current				79.0	73.1	58.6
22.1	21.4	18.4	Fixed Assets (net)				12.4	17.1	22.9
5.8	8.9	6.7	Intangibles (net)				.4	5.3	9.7
7.4	8.3	8.1	All Other Non-Current				8.1	4.5	8.8
100.0	100.0	100.0	Total				100.0	100.0	100.0
			LIABILITIES						
10.8	9.3	9.5	Notes Payable-Short Term				8.6	9.9	6.7
3.8	4.1	4.9	Cur. Mat.-L.T.D.				3.6	2.3	8.5
15.2	14.3	15.5	Trade Payables				27.0	15.4	12.6
.0	.4	.2	Income Taxes Payable				.1	.1	.3
7.4	7.6	8.5	All Other Current				5.1	8.6	8.9
37.1	35.7	38.5	Total Current				44.4	36.3	37.0
13.6	14.5	11.4	Long-Term Debt				8.8	4.8	12.9
.7	1.1	.7	Deferred Taxes				.2	1.0	1.3
6.4	8.8	8.1	All Other Non-Current				8.2	5.9	11.3
42.2	39.8	41.3	Net Worth				38.4	52.1	37.6
100.0	100.0	100.0	Total Liabilities & Net Worth				100.0	100.0	100.0
			INCOME DATA						
100.0	100.0	100.0	Net Sales				100.0	100.0	100.0
29.2	32.8	33.6	Gross Profit				35.5	31.7	27.9
25.0	27.3	27.4	Operating Expenses				31.7	26.0	20.2
4.3	5.5	6.2	Operating Profit				3.8	5.8	7.6
.8	1.1	.6	All Other Expenses (net)				-.2	.4	1.2
3.4	4.4	5.6	Profit Before Taxes				3.9	5.4	6.5
			RATIOS						
3.1	2.7	2.7	Current				2.8	2.8	2.5
1.8	1.9	1.8					2.2	2.1	1.6
1.2	1.3	1.3					1.3	1.5	1.2
2.1	1.5	1.4	Quick				1.4	1.6	1.3
.9	.9	.9					1.0	1.0	.8
.5	.6	.6					.8	.7	.6
30 12.4	39 9.4	33 10.9	Sales/Receivables				39 9.5	31 11.9	36 10.2
39 9.4	47 7.8	44 8.3					44 8.3	43 8.5	45 8.1
49 7.5	52 7.0	55 6.7					49 7.4	62 5.9	60 6.1
39 9.3	50 7.3	55 6.7	Cost of Sales/Inventory				61 6.0	51 7.2	54 6.7
57 6.5	67 5.4	70 5.2					77 4.8	71 5.1	67 5.5
84 4.4	97 3.8	103 3.5					112 3.3	122 3.0	80 4.6
17 21.6	25 14.5	22 16.9	Cost of Sales/Payables				30 12.0	22 16.3	24 15.2
27 13.3	32 11.4	32 11.3					47 7.8	30 12.4	32 11.4
46 7.9	45 8.1	56 6.5					66 5.5	58 6.3	43 8.5
4.7	5.4	4.9	Sales/Working Capital				4.4	4.2	5.1
8.0	7.2	7.4					7.0	5.9	8.0
20.9	22.4	20.2					23.1	12.3	26.1
10.7	12.3	18.4	EBIT/Interest				11.7	30.8	34.6
(69) 3.5	(70) 3.8	(59) 5.9					(13) 5.3	(12) 12.2	(25) 4.6
.8	1.5	2.9					4.0	6.6	2.3
6.9	7.6	5.2	Net Profit + Depr., Dep., Amort./Cur. Mat. L/T/D						5.9
(28) 1.5	(24) 2.8	(19) 2.8							(14) 3.7
.1	1.3	2.1							2.3
.1	.2	.2	Fixed/Worth				.1	.2	.5
.5	.7	.5					.3	.3	.7
1.7	1.6	1.3					.7	.7	1.9
.7	.8	.6	Debt/Worth				.6	.7	.9
1.4	1.9	1.7					2.1	1.2	2.2
3.8	4.9	3.3					2.7	2.2	5.8
45.5	41.6	54.8	% Profit Before Taxes/Tangible Net Worth				55.1	40.4	63.0
(73) 17.0	(68) 20.6	(62) 31.4					(14) 15.8	31.6	(23) 35.7
2.5	5.5	11.1					1.6	11.8	20.3
16.2	14.9	18.6	% Profit Before Taxes/Total Assets				14.6	14.4	20.7
6.1	6.1	8.3					6.1	9.9	10.9
.1	1.9	3.9					1.4	7.2	4.4
30.2	23.6	41.0	Sales/Net Fixed Assets				115.8	24.3	14.8
11.4	10.9	14.6					41.8	16.0	9.4
6.6	6.0	7.1					10.7	10.2	6.5
2.9	2.5	2.6	Sales/Total Assets				3.4	3.0	2.4
2.3	2.0	2.1					2.6	1.9	2.1
1.8	1.6	1.6					1.9	1.6	1.5
.7	.8	.9	% Depr., Dep., Amort./Sales				.3	.8	1.3
(70) 1.5	(61) 1.7	(54) 1.4					(11) 1.2	1.4	(24) 1.5
2.5	2.5	2.1					1.7	1.7	2.7
2.1	3.0	2.8	% Officers', Directors', Owners' Comp/Sales				3.7		
(20) 5.4	(20) 6.1	(26) 4.3					(13) 4.4		
8.7	8.6	7.8					11.6		
2984928M	2598491M	2289217M	Net Sales ($)	934M	13410M	19130M	106737M	224759M	1924247M
1484127M	1634189M	1275718M	Total Assets ($)	566M	6618M	13695M	40829M	113669M	1100341M

M = $ thousand   MM = $ million
See Pages 9 through 22 for Explanation of Ratios and Data

Current Data Sorted by Assets   Comparative Historical Data

Type of Statement	0-500M	500M-2MM	2-10MM	10-50MM	50-100MM	100-250MM		4/1/06-3/31/07 ALL	4/1/07-3/31/08 ALL
Unqualified			2	1				12	7
Reviewed			11	2				12	10
Compiled			6	6				6	3
Tax Returns	4	7		10				4	5
Other	1	3	10	9	3	3		21	18
			13 (4/1-9/30/10)	55 (10/1/10-3/31/11)					
NUMBER OF STATEMENTS	5	10	35	12	3	3		55	43

	0-500M %	500M-2MM %	2-10MM %	10-50MM %	50-100MM %	100-250MM %		4/1/06-3/31/07 ALL %	4/1/07-3/31/08 ALL %
ASSETS									
Cash & Equivalents		15.3	8.0	1.5				6.4	7.2
Trade Receivables (net)		28.1	23.6	28.1				25.9	28.8
Inventory		18.3	32.5	27.3				28.8	28.7
All Other Current		1.1	2.4	1.2				2.3	2.3
Total Current		62.8	66.3	58.1				63.4	67.1
Fixed Assets (net)		30.7	20.9	24.1				22.8	20.6
Intangibles (net)		2.5	5.1	12.6				6.6	6.5
All Other Non-Current		4.0	7.7	5.1				7.1	5.9
Total		100.0	100.0	100.0				100.0	100.0
LIABILITIES									
Notes Payable-Short Term		15.6	10.0	13.7				12.4	13.6
Cur. Mat.-L.T.D.		4.4	3.4	8.4				3.7	3.0
Trade Payables		16.8	15.5	17.0				17.5	18.7
Income Taxes Payable		.0	.1	.0				.1	.1
All Other Current		8.4	7.3	4.6				8.8	8.1
Total Current		45.2	36.4	43.8				42.5	43.6
Long-Term Debt		29.6	12.1	13.1				15.7	12.5
Deferred Taxes		.0	.1	.1				.5	.3
All Other Non-Current		.0	6.0	8.6				7.0	6.2
Net Worth		25.1	45.5	34.4				34.3	37.4
Total Liabilities & Net Worth		100.0	100.0	100.0				100.0	100.0
INCOME DATA									
Net Sales		100.0	100.0	100.0				100.0	100.0
Gross Profit		51.7	39.0	25.7				37.5	33.3
Operating Expenses		41.5	32.8	19.3				32.1	28.4
Operating Profit		10.2	6.3	6.4				5.4	5.0
All Other Expenses (net)		1.9	.4	.4				1.4	1.4
Profit Before Taxes		8.4	5.8	6.0				4.0	3.5
RATIOS									
Current		4.3	2.4	1.7				2.3	2.7
		1.8	1.7	1.5				1.5	1.6
		1.0	1.4	.9				1.0	1.1
Quick		3.3	1.0	1.0				1.2	1.4
		1.4	.9	.8				.7	.8
		.7	.5	.4				.4	.5
Sales/Receivables		30 12.3	24 14.9	40 9.2				28 12.9	35 10.3
		40 9.1	32 11.3	49 7.5				39 9.4	43 8.5
		51 7.1	44 8.4	55 6.6				45 8.1	54 6.8
Cost of Sales/Inventory		30 12.0	46 7.9	30 12.2				41 8.9	40 9.2
		56 6.5	78 4.7	55 6.7				65 5.6	60 6.0
		111 3.3	117 3.1	90 4.1				96 3.8	89 4.1
Cost of Sales/Payables		9 42.1	17 20.9	22 16.5				28 13.1	26 14.2
		33 11.2	35 10.5	37 9.8				40 9.0	40 9.1
		72 5.1	50 7.3	54 6.8				61 6.0	65 5.6
Sales/Working Capital		5.5	4.3	7.6				5.9	5.0
		6.7	9.1	15.0				12.2	9.5
		NM	17.8	NM				-219.6	45.0
EBIT/Interest		20.6	24.7	19.1				14.9	10.4
		3.6	(33) 5.7	7.4				(51) 3.9	(38) 3.7
		1.0	3.1	3.0				1.0	1.1
Net Profit + Depr., Dep., Amort./Cur. Mat. L/T/D			4.6					8.5	
			(11) 2.8					(13) 2.2	
			1.1					.4	
Fixed/Worth		.1	.2	.4				.2	.2
		1.4	.4	.9				.7	.5
		NM	1.0	NM				2.9	2.0
Debt/Worth		1.2	.7	1.4				.8	.6
		2.3	1.2	2.1				1.6	2.0
		NM	1.8	NM				13.2	7.7
% Profit Before Taxes/Tangible Net Worth			71.8					50.0	45.8
			27.3					(45) 30.1	(35) 16.6
			5.5					7.4	4.6
% Profit Before Taxes/Total Assets		28.2	20.5	16.7				18.6	19.0
		4.8	8.3	12.4				9.0	5.4
		.6	2.9	6.7				.4	.6
Sales/Net Fixed Assets		110.9	42.3	20.7				27.1	53.7
		12.6	16.3	10.4				11.8	14.6
		3.9	6.3	6.3				6.2	5.2
Sales/Total Assets		3.4	2.9	2.8				3.1	3.3
		2.4	2.3	2.1				2.4	2.2
		1.7	1.8	1.6				1.7	1.6
% Depr., Dep., Amort./Sales			.8	1.3				.9	.8
			(31) 1.0	2.3				(46) 1.6	(36) 1.3
			2.5	4.4				2.5	2.0
% Officers', Directors' Owners' Comp/Sales			1.3					3.1	2.7
			(19) 2.6					(17) 4.2	(13) 5.0
			5.8					6.5	6.0
Net Sales ($)	2995M	23541M	411615M	537229M	579601M	494865M		1513028M	1441986M
Total Assets ($)	909M	10440M	161632M	270211M	211562M	461120M		755644M	906557M

M = $ thousand   MM = $ million
See Pages 9 through 22 for Explanation of Ratios and Data

Comparative Historical Data | | | | ## Current Data Sorted by Sales

			Type of Statement						
10	6	3	Unqualified					2	1
7	9	13	Reviewed		1		5	6	1
5	5	6	Compiled			1	2	3	
10	13	17	Tax Returns	4	6	1	3	3	
22	26	29	Other	1	2	2	5	5	14
4/1/08-3/31/09 ALL	4/1/09-3/31/10 ALL	4/1/10-3/31/11 ALL		0-1MM	1-3MM	3-5MM	5-10MM	10-25MM	25MM & OVER
					13 (4/1-9/30/10)			55 (10/1/10-3/31/11)	
54	59	68	**NUMBER OF STATEMENTS**	5	9	4	15	19	16
%	%	%	**ASSETS**	%	%	%	%	%	%
5.6	8.0	7.4	Cash & Equivalents				12.7	3.1	3.8
24.5	25.7	23.5	Trade Receivables (net)				17.8	28.9	26.2
29.6	26.4	28.5	Inventory				33.7	31.0	25.0
3.0	2.4	1.8	All Other Current				2.7	2.5	1.5
62.7	62.5	61.2	Total Current				66.9	65.5	56.5
21.4	22.8	25.4	Fixed Assets (net)				19.8	25.8	21.3
11.9	7.3	7.7	Intangibles (net)				3.5	2.8	18.0
4.0	7.4	5.8	All Other Non-Current				9.8	5.9	4.2
100.0	100.0	100.0	Total				100.0	100.0	100.0
			LIABILITIES						
14.3	11.8	11.0	Notes Payable-Short Term				5.9	14.3	10.0
3.8	7.1	5.2	Cur. Mat.-L.T.D.				3.5	4.0	6.4
17.4	15.0	15.8	Trade Payables				14.3	15.1	19.6
.2	.1	.1	Income Taxes Payable				.1	.1	.1
8.2	10.1	7.4	All Other Current				8.0	7.0	6.5
43.9	44.2	39.4	Total Current				31.7	40.6	42.7
17.0	15.6	17.7	Long-Term Debt				15.6	9.2	11.0
.2	.6	.3	Deferred Taxes				.1	.0	1.3
3.2	3.9	6.4	All Other Non-Current				8.7	7.0	6.7
35.6	35.7	36.2	Net Worth				43.8	43.1	38.2
100.0	100.0	100.0	Total Liabilties & Net Worth				100.0	100.0	100.0
			INCOME DATA						
100.0	100.0	100.0	Net Sales				100.0	100.0	100.0
35.7	42.2	38.7	Gross Profit				39.6	36.3	23.5
31.1	34.4	32.8	Operating Expenses				33.8	30.2	18.6
4.7	7.7	5.9	Operating Profit				5.8	6.0	4.9
2.0	1.0	1.0	All Other Expenses (net)				.3	.5	1.0
2.7	6.8	4.9	Profit Before Taxes				5.4	5.6	3.8
			RATIOS						
2.6	2.8	2.7	Current				3.2	2.1	1.8
1.4	1.8	1.6					1.9	1.5	1.4
1.1	1.0	1.2					1.5	1.4	1.0
1.5	1.9	1.4	Quick				2.0	1.0	1.0
.7	.9	.9					.9	.9	.6
.4	.5	.5					.5	.7	.5
25 14.8	31 11.9	27 13.7	Sales/Receivables				18 20.1	31 11.8	37 9.8
33 11.1	40 9.2	37 9.9					30 12.0	39 9.4	41 9.0
41 8.9	50 7.3	49 7.5					42 8.8	50 7.3	55 6.6
37 9.8	39 9.4	38 9.5	Cost of Sales/Inventory				59 6.2	35 10.3	34 10.7
61 6.0	68 5.3	66 5.5					99 3.7	63 5.8	49 7.4
89 4.1	113 3.2	109 3.3					158 2.3	107 3.4	72 5.1
19 19.1	21 17.5	20 18.7	Cost of Sales/Payables				20 18.7	16 22.4	31 11.7
37 9.8	36 10.0	36 10.0					38 9.7	22 16.6	37 9.8
48 7.7	59 6.2	52 7.0					74 4.9	47 7.8	54 6.8
6.1	4.4	5.4	Sales/Working Capital				3.9	7.4	7.6
15.3	10.0	9.9					5.2	14.4	16.0
40.6	-999.8	24.6					12.9	18.8	NM
12.0	17.4	19.8	EBIT/Interest				22.6	24.8	17.6
(49) 3.5	(52) 4.9	(66) 5.0					(14) 4.7	7.1	(15) 5.1
.3	2.5	2.5					2.1	3.6	2.8
	4.4	3.7	Net Profit + Depr., Dep., Amort./Cur. Mat. L/T/D						
	(15) 1.8	(16) 1.8							
	1.1	1.0							
.2	.2	.3	Fixed/Worth				.2	.3	.4
.7	.6	.8					.6	.8	1.0
2.9	2.4	2.4					1.0	1.2	NM
.9	.9	1.0	Debt/Worth				.7	.7	1.4
2.4	2.0	1.6					1.4	1.2	2.6
6.6	4.3	6.5					1.8	2.6	NM
48.4	79.0	67.9	% Profit Before Taxes/Tangible Net Worth				75.3	66.7	61.7
(43) 17.9	(50) 30.0	(58) 29.6					17.2	(18) 27.0	(12) 28.9
1.4	8.8	10.3					2.2	5.5	20.1
17.4	22.1	19.0	% Profit Before Taxes/Total Assets				21.3	20.5	13.6
5.3	8.6	7.4					5.7	13.0	8.9
-2.1	3.3	2.6					1.9	2.9	3.5
36.6	33.7	31.4	Sales/Net Fixed Assets				38.0	42.3	18.7
13.8	14.6	12.4					12.8	13.0	10.9
6.9	6.3	6.1					6.1	6.1	7.4
3.6	2.9	2.9	Sales/Total Assets				2.7	3.4	2.9
2.5	2.2	2.3					2.1	2.4	2.1
1.7	1.7	1.8					1.7	2.1	1.6
1.0	1.1	1.0	% Depr., Dep., Amort./Sales				.4	.9	1.3
(44) 1.8	(46) 1.9	(61) 1.8					(14) 1.4	(17) 1.2	2.2
2.9	3.1	3.1					2.5	2.6	3.7
3.3	1.7	1.4	% Officers', Directors' Owners' Comp/Sales						1.8
(15) 5.3	(24) 3.5	(30) 4.4						(10) 2.7	
7.6	6.0	6.9						6.1	
1867735M	1479425M	2049846M	Net Sales ($)	1968M	19916M	15868M	114535M	309420M	1588139M
919395M	737978M	1115874M	Total Assets ($)	1667M	10130M	6902M	57090M	123875M	916210M

M = $ thousand   MM = $ million
See Pages 9 through 22 for Explanation of Ratios and Data

Current Data Sorted by Assets   **Comparative Historical Data**

0-500M	500M-2MM	2-10MM	10-50MM	50-100MM	100-250MM	Type of Statement	4/1/06-3/31/07 ALL	4/1/07-3/31/08 ALL
		1	8	6	1	Unqualified	15	18
	1	8	5	2		Reviewed	14	13
	2	7	2			Compiled	10	7
3	7	6				Tax Returns	8	8
1	2		5			Other	21	16
	7 (4/1-9/30/10)		60 (10/1/10-3/31/11)					
4	12	22	20	8	1	NUMBER OF STATEMENTS	68	62
%	%	%	%	%	%		%	%
	7.4	8.8	13.1			ASSETS — Cash & Equivalents	7.0	9.2
	30.0	30.1	23.2			Trade Receivables (net)	31.7	31.0
	23.5	30.6	27.7			Inventory	27.2	26.0
	.4	2.3	2.9			All Other Current	3.5	2.5
	61.4	71.8	66.9			Total Current	69.4	68.7
	28.0	15.4	23.3			Fixed Assets (net)	18.4	21.4
	.7	8.0	7.1			Intangibles (net)	6.2	4.7
	10.0	4.8	2.7			All Other Non-Current	6.0	5.3
	100.0	100.0	100.0			Total	100.0	100.0
	7.6	12.7	7.9			LIABILITIES — Notes Payable-Short Term	13.3	9.9
	2.8	2.3	2.9			Cur. Mat.-L.T.D.	3.0	3.1
	14.0	17.6	13.3			Trade Payables	19.2	19.4
	.0	.1	.6			Income Taxes Payable	.2	.5
	11.8	9.4	7.7			All Other Current	9.5	8.7
	36.2	42.1	32.3			Total Current	45.2	41.6
	14.7	8.6	8.7			Long-Term Debt	15.6	13.4
	.0	.3	.6			Deferred Taxes	.4	.6
	3.4	3.8	2.9			All Other Non-Current	6.6	2.9
	45.7	45.2	55.6			Net Worth	32.3	41.5
	100.0	100.0	100.0			Total Liabilities & Net Worth	100.0	100.0
	100.0	100.0	100.0			INCOME DATA — Net Sales	100.0	100.0
	49.8	44.8	33.3			Gross Profit	39.1	40.5
	50.2	40.0	24.3			Operating Expenses	33.7	34.8
	-.4	4.8	9.0			Operating Profit	5.4	5.7
	.4	.7	.3			All Other Expenses (net)	1.1	.7
	-.8	4.1	8.7			Profit Before Taxes	4.3	5.0
	4.1	2.2	3.9			RATIOS — Current	2.8	2.9
	2.5	1.5	1.8				1.7	1.8
	.6	1.3	1.5				1.1	1.3
	3.3	1.4	2.6			Quick	1.5	1.5
	1.4	.9	1.0				.9	1.0
	.3	.6	.6				.5	.7
	26 14.1	29 12.5	32 11.4			Sales/Receivables	36 10.2	33 11.0
	37 10.0	37 9.8	39 9.4				41 8.9	40 9.0
	53 6.9	49 7.5	44 8.4				50 7.3	47 7.8
	39 9.3	54 6.8	49 7.5			Cost of Sales/Inventory	45 8.2	42 8.7
	55 6.6	67 5.5	59 6.1				59 6.2	60 6.1
	94 3.9	87 4.2	119 3.1				94 3.9	79 4.6
	13 28.7	24 15.1	17 21.0			Cost of Sales/Payables	23 15.6	22 16.4
	26 14.3	42 8.6	29 12.6				34 10.8	35 10.5
	58 6.3	62 5.9	39 9.3				59 6.2	51 7.2
	6.5	6.3	3.3			Sales/Working Capital	5.6	5.7
	7.5	10.2	7.7				9.1	9.0
	-7.7	19.3	12.8				24.4	23.0
	14.0	23.8	36.4			EBIT/Interest	11.0	7.6
	(11) 5.6	(21) 4.7	(16) 16.6				(60) 3.6	(54) 4.5
	-13.1	3.0	4.2				1.7	2.1
						Net Profit + Depr., Dep., Amort./Cur. Mat. L/T/D	11.4	6.8
							(19) 3.0	(23) 3.3
							2.0	1.8
	.2	.2	.2			Fixed/Worth	.2	.2
	.4	.4	.5				.6	.5
	1.1	.9	1.0				NM	1.0
	.7	.8	.3			Debt/Worth	.7	.6
	1.2	1.9	1.0				1.8	1.3
	1.9	4.9	2.2				NM	3.7
	48.7	56.5	51.0			% Profit Before Taxes/Tangible Net Worth	54.0	45.2
	(11) -.6	(20) 26.2	(19) 26.2				(51) 25.6	(57) 26.5
	-33.7	4.8	19.7				7.6	9.4
	24.2	17.4	26.1			% Profit Before Taxes/Total Assets	16.5	18.7
	7.1	9.1	15.8				6.0	7.7
	-10.9	3.5	6.5				2.7	3.3
	38.2	54.0	21.1			Sales/Net Fixed Assets	34.6	36.5
	12.4	18.3	10.5				14.7	12.5
	3.3	13.9	5.2				8.5	8.1
	3.9	3.3	2.4			Sales/Total Assets	3.1	3.4
	3.0	2.9	2.1				2.6	2.5
	1.6	2.2	1.5				2.0	2.0
	.6	1.0	1.2			% Depr., Dep., Amort./Sales	.7	.8
	(11) 1.3	(18) 1.3	1.9				(60) 1.5	(52) 1.4
	2.7	1.9	2.5				2.6	2.3
						% Officers', Directors' Owners' Comp/Sales	2.3	1.7
							(22) 4.2	(19) 3.1
							6.4	3.9
2003M	35313M	300421M	887061M	1033407M	203148M	Net Sales ($)	2025244M	3090790M
1150M	12868M	107966M	424309M	567120M	103700M	Total Assets ($)	902318M	1384852M

M = $ thousand   MM = $ million
See Pages 9 through 22 for Explanation of Ratios and Data

Comparative Historical Data   Current Data Sorted by Sales

4/1/08-3/31/09 ALL	4/1/09-3/31/10 ALL	4/1/10-3/31/11 ALL	Type of Statement	0-1MM	1-3MM	3-5MM	5-10MM	10-25MM	25MM & OVER
17	14	16	Unqualified			1			15
17	21	16	Reviewed				4	5	7
8	7	11	Compiled		2	1		7	1
2	7	10	Tax Returns	3	2	5			
21	18	14	Other	2	1	1	3	3	4
				7 (4/1-9/30/10)			60 (10/1/10-3/31/11)		
65	67	67	**NUMBER OF STATEMENTS**	5	5	8	7	15	27
%	%	%	**ASSETS**	%	%	%	%	%	%
9.3	9.8	11.4	Cash & Equivalents					10.1	12.4
27.3	28.5	27.4	Trade Receivables (net)					31.9	25.1
28.6	25.2	26.9	Inventory					27.6	27.7
2.1	2.0	2.0	All Other Current					1.2	3.4
67.2	65.5	67.7	Total Current					70.7	68.5
21.2	18.6	20.2	Fixed Assets (net)					19.1	20.5
5.3	7.4	6.8	Intangibles (net)					4.5	7.1
6.3	8.5	5.3	All Other Non-Current					5.7	4.0
100.0	100.0	100.0	Total					100.0	100.0
			LIABILITIES						
11.9	10.9	9.2	Notes Payable-Short Term					13.5	8.1
3.4	2.3	2.4	Cur. Mat.-L.T.D.					2.1	2.6
18.0	16.3	15.4	Trade Payables					16.1	14.8
.2	.1	.2	Income Taxes Payable					.0	.5
8.3	8.0	8.6	All Other Current					11.2	7.5
41.7	37.7	35.9	Total Current					43.0	33.5
15.7	12.5	10.6	Long-Term Debt					5.1	8.4
.3	.3	.3	Deferred Taxes					.4	.5
10.0	13.8	4.3	All Other Non-Current					3.6	4.3
32.2	35.6	49.0	Net Worth					47.9	53.3
100.0	100.0	100.0	Total Liabilities & Net Worth					100.0	100.0
			INCOME DATA						
100.0	100.0	100.0	Net Sales					100.0	100.0
35.7	37.9	40.7	Gross Profit					43.1	30.0
32.2	32.1	34.9	Operating Expenses					37.8	22.7
3.5	5.8	5.7	Operating Profit					5.3	7.3
1.1	.9	.6	All Other Expenses (net)					.3	.4
2.5	4.9	5.1	Profit Before Taxes					5.0	6.9
			RATIOS						
2.5	2.7	3.7	Current					2.6	3.8
1.8	1.8	1.8						1.5	1.8
1.2	1.3	1.2						1.2	1.5
1.5	1.8	2.5	Quick					1.6	2.5
.8	1.0	1.0						.9	.8
.6	.6	.6						.6	.6
29 12.4	34 10.8	31 11.9	Sales/Receivables					29 12.7	32 11.4
39 9.3	41 8.9	39 9.4						37 9.8	37 9.9
48 7.7	47 7.7	50 7.3						50 7.3	48 7.6
43 8.6	41 8.8	48 7.5	Cost of Sales/Inventory					51 7.2	48 7.6
67 5.5	63 5.8	62 5.9						62 5.9	58 6.3
91 4.0	84 4.3	102 3.6						69 5.3	88 4.1
21 17.7	19 19.1	16 22.4	Cost of Sales/Payables					17 21.4	18 20.1
35 10.6	35 10.3	32 11.3						38 9.6	29 12.4
53 6.9	50 7.2	49 7.5						49 7.5	40 9.2
5.6	5.6	4.2	Sales/Working Capital					6.2	2.9
9.1	8.0	8.5						13.8	8.5
28.1	22.2	18.7						28.0	15.4
13.0	12.3	24.0	EBIT/Interest					29.3	30.4
(57) 4.8	(59) 7.7	(57) 6.9						(13) 4.7	(22) 15.6
-.2	2.6	3.0						3.7	3.4
7.1	8.5	4.8	Net Profit + Depr., Dep., Amort./Cur. Mat. L/T/D						21.6
(19) 2.4	(20) 3.7	(15) 2.5							(10) 2.9
1.0	1.1	1.0							.9
.2	.2	.2	Fixed/Worth					.3	.2
.5	.5	.4						.4	.5
1.2	1.0	1.0						.8	.7
.6	.7	.5	Debt/Worth					.7	.4
1.3	1.6	1.1						1.0	1.1
3.2	4.4	2.3						2.3	2.3
41.6	46.3	49.3	% Profit Before Taxes/Tangible Net Worth					62.8	43.2
(56) 14.8	(58) 24.3	(60) 24.7						28.9	(25) 26.2
-1.3	9.5	7.4						9.4	12.6
16.4	24.5	19.3	% Profit Before Taxes/Total Assets					16.3	18.0
6.3	9.8	10.5						10.5	9.7
-2.3	2.8	4.2						4.7	5.4
35.1	30.4	36.8	Sales/Net Fixed Assets					36.8	20.6
14.7	16.6	14.6						18.7	10.4
8.9	9.1	7.2						12.7	6.0
3.1	3.1	3.2	Sales/Total Assets					3.2	3.2
2.6	2.4	2.4						2.9	2.1
1.8	1.7	1.5						2.2	1.5
.9	1.1	1.1	% Depr., Dep., Amort./Sales					1.1	1.0
(58) 1.4	(57) 1.4	(59) 1.5						(14) 1.5	1.5
2.1	2.2	2.4						2.2	2.4
1.0	1.7	2.9	% Officers', Directors' Owners' Comp/Sales						
(15) 2.8	(22) 3.2	(23) 5.0							
4.1	8.2	8.8							
2804520M	2881152M	2461353M	Net Sales ($)	2764M	9458M	30626M	56013M	257725M	2104767M
1266703M	1388903M	1217113M	Total Assets ($)	2420M	4872M	15033M	25414M	109519M	1059855M

© RMA 2011

M = $ thousand   MM = $ million
See Pages 9 through 22 for Explanation of Ratios and Data

Current Data Sorted by Assets   Comparative Historical Data

0-500M	500M-2MM	2-10MM	10-50MM	50-100MM	100-250MM	Type of Statement	ALL 4/1/06-3/31/07	ALL 4/1/07-3/31/08
		1	10	1	4	Unqualified	17	20
		6	8	1		Reviewed	16	23
	2	7				Compiled	7	9
	1	5				Tax Returns	2	2
1	5	17	19	5	2	Other	38	36
	15 (4/1-9/30/10)		80 (10/1/10-3/31/11)					
1	8	36	37	7	6	**NUMBER OF STATEMENTS**	80	90
%	%	%	%	%	%	**ASSETS**	%	%
		13.5	8.5			Cash & Equivalents	8.7	8.6
		27.7	24.5			Trade Receivables (net)	25.8	26.5
		30.1	30.1			Inventory	30.2	29.8
		2.8	2.1			All Other Current	2.5	3.3
		74.0	65.3			Total Current	67.2	68.1
		16.5	18.7			Fixed Assets (net)	21.3	16.2
		6.0	12.7			Intangibles (net)	4.0	8.6
		3.5	3.3			All Other Non-Current	7.5	7.1
		100.0	100.0			Total	100.0	100.0
						LIABILITIES		
		6.9	11.4			Notes Payable-Short Term	12.7	12.1
		2.8	2.0			Cur. Mat.-L.T.D.	2.4	2.5
		16.2	18.1			Trade Payables	19.1	18.6
		.1	.1			Income Taxes Payable	.2	.4
		9.2	12.6			All Other Current	12.9	9.8
		35.3	44.1			Total Current	47.3	43.4
		11.3	10.2			Long-Term Debt	11.7	12.3
		.1	.4			Deferred Taxes	.1	.2
		9.9	12.4			All Other Non-Current	6.0	5.1
		43.5	32.8			Net Worth	34.9	39.0
		100.0	100.0			Total Liabilities & Net Worth	100.0	100.0
						INCOME DATA		
		100.0	100.0			Net Sales	100.0	100.0
		42.9	37.7			Gross Profit	39.4	41.3
		35.5	32.2			Operating Expenses	34.8	34.3
		7.3	5.5			Operating Profit	4.6	7.0
		.9	2.0			All Other Expenses (net)	1.5	1.8
		6.4	3.5			Profit Before Taxes	3.1	5.2
						RATIOS		
		4.0	2.6			Current	2.4	2.6
		2.4	1.6				1.5	1.6
		1.4	1.1				1.1	1.1
		2.3	1.3			Quick	1.2	1.5
		1.3	.8				.8	.8
		.6	.5				.4	.5
		31 11.8	36 10.1			Sales/Receivables	30 12.1	33 11.0
		45 8.2	44 8.2				47 7.7	48 7.6
		65 5.6	55 6.6				63 5.8	65 5.6
		49 7.4	67 5.4			Cost of Sales/Inventory	53 6.9	64 5.7
		75 4.9	96 3.8				83 4.4	89 4.1
		159 2.3	132 2.8				136 2.7	141 2.6
		15 24.1	29 12.5			Cost of Sales/Payables	26 13.8	31 11.7
		36 10.2	49 7.4				45 8.0	52 7.0
		76 4.8	73 5.0				75 4.9	79 4.6
		3.2	4.0			Sales/Working Capital	5.0	4.6
		-5.9	9.4				8.1	7.9
		10.8	34.8				33.5	29.9
		49.0	21.5			EBIT/Interest	14.0	15.4
		(31) 8.1	(33) 6.2				(73) 3.2	(83) 5.3
		3.6	1.3				.1	1.6
			28.6			Net Profit + Depr., Dep., Amort./Cur. Mat. L/T/D	8.2	8.1
			(12) 10.9				(20) 2.9	(28) 3.2
			4.0				1.0	.4
		.1	.2			Fixed/Worth	.2	.2
		.5	.6				.5	.4
		.9	2.4				2.0	1.4
		.5	.6			Debt/Worth	.7	.7
		1.5	2.1				1.8	2.1
		3.7	15.4				5.8	7.4
		64.7	67.1			% Profit Before Taxes/Tangible Net Worth	54.8	54.5
		(33) 41.2	(29) 29.1				(71) 21.6	(76) 24.2
		8.7	12.8				-1.6	7.3
		25.3	18.1			% Profit Before Taxes/Total Assets	18.1	19.9
		10.4	8.3				8.2	6.3
		3.8	1.1				-2.0	1.2
		45.8	55.7			Sales/Net Fixed Assets	31.7	45.8
		17.5	11.1				13.8	16.1
		8.0	7.1				5.8	7.8
		2.9	2.7			Sales/Total Assets	2.8	2.8
		2.1	2.0				2.1	2.0
		1.4	1.3				1.4	1.3
		.5	.7			% Depr., Dep., Amort./Sales	.6	.5
		(29) 1.2	(34) 1.5				(67) 1.8	(79) 1.4
		3.0	2.0				2.8	2.2
		3.0				% Officers', Directors' Owners' Comp/Sales	1.6	1.6
		(13) 5.0					(28) 2.5	(24) 3.5
		11.3					5.1	7.3
1221M	31025M	403598M	1685444M	716445M	1198472M	Net Sales ($)	3131027M	4615734M
446M	11081M	186682M	891264M	572832M	966464M	Total Assets ($)	1723217M	2856815M

© RMA 2011

M = $ thousand   MM = $ million
See Pages 9 through 22 for Explanation of Ratios and Data

Comparative Historical Data

		4/1/08-3/31/09 ALL		4/1/09-3/31/10 ALL		4/1/10-3/31/11 ALL
Type of Statement						
Unqualified		25		26		16
Reviewed		15		22		15
Compiled		9		5		9
Tax Returns		4		3		6
Other		36		38		49
NUMBER OF STATEMENTS		89		94		95
ASSETS		%		%		%
Cash & Equivalents		7.9		7.0		10.1
Trade Receivables (net)		24.6		25.9		25.2
Inventory		30.1		30.2		29.2
All Other Current		3.1		4.3		2.4
Total Current		65.7		67.4		66.9
Fixed Assets (net)		17.4		16.3		16.7
Intangibles (net)		11.5		10.4		12.5
All Other Non-Current		5.4		5.9		3.9
Total		100.0		100.0		100.0
LIABILITIES						
Notes Payable-Short Term		11.2		13.2		9.3
Cur. Mat.-L.T.D.		3.1		2.8		2.3
Trade Payables		16.8		21.1		16.5
Income Taxes Payable		.4		.4		.2
All Other Current		10.7		9.4		10.0
Total Current		42.2		46.9		38.2
Long-Term Debt		13.7		10.4		11.8
Deferred Taxes		.3		.4		.5
All Other Non-Current		6.9		3.6		9.7
Net Worth		36.9		38.8		39.7
Total Liabilities & Net Worth		100.0		100.0		100.0
INCOME DATA						
Net Sales		100.0		100.0		100.0
Gross Profit		39.2		37.4		40.0
Operating Expenses		32.5		31.5		33.8
Operating Profit		6.6		5.9		6.2
All Other Expenses (net)		1.9		1.3		1.5
Profit Before Taxes		4.8		4.6		4.7
RATIOS						
Current		2.9		2.1		2.9
		1.6		1.5		1.9
		1.1		1.1		1.3
Quick		1.7		1.2		1.6
		.7		.8		.8
		.5		.5		.6
Sales/Receivables	**33**	11.0	**31**	11.9	**31**	11.8
	45	8.1	**43**	8.4	**44**	8.2
	57	6.4	**60**	6.0	**61**	6.0
Cost of Sales/Inventory	**60**	6.1	**55**	6.6	**60**	6.1
	91	4.0	**92**	4.0	**93**	3.9
	134	2.7	**141**	2.6	**144**	2.5
Cost of Sales/Payables	**25**	14.7	**32**	11.4	**24**	15.0
	48	7.5	**50**	7.3	**43**	8.5
	73	5.0	**77**	4.7	**73**	5.0
Sales/Working Capital		4.4		5.2		3.9
		8.3		10.1		6.3
		31.6		29.9		12.9
EBIT/Interest		15.6		17.5		22.7
	(84)	3.9	(87)	5.2	(85)	6.6
		1.4		1.5		1.8
Net Profit + Depr., Dep., Amort./Cur. Mat. L/T/D		21.4		13.3		18.0
	(26)	5.7	(21)	5.9	(18)	8.1
		-.1		2.2		1.7
Fixed/Worth		.3		.2		.2
		.6		.7		.5
		2.4		1.5		2.0
Debt/Worth		.7		1.1		.6
		2.2		2.3		1.8
		14.0		4.8		5.1
% Profit Before Taxes/Tangible Net Worth		55.4		53.8		54.6
	(71)	17.8	(79)	28.2	(77)	29.4
		6.9		8.0		11.3
% Profit Before Taxes/Total Assets		15.4		14.6		18.9
		6.8		8.1		7.4
		1.2		1.1		1.3
Sales/Net Fixed Assets		23.5		36.3		35.1
		14.0		15.4		14.2
		7.8		7.6		7.7
Sales/Total Assets		2.6		2.6		2.8
		2.1		2.0		2.0
		1.3		1.4		1.2
% Depr., Dep., Amort./Sales		1.1		.8		.7
	(78)	1.7	(77)	1.8	(79)	1.5
		2.6		3.0		2.4
% Officers', Directors' Owners' Comp/Sales		1.6		1.3		2.1
	(20)	2.5	(25)	3.2	(26)	4.2
		5.1		5.3		7.6
Net Sales ($)		4733329M		4223748M		4036205M
Total Assets ($)		3116788M		2642988M		2628769M

Current Data Sorted by Sales

	15 (4/1-9/30/10)		80 (10/1/10-3/31/11)							
	0-1MM	1-3MM		3-5MM		5-10MM		10-25MM		25MM & OVER
Type of Statement										
Unqualified						1		4		11
Reviewed						4		4		7
Compiled		1		2		4		2		
Tax Returns		2		2		1		1		
Other		3		6		4		12		24
NUMBER OF STATEMENTS		6		10		14		23		42
ASSETS	%	%		%		%		%		%
Cash & Equivalents	DATA NOT AVAILABLE			14.8		14.2		9.9		7.8
Trade Receivables (net)				21.7		24.8		29.6		23.5
Inventory				21.5		26.4		31.6		29.4
All Other Current				6.7		.4		1.6		2.7
Total Current				64.6		65.8		72.8		63.4
Fixed Assets (net)				28.1		14.7		18.0		14.7
Intangibles (net)				2.3		13.1		7.5		17.2
All Other Non-Current				5.0		6.4		1.7		4.6
Total				100.0		100.0		100.0		100.0
LIABILITIES										
Notes Payable-Short Term				4.7		7.5		9.8		9.2
Cur. Mat.-L.T.D.				2.4		3.7		2.8		1.7
Trade Payables				10.1		14.1		17.7		18.3
Income Taxes Payable				.0		.0		.1		.3
All Other Current				9.1		5.4		9.1		13.1
Total Current				26.2		30.7		39.5		42.6
Long-Term Debt				20.1		11.5		8.3		11.7
Deferred Taxes				.0		.0		.2		1.0
All Other Non-Current				6.1		15.7		.3		12.8
Net Worth				47.6		42.1		51.7		31.9
Total Liabilities & Net Worth				100.0		100.0		100.0		100.0
INCOME DATA										
Net Sales				100.0		100.0		100.0		100.0
Gross Profit				55.4		40.4		39.4		37.5
Operating Expenses				49.8		32.6		30.9		31.5
Operating Profit				5.6		7.8		8.4		6.1
All Other Expenses (net)				.3		1.5		.8		2.0
Profit Before Taxes				5.3		6.3		7.6		4.1
RATIOS										
Current				5.4		3.1		3.0		2.4
				2.9		2.3		1.9		1.6
				1.6		1.5		1.3		1.2
Quick				3.1		2.1		1.9		1.1
				1.6		1.2		.9		.8
				.7		.6		.7		.5
Sales/Receivables			**17**	21.9	**35**	10.4	**29**	12.6	**32**	11.5
			44	8.3	**45**	8.1	**50**	7.3	**44**	8.3
			80	4.5	**54**	6.7	**66**	5.6	**55**	6.6
Cost of Sales/Inventory			**50**	7.4	**45**	8.1	**49**	7.5	**66**	5.5
			65	5.6	**75**	4.9	**91**	4.0	**94**	3.9
			152	2.4	**150**	2.4	**142**	2.6	**137**	2.7
Cost of Sales/Payables			**14**	26.4	**18**	19.8	**15**	23.9	**37**	10.0
			25	14.5	**30**	12.0	**39**	9.4	**48**	7.6
			74	4.9	**76**	4.8	**74**	4.9	**70**	5.2
Sales/Working Capital				2.6		3.0		4.0		4.5
				5.0		4.5		7.6		8.9
				12.0		15.4		10.9		29.2
EBIT/Interest						42.4		49.0		21.4
					(13)	7.6	(19)	12.7	(38)	5.0
						2.1		2.8		1.0
Net Profit + Depr., Dep., Amort./Cur. Mat. L/T/D										27.7
									(15)	8.1
										2.6
Fixed/Worth				.2		.1		.1		.2
				.8		.5		.3		.7
				1.5		NM		.6		-1.7
Debt/Worth				.3		.5		.7		.6
				1.1		1.6		1.4		2.7
				4.1		NM		2.4		-7.8
% Profit Before Taxes/Tangible Net Worth				41.6		77.4		62.8		57.4
				27.2	(11)	50.3		31.1	(29)	29.1
				12.3		6.3		17.8		12.8
% Profit Before Taxes/Total Assets				17.2		33.8		25.1		15.9
				7.6		14.1		13.0		6.6
				4.3		3.5		4.3		.2
Sales/Net Fixed Assets				18.3		84.9		38.4		31.1
				7.1		26.6		14.2		13.6
				4.3		7.6		8.3		7.6
Sales/Total Assets				2.9		2.9		3.1		2.7
				1.6		1.8		2.2		2.1
				1.1		1.4		1.7		1.2
% Depr., Dep., Amort./Sales						.3		.6		.7
					(11)	1.3	(19)	1.2	(36)	1.5
						3.3		2.7		2.2
% Officers', Directors' Owners' Comp/Sales										
Net Sales ($)		12270M		40959M		112921M		426300M		3443755M
Total Assets ($)		12484M		27785M		79501M		257506M		2251493M

M = $ thousand MM = $ million

See Pages 9 through 22 for Explanation of Ratios and Data

Current Data Sorted by Assets   Comparative Historical Data

0-500M	500M-2MM	2-10MM	10-50MM	50-100MM	100-250MM	Type of Statement	4/1/06-3/31/07 ALL	4/1/07-3/31/08 ALL
			6	1	1	Unqualified	8	8
	1	7	1			Reviewed	6	10
1	1	3				Compiled	6	5
1	1	1				Tax Returns	1	3
1	2	6	3		1	Other	14	14
	8 (4/1-9/30/10)		28 (10/1/10-3/31/11)					
2	4	17	10	1	2	**NUMBER OF STATEMENTS**	35	40
%	%	%	%	%	%	**ASSETS**	%	%
		4.4	4.3			Cash & Equivalents	6.7	5.9
		34.8	21.5			Trade Receivables (net)	27.9	27.2
		29.4	30.5			Inventory	29.8	33.2
		2.0	2.1			All Other Current	3.1	2.5
		70.6	58.4			Total Current	67.5	68.8
		20.3	18.7			Fixed Assets (net)	21.0	20.3
		3.6	21.9			Intangibles (net)	9.0	7.0
		5.5	1.0			All Other Non-Current	2.6	3.9
		100.0	100.0			Total	100.0	100.0
						LIABILITIES		
		10.0	9.5			Notes Payable-Short Term	10.2	10.8
		2.2	2.7			Cur. Mat.-L.T.D.	2.7	2.8
		20.5	12.0			Trade Payables	16.9	16.4
		.3	.0			Income Taxes Payable	.5	.4
		8.1	9.2			All Other Current	11.7	13.8
		41.0	33.5			Total Current	42.0	44.2
		20.7	7.7			Long-Term Debt	16.1	8.9
		.6	1.7			Deferred Taxes	.7	.3
		4.9	1.0			All Other Non-Current	6.4	5.7
		32.8	56.1			Net Worth	34.7	40.9
		100.0	100.0			Total Liabilties & Net Worth	100.0	100.0
						INCOME DATA		
		100.0	100.0			Net Sales	100.0	100.0
		34.6	31.0			Gross Profit	35.8	31.6
		28.8	25.2			Operating Expenses	29.9	26.5
		5.8	5.7			Operating Profit	5.9	5.1
		.9	1.8			All Other Expenses (net)	.8	.9
		4.8	3.9			Profit Before Taxes	5.1	4.2
						RATIOS		
		2.5	2.9			Current	2.3	2.5
		2.2	2.1				1.7	1.7
		1.2	1.1				1.1	1.1
		2.0	1.4			Quick	1.0	1.2
		.9	.8				.8	.7
		.5	.5				.6	.6
		37 9.9	38 9.5			Sales/Receivables	39 9.4	37 9.9
		50 7.4	43 8.5				47 7.8	43 8.6
		62 5.9	47 7.7				54 6.7	49 7.4
		22 16.5	65 5.6			Cost of Sales/Inventory	49 7.5	56 6.5
		67 5.4	83 4.4				81 4.5	76 4.8
		115 3.2	140 2.6				114 3.2	113 3.2
		19 19.5	24 15.5			Cost of Sales/Payables	27 13.4	23 16.0
		30 12.1	32 11.3				36 10.2	35 10.4
		65 5.7	45 8.0				51 7.2	50 7.3
		5.4	4.4			Sales/Working Capital	5.5	5.4
		10.5	5.9				8.4	8.5
		15.7	83.2				35.0	39.8
		23.2	37.2			EBIT/Interest	13.8	21.9
		4.5	14.8				(31) 8.8	(35) 7.2
		2.5	3.1				1.4	2.6
						Net Profit + Depr., Dep.,	22.4	9.8
						Amort./Cur. Mat. L/T/D	(13) 5.9	(13) 3.6
							1.6	1.6
		.3	.4			Fixed/Worth	.4	.3
		.8	.5				.7	.5
		1.9	1.4				5.7	1.2
		.7	.5			Debt/Worth	1.0	.7
		3.4	1.7				1.7	1.7
		8.6	4.0				23.0	6.2
		49.0				% Profit Before Taxes/Tangible	49.9	48.2
		(15) 33.6				Net Worth	(27) 31.5	(36) 20.1
		11.3					3.0	7.4
		22.1	19.9			% Profit Before Taxes/Total	20.2	15.3
		9.8	11.1			Assets	12.1	8.1
		2.5	-1.7				.6	3.4
		32.1	22.7			Sales/Net Fixed Assets	24.7	23.4
		11.0	12.1				14.1	14.5
		7.1	4.9				7.9	7.5
		3.0	2.3			Sales/Total Assets	3.0	2.8
		2.4	1.7				2.2	2.3
		2.1	1.5				1.6	1.7
		.9				% Depr., Dep., Amort./Sales	1.0	1.0
		(15) 1.5					(32) 1.6	(37) 1.6
		2.4					2.2	2.2
						% Officers', Directors'	1.1	1.0
						Owners' Comp/Sales	(11) 3.0	(10) 2.3
							8.5	3.0
592M	9560M	213872M	379793M	114102M	673246M	Net Sales ($)	1307642M	1707998M
369M	4601M	81495M	197766M	70018M	355589M	Total Assets ($)	705280M	905877M

Comparative Historical Data | Current Data Sorted by Sales

12	8	8	Type of Statement					3	5
12	8	8	Unqualified					3	5
14	10	9	Reviewed			1	1	6	1
	3	5	Compiled	1	1		3		
9	12	2	Tax Returns	1	1				1
16	17	12	Other	1		1	3	1	4
4/1/08-3/31/09 ALL	4/1/09-3/31/10 ALL	4/1/10-3/31/11 ALL		8 (4/1-9/30/10)			28 (10/1/10-3/31/11)		
				0-1MM	1-3MM	3-5MM	5-10MM	10-25MM	25MM & OVER
51	50	36	NUMBER OF STATEMENTS	3	2	3	7	10	11
%	%	%	ASSETS	%	%	%	%	%	%
10.7	10.8	6.3	Cash & Equivalents					3.8	3.8
25.5	27.5	31.2	Trade Receivables (net)					26.1	26.7
30.2	27.5	27.2	Inventory					31.4	31.4
3.2	1.9	2.3	All Other Current					1.8	3.7
69.6	67.7	67.1	Total Current					63.1	65.6
19.3	19.8	17.6	Fixed Assets (net)					23.5	19.4
7.0	4.6	9.7	Intangibles (net)					11.9	10.7
4.2	7.9	5.5	All Other Non-Current					1.5	4.3
100.0	100.0	100.0	Total					100.0	100.0
			LIABILITIES						
11.1	9.1	11.1	Notes Payable-Short Term					10.3	13.8
3.1	1.9	2.0	Cur. Mat.-L.T.D.					2.3	2.4
16.8	18.2	18.6	Trade Payables					15.1	18.3
.1	.2	.2	Income Taxes Payable					.4	.1
11.3	8.8	8.0	All Other Current					7.8	9.2
42.4	38.1	39.9	Total Current					36.0	43.8
13.7	12.2	18.7	Long-Term Debt					16.4	5.7
.3	1.4	.8	Deferred Taxes					2.3	.6
5.5	3.7	3.6	All Other Non-Current					2.0	2.7
38.1	44.7	36.9	Net Worth					43.3	47.2
100.0	100.0	100.0	Total Liabilities & Net Worth					100.0	100.0
			INCOME DATA						
100.0	100.0	100.0	Net Sales					100.0	100.0
31.9	36.7	32.9	Gross Profit					30.3	27.9
27.2	29.7	26.8	Operating Expenses					27.9	21.1
4.6	7.0	6.0	Operating Profit					2.5	6.8
1.0	.4	1.1	All Other Expenses (net)					1.8	.5
3.7	6.6	4.9	Profit Before Taxes					.6	6.3
			RATIOS						
2.7	2.9	2.5	Current					2.6	2.2
1.7	1.7	1.8						2.4	1.5
1.2	1.2	1.2						1.1	1.2
1.7	1.5	1.6	Quick					1.5	.9
.9	.9	.8						1.1	.7
.5	.7	.5						.5	.6
34 10.9	32 11.4	39 9.3	Sales/Receivables					41 8.9	39 9.3
41 8.9	42 8.8	46 8.0						51 7.2	42 8.7
49 7.4	52 7.0	58 6.3						58 6.3	46 8.0
47 7.8	34 10.8	29 12.7	Cost of Sales/Inventory					38 9.7	55 6.6
65 5.6	59 6.1	74 4.9						89 4.1	71 5.1
88 4.1	107 3.4	109 3.3						127 2.9	87 4.2
17 21.5	20 18.5	23 15.9	Cost of Sales/Payables					19 19.3	26 13.8
32 11.3	33 11.0	32 11.5						29 12.6	33 11.0
53 6.9	55 6.6	57 6.4						63 5.8	53 6.9
5.4	4.9	4.7	Sales/Working Capital					4.1	6.6
8.3	7.4	9.2						6.7	10.5
22.4	22.3	18.8						NM	29.3
13.4	21.5	27.4	EBIT/Interest					16.3	28.0
(46) 3.8	(47) 7.7	(35) 6.1						3.8	20.4
.9	3.0	2.3						-.2	5.4
21.6	15.4	26.4	Net Profit + Depr., Dep., Amort./Cur. Mat. L/T/D						
(16) 4.1	(15) 3.7	(12) 4.7							
1.8	1.6	2.8							
.3	.2	.3	Fixed/Worth					.4	.4
.5	.5	.6						.6	.5
1.3	1.0	1.5						3.4	.9
.8	.5	.8	Debt/Worth					.5	.8
2.4	1.2	3.2						1.7	1.5
4.9	3.5	5.8						10.6	3.4
36.6	69.4	45.1	% Profit Before Taxes/Tangible Net Worth						55.5
(46) 22.2	(46) 25.0	(31) 30.2							(10) 36.1
.1	5.9	7.5							12.7
16.4	19.8	17.1	% Profit Before Taxes/Total Assets					11.3	23.3
4.4	10.5	9.1						1.9	11.5
-.2	3.7	1.4						-3.3	5.3
35.1	33.1	39.3	Sales/Net Fixed Assets					19.2	21.0
14.6	16.9	12.5						7.8	12.4
7.0	7.2	7.0						5.4	6.8
2.9	3.4	2.6	Sales/Total Assets					2.4	2.8
2.4	2.2	2.2						1.8	2.1
1.7	1.8	1.6						1.5	1.7
1.1	.9	.9	% Depr., Dep., Amort./Sales					1.0	
(42) 1.5	(38) 1.4	(30) 1.6						2.6	
2.7	3.5	2.6						3.5	
	1.6	1.5	% Officers', Directors', Owners' Comp/Sales						
	(16) 4.9	(10) 4.2							
	12.2	8.0							
1984967M	1677961M	1391165M	Net Sales ($)	1227M	4112M	11428M	53922M	164074M	1156402M
1184116M	866795M	709838M	Total Assets ($)	955M	4213M	4180M	21923M	96569M	581998M

© RMA 2011

M = $ thousand   MM = $ million
See Pages 9 through 22 for Explanation of Ratios and Data

Current Data Sorted by Assets   Comparative Historical Data

						Type of Statement		
1	1	3	2			Unqualified	5	7
		1				Reviewed	4	2
2		1				Compiled	3	3
	2					Tax Returns		
3	6	5	1			Other	12	10
							4/1/06-	4/1/07-
							3/31/07	3/31/08
0-500M	4 (4/1-9/30/10) 500M-2MM	2-10MM	24 (10/1/10-3/31/11) 10-50MM	50-100MM	100-250MM		ALL	ALL
6		9	10		3	NUMBER OF STATEMENTS	24	22
%	%	%	%	%	%	ASSETS	%	%
D			9.1	D		Cash & Equivalents	3.4	5.3
A			26.2	A		Trade Receivables (net)	24.6	29.7
T			26.4	T		Inventory	25.9	17.1
A			1.9	A		All Other Current	2.7	4.0
			63.6			Total Current	56.6	56.1
N			27.9	N		Fixed Assets (net)	35.1	34.0
O			4.4	O		Intangibles (net)	4.0	2.4
T			4.2	T		All Other Non-Current	4.3	7.5
			100.0			Total	100.0	100.0
A				A		LIABILITIES		
V			9.2	V		Notes Payable-Short Term	13.6	13.0
A			2.1	A		Cur. Mat.-L.T.D.	2.6	1.6
I			20.6	I		Trade Payables	17.0	14.9
L			.2	L		Income Taxes Payable	.0	.1
A			7.9	A		All Other Current	5.5	8.8
B			40.0	B		Total Current	38.7	38.4
L			14.5	L		Long-Term Debt	18.2	10.9
E			.6	E		Deferred Taxes	.2	.1
			5.2			All Other Non-Current	6.0	6.7
			39.7			Net Worth	36.9	43.9
			100.0			Total Liabilities & Net Worth	100.0	100.0
						INCOME DATA		
			100.0			Net Sales	100.0	100.0
			16.6			Gross Profit	27.0	24.8
			9.4			Operating Expenses	22.9	18.7
			7.2			Operating Profit	4.1	6.2
			.7			All Other Expenses (net)	1.5	1.5
			6.5			Profit Before Taxes	2.6	4.7
						RATIOS		
			2.4				2.2	2.3
			1.5			Current	1.7	1.7
			1.0				1.2	1.4
			1.4				1.3	1.6
			.8			Quick	1.0	1.1
			.4				.5	.9
		32	11.3				36 10.1	31 11.8
		41	8.9			Sales/Receivables	42 8.7	45 8.2
		52	7.0				48 7.6	69 5.3
		29	12.6				37 9.9	10 36.2
		43	8.6			Cost of Sales/Inventory	52 7.0	40 9.2
		74	4.9				70 5.2	54 6.8
		21	17.0				24 15.4	17 22.0
		39	9.3			Cost of Sales/Payables	31 11.7	26 14.2
		66	5.5				52 7.0	41 8.9
			5.9				6.7	6.7
			13.4			Sales/Working Capital	10.3	9.0
			NM				35.8	26.1
							11.5	15.1
						EBIT/Interest	(23) 3.9	(18) 4.5
							1.2	1.2
						Net Profit + Depr., Dep., Amort./Cur. Mat. L/T/D		
			.4				.7	.6
			.5			Fixed/Worth	1.4	.7
			1.8				2.8	2.1
			.8				1.1	.3
			2.2			Debt/Worth	2.5	1.3
			3.9				5.1	4.3
			79.6				43.3	32.8
			30.7			% Profit Before Taxes/Tangible Net Worth	27.5 (20)	24.2
			10.5				3.2	4.4
			22.9				11.4	12.0
			7.5			% Profit Before Taxes/Total Assets	7.3	9.4
			1.5				.3	1.1
			16.2				12.5	18.8
			9.5			Sales/Net Fixed Assets	6.4	7.5
			5.4				3.7	3.9
			2.7				3.3	3.2
			2.3			Sales/Total Assets	2.1	2.1
			1.6				1.7	1.5
							1.9	1.3
						% Depr., Dep., Amort./Sales	(20) 2.8	(19) 1.7
							3.9	3.5
						% Officers', Directors' Owners' Comp/Sales		
	21333M	108833M	697673M		727558M	Net Sales ($)	1844283M	2091969M
	7813M	46674M	286902M		542965M	Total Assets ($)	908471M	998813M

M = $ thousand   MM = $ million
See Pages 9 through 22 for Explanation of Ratios and Data

Comparative Historical Data				Current Data Sorted by Sales					
			Type of Statement						
6	7	7	Unqualified				1	1	5
3	4	1	Reviewed					1	
4	2	3	Compiled		1		1		1
5	4	2	Tax Returns			1	1		
11	13	15	Other		2	1	2	4	6
4/1/08-3/31/09 ALL	**4/1/09-3/31/10 ALL**	**4/1/10-3/31/11 ALL**			**4 (4/1-9/30/10)**		**24 (10/1/10-3/31/11)**		
				0-1MM	**1-3MM**	**3-5MM**	**5-10MM**	**10-25MM**	**25MM & OVER**
29	30	28	**NUMBER OF STATEMENTS**		3	2	5	6	12
%	%	%	**ASSETS**	%	%	%	%	%	%
7.5	6.6	9.2	Cash & Equivalents	**DATA NOT AVAILABLE**					11.2
24.4	24.2	28.2	Trade Receivables (net)						25.3
22.2	18.1	23.3	Inventory						24.5
6.2	2.0	2.3	All Other Current						2.2
60.3	50.9	63.0	Total Current						63.3
30.6	39.7	26.1	Fixed Assets (net)						26.1
5.4	5.5	5.5	Intangibles (net)						3.4
3.8	3.9	5.3	All Other Non-Current						7.2
100.0	100.0	100.0	Total						100.0
			LIABILITIES						
10.1	9.1	9.4	Notes Payable-Short Term						7.2
4.6	6.3	2.6	Cur. Mat.-L.T.D.						1.3
23.8	15.3	19.5	Trade Payables						18.0
.1	.6	.2	Income Taxes Payable						.2
7.5	4.8	6.1	All Other Current						7.1
46.1	36.1	37.8	Total Current						33.9
20.4	19.7	14.6	Long-Term Debt						10.0
.1	.3	.5	Deferred Taxes						.5
8.2	3.5	8.2	All Other Non-Current						3.8
25.2	40.4	38.9	Net Worth						51.8
100.0	100.0	100.0	Total Liabilties & Net Worth						100.0
			INCOME DATA						
100.0	100.0	100.0	Net Sales						100.0
30.3	25.5	28.3	Gross Profit						17.7
25.9	21.4	20.8	Operating Expenses						9.4
4.3	4.2	7.5	Operating Profit						8.2
1.4	1.3	.8	All Other Expenses (net)						.2
3.0	2.9	6.7	Profit Before Taxes						8.0
			RATIOS						
2.2	2.3	2.4							3.6
1.9	1.4	1.9	Current						2.1
1.2	.8	1.1							1.3
1.6	1.4	1.5							2.0
.7	.7	1.1	Quick						1.2
.4	.4	.5							.5
26 14.3	**37** 9.9	**33** 11.1							**35** 10.3
34 10.9	**54** 6.8	**42** 8.6	Sales/Receivables						**43** 8.4
45 8.1	**64** 5.7	**60** 6.1							**55** 6.7
33 11.1	**33** 11.2	**37** 9.9							**23** 16.1
43 8.5	**46** 8.0	**58** 6.3	Cost of Sales/Inventory						**50** 7.3
65 5.6	**76** 4.8	**77** 4.8							**80** 4.5
19 18.9	**26** 14.2	**23** 15.9							**19** 18.9
31 11.7	**42** 8.7	**40** 9.2	Cost of Sales/Payables						**32** 11.2
43 8.5	**61** 5.9	**68** 5.4							**61** 6.0
6.3	5.7	6.3							4.4
10.5	15.6	7.7	Sales/Working Capital						6.6
32.2	-13.4	59.5							22.1
5.4	8.0	38.8							39.2
(23) 3.8	(28) 1.7	(24) 7.3	EBIT/Interest						(10) 14.5
1.4	-.2	1.5							2.3
			Net Profit + Depr., Dep., Amort./Cur. Mat. L/T/D						
.3	.6	.4							.4
1.1	1.0	.6	Fixed/Worth						.5
2.4	2.8	3.0							.7
1.0	.7	.8							.4
1.6	1.7	1.3	Debt/Worth						1.1
8.2	3.8	8.9							3.2
31.5	20.9	76.9							64.5
(26) 17.4	(27) 5.2	(24) 35.3	% Profit Before Taxes/Tangible Net Worth						28.9
3.1	-10.7	12.4							12.4
11.1	9.1	29.7							17.8
7.4	3.1	16.6	% Profit Before Taxes/Total Assets						13.5
1.4	-3.1	3.1							7.0
18.0	9.1	17.8							13.4
11.4	4.7	9.7	Sales/Net Fixed Assets						9.5
4.4	1.9	5.1							5.0
3.3	2.3	3.0							2.6
2.5	1.5	2.4	Sales/Total Assets						2.2
1.8	1.1	1.6							1.5
1.5	1.9	1.9							1.4
(26) 2.2	(25) 4.5	(20) 2.7	% Depr., Dep., Amort./Sales						(10) 2.6
3.4	8.1	3.6							2.9
2.6	1.4	2.3							
(13) 5.9	(12) 3.8	(11) 5.2	% Officers', Directors' Owners' Comp/Sales						
13.6	6.6	6.7							
1832262M	**1335316M**	**1555397M**	Net Sales ($)		**5751M**	**8227M**	**34419M**	**102206M**	**1404794M**
831723M	**809849M**	**884354M**	Total Assets ($)		**2437M**	**5043M**	**10866M**	**49027M**	**816981M**

M = $ thousand MM = $ million

See Pages 9 through 22 for Explanation of Ratios and Data

Current Data Sorted by Assets   **Comparative Historical Data**

0-500M	500M-2MM	2-10MM	10-50MM	50-100MM	100-250MM	Type of Statement	4/1/06-3/31/07 ALL	4/1/07-3/31/08 ALL
		5	18	8	4	Unqualified	50	41
1	8	28	9	2		Reviewed	38	40
2	7	7				Compiled	19	21
3	13	5	1			Tax Returns	22	17
6	19	26	39	12	6	Other	91	84
	48 (4/1-9/30/10)		181 (10/1/10-3/31/11)					
12	47	71	67	22	10	NUMBER OF STATEMENTS	220	203
%	%	%	%	%	%	**ASSETS**	%	%
4.9	11.3	10.3	7.3	8.9	4.5	Cash & Equivalents	8.0	7.7
24.2	33.4	31.0	27.7	19.4	13.7	Trade Receivables (net)	28.7	28.4
36.9	28.0	23.7	26.4	18.2	23.0	Inventory	24.0	25.8
2.6	3.3	2.4	3.0	2.7	1.9	All Other Current	2.8	3.4
68.7	76.0	67.2	64.3	49.1	43.0	Total Current	63.4	65.2
10.9	17.4	22.5	21.8	34.6	33.5	Fixed Assets (net)	23.3	23.2
5.0	2.1	2.7	8.7	11.5	20.3	Intangibles (net)	7.5	6.7
15.4	4.5	7.5	5.2	4.8	3.2	All Other Non-Current	5.7	4.9
100.0	100.0	100.0	100.0	100.0	100.0	Total	100.0	100.0
						LIABILITIES		
21.8	11.3	8.9	8.9	2.1	4.3	Notes Payable-Short Term	11.9	11.7
5.2	4.1	4.0	2.3	3.5	3.5	Cur. Mat.-L.T.D.	3.3	3.5
11.5	19.4	16.9	13.9	10.6	12.0	Trade Payables	18.0	18.3
.5	.1	.4	.4	.3	.1	Income Taxes Payable	.3	.4
8.3	7.5	8.4	9.6	7.8	13.5	All Other Current	10.2	11.4
47.3	42.4	38.6	35.0	24.3	33.4	Total Current	43.6	45.3
31.2	15.1	10.2	12.7	16.8	23.7	Long-Term Debt	15.5	16.3
.0	.5	.3	1.0	1.9	1.9	Deferred Taxes	.7	.7
14.7	5.1	8.7	4.7	10.6	2.3	All Other Non-Current	6.8	5.9
6.8	37.1	42.2	46.6	46.4	38.6	Net Worth	33.5	31.8
100.0	100.0	100.0	100.0	100.0	100.0	Total Liabilities & Net Worth	100.0	100.0
						INCOME DATA		
100.0	100.0	100.0	100.0	100.0	100.0	Net Sales	100.0	100.0
49.4	38.3	39.0	29.6	25.5	22.7	Gross Profit	33.0	33.0
47.5	30.9	32.7	20.3	17.5	16.4	Operating Expenses	27.6	27.0
1.8	7.4	6.3	9.3	8.0	6.4	Operating Profit	5.4	5.9
1.1	.4	.4	.7	1.9	4.7	All Other Expenses (net)	1.2	1.8
.8	7.0	5.9	8.6	6.1	1.6	Profit Before Taxes	4.2	4.1
						RATIOS		
2.7	3.4	3.4	2.8	3.0	2.0	Current	2.4	2.4
2.3	1.7	1.7	1.9	2.1	1.7		1.6	1.5
1.6	1.2	1.3	1.3	1.6	1.0		1.1	1.0
2.0	2.5	2.3	1.8	1.6	1.2	Quick	1.4	1.3
1.0	1.0	1.0	1.0	1.1	.8		.9	.8
.1	.6	.7	.6	.6	.2		.6	.5
6 56.3	23 15.9	37 9.9	34 10.6	32 11.5	13 27.7	Sales/Receivables	34 10.8	32 11.3
44 8.2	36 10.2	44 8.3	45 8.0	48 7.6	37 9.7		46 8.0	42 8.7
56 6.6	47 7.8	55 6.6	56 6.5	55 6.7	68 5.4		60 6.1	52 7.1
40 9.0	22 16.6	39 9.3	42 8.8	33 10.9	39 9.5	Cost of Sales/Inventory	32 11.4	33 10.9
78 4.7	40 9.2	58 6.3	63 5.8	48 7.7	74 4.9		55 6.6	55 6.6
199 1.8	94 3.9	90 4.0	100 3.7	96 3.8	115 3.2		98 3.7	101 3.6
2 153.8	16 22.2	24 15.4	21 17.7	23 16.2	17 21.6	Cost of Sales/Payables	23 15.9	21 17.2
31 11.7	28 13.1	38 9.6	32 11.5	26 13.9	44 8.3		39 9.3	37 10.0
49 7.4	53 6.9	54 6.8	50 7.3	34 10.6	78 4.7		62 5.9	56 6.5
3.7	5.0	5.3	4.3	4.2	6.8	Sales/Working Capital	5.5	6.1
7.5	10.3	9.7	7.2	6.7	8.0		10.5	12.3
14.8	25.7	24.0	15.4	10.6	NM		64.1	92.1
	23.0	17.6	32.1	21.6	17.9	EBIT/Interest	10.0	9.6
	(39) 6.3	(59) 5.7	(59) 10.0	6.2	4.7		(194) 3.9	(179) 3.4
	2.8	2.8	2.9	3.0	2.5		1.6	1.5
		9.7	11.8	8.7		Net Profit + Depr., Dep., Amort./Cur. Mat. L/T/D	8.4	8.8
		(18) 3.0	(19) 5.5	(13) 4.0			(68) 3.5	(65) 3.1
		1.0	2.2	2.6			1.1	1.7
.0	.1	.2	.2	.6	1.0	Fixed/Worth	.2	.2
.1	.4	.6	.5	1.1	1.4		.7	.8
NM	1.7	1.3	1.1	5.2	NM		3.2	2.5
.6	.5	.6	.7	.8	1.1	Debt/Worth	.9	1.0
1.4	2.3	1.5	1.5	1.1	3.8		2.0	2.2
-3.0	6.4	4.8	3.9	9.3	NM		10.1	12.3
	76.5	57.3	69.3	52.1		% Profit Before Taxes/Tangible Net Worth	54.4	58.8
	(43) 46.7	(67) 29.4	(61) 34.8	(19) 30.6			(182) 26.9	(171) 29.0
	13.8	12.6	14.7	6.8			6.4	9.5
21.6	38.0	21.1	26.1	20.3	9.9	% Profit Before Taxes/Total Assets	15.6	16.8
6.9	13.2	9.8	11.6	11.1	7.1		7.0	7.2
-4.1	4.9	4.1	5.4	3.5	.6		1.8	1.8
UND	136.3	44.8	28.1	8.1	18.2	Sales/Net Fixed Assets	38.7	43.6
53.7	29.7	12.3	10.5	4.3	4.1		11.4	12.7
23.9	10.1	5.4	5.1	2.8	2.2		5.4	5.9
4.5	4.3	3.1	2.7	2.0	1.5	Sales/Total Assets	3.1	3.3
2.6	3.0	2.3	1.9	1.5	1.0		2.1	2.3
1.7	2.3	1.6	1.5	1.1	.8		1.4	1.7
	.2	.7	.8	2.3		% Depr., Dep., Amort./Sales	.8	.6
	(37) .8	(59) 1.5	(63) 1.9	4.1			(176) 1.6	(178) 1.6
	2.3	3.3	3.1	5.2			3.3	3.0
	2.6	1.3				% Officers', Directors' Owners' Comp/Sales	2.0	1.6
	(27) 5.5	(24) 2.9					(55) 3.4	(53) 3.3
	8.5	3.9					6.4	6.3
9881M	202852M	1702322M	3295102M	2517919M	2186142M	Net Sales ($)	9519079M	9621034M
3531M	59066M	375211M	1675340M	1655908M	1714758M	Total Assets ($)	5509255M	4880927M

M = $ thousand   MM = $ million
See Pages 9 through 22 for Explanation of Ratios and Data

Comparative Historical Data · Current Data Sorted by Sales

Type of Statement

4/1/08-3/31/09 ALL	4/1/09-3/31/10 ALL	4/1/10-3/31/11 ALL	Type of Statement	0-1MM	1-3MM	3-5MM	5-10MM	10-25MM	25MM & OVER
41	48	35	Unqualified					5	30
43	43	48	Reviewed		1	9	10	17	11
18	19	16	Compiled	3	1	4	4	3	1
23	21	22	Tax Returns	2	7	5	5	2	1
94	95	108	Other	4	11	10	12	15	56
				48 (4/1-9/30/10)		181 (10/1/10-3/31/11)			
219	**226**	**229**	**NUMBER OF STATEMENTS**	**9**	**20**	**28**	**31**	**42**	**99**

ASSETS

%	%	%		%	%	%	%	%	%
7.6	9.4	8.9	Cash & Equivalents		11.7	14.7	7.6	8.7	7.8
25.9	26.5	28.3	Trade Receivables (net)		27.1	30.8	31.0	31.3	26.8
26.1	23.3	25.5	Inventory		30.3	20.3	28.2	26.3	23.2
2.7	3.5	2.8	All Other Current		5.0	3.9	1.9	2.7	2.4
62.2	62.8	65.5	Total Current		74.1	69.7	68.7	69.0	60.3
23.1	25.8	22.3	Fixed Assets (net)		13.5	25.4	22.6	19.2	25.2
7.5	5.6	6.1	Intangibles (net)		5.4	.7	2.2	4.4	9.8
7.2	5.8	6.2	All Other Non-Current		6.9	4.2	6.5	7.4	4.6
100.0	100.0	100.0	Total		100.0	100.0	100.0	100.0	100.0

LIABILITIES

10.7	10.9	9.2	Notes Payable-Short Term		16.6	11.0	9.6	9.8	7.0
3.8	3.8	3.5	Cur. Mat.-L.T.D.		1.8	6.5	4.9	2.7	2.6
16.2	15.8	15.4	Trade Payables		12.5	16.5	18.4	17.7	14.4
.2	.2	.3	Income Taxes Payable		.3	.3	.4	.2	.3
10.3	10.5	8.7	All Other Current		3.7	7.9	8.9	7.5	9.8
41.3	41.1	37.2	Total Current		34.7	42.2	42.2	37.9	34.1
14.6	15.1	14.3	Long-Term Debt		12.0	22.8	9.8	7.1	14.3
.5	.7	.7	Deferred Taxes		.1	.6	.3	.2	1.4
5.4	6.2	7.0	All Other Non-Current		6.9	3.2	7.3	9.7	5.6
38.1	36.9	40.8	Net Worth		46.3	31.3	40.5	45.1	44.6
100.0	100.0	100.0	Total Liabilities & Net Worth		100.0	100.0	100.0	100.0	100.0

INCOME DATA

100.0	100.0	100.0	Net Sales		100.0	100.0	100.0	100.0	100.0
32.7	33.3	34.7	Gross Profit		45.6	42.5	36.4	36.3	27.4
26.2	27.7	27.3	Operating Expenses		34.5	34.9	31.0	29.9	19.1
6.4	5.5	7.3	Operating Profit		11.1	7.6	5.4	6.4	8.4
1.1	1.1	.8	All Other Expenses (net)		.2	.6	.4	.4	1.3
5.3	4.4	6.5	Profit Before Taxes		10.9	7.0	5.0	5.9	7.0

RATIOS

2.3	2.7	3.0	Current		5.3	3.0	3.4	3.1	2.7
1.5	1.7	1.8			2.7	1.7	1.5	1.9	1.8
1.1	1.2	1.3			1.7	1.1	1.2	1.4	1.3
1.3	1.6	1.8	Quick		3.4	2.3	2.4	2.1	1.6
.8	.9	1.0			1.2	1.0	.9	.9	1.1
.5	.6	.6			.5	.6	.6	.7	.6
26 13.8	29 12.7	31 11.6	Sales/Receivables		17 21.4	30 12.4	31 11.9	34 10.8	32 11.2
39 9.4	42 8.7	44 8.3			34 10.8	42 8.6	43 8.4	43 8.4	45 8.0
49 7.5	54 6.7	55 6.6			61 6.0	56 6.6	56 6.5	54 6.8	56 6.6
28 13.2	28 13.1	35 10.5	Cost of Sales/Inventory		0 UND	25 14.7	31 11.6	40 9.2	33 10.9
61 5.9	57 6.4	56 6.5			64 5.7	47 7.8	55 6.6	63 5.8	56 6.5
100 3.7	93 3.9	96 3.8			116 3.1	80 4.5	90 4.0	89 4.1	96 3.8
18 20.1	20 18.6	21 17.7	Cost of Sales/Payables		5 79.1	23 15.6	15 23.6	21 15.8	21 17.3
31 11.7	31 11.6	32 11.5			24 15.4	40 9.1	31 11.7	34 10.6	30 12.3
52 7.1	50 7.3	52 7.1			72 5.1	60 6.1	52 7.0	51 7.1	47 7.7
6.3	4.9	4.6	Sales/Working Capital		3.4	5.1	6.0	5.2	4.5
12.5	10.0	8.7			4.4	10.3	11.2	9.1	8.1
63.4	26.8	18.9			14.0	37.4	24.5	15.4	19.8
11.8	18.0	22.0	EBIT/Interest		9.1	22.3	28.4	25.6	27.6
(200) 4.2	(197) 5.3	(197) 6.3			(14) 6.0	(26) 6.6	(28) 4.4	(33) 6.1	(90) 7.4
1.4	1.5	2.9			3.8	4.0	2.7	3.0	3.1
7.2	13.9	9.6	Net Profit + Depr., Dep., Amort./Cur. Mat. L/T/D					39.1	9.8
(68) 2.4	(55) 3.0	(63) 3.4					(10) 8.5	(34) 4.4	
.9	1.1	1.8						1.5	2.3
.2	.3	.2	Fixed/Worth		.0	.1	.2	.1	.3
.7	.7	.5			.2	.4	.7	.5	.6
2.1	1.6	1.5			2.3	1.7	1.4	1.1	1.5
1.0	.7	.7	Debt/Worth		.2	.6	.5	.6	.8
2.0	1.6	1.5			1.0	1.4	1.7	1.4	1.5
5.4	4.6	5.4			7.1	6.2	7.4	3.8	5.0
53.1	50.0	61.4	% Profit Before Taxes/Tangible Net Worth		81.8	85.2	57.7	58.1	67.1
(191) 20.4	(190) 25.6	(206) 32.6			(17) 53.3	(26) 34.6	(28) 34.0	(41) 30.7	(88) 31.0
2.7	5.8	13.6			14.9	10.6	17.1	14.1	14.6
20.6	20.8	22.1	% Profit Before Taxes/Total Assets		40.7	21.9	25.2	20.9	22.2
7.2	8.5	10.8			14.4	13.7	9.4	11.3	10.7
1.6	1.2	4.2			5.6	4.7	3.4	5.2	4.3
43.8	30.8	42.9	Sales/Net Fixed Assets		216.5	44.5	55.1	49.5	31.2
14.2	10.4	12.1			32.3	22.6	11.0	15.3	8.7
5.4	4.3	5.2			6.6	4.5	6.2	7.7	4.1
3.4	3.0	3.0	Sales/Total Assets		3.0	3.4	3.6	3.3	2.7
2.3	2.1	2.2			2.4	2.5	2.6	2.4	1.8
1.5	1.4	1.5			1.5	1.6	1.8	2.1	1.3
.6	.8	.7	% Depr., Dep., Amort./Sales		.6	.6	.7	.6	.9
(181) 1.7	(185) 1.8	(193) 1.8			(14) 1.6	(22) .9	(27) 1.9	(35) .9	(90) 2.3
3.3	3.9	3.3			4.5	3.2	2.9	2.8	4.1
1.5	2.0	1.9	% Officers', Directors' Owners' Comp/Sales		4.4	2.4	1.8	1.3	
(59) 3.2	(56) 4.7	(60) 3.7			(11) 6.5	(10) 4.9	(17) 3.7	(14) 2.6	
5.2	8.2	6.8			11.7	8.9	4.9	5.0	
15154316M	10746757M	9914218M	Net Sales ($)	5200M	38039M	110777M	220200M	719772M	8820230M
6007778M	6177397M	5483814M	Total Assets ($)	3375M	21066M	52568M	104948M	308969M	4992888M

Current Data Sorted by Assets   Comparative Historical Data

Date ranges for Current Data: **5 (4/1-9/30/10)** (500M-2MM column) and **53 (10/1/10-3/31/11)** (10-50MM column).

Type of Statement	0-500M	500M-2MM	2-10MM	10-50MM	50-100MM	100-250MM		6 / 6 / 5 / — / 11 4/1/06-3/31/07 ALL	6 / 5 / 4 / 4 / 10 4/1/07-3/31/08 ALL
Unqualified	1			6	1	1		6	6
Reviewed			7	2				6	5
Compiled		2	2					5	4
Tax Returns	4	5	4						4
Other	1	4	8	8	1	1		11	10
NUMBER OF STATEMENTS	6	11	21	16	2	2		28	29
	%	%	%	%	%	%		%	%
ASSETS									
Cash & Equivalents		8.3	9.9	1.8				5.6	6.6
Trade Receivables (net)		34.2	27.5	22.2				24.8	27.7
Inventory		29.4	24.4	24.0				21.8	23.1
All Other Current		1.1	3.9	3.2				1.4	.9
Total Current		73.0	65.7	51.1				53.6	58.4
Fixed Assets (net)		18.7	25.0	37.2				35.7	31.4
Intangibles (net)		2.1	4.6	7.3				5.1	3.5
All Other Non-Current		6.3	4.7	4.4				5.7	6.8
Total		100.0	100.0	100.0				100.0	100.0
LIABILITIES									
Notes Payable-Short Term		15.4	7.6	11.1				12.5	15.6
Cur. Mat.-L.T.D.		10.0	2.8	9.7				5.9	3.4
Trade Payables		19.9	23.3	14.3				15.8	20.4
Income Taxes Payable		.0	.2	.7				.8	.3
All Other Current		4.1	2.5	5.3				7.5	5.8
Total Current		49.4	36.4	41.1				42.6	45.6
Long-Term Debt		21.2	16.3	16.8				19.9	18.8
Deferred Taxes		.7	.6	.8				1.2	1.2
All Other Non-Current		8.7	7.7	3.9				2.6	4.7
Net Worth		19.9	39.0	37.4				33.8	29.7
Total Liabilities & Net Worth		100.0	100.0	100.0				100.0	100.0
INCOME DATA									
Net Sales		100.0	100.0	100.0				100.0	100.0
Gross Profit		35.7	25.6	21.4				21.5	19.5
Operating Expenses		29.8	21.1	15.2				16.4	16.5
Operating Profit		6.0	4.5	6.2				5.1	3.0
All Other Expenses (net)		3.5	.9	.8				1.6	1.4
Profit Before Taxes		2.5	3.6	5.3				3.4	1.5
RATIOS									
Current		7.1 / 2.0 / .8	3.1 / 1.9 / 1.1	1.7 / 1.3 / 1.0				2.1 / 1.2 / 1.0	1.6 / 1.2 / 1.0
Quick		3.2 / 1.4 / .4	1.9 / 1.0 / .5	.8 / .7 / .5				1.0 / .6 / .5	1.3 / .6 / .5
Sales/Receivables		21 17.2 / 40 9.2 / 48 7.6	28 13.1 / 35 10.3 / 50 7.4	38 9.6 / 42 8.7 / 53 6.8				33 10.9 / 39 9.4 / 48 7.5	34 10.7 / 40 9.2 / 51 7.1
Cost of Sales/Inventory		21 17.1 / 45 8.0 / 64 5.7	30 12.1 / 44 8.3 / 76 4.8	37 9.9 / 58 6.3 / 75 4.9				27 13.4 / 46 7.9 / 62 5.9	26 13.9 / 44 8.3 / 58 6.3
Cost of Sales/Payables		12 30.3 / 27 13.4 / 51 7.2	20 18.4 / 44 8.3 / 57 6.4	22 16.6 / 36 10.2 / 47 7.8				18 20.0 / 33 11.2 / 51 7.2	16 22.3 / 45 8.1 / 59 6.2
Sales/Working Capital		4.8 / 8.9 / -16.6	5.4 / 7.6 / 26.7	11.3 / 15.3 / 102.7				7.7 / 37.5 / UND	8.0 / 30.5 / NM
EBIT/Interest			8.9 / (20) 3.7 / 1.3	8.4 / 4.3 / 2.1				5.4 / (27) 2.5 / .8	5.4 / 1.8 / 1.2
Net Profit + Depr., Dep., Amort./Cur. Mat. L/T/D			(10) 3.8 / 2.5 / 1.5					2.4 / (11) 1.6 / .5	2.1 / (13) 1.8 / 1.3
Fixed/Worth		.2 / .7 / -.3	.2 / .6 / 1.6	.9 / 1.4 / 3.4				.8 / 1.2 / 2.7	.7 / 1.2 / 7.4
Debt/Worth		.9 / 2.5 / -5.4	.7 / 1.8 / 4.9	1.2 / 1.7 / 7.8				1.1 / 2.8 / 6.8	1.2 / 3.2 / 19.4
% Profit Before Taxes/Tangible Net Worth			45.2 / (19) 24.7 / .3	50.4 / (14) 23.0 / 13.7				30.1 / (23) 13.1 / 3.4	28.2 / (25) 16.1 / 5.8
% Profit Before Taxes/Total Assets		26.7 / 9.5 / -2.4	12.3 / 7.9 / .1	11.5 / 6.4 / 3.6				12.8 / 4.0 / -.5	9.2 / 3.9 / .8
Sales/Net Fixed Assets		91.8 / 31.3 / 20.4	33.0 / 13.8 / 5.5	9.9 / 6.4 / 4.4				12.2 / 6.0 / 4.3	22.9 / 7.8 / 4.5
Sales/Total Assets		4.6 / 3.8 / 2.8	3.2 / 2.5 / 1.9	2.3 / 1.9 / 1.3				2.6 / 2.2 / 1.7	3.3 / 2.3 / 1.8
% Depr., Dep., Amort./Sales		.4 / (10) 1.1 / 1.5	.5 / (18) 2.3 / 3.3	1.8 / 2.9 / 3.4				1.4 / (25) 2.6 / 3.9	1.1 / (28) 1.6 / 3.5
% Officers', Directors', Owners' Comp/Sales								1.5 / (10) 2.7 / 3.9	1.7 / (12) 3.1 / 4.8
Net Sales ($)	7773M	41343M	215758M	744895M	262072M	431059M		1976986M	1182272M
Total Assets ($)	1696M	11578M	89778M	423682M	141452M	255529M		1098782M	558422M

© RMA 2011

M = $ thousand   MM = $ million
See Pages 9 through 22 for Explanation of Ratios and Data

Comparative Historical Data

Current Data Sorted by Sales

			Type of Statement						
10	9	9	Unqualified	1					8
3	3	9	Reviewed		1		4	4	
5	5	4	Compiled			2		2	
3	6	13	Tax Returns	3	3	2	2	3	9
15	21	23	Other	3	3	4	2	5	
4/1/08-	4/1/09-	4/1/10-			5 (4/1-9/30/10)		53 (10/1/10-3/31/11)		
3/31/09	3/31/10	3/31/11							
ALL	ALL	ALL		0-1MM	1-3MM	3-5MM	5-10MM	10-25MM	25MM & OVER
36	44	58	**NUMBER OF STATEMENTS**	4	6	9	8	14	17
%	%	%	**ASSETS**	%	%	%	%	%	%
3.3	3.5	6.9	Cash & Equivalents					10.2	1.4
28.2	29.5	28.0	Trade Receivables (net)					29.8	21.6
26.7	24.0	23.8	Inventory					29.3	24.4
2.7	2.7	3.5	All Other Current					5.8	2.8
60.9	59.7	62.1	Total Current					75.2	50.3
30.5	30.9	27.0	Fixed Assets (net)					18.7	36.7
3.6	4.3	4.7	Intangibles (net)					1.6	8.7
5.0	5.1	6.3	All Other Non-Current					4.4	4.3
100.0	100.0	100.0	Total					100.0	100.0
			LIABILITIES						
18.9	18.4	10.1	Notes Payable-Short Term					9.2	9.9
4.0	3.7	6.9	Cur. Mat.-L.T.D.					2.2	8.7
18.3	19.6	19.0	Trade Payables					26.2	13.2
.4	.1	.3	Income Taxes Payable					.2	.7
4.5	7.7	4.1	All Other Current					2.5	6.9
46.0	49.6	40.5	Total Current					40.3	39.4
16.7	16.2	17.2	Long-Term Debt					14.3	14.7
1.1	.6	.8	Deferred Taxes					.2	1.5
5.3	3.3	6.0	All Other Non-Current					11.2	4.3
30.9	30.2	35.5	Net Worth					34.0	40.1
100.0	100.0	100.0	Total Liabilities & Net Worth					100.0	100.0
			INCOME DATA						
100.0	100.0	100.0	Net Sales					100.0	100.0
20.7	26.5	27.7	Gross Profit					21.1	20.5
17.9	22.0	22.4	Operating Expenses					17.9	15.3
2.8	4.5	5.3	Operating Profit					3.2	5.2
1.5	1.5	1.4	All Other Expenses (net)					.8	1.2
1.2	3.0	3.9	Profit Before Taxes					2.5	4.1
			RATIOS						
1.6	1.9	2.5						3.0	1.9
1.2	1.3	1.7	Current					1.9	1.4
1.1	1.0	1.1						1.3	1.1
.9	1.1	1.6						1.7	.9
.6	.6	.8	Quick					1.0	.7
.5	.4	.5						.6	.6

											Sales/Receivables										
32	11.2	34	10.8	28	13.3													26	14.1	39	9.5
38	9.5	42	8.7	41	9.0	Sales/Receivables												36	10.2	42	8.7
45	8.2	52	7.0	48	7.6													49	7.5	47	7.8
37	9.8	32	11.5	30	12.1													28	12.9	39	9.4
46	7.9	52	7.0	49	7.4	Cost of Sales/Inventory												53	6.9	57	6.4
63	5.8	69	5.3	73	5.0													76	4.8	74	4.9
20	18.2	25	14.4	19	19.7													19	18.9	23	16.2
26	13.9	35	10.4	33	11.2	Cost of Sales/Payables												44	8.3	30	12.2
46	7.9	50	7.2	51	7.1													53	6.8	45	8.1

10.5	10.7	5.9	Sales/Working Capital		5.2	8.6
31.6	21.8	12.0			8.4	14.1
49.5	269.2	50.0			13.2	38.1
4.3	10.0	11.1	EBIT/Interest		8.2	7.8
2.1 (43)	2.4 (54)	4.3			3.7 (16)	4.3
.8	1.4	2.0			1.1	2.1
6.6	4.0	3.5	Net Profit + Depr., Dep.,			
2.9 (15)	2.5 (15)	2.5 (16)	Amort./Cur. Mat. L/T/D			
1.3	1.2	1.2				
.8	.5	.3			.1	.9
1.0	1.1	.9	Fixed/Worth		.6	1.0
2.9	3.3	2.6			11.4	1.6
1.2	.9	.9			.8	1.2
2.2	2.9	1.7	Debt/Worth		1.9	1.7
13.5	9.0	5.3			33.8	3.0
31.9	35.6	42.1	% Profit Before Taxes/Tangible		42.7	24.4
18.7 (31)	18.2 (38)	23.9 (49)	Net Worth		27.4 (12)	21.0 (15)
1.7	6.4	7.7			1.2	13.2
9.4	13.5	17.6	% Profit Before Taxes/Total		12.1	9.8
3.5	4.6	8.6	Assets		6.5	6.7
-.9	1.1	2.1			.2	3.8
17.8	17.4	33.8	Sales/Net Fixed Assets		42.8	8.8
7.5	7.4	11.9			17.5	6.2
5.7	4.7	5.7			8.1	3.8
3.1	2.9	3.7	Sales/Total Assets		3.6	2.3
2.4	2.3	2.3			2.5	1.9
2.0	1.8	1.7			2.3	1.3
1.2	1.4	.8	% Depr., Dep., Amort./Sales		.4	2.7
2.2 (34)	2.8 (40)	2.0 (51)			1.3 (12)	3.0 (16)
3.4	3.6	3.2			2.3	3.6
	1.7	1.4	% Officers', Directors'			
(16)	4.5 (23)	3.0	Owners' Comp/Sales			
	7.8	4.6				

2330457M	1491034M	1702900M	Net Sales ($)	1992M	14273M	36691M	66824M	202142M	1380978M
1023726M	735641M	923715M	Total Assets ($)	1947M	4667M	12545M	37703M	78831M	788022M

M = $ thousand   MM = $ million
See Pages 9 through 22 for Explanation of Ratios and Data

| Current Data Sorted by Assets | | | | | | | | Comparative Historical Data | |

Type of Statement

	0-500M	500M-2MM	2-10MM	10-50MM	50-100MM	100-250MM		4/1/06-3/31/07 ALL	4/1/07-3/31/08 ALL
Unqualified			1	5	3	3		8	8
Reviewed			6	2				2	2
Compiled		1	1	1					1
Tax Returns	1	1	1					2	4
Other	1	1	3	5	5	3		8	7
	10 (4/1-9/30/10)			34 (10/1/10-3/31/11)				ALL	ALL
NUMBER OF STATEMENTS	1	3	12	13	8	7		20	22
	%	%	%	%	%	%		%	%

ASSETS

	2-10MM	10-50MM		4/1/06-3/31/07 ALL	4/1/07-3/31/08 ALL
Cash & Equivalents	10.0	7.0		5.2	4.4
Trade Receivables (net)	33.7	25.3		36.4	23.9
Inventory	24.6	30.6		20.0	23.7
All Other Current	1.1	2.3		1.3	2.2
Total Current	69.4	65.2		62.9	54.2
Fixed Assets (net)	28.1	23.9		28.1	38.8
Intangibles (net)	.0	4.1		4.9	2.1
All Other Non-Current	2.5	6.8		4.2	5.0
Total	100.0	100.0		100.0	100.0

LIABILITIES

	2-10MM	10-50MM		4/1/06-3/31/07 ALL	4/1/07-3/31/08 ALL
Notes Payable-Short Term	10.1	11.2		11.4	6.7
Cur. Mat.-L.T.D.	2.3	2.0		3.4	6.1
Trade Payables	22.7	17.9		20.7	17.6
Income Taxes Payable	.0	.6		.2	.1
All Other Current	5.2	11.1		6.4	6.5
Total Current	40.3	42.8		42.0	37.1
Long-Term Debt	14.6	11.6		24.8	28.3
Deferred Taxes	.5	.6		.6	.7
All Other Non-Current	.5	13.5		2.0	3.0
Net Worth	44.1	31.5		30.6	30.9
Total Liabilities & Net Worth	100.0	100.0		100.0	100.0

INCOME DATA

	2-10MM	10-50MM		4/1/06-3/31/07 ALL	4/1/07-3/31/08 ALL
Net Sales	100.0	100.0		100.0	100.0
Gross Profit	27.9	24.5		25.5	25.6
Operating Expenses	20.4	20.4		21.6	22.7
Operating Profit	7.6	4.1		4.0	2.9
All Other Expenses (net)	-.4	1.7		1.2	.8
Profit Before Taxes	8.0	2.5		2.8	2.1

RATIOS

	2-10MM	10-50MM		4/1/06-3/31/07 ALL	4/1/07-3/31/08 ALL
Current	2.9	2.5		2.0	2.5
	1.5	1.8		1.6	1.8
	1.1	1.1		1.2	1.2
Quick	2.0	1.2		1.3	1.3
	1.0	.7		.9	.9
	.7	.5		.7	.6
Sales/Receivables	35 10.4	37 9.9		40 9.2	30 12.0
	42 8.7	45 8.2		49 7.5	35 10.3
	49 7.4	56 6.5		64 5.7	45 8.2
Cost of Sales/Inventory	31 11.6	52 7.0		29 12.6	39 9.4
	56 6.6	74 4.9		45 8.0	52 7.0
	84 4.3	119 3.1		58 6.3	68 5.4
Cost of Sales/Payables	24 15.1	24 15.1		19 19.3	17 21.5
	27 13.6	30 12.0		33 11.1	37 9.8
	46 7.9	50 7.3		69 5.3	59 6.2
Sales/Working Capital	5.4	4.4		7.1	5.6
	8.7	6.5		10.9	9.3
	48.3	NM		44.4	42.9
EBIT/Interest		36.5		10.7	10.7
		(12) 5.9		5.1	3.4
		2.7		.6	1.1
Net Profit + Depr., Dep., Amort./Cur. Mat. L/T/D					
Fixed/Worth	.2	.3		.4	.5
	.6	.4		1.1	.9
	2.6	NM		UND	3.3
Debt/Worth	.3	.5		1.0	.8
	1.2	1.3		1.8	1.6
	6.2	NM		UND	6.2
% Profit Before Taxes/Tangible Net Worth	62.6	58.8		58.0	40.9
	41.9	(10) 25.2		(16) 29.5	(19) 24.1
	16.3	14.9		6.3	6.7
% Profit Before Taxes/Total Assets	27.9	17.5		15.6	11.4
	12.5	9.9		7.0	5.0
	7.1	2.8		-1.8	.8
Sales/Net Fixed Assets	24.5	9.8		25.5	8.3
	9.4	7.4		7.4	4.3
	4.7	6.0		5.4	2.6
Sales/Total Assets	3.2	2.3		3.1	2.6
	2.4	1.8		2.4	1.9
	1.7	1.5		1.6	1.5
% Depr., Dep., Amort./Sales	.8	1.8		.8	2.0
	2.4	2.5		(18) 2.8	(16) 3.2
	3.7	3.9		3.7	4.5
% Officers', Directors' Owners' Comp/Sales					

	0-500M	500M-2MM	2-10MM	10-50MM	50-100MM	100-250MM		4/1/06-3/31/07 ALL	4/1/07-3/31/08 ALL
Net Sales ($)	905M	10651M	198230M	582666M	987969M	3411530M		1446480M	1531812M
Total Assets ($)	166M	3334M	71813M	297163M	527499M	1276494M		721593M	855200M

Comparative Historical Data

Current Data Sorted by Sales

			Type of Statement						
5	8	12	Unqualified				1	1	11
4	8	8	Reviewed		2		4		2
1	1	3	Compiled		1	1			1
3	2	4	Tax Returns	1	1	1			1
12	11	17	Other	1			4		12
4/1/08-3/31/09 ALL	4/1/09-3/31/10 ALL	4/1/10-3/31/11 ALL		0-1MM	10 (4/1-9/30/10) 1-3MM	3-5MM	34 (10/1/10-3/31/11) 5-10MM	10-25MM	25MM & OVER
25	30	44	**NUMBER OF STATEMENTS**	1	1	2	4	9	27
%	%	%	**ASSETS**	%	%	%	%	%	%
3.5	7.5	6.8	Cash & Equivalents						5.9
27.3	28.9	27.7	Trade Receivables (net)						24.6
28.6	21.7	25.9	Inventory						25.1
3.4	2.6	2.7	All Other Current						3.7
62.7	60.7	63.0	Total Current						59.3
31.7	27.2	26.4	Fixed Assets (net)						26.2
2.3	4.4	5.9	Intangibles (net)						9.6
3.4	7.7	4.6	All Other Non-Current						5.0
100.0	100.0	100.0	Total						100.0
			LIABILITIES						
12.4	11.5	9.5	Notes Payable-Short Term						8.6
3.8	4.7	2.1	Cur. Mat.-L.T.D.						2.3
17.4	16.0	19.1	Trade Payables						17.2
.0	.4	.3	Income Taxes Payable						.5
5.3	6.8	10.9	All Other Current						9.0
38.8	39.4	41.9	Total Current						37.6
20.1	16.4	20.4	Long-Term Debt						17.9
.9	.7	1.0	Deferred Taxes						1.4
2.8	8.8	8.7	All Other Non-Current						6.0
37.4	34.9	28.0	Net Worth						37.1
100.0	100.0	100.0	Total Liabilties & Net Worth						100.0
			INCOME DATA						
100.0	100.0	100.0	Net Sales						100.0
20.4	25.9	24.8	Gross Profit						20.8
16.8	21.5	19.4	Operating Expenses						15.4
3.6	4.4	5.4	Operating Profit						5.3
1.2	1.7	1.1	All Other Expenses (net)						1.6
2.4	2.8	4.3	Profit Before Taxes						3.7
			RATIOS						
3.2	2.6	2.5							2.5
1.6	1.8	1.6	Current						1.8
1.2	1.1	1.1							1.1
1.5	1.5	1.5							1.2
.7	.8	.8	Quick						.8
.5	.6	.6							.6
30 12.3	33 11.2	37 10.0						38	9.7
40 9.0	45 8.1	43 8.5	Sales/Receivables					44	8.3
45 8.1	53 6.9	49 7.4						49	7.5
33 11.1	33 10.9	43 8.4						45	8.2
43 8.5	49 7.5	56 6.5	Cost of Sales/Inventory					56	6.5
62 5.9	68 5.4	77 4.8						74	4.9
18 20.2	22 16.8	24 15.1						23	15.8
30 12.1	36 10.2	33 11.2	Cost of Sales/Payables					32	11.3
44 8.3	52 7.0	50 7.3						46	8.0
5.8	7.2	4.8							4.6
10.2	9.3	9.1	Sales/Working Capital						7.6
44.1	55.5	33.6							35.7
6.7	24.5	18.4							17.3
(24) 3.3	(28) 4.4	(39) 5.5	EBIT/Interest					(26)	4.2
1.1	1.8	2.0							1.4
3.8	16.9	15.7	Net Profit + Depr., Dep.,						17.0
(11) 2.2	(12) 5.5	(16) 4.6	Amort./Cur. Mat. L/T/D					(13)	4.7
1.2	1.0	1.4							1.3
.5	.3	.4							.4
.8	.8	.7	Fixed/Worth						.7
1.8	3.3	7.0							7.8
.9	.7	.8							.8
1.8	1.9	2.3	Debt/Worth						2.1
3.3	8.6	13.2							13.7
37.6	68.3	63.6	% Profit Before Taxes/Tangible						52.7
(23) 19.4	(26) 25.3	(35) 33.5	Net Worth					(21)	25.4
4.2	8.0	15.9							11.7
10.1	17.6	18.2	% Profit Before Taxes/Total						12.9
5.9	6.7	8.1	Assets						6.9
.5	.7	3.7							2.0
14.3	18.4	11.6							10.8
7.2	7.3	7.4	Sales/Net Fixed Assets						6.7
4.6	4.3	5.7							5.3
3.2	2.7	2.6							2.2
2.2	2.0	2.0	Sales/Total Assets						1.8
1.8	1.4	1.5							1.5
1.8	1.1	1.8							1.8
(18) 2.7	(24) 1.8	(40) 2.5	% Depr., Dep., Amort./Sales					(24)	2.6
3.9	4.4	3.5							3.5
		1.6	% Officers', Directors'						
		(12) 3.9	Owners' Comp/Sales						
		6.2							
1965843M	2409572M	5191951M	Net Sales ($)	905M	2989M	7662M	36499M	144259M	4999637M
931092M	1359816M	2176469M	Total Assets ($)	166M	1081M	2253M	18006M	76644M	2078319M

M = $ thousand   MM = $ million
See Pages 9 through 22 for Explanation of Ratios and Data

Current Data Sorted by Assets

Comparative Historical Data

0-500M	500M-2MM	2-10MM	10-50MM	50-100MM	100-250MM	Type of Statement	4/1/06-3/31/07 ALL	4/1/07-3/31/08 ALL
1		1	9	4	4	Unqualified	31	21
	1	13	10			Reviewed	25	19
1	3	3				Compiled	14	9
1	8	7				Tax Returns	4	5
2	2	13	15	3	1	Other	29	35
	19 (4/1-9/30/10)		83 (10/1/10-3/31/11)					
5	14	37	34	7	5	**NUMBER OF STATEMENTS**	103	89
%	%	%	%	%	%		%	%
						ASSETS		
	8.5	10.8	4.4			Cash & Equivalents	4.7	5.7
	36.7	28.7	24.3			Trade Receivables (net)	29.1	26.1
	28.4	27.2	30.3			Inventory	28.0	28.1
	.4	2.6	2.6			All Other Current	1.8	1.7
	74.0	69.3	61.6			Total Current	63.6	61.6
	20.8	25.2	33.0			Fixed Assets (net)	28.3	29.2
	1.0	.4	1.8			Intangibles (net)	3.2	4.3
	4.3	5.1	3.6			All Other Non-Current	4.9	4.9
	100.0	100.0	100.0			Total	100.0	100.0
						LIABILITIES		
	4.3	10.9	8.9			Notes Payable-Short Term	14.0	11.2
	6.4	2.8	3.2			Cur. Mat.-L.T.D.	3.6	4.1
	17.4	16.0	16.0			Trade Payables	19.2	18.0
	.2	.3	.4			Income Taxes Payable	.3	.3
	9.0	14.3	7.8			All Other Current	8.1	7.5
	37.3	44.3	36.2			Total Current	45.2	41.0
	14.2	13.2	17.8			Long-Term Debt	15.8	16.2
	.0	.4	.7			Deferred Taxes	.6	.6
	13.4	.9	2.8			All Other Non-Current	8.7	5.7
	35.1	41.0	42.5			Net Worth	29.7	36.4
	100.0	100.0	100.0			Total Liabilties & Net Worth	100.0	100.0
						INCOME DATA		
	100.0	100.0	100.0			Net Sales	100.0	100.0
	29.4	25.5	20.5			Gross Profit	22.8	23.8
	25.4	19.7	13.7			Operating Expenses	18.4	19.4
	4.0	5.8	6.8			Operating Profit	4.4	4.4
	.1	.5	.9			All Other Expenses (net)	1.2	1.5
	3.8	5.3	5.9			Profit Before Taxes	3.2	2.9
						RATIOS		
	3.9	3.0	2.3				2.3	2.5
	2.2	1.6	1.9			Current	1.6	1.6
	1.1	1.2	1.2				1.0	1.1
	2.3	2.0	1.3				1.2	1.2
	1.5	1.0	.8			Quick	.8	.8
	.5	.6	.4				.5	.5
	26 14.0	32 11.3	31 12.0				34 10.7	35 10.5
	35 10.4	46 8.0	39 9.3			Sales/Receivables	42 8.6	44 8.3
	44 8.4	52 7.0	47 7.7				52 7.1	53 6.9
	28 12.8	30 12.2	41 9.0				37 9.7	42 8.7
	39 9.5	52 7.0	60 6.1			Cost of Sales/Inventory	51 7.1	56 6.5
	54 6.8	71 5.2	87 4.2				73 5.0	81 4.5
	18 20.0	14 26.5	24 15.3				21 17.7	23 15.6
	24 15.4	28 13.2	33 11.2			Cost of Sales/Payables	33 11.0	35 10.4
	34 10.9	47 7.7	44 8.4				51 7.1	51 7.1
	4.9	6.4	5.2				5.9	5.8
	8.7	8.8	8.4			Sales/Working Capital	11.5	10.6
	110.6	25.4	19.2				131.4	42.0
	16.6	25.4	17.2				10.1	9.5
	(10) 7.6	(30) 4.8	(33) 6.1			EBIT/Interest	(99) 3.6	(83) 3.3
	3.7	2.2	1.7				1.3	1.8
			4.9				5.0	3.5
		(15) 3.9				Net Profit + Depr., Dep., Amort./Cur. Mat. L/T/D	(31) 2.7	(26) 2.3
			2.0				1.5	1.2
	.1	.2	.5				.5	.4
	.4	.5	.9			Fixed/Worth	.9	.9
	3.9	1.3	1.4				2.3	2.0
	.4	.4	.9				1.1	.9
	.8	1.3	1.5			Debt/Worth	2.7	2.1
	6.8	3.7	2.7				5.6	4.6
	61.5	39.5	42.7				56.0	39.2
	(12) 23.9	(33) 22.8	(33) 26.6			% Profit Before Taxes/Tangible Net Worth	(88) 23.1	(79) 22.8
	9.1	10.0	7.3				8.0	7.9
	23.3	16.8	21.3				14.3	14.9
	7.1	9.7	10.0			% Profit Before Taxes/Total Assets	6.7	6.6
	4.2	4.4	1.8				1.1	2.0
	65.4	41.2	12.4				15.6	16.7
	27.8	12.9	6.6			Sales/Net Fixed Assets	9.1	8.7
	11.3	6.3	4.4				5.2	4.7
	5.2	3.2	2.6				3.0	2.8
	3.1	2.5	2.0			Sales/Total Assets	2.5	2.2
	2.1	2.0	1.7				1.8	1.7
	.2	.6	1.4				1.2	1.2
	(12) 1.0	(29) 2.1	(31) 2.3			% Depr., Dep., Amort./Sales	(89) 2.1	(78) 2.3
	2.9	3.4	4.3				3.5	3.8
		1.4					1.4	1.9
		(17) 2.4				% Officers', Directors' Owners' Comp/Sales	(24) 2.6	(21) 4.0
		4.4					6.8	6.1
2921M	64020M	459194M	1492666M	739637M	1154046M	Net Sales ($)	4463622M	3946948M
1286M	17053M	175879M	726568M	443028M	757302M	Total Assets ($)	2296095M	2237107M

M = $ thousand   MM = $ million
See Pages 9 through 22 for Explanation of Ratios and Data

Comparative Historical Data

Current Data Sorted by Sales

4/1/08-3/31/09 ALL	4/1/09-3/31/10 ALL	4/1/10-3/31/11 ALL	Type of Statement	0-1MM	1-3MM	3-5MM	5-10MM	10-25MM	25MM & OVER
21	21	19	Unqualified	1			1	1	16
22	23	24	Reviewed				3	15	6
10	10	7	Compiled	2	1		1	3	
14	21	16	Tax Returns		4	4	5	3	
32	41	36	Other	2	2	2	7	6	17
					19 (4/1-9/30/10)			83 (10/1/10-3/31/11)	
99	116	102	NUMBER OF STATEMENTS	5	7	6	17	28	39
%	%	%	**ASSETS**	%	%	%	%	%	%
7.7	8.3	7.4	Cash & Equivalents				3.8	10.8	3.3
25.7	27.3	27.1	Trade Receivables (net)				31.6	29.7	22.9
26.4	23.9	27.5	Inventory				30.2	27.7	27.5
1.6	2.4	2.5	All Other Current				1.6	.9	3.6
61.4	61.8	64.6	Total Current				67.1	69.0	57.3
29.3	30.0	28.6	Fixed Assets (net)				27.3	24.6	35.0
2.8	3.1	2.6	Intangibles (net)				.3	1.2	4.1
6.4	5.1	4.3	All Other Non-Current				5.4	5.2	3.6
100.0	100.0	100.0	Total				100.0	100.0	100.0
			LIABILITIES						
10.5	9.0	8.4	Notes Payable-Short Term				10.5	9.5	8.9
4.3	4.4	3.4	Cur. Mat.-L.T.D.				4.4	3.1	2.9
16.4	17.4	15.9	Trade Payables				19.1	15.5	15.4
.2	.3	.3	Income Taxes Payable				.3	.3	.2
7.5	9.3	16.0	All Other Current				15.0	11.4	8.5
38.8	40.4	43.9	Total Current				49.2	39.8	35.9
16.7	14.1	17.1	Long-Term Debt				18.1	10.2	19.9
.8	.5	.5	Deferred Taxes				.4	.4	.9
4.2	3.8	3.8	All Other Non-Current				7.9	3.8	3.0
39.5	41.1	34.6	Net Worth				24.4	45.8	40.3
100.0	100.0	100.0	Total Liabilities & Net Worth				100.0	100.0	100.0
			INCOME DATA						
100.0	100.0	100.0	Net Sales				100.0	100.0	100.0
22.9	27.0	25.3	Gross Profit				29.0	21.5	20.3
18.0	21.6	19.4	Operating Expenses				23.2	15.1	14.8
4.8	5.4	5.8	Operating Profit				5.7	6.5	5.6
1.1	.7	1.0	All Other Expenses (net)				.8	.6	1.1
3.7	4.7	4.9	Profit Before Taxes				5.0	5.8	4.5
			RATIOS						
2.4	2.3	2.7	Current				2.4	2.9	2.3
1.6	1.6	1.9					1.6	2.0	1.8
1.2	1.1	1.2					1.1	1.3	1.2
1.4	1.6	1.7	Quick				1.5	2.0	1.2
.9	.9	.9					.9	1.2	.8
.5	.6	.5					.5	.6	.5
30 12.1	34 10.8	32 11.3	Sales/Receivables				29 12.6	32 11.6	31 11.7
38 9.7	45 8.2	41 8.8					43 8.6	40 9.1	41 8.9
49 7.5	54 6.8	52 7.0					53 6.8	50 7.3	51 7.2
31 11.8	36 10.2	37 9.9	Cost of Sales/Inventory				30 12.3	30 12.0	41 9.0
51 7.2	54 6.8	54 6.8					50 7.2	52 7.0	59 6.2
76 4.8	73 5.0	72 5.1					82 4.4	69 5.3	74 4.9
19 19.7	23 16.2	18 20.8	Cost of Sales/Payables				17 21.3	13 28.1	21 17.3
26 14.2	37 9.8	29 12.6					27 13.4	26 13.9	33 11.1
45 8.0	51 7.2	44 8.4					49 7.5	38 9.7	43 8.4
5.7	5.6	5.7	Sales/Working Capital				7.9	5.5	6.5
10.8	11.0	8.6					9.9	8.1	9.6
28.0	41.7	23.5					77.1	19.9	22.3
11.0	21.7	14.8	EBIT/Interest				27.4	20.7	14.0
(92) 3.0	(105) 4.9	(89) 5.5					(15) 4.7	(23) 6.9	5.1
1.1	2.1	2.0					2.3	2.4	1.0
4.0	5.4	5.4	Net Profit + Depr., Dep., Amort./Cur. Mat. L/T/D						8.4
(32) 2.1	(34) 2.4	(28) 3.9							(18) 3.8
.5	.4	2.0							1.6
.5	.3	.3	Fixed/Worth				.4	.2	.6
.8	.7	.8					.8	.5	1.0
2.3	1.3	1.7					NM	1.0	1.8
.6	.7	.7	Debt/Worth				.7	.5	1.0
1.8	1.6	1.6					2.1	1.2	1.7
5.7	3.7	3.6					NM	2.5	3.1
43.3	38.7	40.8	% Profit Before Taxes/Tangible Net Worth				52.6	39.3	38.7
(90) 22.5	(110) 20.8	(90) 25.0					(13) 26.0	(26) 30.4	(37) 24.1
1.0	5.4	9.0					6.6	11.8	2.9
15.3	16.0	17.6	% Profit Before Taxes/Total Assets				17.2	21.7	15.9
6.4	7.0	8.2					7.4	13.2	7.3
.3	2.2	3.0					2.8	5.3	.0
16.7	25.1	20.7	Sales/Net Fixed Assets				29.6	54.5	9.8
8.9	8.3	9.4					14.9	10.6	6.5
4.7	4.0	5.1					5.1	5.5	3.5
2.8	2.8	3.0	Sales/Total Assets				3.8	3.3	2.5
2.3	2.2	2.3					2.7	2.6	2.0
1.9	1.6	1.7					1.8	1.8	1.5
1.2	1.3	1.1	% Depr., Dep., Amort./Sales				.8	.5	1.5
(87) 2.6	(98) 2.4	(86) 2.2					(13) 1.7	(23) 2.3	(37) 2.5
4.4	4.1	3.8					3.4	4.0	4.6
1.5	1.2	1.1	% Officers', Directors' Owners' Comp/Sales					1.3	
(30) 3.0	(46) 2.6	(28) 2.3						(11) 2.3	
4.9	4.6	5.3						4.2	
5829730M	5303131M	3912484M	Net Sales ($)	2427M	13876M	25934M	127493M	510735M	3232019M
3047510M	3044119M	2121116M	Total Assets ($)	1425M	9563M	10049M	51906M	229770M	1818403M

M = $ thousand   MM = $ million
See Pages 9 through 22 for Explanation of Ratios and Data

Current Data Sorted by Assets   Comparative Historical Data

0-500M	500M-2MM	2-10MM	10-50MM	50-100MM	100-250MM	Type of Statement	ALL 4/1/06-3/31/07	ALL 4/1/07-3/31/08
1	1	4	7	2	1	Unqualified	14	15
	2	12	5			Reviewed	16	20
	2	4	1			Compiled	17	20
2	3	4				Tax Returns	7	3
	3	11	2	3		Other	31	22
	11 (4/1-9/30/10)		59 (10/1/10-3/31/11)					
3	11	35	15	5	1	NUMBER OF STATEMENTS	85	80
%	%	%	%	%	%	ASSETS	%	%
	3.6	7.8	9.4			Cash & Equivalents	8.3	7.3
	26.7	23.6	20.5			Trade Receivables (net)	25.4	26.1
	27.6	23.8	26.2			Inventory	25.0	24.8
	5.4	1.3	.7			All Other Current	1.5	1.3
	63.3	56.5	56.8			Total Current	60.2	59.5
	24.1	29.7	33.9			Fixed Assets (net)	31.3	32.9
	4.7	4.4	2.9			Intangibles (net)	3.4	1.8
	7.8	9.4	6.4			All Other Non-Current	5.1	5.8
	100.0	100.0	100.0			Total	100.0	100.0
						LIABILITIES		
	17.0	10.8	11.3			Notes Payable-Short Term	9.3	11.9
	6.3	2.9	5.3			Cur. Mat.-L.T.D.	5.3	4.6
	19.6	14.6	12.3			Trade Payables	15.3	16.0
	.0	.2	.1			Income Taxes Payable	.0	.3
	8.6	4.3	5.7			All Other Current	9.3	8.1
	51.5	32.8	34.6			Total Current	39.3	40.9
	15.2	14.5	13.5			Long-Term Debt	19.3	18.2
	.5	.7	.5			Deferred Taxes	.8	.4
	17.2	7.0	7.2			All Other Non-Current	6.2	6.0
	15.6	45.1	44.2			Net Worth	34.5	34.6
	100.0	100.0	100.0			Total Liabilities & Net Worth	100.0	100.0
						INCOME DATA		
	100.0	100.0	100.0			Net Sales	100.0	100.0
	33.5	30.7	26.4			Gross Profit	28.4	25.6
	33.6	24.4	21.7			Operating Expenses	23.0	22.1
	-.2	6.3	4.7			Operating Profit	5.4	3.5
	.5	1.4	.8			All Other Expenses (net)	1.4	1.0
	-.7	5.0	3.9			Profit Before Taxes	4.0	2.5
						RATIOS		
	1.9	3.1	2.2			Current	3.1	2.3
	1.1	1.7	1.5				1.6	1.6
	.9	1.1	1.1				1.0	1.0
	.8	1.6	1.8			Quick	1.7	1.3
	.6	.8	.8				1.0	.8
	.3	.6	.5				.4	.5
	26 14.1	36 10.2	38 9.5			Sales/Receivables	31 11.8	33 11.1
	34 10.7	51 7.2	42 8.6				38 9.5	41 8.9
	64 5.7	55 6.7	53 6.9				53 7.0	52 7.0
	36 10.2	44 8.3	42 8.6			Cost of Sales/Inventory	35 10.5	39 9.5
	60 6.1	63 5.8	73 5.0				59 6.2	52 7.1
	82 4.5	89 4.1	106 3.4				91 4.0	75 4.9
	12 29.7	21 17.1	22 16.7			Cost of Sales/Payables	17 21.1	18 20.5
	52 7.0	31 11.9	35 10.3				28 13.0	33 11.0
	67 5.5	50 7.3	48 7.6				54 6.7	48 7.5
	11.9	3.9	5.6			Sales/Working Capital	5.0	6.1
	26.3	6.9	9.0				11.1	10.7
	-30.7	81.8	56.5				-237.6	-131.9
	12.8	9.6	11.8			EBIT/Interest	10.5	8.0
(10)	5.3	(31) 4.3	(14) 2.9				(77) 2.9	(72) 2.1
	.8	1.3	-4.2				1.1	.4
		4.8				Net Profit + Depr., Dep., Amort./Cur. Mat. L/T/D	7.4	4.2
		(11) 3.4					(17) 3.8	(22) 1.8
		1.9					1.3	.1
	.5	.2	.2			Fixed/Worth	.4	.3
	.9	.8	.9				1.1	.9
	-.9	1.6	1.9				4.5	2.4
	1.0	.5	.4			Debt/Worth	.8	.7
	2.3	1.0	1.1				2.3	1.6
	-3.7	4.0	3.0				9.6	5.1
		47.3	38.9			% Profit Before Taxes/Tangible Net Worth	43.1	37.2
		(34) 17.7	(14) 20.4				(70) 20.6	(69) 10.4
		3.1	2.0				4.5	.8
	22.8	12.9	17.5			% Profit Before Taxes/Total Assets	17.2	13.4
	6.8	7.5	4.3				6.0	3.9
	-1.6	1.6	-1.7				.2	-.5
	23.8	24.4	8.8			Sales/Net Fixed Assets	18.0	18.2
	10.1	7.2	5.7				6.2	6.9
	4.8	3.4	3.2				3.5	3.3
	3.8	2.6	2.1			Sales/Total Assets	2.9	2.8
	2.3	1.6	1.9				2.1	2.2
	1.9	1.2	1.1				1.5	1.5
		1.3	2.1			% Depr., Dep., Amort./Sales	1.7	1.8
		(32) 2.3	3.3				(72) 2.9	(73) 2.9
		3.8	5.7				4.5	4.6
		2.6				% Officers', Directors' Owners' Comp/Sales	2.1	2.1
		(16) 5.5					(33) 3.7	(30) 3.5
		7.5					6.9	7.0
2292M	37328M	315858M	510141M	474870M	89325M	Net Sales ($)	2217994M	2412150M
1017M	14277M	177120M	288766M	369222M	158546M	Total Assets ($)	1469436M	1479683M

M = $ thousand   MM = $ million
See Pages 9 through 22 for Explanation of Ratios and Data

Comparative Historical Data | Current Data Sorted by Sales

Hist 1	Hist 2	Hist 3	Type of Statement	0-1MM	1-3MM	3-5MM	5-10MM	10-25MM	25MM & OVER
16	16	16	Unqualified	1		1	2	5	7
17	16	19	Reviewed		2		8	8	1
14	10	7	Compiled		2	1	2	1	1
10	5	9	Tax Returns	2	1	3	1	2	
21	28	19	Other		2	3	5	4	5
4/1/08-3/31/09 ALL	4/1/09-3/31/10 ALL	4/1/10-3/31/11 ALL		11 (4/1-9/30/10)			59 (10/1/10-3/31/11)		
78	75	70	NUMBER OF STATEMENTS	3	7	8	18	20	14
%	%	%	ASSETS	%	%	%	%	%	%
6.6	7.4	7.5	Cash & Equivalents				7.0	10.6	6.6
25.5	22.0	22.4	Trade Receivables (net)				19.9	25.2	20.7
24.2	22.8	23.7	Inventory				25.5	24.4	23.6
1.8	1.4	1.8	All Other Current				3.5	1.4	1.0
58.2	53.6	55.4	Total Current				56.0	61.6	51.9
32.0	32.0	30.3	Fixed Assets (net)				29.8	26.9	33.7
3.0	6.2	5.9	Intangibles (net)				5.7	2.3	8.5
6.8	8.2	8.3	All Other Non-Current				8.5	9.2	5.9
100.0	100.0	100.0	Total				100.0	100.0	100.0
			LIABILITIES						
10.7	11.4	11.0	Notes Payable-Short Term				9.9	10.6	9.1
4.8	5.0	4.2	Cur. Mat.-L.T.D.				4.9	3.7	4.3
14.7	13.0	13.9	Trade Payables				12.2	15.6	12.9
.3	.3	.1	Income Taxes Payable				.3	.0	.0
10.5	6.9	5.4	All Other Current				4.3	5.6	6.2
40.9	36.6	34.6	Total Current				31.5	35.6	32.6
17.1	17.1	16.9	Long-Term Debt				16.3	9.8	20.2
.6	.8	.7	Deferred Taxes				.3	1.0	1.3
5.5	5.2	8.2	All Other Non-Current				10.3	8.3	3.0
35.9	40.3	39.5	Net Worth				41.6	45.3	42.9
100.0	100.0	100.0	Total Liabilities & Net Worth				100.0	100.0	100.0
			INCOME DATA						
100.0	100.0	100.0	Net Sales				100.0	100.0	100.0
27.0	30.3	32.3	Gross Profit				30.0	28.0	27.4
23.4	26.8	26.5	Operating Expenses				20.8	24.5	20.1
3.6	3.5	5.8	Operating Profit				9.2	3.5	7.3
.7	1.3	1.4	All Other Expenses (net)				1.6	.4	1.3
2.9	2.2	4.3	Profit Before Taxes				7.6	3.1	6.0
			RATIOS						
2.6	2.7	2.4	Current				3.3	3.0	2.3
1.5	1.6	1.5					1.8	1.5	1.6
1.0	1.1	1.1					1.0	1.1	1.2
1.4	1.6	1.3	Quick				1.9	1.7	1.3
.7	.9	.8					.6	.9	.8
.5	.5	.5					.5	.6	.6
25 14.8	35 10.6	34 10.6	Sales/Receivables				34 10.6	35 10.4	38 9.7
38 9.7	42 8.7	45 8.1					50 7.3	42 8.7	45 8.2
49 7.4	52 7.0	53 6.9					54 6.7	52 7.0	54 6.7
35 10.4	48 7.6	43 8.4	Cost of Sales/Inventory				52 7.0	38 9.6	44 8.4
50 7.3	68 5.4	68 5.4					80 4.6	68 5.4	68 5.4
75 4.8	110 3.3	97 3.8					108 3.4	89 4.1	90 4.1
17 21.7	20 18.1	20 18.5	Cost of Sales/Payables				14 26.0	25 14.7	15 23.8
27 13.8	37 9.9	34 10.7					28 13.2	30 12.0	39 9.5
48 7.6	51 7.1	55 6.7					53 6.9	43 8.5	53 6.9
7.0	4.8	4.5	Sales/Working Capital				3.6	4.0	4.9
13.4	9.5	9.7					5.0	9.7	9.2
NM	54.9	79.0					NM	34.8	27.3
6.5	7.0	10.6	EBIT/Interest				14.8	10.8	24.3
(68) 2.3	(69) 2.5	(62) 3.7					(17) 3.6	(17) 4.6	(13) 3.9
.8	.6	1.3					1.6	-.8	.8
4.1	4.1	4.1	Net Profit + Depr., Dep., Amort./Cur. Mat. L/T/D						
(20) 2.9	(22) 2.1	(22) 3.0							
1.6	.9	1.8							
.5	.4	.3	Fixed/Worth				.1	.2	.7
1.0	.9	.9					.8	.6	.9
2.3	2.1	2.2					1.9	1.8	2.2
.7	.6	.7	Debt/Worth				.7	.4	.7
1.6	1.4	1.5					1.0	1.1	2.2
5.6	4.8	4.5					5.0	3.6	4.8
26.4	34.9	49.7	% Profit Before Taxes/Tangible Net Worth				56.6	59.8	67.1
(68) 10.5	(66) 14.5	(63) 19.7					(17) 21.8	(19) 15.8	21.5
1.9	-3.2	3.2					7.4	.7	3.5
10.9	10.8	13.7	% Profit Before Taxes/Total Assets				18.3	12.3	17.1
3.5	4.2	6.4					9.4	4.6	5.8
.1	-1.5	1.5					2.5	.4	1.1
15.2	13.2	16.8	Sales/Net Fixed Assets				22.9	18.7	7.6
7.6	5.6	7.0					6.7	9.0	4.9
4.6	3.7	3.4					2.7	5.4	3.3
3.4	2.2	2.4	Sales/Total Assets				2.3	2.9	2.2
2.2	1.8	1.7					1.4	1.9	1.6
1.5	1.1	1.2					1.1	1.2	1.4
1.6	1.8	1.4	% Depr., Dep., Amort./Sales				1.3	.6	2.0
(67) 2.5	(63) 3.3	(63) 3.2					(15) 2.5	(19) 2.6	3.6
4.1	5.1	4.6					5.9	4.0	7.1
2.4	1.9	3.2	% Officers', Directors' Owners' Comp/Sales						
(31) 5.4	(29) 3.7	(28) 5.8							
6.7	7.4	7.5							
2274218M	2066496M	1429814M	Net Sales ($)	1232M	17017M	31695M	117270M	292051M	970549M
1369138M	1574492M	1008948M	Total Assets ($)	1246M	8893M	22537M	83032M	162461M	730779M

M = $ thousand   MM = $ million
See Pages 9 through 22 for Explanation of Ratios and Data

Current Data Sorted by Assets   Comparative Historical Data

Type of Statement		
Unqualified	28	31
Reviewed	22	32
Compiled	22	18
Tax Returns	5	5
Other	40	45

0-500M	500M-2MM	2-10MM	10-50MM	50-100MM	100-250MM		4/1/06-3/31/07 ALL	4/1/07-3/31/08 ALL
1		6	10	3	7	Unqualified		
	4	16	3			Reviewed		
2	10	10	1	1		Compiled		
1	1					Tax Returns		
	5	12	6	6	2	Other		
		17 (4/1-9/30/10)	90 (10/1/10-3/31/11)					
4	20	44	20	10	9	**NUMBER OF STATEMENTS**	117	131
%	%	%	%	%	%	**ASSETS**	%	%
	10.0	8.3	6.9	4.9		Cash & Equivalents	7.6	5.7
	27.9	25.3	22.8	27.7		Trade Receivables (net)	25.1	26.6
	30.4	26.3	29.2	31.2		Inventory	24.7	24.9
	.3	.7	1.3	4.0		All Other Current	2.3	1.8
	68.5	60.5	60.2	67.7		Total Current	59.7	59.1
	22.9	31.0	32.0	27.0		Fixed Assets (net)	31.6	30.5
	1.1	3.2	.8	2.8		Intangibles (net)	3.8	4.9
	7.5	5.3	6.9	2.5		All Other Non-Current	4.9	5.6
	100.0	100.0	100.0	100.0		Total	100.0	100.0
						LIABILITIES		
	22.7	9.6	8.7	10.3		Notes Payable-Short Term	10.7	10.4
	5.5	4.2	5.9	1.1		Cur. Mat.-L.T.D.	3.8	5.1
	12.9	13.4	11.2	15.1		Trade Payables	14.3	14.2
	.0	.1	.0	.1		Income Taxes Payable	.2	.2
	6.5	7.8	7.1	14.9		All Other Current	8.1	8.1
	47.6	35.1	32.9	41.4		Total Current	37.1	38.0
	16.1	16.3	16.7	8.7		Long-Term Debt	14.5	16.9
	.4	1.1	.5	.2		Deferred Taxes	1.0	.8
	10.1	10.7	2.9	7.8		All Other Non-Current	6.0	6.5
	25.9	36.8	47.0	41.9		Net Worth	41.3	37.8
	100.0	100.0	100.0	100.0		Total Liabilities & Net Worth	100.0	100.0
						INCOME DATA		
	100.0	100.0	100.0	100.0		Net Sales	100.0	100.0
	24.7	29.0	29.0	22.1		Gross Profit	27.0	24.7
	24.9	23.1	22.1	16.2		Operating Expenses	21.1	20.2
	-.1	5.9	7.0	5.8		Operating Profit	5.9	4.5
	-.6	1.7	.9	.1		All Other Expenses (net)	.8	1.4
	.4	4.2	6.1	5.7		Profit Before Taxes	5.1	3.1
						RATIOS		
	4.0	3.3	4.1	3.5			2.9	2.7
	1.5	1.6	2.1	1.6	Current	1.7	1.6
	1.2	1.2	1.3	1.2		1.1	1.1
	3.0	1.4	2.3	1.3			1.5	1.5
	.9	.9	.9	.7	Quick	.9	.9
	.5	.6	.6	.6		.5	.5
	34 10.9	33 10.9	39 9.3	42 8.7			28 12.9	31 11.6
	45 8.2	41 8.8	45 8.1	56 6.5	Sales/Receivables	38 9.7	45 8.1
	61 6.0	63 5.8	62 5.9	70 5.2		52 7.0	57 6.4
	30 12.1	47 7.8	44 8.3	37 9.9			35 10.3	32 11.4
	56 6.5	56 6.5	72 5.1	94 3.9	Cost of Sales/Inventory	50 7.3	53 6.9
	101 3.6	84 4.3	135 2.7	137 2.7		83 4.4	76 4.8
	4 101.1	15 23.7	18 20.4	16 23.2			14 26.5	17 22.0
	25 14.4	29 12.6	35 10.5	37 9.8	Cost of Sales/Payables	25 14.4	32 11.6
	33 11.0	42 8.7	50 7.2	62 5.8		44 8.2	45 8.2
	4.8	4.0	3.2	3.4			5.3	5.3
	9.3	10.8	7.1	7.7	Sales/Working Capital	9.3	9.0
	18.4	26.3	16.2	17.2		46.1	60.9
	13.5	7.2	27.4				14.0	11.8
	(17) 2.3	(40) 3.5	(18) 6.4			EBIT/Interest	(108) 5.8	(122) 3.1
	-.8	1.5	2.1				1.8	.9
		8.8				Net Profit + Depr., Dep.,	7.0	8.0
		(14) 2.6				Amort./Cur. Mat. L/T/D	(37) 4.1	(41) 2.5
		.8					1.5	1.5
	.3	.4	.3	.5			.4	.4
	.7	.7	.7	.7	Fixed/Worth	.7	.7
	2.6	1.7	1.5	1.0		1.5	2.6
	.6	.8	.3	.7			.7	.7
	1.2	1.5	.7	1.4	Debt/Worth	1.3	1.3
	8.5	3.3	2.4	3.8		3.2	6.0
	61.8	29.1	37.6	47.7		% Profit Before Taxes/Tangible	49.8	35.6
	(17) 5.4	(41) 14.4	(18) 16.2	27.9		Net Worth	(107) 23.4	(112) 17.9
	.4	4.5	11.7	3.5			5.7	1.4
	14.7	13.6	18.6	16.8		% Profit Before Taxes/Total	20.1	15.1
	1.7	7.8	8.5	5.3		Assets	9.5	6.9
	-.4	1.4	4.2	1.5			1.6	.2
	19.3	14.3	7.3	8.3			12.9	14.9
	10.4	6.7	5.4	6.2	Sales/Net Fixed Assets	7.2	7.8
	6.4	3.7	3.9	4.7		4.4	4.0
	2.8	2.4	2.1	2.0			2.9	2.7
	2.3	2.0	1.8	1.7	Sales/Total Assets	2.1	2.0
	1.7	1.4	1.4	1.4		1.6	1.6
	2.0	1.5	1.5				1.7	1.6
	(17) 3.1	(40) 2.8	(19) 2.9			% Depr., Dep., Amort./Sales	(102) 2.8	(116) 2.8
	5.1	5.3	3.8				4.4	4.2
	3.1	1.3				% Officers', Directors'	1.4	1.4
	(14) 5.2	(21) 4.3				Owners' Comp/Sales	(42) 3.3	(45) 3.8
	7.4	4.9					6.7	7.3
3442M	50796M	449017M	876451M	1249144M	1799167M	Net Sales ($)	5901083M	5760168M
967M	22463M	218586M	507325M	709166M	1439827M	Total Assets ($)	3465145M	3190810M

Comparative Historical Data | Current Data Sorted by Sales

			Type of Statement						
28	30	27	Unqualified	1			1	6	19
27	19	23	Reviewed		3	4	8	5	3
14	22	24	Compiled	2	7	6	4	3	2
4	6	2	Tax Returns		2				
40	38	31	Other	1	5	1	4	6	14
4/1/08-3/31/09 ALL	4/1/09-3/31/10 ALL	4/1/10-3/31/11 ALL		0-1MM	1-3MM	3-5MM	5-10MM	10-25MM	25MM & OVER
				17 (4/1-9/30/10)			90 (10/1/10-3/31/11)		
113	115	107	NUMBER OF STATEMENTS	4	17	11	17	20	38
%	%	%	**ASSETS**	%	%	%	%	%	%
5.9	7.6	7.9	Cash & Equivalents		6.3	12.4	8.2	9.3	6.1
21.4	23.0	24.4	Trade Receivables (net)		24.2	23.3	24.1	27.7	23.7
25.6	26.5	27.3	Inventory		30.5	23.8	24.6	32.8	25.3
1.8	2.8	1.1	All Other Current		.1	.5	.7	.7	2.3
54.8	59.9	60.7	Total Current		61.1	60.0	57.6	70.5	57.4
31.9	29.2	29.0	Fixed Assets (net)		33.0	22.4	33.9	23.9	29.0
6.4	4.5	5.0	Intangibles (net)		1.1	7.8	1.4	1.9	9.0
7.0	6.4	5.3	All Other Non-Current		4.8	9.9	7.1	3.7	4.6
100.0	100.0	100.0	Total		100.0	100.0	100.0	100.0	100.0
			LIABILITIES						
13.2	12.3	11.2	Notes Payable-Short Term		21.2	5.9	11.2	10.9	8.0
5.0	3.7	4.6	Cur. Mat.-L.T.D.		6.3	3.6	4.3	3.7	4.9
10.8	12.6	12.4	Trade Payables		12.3	9.1	14.0	14.0	11.8
.0	.1	.1	Income Taxes Payable		.0	.0	.1	.1	.0
9.2	8.5	8.6	All Other Current		5.3	6.6	5.9	10.1	10.3
38.3	37.2	36.9	Total Current		45.0	25.2	35.4	38.8	35.1
18.1	14.5	15.9	Long-Term Debt		13.9	8.2	25.3	8.0	13.8
.7	.7	.8	Deferred Taxes		.4	.6	1.0	1.0	.9
7.5	8.5	8.4	All Other Non-Current		3.7	22.3	4.1	14.3	6.2
35.3	39.2	37.9	Net Worth		36.9	43.7	34.2	37.9	44.0
100.0	100.0	100.0	Total Liabilities & Net Worth		100.0	100.0	100.0	100.0	100.0
			INCOME DATA						
100.0	100.0	100.0	Net Sales		100.0	100.0	100.0	100.0	100.0
24.9	24.2	26.9	Gross Profit		28.2	29.4	32.0	26.6	24.8
21.0	22.9	22.0	Operating Expenses		24.7	26.2	24.8	21.4	18.8
3.9	1.3	4.9	Operating Profit		3.5	3.2	7.2	5.2	6.0
1.3	1.5	1.0	All Other Expenses (net)		1.1	.6	1.1	1.2	1.2
2.5	-.3	3.9	Profit Before Taxes		2.4	2.6	6.1	3.9	4.8
			RATIOS						
2.8	3.3	3.4			4.2	4.3	3.6	4.6	3.0
1.5	1.7	1.6	Current		1.4	2.4	1.8	1.6	1.6
1.0	1.1	1.2			1.0	1.3	1.2	1.3	1.2
1.4	1.8	1.8			1.7	3.3	2.0	1.7	1.6
.7	.8	.9	Quick		.6	1.3	1.0	.9	.9
.5	.5	.5			.5	.5	.6	.6	.5
27 13.5	36 10.2	36 10.2		34 10.7	31 12.0	26 14.3	35 10.4	41 9.0	
35 10.3	48 7.7	43 8.4	Sales/Receivables	42 8.7	41 8.8	56 6.6	38 9.7	47 7.7	
47 7.7	63 5.8	59 6.2		55 6.7	55 6.7	64 5.7	57 6.4	60 6.1	
37 9.9	41 8.8	43 8.6		33 11.0	45 8.0	46 7.9	47 7.8	40 9.1	
56 6.5	64 5.7	59 6.2	Cost of Sales/Inventory	61 6.0	58 6.3	59 6.2	50 7.3	70 6.2	
95 3.8	98 3.7	106 3.4		121 3.0	81 4.5	91 4.0	102 3.6	115 3.2	
12 29.4	17 21.4	15 24.4		9 38.9	9 40.1	19 19.2	8 43.0	17 21.0	
22 16.8	30 12.1	27 13.8	Cost of Sales/Payables	24 15.1	25 14.5	30 12.0	23 15.9	31 11.8	
35 10.3	43 8.4	41 8.8		35 10.4	34 10.6	67 5.4	41 8.9	43 8.5	
5.1	4.2	4.1			5.3	3.2	4.7	3.7	3.9
11.7	7.6	9.5	Sales/Working Capital		13.6	6.7	7.2	12.8	10.0
230.8	25.5	22.3			NM	16.4	31.6	17.8	18.0
7.1	6.4	9.4			10.7	6.3	9.4	12.2	11.2
(106) 2.6	(107) 1.2	(97) 3.9	EBIT/Interest		(14) 2.2	3.5	4.8	(16) 4.9	(35) 3.9
.3	-5.3	1.3			1.0	1.6	1.8	2.2	1.0
4.0	3.1	7.4							7.0
(31) 1.9	(34) 1.3	(31) 3.5	Net Profit + Depr., Dep., Amort./Cur. Mat. L/T/D						(16) 3.6
.8	.0	1.6							1.8
.4	.3	.4			.5	.2	.5	.2	.5
1.0	.7	.8	Fixed/Worth		.8	1.2	1.0	.6	.8
3.9	1.8	1.7			1.4	51.0	1.9	1.1	1.6
.5	.4	.6			.7	.3	.9	.5	.5
1.6	1.5	1.5	Debt/Worth		1.3	1.2	1.6	1.1	1.6
9.4	4.6	3.4			3.2	911.0	5.3	2.2	4.5
29.2	24.4	33.7			59.5		30.5	29.4	42.4
(91) 12.1	(100) 1.8	(95) 16.4	% Profit Before Taxes/Tangible Net Worth		(16) 4.8		(16) 23.4	(19) 14.5	(33) 16.4
-1.7	-19.6	3.8			.4		9.0	6.6	2.4
13.0	9.6	13.8			16.1	14.3	18.3	18.3	11.3
4.2	.9	6.6	% Profit Before Taxes/Total Assets		1.9	5.5	9.1	8.3	5.9
-1.6	-9.4	1.2			.2	.4	2.7	1.6	1.5
13.7	13.1	13.1			13.2	58.0	8.5	23.8	8.3
6.2	6.4	6.6	Sales/Net Fixed Assets		7.9	17.2	5.8	9.3	5.6
3.9	3.6	4.2			4.4	2.9	3.4	5.5	4.0
2.6	2.2	2.4			2.8	2.7	2.3	2.7	2.0
2.0	1.7	1.9	Sales/Total Assets		2.2	1.6	1.7	2.2	1.7
1.4	1.3	1.4			1.6	1.3	1.5	2.0	1.2
1.8	1.8	1.6			2.2		1.7	1.5	1.5
(101) 2.9	(103) 3.4	(94) 2.9	% Depr., Dep., Amort./Sales		(15) 4.3		3.9	(17) 2.0	(32) 2.9
4.4	5.4	4.5			5.4		5.5	4.3	3.7
1.7	1.9	1.7			3.2				
(39) 3.8	(34) 4.2	(40) 4.3	% Officers', Directors' Owners' Comp/Sales		(11) 5.3				
6.9	5.8	6.3			7.9				
5166648M	4101749M	4428017M	Net Sales ($)	2310M	39417M	41140M	126478M	308705M	3909967M
3023015M	2980570M	2898334M	Total Assets ($)	1335M	21091M	24579M	72300M	138737M	2640292M

M = $ thousand   MM = $ million
See Pages 9 through 22 for Explanation of Ratios and Data

Current Data Sorted by Assets / Comparative Historical Data

Type of Statement	0-500M	500M-2MM	2-10MM	10-50MM	50-100MM	100-250MM		4/1/06-3/31/07 ALL	4/1/07-3/31/08 ALL
Unqualified			2	7	2	2		15	11
Reviewed		2	8	4				6	12
Compiled			2					3	4
Tax Returns	1	1	3					2	8
Other	2		4	4	5			15	16
	9 (4/1-9/30/10)		40 (10/1/10-3/31/11)						
NUMBER OF STATEMENTS	3	3	19	15	7	2		41	51
ASSETS	%	%	%	%	%	%		%	%
Cash & Equivalents			7.7	5.1				8.4	7.6
Trade Receivables (net)			29.3	17.2				23.2	23.7
Inventory			34.3	23.4				21.3	25.9
All Other Current			1.1	2.6				1.4	2.2
Total Current			72.4	48.2				54.2	59.3
Fixed Assets (net)			22.3	36.1				34.9	27.7
Intangibles (net)			.8	5.9				4.0	6.0
All Other Non-Current			4.5	9.7				6.9	6.9
Total			100.0	100.0				100.0	100.0
LIABILITIES									
Notes Payable-Short Term			11.5	7.9				6.7	12.3
Cur. Mat.-L.T.D.			3.8	3.2				4.5	4.9
Trade Payables			12.9	12.1				18.3	15.7
Income Taxes Payable			.4	.1				.3	.2
All Other Current			6.9	3.7				9.9	8.2
Total Current			35.4	27.0				39.8	41.3
Long-Term Debt			14.0	16.4				17.0	18.7
Deferred Taxes			.8	.4				1.4	1.0
All Other Non-Current			2.7	9.8				6.8	8.0
Net Worth			47.1	46.4				35.1	31.0
Total Liabilities & Net Worth			100.0	100.0				100.0	100.0
INCOME DATA									
Net Sales			100.0	100.0				100.0	100.0
Gross Profit			26.0	25.1				22.4	23.7
Operating Expenses			20.2	20.6				19.0	19.5
Operating Profit			5.8	4.5				3.4	4.3
All Other Expenses (net)			.6	2.0				1.5	1.8
Profit Before Taxes			5.2	2.5				1.9	2.5
RATIOS									
Current			2.7	3.9				2.2	2.4
			2.0	1.7				1.3	1.5
			1.6	1.2				1.1	1.2
Quick			1.8	1.6				1.3	1.5
			1.2	1.0				.9	.9
			.6	.5				.4	.5
Sales/Receivables			39 9.4	24 15.0				27 13.3	29 12.6
			43 8.6	42 8.7				39 9.4	41 8.9
			47 7.7	57 6.4				50 7.3	50 7.3
Cost of Sales/Inventory			39 9.4	42 8.7				34 10.8	31 11.7
			65 5.6	55 6.6				41 8.9	52 7.0
			112 3.2	106 3.4				71 5.1	91 4.0
Cost of Sales/Payables			17 21.6	22 16.5				26 14.3	22 16.8
			25 14.6	31 11.9				37 9.9	32 11.4
			35 10.3	64 5.7				47 7.7	47 7.8
Sales/Working Capital			5.5	3.8				7.2	6.3
			6.6	10.6				16.9	11.5
			10.2	24.0				94.4	30.7
EBIT/Interest			24.8	12.6				9.1	14.2
			(18) 3.3	(14) 1.6				(38) 4.1	(47) 3.7
			1.9	-1.5				1.4	1.0
Net Profit + Depr., Dep., Amort./Cur. Mat. L/T/D								4.1	3.7
								(15) 2.4	(18) 2.4
								1.8	.7
Fixed/Worth			.3	.4				.5	.4
			.5	1.1				1.0	1.0
			.7	2.1				3.3	3.3
Debt/Worth			.5	.3				.8	.9
			1.5	1.3				1.8	2.4
			1.9	4.1				5.5	9.2
% Profit Before Taxes/Tangible Net Worth			51.5	26.8				49.2	48.5
			13.2	(13) 8.6				(34) 19.3	(40) 17.6
			4.3	-12.2				5.2	5.1
% Profit Before Taxes/Total Assets			25.8	10.0				13.3	14.6
			6.3	2.0				5.5	6.2
			1.9	-4.1				.6	.1
Sales/Net Fixed Assets			20.4	8.9				13.0	17.9
			10.7	3.8				6.7	8.2
			6.5	2.6				3.5	4.9
Sales/Total Assets			2.5	1.7				3.0	2.5
			2.1	1.5				2.0	2.1
			1.9	1.3				1.5	1.5
% Depr., Dep., Amort./Sales			.8	2.0				1.6	1.5
			(16) 1.5	3.7				(36) 2.8	(46) 2.6
			3.7	4.7				4.7	4.5
% Officers', Directors' Owners' Comp/Sales			.7					.9	1.2
			(13) 3.5					(12) 3.4	(17) 1.9
			5.1					5.0	6.3
Net Sales ($)	2236M	35078M	215072M	427267M	823014M	406530M		2313399M	1751145M
Total Assets ($)	831M	4882M	94261M	287381M	450813M	339532M		1297650M	1053354M

M = $ thousand   MM = $ million
See Pages 9 through 22 for Explanation of Ratios and Data

Comparative Historical Data / Current Data Sorted by Sales

11 9 3 4 21 4/1/08- 3/31/09 ALL	10 13 8 2 23 4/1/09- 3/31/10 ALL	13 14 2 4 16 4/1/10- 3/31/11 ALL	Type of Statement Unqualified Reviewed Compiled Tax Returns Other	1 1 0-1MM	9 (4/1-9/30/10) 1 1-3MM	1 1 3-5MM	4 1 1 3 5-10MM	2 8 1 1 5 40 (10/1/10-3/31/11) 10-25MM	11 1 1 1 6 25MM & OVER
48	56	49	**NUMBER OF STATEMENTS**	2	1	2	9	17	18
%	%	%	**ASSETS**	%	%	%	%	%	%
4.5	4.4	7.5	Cash & Equivalents					10.5	4.1
21.5	23.5	23.3	Trade Receivables (net)					23.0	20.4
31.7	26.6	29.3	Inventory					25.6	25.1
2.3	1.4	2.5	All Other Current					5.4	1.1
60.0	55.9	62.6	Total Current					64.5	50.6
28.2	26.5	26.4	Fixed Assets (net)					27.1	31.6
6.7	12.3	5.1	Intangibles (net)					2.2	11.7
5.1	5.3	5.9	All Other Non-Current					6.3	6.0
100.0	100.0	100.0	Total					100.0	100.0
			LIABILITIES						
10.8	9.4	9.1	Notes Payable-Short Term					7.1	8.2
5.6	8.3	3.7	Cur. Mat.-L.T.D.					4.1	2.0
15.9	15.3	14.2	Trade Payables					10.8	15.2
.1	.2	.4	Income Taxes Payable					.6	.4
7.0	7.1	6.5	All Other Current					7.3	4.4
39.4	40.4	33.9	Total Current					29.9	30.2
24.7	22.2	18.7	Long-Term Debt					15.3	23.7
.9	.9	1.1	Deferred Taxes					.2	1.7
7.0	7.3	6.8	All Other Non-Current					.8	15.4
28.0	29.3	39.5	Net Worth					53.8	29.0
100.0	100.0	100.0	Total Liabilities & Net Worth					100.0	100.0
			INCOME DATA						
100.0	100.0	100.0	Net Sales					100.0	100.0
28.2	27.8	27.4	Gross Profit					26.4	23.5
23.2	23.2	22.0	Operating Expenses					18.1	19.7
5.0	4.6	5.4	Operating Profit					8.3	3.9
2.3	1.7	1.7	All Other Expenses (net)					1.2	3.1
2.7	2.9	3.7	Profit Before Taxes					7.2	.8
			RATIOS						
2.9	2.4	2.5	Current					4.4	2.4
1.6	1.3	1.9						2.0	1.9
1.1	1.0	1.3						1.5	1.3
1.3	1.4	1.6	Quick					2.3	1.4
.8	.7	1.0						1.2	.9
.4	.5	.5						.5	.5
23 16.2	32 11.5	29 12.4	Sales/Receivables					28 13.3	34 10.8
37 9.9	40 9.2	42 8.8						39 9.4	44 8.2
51 7.2	51 7.1	54 6.7						47 7.7	65 5.6
39 9.3	39 9.3	43 8.5	Cost of Sales/Inventory					31 11.9	44 8.4
71 5.2	57 6.5	65 5.6						55 6.6	71 5.2
108 3.4	100 3.6	116 3.2						81 4.5	119 3.1
21 17.1	20 18.1	20 18.0	Cost of Sales/Payables					16 23.3	27 13.6
31 11.8	35 10.4	30 12.3						24 15.3	42 8.6
43 8.5	48 7.6	51 7.2						33 11.1	54 6.7
5.4	5.2	5.3	Sales/Working Capital					5.9	4.9
11.7	14.6	7.7						9.9	7.9
58.1	536.7	12.7						13.4	14.9
8.3	4.2	15.8	EBIT/Interest					24.6	4.4
(46) 1.8	(50) 1.7	(46) 3.0						(15) 5.6	(17) 2.0
-.5	.9	.7						.3	-1.7
3.5	2.8	6.4	Net Profit + Depr., Dep., Amort./Cur. Mat. L/T/D						
(14) 1.1	(18) 1.6	(19) 2.0							
.0	.2	1.4							
.6	.6	.4	Fixed/Worth					.2	.5
1.4	1.3	.6						.5	1.8
-8.0	-5.2	2.1						1.3	-8.1
1.0	1.2	.7	Debt/Worth					.3	1.1
3.4	3.3	1.6						1.3	3.0
-20.6	-15.4	10.4						1.7	-28.1
41.7	41.4	48.8	% Profit Before Taxes/Tangible Net Worth					51.9	23.2
(34) 17.7	(40) 15.0	(42) 14.6						(16) 33.9	(13) 8.6
-14.1	2.7	2.9						8.9	-13.7
16.4	8.7	16.5	% Profit Before Taxes/Total Assets					27.7	8.9
4.0	3.1	6.3						14.1	2.1
-4.1	.1	.4						.6	-2.9
16.1	17.1	18.4	Sales/Net Fixed Assets					24.9	9.3
7.5	7.8	8.9						9.7	4.9
4.6	4.8	3.6						3.6	3.1
2.7	2.5	2.4	Sales/Total Assets					3.0	1.9
2.2	2.0	1.9						2.0	1.5
1.6	1.5	1.5						1.5	1.2
1.2	1.4	1.2	% Depr., Dep., Amort./Sales					.8	1.7
(44) 2.3	(48) 2.3	(43) 2.3						(16) 2.2	3.0
3.6	4.2	4.3						4.3	6.3
1.7	1.8	.4	% Officers', Directors' Owners' Comp/Sales						
(15) 2.7	(18) 4.3	(18) 2.7							
7.5	6.0	4.9							
2624494M	2017690M	1909197M	Net Sales ($)	1204M	1032M	7926M	64171M	290196M	1544668M
1674757M	1342283M	1177700M	Total Assets ($)	596M	235M	3680M	30509M	141974M	1000706M

M = $ thousand   MM = $ million
See Pages 9 through 22 for Explanation of Ratios and Data

Current Data Sorted by Assets / Comparative Historical Data

Type of Statement						
Unqualified						25 / 20
Reviewed						19 / 18
Compiled						11 / 8
Tax Returns						6 / 3
Other						34 / 31

	0-500M	500M-2MM	2-10MM	10-50MM	50-100MM	100-250MM		4/1/06-3/31/07 ALL	4/1/07-3/31/08 ALL
Unqualified	2	2	3		2	3		25	20
Reviewed	1	3	7	7	1	1		19	18
Compiled		1	1	3	1			11	8
Tax Returns		1	1					6	3
Other		6	13	12	1	1		34	31
		13 (4/1-9/30/10)		57 (10/1/10-3/31/11)					
NUMBER OF STATEMENTS	3	12	25	22	5	3		95	80
	%	%	%	%	%	%		%	%
ASSETS									
Cash & Equivalents		8.2	5.9	3.4				8.1	8.5
Trade Receivables (net)		34.5	26.5	25.4				28.2	25.7
Inventory		32.9	20.6	20.9				21.3	20.7
All Other Current		1.1	1.6	1.5				1.8	3.1
Total Current		76.7	54.5	51.3				59.4	58.1
Fixed Assets (net)		19.0	32.7	33.3				30.7	33.6
Intangibles (net)		.1	3.8	9.3				4.1	2.3
All Other Non-Current		4.2	8.9	6.2				5.9	6.0
Total		100.0	100.0	100.0				100.0	100.0
LIABILITIES									
Notes Payable-Short Term		13.5	12.1	7.9				9.8	5.9
Cur. Mat.-L.T.D.		7.9	3.5	3.8				3.7	3.3
Trade Payables		24.6	13.9	13.6				16.2	14.7
Income Taxes Payable		.0	.0	.0				.1	.1
All Other Current		12.3	7.2	7.9				7.6	7.7
Total Current		58.3	36.8	33.3				37.4	31.6
Long-Term Debt		11.7	18.5	20.8				21.0	22.1
Deferred Taxes		.0	.4	1.1				.5	.4
All Other Non-Current		6.3	6.1	5.4				5.7	5.2
Net Worth		23.7	38.2	39.4				35.4	40.6
Total Liabilties & Net Worth		100.0	100.0	100.0				100.0	100.0
INCOME DATA									
Net Sales		100.0	100.0	100.0				100.0	100.0
Gross Profit		23.6	27.9	23.5				25.3	23.2
Operating Expenses		19.1	22.5	17.7				20.3	18.3
Operating Profit		4.5	5.4	5.8				5.0	4.9
All Other Expenses (net)		1.7	.8	1.3				.8	1.1
Profit Before Taxes		2.8	4.6	4.5				4.2	3.8
RATIOS									
Current		2.3	2.4	1.8				2.6	2.7
		1.5	1.5	1.4				1.7	1.8
		1.0	1.1	1.2				1.1	1.2
Quick		1.2	1.5	1.1				1.6	1.6
		.7	.7	.8				.9	1.1
		.4	.6	.6				.6	.6
Sales/Receivables	27 13.7	37 9.9	31 11.9					31 11.8	30 12.1
	42 8.6	48 7.6	44 8.2					39 9.3	42 8.8
	59 6.2	57 6.4	51 7.2					55 6.6	52 7.1
Cost of Sales/Inventory	35 10.6	29 12.4	34 10.6					27 13.5	24 15.3
	58 6.3	45 8.2	43 8.5					43 8.4	40 9.1
	102 3.6	81 4.5	58 6.3					61 6.0	57 6.5
Cost of Sales/Payables	23 15.8	21 17.7	13 28.4					17 20.9	16 22.5
	33 11.0	35 10.4	30 12.2					27 13.8	28 13.3
	57 6.4	44 8.3	42 8.7					43 8.5	39 9.4
Sales/Working Capital		6.8	5.1	7.6				6.8	6.0
		10.8	10.8	16.1				12.5	10.3
		NM	97.1	31.5				47.0	24.3
EBIT/Interest		13.7	13.5	14.1				10.4	7.7
		(11) 6.1	2.0	5.7				(88) 4.1	(74) 3.9
		-.8	.8	2.2				1.8	.7
Net Profit + Depr., Dep., Amort./Cur. Mat. L/T/D				4.9				6.2	5.5
			(11)	3.5				(27) 3.7	(27) 2.5
				1.5				1.7	1.3
Fixed/Worth		.4	.4	.6				.4	.4
		.7	1.4	1.0				.8	.9
		2.5	8.1	2.5				2.5	1.8
Debt/Worth		.8	.6	.9				.8	.5
		4.0	2.1	1.4				1.8	1.4
		7.8	18.6	3.6				6.8	4.8
% Profit Before Taxes/Tangible Net Worth		68.6	34.0	49.6				53.0	36.1
		(10) 24.6	(20) 11.0	(19) 19.2				(84) 27.3	(73) 20.0
		-1.2	-5.6	3.1				8.9	.3
% Profit Before Taxes/Total Assets		12.0	11.9	16.1				17.5	16.0
		9.4	4.6	8.3				7.7	7.9
		-1.7	-.5	1.3				2.7	-.7
Sales/Net Fixed Assets		35.2	12.1	12.1				15.0	13.7
		18.4	6.7	5.2				8.2	7.4
		6.9	3.3	4.1				5.1	3.5
Sales/Total Assets		4.4	2.4	2.5				3.2	3.0
		2.8	1.8	1.9				2.4	2.3
		1.6	1.7	1.7				1.7	1.5
% Depr., Dep., Amort./Sales		.3	1.5	2.7				1.5	1.5
		(11) 1.1	(21) 2.6	(20) 3.2				(80) 2.4	(74) 2.7
		2.5	5.3	4.5				3.8	4.4
% Officers', Directors' Owners' Comp/Sales								1.0	1.0
								(30) 3.3	(22) 2.7
								6.6	4.7
Net Sales ($)	2675M	49540M	250786M	1099554M	508302M	785210M		4848850M	4432832M
Total Assets ($)	778M	15869M	124522M	551152M	361404M	424666M		2394881M	2227113M

M = $ thousand   MM = $ million
See Pages 9 through 22 for Explanation of Ratios and Data

Comparative Historical Data   Current Data Sorted by Sales

Type of Statement

	Hist 1	Hist 2	Hist 3		0-1MM	1-3MM	3-5MM	5-10MM	10-25MM	25MM & OVER
Unqualified	20	18	15					1	2	12
Reviewed	13	14	13				2	3	5	3
Compiled	13	8	5			1	2	1		1
Tax Returns	3	3	4		1	1		2		
Other	40	23	33		1	5	5	4	7	11
	4/1/08-3/31/09 ALL	4/1/09-3/31/10 ALL	4/1/10-3/31/11 ALL		13 (4/1-9/30/10)			57 (10/1/10-3/31/11)		
NUMBER OF STATEMENTS	89	66	70		2	7	9	11	14	27

ASSETS

	Hist 1 %	Hist 2 %	Hist 3 %		0-1MM %	1-3MM %	3-5MM %	5-10MM %	10-25MM %	25MM & OVER %
Cash & Equivalents	4.8	7.5	6.0					4.7	6.4	5.7
Trade Receivables (net)	25.9	25.1	26.4					30.4	28.9	23.6
Inventory	24.0	19.8	22.0					24.7	18.6	18.9
All Other Current	4.1	2.6	1.9					2.0	2.2	2.7
Total Current	58.8	55.0	56.3					61.9	56.2	50.9
Fixed Assets (net)	33.2	34.0	30.8					27.8	38.4	32.0
Intangibles (net)	3.2	5.5	5.9					4.2	1.0	9.5
All Other Non-Current	4.8	5.5	7.1					6.1	4.4	7.6
Total	100.0	100.0	100.0					100.0	100.0	100.0

LIABILITIES

	Hist 1	Hist 2	Hist 3		0-1MM	1-3MM	3-5MM	5-10MM	10-25MM	25MM & OVER
Notes Payable-Short Term	12.0	9.0	12.1					8.2	10.3	7.0
Cur. Mat.-L.T.D.	4.7	6.0	4.5					9.9	4.7	3.2
Trade Payables	14.4	14.5	16.9					19.5	14.2	13.7
Income Taxes Payable	.1	.0	.0					.0	.0	.1
All Other Current	7.5	7.0	8.5					13.4	8.3	7.5
Total Current	38.7	36.6	42.1					51.0	37.7	31.5
Long-Term Debt	19.5	17.0	19.3					15.8	22.1	17.2
Deferred Taxes	.6	.5	.7					.2	.5	1.5
All Other Non-Current	6.5	8.6	8.8					5.8	6.7	6.2
Net Worth	34.8	37.2	29.1					27.2	33.0	43.6
Total Liabilities & Net Worth	100.0	100.0	100.0					100.0	100.0	100.0

INCOME DATA

	Hist 1	Hist 2	Hist 3		0-1MM	1-3MM	3-5MM	5-10MM	10-25MM	25MM & OVER
Net Sales	100.0	100.0	100.0					100.0	100.0	100.0
Gross Profit	23.6	25.8	26.0					26.0	26.8	19.5
Operating Expenses	21.3	23.4	21.0					23.0	22.1	15.2
Operating Profit	2.2	2.4	5.0					3.0	4.6	4.3
All Other Expenses (net)	1.1	1.6	1.2					.9	1.0	1.5
Profit Before Taxes	1.1	.8	3.8					2.1	3.7	2.8

RATIOS

	Hist 1	Hist 2	Hist 3		0-1MM	1-3MM	3-5MM	5-10MM	10-25MM	25MM & OVER
Current	2.6	2.8	2.4					2.1	2.7	2.4
	1.5	1.6	1.5					1.3	1.2	1.5
	1.2	1.0	1.1					1.0	1.1	1.3
Quick	1.4	1.7	1.3					1.3	1.9	1.2
	.8	.9	.8					.6	.8	.9
	.5	.5	.5					.5	.6	.6
Sales/Receivables	25 14.4	32 11.3	32 11.3					26 13.8	37 9.9	30 12.2
	37 9.9	47 7.8	45 8.2					47 7.7	47 7.8	42 8.6
	50 7.3	57 6.4	53 6.9					55 6.6	54 6.7	48 7.5
Cost of Sales/Inventory	30 12.2	30 12.0	32 11.6					29 12.5	30 12.4	35 10.4
	38 9.7	43 8.5	44 8.3					57 6.4	34 10.8	42 8.7
	67 5.5	67 5.5	72 5.1					73 5.0	48 7.7	51 7.2
Cost of Sales/Payables	14 26.5	15 24.7	20 18.1					15 24.9	15 25.1	18 20.3
	25 14.9	28 13.0	31 11.7					31 11.8	30 12.3	30 12.2
	34 10.6	44 8.3	45 8.1					53 6.9	40 9.2	40 9.0
Sales/Working Capital	6.2	5.3	6.1					4.2	6.2	5.7
	13.1	12.0	12.5					15.5	32.9	14.2
	55.6	NM	45.2					-189.8	85.5	27.6
EBIT/Interest	9.0	8.6	14.3					7.1	17.2	16.5
	(84) 3.3	(57) 2.7	(68) 4.9					(10) 1.6	2.5	(26) 5.1
	-.1	-1.2	1.2					.7	-.1	1.3
Net Profit + Depr., Dep., Amort./Cur. Mat. L/T/D	4.5	7.8	6.4							6.7
	(28) 2.8	(22) 3.7	(23) 3.5							(15) 4.6
	1.7	1.1	1.4							1.5
Fixed/Worth	.5	.5	.5					.6	.4	.5
	.9	1.1	1.1					.9	1.8	.7
	5.3	3.8	3.5					-4.8	NM	3.3
Debt/Worth	.7	.8	.7					.8	.5	.9
	1.9	1.8	1.8					2.9	2.2	1.3
	10.8	8.4	7.2					-19.6	NM	4.7
% Profit Before Taxes/Tangible Net Worth	32.3	42.8	47.9						34.9	48.1
	(76) 14.6	(57) 15.7	(57) 17.7						(11) 17.7	(23) 19.0
	3.3	-8.8	2.5						-10.5	3.1
% Profit Before Taxes/Total Assets	12.8	15.0	12.4					6.7	14.6	10.5
	4.4	3.9	6.5					1.6	5.1	6.4
	-1.8	-10.1	.4					.0	-4.1	.5
Sales/Net Fixed Assets	15.5	13.2	14.5					17.7	12.7	11.4
	8.3	7.1	6.4					14.7	6.0	5.2
	4.1	3.4	4.0					4.0	3.2	4.2
Sales/Total Assets	3.3	2.6	2.6					3.6	2.6	2.4
	2.4	2.0	1.9					2.2	1.8	1.9
	1.7	1.5	1.5					1.7	1.7	1.4
% Depr., Dep., Amort./Sales	1.4	2.2	1.6					1.1	2.1	2.2
	(77) 2.1	(62) 3.1	(63) 2.8					2.0	(13) 2.8	(25) 3.2
	3.9	5.3	4.7					3.8	6.0	4.5
% Officers', Directors' Owners' Comp/Sales	1.7	.7	.9							
	(22) 3.4	(16) 4.4	(17) 2.3							
	4.8	9.0	4.2							
Net Sales ($)	4188094M	2526183M	2696067M		754M	12820M	37333M	83030M	240240M	2321890M
Total Assets ($)	2095623M	1500331M	1478391M		357M	11425M	17331M	36440M	120939M	1291899M

© RMA 2011   M = $ thousand   MM = $ million
See Pages 9 through 22 for Explanation of Ratios and Data

Current Data Sorted by Assets   Comparative Historical Data

0-500M	500M-2MM	2-10MM	10-50MM	50-100MM	100-250MM	Type of Statement	4/1/06-3/31/07 ALL	4/1/07-3/31/08 ALL
		3	7		2	Unqualified	13	10
		4	1			Reviewed	4	7
		1				Compiled		1
			1			Tax Returns	2	
	3	4	6		2	Other	14	10
						7 (4/1-9/30/10) 27 (10/1/10-3/31/11)		
	3	12	15		4	**NUMBER OF STATEMENTS**	33	28
%	%	%	%	%	%	**ASSETS**	%	%
		6.2	4.4			Cash & Equivalents	8.8	7.3
		24.4	21.6			Trade Receivables (net)	22.4	22.8
		20.1	20.6			Inventory	15.4	15.1
		.9	8.2			All Other Current	2.5	1.9
		51.5	54.7			Total Current	49.1	47.1
		35.8	39.8			Fixed Assets (net)	42.2	40.8
		1.6	2.9			Intangibles (net)	4.0	5.1
		11.1	2.6			All Other Non-Current	4.7	7.0
		100.0	100.0			Total	100.0	100.0
						LIABILITIES		
		8.8	11.1			Notes Payable-Short Term	6.7	7.7
		3.1	8.9			Cur. Mat.-L.T.D.	5.6	4.0
		10.9	16.1			Trade Payables	13.2	13.8
		.0	.1			Income Taxes Payable	.2	.1
		5.6	18.5			All Other Current	12.8	6.1
		28.4	54.7			Total Current	38.6	31.7
		20.4	13.3			Long-Term Debt	25.6	27.8
		.2	.8			Deferred Taxes	1.0	1.0
		7.4	5.0			All Other Non-Current	6.4	3.9
		43.6	26.1			Net Worth	28.4	35.6
		100.0	100.0			Total Liabilties & Net Worth	100.0	100.0
						INCOME DATA		
		100.0	100.0			Net Sales	100.0	100.0
		24.3	22.7			Gross Profit	28.3	23.4
		17.5	21.5			Operating Expenses	20.8	16.9
		6.8	1.1			Operating Profit	7.4	6.6
		1.3	.4			All Other Expenses (net)	2.1	1.8
		5.6	.7			Profit Before Taxes	5.4	4.7
						RATIOS		
		2.9	2.1			Current	2.1	1.7
		1.5	1.0				1.3	1.3
		1.0	.6				.8	1.0
		1.4	1.1			Quick	1.4	1.1
		1.0	.4				.8	.7
		.6	.2				.5	.6
		34 10.7	26 14.1			Sales/Receivables	29 12.6	30 12.1
		37 9.8	44 8.4				43 8.6	42 8.6
		40 9.2	69 5.3				66 5.6	54 6.7
		32 11.5	23 16.0			Cost of Sales/Inventory	26 13.8	28 13.2
		43 8.5	35 10.5				39 9.4	35 10.4
		61 6.0	107 3.4				55 6.6	51 7.1
		11 33.8	17 20.9			Cost of Sales/Payables	20 18.0	22 16.3
		22 16.4	36 10.1				33 10.9	33 11.2
		38 9.6	84 4.3				46 7.9	54 6.8
		5.6	9.4			Sales/Working Capital	7.5	8.8
		13.5	404.7				16.1	20.0
		NM	-11.9				-27.5	91.0
		4.8	19.9			EBIT/Interest	10.6	8.0
		(11) 3.3	4.3				(31) 3.5	(27) 2.8
		2.0	2.6				1.2	1.3
						Net Profit + Depr., Dep., Amort./Cur. Mat. L/T/D	6.0	13.7
							(16) 2.4	(12) 3.4
							1.5	1.6
		.2	.5			Fixed/Worth	.6	.6
		.5	2.0				1.8	1.6
		2.4	3.9				11.4	2.5
		.7	1.7			Debt/Worth	1.0	1.3
		1.4	4.2				2.5	2.1
		2.7	11.1				14.4	4.4
		47.9	69.2			% Profit Before Taxes/Tangible Net Worth	42.2	30.2
		(11) 13.7	(13) 33.1				(26) 31.5	(25) 12.8
		6.6	9.4				8.3	1.8
		9.6	14.3			% Profit Before Taxes/Total Assets	21.7	10.9
		5.7	5.8				8.7	4.3
		3.6	1.5				.7	1.0
		74.6	31.2			Sales/Net Fixed Assets	11.1	8.8
		8.3	5.6				4.1	4.3
		2.2	2.5				1.9	2.4
		3.1	3.4			Sales/Total Assets	2.3	2.2
		2.0	2.2				1.8	1.6
		1.2	1.5				1.1	1.1
		.2	1.5			% Depr., Dep., Amort./Sales	2.5	1.6
		(11) 2.9	(14) 2.4				(26) 4.6	(24) 3.9
		5.9	8.0				5.4	5.4
						% Officers', Directors' Owners' Comp/Sales		
	16329M	135361M	868650M		904236M	Net Sales ($)	2138624M	2143560M
	3382M	64241M	308356M		708303M	Total Assets ($)	1304711M	1372486M

Columns 0-500M / 500M-2MM and 50-100MM / 100-250MM are marked "DATA NOT AVAILABLE."

M = $ thousand   MM = $ million
See Pages 9 through 22 for Explanation of Ratios and Data

Comparative Historical Data				Current Data Sorted by Sales					
			Type of Statement						
11	12	12	Unqualified			1	2	2	7
6	7	5	Reviewed				1	3	1
1		1	Compiled				1		
3	2	1	Tax Returns					1	
13	13	15	Other		1	2	2	6	4
					7 (4/1-9/30/10)		27 (10/1/10-3/31/11)		
4/1/08-3/31/09 ALL	**4/1/09-3/31/10 ALL**	**4/1/10-3/31/11 ALL**		**0-1MM**	**1-3MM**	**3-5MM**	**5-10MM**	**10-25MM**	**25MM & OVER**
34	34	34	**NUMBER OF STATEMENTS**		1	3	6	12	12
%	%	%	**ASSETS**	%	%	%	%	%	%
7.0	7.0	7.3	Cash & Equivalents	**DATA NOT AVAILABLE**				10.3	5.2
21.6	18.3	21.9	Trade Receivables (net)					26.8	18.1
16.3	17.2	20.3	Inventory					24.3	21.2
2.0	4.4	4.1	All Other Current					1.5	9.9
46.9	46.9	53.6	Total Current					62.8	54.4
41.3	43.6	37.3	Fixed Assets (net)					29.1	37.6
5.3	5.5	3.2	Intangibles (net)					3.3	4.8
6.5	4.0	5.9	All Other Non-Current					4.8	3.1
100.0	100.0	100.0	Total					100.0	100.0
			LIABILITIES						
7.7	5.0	8.3	Notes Payable-Short Term					9.1	9.2
3.7	4.3	5.6	Cur. Mat.-L.T.D.					2.4	9.6
13.6	11.2	13.6	Trade Payables					13.5	16.0
.1	.2	.0	Income Taxes Payable					.1	.0
7.6	14.2	10.7	All Other Current					5.0	16.9
32.8	34.9	38.1	Total Current					30.1	51.7
21.2	22.1	16.5	Long-Term Debt					9.2	19.5
.9	.7	.5	Deferred Taxes					.2	.8
3.6	1.8	8.9	All Other Non-Current					4.4	6.3
41.5	40.6	36.0	Net Worth					56.1	21.6
100.0	100.0	100.0	Total Liabilties & Net Worth					100.0	100.0
			INCOME DATA						
100.0	100.0	100.0	Net Sales					100.0	100.0
22.6	23.0	24.8	Gross Profit					24.4	20.1
17.7	17.2	18.8	Operating Expenses					17.4	13.0
4.9	5.8	6.0	Operating Profit					7.0	7.1
1.4	1.7	1.2	All Other Expenses (net)					.5	2.4
3.5	4.1	4.9	Profit Before Taxes					6.5	4.8
			RATIOS						
2.4	2.6	2.4						4.5	1.8
1.4	1.3	1.4	Current					2.2	1.0
.9	.9	.9						1.3	.7
1.4	1.3	1.4						2.6	.7
.7	.8	.7	Quick					1.3	.4
.5	.4	.4						.7	.3
24 15.4	**28** 12.9	**27** 13.5						**34** 10.7	**15** 24.9
32 11.4	**37** 10.0	**36** 10.2	Sales/Receivables					**41** 8.8	**29** 12.6
45 8.1	**47** 7.8	**46** 7.9						**45** 8.0	**44** 8.3
23 16.1	**27** 13.6	**24** 15.1						**31** 12.0	**17** 21.1
30 12.1	**39** 9.3	**39** 9.3	Cost of Sales/Inventory					**37** 9.9	**34** 10.8
43 8.4	**77** 4.7	**85** 4.3						**58** 6.3	**104** 3.5
17 22.1	**16** 23.3	**15** 23.6						**12** 30.5	**20** 18.2
30 12.1	**31** 11.9	**24** 15.2	Cost of Sales/Payables					**23** 15.9	**29** 12.5
39 9.4	**44** 8.3	**55** 6.6						**53** 6.9	**52** 7.0
7.3	5.9	6.9						5.3	9.9
12.0	14.0	17.2	Sales/Working Capital					8.4	339.0
-36.8	-74.1	-19.2						24.5	-12.8
10.4	15.9	16.2						65.5	25.7
(32) 1.9	(30) 4.4	(30) 3.7	EBIT/Interest					(10) 5.0	3.6
1.2	1.8	1.9						3.8	1.9
3.3		8.1							
(12) 2.1		(11) 2.3	Net Profit + Depr., Dep., Amort./Cur. Mat. L/T/D						
1.0		1.2							
.4	.7	.2						.2	.5
1.2	1.4	1.5	Fixed/Worth					.5	3.1
2.4	3.2	3.8						1.6	NM
.8	.6	.7						.3	2.4
2.1	2.1	2.1	Debt/Worth					.8	6.9
3.8	6.2	9.1						1.9	NM
36.1	33.8	58.1						44.4	
(31) 6.9	(30) 18.0	(29) 23.5	% Profit Before Taxes/Tangible Net Worth					15.9	
.2	11.5	11.3						12.3	
18.0	16.9	22.4						21.1	22.2
2.8	7.0	6.9	% Profit Before Taxes/Total Assets					9.3	5.8
.8	2.7	3.4						4.5	2.2
17.6	8.2	32.7						76.6	30.4
4.5	3.4	5.7	Sales/Net Fixed Assets					8.3	4.7
2.7	2.1	2.5						4.2	2.8
2.8	2.8	3.4						3.1	3.6
2.0	1.6	2.0	Sales/Total Assets					2.2	2.0
1.5	1.2	1.2						1.6	1.1
1.7	.8	1.1						.4	
(29) 2.9	(22) 2.9	(27) 2.8	% Depr., Dep., Amort./Sales					2.0	
5.2	5.7	5.9						2.9	
			% Officers', Directors' Owners' Comp/Sales						
2587317M	**2406121M**	**1924576M**	Net Sales ($)		**2797M**	**12622M**	**44397M**	**216764M**	**1647996M**
1466133M	**1748470M**	**1084282M**	Total Assets ($)		**792M**	**8971M**	**66899M**	**95802M**	**911818M**

M = $ thousand MM = $ million

See Pages 9 through 22 for Explanation of Ratios and Data

Current Data Sorted by Assets   Comparative Historical Data

0-500M	500M-2MM	2-10MM	10-50MM	50-100MM	100-250MM	Type of Statement	4/1/06-3/31/07 ALL	4/1/07-3/31/08 ALL
			4	1	2	Unqualified	6	4
		2	1			Reviewed	3	4
1	1	2				Compiled	3	1
	1					Tax Returns		2
1		5	3	1	2	Other	6	9
	5 (4/1-9/30/10)		22 (10/1/10-3/31/11)				18	20
2	2	9	8	2	4	NUMBER OF STATEMENTS		
%	%	%	%	%	%	**ASSETS**	%	%
						Cash & Equivalents	6.1	5.7
						Trade Receivables (net)	23.6	17.7
						Inventory	31.6	31.6
						All Other Current	1.9	3.1
						Total Current	63.2	58.1
						Fixed Assets (net)	21.9	29.4
						Intangibles (net)	9.6	8.3
						All Other Non-Current	5.3	4.3
						Total	100.0	100.0
						LIABILITIES		
						Notes Payable-Short Term	4.6	11.4
						Cur. Mat.-L.T.D.	6.0	4.5
						Trade Payables	16.6	15.0
						Income Taxes Payable	.0	.0
						All Other Current	10.3	11.6
						Total Current	37.6	42.5
						Long-Term Debt	27.7	13.4
						Deferred Taxes	.5	.9
						All Other Non-Current	19.1	5.5
						Net Worth	15.1	37.6
						Total Liabilties & Net Worth	100.0	100.0
						INCOME DATA		
						Net Sales	100.0	100.0
						Gross Profit	29.4	24.8
						Operating Expenses	23.3	24.4
						Operating Profit	6.1	.5
						All Other Expenses (net)	1.9	1.9
						Profit Before Taxes	4.2	-1.4
						RATIOS		
						Current	2.8	2.7
							2.1	1.6
							1.2	1.0
						Quick	1.8	1.3
							.9	.6
							.6	.3
						Sales/Receivables	17 22.0	14 25.8
							34 10.7	25 14.5
							55 6.7	39 9.4
						Cost of Sales/Inventory	48 7.5	47 7.7
							60 6.1	64 5.7
							103 3.5	78 4.7
						Cost of Sales/Payables	13 28.5	12 30.3
							23 16.0	23 16.0
							49 7.4	43 8.4
						Sales/Working Capital	5.1	6.9
							8.3	13.3
							27.8	-95.3
						EBIT/Interest	10.1	11.1
							(17) 2.9	(17) .3
							1.2	-2.0
						Net Profit + Depr., Dep., Amort./Cur. Mat. L/T/D		
						Fixed/Worth	.2	.4
							.7	1.4
							-22.2	3.7
						Debt/Worth	.7	.9
							1.9	1.4
							-75.1	6.7
						% Profit Before Taxes/Tangible Net Worth	31.6	42.9
							(13) 23.7	(17) 5.7
							.0	-44.6
						% Profit Before Taxes/Total Assets	21.1	15.5
							9.9	-.2
							1.0	-11.8
						Sales/Net Fixed Assets	29.9	28.0
							10.1	8.3
							7.2	5.6
						Sales/Total Assets	3.2	3.5
							2.7	2.8
							1.9	1.7
						% Depr., Dep., Amort./Sales	1.0	1.2
							(16) 1.9	(17) 2.5
							4.1	4.3
						% Officers', Directors' Owners' Comp/Sales		
1029M	3835M	108810M	279774M	235030M	609661M	Net Sales ($)	872076M	495672M
688M	2376M	40172M	177609M	173694M	731587M	Total Assets ($)	513178M	326018M

Comparative Historical Data | Current Data Sorted by Sales

Hist 4/1/08-3/31/09 ALL	Hist 4/1/09-3/31/10 ALL	Hist 4/1/10-3/31/11 ALL	Type of Statement	0-1MM	1-3MM	3-5MM	5-10MM	10-25MM	25MM & OVER
6	8	7	Unqualified					1	6
3	6	3	Reviewed			1	1	1	
	1	4	Compiled	2			1	1	
2	2	1	Tax Returns			1			
10	14	12	Other	1			2	3	6
				5 (4/1-9/30/10)			22 (10/1/10-3/31/11)		
21	31	27	**NUMBER OF STATEMENTS**	3		2	4	6	12
%	%	%	**ASSETS**	%	%	%	%	%	%

Data not available for 0-1MM through 10-25MM ranges in the ASSETS, LIABILITIES and INCOME DATA sections (marked "DATA NOT AVAILABLE").

Hist1	Hist2	Hist3	Item	25MM & OVER
4.0	6.5	6.5	Cash & Equivalents	6.8
23.5	23.7	18.4	Trade Receivables (net)	19.0
30.8	25.9	25.7	Inventory	16.9
4.0	5.5	3.0	All Other Current	3.2
62.4	61.6	53.6	Total Current	45.9
24.6	24.8	28.0	Fixed Assets (net)	32.0
6.4	8.8	12.4	Intangibles (net)	16.3
6.6	4.8	6.0	All Other Non-Current	5.8
100.0	100.0	100.0	Total	100.0
			LIABILITIES	
11.4	9.8	9.1	Notes Payable-Short Term	5.8
2.4	3.3	3.8	Cur. Mat.-L.T.D.	4.9
12.6	15.4	11.2	Trade Payables	9.3
.8	.2	.6	Income Taxes Payable	.9
8.6	9.7	10.3	All Other Current	6.9
35.8	38.4	34.9	Total Current	27.8
16.9	15.8	18.1	Long-Term Debt	16.3
.1	.3	1.2	Deferred Taxes	2.2
7.2	7.8	11.3	All Other Non-Current	7.7
39.9	37.8	34.5	Net Worth	46.0
100.0	100.0	100.0	Total Liabilities & Net Worth	100.0
			INCOME DATA	
100.0	100.0	100.0	Net Sales	100.0
24.5	29.9	30.6	Gross Profit	29.7
22.6	25.2	25.9	Operating Expenses	20.0
1.9	4.6	4.7	Operating Profit	9.7
1.6	1.0	2.8	All Other Expenses (net)	3.3
.3	3.6	1.9	Profit Before Taxes	6.4

RATIOS

Hist1	Hist2	Hist3	Ratio	25MM & OVER
3.0 / 1.8 / 1.2	2.9 / 1.7 / 1.1	2.4 / 1.7 / 1.2	Current	2.4 / 1.7 / 1.4
1.4 / .7 / .4	1.7 / 1.1 / .5	1.2 / .8 / .4	Quick	1.6 / .8 / .6
23 15.9 / 35 10.6 / 49 7.5	30 12.2 / 40 9.1 / 59 6.2	25 14.7 / 41 9.0 / 52 7.0	Sales/Receivables	46 8.0 / 48 7.6 / 54 6.8
42 8.7 / 56 6.5 / 78 4.7	44 8.4 / 63 5.8 / 79 4.6	43 8.6 / 61 6.0 / 92 4.0	Cost of Sales/Inventory	43 8.4 / 60 6.1 / 84 4.3
10 36.6 / 25 14.6 / 35 10.5	27 13.3 / 32 11.3 / 42 8.7	23 15.8 / 33 11.0 / 48 7.6	Cost of Sales/Payables	26 14.2 / 36 10.0 / 46 8.0
6.1 / 8.3 / 27.4	4.2 / 12.1 / 48.0	4.1 / 7.6 / 27.3	Sales/Working Capital	6.5 / 7.3 / 11.8
(20) 2.7 / -.4 / -3.7	(27) 22.3 / 4.9 / .3	(23) 9.1 / 2.2 / 1.2	EBIT/Interest	(11) 10.8 / 3.2 / 1.8
	(10) 6.7 / 2.6 / .5		Net Profit + Depr., Dep., Amort./Cur. Mat. L/T/D	
.3 / .6 / 233.6	.3 / .9 / 7.3	.4 / 1.1 / -1.9	Fixed/Worth	.5 / 1.0 / NM
.7 / 1.7 / 501.7	.7 / 1.6 / 33.7	.8 / 2.0 / -5.7	Debt/Worth	.9 / 2.2 / NM
(17) 25.9 / -1.7 / -18.0	(24) 50.1 / 22.4 / 3.5	(19) 35.6 / 16.8 / 6.1	% Profit Before Taxes/Tangible Net Worth	
5.9 / -3.4 / -12.9	19.8 / 5.3 / -3.4	12.5 / 3.4 / .5	% Profit Before Taxes/Total Assets	14.5 / 9.9 / 2.4
23.5 / 13.3 / 5.4	16.5 / 8.3 / 6.1	12.5 / 6.4 / 3.7	Sales/Net Fixed Assets	9.6 / 4.6 / 2.4
3.1 / 2.3 / 1.9	2.9 / 2.1 / 1.5	2.5 / 1.7 / 1.2	Sales/Total Assets	1.8 / 1.4 / .8
(19) 1.1 / 1.4 / 2.1	(26) 1.6 / 2.3 / 4.6	(19) 1.4 / 2.6 / 4.5	% Depr., Dep., Amort./Sales	
			% Officers', Directors' Owners' Comp/Sales	

Hist1	Hist2	Hist3		0-1MM	1-3MM	3-5MM	5-10MM	10-25MM	25MM & OVER
1031152M	1402315M	1238139M	Net Sales ($)	1342M		7617M	29016M	104106M	1096058M
518675M	909841M	1126126M	Total Assets ($)	1569M		18056M	12854M	41868M	1051779M

M = $ thousand   MM = $ million
See Pages 9 through 22 for Explanation of Ratios and Data

Current Data Sorted by Assets

Comparative Historical Data

						Type of Statement		
1		26	68	22	20	Unqualified	183	155
1	17	103	55	3		Reviewed	220	178
6	28	47	9	1		Compiled	105	89
14	44	34	3			Tax Returns	60	50
10	40	118	100	26	26	Other	300	300
	150 (4/1-9/30/10)		672 (10/1/10-3/31/11)				4/1/06-3/31/07	4/1/07-3/31/08
0-500M	500M-2MM	2-10MM	10-50MM	50-100MM	100-250MM		ALL	ALL
32	129	328	235	52	46	NUMBER OF STATEMENTS	868	772
%	%	%	%	%	%	ASSETS	%	%
9.1	10.7	8.3	7.9	4.8	3.3	Cash & Equivalents	6.2	7.2
26.1	30.0	26.8	25.7	20.6	17.4	Trade Receivables (net)	26.9	26.2
20.3	23.6	23.6	22.9	19.9	18.1	Inventory	22.6	22.9
4.3	1.0	2.1	2.5	3.4	3.6	All Other Current	2.0	2.3
59.7	65.4	60.8	58.9	48.8	42.5	Total Current	57.6	58.6
29.7	25.2	30.2	32.2	30.5	37.1	Fixed Assets (net)	32.5	31.8
6.0	3.3	4.0	5.3	14.8	15.2	Intangibles (net)	4.5	4.4
4.6	6.0	4.9	3.6	5.9	5.2	All Other Non-Current	5.4	5.1
100.0	100.0	100.0	100.0	100.0	100.0	Total	100.0	100.0
						LIABILITIES		
16.4	11.0	9.8	9.3	6.3	5.1	Notes Payable-Short Term	12.1	10.9
2.8	4.5	4.5	4.2	3.7	2.9	Cur. Mat.-L.T.D.	5.0	5.0
21.0	18.0	14.8	14.6	12.4	11.1	Trade Payables	16.4	16.2
.1	.1	.1	.3	.3	.2	Income Taxes Payable	.2	.2
5.0	8.6	7.5	8.0	8.3	8.0	All Other Current	9.3	8.0
45.2	42.2	36.8	36.4	31.0	27.4	Total Current	43.0	40.4
23.3	21.7	16.0	16.2	16.8	23.4	Long-Term Debt	20.1	19.1
.0	.2	.4	1.0	1.7	1.7	Deferred Taxes	.7	.6
9.0	10.6	6.6	7.2	4.8	9.2	All Other Non-Current	6.8	6.8
22.4	25.3	40.2	39.2	45.8	38.4	Net Worth	29.4	33.1
100.0	100.0	100.0	100.0	100.0	100.0	Total Liabilities & Net Worth	100.0	100.0
						INCOME DATA		
100.0	100.0	100.0	100.0	100.0	100.0	Net Sales	100.0	100.0
40.8	37.1	28.4	24.3	26.1	24.6	Gross Profit	26.3	26.7
36.4	32.3	22.6	17.8	19.2	16.6	Operating Expenses	21.3	21.5
4.4	4.8	5.9	6.5	6.9	8.0	Operating Profit	5.1	5.2
1.3	1.0	1.0	1.2	1.2	3.1	All Other Expenses (net)	1.6	1.5
3.1	3.8	4.9	5.3	5.7	4.9	Profit Before Taxes	3.5	3.7
						RATIOS		
2.7	2.9	2.9	2.9	2.3	2.3	Current	2.2	2.4
1.4	1.7	1.8	1.7	1.6	1.6		1.4	1.5
.9	1.0	1.2	1.2	1.3	1.2		1.0	1.1
1.4	2.0	1.8	1.7	1.3	1.1	Quick	1.3	1.4
.8	.9	1.0	.9	.8	.8	(867)	.8	.8
.4	.6	.6	.6	.6	.6		.5	.5

19	19.4	28	13.0	33	10.9	38	9.6	39	9.3	39	9.4	Sales/Receivables	34	10.7	32	11.4
34	10.9	40	9.2	44	8.3	47	7.7	46	7.9	47	7.8		44	8.3	43	8.5
49	7.5	52	7.0	57	6.4	60	6.1	62	5.9	58	6.2		57	6.4	53	6.9
4	85.9	23	15.8	33	11.1	37	9.7	44	8.2	47	7.8	Cost of Sales/Inventory	32	11.3	32	11.2
41	8.9	42	8.6	51	7.2	52	7.1	59	6.1	68	5.4		49	7.4	51	7.2
76	4.8	79	4.6	76	4.8	83	4.4	85	4.3	95	3.8		70	5.2	76	4.8
15	23.6	16	23.0	18	20.0	20	14.4	25	14.4	26	14.2	Cost of Sales/Payables	20	18.2	20	18.0
40	9.1	29	12.5	30	12.2	30	12.1	40	9.2	33	7.9		33	11.2	32	11.3
60	6.1	54	6.8	47	7.8	45	8.0	52	7.0	46	7.9		50	7.3	47	7.7

5.9	5.6	5.0	4.7	5.3	4.6	Sales/Working Capital	6.2	5.9
18.0	10.3	8.5	8.2	8.1	8.6		13.6	12.1
-55.9	197.1	22.8	21.0	17.8	19.1		999.8	82.2
	8.8		10.2		14.9		20.1		14.9		7.6	EBIT/Interest		8.1		8.5
(24)	1.7	(108)	3.7	(293)	4.8	(218)	6.9	(49)	6.9	(42)	4.3		(804)	3.0	(709)	2.9
	.2		1.0		1.6		2.3		2.5		1.5			1.1		1.1
			5.0		6.1		9.2		7.1		8.8	Net Profit + Depr., Dep., Amort./Cur. Mat. L/T/D		4.6		5.4
		(16)	2.1	(90)	2.8	(106)	3.4	(29)	3.4	(19)	2.5		(241)	2.3	(228)	2.5
			-.8		1.4		2.3		1.9		.7			1.4		1.3
	.1		.2		.4		.4		.6		.8	Fixed/Worth		.5		.5
	1.0		.7		.8		.9		.9		1.8			1.1		1.1
	-29.3		3.7		2.1		1.9		2.2		10.3			4.0		3.7
	.6		.7		.6		.6		.8		1.4	Debt/Worth		.9		.8
	2.2		2.5		1.7		1.4		1.6		2.3			2.3		2.1
	-7.5		13.2		4.0		3.8		6.0		15.3			10.3		8.7

	60.2		66.7		47.9		39.4		30.0		38.8	% Profit Before Taxes/Tangible Net Worth		43.6		42.4
(21)	28.0	(104)	24.4	(299)	23.8	(207)	21.3	(43)	18.4	(38)	21.4		(710)	21.1	(638)	22.4
	-.3		2.2		6.2		11.0		10.4		10.5			5.2		5.2
22.4	17.7	17.9	15.1	11.4	9.9	% Profit Before Taxes/Total Assets	13.7	15.5
5.1	6.2	8.4	8.3	8.6	6.7		6.3	6.2
-2.5	.0	1.6	3.1	4.0	3.0		.4	.5
75.7	37.1	15.1	10.7	8.3	6.1	Sales/Net Fixed Assets	13.1	13.9
16.4	14.2	8.1	5.7	5.5	3.6		6.6	6.9
5.1	6.3	4.1	3.7	3.5	2.5		3.8	4.2
4.2	3.9	2.7	2.4	1.8	1.7	Sales/Total Assets	2.7	2.8
2.7	2.6	2.1	1.8	1.5	1.4		2.1	2.1
2.1	1.8	1.5	1.4	1.1	1.1		1.6	1.6
	1.2		.8		1.5		1.9		2.3		2.9	% Depr., Dep., Amort./Sales		1.7		1.7
(19)	2.8	(101)	1.9	(301)	2.8	(228)	3.2	(49)	3.4	(27)	3.9		(766)	2.8	(684)	2.9
	4.1		4.4		4.5		4.6		5.4		5.6			4.4		4.5
	3.3		3.0		1.6		1.9					% Officers', Directors' Owners' Comp/Sales		1.7		1.4
(15)	5.9	(76)	4.9	(116)	3.1	(45)	3.1						(263)	3.3	(241)	3.2
	12.6		7.4		6.0		4.8							5.9		6.1

29219M	444162M	3472892M	9118785M	5891518M	8721442M	Net Sales ($)	31059173M	28074274M
9250M	157967M	1614074M	4965202M	3884898M	6523345M	Total Assets ($)	17823292M	15758336M

© RMA 2011

M = $ thousand   MM = $ million
See Pages 9 through 22 for Explanation of Ratios and Data

Comparative Historical Data   Current Data Sorted by Sales

			Type of Statement						
152	150	137	Unqualified	1		1	15	22	98
171	187	179	Reviewed	1	11	10	46	71	40
98	76	91	Compiled	5	12	15	34	17	8
72	61	95	Tax Returns	13	30	17	21	11	3
335	311	320	Other	9	27	29	52	70	133
4/1/08-3/31/09 ALL	4/1/09-3/31/10 ALL	4/1/10-3/31/11 ALL		0-1MM 150 (4/1-9/30/10)	1-3MM	3-5MM	5-10MM 672 (10/1/10-3/31/11)	10-25MM	25MM & OVER
828	785	822	**NUMBER OF STATEMENTS**	29	80	72	168	191	282
%	%	%	**ASSETS**	%	%	%	%	%	%
6.6	8.3	8.1	Cash & Equivalents	10.4	10.6	8.9	10.3	7.5	6.0
24.2	24.4	26.1	Trade Receivables (net)	19.4	26.0	27.3	25.9	28.4	24.9
24.5	22.7	22.7	Inventory	20.5	21.4	24.7	22.8	23.3	22.4
2.7	2.3	2.3	All Other Current	3.0	1.7	.8	2.0	2.1	3.0
58.0	57.8	59.1	Total Current	53.5	59.7	61.7	61.0	61.3	56.3
31.6	32.1	30.4	Fixed Assets (net)	31.6	30.8	28.1	29.4	30.7	31.1
5.2	5.3	5.7	Intangibles (net)	7.5	3.4	4.1	5.2	3.5	8.3
5.3	4.9	4.8	All Other Non-Current	7.4	6.1	6.1	4.3	4.5	4.3
100.0	100.0	100.0	Total	100.0	100.0	100.0	100.0	100.0	100.0
			LIABILITIES						
12.2	11.3	9.6	Notes Payable-Short Term	9.0	12.1	12.0	10.5	9.7	7.8
4.8	4.7	4.2	Cur. Mat.-L.T.D.	3.9	5.2	4.6	4.1	4.1	4.0
15.1	14.5	15.1	Trade Payables	15.6	15.4	15.9	13.7	16.7	14.7
.2	.2	.2	Income Taxes Payable	.1	.1	.0	.1	.2	.1
9.3	8.1	7.8	All Other Current	4.8	7.0	8.0	8.3	7.1	8.4
41.6	38.7	37.0	Total Current	33.3	39.8	40.5	36.8	37.8	35.2
17.9	18.2	17.7	Long-Term Debt	22.6	25.0	22.1	15.6	15.6	16.6
.6	.7	.7	Deferred Taxes	.1	.1	.4	.3	.7	1.2
7.0	6.6	7.5	All Other Non-Current	9.6	11.6	10.3	6.0	5.4	7.8
32.9	35.8	37.1	Net Worth	34.3	23.4	26.8	41.4	40.5	39.2
100.0	100.0	100.0	Total Liabilities & Net Worth	100.0	100.0	100.0	100.0	100.0	100.0
			INCOME DATA						
100.0	100.0	100.0	Net Sales	100.0	100.0	100.0	100.0	100.0	100.0
25.3	27.6	28.7	Gross Profit	45.5	38.5	35.7	30.3	24.7	24.3
21.5	23.5	22.7	Operating Expenses	37.6	34.1	31.1	24.1	19.1	17.5
3.8	4.1	6.0	Operating Profit	8.0	4.4	4.6	6.2	5.6	6.8
1.4	1.5	1.2	All Other Expenses (net)	1.8	1.3	1.2	1.1	.7	1.5
2.4	2.6	4.8	Profit Before Taxes	6.1	3.1	3.4	5.1	4.9	5.3
			RATIOS						
2.4	2.5	2.8		4.3	3.3	3.0	3.3	2.6	2.5
1.5	1.6	1.7	Current	1.6	1.8	1.7	1.9	1.7	1.7
1.0	1.1	1.2		.9	.9	1.0	1.2	1.2	1.2
1.3	1.5	1.7		2.5	1.9	2.2	2.2	1.6	1.4
.8	.8	.9	Quick	.8	.9	.8	1.1	.9	.8
.5	.5	.6		.4	.6	.5	.6	.7	.6
30 12.1	34 10.8	34 10.8		23 15.7	26 14.1	33 11.2	33 11.1	34 10.7	38 9.7
40 9.1	46 8.0	44 8.2	Sales/Receivables	44 8.3	40 9.2	44 8.3	44 8.4	43 8.5	47 7.7
51 7.2	59 6.2	58 6.3		59 6.1	58 6.3	55 6.7	56 6.5	55 6.7	59 6.1
34 10.7	36 10.0	33 10.9		15 24.7	23 15.6	34 10.6	33 11.2	32 11.5	38 9.7
52 7.0	57 6.5	52 7.0	Cost of Sales/Inventory	58 6.3	47 7.8	64 5.7	52 7.1	47 7.8	55 6.7
79 4.6	84 4.3	80 4.6		99 3.7	88 4.1	94 3.9	82 4.5	68 5.4	80 4.6
18 20.1	20 18.1	19 19.3		16 23.5	14 26.7	18 20.0	17 21.7	20 18.0	22 16.3
29 12.5	33 11.2	31 11.9	Cost of Sales/Payables	36 10.0	30 12.2	32 11.3	27 13.3	32 11.5	32 11.5
44 8.3	49 7.4	47 7.7		71 5.1	54 6.7	57 6.4	48 7.7	46 7.9	46 7.9
5.8	5.0	5.1		4.4	4.2	5.0	4.7	5.5	5.2
12.4	9.8	8.8	Sales/Working Capital	13.5	8.0	8.3	8.1	10.3	9.0
999.8	43.6	27.2		-42.6	-57.8	92.5	23.0	24.8	20.0
7.7	8.9	14.6		8.3	10.5	6.8	14.7	16.5	16.8
(769) 2.6	(716) 3.2	(734) 4.8	EBIT/Interest	(21) 4.6	(69) 2.3	(65) 3.5	(138) 4.0	(175) 5.6	(266) 6.7
.7	.7	1.7		.4	.1	.8	1.7	2.0	2.3
4.3	5.6	6.8			6.5	3.7	5.0	6.0	9.2
(267) 2.4	(244) 2.3	(260) 3.1	Net Profit + Depr., Dep., Amort./Cur. Mat. L/T/D	(12) 2.7	(12) 1.9	(39) 2.6	(68) 2.9	(129) 3.7
1.0	.9	1.7			-.4	.2	1.4	1.7	2.0
.4	.4	.4		.2	.3	.4	.3	.4	.4
1.1	1.0	.9	Fixed/Worth	1.0	1.0	1.2	.8	.8	.9
3.5	2.8	2.3		42.8	NM	2.7	2.2	1.9	2.2
.9	.7	.7		.4	.7	1.1	.4	.7	.7
2.0	1.9	1.7	Debt/Worth	1.5	2.9	2.7	1.6	1.6	1.7
7.7	6.0	5.1		NM	-35.1	7.0	4.0	3.7	4.6
34.9	35.5	45.8		60.1	52.7	44.7	46.3	48.8	39.9
(682) 15.6	(664) 14.2	(712) 22.5	% Profit Before Taxes/Tangible Net Worth	(22) 29.6	(59) 18.0	(62) 23.8	(150) 24.7	(178) 23.1	(241) 21.2
.7	.7	8.2		-.1	.0	4.0	6.4	9.4	12.5
12.0	12.8	15.7		22.9	14.6	12.7	17.7	17.7	14.2
4.6	4.3	7.8	% Profit Before Taxes/Total Assets	5.7	3.7	5.7	7.5	10.0	8.3
-1.0	-1.0	2.0		-.3	-1.4	.1	1.7	2.5	3.7
14.5	13.0	15.1		39.2	35.8	17.7	16.7	13.6	10.8
6.9	5.9	7.2	Sales/Net Fixed Assets	5.7	8.9	8.5	8.4	7.6	5.9
4.0	3.4	4.0		2.8	3.5	3.9	4.1	4.3	3.7
2.8	2.5	2.6		2.7	3.4	2.9	2.6	2.9	2.4
2.1	1.8	2.0	Sales/Total Assets	1.8	2.1	1.9	2.0	2.2	1.8
1.5	1.3	1.5		1.0	1.3	1.5	1.5	1.7	1.3
1.7	1.8	1.9		1.7	1.2	1.4	1.4	1.5	1.9
(724) 3.0	(670) 3.3	(725) 3.0	% Depr., Dep., Amort./Sales	(19) 3.6	(65) 2.8	(58) 2.8	(153) 2.8	(178) 2.8	(252) 3.1
4.6	5.2	4.7		8.8	5.4	4.5	4.9	4.3	4.7
1.7	2.0	2.0		2.0	3.6	3.1	1.9	1.4	1.6
(242) 3.8	(223) 3.9	(257) 3.8	% Officers', Directors' Owners' Comp/Sales	(13) 5.8	(42) 5.8	(34) 5.4	(72) 3.7	(61) 2.3	(35) 3.5
6.2	7.0	6.4		16.4	9.9	7.3	6.0	4.6	4.9
31305117M	25551409M	27678018M	Net Sales ($)	17444M	167940M	282095M	1230800M	3104792M	22874947M
18684007M	16177132M	17154736M	Total Assets ($)	11580M	93102M	165111M	674880M	1559884M	14650179M

Current Data Sorted by Assets   Comparative Historical Data

0-500M	500M-2MM	2-10MM	10-50MM	50-100MM	100-250MM	Type of Statement	4/1/06-3/31/07 ALL	4/1/07-3/31/08 ALL
	1	1	1		1	Unqualified	2	3
	1	7	1	1		Reviewed	7	5
	1	3				Compiled	7	9
2	6	3	1			Tax Returns	10	6
	2	3	1	3	2	Other	14	16
	3 (4/1-9/30/10)		37 (10/1/10-3/31/11)					
2	11	17	6	1	3	NUMBER OF STATEMENTS	40	39
%	%	%	%	%	%	**ASSETS**	%	%
	25.8	4.3				Cash & Equivalents	8.4	8.3
	10.8	27.6				Trade Receivables (net)	27.2	26.3
	28.8	37.0				Inventory	31.6	31.6
	2.0	2.7				All Other Current	2.8	2.4
	67.4	71.7				Total Current	69.9	68.7
	19.7	22.4				Fixed Assets (net)	24.3	27.2
	5.9	.5				Intangibles (net)	2.4	1.4
	7.0	5.5				All Other Non-Current	3.4	2.8
	100.0	100.0				Total	100.0	100.0
						LIABILITIES		
	2.2	11.4				Notes Payable-Short Term	8.2	10.7
	5.7	2.1				Cur. Mat.-L.T.D.	2.9	3.5
	26.5	32.5				Trade Payables	38.2	28.3
	.1	.1				Income Taxes Payable	.4	.2
	4.7	6.7				All Other Current	7.8	9.1
	39.1	52.8				Total Current	57.5	51.8
	19.4	17.4				Long-Term Debt	11.8	15.5
	.0	.4				Deferred Taxes	.7	.5
	3.2	2.4				All Other Non-Current	5.3	3.7
	38.2	27.1				Net Worth	24.6	28.4
	100.0	100.0				Total Liabilities & Net Worth	100.0	100.0
						INCOME DATA		
	100.0	100.0				Net Sales	100.0	100.0
	34.2	29.0				Gross Profit	32.3	34.5
	29.9	26.7				Operating Expenses	29.2	30.3
	4.3	2.3				Operating Profit	3.1	4.2
	.3	.3				All Other Expenses (net)	-.1	.9
	4.0	2.0				Profit Before Taxes	3.2	3.3
						RATIOS		
	3.4	1.8					1.8	1.6
	1.7	1.4				Current	1.4	1.3
	1.2	1.0					1.0	1.0
	2.5	.9					1.0	1.0
	1.0	.6				Quick	.7	.7
	.3	.4					.4	.4
	1 391.1	27 13.5					15 24.9	21 17.5
	3 107.2	36 10.2				Sales/Receivables	35 10.3	35 10.6
	27 13.3	41 8.9					49 7.4	50 7.3
	20 18.0	43 8.6					38 9.5	54 6.7
	42 8.8	60 6.0				Cost of Sales/Inventory	61 6.0	67 5.5
	94 3.9	90 4.1					80 4.6	95 3.8
	16 22.3	32 11.4					30 12.3	27 13.5
	40 9.2	62 5.8				Cost of Sales/Payables	54 6.8	66 5.6
	84 4.4	76 4.8					72 5.1	83 4.4
	5.7	9.1					8.6	10.7
	11.0	16.9				Sales/Working Capital	16.7	19.6
	41.6	98.2					107.8	-122.8
		11.4					14.3	8.6
		7.1				EBIT/Interest	(37) 4.6	(35) 3.1
		2.9					2.3	1.3
							4.2	3.7
						Net Profit + Depr., Dep., Amort./Cur. Mat. L/T/D	(12) 2.8	(13) 1.7
							1.2	1.0
	.2	.3					.3	.4
	.4	.5				Fixed/Worth	1.0	.9
	2.1	NM					1.6	3.4
	.8	.9					1.1	1.2
	1.3	2.1				Debt/Worth	2.8	3.3
	6.5	NM					4.9	9.7
	102.0	48.4					47.6	69.3
	(10) 32.3	(13) 17.1				% Profit Before Taxes/Tangible Net Worth	(35) 25.7	(34) 22.4
	8.5	5.3					9.9	10.8
	19.5	8.8					12.5	9.7
	9.2	5.2				% Profit Before Taxes/Total Assets	5.3	4.9
	4.1	1.7					1.6	1.4
	42.9	30.1					31.0	26.3
	17.8	17.3				Sales/Net Fixed Assets	12.4	10.3
	10.9	7.0					6.3	5.5
	3.3	3.5					3.6	3.2
	2.6	2.8				Sales/Total Assets	2.9	2.5
	2.3	1.4					2.2	1.9
		.6					1.1	1.2
	(16)	1.5				% Depr., Dep., Amort./Sales	(37) 2.1	(36) 2.0
		2.4					2.7	3.1
							.6	.6
						% Officers', Directors' Owners' Comp/Sales	(17) 1.6	(17) .9
							3.4	4.3
2571M	36572M	229462M	391820M	153108M	612427M	Net Sales ($)	890828M	989823M
831M	11782M	83294M	146268M	68060M	395697M	Total Assets ($)	343679M	418367M

© RMA 2011

M = $ thousand   MM = $ million
See Pages 9 through 22 for Explanation of Ratios and Data

Comparative Historical Data

Current Data Sorted by Sales

			Type of Statement						
5	4	4	Unqualified	1			1	1	2
4	4	10	Reviewed	2		1	2	5	2
6	8	4	Compiled		1	2	1	1	
11	14	12	Tax Returns	6	3	1	1	2	
12	13	10	Other	2		1	1	1	6
4/1/08-3/31/09 ALL	4/1/09-3/31/10 ALL	4/1/10-3/31/11 ALL		0-1MM	3 (4/1-9/30/10) 1-3MM	3-5MM	37 (10/1/10-3/31/11) 5-10MM	10-25MM	25MM & OVER
38	43	40	**NUMBER OF STATEMENTS**	9	6	5	10	10	
%	%	%	**ASSETS**	%	%	%	%	%	%
5.3	9.5	11.5	Cash & Equivalents					7.6	2.2
25.4	22.4	20.4	Trade Receivables (net)	D				27.9	21.1
40.3	34.5	32.0	Inventory	A				43.2	30.2
1.7	1.4	2.7	All Other Current	T				1.5	3.8
72.7	67.9	66.7	Total Current	A				80.1	57.3
19.6	20.5	24.0	Fixed Assets (net)					17.6	30.9
4.2	4.1	4.0	Intangibles (net)	N				.6	7.5
3.6	7.5	5.3	All Other Non-Current	O				1.7	4.3
100.0	100.0	100.0	Total	T				100.0	100.0
			LIABILITIES	A					
11.1	8.2	7.8	Notes Payable-Short Term	V				9.2	10.9
2.2	4.4	3.1	Cur. Mat.-L.T.D.	A				2.9	2.7
27.1	26.6	29.4	Trade Payables	I				44.4	28.6
.0	.1	.1	Income Taxes Payable	L				.2	.2
9.3	9.1	5.9	All Other Current	A				5.2	4.9
49.7	48.4	46.3	Total Current	B				61.9	47.3
13.0	20.2	18.5	Long-Term Debt	L				7.7	20.6
.2	.1	.2	Deferred Taxes	E				.6	.1
5.6	4.6	4.7	All Other Non-Current					2.5	4.1
31.5	26.7	30.3	Net Worth					27.2	27.9
100.0	100.0	100.0	Total Liabilities & Net Worth					100.0	100.0
			INCOME DATA						
100.0	100.0	100.0	Net Sales					100.0	100.0
31.0	31.2	31.7	Gross Profit					24.2	32.4
28.8	29.0	28.9	Operating Expenses					21.1	31.2
2.2	2.2	2.8	Operating Profit					3.1	1.2
-.3	.5	.1	All Other Expenses (net)					.2	-.8
2.5	1.7	2.7	Profit Before Taxes					2.9	2.0
			RATIOS						
2.0	2.2	1.8						1.7	1.5
1.3	1.4	1.4	Current					1.3	1.3
1.2	1.0	1.1						1.1	1.0
.8	1.3	1.0						.8	.6
.5	.6	.6	Quick					.5	.5
.4	.3	.4						.4	.4
21 17.5	12 29.6	19 18.8						24 15.2	15 23.7
34 10.7	32 11.6	30 12.1	Sales/Receivables					32 11.4	28 12.8
46 7.9	46 7.9	39 9.4						36 10.1	41 8.8
59 6.2	33 11.2	41 9.0						49 7.5	52 7.0
79 4.6	64 5.7	60 6.1	Cost of Sales/Inventory					63 5.8	75 4.9
116 3.1	97 3.7	91 4.0						88 4.2	93 3.9
29 12.5	31 11.8	33 11.1						46 7.9	41 8.9
52 7.0	54 6.7	63 5.8	Cost of Sales/Payables					66 5.5	67 5.5
73 5.0	76 4.8	78 4.7						78 4.7	81 4.5
7.6	6.8	8.4						9.6	14.6
15.4	16.4	15.6	Sales/Working Capital					18.8	19.4
25.8	106.0	42.4						45.6	83.6
6.7	8.6	11.8						19.9	
(36) 2.7	(38) 2.7	(34) 5.2	EBIT/Interest					9.3	
1.0	.8	3.0						4.3	
6.5	4.1	16.2							
(11) 1.7	(10) 1.0	(10) 7.3	Net Profit + Depr., Dep., Amort./Cur. Mat. L/T/D						
1.2	.4	3.2							
.3	.2	.3						.3	.8
.6	.5	.8	Fixed/Worth					.5	1.3
1.6	6.8	4.0						1.5	6.0
1.3	.8	1.0						.9	2.3
2.8	2.7	2.3	Debt/Worth					2.1	4.4
6.6	12.3	9.3						11.0	11.2
40.0	42.7	41.9							30.1
(34) 18.3	(37) 10.2	(34) 17.1	% Profit Before Taxes/Tangible Net Worth						16.6
2.4	1.2	8.5							4.5
9.7	9.0	9.2						10.8	7.6
3.2	3.1	5.3	% Profit Before Taxes/Total Assets					8.3	3.3
.0	.3	2.4						5.1	1.7
37.1	37.1	27.7						89.9	19.4
15.9	14.4	14.9	Sales/Net Fixed Assets					19.3	9.8
8.2	7.2	7.0						8.6	4.8
3.3	3.9	3.2						3.9	3.0
2.7	2.8	2.7	Sales/Total Assets					3.0	2.3
2.0	1.9	1.9						2.6	1.8
.8	.8	.7							
(33) 1.5	(37) 1.6	(35) 1.5	% Depr., Dep., Amort./Sales						
2.4	2.8	2.6							
.5	.7	.8							
(17) 1.0	(16) 1.3	(16) 1.5	% Officers', Directors' Owners' Comp/Sales						
2.0	3.0	2.3							
1510190M	1411025M	1425960M	Net Sales ($)	16668M	24490M	38342M	179831M	1166629M	
615928M	552404M	705932M	Total Assets ($)	8437M	11297M	18381M	60969M	606848M	

© RMA 2011

M = $ thousand   MM = $ million
See Pages 9 through 22 for Explanation of Ratios and Data

Current Data Sorted by Assets   **Comparative Historical Data**

0-500M	500M-2MM	2-10MM	10-50MM	50-100MM	100-250MM	Type of Statement	4/1/06-3/31/07 ALL	4/1/07-3/31/08 ALL
		1	1	4	4	Unqualified	11	15
	5	6		1		Reviewed	10	10
	2	3	1			Compiled	7	2
	1	2	1			Tax Returns	3	2
	1	5	8	3	1	Other	15	13
	2							
5 (4/1-9/30/10)		**47 (10/1/10-3/31/11)**						
	5	17	17	8	5	**NUMBER OF STATEMENTS**	46	42
%	%	%	%	%	%	**ASSETS**	%	%
		10.8	10.6			Cash & Equivalents	6.9	9.6
		24.2	19.7			Trade Receivables (net)	26.0	24.3
		31.2	27.3			Inventory	31.0	32.8
		.8	2.3			All Other Current	1.8	2.6
		66.9	59.9			Total Current	65.7	69.3
		24.3	18.0			Fixed Assets (net)	22.5	18.4
		5.6	11.7			Intangibles (net)	5.7	5.8
		3.2	10.3			All Other Non-Current	6.0	6.4
		100.0	100.0			Total	100.0	100.0
						LIABILITIES		
		8.7	4.4			Notes Payable-Short Term	8.4	7.2
		3.4	2.9			Cur. Mat.-L.T.D.	3.2	3.0
		12.8	12.3			Trade Payables	14.1	12.7
		.1	.2			Income Taxes Payable	.5	.2
		8.7	8.7			All Other Current	9.1	10.5
		33.7	28.5			Total Current	35.3	33.7
		9.8	10.4			Long-Term Debt	14.2	15.5
		.3	.6			Deferred Taxes	.4	.6
		3.6	7.4			All Other Non-Current	6.4	7.0
		52.5	53.2			Net Worth	43.7	43.2
		100.0	100.0			Total Liabilities & Net Worth	100.0	100.0
						INCOME DATA		
		100.0	100.0			Net Sales	100.0	100.0
		33.3	27.6			Gross Profit	31.5	30.6
		24.4	18.5			Operating Expenses	24.6	24.1
		8.9	9.1			Operating Profit	6.9	6.6
		.8	1.2			All Other Expenses (net)	.9	.9
		8.1	8.0			Profit Before Taxes	6.1	5.7
						RATIOS		
		3.8	3.8			Current	3.0	3.2
		2.2	2.0				2.2	2.4
		1.1	1.3				1.3	1.7
		2.1	2.3			Quick	1.5	1.9
		1.2	1.0				1.0	1.2
		.5	.4				.7	.7
	35	10.6	35 10.5			Sales/Receivables	35 10.5	35 10.3
	44	8.3	45 8.2				45 8.0	43 8.5
	55	6.6	51 7.1				60 6.1	52 7.0
	56	6.5	63 5.8			Cost of Sales/Inventory	46 8.0	55 6.6
	72	5.1	81 4.5				66 5.5	67 5.4
	116	3.2	107 3.4				109 3.4	113 3.2
	18	20.8	16 23.5			Cost of Sales/Payables	22 16.7	15 23.9
	31	11.9	34 10.8				32 11.4	29 12.7
	57	6.4	42 8.6				48 7.7	38 9.5
		3.9	3.2			Sales/Working Capital	4.4	3.0
		6.9	7.0				6.1	5.7
		251.0	16.3				14.8	10.1
		29.8	35.3			EBIT/Interest	23.8	16.8
	(16)	13.3	(15) 9.2				(44) 7.9	(38) 3.6
		4.0	3.6				1.9	2.2
						Net Profit + Depr., Dep., Amort./Cur. Mat. L/T/D	11.9	10.0
							(17) 3.7	(18) 4.7
							1.0	2.1
		.2	.2			Fixed/Worth	.2	.2
		.4	.6				.5	.5
		1.7	.9				1.2	1.0
		.4	.4			Debt/Worth	.7	.5
		.8	1.4				1.0	1.4
		3.1	2.5				3.5	3.7
		50.3	42.1			% Profit Before Taxes/Tangible Net Worth	55.8	36.9
	(16)	25.9	(16) 22.6				(41) 22.6	(36) 24.0
		11.5	18.4				3.0	10.7
		24.2	15.0			% Profit Before Taxes/Total Assets	17.9	18.7
		11.4	12.7				10.9	8.1
		4.4	4.7				1.7	3.4
		18.5	16.9			Sales/Net Fixed Assets	22.7	27.8
		7.2	9.6				10.3	10.7
		5.6	7.8				5.9	6.9
		2.8	2.3			Sales/Total Assets	2.6	2.8
		2.0	1.8				2.0	1.9
		1.2	1.2				1.5	1.4
		1.3	.5			% Depr., Dep., Amort./Sales	.9	.5
	(16)	1.8	1.7				(43) 1.8	(37) 1.6
		2.6	2.6				2.9	2.8
						% Officers', Directors' Owners' Comp/Sales	2.4	2.3
	(18)						(18) 3.9	(10) 3.9
							7.0	9.8
17576M	160227M	545485M	855374M	1238151M		Net Sales ($)	1660319M	1959491M
5997M	77239M	360487M	593204M	755133M		Total Assets ($)	810816M	1152968M

M = $ thousand   MM = $ million
See Pages 9 through 22 for Explanation of Ratios and Data

Comparative Historical Data | Current Data Sorted by Sales

Type of Statement	H: 4/1/08-3/31/09 ALL	H: 4/1/09-3/31/10 ALL	H: 4/1/10-3/31/11 ALL		0-1MM	1-3MM	3-5MM	5-10MM	10-25MM	25MM & OVER
Unqualified	13	11	12			1	1	1		9
Reviewed	8	6	12			1		2	4	5
Compiled	7	5	6			1		2	3	
Tax Returns	4	2	4			1		1	2	
Other	16	16	18		1	1		2	6	8
					5 (4/1-9/30/10)			47 (10/1/10-3/31/11)		
NUMBER OF STATEMENTS	48	40	52		1	4	2	8	15	22
ASSETS	%	%	%		%	%	%	%	%	%
Cash & Equivalents	8.4	8.1	9.3						10.4	8.8
Trade Receivables (net)	22.3	22.8	22.5						19.4	22.4
Inventory	29.1	29.7	28.7						25.6	30.6
All Other Current	3.0	4.1	1.7						1.2	2.7
Total Current	62.8	64.6	62.2						56.6	64.5
Fixed Assets (net)	21.0	20.7	22.3						22.0	21.5
Intangibles (net)	7.7	6.4	9.6						13.9	9.8
All Other Non-Current	8.5	8.3	5.9						7.5	4.2
Total	100.0	100.0	100.0						100.0	100.0
LIABILITIES										
Notes Payable-Short Term	10.2	9.0	7.9						7.0	5.7
Cur. Mat.-L.T.D.	2.7	3.4	4.5						2.9	4.0
Trade Payables	12.0	11.2	13.9						11.0	13.8
Income Taxes Payable	.2	.1	.4						.0	.8
All Other Current	8.5	8.7	8.2						7.7	8.4
Total Current	33.6	32.4	35.0						28.7	32.7
Long-Term Debt	12.8	11.4	11.3						12.4	8.8
Deferred Taxes	.5	.5	.7						.8	1.1
All Other Non-Current	8.7	8.7	5.6						6.4	5.5
Net Worth	44.4	47.0	47.4						51.7	51.9
Total Liabilities & Net Worth	100.0	100.0	100.0						100.0	100.0
INCOME DATA										
Net Sales	100.0	100.0	100.0						100.0	100.0
Gross Profit	29.6	31.7	30.8						30.5	26.9
Operating Expenses	22.1	24.7	22.0						20.7	19.5
Operating Profit	7.5	7.1	8.8						9.8	7.4
All Other Expenses (net)	.9	.8	.5						1.7	-.7
Profit Before Taxes	6.6	6.3	8.3						8.0	8.1
RATIOS										
Current	3.8 / 2.2 / 1.3	3.9 / 2.1 / 1.4	3.1 / 2.1 / 1.2						3.9 / 2.1 / 1.0	3.1 / 2.2 / 1.4
Quick	1.9 / .9 / .5	1.9 / (39) 1.1 / .7	1.8 / .9 / .5						2.3 / 1.1 / .4	1.5 / .9 / .5
Sales/Receivables	30 12.0 / 38 9.5 / 51 7.2	40 9.1 / 48 7.6 / 56 6.5	36 10.2 / 46 8.0 / 53 6.9						27 13.4 / 39 9.3 / 50 7.3	42 8.8 / 46 8.0 / 53 6.9
Cost of Sales/Inventory	51 7.1 / 68 5.4 / 105 3.5	63 5.8 / 99 3.7 / 140 2.6	59 6.2 / 81 4.5 / 118 3.1						59 6.2 / 72 5.1 / 97 3.8	65 5.6 / 99 3.7 / 127 2.9
Cost of Sales/Payables	18 19.9 / 29 12.5 / 41 9.0	18 19.8 / 30 12.3 / 41 9.0	18 19.9 / 35 10.5 / 58 6.3						15 24.5 / 25 14.5 / 44 8.3	24 15.3 / 35 10.5 / 57 6.4
Sales/Working Capital	4.2 / 7.6 / 21.9	2.8 / 6.1 / 10.5	3.4 / 6.9 / 19.9						4.6 / 5.6 / 464.7	3.2 / 6.5 / 10.7
EBIT/Interest	24.9 / (44) 9.4 / 3.0	16.8 / (37) 8.6 / 2.2	34.2 / (48) 11.6 / 3.7						29.2 / (13) 9.2 / 2.5	38.1 / (21) 26.7 / 6.7
Net Profit + Depr., Dep., Amort./Cur. Mat. L/T/D	8.7 / (17) 4.4 / 2.6	6.6 / (15) 4.0 / 2.0	7.5 / (20) 5.2 / 1.2							8.4 / (10) 5.6 / 1.5
Fixed/Worth	.2 / .4 / 1.8	.2 / .5 / .9	.2 / .6 / 1.5						.1 / .6 / 1.7	.3 / .6 / 1.0
Debt/Worth	.5 / 1.4 / 3.7	.7 / 1.2 / 2.4	.5 / 1.4 / 3.7						.6 / 1.4 / 3.4	.5 / 1.3 / 3.4
% Profit Before Taxes/Tangible Net Worth	41.8 / (43) 24.1 / 10.3	39.5 / (35) 21.4 / 5.0	50.2 / (47) 23.1 / 16.2						51.1 / (14) 29.3 / 16.6	53.7 / (21) 25.9 / 18.7
% Profit Before Taxes/Total Assets	16.8 / 10.2 / 4.4	18.4 / 7.2 / 2.1	18.6 / 11.7 / 5.7						18.3 / 11.4 / 5.0	16.4 / 12.4 / 8.8
Sales/Net Fixed Assets	24.9 / 10.1 / 6.5	17.6 / 7.8 / 4.7	16.1 / 8.8 / 5.3						24.7 / 7.7 / 5.1	13.1 / 9.0 / 5.2
Sales/Total Assets	2.6 / 1.9 / 1.4	2.1 / 1.6 / 1.1	2.3 / 1.8 / 1.2						2.5 / 1.6 / 1.2	2.2 / 1.8 / 1.2
% Depr., Dep., Amort./Sales	.5 / (45) 1.1 / 2.5	.7 / (33) 1.5 / 2.6	.9 / (48) 1.7 / 2.6						.6 / 1.8 / 2.6	.9 / (20) 1.7 / 2.7
% Officers', Directors' Owners' Comp/Sales	1.5 / (13) 3.5 / 4.8	1.9 / (12) 3.1 / 5.6	1.8 / (18) 2.5 / 4.1							
Net Sales ($)	1867386M	1495493M	2816813M		775M	9331M	8477M	62529M	232943M	2502758M
Total Assets ($)	1168204M	1050821M	1792060M		518M	6541M	6602M	29659M	200067M	1548673M

M = $ thousand   MM = $ million
See Pages 9 through 22 for Explanation of Ratios and Data

Current Data Sorted by Assets / Comparative Historical Data

0-500M	500M-2MM	2-10MM	10-50MM	50-100MM	100-250MM	Type of Statement	4/1/06-3/31/07 ALL	4/1/07-3/31/08 ALL
		1	2	2	1	Unqualified	12	8
		9				Reviewed	12	8
	1	3		1		Compiled	4	2
	1	1		1		Tax Returns	5	2
1	2	9	2			Other	18	22
	8 (4/1-9/30/10)		29 (10/1/10-3/31/11)					
1	4	23	4	4	1	**NUMBER OF STATEMENTS**	51	42
%	%	%	%	%	%	**ASSETS**	%	%
		9.1				Cash & Equivalents	6.4	8.4
		29.7				Trade Receivables (net)	29.2	27.8
		22.3				Inventory	22.6	20.0
		3.5				All Other Current	3.3	2.0
		64.6				Total Current	61.4	58.1
		28.4				Fixed Assets (net)	31.0	34.1
		2.2				Intangibles (net)	3.2	2.0
		4.8				All Other Non-Current	4.4	5.8
		100.0				Total	100.0	100.0
						LIABILITIES		
		14.6				Notes Payable-Short Term	12.4	18.4
		3.7				Cur. Mat.-L.T.D.	3.0	2.4
		15.5				Trade Payables	15.3	14.3
		.7				Income Taxes Payable	.4	.2
		11.4				All Other Current	9.0	9.4
		45.9				Total Current	40.1	44.8
		10.9				Long-Term Debt	15.9	16.9
		1.3				Deferred Taxes	.9	.8
		9.3				All Other Non-Current	7.3	6.6
		32.6				Net Worth	35.8	30.9
		100.0				Total Liabilities & Net Worth	100.0	100.0
						INCOME DATA		
		100.0				Net Sales	100.0	100.0
		28.5				Gross Profit	27.0	29.3
		19.2				Operating Expenses	22.6	23.4
		9.3				Operating Profit	4.4	6.0
		1.1				All Other Expenses (net)	1.2	1.5
		8.2				Profit Before Taxes	3.2	4.4
						RATIOS		
		2.4					3.0	2.4
		1.6				Current	1.6	1.3
		1.2					1.1	1.0
		1.4					2.0	1.3
		.9				Quick	.8	.7
		.6					.6	.5
	35	10.4					39 9.3	35 10.3
	46	8.0				Sales/Receivables	46 7.9	46 8.0
	56	6.5					56 6.5	54 6.7
	36	10.0					24 15.0	28 12.8
	51	7.2				Cost of Sales/Inventory	44 8.2	39 9.3
	67	5.5					82 4.5	76 4.8
	17	20.9					18 20.8	17 21.1
	28	13.2				Cost of Sales/Payables	25 14.7	26 13.9
	38	9.6					48 7.6	44 8.2
		4.9					5.6	6.6
		9.6				Sales/Working Capital	8.6	20.5
		37.3					60.8	-141.8
		18.9					12.8	11.6
	(22)	7.7				EBIT/Interest	(47) 3.4	(39) 2.9
		5.5					.9	.5
						Net Profit + Depr., Dep.,	7.9	5.5
						Amort./Cur. Mat. L/T/D	(13) 3.0	(10) 2.3
							.9	1.1
		.4					.3	.5
		.7				Fixed/Worth	.9	1.2
		1.5					2.5	2.9
		.7					.7	.8
		1.5				Debt/Worth	2.2	2.5
		4.7					5.0	5.9
		80.9				% Profit Before Taxes/Tangible	44.6	44.9
	(21)	36.5				Net Worth	(43) 19.7	(35) 23.1
		19.8					2.8	-3.4
		25.3				% Profit Before Taxes/Total	13.9	19.5
		13.9				Assets	5.8	7.2
		9.8					-.7	-1.9
		17.8					15.2	14.0
		7.1				Sales/Net Fixed Assets	8.0	5.8
		4.5					4.1	3.5
		2.9					2.9	2.6
		2.1				Sales/Total Assets	2.0	2.0
		1.9					1.6	1.6
		.9					1.6	2.3
	(22)	2.2				% Depr., Dep., Amort./Sales	(37) 2.9	(35) 3.1
		3.7					4.2	4.7
						% Officers', Directors'	3.5	2.6
						Owners' Comp/Sales	(16) 4.9	(12) 8.4
							10.0	11.8
1429M	14302M	273857M	122710M	275493M	276773M	Net Sales ($)	1240735M	1053442M
374M	5114M	114075M	59152M	252271M	138744M	Total Assets ($)	726265M	685534M

© RMA 2011

M = $ thousand   MM = $ million
See Pages 9 through 22 for Explanation of Ratios and Data

Comparative Historical Data

Current Data Sorted by Sales

						Type of Statement								
	7		14		6	Unqualified						1	1	4
	8		4		9	Reviewed						4	5	
	7		5		5	Compiled		1		1		2		1
	2		5		3	Tax Returns		2		1		4	1	
	13		18		14	Other		2			2	4	5	3
	4/1/08-3/31/09 ALL		4/1/09-3/31/10 ALL		4/1/10-3/31/11 ALL			8 (4/1-9/30/10)				29 (10/1/10-3/31/11)		
							0-1MM	1-3MM		3-5MM		5-10MM	10-25MM	25MM & OVER
	37		46		37	NUMBER OF STATEMENTS		3		3		11	12	8
	%		%		%	ASSETS	%	%		%		%	%	%
	7.0		8.0		10.0	Cash & Equivalents						9.9	5.0	
	24.3		25.0		29.2	Trade Receivables (net)	D					27.6	33.5	
	25.5		24.6		21.5	Inventory	A					21.4	25.7	
	1.7		3.8		2.7	All Other Current	T					2.7	3.2	
	58.5		61.5		63.5	Total Current	A					61.6	67.4	
	34.7		27.9		25.1	Fixed Assets (net)						35.0	21.0	
	2.3		3.4		5.7	Intangibles (net)	N					.8	1.6	
	4.5		7.2		5.8	All Other Non-Current	O					2.7	10.1	
	100.0		100.0		100.0	Total	T					100.0	100.0	
						LIABILITIES	A							
	16.1		12.8		11.6	Notes Payable-Short Term	V					8.6	13.1	
	3.1		4.0		4.3	Cur. Mat.-L.T.D.	A					3.3	4.1	
	16.9		13.2		13.2	Trade Payables	I					8.9	19.8	
	.3		.4		.5	Income Taxes Payable	L					.1	1.2	
	12.0		14.1		10.9	All Other Current	A					9.6	10.3	
	48.4		44.6		40.5	Total Current	B					30.6	48.5	
	15.1		9.3		10.6	Long-Term Debt	L					9.7	8.5	
	1.0		.8		1.3	Deferred Taxes	E					1.6	1.2	
	8.1		13.9		7.5	All Other Non-Current						3.6	1.4	
	27.4		31.4		40.1	Net Worth						54.5	40.3	
	100.0		100.0		100.0	Total Liabilties & Net Worth						100.0	100.0	
						INCOME DATA								
	100.0		100.0		100.0	Net Sales						100.0	100.0	
	26.7		33.7		30.3	Gross Profit						26.6	28.2	
	22.0		28.2		20.7	Operating Expenses						16.1	20.2	
	4.7		5.5		9.7	Operating Profit						10.6	8.0	
	1.8		.8		1.1	All Other Expenses (net)						1.6	.6	
	2.9		4.7		8.5	Profit Before Taxes						9.0	7.3	
						RATIOS								
	2.0		3.3		3.5							2.8	1.9	
	1.2		1.4		1.8	Current						2.0	1.4	
	.9		1.0		1.2							1.6	1.1	
	1.1		1.3		2.3							2.0	1.1	
	.6		.7		1.0	Quick						1.3	.7	
	.4		.5		.6							.8	.6	
31	11.9	30	12.3	37	9.9						39	9.4	37	9.9
37	9.8	47	7.8	48	7.6	Sales/Receivables					53	6.9	48	7.7
46	7.9	58	6.3	59	6.2						57	6.4	60	6.1
31	11.8	35	10.3	41	8.9						36	10.0	30	12.1
51	7.1	59	6.2	47	7.8	Cost of Sales/Inventory					51	7.1	51	7.2
65	5.6	82	4.4	65	5.6						67	5.4	81	4.5
20	18.4	17	21.9	17	21.7						16	22.5	23	16.2
26	14.1	29	12.8	24	15.1	Cost of Sales/Payables					18	20.2	31	11.7
43	8.5	46	7.9	38	9.6						28	13.2	39	9.4
	6.5		5.0		4.5							4.5	7.6	
	24.9		13.2		7.6	Sales/Working Capital						5.4	10.0	
	-44.2		-296.1		23.7							14.5	126.1	
	9.6		10.1		18.9							18.4	31.8	
(33)	2.4	(41)	3.6	(34)	7.6	EBIT/Interest						9.6	(11)	13.3
	.3		1.6		5.3							5.5	7.4	
	3.2		8.7		4.5	Net Profit + Depr., Dep.,								
(13)	1.9	(15)	3.6	(13)	3.2	Amort./Cur. Mat. L/T/D								
	.5		.9		1.3									
	.6		.2		.3							.4	.2	
	1.2		1.0		.7	Fixed/Worth						.7	.5	
	2.3		2.5		1.7							.8	1.5	
	.8		.6		.5							.5	.8	
	2.4		2.0		1.5	Debt/Worth						.9	2.2	
	4.6		6.1		3.9							1.5	4.2	
	49.4		44.9		62.7	% Profit Before Taxes/Tangible						36.5	161.9	
(32)	24.8	(37)	17.7	(33)	35.5	Net Worth						25.6	37.0	
	-2.3		4.0		19.8							12.9	21.1	
	14.2		13.7		22.1	% Profit Before Taxes/Total						24.6	23.4	
	5.2		6.7		12.6	Assets						11.1	14.1	
	-3.8		1.1		8.6							9.0	11.7	
	15.8		21.4		17.5							7.1	19.6	
	7.2		8.2		8.2	Sales/Net Fixed Assets						6.2	14.5	
	3.5		3.5		4.8							3.1	5.5	
	2.9		2.6		2.9							2.4	3.7	
	2.0		1.8		2.1	Sales/Total Assets						2.2	2.1	
	1.6		1.3		1.4							1.4	2.0	
	1.3		1.7		1.1							2.2	.8	
(34)	2.8	(37)	3.4	(35)	2.2	% Depr., Dep., Amort./Sales				(10)	3.5	(11)	1.4	
	4.9		5.3		4.4							4.6	2.5	
	1.4				2.6	% Officers', Directors'								
(10)	3.5			(13)	4.1	Owners' Comp/Sales								
	9.7				4.9									
	844131M		728776M		964564M	Net Sales ($)		5464M	12809M		78212M		183517M	684562M	
	523617M		547832M		569730M	Total Assets ($)		2445M	7351M		41080M		86001M	432853M	

M = $ thousand   MM = $ million
See Pages 9 through 22 for Explanation of Ratios and Data

Current Data Sorted by Assets   Comparative Historical Data

Type of Statement	0-500M	500M-2MM	2-10MM	10-50MM	50-100MM	100-250MM		4/1/06-3/31/07 ALL	4/1/07-3/31/08 ALL
Unqualified	1	1	8	8	5	1		21	24
Reviewed		4	21	10				37	34
Compiled	1	5	11	1				18	12
Tax Returns	4	4	2					6	7
Other	2	7	18	9	5	3		34	46
		27 (4/1-9/30/10)		104 (10/1/10-3/31/11)					
NUMBER OF STATEMENTS	8	21	60	28	10	4		116	123
	%	%	%	%	%	%		%	%
ASSETS									
Cash & Equivalents		15.5	9.0	8.7	2.3			7.1	6.9
Trade Receivables (net)		25.9	24.8	29.7	21.4			27.9	27.5
Inventory		23.0	28.5	25.3	27.9			22.2	25.2
All Other Current		3.5	1.7	2.5	8.9			2.0	2.2
Total Current		67.9	64.0	66.3	60.6			59.2	61.9
Fixed Assets (net)		25.1	26.1	23.3	28.5			28.2	26.8
Intangibles (net)		3.8	2.5	4.7	6.6			4.4	4.5
All Other Non-Current		3.2	7.4	5.8	4.3			8.2	6.9
Total		100.0	100.0	100.0	100.0			100.0	100.0
LIABILITIES									
Notes Payable-Short Term		10.4	8.4	10.8	9.9			10.9	11.5
Cur. Mat.-L.T.D.		1.2	2.5	3.0	9.3			2.6	3.0
Trade Payables		14.6	14.8	13.4	8.6			16.2	14.7
Income Taxes Payable		.0	.4	.3	.2			.1	.2
All Other Current		3.8	8.8	7.2	17.4			9.9	9.6
Total Current		30.1	34.9	34.8	45.4			39.6	39.1
Long-Term Debt		16.6	13.0	8.9	12.0			12.2	14.5
Deferred Taxes		.4	1.0	.7	1.3			.7	.6
All Other Non-Current		4.2	9.5	5.8	8.2			5.1	8.0
Net Worth		48.7	41.6	49.8	33.1			42.4	37.8
Total Liabilities & Net Worth		100.0	100.0	100.0	100.0			100.0	100.0
INCOME DATA									
Net Sales		100.0	100.0	100.0	100.0			100.0	100.0
Gross Profit		38.2	30.1	25.0	26.1			26.4	26.6
Operating Expenses		30.9	24.8	18.7	20.2			21.8	22.7
Operating Profit		7.3	5.3	6.3	5.9			4.6	3.9
All Other Expenses (net)		.2	1.4	.5	.8			1.4	1.4
Profit Before Taxes		7.1	4.0	5.9	5.1			3.1	2.6
RATIOS									
Current		5.1	3.6	3.4	1.9			2.7	2.8
		2.5	2.2	2.1	1.6			1.7	1.7
		1.3	1.2	1.3	1.2			1.1	1.1
Quick		3.4	2.3	2.1	1.0			1.6	1.7
		1.2	1.1	1.3	.5			1.0 (122)	.9
		.8	.5	.7	.4			.6	.5
Sales/Receivables	15	24.1	33 11.0	48 7.6	36 10.1			35 10.5	37 10.0
	33	10.9	41 8.8	52 7.0	42 8.7			43 8.4	45 8.1
	48	7.6	53 6.9	60 6.1	59 6.2			53 6.9	56 6.6
Cost of Sales/Inventory	19	18.7	42 8.6	36 10.2	48 7.7			28 13.1	32 11.2
	47	7.8	71 5.1	69 5.3	71 5.2			44 8.2	53 6.9
	98	3.7	123 3.0	98 3.7	117 3.1			84 4.4	97 3.8
Cost of Sales/Payables	14	25.4	19 19.5	24 14.9	17 22.1			17 21.2	18 20.5
	25	14.7	31 11.7	30 12.0	25 14.6			29 12.6	29 12.7
	43	8.5	47 7.7	36 10.1	31 11.9			41 8.9	42 8.6
Sales/Working Capital		4.0	4.3	4.2	6.1			5.6	5.0
		6.0	7.2	6.6	8.2			9.8	9.6
		15.3	20.7	14.8	NM			59.2	32.2
EBIT/Interest		10.7	8.6	54.1	8.9			10.5	9.5
	(19)	4.3	(49) 4.6	(22) 13.4	5.0			(104) 3.1	(108) 2.8
		2.3	1.7	5.5	4.0			1.2	1.0
Net Profit + Depr., Dep., Amort./Cur. Mat. L/T/D			4.1					8.3	5.1
			(15) 2.8					(37) 2.5	(31) 2.0
			1.5					1.2	.8
Fixed/Worth		.2	.2	.3	.7			.3	.2
		.4	.5	.4	.9			.7	.6
		1.4	1.4	.9	2.5			1.6	2.0
Debt/Worth		.3	.4	.4	1.3			.4	.6
		1.1	1.1	1.3	2.6			1.6	1.8
		3.7	3.1	2.8	7.5			4.2	5.9
% Profit Before Taxes/Tangible Net Worth		70.7	25.0	35.1				47.3	42.3
	(19)	29.9	(54) 13.0	(27) 24.4				(103) 15.0	(107) 15.1
		5.2	4.5	8.4				3.8	2.1
% Profit Before Taxes/Total Assets		34.0	12.2	16.7	11.9			15.0	14.0
		12.2	5.6	9.3	6.9			4.9	5.6
		3.6	1.8	6.5	4.3			.4	-.1
Sales/Net Fixed Assets		93.2	30.1	20.6	9.0			21.5	20.4
		13.4	9.8	8.6	5.9			9.7	10.1
		5.7	5.0	5.5	4.3			4.4	4.5
Sales/Total Assets		3.2	2.7	2.3	2.0			3.2	2.9
		2.5	2.1	1.9	1.8			2.0	2.0
		1.7	1.5	1.5	1.4			1.4	1.6
% Depr., Dep., Amort./Sales		.7	1.0	.8				1.0	1.1
	(14)	1.8	(56) 1.9	2.4				(106) 2.1	(105) 2.0
		3.8	3.0	3.8				3.5	3.3
% Officers', Directors' Owners' Comp/Sales		3.5	1.1					1.6	2.8
	(10)	4.7	(20) 3.8					(37) 3.8	(36) 4.2
		6.6	7.9					5.5	6.4
Net Sales ($)	7870M	80714M	641273M	1057771M	1248609M	1277443M		2902188M	3634434M
Total Assets ($)	1706M	27794M	295602M	563792M	715832M	787343M		1587742M	1967695M

M = $ thousand   MM = $ million
See Pages 9 through 22 for Explanation of Ratios and Data

Comparative Historical Data | Current Data Sorted by Sales

			Type of Statement	0-1MM	1-3MM	3-5MM	5-10MM	10-25MM	25MM & OVER
15	25	24	Unqualified	2		1	1	4	16
36	24	35	Reviewed			5	12	9	9
16	14	18	Compiled		3	3	7	4	1
7	14	10	Tax Returns	4	2	2	1	1	
60	45	44	Other	4	4	4	9	9	14
4/1/08-3/31/09 ALL	4/1/09-3/31/10 ALL	4/1/10-3/31/11 ALL		27 (4/1-9/30/10)		104 (10/1/10-3/31/11)			
134	122	131	NUMBER OF STATEMENTS	10	9	15	30	27	40
%	%	%	ASSETS	%	%	%	%	%	%
8.1	9.2	9.4	Cash & Equivalents	9.1		17.1	8.7	14.5	3.9
26.1	26.7	25.0	Trade Receivables (net)	20.0		26.4	22.1	27.0	29.2
24.7	24.2	26.9	Inventory	27.6		26.1	30.2	26.2	26.8
2.3	2.7	2.6	All Other Current	1.0		4.2	1.0	2.3	4.1
61.2	62.9	63.8	Total Current	57.7		73.8	61.9	70.0	64.0
25.8	27.2	25.7	Fixed Assets (net)	33.7		15.6	27.3	21.6	25.5
5.4	4.1	4.4	Intangibles (net)	6.2		1.7	2.5	3.1	6.7
7.5	5.9	6.0	All Other Non-Current	2.5		8.9	8.3	5.2	3.8
100.0	100.0	100.0	Total	100.0		100.0	100.0	100.0	100.0
			LIABILITIES						
12.1	12.5	11.6	Notes Payable-Short Term	15.6		12.8	6.7	5.7	11.6
3.5	3.2	2.8	Cur. Mat.-L.T.D.	.2		2.5	2.8	1.2	5.0
14.6	14.8	13.6	Trade Payables	8.1		15.3	13.3	16.3	14.0
.2	.1	.2	Income Taxes Payable	.0		.3	.2	.5	.2
11.3	7.9	8.1	All Other Current	3.3		5.3	5.9	8.6	12.2
41.7	38.6	36.3	Total Current	27.2		36.1	28.9	32.3	43.1
14.0	16.2	14.0	Long-Term Debt	27.9		6.1	13.4	7.5	12.9
.6	.7	.9	Deferred Taxes	1.0		.3	1.5	.3	.9
8.2	10.2	9.5	All Other Non-Current	19.3		2.3	5.5	4.0	13.6
35.6	34.3	39.3	Net Worth	24.5		55.2	50.6	55.9	29.5
100.0	100.0	100.0	Total Liabilities & Net Worth	100.0		100.0	100.0	100.0	100.0
			INCOME DATA						
100.0	100.0	100.0	Net Sales	100.0		100.0	100.0	100.0	100.0
27.2	29.6	30.8	Gross Profit	44.9		38.9	32.0	26.2	23.2
22.7	25.1	24.6	Operating Expenses	37.5		32.4	26.8	21.9	16.4
4.4	4.5	6.1	Operating Profit	7.4		6.5	5.2	4.3	6.8
1.2	1.6	1.0	All Other Expenses (net)	.9		.6	1.0	.3	.9
3.3	2.9	5.2	Profit Before Taxes	6.5		5.9	4.2	4.0	5.9
			RATIOS						
3.0	3.3	3.6	Current	5.6		4.3	3.6	3.8	2.2
1.7	1.9	2.1		2.6		2.5	2.6	2.7	1.6
1.1	1.2	1.3		1.0		1.3	1.3	1.3	1.2
1.8	2.0	2.1	Quick	2.7		3.7	2.3	2.7	1.3
1.0	1.0	1.0		1.1		1.2	1.0	2.0	.7
.5	.6	.6		.7		.7	.7	.7	.5
31 11.9	35 10.3	33 10.9	Sales/Receivables	16 22.9		32 11.5	32 11.4	37 9.9	39 9.3
40 9.0	45 8.0	43 8.5		32 11.3		39 9.3	40 9.1	45 8.2	48 7.6
50 7.3	56 6.5	53 6.8		59 6.2		45 8.2	49 7.4	56 6.5	59 6.2
31 11.7	34 10.6	35 10.3	Cost of Sales/Inventory	7 51.5		47 7.8	43 8.5	35 10.3	38 9.7
51 7.2	54 6.8	66 5.5		145 2.5		69 5.3	83 4.4	57 6.4	62 5.8
88 4.1	92 4.0	110 3.3		294 1.2		127 2.9	125 2.9	110 3.3	86 4.2
18 20.1	20 18.3	19 19.5	Cost of Sales/Payables	2 193.0		18 20.0	17 21.5	19 19.2	25 14.8
26 13.8	29 12.7	29 12.7		23 15.9		40 9.1	27 13.6	28 13.0	30 12.2
39 9.4	43 8.6	42 8.8		52 7.1		49 7.4	47 7.8	39 9.4	35 10.4
5.2	4.4	4.3	Sales/Working Capital	2.1		4.0	4.5	3.9	5.2
9.9	7.9	7.4		6.3		6.0	6.0	5.6	8.7
59.6	26.9	16.7		NM		12.6	15.8	12.9	17.4
10.5	11.4	13.1	EBIT/Interest			12.4	8.4	56.0	30.4
(120) 3.3	(105) 3.3	(109) 5.4				(12) 4.5	(27) 4.3	(17) 5.8	(37) 7.3
1.2	1.1	2.3				1.4	2.1	1.9	4.0
5.0	7.0	4.5	Net Profit + Depr., Dep., Amort./Cur. Mat. L/T/D				4.0		4.5
(41) 2.8	(32) 3.1	(32) 3.2					(11) 2.1		(13) 3.6
1.6	.6	1.7					1.5		1.9
.2	.3	.2	Fixed/Worth	.4		.1	.3	.1	.3
.6	.8	.5		1.1		.3	.5	.2	.8
3.0	2.6	1.5		-1.5		.6	1.2	1.1	2.5
.5	.5	.4	Debt/Worth	.5		.3	.3	.3	.9
1.6	1.7	1.3		1.4		.5	.9	.7	2.0
14.9	10.1	3.6		-2.8		3.0	3.3	2.0	7.0
37.9	32.8	36.4	% Profit Before Taxes/Tangible Net Worth			66.5	29.7	22.7	45.4
(106) 15.4	(98) 15.6	(117) 18.5				36.8	(28) 14.3	(26) 10.7	(34) 27.7
3.2	.4	7.0				.8	5.1	6.2	14.5
14.6	13.9	14.7	% Profit Before Taxes/Total Assets	17.9		27.6	11.8	12.9	18.3
5.2	5.2	8.6		9.3		10.2	4.8	6.6	10.1
.4	.0	3.2		-.4		.4	2.7	2.4	4.8
21.0	25.3	30.2	Sales/Net Fixed Assets	64.0		86.9	24.7	33.9	17.6
11.2	9.0	9.9		6.9		18.8	10.5	12.7	8.7
5.2	4.7	5.2		1.5		6.1	4.7	5.7	5.3
3.0	2.9	2.8	Sales/Total Assets	3.1		3.0	2.7	2.8	2.7
2.1	2.0	1.9		1.3		2.1	2.0	2.2	2.1
1.7	1.4	1.5		1.0		1.6	1.5	1.5	1.6
1.1	1.3	1.0	% Depr., Dep., Amort./Sales			.7	1.1	.8	.9
(115) 1.9	(101) 2.0	(113) 2.1				(12) 1.3	(28) 2.2	(24) 1.7	(36) 2.0
3.9	4.1	3.4				2.6	3.4	2.7	3.6
1.9	1.9	1.8	% Officers', Directors' Owners' Comp/Sales				1.1		
(38) 3.9	(33) 4.0	(37) 4.4					(10) 4.6		
7.6	6.3	8.7					8.7		
4548540M	4246318M	4313680M	Net Sales ($)	6128M	20163M	56892M	210119M	418421M	3601957M
2324881M	2517611M	2392069M	Total Assets ($)	5417M	15446M	31758M	113228M	222780M	2003440M

M = $ thousand   MM = $ million
See Pages 9 through 22 for Explanation of Ratios and Data

Current Data Sorted by Assets **Comparative Historical Data**

0-500M	500M-2MM	2-10MM	10-50MM	50-100MM	100-250MM	Type of Statement	4/1/06-3/31/07 ALL	4/1/07-3/31/08 ALL
1		1	4	2	2	Unqualified	19	18
		4	3			Reviewed	6	10
	1	1				Compiled	6	4
2			1			Tax Returns	1	3
1	2	2	9	2	3	Other	12	18
	6 (4/1-9/30/10)		35 (10/1/10-3/31/11)					
4	3	8	17	4	5	**NUMBER OF STATEMENTS**	44	53
%	%	%	%	%	%	**ASSETS**	%	%
			5.8			Cash & Equivalents	6.8	8.5
			10.6			Trade Receivables (net)	19.0	20.1
			22.6			Inventory	24.4	23.5
			1.1			All Other Current	2.9	1.5
			40.0			Total Current	53.1	53.7
			46.3			Fixed Assets (net)	35.1	36.2
			2.5			Intangibles (net)	5.4	4.7
			11.3			All Other Non-Current	6.4	5.5
			100.0			Total	100.0	100.0
						LIABILITIES		
			5.8			Notes Payable-Short Term	7.1	6.5
			6.0			Cur. Mat.-L.T.D.	2.6	2.4
			4.5			Trade Payables	10.7	11.9
			.2			Income Taxes Payable	.3	.2
			7.0			All Other Current	6.4	7.1
			23.5			Total Current	27.1	28.0
			24.7			Long-Term Debt	23.4	24.2
			.8			Deferred Taxes	1.3	1.6
			6.9			All Other Non-Current	5.3	3.5
			44.2			Net Worth	42.9	42.6
			100.0			Total Liabilities & Net Worth	100.0	100.0
						INCOME DATA		
			100.0			Net Sales	100.0	100.0
			28.1			Gross Profit	32.8	33.1
			31.9			Operating Expenses	23.9	24.9
			-3.8			Operating Profit	8.9	8.3
			1.4			All Other Expenses (net)	1.6	2.0
			-5.2			Profit Before Taxes	7.3	6.2
						RATIOS		
			6.7				3.9	3.7
			2.2			Current	2.1	2.3
			1.0				1.7	1.4
			2.1				1.8	1.8
			.7			Quick	1.0	.9
			.4				.5	.4
		36	10.1				31 / 11.7	29 / 12.7
		39	9.4			Sales/Receivables	36 / 10.1	37 / 10.0
		47	7.7				45 / 8.1	48 / 7.7
		107	3.4				42 / 8.7	58 / 6.3
		149	2.5			Cost of Sales/Inventory	76 / 4.8	82 / 4.5
		234	1.6				102 / 3.6	152 / 2.4
		11	34.4				17 / 21.3	15 / 23.7
		21	17.1			Cost of Sales/Payables	25 / 14.3	28 / 13.2
		31	11.8				41 / 8.9	45 / 8.0
			1.7				4.0	3.4
			3.5			Sales/Working Capital	6.1	7.0
			NM				11.8	14.6
			1.8				15.8	5.0
			(15) -1.1			EBIT/Interest	(40) 3.7	(47) 2.3
			-1.8				2.1	1.0
						Net Profit + Depr., Dep.,	8.1	4.2
						Amort./Cur. Mat. L/T/D	(15) 2.8	(11) 2.1
							1.5	1.4
			.6				.3	.3
			1.1			Fixed/Worth	.8	1.0
			1.8				2.4	2.3
			.6				.3	.5
			1.2			Debt/Worth	1.4	2.0
			3.9				5.8	3.7
			11.7				47.1	39.4
			(16) -7.0			% Profit Before Taxes/Tangible Net Worth	(39) 24.7	(48) 14.9
			-11.3				12.2	.2
			3.4				19.1	16.5
			-4.4			% Profit Before Taxes/Total Assets	9.5	5.2
			-6.2				4.3	.1
			5.6				19.9	19.1
			1.5			Sales/Net Fixed Assets	4.5	3.4
			.8				2.0	1.4
			1.2				2.3	2.3
			.7			Sales/Total Assets	1.5	1.6
			.5				1.0	.8
			2.7				1.2	1.4
			(15) 6.6			% Depr., Dep., Amort./Sales	(37) 2.8	(44) 3.6
			17.1				5.5	7.2
						% Officers', Directors' Owners' Comp/Sales		1.2
								(12) 3.4
								5.2
1352M	11591M	68600M	343937M	139751M	550378M	Net Sales ($)	1332586M	2268332M
703M	2570M	44004M	432492M	316612M	713880M	Total Assets ($)	1190295M	2250966M

M = $ thousand   MM = $ million
See Pages 9 through 22 for Explanation of Ratios and Data

Comparative Historical Data | Current Data Sorted by Sales

			Type of Statement						
16	12	10	Unqualified	1			1	1	7
9	8	7	Reviewed				4	3	
6	5	2	Compiled		1		1		
2	7	3	Tax Returns	2			1		
1		1	Other	1		2	3	6	7
20	22	19			6 (4/1-9/30/10)		35 (10/1/10-3/31/11)		
4/1/08-	4/1/09-	4/1/10-							
3/31/09	3/31/10	3/31/11							
ALL	ALL	ALL		0-1MM	1-3MM	3-5MM	5-10MM	10-25MM	25MM & OVER
53	54	41	NUMBER OF STATEMENTS	4		3	10	10	14
%	%	%	ASSETS	%	%	%	%	%	%
10.9	8.1	10.8	Cash & Equivalents				18.2	.8	6.5
17.6	15.0	12.9	Trade Receivables (net)		D		12.2	13.0	9.8
25.4	29.7	24.8	Inventory		A		20.7	24.0	22.7
1.8	1.5	1.8	All Other Current		T		.6	3.2	1.1
55.8	54.3	50.3	Total Current		A		51.7	41.0	40.1
35.2	34.2	37.8	Fixed Assets (net)				34.4	46.8	44.8
4.0	5.6	4.3	Intangibles (net)		N		7.2	4.1	4.5
5.0	5.9	7.9	All Other Non-Current		O		6.8	8.2	10.7
100.0	100.0	100.0	Total		T		100.0	100.0	100.0
			LIABILITIES		A				
6.7	6.9	7.1	Notes Payable-Short Term		V		2.2	13.6	2.8
5.2	5.4	3.6	Cur. Mat.-L.T.D.		A		2.5	8.0	2.3
10.0	9.1	7.2	Trade Payables		I		6.5	4.8	5.2
.4	.1	.1	Income Taxes Payable		L		.1	.0	.1
8.4	12.0	8.5	All Other Current		A		2.5	7.2	12.6
30.7	33.5	26.4	Total Current		B		13.7	33.5	23.0
19.8	19.1	21.7	Long-Term Debt		L		21.1	21.0	27.6
1.2	1.1	1.2	Deferred Taxes		E		.2	.9	2.9
6.5	4.7	7.3	All Other Non-Current				10.7	8.5	6.8
41.8	41.6	43.4	Net Worth				54.3	36.2	39.8
100.0	100.0	100.0	Total Liabilties & Net Worth				100.0	100.0	100.0
			INCOME DATA						
100.0	100.0	100.0	Net Sales				100.0	100.0	100.0
29.3	30.5	31.0	Gross Profit				30.3	25.4	26.0
26.1	30.7	31.9	Operating Expenses				30.7	25.1	30.1
3.1	-.3	-1.0	Operating Profit				-.4	.3	-4.1
1.6	1.9	1.5	All Other Expenses (net)				-1.1	3.6	2.2
1.5	-2.2	-2.5	Profit Before Taxes				.7	-3.4	-6.3
			RATIOS						
3.9	3.0	5.7					7.2	8.1	3.0
2.0	1.9	2.3	Current				4.0	1.6	2.1
1.2	1.2	1.2					2.2	.9	1.3
1.8	1.1	2.2					3.5	2.3	.8
1.0	.7	.8	Quick				2.2	.5	.7
.4	.3	.4					.6	.3	.3

							Sales/Receivables					
23	15.7	27	13.3	32	11.6		23	16.1	34	10.6	35	10.4
28	12.9	34	10.6	38	9.6		35	10.5	38	9.6	42	8.6
39	9.3	43	8.4	47	7.8		48	7.7	43	8.6	49	7.4
39	9.3	80	4.6	71	5.1	Cost of Sales/Inventory	43	8.5	79	4.6	96	3.8
90	4.1	115	3.2	117	3.1		140	2.6	125	2.9	118	3.1
158	2.3	233	1.6	217	1.7		223	1.6	225	1.6	221	1.7
15	24.9	13	28.3	12	30.7	Cost of Sales/Payables	9	39.1	12	29.8	14	25.9
21	17.0	24	15.2	22	16.5		15	23.6	17	21.9	23	16.0
33	11.0	38	9.5	32	11.5		28	13.2	25	14.6	32	11.3

3.2	2.6	2.1	Sales/Working Capital	1.2	2.0	2.1
5.8	6.5	4.2		3.1	8.9	4.1
31.5	22.8	19.8		5.5	-752.1	14.1
7.7	4.7	4.7	EBIT/Interest			1.7
(48) 2.2	(48) 1.1	(35) -.8			(13)	-1.8
-.8	-1.4	-2.1				-6.2
			Net Profit + Depr., Dep., Amort./Cur. Mat. L/T/D			
.4	.3	.5	Fixed/Worth	.2	.8	.7
.9	.8	1.0		.5	1.5	1.1
2.4	2.6	2.1		1.3	6.9	2.3
.6	.5	.5	Debt/Worth	.5	.4	.8
1.4	1.6	1.3		.8	1.8	1.7
4.8	4.7	3.1		1.5	8.3	2.8
30.9	21.2	13.6	% Profit Before Taxes/Tangible Net Worth			7.6
(49) 6.3	(47) .6	(35) -.2			(12)	-9.7
-8.4	-31.8	-11.8				-23.7
12.6	5.7	9.2	% Profit Before Taxes/Total Assets	17.0	6.6	3.5
4.0	.2	-.2		1.0	2.0	-3.9
-2.5	-9.9	-6.2		-5.6	-5.6	-8.3
20.9	17.5	16.9	Sales/Net Fixed Assets	34.0	12.4	4.2
5.1	2.9	3.0		1.9	1.1	2.0
1.4	1.0	.8		1.3	.6	.7
2.3	2.1	1.9	Sales/Total Assets	2.1	1.8	1.4
1.4	1.1	1.0		1.0	.7	.7
.8	.6	.5		.5	.4	.4
1.1	1.6	1.8	% Depr., Dep., Amort./Sales		1.2	4.8
(41) 3.7	(38) 5.3	(33) 4.9			9.8 (11)	6.5
8.8	10.6	12.6			19.3	9.0
2.9		2.7	% Officers', Directors' Owners' Comp/Sales			
(13) 4.4	(11)	3.8				
9.3		5.1				

1565121M	1565213M	1115609M	Net Sales ($)	1352M	11591M	74159M	145402M		883105M
1580363M	1894832M	1510261M	Total Assets ($)	703M	2570M	111592M	216332M		1179064M

M = $ thousand   MM = $ million
See Pages 9 through 22 for Explanation of Ratios and Data

Current Data Sorted by Assets　　　　　　　　　　　　**Comparative Historical Data**

Type of Statement (current-column counts, top of page):

	0-500M	500M-2MM	2-10MM	10-50MM	50-100MM	100-250MM
	1	3 2 1	1 5 9	3 2 5		1

Type of Statement								4/1/06-3/31/07 ALL	4/1/07-3/31/08 ALL
Unqualified								7	3
Reviewed								4	3
Compiled								4	4
Tax Returns								2	2
Other								13	15

0-500M	500M-2MM	6 (4/1-9/30/10) 2-10MM	27 (10/1/10-3/31/11) 10-50MM	50-100MM	100-250MM		13	15
1	6	15	10		1	**NUMBER OF STATEMENTS**	30	27
%	%	%	%	%	%	**ASSETS**	%	%
		6.3	7.6			Cash & Equivalents	13.3	9.2
		25.0	24.3			Trade Receivables (net)	24.9	29.5
		19.3	25.8			Inventory	23.4	24.6
		2.9	3.1			All Other Current	1.6	1.5
		53.6	60.8			Total Current	63.2	64.8
		40.4	24.9			Fixed Assets (net)	25.1	24.9
		4.6	9.6			Intangibles (net)	8.1	7.6
		1.4	4.6			All Other Non-Current	3.6	2.7
		100.0	100.0			Total	100.0	100.0
						LIABILITIES		
		8.4	7.3			Notes Payable-Short Term	7.5	9.9
		4.3	2.9			Cur. Mat.-L.T.D.	2.9	2.1
		16.4	12.8			Trade Payables	12.6	16.2
		1.3	.2			Income Taxes Payable	.0	.2
		4.5	6.4			All Other Current	12.6	5.0
		35.0	29.7			Total Current	35.7	33.4
		16.3	13.1			Long-Term Debt	18.9	15.0
		.0	1.3			Deferred Taxes	.5	.3
		11.2	3.5			All Other Non-Current	9.9	3.4
		37.5	52.4			Net Worth	35.1	47.9
		100.0	100.0			Total Liabilities & Net Worth	100.0	100.0
						INCOME DATA		
		100.0	100.0			Net Sales	100.0	100.0
		31.6	29.2			Gross Profit	31.5	36.2
		29.4	23.2			Operating Expenses	24.6	33.1
		2.2	6.0			Operating Profit	7.0	3.1
		1.0	1.2			All Other Expenses (net)	.8	.9
		1.1	4.8			Profit Before Taxes	6.1	2.1
						RATIOS		
		3.4	6.4				3.3	4.4
		2.3	1.8			Current	1.8	2.1
		.9	1.4				1.2	1.2
		2.3	2.3				1.9	3.1
		1.5	1.2			Quick	1.1	1.1
		.6	.7				.7	.7
		23 15.7	23 15.8				28 12.9	27 13.3
		39 9.3	43 8.4			Sales/Receivables	46 7.9	45 8.1
		53 6.9	67 5.5				57 6.4	64 5.7
		16 22.6	24 14.9				23 15.6	22 16.8
		29 12.4	55 6.6			Cost of Sales/Inventory	48 7.6	43 8.6
		44 8.2	146 2.5				107 3.4	120 3.0
		16 22.2	17 22.0				13 27.2	24 15.4
		22 16.5	35 10.4			Cost of Sales/Payables	32 11.6	43 8.5
		50 7.3	52 7.0				42 8.7	49 7.4
		7.6	3.3				3.7	3.1
		9.6	7.3			Sales/Working Capital	9.5	10.0
		-72.4	NM				31.4	21.7
		2.4					11.3	13.6
		(12) -.3				EBIT/Interest	(28) 3.1	(26) 1.8
		-2.9					1.5	-1.4
						Net Profit + Depr., Dep., Amort./Cur. Mat. L/T/D		
		.6	.2				.5	.2
		1.1	.6			Fixed/Worth	1.3	.5
		2.1	1.9				22.6	1.5
		.3	.2				.8	.3
		1.2	1.1			Debt/Worth	3.7	1.9
		2.6	3.2				60.6	6.4
		19.9					55.2	20.0
		(12) 4.2				% Profit Before Taxes/Tangible Net Worth	(24) 27.0	(23) 6.7
		-12.7					14.4	-27.7
		12.3	21.8				13.5	14.0
		1.9	9.3			% Profit Before Taxes/Total Assets	7.8	1.8
		-8.0	3.6				1.2	-11.5
		27.1	33.0				23.1	26.8
		5.8	9.8			Sales/Net Fixed Assets	10.8	12.8
		3.6	3.7				4.4	5.2
		3.2	2.6				2.9	3.5
		2.2	1.6			Sales/Total Assets	1.9	2.0
		1.8	1.3				1.5	1.5
		1.2					1.0	1.3
		(14) 3.9				% Depr., Dep., Amort./Sales	(26) 2.3	(22) 1.6
		6.4					3.4	3.3
						% Officers', Directors' Owners' Comp/Sales		
774M	18000M	220433M	309696M		263549M	Net Sales ($)	1904472M	1287380M
41M	4605M	77878M	157584M		160404M	Total Assets ($)	1057695M	569642M

(Columns 0-500M, 500M-2MM, 50-100MM and 100-250MM percentage data: **DATA NOT AVAILABLE**)

M = $ thousand   MM = $ million
See Pages 9 through 22 for Explanation of Ratios and Data

Comparative Historical Data   Current Data Sorted by Sales

Item	4/1/08-3/31/09 ALL	4/1/09-3/31/10 ALL	4/1/10-3/31/11 ALL	0-1MM	1-3MM	3-5MM	5-10MM	10-25MM	25MM & OVER
Type of Statement					6 (4/1-9/30/10)		27 (10/1/10-3/31/11)		
Unqualified	5	6	4					2	2
Reviewed	3	3	7			1		4	2
Compiled	3	1	4	1	1	2			
Tax Returns	2	6	2		1	1			
Other	9	6	16		1		7	4	4
NUMBER OF STATEMENTS	22	22	33	1	3	4	7	10	8
ASSETS	%	%	%	%	%	%	%	%	%
Cash & Equivalents	9.6	8.9	7.6					7.9	
Trade Receivables (net)	30.3	25.8	26.9					28.9	
Inventory	19.7	18.3	24.1					20.3	
All Other Current	2.2	2.0	2.7					3.3	
Total Current	61.7	55.1	61.4					60.4	
Fixed Assets (net)	30.1	36.9	30.5					26.6	
Intangibles (net)	6.3	5.2	5.3					9.8	
All Other Non-Current	2.0	2.9	2.8					3.2	
Total	100.0	100.0	100.0					100.0	
LIABILITIES									
Notes Payable-Short Term	11.2	6.7	9.8					8.1	
Cur. Mat.-L.T.D.	3.5	5.6	3.5					5.3	
Trade Payables	11.9	15.6	17.0					12.8	
Income Taxes Payable	.4	.2	.7					.7	
All Other Current	6.1	9.5	7.1					4.6	
Total Current	33.2	37.6	38.0					31.7	
Long-Term Debt	15.9	22.7	15.0					17.5	
Deferred Taxes	.3	.7	.4					.2	
All Other Non-Current	8.0	5.2	7.1					12.2	
Net Worth	42.6	33.9	39.5					38.5	
Total Liabilities & Net Worth	100.0	100.0	100.0					100.0	
INCOME DATA									
Net Sales	100.0	100.0	100.0					100.0	
Gross Profit	34.9	34.4	31.4					24.0	
Operating Expenses	29.8	33.6	28.0					22.2	
Operating Profit	5.0	.8	3.3					1.8	
All Other Expenses (net)	1.5	1.3	.9					1.8	
Profit Before Taxes	3.5	-.5	2.4					.0	
RATIOS									
Current	4.9	2.6	3.3					5.8	
	1.7	1.6	1.7					2.1	
	1.1	1.0	1.2					1.4	
Quick	3.3	1.5	2.1					2.3	
	.8	.9	1.2					1.4	
	.6	.6	.7					1.0	
Sales/Receivables	34 10.7	26 14.1	22 16.2					23 16.0	
	46 7.9	34 10.7	39 9.3					44 8.3	
	64 5.7	58 6.3	56 6.5					61 6.0	
Cost of Sales/Inventory	19 18.8	18 20.3	18 20.5					12 29.4	
	44 8.3	32 11.2	34 10.7					31 11.7	
	58 6.3	78 4.7	62 5.9					76 4.8	
Cost of Sales/Payables	14 26.4	18 20.3	18 20.1					16 23.5	
	24 15.0	36 10.0	30 12.1					22 16.7	
	50 7.4	53 6.8	51 7.1					54 6.8	
Sales/Working Capital	5.4	5.9	5.2					4.4	
	9.5	13.3	9.6					7.4	
	39.1	NM	62.5					NM	
EBIT/Interest	8.6	3.9	10.6					24.1	
	3.3	(20) 2.6	(28) 2.2					1.1	
	1.7	-1.7	-1.0					-2.9	
Net Profit + Depr., Dep., Amort./Cur. Mat. L/T/D									
Fixed/Worth	.4	.8	.5					.3	
	1.1	1.3	.7					.8	
	2.7	2.0	1.9					NM	
Debt/Worth	.5	1.1	.4					.4	
	2.0	2.2	1.4					1.3	
	4.8	5.2	3.5					NM	
% Profit Before Taxes/Tangible Net Worth	61.2	24.0	54.6						
	(20) 21.9	(19) 10.6	(29) 11.7						
	7.0	-25.1	-1.2						
% Profit Before Taxes/Total Assets	14.6	8.5	15.0					10.8	
	5.3	3.9	6.1					.8	
	2.2	-7.3	-3.1					-12.8	
Sales/Net Fixed Assets	14.7	22.4	27.7					37.2	
	6.8	6.5	9.7					11.0	
	4.5	3.7	4.0					3.7	
Sales/Total Assets	3.1	3.3	4.0					3.3	
	2.0	2.4	2.2					1.9	
	1.7	1.4	1.6					1.3	
% Depr., Dep., Amort./Sales	2.1	1.7	1.2						
	(17) 2.7	(20) 3.5	(29) 2.5						
	3.5	5.5	5.5						
% Officers', Directors' Owners' Comp/Sales			2.0						
		(10)	6.2						
			10.7						
Net Sales ($)	1252816M	1065927M	812452M	774M	6136M	16703M	49705M	166337M	572797M
Total Assets ($)	530203M	496376M	400512M	41M	2227M	4570M	31616M	96309M	265749M

M = $ thousand   MM = $ million
See Pages 9 through 22 for Explanation of Ratios and Data

Current Data Sorted by Assets | Comparative Historical Data

0-500M	500M-2MM	2-10MM	10-50MM	50-100MM	100-250MM	Type of Statement	4/1/06-3/31/07 ALL	4/1/07-3/31/08 ALL
		16	7		2	Unqualified	10	20
	4	6	6			Reviewed	35	22
1	7	4				Compiled	15	10
6	11	18	15			Tax Returns	17	12
4	12				4	Other	40	38
	20 (4/1-9/30/10)		103 (10/1/10-3/31/11)					
11	34	44	28		6	NUMBER OF STATEMENTS	117	102
%	%	%	%	%	%	ASSETS	%	%
12.5	8.0	10.7	10.1			Cash & Equivalents	9.3	7.9
25.4	32.3	25.7	22.0			Trade Receivables (net)	28.1	24.9
29.5	27.3	20.5	19.9			Inventory	23.5	22.4
.2	2.4	2.6	4.2			All Other Current	3.8	4.0
67.7	70.0	59.5	56.3			Total Current	64.7	59.2
14.2	24.1	35.2	34.2			Fixed Assets (net)	26.8	28.9
7.7	2.3	2.1	4.9			Intangibles (net)	3.4	6.2
10.4	3.5	3.2	4.6			All Other Non-Current	5.1	5.7
100.0	100.0	100.0	100.0			Total	100.0	100.0
						LIABILITIES		
12.8	11.9	5.8	8.3			Notes Payable-Short Term	11.8	8.2
2.6	3.2	3.9	6.9			Cur. Mat.-L.T.D.	3.9	4.5
9.2	16.0	10.7	14.7			Trade Payables	14.7	13.0
.0	.2	.3	.6			Income Taxes Payable	.2	.2
24.2	11.7	8.2	8.1			All Other Current	9.3	10.2
48.9	43.1	28.9	38.6			Total Current	40.0	36.1
19.1	14.4	15.8	20.5			Long-Term Debt	17.1	19.9
.0	.1	.1	.9			Deferred Taxes	.4	.7
32.5	3.4	6.7	5.4			All Other Non-Current	6.3	7.0
-.4	39.1	48.4	34.6			Net Worth	36.2	36.2
100.0	100.0	100.0	100.0			Total Liabilities & Net Worth	100.0	100.0
						INCOME DATA		
100.0	100.0	100.0	100.0			Net Sales	100.0	100.0
43.0	36.7	33.6	25.6			Gross Profit	31.8	34.8
34.9	35.0	30.5	21.3			Operating Expenses	27.0	29.9
8.1	1.7	3.0	4.4			Operating Profit	4.9	4.9
1.3	.6	.3	1.3			All Other Expenses (net)	1.0	1.4
6.8	1.1	2.7	3.1			Profit Before Taxes	3.8	3.5
						RATIOS		
4.0	2.9	4.8	2.5			Current	3.1	3.1
1.4	1.4	2.4	1.9				1.8	1.7
.7	1.2	1.3	1.0				1.1	1.2
1.0	2.1	3.1	1.4			Quick	1.8	1.5
.7	1.0	1.4	.9				.9	1.0
.1	.6	.6	.5				.6	.6
0 UND	36 10.1	36 10.1	40 9.1			Sales/Receivables	34 10.6	30 12.1
15 24.8	45 8.2	45 8.1	46 7.9				43 8.5	42 8.7
46 8.0	55 6.6	56 6.5	60 6.1				57 6.4	52 7.0
0 UND	20 18.2	23 15.8	31 11.7			Cost of Sales/Inventory	18 19.9	24 15.5
7 53.6	50 7.2	41 9.0	50 7.3				47 7.7	51 7.2
200 1.8	100 3.6	105 3.5	75 4.9				89 4.1	84 4.3
0 UND	16 22.5	20 18.6	19 19.0			Cost of Sales/Payables	15 24.6	16 23.1
0 UND	30 12.4	26 14.3	38 9.5				28 13.1	26 13.9
29 12.6	46 7.9	37 9.8	61 6.0				49 7.5	46 7.9
2.7	4.9	3.1	4.5			Sales/Working Capital	4.6	5.3
11.3	13.6	6.7	7.4				8.8	9.7
-36.8	25.4	18.2	NM				31.2	22.5
	14.7	8.9	12.0			EBIT/Interest	15.0	9.7
	(27) 3.6	(39) 3.0	(26) 2.7				(105) 3.6	(92) 3.3
	-.3	-.9	.8				1.1	1.1
		2.9	5.2			Net Profit + Depr., Dep., Amort./Cur. Mat. L/T/D	10.0	5.6
		(12) 1.2	(10) 2.0				(27) 2.4	(27) 2.3
		.4	.5				1.7	.9
.0	.1	.3	.5			Fixed/Worth	.3	.4
.5	.6	.7	1.1				.6	1.1
-.5	1.6	1.7	4.2				2.9	5.6
.5	.7	.3	.7			Debt/Worth	.6	.6
13.5	1.3	1.2	1.6				1.6	1.8
-2.1	5.5	3.0	7.6				6.2	39.8
	36.4	26.4	29.3			% Profit Before Taxes/Tangible Net Worth	42.1	46.0
	(28) 13.5	(42) 10.2	(22) 21.7				(101) 20.8	(81) 20.7
	-1.9	-6.3	-2.8				2.7	4.1
86.5	17.0	13.8	13.2			% Profit Before Taxes/Total Assets	20.0	19.3
13.2	4.9	3.6	3.7				6.5	6.3
.6	-5.7	-2.2	-2.8				.3	.0
UND	45.1	13.0	11.0			Sales/Net Fixed Assets	23.9	16.4
82.8	15.4	5.2	5.1				10.2	9.6
19.3	4.9	3.4	3.1				5.3	4.2
7.6	3.2	2.4	2.0			Sales/Total Assets	3.1	2.9
2.7	2.6	1.8	1.6				2.2	2.2
1.3	1.9	1.4	1.3				1.7	1.5
	.9	1.7	1.9			% Depr., Dep., Amort./Sales	1.1	1.4
	(26) 1.6	(42) 4.1	2.9				(107) 2.1	(87) 2.5
	4.3	5.7	4.5				3.6	4.2
		1.8	2.7			% Officers', Directors' Owners' Comp/Sales	2.3	2.4
		(19) 4.3	(19) 4.2				(40) 3.9	(33) 4.5
		6.7	7.1				9.6	9.4
9730M	101791M	436168M	966358M		1192629M	Net Sales ($)	1981223M	3249674M
2727M	39696M	231537M	603237M		894394M	Total Assets ($)	1002929M	1586902M

Note: Column 50-100MM — DATA NOT AVAILABLE.

M = $ thousand MM = $ million
See Pages 9 through 22 for Explanation of Ratios and Data

	Comparative Historical Data			Current Data Sorted by Sales					
Type of Statement									
Unqualified	21	21	9		4	3	8	1	8
Reviewed	35	32	26					7	4
Compiled	11	10	14	2	4	2	4	2	
Tax Returns	15	18	21	3	10	4	2	2	
Other	42	46	53	4	6	7	8	12	16
	4/1/08-3/31/09 ALL	4/1/09-3/31/10 ALL	4/1/10-3/31/11 ALL		20 (4/1-9/30/10)			103 (10/1/10-3/31/11)	
				0-1MM	1-3MM	3-5MM	5-10MM	10-25MM	25MM & OVER
NUMBER OF STATEMENTS	124	127	123	9	24	16	22	24	28
	%	%	%	%	%	%	%	%	%
ASSETS									
Cash & Equivalents	8.5	8.2	10.2		11.8	7.5	12.9	9.2	9.9
Trade Receivables (net)	26.6	24.7	26.1		27.8	30.7	27.7	26.4	21.5
Inventory	24.2	21.8	22.9		26.0	29.3	16.0	25.0	18.8
All Other Current	2.7	2.4	2.8		1.5	2.3	3.6	2.1	4.8
Total Current	61.9	57.1	62.0		67.1	69.8	60.2	62.7	55.0
Fixed Assets (net)	27.6	31.4	29.5		22.8	23.5	34.3	31.9	32.7
Intangibles (net)	4.0	4.1	3.7		6.0	3.5	.4	1.6	6.9
All Other Non-Current	6.5	7.4	4.8		4.2	3.3	5.2	3.7	5.3
Total	100.0	100.0	100.0		100.0	100.0	100.0	100.0	100.0
LIABILITIES									
Notes Payable-Short Term	9.2	11.1	8.5		11.4	10.3	5.7	6.3	8.2
Cur. Mat.-L.T.D.	4.0	5.1	4.2		2.1	2.7	3.6	5.0	6.5
Trade Payables	12.9	14.2	12.9		12.4	18.0	10.9	11.2	16.0
Income Taxes Payable	.2	.1	.3		.0	.3	.6	.0	.7
All Other Current	9.8	13.7	10.8		15.1	10.1	7.6	6.0	9.9
Total Current	36.1	44.3	36.7		41.0	41.4	28.4	28.4	41.3
Long-Term Debt	18.2	23.4	17.0		9.3	8.5	21.5	18.7	17.6
Deferred Taxes	.4	.5	.4		.0	.0	.1	.0	1.8
All Other Non-Current	6.1	5.6	7.7		9.1	2.9	1.1	12.2	5.5
Net Worth	39.2	26.2	38.2		40.6	47.2	48.9	40.7	33.9
Total Liabilties & Net Worth	100.0	100.0	100.0		100.0	100.0	100.0	100.0	100.0
INCOME DATA									
Net Sales	100.0	100.0	100.0		100.0	100.0	100.0	100.0	100.0
Gross Profit	32.3	31.6	33.3		36.6	38.4	34.6	31.6	23.6
Operating Expenses	27.8	30.2	29.7		33.8	37.2	29.2	27.9	20.4
Operating Profit	4.6	1.4	3.5		2.8	1.2	5.4	3.7	3.2
All Other Expenses (net)	.7	1.0	.8		.2	.2	.4	.9	1.1
Profit Before Taxes	3.9	.5	2.8		2.6	1.1	5.0	2.8	2.0
RATIOS									
Current	3.1	2.6	3.7		3.9	3.8	5.2	5.2	2.5
	1.8	1.5	1.8		1.5	1.6	2.2	2.2	1.5
	1.2	.9	1.2		1.2	1.2	1.1	1.2	.8
Quick	1.7	1.4	2.2		3.4	3.0	3.4	2.4	1.3
	1.0	.8	1.0		1.0	.9	1.3	1.4	1.0
	.6	.4	.6		.5	.5	.7	.4	.4
Sales/Receivables	30 12.1	31 11.9	35 10.5		31 11.7	27 13.4	38 9.6	37 9.9	29 12.7
	42 8.7	42 8.8	44 8.3		46 7.9	36 10.1	44 8.3	41 8.9	45 8.1
	60 6.1	55 6.7	55 6.6		53 7.0	58 6.3	51 7.2	55 6.6	58 6.3
Cost of Sales/Inventory	23 16.2	23 16.1	24 15.5		8 47.6	32 11.3	14 26.0	31 11.6	31 11.9
	48 7.6	47 7.7	47 7.7		52 7.0	56 6.5	41 9.0	45 8.0	45 8.2
	100 3.6	91 4.0	95 3.8		131 2.8	131 2.8	78 4.7	111 3.3	74 4.9
Cost of Sales/Payables	15 24.6	14 26.1	17 22.0		13 27.0	22 17.0	9 38.7	21 17.2	27 13.5
	26 14.1	29 12.7	29 12.6		23 15.7	27 13.5	25 14.6	28 12.9	39 9.4
	45 8.2	49 7.4	45 8.1		32 11.5	44 8.3	48 7.6	38 9.6	64 5.7
Sales/Working Capital	4.6	5.0	4.1		4.2	4.0	4.1	3.3	5.2
	9.5	14.4	8.0		10.4	10.3	8.6	6.2	9.7
	33.0	-36.6	32.2		26.6	42.7	NM	21.0	-32.0
EBIT/Interest	11.8	7.3	9.5		10.4	7.2	11.3	9.8	6.0
	(112) 3.4	(116) 1.9	(104) 2.9		(19) 3.6	(14) 2.7	(17) 4.0	(23) 2.6	(25) 2.1
	.4	-1.8	-.2		.6	-8.1	-.1	-.6	-.4
Net Profit + Depr., Dep., Amort./Cur. Mat. L/T/D	6.5	3.3	3.8						4.2
	(36) 1.5	(32) 1.5	(29) 1.7					(10) 2.0	
	.3	.4	.4						1.0
Fixed/Worth	.3	.5	.3		.1	.3	.2	.4	.5
	.8	1.1	.7		.5	.5	.6	.8	1.2
	2.0	19.5	2.0		1.4	.9	2.0	1.7	5.4
Debt/Worth	.6	.8	.6		.3	.4	.2	.5	1.0
	1.8	2.2	1.5		1.4	1.0	1.2	1.5	1.8
	5.1	73.6	4.7		5.1	2.2	3.3	4.0	14.5
% Profit Before Taxes/Tangible Net Worth	38.3	36.2	30.5		71.4	20.5	35.3	29.2	29.5
	(108) 19.6	(97) 11.9	(104) 13.6		(19) 4.2	(14) 8.7	(21) 22.6	(23) 11.7	(22) 18.2
	-1.9	-6.1	-3.3		-1.6	-5.2	3.4	-7.0	-10.5
% Profit Before Taxes/Total Assets	16.1	10.8	15.4		21.4	13.4	18.2	14.0	10.5
	6.4	3.1	4.1		3.7	4.3	8.6	3.3	3.1
	-1.3	-8.0	-2.0		-.6	-4.4	-.2	-3.0	-3.9
Sales/Net Fixed Assets	20.3	17.1	21.4		90.8	22.0	24.7	14.0	9.6
	9.4	7.2	8.3		37.9	9.6	4.9	7.2	5.4
	5.1	3.5	3.9		4.5	6.0	3.2	3.6	3.8
Sales/Total Assets	2.8	2.8	2.5		3.2	3.5	2.7	2.3	2.3
	2.2	1.9	1.9		2.7	2.1	2.0	1.9	1.6
	1.6	1.3	1.4		1.8	1.8	1.5	1.4	1.2
% Depr., Dep., Amort./Sales	1.3	1.3	1.5		.7	1.1	1.4	2.1	1.9
	(112) 2.3	(112) 2.7	(101) 2.9		(17) 1.6	(13) 2.1	(20) 3.6	(22) 3.7	(25) 2.9
	3.5	5.6	4.9		4.1	5.2	5.4	4.7	4.3
% Officers', Directors' Owners' Comp/Sales	2.0	2.1	2.0		2.0	2.0			
	(43) 3.0	(36) 3.6	(44) 4.1		(13) 3.8	(12) 4.9			
	6.0	7.7	6.9		7.0	6.8			
Net Sales ($)	4104065M	3541699M	2706676M	3566M	45879M	64079M	152238M	384747M	2056167M
Total Assets ($)	2234772M	2366352M	1771591M	4086M	23809M	28640M	87683M	215027M	1412346M

M = $ thousand   MM = $ million
See Pages 9 through 22 for Explanation of Ratios and Data

Current Data Sorted by Assets   **Comparative Historical Data**

0-500M	500M-2MM	2-10MM	10-50MM	50-100MM	100-250MM	Type of Statement	4/1/06-3/31/07 ALL	4/1/07-3/31/08 ALL
		5	16	10	7	Unqualified	65	44
	4	22	13	1		Reviewed	53	55
	10	13	3		1	Compiled	37	50
6	11	13	37	3	7	Tax Returns	35	34
4	14			30		Other	86	78
	30 (4/1-9/30/10)		200 (10/1/10-3/31/11)					
10	39	90	62	14	15	NUMBER OF STATEMENTS	276	261

0-500M %	500M-2MM %	2-10MM %	10-50MM %	50-100MM %	100-250MM %	ASSETS	%	%
13.7	12.2	8.5	11.2	5.2	6.5	Cash & Equivalents	9.2	8.6
20.4	24.6	25.1	18.2	13.4	14.8	Trade Receivables (net)	24.2	22.9
6.6	8.1	7.3	10.1	9.0	7.6	Inventory	7.4	7.1
3.0	2.6	3.0	3.4	2.6	4.1	All Other Current	2.8	2.8
43.7	47.5	43.9	43.0	30.2	33.0	Total Current	43.6	41.4
45.5	42.0	45.4	44.7	52.3	53.7	Fixed Assets (net)	45.7	48.2
.7	2.6	1.8	5.4	7.4	7.7	Intangibles (net)	4.0	2.8
10.0	7.9	8.9	6.9	10.0	5.6	All Other Non-Current	6.7	7.5
100.0	100.0	100.0	100.0	100.0	100.0	Total	100.0	100.0
						LIABILITIES		
11.4	5.6	9.4	5.8	7.3	2.7	Notes Payable-Short Term	5.6	4.9
7.8	6.2	5.4	6.4	4.4	6.2	Cur. Mat.-L.T.D.	5.3	5.6
19.7	11.2	17.0	8.9	6.5	5.4	Trade Payables	14.2	11.8
.2	.1	.2	.1	.6	.1	Income Taxes Payable	.2	.2
3.4	8.9	9.1	7.2	6.6	6.9	All Other Current	6.4	6.5
42.5	32.1	41.1	28.3	25.3	21.3	Total Current	31.7	29.0
38.9	30.2	22.1	23.5	12.4	21.7	Long-Term Debt	23.2	24.5
.0	.1	.4	1.1	4.1	1.4	Deferred Taxes	1.2	1.0
8.8	3.2	5.4	6.1	6.4	5.4	All Other Non-Current	3.2	3.5
9.8	34.4	31.1	41.0	51.8	50.3	Net Worth	40.7	42.0
100.0	100.0	100.0	100.0	100.0	100.0	Total Liabilities & Net Worth	100.0	100.0
						INCOME DATA		
100.0	100.0	100.0	100.0	100.0	100.0	Net Sales	100.0	100.0
39.5	31.9	29.9	21.3	12.9	13.2	Gross Profit	30.0	29.3
30.3	31.6	30.6	20.1	17.5	12.9	Operating Expenses	25.1	25.1
9.2	.2	-.7	1.3	-4.6	.3	Operating Profit	4.9	4.1
1.4	.6	.5	2.2	1.0	-.4	All Other Expenses (net)	.5	.8
7.9	-.3	-1.2	-.9	-5.6	.7	Profit Before Taxes	4.4	3.3

RATIOS

0-500M	500M-2MM	2-10MM	10-50MM	50-100MM	100-250MM		4/1/06-3/31/07	4/1/07-3/31/08
1.3	4.8	2.5	2.7	2.1	2.6		2.2	2.4
1.0	2.5	1.2	1.5	1.2	1.8	Current	1.4	1.5
.6	1.1	.7	1.0	.6	1.1		1.0	1.0
1.1	3.8	1.9	1.9	1.4	1.5		1.7	1.7
.6	2.1	.9	1.0	.7	1.2	Quick	1.1 (260)	1.1
.5	.9	.6	.5	.4	.5		.7	.7
11 33.0	18 19.8	32 11.2	34 10.6	33 11.2	32 11.4		33 11.0	29 12.5
23 15.8	37 9.8	43 8.5	44 8.2	47 7.8	49 7.4	Sales/Receivables	43 8.5	38 9.6
31 11.8	55 6.6	59 6.2	55 6.6	63 5.8	65 5.6		54 6.7	51 7.1
0 UND	1 519.0	6 59.6	11 33.9	19 18.8	16 22.9		6 63.8	6 59.1
3 130.7	12 30.2	12 30.1	26 13.8	35 10.4	25 14.9	Cost of Sales/Inventory	14 25.7	12 30.0
22 16.8	26 14.1	27 13.6	52 7.1	63 5.8	41 9.0		31 11.6	30 12.0
9 41.0	8 47.1	22 16.3	16 22.7	16 22.4	13 27.6		20 18.3	16 22.3
37 9.9	14 25.4	37 9.9	28 12.9	21 17.2	18 19.9	Cost of Sales/Payables	30 12.3	25 14.4
65 5.6	37 9.9	68 5.3	37 9.9	40 9.0	30 12.3		44 8.2	41 9.0
39.0	5.0	6.2	5.0	5.9	4.1		7.4	7.6
NM	11.3	31.6	10.6	23.2	9.2	Sales/Working Capital	15.8	15.9
-20.9	47.8	-12.7	-775.5	-6.3	59.2		469.5	-616.1
	10.6	5.8	4.0	2.3	11.5		10.5	9.3
	(35) 1.9	(84) 1.4	(56) 1.5	.7	(14) 1.9	EBIT/Interest	(257) 3.9	(237) 2.7
	-2.2	-3.0	-1.2	-3.0	-5.7		1.6	1.1
		4.0	2.1			Net Profit + Depr., Dep.,	5.5	3.7
		(13) 1.6	(19) 1.0			Amort./Cur. Mat. L/T/D	(82) 2.5	(67) 1.7
		.9	-.3				1.2	1.2
1.0	.6	.5	.7	.8	.8		.7	.6
NM	.9	1.3	1.2	1.2	1.1	Fixed/Worth	1.2	1.3
-3.8	6.0	7.5	2.2	1.6	1.8		2.3	2.5
1.9	.4	.5	.7	.7	.5		.7	.6
NM	1.6	1.6	1.2	.8	1.1	Debt/Worth	1.6	1.4
-17.2	15.6	17.3	2.6	1.9	3.5		3.9	3.5
	39.6	27.7	12.2	4.4	27.8	% Profit Before Taxes/Tangible	41.2	36.2
	(32) 11.4	(71) 5.3	(54) 3.5	-.9	3.7	Net Worth	(252) 18.8	(237) 13.7
	-14.8	-7.7	-5.8	-35.5	-42.3		7.1	1.3
31.4	15.9	7.2	3.5	2.4	9.4	% Profit Before Taxes/Total	14.9	14.2
15.5	2.5	1.4	.9	-.4	2.7	Assets	6.6	4.3
.0	-9.2	-7.6	-3.8	-7.4	-15.1		1.7	.1
14.8	9.1	8.0	5.6	3.2	2.5		6.9	6.1
8.8	6.0	4.2	3.1	1.8	1.9	Sales/Net Fixed Assets	4.4	4.0
5.5	3.2	2.3	1.7	1.0	1.6		2.8	2.6
5.3	3.0	2.5	1.7	1.3	1.3		2.5	2.5
3.7	2.1	1.7	1.3	1.1	1.0	Sales/Total Assets	2.0	1.8
1.0	1.4	1.2	.9	.9	.9		1.4	1.5
	2.4	3.6	3.9	6.2	2.6		3.1	3.2
	(36) 4.7	(85) 5.9	(58) 5.8	8.1	(12) 6.2	% Depr., Dep., Amort./Sales	(245) 4.6	(232) 4.8
	8.1	8.6	8.0	10.3	7.1		6.2	6.4
	1.7	1.9	.5				1.5	1.3
	(17) 2.6	(35) 3.1	(13) .8			% Officers', Directors' Owners' Comp/Sales	(89) 3.2	(91) 2.4
	7.3	6.3	1.6				5.8	4.7
10159M	125124M	827882M	2054827M	989884M	2244337M	Net Sales ($)	11752949M	11205252M
3001M	52665M	437700M	1527715M	1004824M	1970194M	Total Assets ($)	7375872M	7046906M

M = $ thousand   MM = $ million
See Pages 9 through 22 for Explanation of Ratios and Data

Comparative Historical Data   Current Data Sorted by Sales

	4/1/08-3/31/09 ALL	4/1/09-3/31/10 ALL	4/1/10-3/31/11 ALL	0-1MM	1-3MM	3-5MM	5-10MM	10-25MM	25MM & OVER
Type of Statement									
Unqualified	49	46	38			2		9	27
Reviewed	58	53	40	1		4	18	8	9
Compiled	41	43	27		6	7	5	5	4
Tax Returns	26	24	30	5	11	6	6	2	
Other	101	69	95	3	12	7	22	24	27
				30 (4/1-9/30/10)			200 (10/1/10-3/31/11)		
NUMBER OF STATEMENTS	275	235	230	9	29	26	51	48	67
	%	%	%	%	%	%	%	%	%
ASSETS									
Cash & Equivalents	8.3	10.7	9.8		11.6	10.5	8.0	11.1	9.3
Trade Receivables (net)	23.1	20.2	21.6		19.0	23.7	24.0	27.7	17.1
Inventory	8.6	8.3	8.3		9.1	8.6	5.6	8.8	9.8
All Other Current	2.9	2.6	3.1		4.5	3.8	1.5	3.4	3.3
Total Current	43.0	41.8	42.7		44.2	46.7	39.1	51.0	39.6
Fixed Assets (net)	46.5	46.6	45.6		46.2	41.8	48.8	39.7	46.9
Intangibles (net)	3.2	4.1	3.6		3.6	2.2	1.4	3.4	6.3
All Other Non-Current	7.3	7.6	8.1		5.9	9.3	10.7	5.9	7.2
Total	100.0	100.0	100.0		100.0	100.0	100.0	100.0	100.0
LIABILITIES									
Notes Payable-Short Term	5.6	5.7	7.3		7.8	11.2	7.8	6.7	5.8
Cur. Mat.-L.T.D.	6.5	5.8	5.9		5.7	6.0	5.7	7.2	4.8
Trade Payables	13.2	10.2	12.6		13.5	11.1	16.9	16.4	7.6
Income Taxes Payable	.1	.2	.2		.1	.2	.1	.2	.2
All Other Current	7.4	7.3	8.0		9.6	14.7	6.7	6.4	7.5
Total Current	32.8	29.2	33.9		36.7	43.2	37.2	37.0	25.8
Long-Term Debt	24.8	26.0	23.9		32.0	23.3	26.5	17.9	21.8
Deferred Taxes	1.1	.7	.8		.0	.4	.6	.6	1.7
All Other Non-Current	4.8	4.3	5.4		4.3	5.2	4.5	7.8	4.5
Net Worth	36.5	39.7	35.9		27.0	27.9	31.2	36.7	46.2
Total Liabilties & Net Worth	100.0	100.0	100.0		100.0	100.0	100.0	100.0	100.0
INCOME DATA									
Net Sales	100.0	100.0	100.0		100.0	100.0	100.0	100.0	100.0
Gross Profit	25.0	27.5	26.2		39.4	29.2	29.3	23.4	18.0
Operating Expenses	24.8	28.3	26.0		36.8	30.3	30.1	23.2	17.7
Operating Profit	.2	-.8	.2		2.6	-1.0	-.9	.3	.3
All Other Expenses (net)	.7	.8	1.0		1.7	1.0	.5	1.4	.5
Profit Before Taxes	-.4	-1.5	-.7		.9	-2.0	-1.3	-1.1	-.2
RATIOS									
Current	2.3	3.0	2.8		4.0	4.4	2.7	2.1	2.6
	1.4	1.5	1.4		1.9	1.8	1.1	1.5	1.5
	.9	.9	.9		.6	.9	.6	1.0	1.1
Quick	1.5	2.1	2.0		2.8	3.8	1.9	1.8	1.7
	.9	1.0	1.0		1.0	1.3	.8	1.0	1.1
	.6	.6	.6		.5	.7	.5	.6	.6
Sales/Receivables	29 12.6	30 12.3	30 12.2		17 21.7	27 13.7	33 11.0	33 11.0	32 11.4
	40 9.1	42 8.6	42 8.6		32 11.5	43 8.5	44 8.3	47 7.8	42 8.6
	51 7.1	57 6.4	58 6.3		51 7.1	64 5.7	57 6.4	60 6.1	57 6.4
Cost of Sales/Inventory	7 52.6	7 49.4	7 49.1		0 UND	2 213.8	5 81.1	8 45.4	14 25.2
	15 23.7	20 18.7	17 21.9		10 37.0	16 22.3	11 33.0	17 21.8	27 13.3
	33 11.0	39 9.3	35 10.3		35 10.3	37 9.9	21 17.0	32 11.4	50 7.3
Cost of Sales/Payables	14 25.5	14 26.6	15 24.4		9 38.8	11 31.8	23 15.9	17 21.0	15 25.1
	24 15.3	26 14.1	29 12.7		32 11.5	28 12.8	44 8.3	31 11.9	21 17.6
	41 8.9	43 8.5	53 6.9		66 5.5	53 6.9	68 5.4	61 5.9	34 10.8
Sales/Working Capital	7.0	5.3	5.7		3.3	4.1	8.4	6.2	5.7
	16.5	13.1	16.5		20.4	14.8	50.5	13.1	9.5
	-41.7	-43.9	-33.7		-13.8	-56.0	-11.1	NM	85.9
EBIT/Interest	4.9	3.9	5.1		6.1	8.5	3.6	6.4	5.3
	(253) 1.4	(213) 1.1	(212) 1.4		(24) 2.0	(24) .4	(50) 1.1	(43) 1.8	(63) 1.7
	-1.5	-1.9	-2.1		-1.1	-3.8	-1.8	-1.3	-1.9
Net Profit + Depr., Dep., Amort./Cur. Mat. L/T/D	3.3	3.1	2.4					3.2	2.3
	(72) 1.6	(60) 1.3	(51) 1.2				(10) .9	(25) 1.3	
	.6	.4	.4					-.3	.4
Fixed/Worth	.7	.6	.6		.6	.3	.7	.5	.8
	1.3	1.2	1.2		1.7	.8	1.7	1.1	1.2
	2.8	3.3	3.6		-15.6	NM	4.0	3.6	1.7
Debt/Worth	.7	.5	.6		.8	.2	.4	.7	.7
	1.5	1.4	1.4		2.4	1.1	2.1	1.3	1.2
	4.8	5.5	5.4		-23.6	NM	12.0	4.7	2.6
% Profit Before Taxes/Tangible Net Worth	18.1	16.1	23.9		41.6	21.8	22.5	26.6	14.9
	(232) 4.3	(199) 2.2	(191) 3.8		(21) 9.1	(20) 2.1	(42) 2.2	(41) 6.0	(61) 3.5
	-13.6	-14.9	-8.2		-17.2	-10.5	-9.3	-7.3	-6.8
% Profit Before Taxes/Total Assets	6.8	5.3	8.0		14.0	15.4	7.1	9.9	5.6
	.8	.4	1.3		2.1	.5	.2	1.9	1.5
	-6.4	-7.0	-5.9		-8.3	-10.8	-10.2	-4.0	-4.4
Sales/Net Fixed Assets	7.1	6.1	7.2		8.6	9.7	5.8	9.5	5.0
	3.9	3.2	3.7		4.7	5.4	3.5	4.5	2.9
	2.5	1.9	2.0		2.4	2.0	2.3	2.9	1.7
Sales/Total Assets	2.6	2.0	2.2		2.9	2.6	2.5	2.8	1.7
	1.8	1.5	1.5		1.5	1.7	1.7	1.9	1.3
	1.3	1.1	1.1		1.0	1.2	1.2	1.2	.9
% Depr., Dep., Amort./Sales	3.2	3.5	3.6		3.2	2.4	3.7	3.2	3.9
	(240) 5.0	(210) 5.8	(212) 5.9		(26) 5.7	(25) 6.1	(49) 5.5	(44) 5.8	(61) 6.3
	7.3	8.9	8.3		9.1	11.9	7.8	8.5	7.8
% Officers', Directors' Owners' Comp/Sales	1.0	1.3	1.4		3.1	2.4	1.5	.8	
	(84) 2.4	(72) 2.8	(70) 2.6		(11) 4.9	(13) 2.9	(22) 2.8	(14) 1.9	
	4.1	6.6	5.6		7.0	8.1	6.5	3.7	
Net Sales ($)	11302451M	7509555M	6252213M	5020M	57798M	102547M	393209M	800428M	4893211M
Total Assets ($)	7403917M	6044683M	4996099M	4807M	60739M	67599M	265728M	516571M	4080655M

M = $ thousand   MM = $ million
See Pages 9 through 22 for Explanation of Ratios and Data

Current Data Sorted by Assets / Comparative Historical Data

0-500M	500M-2MM 10 (4/1-9/30/10)	2-10MM	10-50MM 97 (10/1/10-3/31/11)	50-100MM	100-250MM	Type of Statement	4/1/06-3/31/07 ALL	4/1/07-3/31/08 ALL
		1	6	3	4	Unqualified	35	33
	3	15	8	1		Reviewed	32	19
	6	4	2			Compiled	13	14
	5	4				Tax Returns	9	9
3	5	11	17	4	5	Other	47	55
3	19	35	33	8	9	NUMBER OF STATEMENTS	136	130
%	%	%	%	%	%	ASSETS	%	%
	6.4	9.3	8.4			Cash & Equivalents	6.9	9.2
	17.2	21.3	12.9			Trade Receivables (net)	18.5	16.3
	19.0	20.3	16.9			Inventory	19.3	18.6
	2.6	4.0	1.1			All Other Current	2.9	3.7
	45.3	54.8	39.3			Total Current	47.6	47.8
	42.2	36.8	55.7			Fixed Assets (net)	43.1	43.3
	1.8	1.6	2.9			Intangibles (net)	2.9	2.9
	10.7	6.7	2.1			All Other Non-Current	6.5	5.9
	100.0	100.0	100.0			Total	100.0	100.0
						LIABILITIES		
	13.6	6.2	8.0			Notes Payable-Short Term	8.0	6.3
	2.7	4.3	8.0			Cur. Mat.-L.T.D.	4.4	5.3
	14.9	9.7	6.8			Trade Payables	10.3	8.5
	.1	.1	.0			Income Taxes Payable	.2	.2
	14.1	6.5	6.3			All Other Current	7.3	9.8
	45.4	26.9	29.2			Total Current	30.2	30.0
	27.8	17.3	24.4			Long-Term Debt	22.5	22.6
	.0	.4	.5			Deferred Taxes	.5	.7
	10.4	10.1	3.9			All Other Non-Current	5.3	7.9
	16.4	45.4	42.1			Net Worth	41.5	38.7
	100.0	100.0	100.0			Total Liabilities & Net Worth	100.0	100.0
						INCOME DATA		
	100.0	100.0	100.0			Net Sales	100.0	100.0
	30.8	31.1	28.4			Gross Profit	32.2	31.9
	29.9	27.9	29.2			Operating Expenses	24.1	25.0
	.9	3.2	-.8			Operating Profit	8.1	6.9
	1.2	2.3	3.5			All Other Expenses (net)	1.5	2.2
	-.3	1.0	-4.3			Profit Before Taxes	6.6	4.7
						RATIOS		
	2.5	4.2	3.3			Current	2.5	3.4
	1.3	2.1	1.6				1.6	1.7
	.7	1.3	1.1				1.1	1.0
	1.3	2.6	1.7			Quick	1.6	1.6
	.5	1.1	.8				.9	.9
	.2	.5	.4				.4	.4
	10 36.9	33 11.0	31 11.7			Sales/Receivables	27 13.4	25 14.9
	27 13.7	47 7.7	39 9.3				37 9.9	35 10.3
	55 6.6	61 5.9	57 6.4				49 7.5	47 7.8
	16 23.3	35 10.3	61 5.9			Cost of Sales/Inventory	31 11.6	36 10.1
	48 7.6	73 5.0	87 4.2				59 6.2	68 5.4
	110 3.3	110 3.3	122 3.0				97 3.8	93 3.9
	10 37.9	10 35.2	18 20.3			Cost of Sales/Payables	20 18.6	15 24.9
	26 14.2	25 14.4	27 13.4				27 13.5	25 14.4
	40 9.1	55 6.6	38 9.5				43 8.5	37 9.9
	6.4	3.4	4.1			Sales/Working Capital	5.9	4.4
	27.0	5.3	8.9				10.4	9.2
	-17.0	19.6	-54.5				40.0	NM
	5.4	4.9	6.0			EBIT/Interest	17.5	7.4
	(16) .6	(30) 1.6	(29) 2.0				(128) 4.5	(112) 2.3
	-3.3	-.3	-1.0				1.6	1.0
						Net Profit + Depr., Dep., Amort./Cur. Mat. L/T/D	7.8	3.0
							(37) 3.6	(37) 1.9
							1.9	.7
	.8	.4	.8			Fixed/Worth	.6	.6
	2.3	.8	1.6				1.0	1.2
	-.8	2.0	2.7				2.3	2.8
	.8	.4	.6			Debt/Worth	.6	.5
	2.9	1.2	1.6				1.4	1.5
	-5.2	3.9	5.3				3.2	4.8
	10.3	23.1	11.9			% Profit Before Taxes/Tangible Net Worth	38.8	33.9
	(12) -5.9	(31) 3.1	(29) 7.1				(124) 24.8	(113) 14.0
	-20.5	-3.4	-9.9				10.2	4.4
	8.5	8.7	5.9			% Profit Before Taxes/Total Assets	16.8	12.5
	-3.6	2.2	1.7				8.1	5.3
	-10.2	-2.5	-5.9				3.0	.0
	13.5	9.8	2.9			Sales/Net Fixed Assets	7.2	7.5
	4.7	4.3	1.7				3.6	3.9
	2.2	2.2	1.0				2.2	2.4
	3.8	2.0	1.3			Sales/Total Assets	2.2	2.1
	1.5	1.4	.9				1.6	1.5
	1.0	1.0	.6				1.1	1.1
	2.8	1.9	4.2			% Depr., Dep., Amort./Sales	2.1	2.2
	(16) 5.3	(33) 4.2	(28) 5.9				(122) 3.7	(117) 3.8
	7.7	6.7	12.2				5.7	5.9
		(11) 1.7				% Officers', Directors' Owners' Comp/Sales	2.1	1.7
		3.5					(28) 2.9	(33) 3.4
		3.6					4.2	5.2
2802M	61034M	236572M	769058M	458668M	1277219M	Net Sales ($)	4625493M	4093921M
1155M	24223M	158301M	803042M	573052M	1256249M	Total Assets ($)	3267613M	3186357M

M = $ thousand   MM = $ million
See Pages 9 through 22 for Explanation of Ratios and Data

Comparative Historical Data | | | | Current Data Sorted by Sales

4/1/08-3/31/09 ALL	4/1/09-3/31/10 ALL	4/1/10-3/31/11 ALL	Type of Statement	0-1MM	1-3MM	3-5MM	5-10MM	10-25MM	25MM & OVER
23	16	14	Unqualified					4	10
23	23	27	Reviewed	1	2	2	15	5	2
15	15	12	Compiled	2	3	2	3	2	
10	11	9	Tax Returns	1	2	2	2	2	
52	55	45	Other	4	7	5	4	7	18
				10 (4/1-9/30/10)			97 (10/1/10-3/31/11)		
123	120	107	**NUMBER OF STATEMENTS**	8	14	11	24	20	30
%	%	%	**ASSETS**	%	%	%	%	%	%
7.6	8.5	8.1	Cash & Equivalents		5.2	12.7	8.6	10.7	7.0
16.5	16.3	16.4	Trade Receivables (net)		17.4	19.1	20.0	16.6	13.4
23.3	21.6	18.1	Inventory		16.6	26.2	16.0	17.5	18.4
3.4	4.1	2.9	All Other Current		4.7	1.4	.6	1.5	3.1
50.8	50.6	45.4	Total Current		43.9	59.3	45.2	46.3	41.9
39.5	40.1	45.0	Fixed Assets (net)		45.4	32.6	48.6	45.8	48.3
2.7	3.2	3.9	Intangibles (net)		3.6	1.0	.2	4.4	5.7
7.0	6.2	5.7	All Other Non-Current		7.1	7.1	6.0	3.4	4.0
100.0	100.0	100.0	Total		100.0	100.0	100.0	100.0	100.0
			LIABILITIES						
8.6	8.3	7.9	Notes Payable-Short Term		9.0	3.9	11.0	7.1	7.3
5.5	7.1	4.8	Cur. Mat.-L.T.D.		3.2	.9	9.4	6.3	2.5
10.3	9.5	9.4	Trade Payables		8.4	8.6	12.9	10.6	8.0
.1	.0	.1	Income Taxes Payable		.0	.1	.1	.0	.1
6.5	8.1	8.3	All Other Current		8.9	18.7	7.6	7.3	4.5
31.0	33.0	30.4	Total Current		29.6	32.2	41.1	31.3	22.3
22.2	24.2	23.5	Long-Term Debt		36.0	13.8	21.6	14.2	24.7
.9	.6	.4	Deferred Taxes		.0	.0	.6	.5	.5
6.2	9.2	8.1	All Other Non-Current		17.6	6.2	8.7	4.8	8.0
39.7	32.9	37.6	Net Worth		16.7	47.7	28.0	49.2	44.5
100.0	100.0	100.0	Total Liabilties & Net Worth		100.0	100.0	100.0	100.0	100.0
			INCOME DATA						
100.0	100.0	100.0	Net Sales		100.0	100.0	100.0	100.0	100.0
31.6	33.4	29.9	Gross Profit		33.9	30.7	31.9	23.9	28.3
29.0	32.0	28.5	Operating Expenses		30.8	31.7	35.0	22.6	24.9
2.6	1.4	1.5	Operating Profit		3.1	-1.0	-3.1	1.3	3.4
1.8	2.2	2.5	All Other Expenses (net)		2.7	-.1	3.2	1.1	1.9
.9	-.8	-1.0	Profit Before Taxes		.4	-.9	-6.3	.2	1.4
			RATIOS						
3.3	3.9	3.2	Current		2.9	10.1	2.4	6.1	3.0
1.9	1.9	1.9			2.1	1.8	1.3	2.1	2.3
1.1	1.1	1.1			1.2	.7	.7	.9	1.3
1.7	1.9	2.0	Quick		1.4	4.3	1.9	3.0	1.7
.9	.8	.9			1.0	1.1	.7	1.3	.9
.4	.3	.4			.5	.2	.3	.5	.5
23 15.9	26 14.0	27 13.8	Sales/Receivables		20 18.5	27 13.8	18 20.0	28 13.0	34 10.8
31 11.8	36 10.1	40 9.1			49 7.4	45 8.0	42 8.7	39 9.4	40 9.1
48 7.7	53 6.9	57 6.4			57 6.5	61 5.9	59 6.2	57 6.4	52 7.0
44 8.3	40 9.2	44 8.4	Cost of Sales/Inventory		21 17.4	34 10.8	36 10.0	26 14.1	59 6.2
78 4.7	78 4.7	78 4.7			71 5.2	85 4.3	57 6.4	75 4.9	83 4.4
112 3.2	127 2.9	115 3.2			89 4.1	130 2.8	109 3.4	118 3.1	110 3.3
13 27.3	14 26.3	17 22.1	Cost of Sales/Payables		9 39.3	10 35.2	17 22.7	16 22.7	20 17.8
21 17.2	26 14.0	26 14.0			21 17.1	18 20.4	30 12.1	24 15.1	30 12.1
42 8.7	43 8.4	43 8.4			38 9.6	70 5.2	54 6.7	37 9.8	49 7.4
4.6	3.2	4.0	Sales/Working Capital		4.6	2.2	5.4	3.5	3.5
7.8	6.1	7.3			7.0	8.5	21.8	7.2	5.7
44.5	62.8	45.4			38.5	-7.5	-13.2	NM	12.1
5.4	4.4	4.8	EBIT/Interest		4.8		2.3	22.0	5.3
(114) 1.3	(105) 1.5	(93) 1.1			(13) .3		(21) .9	(17) 3.6	(29) 2.0
-1.0	-1.6	-1.7			-2.8		-2.6	1.3	.1
4.1	2.7	8.3	Net Profit + Depr., Dep., Amort./Cur. Mat. L/T/D						
(32) 1.8	(28) 1.4	(21) 2.2							
.4	.2	1.1							
.5	.5	.7	Fixed/Worth		1.2	.1	.5	.5	.9
1.0	1.2	1.4			2.9	1.4	1.5	.8	1.4
2.2	3.6	3.3			-1.0	2.0	190.4	5.8	1.7
.5	.5	.6	Debt/Worth		1.0	.3	.8	.2	.8
1.4	1.6	1.6			5.4	1.2	2.2	.8	1.5
4.3	6.1	7.1			-6.0	2.7	264.2	13.8	2.1
18.1	16.2	14.2	% Profit Before Taxes/Tangible Net Worth		19.5		23.2	18.7	13.4
(108) 5.5	(101) 5.5	(88) 3.3			(10) 1.7		(19) -.4	(16) 7.2	(28) 7.3
-7.9	-10.0	-11.1			-11.0		-27.6	2.9	-11.0
7.7	6.1	6.4	% Profit Before Taxes/Total Assets		9.4	8.7	2.6	7.2	9.0
1.1	1.6	.2			-1.2	.2	-.9	3.1	1.9
-4.9	-6.5	-6.1			-7.0	-6.1	-15.9	-2.4	-3.7
8.8	8.1	5.1	Sales/Net Fixed Assets		5.0	25.0	8.3	10.3	3.0
4.1	3.6	2.6			2.8	11.9	4.3	2.3	2.0
2.1	1.8	1.5			2.1	1.3	1.3	1.3	1.7
2.1	1.9	1.8	Sales/Total Assets		2.2	2.3	2.8	1.7	1.3
1.4	1.2	1.1			1.1	1.4	1.7	1.0	1.1
1.0	.9	.8			1.0	.6	.9	.7	.8
2.4	2.7	3.1	% Depr., Dep., Amort./Sales		3.7		3.1	2.7	4.4
(112) 4.0	(105) 4.9	(87) 5.7			(13) 6.7		(23) 4.4	(16) 5.0	(21) 5.9
5.9	7.6	7.7			7.7		13.6	6.6	8.5
1.9	2.1	1.5	% Officers', Directors' Owners' Comp/Sales						
(38) 3.1	(36) 3.4	(30) 2.8							
5.3	5.5	4.9							
3246691M	3167171M	2805353M	Net Sales ($)	5026M	29783M	42324M	168283M	325636M	2234301M
2849871M	3304976M	2816022M	Total Assets ($)	12160M	25446M	43314M	172374M	349701M	2213027M

M = $ thousand   MM = $ million
See Pages 9 through 22 for Explanation of Ratios and Data

Current Data Sorted by Assets   Comparative Historical Data

							Type of Statement			
			3	3	3		Unqualified		8	5
		3					Reviewed		6	6
	2	3					Compiled		5	4
		1					Tax Returns		2	
	4	2	5	2	1		Other		14	16
	7 (4/1-9/30/10)		22 (10/1/10-3/31/11)						4/1/06-3/31/07	4/1/07-3/31/08
0-500M	500M-2MM	2-10MM	10-50MM	50-100MM	100-250MM				ALL	ALL
	6	9	8	5	1		NUMBER OF STATEMENTS		35	31
%	%	%	%	%	%				%	%
							ASSETS			
							Cash & Equivalents		7.3	8.5
							Trade Receivables (net)		26.4	20.9
							Inventory		17.2	17.2
							All Other Current		2.2	2.2
							Total Current		53.1	48.9
							Fixed Assets (net)		38.9	44.6
							Intangibles (net)		4.8	3.0
							All Other Non-Current		3.2	3.5
							Total		100.0	100.0
							LIABILITIES			
							Notes Payable-Short Term		6.1	6.5
							Cur. Mat.-L.T.D.		4.5	5.6
							Trade Payables		11.4	7.9
							Income Taxes Payable		.3	.0
							All Other Current		7.2	6.5
							Total Current		29.4	26.6
							Long-Term Debt		18.3	19.7
							Deferred Taxes		.8	1.1
							All Other Non-Current		7.3	6.4
							Net Worth		44.2	46.2
							Total Liabilties & Net Worth		100.0	100.0
							INCOME DATA			
							Net Sales		100.0	100.0
							Gross Profit		25.2	29.1
							Operating Expenses		17.5	22.2
							Operating Profit		7.7	6.9
							All Other Expenses (net)		1.2	1.4
							Profit Before Taxes		6.5	5.5
							RATIOS			
							Current		3.1	3.4
									1.8	2.2
									1.2	1.2
							Quick		2.0	2.7
									1.0	1.1
									.8	.6
							Sales/Receivables	36	10.2	33	11.1
								43	8.4	37	9.8
								66	5.5	57	6.4
							Cost of Sales/Inventory	18	19.8	22	16.7
								36	10.0	64	5.7
								68	5.4	93	3.9
							Cost of Sales/Payables	17	21.5	18	20.7
								23	15.8	24	15.2
								34	10.7	35	10.6
							Sales/Working Capital		4.8	4.7
									9.1	7.2
									19.3	20.0
							EBIT/Interest		15.9	11.1
								(33)	5.0	(30)	3.6
									1.5	.7
							Net Profit + Depr., Dep., Amort./Cur. Mat. L/T/D		6.4	6.7
								(15)	4.2	(14)	3.7
									1.4	2.1
							Fixed/Worth		.5	.6
									1.1	1.0
									2.2	1.9
							Debt/Worth		.6	.6
									1.7	1.3
									5.2	3.0
							% Profit Before Taxes/Tangible Net Worth		31.8	33.8
								(32)	24.4		22.2
									8.7	-1.1
							% Profit Before Taxes/Total Assets		20.0	19.9
									9.4	10.0
									2.0	-.5
							Sales/Net Fixed Assets		9.5	4.9
									5.1	3.7
									2.8	2.3
							Sales/Total Assets		2.3	1.9
									1.9	1.6
									1.4	1.2
							% Depr., Dep., Amort./Sales		1.3	2.6
								(32)	3.4	(30)	3.6
									4.8	5.7
							% Officers', Directors' Owners' Comp/Sales		.7	.8
								(17)	2.6	(13)	1.7
									5.1	4.3
20505M	49797M	310381M	387344M	326806M			Net Sales ($)		1387999M	1089860M
8698M	35309M	242873M	359786M	208386M			Total Assets ($)		871298M	897547M

(Left-side columns 0-500M, 500M-2MM, 2-10MM, 10-50MM, 50-100MM, 100-250MM marked: DATA NOT AVAILABLE)

M = $ thousand   MM = $ million
See Pages 9 through 22 for Explanation of Ratios and Data

Comparative Historical Data / Current Data Sorted by Sales

	4/1/08-3/31/09 ALL		4/1/09-3/31/10 ALL		4/1/10-3/31/11 ALL	Type of Statement	0-1MM	1-3MM	3-5MM	5-10MM	10-25MM		25MM & OVER
	5		6		6	Unqualified							6
	4		3		3	Reviewed			1	1	1		
	4		5		5	Compiled		2	2	1			
			1		1	Tax Returns				1			
	13		8		14	Other		2	2	2	1		7
								7 (4/1-9/30/10)		22 (10/1/10-3/31/11)			
	26		23		29	NUMBER OF STATEMENTS		4	5	5	2		13
	%		%		%	**ASSETS**	%	%	%	%	%		%
	7.2		9.7		9.7	Cash & Equivalents	DATA NOT AVAILABLE						5.0
	23.4		21.1		20.1	Trade Receivables (net)							18.3
	16.7		17.4		20.5	Inventory							19.0
	2.0		1.4		2.2	All Other Current							2.5
	49.2		49.6		52.5	Total Current							44.8
	43.9		41.3		34.8	Fixed Assets (net)							37.5
	2.5		3.7		6.1	Intangibles (net)							8.1
	4.3		5.4		6.6	All Other Non-Current							9.6
	100.0		100.0		100.0	Total							100.0
						LIABILITIES							
	7.1		4.8		9.4	Notes Payable-Short Term							4.7
	5.8		3.3		3.2	Cur. Mat.-L.T.D.							3.8
	9.0		9.1		9.3	Trade Payables							8.7
	.2		.2		.0	Income Taxes Payable							.0
	5.1		3.7		5.2	All Other Current							5.8
	27.1		21.1		27.1	Total Current							22.9
	20.3		25.3		16.0	Long-Term Debt							20.7
	2.0		.6		1.2	Deferred Taxes							1.9
	5.1		4.6		9.5	All Other Non-Current							11.7
	45.5		48.3		46.2	Net Worth							42.8
	100.0		100.0		100.0	Total Liabilties & Net Worth							100.0
						INCOME DATA							
	100.0		100.0		100.0	Net Sales							100.0
	21.6		25.4		24.5	Gross Profit							23.6
	21.8		23.9		23.5	Operating Expenses							22.0
	-.2		1.5		1.0	Operating Profit							1.6
	1.6		1.2		2.0	All Other Expenses (net)							5.4
	-1.8		.3		-1.0	Profit Before Taxes							-3.8
						RATIOS							
	3.7		4.6		4.0								3.0
	2.0		2.6		2.3	Current							2.1
	1.3		1.5		1.4								1.4
	2.3		3.4		2.1								1.5
	1.1		1.1		1.0	Quick							1.0
	.5		.7		.6								.7
24	15.0	**39**	9.5	**37**	9.8							**39**	9.3
49	7.5	**51**	7.1	**50**	7.3	Sales/Receivables						**59**	6.2
67	5.4	**61**	6.0	**67**	5.5							**65**	5.6
18	20.3	**41**	8.9	**44**	8.3							**49**	7.5
65	5.6	**74**	4.9	**73**	5.0	Cost of Sales/Inventory						**73**	5.0
89	4.1	**92**	4.0	**91**	4.0							**91**	4.0
13	27.7	**13**	28.7	**14**	26.7							**19**	19.7
19	19.3	**23**	15.9	**26**	14.2	Cost of Sales/Payables						**27**	13.6
30	12.1	**42**	8.8	**37**	9.8							**43**	8.5
	4.4		3.2		3.5								4.4
	7.5		4.5		5.7	Sales/Working Capital							5.7
	28.9		10.4		14.7								10.4
	4.5		5.2		4.6								4.5
(24)	2.2		1.0	(28)	.2	EBIT/Interest						(12)	.6
	-3.3		-.1		-2.0								-1.8
	6.2				19.3								
(13)	3.6			(10)	2.1	Net Profit + Depr., Dep., Amort./Cur. Mat. L/T/D							
	1.6				.5								
	.7		.5		.6								.7
	1.0		1.1		1.0	Fixed/Worth							1.0
	1.7		1.6		1.6								2.1
	.6		.4		.6								.7
	1.3		1.0		.8	Debt/Worth							.8
	2.7		3.5		3.4								7.5
	14.3		21.2		20.2								22.8
(23)	8.2	(22)	1.0	(25)	-.7	% Profit Before Taxes/Tangible Net Worth						(11)	-.6
	.1		-9.7		-8.5								-7.4
	6.4		5.7		9.8								5.4
	4.0		.1		-.7	% Profit Before Taxes/Total Assets							-.4
	-7.2		-2.9		-4.9								-4.8
	4.6		4.7		8.1								5.9
	3.8		3.3		4.0	Sales/Net Fixed Assets							3.5
	1.9		2.0		2.2								1.7
	2.3		1.8		2.1								1.9
	1.2		1.4		1.6	Sales/Total Assets							1.2
	1.0		1.0		.9								.7
	3.8		3.4		2.9								3.4
(24)	5.0	(22)	5.0	(26)	4.8	% Depr., Dep., Amort./Sales						(12)	5.3
	7.1		7.2		5.8								5.7
			1.2		1.5								
		(12)	2.2	(10)	2.6	% Officers', Directors' Owners' Comp/Sales							
			4.8		5.7								
	747309M		700018M		1094833M	Net Sales ($)		9422M	19018M	31219M	35377M		999797M
	618164M		568819M		855052M	Total Assets ($)		4976M	17735M	16306M	26297M		789738M

M = $ thousand MM = $ million

See Pages 9 through 22 for Explanation of Ratios and Data

Current Data Sorted by Assets

Comparative Historical Data

0-500M	500M-2MM	2-10MM	10-50MM	50-100MM	100-250MM		4/1/06-3/31/07 ALL	4/1/07-3/31/08 ALL
		5	12	4	4	**Type of Statement** Unqualified	35	33
	6	16	8			Reviewed	37	41
3	8	13	1			Compiled	29	23
6	11	2				Tax Returns	25	16
	6	22	13	4	7	Other	44	52
	24 (4/1-9/30/10)		**127 (10/1/10-3/31/11)**					
9	31	58	34	8	11	**NUMBER OF STATEMENTS**	170	165
%	%	%	%	%	%	**ASSETS**	%	%
	8.7	13.8	11.1		6.8	Cash & Equivalents	8.6	7.1
	28.1	23.7	26.4		17.4	Trade Receivables (net)	27.3	28.6
	16.0	13.8	14.0		16.2	Inventory	16.3	15.4
	1.8	4.2	3.7		6.9	All Other Current	2.9	2.5
	54.6	55.5	55.3		47.3	Total Current	55.1	53.6
	33.1	34.9	36.8		43.4	Fixed Assets (net)	34.2	35.3
	2.7	4.9	.7		5.1	Intangibles (net)	3.3	3.2
	9.6	4.8	7.2		4.2	All Other Non-Current	7.4	7.9
	100.0	100.0	100.0		100.0	Total	100.0	100.0
						LIABILITIES		
	15.4	7.9	5.1		5.8	Notes Payable-Short Term	5.9	7.6
	5.9	3.4	5.8		1.9	Cur. Mat.-L.T.D.	4.3	4.7
	15.5	12.5	10.3		6.2	Trade Payables	12.4	11.7
	.0	.5	.7		.0	Income Taxes Payable	.3	.3
	4.2	6.2	10.2		14.9	All Other Current	8.5	9.7
	41.0	30.5	32.1		28.7	Total Current	31.5	34.0
	29.1	21.0	12.6		15.9	Long-Term Debt	23.6	19.9
	.2	.3	.6		.8	Deferred Taxes	.7	.7
	4.8	4.0	4.9		3.6	All Other Non-Current	4.8	4.0
	25.0	44.2	49.8		51.0	Net Worth	39.5	41.3
	100.0	100.0	100.0		100.0	Total Liabilities & Net Worth	100.0	100.0
						INCOME DATA		
	100.0	100.0	100.0		100.0	Net Sales	100.0	100.0
	38.5	35.2	24.6		14.3	Gross Profit	33.7	32.1
	35.2	30.1	20.5		14.6	Operating Expenses	26.4	26.1
	3.3	5.2	4.1		-.3	Operating Profit	7.3	6.0
	1.7	1.0	.5		.4	All Other Expenses (net)	1.1	1.3
	1.7	4.2	3.6		-.6	Profit Before Taxes	6.2	4.7
						RATIOS		
	3.2	3.6	3.2		3.1		3.3	3.0
	1.3	1.7	1.5		2.4	Current	1.9	1.7
	.8	1.1	1.3		1.8		1.2	1.1
	1.7	2.5	2.3		2.5		2.0	1.8
	.9	1.1	1.1		.9	Quick	1.1	1.1
	.5	.7	.8		.7		.7	.7
	27 13.5	34 10.8	48 7.6		32 11.5		34 10.8	34 10.6
	42 8.7	56 6.5	58 6.3		53 6.9	Sales/Receivables	46 7.9	50 7.3
	64 5.7	68 5.3	75 4.8		75 4.8		71 5.1	72 5.1
	11 34.5	17 21.1	17 21.0		16 22.5		11 32.2	16 22.5
	50 7.3	38 9.6	47 7.8		71 5.1	Cost of Sales/Inventory	38 9.7	35 10.3
	88 4.2	71 5.1	74 4.9		130 2.8		74 5.0	76 4.8
	17 21.2	14 26.8	20 18.1		12 31.0		17 21.9	16 22.8
	33 11.1	34 10.6	31 11.7		16 23.4	Cost of Sales/Payables	29 12.8	25 14.6
	63 5.8	61 6.0	42 8.7		30 12.2		46 7.9	39 9.3
	5.9	4.0	3.2		3.2		4.8	5.1
	26.7	6.8	7.2		5.0	Sales/Working Capital	9.0	8.4
	-21.1	34.8	11.9		8.1		31.7	39.3
	3.5	10.3	17.6		7.6		10.6	11.6
	(29) 1.3	(48) 2.2	(32) 5.4		(10) 3.8	EBIT/Interest	(150) 4.9	(156) 3.7
	-1.3	-.6	.4		-7.3		1.7	1.4
		4.2	5.2				11.1	9.5
		(14) 2.2	(11) 1.6			Net Profit + Depr., Dep., Amort./Cur. Mat. L/T/D	(41) 3.9	(49) 3.4
		.7	.3				1.6	1.6
	.5	.3	.5		.5		.4	.4
	1.9	.7	.7		.9	Fixed/Worth	.9	.9
	-11.0	3.2	1.2		1.7		2.1	2.3
	.9	.4	.5		.8		.8	.7
	4.1	1.2	.9		.9	Debt/Worth	1.5	1.4
	-20.8	5.5	2.5		3.0		4.0	3.3
	34.9	39.7	27.8		19.4		54.5	43.0
	(23) 8.2	(51) 15.6	(32) 8.9		4.6	% Profit Before Taxes/Tangible Net Worth	(149) 28.3	(147) 22.0
	-1.5	-5.4	-4.6		-12.9		9.8	6.7
	10.1	14.6	13.7		10.6		21.8	16.4
	2.0	4.9	4.5		3.1	% Profit Before Taxes/Total Assets	11.4	7.1
	-1.8	-1.3	-1.8		-6.0		2.7	1.3
	15.9	11.0	6.8		4.1		12.6	10.2
	6.9	5.0	4.1		2.8	Sales/Net Fixed Assets	6.1	5.6
	3.1	2.6	2.7		2.4		3.7	3.6
	3.3	2.1	1.9		1.5		2.6	2.5
	1.9	1.6	1.5		1.3	Sales/Total Assets	1.9	1.9
	1.3	1.1	1.1		1.1		1.4	1.3
	3.5	2.1	2.3				1.9	1.8
	(23) 4.3	(55) 3.7	(33) 3.9			% Depr., Dep., Amort./Sales	(146) 3.1	(152) 3.0
	7.5	5.8	6.0				4.9	4.8
	1.6	1.5					1.6	2.0
	(18) 5.0	(26) 3.0				% Officers', Directors' Owners' Comp/Sales	(62) 2.9	(59) 3.2
	7.6	4.4					5.3	5.6
10326M	83861M	490786M	1087386M	769581M	2432776M	Net Sales ($)	5778113M	6143799M
2943M	38254M	298297M	767282M	552695M	2002431M	Total Assets ($)	3342519M	3940422M

M = $ thousand   MM = $ million
See Pages 9 through 22 for Explanation of Ratios and Data

Comparative Historical Data

Current Data Sorted by Sales

			Type of Statement						
29	29	25	Unqualified			1		7	17
41	35	30	Reviewed	1	2	4	11	8	4
23	23	25	Compiled	1	11	3	7	2	1
14	16	19	Tax Returns	5	10	4			
53	65	52	Other		6	4	13	9	20
4/1/08-3/31/09 ALL	4/1/09-3/31/10 ALL	4/1/10-3/31/11 ALL		24 (4/1-9/30/10)			127 (10/1/10-3/31/11)		
				0-1MM	1-3MM	3-5MM	5-10MM	10-25MM	25MM & OVER
160	168	151	NUMBER OF STATEMENTS	7	29	16	31	26	42
%	%	%	ASSETS	%	%	%	%	%	%
7.9	10.2	12.1	Cash & Equivalents		9.3	6.2	18.2	10.3	9.8
27.1	24.5	24.8	Trade Receivables (net)		18.6	28.2	24.9	30.6	25.1
17.0	17.0	14.8	Inventory		17.5	14.7	13.5	13.6	14.8
3.2	3.0	3.6	All Other Current		.2	2.5	4.1	4.2	5.2
55.1	54.6	55.3	Total Current		45.7	51.5	60.7	58.7	54.9
36.0	36.4	35.4	Fixed Assets (net)		35.5	41.4	33.0	33.8	36.7
2.7	2.6	3.1	Intangibles (net)		8.0	2.0	2.6	2.0	1.8
6.2	6.4	6.2	All Other Non-Current		10.8	5.1	3.7	5.5	6.7
100.0	100.0	100.0	Total		100.0	100.0	100.0	100.0	100.0
			LIABILITIES						
8.8	9.1	8.9	Notes Payable-Short Term		14.5	14.8	8.5	9.2	3.5
4.1	5.4	4.4	Cur. Mat.-L.T.D.		6.4	2.8	4.2	4.5	4.2
12.6	12.4	12.0	Trade Payables		10.3	14.2	13.5	13.8	10.3
.2	.4	.4	Income Taxes Payable		.0	.0	.6	.3	.8
8.5	11.0	7.9	All Other Current		4.1	3.2	6.1	8.3	13.3
34.2	38.3	33.7	Total Current		35.3	35.1	32.9	36.1	32.0
20.8	18.3	20.4	Long-Term Debt		40.6	22.7	14.9	13.4	11.8
.6	.5	.4	Deferred Taxes		.2	.0	.5	.3	.9
6.0	5.2	4.8	All Other Non-Current		2.8	8.5	3.6	2.9	5.4
38.5	37.7	40.7	Net Worth		21.1	33.7	48.1	47.2	50.0
100.0	100.0	100.0	Total Liabilties & Net Worth		100.0	100.0	100.0	100.0	100.0
			INCOME DATA						
100.0	100.0	100.0	Net Sales		100.0	100.0	100.0	100.0	100.0
30.3	31.1	31.9	Gross Profit		40.3	36.3	34.9	32.0	19.4
25.9	28.1	28.0	Operating Expenses		37.2	33.3	29.3	25.5	17.6
4.4	3.1	3.8	Operating Profit		3.0	3.0	5.5	6.5	1.8
1.3	1.2	.8	All Other Expenses (net)		2.7	.6	.6	.6	-.1
3.1	1.9	3.0	Profit Before Taxes		.4	2.4	4.9	5.9	1.9
			RATIOS						
2.8	2.7	3.2			2.5	3.7	3.7	3.5	2.9
1.7	1.7	1.7	Current		1.2	1.6	2.1	1.6	1.9
1.2	1.1	1.1			.8	.9	1.1	1.0	1.4
1.7	2.1	2.2			1.5	2.4	2.9	2.6	2.0
1.1	1.0	1.1	Quick		.8	.9	1.4	1.1	1.1
.6	.5	.6			.5	.5	.7	.7	.7
38 9.7	33 11.0	36 10.2			27 13.7	32 11.5	23 15.9	41 8.9	49 7.5
47 7.7	46 8.0	54 6.8	Sales/Receivables		43 8.4	56 6.5	51 7.1	59 6.1	58 6.3
68 5.4	68 5.4	71 5.2			63 5.8	78 4.7	71 5.2	66 5.5	75 4.9
16 23.0	19 19.7	14 25.2			27 13.4	11 34.4	16 22.3	14 26.1	15 23.6
45 8.1	44 8.3	44 8.2	Cost of Sales/Inventory		73 5.0	43 8.4	35 10.5	30 12.3	48 7.6
88 4.1	89 4.1	85 4.3			96 3.8	90 4.0	67 5.5	55 6.6	85 4.3
16 22.5	16 22.6	16 23.2			16 22.4	16 22.9	13 28.0	15 23.7	15 23.8
27 13.7	29 12.6	31 11.8	Cost of Sales/Payables		33 11.1	35 10.5	29 12.5	36 10.0	27 13.3
51 7.1	46 8.0	51 7.2			51 7.1	74 4.9	54 6.9	54 6.7	38 9.7
5.1	4.3	3.9			5.4	4.3	3.7	3.8	3.6
7.7	8.1	7.3	Sales/Working Capital		27.1	6.6	6.7	10.1	7.0
21.3	47.9	48.1			-21.6	NM	30.4	110.3	10.5
7.5	9.0	8.8			2.7	2.4	10.1	20.2	12.3
(147) 2.4	(150) 2.1	(134) 2.1	EBIT/Interest		(27) .7	(12) 1.1	(24) 2.0	(25) 5.1	(40) 4.1
.1	-.2	-.6			-1.1	-2.4	-1.9	1.7	.0
10.3	7.7	5.1						3.0	14.4
(41) 2.7	(42) 1.8	(32) 2.0	Net Profit + Depr., Dep., Amort./Cur. Mat. L/T/D					(10) 2.3	(11) 2.5
1.5	.8	.4						1.0	.3
.4	.5	.4			.5	.3	.1	.4	.5
.9	.8	.8	Fixed/Worth		2.8	1.2	.7	.7	.7
2.2	3.0	2.6			-7.0	35.4	2.6	1.8	1.1
.7	.6	.6			1.2	.6	.3	.4	.6
1.5	1.2	1.2	Debt/Worth		5.7	1.2	1.0	1.2	1.0
4.8	5.5	4.6			-13.3	69.1	5.4	3.6	1.9
29.4	28.3	33.8			32.1	20.0	35.3	44.4	22.0
(142) 11.3	(143) 8.9	(132) 9.6	% Profit Before Taxes/Tangible Net Worth		(21) 3.6	(13) 10.6	(28) 13.6	(23) 18.4	(41) 9.5
-1.2	-3.6	-4.8			-31.5	-2.9	-4.0	3.0	-5.7
10.7	12.3	12.4			9.8	9.3	20.6	19.1	11.7
4.7	2.4	3.5	% Profit Before Taxes/Total Assets		.0	3.3	5.3	6.1	3.9
-2.3	-2.5	-1.8			-6.2	-3.3	-4.0	1.4	-2.8
10.0	9.2	10.9			17.9	10.2	15.8	9.7	5.8
4.8	4.5	4.8	Sales/Net Fixed Assets		4.1	5.5	5.7	5.1	3.8
3.0	2.8	2.7			2.1	2.3	2.6	3.6	2.7
2.3	2.1	2.1			2.2	2.2	2.8	2.2	1.6
1.8	1.6	1.6	Sales/Total Assets		1.4	1.8	1.6	1.8	1.4
1.3	1.2	1.1			1.0	1.2	1.0	1.4	1.1
1.9	2.1	2.3			1.7	3.7	1.7	1.8	2.5
(136) 3.2	(142) 3.5	(130) 3.8	% Depr., Dep., Amort./Sales		(23) 4.8	(14) 4.0	(28) 3.7	3.2	(36) 3.8
5.0	5.5	5.8			8.8	6.4	6.0	4.6	5.0
1.8	2.1	1.5			1.6	2.6	1.5		
(49) 3.4	(45) 4.5	(54) 3.3	% Officers', Directors' Owners' Comp/Sales		(15) 3.8	(10) 3.5	(14) 2.6		
5.1	5.9	5.7			7.4	4.7	4.8		
6644540M	5775116M	4874716M	Net Sales ($)	4529M	55038M	59832M	222783M	427874M	4104660M
4132100M	3950254M	3661902M	Total Assets ($)	2587M	43489M	42460M	152844M	288501M	3132021M

M = $ thousand   MM = $ million
See Pages 9 through 22 for Explanation of Ratios and Data

Current Data Sorted by Assets   Comparative Historical Data

0-500M	500M-2MM	2-10MM	10-50MM	50-100MM	100-250MM	Type of Statement	4/1/06-3/31/07 ALL	4/1/07-3/31/08 ALL
		3	4		2	Unqualified	10	15
	5	12	4			Reviewed	16	11
	6	6				Compiled	6	8
	2	2	1			Tax Returns		4
2	8	8	7	3		Other	22	19
0-500M	14 (4/1-9/30/10)		61 (10/1/10-3/31/11)					
2	21	31	16	3	2	NUMBER OF STATEMENTS	54	57
%	%	%	%	%	%	**ASSETS**	%	%
	7.6	15.1	4.9			Cash & Equivalents	7.0	8.6
	35.0	26.0	23.6			Trade Receivables (net)	24.9	24.0
	27.7	25.6	35.9			Inventory	32.3	30.6
	.8	1.7	1.6			All Other Current	1.4	3.6
	71.2	68.5	66.1			Total Current	65.6	66.9
	25.5	20.2	26.6			Fixed Assets (net)	27.1	23.0
	.5	4.2	1.8			Intangibles (net)	1.2	4.4
	2.8	7.0	5.5			All Other Non-Current	6.2	5.7
	100.0	100.0	100.0			Total	100.0	100.0
						LIABILITIES		
	17.1	7.0	12.4			Notes Payable-Short Term	12.3	10.6
	6.9	4.5	2.5			Cur. Mat.-L.T.D.	2.8	3.1
	18.4	12.6	13.8			Trade Payables	17.1	16.9
	.1	.0	.7			Income Taxes Payable	.3	.2
	4.9	8.8	6.7			All Other Current	7.0	7.2
	47.5	32.9	36.0			Total Current	39.6	38.0
	16.5	11.2	12.8			Long-Term Debt	13.9	11.1
	.0	.4	.5			Deferred Taxes	.3	.5
	2.1	14.5	5.8			All Other Non-Current	4.6	4.6
	34.0	40.9	44.8			Net Worth	41.6	45.8
	100.0	100.0	100.0			Total Liabilities & Net Worth	100.0	100.0
						INCOME DATA		
	100.0	100.0	100.0			Net Sales	100.0	100.0
	31.6	34.6	25.4			Gross Profit	28.1	28.4
	25.9	26.0	16.8			Operating Expenses	21.9	21.1
	5.7	8.5	8.6			Operating Profit	6.2	7.3
	1.1	.4	1.0			All Other Expenses (net)	.8	1.3
	4.6	8.1	7.6			Profit Before Taxes	5.4	6.0
						RATIOS		
	2.2	4.1	3.8			Current	2.9	2.7
	1.7	2.1	2.0				1.8	1.7
	1.2	1.4	1.4				1.2	1.3
	1.9	2.5	1.5			Quick	1.6	1.4
	1.0	1.2	.7				.9	.9
	.6	.8	.5				.5	.5
	37 9.7	36 10.1	28 13.1			Sales/Receivables	34 10.9	31 11.8
	50 7.3	44 8.4	43 8.5				41 9.0	37 9.9
	57 6.4	58 6.3	49 7.4				53 6.9	50 7.4
	21 17.3	36 10.1	54 6.8			Cost of Sales/Inventory	55 6.6	42 8.7
	74 4.9	53 6.9	94 3.9				68 5.3	75 4.9
	106 3.4	113 3.2	124 2.9				91 4.0	101 3.6
	13 27.2	17 21.4	16 23.1			Cost of Sales/Payables	18 19.7	19 19.4
	35 10.6	27 13.4	30 12.4				33 11.1	31 11.8
	53 6.9	44 8.3	43 8.5				50 7.2	47 7.8
	6.3	3.4	3.8			Sales/Working Capital	5.0	4.4
	10.6	5.0	7.0				7.1	7.9
	30.9	11.6	15.2				36.2	21.3
	9.6	27.3	19.8			EBIT/Interest	20.3	25.6
	(18) 5.9	(30) 8.8	(14) 8.7				(51) 5.9	(53) 7.0
	.8	2.2	2.1				1.9	2.2
						Net Profit + Depr., Dep., Amort./Cur. Mat. L/T/D	5.5	6.9
							(15) 3.1	(15) 2.2
							1.2	1.1
	.2	.1	.2			Fixed/Worth	.3	.2
	.8	.3	.6				.6	.5
	2.0	.8	2.5				1.4	1.1
	.8	.4	.6			Debt/Worth	.5	.6
	1.5	.9	1.2				1.4	1.3
	20.0	2.3	3.4				3.2	2.9
	75.4	42.0	52.7			% Profit Before Taxes/Tangible Net Worth	39.2	46.0
	(17) 31.2	(29) 19.2	(15) 39.4				(49) 24.1	(50) 23.6
	-2.8	5.7	4.8				10.7	9.9
	26.4	19.2	20.9			% Profit Before Taxes/Total Assets	21.0	23.2
	5.9	11.1	13.5				11.1	9.6
	-.5	2.0	4.1				2.8	4.2
	56.1	34.7	18.0			Sales/Net Fixed Assets	17.7	21.4
	12.1	10.5	11.5				9.0	11.4
	5.8	6.1	3.9				4.7	5.3
	3.5	2.6	2.5			Sales/Total Assets	2.8	2.8
	2.5	1.8	1.9				2.0	2.0
	1.7	1.6	1.5				1.7	1.6
	.5	.8	.8			% Depr., Dep., Amort./Sales	1.0	.9
	(19) 1.4	(27) 1.6	(15) 1.8				(50) 1.9	(49) 1.7
	3.3	2.9	3.1				3.2	2.7
	.8	2.1				% Officers', Directors' Owners' Comp/Sales	.9	1.1
	(10) 4.7	(12) 5.5					(14) 2.6	(22) 2.6
	6.9	7.4					9.1	7.2
1870M	69566M	289013M	688356M	233034M	833999M	Net Sales ($)	1451193M	1608811M
654M	26056M	151186M	321444M	177007M	417530M	Total Assets ($)	843084M	1148738M

M = $ thousand   MM = $ million
See Pages 9 through 22 for Explanation of Ratios and Data

Comparative Historical Data | | | Current Data Sorted by Sales

			Type of Statement						
13	8	9	Unqualified				1	2	6
12	12	21	Reviewed		3	2	7	7	2
7	6	12	Compiled		5	1	3	3	
5	5	5	Tax Returns		1	1	2	1	
14	27	28	Other	3	3	5	5	3	9
4/1/08-3/31/09 ALL	4/1/09-3/31/10 ALL	4/1/10-3/31/11 ALL			14 (4/1-9/30/10)		61 (10/1/10-3/31/11)		
				0-1MM	1-3MM	3-5MM	5-10MM	10-25MM	25MM & OVER
51	58	75	NUMBER OF STATEMENTS	3	12	9	18	16	17
%	%	%	ASSETS	%	%	%	%	%	%
7.7	7.8	11.5	Cash & Equivalents		15.4		14.7	7.9	7.8
19.1	23.5	28.0	Trade Receivables (net)		27.1		29.9	24.3	25.0
30.3	30.4	27.8	Inventory		31.4		22.8	31.3	34.4
3.3	4.3	2.0	All Other Current		1.1		1.8	1.5	4.1
60.4	65.9	69.4	Total Current		74.9		69.3	65.1	71.4
27.1	22.1	22.7	Fixed Assets (net)		23.3		22.6	25.7	21.3
3.9	3.6	2.6	Intangibles (net)		.5		.6	6.3	1.5
8.6	8.3	5.4	All Other Non-Current		1.4		7.5	2.9	5.8
100.0	100.0	100.0	Total		100.0		100.0	100.0	100.0
			LIABILITIES						
11.8	13.1	10.6	Notes Payable-Short Term		6.4		8.3	5.4	13.2
4.2	4.5	4.4	Cur. Mat.-L.T.D.		8.6		5.4	3.6	1.4
10.7	13.1	14.8	Trade Payables		18.1		13.7	11.3	15.5
.5	.7	.2	Income Taxes Payable		.2		.0	.0	.8
7.9	7.5	7.8	All Other Current		3.6		6.5	10.1	8.2
35.1	38.8	37.8	Total Current		37.0		34.0	30.4	39.1
15.0	12.0	12.2	Long-Term Debt		16.7		14.3	10.6	6.6
.4	.5	.3	Deferred Taxes		.0		.5	.6	.4
5.3	7.5	8.6	All Other Non-Current		1.1		24.9	2.9	6.1
44.2	41.2	41.2	Net Worth		45.3		26.4	55.5	47.8
100.0	100.0	100.0	Total Liabilities & Net Worth		100.0		100.0	100.0	100.0
			INCOME DATA						
100.0	100.0	100.0	Net Sales		100.0		100.0	100.0	100.0
28.2	28.5	31.0	Gross Profit		26.7		34.4	28.7	24.0
23.7	26.7	23.6	Operating Expenses		22.3		25.3	22.4	16.9
4.5	1.8	7.5	Operating Profit		4.4		9.1	6.3	7.1
.9	1.3	.8	All Other Expenses (net)		.4		.5	.2	.8
3.6	.5	6.7	Profit Before Taxes		3.9		8.5	6.1	6.3
			RATIOS						
3.7	2.9	3.5			3.1		4.3	3.9	3.8
1.8	1.9	1.9	Current		1.9		2.2	2.2	1.9
1.2	1.2	1.4			1.4		1.5	1.5	1.4
1.6	1.6	2.2			2.3		4.0	2.2	1.8
.8	.9	1.0	Quick		.9		1.4	1.3	.8
.5	.5	.7			.6		.8	.6	.5
29 12.8	32 11.4	35 10.4			30 12.1		38 9.7	29 12.5	27 13.5
35 10.3	51 7.2	46 8.0	Sales/Receivables		50 7.3		45 8.2	41 8.9	43 8.5
45 8.1	64 5.7	57 6.5			56 6.6		71 5.1	49 7.4	53 6.8
35 10.3	47 7.7	36 10.1			14 26.2		30 12.3	47 7.7	48 7.6
81 4.5	91 4.0	69 5.3	Cost of Sales/Inventory		97 3.8		40 9.2	81 4.5	90 4.1
115 3.2	143 2.6	115 3.2			118 3.1		129 2.8	114 3.2	126 2.9
14 25.2	16 22.8	17 22.1			19 18.9		16 22.8	18 20.7	13 28.1
22 16.5	27 13.6	30 12.0	Cost of Sales/Payables		36 10.2		28 13.1	24 14.9	17 21.2
38 9.7	46 8.0	44 8.3			51 7.1		48 7.6	32 11.3	54 6.8
4.6	3.0	3.6			3.2		4.0	3.2	3.4
9.3	6.9	7.1	Sales/Working Capital		7.3		4.9	5.1	8.2
36.2	16.2	16.5			15.5		14.6	10.8	13.3
10.8	15.2	22.5			9.2		15.1	41.9	25.2
(47) 3.7	(53) 2.9	(66) 7.6	EBIT/Interest		(10) 2.7		8.2	(14) 12.0	(15) 12.1
.8	-2.0	1.7			-1.5		3.1	1.9	2.3
5.6	3.6	10.8							
(14) 2.3	(13) .1	(20) 2.8	Net Profit + Depr., Dep., Amort./Cur. Mat. L/T/D						
.2	-1.1	2.1							
.2	.2	.2			.1		.1	.1	.2
.6	.4	.4	Fixed/Worth		.4		.3	.3	.4
1.6	2.1	1.2			1.4		1.5	1.3	.8
.5	.4	.5			.3		.6	.4	.5
1.3	1.2	1.1	Debt/Worth		1.1		1.5	1.0	1.0
4.4	5.0	3.3			3.4		2.4	2.4	3.0
39.0	22.5	47.6			35.2		57.2	42.2	47.5
(46) 12.4	(50) 5.5	(68) 22.3	% Profit Before Taxes/Tangible Net Worth		(11) 2.4		(17) 25.2	18.0	(16) 23.0
1.5	-5.9	4.6			-4.0		10.7	3.9	4.5
14.5	9.2	19.9			22.6		25.6	19.2	19.7
6.4	1.8	9.8	% Profit Before Taxes/Total Assets		1.2		13.7	11.0	9.8
-.8	-4.2	1.6			-6.0		6.2	1.4	3.7
16.4	18.9	34.7			56.9		57.2	26.4	19.9
10.8	9.1	11.4	Sales/Net Fixed Assets		9.4		10.8	11.8	11.4
4.1	4.5	6.0			4.0		4.8	5.2	6.0
2.5	2.2	2.7			3.2		2.7	2.4	2.7
1.9	1.5	2.1	Sales/Total Assets		2.0		2.0	1.8	2.2
1.4	1.1	1.5			1.5		1.5	1.5	1.4
1.0	1.2	.7			.4		.8	.7	1.0
(45) 1.7	(49) 2.2	(67) 1.6	% Depr., Dep., Amort./Sales		(11) .7		(17) 1.6	(14) 1.8	1.8
3.4	4.4	3.0			3.0		3.1	3.1	3.2
1.9	2.3	2.0							
(12) 3.7	(21) 5.0	(27) 5.3	% Officers', Directors' Owners' Comp/Sales						
8.1	9.3	7.4							
1605590M	1013674M	2115838M	Net Sales ($)	2750M	27017M	35517M	128304M	231411M	1690839M
1088780M	824788M	1093877M	Total Assets ($)	1173M	15802M	16640M	72119M	121747M	866396M

M = $ thousand   MM = $ million
See Pages 9 through 22 for Explanation of Ratios and Data

Current Data Sorted by Assets   Comparative Historical Data

0-500M	500M-2MM	2-10MM	10-50MM	50-100MM	100-250MM	Type of Statement	11	'10
	1	1	4	1	2	Unqualified	11	10
1	1	12	4			Reviewed	18	20
1	7	5				Compiled	26	22
7	8	5				Tax Returns	25	25
4	13	13	8	3	1	Other	47	46
	13 (4/1-9/30/10)		89 (10/1/10-3/31/11)				4/1/06-3/31/07	4/1/07-3/31/08
0-500M	500M-2MM	2-10MM	10-50MM	50-100MM	100-250MM		ALL	ALL
13	30	36	16	4	3	NUMBER OF STATEMENTS	127	123
%	%	%	%	%	%	ASSETS	%	%
5.4	4.3	7.5	11.0			Cash & Equivalents	6.9	7.2
15.0	19.8	18.2	14.3			Trade Receivables (net)	26.3	23.1
28.4	26.0	33.0	18.4			Inventory	23.4	22.9
2.2	2.7	1.7	9.7			All Other Current	4.0	2.5
51.0	52.8	60.4	53.4			Total Current	60.6	55.7
29.7	30.2	28.2	33.5			Fixed Assets (net)	32.4	35.3
.8	5.5	3.1	8.6			Intangibles (net)	1.9	3.0
18.4	11.5	8.4	4.6			All Other Non-Current	5.1	6.0
100.0	100.0	100.0	100.0			Total	100.0	100.0
						LIABILITIES		
18.8	14.2	13.1	3.8			Notes Payable-Short Term	10.5	10.0
4.8	8.6	4.1	2.8			Cur. Mat.-L.T.D.	3.8	4.1
15.9	17.1	12.5	7.2			Trade Payables	15.8	14.3
.0	.3	.2	2.3			Income Taxes Payable	.3	.4
19.0	11.9	9.8	10.8			All Other Current	9.5	10.2
58.5	52.1	39.6	26.8			Total Current	39.8	39.0
40.6	39.6	11.9	15.9			Long-Term Debt	26.8	22.6
.0	.0	.3	.8			Deferred Taxes	.3	.6
23.6	5.7	4.7	4.3			All Other Non-Current	8.6	5.6
-22.7	2.5	43.5	52.2			Net Worth	24.5	32.2
100.0	100.0	100.0	100.0			Total Liabilties & Net Worth	100.0	100.0
						INCOME DATA		
100.0	100.0	100.0	100.0			Net Sales	100.0	100.0
51.6	34.8	32.2	31.1			Gross Profit	36.9	35.5
48.2	34.9	30.3	23.3			Operating Expenses	31.0	30.0
3.4	.0	1.8	7.8			Operating Profit	5.8	5.4
.1	1.6	.9	1.9			All Other Expenses (net)	1.4	1.6
3.3	-1.7	.9	5.9			Profit Before Taxes	4.4	3.8
						RATIOS		
2.0	1.3	2.8	4.7				2.5	2.7
1.0	1.1	1.9	2.5			Current	1.6	1.5
.4	.8	1.2	1.1				1.1	.9
.9	1.0	1.2	3.0				1.7	1.4
.3	.4	.7	.8			Quick	.8	.7
.1	.2	.3	.6				.4	.4
0 UND	17 21.1	25 14.6	29 12.4				22 16.4	20 17.8
14 26.8	34 10.7	36 10.1	39 9.3			Sales/Receivables	38 9.5	35 10.4
23 16.2	46 8.0	60 6.1	47 7.7				55 6.6	54 6.8
17 21.6	20 18.4	44 8.2	43 8.5				15 24.1	21 17.6
46 7.9	66 5.5	94 3.9	57 6.4			Cost of Sales/Inventory	54 6.8	49 7.5
88 4.1	114 3.2	200 1.8	119 3.1				114 3.2	118 3.1
17 21.3	12 31.4	13 28.7	25 14.7				16 23.4	13 28.1
30 12.1	39 9.3	21 17.8	32 11.5			Cost of Sales/Payables	31 11.9	30 12.2
44 8.2	62 5.9	42 8.7	40 9.0				55 6.7	47 7.8
9.7	10.3	3.3	2.7				6.9	6.0
UND	42.4	7.8	5.1			Sales/Working Capital	12.0	11.7
-7.8	-13.2	19.7	56.7				57.7	-141.7
5.7	.9	14.9	33.6				10.0	11.1
(12) 2.3	(28) -.7	(31) 2.0	(15) 9.0			EBIT/Interest	(116) 3.7	(116) 3.0
1.3	-1.9	-.3	1.8				1.4	1.1
		3.3					5.8	9.0
	(11) 1.2					Net Profit + Depr., Dep., Amort./Cur. Mat. L/T/D	(30) 2.6	(29) 3.2
		.0					1.5	1.3
.5	.8	.3	.3				.5	.4
9.2	4.3	.6	.6			Fixed/Worth	1.2	1.1
-.2	-3.7	1.8	2.5				4.3	3.4
1.3	2.3	.6	.3				1.0	.9
15.4	10.4	1.5	1.1			Debt/Worth	2.3	2.0
-1.8	-8.1	4.1	3.6				11.8	5.9
	29.3	27.8	30.8				54.7	47.0
	(21) -30.0	(33) 7.5	(14) 15.9			% Profit Before Taxes/Tangible Net Worth	(104) 20.5	(104) 21.5
	-88.6	-5.6	1.7				7.3	6.9
14.0	3.9	10.3	17.9				20.5	16.0
2.4	-6.2	3.6	5.9			% Profit Before Taxes/Total Assets	8.4	5.0
.6	-9.7	-4.8	1.1				1.9	.3
32.1	17.1	19.8	7.6				18.6	17.1
15.3	8.3	6.0	3.9			Sales/Net Fixed Assets	8.0	7.0
6.9	4.6	3.1	2.0				3.8	3.2
5.1	2.8	2.1	1.6				3.5	3.3
3.3	1.9	1.6	1.1			Sales/Total Assets	2.4	2.1
2.1	1.5	1.0	.8				1.4	1.4
1.6	1.6	1.7	2.2				1.3	1.4
3.3	(24) 3.5	(30) 3.8	(15) 4.9			% Depr., Dep., Amort./Sales	(106) 2.3	(107) 2.5
4.7	6.7	6.8	5.9				4.4	4.9
	2.1	1.5					1.8	1.5
	(19) 4.4	(16) 2.5				% Officers', Directors' Owners' Comp/Sales	(63) 3.2	(66) 2.9
	6.6	3.2					5.8	6.2
14399M	69622M	264373M	361115M	344185M	685466M	Net Sales ($)	2777545M	1884309M
4098M	32653M	168700M	297038M	319431M	477304M	Total Assets ($)	1213093M	1136900M

M = $ thousand   MM = $ million
See Pages 9 through 22 for Explanation of Ratios and Data

Comparative Historical Data | | | Current Data Sorted by Sales

			Type of Statement						
10	8	9	Unqualified	1	3	1 2	2 6	1 5	5 1
25	17	18	Reviewed						
15	17	13	Compiled		7	5	1		
26	20	20	Tax Returns	6	8	1	5		
41	52	42	Other	3	14	5	5	8	7
4/1/08-3/31/09 ALL	4/1/09-3/31/10 ALL	4/1/10-3/31/11 ALL		0-1MM	13 (4/1-9/30/10) 1-3MM	3-5MM	89 (10/1/10-3/31/11) 5-10MM	10-25MM	25MM & OVER
117	114	102	NUMBER OF STATEMENTS	10	32	14	19	14	13
%	%	%	ASSETS	%	%	%	%	%	%
8.0	7.0	6.5	Cash & Equivalents	4.4	4.5	6.1	9.2	7.1	8.9
22.5	19.8	17.6	Trade Receivables (net)	5.8	18.0	20.1	17.5	22.4	17.5
23.4	24.0	27.9	Inventory	28.9	25.2	32.2	33.6	23.3	25.3
1.5	2.8	3.3	All Other Current	1.2	3.0	6.0	1.9	6.4	1.6
55.4	53.7	55.2	Total Current	40.2	50.7	64.3	62.3	59.2	53.2
34.7	34.1	30.7	Fixed Assets (net)	32.7	30.2	27.7	29.4	29.2	37.2
3.7	4.5	4.3	Intangibles (net)	6.9	4.8	.7	3.8	6.1	3.7
6.3	7.7	9.8	All Other Non-Current	20.1	14.3	7.3	4.5	5.4	5.9
100.0	100.0	100.0	Total	100.0	100.0	100.0	100.0	100.0	100.0
			LIABILITIES						
16.7	14.4	12.1	Notes Payable-Short Term	21.0	11.2	14.3	14.1	8.7	5.8
4.1	4.6	5.2	Cur. Mat.-L.T.D.	2.7	7.5	5.1	6.3	1.9	3.4
14.7	12.5	13.1	Trade Payables	12.7	13.3	17.0	13.3	12.7	8.9
.3	.2	.5	Income Taxes Payable	.0	.2	.2	.3	2.6	.1
11.5	10.9	12.0	All Other Current	17.6	10.8	13.5	10.8	11.8	10.9
47.3	42.7	42.9	Total Current	54.0	43.1	50.1	44.7	37.7	29.1
24.9	28.3	24.4	Long-Term Debt	46.1	36.9	17.9	14.5	9.4	14.6
.3	.2	.3	Deferred Taxes	.0	.0	.5	.5	.2	1.1
4.4	6.1	7.2	All Other Non-Current	13.5	11.8	2.6	6.1	3.2	2.1
23.1	22.7	25.2	Net Worth	-13.6	8.2	29.0	34.3	49.5	53.2
100.0	100.0	100.0	Total Liabilities & Net Worth	100.0	100.0	100.0	100.0	100.0	100.0
			INCOME DATA						
100.0	100.0	100.0	Net Sales	100.0	100.0	100.0	100.0	100.0	100.0
34.5	37.0	34.9	Gross Profit	49.2	38.3	38.6	27.2	28.2	30.2
32.9	35.7	32.2	Operating Expenses	49.1	35.8	41.9	24.5	20.3	24.2
1.6	1.3	2.7	Operating Profit	.1	2.6	-3.3	2.7	7.9	6.1
2.0	1.7	1.2	All Other Expenses (net)	1.1	1.5	1.2	1.3	.9	.9
-.4	-.4	1.5	Profit Before Taxes	-1.1	1.1	-4.5	1.4	7.0	5.2
			RATIOS						
2.7	2.5	2.3		2.0	1.9	3.8	2.4	3.3	3.4
1.5	1.5	1.3	Current	.9	1.3	1.1	1.5	2.2	2.0
.8	.9	.9		.3	.8	.8	.9	1.3	1.1
1.3	1.5	1.1		.6	1.0	1.0	.9	1.8	1.5
.7	.7	.6	Quick	.1	.5	.6	.7	1.1	.7
.4	.3	.3		.1	.3	.2	.4	.4	.4
22 16.2	22 16.3	21 17.5		0 UND	22 16.7	23 15.5	20 18.2	38 9.5	33 10.9
37 9.9	34 10.6	36 10.3	Sales/Receivables	2 192.0	35 10.5	43 8.4	29 12.7	45 8.0	41 8.9
51 7.2	51 7.2	49 7.5		16 22.9	43 8.5	59 6.2	57 6.5	61 6.0	55 6.7
19 19.3	22 16.7	41 8.9		0 UND	34 10.7	28 13.1	38 9.7	35 10.5	57 6.4
52 7.1	60 6.1	73 5.0	Cost of Sales/Inventory	77 4.7	71 5.1	117 3.1	73 5.0	50 7.3	93 3.9
126 2.9	144 2.5	142 2.6		247 1.5	113 3.2	361 1.0	167 2.2	132 2.8	140 2.6
10 35.1	12 30.4	16 23.1		5 81.0	14 26.8	11 32.8	13 28.0	19 18.8	21 17.7
19 19.0	25 14.5	28 13.2	Cost of Sales/Payables	39 9.3	31 11.7	25 14.4	20 17.8	29 12.7	26 13.8
40 9.2	47 7.8	51 7.1		70 5.2	54 6.8	62 5.8	46 8.0	44 8.3	48 7.7
5.2	4.6	4.9		30.3	7.5	2.3	3.4	3.4	3.1
15.1	12.9	12.6	Sales/Working Capital	UND	17.1	29.7	9.0	5.5	8.9
-27.6	-38.2	-42.7		-5.6	-67.9	-11.5	-47.0	16.9	47.7
4.4	6.6	9.0			2.1	6.7	9.2	31.5	22.2
(109) 1.3	(107) 1.6	(93) 1.9	EBIT/Interest	(30)	1.3	(12) .3	(15) 2.0	15.4	4.6
-.9	-1.2	-.9			-1.0	-1.9	-1.7	6.8	1.1
5.1	2.0	15.9	Net Profit + Depr., Dep.,						
(23) 2.0	(20) 1.1	(26) 3.7	Amort./Cur. Mat. L/T/D						
1.0	-.1	1.0							
.4	.6	.4		1.0	.8	.4	.3	.2	.4
1.5	1.6	1.1	Fixed/Worth	8.3	2.5	1.1	.7	.5	.9
10.7	-27.2	7.2		-.2	-4.1	5.3	2.7	.8	1.3
.9	1.0	.8		2.2	1.3	.6	.8	.4	.4
2.3	2.7	2.1	Debt/Worth	15.4	7.1	2.1	1.9	1.2	1.0
19.1	-26.6	15.5		-1.7	-8.0	9.5	4.8	2.2	2.1
18.7	26.6	27.8	% Profit Before Taxes/Tangible	15.1	15.3	42.1	34.9	20.5	
(92) 6.3	(84) 6.7	(82) 7.4	Net Worth	(22) 2.4	(12) -11.4	(17) 10.6	(12) 22.4	12.6	
-10.3	-21.8	-14.5		-62.3	-72.8	-22.4	16.8	3.1	
7.2	10.1	8.8	% Profit Before Taxes/Total	8.1	5.1	3.6	13.7	17.3	13.2
1.2	2.0	2.2	Assets	-1.9	.6	-2.6	4.2	9.5	4.4
-5.9	-9.5	-6.4		-18.1	-7.9	-9.6	-5.2	6.0	.5
17.7	14.9	15.7		31.8	16.1	15.4	23.5	27.5	7.6
7.1	6.9	6.2	Sales/Net Fixed Assets	4.5	8.3	6.9	6.6	6.2	3.3
3.2	2.9	3.0		2.1	4.0	3.2	3.3	3.2	2.8
3.2	3.2	2.7		3.2	2.8	3.0	2.8	2.1	1.7
2.0	1.8	1.6	Sales/Total Assets	1.4	1.9	1.7	1.6	1.6	1.3
1.3	1.1	1.1		1.0	1.3	.8	1.4	1.0	1.1
1.5	1.8	1.9			2.2	1.6	1.6	1.5	2.5
(101) 3.4	(104) 3.2	(88) 3.6	% Depr., Dep., Amort./Sales	(26) 3.7	(12) 6.5	(16) 2.5	2.8	(12) 4.7	
5.0	6.1	6.5		6.2	9.4	8.2	4.6	5.8	
1.8	2.6	2.0	% Officers', Directors'		2.9				
(53) 3.0	(45) 4.7	(46) 3.4	Owners' Comp/Sales	(17)	4.9				
5.6	7.1	5.8			6.9				
2231357M	1231173M	1739160M	Net Sales ($)	6103M	61092M	60890M	146072M	215535M	1249468M
1306950M	1010825M	1299224M	Total Assets ($)	4630M	53250M	53304M	93597M	160771M	933672M

© RMA 2011

M = $ thousand   MM = $ million
See Pages 9 through 22 for Explanation of Ratios and Data

Current Data Sorted by Assets							Comparative Historical Data	
						Type of Statement		
			3	1		Unqualified	4	6
1	2	3	2			Reviewed	8	9
1	1					Compiled	5	5
1	1	1				Tax Returns	3	6
		3	8	1		Other	18	13
	5 (4/1-9/30/10)		24 (10/1/10-3/31/11)				4/1/06-3/31/07 ALL	4/1/07-3/31/08 ALL
0-500M	500M-2MM	2-10MM	10-50MM	50-100MM	100-250MM			
3	4	7	13	2		NUMBER OF STATEMENTS	38	39
%	%	%	%	%	%	**ASSETS**	%	%
			11.1		D	Cash & Equivalents	8.6	9.1
			13.5		A	Trade Receivables (net)	26.1	22.9
			20.3		T	Inventory	18.8	22.6
			5.4		A	All Other Current	1.7	2.4
			50.3			Total Current	55.1	56.9
			39.1		N	Fixed Assets (net)	33.0	34.6
			5.6		O	Intangibles (net)	3.0	2.4
			5.0		T	All Other Non-Current	8.8	6.1
			100.0			Total	100.0	100.0
					A	**LIABILITIES**		
			5.0		V	Notes Payable-Short Term	7.2	9.2
			1.9		A	Cur. Mat.-L.T.D.	5.8	3.9
			8.6		I	Trade Payables	15.2	14.9
			.0		L	Income Taxes Payable	.3	.2
			5.9		A	All Other Current	7.1	12.3
			21.4		B	Total Current	35.6	40.4
			15.6		L	Long-Term Debt	19.3	19.2
			3.4		E	Deferred Taxes	.6	.4
			10.6			All Other Non-Current	5.3	5.3
			49.0			Net Worth	39.2	34.7
			100.0			Total Liabilties & Net Worth	100.0	100.0
						INCOME DATA		
			100.0			Net Sales	100.0	100.0
			31.1			Gross Profit	33.8	32.9
			22.8			Operating Expenses	25.9	25.5
			8.4			Operating Profit	7.9	7.4
			.5			All Other Expenses (net)	.6	.8
			7.8			Profit Before Taxes	7.3	6.6
						RATIOS		
			4.3				4.2	3.1
			3.5			Current	1.7	1.9
			2.0				1.0	1.0
			2.0				2.1	2.1
			1.3			Quick	1.1	1.0
			.7				.6	.5
			14 26.0				**35** 10.5	**33** 11.0
			43 8.5			Sales/Receivables	**43** 8.5	**41** 9.0
			61 6.0				**55** 6.6	**55** 6.7
			46 7.9				**20** 18.0	**37** 9.9
			79 4.6			Cost of Sales/Inventory	**42** 8.6	**57** 6.4
			109 3.3				**82** 4.5	**87** 4.2
			16 23.1				**15** 24.0	**20** 18.5
			20 18.0			Cost of Sales/Payables	**25** 14.6	**35** 10.3
			51 7.2				**45** 8.1	**53** 6.9
			2.6				5.4	4.7
			4.4			Sales/Working Capital	10.0	6.8
			5.4				NM	161.4
			24.0				17.1	9.4
			(12) 14.1			EBIT/Interest	(32) 4.4	(34) 4.8
			-3.2				1.7	1.4
								8.3
						Net Profit + Depr., Dep., Amort./Cur. Mat. L/T/D		(16) 3.4
								2.4
			.3				.3	.3
			.9			Fixed/Worth	.9	1.1
			1.3				2.1	2.5
			.4				.5	.6
			1.3			Debt/Worth	1.0	1.4
			2.6				4.9	4.2
			42.1				44.3	43.5
			(12) 23.8			% Profit Before Taxes/Tangible Net Worth	(32) 27.9	(32) 22.3
			-2.3				10.4	11.6
			19.3				25.5	18.5
			11.1			% Profit Before Taxes/Total Assets	11.2	8.5
			-2.0				3.0	2.6
			6.0				13.1	21.7
			3.4			Sales/Net Fixed Assets	6.1	7.7
			1.8				3.8	3.2
			2.0				2.7	2.5
			1.4			Sales/Total Assets	2.3	2.0
			.7				1.5	1.2
			1.9				1.4	1.9
			(12) 3.9			% Depr., Dep., Amort./Sales	(28) 3.3	(31) 3.5
			8.1				4.8	4.7
							.7	1.7
						% Officers', Directors' Owners' Comp/Sales	(14) 5.5	(13) 8.2
							11.1	11.7
3351M	13710M	62066M	303869M	143220M		Net Sales ($)	708117M	893767M
1267M	6264M	45448M	260908M	145103M		Total Assets ($)	419192M	627232M

M = $ thousand MM = $ million

See Pages 9 through 22 for Explanation of Ratios and Data

Comparative Historical Data | Current Data Sorted by Sales

			Type of Statement						
3	6	4	Unqualified					2	2
8	13	8	Reviewed	1	1	1	1	3	1
5	3	2	Compiled	1		1			
3	3	3	Tax Returns		2	1			
22	9	12	Other	2			1	5	4
4/1/08-3/31/09 ALL	4/1/09-3/31/10 ALL	4/1/10-3/31/11 ALL		0-1MM	5 (4/1-9/30/10) 1-3MM	3-5MM	5-10MM	24 (10/1/10-3/31/11) 10-25MM	25MM & OVER
41	34	29	NUMBER OF STATEMENTS	2	5	3	2	10	7
%	%	%	ASSETS	%	%	%	%	%	%
10.3	10.9	12.9	Cash & Equivalents					11.6	
23.1	20.6	17.9	Trade Receivables (net)					14.7	
22.3	22.5	22.4	Inventory					21.5	
1.8	3.5	3.0	All Other Current					1.0	
57.6	57.4	56.1	Total Current					48.9	
26.6	31.1	33.0	Fixed Assets (net)					43.7	
5.2	4.2	5.9	Intangibles (net)					1.9	
10.6	7.3	4.9	All Other Non-Current					5.5	
100.0	100.0	100.0	Total					100.0	
			LIABILITIES						
11.0	8.6	4.6	Notes Payable-Short Term					7.8	
4.0	3.5	2.8	Cur. Mat.-L.T.D.					5.5	
12.9	12.0	11.8	Trade Payables					9.1	
.3	.1	.0	Income Taxes Payable					.0	
17.0	9.9	4.3	All Other Current					3.9	
45.1	34.1	23.6	Total Current					26.3	
13.5	15.6	15.3	Long-Term Debt					10.1	
.7	.3	1.5	Deferred Taxes					.8	
5.1	6.6	9.9	All Other Non-Current					7.0	
35.6	43.4	49.8	Net Worth					55.9	
100.0	100.0	100.0	Total Liabilities & Net Worth					100.0	
			INCOME DATA						
100.0	100.0	100.0	Net Sales					100.0	
28.6	30.0	32.8	Gross Profit					30.4	
22.2	26.3	25.5	Operating Expenses					23.4	
6.4	3.7	7.3	Operating Profit					7.0	
1.0	.5	-.1	All Other Expenses (net)					.7	
5.4	3.2	7.4	Profit Before Taxes					6.3	
			RATIOS						
2.7	3.2	4.3	Current					3.9	
1.4	2.1	2.5						2.4	
1.0	1.2	1.5						1.2	
1.4	2.2	2.3	Quick					2.2	
.8	1.0	1.2						1.3	
.5	.6	.7						.6	
29 12.4	30 12.3	25 14.9	Sales/Receivables					18 19.9	
38 9.5	44 8.3	46 7.9						43 8.4	
53 6.9	60 6.0	63 5.8						61 6.0	
27 13.3	27 13.5	35 10.5	Cost of Sales/Inventory					40 9.2	
62 5.9	65 5.6	76 4.8						74 4.9	
97 3.8	105 3.5	109 3.3						106 3.5	
15 23.6	14 25.7	16 22.2	Cost of Sales/Payables					16 23.0	
26 13.8	18 20.3	29 12.5						25 14.4	
59 6.2	43 8.5	53 6.9						42 8.7	
4.2	3.4	2.7	Sales/Working Capital					2.6	
10.2	7.4	4.7						4.8	
NM	29.2	13.6						53.0	
9.1	20.8	25.2	EBIT/Interest					15.0	
(36) 3.0	(30) 4.7	(24) 6.7						3.7	
-.8	.8	.0						-2.0	
7.4	7.3		Net Profit + Depr., Dep., Amort./Cur. Mat. L/T/D						
(19) 1.9	(10) 3.8								
.1	.5								
.3	.4	.3	Fixed/Worth					.5	
.8	.7	.8						.9	
1.6	1.4	1.4						1.2	
.9	.6	.4	Debt/Worth					.3	
1.7	1.3	1.3						.7	
3.7	3.9	3.3						3.2	
33.1	32.7	39.1	% Profit Before Taxes/Tangible Net Worth					24.7	
(35) 15.5	(29) 14.5	(26) 19.4						15.3	
-2.7	-2.0	-1.9						-15.3	
17.8	13.4	17.3	% Profit Before Taxes/Total Assets					18.5	
5.2	5.9	6.4						5.6	
-2.0	-.3	-1.2						-4.1	
19.2	15.7	15.2	Sales/Net Fixed Assets					5.8	
8.6	6.6	4.6						3.3	
3.9	2.9	3.0						2.0	
2.3	2.5	2.2	Sales/Total Assets					2.0	
1.8	1.6	1.4						1.4	
1.3	.9	.8						.8	
.9	1.5	1.7	% Depr., Dep., Amort./Sales					2.8	
(37) 2.5	(33) 3.3	(26) 2.7						4.7	
3.5	4.2	5.3						7.8	
3.0			% Officers', Directors' Owners' Comp/Sales						
(15) 3.8									
10.9									
1441500M	679323M	526216M	Net Sales ($)	1803M	9375M	11220M	15163M	166142M	322513M
800961M	578745M	458990M	Total Assets ($)	898M	23740M	8822M	9200M	141056M	275274M

M = $ thousand   MM = $ million
See Pages 9 through 22 for Explanation of Ratios and Data

Current Data Sorted by Assets   Comparative Historical Data

Type of Statement

Type of Statement	0-500M	500M-2MM	2-10MM	10-50MM	50-100MM	100-250MM		4/1/06-3/31/07 ALL	4/1/07-3/31/08 ALL
Unqualified		2	6	20	2	5		24	27
Reviewed			15	7	1			22	15
Compiled		4	3	2				15	8
Tax Returns	6	2	2					14	13
Other	3	6	14	17	7	9		40	47
		29 (4/1-9/30/10)		104 (10/1/10-3/31/11)					
NUMBER OF STATEMENTS	9	14	40	46	10	14		115	110

	0-500M %	500M-2MM %	2-10MM %	10-50MM %	50-100MM %	100-250MM %		4/1/06-3/31/07 ALL %	4/1/07-3/31/08 ALL %
ASSETS									
Cash & Equivalents		12.9	7.6	7.2	7.3	8.2		6.7	8.0
Trade Receivables (net)		34.5	28.9	23.1	21.7	16.2		30.9	29.2
Inventory		11.9	26.2	25.3	29.7	26.4		25.1	22.8
All Other Current		2.8	2.5	3.8	3.2	4.9		3.3	2.5
Total Current		62.1	65.3	59.5	61.8	55.7		65.9	62.6
Fixed Assets (net)		29.4	26.4	28.6	24.4	27.3		25.6	28.9
Intangibles (net)		1.7	1.3	2.3	6.3	11.2		2.6	3.4
All Other Non-Current		6.7	7.0	9.6	7.5	5.7		5.8	5.1
Total		100.0	100.0	100.0	100.0	100.0		100.0	100.0
LIABILITIES									
Notes Payable-Short Term		22.2	9.5	14.4	4.0	3.8		12.2	12.2
Cur. Mat.-L.T.D.		5.0	4.1	3.1	2.4	2.0		3.1	3.4
Trade Payables		18.8	18.7	13.0	24.6	10.7		19.4	19.6
Income Taxes Payable		.2	.3	.3	1.4	.1		.2	.2
All Other Current		5.2	11.3	11.7	6.4	8.6		8.1	9.5
Total Current		51.4	44.0	42.4	38.8	25.2		43.0	44.9
Long-Term Debt		9.0	16.4	12.6	16.8	7.5		17.4	15.6
Deferred Taxes		1.8	.5	.5	.7	4.1		.9	.6
All Other Non-Current		31.0	4.5	10.0	4.1	4.1		6.3	6.3
Net Worth		6.8	34.6	34.5	39.6	59.1		32.4	32.8
Total Liabilities & Net Worth		100.0	100.0	100.0	100.0	100.0		100.0	100.0
INCOME DATA									
Net Sales		100.0	100.0	100.0	100.0	100.0		100.0	100.0
Gross Profit		28.0	20.7	15.9	19.4	15.6		23.5	22.2
Operating Expenses		28.2	20.7	12.1	9.3	8.3		17.5	15.8
Operating Profit		-.2	.0	3.8	10.1	7.2		6.0	6.4
All Other Expenses (net)		.5	.9	.6	1.0	.6		1.3	1.1
Profit Before Taxes		-.6	-.9	3.2	9.1	6.6		4.7	5.4
RATIOS									
Current		3.4	3.0	2.6	3.2	3.9		2.3	2.5
		1.4	1.6	1.4	2.0	2.5		1.5	1.4
		.9	.9	1.1	1.2	1.5		1.1	1.0
Quick		2.4	1.9	1.8	1.7	1.8		1.4	1.6
		1.2	.8	.7	1.1	1.1		.9	.9
		.7	.5	.4	.7	.5		.5	.5
Sales/Receivables		33 11.0	34 10.8	31 11.7	25 14.5	28 13.1		30 12.3	32 11.3
		52 7.1	46 8.0	40 9.1	41 8.8	54 6.8		41 8.8	44 8.4
		63 5.8	68 5.3	59 6.2	64 5.7	62 5.9		57 6.5	56 6.5
Cost of Sales/Inventory		0 UND	15 24.8	29 12.4	28 13.2	43 8.5		17 21.1	10 36.5
		10 35.2	48 7.6	57 6.4	60 6.1	85 4.3		45 8.0	39 9.4
		57 6.4	123 3.0	83 4.4	98 3.7	152 2.4		72 5.1	72 5.1
Cost of Sales/Payables		12 31.7	22 16.7	18 20.5	24 15.0	27 13.3		22 16.6	19 18.7
		38 9.6	35 10.3	31 11.8	37 9.8	36 10.2		33 11.1	31 11.8
		54 6.7	51 7.1	38 9.6	57 6.4	47 7.7		55 6.7	46 7.9
Sales/Working Capital		5.1	3.0	5.8	3.6	2.6		6.1	5.8
		18.3	11.0	10.5	6.1	4.5		10.9	13.4
		-56.5	-56.2	32.7	27.8	8.0		78.6	246.9
EBIT/Interest		6.6	10.2	19.3		40.1		13.5	18.5
		(11) .9	(38) 1.7	(43) 4.0		(12) 10.8		(102) 4.7	(101) 4.5
		-11.3	-6.8	1.9		3.6		1.7	1.4
Net Profit + Depr., Dep., Amort./Cur. Mat. L/T/D				5.1				13.4	7.9
			(17) 2.3					(34) 4.8	(24) 1.9
				1.5				1.5	1.2
Fixed/Worth		.1	.3	.5	.1	.4		.3	.3
		1.3	.6	.8	.4	.6		.7	.8
		NM	1.7	1.3	1.9	1.3		3.5	2.6
Debt/Worth		.9	.6	.7	.7	.3		.9	1.0
		8.4	1.8	1.6	2.1	1.0		2.0	2.2
		-3.0	4.0	6.1	4.3	4.9		8.0	6.5
% Profit Before Taxes/Tangible Net Worth		67.2	23.4	40.8		19.3		59.4	58.8
		(10) 1.1	(34) 3.2	(40) 19.0		(12) 13.8		(98) 29.9	(96) 26.4
		-19.8	-17.6	4.8		8.5		13.2	7.0
% Profit Before Taxes/Total Assets		6.5	8.8	14.4	23.1	11.1		21.8	22.2
		-1.6	1.5	5.4	13.5	8.5		9.8	10.1
		-12.5	-9.4	1.6	7.7	3.1		2.6	2.1
Sales/Net Fixed Assets		131.1	22.3	16.9	73.1	5.9		24.9	23.3
		9.0	9.1	8.2	9.5	4.7		12.0	11.5
		5.2	4.9	3.4	4.1	3.3		5.7	4.3
Sales/Total Assets		3.3	2.8	2.4	2.7	1.4		3.1	2.9
		2.4	1.9	1.8	1.5	1.3		2.5	2.3
		1.4	1.3	1.1	1.1	.9		1.8	1.6
% Depr., Dep., Amort./Sales		1.0	.9	1.0	.7			.9	.7
		(10) 2.7	(39) 1.9	(41) 1.8	1.2			(97) 1.6	(98) 1.4
		7.0	3.6	2.9	8.7			2.3	2.7
% Officers', Directors', Owners' Comp/Sales				2.3				1.2	1.2
			(15) 5.4					(33) 2.9	(28) 4.1
				6.8				5.9	6.3
Net Sales ($)	30476M	46462M	538711M	2440693M	1412999M	3316516M		6130458M	6552594M
Total Assets ($)	2845M	19085M	238538M	1251562M	723173M	2566358M		3160940M	3141943M

M = $ thousand   MM = $ million
See Pages 9 through 22 for Explanation of Ratios and Data

Comparative Historical Data | Current Data Sorted by Sales

Type of Statement									
29	36	35	Unqualified	1			5	3	26
27	24	23	Reviewed		1		5	8	8
12	13	9	Compiled	1		2	5	1	
15	5	10	Tax Returns	1	6			3	
60	64	56	Other	2	4		5	7	33

4/1/08-3/31/09 ALL	4/1/09-3/31/10 ALL	4/1/10-3/31/11 ALL		29 (4/1-9/30/10)			104 (10/1/10-3/31/11)		
				0-1MM	1-3MM	3-5MM	5-10MM	10-25MM	25MM & OVER
143	142	133	NUMBER OF STATEMENTS	5	11	8	20	22	67
%	%	%	ASSETS	%	%	%	%	%	%
7.1	8.5	8.5	Cash & Equivalents		17.6		10.2	9.2	6.7
27.4	24.5	25.1	Trade Receivables (net)		20.7		25.5	30.8	23.4
25.4	22.8	23.7	Inventory		9.4		23.9	21.4	28.0
2.9	3.4	3.2	All Other Current		2.5		2.6	3.2	3.8
62.8	59.1	60.6	Total Current		50.2		62.2	64.6	61.9
27.7	30.9	27.2	Fixed Assets (net)		27.6		31.5	27.8	25.3
2.7	3.3	3.7	Intangibles (net)		2.0		.6	2.5	4.6
6.8	6.7	8.6	All Other Non-Current		20.2		5.8	5.2	8.3
100.0	100.0	100.0	Total		100.0		100.0	100.0	100.0
			LIABILITIES						
12.9	10.7	12.6	Notes Payable-Short Term		26.8		10.7	8.1	11.3
3.6	4.6	3.4	Cur. Mat.-L.T.D.		3.5		4.6	3.6	2.6
15.5	14.3	16.0	Trade Payables		12.0		14.6	22.0	14.8
.5	.2	.4	Income Taxes Payable		.0		.1	1.0	.4
9.0	11.1	10.6	All Other Current		16.3		10.5	13.8	9.9
41.5	40.9	43.0	Total Current		58.6		40.5	48.4	38.9
14.6	18.2	13.6	Long-Term Debt		13.5		20.1	15.5	10.4
.6	.9	1.0	Deferred Taxes		.0		1.3	.7	1.2
6.4	7.6	9.9	All Other Non-Current		13.5		3.5	2.6	8.8
36.9	32.3	32.5	Net Worth		14.4		34.7	32.8	40.6
100.0	100.0	100.0	Total Liabilities & Net Worth		100.0		100.0	100.0	100.0
			INCOME DATA						
100.0	100.0	100.0	Net Sales		100.0		100.0	100.0	100.0
22.5	21.5	20.2	Gross Profit		34.6		23.6	18.7	16.0
16.7	20.3	17.1	Operating Expenses		31.7		23.1	18.6	10.3
5.8	1.2	3.0	Operating Profit		2.9		.5	.0	5.7
1.0	1.8	.8	All Other Expenses (net)		1.0		1.6	.0	.7
4.8	-.7	2.3	Profit Before Taxes		1.9		-1.1	.0	5.0
			RATIOS						
2.6 / 1.7 / 1.1	3.1 / 1.4 / 1.0	3.1 / 1.5 / 1.1	Current		2.5 / 1.0 / .4		3.0 / 1.9 / .7	3.0 / 1.5 / .9	3.1 / 1.6 / 1.2
1.4 / .9 / .5	1.6 / .7 / .4	1.7 / .9 / .5	Quick		1.4 / .7 / .4		1.8 / .9 / .6	2.3 / .8 / .4	1.7 / .9 / .5
23 15.6 / 39 9.3 / 57 6.4	31 12.0 / 43 8.6 / 60 6.1	31 11.7 / 43 8.6 / 61 6.0	Sales/Receivables		0 UND / 31 11.7 / 67 5.5		35 10.4 / 52 7.1 / 78 4.7	30 12.0 / 44 8.3 / 80 4.5	30 12.1 / 41 8.9 / 56 6.5
18 20.4 / 45 8.1 / 76 4.8	20 18.2 / 49 7.4 / 84 4.4	18 19.9 / 49 7.5 / 89 4.1	Cost of Sales/Inventory		3 121.9 / 13 29.1 / 27 13.7		4 96.7 / 47 7.8 / 140 2.6	12 29.4 / 47 7.7 / 76 4.8	33 11.0 / 58 6.3 / 91 4.0
12 29.8 / 25 14.8 / 43 8.6	16 23.1 / 30 12.0 / 46 8.0	17 21.7 / 34 10.9 / 47 7.8	Cost of Sales/Payables		0 UND / 42 8.6 / 53 7.0		24 15.3 / 35 10.4 / 66 5.6	13 27.7 / 40 9.1 / 50 7.3	20 18.4 / 30 12.0 / 40 9.0
5.3 / 11.2 / 67.4	4.5 / 10.5 / -478.2	4.5 / 10.2 / 39.2	Sales/Working Capital		12.6 / 170.2 / -20.7		2.6 / 6.2 / -13.6	4.5 / 8.5 / -75.5	4.5 / 8.4 / 28.3
17.3 / (134) 5.6 / 2.0	6.5 / (124) 1.5 / -1.4	14.6 / (120) 4.0 / .2	EBIT/Interest		17.5 / (10) .4 / -6.7		6.2 / .2 / -7.0	10.4 / (17) 3.1 / -.8	23.4 / (63) 7.2 / 2.6
11.8 / (35) 3.7 / 2.3	6.5 / (36) 2.3 / .2	6.0 / (36) 2.2 / 1.2	Net Profit + Depr., Dep., Amort./Cur. Mat. L/T/D						7.8 / (23) 3.9 / 1.5
.3 / .8 / 1.8	.3 / .8 / 2.1	.3 / .7 / 2.3	Fixed/Worth		.4 / 2.4 / -.7		.1 / .6 / 2.1	.3 / .7 / 2.1	.4 / .6 / 1.1
.8 / 1.7 / 4.6	.7 / 1.8 / 5.1	.6 / 1.8 / 10.1	Debt/Worth		1.4 / 2.3 / -3.3		.6 / 1.8 / 4.1	.6 / 1.8 / NM	.6 / 1.4 / 4.5
62.0 / (127) 29.4 / 11.1	23.8 / (118) 6.0 / -8.5	33.8 / (108) 15.1 / 1.1	% Profit Before Taxes/Tangible Net Worth		11.1 / (18) -.3 / -14.2			25.4 / (17) 2.9 / -16.0	42.1 / (59) 23.1 / 11.9
19.3 / 10.8 / 2.6	8.6 / 1.7 / -7.0	12.1 / 4.4 / -2.1	% Profit Before Taxes/Total Assets		44.5 / 2.8 / -19.0		4.8 / -1.2 / -9.4	8.9 / 1.6 / -3.0	14.9 / 9.2 / 3.1
23.7 / 10.8 / 5.5	17.6 / 7.0 / 3.1	21.5 / 8.7 / 4.3	Sales/Net Fixed Assets		45.4 / 14.0 / 8.7		28.7 / 7.6 / 2.5	17.9 / 7.9 / 4.8	21.8 / 8.4 / 3.9
3.3 / 2.4 / 1.7	2.6 / 1.8 / 1.2	2.7 / 1.8 / 1.3	Sales/Total Assets		6.9 / 3.1 / 1.3		2.3 / 1.4 / .9	2.9 / 2.3 / 1.3	2.6 / 1.8 / 1.3
.7 / (127) 1.3 / 2.7	1.0 / (119) 2.2 / 4.2	1.0 / (110) 1.8 / 3.6	% Depr., Dep., Amort./Sales				1.3 / (18) 3.3 / 5.6	1.2 / (20) 1.8 / 2.8	.9 / (55) 1.8 / 2.9
1.1 / (41) 2.8 / 4.7	1.9 / (25) 3.3 / 6.8	1.8 / (31) 3.2 / 6.8	% Officers', Directors' Owners' Comp/Sales						
10441471M / 4322972M	6024034M / 3702847M	7785857M / 4801561M	Net Sales ($) / Total Assets ($)	3263M / 3140M	21854M / 13389M	31790M / 17655M	148648M / 112101M	344318M / 194670M	7235984M / 4460606M

M = $ thousand   MM = $ million
See Pages 9 through 22 for Explanation of Ratios and Data

Current Data Sorted by Assets | Comparative Historical Data

Type of Statement	0-500M	500M-2MM	2-10MM	10-50MM	50-100MM	100-250MM		4/1/06-3/31/07 ALL	4/1/07-3/31/08 ALL
Unqualified		1	2	22	6	5		24	31
Reviewed	1	4	20	13	4	1		17	23
Compiled	3	5	10	7	1			13	17
Tax Returns	5	12	7	1				12	13
Other		11	13	22	5	3		50	50
		27 (4/1-9/30/10)		157 (10/1/10-3/31/11)					
NUMBER OF STATEMENTS	9	33	52	65	16	9		116	134
ASSETS	%	%	%	%	%	%		%	%
Cash & Equivalents		10.0	8.4	6.2	6.9			7.3	7.3
Trade Receivables (net)		38.0	25.6	22.3	19.6			31.4	27.2
Inventory		20.8	24.1	27.9	27.2			33.3	30.9
All Other Current		3.9	3.7	2.3	6.4			2.3	4.7
Total Current		72.7	61.9	58.7	60.2			74.3	70.0
Fixed Assets (net)		19.1	26.5	29.4	28.0			20.4	22.9
Intangibles (net)		2.3	4.7	5.5	5.6			1.9	4.0
All Other Non-Current		5.8	7.0	6.4	6.2			3.4	3.1
Total		100.0	100.0	100.0	100.0			100.0	100.0
LIABILITIES									
Notes Payable-Short Term		9.3	9.1	10.8	12.5			10.9	12.8
Cur. Mat.-L.T.D.		7.9	2.8	3.1	1.1			2.0	2.9
Trade Payables		20.2	16.0	10.9	10.3			19.8	17.6
Income Taxes Payable		.0	.1	.1	.1			.4	.4
All Other Current		10.4	10.3	8.7	12.2			9.3	8.5
Total Current		47.8	38.2	33.6	36.1			42.3	42.2
Long-Term Debt		27.0	12.3	15.1	12.3			13.1	12.8
Deferred Taxes		.0	.6	.4	.9			.8	.3
All Other Non-Current		7.5	6.7	3.6	6.5			4.1	4.0
Net Worth		17.7	42.1	47.3	44.2			39.7	40.7
Total Liabilties & Net Worth		100.0	100.0	100.0	100.0			100.0	100.0
INCOME DATA									
Net Sales		100.0	100.0	100.0	100.0			100.0	100.0
Gross Profit		31.1	29.9	20.7	19.9			22.4	23.7
Operating Expenses		29.8	24.7	14.8	14.9			15.3	17.0
Operating Profit		1.4	5.1	6.0	5.0			7.1	6.7
All Other Expenses (net)		.9	.2	.7	1.2			.5	.9
Profit Before Taxes		.5	5.0	5.3	3.8			6.6	5.8
RATIOS									
Current		4.0	2.9	3.6	3.3			2.9	3.0
		1.8	1.6	1.9	1.6			1.7	1.6
		.9	1.0	1.1	1.1			1.3	1.2
Quick		2.5	1.7	2.0	1.3			1.6	1.4
		1.3	.9	.7	.8			.9	.8
		.5	.4	.4	.3			.6	.5
Sales/Receivables		33 11.0	30 12.2	37 9.8	40 9.1			32 11.3	27 13.4
		49 7.5	40 9.1	47 7.8	56 6.5			48 7.6	38 9.5
		65 5.7	52 7.0	55 6.7	82 4.5			56 6.5	48 7.7
Cost of Sales/Inventory		13 29.1	22 16.4	36 10.2	50 7.3			32 11.5	23 15.8
		42 8.8	54 6.7	69 5.3	93 3.9			66 5.6	57 6.4
		64 5.7	92 4.0	126 2.9	113 3.2			110 3.3	92 4.0
Cost of Sales/Payables		16 22.3	20 17.8	10 34.8	16 22.6			21 17.2	15 24.2
		36 10.0	31 11.8	24 15.2	29 12.6			35 10.4	28 13.1
		57 6.4	51 7.2	42 8.7	40 9.1			48 7.5	41 8.8
Sales/Working Capital		5.8	4.6	4.3	3.9			4.2	5.1
		8.1	10.7	7.5	5.0			7.7	9.6
		-113.9	UND	20.6	277.6			15.8	32.2
EBIT/Interest		6.8	21.4	14.4	25.5			22.8	13.7
		(29) 2.8	(47) 5.6	(60) 3.5	(14) 10.6			(100) 7.7	(116) 5.0
		-.4	1.7	2.0	2.9			2.6	2.0
Net Profit + Depr., Dep., Amort./Cur. Mat. L/T/D				5.0				14.9	12.4
				(14) 1.9				(22) 7.0	(32) 4.7
				1.2				2.4	1.5
Fixed/Worth		.3	.2	.3	.3			.2	.2
		.7	1.0	.7	.8			.5	.5
		-1.6	2.1	1.5	2.1			1.1	1.5
Debt/Worth		1.4	.7	.5	.5			.7	.6
		3.2	1.6	1.1	1.2			1.6	1.6
		-6.3	3.5	3.4	10.0			3.9	4.2
% Profit Before Taxes/Tangible Net Worth		50.3	47.5	35.0	26.0			58.6	59.2
		(23) 13.0	(47) 21.7	(58) 16.7	(13) 17.2			(109) 33.4	(113) 28.3
		-25.7	6.2	6.0	9.0			14.5	11.8
% Profit Before Taxes/Total Assets		12.0	17.1	13.3	11.1			22.3	21.5
		3.7	7.6	5.7	7.8			12.4	10.5
		-9.3	1.7	2.6	5.5			4.4	2.5
Sales/Net Fixed Assets		53.6	27.9	16.7	9.7			42.7	34.8
		18.3	7.2	8.1	4.8			15.3	15.1
		8.2	4.7	3.3	4.0			6.6	7.4
Sales/Total Assets		3.5	2.8	2.3	2.2			3.0	3.4
		2.9	2.1	1.7	1.4			2.3	2.4
		1.9	1.4	1.1	.9			1.7	1.8
% Depr., Dep., Amort./Sales		.7	.8	1.2	1.3			.5	.5
		(27) 1.9	(49) 2.5	(59) 2.3	(13) 2.4			(104) 1.2	(120) 1.1
		3.3	4.1	3.4	3.9			2.4	2.3
% Officers', Directors' Owners' Comp/Sales		2.5	1.7					1.1	1.4
		(20) 3.7	(23) 4.0					(37) 2.4	(47) 2.3
		8.2	8.6					5.7	5.7
Net Sales ($)	9892M	113542M	645768M	2648896M	1791253M	2858989M		6782453M	7484970M
Total Assets ($)	2246M	42450M	300132M	1454616M	1171618M	1672572M		3221173M	3537587M

M = $ thousand   MM = $ million
See Pages 9 through 22 for Explanation of Ratios and Data

Comparative Historical Data | Current Data Sorted by Sales

			Type of Statement	0-1MM	1-3MM	3-5MM	5-10MM	10-25MM	25MM & OVER
37	33	36	Unqualified		1			2	33
26	42	38	Reviewed		3	3	6	17	9
23	14	20	Compiled	1	2	5	4	7	1
15	19	23	Tax Returns	2	6	3	9	2	1
70	73	67	Other	2	9	7	3	17	29
4/1/08- 3/31/09 ALL	4/1/09- 3/31/10 ALL	4/1/10- 3/31/11 ALL		27 (4/1-9/30/10)			157 (10/1/10-3/31/11)		
171	181	184	NUMBER OF STATEMENTS	5	21	18	22	45	73
%	%	%	**ASSETS**	%	%	%	%	%	%
8.2	8.7	8.0	Cash & Equivalents		11.9	11.4	10.3	5.5	7.0
26.1	25.7	25.8	Trade Receivables (net)		31.5	27.4	26.4	25.5	23.4
27.9	26.3	25.3	Inventory		16.0	23.2	17.4	27.6	28.9
4.9	4.3	3.6	All Other Current		10.7	1.4	3.5	1.9	3.5
67.1	65.0	62.8	Total Current		70.1	63.4	57.6	60.5	62.8
23.9	25.9	25.7	Fixed Assets (net)		18.5	25.8	28.9	28.0	25.6
3.9	3.9	4.9	Intangibles (net)		.7	5.4	7.4	4.6	5.4
5.2	5.2	6.7	All Other Non-Current		10.6	5.3	6.1	6.9	6.2
100.0	100.0	100.0	Total		100.0	100.0	100.0	100.0	100.0
			LIABILITIES						
12.3	10.4	10.1	Notes Payable-Short Term		7.6	15.3	3.7	12.7	10.0
2.7	3.9	3.5	Cur. Mat.-L.T.D.		8.1	4.2	4.3	3.1	2.2
15.9	14.1	14.4	Trade Payables		18.0	18.2	11.0	15.6	12.1
.5	.1	.1	Income Taxes Payable		.0	.0	.1	.1	.1
10.3	13.8	12.6	All Other Current		14.4	11.0	8.5	12.2	8.6
41.6	42.2	40.7	Total Current		48.0	48.7	27.6	43.8	33.1
11.6	14.8	17.2	Long-Term Debt		32.6	17.0	15.9	14.4	12.9
.4	.4	.5	Deferred Taxes		.0	.3	1.2	.3	.6
4.6	4.6	5.9	All Other Non-Current		17.0	4.0	4.0	5.1	4.6
41.8	37.9	35.7	Net Worth		2.4	30.0	51.4	36.4	48.9
100.0	100.0	100.0	Total Liabilties & Net Worth		100.0	100.0	100.0	100.0	100.0
			INCOME DATA						
100.0	100.0	100.0	Net Sales		100.0	100.0	100.0	100.0	100.0
24.4	25.8	25.4	Gross Profit		36.0	28.1	28.9	26.6	19.0
17.5	23.3	20.9	Operating Expenses		35.9	25.4	23.8	22.9	12.1
6.9	2.5	4.5	Operating Profit		.1	2.7	5.2	3.7	6.9
1.2	1.3	.6	All Other Expenses (net)		.5	.9	.4	.3	.8
5.7	1.2	3.9	Profit Before Taxes		-.3	1.8	4.7	3.4	6.0
			RATIOS						
3.0	3.1	3.2	Current		4.1	2.7	3.7	2.8	3.6
1.6	1.7	1.7			1.7	1.4	2.2	1.4	1.9
1.1	1.1	1.0			.8	.9	1.3	.9	1.3
1.5	1.6	1.9	Quick		2.1	2.2	2.1	1.3	2.0
.8	.8	.8			1.1	.9	1.3	.7	.9
.5	.5	.4			.5	.4	.6	.4	.5
26 14.1	29 12.6	32 11.3	Sales/Receivables	27 13.4	32 11.5	34 10.7	30 12.1	36 10.1	
37 10.0	43 8.5	45 8.2		52 7.0	39 9.4	40 9.2	49 7.4	43 8.4	
48 7.6	58 6.3	57 6.4		67 5.5	47 7.8	56 6.5	64 5.7	56 6.5	
24 15.5	25 14.4	29 12.4	Cost of Sales/Inventory	0 UND	13 28.4	15 25.0	44 8.3	36 10.2	
45 8.0	60 6.1	53 6.8		50 7.3	43 8.5	43 8.5	62 5.9	61 6.0	
88 4.2	108 3.4	97 3.8		89 4.1	68 5.4	88 4.2	97 3.8	109 3.3	
11 32.6	15 24.0	17 21.7	Cost of Sales/Payables	11 32.4	17 21.8	15 24.9	19 18.9	14 25.3	
26 14.0	27 13.4	29 12.7		42 8.6	27 13.7	28 12.9	29 12.7	27 13.6	
42 8.8	47 7.8	45 8.0		70 5.2	60 6.1	40 9.1	51 7.2	39 9.5	
4.9	4.3	4.7	Sales/Working Capital		4.5	7.3	4.5	4.8	4.3
10.4	8.7	8.1			8.0	11.5	6.9	12.5	7.0
50.2	60.0	154.0			-25.7	-33.9	24.8	-44.8	13.7
24.0	10.5	14.0	EBIT/Interest		6.1	10.2	10.9	14.6	25.0
(142) 5.2	(162) 2.4	(164) 4.0			(17) 2.8	(17) 3.1	(17) 2.4	(42) 5.1	(68) 6.5
1.6	-1.4	1.5			-.4	.2	.9	1.2	2.5
8.0	6.0	4.8	Net Profit + Depr., Dep., Amort./Cur. Mat. L/T/D					5.3	4.9
(39) 4.0	(35) 1.5	(32) 3.1						(11) 2.9	(15) 3.4
1.6	-.1	1.6						1.3	1.9
.2	.2	.3	Fixed/Worth		.1	.5	.2	.3	.3
.6	.7	.8			1.0	1.0	.9	1.0	.6
1.6	2.9	2.1			-.4	NM	2.1	3.0	1.2
.5	.5	.6	Debt/Worth		1.4	.9	.4	.8	.4
1.4	1.7	1.7			36.4	2.3	1.6	1.9	1.1
4.5	7.7	6.1			-4.4	NM	3.1	6.1	2.7
65.9	34.7	39.6	% Profit Before Taxes/Tangible Net Worth		76.6	50.7	23.4	44.8	36.6
(151) 28.4	(152) 8.9	(152) 17.8		(11) 13.0	(14) 22.2	(20) 12.0	(40) 21.7	(65) 17.9	
7.7	-4.6	6.0			-3.2	-3.9	3.5	4.1	8.2
24.3	11.8	14.3	% Profit Before Taxes/Total Assets		12.0	20.3	13.4	13.6	17.2
9.7	3.5	6.6			3.7	3.7	4.7	7.2	7.6
2.0	-3.7	1.6			-3.2	-8.5	.1	.4	4.0
32.1	26.1	25.2	Sales/Net Fixed Assets		57.7	24.6	25.2	30.3	17.1
14.0	8.4	9.0			12.7	10.9	9.3	7.3	8.6
6.2	4.1	4.6			5.7	5.0	3.2	4.0	4.5
3.4	2.7	2.8	Sales/Total Assets		4.0	3.3	3.0	2.6	2.4
2.4	1.8	2.0			2.7	2.4	1.7	2.0	1.9
1.8	1.3	1.4			1.1	1.8	1.3	1.1	1.4
.6	.9	1.0	% Depr., Dep., Amort./Sales		.7	1.8	.7	.8	1.1
(147) 1.4	(148) 2.1	(158) 2.2		(14) 2.1	(16) 2.4	(20) 2.5	(43) 2.4	(64) 1.9	
2.7	4.4	3.4			5.7	4.1	4.0	4.3	2.8
1.9	1.7	1.5	% Officers', Directors' Owners' Comp/Sales		2.4	2.2	1.2		
(50) 2.7	(54) 3.4	(54) 3.7			(11) 3.8	(15) 3.5	(12) 2.9		
7.8	7.3	8.0			7.9	4.9	8.0		
11396480M	7609908M	8068340M	Net Sales ($)	3136M	39580M	73845M	159583M	758656M	7033540M
5027076M	4298495M	4643634M	Total Assets ($)	815M	26467M	32561M	106150M	510367M	3967274M

M = $ thousand   MM = $ million
See Pages 9 through 22 for Explanation of Ratios and Data

Current Data Sorted by Assets   Comparative Historical Data

0-500M	500M-2MM	2-10MM	10-50MM	50-100MM	100-250MM	Type of Statement	4/1/06-3/31/07 ALL	4/1/07-3/31/08 ALL
		4	5	1	1	Unqualified	25	18
	1	7	9	1		Reviewed	18	11
	1	1	2			Compiled	13	10
1	4		1			Tax Returns	6	2
	3	12	22		3	Other	29	34
		16 (4/1-9/30/10)	63 (10/1/10-3/31/11)					
1	9	24	39	2	4	NUMBER OF STATEMENTS	91	75
%	%	%	%	%	%	**ASSETS**	%	%
		6.5	7.2			Cash & Equivalents	7.4	5.3
		27.6	23.8			Trade Receivables (net)	27.7	25.6
		29.4	31.0			Inventory	30.6	29.5
		.4	1.1			All Other Current	2.0	2.0
		63.9	63.1			Total Current	67.7	62.3
		27.9	29.8			Fixed Assets (net)	24.6	29.4
		2.9	2.2			Intangibles (net)	2.8	2.7
		5.3	4.9			All Other Non-Current	4.8	5.7
		100.0	100.0			Total	100.0	100.0
						LIABILITIES		
		20.4	14.6			Notes Payable-Short Term	13.8	13.0
		2.8	4.0			Cur. Mat.-L.T.D.	3.4	3.3
		20.1	13.2			Trade Payables	18.9	18.8
		.0	.1			Income Taxes Payable	.2	.4
		5.1	8.5			All Other Current	8.0	5.8
		48.4	40.3			Total Current	44.4	41.3
		13.6	16.7			Long-Term Debt	15.6	14.0
		.4	.3			Deferred Taxes	.3	.8
		4.4	7.4			All Other Non-Current	6.0	7.5
		33.2	35.3			Net Worth	33.7	36.4
		100.0	100.0			Total Liabilities & Net Worth	100.0	100.0
						INCOME DATA		
		100.0	100.0			Net Sales	100.0	100.0
		25.6	20.0			Gross Profit	21.5	20.3
		20.6	14.0			Operating Expenses	16.0	13.1
		5.0	6.0			Operating Profit	5.6	7.2
		1.2	1.2			All Other Expenses (net)	1.6	1.4
		3.8	4.8			Profit Before Taxes	3.9	5.8
						RATIOS		
		2.0	2.8			Current	2.3	2.4
		1.3	1.4				1.6	1.6
		1.0	1.1				1.1	1.1
		1.6	1.5			Quick	1.2	1.3
		.5	.7				.8	.7
		.4					.5	.5
		39 9.3	35 10.3			Sales/Receivables	32 11.6	33 11.1
		51 7.1	45 8.1				42 8.6	39 9.3
		64 5.7	52 7.0				54 6.7	48 7.6
		26 14.2	37 9.8			Cost of Sales/Inventory	39 9.3	35 10.4
		57 6.4	69 5.3				60 6.1	59 6.2
		76 4.8	92 4.0				89 4.1	80 4.6
		28 12.9	19 19.6			Cost of Sales/Payables	21 17.6	20 18.5
		40 9.1	30 12.1				33 11.1	33 10.9
		53 6.9	40 9.0				49 7.4	41 9.0
		7.7	4.3			Sales/Working Capital	5.7	5.6
		14.3	12.3				10.8	12.3
		NM	32.6				33.5	41.6
		6.3	14.6			EBIT/Interest	9.0	17.1
		(20) 3.2	(38) 4.1				(81) 3.5	(67) 4.4
		1.1	1.8				1.0	1.9
			3.8			Net Profit + Depr., Dep., Amort./Cur. Mat. L/T/D	8.4	8.9
			(12) 3.1				(34) 4.0	(31) 3.0
			1.9				1.7	1.0
		.3	.4			Fixed/Worth	.3	.3
		1.0	.9				.6	.6
		2.4	1.5				2.0	1.6
		1.2	.8			Debt/Worth	.9	.6
		2.4	1.6				2.0	1.5
		5.1	5.1				5.9	3.9
		42.3	40.3			% Profit Before Taxes/Tangible Net Worth	50.3	47.1
		(23) 19.0	(35) 20.2				(75) 22.8	(66) 25.4
		.7	3.5				7.2	9.3
		11.0	13.8			% Profit Before Taxes/Total Assets	14.1	18.8
		5.6	5.6				8.3	8.6
		.4	2.0				.9	2.4
		25.3	13.1			Sales/Net Fixed Assets	24.1	19.4
		9.5	9.1				12.4	8.1
		3.1	3.8				5.6	4.7
		2.3	2.5			Sales/Total Assets	2.9	2.9
		1.9	1.9				2.3	2.2
		1.3	1.3				1.8	1.8
		.5	.9			% Depr., Dep., Amort./Sales	.9	.9
		(22) 1.6	(37) 1.7				(85) 1.6	(67) 1.7
		4.3	3.7				2.9	2.8
						% Officers', Directors' Owners' Comp/Sales	.9	.7
							(21) 2.1	(18) 1.5
							5.0	2.7
1730M	31170M	273090M	1530220M	228067M	867347M	Net Sales ($)	5019590M	4110201M
293M	11149M	116729M	812024M	145576M	441012M	Total Assets ($)	2330996M	1954521M

© RMA 2011

M = $ thousand   MM = $ million
See Pages 9 through 22 for Explanation of Ratios and Data

Comparative Historical Data | Current Data Sorted by Sales

						Type of Statement								
	17		13		7	Unqualified						2		5
	19		21		15	Reviewed		1			1	4		9
	10		11		10	Compiled			1		4	2		3
	8		12		7	Tax Returns		4	2					1
	36		35		40	Other		3	4		3	8		22
	4/1/08-		4/1/09-		4/1/10-			16 (4/1-9/30/10)			63 (10/1/10-3/31/11)			
	3/31/09		3/31/10		3/31/11									
	ALL		ALL		ALL		0-1MM	1-3MM	3-5MM	5-10MM	10-25MM		25MM & OVER	
	90		92		79	NUMBER OF STATEMENTS		8	7	8	16		40	
	%		%		%	ASSETS	%	%	%	%	%		%	
	7.3		9.4		6.6	Cash & Equivalents	D				7.6		6.5	
	25.0		23.4		26.9	Trade Receivables (net)	A				26.5		23.9	
	27.8		28.8		29.9	Inventory	T				30.6		31.8	
	2.1		2.9		.8	All Other Current	A				.7		1.2	
	62.2		64.5		64.2	Total Current					65.4		63.3	
	29.4		27.1		27.5	Fixed Assets (net)	N				24.6		29.1	
	2.4		3.1		2.5	Intangibles (net)	O				2.4		1.5	
	6.0		5.3		5.8	All Other Non-Current	T				7.6		6.1	
	100.0		100.0		100.0	Total					100.0		100.0	
						LIABILITIES	A							
	13.5		11.5		16.0	Notes Payable-Short Term	V				13.3		16.8	
	2.7		3.0		3.0	Cur. Mat.-L.T.D.	A				5.3		2.3	
	18.5		14.4		17.1	Trade Payables	I				15.6		16.0	
	.2		.2		.1	Income Taxes Payable	L				.1		.1	
	6.7		7.0		7.9	All Other Current	A				8.0		7.1	
	41.7		36.2		44.0	Total Current	B				42.3		42.2	
	17.6		12.8		16.0	Long-Term Debt	L				18.4		12.2	
	.4		.7		.4	Deferred Taxes	E				.5		.5	
	6.2		7.0		9.0	All Other Non-Current					2.0		11.7	
	34.1		43.3		30.6	Net Worth					36.8		33.4	
	100.0		100.0		100.0	Total Liabilties & Net Worth					100.0		100.0	
						INCOME DATA								
	100.0		100.0		100.0	Net Sales					100.0		100.0	
	21.2		20.8		22.1	Gross Profit					22.3		16.8	
	15.9		18.3		16.9	Operating Expenses					18.5		11.5	
	5.4		2.4		5.2	Operating Profit					3.8		5.3	
	1.3		1.0		1.2	All Other Expenses (net)					1.9		.9	
	4.0		1.4		4.0	Profit Before Taxes					1.9		4.4	
						RATIOS								
	2.5		3.9		2.3						3.5		2.0	
	1.5		1.8		1.3	Current					1.6		1.4	
	1.1		1.1		1.1						.9		1.2	
	1.4		1.8		1.3						1.9		1.2	
	.7		.8		.7	Quick					.6		.7	
	.5		.5		.4						.4		.4	
27	13.7	29	12.7	38	9.7					40	9.2	31	11.6	
34	10.8	43	8.6	46	7.9	Sales/Receivables				50	7.3	44	8.4	
45	8.1	55	6.7	55	6.7					64	5.7	48	7.6	
23	16.2	33	11.0	36	10.2					37	9.8	37	9.8	
47	7.8	61	6.0	58	6.3	Cost of Sales/Inventory				70	5.2	58	6.3	
77	4.7	86	4.2	87	4.2					149	2.5	84	4.4	
13	27.5	14	25.6	21	17.0					28	12.8	19	19.0	
26	13.8	24	15.1	32	11.5	Cost of Sales/Payables				39	9.3	29	12.7	
43	8.6	44	8.4	47	7.8					44	8.4	41	8.8	
	6.4		3.8		4.9						3.3		7.2	
	12.6		7.9		13.7	Sales/Working Capital					9.3		13.8	
	72.4		52.4		41.4						-25.3		28.2	
	11.1		7.0		9.2						19.3		10.2	
(83)	3.7	(82)	2.2	(73)	3.3	EBIT/Interest				(13)	3.6	(39)	3.2	
	1.6		-1.1		1.5						-7.5		1.7	
	14.9		13.3		4.9	Net Profit + Depr., Dep.,							3.9	
(22)	2.3	(22)	2.8	(16)	3.2	Amort./Cur. Mat. L/T/D					(11)	3.0	
	1.4		.3		1.9								1.9	
	.3		.3		.4						.2		.4	
	.7		.6		.9	Fixed/Worth					.9		.9	
	1.8		1.8		1.9						2.3		1.5	
	.8		.5		.9						.6		.9	
	2.0		1.6		2.0	Debt/Worth					1.7		1.8	
	5.2		3.4		7.3						5.0		5.1	
	45.1		24.0		38.6	% Profit Before Taxes/Tangible					32.4		40.3	
(81)	24.1	(82)	8.6	(69)	19.0	Net Worth				(15)	3.5	(35)	19.6	
	4.7		-7.8		3.8						-7.2		4.1	
	14.7		8.2		13.4	% Profit Before Taxes/Total					12.7		14.8	
	6.8		3.0		5.1	Assets					2.5		5.4	
	.8		-5.0		.8						-3.9		1.4	
	28.4		20.4		22.1						14.6		21.4	
	10.8		8.2		9.8	Sales/Net Fixed Assets					9.5		8.9	
	5.0		4.0		4.1						4.3		4.3	
	3.1		2.7		2.6						2.1		2.7	
	2.5		1.9		2.1	Sales/Total Assets					1.7		2.1	
	1.6		1.4		1.4						1.3		1.7	
	.7		1.0		.8						.8		.8	
(81)	1.4	(76)	1.8	(72)	1.7	% Depr., Dep., Amort./Sales					1.4	(37)	1.9	
	2.7		4.0		3.6						2.4		3.4	
	1.0		1.5		1.4	% Officers', Directors'								
(20)	1.6	(25)	2.3	(16)	2.7	Owners' Comp/Sales								
	3.2		4.2		4.7									
	5016861M		4122993M		2931624M	Net Sales ($)		16842M	28538M	52726M	249270M		2584248M	
	2363393M		2133776M		1526783M	Total Assets ($)		11916M	17101M	28896M	159840M		1309030M	

M = $ thousand   MM = $ million
See Pages 9 through 22 for Explanation of Ratios and Data

Current Data Sorted by Assets | Comparative Historical Data

0-500M	500M-2MM	2-10MM	10-50MM	50-100MM	100-250MM		4/1/06-3/31/07 ALL	4/1/07-3/31/08 ALL
			3	2	1	Type of Statement — Unqualified	12	14
	1	6	5			Reviewed	9	8
1	3	1				Compiled	4	8
	1					Tax Returns	2	1
2	5	4	2			Other	14	17
4 (4/1-9/30/10)			33 (10/1/10-3/31/11)					
1	7	12	12	4	1	NUMBER OF STATEMENTS	41	48
%	%	%	%	%	%	**ASSETS**	%	%
		8.7	3.9			Cash & Equivalents	4.6	8.0
		29.1	25.4			Trade Receivables (net)	25.2	26.5
		43.0	35.2			Inventory	32.8	31.7
		1.1	1.4			All Other Current	1.0	2.3
		82.0	65.9			Total Current	63.6	68.4
		16.0	21.3			Fixed Assets (net)	29.8	22.8
		.2	4.0			Intangibles (net)	1.6	1.4
		1.8	8.8			All Other Non-Current	5.0	7.4
		100.0	100.0			Total	100.0	100.0
						LIABILITIES		
		15.8	16.6			Notes Payable-Short Term	16.7	12.3
		3.0	1.0			Cur. Mat.-L.T.D.	4.0	2.5
		21.7	17.0			Trade Payables	15.4	16.1
		.0	.3			Income Taxes Payable	.2	.3
		11.2	8.4			All Other Current	5.9	5.2
		51.7	43.4			Total Current	42.2	36.3
		8.4	7.7			Long-Term Debt	17.5	9.7
		.3	1.3			Deferred Taxes	.7	.5
		.4	3.5			All Other Non-Current	2.8	3.2
		39.2	44.2			Net Worth	36.8	50.3
		100.0	100.0			Total Liabilities & Net Worth	100.0	100.0
						INCOME DATA		
		100.0	100.0			Net Sales	100.0	100.0
		28.9	15.0			Gross Profit	20.9	20.0
		23.3	10.9			Operating Expenses	16.4	14.5
		5.6	4.0			Operating Profit	4.6	5.5
		.1	.7			All Other Expenses (net)	1.0	.4
		5.6	3.3			Profit Before Taxes	3.6	5.1
						RATIOS		
		2.7	4.1			Current	3.0	4.3
		1.7	1.2				1.4	2.0
		1.0	1.1				1.0	1.3
		1.3	1.6			Quick	1.4	1.8
		.7	.6				.7	1.0
		.5	.4				.5	.5
		42 8.7	37 9.9			Sales/Receivables	31 11.6	37 10.0
		45 8.1	44 8.3				42 8.7	44 8.3
		54 6.8	50 7.2				53 6.9	53 6.9
		57 6.4	49 7.5			Cost of Sales/Inventory	47 7.8	43 8.5
		75 4.8	63 5.8				72 5.1	69 5.3
		137 2.7	117 3.1				98 3.7	100 3.7
		27 13.7	15 24.9			Cost of Sales/Payables	20 18.6	17 21.3
		39 9.2	30 12.1				29 12.8	30 12.0
		64 5.7	49 7.4				44 8.4	45 8.1
		4.5	4.0			Sales/Working Capital	5.3	3.7
		7.6	20.7				10.3	6.0
		128.1	81.9				235.8	14.7
		126.5	13.2			EBIT/Interest	11.4	15.7
		(10) 4.4	(11) 4.6				(38) 2.2	(37) 4.6
		.7	.4				1.3	1.8
						Net Profit + Depr., Dep., Amort./Cur. Mat. L/T/D	5.8	3.5
							(13) 2.5	(12) 1.8
							1.6	.9
		.1	.3			Fixed/Worth	.3	.2
		.5	.7				1.0	.3
		.8	1.6				1.6	1.0
		.6	.3			Debt/Worth	1.0	.4
		1.7	2.3				1.9	1.0
		4.5	5.3				3.9	2.8
		88.0	28.0			% Profit Before Taxes/Tangible Net Worth	28.8	32.6
		38.7	9.2				(38) 14.5	(46) 18.7
		5.4	-3.8				6.3	7.5
		35.6	9.7			% Profit Before Taxes/Total Assets	14.1	20.1
		5.7	3.1				3.3	7.7
		1.2	-.4				1.1	2.7
		162.4	26.7			Sales/Net Fixed Assets	20.1	23.9
		25.8	14.7				8.5	11.7
		7.1	5.6				4.5	5.6
		3.4	3.1			Sales/Total Assets	2.9	2.8
		2.3	1.8				2.2	2.0
		1.8	1.2				1.6	1.4
		.7	1.2			% Depr., Dep., Amort./Sales	1.0	.9
		(10) 1.1	(11) 1.6				(38) 1.7	(41) 1.6
		3.1	2.7				4.0	2.4
						% Officers', Directors' Owners' Comp/Sales	2.4	1.7
							(10) 4.3	(12) 3.7
							5.9	5.2
532M	22491M	180832M	670542M	412656M	235001M	Net Sales ($)	2257938M	2122318M
375M	9354M	74514M	301781M	216763M	102833M	Total Assets ($)	1158928M	1217935M

M = $ thousand   MM = $ million
See Pages 9 through 22 for Explanation of Ratios and Data

Comparative Historical Data | Current Data Sorted by Sales

4/1/08-3/31/09 ALL	4/1/09-3/31/10 ALL	4/1/10-3/31/11 ALL	Type of Statement	0-1MM	1-3MM	3-5MM	5-10MM	10-25MM	25MM & OVER
17	5	6	Unqualified					1	5
10	8	12	Reviewed		1	1	2	4	4
1	4	5	Compiled	1	1	1	2		
4	6	1	Tax Returns		1				
8	18	13	Other	1		1	1	4	6
						4 (4/1-9/30/10)		33 (10/1/10-3/31/11)	
40	41	37	NUMBER OF STATEMENTS	2	3	3	5	9	15
%	%	%	ASSETS	%	%	%	%	%	%
7.8	9.3	7.4	Cash & Equivalents						7.1
24.0	27.2	26.7	Trade Receivables (net)						26.2
35.1	27.3	35.8	Inventory						39.4
3.9	4.4	1.8	All Other Current						1.2
70.8	68.2	71.7	Total Current						74.0
21.6	21.7	22.5	Fixed Assets (net)						20.3
2.2	1.8	1.5	Intangibles (net)						3.2
5.4	8.4	4.4	All Other Non-Current						2.5
100.0	100.0	100.0	Total						100.0
			LIABILITIES						
16.7	14.8	14.7	Notes Payable-Short Term						15.7
4.1	3.1	1.9	Cur. Mat.-L.T.D.						1.3
14.0	17.8	19.4	Trade Payables						18.1
.2	.1	.1	Income Taxes Payable						.3
5.5	5.4	7.8	All Other Current						8.3
40.5	41.1	43.9	Total Current						43.7
10.7	9.2	12.2	Long-Term Debt						9.8
.4	.4	.5	Deferred Taxes						.9
6.7	13.7	3.5	All Other Non-Current						2.0
41.7	35.5	39.9	Net Worth						43.6
100.0	100.0	100.0	Total Liabilities & Net Worth						100.0
			INCOME DATA						
100.0	100.0	100.0	Net Sales						100.0
19.2	21.8	23.4	Gross Profit						14.9
15.7	21.4	18.7	Operating Expenses						9.6
3.5	.3	4.8	Operating Profit						5.3
.6	.2	.6	All Other Expenses (net)						.7
2.9	.1	4.2	Profit Before Taxes						4.6
			RATIOS						
4.9	3.8	3.5	Current						3.4
1.7	1.9	1.5							1.9
1.1	1.1	1.1							1.1
2.1	2.3	1.5	Quick						1.3
.8	.9	.7							.7
.4	.6	.5							.5
26 14.2	34 10.8	37 10.0	Sales/Receivables						34 10.8
36 10.1	41 8.8	46 7.9							38 9.7
50 7.3	54 6.8	53 6.9							50 7.3
39 9.3	34 10.8	49 7.4	Cost of Sales/Inventory						49 7.5
69 5.3	55 6.6	68 5.3							57 6.4
97 3.8	96 3.8	135 2.7							119 3.1
12 31.0	13 28.4	23 15.7	Cost of Sales/Payables						13 28.4
25 14.4	26 14.2	37 9.7							25 14.5
39 9.3	60 6.1	58 6.3							40 9.0
4.6	3.6	4.2	Sales/Working Capital						4.1
8.6	8.2	7.9							7.3
28.4	62.3	78.7							72.2
8.0	11.4	17.6	EBIT/Interest						21.3
(33) 1.8	(33) 2.6	(34) 4.3						(14)	9.2
-1.6	-4.2	1.2							2.0
2.4			Net Profit + Depr., Dep., Amort./Cur. Mat. L/T/D						
(12) 1.0									
.0									
.1	.1	.2	Fixed/Worth						.3
.4	.5	.5							.5
1.0	1.1	1.6							1.1
.4	.5	.6	Debt/Worth						.7
1.6	1.4	1.7							1.4
4.8	4.7	5.8							4.5
37.1	29.4	51.2	% Profit Before Taxes/Tangible Net Worth						44.0
(35) 13.4	(36) 9.7	(36) 17.8							19.6
-4.3	-17.2	1.7							4.6
17.7	7.5	15.5	% Profit Before Taxes/Total Assets						15.7
4.2	2.8	5.0							6.7
-2.1	-10.2	1.0							1.7
57.8	66.4	34.6	Sales/Net Fixed Assets						27.8
14.2	11.6	13.5							14.6
6.7	6.4	5.3							6.5
2.9	3.0	3.0	Sales/Total Assets						3.2
2.2	2.0	2.0							2.3
1.8	1.5	1.5							1.8
.4	.8	1.0	% Depr., Dep., Amort./Sales						.9
(32) 1.5	(31) 1.5	(32) 1.5						(12)	1.5
2.8	2.5	2.9							2.0
			% Officers', Directors' Owners' Comp/Sales						
2521552M	2115329M	1522054M	Net Sales ($)	1343M	7574M	11444M	39815M	167465M	1294413M
1253196M	1295253M	705620M	Total Assets ($)	902M	4316M	4635M	16367M	101608M	577792M

© RMA 2011

M = $ thousand   MM = $ million

See Pages 9 through 22 for Explanation of Ratios and Data

Current Data Sorted by Assets   Comparative Historical Data

Type of Statement

0-500M	500M-2MM	2-10MM	10-50MM	50-100MM	100-250MM	Type of Statement	16 4/1/06- 3/31/07 ALL	10 4/1/07- 3/31/08 ALL
			4	3	1	Unqualified	8	5
		1	2			Reviewed	4	4
			2			Compiled	1	2
						Tax Returns	1	1
	2 (4/1-9/30/10)	2	19 (10/1/10-3/31/11) 3	3		Other	16	10
		3	11	6	1	NUMBER OF STATEMENTS	30	22

Main Data

(Columns 0-500M and 500M-2MM marked vertically: DATA NOT AVAILABLE)

0-500M	500M-2MM	2-10MM	10-50MM	50-100MM	100-250MM		30 %	22 %
%	%	%	%	%	%	**ASSETS**	%	%
			6.6			Cash & Equivalents	7.1	8.0
			31.8			Trade Receivables (net)	34.0	39.6
			26.1			Inventory	25.2	23.9
			2.0			All Other Current	1.1	1.4
			66.5			Total Current	67.3	72.9
			29.5			Fixed Assets (net)	24.5	21.5
			1.5			Intangibles (net)	1.7	1.9
			2.5			All Other Non-Current	6.5	3.7
			100.0			Total	100.0	100.0
						LIABILITIES		
			20.8			Notes Payable-Short Term	16.6	16.7
			3.4			Cur. Mat.-L.T.D.	4.6	1.9
			16.4			Trade Payables	19.6	20.6
			.1			Income Taxes Payable	.2	.1
			6.8			All Other Current	7.7	7.1
			47.6			Total Current	48.7	46.4
			11.4			Long-Term Debt	12.1	14.3
			.2			Deferred Taxes	.5	.2
			3.3			All Other Non-Current	3.9	3.8
			37.5			Net Worth	34.7	35.3
			100.0			Total Liabilities & Net Worth	100.0	100.0
						INCOME DATA		
			100.0			Net Sales	100.0	100.0
			11.4			Gross Profit	21.4	21.6
			7.8			Operating Expenses	15.0	14.8
			3.6			Operating Profit	6.4	6.8
			2.0			All Other Expenses (net)	1.1	1.7
			1.6			Profit Before Taxes	5.3	5.2
						RATIOS		
			2.2			Current	2.8	2.3
			1.1				1.4	1.5
			1.0				1.0	1.2
			1.6			Quick	1.9	1.7
			.7				.8	1.2
			.5				.6	.6
			33 11.0			Sales/Receivables	28 13.1	31 11.7
			38 9.6				37 9.8	45 8.1
			64 5.7				54 6.8	55 6.6
			17 21.7			Cost of Sales/Inventory	16 22.8	10 36.1
			31 11.8				36 10.0	35 10.5
			57 6.5				53 6.9	70 5.2
			13 28.3			Cost of Sales/Payables	14 25.5	17 21.0
			21 17.6				31 11.6	30 12.2
			36 10.2				43 8.5	38 9.6
			4.8			Sales/Working Capital	7.1	8.7
			35.3				16.4	13.4
			-791.7				-339.8	23.0
			6.3			EBIT/Interest	13.4	16.2
			(10) 4.6				(27) 4.0	(20) 5.5
			.5				2.4	1.4
			8.1			Net Profit + Depr., Dep., Amort./Cur. Mat. L/T/D		
			(11) 4.4					
			1.4					
			.3			Fixed/Worth	.3	.3
			.7				.9	.4
			1.8				2.8	1.6
			.7			Debt/Worth	.7	.6
			3.0				3.2	2.2
			4.2				7.3	12.5
			52.9			% Profit Before Taxes/Tangible Net Worth	57.1	46.6
			18.4				(29) 38.0	(19) 40.1
			2.0				20.9	13.6
			10.4			% Profit Before Taxes/Total Assets	19.8	23.3
			4.6				9.6	14.5
			.7				5.5	3.4
			23.4			Sales/Net Fixed Assets	29.3	57.8
			10.2				15.4	18.9
			3.2				8.8	7.9
			3.4			Sales/Total Assets	4.3	4.0
			2.8				3.0	2.8
			1.6				1.8	2.1
			.4			% Depr., Dep., Amort./Sales	.7	.5
			(10) 1.5				(26) 1.0	(20) 1.0
			4.8				2.2	1.8
						% Officers', Directors' Owners' Comp/Sales		
		74763M	739694M	1001177M	194289M	Net Sales ($)	2537308M	1744102M
		20556M	278420M	369990M	181862M	Total Assets ($)	807271M	579780M

M = $ thousand   MM = $ million
See Pages 9 through 22 for Explanation of Ratios and Data

Comparative Historical Data   ## Current Data Sorted by Sales

Type of Statement	7 2 1	10 5 2	8 3 2					1	7 3 2
Unqualified									
Reviewed									
Compiled								2	6
Tax Returns	**10** 4/1/08- 3/31/09 ALL	**11** 4/1/09- 3/31/10 ALL	**8** 4/1/10- 3/31/11 ALL	**2 (4/1-9/30/10)**				**19 (10/1/10-3/31/11)**	
Other				0-1MM	1-3MM	3-5MM	5-10MM	10-25MM	25MM & OVER
NUMBER OF STATEMENTS	20	28	21					3	18
	%	%	%	%	%	%	%	%	%
ASSETS									
Cash & Equivalents	6.8	5.2	4.9	D	D	D	D		4.9
Trade Receivables (net)	37.2	32.0	31.5	A	A	A	A		33.3
Inventory	17.5	20.2	23.8	T	T	T	T		26.0
All Other Current	2.6	3.4	1.6	A	A	A	A		1.5
Total Current	64.1	60.9	61.8						65.8
Fixed Assets (net)	30.1	34.0	35.0	N	N	N	N		30.7
Intangibles (net)	2.2	.9	1.2	O	O	O	O		1.4
All Other Non-Current	3.6	4.2	2.0	T	T	T	T		2.1
Total	100.0	100.0	100.0						100.0
LIABILITIES				A	A	A	A		
Notes Payable-Short Term	18.8	19.0	16.8	V	V	V	V		16.7
Cur. Mat.-L.T.D.	7.4	2.9	2.8	A	A	A	A		2.3
Trade Payables	17.1	18.1	19.2	I	I	I	I		20.7
Income Taxes Payable	.0	.1	.1	L	L	L	L		.1
All Other Current	12.6	7.1	6.1	A	A	A	A		6.1
Total Current	55.9	47.2	45.0	B	B	B	B		45.9
Long-Term Debt	17.5	14.1	16.0	L	L	L	L		15.1
Deferred Taxes	.1	.5	.2	E	E	E	E		.2
All Other Non-Current	5.5	4.0	3.3						3.6
Net Worth	20.9	34.2	35.5						35.1
Total Liabilties & Net Worth	100.0	100.0	100.0						100.0
INCOME DATA									
Net Sales	100.0	100.0	100.0						100.0
Gross Profit	14.6	17.3	13.1						10.1
Operating Expenses	12.9	15.2	10.0						7.3
Operating Profit	1.7	2.1	3.1						2.9
All Other Expenses (net)	1.4	.8	1.5						.8
Profit Before Taxes	.2	1.3	1.6						2.0
RATIOS									
Current	1.9 / 1.1 / .8	2.1 / 1.4 / .9	2.1 / 1.3 / 1.0						2.1 / 1.3 / 1.0
Quick	1.6 / .6 / .4	1.4 / .8 / .4	1.2 / .7 / .5						1.3 / .8 / .5
Sales/Receivables	18 20.4 / 27 13.3 / 41 8.9	39 9.4 / 46 8.0 / 60 6.1	33 11.1 / 43 8.6 / 51 7.1						33 11.0 / 40 9.1 / 50 7.4
Cost of Sales/Inventory	5 75.6 / 13 27.1 / 43 8.5	16 22.9 / 34 10.6 / 63 5.8	23 15.7 / 30 12.3 / 53 6.9						24 15.0 / 30 12.0 / 52 7.1
Cost of Sales/Payables	6 57.0 / 14 26.1 / 29 12.8	14 26.4 / 30 12.2 / 48 7.7	17 21.3 / 28 13.0 / 38 9.5						16 23.1 / 27 13.5 / 41 8.8
Sales/Working Capital	13.6 / 43.2 / -22.8	8.0 / 14.3 / -43.2	8.6 / 24.8 / NM						7.3 / 23.1 / 139.0
EBIT/Interest	8.0 / (19) 2.6 / 1.1	14.7 / (25) 3.4 / -1.9	8.0 / (20) 4.6 / -.3						8.2 / (17) 4.7 / 1.2
Net Profit + Depr., Dep., Amort./Cur. Mat. L/T/D		25.6 / (10) 2.6 / -1.1							
Fixed/Worth	.5 / 1.9 / NM	.5 / 1.0 / 8.8	.5 / 1.0 / 2.1						.4 / .9 / 2.0
Debt/Worth	1.0 / 4.7 / NM	.8 / 2.0 / 10.6	.9 / 2.2 / 5.2						.8 / 2.6 / 4.7
% Profit Before Taxes/Tangible Net Worth	90.0 / (15) 12.3 / 4.0	37.7 / (24) 21.0 / .5	51.3 / (20) 16.9 / .7						53.6 / (17) 23.8 / 2.4
% Profit Before Taxes/Total Assets	15.5 / 4.3 / .2	11.5 / 6.5 / -3.2	10.5 / 4.6 / -1.0						11.3 / 5.0 / .6
Sales/Net Fixed Assets	42.4 / 18.9 / 7.7	15.8 / 7.2 / 4.1	22.9 / 9.1 / 3.1						24.3 / 10.0 / 4.4
Sales/Total Assets	5.7 / 4.0 / 3.3	2.8 / 2.3 / 1.9	3.4 / 2.7 / 1.7						3.4 / 3.0 / 1.8
% Depr., Dep., Amort./Sales	.4 / (18) 1.1 / 1.8	.8 / (26) 1.9 / 3.2	.6 / (18) 1.5 / 3.3						.5 / (15) 1.2 / 2.0
% Officers', Directors' Owners' Comp/Sales									
Net Sales ($)	2878759M	1350586M	2009923M					47946M	1961977M
Total Assets ($)	776183M	593606M	850828M					27653M	823175M

© RMA 2011   **M = $ thousand   MM = $ million**
See Pages 9 through 22 for Explanation of Ratios and Data

Current Data Sorted by Assets

Comparative Historical Data

	0-500M	500M-2MM	2-10MM	10-50MM	50-100MM	100-250MM		4/1/06-3/31/07 ALL	4/1/07-3/31/08 ALL
Type of Statement									
Unqualified			4	9	6	2		37	20
Reviewed		1	7	7				18	8
Compiled	1	3	1					7	4
Tax Returns	1	2		1				7	2
Other	1	4	9	16	7	1		21	44
	15 (4/1-9/30/10)			68 (10/1/10-3/31/11)					
NUMBER OF STATEMENTS	3	10	21	33	13	3		90	78
	%	%	%	%	%	%		%	%
ASSETS									
Cash & Equivalents		11.2	7.2	5.9	5.4			5.6	4.2
Trade Receivables (net)		27.9	31.8	28.0	24.9			27.8	29.9
Inventory		33.2	28.6	24.8	19.7			26.2	24.5
All Other Current		1.4	1.9	1.8	4.0			2.7	2.2
Total Current		73.7	69.5	60.6	54.0			62.3	60.9
Fixed Assets (net)		21.3	25.1	31.9	35.7			29.2	31.8
Intangibles (net)		.7	.6	3.0	3.2			3.8	3.5
All Other Non-Current		4.3	4.8	4.5	7.1			4.7	3.8
Total		100.0	100.0	100.0	100.0			100.0	100.0
LIABILITIES									
Notes Payable-Short Term		14.6	21.3	9.0	6.9			10.5	15.6
Cur. Mat.-L.T.D.		13.1	4.1	3.3	2.4			3.0	4.6
Trade Payables		25.5	15.3	14.8	12.6			18.5	17.5
Income Taxes Payable		.3	.0	.2	.2			.2	.2
All Other Current		15.3	6.6	7.9	8.3			8.5	5.8
Total Current		68.8	47.3	35.2	30.5			40.8	43.7
Long-Term Debt		25.8	12.3	17.6	13.5			16.7	21.6
Deferred Taxes		.0	.5	.4	2.0			1.1	.4
All Other Non-Current		5.3	11.3	3.1	12.1			9.7	5.2
Net Worth		.1	28.6	43.7	41.9			31.9	29.1
Total Liabilities & Net Worth		100.0	100.0	100.0	100.0			100.0	100.0
INCOME DATA									
Net Sales		100.0	100.0	100.0	100.0			100.0	100.0
Gross Profit		30.2	20.5	17.3	17.6			19.8	20.1
Operating Expenses		28.6	16.1	12.6	10.7			14.5	15.3
Operating Profit		1.6	4.3	4.7	7.0			5.4	4.8
All Other Expenses (net)		-.3	.2	.6	.9			1.4	1.6
Profit Before Taxes		1.9	4.1	4.1	6.1			3.9	3.2
RATIOS									
Current		2.1	3.1	2.5	3.3			2.1	2.1
		1.5	1.4	1.8	2.1			1.6	1.5
		.7	1.0	1.4	1.2			1.2	1.1
Quick		1.4	1.6	1.9	1.8			1.2	1.2
		.6	.8	.9	1.4			.8	.9
		.3	.5	.6	.5			.6	.6
Sales/Receivables		16 23.0	33 11.0	37 9.9	33 11.1			29 12.7	34 10.6
		31 12.0	47 7.7	42 8.6	43 8.6			43 8.5	42 8.7
		55 6.6	56 6.5	53 6.9	49 7.5			53 6.9	50 7.3
Cost of Sales/Inventory		7 50.9	24 15.4	31 11.9	23 15.6			28 13.2	20 18.6
		38 9.5	49 7.5	42 8.7	39 9.3			49 7.5	41 8.9
		141 2.6	96 3.8	87 4.2	75 4.9			68 5.4	62 5.9
Cost of Sales/Payables		26 14.0	18 20.5	19 19.6	16 22.3			21 17.5	21 17.3
		40 9.2	25 14.4	27 13.6	22 16.5			30 12.1	27 13.3
		68 5.4	45 8.1	41 9.0	32 11.5			43 8.4	36 10.2
Sales/Working Capital		6.5	4.6	4.9	4.9			6.8	8.2
		13.2	9.8	10.4	6.0			12.4	15.5
		-15.9	NM	13.8	NM			26.8	59.4
EBIT/Interest		13.9	7.8	26.8	85.0			12.8	6.9
		2.0	(19) 5.2	(31) 8.9	15.9			(85) 5.3	(77) 2.9
		.4	1.2	2.9	3.3			2.0	1.0
Net Profit + Depr., Dep., Amort./Cur. Mat. L/T/D								7.9	4.1
								(28) 3.3	(25) 2.4
								2.0	.8
Fixed/Worth		.1	.2	.4	.6			.5	.6
		1.7	.5	.7	1.0			1.0	1.3
		-1.1	1.9	1.2	NM			2.2	2.3
Debt/Worth		1.0	.7	.7	.4			.9	1.4
		4.0	2.2	1.4	1.2			2.0	3.0
		-5.9	4.5	2.6	NM			7.8	7.5
% Profit Before Taxes/Tangible Net Worth			52.2	31.2	42.8			51.8	52.4
			(18) 19.5	(30) 17.9	(10) 30.3			(76) 30.7	(67) 24.6
			9.2	8.2	10.7			12.1	2.8
% Profit Before Taxes/Total Assets		23.1	19.0	12.9	17.0			18.3	12.4
		2.1	5.9	8.1	8.6			8.1	6.9
		-1.8	.6	3.9	3.3			3.4	.2
Sales/Net Fixed Assets		78.1	33.7	9.9	9.0			17.9	19.0
		30.9	10.7	6.8	4.6			8.3	7.4
		9.8	4.6	4.2	3.6			4.7	4.9
Sales/Total Assets		4.4	3.0	2.9	2.5			3.3	3.2
		2.6	2.2	2.3	1.6			2.3	2.5
		1.7	1.6	1.6	1.5			1.7	1.9
% Depr., Dep., Amort./Sales			1.0	1.3	1.4			1.0	.9
			(17) 1.5	(31) 2.2	(12) 2.5			(78) 1.6	(73) 1.7
			3.3	3.3	3.5			2.6	2.8
% Officers', Directors' Owners' Comp/Sales								1.1	.7
								(19) 2.1	(19) 1.5
								3.1	3.5
Net Sales ($)	1767M	40897M	301642M	1437727M	1989260M	589801M		5414080M	4455405M
Total Assets ($)	687M	14134M	128710M	630703M	961327M	600304M		2503556M	1912080M

M = $ thousand   MM = $ million
See Pages 9 through 22 for Explanation of Ratios and Data

Comparative Historical Data | Current Data Sorted by Sales

				Type of Statement	0-1MM	1-3MM	3-5MM	5-10MM	10-25MM	25MM & OVER
	23	24	21	Unqualified					4	17
	8	10	15	Reviewed				4	4	7
	6	3	5	Compiled			2	2		1
	3	3	4	Tax Returns	1			1		1
	46	32	38	Other	1	2	4	5	5	21
	4/1/08-3/31/09 ALL	4/1/09-3/31/10 ALL	4/1/10-3/31/11 ALL		\<15 (4/1-9/30/10)\>			\<68 (10/1/10-3/31/11)\>		
	86	72	83	NUMBER OF STATEMENTS	3	2	7	12	13	46
	%	%	%	ASSETS	%	%	%	%	%	%
	4.6	6.8	6.5	Cash & Equivalents				13.3	5.0	5.1
	25.8	24.2	28.2	Trade Receivables (net)				34.6	26.5	28.5
	26.2	23.7	25.2	Inventory				22.7	28.9	23.3
	3.3	3.6	2.1	All Other Current				2.4	1.8	2.3
	59.8	58.3	62.1	Total Current				72.9	62.3	59.1
	30.5	32.7	31.2	Fixed Assets (net)				22.1	29.2	34.9
	2.6	3.2	2.0	Intangibles (net)				1.5	2.7	1.8
	7.1	5.8	4.7	All Other Non-Current				3.5	5.8	4.3
	100.0	100.0	100.0	Total				100.0	100.0	100.0
				LIABILITIES						
	14.7	14.3	13.2	Notes Payable-Short Term				22.3	16.9	8.9
	3.3	4.5	4.4	Cur. Mat.-L.T.D.				3.4	5.3	2.6
	14.6	14.7	15.9	Trade Payables				18.6	14.4	14.6
	.2	.1	.2	Income Taxes Payable				.0	.1	.2
	7.5	10.6	8.2	All Other Current				9.4	11.2	7.1
	40.5	44.2	41.9	Total Current				53.6	47.8	33.4
	21.3	20.7	17.0	Long-Term Debt				8.1	14.5	15.5
	.8	.7	.8	Deferred Taxes				.9	.1	1.2
	5.3	5.8	7.0	All Other Non-Current				7.2	12.3	5.7
	32.2	28.6	33.3	Net Worth				30.0	25.3	44.3
	100.0	100.0	100.0	Total Liabilities & Net Worth				100.0	100.0	100.0
				INCOME DATA						
	100.0	100.0	100.0	Net Sales				100.0	100.0	100.0
	18.7	20.9	20.2	Gross Profit				25.3	17.6	16.7
	15.7	18.3	16.0	Operating Expenses				24.6	13.8	10.6
	3.0	2.6	4.1	Operating Profit				.7	3.8	6.1
	1.2	.9	.6	All Other Expenses (net)				.3	.2	.8
	1.8	1.7	3.6	Profit Before Taxes				.4	3.6	5.4
				RATIOS						
	2.5	2.4	2.5					3.2	2.5	2.8
	1.7	1.6	1.7	Current				1.4	1.3	1.8
	1.1	.9	1.2					.9	.8	1.4
	1.3	1.4	1.6					2.9	1.5	1.6
	.8	.8	.9	Quick				.9	.7	1.2
	.5	.4	.5					.4	.3	.7
	29 12.6	31 11.9	35 10.6					28 13.0	34 10.6	36 10.2
	36 10.1	41 8.9	43 8.4	Sales/Receivables				47 7.8	39 9.3	43 8.4
	46 8.0	51 7.1	54 6.8					89 4.1	53 6.9	51 7.1
	22 16.4	25 14.6	25 14.4					27 13.7	32 11.5	25 14.4
	33 11.0	42 8.7	42 8.7	Cost of Sales/Inventory				49 7.5	56 6.5	37 9.9
	83 4.4	82 4.4	79 4.6					91 4.0	96 3.8	69 5.3
	14 26.2	15 23.7	19 19.1					19 19.4	16 22.3	19 19.1
	23 16.0	25 14.8	28 12.9	Cost of Sales/Payables				33 11.1	24 14.9	26 14.3
	31 11.9	45 8.1	43 8.5					60 6.1	41 8.9	34 10.6
	6.4	5.8	5.0					6.3	8.4	5.3
	9.9	10.3	9.8	Sales/Working Capital				10.0	11.7	9.4
	57.6	-66.1	34.5					NM	-20.9	13.6
	8.5	7.2	21.2					4.5	9.4	29.5
	(81) 2.8	(68) 2.1	(79) 5.7	EBIT/Interest			(10) 1.6	(12) 3.7	(45) 9.6
	.0	-.6	1.5					.5	1.0	3.6
	6.6	4.2	6.3							6.3
	(27) 2.4	(19) 1.8	(24) 2.9	Net Profit + Depr., Dep., Amort./Cur. Mat. L/T/D						(16) 3.8
	.0	.1	.9							1.8
	.3	.4	.3					.2	.2	.5
	.8	1.2	.8	Fixed/Worth				.5	.9	.8
	2.2	3.7	2.2					1.5	NM	1.5
	.8	.7	.7					.7	.8	.7
	1.9	2.0	1.6	Debt/Worth				2.7	2.2	1.2
	4.7	7.9	4.5					5.7	NM	2.8
	38.8	33.8	36.9					25.8	36.9	40.3
	(75) 14.9	(59) 9.1	(68) 19.2	% Profit Before Taxes/Tangible Net Worth			(10) 10.0	(10) 28.1	(42) 20.8
	1.2	-9.7	7.6					2.4	.7	9.8
	12.5	10.6	15.3					14.6	14.2	16.0
	4.5	2.1	7.4	% Profit Before Taxes/Total Assets				1.5	6.4	8.6
	-2.1	-4.2	1.3					-2.9	-.3	4.9
	21.7	16.7	22.8					39.7	25.1	9.9
	7.8	6.4	7.7	Sales/Net Fixed Assets				19.3	7.6	7.0
	4.5	4.1	4.0					4.9	3.8	3.9
	3.1	2.6	2.9					3.5	2.8	3.1
	2.4	2.1	2.1	Sales/Total Assets				2.3	2.1	2.3
	1.6	1.4	1.6					1.6	1.6	1.6
	.9	1.3	1.1						1.2	1.3
	(76) 1.5	(58) 2.4	(71) 2.0	% Depr., Dep., Amort./Sales				(12) 1.5	(42) 2.1
	3.2	4.2	3.3						4.0	3.1
	.9	1.0	.8							.3
	(21) 2.0	(15) 1.6	(20) 1.8	% Officers', Directors' Owners' Comp/Sales					(10) .8
	5.1	2.7	11.5							2.3
	5506351M	3148993M	4361094M	Net Sales ($)	1767M	3862M	25852M	89958M	235760M	4003895M
	2738973M	1785128M	2335865M	Total Assets ($)	687M	2756M	27476M	63136M	121064M	2120746M

M = $ thousand   MM = $ million
See Pages 9 through 22 for Explanation of Ratios and Data

Current Data Sorted by Assets							Comparative Historical Data	
						Type of Statement		
		2	4	1	2	Unqualified	11	7
	3	1	6			Reviewed	8	10
		1				Compiled	4	1
	2	1				Tax Returns	3	2
		3	8	3	2	Other	17	13
	8 (4/1-9/30/10)		31 (10/1/10-3/31/11)				4/1/06-3/31/07 ALL	4/1/07-3/31/08 ALL
0-500M	500M-2MM	2-10MM	10-50MM	50-100MM	100-250MM			
	5	8	18	4	4	**NUMBER OF STATEMENTS**	43	33
%	%	%	%	%	%	**ASSETS**	%	%
DATA NOT AVAILABLE			7.1			Cash & Equivalents	4.4	5.4
			24.9			Trade Receivables (net)	33.9	31.6
			27.1			Inventory	30.5	31.8
			2.0			All Other Current	1.5	1.2
			61.0			Total Current	70.3	69.9
			24.9			Fixed Assets (net)	23.4	17.8
			5.2			Intangibles (net)	2.4	2.7
			8.9			All Other Non-Current	3.8	9.5
			100.0			Total	100.0	100.0
						LIABILITIES		
			8.0			Notes Payable-Short Term	13.9	16.3
			3.0			Cur. Mat.-L.T.D.	4.8	4.0
			19.7			Trade Payables	21.9	19.4
			.1			Income Taxes Payable	.3	1.6
			8.7			All Other Current	8.0	8.4
			39.4			Total Current	48.9	49.7
			12.0			Long-Term Debt	13.9	11.0
			1.0			Deferred Taxes	.5	.4
			6.3			All Other Non-Current	5.6	7.1
			41.3			Net Worth	31.1	31.8
			100.0			Total Liabilties & Net Worth	100.0	100.0
						INCOME DATA		
			100.0			Net Sales	100.0	100.0
			19.7			Gross Profit	20.0	22.8
			15.3			Operating Expenses	14.5	19.2
			4.4			Operating Profit	5.5	3.6
			1.1			All Other Expenses (net)	1.3	1.1
			3.3			Profit Before Taxes	4.2	2.5
						RATIOS		
			2.4				2.1	2.2
			1.8			Current	1.4	1.6
			1.0				1.1	1.1
			1.2				1.0	1.2
			.9			Quick	.8	.8
			.6				.5	.6
			41 8.8				**34** 10.7	**35** 10.3
			49 7.4			Sales/Receivables	**41** 8.9	**39** 9.3
			56 6.5				**50** 7.4	**48** 7.6
			36 10.2				**28** 13.0	**43** 8.5
			56 6.6			Cost of Sales/Inventory	**53** 6.9	**54** 6.8
			91 4.0				**74** 5.0	**61** 5.9
			18 19.9				**21** 17.3	**19** 19.4
			30 12.2			Cost of Sales/Payables	**34** 10.7	**30** 12.2
			51 7.1				**41** 8.9	**42** 8.6
			5.0				6.3	6.6
			8.9			Sales/Working Capital	12.3	9.8
			-127.6				57.5	46.9
			12.8				15.5	10.8
			(15) 5.8			EBIT/Interest	(41) 3.2	(31) 4.4
			2.9				1.7	1.7
							6.0	9.4
						Net Profit + Depr., Dep., Amort./Cur. Mat. L/T/D	(14) 3.1	(14) 4.4
							1.8	1.9
			.2				.2	.2
			.6			Fixed/Worth	.8	.4
			1.5				1.9	1.4
			.6				1.1	1.2
			1.9			Debt/Worth	3.5	1.8
			4.2				9.2	7.2
			50.5				73.3	67.0
			(17) 29.4			% Profit Before Taxes/Tangible Net Worth	(38) 30.9	(30) 32.5
			8.1				10.9	7.4
			12.2				17.0	15.2
			5.8			% Profit Before Taxes/Total Assets	9.6	8.0
			2.2				2.0	1.9
			87.4				29.6	42.6
			10.3			Sales/Net Fixed Assets	15.6	22.0
			4.6				8.1	8.2
			2.9				3.7	3.6
			1.8			Sales/Total Assets	2.8	3.1
			1.2				2.0	2.1
			1.3				.7	.8
			(13) 3.0			% Depr., Dep., Amort./Sales	(39) 1.3	(30) 1.3
			4.1				2.6	2.1
						% Officers', Directors' Owners' Comp/Sales		
	12525M	69904M	859898M	878567M	1367725M	Net Sales ($)	5357995M	2513937M
	4709M	33646M	400245M	310896M	512160M	Total Assets ($)	1988903M	1129457M

M = $ thousand MM = $ million

See Pages 9 through 22 for Explanation of Ratios and Data

Comparative Historical Data

Current Data Sorted by Sales

							Type of Statement		0-1MM	1-3MM	3-5MM	5-10MM	10-25MM	25MM & OVER
	7		11		9		Unqualified			2			2	5
	12		9		10		Reviewed		2	2			3	3
	2		3		1		Compiled						1	
	2		4		3		Tax Returns						1	
	19		15		16		Other		2			2	3	11
	4/1/08-		4/1/09-		4/1/10-					8 (4/1-9/30/10)			31 (10/1/10-3/31/11)	
	3/31/09		3/31/10		3/31/11									
	ALL		ALL		ALL				0-1MM	1-3MM	3-5MM	5-10MM	10-25MM	25MM & OVER
	42		42		39		**NUMBER OF STATEMENTS**		4	4	2	10	19	
	%		%		%		**ASSETS**	%	%	%	%	%	%	%
	8.6		10.2		7.4		Cash & Equivalents	D					11.4	6.3
	27.1		28.2		30.8		Trade Receivables (net)	A					27.9	33.7
	30.8		26.6		28.6		Inventory	T					22.5	31.6
	2.2		3.9		1.6		All Other Current	A					.4	2.6
	68.7		68.9		68.4		Total Current						62.1	74.3
	19.6		21.5		19.7		Fixed Assets (net)	N					29.0	15.1
	3.2		2.6		4.2		Intangibles (net)	O					5.0	3.9
	8.5		7.0		7.8		All Other Non-Current	T					4.0	6.7
	100.0		100.0		100.0		Total						100.0	100.0
							LIABILITIES	A						
	11.8		10.0		12.8		Notes Payable-Short Term	V					5.7	16.9
	2.6		1.8		2.1		Cur. Mat.-L.T.D.	A					3.2	1.3
	18.1		18.2		18.5		Trade Payables	I					10.9	23.1
	.4		.1		.3		Income Taxes Payable	L					.9	.1
	7.1		10.6		8.2		All Other Current	A					11.6	6.6
	39.9		40.8		41.8		Total Current	B					32.3	48.0
	12.0		14.1		13.2		Long-Term Debt	L					13.6	14.2
	.4		.4		.8		Deferred Taxes	E					.5	1.1
	7.1		6.2		7.0		All Other Non-Current						2.7	6.2
	40.6		38.4		37.3		Net Worth						50.8	30.4
	100.0		100.0		100.0		Total Liabilties & Net Worth						100.0	100.0
							INCOME DATA							
	100.0		100.0		100.0		Net Sales						100.0	100.0
	19.2		21.8		20.9		Gross Profit						28.2	12.9
	16.6		19.0		17.9		Operating Expenses						20.9	10.5
	2.6		2.8		3.1		Operating Profit						7.3	2.4
	.2		1.4		1.1		All Other Expenses (net)						.3	1.6
	2.4		1.4		1.9		Profit Before Taxes						7.0	.8
							RATIOS							
	2.8		3.1		2.7								2.7	3.6
	1.8		1.6		1.6		Current						2.0	1.4
	1.2		1.2		1.1								1.2	1.1
	1.6		1.8		1.6								1.9	2.0
	.9		1.0		.9		Quick						1.1	.8
	.6		.7		.6								.5	.6
24	14.9	33	10.9	41	8.9							39	9.4	41	8.8
33	11.0	50	7.3	52	7.1		Sales/Receivables					53	6.9	50	7.3
41	8.9	60	6.1	62	5.9							74	4.9	62	5.9
21	17.7	32	11.2	36	10.1							41	9.0	36	10.2
47	7.7	70	5.2	54	6.8		Cost of Sales/Inventory					57	6.4	46	7.9
67	5.5	94	3.9	84	4.3							82	4.4	73	5.0
15	24.2	22	16.9	15	24.9							4	89.8	15	24.9
20	17.9	37	9.8	32	11.4		Cost of Sales/Payables					23	16.1	29	12.5
35	10.5	49	7.4	51	7.2							44	8.3	51	7.2
	5.5		3.6		4.2								5.4	3.6
	9.6		7.4		10.7		Sales/Working Capital						7.1	10.7
	28.8		20.8		37.1								NM	45.7
	12.7		11.6		11.5									12.5
	3.8	(38)	2.6	(33)	5.6		EBIT/Interest					(16)	5.7
	1.6		-.4		1.5									1.4
	11.0		7.7		5.9		Net Profit + Depr., Dep.,						
(14)	3.6	(12)	2.6	(10)	4.8		Amort./Cur. Mat. L/T/D						
	1.4		.5		-4.6									
	.1		.2		.1								.1	.2
	.3		.4		.5		Fixed/Worth						.5	.4
	1.0		1.5		1.3								1.3	1.5
	.6		.6		.5								.5	.7
	1.4		2.0		2.2		Debt/Worth						1.2	2.9
	3.7		4.4		7.8								2.8	8.8
	43.5		29.6		48.2		% Profit Before Taxes/Tangible						46.9	50.9
(39)	22.5	(39)	12.4	(36)	26.6		Net Worth						39.9	(17)	21.4
	5.5		-2.8		8.0								24.0	6.3
	15.4		8.1		9.7		% Profit Before Taxes/Total						30.5	6.8
	7.3		3.6		4.8		Assets						16.6	4.7
	1.6		-1.8		2.3								3.3	1.4
	48.0		36.6		62.1								45.4	89.8
	26.6		16.3		22.3		Sales/Net Fixed Assets						18.4	12.5
	10.3		4.7		5.2								3.2	7.8
	4.3		2.8		3.2								2.7	3.6
	3.0		2.0		2.1		Sales/Total Assets						1.8	2.6
	1.8		1.3		1.4								1.4	1.5
	.6		1.0		.5									.3
(36)	.9	(33)	1.6	(31)	1.7		% Depr., Dep., Amort./Sales					(14)	1.3
	2.3		4.1		3.1									3.2
	2.1		2.5		3.4		% Officers', Directors'						
(11)	4.6	(13)	3.6	(11)	4.2		Owners' Comp/Sales						
	8.3		7.0		9.5									
	5822310M		2779704M		3188619M		Net Sales ($)		9118M	15133M	12658M	158573M	2993137M
	1828683M		1400287M		1261656M		Total Assets ($)		3769M	13145M	14149M	99420M	1131173M

© RMA 2011

M = $ thousand   MM = $ million
See Pages 9 through 22 for Explanation of Ratios and Data

Current Data Sorted by Assets   Comparative Historical Data

0-500M	500M-2MM	2-10MM	10-50MM	50-100MM	100-250MM	Type of Statement	4/1/06-3/31/07 ALL	4/1/07-3/31/08 ALL
		2	3	1	2	Unqualified	9	7
	1	6	3			Reviewed	10	7
	2	2				Compiled	3	
1	1					Tax Returns	4	2
1	4	5	5	3	3	Other	12	12
	8 (4/1-9/30/10)		36 (10/1/10-3/31/11)					
1	8	15	11	4	5	NUMBER OF STATEMENTS	38	28
%	%	%	%	%	%	**ASSETS**	%	%
		8.6	11.4			Cash & Equivalents	5.2	9.8
		24.9	22.6			Trade Receivables (net)	27.0	25.0
		28.2	27.5			Inventory	32.3	32.0
		.7	3.1			All Other Current	3.4	3.5
		62.4	64.6			Total Current	67.9	70.3
		21.4	25.8			Fixed Assets (net)	26.1	21.9
		14.2	2.5			Intangibles (net)	3.1	5.0
		2.0	7.0			All Other Non-Current	2.9	2.8
		100.0	100.0			Total	100.0	100.0
						LIABILITIES		
		14.3	11.6			Notes Payable-Short Term	16.1	14.0
		6.1	5.7			Cur. Mat.-L.T.D.	2.9	3.0
		13.2	13.3			Trade Payables	16.5	14.0
		.3	.4			Income Taxes Payable	1.2	.3
		9.3	6.0			All Other Current	7.9	8.3
		43.3	37.0			Total Current	44.7	39.6
		12.2	13.9			Long-Term Debt	13.9	9.6
		1.6	1.4			Deferred Taxes	.4	.3
		11.0	10.3			All Other Non-Current	5.5	7.7
		31.9	37.4			Net Worth	35.5	42.8
		100.0	100.0			Total Liabilities & Net Worth	100.0	100.0
						INCOME DATA		
		100.0	100.0			Net Sales	100.0	100.0
		28.7	21.9			Gross Profit	23.6	24.9
		24.1	12.4			Operating Expenses	16.0	17.0
		4.7	9.5			Operating Profit	7.5	7.9
		1.2	1.7			All Other Expenses (net)	.8	1.0
		3.5	7.8			Profit Before Taxes	6.8	6.9
						RATIOS		
		1.9	4.0				2.4	3.4
		1.3	1.8			Current	1.5	2.0
		.7	1.2				1.1	1.2
		.9	2.4				1.2	1.7
		.6	1.3			Quick	.7	.8
		.4	.6				.4	.5
		36 10.2	17 21.4				35 10.5	30 12.1
		46 8.0	42 8.7			Sales/Receivables	44 8.2	36 10.2
		52 7.0	56 6.5				60 6.1	47 7.7
		29 12.8	26 14.2				29 12.7	27 13.5
		69 5.3	64 5.7			Cost of Sales/Inventory	80 4.6	54 6.8
		142 2.6	96 3.8				106 3.4	112 3.2
		22 16.6	17 21.5				18 19.9	13 28.0
		37 9.9	27 13.3			Cost of Sales/Payables	36 10.1	22 16.9
		48 7.6	53 6.9				51 7.1	42 8.8
		4.0	3.8				4.3	3.6
		9.8	8.6			Sales/Working Capital	9.3	7.2
		-14.8	17.5				28.8	21.8
		18.3	12.5				11.0	15.1
		(14) 5.9	(10) 3.1			EBIT/Interest	(36) 4.4	(25) 7.3
		-1.1	2.2				1.2	1.0
						Net Profit + Depr., Dep.,	13.7	4.2
						Amort./Cur. Mat. L/T/D	(11) -3.3	(11) 2.0
							1.6	.7
		.3	.4				.2	.3
		.6	.6			Fixed/Worth	.5	.5
		-7.0	2.0				2.2	2.9
		1.2	.3				.9	.6
		3.6	2.1			Debt/Worth	1.8	1.2
		-17.0	4.0				6.9	13.1
		72.4	51.9			% Profit Before Taxes/Tangible	50.6	63.0
		(11) 29.7	(10) 22.6			Net Worth	(32) 27.4	(23) 26.0
		15.5	13.9				9.9	16.7
		17.7	14.6			% Profit Before Taxes/Total	22.8	25.6
		7.3	8.7			Assets	7.9	10.7
		-4.3	3.6				1.4	.3
		22.7	14.5				33.7	34.4
		15.2	10.0			Sales/Net Fixed Assets	8.7	12.7
		6.7	3.5				4.5	5.9
		2.6	3.2				2.8	3.6
		1.6	2.1			Sales/Total Assets	1.9	2.1
		1.3	1.4				1.4	1.5
		.7	1.0				.4	.9
		(11) 1.3	1.7			% Depr., Dep., Amort./Sales	(37) 1.9	(27) 1.6
		1.7	3.8				3.4	2.4
						% Officers', Directors'	.8	.8
						Owners' Comp/Sales	(12) 3.8	(10) 1.4
							6.0	9.0
888M	22254M	165355M	486490M	441486M	1273421M	Net Sales ($)	1459571M	1494817M
284M	9810M	81726M	237313M	280549M	918123M	Total Assets ($)	775521M	912634M

M = $ thousand   MM = $ million
See Pages 9 through 22 for Explanation of Ratios and Data

Comparative Historical Data / Current Data Sorted by Sales

4/1/08-3/31/09 ALL	4/1/09-3/31/10 ALL	4/1/10-3/31/11 ALL	Type of Statement	0-1MM	1-3MM	3-5MM	5-10MM	10-25MM	25MM & OVER
8	4	8	Unqualified			3		1	7
13	14	10	Reviewed		1			5	2
4	4	4	Compiled			2	1		
2	6	2	Tax Returns			1			
20	21	20	Other	1	2	4	1	2	11
						8 (4/1-9/30/10)		36 (10/1/10-3/31/11)	
47	49	44	NUMBER OF STATEMENTS	1	3	10	2	8	20
%	%	%	**ASSETS**	%	%	%	%	%	%
7.1	10.9	8.2	Cash & Equivalents			9.5			7.1
22.8	23.8	23.7	Trade Receivables (net)			26.9			21.5
30.6	26.9	27.7	Inventory			26.7			26.0
3.1	2.8	2.6	All Other Current			.5			5.5
63.5	64.4	62.2	Total Current			63.6			60.1
28.7	26.7	24.5	Fixed Assets (net)			12.4			27.3
3.2	3.7	7.9	Intangibles (net)			14.8			7.1
4.6	5.1	5.4	All Other Non-Current			9.2			5.5
100.0	100.0	100.0	Total			100.0			100.0
			LIABILITIES						
12.5	14.2	13.1	Notes Payable-Short Term			17.9			9.7
2.4	2.9	4.6	Cur. Mat.-L.T.D.			3.5			3.9
14.1	15.4	15.3	Trade Payables			20.7			12.6
.2	.2	.6	Income Taxes Payable			.1			.8
10.3	7.6	7.4	All Other Current			6.5			8.1
39.6	40.4	40.9	Total Current			48.8			35.0
15.8	14.6	15.5	Long-Term Debt			18.6			11.7
.7	1.0	2.0	Deferred Taxes			.1			2.9
5.4	19.8	8.8	All Other Non-Current			13.9			6.0
38.5	24.2	32.8	Net Worth			18.6			44.4
100.0	100.0	100.0	Total Liabilities & Net Worth			100.0			100.0
			INCOME DATA						
100.0	100.0	100.0	Net Sales			100.0			100.0
23.4	23.4	26.3	Gross Profit			28.9			18.4
17.0	20.0	20.3	Operating Expenses			24.7			11.6
6.4	3.4	6.0	Operating Profit			4.2			6.9
1.5	.6	1.6	All Other Expenses (net)			-.2			2.5
4.9	2.8	4.4	Profit Before Taxes			4.4			4.4
			RATIOS						
2.8	2.7	3.0	Current			2.9			3.4
1.7	1.6	1.4				1.1			2.0
1.1	1.2	1.0				.7			1.2
1.2	1.5	1.3	Quick			1.5			1.8
.7	.9	.7				.6			1.0
.5	.5	.4				.4			.5
22 16.3	29 12.5	35 10.5	Sales/Receivables			41 9.0			30 12.3
33 10.9	45 8.1	44 8.2				52 7.0			40 9.2
44 8.4	53 6.8	52 7.0				57 6.4			48 7.6
20 18.6	33 11.1	39 9.3	Cost of Sales/Inventory			4 96.4			41 8.9
48 7.6	55 6.6	69 5.3				47 7.8			64 5.7
111 3.3	109 3.4	101 3.6				116 3.1			93 3.9
11 33.6	14 26.9	22 16.3	Cost of Sales/Payables			23 16.1			14 26.1
22 16.6	27 13.7	33 10.9				43 8.4			30 12.2
42 8.6	44 8.3	51 7.2				73 5.0			46 7.9
4.7	3.5	4.8	Sales/Working Capital			2.8			4.5
10.4	9.6	10.2				29.7			7.5
60.0	21.8	67.5				-14.0			24.3
13.8	14.1	9.3	EBIT/Interest						10.0
(42) 7.2	(46) 2.0	(40) 3.2						(18)	3.4
.1	.1	1.8							2.5
7.7	3.9	5.0	Net Profit + Depr., Dep., Amort./Cur. Mat. L/T/D						
(13) 4.3	(12) .6	(13) 2.2							
-.2	.1	.6							
.4	.3	.3	Fixed/Worth			.1			.4
.9	.7	.7				.9			.7
2.7	2.7	2.0				-5.3			1.1
.7	.7	.8	Debt/Worth			2.5			.6
1.9	1.8	2.2				6.8			1.4
5.3	6.0	5.9				-13.4			2.4
50.3	34.7	44.8	% Profit Before Taxes/Tangible Net Worth						39.8
(41) 27.5	(40) 10.2	(37) 20.4						(19)	20.4
7.5	-4.4	9.8							10.1
19.3	12.8	12.0	% Profit Before Taxes/Total Assets			20.8			11.6
8.8	3.0	6.7				5.0			7.7
-.2	-2.7	2.1				-1.9			3.8
21.9	32.0	20.2	Sales/Net Fixed Assets			53.4			18.2
7.5	9.3	12.3				26.7			9.0
4.9	4.4	4.1				12.1			3.1
3.3	2.9	2.8	Sales/Total Assets			2.3			3.1
2.3	1.9	1.9				1.5			2.2
1.2	1.2	1.3				1.2			1.0
.8	.5	.9	% Depr., Dep., Amort./Sales						1.0
(40) 2.3	(39) 1.7	(34) 1.3						(17)	1.3
3.4	3.6	2.1							3.2
1.1	2.4		% Officers', Directors' Owners' Comp/Sales						
(15) 2.5	(11) 4.0								
5.4	6.5								
2615226M	2154322M	2389894M	Net Sales ($)	888M	5755M	35943M	11851M	119646M	2215811M
1510743M	1331559M	1527805M	Total Assets ($)	284M	2852M	24403M	9422M	74376M	1416468M

M = $ thousand   MM = $ million
See Pages 9 through 22 for Explanation of Ratios and Data

Current Data Sorted by Assets   Comparative Historical Data

0-500M	500M-2MM	2-10MM	10-50MM	50-100MM	100-250MM	Type of Statement	4/1/06-3/31/07 ALL	4/1/07-3/31/08 ALL
			8	2	4	Unqualified	15	17
		3	2			Reviewed	9	7
	1	2			1	Compiled	9	6
	2	1				Tax Returns	3	7
1	2	2	10	4	4	Other	22	25
7 (4/1-9/30/10)			42 (10/1/10-3/31/11)					
1	**5**	**8**	**20**	**6**	**9**	NUMBER OF STATEMENTS	**58**	**62**
%	%	%	%	%	%	ASSETS	%	%
			5.4			Cash & Equivalents	5.9	8.0
			25.1			Trade Receivables (net)	30.7	25.6
			32.4			Inventory	34.4	32.2
			4.6			All Other Current	2.5	4.2
			67.6			Total Current	73.5	70.0
			24.7			Fixed Assets (net)	18.9	19.8
			2.6			Intangibles (net)	2.7	2.3
			5.1			All Other Non-Current	4.8	7.9
			100.0			Total	100.0	100.0
						LIABILITIES		
			19.6			Notes Payable-Short Term	17.3	16.0
			3.4			Cur. Mat.-L.T.D.	3.5	2.3
			17.9			Trade Payables	23.2	17.9
			.1			Income Taxes Payable	.8	.4
			9.0			All Other Current	10.2	13.1
			50.0			Total Current	54.9	49.8
			11.8			Long-Term Debt	13.6	12.4
			.5			Deferred Taxes	.5	.4
			2.0			All Other Non-Current	1.5	2.8
			35.7			Net Worth	29.4	34.6
			100.0			Total Liabilities & Net Worth	100.0	100.0
						INCOME DATA		
			100.0			Net Sales	100.0	100.0
			11.8			Gross Profit	16.6	18.9
			9.4			Operating Expenses	11.4	12.6
			2.4			Operating Profit	5.2	6.2
			.9			All Other Expenses (net)	1.1	.7
			1.5			Profit Before Taxes	4.1	5.6
						RATIOS		
			2.0			Current	2.1	2.5
			1.5			Current	1.5	1.4
			.9				1.0	1.1
			.9			Quick	1.2	1.2
			.6			Quick	.8	.7
			.2				.3	.4
		32	11.5			Sales/Receivables	18 · 20.7	14 · 26.2
		42	8.6			Sales/Receivables	37 · 9.9	35 · 10.5
		47	7.8				48 · 7.5	44 · 8.4
		26	14.2			Cost of Sales/Inventory	23 · 15.7	16 · 22.4
		57	6.4			Cost of Sales/Inventory	45 · 8.0	36 · 10.1
		83	4.4				74 · 4.9	66 · 5.5
		9	38.6			Cost of Sales/Payables	15 · 24.1	8 · 46.0
		34	10.8			Cost of Sales/Payables	25 · 14.7	24 · 15.1
		52	7.0				48 · 7.6	43 · 8.5
			5.9			Sales/Working Capital	8.1	6.9
			14.1			Sales/Working Capital	19.1	16.4
			NM				-814.3	50.7
			36.1			EBIT/Interest	11.1	19.5
		(19)	5.5			EBIT/Interest	(53) 6.3	(57) 6.6
			2.4				1.9	3.1
						Net Profit + Depr., Dep.,	12.7	12.5
						Amort./Cur. Mat. L/T/D	(19) 3.8	(14) 6.2
							1.4	2.7
			.1			Fixed/Worth	.2	.2
			.6			Fixed/Worth	.5	.4
			4.3				1.9	1.2
			.9			Debt/Worth	1.0	1.0
			1.8			Debt/Worth	2.1	2.2
			8.8				8.8	4.1
			76.9			% Profit Before Taxes/Tangible	68.2	69.3
			26.0			Net Worth	(49) 36.7	(58) 35.0
			10.0				15.0	20.5
			16.5			% Profit Before Taxes/Total	23.1	21.7
			10.1			Assets	9.0	12.1
			3.1				3.4	5.8
			45.3			Sales/Net Fixed Assets	71.7	85.3
			12.8			Sales/Net Fixed Assets	24.0	34.4
			5.3				9.9	7.5
			3.4			Sales/Total Assets	4.5	4.6
			2.5			Sales/Total Assets	3.4	3.3
			1.7				2.3	1.7
			.3			% Depr., Dep., Amort./Sales	.3	.2
		(18)	.9			% Depr., Dep., Amort./Sales	(51) 1.1	(55) .6
			1.7				1.9	2.4
						% Officers', Directors'	.4	1.1
						Owners' Comp/Sales	(17) 1.3	(17) 2.0
							4.4	5.4
1086M	21385M	171566M	1091375M	1267791M	3929421M	Net Sales ($)	5135752M	5777088M
143M	4604M	42821M	437439M	410683M	1418962M	Total Assets ($)	1796972M	1827655M

© RMA 2011

M = $ thousand   MM = $ million
See Pages 9 through 22 for Explanation of Ratios and Data

Comparative Historical Data   Current Data Sorted by Sales

					Type of Statement							
	16		17		14	Unqualified					1	13
	8		7		5	Reviewed				3	3	2
	1		2		4	Compiled			3			1
	2		2		4	Tax Returns			1		1	
	17		21		22	Other	2	1		2	2	18
	4/1/08-		4/1/09-		4/1/10-		1					
	3/31/09		3/31/10		3/31/11		7 (4/1-9/30/10)			42 (10/1/10-3/31/11)		
	ALL		ALL		ALL		0-1MM	1-3MM	3-5MM	5-10MM	10-25MM	25MM & OVER
	44		49		49	NUMBER OF STATEMENTS	3			4	7	34
	%		%		%	ASSETS	%	%	%	%	%	%
	11.4		9.2		8.5	Cash & Equivalents						6.4
	25.7		24.3		25.4	Trade Receivables (net)						26.4
	35.6		31.5		34.5	Inventory						36.4
	1.7		4.0		4.8	All Other Current						5.6
	74.4		68.9		73.1	Total Current						74.7
	17.6		21.3		20.4	Fixed Assets (net)						18.2
	2.2		2.7		2.3	Intangibles (net)						2.2
	5.8		7.1		4.2	All Other Non-Current						4.9
	100.0		100.0		100.0	Total						100.0
						LIABILITIES						
	20.6		17.8		20.0	Notes Payable-Short Term						22.0
	1.5		2.9		2.1	Cur. Mat.-L.T.D.						.9
	15.8		17.3		14.9	Trade Payables						16.3
	.4		.2		.2	Income Taxes Payable						.3
	9.0		11.2		10.9	All Other Current						10.1
	47.1		49.6		48.2	Total Current						49.5
	8.2		9.8		13.5	Long-Term Debt						7.9
	.6		.5		.3	Deferred Taxes						.4
	3.8		4.6		6.9	All Other Non-Current						4.0
	40.2		35.5		31.2	Net Worth						38.2
	100.0		100.0		100.0	Total Liabilities & Net Worth						100.0
						INCOME DATA						
	100.0		100.0		100.0	Net Sales						100.0
	13.8		16.7		18.2	Gross Profit						15.4
	9.3		13.3		12.9	Operating Expenses						9.3
	4.5		3.4		5.3	Operating Profit						6.1
	.6		.0		.6	All Other Expenses (net)						.4
	4.0		3.4		4.6	Profit Before Taxes						5.6
						RATIOS						
	2.1		2.6		2.4							2.5
	1.5		1.5		1.6	Current						1.7
	1.2		1.1		1.2							1.2
	1.1		1.3		1.1							1.1
	.8		.7		.7	Quick						.8
	.5		.5		.4							.3
15	24.3	20	18.6	14	26.8						19	19.3
24	15.4	36	10.2	43	8.5	Sales/Receivables					43	8.5
39	9.5	53	6.9	56	6.6						53	6.9
16	22.6	26	14.0	23	15.8						24	15.3
38	9.5	43	8.4	52	7.0	Cost of Sales/Inventory					53	6.9
63	5.8	69	5.3	78	4.7						79	4.6
9	40.0	10	35.1	9	42.8						9	42.2
15	24.1	24	15.4	24	15.2	Cost of Sales/Payables					22	16.5
33	11.0	43	8.5	39	9.4						39	9.5
	8.7		5.0		5.6							5.0
	15.9		13.1		12.0	Sales/Working Capital						10.5
	51.5		86.1		38.9							43.9
	15.2		18.4		33.2							42.4
(43)	6.3	(47)	4.0	(46)	9.7	EBIT/Interest					(32)	17.5
	1.9		-.4		3.7							4.9
	11.0		10.9		27.5	Net Profit + Depr., Dep.,						31.1
(20)	5.7	(16)	1.6	(12)	13.5	Amort./Cur. Mat. L/T/D					(10)	16.9
	2.5		.2		2.3							6.7
	.2		.2		.1							.1
	.4		.5		.5	Fixed/Worth						.5
	1.1		1.3		1.7							1.0
	.9		.7		1.0							.7
	1.7		2.0		2.3	Debt/Worth						1.3
	4.3		5.7		8.2							6.6
	66.7		46.7		93.9	% Profit Before Taxes/Tangible						88.1
(43)	33.6	(43)	20.5	(46)	37.4	Net Worth					(33)	37.1
	6.2		-.2		18.1							20.7
	20.1		16.8		20.2	% Profit Before Taxes/Total						22.1
	10.9		6.5		13.4	Assets						13.8
	2.9		-2.6		6.4							7.8
	77.4		55.0		53.6							49.8
	31.8		14.7		15.4	Sales/Net Fixed Assets						18.2
	11.5		6.8		7.7							8.0
	5.9		3.9		4.1							4.5
	3.4		2.7		2.6	Sales/Total Assets						2.6
	2.2		1.5		1.7							1.8
	.3		.4		.2							.3
(41)	.5	(44)	1.2	(44)	.7	% Depr., Dep., Amort./Sales					(30)	.9
	1.4		3.0		2.2							1.7
	.4				1.5	% Officers', Directors'						
(13)	1.6			(11)	3.7	Owners' Comp/Sales						
	3.0				5.5							
	6628877M		6001347M		6482624M	Net Sales ($)	5300M	4106M	27850M	97206M	6348162M
	1748066M		1944277M		2314652M	Total Assets ($)	1542M	1221M	7208M	73141M	2231540M

In the ASSETS/LIABILITIES sections under the 0-1MM, 1-3MM, 3-5MM, 5-10MM, 10-25MM columns: **DATA NOT AVAILABLE**

M = $ thousand   MM = $ million
See Pages 9 through 22 for Explanation of Ratios and Data

Current Data Sorted by Assets

Comparative Historical Data

0-500M	500M-2MM 17 (4/1-9/30/10)	2-10MM	10-50MM 47 (10/1/10-3/31/11)	50-100MM	100-250MM	Type of Statement	4/1/06-3/31/07 ALL	4/1/07-3/31/08 ALL
		2	12	1	3	Unqualified	20	19
	1	5	3			Reviewed	15	13
	3	6				Compiled	10	8
		1				Tax Returns	2	2
1		12	11	1	2	Other	23	31
1	4	26	26	2	5	**NUMBER OF STATEMENTS**	70	73
%	%	%	%	%	%		%	%
						ASSETS		
		12.4	6.6			Cash & Equivalents	8.2	8.2
		28.7	27.7			Trade Receivables (net)	26.4	26.0
		20.3	16.2			Inventory	18.2	16.9
		1.6	3.7			All Other Current	2.3	2.0
		63.1	54.3			Total Current	55.1	53.1
		29.4	35.7			Fixed Assets (net)	35.7	36.2
		3.0	2.1			Intangibles (net)	3.5	5.0
		4.5	7.9			All Other Non-Current	5.7	5.6
		100.0	100.0			Total	100.0	100.0
						LIABILITIES		
		9.1	8.6			Notes Payable-Short Term	7.7	7.8
		5.9	4.1			Cur. Mat.-L.T.D.	3.5	3.6
		17.0	13.8			Trade Payables	15.9	13.9
		.1	.1			Income Taxes Payable	.4	.3
		7.5	8.8			All Other Current	6.0	7.4
		39.6	35.4			Total Current	33.5	32.9
		14.5	11.0			Long-Term Debt	17.3	16.2
		.2	1.4			Deferred Taxes	1.4	1.2
		2.8	2.7			All Other Non-Current	3.4	6.8
		42.9	49.6			Net Worth	44.3	42.9
		100.0	100.0			Total Liabilities & Net Worth	100.0	100.0
						INCOME DATA		
		100.0	100.0			Net Sales	100.0	100.0
		21.4	19.6			Gross Profit	22.2	21.9
		16.8	13.6			Operating Expenses	15.7	15.9
		4.6	6.0			Operating Profit	6.5	6.0
		.5	.6			All Other Expenses (net)	1.0	1.3
		4.1	5.4			Profit Before Taxes	5.5	4.7
						RATIOS		
		3.1	2.6				2.5	2.5
		1.9	1.9			Current	1.7	1.6
		.9	1.0				1.1	1.1
		2.3	1.9				1.7	1.8
		1.1	1.0			Quick	1.1	1.1
		.5	.6				.7	.7
		49 7.5	43 8.4				39 9.4	38 9.6
		54 6.8	55 6.6			Sales/Receivables	45 8.1	46 7.9
		65 5.6	76 4.8				54 6.7	55 6.6
		23 16.2	23 15.5				20 18.2	19 19.3
		41 8.8	41 9.0			Cost of Sales/Inventory	33 11.0	32 11.6
		65 5.6	63 5.8				62 5.9	59 6.2
		23 15.8	25 14.8				19 18.7	18 20.4
		31 11.8	31 11.6			Cost of Sales/Payables	31 11.9	29 12.7
		60 6.1	44 8.3				39 9.2	40 9.1
		3.4	3.9				5.4	5.9
		9.4	8.9			Sales/Working Capital	10.8	11.1
		-37.0	NM				40.7	67.2
		28.6	12.8				12.6	13.9
		(25) 4.1	(23) 4.2			EBIT/Interest	(66) 4.0	(65) 4.2
		1.4	1.2				2.7	1.3
			6.0				6.8	10.2
			(10) 3.3			Net Profit + Depr., Dep., Amort./Cur. Mat. L/T/D	(33) 3.8	(31) 3.3
			2.2				1.7	1.5
		.3	.3				.5	.5
		1.0	.9			Fixed/Worth	.9	.9
		1.8	1.6				1.6	2.7
		.6	.5				.6	.7
		1.6	.9			Debt/Worth	1.2	1.3
		4.9	2.5				3.2	3.9
		46.2	33.8			% Profit Before Taxes/Tangible Net Worth	47.2	36.7
		(25) 16.3	17.7				(63) 23.1	(66) 17.5
		2.4	6.0				10.0	5.0
		12.5	15.0			% Profit Before Taxes/Total Assets	17.4	16.6
		6.7	6.8				8.9	7.4
		1.0	1.2				3.8	1.9
		12.5	9.3			Sales/Net Fixed Assets	9.4	10.5
		7.1	5.2				6.1	5.3
		3.6	3.4				3.6	3.2
		2.2	1.8			Sales/Total Assets	2.7	2.5
		1.7	1.7				2.1	2.0
		1.4	1.4				1.5	1.3
		1.5	2.5			% Depr., Dep., Amort./Sales	1.5	1.7
		(25) 2.7	3.5				(64) 2.4	(63) 2.6
		3.9	4.9				4.1	4.2
						% Officers', Directors' Owners' Comp/Sales	1.2	1.3
							(19) 2.0	(18) 2.5
							5.4	5.3
689M	16165M	239310M	851279M	146655M	829712M	Net Sales ($)	2812039M	4116715M
448M	6171M	129187M	521119M	135566M	693614M	Total Assets ($)	1887142M	2470641M

M = $ thousand   MM = $ million
See Pages 9 through 22 for Explanation of Ratios and Data

Comparative Historical Data

Current Data Sorted by Sales

H1	H2	H3	Type of Statement	0-1MM	1-3MM	3-5MM	5-10MM	10-25MM	25MM & OVER
20	13	18	Unqualified					5	13
15	11	9	Reviewed				1	3	5
4	6	9	Compiled		3	2	4		
2	1	1	Tax Returns			1			
20	27	27	Other	1	2	2	5	12	5
4/1/08-3/31/09	4/1/09-3/31/10	4/1/10-3/31/11					17 (4/1-9/30/10)	47 (10/1/10-3/31/11)	
ALL	ALL	ALL							
61	58	64	**NUMBER OF STATEMENTS**	1	5	5	10	20	23
%	%	%	**ASSETS**	%	%	%	%	%	%
8.7	7.6	8.5	Cash & Equivalents				12.0	9.3	5.8
24.9	21.2	27.6	Trade Receivables (net)				29.8	26.3	27.2
18.8	18.2	17.7	Inventory				25.5	21.5	14.4
1.9	3.5	2.8	All Other Current				.0	2.5	4.2
54.3	50.5	56.6	Total Current				67.3	59.6	51.6
36.1	36.9	32.2	Fixed Assets (net)				27.3	34.8	30.3
3.9	4.3	4.3	Intangibles (net)				2.3	.2	8.1
5.8	8.2	6.9	All Other Non-Current				3.1	5.3	10.0
100.0	100.0	100.0	Total				100.0	100.0	100.0
			LIABILITIES						
10.3	10.6	8.4	Notes Payable-Short Term				10.8	8.8	6.8
3.5	4.4	4.6	Cur. Mat.-L.T.D.				3.9	5.5	2.0
14.2	11.0	14.2	Trade Payables				20.4	13.2	13.8
.2	.1	.3	Income Taxes Payable				.0	.2	.6
6.1	7.9	9.0	All Other Current				2.8	7.1	10.6
34.3	34.1	36.4	Total Current				38.0	34.7	33.8
14.2	13.9	15.1	Long-Term Debt				18.8	12.3	12.3
1.2	1.0	.7	Deferred Taxes				.0	.8	1.3
4.7	6.2	3.5	All Other Non-Current				.6	5.0	4.8
45.6	44.8	44.2	Net Worth				42.6	47.2	47.7
100.0	100.0	100.0	Total Liabilities & Net Worth				100.0	100.0	100.0
			INCOME DATA						
100.0	100.0	100.0	Net Sales				100.0	100.0	100.0
17.7	20.6	21.4	Gross Profit				27.6	20.5	20.2
12.6	19.6	15.5	Operating Expenses				19.8	15.3	13.6
5.0	1.0	5.8	Operating Profit				7.8	5.2	6.6
1.1	1.5	1.0	All Other Expenses (net)				.4	.7	1.5
3.9	-.5	4.9	Profit Before Taxes				7.4	4.5	5.1
			RATIOS						
2.9	3.5	2.9					4.1	2.9	3.1
1.6	1.8	1.9	Current				2.1	1.9	2.1
1.1	1.0	1.0					1.1	1.1	1.0
1.7	1.8	2.0					2.9	2.0	2.0
1.0	.8	1.0	Quick				1.6	1.0	1.0
.7	.5	.6					.6	.7	.6
32 11.4	38 9.5	44 8.3					30 12.2	43 8.6	51 7.2
42 8.7	44 8.3	55 6.7	Sales/Receivables				52 7.0	50 7.3	59 6.2
57 6.5	53 6.9	67 5.5					55 6.7	64 5.7	67 5.5
21 17.7	25 14.4	23 15.7					27 13.5	26 13.9	20 17.8
33 11.2	45 8.2	42 8.7	Cost of Sales/Inventory				42 8.7	45 8.1	42 8.7
62 5.9	70 5.2	63 5.8					69 5.3	66 5.6	62 5.9
14 25.9	15 24.9	24 15.4					21 17.3	20 18.3	27 13.6
27 13.8	21 17.2	31 11.6	Cost of Sales/Payables				29 12.6	28 13.2	32 11.5
34 10.8	36 10.1	45 8.1					53 6.9	43 8.5	44 8.3
5.4	3.3	3.8					3.6	3.4	3.9
11.4	10.5	9.0	Sales/Working Capital				8.7	9.0	8.0
50.5	-193.3	-851.2					43.9	53.8	-801.7
13.1	4.9	23.4					45.9	7.7	75.1
(57) 4.3	(50) 1.4	(58) 4.6	EBIT/Interest				9.2	(19) 4.7	(19) 5.4
1.5	-1.3	1.5					2.3	2.0	2.3
9.7	4.7	7.7	Net Profit + Depr., Dep.,						
(24) 3.0	(16) 2.9	(20) 3.7	Amort./Cur. Mat. L/T/D						
.8	.9	2.5							
.4	.4	.3					.4	.2	.3
1.0	.9	.9	Fixed/Worth				.8	1.0	.6
1.8	3.3	1.7					1.3	1.7	1.7
.4	.4	.6					.5	.6	.3
1.2	1.1	1.2	Debt/Worth				1.4	.9	1.0
3.7	8.4	4.3					13.2	2.5	3.6
34.4	19.5	37.4	% Profit Before Taxes/Tangible				59.7	34.5	36.5
(57) 16.9	(52) 3.0	(60) 18.9	Net Worth				32.3	21.1	(21) 18.7
3.3	-10.5	4.7					15.8	2.9	8.0
15.3	8.9	16.0	% Profit Before Taxes/Total				26.4	11.4	16.9
5.1	.7	8.1	Assets				16.1	7.7	8.4
1.4	-6.3	1.2					3.2	1.7	1.4
10.2	7.7	9.4					13.9	15.1	8.8
6.2	4.8	6.2	Sales/Net Fixed Assets				8.5	6.2	5.6
3.8	2.6	3.3					6.8	3.2	3.9
2.5	2.0	2.0					3.1	2.1	1.8
2.0	1.6	1.7	Sales/Total Assets				2.1	1.7	1.7
1.4	1.0	1.3					1.8	1.4	1.2
1.5	1.7	2.1						1.8	2.3
(57) 2.7	(52) 3.7	(59) 3.0	% Depr., Dep., Amort./Sales					2.7	(20) 3.1
4.0	5.2	4.8						5.0	3.9
.8	1.4	.8	% Officers', Directors'						
(14) 1.9	(15) 3.3	(15) 2.6	Owners' Comp/Sales						
5.9	5.3	4.6							
2743167M	2036623M	2083810M	Net Sales ($)	689M	12086M	20833M	73175M	337944M	1639083M
1810612M	1820589M	1486105M	Total Assets ($)	448M	11935M	15520M	33756M	203119M	1221327M

M = $ thousand   MM = $ million
See Pages 9 through 22 for Explanation of Ratios and Data

Current Data Sorted by Assets   Comparative Historical Data

						Type of Statement		
			5	3	1	Unqualified	13	8
		12	3	1		Reviewed	17	13
	3	3	1			Compiled	9	5
		1				Tax Returns	5	2
1	1	1	3	1	1	Other	26	12
		4					4/1/06-3/31/07	4/1/07-3/31/08
0-500M	5 (4/1-9/30/10) 500M-2MM	2-10MM	39 (10/1/10-3/31/11) 10-50MM	50-100MM	100-250MM		ALL	ALL
1	4	20	12	5	2	NUMBER OF STATEMENTS	70	40
%	%	%	%	%	%	ASSETS	%	%
		9.6	6.7			Cash & Equivalents	7.3	7.3
		36.5	26.9			Trade Receivables (net)	34.1	27.6
		22.0	38.2			Inventory	21.3	23.7
		3.2	1.6			All Other Current	3.4	2.8
		71.2	73.4			Total Current	66.2	61.3
		22.8	25.1			Fixed Assets (net)	27.3	32.6
		2.7	.4			Intangibles (net)	3.0	1.7
		3.4	1.2			All Other Non-Current	3.6	4.4
		100.0	100.0			Total	100.0	100.0
						LIABILITIES		
		9.6	12.8			Notes Payable-Short Term	12.0	9.3
		2.2	2.9			Cur. Mat.-L.T.D.	3.0	2.7
		20.7	13.2			Trade Payables	22.4	15.4
		.0	.1			Income Taxes Payable	.2	.1
		12.4	14.4			All Other Current	11.1	13.1
		44.8	43.3			Total Current	48.7	40.6
		13.3	7.9			Long-Term Debt	14.6	16.6
		.4	.0			Deferred Taxes	.4	.5
		2.6	8.9			All Other Non-Current	5.5	5.2
		38.9	39.9			Net Worth	30.8	37.2
		100.0	100.0			Total Liabilities & Net Worth	100.0	100.0
						INCOME DATA		
		100.0	100.0			Net Sales	100.0	100.0
		25.7	22.5			Gross Profit	23.7	24.1
		21.7	17.6			Operating Expenses	16.7	17.6
		4.0	4.9			Operating Profit	7.1	6.5
		.6	.9			All Other Expenses (net)	1.0	1.1
		3.3	4.0			Profit Before Taxes	6.1	5.4
						RATIOS		
		2.6	3.2				1.9	2.3
		1.5	1.8			Current	1.5	1.6
		1.1	1.3				1.1	1.1
		1.6	1.2				1.3	1.4
		1.1	.8			Quick	.9	.9
		.6	.5				.6	.6
		42 8.6	42 8.7				41 9.0	34 10.6
		62 5.8	57 6.4			Sales/Receivables	48 7.6	43 8.5
		78 4.7	69 5.3				61 6.0	52 7.0
		29 12.7	50 7.2				13 27.7	17 21.0
		39 9.3	82 4.4			Cost of Sales/Inventory	36 10.3	40 9.0
		68 5.3	145 2.5				56 6.5	82 4.4
		29 12.6	19 19.7				24 15.2	16 22.1
		47 7.7	33 11.1			Cost of Sales/Payables	36 10.2	30 12.3
		58 6.3	44 8.4				49 7.5	38 9.5
		4.3	3.1				6.6	6.1
		8.1	6.2			Sales/Working Capital	12.7	9.4
		40.4	10.5				50.5	28.1
		10.4	17.9				13.6	16.7
		(15) 4.4	8.2			EBIT/Interest	(66) 6.0	(38) 4.2
		.2	3.6				2.3	2.1
						Net Profit + Depr., Dep., Amort./Cur. Mat. L/T/D	18.1	7.3
							(21) 5.7	(12) 4.4
							2.7	2.6
		.2	.3				.4	.4
		.6	.6			Fixed/Worth	.8	.8
		1.3	1.3				1.7	1.9
		.8	.8				1.0	.8
		2.5	1.3			Debt/Worth	1.8	1.7
		5.0	5.2				6.3	3.7
		41.1	35.8				61.1	52.8
		25.1	(11) 11.3			% Profit Before Taxes/Tangible Net Worth	(64) 39.1	(37) 25.8
		-9.1	6.8				11.9	9.0
		13.8	11.7				20.7	18.0
		6.2	8.3			% Profit Before Taxes/Total Assets	10.5	8.5
		-2.1	2.9				4.7	3.0
		26.0	9.8				20.4	12.5
		17.3	8.8			Sales/Net Fixed Assets	10.4	.7.7
		4.9	5.9				5.1	5.6
		2.8	2.3				2.9	3.0
		2.3	1.8			Sales/Total Assets	2.4	2.6
		1.7	1.4				1.8	1.8
		.7	1.5				.9	1.0
		(18) 1.2	2.2			% Depr., Dep., Amort./Sales	(63) 1.7	(38) 1.9
		2.2	2.7				3.0	3.2
						% Officers', Directors' Owners' Comp/Sales	1.4	3.2
							(18) 3.3	(11) 4.0
							4.0	6.1
398M	22234M	193586M	393712M	834007M	490736M	Net Sales ($)	4018832M	2269488M
180M	6109M	92584M	231203M	436659M	270396M	Total Assets ($)	1998727M	1128733M

M = $ thousand   MM = $ million
See Pages 9 through 22 for Explanation of Ratios and Data

Comparative Historical Data | Current Data Sorted by Sales

				Type of Statement	0-1MM	1-3MM	3-5MM	5-10MM	10-25MM	25MM & OVER
	10		9	9	Unqualified				6	1	8
	14		14	16	Reviewed					5	4
	7		8	7	Compiled		1	1	3	2	
	2		1	2	Tax Returns					1	
	18		14	10	Other	1			4	3	3
	4/1/08-3/31/09 ALL		4/1/09-3/31/10 ALL	4/1/10-3/31/11 ALL				5 (4/1-9/30/10)		39 (10/1-3/31/11)	
	51		46	44	**NUMBER OF STATEMENTS**	1	1	2	13	12	15
	%		%	%	**ASSETS**	%	%	%	%	%	%
	7.2		9.2	8.4	Cash & Equivalents				7.0	9.0	7.3
	30.1		27.8	31.9	Trade Receivables (net)				32.7	36.5	25.1
	27.2		25.5	25.9	Inventory				24.3	27.1	30.4
	2.8		2.4	2.4	All Other Current				1.2	4.1	1.6
	67.2		64.9	68.6	Total Current				65.2	76.8	64.5
	25.0		28.7	25.0	Fixed Assets (net)				28.9	18.6	25.6
	3.2		2.9	2.1	Intangibles (net)				3.8	.4	2.5
	4.5		3.5	4.4	All Other Non-Current				2.1	4.1	7.3
	100.0		100.0	100.0	Total				100.0	100.0	100.0
					LIABILITIES						
	11.3		9.4	9.3	Notes Payable-Short Term				8.8	13.2	7.5
	2.5		3.8	2.7	Cur. Mat.-L.T.D.				2.5	3.2	2.1
	16.9		16.5	18.0	Trade Payables				20.1	19.0	13.3
	.2		.1	.1	Income Taxes Payable				.0	.0	.1
	10.9		8.7	11.2	All Other Current				8.6	9.7	12.4
	41.8		38.4	41.2	Total Current				40.1	45.1	35.3
	11.6		12.7	13.9	Long-Term Debt				16.3	8.5	10.2
	.4		.1	.4	Deferred Taxes				.2	.4	.7
	9.1		13.6	7.4	All Other Non-Current				7.0	3.2	10.0
	37.1		35.2	37.1	Net Worth				36.3	42.8	43.7
	100.0		100.0	100.0	Total Liabilities & Net Worth				100.0	100.0	100.0
					INCOME DATA						
	100.0		100.0	100.0	Net Sales				100.0	100.0	100.0
	21.0		20.8	25.1	Gross Profit				21.0	31.1	18.5
	17.0		20.6	19.6	Operating Expenses				18.1	24.6	11.2
	4.0		.1	5.5	Operating Profit				2.9	6.4	7.3
	.7		1.2	.8	All Other Expenses (net)				1.0	.6	.7
	3.3		-1.1	4.7	Profit Before Taxes				1.9	5.8	6.6
					RATIOS						
	2.6		2.9	2.8					2.6	2.5	3.9
	1.6		1.8	1.7	Current				1.6	1.6	1.9
	1.2		1.1	1.1					1.1	1.2	1.2
	1.4		1.9	1.5					1.9	1.2	1.4
	.9		1.0	1.1	Quick				1.1	.9	1.2
	.6		.6	.7					.5	.6	.7
33	11.0	35	10.3	41 8.8	Sales/Receivables				34 10.6	46 8.0	36 10.2
44	8.4	51	7.2	57 6.4					59 6.2	61 6.0	46 8.0
58	6.3	58	6.3	70 5.2					85 4.3	66 5.5	69 5.3
22	16.7	27	13.7	30 12.2	Cost of Sales/Inventory				24 15.3	31 11.7	43 8.4
46	7.9	48	7.6	48 7.6					36 10.1	49 7.4	58 6.3
72	5.1	96	3.8	86 4.2					80 4.6	101 3.6	95 3.9
13	28.4	17	21.8	19 19.7	Cost of Sales/Payables				17 21.8	29 12.6	16 23.2
27	13.4	27	13.3	33 11.0					31 11.6	46 8.0	25 14.6
44	8.3	48	7.6	56 6.5					58 6.3	59 6.2	42 8.8
	5.8		4.2	4.2	Sales/Working Capital				4.5	3.9	3.4
	8.5		7.9	6.7					7.2	6.9	5.6
	31.5		27.9	38.2					NM	32.8	33.0
	14.0		7.0	22.3	EBIT/Interest				9.7		56.0
(46)	4.4	(43)	2.6	(38) 7.1					(12) 3.3		17.6
	1.8		-2.8	2.2					-6.9		3.9
	11.5		5.0	8.3	Net Profit + Depr., Dep.,						
(13)	2.4	(13)	1.0	(13) 2.6	Amort./Cur. Mat. L/T/D						
	1.6		-.3	1.5							
	.4		.3	.3	Fixed/Worth				.3	.2	.3
	.7		.6	.6					.8	.5	.6
	1.4		2.1	1.4					2.2	.9	1.3
	.8		.6	.7	Debt/Worth				.7	.8	.3
	1.8		1.5	1.4					2.4	1.7	1.1
	4.2		4.9	5.0					4.9	2.6	6.2
	53.4		19.3	39.5	% Profit Before Taxes/Tangible				46.8	39.5	30.6
(45)	28.0	(40)	5.9	(40) 18.7	Net Worth				(12) 21.1	21.2	(13) 16.0
	2.3		-11.6	6.5					-35.0	6.8	8.5
	16.7		6.6	14.0	% Profit Before Taxes/Total				14.0	13.1	15.3
	8.3		2.0	9.3	Assets				3.3	9.1	11.9
	1.7		-5.5	2.4					-16.2	2.6	3.8
	21.7		16.1	21.5	Sales/Net Fixed Assets				23.5	24.8	9.8
	11.2		7.2	9.7					6.9	17.3	7.9
	6.1		4.7	5.7					3.2	6.0	6.0
	3.2		2.8	2.6	Sales/Total Assets				3.9	2.8	2.3
	2.4		1.8	2.0					1.8	2.2	2.0
	1.8		1.5	1.5					1.4	1.7	1.5
	.7		.9	.8	% Depr., Dep., Amort./Sales				.9	.6	1.5
(47)	1.3	(43)	2.4	(41) 1.8					(11) 2.2	(11) 1.1	1.8
	2.7		3.6	2.6					2.5	2.4	2.7
	.6		2.2	1.8	% Officers', Directors'						
(12)	2.0	(10)	3.8	(12) 3.1	Owners' Comp/Sales						
	4.3		4.9	5.5							
	2662556M		2120873M	1934673M	Net Sales ($)	398M	1978M	9905M	94297M	186030M	1642065M
	1275243M		1130338M	1037131M	Total Assets ($)	180M	1190M	3957M	47714M	110349M	873741M

© RMA 2011

M = $ thousand   MM = $ million
See Pages 9 through 22 for Explanation of Ratios and Data

Current Data Sorted by Assets   Comparative Historical Data

						Type of Statement		
	2	1	6	2	3	Unqualified	10	11
	2	6	2	1		Reviewed	18	16
1	2	8	2			Compiled	10	9
2	3	2				Tax Returns	5	2
	3	8	6	2	1	Other	16	22
	11 (4/1-9/30/10)		52 (10/1/10-3/31/11)				4/1/06-3/31/07	4/1/07-3/31/08
0-500M	500M-2MM	2-10MM	10-50MM	50-100MM	100-250MM		ALL	ALL
3	10	25	16	5	4	NUMBER OF STATEMENTS	59	60
%	%	%	%	%	%	ASSETS	%	%
	5.3	9.4	5.6			Cash & Equivalents	5.4	7.1
	44.0	26.3	30.0			Trade Receivables (net)	31.5	29.8
	22.1	24.7	17.8			Inventory	19.7	21.1
	1.1	1.3	2.3			All Other Current	1.2	1.6
	72.4	61.7	55.7			Total Current	57.7	59.7
	21.7	27.4	35.0			Fixed Assets (net)	33.9	33.5
	3.1	4.0	3.6			Intangibles (net)	2.8	.8
	2.8	6.9	5.7			All Other Non-Current	5.6	5.9
	100.0	100.0	100.0			Total	100.0	100.0
						LIABILITIES		
	16.4	11.9	8.5			Notes Payable-Short Term	7.9	9.6
	2.4	4.2	5.5			Cur. Mat.-L.T.D.	3.9	3.1
	23.8	13.2	15.5			Trade Payables	16.3	16.2
	.1	.1	.2			Income Taxes Payable	.2	.2
	6.9	7.3	9.6			All Other Current	9.7	9.5
	49.6	36.8	39.3			Total Current	37.9	38.6
	10.7	12.8	20.8			Long-Term Debt	18.1	16.4
	.0	.5	.3			Deferred Taxes	.5	.6
	1.0	4.0	7.6			All Other Non-Current	5.3	5.2
	38.7	45.8	32.0			Net Worth	38.2	39.2
	100.0	100.0	100.0			Total Liabilities & Net Worth	100.0	100.0
						INCOME DATA		
	100.0	100.0	100.0			Net Sales	100.0	100.0
	34.1	22.9	15.1			Gross Profit	19.5	21.1
	29.6	18.0	9.8			Operating Expenses	15.7	15.9
	4.5	4.9	5.3			Operating Profit	3.8	5.2
	.3	.9	.8			All Other Expenses (net)	1.0	1.1
	4.2	4.0	4.5			Profit Before Taxes	2.8	4.0
						RATIOS		
	3.1	2.7	2.5				2.4	2.6
	1.6	1.8	1.6			Current	1.5	1.6
	1.0	1.2	.9				1.2	1.0
	2.3	1.9	1.5				1.7	1.8
	.9	.8	.9			Quick	.9	.9
	.5	.6	.6				.6	.6

30	12.1	40	9.2	53	6.9			Sales/Receivables	45	8.1	40	9.2
53	6.9	52	7.1	59	6.2				57	6.4	51	7.2
68	5.4	66	5.5	71	5.2				66	5.6	58	6.2
6	65.8	36	10.1	28	12.9			Cost of Sales/Inventory	24	15.5	25	14.6
23	16.0	49	7.5	41	8.9				37	9.9	43	8.5
76	4.8	95	3.8	56	6.6				61	6.0	68	5.4
20	18.6	17	21.0	23	15.7			Cost of Sales/Payables	18	20.4	15	24.2
33	10.9	25	14.3	37	9.8				33	11.2	31	11.8
59	6.2	43	8.6	45	8.2				51	7.2	46	7.9

	7.0	5.2	4.9			Sales/Working Capital	5.5	5.7
	10.4	8.6	9.7				10.4	9.5
	NM	26.3	-34.9				30.4	103.1

	36.6	13.1	35.0			EBIT/Interest		8.2	4.7
	17.6	(23) 3.5	(15) 4.6				(53)	3.0 (53)	2.4
	1.4	2.3	1.8					.9	1.2

						Net Profit + Depr., Dep.,		9.9	5.2
						Amort./Cur. Mat. L/T/D	(20)	3.6 (21)	3.0
								.5	1.8

	.2	.3	.6			Fixed/Worth	.4	.4
	.8	.6	1.3				.9	.9
	NM	1.1	6.4				2.0	2.1
	.4	.6	1.0			Debt/Worth	.8	.6
	1.3	1.2	1.9				1.4	1.6
	NM	3.5	15.7				3.8	4.6

		26.2	56.1			% Profit Before Taxes/Tangible		35.2	37.3
	(23)	14.1 (13)	20.0			Net Worth	(53)	15.7 (56)	13.6
		8.4	15.1					1.8	5.4

	21.2	9.9	10.3			% Profit Before Taxes/Total	12.5	13.4
	13.5	6.4	8.7			Assets	5.2	5.4
	1.2	2.7	3.2				.0	1.2
	25.9	16.0	7.8			Sales/Net Fixed Assets	13.1	13.5
	18.5	7.6	5.6				7.3	7.3
	7.5	3.4	3.6				3.4	4.1
	4.2	2.6	2.1			Sales/Total Assets	2.4	2.7
	2.9	1.6	1.7				2.0	2.1
	2.2	1.4	1.5				1.7	1.5

		1.1	2.0			% Depr., Dep., Amort./Sales		1.4	1.1
	(24)	2.0 (15)	3.7				(54)	2.4 (54)	2.4
		3.3	4.1					4.3	4.3

		.7				% Officers', Directors'		1.4	1.9
	(13)	1.8				Owners' Comp/Sales	(27)	1.9 (21)	2.6
		4.2						3.7	4.3

1777M	36676M	240159M	710802M	652534M	1464723M	Net Sales ($)	2392127M	2776002M
524M	12999M	135173M	381222M	308439M	647265M	Total Assets ($)	1340437M	1480244M

M = $ thousand   MM = $ million
See Pages 9 through 22 for Explanation of Ratios and Data

Comparative Historical Data | Current Data Sorted by Sales

Type of Statement	4/1/08-3/31/09 ALL	4/1/09-3/31/10 ALL	4/1/10-3/31/11 ALL	0-1MM	1-3MM	3-5MM	5-10MM	10-25MM	25MM & OVER
Unqualified	12	10	12				1	2	9
Reviewed	11	12	11		1		3	2	3
Compiled	10	12	13	1		2	4	6	
Tax Returns	4	4	7		1	2	2		
Other	16	16	20	2	2	1	5	5	7
	11 (4/1-9/30/10)						52 (10/1/10-3/31/11)		
NUMBER OF STATEMENTS	53	54	63	3	4	7	15	15	19

ASSETS (%)

	08-09	09-10	10-11	0-1MM	1-3MM	3-5MM	5-10MM	10-25MM	25MM & OVER
Cash & Equivalents	8.0	10.3	8.2				13.0	6.9	9.5
Trade Receivables (net)	25.7	22.4	29.4				27.8	29.0	28.3
Inventory	21.9	18.3	20.3				20.3	23.5	15.3
All Other Current	2.1	3.4	1.8				1.3	1.4	3.4
Total Current	57.8	54.4	59.8				62.4	60.7	56.5
Fixed Assets (net)	31.6	35.9	30.1				29.6	27.1	37.2
Intangibles (net)	3.7	2.7	3.9				2.7	6.6	1.4
All Other Non-Current	6.9	7.1	6.2				5.2	5.6	4.9
Total	100.0	100.0	100.0				100.0	100.0	100.0

LIABILITIES

	08-09	09-10	10-11	0-1MM	1-3MM	3-5MM	5-10MM	10-25MM	25MM & OVER
Notes Payable-Short Term	11.7	8.5	12.4				7.2	10.4	8.1
Cur. Mat.-L.T.D.	3.7	3.9	4.1				4.8	5.6	2.7
Trade Payables	15.1	12.5	15.8				14.8	12.6	18.7
Income Taxes Payable	.0	.1	.1				.2	.0	.2
All Other Current	8.4	10.4	8.8				8.5	7.3	9.7
Total Current	38.9	35.4	41.2				35.5	35.9	39.4
Long-Term Debt	17.0	21.1	15.6				12.4	11.1	17.1
Deferred Taxes	.3	.8	.4				.7	.5	.3
All Other Non-Current	5.6	8.5	5.1				1.9	4.8	9.2
Net Worth	38.2	34.1	37.7				49.5	47.7	34.0
Total Liabilties & Net Worth	100.0	100.0	100.0				100.0	100.0	100.0

INCOME DATA

	08-09	09-10	10-11	0-1MM	1-3MM	3-5MM	5-10MM	10-25MM	25MM & OVER
Net Sales	100.0	100.0	100.0				100.0	100.0	100.0
Gross Profit	17.6	19.9	23.3				28.0	19.4	14.7
Operating Expenses	15.3	18.0	18.1				23.4	14.2	9.0
Operating Profit	2.2	1.9	5.2				4.6	5.2	5.7
All Other Expenses (net)	.9	1.6	.9				.4	.5	1.2
Profit Before Taxes	1.3	.3	4.4				4.2	4.7	4.5

RATIOS

	08-09	09-10	10-11	0-1MM	1-3MM	3-5MM	5-10MM	10-25MM	25MM & OVER
Current	2.7	3.4	2.9				3.0	2.7	2.1
	1.7	1.6	1.7				2.0	1.9	1.5
	1.1	1.1	1.1				1.2	1.0	.9
Quick	1.7	1.9	2.2				2.6	1.9	1.4
	.8	.9	.9				1.4	.9	1.0
	.6	.6	.6				.7	.7	.6
Sales/Receivables	31 11.7	38 9.6	35 10.3				39 9.3	42 8.7	34 10.9
	49 7.5	50 7.2	54 6.8				52 7.1	60 6.1	54 6.8
	59 6.2	67 5.4	62 5.9				59 6.2	70 5.2	62 5.9
Cost of Sales/Inventory	27 13.6	29 12.4	24 14.9				32 11.4	39 9.3	20 18.3
	36 10.0	48 7.6	45 8.1				47 7.8	48 7.6	31 11.9
	57 6.4	81 4.5	64 5.7				83 4.4	63 5.8	43 8.5
Cost of Sales/Payables	15 24.3	15 23.8	17 21.7				18 20.4	14 25.9	23 15.7
	23 15.8	29 12.8	32 11.3				32 11.3	25 14.3	38 9.6
	42 8.6	48 7.7	45 8.2				50 7.3	41 9.0	45 8.2
Sales/Working Capital	5.2	4.9	5.1				4.9	4.7	5.4
	11.3	7.8	9.4				8.8	6.3	11.6
	40.6	31.2	41.6				12.9	205.5	-61.9
EBIT/Interest	4.3	6.6	15.7				32.1	20.9	22.6
	(48) 2.0	(60) 1.9	4.8				(14) 4.1	(14) 5.3	(18) 4.3
	-2.8	-.9	2.0				2.8	3.9	1.6
Net Profit + Depr., Dep., Amort./Cur. Mat. L/T/D	5.3	6.6	9.5						
	(23) 1.3	(17) 2.7	(17) 2.4						
	.2	.0	2.0						
Fixed/Worth	.3	.5	.4				.4	.4	.6
	.8	1.1	.8				.7	.6	1.0
	2.4	2.6	1.8				1.1	1.5	3.1
Debt/Worth	.5	.5	.6				.5	.5	1.1
	1.3	1.8	1.6				1.2	.9	2.2
	6.6	9.0	5.5				2.0	5.9	6.8
% Profit Before Taxes/Tangible Net Worth	24.8	13.7	29.0				30.5	35.6	29.7
	(44) 9.8	(45) 3.9	(54) 17.8				(14) 11.4	(14) 23.4	(16) 18.6
	-.6	-5.7	8.9				6.1	13.7	10.1
% Profit Before Taxes/Total Assets	7.5	4.9	14.0				18.4	11.9	14.0
	3.3	1.5	7.9				8.0	8.4	7.9
	-3.2	-4.9	2.9				2.9	6.4	1.7
Sales/Net Fixed Assets	14.3	10.7	12.7				19.4	10.2	8.3
	6.6	3.7	6.9				6.3	6.3	5.4
	4.1	2.4	4.0				3.3	4.5	3.6
Sales/Total Assets	2.6	2.0	2.7				2.9	2.1	2.2
	1.9	1.6	1.9				2.2	1.6	1.8
	1.4	1.1	1.5				1.4	1.5	1.5
% Depr., Dep., Amort./Sales	1.3	2.2	1.4				1.0	1.6	3.2
	(49) 2.4	(46) 3.7	(56) 2.4				(14) 1.4	(14) 1.9	(17) 3.8
	4.0	5.9	3.7				2.4	2.6	4.8
% Officers', Directors' Owners' Comp/Sales	1.4	1.9	1.4						
	(26) 3.8	(22) 3.7	(26) 2.7						
	5.5	5.2	4.6						
Net Sales ($)	2180097M	1963616M	3106671M	1777M	9069M	29104M	108264M	259040M	2699417M
Total Assets ($)	1297251M	1458891M	1485622M	524M	4859M	17696M	60480M	147530M	1254533M

Current Data Sorted by Assets   **Comparative Historical Data**

Type of Statement	0-500M	500M-2MM	2-10MM	10-50MM	50-100MM	100-250MM		4/1/06-3/31/07 ALL	4/1/07-3/31/08 ALL
Unqualified			3					4	4
Reviewed		1	5	2				8	5
Compiled	1	2	1					6	5
Tax Returns	1	1	1					1	2
Other		2	6	2				13	13
		9 (4/1-9/30/10)		19 (10/1/10-3/31/11)					
NUMBER OF STATEMENTS	2	6	16	4				32	29
ASSETS	%	%	%	%	%	%		%	%
Cash & Equivalents			9.0		DATA	DATA		6.0	5.2
Trade Receivables (net)			32.6		NOT	NOT		30.5	33.8
Inventory			16.9		AVAILABLE	AVAILABLE		18.5	20.2
All Other Current			1.2					.9	1.9
Total Current			59.7					55.9	61.1
Fixed Assets (net)			34.5					38.7	31.1
Intangibles (net)			2.0					1.7	2.7
All Other Non-Current			3.8					3.7	5.1
Total			100.0					100.0	100.0
LIABILITIES									
Notes Payable-Short Term			8.7					10.7	24.1
Cur. Mat.-L.T.D.			4.0					4.5	4.9
Trade Payables			16.6					14.5	20.9
Income Taxes Payable			.4					.0	.1
All Other Current			9.6					7.7	8.6
Total Current			39.2					37.3	58.6
Long-Term Debt			15.3					21.9	16.5
Deferred Taxes			.6					.3	.4
All Other Non-Current			3.8					4.4	5.8
Net Worth			41.0					36.0	18.6
Total Liabilties & Net Worth			100.0					100.0	100.0
INCOME DATA									
Net Sales			100.0					100.0	100.0
Gross Profit			24.1					26.1	23.8
Operating Expenses			17.0					20.4	18.6
Operating Profit			7.1					5.7	5.2
All Other Expenses (net)			1.3					1.3	1.3
Profit Before Taxes			5.8					4.4	4.0
RATIOS									
Current			2.7					2.6	2.2
			1.6					1.5	1.2
			1.0					1.0	.9
Quick			1.9					1.8	1.5
			1.0					.9	.7
			.6					.6	.5
Sales/Receivables		40	9.2					41 8.9	40 9.2
		58	6.3					49 7.5	53 6.9
		71	5.2					60 6.1	59 6.1
Cost of Sales/Inventory		30	12.3					24 15.3	20 18.5
		46	7.9					40 9.2	35 10.3
		66	5.5					56 6.5	62 5.9
Cost of Sales/Payables		24	15.4					15 24.7	18 20.1
		32	11.4					28 13.0	39 9.4
		61	6.0					51 7.1	59 6.2
Sales/Working Capital			5.9					6.1	7.2
			9.3					12.0	15.4
			NM					108.4	-28.7
EBIT/Interest			16.3					8.6	14.7
		(13)	4.6					(29) 2.9	(28) 2.1
			1.2					1.2	.6
Net Profit + Depr., Dep., Amort./Cur. Mat. L/T/D									
Fixed/Worth			.4					.6	.5
			.7					1.3	1.6
			2.8					2.0	NM
Debt/Worth			.7					.9	.6
			1.2					2.5	3.1
			6.0					4.8	NM
% Profit Before Taxes/Tangible Net Worth			38.9					47.9	48.6
		(14)	24.2					(30) 20.9	(22) 19.3
			6.3					4.5	5.5
% Profit Before Taxes/Total Assets			17.9					17.3	12.4
			7.5					5.4	2.2
			1.3					1.1	-1.8
Sales/Net Fixed Assets			11.9					11.0	23.3
			6.8					5.7	7.8
			3.1					3.3	3.8
Sales/Total Assets			2.6					2.9	3.4
			2.1					2.0	2.0
			1.5					1.5	1.6
% Depr., Dep., Amort./Sales			1.4					1.8	.7
		(15)	2.8					(29) 2.8	(26) 2.0
			4.9					5.8	4.0
% Officers', Directors' Owners' Comp/Sales								1.5	1.6
								(10) 2.8	(11) 7.3
								8.7	13.2
Net Sales ($)	1988M	18900M	160462M	83416M				598277M	562757M
Total Assets ($)	523M	8258M	77439M	73109M				270705M	256681M

© RMA 2011

M = $ thousand   MM = $ million
See Pages 9 through 22 for Explanation of Ratios and Data

Comparative Historical Data | | | Current Data Sorted by Sales

				0-1MM	1-3MM	3-5MM	5-10MM	10-25MM	25MM & OVER
			Type of Statement						
3	4	3	Unqualified		2	1	1	2	
9	11	8	Reviewed		1	1	1	3	1
4	6	5	Compiled	1	1		2	1	
4	3	2	Tax Returns	1		1			
12	9	10	Other		2	1	3	3	1
4/1/08-3/31/09 ALL	4/1/09-3/31/10 ALL	4/1/10-3/31/11 ALL			9 (4/1-9/30/10)		19 (10/1/10-3/31/11)		
32	33	28	**NUMBER OF STATEMENTS**	2	5	3	7	9	2
%	%	%	**ASSETS**	%	%	%	%	%	%
11.6	12.1	9.8	Cash & Equivalents						
28.7	25.5	29.4	Trade Receivables (net)						
20.2	17.0	16.3	Inventory						
2.3	1.3	1.1	All Other Current						
62.8	55.9	56.6	Total Current						
31.1	38.2	35.2	Fixed Assets (net)						
1.7	2.8	3.0	Intangibles (net)						
4.4	3.1	5.1	All Other Non-Current						
100.0	100.0	100.0	Total						
			LIABILITIES						
10.8	8.7	15.0	Notes Payable-Short Term						
4.8	5.1	3.9	Cur. Mat.-L.T.D.						
15.8	13.3	14.5	Trade Payables						
.0	.0	.2	Income Taxes Payable						
12.1	6.9	7.0	All Other Current						
43.6	34.0	40.6	Total Current						
17.0	20.9	16.6	Long-Term Debt						
.8	.7	.9	Deferred Taxes						
2.1	1.8	4.0	All Other Non-Current						
36.6	42.7	37.9	Net Worth						
100.0	100.0	100.0	Total Liabilties & Net Worth						
			INCOME DATA						
100.0	100.0	100.0	Net Sales						
24.3	24.6	27.6	Gross Profit						
16.3	21.9	21.5	Operating Expenses						
8.0	2.7	6.1	Operating Profit						
.6	1.2	1.4	All Other Expenses (net)						
7.4	1.5	4.7	Profit Before Taxes						
			RATIOS						
2.9	3.4	3.0							
1.5	2.1	1.9	Current						
1.0	1.2	1.0							
1.6	2.5	2.4							
1.0	1.4	1.2	Quick						
.5	.6	.6							
35 10.3	38 9.6	40 9.2							
45 8.1	45 8.2	53 6.8	Sales/Receivables						
62 5.9	65 5.6	70 5.2							
19 19.2	29 12.5	28 13.2							
40 9.1	40 9.2	42 8.7	Cost of Sales/Inventory						
56 6.5	57 6.4	66 5.5							
17 21.1	13 28.1	19 19.2							
27 13.5	24 15.1	29 12.5	Cost of Sales/Payables						
54 6.8	39 9.4	54 6.8							
5.2	4.3	5.3							
11.6	8.2	9.0	Sales/Working Capital						
NM	386.1	NM							
32.1	13.1	21.1							
(31) 5.3	(31) 2.6	(25) 4.2	EBIT/Interest						
2.1	1.1	1.2							
			Net Profit + Depr., Dep., Amort./Cur. Mat. L/T/D						
.4	.4	.4							
.7	.8	.7	Fixed/Worth						
2.6	2.3	2.1							
.5	.4	.4							
2.3	1.6	1.5	Debt/Worth						
6.2	3.8	4.2							
62.2	23.7	32.9							
(30) 29.3	(28) 7.4	(24) 20.9	% Profit Before Taxes/Tangible Net Worth						
19.5	.2	2.6							
23.5	10.7	16.1							
11.8	1.9	6.9	% Profit Before Taxes/Total Assets						
2.7	-1.0	.6							
20.1	12.1	12.6							
7.9	5.1	6.8	Sales/Net Fixed Assets						
4.4	2.7	3.7							
3.0	2.5	2.6							
2.2	1.8	2.1	Sales/Total Assets						
1.6	1.2	1.4							
.9	2.4	1.8							
(26) 2.5	(32) 3.5	(26) 3.1	% Depr., Dep., Amort./Sales						
4.8	5.9	5.0							
	2.3								
	(11) 5.8		% Officers', Directors' Owners' Comp/Sales						
	10.5								
778545M	406035M	264766M	Net Sales ($)	1770M	11856M	12486M	46000M	138896M	53758M
308547M	236574M	159329M	Total Assets ($)	864M	7486M	8767M	21068M	69800M	51344M

M = $ thousand   MM = $ million
See Pages 9 through 22 for Explanation of Ratios and Data

Current Data Sorted by Assets | Comparative Historical Data

Date spans for current data: **4 (4/1-9/30/10)** covers the smaller asset groups; **19 (10/1/10-3/31/11)** covers the larger asset groups.

Type of Statement

Type of Statement	0-500M	500M-2MM	2-10MM	10-50MM	50-100MM	100-250MM	4/1/06-3/31/07 ALL	4/1/07-3/31/08 ALL
Unqualified			3	2			7	9
Reviewed			5	2			8	11
Compiled		1	2				7	6
Tax Returns			1				4	
Other			1	5	1		11	12
NUMBER OF STATEMENTS		1	12	9	1		37	38

Main Data

(Columns 0-500M and 100-250MM are marked "DATA NOT AVAILABLE".)

	0-500M	500M-2MM	2-10MM %	10-50MM	50-100MM	100-250MM	4/1/06-3/31/07 ALL %	4/1/07-3/31/08 ALL %
ASSETS								
Cash & Equivalents			4.1				8.1	6.3
Trade Receivables (net)			34.3				29.6	29.6
Inventory			20.2				23.7	22.7
All Other Current			2.9				1.4	1.8
Total Current			61.5				62.7	60.5
Fixed Assets (net)			28.0				30.5	31.3
Intangibles (net)			6.9				3.5	2.2
All Other Non-Current			3.5				3.3	6.1
Total			100.0				100.0	100.0
LIABILITIES								
Notes Payable-Short Term			12.0				10.6	15.2
Cur. Mat.-L.T.D.			3.9				3.2	4.6
Trade Payables			15.0				18.4	17.2
Income Taxes Payable			1.6				.1	.2
All Other Current			12.1				9.0	8.8
Total Current			44.6				41.3	45.9
Long-Term Debt			7.2				14.6	14.0
Deferred Taxes			.0				.7	.4
All Other Non-Current			.2				4.4	2.6
Net Worth			48.0				39.0	37.1
Total Liabilities & Net Worth			100.0				100.0	100.0
INCOME DATA								
Net Sales			100.0				100.0	100.0
Gross Profit			30.2				23.7	21.8
Operating Expenses			26.6				15.7	15.9
Operating Profit			3.6				8.0	6.0
All Other Expenses (net)			.2				.9	1.1
Profit Before Taxes			3.4				7.1	4.9

Ratios

Ratio	2-10MM	4/1/06-3/31/07 ALL	4/1/07-3/31/08 ALL
Current	1.8	2.0	2.0
	1.4	1.5	1.4
	.9	1.1	1.0
Quick	1.3	1.4	1.3
	.9	.8	.8
	.5	.6	.5
Sales/Receivables	38 9.7	40 9.2	30 12.0
	49 7.5	53 6.9	50 7.4
	69 5.3	64 5.7	63 5.8
Cost of Sales/Inventory	14 26.3	25 14.6	24 15.3
	48 7.5	47 7.8	48 7.6
	82 4.5	67 5.4	69 5.3
Cost of Sales/Payables	24 15.5	25 14.6	20 17.9
	29 12.7	35 10.3	29 12.5
	40 9.1	57 6.4	39 9.4
Sales/Working Capital	6.8	4.9	8.2
	19.6	11.8	18.4
	NM	36.6	-135.6
EBIT/Interest	38.6	9.9	11.0
	7.8	(33) 5.3	(37) 4.0
	4.5	2.1	2.0
Net Profit + Depr., Dep., Amort./Cur. Mat. L/T/D		6.9	10.2
		(10) 2.3	(11) 3.8
		1.9	2.7
Fixed/Worth	.3	.4	.4
	.6	1.0	1.1
	1.6	1.9	1.8
Debt/Worth	.6	1.0	1.0
	1.0	2.3	1.9
	3.3	5.2	4.0
% Profit Before Taxes/Tangible Net Worth	51.2	57.8	49.8
	(11) 18.1	(34) 36.5	(35) 26.1
	6.8	13.5	10.4
% Profit Before Taxes/Total Assets	12.1	20.7	16.0
	9.9	9.4	8.9
	3.8	3.4	2.8
Sales/Net Fixed Assets	15.1	14.2	21.1
	9.4	7.2	6.9
	4.6	3.9	4.6
Sales/Total Assets	2.7	2.6	3.0
	2.1	2.0	2.3
	1.5	1.5	1.5
% Depr., Dep., Amort./Sales	1.5	1.6	.9
	2.2	(34) 2.8	(34) 2.2
	4.5	4.5	4.3
% Officers', Directors' Owners' Comp/Sales		2.8	1.4
		(10) 5.0	(12) 3.1
		6.6	5.2

	0-500M	500M-2MM	2-10MM	10-50MM	50-100MM/100-250MM	4/1/06-3/31/07 ALL	4/1/07-3/31/08 ALL
Net Sales ($)	1986M	147565M	564340M	426248M		759233M	1120342M
Total Assets ($)	1874M	57635M	239926M	88583M		514812M	531872M

M = $ thousand   MM = $ million
See Pages 9 through 22 for Explanation of Ratios and Data

Comparative Historical Data | **Current Data Sorted by Sales**

						Type of Statement						
	5		5		5	Unqualified				2	2	1
	14		11		7	Reviewed			1	1	2	3
	3		3		3	Compiled		1	2			
	6		1		1	Tax Returns					1	
	12		10		7	Other					2	5
	4/1/08-3/31/09 ALL		**4/1/09-3/31/10 ALL**		**4/1/10-3/31/11 ALL**			**4 (4/1-9/30/10)**		**19 (10/1/10-3/31/11)**		
							0-1MM	**1-3MM**	**3-5MM**	**5-10MM**	**10-25MM**	**25MM & OVER**
	40		30		23	**NUMBER OF STATEMENTS**		1	3	3	7	9
	%		%		%	**ASSETS**	%	%	%	%	%	%
	8.9		9.4		7.2	Cash & Equivalents	DATA NOT AVAILABLE					
	31.2		28.2		29.4	Trade Receivables (net)						
	25.2		24.0		25.8	Inventory						
	3.6		2.2		2.4	All Other Current						
	68.8		63.8		64.8	Total Current						
	26.6		29.7		26.3	Fixed Assets (net)						
	.9		1.4		3.8	Intangibles (net)						
	3.6		5.1		5.0	All Other Non-Current						
	100.0		100.0		100.0	Total						
						LIABILITIES						
	10.2		9.5		12.9	Notes Payable-Short Term						
	3.2		6.1		2.7	Cur. Mat.-L.T.D.						
	13.6		18.0		14.8	Trade Payables						
	1.1		.1		1.0	Income Taxes Payable						
	11.2		7.4		8.8	All Other Current						
	39.4		41.1		40.3	Total Current						
	11.9		10.1		6.4	Long-Term Debt						
	.6		.3		.1	Deferred Taxes						
	4.1		3.8		4.3	All Other Non-Current						
	44.0		44.7		48.9	Net Worth						
	100.0		100.0		100.0	Total Liabilties & Net Worth						
						INCOME DATA						
	100.0		100.0		100.0	Net Sales						
	21.5		18.8		26.6	Gross Profit						
	15.9		17.5		21.5	Operating Expenses						
	5.6		1.3		5.1	Operating Profit						
	.2		1.2		1.0	All Other Expenses (net)						
	5.4		.1		4.2	Profit Before Taxes						
						RATIOS						
	2.7		3.1		3.4							
	1.9		1.7		1.6	Current						
	1.3		1.0		1.1							
	1.5		1.8		1.4							
	1.0		1.1		1.1	Quick						
	.7		.5		.6							
32	11.3	**36**	10.1	**35**	10.4							
45	8.1	**49**	7.5	**45**	8.1	Sales/Receivables						
55	6.7	**62**	5.9	**64**	5.7							
22	16.9	**32**	11.4	**22**	16.4							
45	8.1	**55**	6.6	**55**	6.6	Cost of Sales/Inventory						
77	4.8	**80**	4.6	**108**	3.4							
13	27.5	**18**	20.1	**21**	17.5							
20	18.1	**27**	13.6	**27**	13.5	Cost of Sales/Payables						
32	11.5	**63**	5.8	**41**	8.8							
	4.6		4.3		4.9							
	8.3		9.1		9.1	Sales/Working Capital						
	25.1		-199.9		29.7							
	20.9		36.0		13.9							
(39)	6.2	(29)	2.9	(21)	7.3	EBIT/Interest						
	.9		-2.3		3.6							
	13.8											
(10)	3.3					Net Profit + Depr., Dep., Amort./Cur. Mat. L/T/D						
	.7											
	.3		.3		.3							
	.5		.6		.5	Fixed/Worth						
	1.3		1.6		.9							
	.6		.5		.5							
	1.1		1.0		.9	Debt/Worth						
	2.5		4.9		2.8							
	51.0		20.8		42.2							
(38)	20.8	(28)	6.0	(21)	18.1	% Profit Before Taxes/Tangible Net Worth						
	-.1		-12.8		6.2							
	25.4		10.8		16.5							
	11.6		1.0		8.6	% Profit Before Taxes/Total Assets						
	-.2		-6.1		2.8							
	20.9		14.8		14.3							
	8.7		7.1		8.5	Sales/Net Fixed Assets						
	5.3		4.1		6.3							
	3.2		2.3		3.4							
	2.5		1.7		2.2	Sales/Total Assets						
	1.8		1.4		1.5							
	.5		.9		1.1							
(34)	1.5	(24)	2.2		2.1	% Depr., Dep., Amort./Sales						
	3.8		5.1		3.0							
	2.8											
(15)	4.8					% Officers', Directors' Owners' Comp/Sales						
	8.0											
	904472M		**1917370M**		**1140139M**	Net Sales ($)		**1986M**	**13375M**	**23350M**	**103857M**	**997571M**
	415072M		**871603M**		**388018M**	Total Assets ($)		**1874M**	**9796M**	**13383M**	**57734M**	**305231M**

M = $ thousand MM = $ million

See Pages 9 through 22 for Explanation of Ratios and Data

Current Data Sorted by Assets   Comparative Historical Data

0-500M	500M-2MM	2-10MM	10-50MM	50-100MM	100-250MM	Type of Statement	4/1/06-3/31/07 ALL	4/1/07-3/31/08 ALL
		5	13	1	3	Unqualified	26	22
	1	11	9			Reviewed	25	18
1	1	5	4			Compiled	10	11
1	5	6				Tax Returns	8	10
1	3	18	21	8	3	Other	26	46
	24 (4/1-9/30/10)		96 (10/1/10-3/31/11)					
3	10	45	47	9	6	**NUMBER OF STATEMENTS**	95	107
%	%	%	%	%	%	**ASSETS**	%	%
	6.4	6.5	7.7			Cash & Equivalents	7.3	5.5
	35.4	24.8	21.8			Trade Receivables (net)	24.7	26.1
	17.7	30.7	29.5			Inventory	27.3	27.2
	.2	1.0	1.7			All Other Current	2.4	3.5
	59.7	63.1	60.7			Total Current	61.7	62.3
	37.6	28.1	29.0			Fixed Assets (net)	30.9	29.9
	1.6	2.3	6.1			Intangibles (net)	3.3	2.9
	1.1	6.5	4.3			All Other Non-Current	4.1	4.9
	100.0	100.0	100.0			Total	100.0	100.0
						LIABILITIES		
	9.9	12.1	7.0			Notes Payable-Short Term	8.7	9.7
	8.4	2.7	4.6			Cur. Mat.-L.T.D.	3.5	3.2
	18.8	15.1	12.5			Trade Payables	15.5	15.5
	.0	.1	.1			Income Taxes Payable	.2	.2
	16.9	9.7	11.0			All Other Current	10.3	10.7
	53.9	39.7	35.2			Total Current	38.3	39.2
	13.6	13.2	15.3			Long-Term Debt	20.8	20.6
	.0	.4	1.4			Deferred Taxes	.4	.4
	3.2	9.5	14.8			All Other Non-Current	4.8	8.6
	29.2	37.2	33.2			Net Worth	35.8	31.2
	100.0	100.0	100.0			Total Liabilities & Net Worth	100.0	100.0
						INCOME DATA		
	100.0	100.0	100.0			Net Sales	100.0	100.0
	29.0	25.1	22.3			Gross Profit	25.6	25.1
	28.1	20.4	14.3			Operating Expenses	18.7	18.1
	.9	4.7	8.0			Operating Profit	6.9	7.0
	.6	1.6	2.0			All Other Expenses (net)	.8	1.3
	.3	3.1	6.0			Profit Before Taxes	6.1	5.7
						RATIOS		
	6.1	2.8	2.8				2.5	2.6
	2.0	1.7	1.8			Current	1.7	1.9
	.6	1.0	1.2				1.2	1.2
	4.1	1.4	1.3				1.4	1.4
	1.4	.7	.8			Quick	.9	.9
	.4	.5	.5				.6	.5
43 8.4	36 10.2	37 9.8					33 10.9	36 10.1
50 7.3	46 8.0	52 7.0				Sales/Receivables	45 8.1	47 7.8
59 6.2	55 6.7	61 5.9					57 6.4	54 6.7
11 32.6	44 8.3	54 6.7					29 12.4	29 12.4
31 11.8	73 5.0	88 4.2				Cost of Sales/Inventory	60 6.1	58 6.3
83 4.4	129 2.8	124 2.9					107 3.4	93 3.9
20 18.7	19 18.9	22 16.5					22 16.3	21 17.3
35 10.4	34 10.8	33 11.1				Cost of Sales/Payables	32 11.5	33 11.2
44 8.3	45 8.0	48 7.5					51 7.2	47 7.8
	4.1	4.7	3.7				5.1	5.0
	8.3	9.3	6.6			Sales/Working Capital	8.7	8.6
	-10.2	-94.7	15.9				24.2	21.7
		13.3	15.5				11.7	19.7
		(43) 3.4	(44) 5.6			EBIT/Interest	(86) 4.1	(100) 4.5
		1.0	1.5				1.9	1.8
			4.3			Net Profit + Depr., Dep.,	11.1	9.5
		(16) 2.1				Amort./Cur. Mat. L/T/D	(33) 3.1	(36) 4.2
			1.1				2.0	2.4
	.4	.3	.5				.4	.4
	.6	.6	1.0			Fixed/Worth	.8	.8
	-2.1	2.4	2.7				2.2	2.9
	.3	.9	.8				.8	.9
	1.0	1.9	1.9			Debt/Worth	1.8	1.8
	-6.0	7.9	4.4				4.0	7.5
		42.1	44.7			% Profit Before Taxes/Tangible	46.9	65.8
		(41) 12.5	(39) 25.0			Net Worth	(84) 25.1	(92) 35.2
		1.8	7.6				9.9	10.6
	20.0	14.0	17.4			% Profit Before Taxes/Total	19.0	23.9
	12.8	3.8	5.9			Assets	9.2	9.5
	-7.4	.1	.8				2.5	3.0
	10.4	17.4	14.7				14.6	15.7
	7.4	10.1	6.1			Sales/Net Fixed Assets	6.2	7.7
	3.7	3.6	3.2				3.8	4.4
	2.8	2.4	2.0				2.5	2.6
	2.3	2.1	1.6			Sales/Total Assets	2.0	2.0
	1.6	1.3	1.2				1.5	1.5
	1.0	1.5	1.3				1.4	1.3
	2.3	(38) 2.6	2.9			% Depr., Dep., Amort./Sales	(85) 2.7	(91) 2.3
	4.1	5.0	4.8				4.1	4.3
		1.4				% Officers', Directors'	1.3	1.9
		(19) 2.1				Owners' Comp/Sales	(26) 3.0	(27) 3.2
		4.4					7.3	6.4
5074M	30360M	482469M	1600043M	955896M	1590024M	Net Sales ($)	3606235M	5127544M
1068M	13146M	247657M	1033149M	677835M	1026689M	Total Assets ($)	2222800M	2909387M

M = $ thousand   MM = $ million
See Pages 9 through 22 for Explanation of Ratios and Data

Comparative Historical Data   **Current Data Sorted by Sales**

Type of Statement

	4/1/08-3/31/09 ALL	4/1/09-3/31/10 ALL	4/1/10-3/31/11 ALL	0-1MM	1-3MM	3-5MM	5-10MM	10-25MM	25MM & OVER
Unqualified	23	20	22		1	2	3	7	12
Reviewed	13	19	21		1	2	5	5	8
Compiled	15	12	11		3	2	5	1	3
Tax Returns	10	11	12	1	3	3	4	1	
Other	44	60	54		4	2	4	20	24
					24 (4/1-9/30/10)		96 (10/1/10-3/31/11)		
NUMBER OF STATEMENTS	105	122	120	1	11	9	18	34	47

ASSETS

H: 4/1/08-3/31/09	H: 4/1/09-3/31/10	H: 4/1/10-3/31/11		0-1MM	1-3MM	3-5MM	5-10MM	10-25MM	25MM & OVER
%	%	%	**ASSETS**	%	%	%	%	%	%
7.8	9.8	8.0	Cash & Equivalents		10.8		4.7	8.9	8.0
23.1	21.7	23.8	Trade Receivables (net)		22.4		23.1	25.8	22.3
29.5	24.2	28.0	Inventory		19.8		33.5	33.1	26.2
2.3	3.0	1.4	All Other Current		.3		.6	1.7	2.1
62.8	58.7	61.2	Total Current		53.3		61.9	69.4	58.6
28.3	32.0	29.9	Fixed Assets (net)		33.3		32.1	22.5	31.6
4.3	4.5	4.2	Intangibles (net)		1.4		1.2	3.1	6.2
4.6	4.8	4.7	All Other Non-Current		12.0		4.8	4.9	3.6
100.0	100.0	100.0	Total		100.0		100.0	100.0	100.0

LIABILITIES

H: 4/1/08-3/31/09	H: 4/1/09-3/31/10	H: 4/1/10-3/31/11		0-1MM	1-3MM	3-5MM	5-10MM	10-25MM	25MM & OVER
10.4	10.3	9.4	Notes Payable-Short Term		19.8		8.5	10.6	5.7
3.6	3.5	3.8	Cur. Mat.-L.T.D.		8.5		2.4	3.8	3.2
12.4	10.8	14.0	Trade Payables		12.6		13.9	14.7	13.6
.1	.1	.1	Income Taxes Payable		.0		.0	.2	.1
7.9	10.0	10.9	All Other Current		23.4		5.5	12.5	9.3
34.4	34.8	38.2	Total Current		64.2		30.4	41.9	31.9
14.3	18.8	14.0	Long-Term Debt		21.8		9.1	10.2	15.1
.8	.8	1.0	Deferred Taxes		.0		.4	.3	2.0
9.2	10.7	11.7	All Other Non-Current		5.5		10.1	9.6	13.6
41.4	35.0	35.2	Net Worth		8.5		50.0	38.0	37.4
100.0	100.0	100.0	Total Liabilities & Net Worth		100.0		100.0	100.0	100.0

INCOME DATA

H: 4/1/08-3/31/09	H: 4/1/09-3/31/10	H: 4/1/10-3/31/11		0-1MM	1-3MM	3-5MM	5-10MM	10-25MM	25MM & OVER
100.0	100.0	100.0	Net Sales		100.0		100.0	100.0	100.0
25.6	26.1	24.3	Gross Profit		30.3		26.2	23.9	20.6
18.8	21.4	18.4	Operating Expenses		31.9		21.5	17.0	13.4
6.9	4.7	5.9	Operating Profit		-1.6		4.7	6.9	7.3
1.1	1.3	1.6	All Other Expenses (net)		2.3		1.3	1.3	2.0
5.8	3.3	4.2	Profit Before Taxes		-3.8		3.4	5.6	5.3

RATIOS

H: 4/1/08-3/31/09	H: 4/1/09-3/31/10	H: 4/1/10-3/31/11		0-1MM	1-3MM	3-5MM	5-10MM	10-25MM	25MM & OVER
3.1	3.4	2.9	Current		3.2		3.6	2.8	3.4
2.0	1.9	1.8			.8		2.2	1.6	1.9
1.3	1.2	1.2			.5		1.4	1.2	1.3
1.7	2.1	1.8	Quick		1.5		1.9	1.9	1.6
.8	.9	.8			.4		.8	.7	1.0
.5	.6	.5			.2				.6
(30) 12.0	(33) 11.1	(37) 9.8	Sales/Receivables		(31) 11.8		(35) 10.5	(41) 8.8	(37) 9.8
(41) 8.8	(44) 8.4	(48) 7.6			(40) 9.2		(45) 8.1	(49) 7.4	(48) 7.6
(49) 7.4	(60) 6.1	(58) 6.3			(56) 6.5		(59) 6.2	(59) 6.2	(59) 6.2
(37) 9.9	(35) 10.4	(44) 8.4	Cost of Sales/Inventory		(5) 68.3		(44) 8.3	(52) 7.0	(41) 8.9
(68) 5.3	(59) 6.2	(75) 4.9			(58) 6.3		(76) 4.8	(91) 4.0	(64) 5.7
(108) 3.4	(111) 3.3	(123) 3.0			(131) 2.8		(146) 2.5	(135) 2.7	(118) 3.1
(16) 22.9	(15) 24.6	(22) 16.9	Cost of Sales/Payables		(22) 16.8		(12) 29.8	(22) 16.3	(26) 13.9
(24) 14.9	(26) 13.8	(33) 10.9			(43) 8.5		(29) 12.5	(31) 11.6	(35) 10.3
(41) 8.8	(42) 8.6	(47) 7.8			(48) 7.6		(37) 9.8	(51) 7.1	(48) 7.5
4.5	3.7	3.8	Sales/Working Capital		5.6		3.9	3.6	3.6
7.3	7.2	7.3			-13.1		7.0	7.4	6.0
16.8	27.9	18.8			-4.5		12.6	13.7	15.9
24.5	14.6	17.2	EBIT/Interest				16.8	16.8	20.0
(95) 5.5	(113) 2.6	(111) 5.0					(17) 3.8	(32) 5.1	(44) 5.7
1.3	-.5	1.1					1.4	1.5	2.4
12.3	4.1	5.4	Net Profit + Depr., Dep., Amort./Cur. Mat. L/T/D						8.9
(31) 4.2	(28) 1.6	(29) 2.1						(19) 2.5	
1.7	.5	1.3							1.4
.3	.4	.4	Fixed/Worth		.4		.3	.3	.4
.7	.7	.8			1.3		.5	.7	.8
2.3	3.2	2.7			-1.6		1.2	1.2	2.7
.6	.7	.6	Debt/Worth		.8		.4	.9	.5
1.3	1.5	1.8			32.8		1.0	1.9	1.5
5.7	7.1	7.1			-4.9		2.0	4.6	4.4
55.4	39.9	41.3	% Profit Before Taxes/Tangible Net Worth				32.8	37.7	44.4
(90) 30.6	(102) 14.5	(101) 19.5					(17) 10.6	(33) 22.6	(39) 20.7
3.0	-6.0	4.5					1.8	5.1	5.8
24.7	14.5	17.0	% Profit Before Taxes/Total Assets		14.4		13.2	15.1	17.8
11.2	3.3	5.5			-2.9		6.0	6.2	5.9
.4	-4.6	.2			-7.6		.6	1.3	2.4
16.9	11.1	13.1	Sales/Net Fixed Assets		52.4		16.0	32.1	10.3
7.4	5.3	6.8			3.9		7.4	10.6	5.8
4.3	3.4	3.5			2.6		3.0	4.2	3.5
2.7	2.2	2.2	Sales/Total Assets		2.8		2.4	2.2	2.0
2.1	1.6	1.8			1.5		2.1	1.8	1.7
1.4	1.2	1.2			1.0		1.2	1.3	1.2
1.2	1.7	1.5	% Depr., Dep., Amort./Sales				1.5	1.3	1.5
(94) 2.1	(103) 3.0	(110) 2.8					2.5	(30) 2.5	(44) 2.9
4.3	5.2	4.7					5.4	4.2	4.6
1.8	1.8	1.4	% Officers', Directors' Owners' Comp/Sales					1.5	
(30) 2.9	(34) 3.8	(33) 2.7						(11) 3.6	
7.4	8.2	4.6						4.4	
5005417M	5149694M	4663866M	Net Sales ($)	953M	24445M	35724M	139231M	586112M	3877401M
2671541M	3388856M	2999544M	Total Assets ($)	443M	16265M	23210M	88204M	361735M	2509687M

M = $ thousand   MM = $ million
See Pages 9 through 22 for Explanation of Ratios and Data

Current Data Sorted by Assets   **Comparative Historical Data**

	0-500M	500M-2MM	2-10MM	10-50MM	50-100MM	100-250MM	Type of Statement	4/1/06-3/31/07 ALL	4/1/07-3/31/08 ALL
Unqualified			3	19	7	1		47	42
Reviewed	2	7	47	23	2			91	83
Compiled	1	7	27	2				54	47
Tax Returns	7	11	11	1				26	17
Other	3	9	37	37	9	4		103	96
		52 (4/1-9/30/10)		223 (10/1/10-3/31/11)					
NUMBER OF STATEMENTS	13	34	125	82	16	5		321	285

0-500M	500M-2MM	2-10MM	10-50MM	50-100MM	100-250MM		4/1/06-3/31/07	4/1/07-3/31/08
%	%	%	%	%	%	**ASSETS**	%	%
12.4	9.5	7.8	6.9	5.7		Cash & Equivalents	6.9	7.3
29.8	27.5	27.1	23.9	18.5		Trade Receivables (net)	27.1	25.9
27.5	27.6	24.1	22.7	13.9		Inventory	23.1	22.5
1.7	.8	1.5	1.3	4.8		All Other Current	1.8	1.5
71.3	65.3	60.4	54.9	42.9		Total Current	58.9	57.2
26.9	30.6	29.8	35.2	32.4		Fixed Assets (net)	31.1	32.2
.1	.3	2.7	4.3	9.4		Intangibles (net)	4.1	5.0
1.6	3.8	7.1	5.5	15.3		All Other Non-Current	5.9	5.6
100.0	100.0	100.0	100.0	100.0		Total	100.0	100.0
						LIABILITIES		
29.5	14.1	7.8	9.7	5.1		Notes Payable-Short Term	9.4	9.6
1.9	6.5	4.8	3.9	1.8		Cur. Mat.-L.T.D.	4.7	4.9
30.2	15.8	14.1	13.4	8.7		Trade Payables	14.7	14.5
.0	.0	.2	.1	.1		Income Taxes Payable	.3	.1
19.2	8.6	6.7	7.2	7.2		All Other Current	8.3	7.7
80.8	44.9	33.6	34.2	22.9		Total Current	37.3	36.8
25.6	22.8	13.4	15.5	14.5		Long-Term Debt	17.5	16.6
.0	.0	.5	.8	.9		Deferred Taxes	.5	.4
5.2	5.5	5.8	5.5	7.6		All Other Non-Current	7.1	6.4
-11.6	26.7	46.7	44.0	54.1		Net Worth	37.6	39.8
100.0	100.0	100.0	100.0	100.0		Total Liabilities & Net Worth	100.0	100.0
						INCOME DATA		
100.0	100.0	100.0	100.0	100.0		Net Sales	100.0	100.0
43.8	28.1	27.0	20.9	22.4		Gross Profit	25.0	23.8
39.1	24.5	21.6	14.1	14.7		Operating Expenses	20.0	18.8
4.7	3.6	5.3	6.7	7.7		Operating Profit	4.9	5.0
1.6	.6	.3	1.1	3.2		All Other Expenses (net)	.9	1.1
3.1	2.9	5.0	5.6	4.5		Profit Before Taxes	4.0	4.0
						RATIOS		
2.9	3.1	3.4	2.8	2.9			2.6	2.7
1.0	2.0	1.9	1.6	1.4		Current	1.6	1.6
.6	1.0	1.2	1.1	1.2			1.1	1.1
1.5	1.9	2.1	1.4	1.7			1.5	1.5
.6	1.2	1.1	.9	.9		Quick	.9	.9
.4	.6	.7	.6	.6			.6	.6
15 23.9	32 11.5	38 9.6	42 8.7	38 9.5			35 10.3	36 10.3
32 11.6	46 8.0	47 7.8	50 7.3	50 7.2		Sales/Receivables	45 8.2	45 8.2
49 7.4	54 6.7	60 6.1	60 6.1	60 6.0			56 6.5	55 6.7
0 UND	24 14.9	38 9.7	45 8.1	39 9.4			30 12.3	30 12.3
40 9.1	51 7.1	53 6.9	57 6.4	54 6.8		Cost of Sales/Inventory	48 7.7	48 7.6
83 4.4	101 3.6	82 4.5	84 4.3	87 4.2			71 5.2	72 5.1
8 43.3	19 18.9	19 19.4	21 17.6	17 21.8			19 19.6	19 19.7
55 6.6	31 11.9	32 11.6	32 11.5	31 11.9		Cost of Sales/Payables	30 12.3	29 12.7
96 3.8	43 8.4	48 7.7	43 8.4	51 7.1			42 8.7	42 8.8
6.9	4.8	4.4	4.8	4.5			5.8	5.5
-185.0	7.0	7.9	9.6	12.9		Sales/Working Capital	10.7	10.5
-15.0	294.8	26.4	33.1	20.6			44.7	71.8
	10.3	17.1	12.8	42.6			9.0	8.7
	(28) 3.0	(113) 7.0	(73) 4.4	(13) 4.5		EBIT/Interest	(298) 3.3	(269) 3.1
	.4	2.5	2.3	1.3			1.4	1.2
		8.1	8.7				4.4	6.0
	(30) 4.7	(29) 3.6				Net Profit + Depr., Dep., Amort./Cur. Mat. L/T/D	(88) 2.2	(79) 2.7
	2.0	1.8					1.2	.8
.3	.3	.3	.6	.3			.5	.4
9.0	1.0	.6	.9	.6		Fixed/Worth	.9	.9
-1.2	3.2	1.5	1.5	2.3			2.7	2.3
.6	.7	.5	.6	.4			.7	.7
57.0	2.1	1.1	1.5	.8		Debt/Worth	1.8	1.7
-2.9	7.0	2.8	3.5	3.2			6.3	5.2
	48.1	35.8	42.7	21.3			49.0	41.5
	(28) 14.5	(117) 17.2	(78) 25.5	(14) 17.4		% Profit Before Taxes/Tangible Net Worth	(280) 21.7	(252) 19.0
	-5.8	4.4	10.8	9.2			5.5	3.4
26.7	15.6	15.6	14.2	12.1			15.9	14.1
4.8	8.1	7.3	10.5	7.0		% Profit Before Taxes/Total Assets	6.1	6.0
-4.3	-.2	2.4	2.8	2.5			1.2	.5
59.1	28.6	13.4	8.4	5.3			14.1	12.4
11.0	10.2	7.6	5.0	4.7		Sales/Net Fixed Assets	7.0	6.5
7.7	4.2	4.2	3.9	3.0			4.7	4.4
5.0	2.7	2.5	2.1	1.6			2.7	2.6
4.0	2.3	1.9	1.7	1.4		Sales/Total Assets	2.1	2.0
2.3	1.7	1.5	1.4	.9			1.7	1.7
	1.1	1.7	2.2	3.1			1.7	1.8
	(33) 2.7	(114) 2.9	(77) 3.1	(14) 3.6		% Depr., Dep., Amort./Sales	(295) 2.6	(260) 2.7
	4.4	4.6	4.8	5.0			3.8	4.2
3.2	2.3	2.1	1.6				1.8	1.4
(11) 7.1	(16) 3.5	(56) 3.4	(15) 1.9			% Officers', Directors' Owners' Comp/Sales	(122) 3.9	(99) 3.2
11.8	7.1	5.6	3.9				7.4	5.3
11337M	103140M	1204770M	2949616M	1385793M	1468995M	Net Sales ($)	7631524M	8015387M
3114M	41270M	608128M	1749246M	1067780M	938599M	Total Assets ($)	4258545M	4412735M

© RMA 2011

M = $ thousand   MM = $ million
See Pages 9 through 22 for Explanation of Ratios and Data

Comparative Historical Data | Current Data Sorted by Sales

	4/1/08-3/31/09 ALL	4/1/09-3/31/10 ALL	4/1/10-3/31/11 ALL	Type of Statement	0-1MM	1-3MM	3-5MM	5-10MM	10-25MM	25MM & OVER
	36	34	30	Unqualified	3	6	9	18	8	22
	80	72	79	Reviewed					24	19
	37	31	37	Compiled	1	8	7	15	5	1
	20	19	30	Tax Returns	8	5	5	5	6	1
	126	116	99	Other	2	9	4	20	29	35
					52 (4/1-9/30/10)			223 (10/1/10-3/31/11)		
	299	272	275	NUMBER OF STATEMENTS	14	28	25	58	72	78
	%	%	%	**ASSETS**	%	%	%	%	%	%
	7.4	7.2	7.8	Cash & Equivalents	9.6	7.3	10.2	9.8	6.9	6.2
	23.0	23.5	25.8	Trade Receivables (net)	24.2	23.1	25.0	26.5	27.4	25.5
	25.0	22.5	23.5	Inventory	18.0	32.8	21.6	22.3	25.6	20.7
	1.9	2.9	1.6	All Other Current	1.6	1.1	1.0	1.3	1.8	1.9
	57.3	56.0	58.7	Total Current	53.4	64.3	57.8	59.9	61.7	54.3
	32.5	33.7	31.6	Fixed Assets (net)	44.4	27.8	32.8	30.1	28.3	34.3
	4.0	5.0	3.4	Intangibles (net)	.2	.7	2.4	2.9	3.7	5.3
	6.1	5.3	6.3	All Other Non-Current	1.9	7.2	7.0	7.1	6.2	6.1
	100.0	100.0	100.0	Total	100.0	100.0	100.0	100.0	100.0	100.0
				LIABILITIES						
	10.7	11.2	9.9	Notes Payable-Short Term	29.9	12.8	7.0	6.1	10.3	8.8
	4.2	4.7	4.4	Cur. Mat.-L.T.D.	4.5	6.2	4.7	5.7	3.7	3.3
	12.6	13.7	14.7	Trade Payables	23.6	13.8	15.2	13.5	14.9	14.0
	.2	.1	.1	Income Taxes Payable	.0	.0	.0	.3	.1	.1
	7.0	7.8	7.6	All Other Current	19.0	9.1	5.7	7.6	6.0	7.2
	34.7	37.6	36.8	Total Current	77.0	41.8	32.5	33.1	35.1	33.4
	18.0	18.5	16.2	Long-Term Debt	35.0	20.0	19.3	12.1	14.1	15.4
	.5	.4	.5	Deferred Taxes	.0	.1	.7	.4	.4	1.0
	6.6	7.9	5.9	All Other Non-Current	1.8	12.7	2.9	3.0	6.8	6.5
	40.3	35.5	40.6	Net Worth	-13.8	25.4	44.5	51.3	43.6	43.7
	100.0	100.0	100.0	Total Liabilities & Net Worth	100.0	100.0	100.0	100.0	100.0	100.0
				INCOME DATA						
	100.0	100.0	100.0	Net Sales	100.0	100.0	100.0	100.0	100.0	100.0
	24.2	23.4	25.6	Gross Profit	47.3	29.9	26.2	27.2	23.7	20.4
	19.6	21.5	20.0	Operating Expenses	35.7	28.2	24.2	22.1	17.3	13.8
	4.6	1.9	5.6	Operating Profit	11.6	1.6	2.1	5.1	6.4	6.6
	1.1↑	1.0	.9	All Other Expenses (net)	3.8	.8	.2	.0	.6	1.4
	3.4	.9	4.7	Profit Before Taxes	7.8	.8	1.9	5.1	5.7	5.2
				RATIOS						
	2.7	2.7	3.0	Current	1.3	3.5	2.9	4.0	3.0	2.5
	1.7	1.5	1.7		.8	2.4	1.7	2.2	1.7	1.6
	1.1	1.0	1.1		.4	1.1	1.3	1.2	1.1	1.1
	1.4	1.6	1.8	Quick	.8	1.5	1.8	2.2	1.9	1.3
	.8	.8	1.0		.5	1.2	1.0	1.3	.9	.9
	.5	.5	.6		.3	.5	.6	.7	.6	.6
	30 12.2	35 10.3	38 9.6	Sales/Receivables	0 UND	37 9.8	38 9.7	38 9.6	40 9.2	42 8.7
	40 9.2	50 7.3	48 7.7		33 11.0	46 8.0	54 6.7	46 7.9	47 7.8	51 7.2
	51 7.1	64 5.7	60 6.1		54 6.7	53 6.9	62 5.9	57 6.4	58 6.3	61 6.0
	35 10.5	36 10.1	38 9.7	Cost of Sales/Inventory	0 UND	38 9.6	38 9.6	37 9.8	42 8.8	37 9.9
	55 6.7	58 6.3	54 6.7		36 10.3	82 4.5	60 6.1	52 7.0	59 6.2	52 7.0
	80 4.6	86 4.3	80 4.5		75 4.9	153 2.4	76 4.8	75 4.9	93 3.9	69 5.3
	16 23.3	19 19.1	20 18.2	Cost of Sales/Payables	0 UND	20 18.3	30 12.3	19 19.5	18 19.9	21 17.6
	24 14.9	30 12.1	32 11.4		37 10.0	33 11.0	41 9.0	29 12.6	32 11.4	31 11.9
	39 9.5	50 7.3	47 7.7		89 4.1	46 7.9	57 6.4	44 8.3	48 7.6	43 8.5
	5.5	4.6	4.7	Sales/Working Capital	345.0	3.9	4.2	4.6	3.8	5.2
	9.7	9.9	8.9		-21.5	6.4	10.2	7.0	8.6	9.8
	46.6	306.2	36.1		-5.0	26.5	15.2	30.3	41.3	28.5
	10.0	6.5	13.0	EBIT/Interest	4.5	6.5	12.7	15.6	16.6	12.9
	(273) 3.5	(254) 1.6	(241) 5.2		(10) 2.1	(24) 1.9	(22) 3.4	(49) 5.3	(67) 7.0	(69) 5.7
	1.1	-1.0	1.8		.2	-.1	.8	2.5	2.7	2.6
	5.3	3.5	7.9	Net Profit + Depr., Dep., Amort./Cur. Mat. L/T/D				7.3	5.9	9.2
	(85) 2.4	(59) 1.6	(64) 3.8					(14) 3.4	(18) 3.8	(27) 4.1
	1.2	.6	1.9					1.8	1.5	2.2
	.4	.5	.4	Fixed/Worth	1.3	.3	.3	.3	.3	.5
	.9	1.0	.8		5.8	.9	.7	.6	.7	1.0
	2.0	2.6	1.8		-1.5	2.5	2.5	1.4	1.7	1.7
	.6	.6	.5	Debt/Worth	1.8	.7	.5	.4	.6	.5
	1.6	1.7	1.5		21.9	1.4	1.5	.9	1.7	1.6
	3.7	5.8	3.6		-3.2	6.3	4.1	2.4	3.6	3.5
	36.5	24.8	37.5	% Profit Before Taxes/Tangible Net Worth		41.4	14.2	33.3	39.2	43.5
	(266) 15.0	(236) 6.5	(246) 19.2			(23) 9.3	(24) 4.2	(53) 15.5	(66) 24.2	(71) 25.5
	2.2	-10.8	4.7			-9.0	-5.8	5.3	9.6	13.8
	13.7	8.3	14.5	% Profit Before Taxes/Total Assets	26.6	14.0	10.4	16.1	17.5	14.5
	5.9	1.4	8.4		7.3	3.2	3.1	7.2	9.1	10.8
	.2	-5.1	2.0		-3.0	-3.5	-1.0	2.4	3.6	5.0
	13.1	10.7	11.8	Sales/Net Fixed Assets	19.9	23.3	19.0	12.0	15.4	8.7
	6.5	5.2	6.1		7.7	9.4	4.2	6.9	6.7	5.0
	4.3	3.2	4.2		3.1	4.5	3.4	4.3	4.4	3.9
	2.5	2.2	2.4	Sales/Total Assets	4.8	2.4	2.6	2.4	2.5	2.2
	2.0	1.7	1.9		2.3	2.1	1.7	1.9	1.9	1.8
	1.6	1.2	1.4		1.3	1.3	1.3	1.6	1.5	1.4
	1.7	2.2	1.9	% Depr., Dep., Amort./Sales	.8	1.6	1.6	1.5	1.9	2.3
	(273) 2.7	(237) 3.8	(247) 3.1		(11) 6.1	(25) 4.2	(24) 3.6	(52) 2.9	(64) 2.7	(71) 3.2
	4.5	5.9	4.6		12.3	4.5	4.9	4.6	3.8	4.7
	1.6	2.1	2.0	% Officers', Directors' Owners' Comp/Sales	3.2	3.3	1.5	2.2	1.7	1.0
	(99) 3.6	(87) 3.7	(99) 3.3		(11) 8.2	(13) 4.9	(13) 3.7	(26) 3.3	(24) 2.8	(12) 1.9
	7.1	7.1	6.3		11.8	7.0	5.1	5.8	5.2	3.7
	7614453M	5747250M	7123651M	Net Sales ($)	8650M	58336M	105699M	429290M	1177769M	5343907M
	4141483M	4010216M	4408137M	Total Assets ($)	7680M	34688M	69571M	245415M	731025M	3319758M

M = $ thousand   MM = $ million
See Pages 9 through 22 for Explanation of Ratios and Data

Current Data Sorted by Assets   Comparative Historical Data

0-500M	500M-2MM	2-10MM	10-50MM	50-100MM	100-250MM	Type of Statement	4/1/06-3/31/07 ALL	4/1/07-3/31/08 ALL
		2	3	1		Unqualified	2	7
	1	6	2			Reviewed	11	6
1	5	6	2			Compiled	4	5
2	1					Tax Returns	2	3
	4	3	7			Other	10	10
20 (4/1-9/30/10)			26 (10/1/10-3/31/11)					
3	11	17	14	1		NUMBER OF STATEMENTS	29	31
%	%	%	%	%	%	**ASSETS**	%	%
	4.6	8.4	7.2			Cash & Equivalents	8.8	8.8
	34.7	24.8	19.1			Trade Receivables (net)	25.8	27.1
	21.5	22.9	29.3			Inventory	29.8	24.6
	.9	1.2	.3			All Other Current	3.2	1.6
	61.7	57.3	56.0			Total Current	67.6	62.1
	28.1	34.2	25.7			Fixed Assets (net)	22.9	25.9
	8.1	5.3	8.3			Intangibles (net)	2.2	6.3
	2.2	3.3	10.0			All Other Non-Current	7.3	5.8
	100.0	100.0	100.0			Total	100.0	100.0
						LIABILITIES		
	8.2	5.7	6.6			Notes Payable-Short Term	11.9	7.6
	5.2	4.4	1.6			Cur. Mat.-L.T.D.	3.2	5.1
	21.1	12.6	13.7			Trade Payables	13.1	13.7
	.0	.3	1.0			Income Taxes Payable	.0	.0
	10.3	4.5	4.7			All Other Current	13.9	7.9
	44.8	27.6	27.6			Total Current	42.1	34.3
	40.7	27.0	7.2			Long-Term Debt	11.4	20.7
	.0	.0	1.6			Deferred Taxes	.0	.7
	5.2	6.8	9.8			All Other Non-Current	5.0	4.8
	9.4	38.6	53.8			Net Worth	41.5	39.6
	100.0	100.0	100.0			Total Liabilities & Net Worth	100.0	100.0
						INCOME DATA		
	100.0	100.0	100.0			Net Sales	100.0	100.0
	30.9	26.8	26.8			Gross Profit	28.0	27.5
	35.1	19.8	19.6			Operating Expenses	21.5	18.5
	-4.2	7.0	7.1			Operating Profit	6.5	9.0
	2.3	1.5	1.9			All Other Expenses (net)	.7	.9
	-6.4	5.5	5.2			Profit Before Taxes	5.8	8.1
						RATIOS		
	2.1	3.6	4.4			Current	3.2	2.7
	1.5	2.2	2.6				1.9	2.0
	.8	1.4	1.1				1.4	1.2
	1.4	2.2	2.4			Quick	1.9	1.8
	.9	1.2	1.3				.9	1.1
	.5	.8	.4				.6	.7
	39 9.3	32 11.3	30 12.0			Sales/Receivables	34 10.7	33 11.0
	58 6.3	46 8.0	56 6.5				37 9.8	47 7.7
	61 6.0	56 6.6	77 4.7				55 6.7	67 5.4
	24 15.1	33 11.2	83 4.4			Cost of Sales/Inventory	32 11.5	35 10.4
	58 6.3	59 6.2	110 3.3				68 5.4	67 5.5
	65 5.6	94 3.9	146 2.5				85 4.3	91 4.0
	31 11.8	20 18.3	20 18.2			Cost of Sales/Payables	14 27.0	17 20.9
	62 5.8	39 9.5	50 7.2				29 12.7	29 12.7
	85 4.3	50 7.3	78 4.7				44 8.2	49 7.5
	6.1	3.8	2.5			Sales/Working Capital	4.2	3.6
	10.2	5.0	4.9				7.3	6.6
	-12.5	14.2	30.5				17.6	17.8
	2.9	9.9	102.1			EBIT/Interest	15.0	18.0
	(10) .2	(16) 7.0	2.5				(26) 5.4	(28) 4.5
	-6.5	1.7	-1.4				1.4	2.6
						Net Profit + Depr., Dep., Amort./Cur. Mat. L/T/D		10.2
							(10)	3.9
								1.9
	.4	.4	.3			Fixed/Worth	.2	.3
	3.8	.9	.5				.5	.7
	-.2	3.8	1.7				1.3	1.5
	1.5	.6	.3			Debt/Worth	.5	.6
	7.2	1.8	.6				1.2	1.4
	-3.5	11.2	4.6				3.3	5.4
		74.6	27.7			% Profit Before Taxes/Tangible Net Worth	41.3	45.8
		(15) 20.8	(12) 13.1				(26) 22.3	(26) 23.6
		3.5	-6.0				1.8	15.0
	8.5	14.0	15.1			% Profit Before Taxes/Total Assets	20.6	16.8
	-3.2	5.6	4.7				11.3	13.1
	-17.9	2.4	-3.3				.8	4.0
	63.9	9.8	9.4			Sales/Net Fixed Assets	21.5	16.3
	16.4	6.2	5.7				13.4	7.6
	2.3	2.8	3.5				6.0	4.8
	3.0	2.6	1.5			Sales/Total Assets	2.7	2.4
	2.2	1.7	1.3				2.1	2.0
	1.4	1.1	1.1				1.7	1.4
		2.4	2.2			% Depr., Dep., Amort./Sales	1.2	1.5
		(15) 3.6	3.8				(25) 2.1	(27) 2.7
		5.0	5.6				2.8	3.9
						% Officers', Directors' Owners' Comp/Sales		
3087M	24866M	157145M	444606M	65308M		Net Sales ($)	491673M	913778M
943M	11684M	94580M	318973M	63550M		Total Assets ($)	258346M	641629M

© RMA 2011

M = $ thousand   MM = $ million
See Pages 9 through 22 for Explanation of Ratios and Data

Comparative Historical Data | Current Data Sorted by Sales

© RMA 2011   M = $ thousand   MM = $ million
See Pages 9 through 22 for Explanation of Ratios and Data

4/1/08-3/31/09 ALL	4/1/09-3/31/10 ALL	4/1/10-3/31/11 ALL	Type of Statement	0-1MM	1-3MM	3-5MM	5-10MM	10-25MM	25MM & OVER
					20 (4/1-9/30/10)			26 (10/1/10-3/31/11)	
6	4	6	Unqualified			1		2	3
8	2	9	Reviewed	1		2	1	5	
13	13	14	Compiled		4	4	2	4	
6	6	3	Tax Returns	2	1			1	
10	12	14	Other		3	1	1	5	4
43	37	46	NUMBER OF STATEMENTS	3	8	8	4	16	7
%	%	%	ASSETS	%	%	%	%	%	%
8.4	12.8	7.8	Cash & Equivalents					10.2	
24.1	23.2	24.3	Trade Receivables (net)					23.4	
23.2	17.8	23.4	Inventory					25.3	
2.2	.5	.8	All Other Current					.7	
57.9	54.4	56.3	Total Current					59.7	
32.0	31.7	31.6	Fixed Assets (net)					28.4	
4.7	9.1	6.5	Intangibles (net)					6.1	
5.4	4.8	5.7	All Other Non-Current					5.8	
100.0	100.0	100.0	Total					100.0	
			LIABILITIES						
7.6	4.8	7.2	Notes Payable-Short Term					3.1	
3.8	4.9	4.6	Cur. Mat.-L.T.D.					2.3	
15.3	14.7	16.1	Trade Payables					11.4	
.0	.0	.4	Income Taxes Payable					.4	
5.0	4.9	5.9	All Other Current					4.7	
31.7	29.2	34.3	Total Current					21.9	
25.2	30.3	26.5	Long-Term Debt					15.5	
.2	.8	.5	Deferred Taxes					.9	
9.3	15.3	7.8	All Other Non-Current					9.9	
33.5	24.5	31.0	Net Worth					51.8	
100.0	100.0	100.0	Total Liabilities & Net Worth					100.0	
			INCOME DATA						
100.0	100.0	100.0	Net Sales					100.0	
28.9	28.8	28.4	Gross Profit					25.5	
22.6	27.2	24.4	Operating Expenses					18.7	
6.3	1.6	4.0	Operating Profit					6.8	
.7	2.2	1.9	All Other Expenses (net)					1.9	
5.6	-.6	2.2	Profit Before Taxes					4.9	
			RATIOS						
3.2	4.2	3.1						5.9	
2.2	2.5	1.8	Current					3.1	
1.4	1.4	1.1						1.7	
2.1	3.4	1.8						3.7	
1.1	1.5	1.1	Quick					1.6	
.7	.9	.5						1.1	
29 12.6	31 11.9	33 11.2						36 10.1	
39 9.4	45 8.0	52 7.0	Sales/Receivables					54 6.7	
55 6.7	56 6.5	62 5.9						72 5.1	
33 11.2	17 21.0	35 10.5						37 9.9	
65 5.7	52 7.0	64 5.7	Cost of Sales/Inventory					85 4.3	
88 4.1	89 4.1	117 3.1						102 3.6	
13 28.2	10 35.3	20 18.2						17 21.4	
31 11.9	26 14.1	41 8.9	Cost of Sales/Payables					29 12.5	
49 7.4	42 8.7	70 5.2						50 7.4	
4.3	3.5	4.1						2.5	
7.8	6.1	7.7	Sales/Working Capital					4.2	
18.1	17.2	30.5						8.6	
11.5	5.3	12.0						16.1	
(38) 4.1	(33) .5	(44) 2.5	EBIT/Interest					(15) 7.8	
1.7	-1.7	.3						1.4	
			Net Profit + Depr., Dep., Amort./Cur. Mat. L/T/D						
.4	.3	.4						.3	
.7	1.0	1.0	Fixed/Worth					.6	
2.3	-10.2	NM						1.2	
.5	.4	.5						.2	
1.4	2.2	2.0	Debt/Worth					.7	
6.9	-15.7	NM						4.6	
66.6	33.3	32.3						42.5	
(37) 28.5	(26) 12.7	(35) 13.0	% Profit Before Taxes/Tangible Net Worth					(14) 20.7	
5.8	-7.8	-6.1						.6	
16.8	10.8	13.5						16.5	
7.8	-.6	3.9	% Profit Before Taxes/Total Assets					6.2	
2.1	-7.3	-3.0						2.0	
15.7	13.7	13.3						8.2	
6.0	6.2	6.3	Sales/Net Fixed Assets					6.3	
3.9	3.2	3.3						3.7	
2.6	2.6	2.5						2.4	
1.9	1.9	1.6	Sales/Total Assets					1.5	
1.4	1.0	1.2						1.1	
1.1	2.1	2.0						2.6	
(39) 2.4	(29) 4.1	(42) 3.6	% Depr., Dep., Amort./Sales					(15) 3.5	
3.3	7.0	6.2						4.8	
1.7	3.0	2.3							
(17) 2.5	(12) 3.9	(14) 3.4	% Officers', Directors' Owners' Comp/Sales						
4.4	9.1	11.9							
845918M	579752M	695012M	Net Sales ($)	1875M	13613M	32969M	27822M	245215M	373518M
512627M	533166M	489730M	Total Assets ($)	2121M	5957M	34451M	12165M	173493M	261543M

Current Data Sorted by Assets | Comparative Historical Data

0-500M	500M-2MM	2-10MM	10-50MM	50-100MM	100-250MM	Type of Statement	4/1/06-3/31/07 ALL	4/1/07-3/31/08 ALL
	3	3	8	2	1	Unqualified	17	13
	3	16	6	1		Reviewed	24	18
1	3	2				Compiled	16	17
3	3	2				Tax Returns	8	9
	5	12	4	5	1	Other	32	30
	20 (4/1-9/30/10)		61 (10/1/10-3/31/11)					
4	14	35	18	8	2	**NUMBER OF STATEMENTS**	97	87
%	%	%	%	%	%	**ASSETS**	%	%
	7.2	9.6	9.5			Cash & Equivalents	6.7	8.5
	24.0	19.4	19.7			Trade Receivables (net)	24.5	23.9
	33.2	37.5	31.8			Inventory	30.6	34.6
	.7	.9	4.9			All Other Current	1.7	1.4
	65.1	67.4	65.8			Total Current	63.5	68.3
	31.1	23.1	17.5			Fixed Assets (net)	22.2	21.7
	.6	3.9	4.8			Intangibles (net)	7.6	4.8
	3.0	5.5	11.9			All Other Non-Current	6.7	5.2
	100.0	100.0	100.0			Total	100.0	100.0
						LIABILITIES		
	12.7	6.9	4.5			Notes Payable-Short Term	12.4	12.1
	6.2	3.4	1.2			Cur. Mat.-L.T.D.	3.3	3.0
	15.7	9.9	8.9			Trade Payables	13.2	10.7
	.2	.0	.3			Income Taxes Payable	.2	.2
	13.2	9.4	3.5			All Other Current	9.1	9.3
	48.0	29.6	18.4			Total Current	38.1	35.3
	14.7	14.7	8.1			Long-Term Debt	22.2	13.8
	.0	.7	1.2			Deferred Taxes	.5	.7
	9.9	2.7	7.8			All Other Non-Current	4.8	6.6
	27.4	52.4	64.6			Net Worth	34.4	43.7
	100.0	100.0	100.0			Total Liabilities & Net Worth	100.0	100.0
						INCOME DATA		
	100.0	100.0	100.0			Net Sales	100.0	100.0
	39.0	34.6	31.8			Gross Profit	36.1	35.8
	36.8	28.7	24.2			Operating Expenses	29.4	30.3
	2.3	5.9	7.6			Operating Profit	6.6	5.5
	1.7	1.2	.4			All Other Expenses (net)	1.6	1.5
	.6	4.7	7.2			Profit Before Taxes	5.0	4.0
						RATIOS		
	2.5	4.0	6.6			Current	2.9	4.4
	1.4	2.4	3.6				1.8	2.1
	1.1	1.7	2.6				1.2	1.3
	1.6	2.0	3.3			Quick	1.5	2.1
	.8	.9	1.6				.9	1.0
	.4	.5	1.0				.6	.6
	29 12.4	28 13.2	39 9.4			Sales/Receivables	32 11.3	29 12.4
	44 8.3	42 8.6	51 7.2				43 8.5	40 9.2
	58 6.3	54 6.8	59 6.1				58 6.2	57 6.4
	62 5.9	65 5.6	84 4.4			Cost of Sales/Inventory	53 6.9	60 6.1
	79 4.6	123 3.0	118 3.1				92 4.0	98 3.7
	149 2.5	193 1.9	162 2.3				138 2.6	154 2.4
	21 17.3	11 32.6	17 21.3			Cost of Sales/Payables	16 22.7	15 23.6
	38 9.6	23 15.7	26 14.2				30 12.4	24 15.2
	60 6.1	50 7.3	49 7.4				53 6.8	45 8.1
	4.9	3.0	2.3			Sales/Working Capital	4.0	3.7
	11.7	4.2	2.9				7.1	5.3
	NM	8.2	5.0				16.9	14.8
	6.3	15.1	34.8			EBIT/Interest	8.9	9.8
	2.7	(33) 4.5	(17) 16.6				(90) 2.9	(77) 2.9
	.7	1.8	3.6				1.3	1.0
			14.9			Net Profit + Depr., Dep., Amort./Cur. Mat. L/T/D	4.5	5.3
		(10)	8.4				(27) 1.8	(26) 2.5
			3.2				1.1	1.4
	.4	.1	.1			Fixed/Worth	.2	.2
	.7	.4	.3				.7	.5
	2.0	1.1	.6				2.5	1.2
	1.2	.5	.2			Debt/Worth	.7	.6
	3.0	1.0	.5				1.8	1.3
	6.2	1.9	1.1				10.3	4.2
	38.7	26.5	30.0			% Profit Before Taxes/Tangible Net Worth	37.6	34.2
	(12) 12.3	(34) 11.5	(17) 12.4				(79) 15.6	(79) 15.0
	2.5	3.5	3.7				4.0	3.4
	9.3	12.2	16.8			% Profit Before Taxes/Total Assets	15.7	13.7
	3.1	7.0	9.7				5.8	6.5
	-1.3	1.6	2.2				1.7	.5
	24.3	21.1	28.3			Sales/Net Fixed Assets	28.1	24.9
	7.0	9.7	9.3				11.7	11.2
	5.3	3.5	4.8				4.8	5.3
	2.6	1.9	1.7			Sales/Total Assets	2.5	2.6
	1.9	1.6	1.5				1.8	1.9
	1.6	1.3	1.1				1.4	1.5
	.7	1.8	.9			% Depr., Dep., Amort./Sales	1.2	1.5
	3.2	(27) 3.1	(16) 1.9				(81) 2.2	(74) 2.4
	5.3	5.1	3.6				4.1	4.1
		2.9				% Officers', Directors' Owners' Comp/Sales	2.4	2.2
		(16) 3.5					(31) 4.6	(31) 4.4
		5.0					7.7	7.4
3338M	36947M	266855M	542926M	685973M	258120M	Net Sales ($)	2488513M	1814444M
1113M	16925M	165312M	381893M	572624M	236937M	Total Assets ($)	1537664M	1188162M

M = $ thousand   MM = $ million
See Pages 9 through 22 for Explanation of Ratios and Data

Comparative Historical Data / Current Data Sorted by Sales

				Type of Statement						
13		18	14	Unqualified				2	4	8
21		21	26	Reviewed		3	3	10	8	2
16		8	6	Compiled	1	3	1	1		
6		8	8	Tax Returns	2	3	2		1	
34		28	27	Other	1	3	3	6	6	8
4/1/08-		4/1/09-	4/1/10-			20 (4/1-9/30/10)		61 (10/1/10-3/31/11)		
3/31/09		3/31/10	3/31/11							
ALL		ALL	ALL		0-1MM	1-3MM	3-5MM	5-10MM	10-25MM	25MM & OVER
90		83	81	NUMBER OF STATEMENTS	4	12	9	19	19	18
%		%	%	ASSETS	%	%	%	%	%	%
6.2		7.0	9.0	Cash & Equivalents		8.9		7.5	10.2	8.2
23.1		20.5	19.8	Trade Receivables (net)		18.9		22.4	20.7	17.6
33.7		36.5	32.5	Inventory		35.0		37.0	31.0	27.1
2.3		2.1	1.9	All Other Current		.7		.8	2.1	4.1
65.2		66.1	63.2	Total Current		63.5		67.8	64.0	57.2
22.9		21.4	24.8	Fixed Assets (net)		30.7		22.4	20.3	23.3
6.1		7.3	4.1	Intangibles (net)		.8		5.7	5.1	6.3
5.8		5.2	7.9	All Other Non-Current		5.0		4.2	10.6	13.3
100.0		100.0	100.0	Total		100.0		100.0	100.0	100.0
				LIABILITIES						
12.1		8.6	6.9	Notes Payable-Short Term		8.9		6.8	6.0	4.1
3.2		3.0	3.0	Cur. Mat.-L.T.D.		3.5		4.2	1.7	1.5
12.0		9.5	11.6	Trade Payables		10.6		14.8	7.9	8.6
.0		.3	.1	Income Taxes Payable		.2		.0	.3	.0
8.5		9.0	9.2	All Other Current		14.8		9.1	7.6	5.0
35.9		30.4	30.8	Total Current		38.1		35.0	23.6	19.2
17.5		15.9	13.6	Long-Term Debt		14.8		12.2	12.2	10.6
.7		.7	.6	Deferred Taxes		.4		.6	.3	1.1
7.6		9.1	5.5	All Other Non-Current		7.4		4.0	6.0	7.0
38.4		43.9	49.4	Net Worth		39.3		48.3	58.0	62.0
100.0		100.0	100.0	Total Liabilities & Net Worth		100.0		100.0	100.0	100.0
				INCOME DATA						
100.0		100.0	100.0	Net Sales		100.0		100.0	100.0	100.0
34.7		35.0	34.4	Gross Profit		46.0		33.1	35.5	28.2
30.6		32.3	29.2	Operating Expenses		42.8		26.9	28.8	21.2
4.0		2.7	5.2	Operating Profit		3.2		6.2	6.7	7.0
1.8		1.3	1.1	All Other Expenses (net)		1.4		.8	1.1	.6
2.2		1.5	4.2	Profit Before Taxes		1.8		5.4	5.6	6.4
				RATIOS						
3.8		4.0	4.0			4.6		2.9	5.1	5.5
1.9		2.3	2.6	Current		1.9		2.1	3.0	2.9
1.3		1.5	1.5			1.2		1.3	2.0	2.1
1.5		1.6	2.1			2.0		1.5	3.1	2.8
.8		.9	1.0	Quick		.8		.8	1.5	1.3
.4		.5	.5			.4		.4	1.0	.8

27	13.5	33	11.2	31	11.8	Sales/Receivables	27	13.6	27	13.4	40	9.2	40	9.2
41	8.9	42	8.6	43	8.4		48	7.6	37	9.8	48	7.7	46	7.9
51	7.1	55	6.7	57	6.4		62	5.9	54	6.8	59	6.2	59	6.2
50	7.3	79	4.6	65	5.6	Cost of Sales/Inventory	55	6.6	48	7.6	90	4.0	65	5.6
99	3.7	133	2.8	102	3.6		100	3.6	90	4.1	123	3.0	92	4.0
164	2.2	193	1.9	166	2.2		255	1.4	172	2.1	148	2.5	154	2.4
14	26.5	16	23.2	16	23.3	Cost of Sales/Payables	14	26.5	17	22.0	12	30.0	17	21.3
26	14.1	24	15.3	30	12.4		47	7.7	32	11.4	30	12.4	24	15.4
48	7.5	41	8.8	50	7.3		65	5.6	50	7.3	44	8.4	39	9.3

3.6		2.8	2.8	Sales/Working Capital		2.2		4.1	2.8	2.1
6.4		5.1	4.8			5.2		5.3	3.2	5.0
13.2		9.1	10.0			29.7		19.2	5.2	5.6

	6.0		8.6		17.6	EBIT/Interest		6.3		15.8		29.4		35.4
(83)	1.7	(76)	2.8	(77)	5.1			2.8	(18)	5.1		7.1	(16)	13.9
	.0		-.3		1.8			.9		1.9		2.8		2.6

	5.8		5.1		11.2	Net Profit + Depr., Dep.,
(31)	1.2	(26)	1.7	(23)	7.1	Amort./Cur. Mat. L/T/D
	.1		.4		1.8	

.3		.2	.1	Fixed/Worth		.2		.1	.1	.1
.6		.6	.5			.5		.6	.4	.5
1.6		1.7	.9			1.4		.9	.9	.7
.7		.6	.5	Debt/Worth		.6		.6	.4	.2
1.6		1.3	1.0			1.2		1.2	.9	.6
5.4		4.8	2.2			3.9		2.5	1.6	1.7

	37.6		21.8		26.5	% Profit Before Taxes/Tangible		15.2		37.4		23.1		37.1
(78)	11.2	(68)	8.2	(74)	11.3	Net Worth	(11)	2.9	(18)	19.8	(18)	8.3	(17)	12.4
	-6.6		-3.7		3.3			1.8		6.8		5.6		6.4

10.8		10.1	12.0	% Profit Before Taxes/Total		7.5		16.1	11.3	16.0
2.7		3.6	6.3	Assets		1.5		8.5	5.2	6.8
-2.9		-3.4	1.7			-2.2		2.4	3.2	2.1
21.0		31.2	19.7	Sales/Net Fixed Assets		28.2		46.6	25.3	13.3
9.8		8.8	8.2			6.9		12.4	8.2	6.5
4.7		4.7	4.1			4.8		3.9	4.3	3.4
2.4		2.2	1.9	Sales/Total Assets		2.2		2.2	1.8	1.7
1.7		1.6	1.6			1.8		1.9	1.6	1.4
1.3		1.1	1.1			1.1		1.4	1.2	.8

	1.2		1.4		1.6	% Depr., Dep., Amort./Sales		1.7		.9		1.3		2.3
(80)	2.7	(68)	2.8	(69)	3.1		(11)	3.1	(15)	2.5	(16)	2.0	(16)	4.2
	3.9		4.8		4.6			6.0		3.9		4.0		4.8

	1.9		3.1		2.6	% Officers', Directors'
(35)	5.6	(22)	5.5	(31)	3.5	Owners' Comp/Sales
	8.0		9.0		5.8	

1975566M		2000748M	1794159M	Net Sales ($)	2372M	23774M	35926M	127565M	320345M	1284177M
1428892M		1653543M	1374804M	Total Assets ($)	1812M	16906M	23750M	72530M	224972M	1034834M

M = $ thousand   MM = $ million
See Pages 9 through 22 for Explanation of Ratios and Data

Current Data Sorted by Assets   **Comparative Historical Data**

0-500M	500M-2MM	2-10MM	10-50MM	50-100MM	100-250MM		4/1/06-3/31/07 ALL	4/1/07-3/31/08 ALL
						Type of Statement		
1	3	3	7	3	2	Unqualified	23	21
1	3	11	4			Reviewed	17	20
1	3	4	1			Compiled	14	11
4	5	4	1			Tax Returns	11	11
2	9	12	10	2	3	Other	27	32
	17 (4/1-9/30/10)		78 (10/1/10-3/31/11)					
8	20	34	23	5	5	**NUMBER OF STATEMENTS**	92	95
%	%	%	%	%	%	**ASSETS**	%	%
	15.1	12.5	10.5			Cash & Equivalents	7.3	11.0
	29.5	29.0	22.5			Trade Receivables (net)	30.9	27.8
	21.5	27.5	18.8			Inventory	25.7	24.1
	2.7	2.2	3.8			All Other Current	4.5	4.1
	68.7	71.1	55.6			Total Current	68.4	67.0
	22.3	19.8	34.7			Fixed Assets (net)	23.7	25.1
	3.4	3.3	5.6			Intangibles (net)	3.0	2.7
	5.6	5.7	4.1			All Other Non-Current	4.8	5.2
	100.0	100.0	100.0			Total	100.0	100.0
						LIABILITIES		
	10.1	7.1	11.2			Notes Payable-Short Term	8.5	12.7
	2.3	2.3	11.6			Cur. Mat.-L.T.D.	2.6	3.8
	21.9	14.4	13.8			Trade Payables	17.8	14.0
	.1	.5	.1			Income Taxes Payable	.4	.3
	11.9	10.3	10.9			All Other Current	18.6	19.3
	46.4	34.6	47.7			Total Current	48.0	50.2
	14.6	15.4	20.1			Long-Term Debt	13.3	13.9
	.2	.3	.3			Deferred Taxes	.4	.2
	6.8	2.9	7.5			All Other Non-Current	5.5	3.1
	32.1	46.7	24.5			Net Worth	32.9	32.6
	100.0	100.0	100.0			Total Liabilities & Net Worth	100.0	100.0
						INCOME DATA		
	100.0	100.0	100.0			Net Sales	100.0	100.0
	26.8	29.8	23.8			Gross Profit	27.0	29.1
	25.0	26.4	24.6			Operating Expenses	20.4	23.3
	1.8	3.4	-.8			Operating Profit	6.6	5.8
	.1	1.3	.8			All Other Expenses (net)	.9	1.3
	1.7	2.0	-1.6			Profit Before Taxes	5.6	4.5
						RATIOS		
	3.5	3.7	3.0				2.1	2.2
	1.4	2.5	1.7			Current	1.5	1.5
	1.0	1.4	.8				1.2	1.1
	2.2	2.1	1.5				1.2	1.4
	1.2	1.1	.7			Quick	.9	.8
	.6	.6	.4				.5	.6
	17 21.7	33 11.2	36 10.2				27 13.6	24 15.2
	31 11.9	46 7.9	69 5.3			Sales/Receivables	43 8.5	38 9.7
	50 7.3	63 5.8	79 4.6				66 5.5	62 5.8
	12 30.9	36 10.2	15 25.1				24 15.3	17 21.7
	33 11.2	60 6.1	36 10.0			Cost of Sales/Inventory	46 8.0	41 9.0
	47 7.7	114 3.2	150 2.4				76 4.8	81 4.5
	18 19.7	19 19.3	23 15.8				20 18.6	16 23.2
	27 13.6	30 12.0	38 9.7			Cost of Sales/Payables	30 12.2	26 14.2
	53 6.9	42 8.6	62 5.9				44 8.3	39 9.3
	6.1	3.2	2.6				6.8	6.2
	16.3	5.2	6.8			Sales/Working Capital	10.8	12.0
	141.5	15.7	-20.1				29.4	104.6
	19.5	18.4	21.5				16.1	19.7
	(17) 4.4	(31) 1.9	(20) 1.3			EBIT/Interest	(85) 6.5	(85) 5.2
	-3.3	.3	-4.0				3.1	1.4
						Net Profit + Depr., Dep.,	17.6	14.9
						Amort./Cur. Mat. L/T/D	(32) 5.6	(30) 4.2
							2.6	1.5
	.3	.1	.5				.3	.2
	.6	.4	1.5			Fixed/Worth	.7	.6
	1.9	1.1	206.8				1.5	1.6
	.6	.4	.5				1.0	.9
	2.2	1.1	3.0			Debt/Worth	1.7	1.7
	6.4	3.7	289.4				3.1	4.7
	59.2	28.9	20.2				54.6	54.5
	(16) 9.1	(32) 7.6	(19) 3.8			% Profit Before Taxes/Tangible Net Worth	(83) 27.1	(85) 30.3
	-13.3	-1.5	-34.1				14.9	8.2
	19.1	16.2	7.6				17.7	19.9
	6.5	2.3	.8			% Profit Before Taxes/Total Assets	11.4	9.9
	-5.8	-1.5	-12.9				5.4	.8
	39.2	32.3	9.1				25.9	33.4
	18.0	13.6	5.5			Sales/Net Fixed Assets	10.7	12.5
	10.0	5.7	2.2				6.6	6.4
	4.4	2.6	1.8				3.5	3.3
	3.1	1.8	1.4			Sales/Total Assets	2.4	2.4
	2.6	1.5	.9				1.8	1.7
	.4	.7	2.0				.8	.8
	(13) 1.1	(28) 1.6	3.5			% Depr., Dep., Amort./Sales	(86) 1.5	(84) 1.4
	2.2	2.7	4.0				2.1	2.2
	3.7	2.1					2.3	1.4
	(10) 6.8	(14) 3.6				% Officers', Directors' Owners' Comp/Sales	(24) 4.9	(22) 3.5
	10.3	4.5					6.4	6.2
10596M	79178M	369633M	623759M	910835M	1163081M	Net Sales ($)	5852125M	4315287M
1564M	24491M	176306M	461736M	420128M	694790M	Total Assets ($)	2522908M	1820120M

M = $ thousand   MM = $ million
See Pages 9 through 22 for Explanation of Ratios and Data

Comparative Historical Data | Current Data Sorted by Sales

					Type of Statement						
	17		16	15	Unqualified				2	3	10
	14		11	19	Reviewed	1		4	6	7	1
	10		12	9	Compiled		1	3	5		
	10		11	14	Tax Returns	1	6		2	4	1
	40		39	38	Other	1	5	4	8	9	11
	4/1/08-3/31/09 ALL		4/1/09-3/31/10 ALL	4/1/10-3/31/11 ALL			17 (4/1-9/30/10)			78 (10/1/10-3/31/11)		
						0-1MM	1-3MM	3-5MM	5-10MM	10-25MM	25MM & OVER
	91		89	95	NUMBER OF STATEMENTS	3	12	11	23	23	23
	%		%	%	ASSETS	%	%	%	%	%	%
	12.8		14.9	13.4	Cash & Equivalents	17.1	18.4	10.5	15.8	9.3	
	28.1		22.8	25.6	Trade Receivables (net)	27.2	24.8	27.3	26.1	24.3	
	25.9		25.2	23.5	Inventory	17.9	15.5	28.4	26.1	23.6	
	3.8		3.2	2.8	All Other Current	1.7	2.5	1.3	2.9	5.2	
	70.6		66.1	65.3	Total Current	64.0	61.2	67.6	70.9	62.4	
	21.4		25.1	26.3	Fixed Assets (net)	22.7	34.1	26.2	17.0	30.4	
	1.8		2.3	3.6	Intangibles (net)	7.8	.0	1.5	5.7	3.6	
	6.1		6.5	4.8	All Other Non-Current	5.6	4.6	4.7	6.4	3.6	
	100.0		100.0	100.0	Total	100.0	100.0	100.0	100.0	100.0	
					LIABILITIES						
	15.8		10.2	9.7	Notes Payable-Short Term	21.5	1.2	9.5	8.2	7.1	
	3.0		4.0	6.5	Cur. Mat.-L.T.D.	5.4	6.3	2.2	3.3	10.0	
	16.6		15.0	16.6	Trade Payables	29.4	9.9	16.4	13.7	18.2	
	.3		.2	.3	Income Taxes Payable	.0	1.3	.2	.1	.3	
	19.6		13.2	13.6	All Other Current	28.7	10.5	9.4	11.2	15.2	
	55.4		42.7	46.7	Total Current	85.0	29.1	37.7	36.4	50.8	
	15.3		17.3	16.1	Long-Term Debt	25.8	15.2	17.0	13.6	15.2	
	.4		.7	.3	Deferred Taxes	.0	.0	.6	.3	.3	
	3.2		11.2	4.6	All Other Non-Current	3.4	4.0	4.9	2.5	7.8	
	25.7		28.0	32.2	Net Worth	-14.2	51.7	39.8	47.3	25.8	
	100.0		100.0	100.0	Total Liabilities & Net Worth	100.0	100.0	100.0	100.0	100.0	
					INCOME DATA						
	100.0		100.0	100.0	Net Sales	100.0	100.0	100.0	100.0	100.0	
	27.5		32.2	27.7	Gross Profit	24.7	25.7	31.7	29.2	20.0	
	24.1		30.1	25.8	Operating Expenses	26.5	24.1	29.1	24.9	20.2	
	3.4		2.1	1.8	Operating Profit	-1.8	1.6	2.6	4.3	-.2	
	.5		1.7	.6	All Other Expenses (net)	.9	.2	2.2	.3	-.3	
	2.9		.5	1.2	Profit Before Taxes	-2.6	1.5	.5	4.0	.1	
					RATIOS						
	2.9		3.5	3.3		1.5	3.5	3.0	4.1	2.1	
	1.5		1.7	1.8	Current	1.2	2.1	2.0	2.5	1.7	
	1.1		1.2	1.1		.5	1.4	1.4	1.1	1.0	
	1.5		2.3	2.0		1.3	2.9	2.0	2.3	1.4	
	.7		1.0	.9	Quick	.8	1.4	1.0	1.2	.7	
	.5		.4	.5		.2	.9	.5	.7	.5	

21	17.5	19	19.7	24	15.5		13	28.9	28	13.2	20	18.0	35	10.3	29	12.4	
36	10.3	36	10.3	42	8.7	Sales/Receivables	21	17.8	34	10.7	48	7.7	54	6.7	40	9.2	
51	7.1	58	6.3	67	5.4		56	6.5	67	5.4	47	4.7	70	5.2	69	5.3	
24	14.9	21	17.4	18	20.1		13	29.0	0	UND	37	9.9	27	13.4	16	23.3	
50	7.3	48	7.6	43	8.6	Cost of Sales/Inventory	31	11.7	18	20.4	60	6.1	56	6.6	40	9.2	
86	4.3	107	3.4	104	3.5		43	8.6	80	4.6	147	2.5	118	3.1	106	3.5	
12	29.3	14	26.1	19	19.7		19	19.4	13	27.2	19	19.2	9	40.5	23	15.8	
26	14.3	29	12.7	31	11.8	Cost of Sales/Payables	40	9.1	24	15.1	35	10.4	24	15.5	36	10.3	
40	9.2	50	7.3	49	7.4		73	5.0	39	9.4	52	7.0	42	8.8	56	6.5	
	5.0		3.8		3.6			16.4		4.3		3.2		2.1		5.6	
	12.1		7.5		7.8	Sales/Working Capital		24.0		5.6		6.0		3.6		8.5	
	73.2		31.1		136.6			NM		91.8		11.6		65.0		449.1	
	13.1		9.1		23.0			10.4				12.1		31.3		41.9	
(79)	4.1	(81)	1.4	(84)	3.5	EBIT/Interest	(11)	2.7	(20)	1.8	(20)	5.7	(22)	4.6		
	1.3		-2.5		-.4			-2.9				-2.6		-.2		-1.0	
	10.7		16.7		4.9												
(23)	4.6	(26)	2.8	(22)	1.5	Net Profit + Depr., Dep., Amort./Cur. Mat. L/T/D											
	1.6		.8		.6												
	.2		.3		.3			.5		.3		.4		.2		.5	
	.7		.7		.7	Fixed/Worth		1.1		.6		.5		.3		.8	
	2.1		1.5		1.9			-128.2		.9		1.3		3.4		1.6	
	.7		.7		.5			3.2		.5		.4		.2		1.1	
	2.3		1.8		2.0	Debt/Worth		5.4		.9		1.2		.6		2.1	
	4.5		5.3		5.1			-195.2		1.7		3.7		6.6		3.2	
	47.8		27.5		38.3					39.8		22.4		40.2		23.0	
(79)	27.8	(75)	6.1	(82)	9.1	% Profit Before Taxes/Tangible Net Worth			(21)	8.4	(19)	5.7	(21)	17.4		12.9	
	5.9		-13.3		-3.2					-16.5		-7.6		-1.7		-5.5	
	19.9		11.5		15.7			14.8		19.3		7.8		17.2		11.6	
	6.4		1.6		4.4	% Profit Before Taxes/Total Assets		4.7		4.4		1.6		4.4		3.1	
	.9		-7.4		-3.9			-37.2		-3.9		-6.5		-3.4		-4.7	
	38.4		25.2		21.0			80.9		20.0		23.8		31.7		10.1	
	14.3		11.3		9.9	Sales/Net Fixed Assets		29.6		10.0		10.0		13.6		8.1	
	7.5		6.0		5.4			7.3		4.4		4.5		8.7		4.0	
	3.3		3.0		3.0			4.1		4.7		3.1		2.3		2.3	
	2.6		2.1		2.1	Sales/Total Assets		3.0		2.7		2.0		1.8		2.0	
	1.9		1.6		1.4			2.5		1.3		1.2		1.4		1.5	
	.7		.7		.9							1.1		.7		2.0	
(75)	1.3	(76)	1.8	(78)	2.1	% Depr., Dep., Amort./Sales					(21)	2.1	(20)	1.4	(22)	2.3	
	1.9		2.9		3.5							3.4		3.1		3.6	
	2.1		2.4		2.1							2.8		2.0			
(24)	3.6	(32)	6.0	(37)	3.7	% Officers', Directors' Owners' Comp/Sales					(10)	4.2	(11)	3.5			
	6.0		9.5		7.0							5.3		4.6			

5042422M		3756233M	3157082M	Net Sales ($)	853M	23411M	43779M	160509M	330461M	2598069M
2279140M		1957229M	1779015M	Total Assets ($)	275M	8142M	22087M	119041M	208053M	1421417M

M = $ thousand   MM = $ million
See Pages 9 through 22 for Explanation of Ratios and Data

Current Data Sorted by Assets   Comparative Historical Data

Type of Statement	0-500M	500M-2MM	2-10MM	10-50MM	50-100MM	100-250MM	4/1/06-3/31/07 ALL	4/1/07-3/31/08 ALL
Unqualified		4	12	35	5	8	83	81
Reviewed	1	29	86	32	2		157	139
Compiled	9	29	23	3			73	64
Tax Returns	8	31	28	1			49	44
Other	9	36	65	36	3	6	131	174
		99 (4/1-9/30/10)			402 (10/1/10-3/31/11)			
NUMBER OF STATEMENTS	27	129	214	107	10	14	493	502
ASSETS	%	%	%	%	%	%	%	%
Cash & Equivalents	14.6	10.7	12.1	15.4	14.2	7.6	8.1	10.6
Trade Receivables (net)	23.9	31.0	31.2	29.6	25.9	25.7	37.1	34.4
Inventory	9.5	20.6	19.2	15.8	23.5	14.2	18.7	18.5
All Other Current	3.4	4.0	4.9	6.5	8.2	12.4	5.0	5.3
Total Current	51.4	66.4	67.5	67.4	71.9	59.8	68.9	68.8
Fixed Assets (net)	33.5	25.3	26.3	23.8	18.8	24.9	23.7	23.4
Intangibles (net)	1.4	2.2	1.4	3.8	4.5	9.6	1.8	2.4
All Other Non-Current	13.7	6.1	4.7	5.0	4.8	5.7	5.6	5.5
Total	100.0	100.0	100.0	100.0	100.0	100.0	100.0	100.0
LIABILITIES								
Notes Payable-Short Term	43.0	12.2	9.8	8.8	1.4	2.0	11.1	9.7
Cur. Mat.-L.T.D.	4.5	4.1	3.5	3.3	1.5	2.6	3.4	4.3
Trade Payables	16.5	14.8	15.1	12.9	10.5	10.5	18.6	17.3
Income Taxes Payable	.2	.2	.4	.2	.3	.3	.5	.4
All Other Current	9.8	7.9	7.7	10.1	26.3	17.4	11.8	13.9
Total Current	73.9	39.3	36.4	35.3	40.1	32.8	45.4	45.6
Long-Term Debt	26.7	17.4	11.9	10.5	5.5	17.4	15.0	14.2
Deferred Taxes	.0	.1	.4	.6	.5	1.5	.4	.3
All Other Non-Current	9.4	5.2	5.2	2.7	4.8	1.3	3.1	3.0
Net Worth	-9.9	37.9	46.0	50.9	49.1	47.0	36.1	36.9
Total Liabilties & Net Worth	100.0	100.0	100.0	100.0	100.0	100.0	100.0	100.0
INCOME DATA								
Net Sales	100.0	100.0	100.0	100.0	100.0	100.0	100.0	100.0
Gross Profit	39.4	30.7	23.7	22.7	21.6	16.7	25.9	27.1
Operating Expenses	41.6	31.3	21.2	18.3	12.5	11.9	20.1	20.4
Operating Profit	-2.2	-.6	2.4	4.3	9.2	4.8	5.8	6.7
All Other Expenses (net)	.7	.6	.8	1.0	-.3	.6	.6	.7
Profit Before Taxes	-2.8	-1.2	1.6	3.4	9.4	4.2	5.2	6.0
RATIOS								
Current	2.0	3.9	3.6	3.3	2.8	2.2	2.3	2.4
	1.0	1.8	2.1	1.7	1.5	1.9	1.5	1.6
	.5	1.2	1.3	1.3	1.3	1.5	1.1	1.2
Quick	1.7	2.4	2.5	2.4	1.7	1.3	1.5	1.6
	.7	1.1	1.2	1.1	1.0	.9	1.0 (501)	1.0
	.4	.6	.7	.7	.7	.8	.7	.7
Sales/Receivables	12 29.4	28 13.2	39 9.4	49 7.4	47 7.7	49 7.5	37 9.9	35 10.4
	26 13.8	48 7.6	54 6.7	64 5.7	61 6.0	62 5.9	55 6.7	49 7.5
	44 8.3	73 5.0	75 4.9	85 4.3	77 4.8	95 3.8	74 5.0	66 5.5
Cost of Sales/Inventory	0 UND	7 54.7	18 20.4	16 23.5	39 9.5	12 30.6	10 38.1	9 42.7
	13 29.1	36 10.2	39 9.3	42 8.7	68 5.3	26 14.2	32 11.4	31 11.7
	29 12.8	91 4.0	70 5.2	80 4.6	115 3.2	58 6.3	62 5.9	65 5.6
Cost of Sales/Payables	9 39.0	12 31.3	18 20.0	23 15.7	18 20.6	21 17.1	19 18.9	18 20.0
	21 17.0	26 14.3	32 11.5	36 10.2	25 14.8	34 10.8	33 11.2	29 12.6
	55 6.6	47 7.8	48 7.6	52 7.1	37 9.9	43 8.5	49 7.5	45 8.2
Sales/Working Capital	7.7	4.3	3.4	3.0	3.1	3.6	5.8	5.8
	-132.0	7.8	6.5	5.8	5.0	5.8	10.2	9.7
	-13.8	42.8	16.0	11.2	12.4	9.6	31.1	23.9
EBIT/Interest	6.9	6.9	13.6	16.5		34.1	17.1	19.0
	(23) -2.7	(108) 1.6	(189) 3.8	(101) 5.7		11.2	(458) 5.7	(458) 5.8
	-6.2	-6.6	-.1	1.5		2.1	2.1	2.4
Net Profit + Depr., Dep., Amort./Cur. Mat. L/T/D		2.7	3.4	4.4		22.5	8.8	9.1
		(16) .7	(47) 1.3	(37) 2.4		(10) 3.5	(128) 4.2	(132) 3.4
		-3.1	.1	.6		1.4	2.0	1.5
Fixed/Worth	.4	.2	.2	.2	.3	.5	.3	.2
	1.6	.5	.5	.5	.5	.6	.6	.5
	-4.4	1.5	1.4	.9	.6	1.0	1.6	1.3
Debt/Worth	1.2	.4	.4	.5	.6	.8	.9	.8
	8.8	1.5	1.1	1.1	1.2	1.1	1.8	1.6
	-3.7	4.3	2.7	2.3	2.1	1.8	4.4	4.0
% Profit Before Taxes/Tangible Net Worth	74.7	41.3	25.7	28.7		23.4	49.6	58.3
	(16) -6.3	(113) 7.2	(199) 9.1	(101) 13.0		(12) 12.7	(455) 30.2	(448) 32.6
	-146.0	-16.4	-1.7	2.6		4.6	14.5	14.2
% Profit Before Taxes/Total Assets	13.9	13.4	11.6	11.6	21.8	11.6	18.9	24.3
	-4.9	1.6	4.0	5.0	14.2	3.2	10.2	11.4
	-28.1	-10.0	-3.0	.9	3.2	.6	3.6	4.1
Sales/Net Fixed Assets	37.8	31.1	16.0	14.1	14.4	8.9	27.2	26.5
	9.0	13.5	8.6	6.8	8.6	6.4	14.0	13.4
	6.4	6.0	5.0	4.0	7.4	4.6	6.9	6.9
Sales/Total Assets	4.9	3.1	2.5	2.0	1.8	1.7	3.1	3.1
	3.7	2.3	2.0	1.5	1.6	1.5	2.4	2.5
	2.4	1.7	1.5	1.2	1.2	1.1	1.9	1.9
% Depr., Dep., Amort./Sales	.9	.8	1.0	1.2	1.2	1.7	.8	.7
	(21) 1.9	(110) 2.1	(196) 1.9	2.0	2.0	(12) 2.3	(440) 1.4	(441) 1.3
	5.0	3.9	3.7	3.5	2.6	3.6	2.5	2.4
% Officers', Directors' Owners' Comp/Sales	7.8	3.5	1.7	.9			1.7	1.7
	(16) 10.1	(67) 5.6	(93) 2.7	(23) 1.7			(179) 3.1	(201) 3.1
	20.4	8.9	6.3	5.0			6.0	6.7
Net Sales ($)	30535M	387752M	2123970M	3438873M	1336812M	3424661M	16043368M	16970525M
Total Assets ($)	8344M	165455M	1082109M	2245277M	840803M	2350475M	7296738M	7847073M

M = $ thousand   MM = $ million
See Pages 9 through 22 for Explanation of Ratios and Data

Comparative Historical Data | Current Data Sorted by Sales

Type of Statement	4/1/08-3/31/09 ALL	4/1/09-3/31/10 ALL	4/1/10-3/31/11 ALL	0-1MM	1-3MM	3-5MM	5-10MM	10-25MM	25MM & OVER
Unqualified	81	61	64		2	2	4	21	35
Reviewed	148	126	150		17	27	33	54	19
Compiled	66	50	64	4	19	15	18	8	
Tax Returns	47	50	68	9	21	14	15	9	
Other	180	146	155	9	24	22	29	38	33
					99 (4/1-9/30/10)		402 (10/1/10-3/31/11)		
NUMBER OF STATEMENTS	522	433	501	22	83	80	99	130	87
ASSETS	%	%	%	%	%	%	%	%	%
Cash & Equivalents	10.3	14.2	12.5	11.8	11.4	12.3	14.1	12.7	11.7
Trade Receivables (net)	34.2	29.7	30.2	18.8	28.4	31.1	30.5	32.1	30.6
Inventory	19.2	18.1	18.3	13.5	18.7	17.7	19.4	18.8	17.7
All Other Current	5.3	5.0	5.2	2.9	4.5	4.2	4.3	5.3	8.3
Total Current	69.0	66.9	66.2	47.1	63.0	65.2	68.3	69.0	68.3
Fixed Assets (net)	23.7	25.6	25.7	36.8	28.6	27.3	24.1	24.4	22.7
Intangibles (net)	2.4	2.7	2.4	1.8	1.4	2.3	2.5	2.0	4.4
All Other Non-Current	5.0	4.7	5.7	14.3	7.0	5.2	5.1	4.7	4.7
Total	100.0	100.0	100.0	100.0	100.0	100.0	100.0	100.0	100.0
LIABILITIES									
Notes Payable-Short Term	10.2	9.9	11.6	41.0	15.1	10.3	9.2	10.2	7.0
Cur. Mat.-L.T.D.	3.2	3.4	3.6	3.1	5.1	2.9	4.4	3.1	2.7
Trade Payables	15.9	13.5	14.4	12.6	14.7	13.5	15.6	15.1	13.0
Income Taxes Payable	.4	.3	.3	.0	.2	.3	.1	.6	.2
All Other Current	13.1	10.9	9.0	1.9	10.3	6.7	7.9	8.8	13.3
Total Current	42.8	38.0	38.9	58.7	45.4	33.7	37.2	37.7	36.2
Long-Term Debt	14.0	12.9	13.9	36.1	18.1	15.0	12.2	10.7	9.8
Deferred Taxes	.4	.5	.4	.0	.0	.3	.4	.5	.7
All Other Non-Current	2.7	4.2	4.8	10.4	7.5	4.2	5.3	2.5	3.9
Net Worth	40.1	44.4	42.1	-5.3	29.0	46.8	44.8	48.5	49.4
Total Liabilities & Net Worth	100.0	100.0	100.0	100.0	100.0	100.0	100.0	100.0	100.0
INCOME DATA									
Net Sales	100.0	100.0	100.0	100.0	100.0	100.0	100.0	100.0	100.0
Gross Profit	26.1	25.1	25.9	42.6	31.7	28.1	25.2	22.9	19.5
Operating Expenses	20.1	22.8	23.9	45.0	33.7	27.3	23.3	19.0	14.0
Operating Profit	6.0	2.4	2.0	-2.3	-2.0	.8	1.9	3.9	5.5
All Other Expenses (net)	.7	.7	.8	2.5	.7	.9	.3	.6	1.1
Profit Before Taxes	5.3	1.7	1.3	-4.9	-2.7	-.1	1.6	3.3	4.4
RATIOS									
Current	2.6	3.3	3.4	3.7	3.6	4.3	3.6	3.3	2.9
	1.7	1.8	1.9	1.2	1.5	2.2	2.0	2.0	1.7
	1.2	1.3	1.2	.5	.9	1.2	1.2	1.3	1.3
Quick	1.7	2.1	2.3	2.3	2.3	2.7	2.2	2.4	1.8
	1.0	1.1	1.1	.8	.9	1.1	1.1	1.3	1.0
	.7	.7	.7	.3	.5	.7	.7	.8	.7
Sales/Receivables	32 11.3	34 10.8	38 9.7	14 27.0	29 12.4	36 10.2	33 11.2	42 8.6	48 7.5
	49 7.4	49 7.4	54 6.8	27 13.3	47 7.8	52 7.0	49 7.4	56 6.5	62 5.8
	67 5.4	70 5.2	75 4.8	53 6.8	80 4.6	74 4.9	77 4.7	74 4.9	78 4.7
Cost of Sales/Inventory	10 36.6	11 32.8	13 28.1	0 UND	8 46.1	6 59.1	19 19.0	19 19.5	16 23.5
	32 11.5	35 10.3	37 9.8	27 13.6	33 11.2	33 11.0	37 10.0	41 9.0	42 8.8
	63 5.8	70 5.2	72 5.1	64 5.7	84 4.3	73 5.0	67 5.4	71 5.1	72 5.1
Cost of Sales/Payables	16 22.6	15 24.4	17 20.9	9 42.0	12 30.2	17 21.9	19 19.6	17 20.9	22 16.7
	27 13.6	26 14.0	32 11.6	28 12.8	33 11.0	25 14.4	32 11.3	33 10.9	32 11.5
	42 8.7	41 8.8	48 7.6	72 5.0	63 5.8	41 8.9	49 7.5	50 7.4	41 9.0
Sales/Working Capital	5.3	4.0	3.7	5.8	3.9	3.7	3.1	3.6	3.7
	8.7	7.4	6.9	171.8	7.8	7.2	6.6	6.6	5.9
	21.9	19.6	18.3	-11.5	-56.2	23.9	23.9	12.1	11.1
EBIT/Interest	20.2	13.0	13.4	2.8	6.0	8.9	13.3	19.3	21.0
	(476) 6.5	(389) 3.3	(444) 3.8	(16) -3.0	(70) .8	(71) 1.0	(86) 4.1	(118) 5.2	(83) 7.9
	2.4	-.1	-1.0	-5.7	-6.9	-6.2	1.3	1.0	2.1
Net Profit + Depr., Dep., Amort./Cur. Mat. L/T/D	10.4	8.6	4.1		2.6	1.3	2.0	6.4	5.9
	(134) 3.9	(114) 2.0	(114) 1.7		(13) .3	(12) .6	(20) .7	(31) 2.0	(38) 2.7
	1.7	.7	.2		-1.9	-3.4	-4.4	.6	1.2
Fixed/Worth	.2	.2	.2	.3	.2	.2	.2	.2	.3
	.5	.5	.5	3.0	.6	.5	.5	.4	.6
	1.3	1.4	1.4	-2.1	2.3	1.4	1.6	1.0	.8
Debt/Worth	.6	.5	.5	.9	.4	.5	.4	.5	.6
	1.5	1.2	1.2	8.2	1.9	1.1	1.2	1.0	1.2
	3.6	3.1	3.2	-4.2	7.6	2.5	3.2	2.1	2.1
% Profit Before Taxes/Tangible Net Worth	52.2	30.1	29.6	16.4	29.7	42.9	24.1	28.4	31.0
	(469) 26.2	(392) 10.7	(450) 9.7	(13) -32.7	(68) 6.7	(74) 2.2	(90) 9.3	(122) 9.4	(83) 17.2
	9.8	-.9	-4.6	-154.4	-19.0	-9.7	.5	1.0	4.8
% Profit Before Taxes/Total Assets	19.5	12.5	12.0	10.0	10.1	15.8	9.5	13.6	13.9
	9.4	4.4	3.9	-4.3	.4	.9	4.4	4.6	6.5
	3.1	-2.6	-3.8	-21.6	-15.1	-6.2	.1	.2	2.0
Sales/Net Fixed Assets	26.7	21.3	18.1	13.8	21.6	34.5	15.9	17.7	14.5
	12.4	9.7	8.8	6.8	8.7	12.1	9.9	9.5	8.4
	6.7	4.7	5.0	2.6	4.3	4.6	5.7	5.2	4.9
Sales/Total Assets	3.1	2.6	2.5	3.5	2.7	3.1	2.5	2.5	2.1
	2.3	2.0	2.0	1.9	2.0	2.2	2.1	2.0	1.6
	1.8	1.5	1.4	1.2	1.3	1.5	1.4	1.5	1.3
% Depr., Dep., Amort./Sales	.8	.9	1.1	.9	.8	1.2	.9	1.2	1.2
	(457) 1.4	(386) 1.8	(456) 2.0	(17) 2.8	(74) 2.3	(67) 2.3	(88) 1.7	(126) 1.9	(84) 2.0
	2.5	3.6	3.7	10.0	5.4	4.4	3.5	3.3	3.1
% Officers', Directors' Owners' Comp/Sales	1.7	1.8	2.1	7.6	4.2	2.1	1.9	1.6	
	(202) 3.2	(175) 3.9	(200) 4.2	(11) 10.2	(43) 6.6	(40) 4.1	(48) 3.3	(49) 2.6	
	6.1	7.3	7.4	20.9	11.2	7.8	6.7	5.7	
Net Sales ($)	18167322M	12949647M	10742603M	13213M	174842M	309144M	721912M	2061895M	7461597M
Total Assets ($)	8290672M	7552121M	6692463M	11817M	102511M	184998M	431237M	1183928M	4777972M

© RMA 2011

M = $ thousand   MM = $ million
See Pages 9 through 22 for Explanation of Ratios and Data

Current Data Sorted by Assets   Comparative Historical Data

0-500M	500M-2MM	2-10MM	10-50MM	50-100MM	100-250MM	Type of Statement	4/1/06-3/31/07 ALL	4/1/07-3/31/08 ALL
		8	11	4	1	Unqualified	29	22
	2	24	4			Reviewed	30	35
	6	10				Compiled	18	20
	8	1				Tax Returns	10	8
3	3	18	20	5		Other	42	42
3	24 (4/1-9/30/10)	107 (10/1/10-3/31/11)						
6	19	61	35	9	1	**NUMBER OF STATEMENTS**	129	127
%	%	%	%	%	%	**ASSETS**	%	%
	11.3	13.5	13.5			Cash & Equivalents	9.5	9.2
	25.4	26.0	21.6			Trade Receivables (net)	29.4	26.7
	23.4	22.5	25.5			Inventory	22.1	22.0
	2.0	5.0	4.9			All Other Current	4.5	5.2
	62.1	66.9	65.6			Total Current	65.5	63.1
	30.0	24.3	25.3			Fixed Assets (net)	25.4	27.2
	.3	2.3	4.7			Intangibles (net)	3.3	2.4
	7.7	6.5	4.4			All Other Non-Current	5.8	7.2
	100.0	100.0	100.0			Total	100.0	100.0
						LIABILITIES		
	7.3	11.0	6.6			Notes Payable-Short Term	9.1	7.9
	6.8	3.2	3.7			Cur. Mat.-L.T.D.	2.4	2.9
	16.3	12.2	11.7			Trade Payables	14.9	13.6
	.1	.2	.2			Income Taxes Payable	.4	.2
	9.5	10.6	13.2			All Other Current	17.4	14.3
	40.0	37.1	35.5			Total Current	44.1	39.0
	15.7	10.9	14.1			Long-Term Debt	14.4	16.6
	.0	.2	.6			Deferred Taxes	.5	.3
	12.1	5.7	3.8			All Other Non-Current	7.1	6.0
	32.2	46.1	46.0			Net Worth	33.9	38.1
	100.0	100.0	100.0			Total Liabilities & Net Worth	100.0	100.0
						INCOME DATA		
	100.0	100.0	100.0			Net Sales	100.0	100.0
	41.5	27.0	25.9			Gross Profit	25.7	26.3
	38.9	22.5	19.8			Operating Expenses	19.3	19.7
	2.6	4.5	6.1			Operating Profit	6.4	6.7
	-.2	.5	1.5			All Other Expenses (net)	.7	1.0
	2.8	4.0	4.6			Profit Before Taxes	5.7	5.7
						RATIOS		
	2.7	3.6	3.0			Current	2.4	2.8
	1.7	1.9	2.2				1.6	1.7
	.7	1.3	1.2				1.2	1.2
	1.6	2.6	2.1			Quick	1.5	1.5
	.8	1.0	.9				.8	.9
	.5	.7	.5				.6	.6
	24 14.9	38 9.7	36 10.1			Sales/Receivables	33 11.1	28 13.1
	35 10.5	47 7.8	46 8.0				46 8.0	43 8.6
	48 7.6	60 6.0	58 6.2				63 5.8	62 5.9
	17 21.7	22 16.8	25 14.8			Cost of Sales/Inventory	21 17.6	23 15.8
	35 10.4	52 7.0	81 4.5				47 7.7	47 7.8
	106 3.4	112 3.3	122 3.0				81 4.5	85 4.3
	17 21.5	16 23.3	21 17.1			Cost of Sales/Payables	17 21.5	16 22.2
	29 12.7	27 13.7	31 11.6				32 11.3	27 13.3
	54 6.8	42 8.8	42 8.8				46 8.0	46 8.0
	5.7	3.4	2.6			Sales/Working Capital	5.3	4.4
	10.6	5.8	6.0				9.9	7.6
	-26.5	16.3	13.6				24.5	20.9
	14.7	13.1	14.0			EBIT/Interest	17.1	16.0
	(17) 5.3	(54) 4.2	(30) 4.5				(115) 5.2	(112) 4.8
	.4	.8	2.1				1.7	1.4
		4.4	9.9			Net Profit + Depr., Dep., Amort./Cur. Mat. L/T/D	8.0	28.1
		(14) 2.2	(14) 1.9				(32) 3.2	(29) 5.7
		.8	.9				1.3	1.8
	.3	.2	.3			Fixed/Worth	.3	.3
	.6	.4	.6				.6	.7
	1.3	1.0	1.6				1.9	1.3
	.9	.4	.6			Debt/Worth	.7	.7
	1.4	1.2	1.1				1.8	1.3
	3.8	2.6	3.7				5.3	3.2
	66.2	27.8	28.0			% Profit Before Taxes/Tangible Net Worth	55.7	52.5
	(17) 27.4	(56) 13.0	(32) 17.1				(112) 25.8	(111) 27.2
	-.2	2.2	8.1				11.7	10.4
	23.3	12.1	14.0			% Profit Before Taxes/Total Assets	19.9	21.1
	11.4	6.3	8.2				9.0	9.3
	-.7	.2	2.3				2.4	1.3
	28.6	19.9	10.9			Sales/Net Fixed Assets	20.2	16.7
	9.2	8.2	8.3				9.9	8.5
	5.4	4.2	3.9				5.3	4.9
	3.8	2.3	2.3			Sales/Total Assets	2.7	2.5
	2.6	1.8	1.6				2.2	2.0
	1.9	1.2	1.1				1.6	1.6
	.8	1.6	1.9			% Depr., Dep., Amort./Sales	.9	.9
	(14) 2.1	(55) 2.4	(34) 2.3				(115) 1.6	(114) 1.6
	7.3	3.2	4.9				2.5	3.0
		1.8				% Officers', Directors' Owners' Comp/Sales	1.8	2.0
		(20) 3.5					(58) 4.3	(50) 4.2
		5.1					7.3	6.2
4529M	61307M	560614M	1300452M	679685M	277100M	Net Sales ($)	5459858M	3472589M
2004M	21633M	311857M	810421M	608543M	234268M	Total Assets ($)	2525986M	1805743M

M = $ thousand   MM = $ million
See Pages 9 through 22 for Explanation of Ratios and Data

Comparative Historical Data / Current Data Sorted by Sales

				Type of Statement						
26		19	24	Unqualified			1	5	5	13
35		27	30	Reviewed		2	5	11	9	3
23		24	16	Compiled		1	7	6	2	
12		15	12	Tax Returns	3	6	2	1		
45		49	49	Other	2	5	2	9	11	20
4/1/08-		4/1/09-	4/1/10-			24 (4/1-9/30/10)		107 (10/1/10-3/31/11)		
3/31/09		3/31/10	3/31/11							
ALL		ALL	ALL		0-1MM	1-3MM	3-5MM	5-10MM	10-25MM	25MM & OVER
141		134	131	**NUMBER OF STATEMENTS**	5	14	17	32	27	36
%		%	%	**ASSETS**	%	%	%	%	%	%
11.8		14.1	13.3	Cash & Equivalents		13.2	11.0	18.1	12.6	12.0
26.0		21.1	23.4	Trade Receivables (net)		17.7	25.3	24.7	27.1	22.3
22.1		18.9	23.7	Inventory		18.2	26.8	21.9	24.0	24.4
4.1		4.1	4.1	All Other Current		3.3	2.7	3.9	4.0	5.3
63.9		58.2	64.5	Total Current		52.4	65.7	68.6	67.6	63.9
26.9		30.7	25.5	Fixed Assets (net)		40.0	20.3	23.4	27.0	22.6
3.8		3.4	3.5	Intangibles (net)		.6	2.3	2.6	1.7	7.9
5.4		7.7	6.5	All Other Non-Current		7.0	11.7	5.3	3.7	5.6
100.0		100.0	100.0	Total		100.0	100.0	100.0	100.0	100.0
				LIABILITIES						
8.7		7.3	10.2	Notes Payable-Short Term		8.6	7.6	10.1	9.3	7.9
4.4		4.2	4.0	Cur. Mat.-L.T.D.		4.7	6.1	3.7	3.6	3.4
13.3		10.8	12.6	Trade Payables		11.1	12.4	12.5	13.0	12.3
.2		.2	.2	Income Taxes Payable		.1	.1	.3	.1	.2
13.1		11.2	11.5	All Other Current		9.3	10.0	11.3	11.7	13.7
39.7		33.7	38.5	Total Current		33.8	36.2	37.8	37.7	37.5
16.4		17.1	13.2	Long-Term Debt		25.6	6.7	9.1	10.9	14.2
.4		.3	.3	Deferred Taxes		.3	.0	.2	.2	.6
6.0		8.9	6.0	All Other Non-Current		14.5	10.0	3.7	5.8	3.5
37.5		39.9	41.9	Net Worth		25.8	47.2	49.1	45.5	44.1
100.0		100.0	100.0	Total Liabilties & Net Worth		100.0	100.0	100.0	100.0	100.0
				INCOME DATA						
100.0		100.0	100.0	Net Sales		100.0	100.0	100.0	100.0	100.0
28.4		29.5	29.2	Gross Profit		41.5	31.9	29.0	22.3	26.7
21.5		26.9	24.4	Operating Expenses		40.7	26.6	25.3	18.5	18.7
6.9		2.6	4.8	Operating Profit		.8	5.3	3.7	3.7	8.0
.8		1.2	1.0	All Other Expenses (net)		-.1	.2	.4	1.0	1.8
6.1		1.4	3.8	Profit Before Taxes		.9	5.1	3.3	2.8	6.2
				RATIOS						
2.7		3.4	3.2			2.9	3.2	5.1	2.7	2.8
1.9		2.0	1.8	Current		1.8	1.9	1.7	1.8	2.1
1.3		1.1	1.2			.7	1.6	1.2	1.3	1.3
1.7		2.0	2.0			2.2	2.1	3.2	1.7	1.6
1.0		1.1	.9	Quick		.8	1.0	1.1	1.1	.9
.6		.5	.5			.4	.7	.6	.5	.5

												Sales/Receivables												

n	val	n	val	n	val	ratio	n	val	n	val	n	val	n	val	n	val
29	12.7	26	13.8	34	10.6	Sales/Receivables	0	UND	31	11.9	35	10.5	37	9.8	35	10.3
40	9.2	44	8.4	45	8.2		36	10.1	44	8.3	44	8.2	48	7.6	47	7.8
51	7.2	58	6.2	58	6.3		56	6.5	57	6.4	60	6.1	63	5.8	57	6.4
18	20.2	22	16.7	26	13.8	Cost of Sales/Inventory	0	UND	29	12.5	17	21.0	26	13.8	25	14.9
48	7.6	49	7.5	60	6.1		43	8.4	39	9.4	55	6.6	76	4.8	75	4.9
84	4.3	92	3.9	115	3.2		138	2.6	114	3.2	96	3.8	122	3.0	100	3.7
15	24.0	15	25.0	18	20.4	Cost of Sales/Payables	0	UND	13	27.9	16	22.4	19	19.1	21	17.3
23	16.0	25	14.5	30	12.2		27	13.7	27	13.7	27	13.5	30	12.3	33	11.2
39	9.4	43	8.4	43	8.6		57	6.4	35	10.4	39	9.3	43	8.5	43	8.6

4.6		3.4	3.4	Sales/Working Capital		4.3	4.1	2.8	4.4	3.5
7.8		6.0	6.3			10.0	5.1	6.4	6.4	6.1
16.2		146.6	17.2			-24.9	11.6	20.8	16.6	14.5

n	val	n	val	n	val		n	val	n	val		val		val	n	val
	16.6		10.9		13.6	EBIT/Interest		10.3		24.6		13.0		12.8		28.2
(126)	5.2	(116)	2.2	(114)	4.4		(13)	1.4	(15)	7.9	(26)	4.2	(24)	2.8	(32)	5.0
	1.9		-1.5		1.3			-.8		1.8		-2.3		1.6		2.4
	10.4		9.1		5.0	Net Profit + Depr., Dep.,										6.8
(37)	5.2	(30)	2.0	(33)	2.2	Amort./Cur. Mat. L/T/D									(13)	2.2
	1.8		.6		.8											1.0
	.3		.2		.2	Fixed/Worth		.5		.1		.3		.1		.2
	.6		.7		.7			1.0		.3		.4		.5		.6
	2.1		1.8		1.4			4.4		.8		1.0		1.0		1.8
	.7		.5		.6	Debt/Worth		.8		.6		.3		.6		.5
	1.4		1.3		1.4			1.5		1.1		1.2		1.4		1.4
	4.4		3.9		3.3			11.7		2.1		3.1		2.5		4.5
	57.9		36.3		30.9	% Profit Before Taxes/Tangible		56.8		57.5		27.4		27.1		42.5
(119)	32.0	(113)	11.3	(115)	16.0	Net Worth	(12)	9.2	(15)	17.0	(30)	14.0	(25)	14.0	(30)	17.5
	8.4		-2.5		4.9			-20.8		2.1		-1.3		4.9		10.3
	22.0		12.1		13.7	% Profit Before Taxes/Total		17.3		18.9		12.8		11.3		16.0
	9.3		3.3		6.6	Assets		.1		9.0		6.1		5.8		8.4
	1.9		-4.3		1.3			-5.8		1.8		-1.4		1.3		3.1
	22.4		16.1		18.2	Sales/Net Fixed Assets		15.6		27.7		19.5		19.1		14.5
	9.2		6.4		8.5			6.0		15.8		10.3		7.0		8.4
	5.3		3.1		4.3			2.5		6.0		5.7		4.1		4.7
	3.0		2.3		2.4	Sales/Total Assets		2.6		3.3		2.4		2.3		2.4
	2.1		1.6		1.8			2.1		2.4		1.8		1.8		1.6
	1.6		1.1		1.2			1.2		1.2		1.2		1.5		1.2
	1.1		1.3		1.6	% Depr., Dep., Amort./Sales		2.2		1.1		2.0		1.1		2.1
(118)	2.0	(115)	2.9	(117)	2.4		(11)	4.3	(14)	2.1	(28)	2.7	(26)	1.9	(34)	2.5
	3.8		4.5		4.0			7.6		2.7		3.4		3.2		4.8
	2.1		2.8		2.1	% Officers', Directors'		2.7				1.8				
(49)	3.2	(43)	5.6	(41)	3.9	Owners' Comp/Sales	(10)	5.2			(11)	3.5				
	7.2		8.3		7.0			10.3				4.8				

5158448M		2909449M	2883687M	Net Sales ($)	2828M	29373M	70232M	240808M	396570M	2143876M
2632063M		1970590M	1988726M	Total Assets ($)	1891M	16997M	44304M	171778M	271284M	1482472M

Current Data Sorted by Assets | Comparative Historical Data

	0-500M	500M-2MM	2-10MM	10-50MM	50-100MM	100-250MM		4/1/06-3/31/07 ALL	4/1/07-3/31/08 ALL
Type of Statement									
Unqualified		1	3	10	2	4		24	20
Reviewed		2	23	9				43	38
Compiled	1	3	6					10	11
Tax Returns	1	6	3					17	15
Other	2	7	26	17	4	1		59	58
		20 (4/1-9/30/10)		111 (10/1/10-3/31/11)					
NUMBER OF STATEMENTS	4	19	61	36	6	5		153	142
	%	%	%	%	%	%		%	%
ASSETS									
Cash & Equivalents		10.0	10.0	8.8				8.3	7.4
Trade Receivables (net)		33.0	31.3	27.1				32.2	31.7
Inventory		29.1	26.6	21.7				23.4	22.5
All Other Current		2.0	2.9	3.0				3.3	3.5
Total Current		74.1	70.8	60.6				67.3	65.1
Fixed Assets (net)		14.7	20.8	30.6				24.3	25.5
Intangibles (net)		5.8	3.8	3.4				3.7	4.8
All Other Non-Current		5.4	4.6	5.3				4.7	4.6
Total		100.0	100.0	100.0				100.0	100.0
LIABILITIES									
Notes Payable-Short Term		11.2	8.6	9.6				14.2	12.4
Cur. Mat.-L.T.D.		4.7	3.5	3.1				2.6	3.0
Trade Payables		21.0	13.8	11.6				15.9	14.9
Income Taxes Payable		.0	.2	.5				.2	.1
All Other Current		10.0	12.3	11.9				10.7	10.5
Total Current		46.9	38.3	36.8				43.6	40.9
Long-Term Debt		6.9	11.6	17.0				15.5	18.8
Deferred Taxes		.3	.4	.3				.4	.6
All Other Non-Current		12.7	2.9	11.6				4.7	4.6
Net Worth		33.1	46.8	34.3				35.7	35.2
Total Liabilities & Net Worth		100.0	100.0	100.0				100.0	100.0
INCOME DATA									
Net Sales		100.0	100.0	100.0				100.0	100.0
Gross Profit		32.0	30.1	28.0				29.1	29.2
Operating Expenses		31.4	27.4	24.4				25.1	24.8
Operating Profit		.6	2.6	3.6				4.0	4.4
All Other Expenses (net)		.1	.5	1.4				.7	1.7
Profit Before Taxes		.4	2.1	2.2				3.3	2.8
RATIOS									
Current		4.6	3.5	2.5				2.6	2.7
		1.9	1.9	1.6				1.6	1.6
		1.3	1.3	1.2				1.2	1.1
Quick		3.0	2.4	1.8				1.5	1.7
		1.1	1.1	.9				.9	.9
		.4	.6	.6				.6	.6
Sales/Receivables	29	12.6	32 11.3	36 10.2				27 13.4	30 12.3
	41	8.9	48 7.6	43 8.4				42 8.7	44 8.3
	58	6.3	67 5.4	67 5.5				63 5.8	65 5.6
Cost of Sales/Inventory	21	17.2	31 11.8	35 10.4				29 12.4	24 15.5
	56	6.5	54 6.7	48 7.6				47 7.7	45 8.2
	87	4.2	79 4.6	79 4.6				68 5.4	69 5.3
Cost of Sales/Payables	11	34.0	15 24.6	17 22.1				16 23.5	16 22.7
	33	11.2	26 13.9	25 14.6				25 14.9	28 13.1
	58	6.3	39 9.3	39 9.4				44 8.3	44 8.2
Sales/Working Capital		4.6	4.8	3.8				5.7	5.5
		8.7	6.7	10.5				10.8	9.7
		18.3	16.9	23.1				34.9	34.1
EBIT/Interest		8.5	20.2	17.9				9.3	7.1
		(17) 3.2	(56) 3.9	3.4				(140) 3.5	(126) 2.9
		-2.6	1.2	-.3				1.4	1.0
Net Profit + Depr., Dep., Amort./Cur. Mat. L/T/D			5.0	6.4				4.6	6.3
			(20) 2.4	(14) 2.2				(44) 2.5	(45) 2.3
			.2	.8				.9	1.4
Fixed/Worth		.2	.2	.4				.2	.3
		.4	.4	1.1				.7	.8
		-23.0	1.0	1.7				1.6	2.0
Debt/Worth		.4	.4	1.0				.8	1.0
		3.5	1.0	2.5				1.9	1.9
		-334.8	2.6	3.9				5.4	6.4
% Profit Before Taxes/Tangible Net Worth		21.9	35.7	25.1				46.3	44.9
		(14) 7.1	(56) 12.3	(34) 18.1				(136) 22.0	(119) 19.5
		-23.6	1.8	-7.4				7.0	4.5
% Profit Before Taxes/Total Assets		5.5	11.7	12.2				15.8	11.8
		1.5	4.5	5.1				7.6	6.0
		-3.0	.5	-3.4				1.2	.6
Sales/Net Fixed Assets		61.5	28.4	12.2				32.9	25.1
		23.7	15.6	6.7				13.2	12.1
		16.8	8.2	3.8				5.9	6.0
Sales/Total Assets		3.8	3.1	2.6				3.2	2.9
		2.9	2.5	1.8				2.6	2.4
		2.3	1.8	1.5				1.9	1.8
% Depr., Dep., Amort./Sales		.4	.8	1.3				.8	.8
		(15) .7	(54) 1.4	2.2				(134) 1.5	(128) 1.8
		2.1	2.5	3.4				2.4	2.7
% Officers', Directors', Owners' Comp/Sales			2.8	2.1				1.9	1.9
			(11) 3.7	(19) 2.6				(51) 2.7	(45) 2.9
			5.9	4.8				5.4	5.9
Net Sales ($)	3498M	59867M	751656M	1432085M	571511M	1329239M		6021998M	4570846M
Total Assets ($)	1391M	20797M	303231M	764522M	386092M	834752M		2727447M	2417488M

M = $ thousand   MM = $ million
See Pages 9 through 22 for Explanation of Ratios and Data

Comparative Historical Data / Current Data Sorted by Sales

			Type of Statement						
27	23	20	Unqualified	1			2	2	15
30	34	34	Reviewed			4	9	15	6
13	16	10	Compiled		3		2	4	1
16	11	10	Tax Returns	1	3	4	1	1	
65	53	57	Other	1	6	4	10	18	18
4/1/08-3/31/09 ALL	4/1/09-3/31/10 ALL	4/1/10-3/31/11 ALL		20 (4/1-9/30/10)			111 (10/1/10-3/31/11)		
				0-1MM	1-3MM	3-5MM	5-10MM	10-25MM	25MM & OVER
151	137	131	NUMBER OF STATEMENTS	3	12	12	24	40	40
%	%	%	ASSETS	%	%	%	%	%	%
7.6	11.7	10.1	Cash & Equivalents		16.6	12.4	10.1	8.7	9.4
28.9	25.9	29.0	Trade Receivables (net)		27.4	30.0	32.7	32.5	25.3
24.8	22.0	24.7	Inventory		27.0	30.6	19.7	28.7	20.6
3.7	3.9	2.7	All Other Current		.8	3.4	4.7	2.0	2.6
65.0	63.5	66.5	Total Current		71.8	76.4	67.2	71.9	57.9
23.9	26.4	22.9	Fixed Assets (net)		13.9	20.0	22.5	21.6	28.5
5.7	4.6	4.9	Intangibles (net)		4.1	.3	5.9	1.8	5.2
5.3	5.5	5.7	All Other Non-Current		10.2	3.3	4.5	4.7	5.3
100.0	100.0	100.0	Total		100.0	100.0	100.0	100.0	100.0
			LIABILITIES						
13.1	11.6	9.0	Notes Payable-Short Term		9.8	11.4	6.8	11.0	6.0
3.8	3.3	3.3	Cur. Mat.-L.T.D.		6.6	2.1	2.5	3.8	3.0
14.2	12.5	13.4	Trade Payables		18.7	17.0	12.4	13.9	11.5
.1	.1	.2	Income Taxes Payable		.0	.1	.0	.3	.5
12.4	9.5	11.8	All Other Current		15.6	10.4	13.2	11.8	11.1
43.6	37.1	37.8	Total Current		50.7	41.0	34.9	40.8	32.0
15.5	20.0	13.2	Long-Term Debt		7.7	9.2	11.5	12.9	17.7
.4	.6	.5	Deferred Taxes		.0	1.2	.2	.3	.9
5.8	9.6	6.7	All Other Non-Current		4.1	11.6	5.4	5.5	8.4
34.6	32.7	41.7	Net Worth		37.4	37.1	48.1	40.5	41.1
100.0	100.0	100.0	Total Liabilities & Net Worth		100.0	100.0	100.0	100.0	100.0
			INCOME DATA						
100.0	100.0	100.0	Net Sales		100.0	100.0	100.0	100.0	100.0
30.9	31.2	30.3	Gross Profit		32.8	35.4	32.5	28.5	28.2
27.1	28.3	27.3	Operating Expenses		29.2	32.3	29.9	26.4	24.1
3.8	3.0	3.0	Operating Profit		3.6	3.2	2.6	2.0	4.0
1.6	1.5	.9	All Other Expenses (net)		-.4	1.2	.5	.6	1.7
2.1	1.4	2.1	Profit Before Taxes		4.0	1.9	2.1	1.5	2.3
			RATIOS						
2.8	3.8	3.4	Current		11.3	4.1	5.1	3.0	3.0
1.5	1.9	1.9			2.1	1.7	2.4	1.8	1.9
1.1	1.2	1.3			.7	1.3	1.3	1.2	1.3
1.7	2.2	2.2	Quick		4.8	1.7	3.3	2.0	2.2
.8	1.1	1.1			1.0	.9	1.1	1.0	1.0
.5	.6	.6			.4	.4	.7	.6	.7
29 12.8	31 11.7	31 11.7	Sales/Receivables		24 15.3	26 14.3	43 8.6	33 11.0	34 10.9
42 8.8	40 9.2	44 8.4			33 11.1	47 7.8	51 7.2	47 7.7	42 8.8
59 6.2	57 6.4	62 5.8			65 5.6	62 5.9	65 5.6	68 5.4	56 6.5
29 12.8	26 14.1	33 11.1	Cost of Sales/Inventory		22 16.6	37 9.7	19 19.6	35 10.4	33 11.1
48 7.7	50 7.3	51 7.1			53 6.9	79 4.6	44 8.3	54 6.7	46 7.9
83 4.4	78 4.7	81 4.5			80 4.6	141 2.6	75 4.9	81 4.5	63 5.8
14 27.0	11 33.1	14 25.2	Cost of Sales/Payables		9 41.0	26 13.9	10 34.8	16 22.8	15 25.2
22 16.2	23 15.8	25 14.8			18 20.0	37 9.7	23 15.7	24 15.3	24 15.2
40 9.2	37 9.8	40 9.0			48 7.6	53 6.9	44 8.3	39 9.3	35 10.5
5.9	4.1	4.7	Sales/Working Capital		3.6	6.0	3.6	4.6	4.9
9.7	8.3	7.2			7.6	8.3	6.4	6.9	9.3
76.1	24.1	18.3			-14.3	11.4	15.0	22.9	18.0
9.3	12.3	16.4	EBIT/Interest		13.0		17.1	20.2	17.9
(137) 2.3	(123) 2.6	(120) 3.6			(11) 6.2		(23) 1.8	(36) 5.1	3.4
-.1	.5	.1			-.2		-3.5	1.6	-.2
3.7	4.8	6.0	Net Profit + Depr., Dep., Amort./Cur. Mat. L/T/D					4.3	6.7
(44) 2.2	(37) 1.7	(40) 2.3						(15) 2.2	(13) 2.7
.5	-.1	.4						.2	1.0
.3	.3	.3	Fixed/Worth		.1	.2	.2	.2	.4
.8	.7	.6			.3	.6	.5	.4	1.0
3.1	5.7	1.7			NM	1.6	1.7	1.6	1.7
.9	.6	.6	Debt/Worth		.1	.3	.3	.7	.8
1.9	1.7	1.6			2.1	2.3	1.0	1.3	2.3
7.7	13.4	4.1			NM	7.3	2.3	3.3	4.2
36.1	36.0	35.2	% Profit Before Taxes/Tangible Net Worth		19.5		26.6	35.0	39.8
(123) 11.5	(109) 13.9	(118) 13.1			(11) 13.2		(20) 3.9	(38) 12.8	(37) 15.2
-5.8	-2.5	.8			.9		-8.7	3.1	-6.9
12.8	13.0	11.9	% Profit Before Taxes/Total Assets		28.0	10.2	15.1	10.8	12.6
3.1	5.6	4.2			2.1	4.0	1.5	5.1	4.5
-3.1	-1.7	-1.5			-1.0	-2.1	-5.1	1.1	-2.5
28.7	24.5	27.1	Sales/Net Fixed Assets		182.3	68.3	27.4	27.4	12.2
12.0	12.3	12.1			32.8	13.9	13.1	15.4	7.5
6.3	4.8	5.7			17.5	5.3	6.4	7.6	4.2
3.1	3.1	2.9	Sales/Total Assets		3.1	3.8	3.0	3.1	2.7
2.3	2.2	2.3			2.5	2.1	2.3	2.6	2.0
1.7	1.5	1.7			2.0	1.5	1.6	2.1	1.6
.9	.8	.9	% Depr., Dep., Amort./Sales			.6	1.1	.9	1.2
(133) 1.5	(120) 1.7	(114) 1.6				(10) 1.2	2.0	(34) 1.4	(35) 2.3
2.6	3.0	2.8				2.2	3.5	2.3	3.4
1.5	1.7	2.1	% Officers', Directors' Owners' Comp/Sales						
(47) 3.2	(38) 3.7	(32) 2.7							
6.1	6.0	5.7							
5411060M	3845685M	4147856M	Net Sales ($)	2170M	24204M	47412M	177899M	670599M	3225572M
2571153M	2388586M	2310785M	Total Assets ($)	1854M	12467M	24879M	91752M	313946M	1865887M

© RMA 2011

M = $ thousand   MM = $ million

See Pages 9 through 22 for Explanation of Ratios and Data

Current Data Sorted by Assets   Comparative Historical Data

0-500M	500M-2MM	2-10MM	10-50MM	50-100MM	100-250MM	Type of Statement	4/1/06-3/31/07 ALL	4/1/07-3/31/08 ALL
2	14	7	13	4		Unqualified	49	39
4	24	69	10			Reviewed	96	93
11	26	23	4	1		Compiled	69	59
3	27	17				Tax Returns	29	41
		33	20	5	3	Other	92	87
	66 (4/1-9/30/10)		254 (10/1/10-3/31/11)					
20	91	149	47	10	3	**NUMBER OF STATEMENTS**	335	319
%	%	%	%	%	%	**ASSETS**	%	%
14.4	9.3	10.1	12.4	16.5		Cash & Equivalents	8.0	8.9
27.5	35.0	28.3	28.6	19.3		Trade Receivables (net)	31.7	32.1
21.3	15.1	20.3	16.4	23.3		Inventory	20.6	21.3
1.7	2.6	2.6	3.5	1.8		All Other Current	2.4	2.5
64.9	62.0	61.2	61.0	60.9		Total Current	62.7	64.8
21.4	28.1	30.4	26.0	26.6		Fixed Assets (net)	28.7	26.5
3.0	1.9	2.9	7.5	6.8		Intangibles (net)	3.2	3.0
10.7	8.1	5.4	5.5	5.7		All Other Non-Current	5.4	5.8
100.0	100.0	100.0	100.0	100.0		Total	100.0	100.0
						LIABILITIES		
46.0	12.8	8.4	10.0	6.1		Notes Payable-Short Term	10.6	10.8
4.7	4.4	3.7	3.1	2.3		Cur. Mat.-L.T.D.	4.1	4.1
32.5	16.3	12.6	12.2	7.1		Trade Payables	14.6	14.7
.2	.3	.1	.6	.2		Income Taxes Payable	.3	.2
14.7	6.9	8.0	8.1	12.2		All Other Current	11.3	9.3
98.2	40.7	32.7	34.0	28.0		Total Current	40.8	39.1
18.1	17.6	16.9	16.5	16.9		Long-Term Debt	17.8	16.3
.1	.3	.3	1.0	.7		Deferred Taxes	.5	.4
18.6	4.9	5.7	4.1	8.7		All Other Non-Current	4.9	5.2
-35.3	36.5	44.4	44.5	45.7		Net Worth	36.0	38.9
100.0	100.0	100.0	100.0	100.0		Total Liabilities & Net Worth	100.0	100.0
						INCOME DATA		
100.0	100.0	100.0	100.0	100.0		Net Sales	100.0	100.0
40.2	35.8	27.5	22.5	28.2		Gross Profit	28.0	27.9
34.4	33.1	23.1	17.1	21.6		Operating Expenses	21.9	22.5
5.9	2.7	4.4	5.4	6.6		Operating Profit	6.1	5.4
1.0	.7	.7	1.0	1.1		All Other Expenses (net)	.9	.9
4.8	2.0	3.7	4.4	5.5		Profit Before Taxes	5.2	4.5
						RATIOS		
2.7	2.9	3.1	3.5	7.5			2.6	2.7
.9	1.7	1.8	1.8	2.3		Current	1.6	1.7
.4	1.1	1.3	1.3	1.3			1.2	1.2
2.2	2.3	2.1	2.1	6.3			1.7	1.8
.5	1.2	1.1	1.1	1.2		Quick	1.0	1.0
.2	.7	.7	.7	.6			.7	.6
0 UND	33 11.0	33 11.1	42 8.7	42 8.8			31 11.7	33 11.2
25 14.4	46 8.0	49 7.5	51 7.2	51 7.2		Sales/Receivables	43 8.4	44 8.3
49 7.5	66 5.5	62 5.9	77 4.7	54 6.8			57 6.4	60 6.1
1 327.0	5 66.8	20 17.8	15 24.1	49 7.5			14 26.3	17 21.4
31 11.8	26 13.9	49 7.4	49 7.4	85 4.3		Cost of Sales/Inventory	37 9.8	42 8.8
92 3.9	56 6.6	79 4.6	75 4.9	115 3.2			68 5.4	71 5.2
0 UND	19 19.7	17 22.0	16 22.5	6 60.2			16 22.4	16 22.7
28 13.3	33 11.0	26 14.0	31 11.8	23 15.8		Cost of Sales/Payables	26 13.8	28 13.0
38 9.6	55 6.6	41 9.0	41 8.8	32 11.5			37 9.9	42 8.7
10.9	5.3	4.2	3.9	2.5			6.3	5.5
NM	12.9	7.4	7.2	5.1		Sales/Working Capital	11.1	9.6
-5.0	65.1	19.2	13.2	13.7			29.2	26.9
13.0	8.0	11.7	17.3				12.8	12.3
(16) 3.8	(81) 2.7	(136) 5.3	(41) 4.9			EBIT/Interest	(308) 4.6	(292) 4.7
.9	-.4	1.1	1.6				1.8	1.6
	3.5	5.5	8.3			Net Profit + Depr., Dep.,	6.5	7.1
	(13) 1.4	(30) 3.1	(15) 3.4			Amort./Cur. Mat. L/T/D	(94) 3.0	(79) 2.8
	.4	1.4	1.2				1.6	1.7
.4	.2	.3	.4	.4			.3	.3
-1.0	.6	.7	.8	1.1		Fixed/Worth	.7	.6
-.2	1.5	1.5	1.7	NM			2.0	1.7
1.3	.5	.6	.6	.2			.7	.7
-4.7	1.7	1.2	1.7	2.5		Debt/Worth	1.8	1.6
-2.4	4.3	3.6	4.3	NM			4.4	4.8
	37.5	48.1	34.4			% Profit Before Taxes/Tangible	50.4	48.5
	(76) 14.9	(139) 14.6	(42) 13.0			Net Worth	(299) 27.0	(284) 21.4
	-1.6	3.3	6.5				10.0	7.4
44.5	16.5	14.9	10.6	22.7		% Profit Before Taxes/Total	21.4	19.4
14.4	4.8	6.0	6.1	11.4		Assets	9.1	7.9
-.3	-4.9	.6	1.7	-4.3			2.6	2.4
112.7	34.1	14.8	17.4	12.7			18.6	21.5
37.5	9.7	7.6	9.2	5.1		Sales/Net Fixed Assets	10.0	11.1
16.2	5.3	3.9	3.0	2.4			5.8	5.8
8.8	3.4	2.5	2.2	2.1			3.1	3.1
4.2	2.5	2.0	1.6	1.3		Sales/Total Assets	2.5	2.3
2.3	1.7	1.5	1.1	1.0			1.9	1.8
.6	1.0	1.6	.8				1.2	1.1
(13) 1.2	(76) 2.3	(139) 2.8	(45) 2.3			% Depr., Dep., Amort./Sales	(313) 2.2	(290) 2.0
2.8	4.8	4.5	4.1				3.8	3.5
2.9	2.5	1.6					2.2	2.1
(10) 5.0	(54) 4.5	(73) 3.0				% Officers', Directors' Owners' Comp/Sales	(152) 3.7	(159) 3.8
14.4	7.2	5.7					7.4	6.6
27418M	285006M	1427429M	1684887M	1159147M	751357M	Net Sales ($)	7056412M	6278311M
5728M	109199M	717614M	1003738M	780445M	404998M	Total Assets ($)	3226870M	2906512M

Comparative Historical Data — Current Data Sorted by Sales

			Type of Statement						
34	28	24	Unqualified			2	4	4	14
78	79	95	Reviewed	2	11	13	26	36	7
61	54	56	Compiled	3	14	11	19	7	2
52	52	54	Tax Returns	7	13	22	11	1	
101	87	91	Other	6	10	17	19	18	21
4/1/08-3/31/09 ALL	4/1/09-3/31/10 ALL	4/1/10-3/31/11 ALL		0-1MM	1-3MM	3-5MM	5-10MM	10-25MM	25MM & OVER
				66 (4/1-9/30/10)			254 (10/1/10-3/31/11)		
326	300	320	NUMBER OF STATEMENTS	18	48	65	79	66	44
%	%	%	**ASSETS**	%	%	%	%	%	%
9.4	10.8	10.6	Cash & Equivalents	9.3	8.6	9.8	11.4	11.7	11.6
29.4	27.7	29.9	Trade Receivables (net)	25.8	31.5	27.5	30.5	32.9	27.8
22.1	20.3	18.6	Inventory	17.8	14.4	17.6	19.6	19.9	21.1
2.7	3.3	2.6	All Other Current	3.7	1.7	2.2	2.6	3.0	3.2
63.7	62.0	61.7	Total Current	56.5	56.2	57.1	64.1	67.6	63.6
27.4	28.5	28.3	Fixed Assets (net)	31.9	30.0	31.9	27.4	24.7	26.8
3.4	3.4	3.5	Intangibles (net)	4.8	2.3	3.6	1.9	4.3	5.7
5.5	6.2	6.5	All Other Non-Current	6.8	11.5	7.4	6.6	3.5	3.8
100.0	100.0	100.0	Total	100.0	100.0	100.0	100.0	100.0	100.0
			LIABILITIES						
11.2	11.3	12.2	Notes Payable-Short Term	45.9	13.8	11.6	7.5	9.2	10.7
4.1	4.8	3.8	Cur. Mat.-L.T.D.	3.8	4.4	4.8	3.6	2.9	3.5
15.3	12.9	14.7	Trade Payables	25.9	15.4	13.8	14.1	13.8	12.8
.3	.1	.2	Income Taxes Payable	.0	.4	.2	.1	.3	.4
8.5	8.1	8.2	All Other Current	12.3	5.9	7.8	6.8	9.7	10.0
39.3	37.2	39.2	Total Current	87.9	39.9	38.2	32.0	35.9	37.5
17.2	18.8	17.0	Long-Term Debt	15.7	20.4	21.5	16.3	12.9	14.8
.5	.4	.4	Deferred Taxes	.0	.4	.3	.2	.6	.9
7.1	8.5	6.1	All Other Non-Current	18.4	6.2	4.7	4.4	7.5	4.0
35.9	35.0	37.3	Net Worth	-22.2	33.2	35.3	47.0	43.2	42.7
100.0	100.0	100.0	Total Liabilities & Net Worth	100.0	100.0	100.0	100.0	100.0	100.0
			INCOME DATA						
100.0	100.0	100.0	Net Sales	100.0	100.0	100.0	100.0	100.0	100.0
27.8	29.7	29.9	Gross Profit	45.5	35.8	33.5	28.9	24.6	21.4
23.2	27.0	25.7	Operating Expenses	39.7	33.0	30.6	24.8	18.7	16.6
4.5	2.7	4.2	Operating Profit	5.9	2.8	2.8	4.0	5.9	4.8
.8	1.0	.8	All Other Expenses (net)	1.1	1.0	.9	.1	1.3	.6
3.7	1.7	3.4	Profit Before Taxes	4.8	1.8	1.9	3.9	4.7	4.1
			RATIOS						
2.9	3.7	3.2	Current	1.5	2.9	3.5	3.3	3.4	3.2
1.7	1.8	1.7		.8	1.7	1.6	2.1	1.7	1.7
1.1	1.2	1.2		.4	1.0	1.1	1.4	1.3	1.2
1.8	2.2	2.1	Quick	1.3	2.3	2.2	2.2	2.2	1.7
1.0	1.1	1.1		.5	1.0	1.1	1.3	1.1	1.0
.6	.6	.7		.2	.6	.6	.8	.8	.6
29 12.5	29 12.6	33 11.0	Sales/Receivables	0 UND	28 12.9	31 11.9	36 10.2	37 10.0	38 9.5
41 8.9	42 8.6	48 7.5		46 7.9	51 7.1	40 9.2	50 7.3	49 7.4	50 7.3
54 6.8	57 6.4	64 5.7		80 4.5	70 5.2	57 6.4	64 5.7	67 5.4	57 6.3
19 19.5	17 21.4	14 26.5	Cost of Sales/Inventory	0 UND	9 42.3	14 25.9	16 22.3	16 22.6	29 12.5
40 9.0	42 8.6	43 8.5		31 11.8	28 13.1	41 9.0	44 8.3	45 8.1	52 7.1
72 5.1	73 5.0	75 4.9		126 2.9	60 6.1	85 4.3	76 4.8	65 5.6	97 3.8
14 25.2	13 27.9	17 21.9	Cost of Sales/Payables	10 36.3	20 18.3	14 26.2	16 22.8	17 22.0	15 23.8
25 14.3	22 16.4	27 13.3		37 9.8	35 10.5	24 15.3	26 13.9	26 14.0	28 12.9
41 8.8	40 9.2	43 8.5		85 4.3	57 6.4	39 9.4	45 8.2	39 9.4	41 8.9
5.8	5.0	4.6	Sales/Working Capital	8.9	5.5	4.3	4.6	4.2	4.1
10.0	9.0	8.8		-16.1	12.6	13.2	7.0	7.6	7.8
33.2	26.2	26.9		-3.9	110.7	56.3	14.4	17.5	25.7
13.7	9.1	12.3	EBIT/Interest	9.1	7.6	8.6	13.7	18.4	18.0
(306) 4.0	(274) 2.7	(285) 4.2		(14) 2.3	(43) 3.0	(60) 2.4	(71) 5.5	(57) 5.9	(40) 5.9
1.3	-.4	.9		-.7	-.5	-.6	1.1	1.6	2.2
7.7	7.5	4.6	Net Profit + Depr., Dep., Amort./Cur. Mat. L/T/D				5.1	7.4	7.5
(103) 3.8	(72) 2.4	(67) 2.8					(14) 2.5	(20) 3.6	(16) 3.4
1.7	.9	1.2					1.1	1.8	1.5
.3	.3	.3	Fixed/Worth	.6	.4	.3	.2	.3	.4
.8	.7	.7		-33.7	.8	.9	.5	.6	.9
1.9	2.6	1.8		-.3	NM	2.2	1.5	1.4	1.7
.7	.7	.6	Debt/Worth	.5	.6	.6	.4	.7	.6
1.9	1.7	1.6		-5.5	1.6	1.7	1.0	1.5	1.9
4.8	6.7	4.6		-2.6	NM	4.9	3.7	3.1	4.1
44.9	38.1	40.6	% Profit Before Taxes/Tangible Net Worth		38.2	29.8	48.1	43.7	38.7
(290) 21.5	(250) 13.6	(275) 14.8			(36) 11.9	(56) 14.0	(75) 18.6	(61) 15.4	(40) 14.1
6.8	-.3	3.2			-2.4	-.7	2.0	6.6	4.7
15.9	13.7	15.2	% Profit Before Taxes/Total Assets	20.8	13.8	15.1	16.5	14.9	13.4
7.8	4.0	6.1		10.9	4.7	3.3	7.3	6.9	7.0
1.2	-2.0	.1		-2.4	-5.2	-4.4	.2	1.6	3.1
19.5	23.8	23.8	Sales/Net Fixed Assets	38.3	37.5	19.4	23.9	22.3	16.0
10.1	9.6	8.7		5.8	7.7	7.0	8.8	11.0	8.8
5.5	4.4	4.3		3.4	4.9	3.8	4.2	4.7	4.6
3.1	3.0	2.8	Sales/Total Assets	3.1	3.0	3.1	2.8	2.7	2.3
2.4	2.2	2.1		1.6	2.2	2.1	2.1	2.2	2.0
1.8	1.6	1.5		1.0	1.5	1.5	1.4	1.5	1.5
1.3	1.1	1.1	% Depr., Dep., Amort./Sales	.6	1.4	1.4	1.3	.9	1.5
(290) 2.1	(266) 2.5	(285) 2.6		(11) 1.1	(40) 3.3	(61) 2.6	(70) 2.7	(61) 1.8	(42) 2.5
3.7	4.4	4.4		4.1	5.3	4.8	4.4	3.9	3.5
2.4	2.6	2.0	% Officers', Directors', Owners' Comp/Sales		2.8	2.3	1.7	1.4	
(146) 4.0	(147) 4.4	(147) 3.3			(29) 4.8	(38) 3.7	(42) 3.2	(25) 2.2	
6.4	8.5	6.0			7.7	6.1	5.9	3.4	
11372069M	5258063M	5335244M	Net Sales ($)	11939M	97105M	259074M	565572M	1046317M	3355237M
3832592M	2775498M	3021722M	Total Assets ($)	8661M	49345M	147651M	315035M	572807M	1928223M

© RMA 2011

M = $ thousand   MM = $ million
See Pages 9 through 22 for Explanation of Ratios and Data

Current Data Sorted by Assets   Comparative Historical Data

0-500M	500M-2MM	2-10MM	10-50MM	50-100MM	100-250MM	Type of Statement	4/1/06-3/31/07 ALL	4/1/07-3/31/08 ALL
1	1	1	4	1		Unqualified	10	8
1		18	4			Reviewed	25	29
1	3	4				Compiled	12	12
4	5	3				Tax Returns	15	11
4	8	9	8	2	2	Other	26	21
9 (4/1-9/30/10)			75 (10/1/10-3/31/11)					
11	17	35	16	3	2	NUMBER OF STATEMENTS	88	81
%	%	%	%	%	%	ASSETS	%	%
12.0	7.6	6.1	13.2			Cash & Equivalents	8.1	9.5
17.6	29.1	35.3	27.1			Trade Receivables (net)	40.6	34.4
12.9	23.1	16.0	17.1			Inventory	19.0	23.0
7.6	3.8	7.8	5.2			All Other Current	4.9	4.9
50.1	63.6	65.2	62.6			Total Current	72.6	71.7
25.0	20.8	23.8	19.7			Fixed Assets (net)	17.1	20.5
7.1	10.9	4.3	10.4			Intangibles (net)	4.6	2.1
17.8	4.7	6.8	7.3			All Other Non-Current	5.6	5.6
100.0	100.0	100.0	100.0			Total	100.0	100.0
						LIABILITIES		
32.7	13.1	12.2	6.4			Notes Payable-Short Term	10.6	9.7
2.5	1.2	2.9	2.4			Cur. Mat.-L.T.D.	2.7	3.8
6.0	17.7	16.3	10.9			Trade Payables	15.1	15.0
.2	.0	.7	.1			Income Taxes Payable	.8	.5
11.7	13.5	10.5	10.4			All Other Current	16.4	17.7
53.1	45.6	42.6	30.2			Total Current	45.6	46.7
15.1	27.1	15.5	18.1			Long-Term Debt	12.2	12.0
.0	.0	.1	.2			Deferred Taxes	.3	.6
1.5	3.3	9.2	13.0			All Other Non-Current	8.7	5.6
30.3	24.0	32.6	38.6			Net Worth	33.2	35.1
100.0	100.0	100.0	100.0			Total Liabilities & Net Worth	100.0	100.0
						INCOME DATA		
100.0	100.0	100.0	100.0			Net Sales	100.0	100.0
47.8	36.2	29.0	31.1			Gross Profit	33.3	33.8
41.1	37.0	28.1	23.8			Operating Expenses	27.1	26.9
6.7	-.9	.9	7.3			Operating Profit	6.2	6.9
.1	1.3	1.1	2.5			All Other Expenses (net)	.6	.7
6.6	-2.1	-.3	4.8			Profit Before Taxes	5.6	6.2
						RATIOS		
2.8	2.3	2.5	3.8			Current	2.4	2.6
1.8	1.6	1.5	2.1				1.6	1.6
.2	1.4	1.2	1.3				1.2	1.2
2.8	1.5	1.5	2.6			Quick	1.6	1.6
.6	1.0	1.0	1.1				1.1	.9
.2	.6	.6	.6				.8	.6
0 UND	24 15.4	41 9.0	38 9.5			Sales/Receivables	37 9.8	35 10.3
24 15.1	35 10.3	51 7.1	52 7.0				58 6.3	50 7.4
31 11.8	65 5.6	81 4.5	67 5.5				81 4.5	71 5.2
0 UND	8 43.5	10 37.2	30 12.3			Cost of Sales/Inventory	5 76.8	15 24.3
0 UND	63 5.8	36 10.1	59 6.2				37 9.9	46 7.9
55 6.7	112 3.2	64 5.7	85 4.3				76 4.8	80 4.6
0 UND	24 15.2	21 17.4	17 21.3			Cost of Sales/Payables	19 19.4	15 24.3
8 43.0	28 13.2	37 9.8	27 13.5				31 11.6	27 13.5
13 28.1	76 4.8	59 6.2	35 10.4				48 7.6	44 8.3
8.2	5.1	5.9	3.6			Sales/Working Capital	5.1	5.5
18.0	11.2	11.9	7.2				8.3	9.2
-8.7	24.4	16.2	14.9				21.6	23.1
	2.7	9.3	13.0			EBIT/Interest	11.8	20.4
	(14) .7	(32) 2.8	3.9				(77) 5.3	(71) 5.6
	-12.8	-1.9	1.2				1.6	2.1
		3.6				Net Profit + Depr., Dep., Amort./Cur. Mat. L/T/D	7.8	14.2
		(11) .7					(20) 3.0	(23) 4.0
		-1.5					1.6	1.7
.1	.2	.3	.2			Fixed/Worth	.2	.2
3.0	.9	.7	.8				.5	.7
18.0	-1.2	3.2	NM				1.4	1.9
.6	1.3	.8	.6			Debt/Worth	.9	.7
3.2	2.4	2.9	2.6				2.4	2.2
36.8	-5.4	10.9	NM				5.4	6.3
	20.8	73.7	102.1			% Profit Before Taxes/Tangible Net Worth	78.0	77.8
	(10) 4.8	(31) 10.2	(12) 18.3				(78) 36.1	(69) 38.5
	-11.8	-13.2	2.8				13.9	22.0
43.4	6.4	11.2	17.3			% Profit Before Taxes/Total Assets	23.7	23.4
22.6	1.4	3.1	6.6				11.4	13.0
.8	-11.9	-4.6	.6				2.7	4.3
151.9	33.0	30.2	36.4			Sales/Net Fixed Assets	37.3	37.2
39.1	13.7	8.8	11.0				19.3	13.3
18.1	7.3	5.0	4.1				8.9	8.2
5.0	2.9	2.7	2.0			Sales/Total Assets	3.0	3.2
3.2	2.2	2.1	1.7				2.4	2.5
2.4	2.0	1.4	1.1				2.0	1.8
	.9	.7	.6			% Depr., Dep., Amort./Sales	.7	.6
	(14) 2.3	(34) 1.6	(15) 2.4				(72) 1.1	(72) 1.2
	4.1	3.4	3.1				1.8	2.2
		1.7				% Officers', Directors' Owners' Comp/Sales	2.3	1.9
		(15) 2.6					(38) 4.4	(43) 3.5
		6.7					7.2	6.9
12331M	50312M	376492M	521667M	302961M	666432M	Net Sales ($)	1681839M	2186388M
2998M	20801M	171983M	319239M	241688M	335297M	Total Assets ($)	838829M	1054245M

M = $ thousand   MM = $ million
See Pages 9 through 22 for Explanation of Ratios and Data

Comparative Historical Data | Current Data Sorted by Sales

			Type of Statement	0-1MM	1-3MM	3-5MM	5-10MM	10-25MM	25MM & OVER
9	5	8	Unqualified		1		1	3	3
22	29	23	Reviewed	1		4	4	12	2
10	7	8	Compiled		4	1	1	2	
11	5	12	Tax Returns	2	6	2	1	1	
36	42	33	Other	4	5	5	5	6	8
4/1/08-3/31/09 ALL	4/1/09-3/31/10 ALL	4/1/10-3/31/11 ALL			9 (4/1-9/30/10)			75 (10/1/10-3/31/11)	
88	88	84	NUMBER OF STATEMENTS	7	16	12	12	24	13
%	%	%	**ASSETS**	%	%	%	%	%	%
8.5	8.0	8.9	Cash & Equivalents		9.0	3.8	8.3	8.6	12.8
37.1	32.1	29.2	Trade Receivables (net)		27.2	34.9	31.9	30.1	33.3
19.0	18.7	17.6	Inventory		21.7	9.2	18.5	18.3	20.7
4.7	5.8	6.2	All Other Current		7.0	5.3	10.6	5.2	7.2
69.3	64.6	61.9	Total Current		64.8	53.2	69.4	62.3	74.0
20.0	23.6	22.7	Fixed Assets (net)		24.1	26.0	18.4	23.4	19.3
5.2	3.9	7.0	Intangibles (net)		2.4	13.0	4.2	7.2	.7
5.5	8.0	8.4	All Other Non-Current		8.7	7.8	8.0	7.0	6.1
100.0	100.0	100.0	Total		100.0	100.0	100.0	100.0	100.0
			LIABILITIES						
13.1	10.0	13.6	Notes Payable-Short Term		21.1	7.8	14.3	12.1	6.3
4.8	3.1	2.3	Cur. Mat.-L.T.D.		1.3	2.7	2.8	2.6	1.5
15.2	14.1	14.0	Trade Payables		14.3	16.5	12.5	14.5	16.7
.5	.5	.3	Income Taxes Payable		.1	.1	1.7	.1	.1
14.0	13.9	11.3	All Other Current		14.8	5.6	9.8	12.6	11.5
47.6	41.6	41.5	Total Current		51.7	32.7	41.0	41.9	36.1
15.0	16.2	17.6	Long-Term Debt		22.5	25.3	11.7	14.3	11.8
.5	.9	.2	Deferred Taxes		.0	.0	.1	.1	.8
6.3	7.5	7.4	All Other Non-Current		4.0	5.2	6.9	9.0	14.2
30.7	33.9	33.3	Net Worth		21.9	36.7	40.3	34.7	37.1
100.0	100.0	100.0	Total Liabilities & Net Worth		100.0	100.0	100.0	100.0	100.0
			INCOME DATA						
100.0	100.0	100.0	Net Sales		100.0	100.0	100.0	100.0	100.0
32.5	33.7	33.2	Gross Profit		38.0	28.1	29.8	31.3	26.3
27.7	31.1	30.3	Operating Expenses		35.5	32.0	28.8	26.3	20.4
4.8	2.6	2.9	Operating Profit		2.4	-3.9	.9	5.0	5.9
.9	1.2	1.2	All Other Expenses (net)		.9	1.1	1.1	1.8	.3
3.9	1.4	1.7	Profit Before Taxes		1.5	-5.1	-.2	3.2	5.5
			RATIOS						
2.3	2.5	2.7			2.7	2.4	2.3	3.4	3.1
1.7	1.6	1.6	Current		1.9	1.6	1.5	1.4	1.8
1.2	1.2	1.2			1.1	1.2	1.3	1.1	1.5
1.6	1.7	1.7			1.5	1.9	1.3	1.6	1.9
1.0	.9	1.0	Quick		1.1	1.2	.9	.9	1.2
.6	.6	.6			.4	.7	.5	.6	.8
33 11.2	34 10.8	31 11.7		22 16.3	41 8.9	28 13.0	38 9.7		37 9.9
47 7.8	50 7.2	47 7.8	Sales/Receivables	32 11.3	56 6.6	55 6.7	49 7.4		51 7.2
68 5.4	69 5.3	68 5.4		66 5.5	99 3.7	92 4.0	59 6.2		64 5.7
10 38.4	13 28.7	9 38.6		1 577.9	2 160.4	11 33.6	29 12.8		25 14.6
36 10.2	46 7.9	45 8.1	Cost of Sales/Inventory	31 11.7	10 35.8	36 10.1	51 7.1		59 6.2
65 5.6	86 4.2	75 4.9		114 3.2	64 5.7	79 4.6	75 4.9		71 5.2
16 22.1	17 21.7	17 21.1		13 28.0	24 15.2	16 22.9	18 20.8		23 15.6
27 13.3	28 13.1	28 13.3	Cost of Sales/Payables	26 14.1	35 14.3	29 12.6	27 13.6		33 11.0
39 9.3	48 7.5	49 7.5		62 5.9	79 4.6	51 7.2	49 7.5		49 7.5
6.2	4.7	4.9			5.0	5.7	3.7	5.6	4.2
9.5	8.4	10.1	Sales/Working Capital		10.5	12.5	8.6	13.8	7.1
32.0	47.8	21.2			NM	24.1	15.1	39.9	7.7
10.5	8.4	11.2			2.6	2.8	11.4	14.8	39.5
(79) 3.6	(80) 3.1	(76) 3.4	EBIT/Interest	(13) 1.3	(11) -.7	(10) 3.8	(23) 3.9		7.5
1.5	.4	.0			-1.4	-43.4	-3.0	.8	4.7
10.9	7.2	4.7	Net Profit + Depr., Dep.,						
(16) 2.2	(18) 1.5	(16) 1.1	Amort./Cur. Mat. L/T/D						
1.5	.4	.1							
.2	.3	.2			.1	.1	.3	.4	.1
.6	.7	.7	Fixed/Worth		1.8	.9	.4	.8	.7
6.7	3.3	14.2			-1.1	169.0	.8	3.8	NM
.9	.7	.7			.8	.6	1.0	.8	.5
2.3	1.8	2.3	Debt/Worth		2.6	3.1	2.2	4.0	1.4
28.9	11.9	34.8			-5.1	342.4	4.4	10.7	NM
65.8	34.6	59.3	% Profit Before Taxes/Tangible		35.3	28.8	42.3	123.7	35.3
(70) 25.3	(73) 11.6	(67) 18.6	Net Worth	(10) 2.8	(10) 4.2	8.0	(20) 26.6		(10) 25.1
9.8	.3	1.6			-11.8	-34.7	-17.5	2.8	15.1
18.5	11.1	14.8	% Profit Before Taxes/Total		12.8	2.0	8.8	17.7	14.9
8.1	4.4	5.3	Assets		1.2	-1.2	4.7	6.8	7.6
1.2	-3.0	-2.1			-2.8	-12.7	-4.6	-.9	6.4
41.3	25.3	31.7			38.6	175.7	39.0	30.2	32.9
19.4	10.1	12.3	Sales/Net Fixed Assets		16.2	8.0	15.8	8.8	9.3
7.1	5.7	5.5			6.2	3.4	5.8	4.6	6.3
3.6	2.7	2.8			4.3	2.4	2.7	2.7	3.1
2.6	2.0	2.1	Sales/Total Assets		2.2	1.7	2.0	2.0	2.0
1.9	1.4	1.6			1.9	1.4	1.4	1.6	1.7
.7	1.1	.8			.7	1.4	.7	.9	.6
(69) 1.4	(71) 1.7	(74) 2.0	% Depr., Dep., Amort./Sales	(14) 1.9	(10) 4.0	(11) 1.7	2.4		(11) 2.0
2.9	3.4	3.1			3.5	6.9	3.1	3.3	2.6
1.8	2.5	2.1	% Officers', Directors'		3.5				
(30) 4.0	(32) 4.0	(32) 5.5	Owners' Comp/Sales	(10) 7.6					
7.0	7.3	8.4			10.7				
2430094M	2212404M	1930195M	Net Sales ($)	5162M	32208M	49858M	77051M	413826M	1352090M
1180874M	1262990M	1092006M	Total Assets ($)	2645M	15469M	36563M	44090M	263682M	729557M

Current Data Sorted by Assets   Comparative Historical Data

						Type of Statement		
		4	7	1		Unqualified	13	10
	2	8	1			Reviewed	10	7
1	3	6	3	1		Compiled	4	6
1	4	3	1			Tax Returns	9	5
	5	8	7	3	3	Other	18	17
	12 (4/1-9/30/10)		56 (10/1/10-3/31/11)				4/1/06-3/31/07	4/1/07-3/31/08
0-500M	500M-2MM	2-10MM	10-50MM	50-100MM	100-250MM		ALL	ALL
2	14	29	16	4	3	**NUMBER OF STATEMENTS**	54	45
%	%	%	%	%	%	**ASSETS**	%	%
	12.3	10.9	6.5			Cash & Equivalents	6.3	9.1
	23.9	29.9	21.9			Trade Receivables (net)	28.5	26.9
	21.8	28.3	21.7			Inventory	25.8	22.6
	1.2	2.5	2.6			All Other Current	2.9	1.9
	59.1	71.5	52.8			Total Current	63.6	60.5
	36.9	20.1	28.1			Fixed Assets (net)	25.9	29.1
	1.4	4.1	14.3			Intangibles (net)	6.6	6.6
	2.5	4.3	4.8			All Other Non-Current	3.8	3.8
	100.0	100.0	100.0			Total	100.0	100.0
						LIABILITIES		
	4.9	16.2	5.9			Notes Payable-Short Term	8.1	15.4
	4.2	2.0	8.0			Cur. Mat.-L.T.D.	3.7	4.2
	12.2	16.9	9.9			Trade Payables	16.5	15.0
	.0	.5	.0			Income Taxes Payable	.7	1.0
	17.2	8.4	14.8			All Other Current	12.1	8.5
	38.4	44.1	38.7			Total Current	41.1	44.2
	25.9	13.5	15.8			Long-Term Debt	21.3	20.7
	.1	.3	1.0			Deferred Taxes	.6	.5
	.0	3.8	9.1			All Other Non-Current	4.1	6.7
	35.6	38.3	35.5			Net Worth	32.9	27.9
	100.0	100.0	100.0			Total Liabilities & Net Worth	100.0	100.0
						INCOME DATA		
	100.0	100.0	100.0			Net Sales	100.0	100.0
	32.3	28.0	26.7			Gross Profit	28.1	32.7
	27.6	24.1	22.5			Operating Expenses	22.4	23.8
	4.6	3.9	4.1			Operating Profit	5.8	8.8
	.4	.5	2.3			All Other Expenses (net)	1.3	1.8
	4.2	3.4	1.8			Profit Before Taxes	4.5	7.0
						RATIOS		
	3.6	2.3	2.2				2.5	2.1
	2.1	1.5	1.5			Current	1.6	1.6
	1.3	1.3	1.0				1.1	1.2
	2.1	1.5	1.4				1.4	1.4
	1.3	1.0	.9			Quick	.8	.9
	.6	.6	.4				.5	.5
1 331.2		35 10.4	40 9.1				34 10.7	32 11.5
42 8.6		44 8.2	48 7.7			Sales/Receivables	45 8.1	44 8.3
49 7.4		58 6.2	71 5.1				56 6.5	55 6.6
20 17.9		32 11.5	37 10.0				31 11.9	26 14.0
36 10.0		58 6.3	73 5.0			Cost of Sales/Inventory	55 6.7	54 6.8
90 4.1		107 3.4	109 3.3				83 4.4	83 4.4
0 UND		23 16.0	11 33.8				18 19.8	22 16.4
20 18.6		34 10.7	26 13.8			Cost of Sales/Payables	30 12.1	28 12.9
38 9.5		51 7.1	56 6.5				47 7.8	41 9.0
	5.0	3.9	5.4				5.8	6.6
	7.9	9.7	10.5			Sales/Working Capital	10.1	11.6
	54.8	17.4	NM				68.1	22.4
	12.9	22.5	9.2				10.7	14.5
	(13) 6.3	(26) 5.2	(14) 2.4			EBIT/Interest	(50) 4.5	(44) 7.1
	1.6	1.3	1.3				2.4	2.6
						Net Profit + Depr., Dep.,	7.9	7.9
						Amort./Cur. Mat. L/T/D	(20) 2.0	(15) 3.1
							1.1	1.6
	.2	.2	.5				.3	.4
	.5	.4	1.0			Fixed/Worth	.6	.8
	4.4	1.9	11.2				4.2	3.5
	.5	.7	1.0				.8	.8
	1.2	1.9	2.4			Debt/Worth	1.7	1.6
	7.5	6.2	26.7				9.0	6.3
	63.3	42.1	26.3			% Profit Before Taxes/Tangible	48.1	55.2
	(12) 29.4	(24) 11.7	(13) 6.7			Net Worth	(43) 25.5	(37) 22.6
	10.2	2.2	-6.0				12.0	12.5
	19.9	10.2	7.8			% Profit Before Taxes/Total	17.7	24.1
	12.3	5.4	3.8			Assets	8.1	9.1
	1.7	1.2	-.5				3.0	4.5
	17.7	25.4	11.1				22.8	20.6
	11.2	11.6	6.5			Sales/Net Fixed Assets	11.4	9.7
	4.7	8.5	3.0				4.8	4.9
	4.2	2.8	1.9				3.1	3.4
	2.4	2.1	1.4			Sales/Total Assets	2.4	2.3
	1.9	1.5	1.1				1.8	1.4
	1.7	.8	1.8				1.1	1.0
	(10) 2.4	(27) 1.7	(14) 2.7			% Depr., Dep., Amort./Sales	(47) 1.7	(41) 2.4
	5.1	2.6	4.0				3.3	3.8
		1.0				% Officers', Directors'	2.5	1.5
		(12) 3.4				Owners' Comp/Sales	(17) 4.9	(17) 3.7
		11.3					7.9	4.5
2236M	48684M	313718M	683009M	534200M	475267M	Net Sales ($)	1923417M	1506243M
578M	18461M	142976M	446378M	236577M	510783M	Total Assets ($)	1142326M	959894M

M = $ thousand   MM = $ million
See Pages 9 through 22 for Explanation of Ratios and Data

Comparative Historical Data | Type of Statement | Current Data Sorted by Sales

			Type of Statement	0-1MM	1-3MM	3-5MM	5-10MM	10-25MM	25MM & OVER
12	11	12	Unqualified				1	4	7
12	7	11	Reviewed			3	5	2	1
7	6	10	Compiled		2	2	2	4	
6	7	9	Tax Returns		1	2	3	1	1
29	27	26	Other	1	3	3	5	4	11
4/1/08-3/31/09 ALL	4/1/09-3/31/10 ALL	4/1/10-3/31/11 ALL		12 (4/1-9/30/10)			56 (10/1/10-3/31/11)		
66	58	68	**NUMBER OF STATEMENTS**	1	6	10	16	15	20

H1 %	H2 %	H3 %		0-1MM	1-3MM	3-5MM %	5-10MM %	10-25MM %	25MM& %
			ASSETS						
7.3	7.5	9.7	Cash & Equivalents			11.4	11.1	9.2	5.8
25.2	25.6	26.0	Trade Receivables (net)			20.6	26.2	32.1	22.2
25.2	22.3	24.6	Inventory			33.1	28.5	20.1	24.0
3.1	4.0	2.3	All Other Current			.2	2.8	2.7	3.0
60.9	59.4	62.6	Total Current			65.3	68.5	64.1	55.1
26.8	28.1	27.3	Fixed Assets (net)			28.5	22.6	24.0	29.9
6.5	8.7	6.2	Intangibles (net)			2.5	5.1	4.7	12.2
5.9	3.7	3.9	All Other Non-Current			3.7	3.8	7.2	2.8
100.0	100.0	100.0	Total			100.0	100.0	100.0	100.0
			LIABILITIES						
10.6	8.1	9.9	Notes Payable-Short Term			7.5	14.5	14.0	5.6
2.9	3.6	3.8	Cur. Mat.-L.T.D.			4.7	2.3	5.2	3.9
12.2	13.5	14.9	Trade Payables			17.2	11.6	18.2	12.4
.3	.2	.2	Income Taxes Payable			.0	.2	.8	.0
11.3	8.9	13.5	All Other Current			3.9	9.4	9.2	12.6
37.2	34.2	42.4	Total Current			33.4	38.0	47.3	34.5
16.9	18.2	20.1	Long-Term Debt			29.9	14.8	10.4	14.5
.9	1.0	.8	Deferred Taxes			.1	.5	.1	2.3
6.0	6.3	4.1	All Other Non-Current			2.5	3.4	2.5	8.1
39.0	40.3	32.6	Net Worth			34.2	43.4	39.7	40.6
100.0	100.0	100.0	Total Liabilities & Net Worth			100.0	100.0	100.0	100.0
			INCOME DATA						
100.0	100.0	100.0	Net Sales			100.0	100.0	100.0	100.0
28.2	29.0	28.7	Gross Profit			31.3	30.6	25.9	27.4
21.7	25.2	24.3	Operating Expenses			27.7	26.0	24.2	19.4
6.5	3.8	4.4	Operating Profit			3.6	4.6	1.7	8.0
1.2	1.8	1.0	All Other Expenses (net)			.7	.5	.5	2.2
5.3	2.1	3.4	Profit Before Taxes			2.9	4.0	1.2	5.8
			RATIOS						
2.5	3.2	2.3	Current			3.6	3.2	1.7	2.2
1.6	1.6	1.6				1.7	2.1	1.3	1.6
1.2	1.2	1.2				1.3	1.3	1.0	1.2
1.3	1.8	1.5	Quick			2.1	1.5	1.3	1.4
.9	.9	.9				1.0	1.2	1.0	.8
.6	.6	.5				.3	.6	.7	.4
30 12.0	37 9.7	34 10.8	Sales/Receivables			1 331.2	31 11.9	44 8.3	38 9.6
40 9.2	50 7.4	44 8.3				44 8.3	35 10.4	49 7.4	43 8.5
51 7.2	60 6.1	57 6.4				49 7.5	70 5.2	72 5.1	56 6.6
31 11.8	29 12.6	32 11.6	Cost of Sales/Inventory			38 9.7	35 10.3	28 13.1	36 10.1
55 6.6	51 7.1	52 7.1				91 4.0	80 4.6	43 8.5	63 5.8
87 4.2	100 3.7	102 3.6				153 2.4	120 3.0	62 5.9	105 3.5
12 31.7	19 18.8	17 21.5	Cost of Sales/Payables			17 21.7	17 21.6	19 19.2	18 20.3
21 17.1	32 11.6	31 11.9				33 11.0	26 13.8	36 10.1	31 11.8
36 10.1	49 7.5	52 7.0				68 5.4	35 10.4	57 6.4	51 7.2
5.2	4.1	5.6	Sales/Working Capital			3.6	2.8	7.1	6.1
9.9	9.3	10.1				7.6	6.9	13.0	10.1
21.4	20.0	21.2				54.8	11.6	102.4	19.5
18.9	5.5	16.8	EBIT/Interest				26.3	12.0	37.2
(61) 4.5	(55) 2.4	(62) 4.9					(14) 5.9	(13) 2.6	6.0
2.2	-1.3	1.5					2.0	.4	2.4
18.5	6.1	7.4	Net Profit + Depr., Dep., Amort./Cur. Mat. L/T/D						
(19) 6.0	(14) 2.1	(13) 4.5							
3.1	-.1	.9							
.3	.4	.3	Fixed/Worth			.2	.1	.4	.4
.8	.9	.7				.7	.6	.6	1.0
2.3	1.8	2.4				NM	2.0	1.6	4.6
.8	.9	.7	Debt/Worth			.4	.6	.7	.8
1.7	1.7	1.7				1.6	1.6	1.9	1.6
6.3	6.7	6.4				NM	3.6	7.8	6.4
45.7	36.8	39.7	% Profit Before Taxes/Tangible Net Worth				42.0	22.9	38.6
(54) 24.6	(49) 14.2	(57) 12.7					(13) 9.0	(14) 8.6	(17) 20.7
11.2	-2.0	3.1					6.4	-12.1	8.0
19.1	11.6	10.0	% Profit Before Taxes/Total Assets			16.2	10.3	6.5	9.6
8.0	2.7	6.4				7.8	5.9	5.0	7.3
3.8	-2.2	1.3				.9	3.4	-1.9	4.2
24.4	16.8	17.5	Sales/Net Fixed Assets			22.5	23.8	15.4	11.9
9.7	7.4	10.7				11.2	13.0	10.6	6.9
5.6	3.7	5.7				7.1	6.8	6.3	3.8
3.0	2.5	2.7	Sales/Total Assets			2.6	2.8	2.9	2.3
2.2	1.8	2.0				2.0	2.2	2.1	1.7
1.6	1.2	1.4				1.6	1.2	1.5	1.1
.9	1.4	1.0	% Depr., Dep., Amort./Sales				1.0	.7	1.3
(53) 1.5	(48) 2.6	(60) 2.1					(14) 2.3	(13) 1.5	(19) 2.5
3.4	4.2	3.3					4.0	2.8	3.8
1.9	1.3	1.3	% Officers', Directors' Owners' Comp/Sales						
(20) 4.0	(15) 7.4	(21) 3.6							
8.6	11.6	11.1							
3333095M	2050580M	2057114M	Net Sales ($)	481M	13157M	37428M	98499M	232311M	1675238M
1515239M	1537366M	1355753M	Total Assets ($)	113M	5468M	17801M	59952M	118367M	1154052M

Current Data Sorted by Assets   **Comparative Historical Data**

0-500M	500M-2MM	2-10MM	10-50MM	50-100MM	100-250MM	Type of Statement	4/1/06-3/31/07 ALL	4/1/07-3/31/08 ALL
		3	12	6	3	Unqualified	20	14
	1	11	3			Reviewed	27	22
2	7	6	1			Compiled	17	12
4	8	5				Tax Returns	12	21
2	7	14	13	2		Other	25	36
	14 (4/1-9/30/10)		96 (10/1/10-3/31/11)					
8	23	39	29	8	3	**NUMBER OF STATEMENTS**	101	105
%	%	%	%	%	%	**ASSETS**	%	%
	8.2	7.9	7.4			Cash & Equivalents	7.7	7.5
	24.0	20.2	24.6			Trade Receivables (net)	23.3	24.7
	30.7	42.7	26.3			Inventory	33.4	31.8
	1.8	3.5	3.5			All Other Current	1.4	1.1
	64.7	74.3	61.8			Total Current	65.8	65.2
	19.3	17.1	23.4			Fixed Assets (net)	22.8	22.9
	1.7	3.9	9.4			Intangibles (net)	4.4	5.7
	14.3	4.7	5.5			All Other Non-Current	7.0	6.3
	100.0	100.0	100.0			Total	100.0	100.0
						LIABILITIES		
	17.6	12.0	7.2			Notes Payable-Short Term	10.3	10.1
	2.8	2.9	3.3			Cur. Mat.-L.T.D.	3.0	3.3
	12.0	12.1	10.3			Trade Payables	13.4	15.6
	.0	.1	.5			Income Taxes Payable	.2	.2
	10.8	6.2	6.7			All Other Current	10.4	7.7
	43.3	33.3	28.0			Total Current	37.3	36.9
	24.1	12.8	12.5			Long-Term Debt	15.9	17.4
	.0	.3	.8			Deferred Taxes	.6	.5
	5.7	1.8	13.8			All Other Non-Current	8.0	9.5
	26.9	51.8	44.9			Net Worth	38.2	35.7
	100.0	100.0	100.0			Total Liabilities & Net Worth	100.0	100.0
						INCOME DATA		
	100.0	100.0	100.0			Net Sales	100.0	100.0
	29.0	35.9	29.0			Gross Profit	34.5	31.5
	26.1	29.2	22.2			Operating Expenses	28.5	25.4
	2.9	6.8	6.9			Operating Profit	6.1	6.2
	1.2	.5	1.3			All Other Expenses (net)	1.1	1.5
	1.7	6.3	5.5			Profit Before Taxes	5.0	4.7
						RATIOS		
	2.5	5.5	3.7				3.2	3.4
	1.7	2.2	2.6			Current	2.1	2.1
	.8	1.6	1.7				1.3	1.2
	2.1	2.3	2.0				1.5	1.7
	.7	.7	1.4			Quick	.9	.9
	.3	.5	.9				.5	.6
	22 16.8	27 13.4	39 9.4				28 13.0	30 12.0
	34 10.8	37 9.8	48 7.6			Sales/Receivables	39 9.3	38 9.6
	51 7.2	47 7.7	60 6.1				48 7.5	48 7.5
	39 9.4	84 4.3	50 7.3				47 7.7	51 7.1
	74 4.9	126 2.9	73 5.0			Cost of Sales/Inventory	86 4.3	82 4.5
	118 3.1	173 2.1	124 2.9				147 2.5	133 2.7
	11 34.2	17 21.5	18 20.8				15 24.3	15 24.0
	31 11.9	27 13.4	29 12.6			Cost of Sales/Payables	28 13.2	29 12.4
	43 8.5	43 8.5	38 9.6				46 7.9	51 7.1
	5.1	2.9	3.6				3.9	4.0
	10.5	4.6	5.0			Sales/Working Capital	6.4	7.1
	-20.8	7.6	7.2				18.6	19.5
	5.6	18.9	13.4				13.6	11.1
	(20) 2.6	(32) 5.7	(26) 6.1			EBIT/Interest	(90) 4.7	(93) 3.7
	.6	1.8	1.8				2.0	1.5
		4.7					7.7	11.2
		(10) 2.1				Net Profit + Depr., Dep., Amort./Cur. Mat. L/T/D	(30) 3.9	(24) 2.8
		.3					1.6	1.7
	.0	.1	.3				.3	.3
	.4	.4	.5			Fixed/Worth	.6	.5
	4.0	.6	1.0				1.7	2.1
	.7	.2	.6				.6	.6
	2.5	1.1	.9			Debt/Worth	1.6	2.2
	16.2	2.2	4.2				5.6	6.4
	105.6	28.9	50.6				47.4	43.9
	(21) 18.2	(35) 16.7	(27) 18.1			% Profit Before Taxes/Tangible Net Worth	(87) 23.1	(86) 19.6
	-1.0	7.3	7.0				9.8	6.5
	12.9	16.4	15.0				17.2	15.3
	4.8	8.3	8.2			% Profit Before Taxes/Total Assets	7.9	5.7
	-1.8	2.1	2.1				2.3	1.2
	117.9	35.8	15.5				25.7	28.4
	13.2	12.5	9.8			Sales/Net Fixed Assets	10.5	12.4
	5.1	8.0	4.0				5.3	5.7
	3.3	2.3	2.2				2.9	2.6
	2.5	1.8	1.7			Sales/Total Assets	1.9	2.0
	.9	1.5	1.4				1.5	1.5
	.8	.6	1.4				.8	.8
	(15) 1.9	(34) 1.7	(26) 2.0			% Depr., Dep., Amort./Sales	(91) 2.0	(84) 2.2
	3.8	3.5	3.4				2.7	3.1
	2.7	2.9					2.7	1.8
	(13) 3.5	(16) 3.4				% Officers', Directors' Owners' Comp/Sales	(30) 3.7	(40) 2.8
	7.0	4.3					6.1	5.5
16820M	61022M	369938M	1112181M	721837M	425258M	Net Sales ($)	3109317M	2440692M
1969M	26400M	200988M	650638M	570835M	467630M	Total Assets ($)	1869020M	1534982M

M = $ thousand   MM = $ million
See Pages 9 through 22 for Explanation of Ratios and Data

Comparative Historical Data   Current Data Sorted by Sales

Current Data groupings: **14 (4/1-9/30/10)** covers 0-1MM and 1-3MM; **96 (10/1/10-3/31/11)** covers 3-5MM through 25MM & OVER.

4/1/08-3/31/09 ALL	4/1/09-3/31/10 ALL	4/1/10-3/31/11 ALL		0-1MM	1-3MM	3-5MM	5-10MM	10-25MM	25MM & OVER
			Type of Statement						
18	18	24	Unqualified				1	7	16
20	14	15	Reviewed			3	5	5	2
14	20	16	Compiled	2	2	5	5	2	
16	16	17	Tax Returns	3	6	3	3	2	
39	37	38	Other	4	3	2	8	8	13
107	105	110	**NUMBER OF STATEMENTS**	9	11	13	22	24	31
%	%	%	**ASSETS**	%	%	%	%	%	%
8.5	9.3	8.0	Cash & Equivalents		8.8	6.9	9.2	8.0	7.0
25.3	22.4	21.5	Trade Receivables (net)		21.0	21.8	23.3	18.8	24.2
33.9	34.5	32.8	Inventory		36.9	37.9	41.5	34.8	25.7
2.0	2.3	2.8	All Other Current		2.6	2.6	2.3	3.5	3.7
69.7	68.6	65.2	Total Current		69.2	69.2	76.3	65.1	60.6
20.9	20.3	19.5	Fixed Assets (net)		19.5	14.6	17.6	21.5	20.4
4.0	4.0	6.4	Intangibles (net)		.7	4.7	2.3	6.3	11.0
5.4	7.2	8.9	All Other Non-Current		10.7	11.4	3.8	7.1	8.0
100.0	100.0	100.0	Total		100.0	100.0	100.0	100.0	100.0
			LIABILITIES						
13.5	13.0	11.6	Notes Payable-Short Term		12.1	17.5	6.5	15.5	5.6
3.4	3.2	2.7	Cur. Mat.-L.T.D.		4.4	2.0	2.8	3.5	2.5
13.6	11.8	11.4	Trade Payables		7.5	13.8	11.6	11.2	10.6
.2	.3	.2	Income Taxes Payable		.0	.0	.0	.1	.6
9.1	10.9	7.8	All Other Current		10.2	12.9	7.0	5.8	7.7
39.8	39.2	33.7	Total Current		34.3	46.2	27.8	36.1	27.0
15.6	12.6	14.4	Long-Term Debt		19.1	22.9	9.7	13.4	13.0
.4	.5	.5	Deferred Taxes		.0	.0	.4	1.0	.8
5.2	8.9	7.2	All Other Non-Current		3.6	2.0	3.9	3.0	16.2
39.0	38.9	44.1	Net Worth		42.9	28.9	58.3	46.4	43.0
100.0	100.0	100.0	Total Liabilities & Net Worth		100.0	100.0	100.0	100.0	100.0
			INCOME DATA						
100.0	100.0	100.0	Net Sales		100.0	100.0	100.0	100.0	100.0
30.7	32.4	32.5	Gross Profit		38.6	28.1	38.0	32.5	29.0
25.1	29.4	26.6	Operating Expenses		37.5	23.9	31.2	25.7	21.4
5.6	3.0	5.8	Operating Profit		1.1	4.2	6.8	6.8	7.6
1.4	1.5	1.1	All Other Expenses (net)		.3	1.3	.3	1.0	1.9
4.2	1.5	4.7	Profit Before Taxes		.8	2.8	6.6	5.8	5.6
			RATIOS						
3.8	3.8	3.9			4.4	3.9	6.0	3.4	3.2
2.1	2.4	2.2	Current		2.0	1.7	3.4	1.7	2.3
1.3	1.3	1.3			1.1	1.2	2.1	1.2	1.8
1.9	1.8	2.0			1.5	1.8	2.5	1.9	1.9
.8	.9	.9	Quick		.9	.7	1.0	.7	1.4
.5	.5	.5			.4	.4	.7	.4	.9
25 14.9	27 13.7	27 13.4			21 17.6	25 14.6	27 13.4	29 12.4	37 9.9
36 10.2	39 9.5	39 9.3	Sales/Receivables		39 9.3	34 10.8	36 10.3	41 9.0	48 7.6
57 6.4	50 7.2	52 7.0			51 7.2	41 9.0	51 7.1	52 7.0	65 5.6
44 8.3	50 7.3	58 6.3			39 9.4	48 7.6	59 6.2	77 4.8	52 7.1
75 4.9	87 4.2	94 3.9	Cost of Sales/Inventory		61 6.0	97 3.8	134 2.7	118 3.1	68 5.4
154 2.4	167 2.2	148 2.5			194 1.9	155 2.4	255 1.4	154 2.4	107 3.4
10 34.9	12 30.4	14 25.5			1 418.0	10 36.3	11 33.7	15 24.3	18 20.8
24 15.3	24 15.4	29 12.6	Cost of Sales/Payables		22 16.8	21 17.6	28 13.0	26 13.8	33 11.2
42 8.7	50 7.3	43 8.6			39 9.2	52 7.1	38 9.6	43 8.5	44 8.3
4.1	3.3	3.6			4.8	4.8	2.4	3.6	3.7
6.4	5.3	6.0	Sales/Working Capital		9.8	6.3	3.7	6.1	5.0
16.4	12.9	11.6			26.8	NM	6.7	12.8	7.2
12.5	9.6	12.0				7.0	22.1	10.8	25.7
(91) 3.2	(91) 2.6	(89) 5.7	EBIT/Interest		(10) 3.9	(17) 4.6	(21) 4.7	(25) 8.1	
.9	.1	1.8				2.3	.9	1.8	5.6
12.9	45.8	11.4						4.1	
(21) 1.1	(20) 3.6	(23) 2.6	Net Profit + Depr., Dep., Amort./Cur. Mat. L/T/D				(10) 1.9		
.1	.6	1.1						1.0	
.2	.2	.2			.1	.2	.1	.1	.3
.5	.4	.4	Fixed/Worth		.3	.4	.3	.4	.5
1.5	1.0	.9			.9	12.7	.5	2.8	.8
.5	.5	.5			.7	1.0	.2	.6	.5
1.8	1.3	1.1	Debt/Worth		.9	2.2	.8	1.2	.9
5.5	4.1	3.6			4.3	52.2	1.6	5.1	3.7
50.8	31.0	49.3			40.0	125.9	45.7	43.5	50.5
(91) 17.7	(96) 9.1	(99) 18.1	% Profit Before Taxes/Tangible Net Worth		7.1	(11) 27.0	15.5	(21) 18.1	(27) 20.1
1.0	.8	7.0			-28.2	8.7	2.5	7.4	12.3
16.2	11.1	15.8			12.9	15.8	16.1	17.8	14.3
6.7	3.9	7.8	% Profit Before Taxes/Total Assets		2.9	4.8	8.6	7.8	9.7
-.7	-.6	1.7			-14.6	2.0	.5	2.0	5.4
40.1	26.8	28.8			38.2	82.3	45.7	31.0	15.0
12.2	10.7	11.6	Sales/Net Fixed Assets		22.5	11.6	12.0	11.8	10.8
5.5	5.5	5.3			5.3	9.3	6.9	4.5	4.7
2.8	2.7	2.4			3.4	3.3	2.5	2.4	2.1
2.0	1.8	1.7	Sales/Total Assets		2.9	2.1	1.6	1.8	1.6
1.5	1.3	1.3			1.7	1.6	1.5	1.4	1.3
.9	1.0	1.0					1.3	.5	1.4
(91) 1.7	(88) 2.3	(90) 1.9	% Depr., Dep., Amort./Sales				(16) 2.4	(23) 1.8	(26) 2.1
3.1	4.0	3.3					4.4	4.0	3.2
2.3	1.9	2.7					3.1		
(43) 3.2	(48) 3.8	(36) 3.5	% Officers', Directors' Owners' Comp/Sales				(11) 3.6		
4.9	7.4	5.2					4.4		
2885470M	2621460M	2707056M	Net Sales ($)	4910M	20180M	50169M	173261M	364879M	2093657M
1712372M	1767648M	1918460M	Total Assets ($)	5141M	9371M	24460M	96836M	223646M	1559006M

M = $ thousand   MM = $ million

See Pages 9 through 22 for Explanation of Ratios and Data

Current Data Sorted by Assets							Comparative Historical Data	
						Type of Statement		
		2	3			Unqualified	9	8
	1	8	2			Reviewed	11	10
	2	5	1			Compiled	6	11
2	3	1				Tax Returns	5	2
		6	2	1		Other	9	14
	9 (4/1-9/30/10)		30 (10/1/10-3/31/11)				4/1/06-3/31/07 ALL	4/1/07-3/31/08 ALL
0-500M	500M-2MM	2-10MM	10-50MM	50-100MM	100-250MM			
2	6	22	8	1		NUMBER OF STATEMENTS	40	45
%	%	%	%	%	%	**ASSETS**	%	%
		11.8			D A T A	Cash & Equivalents	6.5	8.3
		19.5				Trade Receivables (net)	25.3	23.0
		23.3				Inventory	25.1	24.0
		2.3				All Other Current	1.9	.9
		56.9				Total Current	58.8	56.1
		32.9			N O T	Fixed Assets (net)	30.0	29.1
		3.6				Intangibles (net)	4.1	6.7
		6.5				All Other Non-Current	7.1	8.1
		100.0				Total	100.0	100.0
					A V A I L A B L E	**LIABILITIES**		
		5.8				Notes Payable-Short Term	9.3	9.1
		3.7				Cur. Mat.-L.T.D.	5.9	3.4
		8.4				Trade Payables	12.9	8.2
		.1				Income Taxes Payable	.1	.1
		5.9				All Other Current	10.3	7.0
		23.9				Total Current	38.5	27.7
		20.3				Long-Term Debt	15.1	17.2
		.5				Deferred Taxes	.8	.7
		6.4				All Other Non-Current	5.2	5.0
		48.9				Net Worth	40.5	49.5
		100.0				Total Liabilties & Net Worth	100.0	100.0
						INCOME DATA		
		100.0				Net Sales	100.0	100.0
		31.9				Gross Profit	28.0	26.4
		23.2				Operating Expenses	23.4	20.5
		8.7				Operating Profit	4.6	5.8
		.9				All Other Expenses (net)	1.3	1.0
		7.8				Profit Before Taxes	3.3	4.8
						RATIOS		
		3.6					2.5	3.0
		2.6				Current	1.9	2.3
		1.8					1.4	1.4
		2.3					1.6	2.1
		1.4				Quick	.9	1.1
		.7					.6	.7
		41 8.9					**36** 10.1	**37** 9.9
		47 7.8				Sales/Receivables	**47** 7.7	**46** 7.9
		51 7.1					**56** 6.6	**54** 6.7
		58 6.3					**38** 9.6	**35** 10.3
		70 5.2				Cost of Sales/Inventory	**63** 5.8	**56** 6.5
		102 3.6					**88** 4.1	**83** 4.4
		13 28.7					**15** 24.2	**11** 34.1
		19 18.8				Cost of Sales/Payables	**24** 15.4	**20** 18.5
		38 9.6					**38** 9.6	**29** 12.7
		3.2					5.3	4.9
		4.7				Sales/Working Capital	7.5	7.1
		7.7					14.2	15.2
		14.5					16.1	9.9
		(20) 3.7				EBIT/Interest	(39) 6.2	(42) 3.9
		2.6					1.3	1.4
							8.5	4.0
						Net Profit + Depr., Dep., Amort./Cur. Mat. L/T/D	(14) 5.8	(11) 3.2
							1.4	2.7
		.4					.4	.4
		.7				Fixed/Worth	.7	.7
		1.7					2.6	1.2
		.4					.6	.5
		1.0				Debt/Worth	.9	1.1
		2.8					6.4	2.6
		39.3					36.2	31.6
		(20) 19.3				% Profit Before Taxes/Tangible Net Worth	(33) 18.4	(41) 15.2
		13.3					4.3	4.3
		16.4					16.2	12.8
		8.5				% Profit Before Taxes/Total Assets	5.8	8.3
		4.7					1.1	1.3
		9.4					17.5	11.5
		5.1				Sales/Net Fixed Assets	7.1	7.0
		3.1					4.3	4.4
		1.9					2.7	2.3
		1.6				Sales/Total Assets	1.9	1.9
		1.3					1.5	1.6
		2.4					2.3	2.3
		(21) 3.6				% Depr., Dep., Amort./Sales	(34) 3.4	(43) 3.0
		5.0					5.3	4.4
		2.1					2.3	1.9
		(10) 5.6				% Officers', Directors' Owners' Comp/Sales	(15) 6.2	(14) 5.3
		10.7					10.7	8.5
3457M	**16028M**	**208010M**	**332747M**	**84557M**		Net Sales ($)	**721788M**	**846020M**
845M	**6040M**	**129933M**	**222513M**	**52675M**		Total Assets ($)	**411140M**	**480793M**

M = $ thousand MM = $ million

See Pages 9 through 22 for Explanation of Ratios and Data

Comparative Historical Data | Current Data Sorted by Sales

	4/1/08-3/31/09 ALL	4/1/09-3/31/10 ALL	4/1/10-3/31/11 ALL		0-1MM	1-3MM	3-5MM	5-10MM	10-25MM	25MM & OVER
Type of Statement										
Unqualified	8	7	5					1	1	3
Reviewed	10	12	11				1	4	4	2
Compiled	9	9	8			1	1	4	2	
Tax Returns	6	6	6		1	4		1		
Other	12	12	9			1		3	2	3
	4/1/08- 3/31/09 ALL	4/1/09- 3/31/10 ALL	4/1/10- 3/31/11 ALL		9 (4/1-9/30/10)			30 (10/1/10-3/31/11)		
NUMBER OF STATEMENTS	45	46	39		1	4	2	13	9	8
	%	%	%		%	%	%	%	%	%
ASSETS										
Cash & Equivalents	6.8	10.1	11.1					12.8		
Trade Receivables (net)	21.7	22.4	21.7					18.1		
Inventory	32.3	24.4	24.1					19.9		
All Other Current	1.1	3.1	2.0					2.5		
Total Current	62.0	60.0	58.9					53.2		
Fixed Assets (net)	28.2	29.5	31.3					32.4		
Intangibles (net)	2.6	5.9	4.3					5.6		
All Other Non-Current	7.3	4.6	5.5					8.8		
Total	100.0	100.0	100.0					100.0		
LIABILITIES										
Notes Payable-Short Term	12.5	10.6	10.6					6.8		
Cur. Mat.-L.T.D.	4.2	4.7	3.0					4.4		
Trade Payables	11.1	8.5	10.2					9.5		
Income Taxes Payable	.0	.1	.2					.0		
All Other Current	7.9	5.1	5.5					5.2		
Total Current	35.8	29.1	29.5					25.8		
Long-Term Debt	20.2	15.5	17.4					26.0		
Deferred Taxes	.4	.3	.5					.0		
All Other Non-Current	7.1	8.0	7.2					7.7		
Net Worth	36.5	47.1	45.5					40.4		
Total Liabilties & Net Worth	100.0	100.0	100.0					100.0		
INCOME DATA										
Net Sales	100.0	100.0	100.0					100.0		
Gross Profit	25.1	29.4	33.9					31.5		
Operating Expenses	21.8	24.6	25.9					23.4		
Operating Profit	3.2	4.8	8.0					8.1		
All Other Expenses (net)	.8	1.5	.7					1.1		
Profit Before Taxes	2.4	3.3	7.3					6.9		
RATIOS										
Current	2.9	4.7	3.6					3.5		
	2.2	2.3	2.0					2.3		
	1.3	1.4	1.4					1.6		
Quick	1.7	2.9	2.3					2.3		
	.9	1.2	1.1					1.1		
	.6	.7	.7					.6		
Sales/Receivables	31 11.8	38 9.6	34 10.9					37 9.8		
	40 9.1	48 7.6	46 7.9					49 7.4		
	48 7.6	61 5.9	52 7.0					51 7.1		
Cost of Sales/Inventory	44 8.3	50 7.3	48 7.5					54 6.8		
	70 5.2	71 5.2	67 5.4					69 5.3		
	102 3.6	98 3.7	99 3.7					95 3.9		
Cost of Sales/Payables	12 29.3	13 28.0	15 24.0					14 25.2		
	17 21.1	23 15.9	23 16.2					20 18.6		
	31 11.8	35 10.5	38 9.7					41 9.0		
Sales/Working Capital	4.5	3.5	3.5					3.8		
	7.1	6.0	6.3					5.3		
	15.6	14.0	12.2					11.2		
EBIT/Interest	6.4	10.0	14.9					6.5		
	(42) 2.7	(39) 2.0	(35) 5.1					(12) 3.3		
	.3	-.3	2.7					2.6		
Net Profit + Depr., Dep., Amort./Cur. Mat. L/T/D	4.5	31.8	14.2							
	(14) 2.6	(12) 3.3	(10) 3.8							
	1.2	1.2	2.1							
Fixed/Worth	.3	.4	.4					.5		
	.8	1.0	.7					.7		
	1.7	1.7	2.3					3.8		
Debt/Worth	.5	.3	.4					.5		
	2.0	1.8	1.4					2.0		
	4.3	4.5	3.8					6.4		
% Profit Before Taxes/Tangible Net Worth	29.2	26.6	41.7					42.0		
	(40) 8.6	(41) 5.8	(35) 23.2					(11) 24.3		
	-2.6	-7.8	13.0					2.4		
% Profit Before Taxes/Total Assets	12.1	7.7	16.4					15.5		
	3.6	2.2	10.0					8.0		
	-.9	-2.7	5.6					2.7		
Sales/Net Fixed Assets	16.2	11.3	10.3					9.2		
	7.5	6.0	5.7					4.7		
	5.1	3.4	3.5					3.0		
Sales/Total Assets	2.6	2.2	2.2					1.9		
	1.9	1.6	1.7					1.5		
	1.7	1.2	1.5					1.1		
% Depr., Dep., Amort./Sales	1.5	2.2	2.0					2.6		
	(43) 2.8	(43) 3.3	(37) 3.1					(12) 3.8		
	4.4	5.4	4.4					6.7		
% Officers', Directors' Owners' Comp/Sales	1.8	3.6	2.0							
	(14) 3.7	(17) 6.9	(18) 4.7							
	10.6	10.0	8.3							
Net Sales ($)	923729M	671457M	644799M		876M	11605M	8417M	97113M	127431M	399357M
Total Assets ($)	483366M	443438M	412006M		517M	5762M	2750M	70251M	69902M	262824M

© RMA 2011

M = $ thousand   MM = $ million

See Pages 9 through 22 for Explanation of Ratios and Data

Current Data Sorted by Assets   **Comparative Historical Data**

0-500M	500M-2MM	2-10MM	10-50MM	50-100MM	100-250MM	Type of Statement	ALL 4/1/06-3/31/07	ALL 4/1/07-3/31/08
	5	5	8	4		Unqualified	51	36
	4	20	10			Reviewed	36	33
	6	2	2			Compiled	24	26
2	9	4				Tax Returns	13	18
3		17	17	7	1	Other	58	77
	30 (4/1-9/30/10)		96 (10/1/10-3/31/11)					
5	24	48	37	11	1	**NUMBER OF STATEMENTS**	182	190
%	%	%	%	%	%	**ASSETS**	%	%
	10.4	8.7	6.2	4.8		Cash & Equivalents	7.5	7.2
	24.5	26.9	28.3	22.1		Trade Receivables (net)	29.1	27.7
	24.2	33.2	33.4	22.7		Inventory	29.2	32.8
	1.7	1.7	1.9	11.5		All Other Current	1.6	2.2
	60.9	70.5	69.9	61.0		Total Current	67.4	69.8
	27.0	20.0	23.5	28.3		Fixed Assets (net)	24.0	21.5
	3.0	3.2	2.6	3.1		Intangibles (net)	3.5	3.2
	9.1	6.2	4.1	7.5		All Other Non-Current	5.0	5.5
	100.0	100.0	100.0	100.0		Total	100.0	100.0
						LIABILITIES		
	10.2	13.7	16.6	7.8		Notes Payable-Short Term	11.8	13.5
	4.1	3.8	1.9	.9		Cur. Mat.-L.T.D.	3.2	3.8
	17.6	18.0	14.2	13.7		Trade Payables	17.2	18.5
	.0	.2	.4	.3		Income Taxes Payable	.4	.2
	6.9	11.8	5.4	10.6		All Other Current	10.1	10.5
	38.9	47.4	38.5	33.4		Total Current	42.6	46.5
	17.1	10.7	12.5	9.5		Long-Term Debt	14.4	13.0
	.0	.3	.8	.7		Deferred Taxes	.6	.4
	6.8	2.0	4.0	5.1		All Other Non-Current	4.6	5.0
	37.3	39.7	44.3	51.3		Net Worth	37.8	35.1
	100.0	100.0	100.0	100.0		Total Liabilities & Net Worth	100.0	100.0
						INCOME DATA		
	100.0	100.0	100.0	100.0		Net Sales	100.0	100.0
	29.4	27.6	20.4	23.2		Gross Profit	26.7	25.6
	26.8	24.3	14.8	17.5		Operating Expenses	20.3	21.0
	2.6	3.2	5.6	5.7		Operating Profit	6.4	4.6
	-.2	.8	.8	.2		All Other Expenses (net)	.9	1.0
	2.8	2.5	4.8	5.5		Profit Before Taxes	5.5	3.6
						RATIOS		
	3.2	2.9	2.3	3.0		Current	2.4	2.5
	1.4	1.5	1.8	1.6			1.7	1.6
	1.1	1.1	1.4	1.4			1.2	1.1
	1.8	1.6	1.2	1.2		Quick	1.4	1.3
	.7	.8	.8	.8			.9	.8
	.5	.4	.6	.6			.6	.5
	29 12.6	31 11.6	42 8.7	37 9.9		Sales/Receivables	34 10.8	33 11.1
	48 7.5	40 9.1	47 7.8	43 8.5			44 8.2	42 8.8
	54 6.7	54 6.8	56 6.5	51 7.2			58 6.3	52 7.0
	19 18.7	40 9.2	44 8.3	36 10.2		Cost of Sales/Inventory	35 10.6	38 9.5
	60 6.0	69 5.3	75 4.9	75 4.9			62 5.8	65 5.6
	94 3.9	98 3.7	137 2.7	83 4.4			89 4.1	99 3.7
	27 13.6	17 21.5	18 20.8	20 18.6		Cost of Sales/Payables	18 20.2	18 20.8
	40 9.1	28 13.1	25 14.5	30 12.0			30 12.1	31 11.7
	52 7.0	58 6.2	38 9.6	39 9.2			46 8.0	49 7.4
	4.0	4.9	4.0	4.4		Sales/Working Capital	5.1	5.0
	12.2	8.5	7.0	9.3			7.9	9.1
	125.6	35.9	14.7	10.8			22.9	37.7
	5.5	11.1	17.8	12.9		EBIT/Interest	11.0	9.1
	(18) 2.4	(43) 3.4	(36) 5.7	12.4			(167) 3.7	(172) 2.4
	.3	1.5	1.9	3.1			1.8	.9
		6.5	18.1			Net Profit + Depr., Dep., Amort./Cur. Mat. L/T/D	6.6	3.2
		(14) 3.1	(11) 3.7				(60) 2.1	(47) 2.1
		1.3	1.5				1.3	.8
	.2	.2	.3	.3		Fixed/Worth	.3	.2
	.6	.5	.5	.5			.5	.6
	.9	1.6	1.0	1.0			1.5	1.9
	.6	.5	.7	.4		Debt/Worth	.6	.7
	1.7	1.5	1.3	1.3			1.3	1.8
	5.7	14.4	3.1	1.7			5.7	7.3
	59.2	31.4	41.2	31.4		% Profit Before Taxes/Tangible Net Worth	46.6	42.2
	(21) 8.3	(41) 20.6	(35) 20.3	20.7			(162) 20.6	(162) 19.6
	1.0	2.8	7.3	10.0			8.2	2.8
	8.7	11.8	15.1	15.0		% Profit Before Taxes/Total Assets	16.6	15.2
	3.4	6.5	8.3	9.7			8.0	4.5
	-1.6	.1	1.7	5.7			2.0	-.1
	22.4	40.0	16.1	18.9		Sales/Net Fixed Assets	30.8	37.7
	8.2	14.3	8.6	6.3			10.6	13.0
	3.2	8.0	5.9	4.1			4.7	6.2
	2.7	2.9	2.7	2.1		Sales/Total Assets	2.8	3.0
	1.9	2.0	1.8	2.0			2.1	2.2
	1.3	1.6	1.5	1.3			1.6	1.7
	1.7	1.1	.8	1.0		% Depr., Dep., Amort./Sales	.9	.8
	(20) 2.5	(42) 2.0	(36) 1.5	1.6			(162) 1.7	(160) 1.5
	3.2	2.7	2.7	4.1			3.2	2.8
	2.7	2.8				% Officers', Directors' Owners' Comp/Sales	2.1	2.1
	(14) 7.5	(19) 5.1					(55) 4.9	(61) 3.9
	11.0	8.7					7.5	8.0
6306M	55561M	604691M	1813595M	5630499M	222691M	Net Sales ($)	8325512M	7328735M
1320M	28821M	256352M	862257M	749288M	190270M	Total Assets ($)	3286362M	3467814M

Comparative Historical Data / Current Data Sorted by Sales

	4/1/08-3/31/09 ALL	4/1/09-3/31/10 ALL	4/1/10-3/31/11 ALL	0-1MM	30 (4/1-9/30/10) 1-3MM	3-5MM	96 (10/1/10-3/31/11) 5-10MM	10-25MM	25MM & OVER
Type of Statement									
Unqualified	25	24	17				1	4	12
Reviewed	21	33	35	1	3	2	8	12	9
Compiled	19	14	8	1	1	2	1	3	
Tax Returns	8	9	12	2	5	1	1	2	1
Other	44	52	54	1	9	7	5	10	22
NUMBER OF STATEMENTS	117	132	126	5	18	12	16	31	44
	%	%	%	%	%	%	%	%	%
ASSETS									
Cash & Equivalents	7.4	8.0	8.7		13.0	2.7	11.1	10.6	4.2
Trade Receivables (net)	25.5	24.5	26.4		26.5	22.9	27.5	28.8	26.5
Inventory	32.9	31.3	30.3		22.2	36.9	29.9	32.1	30.9
All Other Current	2.0	3.3	2.6		2.0	1.4	1.8	1.0	4.9
Total Current	67.7	67.0	68.1		63.8	63.9	70.3	72.5	66.6
Fixed Assets (net)	24.4	25.4	22.9		25.7	20.5	20.2	21.1	25.6
Intangibles (net)	3.7	3.4	2.8		2.4	5.2	4.3	1.8	2.9
All Other Non-Current	4.2	4.2	6.1		8.1	10.3	5.2	4.6	4.9
Total	100.0	100.0	100.0		100.0	100.0	100.0	100.0	100.0
LIABILITIES									
Notes Payable-Short Term	15.1	13.8	13.0		12.3	15.7	16.1	8.7	15.4
Cur. Mat.-L.T.D.	2.5	4.1	3.0		4.6	3.5	3.8	3.6	1.8
Trade Payables	15.6	15.4	16.6		21.1	15.5	14.8	17.7	15.2
Income Taxes Payable	.5	.3	.2		.1	.0	.2	.2	.5
All Other Current	10.1	6.7	8.7		6.0	9.2	16.4	8.4	7.8
Total Current	43.8	40.3	41.5		44.1	43.9	51.3	38.6	40.7
Long-Term Debt	13.1	13.6	12.8		23.7	4.2	12.2	12.0	10.9
Deferred Taxes	.7	.4	.4		.0	.4	.2	.2	.8
All Other Non-Current	4.1	8.0	4.1		6.5	6.1	5.0	.5	4.6
Net Worth	38.3	37.7	41.3		25.8	45.5	31.4	48.7	43.0
Total Liabilities & Net Worth	100.0	100.0	100.0		100.0	100.0	100.0	100.0	100.0
INCOME DATA									
Net Sales	100.0	100.0	100.0		100.0	100.0	100.0	100.0	100.0
Gross Profit	24.5	23.8	26.0		30.3	37.2	24.7	27.2	19.8
Operating Expenses	20.0	22.5	22.1		27.4	34.8	22.5	22.0	15.0
Operating Profit	4.6	1.3	3.9		2.9	2.4	2.2	5.3	4.8
All Other Expenses (net)	.9	1.1	.6		-.2	.3	1.5	.4	.7
Profit Before Taxes	3.6	.2	3.3		3.1	2.1	.7	4.8	4.1
RATIOS									
Current	2.8	2.6	2.9		2.6	1.7	3.0	4.3	2.2
	1.7	1.8	1.6		1.3	1.4	1.8	1.8	1.6
	1.1	1.2	1.3		1.0	1.2	1.0	1.3	1.4
Quick	1.4	1.3	1.3		1.6	1.1	1.6	2.1	1.1
	.7	.8	.8		.8	.5	.9	1.1	.8
	.4	.5	.5		.5	.3	.4	.6	.6
Sales/Receivables	28 12.9	32 11.3	34 10.8		27 13.5	30 12.2	32 11.5	35 10.5	38 9.7
	39 9.3	43 8.6	43 8.5		42 8.6	41 9.0	42 8.7	43 8.5	44 8.3
	48 7.5	57 6.4	54 6.8		52 7.0	55 6.6	71 5.2	54 6.7	50 7.3
Cost of Sales/Inventory	43 8.4	43 8.4	35 10.3		6 60.4	67 5.5	43 8.5	39 9.4	37 9.9
	64 5.7	75 4.9	65 5.6		51 7.2	92 4.0	64 5.7	75 4.9	68 5.4
	108 3.4	113 3.2	111 3.3		66 5.6	281 1.3	97 3.8	113 3.2	112 3.3
Cost of Sales/Payables	17 22.0	17 21.1	18 19.9		26 14.1	22 16.6	19 19.2	15 24.9	19 19.6
	28 13.2	30 12.3	31 11.7		44 8.3	35 10.4	28 12.9	24 15.2	29 12.7
	43 8.5	47 7.8	49 7.4		58 6.3	77 4.7	41 9.0	55 6.6	38 9.6
Sales/Working Capital	4.5	4.0	4.4		4.3	4.6	3.7	4.9	4.4
	10.0	6.7	8.6		19.7	11.8	8.5	6.0	8.9
	34.3	27.5	19.6		160.7	18.0	NM	19.0	17.5
EBIT/Interest	10.6	8.6	12.3		6.7	12.1	11.6	21.7	15.0
	(110) 3.3	(123) 1.6	(112) 4.0		(14) 2.0	(10) 2.9	2.4	(26) 6.6	5.8
	1.0	-1.3	1.7		-.9	.3	-.2	2.7	2.3
Net Profit + Depr., Dep., Amort./Cur. Mat. L/T/D	5.4	3.6	11.4						21.7
	(41) 2.6	(38) 1.5	(37) 3.2					(21)	4.6
	.9	.2	1.6						2.4
Fixed/Worth	.3	.3	.2		.2	.1	.2	.2	.3
	.8	.6	.5		.8	.6	.5	.4	.6
	1.7	1.4	1.1		NM	.8	-7.5	.7	1.1
Debt/Worth	.6	.6	.6		.7	.6	.5	.3	.7
	1.8	1.7	1.5		3.2	1.6	1.3	1.3	1.5
	6.0	3.9	4.1		NM	3.3	-17.3	2.8	3.0
% Profit Before Taxes/Tangible Net Worth	32.6	21.9	35.5		170.7	33.1	22.7	35.6	33.0
	(103) 15.4	(115) 6.1	(112) 19.4		(14) 18.2	(11) 6.0	(11) 9.2	(29) 24.4	(42) 20.5
	3.0	-10.9	5.4		3.5	.1	.8	10.7	8.0
% Profit Before Taxes/Total Assets	13.3	8.5	12.7		11.5	8.8	9.5	15.3	15.0
	5.2	1.5	6.5		2.6	4.0	2.1	10.2	8.4
	.6	-7.2	1.2		-8.5	.6	-3.9	1.5	2.6
Sales/Net Fixed Assets	20.2	17.9	23.7		40.5	16.5	29.3	27.4	17.0
	11.2	8.4	10.4		15.7	10.6	10.5	14.7	8.8
	5.3	4.4	5.2		3.2	6.2	8.0	6.7	5.2
Sales/Total Assets	3.1	2.4	2.8		3.4	2.5	2.6	3.0	2.9
	2.3	1.8	2.0		2.1	1.9	2.0	2.2	1.9
	1.6	1.4	1.5		1.3	1.3	1.3	1.7	1.6
% Depr., Dep., Amort./Sales	1.0	1.5	1.1		1.1	1.8	1.1	.9	1.1
	(107) 1.8	(113) 2.4	(112) 2.0		(13) 1.8	(11) 2.5	(15) 2.3	(28) 1.5	(42) 1.6
	2.6	4.0	2.9		2.9	4.3	3.3	2.3	3.0
% Officers', Directors' Owners' Comp/Sales	2.4	2.0	2.8		2.8				2.9
	(39) 4.6	(42) 3.0	(43) 5.3		(11) 8.3			(13) 5.1	
	7.8	7.9	8.3		11.2				8.7
Net Sales ($)	4628051M	4196284M	8333343M	3368M	35026M	47639M	129897M	494256M	7623157M
Total Assets ($)	2157112M	2581220M	2088308M	3270M	17293M	27759M	72331M	238835M	1728820M

M = $ thousand   MM = $ million
See Pages 9 through 22 for Explanation of Ratios and Data

Current Data Sorted by Assets   Comparative Historical Data

	0-500M	500M-2MM	2-10MM	10-50MM	50-100MM	100-250MM		4/1/06-3/31/07 ALL	4/1/07-3/31/08 ALL
Type of Statement									
Unqualified		1	4	22	2	3		58	41
Reviewed	2	31	92	29	2			157	131
Compiled	18	79	74	4				201	180
Tax Returns	55	113	51	1				197	169
Other	24	82	128	57	6	4		244	259
		166 (4/1-9/30/10)		718 (10/1/10-3/31/11)					
NUMBER OF STATEMENTS	99	306	349	113	10	7		857	780
ASSETS	%	%	%	%	%	%		%	%
Cash & Equivalents	18.4	10.5	9.0	8.7	7.6			8.8	9.8
Trade Receivables (net)	26.8	28.7	24.5	20.6	20.6			25.3	24.6
Inventory	9.1	15.0	20.5	24.2	29.7			18.1	18.1
All Other Current	1.8	1.3	1.7	3.0	7.2			2.0	1.8
Total Current	56.1	55.5	55.7	56.5	65.2			54.3	54.4
Fixed Assets (net)	34.2	35.2	36.7	32.4	23.9			36.6	37.2
Intangibles (net)	1.5	2.9	3.2	7.0	8.2			3.5	3.0
All Other Non-Current	8.2	6.4	4.5	4.1	2.7			5.5	5.4
Total	100.0	100.0	100.0	100.0	100.0			100.0	100.0
LIABILITIES									
Notes Payable-Short Term	16.2	9.6	7.3	7.4	5.6			9.5	8.1
Cur. Mat.-L.T.D.	9.2	7.3	6.4	5.0	2.4			6.5	6.3
Trade Payables	10.3	11.1	10.4	11.4	10.3			12.2	11.2
Income Taxes Payable	.0	.1	.2	.1	.0			.2	.3
All Other Current	5.9	5.8	6.6	8.0	8.5			7.5	7.6
Total Current	41.6	33.9	30.9	31.9	26.8			35.9	33.4
Long-Term Debt	46.6	24.6	20.7	17.4	9.8			25.6	26.2
Deferred Taxes	.4	.3	.8	.9	1.2			.4	.4
All Other Non-Current	7.8	6.4	4.7	6.1	8.2			5.9	5.5
Net Worth	3.5	34.9	42.9	43.7	54.1			32.2	34.4
Total Liabilities & Net Worth	100.0	100.0	100.0	100.0	100.0			100.0	100.0
INCOME DATA									
Net Sales	100.0	100.0	100.0	100.0	100.0			100.0	100.0
Gross Profit	57.8	40.3	32.6	23.2	23.6			35.4	35.7
Operating Expenses	48.7	35.0	25.4	15.4	11.9			28.2	28.2
Operating Profit	9.1	5.3	7.1	7.7	11.7			7.2	7.6
All Other Expenses (net)	1.4	1.2	1.3	1.0	2.6			1.6	1.5
Profit Before Taxes	7.7	4.1	5.8	6.7	9.1			5.6	6.0
RATIOS									
Current	4.4	3.4	3.2	2.9	8.9			2.6	2.9
	1.4	1.7	1.8	1.7	2.2			1.6	1.7
	.8	1.0	1.2	1.2	1.1			1.1	1.1
Quick	4.1	2.8	2.1	1.6	3.2			1.7	2.0
	1.1	1.1	1.1	.8	1.2			1.0	1.0
	.5	.6	.7	.6	.6			.6	.6
Sales/Receivables	8 47.6	33 11.1	34 10.7	37 10.0	32 11.4			29 12.6	30 12.0
	37 9.9	45 8.0	49 7.4	51 7.2	47 7.7			44 8.4	43 8.4
	52 7.0	60 6.1	62 5.9	65 5.6	60 6.1			56 6.5	56 6.5
Cost of Sales/Inventory	0 UND	5 68.2	25 14.3	41 9.0	47 7.8			11 34.1	14 26.3
	3 121.6	28 13.0	55 6.6	64 5.7	72 5.1			36 10.1	40 9.1
	50 7.3	69 5.3	98 3.7	102 3.6	127 2.9			70 5.2	77 4.7
Cost of Sales/Payables	0 UND	12 30.5	15 23.8	19 19.2	19 19.3			13 25.9	14 25.9
	19 19.2	24 15.1	28 13.1	29 12.5	28 13.1			25 14.7	26 14.2
	42 8.8	40 9.0	41 8.9	41 9.0	37 9.7			43 8.6	41 8.9
Sales/Working Capital	5.4	5.2	4.3	3.5	2.0			5.8	5.4
	20.1	10.0	8.1	7.2	5.0			11.8	10.0
	-47.2	213.4	25.0	16.6	32.5			68.6	45.6
EBIT/Interest	15.0	8.9	13.6	24.7	999.8			9.9	9.6
	(78) 4.7	(276) 3.8	(325) 4.3	(106) 5.6	17.2			(793) 3.9	(710) 4.2
	1.3	1.1	1.7	2.5	3.1			1.7	1.6
Net Profit + Depr., Dep., Amort./Cur. Mat. L/T/D		3.0	3.9	8.3				4.5	5.1
		(33) 1.6	(72) 2.1	(33) 2.2				(181) 2.3	(174) 2.5
		.9	1.3	1.4				1.2	1.4
Fixed/Worth	.3	.5	.4	.4	.1			.5	.5
	1.5	1.1	.9	.9	.7			1.1	1.1
	-1.9	3.1	2.0	1.7	NM			3.1	2.8
Debt/Worth	.6	.7	.5	.7	.1			.9	.8
	2.5	1.9	1.4	1.3	1.1			1.9	2.0
	-5.8	7.1	3.4	3.3	NM			6.3	5.0
% Profit Before Taxes/Tangible Net Worth	89.3	57.0	41.2	29.3				60.5	57.3
	(67) 46.1	(256) 20.9	(318) 18.8	(97) 18.3				(731) 27.6	(676) 28.6
	9.2	2.3	7.1	11.3				7.8	8.6
% Profit Before Taxes/Total Assets	35.2	18.4	14.1	15.0	26.3			18.7	21.0
	14.4	6.5	7.3	8.1	12.4			8.1	9.7
	.6	.3	2.2	3.7	6.2			2.5	2.1
Sales/Net Fixed Assets	26.3	15.7	10.4	8.3	21.7			12.8	11.4
	10.4	6.9	5.2	4.9	7.0			6.1	5.8
	5.4	3.8	3.1	3.0	3.3			3.6	3.5
Sales/Total Assets	4.6	3.0	2.3	1.9	2.2			2.8	2.7
	2.7	2.2	1.8	1.5	1.7			2.0	2.0
	1.9	1.6	1.3	1.1	1.1			1.5	1.5
% Depr., Dep., Amort./Sales	1.5	2.1	2.4	2.2	1.2			2.1	2.1
	(66) 3.5	(247) 4.0	(321) 4.1	(108) 4.1	3.7			(758) 3.8	(695) 3.8
	5.8	7.5	6.5	6.0	5.5			5.9	6.3
% Officers', Directors' Owners' Comp/Sales	5.2	3.6	2.2	1.3				2.7	2.8
	(66) 9.2	(202) 6.0	(169) 3.9	(26) 3.0				(452) 4.9	(434) 4.8
	14.4	10.6	7.0	4.6				8.7	8.8
Net Sales ($)	93001M	829505M	2747332M	3708600M	1278825M	1540914M		11007224M	9680374M
Total Assets ($)	27781M	348337M	1536527M	2266362M	785402M	1201720M		5603292M	4901691M

M = $ thousand   MM = $ million
See Pages 9 through 22 for Explanation of Ratios and Data

Comparative Historical Data   Current Data Sorted by Sales

Hist 1	Hist 2	Hist 3	Type of Statement	0-1MM	1-3MM	3-5MM	5-10MM	10-25MM	25MM & OVER
30	38	32	Unqualified	2	26	2	3	11	16
117	141	156	Reviewed			20	46	47	15
149	155	175	Compiled	17	56	39	45	17	1
160	170	220	Tax Returns	41	90	45	32	11	1
200	245	301	Other	29	60	57	61	55	39
4/1/08-3/31/09 ALL	4/1/09-3/31/10 ALL	4/1/10-3/31/11 ALL		166 (4/1-9/30/10)			718 (10/1/10-3/31/11)		
656	749	884	NUMBER OF STATEMENTS	89	232	163	187	141	72
%	%	%	ASSETS	%	%	%	%	%	%
9.8	10.3	10.5	Cash & Equivalents	15.9	10.9	9.8	9.4	10.4	7.0
23.2	21.9	25.6	Trade Receivables (net)	19.6	28.7	24.6	27.1	24.5	23.5
17.4	18.3	17.8	Inventory	10.6	14.0	18.0	20.4	21.5	25.1
1.9	2.1	1.8	All Other Current	1.5	1.2	1.4	2.0	2.3	3.6
52.3	52.6	55.7	Total Current	47.6	54.8	53.8	58.8	58.6	59.3
39.2	38.0	35.2	Fixed Assets (net)	38.0	36.1	38.1	33.7	32.7	31.1
3.2	3.5	3.6	Intangibles (net)	4.6	2.7	2.9	2.9	4.5	6.4
5.3	5.9	5.5	All Other Non-Current	9.7	6.3	5.2	4.6	4.1	3.3
100.0	100.0	100.0	Total	100.0	100.0	100.0	100.0	100.0	100.0
			LIABILITIES						
9.8	10.0	9.1	Notes Payable-Short Term	14.6	10.0	8.7	8.0	6.6	8.3
6.4	6.3	6.8	Cur. Mat.-L.T.D.	6.8	7.6	8.5	6.1	5.2	4.6
10.3	10.1	10.8	Trade Payables	7.6	10.4	10.0	11.5	11.5	14.2
.2	.2	.1	Income Taxes Payable	.0	.1	.2	.3	.1	.1
6.6	7.7	6.5	All Other Current	6.1	5.7	4.9	7.0	8.1	8.3
33.3	34.2	33.3	Total Current	35.1	33.8	32.3	32.8	31.6	35.6
26.8	26.0	24.4	Long-Term Debt	45.9	26.3	28.0	19.0	15.5	15.0
.5	.6	.6	Deferred Taxes	.3	.4	.4	.7	.9	.7
5.5	7.0	5.8	All Other Non-Current	9.2	5.9	5.6	5.1	3.6	8.3
33.9	32.3	35.9	Net Worth	9.4	33.5	33.6	42.4	48.3	40.4
100.0	100.0	100.0	Total Liabilities & Net Worth	100.0	100.0	100.0	100.0	100.0	100.0
			INCOME DATA						
100.0	100.0	100.0	Net Sales	100.0	100.0	100.0	100.0	100.0	100.0
35.1	34.7	36.7	Gross Profit	57.4	41.9	37.3	31.0	29.6	21.5
28.9	31.6	29.9	Operating Expenses	49.7	36.3	30.4	24.7	21.4	13.7
6.2	3.0	6.8	Operating Profit	7.7	5.7	6.9	6.3	8.2	7.8
1.2	1.5	1.3	All Other Expenses (net)	1.8	1.5	1.3	1.0	1.0	1.0
5.0	1.5	5.6	Profit Before Taxes	5.9	4.2	5.5	5.4	7.2	6.8
			RATIOS						
3.2	3.2	3.3	Current	4.4	3.5	2.9	3.3	3.3	2.7
1.7	1.6	1.7		1.4	1.8	1.6	1.9	1.9	1.6
1.1	1.0	1.1		.8	1.0	1.1	1.3	1.3	1.2
2.2	2.1	2.2	Quick	4.1	2.9	1.9	2.3	1.9	1.4
1.0	1.0	1.1		1.0	1.1	1.1	1.1	1.2	.8
.5	.5	.6		.4	.7	.6	.6	.6	.6
27 13.5	29 12.6	33 11.2	Sales/Receivables	13 28.3	35 10.4	31 11.9	34 10.8	33 11.1	32 11.6
40 9.1	43 8.5	47 7.8		40 9.1	46 7.9	47 7.7	47 7.8	47 7.8	48 7.7
53 6.8	58 6.2	61 6.0		63 5.8	60 6.1	63 5.8	62 5.9	61 6.0	57 6.5
10 38.1	14 25.5	13 28.1	Cost of Sales/Inventory	0 UND	5 70.1	7 48.8	20 17.9	27 13.7	40 9.2
36 10.0	45 8.0	43 8.4		14 25.3	30 12.2	44 8.3	46 7.9	53 6.9	55 6.7
70 5.2	91 4.0	84 4.3		101 3.6	76 4.8	83 4.4	86 4.2	93 3.9	90 4.0
11 32.1	13 28.7	13 27.5	Cost of Sales/Payables	2 161.5	12 29.7	12 31.0	14 26.8	17 21.5	22 17.0
23 16.1	23 15.9	27 13.6		27 13.5	24 15.4	26 13.9	27 13.6	27 13.4	33 11.0
39 9.3	42 8.8	41 9.0		48 7.6	41 8.9	39 9.3	41 9.0	41 9.0	41 9.0
5.5	4.5	4.7	Sales/Working Capital	4.2	5.0	4.9	4.4	4.2	4.7
11.4	9.6	9.1		15.7	9.3	9.9	7.9	8.2	8.9
87.1	160.3	42.3		-21.4	214.1	42.8	22.4	17.0	24.2
9.8	6.6	12.5	EBIT/Interest	11.7	8.2	8.3	19.9	24.8	34.3
(595) 4.1	(686) 2.0	(802) 4.2		(70) 2.7	(208) 3.2	(149) 3.8	(176) 4.9	(129) 6.0	(70) 8.2
1.3	-.7	1.5		.5	.9	1.3	2.0	2.3	2.8
4.1	3.3	4.5	Net Profit + Depr., Dep., Amort./Cur. Mat. L/T/D		3.3	2.7	5.8	2.9	9.0
(114) 2.1	(151) 1.6	(151) 2.0			(25) 1.8	(24) 1.3	(40) 2.3	(36) 2.1	(23) 4.5
1.1	.4	1.2			.2	1.0	1.3	1.6	1.7
.5	.5	.4	Fixed/Worth	.6	.5	.5	.4	.4	.5
1.1	1.1	1.0		2.0	1.0	1.2	.8	.8	.9
2.8	3.5	2.6		-12.3	3.7	3.4	2.4	1.4	1.8
.7	.7	.6	Debt/Worth	.9	.6	.7	.5	.5	.7
1.7	1.9	1.6		2.8	1.8	1.8	1.2	1.2	1.5
5.8	7.4	5.4		-21.7	7.4	6.3	4.6	2.8	3.6
55.8	35.5	47.4	% Profit Before Taxes/Tangible Net Worth	89.1	47.1	49.1	42.2	36.8	53.7
(558) 26.7	(618) 8.9	(750) 20.6		(64) 30.5	(190) 21.0	(140) 21.8	(164) 16.6	(132) 21.5	(60) 23.3
6.0	-7.0	5.8		-1.8	2.3	4.4	7.6	10.7	14.1
19.8	12.4	18.3	% Profit Before Taxes/Total Assets	29.2	18.3	16.4	15.2	18.6	18.0
9.2	3.0	7.5		6.5	6.2	7.4	7.4	8.7	9.7
1.1	-4.6	1.3		-3.0	.0	1.3	1.7	4.0	4.7
12.0	10.4	12.7	Sales/Net Fixed Assets	16.8	15.2	12.2	14.1	10.8	9.2
5.6	4.9	6.1		5.1	6.3	5.6	6.6	6.0	6.6
3.2	2.8	3.3		2.2	3.4	3.1	3.7	3.3	3.7
2.8	2.4	2.6	Sales/Total Assets	2.7	2.9	2.7	2.6	2.5	2.4
2.0	1.7	1.9		1.6	2.1	2.0	2.0	1.7	1.8
1.5	1.2	1.4		1.1	1.5	1.4	1.5	1.4	1.4
2.0	2.3	2.2	% Depr., Dep., Amort./Sales	2.1	2.2	2.4	2.1	2.3	2.0
(562) 3.7	(682) 4.5	(756) 4.0		(65) 5.1	(188) 4.6	(143) 4.2	(158) 3.7	(136) 3.8	(66) 3.7
6.2	7.6	6.4		8.9	8.3	6.4	6.1	5.9	4.9
2.5	2.7	2.6	% Officers', Directors' Owners' Comp/Sales	6.4	4.0	2.9	2.2	1.8	.8
(359) 4.8	(405) 5.4	(463) 5.1		(49) 10.5	(153) 6.4	(91) 4.9	(100) 3.9	(55) 3.2	(15) 2.2
7.8	9.2	9.4		15.1	10.9	8.8	7.1	5.7	4.0
7702159M	8498431M	10198177M	Net Sales ($)	51664M	451748M	632662M	1310513M	2192662M	5558928M
4387194M	5087063M	6166129M	Total Assets ($)	57514M	248539M	376108M	760440M	1362981M	3360547M

© RMA 2011

M = $ thousand   MM = $ million

See Pages 9 through 22 for Explanation of Ratios and Data

Current Data Sorted by Assets | Comparative Historical Data

						Type of Statement		
		3		7	3	Unqualified	18	16
	7	38		14		Reviewed	67	60
3	21	21				Compiled	40	36
3	8	9				Tax Returns	14	18
4	8	25		25	2	Other	61	55
	48 (4/1-9/30/10)		153 (10/1/10-3/31/11)				4/1/06-3/31/07	4/1/07-3/31/08
0-500M	500M-2MM	2-10MM	10-50MM	50-100MM	100-250MM		ALL	ALL
10	44	96	46	3	2	NUMBER OF STATEMENTS	200	185
%	%	%	%	%	%	ASSETS	%	%
16.1	9.6	7.0	5.0			Cash & Equivalents	6.7	7.5
24.5	28.6	26.0	20.3			Trade Receivables (net)	25.0	22.8
12.8	27.0	24.3	27.2			Inventory	22.5	23.1
.3	.5	1.0	1.8			All Other Current	1.2	1.4
53.7	65.7	58.2	54.3			Total Current	55.4	54.8
39.0	27.6	32.1	36.3			Fixed Assets (net)	36.8	36.9
1.4	2.3	3.9	4.4			Intangibles (net)	2.7	2.8
5.9	4.3	5.8	5.0			All Other Non-Current	5.1	5.6
100.0	100.0	100.0	100.0			Total	100.0	100.0
						LIABILITIES		
9.9	7.9	7.8	13.9			Notes Payable-Short Term	9.9	9.0
16.2	6.8	4.6	5.1			Cur. Mat.-L.T.D.	7.5	6.2
12.8	12.5	14.3	12.1			Trade Payables	13.0	12.3
.0	.4	.3	.1			Income Taxes Payable	.2	.1
12.3	6.3	7.3	6.9			All Other Current	6.3	6.3
51.3	33.9	34.3	38.1			Total Current	37.0	33.9
56.1	18.7	18.1	16.4			Long-Term Debt	21.9	23.3
.0	.4	.7	1.4			Deferred Taxes	.7	1.0
8.2	7.4	3.4	8.3			All Other Non-Current	4.5	4.7
-15.7	39.6	43.6	35.9			Net Worth	35.8	37.1
100.0	100.0	100.0	100.0			Total Liabilities & Net Worth	100.0	100.0
						INCOME DATA		
100.0	100.0	100.0	100.0			Net Sales	100.0	100.0
34.8	36.2	26.2	23.1			Gross Profit	27.2	28.3
36.1	31.6	20.9	16.3			Operating Expenses	22.0	23.3
-1.2	4.5	5.3	6.8			Operating Profit	5.2	5.0
1.1	.9	1.1	1.6			All Other Expenses (net)	1.6	1.4
-2.3	3.6	4.2	5.2			Profit Before Taxes	3.6	3.6
						RATIOS		
1.9	3.0	2.4	2.8			Current	2.2	2.5
1.0	1.9	1.6	1.3				1.5	1.6
.6	1.3	1.3	1.1				1.0	1.1
1.6	2.0	1.5	1.3			Quick	1.3	1.6
.8	1.0	.9	.6				.8	.9
.4	.6	.6	.4				.5	.5
10 38.2	36 10.2	38 9.5	34 10.7			Sales/Receivables	35 10.4	33 11.0
33 11.0	53 6.9	48 7.6	48 7.7				43 8.4	44 8.4
42 8.6	72 5.1	61 5.1	61 6.0				56 6.5	53 6.9
0 UND	41 9.0	33 11.2	46 7.9			Cost of Sales/Inventory	31 11.6	31 11.9
13 29.0	60 6.1	55 6.7	71 5.1				55 6.7	54 6.7
51 7.1	99 3.7	97 3.8	117 3.1				80 4.5	93 3.9
5 77.6	17 22.0	21 17.5	21 17.6			Cost of Sales/Payables	15 23.9	16 23.0
17 22.1	31 12.0	32 11.3	35 10.4				27 13.7	27 13.6
29 12.5	41 8.8	47 7.8	47 7.7				42 8.8	40 9.2
15.0	4.7	4.6	5.5			Sales/Working Capital	5.9	5.5
160.6	6.4	10.0	11.7				11.7	10.0
-13.5	16.1	16.5	39.8				557.2	36.3
	9.2	18.5	7.9			EBIT/Interest	6.1	6.1
	(40) 3.3	4.6	(42) 3.6				(178) 2.7	(171) 2.6
	-.2	1.7	1.6				1.5	1.0
	2.2	3.0	6.0			Net Profit + Depr., Dep., Amort./Cur. Mat. L/T/D	4.4	4.0
	(11) 1.3	(33) 1.8	(18) 2.8				(65) 1.9	(63) 2.3
	.7	1.1	1.5				1.2	1.4
1.2	.3	.4	.7			Fixed/Worth	.5	.6
2.4	.6	.8	1.3				1.1	1.0
-.9	1.4	1.6	2.8				2.6	2.2
3.1	.7	.8	1.3			Debt/Worth	.8	.8
NM	1.5	1.2	2.0				1.8	1.7
-2.3	2.7	3.3	5.4				4.9	4.5
	51.6	43.8	40.5			% Profit Before Taxes/Tangible Net Worth	33.2	35.5
	(41) 17.3	(92) 16.8	(40) 19.8				(169) 16.4	(161) 14.6
	-2.2	4.7	7.4				5.6	.9
23.0	19.4	14.1	11.5			% Profit Before Taxes/Total Assets	12.5	14.6
-2.3	6.7	5.1	7.8				5.4	6.1
-29.8	-1.4	1.3	2.6				1.3	.0
28.9	20.1	11.8	7.6			Sales/Net Fixed Assets	12.7	10.7
9.6	8.5	6.2	4.2				5.3	5.6
4.7	4.3	4.0	3.0				3.1	3.2
5.8	2.7	2.5	1.9			Sales/Total Assets	2.7	2.6
3.4	2.1	1.9	1.6				1.8	1.9
2.3	1.6	1.4	1.4				1.4	1.3
	2.2	2.0	2.5			% Depr., Dep., Amort./Sales	2.0	1.7
	(36) 4.0	(88) 4.2	4.0				(183) 4.4	(174) 3.8
	7.3	6.4	6.1				6.2	6.4
	2.2	1.8	1.4			% Officers', Directors' Owners' Comp/Sales	2.0	2.1
	(23) 3.8	(49) 3.7	(13) 1.6				(87) 3.5	(91) 3.9
	10.4	6.2	3.7				6.4	7.0
11861M	117895M	882176M	1316902M	355878M	479076M	Net Sales ($)	2710579M	2565289M
3199M	54266M	447257M	803236M	205834M	342637M	Total Assets ($)	1609167M	1510989M

M = $ thousand   MM = $ million
See Pages 9 through 22 for Explanation of Ratios and Data

Comparative Historical Data

Current Data Sorted by Sales

					Type of Statement						
13		14		13	Unqualified		6	7	2 21	3 20	8 5
56		56		59	Reviewed						
37		35		45	Compiled	4	14	8	14	5	
16		21		20	Tax Returns	2	7	6	5		
55		48		64	Other	2	9	5	8	21	19
4/1/08- 3/31/09 ALL		4/1/09- 3/31/10 ALL		4/1/10- 3/31/11 ALL			48 (4/1-9/30/10)		153 (10/1/10-3/31/11)		
						0-1MM	1-3MM	3-5MM	5-10MM	10-25MM	25MM & OVER
177		174		201	NUMBER OF STATEMENTS	8	36	26	50	49	32
%		%		%	**ASSETS**	%	%	%	%	%	%
6.4		7.7		7.6	Cash & Equivalents		11.5	7.4	8.1	7.3	3.8
21.5		20.5		25.2	Trade Receivables (net)		26.2	23.7	24.3	26.2	25.6
24.6		24.1		25.0	Inventory		23.6	22.2	24.3	26.1	27.1
1.3		1.8		1.0	All Other Current		.5	.6	1.2	1.5	1.2
53.9		54.2		58.7	Total Current		61.8	53.9	57.9	61.0	57.7
36.6		37.1		32.5	Fixed Assets (net)		29.0	34.0	33.4	32.7	32.0
4.6		3.2		3.5	Intangibles (net)		4.1	6.0	2.6	2.1	5.1
4.9		5.5		5.3	All Other Non-Current		5.1	6.1	6.2	4.1	5.2
100.0		100.0		100.0	Total		100.0	100.0	100.0	100.0	100.0
					LIABILITIES						
12.8		10.2		9.2	Notes Payable-Short Term		9.9	6.1	6.7	10.3	13.6
6.7		7.4		5.8	Cur. Mat.-L.T.D.		7.2	5.6	5.3	4.5	4.9
11.6		10.8		13.3	Trade Payables		11.3	10.4	12.9	15.1	16.0
.2		.2		.2	Income Taxes Payable		.4	.2	.3	.1	.2
5.5		6.1		7.3	All Other Current		5.6	7.6	8.5	6.3	7.8
36.7		34.8		35.9	Total Current		34.4	29.9	33.6	36.4	42.3
25.0		22.3		19.6	Long-Term Debt		24.7	25.0	19.6	15.0	13.7
.7		.8		.7	Deferred Taxes		.5	1.0	.4	.8	1.2
5.0		8.4		5.7	All Other Non-Current		4.8	1.9	2.7	6.5	7.7
32.6		33.7		38.1	Net Worth		35.6	42.2	43.7	41.4	35.1
100.0		100.0		100.0	Total Liabilties & Net Worth		100.0	100.0	100.0	100.0	100.0
					INCOME DATA						
100.0		100.0		100.0	Net Sales		100.0	100.0	100.0	100.0	100.0
26.4		28.0		28.0	Gross Profit		34.7	32.7	25.6	24.1	23.1
22.8		26.3		22.8	Operating Expenses		29.7	27.1	21.4	17.4	16.6
3.6		1.8		5.2	Operating Profit		5.0	5.6	4.2	6.7	6.5
1.4		1.6		1.2	All Other Expenses (net)		1.0	2.0	.5	1.2	1.2
2.2		.2		4.0	Profit Before Taxes		4.0	3.6	3.7	5.4	5.2
					RATIOS						
2.5		2.6		2.6			3.0	2.7	2.5	2.6	1.7
1.6		1.6		1.6	Current		1.8	1.6	1.6	1.7	1.3
1.1		1.1		1.2			1.1	1.2	1.3	1.3	1.1
1.5		1.5		1.5			2.0	1.6	1.3	1.5	1.2
.8	(173)	.8		.9	Quick		1.0	1.0	.8	.9	.7
.5		.4		.5			.6	.6	.6	.5	.4

29	12.4	30	12.1	36	10.3	Sales/Receivables	35	10.3	38	9.7	29	12.4	38	9.7	37	10.0
40	9.1	44	8.3	49	7.5		46	7.9	54	6.7	45	8.1	49	7.4	49	7.5
52	7.1	59	6.2	61	6.0		68	5.4	72	5.0	59	6.2	59	6.2	63	5.8
33	11.2	42	8.7	35	10.5	Cost of Sales/Inventory	17	21.3	28	12.9	34	10.8	37	10.0	42	8.6
59	6.2	66	5.5	59	6.2		54	6.7	63	5.8	55	6.7	54	6.8	73	5.0
90	4.0	106	3.4	98	3.7		121	3.0	96	3.8	97	3.8	87	4.2	101	3.6
14	26.5	13	27.6	20	18.2	Cost of Sales/Payables	11	33.1	19	19.0	19	19.5	25	14.7	27	13.3
25	14.5	27	13.6	32	11.2		25	14.8	32	11.2	28	12.9	35	10.6	39	9.5
39	9.3	48	7.6	45	8.1		48	7.6	48	7.7	40	9.1	44	8.3	53	6.9

5.7		4.6		4.9	Sales/Working Capital		4.4	4.3	4.6	4.9	8.4
9.5		8.4		10.0			6.6	8.1	9.6	10.0	11.7
52.2		46.4		21.0			28.7	30.5	16.6	15.4	81.6
	5.6		3.6		11.5	EBIT/Interest		6.7	10.8	18.5	23.4	12.7
(167)	2.2	(162)	.7	(192)	3.8		(31)	3.3	2.8	3.5	(47) 6.3	(30) 5.8
	.4		-2.1		1.4			-1.0	.9	1.8	1.8	2.1
	4.2		3.1		3.9	Net Profit + Depr., Dep., Amort./Cur. Mat. L/T/D				2.1	5.5	8.5
(51)	1.9	(51)	1.3	(65)	1.8				(17) 1.3	(19) 2.4	(15) 4.5
	1.3		.5		1.2					.7	1.6	1.8
.6		.6		.5	Fixed/Worth		.3	.5	.4	.4	.6
1.2		1.2		.9			.7	.9	.7	.9	1.2
2.9		2.6		1.7			1.5	2.4	1.8	1.4	1.7
.8		.8		.8	Debt/Worth		.9	.7	.7	.9	1.3
1.8		1.8		1.5			1.6	1.7	1.3	1.4	2.2
6.0		6.2		3.7			4.8	5.3	3.2	3.5	4.0
	32.7		21.2		41.3	% Profit Before Taxes/Tangible Net Worth		60.5	37.7	35.2	45.2	49.0
(147)	11.1	(145)	1.3	(183)	17.4		(31)	3.5	(24) 12.8	(48) 15.2	(47) 22.3	(28) 24.5
	-2.6		-17.0		3.2			-16.8	.7	4.3	10.6	13.9
11.8		7.7		14.5	% Profit Before Taxes/Total Assets		25.3	10.8	14.0	14.9	14.6
3.4		.3		6.1			4.8	3.9	4.9	8.6	8.2
-2.5		-7.0		.5			-6.2	-.2	1.2	3.1	2.7
10.3		9.3		11.8	Sales/Net Fixed Assets		23.4	10.6	10.6	12.7	9.4
5.3		4.6		6.1			8.1	5.5	6.9	5.6	5.4
3.2		2.8		3.6			4.2	2.5	3.6	3.5	3.5
2.7		2.1		2.4	Sales/Total Assets		2.8	2.1	2.6	2.5	2.1
1.9		1.6		1.8			2.0	1.5	1.9	1.8	1.8
1.4		1.2		1.4			1.6	1.0	1.5	1.5	1.5
	2.1		3.2		2.2	% Depr., Dep., Amort./Sales		2.3	3.7	2.2	2.1	2.2
(165)	4.0	(155)	5.1	(181)	4.0		(27)	4.9	(24) 4.8	(47) 4.3	(45) 3.2	(31) 3.5
	6.4		7.2		6.3			8.4	8.0	5.7	5.7	5.7
	2.3		1.9		1.8	% Officers', Directors' Owners' Comp/Sales		2.2	3.1	2.2	1.4	
(83)	3.7	(90)	4.2	(90)	3.6		(18)	4.4	(13) 4.3	(24) 5.1	(23) 1.8	
	6.3		8.1		6.1			6.9	9.6	6.9	3.7	
2435181M		2094630M		3163788M	Net Sales ($)	6336M	71865M	103371M	359526M	803000M	1819690M
1536238M		1572376M		1856429M	Total Assets ($)	4753M	39108M	76736M	194034M	459491M	1082307M

M = $ thousand   MM = $ million
See Pages 9 through 22 for Explanation of Ratios and Data

Current Data Sorted by Assets / Comparative Historical Data

Type of Statement

			7	9	3		Type of Statement	26	22
	6		15	9			Unqualified	37	36
1	1		8	1			Reviewed	19	16
3	5		3				Compiled	8	12
3	4		22	14	3	1	Tax Returns	43	36
	27 (4/1-9/30/10)			91 (10/1/10-3/31/11)			Other		
0-500M	500M-2MM		2-10MM	10-50MM	50-100MM	100-250MM		4/1/06-3/31/07 ALL	4/1/07-3/31/08 ALL
7	16		55	33	6	1	NUMBER OF STATEMENTS	133	122
%	%		%	%	%	%	**ASSETS**	%	%
	8.9		6.1	7.8			Cash & Equivalents	5.5	6.6
	28.8		23.7	22.5			Trade Receivables (net)	25.3	24.8
	23.0		33.9	28.8			Inventory	33.4	33.5
	.6		2.0	2.6			All Other Current	1.7	2.1
	61.2		65.8	61.8			Total Current	65.8	67.0
	27.9		26.7	25.1			Fixed Assets (net)	26.0	24.4
	1.7		1.7	7.4			Intangibles (net)	3.0	2.4
	9.2		5.8	5.7			All Other Non-Current	5.1	6.2
	100.0		100.0	100.0			Total	100.0	100.0
							LIABILITIES		
	8.8		10.7	7.0			Notes Payable-Short Term	11.3	13.5
	5.6		5.0	3.1			Cur. Mat.-L.T.D.	5.0	3.5
	22.2		13.2	11.4			Trade Payables	15.1	14.5
	.3		.3	.4			Income Taxes Payable	.3	.3
	6.4		6.2	5.8			All Other Current	8.5	5.9
	43.3		35.6	27.6			Total Current	40.2	37.8
	19.8		17.8	12.7			Long-Term Debt	15.9	14.2
	.8		.5	1.1			Deferred Taxes	.6	.7
	14.9		6.1	11.8			All Other Non-Current	6.3	4.8
	21.1		40.1	46.8			Net Worth	36.9	42.5
	100.0		100.0	100.0			Total Liabilties & Net Worth	100.0	100.0
							INCOME DATA		
	100.0		100.0	100.0			Net Sales	100.0	100.0
	38.3		27.6	25.3			Gross Profit	28.2	28.3
	34.7		22.2	17.8			Operating Expenses	22.8	22.6
	3.5		5.5	7.5			Operating Profit	5.5	5.7
	.9		1.3	1.8			All Other Expenses (net)	1.3	1.3
	2.6		4.2	5.7			Profit Before Taxes	4.2	4.4
							RATIOS		
	2.1		2.7	4.6				3.0	2.8
	1.5		1.9	2.2			Current	1.7	1.9
	.9		1.4	1.6				1.2	1.2
	1.3		1.4	2.2				1.2	1.5
	.7		.8	1.3			Quick	.8	.8
	.6		.5	.7				.5	.5
38 9.7	39 9.3		39 9.3					37 9.9	35 10.5
44 8.3	45 8.1		51 7.2				Sales/Receivables	44 8.2	44 8.3
56 6.6	54 6.7		61 6.0					53 6.9	54 6.8
25 14.5	55 6.6		57 6.4					56 6.6	54 6.8
42 8.7	85 4.3		82 4.4				Cost of Sales/Inventory	86 4.2	83 4.4
135 2.7	141 2.6		134 2.7					119 3.1	124 3.0
17 21.8	20 18.3		18 20.8					18 20.1	19 19.0
36 10.1	30 12.1		34 10.9				Cost of Sales/Payables	33 10.9	31 11.9
76 4.8	49 7.5		48 7.6					48 7.6	46 7.9
	5.0		3.7	2.7				4.3	4.9
	11.5		6.4	4.8			Sales/Working Capital	6.8	7.3
	-63.1		11.7	8.3				26.6	16.7
	47.2		9.8	21.1				8.0	9.4
	(14) 1.7		(53) 4.1	(30) 7.6			EBIT/Interest	(124) 3.0	(113) 3.5
	-1.8		1.3	2.9				1.6	1.3
			8.7	9.1				5.1	4.1
			(19) 2.4	(14) 4.5			Net Profit + Depr., Dep., Amort./Cur. Mat. L/T/D	(44) 3.0	(37) 2.7
			.8	2.5				1.2	1.6
	.2		.3	.3				.3	.3
	1.2		.8	.7			Fixed/Worth	.7	.6
	NM		1.6	1.4				1.9	1.2
	.7		.7	.3				.6	.6
	2.7		1.4	1.1			Debt/Worth	1.7	1.3
	NM		3.9	4.0				5.4	4.3
	24.7		44.0	43.7				45.5	46.5
	(12) 14.4		(53) 12.3	(30) 21.3			% Profit Before Taxes/Tangible Net Worth	(118) 18.8	(113) 19.7
	-50.1		2.6	7.7				6.6	4.5
	19.4		12.7	13.9				15.0	16.0
	1.8		4.7	8.5			% Profit Before Taxes/Total Assets	5.7	6.3
	-10.2		1.0	3.9				2.1	1.0
	19.9		13.8	9.9				16.1	20.1
	14.1		7.3	7.1			Sales/Net Fixed Assets	8.4	9.5
	4.2		3.6	3.9				4.7	5.2
	2.7		2.3	2.0				2.5	2.6
	2.3		2.0	1.6			Sales/Total Assets	2.0	2.0
	1.6		1.4	1.2				1.6	1.5
	1.2		1.2	1.7				1.3	1.3
	(14) 2.1		(50) 2.2	2.6			% Depr., Dep., Amort./Sales	(121) 2.4	(114) 2.1
	7.4		3.6	4.6				3.8	3.2
	4.1		1.7					2.3	1.8
	(10) 8.4		(16) 3.1				% Officers', Directors' Owners' Comp/Sales	(49) 3.6	(51) 3.3
	11.4		9.0					8.4	7.9
5000M	50072M		514292M	1247789M	622294M	301894M	Net Sales ($)	3009329M	2905891M
2457M	20361M		276435M	815116M	389758M	216900M	Total Assets ($)	1764976M	1602136M

M = $ thousand   MM = $ million
See Pages 9 through 22 for Explanation of Ratios and Data

Comparative Historical Data | Current Data Sorted by Sales

	Comparative Historical Data				Current Data Sorted by Sales				
Type of Statement									
Unqualified	27	15	19		4	5	2	6	11
Reviewed	37	25	30				8	6	7
Compiled	15	8	11	1	1	3	3	2	1
Tax Returns	12	11	11	3	3	2	3		
Other	41	49	47	2	5	4	11	14	11
	4/1/08-3/31/09 ALL	4/1/09-3/31/10 ALL	4/1/10-3/31/11 ALL	0-1MM	27 (4/1-9/30/10) 1-3MM	3-5MM	5-10MM	91 (10/1/10-3/31/11) 10-25MM	25MM & OVER
NUMBER OF STATEMENTS	132	108	118	6	13	14	27	28	30
ASSETS	%	%	%	%	%	%	%	%	%
Cash & Equivalents	6.3	9.1	6.7		9.2	7.8	5.2	7.7	5.9
Trade Receivables (net)	23.2	21.6	24.0		25.2	22.0	22.6	27.1	24.0
Inventory	32.5	31.9	29.7		30.4	30.9	32.3	28.9	30.4
All Other Current	1.7	2.4	1.8		1.1	.2	1.3	3.7	2.0
Total Current	63.7	64.9	62.2		66.0	61.0	61.5	67.4	62.4
Fixed Assets (net)	26.8	24.7	27.2		27.3	33.9	27.3	22.2	25.2
Intangibles (net)	3.8	4.4	3.5		.9	1.4	2.2	5.0	5.1
All Other Non-Current	5.7	6.0	7.1		5.8	3.7	9.0	5.3	7.4
Total	100.0	100.0	100.0		100.0	100.0	100.0	100.0	100.0
LIABILITIES									
Notes Payable-Short Term	11.7	13.3	9.2		10.8	5.5	13.7	9.0	7.3
Cur. Mat.-L.T.D.	3.3	3.2	4.5		5.1	8.6	4.4	2.5	3.1
Trade Payables	11.7	12.5	14.1		17.1	10.6	16.9	12.8	13.1
Income Taxes Payable	.4	.3	.3		.1	.6	.3	.5	.3
All Other Current	5.1	7.4	6.0		5.4	7.9	6.2	5.6	6.3
Total Current	32.1	36.6	34.0		38.6	33.1	41.5	30.4	30.1
Long-Term Debt	14.7	13.3	17.9		19.6	28.4	15.4	14.0	14.9
Deferred Taxes	.6	.8	.7		.7	.8	.4	1.0	.6
All Other Non-Current	5.8	4.4	9.2		6.0	3.6	5.4	6.9	13.4
Net Worth	46.8	44.9	38.2		35.1	34.1	37.3	47.7	41.0
Total Liabilities & Net Worth	100.0	100.0	100.0		100.0	100.0	100.0	100.0	100.0
INCOME DATA									
Net Sales	100.0	100.0	100.0		100.0	100.0	100.0	100.0	100.0
Gross Profit	25.7	29.4	29.8		32.2	32.3	28.8	26.6	24.0
Operating Expenses	20.7	27.3	24.2		31.4	26.0	24.9	17.8	18.4
Operating Profit	5.0	2.1	5.6		.8	6.3	3.9	8.9	5.6
All Other Expenses (net)	1.0	1.3	1.4		1.5	1.3	1.5	1.6	1.1
Profit Before Taxes	4.0	.9	4.2		-.7	5.0	2.4	7.3	4.5
RATIOS									
Current	3.6	4.1	2.9		2.8	3.0	2.3	3.4	3.3
	2.0	1.9	1.9		1.7	2.0	1.6	2.4	2.2
	1.3	1.2	1.3		1.2	1.3	1.2	1.7	1.6
Quick	1.8	1.9	1.6		2.2	1.6	1.1	1.9	1.6
	.9	.8	1.0		.7	.9	.6	1.3	1.0
	.5	.4	.5		.4	.5	.4	.7	.7
Sales/Receivables	31 / 11.6	36 / 10.2	39 / 9.3		37 / 9.7	41 / 9.0	35 / 10.5	42 / 8.7	40 / 9.2
	40 / 9.1	48 / 7.7	46 / 7.9		45 / 8.1	43 / 8.5	45 / 8.1	50 / 7.3	53 / 6.9
	49 / 7.5	60 / 6.0	58 / 6.3		58 / 6.3	47 / 7.7	52 / 7.1	62 / 5.9	59 / 6.1
Cost of Sales/Inventory	48 / 7.6	58 / 6.2	53 / 6.9		30 / 12.3	45 / 8.2	53 / 6.8	56 / 6.6	
	80 / 4.5	102 / 3.6	82 / 4.4		95 / 3.8	93 / 3.9	88 / 4.1	72 / 5.1	84 / 4.3
	123 / 3.0	138 / 2.6	125 / 2.9		176 / 2.1	159 / 2.3	141 / 2.6	91 / 4.0	125 / 2.9
Cost of Sales/Payables	12 / 29.3	15 / 23.9	19 / 19.1		20 / 18.6	16 / 23.2	29 / 12.8	19 / 18.8	19 / 19.7
	23 / 16.0	31 / 11.7	32 / 11.4		33 / 11.0	20 / 18.7	27 / 9.9	38 / 13.3	38 / 9.6
	41 / 8.8	46 / 7.9	50 / 7.2		83 / 4.4	35 / 10.6	57 / 6.4	44 / 8.3	48 / 7.6
Sales/Working Capital	4.0	3.5	4.0		4.2	3.7	5.3	3.4	3.8
	6.0	6.0	6.1		6.2	5.2	10.0	5.9	5.1
	14.3	18.0	14.2		17.5	15.1	31.1	8.1	9.0
EBIT/Interest	13.3	8.1	16.2		3.5	27.5	6.0	46.5	18.9
	(121) 3.6	(92) 1.4	(109) 4.1		(11) 1.5	3.9	2.2	(26) 7.2	(27) 7.1
	.8	-2.1	1.1		-2.7	1.1	-.2	2.9	3.1
Net Profit + Depr., Dep., Amort./Cur. Mat. L/T/D	8.5	6.0	8.2					29.2	8.9
	(51) 3.2	(32) 2.6	(40) 2.5					(10) 11.2	(15) 3.6
	1.6	1.0	.9					2.5	1.1
Fixed/Worth	.3	.2	.3		.2	.4	.3	.2	.4
	.6	.6	.8		.9	1.1	.9	.4	.7
	1.2	1.3	2.1		2.5	4.0	2.2	1.2	1.5
Debt/Worth	.5	.3	.5		.6	.6	.9	.4	.5
	1.2	1.3	1.4		2.6	2.0	1.4	.9	1.2
	3.6	4.8	5.9		5.5	13.8	6.3	2.7	4.9
% Profit Before Taxes/Tangible Net Worth	37.2	23.2	42.4		23.4	44.8	29.3	49.9	37.7
	(125) 11.5	(96) 1.5	(106) 14.5		(12) 5.7	(12) 27.3	(26) 9.2	(26) 36.6	(27) 21.2
	1.4	-8.1	3.8		-7.0	13.3	-8.7	6.8	4.9
% Profit Before Taxes/Total Assets	14.9	9.3	13.0		8.5	13.8	6.5	26.6	10.8
	4.7	.4	6.1		1.6	8.4	3.5	10.8	8.3
	-.4	-4.9	.5		-8.6	.4	-1.6	3.6	3.5
Sales/Net Fixed Assets	16.5	14.9	13.7		21.2	12.0	13.8	17.6	11.7
	7.5	7.8	7.4		8.1	4.2	7.6	9.4	7.3
	4.2	4.1	3.8		3.2	3.0	4.2	4.7	3.8
Sales/Total Assets	2.5	2.2	2.3		2.6	2.3	2.6	2.3	2.1
	2.0	1.6	1.8		1.7	1.8	1.9	2.1	1.7
	1.5	1.3	1.3		1.4	1.3	1.5	1.6	1.2
% Depr., Dep., Amort./Sales	1.0	1.2	1.4		.8	2.1	1.3	1.0	1.6
	(123) 2.2	(94) 2.5	(110) 2.5		(12) 1.7	(13) 3.3	(25) 2.6	(25) 1.5	2.5
	3.7	4.9	4.7		4.7	6.3	4.3	3.8	4.4
% Officers', Directors' Owners' Comp/Sales	1.5	2.5	2.4						
	(48) 4.3	(34) 6.4	(36) 5.4						
	8.0	11.1	11.3						
Net Sales ($)	3561606M	2876032M	2741341M	3143M	27790M	58051M	208967M	486336M	1957054M
Total Assets ($)	2102480M	1778024M	1721027M	2163M	18926M	35472M	120575M	290666M	1253225M

M = $ thousand   MM = $ million
See Pages 9 through 22 for Explanation of Ratios and Data

Current Data Sorted by Assets   Comparative Historical Data

Type of Statement

0-500M	500M-2MM	2-10MM	10-50MM	50-100MM	100-250MM		4/1/06-3/31/07 ALL	4/1/07-3/31/08 ALL
		2	4	2		Unqualified	7	9
	2	8	5			Reviewed	23	14
	7	9				Compiled	17	17
3	6	3				Tax Returns	6	5
2	7	8	13		2	Other	31	27
	16 (4/1-9/30/10)		67 (10/1/10-3/31/11)					
5	22	30	22	2	2	NUMBER OF STATEMENTS	84	72

0-500M %	500M-2MM %	2-10MM %	10-50MM %	50-100MM %	100-250MM %		%	%
						ASSETS		
	8.6	12.6	10.7			Cash & Equivalents	6.7	8.4
	35.1	24.3	17.8			Trade Receivables (net)	28.7	26.9
	6.0	5.1	12.0			Inventory	7.9	10.8
	1.7	1.2	3.2			All Other Current	1.7	1.6
	51.3	43.3	43.8			Total Current	45.1	47.8
	33.4	46.9	42.7			Fixed Assets (net)	43.0	41.5
	7.3	4.0	7.9			Intangibles (net)	5.0	5.2
	7.9	5.8	5.7			All Other Non-Current	7.0	5.5
	100.0	100.0	100.0			Total	100.0	100.0
						LIABILITIES		
	7.8	5.9	4.3			Notes Payable-Short Term	7.4	6.3
	6.0	6.3	6.0			Cur. Mat.-L.T.D.	6.3	7.7
	12.6	9.0	7.7			Trade Payables	11.0	10.7
	.2	.2	.0			Income Taxes Payable	.5	.2
	5.9	7.5	6.6			All Other Current	14.4	10.7
	32.4	28.8	24.6			Total Current	39.6	35.5
	31.7	20.3	22.5			Long-Term Debt	23.5	25.1
	.0	.9	2.0			Deferred Taxes	.6	1.4
	9.3	6.3	10.8			All Other Non-Current	7.9	6.6
	26.6	43.7	40.0			Net Worth	28.3	31.4
	100.0	100.0	100.0			Total Liabilities & Net Worth	100.0	100.0
						INCOME DATA		
	100.0	100.0	100.0			Net Sales	100.0	100.0
	43.8	40.3	36.0			Gross Profit	36.2	36.5
	36.9	30.8	27.1			Operating Expenses	29.6	28.3
	6.9	9.5	8.9			Operating Profit	6.7	8.3
	.7	1.3	2.8			All Other Expenses (net)	1.8	2.3
	6.3	8.2	6.2			Profit Before Taxes	4.8	6.0
						RATIOS		
	2.6	3.2	2.5			Current	2.4	3.2
	1.4	1.9	1.6				1.4	1.7
	1.0	1.0	1.3				.8	.8
	2.2	3.2	1.9			Quick	2.1	2.2
	1.3	1.8	1.1				1.0	1.1
	.8	.8	.7				.6	.7
	38 9.5	38 9.7	42 8.7			Sales/Receivables	43 8.6	43 8.5
	53 6.9	50 7.4	50 7.3				51 7.1	50 7.3
	65 5.6	61 6.0	63 5.8				60 6.1	62 5.9
	0 UND	0 UND	0 UND			Cost of Sales/Inventory	0 UND	0 UND
	0 UND	0 UND	36 10.2				6 60.7	9 41.1
	15 23.7	14 25.4	69 5.3				35 10.5	53 6.8
	15 24.1	14 27.0	21 17.6			Cost of Sales/Payables	16 23.5	16 23.0
	32 11.5	23 15.6	27 13.3				25 14.5	27 13.3
	48 7.6	51 7.2	50 7.3				35 10.3	42 8.7
	7.8	5.8	3.7			Sales/Working Capital	7.7	4.7
	14.8	9.8	10.6				16.4	12.4
	NM	130.4	19.7				-29.5	-25.4
	9.1	35.0	20.8			EBIT/Interest	9.1	6.7
	(20) 4.1	(28) 8.9	(19) 5.3				(78) 2.6	(66) 2.3
	2.4	2.3	1.9				1.1	.4
						Net Profit + Depr., Dep., Amort./Cur. Mat. L/T/D	4.1	1.9
							(24) 2.6	(17) 1.3
							1.5	.6
	.4	.5	.5			Fixed/Worth	.8	.6
	1.8	1.1	1.0				1.6	1.5
	11.9	2.5	2.8				5.7	12.6
	1.1	.4	.5			Debt/Worth	.7	.7
	4.1	1.1	.9				1.8	1.9
	29.1	3.1	3.5				20.6	28.5
	76.5	68.1	40.6			% Profit Before Taxes/Tangible Net Worth	53.3	55.3
	(18) 26.2	(28) 30.5	(19) 19.9				(66) 25.2	(55) 25.0
	18.1	7.7	8.7				10.3	-.1
	21.3	25.1	18.7			% Profit Before Taxes/Total Assets	14.8	15.5
	8.3	14.2	10.3				7.2	6.7
	5.2	3.5	2.0				.8	-.9
	14.4	6.0	5.7			Sales/Net Fixed Assets	11.3	11.3
	8.0	4.0	3.7				4.3	4.2
	4.0	2.4	1.4				2.6	2.0
	3.3	2.4	1.7			Sales/Total Assets	2.8	2.7
	2.5	1.8	1.1				1.9	1.8
	1.6	1.2	.8				1.2	1.1
	2.1	3.0	4.1			% Depr., Dep., Amort./Sales	2.3	2.5
	(17) 3.9	(26) 5.2	(18) 5.7				(82) 4.3	(64) 4.6
	5.6	7.8	10.3				6.8	6.9
	3.2	5.1				% Officers', Directors' Owners' Comp/Sales	3.9	2.6
	(14) 5.6	(12) 6.2					(36) 6.1	(27) 4.6
	9.4	10.7					8.4	9.7
4547M	66615M	254503M	633459M	133101M	323175M	Net Sales ($)	1000243M	1613019M
1334M	26110M	137633M	495676M	130167M	392169M	Total Assets ($)	652105M	1239084M

© RMA 2011

M = $ thousand   MM = $ million
See Pages 9 through 22 for Explanation of Ratios and Data

Comparative Historical Data | Current Data Sorted by Sales

Type of Statement

08-09	09-10	10-11	Type of Statement	0-1MM	1-3MM	3-5MM	5-10MM	10-25MM	25MM & OVER
10	4	8	Unqualified					1	7
20	20	15	Reviewed		1	1	5	8	
13	17	16	Compiled	1	3	7	5		
6	7	12	Tax Returns	1	6	4		1	
26	40	32	Other	1	8	1	6	7	9
4/1/08-3/31/09 ALL	4/1/09-3/31/10 ALL	4/1/10-3/31/11 ALL			16 (4/1-9/30/10)			67 (10/1/10-3/31/11)	

08-09 ALL	09-10 ALL	10-11 ALL		0-1MM	1-3MM	3-5MM	5-10MM	10-25MM	25MM & OVER
75	88	83	**NUMBER OF STATEMENTS**	3	18	13	16	17	16
%	%	%	**ASSETS**	%	%	%	%	%	%
8.2	9.4	11.1	Cash & Equivalents		10.1	11.0	11.3	14.9	10.0
25.1	22.4	25.6	Trade Receivables (net)		26.7	38.2	24.4	22.3	20.2
6.4	9.4	7.6	Inventory		3.9	2.4	7.2	6.8	15.2
1.2	3.3	2.2	All Other Current		1.5	1.4	1.1	3.3	3.7
41.0	44.6	46.5	Total Current		42.2	53.1	43.9	47.4	49.1
45.3	43.5	40.4	Fixed Assets (net)		43.7	31.2	45.4	45.2	33.3
5.7	6.4	6.4	Intangibles (net)		2.4	8.7	5.7	2.4	11.7
8.1	5.5	6.7	All Other Non-Current		11.7	7.0	4.9	5.0	5.9
100.0	100.0	100.0	Total		100.0	100.0	100.0	100.0	100.0
			LIABILITIES						
6.6	9.4	9.3	Notes Payable-Short Term		21.2	9.3	8.0	3.3	4.4
7.0	6.4	6.2	Cur. Mat.-L.T.D.		6.9	2.9	8.7	6.1	2.9
8.8	9.5	9.4	Trade Payables		7.7	12.8	10.8	7.6	8.7
.1	.1	.3	Income Taxes Payable		1.0	.3	.2	.0	.1
5.8	8.1	6.9	All Other Current		2.4	7.1	7.2	8.7	9.7
28.4	33.5	32.1	Total Current		39.3	32.4	34.9	25.9	25.7
22.9	24.9	29.0	Long-Term Debt		36.9	31.1	16.1	16.6	32.3
1.0	1.0	.9	Deferred Taxes		.6	.0	1.2	1.0	1.8
7.3	11.6	8.1	All Other Non-Current		8.6	8.4	10.8	11.6	2.3
40.5	29.0	29.9	Net Worth		14.6	28.2	37.1	44.9	37.8
100.0	100.0	100.0	Total Liabilities & Net Worth		100.0	100.0	100.0	100.0	100.0
			INCOME DATA						
100.0	100.0	100.0	Net Sales		100.0	100.0	100.0	100.0	100.0
36.0	35.2	39.7	Gross Profit		47.9	43.1	38.8	38.0	30.4
30.2	35.5	31.4	Operating Expenses		40.2	37.7	30.1	29.2	18.5
5.8	-.3	8.4	Operating Profit		7.7	5.4	8.7	8.8	11.9
1.3	1.9	1.9	All Other Expenses (net)		1.5	.6	1.3	2.4	3.3
4.5	-2.1	6.5	Profit Before Taxes		6.2	4.8	7.3	6.4	8.6
			RATIOS						
2.5	2.6	2.6	Current		2.6	2.7	3.5	2.8	2.0
1.5	1.4	1.7			1.3	1.6	1.6	1.9	1.6
.8	.8	1.1			1.0	1.1	.6	1.5	1.4
2.1	2.0	2.1	Quick		2.1	2.5	3.5	2.8	1.6
1.0	.9	1.2			1.2	1.6	1.5	1.8	.9
.7	.6	.7			.7	.9	.4	1.1	.7
38 9.6	34 10.6	40 9.2	Sales/Receivables	45 8.2	32 11.4	33 10.9	43 8.6	41 9.0	
48 7.6	46 7.9	51 7.2		58 6.3	53 6.9	42 8.7	49 7.4	48 7.6	
58 6.3	57 6.4	62 5.9		73 5.0	61 6.0	61 6.0	62 5.9	58 6.3	
0 UND	0 UND	0 UND	Cost of Sales/Inventory	0 UND	0 UND	0 UND	0 UND	12 29.2	
7 50.1	6 59.7	3 121.3		0 UND	0 UND	5 80.3	0 UND	47 7.8	
28 12.8	35 10.5	41 8.9		14 25.4	5 74.2	27 13.5	31 11.6	93 3.9	
15 24.6	14 26.8	16 23.3	Cost of Sales/Payables	12 30.2	14 25.3	17 21.8	15 23.6	16 22.5	
24 15.2	24 15.5	24 14.9		34 10.8	23 15.6	25 14.5	24 14.9	24 15.1	
40 9.1	41 8.9	48 7.6		58 6.3	48 7.6	50 7.2	36 10.2	46 8.0	
6.7	5.5	5.4	Sales/Working Capital		6.2	6.0	5.3	4.8	3.9
13.8	30.1	11.9			14.4	16.3	11.3	7.3	10.9
-22.9	-18.5	33.7			NM	NM	-12.9	17.3	18.4
9.9	4.8	24.2	EBIT/Interest		6.9	25.6	29.9	40.0	30.4
(68) 2.6	(79) .6	(74) 4.5		(15) 2.9	4.0	4.5	(16) 10.2	(12) 5.1	
.2	-4.7	2.1			1.2	2.4	1.9	4.2	1.7
3.6	3.3	4.8	Net Profit + Depr., Dep., Amort./Cur. Mat. L/T/D						
(30) 1.9	(22) 1.9	(18) 2.1							
1.2	.7	1.4							
.6	.6	.5	Fixed/Worth		.7	.4	.8	.5	.4
1.3	1.3	1.1			2.6	1.7	1.2	.9	.9
3.2	21.3	4.5			13.4	NM	3.3	1.2	NM
.5	.5	.5	Debt/Worth		1.0	.6	.5	.5	.5
1.3	1.3	1.7			3.1	2.3	2.1	.8	1.2
7.0	NM	7.1			29.1	NM	4.2	2.0	NM
39.5	17.1	64.0	% Profit Before Taxes/Tangible Net Worth		46.1	81.3	75.3	41.2	74.5
(65) 16.3	(66) 3.2	(69) 24.7		(15) 20.9	(10) 32.9	(15) 22.5	(16) 30.2	(12) 31.5	
-1.5	-13.6	10.2			4.0	17.4	7.0	10.6	18.1
16.4	7.7	21.5	% Profit Before Taxes/Total Assets		25.6	15.8	25.8	20.7	22.0
6.8	.7	10.0			6.7	8.5	10.9	10.8	12.0
-1.2	-10.6	2.8			.8	6.8	1.9	6.0	3.3
7.3	7.9	8.4	Sales/Net Fixed Assets		8.6	29.0	6.7	6.8	9.5
4.0	4.1	4.5			3.8	9.6	4.3	4.2	4.7
1.9	1.8	2.5			2.0	4.2	1.8	1.9	2.8
3.0	2.7	2.7	Sales/Total Assets		2.2	4.1	2.6	2.5	2.1
1.8	1.5	1.7			1.6	2.8	1.8	1.4	1.5
1.0	1.0	1.0			1.1	1.6	1.0	.9	.9
2.9	2.8	2.9	% Depr., Dep., Amort./Sales		2.4	1.8	4.7	4.7	1.5
(68) 4.8	(73) 4.7	(66) 4.7		(14) 3.6	(11) 2.4	(14) 6.5	(13) 6.2	(11) 4.6	
7.8	9.9	7.6			6.5	7.7	9.1	8.4	7.9
2.4	4.6	2.8	% Officers', Directors' Owners' Comp/Sales		5.3	4.7			
(28) 4.5	(27) 6.1	(32) 5.3		(11) 6.9	(10) 5.5				
8.3	11.6	9.4			11.0	11.1			
1110014M	1297227M	1415400M	Net Sales ($)	1663M	33837M	49115M	117447M	245806M	967532M
864420M	1122232M	1183089M	Total Assets ($)	1854M	25597M	21433M	94284M	188937M	850984M

© RMA 2011

M = $ thousand   MM = $ million
See Pages 9 through 22 for Explanation of Ratios and Data

Current Data Sorted by Assets | **Comparative Historical Data**

Type of Statement	0-500M	500M-2MM	2-10MM	10-50MM	50-100MM	100-250MM	4/1/06-3/31/07 ALL	4/1/07-3/31/08 ALL
Unqualified		1	5	4	1	1	19	11
Reviewed	4	8	18	5			40	33
Compiled	7	9	10	4			20	23
Tax Returns	4	6	4				13	16
Other		14	15	14	2	2	54	52

Sub-period labels (current data): **30 (4/1-9/30/10)** and **104 (10/1/10-3/31/11)**

	0-500M	500M-2MM	2-10MM	10-50MM	50-100MM	100-250MM	4/1/06-3/31/07 ALL	4/1/07-3/31/08 ALL
NUMBER OF STATEMENTS	15	38	52	23	3	3	146	135
	%	%	%	%	%	%	%	%
ASSETS								
Cash & Equivalents	11.1	12.3	11.8	12.9			7.0	8.1
Trade Receivables (net)	32.7	37.2	23.1	26.0			28.8	28.8
Inventory	7.0	10.1	13.2	19.1			13.7	13.3
All Other Current	1.2	3.2	1.9	3.3			2.8	2.7
Total Current	51.9	62.8	49.9	61.2			52.3	52.9
Fixed Assets (net)	38.3	25.5	40.0	28.9			36.5	33.4
Intangibles (net)	5.4	5.6	4.2	2.5			4.6	4.9
All Other Non-Current	4.5	6.1	5.9	7.4			6.7	8.7
Total	100.0	100.0	100.0	100.0			100.0	100.0
LIABILITIES								
Notes Payable-Short Term	26.6	13.5	7.0	5.9			10.6	10.6
Cur. Mat.-L.T.D.	6.2	2.9	3.5	3.7			4.7	3.9
Trade Payables	14.6	14.6	9.0	12.2			13.5	12.3
Income Taxes Payable	.0	.1	.2	.2			.2	.5
All Other Current	23.8	8.1	5.4	7.3			11.6	10.7
Total Current	71.1	39.2	25.0	29.3			40.7	38.1
Long-Term Debt	53.3	15.2	21.4	13.2			18.4	23.6
Deferred Taxes	.0	.3	.6	.4			.5	.4
All Other Non-Current	16.1	17.2	4.7	2.9			7.9	5.2
Net Worth	-40.6	28.1	48.2	54.2			32.4	32.8
Total Liabilities & Net Worth	100.0	100.0	100.0	100.0			100.0	100.0
INCOME DATA								
Net Sales	100.0	100.0	100.0	100.0			100.0	100.0
Gross Profit	44.6	44.0	31.1	27.6			30.5	31.4
Operating Expenses	39.6	40.6	25.0	18.7			24.2	25.4
Operating Profit	5.0	3.4	6.2	8.9			6.2	5.9
All Other Expenses (net)	.7	.1	1.2	.5			1.4	1.5
Profit Before Taxes	4.3	3.3	4.9	8.4			4.8	4.4
RATIOS								
Current	7.7	3.8	3.2	4.4			2.3	2.5
	.9	2.0	2.0	2.0			1.4	1.6
	.4	1.0	1.4	1.3			.9	1.0
Quick	6.0	3.2	2.6	3.1			1.5	1.9
	.8	1.7	1.5	1.1			1.0	1.0
	.4	.7	.7	.7			.6	.6
Sales/Receivables	17 20.9	37 10.0	39 9.4	39 9.4			37 9.9	37 9.8
	33 11.2	46 7.9	45 8.1	49 7.4			48 7.6	46 8.0
	51 7.2	64 5.7	54 6.7	61 6.0			61 6.0	56 6.5
Cost of Sales/Inventory	0 UND	2 147.4	12 31.4	28 13.2			10 35.9	7 49.5
	7 49.2	20 18.6	28 12.9	45 8.1			22 16.8	25 14.7
	24 15.3	44 8.3	57 6.4	67 5.5			48 7.6	55 6.6
Cost of Sales/Payables	0 UND	7 51.9	16 23.5	14 26.7			15 23.8	16 22.7
	19 19.4	28 13.1	25 14.8	30 12.0			26 13.9	25 14.4
	31 11.6	41 8.8	34 10.6	42 8.8			40 9.1	40 9.0
Sales/Working Capital	7.7	5.1	4.9	2.7			6.6	6.5
	-37.3	10.1	7.4	8.1			15.1	13.8
	-6.9	NM	12.3	15.8			-103.2	-229.0
EBIT/Interest	24.2	21.2	12.6	54.3			9.7	13.5
	(14) 2.8	(34) 5.1	(48) 4.4	(21) 18.0			(133) 3.8	(122) 4.5
	.6	-.3	1.9	7.4			1.2	1.4
Net Profit + Depr., Dep., Amort./Cur. Mat. L/T/D			4.3	11.0			3.9	2.5
		(13) 3.4	(10) 5.0				(36) 2.1	(28) 1.8
			2.1	2.1			.8	.8
Fixed/Worth	.6	.2	.5	.2			.5	.4
	-4.6	.6	.8	.7			1.1	1.0
	-.2	-24.7	2.1	1.1			3.3	3.5
Debt/Worth	.8	.3	.5	.3			.6	.7
	-14.3	1.5	1.1	1.0			1.9	1.8
	-1.7	-91.1	2.9	2.0			8.8	6.8
% Profit Before Taxes/Tangible Net Worth		53.4	39.0	62.6			62.5	56.7
	(28) 24.9	(49) 24.3	(22) 24.6				(123) 25.6	(115) 25.7
		1.3	4.4	15.4			7.2	4.0
% Profit Before Taxes/Total Assets	42.0	23.3	16.6	24.5			17.1	20.9
	11.5	6.6	7.1	16.2			9.5	8.1
	-.6	-1.5	2.3	7.7			.9	.8
Sales/Net Fixed Assets	28.9	31.5	11.4	13.3			13.7	18.0
	10.1	10.2	4.4	6.7			6.3	6.8
	7.0	6.6	2.5	4.4			3.5	3.8
Sales/Total Assets	4.1	3.5	2.3	2.5			2.9	2.9
	3.6	2.7	1.6	2.0			2.2	1.9
	2.5	1.9	1.2	1.4			1.5	1.4
% Depr., Dep., Amort./Sales	.9	1.0	2.1	1.1			1.8	1.3
	(12) 2.2	(30) 2.5	(49) 3.7	1.8			(124) 3.1	(114) 2.8
	3.4	3.8	6.8	2.9			4.5	4.4
% Officers', Directors' Owners' Comp/Sales		4.0	3.1				3.1	3.4
		(20) 7.1	(19) 4.7				(47) 4.9	(39) 5.2
		9.9	8.6				8.5	8.3
Net Sales ($)	17482M	126224M	400956M	1032121M	300296M	758317M	3781106M	3540245M
Total Assets ($)	4488M	47185M	238728M	523594M	244080M	519156M	2163090M	2207264M

© RMA 2011

M = $ thousand   MM = $ million
See Pages 9 through 22 for Explanation of Ratios and Data

Comparative Historical Data | Current Data Sorted by Sales

Hist 1	Hist 2	Hist 3	Type of Statement	0-1MM	1-3MM	3-5MM	5-10MM	10-25MM	25MM & OVER
11	17	12	Unqualified		1		2	2	7
27	23	31	Reviewed		5	5	13	6	2
21	22	23	Compiled	3	8	5	6	1	
20	17	17	Tax Returns	4	5	5	3		
48	53	51	Other	2	11	8	8	6	16
4/1/08-3/31/09 ALL	4/1/09-3/31/10 ALL	4/1/10-3/31/11 ALL		30 (4/1-9/30/10)			104 (10/1/10-3/31/11)		
127	132	134	**NUMBER OF STATEMENTS**	9	30	23	32	15	25

ASSETS

Hist 1	Hist 2	Hist 3		0-1MM	1-3MM	3-5MM	5-10MM	10-25MM	25MM & OVER
%	%	%		%	%	%	%	%	%
7.9	10.7	12.0	Cash & Equivalents		11.0	11.6	13.0	13.2	10.8
26.2	26.6	28.4	Trade Receivables (net)		28.6	31.6	29.9	21.7	25.9
11.1	11.6	12.3	Inventory		6.7	11.3	12.3	18.5	16.9
3.5	2.9	2.4	All Other Current		2.3	3.0	1.8	1.4	3.4
48.7	51.7	55.2	Total Current		48.6	57.5	56.9	54.8	57.0
40.5	35.4	34.1	Fixed Assets (net)		36.5	35.9	31.7	37.3	31.0
3.8	5.2	4.7	Intangibles (net)		6.6	4.0	4.0	3.2	5.0
7.0	7.7	6.0	All Other Non-Current		8.3	2.6	7.4	4.6	6.9
100.0	100.0	100.0	Total		100.0	100.0	100.0	100.0	100.0

LIABILITIES

Hist 1	Hist 2	Hist 3		0-1MM	1-3MM	3-5MM	5-10MM	10-25MM	25MM & OVER
12.2	12.4	10.5	Notes Payable-Short Term		8.3	12.0	7.9	12.3	6.3
5.4	4.3	3.6	Cur. Mat.-L.T.D.		4.1	2.0	3.7	3.3	3.6
10.5	10.2	11.7	Trade Payables		7.7	12.0	14.4	10.2	12.4
.2	.2	.2	Income Taxes Payable		.1	.0	.1	.2	.5
11.3	9.0	9.0	All Other Current		9.8	7.4	5.8	4.9	9.8
39.6	36.1	35.1	Total Current		30.0	33.5	31.9	30.9	32.6
21.8	24.1	22.2	Long-Term Debt		20.0	28.0	17.4	14.1	17.8
.4	.5	.5	Deferred Taxes		.2	.7	.4	.8	.6
4.5	5.1	9.4	All Other Non-Current		20.4	8.7	6.4	.2	4.8
33.7	34.2	32.9	Net Worth		29.4	29.1	43.9	53.9	44.2
100.0	100.0	100.0	Total Liabilities & Net Worth		100.0	100.0	100.0	100.0	100.0

INCOME DATA

Hist 1	Hist 2	Hist 3		0-1MM	1-3MM	3-5MM	5-10MM	10-25MM	25MM & OVER
100.0	100.0	100.0	Net Sales		100.0	100.0	100.0	100.0	100.0
34.5	34.6	35.3	Gross Profit		48.2	35.8	31.1	27.2	23.8
30.3	31.5	29.5	Operating Expenses		46.0	29.7	26.3	17.3	15.1
4.2	3.0	5.8	Operating Profit		2.2	6.2	4.8	9.8	8.7
1.4	1.6	.9	All Other Expenses (net)		.7	.8	.6	.9	1.7
2.8	1.5	4.9	Profit Before Taxes		1.5	5.4	4.2	8.9	7.0

RATIOS

Hist 1	Hist 2	Hist 3		0-1MM	1-3MM	3-5MM	5-10MM	10-25MM	25MM & OVER
2.6 / 1.3 / .8	3.4 / 1.7 / .9	3.2 / 1.8 / 1.2	Current		7.7 / 2.4 / .9	3.2 / 2.3 / 1.3	2.9 / 1.9 / 1.3	3.0 / 2.0 / 1.1	2.6 / 1.6 / 1.2
1.7 / .9 / .5	2.4 / 1.2 / .6	2.7 / 1.3 / .7	Quick		7.2 / 2.1 / .7	2.3 / 1.7 / .9	2.7 / 1.4 / .8	2.4 / .9 / .5	1.4 / .9 / .7
32 11.4 / 43 8.4 / 54 6.8	35 10.4 / 43 8.4 / 56 6.5	37 9.9 / 45 8.1 / 57 6.4	Sales/Receivables		32 11.6 / 42 8.7 / 65 5.6	36 10.2 / 48 7.7 / 59 6.2	40 9.2 / 49 7.5 / 58 6.2	36 10.2 / 43 8.4 / 53 6.9	39 9.4 / 46 7.9 / 55 6.6
8 44.6 / 21 17.1 / 49 7.5	3 109.8 / 22 16.5 / 46 7.9	9 38.4 / 26 14.2 / 50 7.3	Cost of Sales/Inventory		0 UND / 17 22.0 / 45 8.2	3 132.6 / 19 19.3 / 53 6.9	10 36.2 / 23 15.8 / 50 7.3	10 35.9 / 32 11.5 / 119 3.1	20 18.0 / 42 8.6 / 51 7.1
14 25.2 / 25 14.8 / 41 8.8	12 31.0 / 24 15.5 / 42 8.8	12 31.5 / 26 14.2 / 38 9.6	Cost of Sales/Payables		3 120.0 / 19 18.8 / 41 8.8	16 23.2 / 22 16.5 / 36 10.1	16 22.4 / 27 13.3 / 35 10.3	10 35.4 / 30 12.4 / 42 8.8	14 26.5 / 30 12.0 / 43 8.6
6.5 / 21.1 / -15.7	5.0 / 10.8 / -53.6	4.9 / 9.1 / 27.1	Sales/Working Capital		4.4 / 9.5 / -42.5	6.6 / 8.9 / 15.1	4.9 / 9.4 / 14.6	4.7 / 7.9 / 50.4	5.7 / 12.1 / 21.4
9.8 / (111) 3.7 / 1.1	9.2 / (121) 2.4 / -.7	21.0 / (122) 5.7 / 1.5	EBIT/Interest		22.3 / (27) 1.3 / -2.4	19.8 / (22) 4.8 / 1.6	10.1 / (30) 6.1 / 2.4	29.7 / (13) 11.6 / 2.5	35.4 / (23) 11.9 / 2.8
2.5 / (22) 1.6 / .9	2.9 / (26) 1.6 / .2	5.9 / (31) 3.4 / 2.2	Net Profit + Depr., Dep., Amort./Cur. Mat. L/T/D						
.5 / 1.1 / 3.2	.4 / .9 / 7.1	.3 / .8 / 2.9	Fixed/Worth		.3 / 1.1 / -1.2	.5 / .9 / 2.6	.3 / .7 / 1.8	.5 / .6 / 2.6	.3 / .7 / 1.5
.7 / 1.9 / 5.9	.5 / 1.4 / 9.9	.5 / 1.3 / 5.9	Debt/Worth		.3 / 1.3 / -78.0	.5 / 1.7 / 4.6	.7 / 1.3 / 4.4	.3 / .7 / 4.2	.8 / 1.1 / 3.1
45.3 / (106) 18.1 / .7	32.6 / (104) 13.6 / -3.7	45.5 / (110) 24.8 / 6.7	% Profit Before Taxes/Tangible Net Worth		47.0 / (22) 12.8 / -3.5	41.4 / (20) 24.5 / 4.0	40.1 / (29) 25.1 / 5.4	50.5 / (13) 23.2 / 12.3	63.2 / (22) 28.4 / 13.8
15.8 / 5.5 / -.2	15.6 / 4.4 / -6.1	19.2 / 8.1 / 1.3	% Profit Before Taxes/Total Assets		23.3 / 2.6 / -4.3	17.6 / 6.3 / 1.1	16.2 / 7.1 / 2.8	25.8 / 14.4 / 5.1	23.2 / 12.4 / 3.9
11.6 / 5.4 / 3.1	14.3 / 6.9 / 2.8	15.2 / 7.1 / 2.9	Sales/Net Fixed Assets		19.5 / 9.5 / 2.9	20.8 / 7.6 / 3.1	25.8 / 7.1 / 3.2	11.2 / 4.8 / 2.7	14.4 / 6.2 / 3.6
3.0 / 2.0 / 1.3	2.9 / 2.0 / 1.2	2.9 / 2.1 / 1.4	Sales/Total Assets		3.5 / 2.3 / 1.5	3.5 / 1.9 / 1.3	3.0 / 2.1 / 1.3	2.3 / 1.7 / 1.3	2.5 / 2.0 / 1.5
1.6 / (102) 3.0 / 5.5	1.8 / (110) 3.3 / 6.1	1.4 / (117) 2.7 / 4.6	% Depr., Dep., Amort./Sales		1.5 / (24) 3.4 / 6.0	2.2 / (21) 2.7 / 4.0	1.6 / (29) 3.5 / 6.0	1.3 / 2.4 / 4.8	.9 / (22) 1.8 / 3.2
2.7 / (46) 5.7 / 7.4	3.6 / (48) 5.7 / 10.1	3.3 / (47) 6.7 / 9.5	% Officers', Directors' Owners' Comp/Sales		7.4 / (13) 8.6 / 10.5	3.4 / (15) 4.8 / 8.6	2.9 / (12) 4.1 / 7.6		
2990099M	2170995M	2635396M	Net Sales ($)	4927M	62232M	91546M	226064M	197549M	2053078M
1944148M	1546595M	1577231M	Total Assets ($)	2688M	36621M	50299M	136081M	121174M	1230368M

M = $ thousand   MM = $ million
See Pages 9 through 22 for Explanation of Ratios and Data

Current Data Sorted by Assets   Comparative Historical Data

		4	2	1	1	Type of Statement		15	8
	2	18	3	1		Unqualified		40	30
1	20	15	1			Reviewed		33	35
9	5	6	1			Compiled		23	14
4	14	19	7	1	1	Tax Returns		60	59
	33 (4/1-9/30/10)		103 (10/1/10-3/31/11)			Other		4/1/06-3/31/07	4/1/07-3/31/08
0-500M	500M-2MM	2-10MM	10-50MM	50-100MM	100-250MM			ALL	ALL
14	41	62	14	3	2	NUMBER OF STATEMENTS		171	146
%	%	%	%	%	%	ASSETS		%	%
11.2	8.5	11.0	3.5			Cash & Equivalents		8.2	9.2
32.0	35.0	28.1	22.3			Trade Receivables (net)		29.6	29.3
10.2	9.1	9.5	21.4			Inventory		10.5	9.4
4.4	2.3	2.6	1.1			All Other Current		1.5	2.5
57.8	54.8	51.1	48.4			Total Current		49.8	50.3
26.4	34.2	36.6	36.8			Fixed Assets (net)		40.9	39.4
7.2	2.7	4.3	7.7			Intangibles (net)		3.1	4.0
8.5	8.3	7.9	7.1			All Other Non-Current		6.2	6.3
100.0	100.0	100.0	100.0			Total		100.0	100.0
						LIABILITIES			
10.7	9.6	6.4	12.8			Notes Payable-Short Term		10.2	12.4
2.7	4.0	3.3	5.7			Cur. Mat.-L.T.D.		5.2	5.2
10.9	17.2	10.2	14.7			Trade Payables		14.2	14.0
.0	.0	.3	.0			Income Taxes Payable		.4	.1
22.9	11.7	7.3	7.3			All Other Current		9.3	10.0
47.3	42.5	27.5	40.5			Total Current		39.3	41.7
37.2	34.6	14.9	15.9			Long-Term Debt		23.3	17.9
.0	.7	.7	.8			Deferred Taxes		.5	.6
8.6	3.2	5.9	7.6			All Other Non-Current		9.1	10.7
6.9	19.0	51.0	35.1			Net Worth		27.8	29.1
100.0	100.0	100.0	100.0			Total Liabilties & Net Worth		100.0	100.0
						INCOME DATA			
100.0	100.0	100.0	100.0			Net Sales		100.0	100.0
50.7	42.5	30.9	24.5			Gross Profit		33.0	31.0
45.4	35.5	24.0	17.8			Operating Expenses		27.4	25.8
5.3	7.0	6.9	6.7			Operating Profit		5.6	5.3
3.0	2.1	.7	2.0			All Other Expenses (net)		1.8	1.4
2.3	4.8	6.2	4.7			Profit Before Taxes		3.8	3.8
						RATIOS			
4.9	4.0	3.5	1.6					2.6	2.2
1.5	1.3	1.9	1.4			Current		1.3	1.3
.9	.8	1.2	.9					.9	.9
3.3	2.7	2.7	1.1					2.0	1.6
1.1	1.0	1.5	.6			Quick		1.0	1.0
.8	.7	.9	.5					.6	.6
0 UND	40 9.2	44 8.3	41 8.9					37 9.8	38 9.7
36 10.2	50 7.3	52 7.0	54 6.8			Sales/Receivables		47 7.8	46 7.9
54 6.8	63 5.8	60 6.1	60 6.1					55 6.7	55 6.6
0 UND	4 83.0	7 54.1	20 18.1					4 81.9	4 100.9
13 27.9	14 26.1	14 26.3	54 6.8			Cost of Sales/Inventory		14 25.5	12 30.7
28 13.0	26 14.3	40 9.1	107 3.4					39 9.3	29 12.4
0 UND	6 57.4	12 29.3	17 22.0					13 27.1	15 24.0
22 16.4	25 14.6	23 16.1	32 11.3			Cost of Sales/Payables		28 13.1	25 14.5
55 6.6	58 6.2	36 10.1	50 7.3					42 8.6	38 9.6
5.4	5.4	4.5	5.7					8.0	8.4
27.6	24.1	8.6	15.3			Sales/Working Capital		18.3	22.4
NM	-32.7	28.6	-26.6					-37.7	-61.0
21.2	18.0	21.4	14.3					9.6	10.4
(12) 4.6	(39) 2.3	(55) 7.1	4.4			EBIT/Interest		(156) 3.7	(134) 3.4
-.1	.0	2.2	2.3					1.0	1.0
		9.4				Net Profit + Depr., Dep.,		8.7	5.5
	(23) 4.4					Amort./Cur. Mat. L/T/D	(48) 2.9	(42) 2.4
		2.0						1.1	.9
.1	.7	.5	.6					.6	.6
1.0	1.4	.7	1.6			Fixed/Worth		1.3	1.0
-32.3	-.9	1.3	3.3					9.6	3.8
.7	.8	.3	1.3					.8	.7
1.9	2.3	1.2	3.9			Debt/Worth		2.0	1.9
-2.1	-4.8	-2.5	5.4					29.3	10.0
	46.1	37.0	64.1			% Profit Before Taxes/Tangible		49.6	40.6
(27) 12.8	(57) 19.4	(12) 42.9			Net Worth	(133) 22.4	(118) 19.5
	-.3	7.3	21.3					3.3	4.1
23.3	21.0	23.0	19.1					16.1	14.9
4.4	6.9	10.8	8.7			% Profit Before Taxes/Total Assets		7.1	6.2
-5.5	-1.8	3.0	4.3					.2	.2
124.1	23.3	13.2	9.5					12.0	12.0
21.3	7.2	5.1	4.7			Sales/Net Fixed Assets		5.6	6.1
8.2	3.9	2.8	2.7					3.3	3.4
5.1	3.0	2.8	2.0					3.3	3.0
3.6	2.4	1.9	1.4			Sales/Total Assets		2.2	2.2
1.9	1.6	1.3	1.2					1.5	1.6
	1.5	1.6	.8					1.5	1.6
(35) 2.8	(60) 2.6	(13) 2.6			% Depr., Dep., Amort./Sales	(163) 3.0	(134) 2.9
	4.5	4.9	3.9					4.8	4.8
6.8	2.9	1.5						3.3	2.1
(10) 8.8	(21) 7.0	(25) 3.7				% Officers', Directors' Owners' Comp/Sales	(79) 5.3	(71) 4.9
17.3	11.2	7.4						8.4	7.7
14458M	119651M	555835M	448709M	274426M	847144M	Net Sales ($)		2260219M	2076297M
4022M	45657M	279478M	283004M	225748M	292966M	Total Assets ($)		1144396M	1045949M

© RMA 2011

M = $ thousand   MM = $ million
See Pages 9 through 22 for Explanation of Ratios and Data

Comparative Historical Data / Current Data Sorted by Sales

Hist 1		Hist 2		Hist 3		Type of Statement	0-1MM	1-3MM	3-5MM	5-10MM	10-25MM	25MM & OVER
	13		11		8	Unqualified				1	3	4
	36		28		24	Reviewed		1		14	4	3
	32		23		37	Compiled	1	12	10	11	3	
	15		15		21	Tax Returns	4	9	2	3	3	
	64		53		46	Other	5	10	5	10	9	7
	4/1/08-3/31/09 ALL		4/1/09-3/31/10 ALL		4/1/10-3/31/11 ALL			33 (4/1-9/30/10)			103 (10/1/10-3/31/11)	
	160		130		136	**NUMBER OF STATEMENTS**	10	32	19	39	22	14
	%		%		%	**ASSETS**	%	%	%	%	%	%
	8.1		7.0		9.2	Cash & Equivalents	11.0	9.8	8.2	9.9	10.3	3.9
	26.5		27.3		29.7	Trade Receivables (net)	32.4	26.4	37.8	29.1	32.0	22.4
	14.2		12.5		11.3	Inventory	9.0	9.2	7.0	9.8	14.7	22.2
	3.3		3.3		2.5	All Other Current	3.2	3.3	.9	2.1	3.7	1.4
	52.0		50.2		52.7	Total Current	55.7	48.8	53.9	50.9	60.6	49.9
	37.6		38.1		34.6	Fixed Assets (net)	28.7	34.4	37.4	38.4	29.5	33.2
	4.4		3.9		4.8	Intangibles (net)	4.0	7.2	4.2	2.8	3.4	8.3
	5.9		7.8		7.9	All Other Non-Current	11.6	9.7	4.4	7.9	6.4	8.6
	100.0		100.0		100.0	Total	100.0	100.0	100.0	100.0	100.0	100.0
						LIABILITIES						
	11.4		12.1		8.4	Notes Payable-Short Term	14.3	6.2	11.3	7.0	6.6	12.1
	5.7		5.0		3.8	Cur. Mat.-L.T.D.	2.0	3.6	3.6	3.6	4.2	5.5
	14.1		14.4		13.0	Trade Payables	9.6	8.0	17.1	14.5	13.6	16.1
	.1		.0		.1	Income Taxes Payable	.0	.0	.3	.2	.1	.2
	7.5		8.6		10.2	All Other Current	29.9	8.6	9.7	9.5	7.2	7.3
	38.8		40.2		35.5	Total Current	55.8	26.4	42.0	34.7	31.8	41.1
	20.3		21.0		23.5	Long-Term Debt	44.4	42.7	19.0	12.9	12.7	17.5
	.6		.7		.7	Deferred Taxes	.0	.0	1.7	.9	.6	.7
	8.0		10.0		5.6	All Other Non-Current	12.3	3.4	2.9	6.9	3.2	9.8
	32.2		28.1		34.7	Net Worth	-12.4	27.5	34.4	44.6	51.7	30.9
	100.0		100.0		100.0	Total Liabilities & Net Worth	100.0	100.0	100.0	100.0	100.0	100.0
						INCOME DATA						
	100.0		100.0		100.0	Net Sales	100.0	100.0	100.0	100.0	100.0	100.0
	30.1		33.5		35.5	Gross Profit	52.7	48.3	33.9	29.3	32.0	19.1
	25.0		30.8		28.8	Operating Expenses	46.4	39.4	30.1	23.8	22.2	14.6
	5.1		2.7		6.7	Operating Profit	6.3	8.9	3.8	5.5	9.7	4.5
	1.5		1.4		1.6	All Other Expenses (net)	5.2	2.5	1.1	.2	1.0	2.2
	3.6		1.3		5.1	Profit Before Taxes	1.1	6.4	2.8	5.3	8.7	2.2
						RATIOS						
	2.4		2.7		3.4		4.9	4.5	2.3	3.1	4.4	2.1
	1.3		1.2		1.5	Current	1.4	2.3	1.3	1.5	2.1	1.1
	.9		.9		1.1		.6	1.0	.9	1.1	1.5	.9
	1.7		1.8		2.5		4.4	2.9	2.0	2.3	3.6	1.0
	.9		.9		1.1	Quick	1.0	1.2	1.0	1.1	1.5	.6
	.6		.6		.7		.5	.8	.8	.8	.9	.4
31	11.7	38	9.7	40	9.2		30 12.3	26 14.1	41 8.9	42 8.7	46 8.0	36 10.3
42	8.7	47	7.8	50	7.3	Sales/Receivables	51 7.2	47 7.8	52 7.0	49 7.4	54 6.7	45 8.2
53	6.9	58	6.3	60	6.0		69 5.3	63 5.8	63 5.8	59 6.1	60 6.0	61 6.0
8	44.1	8	45.5	7	55.0		0 UND	4 86.3	3 141.8	9 41.2	6 64.2	11 32.8
21	17.5	18	20.7	16	23.3	Cost of Sales/Inventory	13 27.9	12 29.6	15 23.7	16 22.8	16 22.8	50 7.2
46	7.9	45	8.1	47	7.7		133 2.8	32 11.6	26 13.9	41 9.0	40 9.2	66 5.6
13	27.3	17	20.9	12	29.8		3 137.5	4 92.3	7 49.0	16 22.1	15 25.0	17 21.0
25	14.5	32	11.4	25	14.7	Cost of Sales/Payables	19 19.1	20 18.6	22 16.7	26 14.2	22 16.9	32 11.3
41	8.9	46	8.0	41	8.9		73 5.0	33 11.0	58 6.3	39 9.4	39 9.2	50 7.3
	7.1		6.4		5.0		2.5	5.0	6.3	4.8	4.5	9.1
	21.3		22.1		11.7	Sales/Working Capital	23.0	10.9	23.3	13.2	7.2	67.3
	-138.9		-33.5		95.1		-8.5	NM	-51.1	70.5	13.5	-26.6
	7.6		6.9		19.0			19.6	6.3	26.6	31.9	8.2
(144)	2.7	(120)	2.4	(125)	4.2	EBIT/Interest	(30) 4.0	(17) 1.6	(37) 7.3	(19) 9.8		3.0
	1.0		-.4		1.4			1.0	-2.2	1.3	3.3	2.0
	4.9		3.7		6.4					9.4		
(41)	1.9	(29)	1.6	(36)	2.4	Net Profit + Depr., Dep., Amort./Cur. Mat. L/T/D				(15) 3.4		
	1.1		.6		1.6					1.7		
	.5		.6		.5		.6	.4	.6	.6	.2	.7
	1.0		1.2		1.0	Fixed/Worth	9.0	1.2	1.2	.8	.6	2.2
	3.7		7.4		2.9		-.1	-1.3	-73.0	1.4	.9	NM
	.7		.8		.5		.7	.5	.7	.4	.2	1.3
	1.9		2.0		1.6	Debt/Worth	11.4	2.1	1.7	1.4	.7	4.8
	9.0		15.9		5.0		-1.8	-5.3	-95.7	2.5	3.0	NM
	40.1		31.5		47.9			51.8	29.3	47.1	46.9	63.4
(126)	18.0	(103)	8.5	(109)	20.4	% Profit Before Taxes/Tangible Net Worth		(21) 12.8	(14) 16.6	(35) 14.6	(21) 30.3	(11) 21.6
	2.9		-.5		5.9			-5.3	2.9	4.9	20.8	9.9
	13.3		8.8		21.9		8.1	24.2	15.2	23.4	24.7	10.7
	5.0		3.2		8.1	% Profit Before Taxes/Total Assets	4.1	7.2	3.5	9.8	14.5	8.1
	-.8		-2.9		1.8		-4.6	-.7	-9.5	1.6	7.8	3.1
	13.2		10.8		17.0		53.0	25.8	19.7	12.0	20.0	10.2
	6.2		5.3		6.0	Sales/Net Fixed Assets	11.2	7.9	5.9	5.3	12.8	5.2
	3.4		2.9		3.2		5.1	3.0	2.8	2.6	3.6	3.2
	3.1		2.8		3.0		2.5	3.1	3.0	2.9	3.4	3.1
	2.1		1.9		2.0	Sales/Total Assets	1.8	2.0	2.3	2.1	1.9	1.5
	1.5		1.4		1.4		1.1	1.5	1.4	1.4	1.5	1.2
	1.4		1.3		1.3			1.3	1.7	1.9	1.1	1.1
(147)	2.5	(113)	3.3	(120)	2.5	% Depr., Dep., Amort./Sales		(24) 2.2	3.3	(37) 2.9	(21) 1.6	(12) 3.6
	4.4		5.2		4.6			3.9	6.0	5.6	3.0	5.1
	2.6		2.6		2.6			6.4		1.7	2.0	
(62)	4.8	(62)	5.5	(61)	6.0	% Officers', Directors' Owners' Comp/Sales		(17) 8.6		(18) 3.7	(10) 5.8	
	8.1		7.8		9.9			13.1		7.3	7.5	
	2702961M		1175684M		2260223M	Net Sales ($)	5271M	58551M	74536M	291726M	323744M	1506395M
	1342564M		728761M		1130875M	Total Assets ($)	3351M	30645M	36803M	162444M	168698M	728934M

M = $ thousand   MM = $ million
See Pages 9 through 22 for Explanation of Ratios and Data

Current Data Sorted by Assets

Comparative Historical Data

Type of Statement

	0-500M	500M-2MM	2-10MM	10-50MM	50-100MM	100-250MM		4/1/06-3/31/07 ALL	4/1/07-3/31/08 ALL
Unqualified			1	5	3	2		17	16
Reviewed		2	11	6	1			10	10
Compiled	2	13	12	1				9	10
Tax Returns	10	15	13					13	8
Other	7	22	28	15	3	2		36	25
		26 (4/1-9/30/10)		148 (10/1/10-3/31/11)					
NUMBER OF STATEMENTS	19	52	65	27	7	4		85	69

ASSETS	%	%	%	%	%	%		%	%
Cash & Equivalents	11.4	10.2	9.9	11.6				7.8	6.2
Trade Receivables (net)	29.7	26.3	28.5	21.4				28.0	28.2
Inventory	13.5	22.3	27.3	36.6				30.1	32.3
All Other Current	2.2	1.8	2.2	1.7				2.0	2.7
Total Current	56.9	60.4	67.8	71.4				67.9	69.5
Fixed Assets (net)	28.6	27.3	26.4	20.3				22.8	21.0
Intangibles (net)	12.1	4.6	1.7	3.8				3.6	4.1
All Other Non-Current	2.1	7.7	4.1	4.5				5.7	5.5
Total	100.0	100.0	100.0	100.0				100.0	100.0

LIABILITIES									
Notes Payable-Short Term	28.7	10.8	10.4	9.2				11.2	10.0
Cur. Mat.-L.T.D.	3.7	5.1	5.9	4.9				4.1	3.7
Trade Payables	14.0	14.1	13.0	10.0				14.2	12.9
Income Taxes Payable	.0	.1	.3	.5				.2	1.2
All Other Current	7.2	9.0	10.3	8.6				9.7	9.8
Total Current	53.6	39.1	40.0	33.2				39.5	37.6
Long-Term Debt	16.8	32.0	13.6	11.9				15.3	16.9
Deferred Taxes	.0	.4	.2	.0				.4	.8
All Other Non-Current	28.5	13.3	6.0	4.5				4.3	3.5
Net Worth	.7	15.3	40.2	50.4				40.5	41.2
Total Liabilities & Net Worth	100.0	100.0	100.0	100.0				100.0	100.0

INCOME DATA									
Net Sales	100.0	100.0	100.0	100.0				100.0	100.0
Gross Profit	54.7	37.3	37.9	33.2				33.7	34.4
Operating Expenses	49.0	34.6	29.3	20.3				24.9	24.3
Operating Profit	5.7	2.7	8.7	12.9				8.8	10.1
All Other Expenses (net)	1.3	1.1	.9	1.5				1.1	.7
Profit Before Taxes	4.4	1.6	7.8	11.4				7.6	9.4

RATIOS									
Current	2.4	2.6	4.4	4.3				2.8	3.1
	1.4	1.7	1.9	3.1				1.9	2.0
	.4	.9	1.1	1.5				1.2	1.3
Quick	1.8	1.7	2.2	2.3				1.6	1.7
	.7	1.1	1.0	1.1				.9	1.0
	.2	.5	.6	.5				.5	.6
Sales/Receivables	4 97.0	22 16.6	36 10.1	40 9.0				41 8.9	40 9.1
	39 9.4	41 8.9	52 7.0	45 8.2				49 7.5	51 7.2
	61 6.0	55 6.6	68 5.4	56 6.6				61 6.0	63 5.8
Cost of Sales/Inventory	0 UND	15 24.0	30 12.2	95 3.8				42 8.8	47 7.8
	3 109.3	41 8.9	73 5.0	141 2.6				84 4.3	96 3.8
	52 7.0	92 4.0	123 3.0	160 2.3				139 2.6	150 2.4
Cost of Sales/Payables	0 UND	18 20.7	20 18.1	20 18.2				14 25.5	19 19.7
	20 18.0	31 11.8	31 11.7	31 11.8				31 11.7	33 11.2
	81 4.5	53 6.9	53 6.9	48 7.6				49 7.4	50 7.2
Sales/Working Capital	6.7	4.9	3.2	2.3				3.9	3.2
	13.2	10.5	5.7	3.7				8.0	5.7
	-10.8	-42.7	26.5	7.4				24.7	14.1
EBIT/Interest	11.3	6.1	18.9	50.6				10.0	15.8
	(16) 4.7	(49) 2.4	(56) 5.1	(23) 12.5				(77) 6.2	(63) 5.7
	-5.1	.3	1.9	5.2				2.9	2.6
Net Profit + Depr., Dep., Amort./Cur. Mat. L/T/D								5.9	3.6
								(26) 2.8	(22) 2.5
								1.4	1.3
Fixed/Worth	.3	.2	.2	.2				.2	.2
	2.1	2.0	.6	.4				.5	.6
	-1.0	-3.7	2.5	1.1				1.3	1.3
Debt/Worth	1.0	.9	.4	.4				.8	.7
	6.2	5.8	1.8	.9				1.8	1.5
	-3.2	-10.6	4.9	3.9				4.1	4.6
% Profit Before Taxes/Tangible Net Worth	140.7	79.4	62.7	90.5				59.7	48.8
	(13) 45.1	(36) 25.4	(58) 30.8	(26) 31.8				(76) 27.6	(59) 36.9
	-1.5	1.7	14.0	15.8				17.5	20.2
% Profit Before Taxes/Total Assets	26.9	14.3	24.2	25.4				20.1	22.8
	15.6	5.8	11.5	14.8				11.6	13.6
	-21.5	-.1	3.2	7.9				4.9	4.9
Sales/Net Fixed Assets	24.0	23.0	17.6	19.9				33.6	28.5
	15.2	9.7	8.3	9.7				11.3	12.6
	4.4	5.2	4.7	5.3				5.5	5.5
Sales/Total Assets	4.7	3.0	2.5	2.1				2.8	2.5
	3.0	2.2	1.8	1.6				1.9	1.8
	2.1	1.6	1.6	1.3				1.4	1.5
% Depr., Dep., Amort./Sales	1.0	1.5	1.1	1.0				1.1	1.0
	(16) 2.2	(41) 2.7	(57) 2.2	(26) 1.7				(73) 2.3	(59) 1.8
	5.3	6.4	4.0	3.5				3.4	2.9
% Officers', Directors' Owners' Comp/Sales	5.2	3.2	1.7					1.7	1.6
	(11) 9.2	(30) 4.5	(31) 3.1					(32) 3.2	(23) 4.0
	19.6	7.7	5.8					5.6	7.2
Net Sales ($)	13953M	147818M	578751M	908537M	727567M	534342M		2478571M	2051014M
Total Assets ($)	4793M	60447M	294933M	578261M	522154M	561892M		1526789M	1391976M

M = $ thousand   MM = $ million
See Pages 9 through 22 for Explanation of Ratios and Data

Comparative Historical Data | Current Data Sorted by Sales

4/1/08-3/31/09 ALL	4/1/09-3/31/10 ALL	4/1/10-3/31/11 ALL	Type of Statement	0-1MM	1-3MM	3-5MM	5-10MM	10-25MM	25MM & OVER
					26 (4/1-9/30/10)		148 (10/1/10-3/31/11)		
8	13	11	Unqualified			3	7	3	8
11	23	20	Reviewed	2	13	3	8	3	7
18	32	28	Compiled	8	12	5	6	2	
25	42	38	Tax Returns					7	
39	63	77	Other	5	17	12	14	14	15
101	173	174	**NUMBER OF STATEMENTS**	15	42	23	35	29	30
%	%	%	**ASSETS**	%	%	%	%	%	%
8.8	10.2	10.3	Cash & Equivalents	6.6	12.4	8.0	9.5	13.3	9.1
26.0	23.0	26.4	Trade Receivables (net)	21.3	24.5	30.5	30.8	27.2	22.5
30.5	25.9	26.1	Inventory	21.8	19.7	24.6	26.4	27.5	36.6
1.5	2.2	2.0	All Other Current	.8	1.7	1.8	2.8	2.3	2.1
66.9	61.2	64.8	Total Current	50.5	58.3	65.0	69.4	70.3	70.4
24.2	28.7	25.7	Fixed Assets (net)	35.5	28.1	27.9	25.1	21.5	20.5
3.1	3.8	4.5	Intangibles (net)	10.8	5.4	3.6	1.6	3.2	5.5
5.8	6.3	4.9	All Other Non-Current	2.8	8.2	3.5	3.9	4.9	3.6
100.0	100.0	100.0	Total	100.0	100.0	100.0	100.0	100.0	100.0
			LIABILITIES						
12.1	11.1	11.9	Notes Payable-Short Term	25.3	12.9	10.4	10.8	8.8	9.3
3.4	5.3	5.2	Cur. Mat.-L.T.D.	2.3	6.8	4.3	4.2	7.2	4.3
16.4	13.1	12.7	Trade Payables	13.4	11.0	19.5	11.1	13.8	10.5
.3	.3	.2	Income Taxes Payable	.0	.2	.3	.4	.2	.4
14.2	11.1	9.5	All Other Current	5.8	8.8	7.5	9.1	13.1	10.6
46.4	40.9	39.6	Total Current	46.7	39.8	41.9	35.6	43.1	35.1
15.4	24.0	19.3	Long-Term Debt	27.5	31.1	25.6	12.5	8.7	12.3
.7	.2	.3	Deferred Taxes	.0	.3	.6	.2	.1	.3
5.1	9.8	10.3	All Other Non-Current	36.9	16.0	7.1	3.0	6.3	4.1
32.5	25.1	30.5	Net Worth	-11.6	12.8	24.7	48.7	41.9	48.2
100.0	100.0	100.0	Total Liabilities & Net Worth	100.0	100.0	100.0	100.0	100.0	100.0
			INCOME DATA						
100.0	100.0	100.0	Net Sales	100.0	100.0	100.0	100.0	100.0	100.0
35.5	37.7	38.6	Gross Profit	50.1	45.5	32.4	39.5	33.9	31.5
28.7	33.0	31.3	Operating Expenses	47.4	39.6	28.9	29.3	26.8	20.2
6.9	4.6	7.3	Operating Profit	2.7	5.9	3.5	10.2	7.1	11.3
1.0	1.4	1.2	All Other Expenses (net)	2.1	1.6	.5	.7	1.0	1.6
5.8	3.3	6.1	Profit Before Taxes	.7	4.2	3.1	9.5	6.2	9.7
			RATIOS						
3.1	2.9	3.6		3.5	3.1	2.7	4.1	4.8	3.7
1.9	1.7	1.9	Current	1.8	1.6	1.8	2.1	2.1	1.9
1.1	1.1	1.1		.4	.9	1.1	1.3	1.0	1.3
1.8	1.7	1.9		1.7	1.9	1.8	2.8	2.5	1.6
.8	.8	1.1	Quick	.4	1.0	.9	1.3	1.1	1.0
.5	.5	.5		.2	.5	.6	.7	.5	.5
30 12.2	28 13.0	33 11.0		8 47.3	20 18.5	33 11.0	40 9.2	36 10.1	41 9.0
40 9.0	44 8.2	48 7.6	Sales/Receivables	32 11.5	39 9.4	50 7.3	54 6.7	43 8.4	50 7.3
51 7.2	58 6.3	61 6.0		80 4.6	57 6.4	60 6.0	66 5.5	58 6.3	60 6.1
26 14.0	24 15.2	23 15.9		0 UND	5 73.5	18 20.0	29 12.5	25 14.6	73 5.0
85 4.3	72 5.1	68 5.4	Cost of Sales/Inventory	27 13.4	52 7.0	31 11.9	66 5.5	102 3.6	135 2.7
147 2.5	129 2.8	138 2.6		101 3.6	94 3.9	93 3.9	109 3.3	152 2.4	187 1.9
16 22.2	15 24.2	18 20.1		0 UND	15 24.3	31 11.8	16 23.3	20 18.7	24 15.3
30 12.3	29 12.6	31 11.8	Cost of Sales/Payables	27 13.4	31 11.9	38 9.5	28 13.0	30 12.2	31 11.9
45 8.2	50 7.3	53 7.0		81 4.5	59 6.2	50 7.3	40 9.2	57 6.4	42 8.8
4.3	4.1	3.5		2.0	4.8	5.1	3.9	2.7	2.3
7.8	8.3	7.0	Sales/Working Capital	12.5	11.3	10.8	5.5	5.5	4.5
40.5	80.1	68.3		-10.8	-35.7	61.6	15.4	NM	9.3
16.5	8.7	15.7		4.0	6.8	5.3	18.3	38.1	47.8
(91) 5.1	(162) 2.8	(154) 4.7	EBIT/Interest	(13) .5	(37) 2.4	2.6	(29) 5.1	(24) 10.3	(28) 10.1
2.2	.1	1.6		-9.8	.1	1.6	3.4	2.0	4.0
4.1	5.7	7.9	Net Profit + Depr., Dep., Amort./Cur. Mat. L/T/D						
(23) 2.5	(35) 1.8	(25) 3.4							
.8	.9	2.0							
.2	.3	.2		.3	.2	.4	.1	.2	.2
.7	.8	.8	Fixed/Worth	30.4	2.1	1.4	.4	.5	.4
4.0	5.6	4.8		-.4	-2.0	10.1	1.4	3.5	1.1
.6	.8	.6		1.0	.7	1.2	.4	.4	.4
1.8	2.3	2.0	Debt/Worth	35.1	6.2	4.7	1.1	1.3	1.3
24.7	9.5	18.5		-3.2	-5.5	-16.5	3.0	11.1	3.2
62.1	51.7	72.9			89.1	117.6	57.3	84.9	52.9
(80) 30.8	(136) 21.3	(143) 31.4	% Profit Before Taxes/Tangible Net Worth	(29) 33.5	(17) 28.1	(33) 30.1	(26) 30.2	(29) 32.3	
11.9	-.1	11.2		7.0	5.4	13.3	11.8	17.3	
22.0	19.4	22.4		15.6	24.1	12.4	24.4	24.2	23.0
9.1	5.1	10.7	% Profit Before Taxes/Total Assets	-2.4	8.2	7.2	12.8	12.4	11.8
2.8	-2.7	1.9		-21.5	-2.4	1.9	7.4	4.0	7.2
26.2	18.2	18.5		15.3	19.1	23.0	19.2	26.3	18.2
12.0	9.4	9.3	Sales/Net Fixed Assets	6.0	9.5	7.8	11.2	11.9	8.6
5.6	4.4	4.9		2.2	5.0	3.8	5.2	5.5	5.6
3.0	2.5	2.7		3.0	3.2	3.0	2.7	2.4	2.2
2.1	1.9	2.0	Sales/Total Assets	1.5	2.1	2.2	2.2	1.7	1.5
1.5	1.3	1.4		.8	1.5	1.8	1.6	1.4	1.3
1.0	1.3	1.1		1.3	1.4	1.9	1.1	1.0	1.0
(85) 2.0	(142) 2.6	(151) 2.3	% Depr., Dep., Amort./Sales	(13) 2.7	(34) 2.8	(18) 2.8	(29) 2.0	(28) 2.3	(29) 1.6
3.0	4.8	4.5		8.0	5.8	5.8	3.8	4.4	3.0
2.4	2.7	2.4			3.7	2.8	1.7	1.5	
(43) 5.3	(89) 4.5	(75) 4.5	% Officers', Directors' Owners' Comp/Sales	(21) 7.2	(13) 3.6	(19) 3.0	(11) 3.0		
7.9	7.9	7.8		10.8	5.6	6.8	8.3		
1984905M	4124465M	2910968M	Net Sales ($)	7325M	78383M	91260M	248166M	440666M	2045168M
1202179M	2340692M	2022480M	Total Assets ($)	7401M	42293M	46031M	126892M	260869M	1538994M

M = $ thousand   MM = $ million
See Pages 9 through 22 for Explanation of Ratios and Data

Current Data Sorted by Assets   Comparative Historical Data

0-500M	500M-2MM	2-10MM	10-50MM	50-100MM	100-250MM	Type of Statement	4/1/06-3/31/07 ALL	4/1/07-3/31/08 ALL
1		1	5	2	4	Unqualified	9	6
	2	9	4	2		Reviewed	16	13
	2	6		1		Compiled	5	7
	2	1	1			Tax Returns	6	3
1	3	9	8	1	1	Other	25	29
	12 (4/1-9/30/10)		54 (10/1/10-3/31/11)					
2	9	26	18	6	5	NUMBER OF STATEMENTS	61	58
%	%	%	%	%	%	ASSETS	%	%
		6.6	11.8			Cash & Equivalents	6.5	7.3
		27.8	18.7			Trade Receivables (net)	24.3	26.6
		34.7	27.0			Inventory	32.1	32.6
		4.7	2.7			All Other Current	4.8	4.1
		73.9	60.1			Total Current	67.7	70.7
		19.5	29.7			Fixed Assets (net)	23.7	20.9
		3.7	1.3			Intangibles (net)	3.8	2.5
		2.9	8.9			All Other Non-Current	4.8	5.9
		100.0	100.0			Total	100.0	100.0
						LIABILITIES		
		13.7	6.7			Notes Payable-Short Term	12.5	10.8
		4.0	3.4			Cur. Mat.-L.T.D.	3.6	3.3
		11.2	7.5			Trade Payables	12.6	12.5
		.7	.0			Income Taxes Payable	.5	.7
		10.3	5.8			All Other Current	10.1	8.2
		39.9	23.4			Total Current	39.2	35.6
		9.3	9.3			Long-Term Debt	15.1	12.6
		.2	.6			Deferred Taxes	.4	.5
		1.7	5.6			All Other Non-Current	9.0	8.2
		49.0	61.0			Net Worth	36.3	43.0
		100.0	100.0			Total Liabilities & Net Worth	100.0	100.0
						INCOME DATA		
		100.0	100.0			Net Sales	100.0	100.0
		35.7	32.8			Gross Profit	32.0	30.1
		27.7	24.1			Operating Expenses	25.7	21.7
		8.0	8.8			Operating Profit	6.3	8.5
		1.1	.8			All Other Expenses (net)	1.2	1.4
		6.9	8.0			Profit Before Taxes	5.1	7.1
						RATIOS		
		4.3	7.6				3.2	3.3
		2.0	2.7			Current	1.9	2.1
		1.2	1.6				1.3	1.4
		1.9	3.4				1.2	1.9
		.8	1.1			Quick	.8	.9
		.5	.5				.6	.6
		33 11.0	34 10.7				38 9.5	36 10.1
		49 7.5	51 7.2			Sales/Receivables	48 7.6	47 7.7
		62 5.9	59 6.2				59 6.2	61 6.0
		47 7.7	40 9.1				40 9.2	51 7.1
		85 4.3	108 3.4			Cost of Sales/Inventory	93 3.9	94 3.9
		138 2.6	148 2.5				142 2.6	135 2.7
		17 21.0	14 25.4				19 19.6	20 18.1
		26 14.0	31 11.7			Cost of Sales/Payables	33 11.2	29 12.6
		38 9.5	43 8.5				51 7.2	39 9.3
		3.5	2.3				3.7	3.1
		7.5	4.1			Sales/Working Capital	5.5	5.0
		28.8	10.0				14.0	11.9
		23.4	13.8				9.7	16.8
		(24) 13.3	(13) 6.7			EBIT/Interest	(55) 4.5	(52) 5.7
		5.0	4.0				1.4	2.1
						Net Profit + Depr., Dep.,	6.9	11.0
						Amort./Cur. Mat. L/T/D	(23) 3.8	(23) 3.4
							2.0	1.7
		.1	.3				.2	.2
		.4	.4			Fixed/Worth	.6	.5
		1.1	1.0				1.1	1.0
		.5	.2				.8	.6
		1.1	.7			Debt/Worth	1.4	1.2
		3.0	1.2				3.1	2.6
		48.5	25.0			% Profit Before Taxes/Tangible	38.2	42.9
		(24) 32.3	(17) 20.4			Net Worth	(56) 21.3	(52) 25.6
		19.0	8.2				10.1	10.3
		24.1	16.0			% Profit Before Taxes/Total	14.4	20.2
		13.9	10.4			Assets	8.1	12.1
		8.0	6.9				2.6	3.9
		62.8	13.6				20.1	28.7
		20.4	5.1			Sales/Net Fixed Assets	9.7	10.2
		6.1	2.9				4.2	5.7
		2.8	1.7				2.3	2.4
		2.2	1.3			Sales/Total Assets	1.9	1.9
		1.5	1.0				1.3	1.4
		1.1	2.6				1.3	.7
		(21) 1.8	(15) 3.8			% Depr., Dep., Amort./Sales	(59) 2.1	(55) 1.9
		3.7	6.5				3.3	3.9
		1.5				% Officers', Directors'	1.7	1.6
		(13) 2.0				Owners' Comp/Sales	(23) 5.0	(21) 2.9
		3.4					8.2	6.8
1910M	34528M	279774M	614428M	626509M	920975M	Net Sales ($)	2232236M	2511986M
205M	11130M	126211M	424958M	451111M	847079M	Total Assets ($)	1683603M	1563332M

M = $ thousand   MM = $ million
See Pages 9 through 22 for Explanation of Ratios and Data

Comparative Historical Data

Current Data Sorted by Sales

			Type of Statement						
7	8	12	Unqualified				5	3	9
15	14	18	Reviewed	1	1	2	5	6	3
13	7	9	Compiled		1		5	2	1
9	10	4	Tax Returns		1		3		
22	15	23	Other	1	2	2	1	9	8
4/1/08-3/31/09 ALL	4/1/09-3/31/10 ALL	4/1/10-3/31/11 ALL		12 (4/1-9/30/10)			54 (10/1/10-3/31/11)		
				0-1MM	1-3MM	3-5MM	5-10MM	10-25MM	25MM & OVER
66	54	66	**NUMBER OF STATEMENTS**	2	5	4	14	20	21
%	%	%	**ASSETS**	%	%	%	%	%	%
11.0	13.1	11.1	Cash & Equivalents				7.4	9.0	13.0
23.1	25.5	25.7	Trade Receivables (net)				29.4	27.2	18.5
30.7	31.3	29.5	Inventory				34.9	31.6	24.0
3.3	3.9	3.4	All Other Current				.4	4.5	3.6
68.1	73.8	69.7	Total Current				72.2	72.3	59.1
21.9	17.0	21.7	Fixed Assets (net)				21.3	21.4	27.8
3.5	3.0	3.5	Intangibles (net)				3.1	1.4	5.5
6.5	6.2	5.0	All Other Non-Current				3.4	4.9	7.6
100.0	100.0	100.0	Total				100.0	100.0	100.0
			LIABILITIES						
8.4	6.9	9.3	Notes Payable-Short Term				15.2	10.9	5.4
3.2	3.2	2.9	Cur. Mat.-L.T.D.				2.8	5.4	1.6
10.7	10.7	10.9	Trade Payables				10.6	11.8	7.8
.6	.5	.5	Income Taxes Payable				.1	.3	.5
8.5	10.7	8.8	All Other Current				8.9	9.4	5.9
31.4	31.9	32.3	Total Current				37.6	37.8	21.3
10.4	7.9	8.7	Long-Term Debt				9.4	8.9	10.9
.4	.4	.7	Deferred Taxes				.1	.1	1.8
5.2	5.8	3.9	All Other Non-Current				1.0	5.1	4.6
52.6	54.0	54.4	Net Worth				51.8	48.1	61.4
100.0	100.0	100.0	Total Liabilities & Net Worth				100.0	100.0	100.0
			INCOME DATA						
100.0	100.0	100.0	Net Sales				100.0	100.0	100.0
33.5	34.8	35.0	Gross Profit				38.7	32.5	31.5
24.9	27.9	25.3	Operating Expenses				31.0	24.6	21.6
8.7	6.9	9.7	Operating Profit				7.7	7.8	9.9
1.0	.9	.9	All Other Expenses (net)				.9	.3	1.2
7.7	6.1	8.8	Profit Before Taxes				6.8	7.6	8.8
			RATIOS						
4.1	6.3	4.5					4.5	4.4	4.5
2.3	2.8	2.5	Current				2.5	2.0	2.9
1.6	1.6	1.4					1.1	1.3	2.0
2.1	3.6	2.4					2.0	1.6	2.4
.9	1.1	1.2	Quick				1.2	.8	1.8
.6	.7	.6					.6	.5	.6
33 11.0	36 10.1	36 10.1					32 11.3	35 10.3	40 9.1
42 8.7	46 7.9	50 7.3	Sales/Receivables				40 9.1	50 7.3	54 6.7
52 7.1	60 6.1	60 6.1					55 6.7	62 5.9	60 6.0
43 8.5	53 6.9	44 8.2					47 7.8	37 10.0	43 8.4
89 4.1	95 3.8	93 3.9	Cost of Sales/Inventory				88 4.1	79 4.6	104 3.5
136 2.7	150 2.4	140 2.6					152 2.4	132 2.8	134 2.7
16 23.2	13 28.0	17 21.0					15 25.2	20 18.4	19 19.6
23 15.6	22 16.3	28 13.0	Cost of Sales/Payables				24 15.4	32 11.3	28 13.2
39 9.4	37 10.0	42 8.6					39 9.3	43 8.6	43 8.4
3.3	2.5	2.5					2.9	3.4	2.2
5.1	4.0	4.8	Sales/Working Capital				9.1	6.4	3.4
10.2	9.2	11.3					58.9	11.7	6.0
23.9	17.4	21.4					28.6	38.0	18.5
(59) 8.8	(46) 3.8	(52) 11.1	EBIT/Interest				6.6 (17)	11.9 (16)	10.0
3.0	-.4	4.6					2.3	5.0	4.6
14.6	3.5	12.7	Net Profit + Depr., Dep.,						
(26) 4.2	(15) 2.1	(17) 5.8	Amort./Cur. Mat. L/T/D						
2.2	.4	1.9							
.1	.1	.2					.2	.0	.3
.4	.3	.4	Fixed/Worth				.4	.3	.5
.7	.6	.9					1.1	1.2	.8
.5	.3	.3					.3	.6	.3
1.0	1.1	.8	Debt/Worth				1.0	1.1	.7
1.6	2.0	1.9					2.8	2.2	1.3
48.6	37.1	43.3	% Profit Before Taxes/Tangible				65.1	44.7	31.9
(63) 29.6	(53) 17.6	(62) 26.5	Net Worth		(13) 35.7	(18) 29.0			20.4
9.7	-1.7	17.2					15.0	23.7	16.4
25.2	21.1	23.6	% Profit Before Taxes/Total				28.6	23.0	14.3
14.3	8.0	12.6	Assets				15.5	13.4	12.1
2.9	-1.4	8.8					2.7	9.8	8.9
26.3	40.3	28.2					29.2	75.1	9.4
12.7	13.7	10.1	Sales/Net Fixed Assets				10.7	21.0	5.1
5.7	6.5	4.3					4.8	4.2	3.3
2.7	2.4	2.4					3.1	2.9	1.5
2.0	1.6	1.6	Sales/Total Assets				2.1	2.2	1.2
1.5	1.3	1.2					1.5	1.5	1.0
.7	.6	1.4					1.4	.7	2.8
(56) 2.0	(44) 1.5	(53) 2.7	% Depr., Dep., Amort./Sales		(13) 2.2	(16) 2.2		(17) 3.8	
3.5	3.0	4.3					5.1	6.3	4.4
1.8	1.7	1.7	% Officers', Directors'						
(15) 3.1	(12) 3.5	(17) 2.1	Owners' Comp/Sales						
16.6	9.9	3.8							
3114674M	1570930M	2478124M	Net Sales ($)	1157M	9151M	14401M	98784M	328690M	2025941M
2067730M	1160848M	1860694M	Total Assets ($)	1352M	5500M	7881M	53172M	173828M	1618961M

M = $ thousand   MM = $ million
See Pages 9 through 22 for Explanation of Ratios and Data

Current Data Sorted by Assets   Comparative Historical Data

	0-500M	500M-2MM 7 (4/1-9/30/10)	2-10MM	10-50MM 24 (10/1/10-3/31/11)	50-100MM	100-250MM	4/1/06-3/31/07 ALL	4/1/07-3/31/08 ALL
Type of Statement								
Unqualified			2	2	1	3	12	14
Reviewed			5	3			7	3
Compiled	1		1	1			3	1
Tax Returns	1			1			1	1
Other		1	3	3		3	10	10
NUMBER OF STATEMENTS	2	1	11	10	1	6	33	29
	%	%	%	%	%	%	%	%
ASSETS								
Cash & Equivalents			8.8	3.2			11.1	8.4
Trade Receivables (net)			29.0	22.1			26.2	23.6
Inventory			32.0	34.6			34.5	35.7
All Other Current			6.5	3.9			1.8	3.3
Total Current			76.2	63.8			73.6	70.9
Fixed Assets (net)			19.0	18.6			15.3	16.8
Intangibles (net)			1.7	10.7			3.8	7.1
All Other Non-Current			3.1	6.9			7.4	5.2
Total			100.0	100.0			100.0	100.0
LIABILITIES								
Notes Payable-Short Term			10.2	11.1			11.0	12.5
Cur. Mat.-L.T.D.			2.8	2.4			3.5	2.7
Trade Payables			12.4	6.3			10.8	11.7
Income Taxes Payable			.4	1.1			.8	.7
All Other Current			9.3	7.5			13.0	11.7
Total Current			35.0	28.5			39.1	39.2
Long-Term Debt			12.5	18.3			16.1	23.4
Deferred Taxes			.7	1.3			.4	.1
All Other Non-Current			5.3	6.2			3.5	6.2
Net Worth			46.5	45.8			40.9	31.1
Total Liabilties & Net Worth			100.0	100.0			100.0	100.0
INCOME DATA								
Net Sales			100.0	100.0			100.0	100.0
Gross Profit			32.3	32.4			37.8	36.3
Operating Expenses			29.4	27.2			29.5	29.0
Operating Profit			3.0	5.2			8.3	7.2
All Other Expenses (net)			-.3	.7			1.0	1.8
Profit Before Taxes			3.3	4.4			7.3	5.4
RATIOS								
Current			5.9	4.7			3.9	3.2
			3.7	2.3			1.9	2.5
			1.3	1.7			1.4	1.5
Quick			2.8	1.5			2.1	1.7
			1.3	.9			1.0	.9
			.5	.6			.5	.6
Sales/Receivables			36 10.1	30 12.3			38 9.5	31 11.7
			42 8.8	43 8.5			45 8.1	46 7.9
			57 6.4	67 5.4			58 6.3	56 6.5
Cost of Sales/Inventory			44 8.4	59 6.2			74 4.9	79 4.6
			87 4.2	144 2.5			100 3.7	98 3.7
			113 3.2	173 2.1			145 2.5	124 3.0
Cost of Sales/Payables			20 18.5	6 62.9			14 25.4	17 21.6
			28 12.9	15 25.0			31 11.7	34 10.7
			39 9.3	26 14.2			42 8.7	49 7.4
Sales/Working Capital			3.0	2.6			4.0	4.2
			4.0	4.5			6.2	5.2
			18.9	7.8			14.8	9.0
EBIT/Interest			14.5				22.4	8.5
			(10) 5.6				(29) 3.9	(25) 3.1
			.7				1.7	1.3
Net Profit + Depr., Dep., Amort./Cur. Mat. L/T/D							11.9	
							(11) 2.5	
							2.3	
Fixed/Worth			.2	.2			.2	.2
			.3	.5			.3	.7
			1.2	NM			1.1	8.5
Debt/Worth			.2	.9			.6	.9
			1.6	1.2			1.5	2.9
			3.1	NM			3.7	33.5
% Profit Before Taxes/Tangible Net Worth			27.4				62.8	61.1
			(10) 15.8				(30) 35.6	(23) 37.8
			6.8				16.7	15.8
% Profit Before Taxes/Total Assets			11.3	21.8			18.4	19.0
			6.8	7.6			12.0	11.9
			1.1	-3.4			3.3	3.1
Sales/Net Fixed Assets			33.2	20.1			32.2	22.7
			17.2	12.7			14.7	14.8
			6.8	7.3			8.8	7.7
Sales/Total Assets			2.5	2.2			2.4	2.3
			2.1	1.6			2.1	1.9
			1.8	1.2			1.6	1.6
% Depr., Dep., Amort./Sales							.6	1.1
							(30) 1.0	(23) 1.8
							1.6	2.7
% Officers', Directors' Owners' Comp/Sales								
Net Sales ($)	1603M	541M	143121M	356723M	85284M	1098549M	2008389M	1978979M
Total Assets ($)	743M	522M	67670M	205959M	75096M	820918M	1231551M	1127025M

M = $ thousand   MM = $ million
See Pages 9 through 22 for Explanation of Ratios and Data

Comparative Historical Data / Current Data Sorted by Sales

4/1/08-3/31/09 ALL	4/1/09-3/31/10 ALL	4/1/10-3/31/11 ALL	Type of Statement	0-1MM	1-3MM	3-5MM	5-10MM	10-25MM	25MM & OVER
10	11	8	Unqualified					3	5
10	8	8	Reviewed				1	6	1
1		2	Compiled	1					1
6	2	3	Tax Returns	1			1	1	
9	11	10	Other	1			2	2	5
				7 (4/1-9/30/10)			24 (10/1/10-3/31/11)		
36	32	31	NUMBER OF STATEMENTS	3			4	12	12
%	%	%	**ASSETS**	%	%	%	%	%	%
6.2	11.1	8.9	Cash & Equivalents		DATA NOT AVAILABLE	DATA NOT AVAILABLE		6.2	7.2
23.0	21.8	22.7	Trade Receivables (net)					29.1	22.2
38.3	31.2	28.6	Inventory					30.9	24.2
3.2	4.3	4.3	All Other Current					7.3	3.6
70.7	68.3	64.6	Total Current					73.5	57.3
18.4	19.5	17.5	Fixed Assets (net)					20.3	16.0
6.4	7.2	10.2	Intangibles (net)					1.8	19.4
4.5	4.9	7.7	All Other Non-Current					4.5	7.3
100.0	100.0	100.0	Total					100.0	100.0
			LIABILITIES						
9.9	9.8	12.0	Notes Payable-Short Term					11.6	6.3
3.1	2.4	3.4	Cur. Mat.-L.T.D.					2.6	1.8
11.9	10.6	8.6	Trade Payables					10.7	7.4
.4	.5	.5	Income Taxes Payable					.4	1.0
10.8	9.8	8.7	All Other Current					9.8	10.6
36.0	33.2	33.2	Total Current					35.1	27.0
15.0	16.2	18.2	Long-Term Debt					9.9	18.8
.4	.2	.7	Deferred Taxes					.9	.9
7.4	6.7	12.4	All Other Non-Current					6.3	10.0
41.2	43.7	35.5	Net Worth					47.8	43.2
100.0	100.0	100.0	Total Liabilties & Net Worth					100.0	100.0
			INCOME DATA						
100.0	100.0	100.0	Net Sales					100.0	100.0
29.9	34.7	35.2	Gross Profit					31.4	29.0
27.5	30.7	31.6	Operating Expenses					28.8	23.0
2.4	4.0	3.6	Operating Profit					2.6	6.0
.6	1.3	.7	All Other Expenses (net)					-.5	2.0
1.8	2.7	2.9	Profit Before Taxes					3.1	4.0
			RATIOS						
3.7	4.4	4.8						5.7	4.3
2.1	2.2	2.3	Current					3.2	1.9
1.6	1.4	1.3						1.3	1.3
1.5	2.2	2.3						2.7	2.0
.7	.7	1.1	Quick					1.4	.9
.5	.6	.5						.4	.5
26 13.8	36 10.0	35 10.4						37 9.8	33 11.0
35 10.5	44 8.3	43 8.5	Sales/Receivables					44 8.3	43 8.5
53 6.9	54 6.8	57 6.4						60 6.1	65 5.6
73 5.0	68 5.4	52 7.0						48 7.6	52 7.1
97 3.8	102 3.6	87 4.2	Cost of Sales/Inventory					91 4.0	59 6.2
147 2.5	134 2.7	159 2.3						166 2.2	116 3.2
12 29.6	21 17.4	11 34.4						16 22.9	10 35.0
24 14.9	25 14.3	23 15.7	Cost of Sales/Payables					26 13.9	23 15.7
39 9.4	37 9.8	34 10.8						35 10.5	32 11.4
3.4	3.1	2.9						3.1	3.2
5.5	4.9	4.5	Sales/Working Capital					4.2	7.2
8.6	10.8	17.7						18.6	13.7
13.7	16.5	12.3						18.3	12.5
(32) 2.1	(29) 2.6	(27) 3.0	EBIT/Interest					(11) 2.3	(11) 4.3
-1.3	1.1	-.1						-1.8	.7
4.6	9.0								
(11) 2.1	(16) 4.0		Net Profit + Depr., Dep., Amort./Cur. Mat. L/T/D						
.6	.8								
.2	.2	.2						.2	.3
.5	.6	.5	Fixed/Worth					.4	.5
1.1	2.0	11.9						1.0	NM
.6	.5	.6						.3	1.0
1.5	1.7	1.8	Debt/Worth					1.4	1.9
5.1	7.8	26.5						3.1	NM
23.5	33.3	34.0						31.3	
(31) 17.1	(27) 13.6	(24) 20.8	% Profit Before Taxes/Tangible Net Worth					(11) 13.9	
-.7	3.0	9.0						-4.7	
13.9	14.1	13.6						13.0	13.5
4.6	4.4	6.7	% Profit Before Taxes/Total Assets					5.5	7.7
-3.3	.7	-3.3						-7.2	-.2
20.7	16.8	27.4						31.3	24.9
11.9	9.9	12.6	Sales/Net Fixed Assets					12.5	11.2
8.4	6.2	7.0						5.6	7.0
2.7	2.2	2.3						2.3	2.3
2.0	1.9	1.8	Sales/Total Assets					2.0	1.6
1.5	1.3	1.2						1.5	1.2
.7	1.2	.9						.8	
(33) 1.4	(28) 2.0	(22) 1.7	% Depr., Dep., Amort./Sales					(11) 1.7	
2.4	3.3	2.7						2.9	
			% Officers', Directors' Owners' Comp/Sales						
2332914M	2084224M	1685821M	Net Sales ($)	2144M			27551M	202255M	1453871M
1333520M	1377117M	1170908M	Total Assets ($)	1265M			26002M	112726M	1030915M

M = $ thousand MM = $ million

See Pages 9 through 22 for Explanation of Ratios and Data

Current Data Sorted by Assets   Comparative Historical Data

0-500M	500M-2MM	2-10MM	10-50MM	50-100MM	100-250MM		ALL 4/1/06-3/31/07	ALL 4/1/07-3/31/08
						Type of Statement		
	1	4	12	3	3	Unqualified	33	25
	2	7	3			Reviewed	13	10
	2	5	2			Compiled	10	9
	2	7				Tax Returns	5	3
3	7	19	11	2	4	Other	34	34
	26 (4/1-9/30/10)		73 (10/1/10-3/31/11)					
3	14	42	28	5	7	**NUMBER OF STATEMENTS**	95	81
%	%	%	%	%	%	**ASSETS**	%	%
	10.9	9.3	12.4			Cash & Equivalents	7.8	8.4
	34.7	26.6	22.0			Trade Receivables (net)	26.9	23.0
	25.2	34.0	29.7			Inventory	31.7	32.0
	2.3	1.3	2.4			All Other Current	2.3	3.0
	73.2	71.2	66.5			Total Current	68.6	66.5
	15.3	21.2	19.4			Fixed Assets (net)	19.1	20.5
	7.4	2.3	7.8			Intangibles (net)	5.3	6.9
	4.1	5.3	6.3			All Other Non-Current	7.0	6.1
	100.0	100.0	100.0			Total	100.0	100.0
						LIABILITIES		
	10.9	11.9	4.2			Notes Payable-Short Term	12.3	9.3
	2.4	3.5	4.2			Cur. Mat.-L.T.D.	3.1	3.5
	17.5	13.2	11.8			Trade Payables	16.3	11.8
	.5	.3	.3			Income Taxes Payable	.5	.4
	5.2	7.4	6.2			All Other Current	9.5	7.7
	36.4	36.3	26.6			Total Current	41.7	32.7
	8.5	14.7	11.3			Long-Term Debt	13.7	15.2
	.0	.2	.4			Deferred Taxes	.4	.4
	.7	4.0	8.0			All Other Non-Current	3.2	7.7
	54.3	44.7	53.7			Net Worth	40.9	44.0
	100.0	100.0	100.0			Total Liabilities & Net Worth	100.0	100.0
						INCOME DATA		
	100.0	100.0	100.0			Net Sales	100.0	100.0
	33.5	32.6	30.6			Gross Profit	32.1	33.2
	29.9	25.3	25.2			Operating Expenses	25.6	25.3
	3.5	7.3	5.3			Operating Profit	6.4	7.9
	.8	.7	1.1			All Other Expenses (net)	1.0	1.3
	2.7	6.5	4.2			Profit Before Taxes	5.5	6.6
						RATIOS		
	4.3	3.4	3.8				3.1	4.3
	1.8	1.9	2.9			Current	1.7	2.1
	1.5	1.3	1.4				1.2	1.3
	2.2	1.9	2.1				1.8	1.8
	1.3	.9	1.2			Quick	.9	1.0
	.6	.6	.8				.5	.6
	41 8.9	35 10.5	39 9.3				34 10.9	35 10.6
	50 7.3	55 6.7	51 7.2			Sales/Receivables	45 8.1	45 8.2
	84 4.3	70 5.2	61 6.0				58 6.3	56 6.5
	1 256.9	49 7.4	75 4.9				45 8.0	65 5.6
	79 4.6	110 3.3	90 4.1			Cost of Sales/Inventory	81 4.5	91 4.0
	121 3.0	165 2.2	113 3.2				121 3.0	124 2.9
	23 15.7	16 23.5	23 15.7				16 23.1	16 22.1
	42 8.8	36 10.2	37 9.8			Cost of Sales/Payables	31 11.8	29 12.6
	63 5.8	64 5.7	50 7.4				54 6.8	41 8.9
	3.0	2.6	2.9				4.5	3.5
	4.5	5.8	4.4			Sales/Working Capital	6.4	6.0
	9.9	12.8	9.0				21.0	12.4
	15.6	12.5	35.1				18.9	19.5
	(10) 4.5	(36) 4.9	(25) 5.6			EBIT/Interest	(84) 5.2	(74) 6.3
	-3.3	1.1	.3				2.0	2.0
		4.9	15.8				11.9	11.6
		(12) 2.4	(13) 2.4			Net Profit + Depr., Dep., Amort./Cur. Mat. L/T/D	(35) 4.3	(28) 3.5
		1.1	.2				1.8	1.3
	.0	.2	.2				.2	.2
	.2	.4	.4			Fixed/Worth	.4	.5
	.7	1.1	.9				1.4	1.4
	.3	.6	.3				.5	.4
	.9	1.3	1.1			Debt/Worth	1.9	1.4
	2.6	3.2	2.9				5.5	5.6
	24.3	38.2	26.8				46.8	55.0
	(13) 11.5	(39) 13.1	(26) 16.1			% Profit Before Taxes/Tangible Net Worth	(82) 27.6	(70) 28.8
	-1.0	2.8	2.4				7.6	10.1
	12.4	19.1	13.9				17.4	20.5
	5.6	6.7	6.4			% Profit Before Taxes/Total Assets	7.9	12.1
	-2.3	1.3	-.8				3.6	3.2
	UND	24.3	18.1				26.7	24.1
	45.9	9.5	9.6			Sales/Net Fixed Assets	11.3	10.2
	6.3	4.6	7.0				7.5	5.9
	2.3	2.0	2.0				2.6	2.3
	2.0	1.8	1.6			Sales/Total Assets	2.1	1.9
	1.5	1.4	1.2				1.5	1.5
		.9	1.6				1.0	1.1
		(35) 2.1	(26) 2.6			% Depr., Dep., Amort./Sales	(80) 1.9	(73) 2.0
		3.2	3.8				3.1	3.4
		1.6					.9	1.2
		(13) 2.9				% Officers', Directors' Owners' Comp/Sales	(23) 2.8	(18) 2.5
		11.8					9.4	7.0
4166M	31161M	373348M	983495M	459788M	1762225M	Net Sales ($)	3654539M	2725889M
901M	16255M	222082M	600384M	359329M	1152433M	Total Assets ($)	2133352M	1589412M

© RMA 2011

M = $ thousand   MM = $ million
See Pages 9 through 22 for Explanation of Ratios and Data

Comparative Historical Data | **Current Data Sorted by Sales**

Hist 4/1/08-3/31/09 ALL	Hist 4/1/09-3/31/10 ALL	Hist 4/1/10-3/31/11 ALL	Type of Statement	0-1MM	1-3MM	3-5MM	5-10MM	10-25MM	25MM & OVER
28	20	23	Unqualified		1		3	6	13
15	16	12	Reviewed	1	1		2	7	1
9	11	9	Compiled		1	2	2	4	
9	13	15	Tax Returns	2	4	5	3	1	
35	38	40	Other		5	3	7	9	16
					26 (4/1-9/30/10)		73 (10/1/10-3/31/11)		
96	98	99	NUMBER OF STATEMENTS	3	12	10	17	27	30
%	%	%	**ASSETS**	%	%	%	%	%	%
9.2	9.7	11.1	Cash & Equivalents		9.6	4.6	11.4	11.3	11.6
22.2	23.1	25.8	Trade Receivables (net)		30.0	32.4	26.9	23.1	23.6
31.7	28.1	30.2	Inventory		18.4	32.8	36.9	32.2	27.5
3.2	2.7	2.2	All Other Current		2.7	.5	1.1	2.2	3.3
66.4	63.5	69.3	Total Current		60.7	70.3	76.4	68.9	66.0
20.2	23.8	20.7	Fixed Assets (net)		26.1	24.5	15.1	21.4	21.7
7.5	6.3	4.4	Intangibles (net)		6.9	3.2	3.6	3.0	5.8
5.9	6.3	5.6	All Other Non-Current		6.3	2.0	4.9	6.7	6.5
100.0	100.0	100.0	Total		100.0	100.0	100.0	100.0	100.0
			LIABILITIES						
9.1	7.5	8.7	Notes Payable-Short Term		18.2	14.2	9.4	6.8	4.6
3.2	5.4	3.2	Cur. Mat.-L.T.D.		2.2	5.2	1.8	4.3	3.0
13.1	11.3	12.5	Trade Payables		10.3	10.9	13.4	13.0	11.6
.5	.1	.3	Income Taxes Payable		.6	.1	.5	.2	.2
8.8	7.1	7.8	All Other Current		10.4	5.8	9.8	6.2	8.5
34.7	31.4	32.5	Total Current		41.7	36.2	34.8	30.4	27.9
13.6	22.8	13.8	Long-Term Debt		13.7	17.9	11.1	14.1	12.2
.5	.4	.4	Deferred Taxes		.0	.2	.3	.5	.8
7.3	7.5	4.8	All Other Non-Current		2.5	3.5	5.6	5.1	6.0
43.9	37.8	48.5	Net Worth		42.1	42.2	48.1	49.9	53.1
100.0	100.0	100.0	Total Liabilities & Net Worth		100.0	100.0	100.0	100.0	100.0
			INCOME DATA						
100.0	100.0	100.0	Net Sales		100.0	100.0	100.0	100.0	100.0
34.1	31.4	31.3	Gross Profit		37.1	34.4	30.8	31.3	27.9
25.1	27.1	25.1	Operating Expenses		31.6	29.2	25.1	23.8	21.7
8.9	4.4	6.3	Operating Profit		5.6	5.2	5.7	7.5	6.2
1.0	1.4	.7	All Other Expenses (net)		1.0	1.6	.7	.6	.1
7.9	3.0	5.6	Profit Before Taxes		4.5	3.6	5.0	6.9	6.1
			RATIOS						
3.2	3.6	3.8	Current		3.4	5.5	5.6	4.1	3.7
2.0	2.1	2.1			1.5	1.6	2.4	2.1	2.7
1.3	1.4	1.4			.6	1.2	1.4	1.3	1.7
1.9	2.0	2.1	Quick		2.0	3.2	2.8	2.3	2.0
.9	1.1	1.2			.9	.8	1.1	1.0	1.3
.5	.6	.7			.4	.5	.7	.6	.8
30 12.1	35 10.5	37 9.8	Sales/Receivables	37 9.9	48 7.5	36 10.1	32 11.3	42 8.7	
39 9.5	45 8.1	51 7.1		45 8.0	61 6.0	57 6.4	43 8.4	52 7.0	
51 7.2	60 6.1	66 5.5		114 3.2	82 4.5	71 5.1	61 5.9	60 6.1	
62 5.9	47 7.7	54 6.7	Cost of Sales/Inventory	0 UND	60 6.1	61 6.0	47 7.8	71 5.1	
99 3.7	85 4.3	96 3.8		55 6.7	100 3.7	121 3.0	106 3.5	89 4.1	
133 2.7	142 2.6	131 2.8		118 3.1	165 2.2	194 1.9	156 2.3	109 3.4	
14 25.3	17 21.2	19 18.8	Cost of Sales/Payables	19 19.0	21 17.4	11 31.8	17 21.7	23 16.1	
27 13.6	28 13.2	34 10.8		44 8.3	29 12.7	31 11.9	36 10.2	32 11.3	
42 8.8	43 8.4	52 7.0		82 4.4	48 7.6	63 5.8	58 6.3	41 9.0	
4.3	3.7	2.7	Sales/Working Capital		3.2	2.7	2.3	2.7	2.9
7.1	5.3	4.8			8.5	7.8	3.3	4.9	4.2
14.1	14.2	10.5			-19.7	12.4	8.2	11.8	8.6
21.7	10.5	21.1	EBIT/Interest				7.8	20.1	42.3
(81) 7.0	(87) 3.7	(85) 5.4					(15) 4.5	(24) 6.5	(26) 7.9
3.0	.7	1.2					1.0	1.4	2.1
9.8	6.7	9.2	Net Profit + Depr., Dep., Amort./Cur. Mat. L/T/D					5.4	24.9
(42) 3.5	(42) 2.0	(32) 2.8						(10) 1.8	(14) 4.8
1.7	.7	1.3						1.0	1.5
.2	.2	.2	Fixed/Worth		.1	.2	.2	.2	.2
.5	.6	.4			.7	.6	.3	.5	.4
1.7	2.2	1.0			8.5	2.3	.4	1.0	1.0
.6	.7	.5	Debt/Worth		.5	.5	.6	.3	.5
1.5	1.6	1.1			2.9	1.4	1.0	1.1	.9
3.8	6.8	3.0			10.1	6.6	2.4	3.0	2.0
58.4	40.2	27.8	% Profit Before Taxes/Tangible Net Worth	93.1			19.0	52.2	27.0
(80) 27.4	(82) 17.8	(92) 16.4		(10) 16.3			(16) 10.7	(25) 24.5	(29) 18.6
10.6	-1.6	3.3		1.1			.3	6.2	12.0
23.3	12.8	14.0	% Profit Before Taxes/Total Assets		20.5	11.3	15.5	19.0	14.5
10.1	6.0	6.7			3.9	5.6	6.6	8.5	9.9
4.0	-1.4	1.9			-.8	1.7	.1	2.5	5.6
31.9	17.4	23.7	Sales/Net Fixed Assets		65.3	41.0	24.6	17.0	18.6
10.8	8.4	9.6			7.9	17.3	9.8	10.0	9.4
6.4	4.7	5.1			4.7	2.7	6.5	5.3	4.8
2.4	2.3	2.0	Sales/Total Assets		2.5	2.0	2.1	2.0	2.0
1.9	1.8	1.6			1.9	1.7	1.8	1.7	1.5
1.3	1.2	1.3			.9	1.2	1.3	1.5	1.3
.6	1.1	1.0	% Depr., Dep., Amort./Sales				.9	1.3	1.5
(84) 1.5	(88) 2.0	(79) 2.3					(13) 2.0	(25) 2.3	(26) 2.5
3.2	5.3	3.5					3.0	3.6	3.6
1.2	1.3	1.6	% Officers', Directors' Owners' Comp/Sales						
(18) 3.8	(30) 4.7	(21) 4.7							
6.6	8.2	9.6							
4034028M	2674664M	3614183M	Net Sales ($)	1731M	23426M	38023M	127192M	410164M	3013647M
2447944M	1749954M	2351384M	Total Assets ($)	1432M	16995M	25625M	83754M	257870M	1965708M

M = $ thousand   MM = $ million
See Pages 9 through 22 for Explanation of Ratios and Data

Current Data Sorted by Assets   Comparative Historical Data

Type of Statement

Type of Statement	500M-2MM	2-10MM	10-50MM	50-100MM	100-250MM	34 — 4/1/06-3/31/07 ALL	30 — 4/1/07-3/31/08 ALL
Unqualified		1	2	1	2	10	8
Reviewed		3	2	1		9	6
Compiled	1	1	1			6	2
Tax Returns	2		1				5
Other		3	6	2	1	9	9

Sorting key for current data: **3 (4/1-9/30/10)**   **26 (10/1/10-3/31/11)**

	0-500M	500M-2MM	2-10MM	10-50MM	50-100MM	100-250MM		34 ALL	30 ALL
NUMBER OF STATEMENTS		3	8	11	4	3		34	30
ASSETS	%	%	%	%	%	%		%	%
Cash & Equivalents				3.7				7.0	12.2
Trade Receivables (net)				22.6				23.9	25.1
Inventory				29.0				31.0	32.1
All Other Current				3.1				3.2	3.4
Total Current				58.4				65.2	72.7
Fixed Assets (net)				31.2				22.7	18.9
Intangibles (net)				9.8				2.9	3.3
All Other Non-Current				.6				9.2	5.0
Total				100.0				100.0	100.0
LIABILITIES									
Notes Payable-Short Term				20.1				12.3	10.7
Cur. Mat.-L.T.D.				3.6				2.8	2.0
Trade Payables				13.4				11.4	13.3
Income Taxes Payable				.3				.2	.4
All Other Current				5.7				10.7	12.1
Total Current				43.0				37.4	38.5
Long-Term Debt				11.9				9.7	9.7
Deferred Taxes				.2				.4	.4
All Other Non-Current				2.9				6.9	8.7
Net Worth				42.0				45.6	42.8
Total Liabilities & Net Worth				100.0				100.0	100.0
INCOME DATA									
Net Sales				100.0				100.0	100.0
Gross Profit				27.4				27.5	29.6
Operating Expenses				18.2				19.8	20.3
Operating Profit				9.1				7.7	9.3
All Other Expenses (net)				1.6				2.0	1.8
Profit Before Taxes				7.6				5.7	7.5

(Note: Columns 0-500M, 500M-2MM, 2-10MM, 50-100MM and 100-250MM are marked **DATA NOT AVAILABLE** for the sections above.)

RATIOS

Ratio	10-50MM	34 ALL	30 ALL
Current	2.5	3.5	4.4
	1.1	1.8	2.2
	.9	1.2	1.4
Quick	.9	1.7	1.8
	.5	.8	.9
	.4	.5	.6
Sales/Receivables	43 8.6	41 8.8	36 10.2
	44 8.3	53 6.9	45 8.0
	54 6.8	62 5.9	53 6.8
Cost of Sales/Inventory	42 8.8	54 6.8	43 8.6
	120 3.1	96 3.8	93 3.9
	137 2.7	139 2.6	131 2.8
Cost of Sales/Payables	14 26.4	15 24.6	17 21.3
	33 11.1	33 11.0	30 12.1
	50 7.3	51 7.2	47 7.8
Sales/Working Capital	4.9	3.1	3.1
	29.2	5.5	4.3
	-18.0	18.6	10.5
EBIT/Interest	18.0	18.7	18.1
	2.6	(31) 4.4	(27) 7.2
	1.3	2.1	2.6
Net Profit + Depr., Dep., Amort./Cur. Mat. L/T/D		8.9	51.2
		(11) 4.9	(12) 8.1
		1.1	2.7
Fixed/Worth	.3	.1	.1
	1.4	.5	.4
	2.8	.9	1.4
Debt/Worth	.8	.5	.4
	2.4	1.4	1.5
	4.2	2.9	3.8
% Profit Before Taxes/Tangible Net Worth		38.9	42.4
		(31) 21.1	(26) 24.5
		2.5	12.2
% Profit Before Taxes/Total Assets	19.2	15.3	16.5
	7.1	7.2	11.5
	1.4	2.1	3.1
Sales/Net Fixed Assets	13.8	20.9	42.3
	6.0	7.0	9.4
	4.2	4.3	5.4
Sales/Total Assets	2.2	2.1	2.3
	1.7	1.7	1.6
	1.2	1.3	1.3
% Depr., Dep., Amort./Sales	1.1	1.4	.9
	1.7	(29) 2.3	(24) 1.9
	3.7	3.8	3.0
% Officers', Directors' Owners' Comp/Sales			

	500M-2MM	2-10MM	10-50MM	50-100MM	100-250MM	34 ALL	30 ALL
Net Sales ($)	8014M	112270M	483866M	398698M	680682M	1497887M	1087561M
Total Assets ($)	3648M	47284M	266353M	241749M	467345M	918297M	772286M

© RMA 2011

M = $ thousand   MM = $ million
See Pages 9 through 22 for Explanation of Ratios and Data

Comparative Historical Data

Current Data Sorted by Sales

						Type of Statement						
	7		12		6	Unqualified						6
	7		6		6	Reviewed			2	2		2
	4		1		2	Compiled			2			1
	2		3		3	Tax Returns	1				1	
	14		14		12	Other	1	1	2	2	1	8
	4/1/08- 3/31/09 ALL		4/1/09- 3/31/10 ALL		4/1/10- 3/31/11 ALL		0-1MM	3 (4/1-9/30/10) 1-3MM	3-5MM	26 (10/1/10-3/31/11) 5-10MM	10-25MM	25MM & OVER
	34		36		29	**NUMBER OF STATEMENTS**	2	1	4	5		17
	%		%		%	**ASSETS**	%	%	%	%	%	%
	8.9		10.9		9.3	Cash & Equivalents						6.1
	22.4		21.5		24.0	Trade Receivables (net)	D					21.9
	31.7		28.2		31.4	Inventory	A					30.7
	1.8		2.8		2.1	All Other Current	T					.9
	64.8		63.3		66.8	Total Current	A					59.7
	20.9		24.2		22.1	Fixed Assets (net)						27.9
	4.8		4.2		8.4	Intangibles (net)	N					9.7
	9.6		8.3		2.8	All Other Non-Current	O					2.7
	100.0		100.0		100.0	Total	T					100.0
						LIABILITIES	A					
	10.1		9.3		11.8	Notes Payable-Short Term	V					15.2
	1.9		3.0		2.9	Cur. Mat.-L.T.D.	A					3.1
	9.9		9.3		14.3	Trade Payables	I					15.4
	.2		.0		.1	Income Taxes Payable	L					.2
	9.7		9.4		6.1	All Other Current	A					5.3
	31.7		31.0		35.2	Total Current	B					39.2
	9.9		14.6		9.3	Long-Term Debt	L					11.2
	.4		.6		.2	Deferred Taxes	E					.4
	7.3		4.4		5.4	All Other Non-Current						6.1
	50.9		49.4		49.8	Net Worth						43.1
	100.0		100.0		100.0	Total Liabilities & Net Worth						100.0
						INCOME DATA						
	100.0		100.0		100.0	Net Sales						100.0
	28.7		26.4		28.0	Gross Profit						25.4
	19.4		22.0		20.1	Operating Expenses						18.0
	9.3		4.4		7.9	Operating Profit						7.4
	.9		1.7		1.6	All Other Expenses (net)						1.3
	8.4		2.7		6.4	Profit Before Taxes						6.1
						RATIOS						
	4.5		4.2		3.6							2.4
	2.1		2.1		1.8	Current						1.4
	1.5		1.2		1.1							1.0
	2.3		2.5		2.0							.9
	1.0		.9		.8	Quick						.7
	.4		.4		.5							.4
40	9.1	30	12.0	40	9.1						40	9.1
45	8.1	47	7.8	47	7.8	Sales/Receivables					45	8.1
58	6.3	66	5.5	58	6.2						54	6.8
42	8.7	46	7.9	51	7.2						48	7.6
115	3.2	81	4.5	85	4.3	Cost of Sales/Inventory					85	4.3
159	2.3	147	2.5	143	2.6						130	2.8
17	21.2	12	29.6	20	18.0						24	15.2
29	12.6	26	14.1	33	11.1	Cost of Sales/Payables					39	9.3
42	8.7	46	8.0	50	7.2						51	7.2
	3.0		2.8		3.5							5.1
	4.2		5.2		8.3	Sales/Working Capital						11.4
	13.6		13.8		27.8							NM
	28.5		12.5		27.3							16.0
(29)	6.1	(33)	2.9		4.6	EBIT/Interest						3.4
	2.7		.4		1.6							1.6
	13.6		2.9									
(11)	2.6	(10)	1.1			Net Profit + Depr., Dep., Amort./Cur. Mat. L/T/D						
	1.4		.4									
	.1		.2		.2							.3
	.5		.6		.4	Fixed/Worth						1.3
	1.2		1.5		1.6							1.7
	.3		.3		.5							.8
	1.6		1.9		1.4	Debt/Worth						2.4
	2.5		2.6		3.0							3.8
	49.8		16.7		33.7	% Profit Before Taxes/Tangible						60.5
(32)	20.2	(34)	4.5	(27)	16.5	Net Worth					(15)	18.0
	14.4		-5.6		7.3							5.9
	15.9		9.0		15.2							17.3
	7.8		1.8		7.6	% Profit Before Taxes/Total						7.6
	4.2		-1.2		1.6	Assets						1.6
	17.4		14.1		22.2							22.2
	8.0		5.5		12.3	Sales/Net Fixed Assets						7.6
	4.6		4.2		5.2							4.6
	1.9		1.9		2.4							2.4
	1.7		1.4		1.7	Sales/Total Assets						1.7
	1.1		1.1		1.3							1.4
	1.0		1.8		1.1							1.0
(29)	1.9	(31)	2.6	(27)	1.9	% Depr., Dep., Amort./Sales					(16)	1.8
	3.4		3.3		3.5							3.2
						% Officers', Directors' Owners' Comp/Sales						
	1257695M		1843572M		1683530M	Net Sales ($)	3069M	4945M	26930M	81618M		1566968M
	1046857M		1483999M		1026379M	Total Assets ($)	1748M	1900M	21275M	43802M		957654M

© RMA 2011

M = $ thousand   MM = $ million

See Pages 9 through 22 for Explanation of Ratios and Data

Current Data Sorted by Assets							Comparative Historical Data	

Type of Statement

0-500M	500M-2MM	2-10MM	10-50MM	50-100MM	100-250MM		4/1/06-3/31/07 ALL	4/1/07-3/31/08 ALL
		4	8	7	2	Unqualified	22	16
	2	9	6			Reviewed	23	18
	7	3	2	1		Compiled	21	18
1	4	2	1			Tax Returns	5	9
3	4	19	9	2	1	Other	25	31
	19 (4/1-9/30/10)		78 (10/1/10-3/31/11)					
4	17	37	26	10	3	**NUMBER OF STATEMENTS**	96	92

0-500M %	500M-2MM %	2-10MM %	10-50MM %	50-100MM %	100-250MM %	ASSETS	%	%
	15.8	10.7	8.9	24.9		Cash & Equivalents	9.6	11.3
	27.6	29.3	25.6	16.0		Trade Receivables (net)	35.4	32.5
	24.7	31.1	19.5	20.2		Inventory	25.1	21.3
	2.8	4.6	3.0	1.3		All Other Current	3.2	5.3
	70.9	75.8	57.0	62.5		Total Current	73.3	70.3
	19.4	19.7	26.6	17.3		Fixed Assets (net)	20.8	22.4
	1.1	1.8	10.4	12.8		Intangibles (net)	1.9	3.3
	8.6	2.8	6.0	7.4		All Other Non-Current	4.0	4.0
	100.0	100.0	100.0	100.0		Total	100.0	100.0
						LIABILITIES		
	12.5	10.0	7.0	4.7		Notes Payable-Short Term	12.0	9.2
	3.4	2.6	2.6	1.4		Cur. Mat.-L.T.D.	3.4	4.0
	12.6	14.9	10.0	7.2		Trade Payables	16.4	14.9
	.6	.5	.1	.0		Income Taxes Payable	.3	.5
	14.0	9.4	8.9	14.0		All Other Current	8.5	13.0
	43.1	37.4	28.6	27.3		Total Current	40.6	41.5
	7.2	10.2	16.3	7.4		Long-Term Debt	14.8	15.5
	.2	.4	1.3	1.5		Deferred Taxes	.5	.6
	6.2	1.3	4.8	14.8		All Other Non-Current	4.4	4.7
	43.4	50.7	49.0	49.1		Net Worth	39.7	37.6
	100.0	100.0	100.0	100.0		Total Liabilities & Net Worth	100.0	100.0
						INCOME DATA		
	100.0	100.0	100.0	100.0		Net Sales	100.0	100.0
	29.3	30.3	28.8	27.1		Gross Profit	28.0	29.6
	29.0	24.9	19.7	11.1		Operating Expenses	19.9	21.0
	.3	5.4	9.1	16.0		Operating Profit	8.1	8.6
	.7	.4	2.0	.0		All Other Expenses (net)	.9	1.3
	-.4	5.0	7.1	15.9		Profit Before Taxes	7.3	7.3
						RATIOS		
	3.9	3.1	3.5	4.3		Current	3.1	2.9
	2.2	2.3	2.0	2.7			1.9	1.7
	.8	1.4	1.3	1.7			1.3	1.2
	3.5	2.0	1.9	3.1		Quick	1.9	1.8
	1.1	1.1	1.3	1.5			1.1	1.0
	.7	.6	.8	.7			.7	.7
	34 10.7	36 10.1	44 8.2	36 10.1		Sales/Receivables	40 9.1	35 10.5
	48 7.6	47 7.8	61 6.0	50 7.3			51 7.2	47 7.7
	60 6.1	58 6.2	76 4.8	82 4.5			65 5.6	66 5.6
	12 29.6	34 10.6	42 8.8	54 6.8		Cost of Sales/Inventory	21 17.7	19 19.5
	68 5.3	78 4.7	56 6.5	70 5.2			58 6.3	41 8.9
	115 3.2	133 2.7	92 4.0	147 2.5			87 4.2	69 5.3
	7 52.4	20 17.8	16 22.8	14 25.8		Cost of Sales/Payables	15 24.0	16 22.8
	29 12.8	35 10.5	29 12.5	27 13.6			29 12.6	26 14.1
	43 8.4	48 7.6	41 8.8	41 8.9			53 6.9	46 7.9
	4.6	3.5	3.8	1.7		Sales/Working Capital	4.4	4.7
	7.6	6.1	6.1	3.5			7.1	8.2
	-20.1	11.1	12.5	4.9			13.8	22.5
	11.8	20.6	10.3			EBIT/Interest	18.5	19.3
	(15) 1.8	(29) 6.6	(22) 3.9				(87) 6.8	(84) 6.2
	-3.2	3.5	2.0				2.9	2.2
			5.6			Net Profit + Depr., Dep., Amort./Cur. Mat. L/T/D	17.7	10.8
		(10) 2.9					(31) 5.2	(28) 4.2
			1.1				2.2	1.8
	.2	.1	.3	.2		Fixed/Worth	.2	.2
	.3	.3	.7	.4			.4	.5
	1.9	.6	4.1	.9			.9	1.6
	.4	.4	.6	.6		Debt/Worth	.5	.7
	1.3	.8	1.1	1.4			1.3	1.6
	5.3	2.6	8.3	4.7			3.2	5.4
	26.6	36.2	43.1			% Profit Before Taxes/Tangible Net Worth	60.3	59.8
	(16) 10.4	(35) 15.5	(22) 17.3				(86) 32.0	(81) 42.9
	-15.1	6.2	5.3				14.6	12.6
	14.9	19.0	14.3	26.7		% Profit Before Taxes/Total Assets	23.1	25.0
	1.8	9.2	6.8	17.6			13.7	13.2
	-6.1	2.6	3.0	11.8			5.0	4.5
	41.0	32.2	13.7	12.5		Sales/Net Fixed Assets	32.3	33.0
	19.8	12.7	7.2	4.8			14.1	13.3
	7.8	7.5	3.9	4.6			7.9	7.1
	3.4	2.8	1.9	1.3		Sales/Total Assets	3.3	3.1
	2.2	2.2	1.6	.9			2.2	2.3
	1.5	1.6	1.1	.8			1.7	1.6
	.6	1.1	1.8	1.9		% Depr., Dep., Amort./Sales	.8	.7
	(14) 1.5	(34) 1.5	(24) 2.6	3.0			(85) 1.6	(83) 1.4
	2.4	4.0	3.9	4.3			2.8	2.5
		1.9				% Officers', Directors' Owners' Comp/Sales	1.6	2.0
		(11) 2.6					(32) 2.9	(35) 3.0
		4.1					6.3	8.3
4201M	55428M	406330M	892373M	733595M	569312M	Net Sales ($)	3364256M	4012676M
1116M	21449M	189880M	555769M	691851M	424661M	Total Assets ($)	1756949M	1954561M

M = $ thousand   MM = $ million
See Pages 9 through 22 for Explanation of Ratios and Data

Comparative Historical Data | Current Data Sorted by Sales

Type of Statement					19 (4/1-9/30/10)			78 (10/1/10-3/31/11)		
					0-1MM	1-3MM	3-5MM	5-10MM	10-25MM	25MM & OVER
Unqualified	28	22	21		3		4	6	11
Reviewed	18	18	17				2	10	2
Compiled	16	7	13		4	2	3	2	2
Tax Returns	10	4	8	1	2	1	2	1	1
Other	37	42	38	1	5	4	4	16	8
	4/1/08-3/31/09 ALL	4/1/09-3/31/10 ALL	4/1/10-3/31/11 ALL						
NUMBER OF STATEMENTS	109	93	97	2	14	7	15	35	24
	%	%	%	%	%	%	%	%	%
ASSETS									
Cash & Equivalents	11.5	11.1	12.7		14.3		14.6	10.3	15.0
Trade Receivables (net)	28.5	26.6	26.6		28.2		28.1	28.2	22.7
Inventory	26.3	24.0	24.6		20.5		33.1	24.6	20.6
All Other Current	4.0	4.6	3.4		4.3		2.4	5.0	2.5
Total Current	70.4	66.4	67.4		67.3		78.3	68.0	60.9
Fixed Assets (net)	23.2	24.6	22.0		19.2		19.9	22.1	22.8
Intangibles (net)	2.5	4.5	5.1		1.1		.6	5.8	9.7
All Other Non-Current	3.9	4.5	5.5		12.3		1.3	4.0	6.7
Total	100.0	100.0	100.0		100.0		100.0	100.0	100.0
LIABILITIES									
Notes Payable-Short Term	10.3	11.3	9.8		21.4		13.2	5.7	6.0
Cur. Mat.-L.T.D.	4.1	3.1	2.6		4.1		3.5	2.3	1.6
Trade Payables	14.0	12.6	12.6		15.9		13.6	13.2	9.5
Income Taxes Payable	.5	.6	.4		.5		.0	.8	.2
All Other Current	10.6	9.7	10.5		16.9		12.9	8.7	10.6
Total Current	39.5	37.3	35.9		58.7		43.2	30.7	27.9
Long-Term Debt	13.6	12.0	10.9		10.9		9.7	10.4	13.7
Deferred Taxes	.5	.6	.7		.2		.3	.7	1.6
All Other Non-Current	4.5	4.3	4.5		1.6		4.6	3.7	8.1
Net Worth	41.8	45.7	48.0		28.5		42.2	54.5	48.7
Total Liabilities & Net Worth	100.0	100.0	100.0		100.0		100.0	100.0	100.0
INCOME DATA									
Net Sales	100.0	100.0	100.0		100.0		100.0	100.0	100.0
Gross Profit	28.7	27.2	30.9		33.7		34.0	29.0	27.2
Operating Expenses	20.1	21.0	24.6		36.6		27.7	21.9	16.5
Operating Profit	8.6	6.2	6.4		-2.9		6.3	7.1	10.7
All Other Expenses (net)	1.0	.9	.9		.9		.6	1.0	1.1
Profit Before Taxes	7.7	5.3	5.4		-3.8		5.7	6.1	9.6
RATIOS									
Current	3.0	3.0	3.3		6.7		3.1	3.2	3.6
	1.9	1.9	2.3		1.2		2.3	2.3	2.7
	1.2	1.2	1.3		.8		1.2	1.6	1.4
Quick	2.1	1.9	2.0		4.1		2.0	1.9	2.1
	.9	1.0	1.2		.8		.6	1.2	1.5
	.6	.6	.7		.3		.4	.9	.8
Sales/Receivables	31 11.7	34 10.9	37 9.7		38 9.7		32 11.3	35 10.3	41 8.8
	40 9.1	49 7.5	51 7.1		53 6.8		44 8.3	51 7.2	53 6.8
	54 6.8	62 5.9	67 5.4		71 5.2		58 6.3	74 4.9	67 5.5
Cost of Sales/Inventory	28 13.3	31 11.8	35 10.4		17 22.1		22 16.7	37 9.8	46 7.9
	50 7.4	56 6.5	63 5.8		57 6.4		108 3.4	58 6.3	62 5.9
	93 3.9	96 3.8	114 3.2		119 3.1		131 2.8	98 3.7	102 3.6
Cost of Sales/Payables	15 24.9	14 25.2	18 20.6		8 46.4		19 19.2	21 17.1	17 22.1
	24 15.2	24 15.1	31 11.8		32 11.2		35 10.5	33 11.1	29 12.7
	43 8.5	40 9.1	45 8.1		69 5.3		44 8.2	45 8.0	43 8.5
Sales/Working Capital	5.0	4.3	3.5		3.7		5.3	3.5	3.2
	8.4	7.2	5.9		UND		6.8	5.3	4.5
	23.6	25.7	13.2		-8.8		16.9	10.1	10.1
EBIT/Interest	22.2	14.1	20.5		3.3		118.3	19.2	49.3
	(97) 5.8	(85) 4.5	(78) 6.1	(11) .9	(14) 8.0		(28) 6.2	(18) 10.2
	2.1	1.5	1.7		-16.7		3.3	2.5	-2.7
Net Profit + Depr., Dep., Amort./Cur. Mat. L/T/D	17.2	8.0	6.2						
	(33) 4.2	(28) 2.5	(23) 3.1						
	2.1	1.6	1.1						
Fixed/Worth	.2	.2	.2		.2		.1	.2	.3
	.4	.5	.4		.8		.4	.4	.5
	1.3	1.6	1.0		2.8		1.0	.8	1.7
Debt/Worth	.5	.6	.4		.2		.4	.5	.5
	1.4	1.4	1.1		4.5		1.5	.8	1.2
	3.0	3.3	4.1		50.9		4.2	1.9	5.9
% Profit Before Taxes/Tangible Net Worth	64.1	54.3	38.9		21.3		45.7	40.4	46.2
	(100) 37.5	(86) 20.5	(88) 18.7	(12) 2.9	(14) 15.4		(33) 16.7	(21) 32.0
	14.2	4.1	4.6		-14.5		.0	6.5	13.0
% Profit Before Taxes/Total Assets	26.3	21.2	17.6		8.5		14.7	15.1	21.0
	12.8	7.6	8.9		.4		9.7	8.9	13.8
	4.9	.9	1.8		-14.3		.2	3.5	5.3
Sales/Net Fixed Assets	26.3	23.8	29.4		42.4		45.7	22.7	16.0
	11.8	9.1	11.5		16.5		18.4	11.3	6.4
	6.3	4.5	4.8		4.4		6.8	6.1	4.6
Sales/Total Assets	3.2	2.9	2.6		3.0		3.6	2.4	2.0
	2.3	2.0	1.9		1.6		2.6	1.8	1.5
	1.7	1.4	1.3		1.4		1.2	1.5	.9
% Depr., Dep., Amort./Sales	.6	1.0	1.2		.5		1.1	1.3	1.7
	(94) 1.7	(84) 2.2	(85) 2.1	(11) 1.7	(13) 1.6		(31) 1.8	(22) 2.6
	2.9	3.2	3.5		2.8		4.0	3.4	3.2
% Officers', Directors' Owners' Comp/Sales	1.5	2.1	1.8					2.3	
	(39) 3.4	(28) 3.1	(24) 3.1					(12) 2.7	
	5.2	5.7	4.8					4.1	
Net Sales ($)	5355596M	5533458M	2661239M	1190M	26042M	28820M	116050M	563193M	1925944M
Total Assets ($)	2467769M	2251811M	1884726M	279M	15817M	14833M	65534M	334600M	1453663M

© RMA 2011

M = $ thousand   MM = $ million
See Pages 9 through 22 for Explanation of Ratios and Data

Current Data Sorted by Assets | Comparative Historical Data

Type of Statement	0-500M	500M-2MM	2-10MM	10-50MM	50-100MM	100-250MM	ALL	ALL
Unqualified		1	9	31	10	5	69	66
Reviewed	1	10	75	32			118	114
Compiled	6	33	41	3		2	86	92
Tax Returns	31	54	19	2	7	5	98	84
Other	8	42	88	42		5	192	186
	106 (4/1-9/30/10)			451 (10/1/10-3/31/11)			4/1/06-3/31/07	4/1/07-3/31/08
NUMBER OF STATEMENTS	46	140	232	110	17	12	563	542

ASSETS	%	%	%	%	%	%	%	%
Cash & Equivalents	10.7	12.9	8.1	10.5	7.6	9.4	8.2	9.0
Trade Receivables (net)	32.9	28.9	24.6	23.7	23.4	21.6	27.4	26.6
Inventory	19.1	19.2	25.9	24.8	18.6	15.2	24.7	24.5
All Other Current	2.2	2.6	2.6	2.7	1.3	4.9	3.0	2.5
Total Current	64.8	63.5	61.2	61.8	51.0	51.0	63.3	62.6
Fixed Assets (net)	21.7	26.9	30.1	25.5	27.3	31.3	28.3	27.6
Intangibles (net)	7.4	3.3	3.5	7.9	19.6	13.0	3.1	3.9
All Other Non-Current	6.1	6.2	5.1	4.8	2.1	4.6	5.3	5.9
Total	100.0	100.0	100.0	100.0	100.0	100.0	100.0	100.0

LIABILITIES								
Notes Payable-Short Term	25.6	10.9	10.8	6.4	10.5	3.2	11.1	11.4
Cur. Mat.-L.T.D.	4.8	6.3	4.1	4.0	2.1	5.5	5.3	3.7
Trade Payables	23.2	15.2	13.5	12.5	9.0	23.1	15.3	13.6
Income Taxes Payable	.2	.2	.2	.1	.6	.4	.3	.3
All Other Current	7.5	6.5	8.2	10.4	9.6	7.8	9.6	10.0
Total Current	61.3	39.1	36.8	33.5	31.8	40.0	41.7	39.1
Long-Term Debt	14.3	23.3	15.8	15.1	20.5	22.3	17.8	17.8
Deferred Taxes	.0	.3	.6	.8	.1	1.2	.4	.4
All Other Non-Current	19.7	6.4	5.3	5.4	13.6	28.6	6.9	6.2
Net Worth	4.7	30.9	41.5	45.2	34.0	7.8	33.2	36.5
Total Liabilities & Net Worth	100.0	100.0	100.0	100.0	100.0	100.0	100.0	100.0

INCOME DATA								
Net Sales	100.0	100.0	100.0	100.0	100.0	100.0	100.0	100.0
Gross Profit	37.8	38.8	30.3	25.8	24.8	33.1	30.2	32.0
Operating Expenses	37.0	33.8	25.1	19.9	16.4	27.1	24.3	25.3
Operating Profit	.8	5.0	5.1	5.9	8.4	6.0	5.9	6.7
All Other Expenses (net)	.7	.8	.9	1.1	2.7	1.6	1.2	1.2
Profit Before Taxes	.1	4.2	4.2	4.8	5.7	4.5	4.6	5.4

RATIOS	0-500M	500M-2MM	2-10MM	10-50MM	50-100MM	100-250MM	ALL	ALL
Current	3.2	3.0	2.9	3.2	2.0	2.9	2.9	2.9
	1.2	1.9	1.7	2.0	1.6	1.9	1.7	1.7
	.6	1.1	1.2	1.4	1.3	1.0	1.1	1.2
Quick	1.8	2.1	1.7	1.8	1.5	1.4	1.6	1.7
	1.0	1.1	.8	1.1	1.0	.9	(562) .9	.9
	.4	.6	.5	.7	.7	.7	.5	.6
Sales/Receivables	16 22.5	28 12.9	33 10.9	37 10.0	35 10.3	25 14.5	28 13.0	29 12.6
	34 10.6	42 8.6	43 8.6	48 7.6	45 8.1	45 8.0	42 8.6	42 8.8
	53 6.9	56 6.5	57 6.4	61 6.0	51 7.1	59 6.2	58 6.3	56 6.5
Cost of Sales/Inventory	5 77.7	13 28.4	31 11.7	37 9.8	36 10.2	24 15.5	22 16.4	23 15.7
	22 16.8	35 10.4	63 5.8	65 5.6	52 7.0	53 6.9	51 7.2	53 6.9
	43 8.6	72 5.0	109 3.4	103 3.5	71 5.1	96 3.8	83 4.4	91 4.0
Cost of Sales/Payables	12 30.3	16 22.2	18 20.4	17 21.4	15 24.6	24 15.4	16 23.3	15 23.6
	28 13.0	31 11.9	30 12.0	28 13.2	27 13.6	35 10.4	29 12.8	27 13.5
	58 6.3	52 7.0	45 8.1	42 8.8	43 8.4	47 7.8	46 7.9	43 8.5
Sales/Working Capital	7.3	5.1	4.3	3.9	5.7	3.5	5.4	5.3
	35.0	9.0	8.3	6.4	9.8	5.3	9.2	9.0
	-10.1	52.1	24.6	12.6	16.7	NM	39.6	29.8
EBIT/Interest	9.5	12.1	10.3	15.7	15.6	31.7	12.8	12.8
	(38) 1.4	(127) 4.0	(216) 3.8	(97) 5.4	(15) 9.7	(11) 3.7	(513) 4.2	(491) 4.0
	-4.8	1.0	1.1	1.8	2.6	.3	1.6	1.7
Net Profit + Depr., Dep., Amort./Cur. Mat. L/T/D		4.4	3.9	5.4			7.2	8.5
		(24) 2.2	(57) 2.1	(35) 2.0			(144) 3.1	(139) 3.1
		1.3	.6	1.3			1.5	1.4
Fixed/Worth	.2	.3	.3	.3	.6	.5	.3	.3
	2.2	.7	.7	.6	4.5	1.1	.7	.7
	-1.0	4.4	2.1	1.6	-1.9	-1.6	2.3	2.0
Debt/Worth	.5	.6	.6	.6	.8	1.1	.7	.7
	26.7	1.4	1.8	1.2	16.8	1.4	1.8	1.7
	-3.5	21.4	4.2	3.3	-6.6	-5.0	6.0	5.3
% Profit Before Taxes/Tangible Net Worth	67.1	51.9	46.1	38.8	93.1		49.0	53.7
	(25) 23.1	(109) 23.5	(210) 19.8	(96) 17.1	(10) 32.4		(492) 24.7	(470) 25.4
	-32.6	1.9	1.9	8.0	14.4		8.2	8.5
% Profit Before Taxes/Total Assets	23.2	18.0	15.2	13.7	12.1	14.3	18.9	19.6
	5.5	8.8	6.2	7.2	10.2	4.7	8.5	7.9
	-13.0	.3	.5	2.4	4.5	-2.9	2.0	2.6
Sales/Net Fixed Assets	100.6	24.3	18.1	14.5	9.3	13.9	21.9	23.5
	19.8	11.3	7.3	6.9	7.0	6.1	9.2	10.0
	8.2	6.0	3.6	4.2	3.9	4.0	5.1	5.0
Sales/Total Assets	4.7	3.2	2.5	2.2	2.2	2.5	3.1	2.9
	3.5	2.3	1.9	1.7	1.6	1.6	2.2	2.2
	2.4	1.6	1.5	1.2	1.1	1.2	1.6	1.6
% Depr., Dep., Amort./Sales	.6	1.3	1.2	1.5	2.1		1.0	1.1
	(31) 2.1	(114) 2.7	(210) 2.4	(104) 2.5	3.1		(479) 2.2	(466) 2.2
	4.3	4.8	4.7	4.0	4.9		4.0	4.1
% Officers', Directors' Owners' Comp/Sales	3.1	3.3	2.2	1.2			2.2	2.3
	(27) 6.1	(69) 5.0	(98) 3.5	(20) 2.5			(240) 4.0	(225) 4.2
	11.1	9.6	5.5	4.1			6.9	7.5
Net Sales ($)	48091M	434361M	2363934M	3963899M	2086283M	8038157M	15580360M	14233757M
Total Assets ($)	12947M	163607M	1170874M	2213215M	1229071M	1971009M	7417099M	7243192M

Comparative Historical Data | Current Data Sorted by Sales

55	57	56	Type of Statement						
121	109	118	Unqualified			1	6	15	34
79	90	83	Reviewed		7	16	25	53	17
83	107	108	Compiled	7	21	16	25	11	3
199	173	192	Tax Returns	19	41	24	14	3	7
			Other	10	27	24	38	55	38
4/1/08-	4/1/09-	4/1/10-			106 (4/1-9/30/10)		451 (10/1/10-3/31/11)		
3/31/09	3/31/10	3/31/11							
ALL	ALL	ALL		0-1MM	1-3MM	3-5MM	5-10MM	10-25MM	25MM & OVER
537	536	557	**NUMBER OF STATEMENTS**	36	96	81	108	137	99
%	%	%	**ASSETS**	%	%	%	%	%	%
9.1	10.4	10.0	Cash & Equivalents	13.5	12.3	9.8	8.5	8.7	9.9
25.5	22.2	26.1	Trade Receivables (net)	26.8	26.5	24.9	25.7	26.9	25.9
25.6	23.4	23.0	Inventory	13.2	20.3	20.7	24.8	26.4	24.4
2.9	2.9	2.6	All Other Current	2.8	3.3	1.3	2.4	2.8	2.8
63.1	58.8	61.7	Total Current	56.3	62.5	56.6	61.5	64.7	63.0
27.3	28.9	27.7	Fixed Assets (net)	26.2	25.3	34.3	30.2	25.4	25.5
3.9	6.0	5.4	Intangibles (net)	10.0	5.0	3.0	3.4	5.6	7.7
5.8	6.3	5.3	All Other Non-Current	7.5	7.2	6.1	4.9	4.3	3.9
100.0	100.0	100.0	Total	100.0	100.0	100.0	100.0	100.0	100.0
			LIABILITIES						
12.3	11.9	11.0	Notes Payable-Short Term	20.2	14.4	9.5	9.7	10.8	7.4
4.0	4.6	4.7	Cur. Mat.-L.T.D.	4.2	5.6	6.4	4.2	4.5	3.3
13.3	12.0	14.6	Trade Payables	20.8	14.8	11.5	13.4	15.0	15.4
.2	.2	.2	Income Taxes Payable	.1	.1	.2	.2	.2	.3
10.0	8.8	8.2	All Other Current	8.4	6.1	6.1	8.8	8.1	11.3
39.9	37.5	38.7	Total Current	53.7	41.1	33.7	36.3	38.6	37.7
16.5	19.5	17.7	Long-Term Debt	27.5	22.4	20.1	15.4	12.9	16.8
.5	.6	.5	Deferred Taxes	.0	.1	.5	.8	.6	.6
5.4	7.9	7.6	All Other Non-Current	15.8	10.2	6.9	5.3	4.4	9.4
37.7	34.6	35.6	Net Worth	3.0	26.2	38.8	42.2	43.5	35.6
100.0	100.0	100.0	Total Liabilities & Net Worth	100.0	100.0	100.0	100.0	100.0	100.0
			INCOME DATA						
100.0	100.0	100.0	Net Sales	100.0	100.0	100.0	100.0	100.0	100.0
29.2	31.0	32.0	Gross Profit	42.9	40.4	35.9	29.2	28.1	25.3
23.7	27.4	27.0	Operating Expenses	40.9	35.6	30.8	25.4	22.2	18.9
5.5	3.6	5.0	Operating Profit	2.1	4.8	5.0	3.9	5.9	6.4
1.0	1.7	1.0	All Other Expenses (net)	1.7	.8	.8	.9	.8	1.2
4.5	1.9	4.1	Profit Before Taxes	.4	4.0	4.2	2.9	5.1	5.2
			RATIOS						
3.0	3.3	2.9		3.3	3.4	3.6	2.8	3.0	2.6
1.7	1.8	1.8	Current	1.3	2.0	2.0	1.8	1.7	1.9
1.1	1.1	1.2		.6	1.1	1.1	1.2	1.2	1.4
1.8	2.0	1.8		2.4	2.4	2.3	1.5	1.6	1.5
.8	.9	1.0	Quick	.9	1.0	1.1	.9	.9	1.1
.5	.5	.6		.4	.5	.6	.5	.5	.7
26 14.1	27 13.5	31 11.7		20 18.5	24 14.9	33 11.0	28 13.2	37 9.9	31 11.6
38 9.6	39 9.3	43 8.4	Sales/Receivables	33 11.0	43 8.4	44 8.2	42 8.7	45 8.2	45 8.1
52 7.0	52 7.0	57 6.4		59 6.1	58 6.3	55 6.7	56 6.5	58 6.3	56 6.5
22 16.8	26 14.1	24 15.3		5 75.5	14 25.6	21 17.1	22 17.0	37 9.9	35 10.5
50 7.3	57 6.4	54 6.8	Cost of Sales/Inventory	22 16.9	36 10.2	52 7.0	59 6.2	64 5.7	55 6.6
94 3.9	100 3.6	96 3.8		51 7.1	96 3.8	96 3.8	104 3.5	105 3.5	85 4.3
13 28.4	13 27.3	17 21.1		14 26.0	15 24.0	16 22.4	17 22.0	18 20.2	18 20.3
23 15.6	24 15.5	30 12.2	Cost of Sales/Payables	30 12.2	30 12.0	27 13.6	29 12.7	31 11.6	30 12.3
38 9.6	40 9.1	45 8.1		101 3.6	57 6.4	42 8.7	40 9.1	45 8.1	43 8.4
5.3	4.1	4.5		4.5	4.5	4.3	4.6	4.4	4.7
9.6	8.1	8.4	Sales/Working Capital	34.8	8.0	7.7	8.8	8.0	7.3
31.7	42.1	30.9		-8.3	84.1	60.3	35.6	24.3	15.1
12.4	8.5	11.7		6.2	11.2	8.8	9.3	15.9	19.0
(493) 3.9	(477) 2.2	(504) 4.0	EBIT/Interest	(31) 1.9	(85) 3.7	(75) 3.5	(101) 3.0	(123) 5.4	(89) 7.5
1.2	-1.0	1.0		-2.8	.1	1.0	.6	1.8	2.5
6.6	5.1	5.1				4.5	3.7		10.6
(145) 2.8	(135) 2.1	(126) 2.0	Net Profit + Depr., Dep., Amort./Cur. Mat. L/T/D		(17) 1.9	(25) 1.8	(42) 1.8	(30) 3.6
1.1	.5	.9				1.4	.3	.6	1.7
.3	.3	.3		.2	.3	.4	.3	.3	.3
.7	.8	.7	Fixed/Worth	NM	1.0	.8	.7	.7	.6
1.7	3.6	2.8		-1.0	-21.8	2.8	1.7	2.3	1.7
.7	.6	.6		.4	.7	.6	.5	.6	.7
1.6	1.7	1.5	Debt/Worth	-24.0	2.6	1.2	1.4	1.7	1.4
4.3	14.4	8.3		-3.4	-58.8	5.1	2.9	5.5	9.1
49.3	35.4	46.4		31.6	61.9	41.3	40.5	45.5	46.7
(471) 21.9	(422) 11.2	(458) 20.2	% Profit Before Taxes/Tangible Net Worth	(16) 5.8	(70) 23.8	(70) 17.3	(99) 10.2	(121) 24.7	(82) 19.9
6.0	-5.2	2.4		-3.7	.6	-.3	-.2	7.9	10.7
17.9	12.7	16.0		14.8	18.6	15.5	13.8	16.9	14.4
7.7	3.0	7.1	% Profit Before Taxes/Total Assets	4.2	9.8	6.9	3.1	10.1	8.2
1.0	-4.7	.4		-12.2	-1.6	.0	-.3	2.0	3.0
23.1	18.6	19.3		45.4	24.3	13.1	18.4	18.7	18.8
9.4	8.2	8.4	Sales/Net Fixed Assets	15.4	11.1	7.5	7.1	8.6	8.1
5.1	3.9	4.3		4.3	5.4	3.4	3.7	4.9	4.7
3.0	2.6	2.7		3.8	3.2	2.6	2.7	2.5	2.6
2.2	1.8	2.0	Sales/Total Assets	2.2	2.2	1.9	2.0	2.0	2.0
1.6	1.3	1.4		1.1	1.4	1.5	1.5	1.5	1.5
1.2	1.3	1.3		.7	1.2	1.9	1.2	1.2	1.2
(446) 2.3	(460) 2.8	(483) 2.5	% Depr., Dep., Amort./Sales	(23) 2.8	(75) 2.2	(72) 3.9	(100) 2.4	(125) 2.4	(88) 2.4
4.1	5.5	4.6		8.4	4.5	6.7	4.7	4.1	3.6
1.9	2.5	2.6		5.2	4.3	3.0	2.2	1.5	1.3
(209) 3.7	(224) 4.9	(217) 4.2	% Officers', Directors' Owners' Comp/Sales	(15) 8.5	(53) 5.7	(41) 4.9	(44) 3.9	(49) 2.9	(15) 3.1
7.6	8.2	7.4		11.4	10.5	7.4	5.4	4.4	7.2
14298619M	12005939M	16934725M	Net Sales ($)	22021M	179311M	311300M	782393M	2151852M	13487848M
7686824M	7997394M	6760723M	Total Assets ($)	12407M	94914M	193471M	437448M	1256589M	4765894M

© RMA 2011

M = $ thousand   MM = $ million
See Pages 9 through 22 for Explanation of Ratios and Data

Current Data Sorted by Assets   Comparative Historical Data

	0-500M	500M-2MM	2-10MM	10-50MM	50-100MM	100-250MM	Type of Statement	4/1/06-3/31/07 ALL	4/1/07-3/31/08 ALL
			5	14	7	3	Unqualified	34	33
		1	11	9	1		Reviewed	32	32
		4	15	2			Compiled	24	23
		11	10	1			Tax Returns	11	12
	1	8	20	20	3	2	Other	46	41
		34 (4/1-9/30/10)		114 (10/1/10-3/31/11)					
NUMBER OF STATEMENTS	1	24	61	46	11	5		147	141

	0-500M	500M-2MM	2-10MM	10-50MM	50-100MM	100-250MM		4/1/06-3/31/07	4/1/07-3/31/08
	%	%	%	%	%	%	**ASSETS**	%	%
		10.3	8.0	12.0	6.4		Cash & Equivalents	6.0	5.4
		20.7	22.2	19.2	21.5		Trade Receivables (net)	18.0	20.0
		46.4	38.5	41.9	37.5		Inventory	47.2	43.6
		.2	1.3	2.0	2.2		All Other Current	2.5	3.2
		77.6	70.0	75.0	67.6		Total Current	73.7	72.2
		12.4	20.2	18.5	20.8		Fixed Assets (net)	18.1	18.8
		2.0	3.4	1.5	9.8		Intangibles (net)	3.8	4.6
		8.0	6.4	5.0	1.9		All Other Non-Current	4.4	4.5
		100.0	100.0	100.0	100.0		Total	100.0	100.0
							LIABILITIES		
		17.5	12.7	12.9	6.7		Notes Payable-Short Term	16.9	16.5
		2.7	2.8	1.6	3.1		Cur. Mat.-L.T.D.	2.9	2.5
		10.4	10.2	8.1	15.9		Trade Payables	10.8	11.5
		.0	.3	.3	.2		Income Taxes Payable	.2	.2
		8.8	9.1	14.4	13.2		All Other Current	10.2	10.2
		39.3	35.0	37.4	39.3		Total Current	41.0	40.9
		16.4	15.4	8.7	7.4		Long-Term Debt	14.4	13.8
		.0	.3	.2	.9		Deferred Taxes	.3	.3
		4.5	7.6	1.8	22.0		All Other Non-Current	6.2	3.8
		39.8	41.8	52.0	30.4		Net Worth	38.0	41.1
		100.0	100.0	100.0	100.0		Total Liabilities & Net Worth	100.0	100.0
							INCOME DATA		
		100.0	100.0	100.0	100.0		Net Sales	100.0	100.0
		36.2	30.1	24.4	24.8		Gross Profit	26.6	26.6
		30.9	25.0	18.6	19.8		Operating Expenses	21.8	21.0
		5.3	5.1	5.7	4.9		Operating Profit	4.9	5.6
		.2	1.2	.6	2.2		All Other Expenses (net)	1.4	1.2
		5.1	3.9	5.2	2.8		Profit Before Taxes	3.4	4.4
							RATIOS		
		3.6	3.7	3.8	2.7		Current	2.8	2.8
		2.1	2.0	2.1	1.6			1.8	1.9
		1.3	1.4	1.4	1.2			1.3	1.2
		2.2	1.6	1.6	1.3		Quick	1.1	1.2
		.7	.8	1.0	.6			.6 (140)	.7
		.4	.5	.5	.5			.3	.3
	21	17.7	27 / 13.5	28 / 13.0	25 / 14.6		Sales/Receivables	17 / 21.2	20 / 17.9
	34	10.8	41 / 9.0	38 / 9.6	31 / 11.9			34 / 10.6	33 / 11.2
	46	8.0	54 / 6.7	55 / 6.6	76 / 4.8			56 / 6.5	54 / 6.8
	69	5.3	62 / 5.9	72 / 5.1	88 / 4.2		Cost of Sales/Inventory	82 / 4.5	70 / 5.2
	118	3.1	102 / 3.6	113 / 3.2	100 / 3.7			120 / 3.0	106 / 3.4
	190	1.9	174 / 2.1	187 / 1.9	148 / 2.5			197 / 1.9	164 / 2.2
	15	24.4	14 / 26.4	8 / 44.9	25 / 14.5		Cost of Sales/Payables	13 / 28.5	14 / 25.7
	27	13.3	22 / 16.3	16 / 22.2	30 / 12.3			25 / 14.8	25 / 14.4
	40	9.1	40 / 9.2	30 / 12.1	46 / 8.0			40 / 9.1	39 / 9.3
		2.9	3.2	2.9	3.6		Sales/Working Capital	3.6	3.7
		4.3	5.0	4.1	5.5			5.8	6.3
		18.4	11.0	10.8	17.0			12.1	14.0
		13.4	16.3	33.1	16.7		EBIT/Interest	5.9	8.8
	(20)	4.2	(56) / 4.7	(41) / 6.2	12.3			(138) / 2.8	(135) / 3.7
		1.4	1.5	2.8	2.7			1.3	1.6
							Net Profit + Depr., Dep., Amort./Cur. Mat. L/T/D	4.3	5.7
								(34) 2.6	(42) 2.6
								1.4	1.9
		.0	.1	.1	.3		Fixed/Worth	.2	.2
		.2	.3	.4	.5			.5	.5
		1.0	.9	.7	1.0			1.0	1.1
		.4	.4	.4	.4		Debt/Worth	.9	.7
		1.4	1.2	.9	1.4			1.7	1.5
		5.6	2.7	2.1	2.9			5.1	3.9
		58.2	41.6	35.5			% Profit Before Taxes/Tangible Net Worth	31.5	42.5
	(20)	11.0	(59) / 17.5	22.1				(137) / 15.2	(129) / 19.4
		1.8	2.2	8.5				3.8	6.2
		19.5	16.5	17.1	15.0		% Profit Before Taxes/Total Assets	10.9	13.6
		6.7	6.9	10.2	7.2			4.3	7.4
		.6	1.2	3.4	2.6			.9	2.1
		214.9	49.2	21.7	13.3		Sales/Net Fixed Assets	32.8	30.7
		23.5	13.3	12.0	9.5			11.4	10.7
		8.0	4.2	5.7	5.7			6.6	6.4
		2.5	2.4	2.4	2.0		Sales/Total Assets	2.3	2.4
		2.0	1.6	1.7	1.9			1.8	1.8
		1.5	1.1	1.2	1.6			1.3	1.4
		1.3	.8	.8	1.5		% Depr., Dep., Amort./Sales	.9	.8
	(14)	2.5	(52) / 2.1	(43) / 1.5	2.0			(124) / 1.5	(123) / 1.4
		4.0	3.8	2.8	2.3			2.4	2.3
		2.9	1.2	.7			% Officers', Directors' Owners' Comp/Sales	1.0	1.2
	(12)	3.8	(19) / 2.5	(11) / 1.5				(43) / 2.5	(36) / 2.4
		8.3	4.3	2.8				4.6	4.4
	1096M	60951M	508980M	1942391M	1460301M	1015700M	Net Sales ($)	4738641M	5004293M
	232M	27592M	297405M	1074790M	821614M	828544M	Total Assets ($)	3078298M	3307552M

M = $ thousand   MM = $ million
See Pages 9 through 22 for Explanation of Ratios and Data

Comparative Historical Data | **Current Data Sorted by Sales**

4/1/08-3/31/09 ALL	4/1/09-3/31/10 ALL	4/1/10-3/31/11 ALL	Type of Statement	0-1MM	1-3MM	3-5MM	5-10MM	10-25MM	25MM & OVER
37	31	29	Unqualified		1		2	8	18
30	30	22	Reviewed		1	1		6	9
25	29	21	Compiled		3	5	5	8	
14	9	22	Tax Returns	4	7	5	5		1
44	42	54	Other	1	7	5	7	16	18
				34 (4/1-9/30/10)		114 (10/1/10-3/31/11)			
150	141	148	NUMBER OF STATEMENTS	5	19	16	24	38	46
%	%	%	ASSETS	%	%	%	%	%	%
5.4	7.5	9.9	Cash & Equivalents		10.1	11.5	8.0	9.5	10.4
20.9	19.4	20.6	Trade Receivables (net)		12.9	21.8	18.3	24.5	20.0
45.8	42.3	40.4	Inventory		47.3	34.7	37.9	40.7	40.8
2.2	2.1	1.6	All Other Current		1.5	.9	.9	1.8	2.3
74.3	71.3	72.5	Total Current		71.8	68.9	65.1	76.4	73.4
18.3	19.6	18.6	Fixed Assets (net)		15.4	21.1	23.9	17.3	18.3
2.5	3.8	3.0	Intangibles (net)		4.0	4.4	2.9	1.5	3.7
4.8	5.3	5.9	All Other Non-Current		8.8	5.7	8.1	4.8	4.6
100.0	100.0	100.0	Total		100.0	100.0	100.0	100.0	100.0
			LIABILITIES						
15.6	14.7	12.6	Notes Payable-Short Term		10.4	18.8	10.7	12.8	12.6
3.3	3.1	2.3	Cur. Mat.-L.T.D.		2.5	3.8	3.2	1.7	2.0
11.6	9.5	10.0	Trade Payables		10.0	7.9	11.5	8.6	11.0
.3	.3	.3	Income Taxes Payable		.0	.8	.3	.2	.3
11.5	11.6	11.3	All Other Current		8.5	9.7	11.0	9.4	14.6
42.3	39.2	36.5	Total Current		31.4	41.0	36.5	32.6	40.6
11.4	13.9	12.5	Long-Term Debt		12.7	19.2	12.4	15.5	7.8
.5	.6	.2	Deferred Taxes		.0	.0	.4	.2	.3
3.6	6.0	6.2	All Other Non-Current		7.2	2.3	13.7	1.9	7.3
42.3	40.4	44.6	Net Worth		48.6	37.4	37.0	49.8	44.0
100.0	100.0	100.0	Total Liabilities & Net Worth		100.0	100.0	100.0	100.0	100.0
			INCOME DATA						
100.0	100.0	100.0	Net Sales		100.0	100.0	100.0	100.0	100.0
27.5	29.4	29.2	Gross Profit		34.5	34.4	33.1	26.2	24.9
21.6	25.8	23.8	Operating Expenses		35.7	27.7	27.3	20.1	18.8
5.9	3.7	5.4	Operating Profit		-1.2	6.7	5.8	6.1	6.0
.8	1.0	.8	All Other Expenses (net)		-.2	1.3	.7	1.0	.7
5.1	2.6	4.6	Profit Before Taxes		-1.1	5.3	5.1	5.1	5.3
			RATIOS						
2.6	3.1	3.5	Current		4.9	8.7	3.3	4.1	2.8
1.8	2.0	2.1			2.7	1.4	1.9	2.3	1.9
1.4	1.3	1.4			1.3	1.1	1.3	1.9	1.3
1.2	1.3	1.6	Quick		2.9	3.7	1.5	1.6	1.4
.7	.7	.8			.5	.9	.7	1.0	.8
.4	.4	.4			.3	.4	.3	.7	.4
19 18.8	19 19.2	25 14.5	Sales/Receivables		20 17.9	27 13.7	14 26.2	34 10.7	24 14.9
34 10.8	34 10.6	38 9.6			33 11.0	39 9.4	33 11.0	48 7.7	32 11.3
55 6.6	56 6.5	56 6.5			42 8.7	66 5.5	42 8.7	64 5.7	56 6.5
68 5.4	70 5.2	67 5.5	Cost of Sales/Inventory		81 4.5	44 8.4	56 6.6	70 5.2	67 5.5
111 3.3	126 2.9	113 3.2			172 2.1	118 3.1	107 3.4	124 2.9	105 3.5
164 2.2	209 1.7	177 2.1			331 1.1	173 2.1	152 2.4	198 1.8	148 2.5
11 31.8	11 31.8	13 28.7	Cost of Sales/Payables		15 24.0	9 38.6	13 27.2	14 25.7	11 32.1
23 15.7	20 18.0	23 15.9			34 10.7	18 20.0	23 15.8	19 19.2	24 15.0
37 9.9	35 10.3	35 10.5			41 8.9	47 7.8	38 9.6	32 11.4	36 10.2
3.9	3.2	3.1	Sales/Working Capital		2.2	3.9	4.4	2.9	3.3
6.7	5.5	4.6			3.3	10.7	7.7	3.5	5.5
13.1	11.1	11.2			11.3	45.5	12.3	6.3	15.4
16.3	10.8	20.3	EBIT/Interest		3.8	20.3	13.1	45.5	27.7
(144) 5.6	(129) 3.7	(134) 5.7		(15) 1.4	(14) 6.6	(22) 5.1	(35) 8.6	(43) 10.1	
2.1	.9	1.8			-6.0	2.6	2.8	1.8	3.2
7.7	16.7	19.1	Net Profit + Depr., Dep., Amort./Cur. Mat. L/T/D						22.1
(38) 3.2	(34) 4.2	(28) 5.5						(16) 6.1	
.8	1.6	2.7							3.7
.2	.2	.1	Fixed/Worth		.1	.1	.1	.1	.2
.4	.4	.4			.4	.5	.4	.2	.4
.9	1.0	.8			1.0	3.7	1.4	.5	.7
.7	.6	.4	Debt/Worth		.2	.4	.7	.3	.4
1.4	1.1	1.1			1.4	1.6	1.4	.9	1.0
3.2	3.5	2.6			3.5	11.3	4.0	1.4	2.9
43.7	29.8	41.0	% Profit Before Taxes/Tangible Net Worth		11.0	48.3	49.6	36.0	40.4
(142) 24.0	(127) 12.1	(140) 19.2		(17) 2.2	(14) 20.4	(23) 18.2	(37) 18.0	(44) 23.1	
6.6	1.2	5.6			-13.6	3.6	7.8	4.4	13.4
16.8	11.4	16.8	% Profit Before Taxes/Total Assets		6.7	20.0	13.5	17.1	17.3
8.7	5.2	7.5			.5	9.0	8.5	8.4	10.8
2.6	-.3	1.6			-7.5	4.7	2.2	1.6	4.2
36.6	33.8	29.7	Sales/Net Fixed Assets		42.3	27.7	54.6	34.0	16.2
13.4	11.1	12.0			13.3	13.6	7.4	14.1	11.2
6.8	5.1	5.3			7.4	6.1	3.7	4.6	7.5
2.5	2.2	2.4	Sales/Total Assets		2.3	2.5	2.7	2.4	2.4
1.9	1.6	1.8			1.5	1.9	2.0	1.6	1.9
1.5	1.2	1.2			1.0	1.3	1.3	1.2	1.5
.9	1.1	1.0	% Depr., Dep., Amort./Sales		1.4	1.1	.9	.7	1.4
(127) 1.4	(126) 1.9	(125) 1.8		(11) 2.7	(15) 2.5	(19) 2.9	(35) 1.5	(43) 1.7	
2.3	3.2	3.0			8.0	3.8	4.5	2.7	2.4
1.0	1.5	1.2	% Officers', Directors' Owners' Comp/Sales				1.3	.8	
(51) 2.1	(39) 2.8	(43) 2.7				(10) 3.5	(11) 1.2		
4.5	5.9	4.3					5.9	2.9	
5953923M	4407935M	4989419M	Net Sales ($)	3698M	36477M	66760M	178345M	599156M	4104983M
3266627M	2889923M	3050177M	Total Assets ($)	6113M	28379M	40165M	103745M	436303M	2435472M

M = $ thousand   MM = $ million
See Pages 9 through 22 for Explanation of Ratios and Data

Current Data Sorted by Assets | Comparative Historical Data

0-500M	500M-2MM	2-10MM	10-50MM	50-100MM	100-250MM	Type of Statement	4/1/06-3/31/07 ALL	4/1/07-3/31/08 ALL
	1		2	1	1	Unqualified	8	8
		5	1			Reviewed	9	9
	3	3				Compiled	4	5
	1	1				Tax Returns	7	4
	1	6	6	1	1	Other	16	24
	10 (4/1-9/30/10)		24 (10/1/10-3/31/11)				44	50
	6	15	9	2	2	NUMBER OF STATEMENTS	ALL	ALL

0-500M %	500M-2MM %	2-10MM %	10-50MM %	50-100MM %	100-250MM %	ASSETS	%	%
		7.8				Cash & Equivalents	8.2	5.7
		22.5				Trade Receivables (net)	18.9	22.5
		39.8				Inventory	40.8	44.3
		3.0				All Other Current	3.2	1.5
		73.1				Total Current	71.1	74.0
		19.1				Fixed Assets (net)	19.3	15.8
		1.4				Intangibles (net)	5.0	5.9
		6.4				All Other Non-Current	4.7	4.4
		100.0				Total	100.0	100.0

(DATA NOT AVAILABLE for 0-500M and 500M-2MM columns)

		2-10MM				LIABILITIES		
		24.2				Notes Payable-Short Term	22.1	19.6
		2.6				Cur. Mat.-L.T.D.	1.8	3.2
		19.2				Trade Payables	17.5	17.6
		.0				Income Taxes Payable	.5	.4
		8.1				All Other Current	9.6	9.4
		54.1				Total Current	51.5	50.2
		8.7				Long-Term Debt	11.4	13.6
		.3				Deferred Taxes	.4	.3
		6.0				All Other Non-Current	5.3	9.6
		30.9				Net Worth	31.4	26.4
		100.0				Total Liabilities & Net Worth	100.0	100.0

		2-10MM				INCOME DATA		
		100.0				Net Sales	100.0	100.0
		32.5				Gross Profit	28.3	28.1
		27.2				Operating Expenses	25.0	24.6
		5.2				Operating Profit	3.2	3.6
		1.0				All Other Expenses (net)	1.6	2.0
		4.2				Profit Before Taxes	1.7	1.6

		2-10MM				RATIOS		
		1.6					2.5	3.1
		1.3				Current	1.6	1.6
		1.1					1.2	1.1
		.9					1.1	1.5
		.5				Quick	.6	.5
		.3					.3	.3
		18 19.8					17 21.3	24 15.0
		41 9.0				Sales/Receivables	36 10.1	37 9.9
		77 4.8					53 6.8	58 6.3
		59 6.2					72 5.1	69 5.3
		120 3.0				Cost of Sales/Inventory	100 3.7	101 3.6
		186 2.0					134 2.7	156 2.3
		23 15.8					16 23.3	16 22.3
		43 8.4				Cost of Sales/Payables	32 11.4	34 10.7
		69 5.3					60 6.1	54 6.7
		5.5					4.4	4.0
		12.5				Sales/Working Capital	8.2	8.6
		51.1					18.4	30.4
		19.4					4.7	5.3
		3.5				EBIT/Interest	(42) 1.4	(46) 1.7
		-.2					.6	.2
							22.0	
						Net Profit + Depr., Dep., Amort./Cur. Mat. L/T/D	(10) 1.7	
							.9	
		.1					.3	.2
		.5				Fixed/Worth	.5	.5
		1.8					1.1	NM
		1.1					.7	.7
		3.4				Debt/Worth	1.9	2.0
		6.7					5.4	-11.3
		120.4					27.3	32.3
	(14)	44.3				% Profit Before Taxes/Tangible Net Worth	(35) 11.3	(37) 17.3
		-10.3					-3.0	4.0
		27.9					11.9	10.4
		7.9				% Profit Before Taxes/Total Assets	3.2	5.0
		-3.7					-1.0	-2.5
		60.4					25.2	43.7
		17.8				Sales/Net Fixed Assets	12.6	18.0
		4.8					6.7	8.3
		2.2					2.6	2.7
		1.9				Sales/Total Assets	2.0	2.0
		1.2					1.4	1.5
		.6					1.3	.6
	(13)	1.4				% Depr., Dep., Amort./Sales	(39) 1.7	(38) 1.5
		1.9					2.7	2.5
							1.5	1.7
						% Officers', Directors' Owners' Comp/Sales	(10) 2.3	(10) 2.6
							5.3	4.4

0-500M	500M-2MM	2-10MM	10-50MM	50-100MM	100-250MM		4/1/06-3/31/07	4/1/07-3/31/08
	12212M	151942M	348539M	185233M	868783M	Net Sales ($)	2190445M	1921653M
	5607M	74478M	223554M	104515M	321705M	Total Assets ($)	1206273M	1011123M

M = $ thousand   MM = $ million
See Pages 9 through 22 for Explanation of Ratios and Data

Comparative Historical Data   **Current Data Sorted by Sales**

						Type of Statement							
	10		8		5	Unqualified	1				2	3	4
	3		6		6	Reviewed							1
	5		5		6	Compiled		3	1	1	1	1	
	6		4		2	Tax Returns		1		1			
	20		16		15	Other		1	2	2	2	1	9
	4/1/08-		4/1/09-		4/1/10-			10 (4/1-9/30/10)			24 (10/1/10-3/31/11)		
	3/31/09		3/31/10		3/31/11								
	ALL		ALL		ALL		0-1MM	1-3MM	3-5MM	5-10MM	10-25MM	25MM & OVER	
	44		39		34	NUMBER OF STATEMENTS	1	5	3	6	5	14	
	%		%		%	ASSETS	%	%	%	%	%	%	
	7.6		10.4		11.1	Cash & Equivalents						15.8	
	15.3		14.8		17.3	Trade Receivables (net)						12.5	
	48.8		42.7		40.8	Inventory						40.3	
	2.4		1.9		2.7	All Other Current						3.7	
	74.1		69.8		71.9	Total Current						72.3	
	15.7		17.6		18.2	Fixed Assets (net)						21.2	
	6.3		5.0		6.0	Intangibles (net)						4.2	
	3.9		7.7		4.0	All Other Non-Current						2.3	
	100.0		100.0		100.0	Total						100.0	
						LIABILITIES							
	17.8		17.5		15.0	Notes Payable-Short Term						7.8	
	3.0		3.3		2.6	Cur. Mat.-L.T.D.						2.6	
	16.8		17.4		17.3	Trade Payables						12.9	
	.1		.4		.5	Income Taxes Payable						1.1	
	8.5		10.6		7.6	All Other Current						10.2	
	46.3		49.2		42.9	Total Current						34.6	
	11.9		8.1		12.2	Long-Term Debt						11.7	
	.1		.3		.3	Deferred Taxes						.2	
	5.9		10.7		4.2	All Other Non-Current						1.9	
	35.8		31.7		40.4	Net Worth						51.6	
	100.0		100.0		100.0	Total Liabilties & Net Worth						100.0	
						INCOME DATA							
	100.0		100.0		100.0	Net Sales						100.0	
	29.7		30.9		29.1	Gross Profit						23.0	
	27.7		28.9		24.1	Operating Expenses						18.5	
	2.0		2.0		5.0	Operating Profit						4.6	
	1.3		1.4		.8	All Other Expenses (net)						-.2	
	.7		.6		4.2	Profit Before Taxes						4.8	
						RATIOS							
	2.8		5.5		2.9							3.0	
	1.5		1.5		1.5	Current						1.8	
	1.1		1.2		1.2							1.5	
	.9		1.6		1.3							1.4	
	.5		.6		.6	Quick						.7	
	.3		.2		.3							.4	
17	21.7	8	48.4	13	29.0							17	21.8
34	10.9	27	13.6	36	10.2	Sales/Receivables						29	12.6
45	8.2	47	7.8	49	7.5							37	10.0
100	3.7	69	5.3	81	4.5							81	4.5
134	2.7	120	3.0	107	3.4	Cost of Sales/Inventory						93	3.9
195	1.9	178	2.0	166	2.2							140	2.6
18	19.8	11	33.5	22	16.8							14	26.0
31	11.7	20	18.6	38	9.7	Cost of Sales/Payables						29	12.4
71	5.1	48	7.6	55	6.6							46	8.0
	3.4		3.5		4.3							2.6	
	7.8		7.2		8.2	Sales/Working Capital						6.9	
	31.5		20.2		17.1							10.4	
	5.5		10.3		18.2							58.5	
(41)	2.3	(37)	1.6	(33)	6.0	EBIT/Interest						7.6	
	.4		-1.9		1.1							1.1	
	4.0					Net Profit + Depr., Dep.,							
(15)	2.9					Amort./Cur. Mat. L/T/D							
	2.3												
	.2		.1		.1							.1	
	.4		.4		.4	Fixed/Worth						.3	
	1.3		1.1		1.3							.7	
	.6		.7		.7							.6	
	1.9		1.2		1.8	Debt/Worth						.9	
	12.9		2.7		4.4							2.4	
	27.7		19.2		81.5	% Profit Before Taxes/Tangible						43.1	
(35)	14.4	(34)	3.9	(31)	18.7	Net Worth						17.6	
	2.6		-19.1		.3							.3	
	9.3		9.6		15.7	% Profit Before Taxes/Total						13.7	
	4.0		1.1		7.1	Assets						9.5	
	-1.2		-6.8		.2							.2	
	34.3		51.8		52.8							50.0	
	13.7		15.6		21.6	Sales/Net Fixed Assets						18.4	
	8.4		6.1		5.5							4.8	
	2.3		2.6		2.3							2.5	
	1.7		1.7		1.7	Sales/Total Assets						1.7	
	1.3		1.3		1.2							1.2	
	.8		.6		.6							.6	
(37)	1.7	(38)	1.5	(27)	1.4	% Depr., Dep., Amort./Sales						(12)	1.2
	2.3		2.4		1.9							2.7	
	1.6		1.7		1.1								
(10)	2.9	(16)	3.0	(14)	2.4	% Officers', Directors'							
	7.4		6.8		3.6	Owners' Comp/Sales							
1927255M		1634538M		1566709M		Net Sales ($)	611M	11601M	10737M	36891M	63223M	1443646M	
1040757M		808964M		729859M		Total Assets ($)	581M	5026M	7338M	26132M	31909M	658873M	

© RMA 2011

M = $ thousand   MM = $ million
See Pages 9 through 22 for Explanation of Ratios and Data

Current Data Sorted by Assets   **Comparative Historical Data**

M = $ thousand   MM = $ million
See Pages 9 through 22 for Explanation of Ratios and Data

Type of Statement	0-500M	500M-2MM	2-10MM	10-50MM	50-100MM	100-250MM	4/1/06-3/31/07 ALL	4/1/07-3/31/08 ALL
Unqualified		1	4	11	7	3	38	37
Reviewed	1	3	9	10			27	24
Compiled		2	7	2			13	16
Tax Returns	3	3					9	7
Other		5	16	19	6	7	38	44
		25 (4/1-9/30/10)	94 (10/1/10-3/31/11)					
NUMBER OF STATEMENTS	4	14	36	42	13	10	125	128
ASSETS	%	%	%	%	%	%	%	%
Cash & Equivalents		12.0	6.7	8.5	16.3	21.6	8.1	7.2
Trade Receivables (net)		24.9	23.4	19.1	12.4	16.2	23.9	22.8
Inventory		16.5	33.5	38.2	28.8	24.6	32.3	31.9
All Other Current		3.9	3.3	3.0	4.6	7.8	4.0	4.5
Total Current		57.3	66.9	68.7	62.1	70.2	68.4	66.4
Fixed Assets (net)		29.8	24.3	23.7	21.6	13.9	23.3	24.4
Intangibles (net)		6.5	4.8	3.1	11.5	4.9	3.5	4.3
All Other Non-Current		6.4	4.0	4.4	4.8	11.0	4.8	5.0
Total		100.0	100.0	100.0	100.0	100.0	100.0	100.0
LIABILITIES								
Notes Payable-Short Term		17.3	14.8	11.6	2.2	10.7	12.7	14.9
Cur. Mat.-L.T.D.		6.6	3.6	2.3	1.1	.6	2.8	4.5
Trade Payables		16.6	13.1	9.2	6.4	9.7	14.9	12.2
Income Taxes Payable		.1	.3	.2	.0	1.0	.4	.3
All Other Current		20.5	9.3	11.3	23.4	11.6	12.4	12.3
Total Current		61.0	41.1	34.7	33.1	33.7	43.2	44.2
Long-Term Debt		20.5	11.9	8.3	8.5	7.4	15.7	15.8
Deferred Taxes		.3	.5	.7	.1	.7	.4	.3
All Other Non-Current		16.4	2.6	3.1	6.6	7.1	5.5	4.1
Net Worth		1.9	43.9	53.2	51.7	51.1	35.1	35.6
Total Liabilities & Net Worth		100.0	100.0	100.0	100.0	100.0	100.0	100.0
INCOME DATA								
Net Sales		100.0	100.0	100.0	100.0	100.0	100.0	100.0
Gross Profit		33.5	31.1	26.2	29.3	22.1	27.0	29.7
Operating Expenses		31.1	26.9	22.3	23.4	18.3	20.2	22.9
Operating Profit		2.4	4.2	3.9	5.9	3.8	6.8	6.7
All Other Expenses (net)		.3	.7	.7	1.3	-.1	1.0	1.3
Profit Before Taxes		2.1	3.5	3.2	4.6	3.9	5.7	5.4
RATIOS								
Current		2.9	2.3	3.5	6.3	5.0	2.2	2.4
		1.2	1.7	2.0	2.3	2.2	1.6	1.6
		.4	1.1	1.4	1.2	1.3	1.2	1.1
Quick		2.1	1.1	1.4	3.4	3.2	1.2	1.2
		.5	.7	.7	.9	.9	.7	.6
		.3	.5	.5	.5	.8	.5	.3
Sales/Receivables		23 15.7	28 13.2	42 8.8	27 13.7	24 15.0	29 12.7	26 14.1
		38 9.7	45 8.2	52 7.1	47 7.7	57 6.4	42 8.6	41 8.9
		53 6.9	57 6.4	61 5.9	61 6.0	81 4.5	61 6.0	57 6.3
Cost of Sales/Inventory		0 UND	42 8.7	108 3.4	92 4.0	83 4.4	42 8.6	35 10.3
		25 14.4	107 3.4	142 2.6	178 2.0	132 2.8	91 4.0	91 4.0
		56 6.6	162 2.3	188 1.9	285 1.3	160 2.3	126 2.9	149 2.4
Cost of Sales/Payables		9 42.0	26 14.3	18 20.4	17 22.1	24 15.3	19 19.7	16 22.5
		26 13.9	37 10.0	29 12.6	24 15.3	51 7.1	28 13.1	29 12.8
		46 7.9	48 7.7	45 8.1	45 8.1	69 5.3	48 7.5	44 8.4
Sales/Working Capital		5.3	3.8	2.8	1.7	1.2	4.9	4.7
		NM	7.1	3.6	3.1	3.5	8.6	9.3
		-7.1	24.3	7.3	508.1	8.0	18.7	24.4
EBIT/Interest		7.6	12.0	14.2	999.8		12.2	10.0
		(12) 3.3	(33) 4.5	(38) 3.7	(11) 4.0		(116) 4.9	(121) 4.1
		1.3	1.8	2.0	-1.6		2.1	1.3
Net Profit + Depr., Dep., Amort./Cur. Mat. L/T/D				6.3			5.7	7.4
			(16) 2.3				(34) 2.4	(45) 2.6
				1.0			1.5	1.0
Fixed/Worth		.5	.3	.2	.2	.1	.3	.2
		NM	.6	.5	.3	.3	.6	.5
		-.4	1.3	.7	2.8	.8	1.6	1.7
Debt/Worth		.6	.8	.4	.2	.4	1.0	.8
		NM	1.5	.9	1.3	1.0	2.1	2.2
		-3.0	2.7	1.7	4.5	4.5	5.2	5.2
% Profit Before Taxes/Tangible Net Worth			39.4	18.0	13.8	45.0	66.3	44.3
		(35) 17.5	(40) 9.9	(11) 10.5	7.4		(113) 25.4	(116) 22.0
			5.5	2.9	-1.2	-1.0	12.9	5.3
% Profit Before Taxes/Total Assets		13.9	13.3	8.6	8.8	8.3	17.0	15.7
		5.5	7.1	4.6	5.8	3.4	8.7	7.5
		1.1	1.3	1.2	-.9	.8	3.1	1.5
Sales/Net Fixed Assets		23.0	15.7	12.2	11.6	28.8	22.2	25.3
		10.8	8.6	7.6	8.6	8.1	9.5	10.1
		4.6	5.3	2.5	2.6	3.6	6.0	5.1
Sales/Total Assets		3.4	2.4	1.7	1.2	1.2	2.6	2.5
		2.4	1.9	1.4	.9	1.0	1.9	1.7
		1.5	1.3	.9	.6	.7	1.5	1.2
% Depr., Dep., Amort./Sales		1.7	1.4	1.1	1.8		.8	.9
		(12) 3.3	(30) 2.0	(38) 2.1	(12) 2.2		(108) 1.7	(108) 1.9
		6.5	3.7	4.1	4.4		2.9	3.4
% Officers', Directors' Owners' Comp/Sales			1.1				2.4	2.2
			(15) 2.4				(27) 3.6	(25) 3.8
			7.2				5.0	5.4
Net Sales ($)		3125M	34012M	306581M	1138637M	934492M	1617125M	5486966M	5064454M
Total Assets ($)		1273M	14513M	158149M	896935M	1005300M	1591835M	3296535M	3197587M

© RMA 2011

	Comparative Historical Data			Current Data Sorted by Sales					
Type of Statement									
Unqualified	44	36	26		1		1	10	14
Reviewed	22	20	23	1	3	1	3	12	3
Compiled	14	9	11		3	3	3		2
Tax Returns	7	9	6	2	3	1			
Other	56	59	53	1	3	7	6	13	23
	4/1/08-3/31/09 ALL	4/1/09-3/31/10 ALL	4/1/10-3/31/11 ALL	\<— 25 (4/1-9/30/10) —\>			\<— 94 (10/1/10-3/31/11) —\>		
				0-1MM	1-3MM	3-5MM	5-10MM	10-25MM	25MM & OVER
NUMBER OF STATEMENTS	143	133	119	4	13	12	13	35	42
ASSETS	%	%	%	%	%	%	%	%	%
Cash & Equivalents	6.3	10.9	10.2		13.2	2.5	5.6	10.2	13.5
Trade Receivables (net)	18.7	18.5	20.2		19.2	27.3	25.1	18.8	18.7
Inventory	38.3	34.1	32.2		18.5	31.2	41.0	30.7	35.0
All Other Current	4.1	4.8	3.7		1.9	3.4	3.2	4.1	4.4
Total Current	67.3	68.3	66.3		52.8	64.5	74.8	63.7	71.6
Fixed Assets (net)	23.2	23.5	23.6		34.2	26.3	19.0	26.0	18.0
Intangibles (net)	5.4	3.0	5.1		4.6	7.0	1.9	5.1	5.2
All Other Non-Current	4.1	5.3	5.0		8.4	2.2	4.3	5.2	5.1
Total	100.0	100.0	100.0		100.0	100.0	100.0	100.0	100.0
LIABILITIES									
Notes Payable-Short Term	14.9	12.5	12.5		7.1	22.9	20.2	9.4	10.2
Cur. Mat.-L.T.D.	2.7	2.8	3.6		2.7	7.3	5.7	2.0	1.7
Trade Payables	11.3	10.6	11.2		13.4	13.5	14.7	10.5	9.1
Income Taxes Payable	.3	.2	.3		.1	.5	.4	.2	.3
All Other Current	12.6	14.2	13.0		12.4	6.0	9.2	14.0	13.6
Total Current	41.7	40.3	40.5		35.6	50.1	50.1	36.1	34.9
Long-Term Debt	15.1	13.1	11.5		15.2	25.2	10.8	8.4	8.0
Deferred Taxes	.6	.4	.5		.3	.6	.2	.6	.5
All Other Non-Current	5.1	6.3	5.8		14.9	7.4	.3	2.0	6.1
Net Worth	37.4	39.8	41.7		34.0	16.6	38.5	52.8	50.5
Total Liabilities & Net Worth	100.0	100.0	100.0		100.0	100.0	100.0	100.0	100.0
INCOME DATA									
Net Sales	100.0	100.0	100.0		100.0	100.0	100.0	100.0	100.0
Gross Profit	27.2	26.5	28.7		30.4	33.8	30.5	28.0	25.5
Operating Expenses	23.1	26.6	24.8		26.3	29.2	27.4	24.1	20.8
Operating Profit	4.1	-.1	4.0		4.1	4.6	3.1	3.9	4.8
All Other Expenses (net)	1.1	.6	.7		.4	1.0	.5	.6	.7
Profit Before Taxes	3.0	-.7	3.3		3.6	3.6	2.6	3.3	4.1
RATIOS									
Current	2.9	3.5	3.4		5.5	2.2	2.8	3.4	3.7
	1.6	1.8	1.8		1.8	1.7	1.7	1.9	2.0
	1.1	1.2	1.3		.7	1.1	1.1	1.3	1.4
Quick	1.0	1.5	1.5		2.7	1.1	1.2	1.6	1.8
	.6	.7	.7		.8	.6	.5	.7	.8
	.3	.3	.5		.4	.4	.4	.6	.5
Sales/Receivables	23 16.0	29 12.6	34 10.7		20 18.2	35 10.3	22 16.3	34 10.7	40 9.1
	37 10.0	45 8.2	48 7.6		48 7.6	46 8.0	48 7.7	51 7.2	48 7.6
	56 6.6	62 5.9	59 6.2		63 5.8	52 7.1	62 5.9	65 5.6	57 6.4
Cost of Sales/Inventory	65 5.6	68 5.3	58 6.2		1 269.6	31 11.7	52 7.0	62 5.9	82 4.5
	107 3.4	118 3.1	122 3.0		34 10.8	105 3.5	108 3.4	136 2.7	140 2.6
	170 2.1	199 1.8	178 2.0		112 3.3	190 1.9	182 2.0	185 2.0	180 2.0
Cost of Sales/Payables	15 24.8	16 23.5	18 19.9		6 64.9	23 15.9	27 13.7	19 19.0	18 20.8
	27 13.6	23 15.6	33 10.9		20 17.9	31 11.9	37 9.9	36 10.1	29 12.6
	41 9.0	46 8.0	50 7.3		42 8.7	50 7.3	56 6.5	51 7.2	44 8.3
Sales/Working Capital	4.1	2.6	3.0		3.0	4.0	3.7	2.9	1.9
	6.7	5.3	5.1		6.0	9.1	7.4	4.0	3.7
	21.9	13.2	14.8		-11.6	23.5	93.8	13.8	8.0
EBIT/Interest	10.2	6.7	12.2		10.4	6.0	12.7	16.5	17.5
	(132) 3.2	(120) 2.3	(106) 3.6		(11) 6.0	(11) 2.4	(12) 4.0	(32) 4.9	(36) 3.6
	.4	-2.9	1.8		2.0	1.1	1.7	2.2	2.1
Net Profit + Depr., Dep., Amort./Cur. Mat. L/T/D	6.5	6.2	9.5					13.3	12.5
	(44) 3.0	(37) 1.4	(34) 3.5					(10) 4.0	(18) 5.0
	.7	.0	.9					1.2	.9
Fixed/Worth	.2	.2	.2		.2	.5	.3	.3	.1
	.5	.6	.5		1.2	.7	.5	.6	.3
	1.9	1.8	1.3		-10.1	2.1	2.3	1.0	.8
Debt/Worth	.6	.6	.5		.3	.9	.6	.5	.4
	1.8	1.4	1.3		1.8	1.7	1.4	.9	1.2
	7.7	4.1	2.8		-20.9	2.5	6.4	2.1	2.9
% Profit Before Taxes/Tangible Net Worth	36.4	21.1	25.5		19.2	54.8		21.9	18.7
	(122) 16.4	(119) 5.2	(105) 11.1		(10) 8.0	(12) 22.2		(34) 9.4	(39) 10.5
	1.8	-8.4	3.1		2.1	10.3		4.4	2.5
% Profit Before Taxes/Total Assets	13.2	7.3	9.6		14.5	7.8	18.5	12.4	8.8
	5.3	2.1	4.9		11.8	2.8	7.3	4.9	5.0
	-.8	-5.0	1.2		3.2	.7	1.9	1.2	1.5
Sales/Net Fixed Assets	18.7	18.2	13.9		24.7	20.4	22.2	10.1	15.6
	9.9	7.5	8.8		6.2	9.4	9.6	6.7	9.9
	5.1	3.7	4.6		2.7	5.2	6.2	2.3	5.3
Sales/Total Assets	2.4	2.1	2.2		2.4	3.1	2.7	1.9	1.7
	1.6	1.3	1.4		1.6	1.5	2.2	1.4	1.2
	1.2	.9	1.0		1.4	1.0	1.4	.8	.9
% Depr., Dep., Amort./Sales	1.0	1.3	1.5		2.4	1.2		1.2	1.3
	(121) 1.8	(112) 2.3	(104) 2.2		(12) 3.9	(10) 1.8		(32) 2.3	(37) 2.1
	3.4	4.0	4.1		6.9	3.0		3.7	4.1
% Officers', Directors' Owners' Comp/Sales	1.1	1.2	1.9						
	(23) 3.1	(26) 2.9	(33) 3.5						
	5.7	7.1	5.8						
Net Sales ($)	6771288M	4111564M	4033972M	2338M	26391M	45384M	91673M	572594M	3295592M
Total Assets ($)	4623437M	3820166M	3668005M	1333M	16451M	30659M	48824M	607991M	2962747M

M = $ thousand   MM = $ million
See Pages 9 through 22 for Explanation of Ratios and Data

Current Data Sorted by Assets / Comparative Historical Data

	0-500M	500M-2MM	2-10MM	10-50MM	50-100MM	100-250MM	4/1/06-3/31/07 ALL	4/1/07-3/31/08 ALL
Type of Statement								
Unqualified		1	1	6	2	1	9	12
Reviewed			4	5	1		18	12
Compiled		4	4	1			9	9
Tax Returns		1	2					3
Other		2	9	8	4	3	19	15
	14 (4/1-9/30/10)			45 (10/1/10-3/31/11)				
NUMBER OF STATEMENTS		8	20	20	7	4	55	51
ASSETS	%	%	%	%	%	%	%	%
Cash & Equivalents	D		5.3	8.3			6.7	6.3
Trade Receivables (net)	A		25.5	21.0			25.0	24.1
Inventory	T		33.1	34.8			35.4	33.0
All Other Current	A		7.5	2.6			3.6	3.6
Total Current			71.5	66.6			70.7	67.0
Fixed Assets (net)	N		20.6	27.9			19.8	23.2
Intangibles (net)	O		.8	2.6			3.4	3.2
All Other Non-Current	T		7.1	2.8			6.1	6.5
Total			100.0	100.0			100.0	100.0
LIABILITIES	A							
Notes Payable-Short Term	V		9.2	12.7			10.7	10.4
Cur. Mat.-L.T.D.	A		6.7	3.5			2.8	3.3
Trade Payables	I		16.0	11.4			17.0	15.3
Income Taxes Payable	L		.3	.9			.3	.1
All Other Current	A		7.5	11.1			13.4	14.8
Total Current	B		39.7	39.5			44.2	43.9
Long-Term Debt	L		14.1	15.5			13.7	18.3
Deferred Taxes	E		.4	.9			.4	.3
All Other Non-Current			6.1	.6			7.4	4.0
Net Worth			39.7	43.5			34.4	33.4
Total Liabilties & Net Worth			100.0	100.0			100.0	100.0
INCOME DATA								
Net Sales			100.0	100.0			100.0	100.0
Gross Profit			37.8	30.0			30.7	29.0
Operating Expenses			29.3	24.3			23.9	22.0
Operating Profit			8.5	5.7			6.9	7.0
All Other Expenses (net)			.3	2.6			.8	.8
Profit Before Taxes			8.1	3.1			6.0	6.2
RATIOS								
Current			2.5	2.9			2.6	2.7
			1.6	1.4			1.7	1.9
			1.4	1.0			1.2	1.3
Quick			1.4	1.5			1.2	1.2
			.7	.6			.8	.8
			.4	.4			.5	.5
Sales/Receivables			37 9.9	48 7.6			29 12.7	31 11.8
			46 8.0	59 6.2			42 8.6	49 7.5
			66 5.5	66 5.5			61 6.0	61 5.9
Cost of Sales/Inventory			65 5.6	88 4.2			46 7.9	45 8.1
			101 3.6	133 2.7			90 4.0	69 5.3
			125 2.9	174 2.1			155 2.4	155 2.4
Cost of Sales/Payables			21 17.1	32 11.4			20 18.3	18 20.2
			44 8.2	42 8.7			36 10.2	32 11.5
			73 5.0	59 6.2			55 6.6	63 5.8
Sales/Working Capital			4.7	3.0			3.9	3.4
			6.7	7.6			6.4	6.2
			10.4	NM			19.0	14.4
EBIT/Interest			25.7	33.3			30.4	15.0
			(18) 6.1	(18) 7.0			(53) 6.9	(50) 5.9
			3.1	2.6			2.1	1.5
Net Profit + Depr., Dep., Amort./Cur. Mat. L/T/D				18.3			25.0	5.0
				(10) 4.8			(13) 5.7	(15) 2.9
				1.0			3.8	.3
Fixed/Worth			.2	.2			.2	.3
			.6	.6			.4	.6
			.9	2.2			2.1	1.8
Debt/Worth			.7	.6			.8	.9
			1.7	1.6			1.5	2.0
			3.0	2.8			6.0	5.2
% Profit Before Taxes/Tangible Net Worth			54.1	32.9			49.8	49.6
			(19) 31.5	(18) 23.3			(46) 28.3	(44) 25.9
			14.5	5.5			13.6	13.2
% Profit Before Taxes/Total Assets			20.7	15.1			22.5	21.3
			11.9	8.6			10.3	10.1
			5.8	1.6			2.3	1.0
Sales/Net Fixed Assets			27.9	15.8			37.7	28.4
			12.4	6.5			10.8	12.4
			5.6	3.4			7.0	4.5
Sales/Total Assets			2.5	1.8			2.4	2.5
			2.0	1.4			1.9	2.0
			1.1	1.0			1.6	1.4
% Depr., Dep., Amort./Sales			1.1	1.3			.7	.9
			(18) 2.6	(18) 1.8			(49) 1.3	(47) 1.6
			4.4	4.4			2.6	3.2
% Officers', Directors' Owners' Comp/Sales							2.1	1.5
							(15) 3.9	(13) 2.2
							7.6	4.1
Net Sales ($)		19268M	176261M	544085M	592041M	685433M	2445335M	2025816M
Total Assets ($)		8327M	94182M	406852M	528165M	652745M	1300492M	1112012M

M = $ thousand MM = $ million

See Pages 9 through 22 for Explanation of Ratios and Data

Comparative Historical Data | Current Data Sorted by Sales

9	12	11	Type of Statement						
9	12	11	Unqualified	1			1	1	8
14	13	10	Reviewed				3	5	2
8	2	9	Compiled	3	1		4	1	
3	3	3	Tax Returns	2				1	
22	24	26	Other	2	2		5	7	10
4/1/08-3/31/09 ALL	4/1/09-3/31/10 ALL	4/1/10-3/31/11 ALL			14 (4/1-9/30/10)			45 (10/1/10-3/31/11)	
				0-1MM	1-3MM	3-5MM	5-10MM	10-25MM	25MM & OVER
56	54	59	**NUMBER OF STATEMENTS**	8	3		13	15	20
%	%	%	**ASSETS**	%	%	%	%	%	%
7.1	7.4	9.3	Cash & Equivalents				6.0	7.4	9.2
23.9	20.2	22.5	Trade Receivables (net)				27.6	21.9	22.0
33.2	36.2	29.7	Inventory				35.2	29.7	29.5
2.4	4.3	4.7	All Other Current		DATA		7.5	1.5	5.4
66.7	68.2	66.2	Total Current		NOT		76.2	60.5	66.0
22.8	24.1	24.6	Fixed Assets (net)		AVAILABLE		20.4	31.9	20.3
5.1	4.0	3.1	Intangibles (net)				1.1	3.5	5.7
5.5	3.7	6.1	All Other Non-Current				2.3	4.1	8.0
100.0	100.0	100.0	Total				100.0	100.0	100.0
			LIABILITIES						
12.7	12.0	9.7	Notes Payable-Short Term				9.7	12.2	8.1
4.3	4.5	4.5	Cur. Mat.-L.T.D.				3.6	5.2	2.3
15.0	11.6	13.9	Trade Payables				19.0	13.5	10.7
.5	.9	.5	Income Taxes Payable				.3	1.3	.3
10.2	10.3	10.6	All Other Current				6.3	7.5	13.8
42.7	39.3	39.3	Total Current				39.0	39.7	35.2
16.6	14.6	17.6	Long-Term Debt				16.2	18.1	8.1
.2	.6	.6	Deferred Taxes				.1	.8	.8
4.2	7.0	3.3	All Other Non-Current				4.1	1.4	2.2
36.4	38.6	39.2	Net Worth				40.6	40.0	53.6
100.0	100.0	100.0	Total Liabilities & Net Worth				100.0	100.0	100.0
			INCOME DATA						
100.0	100.0	100.0	Net Sales				100.0	100.0	100.0
29.5	28.9	32.5	Gross Profit				31.5	37.7	28.8
24.2	25.1	26.2	Operating Expenses				22.8	32.6	20.6
5.2	3.8	6.2	Operating Profit				8.7	5.0	8.2
1.5	.7	1.6	All Other Expenses (net)				.6	2.7	1.0
3.7	3.0	4.7	Profit Before Taxes				8.1	2.4	7.2
			RATIOS						
2.1	2.6	2.7					3.6	2.5	2.9
1.6	1.7	1.5	Current				1.6	1.5	2.0
1.2	1.3	1.2					1.4	1.0	1.2
1.1	1.5	1.6					2.0	1.2	1.7
.7	.7	.8	Quick				.8	.9	.9
.5	.3	.4					.5	.4	.5
28 12.8	29 12.5	37 9.9					28 13.2	39 9.4	49 7.5
39 9.4	41 8.9	52 7.0	Sales/Receivables				39 9.4	56 6.5	64 5.7
53 6.9	62 5.9	66 5.5					62 5.9	62 5.9	72 5.0
35 10.5	56 6.5	62 5.9					35 10.5	52 7.0	78 4.7
76 4.8	110 3.3	98 3.7	Cost of Sales/Inventory				104 3.5	95 3.8	98 3.7
136 2.7	202 1.8	158 2.3					157 2.3	163 2.2	159 2.3
14 25.7	19 19.2	23 15.8					15 24.1	34 10.6	26 14.0
29 12.5	30 12.0	42 8.7	Cost of Sales/Payables				33 11.0	45 8.0	42 8.7
51 7.2	51 7.2	63 5.8					85 4.3	63 5.8	57 6.4
4.7	3.0	3.2					2.6	5.8	2.5
9.5	5.8	7.0	Sales/Working Capital				5.5	11.2	4.3
21.6	15.6	16.9					13.4	-133.4	14.8
18.7	16.0	16.7					168.8	31.7	29.9
(52) 5.3	(50) 3.6	(53) 5.8	EBIT/Interest		(11) 9.5	(13) 6.3			(18) 6.8
1.7	-.7	2.0					1.9	3.9	3.6
7.5	13.9	18.4							30.8
(20) 2.6	(18) 3.6	(19) 2.4	Net Profit + Depr., Dep., Amort./Cur. Mat. L/T/D						(12) 7.4
.7	1.3	1.1							1.6
.3	.3	.3					.1	.4	.3
.7	.7	.6	Fixed/Worth				.5	.7	.4
1.4	1.5	1.2					.9	2.5	.8
1.0	.7	.6					.7	.6	.4
1.7	1.9	1.6	Debt/Worth				1.2	1.7	1.1
3.8	3.2	4.1					4.1	4.5	1.9
59.8	37.9	37.1					51.8	37.7	29.2
(46) 31.5	(48) 18.4	(52) 21.6	% Profit Before Taxes/Tangible Net Worth		(12) 28.2	(13) 32.8			(19) 19.0
5.5	2.8	13.3					13.8	17.3	13.3
20.5	16.1	14.3					22.2	14.1	14.2
7.3	5.3	7.9	% Profit Before Taxes/Total Assets				11.9	9.8	8.5
-.8	-3.7	2.1					4.3	4.3	5.1
27.9	13.4	19.5					64.0	19.5	13.5
10.9	7.0	7.1	Sales/Net Fixed Assets				20.3	5.4	7.0
5.4	4.2	4.4					5.7	3.0	4.8
2.9	2.1	2.1					2.1	2.6	1.6
2.1	1.6	1.5	Sales/Total Assets				2.0	1.8	1.3
1.5	1.0	1.1					1.4	1.0	1.2
1.1	1.5	1.4					.6	1.1	1.6
(50) 1.7	(50) 2.8	(53) 2.2	% Depr., Dep., Amort./Sales		(12) 2.2	(12) 2.6			(19) 2.0
2.7	4.4	3.8					3.4	4.6	3.3
1.4		.9							
(14) 1.7		(14) 1.5	% Officers', Directors' Owners' Comp/Sales						
6.3		2.6							
2177751M	2032245M	2017088M	Net Sales ($)	15004M	11883M		94644M	278760M	1616797M
1224053M	1260229M	1690271M	Total Assets ($)	11605M	7893M		58420M	202472M	1409881M

M = $ thousand   MM = $ million
See Pages 9 through 22 for Explanation of Ratios and Data

Current Data Sorted by Assets							Comparative Historical Data	
0-500M	500M-2MM	2-10MM	10-50MM	50-100MM	100-250MM	**Type of Statement**		
		3	12	6	4	Unqualified	13	11
1		8	4	1		Reviewed	6	17
	2	2	3		1	Compiled	14	17
1	5	6				Tax Returns	4	5
1	6	28	14	8	3	Other	41	47
	20 (4/1-9/30/10)		99 (10/1/10-3/31/11)				4/1/06-3/31/07 ALL	4/1/07-3/31/08 ALL
3	13	47	33	15	8	**NUMBER OF STATEMENTS**	78	97
%	%	%	%	%	%	**ASSETS**	%	%
	22.7	11.2	9.6	16.0		Cash & Equivalents	7.3	8.2
	32.3	26.2	21.0	14.9		Trade Receivables (net)	28.5	28.8
	18.1	22.8	28.7	14.1		Inventory	25.3	24.4
	2.6	9.1	4.2	3.1		All Other Current	5.1	8.0
	75.7	69.3	63.5	48.1		Total Current	66.3	69.3
	17.8	20.1	25.8	28.4		Fixed Assets (net)	26.0	22.1
	2.3	3.7	6.3	11.4		Intangibles (net)	4.5	3.7
	4.2	6.9	4.5	12.1		All Other Non-Current	3.2	4.9
	100.0	100.0	100.0	100.0		Total	100.0	100.0
						LIABILITIES		
	7.6	10.5	5.4	1.2		Notes Payable-Short Term	8.0	9.3
	5.8	1.8	5.3	2.8		Cur. Mat.-L.T.D.	3.0	2.9
	14.2	13.0	11.4	10.5		Trade Payables	15.6	15.5
	.0	.4	.3	.5		Income Taxes Payable	.3	.8
	3.7	9.9	10.1	11.4		All Other Current	13.4	11.7
	31.4	35.7	32.5	26.4		Total Current	40.3	40.2
	5.4	9.7	15.3	15.2		Long-Term Debt	15.8	13.1
	.5	.9	1.4	2.8		Deferred Taxes	.6	.7
	18.4	1.9	2.4	9.9		All Other Non-Current	5.4	1.9
	44.4	51.8	48.4	45.8		Net Worth	37.9	44.1
	100.0	100.0	100.0	100.0		Total Liabilities & Net Worth	100.0	100.0
						INCOME DATA		
	100.0	100.0	100.0	100.0		Net Sales	100.0	100.0
	41.5	37.1	35.4	39.5		Gross Profit	35.1	37.1
	36.7	28.3	27.3	23.2		Operating Expenses	24.9	25.1
	4.8	8.8	8.1	16.2		Operating Profit	10.3	12.0
	-.3	1.4	1.6	2.6		All Other Expenses (net)	1.3	1.5
	5.1	7.4	6.5	13.6		Profit Before Taxes	9.0	10.5
						RATIOS		
	5.3	3.3	3.6	2.9			2.3	2.7
	2.2	2.1	2.3	1.9		Current	1.6	1.8
	1.9	1.3	1.3	1.5			1.3	1.3
	4.1	2.2	1.7	1.7			1.6	1.6
	2.1	1.0	.9	1.0		Quick	.8	1.0
	1.0	.5	.7	.7			.5	.6
43 8.6	34 10.8	40 9.2	45 8.2			Sales/Receivables	38 9.5	38 9.7
59 6.2	56 6.5	57 6.4	67 5.5				56 6.5	57 6.4
83 4.4	69 5.3	71 5.1	92 4.0				71 5.2	69 5.3
0 UND	4 95.8	63 5.8	71 5.1			Cost of Sales/Inventory	30 12.1	18 19.8
40 9.1	44 8.2	115 3.2	81 4.5				70 5.2	66 5.5
99 3.7	166 2.2	195 1.9	162 2.2				148 2.5	145 2.5
13 27.2	18 20.2	29 12.8	19 19.0			Cost of Sales/Payables	21 17.1	22 16.7
37 9.8	33 11.0	46 7.9	66 5.5				47 7.8	40 9.2
69 5.3	48 7.6	67 5.4	89 4.1				68 5.3	60 6.1
	3.0	2.9	2.7	2.5		Sales/Working Capital	4.5	4.5
	5.8	4.7	4.9	4.6			8.0	7.3
	9.3	11.4	9.7	5.7			14.6	18.2
		22.5	14.7	23.2		EBIT/Interest	13.5	23.4
	(39) 7.5	(30) 4.0	(13) 9.1				(72) 6.3	(85) 8.2
	1.8	1.2	4.6				3.2	3.2
			6.0			Net Profit + Depr., Dep., Amort./Cur. Mat. L/T/D	16.2	29.2
		(10) 2.8					(22) 5.1	(26) 5.2
		1.2					2.0	2.7
	.0	.1	.3	.3		Fixed/Worth	.3	.2
	.2	.3	.5	.4			.9	.5
	1.7	.9	2.2	3.4			1.6	1.2
	.4	.4	.5	.6		Debt/Worth	1.0	.7
	1.0	1.0	1.5	1.5			1.9	1.4
	5.4	2.5	3.0	5.5			4.9	3.7
	100.0	64.2	34.9	71.9		% Profit Before Taxes/Tangible Net Worth	60.7	75.7
	(11) 32.5	(46) 13.3	(29) 18.0	(13) 20.1			(72) 38.9	(94) 42.7
	9.8	1.1	6.3	15.6			18.6	22.5
	29.0	21.2	17.0	13.9		% Profit Before Taxes/Total Assets	21.5	28.5
	11.0	6.5	8.9	9.1			11.1	15.7
	1.4	.3	1.0	4.8			6.8	5.7
	705.1	58.4	10.7	9.0		Sales/Net Fixed Assets	19.8	32.6
	11.4	12.3	6.9	5.3			7.7	9.6
	6.7	5.4	4.3	1.6			4.5	5.5
	2.5	2.6	1.7	1.1		Sales/Total Assets	2.5	2.7
	2.1	1.7	1.3	.8			1.7	1.8
	1.6	1.1	1.0	.5			1.3	1.3
		.7	2.0	4.0		% Depr., Dep., Amort./Sales	1.1	.5
	(35)	1.6	(29) 3.0	(10) 5.1			(66) 2.1	(77) 1.8
		4.5	4.0	7.0			3.0	4.1
		1.7				% Officers', Directors' Owners' Comp/Sales	1.7	1.4
	(11)	4.1					(18) 2.4	(24) 3.4
		6.9					5.6	7.7
3373M	39583M	399441M	953451M	940889M	1119370M	Net Sales ($)	2791109M	3450700M
1109M	16181M	225987M	697797M	1134580M	1320676M	Total Assets ($)	1931830M	2435625M

Comparative Historical Data | Current Data Sorted by Sales

4/1/08-3/31/09 ALL	4/1/09-3/31/10 ALL	4/1/10-3/31/11 ALL	Type of Statement	0-1MM	1-3MM	3-5MM	5-10MM	10-25MM	25MM & OVER
19	18	25	Unqualified			1	2	6	16
11	8	14	Reviewed	1		5	5	5	2
9	10	8	Compiled			3	1	3	1
6	7	12	Tax Returns	2		2	2	2	
60	51	60	Other		4	6	11	17	18
					20 (4/1-9/30/10)		99 (10/1/10-3/31/11)		
105	94	119	**NUMBER OF STATEMENTS**	3	10	15	21	33	37
%	%	%	**ASSETS**	%	%	%	%	%	%
9.9	12.1	12.1	Cash & Equivalents		10.3	12.9	13.5	14.8	9.3
23.2	18.2	23.4	Trade Receivables (net)		31.4	27.2	25.1	22.6	19.6
24.7	21.8	22.3	Inventory		18.9	21.9	22.1	25.7	20.5
6.3	5.8	6.2	All Other Current		16.1	5.5	4.3	6.6	5.1
64.1	58.0	64.0	Total Current		76.6	67.5	65.0	69.7	54.5
23.2	24.8	22.8	Fixed Assets (net)		16.4	21.6	24.2	19.9	27.4
6.7	9.2	6.6	Intangibles (net)		.7	6.7	2.1	6.2	11.7
5.9	8.0	6.6	All Other Non-Current		6.3	4.2	8.7	4.2	6.4
100.0	100.0	100.0	Total		100.0	100.0	100.0	100.0	100.0
			LIABILITIES						
9.0	6.3	6.7	Notes Payable-Short Term		16.8	12.7	7.3	6.3	2.1
2.9	2.6	3.5	Cur. Mat.-L.T.D.		.8	6.2	2.6	4.6	2.8
11.9	9.0	12.5	Trade Payables		14.4	14.4	13.0	12.8	10.1
.8	.4	.4	Income Taxes Payable		.0	.9	.2	.2	.7
12.2	9.6	9.3	All Other Current		5.1	6.4	8.1	14.1	8.9
36.9	28.0	32.5	Total Current		37.1	40.6	31.1	38.1	24.6
12.6	16.8	13.4	Long-Term Debt		7.0	10.5	10.6	14.1	15.1
1.4	1.3	1.2	Deferred Taxes		.7	1.0	.2	1.8	1.6
3.8	6.2	5.4	All Other Non-Current		21.7	4.5	2.0	1.6	5.6
45.4	47.7	47.5	Net Worth		33.4	43.4	56.1	44.4	53.0
100.0	100.0	100.0	Total Liabilities & Net Worth		100.0	100.0	100.0	100.0	100.0
			INCOME DATA						
100.0	100.0	100.0	Net Sales		100.0	100.0	100.0	100.0	100.0
37.5	35.1	37.5	Gross Profit		44.8	43.9	39.1	33.8	35.9
25.2	29.3	28.5	Operating Expenses		37.1	39.5	28.2	26.9	23.2
12.3	5.8	8.9	Operating Profit		7.7	4.5	10.9	6.9	12.7
1.5	1.9	1.7	All Other Expenses (net)		-.5	.9	1.4	1.8	2.8
10.7	4.0	7.2	Profit Before Taxes		8.1	3.5	9.5	5.1	9.9
			RATIOS						
2.6	3.6	3.3	Current		6.4	3.0	3.6	3.4	3.2
1.8	2.2	2.1			2.6	1.9	2.7	2.0	2.3
1.2	1.3	1.4			1.5	1.3	1.3	1.1	1.5
1.6	2.0	2.0	Quick		2.3	2.2	2.5	1.9	1.7
.9	1.0	1.0			1.2	1.0	1.1	.9	1.0
.5	.5	.7			.5	.6	.6	.5	.7
39 9.4	28 13.3	38 9.7	Sales/Receivables	48 7.6	43 8.4	27 13.3	35 10.4	46 7.9	
54 6.8	50 7.3	57 6.4		63 5.8	53 6.9	57 6.4	56 6.5	60 6.1	
72 5.1	66 5.5	74 4.9		83 4.4	69 5.3	75 4.9	69 5.3	80 4.6	
16 23.5	16 22.8	13 27.8	Cost of Sales/Inventory	0 UND	0 UND	4 103.8	21 17.2	60 6.1	
83 4.4	88 4.1	78 4.7		15 23.9	113 3.2	34 10.8	84 4.4	81 4.5	
154 2.4	165 2.2	166 2.2		99 3.7	166 2.2	181 2.0	177 2.1	172 2.1	
20 18.4	14 26.7	20 18.2	Cost of Sales/Payables	10 36.0	28 12.8	10 36.4	20 18.6	21 17.3	
34 10.7	26 14.0	42 8.7		36 10.2	40 9.2	31 11.8	43 8.6	46 7.9	
62 5.9	50 7.3	66 5.5		52 7.0	55 6.7	68 5.3	66 5.5	72 5.0	
3.6	2.8	2.9	Sales/Working Capital		1.5	4.0	3.0	2.9	2.8
6.2	4.7	4.8			3.1	6.3	4.7	4.9	4.6
14.3	11.7	10.1			NM	8.6	19.4	15.2	7.8
44.7	23.1	23.1	EBIT/Interest		*	47.2	22.5	14.5	36.7
(94) 12.3	(81) 4.7	(101) 7.9			(11) 14.5	(19) 8.0	(29) 3.9	(33) 8.7	
4.4	1.2	1.3			1.1	2.4	-.2	1.8	
20.1	6.4	11.4	Net Profit + Depr., Dep., Amort./Cur. Mat. L/T/D					11.3	
(33) 3.3	(20) 1.8	(26) 3.2					(11)	3.8	
1.5	.2	1.7						2.9	
.2	.2	.2	Fixed/Worth		.1	.2	.1	.1	.3
.4	.5	.4			.4	.4	.4	.5	.4
1.4	1.3	1.4			NM	1.7	.9	1.2	2.1
.7	.4	.5	Debt/Worth		.5	.7	.4	.6	.5
1.4	1.1	1.2			4.1	1.0	.6	1.5	1.5
3.2	3.7	3.9			NM	4.1	2.2	4.6	3.0
64.6	30.1	55.4	% Profit Before Taxes/Tangible Net Worth			86.6	92.9	26.9	57.1
(93) 35.0	(82) 14.9	(106) 17.3			(13) 32.5	19.2	(29) 16.7	(33) 18.0	
19.3	2.4	4.4			4.0	3.5	-5.8	12.2	
27.6	14.3	18.2	% Profit Before Taxes/Total Assets		25.3	20.9	35.6	14.9	19.5
13.4	6.2	8.9			8.3	6.6	11.2	6.0	9.8
7.1	.4	.7			-.3	.2	2.0	-6.0	2.6
28.1	15.6	23.3	Sales/Net Fixed Assets		40.7	32.8	51.8	23.7	11.7
9.2	7.0	7.7			9.6	10.6	7.7	8.3	6.3
4.3	3.0	4.2			6.0	3.3	3.7	4.8	3.0
2.2	1.8	2.1	Sales/Total Assets		2.2	2.3	2.7	2.0	1.7
1.7	1.3	1.4			1.4	1.7	1.6	1.5	1.0
1.0	.7	1.0			.7	1.4	1.1	1.1	.8
.7	1.2	1.2	% Depr., Dep., Amort./Sales				.8	1.1	2.6
(82) 2.6	(77) 3.0	(88) 2.6				(14) 2.0	(27) 2.0	(27) 4.0	
5.1	6.3	4.9				6.5	4.1	5.3	
1.6	2.6	1.8	% Officers', Directors', Owners' Comp/Sales						
(27) 3.4	(25) 4.3	(21) 4.1							
8.0	7.6	7.3							
4239960M	2948531M	3456107M	Net Sales ($)	1731M	21147M	61042M	153378M	512755M	2706054M
3618243M	3056738M	3396330M	Total Assets ($)	1269M	20270M	44010M	98828M	413470M	2818483M

M = $ thousand   MM = $ million
See Pages 9 through 22 for Explanation of Ratios and Data

Current Data Sorted by Assets							Comparative Historical Data	
		4	4		1	**Type of Statement** Unqualified	13	8
	1	13	2			Reviewed	12	16
	2	4	1			Compiled	5	6
2	6	3				Tax Returns	3	2
	8	7	10			Other	12	16
	7 (4/1-9/30/10)		61 (10/1/10-3/31/11)				**4/1/06-3/31/07**	**4/1/07-3/31/08**
0-500M	**500M-2MM**	**2-10MM**	**10-50MM**	**50-100MM**	**100-250MM**		**ALL**	**ALL**
2	17	31	17		1	**NUMBER OF STATEMENTS**	45	48
%	%	%	%	%	%	**ASSETS**	%	%
	18.0	10.1	5.1	**DATA NOT AVAILABLE**		Cash & Equivalents	7.9	6.6
	28.7	22.4	26.6			Trade Receivables (net)	22.2	25.6
	13.1	27.7	26.3			Inventory	24.7	24.7
	.0	.7	1.2			All Other Current	3.1	2.1
	59.7	61.0	59.2			Total Current	57.9	59.1
	34.4	25.7	30.1			Fixed Assets (net)	30.3	29.1
	.2	5.7	4.8			Intangibles (net)	6.2	5.0
	5.7	7.7	5.9			All Other Non-Current	5.6	6.9
	100.0	100.0	100.0			Total	100.0	100.0
						LIABILITIES		
	4.2	10.3	7.5			Notes Payable-Short Term	11.7	9.8
	1.2	5.7	5.3			Cur. Mat.-L.T.D.	4.3	3.8
	12.5	13.6	11.3			Trade Payables	15.9	15.5
	.0	.1	.0			Income Taxes Payable	.1	.1
	18.3	11.3	15.6			All Other Current	10.1	10.7
	36.2	41.0	39.8			Total Current	42.1	39.8
	27.2	18.7	14.6			Long-Term Debt	13.6	16.4
	.1	.4	1.3			Deferred Taxes	.5	.2
	8.1	4.6	8.0			All Other Non-Current	6.0	4.0
	28.4	35.3	36.3			Net Worth	37.9	39.5
	100.0	100.0	100.0			Total Liabilties & Net Worth	100.0	100.0
						INCOME DATA		
	100.0	100.0	100.0			Net Sales	100.0	100.0
	37.7	28.9	24.9			Gross Profit	25.6	28.8
	27.8	22.0	20.0			Operating Expenses	19.1	22.2
	9.9	6.9	4.8			Operating Profit	6.5	6.7
	4.5	.6	1.5			All Other Expenses (net)	1.3	1.3
	5.5	6.3	3.3			Profit Before Taxes	5.2	5.3
						RATIOS		
	8.2	2.6	2.6				2.1	2.0
	2.8	1.6	1.6			Current	1.2	1.5
	.8	1.0	1.1				1.0	1.1
	5.8	1.5	1.5				.9	1.1
	2.1	.8	.9			Quick	.6	.8
	.7	.4	.5				.4	.6
	26 14.3	**33** 11.0	**37** 10.0				**30** 12.2	**34** 10.6
	48 7.6	**40** 9.0	**56** 6.5			Sales/Receivables	**46** 8.0	**46** 7.9
	70 5.2	**50** 7.3	**88** 4.2				**59** 6.1	**58** 6.3
	0 UND	**44** 8.2	**43** 8.4				**40** 9.2	**35** 10.3
	30 12.3	**68** 5.4	**81** 4.5			Cost of Sales/Inventory	**61** 6.0	**59** 6.2
	51 7.2	**124** 2.9	**125** 2.9				**89** 4.1	**81** 4.5
	10 35.9	**22** 16.3	**18** 20.1				**22** 16.4	**22** 16.7
	22 16.7	**31** 11.7	**38** 9.7			Cost of Sales/Payables	**34** 10.7	**32** 11.3
	56 6.5	**51** 7.2	**55** 6.6				**46** 7.9	**53** 6.9
	2.8	5.2	4.7				5.5	6.7
	4.9	7.9	7.7			Sales/Working Capital	20.6	12.0
	-46.3	-138.6	44.2				-150.6	33.4
	7.5	23.0	20.0				10.0	10.8
	(14) 2.8	(27) 2.3	3.3			EBIT/Interest	(39) 3.4	(44) 3.3
	.5	2.0	1.9				1.5	1.4
		2.5	5.2				2.7	3.0
		(12) 1.7	(10) 1.4			Net Profit + Depr., Dep., Amort./Cur. Mat. L/T/D	(11) 1.3	(11) 2.1
		1.3	.5				.4	1.8
	.4	.3	.5				.4	.4
	1.2	.8	1.1			Fixed/Worth	1.2	.9
	3.7	4.5	1.7				2.4	1.7
	.8	.7	.8				.9	.9
	2.8	2.2	2.0			Debt/Worth	2.3	2.0
	4.2	11.8	3.8				6.4	3.7
	75.0	56.2	29.4				52.2	35.3
	(15) 10.7	(27) 25.8	(14) 17.7			% Profit Before Taxes/Tangible Net Worth	(42) 23.7	(42) 21.1
	-.3	6.5	8.3				4.0	9.1
	18.3	18.5	12.2				14.2	14.9
	7.1	7.1	5.8			% Profit Before Taxes/Total Assets	6.9	6.7
	-.6	1.7	2.2				2.3	1.7
	28.3	14.6	17.0				16.3	15.2
	8.9	9.6	4.8			Sales/Net Fixed Assets	5.8	6.8
	1.8	5.1	2.6				3.2	3.4
	2.8	2.4	2.1				2.5	2.5
	2.2	1.9	1.7			Sales/Total Assets	1.8	1.9
	.7	1.3	.9				1.3	1.4
	.6	1.7	1.3				1.9	1.1
	(15) 1.5	(27) 2.5	(16) 3.7			% Depr., Dep., Amort./Sales	(38) 2.9	(44) 2.5
	4.2	3.9	7.2				4.7	4.4
		2.9					1.4	2.1
		(12) 4.0				% Officers', Directors' Owners' Comp/Sales	(13) 3.1	(11) 3.7
		4.6					8.7	17.1
2595M	**42069M**	**307811M**	**561459M**		**231056M**	Net Sales ($)	**1440879M**	**1166512M**
671M	**22581M**	**154772M**	**376071M**		**158927M**	Total Assets ($)	**1044502M**	**768371M**

M = $ thousand MM = $ million

See Pages 9 through 22 for Explanation of Ratios and Data

Comparative Historical Data | | Current Data Sorted by Sales

4/1/08-3/31/09 ALL	4/1/09-3/31/10 ALL	4/1/10-3/31/11 ALL	Type of Statement	0-1MM	1-3MM	3-5MM	5-10MM	10-25MM	25MM & OVER
15	11	9	Unqualified			1	1	6	2
17	17	16	Reviewed	1		3	7	5	
3	4	7	Compiled		1		4	1	1
7	9	11	Tax Returns	3	5	1	2		
21	28	25	Other	1	2	7	1	7	7
				7 (4/1-9/30/10)			61 (10/1/10-3/31/11)		
63	69	68	**NUMBER OF STATEMENTS**	5	8	11	15	19	10
%	%	%	**ASSETS**	%	%	%	%	%	%
7.4	9.7	11.0	Cash & Equivalents			11.4	11.8	7.8	5.9
24.7	21.9	24.4	Trade Receivables (net)			29.0	22.6	27.1	23.9
23.7	25.9	23.0	Inventory			21.8	27.8	25.9	26.4
2.6	2.9	.7	All Other Current			.6	.4	1.0	1.7
58.4	60.4	59.0	Total Current			62.8	62.5	61.7	57.8
26.2	25.2	29.1	Fixed Assets (net)			24.5	24.6	30.0	27.1
6.4	5.3	3.9	Intangibles (net)			4.8	5.7	3.0	6.3
9.0	9.0	8.1	All Other Non-Current			8.0	7.1	5.3	8.8
100.0	100.0	100.0	Total			100.0	100.0	100.0	100.0
			LIABILITIES						
10.4	12.9	9.1	Notes Payable-Short Term			6.4	8.3	9.8	6.7
3.7	3.4	4.2	Cur. Mat.-L.T.D.			5.0	6.5	3.2	5.9
14.1	12.4	12.4	Trade Payables			13.1	14.5	12.0	12.6
.1	.1	.1	Income Taxes Payable			.0	.1	.0	.0
13.2	16.8	14.1	All Other Current			5.4	14.8	12.5	17.1
41.4	45.7	39.9	Total Current			30.0	44.3	37.5	42.3
17.5	15.9	20.4	Long-Term Debt			27.8	14.5	17.3	13.9
.8	.8	.6	Deferred Taxes			.0	.1	1.6	.4
4.9	5.8	6.4	All Other Non-Current			10.2	4.3	3.4	12.1
35.4	31.9	32.7	Net Worth			32.1	36.7	40.3	31.3
100.0	100.0	100.0	Total Liabilities & Net Worth			100.0	100.0	100.0	100.0
			INCOME DATA						
100.0	100.0	100.0	Net Sales			100.0	100.0	100.0	100.0
29.0	30.4	30.4	Gross Profit			39.6	29.3	24.0	22.1
23.7	26.5	23.2	Operating Expenses			33.4	23.2	16.8	18.4
5.3	3.9	7.2	Operating Profit			6.2	6.1	7.2	3.6
1.8	1.4	1.9	All Other Expenses (net)			.8	.3	1.0	1.8
3.5	2.5	5.3	Profit Before Taxes			5.4	5.8	6.2	1.9
			RATIOS						
2.0	1.9	3.0	Current			9.8	2.6	2.6	2.4
1.4	1.4	1.6				1.6	1.6	1.9	1.6
1.1	.9	1.0				.9	1.0	1.3	.9
1.2	1.1	1.7	Quick			6.9	1.5	1.6	1.2
.8	.6	1.0				.9	.8	1.1	.9
.6	.4	.4				.4	.5	.4	.3
31 11.7	37 10.0	33 11.2	Sales/Receivables			34 10.8	29 12.7	37 9.8	31 11.7
44 8.3	49 7.5	43 8.5				48 7.6	40 9.0	48 7.7	37 9.8
55 6.6	64 5.7	64 5.7				66 5.5	49 7.5	62 5.9	73 5.0
30 12.0	39 9.4	34 10.6	Cost of Sales/Inventory			30 12.3	40 9.1	43 8.4	39 9.4
54 6.8	70 5.2	50 7.3				62 5.9	68 5.4	50 7.3	58 6.3
91 4.0	147 2.5	113 3.2				107 3.4	124 2.9	112 3.2	113 3.2
17 21.1	16 22.2	17 21.1	Cost of Sales/Payables			12 29.5	24 15.4	21 17.1	20 17.8
35 10.6	37 9.9	30 12.3				24 15.0	24 8.4	28 13.2	33 11.2
43 8.4	61 6.0	49 7.5				87 4.2	51 7.2	39 9.3	45 8.1
6.9	4.9	4.2	Sales/Working Capital			4.8	5.2	3.7	6.5
11.6	9.9	7.7				7.6	6.7	7.5	10.7
44.1	-49.9	NM				-25.7	191.5	9.7	-52.4
9.5	6.6	17.0	EBIT/Interest				9.6	25.4	23.2
(58) 4.0	(61) 1.5	(61) 3.3				(13) 2.2	12.3	3.2	
1.6	-.7	1.9					1.9	1.9	.8
8.8	2.9	4.9	Net Profit + Depr., Dep., Amort./Cur. Mat. L/T/D					10.3	
(19) 3.3	(22) 1.2	(23) 1.6					(10) 3.6		
2.5	-.4	1.0						1.6	
.4	.3	.4	Fixed/Worth			.2	.3	.4	.4
1.0	.9	.9				.7	.8	.8	1.0
2.3	UND	3.7				10.7	2.0	1.6	-1.8
.9	.7	.8	Debt/Worth			1.6	.9	.6	.9
2.8	2.8	2.4				2.5	2.4	2.0	1.5
6.9	UND	7.8				27.9	8.3	2.7	-15.4
59.8	32.8	54.4	% Profit Before Taxes/Tangible Net Worth				68.0	52.1	
(57) 23.3	(53) 7.0	(58) 21.4				(14) 32.9	(18) 23.2		
6.4	-4.5	6.3					2.6	9.0	
14.6	10.6	18.3	% Profit Before Taxes/Total Assets			23.8	14.8	23.9	20.7
5.5	1.6	6.8				4.7	5.0	7.5	7.3
1.5	-4.7	1.6				2.7	1.6	3.9	-.2
18.5	14.8	17.0	Sales/Net Fixed Assets			29.2	13.6	14.9	17.0
8.7	7.1	8.1				12.5	10.5	5.9	6.3
4.5	3.7	3.4				2.9	5.1	3.4	3.0
2.3	1.9	2.5	Sales/Total Assets			3.3	2.4	2.4	3.0
1.9	1.4	1.9				2.0	2.1	1.9	1.9
1.5	1.0	1.2				1.1	1.4	1.4	1.0
1.1	1.4	1.1	% Depr., Dep., Amort./Sales				1.7	1.4	
(58) 2.6	(61) 2.3	(60) 2.6				(13) 2.5	(17) 2.6		
4.3	5.2	4.8					4.0	3.8	
1.2	2.1	2.9	% Officers', Directors' Owners' Comp/Sales						
(15) 2.6	(18) 4.8	(24) 4.2							
10.3	10.8	6.8							
1649618M	1131458M	1144990M	Net Sales ($)	2660M	16958M	44262M	114550M	311504M	655056M
1052100M	831614M	713022M	Total Assets ($)	5519M	11418M	26344M	63071M	190574M	416096M

M = $ thousand   MM = $ million
See Pages 9 through 22 for Explanation of Ratios and Data

Current Data Sorted by Assets   Comparative Historical Data

0-500M	500M-2MM	2-10MM	10-50MM	50-100MM	100-250MM	Type of Statement	4/1/06-3/31/07 ALL	4/1/07-3/31/08 ALL
	1	5		1	2	Unqualified	8	5
	2	3				Reviewed	12	6
	1					Compiled	6	4
						Tax Returns	4	2
	1	7	7	1	3	Other	9	12
	7 (4/1-9/30/10)		27 (10/1/10-3/31/11)					
5	15	7	2	5		NUMBER OF STATEMENTS	39	29
%	%	%	%	%	%	**ASSETS**	%	%
		8.9				Cash & Equivalents	13.0	10.1
		22.8				Trade Receivables (net)	29.7	23.7
		34.7				Inventory	29.3	32.5
		6.4				All Other Current	2.6	3.9
		72.7				Total Current	74.5	70.2
		19.9				Fixed Assets (net)	17.7	19.8
		3.9				Intangibles (net)	3.6	6.8
		3.5				All Other Non-Current	4.1	3.2
		100.0				Total	100.0	100.0
						LIABILITIES		
		14.3				Notes Payable-Short Term	7.7	5.0
		1.7				Cur. Mat.-L.T.D.	2.8	3.9
		13.4				Trade Payables	17.2	17.2
		.1				Income Taxes Payable	.3	.5
		12.4				All Other Current	21.9	22.4
		41.9				Total Current	50.0	49.1
		8.8				Long-Term Debt	7.4	9.7
		1.2				Deferred Taxes	.1	.5
		8.9				All Other Non-Current	4.5	4.2
		39.3				Net Worth	38.0	36.6
		100.0				Total Liabilities & Net Worth	100.0	100.0
						INCOME DATA		
		100.0				Net Sales	100.0	100.0
		36.0				Gross Profit	28.8	28.6
		28.9				Operating Expenses	23.8	23.1
		7.1				Operating Profit	5.0	5.5
		1.0				All Other Expenses (net)	1.6	.9
		6.1				Profit Before Taxes	3.4	4.6
						RATIOS		
		4.4				Current	2.3	2.3
		2.3					1.6	1.8
		1.1					1.1	1.0
		1.8				Quick	1.5	1.3
		.8					.8	.7
		.5					.6	.3
		26 13.9				Sales/Receivables	36 10.3	38 9.5
		55 6.6					48 7.6	49 7.4
		60 6.1					58 6.2	59 6.2
		56 6.6				Cost of Sales/Inventory	32 11.3	52 7.1
		90 4.1					64 5.7	81 4.5
		151 2.4					110 3.3	181 2.0
		21 17.2				Cost of Sales/Payables	13 27.2	20 18.4
		32 11.5					33 11.1	41 8.9
		56 6.5					49 7.4	63 5.8
		3.4				Sales/Working Capital	4.2	3.4
		4.9					10.5	9.4
		10.6					27.5	NM
		7.7				EBIT/Interest	23.3	34.4
		(12) 3.8					(33) 5.7	(23) 7.4
		2.4					2.2	.4
						Net Profit + Depr., Dep., Amort./Cur. Mat. L/T/D		
		.1				Fixed/Worth	.2	.2
		.4					.4	.6
		2.9					1.2	4.7
		.4				Debt/Worth	.6	.6
		2.1					1.6	2.6
		9.5					4.1	10.7
		35.6				% Profit Before Taxes/Tangible Net Worth	55.1	60.8
		(13) 20.2					(35) 20.9	(23) 18.8
		7.2					7.6	-5.3
		12.5				% Profit Before Taxes/Total Assets	17.4	14.6
		6.4					8.3	8.0
		4.3					3.9	-1.4
		27.3				Sales/Net Fixed Assets	44.6	35.4
		8.6					12.6	10.9
		5.8					7.8	3.7
		2.3				Sales/Total Assets	3.0	2.3
		1.7					2.1	1.7
		1.4					1.6	1.1
		1.1				% Depr., Dep., Amort./Sales	.6	.5
		(11) 1.5					(38) 1.0	1.4
		2.1					2.4	3.5
						% Officers', Directors' Owners' Comp/Sales	1.7	
							(12) 2.4	
							3.8	
	13722M	112069M	396734M	85117M	822876M	Net Sales ($)	1205785M	923136M
	7074M	62306M	198895M	138746M	840298M	Total Assets ($)	798657M	934191M

Note: columns 0-500M and 500M-2MM are marked **DATA NOT AVAILABLE** for the ASSETS, LIABILITIES, INCOME DATA and RATIOS percentage sections.

M = $ thousand   MM = $ million
See Pages 9 through 22 for Explanation of Ratios and Data

Comparative Historical Data				Current Data Sorted by Sales					
			Type of Statement						
	5	3	Unqualified						3
7	6	6	Reviewed		1	1	2	2	
7	4	5	Compiled		1	3	1		
2	1	1	Tax Returns			1			
15	16	19	Other		1	2	2	3	11
4/1/08-3/31/09 ALL	**4/1/09-3/31/10 ALL**	**4/1/10-3/31/11 ALL**			**7 (4/1-9/30/10)**		**27 (10/1/10-3/31/11)**		
				0-1MM	**1-3MM**	**3-5MM**	**5-10MM**	**10-25MM**	**25MM & OVER**
31	32	34	**NUMBER OF STATEMENTS**		3	7	5	5	14
%	%	%	**ASSETS**	%	%	%	%	%	%
10.4	15.2	11.4	Cash & Equivalents	DATA NOT AVAILABLE					14.1
25.2	20.6	23.5	Trade Receivables (net)						22.6
32.6	30.7	28.5	Inventory						21.8
3.5	2.5	6.0	All Other Current						7.4
71.8	68.9	69.4	Total Current						65.8
20.6	22.2	17.7	Fixed Assets (net)						16.4
4.2	3.5	7.1	Intangibles (net)						9.5
3.5	5.4	5.8	All Other Non-Current						8.3
100.0	100.0	100.0	Total						100.0
			LIABILITIES						
10.6	9.9	11.6	Notes Payable-Short Term						6.8
3.3	1.9	1.7	Cur. Mat.-L.T.D.						1.6
17.2	12.2	12.1	Trade Payables						12.5
.1	.0	.1	Income Taxes Payable						.1
18.8	17.3	16.4	All Other Current						22.0
50.0	41.3	41.9	Total Current						43.0
12.3	11.2	9.1	Long-Term Debt						6.4
.6	.8	.8	Deferred Taxes						.7
6.3	6.1	9.5	All Other Non-Current						5.3
30.9	40.6	38.8	Net Worth						44.6
100.0	100.0	100.0	Total Liabilties & Net Worth						100.0
			INCOME DATA						
100.0	100.0	100.0	Net Sales						100.0
30.4	29.9	30.8	Gross Profit						26.8
26.0	28.1	25.6	Operating Expenses						21.5
4.4	1.8	5.3	Operating Profit						5.3
.7	.5	.8	All Other Expenses (net)						.9
3.7	1.3	4.4	Profit Before Taxes						4.4
			RATIOS						
2.4	3.8	3.3							2.4
1.3	1.7	1.5	Current						1.4
.9	1.1	1.0							1.0
1.3	2.0	1.7							1.6
.6	.7	.8	Quick						.7
.4	.4	.5							.4
30 12.2	**38** 9.7	**35** 10.5							**37** 9.8
39 9.5	**44** 8.4	**51** 7.2	Sales/Receivables						**51** 7.2
49 7.5	**57** 6.4	**60** 6.1							**69** 5.3
43 8.6	**42** 8.7	**54** 6.7							**54** 6.7
71 5.1	**92** 4.0	**79** 4.6	Cost of Sales/Inventory						**79** 4.6
111 3.3	**164** 2.2	**116** 3.1							**93** 3.9
20 18.6	**17** 21.6	**21** 17.4							**21** 17.6
31 11.7	**32** 11.3	**32** 11.3	Cost of Sales/Payables						**38** 9.6
52 7.0	**54** 6.8	**53** 6.9							**61** 6.0
5.0	2.6	3.3							2.4
11.1	6.0	6.3	Sales/Working Capital						9.5
-75.7	28.8	181.9							NM
20.5	8.7	19.0							78.4
(27) 3.5	(28) 1.6	(28) 3.4	EBIT/Interest						(12) 9.6
.1	-1.1	1.3							1.2
			Net Profit + Depr., Dep., Amort./Cur. Mat. L/T/D						
.2	.2	.2							.2
.6	.4	.4	Fixed/Worth						.4
-4.9	3.3	3.2							1.2
.9	.5	.5							.6
2.9	1.0	2.2	Debt/Worth						2.2
-38.8	32.9	10.6							6.5
55.5	17.4	37.7							40.4
(23) 19.3	(26) 3.6	(27) 20.2	% Profit Before Taxes/Tangible Net Worth						(12) 20.3
8.4	-4.9	6.8							6.1
13.5	5.2	9.5							8.7
7.5	1.6	6.4	% Profit Before Taxes/Total Assets						6.5
.2	-3.9	.9							.0
26.9	18.5	23.8							16.1
13.0	8.0	9.4	Sales/Net Fixed Assets						9.1
7.7	5.2	5.8							5.4
3.5	1.9	2.2							2.2
2.1	1.5	1.6	Sales/Total Assets						1.4
1.7	1.1	1.2							.8
.5	.9	1.0							1.2
(24) 1.0	(29) 1.6	(28) 1.5	% Depr., Dep., Amort./Sales						1.5
2.1	2.3	2.4							2.9
			% Officers', Directors' Owners' Comp/Sales						
817392M	934233M	1430518M	Net Sales ($)		6858M	27279M	38396M	53258M	1304727M
497241M	857064M	1247319M	Total Assets ($)		4335M	18313M	23566M	23166M	1177939M

M = $ thousand MM = $ million

See Pages 9 through 22 for Explanation of Ratios and Data

Current Data Sorted by Assets | Comparative Historical Data

Type of Statement	0-500M	500M-2MM	2-10MM	10-50MM	50-100MM	100-250MM		4/1/06-3/31/07 ALL	4/1/07-3/31/08 ALL
Unqualified			1		1			12	8
Reviewed		1	8					14	18
Compiled		1	4					7	7
Tax Returns	1	2	2					7	5
Other	1	1	4					18	26
		6 (4/1-9/30/10)		31 (10/1/10-3/31/11)					
NUMBER OF STATEMENTS	2	4	19	5	4	3		58	64
ASSETS	%	%	%	%	%	%		%	%
Cash & Equivalents			9.9					7.7	7.9
Trade Receivables (net)			26.0					25.4	27.2
Inventory			23.8					29.1	29.0
All Other Current			5.0					2.0	2.7
Total Current			64.7					64.2	66.8
Fixed Assets (net)			22.3					23.8	23.3
Intangibles (net)			6.7					5.9	2.5
All Other Non-Current			6.4					6.0	7.4
Total			100.0					100.0	100.0
LIABILITIES									
Notes Payable-Short Term			9.3					10.3	8.3
Cur. Mat.-L.T.D.			10.9					4.4	4.1
Trade Payables			14.3					16.2	18.3
Income Taxes Payable			.1					.2	.2
All Other Current			10.3					21.2	18.5
Total Current			45.0					52.3	49.5
Long-Term Debt			8.4					22.6	16.2
Deferred Taxes			.5					.3	.0
All Other Non-Current			8.2					7.1	4.6
Net Worth			37.9					17.8	29.7
Total Liabilties & Net Worth			100.0					100.0	100.0
INCOME DATA									
Net Sales			100.0					100.0	100.0
Gross Profit			34.6					34.7	35.0
Operating Expenses			28.2					29.1	30.4
Operating Profit			6.4					5.6	4.6
All Other Expenses (net)			1.3					2.1	1.2
Profit Before Taxes			5.1					3.5	3.4
RATIOS									
Current			2.4					1.9	2.4
			1.6					1.4	1.6
			.9					.9	1.0
Quick			2.0					1.1	1.1
			.7					.7	.8
			.4					.4	.4
Sales/Receivables		38	9.6					30 12.0	32 11.4
		44	8.4					46 7.9	47 7.8
		59	6.2					61 6.0	59 6.2
Cost of Sales/Inventory		18	20.6					36 10.0	28 13.1
		58	6.3					74 4.9	64 5.7
		112	3.3					127 2.9	116 3.2
Cost of Sales/Payables		24	15.3					19 18.9	22 16.3
		34	10.7					36 10.2	37 10.0
		54	6.8					55 6.7	55 6.6
Sales/Working Capital			4.5					5.5	5.6
			8.0					11.3	8.7
			-17.1					-66.2	107.0
EBIT/Interest			10.4					9.4	9.9
			3.5					(57) 3.1	(61) 3.1
			1.4					1.1	1.0
Net Profit + Depr., Dep., Amort./Cur. Mat. L/T/D								14.8	12.7
								(12) 3.7	(17) 7.2
								.4	1.1
Fixed/Worth			.2					.3	.2
			.3					1.1	.6
			2.6					-8.9	2.4
Debt/Worth			.8					1.7	.8
			1.5					5.5	2.4
			24.0					-75.3	11.8
% Profit Before Taxes/Tangible Net Worth			41.3					61.4	47.4
			(16) 17.9					(42) 23.6	(54) 15.5
			1.7					3.7	2.1
% Profit Before Taxes/Total Assets			16.3					14.5	12.9
			8.9					4.7	3.8
			.8					.8	.2
Sales/Net Fixed Assets			31.4					33.9	51.8
			11.2					10.6	13.7
			5.2					6.2	5.9
Sales/Total Assets			2.3					2.6	2.8
			1.9					1.9	2.2
			1.3					1.4	1.5
% Depr., Dep., Amort./Sales			.5					.7	.7
			(17) 3.0					(51) 1.6	(59) 1.2
			4.0					3.6	3.7
% Officers', Directors' Owners' Comp/Sales								2.4	1.7
								(18) 5.2	(16) 6.0
								7.4	8.4
Net Sales ($)	2514M	13250M	154402M	216755M	350440M	621058M		2201639M	2113365M
Total Assets ($)	780M	3850M	77819M	127069M	307044M	395792M		1496359M	1228451M

© RMA 2011

M = $ thousand   MM = $ million
See Pages 9 through 22 for Explanation of Ratios and Data

Comparative Historical Data   **Current Data Sorted by Sales**

C1	C2	C3	Type of Statement	0-1MM	1-3MM	3-5MM	5-10MM	10-25MM	25MM & OVER
6	8	2	Unqualified					1	1
11	11	8	Reviewed		1	1	5		1
3	2	5	Compiled			1	3	1	
9	8	5	Tax Returns	1	2	2			
27	23	17	Other		1	1	3	3	9
4/1/08-3/31/09 ALL	4/1/09-3/31/10 ALL	4/1/10-3/31/11 ALL			6 (4/1-9/30/10)		31 (10/1/10-3/31/11)		
56	52	37	**NUMBER OF STATEMENTS**	1	4	5	11	5	11
%	%	%	**ASSETS**	%	%	%	%	%	%
8.1	9.9	9.3	Cash & Equivalents				9.4		8.0
21.9	21.9	25.0	Trade Receivables (net)				29.5		21.4
30.1	30.2	25.1	Inventory				20.6		25.4
2.3	2.9	4.2	All Other Current				.6		3.4
62.5	64.9	63.7	Total Current				60.1		58.1
23.1	20.6	18.0	Fixed Assets (net)				25.8		11.2
6.9	7.9	11.0	Intangibles (net)				5.1		23.6
7.5	6.6	7.4	All Other Non-Current				9.1		7.1
100.0	100.0	100.0	Total				100.0		100.0
			LIABILITIES						
11.2	8.4	9.2	Notes Payable-Short Term				8.9		5.6
4.1	7.0	6.5	Cur. Mat.-L.T.D.				11.0		4.5
12.7	18.6	13.1	Trade Payables				17.0		10.3
.3	.2	.2	Income Taxes Payable				.0		.3
20.9	13.3	17.9	All Other Current				13.9		20.6
49.2	47.5	46.9	Total Current				50.9		41.3
18.8	23.3	10.0	Long-Term Debt				6.5		11.1
.1	.3	.5	Deferred Taxes				.3		.7
8.3	6.4	10.5	All Other Non-Current				10.8		7.1
23.7	22.5	32.2	Net Worth				31.5		39.8
100.0	100.0	100.0	Total Liabilities & Net Worth				100.0		100.0
			INCOME DATA						
100.0	100.0	100.0	Net Sales				100.0		100.0
34.1	34.2	35.1	Gross Profit				37.1		27.4
29.5	34.1	29.0	Operating Expenses				30.9		25.1
4.6	.1	6.1	Operating Profit				6.1		2.3
1.5	1.9	1.4	All Other Expenses (net)				1.2		1.6
3.1	-1.8	4.7	Profit Before Taxes				5.0		.7
			RATIOS						
2.9	2.2	2.3	Current				1.8		1.7
1.6	1.5	1.5					1.2		1.5
1.0	1.1	.9					.8		.9
1.4	1.4	1.0	Quick				1.1		1.0
.7	.7	.7					.7		.7
.3	.4	.5					.6		.5
(19) 19.7	(32) 11.5	(38) 9.5	Sales/Receivables				(40) 9.2		(44) 8.3
(44) 8.3	(49) 7.5	(46) 8.0					(47) 7.7		(50) 7.3
(55) 6.7	(61) 6.0	(59) 6.2					(59) 6.2		(56) 6.5
(31) 11.8	(43) 8.5	(35) 10.3	Cost of Sales/Inventory				(16) 22.6		(51) 7.1
(75) 4.9	(77) 4.7	(68) 5.4					(51) 7.2		(74) 4.9
(97) 3.8	(159) 2.3	(105) 3.5					(68) 5.4		(102) 3.6
(13) 27.7	(21) 17.5	(24) 15.3	Cost of Sales/Payables				(25) 14.8		(21) 17.0
(26) 13.9	(39) 9.3	(34) 10.7					(34) 10.7		(25) 14.5
(39) 9.4	(54) 6.8	(53) 6.9					(52) 7.1		(48) 7.6
5.1	4.6	5.3	Sales/Working Capital				7.4		5.8
7.7	8.6	11.4					17.7		11.7
288.3	43.2	-28.0					-12.2		-41.2
6.5	11.1	13.3	EBIT/Interest				51.2		10.2
(51) 2.9	(50) 2.1	(36) 3.4					3.9		(10) 2.4
.6	-.7	1.4					1.4		.7
13.9	5.7		Net Profit + Depr., Dep., Amort./Cur. Mat. L/T/D						
(18) 3.5	(16) 1.2								
1.2	-1.9								
.3	.3	.2	Fixed/Worth				.3		.2
.7	.6	.5					.4		.9
NM	5.1	21.5					2.6		-1.5
1.0	1.0	.8	Debt/Worth				.9		.8
3.6	2.5	3.2					2.2		16.3
NM	54.5	NM					4.1		-4.4
38.8	38.9	69.7	% Profit Before Taxes/Tangible Net Worth				51.6		
(42) 9.7	(40) 14.6	(28) 29.2					(10) 20.1		
-3.8	-26.0	1.8					-1.0		
11.1	11.8	15.0	% Profit Before Taxes/Total Assets				19.5		5.7
3.4	1.8	4.3					10.0		1.3
-1.5	-9.4	.5					.4		-.6
48.1	33.8	44.1	Sales/Net Fixed Assets				31.4		27.6
12.2	10.4	13.3					11.2		15.0
6.9	5.6	6.3					3.7		9.7
2.7	2.1	2.3	Sales/Total Assets				2.3		2.3
2.1	1.7	1.8					2.1		1.3
1.5	1.2	1.3					1.4		1.1
.7	1.2	.6	% Depr., Dep., Amort./Sales				.6		.6
(50) 1.7	(43) 3.0	(32) 2.2					3.0		(10) 2.2
3.4	4.7	3.7					4.4		3.4
2.0	1.9	1.6	% Officers', Directors' Owners' Comp/Sales						
(16) 4.6	(16) 5.7	(11) 2.9							
6.7	7.1	10.0							
2050886M	1647637M	1358419M	Net Sales ($)	912M	6879M	20482M	73488M	72731M	1183927M
1277343M	1241141M	912354M	Total Assets ($)	337M	5339M	14290M	38524M	43841M	810023M

M = $ thousand   MM = $ million
See Pages 9 through 22 for Explanation of Ratios and Data

Current Data Sorted by Assets — Comparative Historical Data

		2-10MM	10-50MM	50-100MM	100-250MM	Type of Statement		
		4	5		3	Unqualified	15	10
		13	7	1		Reviewed	26	18
	2	2				Compiled	12	13
1	1	3	1			Tax Returns	5	6
2	2	17	17	5	4	Other	33	35
	13 (4/1-9/30/10)		77 (10/1/10-3/31/11)				4/1/06-3/31/07 ALL	4/1/07-3/31/08 ALL
0-500M	500M-2MM	2-10MM	10-50MM	50-100MM	100-250MM	NUMBER OF STATEMENTS	91	82
3	5	39	30	6	7			

0-500M %	500M-2MM %	2-10MM %	10-50MM %	50-100MM %	100-250MM %		ALL %	ALL %
						ASSETS		
		11.5	14.7			Cash & Equivalents	10.4	9.5
		25.8	21.2			Trade Receivables (net)	24.5	24.9
		35.0	24.5			Inventory	31.1	29.6
		3.3	5.9			All Other Current	2.8	4.7
		75.6	66.2			Total Current	68.8	68.6
		13.3	19.6			Fixed Assets (net)	18.9	19.5
		4.1	9.8			Intangibles (net)	5.8	5.4
		7.0	4.4			All Other Non-Current	6.5	6.5
		100.0	100.0			Total	100.0	100.0
						LIABILITIES		
		5.8	2.4			Notes Payable-Short Term	6.0	6.8
		2.1	1.2			Cur. Mat.-L.T.D.	2.9	3.3
		13.5	10.2			Trade Payables	12.6	15.7
		.3	.3			Income Taxes Payable	.3	.2
		25.3	25.7			All Other Current	18.9	17.3
		47.0	39.8			Total Current	40.8	43.3
		8.4	8.8			Long-Term Debt	13.4	14.7
		.3	.3			Deferred Taxes	.3	.1
		6.7	2.1			All Other Non-Current	3.3	3.0
		37.6	48.9			Net Worth	42.2	38.9
		100.0	100.0			Total Liabilities & Net Worth	100.0	100.0
						INCOME DATA		
		100.0	100.0			Net Sales	100.0	100.0
		33.0	31.4			Gross Profit	36.1	35.0
		28.1	26.2			Operating Expenses	29.7	28.7
		4.9	5.1			Operating Profit	6.5	6.2
		.6	1.4			All Other Expenses (net)	.9	.2
		4.3	3.8			Profit Before Taxes	5.6	6.0

RATIOS

2-10MM	10-50MM	Ratio	Hist ALL	Hist ALL
2.7	3.2	Current	2.9	2.7
1.5	1.9		1.8	1.5
1.2	1.2		1.2	1.2
1.3	1.8	Quick	1.5	1.5
.7	1.1		.9	.7
.5	.6		.5	.5
33 11.2	33 11.0	Sales/Receivables	32 11.5	31 11.9
43 8.6	47 7.8		41 8.9	39 9.3
61 6.0	64 5.7		52 7.0	50 7.4
41 9.0	71 5.1	Cost of Sales/Inventory	52 7.0	43 8.5
90 4.1	107 3.4		88 4.1	76 4.8
170 2.1	146 2.5		145 2.5	117 3.1
16 23.4	21 17.1	Cost of Sales/Payables	21 17.2	22 16.8
27 13.3	31 11.8		31 11.6	36 10.1
45 8.2	49 7.4		43 8.4	55 6.7
5.0	3.1	Sales/Working Capital	4.3	4.8
7.6	5.4		6.4	8.8
13.9	16.4		17.7	27.2
26.8	65.6	EBIT/Interest	20.8	15.9
(31) 3.0	(29) 13.1		(77) 5.1	(74) 7.1
.4	2.6		2.4	2.9
7.4	23.8	Net Profit + Depr., Dep., Amort./Cur. Mat. L/T/D	10.8	10.5
(10) 1.9	(11) 6.7		(27) 7.3	(25) 5.4
1.5	3.7		2.3	1.0
.1	.1	Fixed/Worth	.2	.1
.3	.6		.4	.5
.9	1.1		1.1	1.3
.9	.6	Debt/Worth	.7	.7
2.1	.9		1.7	1.7
5.4	4.1		4.0	5.0
47.2	36.0	% Profit Before Taxes/Tangible Net Worth	49.2	55.5
(35) 21.9	(26) 24.3		(82) 21.9	(75) 32.5
1.7	8.4		8.7	12.7
20.4	13.6	% Profit Before Taxes/Total Assets	18.3	16.4
6.4	8.6		8.4	9.8
.0	1.3		3.1	3.6
52.7	23.2	Sales/Net Fixed Assets	30.4	44.5
19.3	11.1		13.7	14.3
9.9	4.9		6.3	6.9
2.7	1.9	Sales/Total Assets	2.6	2.9
2.0	1.4		1.9	2.0
1.4	.9		1.6	1.5
.4	.9	% Depr., Dep., Amort./Sales	.7	.7
(31) 1.0	(26) 1.4		(75) 1.3	(69) 1.5
2.0	2.7		2.0	2.5
1.0		% Officers', Directors' Owners' Comp/Sales	2.7	2.6
(11) 1.9			(24) 5.0	(22) 4.6
4.6			9.4	8.6

0-500M	500M-2MM	2-10MM	10-50MM	50-100MM	100-250MM		Hist ALL	Hist ALL
1711M	19211M	437676M	956149M	619866M	1674800M	Net Sales ($)	2850213M	2818427M
469M	7212M	206607M	702792M	434358M	1154340M	Total Assets ($)	1727455M	1528821M

M = $ thousand   MM = $ million
See Pages 9 through 22 for Explanation of Ratios and Data

Comparative Historical Data   Current Data Sorted by Sales

			Type of Statement	0-1MM	1-3MM	3-5MM	5-10MM	10-25MM	25MM & OVER
14	11	12	Unqualified				2	2	8
19	20	21	Reviewed				4	10	7
7	8	4	Compiled		1	1	1	1	
6	9	6	Tax Returns		1		4	1	
37	28	47	Other	2	3	4	6	13	19
4/1/08-3/31/09 ALL	4/1/09-3/31/10 ALL	4/1/10-3/31/11 ALL		13 (4/1-9/30/10)			77 (10/1/10-3/31/11)		
83	76	90	NUMBER OF STATEMENTS	2	5	5	17	27	34
%	%	%	ASSETS	%	%	%	%	%	%
9.9	14.0	12.5	Cash & Equivalents				8.5	13.4	15.3
23.1	18.1	23.4	Trade Receivables (net)				25.5	27.0	21.4
31.7	29.4	28.9	Inventory				37.1	28.1	24.1
4.7	3.3	4.0	All Other Current				2.6	4.0	3.4
69.4	64.8	68.9	Total Current				73.6	72.5	64.2
19.1	20.1	17.8	Fixed Assets (net)				14.6	16.5	19.4
4.6	8.9	7.4	Intangibles (net)				5.0	4.0	12.4
6.8	6.2	6.0	All Other Non-Current				6.7	7.0	4.0
100.0	100.0	100.0	Total				100.0	100.0	100.0
			LIABILITIES						
7.7	6.3	4.6	Notes Payable-Short Term				7.1	4.9	2.6
2.1	2.6	2.2	Cur. Mat.-L.T.D.				1.7	1.1	2.2
12.9	11.3	12.1	Trade Payables				13.1	11.8	11.8
.5	.3	.4	Income Taxes Payable				.1	.5	.3
20.6	16.1	24.3	All Other Current				24.9	26.8	22.5
43.8	36.7	43.6	Total Current				46.9	45.1	39.3
11.4	13.6	10.2	Long-Term Debt				9.8	7.6	11.2
.4	.4	.4	Deferred Taxes				.1	.4	.8
4.4	10.6	4.9	All Other Non-Current				7.5	3.0	3.3
40.0	38.8	41.0	Net Worth				35.7	43.9	45.4
100.0	100.0	100.0	Total Liabilities & Net Worth				100.0	100.0	100.0
			INCOME DATA						
100.0	100.0	100.0	Net Sales				100.0	100.0	100.0
32.6	35.5	32.8	Gross Profit				30.2	31.4	33.3
28.0	32.2	27.5	Operating Expenses				28.4	27.7	25.3
4.6	3.3	5.3	Operating Profit				1.8	3.7	8.0
.7	1.2	1.0	All Other Expenses (net)				1.5	.3	1.2
3.8	2.1	4.3	Profit Before Taxes				.2	3.4	6.7
			RATIOS						
2.6	2.9	2.6					2.6	3.2	2.4
1.5	1.9	1.5	Current				1.4	1.7	1.5
1.2	1.4	1.2					1.1	1.2	1.2
1.4	1.8	1.3					1.2	1.6	1.4
.7	.9	.8	Quick				.6	1.0	.9
.4	.5	.5					.5	.7	.6
26 14.0	27 13.3	34 10.7					36 10.2	39 9.4	35 10.5
38 9.7	38 9.7	43 8.5	Sales/Receivables				41 8.9	43 8.6	47 7.8
48 7.6	48 7.7	61 6.0					63 5.8	61 5.9	57 6.4
40 9.1	50 7.3	43 8.4					60 6.1	41 9.0	42 8.8
80 4.5	92 4.0	93 3.9	Cost of Sales/Inventory				118 3.1	72 5.1	81 4.5
129 2.8	146 2.5	147 2.5					186 2.0	120 3.0	126 2.9
18 20.0	16 23.0	20 18.0					20 18.6	13 27.5	24 15.4
28 13.2	29 12.8	31 11.8	Cost of Sales/Payables				35 10.4	27 13.3	31 11.8
43 8.5	48 7.6	56 6.5					66 5.5	40 9.2	48 7.6
5.1	4.1	4.2					5.8	3.8	3.7
8.0	6.2	7.1	Sales/Working Capital				6.5	5.6	7.1
25.9	10.7	17.7					15.0	19.8	17.1
20.8	23.5	31.7					23.1	33.5	69.3
(73) 6.1	(67) 6.7	(77) 12.3	EBIT/Interest				(14) 1.1	(21) 4.7	(32) 14.6
2.0	1.3	1.3					-1.0	1.2	6.3
18.7	13.4	12.0	Net Profit + Depr., Dep.,					7.4	23.8
(24) 4.7	(20) 4.1	(29) 5.2	Amort./Cur. Mat. L/T/D					(10) 4.8	(15) 9.9
2.7	2.5	1.9						1.7	2.9
.2	.2	.2					.1	.1	.2
.5	.5	.4	Fixed/Worth				.8	.3	.6
1.3	1.3	1.8					NM	.8	2.1
.6	.6	.7					.7	.6	.7
1.6	1.3	1.7	Debt/Worth				1.9	1.0	1.5
4.1	4.7	5.9					NM	5.4	8.6
42.3	29.4	39.2	% Profit Before Taxes/Tangible				41.2	40.0	41.4
(76) 23.2	(65) 15.5	(78) 23.4	Net Worth				(13) 24.2	(24) 19.3	(30) 27.3
5.3	4.9	4.1					-1.8	1.3	9.6
18.2	13.2	15.6	% Profit Before Taxes/Total				13.8	14.6	16.0
7.8	6.2	7.2	Assets				2.6	6.4	10.8
2.3	.1	.3					-4.5	.2	5.0
34.9	22.8	32.4					48.5	52.7	22.5
14.6	9.4	13.3	Sales/Net Fixed Assets				14.4	19.3	9.2
6.5	4.8	5.6					5.5	9.9	5.1
2.7	2.2	2.4					2.8	2.7	2.0
2.0	1.6	1.6	Sales/Total Assets				1.5	2.0	1.4
1.5	1.2	1.3					1.1	1.6	1.3
.7	1.0	.6					.6	.5	.7
(69) 1.3	(64) 2.0	(71) 1.4	% Depr., Dep., Amort./Sales				(14) 1.3	(23) 1.3	(27) 1.3
2.3	3.1	2.9					1.8	2.8	3.3
1.8	3.3	1.8							
(24) 3.7	(22) 4.5	(21) 4.2	% Officers', Directors' Owners' Comp/Sales						
6.3	9.6	5.1							
3724888M	2510089M	3709413M	Net Sales ($)	49M	9442M	19652M	131934M	419199M	3129137M
1984808M	1706534M	2505778M	Total Assets ($)	71M	7470M	27810M	96532M	245522M	2128373M

Current Data Sorted by Assets   **Comparative Historical Data**

0-500M	500M-2MM	2-10MM	10-50MM	50-100MM	100-250MM	Type of Statement		4/1/06-3/31/07 ALL	4/1/07-3/31/08 ALL
		10	11	10	4	Unqualified		38	36
	6	24	10	3		Reviewed		40	38
	10	17	1	1	1	Compiled		41	29
	12	7	2			Tax Returns		20	14
4	11	32	25	6	8	Other		62	75
	48 (4/1-9/30/10)		167 (10/1/10-3/31/11)						
4	39	90	49	20	13	**NUMBER OF STATEMENTS**		201	192
%	%	%	%	%	%	**ASSETS**		%	%
	10.0	12.7	16.8	16.4	21.3	Cash & Equivalents		12.4	11.7
	25.8	26.7	21.6	21.4	16.7	Trade Receivables (net)		27.0	26.4
	31.5	28.3	20.0	20.1	19.3	Inventory		26.7	25.8
	3.8	3.5	6.6	5.8	6.5	All Other Current		3.7	4.6
	71.2	71.3	65.0	63.7	63.7	Total Current		69.8	68.4
	19.1	19.2	20.4	22.2	14.6	Fixed Assets (net)		19.6	19.9
	5.1	3.2	6.8	5.3	15.8	Intangibles (net)		4.4	5.9
	4.6	6.3	7.8	8.9	5.9	All Other Non-Current		6.2	5.7
	100.0	100.0	100.0	100.0	100.0	Total		100.0	100.0
						LIABILITIES			
	8.1	9.7	4.1	2.2	1.8	Notes Payable-Short Term		9.2	9.4
	6.6	2.8	1.8	2.7	4.9	Cur. Mat.-L.T.D.		2.9	3.1
	17.2	15.8	9.0	9.4	9.2	Trade Payables		13.9	16.1
	.2	.3	.8	.4	.5	Income Taxes Payable		.2	.2
	18.9	16.8	18.0	23.0	16.7	All Other Current		16.9	17.2
	50.9	45.4	33.7	37.7	33.0	Total Current		43.2	46.1
	15.2	9.8	7.9	9.6	2.9	Long-Term Debt		14.0	13.6
	.0	.5	.5	.5	.9	Deferred Taxes		.4	.3
	16.7	5.2	7.7	11.2	5.9	All Other Non-Current		5.7	6.6
	17.2	39.1	50.2	41.0	57.4	Net Worth		36.8	33.5
	100.0	100.0	100.0	100.0	100.0	Total Liabilities & Net Worth		100.0	100.0
						INCOME DATA			
	100.0	100.0	100.0	100.0	100.0	Net Sales		100.0	100.0
	38.6	34.7	30.0	31.3	35.9	Gross Profit		34.2	31.7
	37.5	30.4	22.7	21.9	31.0	Operating Expenses		26.9	25.9
	1.2	4.3	7.2	9.4	4.9	Operating Profit		7.3	5.7
	.4	1.1	1.4	1.5	1.0	All Other Expenses (net)		1.1	1.3
	.8	3.2	5.9	7.9	3.9	Profit Before Taxes		6.2	4.4
						RATIOS			
	2.2	3.0	3.0	2.6	3.6	Current		2.8	2.3
	1.5	1.5	2.0	1.6	2.3			1.7	1.4
	.9	1.1	1.5	1.2	1.1			1.2	1.1
	1.2	1.6	1.9	1.6	2.0	Quick		1.5	1.4
	.7	.9	1.2	.9	1.1			.9 (191)	.8
	.5	.5	.7	.7	.7			.6	.5
	26 14.3	35 10.5	36 10.2	43 8.6	46 7.9	Sales/Receivables		34 10.7	35 10.6
	41 9.0	47 7.8	48 7.6	56 6.5	73 5.0			47 7.8	47 7.7
	63 5.8	67 5.5	66 4.9	74 4.9	78 4.7			61 5.9	63 5.8
	29 12.7	39 9.4	30 12.4	55 6.7	81 4.5	Cost of Sales/Inventory		34 10.7	33 10.9
	96 3.8	86 4.3	73 5.0	96 3.8	117 3.1			75 4.9	76 4.8
	203 1.8	136 2.7	105 3.5	133 2.7	189 1.9			124 2.9	116 3.1
	21 17.4	26 14.2	19 19.6	22 16.6	40 9.2	Cost of Sales/Payables		16 22.4	21 17.1
	36 10.2	37 9.9	25 14.5	30 12.2	54 6.8			34 10.8	35 10.4
	61 6.0	63 5.8	46 8.0	45 8.1	71 5.1			53 6.9	54 6.7
	4.0	3.7	3.4	2.9	1.3	Sales/Working Capital		4.3	4.5
	10.3	7.5	5.0	5.7	2.7			7.6	9.8
	-46.7	52.0	7.2	16.5	NM			23.6	47.0
	7.3	30.8	37.7	25.4		EBIT/Interest		20.1	11.3
	(37) 1.9	(82) 7.4	(37) 7.5	(19) 17.0				(169) 5.0	(164) 4.2
	-2.4	2.0	2.2	2.5				1.7	1.1
		6.3	26.3	13.0		Net Profit + Depr., Dep., Amort./Cur. Mat. L/T/D		8.2	11.7
		(18) 2.1	(16) 6.0	(11) 4.4				(51) 3.4	(55) 3.7
		.9	2.8	1.7				1.5	1.4
	.2	.2	.2	.2	.2	Fixed/Worth		.2	.2
	.7	.4	.5	.5	.3			.5	.6
	-1.3	1.3	1.2	2.4	NM			1.5	2.4
	1.1	.7	.4	.7	.5	Debt/Worth		.7	1.0
	2.5	1.7	.8	1.4	.8			1.8	2.4
	-4.4	6.9	3.9	3.3	NM			5.8	6.4
	29.8	50.9	31.8	48.2	22.3	% Profit Before Taxes/Tangible Net Worth		57.4	55.0
	(28) 9.8	(84) 24.2	(42) 18.5	(18) 21.0	(10) 11.1			(175) 27.4	(164) 26.7
	-11.8	7.0	7.1	5.7	-5.4			9.6	6.6
	10.4	17.3	13.8	16.6	11.6	% Profit Before Taxes/Total Assets		19.8	19.1
	2.6	6.7	7.9	6.1	6.7			10.7	7.4
	-5.0	2.4	2.9	2.3	-2.5			2.0	.8
	71.2	29.3	24.7	16.0	10.9	Sales/Net Fixed Assets		30.3	34.1
	20.6	12.4	7.5	7.1	7.1			13.1	12.3
	6.0	6.9	4.9	3.7	4.3			6.2	5.3
	3.0	2.4	1.7	1.4	1.2	Sales/Total Assets		2.7	2.6
	1.9	1.9	1.5	1.2	.9			1.8	1.8
	1.2	1.3	1.1	1.0	.8			1.4	1.3
	.5	.7	.9	1.3	2.0	% Depr., Dep., Amort./Sales		.6	.7
	(31) 1.6	(81) 1.4	(40) 2.4	(19) 2.6	(11) 2.8			(173) 1.5	(161) 1.5
	3.6	3.9	3.6	7.7	4.3			2.9	3.1
	4.0	2.3				% Officers', Directors' Owners' Comp/Sales		2.6	2.6
	(21) 5.9	(32) 3.0						(68) 4.5	(51) 4.4
	9.4	7.8						8.4	7.6
5899M	117055M	890925M	1461590M	1672692M	1882170M	Net Sales ($)		5724554M	5849345M
960M	46053M	471662M	1006741M	1384127M	2032376M	Total Assets ($)		3623483M	4289625M

© RMA 2011   M = $ thousand   MM = $ million
See Pages 9 through 22 for Explanation of Ratios and Data

Comparative Historical Data | Current Data Sorted by Sales

4/1/08-3/31/09 ALL	4/1/09-3/31/10 ALL	4/1/10-3/31/11 ALL	Type of Statement	0-1MM	1-3MM	3-5MM	5-10MM	10-25MM	25MM & OVER
47	48	35	Unqualified		1	1	4	9	20
45	48	43	Reviewed		3	5	10	16	9
27	27	30	Compiled		7	8	7	5	3
27	23	21	Tax Returns	2	7	3	6	1	2
90	89	86	Other	5	8	3	20	23	27
					48 (4/1-9/30/10)		167 (10/1/10-3/31/11)		
236	235	215	NUMBER OF STATEMENTS	7	26	20	47	54	61
%	%	%	**ASSETS**	%	%	%	%	%	%
9.9	13.3	14.2	Cash & Equivalents		10.1	11.3	11.1	14.0	19.5
25.6	23.3	24.2	Trade Receivables (net)		18.4	34.0	28.2	23.1	22.6
25.9	25.9	25.8	Inventory		32.3	26.8	29.0	25.4	19.0
5.4	5.4	4.6	All Other Current		.7	4.3	3.1	5.2	6.5
66.7	67.9	68.7	Total Current		61.5	76.4	71.5	67.7	67.7
20.3	19.8	19.4	Fixed Assets (net)		23.2	18.1	19.8	19.8	18.0
6.0	5.1	5.3	Intangibles (net)		5.6	1.1	3.5	5.4	7.3
6.9	7.2	6.6	All Other Non-Current		9.6	4.5	5.2	7.1	7.0
100.0	100.0	100.0	Total		100.0	100.0	100.0	100.0	100.0
			LIABILITIES						
11.0	9.6	7.4	Notes Payable-Short Term		11.3	14.9	9.8	5.8	3.1
3.8	3.2	3.4	Cur. Mat.-L.T.D.		7.5	4.3	2.6	2.9	2.4
13.4	13.0	13.6	Trade Payables		12.1	20.1	16.5	12.5	11.1
.3	.4	.4	Income Taxes Payable		.1	.2	.1	.4	.8
16.5	16.4	17.8	All Other Current		16.8	20.5	15.9	16.6	20.4
44.9	42.6	42.6	Total Current		47.7	59.9	45.0	38.2	37.8
13.4	13.0	10.3	Long-Term Debt		18.8	12.8	9.0	10.0	6.3
.3	.4	.4	Deferred Taxes		.2	.2	.3	.8	.5
6.6	8.0	9.0	All Other Non-Current		25.9	4.4	6.1	5.2	8.5
34.7	35.9	37.7	Net Worth		7.4	22.7	39.6	45.8	46.9
100.0	100.0	100.0	Total Liabilties & Net Worth		100.0	100.0	100.0	100.0	100.0
			INCOME DATA						
100.0	100.0	100.0	Net Sales		100.0	100.0	100.0	100.0	100.0
30.8	31.1	34.2	Gross Profit		40.7	33.1	36.9	29.9	32.5
25.7	28.0	29.2	Operating Expenses		41.4	31.8	32.4	23.6	24.6
5.0	3.1	5.0	Operating Profit		-.7	1.3	4.5	6.3	7.8
1.1	1.4	1.1	All Other Expenses (net)		.8	.3	.6	1.7	1.2
4.0	1.7	4.0	Profit Before Taxes		-1.5	1.1	3.9	4.6	6.6
			RATIOS						
2.3	2.7	2.8			3.1	1.9	3.3	3.0	2.8
1.6	1.6	1.7	Current		1.4	1.4	1.5	2.0	1.8
1.1	1.1	1.2			.8	.9	1.1	1.4	1.3
1.3	1.5	1.6			1.2	1.2	1.4	1.9	1.7
.8	.8	1.0	Quick		.7	.7	.9	1.0	1.1
.5	.5	.6			.3	.5	.6	.6	.7
31 11.9	28 13.0	34 10.6		26 13.8	34 10.6	38 9.6	30 12.2	40 9.1	
45 8.0	45 8.1	49 7.5	Sales/Receivables	42 8.7	55 6.6	53 6.9	45 8.1	55 6.6	
59 6.2	61 6.0	69 5.3		71 5.2	65 5.6	71 5.2	63 5.8	75 4.9	
30 12.1	33 11.0	36 10.2		37 9.9	22 16.8	41 9.0	30 12.0	42 8.6	
66 5.5	75 4.9	87 4.2	Cost of Sales/Inventory	115 3.2	48 7.6	96 3.8	73 5.0	88 4.1	
111 3.3	143 2.6	140 2.6		232 1.6	153 2.4	133 2.7	113 3.2	117 3.1	
17 22.0	16 22.4	22 16.9		21 17.6	21 17.7	26 14.2	20 18.7	22 16.7	
29 12.5	27 13.6	33 11.2	Cost of Sales/Payables	31 11.9	40 9.0	41 8.8	27 13.4	37 9.8	
44 8.2	52 7.0	57 6.4		57 6.4	76 4.8	65 5.6	41 8.9	57 6.4	
4.4	3.6	3.5			2.8	4.6	3.7	3.7	2.9
8.8	7.2	5.8	Sales/Working Capital		8.9	13.9	9.1	5.4	5.0
40.7	23.8	21.0			-10.2	-46.3	118.4	12.4	14.2
16.8	12.0	25.1			7.3	10.8	28.0	48.6	54.3
(202) 3.7	(203) 2.6	(187) 6.7	EBIT/Interest	(25) 2.5	(19) 2.2	(42) 7.8	(45) 7.5	(51) 15.9	
1.1	-.2	1.3			-2.4	-.1	2.6	1.9	2.0
10.1	7.0	12.6	Net Profit + Depr., Dep.,					12.0	23.7
(59) 3.3	(75) 2.1	(57) 3.0	Amort./Cur. Mat. L/T/D					(20) 3.8	(22) 6.5
1.0	-.1	1.3						1.5	1.6
.2	.2	.2			.3	.2	.2	.2	.2
.6	.5	.5	Fixed/Worth		1.3	.5	.4	.5	.4
2.1	2.3	1.4			-.7	1.2	1.7	1.2	1.2
.7	.6	.6			.8	1.7	.5	.5	.5
2.1	1.4	1.5	Debt/Worth		2.3	2.7	1.7	1.2	1.0
8.3	10.2	6.2			-3.8	13.3	9.0	4.8	3.7
42.2	31.5	43.0	% Profit Before Taxes/Tangible	23.4	36.8	53.7	42.4	39.8	
(191) 21.2	(193) 10.1	(185) 18.5	Net Worth	(17) 10.0	(17) 8.7	(43) 27.8	(49) 18.9	(53) 20.5	
5.0	-3.7	5.0			-16.4	-13.5	9.6	6.9	6.8
16.7	11.4	15.6	% Profit Before Taxes/Total		9.5	11.7	16.7	17.1	16.3
7.2	2.8	6.6	Assets		2.4	2.5	6.7	7.8	8.5
.4	-3.1	.9			-7.8	-4.1	2.4	2.7	2.3
31.7	28.0	28.2			49.3	57.6	24.8	31.2	25.0
13.2	11.7	11.4	Sales/Net Fixed Assets		15.1	18.0	12.6	10.7	9.4
5.8	5.6	5.8			2.8	6.8	6.9	5.9	5.6
2.6	2.4	2.2			2.1	2.9	2.3	2.3	1.7
1.9	1.6	1.6	Sales/Total Assets		1.6	2.1	1.8	1.8	1.3
1.4	1.2	1.2			.9	1.5	1.3	1.2	1.0
.8	.9	.8			.9	.5	.6	.8	1.1
(192) 1.6	(190) 1.8	(183) 1.8	% Depr., Dep., Amort./Sales	(20) 3.6	(18) 1.0	(43) 1.4	(47) 1.8	(51) 2.3	
3.0	4.4	3.7			11.3	2.5	3.3	3.5	3.6
2.5	2.2	2.4	% Officers', Directors'		3.6		2.4	2.2	
(75) 3.4	(72) 4.7	(62) 4.5	Owners' Comp/Sales		(15) 6.8		(20) 3.4	(10) 4.1	
6.0	9.0	8.6			9.2		7.8	7.7	
7804340M	6517825M	6030331M	Net Sales ($)	5149M	48949M	78467M	339846M	889287M	4668633M
4824063M	4647450M	4941919M	Total Assets ($)	3805M	43545M	41276M	204962M	584150M	4064181M

© RMA 2011

M = $ thousand   MM = $ million
See Pages 9 through 22 for Explanation of Ratios and Data

Current Data Sorted by Assets   Comparative Historical Data

Type of Statement							4/1/06-3/31/07 ALL	4/1/07-3/31/08 ALL
Unqualified		2	5	4	3		13	10
Reviewed	4	12	3				13	7
Compiled	1	3	1				11	7
Tax Returns	1	4	1				5	4
Other	3 3	8	9	3			15	30

0-500M	500M-2MM	2-10MM	10-50MM	50-100MM	100-250MM			
		17 (4/1-9/30/10)		53 (10/1/10-3/31/11)				
3	9	29	19	7	3	**NUMBER OF STATEMENTS**	57	58
%	%	%	%	%	%	**ASSETS**	%	%
		16.1	7.1			Cash & Equivalents	11.3	13.0
		24.6	18.7			Trade Receivables (net)	23.0	20.9
		24.7	25.1			Inventory	27.2	25.4
		2.7	2.0			All Other Current	3.2	3.6
		68.1	52.9			Total Current	64.7	62.8
		23.1	22.9			Fixed Assets (net)	26.8	26.6
		4.4	14.2			Intangibles (net)	3.9	3.8
		4.4	10.0			All Other Non-Current	4.6	6.7
		100.0	100.0			Total	100.0	100.0
						LIABILITIES		
		5.7	7.3			Notes Payable-Short Term	14.6	5.1
		2.2	1.4			Cur. Mat.-L.T.D.	4.4	4.5
		12.9	9.6			Trade Payables	15.2	14.4
		.4	.4			Income Taxes Payable	.1	.2
		11.4	11.4			All Other Current	9.9	9.3
		32.6	29.9			Total Current	44.3	33.6
		18.6	9.2			Long-Term Debt	15.2	14.8
		.0	1.6			Deferred Taxes	.6	.6
		7.1	10.0			All Other Non-Current	6.3	4.8
		41.8	49.3			Net Worth	33.5	46.3
		100.0	100.0			Total Liabilities & Net Worth	100.0	100.0
						INCOME DATA		
		100.0	100.0			Net Sales	100.0	100.0
		39.7	41.1			Gross Profit	39.0	41.8
		32.7	31.7			Operating Expenses	33.0	35.2
		7.0	9.5			Operating Profit	6.1	6.5
		.9	.8			All Other Expenses (net)	1.4	1.4
		6.1	8.6			Profit Before Taxes	4.6	5.1
						RATIOS		
		3.4	3.3			Current	2.7	3.4
		1.9	2.0				1.6	1.9
		1.5	1.1				1.2	1.4
		2.1	2.1			Quick	1.3	1.6
		1.2	.8				.9	1.0
		.7	.6				.5	.6
		37 9.9	40 9.2			Sales/Receivables	33 10.9	28 12.8
		48 7.6	52 7.1				41 9.0	42 8.7
		58 6.2	61 5.9				55 6.7	56 6.5
		31 11.9	85 4.3			Cost of Sales/Inventory	33 11.0	45 8.1
		78 4.7	120 3.0				89 4.1	91 4.0
		121 3.0	179 2.0				131 2.8	130 2.8
		24 15.3	13 27.6			Cost of Sales/Payables	20 18.5	23 15.9
		41 8.9	24 15.3				35 10.5	37 9.8
		54 6.7	75 4.9				50 7.4	59 6.1
		3.4	3.5			Sales/Working Capital	4.1	3.6
		5.7	4.3				7.8	7.2
		11.6	23.5				30.4	15.5
		25.2	7.2			EBIT/Interest	8.2	8.6
		(27) 4.7	(16) 6.3				(48) 3.5	(45) 3.6
		1.3	1.9				1.7	1.1
			10.5			Net Profit + Depr., Dep., Amort./Cur. Mat. L/T/D	2.6	2.6
			(11) 6.3				(17) 1.8	(20) 2.2
			5.1				1.3	1.1
		.2	.2			Fixed/Worth	.2	.2
		.5	.5				.7	.6
		1.4	1.5				1.5	1.5
		.5	.7			Debt/Worth	1.0	.5
		1.0	1.2				1.5	1.1
		2.7	5.0				3.8	3.3
		55.0	58.4			% Profit Before Taxes/Tangible Net Worth	53.6	45.6
		(27) 17.0	(17) 26.6				(51) 26.9	(52) 13.3
		.9	11.7				8.9	.9
		17.3	22.6			% Profit Before Taxes/Total Assets	16.1	18.1
		10.1	9.8				6.3	5.3
		.7	2.5				2.7	.5
		28.9	27.3			Sales/Net Fixed Assets	27.3	39.0
		9.7	6.4				9.4	8.5
		4.8	3.7				4.2	3.9
		2.3	1.6			Sales/Total Assets	2.5	2.7
		1.8	1.4				2.0	1.8
		1.6	1.2				1.3	1.2
		1.1	1.4			% Depr., Dep., Amort./Sales	1.6	.8
		(23) 2.3	3.6				(48) 3.4	(53) 3.0
		7.9	5.8				5.2	5.0
		2.2				% Officers', Directors' Owners' Comp/Sales	2.8	2.2
		(13) 3.3					(15) 5.8	(18) 3.1
		4.7					6.4	5.7
4393M	40283M	309979M	531261M	692935M	792720M	Net Sales ($)	1203352M	1946228M
1230M	14458M	163708M	408002M	503706M	524334M	Total Assets ($)	831219M	1332204M

M = $ thousand   MM = $ million
See Pages 9 through 22 for Explanation of Ratios and Data

Comparative Historical Data | Current Data Sorted by Sales

11 / 10 / 5 / 4 / 26 (4/1/08-3/31/09 ALL)	13 / 16 / 5 / 5 / 23 (4/1/09-3/31/10 ALL)	14 / 19 / 5 / 6 / 26 (4/1/10-3/31/11 ALL)	Type of Statement	0-1MM	1-3MM	3-5MM	5-10MM	10-25MM	25MM & OVER
			Unqualified					4	10
			Reviewed			3	6	9	1
			Compiled			1	2	2	
			Tax Returns		1	1	3	2	
			Other	2	3	1	4	7	9
					17 (4/1-9/30/10)		53 (10/1/10-3/31/11)		
56	62	70	NUMBER OF STATEMENTS	2	4	6	15	23	20
%	%	%	ASSETS	%	%	%	%	%	%
8.2	11.2	11.8	Cash & Equivalents				13.3	13.3	8.7
22.2	21.6	21.7	Trade Receivables (net)				24.3	23.5	19.8
29.4	28.6	25.6	Inventory				27.1	27.8	25.5
2.6	2.7	2.7	All Other Current				2.5	2.2	4.7
62.3	64.1	61.7	Total Current				67.2	66.6	58.7
23.1	22.9	22.2	Fixed Assets (net)				24.2	21.1	19.9
9.1	8.5	8.5	Intangibles (net)				2.4	4.2	15.2
5.4	4.4	7.6	All Other Non-Current				6.1	8.0	6.3
100.0	100.0	100.0	Total				100.0	100.0	100.0
			LIABILITIES						
7.5	7.8	6.9	Notes Payable-Short Term				8.6	4.0	7.5
3.1	2.9	2.1	Cur. Mat.-L.T.D.				2.2	1.3	2.0
14.6	12.4	11.6	Trade Payables				15.8	10.6	10.3
.2	.2	.3	Income Taxes Payable				.3	.5	.2
11.7	10.9	12.2	All Other Current				8.7	14.1	11.0
37.0	34.2	33.1	Total Current				35.6	30.5	31.1
13.2	11.3	14.8	Long-Term Debt				15.7	13.4	12.0
.5	.9	.5	Deferred Taxes				.0	.3	1.4
6.1	6.0	9.9	All Other Non-Current				7.6	5.2	14.2
43.2	47.6	41.7	Net Worth				41.2	50.6	41.3
100.0	100.0	100.0	Total Liabilties & Net Worth				100.0	100.0	100.0
			INCOME DATA						
100.0	100.0	100.0	Net Sales				100.0	100.0	100.0
38.2	36.8	40.3	Gross Profit				38.6	38.5	39.2
31.1	31.8	33.0	Operating Expenses				34.8	28.3	33.8
7.1	5.0	7.2	Operating Profit				3.8	10.1	5.4
1.3	1.5	.9	All Other Expenses (net)				.9	.5	1.2
5.7	3.4	6.3	Profit Before Taxes				3.0	9.7	4.2
			RATIOS						
2.5	3.4	3.4	Current				2.3	4.3	3.2
1.6	2.0	1.9					1.8	1.9	2.0
1.3	1.4	1.4					1.6	1.4	1.4
1.2	1.6	1.8	Quick				1.7	2.8	1.5
.8	1.0	1.0					.9	1.3	.8
.6	.6	.6					.7	.7	.6
35 10.5	34 10.7	36 10.1	Sales/Receivables				36 10.0	40 9.2	36 10.1
47 7.8	42 8.6	49 7.5					48 7.6	48 7.6	54 6.8
56 6.5	53 6.9	59 6.2					59 6.2	59 6.2	69 5.3
59 6.2	53 6.9	51 7.2	Cost of Sales/Inventory				23 15.7	56 6.6	85 4.3
93 3.9	92 4.0	92 4.0					106 3.4	78 4.7	123 3.0
140 2.6	140 2.6	135 2.7					131 2.8	143 2.6	158 2.3
19 18.8	14 26.5	20 18.1	Cost of Sales/Payables				38 9.5	16 23.5	24 15.4
36 10.0	29 12.7	39 9.5					54 6.7	27 13.4	40 9.1
63 5.8	49 7.4	56 6.5					62 5.9	46 8.0	66 5.5
3.9	3.6	3.4	Sales/Working Capital				3.4	3.1	3.5
8.3	6.2	5.8					5.9	5.7	4.3
19.6	10.9	16.3					11.3	12.9	9.4
11.4	8.9	14.2	EBIT/Interest				13.5	258.5	9.3
(48) 4.2	(49) 3.8	(57) 6.2					(14) 4.0	(19) 13.1	(17) 6.3
1.5	2.5	1.7					.4	1.8	1.1
4.0	3.4	11.1	Net Profit + Depr., Dep., Amort./Cur. Mat. L/T/D						57.3
(19) 2.3	(16) 2.7	(22) 5.9						(10)	6.3
1.6	1.6	2.6							3.6
.2	.2	.2	Fixed/Worth				.1	.1	.3
.7	.5	.5					.6	.2	.8
1.6	1.2	1.6					1.4	.8	7.1
.9	.5	.7	Debt/Worth				.7	.3	1.0
1.6	1.2	1.2					1.2	.7	1.3
3.8	3.0	3.8					3.4	1.5	27.9
46.3	38.3	48.9	% Profit Before Taxes/Tangible Net Worth				62.4	52.5	27.5
(48) 19.9	(59) 15.5	(61) 21.6					15.2	(22) 24.5	(16) 20.5
3.3	3.3	5.2					.7	5.2	9.9
16.3	9.5	17.3	% Profit Before Taxes/Total Assets				17.3	25.5	9.9
6.7	6.0	9.7					5.1	11.2	7.1
1.9	.9	1.8					.2	4.7	-2.9
28.2	29.5	28.5	Sales/Net Fixed Assets				48.9	29.7	26.2
9.7	10.1	8.7					8.2	9.7	7.5
5.2	4.2	4.9					4.5	4.3	4.3
2.3	2.3	2.1	Sales/Total Assets				2.1	2.3	1.7
1.8	1.8	1.7					1.8	1.8	1.3
1.3	1.2	1.3					1.4	1.5	1.0
.7	1.5	1.4	% Depr., Dep., Amort./Sales				.5	1.2	1.1
(45) 2.2	(50) 3.3	(57) 2.6					(13) 3.3	(20) 1.8	(17) 4.1
4.1	4.8	5.8					10.9	5.2	5.9
1.3	1.5	2.9	% Officers', Directors' Owners' Comp/Sales						
(14) 3.5	(20) 5.0	(25) 4.3							
11.6	8.8	7.2							
2396070M	2381115M	2371571M	Net Sales ($)	1414M	9197M	24574M	114194M	358150M	1864042M
1516911M	1425778M	1615438M	Total Assets ($)	748M	4859M	12837M	69163M	200815M	1327016M

M = $ thousand   MM = $ million
See Pages 9 through 22 for Explanation of Ratios and Data

Current Data Sorted by Assets   Comparative Historical Data

0-500M	500M-2MM	2-10MM	10-50MM	50-100MM	100-250MM	Type of Statement	4/1/06-3/31/07 ALL	4/1/07-3/31/08 ALL
		11	12	6	4	Unqualified	33	31
	2	29	8			Reviewed	46	44
1	9	17				Compiled	45	34
5	10	9	3			Tax Returns	22	15
5	27	27	22	3	3	Other	62	63
	35 (4/1-9/30/10)		178 (10/1/10-3/31/11)					
11	48	93	45	9	7	**NUMBER OF STATEMENTS**	208	187
%	%	%	%	%	%	**ASSETS**	%	%
19.2	12.2	11.1	9.6			Cash & Equivalents	7.9	9.5
35.4	29.2	26.6	26.6			Trade Receivables (net)	29.2	27.0
14.0	22.8	26.3	26.3			Inventory	28.2	28.2
6.0	3.3	4.0	7.5			All Other Current	3.1	3.8
74.6	67.4	67.9	70.0			Total Current	68.4	68.5
16.0	22.6	19.6	17.9			Fixed Assets (net)	18.1	18.5
.0	5.3	4.4	4.8			Intangibles (net)	5.8	6.1
9.4	4.7	8.1	7.3			All Other Non-Current	7.7	6.9
100.0	100.0	100.0	100.0			Total	100.0	100.0
						LIABILITIES		
16.6	15.7	7.6	6.3			Notes Payable-Short Term	11.9	11.7
1.3	3.0	3.9	2.1			Cur. Mat.-L.T.D.	3.9	5.4
5.9	17.1	15.9	11.4			Trade Payables	14.4	16.4
.0	.2	.3	.1			Income Taxes Payable	.3	.3
6.6	21.2	12.2	14.0			All Other Current	15.0	16.7
30.4	57.1	39.9	33.8			Total Current	45.4	50.5
24.0	22.0	10.0	8.7			Long-Term Debt	13.7	17.9
.0	.1	.5	.3			Deferred Taxes	.5	.4
7.8	15.9	4.7	3.2			All Other Non-Current	5.4	5.4
37.7	4.8	44.9	54.0			Net Worth	34.9	25.8
100.0	100.0	100.0	100.0			Total Liabilities & Net Worth	100.0	100.0
						INCOME DATA		
100.0	100.0	100.0	100.0			Net Sales	100.0	100.0
54.4	36.8	32.7	32.2			Gross Profit	32.4	31.8
42.2	34.5	27.1	24.9			Operating Expenses	26.2	27.9
12.3	2.3	5.6	7.3			Operating Profit	6.2	4.0
.8	.9	.8	-.1			All Other Expenses (net)	1.2	1.2
11.4	1.4	4.8	7.4			Profit Before Taxes	5.0	2.8
						RATIOS		
22.0	2.6	2.9	3.5				2.4	2.2
7.8	1.4	1.7	1.9			Current	1.7	1.5
1.4	.9	1.2	1.5				1.1	1.1
14.3	1.5	1.6	2.0				1.4	1.3
3.5	.8	.9	1.1			Quick	(207) .8	(186) .8
.9	.5	.6	.7				.5	.5
0 UND	19 19.3	30 12.2	30 12.2				29 12.5	29 12.6
25 14.8	35 10.3	47 7.7	48 7.5			Sales/Receivables	44 8.3	43 8.5
69 5.3	52 7.0	69 5.3	63 5.8				61 6.0	58 6.3
0 UND	11 33.3	31 11.9	33 11.0				30 12.3	29 12.5
1 421.0	42 8.6	53 6.9	72 5.1			Cost of Sales/Inventory	62 5.9	64 5.7
22 16.4	84 4.4	111 3.3	131 2.8				101 3.6	102 3.6
0 UND	15 24.0	18 20.8	16 23.0				17 20.9	18 20.5
3 109.7	31 11.8	30 12.1	26 14.0			Cost of Sales/Payables	29 12.8	33 11.1
50 7.4	55 6.7	52 7.0	48 7.6				45 8.1	53 6.9
3.8	7.2	4.4	3.4				5.2	5.7
10.1	19.0	7.9	5.4			Sales/Working Capital	8.3	9.7
24.4	-25.2	19.2	10.0				30.2	42.7
	13.1	25.9	77.4				13.6	11.7
	(42) 3.8	(75) 6.0	(40) 20.3			EBIT/Interest	(178) 4.7	(168) 3.3
	.9	1.9	3.3				2.0	.8
		3.5	32.4			Net Profit + Depr., Dep.,	10.5	6.8
		(24) 1.9	(15) 10.7			Amort./Cur. Mat. L/T/D	(57) 3.5	(58) 2.9
		.6	3.0				1.2	.8
.1	.2	.1	.2				.2	.2
.3	1.2	.4	.3			Fixed/Worth	.5	.6
.6	-2.7	1.1	.6				1.5	2.2
.2	1.7	.5	.5				.8	1.0
.5	5.5	1.2	.9			Debt/Worth	1.8	2.5
11.9	-7.2	3.5	1.4				5.3	11.1
301.8	88.3	46.8	54.3				58.1	54.7
(10) 129.9	(33) 30.6	(86) 19.3	(44) 22.4			% Profit Before Taxes/Tangible Net Worth	(177) 25.5	(148) 21.2
44.4	7.3	7.4	8.2				8.0	2.6
100.4	17.8	18.4	25.9				20.4	16.7
30.2	8.0	7.4	11.3			% Profit Before Taxes/Total Assets	7.9	6.4
11.8	-.4	2.1	2.1				3.2	-.4
202.9	74.0	41.9	27.8				36.5	36.4
39.0	20.6	16.0	13.4			Sales/Net Fixed Assets	16.2	15.9
7.7	8.1	6.3	7.0				6.9	7.2
8.9	3.9	2.6	2.6				3.0	2.9
3.3	2.6	1.9	1.8			Sales/Total Assets	2.2	2.2
2.7	2.1	1.5	1.3				1.7	1.5
	1.0	.9	1.0				.7	.8
	(31) 1.8	(80) 1.4	(42) 1.5			% Depr., Dep., Amort./Sales	(176) 1.4	(157) 1.5
	3.2	2.6	2.2				2.7	2.8
	3.7	2.5	.8				2.6	1.9
	(18) 5.8	(36) 4.6	(10) 2.2			% Officers', Directors' Owners' Comp/Sales	(77) 4.4	(56) 4.5
	9.1	7.2	9.1				7.6	10.2
16541M	165819M	1002061M	1869746M	818834M	1754785M	Net Sales ($)	6396161M	4785446M
3050M	56579M	447466M	899733M	562287M	1126238M	Total Assets ($)	3501112M	2715591M

© RMA 2011

M = $ thousand   MM = $ million
See Pages 9 through 22 for Explanation of Ratios and Data

Comparative Historical Data				Current Data Sorted by Sales					
			Type of Statement						
39	35	33	Unqualified			3	2	7	21
50	59	39	Reviewed		1	6	9	18	5
43	51	27	Compiled	1	5	10	7	4	
49	67	27	Tax Returns	1	9	7	5	4	1
88	107	87	Other	4	19	12	11	21	20
4/1/08-3/31/09 ALL	4/1/09-3/31/10 ALL	4/1/10-3/31/11 ALL		35 (4/1-9/30/10)		178 (10/1/10-3/31/11)			
				0-1MM	1-3MM	3-5MM	5-10MM	10-25MM	25MM & OVER
269	319	213	**NUMBER OF STATEMENTS**	6	34	38	34	54	47
%	%	%	**ASSETS**	%	%	%	%	%	%
9.8	10.6	11.1	Cash & Equivalents		14.2	9.5	10.9	13.1	8.2
26.5	27.2	27.3	Trade Receivables (net)		24.6	29.0	25.2	28.3	27.4
28.2	25.9	24.4	Inventory		19.4	22.2	29.6	25.9	25.4
3.0	3.3	4.8	All Other Current		6.4	2.8	3.0	5.7	5.8
67.6	66.9	67.6	Total Current		64.6	63.4	68.8	73.1	66.7
20.2	20.6	19.9	Fixed Assets (net)		22.5	21.4	18.7	17.2	18.6
5.8	4.8	5.4	Intangibles (net)		6.3	6.9	2.4	4.4	7.3
6.4	7.7	7.1	All Other Non-Current		6.6	8.2	10.1	5.2	7.3
100.0	100.0	100.0	Total		100.0	100.0	100.0	100.0	100.0
			LIABILITIES						
10.4	10.4	9.5	Notes Payable-Short Term		11.2	14.5	9.7	6.2	7.2
5.4	3.6	3.1	Cur. Mat.-L.T.D.		2.7	4.2	5.4	1.6	2.7
16.1	15.1	14.1	Trade Payables		10.5	15.8	14.7	17.8	12.0
.4	.2	.2	Income Taxes Payable		.1	.4	.2	.2	.2
13.7	11.4	14.8	All Other Current		18.2	16.5	12.1	14.0	15.4
46.0	40.8	41.7	Total Current		42.8	51.5	42.1	39.8	37.6
15.4	15.2	13.6	Long-Term Debt		19.9	15.3	10.5	9.9	9.5
.4	.3	.3	Deferred Taxes		.2	.2	.2	.5	.5
5.2	5.8	7.2	All Other Non-Current		7.2	18.2	3.8	.9	5.1
33.0	37.9	37.1	Net Worth		29.8	14.8	43.4	48.9	47.2
100.0	100.0	100.0	Total Liabilities & Net Worth		100.0	100.0	100.0	100.0	100.0
			INCOME DATA						
100.0	100.0	100.0	Net Sales		100.0	100.0	100.0	100.0	100.0
32.3	33.9	34.8	Gross Profit		38.9	39.4	32.0	29.4	34.0
28.7	31.3	29.0	Operating Expenses		34.7	33.7	28.2	23.4	25.7
3.7	2.6	5.8	Operating Profit		4.2	5.7	3.8	6.0	8.3
1.2	.8	.7	All Other Expenses (net)		.8	1.7	.5	.0	.6
2.5	1.9	5.0	Profit Before Taxes		3.4	4.0	3.3	6.1	7.6
			RATIOS						
2.6	2.8	3.1			5.1	2.3	3.0	2.9	2.9
1.6	1.7	1.7	Current		1.5	1.5	1.6	1.8	1.7
1.1	1.1	1.2			.8	1.1	1.0	1.3	1.4
1.5	1.7	1.9			2.8	1.6	1.3	1.9	1.6
.8	.9	.9	Quick		.9	.9	.9	1.0	1.1
.5	.6	.6			.5	.4	.5	.6	.7
28 12.8	30 12.1	28 12.8		4 81.6	22 16.7	33 10.9	30 12.0	31 12.0	
41 9.0	42 8.7	44 8.2	Sales/Receivables	35 10.4	40 9.1	46 8.0	46 7.9	48 7.6	
55 6.6	56 6.5	65 5.7		79 4.6	58 6.2	63 5.8	60 6.1	64 5.7	
29 12.5	28 13.2	22 16.3		3 133.0	29 12.6	23 16.2	25 14.7	33 11.1	
61 6.0	62 5.9	53 6.9	Cost of Sales/Inventory	44 8.2	55 6.7	69 5.3	49 7.5	62 5.9	
103 3.5	114 3.2	102 3.6		92 4.0	100 3.6	154 2.4	78 4.7	92 4.0	
16 23.0	17 21.7	16 23.2		8 47.1	17 22.1	21 17.6	18 20.7	16 22.8	
30 12.2	30 12.2	29 12.5	Cost of Sales/Payables	24 15.2	34 10.8	38 9.5	28 13.0	25 14.5	
48 7.7	52 7.0	50 7.4		42 8.7	59 6.1	56 6.6	48 7.7	45 8.1	
5.2	4.7	4.5			4.1	6.4	4.4	4.1	4.5
9.6	8.3	8.8	Sales/Working Capital		15.2	12.2	5.8	7.5	8.5
79.2	27.9	21.5			-21.0	NM	NM	15.6	12.4
13.9	9.6	31.0			10.3	26.2	20.5	36.8	85.7
(234) 3.8	(273) 2.9	(177) 6.9	EBIT/Interest	(24) 3.0	(36) 5.2	(30) 5.2	(40) 12.2	(43) 15.2	
.8	.2	1.6			.5	1.2	1.3	3.1	4.3
7.1	7.5	16.8						18.4	32.4
(71) 1.6	(61) 2.3	(45) 2.8	Net Profit + Depr., Dep., Amort./Cur. Mat. L/T/D					(15) 2.8	(15) 7.1
.4	.5	1.3						1.4	2.2
.2	.2	.2			.2	.1	.1	.1	.2
.5	.5	.5	Fixed/Worth		.6	.9	.4	.3	.5
2.0	1.5	1.5			3.8	-2.9	1.1	.6	.9
.8	.7	.6			1.1	.8	.5	.5	.6
2.1	1.8	1.6	Debt/Worth		3.2	2.6	1.6	1.1	1.0
6.9	4.7	4.4			22.5	-10.5	3.7	2.4	2.9
45.2	36.6	55.7			93.2	66.4	43.7	46.7	62.4
(222) 22.3	(276) 15.2	(187) 24.3	% Profit Before Taxes/Tangible Net Worth	(28) 35.5	(27) 19.8	(33) 15.2	(52) 28.2	(43) 28.7	
8.3	.5	8.2			1.0	5.8	2.3	10.0	14.1
14.4	12.1	20.3			23.7	17.4	16.9	20.8	29.4
6.4	4.1	8.8	% Profit Before Taxes/Total Assets		6.9	6.6	6.8	9.7	9.5
-.4	-1.6	1.7			-1.2	.7	.4	4.0	3.6
36.6	35.7	37.0			70.4	53.9	34.0	38.9	27.3
16.0	15.8	15.1	Sales/Net Fixed Assets		12.9	20.6	11.4	16.5	11.4
7.5	6.1	6.5			4.5	5.1	6.7	8.6	6.5
3.0	2.9	2.8			3.0	3.7	2.5	2.8	2.7
2.3	2.0	2.1	Sales/Total Assets		2.2	2.0	1.9	2.2	1.9
1.6	1.4	1.5			1.3	1.5	1.5	1.7	1.4
.8	.8	1.0			1.4	1.0	1.2	.6	1.1
(224) 1.4	(250) 1.9	(171) 1.6	% Depr., Dep., Amort./Sales	(22) 2.4	(31) 1.6	(28) 1.5	(46) 1.1	(41) 1.6	
2.8	3.6	2.6			6.8	3.2	2.6	2.1	2.3
2.5	2.5	2.7			4.0	3.5	3.1	1.4	
(100) 4.9	(130) 4.6	(71) 4.6	% Officers', Directors' Owners' Comp/Sales	(16) 5.9	(18) 5.2	(13) 5.7	(15) 3.2		
8.5	7.8	7.9			6.9	9.7	8.8	6.3	
7543137M	6335437M	5627786M	Net Sales ($)	2901M	75670M	153629M	251229M	854596M	4289761M
4072850M	3752214M	3095353M	Total Assets ($)	1646M	47088M	80323M	149301M	428871M	2388124M

M = $ thousand   MM = $ million
See Pages 9 through 22 for Explanation of Ratios and Data

Current Data Sorted by Assets　　　　　　　Comparative Historical Data

						Type of Statement		
			1	5		Unqualified	2	6
1	1	1	4		2	Reviewed	3	6
1	1	3				Compiled	2	3
1	3		1			Tax Returns	3	2
		1		3	1	1	Other	9	7
	5 (4/1-9/30/10)			25 (10/1/10-3/31/11)				4/1/06- 3/31/07 ALL	4/1/07- 3/31/08 ALL
0-500M	500M-2MM	2-10MM	10-50MM	50-100MM	100-250MM			
3	6	9	8	1	3	NUMBER OF STATEMENTS	19	24
%	%	%	%	%	%	ASSETS	%	%
						Cash & Equivalents	12.3	8.2
						Trade Receivables (net)	34.6	27.2
						Inventory	20.0	23.7
						All Other Current	6.7	6.2
						Total Current	73.5	65.3
						Fixed Assets (net)	17.4	18.2
						Intangibles (net)	5.4	7.8
						All Other Non-Current	3.6	8.7
						Total	100.0	100.0
						LIABILITIES		
						Notes Payable-Short Term	8.5	9.6
						Cur. Mat.-L.T.D.	1.9	2.8
						Trade Payables	15.3	16.4
						Income Taxes Payable	.4	.6
						All Other Current	13.7	13.5
						Total Current	39.7	42.9
						Long-Term Debt	20.9	18.6
						Deferred Taxes	.5	1.1
						All Other Non-Current	3.9	4.9
						Net Worth	35.0	32.5
						Total Liabilties & Net Worth	100.0	100.0
						INCOME DATA		
						Net Sales	100.0	100.0
						Gross Profit	32.5	35.6
						Operating Expenses	25.0	25.8
						Operating Profit	7.5	9.8
						All Other Expenses (net)	-.2	2.1
						Profit Before Taxes	7.7	7.7
						RATIOS		
							3.1	2.8
						Current	2.2	1.9
							1.3	1.0
							1.9	1.6
						Quick	1.6	.8
							.7	.4
						Sales/Receivables	28　13.0	34　10.7
							49　7.4	50　7.4
							70　5.2	63　5.8
						Cost of Sales/Inventory	23　15.7	27　13.6
							34　10.6	51　7.2
							80　4.6	87　4.2
						Cost of Sales/Payables	15　24.7	15　24.8
							24　15.1	44　8.3
							39　9.4	58　6.2
						Sales/Working Capital	4.8	4.7
							7.6	7.7
							18.3	NM
						EBIT/Interest	20.7	16.2
							(17)　8.2	(22)　5.5
							2.5	1.7
						Net Profit + Depr., Dep., Amort./Cur. Mat. L/T/D		
						Fixed/Worth	.3	.2
							.6	.6
							1.7	NM
						Debt/Worth	.9	.7
							2.7	2.5
							4.5	NM
						% Profit Before Taxes/Tangible Net Worth	74.5	70.0
							(16)　41.0	(18)　34.4
							23.1	19.2
						% Profit Before Taxes/Total Assets	30.2	20.9
							19.7	13.6
							6.0	3.6
						Sales/Net Fixed Assets	45.7	42.4
							25.8	10.6
							6.7	6.0
						Sales/Total Assets	3.5	2.5
							2.7	2.1
							1.7	1.3
						% Depr., Dep., Amort./Sales	.6	.5
							(17)　1.4	(22)　1.5
							1.8	2.3
						% Officers', Directors' Owners' Comp/Sales		
1874M	16918M	96080M	399492M	120674M	759032M	Net Sales ($)	504241M	1294773M
610M	6454M	45638M	193969M	89004M	447572M	Total Assets ($)	231981M	767970M

M = $ thousand　　MM = $ million
See Pages 9 through 22 for Explanation of Ratios and Data

Comparative Historical Data | Current Data Sorted by Sales

	4/1/08-3/31/09 ALL	4/1/09-3/31/10 ALL	4/1/10-3/31/11 ALL	Type of Statement	0-1MM	1-3MM	3-5MM	5-10MM	10-25MM	25MM & OVER
	5	3	8	Unqualified					2	6
	3	4	6	Reviewed	1		1	4		
	3	2	5	Compiled	1		1	2	1	
	4	2	4	Tax Returns	1					
	10	6	7	Other		3	1	1	1	4
					5 (4/1-9/30/10)		25 (10/1/10-3/31/11)			
	25	17	30	NUMBER OF STATEMENTS	3	4	2	7	4	10
	%	%	%	**ASSETS**	%	%	%	%	%	%
	9.0	9.5	16.4	Cash & Equivalents						7.1
	29.4	23.6	26.1	Trade Receivables (net)						22.1
	19.7	26.5	23.0	Inventory						21.5
	4.9	4.0	5.6	All Other Current						4.3
	63.1	63.7	71.0	Total Current						55.0
	17.3	19.3	15.9	Fixed Assets (net)						26.7
	14.1	5.4	5.8	Intangibles (net)						12.9
	5.5	11.7	7.3	All Other Non-Current						5.4
	100.0	100.0	100.0	Total						100.0
				LIABILITIES						
	11.8	6.2	4.9	Notes Payable-Short Term						5.1
	4.9	1.9	1.4	Cur. Mat.-L.T.D.						2.0
	13.6	11.4	11.8	Trade Payables						11.0
	1.8	.6	.3	Income Taxes Payable						.5
	8.9	7.1	14.6	All Other Current						12.5
	41.0	27.1	33.1	Total Current						31.1
	15.5	19.0	15.0	Long-Term Debt						20.1
	.9	1.0	.7	Deferred Taxes						.8
	3.3	4.7	3.4	All Other Non-Current						5.0
	39.4	48.1	47.9	Net Worth						42.9
	100.0	100.0	100.0	Total Liabilities & Net Worth						100.0
				INCOME DATA						
	100.0	100.0	100.0	Net Sales						100.0
	31.0	33.9	33.6	Gross Profit						28.7
	25.0	27.8	26.7	Operating Expenses						22.2
	6.0	6.0	6.9	Operating Profit						6.5
	1.4	.7	.3	All Other Expenses (net)						1.0
	4.6	5.4	6.7	Profit Before Taxes						5.5
				RATIOS						
	3.6	5.2	3.3	Current						2.6
	1.4	2.2	2.0							2.0
	1.0	1.4	1.4							1.4
	1.5	2.7	1.7	Quick						1.5
	.8	1.0	1.3							1.2
	.5	.5	.7							.6
	26 14.0	23 16.1	29 12.5	Sales/Receivables						23 16.1
	48 7.7	48 7.7	46 7.9							51 7.2
	60 6.0	61 5.9	60 6.1							59 6.2
	17 22.0	38 9.6	19 19.5	Cost of Sales/Inventory						11 34.0
	50 7.3	63 5.8	63 5.8							36 10.2
	77 4.7	93 3.9	96 3.8							83 4.4
	14 26.4	13 28.4	14 25.9	Cost of Sales/Payables						18 20.4
	29 12.6	22 16.5	31 11.9							28 12.9
	45 8.2	51 7.2	48 7.6							42 8.6
	4.2	4.0	3.0	Sales/Working Capital						4.2
	12.5	5.6	6.1							7.4
	NM	11.0	13.1							16.3
	13.9	17.0	24.7	EBIT/Interest						
	(22) 5.2	(15) 5.6	(23) 3.3							
	1.2	1.5	.9							
				Net Profit + Depr., Dep., Amort./Cur. Mat. L/T/D						
	.2	.2	.0	Fixed/Worth						.4
	.7	.3	.2							.6
	-4.8	1.7	1.1							2.8
	.7	.3	.4	Debt/Worth						.8
	3.7	1.2	1.2							2.1
	-11.9	4.8	3.5							6.5
	48.0	28.4	37.6	% Profit Before Taxes/Tangible Net Worth						
	(18) 22.4	(14) 20.2	(27) 18.1							
	10.8	11.7	5.2							
	15.7	12.0	15.7	% Profit Before Taxes/Total Assets						18.2
	6.8	7.1	8.7							6.7
	2.3	3.8	1.4							-.6
	54.0	39.8	73.3	Sales/Net Fixed Assets						7.8
	10.7	8.6	13.5							6.7
	7.1	4.6	7.1							5.9
	2.9	2.8	2.8	Sales/Total Assets						2.7
	2.0	1.9	1.9							2.1
	1.3	1.0	1.3							1.4
	.7	.6	.3	% Depr., Dep., Amort./Sales						
	(21) 1.6	(13) 1.4	(25) 1.5							
	2.3	2.9	2.3							
			1.6	% Officers', Directors' Owners' Comp/Sales						
		(10) 5.6								
			8.4							
	1527618M	558891M	1394070M	Net Sales ($)	1874M	7124M	8398M	56781M	52362M	1267531M
	926749M	477347M	783247M	Total Assets ($)	610M	4321M	6088M	28603M	41178M	702447M

M = $ thousand   MM = $ million
See Pages 9 through 22 for Explanation of Ratios and Data

Current Data Sorted by Assets | Comparative Historical Data

0-500M	500M-2MM	2-10MM	10-50MM	50-100MM	100-250MM	Type of Statement	4/1/06-3/31/07 ALL	4/1/07-3/31/08 ALL
	1	3	1		4	Unqualified	16	14
	1	4	1			Reviewed	6	7
		3				Compiled	9	8
1	2	5				Tax Returns	3	4
1	2	8	7	1	3	Other	21	13
							12 (4/1-9/30/10)	36 (10/1/10-3/31/11)
2	6	23	9	1	7	NUMBER OF STATEMENTS	55	46
%	%	%	%	%	%		%	%
						ASSETS		
		10.5				Cash & Equivalents	10.1	9.8
		36.8				Trade Receivables (net)	30.4	27.8
		24.6				Inventory	21.1	21.3
		3.7				All Other Current	5.9	3.2
		75.7				Total Current	67.6	62.1
		15.8				Fixed Assets (net)	20.8	24.4
		4.0				Intangibles (net)	6.7	7.3
		4.5				All Other Non-Current	4.9	6.3
		100.0				Total	100.0	100.0
						LIABILITIES		
		8.8				Notes Payable-Short Term	7.5	7.5
		3.6				Cur. Mat.-L.T.D.	2.0	2.2
		13.0				Trade Payables	14.7	14.7
		.5				Income Taxes Payable	.5	.5
		16.7				All Other Current	15.6	15.1
		42.6				Total Current	40.4	40.0
		7.7				Long-Term Debt	12.4	13.7
		.5				Deferred Taxes	.4	.8
		6.7				All Other Non-Current	8.2	7.1
		42.5				Net Worth	38.5	38.4
		100.0				Total Liabilities & Net Worth	100.0	100.0
						INCOME DATA		
		100.0				Net Sales	100.0	100.0
		34.1				Gross Profit	30.8	29.0
		25.7				Operating Expenses	22.1	22.5
		8.5				Operating Profit	8.7	6.5
		.5				All Other Expenses (net)	.8	1.2
		8.0				Profit Before Taxes	7.9	5.3
						RATIOS		
		3.3				Current	2.5	2.3
		2.0					1.8	1.6
		1.3					1.3	1.2
		1.7				Quick	1.6	1.4
		1.1					1.0	.9
		.9					.8	.6
		46 7.9				Sales/Receivables	40 9.2	37 10.0
		51 7.1					54 6.8	53 6.9
		84 4.4					73 5.0	72 5.1
		30 12.1				Cost of Sales/Inventory	34 10.6	31 11.9
		81 4.5					52 7.0	48 7.6
		102 3.6					81 4.5	86 4.3
		17 22.0				Cost of Sales/Payables	21 17.8	17 21.8
		26 13.9					33 10.9	35 10.5
		42 8.6					49 7.4	52 7.0
		3.4				Sales/Working Capital	5.0	5.6
		6.1					7.5	9.2
		12.7					15.4	19.8
		40.4				EBIT/Interest	31.0	20.8
		(21) 11.4					(45) 8.8	(41) 5.5
		4.0					2.8	1.7
						Net Profit + Depr., Dep.,	9.8	8.6
						Amort./Cur. Mat. L/T/D	(21) 3.7	(17) 3.1
							1.6	1.6
		.1				Fixed/Worth	.3	.2
		.4					.5	.6
		1.0					1.2	1.4
		.5				Debt/Worth	1.0	1.0
		2.2					1.5	1.6
		7.6					3.5	2.9
		55.3				% Profit Before Taxes/Tangible Net Worth	58.0	49.6
		(21) 23.4					(47) 34.4	(40) 29.8
		9.0					19.4	9.1
		18.3				% Profit Before Taxes/Total Assets	21.6	19.5
		9.5					11.3	10.5
		4.7					5.2	1.6
		42.8				Sales/Net Fixed Assets	26.5	28.5
		14.1					10.4	9.6
		6.4					6.1	4.5
		2.6				Sales/Total Assets	2.5	2.3
		2.2					2.0	1.8
		1.5					1.6	1.3
		1.0				% Depr., Dep., Amort./Sales	.9	.9
		(19) 1.6					(49) 1.5	(41) 1.6
		2.6					2.3	2.1
		3.1				% Officers', Directors' Owners' Comp/Sales		
		(12) 4.7						
		8.1						
1136M	24469M	222227M	404876M	74920M	1696837M	Net Sales ($)	2535000M	1962418M
336M	9075M	112082M	237765M	52957M	1110907M	Total Assets ($)	1376943M	1189963M

© RMA 2011

M = $ thousand   MM = $ million
See Pages 9 through 22 for Explanation of Ratios and Data

Comparative Historical Data | | | | Current Data Sorted by Sales

			Type of Statement						
8	10	9	Unqualified				2	2	5
10	8	6	Reviewed		1		3	1	1
9	3	3	Compiled				2	1	
8	8	8	Tax Returns			1	3	2	
21	20	22	Other	2	1	1	5	3	10
4/1/08-3/31/09 ALL	4/1/09-3/31/10 ALL	4/1/10-3/31/11 ALL			12 (4/1-9/30/10)		36 (10/1/10-3/31/11)		
				0-1MM	1-3MM	3-5MM	5-10MM	10-25MM	25MM & OVER
56	49	48	NUMBER OF STATEMENTS	3	2	3	15	9	16
%	%	%	ASSETS	%	%	%	%	%	%
12.2	13.8	12.3	Cash & Equivalents				13.2		10.6
27.6	24.2	33.7	Trade Receivables (net)				37.7		26.5
23.6	22.6	21.3	Inventory				23.7		17.9
2.1	3.8	4.5	All Other Current				2.9		6.8
65.5	64.5	71.9	Total Current				77.5		61.9
24.1	22.5	18.8	Fixed Assets (net)				14.3		27.2
6.0	6.7	5.0	Intangibles (net)				1.9		5.6
4.3	6.3	4.4	All Other Non-Current				6.3		5.3
100.0	100.0	100.0	Total				100.0		100.0
			LIABILITIES						
9.0	5.8	6.9	Notes Payable-Short Term				12.3		6.0
1.6	1.7	2.5	Cur. Mat.-L.T.D.				3.9		1.2
14.4	9.8	14.0	Trade Payables				13.3		11.4
.4	.2	.5	Income Taxes Payable				.5		.8
13.7	13.3	16.2	All Other Current				17.4		11.9
39.1	30.8	40.1	Total Current				47.4		31.3
14.9	10.0	8.9	Long-Term Debt				6.1		11.4
.5	.6	.7	Deferred Taxes				.6		1.3
8.9	5.8	5.4	All Other Non-Current				.5		4.8
36.6	52.8	44.9	Net Worth				45.3		51.3
100.0	100.0	100.0	Total Liabilities & Net Worth				100.0		100.0
			INCOME DATA						
100.0	100.0	100.0	Net Sales				100.0		100.0
30.6	36.4	32.6	Gross Profit				33.1		27.6
25.1	29.9	25.8	Operating Expenses				26.8		20.9
5.5	6.5	6.8	Operating Profit				6.3		6.8
.4	.4	.8	All Other Expenses (net)				.3		1.4
5.1	6.1	6.0	Profit Before Taxes				6.0		5.4
			RATIOS						
2.7	4.2	2.7	Current				2.7		3.6
1.6	2.1	1.9					1.8		1.9
1.2	1.4	1.3					1.1		1.4
1.7	2.0	1.7	Quick				1.7		1.9
1.0	1.2	1.1					1.1		1.2
.7	.9	.9					.9		.8
29 12.8	34 10.8	47 7.8	Sales/Receivables				45 8.2		51 7.1
44 8.4	46 7.9	56 6.5					51 7.1		60 6.1
59 6.2	61 6.0	73 5.0					84 4.4		66 5.5
28 12.9	35 10.5	26 13.8	Cost of Sales/Inventory				13 28.8		38 9.7
55 6.7	72 5.1	64 5.7					55 6.6		49 7.4
79 4.6	94 3.9	92 4.0					92 4.0		86 4.2
13 28.2	13 27.4	23 15.8	Cost of Sales/Payables				20 17.8		24 15.4
23 16.1	29 12.7	31 11.9					30 12.4		32 11.4
39 9.4	40 9.1	48 7.6					42 8.6		48 7.6
5.5	3.6	3.9	Sales/Working Capital				4.2		3.9
9.6	5.9	6.2					6.5		5.9
19.4	11.3	12.3					28.0		10.9
24.1	27.6	41.2	EBIT/Interest				40.5		46.6
(49) 7.2	(45) 9.4	(41) 11.3					(12) 18.0	(14)	7.0
2.4	2.3	3.2					3.5		2.6
12.7	13.7	9.3	Net Profit + Depr., Dep., Amort./Cur. Mat. L/T/D						
(19) 6.1	(13) 8.4	(13) 4.2							
2.3	1.9	1.5							
.3	.2	.2	Fixed/Worth				.1		.4
.6	.5	.4					.2		.6
2.6	.8	1.0					.7		.9
.7	.4	.6	Debt/Worth				.6		.4
1.9	1.1	1.2					1.1		1.0
19.4	2.3	4.3					3.9		2.7
48.8	34.7	55.3	% Profit Before Taxes/Tangible Net Worth				57.7		40.2
(44) 24.0	(46) 19.4	(45) 23.4					15.9	(15)	21.9
12.3	7.0	8.9					9.2		3.0
17.9	16.4	18.6	% Profit Before Taxes/Total Assets				22.7		15.6
10.4	7.9	9.7					9.9		8.9
4.0	2.5	3.4					4.7		1.8
27.3	23.0	35.8	Sales/Net Fixed Assets				42.8		10.9
10.9	9.9	10.6					20.7		5.1
5.5	5.0	4.9					8.0		3.9
2.8	2.5	2.6	Sales/Total Assets				2.7		2.1
2.4	1.8	2.1					2.2		1.5
1.7	1.4	1.4					1.9		1.3
.9	1.4	1.0	% Depr., Dep., Amort./Sales				.9		1.7
(49) 1.4	(41) 1.8	(40) 1.7					(10) 1.3	(13)	2.4
2.2	2.7	2.8					2.4		3.4
	3.6	3.1	% Officers', Directors' Owners' Comp/Sales						
	(14) 5.1	(16) 4.8							
	6.5	8.0							
2503145M	2027850M	2424465M	Net Sales ($)	1912M	4179M	11805M	105432M	136424M	2164713M
1263358M	1323571M	1523122M	Total Assets ($)	5085M	3685M	5074M	51526M	68807M	1388945M

M = $ thousand   MM = $ million
See Pages 9 through 22 for Explanation of Ratios and Data

Current Data Sorted by Assets							Comparative Historical Data	

0-500M	500M-2MM	2-10MM	10-50MM	50-100MM	100-250MM	Type of Statement	4/1/06-3/31/07 ALL	4/1/07-3/31/08 ALL
		6	12	4	1	Unqualified	30	22
	2	14	5	1		Reviewed	16	20
	1	4	3			Compiled	12	8
	2	4				Tax Returns	6	6
2	3	7	8	1	2	Other	25	20
		22 (4/1-9/30/10)		60 (10/1/10-3/31/11)				
2	8	35	28	6	3	**NUMBER OF STATEMENTS**	89	76
%	%	%	%	%	%	**ASSETS**	%	%
		9.7	7.9			Cash & Equivalents	11.9	8.7
		33.2	29.8			Trade Receivables (net)	26.9	26.4
		29.6	28.7			Inventory	31.1	32.6
		2.7	4.0			All Other Current	3.6	4.9
		75.2	70.4			Total Current	73.5	72.6
		12.8	16.1			Fixed Assets (net)	16.2	15.9
		2.9	6.2			Intangibles (net)	4.4	4.9
		9.1	7.3			All Other Non-Current	5.8	6.6
		100.0	100.0			Total	100.0	100.0
						LIABILITIES		
		10.4	8.6			Notes Payable-Short Term	9.7	9.9
		2.6	2.8			Cur. Mat.-L.T.D.	2.6	3.5
		15.6	16.8			Trade Payables	15.7	15.2
		.6	.1			Income Taxes Payable	.4	.3
		14.4	15.4			All Other Current	12.3	16.1
		43.7	43.7			Total Current	40.7	45.1
		8.4	6.4			Long-Term Debt	11.0	12.3
		.0	.9			Deferred Taxes	.4	.5
		4.8	12.3			All Other Non-Current	8.0	5.5
		43.1	36.6			Net Worth	39.9	36.6
		100.0	100.0			Total Liabilities & Net Worth	100.0	100.0
						INCOME DATA		
		100.0	100.0			Net Sales	100.0	100.0
		35.3	31.1			Gross Profit	30.6	30.4
		27.6	25.7			Operating Expenses	25.3	25.2
		7.6	5.4			Operating Profit	5.3	5.2
		.7	1.2			All Other Expenses (net)	1.2	1.5
		6.9	4.1			Profit Before Taxes	4.2	3.7
						RATIOS		
		3.0	2.3			Current	3.2	2.6
		1.6	1.9				1.9	1.7
		1.2	1.1				1.3	1.2
		1.4	1.6			Quick	1.8	1.2
		.8	.9				.9	.8
		.5	.5				.5	.5
		34 10.8	43 8.5			Sales/Receivables	36 10.1	36 10.3
		49 7.4	53 6.9				44 8.4	49 7.5
		68 5.3	72 5.1				60 6.1	63 5.8
		30 12.0	51 7.1			Cost of Sales/Inventory	39 9.4	51 7.2
		82 4.5	73 5.0				77 4.7	88 4.1
		120 3.0	103 3.5				130 2.8	131 2.8
		15 23.7	26 13.8			Cost of Sales/Payables	18 20.3	20 18.5
		31 11.8	39 9.4				33 10.9	37 9.9
		54 6.7	55 6.6				49 7.4	53 6.9
		5.0	3.9			Sales/Working Capital	4.1	4.1
		7.4	6.2				6.4	7.8
		18.1	28.1				15.2	19.2
		24.5	19.3			EBIT/Interest	13.0	13.1
		(30) 7.1	(27) 8.4				(73) 4.5	(69) 5.0
		2.6	4.4				.8	1.0
			9.6			Net Profit + Depr., Dep., Amort./Cur. Mat. L/T/D	6.7	19.8
		(12)	6.0				(27) 2.3	(30) 3.8
			1.9				.7	.9
		.1	.2			Fixed/Worth	.1	.2
		.3	.5				.3	.4
		1.1	1.1				1.4	1.4
		.8	.7			Debt/Worth	.7	.9
		1.5	2.3				1.5	2.2
		4.0	7.6				5.1	4.5
		70.4	48.3			% Profit Before Taxes/Tangible Net Worth	54.6	48.3
		(33) 19.1	(25) 24.8				(78) 29.3	(67) 18.1
		8.7	6.9				5.6	.3
		20.2	13.8			% Profit Before Taxes/Total Assets	21.3	15.9
		8.3	7.6				7.6	5.6
		3.1	1.6				1.0	.0
		49.9	36.7			Sales/Net Fixed Assets	46.7	41.1
		21.9	22.1				17.2	16.6
		14.6	7.5				6.2	6.3
		2.8	2.7			Sales/Total Assets	2.8	2.7
		2.2	2.0				2.1	1.9
		1.4	1.3				1.5	1.4
		.7	.8			% Depr., Dep., Amort./Sales	.6	.7
		(28) 1.1	(26) 1.2				(73) 1.2	(67) 1.3
		2.2	2.6				1.9	2.4
		1.6				% Officers', Directors' Owners' Comp/Sales	1.8	1.7
		(11) 4.2					(22) 6.7	(15) 2.8
		9.7					13.5	6.1
1876M	29334M	402206M	1208054M	531968M	585204M	Net Sales ($)	3616266M	3529520M
621M	9760M	175934M	652266M	363559M	351150M	Total Assets ($)	2182365M	2123172M

M = $ thousand   MM = $ million
See Pages 9 through 22 for Explanation of Ratios and Data

Comparative Historical Data | Current Data Sorted by Sales

			Type of Statement						
19	19	23	Unqualified			1		6	16
17	23	22	Reviewed	1	2		9	4	6
13	6	8	Compiled	1	2	2	2	1	2
7	4	6	Tax Returns		1	1	2	2	
37	30	23	Other	2	3		3	4	11
4/1/08-3/31/09	4/1/09-3/31/10	4/1/10-3/31/11		22 (4/1-9/30/10)			60 (10/1/10-3/31/11)		
ALL	ALL	ALL		0-1MM	1-3MM	3-5MM	5-10MM	10-25MM	25MM & OVER
93	82	82	**NUMBER OF STATEMENTS**	2	6	6	16	17	35
%	%	%	**ASSETS**	%	%	%	%	%	%
9.9	10.5	10.8	Cash & Equivalents				9.9	10.0	10.2
27.2	26.6	30.6	Trade Receivables (net)				33.7	32.6	30.7
29.5	31.8	27.9	Inventory				19.3	28.4	25.9
4.1	3.7	3.7	All Other Current				3.9	3.2	5.1
70.8	72.6	73.1	Total Current				66.7	74.2	71.9
19.2	17.4	14.6	Fixed Assets (net)				16.6	11.8	16.7
3.3	3.6	5.1	Intangibles (net)				3.7	6.4	6.3
6.7	6.4	7.1	All Other Non-Current				13.0	7.6	5.1
100.0	100.0	100.0	Total				100.0	100.0	100.0
			LIABILITIES						
13.6	12.1	10.5	Notes Payable-Short Term				16.0	8.2	7.5
2.6	2.5	2.9	Cur. Mat.-L.T.D.				1.3	3.9	3.0
12.8	13.2	15.8	Trade Payables				15.3	13.1	17.9
.4	.2	.4	Income Taxes Payable				1.3	.1	.2
14.4	12.8	13.9	All Other Current				13.4	17.8	15.2
43.9	40.8	43.4	Total Current				47.2	43.1	43.8
11.2	10.8	7.8	Long-Term Debt				4.6	10.4	7.1
.4	.5	.4	Deferred Taxes				.0	.3	.7
6.9	8.1	9.1	All Other Non-Current				8.0	6.7	11.0
37.6	39.7	39.4	Net Worth				40.1	39.5	37.4
100.0	100.0	100.0	Total Liabilities & Net Worth				100.0	100.0	100.0
			INCOME DATA						
100.0	100.0	100.0	Net Sales				100.0	100.0	100.0
30.6	32.2	32.8	Gross Profit				33.6	37.2	28.7
25.4	26.9	26.8	Operating Expenses				27.0	28.2	23.6
5.2	5.3	6.0	Operating Profit				6.6	9.0	5.1
1.0	1.1	1.0	All Other Expenses (net)				.6	.6	1.3
4.2	4.2	5.0	Profit Before Taxes				5.9	8.4	3.7
			RATIOS						
2.6	3.0	2.5					2.3	2.8	2.3
1.7	2.0	1.8	Current				1.4	1.9	1.8
1.3	1.3	1.2					1.0	1.3	1.2
1.3	1.7	1.7					1.9	1.7	1.4
.9	.9	.9	Quick				1.0	1.1	.9
.5	.5	.5					.5	.5	.5
31 / 11.8	34 / 10.8	37 / 9.8					33 / 11.0	36 / 10.2	40 / 9.1
44 / 8.4	44 / 8.4	50 / 7.4	Sales/Receivables				48 / 7.7	50 / 7.2	50 / 7.3
60 / 6.1	57 / 6.4	67 / 5.5					69 / 5.3	70 / 5.2	64 / 5.7
45 / 8.1	46 / 8.0	34 / 10.8					7 / 55.6	48 / 7.7	33 / 10.9
73 / 5.0	94 / 3.9	69 / 5.3	Cost of Sales/Inventory				42 / 8.8	82 / 4.4	63 / 5.8
111 / 3.3	129 / 2.8	107 / 3.4					116 / 3.2	107 / 3.4	90 / 4.0
12 / 29.4	18 / 20.1	19 / 19.6					19 / 19.7	15 / 24.4	26 / 14.2
27 / 13.4	28 / 13.1	33 / 11.2	Cost of Sales/Payables				30 / 12.3	26 / 13.9	37 / 10.0
41 / 9.0	44 / 8.3	53 / 6.9					53 / 6.8	43 / 8.6	53 / 6.9
4.6	3.7	3.9					7.1	5.1	4.8
7.3	6.3	7.0	Sales/Working Capital				10.7	7.0	6.4
17.6	12.4	23.4					NM	21.3	23.2
12.3	20.8	19.5					21.8	40.4	23.9
(83) 3.6	(75) 5.4	(72) 7.3	EBIT/Interest				(13) 3.8	10.8	(33) 7.9
1.5	1.6	2.0					1.2	5.2	2.0
5.5	9.6	8.8							11.6
(22) 2.7	(20) 2.4	(22) 4.0	Net Profit + Depr., Dep., Amort./Cur. Mat. L/T/D						(16) 5.9
1.3	.5	.7							.9
.2	.2	.1					.1	.2	.2
.5	.5	.5	Fixed/Worth				.3	.4	.5
1.2	1.1	1.1					1.0	7.7	1.4
.8	.6	.7					.7	.8	.7
1.6	1.6	1.6	Debt/Worth				2.3	1.2	1.9
4.2	5.6	5.4					3.5	95.0	7.9
48.8	44.0	51.0					28.9	83.9	51.1
(85) 16.6	(72) 10.6	(73) 19.1	% Profit Before Taxes/Tangible Net Worth				(15) 15.4	(14) 42.0	(32) 26.3
4.1	3.1	7.8					3.8	16.9	7.7
14.0	17.0	15.2					14.5	23.5	15.0
6.2	4.4	7.6	% Profit Before Taxes/Total Assets				6.6	8.9	7.6
1.1	.9	1.1					.7	6.3	1.1
35.1	31.8	63.9					59.1	42.6	37.2
18.4	16.3	23.6	Sales/Net Fixed Assets				17.0	31.3	22.4
5.8	5.0	7.9					6.3	14.2	7.4
2.8	2.7	2.7					2.7	2.9	2.7
2.0	1.8	2.1	Sales/Total Assets				2.4	2.2	2.2
1.5	1.3	1.4					1.2	1.8	1.5
.6	.8	.7					1.1	.8	.7
(82) 1.2	(68) 1.4	(69) 1.1	% Depr., Dep., Amort./Sales				(12) 1.6	(15) 1.1	(32) 1.1
2.6	2.6	2.5					3.0	1.5	2.6
2.7	1.1	1.6							
(20) 4.1	(17) 3.2	(20) 3.7	% Officers', Directors' Owners' Comp/Sales						
7.5	5.0	9.2							
3643920M	3527014M	2758642M	Net Sales ($)	1264M	10755M	24578M	121356M	285281M	2315408M
1880668M	1998068M	1553290M	Total Assets ($)	1087M	7560M	15251M	102098M	154847M	1272447M

© RMA 2011   M = $ thousand   MM = $ million
See Pages 9 through 22 for Explanation of Ratios and Data

Current Data Sorted by Assets   Comparative Historical Data

Type of Statement

	0-500M	500M-2MM	2-10MM	10-50MM	50-100MM	100-250MM	4/1/06-3/31/07 ALL	4/1/07-3/31/08 ALL
Unqualified		2	2	18	2	5	43	33
Reviewed		4	19	5	1		21	16
Compiled		3	8			1	16	9
Tax Returns	1	3	2				9	7
Other		3	20	21	1	3	32	46
		21 (4/1-9/30/10)	103 (10/1/10-3/31/11)					
NUMBER OF STATEMENTS	1	15	51	44	4	9	121	111

	0-500M	500M-2MM	2-10MM	10-50MM	50-100MM	100-250MM	4/1/06-3/31/07 ALL	4/1/07-3/31/08 ALL
	%	%	%	%	%	%	%	%
ASSETS								
Cash & Equivalents		10.4	11.2	9.0			9.6	7.9
Trade Receivables (net)		40.3	33.5	25.1			31.3	31.3
Inventory		18.7	29.9	24.5			25.6	27.8
All Other Current		5.9	3.6	3.8			2.9	3.4
Total Current		75.4	78.3	62.4			69.3	70.4
Fixed Assets (net)		12.2	13.6	24.5			19.0	17.7
Intangibles (net)		4.5	4.3	7.8			6.2	5.4
All Other Non-Current		8.0	3.9	5.3			5.5	6.5
Total		100.0	100.0	100.0			100.0	100.0
LIABILITIES								
Notes Payable-Short Term		13.0	10.4	5.7			10.7	8.9
Cur. Mat.-L.T.D.		4.4	2.3	1.7			2.2	2.4
Trade Payables		25.0	17.0	12.8			17.2	15.9
Income Taxes Payable		1.0	1.0	.1			.6	.2
All Other Current		11.0	14.0	11.6			13.4	12.2
Total Current		54.3	44.7	31.9			44.2	39.6
Long-Term Debt		13.7	10.6	10.7			14.7	14.2
Deferred Taxes		.5	.4	.4			.7	.9
All Other Non-Current		4.2	4.2	8.0			6.0	4.7
Net Worth		27.2	40.1	49.0			34.4	40.7
Total Liabilities & Net Worth		100.0	100.0	100.0			100.0	100.0
INCOME DATA								
Net Sales		100.0	100.0	100.0			100.0	100.0
Gross Profit		31.7	29.9	27.5			28.4	29.0
Operating Expenses		28.3	23.5	22.0			22.8	22.9
Operating Profit		3.4	6.4	5.4			5.6	6.1
All Other Expenses (net)		1.0	.9	1.0			1.1	1.1
Profit Before Taxes		2.4	5.6	4.4			4.4	5.0
RATIOS								
Current		1.9	3.3	3.3			2.4	2.9
		1.5	1.8	1.9			1.6	1.9
		1.2	1.2	1.3			1.2	1.3
Quick		1.3	2.1	2.0			1.5	1.5
		.9	1.1	1.0			1.0	1.0
		.7	.5	.5			.6	.6
Sales/Receivables	22 16.9	31 11.8	34 10.8				34 10.9	33 11.1
	40 9.2	46 7.9	44 8.4				45 8.1	47 7.8
	73 5.0	68 5.4	68 5.3				58 6.3	62 5.9
Cost of Sales/Inventory	4 102.6	26 13.8	43 8.5				23 15.7	31 11.6
	26 14.2	71 5.1	62 5.9				54 6.7	63 5.8
	40 9.1	103 3.6	104 3.5				91 4.0	102 3.6
Cost of Sales/Payables	17 21.7	21 17.0	14 25.7				17 21.1	19 19.5
	34 10.6	32 11.4	26 13.9				31 11.9	27 13.3
	46 7.9	56 6.6	40 9.1				46 7.9	44 8.4
Sales/Working Capital		7.2	3.8	3.6			5.4	4.5
		13.4	7.0	7.3			9.5	7.5
		28.6	21.1	17.3			26.9	13.4
EBIT/Interest		10.5	29.3	50.5			13.9	21.0
	(14) 3.4	(43) 7.0	(39) 8.3				(107) 5.4	(101) 4.9
		1.4	2.0	1.8			1.8	1.5
Net Profit + Depr., Dep., Amort./Cur. Mat. L/T/D				16.5			11.7	11.4
			(16) 5.9				(45) 4.6	(41) 3.2
				1.8			1.4	1.1
Fixed/Worth		.1	.1	.3			.2	.2
		.5	.3	.6			.5	.4
		3.8	.9	1.2			1.8	1.2
Debt/Worth		1.0	.7	.4			.8	.6
		1.7	1.7	1.3			1.8	1.8
		30.7	5.0	2.8			6.8	4.1
% Profit Before Taxes/Tangible Net Worth		108.2	46.8	36.2			60.5	57.9
	(12) 37.6	(46) 28.0	(40) 17.5				(99) 31.5	(95) 24.4
		4.9	10.4	4.3			16.0	8.4
% Profit Before Taxes/Total Assets		15.9	17.7	14.9			19.5	18.0
		4.6	8.0	6.9			9.1	9.5
		1.6	2.4	1.6			2.9	1.9
Sales/Net Fixed Assets		78.9	48.0	21.5			41.6	43.5
		23.5	24.9	10.6			15.2	14.7
		16.7	9.7	3.3			7.1	6.7
Sales/Total Assets		4.5	2.9	2.6			3.4	3.2
		3.6	2.4	1.9			2.4	2.2
		2.3	1.7	1.2			1.6	1.5
% Depr., Dep., Amort./Sales		.4	.6	.9			.5	.5
	(10) .9	(43) 1.0	(41) 1.6				(112) 1.3	(97) 1.3
		1.2	1.9	2.5			2.2	2.0
% Officers', Directors' Owners' Comp/Sales			1.1				.8	.8
		(18) 2.3					(31) 2.1	(26) 1.8
			3.7				4.5	5.2
Net Sales ($)	700M	51959M	536819M	1916219M	354365M	2796485M	5283228M	5492622M
Total Assets ($)	405M	16569M	227223M	962955M	250995M	1688568M	3234142M	3049924M

M = $ thousand   MM = $ million
See Pages 9 through 22 for Explanation of Ratios and Data

Comparative Historical Data | Current Data Sorted by Sales

4/1/08-3/31/09 ALL	4/1/09-3/31/10 ALL	4/1/10-3/31/11 ALL	Type of Statement	0-1MM	1-3MM	3-5MM	5-10MM	10-25MM	25MM & OVER
26	26	29	Unqualified		3			7	19
34	22	29	Reviewed		1	5	8	8	7
12	19	12	Compiled		2	2	5	2	1
12	9	6	Tax Returns	1	1	2	2		
50	44	48	Other		4	5	8	12	19
					21 (4/1-9/30/10)		103 (10/1/10-3/31/11)		
134	120	124	**NUMBER OF STATEMENTS**	1	11	14	23	29	46
%	%	%	**ASSETS**	%	%	%	%	%	%
8.3	13.7	9.5	Cash & Equivalents		8.1	13.6	10.0	10.0	8.1
28.4	29.5	30.5	Trade Receivables (net)		31.1	36.2	35.2	27.4	28.3
30.1	25.7	26.3	Inventory		22.0	19.9	28.8	28.6	25.8
4.0	3.3	3.8	All Other Current		6.9	2.3	3.7	3.0	4.2
70.8	72.2	70.1	Total Current		68.2	72.0	77.7	69.1	66.5
19.5	17.7	18.4	Fixed Assets (net)		13.7	16.9	15.3	19.7	20.9
6.0	5.6	6.0	Intangibles (net)		13.0	4.7	1.6	7.8	6.0
3.8	4.4	5.5	All Other Non-Current		5.1	6.4	5.4	3.4	6.7
100.0	100.0	100.0	Total		100.0	100.0	100.0	100.0	100.0
			LIABILITIES						
9.7	7.1	8.5	Notes Payable-Short Term		8.2	9.7	11.5	9.3	6.3
4.0	3.2	2.4	Cur. Mat.-L.T.D.		3.4	3.5	3.1	1.7	1.5
14.0	13.3	16.1	Trade Payables		23.0	14.3	19.0	13.3	15.5
.4	.7	.6	Income Taxes Payable		.2	3.8	.3	.3	.1
11.9	12.1	12.5	All Other Current		8.1	13.4	12.5	11.7	13.8
40.0	36.5	40.0	Total Current		42.9	44.8	46.4	36.4	37.1
12.5	11.4	11.3	Long-Term Debt		20.6	7.9	10.8	10.9	9.9
.7	.9	.5	Deferred Taxes		.7	.8	.3	.4	.6
4.8	7.5	6.6	All Other Non-Current		7.7	3.5	3.1	5.5	9.9
42.1	43.7	41.6	Net Worth		28.1	43.0	39.4	46.8	42.5
100.0	100.0	100.0	Total Liabilities & Net Worth		100.0	100.0	100.0	100.0	100.0
			INCOME DATA						
100.0	100.0	100.0	Net Sales		100.0	100.0	100.0	100.0	100.0
30.7	30.1	28.7	Gross Profit		41.4	32.0	28.1	28.3	25.2
24.3	24.7	23.2	Operating Expenses		30.5	26.6	23.7	22.5	20.1
6.5	5.4	5.6	Operating Profit		10.9	5.4	4.4	5.8	5.1
1.0	.7	1.0	All Other Expenses (net)		2.5	1.3	.4	.9	.8
5.5	4.7	4.6	Profit Before Taxes		8.5	4.1	4.0	4.9	4.2
			RATIOS						
2.6	3.6	2.7	Current		2.0	3.8	2.7	3.2	2.5
1.8	2.0	1.8			1.8	1.7	1.7	2.0	1.8
1.4	1.4	1.3			1.4	1.0	1.3	1.2	1.2
1.4	2.3	1.5	Quick		1.3	3.0	2.1	1.6	1.5
.9	1.2	1.0			.9	1.1	1.1	1.0	1.0
.5	.8	.5			.5	.5	.4	.6	.6
28 12.9	31 11.7	33 11.0	Sales/Receivables	30 12.3	25 14.5	34 10.7	38 9.7	31 11.7	
39 9.5	42 8.6	46 7.9		49 7.4	43 8.5	57 6.4	46 7.9	45 8.2	
57 6.4	54 6.7	69 5.3		73 5.0	85 4.3	73 5.0	71 5.2	61 6.0	
30 12.1	26 14.1	32 11.3	Cost of Sales/Inventory	5 74.6	5 74.0	35 10.4	50 7.3	36 10.1	
64 5.7	57 6.3	65 5.6		68 5.3	39 9.3	71 5.1	77 4.7	59 6.2	
109 3.3	100 3.6	99 3.7		138 2.6	92 4.0	96 3.8	109 3.4	83 4.4	
16 22.9	14 26.5	19 19.3	Cost of Sales/Payables	46 7.9	14 26.2	22 16.4	22 16.9	17 21.6	
28 13.1	28 13.1	30 12.2		50 7.4	33 11.2	32 11.4	30 12.1	26 13.9	
41 9.0	37 10.0	48 7.7		156 2.3	41 9.0	59 6.2	43 8.5	46 8.0	
4.7	3.7	4.0	Sales/Working Capital		5.7	3.5	4.0	3.9	4.4
7.9	7.2	7.7			9.2	8.5	7.0	5.5	8.4
16.9	15.9	17.3			15.6	-494.4	12.8	16.8	16.2
23.4	22.6	25.1	EBIT/Interest			19.3	10.1	33.2	37.7
(120) 7.0	(104) 7.2	(110) 7.0			(13) 7.5	(18) 4.1	(26) 5.4		(43) 9.2
2.6	1.3	1.7				1.2	1.7	1.5	3.0
14.3	12.8	10.8	Net Profit + Depr., Dep., Amort./Cur. Mat. L/T/D						15.9
(41) 5.6	(32) 3.5	(38) 4.2						(21)	8.3
1.8	1.0	1.8							2.8
.2	.2	.2	Fixed/Worth		.1	.2	.2	.1	.3
.5	.4	.5			.6	.4	.3	.5	.5
1.2	1.1	1.2			-.3	1.4	.9	1.1	1.1
.7	.5	.7	Debt/Worth		1.0	.5	.6	.6	.7
1.6	1.4	1.5			4.5	1.5	1.6	1.5	1.4
3.2	3.7	3.8			-3.6	5.1	7.5	3.9	2.9
57.6	46.5	40.6	% Profit Before Taxes/Tangible Net Worth			44.1	34.8	40.2	49.7
(120) 27.8	(107) 19.2	(110) 21.8			(13) 24.5	(20) 22.6	(27) 15.0	(41) 21.5	
11.5	5.1	7.2				4.8	6.9	3.8	10.0
18.9	18.4	15.6	% Profit Before Taxes/Total Assets		15.9	17.6	13.5	15.6	15.7
10.2	7.9	6.7			10.2	5.7	4.3	7.0	9.5
3.4	.9	2.2			2.1	1.6	1.6	1.0	4.4
36.5	40.2	36.0	Sales/Net Fixed Assets		36.1	61.1	43.2	39.4	24.7
15.1	17.1	14.7			18.5	15.3	29.3	14.9	11.3
7.0	8.1	7.7			8.1	5.7	9.7	3.0	7.5
3.1	3.1	2.9	Sales/Total Assets		3.6	4.0	2.9	2.7	3.0
2.2	2.2	2.1			1.6	2.1	2.2	2.1	2.1
1.6	1.6	1.4			.5	1.4	1.8	1.2	1.5
.6	.6	.7	% Depr., Dep., Amort./Sales			.3	.6	.7	.9
(116) 1.2	(99) 1.3	(108) 1.3			(12) .9	(19) 1.2	(26) 1.3	(44) 1.5	
2.1	2.5	2.2				1.6	2.4	2.1	2.5
1.1	1.7	1.3	% Officers', Directors' Owners' Comp/Sales				1.2		
(19) 2.3	(30) 2.9	(31) 2.8				(10)	2.3		
7.3	5.1	6.0					3.2		
5512865M	4427381M	5656547M	Net Sales ($)	700M	26781M	55904M	186473M	468358M	4918331M
2921438M	2383913M	3146715M	Total Assets ($)	405M	28068M	27369M	90079M	302683M	2698111M

M = $ thousand   MM = $ million
See Pages 9 through 22 for Explanation of Ratios and Data

Current Data Sorted by Assets   Comparative Historical Data

0-500M	500M-2MM	2-10MM	10-50MM	50-100MM	100-250MM		4/1/06-3/31/07 ALL	4/1/07-3/31/08 ALL
			4	1		Type of Statement		
						Unqualified	16	10
	6	21	15			Reviewed	51	41
5	15	16	1			Compiled	26	28
8	2	6				Tax Returns	18	17
5	16	14	9	3	1	Other	55	35
36 (4/1-9/30/10)			112 (10/1/10-3/31/11)					
18	39	57	29	4	1	NUMBER OF STATEMENTS	166	131
%	%	%	%	%	%	ASSETS	%	%
14.8	8.5	10.4	6.6			Cash & Equivalents	8.0	7.1
26.9	27.9	28.7	25.5			Trade Receivables (net)	28.6	26.8
20.0	19.1	21.0	17.2			Inventory	17.0	16.9
.8	4.0	1.6	6.1			All Other Current	3.7	2.7
62.5	59.5	61.7	55.4			Total Current	57.2	53.5
31.2	33.1	30.4	36.8			Fixed Assets (net)	35.2	37.3
.1	2.4	3.7	4.2			Intangibles (net)	2.9	3.4
6.2	5.0	4.2	3.6			All Other Non-Current	4.7	5.8
100.0	100.0	100.0	100.0			Total	100.0	100.0
						LIABILITIES		
22.9	13.1	8.5	9.3			Notes Payable-Short Term	9.2	9.1
5.3	4.5	4.5	5.5			Cur. Mat.-L.T.D.	4.9	5.9
10.8	11.9	13.5	11.3			Trade Payables	12.7	12.5
.6	.2	.4	.1			Income Taxes Payable	.2	.2
8.5	7.7	10.5	11.9			All Other Current	11.8	10.5
48.2	37.3	37.4	38.1			Total Current	38.7	38.2
25.2	21.3	15.1	18.9			Long-Term Debt	19.6	22.1
.0	.4	.4	.8			Deferred Taxes	.8	1.0
17.0	14.1	6.8	2.0			All Other Non-Current	5.9	6.8
9.6	26.8	40.3	40.1			Net Worth	35.0	32.0
100.0	100.0	100.0	100.0			Total Liabilities & Net Worth	100.0	100.0
						INCOME DATA		
100.0	100.0	100.0	100.0			Net Sales	100.0	100.0
46.5	29.0	26.8	21.9			Gross Profit	28.8	28.0
45.0	26.8	22.6	15.3			Operating Expenses	23.7	24.4
1.5	2.2	4.2	6.6			Operating Profit	5.1	3.6
.4	.8	.6	2.6			All Other Expenses (net)	1.3	1.5
1.1	1.4	3.6	4.0			Profit Before Taxes	3.9	2.1
						RATIOS		
3.0	2.2	2.7	2.8				2.2	1.9
1.8	1.5	1.8	1.5			Current	1.5	1.5
.8	1.1	1.3	1.1				1.1	1.0
3.1	1.4	1.7	1.8				1.5	1.2
(17) 1.2	1.0	1.2	.9			Quick	.9	.9
.4	.6	.7	.5				.6	.6
0 UND	37 10.0	37 9.9	46 8.0				35 10.5	33 10.9
40 9.2	48 7.6	58 6.3	63 5.8			Sales/Receivables	49 7.4	47 7.7
51 7.2	64 5.7	77 4.7	94 3.9				63 5.8	63 5.8
0 UND	19 18.8	24 15.0	32 11.4				17 21.7	16 22.3
14 26.6	34 10.8	42 8.6	45 8.1			Cost of Sales/Inventory	39 9.3	38 9.5
53 6.9	53 6.9	90 4.1	78 4.7				66 5.6	59 6.2
0 UND	14 25.9	17 21.1	20 18.7				15 24.6	15 24.3
14 26.2	26 13.8	28 12.9	38 9.7			Cost of Sales/Payables	25 14.3	26 13.8
39 9.5	34 10.6	49 7.4	57 6.4				40 9.2	43 8.5
9.3	5.1	3.7	4.3				6.3	6.7
14.9	11.8	6.3	7.4			Sales/Working Capital	11.9	13.8
-17.8	82.1	24.4	22.5				72.9	343.4
6.0	5.6	11.8	13.1				8.4	5.9
(15) 1.6	(34) 3.0	(52) 4.7	3.8			EBIT/Interest	(154) 2.8	(126) 2.3
1.0	1.2	1.1	1.9				1.3	.1
		3.9	3.4				4.2	3.2
		(17) 2.2	(13) 2.0			Net Profit + Depr., Dep., Amort./Cur. Mat. L/T/D	(43) 2.0	(37) 2.0
		.9	1.2				1.4	1.3
.1	.3	.4	.6				.6	.6
2.0	1.0	.7	1.2			Fixed/Worth	1.2	1.4
-.7	3.9	1.8	2.1				2.4	3.6
.9	1.0	.6	.7				1.0	1.0
3.6	2.5	1.2	2.5			Debt/Worth	2.1	2.1
-3.8	-12.7	3.5	4.9				5.8	7.5
18.2	60.2	41.0	32.7				42.1	37.6
(11) 4.1	(34) 22.8	(50) 17.1	14.9			% Profit Before Taxes/Tangible Net Worth	(151) 18.7	(108) 11.8
-18.1	-11.3	5.5	5.9				3.6	-1.2
13.7	16.2	16.8	10.7				14.1	11.9
1.4	3.7	6.6	5.2			% Profit Before Taxes/Total Assets	4.7	3.7
-1.4	-4.7	.7	1.6				.7	-1.6
UND	23.0	10.3	5.2				12.7	11.4
9.6	7.6	5.7	4.2			Sales/Net Fixed Assets	5.6	5.7
5.2	3.3	3.8	2.1				3.4	3.1
4.8	2.7	2.4	1.5				2.6	2.5
3.2	2.1	1.8	1.2			Sales/Total Assets	1.9	1.8
2.4	1.6	1.2	1.0				1.4	1.4
1.3	.8	2.4	2.4				2.2	2.1
(13) 3.3	(34) 2.9	(54) 3.7	4.0			% Depr., Dep., Amort./Sales	(149) 3.7	(125) 3.8
10.7	7.7	5.9	5.0				5.4	6.3
5.5	3.0	1.7	.8				2.4	2.7
(11) 8.1	(22) 4.9	(25) 3.1	(11) 2.4			% Officers', Directors' Owners' Comp/Sales	(85) 4.5	(64) 5.1
15.4	9.8	5.3	5.6				7.4	7.8
17035M	105658M	435961M	655041M	421878M	267932M	Net Sales ($)	2173992M	1275390M
5070M	47942M	243038M	531927M	292619M	234520M	Total Assets ($)	1260816M	747340M

M = $ thousand   MM = $ million
See Pages 9 through 22 for Explanation of Ratios and Data

Comparative Historical Data | Current Data Sorted by Sales

4/1/08-3/31/09 ALL	4/1/09-3/31/10 ALL	4/1/10-3/31/11 ALL	Type of Statement	0-1MM	1-3MM	3-5MM	5-10MM	10-25MM	25MM & OVER
9	7	5	Unqualified					2	3
35	38	42	Reviewed		7	10	7	15	3
23	21	37	Compiled	7	8	9	6	7	
10	12	16	Tax Returns	5	6	3	2		
54	33	48	Other	3	12	5	9	10	9
				36 (4/1-9/30/10)			112 (10/1/10-3/31/11)		
131	111	148	NUMBER OF STATEMENTS	15	33	27	24	34	15
%	%	%	**ASSETS**	%	%	%	%	%	%
9.3	8.5	9.5	Cash & Equivalents	15.1	10.0	7.7	10.2	10.4	3.3
26.2	24.9	27.2	Trade Receivables (net)	22.6	27.6	27.9	27.2	29.4	24.7
18.0	19.1	19.5	Inventory	12.8	19.8	22.0	23.5	17.8	18.8
2.2	1.7	3.1	All Other Current	1.4	3.7	2.3	1.6	3.4	6.4
55.7	54.2	59.4	Total Current	51.9	61.1	59.9	62.4	61.0	53.3
34.7	36.5	33.1	Fixed Assets (net)	40.8	30.7	30.5	31.4	32.8	39.3
3.7	3.9	2.9	Intangibles (net)	.3	1.8	6.4	3.3	2.0	3.2
5.9	5.4	4.6	All Other Non-Current	7.0	6.5	3.1	2.9	4.2	4.2
100.0	100.0	100.0	Total	100.0	100.0	100.0	100.0	100.0	100.0
			LIABILITIES						
9.4	11.9	11.4	Notes Payable-Short Term	21.6	13.2	8.4	9.9	8.9	10.8
5.5	6.9	4.7	Cur. Mat.-L.T.D.	4.5	4.9	5.6	6.4	3.5	3.1
11.4	12.0	12.0	Trade Payables	11.3	9.0	12.6	10.0	16.6	11.0
.2	.1	.3	Income Taxes Payable	.7	.2	.2	.1	.4	.2
13.1	9.6	9.9	All Other Current	7.7	7.8	9.3	12.3	11.3	10.5
39.6	40.5	38.3	Total Current	45.7	35.1	36.0	38.7	40.8	35.5
23.7	23.5	19.0	Long-Term Debt	30.4	22.6	17.9	10.8	17.0	19.0
.7	.7	.4	Deferred Taxes	.0	.2	.4	.7	.6	.5
7.4	6.4	8.9	All Other Non-Current	23.6	14.5	6.2	6.8	3.4	2.5
28.6	28.9	33.4	Net Worth	.4	27.6	39.4	43.0	38.1	42.5
100.0	100.0	100.0	Total Liabilities & Net Worth	100.0	100.0	100.0	100.0	100.0	100.0
			INCOME DATA						
100.0	100.0	100.0	Net Sales	100.0	100.0	100.0	100.0	100.0	100.0
28.1	27.2	28.8	Gross Profit	44.1	33.9	27.2	29.3	21.1	21.7
25.0	26.2	24.7	Operating Expenses	46.4	30.1	25.3	23.4	15.6	12.7
3.1	1.0	4.1	Operating Profit	-2.3	3.8	1.9	5.9	5.5	9.0
1.3	1.5	1.0	All Other Expenses (net)	1.3	.9	.8	.8	.9	2.0
1.8	-.5	3.1	Profit Before Taxes	-3.6	2.8	1.1	5.1	4.6	7.0
			RATIOS						
2.6	2.3	2.7	Current	2.9	2.7	2.2	2.8	2.4	3.8
1.5	1.4	1.7		1.5	2.0	1.8	2.0	1.5	1.5
1.0	1.0	1.1		.4	1.1	1.0	1.1	1.2	1.1
1.6	1.3	1.7	Quick	2.9	2.4	1.7	1.6	1.7	2.0
.9	.8	(147) 1.1		(32) 1.2	1.2	1.0	1.2	1.1	.8
.6	.6	.6		.3	.7	.5	.7	.8	.5
31 11.6	33 11.1	37 9.9	Sales/Receivables	8 47.0	26 13.8	38 9.6	47 7.8	37 9.9	46 7.9
47 7.7	44 8.3	53 6.9		48 7.6	49 7.4	59 6.2	56 6.5	50 7.3	65 5.6
61 6.0	69 5.3	69 5.3		54 6.0	73 5.0	77 4.7	63 5.7	64 5.7	78 4.7
19 18.8	22 16.8	20 18.0	Cost of Sales/Inventory	4 86.0	13 28.3	29 12.7	27 13.4	24 15.0	35 10.3
39 9.4	40 9.2	37 9.9		15 25.1	36 10.0	41 9.0	71 5.1	33 10.9	51 7.2
69 5.3	79 4.6	76 4.8		34 10.8	85 4.3	63 5.8	105 3.5	52 7.0	74 4.9
13 28.9	13 28.4	15 25.1	Cost of Sales/Payables	12 31.4	6 56.3	13 27.7	21 17.7	19 18.9	14 25.3
22 16.5	27 13.4	27 13.4		31 11.8	26 14.4	25 14.6	23 15.6	33 10.9	30 12.0
36 10.1	46 7.9	43 8.4		49 7.5	33 10.9	51 7.1	44 8.3	55 6.7	47 7.8
5.8	5.2	4.7	Sales/Working Capital	8.8	4.0	4.7	4.2	4.5	5.4
13.4	13.8	9.5		14.3	9.5	10.0	6.1	10.0	8.3
151.7	-135.8	36.2		-8.3	71.6	147.9	35.3	18.5	50.9
5.9	5.4	9.8	EBIT/Interest	1.5	4.8	6.2	17.4	13.2	14.3
(119) 3.2	(103) 1.9	(135) 3.8		(12) 1.1	(30) 2.7	(25) 2.7	(23) 5.8	(30) 5.5	5.8
-.1	-2.2	1.2		-6.0	1.3	-1.3	1.3	2.1	2.6
6.8	2.1	3.8	Net Profit + Depr., Dep., Amort./Cur. Mat. L/T/D				3.8	5.8	
(33) 2.7	(34) 1.4	(41) 2.3					(10) 1.0	(13) 3.0	
1.7	.6	1.0					.1	1.7	
.6	.6	.4	Fixed/Worth	.2	.4	.3	.4	.5	.8
1.4	1.4	1.0		362.0	1.0	.8	.7	1.0	1.1
3.7	3.2	2.5		-.9	2.7	3.2	1.5	1.7	1.9
.9	.9	.8	Debt/Worth	1.9	.9	.7	.6	.7	.9
2.5	2.1	1.9		606.0	2.6	1.7	.9	1.8	1.5
11.1	8.3	6.2		-4.2	7.7	6.1	2.3	3.9	3.8
42.2	31.8	41.7	% Profit Before Taxes/Tangible Net Worth		60.6	33.8	34.2	45.7	59.1
(106) 17.7	(92) 5.8	(129) 17.3			(29) 12.7	(24) 17.3	(22) 11.6	(31) 18.5	25.1
-.5	-13.2	3.8			-5.7	-11.6	4.3	8.4	6.7
13.5	7.4	13.2	% Profit Before Taxes/Total Assets	3.9	13.2	10.4	18.6	13.7	15.8
5.0	1.7	4.7		.6	3.6	7.0	5.0	7.8	9.8
-2.1	-6.4	.4		-27.2	.4	-4.7	.7	2.2	3.9
11.1	10.3	11.4	Sales/Net Fixed Assets	38.3	21.3	11.4	11.4	9.6	5.9
5.6	4.8	5.3		4.9	7.6	5.2	6.6	5.2	3.0
3.6	2.8	3.3		2.6	4.7	3.6	3.5	3.5	2.4
2.5	2.4	2.5	Sales/Total Assets	3.5	2.8	2.4	2.5	2.7	1.9
1.9	1.7	1.8		2.2	2.0	1.9	1.8	1.6	1.4
1.3	1.3	1.2		1.4	1.2	1.2	1.2	1.2	1.1
1.8	2.3	2.2	% Depr., Dep., Amort./Sales	2.6	.7	2.7	2.4	2.3	2.2
(120) 3.6	(105) 4.3	(134) 3.6		(11) 7.0	(30) 2.7	(26) 4.5	(20) 3.6	(33) 3.5	(14) 4.0
5.9	7.3	6.1		12.1	8.4	5.9	7.8	4.9	5.7
2.5	2.0	2.3	% Officers', Directors', Owners' Comp/Sales		3.0	1.9		1.0	
(58) 4.5	(57) 4.2	(69) 4.2			(19) 5.5	(14) 3.4		(16) 2.6	
7.5	6.3	6.5			14.8	5.3		5.1	
1737766M	1508111M	1903505M	Net Sales ($)	9040M	64777M	106171M	158018M	509465M	1056034M
1128144M	1074581M	1355116M	Total Assets ($)	6118M	38620M	87913M	110947M	324920M	786598M

M = $ thousand   MM = $ million
See Pages 9 through 22 for Explanation of Ratios and Data

Current Data Sorted by Assets   Comparative Historical Data

0-500M	500M-2MM	2-10MM	10-50MM	50-100MM	100-250MM	Type of Statement	ALL 4/1/06-3/31/07	ALL 4/1/07-3/31/08
1		6	11	3	1	Unqualified	24	27
1	7	41	6			Reviewed	61	54
3	22	14	3	1		Compiled	51	32
5	12	7				Tax Returns	28	19
1	13	17	14	6	1	Other	66	73
	44 (4/1-9/30/10)		152 (10/1/10-3/31/11)					
11	54	85	34	10	2	**NUMBER OF STATEMENTS**	230	205
%	%	%	%	%	%	**ASSETS**	%	%
13.6	9.1	7.8	10.4	7.7		Cash & Equivalents	10.1	8.3
25.6	29.5	25.1	18.6	20.7		Trade Receivables (net)	25.6	25.7
23.2	20.6	25.6	25.0	21.2		Inventory	20.1	22.1
1.2	1.2	2.0	6.6	8.8		All Other Current	2.3	3.0
63.6	60.4	60.4	60.6	58.4		Total Current	58.2	59.0
33.7	32.1	31.6	26.8	29.2		Fixed Assets (net)	34.2	32.4
.1	2.2	1.5	6.5	9.8		Intangibles (net)	2.1	3.6
2.6	5.3	6.5	6.1	2.6		All Other Non-Current	5.5	5.0
100.0	100.0	100.0	100.0	100.0		Total	100.0	100.0
						LIABILITIES		
39.3	13.9	10.8	6.1	12.0		Notes Payable-Short Term	8.1	10.3
8.6	6.5	5.1	4.0	3.2		Cur. Mat.-L.T.D.	5.3	4.8
26.2	13.8	12.7	11.6	5.5		Trade Payables	11.8	11.6
.0	.1	.1	.1	.3		Income Taxes Payable	.1	.1
60.8	6.5	11.3	8.9	20.8		All Other Current	10.5	13.3
134.9	40.8	40.0	30.7	41.7		Total Current	35.8	40.1
19.2	28.0	14.9	13.8	6.6		Long-Term Debt	20.2	22.2
.0	.7	.4	1.0	2.7		Deferred Taxes	.5	.6
11.3	7.7	6.7	7.0	4.4		All Other Non-Current	4.7	5.7
-65.4	22.8	38.1	47.5	44.6		Net Worth	38.8	31.5
100.0	100.0	100.0	100.0	100.0		Total Liabilties & Net Worth	100.0	100.0
						INCOME DATA		
100.0	100.0	100.0	100.0	100.0		Net Sales	100.0	100.0
39.0	39.2	30.2	27.7	32.7		Gross Profit	33.2	33.8
42.3	34.9	25.8	20.6	28.0		Operating Expenses	27.1	27.5
-3.3	4.2	4.4	7.1	4.7		Operating Profit	6.1	6.3
.2	1.2	.6	1.1	2.5		All Other Expenses (net)	1.1	1.3
-3.4	3.1	3.8	6.0	2.1		Profit Before Taxes	5.0	4.9
						RATIOS		
1.5	2.2	2.4	2.8	2.5		Current	2.8	2.5
.7	1.5	1.5	2.1	1.6			1.6	1.6
.2	1.1	1.1	1.3	1.0			1.1	1.1
.8	1.5	1.4	1.6	1.4		Quick	1.7	1.7
.4	1.1	.8	1.0	.8			1.0	.9
.0	.7	.6	.5	.5			.6	.6
0 UND	34 10.9	38 9.6	32 11.5	47 7.8		Sales/Receivables	37 9.8	34 10.6
25 14.8	52 7.0	50 7.3	50 7.4	61 6.0			47 7.8	47 7.7
68 5.4	66 5.5	61 6.0	61 5.9	80 4.6			61 6.0	59 6.2
0 UND	10 36.9	37 9.9	45 8.1	44 8.2		Cost of Sales/Inventory	15 25.1	16 23.3
17 21.3	44 8.2	67 5.5	83 4.4	97 3.8			42 8.7	47 7.7
96 3.8	101 3.6	104 3.5	126 2.9	168 2.2			97 3.8	103 3.5
14 25.4	18 19.8	20 18.1	20 17.9	8 43.7		Cost of Sales/Payables	16 22.3	15 24.7
36 10.1	39 9.4	32 11.4	32 11.3	21 17.6			29 12.6	27 13.4
89 4.1	59 6.2	51 7.1	54 6.8	40 9.0			42 8.6	42 8.7
9.0	5.5	4.7	2.6	3.0		Sales/Working Capital	4.9	5.1
-14.6	11.7	8.0	4.5	3.8			9.2	9.3
-6.8	57.8	35.1	13.3	-75.2			37.8	28.2
	6.4	11.6	20.9			EBIT/Interest	10.2	9.0
	(53) 2.5	(82) 2.8	(33) 5.2				(213) 3.6	(187) 3.8
	1.2	1.2	1.8				1.3	1.7
	3.3	6.6	4.1			Net Profit + Depr., Dep., Amort./Cur. Mat. L/T/D	4.6	5.4
	(10) 1.3	(23) 1.9	(12) 2.1				(51) 2.2	(48) 2.1
	.6	1.1	1.5				1.3	1.4
.2	.4	.4	.2	.3		Fixed/Worth	.4	.4
5.2	1.4	.8	.6	1.1			.7	.9
-.3	21.8	1.8	1.9	3.4			2.0	2.3
2.0	1.5	.7	.5	.5		Debt/Worth	.8	.8
51.0	2.7	1.7	1.1	2.3			1.7	2.0
-1.4	54.3	3.3	3.9	22.3			3.4	5.4
	66.2	29.5	27.6			% Profit Before Taxes/Tangible Net Worth	43.3	47.0
	(43) 15.6	(78) 13.3	(32) 13.0				(215) 21.3	(175) 24.4
	4.3	2.9	1.3				5.2	6.6
24.3	9.9	11.5	8.5	8.6		% Profit Before Taxes/Total Assets	15.0	15.9
3.8	2.9	4.1	6.3	2.1			7.3	7.6
-61.9	1.0	.7	.7	-2.5			1.2	1.7
66.7	24.4	12.8	12.9	15.2		Sales/Net Fixed Assets	14.8	16.1
18.1	6.8	6.1	5.9	4.6			6.7	6.7
5.6	3.1	3.6	3.8	1.8			3.4	3.7
7.9	2.6	2.2	1.8	1.5		Sales/Total Assets	2.5	2.4
2.8	2.0	1.8	1.2	1.1			1.9	1.8
2.2	1.5	1.3	.9	.7			1.3	1.3
	1.5	1.4	2.0			% Depr., Dep., Amort./Sales	1.3	1.4
	(44) 3.1	(79) 3.3	(32) 3.2				(217) 2.8	(185) 3.0
	6.9	5.9	5.5				5.8	5.1
	3.8	2.1				% Officers', Directors' Owners' Comp/Sales	2.6	3.0
	(28) 6.3	(33) 3.4					(92) 4.8	(83) 5.6
	9.1	5.3					8.3	10.8
11105M	123354M	675848M	1003390M	822329M	323033M	Net Sales ($)	5315508M	3798528M
3027M	61297M	381613M	754377M	742275M	296459M	Total Assets ($)	3006020M	2318095M

M = $ thousand   MM = $ million
See Pages 9 through 22 for Explanation of Ratios and Data

Comparative Historical Data / Current Data Sorted by Sales

			Type of Statement						
29	24	22	Unqualified		1	1	1	8	11
50	63	55	Reviewed	1	6	7	26	13	2
35	36	43	Compiled	3	17	14	4	2	3
22	24	24	Tax Returns	5	11	3	3	2	
65	60	52	Other	2	12	8	6	11	13
4/1/08-3/31/09 ALL	4/1/09-3/31/10 ALL	4/1/10-3/31/11 ALL		0-1MM	44 (4/1-9/30/10) 1-3MM	3-5MM	5-10MM	152 (10/1/10-3/31/11) 10-25MM	25MM & OVER
201	207	196	NUMBER OF STATEMENTS	11	47	33	40	36	29
%	%	%	ASSETS	%	%	%	%	%	%
7.9	8.7	9.0	Cash & Equivalents	8.6	9.7	9.6	10.6	6.8	7.9
23.7	23.2	25.0	Trade Receivables (net)	23.1	26.9	26.9	23.3	27.0	20.4
24.4	24.1	23.8	Inventory	32.2	17.7	20.8	30.0	23.4	25.8
2.9	4.7	2.9	All Other Current	1.2	1.5	1.4	.9	4.1	8.6
58.9	60.7	60.7	Total Current	65.1	55.8	58.7	64.9	61.3	62.8
33.0	30.3	30.7	Fixed Assets (net)	31.3	35.6	31.4	29.4	29.7	24.6
2.8	3.9	2.9	Intangibles (net)	.4	2.5	1.1	.7	4.5	7.5
5.3	5.1	5.8	All Other Non-Current	3.1	6.2	8.8	5.1	4.5	5.2
100.0	100.0	100.0	Total	100.0	100.0	100.0	100.0	100.0	100.0
			LIABILITIES						
11.9	11.2	12.5	Notes Payable-Short Term	33.7	15.4	12.7	8.6	8.5	9.6
5.3	3.9	5.3	Cur. Mat.-L.T.D.	11.4	6.2	6.4	3.9	4.2	3.9
11.1	11.5	13.2	Trade Payables	24.3	11.8	12.3	14.6	13.9	9.5
.0	.2	.1	Income Taxes Payable	.0	.0	.1	.2	.1	.1
11.4	10.4	12.8	All Other Current	30.7	12.9	9.7	11.3	11.1	13.6
39.7	37.2	43.9	Total Current	100.0	46.3	41.2	38.6	37.7	36.7
19.4	16.9	18.0	Long-Term Debt	19.8	29.0	17.9	15.0	13.4	9.2
.6	.7	.7	Deferred Taxes	.0	.5	.7	.5	.5	1.8
6.1	5.9	7.1	All Other Non-Current	13.5	8.9	9.0	2.8	5.4	7.8
34.1	39.5	30.3	Net Worth	-33.2	15.3	31.1	43.1	42.9	44.4
100.0	100.0	100.0	Total Liabilities & Net Worth	100.0	100.0	100.0	100.0	100.0	100.0
			INCOME DATA						
100.0	100.0	100.0	Net Sales	100.0	100.0	100.0	100.0	100.0	100.0
32.7	30.3	32.9	Gross Profit	44.7	38.8	36.2	29.9	25.9	27.9
28.4	29.4	28.5	Operating Expenses	45.3	34.3	32.1	24.9	19.8	24.5
4.2	.9	4.4	Operating Profit	-.6	4.5	4.1	5.0	6.1	3.4
1.0	.9	.9	All Other Expenses (net)	.3	1.5	1.0	.2	.9	1.4
3.2	.0	3.5	Profit Before Taxes	-.9	3.0	3.1	4.8	5.2	2.0
			RATIOS						
2.6 / 1.7 / 1.1	2.6 / 1.7 / 1.1	2.5 / 1.6 / 1.1	Current	2.0 / 1.5 / .6	2.2 / 1.4 / 1.0	2.4 / 1.6 / 1.0	2.5 / 1.7 / 1.2	2.5 / 1.8 / 1.2	2.9 / 1.9 / 1.1
1.4 / .8 / .5	1.5 / .8 / .6	1.4 / .9 / .6	Quick	.8 / .4 / .0	1.6 / 1.0 / .5	1.6 / .9 / .7	1.1 / .8 / .6	1.6 / 1.0 / .6	1.5 / .8 / .5
31 11.6 / 41 8.8 / 56 6.5	35 10.5 / 47 7.8 / 61 6.0	36 10.3 / 51 7.2 / 64 5.7	Sales/Receivables	3 134.6 / 50 7.3 / 69 5.3	28 12.8 / 43 8.4 / 70 5.2	39 9.4 / 53 6.9 / 61 6.0	38 9.7 / 47 7.8 / 57 6.5	39 9.4 / 55 6.7 / 64 5.7	37 9.8 / 55 6.7 / 75 4.9
20 18.7 / 62 5.9 / 108 3.4	29 12.4 / 63 5.8 / 110 3.3	31 11.9 / 64 5.7 / 111 3.3	Cost of Sales/Inventory	0 UND / 49 7.5 / 179 2.0	7 55.7 / 37 9.8 / 89 4.1	28 13.1 / 52 7.1 / 109 3.3	42 8.7 / 78 4.7 / 120 3.1	44 8.3 / 54 6.7 / 87 4.2	50 7.3 / 94 3.9 / 160 2.3
14 26.6 / 26 14.3 / 41 8.9	16 23.3 / 28 13.3 / 44 8.3	20 18.7 / 33 11.0 / 53 6.9	Cost of Sales/Payables	28 13.0 / 59 6.2 / 98 3.7	13 27.1 / 33 11.0 / 51 7.2	22 16.4 / 36 10.2 / 41 8.8	20 18.0 / 32 11.3 / 59 6.2	22 16.5 / 31 11.6 / 53 6.9	18 20.0 / 31 12.0 / 49 7.4
4.8 / 8.9 / 47.7	4.1 / 7.4 / 45.1	4.3 / 8.1 / 46.4	Sales/Working Capital	4.3 / 15.6 / -7.5	6.1 / 11.7 / 147.6	5.5 / 9.1 / -66.4	4.5 / 7.6 / 28.5	4.5 / 7.7 / 30.6	2.7 / 4.4 / 32.6
7.2 / (187) 3.1 / 1.0	6.3 / (194) 1.6 / -2.9	9.9 / (187) 2.9 / 1.2	EBIT/Interest	10.5 / (10) 3.0 / -2.2	4.9 / (45) 2.2 / 1.0	12.8 / 2.3 / 1.4	16.7 / (38) 3.5 / 1.3	14.6 / (35) 5.2 / 1.6	11.0 / (26) 2.8 / -.5
5.9 / (53) 2.1 / .9	3.5 / (59) 1.0 / .4	4.6 / (50) 1.8 / 1.2	Net Profit + Depr., Dep., Amort./Cur. Mat. L/T/D		4.4 / (12) 1.3 / .7			7.8 / (11) 2.2 / 1.8	19.4 / (12) 1.4 / 1.2
.4 / .9 / 2.0	.3 / .8 / 2.2	.3 / .9 / 2.8	Fixed/Worth	.1 / .4 / -2.7	.6 / 1.5 / 193.8	.4 / .8 / 3.2	.3 / .7 / 1.3	.3 / .7 / 1.5	.2 / .6 / 3.4
.8 / 1.9 / 5.0	.7 / 1.7 / 4.6	.8 / 1.9 / 6.6	Debt/Worth	1.8 / 6.3 / -8.8	1.7 / 3.3 / 297.8	.7 / 2.2 / 8.5	.6 / 1.4 / 2.3	.7 / 1.4 / 3.1	.5 / 1.0 / 8.2
40.3 / (172) 17.2 / 1.9	23.9 / (190) 3.8 / -18.3	36.6 / (170) 14.3 / 3.1	% Profit Before Taxes/Tangible Net Worth		63.8 / (36) 18.1 / 4.4	34.3 / (28) 13.7 / 7.0	24.3 / (39) 13.4 / 5.3	36.9 / (33) 16.9 / 2.2	33.1 / (27) 7.1 / -3.2
14.9 / 5.2 / .3	8.9 / 1.1 / -6.7	10.3 / 3.9 / .6	% Profit Before Taxes/Total Assets	24.3 / 1.6 / -42.6	9.6 / 2.9 / -1.0	9.8 / 3.7 / 1.6	12.5 / 4.8 / 1.1	13.0 / 6.4 / .9	7.3 / 3.0 / -1.3
13.8 / 7.1 / 3.4	13.8 / 6.3 / 3.7	15.2 / 6.2 / 3.6	Sales/Net Fixed Assets	56.4 / 15.0 / 5.6	15.3 / 5.9 / 2.9	17.8 / 7.6 / 2.8	19.0 / 6.9 / 3.7	12.6 / 6.2 / 4.5	21.4 / 5.6 / 3.9
2.5 / 1.9 / 1.3	2.2 / 1.6 / 1.1	2.3 / 1.8 / 1.2	Sales/Total Assets	3.6 / 2.2 / 1.8	2.4 / 1.8 / 1.3	2.5 / 1.8 / 1.2	2.2 / 1.8 / 1.3	2.3 / 1.9 / 1.2	1.8 / 1.3 / .9
1.3 / (175) 2.7 / 4.8	1.3 / (188) 3.2 / 5.9	1.5 / (169) 3.3 / 6.0	% Depr., Dep., Amort./Sales		1.6 / (37) 3.7 / 9.2	1.5 / (30) 3.7 / 7.7	1.4 / (37) 2.9 / 5.4	1.8 / (34) 3.2 / 5.7	1.6 / (26) 3.4 / 4.7
2.4 / (74) 4.2 / 6.8	3.0 / (86) 5.0 / 8.2	2.7 / (75) 4.5 / 7.9	% Officers', Directors' Owners' Comp/Sales		3.6 / (22) 5.5 / 8.9	2.9 / (16) 6.1 / 8.9	2.5 / (18) 3.7 / 4.8		
3941084M	3961256M	2959059M	Net Sales ($)	8949M	90980M	134777M	291460M	579721M	1853172M
2416030M	3072880M	2239048M	Total Assets ($)	4386M	55350M	85027M	199152M	374878M	1520255M

M = $ thousand   MM = $ million
See Pages 9 through 22 for Explanation of Ratios and Data

Current Data Sorted by Assets | **Comparative Historical Data**

0-500M	500M-2MM	2-10MM	10-50MM	50-100MM	100-250MM	Type of Statement	4/1/06-3/31/07 ALL	4/1/07-3/31/08 ALL
	1	5	7	3		Unqualified	16	17
1	4	13	3	1		Reviewed	25	22
	5	5	2			Compiled	22	20
3	8	3				Tax Returns	10	6
4	7	17	12	5		Other	44	37
	15 (4/1-9/30/10)		94 (10/1/10-3/31/11)					
8	25	43	24	9		NUMBER OF STATEMENTS	117	102
%	%	%	%	%	%	**ASSETS**	%	%
	8.7	12.1	13.1		DATA NOT AVAILABLE	Cash & Equivalents	8.9	10.0
	27.4	28.5	18.9			Trade Receivables (net)	28.3	26.5
	29.9	25.4	23.3			Inventory	24.0	25.1
	2.6	1.3	6.3			All Other Current	4.0	4.0
	68.6	67.4	61.7			Total Current	65.2	65.6
	26.3	25.1	22.4			Fixed Assets (net)	25.5	25.2
	1.8	2.6	8.2			Intangibles (net)	2.9	3.4
	3.3	4.9	7.8			All Other Non-Current	6.4	5.8
	100.0	100.0	100.0			Total	100.0	100.0
						LIABILITIES		
	15.7	10.9	6.6			Notes Payable-Short Term	11.6	9.6
	3.0	2.9	3.0			Cur. Mat.-L.T.D.	3.5	4.0
	13.1	12.1	7.6			Trade Payables	15.5	12.3
	.2	.1	.0			Income Taxes Payable	.3	.1
	12.9	10.4	12.7			All Other Current	13.9	12.5
	45.0	36.4	29.9			Total Current	44.7	38.5
	16.7	13.6	13.1			Long-Term Debt	14.7	17.4
	.0	.3	.5			Deferred Taxes	.2	.4
	8.2	3.1	7.6			All Other Non-Current	7.6	5.2
	30.2	46.7	48.9			Net Worth	32.7	38.6
	100.0	100.0	100.0			Total Liabilties & Net Worth	100.0	100.0
						INCOME DATA		
	100.0	100.0	100.0			Net Sales	100.0	100.0
	39.6	29.1	24.8			Gross Profit	28.3	30.0
	34.1	21.2	16.1			Operating Expenses	21.7	23.0
	5.5	7.8	8.7			Operating Profit	6.6	7.0
	.7	.5	1.8			All Other Expenses (net)	1.3	.9
	4.9	7.4	6.9			Profit Before Taxes	5.3	6.1
						RATIOS		
	3.2	2.8	3.9				2.5	3.1
	1.5	1.9	2.4			Current	1.5	1.8
	1.1	1.2	1.4				1.1	1.3
	1.7	1.7	2.1				1.5	1.9
	.9	1.0	1.1			Quick	.9	1.0
	.5	.7	.5				.5	.6
	28 13.0	**36** 10.1	**45** 8.2				**36** 10.3	**35** 10.4
	35 10.3	**51** 7.2	**55** 6.7			Sales/Receivables	**48** 7.6	**43** 8.4
	58 6.3	**81** 4.5	**70** 5.2				**63** 5.8	**60** 6.1
	21 17.6	**36** 10.1	**31** 11.8				**25** 14.8	**23** 15.9
	56 6.5	**65** 5.6	**86** 4.3			Cost of Sales/Inventory	**55** 6.6	**68** 5.4
	138 2.6	**123** 3.0	**149** 2.4				**96** 3.8	**109** 3.4
	18 20.3	**18** 20.2	**17** 21.2				**17** 21.3	**17** 21.8
	35 10.5	**29** 12.6	**31** 11.9			Cost of Sales/Payables	**29** 12.7	**28** 13.3
	50 7.4	**43** 8.5	**43** 8.6				**47** 7.8	**45** 8.2
	6.1	3.4	2.2				4.8	3.6
	11.8	5.3	4.9			Sales/Working Capital	11.0	8.1
	61.7	17.7	8.0				46.8	14.6
	13.5	32.7	22.4				12.2	12.3
	(22) 5.5	(38) 9.8	(23) 8.8			EBIT/Interest	(103) 4.6	(88) 5.0
	-.5	3.3	2.4				1.4	2.1
							8.9	6.1
						Net Profit + Depr., Dep., Amort./Cur. Mat. L/T/D	(27) 1.9	(27) 3.5
							.8	1.3
	.3	.2	.3				.3	.2
	.9	.4	.5			Fixed/Worth	.6	.7
	4.3	1.1	1.1				3.0	1.6
	.6	.7	.6				.7	.6
	2.2	1.5	1.3			Debt/Worth	1.9	1.7
	9.0	2.2	2.9				11.2	4.5
	48.9	66.7	30.4				65.7	52.3
	(21) 26.7	(41) 26.0	(22) 17.0			% Profit Before Taxes/Tangible Net Worth	(98) 36.2	(92) 27.0
	-2.7	11.0	5.9				11.3	10.6
	22.0	24.3	13.2				19.3	17.6
	13.4	11.5	6.8			% Profit Before Taxes/Total Assets	8.1	9.1
	-.3	6.0	4.2				1.9	3.6
	27.2	17.0	9.9				26.0	18.7
	11.9	8.2	5.2			Sales/Net Fixed Assets	10.4	8.8
	6.2	5.2	3.7				4.7	5.3
	3.2	2.3	1.5				2.6	2.4
	2.5	1.8	1.1			Sales/Total Assets	1.9	1.9
	2.0	1.4	.8				1.4	1.5
	1.1	1.3	1.6				1.2	1.1
	(21) 2.4	(38) 2.4	(20) 2.9			% Depr., Dep., Amort./Sales	(102) 1.9	(92) 2.0
	5.5	4.5	4.5				3.7	4.2
	1.8	1.1					1.4	2.6
	(13) 3.5	(17) 2.3				% Officers', Directors' Owners' Comp/Sales	(41) 3.3	(38) 3.4
	9.2	2.7					10.5	9.9
9152M	**68894M**	**411203M**	**576512M**	**669267M**		Net Sales ($)	**2407134M**	**1985266M**
2221M	**27822M**	**221281M**	**498628M**	**605147M**		Total Assets ($)	**1514840M**	**1270384M**

M = $ thousand MM = $ million

See Pages 9 through 22 for Explanation of Ratios and Data

Comparative Historical Data   Current Data Sorted by Sales

			Type of Statement						
16	10	16	Unqualified			1	2	6	7
14	18	22	Reviewed	1	4	3	7	5	2
15	15	12	Compiled		3	3	2	4	
9	9	14	Tax Returns	2	6	4	2		
42	30	45	Other	1	8	3	12	10	11
4/1/08-3/31/09 ALL	4/1/09-3/31/10 ALL	4/1/10-3/31/11 ALL			15 (4/1-9/30/10)		94 (10/1/10-3/31/11)		
				0-1MM	1-3MM	3-5MM	5-10MM	10-25MM	25MM & OVER
96	82	109	NUMBER OF STATEMENTS	4	21	14	25	25	20
%	%	%	ASSETS	%	%	%	%	%	%
9.6	9.4	11.1	Cash & Equivalents		11.3	13.0	10.6	12.0	10.0
25.3	23.8	26.8	Trade Receivables (net)		28.7	31.5	29.0	23.7	19.5
26.2	27.0	24.9	Inventory		27.7	17.1	30.9	23.4	22.8
3.3	5.6	2.8	All Other Current		2.9	.8	1.7	2.9	5.7
64.4	65.8	65.6	Total Current		70.7	62.4	72.2	62.1	58.0
26.3	26.2	23.9	Fixed Assets (net)		23.6	29.4	18.4	26.5	24.7
4.0	3.0	4.9	Intangibles (net)		2.8	.5	2.9	7.0	9.0
5.4	5.0	5.6	All Other Non-Current		3.0	7.7	6.5	4.4	8.3
100.0	100.0	100.0	Total		100.0	100.0	100.0	100.0	100.0
			LIABILITIES						
9.9	13.1	10.1	Notes Payable-Short Term		14.7	12.0	12.9	9.7	2.3
4.3	4.9	3.2	Cur. Mat.-L.T.D.		4.9	3.3	1.5	3.6	3.0
14.2	11.4	11.1	Trade Payables		11.7	10.4	12.1	11.1	7.5
.4	.3	.1	Income Taxes Payable		.2	.4	.0	.1	.1
13.9	14.0	12.9	All Other Current		13.6	11.4	10.5	11.3	16.6
42.6	43.7	37.3	Total Current		45.1	37.4	37.1	35.8	29.5
15.4	12.1	15.1	Long-Term Debt		19.0	13.5	12.1	11.8	14.9
.4	.2	.3	Deferred Taxes		.2	.0	.3	.2	.6
12.7	6.5	7.9	All Other Non-Current		9.9	3.6	6.1	3.7	10.5
28.9	37.4	39.5	Net Worth		25.8	45.5	44.4	48.4	44.4
100.0	100.0	100.0	Total Liabilties & Net Worth		100.0	100.0	100.0	100.0	100.0
			INCOME DATA						
100.0	100.0	100.0	Net Sales		100.0	100.0	100.0	100.0	100.0
31.2	31.1	32.3	Gross Profit		38.9	38.6	30.5	26.6	26.1
25.7	28.8	25.1	Operating Expenses		32.4	33.0	23.7	16.2	19.9
5.6	2.3	7.1	Operating Profit		6.5	5.7	6.8	10.4	6.2
1.5	2.0	1.0	All Other Expenses (net)		.4	.2	1.1	1.1	2.0
4.1	.2	6.1	Profit Before Taxes		6.1	5.4	5.7	9.3	4.2
			RATIOS						
2.7	2.9	3.0			3.2	2.9	2.6	3.8	2.8
1.7	1.9	1.8	Current		1.6	2.2	1.8	1.9	1.9
1.1	1.1	1.2			1.0	1.1	1.4	1.1	1.4
1.6	1.6	1.7			1.6	2.4	1.6	1.9	1.2
.8	.8	1.0	Quick		.9	1.7	1.0	1.2	.9
.5	.5	.6			.5	.7	.7	.5	.6

							Sales/Receivables											
31	11.6	32	11.4	35	10.4			28	13.0	29	12.6	42	8.7	36	10.0	42	8.7
43	8.4	46	8.0	51	7.2	Sales/Receivables		35	10.3	46	7.9	52	7.0	54	6.8	51	7.1
55	6.6	64	5.7	68	5.3			54	6.8	67	5.5	84	4.3	69	5.3	69	5.3
25	14.8	42	8.7	30	12.0			0	UND	11	32.4	47	7.7	20	18.5	47	7.7
65	5.6	70	5.2	68	5.3	Cost of Sales/Inventory		48	7.6	45	8.1	85	4.3	65	5.6	81	4.5
119	3.1	126	2.9	127	2.9			153	2.4	64	5.7	149	2.5	130	2.8	123	3.0
16	22.6	14	26.9	18	20.4			5	73.6	14	26.1	17	21.0	20	18.2	17	21.6
29	12.7	26	14.3	29	12.6	Cost of Sales/Payables		24	14.9	31	11.7	29	12.6	31	11.9	28	13.0
48	7.6	45	8.1	44	8.2			51	7.1	41	8.9	48	7.6	46	8.0	41	8.9

3.9	3.5	3.5	Sales/Working Capital		3.5	5.5	3.4	2.7	4.2
7.9	8.4	6.3			10.3	9.6	5.2	5.1	5.2
90.6	54.0	24.4			174.6	64.3	10.0	121.8	8.5

							EBIT/Interest						
	13.8		10.2		22.3				15.2		17.0	26.2		72.3		22.4
(88)	4.8	(73)	2.5	(99)	6.6	EBIT/Interest	(19)	3.1	(12)	6.4	(21)	5.3	(24)	14.0	(19)	4.7
	1.0		-2.7		2.0				.3		2.8	2.9		5.0		.2

						Net Profit + Depr., Dep., Amort./Cur. Mat. L/T/D
	10.4		3.7		5.1	
(22)	2.8	(15)	2.1	(16)	2.2	Net Profit + Depr., Dep., Amort./Cur. Mat. L/T/D
	1.2		.5		-.3	

.3	.2	.3	Fixed/Worth		.2	.3	.2	.3	.4
.9	.6	.6			.9	.6	.4	.5	.8
3.1	1.8	1.5			NM	1.0	.8	1.5	1.6
.8	.6	.7	Debt/Worth		.7	.6	.9	.5	.6
1.5	1.4	1.6			2.5	.9	1.6	1.5	1.5
8.8	3.9	3.8			NM	3.4	2.2	2.3	5.1

							% Profit Before Taxes/Tangible Net Worth					
	51.0		29.1		54.6			60.5	59.2	65.2	53.3	30.2
(79)	22.8	(74)	9.5	(96)	21.2	% Profit Before Taxes/Tangible Net Worth	(16)	21.9	27.5 (24)	22.1 (23)	23.9 (17)	12.1
	3.8		-13.7		9.3			-2.2	12.2	2.8	15.3	-6.7

17.9	13.9	20.5	% Profit Before Taxes/Total Assets		22.5	20.6	21.4	21.2	13.0
7.6	2.8	7.8			6.5	11.0	8.4	10.5	6.1
.0	-6.7	1.9			-.6	6.8	1.2	5.4	-1.8
22.2	17.9	20.0	Sales/Net Fixed Assets		37.7	13.8	25.7	10.1	9.5
7.6	9.6	8.0			13.5	6.6	13.9	6.2	5.9
4.6	4.5	4.8			6.5	5.5	6.1	4.1	3.8
2.7	2.4	2.5	Sales/Total Assets		3.4	2.6	2.5	2.1	1.5
1.8	1.7	1.7			2.3	2.1	1.7	1.6	1.2
1.4	1.3	1.2			1.7	1.5	1.2	1.2	1.1

						% Depr., Dep., Amort./Sales								
	1.2		1.2		1.3			1.0		1.4		.8	1.6		1.7
(82)	2.5	(69)	2.5	(92)	2.5	% Depr., Dep., Amort./Sales	(18)	2.0	(12)	2.9	(19)	1.8	(23)	3.2	(17)	3.0
	3.7		4.5		4.5			4.8		6.0		3.5	4.7		5.1

						% Officers', Directors' Owners' Comp/Sales					
	1.9		2.6		1.3			2.2		1.5	
(36)	3.4	(34)	5.1	(38)	2.5	% Officers', Directors' Owners' Comp/Sales	(10)	6.6	(10)	2.6	
	9.9		11.4		4.0			9.3		3.5	

1733339M	1135870M	1735028M	Net Sales ($)	2251M	43453M	51652M	189692M	381232M	1066748M
1185835M	822409M	1355099M	Total Assets ($)	721M	19724M	26194M	132111M	274023M	902326M

M = $ thousand   MM = $ million
See Pages 9 through 22 for Explanation of Ratios and Data

Current Data Sorted by Assets							Comparative Historical Data	
						Type of Statement		
	1	7	13	3	2	Unqualified	34	36
1	18	50	19	1		Reviewed	126	87
8	29	25	4			Compiled	116	93
10	27	8				Tax Returns	33	24
4	25	27	23	4	2	Other	100	96
	68 (4/1-9/30/10)		243 (10/1/10-3/31/11)				**4/1/06-3/31/07**	**4/1/07-3/31/08**
0-500M	**500M-2MM**	**2-10MM**	**10-50MM**	**50-100MM**	**100-250MM**		**ALL**	**ALL**
23	100	117	59	8	4	**NUMBER OF STATEMENTS**	409	336
%	%	%	%	%	%	**ASSETS**	%	%
10.8	12.2	10.2	4.6			Cash & Equivalents	7.7	7.6
30.2	33.9	29.4	27.1			Trade Receivables (net)	30.1	30.0
11.9	13.3	20.0	16.1			Inventory	16.9	17.7
3.0	2.1	3.0	7.5			All Other Current	2.8	3.4
55.8	61.4	62.5	55.4			Total Current	57.6	58.6
36.4	31.8	30.2	32.3			Fixed Assets (net)	33.2	33.4
3.6	1.6	2.3	4.0			Intangibles (net)	3.6	2.6
4.2	5.2	4.9	8.3			All Other Non-Current	5.6	5.3
100.0	100.0	100.0	100.0			Total	100.0	100.0
						LIABILITIES		
15.6	7.9	10.6	9.4			Notes Payable-Short Term	12.7	13.1
12.6	5.1	4.7	5.0			Cur. Mat.-L.T.D.	6.2	5.7
14.0	13.8	12.4	11.2			Trade Payables	11.5	13.0
.0	.1	.2	.1			Income Taxes Payable	.2	.2
15.8	12.2	8.9	9.2			All Other Current	10.1	10.1
57.9	39.1	36.8	34.9			Total Current	40.7	42.0
31.6	17.8	12.9	14.3			Long-Term Debt	18.5	18.3
.0	.4	.8	1.1			Deferred Taxes	.6	.6
7.5	7.9	5.2	3.9			All Other Non-Current	7.5	7.0
2.9	34.8	44.3	45.8			Net Worth	32.7	32.1
100.0	100.0	100.0	100.0			Total Liabilities & Net Worth	100.0	100.0
						INCOME DATA		
100.0	100.0	100.0	100.0			Net Sales	100.0	100.0
39.5	33.1	26.5	20.6			Gross Profit	28.8	27.0
36.7	28.2	20.6	15.8			Operating Expenses	23.8	22.4
2.8	4.8	5.9	4.9			Operating Profit	5.0	4.7
1.4	.8	.6	.6			All Other Expenses (net)	1.3	1.1
1.4	4.1	5.3	4.3			Profit Before Taxes	3.7	3.6
						RATIOS		
2.2	3.4	3.6	3.2				2.6	2.5
1.1	1.7	1.8	1.6			Current	1.5	1.4
.8	1.0	1.1	1.1				1.0	1.0
1.4	2.7	2.6	1.7				1.7	1.5
.8	1.1	1.1	.9			Quick	.9	.9
.5	.8	.6	.6				.6	.6
26 14.3	**40** 9.2	**40** 9.0	**50** 7.3				**37** 9.9	**39** 9.4
37 10.0	**53** 6.8	**52** 7.0	**60** 6.0			Sales/Receivables	**51** 7.1	**52** 7.0
53 6.9	**71** 5.1	**72** 5.1	**104** 3.5				**65** 5.6	**68** 5.4
0 UND	**7** 52.8	**29** 12.7	**22** 16.6				**14** 27.0	**16** 22.2
16 22.6	**23** 16.0	**43** 8.5	**49** 7.4			Cost of Sales/Inventory	**35** 10.4	**40** 9.2
38 9.5	**47** 7.8	**73** 5.0	**66** 5.6				**62** 5.9	**69** 5.3
8 45.5	**14** 25.8	**15** 24.7	**20** 18.4				**13** 28.7	**14** 25.4
25 14.9	**28** 13.2	**27** 13.6	**32** 11.5			Cost of Sales/Payables	**24** 15.3	**27** 13.6
39 9.3	**44** 8.3	**43** 8.6	**48** 7.6				**38** 9.6	**43** 8.4
8.0	4.7	3.4	3.6				5.4	4.7
71.1	8.5	7.8	6.4			Sales/Working Capital	11.1	11.3
-32.7	-302.1	46.3	28.3				104.5	UND
6.0	10.7	17.5	9.8				7.4	6.7
(22) 2.6	(88) 3.2	(108) 5.2	(56) 5.4			EBIT/Interest	(373) 2.9	(314) 2.9
-1.5	.2	1.9	1.5				1.3	1.0
	4.6	3.9	4.0				3.7	3.1
	(15) 2.3	(30) 2.0	(20) 2.2			Net Profit + Depr., Dep., Amort./Cur. Mat. L/T/D	(107) 2.0	(84) 1.9
	.6	1.0	1.0				1.0	.8
.6	.3	.3	.4				.4	.4
1.3	.8	.7	.7			Fixed/Worth	1.0	1.0
-3.5	4.3	1.5	1.7				2.9	2.8
1.1	.5	.4	.5				.7	.7
6.1	1.3	1.2	1.5			Debt/Worth	1.8	2.1
-7.5	13.2	3.4	3.0				7.2	6.5
138.6	52.8	41.5	30.5				39.2	34.7
(16) 26.1	(79) 16.5	(107) 21.4	(58) 9.3			% Profit Before Taxes/Tangible Net Worth	(340) 17.4	(288) 14.7
2.0	-.3	6.0	3.1				3.0	2.5
20.5	14.9	16.5	9.2				14.7	12.7
8.0	6.1	7.2	4.8			% Profit Before Taxes/Total Assets	5.4	5.1
-8.9	-.9	2.4	1.1				.6	.3
28.3	14.8	12.2	7.5				13.3	12.3
9.2	8.5	6.7	4.0			Sales/Net Fixed Assets	6.7	5.9
5.7	4.1	4.0	2.7				3.8	3.5
3.9	2.8	2.4	1.7				2.7	2.6
3.0	2.3	1.8	1.3			Sales/Total Assets	1.9	1.9
2.7	1.5	1.3	.9				1.4	1.3
1.1	1.7	1.9	2.7				2.0	2.0
(19) 2.6	(88) 3.2	(106) 3.6	(56) 4.5			% Depr., Dep., Amort./Sales	(370) 3.5	(308) 3.5
8.2	6.0	5.5	5.9				5.7	5.5
7.1	4.2	2.0	1.8				2.5	2.5
(15) 13.2	(78) 5.9	(66) 3.0	(14) 2.6			% Officers', Directors' Owners' Comp/Sales	(206) 4.3	(180) 4.8
16.0	11.0	5.6	3.2				7.4	7.6
23786M	**244969M**	**970618M**	**1472530M**	**689605M**	**810749M**	Net Sales ($)	**5560509M**	**4844617M**
6789M	**113485M**	**510716M**	**1113325M**	**541609M**	**692004M**	Total Assets ($)	**3543094M**	**3107992M**

M = $ thousand MM = $ million

See Pages 9 through 22 for Explanation of Ratios and Data

Comparative Historical Data | Current Data Sorted by Sales

Type of Statement									
Unqualified	37	26	26			2	3	7	14
Reviewed	90	85	89	1	17	11	25	27	8
Compiled	65	57	66	6	27	18	8	5	2
Tax Returns	34	30	45	10	14	14	3	4	
Other	118	89	85	3	18	13	12	24	15
	4/1/08-3/31/09 ALL	4/1/09-3/31/10 ALL	4/1/10-3/31/11 ALL	68 (4/1-9/30/10)			243 (10/1/10-3/31/11)		
				0-1MM	1-3MM	3-5MM	5-10MM	10-25MM	25MM & OVER
NUMBER OF STATEMENTS	344	287	311	20	76	58	51	67	39
ASSETS	%	%	%	%	%	%	%	%	%
Cash & Equivalents	8.2	10.1	9.7	9.8	10.8	13.7	10.5	6.8	5.4
Trade Receivables (net)	28.7	27.3	30.1	27.8	32.8	28.8	31.2	29.7	27.5
Inventory	18.2	17.3	16.3	10.1	12.4	20.2	19.1	15.9	18.3
All Other Current	2.8	4.4	3.7	3.8	1.3	4.0	1.7	7.5	4.2
Total Current	58.0	59.1	59.9	51.5	57.3	66.6	62.5	60.0	55.4
Fixed Assets (net)	32.3	33.2	31.7	43.4	33.8	28.5	27.2	31.9	31.9
Intangibles (net)	3.7	2.7	2.6	2.5	2.3	.8	3.7	2.4	4.8
All Other Non-Current	6.0	5.0	5.8	2.6	6.6	4.1	6.6	5.7	7.8
Total	100.0	100.0	100.0	100.0	100.0	100.0	100.0	100.0	100.0
LIABILITIES									
Notes Payable-Short Term	12.2	10.7	9.6	14.1	10.6	8.1	8.1	9.7	9.4
Cur. Mat.-L.T.D.	5.9	6.0	5.4	9.0	6.1	5.1	5.2	4.4	4.7
Trade Payables	12.6	10.9	12.8	14.0	12.2	11.9	12.6	12.7	15.1
Income Taxes Payable	.2	.1	.1	.0	.1	.1	.1	.2	.3
All Other Current	8.8	9.6	10.6	17.4	8.1	14.0	7.0	10.6	11.4
Total Current	39.7	37.4	38.6	54.4	37.0	39.3	33.0	37.7	40.9
Long-Term Debt	19.6	19.7	16.3	29.4	20.4	16.8	9.6	14.9	11.8
Deferred Taxes	.7	.7	.7	.0	.4	.4	1.2	.8	1.2
All Other Non-Current	6.5	6.3	6.0	8.3	8.3	6.2	4.9	3.9	4.7
Net Worth	33.6	36.0	38.5	7.8	33.8	37.3	51.2	42.6	41.4
Total Liabilities & Net Worth	100.0	100.0	100.0	100.0	100.0	100.0	100.0	100.0	100.0
INCOME DATA									
Net Sales	100.0	100.0	100.0	100.0	100.0	100.0	100.0	100.0	100.0
Gross Profit	26.5	25.6	28.3	40.9	33.6	29.1	28.0	23.6	19.1
Operating Expenses	22.7	25.7	23.2	36.6	30.3	24.2	20.8	17.2	14.2
Operating Profit	3.7	-.1	5.2	4.2	3.3	4.9	7.1	6.4	4.9
All Other Expenses (net)	.9	1.1	.8	1.9	.8	.7	.1	.6	1.4
Profit Before Taxes	2.8	-1.2	4.4	2.3	2.5	4.2	7.0	5.8	3.5
RATIOS									
Current	2.7	3.3	3.2	2.2	3.5	3.5	3.9	3.3	2.0
	1.6	1.7	1.7	1.0	1.6	2.5	2.2	1.8	1.5
	1.1	1.1	1.1	.8	1.0	1.3	1.1	1.2	1.0
Quick	1.7	2.2	2.2	1.4	2.6	2.8	2.8	1.9	1.2
	(343) .9	1.0	1.0	.8	1.0	1.2	1.1	1.1	.9
	.6	.6	.7	.4	.7	.6	.7	.6	.6
Sales/Receivables	36 10.2	41 9.0	41 8.9	32 11.3	38 9.7	38 9.6	40 9.1	47 7.7	47 7.8
	49 7.4	54 6.7	54 6.8	53 6.9	54 6.7	48 7.6	49 7.5	58 6.3	55 6.7
	67 5.5	75 4.8	72 5.1	72 5.1	77 4.8	68 5.4	69 5.3	83 4.4	66 5.6
Cost of Sales/Inventory	17 21.2	21 17.5	15 25.1	4 89.3	7 52.8	14 26.1	31 11.7	20 18.2	22 16.6
	39 9.4	45 8.2	36 10.2	23 15.8	23 16.0	33 11.0	42 8.7	42 8.7	42 8.7
	71 5.1	72 5.1	63 5.8	44 8.4	47 7.8	88 4.2	70 5.2	63 5.8	70 5.2
Cost of Sales/Payables	15 25.0	15 23.6	16 22.2	24 14.9	11 32.2	14 25.8	14 26.1	18 20.5	21 17.7
	26 14.2	26 14.2	28 13.0	38 9.7	27 13.4	26 13.8	26 14.2	32 11.4	28 12.9
	39 9.4	42 8.7	43 8.5	56 6.5	41 8.9	40 9.2	35 10.3	48 7.5	44 8.3
Sales/Working Capital	4.8	3.4	4.0	4.8	4.5	3.3	3.6	3.6	4.8
	10.2	7.4	8.0	UND	9.8	5.9	6.9	7.8	9.5
	62.5	75.2	77.9	-18.9	-244.8	24.6	32.3	17.9	-137.7
EBIT/Interest	7.2	5.5	12.2	6.0	4.7	14.0	20.8	13.5	9.9
	(325) 2.9	(266) 1.8	(285) 4.1	(18) 2.3	(65) 2.0	(55) 3.3	(46) 7.4	(64) 6.1	(37) 5.1
	.5	-1.2	1.3	-.6	-1.1	1.4	3.7	2.1	1.5
Net Profit + Depr., Dep., Amort./Cur. Mat. L/T/D	3.4	2.6	4.1			5.3	3.2	3.9	5.6
	(95) 1.7	(81) 1.6	(72) 2.4		(14) 1.9	(12) 1.9	(18) 2.3	(18) 3.3
	.9	.5	1.1			.7	.9	1.5	1.3
Fixed/Worth	.4	.3	.3	.6	.3	.2	.3	.4	.4
	.9	.9	.8	1.5	.9	.7	.9	.8	.9
	2.9	2.6	1.8	-3.3	4.3	1.8	1.4	1.7	1.9
Debt/Worth	.8	.6	.5	1.2	.5	.4	.4	.5	.7
	2.1	1.7	1.4	2.6	1.4	1.2	.8	1.5	1.9
	7.2	5.9	4.6	-5.4	13.8	4.8	2.7	3.6	3.0
% Profit Before Taxes/Tangible Net Worth	33.8	17.7	40.2	68.6	37.8	39.1	48.0	41.8	30.6
	(291) 14.2	(249) 4.7	(271) 17.0	(14) 15.6	(61) 9.4	(48) 16.4	(47) 23.1	(64) 21.1	(37) 11.9
	-.3	-12.3	3.6	-8.5	-2.9	3.4	8.7	6.8	4.0
% Profit Before Taxes/Total Assets	11.9	6.6	14.3	18.7	12.8	17.6	17.6	13.6	10.7
	4.3	1.4	6.4	8.0	2.5	4.2	10.0	6.8	4.9
	-1.0	-6.7	.9	-7.0	-3.6	.8	5.1	2.8	1.6
Sales/Net Fixed Assets	12.8	10.8	12.4	9.1	14.8	14.1	12.6	9.3	7.5
	6.1	5.4	6.4	5.5	6.6	8.7	9.0	5.2	5.4
	3.6	2.9	3.5	2.3	3.8	4.5	4.2	2.9	3.3
Sales/Total Assets	2.6	2.1	2.5	2.8	2.6	2.8	2.6	2.3	2.4
	1.8	1.5	1.8	1.6	2.2	1.9	1.8	1.6	1.6
	1.3	1.1	1.3	1.3	1.4	1.3	1.4	1.1	1.1
% Depr., Dep., Amort./Sales	1.9	2.5	2.0	1.9	1.6	1.9	1.6	2.3	2.3
	(307) 3.5	(259) 4.5	(279) 3.8	(19) 5.0	(67) 4.2	(52) 3.6	(44) 3.4	(60) 3.8	(37) 4.0
	5.1	6.7	5.9	8.2	6.9	5.7	5.3	5.2	5.6
% Officers', Directors' Owners' Comp/Sales	2.4	2.5	2.4	6.8	4.2	2.2	2.2	1.9	
	(177) 4.6	(138) 4.5	(173) 4.7	(14) 9.9	(58) 6.0	(38) 4.7	(24) 3.0	(34) 3.0	
	8.3	8.1	9.0	14.1	12.3	7.9	7.1	4.1	
Net Sales ($)	4808539M	3883346M	4212257M	14269M	143968M	226211M	353285M	1021813M	2452711M
Total Assets ($)	3407732M	3093038M	2977928M	8213M	85034M	135034M	197837M	809615M	1742195M

M = $ thousand   MM = $ million
See Pages 9 through 22 for Explanation of Ratios and Data

Current Data Sorted by Assets   Comparative Historical Data

0-500M	500M-2MM	2-10MM	10-50MM	50-100MM	100-250MM	Type of Statement	4/1/06-3/31/07 ALL	4/1/07-3/31/08 ALL
	5	12	3		4	Unqualified	22	11
2	8	12	8			Reviewed	52	48
4	4	2	1			Compiled	21	15
1	10	18	1			Tax Returns	17	15
			10	3	4	Other	43	43
	30 (4/1-9/30/10)		82 (10/1/10-3/31/11)					
7	27	44	23	7	4	**NUMBER OF STATEMENTS**	155	132
%	%	%	%	%	%	**ASSETS**	%	%
	6.0	9.6	8.9			Cash & Equivalents	6.8	6.6
	25.4	22.5	22.1			Trade Receivables (net)	26.3	26.4
	22.7	28.8	23.7			Inventory	28.8	27.2
	4.0	.8	4.9			All Other Current	1.6	2.4
	58.1	61.7	59.4			Total Current	63.5	62.6
	33.3	27.5	28.3			Fixed Assets (net)	27.2	27.5
	4.0	4.3	6.8			Intangibles (net)	2.8	3.2
	4.5	6.5	5.5			All Other Non-Current	6.5	6.7
	100.0	100.0	100.0			Total	100.0	100.0
						LIABILITIES		
	11.2	9.8	5.9			Notes Payable-Short Term	12.0	11.7
	9.1	4.7	7.8			Cur. Mat.-L.T.D.	5.0	4.9
	10.2	11.1	10.1			Trade Payables	12.7	13.5
	.0	.1	.1			Income Taxes Payable	.2	.4
	10.3	6.5	8.6			All Other Current	8.8	9.1
	40.9	32.2	32.4			Total Current	38.7	39.6
	18.0	15.2	14.0			Long-Term Debt	16.1	17.9
	.6	.7	.7			Deferred Taxes	.4	.7
	15.8	8.0	3.6			All Other Non-Current	9.2	5.0
	24.7	44.0	49.2			Net Worth	35.7	36.9
	100.0	100.0	100.0			Total Liabilities & Net Worth	100.0	100.0
						INCOME DATA		
	100.0	100.0	100.0			Net Sales	100.0	100.0
	34.8	33.4	29.2			Gross Profit	33.3	34.6
	30.0	26.1	22.7			Operating Expenses	27.7	29.4
	4.8	7.2	6.6			Operating Profit	5.6	5.2
	.5	1.4	1.5			All Other Expenses (net)	1.5	1.7
	4.3	5.8	5.0			Profit Before Taxes	4.0	3.5
						RATIOS		
	2.2	3.3	4.1				2.7	2.4
	1.3	2.1	2.2			Current	1.8	1.5
	.9	1.5	1.2				1.2	1.1
	1.0	1.8	2.4				1.5	1.4
	.7	1.0	1.2			Quick	.9	.8
	.4	.6	.6				.5	.5
37 9.8	43 8.4	42 8.6					37 9.8	35 10.3
49 7.5	52 7.0	49 7.4				Sales/Receivables	46 8.0	47 7.8
57 6.4	61 6.0	66 5.5					58 6.3	62 5.9
27 13.7	50 7.3	50 7.4					37 9.9	36 10.2
53 6.8	107 3.4	82 4.4				Cost of Sales/Inventory	77 4.8	76 4.8
84 4.4	175 2.1	195 1.9					129 2.8	128 2.9
18 20.4	20 18.1	28 13.1					17 21.9	20 17.9
30 12.0	37 10.0	34 10.7				Cost of Sales/Payables	28 13.3	32 11.4
40 9.0	46 7.9	49 7.5					44 8.3	47 7.8
	6.6	2.6	2.5				4.7	5.2
	14.3	5.0	4.8			Sales/Working Capital	7.5	10.2
	-28.9	9.9	13.7				17.0	24.2
	5.8	10.8	22.3				7.4	6.9
(25) 2.5	(40) 3.7	(21) 5.4				EBIT/Interest	(142) 2.8	(117) 2.2
	.9	1.7	2.2				1.0	.9
		3.3					3.9	2.2
	(14) 1.8					Net Profit + Depr., Dep., Amort./Cur. Mat. L/T/D	(53) 2.1	(42) 1.3
		.6					1.1	.7
	.3	.2	.4				.4	.3
	1.5	.9	.6			Fixed/Worth	.7	.7
	6.5	1.4	1.2				1.7	1.6
	.9	.6	.3				.7	.9
	3.2	1.7	1.2			Debt/Worth	1.7	1.8
	9.6	3.9	3.3				5.1	4.6
	71.6	51.7	32.6				29.8	35.4
	(22) 10.4	(40) 21.9	(22) 16.7			% Profit Before Taxes/Tangible Net Worth	(140) 16.1	(115) 14.4
	-2.1	3.5	6.4				1.3	.1
	14.7	15.2	11.8				14.7	13.9
	3.3	5.3	8.8			% Profit Before Taxes/Total Assets	4.7	4.9
	-.9	1.3	4.6				.2	-.2
	13.7	16.1	9.4				15.9	17.2
	6.9	5.6	4.5			Sales/Net Fixed Assets	7.1	8.1
	4.1	3.1	3.2				4.6	4.3
	2.6	1.9	1.7				2.5	2.5
	1.9	1.6	1.3			Sales/Total Assets	1.9	2.0
	1.3	1.2	1.0				1.5	1.4
	2.3	1.3	1.8				1.4	1.2
	(23) 4.0	(43) 2.4	(21) 3.3			% Depr., Dep., Amort./Sales	(141) 2.8	(117) 2.6
	7.3	4.7	4.9				4.2	4.9
	6.5	1.3					3.2	2.5
	(14) 8.3	(18) 3.2				% Officers', Directors' Owners' Comp/Sales	(64) 4.6	(52) 5.4
	10.6	6.3					8.1	8.1
7285M	57711M	357737M	704960M	718599M	631501M	Net Sales ($)	3489318M	2657695M
1538M	30065M	238745M	526090M	520654M	700667M	Total Assets ($)	2202379M	1623446M

M = $ thousand   MM = $ million
See Pages 9 through 22 for Explanation of Ratios and Data

Comparative Historical Data | Current Data Sorted by Sales

Type of Statement	15	13	7					2	5
Unqualified	15	13	7					2	5
Reviewed	41	31	25		4	2	6	10	3
Compiled	22	29	23	1	11	4	5	1	1
Tax Returns	13	15	11	3	3	3	1	1	
Other	36	47	46	3	10	4	6	10	13
	4/1/08-3/31/09 ALL	4/1/09-3/31/10 ALL	4/1/10-3/31/11 ALL	30 (4/1-9/30/10)			82 (10/1/10-3/31/11)		
				0-1MM	1-3MM	3-5MM	5-10MM	10-25MM	25MM & OVER
NUMBER OF STATEMENTS	127	135	112	7	28	13	18	24	22
ASSETS	%	%	%	%	%	%	%	%	%
Cash & Equivalents	7.4	8.7	8.4		9.6	4.5	13.8	7.1	6.7
Trade Receivables (net)	23.5	21.2	23.9		23.8	31.3	22.5	24.8	20.6
Inventory	31.0	27.1	24.9		24.0	21.4	26.8	26.6	25.2
All Other Current	1.7	3.0	2.5		2.2	1.9	.5	3.7	3.0
Total Current	63.6	60.0	59.7		59.7	59.1	63.7	62.2	55.5
Fixed Assets (net)	28.0	26.3	28.3		34.4	29.0	23.1	30.8	25.4
Intangibles (net)	2.4	6.0	5.4		3.0	6.0	5.1	3.5	8.9
All Other Non-Current	5.9	7.7	6.6		2.9	5.9	8.1	3.6	10.2
Total	100.0	100.0	100.0		100.0	100.0	100.0	100.0	100.0
LIABILITIES									
Notes Payable-Short Term	13.0	11.0	9.7		13.5	7.6	9.4	11.2	4.1
Cur. Mat.-L.T.D.	5.1	5.4	5.9		6.2	7.3	4.0	7.3	5.4
Trade Payables	11.1	9.7	11.7		10.9	11.0	8.5	13.2	9.6
Income Taxes Payable	.2	.1	.1		.0	.0	.2	.1	.1
All Other Current	8.1	8.5	8.4		9.1	6.0	5.4	9.6	10.0
Total Current	37.5	34.7	35.8		39.7	32.0	27.5	41.4	29.1
Long-Term Debt	15.8	16.3	16.2		16.9	18.1	13.2	13.6	15.7
Deferred Taxes	.8	.8	.7		.5	.3	1.2	.9	.8
All Other Non-Current	8.1	12.6	9.5		17.4	8.5	7.1	1.4	9.2
Net Worth	37.8	35.5	37.8		25.5	41.1	51.0	42.7	45.1
Total Liabilities & Net Worth	100.0	100.0	100.0		100.0	100.0	100.0	100.0	100.0
INCOME DATA									
Net Sales	100.0	100.0	100.0		100.0	100.0	100.0	100.0	100.0
Gross Profit	33.6	33.5	34.3		36.3	28.1	36.0	31.5	30.6
Operating Expenses	28.9	33.6	28.0		31.7	21.7	27.8	24.7	24.7
Operating Profit	4.7	-.1	6.2		4.6	6.4	8.2	6.8	5.9
All Other Expenses (net)	1.1	1.7	1.3		.6	1.1	1.8	1.1	1.9
Profit Before Taxes	3.6	-1.8	5.0		4.0	5.3	6.4	5.7	4.0

RATIOS

Ratio	H 08-09	H 09-10	H 10-11	0-1MM	1-3MM	3-5MM	5-10MM	10-25MM	25MM & OVER
Current	2.8	3.4	3.1		2.9	3.8	4.7	2.4	4.1
	1.7	1.8	1.7		1.6	2.4	2.2	1.6	2.0
	1.2	1.2	1.2		1.1	1.1	1.7	1.2	1.2
Quick	1.4	1.8	1.5		1.8	2.0	2.7	1.2	2.2
	.8	.8	.9		.9	1.3	1.2	.8	1.1
	.5	.5	.6		.6	.9	.7	.5	.6
Sales/Receivables	32 11.4	36 10.0	42 8.7		36 10.0	43 8.5	42 8.7	40 9.2	47 7.8
	41 9.0	48 7.6	50 7.3		50 7.3	59 6.2	47 7.8	54 6.8	52 7.1
	50 7.3	62 5.9	62 5.9		57 6.5	86 4.3	56 6.5	70 5.2	63 5.8
Cost of Sales/Inventory	37 9.9	39 9.3	38 9.6		25 14.7	23 16.0	36 10.2	53 6.8	53 6.9
	84 4.4	99 3.7	76 4.8		55 6.6	42 8.7	81 4.5	98 3.7	82 4.4
	145 2.5	162 2.2	135 2.7		103 3.5	139 2.6	186 2.0	131 2.8	134 2.7
Cost of Sales/Payables	15 25.1	15 25.1	22 16.9		19 19.3	13 27.6	14 25.8	33 11.1	29 12.8
	27 13.4	27 13.6	35 10.5		26 14.0	36 10.2	28 13.2	44 8.4	35 10.5
	44 8.3	43 8.5	47 7.8		43 8.5	39 9.3	41 9.0	54 6.8	45 8.0
Sales/Working Capital	4.4	2.9	2.9		3.7	3.1	2.4	4.9	2.5
	7.6	5.8	7.2		12.0	7.9	3.8	7.5	5.0
	17.7	30.2	18.3		58.4	22.8	11.0	16.2	12.5
EBIT/Interest	9.5	5.7	11.1		7.7	11.9	15.3	10.5	26.0
	(118) 3.4	(121) 1.4	(103) 3.6		(26) 1.8	4.5	(14) 4.2	(22) 4.3	(21) 2.9
	1.0	-2.8	1.4		-.1	1.8	2.5	2.0	.8
Net Profit + Depr., Dep., Amort./Cur. Mat. L/T/D	4.1	1.9	3.4					2.2	11.1
	(50) 1.3	(41) 1.1	(34) 1.6					(10) 1.5	(10) 2.8
	.4	-.4	.9					.5	1.2
Fixed/Worth	.4	.3	.4		.7	.5	.2	.4	.4
	.7	.7	.9		1.5	1.2	.6	.8	.5
	1.6	2.2	1.8		5.3	134.0	1.3	1.2	1.3
Debt/Worth	.8	.6	.6		1.0	.5	.3	.9	.3
	1.6	1.6	1.8		3.3	2.6	1.3	1.8	1.3
	4.2	9.0	4.2		19.3	233.8	3.3	2.4	3.9
% Profit Before Taxes/Tangible Net Worth	39.2	16.0	39.9		71.4	67.3	62.8	35.6	16.9
	(116) 15.4	(113) 3.6	(96) 15.9		(22) 4.1	(11) 33.6	27.1	(23) 19.9	(19) 13.4
	1.8	-13.0	3.3		-6.1	7.0	8.7	6.6	2.6
% Profit Before Taxes/Total Assets	14.6	6.1	14.5		15.7	18.5	22.7	13.4	10.9
	6.2	.8	5.3		2.8	5.4	8.3	7.7	4.5
	.2	-5.9	.7		-3.2	1.1	3.6	2.1	-.1
Sales/Net Fixed Assets	15.9	14.7	14.5		13.5	26.6	21.5	10.2	10.4
	7.3	6.9	5.8		5.5	6.2	14.1	4.4	4.7
	4.2	3.3	3.6		2.6	3.5	4.1	3.9	3.3
Sales/Total Assets	2.4	1.9	2.0		2.7	3.1	2.1	1.9	1.9
	1.9	1.4	1.6		1.7	2.1	1.8	1.5	1.3
	1.4	1.0	1.1		1.2	.9	1.4	1.2	1.0
% Depr., Dep., Amort./Sales	1.3	1.7	1.7		2.2	.8	1.3	1.5	2.0
	(118) 2.9	(121) 3.6	(102) 3.1		(26) 4.0	(12) 1.6	2.0	(23) 3.6	(20) 2.9
	4.9	5.8	5.3		7.0	6.4	4.4	5.4	4.0
% Officers', Directors', Owners' Comp/Sales	2.3	2.8	2.5		4.8				
	(57) 4.7	(57) 5.9	(42) 6.7		(18) 8.9				
	9.2	9.6	9.9		11.1				
Net Sales ($)	1993863M	2146988M	2477793M	4594M	55179M	50967M	134884M	393449M	1838720M
Total Assets ($)	1371120M	1777538M	2017759M	6692M	42828M	39212M	89901M	273007M	1566119M

M = $ thousand   MM = $ million
See Pages 9 through 22 for Explanation of Ratios and Data

Current Data Sorted by Assets   Comparative Historical Data

Type of Statement

	0-500M	500M-2MM	2-10MM	10-50MM	50-100MM	100-250MM	Type of Statement	4/1/06-3/31/07 ALL	4/1/07-3/31/08 ALL
		7	2	2	1	3	Unqualified	5	5
		3	10	7			Reviewed	24	19
	1	8	5				Compiled	10	12
	3	5	4				Tax Returns	12	7
	3		9	3	1		Other	26	18

Current period splits: 14 (4/1-9/30/10)   63 (10/1/10-3/31/11)

	0-500M	500M-2MM	2-10MM	10-50MM	50-100MM	100-250MM		4/1/06-3/31/07 ALL	4/1/07-3/31/08 ALL
	7	23	30	12	2	3	NUMBER OF STATEMENTS	77	61
	%	%	%	%	%	%		%	%
		19.2	13.1	10.2			Cash & Equivalents	10.3	6.7
		25.9	22.1	13.9			Trade Receivables (net)	28.5	27.8
		15.4	29.4	18.1			Inventory	24.8	25.4
		5.8	3.8	18.5			All Other Current	3.4	4.3
		66.2	68.4	60.7			Total Current	66.9	64.2
		26.5	22.1	23.7			Fixed Assets (net)	23.0	25.9
		1.5	3.7	10.3			Intangibles (net)	5.7	6.7
		5.7	5.7	5.3			All Other Non-Current	4.4	3.2
		100.0	100.0	100.0			Total	100.0	100.0
							LIABILITIES		
		12.2	5.6	2.8			Notes Payable-Short Term	10.6	9.9
		4.3	4.9	3.4			Cur. Mat.-L.T.D.	5.1	6.3
		16.9	12.6	12.5			Trade Payables	14.0	10.7
		.1	.1	.3			Income Taxes Payable	.4	.1
		11.9	12.8	9.4			All Other Current	12.5	12.6
		45.3	36.1	28.4			Total Current	42.5	39.6
		21.9	16.7	14.0			Long-Term Debt	15.8	19.2
		.1	.1	.6			Deferred Taxes	.5	.2
		8.3	6.0	4.7			All Other Non-Current	6.9	8.2
		24.3	41.1	52.3			Net Worth	34.3	32.8
		100.0	100.0	100.0			Total Liabilities & Net Worth	100.0	100.0
							INCOME DATA		
		100.0	100.0	100.0			Net Sales	100.0	100.0
		28.3	29.8	28.4			Gross Profit	30.9	29.5
		27.5	24.5	16.4			Operating Expenses	24.9	25.9
		.8	5.3	11.9			Operating Profit	6.0	3.6
		1.0	1.0	.3			All Other Expenses (net)	1.4	1.8
		-.3	4.2	11.6			Profit Before Taxes	4.6	1.8
							RATIOS		
		3.0	4.1	5.8			Current	2.7	2.8
		1.4	1.9	3.0				1.6	1.9
		1.1	1.2	1.2				1.1	1.1
		2.9	1.6	2.3			Quick	1.6	1.5
		1.0	.9	1.3				.9	.9
		.5	.6	.5				.6	.6
		24 15.2	24 15.0	21 17.5			Sales/Receivables	33 11.2 40 9.1	
		48 7.6	40 9.0	41 8.9				46 7.9 52 7.1	
		57 6.4	50 7.2	82 4.4				62 5.8 65 5.6	
		6 59.4	19 19.3	9 38.5			Cost of Sales/Inventory	18 20.1 23 15.8	
		32 11.4	69 5.3	103 3.5				64 5.7 71 5.1	
		65 5.6	123 3.0	155 2.4				109 3.3 129 2.8	
		8 46.0	16 23.5	16 22.6			Cost of Sales/Payables	18 20.5 14 25.8	
		28 13.1	25 14.4	31 11.6				30 12.0 27 13.6	
		59 6.2	43 8.5	58 6.3				49 7.5 46 8.0	
		4.9	3.1	1.5			Sales/Working Capital	4.5	4.5
		9.8	6.0	2.6				8.4	6.6
		56.3	23.4	13.4				28.9	27.4
		6.8	17.8	107.7			EBIT/Interest	13.8	11.2
		(21) 2.2	(26) 4.2	(10) 19.7				(70) 3.3 (55) 2.9	
		-1.2	1.2	4.1				.7	.8
							Net Profit + Depr., Dep., Amort./Cur. Mat. L/T/D	3.2	11.3
								(19) 2.0 (14) 2.5	
								.6	.7
		.4	.1	.2			Fixed/Worth	.2	.3
		1.0	.3	.4				.6	.9
		-5.3	1.0	1.4				-8.2	17.8
		.8	.4	.3			Debt/Worth	.7	.8
		2.4	1.0	1.3				1.6	2.0
		-63.7	3.6	3.2				-25.7	99.4
		49.0	37.2	30.0			% Profit Before Taxes/Tangible Net Worth	50.3	35.7
		(17) 18.0	(27) 16.9	(11) 13.5				(56) 21.7 (47) 14.3	
		.7	2.3	8.5				4.5	3.1
		14.7	16.5	12.8			% Profit Before Taxes/Total Assets	19.2	13.0
		2.8	5.9	8.0				8.2	4.4
		-1.4	.5	4.2				.1	-.5
		50.8	53.6	34.2			Sales/Net Fixed Assets	34.2	31.6
		18.4	8.9	3.7				12.9	7.3
		2.9	5.7	1.6				4.4	4.2
		3.8	2.5	1.4			Sales/Total Assets	2.7	2.5
		1.9	1.9	.7				1.9	1.7
		1.3	1.3	.5				1.4	1.4
		1.1	.5	.8			% Depr., Dep., Amort./Sales	1.0	1.0
		(18) 2.1	(25) 2.4	(10) 3.3				(62) 2.2 (56) 2.4	
		5.2	5.9	7.1				5.0	4.7
		3.8					% Officers', Directors' Owners' Comp/Sales	2.8	2.0
		(12) 5.5						(33) 5.2 (21) 4.6	
		8.4						8.5	8.1
	8768M	75411M	278824M	212967M	172484M	646269M	Net Sales ($)	1598746M	939716M
	2476M	28661M	143804M	246538M	138107M	510859M	Total Assets ($)	1070429M	705096M

M = $ thousand   MM = $ million
See Pages 9 through 22 for Explanation of Ratios and Data

Comparative Historical Data | Current Data Sorted by Sales

10	7	8	Type of Statement				1	2	5
10	7	8	Unqualified				1	2	5
21	12	24	Reviewed	1	4	3	7	8	1
16	13	9	Compiled	1	1	4	1	2	
8	13	15	Tax Returns	2	6	4	2	1	
27	26	21	Other	2	7	1	6	3	2
4/1/08-3/31/09 ALL	4/1/09-3/31/10 ALL	4/1/10-3/31/11 ALL		0-1MM	14 (4/1-9/30/10) 1-3MM	3-5MM	63 (10/1/10-3/31/11) 5-10MM	10-25MM	25MM & OVER
82	71	77	**NUMBER OF STATEMENTS**	6	18	12	17	16	8
%	%	%	**ASSETS**	%	%	%	%	%	%
7.1	13.0	15.6	Cash & Equivalents		25.4	17.9	10.1	14.8	
24.5	21.8	23.1	Trade Receivables (net)		22.2	23.2	20.1	27.0	
28.2	21.2	21.0	Inventory		17.3	19.2	28.0	19.7	
4.4	4.7	6.3	All Other Current		2.4	1.9	7.8	7.8	
64.3	60.7	66.1	Total Current		67.4	62.2	66.0	69.4	
22.8	28.9	22.8	Fixed Assets (net)		22.5	30.0	23.7	20.7	
6.4	5.8	5.2	Intangibles (net)		4.4	1.8	4.3	5.7	
6.5	4.6	5.9	All Other Non-Current		5.7	6.0	6.0	4.3	
100.0	100.0	100.0	Total		100.0	100.0	100.0	100.0	
			LIABILITIES						
7.5	8.1	7.1	Notes Payable-Short Term		9.9	7.0	6.3	4.9	
5.0	4.0	4.0	Cur. Mat.-L.T.D.		5.1	4.2	4.7	3.9	
11.1	12.4	14.0	Trade Payables		15.1	9.4	12.5	23.3	
.2	.1	.1	Income Taxes Payable		.1	.0	.1	.1	
13.8	13.9	11.9	All Other Current		14.5	5.1	9.1	14.1	
37.7	38.4	37.2	Total Current		44.7	25.8	32.8	46.3	
17.6	24.7	22.3	Long-Term Debt		46.5	13.5	23.0	9.9	
.3	.2	.3	Deferred Taxes		.1	.1	.1	.2	
8.6	9.3	6.8	All Other Non-Current		6.8	3.3	5.2	2.4	
35.9	27.3	33.5	Net Worth		2.0	57.3	38.9	41.2	
100.0	100.0	100.0	Total Liabilities & Net Worth		100.0	100.0	100.0	100.0	
			INCOME DATA						
100.0	100.0	100.0	Net Sales		100.0	100.0	100.0	100.0	
30.9	32.4	30.7	Gross Profit		27.8	32.3	28.5	26.9	
24.6	30.3	25.9	Operating Expenses		28.2	27.0	20.3	19.8	
6.3	2.1	4.8	Operating Profit		-.4	5.3	8.3	7.1	
1.2	1.5	.8	All Other Expenses (net)		.2	1.0	.9	.8	
5.1	.5	4.1	Profit Before Taxes		-.6	4.3	7.4	6.3	
			RATIOS						
3.0	4.3	3.7	Current		3.3	6.9	3.2	3.8	
1.8	1.9	1.6			1.5	2.1	2.0	1.4	
1.2	1.1	1.2			1.1	1.3	1.2	1.1	
1.4	1.9	1.9	Quick		2.9	2.4	1.5	2.2	
.9	1.0	1.0			1.2	1.3	1.0	.9	
.6	.6	.6			.4	1.0	.5	.6	
31 11.6	24 15.4	24 14.9	Sales/Receivables	25 14.6	26 14.1	19 19.3	30 12.2		
43 8.5	39 9.3	42 8.6		39 9.4	51 7.1	33 11.1	42 8.8		
57 6.4	57 6.4	60 6.1		52 7.1	63 5.8	67 5.5	49 7.5		
20 18.1	13 27.4	8 47.5	Cost of Sales/Inventory	0 UND	5 77.2	21 17.4	6 56.6		
78 4.7	50 7.3	45 8.2		37 10.0	22 16.7	97 3.8	39 9.3		
128 2.9	110 3.3	111 3.3		88 4.2	96 3.8	153 2.4	84 4.3		
14 26.9	10 38.2	16 23.3	Cost of Sales/Payables	10 35.6	9 41.5	16 23.1	16 22.6		
25 14.4	21 17.4	29 12.7		30 12.3	23 15.8	23 15.8	28 13.1		
38 9.6	40 9.1	47 7.7		55 6.6	40 9.1	49 7.5	52 7.0		
4.5	3.3	3.1	Sales/Working Capital		4.3	2.6	2.3	4.4	
7.4	7.0	8.0			9.3	8.8	5.2	13.8	
18.7	88.4	22.5			54.9	14.9	23.7	49.4	
11.9	6.8	14.4	EBIT/Interest		5.4	20.0	14.0	61.2	
(71) 4.8	(62) 2.0	(65) 4.0		(16) 1.8	(10) 5.4	(16) 5.0	(12) 6.5		
1.5	-.8	1.2			-2.5	1.4	2.3	1.5	
10.4	6.1	3.1	Net Profit + Depr., Dep., Amort./Cur. Mat. L/T/D						
(20) 2.2	(14) 2.2	(11) 1.5							
1.1	.8	.8							
.3	.3	.2	Fixed/Worth		.1	.2	.3	.1	
.6	1.1	.6			1.6	.4	.6	.5	
2.8	26.4	1.9			-4.1	.8	1.3	1.5	
.7	.8	.6	Debt/Worth		.8	.3	.6	.6	
1.8	1.6	1.4			7.0	.7	.9	2.3	
6.2	236.0	6.4			-9.2	2.1	4.4	3.7	
37.9	25.8	40.0	% Profit Before Taxes/Tangible Net Worth		42.5	35.7	45.3	100.8	
(66) 21.5	(54) 9.2	(65) 16.9		(12) 11.6	13.9	(16) 15.8	(14) 18.1		
7.7	-2.0	2.4			-18.5	1.7	8.3	8.1	
15.7	9.2	15.3	% Profit Before Taxes/Total Assets		12.8	15.6	16.0	19.2	
8.7	1.8	5.9			2.9	3.8	7.5	9.7	
1.5	-2.9	1.1			-8.2	1.6	3.2	4.7	
26.9	23.7	43.0	Sales/Net Fixed Assets		183.4	17.7	28.0	148.0	
11.8	7.7	9.5			24.8	8.6	6.3	19.8	
5.9	3.4	4.1			4.3	3.9	3.3	6.5	
2.7	2.6	2.6	Sales/Total Assets		3.7	2.5	2.3	3.0	
1.8	1.5	1.7			1.6	1.7	1.5	2.4	
1.3	.9	1.1			1.3	1.3	.7	1.5	
1.1	1.0	.8	% Depr., Dep., Amort./Sales		2.0	1.1	1.0	.3	
(71) 2.0	(60) 2.8	(59) 2.8		(10) 3.3	(11) 2.3	(15) 3.4	(14) .6		
3.9	5.7	5.5			6.9	7.3	6.9	4.8	
2.7	2.2	3.3	% Officers', Directors' Owners' Comp/Sales						
(34) 4.9	(30) 4.6	(27) 5.5							
6.7	7.7	8.9							
2005985M	950566M	1394723M	Net Sales ($)	3668M	37829M	44906M	129019M	243444M	935857M
1413567M	922060M	1070445M	Total Assets ($)	4705M	21245M	30968M	131527M	149831M	732169M

M = $ thousand   MM = $ million
See Pages 9 through 22 for Explanation of Ratios and Data

Current Data Sorted by Assets / Comparative Historical Data

0-500M	500M-2MM	2-10MM	10-50MM	50-100MM	100-250MM		4/1/06-3/31/07 ALL	4/1/07-3/31/08 ALL
						Type of Statement		
		4	4		2	Unqualified	7	7
	3	5	2			Reviewed	9	4
		2	1			Compiled	6	2
		2	1			Tax Returns	1	1
		3	5	1		Other	7	11
	6 (4/1-9/30/10)		29 (10/1/10-3/31/11)					
	3	16	13	1	2	NUMBER OF STATEMENTS	30	25
%	%	%	%	%	%	**ASSETS**	%	%
DATA NOT AVAILABLE		10.1	5.1			Cash & Equivalents	5.3	5.8
		23.1	19.4			Trade Receivables (net)	22.0	23.9
		27.8	34.3			Inventory	30.0	32.7
		2.7	1.8			All Other Current	1.0	1.4
		63.7	60.6			Total Current	58.4	63.7
		28.0	33.7			Fixed Assets (net)	29.2	29.0
		2.8	1.8			Intangibles (net)	4.8	3.5
		5.5	3.9			All Other Non-Current	7.7	3.8
		100.0	100.0			Total	100.0	100.0
						LIABILITIES		
		3.5	1.0			Notes Payable-Short Term	9.6	9.1
		6.9	4.0			Cur. Mat.-L.T.D.	4.3	3.5
		9.3	15.6			Trade Payables	10.4	16.1
		.3	.0			Income Taxes Payable	.2	2.2
		5.9	7.8			All Other Current	10.3	9.4
		25.9	28.4			Total Current	34.9	40.3
		20.9	23.7			Long-Term Debt	17.8	14.5
		.0	1.4			Deferred Taxes	.4	.5
		8.3	11.2			All Other Non-Current	5.9	4.0
		45.0	35.3			Net Worth	41.1	40.8
		100.0	100.0			Total Liabilties & Net Worth	100.0	100.0
						INCOME DATA		
		100.0	100.0			Net Sales	100.0	100.0
		32.1	19.2			Gross Profit	27.6	33.7
		25.6	13.5			Operating Expenses	20.2	24.4
		6.5	5.8			Operating Profit	7.4	9.3
		1.1	2.3			All Other Expenses (net)	1.2	1.0
		5.4	3.4			Profit Before Taxes	6.2	8.3
						RATIOS		
		6.2	3.8				2.1	3.2
		3.1	2.0			Current	1.6	1.8
		1.6	1.6				1.3	1.0
		3.1	1.5				1.2	1.5
		1.6	.8			Quick	.8	1.0
		.8	.7				.6	.5
		41 9.0	**39** 9.3				**42** 8.6	**37** 9.9
		49 7.4	**54** 6.8			Sales/Receivables	**52** 7.1	**52** 7.0
		57 6.4	**66** 5.5				**59** 6.2	**62** 5.9
		55 6.6	**92** 4.0				**68** 5.4	**73** 5.0
		92 4.0	**104** 3.5			Cost of Sales/Inventory	**99** 3.7	**99** 3.7
		125 2.9	**121** 3.0				**115** 3.2	**116** 3.1
		14 25.3	**21** 17.6				**12** 29.5	**17** 21.0
		22 16.5	**40** 9.2			Cost of Sales/Payables	**30** 12.1	**36** 10.3
		46 7.9	**53** 6.8				**42** 8.6	**70** 5.2
		2.9	2.9				5.0	3.8
		4.3	4.5			Sales/Working Capital	7.8	6.0
		8.3	7.6				14.9	NM
		8.9	4.6				8.8	11.3
		(15) 3.8	2.8			EBIT/Interest	5.9	(23) 7.1
		.7	.9				3.1	4.5
							4.9	
						Net Profit + Depr., Dep., Amort./Cur. Mat. L/T/D	(10) 2.4	
							.9	
		.2	.4				.4	.4
		.4	1.1			Fixed/Worth	.9	.9
		1.4	1.9				2.0	6.2
		.5	1.2				1.0	.5
		1.5	2.6			Debt/Worth	2.0	1.5
		3.4	3.4				3.6	33.6
		37.1	33.1				50.8	46.7
		20.0	10.0			% Profit Before Taxes/Tangible Net Worth	(26) 20.1	(20) 27.7
		-1.6	-1.9				3.7	16.2
		15.4	9.2				15.6	20.3
		6.5	2.9			% Profit Before Taxes/Total Assets	9.7	13.6
		-.3	-.4				4.2	7.4
		23.7	15.8				11.3	11.9
		7.4	2.6			Sales/Net Fixed Assets	5.3	5.5
		3.4	2.0				3.5	3.5
		2.2	2.1				2.0	2.1
		1.6	1.2			Sales/Total Assets	1.6	1.7
		1.3	.9				1.2	1.2
		2.0	1.7				2.2	2.1
		2.8	(12) 4.5			% Depr., Dep., Amort./Sales	3.7	(23) 3.0
		5.1	7.5				5.1	4.7
							1.9	
						% Officers', Directors' Owners' Comp/Sales	(13) 5.7	
							8.0	
	10377M	118740M	430517M	52585M	508022M	Net Sales ($)	672328M	909489M
	4757M	67570M	306338M	74642M	406925M	Total Assets ($)	507976M	579729M

M = $ thousand MM = $ million

See Pages 9 through 22 for Explanation of Ratios and Data

Comparative Historical Data

Current Data Sorted by Sales

						Type of Statement						
	12		7		10	Unqualified			1		1	5	4
	6		6		10	Reviewed		3		3	2	1
	4		5		3	Compiled			1		1	1	
	3		2		3	Tax Returns		2				1
	14		13		9	Other			1		3	3
	4/1/08-3/31/09 ALL		4/1/09-3/31/10 ALL		4/1/10-3/31/11 ALL			6 (4/1-9/30/10)			29 (10/1/10-3/31/11)		
							0-1MM	1-3MM	3-5MM	5-10MM	10-25MM	25MM & OVER
	39		33		35	**NUMBER OF STATEMENTS**		3	5	7	11	9
	%		%		%	**ASSETS**	%	%	%	%	%	%
	4.9		8.9		8.1	Cash & Equivalents					9.6	
	23.9		20.5		21.6	Trade Receivables (net)					20.7	
	32.8		29.9		29.9	Inventory					31.6	
	1.9		2.2		2.2	All Other Current					1.8	
	63.5		61.4		61.7	Total Current					63.7	
	23.7		29.1		30.8	Fixed Assets (net)					32.8	
	6.3		3.9		1.9	Intangibles (net)					.9	
	6.5		5.6		5.6	All Other Non-Current					2.7	
	100.0		100.0		100.0	Total					100.0	
						LIABILITIES						
	13.1		11.6		3.6	Notes Payable-Short Term					1.2	
	3.9		3.4		5.0	Cur. Mat.-L.T.D.					4.1	
	16.7		12.0		12.1	Trade Payables					7.8	
	.4		.1		.2	Income Taxes Payable					.5	
	9.1		10.7		7.0	All Other Current					7.1	
	43.3		37.9		27.9	Total Current					20.8	
	14.8		18.3		22.3	Long-Term Debt					22.0	
	.7		.7		.7	Deferred Taxes					1.5	
	12.7		9.6		8.3	All Other Non-Current					7.3	
	28.6		33.4		40.8	Net Worth					48.4	
	100.0		100.0		100.0	Total Liabilties & Net Worth					100.0	
						INCOME DATA						
	100.0		100.0		100.0	Net Sales					100.0	
	29.5		26.9		26.9	Gross Profit					22.8	
	23.0		27.6		20.6	Operating Expenses					14.8	
	6.5		-.7		6.3	Operating Profit					7.9	
	1.3		1.2		1.7	All Other Expenses (net)					1.0	
	5.2		-2.0		4.6	Profit Before Taxes					6.9	
						RATIOS						
	2.7		4.1		3.6	Current					5.0	
	1.5		2.0		2.5						3.4	
	1.1		1.2		1.6						2.0	
	1.0		1.8		1.7	Quick					2.3	
	.7		1.0		1.3						1.6	
	.4		.5		.7						.8	
35	10.6	35	10.3	40	9.1	Sales/Receivables				40	9.1	
43	8.5	47	7.8	52	7.0					54	6.8	
55	6.7	53	6.9	62	5.9					65	5.6	
70	5.2	57	6.4	82	4.4	Cost of Sales/Inventory				91	4.0	
85	4.3	98	3.7	96	3.8					101	3.6	
106	3.4	124	2.9	119	3.1					119	3.1	
19	18.9	11	31.8	17	21.0	Cost of Sales/Payables				10	35.5	
31	11.7	25	14.7	31	11.6					27	13.3	
69	5.3	54	6.8	47	7.7					43	8.5	
	4.9		2.9		3.0	Sales/Working Capital					2.6	
	7.8		4.9		4.4						3.7	
	53.0		32.0		7.2						5.0	
	16.6		5.4		9.0	EBIT/Interest					15.9	
(37)	5.0	(29)	1.2	(34)	3.3					(10)	3.2	
	1.6		-1.7		1.1						1.7	
	5.6		3.5		19.9	Net Profit + Depr., Dep., Amort./Cur. Mat. L/T/D						
(10)	2.9	(11)	1.0	(11)	2.9							
	1.8		-1.4		1.6							
	.5		.4		.3	Fixed/Worth					.2	
	.8		.9		.8						.5	
	3.9		2.6		1.8						1.9	
	.9		.9		.9	Debt/Worth					.4	
	2.2		2.3		1.7						1.4	
	7.1		4.1		3.3						3.0	
	53.3		15.9		37.3	% Profit Before Taxes/Tangible Net Worth					36.6	
(31)	22.9	(27)	.0		12.5						10.3	
	3.8		-35.7		1.3						1.5	
	21.7		9.5		12.2	% Profit Before Taxes/Total Assets					17.6	
	9.3		.1		5.5						4.7	
	2.8		-9.1		.5						1.2	
	20.9		22.6		15.4	Sales/Net Fixed Assets					16.3	
	11.5		6.8		5.2						2.8	
	4.3		2.1		2.3						2.3	
	2.5		2.1		2.1	Sales/Total Assets					2.0	
	2.0		1.5		1.5						1.3	
	1.3		1.0		1.1						1.0	
	1.0		1.6		1.9	% Depr., Dep., Amort./Sales					2.1	
(31)	2.2	(29)	3.2	(33)	3.1					(10)	2.8	
	5.3		5.3		6.6						6.3	
	1.6					% Officers', Directors' Owners' Comp/Sales						
(10)	4.5											
	7.8											
	1689273M		1021026M		1120241M	Net Sales ($)		5888M	18163M	43045M	188117M	865028M
	1159657M		752441M		860232M	Total Assets ($)		6593M	10924M	25691M	143338M	673686M

Note: For the Current Data Sorted by Sales, the columns 0-1MM, 1-3MM, 3-5MM are marked "DATA NOT AVAILABLE" for the Assets, Liabilities, Income Data, and ratio percentage rows.

M = $ thousand   MM = $ million
See Pages 9 through 22 for Explanation of Ratios and Data

Current Data Sorted by Assets   **Comparative Historical Data**

		2-10MM	10-50MM	50-100MM	100-250MM	Type of Statement		
		2	5	2	1	Unqualified	12	11
	2	10	3			Reviewed	10	7
	1	3	2			Compiled	4	4
		1				Tax Returns	5	1
	2	11	4	1	1	Other	15	22
		12 (4/1-9/30/10)	39 (10/1/10-3/31/11)				4/1/06-3/31/07 ALL	4/1/07-3/31/08 ALL
0-500M	500M-2MM	2-10MM	10-50MM	50-100MM	100-250MM			

0-500M	500M-2MM	2-10MM	10-50MM	50-100MM	100-250MM		4/1/06-3/31/07 ALL	4/1/07-3/31/08 ALL
	5	27	14	3	2	**NUMBER OF STATEMENTS**	46	45
%	%	%	%	%	%	**ASSETS**	%	%
		9.2	7.1			Cash & Equivalents	5.8	4.0
		29.0	27.1			Trade Receivables (net)	25.8	27.1
		36.3	30.5			Inventory	30.9	30.6
		1.3	1.6			All Other Current	3.5	4.7
		75.8	66.3			Total Current	66.0	66.4
		18.5	24.1			Fixed Assets (net)	25.4	24.4
		1.3	1.3			Intangibles (net)	2.8	4.0
		4.4	8.2			All Other Non-Current	5.8	5.2
		100.0	100.0			Total	100.0	100.0
						LIABILITIES		
		6.8	5.2			Notes Payable-Short Term	24.6	19.1
		2.8	10.1			Cur. Mat.-L.T.D.	4.2	3.6
		12.8	10.7			Trade Payables	14.2	13.3
		.7	.0			Income Taxes Payable	.3	.5
		11.7	17.6			All Other Current	9.5	12.8
		34.7	43.5			Total Current	52.9	49.3
		9.0	13.4			Long-Term Debt	19.8	15.6
		1.2	.7			Deferred Taxes	.5	.7
		1.5	5.9			All Other Non-Current	6.5	5.7
		53.6	36.4			Net Worth	20.3	28.6
		100.0	100.0			Total Liabilities & Net Worth	100.0	100.0
						INCOME DATA		
		100.0	100.0			Net Sales	100.0	100.0
		31.5	36.1			Gross Profit	33.6	33.5
		22.6	24.3			Operating Expenses	25.7	25.7
		9.0	11.8			Operating Profit	7.9	7.8
		.3	1.7			All Other Expenses (net)	2.2	.9
		8.6	10.1			Profit Before Taxes	5.7	7.0
						RATIOS		
		3.4	2.9				2.9	2.8
		2.2	1.9			Current	1.7	1.9
		1.6	1.2				1.2	1.2
		1.8	1.7				1.3	1.2
		1.0	1.0			Quick	.9	.7
		.7	.4				.5	.6
		37 9.9	49 7.5				40 9.2	40 9.2
		47 7.7	57 6.4			Sales/Receivables	50 7.3	47 7.8
		65 5.6	70 5.2				61 6.0	60 6.1
		67 5.5	50 7.3				37 9.9	42 8.8
		80 4.6	100 3.6			Cost of Sales/Inventory	79 4.6	89 4.1
		180 2.0	139 2.6				143 2.6	144 2.5
		19 19.7	23 15.9				20 18.6	17 22.0
		29 12.8	32 11.5			Cost of Sales/Payables	31 11.8	29 12.8
		47 7.7	53 6.9				55 6.7	44 8.3
		3.2	3.7				3.7	3.9
		4.3	5.6			Sales/Working Capital	8.2	6.0
		8.0	20.5				20.6	14.9
		58.7	22.7				16.6	15.2
		(24) 14.7	(11) 7.3			EBIT/Interest	(43) 6.0	(38) 6.7
		5.2	3.5				2.6	3.3
						Net Profit + Depr., Dep.,	7.4	8.1
						Amort./Cur. Mat. L/T/D	(19) 3.0	(18) 4.2
							1.9	1.8
		.1	.3				.3	.3
		.3	.6			Fixed/Worth	.6	.7
		.6	.8				1.5	1.1
		.4	.6				.6	.6
		1.1	1.0			Debt/Worth	1.7	1.6
		1.5	3.5				3.9	8.5
		42.6	58.2			% Profit Before Taxes/Tangible	36.9	62.0
		24.8	(13) 31.9			Net Worth	(38) 20.8	(39) 23.8
		14.1	19.1				10.8	14.2
		22.0	21.5			% Profit Before Taxes/Total	18.2	16.7
		11.7	12.9			Assets	10.3	10.4
		8.6	7.9				4.9	5.4
		56.6	14.0				21.5	19.4
		15.6	7.6			Sales/Net Fixed Assets	8.2	9.1
		5.2	3.5				4.4	4.0
		2.2	2.0				2.4	2.3
		1.8	1.6			Sales/Total Assets	1.9	1.9
		1.5	1.3				1.5	1.5
		.7	1.5				1.1	1.2
		(25) 2.0	(13) 2.0			% Depr., Dep., Amort./Sales	(39) 2.4	(39) 1.9
		3.4	4.9				4.1	2.9
						% Officers', Directors' Owners' Comp/Sales		
	11555M	270618M	434547M	209895M	314232M	Net Sales ($)	1184947M	1206163M
	4735M	143602M	250543M	171779M	353400M	Total Assets ($)	733707M	811377M

(Left columns 0-500M and 500M-2MM display "DATA NOT AVAILABLE" for the statement and ratio sections.)

© RMA 2011

M = $ thousand   MM = $ million
See Pages 9 through 22 for Explanation of Ratios and Data

Comparative Historical Data | Current Data Sorted by Sales

Type of Statement	4/1/08-3/31/09 ALL	4/1/09-3/31/10 ALL	4/1/10-3/31/11 ALL	0-1MM	1-3MM	3-5MM	5-10MM	10-25MM	25MM & OVER
Unqualified	13	12	10		2	4	4	7	3
Reviewed	7	7	15	1		1		3	2
Compiled	1	2	6				2	2	
Tax Returns	2	2	1				1		
Other	20	19	19		1	1	1	11	5
					12 (4/1-9/30/10)			39 (10/1/10-3/31/11)	
NUMBER OF STATEMENTS	43	42	51	1	3	6	8	23	10
ASSETS	%	%	%	%	%	%	%	%	%
Cash & Equivalents	4.6	7.5	8.8					9.4	7.6
Trade Receivables (net)	25.3	21.3	26.2					28.4	26.9
Inventory	31.8	33.9	33.6					31.6	29.2
All Other Current	3.2	4.2	1.3					1.9	1.1
Total Current	65.0	66.9	69.9					71.3	64.9
Fixed Assets (net)	29.8	21.1	21.2					20.4	25.7
Intangibles (net)	1.7	5.7	1.9					1.7	2.9
All Other Non-Current	3.6	6.3	6.9					6.6	6.5
Total	100.0	100.0	100.0					100.0	100.0
LIABILITIES									
Notes Payable-Short Term	21.0	13.0	6.6					4.9	9.7
Cur. Mat.-L.T.D.	3.8	4.1	5.0					5.6	4.8
Trade Payables	10.0	9.6	11.7					11.7	11.1
Income Taxes Payable	.1	.2	.4					.6	.1
All Other Current	14.7	13.0	12.4					16.3	13.2
Total Current	49.5	39.8	36.0					39.2	38.9
Long-Term Debt	16.9	12.1	12.5					10.9	7.3
Deferred Taxes	1.0	1.1	.9					.8	.5
All Other Non-Current	1.7	10.3	4.9					3.6	6.9
Net Worth	30.9	36.6	45.6					45.5	46.4
Total Liabilities & Net Worth	100.0	100.0	100.0					100.0	100.0
INCOME DATA									
Net Sales	100.0	100.0	100.0					100.0	100.0
Gross Profit	30.4	33.7	33.9					30.6	31.5
Operating Expenses	22.8	29.1	25.3					20.0	23.1
Operating Profit	7.5	4.6	8.6					10.6	8.3
All Other Expenses (net)	.8	1.5	.7					.4	1.5
Profit Before Taxes	6.7	3.1	7.8					10.2	6.8
RATIOS									
Current	2.6	3.2	3.3					3.4	3.5
	1.7	1.9	2.0					1.9	1.7
	1.2	1.3	1.5					1.4	1.2
Quick	1.3	1.5	2.1					1.6	2.2
	.8	.8	1.0					1.1	.7
	.4	.4	.6					.6	.5
Sales/Receivables	33 11.2	34 10.8	37 9.9					38 9.6	49 7.5
	44 8.3	47 7.8	53 6.9					54 6.7	63 5.8
	61 6.0	69 5.3	66 5.5					70 5.2	69 5.3
Cost of Sales/Inventory	46 7.9	52 7.0	62 5.9					56 6.6	92 4.0
	70 5.2	119 3.1	92 4.0					76 4.8	101 3.6
	148 2.5	247 1.5	163 2.2					179 2.0	134 2.7
Cost of Sales/Payables	16 23.1	21 17.4	23 15.7					19 19.7	24 15.3
	27 13.5	29 12.7	29 12.5					29 12.5	29 12.7
	38 9.6	41 8.9	49 7.5					47 7.8	49 7.4
Sales/Working Capital	4.3	2.6	3.0					3.2	2.7
	7.5	5.0	4.5					4.3	6.3
	18.7	13.5	12.6					14.6	14.4
EBIT/Interest	13.3	14.3	23.0					53.1	
	(41) 5.3	(35) 3.0	(44) 8.4					(18) 17.9	
	1.3	-.6	3.3					4.7	
Net Profit + Depr., Dep., Amort./Cur. Mat. L/T/D	11.0	6.3	4.6						
	(20) 4.4	(12) 3.1	(17) 3.2						
	1.7	.8	2.2						
Fixed/Worth	.4	.2	.2					.1	.4
	.8	.5	.5					.4	.6
	1.1	1.0	.7					.6	1.3
Debt/Worth	.9	.6	.6					.6	.5
	1.5	1.3	1.1					1.1	1.5
	2.8	3.3	2.1					1.7	2.9
% Profit Before Taxes/Tangible Net Worth	65.5	38.3	37.2					45.0	52.2
	(41) 20.8	(37) 14.0	(49) 23.4					(22) 24.3	15.4
	1.6	-.4	12.0					14.9	5.7
% Profit Before Taxes/Total Assets	19.3	16.9	19.1					19.7	16.8
	10.8	5.6	10.0					13.0	7.3
	.8	-4.5	5.3					8.6	2.0
Sales/Net Fixed Assets	11.5	24.0	21.7					25.5	14.5
	8.1	6.9	9.8					9.3	5.8
	3.4	3.6	3.9					3.8	3.0
Sales/Total Assets	2.2	2.0	2.1					2.0	2.1
	2.0	1.3	1.7					1.6	1.6
	1.4	.9	1.3					1.3	1.0
% Depr., Dep., Amort./Sales	1.4	1.6	1.0					.9	1.5
	(41) 2.0	(34) 2.9	(47) 2.0					(20) 1.9	2.5
	3.9	5.7	4.5					4.2	4.8
% Officers', Directors' Owners' Comp/Sales			1.3						
		(11)	3.0						
			6.4						
Net Sales ($)	1425466M	1153264M	1240847M	379M	6414M	24688M	61244M	371858M	776264M
Total Assets ($)	844326M	1106907M	924059M	886M	2726M	16439M	28039M	232702M	643267M

© RMA 2011

M = $ thousand   MM = $ million

See Pages 9 through 22 for Explanation of Ratios and Data

Current Data Sorted by Assets   Comparative Historical Data

0-500M	500M-2MM	2-10MM	10-50MM	50-100MM	100-250MM	Type of Statement	4/1/06-3/31/07 ALL	4/1/07-3/31/08 ALL
		2	16	6		Unqualified	21	25
1	2	16	14		1	Reviewed	21	23
1	4	7	14			Compiled	10	17
1	4	14	1			Tax Returns	8	13
	8	12	17	2	1	Other	23	31
	29 (4/1-9/30/10)		101 (10/1/10-3/31/11)					
3	18	51	48	8	2	NUMBER OF STATEMENTS	83	109
%	%	%	%	%	%	ASSETS	%	%
	7.8	10.5	9.6			Cash & Equivalents	6.9	9.2
	22.0	26.3	25.7			Trade Receivables (net)	27.3	28.2
	38.7	35.4	27.7			Inventory	33.8	33.2
	1.7	2.5	5.5			All Other Current	2.4	2.7
	70.2	74.7	68.5			Total Current	70.5	73.3
	20.3	19.0	21.9			Fixed Assets (net)	19.4	18.8
	4.6	1.2	4.2			Intangibles (net)	4.2	3.8
	4.9	5.1	5.4			All Other Non-Current	5.9	4.2
	100.0	100.0	100.0			Total	100.0	100.0
						LIABILITIES		
	7.2	5.7	6.2			Notes Payable-Short Term	7.5	8.9
	2.2	2.9	1.9			Cur. Mat.-L.T.D.	2.4	2.9
	17.1	18.2	9.5			Trade Payables	14.3	14.1
	.0	.3	.4			Income Taxes Payable	.5	.3
	16.3	12.3	12.8			All Other Current	12.0	9.6
	42.8	39.5	30.8			Total Current	36.8	35.7
	25.8	10.2	8.5			Long-Term Debt	11.3	12.8
	.0	.6	.9			Deferred Taxes	.5	.5
	4.9	5.3	3.1			All Other Non-Current	6.3	3.8
	26.5	44.4	56.8			Net Worth	45.1	47.1
	100.0	100.0	100.0			Total Liabilities & Net Worth	100.0	100.0
						INCOME DATA		
	100.0	100.0	100.0			Net Sales	100.0	100.0
	34.7	34.8	33.6			Gross Profit	32.3	34.1
	30.4	27.4	26.0			Operating Expenses	24.6	25.5
	4.2	7.3	7.6			Operating Profit	7.6	8.6
	.0	.3	.4			All Other Expenses (net)	.6	.6
	4.3	7.1	7.1			Profit Before Taxes	7.0	7.9
						RATIOS		
	3.0	3.2	4.1				3.0	3.1
	1.8	1.8	2.3			Current	2.1	2.0
	1.2	1.5	1.5				1.5	1.4
	1.8	1.9	2.3				1.6	1.7
	.6	1.0	1.1			Quick	.9	.9
	.5	.6	.7				.7	.7
	17 21.8	35 10.5	44 8.3				38 9.6	38 9.6
	29 12.8	45 8.1	56 6.5			Sales/Receivables	47 7.7	49 7.4
	49 7.4	60 6.0	71 5.1				61 6.0	60 6.0
	35 10.6	57 6.4	59 6.2				58 6.3	52 7.1
	110 3.3	83 4.4	95 3.9			Cost of Sales/Inventory	87 4.2	87 4.2
	144 2.5	154 2.4	147 2.5				123 3.0	140 2.6
	17 21.8	16 22.1	17 21.1				20 18.6	20 18.5
	38 9.5	42 8.7	24 15.2			Cost of Sales/Payables	29 12.6	32 11.2
	63 5.8	55 6.7	38 9.7				47 7.7	48 7.6
	4.0	4.1	3.0				3.8	3.5
	6.8	6.0	3.7			Sales/Working Capital	6.5	6.0
	24.9	12.8	9.3				10.6	11.2
	20.3	31.4	40.6				36.3	23.2
	(17) 8.1	(49) 7.7	(41) 6.5			EBIT/Interest	(79) 7.1	(101) 6.4
	1.4	2.9	3.3				2.7	2.7
		53.2	12.9				9.1	10.0
		(13) 4.6	(23) 4.3			Net Profit + Depr., Dep., Amort./Cur. Mat. L/T/D	(27) 5.1	(38) 3.2
		2.3	1.3				1.6	1.5
	.2	.1	.2				.2	.1
	.4	.3	.4			Fixed/Worth	.3	.3
	NM	.9	.8				1.0	.9
	.9	.4	.4				.6	.6
	1.4	1.2	.9			Debt/Worth	1.2	1.4
	NM	2.4	1.6				2.9	2.9
	47.4	41.3	30.5				49.3	58.7
	(14) 12.3	(48) 24.7	(47) 14.2			% Profit Before Taxes/Tangible Net Worth	(80) 27.8	(105) 34.8
	5.6	4.6	6.1				15.6	14.4
	19.0	20.5	16.6				21.6	24.1
	3.5	10.5	8.1			% Profit Before Taxes/Total Assets	10.7	12.2
	.8	2.4	3.1				6.2	5.2
	38.3	45.6	14.6				39.0	48.9
	20.8	14.2	8.1			Sales/Net Fixed Assets	12.3	12.9
	6.7	6.2	5.4				6.3	5.8
	2.7	2.6	2.0				2.5	2.7
	1.9	2.1	1.5			Sales/Total Assets	2.0	2.1
	1.5	1.7	1.3				1.5	1.5
	.6	.6	1.4				.7	.7
	(14) 1.4	(43) 1.3	(46) 1.8			% Depr., Dep., Amort./Sales	(72) 1.4	(90) 1.3
	3.3	2.5	3.0				2.2	2.2
		1.5					1.7	1.8
		(24) 3.0				% Officers', Directors' Owners' Comp/Sales	(27) 3.5	(39) 3.5
		6.2					6.5	8.2
4287M	54454M	544246M	1942957M	869827M	481936M	Net Sales ($)	2991531M	2843777M
1171M	23818M	263246M	1163693M	564150M	282781M	Total Assets ($)	1595522M	1680249M

M = $ thousand   MM = $ million
See Pages 9 through 22 for Explanation of Ratios and Data

Comparative Historical Data   Current Data Sorted by Sales

			Type of Statement						
26	26	24	Unqualified		1			2	21
24	25	34	Reviewed		2	1	9	16	6
13	14	12	Compiled		2	2	6	2	
10	14	20	Tax Returns	1	4	2	7	6	
35	38	40	Other		5	2	5	9	19
4/1/08-3/31/09	4/1/09-3/31/10	4/1/10-3/31/11			29 (4/1-9/30/10)		101 (10/1/10-3/31/11)		
ALL	ALL	ALL		0-1MM	1-3MM	3-5MM	5-10MM	10-25MM	25MM & OVER
108	117	130	**NUMBER OF STATEMENTS**	1	13	8	27	35	46
%	%	%	**ASSETS**	%	%	%	%	%	%
8.9	10.2	10.6	Cash & Equivalents		8.9		8.9	14.0	9.2
25.1	25.5	25.6	Trade Receivables (net)		24.9		23.5	27.3	26.4
33.6	31.8	31.6	Inventory		30.3		33.7	29.4	28.8
3.5	3.4	3.8	All Other Current		1.4		1.1	4.3	6.1
71.1	70.9	71.5	Total Current		65.5		67.2	74.9	70.5
20.0	20.1	20.3	Fixed Assets (net)		24.5		24.4	16.6	21.6
4.2	3.5	2.9	Intangibles (net)		6.9		3.1	1.8	3.2
4.7	5.5	5.3	All Other Non-Current		3.1		5.3	6.7	4.7
100.0	100.0	100.0	Total		100.0		100.0	100.0	100.0
			LIABILITIES						
9.8	8.1	5.6	Notes Payable-Short Term		5.8		4.6	4.3	5.7
2.7	3.9	2.6	Cur. Mat.-L.T.D.		6.1		3.7	1.9	1.9
12.9	13.3	13.9	Trade Payables		11.2		17.0	16.3	10.6
.3	.4	.3	Income Taxes Payable		.6		.1	.3	.5
11.0	14.7	13.3	All Other Current		20.5		13.1	13.0	12.0
36.8	40.4	35.7	Total Current		44.2		38.4	35.8	30.7
11.6	11.6	11.5	Long-Term Debt		32.3		13.6	7.5	8.5
.5	.9	.6	Deferred Taxes		.0		.6	.2	1.0
5.5	3.0	5.3	All Other Non-Current		19.2		5.1	3.8	2.9
45.5	44.2	46.8	Net Worth		4.3		42.3	52.7	56.8
100.0	100.0	100.0	Total Liabilities & Net Worth		100.0		100.0	100.0	100.0
			INCOME DATA						
100.0	100.0	100.0	Net Sales		100.0		100.0	100.0	100.0
32.8	34.2	34.7	Gross Profit		36.8		39.0	34.3	31.5
26.2	29.2	27.3	Operating Expenses		33.3		32.2	26.5	23.0
6.6	5.1	7.3	Operating Profit		3.5		6.8	7.7	8.5
.7	1.0	.3	All Other Expenses (net)		.1		.6	.0	.2
6.0	4.1	7.1	Profit Before Taxes		3.4		6.2	7.7	8.3
			RATIOS						
3.2	4.0	3.8			3.6		3.5	4.2	3.9
2.0	2.0	2.1	Current		1.7		2.4	1.9	2.3
1.4	1.3	1.4			.8		1.4	1.3	1.5
1.6	2.0	2.0			2.1		2.3	2.3	1.8
1.0	1.0	1.0	Quick		.7		1.0	1.1	1.1
.6	.6	.6			.5		.5	.7	.7

												Sales/Receivables											

32	11.4	33	11.2	35	10.5	Sales/Receivables	16	23.5			30	12.2	39	9.3	42	8.7
46	7.9	47	7.7	47	7.7		34	10.7			39	9.4	49	7.5	55	6.7
57	6.4	65	5.6	66	5.6		54	6.7			55	6.6	65	5.6	70	5.2
57	6.4	47	7.7	55	6.6	Cost of Sales/Inventory	32	11.4			58	6.3	48	7.5	60	6.1
90	4.1	87	4.2	91	4.0		82	4.4			83	4.4	71	5.1	91	4.0
139	2.6	146	2.5	145	2.5		132	2.8			162	2.3	127	2.9	145	2.5
18	20.0	17	21.7	17	21.4	Cost of Sales/Payables	16	22.8			14	25.6	22	16.9	17	21.6
29	12.7	28	12.9	33	11.1		20	18.4			41	8.8	38	9.7	26	13.8
43	8.4	47	7.8	51	7.2		47	7.8			75	4.9	52	7.1	39	9.3

												Sales/Working Capital					
3.7		3.0		3.2		Sales/Working Capital	4.9			4.1		3.0		2.9	
6.9		5.9		5.4			6.7			6.0		5.3		3.7	
13.5		13.5		11.8			-21.1			13.5		12.8		9.8	

												EBIT/Interest											
	16.4		26.6		31.8	EBIT/Interest		19.3				21.4		56.8		70.5
(94)	5.3	(108)	5.8	(116)	8.0		(12)	5.1	(25)			5.4	(32)	9.2	(38)	9.4
	1.7		1.0		2.8			.1				2.0		4.3		3.1

						Net Profit + Depr., Dep., Amort./Cur. Mat. L/T/D										
	10.3		9.4		16.9	Net Profit + Depr., Dep., Amort./Cur. Mat. L/T/D								8.6		17.4
(36)	3.1	(44)	2.8	(38)	5.1							(10)	5.1	(21)	6.0
	1.2		.9		1.4								3.0		1.3

						Fixed/Worth						
.2		.2		.2		Fixed/Worth	.3		.2		.1		.2
.4		.4		.3			2.2		.5		.3		.3
1.1		1.0		.9			-.2		1.7		.7		.7

						Debt/Worth						
.6		.4		.4		Debt/Worth	.7		.6		.4		.3
1.2		1.4		1.1			5.3		1.5		.6		.9
3.3		2.5		2.1			-2.1		2.5		1.9		1.4

						% Profit Before Taxes/Tangible Net Worth									
	43.4		34.3		34.5	% Profit Before Taxes/Tangible Net Worth						31.7		40.7		30.8
(97)	21.8	(106)	15.7	(120)	18.2				(26)	18.3	(33)	24.9	(44)	20.5
	7.2		3.6		6.2					3.1		9.1		10.6

						% Profit Before Taxes/Total Assets						
17.4		15.3		19.6		% Profit Before Taxes/Total Assets	23.6		15.3		28.4		19.9
8.3		7.0		10.0			4.2		9.4		10.5		11.3
2.5		.0		2.3			-3.0		1.1		3.4		4.0

						Sales/Net Fixed Assets						
34.5		25.2		25.9		Sales/Net Fixed Assets	41.1		18.5		45.6		14.8
13.8		13.0		11.7			12.5		10.9		19.0		8.4
6.5		5.6		6.2			4.5		5.8		6.9		6.3

						Sales/Total Assets						
2.6		2.5		2.4		Sales/Total Assets	3.1		2.5		2.7		2.0
2.0		1.8		1.9			1.9		2.1		2.0		1.6
1.4		1.3		1.4			1.5		1.5		1.5		1.3

						% Depr., Dep., Amort./Sales									
	.8		.8		.9	% Depr., Dep., Amort./Sales		.8		1.3		.6		1.2
(90)	1.6	(98)	1.6	(115)	1.7		(11)	1.7	(22)	2.1	(32)	1.0	(44)	1.7
	2.6		2.9		2.7			3.8		3.2		2.4		2.6

						% Officers', Directors' Owners' Comp/Sales							
	2.0		1.9		.8	% Officers', Directors' Owners' Comp/Sales				.6		1.6	
(30)	3.9	(36)	4.1	(35)	2.6				(10)	2.2	(12)	4.1	
	8.7		8.4		6.0					3.6		6.6	

3850714M	3632628M	3897707M	Net Sales ($)	754M	24033M	31460M	204657M	542573M	3094230M
2306591M	2475141M	2298859M	Total Assets ($)	730M	12616M	17228M	117334M	319863M	1831088M

© RMA 2011

M = $ thousand   MM = $ million
See Pages 9 through 22 for Explanation of Ratios and Data

Current Data Sorted by Assets   Comparative Historical Data

0-500M	500M-2MM	2-10MM	10-50MM	50-100MM	100-250MM		4/1/06-3/31/07 ALL	4/1/07-3/31/08 ALL
			8 (4/1-9/30/10)		**27 (10/1/10-3/31/11)**			
						Type of Statement		
			4		2	Unqualified	6	9
	3	4	5			Reviewed	8	5
2		2				Compiled	2	4
						Tax Returns		1
	3	1	4	3	2	Other	11	12
2	6	7	13	3	4	**NUMBER OF STATEMENTS**	27	31
%	%	%	%	%	%	**ASSETS**	%	%
			8.1			Cash & Equivalents	3.1	7.3
			27.2			Trade Receivables (net)	22.7	22.5
			31.7			Inventory	34.0	30.0
			3.5			All Other Current	4.1	1.6
			70.4			Total Current	63.9	61.4
			18.3			Fixed Assets (net)	22.9	25.1
			3.9			Intangibles (net)	9.1	10.5
			7.4			All Other Non-Current	4.2	3.0
			100.0			Total	100.0	100.0
						LIABILITIES		
			7.7			Notes Payable-Short Term	14.5	10.4
			1.6			Cur. Mat.-L.T.D.	4.6	4.0
			12.3			Trade Payables	12.7	14.4
			.1			Income Taxes Payable	.2	.2
			20.1			All Other Current	11.8	11.9
			41.7			Total Current	43.7	40.9
			9.0			Long-Term Debt	15.5	15.7
			.9			Deferred Taxes	1.4	1.4
			3.5			All Other Non-Current	13.0	4.2
			44.9			Net Worth	26.5	37.8
			100.0			Total Liabilties & Net Worth	100.0	100.0
						INCOME DATA		
			100.0			Net Sales	100.0	100.0
			26.5			Gross Profit	33.7	33.5
			19.3			Operating Expenses	23.7	25.2
			7.2			Operating Profit	10.0	8.3
			.8			All Other Expenses (net)	3.4	2.3
			6.4			Profit Before Taxes	6.6	6.0
						RATIOS		
			2.8				1.8	2.4
			1.9			Current	1.5	1.4
			1.1				1.3	1.0
			1.2				.9	1.3
			1.0			Quick	.6	.7
			.6				.5	.4
			35 10.3				37 9.9	34 10.7
			50 7.3			Sales/Receivables	46 7.9	50 7.3
			83 4.4				63 5.8	65 5.6
			57 6.4				72 5.0	63 5.8
			104 3.5			Cost of Sales/Inventory	93 3.9	98 3.7
			118 3.1				115 3.2	144 2.5
			19 19.4				23 16.0	31 11.7
			29 12.5			Cost of Sales/Payables	33 11.1	47 7.7
			41 9.0				49 7.5	59 6.1
			3.2				4.7	4.5
			4.4			Sales/Working Capital	8.2	8.1
			30.4				14.4	62.7
			37.8				8.4	9.3
			(12) 18.7			EBIT/Interest	(24) 3.7	(27) 3.7
			3.3				1.7	1.1
			7.7					5.3
			(13) 4.6			Net Profit + Depr., Dep., Amort./Cur. Mat. L/T/D		(10) 3.1
			2.9					-.4
			.2				.3	.4
			.5			Fixed/Worth	1.4	.7
			.6				7.5	2.9
			.6				1.4	.9
			1.4			Debt/Worth	3.6	2.6
			4.0				-44.9	6.6
			42.7				92.8	77.7
			30.3			% Profit Before Taxes/Tangible Net Worth	(20) 44.2	(29) 21.4
			13.5				15.9	3.9
			15.0				18.3	16.3
			9.9			% Profit Before Taxes/Total Assets	9.5	8.8
			5.5				2.7	1.1
			27.4				21.9	17.0
			9.5			Sales/Net Fixed Assets	9.5	8.0
			6.1				5.8	5.1
			1.9				2.3	2.1
			1.7			Sales/Total Assets	1.9	1.5
			1.2				1.0	1.1
			.8				.8	1.2
			(12) 2.0			% Depr., Dep., Amort./Sales	(24) 2.1	(28) 1.9
			3.2				3.1	2.9
								1.5
						% Officers', Directors' Owners' Comp/Sales		(10) 4.5
								12.4
2605M	20828M	52523M	547273M	406262M	256499M	Net Sales ($)	552890M	700916M
684M	7604M	36815M	309606M	184429M	631029M	Total Assets ($)	437737M	539778M

M = $ thousand   MM = $ million
See Pages 9 through 22 for Explanation of Ratios and Data

Comparative Historical Data

Current Data Sorted by Sales

					Type of Statement						
	7		4	6	Unqualified					1	5
	4		5	12	Reviewed		1	1	4	3	3
	3		2		Compiled						
	1		2	4	Tax Returns		2		1	1	
	15		18	13	Other	1	2	1			9
	4/1/08-3/31/09		4/1/09-3/31/10	4/1/10-3/31/11			8 (4/1-9/30/10)		27 (10/1/10-3/31/11)		
	ALL		ALL	ALL		0-1MM	1-3MM	3-5MM	5-10MM	10-25MM	25MM & OVER
	30		31	35	NUMBER OF STATEMENTS	1	5	2	5	5	17
	%		%	%	ASSETS	%	%	%	%	%	%
	4.8		9.7	10.8	Cash & Equivalents						11.6
	23.6		22.9	24.4	Trade Receivables (net)						24.1
	33.7		29.7	27.4	Inventory						23.3
	3.4		4.8	2.4	All Other Current						3.9
	65.5		67.2	65.0	Total Current						62.9
	24.8		22.3	18.4	Fixed Assets (net)						19.1
	4.1		4.3	8.9	Intangibles (net)						7.8
	5.6		6.2	7.6	All Other Non-Current						10.2
	100.0		100.0	100.0	Total						100.0
					LIABILITIES						
	14.6		11.4	10.3	Notes Payable-Short Term						9.2
	3.4		3.8	3.7	Cur. Mat.-L.T.D.						1.1
	14.7		11.1	14.3	Trade Payables						13.1
	.2		.1	.1	Income Taxes Payable						.2
	9.1		12.0	12.7	All Other Current						17.4
	42.0		38.4	41.2	Total Current						41.0
	14.0		12.7	8.1	Long-Term Debt						7.7
	1.8		1.5	1.2	Deferred Taxes						1.8
	5.4		7.6	3.6	All Other Non-Current						2.9
	36.8		39.8	46.0	Net Worth						46.7
	100.0		100.0	100.0	Total Liabilities & Net Worth						100.0
					INCOME DATA						
	100.0		100.0	100.0	Net Sales						100.0
	31.6		35.0	36.4	Gross Profit						31.3
	23.9		28.6	28.4	Operating Expenses						22.8
	7.6		6.4	8.0	Operating Profit						8.5
	1.7		.6	3.0	All Other Expenses (net)						3.8
	5.9		5.8	5.0	Profit Before Taxes						4.7
					RATIOS						
	2.5		3.4	2.7							2.8
	1.7		2.2	1.6	Current						1.6
	1.0		1.2	1.2							1.1
	1.2		1.7	1.5							1.4
	.6		1.0	1.0	Quick						1.0
	.4		.5	.6							.7
37	9.8	35	10.6	30	12.4	Sales/Receivables				33	11.0
49	7.5	46	8.0	46	8.0					47	7.8
62	5.9	59	6.2	69	5.3					80	4.5
67	5.4	62	5.9	50	7.3	Cost of Sales/Inventory				51	7.1
97	3.8	92	4.0	100	3.6					107	3.4
128	2.8	141	2.6	124	2.9					134	2.7
21	17.0	20	18.5	18	20.2	Cost of Sales/Payables				19	19.4
37	9.8	25	14.4	33	11.0					35	10.3
60	6.1	49	7.5	60	6.1					52	7.1
	4.5		3.1	3.3	Sales/Working Capital						3.0
	8.1		5.3	6.7							4.7
	64.0		26.0	16.6							33.9
	14.0		19.1	87.8	EBIT/Interest						112.8
(27)	4.6	(27)	5.4	(32)	12.5					(16)	25.5
	1.5		3.1	2.1							5.5
	10.0				Net Profit + Depr., Dep.,						
(12)	2.3				Amort./Cur. Mat. L/T/D						
	1.7										
	.3		.2	.2	Fixed/Worth						.2
	.7		.4	.3							.3
	2.2		2.5	.8							.7
	1.0		.5	.6	Debt/Worth						.5
	2.2		1.7	1.4							1.4
	3.5		3.2	3.2							5.0
	44.7		34.3	40.1	% Profit Before Taxes/Tangible Net Worth						38.9
(27)	20.3	(27)	14.1	(31)	25.6					(16)	21.0
	9.2		4.9	12.2							12.4
	15.0		16.0	15.0	% Profit Before Taxes/Total Assets						11.5
	10.7		6.3	8.0							8.9
	2.1		2.9	2.2							2.6
	18.9		31.3	43.0	Sales/Net Fixed Assets						15.5
	8.9		8.9	11.4							9.5
	4.0		4.0	7.3							6.9
	2.1		2.2	2.0	Sales/Total Assets						1.9
	1.7		1.7	1.7							1.5
	1.3		1.1	1.0							1.0
	.9		1.1	.8	% Depr., Dep., Amort./Sales						.7
(26)	1.8	(24)	1.9	(29)	1.8					(14)	1.8
	2.9		3.4	3.1							3.2
			.8	1.4	% Officers', Directors' Owners' Comp/Sales						
		(14)	2.1	(10)	2.7						
			9.7	9.7							
	1022799M		848497M	1285990M	Net Sales ($)	619M	8121M	8717M	32859M	79523M	1156151M
	853880M		707836M	1170167M	Total Assets ($)	840M	5978M	7385M	17607M	48737M	1089620M

M = $ thousand   MM = $ million
See Pages 9 through 22 for Explanation of Ratios and Data

Current Data Sorted by Assets   Comparative Historical Data

0-500M	500M-2MM	2-10MM	10-50MM	50-100MM	100-250MM	Type of Statement	4/1/06-3/31/07 ALL	4/1/07-3/31/08 ALL
	1		7	5	2	Unqualified	21	26
	3	24	11			Reviewed	41	27
1	6	8	2			Compiled	20	15
1	1	2				Tax Returns	6	4
1	3	20	13	1	1	Other	37	35
	28 (4/1-9/30/10)		85 (10/1/10-3/31/11)					
3	14	54	33	6	3	**NUMBER OF STATEMENTS**	125	107
%	%	%	%	%	%	**ASSETS**	%	%
	11.7	10.0	19.0			Cash & Equivalents	9.5	14.7
	38.1	33.0	26.2			Trade Receivables (net)	32.3	33.7
	26.9	24.1	25.4			Inventory	26.8	22.7
	3.9	3.1	3.2			All Other Current	3.7	3.2
	80.6	70.3	73.7			Total Current	72.3	74.4
	13.8	20.3	14.7			Fixed Assets (net)	17.7	16.7
	.9	3.1	7.0			Intangibles (net)	2.8	3.8
	4.7	6.4	4.6			All Other Non-Current	7.3	5.1
	100.0	100.0	100.0			Total	100.0	100.0
						LIABILITIES		
	18.0	7.6	4.7			Notes Payable-Short Term	9.9	8.8
	5.1	3.0	2.2			Cur. Mat.-L.T.D.	2.1	2.1
	24.2	15.2	11.1			Trade Payables	19.6	17.1
	.0	.2	.3			Income Taxes Payable	.3	.7
	18.0	20.7	17.8			All Other Current	19.4	17.7
	65.3	46.6	36.2			Total Current	51.4	46.5
	12.9	8.2	9.5			Long-Term Debt	12.3	9.9
	.1	.3	.4			Deferred Taxes	.3	.4
	2.4	3.6	9.1			All Other Non-Current	5.6	5.5
	19.4	41.2	44.8			Net Worth	30.3	37.8
	100.0	100.0	100.0			Total Liabilties & Net Worth	100.0	100.0
						INCOME DATA		
	100.0	100.0	100.0			Net Sales	100.0	100.0
	38.7	30.8	30.9			Gross Profit	29.9	29.9
	36.8	26.8	25.1			Operating Expenses	25.2	23.9
	1.9	4.0	5.8			Operating Profit	4.7	6.0
	1.2	.5	.9			All Other Expenses (net)	1.0	.8
	.6	3.5	4.9			Profit Before Taxes	3.7	5.2
						RATIOS		
	1.9	2.3	3.2				2.1	2.5
	1.5	1.5	1.8			Current	1.5	1.6
	.8	1.1	1.5				1.1	1.2
	1.5	1.3	2.0				1.2	1.8
	.7	.9	1.3			Quick	.8	1.0
	.4	.6	.8				.6	.7
	28 13.1	43 8.6	44 8.3				40 9.1	39 9.5
	50 7.3	55 6.6	57 6.4			Sales/Receivables	51 7.2	52 7.0
	88 4.1	72 5.1	71 5.1				67 5.5	68 5.4
	12 29.4	43 8.5	35 10.6				34 10.9	23 15.8
	52 7.1	59 6.2	72 5.1			Cost of Sales/Inventory	58 6.3	56 6.5
	99 3.7	99 3.7	131 2.8				112 3.3	83 4.4
	30 12.2	21 17.7	25 14.5				26 13.8	22 16.8
	40 9.1	33 11.1	34 10.8			Cost of Sales/Payables	40 9.1	35 10.3
	56 6.6	51 7.1	43 8.5				56 6.5	60 6.1
	4.2	4.9	3.0				5.2	4.4
	13.7	8.6	4.8			Sales/Working Capital	9.5	7.6
	-18.3	26.0	8.3				48.8	20.9
	8.5	18.7	32.7				17.2	24.8
	(13) 3.6	(48) 4.2	(27) 3.8			EBIT/Interest	(113) 4.0	(86) 7.3
	-1.7	.1	2.5				1.6	1.8
		14.5	4.9				9.3	18.0
		(13) 4.6	(10) 2.5			Net Profit + Depr., Dep., Amort./Cur. Mat. L/T/D	(37) 2.8	(26) 6.7
		.4	.9				1.7	2.1
	.1	.2	.2				.2	.2
	.3	.5	.3			Fixed/Worth	.5	.4
	-4.1	1.0	.8				1.4	1.4
	.9	.8	.4				1.0	.6
	3.3	1.9	1.2			Debt/Worth	2.4	1.9
	-15.8	3.8	3.4				7.3	5.5
	44.5	47.6	31.9				47.2	63.3
	(10) 8.6	(52) 12.8	(28) 14.7			% Profit Before Taxes/Tangible Net Worth	(108) 22.1	(93) 23.0
	-11.2	-1.5	4.6				3.8	5.3
	13.6	13.0	15.0				14.8	20.2
	3.5	3.1	8.2			% Profit Before Taxes/Total Assets	6.8	9.0
	-.1	-.7	1.8				.9	1.2
	70.4	33.2	22.6				37.3	32.3
	22.2	12.6	11.3			Sales/Net Fixed Assets	15.1	15.7
	10.3	6.6	7.4				6.9	9.1
	3.5	2.5	2.0				2.7	2.7
	2.3	1.9	1.6			Sales/Total Assets	2.1	2.1
	1.9	1.6	1.3				1.7	1.6
	.6	.8	1.1				.7	.6
	(10) .7	(49) 1.4	(30) 1.7			% Depr., Dep., Amort./Sales	(114) 1.4	(96) 1.4
	1.8	2.9	2.3				2.1	2.1
		1.8	.6				2.2	2.1
		(12) 2.2	(11) 2.6			% Officers', Directors' Owners' Comp/Sales	(32) 4.5	(33) 4.2
		4.6	4.5				9.6	6.9
1847M	50365M	600007M	1293055M	622852M	700006M	Net Sales ($)	3615137M	4585537M
804M	19057M	292466M	743294M	412211M	366150M	Total Assets ($)	2155352M	2567486M

M = $ thousand   MM = $ million
See Pages 9 through 22 for Explanation of Ratios and Data

Comparative Historical Data | Current Data Sorted by Sales

	4/1/08-3/31/09 ALL	4/1/09-3/31/10 ALL	4/1/10-3/31/11 ALL	Type of Statement	0-1MM	1-3MM	3-5MM	5-10MM	10-25MM	25MM & OVER
	23	21	15	Unqualified			1	1	1	12
	39	43	38	Reviewed			5	10	17	6
	17	13	17	Compiled	1	4	3	5	2	2
	6	3	4	Tax Returns	1	1		2		
	32	35	39	Other	1	2	2	8	15	11
						28 (4/1-9/30/10)		85 (10/1/10-3/31/11)		
NUMBER OF STATEMENTS	117	115	113		3	7	11	26	35	31
	%	%	%	**ASSETS**	%	%	%	%	%	%
Cash & Equivalents	10.3	11.3	13.2				9.7	12.1	11.8	16.5
Trade Receivables (net)	32.2	26.9	31.3				28.1	38.4	27.3	30.9
Inventory	26.5	24.9	25.1				34.7	20.0	25.6	22.8
All Other Current	5.4	5.0	3.5				1.2	4.8	3.0	4.6
Total Current	74.5	68.1	73.1				73.7	75.2	67.7	74.7
Fixed Assets (net)	15.9	20.0	17.2				18.0	14.6	20.9	15.2
Intangibles (net)	3.6	5.3	4.3				4.0	3.2	3.7	7.4
All Other Non-Current	6.0	6.6	5.3				4.4	7.0	7.7	2.6
Total	100.0	100.0	100.0				100.0	100.0	100.0	100.0
				LIABILITIES						
Notes Payable-Short Term	11.0	11.1	8.1				10.2	9.8	7.5	3.6
Cur. Mat.-L.T.D.	2.6	2.6	2.9				2.3	2.1	3.9	1.3
Trade Payables	16.7	13.2	15.9				19.0	16.7	10.9	16.6
Income Taxes Payable	.4	.3	.2				.0	.4	.0	.4
All Other Current	18.9	15.6	18.9				12.6	22.2	19.0	19.4
Total Current	49.6	42.8	46.0				44.0	51.2	41.3	41.4
Long-Term Debt	10.3	10.0	9.6				13.4	5.3	7.0	11.5
Deferred Taxes	.4	.3	.3				.1	.0	.6	.5
All Other Non-Current	5.2	6.0	5.2				4.6	1.3	4.5	8.4
Net Worth	34.5	41.0	38.8				37.9	42.2	46.6	38.3
Total Liabilities & Net Worth	100.0	100.0	100.0				100.0	100.0	100.0	100.0
				INCOME DATA						
Net Sales	100.0	100.0	100.0				100.0	100.0	100.0	100.0
Gross Profit	29.5	30.1	31.6				39.1	29.3	31.8	29.1
Operating Expenses	24.5	27.8	27.3				35.5	25.6	26.7	22.6
Operating Profit	5.0	2.3	4.2				3.6	3.7	5.1	6.5
All Other Expenses (net)	.7	1.3	.7				1.5	.2	.4	1.0
Profit Before Taxes	4.3	1.0	3.5				2.1	3.5	4.7	5.5
				RATIOS						
Current	2.5	2.7	2.5				2.1	3.0	2.6	2.8
	1.6	1.7	1.6				1.6	1.5	1.6	1.8
	1.1	1.2	1.2				1.5	1.1	1.2	1.4
Quick	1.4	1.6	1.7				1.1	2.0	1.3	1.7
	.8	.9	1.0				.8	1.0	.9	1.3
	.5	.6	.6				.6	.6	.7	.8
Sales/Receivables	37 · 9.8	35 · 10.4	43 · 8.4				40 · 9.0	51 · 7.2	38 · 9.7	51 · 7.1
	52 · 7.1	49 · 7.4	56 · 6.5				53 · 6.9	71 · 5.2	58 · 7.1	58 · 6.2
	71 · 5.1	71 · 5.1	75 · 4.9				57 · 6.4	88 · 4.1	64 · 5.7	71 · 5.1
Cost of Sales/Inventory	31 · 11.9	35 · 10.4	34 · 10.6				45 · 8.0	18 · 20.2	44 · 8.2	22 · 16.6
	59 · 6.2	60 · 6.1	61 · 6.0				97 · 3.7	58 · 6.3	61 · 6.0	56 · 6.5
	109 · 3.4	105 · 3.5	108 · 3.4				149 · 2.4	106 · 3.5	92 · 4.0	114 · 3.2
Cost of Sales/Payables	20 · 17.9	17 · 22.0	26 · 14.1				29 · 12.7	32 · 11.6	19 · 19.6	31 · 11.7
	35 · 10.5	30 · 12.2	36 · 10.2				33 · 11.1	41 · 9.0	27 · 13.7	41 · 8.9
	58 · 6.2	52 · 7.1	53 · 6.9				45 · 8.2	56 · 6.5	39 · 9.3	68 · 5.3
Sales/Working Capital	4.3	4.1	3.9				4.7	3.8	4.2	3.4
	7.4	6.9	6.8				6.7	8.6	7.4	5.2
	29.4	20.9	18.8				12.9	29.1	19.1	8.4
EBIT/Interest	22.8	8.0	17.3				7.6	41.4	22.4	42.5
	(97) 5.1	(103) 2.6	(98) 3.9				(10) 3.0	(21) 8.1	(31) 4.9	(27) 3.8
	1.3	-.7	1.0				-.4	1.5	1.1	
Net Profit + Depr., Dep., Amort./Cur. Mat. L/T/D	9.9	3.8	10.2						6.6	25.7
	(36) 4.2	(34) 1.4	(29) 2.5					(12) 2.3	(10) 4.3	
	1.9	.2	1.0						.2	1.8
Fixed/Worth	.1	.2	.2				.1	.1	.2	.2
	.4	.5	.4				.3	.3	.5	.3
	1.0	1.3	1.0				2.3	.8	.9	1.3
Debt/Worth	.8	.6	.7				.9	.4	.7	.6
	2.2	1.9	1.6				2.6	1.7	1.3	1.4
	6.5	4.1	4.3				3.9	5.2	3.0	7.4
% Profit Before Taxes/Tangible Net Worth	49.5	29.9	40.1					60.5	29.1	47.6
	(100) 21.2	(104) 8.9	(99) 13.9					(25) 24.2	(34) 13.6	(25) 16.8
	5.0	-3.4	2.5					-6.9	5.8	5.5
% Profit Before Taxes/Total Assets	16.5	10.6	15.0				15.6	14.1	15.1	16.6
	7.7	2.2	5.0				3.9	4.5	6.6	10.6
	.9	-1.7	.1				-2.2	-2.7	1.4	1.8
Sales/Net Fixed Assets	36.6	26.3	32.9				98.5	42.8	19.0	26.5
	17.8	12.0	12.6				21.5	13.5	10.0	12.0
	9.0	5.7	6.9				8.0	6.0	6.9	7.6
Sales/Total Assets	2.7	2.5	2.4				2.9	2.3	2.5	2.3
	2.1	1.9	1.8				2.2	1.8	2.1	1.7
	1.5	1.3	1.4				1.6	1.4	1.6	1.5
% Depr., Dep., Amort./Sales	.8	.9	.8					.7	.8	1.1
	(106) 1.2	(98) 1.6	(98) 1.6					(23) 1.4	(34) 1.3	(27) 1.7
	2.3	2.8	2.7					2.6	2.9	2.4
% Officers', Directors' Owners' Comp/Sales	2.2	2.0	1.8						2.1	
	(25) 3.4	(23) 4.1	(28) 2.9						(10) 4.2	
	6.3	6.1	8.6						6.7	
Net Sales ($)	4516392M	3651681M	3268132M		1847M	14259M	45076M	190637M	573484M	2442829M
Total Assets ($)	2479482M	2283906M	1833982M		804M	9329M	24670M	135324M	335000M	1328855M

© RMA 2011

M = $ thousand   MM = $ million
See Pages 9 through 22 for Explanation of Ratios and Data

Current Data Sorted by Assets   **Comparative Historical Data**

						Type of Statement		
						Unqualified	7	8
	2	4	2	2	2	Reviewed	14	9
	4	5	3		1	Compiled	9	11
		1				Tax Returns	7	2
	5	7	3		1	Other	11	16
	10 (4/1-9/30/10)	32 (10/1/10-3/31/11)					4/1/06-3/31/07 ALL	4/1/07-3/31/08 ALL
0-500M	500M-2MM	2-10MM	10-50MM	50-100MM	100-250MM	NUMBER OF STATEMENTS	48	46
	11	17	8	2	4			

0-500M	500M-2MM	2-10MM	10-50MM	50-100MM	100-250MM		4/1/06-3/31/07	4/1/07-3/31/08
%	%	%	%	%	%	**ASSETS**	%	%
	10.9	6.6				Cash & Equivalents	8.3	10.9
	51.1	35.9				Trade Receivables (net)	32.8	31.8
	19.2	31.6				Inventory	28.1	27.8
	2.5	3.4				All Other Current	6.6	5.2
	83.8	77.5				Total Current	75.8	75.7
	11.6	15.6				Fixed Assets (net)	18.1	16.2
	.7	1.6				Intangibles (net)	2.2	2.9
	3.9	5.3				All Other Non-Current	3.9	5.2
	100.0	100.0				Total	100.0	100.0
						LIABILITIES		
	13.8	9.3				Notes Payable-Short Term	8.9	7.3
	2.4	3.0				Cur. Mat.-L.T.D.	2.4	1.7
	26.7	13.3				Trade Payables	18.2	17.5
	.0	.0				Income Taxes Payable	.6	.3
	19.5	12.3				All Other Current	16.0	17.1
	62.4	37.9				Total Current	46.1	43.8
	14.7	5.5				Long-Term Debt	11.8	9.2
	-.4	.9				Deferred Taxes	.1	.1
	4.2	6.3				All Other Non-Current	5.0	4.1
	18.2	49.5				Net Worth	37.0	42.8
	100.0	100.0				Total Liabilities & Net Worth	100.0	100.0
						INCOME DATA		
	100.0	100.0				Net Sales	100.0	100.0
	30.5	30.8				Gross Profit	31.0	30.0
	29.9	28.1				Operating Expenses	22.6	22.5
	.6	2.7				Operating Profit	8.4	7.5
	.7	.3				All Other Expenses (net)	1.2	.5
	-.1	2.4				Profit Before Taxes	7.3	7.0
						RATIOS		
	2.0	4.2					2.4	2.6
	1.3	1.9				Current	1.7	1.6
	1.1	1.6					1.2	1.3
	1.0	2.2					1.3	1.7
	.9	1.0				Quick	.9	1.0
	.8	.7					.6	.7
	51 7.2	49 7.4					38 9.7	36 10.2
	60 6.1	67 5.5				Sales/Receivables	56 6.5	46 7.9
	70 5.2	80 4.6					69 5.3	62 5.8
	24 15.0	36 10.0					27 13.5	34 10.7
	32 11.4	76 4.8				Cost of Sales/Inventory	61 6.0	61 6.0
	43 8.4	163 2.2					87 4.2	106 3.4
	27 13.6	19 19.1					24 15.3	21 17.6
	41 8.8	33 10.9				Cost of Sales/Payables	34 10.9	30 12.2
	59 6.2	49 7.4					50 7.4	45 8.2
	8.5	3.4					4.1	4.4
	16.1	4.4				Sales/Working Capital	6.8	7.7
	43.0	8.5					19.7	16.3
	8.1	10.0					22.0	31.3
	(10) .6	(15) 3.9				EBIT/Interest	(42) 5.7	(42) 7.0
	-13.2	1.1					3.2	3.5
						Net Profit + Depr., Dep.,	37.4	96.3
						Amort./Cur. Mat. L/T/D	(11) 24.8	(13) 9.8
							3.8	3.1
	.2	.1					.1	.1
	.5	.5				Fixed/Worth	.3	.2
	3.6	.6					1.3	.5
	1.1	.4					.8	.7
	5.0	1.4				Debt/Worth	2.0	1.7
	17.5	4.4					4.1	2.9
		21.5				% Profit Before Taxes/Tangible	58.2	56.0
		9.3				Net Worth	(43) 30.1	(44) 40.9
		.6					11.6	19.6
	7.1	6.7					20.0	20.0
	-.1	3.5				% Profit Before Taxes/Total Assets	11.1	12.9
	-11.0	.1					4.6	6.5
	100.3	28.8					50.7	40.6
	40.1	25.5				Sales/Net Fixed Assets	22.6	22.4
	15.7	7.8					10.7	12.8
	3.6	2.6					3.0	2.8
	3.0	2.0				Sales/Total Assets	2.4	2.4
	2.9	1.4					1.7	1.9
		1.3					.7	.5
		(16) 1.6				% Depr., Dep., Amort./Sales	(42) .9	(38) 1.0
		2.8					1.7	1.5
						% Officers', Directors'	2.2	1.7
						Owners' Comp/Sales	(22) 4.4	(15) 3.8
							6.0	5.6
	45437M	158316M	258591M	226946M	677665M	Net Sales ($)	1480020M	1255829M
	13944M	81566M	157623M	122227M	721861M	Total Assets ($)	823648M	744796M

(0-500M column: DATA NOT AVAILABLE)

M = $ thousand   MM = $ million
See Pages 9 through 22 for Explanation of Ratios and Data

Comparative Historical Data | Current Data Sorted by Sales

Type of Statement

4/1/08-3/31/09 ALL	4/1/09-3/31/10 ALL	4/1/10-3/31/11 ALL	Type of Statement	0-1MM	1-3MM	3-5MM	5-10MM	10-25MM	25MM & OVER
7	5	6	Unqualified						6
11	8	10	Reviewed			1	2	3	4
8	8	9	Compiled	2	2	4	1		
3	3	1	Tax Returns				1		
15	17	16	Other	2	5	2	5		2
				10 (4/1-9/30/10)		32 (10/1/10-3/31/11)			
44	41	42	NUMBER OF STATEMENTS		4	8,	8	10	12

(Right-side ASSETS / LIABILITIES data not available for 0-1MM, 1-3MM, 3-5MM, 5-10MM columns.)

ASSETS (%)

4/1/08-3/31/09	4/1/09-3/31/10	4/1/10-3/31/11		10-25MM	25MM & OVER
9.4	16.0	9.2	Cash & Equivalents	7.5	12.3
30.7	23.4	35.5	Trade Receivables (net)	39.2	23.6
28.6	27.9	27.3	Inventory	30.3	24.8
6.2	4.9	4.0	All Other Current	4.2	6.8
74.9	72.2	76.0	Total Current	81.2	67.5
17.4	17.5	15.4	Fixed Assets (net)	14.7	17.9
3.4	3.8	4.3	Intangibles (net)	1.7	11.7
4.3	6.6	4.3	All Other Non-Current	2.5	2.9
100.0	100.0	100.0	Total	100.0	100.0

LIABILITIES

4/1/08-3/31/09	4/1/09-3/31/10	4/1/10-3/31/11		10-25MM	25MM & OVER
10.3	14.3	8.9	Notes Payable-Short Term	5.0	5.1
1.9	2.1	2.1	Cur. Mat.-L.T.D.	3.3	.9
16.4	10.0	17.1	Trade Payables	16.1	12.5
.0	.0	.0	Income Taxes Payable	.0	.1
17.1	14.5	16.8	All Other Current	24.6	11.6
45.7	40.9	44.9	Total Current	49.1	30.1
10.2	9.1	8.7	Long-Term Debt	5.3	9.1
.2	.7	.8	Deferred Taxes	.7	1.3
2.6	2.3	3.8	All Other Non-Current	.7	.5
41.3	47.0	41.8	Net Worth	44.2	59.0
100.0	100.0	100.0	Total Liabilities & Net Worth	100.0	100.0

INCOME DATA

4/1/08-3/31/09	4/1/09-3/31/10	4/1/10-3/31/11		10-25MM	25MM & OVER
100.0	100.0	100.0	Net Sales	100.0	100.0
29.5	29.1	30.1	Gross Profit	23.1	30.4
23.0	24.9	27.7	Operating Expenses	24.0	23.9
6.5	4.2	2.4	Operating Profit	-.9	6.4
.7	2.1	1.2	All Other Expenses (net)	1.2	1.9
5.8	2.1	1.2	Profit Before Taxes	-2.1	4.5

RATIOS

4/1/08-3/31/09	4/1/09-3/31/10	4/1/10-3/31/11		10-25MM	25MM & OVER
3.0	4.7	3.4	Current	5.2	3.4
1.6	2.1	1.8		1.8	2.3
1.2	1.3	1.3		1.3	1.4
1.4	2.5	1.8	Quick	3.1	2.4
.8	1.1	1.0		1.1	1.5
.4	.6	.7		.6	.6
33 11.2	28 12.8	49 7.5	Sales/Receivables	49 7.5	47 7.8
52 7.0	41 8.9	59 6.1		67 5.5	60 6.1
61 6.0	56 6.6	74 4.9		77 4.7	70 5.2
17 21.7	26 14.3	32 11.3	Cost of Sales/Inventory	23 16.0	55 6.6
68 5.4	60 6.1	60 6.1		50 7.4	84 4.3
118 3.1	129 2.8	113 3.2		117 3.1	114 3.2
19 19.0	11 32.1	25 14.4	Cost of Sales/Payables	19 19.0	23 16.2
33 11.2	22 16.8	41 9.0		29 12.8	44 8.3
55 6.6	38 9.6	57 6.4		49 7.5	62 5.8
4.3	3.0	3.7	Sales/Working Capital	3.8	2.5
9.0	6.1	7.3		8.2	4.7
22.0	18.8	15.4		12.4	8.5
34.9	13.9	13.3	EBIT/Interest		154.3
(40) 9.6	(34) 4.2	(37) 1.9			(10) 29.6
3.9	1.0	-.1			.5
	44.8		Net Profit + Depr., Dep., Amort./Cur. Mat. L/T/D		
	(12) 10.4				
	1.6				
.2	.1	.2	Fixed/Worth	.1	.1
.3	.4	.4		.4	.3
.8	1.0	.8		.7	1.1
.6	.3	.4	Debt/Worth	.3	.3
1.5	1.2	1.5		1.0	.8
4.1	3.2	4.9		4.5	3.1
58.8	34.1	28.1	% Profit Before Taxes/Tangible Net Worth		33.4
(41) 35.6	(38) 10.8	(38) 9.7			(11) 13.9
11.8	.9	-4.4			-5.2
21.0	12.7	8.5	% Profit Before Taxes/Total Assets	9.4	13.5
11.6	5.8	3.0		2.2	8.1
4.1	.0	-1.7		-6.7	-.8
34.1	38.2	34.3	Sales/Net Fixed Assets	30.7	22.0
21.6	16.7	17.8		22.1	9.7
8.1	7.2	8.6		10.8	7.1
3.0	3.2	2.9	Sales/Total Assets	2.6	2.0
2.5	2.1	2.0		2.1	1.5
1.7	1.4	1.5		1.8	.9
.5	.9	.6	% Depr., Dep., Amort./Sales		.8
(40) 1.0	(34) 1.5	(37) 1.3			(10) 1.2
1.5	2.5	2.3			2.6
1.5	1.9	2.3	% Officers', Directors' Owners' Comp/Sales		
(14) 2.6	(14) 3.1	(14) 4.8			
5.7	8.0	7.8			

Net Sales / Total Assets

4/1/08-3/31/09	4/1/09-3/31/10	4/1/10-3/31/11		0-1MM	1-3MM	3-5MM	5-10MM	10-25MM	25MM & OVER
1535551M	1402363M	1366955M	Net Sales ($)		9029M	32497M	53287M	146741M	1125401M
805443M	1016205M	1097221M	Total Assets ($)		6186M	13102M	29128M	75157M	973648M

M = $ thousand   MM = $ million
See Pages 9 through 22 for Explanation of Ratios and Data

Current Data Sorted by Assets | Comparative Historical Data

0-500M	500M-2MM	2-10MM	10-50MM	50-100MM	100-250MM	Type of Statement	4/1/06-3/31/07 ALL	4/1/07-3/31/08 ALL
	1	1	7	4	1	Unqualified	17	17
		6				Reviewed	10	11
	3	3				Compiled	10	10
	2	4	1			Tax Returns	8	6
	5	9	4		1	Other	19	29
	11 (4/1-9/30/10)		40 (10/1/10-3/31/11)					
0-500M	11	23	12	4	1	**NUMBER OF STATEMENTS**	64	73
%	%	%	%	%	%	**ASSETS**	%	%
D	8.2	7.0	2.5			Cash & Equivalents	5.6	7.1
A	25.0	20.5	26.0			Trade Receivables (net)	22.8	24.3
T	37.0	43.7	36.2			Inventory	34.8	35.2
A	1.5	3.1	3.4			All Other Current	4.3	3.5
	71.8	74.3	68.1			Total Current	67.5	70.1
N	18.1	18.6	23.3			Fixed Assets (net)	22.8	23.2
O	.5	4.8	4.9			Intangibles (net)	3.1	3.7
T	9.7	2.4	3.8			All Other Non-Current	6.7	3.0
	100.0	100.0	100.0			Total	100.0	100.0
A						**LIABILITIES**		
V	21.9	9.4	18.0			Notes Payable-Short Term	14.4	14.2
A	2.2	2.5	4.2			Cur. Mat.-L.T.D.	4.5	3.9
I	28.2	16.4	15.3			Trade Payables	14.3	15.5
L	.0	.1	.0			Income Taxes Payable	.4	.4
A	14.2	8.4	10.8			All Other Current	16.7	9.8
B	66.5	36.8	48.4			Total Current	50.3	43.9
L	12.0	18.5	11.9			Long-Term Debt	17.3	17.3
E	.0	.3	.9			Deferred Taxes	.4	.3
	21.1	8.7	4.2			All Other Non-Current	4.4	4.3
	.3	35.8	34.7			Net Worth	27.6	34.2
	100.0	100.0	100.0			Total Liabilties & Net Worth	100.0	100.0
						INCOME DATA		
	100.0	100.0	100.0			Net Sales	100.0	100.0
	24.1	24.8	22.0			Gross Profit	24.0	24.9
	20.9	22.9	20.5			Operating Expenses	18.8	18.9
	3.2	1.9	1.4			Operating Profit	5.2	6.0
	.5	.7	.5			All Other Expenses (net)	1.2	1.0
	2.7	1.2	.9			Profit Before Taxes	4.0	5.0
						RATIOS		
	2.5	3.0	1.9				2.3	2.4
	1.6	2.1	1.5			Current	1.3	1.5
	.8	1.6	1.0				.9	1.1
	1.0	1.1	1.1				1.2	1.1
	.7	.7	.5			Quick	.5	.6
	.2	.5	.4				.4	.4
	12 29.9	22 16.5	38 9.6				24 15.5	24 15.2
	32 11.3	41 9.0	45 8.1			Sales/Receivables	37 9.9	37 9.8
	43 8.4	62 5.9	53 6.9				49 7.4	51 7.2
	26 14.1	77 4.7	50 7.3				43 8.5	42 8.8
	83 4.4	97 3.7	71 5.1			Cost of Sales/Inventory	70 5.2	66 5.5
	104 3.5	118 3.1	142 2.6				127 2.9	97 3.8
	13 28.5	19 19.7	20 18.3				15 23.8	13 28.4
	22 16.9	37 9.9	32 11.3			Cost of Sales/Payables	27 13.6	27 13.4
	82 4.4	55 6.7	54 6.7				40 9.0	42 8.6
	5.6	3.8	5.1				6.5	5.8
	14.9	6.3	12.3			Sales/Working Capital	15.3	10.3
	-7.7	7.7	564.5				-79.9	59.0
		6.6	37.3				7.0	8.3
		3.1	5.5			EBIT/Interest	(59) 2.9	(63) 3.2
		-.7	-1.8				1.4	1.2
						Net Profit + Depr., Dep.,	3.5	9.7
						Amort./Cur. Mat. L/T/D	(26) 2.2	(17) 3.2
							1.2	.9
	.3	.2	.4				.3	.2
	1.1	.4	.6			Fixed/Worth	.9	.6
	-.2	-4.0	1.2				4.2	3.7
	.4	.6	1.1				1.1	.7
	5.2	1.9	2.1			Debt/Worth	2.7	2.4
	-3.2	-69.2	4.5				13.4	11.2
		22.8	52.1			% Profit Before Taxes/Tangible	46.7	52.1
	(17) 9.5	(10) 22.9				Net Worth	(54) 27.5	(60) 23.3
		-4.3	6.9				14.8	9.4
	23.5	10.5	17.6			% Profit Before Taxes/Total	14.9	16.7
	4.4	2.8	6.6			Assets	6.6	7.0
	-6.0	-5.1	-7.6				1.7	.8
	89.4	25.9	41.7				29.2	50.2
	22.1	10.1	10.5			Sales/Net Fixed Assets	13.7	13.2
	8.0	6.2	3.4				6.1	6.8
	3.7	2.6	2.8				2.9	3.1
	3.0	2.1	2.2			Sales/Total Assets	2.1	2.4
	2.4	1.4	1.0				1.5	1.6
		.8	.5				.6	.6
	(21) 1.5	(11) 1.3				% Depr., Dep., Amort./Sales	(60) 1.4	(63) 1.1
		2.4	3.7				3.1	2.0
		1.5				% Officers', Directors',	1.5	.9
	(10) 3.1					Owners' Comp/Sales	(21) 3.6	(20) 2.7
		4.4					5.3	4.2
	41702M	221986M	474007M	367937M	95875M	Net Sales ($)	2511599M	2793468M
	14062M	112404M	212077M	269624M	105517M	Total Assets ($)	1127744M	1312721M

M = $ thousand   MM = $ million
See Pages 9 through 22 for Explanation of Ratios and Data

Comparative Historical Data | **Current Data Sorted by Sales**

4/1/08-3/31/09 ALL	4/1/09-3/31/10 ALL	4/1/10-3/31/11 ALL	Type of Statement	0-1MM	1-3MM	3-5MM	5-10MM	10-25MM	25MM & OVER
9	9	13	Unqualified					1	12
10	10	7	Reviewed				3	4	
9	6	6	Compiled			4	2		
6	6	7	Tax Returns		2	1	1	3	
39	28	18	Other		3	5	3	5	2
					11 (4/1-9/30/10)		40 (10/1/10-3/31/11)		
73	59	51	NUMBER OF STATEMENTS		5	10	9	13	14
%	%	%	**ASSETS**	%	%	%	%	%	%
5.9	7.8	6.5	Cash & Equivalents	DATA NOT AVAILABLE		8.8		2.4	5.2
20.4	18.5	22.9	Trade Receivables (net)			17.9		21.1	26.6
38.4	33.9	38.0	Inventory			41.7		44.3	29.2
2.5	3.8	2.7	All Other Current			3.8		2.6	2.4
67.1	64.0	70.1	Total Current			72.3		70.3	63.3
20.6	25.1	20.0	Fixed Assets (net)			19.2		24.4	22.6
7.7	6.2	5.0	Intangibles (net)			5.6		3.0	8.2
4.5	4.7	4.8	All Other Non-Current			2.9		2.3	5.9
100.0	100.0	100.0	Total			100.0		100.0	100.0
			LIABILITIES						
13.8	9.7	13.7	Notes Payable-Short Term			10.5		13.7	9.6
4.8	4.4	2.9	Cur. Mat.-L.T.D.			.6		3.3	3.8
12.2	9.7	18.1	Trade Payables			19.8		15.9	14.1
.3	.3	.1	Income Taxes Payable			.1		.0	.3
15.6	12.2	10.4	All Other Current			9.5		8.1	11.5
46.8	36.3	45.3	Total Current			40.6		41.0	39.3
15.8	16.7	15.8	Long-Term Debt			21.6		15.4	16.9
.6	.4	.6	Deferred Taxes			.0		1.1	1.1
4.1	5.8	10.8	All Other Non-Current			18.3		1.8	9.4
32.6	40.7	27.5	Net Worth			19.5		40.7	33.3
100.0	100.0	100.0	Total Liabilities & Net Worth			100.0		100.0	100.0
			INCOME DATA						
100.0	100.0	100.0	Net Sales			100.0		100.0	100.0
23.6	23.8	24.2	Gross Profit			22.9		24.3	26.3
21.9	23.7	21.3	Operating Expenses			20.8		24.8	18.0
1.6	.2	2.9	Operating Profit			2.1		-.5	8.2
1.2	1.5	.7	All Other Expenses (net)			1.1		.9	.7
.4	-1.3	2.2	Profit Before Taxes			1.0		-1.4	7.5
			RATIOS						
2.1	3.1	2.5	Current			3.0		2.5	2.2
1.4	1.8	1.8				2.1		1.9	1.7
1.1	1.2	1.2				1.3		1.1	1.4
.9	1.5	1.0	Quick			1.8		.9	1.1
.5	.7	.7				.7		.5	.9
.3	.4	.4				.2		.4	.6
18 20.1	**21** 17.0	**23** 15.8	Sales/Receivables			**22** 16.8		**22** 16.4	**36** 10.1
33 11.2	**36** 10.2	**41** 9.0				**57** 6.4		**41** 9.0	**44** 8.4
51 7.2	**57** 6.4	**55** 6.6				**71** 5.1		**56** 6.5	**57** 6.4
52 7.0	**51** 7.1	**63** 5.8	Cost of Sales/Inventory			**69** 5.3		**71** 5.1	**44** 8.3
82 4.5	**90** 4.1	**88** 4.2				**105** 3.5		**88** 4.2	**77** 4.8
141 2.6	**144** 2.5	**113** 3.2				**163** 2.2		**150** 2.4	**114** 3.2
10 35.9	**13** 28.5	**19** 19.1	Cost of Sales/Payables			**15** 23.9		**22** 16.3	**19** 18.8
26 13.8	**23** 16.2	**35** 10.3				**50** 7.2		**38** 9.7	**32** 11.3
41 9.0	**36** 10.1	**58** 6.3				**70** 5.2		**57** 6.4	**48** 7.6
5.4	3.1	4.4	Sales/Working Capital			2.6		4.9	4.4
10.9	7.4	7.5				4.9		7.7	8.4
28.1	23.0	19.9				19.9		23.3	17.1
7.6	6.2	8.7	EBIT/Interest			5.8		9.7	44.1
(65) 1.7	(54) 1.7	(49) 3.4				2.9		2.6	5.5
-2.7	-3.2	-.9				-1.6		-2.4	3.6
7.9	10.6	3.5	Net Profit + Depr., Dep., Amort./Cur. Mat. L/T/D						
(15) 5.6	(20) 3.4	(17) 2.4							
2.2	.3	1.1							
.2	.2	.2	Fixed/Worth			.3		.2	.4
.7	.7	.6				1.0		.6	.8
5.8	1.8	-69.6				-.4		1.8	2.0
1.1	.6	.7	Debt/Worth			1.5		.7	1.1
2.8	1.6	2.3				3.8		1.3	2.9
143.8	9.3	-325.7				-4.7		4.8	8.7
44.7	17.2	42.6	% Profit Before Taxes/Tangible Net Worth					25.2	55.2
(56) 10.4	(51) 6.2	(38) 19.3						(11) 14.0	(12) 34.6
-9.3	-11.0	5.4						-11.6	20.8
11.6	5.8	13.9	% Profit Before Taxes/Total Assets			8.8		11.1	18.7
2.3	1.3	4.6				1.8		4.0	10.0
-7.0	-8.0	-5.1				-6.9		-10.0	5.5
39.0	19.9	29.1	Sales/Net Fixed Assets			37.0		17.4	24.4
12.6	8.4	10.5				8.1		9.4	9.8
6.6	4.4	5.8				4.5		5.4	4.0
3.0	2.6	2.8	Sales/Total Assets			2.5		2.5	2.8
2.2	1.8	2.1				1.4		2.1	2.1
1.4	1.2	1.4				.8		1.2	1.1
.8	1.2	.8	% Depr., Dep., Amort./Sales					1.0	.9
(60) 1.3	(52) 2.7	(46) 1.5						(11) 1.7	2.1
2.8	4.3	2.8						5.5	3.4
1.1	1.8	1.2	% Officers', Directors' Owners' Comp/Sales						
(14) 2.9	(14) 2.9	(15) 2.2							
5.0	4.0	4.3							
3165029M	1940310M	1201507M	Net Sales ($)		10587M	42960M	61306M	187444M	899210M
1566961M	1280121M	713684M	Total Assets ($)		5060M	33895M	23215M	112543M	538971M

M = $ thousand MM = $ million

See Pages 9 through 22 for Explanation of Ratios and Data

Current Data Sorted by Assets   **Comparative Historical Data**

Type of Statement

	0-500M	500M-2MM	2-10MM	10-50MM	50-100MM	100-250MM		4/1/06-3/31/07 ALL	4/1/07-3/31/08 ALL
Unqualified		1	5	9				5	2
Reviewed		6	11	7				13	17
Compiled			3					8	7
Tax Returns	1	4	4					5	2
Other	2		9	9				14	21

Date range labels: 13 (4/1-9/30/10)   60 (10/1/10-3/31/11)

0-500M	500M-2MM	2-10MM	10-50MM	50-100MM	100-250MM		4/1/06-3/31/07 ALL	4/1/07-3/31/08 ALL
3	11	32	25	1	1	**NUMBER OF STATEMENTS**	45	49
%	%	%	%	%	%	**ASSETS**	%	%
	11.7	9.6	10.1			Cash & Equivalents	11.8	8.1
	37.8	22.8	26.2			Trade Receivables (net)	26.6	27.6
	31.8	29.9	21.7			Inventory	26.7	28.6
	1.1	4.9	6.3			All Other Current	2.7	3.8
	82.4	67.3	64.4			Total Current	67.8	68.1
	13.4	20.7	19.7			Fixed Assets (net)	21.3	23.9
	.5	2.7	8.2			Intangibles (net)	2.2	1.9
	3.7	9.4	7.8			All Other Non-Current	8.6	6.0
	100.0	100.0	100.0			Total	100.0	100.0
						LIABILITIES		
	9.2	8.9	8.6			Notes Payable-Short Term	10.1	13.5
	2.2	2.7	3.1			Cur. Mat.-L.T.D.	2.6	2.8
	23.4	9.6	8.0			Trade Payables	13.0	14.5
	.0	.1	.3			Income Taxes Payable	.1	.1
	9.8	10.9	19.4			All Other Current	13.2	13.1
	44.7	32.1	39.3			Total Current	39.0	44.0
	10.6	12.1	4.1			Long-Term Debt	10.5	11.9
	.0	.7	1.4			Deferred Taxes	.3	.5
	5.1	7.3	8.8			All Other Non-Current	5.1	5.8
	39.6	47.7	46.5			Net Worth	45.1	37.8
	100.0	100.0	100.0			Total Liabilities & Net Worth	100.0	100.0
						INCOME DATA		
	100.0	100.0	100.0			Net Sales	100.0	100.0
	35.2	36.4	27.5			Gross Profit	35.6	31.3
	29.4	29.2	21.1			Operating Expenses	28.7	26.8
	5.8	7.2	6.4			Operating Profit	6.9	4.5
	.7	2.5	2.1			All Other Expenses (net)	.6	1.1
	5.2	4.7	4.3			Profit Before Taxes	6.3	3.4
						RATIOS		
	4.0	3.3	2.7				2.7	2.4
	1.5	2.1	1.8			Current	1.9	1.7
	1.3	1.5	1.1				1.2	1.1
	3.0	1.9	1.9				1.6	1.4
	1.1	1.0	.9			Quick	1.1	1.0
	.7	.6	.5				.7	.4
	45 8.2	37 9.8	45 8.2				35 10.5	37 9.8
	62 5.9	55 6.7	63 5.8			Sales/Receivables	47 7.8	49 7.5
	80 4.6	71 5.2	75 4.8				62 5.9	73 5.0
	26 14.0	69 5.3	39 9.4				30 12.2	41 8.8
	84 4.3	119 3.1	61 5.9			Cost of Sales/Inventory	66 5.5	78 4.7
	137 2.7	159 2.3	127 2.9				117 3.1	138 2.6
	27 13.6	20 18.1	20 18.5				21 17.3	16 22.9
	56 6.5	25 14.5	24 15.4			Cost of Sales/Payables	26 14.2	29 12.5
	73 5.0	50 7.3	42 8.7				46 8.0	51 7.2
	2.8	2.9	3.0				3.3	3.9
	9.9	3.9	6.3			Sales/Working Capital	6.5	9.4
	17.1	7.6	NM				12.3	36.9
	68.9	33.2	10.7				15.8	10.2
	(10) 16.8	(31) 6.8	(22) 4.5			EBIT/Interest	(34) 4.8	(40) 5.1
	1.9	2.1	1.9				2.1	1.8
			26.8			Net Profit + Depr., Dep.,	6.1	7.4
			(13) 3.4			Amort./Cur. Mat. L/T/D	(10) 3.2	(10) 3.5
			.9				2.0	1.9
	.1	.2	.2				.1	.2
	.2	.5	.6			Fixed/Worth	.4	.6
	1.1	.9	2.7				.9	1.3
	.8	.6	.5				.6	.8
	1.4	1.1	.8			Debt/Worth	1.3	1.7
	3.7	2.9	6.6				2.6	4.6
	63.3	40.7	25.3			% Profit Before Taxes/Tangible	53.8	57.1
	(10) 17.1	16.2	(21) 10.9			Net Worth	(42) 30.2	(45) 31.6
	-.3	3.7	3.4				10.1	6.8
	22.5	17.6	12.7			% Profit Before Taxes/Total	20.8	18.0
	8.5	6.9	5.7			Assets	9.2	7.8
	2.2	1.9	1.6				3.6	1.9
	51.6	19.2	17.5				39.8	28.1
	25.8	9.4	7.3			Sales/Net Fixed Assets	11.6	9.8
	17.2	5.9	5.1				6.4	4.8
	2.7	1.9	1.8				2.8	2.5
	2.5	1.6	1.4			Sales/Total Assets	2.0	2.0
	1.8	1.1	1.1				1.4	1.4
		1.2	1.2				.7	.5
		(26) 1.8	(22) 2.1			% Depr., Dep., Amort./Sales	(35) 1.4	(42) .9
		2.9	3.4				2.6	2.5
		.9					1.7	1.0
		(12) 3.7				% Officers', Directors'	(14) 3.5	(15) 2.9
		6.0				Owners' Comp/Sales	13.1	6.2
2956M	37454M	232446M	813888M	150773M	220500M	Net Sales ($)	910158M	873289M
857M	15393M	152167M	565002M	76680M	127169M	Total Assets ($)	609185M	455562M

M = $ thousand   MM = $ million
See Pages 9 through 22 for Explanation of Ratios and Data

Comparative Historical Data | | | Current Data Sorted by Sales

			Type of Statement						
5	7	14	Unqualified			2		7	5
14	9	19	Reviewed		1	4	6	4	4
4	5	3	Compiled			1	2		
5	4	11	Tax Returns	1	3	4	3		
26	23	26	Other	1	3	3	5	7	7
4/1/08-3/31/09 ALL	4/1/09-3/31/10 ALL	4/1/10-3/31/11 ALL		\<— 13 (4/1-9/30/10) —\>		\<— 60 (10/1/10-3/31/11) —\>			
				0-1MM	1-3MM	3-5MM	5-10MM	10-25MM	25MM & OVER
54	48	73	NUMBER OF STATEMENTS	2	7	14	16	18	16
%	%	%	**ASSETS**	%	%	%	%	%	%
9.2	11.6	11.2	Cash & Equivalents			8.5	9.4	9.5	11.4
26.0	26.0	27.1	Trade Receivables (net)			33.6	24.8	22.6	30.5
28.7	24.2	26.1	Inventory			29.0	32.4	24.7	20.6
3.1	4.9	4.8	All Other Current			4.0	2.2	6.5	7.2
67.1	66.7	69.3	Total Current			75.2	68.8	63.3	69.7
18.6	21.5	19.0	Fixed Assets (net)			18.1	17.7	21.0	17.6
4.8	4.6	4.1	Intangibles (net)			2.6	1.0	10.3	4.0
9.5	7.3	7.5	All Other Non-Current			4.0	12.5	5.4	8.6
100.0	100.0	100.0	Total			100.0	100.0	100.0	100.0
			LIABILITIES						
13.4	13.0	8.8	Notes Payable-Short Term			9.5	10.9	9.3	6.1
2.2	4.7	2.6	Cur. Mat.-L.T.D.			3.1	3.1	3.6	1.3
13.5	14.1	12.3	Trade Payables			16.3	8.8	9.8	12.4
.1	.4	.1	Income Taxes Payable			.1	.1	.2	.2
8.8	9.4	13.4	All Other Current			9.8	9.9	16.2	22.0
38.0	41.6	37.1	Total Current			38.7	32.8	39.0	42.0
7.6	11.4	9.2	Long-Term Debt			12.5	12.4	4.6	3.2
.7	.7	.8	Deferred Taxes			.0	.9	1.5	.6
6.7	9.1	7.1	All Other Non-Current			11.3	2.0	9.1	8.1
47.0	37.3	45.7	Net Worth			37.4	51.9	45.9	46.0
100.0	100.0	100.0	Total Liabilities & Net Worth			100.0	100.0	100.0	100.0
			INCOME DATA						
100.0	100.0	100.0	Net Sales			100.0	100.0	100.0	100.0
28.7	28.8	32.6	Gross Profit			34.5	34.8	30.1	26.3
23.0	27.2	26.0	Operating Expenses			25.5	30.3	23.0	20.0
5.7	1.5	6.5	Operating Profit			9.1	4.5	7.1	6.3
.7	1.5	1.9	All Other Expenses (net)			3.6	1.5	2.2	1.4
5.0	.0	4.6	Profit Before Taxes			5.5	3.0	4.9	4.9
			RATIOS						
2.9	2.9	3.2	Current			3.5	3.1	3.8	2.6
1.9	1.7	1.9				2.2	2.0	1.5	1.9
1.3	1.1	1.3				1.4	1.7	1.1	1.2
1.5	2.0	2.0	Quick			2.5	1.9	2.0	1.9
1.0	.8	1.0				1.0	1.3	.8	1.0
.6	.4	.6				.7	.6	.4	.6

Ratios with observation counts

4/1/08-3/31/09	4/1/09-3/31/10	4/1/10-3/31/11		3-5MM	5-10MM	10-25MM	25MM & OVER
25 / 14.5	41 / 8.8	41 / 9.0	Sales/Receivables	50 / 7.2	41 / 8.8	35 / 10.4	40 / 9.2
41 / 8.8	62 / 5.9	58 / 6.3		75 / 4.9	54 / 6.8	58 / 6.3	58 / 6.3
56 / 6.5	67 / 5.4	73 / 5.0		93 / 3.9	64 / 5.7	76 / 5.4	76 / 4.8
31 / 11.9	28 / 12.9	43 / 8.5	Cost of Sales/Inventory	29 / 12.5	77 / 4.7	33 / 11.1	44 / 8.4
69 / 5.3	80 / 4.6	83 / 4.4		70 / 5.2	103 / 3.5	115 / 3.2	53 / 6.9
117 / 3.1	146 / 2.5	142 / 2.6		149 / 2.5	169 / 2.2	137 / 2.7	83 / 4.4
17 / 21.4	15 / 25.0	20 / 18.2	Cost of Sales/Payables	30 / 12.1	16 / 22.8	20 / 18.2	19 / 18.8
24 / 15.3	27 / 13.6	27 / 13.6		48 / 7.6	24 / 15.4	23 / 15.9	26 / 14.1
38 / 9.7	45 / 8.1	54 / 6.8		59 / 6.2	36 / 10.2	43 / 8.5	44 / 8.3

4/1/08-3/31/09	4/1/09-3/31/10	4/1/10-3/31/11		3-5MM	5-10MM	10-25MM	25MM & OVER
3.5	2.8	2.9	Sales/Working Capital	2.5	3.3	2.9	3.0
6.2	6.3	5.7		3.8	4.6	7.3	6.5
18.4	34.7	16.0		15.5	7.6	NM	18.5
11.7	5.5	20.9	EBIT/Interest	33.2	12.5	42.2	15.7
(45) 5.3	(44) .5	(67) 6.8		8.7	(15) 5.4	(17) 9.0	(14) 6.9
1.6	-6.9	2.1		3.3	-1.9	2.3	2.8
6.3	2.1	11.8	Net Profit + Depr., Dep., Amort./Cur. Mat. L/T/D				
(11) 4.1	(10) .2	(19) 2.2					
1.4	-2.3	.5					
.1	.2	.2	Fixed/Worth	.2	.1	.3	.2
.4	.6	.4		.3	.3	.8	.5
1.3	5.0	1.1		1.2	.7	2.3	.9
.5	.6	.6	Debt/Worth	.8	.5	.7	.5
1.3	1.5	1.2		1.3	1.1	2.5	.7
3.4	19.0	3.8		8.2	2.5	5.7	6.7
51.8	23.0	45.2	% Profit Before Taxes/Tangible Net Worth	80.0	18.8	66.6	24.0
(49) 25.1	(39) .5	(68) 15.3		(13) 19.7	14.0	(17) 22.8	(13) 13.5
6.5	-23.7	3.5		6.2	-5.9	3.7	6.3
17.0	9.5	15.7	% Profit Before Taxes/Total Assets	17.3	9.8	17.9	13.1
8.1	-.9	6.5		6.7	6.2	6.3	6.3
2.1	-11.0	1.9		2.8	-2.5	1.6	1.9
35.7	20.5	21.7	Sales/Net Fixed Assets	37.7	28.1	19.1	20.9
12.8	8.9	10.3		13.8	11.2	8.3	10.7
7.9	5.6	6.2		7.8	6.4	4.5	6.3
2.7	2.2	2.1	Sales/Total Assets	2.6	2.3	1.7	2.3
2.1	1.5	1.6		1.7	1.5	1.5	1.7
1.5	1.2	1.2		1.2	1.1	1.2	1.4
.5	1.2	1.1	% Depr., Dep., Amort./Sales	.6	1.2	1.1	.8
(44) 1.1	(40) 2.4	(58) 1.8		(12) 1.6	(11) 1.9	(17) 1.7	(13) 2.0
2.1	3.9	3.2		3.3	2.7	4.6	2.8
1.1	1.8	1.8	% Officers', Directors' Owners' Comp/Sales				
(15) 2.0	(16) 2.9	(18) 4.8					
4.8	5.4	6.1					

4/1/08-3/31/09	4/1/09-3/31/10	4/1/10-3/31/11		0-1MM	1-3MM	3-5MM	5-10MM	10-25MM	25MM & OVER
1320905M	1487270M	1458017M	Net Sales ($)	1107M	16611M	54989M	110440M	298839M	976031M
724545M	833306M	937268M	Total Assets ($)	433M	10501M	38772M	76156M	222504M	588902M

© RMA 2011

M = $ thousand   MM = $ million

See Pages 9 through 22 for Explanation of Ratios and Data

Current Data Sorted by Assets   **Comparative Historical Data**

0-500M	500M-2MM	2-10MM	10-50MM	50-100MM	100-250MM	Type of Statement	4/1/06-3/31/07 ALL	4/1/07-3/31/08 ALL
		4	8	2	2	Unqualified	24	14
	2	15	9			Reviewed	25	20
1	1	4	1			Compiled	11	9
1	7	6				Tax Returns	6	6
4	4	16	8	1		Other	22	25
	18 (4/1-9/30/10)		78 (10/1/10-3/31/11)					
6	14	45	26	3	2	**NUMBER OF STATEMENTS**	88	74
%	%	%	%	%	%	**ASSETS**	%	%
	10.6	13.0	14.4			Cash & Equivalents	10.9	11.9
	27.5	22.8	21.1			Trade Receivables (net)	27.7	26.9
	30.9	32.4	34.2			Inventory	32.7	32.7
	1.0	5.8	5.3			All Other Current	3.6	4.6
	70.0	74.0	75.0			Total Current	75.0	76.0
	17.3	16.1	13.9			Fixed Assets (net)	15.0	13.3
	.4	3.7	5.0			Intangibles (net)	4.4	6.5
	12.3	6.2	6.1			All Other Non-Current	5.6	4.2
	100.0	100.0	100.0			Total	100.0	100.0
						LIABILITIES		
	5.1	8.0	3.5			Notes Payable-Short Term	6.6	9.9
	3.2	3.1	1.8			Cur. Mat.-L.T.D.	2.1	3.3
	13.8	17.5	8.9			Trade Payables	16.2	19.5
	.5	.5	.6			Income Taxes Payable	.3	.3
	19.8	25.8	26.5			All Other Current	28.2	24.2
	42.4	54.9	41.2			Total Current	53.4	57.3
	7.6	5.6	4.2			Long-Term Debt	9.1	8.7
	.0	.2	.8			Deferred Taxes	.3	.4
	12.0	4.1	5.9			All Other Non-Current	10.8	6.3
	38.0	35.2	47.9			Net Worth	26.3	27.3
	100.0	100.0	100.0			Total Liabilities & Net Worth	100.0	100.0
						INCOME DATA		
	100.0	100.0	100.0			Net Sales	100.0	100.0
	46.0	33.3	28.4			Gross Profit	31.4	30.6
	40.7	28.8	22.3			Operating Expenses	27.7	26.7
	5.3	4.6	6.1			Operating Profit	3.7	3.8
	.2	.9	.3			All Other Expenses (net)	.5	.7
	5.1	3.7	5.7			Profit Before Taxes	3.2	3.2
						RATIOS		
	3.2	2.1	2.8			Current	2.2	2.1
	2.1	1.4	1.9				1.6	1.4
	.9	1.0	1.3				1.2	1.1
	2.3	1.2	1.3			Quick	1.0	1.0
	.8	.7	1.0				.7	.7
	.4	.4	.5				.5	.5
19	18.9	30 12.1	27 13.5			Sales/Receivables	33 11.2	29 12.8
36	10.0	38 9.6	46 8.0				42 8.6	41 9.0
52	7.0	52 7.0	64 5.7				54 6.7	56 6.5
21	17.1	53 6.9	55 6.7			Cost of Sales/Inventory	43 8.5	42 8.6
53	6.9	83 4.4	107 3.4				84 4.4	86 4.3
145	2.5	137 2.7	148 2.5				127 2.9	137 2.7
11	33.8	18 20.0	13 28.3			Cost of Sales/Payables	17 21.8	15 23.9
38	9.6	36 10.1	23 16.2				28 12.9	32 11.3
78	4.7	63 5.8	32 11.3				51 7.2	49 7.4
	4.9	3.8	3.2			Sales/Working Capital	4.7	4.6
	10.5	9.2	5.5				8.0	9.5
	-24.4	85.0	10.0				22.0	50.3
	51.9	26.6	171.1			EBIT/Interest	16.0	16.0
	(12) 26.0	(38) 7.2	(25) 9.0				(72) 4.1	(66) 2.6
	1.4	2.6	5.2				1.4	1.5
		6.8				Net Profit + Depr., Dep., Amort./Cur. Mat. L/T/D	11.0	8.3
		(11) 2.6					(30) 3.6	(31) 3.2
		1.0					1.7	.6
	.1	.1	.1			Fixed/Worth	.2	.2
	.3	.5	.3				.4	.5
	.7	1.2	.5				1.3	2.1
	.7	.8	.5			Debt/Worth	.9	.8
	1.7	1.9	1.2				2.5	2.2
	3.4	4.1	3.1				7.7	8.7
	49.4	63.2	42.4			% Profit Before Taxes/Tangible Net Worth	36.0	37.2
	(13) 31.9	(41) 18.8	25.1				(72) 19.6	(59) 20.6
	5.3	5.9	10.7				3.7	5.1
	21.9	17.5	13.3			% Profit Before Taxes/Total Assets	13.3	15.1
	11.5	8.1	8.5				5.1	5.7
	-.2	1.8	4.4				.7	.7
	77.6	54.2	28.0			Sales/Net Fixed Assets	39.6	45.6
	25.9	20.0	14.5				20.6	21.1
	11.7	8.0	10.3				10.3	11.3
	3.9	2.8	1.9			Sales/Total Assets	2.7	2.8
	2.6	2.1	1.6				2.1	2.1
	1.6	1.3	1.2				1.6	1.6
	.6	.7	1.0			% Depr., Dep., Amort./Sales	.6	.5
	(12) 1.0	(37) 1.4	(22) 1.6				(79) 1.0	(66) 1.1
	1.4	2.3	2.7				2.5	1.7
		2.2				% Officers', Directors' Owners' Comp/Sales	2.1	2.5
		(15) 3.2					(21) 3.1	(20) 3.5
		4.8					4.3	6.0
6158M	49245M	478644M	890686M	259205M	505646M	Net Sales ($)	2157239M	1816315M
1769M	17676M	226692M	565262M	243115M	406218M	Total Assets ($)	1127056M	951276M

M = $ thousand   MM = $ million
See Pages 9 through 22 for Explanation of Ratios and Data

Comparative Historical Data						Type of Statement		Current Data Sorted by Sales					
	17		15		16	Unqualified				1	2	13	
	17		20		26	Reviewed		1	2	10	9	4	
	13		6		7	Compiled		2	2	2		1	
	5		5		14	Tax Returns	1	6	3	2	2		
	18		22		33	Other	2	2	4	7	11	7	
	4/1/08-3/31/09		4/1/09-3/31/10		4/1/10-3/31/11			18 (4/1-9/30/10)		78 (10/1/10-3/31/11)			
	ALL		ALL		ALL		0-1MM	1-3MM	3-5MM	5-10MM	10-25MM	25MM & OVER	
	70		68		96	NUMBER OF STATEMENTS	3	11	11	22	24	25	
	%		%		%	ASSETS	%	%	%	%	%	%	
	12.0		11.6		13.4	Cash & Equivalents		6.0	18.1	12.1	13.9	13.1	
	24.9		19.7		23.2	Trade Receivables (net)		25.0	21.0	26.3	20.5	23.9	
	31.9		35.6		31.4	Inventory		23.3	37.6	31.9	31.6	30.2	
	4.3		4.4		5.0	All Other Current		6.8	1.0	3.5	5.4	6.9	
	73.2		71.3		72.9	Total Current		61.1	77.7	73.8	71.4	74.1	
	14.5		15.4		15.8	Fixed Assets (net)		27.6	11.1	17.0	16.8	12.6	
	6.5		5.0		4.6	Intangibles (net)		.4	1.8	5.1	3.9	8.5	
	5.8		8.3		6.6	All Other Non-Current		10.8	9.4	4.1	7.9	4.7	
	100.0		100.0		100.0	Total		100.0	100.0	100.0	100.0	100.0	
						LIABILITIES							
	10.7		8.1		5.9	Notes Payable-Short Term		3.9	3.2	8.5	6.6	4.2	
	2.8		2.2		3.9	Cur. Mat.-L.T.D.		9.6	1.6	4.3	2.0	4.2	
	16.5		11.0		14.3	Trade Payables		20.7	19.6	18.1	11.2	9.7	
	.4		.3		.5	Income Taxes Payable		.6	.4	.2	.5	.7	
	24.2		24.2		30.3	All Other Current		17.8	12.4	27.5	26.0	29.5	
	54.6		45.8		54.9	Total Current		52.7	37.2	58.6	46.3	48.3	
	6.9		6.2		6.6	Long-Term Debt		14.3	7.2	4.4	7.5	4.9	
	.5		.4		.4	Deferred Taxes		.0	.0	.0	.8	.7	
	4.6		8.6		12.9	All Other Non-Current		69.4	10.7	3.1	3.6	5.8	
	33.5		39.0		25.2	Net Worth		-36.4	44.9	33.9	41.7	40.3	
	100.0		100.0		100.0	Total Liabilities & Net Worth		100.0	100.0	100.0	100.0	100.0	
						INCOME DATA							
	100.0		100.0		100.0	Net Sales		100.0	100.0	100.0	100.0	100.0	
	29.6		34.7		34.3	Gross Profit		55.2	33.2	34.6	30.1	29.5	
	26.1		32.7		29.3	Operating Expenses		50.2	27.7	28.8	26.4	22.1	
	3.5		2.0		4.9	Operating Profit		5.0	5.4	5.8	3.7	7.4	
	.5		.9		.7	All Other Expenses (net)		2.6	.0	.6	.4	.6	
	3.0		1.1		4.2	Profit Before Taxes		2.5	5.4	5.2	3.4	6.8	
						RATIOS							
	2.1		2.7		2.5			3.1	3.2	2.0	2.0	2.4	
	1.5		1.6		1.6	Current		1.5	2.6	1.4	1.5	1.6	
	1.1		1.1		1.1			.7	1.5	1.0	1.1	1.2	
	1.0		1.3		1.3			2.2	2.1	1.3	1.2	1.3	
	.7		.7		.7	Quick		.7	1.7	.7	.8	.6	
	.4		.4		.5			.3	.5	.4	.5	.5	
26	13.8	28	12.8	28	13.1		15 24.3	18 20.2	33 11.0	25 14.8	32 11.5	
38	9.7	39	9.5	42	8.8	Sales/Receivables	50 7.3	46 7.9	41 9.0	36 10.2	48 7.6	
54	6.8	58	6.3	54	6.8		54 6.7	53 6.9	47 7.8	52 7.0	62 5.9	
39	9.5	55	6.6	46	7.9		1 251.4	61 6.0	49 7.5	47 7.8	51 7.2	
78	4.7	126	2.9	78	4.7	Cost of Sales/Inventory	17 21.9	88 4.2	87 4.2	70 5.2	77 4.7	
128	2.8	189	1.9	141	2.6		447 .8	123 3.0	135 2.7	173 2.1	120 3.0	
15	24.3	11	32.6	15	23.9		21 17.7	10 35.7	21 17.6	15 23.9	11 31.8	
26	13.9	24	15.1	30	12.0	Cost of Sales/Payables	66 5.5	39 9.3	35 10.6	25 14.4	22 16.3	
46	8.0	50	7.4	52	7.0		174 2.1	88 4.2	57 6.4	42 8.7	36 10.2	
	4.5		3.7		4.1			3.4	3.1	5.4	4.5	4.3	
	10.3		6.5		8.2	Sales/Working Capital		13.3	4.4	14.3	8.7	6.8	
	25.9		44.2		45.1			-13.9	7.3	NM	46.7	13.5	
	20.2		22.8		51.6			40.9		77.3	14.6	186.3	
(60)	5.2	(58)	5.1	(82)	8.2	EBIT/Interest	(10) 12.8		(18) 10.3	(20) 6.0	(23) 16.8	
	1.3		.1		2.6			1.0		2.3	2.9	6.6	
	17.2		14.3		8.4							36.5	
(15)	5.0	(13)	1.3	(24)	2.6	Net Profit + Depr., Dep., Amort./Cur. Mat. L/T/D					(10) 5.4	
	.0		-.8		.6							1.2	
	.2		.1		.1			.1	.1	.2	.1	.1	
	.4		.4		.4	Fixed/Worth		.7	.2	.5	.4	.3	
	1.6		1.4		.9			1.7	.7	1.2	1.1	.8	
	.8		.6		.7			.7	.4	1.1	.7	.6	
	2.2		1.8		1.8	Debt/Worth		2.1	.9	1.8	1.5	1.7	
	11.5		5.2		4.2			6.1	2.5	3.2	4.2	4.6	
	49.3		27.9		49.4					52.8	68.8	45.1	
(57)	19.1	(59)	15.6	(86)	23.4	% Profit Before Taxes/Tangible Net Worth			(21) 22.0	15.5	(22) 30.2	
	3.4		.9		8.8					5.9	2.6	20.6	
	14.6		11.2		17.6			23.0	19.7	17.6	13.6	19.0	
	7.0		4.6		8.7	% Profit Before Taxes/Total Assets		14.6	10.4	6.8	6.6	10.8	
	.6		-.4		2.1			.1	3.0	1.2	1.7	6.8	
	41.9		39.1		53.8			42.1	59.4	66.1	27.8	29.5	
	19.9		15.3		19.9	Sales/Net Fixed Assets		18.9	35.6	18.4	13.7	21.7	
	9.0		7.7		9.1			5.4	12.6	7.1	7.5	12.4	
	3.0		2.1		2.6			2.9	2.8	2.9	2.5	2.1	
	2.0		1.7		1.9	Sales/Total Assets		2.4	2.3	2.1	1.9	1.7	
	1.5		1.2		1.3			1.1	1.4	1.3	1.3	1.3	
	.6		.8		.8					.5	1.2	.8	
(61)	1.0	(60)	1.3	(78)	1.4	% Depr., Dep., Amort./Sales			(19) 1.4	(20) 1.7	(20) 1.4	
	1.7		1.8		2.4					2.7	2.8	2.6	
	1.9		2.2		2.5								
(16)	4.1	(20)	4.2	(30)	4.0	% Officers', Directors' Owners' Comp/Sales						
	6.7		6.8		6.9								
2081778M		1534465M		2189584M		Net Sales ($)	2087M	20377M	43772M	164456M	364403M	1594489M	
1176255M		1031965M		1460732M		Total Assets ($)	1735M	12969M	22657M	91067M	233739M	1098565M	

M = $ thousand   MM = $ million
See Pages 9 through 22 for Explanation of Ratios and Data

Current Data Sorted by Assets   Comparative Historical Data

Current data date ranges: 14 (4/1-9/30/10) · 32 (10/1/10-3/31/11)

0-500M	500M-2MM	2-10MM	10-50MM	50-100MM	100-250MM	Type of Statement	4/1/06-3/31/07 ALL	4/1/07-3/31/08 ALL
	1	4	7	1	1	Unqualified	7	9
	2	7	4			Reviewed	15	18
	1	2				Compiled	8	5
1	5	1				Tax Returns	4	2
2	1	4	1		1	Other	11	13
3	10	18	12	1	2	NUMBER OF STATEMENTS	45	47
%	%	%	%	%	%	**ASSETS**	%	%
	17.9	19.1	16.7			Cash & Equivalents	13.2	13.9
	39.3	28.8	31.8			Trade Receivables (net)	35.7	35.3
	24.2	16.4	15.6			Inventory	20.8	15.3
	.4	4.6	9.3			All Other Current	6.4	8.2
	81.7	69.1	73.4			Total Current	76.1	72.7
	9.2	19.8	13.6			Fixed Assets (net)	16.4	16.3
	4.1	5.4	9.6			Intangibles (net)	3.8	5.8
	5.0	5.8	3.3			All Other Non-Current	3.7	5.2
	100.0	100.0	100.0			Total	100.0	100.0
						LIABILITIES		
	15.3	10.3	6.4			Notes Payable-Short Term	8.8	10.6
	5.9	2.1	4.1			Cur. Mat.-L.T.D.	3.0	2.3
	14.8	16.2	12.6			Trade Payables	20.1	17.2
	.0	.2	.9			Income Taxes Payable	.4	.7
	13.0	20.4	26.1			All Other Current	27.4	21.3
	49.0	49.2	50.1			Total Current	59.7	52.2
	18.7	13.0	9.8			Long-Term Debt	7.8	8.0
	.0	.3	.4			Deferred Taxes	.2	.3
	9.4	5.7	4.5			All Other Non-Current	7.3	5.9
	22.9	31.8	35.1			Net Worth	25.0	33.7
	100.0	100.0	100.0			Total Liabilties & Net Worth	100.0	100.0
						INCOME DATA		
	100.0	100.0	100.0			Net Sales	100.0	100.0
	36.4	30.4	30.7			Gross Profit	29.5	31.8
	28.5	24.8	24.3			Operating Expenses	24.1	26.0
	7.9	5.6	6.3			Operating Profit	5.4	5.8
	.5	.3	.7			All Other Expenses (net)	1.0	.6
	7.4	5.3	5.7			Profit Before Taxes	4.5	5.3
						RATIOS		
	3.2	2.9	1.9			Current	2.1	2.1
	2.1	1.3	1.4				1.3	1.5
	1.6	.9	1.1				1.0	1.0
	2.4	2.2	1.1			Quick	1.3	1.4
	1.7	1.0	.9				.9	1.0
	.9	.6	.6				.6	.7
35	10.4	42 8.8	47 7.8			Sales/Receivables	31 11.8	35 10.4
45	8.1	56 6.5	65 5.7				49 7.4	53 6.9
79	4.6	74 4.9	85 4.3				60 6.0	66 5.5
0	UND	18 20.3	6 62.9			Cost of Sales/Inventory	10 37.3	7 49.9
50	7.4	38 9.5	49 7.4				34 10.6	24 15.3
77	4.7	68 5.4	87 4.2				81 4.5	63 5.8
12	29.6	23 15.7	20 18.3			Cost of Sales/Payables	19 19.0	21 17.2
25	14.5	42 8.8	42 8.6				32 11.5	33 11.0
42	8.6	59 6.2	60 6.1				52 7.0	45 8.2
	3.1	4.1	6.1			Sales/Working Capital	6.2	6.2
	7.1	12.8	9.5				17.0	9.4
	9.1	-75.8	41.3				-48.8	146.4
		15.9	32.8			EBIT/Interest	13.9	27.0
		(15) 9.9	(10) 5.4				(39) 6.0	(43) 10.3
		.2	2.4				1.2	1.9
						Net Profit + Depr., Dep., Amort./Cur. Mat. L/T/D	9.1	18.6
							(11) 2.1	(10) 6.4
							1.0	2.5
	.0	.2	.1			Fixed/Worth	.3	.2
	.2	.8	.6				.6	.5
	.5	2.9	2.6				1.6	2.2
	.9	1.0	1.0			Debt/Worth	1.0	1.1
	2.0	3.4	4.4				2.5	2.1
	3.9	9.4	8.8				12.6	8.1
		76.2	64.4			% Profit Before Taxes/Tangible Net Worth	53.9	81.6
		(16) 22.5	(10) 19.1				(38) 30.0	(40) 27.3
		-3.3	8.1				8.2	5.8
	33.0	19.0	17.8			% Profit Before Taxes/Total Assets	18.4	16.9
	11.3	9.0	4.0				3.9	9.2
	.7	.7	2.9				.5	1.9
	235.2	51.1	47.4			Sales/Net Fixed Assets	74.9	48.6
	50.3	14.2	15.1				27.4	21.2
	14.6	5.2	10.3				10.5	9.8
	3.5	2.9	2.6			Sales/Total Assets	3.5	3.2
	2.9	1.9	1.5				2.5	2.4
	1.5	1.3	1.1				1.8	1.6
		.4	.6			% Depr., Dep., Amort./Sales	.4	.4
		(15) 1.3	(11) 1.2				(40) 1.0	(40) 1.0
		3.6	1.9				2.0	2.2
						% Officers', Directors' Owners' Comp/Sales	3.2	2.3
							(11) 3.7	(12) 3.5
							8.8	6.8
2453M	39169M	148851M	418288M	91533M	457958M	Net Sales ($)	1082283M	1120977M
635M	15385M	83597M	233872M	64221M	296732M	Total Assets ($)	645298M	565281M

M = $ thousand   MM = $ million
See Pages 9 through 22 for Explanation of Ratios and Data

Comparative Historical Data | Current Data Sorted by Sales

	08-09	09-10	10-11		Type of Statement		0-1MM	1-3MM	3-5MM	5-10MM	10-25MM	25MM & OVER
	8	8	14		Unqualified			1	3	1	3	6
	11	13	13		Reviewed				4	3	3	3
	9	5	3		Compiled			1		2		
	2	2	7		Tax Returns			3	2	2		
	13	12	9		Other		2	1		2	2	2
	4/1/08- 3/31/09	4/1/09- 3/31/10	4/1/10- 3/31/11					14 (4/1-9/30/10)		32 (10/1/10-3/31/11)		
	ALL	ALL	ALL				0-1MM	1-3MM	3-5MM	5-10MM	10-25MM	25MM & OVER
	43	40	46		NUMBER OF STATEMENTS		2	6	9	10	8	11
	%	%	%		ASSETS		%	%	%	%	%	%
	11.9	15.1	18.3		Cash & Equivalents					20.4		14.8
	32.9	29.3	32.5		Trade Receivables (net)					33.1		35.0
	20.5	20.3	17.7		Inventory					21.2		15.8
	6.0	4.9	5.0		All Other Current					2.9		9.0
	71.3	69.5	73.5		Total Current					77.5		74.6
	15.4	17.9	15.3		Fixed Assets (net)					10.2		10.6
	4.9	4.9	6.5		Intangibles (net)					5.1		10.3
	8.5	7.7	4.7		All Other Non-Current					7.2		4.5
	100.0	100.0	100.0		Total					100.0		100.0
					LIABILITIES							
	13.0	12.2	9.9		Notes Payable-Short Term					14.3		5.6
	2.3	4.0	3.2		Cur. Mat.-L.T.D.					1.9		4.1
	19.0	12.3	14.4		Trade Payables					22.2		13.4
	.2	.9	.4		Income Taxes Payable					.0		1.4
	22.8	20.3	27.6		All Other Current					20.8		25.1
	57.3	49.7	55.5		Total Current					59.2		49.6
	8.7	11.3	13.3		Long-Term Debt					8.9		12.9
	.1	.2	.3		Deferred Taxes					.0		.4
	6.0	7.0	6.4		All Other Non-Current					5.7		7.4
	28.0	31.8	24.5		Net Worth					26.2		29.7
	100.0	100.0	100.0		Total Liabilties & Net Worth					100.0		100.0
					INCOME DATA							
	100.0	100.0	100.0		Net Sales					100.0		100.0
	30.4	30.1	34.0		Gross Profit					29.4		29.6
	25.9	26.1	27.4		Operating Expenses					25.3		23.4
	4.5	4.0	6.7		Operating Profit					4.1		6.2
	.7	1.4	.4		All Other Expenses (net)					.2		.2
	3.8	2.7	6.3		Profit Before Taxes					3.9		6.1
					RATIOS							
	2.2	2.0	2.4		Current					2.6		1.9
	1.6	1.5	1.7							1.3		1.6
	1.1	1.1	1.1							.9		1.1
	1.3	1.4	1.9		Quick					1.5		1.2
	.9	.9	1.1							1.0		.9
	.5	.6	.7							.6		.9
	36 10.1	38 9.6	42 8.7		Sales/Receivables					25 14.6		47 7.8
	53 6.9	50 7.2	57 6.5							42 8.6		58 6.3
	68 5.4	71 5.1	75 4.9							76 4.8		74 4.9
	7 50.9	10 35.9	18 20.3		Cost of Sales/Inventory					0 UND		5 69.5
	37 9.8	37 9.8	47 7.8							42 8.8		50 7.2
	84 4.3	101 3.6	81 4.5							62 5.9		82 4.4
	23 15.8	18 19.9	17 21.3		Cost of Sales/Payables					25 14.5		17 21.2
	37 10.0	30 12.0	39 9.4							44 8.3		38 9.6
	60 6.1	43 8.5	59 6.2							64 5.7		46 7.9
	5.3	4.4	3.9		Sales/Working Capital					5.2		5.3
	9.6	10.9	7.5							14.3		7.9
	44.2	56.1	48.5							-27.1		34.3
	29.6	15.7	25.1		EBIT/Interest							49.8
	(37) 3.6	(37) 3.2	(39) 6.8								(10)	7.7
	.7	.8	2.1									2.5
	116.3	5.3			Net Profit + Depr., Dep., Amort./Cur. Mat. L/T/D							
	(10) 3.7	(11) 2.3										
	-3.1	-10.5										
	.2	.2	.1		Fixed/Worth					.0		.1
	.5	.7	.4							.3		.6
	1.4	1.4	1.8							NM		-3.5
	1.0	.9	1.0		Debt/Worth					1.8		.9
	2.9	2.7	2.9							4.4		5.5
	11.9	8.7	8.7							NM		-13.0
	49.9	62.5	59.7		% Profit Before Taxes/Tangible Net Worth							
	(35) 28.3	(37) 10.0	(39) 24.4									
	5.4	.2	10.4									
	15.8	10.7	19.6		% Profit Before Taxes/Total Assets					18.6		15.4
	5.7	2.3	9.3							6.3		9.2
	.8	.0	2.1							.7		3.0
	61.3	43.3	67.2		Sales/Net Fixed Assets					469.9		46.4
	21.4	13.7	15.7							73.4		16.0
	9.0	5.7	9.8							12.6		10.2
	3.2	2.8	3.1		Sales/Total Assets					3.8		2.7
	2.0	1.9	1.8							2.5		1.8
	1.4	1.1	1.3							1.9		1.3
	.6	.7	.7		% Depr., Dep., Amort./Sales							.6
	(35) 1.3	(36) 1.0	(36) 1.3								(10)	1.6
	2.2	2.7	2.8									2.2
	1.9	1.6	2.0		% Officers', Directors' Owners' Comp/Sales							
	(12) 4.9	(13) 4.9	(12) 2.7									
	7.8	6.1	5.4									
	1184984M	866085M	1158252M		Net Sales ($)		1197M	13945M	35974M	73740M	122903M	910493M
	641046M	545403M	694442M		Total Assets ($)		317M	8446M	35358M	30927M	87789M	531605M

© RMA 2011

M = $ thousand   MM = $ million

See Pages 9 through 22 for Explanation of Ratios and Data

Current Data Sorted by Assets

Comparative Historical Data

	0-500M	500M-2MM	2-10MM	10-50MM	50-100MM	100-250MM	Type of Statement	4/1/06-3/31/07 ALL	4/1/07-3/31/08 ALL
	2		10	14	7	4	Unqualified	57	51
	1	9	39	10	1		Reviewed	60	54
	6	7	23	3			Compiled	36	31
	9	18	15	2			Tax Returns	29	21
	2	19	37	20	6	4	Other	66	75
		47 (4/1-9/30/10)		221 (10/1/10-3/31/11)					
	20	53	124	49	14	8	**NUMBER OF STATEMENTS**	248	232
	%	%	%	%	%	%	**ASSETS**	%	%
	12.4	9.5	12.1	12.0	7.9		Cash & Equivalents	8.9	8.6
	27.5	29.9	26.4	26.0	19.5		Trade Receivables (net)	28.9	29.6
	28.2	20.3	25.2	23.6	25.2		Inventory	25.1	24.4
	3.6	7.0	3.9	5.4	6.8		All Other Current	3.6	4.0
	71.7	66.7	67.6	66.9	59.4		Total Current	66.5	66.5
	14.5	24.3	22.9	17.9	22.2		Fixed Assets (net)	23.3	24.5
	5.7	2.2	3.7	9.3	13.7		Intangibles (net)	4.6	4.0
	7.6	6.9	5.8	5.9	4.7		All Other Non-Current	5.6	5.0
	100.0	100.0	100.0	100.0	100.0		Total	100.0	100.0
							LIABILITIES		
	17.6	9.2	9.1	8.1	6.9		Notes Payable-Short Term	9.9	11.6
	10.6	4.7	2.9	3.9	1.2		Cur. Mat.-L.T.D.	3.4	3.5
	21.3	15.2	13.1	10.1	10.4		Trade Payables	15.3	15.3
	.0	.1	.3	.7	.2		Income Taxes Payable	.4	.4
	21.3	13.7	11.5	14.9	17.1		All Other Current	15.1	12.9
	70.7	42.9	36.9	37.6	35.7		Total Current	44.2	43.7
	21.6	16.4	12.6	6.7	10.1		Long-Term Debt	14.6	16.4
	.0	.3	.4	1.1	1.0		Deferred Taxes	.4	.4
	13.7	14.3	6.2	12.8	12.8		All Other Non-Current	5.8	6.1
	-6.5	26.2	43.9	41.9	40.4		Net Worth	34.9	33.5
	100.0	100.0	100.0	100.0	100.0		Total Liabilities & Net Worth	100.0	100.0
							INCOME DATA		
	100.0	100.0	100.0	100.0	100.0		Net Sales	100.0	100.0
	43.5	40.6	34.2	28.5	31.1		Gross Profit	32.8	32.8
	36.5	32.1	28.0	21.2	23.6		Operating Expenses	26.0	26.6
	7.0	8.5	6.2	7.3	7.5		Operating Profit	6.8	6.2
	1.1	1.5	1.1	1.0	.8		All Other Expenses (net)	1.3	1.2
	5.9	7.0	5.1	6.3	6.7		Profit Before Taxes	5.5	5.0
							RATIOS		
	2.4	3.0	3.4	2.8	4.0		Current	2.5	2.2
	1.1	1.6	1.8	2.0	1.4			1.5	1.6
	.6	1.0	1.3	1.2	1.2			1.1	1.1
	1.2	1.9	2.1	1.8	1.3		Quick	1.4	1.4
	.6	.9	1.0	1.0	.8			.9	.8
	.3	.5	.6	.6	.5			.6	.6
	10 36.5	31 11.8	33 11.2	43 8.5	39 9.3		Sales/Receivables	35 10.5	36 10.1
	32 11.5	47 7.7	47 7.8	57 6.4	51 7.2			48 7.6	48 7.6
	48 7.6	68 5.4	62 5.9	77 4.7	62 5.9			62 5.9	63 5.8
	1 478.7	11 34.5	25 14.4	29 12.7	35 10.3		Cost of Sales/Inventory	29 12.7	22 16.8
	29 12.7	43 8.5	75 4.8	73 5.0	77 4.8			61 6.0	58 6.3
	108 3.4	89 4.1	117 3.1	129 2.8	159 2.3			100 3.6	92 4.0
	2 157.7	14 25.5	20 18.4	19 19.5	28 12.9		Cost of Sales/Payables	21 17.0	21 17.7
	33 11.2	30 12.3	33 11.0	26 14.0	38 9.5			32 11.3	30 12.2
	66 5.6	54 6.7	52 7.1	42 8.6	48 7.6			47 7.8	53 6.9
	12.1	4.4	3.8	2.9	2.8		Sales/Working Capital	4.8	4.9
	48.7	11.9	6.3	4.9	9.7			9.5	10.0
	-12.5	162.6	15.3	13.9	66.0			29.1	26.5
	9.3	15.3	17.3	22.1	26.0		EBIT/Interest	16.9	10.7
	(15) 3.3	(47) 4.2	(108) 6.5	(40) 7.1	(12) 10.3			(218) 6.1	(209) 4.0
	1.5	.8	1.8	1.3	2.6			1.8	1.6
			8.8	14.2			Net Profit + Depr., Dep., Amort./Cur. Mat. L/T/D	9.0	11.9
		(30) 4.0		(12) 3.2				(68) 3.5	(60) 3.5
			1.8	1.6				1.3	1.2
	.0	.1	.2	.2	.5		Fixed/Worth	.3	.3
	.3	1.1	.4	.4	.7			.7	.7
	-3.5	UND	1.1	3.3	-46.5			2.0	3.0
	1.8	.7	.5	.5	.9		Debt/Worth	.8	.9
	UND	1.9	1.3	1.3	1.6			1.8	2.1
	-3.4	-109.5	3.4	10.5	-208.5			6.0	8.5
	617.1	57.6	44.0	38.7	31.6		% Profit Before Taxes/Tangible Net Worth	55.3	59.1
	(10) 66.1	(39) 31.3	(112) 23.0	(39) 13.4	(10) 19.5			(210) 27.0	(201) 26.1
	14.6	8.7	5.7	3.6	14.6			11.4	9.9
	40.1	29.0	19.1	11.5	11.8		% Profit Before Taxes/Total Assets	19.5	17.0
	12.3	7.4	8.4	6.8	7.0			8.8	8.7
	1.4	-.9	1.9	.3	4.3			2.9	2.9
	370.7	53.7	25.6	22.9	11.0		Sales/Net Fixed Assets	25.5	25.0
	72.9	10.4	11.1	11.9	8.1			10.4	10.4
	14.5	4.9	4.8	5.8	4.7			5.9	5.2
	5.6	2.8	2.5	1.7	1.6		Sales/Total Assets	2.8	2.8
	3.4	2.2	1.8	1.4	1.5			2.0	2.1
	2.1	1.5	1.4	1.2	1.0			1.5	1.6
		1.2	1.0	1.2	1.4		% Depr., Dep., Amort./Sales	1.0	.9
		(38) 2.8	(110) 1.7	(44) 2.1	2.2			(225) 1.9	(206) 1.8
		7.0	3.2	3.3	4.0			3.4	3.5
			3.4	2.0	1.8		% Officers', Directors' Owners' Comp/Sales	2.4	3.1
		(27) 7.1	(54) 3.4	(10) 2.1				(85) 4.7	(80) 4.5
		10.3	7.3	3.6				8.3	6.8
	21009M	133718M	1135993M	1445777M	1291027M	1445018M	Net Sales ($)	5498834M	6968061M
	5340M	56849M	561752M	1035260M	904268M	1195700M	Total Assets ($)	3040546M	4012450M

© RMA 2011

M = $ thousand   MM = $ million
See Pages 9 through 22 for Explanation of Ratios and Data

Comparative Historical Data | Current Data Sorted by Sales

4/1/08- 3/31/09 ALL	4/1/09- 3/31/10 ALL	4/1/10- 3/31/11 ALL	Type of Statement	0-1MM	1-3MM	3-5MM	5-10MM	10-25MM	25MM & OVER
62	37	37	Unqualified	2		1	4	11	19
76	58	60	Reviewed	2	3	9	21	21	4
63	39	39	Compiled	5	9	2	18	4	1
46	34	44	Tax Returns	9	10	14	5	4	2
122	86	88	Other	2	18	11	15	18	24
				47 (4/1-9/30/10)			221 (10/1/10-3/31/11)		
369	254	268	NUMBER OF STATEMENTS	20	40	37	63	58	50
%	%	%	ASSETS	%	%	%	%	%	%
9.9	10.5	11.4	Cash & Equivalents	7.3	13.1	7.1	15.3	9.7	12.1
25.7	23.8	26.7	Trade Receivables (net)	26.1	24.5	25.7	25.0	30.8	26.6
22.7	24.2	24.0	Inventory	24.1	21.4	24.9	24.8	25.9	22.2
3.9	4.8	5.0	All Other Current	7.0	2.4	7.0	3.6	3.3	8.5
62.2	63.4	67.1	Total Current	64.4	61.3	64.7	68.7	69.7	69.4
27.0	24.5	21.4	Fixed Assets (net)	17.7	29.0	26.6	21.6	18.9	15.9
4.9	5.8	5.3	Intangibles (net)	5.8	3.7	2.8	3.3	6.8	9.0
5.9	6.4	6.1	All Other Non-Current	11.6	5.9	5.9	6.5	4.6	5.7
100.0	100.0	100.0	Total	100.0	100.0	100.0	100.0	100.0	100.0
			LIABILITIES						
10.6	11.7	9.3	Notes Payable-Short Term	11.8	12.0	10.9	8.1	9.5	6.2
4.4	3.4	3.9	Cur. Mat.-L.T.D.	6.3	6.3	4.5	3.3	3.6	1.5
12.1	12.9	13.4	Trade Payables	15.8	14.5	13.4	12.3	14.7	11.2
.3	.3	.3	Income Taxes Payable	.0	.0	.3	.4	.4	.6
11.9	14.2	13.5	All Other Current	19.4	10.3	13.2	11.9	12.7	17.1
39.4	42.4	40.4	Total Current	53.3	43.1	42.3	36.1	40.8	36.6
17.0	15.2	13.0	Long-Term Debt	17.1	23.7	17.3	11.4	6.7	8.8
.6	.5	.5	Deferred Taxes	.0	.2	.4	.5	.5	1.2
5.6	8.8	10.0	All Other Non-Current	3.1	15.8	9.7	7.6	9.8	11.3
37.3	33.0	36.1	Net Worth	26.0	17.2	30.3	44.4	42.0	42.0
100.0	100.0	100.0	Total Liabilities & Net Worth	100.0	100.0	100.0	100.0	100.0	100.0
			INCOME DATA						
100.0	100.0	100.0	Net Sales	100.0	100.0	100.0	100.0	100.0	100.0
32.3	31.4	35.0	Gross Profit	47.5	41.5	37.9	33.4	30.9	29.3
25.8	28.6	27.9	Operating Expenses	35.3	35.6	33.5	26.1	24.4	20.7
6.4	2.8	7.1	Operating Profit	12.2	5.9	4.3	7.3	6.4	8.6
1.2	1.4	1.1	All Other Expenses (net)	1.1	2.1	1.3	.9	.7	1.1
5.2	1.5	6.0	Profit Before Taxes	11.1	3.8	3.0	6.4	5.8	7.4
			RATIOS						
2.8	3.2	3.2		2.6	3.1	3.5	3.7	2.9	3.0
1.6	1.6	1.8	Current	1.2	1.5	1.6	2.0	1.8	2.1
1.1	1.0	1.2		.6	.8	1.1	1.3	1.3	1.3
1.6	1.9	1.8		1.2	2.1	1.5	2.2	1.7	1.7
.9	.8	1.0	Quick	.7	.8	.8	1.1	1.0	1.1
.5	.5	.6		.4	.4	.4	.7	.6	.7
31 11.7	29 12.4	34 10.8		31 11.9	22 17.0	29 12.5	36 10.2	33 11.0	42 8.8
44 8.3	43 8.4	48 7.5	Sales/Receivables	43 8.5	42 8.6	49 7.5	47 7.8	48 7.6	58 6.3
58 6.3	58 6.3	66 5.6		77 4.7	60 6.1	65 5.6	61 5.9	63 5.8	76 4.8
20 18.3	26 13.9	25 14.7		0 UND	20 18.6	19 19.4	18 20.5	29 12.5	29 12.4
55 6.7	62 5.9	64 5.7	Cost of Sales/Inventory	43 8.5	60 6.1	51 7.1	69 5.3	64 5.7	67 5.4
99 3.7	121 3.0	116 3.1		220 1.7	106 3.5	154 2.4	111 3.0	113 3.2	122 3.0
14 26.7	16 23.5	18 19.9		8 43.2	12 29.3	16 22.3	20 18.2	20 18.6	22 16.8
24 15.2	27 13.7	32 11.1	Cost of Sales/Payables	32 11.5	34 10.8	40 9.2	32 11.6	29 12.6	36 10.3
44 8.3	44 8.3	50 7.3		95 3.8	48 7.7	59 6.1	51 7.1	48 7.7	44 8.3
4.6	4.0	3.6		2.8	4.9	3.6	3.6	4.2	2.9
8.8	9.0	6.8	Sales/Working Capital	23.7	11.9	6.6	5.7	7.6	4.7
45.1	264.5	21.5		-14.6	-25.8	87.5	13.3	15.9	15.9
15.3	8.2	15.7		16.3	10.6	13.2	17.3	27.7	25.0
(337) 4.8	(227) 2.5	(230) 5.5	EBIT/Interest	(13) 5.0	(35) 1.6	(35) 4.3	(56) 6.5	(49) 7.9	(42) 8.8
1.6	-.4	1.5		2.1	-.7	1.3	1.8	1.7	2.9
7.5	5.3	8.8	Net Profit + Depr., Dep.,				4.7	27.9	10.0
(103) 2.5	(53) 1.8	(56) 3.8	Amort./Cur. Mat. L/T/D				(15) 1.9	(14) 8.4	(19) 4.2
1.4	.9	1.8					1.8	2.4	2.1
.3	.2	.2		.0	.4	.2	.2	.2	.2
.7	.7	.5	Fixed/Worth	.1	1.9	.8	.3	.5	.5
2.4	4.0	2.1		7.0	-4.4	8.9	.8	1.1	1.2
.7	.6	.6		.7	.8	.7	.4	.5	.7
1.7	2.1	1.6	Debt/Worth	2.2	3.5	1.7	1.2	1.3	1.4
6.0	18.4	9.0		-10.7	-10.5	32.7	2.5	7.0	4.3
54.3	37.1	48.5	% Profit Before Taxes/Tangible	83.0	93.0	43.2	38.6	53.4	39.5
(311) 25.5	(203) 14.5	(218) 22.6	Net Worth	(14) 36.5	(27) 48.4	(29) 14.0	(59) 18.7	(49) 17.5	(40) 19.5
10.1	-.5	6.6		21.8	-6.1	5.9	2.3	7.9	10.8
17.6	11.7	19.0	% Profit Before Taxes/Total	30.5	30.5	15.0	21.1	19.2	13.9
8.3	3.9	7.5	Assets	17.8	4.1	7.6	9.4	7.3	7.9
2.5	-2.6	1.9		4.8	-6.2	1.3	.7	1.6	4.3
21.5	25.0	28.6		UND	49.9	27.8	21.5	27.6	22.4
8.8	9.9	11.4	Sales/Net Fixed Assets	24.4	7.5	9.2	10.9	18.0	10.5
4.6	4.4	5.4		11.3	3.0	3.8	5.9	6.1	5.9
2.7	2.5	2.4		2.4	2.6	2.5	2.3	3.0	1.9
2.0	1.8	1.7	Sales/Total Assets	1.6	1.9	1.9	1.8	2.0	1.6
1.5	1.2	1.3		1.0	1.3	1.4	1.4	1.4	1.2
1.2	1.0	1.1		.5	2.2	.7	1.1	1.1	1.1
(322) 2.3	(216) 2.3	(221) 2.0	% Depr., Dep., Amort./Sales	(11) 1.6	(29) 3.7	(31) 2.0	(55) 1.7	(50) 1.9	(45) 1.7
4.2	4.3	3.6		3.6	7.7	6.1	3.0	3.1	2.9
2.2	2.5	2.2	% Officers', Directors'		4.3	3.2	1.8	1.8	
(139) 4.4	(86) 4.9	(100) 4.9	Owners' Comp/Sales		(22) 6.8	(20) 6.0	(25) 2.7	(20) 2.7	
7.4	7.6	8.2			11.2	8.5	5.2	4.4	
9479556M	5313990M	5472542M	Net Sales ($)	12862M	72286M	139398M	465876M	943201M	3838919M
5853905M	3509307M	3759169M	Total Assets ($)	9503M	45399M	84884M	290619M	534283M	2794481M

M = $ thousand   MM = $ million
See Pages 9 through 22 for Explanation of Ratios and Data

Current Data Sorted by Assets   Comparative Historical Data

Type of Statement	0-500M	500M-2MM	2-10MM	10-50MM	50-100MM	100-250MM		ALL 4/1/06-3/31/07	ALL 4/1/07-3/31/08
Unqualified			3	4	3	1		13	19
Reviewed		2	6	2				6	4
Compiled		3	5	1				4	5
Tax Returns	3	5	5	1				3	10
Other	4	4	11	5	4			20	27
		17 (4/1-9/30/10)		55 (10/1/10-3/31/11)					
NUMBER OF STATEMENTS	7	14	30	13	7	1		46	65

	0-500M %	500M-2MM %	2-10MM %	10-50MM %	50-100MM %	100-250MM %		ALL %	ALL %
ASSETS									
Cash & Equivalents		15.6	9.8	10.3				15.3	14.4
Trade Receivables (net)		22.0	33.0	34.8				31.7	30.9
Inventory		32.4	34.9	30.4				27.6	23.2
All Other Current		1.3	1.3	1.7				3.1	3.2
Total Current		71.3	79.0	77.1				77.7	71.7
Fixed Assets (net)		9.6	15.4	10.2				11.2	12.8
Intangibles (net)		5.5	1.0	6.4				5.7	9.0
All Other Non-Current		13.6	4.5	6.3				5.4	6.5
Total		100.0	100.0	100.0				100.0	100.0
LIABILITIES									
Notes Payable-Short Term		17.7	17.5	8.5				12.2	11.2
Cur. Mat.-L.T.D.		2.4	1.5	1.8				2.4	2.2
Trade Payables		7.1	22.6	15.0				16.8	19.1
Income Taxes Payable		.2	.2	.5				.6	.2
All Other Current		15.6	9.1	8.7				11.1	12.1
Total Current		43.0	50.7	34.5				43.2	44.8
Long-Term Debt		5.9	9.6	4.2				11.3	9.2
Deferred Taxes		.0	.0	.3				.1	.1
All Other Non-Current		3.4	4.0	2.8				9.8	8.7
Net Worth		47.7	35.7	58.3				35.6	37.1
Total Liabilties & Net Worth		100.0	100.0	100.0				100.0	100.0
INCOME DATA									
Net Sales		100.0	100.0	100.0				100.0	100.0
Gross Profit		49.0	30.6	29.1				31.9	34.8
Operating Expenses		44.0	26.4	22.1				27.2	29.7
Operating Profit		5.0	4.2	7.0				4.7	5.1
All Other Expenses (net)		1.4	.9	.6				1.0	.1
Profit Before Taxes		3.6	3.3	6.4				3.7	5.0
RATIOS									
Current		4.2	1.9	3.6				2.8	3.0
		1.6	1.5	2.3				1.7	1.8
		.9	1.3	1.5				1.3	1.2
Quick		2.1	1.2	2.1				1.9	1.8
		.9	.9	1.2				1.0	1.1
		.3	.5	1.0				.6	.6
Sales/Receivables	17	21.0	32 11.3	45 8.2				32 11.5	30 12.3
	25	14.7	43 8.6	55 6.6				49 7.4	44 8.3
	42	8.6	56 6.5	64 5.7				63 5.8	66 5.5
Cost of Sales/Inventory	22	16.4	48 7.6	55 6.6				22 16.5	27 13.6
	55	6.6	77 4.8	61 6.0				53 6.9	44 8.3
	527	.7	101 3.6	104 3.5				100 3.7	83 4.4
Cost of Sales/Payables	5	75.1	23 16.1	18 20.2				16 22.3	21 17.6
	22	17.0	37 9.8	38 9.5				36 10.2	42 8.6
	50	7.3	72 5.1	49 7.4				61 6.0	72 5.1
Sales/Working Capital		4.6	5.2	3.7				3.6	4.3
		10.7	11.1	5.7				7.7	7.9
		-35.7	13.9	10.1				19.0	27.7
EBIT/Interest		5.3	10.7	36.0				11.5	26.7
	(11)	2.8	(27) 6.2	(10) 11.8				(39) 4.4	(59) 6.3
		.6	1.6	3.2				1.4	1.5
Net Profit + Depr., Dep., Amort./Cur. Mat. L/T/D								9.3	42.3
								(11) 1.8	(16) 6.5
								.9	1.8
Fixed/Worth		.0	.0	.0				.1	.1
		.2	.1	.1				.2	.4
		1.2	.8	.2				.9	1.5
Debt/Worth		.4	1.0	.4				.6	.8
		1.2	1.8	.7				2.0	1.8
		9.4	2.9	1.9				5.1	9.0
% Profit Before Taxes/Tangible Net Worth		47.2	46.4	50.1				51.0	71.6
	(13)	9.0	(28) 17.4	23.6				(41) 21.6	(53) 26.9
		2.4	3.1	9.1				7.3	8.6
% Profit Before Taxes/Total Assets		30.2	13.3	17.6				19.5	21.0
		3.7	5.7	14.2				7.4	11.8
		.0	2.1	6.0				2.2	1.3
Sales/Net Fixed Assets		68.8	303.1	74.0				114.8	71.6
		29.8	58.0	44.9				42.8	27.4
		15.5	8.1	23.6				9.9	12.5
Sales/Total Assets		3.5	3.5	2.7				3.1	3.2
		2.5	2.7	2.2				2.4	2.2
		1.6	1.8	1.6				1.6	1.4
% Depr., Dep., Amort./Sales			.3	.3				.3	.5
			(23) .7	(11) 1.2				(31) .9	(44) 1.3
			1.9	1.4				2.2	2.6
% Officers', Directors' Owners' Comp/Sales									1.5
								(17) 3.6	
									7.1
Net Sales ($)	9492M	42567M	390123M	502324M	865935M	206195M		3522331M	3214682M
Total Assets ($)	2526M	16257M	142358M	227900M	493093M	123854M		2003733M	2078851M

M = $ thousand   MM = $ million
See Pages 9 through 22 for Explanation of Ratios and Data

Comparative Historical Data / Current Data Sorted by Sales

4/1/08-3/31/09 ALL	4/1/09-3/31/10 ALL	4/1/10-3/31/11 ALL	Type of Statement	0-1MM	1-3MM	3-5MM	5-10MM	10-25MM	25MM & OVER
15	14	11	Unqualified					2	9
12	15	10	Reviewed				4	4	2
3	3	9	Compiled		1	4		2	2
12	17	14	Tax Returns	2	5	2	2	2	1
27	35	28	Other	2	5	2	4	6	9
					17 (4/1-9/30/10)		55 (10/1/10-3/31/11)		
69	84	72	**NUMBER OF STATEMENTS**	4	11	8	10	16	23
%	%	%	**ASSETS**	%	%	%	%	%	%
14.7	13.3	12.4	Cash & Equivalents		13.8		11.3	10.9	13.0
26.5	29.3	30.1	Trade Receivables (net)		24.6		35.1	33.0	33.7
26.8	23.9	29.4	Inventory		30.3		30.7	35.3	24.1
5.3	3.3	1.7	All Other Current		1.2		1.2	2.1	2.4
73.3	69.7	73.6	Total Current		69.8		78.3	81.3	73.1
14.7	15.3	12.5	Fixed Assets (net)		11.3		14.4	12.4	8.2
5.0	7.2	5.6	Intangibles (net)		5.2		2.0	1.8	11.5
7.1	7.8	8.3	All Other Non-Current		13.7		5.4	4.6	7.2
100.0	100.0	100.0	Total		100.0		100.0	100.0	100.0
			LIABILITIES						
14.7	14.2	14.5	Notes Payable-Short Term		17.7		19.4	13.1	8.9
2.9	2.9	2.1	Cur. Mat.-L.T.D.		1.5		2.1	2.1	2.5
16.5	14.1	15.5	Trade Payables		11.4		16.9	28.1	13.3
.2	.6	.4	Income Taxes Payable		.1		.3	.1	1.1
9.1	12.4	12.1	All Other Current		11.7		10.3	11.2	13.4
43.5	44.3	44.7	Total Current		42.4		49.1	54.6	39.2
9.2	10.9	13.4	Long-Term Debt		26.9		6.6	10.6	13.5
.2	.3	.1	Deferred Taxes		.0		.1	.0	.4
6.1	6.7	8.1	All Other Non-Current		.7		5.2	7.5	12.2
41.0	37.8	33.7	Net Worth		30.0		39.0	27.3	34.6
100.0	100.0	100.0	Total Liabilities & Net Worth		100.0		100.0	100.0	100.0
			INCOME DATA						
100.0	100.0	100.0	Net Sales		100.0		100.0	100.0	100.0
34.1	40.2	37.3	Gross Profit		51.5		30.3	28.9	33.5
31.3	38.0	32.3	Operating Expenses		52.0		28.6	24.9	25.3
2.8	2.1	5.0	Operating Profit		-.4		1.7	4.0	8.2
1.2	.9	1.4	All Other Expenses (net)		1.2		.1	.9	2.1
1.6	1.3	3.6	Profit Before Taxes		-1.6		1.5	3.1	6.1
			RATIOS						
3.3	2.4	2.6	Current		2.3		2.3	1.8	3.3
1.8	1.5	1.6			1.6		1.6	1.4	1.7
1.2	1.1	1.3			1.0		1.2	1.3	1.3
1.9	1.8	1.4	Quick		1.3		1.3	1.3	2.1
.9	.9	.9			.9		1.0	.7	1.2
.5	.6	.6			.6		.6	.5	.8
25 14.6	33 11.1	29 12.8	Sales/Receivables		21 17.8		23 15.8	24 14.9	40 9.1
38 9.5	47 7.8	42 8.7			27 13.4		39 9.3	45 8.1	54 6.8
52 7.0	62 5.9	57 6.4			40 9.1		61 6.0	61 6.0	64 5.7
29 12.4	26 14.2	31 11.9	Cost of Sales/Inventory		14 26.2		23 15.8	39 9.3	31 11.9
52 7.0	59 6.2	61 6.0			57 6.4		51 7.2	83 4.4	57 6.4
128 2.9	106 3.5	103 3.6			198 1.8		79 4.6	102 3.6	72 5.1
17 21.6	17 20.9	13 27.2	Cost of Sales/Payables		2 210.0		7 50.6	27 13.5	17 21.4
31 11.9	34 10.7	32 11.5			27 13.7		32 11.4	65 5.7	37 10.0
54 6.8	54 6.8	58 6.2			45 8.0		51 7.1	88 4.1	46 8.0
4.4	4.1	5.1	Sales/Working Capital		4.8		6.1	5.8	4.6
9.7	9.0	9.2			16.1		11.0	11.1	7.1
29.3	33.7	20.4			UND		NM	14.6	16.9
10.3	15.1	15.1	EBIT/Interest					11.4	37.5
(55) 2.2	(66) 3.7	(60) 4.7						(15) 6.2	(18) 11.8
-1.4	.4	1.6						2.4	3.2
6.0	12.3	19.8	Net Profit + Depr., Dep., Amort./Cur. Mat. L/T/D						
(13) 2.0	(16) 1.7	(10) 2.0							
.3	-.9	.4							
.0	.1	.1	Fixed/Worth		.0		.1	.0	.0
.3	.3	.2			.1		.4	.1	.1
1.3	1.6	1.0			1.0		2.1	.7	2.1
.6	.8	.6	Debt/Worth		.5		.8	1.3	.4
1.5	2.0	1.7			1.9		1.4	2.1	1.4
5.5	4.6	3.9			49.6		9.7	4.9	4.5
54.3	43.2	48.2	% Profit Before Taxes/Tangible Net Worth					49.2	51.5
(59) 14.7	(74) 13.2	(61) 20.1					(14)	20.9	(18) 31.3
-5.2	-.6	4.8						2.6	9.7
18.8	15.1	16.9	% Profit Before Taxes/Total Assets		32.9		9.1	15.3	17.2
5.1	3.6	7.3			4.2		4.4	6.7	10.2
-4.0	-2.0	2.0			-41.1		-1.5	1.9	3.3
136.7	68.2	130.0	Sales/Net Fixed Assets		999.8		78.0	320.2	141.2
34.3	28.6	42.7			64.4		27.8	58.0	47.3
10.6	10.1	15.4			27.7		13.5	24.2	26.2
3.7	3.5	3.5	Sales/Total Assets		4.3		3.8	3.6	3.3
2.2	2.2	2.5			3.0		3.1	2.5	2.2
1.3	1.2	1.6			2.1		2.6	1.8	1.5
.3	.8	.4	% Depr., Dep., Amort./Sales					.2	.2
(45) 1.5	(52) 1.6	(47) 1.2					(13)	.7	(17) 1.3
3.2	3.2	2.1						1.2	2.1
1.9	1.9	1.2	% Officers', Directors' Owners' Comp/Sales						
(14) 5.0	(27) 3.5	(22) 2.0							
12.6	8.0	4.3							
2506877M	2576889M	2016636M	Net Sales ($)	2241M	19264M	32070M	73078M	242870M	1647113M
1434081M	1760336M	1005988M	Total Assets ($)	3393M	7189M	17959M	24425M	95975M	857047M

M = $ thousand   MM = $ million

See Pages 9 through 22 for Explanation of Ratios and Data

Current Data Sorted by Assets   Comparative Historical Data

0-500M	500M-2MM	2-10MM	10-50MM	50-100MM	100-250MM	Type of Statement	4/1/06-3/31/07 ALL	4/1/07-3/31/08 ALL
		6	9	6	3	Unqualified	33	24
	2	6	5			Reviewed	7	10
	1	1				Compiled	4	6
1	6	6				Tax Returns	11	4
	4	9	16	5	7	Other	38	38
	19 (4/1-9/30/10)		74 (10/1/10-3/31/11)					
1	13	28	30	11	10	**NUMBER OF STATEMENTS**	93	82
%	%	%	%	%	%	**ASSETS**	%	%
	13.2	10.8	17.6	18.4	18.3	Cash & Equivalents	15.5	10.5
	17.4	30.5	23.6	23.2	22.3	Trade Receivables (net)	29.3	28.5
	25.1	34.7	23.0	24.7	17.1	Inventory	23.0	26.2
	3.6	4.1	6.2	4.0	5.3	All Other Current	2.9	5.2
	59.2	80.1	70.3	70.4	63.0	Total Current	70.7	70.4
	23.1	7.5	12.9	7.7	13.7	Fixed Assets (net)	12.2	13.8
	9.7	4.8	8.2	20.7	15.2	Intangibles (net)	9.6	9.7
	7.9	7.6	8.5	1.2	8.1	All Other Non-Current	7.5	6.2
	100.0	100.0	100.0	100.0	100.0	Total	100.0	100.0
						LIABILITIES		
	5.7	14.3	5.0	4.0	2.2	Notes Payable-Short Term	8.5	9.8
	4.1	2.6	1.7	1.3	5.3	Cur. Mat.-L.T.D.	2.5	2.1
	12.0	18.5	12.7	18.3	12.8	Trade Payables	16.0	16.0
	.1	.2	.4	.6	.1	Income Taxes Payable	.4	.5
	4.9	8.5	17.4	14.9	16.7	All Other Current	13.0	11.9
	26.8	44.1	37.2	39.0	37.0	Total Current	40.4	40.3
	23.3	7.3	5.5	5.8	8.4	Long-Term Debt	15.7	14.8
	.0	.7	.4	.8	.8	Deferred Taxes	.4	.4
	4.4	8.2	9.5	12.3	4.3	All Other Non-Current	9.3	7.0
	45.5	39.7	47.4	42.1	49.5	Net Worth	34.2	37.4
	100.0	100.0	100.0	100.0	100.0	Total Liabilities & Net Worth	100.0	100.0
						INCOME DATA		
	100.0	100.0	100.0	100.0	100.0	Net Sales	100.0	100.0
	46.4	35.7	34.5	46.0	31.7	Gross Profit	39.5	38.5
	42.7	34.1	29.9	46.0	32.4	Operating Expenses	36.6	35.8
	3.8	1.7	4.6	.0	-.7	Operating Profit	3.0	2.7
	1.4	.3	.6	1.9	.9	All Other Expenses (net)	.9	1.0
	2.4	1.3	4.0	-1.8	-1.5	Profit Before Taxes	2.1	1.8
						RATIOS		
	4.0	2.6	3.6	4.5	3.5		3.2	2.5
	2.4	1.7	1.7	1.7	2.0	Current	1.7	1.8
	1.5	1.4	1.3	1.4	1.1		1.2	1.2
	2.7	1.2	2.2	2.3	2.9		2.3	1.4
	1.1	.9	1.1	1.3	1.0	Quick	1.1	.9
	.5	.7	.5	.6	.6		.6	.6
11 32.3	30 12.3	46 7.9	44 8.3	61 6.0		Sales/Receivables	34 10.6 35 10.5	
35 10.5	42 8.7	55 6.6	50 7.3	65 5.6			51 7.1 50 7.3	
53 6.9	60 6.1	66 5.5	77 4.7	77 4.8			68 5.4 65 5.6	
16 23.4	58 6.3	27 13.6	60 6.0	33 11.0		Cost of Sales/Inventory	32 11.5 42 8.6	
58 6.3	93 3.9	84 4.3	105 3.5	66 5.6			73 5.0 75 4.8	
137 2.7	133 2.7	150 2.4	304 1.2	84 4.4			105 3.5 122 3.0	
12 31.3	21 17.1	17 21.1	46 8.0	30 12.1		Cost of Sales/Payables	26 14.1 26 13.9	
44 8.3	41 8.9	43 8.4	65 5.6	48 7.6			41 8.8 40 9.2	
73 5.0	60 6.1	62 5.8	139 2.6	56 6.5			65 5.6 61 6.0	
	2.9	4.5	3.2	2.5	2.0	Sales/Working Capital	3.7	3.7
	4.9	6.7	5.5	3.3	5.0		6.9	7.1
	17.8	14.7	9.8	14.5	NM		36.0	22.4
	5.6	11.6	46.7			EBIT/Interest	13.6	12.6
	(12) 2.7	(27) 2.7	(23) 12.6				(73) 3.9 (70) 2.5	
	.2	-1.4	2.8				.9	-.3
		26.5				Net Profit + Depr., Dep.,	16.5	18.7
		(16) 4.7				Amort./Cur. Mat. L/T/D	(21) 3.1 (27) 3.3	
		2.2					2.3	1.0
	.1	.0	.1	.2	.1	Fixed/Worth	.1	.1
	.3	.2	.2	.4	.2		.3	.3
	6.5	.5	1.1	-.4	NM		1.7	1.1
	.6	1.0	.4	1.1	.6	Debt/Worth	.6	.6
	1.0	1.4	1.5	3.3	1.0		1.8	2.0
	14.3	2.4	3.4	-8.4	NM		8.8	5.7
	35.3	39.6	58.1			% Profit Before Taxes/Tangible	51.3	38.8
	(11) 6.6	(25) 15.2	(27) 23.3			Net Worth	(78) 21.6 (72) 15.8	
	2.8	-4.5	14.1				4.5	-8.2
	11.2	12.3	17.2	4.3	7.3	% Profit Before Taxes/Total	13.9	16.0
	3.1	1.9	9.3	2.0	3.2	Assets	6.3	3.9
	-1.0	-2.6	4.2	-5.5	-12.0		-.8	-3.8
	144.1	180.0	38.0	66.2	32.8	Sales/Net Fixed Assets	54.9	67.8
	20.6	44.0	21.3	16.1	11.4		24.4	24.5
	4.0	25.6	9.9	8.4	4.0		10.3	8.1
	3.5	3.4	2.1	1.6	1.7	Sales/Total Assets	2.8	2.9
	1.6	2.2	1.5	1.3	1.2		2.0	2.0
	1.2	1.8	1.1	.9	.9		1.3	1.2
	.9	.2	1.0			% Depr., Dep., Amort./Sales	1.0	.7
	(10) 1.4	(23) 1.0	(26) 1.4				(62) 1.6 (60) 1.6	
	7.3	1.7	3.1				2.4	2.9
		.3				% Officers', Directors'	.6	.9
		(10) 3.0				Owners' Comp/Sales	(12) 3.7 (14) 3.5	
		4.2					8.5	7.7
429M	41877M	427186M	984003M	1092251M	1891715M	Net Sales ($)	5719779M	4491862M
113M	15335M	149223M	665100M	810730M	1559595M	Total Assets ($)	3395226M	2915406M

Comparative Historical Data | Current Data Sorted by Sales

			Type of Statement						
35	26	24	Unqualified		1			8	15
13	11	13	Reviewed		1		1	6	5
4	5	2	Compiled		1			1	
6	3	13	Tax Returns	2	4	1	4	1	1
53	52	41	Other		4	2	4	10	21
4/1/08- 3/31/09 ALL	4/1/09- 3/31/10 ALL	4/1/10- 3/31/11 ALL			19 (4/1-9/30/10)			74 (10/1/10-3/31/11)	
				0-1MM	1-3MM	3-5MM	5-10MM	10-25MM	25MM & OVER
111	97	93	NUMBER OF STATEMENTS	2	11	3	9	26	42
%	%	%	ASSETS	%	%	%	%	%	%
11.6	14.2	15.2	Cash & Equivalents		17.0			16.6	16.5
29.4	26.6	24.5	Trade Receivables (net)		20.4			20.8	27.2
25.0	22.9	26.3	Inventory		25.8			25.2	24.6
6.3	4.7	4.8	All Other Current		3.8			6.3	5.1
72.2	68.3	70.7	Total Current		67.0			68.9	73.4
11.7	13.6	12.2	Fixed Assets (net)		19.6			10.7	10.8
9.1	10.1	9.9	Intangibles (net)		7.8			8.9	11.3
7.0	7.9	7.1	All Other Non-Current		5.6			11.6	4.5
100.0	100.0	100.0	Total		100.0			100.0	100.0
			LIABILITIES						
9.9	9.7	7.7	Notes Payable-Short Term		2.8			5.5	6.1
2.7	2.2	2.6	Cur. Mat.-L.T.D.		2.2			3.3	2.2
16.2	14.1	15.0	Trade Payables		12.9			10.4	17.4
.9	.3	.3	Income Taxes Payable		.2			.2	.4
16.2	13.8	12.8	All Other Current		5.8			11.4	17.0
46.0	40.1	38.4	Total Current		23.9			30.9	43.2
9.1	10.4	9.6	Long-Term Debt		25.9			5.1	7.2
.4	.5	.5	Deferred Taxes		.4			.5	.6
6.7	9.0	8.1	All Other Non-Current		.7			9.8	7.7
37.7	40.0	43.4	Net Worth		49.2			53.8	41.4
100.0	100.0	100.0	Total Liabilities & Net Worth		100.0			100.0	100.0
			INCOME DATA						
100.0	100.0	100.0	Net Sales		100.0			100.0	100.0
38.0	36.6	37.8	Gross Profit		43.3			37.2	34.0
35.1	35.0	35.3	Operating Expenses		39.6			33.8	31.8
2.9	1.6	2.5	Operating Profit		3.7			3.3	2.2
.7	.8	.8	All Other Expenses (net)		1.5			-.2	1.1
2.2	.7	1.7	Profit Before Taxes		2.2			3.5	1.1
			RATIOS						
2.9	3.5	3.3	Current		4.4			3.8	3.2
1.8	1.8	1.7			3.1			2.1	1.7
1.2	1.3	1.4			1.7			1.3	1.3
1.6	2.1	2.0	Quick		3.3			2.6	2.0
1.0	1.0	1.0			2.3			1.1	1.0
.6	.6	.6			.7			.6	.6
38 9.6	36 10.1	35 10.6	Sales/Receivables		25 14.4			33 11.2	42 8.7
51 7.2	49 7.5	52 7.1			36 10.1			49 7.5	57 6.4
64 5.7	60 6.0	63 5.8			56 6.5			64 5.7	67 5.4
33 11.0	31 11.8	45 8.0	Cost of Sales/Inventory		14 25.4			44 8.3	43 8.5
65 5.6	65 5.6	80 4.5			112 3.3			78 4.7	69 5.3
102 3.6	114 3.2	132 2.8			149 2.4			166 2.2	107 3.4
23 15.8	21 17.0	22 17.0	Cost of Sales/Payables		26 14.0			16 23.0	22 16.6
37 9.9	34 10.7	45 8.2			44 8.3			33 11.0	49 7.5
54 6.8	54 6.7	63 5.8			64 5.7			51 7.2	66 5.6
4.2	3.2	3.2	Sales/Working Capital		2.7			2.7	3.3
6.6	6.9	5.6			3.3			4.4	5.9
25.3	18.6	14.0			9.2			11.1	16.2
10.6	12.0	15.8	EBIT/Interest		4.5			37.2	16.7
(91) 3.8	(81) 2.7	(80) 3.0		(10) 2.7			(22) 12.7	(34) 4.5	
.3	.3	.6			.8			.2	1.2
9.5	4.8	6.8	Net Profit + Depr., Dep., Amort./Cur. Mat. L/T/D					10.6	18.1
(36) 2.3	(25) 2.1	(27) 3.2					(10) 3.3	(13) 3.7	
1.2	.8	1.5						1.6	1.8
.1	.1	.1	Fixed/Worth		.0			.1	.1
.3	.4	.2			.2			.2	.2
.9	1.2	.9			.8			.5	1.7
.6	.5	.7	Debt/Worth		.5			.4	.8
1.9	1.8	1.4			.6			1.1	1.7
5.7	4.8	5.4			3.9			2.8	5.6
44.2	31.6	35.4	% Profit Before Taxes/Tangible Net Worth		34.9			52.9	36.4
(95) 13.9	(82) 11.2	(79) 15.2		(10) 5.8			(25) 15.6	(34) 18.8	
.1	.7	1.4			-.2			-7.3	5.1
12.9	9.1	11.9	% Profit Before Taxes/Total Assets		8.9			17.9	11.7
4.7	2.7	5.2			3.1			6.7	5.5
-.8	-2.6	-.4			1.1			-3.5	.9
63.4	45.7	61.3	Sales/Net Fixed Assets		230.8			47.6	57.5
27.7	23.2	24.1			20.6			23.9	21.8
13.0	8.9	9.6			2.9			13.5	9.8
3.0	2.5	2.5	Sales/Total Assets		2.5			2.3	2.5
2.2	1.9	1.7			1.4			1.7	1.6
1.3	1.2	1.1			1.1			1.1	1.1
.8	.9	.8	% Depr., Dep., Amort./Sales					1.0	.5
(83) 1.3	(69) 1.7	(73) 1.4					(23) 1.5	(32) 1.2	
2.5	3.1	3.0						3.6	2.4
3.2	3.7	1.0	% Officers', Directors' Owners' Comp/Sales						
(18) 4.6	(15) 5.6	(20) 4.3							
10.4	8.4	6.6							
7129412M	4272415M	4437461M	Net Sales ($)	1131M	22400M	12583M	69759M	443431M	3888157M
4070890M	2570055M	3200096M	Total Assets ($)	1005M	14312M	5686M	39306M	409654M	2730133M

M = $ thousand   MM = $ million
See Pages 9 through 22 for Explanation of Ratios and Data

Current Data Sorted by Assets   Comparative Historical Data

0-500M	500M-2MM	2-10MM	10-50MM	50-100MM	100-250MM		4/1/06-3/31/07 ALL	4/1/07-3/31/08 ALL
		2	3	2	2	Unqualified	9	8
	1	2				Reviewed	4	3
						Compiled	2	5
	1	2				Tax Returns	6	3
2		9	5	1	4	Other	18	18
			7 (4/1-9/30/10)	29 (10/1/10-3/31/11)				
2	2	15	8	3	6	**NUMBER OF STATEMENTS**	39	37
%	%	%	%	%	%	**ASSETS**	%	%
		13.9				Cash & Equivalents	17.2	16.2
		31.3				Trade Receivables (net)	26.8	26.1
		23.3				Inventory	25.6	21.9
		2.8				All Other Current	3.8	5.3
		71.3				Total Current	73.4	69.5
		10.0				Fixed Assets (net)	11.9	10.5
		7.8				Intangibles (net)	7.2	11.6
		10.8				All Other Non-Current	7.5	8.4
		100.0				Total	100.0	100.0
						LIABILITIES		
		6.8				Notes Payable-Short Term	9.8	7.2
		1.8				Cur. Mat.-L.T.D.	5.1	3.4
		18.4				Trade Payables	16.5	17.1
		.2				Income Taxes Payable	.8	.3
		12.6				All Other Current	14.2	15.9
		39.8				Total Current	46.3	44.0
		7.9				Long-Term Debt	7.4	7.4
		.4				Deferred Taxes	.2	.2
		8.3				All Other Non-Current	3.9	7.0
		43.6				Net Worth	42.2	41.3
		100.0				Total Liabilities & Net Worth	100.0	100.0
						INCOME DATA		
		100.0				Net Sales	100.0	100.0
		41.4				Gross Profit	39.3	38.8
		33.7				Operating Expenses	34.4	36.0
		7.7				Operating Profit	4.9	2.8
		1.5				All Other Expenses (net)	.4	1.4
		6.2				Profit Before Taxes	4.5	1.4
						RATIOS		
		4.9					3.6	3.0
		2.3				Current	1.8	1.5
		1.1					1.1	1.1
		3.6					1.8	1.7
		1.6				Quick	1.0	1.0
		.9					.6	.6
		41 8.9					31 11.9	37 9.9
		47 7.7				Sales/Receivables	61 6.0	58 6.3
		54 6.7					80 4.6	79 4.6
		14 26.6					34 10.7	30 12.1
		89 4.1				Cost of Sales/Inventory	83 4.4	80 4.6
		141 2.6					112 3.3	128 2.9
		15 23.7					21 17.4	27 13.8
		31 11.8				Cost of Sales/Payables	33 11.2	56 6.5
		64 5.7					64 5.7	88 4.2
		3.6					3.0	3.0
		4.1				Sales/Working Capital	6.2	8.3
		45.6					33.7	96.5
		50.0					27.2	11.1
		(11) 5.2				EBIT/Interest	(32) 5.1	(29) 1.0
		2.0					.7	-4.0
						Net Profit + Depr., Dep., Amort./Cur. Mat. L/T/D	16.5	
							(10) 1.8	
							.3	
		.1					.1	.1
		.2				Fixed/Worth	.3	.2
		-2.5					1.1	1.1
		.3					.4	.5
		.7				Debt/Worth	1.5	1.3
		-27.0					7.2	9.8
		86.8				% Profit Before Taxes/Tangible Net Worth	64.2	24.4
		(11) 29.0					(32) 18.4	(31) 5.5
		9.2					5.6	-9.3
		23.1				% Profit Before Taxes/Total Assets	16.4	10.7
		12.9					5.8	.7
		3.3					-.2	-3.7
		174.8					65.1	85.8
		33.6				Sales/Net Fixed Assets	24.1	33.4
		15.2					9.2	9.8
		3.2					3.4	2.3
		2.1				Sales/Total Assets	1.7	1.7
		1.5					1.1	.9
		.2					.5	.4
		(12) .8				% Depr., Dep., Amort./Sales	(33) 1.6	(24) 1.4
		1.4					2.6	4.0
						% Officers', Directors' Owners' Comp/Sales		
2927M	12066M	175614M	357190M	387989M	1273418M	Net Sales ($)	1729221M	2142730M
799M	2116M	76021M	179466M	271096M	1132898M	Total Assets ($)	1283139M	1785362M

M = $ thousand   MM = $ million
See Pages 9 through 22 for Explanation of Ratios and Data

Comparative Historical Data

Current Data Sorted by Sales

						Type of Statement	0-1MM	1-3MM	3-5MM	5-10MM	10-25MM	25MM & OVER
	12		9		9	Unqualified				1	2	6
	1		4		3	Reviewed				3		
	1		2			Compiled						
	7		4		3	Tax Returns		2	1			
	16		22		21	Other	1	1	1	4	3	11
	4/1/08-3/31/09		4/1/09-3/31/10		4/1/10-3/31/11			7 (4/1-9/30/10)			29 (10/1/10-3/31/11)	
	ALL		ALL		ALL							
	37		41		36	NUMBER OF STATEMENTS	1	3	2	8	5	17
	%		%		%	ASSETS	%	%	%	%	%	%
	17.7		19.3		20.0	Cash & Equivalents						22.2
	26.0		29.0		27.7	Trade Receivables (net)						29.0
	22.6		21.4		21.5	Inventory						18.4
	2.7		6.0		2.9	All Other Current						3.0
	69.1		75.6		72.0	Total Current						72.6
	13.8		12.0		11.4	Fixed Assets (net)						9.8
	9.5		6.1		6.6	Intangibles (net)						6.5
	7.7		6.3		10.0	All Other Non-Current						11.1
	100.0		100.0		100.0	Total						100.0
						LIABILITIES						
	9.7		7.5		4.8	Notes Payable-Short Term						3.4
	3.9		5.8		1.8	Cur. Mat.-L.T.D.						1.3
	24.6		17.3		17.3	Trade Payables						21.0
	.1		.1		.2	Income Taxes Payable						.3
	15.7		16.6		16.5	All Other Current						17.5
	54.0		47.4		40.6	Total Current						43.5
	9.4		6.2		6.4	Long-Term Debt						4.9
	.4		.3		.3	Deferred Taxes						.3
	11.4		13.1		8.6	All Other Non-Current						6.1
	24.8		33.1		44.1	Net Worth						45.1
	100.0		100.0		100.0	Total Liabilties & Net Worth						100.0
						INCOME DATA						
	100.0		100.0		100.0	Net Sales						100.0
	40.7		42.2		41.3	Gross Profit						34.6
	41.4		41.3		36.4	Operating Expenses						31.1
	-.8		.9		4.9	Operating Profit						3.5
	.9		1.7		1.5	All Other Expenses (net)						1.6
	-1.7		-.8		3.4	Profit Before Taxes						2.0
						RATIOS						
	4.0		3.2		3.8							2.8
	1.6		1.6		2.1	Current						1.8
	1.0		1.2		1.2							1.2
	2.5		2.0		2.3							2.1
	.9		1.0		1.3	Quick						1.2
	.6		.7		.9							.8
33	11.0	38	9.7	39	9.4						46	7.9
52	7.1	54	6.7	47	7.7	Sales/Receivables					53	6.8
65	5.6	63	5.8	65	5.6						83	4.4
23	16.0	34	10.7	33	11.0						28	13.0
74	4.9	79	4.6	84	4.4	Cost of Sales/Inventory					55	6.6
123	3.0	131	2.8	138	2.6						136	2.7
21	17.1	24	15.0	24	15.1						30	12.2
38	9.6	43	8.4	42	8.7	Cost of Sales/Payables					54	6.7
70	5.2	71	5.2	75	4.9						81	4.5
	3.4		3.2		3.1							2.8
	7.3		7.0		4.3	Sales/Working Capital						5.3
	255.2		31.8		31.9							109.5
	6.2		17.4		36.3							46.7
(31)	1.2	(33)	1.8	(29)	5.2	EBIT/Interest					(15)	8.7
	-7.5		-4.6		1.9							-1.6
			7.5			Net Profit + Depr., Dep.,						
		(13)	3.4			Amort./Cur. Mat. L/T/D						
			-4.4									
	.1		.1		.1							.1
	.2		.2		.2	Fixed/Worth						.2
	1.0		3.5		1.3							1.3
	.4		.5		.4							.4
	2.3		1.5		.9	Debt/Worth						1.0
	11.1		18.8		7.8							6.6
	50.5		25.4		58.5	% Profit Before Taxes/Tangible						66.5
(30)	5.8	(33)	10.3	(30)	21.7	Net Worth					(15)	18.0
	-22.1		-22.0		5.0							-2.0
	10.2		13.4		19.8	% Profit Before Taxes/Total						17.4
	1.3		.9		7.2	Assets						5.6
	-13.8		-16.2		1.4							-1.6
	67.5		52.2		56.3							41.7
	20.4		26.6		29.2	Sales/Net Fixed Assets						24.5
	6.6		12.0		9.2							9.1
	2.8		3.0		3.1							2.7
	1.9		1.8		1.9	Sales/Total Assets						1.8
	1.0		1.0		1.2							1.0
	.9		.8		.6							1.1
(24)	2.0	(31)	1.4	(27)	1.4	% Depr., Dep., Amort./Sales					(13)	1.4
	4.4		2.0		1.8							2.0
	4.4					% Officers', Directors'						
(12)	7.3					Owners' Comp/Sales						
	14.2											
	2045527M		2231526M		2209204M	Net Sales ($)	700M	7547M	8698M	60270M	97109M	2034880M
	1497386M		1724293M		1662396M	Total Assets ($)	392M	5209M	5402M	31336M	67798M	1552259M

M = $ thousand   MM = $ million
See Pages 9 through 22 for Explanation of Ratios and Data

Current Data Sorted by Assets   Comparative Historical Data

0-500M	500M-2MM	2-10MM	10-50MM	50-100MM	100-250MM	Type of Statement		
		1	14	4	9	Unqualified	35	26
		4	2	1		Reviewed	21	18
	1	4	1			Compiled	11	7
	3	2	1			Tax Returns	6	9
	4	15	14	4	3	Other	43	47
	22 (4/1-9/30/10)		65 (10/1/10-3/31/11)				4/1/06-3/31/07 ALL	4/1/07-3/31/08 ALL
8	26	32	9	12		NUMBER OF STATEMENTS	116	107
%	%	%	%	%	%	**ASSETS**	%	%
		15.8	19.0		24.2	Cash & Equivalents	11.2	13.2
		22.3	20.7		19.0	Trade Receivables (net)	27.9	23.8
		31.6	29.2		16.0	Inventory	26.4	26.5
D A T A		2.0	5.0		1.9	All Other Current	3.4	3.0
		71.7	73.9		61.1	Total Current	68.9	66.5
N O T		15.8	12.0		13.4	Fixed Assets (net)	19.8	19.1
		4.6	6.3		14.4	Intangibles (net)	6.0	8.9
		7.9	7.7		11.0	All Other Non-Current	5.3	5.4
A V A		100.0	100.0		100.0	Total	100.0	100.0
I						**LIABILITIES**		
L		10.5	6.2		1.5	Notes Payable-Short Term	8.0	13.6
A		2.7	1.2		1.9	Cur. Mat.-L.T.D.	3.5	3.1
B		12.6	10.7		10.9	Trade Payables	14.1	12.1
L		.2	.3		.9	Income Taxes Payable	.8	.6
E		15.4	13.7		8.5	All Other Current	11.2	10.5
		41.3	32.2		23.7	Total Current	37.6	39.9
		11.4	5.4		17.5	Long-Term Debt	11.7	10.3
		.3	.1		.9	Deferred Taxes	.6	.4
		4.5	5.5		3.6	All Other Non-Current	5.6	5.4
		42.5	56.8		54.4	Net Worth	44.4	44.1
		100.0	100.0		100.0	Total Liabilities & Net Worth	100.0	100.0
						INCOME DATA		
		100.0	100.0		100.0	Net Sales	100.0	100.0
		40.7	41.8		35.4	Gross Profit	37.5	39.8
		36.7	32.4		30.8	Operating Expenses	30.8	32.1
		4.0	9.4		4.6	Operating Profit	6.7	7.7
		1.1	.7		2.0	All Other Expenses (net)	1.1	2.0
		2.9	8.6		2.6	Profit Before Taxes	5.5	5.7
						RATIOS		
		3.0	5.4		4.4		3.7	4.0
		1.8	2.9		2.7	Current	1.9	2.0
		1.1	1.6		1.8		1.3	1.2
		1.8	3.1		3.0		2.3	2.5
		1.0	1.6		1.8	Quick	1.0	1.0
		.5	.6		1.0		.6	.5
		24 15.5	32 11.5		32 11.6		35 10.4	31 11.8
		40 9.2	45 8.1		55 6.7	Sales/Receivables	45 8.0	44 8.3
		58 6.3	66 5.5		62 5.8		62 5.9	59 6.1
		57 6.4	81 4.5		59 6.2		34 10.6	28 13.0
		88 4.1	143 2.5		77 4.7	Cost of Sales/Inventory	80 4.6	71 5.1
		208 1.8	192 1.9		100 3.7		122 3.0	117 3.1
		26 14.1	20 18.1		32 11.3		21 17.0	16 22.1
		34 10.6	38 9.6		37 9.8	Cost of Sales/Payables	35 10.3	31 11.6
		49 7.4	67 5.4		51 7.2		53 6.9	54 6.7
		3.7	2.5		1.9		3.4	3.5
		6.0	3.9		3.4	Sales/Working Capital	6.4	6.4
		36.7	5.5		7.5		15.1	23.1
		13.8	24.3		37.1		20.6	16.1
		(23) 4.2	(25) 6.5		(11) 14.4	EBIT/Interest	(100) 5.3	(93) 6.3
		-.1	-.1		1.5		1.6	1.3
							9.2	15.9
						Net Profit + Depr., Dep., Amort./Cur. Mat. L/T/D	(32) 3.0	(26) 3.8
							.9	-.1
		.1	.1		.2		.1	.1
		.3	.2		.3	Fixed/Worth	.4	.4
		1.0	.4		3.0		1.2	1.0
		.6	.3		.5		.5	.4
		1.7	.5		.8	Debt/Worth	1.2	1.4
		7.0	1.5		31.7		3.4	3.4
		74.6	48.3		15.4		47.0	69.7
		12.5	(30) 13.7		(11) 11.4	% Profit Before Taxes/Tangible Net Worth	(104) 18.4	(93) 24.5
		-2.1	.7		3.9		2.8	3.1
		15.5	21.6		7.6		20.3	23.7
		4.6	5.9		6.0	% Profit Before Taxes/Total Assets	6.8	9.8
		-1.3	-1.4		-5.1		1.1	.8
		82.5	40.8		25.6		35.5	44.9
		18.4	14.4		9.8	Sales/Net Fixed Assets	16.6	18.3
		6.2	7.5		4.5		6.9	6.3
		2.4	2.1		1.8		2.9	2.8
		1.8	1.4		1.1	Sales/Total Assets	2.1	1.9
		1.1	1.2		.7		1.3	1.2
		.6	.5				.7	.6
		(16) 2.2	(29) 1.8			% Depr., Dep., Amort./Sales	(104) 1.6	(82) 1.5
		3.1	3.0				2.5	2.8
							2.5	2.3
						% Officers', Directors' Owners' Comp/Sales	(26) 4.0	(24) 5.5
							9.0	8.1
	21407M	259187M	1133555M	802597M	2994951M	Net Sales ($)	4112645M	3951466M
	8686M	140571M	735303M	573194M	2358399M	Total Assets ($)	3179740M	2820366M

Comparative Historical Data | Current Data Sorted by Sales

			Type of Statement						
38	30	28	Unqualified				1	3	24
11	15	7	Reviewed			1	3		3
7	5	6	Compiled	2	1	2	2	1	
7	5	6	Tax Returns	2		2	1	1	
47	45	40	Other	2	1	4	7	11	15
4/1/08-3/31/09 ALL	4/1/09-3/31/10 ALL	4/1/10-3/31/11 ALL		22 (4/1-9/30/10)			65 (10/1/10-3/31/11)		
				0-1MM	1-3MM	3-5MM	5-10MM	10-25MM	25MM & OVER
110	100	87	**NUMBER OF STATEMENTS**	2	5	6	13	17	44
%	%	%	**ASSETS**	%	%	%	%	%	%
13.2	13.8	17.8	Cash & Equivalents				18.9	21.1	17.8
25.0	22.8	21.5	Trade Receivables (net)				16.4	22.7	21.1
27.9	26.7	26.4	Inventory				29.3	28.4	24.8
3.4	6.0	3.5	All Other Current				2.9	3.6	4.3
69.4	69.3	69.2	Total Current				67.4	75.8	68.1
15.8	16.9	14.5	Fixed Assets (net)				14.0	11.4	12.1
7.8	7.5	8.3	Intangibles (net)				7.3	6.6	11.7
6.9	6.4	8.0	All Other Non-Current				11.4	6.2	8.1
100.0	100.0	100.0	Total				100.0	100.0	100.0
			LIABILITIES						
10.5	11.1	6.3	Notes Payable-Short Term				8.8	9.3	3.3
2.4	3.0	1.7	Cur. Mat.-L.T.D.				2.4	1.3	1.5
13.1	13.5	11.9	Trade Payables				12.3	12.1	11.6
.3	.2	.3	Income Taxes Payable				.1	.2	.5
12.7	10.7	12.7	All Other Current				10.5	16.4	11.4
39.1	38.5	32.9	Total Current				34.1	39.3	28.3
13.2	13.0	11.6	Long-Term Debt				11.1	12.2	10.9
.2	.4	.3	Deferred Taxes				.6	.0	.3
10.7	3.8	4.7	All Other Non-Current				1.0	1.2	6.1
36.7	44.3	50.5	Net Worth				53.3	47.2	54.4
100.0	100.0	100.0	Total Liabilities & Net Worth				100.0	100.0	100.0
			INCOME DATA						
100.0	100.0	100.0	Net Sales				100.0	100.0	100.0
38.9	39.4	41.6	Gross Profit				46.6	42.5	37.2
32.7	34.1	34.6	Operating Expenses				41.1	34.6	30.4
6.2	5.4	7.0	Operating Profit				5.5	7.9	6.8
1.8	2.0	1.4	All Other Expenses (net)				.9	1.3	1.4
4.4	3.4	5.6	Profit Before Taxes				4.6	6.6	5.4
			RATIOS						
3.4	3.5	4.3	Current				5.3	5.5	4.4
2.2	2.0	2.5					2.4	2.0	2.7
1.3	1.3	1.5					1.2	1.3	1.7
1.9	2.0	2.4	Quick				2.3	3.6	2.9
1.2	1.1	1.4					1.4	1.7	1.6
.6	.5	.6					.6	.6	.8
31 11.8	29 12.6	30 12.0	Sales/Receivables			23 15.8	22 16.6	34 10.6	
43 8.5	44 8.4	47 7.8				36 10.2	47 7.8	53 6.9	
65 5.6	62 5.9	64 5.7				54 6.8	63 5.8	66 5.6	
46 7.9	38 9.5	61 6.0	Cost of Sales/Inventory			54 6.7	69 5.3	56 6.5	
86 4.2	87 4.2	90 4.0				207 1.8	112 3.3	82 4.4	
137 2.7	148 2.5	176 2.1				251 1.5	176 2.1	144 2.5	
22 16.4	20 18.4	23 15.8	Cost of Sales/Payables			26 14.1	18 20.5	23 16.0	
36 10.3	34 10.7	37 9.8				35 10.4	39 9.4	36 10.2	
57 6.4	49 7.5	59 6.2				42 8.6	67 5.5	58 6.3	
3.0	2.7	2.9	Sales/Working Capital				2.8	2.6	2.6
5.3	5.1	4.8					5.5	5.6	4.2
13.9	13.8	8.0					8.0	25.3	7.0
17.9	17.8	15.4	EBIT/Interest				12.1	12.3	33.8
(94) 3.8	(80) 2.6	(73) 5.3				(12) 3.8	(13) 4.2	(36) 9.5	
.6	-1.3	.0					-5.0	-10.1	.7
16.3	5.2	8.9	Net Profit + Depr., Dep., Amort./Cur. Mat. L/T/D						34.0
(20) 2.5	(26) 2.6	(20) 2.0						(14) 3.9	
-.1	.4	.4							.7
.1	.1	.1	Fixed/Worth				.2	.0	.1
.3	.3	.3					.3	.2	.3
1.1	1.0	.8					.4	1.0	.4
.4	.4	.4	Debt/Worth				.3	.2	.4
1.3	1.3	1.0					.9	1.7	.8
4.7	4.5	3.1					5.9	7.2	1.5
44.7	35.6	53.1	% Profit Before Taxes/Tangible Net Worth				74.0	77.2	60.5
(96) 18.0	(87) 11.6	(82) 13.2					11.7	(16) 12.3	(40) 14.1
2.4	-6.3	-1.2					-2.9	-3.1	-.5
21.2	13.1	17.8	% Profit Before Taxes/Total Assets				17.3	15.9	22.6
7.9	4.0	6.1					4.4	4.0	7.2
-.4	-3.7	-1.7					-1.7	-3.7	-1.4
47.9	38.9	33.2	Sales/Net Fixed Assets				61.7	52.3	30.3
18.2	14.6	15.7					16.9	23.9	14.4
8.0	6.4	7.3					3.7	10.5	7.5
2.6	2.3	2.3	Sales/Total Assets				2.2	2.3	2.2
1.8	1.7	1.4					1.2	1.5	1.4
1.3	1.2	1.0					.9	1.1	1.1
.8	.8	.8	% Depr., Dep., Amort./Sales					.6	.8
(84) 1.5	(76) 1.8	(64) 2.0						(14) 1.5	(33) 2.2
2.6	3.1	3.3						2.8	3.4
2.0	2.2	1.7	% Officers', Directors' Owners' Comp/Sales						
(18) 4.4	(21) 6.0	(16) 7.2							
8.9	13.7	9.6							
5071150M	4589267M	5211697M	Net Sales ($)	1066M	10498M	24082M	94114M	282891M	4799046M
3317319M	3013765M	3816153M	Total Assets ($)	3830M	6080M	18066M	78954M	206454M	3502769M

© RMA 2011

M = $ thousand   MM = $ million
See Pages 9 through 22 for Explanation of Ratios and Data

Current Data Sorted by Assets

Comparative Historical Data

						Type of Statement		
	2	2	7	1	4	Unqualified	17	16
	3	7	2			Reviewed	18	14
	4	3				Compiled	10	5
1	6	18	12	4	7	Tax Returns	6	9
	14 (4/1-9/30/10)		69 (10/1/10-3/31/11)			Other	35	47
							4/1/06-3/31/07 ALL	4/1/07-3/31/08 ALL
0-500M	500M-2MM	2-10MM	10-50MM	50-100MM	100-250MM			
1	15	30	21	5	11	NUMBER OF STATEMENTS	86	91
%	%	%	%	%	%	**ASSETS**	%	%
	7.8	12.7	9.5		22.7	Cash & Equivalents	11.6	14.8
	41.2	26.8	34.7		21.6	Trade Receivables (net)	32.2	28.6
	31.2	27.1	19.8		18.6	Inventory	25.7	22.7
	.7	7.0	6.5		2.2	All Other Current	3.0	4.7
	81.0	73.7	70.6		65.2	Total Current	72.5	70.8
	11.3	14.2	13.4		17.4	Fixed Assets (net)	16.1	16.8
	.5	7.4	9.0		8.8	Intangibles (net)	6.5	6.2
	7.2	4.6	7.0		8.6	All Other Non-Current	4.8	6.2
	100.0	100.0	100.0		100.0	Total	100.0	100.0
						LIABILITIES		
	17.9	14.8	9.8		1.8	Notes Payable-Short Term	8.9	10.0
	.6	2.7	2.0		3.6	Cur. Mat.-L.T.D.	3.1	2.0
	21.1	20.8	12.1		13.6	Trade Payables	15.9	17.7
	.0	.0	.4		.0	Income Taxes Payable	.2	.6
	5.5	9.6	15.1		14.2	All Other Current	12.2	13.6
	45.1	47.9	39.3		33.1	Total Current	40.3	43.9
	6.7	7.5	9.5		14.8	Long-Term Debt	11.7	12.6
	.0	.3	.2		1.1	Deferred Taxes	.4	.5
	15.4	6.1	5.7		7.1	All Other Non-Current	5.3	10.0
	32.8	38.2	45.2		43.9	Net Worth	42.3	33.0
	100.0	100.0	100.0		100.0	Total Liabilties & Net Worth	100.0	100.0
						INCOME DATA		
	100.0	100.0	100.0		100.0	Net Sales	100.0	100.0
	42.9	42.1	43.2		40.4	Gross Profit	39.7	38.5
	34.8	36.2	33.2		36.9	Operating Expenses	33.4	34.4
	8.1	5.9	10.0		3.5	Operating Profit	6.3	4.1
	1.1	1.4	1.0		1.8	All Other Expenses (net)	1.5	.9
	7.0	4.5	8.9		1.7	Profit Before Taxes	4.8	3.2
						RATIOS		
	3.5	3.6	2.4		3.9		3.1	3.8
	1.9	1.7	2.0		2.3	Current	1.8	2.2
	1.0	1.1	1.5		1.2		1.3	1.3
	2.2	1.9	1.6		3.4		1.7	2.6
	1.2	.9	1.2		1.8	Quick	1.1	1.2
	.7	.5	.6		.6		.7	.8
40 9.2	34 10.7	47 7.8		47 7.8		Sales/Receivables	36 10.2	30 12.0
51 7.1	41 8.8	60 6.1		67 5.5			51 7.1	52 7.0
69 5.3	56 6.5	78 4.7		73 5.0			64 5.3	70 5.2
28 13.1	43 8.4	14 26.3		49 7.5		Cost of Sales/Inventory	32 11.2	26 14.1
65 5.6	83 4.4	64 5.7		82 4.5			61 5.9	59 6.2
130 2.8	133 2.7	88 4.1		126 2.9			119 3.1	101 3.6
18 20.8	22 16.9	21 17.8		41 9.0		Cost of Sales/Payables	23 15.6	20 18.2
43 8.6	50 7.2	32 11.3		45 8.1			33 11.0	31 11.8
75 4.9	88 4.2	52 7.0		93 3.9			53 6.9	57 6.4
	3.6	3.5	4.1		1.8	Sales/Working Capital	4.4	3.5
	7.1	7.4	5.2		3.3		7.7	6.2
	94.2	NM	13.9		15.1		15.1	16.3
	31.0	36.8	18.8				19.0	15.4
(13) 4.0	(25) 2.9	(18) 9.5				EBIT/Interest	(76) 6.0	(70) 5.0
	1.1	-.2	3.7				1.6	-1.1
						Net Profit + Depr., Dep., Amort./Cur. Mat. L/T/D	10.2	6.5
							(28) 3.5	(19) 2.8
							.9	1.8
	.0	.1	.2		.1		.1	.1
	.2	.3	.3		.5	Fixed/Worth	.4	.3
	1.8	3.0	.8		1.6		1.0	1.8
	.7	.5	.6		.3		.6	.5
	2.3	1.5	1.5		1.3	Debt/Worth	1.6	1.5
	21.8	24.8	3.4		11.3		3.3	7.3
	116.0	50.0	65.7			% Profit Before Taxes/Tangible Net Worth	56.7	63.7
(12) 38.7	(25) 13.2	(19) 51.0					(77) 29.0	(77) 25.1
	.5	5.1	24.5				3.1	-1.6
	32.4	18.1	31.3		7.3	% Profit Before Taxes/Total Assets	22.6	22.8
	12.3	5.9	15.1		3.1		11.8	9.1
	.2	-2.7	4.9		-1.0		1.7	-1.9
	214.6	60.7	34.8		29.3	Sales/Net Fixed Assets	45.8	54.8
	53.0	24.1	20.6		10.0		18.8	21.6
	22.3	9.4	11.6		6.0		8.8	9.2
	3.2	2.9	2.6		2.1	Sales/Total Assets	3.1	3.1
	2.7	2.2	1.8		1.0		2.4	2.2
	2.4	1.4	1.4		.6		1.5	1.4
	.3	.9	.7			% Depr., Dep., Amort./Sales	.7	.7
(10) .8	(22) 1.4	(18) 1.4					(70) 1.5	(67) 1.5
	2.4	3.5	1.7				2.7	3.2
		1.7				% Officers', Directors' Owners' Comp/Sales	2.5	3.4
	(12) 4.8						(27) 4.6	(21) 5.7
		9.0					8.4	9.7
1645M	50716M	304405M	986490M	460710M	2640955M	Net Sales ($)	3145340M	2854767M
245M	18620M	132336M	500008M	379888M	1846091M	Total Assets ($)	2214175M	2053880M

M = $ thousand   MM = $ million
See Pages 9 through 22 for Explanation of Ratios and Data

Comparative Historical Data / Current Data Sorted by Sales

			Type of Statement						
21	21	14	Unqualified				1	1	12
15	16	11	Reviewed		2	2	1	4	2
8	5	3	Compiled	1		2			
5	6	7	Tax Returns			1	4	2	
40	38	48	Other		6	4	10	7	21
4/1/08-3/31/09 ALL	4/1/09-3/31/10 ALL	4/1/10-3/31/11 ALL			14 (4/1-9/30/10)		69 (10/1/10-3/31/11)		
				0-1MM	1-3MM	3-5MM	5-10MM	10-25MM	25MM & OVER
89	86	83	NUMBER OF STATEMENTS	1	9	12	14	12	35
%	%	%	ASSETS	%	%	%	%	%	%
11.7	13.5	12.3	Cash & Equivalents			6.8	19.3	6.1	13.8
29.4	30.4	30.5	Trade Receivables (net)			42.5	27.1	29.3	29.6
24.7	24.0	23.9	Inventory			34.8	21.5	29.5	20.1
5.0	4.5	4.9	All Other Current			2.5	5.1	12.7	4.3
70.9	72.4	71.6	Total Current			86.6	73.1	77.6	67.7
15.3	14.6	14.1	Fixed Assets (net)			10.1	14.7	12.3	14.2
6.5	7.6	8.3	Intangibles (net)			.0	8.2	3.9	12.2
7.3	5.4	6.0	All Other Non-Current			3.3	4.0	6.1	5.9
100.0	100.0	100.0	Total			100.0	100.0	100.0	100.0
			LIABILITIES						
8.2	12.0	12.4	Notes Payable-Short Term			15.3	14.0	13.4	7.3
3.0	2.6	2.2	Cur. Mat.-L.T.D.			1.5	1.8	2.5	2.8
14.5	15.9	17.0	Trade Payables			30.7	16.6	16.0	13.4
.4	.2	.1	Income Taxes Payable			.0	.0	.0	.2
10.7	11.0	10.9	All Other Current			3.5	6.9	9.7	16.9
36.8	41.8	42.6	Total Current			51.0	39.5	41.5	40.6
9.0	9.5	9.0	Long-Term Debt			7.3	5.4	7.2	10.3
.5	.4	.4	Deferred Taxes			.0	.4	.2	.7
8.7	7.5	8.2	All Other Non-Current			11.8	9.4	4.1	6.3
45.1	40.8	39.8	Net Worth			29.9	45.3	46.9	42.1
100.0	100.0	100.0	Total Liabilities & Net Worth			100.0	100.0	100.0	100.0
			INCOME DATA						
100.0	100.0	100.0	Net Sales			100.0	100.0	100.0	100.0
38.3	39.5	42.0	Gross Profit			39.9	44.0	44.3	39.1
33.4	34.8	34.9	Operating Expenses			33.5	37.3	36.4	31.9
4.9	4.7	7.1	Operating Profit			6.5	6.7	7.9	7.1
2.1	1.8	1.5	All Other Expenses (net)			.6	.6	1.2	2.1
2.8	2.9	5.6	Profit Before Taxes			5.8	6.1	6.8	5.1
			RATIOS						
3.8	3.1	2.9	Current			3.3	5.6	3.3	2.8
1.8	1.9	2.0				2.0	2.0	1.8	2.0
1.3	1.2	1.2				1.1	1.0	1.4	1.3
2.1	1.9	1.8	Quick			2.6	3.2	1.3	1.8
1.0	1.1	1.1				1.3	1.3	.9	1.3
.6	.6	.6				.6	.6	.6	.6

							Sales/Receivables						
35	10.4	46	8.0	39	9.4			41	9.0	27	13.6	37	10.0	47	7.7

Count/Val							Ratio	0-1MM	1-3MM	3-5MM	5-10MM	10-25MM	25MM & OVER
35 10.4	46 8.0	39 9.4					Sales/Receivables			41 9.0	27 13.6	37 10.0	47 7.7
51 7.1	56 6.6	52 7.0								53 6.9	41 8.8	46 7.9	59 6.2
66 5.5	71 5.1	67 5.4								65 5.6	56 6.5	78 4.7	71 5.2
45 8.0	50 7.3	37 9.8					Cost of Sales/Inventory			30 12.3	12 29.6	25 14.5	43 8.6
79 4.6	78 4.7	78 4.7								71 5.1	60 6.1	76 4.8	78 4.7
109 3.4	109 3.3	122 3.0								146 2.5	125 2.9	106 3.4	102 3.6
19 18.9	24 15.0	23 16.0					Cost of Sales/Payables			16 22.4	15 24.6	27 13.7	27 13.7
35 10.5	39 9.4	43 8.5								63 5.8	59 6.2	39 9.4	41 8.9
49 7.5	62 5.9	73 5.0								89 4.1	78 4.7	67 5.5	54 6.8

3.3	3.0	3.5	Sales/Working Capital			4.0	2.9	4.0	3.3
6.9	6.2	5.9				5.6	5.7	6.3	5.3
16.2	17.0	16.2				74.7	-131.2	12.1	15.1

						EBIT/Interest						
	36.8		12.7		35.8				37.8		199.6		43.5		37.1
(75)	6.6	(71)	3.6	(71)	5.4		(11)	4.0	(10)	3.5	(10)	3.4	(31)	8.9
	2.0		1.0		1.1				1.1		.9		1.9		1.1

						Net Profit + Depr., Dep., Amort./Cur. Mat. L/T/D						
	8.9		9.0		11.6										11.4
(21)	3.7	(22)	4.3	(20)	2.8									(13)	2.1
	.7		1.8		.2										-.5

.1	.1	.1	Fixed/Worth			.0	.1	.1	.2
.3	.4	.3				.2	.3	.3	.4
1.0	1.2	2.0				2.2	3.0	.5	1.6
.4	.5	.6	Debt/Worth			.8	.3	.4	.5
1.3	1.5	1.5				2.1	1.5	1.4	1.5
3.3	8.1	18.5				21.2	24.8	3.3	11.3

						% Profit Before Taxes/Tangible Net Worth						
	45.6		51.4		60.2				129.8		60.7		60.5		58.0
(75)	20.6	(71)	15.0	(67)	32.7		(10)	46.7	(13)	13.2		31.5	(27)	33.3
	3.6		2.7		6.4				25.1		-20.5		9.2		9.6

22.1	20.3	24.8	% Profit Before Taxes/Total Assets			34.0	31.8	13.7	22.5
8.4	6.3	7.3				14.2	5.7	7.0	7.3
-.3	-3.0	.3				.2	-.1	2.6	.2
46.1	53.7	51.2	Sales/Net Fixed Assets			186.1	70.3	49.0	31.9
21.3	17.5	20.6				53.3	30.5	20.3	17.7
9.0	7.2	10.0				23.7	6.4	11.8	9.8
2.8	2.7	2.7	Sales/Total Assets			3.2	2.6	3.4	2.5
2.1	1.8	1.9				2.7	1.9	2.1	1.7
1.4	1.2	1.3				2.3	1.5	1.5	1.1

						% Depr., Dep., Amort./Sales						
	.5		.7		.8						.7				.8
(70)	1.0	(67)	1.5	(60)	1.4				(10)	1.5			(28)	1.5
	2.4		3.6		3.1						4.1				3.1

						% Officers', Directors' Owners' Comp/Sales						
	2.6		2.9		2.0										
(25)	4.9	(18)	5.1	(21)	4.6										
	7.4		8.5		8.1										

4029757M	3855652M	4444921M	Net Sales ($)	979M	21904M	49673M	106768M	189630M	4075967M
2604621M	2760872M	2877188M	Total Assets ($)	581M	14690M	19848M	56733M	90195M	2695141M

M = $ thousand   MM = $ million
See Pages 9 through 22 for Explanation of Ratios and Data

Current Data Sorted by Assets — Comparative Historical Data

0-500M	500M-2MM	2-10MM	10-50MM	50-100MM	100-250MM	Type of Statement	4/1/06-3/31/07 ALL	4/1/07-3/31/08 ALL
	4	3	12	4	2	Unqualified	18	13
	1	5	6			Reviewed	12	15
		3	1			Compiled	6	9
	6	1				Tax Returns	6	7
2	9	16	17	7	6	Other	46	33
	23 (4/1-9/30/10)		82 (10/1/10-3/31/11)					
2	20	28	36	11	8	NUMBER OF STATEMENTS	88	77
%	%	%	%	%	%	**ASSETS**	%	%
	15.1	10.9	9.8	12.5		Cash & Equivalents	10.5	9.9
	27.2	33.2	27.0	28.4		Trade Receivables (net)	32.2	29.6
	35.5	31.8	34.0	29.3		Inventory	33.0	34.2
	2.5	3.8	2.9	4.2		All Other Current	4.0	3.1
	80.3	79.6	73.7	74.4		Total Current	79.8	76.8
	13.7	10.4	12.4	13.9		Fixed Assets (net)	12.9	13.6
	3.8	2.8	9.5	8.0		Intangibles (net)	2.9	4.7
	2.2	7.2	4.5	3.7		All Other Non-Current	4.4	4.9
	100.0	100.0	100.0	100.0		Total	100.0	100.0
						LIABILITIES		
	11.9	5.2	9.7	3.5		Notes Payable-Short Term	13.7	15.4
	2.6	2.5	5.3	3.4		Cur. Mat.-L.T.D.	2.6	1.5
	14.7	21.4	13.1	25.6		Trade Payables	17.0	16.3
	.0	.4	.2	3.3		Income Taxes Payable	.5	.4
	14.9	12.6	8.2	13.4		All Other Current	13.5	9.4
	44.1	42.1	36.4	49.3		Total Current	47.2	43.1
	12.8	3.0	17.2	26.5		Long-Term Debt	8.3	12.2
	.0	.2	.5	.5		Deferred Taxes	.2	.1
	9.7	13.8	4.1	9.8		All Other Non-Current	4.1	7.0
	33.5	41.0	41.8	13.9		Net Worth	40.2	37.6
	100.0	100.0	100.0	100.0		Total Liabilities & Net Worth	100.0	100.0
						INCOME DATA		
	100.0	100.0	100.0	100.0		Net Sales	100.0	100.0
	44.0	39.4	39.7	43.0		Gross Profit	37.9	38.4
	43.0	34.3	31.1	29.0		Operating Expenses	32.3	33.9
	.9	5.1	8.6	13.9		Operating Profit	5.6	4.5
	.1	.0	1.8	4.2		All Other Expenses (net)	1.1	1.4
	.8	5.1	6.8	9.7		Profit Before Taxes	4.5	3.2
						RATIOS		
	4.5	5.2	3.1	2.0		Current	3.4	3.1
	1.9	2.6	2.2	1.4			1.7	1.9
	1.1	1.1	1.5	1.2			1.3	1.3
	2.9	2.3	1.8	.9		Quick	1.6	1.5
	1.0	1.3	.9	.8			1.0	1.0
	.5	.8	.6	.6			.6	.6
	23 15.7	35 10.5	39 9.3	45 8.1		Sales/Receivables	34 10.7	32 11.4
	31 11.7	40 9.1	45 8.1	61 6.0			47 7.8	45 8.2
	49 7.4	87 4.2	55 6.6	85 4.3			66 5.5	62 5.9
	24 15.3	23 15.7	75 4.9	66 5.5		Cost of Sales/Inventory	45 8.1	53 6.9
	101 3.6	111 3.3	109 3.3	121 3.0			92 4.0	94 3.9
	125 2.9	167 2.2	140 2.6	179 2.0			151 2.4	159 2.3
	13 28.7	20 17.8	23 15.6	63 5.8		Cost of Sales/Payables	20 18.0	21 17.0
	30 12.1	41 9.0	38 9.5	89 4.1			33 11.2	38 9.7
	57 6.4	90 4.0	49 7.4	114 3.2			58 6.3	61 6.0
	3.9	2.9	3.8	3.6		Sales/Working Capital	3.8	3.9
	7.5	4.5	5.5	5.9			7.9	6.8
	40.4	25.9	9.0	19.7			15.9	14.9
	9.2	57.9	15.4	52.3		EBIT/Interest	15.5	16.9
	(15) 1.8	(20) 26.6	(33) 4.2	(10) 2.9			(75) 4.0	(70) 2.9
	-8.4	.9	1.1	.2			1.6	.8
			10.1			Net Profit + Depr., Dep., Amort./Cur. Mat. L/T/D	6.0	11.2
			(10) 3.4				(21) 2.6	(16) 5.3
			1.5				1.8	1.6
	.1	.1	.1	.2		Fixed/Worth	.1	.1
	.3	.2	.2	.6			.2	.3
	1.0	.9	.7	-.2			.6	1.4
	.6	.3	.6	1.7		Debt/Worth	.6	.6
	2.2	1.2	1.2	2.7			1.6	1.6
	4.9	8.3	2.4	-4.3			3.8	9.3
	57.1	40.6	46.8			% Profit Before Taxes/Tangible Net Worth	48.7	38.8
	(17) 28.8	(24) 26.5	(30) 17.1				(80) 26.9	(66) 18.1
	3.0	4.0	1.5				9.3	3.6
	21.0	20.6	16.4	27.8		% Profit Before Taxes/Total Assets	18.4	17.9
	7.3	9.9	8.8	12.8			8.1	5.4
	-8.4	-.2	1.3	-2.5			2.4	-.2
	82.3	79.5	94.1	50.9		Sales/Net Fixed Assets	77.8	62.9
	44.6	34.9	29.6	34.5			31.5	25.0
	23.0	11.8	11.6	9.1			13.7	14.1
	3.4	2.7	2.6	2.0		Sales/Total Assets	3.2	2.9
	2.7	2.2	2.1	1.6			2.2	2.2
	2.2	1.4	1.2	1.4			1.7	1.5
	.6	.5	.9			% Depr., Dep., Amort./Sales	.5	.8
	(13) 1.3	(17) .9	(24) 1.5				(64) 1.1	(56) 1.2
	2.3	2.1	2.3				2.1	2.0
	3.9					% Officers', Directors' Owners' Comp/Sales	2.0	2.2
	(13) 5.2						(24) 4.6	(20) 3.7
	7.6						6.1	6.3
4502M	72341M	284878M	1513298M	1335675M	1911832M	Net Sales ($)	5716675M	5550368M
651M	24969M	132521M	758139M	803492M	1202098M	Total Assets ($)	2856616M	2929230M

M = $ thousand   MM = $ million
See Pages 9 through 22 for Explanation of Ratios and Data

Comparative Historical Data | Current Data Sorted by Sales

4/1/08-3/31/09 ALL	4/1/09-3/31/10 ALL	4/1/10-3/31/11 ALL	Type of Statement	0-1MM	1-3MM	3-5MM	5-10MM	10-25MM	25MM & OVER
19	16	21	Unqualified	1		1	2		18
14	9	15	Reviewed	1	3	2	7		2
11	7	5	Compiled	1		2	2		
10	10	9	Tax Returns	3	4	1	1		
37	41	55	Other	7	6	6	11		25
					23 (4/1-9/30/10)		82 (10/1/10-3/31/11)		
91	**83**	**105**	**NUMBER OF STATEMENTS**	**12**	**12**	**13**	**12**	**23**	**45**
%	%	%	**ASSETS**	%	%	%	%	%	%
9.2	13.3	11.6	Cash & Equivalents		14.3	19.7	9.1	10.4	9.9
29.1	29.1	29.3	Trade Receivables (net)	D	19.9	30.1	25.8	30.8	31.6
33.2	31.1	32.7	Inventory	A	34.0	35.6	35.8	25.4	34.4
4.2	3.4	3.1	All Other Current	T	2.9	3.8	1.7	2.7	3.5
75.7	76.9	76.7	Total Current	A	71.1	89.2	72.3	69.4	79.4
13.3	13.0	12.3	Fixed Assets (net)	N	19.1	5.4	11.6	19.0	9.2
5.5	5.5	6.5	Intangibles (net)	O	3.8	.1	12.4	6.7	7.3
5.4	4.6	4.6	All Other Non-Current	T	6.0	5.4	3.7	4.9	4.1
100.0	100.0	100.0	Total		100.0	100.0	100.0	100.0	100.0
			LIABILITIES	A					
15.7	10.4	8.7	Notes Payable-Short Term	V	5.1	11.2	6.5	6.5	10.5
3.1	2.6	4.6	Cur. Mat.-L.T.D.	A	3.0	1.5	4.1	2.9	7.0
14.1	15.8	17.2	Trade Payables	I	10.8	15.3	22.3	16.7	18.3
.3	.2	.5	Income Taxes Payable	L	.8	.0	.2	.1	.9
10.3	14.2	11.6	All Other Current	A	23.9	6.9	11.8	8.5	11.3
43.5	43.2	42.6	Total Current	B	43.5	34.8	44.9	34.7	48.1
11.5	7.9	13.9	Long-Term Debt	L	22.4	6.1	2.9	8.9	19.4
.2	.1	.3	Deferred Taxes	E	.1	.0	.1	.3	.5
4.2	6.4	8.3	All Other Non-Current		9.5	14.7	2.1	5.2	9.4
40.5	42.3	34.9	Net Worth		24.4	44.4	50.0	51.0	22.7
100.0	100.0	100.0	Total Liabilities & Net Worth		100.0	100.0	100.0	100.0	100.0
			INCOME DATA						
100.0	100.0	100.0	Net Sales		100.0	100.0	100.0	100.0	100.0
39.9	41.1	40.0	Gross Profit		42.9	45.4	39.1	37.2	39.2
35.6	37.8	33.5	Operating Expenses		45.5	39.1	35.2	30.8	29.7
4.3	3.3	6.4	Operating Profit		-2.6	6.3	3.9	6.5	9.6
1.4	1.0	1.3	All Other Expenses (net)		-.1	.0	.2	.3	3.0
2.9	2.3	5.1	Profit Before Taxes		-2.5	6.3	3.7	6.2	6.6
			RATIOS						
3.6	3.9	3.3	Current		5.4	14.8	7.1	4.6	2.4
1.7	1.8	2.0			2.6	2.6	1.5	2.7	1.9
1.3	1.3	1.2			.9	1.5	.9	1.1	1.4
1.8	2.0	1.7	Quick		1.6	10.3	2.3	2.4	1.1
.8	1.0	.9			1.1	1.7	.8	1.1	.8
.5	.6	.7			.4	.6	.4	.8	.7
32 11.5	34 10.7	34 10.8	Sales/Receivables	23 15.9	32 11.5	24 15.1	34 10.8		42 8.6
44 8.3	45 8.1	45 8.1		28 12.9	49 7.4	36 10.2	44 8.4		52 7.0
61 6.0	69 5.3	64 5.7		46 7.9	77 4.8	47 7.8	74 4.9		74 4.9
48 7.7	53 6.9	58 6.3	Cost of Sales/Inventory	55 6.7	23 16.0	24 15.0	11 34.6		67 5.4
100 3.7	85 4.3	106 3.4		94 3.9	114 3.2	116 3.1	83 4.4		112 3.3
136 2.7	148 2.5	141 2.6		151 2.4	216 1.7	130 2.8	159 2.3		141 2.6
18 20.5	18 20.0	23 15.6	Cost of Sales/Payables	21 17.7	12 31.3	12 30.9	17 21.8		28 12.9
33 11.2	35 10.5	40 9.2		29 12.5	34 10.8	39 9.5	38 9.6		45 8.1
58 6.3	57 6.5	69 5.3		42 8.7	85 4.3	66 5.5	43 8.5		74 4.9
3.8	3.2	3.6	Sales/Working Capital		2.0	2.3	3.9	3.4	4.4
6.5	7.2	5.6			3.9	5.3	30.0	4.7	5.9
17.2	15.9	15.4			NM	8.9	-27.4	25.2	10.6
14.4	16.0	24.4	EBIT/Interest		24.4			92.7	15.2
(81) 3.6	(69) 3.7	(87) 3.7			(11) 2.7			(21) 4.0	(42) 3.4
1.1	.3	.9			-8.4			.4	.9
8.5	13.8	7.2	Net Profit + Depr., Dep., Amort./Cur. Mat. L/T/D						10.1
(24) 2.9	(19) 3.5	(24) 2.0							(15) 2.3
.6	1.0	.5							.5
.1	.1	.1	Fixed/Worth		.0	.0	.1	.1	.1
.2	.2	.2			.3	.1	.5	.3	.2
.7	.9	1.0			NM	.3	NM	.8	1.4
.5	.4	.6	Debt/Worth		.6	.4	.3	.4	1.0
1.5	1.2	1.6			2.6	1.5	.7	1.2	1.7
5.0	5.2	6.9			NM	3.6	NM	2.9	NM
45.1	29.8	46.7	% Profit Before Taxes/Tangible Net Worth			50.7		44.5	59.4
(78) 17.5	(71) 9.7	(85) 23.2			(12) 32.5		(21) 17.6	(34) 29.8	
4.7	.7	2.0				7.4		-.3	3.2
16.9	11.1	19.2	% Profit Before Taxes/Total Assets		13.8	23.9	20.8	16.2	22.3
6.1	4.6	8.7			2.0	9.8	9.6	7.5	9.5
.3	-.2	.0			-11.4	3.5	.5	-.6	.6
66.4	66.4	78.0	Sales/Net Fixed Assets		87.6	UND	49.6	47.8	84.4
31.8	27.6	35.6			18.0	73.4	37.7	28.7	37.2
11.5	10.3	12.5			5.7	35.9	26.4	5.1	16.3
2.9	2.8	2.7	Sales/Total Assets		3.1	3.2	3.1	2.6	2.5
2.1	2.2	2.1			2.0	2.3	2.4	2.1	2.0
1.6	1.3	1.5			1.0	1.8	1.5	1.2	1.6
.6	.6	.6	% Depr., Dep., Amort./Sales					1.2	.5
(66) 1.3	(57) 1.4	(69) 1.4						(17) 2.1	(31) 1.1
2.1	2.5	2.3						2.7	1.7
3.6	2.7	2.2	% Officers', Directors' Owners' Comp/Sales						
(27) 4.7	(23) 4.7	(26) 4.4							
7.2	6.1	7.6							
4593992M	4158422M	5122526M	Net Sales ($)		23886M	48853M	86354M	348908M	4614525M
2531105M	2403481M	2921870M	Total Assets ($)		17600M	25497M	46060M	246831M	2585882M

M = $ thousand   MM = $ million
See Pages 9 through 22 for Explanation of Ratios and Data

Current Data Sorted by Assets　　　　　　　　　　　Comparative Historical Data

							Type of Statement		
			3	8	2		Unqualified	26	14
	2		13	5			Reviewed	20	18
	11		6	1			Compiled	20	21
2	6		6	1			Tax Returns	11	6
2	6		17	10	1	10	Other	40	57
	16 (4/1-9/30/10)			96 (10/1/10-3/31/11)				4/1/06-3/31/07	4/1/07-3/31/08
0-500M	500M-2MM		2-10MM	10-50MM	50-100MM	100-250MM		ALL	ALL
4	25		45	25	3	10	NUMBER OF STATEMENTS	117	116
%	%		%	%	%	%	ASSETS	%	%
	13.4		9.2	7.8		7.8	Cash & Equivalents	7.5	7.9
	25.7		28.7	27.6		30.6	Trade Receivables (net)	31.2	28.9
	23.4		31.6	27.9		26.4	Inventory	26.0	26.9
	.4		.8	1.7		1.9	All Other Current	1.3	1.8
	62.9		70.3	65.0		66.7	Total Current	65.9	65.6
	28.4		19.2	19.1		19.3	Fixed Assets (net)	22.2	23.7
	2.3		6.0	11.6		9.7	Intangibles (net)	5.3	5.9
	6.4		4.6	4.3		4.3	All Other Non-Current	6.6	4.9
	100.0		100.0	100.0		100.0	Total	100.0	100.0
							LIABILITIES		
	6.6		9.7	11.4		9.0	Notes Payable-Short Term	11.1	10.4
	4.5		5.0	3.2		.8	Cur. Mat.-L.T.D.	4.9	4.7
	14.5		21.5	16.4		22.7	Trade Payables	20.8	18.0
	.3		.2	.3		.5	Income Taxes Payable	.2	.1
	5.8		5.8	6.4		9.1	All Other Current	9.2	9.2
	31.6		42.2	37.7		42.1	Total Current	46.2	42.5
	12.1		8.6	10.0		15.5	Long-Term Debt	15.3	15.4
	.0		.6	.7		.4	Deferred Taxes	.2	.3
	11.8		4.7	6.6		4.7	All Other Non-Current	6.8	4.5
	44.5		44.0	45.0		37.2	Net Worth	31.5	37.4
	100.0		100.0	100.0		100.0	Total Liabilties & Net Worth	100.0	100.0
							INCOME DATA		
	100.0		100.0	100.0		100.0	Net Sales	100.0	100.0
	39.1		28.4	24.1		16.3	Gross Profit	27.0	28.5
	34.0		19.9	16.2		13.1	Operating Expenses	21.5	22.1
	5.1		8.6	7.9		3.2	Operating Profit	5.5	6.4
	.4		.7	.9		-.8	All Other Expenses (net)	1.4	1.2
	4.7		7.9	7.0		4.0	Profit Before Taxes	4.2	5.2
							RATIOS		
	3.6		2.7	2.3		2.5		2.2	2.9
	2.3		1.8	1.7		1.6	Current	1.5	1.6
	1.4		1.3	1.2		1.4		1.1	1.2
	2.3		1.3	1.3		1.2		1.5	1.7
	1.4		.8	.8		1.0	Quick	.9	.8
	.8		.6	.6		.9		.6	.6

											Sales/Receivables				
	26	14.0	37	9.8	44	8.3		53	6.9		Sales/Receivables	39	9.3	35	10.3
	39	9.3	47	7.7	52	7.1		60	6.1			47	7.7	48	7.6
	50	7.2	57	6.4	67	5.5		90	4.0			57	6.4	58	6.3
	11	32.4	37	9.8	42	8.7		47	7.8		Cost of Sales/Inventory	25	14.6	35	10.5
	31	11.8	79	4.6	72	5.1		61	6.0			50	7.2	53	6.9
	91	4.0	109	3.3	94	3.9		102	3.6			79	4.6	87	4.2
	15	25.0	23	15.7	26	14.3		45	8.2		Cost of Sales/Payables	24	15.3	18	20.1
	37	9.9	39	9.3	39	9.3		54	6.8			38	9.7	35	10.6
	52	7.1	66	5.6	56	6.5		65	5.6			54	6.7	56	6.5

	4.0	5.3	4.3		2.6	Sales/Working Capital	5.9	5.4
	8.6	7.7	6.9		7.3		12.6	8.5
	15.9	11.0	18.4		9.3		35.8	34.4

		30.2		26.8	27.3			EBIT/Interest		11.9	11.9
(21)	4.8	(43)	10.0	9.1				(107)	3.4	(107)	4.3
		1.4		4.7	2.0				1.1		.8
				8.0				Net Profit + Depr., Dep., Amort./Cur. Mat. L/T/D		8.0	11.9
		(11)		2.0				(32)	4.0	(28)	2.5
				1.6					1.6		.8

	.2	.2	.3		.2	Fixed/Worth	.3	.3
	.6	.5	.6		.9		.6	.5
	3.9	1.0	1.4		NM		1.6	1.5
	.4	.6	.7		1.3	Debt/Worth	.9	.8
	1.1	1.2	1.7		2.0		2.2	1.9
	5.9	2.9	5.9		NM		6.4	4.2

		64.4		56.2	53.3			% Profit Before Taxes/Tangible Net Worth		47.9	55.9
(21)	21.8	(40)	23.4	(22)	37.1			(100)	21.6	(102)	28.4
		.9		13.9	8.7				1.4		2.7

	25.3	23.7	23.8		11.4	% Profit Before Taxes/Total Assets	16.2	20.9
	8.4	10.1	9.7		8.1		8.1	8.2
	-1.2	4.9	3.1		2.4		.2	.5
	54.3	31.6	27.0		22.5	Sales/Net Fixed Assets	25.1	23.2
	7.9	16.8	16.6		8.3		13.3	12.5
	4.8	7.6	6.0		4.6		6.7	7.3
	3.3	2.7	2.3		2.0	Sales/Total Assets	2.9	2.8
	2.3	2.1	1.9		1.6		2.3	2.2
	1.6	1.8	1.4		1.3		1.8	1.8

		1.3		1.1	1.3			% Depr., Dep., Amort./Sales		1.3	1.2
(19)	2.2	(36)	1.7	1.6				(106)	2.3	(105)	2.1
		4.2		3.2	2.7				4.1		3.8
		2.6		2.1				% Officers', Directors' Owners' Comp/Sales		3.1	3.1
(17)	4.6	(18)	3.6					(32)	4.6	(38)	5.5
		6.1		5.4					8.5		8.3

9176M	85970M		550935M	1003503M	367924M	2264862M	Net Sales ($)	3893947M	3483286M
735M	31920M		244475M	559668M	237131M	1525536M	Total Assets ($)	1866964M	1640985M

M = $ thousand　　MM = $ million
See Pages 9 through 22 for Explanation of Ratios and Data

Comparative Historical Data | | | | Current Data Sorted by Sales

12	14	13	Type of Statement					5	8
22	22	20	Unqualified				5	12	3
18	11	18	Reviewed		5		5	1	1
19	6	15	Compiled	1	5	5	5	1	1
47	49	46	Tax Returns		4	1	5	4	1
4/1/08-3/31/09 ALL	4/1/09-3/31/10 ALL	4/1/10-3/31/11 ALL	Other	2	4	4	6	9	21
				0-1MM	16 (4/1-9/30/10) 1-3MM	3-5MM	96 (10/1/10-3/31/11) 5-10MM	10-25MM	25MM & OVER
118	102	112	NUMBER OF STATEMENTS	3	13	10	21	31	34
%	%	%	ASSETS	%	%	%	%	%	%
10.7	8.0	10.7	Cash & Equivalents		15.9	9.1	17.1	7.8	7.2
28.3	28.9	27.3	Trade Receivables (net)		21.6	27.3	25.6	29.7	29.4
23.8	26.7	27.7	Inventory		25.7	16.3	23.3	34.6	28.2
2.4	1.6	1.0	All Other Current		.5	.4	.6	.9	1.9
65.1	65.1	66.8	Total Current		63.7	53.2	66.5	72.9	66.7
25.4	23.8	21.4	Fixed Assets (net)		29.7	34.4	18.0	20.5	16.5
4.8	5.9	7.0	Intangibles (net)		.4	8.2	6.7	3.2	13.5
4.8	5.2	4.9	All Other Non-Current		6.2	4.2	8.8	3.4	3.3
100.0	100.0	100.0	Total		100.0	100.0	100.0	100.0	100.0
			LIABILITIES						
10.2	11.8	9.9	Notes Payable-Short Term		11.4	6.2	5.6	10.1	12.2
4.1	4.3	3.8	Cur. Mat.-L.T.D.		4.8	4.3	7.3	2.9	2.3
17.1	18.2	18.3	Trade Payables		13.1	12.5	14.4	22.7	20.8
.1	.2	.3	Income Taxes Payable		.6	.0	.2	.2	.4
7.9	8.3	6.3	All Other Current		5.7	4.4	7.2	5.8	7.4
39.5	42.9	38.6	Total Current		35.6	27.4	34.8	41.6	43.1
14.1	12.4	12.7	Long-Term Debt		12.1	18.0	12.9	8.0	10.8
.4	.5	.5	Deferred Taxes		.6	.1	.0	.6	.8
10.6	7.9	8.3	All Other Non-Current		24.9	6.1	4.0	6.8	7.0
35.3	36.3	39.9	Net Worth		26.8	48.4	48.4	42.9	38.4
100.0	100.0	100.0	Total Liabilities & Net Worth		100.0	100.0	100.0	100.0	100.0
			INCOME DATA						
100.0	100.0	100.0	Net Sales		100.0	100.0	100.0	100.0	100.0
27.3	26.8	29.0	Gross Profit		42.1	41.5	34.7	23.5	20.8
22.8	24.4	22.4	Operating Expenses		36.2	36.2	24.7	17.7	14.3
4.5	2.4	6.7	Operating Profit		5.9	5.3	10.1	5.8	6.5
.8	1.5	.4	All Other Expenses (net)		.2	.8	.2	.5	.8
3.7	.9	6.2	Profit Before Taxes		5.7	4.5	9.9	5.3	5.8
			RATIOS						
2.9	2.4	2.8	Current		5.8	2.7	4.9	2.7	2.2
1.9	1.6	1.8			3.1	1.9	2.3	1.9	1.5
1.2	1.2	1.4			.8	1.5	1.4	1.4	1.2
1.9	1.4	1.8	Quick		3.2	1.8	3.8	1.4	1.2
1.0	.9	.9			1.9	1.2	1.1	.8	.9
.6	.6	.6			.4	.9	.7	.6	.6
34 10.9	39 9.4	38 9.7	Sales/Receivables	25 14.3	36 10.1	23 16.0	40 9.1	44 8.3	
41 8.9	48 7.6	48 7.6		38 9.6	43 8.5	44 8.2	49 7.4	54 6.7	
51 7.1	62 5.9	58 6.3		48 7.5	53 6.9	58 6.3	56 6.5	67 5.4	
20 18.5	28 12.9	31 11.6	Cost of Sales/Inventory	19 18.9	8 44.7	5 67.7	38 9.6	47 7.8	
45 8.1	59 6.2	64 5.7		46 7.8	27 13.6	40 9.0	73 5.0	71 5.2	
75 4.8	93 3.9	100 3.6		200 1.8	89 4.1	107 3.4	106 3.4	96 3.8	
18 20.3	21 17.6	22 16.3	Cost of Sales/Payables	15 25.0	15 24.1	9 38.7	24 15.1	37 9.8	
31 11.8	33 11.2	42 8.6		25 14.6	39 9.4	25 14.7	37 9.9	48 7.5	
44 8.3	54 6.7	60 6.0		66 5.6	50 7.3	47 7.8	66 5.6	63 5.8	
5.2	5.3	4.6	Sales/Working Capital		2.9	5.7	5.1	4.8	4.6
9.1	8.9	7.8			5.3	10.3	9.3	7.7	7.6
25.7	20.1	14.7			-38.9	15.4	36.4	10.6	18.0
14.2	6.8	27.1	EBIT/Interest		33.8	37.0	21.1	26.9	27.7
(104) 4.3	(95) 1.9	(103) 8.1			(10) 13.8	9.7	(19) 10.0	(30) 6.8	(32) 6.6
1.0	-.4	2.8			.8	.9	3.7	2.2	3.1
7.2	4.8	9.5	Net Profit + Depr., Dep., Amort./Cur. Mat. L/T/D						10.2
(28) 3.0	(31) 2.3	(26) 2.2							(11) 4.6
1.6	1.3	1.5							1.3
.2	.2	.2	Fixed/Worth		.1	.2	.2	.3	.3
.8	.6	.6			1.4	.7	.4	.5	.6
1.8	1.9	1.8			-1.2	3.2	2.1	.8	3.2
.7	.8	.6	Debt/Worth		.4	.6	.4	.6	1.0
1.7	1.8	1.4			1.4	1.0	1.2	1.1	2.3
4.5	4.8	5.1			-5.7	5.0	7.3	2.7	17.9
43.8	22.4	49.3	% Profit Before Taxes/Tangible Net Worth				89.4	40.7	45.8
(103) 18.4	(88) 7.6	(93) 23.6					(18) 35.0	(28) 19.8	(27) 31.2
5.8	-3.3	8.0					13.3	8.2	14.9
18.0	8.7	23.5	% Profit Before Taxes/Total Assets		26.6	17.4	39.9	17.7	16.0
7.3	2.8	9.3			4.6	11.2	23.4	7.8	9.0
.1	-2.1	3.5			-9.5	-.5	7.6	2.5	4.6
26.4	24.0	31.6	Sales/Net Fixed Assets		61.9	44.7	77.4	24.1	31.7
13.3	13.1	14.8			14.3	7.2	19.5	15.5	16.8
5.5	4.2	5.7			3.4	5.2	8.1	6.1	5.5
3.3	2.5	2.7	Sales/Total Assets		3.5	2.8	3.8	2.7	2.3
2.5	2.0	2.0			2.1	2.4	2.2	2.1	1.8
1.9	1.5	1.6			1.3	1.9	1.7	1.8	1.4
1.3	1.4	1.1	% Depr., Dep., Amort./Sales		.5		1.4	1.1	1.0
(100) 2.2	(89) 2.3	(92) 1.9			(10) 1.7	(14) 3.3	(27) 1.7	(30) 1.6	
3.7	3.8	3.2			2.2		4.4	3.2	2.8
2.0	2.9	2.2	% Officers', Directors', Owners' Comp/Sales				2.2		
(43) 4.0	(30) 4.8	(40) 3.8					(14) 4.0		
6.4	12.6	6.0					5.0		
3519141M	3507220M	4282370M	Net Sales ($)	1957M	25658M	38367M	153650M	490159M	3572579M
1662355M	2235898M	2599465M	Total Assets ($)	1646M	19809M	17378M	67876M	249604M	2243152M

M = $ thousand   MM = $ million
See Pages 9 through 22 for Explanation of Ratios and Data

Current Data Sorted by Assets   **Comparative Historical Data**

0-500M	500M-2MM	2-10MM	10-50MM	50-100MM	100-250MM	Type of Statement	4/1/06-3/31/07 ALL	4/1/07-3/31/08 ALL
	1	3	12	5	5	Unqualified	25	24
	1	6	2			Reviewed	6	7
		1	1			Compiled	2	6
4	7	7				Tax Returns	2	5
2	7	11	13	3	5	Other	32	36
	18 (4/1-9/30/10)		78 (10/1/10-3/31/11)					
6	16	28	28	8	10	**NUMBER OF STATEMENTS**	67	78
%	%	%	%	%	%	**ASSETS**	%	%
	24.0	8.8	18.6		22.2	Cash & Equivalents	18.2	16.1
	32.5	23.7	24.9		18.0	Trade Receivables (net)	23.0	24.6
	13.5	30.4	23.4		21.5	Inventory	23.7	25.5
	2.5	2.1	3.7		7.2	All Other Current	2.5	4.1
	72.6	65.0	70.6		68.8	Total Current	67.3	70.2
	17.9	27.4	16.8		19.6	Fixed Assets (net)	23.1	21.2
	1.9	4.6	9.0		6.3	Intangibles (net)	3.6	4.0
	7.6	3.0	3.7		5.2	All Other Non-Current	5.9	4.6
	100.0	100.0	100.0		100.0	Total	100.0	100.0
						LIABILITIES		
	9.4	6.0	4.9		.9	Notes Payable-Short Term	7.9	7.1
	3.0	2.8	5.8		2.2	Cur. Mat.-L.T.D.	2.1	3.0
	14.9	14.1	11.3		11.5	Trade Payables	11.1	13.6
	.0	.1	.3		.4	Income Taxes Payable	.3	.2
	9.0	10.5	21.3		16.6	All Other Current	11.5	12.2
	36.4	33.6	43.7		31.6	Total Current	32.9	36.2
	7.3	11.1	10.6		7.9	Long-Term Debt	10.1	9.9
	.3	.1	.6		.3	Deferred Taxes	.4	.4
	7.6	6.9	8.4		1.7	All Other Non-Current	10.3	8.8
	48.4	48.3	36.8		58.6	Net Worth	46.3	44.7
	100.0	100.0	100.0		100.0	Total Liabilities & Net Worth	100.0	100.0
						INCOME DATA		
	100.0	100.0	100.0		100.0	Net Sales	100.0	100.0
	52.9	38.9	35.1		32.1	Gross Profit	33.8	35.3
	41.3	30.9	30.3		22.7	Operating Expenses	28.9	29.9
	11.6	8.0	4.7		9.4	Operating Profit	4.8	5.4
	.3	-.3	.9		.1	All Other Expenses (net)	1.1	.8
	11.3	8.2	3.9		9.3	Profit Before Taxes	3.7	4.6
						RATIOS		
	8.2	3.3	3.3		4.7		4.1	3.5
	2.4	2.0	2.2		2.9	Current	2.3	2.3
	1.1	1.4	1.3		1.5		1.4	1.6
	5.3	1.8	1.8		3.0		2.8	2.2
	1.8	1.1	.9		1.4	Quick	1.2	1.3
	.8	.7	.7		.9		.7	.9
34	10.9	33 · 10.9	41 · 8.9		19 · 19.2		36 · 10.1	35 · 10.3
45	8.1	44 · 8.4	56 · 6.5		53 · 6.9	Sales/Receivables	49 · 7.5	49 · 7.5
60	6.1	58 · 6.3	86 · 4.2		64 · 5.7		68 · 5.4	63 · 5.8
0	UND	51 · 7.2	67 · 5.5		56 · 6.5		34 · 10.9	46 · 8.0
7	56.0	91 · 4.0	89 · 4.1		65 · 5.6	Cost of Sales/Inventory	76 · 4.8	82 · 4.5
92	4.0	144 · 2.5	135 · 2.7		104 · 3.5		137 · 2.7	122 · 3.0
18	20.3	23 · 15.8	18 · 20.0		18 · 20.4		20 · 18.3	24 · 15.4
39	9.4	37 · 9.9	31 · 11.7		34 · 10.8	Cost of Sales/Payables	32 · 11.2	38 · 9.7
74	4.9	60 · 6.1	69 · 5.3		58 · 6.2		47 · 7.8	51 · 7.1
	3.9	3.4	2.9		1.8		2.6	2.8
	4.9	5.2	3.7		3.7	Sales/Working Capital	3.9	4.1
	62.3	15.3	10.7		8.1		9.9	9.0
	75.0	39.1	67.6				17.7	27.7
	(11) 5.4	(25) 14.5	(24) 7.0			EBIT/Interest	(53) 5.5	(63) 4.5
	1.5	3.2	1.3				.9	1.2
			81.1			Net Profit + Depr., Dep.,	12.1	12.5
		(11) 3.0				Amort./Cur. Mat. L/T/D	(14) 7.0	(25) 7.5
		1.8					1.7	2.3
	.0	.2	.1		.2		.2	.2
	.2	.6	.5		.4	Fixed/Worth	.4	.4
	.8	1.3	1.5		.7		.9	1.0
	.4	.5	.7		.1		.3	.5
	.9	1.2	1.4		.7	Debt/Worth	.8	1.1
	2.1	2.2	4.2		4.0		1.9	3.7
	62.7	67.2	41.9		46.6	% Profit Before Taxes/Tangible	32.7	43.9
	(14) 43.5	(26) 31.0	(23) 22.6		22.6	Net Worth	(62) 14.8	(70) 14.4
	8.2	7.5	9.3		11.8		-5.8	6.6
	48.1	28.3	15.7		18.6	% Profit Before Taxes/Total	15.9	14.7
	21.1	13.4	6.7		11.1	Assets	5.2	7.6
	3.4	2.6	-3.1		6.1		-3.6	.7
	86.4	22.4	23.8		17.0		18.3	24.4
	25.8	10.0	11.6		9.8	Sales/Net Fixed Assets	8.3	8.7
	8.6	3.3	5.9		3.1		3.0	3.8
	3.0	2.4	1.7		1.8		2.1	2.3
	2.6	1.6	1.3		1.4	Sales/Total Assets	1.3	1.5
	2.0	1.4	1.0		.7		.9	1.0
	.4	1.2	2.2				1.8	1.4
	(10) 1.7	(23) 2.4	(23) 3.5			% Depr., Dep., Amort./Sales	(53) 2.8	(65) 3.2
	5.7	3.9	6.5				4.7	4.8
		2.6				% Officers', Directors'	2.2	1.7
		(10) 4.3				Owners' Comp/Sales	(12) 4.4	(16) 2.7
		8.6					7.4	5.6
8738M	51089M	287018M	906158M	960310M	3100461M	Net Sales ($)	3833387M	5523053M
1287M	18643M	164103M	639247M	548293M	1622398M	Total Assets ($)	2804336M	3407538M

M = $ thousand   MM = $ million
See Pages 9 through 22 for Explanation of Ratios and Data

Comparative Historical Data / Current Data Sorted by Sales

Type of Statement

Type of Statement	4/1/08-3/31/09 ALL	4/1/09-3/31/10 ALL	4/1/10-3/31/11 ALL	0-1MM	1-3MM	3-5MM	5-10MM	10-25MM	25MM & OVER
Unqualified	22	30	26			1	1	6	18
Reviewed	6	7	9		1		3	3	2
Compiled	4	4	2				1		1
Tax Returns	6	9	18	1	9	2	2	4	
Other	40	42	41	1	6	2	8	7	17

18 (4/1-9/30/10) covers 0-1MM, 1-3MM, 3-5MM. 78 (10/1/10-3/31/11) covers 5-10MM, 10-25MM, 25MM & OVER.

NUMBER OF STATEMENTS	78	92	96	2	16	5	15	20	38

Main Data

(# = receivable/inventory/payable turn counts or ratio counts in parentheses)

08-09 #	08-09	09-10 #	09-10	10-11 #	10-11	Item	0-1MM	1-3MM #	1-3MM	3-5MM #	3-5MM	5-10MM #	5-10MM	10-25MM #	10-25MM	25MM&OVER #	25MM&OVER
	%		%		%	**ASSETS**	%		%		%		%		%		%
	19.1		19.1		17.5	Cash & Equivalents			25.7				10.9		17.0		17.2
	20.0		21.4		24.7	Trade Receivables (net)			26.4				18.0		26.4		25.1
	25.8		20.3		24.0	Inventory			15.3				25.4		29.5		23.5
	2.8		3.3		3.4	All Other Current			2.6				2.7		1.9		4.8
	67.6		64.1		69.6	Total Current			70.0				57.1		74.8		70.6
	21.6		22.1		19.8	Fixed Assets (net)			12.9				37.4		16.4		17.7
	5.2		6.4		5.4	Intangibles (net)			6.4				2.1		3.3		7.6
	5.6		7.5		5.1	All Other Non-Current			10.7				3.5		5.5		4.1
	100.0		100.0		100.0	Total			100.0				100.0		100.0		100.0
						LIABILITIES											
	5.7		6.1		5.8	Notes Payable-Short Term			10.1				6.4		4.9		4.2
	2.3		2.4		3.4	Cur. Mat.-L.T.D.			1.3				3.0		3.2		4.1
	11.5		13.5		14.2	Trade Payables			15.0				14.1		13.4		14.4
	.2		.3		.2	Income Taxes Payable			.0				.0		.3		.4
	12.9		13.9		16.9	All Other Current			5.7				14.6		15.7		16.5
	32.6		36.2		40.6	Total Current			32.1				38.1		37.5		39.7
	9.8		9.6		12.8	Long-Term Debt			2.6				16.3		6.6		11.4
	.4		.4		.3	Deferred Taxes			.1				.0		.2		.5
	5.9		6.7		6.9	All Other Non-Current			7.5				8.5		3.8		7.9
	51.2		47.2		39.4	Net Worth			57.7				37.1		51.9		40.5
	100.0		100.0		100.0	Total Liabilities & Net Worth			100.0				100.0		100.0		100.0
						INCOME DATA											
	100.0		100.0		100.0	Net Sales			100.0				100.0		100.0		100.0
	36.2		38.0		38.6	Gross Profit			53.2				38.7		36.8		32.7
	30.9		36.6		31.6	Operating Expenses			41.6				34.0		28.7		25.8
	5.3		1.5		7.0	Operating Profit			11.6				4.6		8.2		6.9
	.5		.8		.4	All Other Expenses (net)			-.3				-.7		.1		1.0
	4.8		.7		6.6	Profit Before Taxes			12.0				5.3		8.0		5.9
						RATIOS											
	4.4		3.8		3.4	Current			10.9				2.5		3.8		3.3
	2.3		2.1		2.2				2.7				1.7		1.8		2.3
	1.5		1.3		1.3				1.4				1.2		1.5		1.4
	2.9		2.2		2.1	Quick			7.7				1.6		2.1		2.1
	1.3		1.3		1.2				2.4				1.1		1.2		1.1
	.7		.8		.7				.7				.4		.7		.7
28	12.9	30	12.1	34	10.9	Sales/Receivables		23	15.8			24	15.5	35	10.5	38	9.6
39	9.3	46	7.9	48	7.7			38	9.6			38	9.6	47	7.7	58	6.2
56	6.6	65	5.6	65	5.6			58	6.3			61	6.0	60	6.0	73	5.0
52	7.0	42	8.7	46	7.9	Cost of Sales/Inventory		0	UND			50	7.3	52	7.0	59	6.2
80	4.5	74	4.9	78	4.7			11	32.8			93	3.9	86	4.3	79	4.6
142	2.6	129	2.8	112	3.3			95	3.8			161	2.3	131	2.8	109	3.3
20	18.2	22	16.8	20	18.7	Cost of Sales/Payables		17	21.0			31	11.9	20	18.6	18	20.0
32	11.4	43	8.4	36	10.0			35	10.5			45	8.2	30	12.3	36	10.0
50	7.2	73	5.0	63	5.8			82	4.5			69	5.3	44	8.2	72	5.1
	2.6		2.6		3.0	Sales/Working Capital			3.6				4.4		2.9		2.8
	4.1		5.2		4.9				5.3				5.3		5.4		3.7
	9.2		14.9		15.3				62.3				16.0		16.0		10.5
	31.6		14.0		36.9	EBIT/Interest							16.2		71.3		28.0
(64)	6.1	(76)	3.3	(73)	9.0							(13)	3.6	(18)	15.3	(29)	7.6
	.7		-3.1		2.5								1.6		5.2		2.9
	21.3		20.9		67.9	Net Profit + Depr., Dep., Amort./Cur. Mat. L/T/D												11.5
(18)	9.3	(18)	5.5	(20)	3.5											(11)	2.6
	2.4		.9		1.3													.4
	.2		.2		.1	Fixed/Worth			.0				.6		.1		.2
	.4		.5		.4				.1				.7		.3		.5
	.9		1.0		1.2				.6				2.5		.9		1.2
	.3		.4		.5	Debt/Worth			.1				.7		.3		.5
	.8		1.1		1.1				.8				1.4		1.3		1.2
	2.3		3.3		3.8				2.3				3.0		2.0		4.6
	42.7		28.6		64.0	% Profit Before Taxes/Tangible Net Worth			84.9				35.9		71.3		41.7
(71)	15.1	(81)	13.3	(84)	27.0			(14)	54.3			(13)	8.5	(19)	31.2	(33)	24.3
	.8		-5.4		8.5				30.3				2.4		9.3		8.5
	21.6		10.3		25.9	% Profit Before Taxes/Total Assets			64.0				13.6		27.0		17.6
	6.6		3.0		9.8				29.9				3.4		15.3		7.6
	-1.3		-4.9		2.0				3.4				1.7		5.7		1.8
	17.6		20.2		30.0	Sales/Net Fixed Assets			UND				11.1		45.1		24.2
	9.5		10.9		13.3				37.3				3.5		20.2		11.0
	4.6		3.8		5.2				11.8				2.1		10.0		5.4
	2.1		1.9		2.4	Sales/Total Assets			3.8				1.6		3.2		2.0
	1.5		1.4		1.6				2.6				1.5		1.7		1.3
	.9		.9		1.2				1.7				.8		1.3		1.0
	1.2		1.3		1.3	% Depr., Dep., Amort./Sales							1.4		.5		1.4
(61)	2.6	(64)	3.1	(70)	2.4							(13)	3.5	(16)	2.2	(30)	2.6
	4.2		7.8		4.8								5.2		2.7		5.1
	2.2		1.8		3.6	% Officers', Directors' Owners' Comp/Sales												
(15)	3.1	(22)	4.4	(22)	7.2												
	6.3		10.7		16.3												
	6481287M		5369432M		5313774M	Net Sales ($)	217M		35665M		21554M		111148M		305690M		4839500M
	4250286M		3782796M		2993971M	Total Assets ($)	59M		18716M		8145M		89808M		188800M		2688443M

M = $ thousand   MM = $ million
See Pages 9 through 22 for Explanation of Ratios and Data

Current Data Sorted by Assets   Comparative Historical Data

0-500M	500M-2MM	2-10MM	10-50MM	50-100MM	100-250MM	Type of Statement	4/1/06-3/31/07 ALL	4/1/07-3/31/08 ALL
			4	1	1	Unqualified	7	7
		5	1			Reviewed	7	6
	1	3	1			Compiled	6	5
		1				Tax Returns	5	8
1	5	4	7	3	2	Other	16	15
		6 (4/1-9/30/10)	34 (10/1/10-3/31/11)				4/1/06-3/31/07	4/1/07-3/31/08
1	6	13	13	4	3	NUMBER OF STATEMENTS	41	41
%	%	%	%	%	%	**ASSETS**	%	%
		11.0	23.2			Cash & Equivalents	13.3	15.5
		25.1	19.2			Trade Receivables (net)	25.1	28.6
		26.7	20.9			Inventory	26.0	23.3
		4.7	5.3			All Other Current	3.9	3.4
		67.6	68.6			Total Current	68.3	70.8
		24.3	8.7			Fixed Assets (net)	19.4	18.8
		6.6	21.5			Intangibles (net)	5.6	5.6
		1.5	1.1			All Other Non-Current	6.6	4.9
		100.0	100.0			Total	100.0	100.0
						LIABILITIES		
		5.8	2.4			Notes Payable-Short Term	7.7	10.4
		10.0	.9			Cur. Mat.-L.T.D.	4.0	2.3
		13.7	7.8			Trade Payables	14.0	14.7
		.1	.3			Income Taxes Payable	.1	.2
		7.0	5.7			All Other Current	9.5	6.7
		36.6	17.0			Total Current	35.3	34.3
		12.4	4.8			Long-Term Debt	15.6	10.5
		1.7	.8			Deferred Taxes	.8	.8
		5.7	5.6			All Other Non-Current	12.0	5.9
		43.6	71.7			Net Worth	36.3	48.4
		100.0	100.0			Total Liabilties & Net Worth	100.0	100.0
						INCOME DATA		
		100.0	100.0			Net Sales	100.0	100.0
		32.5	38.2			Gross Profit	37.5	32.0
		24.9	28.0			Operating Expenses	29.3	24.8
		7.6	10.2			Operating Profit	8.3	7.2
		1.3	.5			All Other Expenses (net)	.6	.1
		6.3	9.7			Profit Before Taxes	7.7	7.1
						RATIOS		
		5.3	7.7			Current	4.1	4.2
		2.2	3.5				2.6	2.0
		1.1	2.6				1.2	1.4
		3.0	5.4			Quick	2.6	3.3
		.9	2.2				1.1	1.1
		.4	1.2				.6	.8
		35 10.5	40 9.2			Sales/Receivables	33 11.0	35 10.5
		45 8.1	44 8.4				41 8.9	44 8.3
		61 6.0	62 5.9				51 7.1	58 6.3
		51 7.1	71 5.1			Cost of Sales/Inventory	52 7.0	30 12.0
		74 5.0	103 3.6				73 5.0	59 6.2
		91 4.0	123 3.0				96 3.8	93 3.9
		15 23.7	19 19.6			Cost of Sales/Payables	22 16.8	20 18.7
		28 13.2	31 11.9				29 12.6	29 12.6
		50 7.4	53 6.9				46 7.9	47 7.8
		3.1	1.9			Sales/Working Capital	3.3	3.9
		7.7	3.1				6.1	6.3
		37.9	4.5				22.0	15.6
		133.0	29.2			EBIT/Interest	73.5	36.7
		(12) 14.8	(11) 16.0				(37) 7.0	(34) 6.2
		3.4	1.2				1.9	1.4
						Net Profit + Depr., Dep., Amort./Cur. Mat. L/T/D		
		.2	.0			Fixed/Worth	.2	.2
		.7	.2				.4	.3
		NM	.2				1.8	1.3
		.3	.2			Debt/Worth	.4	.3
		1.5	.5				1.2	.9
		NM	1.4				5.1	2.7
		63.1	40.5			% Profit Before Taxes/Tangible Net Worth	65.3	57.5
		(10) 26.7	(11) 28.6				(33) 43.2	(34) 24.4
		14.1	17.8				21.3	6.5
		22.7	21.4			% Profit Before Taxes/Total Assets	30.5	29.8
		13.1	14.1				16.2	10.8
		4.8	.6				2.2	2.8
		22.9	59.5			Sales/Net Fixed Assets	22.9	37.1
		9.6	22.6				13.2	18.1
		5.4	8.4				7.4	6.8
		2.7	1.7			Sales/Total Assets	2.9	3.0
		1.9	1.5				2.1	2.3
		1.7	1.1				1.6	1.5
		.5	1.1			% Depr., Dep., Amort./Sales	1.2	.5
		(12) 1.1	(10) 1.8				(31) 1.8	(32) 1.4
		3.1	4.6				3.2	3.0
						% Officers', Directors' Owners' Comp/Sales	3.1	2.3
							(14) 5.0	(18) 3.8
							9.0	6.0
673M	20313M	164288M	459885M	360110M	608958M	Net Sales ($)	1183403M	1306965M
342M	7470M	80024M	360536M	265054M	489282M	Total Assets ($)	698111M	765320M

M = $ thousand   MM = $ million
See Pages 9 through 22 for Explanation of Ratios and Data

Comparative Historical Data | Current Data Sorted by Sales

			Type of Statement	0-1MM	1-3MM	3-5MM	5-10MM	10-25MM	25MM & OVER
12	6	6	Unqualified					1	4
6	4	6	Reviewed				2	3	1
6	11	5	Compiled			3		2	
4	3	1	Tax Returns						1
22	23	22	Other	2	1	3	2	5	9
4/1/08-3/31/09 ALL	4/1/09-3/31/10 ALL	4/1/10-3/31/11 ALL		6 (4/1-9/30/10)			34 (10/1/10-3/31/11)		
50	47	40	NUMBER OF STATEMENTS	2	1	7	4	11	15
%	%	%	ASSETS	%	%	%	%	%	%
10.7	12.9	15.4	Cash & Equivalents					26.9	13.5
27.3	26.8	23.2	Trade Receivables (net)					21.7	20.7
26.1	29.1	25.8	Inventory					23.2	25.0
2.6	2.5	3.6	All Other Current					8.6	2.4
66.8	71.3	68.0	Total Current					80.4	61.6
20.5	18.3	17.2	Fixed Assets (net)					15.8	15.5
8.9	6.4	13.1	Intangibles (net)					2.9	20.6
3.8	4.0	1.7	All Other Non-Current					1.0	2.3
100.0	100.0	100.0	Total					100.0	100.0
			LIABILITIES						
20.3	9.9	4.6	Notes Payable-Short Term					4.4	1.8
4.3	3.1	4.9	Cur. Mat.-L.T.D.					6.7	4.3
13.7	14.3	12.3	Trade Payables					9.5	9.7
.2	.1	.4	Income Taxes Payable					.0	.4
7.4	7.5	6.6	All Other Current					7.5	8.7
46.0	34.9	28.7	Total Current					28.1	24.8
16.8	10.6	16.9	Long-Term Debt					2.7	12.8
1.3	.8	1.1	Deferred Taxes					2.0	1.4
11.5	5.7	5.1	All Other Non-Current					8.1	2.8
24.4	48.0	48.1	Net Worth					59.1	58.2
100.0	100.0	100.0	Total Liabilities & Net Worth					100.0	100.0
			INCOME DATA						
100.0	100.0	100.0	Net Sales					100.0	100.0
34.2	35.3	35.9	Gross Profit					33.7	36.2
26.2	29.5	26.6	Operating Expenses					21.7	26.9
8.0	5.8	9.2	Operating Profit					12.1	9.3
1.4	.2	1.0	All Other Expenses (net)					-.2	1.1
6.6	5.6	8.2	Profit Before Taxes					12.2	8.2
			RATIOS						
3.9	3.6	5.7	Current					8.1	3.5
2.2	2.5	3.1						5.0	3.1
1.3	1.6	1.6						2.4	1.7
1.9	2.1	2.9	Quick					6.0	2.2
1.0	1.2	1.5						2.3	1.5
.7	.6	.7						.5	.9
30 12.2	34 10.8	36 10.0	Sales/Receivables					34 10.9	39 9.3
42 8.8	43 8.4	45 8.1						44 8.4	53 6.8
51 7.2	55 6.6	56 6.5						56 6.5	58 6.3
39 9.3	46 7.9	57 6.4	Cost of Sales/Inventory					40 9.1	81 4.5
70 5.2	89 4.1	87 4.2						66 5.6	100 3.7
96 3.8	112 3.3	125 2.9						115 3.2	127 2.9
16 22.5	22 16.3	21 17.2	Cost of Sales/Payables					16 22.9	25 14.9
28 12.9	33 11.1	33 11.1						25 14.8	33 11.0
37 9.9	52 7.0	47 7.7						31 11.9	47 7.7
4.3	3.5	2.8	Sales/Working Capital					1.9	3.1
6.4	5.4	4.5						2.5	3.7
21.6	11.5	8.7						7.7	5.5
40.6	18.9	59.3	EBIT/Interest						61.9
(45) 7.5	(39) 3.8	(34) 13.8						(14) 16.8	
1.7	1.6	3.5							3.1
18.6	11.3	14.3	Net Profit + Depr., Dep., Amort./Cur. Mat. L/T/D						
(11) 4.3	(14) 5.2	(12) 4.4							
2.1	1.9	2.5							
.2	.1	.1	Fixed/Worth					.1	.2
.4	.2	.3						.1	.3
NM	1.1	1.6						.7	.7
.5	.4	.4	Debt/Worth					.2	.4
1.6	.8	.9						.5	.7
-28.3	3.7	7.1						1.8	5.7
57.5	38.7	46.1	% Profit Before Taxes/Tangible Net Worth					56.5	46.9
(37) 34.1	(41) 26.1	(31) 25.0						(10) 38.1	(12) 24.5
16.8	7.2	14.3						24.8	15.6
24.4	20.3	21.8	% Profit Before Taxes/Total Assets					31.5	17.7
12.7	11.9	13.0						18.8	12.8
2.9	2.1	4.5						13.1	6.7
43.6	61.2	31.4	Sales/Net Fixed Assets					80.5	22.9
16.3	18.3	17.8						22.9	9.4
5.7	6.2	6.5						7.1	6.1
3.3	2.7	2.2	Sales/Total Assets					2.4	1.7
2.2	2.0	1.6						1.7	1.5
1.6	1.6	1.3						1.4	1.3
1.0	.6	.8	% Depr., Dep., Amort./Sales						1.5
(40) 2.5	(36) 2.1	(30) 2.1						(14) 2.6	
4.0	3.7	4.0							4.6
2.3		2.7	% Officers', Directors' Owners' Comp/Sales						
(15) 4.0	(13) 4.6								
10.0		7.7							
1701745M	1353985M	1614227M	Net Sales ($)	1113M	2932M	30229M	34733M	194410M	1350810M
1124499M	908006M	1202708M	Total Assets ($)	1225M	1322M	49664M	25919M	120026M	1004552M

M = $ thousand   MM = $ million
See Pages 9 through 22 for Explanation of Ratios and Data

Current Data Sorted by Assets   **Comparative Historical Data**

0-500M	500M-2MM	2-10MM	10-50MM	50-100MM	100-250MM	Type of Statement	4/1/06-3/31/07 ALL	4/1/07-3/31/08 ALL
		6	14	6	6	Unqualified	45	34
	7	24	11			Reviewed	31	34
1	10	10				Compiled	21	18
1	10	10		1		Tax Returns	14	19
1	16	27	34	11	6	Other	71	71
	45 (4/1-9/30/10)		168 (10/1/10-3/31/11)					
3	43	77	60	18	12	**NUMBER OF STATEMENTS**	182	176
%	%	%	%	%	%	**ASSETS**	%	%
	10.0	10.3	9.4	12.1	10.5	Cash & Equivalents	8.1	11.2
	30.6	28.8	26.2	24.2	26.3	Trade Receivables (net)	30.3	29.6
	32.4	31.7	28.8	24.3	24.8	Inventory	29.9	28.1
	3.7	2.3	2.1	3.0	3.7	All Other Current	3.3	2.7
	76.8	73.2	66.6	63.7	65.3	Total Current	71.6	71.6
	14.8	17.5	16.5	15.3	11.1	Fixed Assets (net)	18.6	18.4
	3.4	3.4	10.6	15.2	16.7	Intangibles (net)	4.5	5.2
	4.9	5.9	6.3	5.9	7.0	All Other Non-Current	5.2	4.8
	100.0	100.0	100.0	100.0	100.0	Total	100.0	100.0
						LIABILITIES		
	12.7	11.1	10.8	3.4	3.6	Notes Payable-Short Term	11.6	10.0
	4.8	2.3	4.5	4.3	1.3	Cur. Mat.-L.T.D.	3.3	2.8
	17.9	15.4	11.9	14.0	17.1	Trade Payables	17.0	15.5
	.1	.1	.2	1.3	.7	Income Taxes Payable	.3	.3
	7.0	10.3	10.6	7.8	14.1	All Other Current	10.3	9.4
	42.5	39.1	38.0	30.9	36.8	Total Current	42.5	38.0
	13.6	10.5	12.4	31.1	10.1	Long-Term Debt	11.7	12.0
	.1	.5	1.1	.8	.8	Deferred Taxes	.3	.2
	8.7	5.3	6.3	4.9	21.0	All Other Non-Current	4.6	5.9
	35.1	44.6	42.2	32.3	31.3	Net Worth	40.9	43.9
	100.0	100.0	100.0	100.0	100.0	Total Liabilties & Net Worth	100.0	100.0
						INCOME DATA		
	100.0	100.0	100.0	100.0	100.0	Net Sales	100.0	100.0
	34.3	37.4	31.0	30.6	26.4	Gross Profit	32.7	33.7
	31.0	29.6	19.9	21.1	22.6	Operating Expenses	26.9	27.0
	3.3	7.7	11.0	9.5	3.8	Operating Profit	5.8	6.7
	.7	.6	1.9	1.4	1.8	All Other Expenses (net)	.8	1.3
	2.6	7.1	9.1	8.1	2.0	Profit Before Taxes	5.0	5.4
						RATIOS		
	3.3	2.9	3.2	3.2	2.5	Current	2.8	3.2
	1.7	2.0	1.9	2.1	2.0		1.8	1.8
	1.3	1.4	1.2	1.4	1.2		1.2	1.4
	1.7	2.0	1.6	2.0	1.2	Quick	1.6	1.9
	1.0	1.0	1.0	1.0	1.0		.9	1.0
	.5	.6	.6	.8	.8		.6	.7
28 13.0	33 11.0	44 8.3	52 7.0	55 6.7		Sales/Receivables	39 9.4	38 9.7
40 9.2	42 8.6	54 6.7	59 6.2	56 6.5			50 7.3	49 7.4
53 6.9	65 5.6	64 5.7	67 5.5	59 6.2			62 5.9	61 6.0
40 9.2	46 8.0	69 5.3	60 6.1	44 8.2		Cost of Sales/Inventory	45 8.1	35 10.4
59 6.1	83 4.4	87 4.2	96 3.8	70 5.2			79 4.6	68 5.3
105 3.5	143 2.6	127 2.9	157 2.3	89 4.1			114 3.2	114 3.2
18 20.0	22 16.4	20 18.1	35 10.4	42 8.7		Cost of Sales/Payables	21 17.4	21 17.5
29 12.7	34 10.7	28 13.1	44 8.3	45 8.2			36 10.1	33 11.2
47 7.7	56 6.6	47 7.8	65 5.6	57 6.4			55 6.6	51 7.2
	4.6	4.1	3.8	2.9	3.9	Sales/Working Capital	4.3	3.9
	8.7	6.2	5.6	4.8	6.1		6.8	6.9
	18.9	11.9	16.8	8.5	14.8		18.4	14.3
	10.4	19.6	22.8	61.4	52.0	EBIT/Interest	16.9	13.4
(36) 5.1	(68) 7.0	(49) 9.5	(17) 6.8	(11) 4.0			(161) 4.9	(142) 4.6
	.3	2.1	2.3	2.5	-3.6		2.0	2.0
		9.5	18.5	3.9		Net Profit + Depr., Dep.,	7.9	6.0
	(20) 2.7	(25) 3.7	(10) 1.7			Amort./Cur. Mat. L/T/D	(46) 3.3	(40) 2.8
		1.5	1.4	.9			1.6	1.1
	.1	.1	.2	.2	.2	Fixed/Worth	.2	.2
	.3	.4	.5	.5	1.1		.4	.4
	1.2	.8	1.7	1.4	-.7		1.2	1.0
	.5	.6	.5	.4	.7	Debt/Worth	.7	.5
	1.7	1.3	1.6	1.5	7.3		1.6	1.3
	4.8	3.9	7.6	6.7	-7.3		4.8	3.0
	47.1	66.4	53.9	56.1		% Profit Before Taxes/Tangible	49.5	52.6
(34) 25.7	(73) 30.3	(49) 33.2	(16) 30.9			Net Worth	(162) 26.1	(156) 25.5
	4.8	4.9	16.4	9.0			6.5	10.6
	27.9	22.4	20.7	17.5	10.1	% Profit Before Taxes/Total	16.7	18.8
	6.5	9.3	12.9	10.0	6.0	Assets	8.2	9.8
	.5	1.8	4.9	3.3	-7.5		1.5	3.8
	100.0	39.5	33.0	14.6	27.2	Sales/Net Fixed Assets	28.3	36.5
	22.9	19.7	13.1	9.5	15.1		14.8	14.8
	13.0	10.4	6.6	5.9	13.3		6.9	7.1
	3.8	2.8	2.1	1.8	2.0	Sales/Total Assets	2.6	2.9
	2.7	2.0	1.7	1.4	1.9		2.0	2.1
	1.8	1.5	1.2	.9	1.3		1.6	1.6
	.4	.7	1.2	1.6		% Depr., Dep., Amort./Sales	.9	.7
(35) 1.0	(68) 1.5	(50) 1.9	(16) 2.5				(148) 1.6	(142) 1.8
	2.8	2.7	3.5	3.6			2.6	3.3
	3.2	4.1				% Officers', Directors'	2.3	2.0
(21) 7.3	(26) 4.9					Owners' Comp/Sales	(51) 6.1	(45) 3.6
	10.8	7.1					11.0	5.8
5161M	149049M	858227M	2277337M	1830596M	3174715M	Net Sales ($)	4320432M	4590926M
1002M	54767M	401187M	1267916M	1215378M	1878635M	Total Assets ($)	2950940M	2853621M

M = $ thousand   MM = $ million
See Pages 9 through 22 for Explanation of Ratios and Data

Comparative Historical Data   Current Data Sorted by Sales

Type of Statement

Type of Statement	4/1/08-3/31/09	4/1/09-3/31/10	4/1/10-3/31/11	0-1MM	1-3MM	3-5MM	5-10MM	10-25MM	25MM & OVER
Unqualified	27	31	32			1		9	22
Reviewed	38	52	42	1	4	3	10	16	8
Compiled	23	18	21	1	5	4	6	5	
Tax Returns	15	17	23		6	7	7	1	2
Other	90	97	95	1	7	12	14	20	41
	ALL	ALL	ALL	0-1MM	1-3MM	3-5MM	5-10MM	10-25MM	25MM & OVER

45 (4/1-9/30/10)   168 (10/1/10-3/31/11)

	4/1/08-3/31/09 ALL	4/1/09-3/31/10 ALL	4/1/10-3/31/11 ALL	0-1MM	1-3MM	3-5MM	5-10MM	10-25MM	25MM & OVER
NUMBER OF STATEMENTS	193	215	213	3	22	27	37	51	73
	%	%	%	%	%	%	%	%	%
ASSETS									
Cash & Equivalents	10.0	11.2	10.1		9.7	11.5	6.9	10.7	11.0
Trade Receivables (net)	26.5	26.6	27.9		22.2	29.7	27.1	30.3	27.7
Inventory	30.8	28.4	30.2		29.1	27.3	35.6	30.6	28.1
All Other Current	2.2	3.2	2.7		2.1	4.5	1.5	2.4	2.8
Total Current	69.6	69.3	70.9		63.1	73.0	71.1	74.1	69.5
Fixed Assets (net)	19.8	18.8	16.1		21.4	19.2	16.2	12.9	15.5
Intangibles (net)	5.5	6.2	7.2		7.7	2.0	8.0	5.9	9.6
All Other Non-Current	5.2	5.7	5.9		7.7	5.7	4.8	7.1	5.3
Total	100.0	100.0	100.0		100.0	100.0	100.0	100.0	100.0
LIABILITIES									
Notes Payable-Short Term	13.3	9.8	10.1		15.7	10.5	10.0	11.4	7.2
Cur. Mat.-L.T.D.	2.8	2.6	3.5		2.4	5.9	2.1	3.2	4.1
Trade Payables	14.0	15.6	14.7		12.5	14.3	16.9	14.9	14.8
Income Taxes Payable	.3	.1	.3		.2	.0	.1	.1	.6
All Other Current	9.2	10.9	10.2		6.1	6.4	8.4	13.0	10.1
Total Current	39.5	39.1	38.7		37.0	37.1	37.5	42.7	36.7
Long-Term Debt	12.8	13.6	13.3		10.6	20.0	11.9	10.3	14.9
Deferred Taxes	.5	.4	.6		.2	.0	.4	1.1	.8
All Other Non-Current	6.8	8.7	7.0		10.4	6.5	4.3	6.4	8.3
Net Worth	40.4	38.2	40.3		41.8	36.4	45.9	39.4	39.4
Total Liabilties & Net Worth	100.0	100.0	100.0		100.0	100.0	100.0	100.0	100.0
INCOME DATA									
Net Sales	100.0	100.0	100.0		100.0	100.0	100.0	100.0	100.0
Gross Profit	32.6	33.0	34.1		40.0	41.2	38.0	31.5	29.1
Operating Expenses	27.5	27.6	26.5		34.4	36.5	28.9	23.6	20.1
Operating Profit	5.2	5.4	7.6		5.6	4.7	9.1	7.9	9.1
All Other Expenses (net)	1.2	1.2	1.1		.9	1.4	1.0	.6	1.6
Profit Before Taxes	3.9	4.3	6.5		4.7	3.4	8.0	7.3	7.5
RATIOS									
Current	3.0	3.2	3.1		2.6	3.8	3.9	2.6	3.1
	1.9	1.9	2.0		1.6	2.0	2.0	1.9	2.0
	1.3	1.3	1.3		1.2	1.5	1.3	1.3	1.4
Quick	1.8	1.7	1.8		1.5	2.7	1.6	1.9	1.7
	.9	1.0	1.0		.9	1.2	.8	1.1	1.0
	.6	.6	.6		.5	.5	.6	.6	.7
Sales/Receivables	34 10.6	37 9.9	36 10.2		30 12.0	26 14.1	30 12.1	39 9.3	45 8.1
	44 8.2	49 7.5	51 7.2		40 9.1	40 9.1	41 9.0	53 6.9	56 6.5
	57 6.4	61 6.0	62 5.9		54 6.8	58 6.3	52 7.0	66 5.5	63 5.8
Cost of Sales/Inventory	46 7.9	43 8.4	49 7.5		35 10.5	27 13.7	50 7.3	54 6.7	55 6.6
	78 4.7	79 4.6	79 4.6		65 5.6	60 6.1	90 4.1	84 4.4	80 4.6
	122 3.0	122 3.0	129 2.8		196 1.9	127 2.9	158 2.3	128 2.9	112 3.3
Cost of Sales/Payables	17 21.9	21 17.3	21 17.0		17 21.4	18 19.8	24 14.9	22 16.4	24 15.5
	29 12.4	33 11.0	33 11.0		32 11.3	28 13.0	36 10.1	32 11.3	37 9.7
	49 7.4	55 6.7	52 7.0		82 4.4	46 7.9	57 6.5	52 7.0	53 6.9
Sales/Working Capital	4.1	3.9	4.0		4.9	3.8	4.2	4.4	3.7
	6.5	6.1	6.3		9.0	6.3	7.5	6.2	5.2
	16.2	13.1	13.9		15.3	18.8	18.3	10.8	11.7
EBIT/Interest	15.8	14.4	19.8		8.6	13.2	18.6	23.4	35.2
	(173) 4.4	(185) 3.6	(182) 7.1		(19) 2.2	(23) 3.0	(31) 7.3	(43) 8.9	(65) 8.6
	1.4	1.1	1.9		1.3	-.6	2.0	2.7	2.6
Net Profit + Depr., Dep., Amort./Cur. Mat. L/T/D	6.4	5.4	8.4					12.4	10.3
	(44) 2.1	(62) 2.8	(64) 2.8					(18) 3.5	(33) 3.4
	1.3	.8	1.3					1.2	1.3
Fixed/Worth	.2	.1	.2		.1	.1	.1	.2	.2
	.4	.5	.4		.5	.3	.4	.4	.4
	1.4	1.4	1.2		3.3	1.4	1.5	.9	1.2
Debt/Worth	.7	.6	.6		.6	.4	.5	.7	.5
	1.4	1.4	1.4		1.6	1.1	1.8	1.7	1.3
	5.0	4.3	5.2		4.2	7.9	5.3	5.0	5.3
% Profit Before Taxes/Tangible Net Worth	46.8	47.1	52.2		33.4	51.0	74.7	82.4	49.9
	(164) 21.6	(186) 15.7	(182) 30.2		(18) 13.0	(22) 19.4	(34) 31.0	(44) 39.4	(62) 29.2
	4.1	2.1	8.1		3.2	4.0	4.2	13.8	12.3
% Profit Before Taxes/Total Assets	16.2	18.9	19.9		11.7	29.5	26.0	20.1	19.3
	7.0	4.5	9.4		5.0	5.9	7.9	12.1	10.8
	.8	.4	2.4		.5	-.2	1.6	4.7	4.1
Sales/Net Fixed Assets	33.6	42.0	38.6		45.5	90.1	47.9	40.7	23.6
	14.9	13.5	17.6		13.8	22.9	21.8	20.6	12.2
	6.3	6.0	8.8		5.1	5.3	12.5	10.5	8.2
Sales/Total Assets	2.8	2.6	2.6		2.7	3.3	3.2	2.4	2.3
	2.0	1.9	1.9		1.8	2.4	2.0	2.0	1.8
	1.5	1.4	1.5		1.4	1.6	1.5	1.5	1.3
% Depr., Dep., Amort./Sales	1.0	.8	.8		.7	.6	.6	.5	1.4
	(155) 2.1	(176) 2.1	(176) 1.6		(17) 2.1	(21) 1.3	(30) 1.3	(46) 1.5	(59) 2.0
	3.2	3.6	2.9		3.2	4.8	2.2	2.7	3.1
% Officers', Directors' Owners' Comp/Sales	2.7	2.3	3.0		4.2		1.7	3.8	
	(55) 4.6	(69) 4.5	(58) 5.2		(14) 7.8	(12) 6.4	(11) 4.7	(12) 4.7	
	8.6	7.4	8.9		12.4	11.8	5.3	9.5	
Net Sales ($)	5475372M	5024340M	8295085M	2320M	49073M	102288M	271750M	822267M	7047387M
Total Assets ($)	3180933M	3299563M	4818885M	2335M	30597M	54332M	165783M	461708M	4104130M

M = $ thousand   MM = $ million
See Pages 9 through 22 for Explanation of Ratios and Data

Current Data Sorted by Assets / Comparative Historical Data

	Type of Statement		
		22	17
Unqualified			
Reviewed		4	4
Compiled		3	1
Tax Returns		1	2
Other		23	31

Type of Statement counts by asset size (Unqualified / Reviewed / Compiled / Tax Returns / Other):

0-500M	500M-2MM	2-10MM	10-50MM	50-100MM	100-250MM
1	2	4	5	1	3
	1	2	2		
1	2	4			
2	5	9	12	3	4

0-500M	500M-2MM 15 (4/1-9/30/10)	2-10MM	10-50MM 48 (10/1/10-3/31/11)	50-100MM	100-250MM		4/1/06-3/31/07 ALL	4/1/07-3/31/08 ALL
4	10	19	19	4	7	**NUMBER OF STATEMENTS**	53	55
%	%	%	%	%	%	**ASSETS**	%	%
	16.5	13.4	20.8			Cash & Equivalents	15.4	15.4
	35.5	27.0	23.0			Trade Receivables (net)	20.9	21.9
	21.4	29.1	18.5			Inventory	22.8	18.4
	3.3	2.3	2.0			All Other Current	3.6	4.1
	76.7	71.9	64.3			Total Current	62.7	59.8
	13.6	11.5	17.6			Fixed Assets (net)	19.4	20.4
	2.6	8.3	13.5			Intangibles (net)	13.2	16.4
	7.1	8.2	4.7			All Other Non-Current	4.7	3.4
	100.0	100.0	100.0			Total	100.0	100.0
						LIABILITIES		
	9.0	5.0	3.7			Notes Payable-Short Term	6.3	8.3
	2.4	1.7	2.0			Cur. Mat.-L.T.D.	2.5	2.3
	14.6	10.5	11.6			Trade Payables	10.2	10.0
	.8	.1	.6			Income Taxes Payable	.5	.3
	11.2	12.1	12.0			All Other Current	10.1	13.2
	38.0	29.3	29.9			Total Current	29.6	34.2
	9.6	10.7	7.6			Long-Term Debt	10.6	10.3
	.0	.7	.6			Deferred Taxes	.5	.5
	2.4	14.4	18.4			All Other Non-Current	3.7	7.0
	50.0	44.9	43.5			Net Worth	55.6	47.9
	100.0	100.0	100.0			Total Liabilities & Net Worth	100.0	100.0
						INCOME DATA		
	100.0	100.0	100.0			Net Sales	100.0	100.0
	47.9	45.0	45.7			Gross Profit	49.1	49.0
	37.1	41.8	40.1			Operating Expenses	42.4	40.8
	10.8	3.1	5.6			Operating Profit	6.7	8.1
	3.4	1.2	1.6			All Other Expenses (net)	1.6	1.3
	7.4	1.9	4.0			Profit Before Taxes	5.1	6.9
						RATIOS		
	7.1	3.9	4.3			Current	4.2	3.2
	2.6	2.7	2.3				2.7	2.2
	1.2	2.0	1.4				1.7	1.1
	4.5	2.8	3.0			Quick	2.3	2.2
	1.9	1.2	1.2				1.5	1.1
	1.0	1.0	.7				.8	.6
	17 22.0	41 8.8	27 13.5			Sales/Receivables	35 10.5	34 10.6
	40 9.1	46 7.9	41 8.8				50 7.3	48 7.7
	93 3.9	70 5.2	63 5.8				73 5.0	75 4.9
	0 UND	97 3.8	53 6.9			Cost of Sales/Inventory	77 4.8	37 9.9
	18 19.9	116 3.1	68 5.4				114 3.2	90 4.1
	116 3.1	149 2.4	104 3.5				158 2.3	144 2.5
	5 69.3	16 22.3	27 13.6			Cost of Sales/Payables	27 13.4	25 14.8
	18 20.7	31 11.6	44 8.2				43 8.5	37 9.8
	49 7.4	64 5.7	67 5.4				72 5.1	67 5.4
	4.5	2.3	2.5			Sales/Working Capital	2.2	2.8
	6.1	3.9	6.1				3.3	5.3
	38.7	6.1	11.1				8.9	25.6
		35.0	92.5			EBIT/Interest	23.5	24.5
		(18) 4.9	(16) 3.1				(43) 4.0	(46) 5.3
		-2.9	-1.5				.5	1.4
						Net Profit + Depr., Dep., Amort./Cur. Mat. L/T/D	22.8	45.2
							(14) 4.1	(18) 7.0
							-.4	1.0
	.1	.1	.1			Fixed/Worth	.2	.2
	.1	.2	.5				.4	.4
	.9	.8	2.6				.6	1.5
	.2	.4	.3			Debt/Worth	.4	.5
	1.9	1.0	.9				.8	1.4
	2.3	35.7	5.8				2.8	4.8
		78.5	44.2			% Profit Before Taxes/Tangible Net Worth	34.4	68.5
		(17) 25.6	(15) 26.4				(50) 17.2	(48) 20.8
		-7.5	-2.8				2.3	8.4
	40.4	17.3	21.8			% Profit Before Taxes/Total Assets	12.6	17.4
	16.9	11.8	4.6				7.1	8.2
	1.3	-7.8	-7.3				.3	1.0
	85.8	46.0	39.0			Sales/Net Fixed Assets	19.5	21.9
	32.5	17.2	14.5				9.3	12.0
	11.8	11.0	5.0				4.5	5.1
	4.3	2.2	2.2			Sales/Total Assets	2.1	2.4
	2.8	1.8	1.5				1.3	1.3
	2.3	1.0	1.2				.8	.8
		.5	1.0			% Depr., Dep., Amort./Sales	1.6	1.4
		(14) 1.3	(12) 4.9				(45) 2.9	(49) 2.9
		3.4	7.4				4.9	5.5
						% Officers', Directors' Owners' Comp/Sales		
5874M	42708M	187040M	702999M	403439M	921516M	Net Sales ($)	3096348M	3006329M
1055M	13500M	113379M	431352M	302105M	1092865M	Total Assets ($)	2928948M	2603989M

M = $ thousand   MM = $ million
See Pages 9 through 22 for Explanation of Ratios and Data

Comparative Historical Data   Current Data Sorted by Sales

Hist 1	Hist 2	Hist 3	Type of Statement	0-1MM	1-3MM	3-5MM	5-10MM	10-25MM	25MM & OVER
17	19	13	Unqualified				1	2	8
7	11	7	Reviewed	1	2	1	1	2	
4	1	1	Compiled			1	1		
4	5	7	Tax Returns			3	3		
22	27	35	Other	2	3	1	4	12	13
4/1/08-3/31/09 ALL	4/1/09-3/31/10 ALL	4/1/10-3/31/11 ALL		15 (4/1-9/30/10)			48 (10/1/10-3/31/11)		
54	63	63	NUMBER OF STATEMENTS	3	4	7	11	15	23
%	%	%	**ASSETS**	%	%	%	%	%	%
14.7	15.6	16.8	Cash & Equivalents				15.5	17.8	18.8
22.4	23.9	26.3	Trade Receivables (net)				31.8	24.8	18.4
21.5	20.2	21.2	Inventory				27.0	23.1	18.5
2.8	3.4	2.9	All Other Current				2.1	1.4	4.4
61.4	63.1	67.2	Total Current				76.3	67.1	60.0
21.5	20.0	15.1	Fixed Assets (net)				9.7	16.0	16.7
11.3	10.4	10.8	Intangibles (net)				7.5	8.6	17.5
5.8	6.4	6.9	All Other Non-Current				6.5	8.3	5.9
100.0	100.0	100.0	Total				100.0	100.0	100.0
			LIABILITIES						
9.6	7.7	5.4	Notes Payable-Short Term				9.7	2.9	2.6
4.5	2.9	1.7	Cur. Mat.-L.T.D.				3.5	1.6	1.9
8.4	10.5	10.8	Trade Payables				11.2	10.1	9.2
.4	.2	.3	Income Taxes Payable				.0	.0	.5
11.7	16.1	13.1	All Other Current				14.8	10.6	13.1
34.5	37.4	31.4	Total Current				39.3	25.2	27.2
13.9	8.6	9.0	Long-Term Debt				8.9	13.5	9.5
.5	.8	.6	Deferred Taxes				1.2	.1	1.0
7.7	8.0	11.5	All Other Non-Current				15.8	2.9	16.7
43.3	45.3	47.5	Net Worth				34.9	58.3	45.5
100.0	100.0	100.0	Total Liabilities & Net Worth				100.0	100.0	100.0
			INCOME DATA						
100.0	100.0	100.0	Net Sales				100.0	100.0	100.0
50.0	44.0	46.8	Gross Profit				41.8	44.4	48.6
47.3	40.5	41.0	Operating Expenses				36.9	41.1	43.7
2.7	3.5	5.8	Operating Profit				4.9	3.3	4.9
1.1	1.3	1.9	All Other Expenses (net)				.8	1.4	2.1
1.6	2.2	3.9	Profit Before Taxes				4.1	1.9	2.9
			RATIOS						
2.9	3.3	4.9	Current				6.1	4.4	5.0
2.0	1.8	2.6					2.0	2.8	2.3
1.3	1.2	1.5					1.3	2.3	1.4
2.0	2.5	3.1	Quick				3.3	3.5	3.5
1.4	1.0	1.4					1.0	1.4	1.3
.6	.5	.8					.9	1.0	.7
29 12.4	35 10.4	33 11.0	Sales/Receivables				36 10.0	41 8.8	28 13.2
44 8.2	46 7.9	47 7.7					46 7.9	57 6.4	43 8.5
59 6.2	57 6.5	67 5.5					55 6.6	67 5.5	63 5.8
51 7.2	49 7.4	49 7.5	Cost of Sales/Inventory				17 21.0	60 6.1	61 6.0
87 4.2	77 4.7	83 4.4					98 3.7	90 4.0	80 4.6
146 2.5	123 3.0	141 2.6					141 2.6	123 3.0	151 2.4
14 26.8	16 23.2	21 17.7	Cost of Sales/Payables				11 32.5	24 15.1	27 13.6
31 11.8	32 11.4	35 10.5					21 17.1	41 8.9	37 9.7
53 6.9	54 6.8	63 5.8					35 10.5	72 5.0	63 5.8
3.2	4.0	2.3	Sales/Working Capital				3.1	2.6	2.0
6.1	6.9	4.8					6.2	3.9	5.4
14.1	18.1	10.8					24.2	6.0	10.8
9.9	14.0	44.9	EBIT/Interest				16.7	298.9	44.9
(42) 2.2	(50) 3.6	(52) 4.9					4.5	(12) 4.5	(20) 8.9
-1.1	.9	-.2					-.4	-2.4	.5
4.4	3.2		Net Profit + Depr., Dep., Amort./Cur. Mat. L/T/D						
(15) 2.4	(15) 2.1								
.9	1.3								
.2	.1	.1	Fixed/Worth				.1	.1	.2
.7	.5	.3					.2	.1	.5
2.2	1.3	1.3					1.3	.4	2.6
.6	.4	.3	Debt/Worth				.7	.2	.3
1.4	1.0	.9					2.1	.5	1.3
9.7	4.8	7.9					57.0	1.3	9.4
37.8	41.3	55.9	% Profit Before Taxes/Tangible Net Worth					42.1	47.7
(45) 10.1	(52) 14.9	(53) 20.5						(13) 15.7	(18) 19.9
-16.9	1.5	-2.9						-11.7	-4.8
15.2	16.0	21.9	% Profit Before Taxes/Total Assets				34.5	17.3	21.4
2.9	3.8	8.8					12.6	3.9	4.6
-7.6	-3.7	-2.2					-3.0	-7.2	-5.3
29.2	39.6	37.3	Sales/Net Fixed Assets				79.6	39.0	22.3
11.3	13.4	17.1					37.3	17.1	13.6
5.3	4.2	8.9					18.1	6.8	5.7
2.2	2.4	2.4	Sales/Total Assets				4.3	2.1	2.2
1.6	1.5	1.6					2.7	1.4	1.1
1.1	1.1	1.1					1.7	1.3	.8
1.1	1.3	.9	% Depr., Dep., Amort./Sales						1.5
(41) 2.0	(50) 2.4	(43) 2.3							(18) 3.1
3.8	5.4	4.9							5.4
2.8	1.3	4.6	% Officers', Directors' Owners' Comp/Sales						
(15) 7.7	(16) 3.1	(10) 7.7							
11.8	10.6	10.4							
1897427M	2249239M	2263576M	Net Sales ($)	1583M	7904M	29618M	79630M	248945M	1895896M
1512811M	1882904M	1954256M	Total Assets ($)	1108M	5259M	18439M	39939M	166132M	1723379M

© RMA 2011

M = $ thousand   MM = $ million

See Pages 9 through 22 for Explanation of Ratios and Data

Current Data Sorted by Assets **Comparative Historical Data**

0-500M	500M-2MM	2-10MM	10-50MM	50-100MM	100-250MM	Type of Statement	4/1/06-3/31/07 ALL	4/1/07-3/31/08 ALL
		2	11	2	3	Unqualified	22	20
	1	9	2			Reviewed	8	5
	1	1				Compiled	7	4
1	1					Tax Returns		3
2	6	9	10	1	8	Other	16	24
	16 (4/1-9/30/10)		57 (10/1/10-3/31/11)					
3	12	21	23	3	11	NUMBER OF STATEMENTS	53	56
%	%	%	%	%	%		%	%
						ASSETS		
	10.2	13.1	12.7		10.7	Cash & Equivalents	13.7	11.6
	26.7	25.8	26.9		16.5	Trade Receivables (net)	26.3	25.5
	36.5	32.5	23.2		21.1	Inventory	25.4	23.3
	2.4	3.0	8.7		5.6	All Other Current	6.3	6.6
	75.7	74.4	71.4		54.0	Total Current	71.7	67.0
	14.3	14.8	15.3		9.7	Fixed Assets (net)	15.2	16.5
	2.7	5.8	6.5		32.5	Intangibles (net)	7.6	10.9
	7.3	5.0	6.8		3.8	All Other Non-Current	5.4	5.7
	100.0	100.0	100.0		100.0	Total	100.0	100.0
						LIABILITIES		
	14.9	7.8	8.6		.8	Notes Payable-Short Term	6.8	6.5
	2.2	4.4	2.0		2.1	Cur. Mat.-L.T.D.	2.5	4.1
	16.1	10.6	11.6		8.8	Trade Payables	10.7	10.9
	.0	.4	1.7		.1	Income Taxes Payable	.8	.3
	10.8	14.8	15.9		11.7	All Other Current	10.4	14.7
	44.0	38.0	39.8		23.6	Total Current	31.1	36.6
	13.1	25.1	8.6		13.4	Long-Term Debt	11.3	15.2
	.0	.3	1.1		3.7	Deferred Taxes	.7	.9
	4.7	8.3	2.9		2.9	All Other Non-Current	9.6	7.4
	38.2	28.3	47.7		56.4	Net Worth	47.2	40.0
	100.0	100.0	100.0		100.0	Total Liabilities & Net Worth	100.0	100.0
						INCOME DATA		
	100.0	100.0	100.0		100.0	Net Sales	100.0	100.0
	52.3	40.6	36.8		28.8	Gross Profit	36.3	37.6
	40.3	36.2	31.1		20.3	Operating Expenses	27.8	28.2
	12.0	4.4	5.7		8.6	Operating Profit	8.5	9.4
	.8	1.2	1.4		3.8	All Other Expenses (net)	1.1	1.5
	11.2	3.3	4.4		4.7	Profit Before Taxes	7.4	7.9
						RATIOS		
	3.9	3.1	3.4		3.0		4.0	3.5
	1.6	2.1	1.9		2.1	Current	2.6	2.0
	1.1	1.6	1.3		1.9		1.5	1.3
	2.1	2.1	1.6		1.2		2.4	1.9
	.8	.9	1.1		1.0	Quick	1.2	1.0
	.4	.6	.6		.8		.8	.6
	31 12.0	27 13.5	36 10.1		50 7.2		43 8.4	38 9.6
	38 9.6	40 9.0	61 6.0		56 6.6	Sales/Receivables	57 6.4	48 7.7
	50 7.3	58 6.3	82 4.5		61 6.0		78 4.7	67 5.4
	31 11.8	60 6.1	19 18.7		80 4.6		39 9.3	28 13.2
	177 2.1	133 2.7	107 3.4		106 3.5	Cost of Sales/Inventory	95 3.8	85 4.3
	237 1.5	191 1.9	166 2.2		140 2.6		150 2.4	146 2.5
	9 42.2	15 24.5	17 20.9		21 17.2		19 18.9	19 18.9
	28 13.1	27 13.5	33 10.9		32 11.3	Cost of Sales/Payables	34 10.7	30 12.2
	58 6.3	57 6.5	71 5.2		41 8.9		51 7.2	52 7.1
	3.4	3.1	2.7		2.1		2.4	2.6
	10.0	4.5	4.2		4.4	Sales/Working Capital	3.8	6.1
	NM	9.7	15.6		5.1		8.2	17.6
		31.7	27.0		28.8		31.8	41.4
		(18) 3.4	(22) 4.8		15.3	EBIT/Interest	(47) 7.4	(50) 11.3
		.1	1.5		1.1		1.3	1.9
						Net Profit + Depr., Dep.,	21.3	28.1
						Amort./Cur. Mat. L/T/D	(23) 6.4	(19) 2.2
							1.3	.4
	.1	.1	.1		.2		.1	.1
	.4	.6	.3		.3	Fixed/Worth	.3	.3
	.8	5.3	.7		-.3		.9	1.5
	.9	.5	.4		.5		.4	.5
	1.6	2.1	1.1		1.3	Debt/Worth	1.2	1.6
	6.1	20.4	2.9		-4.3		2.8	7.8
	86.9	45.3	29.3			% Profit Before Taxes/Tangible	51.3	80.4
	(11) 65.2	(17) 19.3	(20) 21.3			Net Worth	(47) 19.7	(47) 31.6
	44.4	2.4	8.7				4.1	7.6
	40.0	13.8	17.9		10.8	% Profit Before Taxes/Total	20.4	25.3
	22.0	7.0	7.9		4.9	Assets	8.6	11.0
	8.9	.9	2.1		.7		.5	3.8
	108.5	75.6	24.3		19.5		24.8	24.1
	21.2	17.4	16.2		14.7	Sales/Net Fixed Assets	11.4	11.6
	11.9	7.5	7.0		9.0		6.4	7.0
	3.0	2.6	1.8		1.4		2.0	2.3
	2.3	1.9	1.3		1.1	Sales/Total Assets	1.5	1.5
	1.6	1.3	1.0		.8		1.2	1.0
		1.1	1.1				1.1	1.2
		(17) 1.9	(17) 2.0			% Depr., Dep., Amort./Sales	(49) 2.0	(45) 1.9
		2.9	5.4				3.1	2.9
						% Officers', Directors' Owners' Comp/Sales		
2461M	38003M	179881M	753968M	197980M	2050467M	Net Sales ($)	2777228M	3072344M
724M	16436M	95739M	585749M	201451M	1962043M	Total Assets ($)	2177754M	2246521M

© RMA 2011

M = $ thousand   MM = $ million
See Pages 9 through 22 for Explanation of Ratios and Data

Comparative Historical Data / Current Data Sorted by Sales

			Type of Statement			16 (4/1-9/30/10)		57 (10/1/10-3/31/11)	
				0-1MM	1-3MM	3-5MM	5-10MM	10-25MM	25MM & OVER
19	29	18	Unqualified			2		5	11
8	16	12	Reviewed			3	4	4	1
5	2	2	Compiled		1			1	
6	1	5	Tax Returns	1	2	2			
24	21	36	Other	1	1	6	3	7	16
4/1/08-3/31/09 ALL	4/1/09-3/31/10 ALL	4/1/10-3/31/11 ALL							
62	69	73	**NUMBER OF STATEMENTS**	2	6	13	7	17	28
%	%	%	**ASSETS**	%	%	%	%	%	%
10.9	14.0	13.1	Cash & Equivalents			7.8		13.7	14.0
24.8	22.1	23.9	Trade Receivables (net)			31.0		27.1	22.3
26.2	27.8	26.6	Inventory			31.4		28.7	20.4
5.2	6.1	4.9	All Other Current			3.1		9.4	4.9
67.1	70.1	68.5	Total Current			73.2		79.0	61.7
15.6	16.2	16.2	Fixed Assets (net)			18.7		15.0	13.6
10.3	9.6	9.7	Intangibles (net)			3.4		.9	19.3
7.0	4.1	5.6	All Other Non-Current			4.7		5.1	5.4
100.0	100.0	100.0	Total			100.0		100.0	100.0
			LIABILITIES						
7.7	4.9	15.2	Notes Payable-Short Term			16.9		6.3	5.5
2.6	2.7	2.6	Cur. Mat.-L.T.D.			2.1		2.6	2.0
13.3	9.8	11.2	Trade Payables			9.1		11.9	10.9
.3	.9	.7	Income Taxes Payable			.0		1.3	.8
13.5	12.8	15.2	All Other Current			10.4		22.4	12.1
37.3	31.2	44.9	Total Current			38.5		44.6	31.4
13.6	10.0	15.8	Long-Term Debt			11.0		9.6	13.5
1.1	.8	1.0	Deferred Taxes			.2		.4	2.2
4.5	4.8	5.4	All Other Non-Current			9.8		7.3	3.8
43.6	53.2	33.0	Net Worth			40.5		38.1	49.1
100.0	100.0	100.0	Total Liabilties & Net Worth			100.0		100.0	100.0
			INCOME DATA						
100.0	100.0	100.0	Net Sales			100.0		100.0	100.0
37.8	37.7	40.8	Gross Profit			43.5		38.1	34.1
31.2	30.9	33.7	Operating Expenses			37.1		28.7	28.7
6.6	6.8	7.1	Operating Profit			6.4		9.3	5.4
1.0	2.0	1.5	All Other Expenses (net)			.8		.9	2.4
5.6	4.8	5.5	Profit Before Taxes			5.6		8.5	2.9
			RATIOS						
3.8	4.4	3.0	Current			2.6		3.5	3.0
2.2	2.6	2.0				2.1		2.1	2.0
1.3	1.5	1.4				1.4		1.5	1.5
2.0	2.5	2.0	Quick			1.7		2.2	1.6
.9	1.1	.9				.9		1.1	1.0
.6	.6	.7				.6		.5	.8
31 11.7	34 10.6	35 10.4	Sales/Receivables			27 13.3		36 10.1	45 8.1
50 7.4	48 7.6	48 7.5				42 8.7		47 7.8	57 6.5
65 5.6	65 5.6	63 5.8				62 5.9		64 5.7	75 4.9
38 9.5	65 5.7	45 8.2	Cost of Sales/Inventory			31 11.7		16 22.8	67 5.4
103 3.5	123 3.0	107 3.4				116 3.1		89 4.1	105 3.5
149 2.4	163 2.2	169 2.2				176 2.1		187 2.0	142 2.6
19 19.3	18 20.3	18 20.5	Cost of Sales/Payables			12 31.4		18 20.2	20 18.4
31 11.6	28 12.9	30 12.3				29 12.5		29 12.7	33 11.0
54 6.8	51 7.2	55 6.6				46 7.9		57 6.4	71 5.2
3.2	2.4	3.0	Sales/Working Capital			3.5		2.8	2.5
5.6	4.0	4.8				5.6		3.8	4.7
13.5	9.4	11.2				14.9		10.0	6.4
23.5	66.8	28.8	EBIT/Interest			40.5		44.9	26.9
(56) 4.4	(61) 6.5	(65) 5.4				(11) 4.2		(14) 5.0	12.5
1.2	.8	1.5				-4.1		3.3	1.2
18.4	10.1	67.5	Net Profit + Depr., Dep., Amort./Cur. Mat. L/T/D						92.0
(20) 2.8	(19) 2.4	(23) 4.6							(11) 15.6
1.0	1.3	1.5							4.6
.2	.1	.1	Fixed/Worth			.2		.1	.2
.4	.3	.4				.4		.3	.3
1.5	.7	2.3				.8		.6	NM
.5	.4	.5	Debt/Worth			.8		.4	.5
1.4	1.0	1.4				1.2		1.1	1.3
5.1	2.5	12.6				5.3		3.3	NM
57.1	36.6	50.9	% Profit Before Taxes/Tangible Net Worth			71.7		44.9	31.1
(51) 20.4	(61) 13.6	(59) 25.5				(11) 54.1		(15) 26.8	(21) 14.8
4.7	2.1	8.5				21.2		11.7	7.4
19.4	18.2	15.8	% Profit Before Taxes/Total Assets			29.6		20.8	11.1
6.4	7.0	8.3				8.9		8.5	5.9
1.6	-.6	1.2				-3.1		3.2	.8
29.5	23.2	30.7	Sales/Net Fixed Assets			271.8		33.6	22.3
12.6	11.9	16.2				17.6		16.0	15.8
7.9	6.3	7.0				7.9		7.6	6.5
2.7	2.0	2.2	Sales/Total Assets			3.0		2.5	1.5
1.6	1.4	1.5				2.1		1.6	1.2
1.2	1.1	1.1				1.5		1.3	.9
.8	1.2	1.1	% Depr., Dep., Amort./Sales					1.1	1.4
(52) 1.7	(58) 2.1	(54) 2.3						(15) 1.5	(19) 3.0
2.6	3.0	3.3						2.8	4.5
2.8	2.4	2.6	% Officers', Directors' Owners' Comp/Sales						
(18) 5.7	(12) 5.1	(12) 6.9							
10.5	7.8	10.0							
2549041M	3383935M	3222760M	Net Sales ($)	1204M	11412M	51201M	50577M	287769M	2820597M
2096510M	2805987M	2862142M	Total Assets ($)	704M	8701M	27111M	30816M	187197M	2607613M

M = $ thousand   MM = $ million
See Pages 9 through 22 for Explanation of Ratios and Data

Current Data Sorted by Assets   Comparative Historical Data

		3	1	2	1	Type of Statement		11		10
	4	7	2			Unqualified				
	2	4	1			Reviewed		9		12
2	3	1				Compiled		4		5
3	4	8	7		3	Tax Returns		6		5
						Other		9		20
	8 (4/1-9/30/10)		50 (10/1/10-3/31/11)					4/1/06-3/31/07		4/1/07-3/31/08
0-500M	500M-2MM	2-10MM	10-50MM	50-100MM	100-250MM			ALL		ALL
5	13	23	11	2	4	NUMBER OF STATEMENTS		39		52
%	%	%	%	%	%	ASSETS		%		%
	10.8	10.6	9.2			Cash & Equivalents		14.7		13.9
	42.9	34.7	36.2			Trade Receivables (net)		35.2		35.6
	25.6	27.6	15.2			Inventory		24.6		21.0
	3.4	9.0	10.8			All Other Current		2.8		4.7
	82.7	81.8	71.4			Total Current		77.2		75.2
	12.7	11.0	19.4			Fixed Assets (net)		15.0		13.1
	1.7	1.8	1.5			Intangibles (net)		3.6		3.4
	2.9	5.4	7.7			All Other Non-Current		4.2		8.4
	100.0	100.0	100.0			Total		100.0		100.0
						LIABILITIES				
	12.9	11.4	3.5			Notes Payable-Short Term		10.6		11.7
	5.3	2.5	3.0			Cur. Mat.-L.T.D.		2.8		3.1
	15.3	15.2	16.1			Trade Payables		16.0		16.4
	.0	.1	.3			Income Taxes Payable		.2		.3
	10.9	13.1	20.7			All Other Current		13.7		19.6
	44.3	42.2	43.5			Total Current		43.2		51.0
	2.7	8.3	7.4			Long-Term Debt		11.2		10.0
	.2	.4	.3			Deferred Taxes		.4		.2
	2.6	.8	5.2			All Other Non-Current		5.0		7.2
	50.2	48.3	43.6			Net Worth		40.1		31.5
	100.0	100.0	100.0			Total Liabilities & Net Worth		100.0		100.0
						INCOME DATA				
	100.0	100.0	100.0			Net Sales		100.0		100.0
	39.9	38.6	33.3			Gross Profit		36.1		36.7
	31.9	33.6	25.5			Operating Expenses		29.5		30.6
	8.1	5.0	7.8			Operating Profit		6.6		6.1
	.4	-.4	.8			All Other Expenses (net)		.7		.6
	7.7	5.4	7.0			Profit Before Taxes		5.8		5.5
						RATIOS				
	4.0	3.8	3.3					3.4		3.6
	2.2	2.1	1.5			Current		1.7		1.8
	1.3	1.3	1.2					1.3		1.3
	3.0	2.0	2.0					1.8		2.0
	1.1	1.1	1.0			Quick		1.0		1.1
	.7	.7	.7					.8		.8
22	16.7	40 9.2	50 7.3				49	7.4	37	9.9
43	8.4	51 7.2	57 6.4			Sales/Receivables	56	6.6	52	7.0
63	5.8	62 5.8	89 4.1				65	5.6	71	5.1
23	16.0	13 28.8	9 41.2				34	10.8	18	20.2
44	8.2	67 5.5	51 7.1			Cost of Sales/Inventory	64	5.7	54	6.8
69	5.3	154 2.4	-79 4.6				114	3.2	94	3.9
10	35.3	20 18.3	13 28.1				19	19.6	18	20.4
26	14.2	29 12.5	39 9.4			Cost of Sales/Payables	29	12.4	31	11.7
39	9.3	37 10.0	70 5.2				54	6.8	52	7.1
	6.1	3.3	3.4					3.9		4.2
	7.1	5.7	7.5			Sales/Working Capital		7.5		6.6
	20.4	14.7	17.7					16.9		15.7
		62.7						20.0		39.0
	(21)	16.1				EBIT/Interest	(34)	8.0	(44)	8.1
		-.1						1.5		.8
						Net Profit + Depr., Dep.,		5.9		
						Amort./Cur. Mat. L/T/D	(12)	2.9		
								1.4		
	.1	.1	.1					.2		.1
	.2	.1	.6			Fixed/Worth		.3		.3
	.5	1.5	.8					.7		1.0
	.3	.3	.7					.6		.6
	.7	1.2	1.2			Debt/Worth		1.7		1.6
	5.1	3.3	3.0					3.7		7.0
	90.6	57.0	33.9			% Profit Before Taxes/Tangible		79.8		67.7
(12)	44.8	(21) 13.4	18.4			Net Worth	(37)	31.4	(45)	31.3
	13.3	1.9	4.9					8.3		6.0
	53.2	31.5	13.5			% Profit Before Taxes/Total		20.2		24.2
	24.9	8.6	8.4			Assets		11.7		11.3
	5.2	.4	2.6					1.6		1.1
	67.2	61.3	46.3					59.9		35.8
	27.9	19.8	16.9			Sales/Net Fixed Assets		21.6		22.5
	17.7	14.2	5.6					7.9		11.8
	4.5	2.9	2.1					3.5		3.0
	3.6	2.5	1.7			Sales/Total Assets		2.1		2.3
	2.2	1.9	1.2					1.6		1.8
	.9	.4	.9					.5		.5
(11)	1.1	(19) 1.1	(10) 1.3			% Depr., Dep., Amort./Sales	(34)	1.2	(44)	1.3
	1.8	1.8	2.4					3.0		2.2
						% Officers', Directors'		2.2		2.7
						Owners' Comp/Sales	(13)	4.9	(13)	4.1
								7.3		7.4
4428M	49655M	269489M	448637M	208807M	887709M	Net Sales ($)		1386681M		1988884M
1928M	13891M	111928M	197202M	123359M	612175M	Total Assets ($)		844175M		1102314M

M = $ thousand   MM = $ million
See Pages 9 through 22 for Explanation of Ratios and Data

Comparative Historical Data | Current Data Sorted by Sales

Type of Statement	08-09	09-10	10-11	0-1MM	1-3MM	3-5MM	5-10MM	10-25MM	25MM & OVER
Unqualified	8	6	7		1			2	4
Reviewed	11	9	13		3	1	3	6	
Compiled	5	5	7		1	1	2	3	
Tax Returns	4	3	6	1	2	1	1	1	
Other	16	11	25	2	4		4	7	8
	4/1/08-3/31/09 ALL	4/1/09-3/31/10 ALL	4/1/10-3/31/11 ALL		8 (4/1-9/30/10)		50 (10/1/10-3/31/11)		
NUMBER OF STATEMENTS	44	34	58	3	11	3	10	19	12
ASSETS	%	%	%	%	%	%	%	%	%
Cash & Equivalents	14.4	13.7	10.2		13.0		4.9	10.2	10.7
Trade Receivables (net)	38.3	38.3	36.0		39.0		41.3	34.7	32.1
Inventory	19.4	22.0	24.0		24.5		20.4	23.9	19.8
All Other Current	3.5	4.6	6.9		4.1		13.9	8.3	3.4
Total Current	75.6	78.6	77.1		80.5		80.5	77.1	66.0
Fixed Assets (net)	14.5	12.4	13.9		16.5		11.7	13.8	16.7
Intangibles (net)	4.1	4.1	4.1		1.6		1.9	1.4	14.1
All Other Non-Current	5.8	5.0	5.0		1.4		5.9	7.7	3.2
Total	100.0	100.0	100.0		100.0		100.0	100.0	100.0
LIABILITIES									
Notes Payable-Short Term	9.0	9.6	8.4		12.4		16.3	8.6	1.4
Cur. Mat.-L.T.D.	3.9	3.1	3.9		2.8		.7	3.6	4.8
Trade Payables	14.0	13.2	14.3		10.2		19.8	14.7	12.6
Income Taxes Payable	.2	.0	.3		.0		.0	.1	1.1
All Other Current	16.0	16.6	13.6		5.1		8.7	17.9	19.7
Total Current	43.1	42.6	40.5		30.5		45.5	44.9	39.7
Long-Term Debt	8.0	6.5	8.4		2.5		7.2	9.9	6.1
Deferred Taxes	.3	.7	.3		.0		.0	.5	.3
All Other Non-Current	4.6	9.0	2.8		.3		2.0	3.0	3.8
Net Worth	44.0	41.1	48.1		66.6		45.3	41.7	50.1
Total Liabilities & Net Worth	100.0	100.0	100.0		100.0		100.0	100.0	100.0
INCOME DATA									
Net Sales	100.0	100.0	100.0		100.0		100.0	100.0	100.0
Gross Profit	36.0	37.5	37.7		40.5		46.0	35.9	36.9
Operating Expenses	28.5	29.5	31.7		31.5		42.9	30.2	27.4
Operating Profit	7.6	7.9	6.0		9.0		3.2	5.6	9.6
All Other Expenses (net)	.5	.4	.3		.2		.5	-.3	1.1
Profit Before Taxes	7.1	7.5	5.7		8.8		2.7	5.9	8.4

RATIOS

Ratio	08-09	09-10	10-11	0-1MM	1-3MM	3-5MM	5-10MM	10-25MM	25MM & OVER
Current	3.4	3.6	3.3		10.2		4.8	2.7	2.6
	1.8	2.0	2.1		2.6		2.3	1.8	1.6
	1.2	1.2	1.3		1.7		1.2	1.5	1.2
Quick	2.1	2.2	2.0		8.6		1.9	2.0	1.7
	1.4	1.3	1.1		1.6		1.0	1.0	1.1
	.8	.8	.7		1.0		.7	.7	.6
Sales/Receivables	41 8.8	36 10.2	41 8.9		36 10.1		42 8.7	33 11.2	46 8.0
	51 7.1	48 7.6	54 6.8		58 6.3		61 5.9	51 7.2	51 7.1
	68 5.4	62 5.9	65 5.6		63 5.8		71 5.2	61 6.0	65 5.6
Cost of Sales/Inventory	11 31.9	7 51.0	21 17.7		6 56.8		0 UND	13 28.8	38 9.6
	48 7.6	50 7.3	56 6.5		49 7.5		87 4.2	51 7.1	66 5.5
	86 4.3	96 3.8	88 4.2		78 4.7		187 2.0	83 4.4	82 4.5
Cost of Sales/Payables	13 27.0	11 32.7	18 20.6		8 48.0		20 18.0	23 23.6	25 14.8
	31 11.8	24 15.0	31 11.9		22 16.9		32 11.4	29 12.4	33 11.2
	49 7.5	39 9.3	49 7.4		34 10.9		102 3.6	52 7.0	54 6.7
Sales/Working Capital	4.1	4.4	3.9		4.6		2.5	4.2	4.9
	7.3	6.7	6.4		6.4		8.3	5.7	7.0
	21.9	21.2	14.7		8.1		20.4	14.9	27.4
EBIT/Interest	44.3	210.9	34.1				32.5	47.2	
	(39) 16.8	(29) 12.0	(48) 10.9				5.8	(18) 15.5	
	3.5	1.9	1.6				-3.2	.2	
Net Profit + Depr., Dep., Amort./Cur. Mat. L/T/D			6.1						
		(13)	1.9						
			.3						
Fixed/Worth	.1	.1	.1		.1		.1	.1	.2
	.2	.3	.2		.2		.1	.2	.4
	.9	.5	.8		.3		2.4	.9	2.3
Debt/Worth	.5	.6	.4		.2		.3	.7	.5
	1.3	1.0	1.0		.4		1.6	1.2	1.0
	4.8	3.1	3.3		1.1		21.9	3.4	6.1
% Profit Before Taxes/Tangible Net Worth	69.8	57.3	52.1		61.3			57.0	51.2
	(39) 37.5	(32) 30.4	(52) 18.4		16.4			(17) 26.8	(10) 26.7
	14.0	9.1	6.0		12.3			2.4	11.6
% Profit Before Taxes/Total Assets	27.2	32.7	25.8		40.4		9.6	31.5	18.8
	16.4	15.0	9.5		11.5		4.1	13.5	12.8
	5.1	1.1	2.5		9.6		-5.9	.4	5.0
Sales/Net Fixed Assets	43.6	63.6	50.7		28.2		62.1	60.1	31.3
	25.7	25.0	19.9		20.0		16.8	19.9	12.8
	11.4	12.0	13.0		11.9		15.9	13.4	8.0
Sales/Total Assets	3.3	3.5	3.2		3.8		3.9	2.9	2.5
	2.3	2.6	2.1		3.2		2.1	2.3	1.8
	1.7	1.7	1.7		2.1		1.5	1.8	1.4
% Depr., Dep., Amort./Sales	.4	.4	.9					.4	1.0
	(36) 1.1	(27) 1.1	(49) 1.4					(17) 1.4	2.1
	2.1	1.8	2.3					2.3	3.3
% Officers', Directors', Owners' Comp/Sales	3.0	2.8	2.7						
	(12) 4.1	(11) 4.8	(17) 5.6						
	7.3	9.9	7.1						
Net Sales ($)	1202524M	1322198M	1868725M	1849M	23610M	12057M	76906M	280181M	1474122M
Total Assets ($)	664087M	592043M	1060483M	1141M	9603M	3574M	37849M	131270M	877046M

M = $ thousand   MM = $ million
See Pages 9 through 22 for Explanation of Ratios and Data

Current Data Sorted by Assets | | | | | | | **Comparative Historical Data**

0-500M	500M-2MM	2-10MM	10-50MM	50-100MM	100-250MM	Type of Statement	4/1/06-3/31/07 ALL	4/1/07-3/31/08 ALL
1	4	6	13	3	7	Unqualified	26	29
	2	25	4			Reviewed	41	36
	1	9				Compiled	20	12
1	1	5				Tax Returns	8	11
	7	16	17	5	5	Other	56	39
	37 (4/1-9/30/10)		94 (10/1/10-3/31/11)					
2	14	61	34	8	12	**NUMBER OF STATEMENTS**	151	127
%	%	%	%	%	%	**ASSETS**	%	%
	8.1	13.4	16.9		17.1	Cash & Equivalents	9.1	12.4
	32.7	28.9	24.7		18.5	Trade Receivables (net)	30.1	29.6
	29.6	29.0	23.7		19.6	Inventory	28.0	24.1
	2.6	5.5	4.5		3.1	All Other Current	4.3	5.0
	73.1	76.8	69.8		58.4	Total Current	71.5	71.2
	21.1	14.6	14.6		12.3	Fixed Assets (net)	16.0	15.6
	1.4	4.2	6.4		25.9	Intangibles (net)	6.0	6.7
	4.4	4.4	9.1		3.4	All Other Non-Current	6.6	6.5
	100.0	100.0	100.0		100.0	Total	100.0	100.0
						LIABILITIES		
	18.0	7.7	4.7		.6	Notes Payable-Short Term	10.5	12.2
	1.3	2.3	3.3		1.6	Cur. Mat.-L.T.D.	2.8	3.4
	13.4	13.5	8.6		10.5	Trade Payables	12.5	13.4
	.2	.1	.7		.1	Income Taxes Payable	.6	.3
	12.3	17.6	16.3		12.7	All Other Current	14.6	15.0
	45.2	41.1	33.6		25.5	Total Current	41.0	44.2
	8.3	9.1	5.4		14.1	Long-Term Debt	11.6	14.0
	.1	.3	.8		2.2	Deferred Taxes	.5	.4
	10.6	8.0	8.0		5.1	All Other Non-Current	6.3	5.6
	35.8	41.6	52.3		53.1	Net Worth	40.7	35.8
	100.0	100.0	100.0		100.0	Total Liabilities & Net Worth	100.0	100.0
						INCOME DATA		
	100.0	100.0	100.0		100.0	Net Sales	100.0	100.0
	49.1	38.2	39.5		35.3	Gross Profit	41.3	42.3
	45.6	30.4	31.2		29.2	Operating Expenses	34.3	34.0
	3.5	7.8	8.4		6.1	Operating Profit	7.0	8.3
	.4	1.4	.6		1.1	All Other Expenses (net)	1.4	1.5
	3.1	6.4	7.8		5.0	Profit Before Taxes	5.6	6.7
						RATIOS		
	6.3	3.3	3.9		3.2	Current	3.0	3.3
	1.6	2.0	2.4		2.6		2.0	2.0
	1.1	1.4	1.5		1.6		1.4	1.3
	3.6	2.0	2.4		2.0	Quick	1.7	1.8
	.8	1.1	1.4		1.6		(150) 1.1	1.1
	.5	.7	.8		1.0		.7	.7
34 10.7	38 9.6	42 8.7			47 7.8	Sales/Receivables	43 8.5	39 9.5
49 7.5	55 6.7	54 6.8			56 6.5		51 7.2	48 7.6
61 6.0	65 5.6	66 5.6			70 5.2		63 5.8	65 5.6
41 8.9	61 6.0	46 8.0			58 6.3	Cost of Sales/Inventory	57 6.4	43 8.6
86 4.3	87 4.2	99 3.7			102 3.6		91 4.0	79 4.6
108 3.4	116 3.2	137 2.7			154 2.4		134 2.7	112 3.3
13 27.7	19 19.4	18 20.7			32 11.4	Cost of Sales/Payables	22 16.3	23 16.0
32 11.5	36 10.2	25 14.8			46 8.0		35 10.4	35 10.3
66 5.6	57 6.4	40 9.1			52 7.1		51 7.1	57 6.4
	3.9	3.3	2.8		1.9	Sales/Working Capital	3.8	3.6
	8.0	4.6	4.1		4.0		6.1	6.2
	NM	10.0	6.8		7.7		10.5	15.3
	16.3	27.8	73.8		32.5	EBIT/Interest	18.0	14.3
	(12) 8.4	(54) 9.0	(30) 17.7		4.6		(135) 5.4	(111) 3.8
	2.8	2.2	2.8		-1.8		1.5	1.8
		4.2	30.7			Net Profit + Depr., Dep., Amort./Cur. Mat. L/T/D	18.0	13.1
		(15) 1.9	(17) 8.6				(45) 6.0	(36) 4.7
		.8	1.6				1.9	1.9
	.2	.1	.2		.1	Fixed/Worth	.2	.2
	.5	.3	.3		.5		.4	.5
	NM	1.4	.6		NM		1.3	2.4
	.4	.6	.4		.4	Debt/Worth	.6	.5
	1.8	1.1	.9		1.7		1.5	1.8
	NM	5.6	2.7		NM		5.0	13.0
	49.7	65.4	35.0			% Profit Before Taxes/Tangible Net Worth	48.8	51.3
	(11) 22.0	(53) 19.8	(32) 18.3				(133) 24.6	(105) 29.7
	5.8	10.5	12.2				8.8	9.9
	17.0	19.7	16.5		14.2	% Profit Before Taxes/Total Assets	18.3	19.5
	6.7	8.3	8.9		6.1		9.0	8.3
	2.1	3.4	3.8		-1.9		2.0	2.8
	27.8	58.3	20.9		22.6	Sales/Net Fixed Assets	38.9	49.2
	20.7	17.7	11.2		13.7		14.9	15.5
	9.1	8.4	8.6		5.0		7.8	7.5
	3.0	2.3	2.2		1.4	Sales/Total Assets	2.7	2.7
	2.3	1.9	1.5		1.0		1.8	1.9
	2.1	1.4	1.1		.7		1.4	1.4
	.9	.6	1.1			% Depr., Dep., Amort./Sales	.8	.8
	(12) 1.5	(48) 1.2	(28) 1.4				(129) 1.7	(105) 1.5
	2.6	2.1	2.3				3.0	2.3
		2.3				% Officers', Directors' Owners' Comp/Sales	2.4	2.4
		(20) 3.2					(36) 5.6	(31) 5.9
		8.0					9.6	8.6
6038M	43610M	579220M	1183667M	637668M	2227488M	Net Sales ($)	4502077M	4004238M
452M	16676M	310152M	688108M	627749M	1847165M	Total Assets ($)	3352550M	2924124M

M = $ thousand   MM = $ million
See Pages 9 through 22 for Explanation of Ratios and Data

Comparative Historical Data | Current Data Sorted by Sales

	4/1/08-3/31/09 ALL	4/1/09-3/31/10 ALL	4/1/10-3/31/11 ALL	Type of Statement	0-1MM	1-3MM	3-5MM	5-10MM	10-25MM	25MM & OVER
	30	29	29	Unqualified			1		9	19
	27	32	34	Reviewed	1	4	6	10	10	3
	8	9	11	Compiled		1	2	4	4	
	5	3	7	Tax Returns			2	4	1	
	49	50	50	Other	1	4	5	9	12	19
						37 (4/1-9/30/10)			94 (10/1/10-3/31/11)	
NUMBER OF STATEMENTS	119	123	131		2	9	16	27	36	41
	%	%	%	**ASSETS**	%	%	%	%	%	%
Cash & Equivalents	11.9	14.0	14.0				7.7	12.2	17.2	15.0
Trade Receivables (net)	26.9	24.2	26.2				30.7	29.0	27.2	22.6
Inventory	24.9	25.2	25.7				26.5	26.5	29.3	22.1
All Other Current	5.0	5.8	5.4				4.8	6.3	3.9	7.1
Total Current	68.6	69.2	71.3				69.7	74.0	77.6	66.7
Fixed Assets (net)	14.7	15.4	15.9				15.7	18.2	13.9	14.4
Intangibles (net)	8.6	9.0	6.8				6.0	3.8	4.3	12.1
All Other Non-Current	8.1	6.4	5.9				8.6	4.0	4.2	6.8
Total	100.0	100.0	100.0				100.0	100.0	100.0	100.0
				LIABILITIES						
Notes Payable-Short Term	9.0	8.9	8.8				11.9	16.3	6.9	3.9
Cur. Mat.-L.T.D.	2.5	2.6	2.6				1.5	2.3	3.5	3.0
Trade Payables	11.0	9.9	11.2				13.2	17.1	10.1	8.9
Income Taxes Payable	1.0	.9	.3				.0	.1	.4	.3
All Other Current	13.7	11.6	15.8				14.9	21.6	15.0	15.2
Total Current	37.2	33.9	38.8				41.5	57.3	35.9	31.4
Long-Term Debt	11.4	10.8	8.0				7.7	11.9	5.5	7.1
Deferred Taxes	.8	.5	.6				.0	.3	.7	1.1
All Other Non-Current	7.7	9.6	8.3				10.2	6.6	7.2	7.4
Net Worth	42.9	45.2	44.3				40.6	23.9	50.7	52.9
Total Liabilities & Net Worth	100.0	100.0	100.0				100.0	100.0	100.0	100.0
				INCOME DATA						
Net Sales	100.0	100.0	100.0				100.0	100.0	100.0	100.0
Gross Profit	42.2	41.2	39.4				44.8	38.8	40.8	36.4
Operating Expenses	34.6	35.1	31.8				35.2	32.4	32.4	28.3
Operating Profit	7.6	6.2	7.6				9.6	6.4	8.4	8.2
All Other Expenses (net)	1.6	1.4	1.2				2.1	1.5	.7	1.3
Profit Before Taxes	6.0	4.8	6.4				7.5	4.9	7.6	6.9
				RATIOS						
Current	3.5	3.5	3.8				2.6	3.5	3.9	3.8
	2.0	2.3	2.3				1.4	2.0	2.2	2.5
	1.3	1.4	1.4				1.2	1.2	1.5	1.5
Quick	1.8	2.1	2.1				1.9	1.7	2.2	2.2
	1.1	1.3	1.2				.9	1.0	1.3	1.3
	.7	.7	.7				.3	.6	.7	.9
Sales/Receivables	38 · 9.6	40 · 9.1	41 · 8.8				20 · 18.6	38 · 9.5	37 · 9.8	45 · 8.1
	48 · 7.6	51 · 7.2	54 · 6.8				53 · 6.8	53 · 6.9	54 · 6.7	55 · 6.6
	65 · 5.6	64 · 5.7	63 · 5.8				76 · 4.8	64 · 5.7	61 · 6.0	63 · 5.8
Cost of Sales/Inventory	52 · 7.0	56 · 6.5	50 · 7.3				37 · 9.9	49 · 7.4	68 · 5.4	50 · 7.4
	83 · 4.4	88 · 4.1	87 · 4.2				80 · 4.5	75 · 4.9	96 · 3.8	94 · 3.9
	138 · 2.7	126 · 2.9	118 · 3.1				183 · 2.0	118 · 3.1	119 · 3.1	129 · 2.8
Cost of Sales/Payables	20 · 18.6	19 · 19.0	19 · 19.3				27 · 13.6	22 · 16.9	16 · 22.5	21 · 17.6
	32 · 11.4	30 · 12.0	32 · 11.4				36 · 10.1	40 · 9.2	28 · 13.2	32 · 11.5
	48 · 7.6	46 · 8.0	50 · 7.3				103 · 3.5	63 · 5.8	45 · 8.2	46 · 7.9
Sales/Working Capital	3.2	2.9	2.9				3.8	3.3	3.1	2.7
	5.4	4.4	4.5				8.0	5.6	4.4	4.1
	13.4	9.9	9.9				16.5	16.2	8.2	8.4
EBIT/Interest	27.1	26.4	25.4				17.8	15.7	54.5	89.5
	(106) 5.4	(108) 3.1	(115) 8.8				(14) 4.9	(24) 6.7	(30) 13.7	(37) 11.3
	1.6	.9	2.1				1.5	1.2	3.4	1.6
Net Profit + Depr., Dep., Amort./Cur. Mat. L/T/D	15.3	11.1	10.6						9.5	26.1
	(41) 3.3	(41) 3.9	(41) 2.6					(14)	2.9 (18)	3.7
	1.7	1.0	.9						1.0	.9
Fixed/Worth	.1	.1	.1				.1	.2	.1	.2
	.4	.3	.4				.5	.5	.3	.3
	1.9	1.6	1.3				NM	15.3	.9	1.1
Debt/Worth	.5	.4	.4				.7	.5	.4	.4
	1.5	1.2	1.2				1.6	2.3	1.1	.9
	8.9	5.9	4.2				NM	95.7	2.5	3.4
% Profit Before Taxes/Tangible Net Worth	50.0	35.2	49.1				34.0	119.9	52.5	36.4
	(98) 22.6	(101) 17.8	(112) 19.7				(12) 11.9	(21) 17.5	(34) 23.5	(35) 19.6
	7.3	5.2	10.9				5.5	10.8	13.2	11.1
% Profit Before Taxes/Total Assets	19.7	14.5	16.9				10.5	16.9	22.1	14.7
	7.7	5.4	8.5				5.1	8.3	9.6	9.2
	1.4	.7	2.6				2.0	1.3	4.8	2.6
Sales/Net Fixed Assets	28.2	30.6	29.2				38.2	32.8	75.4	22.9
	14.1	13.0	15.6				27.4	16.0	15.1	12.6
	8.1	6.8	7.8				5.9	8.2	8.7	6.9
Sales/Total Assets	2.3	2.1	2.3				2.3	2.3	2.4	2.0
	1.7	1.6	1.8				1.5	1.9	1.9	1.5
	1.4	1.1	1.1				1.0	1.5	1.4	.9
% Depr., Dep., Amort./Sales	1.2	1.1	.9				.8	.5	.7	1.1
	(92) 1.7	(103) 1.6	(105) 1.5				(11) 1.2	(21) 1.5	(28) 1.4	(35) 2.1
	2.5	2.8	2.6				2.3	2.6	2.1	3.4
% Officers', Directors', Owners' Comp/Sales	1.3	2.5							1.8	
	(23) 4.1	(22) 6.7	(29) 3.4						(10) 3.2	
	6.1	9.6	7.8						7.3	
Net Sales ($)	4739494M	4138665M	4677691M		1693M	18482M	64428M	195191M	568580M	3829317M
Total Assets ($)	3553653M	3684322M	3490302M		1134M	13994M	58085M	103653M	351387M	2962049M

© RMA 2011

M = $ thousand   MM = $ million
See Pages 9 through 22 for Explanation of Ratios and Data

Current Data Sorted by Assets   Comparative Historical Data

0-500M	500M-2MM	2-10MM	10-50MM	50-100MM	100-250MM	Type of Statement	4/1/06-3/31/07 ALL	4/1/07-3/31/08 ALL
		1	5	1	1	Unqualified	10	7
	2	5	4			Reviewed	8	9
	2	1				Compiled	6	3
2	1	1				Tax Returns	4	5
1	1	6 (4/1-9/30/10)	5 (10/1/10-3/31/11)			Other	18	17
2	6	14	14	2	2	NUMBER OF STATEMENTS	46	41

2-10MM %	10-50MM %	ASSETS	Hist %	Hist %
9.2	8.3	Cash & Equivalents	9.4	11.8
27.5	20.7	Trade Receivables (net)	29.6	26.8
36.4	23.9	Inventory	30.0	29.7
7.1	8.4	All Other Current	6.4	3.1
80.2	61.3	Total Current	75.4	71.5
13.7	23.3	Fixed Assets (net)	18.1	15.9
3.1	5.8	Intangibles (net)	2.5	6.8
3.1	9.5	All Other Non-Current	4.0	5.9
100.0	100.0	Total	100.0	100.0
		LIABILITIES		
5.8	3.9	Notes Payable-Short Term	10.4	7.3
1.7	1.6	Cur. Mat.-L.T.D.	3.2	3.0
14.1	8.7	Trade Payables	15.3	13.2
.8	.3	Income Taxes Payable	.6	.2
13.9	13.3	All Other Current	8.9	10.6
36.3	27.7	Total Current	38.5	34.3
2.3	23.0	Long-Term Debt	13.1	12.5
.9	1.3	Deferred Taxes	.3	.4
6.3	6.8	All Other Non-Current	6.4	3.7
54.3	41.2	Net Worth	41.6	49.1
100.0	100.0	Total Liabilities & Net Worth	100.0	100.0
		INCOME DATA		
100.0	100.0	Net Sales	100.0	100.0
39.0	34.5	Gross Profit	37.9	40.6
34.0	28.4	Operating Expenses	28.9	34.5
5.0	6.1	Operating Profit	9.0	6.0
.3	3.3	All Other Expenses (net)	.8	.0
4.8	2.7	Profit Before Taxes	8.2	6.1
		RATIOS		
4.1	3.3		3.3	4.1
2.2	2.5	Current	1.9	2.2
1.8	1.7		1.4	1.4
2.3	1.9		1.6	2.3
1.0	1.2	Quick	.9	1.1
.7	.6		.6	.6
37 9.9	36 10.2		39 9.3 35 10.5	
42 8.6	49 7.4	Sales/Receivables	49 7.4 48 7.7	
69 5.3	69 5.3		65 5.6 59 6.2	
85 4.3	69 5.3		43 8.4 67 5.5	
110 3.3	88 4.1	Cost of Sales/Inventory	93 3.9 109 3.4	
141 2.6	141 2.6		130 2.8 141 2.6	
19 18.9	13 29.2		19 18.9 19 18.8	
35 10.5	38 9.5	Cost of Sales/Payables	37 9.9 34 10.9	
46 8.0	55 6.6		59 6.2 51 7.1	
2.7	2.2		3.9	3.5
4.1	4.0	Sales/Working Capital	6.1	5.7
7.6	6.5		9.9	9.9
21.8	49.8		19.9	30.1
(10) 12.1	(12) 3.1	EBIT/Interest	(42) 6.6	(36) 3.9
4.4	-.1		1.9	1.6
		Net Profit + Depr., Dep.,	10.5	10.8
		Amort./Cur. Mat. L/T/D	(13) 5.6 (15) 3.9	
			2.9	1.3
.1	.3		.1	.2
.3	.5	Fixed/Worth	.3	.3
.5	1.2		.9	.8
.4	.6		.5	.3
.8	1.0	Debt/Worth	1.4	.9
1.2	3.3		2.6	3.2
33.2	29.6		63.1	53.0
15.6	(12) 16.5	% Profit Before Taxes/Tangible Net Worth	(41) 25.2 (35) 20.2	
5.1	2.7		6.7	6.9
19.5	10.9		27.4	22.6
8.4	4.2	% Profit Before Taxes/Total Assets	9.0	7.8
3.7	-1.8		2.5	1.7
47.4	14.7		25.9	27.1
21.1	7.0	Sales/Net Fixed Assets	13.9	14.9
7.0	3.0		7.9	7.9
2.6	1.9		2.5	2.4
2.0	1.1	Sales/Total Assets	2.1	1.9
1.6	.8		1.6	1.5
.6	1.3		1.0	1.0
(11) .9	(13) 3.0	% Depr., Dep., Amort./Sales	(36) 1.9 (36) 1.8	
2.2	5.8		2.9	2.8
		% Officers', Directors' Owners' Comp/Sales		

0-500M	500M-2MM	2-10MM	10-50MM	50-100MM	100-250MM		Hist1	Hist2
1630M	15897M	130959M	441231M	279406M	433412M	Net Sales ($)	2153188M	1149490M
448M	8083M	63448M	372552M	146247M	319406M	Total Assets ($)	1052739M	748056M

M = $ thousand   MM = $ million
See Pages 9 through 22 for Explanation of Ratios and Data

Comparative Historical Data | Current Data Sorted by Sales

			Type of Statement	0-1MM	1-3MM	3-5MM	5-10MM	10-25MM	25MM & OVER
6	6	8	Unqualified					2	6
11	10	11	Reviewed		1	2	4	1	3
5	2	3	Compiled	1	1			1	
3	4	4	Tax Returns	2	1		1		
14	13	14	Other		1		3	6	4
4/1/08-3/31/09 ALL	4/1/09-3/31/10 ALL	4/1/10-3/31/11 ALL		6 (4/1-9/30/10)			34 (10/1/10-3/31/11)		
39	35	40	NUMBER OF STATEMENTS	3	4	2	8	10	13
%	%	%	ASSETS	%	%	%	%	%	%
12.8	9.0	10.1	Cash & Equivalents					4.1	10.4
24.6	20.7	24.4	Trade Receivables (net)					29.4	20.3
33.7	34.6	30.2	Inventory					27.4	24.8
4.3	6.7	6.3	All Other Current					10.2	5.2
75.4	70.9	71.0	Total Current					71.1	60.8
16.4	16.9	18.3	Fixed Assets (net)					23.1	21.9
4.1	4.1	4.9	Intangibles (net)					2.4	7.5
4.1	8.1	5.8	All Other Non-Current					3.4	9.8
100.0	100.0	100.0	Total					100.0	100.0
			LIABILITIES						
9.6	10.3	6.3	Notes Payable-Short Term					4.0	3.7
3.3	2.4	2.8	Cur. Mat.-L.T.D.					1.9	1.3
14.0	11.1	13.2	Trade Payables					16.4	6.7
.2	.1	.4	Income Taxes Payable					.1	.4
14.6	12.6	17.2	All Other Current					14.8	16.7
41.8	36.5	39.9	Total Current					37.2	28.8
16.1	6.2	11.3	Long-Term Debt					10.3	18.0
.5	.4	.8	Deferred Taxes					.4	1.2
6.8	9.5	12.3	All Other Non-Current					4.6	7.9
34.8	47.4	35.6	Net Worth					47.5	44.0
100.0	100.0	100.0	Total Liabilities & Net Worth					100.0	100.0
			INCOME DATA						
100.0	100.0	100.0	Net Sales					100.0	100.0
37.3	38.8	38.5	Gross Profit					31.3	37.6
33.8	36.5	32.1	Operating Expenses					25.9	32.1
3.5	2.3	6.5	Operating Profit					5.4	5.5
.7	.4	1.6	All Other Expenses (net)					.6	3.1
2.8	1.9	4.9	Profit Before Taxes					4.9	2.5
			RATIOS						
3.9	3.5	3.3	Current					2.6	3.8
2.0	1.9	2.1						2.1	2.6
1.4	1.5	1.4						1.7	1.7
2.1	1.4	1.7	Quick					1.2	2.4
1.0	1.0	1.0						.8	1.3
.5	.5	.6						.6	.7
30 12.2	37 10.0	36 10.1	Sales/Receivables					37 9.9	31 11.7
41 9.0	49 7.5	43 8.6						58 6.2	46 8.0
49 7.5	63 5.8	65 5.6						109 3.4	63 5.8
86 4.3	75 4.9	78 4.7	Cost of Sales/Inventory					43 8.4	79 4.6
111 3.3	111 3.3	102 3.6						103 3.6	88 4.1
164 2.2	173 2.1	143 2.6						144 2.5	109 3.4
20 17.8	21 17.5	20 18.4	Cost of Sales/Payables					18 20.6	11 33.9
35 10.5	35 10.4	38 9.7						27 13.3	38 9.6
48 7.6	51 7.1	52 7.1						176 2.1	40 9.2
2.6	2.5	2.8	Sales/Working Capital					2.4	2.9
5.9	4.5	5.5						4.8	4.5
11.3	8.2	9.8						11.8	7.7
8.4	8.9	32.0	EBIT/Interest						116.4
(31) 2.7	(26) 3.3	(32) 5.8						(11)	32.0
1.6	.3	2.4							-.2
6.6			Net Profit + Depr., Dep., Amort./Cur. Mat. L/T/D						
(10) 1.4									
-253.1									
.1	.1	.2	Fixed/Worth					.2	.3
.2	.3	.4						.4	.5
1.0	.6	.9						.9	.9
.5	.5	.6	Debt/Worth					.5	.5
1.2	.8	1.0						1.0	1.0
3.7	1.4	4.8						2.5	2.4
41.4	25.0	32.6	% Profit Before Taxes/Tangible Net Worth					33.1	35.5
(35) 13.6	(32) 12.4	(33) 16.7						11.8	(11) 17.8
4.0	1.0	5.9						4.9	-2.3
13.6	11.9	17.3	% Profit Before Taxes/Total Assets					16.2	18.9
5.0	5.0	7.7						4.5	8.3
2.0	-1.3	2.0						2.6	-7.5
43.4	22.3	25.6	Sales/Net Fixed Assets					49.1	12.9
14.8	14.0	12.4						9.4	9.0
7.3	6.9	5.6						4.1	3.9
2.7	2.3	2.4	Sales/Total Assets					2.6	2.1
2.1	1.5	1.8						1.6	1.4
1.5	1.2	1.2						1.0	1.0
1.1	1.1	.9	% Depr., Dep., Amort./Sales						1.7
(32) 1.7	(30) 1.8	(35) 2.1							3.1
2.8	2.9	3.6							4.7
			% Officers', Directors' Owners' Comp/Sales						
1602890M	724305M	1302535M	Net Sales ($)	2604M	10148M	8627M	53855M	158019M	1069282M
841765M	503755M	910184M	Total Assets ($)	1230M	5707M	3722M	29417M	138540M	731568M

© RMA 2011

M = $ thousand   MM = $ million
See Pages 9 through 22 for Explanation of Ratios and Data

Current Data Sorted by Assets

Comparative Historical Data

0-500M	500M-2MM	2-10MM	10-50MM	50-100MM	100-250MM	Type of Statement		4/1/06-3/31/07 ALL		4/1/07-3/31/08 ALL
		1	1		1	Unqualified		19		16
	1	1	8			Reviewed		10		12
1	3	3	2		1	Compiled		8		6
1	2					Tax Returns		3		3
1	1	1	9		10	Other		17		17
		8 (4/1-9/30/10)			41 (10/1/10-3/31/11)					
3	8	20	15	3	3	NUMBER OF STATEMENTS		57		54
%	%	%	%	%	%	ASSETS		%		%
		8.0	8.1			Cash & Equivalents		11.5		14.9
		27.1	18.9	D		Trade Receivables (net)		26.9		23.3
		37.1	18.5	A		Inventory		26.5		26.8
		1.2	17.5	T		All Other Current		2.3		2.7
		73.3	63.1	A		Total Current		67.2		67.7
		17.7	19.8	N		Fixed Assets (net)		15.7		15.9
		2.6	11.4	O		Intangibles (net)		8.7		9.4
		6.3	5.7	T		All Other Non-Current		8.4		7.0
		100.0	100.0			Total		100.0		100.0
				A		LIABILITIES				
		10.2	3.5	V		Notes Payable-Short Term		7.9		5.9
		4.3	2.4	A		Cur. Mat.-L.T.D.		2.2		2.9
		10.5	8.8	I		Trade Payables		10.6		10.0
		.3	.5	L		Income Taxes Payable		.6		.3
		12.0	17.3	A		All Other Current		9.6		11.0
		37.2	32.5	B		Total Current		30.8		30.0
		13.2	10.2	L		Long-Term Debt		10.2		10.0
		.1	.8	E		Deferred Taxes		.5		.1
		8.2	15.4			All Other Non-Current		4.7		4.0
		41.3	41.1			Net Worth		53.8		55.9
		100.0	100.0			Total Liabilities & Net Worth		100.0		100.0
						INCOME DATA				
		100.0	100.0			Net Sales		100.0		100.0
		45.2	41.1			Gross Profit		45.5		46.1
		33.3	29.3			Operating Expenses		38.4		39.2
		11.9	11.8			Operating Profit		7.1		6.9
		1.3	1.4			All Other Expenses (net)		.6		1.0
		10.6	10.4			Profit Before Taxes		6.5		5.9
						RATIOS				
		4.0	2.3					4.2		4.3
		1.9	1.8			Current		2.1		2.2
		1.4	1.5					1.6		1.6
		1.8	1.2					2.7		2.4
		.9	.9			Quick		1.1		1.3
		.5	.7					.7		.8
		38 9.5	41 8.9				43	8.5	33	11.2
		51 7.2	51 7.1			Sales/Receivables	58	6.3	49	7.4
		64 5.7	57 6.4				71	5.1	64	5.7
		92 4.0	40 9.2				63	5.8	68	5.4
		114 3.2	76 4.8			Cost of Sales/Inventory	95	3.8	120	3.0
		150 2.4	119 3.1				137	2.7	162	2.3
		21 17.8	4 82.7				21	17.5	19	19.0
		31 11.8	39 9.3			Cost of Sales/Payables	31	11.8	30	12.3
		54 6.8	57 6.5				51	7.1	48	7.7
		3.2	4.1					3.1		2.9
		5.5	6.5			Sales/Working Capital		5.2		4.4
		7.5	8.4					8.7		7.4
		18.1	99.9					46.1		15.0
		(19) 7.4	(13) 13.1			EBIT/Interest	(46)	4.9	(44)	5.0
		2.3	5.7					1.4		1.1
						Net Profit + Depr., Dep., Amort./Cur. Mat. L/T/D		20.6		8.5
							(16)	3.9	(13)	2.5
								1.0		-18.7
		.1	.3					.1		.1
		.3	.6			Fixed/Worth		.3		.3
		.5	-6.4					.9		.7
		.7	.7					.3		.3
		1.7	1.8			Debt/Worth		1.2		1.0
		2.4	-19.9					2.3		1.8
		65.5	84.1					44.0		35.8
		(18) 39.6	(11) 54.2			% Profit Before Taxes/Tangible Net Worth	(53)	21.3	(50)	13.9
		10.3	20.2					4.3		1.2
		36.2	32.2					21.0		17.8
		12.8	20.4			% Profit Before Taxes/Total Assets		7.4		6.5
		3.3	8.2					1.9		1.0
		44.8	12.7					33.0		28.9
		17.6	9.9			Sales/Net Fixed Assets		13.1		13.2
		8.7	8.0					7.4		7.9
		2.2	2.4					2.3		2.4
		1.9	1.7			Sales/Total Assets		1.7		1.6
		1.5	1.3					1.0		1.0
		.6	1.5					1.0		.7
		(18) 1.7	(13) 1.7			% Depr., Dep., Amort./Sales	(49)	2.0	(43)	1.5
		3.4	4.1					2.9		2.7
						% Officers', Directors' Owners' Comp/Sales		3.7		1.8
							(13)	7.4	(13)	3.5
								11.0		9.4
4744M	31509M	194712M	557001M		340160M	Net Sales ($)		1654460M		1573317M
1198M	11033M	108605M	331531M		320558M	Total Assets ($)		1382760M		1481991M

M = $ thousand   MM = $ million
See Pages 9 through 22 for Explanation of Ratios and Data

Comparative Historical Data				Current Data Sorted by Sales					
			Type of Statement						
13	15	7	Unqualified				1	2	4
15	10	9	Reviewed			1	6	2	
7	6	7	Compiled		4	1	1	1	
2	6	3	Tax Returns		2		1		
20	17	23	Other		2	1	4	8	8
4/1/08-3/31/09	4/1/09-3/31/10	4/1/10-3/31/11			8 (4/1-9/30/10)		41 (10/1/10-3/31/11)		
ALL	ALL	ALL		0-1MM	1-3MM	3-5MM	5-10MM	10-25MM	25MM & OVER
57	54	49	**NUMBER OF STATEMENTS**		8	3	13	13	12
%	%	%	**ASSETS**	%	%	%	%	%	%
16.0	14.4	10.5	Cash & Equivalents	DATA NOT AVAILABLE			7.9	8.7	9.7
28.4	24.6	25.8	Trade Receivables (net)				25.0	27.8	17.9
27.1	27.6	28.2	Inventory				34.8	31.1	15.1
4.8	2.5	6.3	All Other Current				.8	1.1	23.2
76.3	69.2	70.9	Total Current				68.4	68.7	65.9
12.7	15.5	19.0	Fixed Assets (net)				24.5	14.0	21.9
4.9	6.2	5.2	Intangibles (net)				3.5	8.4	8.1
6.1	9.1	4.9	All Other Non-Current				3.6	8.8	4.1
100.0	100.0	100.0	Total				100.0	100.0	100.0
			LIABILITIES						
7.4	7.7	9.1	Notes Payable-Short Term				9.2	9.1	1.4
1.3	3.6	2.6	Cur. Mat.-L.T.D.				4.2	3.8	1.6
11.7	10.7	13.4	Trade Payables				18.1	9.1	10.2
.3	.2	.3	Income Taxes Payable				.2	.4	.7
13.0	11.9	16.2	All Other Current				11.3	10.1	17.3
33.7	34.3	41.7	Total Current				43.1	32.5	31.2
6.2	11.4	11.8	Long-Term Debt				16.0	10.3	15.3
.3	.4	.3	Deferred Taxes				.0	.4	.7
4.1	6.4	8.7	All Other Non-Current				3.5	10.0	15.8
55.6	47.5	37.4	Net Worth				37.5	46.8	36.9
100.0	100.0	100.0	Total Liabilities & Net Worth				100.0	100.0	100.0
			INCOME DATA						
100.0	100.0	100.0	Net Sales				100.0	100.0	100.0
43.2	42.6	45.7	Gross Profit				48.0	45.1	40.5
36.4	37.8	35.6	Operating Expenses				36.9	30.2	32.4
6.8	4.8	10.1	Operating Profit				11.2	14.9	8.1
1.3	1.1	1.3	All Other Expenses (net)				1.2	1.4	1.5
5.6	3.7	8.8	Profit Before Taxes				10.0	13.5	6.5
			RATIOS						
4.4	3.3	2.8					3.7	3.6	2.9
2.3	2.1	1.9	Current				1.4	2.0	2.1
1.8	1.4	1.4					1.0	1.6	1.6
2.5	2.1	1.6					1.9	1.8	1.3
1.5	1.2	.9	Quick				.6	1.1	1.0
.9	.7	.5					.4	.9	.2
39 9.4	34 10.8	39 9.3					27 13.6	41 8.8	0 UND
48 7.6	49 7.4	49 7.5	Sales/Receivables				41 8.9	54 6.7	52 7.0
63 5.8	67 5.4	63 5.8					63 5.8	66 5.5	62 5.9
61 6.0	72 5.1	49 7.4					47 7.7	93 3.9	0 UND
101 3.6	107 3.4	104 3.5	Cost of Sales/Inventory				93 3.9	113 3.2	67 5.5
159 2.3	146 2.5	142 2.6					124 3.0	163 2.2	105 3.5
18 20.4	16 22.3	17 21.2					28 13.3	17 21.7	0 UND
24 15.3	32 11.3	37 10.0	Cost of Sales/Payables				38 9.5	31 11.9	43 8.5
39 9.3	44 8.3	64 5.7					103 3.5	61 6.0	75 4.9
2.9	2.9	3.6					4.0	3.6	3.2
4.3	4.6	6.1	Sales/Working Capital				6.5	5.7	5.4
8.5	10.4	8.7					NM	7.9	8.3
28.1	29.3	25.6					32.8	39.1	28.1
(45) 8.5	(45) 4.4	(40) 7.1	EBIT/Interest				(11) 4.8	(12) 8.2	(11) 8.1
1.5	1.1	3.2					.8	5.7	3.0
21.2	7.5	18.6							
(17) 7.8	(17) 3.0	(13) 5.2	Net Profit + Depr., Dep., Amort./Cur. Mat. L/T/D						
2.1	.8	3.0							
.1	.1	.2					.1	.1	.4
.2	.4	.5	Fixed/Worth				.4	.4	.7
.5	.8	1.0					2.6	.6	1.1
.3	.5	.7					.5	.6	1.0
.8	1.1	1.8	Debt/Worth				2.1	1.5	1.9
1.5	2.9	4.6					8.7	2.5	4.2
44.7	44.0	70.4					65.4	58.3	87.6
(54) 20.1	(47) 14.1	(41) 38.3	% Profit Before Taxes/Tangible Net Worth				(11) 43.4	(11) 40.8	(10) 50.5
4.4	1.4	10.1					2.4	36.1	14.0
26.5	16.1	28.5					39.6	31.4	31.8
11.5	6.3	11.1	% Profit Before Taxes/Total Assets				5.3	20.4	10.4
1.4	.0	3.0					-.6	12.7	3.8
67.8	26.5	29.1					30.1	71.0	11.1
16.7	12.9	13.6	Sales/Net Fixed Assets				18.5	16.7	8.6
10.6	6.5	7.5					7.5	9.6	6.3
2.5	2.3	2.5					2.7	2.2	2.5
1.8	1.6	1.9	Sales/Total Assets				1.9	1.9	1.6
1.4	1.2	1.5					1.6	1.4	1.3
.9	1.1	1.2					.5		1.5
(46) 1.8	(44) 2.1	(42) 1.7	% Depr., Dep., Amort./Sales				1.2		2.7
2.4	3.4	4.0					2.6		5.6
2.3	3.1								
(18) 5.3	(14) 5.9		% Officers', Directors' Owners' Comp/Sales						
9.1	9.6								
1762725M	1390867M	1128126M	Net Sales ($)		15303M	13130M	99370M	216298M	784025M
1316941M	1165929M	772925M	Total Assets ($)		7299M	11926M	51773M	139005M	562922M

M = $ thousand MM = $ million

See Pages 9 through 22 for Explanation of Ratios and Data

Current Data Sorted by Assets   Comparative Historical Data

0-500M	500M-2MM	2-10MM	10-50MM	50-100MM	100-250MM	Type of Statement	4/1/06-3/31/07 ALL	4/1/07-3/31/08 ALL
		4	4	5	5	Unqualified	20	15
		8	3			Reviewed	10	11
1	1	2				Compiled	3	4
	2	5				Tax Returns	5	2
1	3	12	10	2	2	Other	20	20
	13 (4/1-9/30/10)		57 (10/1/10-3/31/11)					
2	6	31	17	7	7	NUMBER OF STATEMENTS	58	52
%	%	%	%	%	%	**ASSETS**	%	%
		13.2	14.4			Cash & Equivalents	11.8	11.3
		28.1	23.9			Trade Receivables (net)	26.6	23.8
		29.3	19.7			Inventory	24.9	25.7
		5.0	3.0			All Other Current	1.7	3.1
		75.5	61.1			Total Current	65.0	63.9
		12.4	23.0			Fixed Assets (net)	13.8	15.5
		5.6	10.2			Intangibles (net)	11.8	14.6
		6.5	5.8			All Other Non-Current	9.4	6.0
		100.0	100.0			Total	100.0	100.0
						LIABILITIES		
		9.2	4.1			Notes Payable-Short Term	8.1	5.0
		2.2	1.5			Cur. Mat.-L.T.D.	1.4	3.0
		14.4	6.4			Trade Payables	11.8	9.6
		.3	.4			Income Taxes Payable	.6	.5
		13.4	12.5			All Other Current	14.3	12.6
		39.4	25.0			Total Current	36.1	30.8
		6.9	10.1			Long-Term Debt	9.4	10.8
		.3	.7			Deferred Taxes	.8	.6
		9.6	1.4			All Other Non-Current	6.5	5.1
		43.8	62.8			Net Worth	47.2	52.7
		100.0	100.0			Total Liabilities & Net Worth	100.0	100.0
						INCOME DATA		
		100.0	100.0			Net Sales	100.0	100.0
		47.6	44.3			Gross Profit	45.6	47.0
		40.1	34.3			Operating Expenses	39.5	41.0
		7.6	10.0			Operating Profit	6.1	6.0
		.9	.7			All Other Expenses (net)	1.1	1.3
		6.6	9.3			Profit Before Taxes	5.0	4.7
						RATIOS		
		3.9	3.5				3.7	3.2
		2.3	3.1			Current	2.2	2.3
		1.2	2.1				1.4	1.6
		2.4	2.4				2.1	1.8
		1.3	2.0			Quick	1.2	1.2
		.5	.7				.7	.9
		39 9.4	45 8.2				46 8.0	46 8.0
		61 6.0	50 7.3			Sales/Receivables	58 6.2	53 6.9
		77 4.7	77 4.7				70 5.2	65 5.6
		69 5.3	47 7.8				62 5.8	72 5.1
		110 3.3	68 5.4			Cost of Sales/Inventory	102 3.6	110 3.3
		166 2.2	119 3.1				146 2.5	151 2.4
		29 12.6	19 18.9				22 16.2	22 16.7
		45 8.1	24 14.9			Cost of Sales/Payables	44 8.4	38 9.5
		80 4.6	36 10.1				62 5.9	57 6.4
		2.5	2.4				3.0	3.1
		3.5	3.7			Sales/Working Capital	4.8	4.4
		18.0	5.2				10.4	9.6
		12.8	69.5				33.4	20.5
		(23) 7.3	(13) 8.8			EBIT/Interest	(50) 6.4	(49) 6.6
		1.9	3.4				2.1	1.8
							40.0	20.2
						Net Profit + Depr., Dep., Amort./Cur. Mat. L/T/D	(18) 5.1	(23) 7.6
							1.2	.9
		.1	.2				.1	.1
		.3	.4			Fixed/Worth	.3	.3
		.7	.6				1.5	1.2
		.6	.3				.4	.5
		1.3	.6			Debt/Worth	1.1	.8
		4.1	1.3				5.0	4.9
		47.1	48.1				36.2	44.4
		(28) 17.7	(16) 24.6			% Profit Before Taxes/Tangible Net Worth	(48) 22.5	(43) 18.9
		8.3	11.0				4.3	2.3
		19.3	17.6				17.0	18.1
		8.2	11.4			% Profit Before Taxes/Total Assets	8.9	8.0
		3.4	5.5				2.4	1.8
		66.6	14.9				28.3	33.7
		20.7	6.7			Sales/Net Fixed Assets	16.6	16.1
		7.8	3.5				7.5	7.4
		2.5	1.8				2.2	2.3
		1.6	1.5			Sales/Total Assets	1.6	1.4
		1.4	1.0				1.1	1.1
		.4	1.3				1.0	.8
		(27) 1.0	2.1			% Depr., Dep., Amort./Sales	(44) 1.7	(45) 1.9
		2.2	2.7				2.7	3.0
							2.1	3.1
						% Officers', Directors' Owners' Comp/Sales	(12) 5.0	(12) 6.9
							12.4	11.5
2307M	21265M	285228M	669723M	487952M	1096872M	Net Sales ($)	2233156M	1977478M
781M	7720M	155026M	436182M	424938M	1112423M	Total Assets ($)	2001228M	1868804M

M = $ thousand   MM = $ million
See Pages 9 through 22 for Explanation of Ratios and Data

Comparative Historical Data / Current Data Sorted by Sales

			Type of Statement	0-1MM	1-3MM	3-5MM	5-10MM	10-25MM	25MM & OVER
14	21	18	Unqualified				3	2	13
3	6	11	Reviewed		2		3	5	1
4	1	4	Compiled	2			2		
7	3	7	Tax Returns		1	1	4	1	
25	25	30	Other	1	2	1	9	6	11
4/1/08-3/31/09 ALL	4/1/09-3/31/10 ALL	4/1/10-3/31/11 ALL		1	13 (4/1-9/30/10)			57 (10/1/10-3/31/11)	
53	56	70	**NUMBER OF STATEMENTS**	1	5	4	21	14	25
%	%	%	**ASSETS**	%	%	%	%	%	%
13.8	17.5	15.9	Cash & Equivalents				13.9	12.9	20.2
25.2	23.6	24.2	Trade Receivables (net)				28.0	31.1	19.8
26.1	24.7	24.5	Inventory				25.7	28.0	16.9
3.0	1.6	3.5	All Other Current				3.7	5.1	2.7
68.2	67.5	68.1	Total Current				71.3	77.0	59.6
17.1	15.3	15.5	Fixed Assets (net)				13.1	14.9	18.1
9.9	11.6	11.2	Intangibles (net)				9.5	4.8	16.9
4.8	5.6	5.2	All Other Non-Current				6.2	3.3	5.4
100.0	100.0	100.0	Total				100.0	100.0	100.0
			LIABILITIES						
5.3	5.6	6.4	Notes Payable-Short Term				8.6	6.0	3.1
3.1	1.6	1.8	Cur. Mat.-L.T.D.				.6	1.9	1.5
8.4	10.3	11.9	Trade Payables				14.8	13.8	7.5
.6	.1	.3	Income Taxes Payable				.4	.5	.1
12.7	10.7	11.7	All Other Current				11.2	16.7	12.3
30.0	28.3	32.1	Total Current				35.6	38.9	24.6
7.7	12.7	7.5	Long-Term Debt				6.0	2.3	10.8
.3	.6	.5	Deferred Taxes				.1	.8	.8
5.2	6.5	6.0	All Other Non-Current				11.9	4.1	3.3
56.8	52.0	54.0	Net Worth				46.4	53.8	60.5
100.0	100.0	100.0	Total Liabilities & Net Worth				100.0	100.0	100.0
			INCOME DATA						
100.0	100.0	100.0	Net Sales				100.0	100.0	100.0
47.1	47.0	46.5	Gross Profit				44.2	43.1	51.0
43.4	41.5	38.5	Operating Expenses				37.4	35.2	41.2
3.7	5.5	8.0	Operating Profit				6.8	7.9	9.8
.9	1.2	.7	All Other Expenses (net)				.6	.5	1.0
2.8	4.3	7.3	Profit Before Taxes				6.1	7.5	8.8
			RATIOS						
4.3	4.5	3.7					4.1	3.5	3.4
2.4	2.7	2.6	Current				2.3	2.6	2.6
1.6	1.8	1.3					1.3	1.2	1.9
2.4	2.7	2.4					2.7	2.2	2.4
1.2	1.6	1.7	Quick				1.3	1.4	2.0
.8	1.0	.7					.5	.7	.9
40 9.2	47 7.8	39 9.3					38 9.6	37 10.0	48 7.6
50 7.3	54 6.8	51 7.2	Sales/Receivables				66 5.5	51 7.2	52 7.1
62 5.9	64 5.7	71 5.1					81 4.5	72 5.1	66 5.5
69 5.3	66 5.6	63 5.8					70 5.2	43 8.6	71 5.2
99 3.7	104 3.5	100 3.6	Cost of Sales/Inventory				110 3.3	66 5.6	97 3.8
152 2.4	149 2.4	147 2.5					161 2.3	158 2.3	128 2.9
23 15.5	25 14.8	24 15.0					25 14.6	17 21.5	25 14.5
33 11.1	35 10.4	38 9.6	Cost of Sales/Payables				44 8.3	29 12.7	38 9.6
50 7.2	60 6.1	64 5.7					64 5.7	67 5.5	51 7.1
3.0	2.4	2.5					2.3	3.1	2.3
4.3	3.8	3.7	Sales/Working Capital				3.2	3.8	3.5
8.0	6.3	14.7					16.4	19.0	5.1
46.9	12.6	21.1					9.5	48.6	43.7
(47) 5.9	(49) 3.2	(53) 8.8	EBIT/Interest				(15) 6.4	(11) 12.5	(20) 7.0
.6	-2.2	2.1					1.9	4.2	-4.9
4.9	5.5	8.0	Net Profit + Depr., Dep.,						
(17) 2.4	(15) 2.4	(15) 4.6	Amort./Cur. Mat. L/T/D						
-.3	-1.5	2.8							
.1	.2	.1					.1	.1	.2
.3	.3	.3	Fixed/Worth				.5	.4	.3
.6	.8	.7					.6	.5	.7
.3	.3	.4					.6	.3	.4
.8	.9	.9	Debt/Worth				1.5	1.1	.7
1.7	2.7	3.1					3.5	2.8	1.2
32.8	36.8	42.8	% Profit Before Taxes/Tangible				47.2	64.4	38.3
(49) 10.0	(48) 8.8	(63) 20.3	Net Worth				(19) 24.3	18.8	(22) 20.7
-7.5	-8.0	6.4					10.2	8.4	-3.6
16.2	13.6	17.3	% Profit Before Taxes/Total				18.3	16.4	18.7
4.4	5.8	10.4	Assets				10.2	10.1	11.4
-2.3	-3.0	3.5					2.8	3.3	1.0
35.0	27.1	34.1					75.5	73.8	14.0
11.0	13.0	13.2	Sales/Net Fixed Assets				18.1	18.5	7.7
5.9	5.1	5.4					5.5	6.9	4.4
2.4	1.9	2.3					2.1	2.7	1.5
1.7	1.5	1.5	Sales/Total Assets				1.5	2.3	1.2
1.1	1.0	1.1					1.2	1.5	1.0
1.2	1.4	.9					.7	.2	1.7
(40) 2.1	(44) 2.3	(55) 2.0	% Depr., Dep., Amort./Sales				(16) 1.8	(13) .8	(20) 2.7
3.8	3.6	3.0					2.3	2.2	3.4
2.6	3.2	2.9	% Officers', Directors'						
(10) 5.2	(12) 6.9	(15) 5.8	Owners' Comp/Sales						
8.1	20.7	13.8							
2085476M	2128205M	2563347M	Net Sales ($)	984M	10835M	12960M	161672M	213863M	2163033M
1847969M	1901666M	2137070M	Total Assets ($)	353M	6654M	7924M	115224M	106748M	1900167M

M = $ thousand   MM = $ million
See Pages 9 through 22 for Explanation of Ratios and Data

Current Data Sorted by Assets   Comparative Historical Data

	0-500M	500M-2MM	2-10MM	10-50MM	50-100MM	100-250MM	Type of Statement	4/1/06-3/31/07 ALL	4/1/07-3/31/08 ALL
			6	8	4	5	Unqualified	27	23
		1	22	9			Reviewed	26	24
		6	6	3			Compiled	11	5
		3	1	1			Tax Returns	1	4
	1	10	12	13	2	3	Other	40	42
		17 (4/1-9/30/10)		99 (10/1/10-3/31/11)					
NUMBER OF STATEMENTS	1	20	47	34	6	8		105	98

ASSETS

Item	500M-2MM %	2-10MM %	10-50MM %	4/1/06-3/31/07 %	4/1/07-3/31/08 %
Cash & Equivalents	13.2	13.2	11.3	12.5	10.1
Trade Receivables (net)	33.9	27.2	27.1	29.5	28.4
Inventory	18.8	24.7	23.7	26.1	27.0
All Other Current	.7	6.1	8.2	3.7	3.6
Total Current	66.5	71.2	70.4	71.7	69.2
Fixed Assets (net)	16.3	16.8	17.9	17.3	14.1
Intangibles (net)	4.5	8.8	6.1	5.9	8.5
All Other Non-Current	12.7	3.3	5.6	5.1	8.2
Total	100.0	100.0	100.0	100.0	100.0

LIABILITIES

Item	500M-2MM	2-10MM	10-50MM	4/1/06-3/31/07	4/1/07-3/31/08
Notes Payable-Short Term	12.0	9.7	5.7	11.5	8.2
Cur. Mat.-L.T.D.	.4	3.1	2.2	3.1	2.8
Trade Payables	10.7	11.2	8.0	12.7	10.7
Income Taxes Payable	.0	.9	.3	.7	.3
All Other Current	20.7	15.3	14.8	14.2	13.6
Total Current	43.8	40.1	31.1	42.3	35.5
Long-Term Debt	9.5	7.1	7.7	9.3	9.0
Deferred Taxes	.3	.5	.6	.4	.4
All Other Non-Current	8.5	4.1	3.2	4.0	4.9
Net Worth	37.9	48.2	57.4	44.0	50.2
Total Liabilities & Net Worth	100.0	100.0	100.0	100.0	100.0

INCOME DATA

Item	500M-2MM	2-10MM	10-50MM	4/1/06-3/31/07	4/1/07-3/31/08
Net Sales	100.0	100.0	100.0	100.0	100.0
Gross Profit	48.6	41.3	36.1	41.4	41.6
Operating Expenses	42.3	32.0	27.9	33.8	31.8
Operating Profit	6.3	9.3	8.1	7.6	9.9
All Other Expenses (net)	.7	1.1	.5	1.0	1.2
Profit Before Taxes	5.6	8.2	7.7	6.6	8.7

RATIOS

Ratio	500M-2MM	2-10MM	10-50MM	4/1/06-3/31/07	4/1/07-3/31/08
Current	3.0	2.7	4.2	3.1	3.8
	1.8	1.9	2.4	1.9	2.3
	1.2	1.3	1.4	1.2	1.4
Quick	2.3	1.7	2.7	2.1	2.4
	1.4	1.0	1.1	1.0	1.2
	.6	.6	.7	.6	.7
Sales/Receivables	(35) 10.5	(38) 9.6	(45) 8.1	(41) 9.0	(39) 9.5
	(44) 8.3	(48) 7.7	(55) 6.7	(59) 6.2	(53) 6.9
	(60) 6.1	(65) 5.7	(78) 4.7	(81) 4.5	(77) 4.7
Cost of Sales/Inventory	(4) 89.3	(48) 7.6	(46) 7.9	(48) 7.6	(44) 8.2
	(40) 9.2	(81) 4.5	(100) 3.7	(104) 3.5	(102) 3.6
	(108) 3.4	(129) 2.8	(140) 2.6	(148) 2.5	(148) 2.5
Cost of Sales/Payables	(15) 24.6	(18) 20.0	(16) 22.5	(19) 18.8	(14) 25.3
	(24) 15.1	(32) 11.3	(26) 14.1	(38) 9.7	(28) 13.2
	(51) 7.1	(49) 7.5	(41) 9.0	(59) 6.2	(46) 7.9
Sales/Working Capital	4.6	3.7	2.6	3.1	3.0
	11.0	6.5	4.3	5.6	5.3
	39.7	12.9	9.8	24.1	12.9
EBIT/Interest	69.0	88.2	27.2	14.9	20.7
	(15) 8.2	(41) 7.4	(27) 9.2	(91) 5.1	(76) 6.1
	.6	2.0	1.9	1.7	2.2
Net Profit + Depr., Dep., Amort./Cur. Mat. L/T/D		8.0	6.5	12.3	14.7
		(17) 3.7	(13) 1.7	(30) 3.5	(26) 5.4
		1.8	.9	1.7	2.0
Fixed/Worth	.0	.2	.1	.2	.1
	.2	.4	.4	.4	.3
	1.6	1.2	.9	.9	.8
Debt/Worth	.4	.6	.3	.5	.4
	.9	1.4	.7	1.5	1.0
	4.1	4.5	1.9	3.9	3.3
% Profit Before Taxes/Tangible Net Worth	85.3	67.5	51.9	42.9	55.1
	(17) 37.5	(45) 29.1	(32) 18.1	(95) 30.4	(86) 26.6
	3.5	5.7	4.0	9.1	12.4
% Profit Before Taxes/Total Assets	42.9	27.2	19.4	17.8	26.2
	9.5	10.8	10.0	9.6	10.9
	-.8	1.9	1.8	2.2	4.1
Sales/Net Fixed Assets	80.2	32.4	19.4	28.4	45.7
	49.5	16.0	11.8	12.7	17.9
	12.1	7.7	5.7	6.8	7.9
Sales/Total Assets	3.6	2.5	1.9	2.4	2.5
	2.6	1.7	1.6	1.6	1.7
	1.6	1.3	1.2	1.3	1.3
% Depr., Dep., Amort./Sales	.5	.8	1.2	.9	.8
	(13) .8	(46) 1.5	(32) 1.3	(85) 1.7	(78) 1.6
	2.1	2.3	1.8	2.8	2.3
% Officers', Directors', Owners' Comp/Sales	4.2	2.5		4.2	2.7
	(10) 6.3	(17) 3.9		(16) 6.2	(17) 4.8
	12.4	5.6		9.4	6.3

	0-500M	500M-2MM	2-10MM	10-50MM	50-100MM	100-250MM		4/1/06-3/31/07	4/1/07-3/31/08
Net Sales ($)	1574M	71512M	468641M	1179019M	446919M	1310759M		2669268M	3079775M
Total Assets ($)	330M	24137M	253773M	769140M	371030M	1228494M		1962524M	2232572M

Comparative Historical Data | | Current Data Sorted by Sales

							Type of Statement						
	18		23		23		Unqualified			1	2	6	14
	27		27		32		Reviewed			4	10	12	6
	12		11		15		Compiled		5	4	2	2	2
	4		8		5		Tax Returns			2	2		1
	51		34		41		Other		6	5	7	11	12
	4/1/08-3/31/09 ALL		4/1/09-3/31/10 ALL		4/1/10-3/31/11 ALL			0-1MM	17 (4/1-9/30/10) 1-3MM	3-5MM	99 (10/1/10-3/31/11) 5-10MM	10-25MM	25MM & OVER
	112		103		116		**NUMBER OF STATEMENTS**	11	16	23	31	35
	%		%		%			%	%	%	%	%	%
	11.0		11.4		12.6		**ASSETS** Cash & Equivalents	13.0	14.1	14.7	13.5	9.5
	24.4		25.1		27.2		Trade Receivables (net)	29.3	33.9	24.1	28.6	24.2
	27.9		25.4		22.3		Inventory	18.1	22.0	24.6	20.8	23.6
	4.8		4.7		6.2		All Other Current	4.3	1.3	7.4	6.3	8.3
	68.1		66.5		68.3		Total Current	64.7	71.4	70.9	69.3	65.6
	16.9		19.1		16.9		Fixed Assets (net)	15.1	16.0	16.3	16.7	18.6
	7.3		9.2		8.9		Intangibles (net)	8.1	5.4	8.1	10.5	9.8
	7.7		5.1		5.8		All Other Non-Current	12.2	7.2	4.7	3.5	6.1
	100.0		100.0		100.0		Total	100.0	100.0	100.0	100.0	100.0
	8.9		9.1		8.3		**LIABILITIES** Notes Payable-Short Term	16.4	10.1	11.6	4.9	5.9
	1.7		2.7		2.1		Cur. Mat.-L.T.D.	.1	4.0	2.0	2.1	2.0
	10.5		10.3		9.7		Trade Payables	8.1	10.6	10.1	11.1	8.4
	.4		1.2		.5		Income Taxes Payable	.1	.0	1.2	.7	.3
	13.6		13.4		16.5		All Other Current	28.8	9.1	14.4	16.5	17.4
	35.0		36.7		37.2		Total Current	53.4	33.7	39.4	35.3	34.0
	9.3		11.3		7.9		Long-Term Debt	11.0	5.7	6.2	9.8	7.4
	.6		.5		.6		Deferred Taxes	.4	1.0	.0	.5	1.0
	4.6		9.3		5.2		All Other Non-Current	7.8	5.7	3.7	6.3	4.1
	50.5		42.2		49.1		Net Worth	27.3	53.9	50.7	48.1	53.5
	100.0		100.0		100.0		Total Liabilities & Net Worth	100.0	100.0	100.0	100.0	100.0
	100.0		100.0		100.0		**INCOME DATA** Net Sales	100.0	100.0	100.0	100.0	100.0
	44.2		42.9		41.3		Gross Profit	56.0	45.1	40.7	39.5	36.8
	36.7		37.8		32.6		Operating Expenses	51.8	37.0	32.3	28.2	28.5
	7.5		5.1		8.7		Operating Profit	4.3	8.1	8.5	11.2	8.3
	1.0		.8		1.0		All Other Expenses (net)	1.8	.7	.9	1.5	.6
	6.5		4.3		7.7		Profit Before Taxes	2.5	7.4	7.5	9.7	7.8

						RATIOS						
	3.7		3.5		3.1		2.5	3.6	3.1	3.1	3.6
	2.2		1.9		2.1	Current	1.5	2.4	1.8	2.1	2.1
	1.3		1.4		1.3		1.1	1.3	1.3	1.4	1.2
	2.3		2.1		2.2		1.9	2.4	1.7	2.4	2.1
	1.1	(102)	1.0		1.0	Quick	1.3	1.5	.9	1.1	.9
	.6		.6		.6		.5	.6	.6	.6	.6
31	11.7	35	10.3	39	9.3		42	8.8	42	8.8	32	11.4	42	8.8	41	9.0
47	7.8	50	7.3	49	7.5	Sales/Receivables	44	8.2	63	5.8	38	9.6	50	7.2	49	7.4
61	6.0	67	5.5	68	5.4		61	6.0	77	4.7	63	5.8	75	4.9	61	5.9
56	6.5	40	9.1	34	10.7		0	UND	31	11.8	48	7.6	30	12.1	44	8.4
117	3.1	94	3.9	78	4.7	Cost of Sales/Inventory	92	4.0	75	4.9	78	4.7	72	5.1	84	4.3
160	2.3	148	2.5	130	2.8		113	3.2	132	2.8	129	2.8	141	2.6	132	2.8
16	22.8	15	25.0	16	22.5		15	24.9	20	18.7	11	33.6	14	26.5	17	21.9
29	12.5	32	11.3	31	11.6	Cost of Sales/Payables	40	9.0	31	11.7	32	11.4	32	11.5	31	11.7
57	6.4	52	7.0	45	8.1		52	7.0	53	6.9	46	7.9	46	8.0	40	9.1
	3.1		3.5		3.5		4.6	3.1	3.7	3.3	2.8
	5.3		5.2		5.7	Sales/Working Capital	8.7	4.9	6.5	5.6	4.5
	17.3		11.1		21.8		26.4	9.2	30.2	12.1	24.1
	27.7		13.7		56.3			86.3	100.3	21.7	44.0
(86)	6.1	(83)	4.0	(96)	7.4	EBIT/Interest	(15)	8.2	(19)	7.3	(25)	9.2	(29)	9.3
	2.4		.8		1.9			1.9	2.2	1.9	1.6
	13.7		5.9		9.7	Net Profit + Depr., Dep., Amort./Cur. Mat. L/T/D				10.8	21.0
(26)	4.0	(22)	2.1	(36)	4.1				(15)	3.6	(14)	4.9
	2.0		1.6		1.6					1.2	1.9
	.1		.1		.1		.0	.0	.1	.2	.2
	.4		.5		.4	Fixed/Worth	.2	.2	.4	.5	.4
	.7		1.5		1.2		1.8	.9	.9	1.4	1.0
	.3		.5		.5		.7	.4	.5	.5	.4
	1.1		1.2		1.1	Debt/Worth	1.8	.7	1.0	1.8	.9
	3.1		3.8		3.7		6.1	2.7	4.5	9.4	3.2
	47.9		33.8		53.5			54.2	90.5	58.2	50.2
(103)	20.9	(87)	14.4	(105)	23.4	% Profit Before Taxes/Tangible Net Worth		17.8	(21)	44.2	(27)	25.4	(32)	21.7
	10.8		1.9		5.6			5.6	5.4	4.0	11.3
	18.9		15.2		22.3		16.4	29.2	34.6	25.9	17.5
	10.5		5.3		10.6	% Profit Before Taxes/Total Assets	2.6	5.2	10.5	12.2	12.7
	3.9		.3		1.6		-2.2	2.3	1.4	1.6	1.9
	34.4		26.4		38.2		68.8	65.0	49.8	23.0	17.5
	14.3		11.9		13.8	Sales/Net Fixed Assets	19.2	29.7	23.1	13.7	9.0
	6.4		6.5		6.8		11.6	7.9	7.7	8.5	4.6
	2.3		2.4		2.4		2.9	2.9	2.8	2.5	2.0
	1.7		1.6		1.6	Sales/Total Assets	1.6	1.9	2.0	1.6	1.6
	1.2		1.2		1.2		1.4	1.1	1.3	1.3	1.1
	.7		1.0		.8			.5	.7	1.0	1.2
(85)	1.6	(83)	1.8	(103)	1.3	% Depr., Dep., Amort./Sales	(13)	1.0	(21)	1.2	(30)	1.2	(32)	1.6
	3.0		2.9		2.3			3.7	2.4	1.7	2.9
	3.4		2.7		2.7				2.7		
(23)	4.2	(27)	4.7	(32)	4.5	% Officers', Directors' Owners' Comp/Sales			(12)	3.6		
	8.8		7.8		6.7				6.2		

3340485M	2876376M	3478424M	Net Sales ($)	22516M	63732M	171149M	517493M	2703534M
2627305M	2433800M	2646904M	Total Assets ($)	12708M	43821M	95771M	372599M	2122005M

M = $ thousand   MM = $ million
See Pages 9 through 22 for Explanation of Ratios and Data

Current Data Sorted by Assets   Comparative Historical Data

Type of Statement	0-500M	500M-2MM	2-10MM	10-50MM	50-100MM	100-250MM	4/1/06-3/31/07 ALL	4/1/07-3/31/08 ALL
Unqualified			1	6	1	2	12	11
Reviewed		1	7	3			3	4
Compiled	1		3				3	3
Tax Returns	2	3	6	4	3	1	5	7
Other							11	10
period label		8 (4/1-9/30/10)		36 (10/1/10-3/31/11)				
NUMBER OF STATEMENTS	3	4	17	13	4	3	34	35
ASSETS	%	%	%	%	%	%	%	%
Cash & Equivalents			9.4	8.8			8.2	11.0
Trade Receivables (net)			19.3	23.8			27.3	24.2
Inventory			38.4	30.9			38.7	40.3
All Other Current			3.9	2.7			1.9	1.4
Total Current			71.0	66.2			76.0	77.0
Fixed Assets (net)			15.3	22.0			17.4	13.9
Intangibles (net)			2.8	5.9			2.3	5.1
All Other Non-Current			10.9	5.9			4.2	4.0
Total			100.0	100.0			100.0	100.0
LIABILITIES								
Notes Payable-Short Term			16.6	10.5			10.3	9.5
Cur. Mat.-L.T.D.			1.4	1.4			2.9	3.1
Trade Payables			13.7	8.3			18.1	14.2
Income Taxes Payable			2.2	.1			.7	.8
All Other Current			11.5	10.7			9.3	11.4
Total Current			45.4	30.9			41.2	39.0
Long-Term Debt			9.7	13.6			14.8	11.3
Deferred Taxes			.1	.4			.3	.3
All Other Non-Current			2.2	4.1			9.3	7.1
Net Worth			42.6	50.9			34.5	42.2
Total Liabilities & Net Worth			100.0	100.0			100.0	100.0
INCOME DATA								
Net Sales			100.0	100.0			100.0	100.0
Gross Profit			42.2	45.5			42.1	42.1
Operating Expenses			37.6	39.5			35.3	35.3
Operating Profit			4.6	5.9			6.8	6.7
All Other Expenses (net)			.9	.7			1.1	1.4
Profit Before Taxes			3.7	5.2			5.6	5.3
RATIOS								
Current			2.9; 1.6; 1.2	3.5; 2.7; 1.6			2.9; 2.0; 1.3	3.3; 2.0; 1.4
Quick			1.1; .6; .3	2.1; .9; .7			1.5; .8; .5	1.3; .9; .7
Sales/Receivables			5 71.6; 34 10.8; 53 6.9	42 8.8; 59 6.2; 64 5.7			32 11.3; 49 7.5; 66 5.6	21 17.8; 43 8.4; 65 5.6
Cost of Sales/Inventory			41 8.9; 108 3.4; 209 1.7	76 4.8; 148 2.5; 175 2.1			60 6.1; 137 2.7; 168 2.2	96 3.8; 130 2.8; 183 2.0
Cost of Sales/Payables			28 12.9; 34 10.6; 58 6.3	24 15.3; 28 13.1; 55 6.6			26 14.2; 48 7.6; 82 4.5	21 17.2; 31 11.9; 54 6.8
Sales/Working Capital			3.7; 6.6; NM	2.2; 4.3; 8.9			4.0; 5.8; 19.2	3.5; 6.0; 8.8
EBIT/Interest			15.0; (16) 1.8; -.1	11.6; (11) 5.4; 1.5			19.1; (30) 4.5; 1.5	20.6; (31) 4.1; 1.3
Net Profit + Depr., Dep., Amort./Cur. Mat. L/T/D								
Fixed/Worth			.1; .2; .7	.2; .6; .9			.1; .4; 1.6	.1; .4; .8
Debt/Worth			.7; 1.9; 3.2	.5; 1.1; 3.1			.7; 1.5; 4.7	.8; 1.6; 3.5
% Profit Before Taxes/Tangible Net Worth			54.1; 8.4; -9.6	56.4; 8.3; 2.9			52.3; (30) 25.7; 10.5	50.8; (32) 27.6; 7.3
% Profit Before Taxes/Total Assets			11.2; 4.0; -2.7	13.1; 4.9; 1.3			23.7; 10.6; 1.1	21.5; 11.9; 1.1
Sales/Net Fixed Assets			64.2; 28.7; 8.5	13.8; 7.0; 5.4			42.7; 18.9; 9.0	49.6; 22.5; 7.6
Sales/Total Assets			2.7; 1.9; 1.3	1.9; 1.7; 1.2			2.4; 2.1; 1.7	2.6; 2.1; 1.5
% Depr., Dep., Amort./Sales			.4; (13) 1.1; 3.0	1.2; 2.7; 3.6			.6; (27) 1.1; 2.8	.8; (27) 1.2; 2.4
% Officers', Directors' Owners' Comp/Sales							1.4; (12) 2.3; 4.5	1.7; (13) 2.6; 5.0
Net Sales ($)	1970M	13199M	177767M	428815M	564578M	485107M	1752679M	1342859M
Total Assets ($)	828M	3732M	87329M	290999M	332426M	369887M	970361M	701190M

M = $ thousand   MM = $ million
See Pages 9 through 22 for Explanation of Ratios and Data

Comparative Historical Data   Current Data Sorted by Sales

Type of Statement	4/1/08-3/31/09 ALL	4/1/09-3/31/10 ALL	4/1/10-3/31/11 ALL		0-1MM	1-3MM	3-5MM	5-10MM	10-25MM	25MM & OVER
Unqualified	10	6	10						3	7
Reviewed	5	6	11				4	2	2	3
Compiled	5	1	4		1	1	1			
Tax Returns	8	8								
Other	15	19	19		2	2		2	5	8
						8 (4/1-9/30/10)			36 (10/1/10-3/31/11)	
NUMBER OF STATEMENTS	43	40	44		3	3	5	5	10	18
ASSETS	%	%	%		%	%	%	%	%	%
Cash & Equivalents	7.3	9.7	8.3						12.4	6.5
Trade Receivables (net)	23.4	21.8	22.9						26.6	26.1
Inventory	41.0	36.2	33.9						29.5	29.3
All Other Current	4.0	4.4	3.1						6.3	3.3
Total Current	75.7	72.1	68.1						74.7	65.3
Fixed Assets (net)	16.1	17.6	17.1						16.1	17.4
Intangibles (net)	4.2	6.1	6.8						2.6	13.2
All Other Non-Current	4.0	4.2	7.9						6.6	4.1
Total	100.0	100.0	100.0						100.0	100.0
LIABILITIES										
Notes Payable-Short Term	12.1	11.9	13.6						12.3	10.6
Cur. Mat.-L.T.D.	3.8	4.8	1.6						1.4	1.6
Trade Payables	15.2	10.6	12.7						12.2	11.1
Income Taxes Payable	.5	.0	1.0						.0	.1
All Other Current	8.5	8.4	11.6						10.0	10.0
Total Current	40.2	35.7	40.5						35.9	33.3
Long-Term Debt	10.8	15.0	17.0						10.0	16.4
Deferred Taxes	.4	.3	.2						.6	.1
All Other Non-Current	6.8	5.4	3.8						2.1	4.6
Net Worth	41.9	43.6	38.4						51.5	45.6
Total Liabilties & Net Worth	100.0	100.0	100.0						100.0	100.0
INCOME DATA										
Net Sales	100.0	100.0	100.0						100.0	100.0
Gross Profit	43.6	41.6	42.4						39.0	37.3
Operating Expenses	38.0	38.4	37.3						32.7	31.1
Operating Profit	5.5	3.2	5.0						6.3	6.1
All Other Expenses (net)	1.5	1.6	1.1						.6	1.0
Profit Before Taxes	4.0	1.6	4.0						5.7	5.2
RATIOS										
Current	3.0	4.4	3.3						4.1	3.6
	1.9	1.9	1.7						2.9	1.7
	1.4	1.2	1.3						1.4	1.4
Quick	1.4	2.3	1.5						2.8	1.8
	.6	.8	.8						1.2	.9
	.4	.4	.4						.5	.7
Sales/Receivables	23 16.1	27 13.5	28 13.2						27 13.4	49 7.4
	39 9.5	44 8.4	49 7.5						45 8.0	53 6.9
	60 6.1	59 6.2	59 6.2						58 6.3	62 5.8
Cost of Sales/Inventory	65 5.6	63 5.8	66 5.5						53 6.8	68 5.3
	132 2.8	112 3.3	111 3.3						87 4.2	114 3.2
	182 2.0	187 1.9	168 2.2						157 2.3	149 2.5
Cost of Sales/Payables	23 15.8	21 17.1	27 13.7						25 14.9	26 14.1
	38 9.6	29 12.6	35 10.5						30 12.2	32 11.4
	70 5.2	45 8.2	63 5.8						32 11.4	61 6.0
Sales/Working Capital	3.4	2.9	3.1						3.8	2.6
	7.0	5.8	7.9						5.7	7.9
	14.0	15.9	17.5						13.8	11.2
EBIT/Interest	9.1	12.6	14.6							16.0
	(39) 2.6	(38) 2.4	(41) 3.8						(17)	4.4
	1.3	-1.7	.4							2.1
Net Profit + Depr., Dep., Amort./Cur. Mat. L/T/D	5.8		25.2							
	(13) 1.2		(14) .9							
	.3		-.4							
Fixed/Worth	.1	.2	.1						.2	.2
	.4	.4	.5						.3	.8
	1.0	.9	1.0						.6	1.1
Debt/Worth	.7	.5	.9						.4	.8
	1.6	1.7	1.9						.9	1.9
	3.2	4.5	3.9						2.4	6.9
% Profit Before Taxes/Tangible Net Worth	48.1	15.4	68.4						48.1	67.2
	(40) 14.5	(35) 4.9	(39) 8.8						7.0	(16) 10.1
	1.6	-14.7	-2.7						-8.7	3.8
% Profit Before Taxes/Total Assets	16.8	6.2	10.6						27.0	10.5
	5.8	3.2	4.6						3.5	5.6
	.9	-4.0	-1.1						-3.5	1.4
Sales/Net Fixed Assets	35.8	47.1	62.1						49.0	25.1
	22.5	12.2	14.4						15.0	10.8
	7.6	6.2	6.0						5.8	5.7
Sales/Total Assets	2.8	2.4	2.2						3.9	1.9
	1.9	1.7	1.7						1.9	1.6
	1.6	1.4	1.4						1.4	1.4
% Depr., Dep., Amort./Sales	.6	.7	.7							1.0
	(34) 1.4	(34) 1.5	(34) 1.6						(15)	2.4
	2.7	2.7	3.5							3.6
% Officers', Directors' Owners' Comp/Sales	1.4	2.0	1.2							
	(16) 2.6	(11) 3.6	(14) 2.6							
	6.0	8.9	3.7							
Net Sales ($)	1413151M	1229861M	1671436M		1970M	5768M	20524M	35704M	166674M	1440796M
Total Assets ($)	733318M	752605M	1085201M		828M	4153M	13584M	19331M	87339M	959966M

Current Data Sorted by Assets | Comparative Historical Data

Type of Statement	0-500M	500M-2MM	2-10MM	10-50MM	50-100MM	100-250MM		4/1/06-3/31/07 ALL	4/1/07-3/31/08 ALL
Unqualified			3	5	2			19	15
Reviewed		2	8	3				12	12
Compiled	3	4	6					6	5
Tax Returns			7					8	7
Other	1	6	5	12	4	2		26	23
	4	18 (4/1-9/30/10)		55 (10/1/10-3/31/11)					
NUMBER OF STATEMENTS	4	12	29	20	6	2		71	62
	%	%	%	%	%	%		%	%
ASSETS									
Cash & Equivalents		13.2	12.0	4.9				5.8	7.2
Trade Receivables (net)		26.7	25.3	27.9				32.8	29.1
Inventory		38.5	36.1	30.0				28.2	29.0
All Other Current		3.4	2.7	3.5				3.8	6.0
Total Current		81.9	76.2	66.4				70.6	71.3
Fixed Assets (net)		17.3	14.9	21.4				17.2	15.8
Intangibles (net)		.6	4.4	8.1				6.7	7.4
All Other Non-Current		.2	4.6	4.1				5.4	5.4
Total		100.0	100.0	100.0				100.0	100.0
LIABILITIES									
Notes Payable-Short Term		15.9	12.6	11.0				11.3	15.4
Cur. Mat.-L.T.D.		1.3	3.9	5.1				3.6	3.3
Trade Payables		17.8	14.9	13.5				18.0	16.2
Income Taxes Payable		.0	.1	.1				.4	.1
All Other Current		16.2	12.6	16.1				12.4	11.7
Total Current		51.2	44.2	45.9				45.8	46.8
Long-Term Debt		6.6	10.4	15.0				16.1	14.1
Deferred Taxes		.0	.4	.9				.4	.5
All Other Non-Current		10.1	6.6	2.6				4.7	6.4
Net Worth		32.1	38.5	35.6				33.0	32.3
Total Liabilities & Net Worth		100.0	100.0	100.0				100.0	100.0
INCOME DATA									
Net Sales		100.0	100.0	100.0				100.0	100.0
Gross Profit		38.1	40.6	35.8				34.6	40.9
Operating Expenses		34.1	35.8	29.1				27.6	33.7
Operating Profit		4.0	4.8	6.6				7.0	7.2
All Other Expenses (net)		2.7	.5	2.1				1.1	2.2
Profit Before Taxes		1.3	4.3	4.6				5.9	5.1
RATIOS									
Current		2.3	2.5	2.5				2.6	2.8
		1.6	2.0	1.8				1.6	1.4
		1.2	1.4	1.3				1.2	1.1
Quick		1.5	1.4	1.2				1.5	1.2
		.8	.8	.8				1.0	.7
		.4	.7	.5				.5	.5
Sales/Receivables		26 13.8	26 13.9	41 8.8				40 9.0	37 10.0
		40 9.0	39 9.2	57 6.4				52 7.0	46 8.0
		57 6.4	54 6.8	70 5.2				60 6.1	58 6.3
Cost of Sales/Inventory		50 7.2	71 5.2	59 6.2				39 9.2	43 8.5
		86 4.2	91 4.0	93 3.9				74 4.9	85 4.3
		148 2.5	144 2.5	148 2.5				107 3.4	112 3.3
Cost of Sales/Payables		28 12.9	16 22.5	26 14.1				25 14.7	25 14.8
		39 9.4	24 15.1	40 9.1				38 9.7	35 10.5
		45 8.1	51 7.1	51 7.1				56 6.5	52 7.0
Sales/Working Capital		3.9	4.1	3.8				5.3	4.8
		8.4	6.8	7.8				8.4	12.1
		46.8	12.5	14.5				21.8	32.7
EBIT/Interest		2.9	13.2	22.9				19.2	14.6
		(11) .1	(23) 4.7	7.6				(69) 4.6	(58) 5.9
		-3.9	2.4	1.4				2.1	2.1
Net Profit + Depr., Dep., Amort./Cur. Mat. L/T/D								6.8	25.1
								(24) 2.6	(18) 4.4
								.6	2.2
Fixed/Worth		.1	.1	.2				.2	.2
		.5	.4	.8				.6	.7
		2.4	1.2	NM				1.5	2.2
Debt/Worth		1.0	.9	.9				1.0	1.3
		2.8	1.6	1.5				2.4	2.9
		12.2	4.5	NM				5.1	12.5
% Profit Before Taxes/Tangible Net Worth		53.3	78.5	48.0				56.0	75.7
		(11) 15.9	(25) 13.5	(15) 22.5				(57) 30.3	(53) 41.7
		-13.2	5.5	5.6				13.5	21.7
% Profit Before Taxes/Total Assets		14.1	14.8	16.4				18.8	15.8
		1.4	5.7	5.8				9.8	11.0
		-12.4	1.7	1.1				3.4	3.0
Sales/Net Fixed Assets		773.3	56.0	22.7				39.0	43.0
		23.9	15.2	15.3				19.5	22.9
		8.5	10.4	5.0				8.9	8.3
Sales/Total Assets		2.9	2.8	2.1				2.9	2.9
		2.4	2.1	1.7				2.2	2.2
		1.9	1.7	1.4				1.7	1.7
% Depr., Dep., Amort./Sales			.8	1.4				.8	.6
			(20) 1.2	(17) 2.0				(59) 1.7	(49) 1.4
			2.0	2.8				2.3	2.2
% Officers', Directors' Owners' Comp/Sales			1.9					1.2	2.8
			(15) 4.6					(25) 3.3	(18) 3.9
			7.9					5.0	5.5
Net Sales ($)	10583M	39484M	326820M	796317M	722482M	542478M		2878658M	2641097M
Total Assets ($)	1093M	15668M	142871M	451166M	332893M	396943M		1658916M	1582876M

M = $ thousand   MM = $ million
See Pages 9 through 22 for Explanation of Ratios and Data

Comparative Historical Data   Current Data Sorted by Sales

Period labels for current data: 18 (4/1-9/30/10) and 55 (10/1/10-3/31/11)

M = $ thousand   MM = $ million

	4/1/08-3/31/09 ALL	4/1/09-3/31/10 ALL	4/1/10-3/31/11 ALL	Type of Statement	0-1MM	1-3MM	3-5MM	5-10MM	10-25MM	25MM & OVER
	14	14	10	Unqualified				6		4
	13	21	11	Reviewed		1	2	7	1	
	6	5	8	Compiled		1	1	5	1	
	12	14	14	Tax Returns		4	4	5	1	
	28	31	30	Other	1	5	2	1	7	15
NUMBER OF STATEMENTS	73	85	73			10	8	13	22	20
	%	%	%	**ASSETS**	%	%	%	%	%	%
	10.5	11.0	11.2	Cash & Equivalents		20.2		14.8	7.6	7.2
	29.4	24.1	26.1	Trade Receivables (net)		16.8		23.4	27.3	32.0
	28.6	29.4	33.3	Inventory		40.7	D	43.6	27.2	30.2
	5.2	2.9	3.7	All Other Current		3.3	A	2.0	2.8	5.8
	73.7	67.5	74.3	Total Current		81.0	T	83.7	64.8	75.1
	15.4	19.6	17.8	Fixed Assets (net)		15.8	A	11.6	22.6	17.4
	4.4	8.0	4.3	Intangibles (net)		.4		1.5	8.6	4.0
	6.6	4.9	3.6	All Other Non-Current		2.8	N	3.1	4.0	3.5
	100.0	100.0	100.0	Total		100.0	O	100.0	100.0	100.0
				LIABILITIES			T			
	13.6	14.0	11.3	Notes Payable-Short Term		13.7		11.1	10.5	10.7
	2.7	2.8	4.0	Cur. Mat.-L.T.D.		1.3	A	.6	6.7	6.0
	16.4	16.3	15.0	Trade Payables		14.1	V	19.1	13.9	16.3
	.3	.1	.1	Income Taxes Payable		.0	A	.0	.1	.2
	11.7	11.6	15.6	All Other Current		18.6	I	13.0	11.5	22.1
	44.6	44.9	46.1	Total Current		47.6	L	43.9	42.8	55.3
	12.5	14.3	10.6	Long-Term Debt		6.3	A	10.2	14.2	11.0
	.1	.4	.4	Deferred Taxes		.0	B	.2	1.0	.1
	5.4	6.7	5.1	All Other Non-Current		14.2	L	8.1	1.5	2.1
	37.3	33.7	37.9	Net Worth		31.9	E	37.7	40.5	31.4
	100.0	100.0	100.0	Total Liabilities & Net Worth		100.0		100.0	100.0	100.0
				INCOME DATA						
	100.0	100.0	100.0	Net Sales		100.0		100.0	100.0	100.0
	38.5	37.5	37.9	Gross Profit		47.0		36.9	37.7	31.1
	32.3	32.9	32.3	Operating Expenses		44.5		32.0	32.8	23.0
	6.2	4.6	5.6	Operating Profit		2.4		4.8	4.9	8.1
	1.1	1.4	1.3	All Other Expenses (net)		3.0		.6	1.0	1.7
	5.1	3.2	4.3	Profit Before Taxes		-.5		4.3	3.9	6.5
				RATIOS						
	2.6	2.6	2.7			3.1		2.9	2.5	2.6
	1.7	1.6	1.9	Current		1.8		2.2	1.8	1.7
	1.2	1.1	1.3			1.2		1.3	1.3	.9
	1.5	1.3	1.4			1.7		1.7	1.3	1.2
	.9	.8	.8	Quick		.9		.8	.9	.8
	.5	.5	.6			.3		.6	.7	.4
	33 11.1	32 11.3	31 11.9			3 143.3		22 16.4	39 9.3	48 7.7
	44 8.3	44 8.3	46 8.0	Sales/Receivables		25 14.6		35 10.5	46 7.9	59 6.2
	57 6.4	59 6.2	59 6.2			51 7.1		47 7.7	57 6.4	74 5.0
	38 9.6	55 6.7	54 6.7			44 8.3		74 4.9	52 7.0	48 7.6
	71 5.1	90 4.1	89 4.1	Cost of Sales/Inventory		115 3.2		96 3.8	79 4.6	69 5.3
	109 3.3	140 2.6	140 2.6			169 2.2		146 2.5	119 3.1	148 2.5
	20 17.8	15 23.8	18 20.6			19 19.5		16 22.8	20 18.3	24 15.4
	33 11.1	36 10.0	33 11.1	Cost of Sales/Payables		41 8.8		32 11.3	33 10.9	35 10.4
	54 6.8	61 6.0	51 7.2			66 5.6		51 7.1	47 7.7	55 6.6
	5.0	3.9	3.9			3.6		3.7	5.3	3.4
	8.7	7.9	7.2	Sales/Working Capital		9.0		4.6	9.1	7.8
	20.5	35.5	16.6			NM		9.7	17.2	-28.2
	16.5	6.7	16.8					11.7	16.5	27.1
	(67) 4.2	(75) 3.0	(63) 4.7	EBIT/Interest				(10) 4.0	(20) 4.1	12.2
	1.9	.7	1.7					1.8	1.5	3.4
	6.8	4.5	3.1	Net Profit + Depr., Dep.,						
	(21) 2.4	(25) 2.1	(18) 1.5	Amort./Cur. Mat. L/T/D						
	1.3	.9	.2							
	.1	.2	.1			.0		.1	.4	.2
	.5	.8	.5	Fixed/Worth		.5		.2	.8	.4
	1.4	2.3	1.3			3.2		.6	NM	3.4
	.7	.9	.9			.7		1.0	.9	.7
	2.1	1.9	1.7	Debt/Worth		3.5		1.6	1.4	2.1
	8.3	9.9	6.5			15.1		4.0	NM	8.7
	76.3	55.6	60.0					81.5	23.2	62.5
	(64) 26.2	(67) 11.3	(62) 17.6	% Profit Before Taxes/Tangible Net Worth				(12) 27.0	(17) 9.3	(16) 32.7
	9.3	-.4	2.1					3.8	1.2	6.2
	17.0	15.0	16.9			21.3		16.9	10.3	21.9
	8.1	3.0	5.7	% Profit Before Taxes/Total Assets		2.2		6.5	5.4	9.0
	2.5	-.5	1.0			-15.3		1.3	.5	1.7
	54.0	36.3	53.0			UND		82.8	15.9	30.0
	23.7	13.6	15.5	Sales/Net Fixed Assets		22.0		38.4	13.1	16.8
	9.9	5.6	6.9			10.2		10.8	5.9	5.8
	3.3	2.4	2.7			5.4		2.9	2.8	2.2
	2.4	2.0	2.1	Sales/Total Assets		2.6		2.1	1.8	1.9
	1.6	1.4	1.6			1.5		1.9	1.5	1.5
	.5	.9	.9						1.1	1.2
	(53) 1.3	(67) 1.8	(54) 1.7	% Depr., Dep., Amort./Sales					(18) 1.5	(18) 1.9
	2.0	2.7	2.7						2.4	2.6
	2.3	3.0	1.9					4.1	1.3	
	(20) 2.8	(29) 3.8	(31) 4.2	% Officers', Directors', Owners' Comp/Sales				(10) 4.6	(10) 1.7	
	4.5	5.6	6.5					8.0	6.6	
	2659525M	2733627M	2438164M	Net Sales ($)		20758M	31487M	100761M	385764M	1899394M
	1442081M	1915509M	1340634M	Total Assets ($)		10158M	13660M	47586M	205002M	1064228M

© RMA 2011   M = $ thousand   MM = $ million

See Pages 9 through 22 for Explanation of Ratios and Data

Current Data Sorted by Assets   Comparative Historical Data

Type of Statement	0-500M	500M-2MM	2-10MM	10-50MM	50-100MM	100-250MM		4/1/06-3/31/07 ALL	4/1/07-3/31/08 ALL
Unqualified			3	4	4	1		6	8
Reviewed		1	7	3				9	8
Compiled		4	3					8	7
Tax Returns		8						3	5
Other	1	3	11	8	2	1		19	21
	4		7 (4/1-9/30/10)		61 (10/1/10-3/31/11)				
NUMBER OF STATEMENTS	5	16	24	15	6	2		45	49
ASSETS	%	%	%	%	%	%		%	%
Cash & Equivalents		16.5	6.4	9.7				9.6	9.9
Trade Receivables (net)		23.0	26.5	22.2				26.6	25.5
Inventory		36.4	39.9	26.2				29.9	32.8
All Other Current		2.2	2.3	7.2				2.5	2.7
Total Current		78.1	75.1	65.2				68.5	70.9
Fixed Assets (net)		13.3	16.6	22.1				17.0	18.0
Intangibles (net)		2.2	3.4	3.5				6.3	6.2
All Other Non-Current		6.3	4.9	9.1				8.2	4.9
Total		100.0	100.0	100.0				100.0	100.0
LIABILITIES									
Notes Payable-Short Term		15.1	18.6	5.7				13.6	14.1
Cur. Mat.-L.T.D.		2.4	2.3	3.9				2.4	2.2
Trade Payables		17.2	15.2	11.8				15.8	16.8
Income Taxes Payable		.0	.1	.5				.2	.1
All Other Current		6.4	11.7	6.0				9.9	8.2
Total Current		41.2	47.9	27.9				41.9	41.5
Long-Term Debt		5.3	14.4	11.0				13.0	13.3
Deferred Taxes		.0	.3	.2				.1	.2
All Other Non-Current		8.1	5.0	5.9				6.8	12.9
Net Worth		45.4	32.4	55.0				38.1	32.0
Total Liabilities & Net Worth		100.0	100.0	100.0				100.0	100.0
INCOME DATA									
Net Sales		100.0	100.0	100.0				100.0	100.0
Gross Profit		45.1	36.9	34.6				35.3	35.0
Operating Expenses		38.2	32.1	24.3				28.0	30.4
Operating Profit		6.9	4.9	10.3				7.3	4.6
All Other Expenses (net)		.6	1.2	1.1				1.2	1.8
Profit Before Taxes		6.3	3.7	9.2				6.1	2.8
RATIOS									
Current		3.6	2.6	4.7				3.3	2.9
		1.8	1.8	2.8				2.1	1.9
		1.2	1.1	1.2				1.1	1.3
Quick		1.9	1.4	2.9				1.6	1.7
		.9	.6	1.4				1.0	.9
		.4	.5	.5				.5	.5
Sales/Receivables	19 18.8	36 10.2	28 12.9					30 12.1	28 13.1
	30 12.1	49 7.5	45 8.2					45 8.0	41 9.0
	39 9.4	58 6.3	63 5.8					58 6.3	56 6.6
Cost of Sales/Inventory	29 12.7	66 5.5	66 5.6					51 7.1	46 8.0
	80 4.5	100 3.6	86 4.3					81 4.5	91 4.0
	189 1.9	172 2.1	126 2.9					109 3.3	129 2.8
Cost of Sales/Payables	4 85.4	23 15.6	18 19.7					18 20.2	24 15.3
	41 8.8	39 9.3	46 7.9					36 10.2	36 10.2
	72 5.1	57 6.4	64 5.7					56 6.5	50 7.3
Sales/Working Capital		3.7	3.7	2.7				3.5	4.0
		9.1	6.5	5.3				5.7	7.1
		18.7	22.7	18.0				46.3	17.6
EBIT/Interest		41.3	12.3	92.2				10.6	13.2
	(12) 11.7	(20) 4.0	(12) 7.2					(39) 5.4	(43) 5.3
		4.0	2.0	2.1				2.8	1.4
Net Profit + Depr., Dep., Amort./Cur. Mat. L/T/D									38.3
									(15) 7.8
									3.3
Fixed/Worth		.0	.1	.2				.2	.2
		.2	.2	.3				.4	.4
		.5	1.9	.9				2.4	1.0
Debt/Worth		.4	.6	.3				.6	.8
		1.2	1.5	.8				1.6	1.7
		2.7	4.1	3.4				17.9	3.5
% Profit Before Taxes/Tangible Net Worth		86.7	35.3	85.6				52.7	51.1
	(14) 26.2	(20) 11.8	(14) 22.3					(38) 24.3	(44) 26.2
		3.8	2.2	3.2				7.4	4.9
% Profit Before Taxes/Total Assets		22.6	13.9	33.2				20.0	19.4
		8.9	5.2	12.5				10.3	8.5
		1.1	1.2	2.3				4.0	1.8
Sales/Net Fixed Assets		74.1	79.0	51.6				42.5	46.9
		34.4	19.1	7.1				19.1	18.2
		19.3	8.9	4.5				6.0	5.6
Sales/Total Assets		3.6	2.7	2.1				2.5	2.8
		2.7	2.0	1.6				2.0	2.2
		2.1	1.3	1.0				1.5	1.5
% Depr., Dep., Amort./Sales		.6	.8	.5				.8	.6
	(12) 1.1	(21) 1.4	(13) 1.8					(39) 1.9	(37) 1.4
		1.6	3.0	3.9				2.4	2.4
% Officers', Directors' Owners' Comp/Sales		5.2	1.6					3.7	2.9
	(12) 7.1	(10) 2.0						(13) 6.0	(15) 4.7
		9.8	4.6					8.3	9.0
Net Sales ($)	3866M	56797M	286203M	563699M	672731M	485324M		1784301M	1350904M
Total Assets ($)	1520M	20428M	134373M	304639M	485356M	328410M		1046430M	743831M

M = $ thousand   MM = $ million
See Pages 9 through 22 for Explanation of Ratios and Data

Comparative Historical Data   Current Data Sorted by Sales

7	10	12	Type of Statement				3	1	8
13	12	11	Unqualified			1	5	5	
5	3	7	Reviewed			3	2	1	
6	8	9	Compiled	1		3	2		
32	18	29	Tax Returns	1	3	3	2	2	
4/1/08-3/31/09	4/1/09-3/31/10	4/1/10-3/31/11	Other	3	4	2	3	8	9
ALL	ALL	ALL		0-1MM	1-3MM	3-5MM	5-10MM	10-25MM	25MM & OVER
					7 (4/1-9/30/10)		61 (10/1/10-3/31/11)		
63	51	68	**NUMBER OF STATEMENTS**	5	7	9	15	15	17
%	%	%	**ASSETS**	%	%	%	%	%	%
9.4	12.9	12.4	Cash & Equivalents				11.1	7.6	11.4
24.4	24.4	22.9	Trade Receivables (net)				26.3	26.9	23.2
32.4	30.3	33.8	Inventory				27.2	40.2	33.2
3.8	2.0	3.4	All Other Current				2.2	.3	2.4
70.0	69.5	72.6	Total Current				66.9	75.1	70.2
22.0	21.2	16.5	Fixed Assets (net)				20.8	15.0	15.5
2.3	2.6	4.7	Intangibles (net)				.6	4.8	9.0
5.7	6.6	6.2	All Other Non-Current				11.7	5.1	5.3
100.0	100.0	100.0	Total				100.0	100.0	100.0
			LIABILITIES						
12.0	14.7	12.3	Notes Payable-Short Term				12.0	16.3	7.6
2.4	2.8	2.4	Cur. Mat.-L.T.D.				2.3	3.0	2.1
15.5	12.7	14.5	Trade Payables				17.6	14.3	11.2
.3	.4	.2	Income Taxes Payable				.3	.4	.1
9.2	6.9	10.4	All Other Current				7.4	6.3	8.7
39.4	37.5	39.9	Total Current				39.6	40.4	29.7
10.4	10.0	10.7	Long-Term Debt				8.2	5.6	10.0
.2	.2	.3	Deferred Taxes				.4	.2	.5
10.0	4.3	5.8	All Other Non-Current				5.1	4.3	9.0
40.1	48.0	43.4	Net Worth				46.6	49.5	50.7
100.0	100.0	100.0	Total Liabilities & Net Worth				100.0	100.0	100.0
			INCOME DATA						
100.0	100.0	100.0	Net Sales				100.0	100.0	100.0
37.2	36.9	39.2	Gross Profit				33.6	35.2	35.1
31.7	32.9	32.9	Operating Expenses				31.0	27.5	25.1
5.4	4.0	6.4	Operating Profit				2.6	7.7	10.1
.6	.8	1.0	All Other Expenses (net)				.5	.5	.9
4.9	3.2	5.4	Profit Before Taxes				2.1	7.2	9.2
			RATIOS						
2.9	3.2	3.7	Current				2.2	3.0	4.3
1.8	2.2	1.9					1.8	2.5	3.1
1.2	1.3	1.2					1.2	1.2	1.6
1.5	1.9	1.7	Quick				1.6	1.4	2.2
.8	1.0	.9					.9	.7	1.3
.5	.5	.5					.5	.5	.7
30 12.2	29 12.5	28 12.8	Sales/Receivables				35 10.4	38 9.6	31 11.8
41 8.9	44 8.3	40 9.2					48 7.6	52 7.0	44 8.3
51 7.1	57 6.4	57 6.4					56 6.5	66 5.5	54 6.7
55 6.6	54 6.8	65 5.6	Cost of Sales/Inventory				20 18.5	71 5.1	71 5.1
93 3.9	84 4.4	96 3.8					74 4.9	107 3.4	93 3.9
126 2.9	128 2.8	159 2.3					101 3.6	174 2.1	145 2.5
22 17.0	15 24.3	18 20.6	Cost of Sales/Payables				21 17.4	27 13.5	19 18.9
32 11.5	30 12.2	37 9.9					39 9.3	43 8.6	27 13.6
55 6.7	43 8.5	57 6.4					61 6.0	54 6.8	42 8.7
3.9	3.0	3.0	Sales/Working Capital				4.0	2.9	2.8
7.2	6.9	5.9					9.5	5.2	5.3
19.8	13.7	17.9					24.0	18.8	10.0
28.1	17.3	36.0	EBIT/Interest				10.8	88.6	119.0
(51) 9.6	(42) 3.9	(55) 7.2					(13) 5.2	(12) 9.0	(16) 9.3
2.4	1.2	2.6					1.8	2.4	5.6
19.6		11.0	Net Profit + Depr., Dep., Amort./Cur. Mat. L/T/D						
(12) 5.2		(10) 3.7							
1.9		2.5							
.2	.2	.1	Fixed/Worth				.2	.1	.1
.5	.5	.3					.3	.2	.3
2.0	1.0	.9					.6	2.0	.8
.5	.4	.5	Debt/Worth				.7	.4	.6
1.1	1.1	1.1					1.1	.6	1.1
3.2	2.3	3.8					3.3	8.0	3.7
53.5	34.0	38.6	% Profit Before Taxes/Tangible Net Worth				21.9	61.8	85.4
(58) 27.1	(47) 11.9	(58) 13.6					7.0	(12) 7.5	(15) 37.5
4.4	1.1	3.1					1.7	3.7	8.5
21.3	13.7	18.8	% Profit Before Taxes/Total Assets				7.7	24.2	31.5
9.4	5.2	5.4					3.3	4.5	16.4
2.1	.7	2.0					.8	2.3	3.5
41.4	38.0	51.2	Sales/Net Fixed Assets				22.4	90.8	50.7
15.6	15.3	19.7					14.5	20.5	13.3
5.5	4.6	6.2					5.3	7.1	4.6
2.7	2.6	2.8	Sales/Total Assets				2.8	2.3	2.9
2.0	2.0	2.0					2.6	2.0	1.7
1.5	1.2	1.3					1.2	1.2	1.4
.7	.8	.6	% Depr., Dep., Amort./Sales				1.3	.9	.7
(49) 1.6	(45) 1.5	(57) 1.4				(14)	1.9	(12) 1.2	(16) 1.5
2.8	3.1	2.9					3.6	3.0	4.3
1.6	2.1	2.0	% Officers', Directors' Owners' Comp/Sales						
(22) 3.8	(13) 5.1	(25) 5.0							
8.9	9.3	8.7							
2220200M	1583344M	2068620M	Net Sales ($)	3592M	13847M	35536M	107169M	246969M	1661507M
1374478M	988559M	1274726M	Total Assets ($)	2661M	8203M	34304M	74871M	141443M	1013244M

M = $ thousand   MM = $ million
See Pages 9 through 22 for Explanation of Ratios and Data

Current Data Sorted by Assets   Comparative Historical Data

0-500M	500M-2MM	2-10MM	10-50MM	50-100MM	100-250MM	Type of Statement	4/1/06-3/31/07 ALL	4/1/07-3/31/08 ALL
		3	11	6	5	Unqualified	18	19
	2	9	4			Reviewed	12	15
	3	3				Compiled	4	2
1		3				Tax Returns	3	5
	4	7	18	2	1	Other	30	24
	14 (4/1-9/30/10)		68 (10/1/10-3/31/11)					
1	9	25	33	8	6	NUMBER OF STATEMENTS	67	65
%	%	%	%	%	%	**ASSETS**	%	%
		6.7	10.0			Cash & Equivalents	6.9	8.8
		33.7	24.4			Trade Receivables (net)	31.3	30.3
		29.0	23.8			Inventory	27.6	28.4
		2.0	5.0			All Other Current	1.3	1.6
		71.4	63.1			Total Current	67.2	69.0
		16.2	21.5			Fixed Assets (net)	18.9	15.7
		5.8	9.6			Intangibles (net)	8.8	9.0
		6.5	5.8			All Other Non-Current	5.2	6.3
		100.0	100.0			Total	100.0	100.0
						LIABILITIES		
		12.9	6.7			Notes Payable-Short Term	9.9	8.7
		2.8	3.0			Cur. Mat.-L.T.D.	2.4	2.2
		16.1	12.3			Trade Payables	18.5	16.5
		.6	.2			Income Taxes Payable	.3	.2
		8.4	10.5			All Other Current	10.6	10.6
		40.9	32.6			Total Current	41.7	38.2
		5.1	14.2			Long-Term Debt	14.6	13.5
		.3	.8			Deferred Taxes	.9	.4
		2.0	4.0			All Other Non-Current	5.0	5.9
		51.7	48.3			Net Worth	37.8	42.1
		100.0	100.0			Total Liabilities & Net Worth	100.0	100.0
						INCOME DATA		
		100.0	100.0			Net Sales	100.0	100.0
		30.5	28.4			Gross Profit	29.0	30.3
		25.3	20.2			Operating Expenses	22.5	21.7
		5.2	8.2			Operating Profit	6.5	8.5
		.6	.9			All Other Expenses (net)	1.9	1.1
		4.6	7.3			Profit Before Taxes	4.6	7.4
						RATIOS		
		3.0	3.4				2.4	2.5
		1.6	2.2			Current	1.7	1.9
		1.4	1.1				1.1	1.3
		1.6	1.9				1.5	1.5
		1.0	1.2			Quick	.9	1.0
		.6	.6				.6	.7
		37 9.7	39 9.4				38 9.7	36 10.2
		51 7.1	55 6.7			Sales/Receivables	52 7.1	49 7.5
		69 5.3	66 5.5				68 5.4	62 5.9
		45 8.1	41 9.0				38 9.6	41 8.9
		77 4.7	74 4.9			Cost of Sales/Inventory	69 5.3	64 5.7
		98 3.7	112 3.3				113 3.2	106 3.5
		20 18.7	17 21.5				27 13.5	20 18.1
		37 10.0	27 13.4			Cost of Sales/Payables	40 9.2	39 9.4
		47 7.7	54 6.7				52 7.0	52 7.0
		4.4	4.0				4.7	5.1
		7.9	5.6			Sales/Working Capital	8.4	7.8
		15.0	30.0				29.8	14.7
		37.7	23.1				9.7	20.4
		(23) 7.5	(28) 8.0			EBIT/Interest	(66) 3.7	(61) 6.5
		2.6	2.7				1.9	2.0
			8.6				31.3	34.0
			(15) 2.7			Net Profit + Depr., Dep., Amort./Cur. Mat. L/T/D	(24) 10.1	(22) 15.6
			.7				3.3	2.9
		.2	.3				.2	.2
		.3	.5			Fixed/Worth	.7	.4
		.5	3.0				1.6	1.0
		.5	.4				.9	.6
		1.1	1.1			Debt/Worth	2.6	1.3
		1.8	11.1				6.3	4.3
		43.7	49.1				57.6	60.0
		(24) 15.2	(27) 25.8			% Profit Before Taxes/Tangible Net Worth	(59) 31.4	(54) 34.5
		8.1	6.7				7.8	14.7
		17.6	16.7				15.5	26.4
		7.4	8.6			% Profit Before Taxes/Total Assets	8.6	12.7
		2.6	2.8				2.2	4.4
		31.6	23.5				29.8	31.9
		15.7	8.8			Sales/Net Fixed Assets	11.4	13.9
		9.4	5.2				8.0	9.2
		3.0	2.4				2.9	3.0
		2.1	1.7			Sales/Total Assets	2.0	2.2
		1.6	1.2				1.4	1.7
		.7	.7				.7	.7
		(24) 1.0	(31) 1.7			% Depr., Dep., Amort./Sales	(59) 1.4	(56) 1.4
		1.8	2.6				2.6	2.1
							1.7	1.6
						% Officers', Directors' Owners' Comp/Sales	(13) 4.0	(15) 3.8
							6.3	7.6
1209M	26790M	289191M	1509545M	849295M	1007139M	Net Sales ($)	2974458M	3680109M
304M	9111M	129592M	807902M	588025M	982819M	Total Assets ($)	1863904M	1970508M

M = $ thousand   MM = $ million
See Pages 9 through 22 for Explanation of Ratios and Data

Comparative Historical Data / Current Data Sorted by Sales

							Type of Statement						
	20		18		25		Unqualified				2	7	16
	20		15		15		Reviewed			1	2	9	3
	2		2		3		Compiled				1	1	1
	3		8		7		Tax Returns				3		
	25		38		32		Other		4	3	5	5	17
	4/1/08-3/31/09 ALL		4/1/09-3/31/10 ALL		4/1/10-3/31/11 ALL				2				
									14 (4/1-9/30/10)		68 (10/1/10-3/31/11)		
								0-1MM	1-3MM	3-5MM	5-10MM	10-25MM	25MM & OVER
	70		81		82		NUMBER OF STATEMENTS	6	4		13	22	37
	%		%		%		ASSETS	%	%	%	%	%	%
	8.8		12.3		10.4		Cash & Equivalents				6.4	8.2	13.0
	29.9		24.1		27.0		Trade Receivables (net)				26.9	24.7	28.4
	30.0		30.5		27.6		Inventory				28.8	25.6	24.2
	2.8		3.0		3.1		All Other Current				.6	4.1	3.8
	71.6		69.8		68.1		Total Current				62.6	62.7	69.4
	16.9		19.4		19.9		Fixed Assets (net)				18.8	19.8	21.2
	6.5		5.6		6.4		Intangibles (net)				10.8	10.6	4.0
	5.0		5.2		5.7		All Other Non-Current				7.8	6.9	5.3
	100.0		100.0		100.0		Total				100.0	100.0	100.0
							LIABILITIES						
	9.8		10.9		9.4		Notes Payable-Short Term				17.5	7.5	4.5
	2.8		2.0		2.6		Cur. Mat.-L.T.D.				5.3	3.8	1.3
	17.1		15.4		14.1		Trade Payables				13.4	13.3	12.4
	.5		.3		.3		Income Taxes Payable				.0	.3	.4
	11.4		12.6		10.9		All Other Current				10.2	7.4	13.3
	41.5		41.3		37.2		Total Current				46.4	32.2	31.9
	9.9		9.4		10.3		Long-Term Debt				9.3	13.2	9.3
	.5		.5		.5		Deferred Taxes				.2	1.2	.3
	4.4		4.7		3.0		All Other Non-Current				1.8	2.6	3.0
	43.7		44.1		49.1		Net Worth				42.2	50.9	55.5
	100.0		100.0		100.0		Total Liabilities & Net Worth				100.0	100.0	100.0
							INCOME DATA						
	100.0		100.0		100.0		Net Sales				100.0	100.0	100.0
	27.3		28.0		28.6		Gross Profit				33.1	32.7	23.3
	19.3		24.0		22.8		Operating Expenses				28.4	25.6	16.7
	7.9		4.0		5.9		Operating Profit				4.7	7.1	6.6
	1.0		1.0		.6		All Other Expenses (net)				.3	1.2	.4
	6.9		2.9		5.2		Profit Before Taxes				4.4	5.9	6.2
							RATIOS						
	2.7		3.3		3.4						2.1	3.0	3.9
	1.7		1.8		2.1		Current				1.5	1.8	2.8
	1.3		1.2		1.4						1.0	1.5	1.5
	1.5		1.9		1.8						1.2	1.9	2.2
	1.0		.9		1.0		Quick				.7	.9	1.3
	.6		.6		.7						.4	.6	.9
31	11.7	30	12.0	38	9.7			34	10.9	40	9.2	38	9.5
44	8.2	42	8.7	51	7.1		Sales/Receivables	53	6.9	52	7.1	55	6.6
59	6.1	53	6.9	66	5.5			70	5.2	70	5.2	66	5.5
43	8.5	44	8.2	47	7.8			69	5.3	47	7.8	34	10.9
66	5.5	66	5.6	76	4.8		Cost of Sales/Inventory	83	4.4	83	4.4	59	6.2
85	4.3	105	3.5	110	3.3			144	2.5	121	3.0	91	4.0
17	21.3	15	24.3	18	20.5			16	22.2	25	14.7	16	22.7
28	12.9	28	13.0	29	12.7		Cost of Sales/Payables	29	12.5	40	9.2	23	16.0
49	7.4	47	7.8	47	7.7			47	7.7	62	5.9	35	10.5
	5.0		4.3		3.9						5.6	4.3	3.6
	8.0		7.4		5.5		Sales/Working Capital				13.1	5.6	5.3
	20.2		17.3		14.4						NM	13.7	10.9
	30.1		20.6		26.9						15.9	37.7	39.1
(65)	9.4	(71)	6.8	(70)	7.3		EBIT/Interest			(19)	5.4	(30)	9.3	7.8
	3.0		1.0		2.3						1.5	2.8	1.1
	20.3		10.1		8.8							9.1	16.5
(26)	8.8	(25)	5.2	(26)	2.5		Net Profit + Depr., Dep., Amort./Cur. Mat. L/T/D			(12)	3.1	(12)	3.3
	2.8		1.3		1.2							.7	1.4
	.2		.2		.2						.2	.2	.2
	.4		.4		.4		Fixed/Worth				.5	.4	.3
	.9		.8		1.0						.8	2.4	.9
	.7		.5		.3						1.2	.4	.3
	1.6		1.2		1.1		Debt/Worth				1.8	.9	.7
	3.2		3.1		1.9						2.7	6.6	1.6
	62.4		50.4		43.1						53.7	36.5	40.2
(62)	31.0	(75)	16.6	(73)	16.1		% Profit Before Taxes/Tangible Net Worth		(12)	20.0	(18)	12.9	(35)	16.1
	10.6		.8		6.3						10.9	7.3	6.7
	23.2		16.0		15.0						10.6	14.9	15.9
	11.3		5.6		7.7		% Profit Before Taxes/Total Assets				7.6	7.0	8.7
	4.4		-.5		2.4						1.0	1.9	3.8
	41.1		38.2		24.5						30.5	24.1	21.6
	17.9		13.4		11.4		Sales/Net Fixed Assets				10.8	9.5	10.7
	9.1		7.5		6.1						4.0	7.0	5.2
	3.2		3.2		2.8						2.7	2.4	2.6
	2.4		2.1		1.8		Sales/Total Assets				1.6	1.7	1.7
	1.8		1.4		1.4						1.1	.8	1.4
	.7		.6		.8						.8	.7	.8
(58)	1.1	(70)	1.4	(76)	1.7		% Depr., Dep., Amort./Sales		(12)	1.3	(20)	1.2	(36)	1.8
	2.1		2.6		2.5						2.5	2.4	2.6
	1.3		2.1		1.9								
(14)	2.6	(15)	3.6	(18)	3.5		% Officers', Directors' Owners' Comp/Sales						
	4.0		5.6		7.3								
	3967326M		3121359M		3683169M		Net Sales ($)		11469M	16049M	88539M	330838M	3236274M
	2166204M		1870953M		2517753M		Total Assets ($)		4190M	5707M	60963M	275164M	2171729M

M = $ thousand   MM = $ million
See Pages 9 through 22 for Explanation of Ratios and Data

Current Data Sorted by Assets / Comparative Historical Data

Type of Statement

	0-500M	500M-2MM	2-10MM	10-50MM	50-100MM	100-250MM		4/1/06-3/31/07 ALL	4/1/07-3/31/08 ALL
Unqualified			2	10	4	2		15	15
Reviewed			3	4				15	13
Compiled		5	3					5	9
Tax Returns		2	1					5	6
Other	1	2	9	11	2	2		30	22
			18 (4/1-9/30/10)	45 (10/1/10-3/31/11)					
NUMBER OF STATEMENTS	1	9	18	25	6	4		70	65

ASSETS

	0-500M %	500M-2MM %	2-10MM %	10-50MM %	50-100MM %	100-250MM %		4/1/06-3/31/07 %	4/1/07-3/31/08 %
Cash & Equivalents			8.2	8.1				9.1	8.6
Trade Receivables (net)			32.2	21.2				28.4	28.8
Inventory			30.9	23.9				29.8	28.9
All Other Current			4.0	5.1				2.6	2.4
Total Current			75.3	58.4				69.8	68.6
Fixed Assets (net)			17.7	29.5				21.3	19.9
Intangibles (net)			3.1	5.0				4.4	7.1
All Other Non-Current			3.9	7.2				4.4	4.4
Total			100.0	100.0				100.0	100.0

LIABILITIES

	2-10MM	10-50MM		4/1/06-3/31/07	4/1/07-3/31/08
Notes Payable-Short Term	9.1	8.1		11.0	10.1
Cur. Mat.-L.T.D.	1.1	2.8		3.6	2.6
Trade Payables	21.6	13.0		13.9	14.8
Income Taxes Payable	.0	.2		.3	.1
All Other Current	14.1	9.4		13.3	15.8
Total Current	45.8	33.5		42.1	43.4
Long-Term Debt	8.4	14.8		14.5	14.6
Deferred Taxes	.5	.7		.5	.3
All Other Non-Current	2.5	1.9		4.9	7.4
Net Worth	42.7	49.1		37.9	34.2
Total Liabilities & Net Worth	100.0	100.0		100.0	100.0

INCOME DATA

	2-10MM	10-50MM		4/1/06-3/31/07	4/1/07-3/31/08
Net Sales	100.0	100.0		100.0	100.0
Gross Profit	30.7	25.0		30.3	30.2
Operating Expenses	25.5	18.6		23.4	25.5
Operating Profit	5.3	6.4		6.9	4.8
All Other Expenses (net)	.8	.6		.7	1.1
Profit Before Taxes	4.4	5.8		6.1	3.7

RATIOS

	500M-2MM	2-10MM	10-50MM (col a)	10-50MM (col b)		Hist 4/1/06-3/31/07 (a)	Hist (b)	Hist 4/1/07-3/31/08 (a)	Hist (b)
Current		3.7		2.4		2.7		2.8	
		1.6		2.0		1.7		1.9	
		1.1		1.4		1.2		1.2	
Quick		1.9		1.2		1.5		1.5	
		.8		.9		.9		.9	
		.6		.6		.6		.6	
Sales/Receivables	33	11.1	41	8.9		42 · 8.6		40 · 9.1	
	47	7.8	46	7.9		52 · 7.0		48 · 7.5	
	64	5.7	57	6.4		61 · 6.0		62 · 5.9	
Cost of Sales/Inventory	41	9.0	53	6.8		54 · 6.8		44 · 8.3	
	55	6.7	70	5.2		72 · 5.1		70 · 5.2	
	110	3.3	95	3.9		101 · 3.6		117 · 3.1	
Cost of Sales/Payables	28	13.0	21	17.0		22 · 16.7		22 · 16.8	
	47	7.8	29	12.6		33 · 10.9		33 · 11.1	
	69	5.3	49	7.4		50 · 7.4		46 · 7.9	
Sales/Working Capital		4.7		3.9		4.9		3.4	
		9.5		6.4		8.1		7.5	
		34.7		11.5		26.2		20.3	
EBIT/Interest		17.2		17.9		16.8		13.3	
	(14)	7.8	(23)	6.3		(62) · 3.7		(57) · 3.7	
		2.0		2.4		1.6		1.4	
Net Profit + Depr., Dep., Amort./Cur. Mat. L/T/D				7.5		5.9		8.3	
		(12)		3.2		(25) · 3.2		(22) · 4.3	
				1.3		.7		2.1	
Fixed/Worth		.2		.4		.3		.3	
		.4		.6		.5		.5	
		1.8		1.2		1.6		1.2	
Debt/Worth		.5		.5		.8		.6	
		1.6		1.2		2.1		1.5	
		3.9		2.7		5.1		5.6	
% Profit Before Taxes/Tangible Net Worth		72.6		31.9		60.1		42.0	
	(17)	32.2	(23)	17.6		(63) · 25.8		(56) · 25.8	
		3.4		5.6		13.1		7.2	
% Profit Before Taxes/Total Assets		30.2		12.4		17.9		14.0	
		6.3		9.2		8.7		8.2	
		2.7		2.9		1.6		1.6	
Sales/Net Fixed Assets		34.7		9.5		29.4		27.0	
		20.4		5.9		12.4		11.8	
		8.6		3.6		5.8		6.2	
Sales/Total Assets		2.9		1.9		2.6		2.6	
		2.5		1.7		2.0		1.9	
		1.9		1.3		1.5		1.3	
% Depr., Dep., Amort./Sales		.6		1.8		1.0		1.2	
		(14) 1.3		2.3		(62) · 1.7		(58) · 2.0	
		2.3		3.1		2.7		3.1	
% Officers', Directors' Owners' Comp/Sales						1.7		1.8	
						(25) · 3.3		(22) · 4.1	
						5.6		6.2	

Net Sales ($) / Total Assets ($)

	0-500M	500M-2MM	2-10MM	10-50MM	50-100MM	100-250MM		4/1/06-3/31/07	4/1/07-3/31/08
Net Sales ($)	2319M	25953M	238146M	792239M	701403M	956846M		2922011M	1974319M
Total Assets ($)	448M	10736M	95388M	515872M	414996M	605137M		1352204M	1107867M

Comparative Historical Data   Current Data Sorted by Sales

		Type of Statement						
12	15	18	Unqualified				1	7	10
12	11	7	Reviewed				1	4	2
7	7	8	Compiled		2	1	4	1	
2	2	3	Tax Returns		1	1	1		
23	20	27	Other	1	2	1	2	8	13

4/1/08-3/31/09 ALL	4/1/09-3/31/10 ALL	4/1/10-3/31/11 ALL		0-1MM	1-3MM	3-5MM	5-10MM	10-25MM	25MM & OVER
					18 (4/1-9/30/10)		45 (10/1/10-3/31/11)		
56	55	63	**NUMBER OF STATEMENTS**	1	5	3	9	20	25
%	%	%	**ASSETS**	%	%	%	%	%	%
8.0	6.4	9.3	Cash & Equivalents					10.9	10.1
25.7	28.5	26.6	Trade Receivables (net)					26.5	25.8
32.7	26.8	28.0	Inventory					22.4	26.1
2.4	2.1	3.7	All Other Current					5.8	2.5
68.7	63.8	67.7	Total Current					65.7	64.5
20.1	23.5	21.9	Fixed Assets (net)					23.0	22.2
5.9	7.2	5.4	Intangibles (net)					3.3	9.2
5.2	5.5	5.0	All Other Non-Current					8.0	4.1
100.0	100.0	100.0	Total					100.0	100.0
			LIABILITIES						
12.0	11.4	9.1	Notes Payable-Short Term					4.6	9.3
2.6	2.6	2.0	Cur. Mat.-L.T.D.					2.3	1.5
13.4	14.5	16.3	Trade Payables					18.4	12.4
.1	.5	.1	Income Taxes Payable					.1	.2
19.5	9.2	11.3	All Other Current					13.3	10.7
47.7	38.3	38.8	Total Current					38.7	34.2
13.1	14.0	11.9	Long-Term Debt					12.1	9.9
.6	.6	.6	Deferred Taxes					.9	.7
5.6	4.5	8.2	All Other Non-Current					1.7	9.4
33.0	42.6	40.4	Net Worth					46.6	45.8
100.0	100.0	100.0	Total Liabilities & Net Worth					100.0	100.0
			INCOME DATA						
100.0	100.0	100.0	Net Sales					100.0	100.0
27.8	29.3	28.1	Gross Profit					27.2	25.8
23.0	24.0	24.2	Operating Expenses					21.3	20.2
4.7	5.3	3.9	Operating Profit					5.9	5.6
1.1	2.3	.7	All Other Expenses (net)					.6	.6
3.7	3.0	3.2	Profit Before Taxes					5.3	5.0
			RATIOS						
2.5	2.4	2.7	Current					2.6	2.7
1.8	1.8	2.1						1.8	2.1
1.3	1.3	1.2						1.2	1.5
1.3	1.4	1.6	Quick					1.6	1.6
.8	.9	1.0						1.0	1.0
.6	.6	.6						.6	.6
32 11.4	40 9.1	39 9.5	Sales/Receivables					44 8.2	42 8.8
45 8.2	49 7.4	47 7.8						52 7.0	47 7.7
56 6.5	57 6.4	58 6.3						61 6.0	57 6.4
52 7.0	51 7.2	50 7.3	Cost of Sales/Inventory					45 8.1	51 7.1
85 4.3	66 5.5	66 5.6						58 6.3	70 5.2
107 3.4	87 4.2	111 3.3						93 3.9	98 3.7
17 21.4	22 17.0	20 18.0	Cost of Sales/Payables					25 14.4	20 18.4
26 14.1	31 11.8	35 10.4						37 9.8	33 11.1
42 8.7	44 8.4	54 6.8						64 5.7	44 8.2
4.3	4.6	3.9	Sales/Working Capital					3.9	3.9
7.2	7.4	6.6						6.5	5.9
16.3	15.9	18.2						29.1	11.5
16.2	11.9	17.8	EBIT/Interest					16.2	100.8
(53) 3.6	(49) 3.9	(56) 6.2						(16) 6.4	(24) 12.6
1.3	-1.3	1.6						1.1	3.2
17.7	6.2	8.6	Net Profit + Depr., Dep., Amort./Cur. Mat. L/T/D						
(18) 4.3	(20) 3.0	(21) 2.6							
.7	.5	1.1							
.4	.3	.3	Fixed/Worth					.3	.3
.6	.6	.6						.6	.5
1.2	1.4	1.6						1.5	1.2
.7	.7	.5	Debt/Worth					.5	.5
1.7	1.3	1.4						1.4	1.2
5.0	3.9	4.8						2.9	4.6
35.3	27.3	39.6	% Profit Before Taxes/Tangible Net Worth					40.7	49.1
(51) 20.1	(48) 10.0	(55) 18.7						14.4	(21) 25.4
3.8	-8.0	5.0						1.6	15.8
13.4	11.8	15.8	% Profit Before Taxes/Total Assets					21.3	17.4
5.7	4.7	6.6						6.2	11.4
1.1	-1.2	1.1						.4	4.9
38.9	16.0	30.7	Sales/Net Fixed Assets					32.4	18.3
9.7	8.6	9.6						8.0	9.8
6.0	6.0	5.4						4.1	5.6
2.9	2.5	2.5	Sales/Total Assets					2.4	2.1
2.0	1.9	1.8						1.7	1.7
1.5	1.5	1.3						1.3	1.3
.9	.9	.9	% Depr., Dep., Amort./Sales					.8	1.1
(53) 1.6	(50) 1.9	(59) 1.8						(18) 1.7	2.0
2.6	2.8	2.9						2.9	2.8
1.6	1.2	1.7	% Officers', Directors' Owners' Comp/Sales						
(15) 5.4	(13) 2.1	(18) 5.1							
7.2	6.1	6.5							
2657124M	2074779M	2716906M	Net Sales ($)	608M	10026M	11383M	64177M	350129M	2280583M
1494710M	1288442M	1642577M	Total Assets ($)	801M	4567M	5177M	29907M	224305M	1377820M

© RMA 2011   M = $ thousand   MM = $ million
See Pages 9 through 22 for Explanation of Ratios and Data

Current Data Sorted by Assets   Comparative Historical Data

0-500M	500M-2MM	2-10MM	10-50MM	50-100MM	100-250MM	Type of Statement	4/1/06-3/31/07 ALL	4/1/07-3/31/08 ALL
		3	2	1	1	Unqualified	6	3
	1	11	2			Reviewed	14	9
3	2	5				Compiled	1	7
1	2	3	1			Tax Returns	1	1
	3	2	2	1	1	Other	12	19
	11 (4/1-9/30/10)		36 (10/1/10-3/31/11)					
4	8	24	7	2	2	NUMBER OF STATEMENTS	34	39
%	%	%	%	%	%	ASSETS	%	%
		10.1				Cash & Equivalents	10.3	8.0
		37.7				Trade Receivables (net)	32.4	35.5
		25.8				Inventory	27.4	28.1
		5.4				All Other Current	3.8	3.6
		78.9				Total Current	73.9	75.3
		14.4				Fixed Assets (net)	16.9	16.1
		1.9				Intangibles (net)	4.7	6.2
		4.9				All Other Non-Current	4.4	2.5
		100.0				Total	100.0	100.0
						LIABILITIES		
		15.2				Notes Payable-Short Term	11.3	14.2
		1.8				Cur. Mat.-L.T.D.	3.1	2.2
		18.0				Trade Payables	17.8	18.3
		.2				Income Taxes Payable	.4	.2
		12.7				All Other Current	9.5	8.5
		48.0				Total Current	42.0	43.5
		5.0				Long-Term Debt	4.7	8.6
		.2				Deferred Taxes	.1	.1
		7.3				All Other Non-Current	4.4	5.9
		39.5				Net Worth	48.8	41.9
		100.0				Total Liabilties & Net Worth	100.0	100.0
						INCOME DATA		
		100.0				Net Sales	100.0	100.0
		27.3				Gross Profit	29.0	32.6
		22.5				Operating Expenses	23.3	24.0
		4.7				Operating Profit	5.7	8.6
		.9				All Other Expenses (net)	1.3	1.0
		3.8				Profit Before Taxes	4.4	7.7
						RATIOS		
		3.0				Current	3.6	2.8
		1.6					1.8	2.0
		1.2					1.3	1.4
		1.9				Quick	1.9	1.9
		1.0					1.1	1.2
		.7					.7	.6
		43 8.5				Sales/Receivables	41 9.0	38 9.6
		59 6.2					48 7.6	55 6.6
		73 5.0					56 6.5	64 5.7
		28 13.0				Cost of Sales/Inventory	35 10.5	31 11.8
		54 6.7					66 5.5	58 6.3
		74 4.9					91 4.0	81 4.5
		22 16.5				Cost of Sales/Payables	23 15.9	20 18.0
		32 11.4					36 10.3	30 12.2
		52 7.0					48 7.6	50 7.2
		5.1				Sales/Working Capital	4.1	4.7
		8.0					7.8	7.4
		15.8					20.6	12.7
		17.4				EBIT/Interest	39.5	39.4
		(22) 5.2					(29) 7.0	(38) 6.4
		2.0					1.5	2.0
						Net Profit + Depr., Dep., Amort./Cur. Mat. L/T/D	26.2	29.3
							(10) 4.3	(13) 4.4
							.2	2.4
		.1				Fixed/Worth	.1	.1
		.3					.3	.3
		.5					.8	.9
		.5				Debt/Worth	.4	.7
		1.6					1.2	1.3
		3.4					2.3	4.8
		30.2				% Profit Before Taxes/Tangible Net Worth	42.3	59.4
		(22) 17.5					(31) 29.0	(36) 39.3
		2.5					11.3	20.5
		12.7				% Profit Before Taxes/Total Assets	16.4	30.5
		7.5					11.9	14.7
		1.0					.9	4.0
		45.5				Sales/Net Fixed Assets	58.6	64.6
		22.1					20.8	16.9
		13.1					7.0	11.9
		2.8				Sales/Total Assets	3.0	3.2
		2.3					2.3	2.5
		1.9					1.6	1.7
		.4				% Depr., Dep., Amort./Sales	.6	.4
		(23) 1.1					(28) 1.7	(33) .9
		1.7					2.4	1.9
		2.0				% Officers', Directors' Owners' Comp/Sales		2.4
		(10) 2.9						(13) 3.6
		12.4						14.5
3225M	33794M	242396M	349293M	204113M	471108M	Net Sales ($)	1369742M	1433960M
1174M	11503M	104115M	157541M	133123M	355575M	Total Assets ($)	851223M	805272M

Comparative Historical Data | | Current Data Sorted by Sales

4/1/08–3/31/09 ALL	4/1/09–3/31/10 ALL	4/1/10–3/31/11 ALL	Type of Statement	0-1MM	1-3MM	3-5MM	5-10MM	10-25MM	25MM & OVER
5	10	7	Unqualified				1	3	3
11	16	14	Reviewed		1	1	6	4	2
8	9	10	Compiled		3	1	4	1	
4	6	7	Tax Returns	1	1	1	2	1	1
14	7	9	Other	1		1	2	2	4
				11 (4/1-9/30/10)			36 (10/1/10-3/31/11)		
42	48	47	**NUMBER OF STATEMENTS**	2	5	4	15	11	10
%	%	%	**ASSETS**	%	%	%	%	%	%
13.3	16.2	13.6	Cash & Equivalents				10.4	14.4	23.3
31.5	30.2	33.4	Trade Receivables (net)				39.6	38.2	28.9
28.9	23.6	23.7	Inventory				26.6	22.4	20.6
3.2	3.7	3.9	All Other Current				4.1	6.0	4.9
77.0	73.7	74.6	Total Current				80.7	81.1	77.8
13.9	17.5	17.0	Fixed Assets (net)				16.2	10.6	15.3
6.0	4.9	2.2	Intangibles (net)				1.1	2.9	3.9
3.1	4.0	6.1	All Other Non-Current				2.0	5.4	3.1
100.0	100.0	100.0	Total				100.0	100.0	100.0
			LIABILITIES						
11.5	14.6	14.4	Notes Payable-Short Term				15.5	11.3	2.7
2.1	2.7	1.8	Cur. Mat.-L.T.D.				1.4	1.7	1.4
14.1	15.7	16.5	Trade Payables				21.4	14.5	10.9
.5	.3	.2	Income Taxes Payable				.2	.2	.5
8.9	9.3	10.4	All Other Current				5.8	17.9	11.0
37.0	42.6	43.3	Total Current				44.3	45.7	26.5
8.0	8.2	7.8	Long-Term Debt				5.4	2.2	8.9
.2	.5	.3	Deferred Taxes				.2	.2	.6
8.7	8.4	5.2	All Other Non-Current				10.7	.6	4.9
46.1	40.3	43.4	Net Worth				39.5	51.3	59.1
100.0	100.0	100.0	Total Liabilities & Net Worth				100.0	100.0	100.0
			INCOME DATA						
100.0	100.0	100.0	Net Sales				100.0	100.0	100.0
31.0	30.0	31.5	Gross Profit				28.2	28.1	35.5
22.3	26.9	25.1	Operating Expenses				23.5	20.7	24.6
8.7	3.1	6.3	Operating Profit				4.7	7.4	10.9
.9	1.1	1.0	All Other Expenses (net)				.9	.4	1.0
7.8	2.1	5.3	Profit Before Taxes				3.8	7.0	9.9
			RATIOS						
3.9	3.6	3.4	Current				4.0	2.7	5.0
2.2	2.2	1.8					1.4	1.7	3.4
1.6	1.4	1.3					1.2	1.3	1.9
2.2	2.5	2.3	Quick				2.5	1.8	3.5
1.5	1.3	1.0					.9	1.0	2.2
.7	.8	.7					.6	.8	1.4
37 10.0	38 9.6	41 8.9	Sales/Receivables				43 8.5	41 8.8	46 7.9
45 8.2	46 7.9	51 7.2					59 6.2	52 7.1	52 7.0
54 6.8	57 6.5	65 5.6					68 5.4	74 4.9	59 6.2
30 12.0	32 11.3	29 12.5	Cost of Sales/Inventory				23 16.1	22 16.7	34 10.8
63 5.8	53 6.9	56 6.5					41 8.8	57 6.5	63 5.8
91 4.0	87 4.2	77 4.7					71 5.2	75 4.9	105 3.5
15 23.6	20 18.1	21 17.6	Cost of Sales/Payables				17 21.5	22 17.0	20 18.2
22 16.3	32 11.2	32 11.5					42 8.7	24 15.0	32 11.5
41 9.0	47 7.7	49 7.4					53 6.9	32 11.5	42 8.7
4.4	4.1	4.3	Sales/Working Capital				4.3	5.0	2.5
5.6	6.4	7.8					9.2	8.0	3.6
9.4	12.0	14.7					23.9	14.1	5.6
23.4	22.1	24.3	EBIT/Interest				17.4		
(35) 9.6	(41) 2.9	(42) 6.0					(14) 4.5		
3.5	-2.5	2.1					2.0		
7.6	10.5	8.7	Net Profit + Depr., Dep., Amort./Cur. Mat. L/T/D						
(11) 5.1	(15) 3.7	(14) 2.9							
1.5	1.8	.8							
.2	.1	.1	Fixed/Worth				.1	.1	.1
.3	.3	.3					.4	.3	.2
.6	.8	.5					.7	.3	.5
.3	.5	.4	Debt/Worth				.4	.4	.3
1.1	1.1	1.4					1.6	1.5	.8
3.0	2.6	3.1					3.1	2.9	1.5
59.3	32.3	35.0	% Profit Before Taxes/Tangible Net Worth				30.5	33.1	43.2
(37) 32.9	(40) 11.5	(42) 18.9					(14) 14.2	20.5	30.9
16.0	-2.9	4.1					2.5	13.2	14.7
29.5	14.2	23.4	% Profit Before Taxes/Total Assets				12.7	23.4	25.7
13.1	3.8	7.9					7.4	7.9	15.1
4.4	-5.7	1.0					1.0	3.1	6.9
61.6	44.6	44.5	Sales/Net Fixed Assets				140.8	53.7	21.0
21.5	16.9	18.4					28.5	28.3	12.5
10.0	7.1	8.9					11.4	17.1	8.4
3.0	2.9	2.8	Sales/Total Assets				3.3	2.8	2.2
2.3	2.1	2.3					2.5	2.4	1.9
1.7	1.4	1.8					2.0	1.8	1.4
.3	.6	.7	% Depr., Dep., Amort./Sales				.2	.2	.9
(32) 1.0	(41) 1.2	(42) 1.2					(12) 1.4	(10) .8	1.8
2.0	2.7	2.3					2.3	1.5	2.6
2.8	1.6	2.1	% Officers', Directors' Owners' Comp/Sales						
(10) 6.3	(18) 4.1	(20) 3.8							
11.9	12.9	11.3							
1580284M	1178867M	1303929M	Net Sales ($)	672M	7335M	15849M	106286M	173149M	1000638M
1018234M	884635M	763031M	Total Assets ($)	232M	3873M	7579M	42563M	79698M	629086M

M = $ thousand   MM = $ million
See Pages 9 through 22 for Explanation of Ratios and Data

Current Data Sorted by Assets   Comparative Historical Data

		1	9	5		Type of Statement	22	19
	5	9	6			Unqualified	22	19
	5	5				Reviewed	16	14
5	6	2				Compiled	12	11
2	5	17	5		3	Tax Returns	7	2
						Other	41	27

0-500M	500M-2MM	2-10MM	10-50MM	50-100MM	100-250MM		4/1/06-3/31/07 ALL	4/1/07-3/31/08 ALL
	23 (4/1-9/30/10)		67 (10/1/10-3/31/11)					
7	21	34	20	8		NUMBER OF STATEMENTS	98	73
%	%	%	%	%	%	**ASSETS**	%	%
	12.8	12.9	14.1			Cash & Equivalents	8.9	10.6
	33.8	29.3	29.6			Trade Receivables (net)	30.9	30.9
	26.7	29.5	24.2			Inventory	30.8	27.4
	6.0	6.0	3.6			All Other Current	2.8	3.9
	79.3	77.8	71.5			Total Current	73.4	72.9
	7.8	14.9	18.2			Fixed Assets (net)	16.8	16.6
	4.9	1.7	7.2			Intangibles (net)	4.2	4.7
	8.0	5.6	3.1			All Other Non-Current	5.7	5.8
	100.0	100.0	100.0			Total	100.0	100.0
						LIABILITIES		
	4.1	7.5	9.7			Notes Payable-Short Term	7.8	7.9
	3.0	2.3	1.8			Cur. Mat.-L.T.D.	2.5	2.2
	17.3	13.2	11.1			Trade Payables	15.3	11.5
	.0	.2	.3			Income Taxes Payable	.3	.2
	14.9	9.9	15.2			All Other Current	13.0	13.9
	39.4	33.0	38.1			Total Current	39.0	35.7
	8.2	9.9	8.0			Long-Term Debt	12.2	11.1
	.0	.2	.8			Deferred Taxes	.2	.3
	1.6	7.0	8.2			All Other Non-Current	6.7	3.4
	50.8	49.8	44.9			Net Worth	42.0	49.5
	100.0	100.0	100.0			Total Liabilities & Net Worth	100.0	100.0
						INCOME DATA		
	100.0	100.0	100.0			Net Sales	100.0	100.0
	38.5	40.4	34.5			Gross Profit	34.5	32.4
	33.1	31.2	25.5			Operating Expenses	27.7	25.0
	5.4	9.2	9.0			Operating Profit	6.8	7.4
	.2	.7	.8			All Other Expenses (net)	.5	.8
	5.2	8.5	8.2			Profit Before Taxes	6.3	6.6
						RATIOS		
	3.4	4.6	3.0				2.9	3.2
	1.9	2.4	2.0			Current	1.9	1.8
	1.4	1.6	1.3				1.4	1.5
	1.7	3.1	2.3				1.6	1.7
	1.1	1.3	1.1			Quick	1.0	1.1
	.8	.7	.6				.7	.7
	25 14.3	35 10.6	50 7.2				39 9.3	42 8.6
	39 9.4	52 7.0	58 6.3			Sales/Receivables	49 7.4	53 6.9
	57 6.4	63 5.8	63 5.8				65 5.6	66 5.5
	5 77.5	43 8.6	47 7.8				39 9.4	38 9.6
	36 10.0	100 3.6	80 4.6			Cost of Sales/Inventory	88 4.2	79 4.6
	115 3.2	157 2.3	130 2.8				145 2.5	118 3.1
	20 18.5	22 16.8	19 19.2				20 18.6	16 22.8
	28 13.1	31 11.8	31 11.8			Cost of Sales/Payables	33 11.1	30 12.0
	46 8.0	60 6.0	48 7.6				54 6.8	40 9.2
	3.7	3.0	3.2				3.6	3.9
	7.9	5.0	5.6			Sales/Working Capital	6.7	5.7
	14.6	7.6	11.6				13.1	9.1
	18.9	83.7	89.3				16.6	14.1
	(14) 5.5	(32) 11.6	13.0			EBIT/Interest	(85) 4.9	(62) 5.3
	-.3	2.1	2.1				1.9	1.3
						Net Profit + Depr., Dep.,	15.3	9.4
						Amort./Cur. Mat. L/T/D	(32) 3.4	(14) 4.6
							1.3	1.7
	.0	.2	.3				.2	.1
	.1	.2	.5			Fixed/Worth	.4	.4
	.4	.5	.8				1.0	.7
	.4	.4	.6				.6	.5
	1.4	1.0	1.9			Debt/Worth	1.4	1.2
	2.0	2.7	2.7				3.6	2.1
	47.0	47.8	56.8				56.4	48.0
	23.8	(32) 23.2	(19) 20.7			% Profit Before Taxes/Tangible Net Worth	(86) 21.2	(69) 25.2
	6.2	9.4	13.0				7.5	9.8
	24.3	26.7	20.1				18.1	19.7
	7.3	10.5	9.6			% Profit Before Taxes/Total Assets	7.9	11.3
	2.0	2.6	3.4				2.6	2.4
	190.5	27.0	16.4				34.1	44.3
	61.8	16.6	10.1			Sales/Net Fixed Assets	15.1	15.9
	24.4	9.0	7.1				7.8	7.0
	3.4	2.7	2.0				2.7	2.7
	2.9	1.9	1.6			Sales/Total Assets	2.0	2.1
	2.1	1.3	1.3				1.5	1.4
	.4	.8	1.3				.8	.8
	(15) .7	(32) 1.4	(19) 2.0			% Depr., Dep., Amort./Sales	(82) 1.6	(62) 1.3
	1.2	2.8	2.6				2.6	2.4
	2.5	.7					2.8	2.8
	(10) 4.9	(10) 2.7				% Officers', Directors' Owners' Comp/Sales	(24) 5.8	(20) 4.8
	9.8	5.5					10.0	9.6
4235M	76705M	398987M	758248M	755033M		Net Sales ($)	3421537M	2115855M
1711M	28281M	183406M	476887M	588785M		Total Assets ($)	2010419M	1332757M

(Vertical note across ASSETS/LIABILITIES columns 0-500M, 50-100MM, 100-250MM: "DATA NOT AVAILABLE")

M = $ thousand   MM = $ million
See Pages 9 through 22 for Explanation of Ratios and Data

Comparative Historical Data | Current Data Sorted by Sales

4/1/08-3/31/09 ALL	4/1/09-3/31/10 ALL	4/1/10-3/31/11 ALL	Type of Statement	0-1MM	1-3MM	3-5MM	5-10MM	10-25MM	25MM & OVER
15	13	15	Unqualified				1	1	13
18	16	20	Reviewed	1	2	1	3	9	4
11	13	10	Compiled		1	4	4	1	
8	7	13	Tax Returns	4	3	3	2	1	
25	23	32	Other	2	3	7	3	8	9
						23 (4/1-9/30/10)		67 (10/1/10-3/31/11)	
77	72	90	NUMBER OF STATEMENTS	7	9	15	13	20	26
%	%	%	ASSETS	%	%	%	%	%	%
9.8	13.4	13.4	Cash & Equivalents			16.6	10.8	13.9	14.0
29.1	26.6	29.7	Trade Receivables (net)			34.5	29.7	34.6	26.6
29.4	28.6	27.0	Inventory			25.4	26.4	28.9	25.3
4.5	3.5	4.9	All Other Current			5.3	8.4	5.2	3.6
72.9	72.1	75.0	Total Current			81.8	75.3	82.6	69.5
14.5	16.1	12.9	Fixed Assets (net)			14.1	14.3	12.2	16.7
6.4	6.4	4.5	Intangibles (net)			.2	3.1	.8	8.9
6.3	5.4	7.7	All Other Non-Current			3.9	7.3	4.4	4.9
100.0	100.0	100.0	Total			100.0	100.0	100.0	100.0
			LIABILITIES						
10.1	9.5	7.2	Notes Payable-Short Term			5.4	6.9	7.8	8.7
3.6	2.6	3.1	Cur. Mat.-L.T.D.			1.8	2.8	1.7	1.6
12.5	10.5	14.2	Trade Payables			14.6	16.9	15.8	9.8
.3	.1	.1	Income Taxes Payable			.0	.0	.3	.3
12.5	11.8	12.4	All Other Current			15.3	11.1	12.3	14.2
39.0	34.4	37.0	Total Current			37.1	37.8	37.9	34.5
8.9	9.9	9.7	Long-Term Debt			13.7	5.4	6.3	7.0
.2	.3	.4	Deferred Taxes			.0	.2	.4	.9
6.5	7.2	7.2	All Other Non-Current			2.9	4.7	7.9	11.1
45.3	48.2	45.7	Net Worth			46.2	52.0	47.5	46.5
100.0	100.0	100.0	Total Liabilities & Net Worth			100.0	100.0	100.0	100.0
			INCOME DATA						
100.0	100.0	100.0	Net Sales			100.0	100.0	100.0	100.0
32.5	35.9	37.7	Gross Profit			33.3	45.5	36.1	33.1
26.9	30.9	30.1	Operating Expenses			27.9	38.3	26.4	24.7
5.5	5.0	7.6	Operating Profit			5.5	7.2	9.7	8.4
1.0	1.0	.6	All Other Expenses (net)			.7	.4	.2	1.1
4.5	4.0	7.0	Profit Before Taxes			4.7	6.8	9.5	7.4
			RATIOS						
3.4	4.2	3.5	Current			6.1	4.1	4.3	3.4
2.1	2.1	2.1				1.9	1.8	2.2	2.1
1.4	1.4	1.4				1.5	1.3	1.6	1.3
2.1	2.4	2.4	Quick			1.8	2.0	3.2	2.4
.9	1.3	1.2				1.4	1.0	1.3	1.2
.6	.7	.7				.7	.7	.7	.6
37 9.8	37 10.0	35 10.6	Sales/Receivables			30 12.1	30 12.4	46 7.9	49 7.5
46 7.9	47 7.7	52 7.1				48 7.5	45 8.1	56 6.5	57 6.5
61 6.0	59 6.1	64 5.7				59 6.2	70 5.2	64 5.7	64 5.7
43 8.5	50 7.3	34 10.7	Cost of Sales/Inventory			7 54.6	37 9.9	38 9.7	49 7.4
82 4.4	95 3.8	80 4.6				42 8.6	105 3.5	73 5.0	89 4.1
117 3.1	132 2.8	140 2.6				122 3.0	162 2.3	132 2.8	125 2.9
15 23.7	13 29.1	22 16.8	Cost of Sales/Payables			24 15.0	20 18.3	25 14.9	18 20.1
28 13.1	23 15.9	30 12.2				28 13.1	43 8.5	32 11.4	30 12.0
40 9.0	40 9.0	49 7.5				36 10.0	67 5.5	64 5.7	41 8.8
4.2	3.7	3.2	Sales/Working Capital			2.6	3.1	3.1	3.2
5.9	5.1	5.6				6.7	6.1	5.2	5.7
13.3	10.8	11.0				10.2	15.5	7.3	11.1
24.4	18.4	40.5	EBIT/Interest			66.8	148.5	78.7	92.9
(67) 5.9	(61) 2.7	(76) 10.3				(12) 7.6	12.7	(19) 12.0	(23) 11.4
1.7	.5	1.9				1.1	3.1	5.5	1.9
9.4	11.8	6.7	Net Profit + Depr., Dep., Amort./Cur. Mat. L/T/D						
(21) 3.2	(17) 4.5	(19) 4.5							
.6	.2	1.6							
.1	.1	.1	Fixed/Worth			.1	.1	.2	.2
.4	.4	.3				.2	.2	.3	.4
1.1	.9	.6				.6	.6	.5	.9
.4	.4	.4	Debt/Worth			.3	.4	.5	.3
1.2	1.0	1.2				1.2	.9	1.0	1.4
3.3	3.5	2.8				4.2	2.3	2.6	3.0
45.0	38.6	49.4	% Profit Before Taxes/Tangible Net Worth			37.4	53.5	49.4	56.7
(67) 22.8	(64) 13.7	(83) 22.8				(14) 15.5	31.5	(19) 25.4	(24) 24.2
5.3	-.3	8.9				5.7	8.0	9.2	14.2
18.4	16.1	22.7	% Profit Before Taxes/Total Assets			23.4	23.9	28.3	20.8
6.3	4.6	8.5				6.6	14.3	11.3	10.1
1.0	-.2	2.3				.5	3.0	4.7	2.2
54.3	40.7	60.8	Sales/Net Fixed Assets			104.7	24.6	33.3	16.8
19.2	16.2	17.5				52.2	14.8	18.0	10.9
9.2	7.2	9.1				7.9	9.1	9.7	7.1
2.8	2.8	2.7	Sales/Total Assets			3.0	2.9	2.7	2.0
2.2	1.9	1.9				2.1	2.3	2.3	1.5
1.5	1.4	1.3				1.5	1.5	1.3	1.3
.6	.6	.8	% Depr., Dep., Amort./Sales			.5	.7	.6	1.3
(62) 1.4	(64) 1.4	(77) 1.3				(11) 1.2	1.6	(19) 1.1	(25) 2.2
2.2	2.4	2.6				3.5	3.4	1.7	2.9
3.1	2.5	2.1	% Officers', Directors' Owners' Comp/Sales						
(27) 6.7	(24) 5.1	(29) 3.4							
10.3	11.2	10.0							
2395640M	1609917M	1993208M	Net Sales ($)	2949M	20501M	60405M	90669M	322136M	1496548M
1383535M	1056357M	1279070M	Total Assets ($)	2080M	11734M	28614M	49659M	160349M	1026634M

Current Data Sorted by Assets | Comparative Historical Data

0-500M	500M-2MM	2-10MM	10-50MM	50-100MM	100-250MM	Type of Statement	4/1/06-3/31/07 ALL	4/1/07-3/31/08 ALL
		2	5	3	3	Unqualified	19	14
		12	4			Reviewed	14	10
1	5	7	1			Compiled	8	7
2	3	3				Tax Returns	7	2
	4	8	5	2	2	Other	33	21
	12 (4/1-9/30/10)		60 (10/1/10-3/31/11)					
3	12	32	15	5	5	**NUMBER OF STATEMENTS**	81	54
%	%	%	%	%	%	**ASSETS**	%	%
	8.3	12.1	17.8			Cash & Equivalents	6.9	7.8
	27.1	27.4	26.1			Trade Receivables (net)	34.0	30.9
	33.1	32.6	24.3			Inventory	29.5	33.0
	.4	3.4	2.8			All Other Current	1.9	2.2
	68.9	75.4	71.0			Total Current	72.3	74.0
	23.2	13.6	19.8			Fixed Assets (net)	16.9	16.8
	5.2	5.7	4.0			Intangibles (net)	6.0	4.7
	2.6	5.2	5.2			All Other Non-Current	4.8	4.4
	100.0	100.0	100.0			Total	100.0	100.0
						LIABILITIES		
	6.4	7.2	16.0			Notes Payable-Short Term	8.9	11.8
	2.6	2.8	1.7			Cur. Mat.-L.T.D.	3.3	2.1
	21.0	15.2	11.6			Trade Payables	19.1	17.7
	.0	.2	.2			Income Taxes Payable	.4	.3
	12.8	7.3	8.1			All Other Current	10.7	7.6
	42.8	32.7	37.6			Total Current	42.4	39.6
	13.3	14.0	5.9			Long-Term Debt	11.1	10.5
	.1	.3	1.2			Deferred Taxes	.4	.4
	3.9	4.4	1.6			All Other Non-Current	4.2	4.8
	40.0	48.5	53.7			Net Worth	42.0	44.8
	100.0	100.0	100.0			Total Liabilities & Net Worth	100.0	100.0
						INCOME DATA		
	100.0	100.0	100.0			Net Sales	100.0	100.0
	37.4	32.7	30.1			Gross Profit	27.0	27.6
	32.4	24.8	20.1			Operating Expenses	20.3	21.9
	5.0	7.9	10.0			Operating Profit	6.7	5.7
	.8	1.1	.5			All Other Expenses (net)	1.0	.9
	4.2	6.7	9.5			Profit Before Taxes	5.7	4.8
						RATIOS		
	3.0	4.1	3.4				2.5	2.7
	2.1	2.6	1.8			Current	1.9	2.0
	1.0	1.6	1.1				1.3	1.4
	1.5	2.2	2.5				1.4	1.6
	1.0	1.3	1.2			Quick	1.0	1.1
	.5	.7	.5				.7	.6
	36 10.3	35 10.4	39 9.3				37 9.9	40 9.1
	51 7.1	41 8.8	46 7.9			Sales/Receivables	51 7.2	48 7.6
	74 4.9	48 7.6	53 6.9				68 5.4	58 6.3
	53 6.9	49 7.5	49 7.5				45 8.2	51 7.1
	86 4.3	79 4.6	85 4.3			Cost of Sales/Inventory	67 5.5	71 5.1
	133 2.8	109 3.4	99 3.7				92 4.0	106 3.5
	33 10.9	20 18.7	13 27.6				22 16.4	24 15.4
	40 9.1	30 12.1	23 15.6			Cost of Sales/Payables	35 10.5	32 11.6
	111 3.3	39 9.4	39 9.4				46 8.0	44 8.4
	4.1	3.5	3.8				4.4	4.6
	8.8	6.6	5.2			Sales/Working Capital	7.5	7.4
	NM	9.7	18.6				24.1	12.5
	8.7	16.5	105.5				15.5	21.3
	(11) 4.2	(24) 7.8	(12) 8.5			EBIT/Interest	(71) 5.9	(49) 4.5
	2.3	3.5	3.9				2.0	1.8
		4.8				Net Profit + Depr., Dep.,	11.0	8.3
		(10) 3.5				Amort./Cur. Mat. L/T/D	(21) 6.5	(20) 3.6
		1.9					2.0	2.2
	.2	.1	.2				.2	.2
	.8	.2	.4			Fixed/Worth	.5	.3
	NM	1.3	1.0				1.0	.9
	.6	.5	.3				.6	.6
	1.7	1.4	1.0			Debt/Worth	1.3	1.5
	NM	5.3	3.5				6.1	3.9
		57.9	47.7				49.1	47.1
		(31) 29.3	(14) 26.5			% Profit Before Taxes/Tangible Net Worth	(69) 29.9	(49) 22.3
		21.4	13.5				12.4	7.1
	14.9	21.6	29.5				19.5	22.6
	7.4	13.8	16.5			% Profit Before Taxes/Total Assets	11.4	9.3
	3.5	7.5	3.1				3.4	2.8
	79.7	74.7	16.6				38.9	40.3
	17.4	26.3	10.5			Sales/Net Fixed Assets	14.3	13.4
	7.5	10.7	4.0				7.9	9.0
	3.4	2.9	2.7				3.0	3.0
	2.5	2.3	1.8			Sales/Total Assets	2.4	2.3
	1.5	1.9	1.4				1.7	1.7
		.7	.9				.7	.7
		(25) 1.2	(14) 1.5			% Depr., Dep., Amort./Sales	(60) 1.4	(45) 1.6
		1.9	2.7				2.0	2.1
		5.8				% Officers', Directors'	1.6	1.8
		(10) 6.9				Owners' Comp/Sales	(20) 3.8	(20) 3.4
		14.5					6.4	5.5
3663M	46288M	389115M	865511M	554457M	1755768M	Net Sales ($)	5021621M	3826778M
1007M	15530M	159778M	405437M	350902M	950596M	Total Assets ($)	2669163M	2011654M

M = $ thousand   MM = $ million
See Pages 9 through 22 for Explanation of Ratios and Data

Comparative Historical Data | Current Data Sorted by Sales

Hist 1	Hist 2	Hist 3	Type of Statement	0-1MM	1-3MM	3-5MM	5-10MM	10-25MM	25MM & OVER
15	15	13	Unqualified					4	9
10	11	16	Reviewed			1	5	5	5
8	11	14	Compiled		3	2	4	4	1
1	4	8	Tax Returns	2		1	2	1	1
21	22	21	Other	1	1	3	4	3	9
4/1/08-3/31/09 ALL	4/1/09-3/31/10 ALL	4/1/10-3/31/11 ALL		12 (4/1-9/30/10)			60 (10/1/10-3/31/11)		
55	63	72	NUMBER OF STATEMENTS	3	5	7	15	17	25
%	%	%	**ASSETS**	%	%	%	%	%	%
10.7	10.6	12.3	Cash & Equivalents				11.4	9.9	14.5
27.6	23.9	27.2	Trade Receivables (net)				27.7	21.6	29.8
31.3	29.3	30.5	Inventory				28.6	35.8	26.1
2.5	2.1	2.4	All Other Current				5.6	2.7	1.1
72.1	65.9	72.5	Total Current				73.3	69.9	71.5
16.1	20.2	17.2	Fixed Assets (net)				10.6	22.5	17.7
5.3	6.5	5.3	Intangibles (net)				9.9	2.1	5.5
6.5	7.4	5.0	All Other Non-Current				6.2	5.5	5.3
100.0	100.0	100.0	Total				100.0	100.0	100.0
			LIABILITIES						
9.1	7.4	10.0	Notes Payable-Short Term				2.5	13.1	12.3
1.9	3.6	2.5	Cur. Mat.-L.T.D.				3.0	3.3	2.2
15.0	12.1	16.5	Trade Payables				12.8	15.1	17.1
.1	.1	.2	Income Taxes Payable				.0	.3	.5
9.3	8.9	11.2	All Other Current				7.4	9.0	8.4
35.4	32.2	40.5	Total Current				25.7	40.8	40.4
11.3	10.3	10.8	Long-Term Debt				16.7	13.2	6.0
.2	1.0	.5	Deferred Taxes				.0	.6	.9
3.2	6.2	4.6	All Other Non-Current				1.9	6.6	4.0
49.9	50.2	43.6	Net Worth				55.7	38.8	48.7
100.0	100.0	100.0	Total Liabilities & Net Worth				100.0	100.0	100.0
			INCOME DATA						
100.0	100.0	100.0	Net Sales				100.0	100.0	100.0
29.8	30.4	32.9	Gross Profit				33.6	33.8	25.2
23.8	25.1	25.9	Operating Expenses				23.0	27.3	18.2
6.0	5.4	7.0	Operating Profit				10.6	6.5	7.0
.4	1.0	1.0	All Other Expenses (net)				1.4	1.0	.9
5.5	4.4	5.9	Profit Before Taxes				9.2	5.5	6.1
			RATIOS						
3.3	3.7	3.4	Current				4.1	3.0	3.0
2.2	2.2	2.0					3.1	2.0	1.8
1.5	1.3	1.3					1.9	1.2	1.1
1.7	2.2	2.0	Quick				2.3	1.4	2.0
1.1	1.2	1.0					1.7	.7	1.0
.7	.6	.5					1.0	.5	.6
28 13.1	33 11.1	37 9.9	Sales/Receivables				37 9.9	33 11.1	41 9.0
40 9.1	46 7.9	45 8.1					43 8.5	39 9.5	48 7.7
49 7.5	52 7.0	52 7.0					48 7.6	46 7.9	56 6.6
43 8.5	53 6.9	49 7.4	Cost of Sales/Inventory				49 7.5	64 5.7	38 9.5
66 5.5	84 4.3	85 4.3					74 4.9	98 3.7	73 5.0
105 3.5	118 3.1	114 3.2					99 3.7	110 3.3	104 3.5
17 22.0	17 21.0	23 16.1	Cost of Sales/Payables				17 21.8	24 15.4	18 20.7
29 12.7	28 13.2	33 11.0					32 11.4	33 10.9	31 11.8
42 8.6	43 8.4	47 7.7					38 9.6	39 9.4	48 7.6
4.5	3.6	3.8	Sales/Working Capital				3.6	4.9	3.8
7.2	6.2	7.1					6.3	7.4	6.8
14.8	13.0	13.2					8.6	21.2	19.4
36.6	16.9	17.1	EBIT/Interest				166.8	11.8	48.6
(47) 7.2	(54) 4.4	(59) 6.8		(10) 9.5				(15) 5.6	(21) 7.6
1.8	.4	2.7					4.0	2.7	2.6
8.5	8.0	4.9	Net Profit + Depr., Dep., Amort./Cur. Mat. L/T/D						
(19) 3.4	(19) 2.9	(19) 3.3							
1.3	.2	2.1							
.1	.2	.1	Fixed/Worth				.1	.2	.2
.3	.5	.4					.2	.6	.4
.8	.9	1.4					.9	1.9	1.1
.5	.5	.5	Debt/Worth				.3	.7	.5
1.2	1.1	1.4					.9	1.4	1.1
2.4	3.3	6.1					2.1	7.3	3.8
54.4	39.9	45.0	% Profit Before Taxes/Tangible Net Worth				82.0	49.9	38.0
(52) 21.6	(57) 14.8	(65) 28.2		(14) 35.8				(16) 31.7	(24) 23.0
6.4	-1.4	12.2					26.5	13.9	7.9
27.6	18.7	20.6	% Profit Before Taxes/Total Assets				27.4	20.0	18.4
11.9	5.9	11.6					20.6	9.8	11.4
2.8	-.2	4.3					9.9	5.7	3.1
57.8	34.6	46.5	Sales/Net Fixed Assets				148.6	26.3	17.8
16.0	12.0	16.1					33.3	15.6	13.2
8.7	5.1	7.4					14.3	6.5	5.5
3.5	2.4	2.7	Sales/Total Assets				3.0	2.6	2.5
2.5	2.0	2.2					2.5	2.1	1.9
1.9	1.4	1.6					1.6	1.8	1.3
.7	.9	.7	% Depr., Dep., Amort./Sales					.8	.7
(47) 1.0	(52) 2.1	(56) 1.4						(16) 1.7	(20) 1.5
2.3	3.4	2.6						2.5	2.8
2.8	2.7	2.9	% Officers', Directors' Owners' Comp/Sales						
(15) 4.2	(19) 4.4	(22) 6.4							
8.0	7.0	9.8							
4308514M	4269545M	3614802M	Net Sales ($)	2410M	7937M	25654M	105800M	262525M	3210476M
1940061M	2479891M	1883250M	Total Assets ($)	2945M	3571M	13629M	47750M	120897M	1694458M

M = $ thousand   MM = $ million
See Pages 9 through 22 for Explanation of Ratios and Data

Current Data Sorted by Assets

Comparative Historical Data

						Type of Statement		
1	9	5 / 30	13 / 8	4	6	Unqualified	45	35
2	11	18	1			Reviewed	30	43
4	21	6	2			Compiled	19	28
6	29	42	27	11	7	Tax Returns	28	26
	43 (4/1-9/30/10)		220 (10/1/10-3/31/11)			Other	78	94
							4/1/06-3/31/07	4/1/07-3/31/08
0-500M	500M-2MM	2-10MM	10-50MM	50-100MM	100-250MM		ALL	ALL
13	70	101	51	15	13	**NUMBER OF STATEMENTS**	200	226
%	%	%	%	%	%	**ASSETS**	%	%
20.7	12.9	11.4	8.0	8.1	12.5	Cash & Equivalents	8.9	9.4
40.4	34.9	27.5	26.5	26.3	20.3	Trade Receivables (net)	31.7	30.7
14.1	30.3	29.7	30.7	23.5	16.5	Inventory	28.6	28.5
2.6	1.7	4.0	3.1	7.8	3.3	All Other Current	3.4	3.3
77.8	79.9	72.7	68.4	65.7	52.6	Total Current	72.6	71.9
9.8	12.2	15.6	14.9	14.3	13.9	Fixed Assets (net)	16.1	15.7
6.4	2.1	4.6	9.8	17.3	27.3	Intangibles (net)	5.0	7.1
6.0	5.9	7.1	6.8	2.7	6.2	All Other Non-Current	6.3	5.3
100.0	100.0	100.0	100.0	100.0	100.0	Total	100.0	100.0
						LIABILITIES		
12.1	12.2	9.6	8.9	3.8	2.9	Notes Payable-Short Term	9.6	11.2
2.5	2.4	2.1	2.1	5.1	2.1	Cur. Mat.-L.T.D.	2.3	2.6
13.2	17.7	16.0	12.1	13.2	12.5	Trade Payables	16.3	15.1
.6	.2	.2	.3	.1	.8	Income Taxes Payable	.4	.5
13.5	7.3	13.6	9.9	10.1	10.7	All Other Current	11.1	11.4
41.8	39.8	41.5	33.3	32.4	28.9	Total Current	39.7	40.8
6.0	10.4	10.4	9.7	12.3	12.9	Long-Term Debt	10.8	12.3
.0	.0	.2	.8	1.2	1.7	Deferred Taxes	.3	.4
6.1	6.4	4.0	3.6	2.8	9.7	All Other Non-Current	5.6	6.9
46.0	43.4	43.9	52.6	51.2	46.8	Net Worth	43.7	39.5
100.0	100.0	100.0	100.0	100.0	100.0	Total Liabilties & Net Worth	100.0	100.0
						INCOME DATA		
100.0	100.0	100.0	100.0	100.0	100.0	Net Sales	100.0	100.0
42.2	36.9	38.4	29.7	28.3	36.1	Gross Profit	34.1	36.0
34.7	30.8	31.5	23.0	22.7	26.9	Operating Expenses	26.4	28.7
7.5	6.1	6.9	6.6	5.6	9.2	Operating Profit	7.7	7.3
.7	.3	.5	1.6	1.4	1.3	All Other Expenses (net)	.7	1.6
6.8	5.7	6.4	5.0	4.2	7.9	Profit Before Taxes	6.9	5.7
						RATIOS		
5.0	3.7	3.1	3.9	3.7	2.5		3.0	3.2
1.9	2.1	1.8	2.2	2.0	1.7	Current	1.9	2.0
1.3	1.3	1.2	1.5	1.5	1.4		1.3	1.3
3.1	2.2	1.5	1.8	2.0	1.9		1.7	1.9
1.3	1.2	.9	1.2	1.0	.9	Quick	1.1	1.1
.9	.7	.6	.7	.6	.7		.7	.6

														Sales/Receivables				
29	12.8	27	13.6	32	11.3	43	8.5	44	8.4	57	6.5			35	10.4	34	10.6
46	8.0	39	9.3	47	7.7	52	7.0	51	7.2	60	6.1		Sales/Receivables	47	7.8	48	7.6
65	5.6	51	7.1	60	6.1	61	5.9	73	5.0	73	5.0			64	5.7	62	5.9
0	UND	16	22.7	43	8.4	62	5.9	45	8.2	64	5.7			33	11.2	43	8.5
33	11.2	58	6.2	86	4.2	100	3.7	68	5.3	72	5.1		Cost of Sales/Inventory	74	5.0	75	4.9
63	5.8	97	3.8	124	3.0	131	2.8	114	3.2	117	3.1			115	3.2	123	3.0
7	49.9	13	27.2	23	15.7	20	18.7	23	15.8	39	9.4			19	19.0	18	20.1
20	18.6	27	13.4	36	10.0	36	10.2	35	10.6	52	7.0		Cost of Sales/Payables	34	10.7	32	11.3
32	11.4	46	7.9	61	5.9	47	7.7	47	7.8	84	4.3			50	7.3	51	7.2

													Sales/Working Capital				
	6.4		4.4		4.0		3.1		3.6		3.0				4.1		3.9
	14.8		8.3		6.7		4.7		6.5		5.9		Sales/Working Capital		6.9		6.5
	36.1		22.9		24.6		8.8		8.8		9.2				13.8		15.0
	19.8		24.1		31.7		30.2		64.1		125.1				19.4		14.7
(11)	6.5	(59)	10.7	(83)	11.0	(42)	8.0	(14)	8.7	(10)	30.4		EBIT/Interest	(177)	6.8	(205)	5.1
	3.0		2.4		2.7		1.6		-.1		.0				2.8		1.7
					5.3		13.8						Net Profit + Depr., Dep.,		14.7		9.1
		(17)	2.3	(17)	3.0								Amort./Cur. Mat. L/T/D	(53)	3.9	(51)	3.7
			1.4		1.0										2.0		1.3
	.0		.0		.1		.2		.3		.3				.1		.1
	.2		.3		.3		.3		.4		.5		Fixed/Worth		.3		.4
	.8		.7		.7		1.0		.7		-1.6				.7		1.2
	.4		.4		.5		.5		.7		.8				.6		.6
	.8		1.4		1.3		1.0		1.4		2.3		Debt/Worth		1.3		1.7
	NM		2.6		3.8		2.5		5.1		-13.7				3.3		5.5
	142.0		67.5		53.2		47.8		40.6				% Profit Before Taxes/Tangible		57.6		58.9
(10)	35.1	(62)	29.7	(91)	29.8	(44)	21.9	(14)	27.1				Net Worth	(183)	30.5	(196)	29.2
	16.3		9.9		8.9		5.2		2.5						11.0		10.4
	32.5		23.7		26.6		18.5		19.5		15.6		% Profit Before Taxes/Total		23.7		19.7
	10.6		12.9		10.0		8.0		7.1		12.2		Assets		11.1		9.8
	5.0		2.8		2.5		2.0		-1.2		-.4				3.6		2.8
	UND		128.6		51.7		33.2		32.5		17.1				51.4		54.8
	38.4		42.7		17.1		14.9		12.8		10.0		Sales/Net Fixed Assets		18.8		18.3
	24.0		15.3		10.3		6.6		7.8		6.3				8.5		8.1
	5.2		4.0		2.8		2.3		2.4		1.8				3.1		3.0
	4.6		3.0		2.1		1.6		1.5		1.1		Sales/Total Assets		2.3		2.2
	1.6		2.3		1.6		1.1		1.0		.7				1.6		1.4
			.3		.7		.8		1.3		1.6				.8		.7
		(43)	1.0	(80)	1.4	(47)	1.4	(14)	2.0	(11)	3.7	% Depr., Dep., Amort./Sales	(167)	1.4	(175)	1.5
			2.2		2.5		2.4		3.8		5.2				2.5		2.3
			.3		.7		.8		1.3				% Officers', Directors'		2.2		2.0
		(40)	4.7	(37)	3.1							Owners' Comp/Sales	(68)	4.5	(74)	4.6
			8.2		5.9										7.9		8.3

15385M	272658M	1039989M	2148429M	2280344M	2387326M	Net Sales ($)	7012109M	6995107M
3318M	83566M	472358M	1234906M	1185610M	1980020M	Total Assets ($)	3844307M	4344424M

Note on the % Officers' section rows: the values .3/.7/.8/1.3 in the top line belong to the % Depr., Dep., Amort./Sales grouping as noted above; the % Officers', Directors' Owners' Comp/Sales shows 3.4/4.7/8.2 and 2.0/3.1/5.9.

M = $ thousand   MM = $ million
See Pages 9 through 22 for Explanation of Ratios and Data

Comparative Historical Data						Type of Statement		Current Data Sorted by Sales					

						Type of Statement							
	35		46		29	Unqualified			1		4	4	20
	31		38		47	Reviewed			2	5	17	15	8
	21		28		32	Compiled	2		6	5	11	6	2
	33		33		33	Tax Returns	2		12	8	8	1	2
	108		101		122	Other	7		19	13	20	25	38
	4/1/08-3/31/09		4/1/09-3/31/10		4/1/10-3/31/11			43 (4/1-9/30/10)			220 (10/1/10-3/31/11)		
	ALL		ALL		ALL		0-1MM	1-3MM	3-5MM	5-10MM	10-25MM	25MM & OVER
	228		246		263	NUMBER OF STATEMENTS	11	40	31	60	51	70
	%		%		%	ASSETS	%	%	%	%	%	%
	8.7		10.5		11.5	Cash & Equivalents	15.9	15.8	10.2	10.2	11.5	10.0
	30.2		26.5		29.5	Trade Receivables (net)	31.4	32.8	24.5	32.9	27.8	28.0
	31.5		29.4		28.3	Inventory	25.6	29.8	33.5	26.5	29.5	26.1
	3.0		3.6		3.3	All Other Current	.7	2.3	5.1	2.4	3.2	4.5
	73.4		70.0		72.6	Total Current	73.7	80.7	73.2	72.0	72.1	68.5
	15.5		17.3		14.1	Fixed Assets (net)	14.1	9.8	16.4	14.7	16.5	13.4
	6.1		7.6		6.9	Intangibles (net)	5.4	3.6	4.4	4.7	5.0	13.4
	5.0		5.2		6.4	All Other Non-Current	6.8	6.0	6.0	8.6	6.4	4.7
	100.0		100.0		100.0	Total	100.0	100.0	100.0	100.0	100.0	100.0
						LIABILITIES						
	12.7		10.9		9.6	Notes Payable-Short Term	15.9	12.1	10.3	11.0	7.4	7.5
	2.4		3.2		2.4	Cur. Mat.-L.T.D.	.5	2.4	3.2	2.3	1.8	2.7
	15.8		14.1		15.2	Trade Payables	11.3	14.7	15.2	19.1	12.3	15.0
	.3		.3		.2	Income Taxes Payable	.6	.1	.3	.1	.2	.4
	11.1		12.1		10.9	All Other Current	9.3	9.5	4.8	14.3	11.0	11.4
	42.2		40.6		38.3	Total Current	37.7	38.8	33.8	46.8	32.7	37.0
	11.9		12.3		10.3	Long-Term Debt	13.2	14.2	7.0	10.3	9.4	9.7
	.4		.3		.4	Deferred Taxes	.0	.0	.3	.2	.2	1.0
	7.0		5.3		4.9	All Other Non-Current	4.4	10.0	4.1	4.2	3.8	3.7
	38.5		41.4		46.1	Net Worth	44.7	37.0	54.8	38.5	53.9	48.5
	100.0		100.0		100.0	Total Liabilties & Net Worth	100.0	100.0	100.0	100.0	100.0	100.0
						INCOME DATA						
	100.0		100.0		100.0	Net Sales	100.0	100.0	100.0	100.0	100.0	100.0
	33.7		34.6		35.8	Gross Profit	51.2	41.0	36.1	35.4	37.5	29.4
	28.1		30.1		29.1	Operating Expenses	42.5	34.7	30.6	30.8	28.7	22.1
	5.6		4.4		6.7	Operating Profit	8.7	6.4	5.5	4.5	8.9	7.3
	1.3		1.3		.8	All Other Expenses (net)	1.3	.6	.1	.5	.9	1.2
	4.3		3.2		5.9	Profit Before Taxes	7.4	5.8	5.5	4.0	7.9	6.2
						RATIOS						
	3.0		3.1		3.6		3.8	4.7	3.7	2.4	4.3	2.9
	1.8		1.8		2.0	Current	2.2	2.3	2.4	1.7	2.5	1.9
	1.2		1.2		1.3		1.1	1.2	1.5	1.1	1.4	1.4
	1.7		1.7		1.9		2.2	3.2	1.6	1.8	2.6	1.6
	.9		.9		1.1	Quick	.8	1.3	.9	1.0	1.3	1.0
	.6		.5		.6		.5	.8	.6	.6	.8	.6

33	11.1	32	11.6	34	10.6		23	15.7	32	11.4	25	14.4	32	11.2	34	10.6	43	8.4
44	8.4	44	8.3	48	7.6	Sales/Receivables	46	8.0	43	8.5	37	9.8	44	8.2	49	7.5	55	6.7
56	6.5	59	6.2	60	6.0		67	5.4	61	5.9	51	7.2	60	6.1	60	6.1	64	5.7
48	7.6	44	8.4	39	9.4		0	UND	29	12.5	50	7.3	22	16.6	38	9.6	50	7.4
76	4.8	75	4.9	72	5.1	Cost of Sales/Inventory	71	5.1	72	5.1	88	4.2	58	6.3	87	4.2	74	4.9
113	3.2	115	3.2	120	3.0		285	1.3	160	2.3	122	3.0	115	3.2	131	2.8	109	3.3
18	19.7	19	19.3	18	19.9		12	31.3	13	28.5	15	24.9	18	20.2	13	27.6	25	14.8
32	11.4	31	11.8	34	10.7	Cost of Sales/Payables	27	13.5	29	12.7	34	10.6	41	8.8	27	13.4	37	10.0
52	7.1	50	7.4	52	7.0		152	2.4	51	7.2	46	8.0	61	6.0	50	7.3	51	7.2
	4.8		3.8		3.8			1.7		3.1		3.7		4.9		3.5		3.6
	7.3		7.6		6.7	Sales/Working Capital		7.4		6.3		5.7		10.0		5.3		6.5
	18.3		18.4		18.0			29.1		19.0		19.0		31.3		11.0		10.1
	22.5		15.8		28.8					11.7		24.3		27.5		55.6		54.8
(203)	5.6	(221)	4.0	(219)	10.5	EBIT/Interest		(32)	4.7	(26)	14.6	(51)	9.5	(43)	19.8	(58)	8.9
	1.3		1.0		2.3					1.6		2.9		2.3		4.8		1.5
	17.5		4.6		5.7									5.9				6.9
(55)	3.5	(56)	2.2	(54)	2.3	Net Profit + Depr., Dep., Amort./Cur. Mat. L/T/D						(12)	2.5			(25)	2.4
	1.2		.4		1.0									1.7				.9
	.1		.2		.1			.0		.0		.0		.2		.1		.2
	.4		.4		.3	Fixed/Worth		.4		.2		.3		.3		.3		.3
	1.2		1.4		.8			-2.0		1.6		.5		.6		.9		.7
	.8		.7		.5			.3		.4		.3		.7		.3		.6
	1.6		1.6		1.3	Debt/Worth		.7		1.9		1.0		1.6		.9		1.4
	5.3		5.3		3.1			-18.2		47.3		1.8		4.0		2.2		3.0
	59.1		45.0		55.0	% Profit Before Taxes/Tangible Net Worth				80.2		46.4		52.0		61.5		52.4
(200)	25.6	(212)	18.5	(230)	28.4			(31)	24.8	(29)	26.3	(53)	23.8	(49)	32.0	(60)	27.5
	7.5		1.9		9.0					9.5		5.0		8.2		16.5		7.5
	19.1		14.9		21.9	% Profit Before Taxes/Total Assets		24.6		20.7		23.7		21.5		29.7		19.2
	8.9		6.2		10.6			7.9		7.2		13.5		9.5		15.8		10.3
	.9		.1		2.5			.3		1.9		2.5		1.7		5.7		2.2
	59.2		51.4		54.9			31.9		236.5		64.6		53.3		54.9		35.6
	19.9		16.0		20.1	Sales/Net Fixed Assets		22.3		38.3		18.7		19.9		15.4		16.1
	8.8		6.7		10.3			17.1		12.9		10.4		11.5		7.0		8.3
	3.1		3.0		3.1			3.1		3.4		3.0		3.5		2.7		2.6
	2.3		2.0		2.1	Sales/Total Assets		1.3		2.5		2.3		2.6		2.0		1.8
	1.6		1.5		1.5			1.0		1.7		1.7		1.8		1.6		1.1
	.6		.7		.6			.3		.5		.7		.7		.7	
(185)	1.6	(195)	1.6	(200)	1.4	% Depr., Dep., Amort./Sales		(22)	1.3	(21)	1.0	(49)	1.3	(39)	1.6	(64)	1.5
	2.6		3.4		2.6					3.3		2.2		2.4		2.8		2.7
	2.0		2.5		2.3					3.7		3.3		2.3		1.8	
(69)	3.9	(73)	4.6	(90)	3.9	% Officers', Directors' Owners' Comp/Sales		(21)	5.5	(17)	4.7	(22)	3.3	(19)	2.4	
	5.6		9.0		6.9					9.4		8.0		5.4		4.1	
7779040M		8400981M		8144131M		Net Sales ($)	5796M	88798M	125612M	435282M	772457M	6716186M
4224101M		4978297M		4959778M		Total Assets ($)	3868M	42028M	61642M	207319M	455341M	4189580M

M = $ thousand   MM = $ million
See Pages 9 through 22 for Explanation of Ratios and Data

Current Data Sorted by Assets

Comparative Historical Data

							Type of Statement				
			2	1	1		Unqualified		14		12
1			1	1			Reviewed		6		7
		3					Compiled		7		7
3	2	3	1				Tax Returns		3		1
1	1	7	4	3	1		Other		20		19
	3 (4/1-9/30/10)		32 (10/1/10-3/31/11)						4/1/06-3/31/07		4/1/07-3/31/08
0-500M	500M-2MM	2-10MM	10-50MM	50-100MM	100-250MM				ALL		ALL
4	3	13	8	5	2		NUMBER OF STATEMENTS		50		46
%	%	%	%	%	%		ASSETS		%		%
		8.1					Cash & Equivalents		7.0		10.4
		20.1					Trade Receivables (net)		23.3		17.8
		34.8					Inventory		29.2		33.6
		6.0					All Other Current		2.7		4.4
		69.0					Total Current		62.2		66.2
		20.0					Fixed Assets (net)		26.2		21.7
		3.6					Intangibles (net)		4.7		4.8
		7.4					All Other Non-Current		6.9		7.3
		100.0					Total		100.0		100.0
							LIABILITIES				
		13.3					Notes Payable-Short Term		11.7		12.8
		7.9					Cur. Mat.-L.T.D.		1.9		5.6
		14.4					Trade Payables		14.9		13.0
		.0					Income Taxes Payable		.1		1.1
		13.5					All Other Current		16.3		14.7
		49.1					Total Current		44.8		47.2
		13.9					Long-Term Debt		14.7		15.3
		.4					Deferred Taxes		.8		.5
		17.3					All Other Non-Current		8.8		11.5
		19.3					Net Worth		30.9		25.6
		100.0					Total Liabilities & Net Worth		100.0		100.0
							INCOME DATA				
		100.0					Net Sales		100.0		100.0
		28.6					Gross Profit		22.5		24.2
		27.2					Operating Expenses		18.1		19.7
		1.4					Operating Profit		4.3		4.6
		1.8					All Other Expenses (net)		1.4		1.0
		-.5					Profit Before Taxes		2.9		3.5
							RATIOS				
		1.9							2.2		2.1
		1.5					Current		1.6		1.4
		1.0							1.0		1.1
		1.3							1.2		1.2
		.4					Quick		.7		.5
		.3							.4		.3
		20	17.9					30	12.1	13	28.4
		46	8.0				Sales/Receivables	44	8.2	27	13.4
		68	5.3					57	6.3	47	7.7
		27	13.5					24	15.0	31	11.7
		59	6.2				Cost of Sales/Inventory	63	5.8	55	6.6
		164	2.2					111	3.3	112	3.3
		17	21.5					26	14.1	14	26.0
		34	10.6				Cost of Sales/Payables	35	10.4	26	14.0
		53	6.9					57	6.4	43	8.5
		5.2							4.5		5.0
		12.6					Sales/Working Capital		9.9		9.9
		NM							-41.6		NM
		9.1							12.7		13.0
		(12)	3.8				EBIT/Interest	(40)	3.4	(42)	3.7
		-3.6							.8		.6
							Net Profit + Depr., Dep.,				3.2
							Amort./Cur. Mat. L/T/D			(16)	1.3
											.7
		.2							.3		.2
		.7					Fixed/Worth		1.5		1.2
		12.0							16.4		-2.5
		1.3							.7		1.2
		2.2					Debt/Worth		3.3		3.6
		28.0							63.5		-14.9
		23.9							54.6		36.8
		(11)	14.6				% Profit Before Taxes/Tangible	(39)	19.3	(34)	23.0
		-66.8					Net Worth		6.9		10.0
		9.1							17.0		14.4
		7.0					% Profit Before Taxes/Total		7.7		6.3
		-3.4					Assets		.7		-1.8
		33.0							21.8		43.5
		12.4					Sales/Net Fixed Assets		10.8		13.7
		7.2							4.1		7.9
		2.6							2.4		3.0
		2.0					Sales/Total Assets		1.8		2.1
		1.5							1.2		1.5
		.9							1.2		.6
		(10)	2.1				% Depr., Dep., Amort./Sales	(42)	2.2	(38)	1.6
		3.1							3.7		4.4
											.9
							% Officers', Directors'			(11)	1.9
							Owners' Comp/Sales				7.1
10043M	3464M	127642M	216588M	595807M	799648M		Net Sales ($)		3168636M		3185472M
1375M	2799M	63947M	163632M	386044M	257168M		Total Assets ($)		1861075M		1750852M

© RMA 2011

M = $ thousand   MM = $ million
See Pages 9 through 22 for Explanation of Ratios and Data

Comparative Historical Data   Current Data Sorted by Sales

4/1/08-3/31/09 ALL	4/1/09-3/31/10 ALL	4/1/10-3/31/11 ALL	Type of Statement	0-1MM	1-3MM	3-5MM	5-10MM	10-25MM	25MM & OVER
10	6	4	Unqualified					1	3
4	9	3	Reviewed				1	1	1
7	3	3	Compiled			1		1	1
4	5	9	Tax Returns		4	1	2	1	1
21	20	16	Other	1	1	2	3	3	7
				3 (4/1-9/30/10)			32 (10/1/10-3/31/11)		
46	43	35	NUMBER OF STATEMENTS	1	5	4	6	7	12
%	%	%	**ASSETS**	%	%	%	%	%	%
10.7	9.9	8.9	Cash & Equivalents						8.6
19.8	20.1	21.4	Trade Receivables (net)						22.2
30.9	30.7	32.8	Inventory						22.1
2.4	5.2	6.1	All Other Current						9.1
63.9	65.7	69.1	Total Current						62.0
25.2	23.2	18.2	Fixed Assets (net)						17.9
3.4	3.3	6.3	Intangibles (net)						13.6
7.6	7.8	6.4	All Other Non-Current						6.5
100.0	100.0	100.0	Total						100.0
			LIABILITIES						
13.1	18.0	15.6	Notes Payable-Short Term						13.0
8.0	4.6	4.4	Cur. Mat.-L.T.D.						1.1
13.9	13.7	13.4	Trade Payables						12.9
.3	.2	.3	Income Taxes Payable						.5
13.5	14.2	14.2	All Other Current						17.2
48.8	50.7	48.0	Total Current						44.8
10.0	9.3	12.1	Long-Term Debt						15.3
.3	.4	.3	Deferred Taxes						.2
16.5	7.9	16.4	All Other Non-Current						15.4
24.4	31.6	23.2	Net Worth						24.3
100.0	100.0	100.0	Total Liabilities & Net Worth						100.0
			INCOME DATA						
100.0	100.0	100.0	Net Sales						100.0
23.2	21.9	28.6	Gross Profit						24.0
21.3	21.5	26.2	Operating Expenses						21.5
1.9	.4	2.4	Operating Profit						2.5
1.6	.9	1.7	All Other Expenses (net)						2.0
.2	-.5	.7	Profit Before Taxes						.5
			RATIOS						
2.2	1.9	2.1							2.4
1.4	1.4	1.8	Current						1.6
.9	1.1	1.1							1.0
1.1	1.0	1.2							1.2
.5	.5	.5	Quick						.6
.3	.2	.3							.2
20 18.7	15 24.7	16 22.8							15 24.2
33 11.1	37 9.8	38 9.5	Sales/Receivables						42 8.7
50 7.3	61 6.0	63 5.8							77 4.7
15 23.9	27 13.6	17 21.7							7 50.0
48 7.6	57 6.4	66 5.5	Cost of Sales/Inventory						36 10.3
105 3.5	118 3.1	169 2.2							114 3.2
13 28.3	15 24.9	14 25.9							15 23.9
36 10.2	31 11.7	23 15.9	Cost of Sales/Payables						29 12.5
59 6.2	53 6.8	46 8.0							48 7.7
5.1	5.6	4.5							5.1
11.0	11.3	7.0	Sales/Working Capital						6.6
-17.2	63.2	18.1							NM
12.3	6.6	9.4							18.5
(41) 2.7	(40) 2.6	(32) 3.7	EBIT/Interest						(11) 4.2
.5	-1.6	-.5							.1
2.5	4.3		Net Profit + Depr., Dep.,						
(10) .7	(13) 1.9		Amort./Cur. Mat. L/T/D						
-1.3	-.1								
.2	.2	.2							.3
.5	.9	.7	Fixed/Worth						1.6
-5.5	2.2	-3.7							-1.0
.8	1.0	1.0							1.4
2.3	2.3	2.6	Debt/Worth						59.2
-8.2	5.8	-71.0							-5.2
36.9	27.2	25.7	% Profit Before Taxes/Tangible						
(34) 19.1	(35) 7.0	(26) 13.2	Net Worth						
6.0	-14.2	-4.1							
16.8	8.3	10.6	% Profit Before Taxes/Total						12.7
3.1	3.1	5.9	Assets						4.5
-1.2	-4.6	-3.3							-4.9
39.9	34.6	41.8							22.5
14.5	13.1	12.4	Sales/Net Fixed Assets						10.5
4.8	4.0	8.5							8.0
2.6	2.6	2.4							2.0
1.9	1.6	1.7	Sales/Total Assets						1.3
1.2	1.1	1.2							1.1
.6	.9	.9							1.3
(36) 1.4	(33) 2.0	(27) 2.0	% Depr., Dep., Amort./Sales					(10)	2.8
3.7	4.7	3.5							4.2
1.0	1.9	1.6	% Officers', Directors'						
(10) 3.7	(10) 3.4	(12) 3.2	Owners' Comp/Sales						
10.9	7.1	6.1							
2853685M	1582955M	1753192M	Net Sales ($)	282M	8251M	17527M	44202M	114861M	1568069M
1685617M	1084126M	874965M	Total Assets ($)	210M	3575M	11734M	25796M	64902M	768748M

© RMA 2011   **M = $ thousand   MM = $ million**
See Pages 9 through 22 for Explanation of Ratios and Data

Current Data Sorted by Assets   Comparative Historical Data

0-500M	500M-2MM	2-10MM	10-50MM	50-100MM	100-250MM	Type of Statement	4/1/06-3/31/07 ALL	4/1/07-3/31/08 ALL
		10	14	6	5	Unqualified	33	40
	2	10	9			Reviewed	27	30
2	8	7				Compiled	26	15
1	9	3				Tax Returns	9	20
4	9	14	12	3	7	Other	69	67
	20 (4/1-9/30/10)		115 (10/1/10-3/31/11)					
7	28	44	35	9	12	NUMBER OF STATEMENTS	164	172
%	%	%	%	%	%	**ASSETS**	%	%
	12.2	8.1	11.8		5.8	Cash & Equivalents	5.9	5.9
	21.6	20.3	22.7		16.1	Trade Receivables (net)	21.9	22.7
	40.8	39.9	33.4		22.6	Inventory	34.9	34.1
	1.8	2.9	3.8		7.3	All Other Current	3.3	2.5
	76.4	71.1	71.7		51.8	Total Current	66.0	65.2
	13.8	20.2	16.1		32.0	Fixed Assets (net)	23.2	24.0
	2.9	1.9	5.8		5.1	Intangibles (net)	5.4	5.2
	6.9	6.9	6.4		11.0	All Other Non-Current	5.4	5.6
	100.0	100.0	100.0		100.0	Total	100.0	100.0
						LIABILITIES		
	19.2	17.0	13.3		4.8	Notes Payable-Short Term	15.9	15.0
	2.7	2.7	1.7		4.5	Cur. Mat.-L.T.D.	3.4	3.6
	19.7	15.4	16.6		12.6	Trade Payables	19.2	17.6
	.1	.1	.3		1.0	Income Taxes Payable	.3	.1
	8.4	13.6	12.9		14.1	All Other Current	12.7	14.0
	50.0	48.7	44.7		37.0	Total Current	51.5	50.3
	8.1	8.6	6.1		10.8	Long-Term Debt	13.8	14.9
	.0	.1	1.2		1.5	Deferred Taxes	.5	.5
	10.9	6.1	6.9		14.5	All Other Non-Current	7.1	6.8
	31.0	36.5	41.1		36.3	Net Worth	27.1	27.5
	100.0	100.0	100.0		100.0	Total Liabilties & Net Worth	100.0	100.0
						INCOME DATA		
	100.0	100.0	100.0		100.0	Net Sales	100.0	100.0
	29.1	24.7	18.6		20.1	Gross Profit	23.3	22.8
	27.3	21.9	12.7		17.0	Operating Expenses	19.9	19.6
	1.8	2.8	5.8		3.1	Operating Profit	3.5	3.2
	.7	1.2	.3		1.0	All Other Expenses (net)	1.1	1.4
	1.1	1.6	5.5		2.1	Profit Before Taxes	2.4	1.8
						RATIOS		
	3.6	2.6	2.4		2.1	Current	2.2	2.3
	1.9	1.6	1.6		1.3		1.4	1.4
	.9	1.1	1.1		1.1		1.0	1.1
	1.8	1.3	1.4		.9	Quick	1.0	1.1
	.8	.6	.9		.5		.6	.6
	.3	.3	.5		.4		.4	.4
	5 70.0	14 26.0	20 18.3		28 13.0	Sales/Receivables	18 19.8	23 16.1
	26 14.2	30 12.0	37 9.8		40 9.1		35 10.4	36 10.0
	49 7.5	52 7.0	52 7.0		51 7.2		52 7.1	50 7.3
	45 8.1	55 6.6	32 11.3		37 9.9	Cost of Sales/Inventory	34 10.8	36 10.1
	63 5.8	85 4.3	62 5.9		69 5.3		60 6.1	61 6.0
	125 2.9	132 2.8	110 3.3		90 4.0		105 3.5	108 3.4
	16 22.4	14 26.8	13 27.8		21 17.1	Cost of Sales/Payables	17 22.0	16 22.8
	27 13.6	28 13.0	24 15.4		32 11.4		31 11.6	31 11.8
	56 6.5	38 9.7	43 8.6		38 9.6		48 7.6	44 8.3
	4.8	4.9	4.2		5.0	Sales/Working Capital	6.0	5.6
	8.9	9.5	6.7		11.6		12.9	12.7
	NM	31.5	33.0		51.8		207.1	64.0
	12.8	5.4	39.0		7.6	EBIT/Interest	6.1	5.5
	(27) 2.9	(39) 2.2	(30) 8.4		(11) 4.5		(151) 2.7	(156) 2.3
	.6	1.0	2.1		-2.0		1.2	.8
			103.2			Net Profit + Depr., Dep., Amort./Cur. Mat. L/T/D	9.3	5.1
			(15) 7.6				(47) 3.8	(54) 3.0
			1.8				1.8	.9
	.0	.1	.2		.4	Fixed/Worth	.3	.3
	.3	.4	.4		.8		.8	.9
	1.3	.9	.7		NM		2.5	3.1
	.6	.7	.6		.6	Debt/Worth	1.2	1.0
	1.4	1.9	1.4		1.2		2.9	2.8
	7.1	4.6	7.7		NM		11.8	13.1
	50.0	31.2	36.5			% Profit Before Taxes/Tangible Net Worth	42.2	37.3
	(24) 11.9	(39) 12.6	(28) 20.9				(135) 19.4	(137) 17.4
	.5	.2	7.4				4.6	2.5
	11.0	11.7	13.7		8.1	% Profit Before Taxes/Total Assets	13.2	11.2
	5.0	3.8	7.5		3.5		5.0	3.6
	-.6	.2	2.9		-3.9		.7	-.4
	191.8	51.7	32.9		10.9	Sales/Net Fixed Assets	35.3	31.5
	65.1	15.8	14.3		6.1		13.4	12.2
	12.6	5.4	8.5		2.8		5.6	5.8
	4.5	2.9	2.8		2.3	Sales/Total Assets	3.1	3.0
	3.0	2.4	2.2		1.8		2.2	2.2
	1.9	1.8	1.5		.8		1.6	1.7
	.1	.6	.7			% Depr., Dep., Amort./Sales	.7	.7
	(21) .8	(37) 1.7	(31) 1.0				(141) 1.4	(145) 1.5
	1.8	3.3	2.4				3.2	3.0
	1.9	1.5					% Officers', Directors' Owners' Comp/Sales	1.4	1.2
	(20) 2.8	(13) 2.2						(48) 2.9	(50) 2.6
	6.5	4.8					5.1	5.3
7571M	107608M	525708M	1895093M	1424448M	2992978M	Net Sales ($)	8967945M	10323874M
2186M	33259M	237099M	893965M	743801M	1874830M	Total Assets ($)	4760275M	5690788M

M = $ thousand   MM = $ million
See Pages 9 through 22 for Explanation of Ratios and Data

Comparative Historical Data / Current Data Sorted by Sales

			Type of Statement	0-1MM	1-3MM	3-5MM	5-10MM	10-25MM	25MM & OVER
32	25	35	Unqualified				1	8	26
37	32	21	Reviewed			3	2	9	7
13	9	17	Compiled	1	5	5	3	3	
10	13	13	Tax Returns	1	5	2	4	1	
59	54	49	Other	2	6	4	8	10	19
4/1/08-3/31/09 ALL	4/1/09-3/31/10 ALL	4/1/10-3/31/11 ALL			20 (4/1-9/30/10)		115 (10/1/10-3/31/11)		
151	133	135	**NUMBER OF STATEMENTS**	4	16	14	18	31	52
%	%	%	**ASSETS**	%	%	%	%	%	%
5.7	8.4	9.7	Cash & Equivalents		9.0	12.4	9.9	8.7	9.5
20.8	20.5	21.6	Trade Receivables (net)		23.1	22.9	17.6	21.1	22.4
37.7	36.0	34.6	Inventory		34.2	31.6	43.0	40.2	30.5
2.4	3.2	3.3	All Other Current		1.0	7.4	3.5	3.5	2.7
66.6	68.1	69.2	Total Current		67.3	74.3	74.0	73.6	65.2
22.4	20.6	19.4	Fixed Assets (net)		21.6	18.3	14.3	17.8	20.7
5.1	5.3	4.0	Intangibles (net)		4.5	.7	1.5	2.4	6.9
5.9	6.0	7.4	All Other Non-Current		6.6	6.6	10.2	6.3	7.2
100.0	100.0	100.0	Total		100.0	100.0	100.0	100.0	100.0
			LIABILITIES						
18.1	15.7	14.1	Notes Payable-Short Term		21.6	18.2	8.8	18.8	10.2
4.2	4.3	3.3	Cur. Mat.-L.T.D.		4.2	3.4	1.6	4.8	2.4
15.2	15.7	17.2	Trade Payables		17.7	19.0	15.9	16.1	17.0
.4	.4	.3	Income Taxes Payable		.1	.0	.0	.1	.6
13.6	16.6	13.6	All Other Current		19.8	5.9	14.2	13.2	14.3
51.5	52.7	48.6	Total Current		63.5	46.6	40.5	53.0	44.6
14.0	13.8	10.9	Long-Term Debt		30.6	8.5	4.0	6.5	10.0
.6	.5	.5	Deferred Taxes		.0	.0	.3	.3	1.1
4.9	7.8	7.7	All Other Non-Current		13.7	4.2	9.9	4.4	8.2
28.9	25.3	32.3	Net Worth		-7.8	40.7	45.4	35.9	36.2
100.0	100.0	100.0	Total Liabilties & Net Worth		100.0	100.0	100.0	100.0	100.0
			INCOME DATA						
100.0	100.0	100.0	Net Sales		100.0	100.0	100.0	100.0	100.0
20.2	20.7	23.8	Gross Profit		33.4	32.1	24.9	21.5	18.5
18.6	20.1	20.4	Operating Expenses		33.8	27.8	20.9	18.9	13.7
1.6	.6	3.4	Operating Profit		-.4	4.3	4.0	2.6	4.8
1.7	1.6	.7	All Other Expenses (net)		1.2	.8	.8	1.1	.5
-.1	-1.0	2.7	Profit Before Taxes		-1.6	3.6	3.2	1.5	4.3
			RATIOS						
2.3	2.1	2.7	Current		4.1	3.1	3.4	2.7	2.2
1.5	1.4	1.6			1.4	2.2	1.6	1.6	1.5
1.1	1.0	1.1			.7	1.3	1.2	1.1	1.1
1.0	1.1	1.4	Quick		1.8	1.8	1.5	1.2	1.1
.6	.5	.7			.6	1.2	.6	.6	.6
.3	.3	.3			.2	.4	.3	.3	.4
21 17.7	15 24.6	18 20.0	Sales/Receivables		5 66.4	14 25.4	4 92.0	18 20.8	27 13.6
33 11.1	37 9.9	32 11.3			29 12.5	34 10.7	20 18.7	30 12.0	38 9.6
43 8.4	49 7.5	51 7.2			57 6.4	60 6.1	40 9.0	53 6.9	52 7.1
42 8.6	43 8.4	42 8.7	Cost of Sales/Inventory		17 21.2	45 8.2	49 7.4	53 6.9	32 11.3
70 5.2	67 5.4	69 5.3			93 3.9	71 5.2	68 5.4	75 4.9	65 5.6
106 3.5	112 3.3	113 3.2			151 2.4	100 3.7	111 3.3	133 2.7	100 3.7
12 29.9	12 29.4	15 25.0	Cost of Sales/Payables		20 18.3	9 39.4	9 38.8	17 21.9	18 20.2
25 14.4	21 17.1	28 13.1			35 10.6	21 17.2	18 20.6	28 11.7	31 11.7
41 8.9	47 7.8	43 8.6			56 6.5	45 8.1	30 12.1	42 8.6	42 8.7
5.6	5.6	4.8	Sales/Working Capital		3.6	4.2	6.0	4.1	5.0
10.8	10.7	9.3			9.7	7.3	9.3	10.4	11.3
56.3	-186.1	38.5			-9.5	20.2	27.8	80.8	33.6
5.8	6.3	12.4	EBIT/Interest		6.5	15.9	16.8	5.4	33.2
(136) 1.5	(117) 1.4	(122) 4.0			(11) 1.3	4.8	3.9	(27) 1.9	(47) 6.7
-1.1	-1.3	1.2			-2.8	-1.1	1.1	.8	2.1
5.4	4.2	7.9	Net Profit + Depr., Dep., Amort./Cur. Mat. L/T/D						10.7
(42) 2.1	(33) 1.4	(33) 2.0						(20)	3.6
-.1	-.2	.7							1.6
.3	.2	.2	Fixed/Worth		.1	.0	.1	.1	.2
.7	.6	.5			.8	.3	.2	.4	.6
7.7	4.1	1.5			-.5	1.2	.6	1.0	3.7
.9	.8	.7	Debt/Worth		1.0	.4	.4	.6	.8
2.4	2.4	2.4			2.9	.9	1.2	2.0	1.7
16.0	22.0	7.9			-2.4	3.0	3.0	5.2	22.6
29.1	30.6	36.8	% Profit Before Taxes/Tangible Net Worth		32.9	41.6	63.3	32.8	43.8
(118) 8.6	(102) 5.2	(111) 13.9			(11) 1.0	(12) 9.1	(17) 16.7	(28) 13.3	(40) 18.7
-8.0	-9.7	4.0			-31.4	3.2	.1	4.4	6.8
9.3	8.3	12.7	% Profit Before Taxes/Total Assets		19.5	12.1	14.0	10.6	12.9
1.7	1.1	5.0			1.5	5.0	6.5	3.9	7.2
-4.9	-6.8	.6			-14.9	-.9	.2	.6	2.3
31.0	34.7	47.3	Sales/Net Fixed Assets		105.4	123.0	207.3	53.1	23.9
13.5	15.1	14.3			14.6	25.1	54.9	17.2	11.5
5.4	5.5	6.7			5.5	4.3	10.5	5.7	6.7
3.1	3.1	3.2	Sales/Total Assets		3.5	4.5	4.3	3.0	2.7
2.2	2.1	2.3			2.3	2.6	3.3	2.4	2.1
1.6	1.3	1.5			1.5	.8	2.0	1.5	1.4
.7	.7	.6	% Depr., Dep., Amort./Sales		.6	.4	.2	.5	.8
(127) 1.3	(109) 1.5	(108) 1.4			(12) 1.6	(10) 2.1	(14) .8	(26) 1.6	(44) 1.4
3.0	3.3	2.6			3.2	3.4	1.0	3.3	2.5
1.1	1.4	1.5	% Officers', Directors' Owners' Comp/Sales					1.2	
(35) 3.3	(44) 2.6	(45) 2.4						(10) 2.7	
4.9	4.4	5.5						6.0	
8280571M	6331370M	6953406M	Net Sales ($)	3026M	29336M	55763M	135691M	457261M	6272329M
4876854M	3622413M	3785140M	Total Assets ($)	2209M	16147M	45714M	47361M	296733M	3376976M

M = $ thousand   MM = $ million
See Pages 9 through 22 for Explanation of Ratios and Data

Current Data Sorted by Assets   **Comparative Historical Data**

						Type of Statement		
	1	2	10	1	4	Unqualified	14	15
		9	4	1		Reviewed	15	14
	5	5	1			Compiled	22	23
2	6					Tax Returns	10	11
2	7	9	7	2	3	Other	31	36
	14 (4/1-9/30/10)		67 (10/1/10-3/31/11)				4/1/06-3/31/07	4/1/07-3/31/08
0-500M	500M-2MM	2-10MM	10-50MM	50-100MM	100-250MM		ALL	ALL
4	19	25	22	4	7	NUMBER OF STATEMENTS	92	99
%	%	%	%	%	%	**ASSETS**	%	%
	8.3	10.7	5.5			Cash & Equivalents	5.8	5.7
	15.8	17.7	14.9			Trade Receivables (net)	19.0	15.7
	42.9	40.0	40.8			Inventory	43.2	44.7
	2.3	4.3	4.2			All Other Current	2.5	2.9
	69.4	72.8	65.4			Total Current	70.5	69.0
	20.9	20.5	24.9			Fixed Assets (net)	22.5	20.9
	3.4	2.2	5.8			Intangibles (net)	3.6	4.9
	6.3	4.5	3.9			All Other Non-Current	3.4	5.2
	100.0	100.0	100.0			Total	100.0	100.0
						LIABILITIES		
	10.6	11.8	13.8			Notes Payable-Short Term	15.0	14.7
	6.9	6.2	2.8			Cur. Mat.-L.T.D.	3.2	3.2
	11.4	15.1	12.6			Trade Payables	15.9	15.0
	.0	.1	.6			Income Taxes Payable	.2	.2
	20.4	11.4	12.9			All Other Current	14.7	10.6
	49.3	44.6	42.7			Total Current	49.0	43.7
	19.0	14.9	12.6			Long-Term Debt	12.5	15.3
	.0	.1	1.2			Deferred Taxes	.3	.3
	5.3	27.8	7.7			All Other Non-Current	4.3	7.9
	26.4	12.6	35.7			Net Worth	33.8	32.8
	100.0	100.0	100.0			Total Liabilities & Net Worth	100.0	100.0
						INCOME DATA		
	100.0	100.0	100.0			Net Sales	100.0	100.0
	27.1	18.1	18.3			Gross Profit	19.1	21.0
	22.8	13.7	12.8			Operating Expenses	15.5	17.4
	4.3	4.4	5.5			Operating Profit	3.5	3.6
	.5	.2	1.1			All Other Expenses (net)	.5	1.0
	3.8	4.2	4.4			Profit Before Taxes	3.0	2.5
						RATIOS		
	7.0	3.5	4.7				2.2	3.0
	2.4	1.9	1.4			Current	1.4	1.6
	1.1	1.2	1.0				1.1	1.1
	2.4	1.1	1.6				.8	.9
	.4	.7	.4			Quick	.5	.4
	.2	.3	.2				.3	.2
	(3) 127.9	(7) 49.4	(10) 37.1				(9) 41.4	(8) 44.0
	(9) 41.4	(21) 17.3	(21) 17.3			Sales/Receivables	(20) 18.5	(18) 20.5
	(29) 12.5	(44) 8.4	(40) 9.2				(32) 11.5	(29) 12.7
	(46) 8.0	(39) 9.4	(55) 6.6				(37) 9.8	(40) 9.1
	(60) 6.1	(62) 5.9	(79) 4.6			Cost of Sales/Inventory	(62) 5.9	(64) 5.7
	(118) 3.1	(101) 3.6	(132) 2.8				(95) 3.8	(99) 3.7
	(3) 108.1	(11) 32.7	(9) 41.0				(9) 40.8	(9) 38.9
	(10) 36.8	(17) 21.1	(29) 12.6			Cost of Sales/Payables	(18) 20.1	(15) 23.8
	(28) 12.8	(40) 9.1	(47) 7.7				(35) 10.4	(32) 11.4
	4.8	4.2	3.6				6.9	7.2
	9.2	7.5	18.2			Sales/Working Capital	14.6	11.0
	97.5	27.7	-61.6				62.3	50.5
	15.1	12.1	16.6				14.1	11.2
	(17) 4.7	(22) 5.9	6.7			EBIT/Interest	(82) 4.8	(92) 3.1
	2.0	.9	1.9				1.3	1.3
						Net Profit + Depr., Dep.,	18.8	11.6
						Amort./Cur. Mat. L/T/D	(18) 9.9 (19) 5.8	
							3.3	1.3
	.2	.1	.3				.3	.2
	.7	.4	.9			Fixed/Worth	.7	.7
	-1.4	1.9	2.3				2.3	2.4
	.4	.8	.6				.7	.8
	2.4	1.2	2.0			Debt/Worth	2.1	2.4
	-20.9	4.9	4.5				6.0	11.6
	40.4	44.7	29.2				61.4	54.4
	(14) 6.5	(20) 14.3	(19) 17.8			% Profit Before Taxes/Tangible Net Worth	(81) 29.9	(83) 19.7
	.5	2.2	2.5				6.6	3.4
	24.1	15.4	16.8				19.0	16.2
	4.1	7.6	8.1			% Profit Before Taxes/Total Assets	10.2	6.9
	1.2	.6	1.7				.7	.2
	67.4	52.2	34.8				51.4	46.2
	29.2	20.8	11.6			Sales/Net Fixed Assets	20.2	17.4
	5.7	6.4	4.3				8.2	8.8
	4.2	3.8	2.8				4.8	4.1
	3.5	2.8	2.2			Sales/Total Assets	3.2	3.0
	1.9	1.9	1.2				2.2	2.1
	.4	.6	1.0				.5	.5
	(14) 1.2	(20) 1.1	(19) 1.4			% Depr., Dep., Amort./Sales	(82) .8	(88) 1.0
	1.9	2.4	2.1				1.6	1.5
	2.3						1.2	.8
	(11) 2.8					% Officers', Directors' Owners' Comp/Sales	(26) 2.2	(30) 1.9
	4.1						5.8	3.8
3465M	80024M	360916M	1056350M	627689M	1919669M	Net Sales ($)	3404664M	4410820M
420M	21033M	126053M	508208M	267113M	1131106M	Total Assets ($)	1289162M	1826745M

Comparative Historical Data / Current Data Sorted by Sales

						Type of Statement	0-1MM	1-3MM	3-5MM	5-10MM	10-25MM	25MM & OVER
	12		8		18	Unqualified				1	2	15
	11		8		14	Reviewed				4	6	4
	19		16		11	Compiled	1	4	2		3	1
	8		6		8	Tax Returns	1	2	4	1		
	28		33		30	Other	3	2	5	1	6	13
	4/1/08-3/31/09 ALL		4/1/09-3/31/10 ALL		4/1/10-3/31/11 ALL				14 (4/1-9/30/10)		67 (10/1/10-3/31/11)	
	78		71		81	NUMBER OF STATEMENTS	5	8	11	7	17	33
	%		%		%	ASSETS	%	%	%	%	%	%
	5.8		7.9		8.3	Cash & Equivalents			6.0		16.0	8.0
	12.8		14.4		16.4	Trade Receivables (net)			20.6		17.5	15.1
	45.6		38.6		38.7	Inventory			50.5		34.3	36.9
	2.3		3.6		3.6	All Other Current			.8		1.2	6.5
	66.5		64.5		67.1	Total Current			77.9		68.9	66.5
	20.9		23.0		21.5	Fixed Assets (net)			17.9		18.0	21.7
	7.5		6.0		5.5	Intangibles (net)			1.3		8.4	7.1
	5.1		6.6		5.9	All Other Non-Current			3.0		4.7	4.7
	100.0		100.0		100.0	Total			100.0		100.0	100.0
						LIABILITIES						
	21.2		15.8		14.7	Notes Payable-Short Term			16.5		7.3	11.9
	3.5		3.8		5.7	Cur. Mat.-L.T.D.			1.1		8.9	2.2
	15.6		15.6		17.7	Trade Payables			12.9		17.9	12.9
	.0		.1		.2	Income Taxes Payable			.0		.1	.4
	11.4		13.7		16.5	All Other Current			10.6		20.2	12.6
	51.7		48.9		54.9	Total Current			41.0		54.4	40.0
	18.4		15.5		19.6	Long-Term Debt			17.0		16.3	11.4
	.5		.8		.6	Deferred Taxes			.0		.7	1.2
	9.1		9.5		15.5	All Other Non-Current			5.8		13.9	11.0
	20.4		25.2		9.5	Net Worth			36.1		14.7	36.3
	100.0		100.0		100.0	Total Liabilities & Net Worth			100.0		100.0	100.0
						INCOME DATA						
	100.0		100.0		100.0	Net Sales			100.0		100.0	100.0
	19.7		18.7		19.5	Gross Profit			27.1		19.6	16.3
	17.6		18.2		15.2	Operating Expenses			22.3		15.2	11.0
	2.1		.4		4.3	Operating Profit			4.8		4.4	5.3
	1.3		1.2		.7	All Other Expenses (net)			.2		.5	.9
	.8		-.8		3.6	Profit Before Taxes			4.6		3.9	4.4
						RATIOS						
	3.0		2.8		3.8				7.0		3.5	3.9
	1.5		1.8		1.7	Current			2.5		1.5	1.6
	1.1		1.1		1.0				1.1		.8	1.1
	.7		1.0		1.2				3.8		1.4	1.2
	.4		.6		.5	Quick			.6		.9	.5
	.3		.2		.2				.1		.4	.3
7	51.2	7	51.4	8	46.1				7 54.3		9 42.0	9 40.0
15	24.0	20	18.3	23	15.8	Sales/Receivables			20 17.9		21 17.3	28 13.1
27	13.6	31	11.7	40	9.1				33 10.9		35 10.6	43 8.5
45	8.1	46	8.0	43	8.4				50 7.3		36 10.1	46 8.0
69	5.3	68	5.4	62	5.9	Cost of Sales/Inventory			58 6.3		51 7.1	70 5.2
115	3.2	108	3.4	104	3.5				101 3.6		80 4.5	84 4.3
7	51.3	9	41.2	9	42.3				5 69.6		12 30.2	8 43.8
15	24.4	17	21.3	18	20.0	Cost of Sales/Payables			10 37.1		29 12.6	18 20.0
33	10.9	34	10.8	40	9.1				25 14.5		50 7.4	42 8.7
	5.5		4.6		4.9				4.9		5.4	4.9
	11.0		9.4		10.9	Sales/Working Capital			9.2		15.0	11.8
	46.8		40.8		NM				42.8		-27.1	49.5
	8.3		10.6		11.3				10.1		38.9	14.2
(72)	1.8	(66)	1.9	(74)	4.8	EBIT/Interest			(10) 4.8		(15) 7.6	(32) 5.7
	-.2		-2.8		1.4				.6		1.2	2.1
	8.5		7.1		12.2	Net Profit + Depr., Dep.,						12.2
(18)	2.3	(12)	2.8	(19)	2.0	Amort./Cur. Mat. L/T/D						(15) 2.1
	1.0		-.2		.4							.4
	.2		.3		.3				.2		.2	.2
	.7		.7		.9	Fixed/Worth			.5		.7	.9
	3.0		5.2		NM				3.2		-2.7	2.4
	.9		.7		.8				.4		.6	.7
	2.0		2.6		2.3	Debt/Worth			2.4		2.3	1.8
	26.1		16.8		NM				5.3		-6.7	7.3
	29.9		27.0		43.9	% Profit Before Taxes/Tangible					59.2	50.0
(60)	8.2	(55)	5.1	(61)	17.8	Net Worth					(11) 15.2	(29) 25.5
	-6.1		-18.9		2.1						9.9	3.0
	9.5		9.9		16.2	% Profit Before Taxes/Total			32.8		26.7	17.6
	2.1		2.2		7.2	Assets			10.9		9.8	7.2
	-3.3		-9.0		1.4				1.2		2.3	2.9
	39.5		39.5		46.4				67.4		162.6	24.6
	15.1		12.3		13.8	Sales/Net Fixed Assets			49.7		22.0	12.6
	7.2		5.5		6.2				6.9		6.3	7.7
	4.1		3.6		3.8				4.2		4.3	3.3
	2.7		2.3		2.6	Sales/Total Assets			3.8		2.8	2.3
	1.8		1.4		1.5				2.5		1.6	1.5
	.7		.8		.8				.2		.5	1.0
(60)	1.2	(57)	1.3	(65)	1.4	% Depr., Dep., Amort./Sales			(10) .8		(10) 1.6	(32) 1.4
	2.1		2.5		2.7				1.2		2.2	2.8
	.9		1.2		1.1	% Officers', Directors'						
(21)	2.0	(19)	3.0	(22)	2.3	Owners' Comp/Sales						
	4.1		4.5		4.0							
	5057652M		3672471M		4048113M	Net Sales ($)	2428M	16293M	44891M	52123M	261943M	3670435M
	2389823M		1970602M		2053933M	Total Assets ($)	4951M	12416M	13807M	23343M	118255M	1881161M

© RMA 2011

M = $ thousand   MM = $ million
See Pages 9 through 22 for Explanation of Ratios and Data

Current Data Sorted by Assets   Comparative Historical Data

Type of Statement

0-500M	500M-2MM	2-10MM	10-50MM	50-100MM	100-250MM	Type of Statement	4/1/06-3/31/07 ALL	4/1/07-3/31/08 ALL
1		1	3	1	2	Unqualified	14	8
	2	4	2			Reviewed	7	8
	4	2				Compiled	11	15
1		1				Tax Returns	5	2
3	4	2	6	1	2	Other	13	23
15 (4/1-9/30/10)			27 (10/1/10-3/31/11)					
5	10	10	11	2	4	NUMBER OF STATEMENTS	50	56

ASSETS

0-500M	500M-2MM	2-10MM	10-50MM	50-100MM	100-250MM		ALL	ALL
%	%	%	%	%	%	ASSETS	%	%
	8.9	12.9	5.9			Cash & Equivalents	9.6	9.0
	17.4	18.1	20.0			Trade Receivables (net)	16.9	16.9
	50.1	50.6	44.0			Inventory	44.1	43.3
	1.6	5.9	4.6			All Other Current	1.9	1.0
	78.0	87.5	74.4			Total Current	72.4	70.2
	13.3	9.4	14.2			Fixed Assets (net)	17.5	16.8
	.2	1.9	3.3			Intangibles (net)	3.5	7.6
	8.4	1.2	8.1			All Other Non-Current	6.6	5.4
	100.0	100.0	100.0			Total	100.0	100.0

LIABILITIES

0-500M	500M-2MM	2-10MM	10-50MM	50-100MM	100-250MM		ALL	ALL
	19.2	10.5	8.7			Notes Payable-Short Term	16.4	18.5
	1.4	.7	4.1			Cur. Mat.-L.T.D.	2.7	1.2
	9.3	15.2	14.6			Trade Payables	18.3	17.7
	.2	.0	.1			Income Taxes Payable	.0	.2
	14.7	20.5	15.4			All Other Current	10.9	13.6
	44.9	47.0	43.0			Total Current	48.3	51.3
	3.3	3.8	11.3			Long-Term Debt	11.2	12.5
	.0	.0	.0			Deferred Taxes	.2	.1
	22.1	28.9	10.7			All Other Non-Current	7.5	10.3
	29.8	20.4	35.0			Net Worth	32.8	25.9
	100.0	100.0	100.0			Total Liabilities & Net Worth	100.0	100.0

INCOME DATA

0-500M	500M-2MM	2-10MM	10-50MM	50-100MM	100-250MM		ALL	ALL
	100.0	100.0	100.0			Net Sales	100.0	100.0
	23.5	14.5	15.3			Gross Profit	17.9	16.0
	21.4	11.4	13.5			Operating Expenses	15.9	14.3
	2.1	3.1	1.8			Operating Profit	2.0	1.6
	.1	.7	.5			All Other Expenses (net)	.8	.9
	2.0	2.4	1.3			Profit Before Taxes	1.2	.8

RATIOS

0-500M	500M-2MM	2-10MM	10-50MM	50-100MM	100-250MM		ALL	ALL
	2.8	5.0	2.7			Current	2.2	2.2
	2.1	1.9	2.1				1.6	1.4
	1.1	1.3	1.1				1.1	1.0
	1.0	1.5	1.1			Quick	.9	1.0
	.7	.8	.8				.5	.5
	.3	.4	.5				.3	.2
	7 50.4	4 100.9	13 27.4			Sales/Receivables	4 87.5	8 45.0
	18 20.3	7 50.9	22 16.3				15 24.2	15 25.0
	49 7.5	45 8.1	32 11.6				21 17.5	26 14.0
	58 6.3	32 11.2	46 8.0			Cost of Sales/Inventory	31 11.7	33 10.9
	81 4.5	45 8.2	53 6.9				48 7.6	49 7.4
	166 2.2	111 3.3	73 5.0				65 4.7	78 4.7
	4 81.4	5 71.9	14 26.7			Cost of Sales/Payables	9 41.5	8 43.6
	12 29.2	10 36.3	16 23.5				14 26.1	22 16.5
	32 11.5	19 19.0	29 12.5				33 11.1	40 9.1
	2.8	7.6	6.0			Sales/Working Capital	9.0	10.3
	8.3	11.5	9.2				19.3	20.0
	53.2	25.0	181.3				69.9	NM
	32.0		17.7			EBIT/Interest	6.6	11.9
	.8		5.3				(46) 2.6	(51) 2.0
	-1.2		.7				.2	.3
						Net Profit + Depr., Dep., Amort./Cur. Mat. L/T/D	13.3	11.5
							(10) 1.0	(10) 7.2
							-3.3	3.0
	.1	.1	.1			Fixed/Worth	.2	.2
	.2	.3	.3				.4	.5
	NM	.8	7.2				2.9	UND
	.7	1.3	.4			Debt/Worth	.8	.8
	1.2	5.5	4.1				1.6	2.4
	NM	NM	22.7				10.9	UND
			127.5			% Profit Before Taxes/Tangible Net Worth	46.5	45.9
			(10) 38.9				(42) 29.1	(43) 13.2
			3.2				1.0	-3.7
	22.0	35.1	13.2			% Profit Before Taxes/Total Assets	16.0	16.7
	-.4	9.6	7.1				7.6	3.7
	-5.9	-2.5	-.3				-1.1	-2.7
	162.9	UND	66.9			Sales/Net Fixed Assets	63.8	58.2
	38.8	66.8	42.7				27.4	25.8
	9.8	49.6	18.0				13.7	13.5
	3.7	4.9	4.6			Sales/Total Assets	5.2	5.4
	2.8	3.7	3.5				3.9	3.4
	1.5	3.3	2.4				2.4	2.2
			.4			% Depr., Dep., Amort./Sales	.3	.4
			(10) .5				(42) .6	(48) .6
			.8				1.0	1.2
						% Officers', Directors' Owners' Comp/Sales	.8	1.4
							(17) 1.6	(17) 2.2
							2.4	4.5
6736M	29537M	206309M	970329M	523549M	1362925M	Net Sales ($)	4031693M	5062746M
1112M	11778M	50516M	288667M	176638M	659370M	Total Assets ($)	1135313M	1633932M

M = $ thousand   MM = $ million
See Pages 9 through 22 for Explanation of Ratios and Data

Comparative Historical Data | | | | Current Data Sorted by Sales

			Type of Statement	0-1MM	1-3MM	3-5MM	5-10MM	10-25MM	25MM & OVER
8	10	8	Unqualified		1				7
5	9	8	Reviewed			1	1	1	5
8	10	6	Compiled	1	3		1	1	
3	2	2	Tax Returns	1				1	
22	11	18	Other	2	3	3			10
4/1/08-3/31/09	4/1/09-3/31/10	4/1/10-3/31/11			15 (4/1-9/30/10)			27 (10/1/10-3/31/11)	
ALL	ALL	ALL							
46	42	42	**NUMBER OF STATEMENTS**	4	7	4	2	3	22
%	%	%	**ASSETS**	%	%	%	%	%	%
12.1	11.2	10.4	Cash & Equivalents						9.5
12.4	13.8	19.4	Trade Receivables (net)						20.2
43.5	48.1	40.5	Inventory						39.1
2.7	3.2	3.3	All Other Current						3.5
70.7	76.3	73.7	Total Current						72.4
16.6	13.0	12.6	Fixed Assets (net)						13.7
6.3	6.0	4.8	Intangibles (net)						7.8
6.4	4.7	8.9	All Other Non-Current						6.1
100.0	100.0	100.0	Total						100.0
			LIABILITIES						
16.8	17.7	11.0	Notes Payable-Short Term						6.9
2.5	3.6	1.8	Cur. Mat.-L.T.D.						2.6
12.0	11.4	12.9	Trade Payables						15.5
.1	.2	.2	Income Taxes Payable						.2
15.0	16.5	16.6	All Other Current						18.9
46.3	49.4	42.4	Total Current						44.1
15.4	15.8	10.1	Long-Term Debt						10.9
.1	.0	.1	Deferred Taxes						.2
6.7	11.1	19.0	All Other Non-Current						10.3
31.5	23.6	28.3	Net Worth						34.5
100.0	100.0	100.0	Total Liabilities & Net Worth						100.0
			INCOME DATA						
100.0	100.0	100.0	Net Sales						100.0
15.6	15.4	17.5	Gross Profit						13.8
16.0	18.5	15.9	Operating Expenses						12.0
-.4	-3.1	1.6	Operating Profit						1.8
1.4	1.5	.5	All Other Expenses (net)						.7
-1.9	-4.6	1.0	Profit Before Taxes						1.2
			RATIOS						
2.5	2.8	2.8							2.4
1.3	1.4	1.9	Current						1.8
1.1	1.0	1.2							1.1
1.1	1.1	1.2							1.0
.4	.5	.8	Quick						.7
.2	.3	.5							.4
4 85.1	6 64.0	5 67.2							13 29.1
10 37.0	14 25.6	18 20.0	Sales/Receivables						22 16.4
17 21.1	31 11.9	33 11.2							31 11.6
30 12.2	48 7.7	36 10.0							36 10.0
46 7.9	70 5.2	54 6.7	Cost of Sales/Inventory						50 7.3
90 4.1	139 2.6	79 4.6							56 6.5
6 65.4	7 54.8	7 49.6							10 37.1
13 29.2	14 26.1	15 24.5	Cost of Sales/Payables						16 23.5
35 10.4	28 13.2	24 14.9							23 15.5
7.5	4.7	5.7							7.1
16.3	21.6	10.6	Sales/Working Capital						12.0
99.5	-687.4	40.0							71.5
9.6	11.6	25.8							22.1
(43) 1.2	(39) -.5	(35) 5.3	EBIT/Interest					(19)	7.4
-3.2	-7.7	.7							1.6
			Net Profit + Depr., Dep., Amort./Cur. Mat. L/T/D						
.2	.2	.1							.1
.6	.8	.3	Fixed/Worth						.5
184.3	3.9	1.8							8.1
.8	1.4	.9							1.2
1.6	6.3	2.8	Debt/Worth						3.6
999.8	86.9	NM							27.1
25.5	80.9	80.5	% Profit Before Taxes/Tangible						102.9
(36) 2.5	(34) .7	(32) 34.3	Net Worth					(18)	26.0
-19.3	-66.2	-.4							.5
14.0	9.9	17.4	% Profit Before Taxes/Total						14.2
.4	-4.3	5.3	Assets						6.5
-9.5	-16.5	-3.7							-.3
68.4	62.1	101.4							62.7
25.5	35.5	47.6	Sales/Net Fixed Assets						42.8
12.0	12.1	17.0							13.7
4.7	3.9	4.5							4.5
3.2	2.8	3.4	Sales/Total Assets						3.5
1.8	1.6	2.0							2.1
.3	.4	.4							.4
(36) .7	(33) 1.0	(35) .6	% Depr., Dep., Amort./Sales					(21)	.6
1.3	1.4	1.1							1.1
1.5	2.2	.8	% Officers', Directors'						
(13) 1.9	(11) 2.8	(10) 2.2	Owners' Comp/Sales						
2.7	3.7	3.6							
3906028M	2309508M	3099385M	Net Sales ($)	3301M	13015M	16674M	14379M	33539M	3018477M
1212954M	964214M	1188081M	Total Assets ($)	1413M	5985M	5992M	4466M	9334M	1160891M

M = $ thousand   MM = $ million
See Pages 9 through 22 for Explanation of Ratios and Data

Current Data Sorted by Assets   Comparative Historical Data

0-500M	500M-2MM	2-10MM	10-50MM	50-100MM	100-250MM	Type of Statement	4/1/06-3/31/07 ALL	4/1/07-3/31/08 ALL
		2	1		1	Unqualified	2	
		2	1			Reviewed	2	3
	1	1				Compiled	2	
	1	3				Tax Returns	1	
2	1	5	5	2	2	Other	6	7
	6 (4/1-9/30/10)		24 (10/1/10-3/31/11)					
2	3	13	7	2	3	**NUMBER OF STATEMENTS**	13	10
%	%	%	%	%	%	**ASSETS**	%	%
		12.1				Cash & Equivalents	5.1	6.1
		32.0				Trade Receivables (net)	28.0	26.4
		31.5				Inventory	29.8	41.1
		3.8				All Other Current	3.8	4.4
		79.5				Total Current	66.7	77.9
		18.7				Fixed Assets (net)	22.9	18.9
		1.2				Intangibles (net)	4.1	1.1
		.5				All Other Non-Current	6.3	2.0
		100.0				Total	100.0	100.0
						LIABILITIES		
		6.8				Notes Payable-Short Term	8.7	15.6
		5.1				Cur. Mat.-L.T.D.	5.2	.3
		17.3				Trade Payables	13.8	13.7
		.0				Income Taxes Payable	.2	.0
		4.4				All Other Current	22.7	27.4
		33.6				Total Current	50.7	57.0
		5.6				Long-Term Debt	16.8	10.9
		.0				Deferred Taxes	.0	.1
		9.8				All Other Non-Current	4.9	1.1
		51.1				Net Worth	27.5	30.9
		100.0				Total Liabilties & Net Worth	100.0	100.0
						INCOME DATA		
		100.0				Net Sales	100.0	100.0
		24.6				Gross Profit	22.1	28.8
		16.2				Operating Expenses	17.8	25.3
		8.3				Operating Profit	4.2	3.5
		1.3				All Other Expenses (net)	.5	.4
		7.1				Profit Before Taxes	3.7	3.1
						RATIOS		
		3.7				Current	2.0	2.1
		2.6					1.6	1.3
		1.9					.9	1.2
		2.5				Quick	.9	.9
		1.3					.7	.6
		.9					.5	.3
		34 10.7				Sales/Receivables	22 16.4	38 9.6
		42 8.8					38 9.6	42 8.7
		61 6.0					56 6.6	50 7.3
		25 14.8				Cost of Sales/Inventory	34 10.9	41 8.9
		61 6.0					67 5.4	97 3.8
		109 3.3					89 4.1	182 2.0
		18 20.6				Cost of Sales/Payables	20 17.9	12 31.5
		38 9.5					27 13.6	31 11.7
		45 8.1					35 10.5	70 5.2
		3.6				Sales/Working Capital	8.2	5.8
		6.3					10.8	13.0
		8.5					-84.3	24.5
		37.3				EBIT/Interest	5.4	16.6
		(10) 16.7					(11) 2.2	5.4
		6.5					.5	1.2
						Net Profit + Depr., Dep., Amort./Cur. Mat. L/T/D		
		.1				Fixed/Worth	.2	.1
		.2					1.0	.5
		1.8					-2.6	2.1
		.3				Debt/Worth	.7	1.1
		.9					3.8	3.3
		3.2					-8.7	9.4
		70.8				% Profit Before Taxes/Tangible Net Worth		36.1
		47.7						22.0
		13.0						-10.3
		40.8				% Profit Before Taxes/Total Assets	19.5	13.9
		12.8					4.6	4.2
		4.8					-.7	.2
		80.9				Sales/Net Fixed Assets	39.2	59.1
		16.2					16.2	25.5
		4.7					6.2	4.8
		3.8				Sales/Total Assets	3.0	2.5
		2.3					2.5	1.9
		1.5					1.7	1.7
		.3				% Depr., Dep., Amort./Sales	1.0	
		(12) 1.8					(12) 2.1	
		2.5					3.1	
						% Officers', Directors' Owners' Comp/Sales		
2248M	4802M	225542M	409532M	215763M	914078M	Net Sales ($)	462301M	631845M
601M	3545M	84166M	180580M	138474M	490348M	Total Assets ($)	205429M	294647M

M = $ thousand   MM = $ million
See Pages 9 through 22 for Explanation of Ratios and Data

Comparative Historical Data / Current Data Sorted by Sales

Type of Statement	15 — 4/1/08-3/31/09 ALL	12 — 4/1/09-3/31/10 ALL	17 — 4/1/10-3/31/11 ALL	0-1MM	1-3MM	3-5MM	5-10MM	10-25MM	25MM & OVER
Unqualified	4	3	4					3	1
Reviewed	4	4	3		1		1	1	1
Compiled	1	2	2		1		2	1	
Tax Returns			4		1	1			
Other			4	1	2			4	10
				1	6 (4/1-9/30/10)		2	24 (10/1/10-3/31/11)	10
NUMBER OF STATEMENTS	24	21	30	1	4	1	3	9	12

	%	%	%	%	%	%	%	%	%
ASSETS									
Cash & Equivalents	6.1	10.2	10.5						6.8
Trade Receivables (net)	25.1	25.8	28.5						27.5
Inventory	27.2	34.1	31.1						32.0
All Other Current	3.9	2.0	4.1						5.7
Total Current	62.4	72.1	74.2						72.0
Fixed Assets (net)	27.7	18.7	16.5						13.6
Intangibles (net)	5.1	4.1	5.8						6.7
All Other Non-Current	4.8	5.0	3.5						7.7
Total	100.0	100.0	100.0						100.0
LIABILITIES									
Notes Payable-Short Term	12.4	9.8	8.5						8.4
Cur. Mat.-L.T.D.	4.3	2.7	2.8						1.3
Trade Payables	16.6	15.1	19.0						20.4
Income Taxes Payable	.2	.0	.1						.3
All Other Current	11.6	6.2	9.2						16.8
Total Current	45.1	33.9	39.6						47.2
Long-Term Debt	15.5	16.0	7.6						6.6
Deferred Taxes	.5	.3	.1						.3
All Other Non-Current	6.0	10.5	8.0						3.3
Net Worth	32.9	39.3	44.6						42.7
Total Liabilties & Net Worth	100.0	100.0	100.0						100.0
INCOME DATA									
Net Sales	100.0	100.0	100.0						100.0
Gross Profit	22.7	30.0	26.8						21.8
Operating Expenses	18.9	27.1	19.4						15.6
Operating Profit	3.8	3.0	7.4						6.2
All Other Expenses (net)	1.5	1.4	1.4						1.7
Profit Before Taxes	2.4	1.5	6.0						4.6
RATIOS									
Current	2.4	4.5	3.2						3.0
	1.4	2.2	2.4						1.7
	1.1	1.3	1.5						1.2
Quick	1.0	1.7	2.0						1.9
	.8	1.2	.9						.7
	.4	.6	.7						.5
Sales/Receivables	29 12.8	35 10.5	35 10.3						36 10.1
	37 9.8	60 6.1	43 8.4						43 8.5
	48 7.5	63 5.8	57 6.4						59 6.2
Cost of Sales/Inventory	30 12.3	61 6.0	31 11.8						29 12.4
	51 7.2	99 3.7	64 5.7						40 9.0
	95 3.8	153 2.4	128 2.8						104 3.5
Cost of Sales/Payables	17 21.8	24 15.1	25 14.5						24 15.1
	31 11.8	40 9.1	39 9.3						39 9.5
	45 8.2	54 6.7	58 6.3						58 6.3
Sales/Working Capital	6.9	2.1	3.6						4.2
	14.8	5.1	6.9						10.5
	69.6	13.3	13.8						18.8
EBIT/Interest	7.1	11.4	42.6						130.9
	(23) 2.5	(19) 2.9	(23) 7.9						(11) 7.3
	-.3	.3	2.2						1.9
Net Profit + Depr., Dep., Amort./Cur. Mat. L/T/D									
Fixed/Worth	.3	.1	.1						.1
	1.1	.4	.4						.3
	2.4	1.4	2.1						1.2
Debt/Worth	.7	.7	.5						.4
	3.4	1.6	1.3						1.2
	11.3	4.5	4.4						5.0
% Profit Before Taxes/Tangible Net Worth	43.4	21.2	66.0						61.7
	(21) 13.8	(19) 6.6	(27) 36.8						(10) 30.3
	-7.8	-5.9	13.6						18.0
% Profit Before Taxes/Total Assets	10.1	9.4	20.6						22.0
	3.6	1.7	12.6						16.1
	-.8	-2.4	4.2						.3
Sales/Net Fixed Assets	23.9	35.8	49.3						51.9
	12.7	10.7	24.0						26.2
	4.2	3.6	6.2						8.7
Sales/Total Assets	2.8	2.1	2.9						3.1
	2.4	1.7	2.1						1.9
	1.9	1.1	1.5						1.6
% Depr., Dep., Amort./Sales	1.0	1.3	.8						.4
	(17) 3.4	(14) 2.4	(25) 1.6						(11) 1.2
	4.3	4.3	3.7						3.6
% Officers', Directors' Owners' Comp/Sales			1.7						
		(10) 3.4							
		4.6							
Net Sales ($)	2428474M	777131M	1771965M	702M	6348M	4170M	21955M	175506M	1563284M
Total Assets ($)	1030585M	571404M	897714M	286M	3860M	6159M	14292M	67644M	805473M

© RMA 2011

M = $ thousand   MM = $ million

See Pages 9 through 22 for Explanation of Ratios and Data

Current Data Sorted by Assets   Comparative Historical Data

0-500M	500M-2MM	2-10MM	10-50MM	50-100MM	100-250MM	Type of Statement	4/1/06-3/31/07 ALL	4/1/07-3/31/08 ALL
		6	5		2	Unqualified	12	7
		1	5	1		Reviewed	7	8
		2				Compiled	7	7
2	2	2				Tax Returns	3	2
5	3	5	10	1	3	Other	20	20
	6 (4/1-9/30/10)		49 (10/1/10-3/31/11)					
7	5	16	20	2	5	**NUMBER OF STATEMENTS**	49	44
%	%	%	%	%	%	**ASSETS**	%	%
		13.9	7.8			Cash & Equivalents	5.9	9.8
		32.2	31.5			Trade Receivables (net)	28.6	28.4
		23.9	25.3			Inventory	30.0	29.7
		1.8	2.6			All Other Current	1.7	2.5
		71.9	67.2			Total Current	66.1	70.4
		15.3	22.9			Fixed Assets (net)	22.2	23.3
		9.7	1.1			Intangibles (net)	8.0	2.9
		3.1	8.8			All Other Non-Current	3.8	3.2
		100.0	100.0			Total	100.0	100.0
						LIABILITIES		
		11.5	13.8			Notes Payable-Short Term	11.0	10.1
		.8	1.9			Cur. Mat.-L.T.D.	2.9	1.0
		17.3	20.2			Trade Payables	17.9	17.5
		.1	.0			Income Taxes Payable	.3	.0
		7.5	15.2			All Other Current	9.4	17.0
		37.2	51.2			Total Current	41.4	45.6
		2.9	7.1			Long-Term Debt	17.8	14.9
		.2	.6			Deferred Taxes	.8	.1
		2.0	5.4			All Other Non-Current	5.8	8.3
		57.7	35.8			Net Worth	34.1	31.1
		100.0	100.0			Total Liabilities & Net Worth	100.0	100.0
						INCOME DATA		
		100.0	100.0			Net Sales	100.0	100.0
		26.4	23.0			Gross Profit	27.6	25.5
		20.7	16.1			Operating Expenses	22.4	21.4
		5.7	6.9			Operating Profit	5.2	4.2
		.5	.7			All Other Expenses (net)	1.2	.7
		5.2	6.2			Profit Before Taxes	3.9	3.4
						RATIOS		
		3.4	2.2				2.7	3.6
		2.7	1.4			Current	1.6	1.7
		1.4	1.1				1.2	1.1
		2.1	1.1				1.5	1.8
		1.8	.8			Quick	.9	.9
		.9	.5				.5	.5
		28 13.2	41 8.8				27 13.7	22 16.8
		45 8.1	47 7.7			Sales/Receivables	41 8.9	40 9.2
		63 5.8	61 6.0				54 6.7	56 6.5
		27 13.5	28 13.2				27 13.4	24 15.2
		45 8.2	44 8.4			Cost of Sales/Inventory	41 8.9	43 8.4
		99 3.7	73 5.0				102 3.6	114 3.2
		18 20.5	16 22.9				15 24.8	13 27.2
		28 12.9	41 8.9			Cost of Sales/Payables	30 12.3	30 12.3
		39 9.4	56 6.6				44 8.4	38 9.7
		4.9	6.2				6.1	4.6
		6.8	15.0			Sales/Working Capital	13.1	10.2
		13.5	25.2				26.2	63.4
		39.5	17.4				14.0	20.8
		(12) 17.8	(18) 6.1			EBIT/Interest	(48) 5.1	(39) 7.3
		4.7	3.3				1.1	1.3
						Net Profit + Depr., Dep.,	8.6	
						Amort./Cur. Mat. L/T/D	(11) 4.5	
							1.9	
		.1	.3				.3	.3
		.3	.5			Fixed/Worth	.7	.5
		.6	1.0				3.1	2.4
		.3	.9				.6	.3
		.5	1.8			Debt/Worth	1.9	1.7
		1.6	3.3				9.3	10.5
		49.6	83.4			% Profit Before Taxes/Tangible	55.7	50.4
		(14) 19.3	(18) 28.6			Net Worth	(40) 29.0	(37) 21.4
		8.0	10.0				7.1	9.6
		18.7	32.2			% Profit Before Taxes/Total	22.4	19.0
		11.9	10.4			Assets	9.7	8.2
		5.3	3.9				1.0	2.0
		31.9	31.0				29.4	36.5
		16.2	14.2			Sales/Net Fixed Assets	14.7	17.3
		9.6	5.4				8.4	6.2
		3.0	2.9				3.8	3.8
		2.5	2.6			Sales/Total Assets	2.5	2.6
		1.8	1.7				1.7	1.6
		1.1	1.0				.8	.6
		(13) 2.0	(19) 1.3			% Depr., Dep., Amort./Sales	(42) 1.6	(40) 1.5
		2.9	2.8				2.7	2.9
						% Officers', Directors'	2.4	1.0
						Owners' Comp/Sales	(15) 3.9	(13) 3.6
							5.9	7.3
11741M	20689M	246652M	1154374M	317965M	1476807M	Net Sales ($)	2566329M	1900503M
1995M	6463M	101867M	473765M	170646M	715900M	Total Assets ($)	1077554M	918341M

M = $ thousand   MM = $ million
See Pages 9 through 22 for Explanation of Ratios and Data

Comparative Historical Data				Current Data Sorted by Sales					
7	14	13	Type of Statement / Unqualified				1	3	9
7	6	7	Reviewed					3	4
7	4	4	Compiled					2	
4	3	4	Tax Returns	1	1	1	1	1	
14	19	27	Other	2	3	3	2	4	13
4/1/08-3/31/09 ALL	4/1/09-3/31/10 ALL	4/1/10-3/31/11 ALL			6 (4/1-9/30/10)			49 (10/1/10-3/31/11)	
				0-1MM	1-3MM	3-5MM	5-10MM	10-25MM	25MM & OVER
39	46	55	NUMBER OF STATEMENTS	2	5	5	4	13	26
%	%	%	ASSETS	%	%	%	%	%	%
8.1	9.0	10.2	Cash & Equivalents					10.7	10.5
26.8	27.2	30.3	Trade Receivables (net)					30.4	30.5
29.8	24.5	27.4	Inventory					26.1	21.2
2.8	2.8	3.3	All Other Current					1.0	3.4
67.6	63.5	71.2	Total Current					68.1	65.6
20.4	23.8	19.3	Fixed Assets (net)					22.6	23.3
4.7	6.1	3.9	Intangibles (net)					4.1	3.8
7.3	6.7	5.6	All Other Non-Current					5.1	7.3
100.0	100.0	100.0	Total					100.0	100.0
			LIABILITIES						
8.1	9.3	12.5	Notes Payable-Short Term					19.8	8.9
2.4	3.8	1.7	Cur. Mat.-L.T.D.					1.4	1.8
16.0	14.1	21.0	Trade Payables					20.0	19.4
.1	.1	.0	Income Taxes Payable					.1	.0
15.4	13.8	10.5	All Other Current					9.7	12.2
42.1	41.1	45.8	Total Current					51.0	42.4
18.3	25.1	5.1	Long-Term Debt					6.1	6.2
.1	.7	.4	Deferred Taxes					.7	.6
4.3	14.3	10.5	All Other Non-Current					3.1	4.8
35.2	18.7	38.2	Net Worth					39.2	46.1
100.0	100.0	100.0	Total Liabilities & Net Worth					100.0	100.0
			INCOME DATA						
100.0	100.0	100.0	Net Sales					100.0	100.0
23.7	22.2	24.7	Gross Profit					24.4	21.2
23.1	21.8	19.2	Operating Expenses					19.6	14.0
.5	.3	5.5	Operating Profit					4.8	7.2
1.7	1.5	.7	All Other Expenses (net)					.9	.6
-1.2	-1.2	4.8	Profit Before Taxes					3.9	6.6
			RATIOS						
2.9	2.9	2.8						2.7	2.5
1.8	1.5	1.4	Current					1.3	1.4
1.1	1.1	1.2						1.0	1.2
1.4	1.3	1.6						2.0	1.4
.9	.9 (54)	.9	Quick					.8	1.0
.5	.5	.6						.5	.7
21 17.5	32 11.2	28 13.3						39 9.3	35 10.4
33 11.1	55 6.6	45 8.1	Sales/Receivables					49 7.5	45 8.2
46 7.9	73 5.0	58 6.3						83 4.4	59 6.2
27 13.7	20 18.3	29 12.6						29 12.7	24 15.3
46 7.9	41 8.9	44 8.4	Cost of Sales/Inventory					47 7.7	39 9.4
86 4.2	98 3.7	64 5.7						106 3.5	61 6.0
15 24.5	15 24.9	18 20.7						16 22.4	21 17.3
23 15.6	32 11.5	34 10.7	Cost of Sales/Payables					37 9.8	35 10.5
38 9.5	58 6.3	51 7.2						85 4.3	47 7.8
5.1	4.9	5.9						5.7	5.9
9.8	11.9	13.9	Sales/Working Capital					13.1	14.2
34.5	54.1	25.6						NM	20.0
15.4	4.0	32.6						23.7	31.2
(37) 1.9	(42) 1.4	(45) 7.6	EBIT/Interest					(11) 3.4	(21) 11.5
-3.4	-3.3	3.4						1.8	5.3
	2.5	32.4	Net Profit + Depr., Dep.,						
	(11) .9	(13) 3.1	Amort./Cur. Mat. L/T/D						
	-1.6	1.5							
.3	.2	.2						.3	.2
.5	.6	.5	Fixed/Worth					.5	.5
2.8	2.5	1.0						NM	.9
.6	.8	.4						.5	.5
2.2	2.0	1.7	Debt/Worth					1.7	1.6
8.4	7.7	3.6						NM	2.4
34.0	28.1	57.5	% Profit Before Taxes/Tangible					21.3	69.1
(34) 5.2	(37) 5.8	(46) 22.4	Net Worth					(10) 11.7	(25) 32.4
-16.0	-10.2	9.3						8.4	14.3
12.7	5.3	18.9	% Profit Before Taxes/Total					13.9	28.2
1.8	1.7	9.7	Assets					4.5	14.1
-10.9	-8.9	3.9						2.4	7.4
37.7	22.5	59.7						16.4	34.5
13.6	11.1	16.3	Sales/Net Fixed Assets					10.5	15.0
7.7	4.8	8.0						6.3	5.1
3.6	2.5	3.0						2.3	3.0
2.9	1.9	2.7	Sales/Total Assets					2.0	2.7
2.0	1.2	2.0						1.6	2.1
.9	1.0	.9						1.4	1.1
(29) 1.4	(36) 2.4	(46) 1.4	% Depr., Dep., Amort./Sales					(12) 2.3	(22) 1.4
3.9	4.6	2.6						3.3	2.5
			% Officers', Directors' Owners' Comp/Sales						
2375292M	2166401M	3228228M	Net Sales ($)	1311M	9646M	21473M	32124M	213545M	2950129M
1127128M	1304020M	1470636M	Total Assets ($)	486M	2141M	5831M	14757M	113667M	1333754M

© RMA 2011

M = $ thousand   MM = $ million
See Pages 9 through 22 for Explanation of Ratios and Data

Current Data Sorted by Assets   **Comparative Historical Data**

						Type of Statement		
		2	5	2	6	Unqualified	23	13
		4	7		1	Reviewed	21	17
		3	1			Compiled	15	6
						Tax Returns	4	2
1	1	9	15	3	5	Other	35	39
	7 (4/1-9/30/10)		58 (10/1/10-3/31/11)				4/1/06-3/31/07	4/1/07-3/31/08
0-500M	500M-2MM	2-10MM	10-50MM	50-100MM	100-250MM		ALL	ALL
1	1	18	28	6	11	NUMBER OF STATEMENTS	98	77
%	%	%	%	%	%	ASSETS	%	%
		6.4	6.7		4.3	Cash & Equivalents	4.6	5.3
		32.0	21.9		26.5	Trade Receivables (net)	29.6	26.2
		22.8	17.2		12.8	Inventory	16.9	17.8
		4.9	1.9		3.8	All Other Current	1.9	2.2
		66.2	47.6		47.4	Total Current	53.0	51.5
		27.7	40.4		45.9	Fixed Assets (net)	37.9	37.8
		1.9	4.4		1.2	Intangibles (net)	3.8	2.9
		4.2	7.6		5.5	All Other Non-Current	5.2	7.8
		100.0	100.0		100.0	Total	100.0	100.0
						LIABILITIES		
		14.9	8.5		13.6	Notes Payable-Short Term	13.5	12.9
		4.0	5.8		3.7	Cur. Mat.-L.T.D.	3.9	4.5
		24.6	14.6		18.0	Trade Payables	17.9	16.1
		.0	.1		.4	Income Taxes Payable	.1	.1
		9.4	7.3		8.3	All Other Current	7.5	7.3
		53.0	36.4		44.1	Total Current	42.9	41.0
		13.2	19.5		15.8	Long-Term Debt	17.4	17.1
		.8	1.1		.7	Deferred Taxes	1.7	.8
		11.1	6.5		4.7	All Other Non-Current	6.7	6.9
		21.8	36.5		34.6	Net Worth	31.3	34.3
		100.0	100.0		100.0	Total Liabilities & Net Worth	100.0	100.0
						INCOME DATA		
		100.0	100.0		100.0	Net Sales	100.0	100.0
		21.6	19.8		12.1	Gross Profit	18.8	18.8
		22.1	12.5		7.7	Operating Expenses	15.6	14.8
		-.5	7.3		4.4	Operating Profit	3.2	4.0
		-1.3	.8		1.3	All Other Expenses (net)	1.3	1.2
		.8	6.5		3.2	Profit Before Taxes	2.0	2.8
						RATIOS		
		1.7	2.2		2.0		2.0	2.2
		1.2	1.3		1.2	Current	1.3	1.3
		1.0	.9		.7		.8	.9
		1.1	1.2		1.0		1.3	1.5
		.8	.7		.8	Quick	.8	.8
		.5	.5		.6		.6	.5
		43 8.6	37 9.7		39 9.3		36 10.2	41 9.0
		54 6.7	47 7.7		57 6.4	Sales/Receivables	50 7.2	49 7.4
		69 5.3	58 6.2		70 5.2		63 5.8	58 6.3
		34 10.6	31 11.7		20 18.4		22 16.7	24 15.3
		46 7.9	42 8.7		32 11.5	Cost of Sales/Inventory	32 11.5	40 9.2
		64 5.7	63 5.8		35 10.3		51 7.1	58 6.3
		30 12.1	23 15.8		31 11.8		20 18.5	23 16.0
		41 8.8	40 9.0		38 9.6	Cost of Sales/Payables	32 11.3	35 10.5
		71 5.1	49 7.4		48 7.5		43 8.4	45 8.1
		7.7	6.1		7.9		8.2	6.8
		25.8	19.4		19.0	Sales/Working Capital	17.1	15.7
		NM	-32.7		-9.6		-27.7	-36.4
		5.7	17.2		7.6		5.7	6.6
		(16) 2.4	(25) 6.5		3.0	EBIT/Interest	(94) 2.3	(73) 2.2
		-1.2	2.4		1.4		.1	.1
			4.2			Net Profit + Depr., Dep.,	4.8	3.7
			(13) 3.2			Amort./Cur. Mat. L/T/D	(33) 2.0	(26) 1.7
			1.3				1.4	1.2
		.4	.8		1.0		.7	.5
		1.2	1.3		1.3	Fixed/Worth	1.2	1.3
		NM	6.7		3.7		3.3	3.5
		1.1	.7		1.0		.9	.8
		3.0	1.9		2.6	Debt/Worth	2.2	2.0
		NM	12.3		4.7		5.5	7.3
		40.6	73.5		31.3	% Profit Before Taxes/Tangible	32.3	41.6
		(14) 10.5	(24) 18.7		(10) 11.8	Net Worth	(84) 11.6	(65) 15.6
		.5	2.7		4.1		-2.9	-.7
		7.6	21.4		9.0	% Profit Before Taxes/Total	9.0	12.3
		3.0	8.8		5.4	Assets	3.2	5.3
		-4.3	2.1		2.1		-1.7	-1.3
		11.3	6.4		6.7		10.2	8.9
		7.3	4.4		4.0	Sales/Net Fixed Assets	5.8	5.1
		5.7	2.4		2.7		3.2	3.2
		2.6	2.3		2.2		2.7	2.3
		2.0	1.5		2.0	Sales/Total Assets	2.0	1.9
		1.6	1.3		1.4		1.5	1.5
		1.7	2.5				2.1	2.2
		2.3	(27) 3.6			% Depr., Dep., Amort./Sales	(90) 3.4	(64) 3.5
		3.3	6.0				4.5	5.1
							1.8	1.6
						% Officers', Directors'	(27) 4.0	(21) 3.1
						Owners' Comp/Sales	7.4	4.7
1750M	3289M	200026M	1112205M	829578M	3095045M	Net Sales ($)	5398039M	4540296M
280M	880M	95667M	634873M	399806M	1674029M	Total Assets ($)	2918904M	2412961M

M = $ thousand   MM = $ million
See Pages 9 through 22 for Explanation of Ratios and Data

Comparative Historical Data | Current Data Sorted by Sales

			Type of Statement						
14	12	15	Unqualified					1	14
12	15	12	Reviewed				2	6	4
11	3	4	Compiled				2	2	
1	2	1	Tax Returns		1				
38	35	33	Other			3	4	7	19
					7 (4/1-9/30/10)			58 (10/1/10-3/31/11)	
4/1/08-3/31/09 ALL	4/1/09-3/31/10 ALL	4/1/10-3/31/11 ALL		0-1MM	1-3MM	3-5MM	5-10MM	10-25MM	25MM & OVER
76	67	65	**NUMBER OF STATEMENTS**		1	3	8	16	37
%	%	%	**ASSETS**	%	%	%	%	%	%
6.4	6.2	5.7	Cash & Equivalents	DATA NOT AVAILABLE				9.1	3.5
23.7	25.1	26.6	Trade Receivables (net)					27.2	26.6
19.0	16.3	17.6	Inventory					18.7	16.1
2.2	2.2	3.0	All Other Current					1.5	2.4
51.3	49.7	52.9	Total Current					56.5	48.6
38.6	40.3	38.1	Fixed Assets (net)					31.6	43.6
2.8	3.7	3.2	Intangibles (net)					6.2	1.7
7.4	6.3	5.8	All Other Non-Current					5.8	6.1
100.0	100.0	100.0	Total					100.0	100.0
			LIABILITIES						
12.2	10.8	12.0	Notes Payable-Short Term					9.4	10.4
5.4	4.6	4.5	Cur. Mat.-L.T.D.					4.8	4.9
15.4	15.3	18.5	Trade Payables					16.5	18.6
.2	.0	.2	Income Taxes Payable					.1	.3
6.7	8.7	8.5	All Other Current					4.6	8.8
39.8	39.4	43.8	Total Current					35.3	43.0
16.5	19.1	16.8	Long-Term Debt					19.4	14.7
.6	.7	.9	Deferred Taxes					1.0	.9
5.8	7.0	7.6	All Other Non-Current					7.0	5.1
37.2	33.8	30.9	Net Worth					37.3	36.4
100.0	100.0	100.0	Total Liabilties & Net Worth					100.0	100.0
			INCOME DATA						
100.0	100.0	100.0	Net Sales					100.0	100.0
19.6	16.2	19.1	Gross Profit					19.9	15.7
17.4	16.9	14.8	Operating Expenses					14.3	10.1
2.2	-.6	4.3	Operating Profit					5.6	5.6
1.0	1.0	.4	All Other Expenses (net)					-.3	1.0
1.3	-1.6	4.0	Profit Before Taxes					5.9	4.7
			RATIOS						
2.0	2.2	1.7						2.6	1.5
1.3	1.2	1.3	Current					1.5	1.2
1.0	.9	.9						1.1	.9
1.3	1.2	1.0						2.1	1.0
.8	.8	.8	Quick					.8	.8
.5	.6	.5						.6	.5
32 11.3	**46** 7.9	**40** 9.2						**49** 7.5	**38** 9.5
45 8.2	**60** 6.1	**52** 7.1	Sales/Receivables					**59** 6.2	**49** 7.5
54 6.7	**69** 5.3	**63** 5.8						**73** 5.0	**58** 6.3
24 15.0	**29** 12.7	**29** 12.8						**35** 10.6	**23** 15.6
42 8.8	**38** 9.6	**35** 10.3	Cost of Sales/Inventory					**45** 8.0	**32** 11.3
66 5.6	**64** 5.7	**53** 6.9						**72** 5.1	**42** 8.6
18 20.8	**24** 15.3	**27** 13.5						**19** 19.7	**29** 12.4
28 12.9	**41** 9.0	**41** 8.9	Cost of Sales/Payables					**37** 9.8	**42** 8.6
47 7.8	**59** 6.2	**52** 7.0						**53** 6.9	**49** 7.4
7.0	5.6	8.6						3.6	12.2
19.3	20.3	24.3	Sales/Working Capital					11.8	33.8
NM	-42.3	-43.4						45.5	-32.1
4.7	4.1	9.7						15.8	11.6
(70) 1.8	(66) .5	(60) 4.8	EBIT/Interest					(13) 2.9	(35) 6.0
-1.7	-2.9	1.6						1.7	2.6
3.0	1.9	4.8							5.1
(26) 1.9	(15) .9	(23) 3.2	Net Profit + Depr., Dep., Amort./Cur. Mat. L/T/D						(14) 2.9
.8	.1	1.6							1.2
.6	.7	.8						.3	.9
1.3	1.3	1.3	Fixed/Worth					1.4	1.2
2.6	2.3	5.5						6.7	2.3
.8	.8	.9						.6	.9
2.2	1.9	2.6	Debt/Worth					5.0	2.0
5.5	4.7	9.3						12.8	4.8
30.2	14.7	37.7						42.8	38.8
(68) 7.0	(60) -.3	(54) 18.3	% Profit Before Taxes/Tangible Net Worth					(14) 10.5	(34) 19.1
-11.2	-19.2	5.1						4.5	8.4
9.4	6.4	12.8						14.0	13.4
1.7	-.6	5.4	% Profit Before Taxes/Total Assets					4.2	7.6
-4.8	-7.6	1.2						1.7	2.4
9.8	7.1	8.2						10.1	6.9
5.7	4.3	5.9	Sales/Net Fixed Assets					6.0	5.4
3.2	2.6	3.3						2.2	2.7
2.5	2.0	2.4						2.0	2.4
2.0	1.5	1.8	Sales/Total Assets					1.5	2.0
1.3	1.0	1.4						1.1	1.4
2.4	2.6	2.4						1.9	2.6
(65) 3.3	(57) 4.3	(59) 3.3	% Depr., Dep., Amort./Sales					2.9	(31) 3.8
4.8	5.9	5.3						3.6	5.6
2.0	2.2	.9							
(23) 3.3	(16) 4.8	(11) 1.8	% Officers', Directors' Owners' Comp/Sales						
5.4	6.4	4.9							
4777342M	**3059438M**	**5241893M**	Net Sales ($)		**1750M**	**11621M**	**57879M**	**273592M**	**4897051M**
2510707M	**2036772M**	**2805535M**	Total Assets ($)		**280M**	**6487M**	**32265M**	**210376M**	**2556127M**

M = $ thousand MM = $ million

See Pages 9 through 22 for Explanation of Ratios and Data

Current Data Sorted by Assets | Comparative Historical Data

Type of Statement	0-500M	500M-2MM	2-10MM	10-50MM	50-100MM	100-250MM		4/1/06-3/31/07 ALL	4/1/07-3/31/08 ALL
Unqualified		1	10	24	4	14		102	69
Reviewed	2	6	37	17				64	66
Compiled	1	12	18	6				57	34
Tax Returns	9	8	10					27	24
Other	4	15	41	46	26	19		151	165
		56 (4/1-9/30/10)		274 (10/1/10-3/31/11)					

	0-500M	500M-2MM	2-10MM	10-50MM	50-100MM	100-250MM		4/1/06-3/31/07 ALL	4/1/07-3/31/08 ALL
NUMBER OF STATEMENTS	16	42	116	93	30	33		401	358
ASSETS	%	%	%	%	%	%		%	%
Cash & Equivalents	18.4	10.3	9.8	8.1	6.1	7.2		5.5	6.8
Trade Receivables (net)	22.0	27.4	23.3	24.5	25.2	21.0		26.1	25.3
Inventory	16.7	30.5	32.5	27.5	21.0	20.9		26.7	29.3
All Other Current	2.7	3.5	1.4	3.5	4.2	4.2		2.7	2.6
Total Current	59.7	71.7	67.1	63.7	56.6	53.2		61.0	64.0
Fixed Assets (net)	25.6	21.6	22.3	28.4	30.3	31.9		29.5	26.3
Intangibles (net)	5.0	3.5	5.0	4.2	6.5	7.4		4.2	4.8
All Other Non-Current	9.7	3.2	5.7	3.7	6.6	7.6		5.3	4.9
Total	100.0	100.0	100.0	100.0	100.0	100.0		100.0	100.0
LIABILITIES									
Notes Payable-Short Term	13.4	15.8	11.2	12.1	5.6	7.5		12.9	12.2
Cur. Mat.-L.T.D.	2.8	4.7	3.5	3.5	2.8	3.7		4.1	4.6
Trade Payables	13.1	14.3	14.9	16.4	16.0	16.8		18.0	17.0
Income Taxes Payable	.0	.0	.1	.4	.4	.5		.3	.2
All Other Current	6.7	7.5	9.1	9.0	14.5	9.7		11.2	10.0
Total Current	36.0	42.3	38.8	41.3	39.2	38.2		46.5	44.1
Long-Term Debt	10.3	13.9	14.6	10.5	18.8	10.7		16.3	16.3
Deferred Taxes	.5	.5	.5	1.1	1.0	1.8		.7	.7
All Other Non-Current	14.7	6.7	6.2	4.4	5.4	5.1		5.6	5.9
Net Worth	38.5	36.7	39.9	42.7	35.6	44.2		30.9	33.0
Total Liabilties & Net Worth	100.0	100.0	100.0	100.0	100.0	100.0		100.0	100.0
INCOME DATA									
Net Sales	100.0	100.0	100.0	100.0	100.0	100.0		100.0	100.0
Gross Profit	52.8	37.9	30.4	22.2	20.0	16.2		25.4	25.3
Operating Expenses	49.3	32.3	24.6	15.9	14.4	11.1		20.8	20.9
Operating Profit	3.5	5.6	5.7	6.4	5.6	5.1		4.6	4.4
All Other Expenses (net)	-.3	1.0	.6	1.0	1.8	.7		1.2	1.5
Profit Before Taxes	3.8	4.6	5.1	5.4	3.8	4.4		3.3	2.9
RATIOS									
Current	4.8	3.7	3.2	2.6	2.5	2.2		2.1	2.3
	2.3	1.9	1.7	1.6	1.4	1.5		1.3	1.5
	1.0	1.3	1.2	1.1	1.0	1.1		1.0	1.1
Quick	2.6	1.7	1.8	1.4	1.2	1.1		1.1	1.2
	1.2	.9	.8	.8	.8	.8		(400) .7	.7
	.5	.5	.5	.5	.5	.4		.5	.4
Sales/Receivables	2 176.8	23 16.2	28 12.9	38 9.7	36 10.2	26 13.9		32 11.5	30 12.2
	22 16.3	39 9.4	42 8.7	46 8.0	51 7.1	43 8.4		46 8.0	44 8.3
	47 7.8	51 7.1	51 7.1	59 6.1	64 5.7	62 5.9		59 6.2	57 6.4
Cost of Sales/Inventory	0 UND	20 17.9	47 7.7	35 10.4	28 13.2	24 15.0		28 13.2	34 10.6
	19 19.3	62 5.9	75 4.9	59 6.2	40 9.2	46 7.9		55 6.6	58 6.3
	67 5.5	110 3.3	130 2.8	113 3.2	107 3.4	74 4.9		93 3.9	115 3.2
Cost of Sales/Payables	8 44.3	13 27.6	17 21.8	23 16.2	23 16.0	25 14.5		22 16.3	22 16.8
	23 15.7	27 13.3	30 12.0	39 9.3	36 10.1	38 9.6		36 10.0	35 10.4
	49 7.4	42 8.6	49 7.4	52 7.0	59 6.2	54 6.7		55 6.6	52 7.0
Sales/Working Capital	6.4	4.6	4.0	4.7	4.8	5.3		6.3	5.2
	22.4	8.3	7.9	9.6	16.1	9.5		15.4	10.9
	-377.5	30.9	22.5	60.7	-114.0	122.0		-136.2	57.6
EBIT/Interest	19.7	14.9	20.1	19.5	38.7	23.1		8.5	8.9
	(10) 3.5	(40) 3.7	(107) 7.3	(88) 5.5	(28) 6.9	(31) 4.6		(360) 3.1	(315) 2.6
	-2.2	1.6	1.9	1.6	1.3	1.8		1.0	1.0
Net Profit + Depr., Dep., Amort./Cur. Mat. L/T/D		4.6	7.6	8.8	90.4	37.9		5.2	4.6
		(13) 1.9	(30) 3.6	(32) 3.5	(10) 5.1	(11) 9.1		(126) 2.6	(92) 2.1
		-.2	1.2	1.4	1.9	1.7		1.0	1.2
Fixed/Worth	.2	.1	.2	.3	.5	.5		.4	.3
	.6	.6	.4	.8	1.0	.9		1.0	.9
	1.9	1.4	1.4	1.6	1.4	1.6		3.0	2.5
Debt/Worth	.3	.5	.4	.6	.7	.8		.9	.8
	1.4	1.8	1.5	1.5	1.9	1.2		2.4	2.3
	UND	5.4	4.0	3.9	5.0	4.8		7.6	7.4
% Profit Before Taxes/Tangible Net Worth	69.1	63.1	40.7	56.5	35.4	27.7		43.7	44.0
	(13) 38.3	(35) 20.6	(99) 25.0	(88) 23.2	(27) 18.3	(30) 15.2		(335) 20.5	(305) 18.3
	23.4	2.6	4.3	6.5	8.2	4.2		5.0	2.2
% Profit Before Taxes/Total Assets	30.5	23.2	17.2	16.3	11.2	10.8		12.9	14.0
	11.9	7.3	7.6	6.8	7.8	5.8		6.0	5.7
	-5.6	1.3	2.3	2.0	.3	2.1		.4	-.1
Sales/Net Fixed Assets	59.7	54.9	30.9	15.8	12.6	12.0		18.4	20.9
	19.5	12.9	11.9	6.4	5.9	5.3		8.2	8.8
	7.4	6.9	5.3	3.9	3.8	3.3		4.4	4.7
Sales/Total Assets	4.1	3.4	2.5	2.3	2.0	2.0		2.7	2.7
	3.4	2.5	2.0	1.7	1.7	1.5		2.1	2.0
	2.3	2.0	1.4	1.4	1.2	1.2		1.5	1.5
% Depr., Dep., Amort./Sales	.6	.5	.9	1.7	2.6	1.4		1.2	1.2
	(12) 1.6	(33) 1.8	(104) 1.9	(80) 3.4	(24) 3.4	(22) 2.6		(342) 2.4	(287) 2.4
	8.8	3.1	3.8	5.4	4.4	4.5		4.2	4.0
% Officers', Directors', Owners' Comp/Sales		3.9	1.7					1.9	1.5
		(19) 6.3	(46) 2.9					(106) 4.0	(92) 3.5
		6.9	5.7					6.8	7.5
Net Sales ($)	13678M	143568M	1199672M	3971585M	3757030M	8805012M		25627169M	21943075M
Total Assets ($)	4070M	52956M	615125M	2086119M	2086502M	4878520M		12943175M	10925804M

M = $ thousand   MM = $ million
See Pages 9 through 22 for Explanation of Ratios and Data

Comparative Historical Data / Current Data Sorted by Sales

Hist 1	Hist 2	Hist 3	Type of Statement	0-1MM	1-3MM	3-5MM	5-10MM	10-25MM	25MM & OVER
77	73	53	Unqualified		1		2	12	38
62	61	62	Reviewed	2	5	5	16	22	12
41	35	37	Compiled	1	7	5	10	10	4
32	20	27	Tax Returns	5	8	3	6	5	
148	161	151	Other	3	7	13	23	20	85
4/1/08-3/31/09 ALL	4/1/09-3/31/10 ALL	4/1/10-3/31/11 ALL		56 (4/1-9/30/10)		274 (10/1/10-3/31/11)			
360	350	330	NUMBER OF STATEMENTS	11	28	26	57	69	139
%	%	%	ASSETS	%	%	%	%	%	%
7.9	8.3	9.2	Cash & Equivalents	20.5	8.4	12.2	10.3	10.1	7.0
23.4	24.0	24.1	Trade Receivables (net)	16.8	25.0	23.8	21.7	26.0	24.5
29.3	27.9	27.9	Inventory	18.1	25.6	24.6	36.1	29.9	25.3
2.5	3.0	2.9	All Other Current	3.6	3.6	2.5	1.4	1.5	4.0
63.1	63.2	64.0	Total Current	59.0	62.7	63.1	69.4	67.5	60.9
26.5	27.0	25.8	Fixed Assets (net)	24.1	27.5	24.1	19.1	24.8	29.1
4.7	4.7	4.9	Intangibles (net)	7.2	6.5	6.9	5.1	3.1	4.9
5.7	5.0	5.3	All Other Non-Current	9.7	3.4	5.9	6.4	4.6	5.1
100.0	100.0	100.0	Total	100.0	100.0	100.0	100.0	100.0	100.0
			LIABILITIES						
14.1	12.5	11.3	Notes Payable-Short Term	10.6	16.8	10.3	12.8	10.6	10.1
4.5	4.1	3.6	Cur. Mat.-L.T.D.	2.1	6.0	4.1	2.1	4.3	3.3
16.2	16.7	15.4	Trade Payables	10.3	12.4	11.9	15.2	15.7	17.1
.2	.1	.2	Income Taxes Payable	.0	.0	.1	.1	.2	.5
9.3	10.1	9.3	All Other Current	6.5	9.7	9.5	7.4	7.8	10.9
44.4	43.4	39.8	Total Current	29.4	45.0	35.8	37.6	38.5	41.9
15.3	15.8	13.1	Long-Term Debt	11.8	13.2	17.4	15.7	13.0	11.4
.6	.6	.8	Deferred Taxes	.7	.3	.7	.5	.5	1.3
6.6	7.4	6.0	All Other Non-Current	21.3	4.7	10.8	4.3	7.0	4.3
33.1	32.8	40.3	Net Worth	36.8	36.7	35.3	41.9	41.0	41.1
100.0	100.0	100.0	Total Liabilities & Net Worth	100.0	100.0	100.0	100.0	100.0	100.0
			INCOME DATA						
100.0	100.0	100.0	Net Sales	100.0	100.0	100.0	100.0	100.0	100.0
25.8	24.9	27.8	Gross Profit	55.7	40.0	37.8	30.1	28.6	19.8
22.7	22.9	22.1	Operating Expenses	49.5	37.3	30.2	26.6	20.8	14.0
3.1	2.0	5.7	Operating Profit	6.2	2.7	7.6	3.5	7.8	5.8
1.1	1.4	.9	All Other Expenses (net)	-.2	1.4	.7	.4	.9	1.0
2.0	.6	4.9	Profit Before Taxes	6.4	1.4	6.8	3.1	6.9	4.8
			RATIOS						
2.5	2.6	2.8	Current	6.6	2.7	5.2	3.4	3.0	2.2
1.5	1.5	1.6		3.1	1.5	2.0	1.9	1.7	1.5
1.0	1.1	1.1		1.2	.9	1.2	1.3	1.2	1.0
1.2	1.3	1.5	Quick	2.8	1.5	3.6	1.8	1.8	1.2
.7	.8	.8		1.5	.8	1.0	.7	.9	.8
.4	.5	.5		.4	.2	.5	.5	.5	.5
25 14.4	30 12.1	29 12.8	Sales/Receivables	2 210.3	20 18.1	29 12.5	26 13.9	31 11.6	34 10.9
38 9.6	46 8.0	43 8.4		18 20.6	41 8.9	39 9.3	37 9.9	44 8.2	46 7.9
53 6.9	63 5.8	56 6.6		52 7.1	57 6.4	52 7.1	52 7.1	56 6.5	59 6.2
31 11.7	36 10.0	34 10.6	Cost of Sales/Inventory	0 UND	11 34.7	22 16.7	56 6.5	37 9.9	31 11.6
61 6.0	66 5.5	64 5.7		35 10.3	67 5.5	54 6.8	81 4.5	70 5.2	49 7.4
108 3.4	109 3.3	112 3.2		102 3.6	120 3.1	109 3.4	145 2.5	112 3.3	102 3.6
18 20.1	19 19.1	18 19.9	Cost of Sales/Payables	7 50.8	9 42.4	16 23.0	16 22.9	19 19.3	23 15.6
32 11.4	35 10.3	33 11.1		26 14.3	17 20.9	31 11.8	28 13.2	32 11.6	38 9.6
49 7.5	54 6.8	51 7.2		61 6.0	50 7.3	43 8.4	47 7.7	55 6.7	53 6.9
5.4	4.5	4.8	Sales/Working Capital	5.9	4.9	3.4	3.8	4.5	5.3
11.1	9.4	9.5		14.6	10.8	10.2	6.4	8.9	10.5
206.9	49.7	47.2		38.5	-246.1	26.1	16.9	23.1	142.6
7.1	6.4	20.1	EBIT/Interest		11.0	11.0	19.8	22.0	22.9
(316) 2.4	(322) 2.2	(304) 5.7			(27) 2.5	(23) 4.4	(52) 4.7	(64) 8.0	(132) 6.5
-.4	-1.0	1.7			.4	1.6	1.6	2.6	1.6
5.1	4.3	8.8	Net Profit + Depr., Dep., Amort./Cur. Mat. L/T/D		7.1		6.4	11.0	15.5
(96) 2.2	(100) 2.0	(97) 3.2			(10) 2.0		(12) 2.8	(19) 3.8	(50) 4.2
.8	.6	1.3			.2		1.0	1.5	1.5
.3	.3	.3	Fixed/Worth	.2	.2	.1	.1	.2	.4
.8	.8	.7		.8	.8	.7	.4	.6	.8
2.2	2.0	1.5		2.2	UND	1.8	1.2	1.8	1.5
.8	.7	.6	Debt/Worth	.3	.6	.7	.4	.5	.7
2.2	2.0	1.5		1.4	UND	2.0	1.2	1.8	1.4
6.9	5.6	4.5		-21.2	UND	4.9	3.6	3.8	4.6
36.3	33.6	46.4	% Profit Before Taxes/Tangible Net Worth		37.1	66.8	30.8	47.8	51.0
(307) 13.5	(293) 7.9	(292) 20.6			(22) 16.3	(22) 15.3	(49) 13.4	(62) 30.7	(129) 19.6
-4.5	-5.7	5.8			1.9	.9	3.4	12.6	5.9
11.2	9.8	16.3	% Profit Before Taxes/Total Assets	33.8	13.6	19.3	13.1	19.9	12.6
3.5	2.3	7.4		19.0	6.1	6.8	5.6	9.5	7.5
-3.2	-4.7	1.8		-3.6	-.9	1.3	1.2	4.4	1.8
24.2	23.3	25.8	Sales/Net Fixed Assets	105.2	32.3	39.1	41.0	27.5	15.1
8.1	7.2	8.7		14.1	9.3	11.7	12.2	9.8	6.4
4.5	3.6	4.5		6.4	5.5	5.2	5.6	4.6	3.9
2.8	2.5	2.6	Sales/Total Assets	4.0	3.5	2.4	2.7	2.5	2.4
2.0	1.8	1.9		2.7	2.3	2.0	2.0	1.9	1.7
1.5	1.3	1.4		2.1	1.6	1.3	1.4	1.5	1.4
1.1	1.2	1.2	% Depr., Dep., Amort./Sales		1.3	.6	.9	1.1	1.5
(288) 2.5	(278) 2.6	(275) 2.6			(24) 2.0	(21) 2.6	(51) 1.5	(60) 2.1	(112) 3.2
4.2	4.9	4.5			3.2	5.7	3.9	4.3	4.9
2.1	2.6	1.7	% Officers', Directors' Owners' Comp/Sales		4.5	2.2	2.4	1.4	
(94) 3.8	(88) 4.2	(83) 3.7			(14) 6.5	(10) 5.8	(22) 3.2	(27) 2.0	
6.8	7.7	6.7			8.5	8.8	5.7	4.9	
20680657M	18713440M	17890545M	Net Sales ($)	6946M	56688M	100783M	405675M	1082902M	16237551M
10336026M	10517118M	9723292M	Total Assets ($)	2379M	35542M	61723M	236173M	583729M	8803746M

M = $ thousand   MM = $ million
See Pages 9 through 22 for Explanation of Ratios and Data

Current Data Sorted by Assets   **Comparative Historical Data**

0-500M	500M-2MM	2-10MM	10-50MM	50-100MM	100-250MM	Type of Statement	4/1/06-3/31/07 ALL	4/1/07-3/31/08 ALL
		7	12	7	3	Unqualified	17	23
1		15	6			Reviewed	21	21
	1	7				Compiled	5	7
1	4	4				Tax Returns	7	7
1	3	27	22	4	4	Other	39	48
	19 (4/1-9/30/10)		110 (10/1/10-3/31/11)					
3	8	60	40	11	7	**NUMBER OF STATEMENTS**	89	106
%	%	%	%	%	%	**ASSETS**	%	%
		9.2	5.6	6.8		Cash & Equivalents	5.3	6.6
		19.8	18.5	14.8		Trade Receivables (net)	20.7	20.8
		35.3	39.2	28.9		Inventory	38.5	38.5
		2.0	2.1	4.8		All Other Current	2.5	4.2
		66.3	65.5	55.3		Total Current	67.0	70.1
		24.0	21.4	30.6		Fixed Assets (net)	25.3	21.2
		4.4	7.4	10.8		Intangibles (net)	3.6	4.3
		5.3	5.8	3.4		All Other Non-Current	4.1	4.4
		100.0	100.0	100.0		Total	100.0	100.0
						LIABILITIES		
		8.5	11.1	10.0		Notes Payable-Short Term	11.4	12.1
		4.4	4.4	1.7		Cur. Mat.-L.T.D.	3.6	3.9
		11.5	11.3	10.3		Trade Payables	14.8	13.9
		.4	.1	.2		Income Taxes Payable	.0	.6
		8.3	9.9	12.2		All Other Current	12.4	12.7
		33.1	36.8	34.4		Total Current	42.3	43.2
		15.0	12.6	21.2		Long-Term Debt	16.8	15.4
		.9	.5	.4		Deferred Taxes	.3	.3
		4.9	8.7	13.3		All Other Non-Current	8.6	6.9
		46.1	41.4	30.7		Net Worth	32.0	34.2
		100.0	100.0	100.0		Total Liabilities & Net Worth	100.0	100.0
						INCOME DATA		
		100.0	100.0	100.0		Net Sales	100.0	100.0
		34.7	23.9	21.1		Gross Profit	29.6	31.6
		26.0	16.8	14.3		Operating Expenses	21.9	22.4
		8.6	7.1	6.8		Operating Profit	7.7	9.3
		1.8	1.2	3.3		All Other Expenses (net)	1.2	2.2
		6.9	5.9	3.5		Profit Before Taxes	6.5	7.1
						RATIOS		
		3.0	2.8	2.5			2.3	2.6
		2.2	1.6	2.0		Current	1.6	1.6
		1.3	1.2	1.1			1.2	1.3
		1.5	1.3	1.1			1.0	1.1
		.8	.5	.6		Quick	.6	.6
		.5	.4	.5			.3	.4
23	15.9	33 11.1	32 11.3			Sales/Receivables	28 13.2	25 14.5
43	8.6	48 7.5	54 6.7				46 8.0	42 8.7
56	6.5	67 5.4	59 6.2				59 6.2	55 6.6
61	6.0	100 3.7	68 5.4			Cost of Sales/Inventory	68 5.4	70 5.2
121	3.0	133 2.7	80 4.6				109 3.3	109 3.4
163	2.2	186 2.0	98 3.7				172 2.1	156 2.3
16	23.4	23 15.7	27 13.6			Cost of Sales/Payables	22 16.5	20 18.7
30	12.1	33 11.0	30 12.3				37 9.9	34 10.7
49	7.5	49 7.4	47 7.7				54 6.8	54 6.7
		3.3	2.5	3.3		Sales/Working Capital	3.8	3.3
		5.4	6.6	6.0			6.1	7.0
		14.4	11.9	18.2			18.3	15.1
		17.0	7.4			EBIT/Interest	9.4	9.7
	(54)	4.4	(37) 3.8				(83) 3.6	(95) 3.9
		2.0	1.9				1.8	2.0
		12.0	3.2			Net Profit + Depr., Dep., Amort./Cur. Mat. L/T/D	8.4	5.9
	(11)	2.5	(15) 1.9				(31) 2.5	(31) 2.5
		.7	.6				1.3	.7
		.1	.2	.7		Fixed/Worth	.3	.2
		.5	.6	1.9			.8	.6
		1.2	1.3	-1.7			2.1	1.7
		.6	.9	1.0		Debt/Worth	1.1	.8
		1.1	1.8	4.2			2.1	1.7
		2.7	3.3	-5.6			5.4	4.6
		46.1	33.0			% Profit Before Taxes/Tangible Net Worth	65.9	70.1
	(56)	20.0	(37) 19.9				(78) 24.7	(93) 28.1
		9.2	4.8				7.7	11.4
		14.0	12.2	10.6		% Profit Before Taxes/Total Assets	17.4	17.6
		8.0	5.1	5.5			7.1	9.6
		1.6	2.4	.2			2.9	3.6
		27.6	16.5	8.8		Sales/Net Fixed Assets	18.2	29.3
		9.3	7.5	5.6			8.8	9.6
		3.7	4.1	2.7			3.9	4.9
		2.2	1.8	1.5		Sales/Total Assets	2.5	2.6
		1.7	1.3	1.1			1.7	1.8
		1.0	1.1	.9			1.3	1.2
		1.2	1.4	2.9		% Depr., Dep., Amort./Sales	1.8	1.3
	(53)	2.2	(38) 2.9	(10) 3.8			(76) 2.9	(88) 2.2
		4.3	3.9	6.9			4.0	3.6
		2.1				% Officers', Directors' Owners' Comp/Sales	1.7	1.6
	(21)	4.1					(23) 5.0	(31) 4.4
		6.9					7.1	9.1
3613M	23421M	550408M	1429607M	942366M	1463730M	Net Sales ($)	2928496M	4435095M
1217M	9448M	336902M	905412M	759525M	983949M	Total Assets ($)	1922681M	2811581M

M = $ thousand   MM = $ million
See Pages 9 through 22 for Explanation of Ratios and Data

Comparative Historical Data   Current Data Sorted by Sales

4/1/08-3/31/09 ALL	4/1/09-3/31/10 ALL	4/1/10-3/31/11 ALL	Type of Statement	0-1MM	1-3MM	3-5MM	5-10MM	10-25MM	25MM & OVER
30	24	29	Unqualified				3	6	20
21	21	22	Reviewed		1	2	5	11	3
5	4	8	Compiled	1	1	2	3	1	
9	10	9	Tax Returns	2		2	4	1	
52	46	61	Other	1	5	3	15	21	16
				0-1MM	1-3MM	3-5MM	5-10MM	10-25MM	25MM & OVER
				19 (4/1-9/30/10)			*110 (10/1/10-3/31/11)*		
117	105	129	**NUMBER OF STATEMENTS**	4	7	9	30	40	39
%	%	%	**ASSETS**	%	%	%	%	%	%
7.0	7.4	9.1	Cash & Equivalents				7.0	5.2	7.9
21.2	20.3	18.2	Trade Receivables (net)				20.1	20.8	18.6
38.7	36.3	34.8	Inventory				34.2	37.5	33.8
2.2	2.4	2.7	All Other Current				1.9	1.6	3.5
69.1	66.4	64.8	Total Current				63.2	65.1	63.8
22.3	24.7	23.8	Fixed Assets (net)				23.3	25.5	22.3
4.9	4.2	6.4	Intangibles (net)				7.3	3.8	9.9
3.7	4.6	5.0	All Other Non-Current				6.2	5.7	3.9
100.0	100.0	100.0	Total				100.0	100.0	100.0
			LIABILITIES						
11.6	12.5	8.9	Notes Payable-Short Term				7.7	10.2	7.6
4.7	3.7	4.1	Cur. Mat.-L.T.D.				4.3	4.2	3.9
12.3	10.4	11.1	Trade Payables				8.4	15.6	11.5
.6	.6	.3	Income Taxes Payable				.5	.3	.4
10.2	8.9	9.1	All Other Current				5.3	9.2	11.1
39.3	36.0	33.5	Total Current				26.2	39.6	34.4
18.2	15.8	15.8	Long-Term Debt				13.6	11.9	20.3
.6	.9	.6	Deferred Taxes				1.0	.7	.5
7.2	4.2	6.8	All Other Non-Current				5.0	4.0	10.9
34.7	43.1	43.2	Net Worth				54.1	43.8	33.8
100.0	100.0	100.0	Total Liabilities & Net Worth				100.0	100.0	100.0
			INCOME DATA						
100.0	100.0	100.0	Net Sales				100.0	100.0	100.0
30.2	26.1	30.5	Gross Profit				34.8	25.4	22.8
22.0	18.9	22.4	Operating Expenses				24.1	20.7	14.6
8.2	7.1	8.0	Operating Profit				10.6	4.7	8.2
1.4	1.6	1.8	All Other Expenses (net)				2.3	1.1	2.4
6.8	5.5	6.2	Profit Before Taxes				8.3	3.6	5.8
			RATIOS						
2.7	3.1	3.1	Current				4.3	2.3	2.8
1.9	1.9	1.9					2.7	1.7	1.7
1.3	1.3	1.3					1.5	1.2	1.3
1.4	1.3	1.4	Quick				2.0	.9	1.3
.7	.7	.7					1.0	.7	.6
.4	.5	.5					.5	.4	.5
29 12.6	32 11.6	25 14.5	Sales/Receivables				26 14.1	26 14.1	35 10.5
42 8.6	42 8.7	44 8.2					47 7.8	45 8.2	53 6.9
56 6.5	55 6.7	58 6.3					62 5.9	55 6.6	61 6.0
61 6.0	62 5.9	68 5.4	Cost of Sales/Inventory				62 5.9	64 5.7	72 5.1
113 3.2	107 3.4	117 3.1					130 2.8	115 3.2	98 3.7
195 1.9	169 2.2	167 2.2					207 1.8	135 2.7	167 2.2
19 19.6	14 26.1	19 18.8	Cost of Sales/Payables				13 28.9	24 15.0	26 14.0
30 12.2	25 14.5	32 11.6					27 13.6	33 10.9	33 10.9
44 8.2	38 9.6	48 7.7					51 7.2	52 7.0	45 8.1
3.2	2.9	3.0	Sales/Working Capital				2.7	3.9	2.7
5.2	5.4	6.0					4.0	6.6	7.1
15.3	12.7	12.8					6.6	18.7	11.0
11.1	11.8	11.6	EBIT/Interest				17.3	16.8	8.0
(100) 4.7	(96) 4.1	(108) 4.0					(28) 4.0	(38) 4.5	(30) 3.5
1.8	1.8	1.9					2.5	1.7	1.9
8.0	6.1	4.4	Net Profit + Depr., Dep., Amort./Cur. Mat. L/T/D						3.4
(34) 2.7	(25) 3.0	(31) 2.3							(15) 2.3
1.2	1.4	.7							.5
.2	.1	.1	Fixed/Worth				.1	.2	.2
.6	.6	.6					.6	.5	.7
1.8	1.5	1.5					1.2	1.5	1.9
.8	.6	.6	Debt/Worth				.5	.8	1.0
2.0	1.6	1.5					.9	1.5	2.1
5.7	3.7	3.4					2.2	2.7	5.4
59.8	44.8	34.1	% Profit Before Taxes/Tangible Net Worth				49.2	31.0	33.5
(100) 25.3	(98) 23.3	(116) 19.0					(29) 18.4	(39) 13.5	(32) 21.5
8.7	8.5	7.3					7.8	2.0	11.1
20.0	16.1	14.0	% Profit Before Taxes/Total Assets				15.9	11.6	14.8
9.4	7.6	6.4					6.9	6.2	5.5
2.8	2.4	1.5					2.2	1.1	2.4
20.6	24.7	24.3	Sales/Net Fixed Assets				30.1	25.1	13.5
9.4	8.2	7.6					8.0	7.3	7.2
4.8	3.4	3.7					3.1	3.8	3.9
2.3	2.1	2.0	Sales/Total Assets				2.1	2.5	1.8
1.6	1.5	1.5					1.2	1.7	1.4
1.2	1.1	1.0					.9	1.2	1.0
1.1	1.2	1.2	% Depr., Dep., Amort./Sales				1.4	1.1	1.4
(103) 1.9	(94) 2.4	(114) 2.7					(27) 2.2	(37) 2.7	(35) 3.0
3.3	4.0	4.1					5.0	4.1	3.9
2.1	2.7	1.9	% Officers', Directors', Owners' Comp/Sales				2.1	1.0	
(22) 4.9	(22) 4.5	(37) 4.0					(11) 4.1	(11) 2.6	
8.0	9.6	6.0					4.9	6.0	
5414105M	4582138M	4413145M	Net Sales ($)	2924M	14554M	35012M	221429M	668337M	3470889M
3676039M	3126932M	2996453M	Total Assets ($)	2526M	15906M	26584M	172451M	473901M	2305085M

M = $ thousand   MM = $ million
See Pages 9 through 22 for Explanation of Ratios and Data

Current Data Sorted by Assets   Comparative Historical Data

	0-500M	500M-2MM	2-10MM	10-50MM	50-100MM	100-250MM	Type of Statement	ALL 4/1/06-3/31/07	ALL 4/1/07-3/31/08
			11	11	2	5	Unqualified	24	24
	1	3	26	18			Reviewed	34	39
	2	4	13	1	1		Compiled	15	18
		5	5	1			Tax Returns	12	23
	4	9	30	30	5	9	Other	65	69
		36 (4/1-9/30/10)		160 (10/1/10-3/31/11)				4/1/06-3/31/07	4/1/07-3/31/08
NUMBER OF STATEMENTS	7	21	85	61	8	14		150	173
	%	%	%	%	%	%	ASSETS	%	%
		14.1	11.7	8.1		4.8	Cash & Equivalents	8.9	10.0
		28.2	21.0	16.2		13.5	Trade Receivables (net)	23.6	22.0
		24.3	32.7	35.7		22.2	Inventory	34.9	33.4
		1.6	3.5	4.1		5.7	All Other Current	3.6	3.7
		68.1	68.9	64.1		46.2	Total Current	71.0	69.2
		21.1	23.6	25.6		19.3	Fixed Assets (net)	21.8	21.2
		5.6	5.0	5.2		30.3	Intangibles (net)	2.9	5.6
		5.2	2.5	5.1		4.2	All Other Non-Current	4.3	4.0
		100.0	100.0	100.0		100.0	Total	100.0	100.0
							LIABILITIES		
		12.8	10.3	6.4		.0	Notes Payable-Short Term	9.3	8.9
		3.6	3.7	4.7		1.9	Cur. Mat.-L.T.D.	3.1	4.8
		13.9	11.4	8.3		6.8	Trade Payables	13.1	11.4
		.3	.2	.2		.4	Income Taxes Payable	.4	.5
		6.1	9.0	10.1		5.9	All Other Current	9.9	9.2
		36.7	34.5	29.5		15.0	Total Current	35.7	34.7
		9.7	13.7	14.8		22.7	Long-Term Debt	14.0	17.6
		.0	1.1	.7		3.3	Deferred Taxes	.5	.4
		10.8	6.0	4.6		11.0	All Other Non-Current	4.9	8.0
		42.8	44.6	50.3		48.0	Net Worth	44.9	39.2
		100.0	100.0	100.0		100.0	Total Liabilities & Net Worth	100.0	100.0
							INCOME DATA		
		100.0	100.0	100.0		100.0	Net Sales	100.0	100.0
		37.5	30.8	28.9		29.3	Gross Profit	31.9	32.2
		31.5	22.7	20.1		19.5	Operating Expenses	22.6	21.9
		6.1	8.1	8.8		9.8	Operating Profit	9.4	10.2
		.8	2.1	2.1		3.5	All Other Expenses (net)	1.6	1.8
		5.3	6.0	6.7		6.3	Profit Before Taxes	7.8	8.5
							RATIOS		
		3.9	3.5	4.8		4.2	Current	3.6	3.6
		2.0	2.2	2.1		2.9		2.1	2.1
		1.2	1.5	1.5		2.6		1.4	1.4
		2.4	2.1	1.5		1.8	Quick	1.6	1.7
		.9	1.0	.8		1.3		.9	.9
		.7	.5	.5		.9		.5	.5
	25	14.4	27 / 13.3	31 / 11.9		48 / 7.7	Sales/Receivables	35 / 10.5	28 / 12.9
	44	8.3	43 / 8.5	40 / 9.1		54 / 6.8		48 / 7.6	44 / 8.2
	54	6.8	62 / 5.9	53 / 6.9		58 / 6.3		63 / 5.8	61 / 6.0
	28	13.2	57 / 6.4	89 / 4.1		96 / 3.8	Cost of Sales/Inventory	56 / 6.5	54 / 6.8
	58	6.3	110 / 3.3	131 / 2.8		121 / 3.0		111 / 3.3	107 / 3.4
	112	3.3	177 / 2.1	166 / 2.2		167 / 2.2		160 / 2.3	168 / 2.2
	14	26.4	15 / 24.6	19 / 19.1		23 / 16.1	Cost of Sales/Payables	21 / 17.8	18 / 19.8
	30	12.0	28 / 13.0	27 / 13.7		35 / 10.4		32 / 11.3	28 / 12.8
	53	6.9	50 / 7.3	42 / 8.6		48 / 7.6		56 / 6.5	47 / 7.8
		4.1	3.0	2.7		2.5	Sales/Working Capital	3.1	3.1
		9.7	4.4	3.9		3.0		5.0	5.0
		32.7	8.0	7.8		4.0		10.3	10.1
		22.6	10.4	15.4		12.8	EBIT/Interest	11.9	12.6
		6.5	(76) 3.2	(54) 7.1		(12) 2.2		(130) 5.0	(158) 5.3
		2.2	1.4	2.5		.9		2.4	2.4
			11.9	6.2			Net Profit + Depr., Dep., Amort./Cur. Mat. L/T/D	7.9	14.2
		(31)	2.3	(23) 2.6				(38) 3.4	(48) 3.1
			1.2	1.4				1.6	1.7
		.2	.2	.3		.3	Fixed/Worth	.2	.2
		.5	.5	.5		1.4		.5	.5
		2.2	1.5	1.0		NM		1.1	1.5
		.5	.6	.5		.6	Debt/Worth	.6	.8
		.9	1.4	1.0		3.6		1.2	1.7
		3.5	4.2	2.0		NM		3.2	4.6
		71.4	37.3	29.1		45.8	% Profit Before Taxes/Tangible Net Worth	47.7	58.6
	(18)	22.4	(80) 15.3	(55) 17.7		(11) 23.1		(136) 27.7	(151) 33.1
		1.7	4.4	10.1		9.1		10.3	13.7
		22.1	15.9	13.7		11.3	% Profit Before Taxes/Total Assets	22.4	22.1
		8.2	5.8	9.7		4.8		9.9	11.3
		2.5	1.1	3.0		.6		4.7	5.2
		37.5	17.2	12.4		10.4	Sales/Net Fixed Assets	22.4	31.3
		15.0	8.7	5.5		5.0		9.1	10.0
		3.9	3.7	3.0		3.6		4.6	4.6
		3.5	2.1	1.7		1.2	Sales/Total Assets	2.3	2.2
		2.0	1.6	1.3		.9		1.7	1.7
		1.3	1.2	1.0		.6		1.2	1.2
		1.0	1.4	1.8			% Depr., Dep., Amort./Sales	1.0	1.0
	(19)	2.5	(77) 3.0	(54) 3.1				(126) 2.1	(151) 2.4
		4.5	5.3	4.5				3.9	4.0
		2.1	1.7	1.5			% Officers', Directors' Owners' Comp/Sales	1.2	2.4
	(13)	4.0	(35) 4.4	(15) 2.2				(49) 3.0	(48) 4.2
		8.9	5.3	4.5				8.0	8.0
	11071M	67527M	819208M	1810293M	659189M	2061768M	Net Sales ($)	3665802M	4790994M
	2515M	29179M	472334M	1373754M	506080M	2179966M	Total Assets ($)	2498599M	3757282M

Comparative Historical Data | | | | ## Current Data Sorted by Sales

			Type of Statement	0-1MM	1-3MM	3-5MM	5-10MM	10-25MM	25MM & OVER
30	35	29	Unqualified			1	4	10	14
35	34	48	Reviewed		4	5	12	20	7
20	20	19	Compiled		2	3	10	3	1
16	18	13	Tax Returns	3	3	2	3	2	
85	92	87	Other	4	9	8	8	25	33
4/1/08-3/31/09 ALL	4/1/09-3/31/10 ALL	4/1/10-3/31/11 ALL			36 (4/1-9/30/10)		160 (10/1/10-3/31/11)		
186	199	196	**NUMBER OF STATEMENTS**	7	18	19	37	60	55
%	%	%	**ASSETS**	%	%	%	%	%	%
8.4	9.9	10.8	Cash & Equivalents		18.9	9.0	11.1	9.4	9.9
19.0	18.9	20.1	Trade Receivables (net)		21.4	20.2	24.1	19.6	17.4
32.7	33.2	30.9	Inventory		22.3	33.6	31.6	35.6	28.4
4.1	3.9	4.2	All Other Current		4.5	1.7	2.3	3.2	7.7
64.3	65.9	66.1	Total Current		67.1	64.6	69.1	67.8	63.5
24.4	23.9	22.9	Fixed Assets (net)		28.3	24.4	22.4	25.1	19.5
7.3	6.3	7.2	Intangibles (net)		3.4	9.0	5.0	2.8	12.7
4.1	3.9	3.9	All Other Non-Current		1.2	2.1	3.5	4.3	4.4
100.0	100.0	100.0	Total		100.0	100.0	100.0	100.0	100.0
			LIABILITIES						
9.6	9.0	8.6	Notes Payable-Short Term		10.1	12.7	10.4	9.2	4.7
3.5	4.3	3.7	Cur. Mat.-L.T.D.		3.9	3.7	3.2	4.0	3.9
9.5	9.4	10.2	Trade Payables		11.0	11.4	12.3	9.2	9.7
.4	.3	.3	Income Taxes Payable		.4	.0	.1	.3	.3
8.9	8.3	9.1	All Other Current		12.2	4.3	6.7	9.7	11.3
31.9	31.4	31.9	Total Current		37.6	32.0	32.8	32.5	29.9
16.7	16.3	13.6	Long-Term Debt		10.4	15.0	12.4	15.6	13.7
.7	.8	1.0	Deferred Taxes		.5	.5	.8	1.3	1.2
8.7	7.3	7.0	All Other Non-Current		5.7	11.4	8.8	5.0	5.3
42.1	44.3	46.5	Net Worth		45.9	41.1	45.2	45.6	49.9
100.0	100.0	100.0	Total Liabilties & Net Worth		100.0	100.0	100.0	100.0	100.0
			INCOME DATA						
100.0	100.0	100.0	Net Sales		100.0	100.0	100.0	100.0	100.0
33.2	31.4	31.1	Gross Profit		36.1	36.6	30.9	30.1	27.8
23.6	23.9	22.7	Operating Expenses		28.4	26.5	25.9	21.1	18.7
9.6	7.5	8.3	Operating Profit		7.7	10.1	5.0	9.1	9.1
1.6	1.7	1.9	All Other Expenses (net)		1.1	1.6	1.7	2.6	1.8
8.0	5.8	6.4	Profit Before Taxes		6.6	8.5	3.3	6.5	7.2
			RATIOS						
3.3	4.1	3.9	Current		8.4	3.4	3.0	4.1	3.4
2.1	2.3	2.2			2.2	2.4	2.2	2.2	2.5
1.5	1.6	1.5			1.3	1.6	1.5	1.4	1.7
1.4	1.9	1.9	Quick		2.9	2.2	1.8	1.6	1.6
.8	.9	1.0			1.7	.9	1.0	.8	1.0
.4	.4	.5			.7	.4	.5	.5	.5
25 14.7	29 12.8	31 11.7	Sales/Receivables		28 12.9	18 20.1	29 12.5	29 12.7	34 10.8
40 9.0	41 8.8	44 8.4			45 8.1	42 8.8	44 8.4	40 9.2	46 7.9
51 7.1	54 6.7	58 6.3			57 6.4	50 7.3	60 6.1	56 6.6	56 6.5
67 5.5	63 5.8	58 6.2	Cost of Sales/Inventory		26 14.3	60 6.1	50 7.3	65 5.6	66 5.6
111 3.3	105 3.5	110 3.3			64 5.7	111 3.3	110 3.3	118 3.1	111 3.3
172 2.1	178 2.1	157 2.3			165 2.2	212 1.7	140 2.6	154 2.4	158 2.3
18 20.7	15 24.0	16 22.6	Cost of Sales/Payables		4 86.8	13 28.2	18 20.1	16 23.3	19 19.2
27 13.3	25 14.6	29 12.8			16 22.2	28 12.9	35 10.5	26 13.9	30 12.3
44 8.2	41 8.9	46 7.9			50 7.3	42 8.6	50 7.2	42 8.6	45 8.1
3.4	2.8	2.8	Sales/Working Capital		2.4	3.1	3.0	2.9	2.5
5.0	4.3	4.5			6.4	5.3	4.6	4.9	3.7
10.0	8.2	9.2			17.4	10.2	9.5	9.0	7.3
18.1	12.0	13.2	EBIT/Interest		15.5	14.1	6.2	14.1	14.1
(172) 5.2	(185) 4.6	(175) 4.9			(17) 5.2	(18) 3.8	(33) 2.2	(56) 5.8	(45) 7.9
1.9	1.9	1.9			-1.6	2.0	1.1	2.9	1.9
9.1	6.2	9.5	Net Profit + Depr., Dep., Amort./Cur. Mat. L/T/D				4.6	16.5	8.0
(66) 3.9	(63) 2.6	(70) 2.6					(16) 2.4	(23) 2.3	(23) 2.6
1.9	1.5	1.4					1.2	1.4	1.4
.2	.2	.2	Fixed/Worth		.2	.1	.2	.3	.3
.6	.6	.5			.6	.7	.6	.5	.5
1.5	1.6	1.5			3.8	1.6	1.8	.9	1.9
.7	.6	.5	Debt/Worth		.3	.8	.5	.5	.5
1.4	1.3	1.3			.8	1.5	1.6	1.3	1.1
3.8	3.7	3.6			5.3	2.7	5.7	2.6	5.1
51.2	33.3	40.2	% Profit Before Taxes/Tangible Net Worth		66.4	67.0	24.8	49.4	34.4
(165) 27.7	(176) 19.7	(177) 17.8			(16) 22.4	(16) 30.8	(35) 10.6	(58) 20.4	(47) 20.9
8.4	7.2	7.1			-7.9	4.8	1.1	9.8	10.1
20.0	15.8	15.3	% Profit Before Taxes/Total Assets		26.2	28.8	11.4	17.2	13.3
10.7	8.9	7.7			7.7	5.7	3.0	9.8	9.8
2.5	2.1	2.2			-4.8	2.9	.8	3.7	2.2
18.0	17.0	19.2	Sales/Net Fixed Assets		18.5	82.6	18.5	16.4	19.6
7.7	6.6	7.6			7.3	5.9	9.0	7.1	7.3
3.8	3.7	3.8			2.5	2.6	4.4	3.5	4.0
2.2	2.1	2.0	Sales/Total Assets		3.5	2.3	2.2	1.9	1.7
1.6	1.4	1.5			1.5	1.5	1.6	1.6	1.2
1.1	1.0	1.0			.9	1.0	1.2	1.2	.9
1.1	1.2	1.5	% Depr., Dep., Amort./Sales		2.2	1.1	1.6	1.5	1.0
(160) 2.4	(164) 2.9	(170) 2.9			(17) 4.2	(16) 2.8	(34) 3.0	(54) 2.7	(44) 2.9
4.5	5.2	4.7			8.8	4.5	6.0	4.4	3.8
1.7	1.7	1.8	% Officers', Directors' Owners' Comp/Sales		2.7		1.7	1.5	
(55) 3.6	(65) 5.0	(67) 4.0			(12) 7.9		(19) 3.1	(23) 2.4	
6.6	8.9	7.4			11.5		6.0	6.4	
6254351M	6134648M	5429056M	Net Sales ($)	4810M	39349M	77600M	263472M	996736M	4047089M
5017101M	5114060M	4563828M	Total Assets ($)	7300M	28194M	55637M	194493M	710834M	3567370M

M = $ thousand   MM = $ million
See Pages 9 through 22 for Explanation of Ratios and Data

Current Data Sorted by Assets | **Comparative Historical Data**

0-500M	500M-2MM	2-10MM	10-50MM	50-100MM	100-250MM	Type of Statement	4/1/06-3/31/07 ALL	4/1/07-3/31/08 ALL
		1	4	3	2	Unqualified	7	10
	1	1	3			Reviewed	7	3
	1					Compiled	4	2
	1	1				Tax Returns	2	4
	2	7	8	3	1	Other	18	23
	6 (4/1-9/30/10)		33 (10/1/10-3/31/11)					
	5	10	15	6	3	NUMBER OF STATEMENTS	38	42
%	%	%	%	%	%	**ASSETS**	%	%
DATA NOT AVAILABLE		8.8	10.5			Cash & Equivalents	8.4	12.2
		31.3	19.3			Trade Receivables (net)	24.5	22.4
		27.9	27.5			Inventory	27.0	23.7
		5.6	4.6			All Other Current	2.6	3.0
		73.6	61.9			Total Current	62.6	61.3
		14.8	25.7			Fixed Assets (net)	22.7	21.4
		1.5	5.1			Intangibles (net)	9.5	10.9
		10.1	7.3			All Other Non-Current	5.1	6.4
		100.0	100.0			Total	100.0	100.0
						LIABILITIES		
		7.1	6.6			Notes Payable-Short Term	8.7	8.0
		1.8	2.4			Cur. Mat.-L.T.D.	2.6	5.1
		14.3	6.9			Trade Payables	14.4	12.6
		.4	.3			Income Taxes Payable	.2	.1
		7.3	12.7			All Other Current	9.2	11.8
		30.9	29.1			Total Current	35.1	37.6
		7.5	11.4			Long-Term Debt	21.3	19.2
		.0	1.0			Deferred Taxes	.4	.7
		17.3	4.9			All Other Non-Current	3.1	2.8
		44.4	53.6			Net Worth	40.0	39.7
		100.0	100.0			Total Liabilities & Net Worth	100.0	100.0
						INCOME DATA		
		100.0	100.0			Net Sales	100.0	100.0
		32.6	31.2			Gross Profit	30.1	34.7
		26.0	20.4			Operating Expenses	20.5	25.3
		6.5	10.9			Operating Profit	9.6	9.4
		.0	.6			All Other Expenses (net)	.8	2.3
		6.5	10.3			Profit Before Taxes	8.8	7.1
						RATIOS		
		10.5	3.5				2.9	3.4
		2.3	2.4			Current	1.7	2.1
		1.7	1.4				1.3	1.2
		6.8	2.0				1.4	2.1
		1.7	1.0			Quick	.7	1.0
		.6	.9				.5	.6
		30 12.1	**38** 9.7				**30** 12.1	**31** 11.9
		54 6.8	**43** 8.6			Sales/Receivables	**42** 8.7	**43** 8.5
		77 4.7	**63** 5.8				**65** 5.6	**56** 6.5
		35 10.5	**50** 7.2				**27** 13.3	**34** 10.9
		62 5.9	**76** 4.8			Cost of Sales/Inventory	**73** 5.0	**65** 5.6
		151 2.4	**171** 2.1				**104** 3.5	**103** 3.6
		9 40.1	**16** 22.1				**20** 18.0	**18** 20.6
		37 9.8	**27** 13.7			Cost of Sales/Payables	**32** 11.4	**29** 12.8
		65 5.6	**39** 9.4				**50** 7.4	**47** 7.7
		3.2	2.2				3.8	3.9
		4.2	5.3			Sales/Working Capital	6.9	7.7
		7.0	11.6				24.7	16.1
			26.5				17.2	19.9
			10.2			EBIT/Interest	(33) 6.1	(37) 8.2
			3.9				2.4	1.7
							10.3	13.9
						Net Profit + Depr., Dep., Amort./Cur. Mat. L/T/D	(12) 5.0	(11) 5.0
							2.2	2.8
		.2	.2				.3	.2
		.4	.5			Fixed/Worth	.9	.7
		1.1	1.2				2.1	2.1
		.3	.4				.9	.6
		1.8	.9			Debt/Worth	1.7	1.5
		4.7	2.0				10.9	5.1
		98.4	45.4				62.1	73.4
		27.2	18.7			% Profit Before Taxes/Tangible Net Worth	(33) 36.5	(34) 29.0
		1.2	13.9				15.7	11.6
		23.6	19.3				21.6	30.7
		14.0	12.3			% Profit Before Taxes/Total Assets	13.8	14.6
		2.2	6.2				3.6	2.6
		21.4	12.6				17.8	21.0
		13.7	5.7			Sales/Net Fixed Assets	9.6	10.6
		10.1	4.6				6.3	6.6
		2.3	1.6				2.5	3.0
		2.0	1.4			Sales/Total Assets	2.0	1.8
		1.0	.9				1.1	1.2
			1.4				1.3	.7
			(14) 2.1			% Depr., Dep., Amort./Sales	(32) 2.1	(34) 1.6
			2.7				3.2	2.5
						% Officers', Directors' Owners' Comp/Sales		
	12776M	112755M	486805M	507302M	379784M	Net Sales ($)	1843496M	2388783M
	6167M	58516M	368478M	404587M	452284M	Total Assets ($)	1056928M	1457006M

M = $ thousand MM = $ million

See Pages 9 through 22 for Explanation of Ratios and Data

Comparative Historical Data | Current Data Sorted by Sales

	14	15	10	Type of Statement	0-1MM	1-3MM	3-5MM	5-10MM	10-25MM	25MM & OVER
	14	15	10	Unqualified				1	2	7
	1	5	5	Reviewed		1			3	1
	2	5	1	Compiled			1	1		
	4	3	2	Tax Returns	1		1			
	18	17	21	Other	1	2	1	2	6	10
	4/1/08-3/31/09 ALL	4/1/09-3/31/10 ALL	4/1/10-3/31/11 ALL			6 (4/1-9/30/10)			33 (10/1/10-3/31/11)	
	39	45	39	NUMBER OF STATEMENTS	1	3	2	4	11	18
	%	%	%	ASSETS	%	%	%	%	%	%
	9.2	9.6	11.1	Cash & Equivalents					11.6	8.5
	19.5	19.9	20.5	Trade Receivables (net)					18.0	20.2
	32.3	25.4	25.2	Inventory					21.7	26.1
	4.4	4.1	5.1	All Other Current					6.3	5.9
	65.5	59.0	61.9	Total Current					57.6	60.6
	23.4	25.0	25.5	Fixed Assets (net)					24.0	30.5
	7.1	8.7	3.3	Intangibles (net)					5.9	2.7
	4.0	7.3	9.4	All Other Non-Current					12.5	6.2
	100.0	100.0	100.0	Total					100.0	100.0
				LIABILITIES						
	9.8	6.9	5.5	Notes Payable-Short Term					6.9	6.2
	3.4	3.3	3.6	Cur. Mat.-L.T.D.					3.6	4.8
	13.8	9.3	10.3	Trade Payables					8.7	9.2
	.2	.4	.5	Income Taxes Payable					.0	.5
	14.5	10.9	10.3	All Other Current					7.4	15.1
	41.8	30.8	30.2	Total Current					26.6	35.8
	11.6	12.4	9.8	Long-Term Debt					16.0	8.6
	.8	1.1	1.4	Deferred Taxes					.2	2.3
	12.2	7.2	7.3	All Other Non-Current					7.0	4.4
	33.6	48.5	51.3	Net Worth					50.2	48.9
	100.0	100.0	100.0	Total Liabilities & Net Worth					100.0	100.0
				INCOME DATA						
	100.0	100.0	100.0	Net Sales					100.0	100.0
	27.0	32.3	30.3	Gross Profit					37.7	27.8
	20.7	24.0	23.0	Operating Expenses					26.4	18.9
	6.3	8.3	7.3	Operating Profit					11.4	8.9
	1.5	1.3	.2	All Other Expenses (net)					.6	.6
	4.8	7.0	7.1	Profit Before Taxes					10.8	8.3
				RATIOS						
	2.4	3.8	3.5	Current					5.7	3.3
	1.6	2.1	2.0						1.8	1.8
	1.1	1.2	1.2						1.2	1.0
	1.2	1.6	2.0	Quick					3.0	1.8
	.8	1.0	1.2						.9	.9
	.3	.5	.6						.7	.4
	(33) 11.1	(29) 12.4	(30) 12.2	Sales/Receivables					(36) 10.2	(37) 9.9
	(38) 9.5	(38) 9.5	(46) 7.9						(47) 7.8	(44) 8.3
	(53) 6.9	(63) 5.8	(56) 6.5						(63) 5.8	(52) 7.1
	(49) 7.4	(30) 12.1	(35) 10.3	Cost of Sales/Inventory					(28) 13.1	(46) 8.0
	(88) 4.1	(77) 4.7	(65) 5.6						(61) 6.0	(63) 5.8
	(171) 2.1	(138) 2.6	(152) 2.4						(171) 2.1	(156) 2.3
	(23) 15.7	(16) 23.4	(17) 21.5	Cost of Sales/Payables					(18) 20.3	(17) 21.6
	(33) 11.0	(27) 13.3	(32) 11.3						(31) 11.7	(35) 10.4
	(43) 8.5	(54) 6.8	(51) 7.2						(57) 6.4	(49) 7.4
	3.7	3.2	2.3	Sales/Working Capital					2.8	2.6
	6.1	6.0	5.3						6.9	6.6
	33.7	12.5	12.6						12.6	NM
	21.5	38.7	38.4	EBIT/Interest					26.5	36.4
	(38) 5.6	(42) 9.8	(36) 11.3						10.2	(17) 13.4
	2.7	2.0	2.4						4.9	2.6
	6.1		12.5	Net Profit + Depr., Dep., Amort./Cur. Mat. L/T/D						
	(14) 2.6		(10) 5.4							
	1.4		1.9							
	.3	.3	.2	Fixed/Worth					.3	.3
	.7	.6	.5						.5	.6
	2.3	1.4	1.0						1.2	1.3
	1.0	.3	.4	Debt/Worth					.3	.6
	2.6	1.7	.9						1.0	.9
	7.2	3.3	2.1						4.5	2.0
	38.2	51.0	34.4	% Profit Before Taxes/Tangible Net Worth					45.4	31.6
	(33) 26.8	(42) 19.4	18.7						21.8	16.3
	13.8	8.6	6.7						15.2	8.0
	16.5	17.8	20.2	% Profit Before Taxes/Total Assets					20.8	19.5
	9.3	6.9	9.8						14.6	9.9
	1.4	2.9	1.8						3.9	2.8
	19.1	14.6	16.0	Sales/Net Fixed Assets					16.0	13.1
	8.7	6.3	7.7						10.0	6.3
	5.2	3.9	3.1						4.6	3.2
	2.2	2.2	2.0	Sales/Total Assets					2.1	1.8
	1.5	1.3	1.4						1.4	1.4
	1.1	.9	.9						.9	.9
	.9	1.2	1.3	% Depr., Dep., Amort./Sales					.9	1.7
	(36) 2.0	(38) 2.4	(35) 2.2						(10) 2.0	(17) 2.4
	3.2	3.9	3.5						2.7	3.3
				% Officers', Directors' Owners' Comp/Sales						
	2530898M	2151704M	1499422M	Net Sales ($)	455M	6862M	6639M	28206M	183063M	1274197M
	2026028M	1857200M	1290032M	Total Assets ($)	659M	4607M	7227M	15330M	168908M	1093301M

© RMA 2011

M = $ thousand   MM = $ million
See Pages 9 through 22 for Explanation of Ratios and Data

Current Data Sorted by Assets   Comparative Historical Data

0-500M	500M-2MM	2-10MM	10-50MM	50-100MM	100-250MM	Type of Statement	4/1/06-3/31/07 ALL	4/1/07-3/31/08 ALL
		2	5	6	4	Unqualified	25	29
		6	4			Reviewed	15	14
	3	4				Compiled	16	6
	4	3				Tax Returns	4	6
3	1	11	13	6	6	Other	19	34
	15 (4/1-9/30/10)		66 (10/1/10-3/31/11)					
3	8	26	22	12	10	**NUMBER OF STATEMENTS**	79	89
%	%	%	%	%	%	**ASSETS**	%	%
		11.8	11.6	10.4	8.9	Cash & Equivalents	13.9	13.5
		24.5	18.4	15.2	18.7	Trade Receivables (net)	19.6	20.5
		13.8	18.1	2.8	12.2	Inventory	13.2	11.9
		8.3	8.8	14.5	8.4	All Other Current	12.0	11.9
		58.4	56.9	43.0	48.2	Total Current	58.7	57.8
		32.8	35.5	42.2	39.3	Fixed Assets (net)	31.4	33.7
		2.4	3.2	7.3	7.3	Intangibles (net)	2.7	3.0
		6.3	4.5	7.6	5.2	All Other Non-Current	7.2	5.4
		100.0	100.0	100.0	100.0	Total	100.0	100.0
						LIABILITIES		
		8.1	6.7	11.4	4.0	Notes Payable-Short Term	10.1	7.7
		3.3	3.4	1.9	2.8	Cur. Mat.-L.T.D.	3.7	3.4
		13.1	13.6	9.5	9.1	Trade Payables	12.4	11.4
		.6	.0	.2	.2	Income Taxes Payable	1.1	.8
		14.7	11.9	9.1	11.4	All Other Current	17.6	19.7
		39.7	35.5	32.1	27.4	Total Current	45.0	42.9
		19.5	18.8	21.4	22.1	Long-Term Debt	14.0	15.5
		1.7	1.2	1.9	4.0	Deferred Taxes	.7	.9
		4.9	3.7	5.9	2.1	All Other Non-Current	4.5	7.2
		34.3	40.8	38.7	44.3	Net Worth	35.8	33.6
		100.0	100.0	100.0	100.0	Total Liabilities & Net Worth	100.0	100.0
						INCOME DATA		
		100.0	100.0	100.0	100.0	Net Sales	100.0	100.0
		29.8	22.9	21.7	19.5	Gross Profit	28.6	25.0
		30.1	15.5	16.1	16.1	Operating Expenses	22.3	18.5
		-.2	7.4	5.6	3.4	Operating Profit	6.3	6.5
		-.6	.9	1.1	.6	All Other Expenses (net)	.7	.4
		.3	6.5	4.5	2.8	Profit Before Taxes	5.6	6.1
						RATIOS		
		2.6	2.0	1.8	2.4		2.2	2.0
		1.5	1.7	1.4	1.8	Current	1.5	1.5
		.9	1.1	.9	1.3		1.0	1.1
		1.8	1.3	1.3	1.6		1.3	1.4
		1.1	1.0	1.0	.9	Quick	.8	.9
		.6	.4	.4	.6		.4	.4
		22 16.5	17 22.1	4 87.0	22 17.0		19 19.2	15 25.1
		46 7.9	30 12.0	31 11.9	34 10.8	Sales/Receivables	37 9.7	31 11.7
		61 5.9	49 7.4	75 4.9	45 8.1		57 6.4	56 6.5
		0 UND	0 UND	2 171.3	3 119.2		1 433.8	0 999.8
		18 20.1	32 11.5	3 115.3	10 35.2	Cost of Sales/Inventory	5 66.7	5 71.1
		84 4.3	89 4.1	26 14.1	66 5.5		56 6.5	53 6.9
		12 31.7	14 26.2	20 17.9	15 25.1		17 21.8	16 22.4
		24 15.5	25 14.5	30 12.1	28 13.2	Cost of Sales/Payables	25 14.5	24 14.9
		50 7.3	40 9.2	39 9.4	37 9.7		41 8.9	35 10.5
		5.6	6.9	5.9	4.6		6.0	6.5
		12.0	8.7	13.4	6.9	Sales/Working Capital	9.0	11.9
		-63.7	39.7	NM	18.3		159.8	59.6
		7.6	22.2	17.7			13.4	17.3
		(25) 2.8	(17) 6.3	(11) 6.4		EBIT/Interest	(68) 3.7	(78) 5.3
		.1	1.7	-.8			2.2	2.1
						Net Profit + Depr., Dep.,	9.3	7.8
						Amort./Cur. Mat. L/T/D	(32) 4.0 (30) 2.6	
							2.4	1.4
		.4	.4	.8	.6		.4	.5
		1.1	1.1	1.5	1.1	Fixed/Worth	.8	1.0
		1.9	2.0	2.5	2.5		1.8	2.4
		.7	1.0	.8	.8		.8	.9
		1.3	1.6	1.9	1.4	Debt/Worth	1.7	1.8
		3.9	3.3	7.1	3.3		4.5	6.0
		21.0	70.3	44.2		% Profit Before Taxes/Tangible	39.6	66.0
		(22) 4.2	41.6	(11) 10.8		Net Worth	(72) 24.8	(82) 31.1
		-10.9	8.0	-13.1			10.0	11.0
		9.4	24.5	10.0	14.0	% Profit Before Taxes/Total	15.1	18.8
		2.1	9.6	4.7	3.8	Assets	6.7	8.6
		-4.6	2.5	-2.9	.6		2.5	3.7
		20.9	19.2	5.5	9.3		12.1	16.2
		6.8	7.4	3.3	3.8	Sales/Net Fixed Assets	5.7	5.8
		2.5	2.8	2.2	1.6		3.1	3.5
		2.3	3.1	1.7	2.0		2.6	2.8
		1.7	1.9	1.4	1.3	Sales/Total Assets	1.6	1.9
		1.2	1.2	1.1	.8		1.2	1.3
		1.1	1.3	2.1			1.0	1.0
		(23) 2.6	(19) 2.1	3.9		% Depr., Dep., Amort./Sales	(77) 2.0	(83) 1.8
		4.5	4.3	4.9			3.1	3.3
							1.7	1.0
						% Officers', Directors' Owners' Comp/Sales	(20) 6.1	(14) 1.9
							10.9	6.9
2555M	26541M	328234M	1050554M	1180598M	2035898M	Net Sales ($)	4063802M	6163786M
807M	11531M	149208M	514954M	867074M	1420348M	Total Assets ($)	2750587M	3875066M

M = $ thousand   MM = $ million
See Pages 9 through 22 for Explanation of Ratios and Data

Comparative Historical Data   Current Data Sorted by Sales

			Type of Statement	0-1MM	1-3MM	3-5MM	5-10MM	10-25MM	25MM & OVER
23	20	17	Unqualified					2	15
10	12	10	Reviewed		1	1	4	2	2
9	11	7	Compiled		2		3	2	
6	6	10	Tax Returns	3	4	2	1		
28	41	37	Other			2	3	8	24
4/1/08-3/31/09 ALL	4/1/09-3/31/10 ALL	4/1/10-3/31/11 ALL			15 (4/1-9/30/10)		66 (10/1/10-3/31/11)		
76	90	81	NUMBER OF STATEMENTS	3	7	5	11	14	41
%	%	%	ASSETS	%	%	%	%	%	%
11.8	11.8	11.5	Cash & Equivalents				13.7	14.4	9.7
18.3	20.0	20.0	Trade Receivables (net)				22.3	25.4	20.4
11.4	11.6	14.9	Inventory				6.4	17.4	11.1
12.6	11.4	8.3	All Other Current				6.8	7.7	11.2
54.1	54.7	54.7	Total Current				49.3	64.9	52.3
36.2	36.7	34.9	Fixed Assets (net)				39.9	30.4	36.3
3.4	2.5	3.9	Intangibles (net)				2.8	2.1	5.6
6.2	6.0	6.5	All Other Non-Current				8.0	2.6	5.8
100.0	100.0	100.0	Total				100.0	100.0	100.0
			LIABILITIES						
9.4	8.5	10.2	Notes Payable-Short Term				3.0	11.7	7.3
2.8	2.9	2.9	Cur. Mat.-L.T.D.				4.1	1.7	2.7
10.1	11.1	13.6	Trade Payables				11.9	19.2	13.3
.6	.4	.2	Income Taxes Payable				.1	.0	.1
15.2	13.3	11.9	All Other Current				11.4	12.4	10.5
38.2	36.1	38.9	Total Current				30.6	45.0	33.9
20.8	21.1	21.0	Long-Term Debt				22.3	13.3	19.2
1.1	1.0	1.6	Deferred Taxes				3.4	.4	2.0
2.9	3.0	5.8	All Other Non-Current				7.2	3.9	3.3
37.0	38.8	32.7	Net Worth				36.4	37.4	41.5
100.0	100.0	100.0	Total Liabilities & Net Worth				100.0	100.0	100.0
			INCOME DATA						
100.0	100.0	100.0	Net Sales				100.0	100.0	100.0
24.6	25.2	26.9	Gross Profit				38.7	25.8	20.7
18.5	20.7	23.4	Operating Expenses				36.4	23.4	15.0
6.1	4.5	3.5	Operating Profit				2.3	2.4	5.7
1.1	.9	.5	All Other Expenses (net)				-2.7	.8	.8
5.0	3.6	3.0	Profit Before Taxes				5.0	1.5	4.9
			RATIOS						
2.1	2.4	2.2					2.9	1.8	2.2
1.4	1.5	1.5	Current				1.8	1.4	1.6
1.0	1.1	1.1					1.3	.9	1.2
1.4	1.5	1.4					2.4	1.4	1.3
.7	.9	1.0	Quick				1.3	.8	1.0
.4	.4	.4					.8	.5	.5
14 26.8	16 23.5	18 20.5					40 9.2	22 16.5	17 21.3
31 11.7	34 10.7	33 11.0	Sales/Receivables				57 6.4	35 10.5	32 11.2
46 7.9	47 7.7	54 6.7					65 5.6	55 6.7	48 7.7
0 999.8	1 476.5	1 696.4					2 220.0	0 UND	1 696.4
8 43.8	5 75.7	17 20.9	Cost of Sales/Inventory				19 19.2	24 14.9	6 57.9
32 11.4	45 8.2	79 4.6					51 7.1	102 3.6	45 8.2
11 34.4	12 30.9	14 25.5					13 28.3	15 24.9	17 21.2
20 18.6	24 15.2	27 13.3	Cost of Sales/Payables				37 10.0	25 14.8	28 12.9
40 9.2	39 9.5	44 8.3					56 6.5	61 6.0	38 9.6
5.5	5.8	5.7					2.8	5.3	6.6
13.4	10.4	10.6	Sales/Working Capital				8.4	8.4	10.6
NM	53.0	117.1					19.8	-64.2	32.4
12.4	12.9	11.5					8.7	15.0	19.8
(69) 6.1	(83) 5.2	(72) 3.0	EBIT/Interest				5.4	(11) 1.8	(35) 6.3
1.6	.8	1.1					2.2	-.5	1.1
6.5	9.2	3.9	Net Profit + Depr., Dep.,						4.4
(27) 4.5	(30) 2.7	(23) 2.0	Amort./Cur. Mat. L/T/D					(14)	2.0
2.1	.9	.8							.7
.6	.5	.6					.5	.2	.6
1.1	.8	1.3	Fixed/Worth				1.3	1.3	1.2
2.5	1.9	2.5					1.9	2.3	2.2
.9	.7	.9					.7	1.1	.9
1.9	1.6	1.8	Debt/Worth				1.1	1.7	1.6
4.5	3.1	5.1					3.1	3.5	3.1
51.8	43.8	48.0	% Profit Before Taxes/Tangible					37.2	57.0
(66) 29.6	(82) 16.3	(69) 11.5	Net Worth					(13) 6.6	(39) 22.6
8.3	1.3	1.7						-15.1	1.9
21.5	15.4	13.6	% Profit Before Taxes/Total				11.3	8.1	23.6
10.5	5.7	3.8	Assets				3.8	2.4	7.5
.9	-.3	.3					.5	-3.1	.6
10.1	13.7	18.2					8.6	74.8	14.0
5.0	5.6	6.0	Sales/Net Fixed Assets				3.8	7.3	4.3
3.0	2.6	2.7					1.9	2.1	2.8
2.4	2.5	2.4					2.3	2.7	2.8
1.9	1.7	1.7	Sales/Total Assets				1.2	1.9	1.7
1.3	1.2	1.1					1.1	1.0	1.2
1.4	1.2	1.2					1.4	.7	1.4
(66) 2.3	(81) 2.4	(72) 2.4	% Depr., Dep., Amort./Sales				(10) 3.3	(11) 2.0	(36) 2.5
3.7	3.6	4.5					5.6	3.2	4.9
1.6	1.1	2.1	% Officers', Directors'						
(21) 2.3	(18) 2.7	(23) 3.9	Owners' Comp/Sales						
5.6	4.1	9.2							
5384796M	5654797M	4624380M	Net Sales ($)	1665M	13792M	21881M	77142M	242120M	4267780M
3313183M	3796277M	2963922M	Total Assets ($)	1030M	10706M	17269M	56182M	154815M	2723920M

M = $ thousand   MM = $ million
See Pages 9 through 22 for Explanation of Ratios and Data

Current Data Sorted by Assets   Comparative Historical Data

0-500M	500M-2MM	2-10MM	10-50MM	50-100MM	100-250MM	Type of Statement	4/1/06-3/31/07 ALL	4/1/07-3/31/08 ALL
		1	10	4		Unqualified	33	23
	2	3		1		Reviewed	16	17
	1	4	1			Compiled	9	7
5	5	2				Tax Returns	7	5
1	4	7	9	6	4	Other	34	40
0-500M	17 (4/1-9/30/10) 500M-2MM	2-10MM	53 (10/1/10-3/31/11) 10-50MM	50-100MM	100-250MM			
6	12	17	20	11	4	NUMBER OF STATEMENTS	99	92
%	%	%	%	%	%		%	%
						ASSETS		
	9.1	11.0	10.5	11.2		Cash & Equivalents	10.4	10.5
	10.1	14.9	8.9	7.8		Trade Receivables (net)	14.0	12.5
	33.5	38.3	25.8	15.0		Inventory	32.1	32.0
	4.4	1.6	7.6	2.0		All Other Current	3.6	3.9
	57.2	65.7	52.8	36.0		Total Current	60.2	59.0
	31.1	26.5	34.3	34.1		Fixed Assets (net)	28.7	29.8
	3.6	5.0	7.6	23.6		Intangibles (net)	6.0	5.9
	8.1	2.8	5.3	6.3		All Other Non-Current	5.1	5.4
	100.0	100.0	100.0	100.0		Total	100.0	100.0
						LIABILITIES		
	13.5	13.3	9.3	5.4		Notes Payable-Short Term	10.2	10.3
	2.3	4.9	3.3	2.1		Cur. Mat.-L.T.D.	2.2	4.3
	16.2	15.1	7.2	6.7		Trade Payables	15.7	14.2
	.6	.0	.1	.0		Income Taxes Payable	.3	.2
	8.1	7.7	14.5	14.2		All Other Current	15.3	16.3
	40.7	41.0	34.2	28.4		Total Current	43.7	45.2
	28.2	18.9	21.1	36.5		Long-Term Debt	17.5	17.1
	.2	.2	.3	1.2		Deferred Taxes	.3	.5
	15.4	21.0	5.7	9.9		All Other Non-Current	7.6	3.8
	15.5	18.9	38.7	23.9		Net Worth	30.8	33.4
	100.0	100.0	100.0	100.0		Total Liabilities & Net Worth	100.0	100.0
						INCOME DATA		
	100.0	100.0	100.0	100.0		Net Sales	100.0	100.0
	33.7	22.0	21.7	22.7		Gross Profit	24.0	21.6
	32.2	19.1	20.4	19.4		Operating Expenses	19.1	18.5
	1.5	3.0	1.3	3.3		Operating Profit	4.9	3.1
	1.9	1.5	1.2	3.9		All Other Expenses (net)	1.1	1.2
	-.3	1.5	.1	-.6		Profit Before Taxes	3.8	1.9
						RATIOS		
	2.3	3.3	2.8	1.8		Current	2.1	2.2
	1.4	1.6	1.6	1.2			1.5	1.4
	1.0	1.2	1.0	.7			1.1	1.1
	.9	1.1	1.2	.7		Quick	1.0	.9
	.4	.6	.7	.5			.6	.5
	.2	.4	.2	.4			.3	.2
8 47.1	20 18.7	5 66.7	14 26.8			Sales/Receivables	9 40.9	6 63.4
14 27.0	24 15.0	13 28.6	17 20.9				17 22.9	16 22.9
27 13.6	37 9.9	34 10.7	37 9.9				34 10.7	26 14.2
40 9.1	43 8.6	34 10.9	41 8.8			Cost of Sales/Inventory	31 11.6	31 11.8
88 4.1	84 4.3	80 4.5	56 6.5				54 6.8	53 6.8
136 2.7	131 2.8	112 3.3	60 6.0				94 4.4	84 4.4
18 20.2	16 22.3	10 38.0	10 37.4			Cost of Sales/Payables	14 25.8	13 28.4
30 12.0	26 13.9	18 20.4	27 13.4				23 16.1	21 17.3
36 10.2	33 10.9	36 10.0	35 10.4				37 9.8	32 11.4
	5.9	4.4	4.3	8.5		Sales/Working Capital	6.9	6.6
	15.9	10.8	8.6	22.5			12.0	13.2
	NM	20.6	NM	-11.7			45.9	265.2
	3.6	18.3	7.7	7.3		EBIT/Interest	10.9	8.7
	(11) -.1	(16) 4.0	(18) 1.1	.4			(94) 4.4	(83) 2.7
	-3.8	1.3	-6.4	-1.0			1.8	.7
						Net Profit + Depr., Dep., Amort./Cur. Mat. L/T/D	19.7	9.1
							(20) 5.8	(21) 1.8
							2.3	-.1
	.3	.5	.4	1.1		Fixed/Worth	.4	.4
	.6	1.5	1.2	-2.7			.9	.9
	NM	NM	18.1	-.2			1.9	2.9
	.5	1.4	.8	1.3		Debt/Worth	1.0	.6
	1.2	4.0	1.3	-4.7			2.1	1.9
	NM	NM	40.1	-2.0			6.8	7.4
		29.5	30.2			% Profit Before Taxes/Tangible Net Worth	59.9	46.4
	(13)	14.1	(17) 6.4				(86) 21.1	(75) 13.0
		2.6	-22.9				10.4	.0
	8.0	8.3	10.2	4.0		% Profit Before Taxes/Total Assets	18.3	13.6
	-3.3	5.6	.5	-3.1			7.3	5.5
	-13.8	.6	-6.7	-8.1			2.8	-1.0
	19.0	16.5	9.4	8.0		Sales/Net Fixed Assets	17.2	21.8
	9.1	9.3	4.4	4.9			9.0	9.4
	4.0	4.1	2.3	2.4			5.0	5.2
	3.1	3.0	1.8	1.6		Sales/Total Assets	3.0	3.2
	2.2	1.9	1.4	1.3			2.3	2.5
	1.6	1.4	1.1	1.0			1.6	1.6
		1.0	1.3			% Depr., Dep., Amort./Sales	.8	.8
		1.9	(17) 2.9				(95) 1.5	(83) 1.3
		3.4	3.7				2.6	2.4
						% Officers', Directors' Owners' Comp/Sales	.9	1.0
							(22) 1.8	(21) 2.0
							3.8	5.8
11145M	35393M	193045M	648397M	972196M	446195M	Net Sales ($)	4504086M	4471746M
1324M	14894M	91877M	420270M	732669M	550435M	Total Assets ($)	2289436M	2424477M

M = $ thousand   MM = $ million
See Pages 9 through 22 for Explanation of Ratios and Data

Comparative Historical Data

Current Data Sorted by Sales

Type of Statement	0-1MM	1-3MM	3-5MM	5-10MM	10-25MM	25MM & OVER
Unqualified					5	10
Reviewed	1		1		3	1
Compiled			4	1	1	
Tax Returns				1	1	
Other	3	4	3	4	5	16

4/1/08-3/31/09 ALL	4/1/09-3/31/10 ALL	4/1/10-3/31/11 ALL		17 (4/1-9/30/10)			53 (10/1/10-3/31/11)		

09	10	11		0-1MM	1-3MM	3-5MM	5-10MM	10-25MM	25MM & OVER
88	64	70	**NUMBER OF STATEMENTS**	5	6	8	9	15	27
%	%	%	**ASSETS**	%	%	%	%	%	%
7.1	9.5	11.3	Cash & Equivalents					7.8	12.8
11.0	10.8	11.0	Trade Receivables (net)					15.1	6.5
37.5	32.3	29.6	Inventory					39.2	21.5
2.5	5.0	5.2	All Other Current					3.7	5.3
58.2	57.6	57.0	Total Current					65.8	46.2
31.4	33.0	29.9	Fixed Assets (net)					26.8	33.7
5.3	4.4	7.8	Intangibles (net)					3.8	13.0
5.2	5.0	5.3	All Other Non-Current					3.7	7.1
100.0	100.0	100.0	Total					100.0	100.0
			LIABILITIES						
13.1	12.3	14.9	Notes Payable-Short Term					15.3	6.9
3.1	2.3	2.9	Cur. Mat.-L.T.D.					2.7	2.1
13.0	10.9	13.6	Trade Payables					13.4	6.5
.1	.4	.1	Income Taxes Payable					.1	.0
11.3	12.4	12.4	All Other Current					13.3	13.5
40.6	38.2	43.9	Total Current					44.8	29.0
21.4	18.5	30.2	Long-Term Debt					20.2	23.2
.3	.1	.4	Deferred Taxes					.6	.5
5.6	7.0	11.7	All Other Non-Current					9.9	6.7
32.1	36.2	13.9	Net Worth					24.6	40.6
100.0	100.0	100.0	Total Liabilities & Net Worth					100.0	100.0
			INCOME DATA						
100.0	100.0	100.0	Net Sales					100.0	100.0
22.2	19.9	23.8	Gross Profit					17.4	19.2
20.9	23.4	21.8	Operating Expenses					17.3	17.4
1.4	-3.5	2.0	Operating Profit					.1	1.8
1.0	1.2	2.1	All Other Expenses (net)					.3	2.0
.3	-4.7	-.1	Profit Before Taxes					-.2	-.2
			RATIOS						
2.5	3.1	2.5	Current					2.4	2.8
1.3	1.5	1.4						1.3	1.7
1.0	1.1	1.0						1.0	1.0
.8	1.2	.9	Quick					.8	1.3
.4	.6	.6						.5	.6
.2	.2	.2						.2	.4
6 58.6	8 46.6	9 40.7	Sales/Receivables					11 34.2	9 40.8
14 25.8	16 22.9	16 22.6						23 15.7	14 25.4
26 13.8	38 9.5	30 12.0						47 7.7	31 11.8
40 9.0	34 10.9	38 9.6	Cost of Sales/Inventory					74 4.9	32 11.3
68 5.4	86 4.2	76 4.8						88 4.1	58 6.3
123 3.0	185 2.0	123 3.0						144 2.5	98 3.7
12 30.8	15 23.6	13 27.9	Cost of Sales/Payables					17 21.2	9 40.0
22 16.8	23 15.6	23 15.7						28 13.0	14 26.2
37 9.9	37 9.9	34 10.7						38 9.7	32 11.5
6.0	3.0	5.0	Sales/Working Capital					5.2	3.7
13.7	9.5	13.2						13.0	10.6
NM	57.9	-108.5						-144.2	-37.8
5.7	2.5	5.6	EBIT/Interest					17.1	5.9
(82) 1.3	(55) -.9	(62) 1.3						(13) 4.0	(25) 1.1
-1.1	-6.0	-.9						-2.1	-1.0
9.7	4.8	4.2	Net Profit + Depr., Dep., Amort./Cur. Mat. L/T/D						
(17) 2.3	(13) 1.7	(12) 1.2							
.4	-4.9	-.3							
.5	.4	.5	Fixed/Worth					.5	.5
1.4	1.0	1.4						1.1	1.3
4.1	6.7	-2.4						35.9	-3.5
1.0	.7	1.0	Debt/Worth					1.4	.6
2.6	1.7	3.0						3.3	1.3
16.0	13.3	-6.6						92.1	-10.3
28.7	19.1	24.3	% Profit Before Taxes/Tangible Net Worth					26.2	24.7
(71) 6.7	(52) -3.8	(49) 7.9						(12) 13.6	(20) 6.7
-15.5	-39.2	-5.9						-25.8	-.1
10.2	5.5	6.1	% Profit Before Taxes/Total Assets					8.5	5.4
1.2	-2.7	.8						2.2	.9
-5.7	-19.7	-7.2						-16.3	-5.9
14.9	11.4	15.3	Sales/Net Fixed Assets					14.8	8.2
7.4	4.2	6.0						6.9	4.6
4.2	2.4	3.3						3.9	2.4
2.9	2.3	2.4	Sales/Total Assets					2.2	1.6
2.1	1.3	1.6						1.7	1.3
1.4	1.0	1.1						1.2	1.0
.9	1.4	1.1	% Depr., Dep., Amort./Sales					1.0	2.3
(79) 1.6	(58) 2.5	(59) 2.6						(13) 1.8	(24) 3.3
3.1	4.9	3.9						3.4	4.6
1.2	1.3	1.6	% Officers', Directors' Owners' Comp/Sales						
(21) 1.6	(18) 2.7	(18) 2.5							
2.5	4.0	7.3							
4080234M	1981851M	2306371M	Net Sales ($)	2762M	12454M	30297M	61758M	232484M	1966616M
2369519M	1688944M	1811469M	Total Assets ($)	1692M	4986M	26057M	29984M	146564M	1602186M

© RMA 2011   M = $ thousand   MM = $ million
See Pages 9 through 22 for Explanation of Ratios and Data

Current Data Sorted by Assets   Comparative Historical Data

0-500M	500M-2MM	2-10MM	10-50MM	50-100MM	100-250MM	Type of Statement	4/1/06-3/31/07 ALL	4/1/07-3/31/08 ALL
		1		1	1	Unqualified	4	4
	1	2				Reviewed	5	4
1		5				Compiled	6	5
3	3	4				Tax Returns	4	6
	3	8	3			Other	16	13
	5 (4/1-9/30/10)	31 (10/1/10-3/31/11)						
4	7	20	3	1	1	NUMBER OF STATEMENTS	35	32
%	%	%	%	%	%		%	%
						ASSETS		
		8.8				Cash & Equivalents	9.7	6.4
		15.7				Trade Receivables (net)	16.5	17.3
		42.6				Inventory	45.9	42.1
		3.1				All Other Current	1.8	1.5
		70.2				Total Current	74.0	67.3
		21.1				Fixed Assets (net)	15.4	14.4
		4.8				Intangibles (net)	5.9	11.4
		3.9				All Other Non-Current	4.7	6.9
		100.0				Total	100.0	100.0
						LIABILITIES		
		13.0				Notes Payable-Short Term	18.8	19.4
		2.9				Cur. Mat.-L.T.D.	6.2	1.4
		11.2				Trade Payables	16.5	12.6
		.0				Income Taxes Payable	.1	.3
		6.5				All Other Current	13.1	13.8
		33.6				Total Current	54.6	47.6
		16.1				Long-Term Debt	13.5	13.7
		.1				Deferred Taxes	.6	.4
		11.6				All Other Non-Current	12.5	11.7
		38.6				Net Worth	18.9	26.6
		100.0				Total Liabilities & Net Worth	100.0	100.0
						INCOME DATA		
		100.0				Net Sales	100.0	100.0
		33.4				Gross Profit	33.5	32.6
		31.0				Operating Expenses	28.0	26.8
		2.5				Operating Profit	5.5	5.8
		1.0				All Other Expenses (net)	2.0	2.0
		1.4				Profit Before Taxes	3.5	3.8
						RATIOS		
		6.3				Current	2.6	2.7
		1.9					1.6	1.4
		1.3					1.1	.9
		1.5				Quick	1.0	1.0
		.8					.5	.6
		.4					.2	.2
		11 34.6				Sales/Receivables	8 45.7	9 42.5
		28 12.8					23 15.8	23 16.0
		37 9.9					42 8.7	60 6.1
		77 4.7				Cost of Sales/Inventory	61 6.0	68 5.4
		115 3.2					98 3.7	102 3.6
		141 2.6					148 2.5	141 2.6
		13 27.4				Cost of Sales/Payables	15 24.0	13 27.1
		23 16.1					30 12.2	24 15.0
		37 9.8					51 7.1	50 7.3
		3.1				Sales/Working Capital	5.4	6.3
		6.8					8.3	11.1
		13.2					39.7	-39.8
		3.9				EBIT/Interest	9.7	12.3
		(19) 2.3					(33) 2.4	(29) 3.3
		.2					1.4	1.6
						Net Profit + Depr., Dep., Amort./Cur. Mat. L/T/D	8.1	
							(10) 1.8	
							.6	
		.1				Fixed/Worth	.2	.2
		.5					.5	.9
		2.2					-13.8	-1.1
		.7				Debt/Worth	.9	1.8
		2.6					4.0	4.4
		6.7					-185.6	-8.4
		23.1				% Profit Before Taxes/Tangible Net Worth	74.0	91.7
		(17) 4.8					(25) 30.6	(22) 37.1
		-25.4					16.8	8.4
		9.0				% Profit Before Taxes/Total Assets	17.0	19.9
		2.3					7.7	7.7
		-2.2					1.9	.0
		67.2				Sales/Net Fixed Assets	57.6	43.1
		23.3					27.2	28.5
		4.2					10.8	10.4
		2.8				Sales/Total Assets	3.6	3.4
		2.0					2.6	1.8
		1.4					1.7	1.2
		.6				% Depr., Dep., Amort./Sales	.5	.8
		(16) 1.4					(31) .9	(26) 1.3
		5.0					3.0	2.6
		2.2				% Officers', Directors' Owners' Comp/Sales	1.7	2.4
		(10) 4.4					(15) 3.6	(12) 5.6
		10.1					6.5	11.0
3398M	33068M	210448M	120997M	85242M	524187M	Net Sales ($)	1107353M	1378295M
972M	8952M	102944M	74750M	58333M	242278M	Total Assets ($)	701787M	909511M

M = $ thousand   MM = $ million
See Pages 9 through 22 for Explanation of Ratios and Data

Comparative Historical Data / Current Data Sorted by Sales

			Type of Statement	0-1MM	1-3MM	3-5MM	5-10MM	10-25MM	25MM & OVER
3	2	3	Unqualified				1		2
6	3	3	Reviewed				2	1	
4	5	6	Compiled				3	2	
11	13	10	Tax Returns	1			4		
14	16	14	Other	2	3	1	4	5	2
4/1/08-3/31/09 ALL	4/1/09-3/31/10 ALL	4/1/10-3/31/11 ALL			5 (4/1-9/30/10)			31 (10/1/10-3/31/11)	
38	39	36	**NUMBER OF STATEMENTS**	3	5	2	14	8	4
%	%	%	**ASSETS**	%	%	%	%	%	%
6.0	9.6	9.1	Cash & Equivalents				11.6		
17.9	14.9	16.3	Trade Receivables (net)				14.5		
41.3	44.7	40.9	Inventory				42.3		
1.7	1.9	4.8	All Other Current				4.0		
66.8	71.1	71.1	Total Current				72.4		
17.1	15.2	16.6	Fixed Assets (net)				20.0		
9.6	10.1	6.1	Intangibles (net)				4.1		
6.5	3.6	6.2	All Other Non-Current				3.5		
100.0	100.0	100.0	Total				100.0		
			LIABILITIES						
22.0	16.7	10.6	Notes Payable-Short Term				7.0		
3.3	3.7	2.3	Cur. Mat.-L.T.D.				4.3		
14.1	12.6	13.4	Trade Payables				13.2		
.2	.1	.2	Income Taxes Payable				.0		
9.5	13.3	10.0	All Other Current				10.5		
49.1	46.4	36.6	Total Current				35.0		
17.6	23.1	18.6	Long-Term Debt				21.8		
.0	.0	.1	Deferred Taxes				.1		
14.0	6.2	13.0	All Other Non-Current				11.0		
19.3	24.2	31.8	Net Worth				32.1		
100.0	100.0	100.0	Total Liabilties & Net Worth				100.0		
			INCOME DATA						
100.0	100.0	100.0	Net Sales				100.0		
31.6	32.9	32.1	Gross Profit				34.1		
27.6	30.2	28.7	Operating Expenses				31.5		
4.0	2.7	3.4	Operating Profit				2.6		
3.3	3.1	.7	All Other Expenses (net)				1.0		
.7	-.4	2.6	Profit Before Taxes				1.6		
			RATIOS						
2.3	3.1	4.1					7.6		
1.5	1.4	1.8	Current				1.8		
1.1	1.0	1.3					1.3		
1.0	1.1	1.3					2.0		
.5	.3	.6	Quick				.7		
.2	.2	.3					.3		
10 36.2	11 32.2	5 76.4					4 90.4		
26 14.0	22 16.9	28 12.8	Sales/Receivables				16 22.9		
51 7.1	38 9.6	38 9.6					31 11.6		
63 5.8	62 5.9	61 6.0					60 6.1		
115 3.2	116 3.1	90 4.1	Cost of Sales/Inventory				89 4.1		
157 2.3	220 1.7	135 2.7					126 2.9		
15 24.2	18 20.8	11 33.0					14 26.1		
27 13.3	28 12.9	23 15.9	Cost of Sales/Payables				23 16.1		
47 7.7	59 6.2	44 8.4					36 10.2		
7.0	4.0	3.7					3.6		
10.6	8.5	9.7	Sales/Working Capital				10.0		
170.0	58.0	19.2					19.9		
7.7	8.2	7.8					4.1		
(37) 1.8	(36) 2.4	(33) 2.3	EBIT/Interest				2.5		
.6	-1.1	.6					.9		
			Net Profit + Depr., Dep., Amort./Cur. Mat. L/T/D						
.1	.2	.1					.1		
.6	.5	.5	Fixed/Worth				.5		
-1.7	-1.3	NM					1.5		
1.0	.9	.9					1.1		
3.9	3.4	2.8	Debt/Worth				2.9		
-6.2	-9.4	NM					8.5		
56.8	56.2	34.9					35.1		
(26) 24.5	(28) 16.7	(27) 5.9	% Profit Before Taxes/Tangible Net Worth				(12) 5.1		
7.3	-1.4	-11.3					-8.4		
15.2	10.2	11.9					8.6		
2.9	4.0	2.7	% Profit Before Taxes/Total Assets				2.3		
.0	-8.1	-2.6					-.7		
98.7	51.9	75.8					155.4		
26.6	18.8	31.9	Sales/Net Fixed Assets				35.9		
9.7	9.5	8.5					3.2		
3.1	2.9	3.6					4.3		
2.0	1.8	2.2	Sales/Total Assets				2.2		
1.3	1.3	1.5					1.5		
.5	1.0	.6					.4		
(28) 1.0	(25) 1.6	(25) 1.4	% Depr., Dep., Amort./Sales				(11) 1.4		
2.9	4.9	4.6					5.6		
3.1	1.8	2.2					2.2		
(14) 4.8	(17) 3.9	(14) 3.6	% Officers', Directors' Owners' Comp/Sales						
10.6	8.9	9.0							
1045256M	1332209M	977340M	Net Sales ($)	1800M	11875M	8766M	104048M	140078M	710773M
730927M	726940M	488229M	Total Assets ($)	663M	5947M	4553M	51503M	68234M	357329M

M = $ thousand   MM = $ million
See Pages 9 through 22 for Explanation of Ratios and Data

Current Data Sorted by Assets   **Comparative Historical Data**

0-500M	500M-2MM	2-10MM	10-50MM	50-100MM	100-250MM	Type of Statement	4/1/06-3/31/07 ALL	4/1/07-3/31/08 ALL
	2	5	3	2	4	Unqualified	10	10
	3	5	5			Reviewed	8	5
2	4	2	2			Compiled	9	7
	6	4	1			Tax Returns	11	11
		1	8		1	Other	23	29
12 (4/1-9/30/10)			48 (10/1/10-3/31/11)					
2	15	17	19	2	5	NUMBER OF STATEMENTS	61	62
%	%	%	%	%	%	ASSETS	%	%
	12.2	13.4	9.2			Cash & Equivalents	6.8	9.8
	23.4	20.5	26.1			Trade Receivables (net)	23.2	22.9
	46.0	45.6	26.9			Inventory	41.2	34.6
	1.4	3.3	2.2			All Other Current	2.7	2.8
	82.9	82.8	64.4			Total Current	73.9	70.0
	9.1	14.2	24.7			Fixed Assets (net)	17.9	16.7
	3.9	.6	4.1			Intangibles (net)	3.9	9.0
	4.0	2.4	6.9			All Other Non-Current	4.3	4.3
	100.0	100.0	100.0			Total	100.0	100.0
						LIABILITIES		
	24.9	16.3	11.9			Notes Payable-Short Term	19.3	13.8
	.9	.8	3.1			Cur. Mat.-L.T.D.	4.0	3.2
	20.6	11.7	16.4			Trade Payables	15.9	16.0
	.0	.1	.1			Income Taxes Payable	.0	.2
	10.2	14.3	17.4			All Other Current	9.7	11.1
	56.5	43.2	49.0			Total Current	48.8	44.3
	2.0	12.6	16.2			Long-Term Debt	12.4	13.3
	.0	.0	.8			Deferred Taxes	.1	.1
	3.2	7.9	6.0			All Other Non-Current	13.8	7.4
	38.3	36.3	28.0			Net Worth	24.9	34.9
	100.0	100.0	100.0			Total Liabilities & Net Worth	100.0	100.0
						INCOME DATA		
	100.0	100.0	100.0			Net Sales	100.0	100.0
	38.5	32.0	20.1			Gross Profit	29.0	31.2
	31.1	31.5	15.9			Operating Expenses	23.4	24.6
	7.4	.6	4.2			Operating Profit	5.6	6.6
	.5	-.2	.6			All Other Expenses (net)	1.4	1.7
	6.9	.8	3.6			Profit Before Taxes	4.2	5.0
						RATIOS		
	2.1	3.3	1.8				2.4	2.7
	1.6	1.8	1.3			Current	1.5	1.5
	1.0	1.5	1.0				1.1	1.0
	1.2	2.1	1.1				1.3	1.4
	.6	.5	.7			Quick	.6	.7
	.2	.3	.4				.3	.4
10 36.5	6 58.4		37 9.8				12 31.3	15 24.4
29 12.7	21 17.3		48 7.6			Sales/Receivables	30 12.2	28 13.1
47 7.8	61 6.0		57 6.4				48 7.6	51 7.2
45 8.2	56 6.5		37 9.8				41 9.0	25 14.5
74 4.9	128 2.9		45 8.1			Cost of Sales/Inventory	72 5.0	62 5.9
136 2.7	191 1.9		76 4.8				123 3.0	99 3.7
8 46.9	12 30.4		12 15.8				12 31.2	11 32.6
24 15.0	26 14.2		31 12.0			Cost of Sales/Payables	30 12.2	29 12.6
50 7.3	45 8.1		44 8.4				45 8.1	42 8.6
	6.4	3.3	6.2				6.7	6.2
	13.9	5.8	11.5			Sales/Working Capital	11.2	12.9
	97.6	9.3	614.5				38.6	119.7
	23.2	3.2	7.8				9.9	21.6
	(11) 7.3	(15) 1.8	(17) 4.0			EBIT/Interest	(56) 3.4	(48) 4.3
	-1.6	-2.4	2.3				1.7	2.1
						Net Profit + Depr., Dep., Amort./Cur. Mat. L/T/D		5.9
								(12) 3.6
								1.8
	.0	.1	.3				.2	.2
	.1	.4	.7			Fixed/Worth	.7	.6
	.4	1.2	3.3				3.5	5.0
	.6	.6	1.3				1.2	.7
	1.8	1.7	2.5			Debt/Worth	3.1	2.7
	6.0	5.6	21.6				16.7	19.8
	109.9	19.2	73.0				70.0	64.3
	(14) 21.1	(16) 8.2	(17) 25.3			% Profit Before Taxes/Tangible Net Worth	(51) 30.6	(49) 27.5
	-19.5	-1.0	3.4				15.7	13.9
	28.5	5.1	10.5				20.7	18.0
	6.1	2.6	7.2			% Profit Before Taxes/Total Assets	8.2	9.0
	-2.4	-6.5	1.5				1.6	3.1
	201.7	72.5	25.0				58.9	39.4
	56.0	20.6	9.6			Sales/Net Fixed Assets	21.0	20.1
	38.9	8.5	4.7				9.6	10.3
	5.1	2.7	3.1				3.5	3.9
	2.8	2.2	1.9			Sales/Total Assets	2.4	2.4
	2.0	1.8	1.3				1.8	1.5
		.8	1.0				.5	.7
	(14)	1.1	(17) 1.7			% Depr., Dep., Amort./Sales	(50) .9	(46) 1.0
		2.0	3.0				1.8	2.4
							2.1	2.1
						% Officers', Directors' Owners' Comp/Sales	(20) 4.7	(16) 3.9
							7.9	6.3
2322M	50418M	159386M	836061M	357817M	1397991M	Net Sales ($)	2110568M	2809477M
488M	15046M	73084M	405055M	124597M	652599M	Total Assets ($)	896320M	1237189M

M = $ thousand   MM = $ million
See Pages 9 through 22 for Explanation of Ratios and Data

Comparative Historical Data | Current Data Sorted by Sales

Type of Statement

			Type of Statement	0-1MM	1-3MM	3-5MM	5-10MM	10-25MM	25MM & OVER
10	9	9	Unqualified						9
15	7	12	Reviewed		1	1	3	4	3
9	6	7	Compiled		1		2	3	1
11	10	11	Tax Returns	1	3	3	3		1
25	32	21	Other	1	3	3	3	3	8
4/1/08-3/31/09 ALL	4/1/09-3/31/10 ALL	4/1/10-3/31/11 ALL		12 (4/1-9/30/10)			48 (10/1/10-3/31/11)		

4/1/08-3/31/09 ALL	4/1/09-3/31/10 ALL	4/1/10-3/31/11 ALL		0-1MM	1-3MM	3-5MM	5-10MM	10-25MM	25MM & OVER
70	64	60	**NUMBER OF STATEMENTS**	2	8	7	11	10	22
%	%	%	**ASSETS**	%	%	%	%	%	%
10.6	8.1	12.8	Cash & Equivalents				9.8	15.5	10.1
20.1	17.7	22.6	Trade Receivables (net)				24.1	24.0	25.6
36.7	35.0	38.7	Inventory				44.0	36.0	33.4
3.5	4.6	2.2	All Other Current				3.8	1.9	2.3
71.0	65.4	76.4	Total Current				81.6	77.3	71.4
19.5	20.7	16.2	Fixed Assets (net)				14.3	21.4	16.7
4.9	7.6	3.1	Intangibles (net)				.7	.5	5.2
4.6	6.3	4.3	All Other Non-Current				3.3	.8	6.8
100.0	100.0	100.0	Total				100.0	100.0	100.0
			LIABILITIES						
16.4	15.5	18.2	Notes Payable-Short Term				10.8	17.2	14.3
3.7	5.4	1.6	Cur. Mat.-L.T.D.				1.1	2.1	2.0
11.4	13.9	15.0	Trade Payables				27.6	8.6	14.8
.1	.5	.1	Income Taxes Payable				.0	.1	.3
10.7	10.4	14.0	All Other Current				11.4	10.8	15.5
42.4	45.7	48.9	Total Current				51.0	38.8	46.8
17.8	19.5	12.0	Long-Term Debt				16.0	10.3	16.1
.2	.1	.5	Deferred Taxes				.0	.1	1.2
8.7	10.8	6.2	All Other Non-Current				10.1	5.1	8.0
31.0	23.7	32.5	Net Worth				22.9	45.7	27.9
100.0	100.0	100.0	Total Liabilities & Net Worth				100.0	100.0	100.0
			INCOME DATA						
100.0	100.0	100.0	Net Sales				100.0	100.0	100.0
25.8	31.0	29.5	Gross Profit				33.1	30.1	19.6
21.6	30.2	25.0	Operating Expenses				31.7	22.6	14.0
4.3	.8	4.5	Operating Profit				1.4	7.5	5.6
.7	1.4	.3	All Other Expenses (net)				.4	-1.0	.7
3.5	-.6	4.2	Profit Before Taxes				1.0	8.6	4.9
			RATIOS						
3.1	2.7	2.3	Current				1.8	2.9	2.4
1.6	1.5	1.6					1.6	1.8	1.5
1.2	1.0	1.2					1.3	1.4	1.1
1.5	1.1	1.2	Quick				1.2	1.9	1.3
.7	.7	.7					.5	1.0	.8
.3	.4	.3					.1	.4	.4
7 48.7	16 23.4	14 25.6	Sales/Receivables				14 26.2	9 41.6	22 16.6
31 11.8	30 12.3	37 9.9					19 19.6	40 9.2	40 9.2
52 7.0	50 7.3	51 7.2					50 7.3	54 6.8	53 6.9
26 14.2	27 13.6	41 8.8	Cost of Sales/Inventory				31 11.8	40 9.0	37 9.9
69 5.3	80 4.6	61 6.0					93 3.9	56 6.5	54 6.8
127 2.9	128 2.9	133 2.7					204 1.8	141 2.6	93 3.9
7 54.4	12 29.5	14 26.5	Cost of Sales/Payables				20 18.3	8 48.5	18 20.8
19 19.2	26 14.0	26 14.1					40 9.0	18 20.8	27 13.7
34 10.7	43 8.4	43 8.4					50 7.3	36 10.1	42 8.7
5.5	3.8	4.8	Sales/Working Capital				3.3	4.2	5.0
10.4	11.1	7.6					8.6	6.2	8.6
37.8	85.6	29.1					24.4	13.6	175.5
13.6	6.1	7.7	EBIT/Interest						9.2
(64) 2.0	(56) 1.8	(51) 2.7						(21)	4.0
.5	-1.3	.9							2.3
6.5	4.3	12.3	Net Profit + Depr., Dep., Amort./Cur. Mat. L/T/D						
(20) 1.6	(15) 2.1	(12) 3.7							
-.2	.4	1.4							
.2	.2	.1	Fixed/Worth				.2	.1	.3
.6	.7	.4					.4	.3	.5
1.9	3.6	1.4					2.1	.9	2.0
.7	1.0	1.1	Debt/Worth				1.6	.5	1.2
2.6	2.5	2.2					2.4	1.4	2.7
7.7	12.9	7.4					15.0	4.0	9.4
48.0	56.6	63.5	% Profit Before Taxes/Tangible Net Worth					87.7	67.2
(61) 15.4	(52) 8.6	(55) 20.8						19.1	(20) 27.2
-1.8	-21.4	2.1						8.5	6.9
15.8	9.3	12.7	% Profit Before Taxes/Total Assets				6.1	25.6	12.0
3.8	1.7	5.0					-.1	5.1	7.2
-.7	-9.5	.7					-14.5	1.9	2.0
38.6	35.2	69.9	Sales/Net Fixed Assets				88.5	94.9	48.4
17.5	12.8	21.8					29.8	22.9	16.5
7.4	5.9	7.3					5.2	4.2	8.4
3.5	3.2	3.2	Sales/Total Assets				5.1	2.8	3.1
2.6	2.0	2.3					2.4	2.4	2.3
1.4	1.1	1.7					1.7	1.8	1.4
.7	1.0	.7	% Depr., Dep., Amort./Sales						.7
(60) 1.2	(51) 1.5	(48) 1.1						(21)	1.3
2.4	3.6	2.2							2.4
1.8	2.1	1.0	% Officers', Directors' Owners' Comp/Sales						
(25) 2.8	(12) 6.7	(20) 2.5							
4.9	15.1	9.6							
3280429M	3654711M	2803995M	Net Sales ($)	849M	15015M	28481M	71664M	153029M	2534957M
1620358M	2044056M	1270869M	Total Assets ($)	1015M	7511M	27861M	35147M	69013M	1130322M

M = $ thousand   MM = $ million
See Pages 9 through 22 for Explanation of Ratios and Data

Current Data Sorted by Assets   Comparative Historical Data

0-500M	500M-2MM	2-10MM	10-50MM	50-100MM	100-250MM	Type of Statement	4/1/06-3/31/07 ALL	4/1/07-3/31/08 ALL
		4	10	3	3	Unqualified	21	25
2	6	19	9			Reviewed	42	30
5	15	15	3		1	Compiled	37	34
21	25	8	1		1	Tax Returns	54	53
14	16	33	8	3	2	Other	80	78
41 (4/1-9/30/10)			186 (10/1/10-3/31/11)					
42	62	79	31	6	7	NUMBER OF STATEMENTS	234	220
%	%	%	%	%	%	ASSETS	%	%
13.3	6.8	7.6	11.8			Cash & Equivalents	9.2	9.2
20.7	28.8	25.5	20.6			Trade Receivables (net)	28.5	26.9
15.6	20.1	27.7	16.1			Inventory	20.3	21.1
1.3	2.3	2.1	1.7			All Other Current	2.1	2.7
50.9	58.0	62.8	50.2			Total Current	60.1	59.9
37.4	30.0	27.3	30.0			Fixed Assets (net)	31.9	29.6
2.6	4.4	3.0	7.0			Intangibles (net)	3.2	4.5
9.0	7.6	6.8	12.8			All Other Non-Current	4.8	6.0
100.0	100.0	100.0	100.0			Total	100.0	100.0
						LIABILITIES		
41.5	13.5	12.5	9.8			Notes Payable-Short Term	10.3	10.5
1.8	4.9	5.0	5.4			Cur. Mat.-L.T.D.	4.2	4.4
21.9	18.1	13.4	8.5			Trade Payables	13.5	13.9
.0	.1	.1	.0			Income Taxes Payable	.2	.2
22.1	12.4	15.6	14.8			All Other Current	15.0	13.9
87.2	49.0	46.6	38.6			Total Current	43.3	43.0
28.9	22.2	15.5	15.9			Long-Term Debt	21.0	20.4
.0	.2	.5	.5			Deferred Taxes	.4	.4
18.3	8.5	6.8	7.5			All Other Non-Current	6.6	6.9
-34.5	20.2	30.6	37.5			Net Worth	28.7	29.3
100.0	100.0	100.0	100.0			Total Liabilities & Net Worth	100.0	100.0
						INCOME DATA		
100.0	100.0	100.0	100.0			Net Sales	100.0	100.0
47.6	34.2	27.8	29.4			Gross Profit	33.1	32.9
47.5	34.0	26.7	25.6			Operating Expenses	28.9	29.3
.1	.2	1.1	3.8			Operating Profit	4.2	3.6
.6	1.1	.9	1.3			All Other Expenses (net)	1.1	1.1
-.5	-.9	.2	2.5			Profit Before Taxes	3.1	2.5
						RATIOS		
1.2	2.2	2.8	2.8			Current	2.9	2.7
.8	1.4	1.4	1.4				1.6	1.5
.5	.7	1.0	1.0				1.0	1.0
1.0	1.5	1.6	1.4			Quick	1.8	1.6
.4	.8	.8	1.0				1.0	.9
.2	.3	.4	.5				.5	.4
0 UND	18 20.3	22 16.2	23 16.2			Sales/Receivables	19 18.9	17 20.9
14 26.6	33 11.2	34 10.6	36 10.1				33 11.2	30 12.2
36 10.2	55 6.7	55 6.6	43 8.4				51 7.1	44 8.3
4 83.1	16 22.2	27 13.5	23 15.9			Cost of Sales/Inventory	14 26.8	16 22.6
17 20.9	29 12.5	47 7.8	36 10.2				32 11.3	31 11.9
51 7.1	54 6.7	80 4.6	55 6.6				54 6.8	56 6.5
4 99.8	14 26.3	12 30.3	11 32.4			Cost of Sales/Payables	9 41.7	9 40.0
27 13.4	30 12.4	25 14.8	17 22.1				18 20.0	20 18.0
55 6.7	48 7.6	43 8.4	33 11.0				37 10.0	39 9.3
37.5	8.1	5.7	5.2			Sales/Working Capital	7.0	7.8
-37.2	16.8	13.6	11.6				14.5	16.2
-9.1	-13.1	-237.0	179.4				623.3	-527.6
5.5	5.0	4.7	8.4			EBIT/Interest	16.7	7.3
(35) 2.9	(53) 1.3	(71) 2.3	(30) 3.1				(207) 4.9	(195) 3.0
-2.3	-1.9	-.2	-.5				1.6	.6
		4.2	25.6			Net Profit + Depr., Dep., Amort./Cur. Mat. L/T/D	11.9	8.7
	(16) 1.5	(10) 3.3					(44) 3.1	(38) 1.9
		-.1	.8				1.2	.9
.7	.3	.4	.3			Fixed/Worth	.4	.4
6.1	1.2	.9	.8				1.0	1.0
-.4	-2.8	3.9	1.9				4.1	6.8
1.9	.9	.9	.5			Debt/Worth	.6	.8
18.1	2.5	2.6	1.8				1.9	2.3
-2.2	-6.9	8.5	7.9				12.6	17.5
82.8	38.4	22.8	29.4			% Profit Before Taxes/Tangible Net Worth	60.8	55.9
(22) 31.9	(44) 5.5	(63) 5.2	(25) 16.4				(187) 28.3	(173) 28.4
.9	-15.9	-7.9	-5.4				8.1	6.9
17.9	6.0	6.7	11.9			% Profit Before Taxes/Total Assets	23.4	18.6
5.7	.6	1.7	4.4				8.2	7.2
-14.3	-11.1	-4.1	-4.7				1.6	-2.2
34.1	38.7	19.4	15.3			Sales/Net Fixed Assets	23.1	31.5
17.4	8.7	9.7	4.7				10.7	11.5
6.0	4.7	4.7	3.8				6.0	6.1
6.3	3.8	3.1	2.1			Sales/Total Assets	3.8	4.0
4.2	2.5	2.4	1.8				3.0	2.8
2.5	1.9	1.5	1.3				2.2	2.1
1.1	1.2	.9	.9			% Depr., Dep., Amort./Sales	1.1	1.0
(35) 2.1	(49) 2.2	(69) 1.9	(29) 3.6				(196) 1.8	(187) 2.0
3.8	3.6	2.9	5.6				2.9	3.2
3.6	1.9	1.8				% Officers', Directors' Owners' Comp/Sales	2.1	1.9
(29) 6.6	(36) 4.0	(34) 2.6					(105) 3.7	(94) 4.2
8.0	7.2	5.2					7.6	7.6
39514M	198035M	891349M	1342414M	647387M	4428207M	Net Sales ($)	7783377M	6531850M
9348M	67855M	374558M	622554M	495500M	1348950M	Total Assets ($)	2863380M	2940134M

M = $ thousand   MM = $ million
See Pages 9 through 22 for Explanation of Ratios and Data

Comparative Historical Data   Current Data Sorted by Sales

Hist 1	Hist 2	Hist 3	Type of Statement	0-1MM	1-3MM	3-5MM	5-10MM	10-25MM	25MM & OVER
18	20	20	Unqualified				1	6	13
39	32	36	Reviewed	2	1	4	6	15	8
36	38	39	Compiled	3	12	9	9	2	4
63	46	56	Tax Returns	11	28	5	7	3	2
85	66	76	Other	13	14	4	20	15	10
4/1/08-3/31/09 ALL	4/1/09-3/31/10 ALL	4/1/10-3/31/11 ALL		41 (4/1-9/30/10)			186 (10/1/10-3/31/11)		
241	202	227	NUMBER OF STATEMENTS	29	55	22	43	41	37
%	%	%	**ASSETS**	%	%	%	%	%	%
7.8	9.4	9.1	Cash & Equivalents	14.1	8.9	5.1	10.4	6.5	9.3
24.0	22.0	24.6	Trade Receivables (net)	19.5	23.8	30.0	26.0	24.7	25.0
21.1	23.3	20.9	Inventory	12.6	22.7	19.4	24.8	25.0	16.6
2.3	1.9	2.0	All Other Current	1.6	2.0	1.2	3.2	.9	2.7
55.2	56.6	56.7	Total Current	47.8	57.4	55.7	64.5	57.2	53.6
33.6	32.1	30.8	Fixed Assets (net)	37.4	31.6	32.7	26.4	28.5	31.2
3.6	3.5	4.4	Intangibles (net)	5.7	3.1	2.1	2.8	4.0	8.7
7.5	7.8	8.1	All Other Non-Current	9.1	7.9	9.4	6.4	10.3	6.5
100.0	100.0	100.0	Total	100.0	100.0	100.0	100.0	100.0	100.0
			LIABILITIES						
14.9	17.5	17.7	Notes Payable-Short Term	40.7	18.6	10.9	13.1	13.3	12.5
4.4	4.6	4.4	Cur. Mat.-L.T.D.	1.4	3.8	4.5	4.8	5.7	5.7
14.3	14.0	15.2	Trade Payables	19.1	16.5	17.4	15.2	13.6	10.4
.4	.1	.1	Income Taxes Payable	.0	.1	.1	.1	.1	.1
16.4	14.8	15.4	All Other Current	20.0	17.9	12.9	14.1	13.3	13.1
50.3	51.1	52.7	Total Current	81.2	56.9	45.9	47.3	46.1	41.8
20.6	20.2	20.5	Long-Term Debt	26.0	23.4	22.4	18.5	14.4	19.8
.3	.6	.3	Deferred Taxes	.0	.1	.5	.4	.4	.6
6.9	11.7	10.0	All Other Non-Current	14.5	11.2	13.3	5.3	5.4	13.1
21.9	16.4	16.5	Net Worth	-21.6	8.5	17.9	28.4	33.7	24.8
100.0	100.0	100.0	Total Liabilities & Net Worth	100.0	100.0	100.0	100.0	100.0	100.0
			INCOME DATA						
100.0	100.0	100.0	Net Sales	100.0	100.0	100.0	100.0	100.0	100.0
32.2	31.2	33.2	Gross Profit	49.8	37.1	34.9	30.0	25.5	25.6
31.4	32.7	32.2	Operating Expenses	49.0	37.8	34.2	27.7	25.1	22.5
.9	-1.5	1.0	Operating Profit	.8	-.7	.7	2.3	.4	3.2
1.2	1.0	1.1	All Other Expenses (net)	.7	.9	1.2	.8	1.3	1.8
-.3	-2.5	-.1	Profit Before Taxes	.1	-1.6	-.5	1.6	-.9	1.4
			RATIOS						
2.4	2.5	2.3	Current	1.4	2.3	2.0	3.4	2.3	2.2
1.2	1.2	1.3		1.0	1.2	1.2	1.7	1.3	1.6
.7	.7	.7		.5	.6	.7	1.0	.8	1.1
1.4	1.3	1.4	Quick	1.2	1.4	1.5	1.7	1.3	1.3
(240) .7	.7	.8		.5	.5	.7	.9	.8	.9
.4	.3	.4		.2	.3	.3	.4	.4	.7
14 25.4	17 21.0	18 20.7	Sales/Receivables	0 UND	14 26.0	19 19.6	22 16.7	19 19.5	26 14.0
28 13.1	31 12.0	32 11.3		20 17.9	25 14.5	32 11.6	36 10.0	33 11.1	40 9.1
44 8.2	46 8.0	52 7.1		54 6.8	49 7.4	56 6.5	57 6.3	44 8.3	51 7.1
16 22.7	24 15.5	20 18.3	Cost of Sales/Inventory	0 UND	13 28.2	20 17.8	27 13.5	23 15.7	24 15.5
32 11.4	39 9.4	36 10.0		15 23.6	29 12.5	30 12.0	42 8.7	43 8.6	34 10.9
60 6.1	76 4.8	61 5.9		61 6.0	63 5.8	58 6.3	76 4.8	86 4.3	49 7.4
9 42.6	9 42.2	11 33.4	Cost of Sales/Payables	4 93.1	10 38.0	20 18.3	15 25.0	10 37.7	12 31.7
19 19.0	21 17.4	24 15.3		31 11.7	23 16.0	32 11.4	28 12.9	20 20.6	16 22.9
34 10.7	41 9.0	45 8.1		69 5.3	45 8.0	59 6.2	48 7.7	39 9.3	30 12.1
8.4	7.3	7.4	Sales/Working Capital	17.1	8.2	8.1	4.0	7.7	6.1
30.3	28.3	19.8		-256.0	61.9	30.8	12.5	18.7	12.4
-17.9	-17.5	-17.7		-6.3	-10.4	-14.4	-237.0	-24.6	110.4
4.9	3.5	5.5	EBIT/Interest	7.4	4.5	4.8	7.9	3.7	8.6
(215) 1.5	(183) .8	(202) 1.7		(21) 3.2	(46) 1.2	1.4	(39) 2.4	(37) .7	2.8
-2.1	-3.1	-1.0		-1.9	-3.6	-1.1	-.8	-2.1	-.5
6.7	5.3	3.4	Net Profit + Depr., Dep., Amort./Cur. Mat. L/T/D					3.1	6.1
(37) 2.1	(36) .7	(36) 1.5						(11) .3	(11) 1.6
.2	-.1	-.1						-6.0	.0
.5	.4	.5	Fixed/Worth	.7	.5	.3	.3	.5	.6
1.5	1.3	1.2		2.1	1.5	1.3	.8	.9	1.3
-7.4	-3.9	-4.6		-.7	-1.9	35.5	-11.4	3.8	NM
.9	.8	.9	Debt/Worth	1.5	1.0	1.4	.5	.7	1.0
3.5	2.7	2.9		8.9	2.8	5.4	2.0	1.9	3.3
-20.9	-10.3	-8.7		-2.3	-6.6	73.7	-35.9	8.6	-307.0
42.6	16.0	34.0	% Profit Before Taxes/Tangible Net Worth	112.7	25.5	44.9	26.2	17.1	48.5
(173) 10.4	(142) 1.8	(163) 7.0		(17) 50.0	(36) 4.1	(18) 5.0	(32) 14.5	(33) -1.6	(27) 17.7
-5.1	-26.9	-9.7		4.5	-19.7	-18.3	.6	-11.2	-10.7
10.3	5.6	9.3	% Profit Before Taxes/Total Assets	17.9	9.3	4.7	9.6	6.8	13.2
2.1	-1.1	1.7		5.5	.4	1.6	3.4	-1.5	4.4
-9.2	-10.0	-8.3		-13.9	-10.9	-7.7	-4.2	-8.7	-5.2
22.3	24.1	26.9	Sales/Net Fixed Assets	32.5	33.8	40.1	20.7	22.4	17.7
9.5	9.8	9.0		10.8	10.8	7.9	10.5	9.0	8.3
4.7	4.7	4.5		4.3	5.3	4.4	4.7	4.5	3.4
3.7	3.5	3.7	Sales/Total Assets	5.2	4.0	3.7	3.2	3.2	3.3
2.7	2.4	2.4		2.6	2.8	2.5	2.5	2.4	1.9
2.0	1.6	1.6		1.4	1.9	1.8	1.5	1.6	1.6
1.2	1.2	1.1	% Depr., Dep., Amort./Sales	1.1	1.2	1.4	.7	1.2	.8
(208) 2.1	(170) 2.3	(188) 2.1		(23) 2.6	(43) 2.2	(18) 2.5	(40) 1.5	(36) 1.8	(28) 2.8
3.8	4.0	3.9		6.0	3.8	3.2	2.6	4.2	5.8
2.1	1.9	1.9	% Officers', Directors' Owners' Comp/Sales	4.2	2.4	2.1	2.3	1.0	
(106) 3.1	(100) 3.5	(108) 3.6		(17) 7.6	(37) 5.4	(11) 2.6	(24) 3.6	(15) 1.4	
6.7	7.6	7.0		8.2	7.0	6.7	5.2	2.1	
5689639M	4307628M	7546906M	Net Sales ($)	14656M	111691M	88941M	296881M	681900M	6352837M
2484522M	1760586M	2918765M	Total Assets ($)	6505M	47713M	35856M	168547M	324322M	2335822M

M = $ thousand   MM = $ million
See Pages 9 through 22 for Explanation of Ratios and Data

Current Data Sorted by Assets   **Comparative Historical Data**

0-500M	500M-2MM	2-10MM	10-50MM	50-100MM	100-250MM	Type of Statement	4/1/06-3/31/07 ALL	4/1/07-3/31/08 ALL
		2	7	5	2	Unqualified	15	14
1	2	7	3			Reviewed	21	19
	4	7				Compiled	14	13
3	3	2				Tax Returns	17	7
1	5	8	13	5	2	Other	29	35
12 (4/1-9/30/10)			70 (10/1/10-3/31/11)					
5	14	26	23	10	4	**NUMBER OF STATEMENTS**	96	88

0-500M %	500M-2MM %	2-10MM %	10-50MM %	50-100MM %	100-250MM %	ASSETS	%	%
	6.8	5.2	9.1	7.6		Cash & Equivalents	7.8	6.9
	25.4	24.3	23.7	16.7		Trade Receivables (net)	23.7	24.0
	34.9	35.6	29.2	36.0		Inventory	36.4	35.2
	6.7	3.4	4.2	4.0		All Other Current	2.8	4.6
	73.9	68.5	66.1	64.3		Total Current	70.6	70.7
	20.3	17.9	19.4	21.8		Fixed Assets (net)	18.6	18.4
	2.3	3.1	1.7	9.3		Intangibles (net)	2.3	2.7
	3.4	10.4	12.7	4.6		All Other Non-Current	8.4	8.2
	100.0	100.0	100.0	100.0		Total	100.0	100.0
						LIABILITIES		
	4.5	20.8	7.6	4.8		Notes Payable-Short Term	11.6	12.9
	2.5	1.9	1.4	3.8		Cur. Mat.-L.T.D.	2.1	2.6
	23.3	16.4	13.2	10.2		Trade Payables	16.5	17.1
	.2	.1	.5	.0		Income Taxes Payable	.2	.2
	21.2	11.7	16.1	11.2		All Other Current	10.5	14.1
	51.6	50.9	38.8	30.1		Total Current	41.0	47.0
	9.5	11.4	28.2	14.2		Long-Term Debt	13.0	16.2
	.0	.2	.6	1.0		Deferred Taxes	.5	.5
	9.2	2.8	7.8	3.6		All Other Non-Current	5.9	5.6
	29.6	34.7	24.5	51.2		Net Worth	39.6	30.7
	100.0	100.0	100.0	100.0		Total Liabilities & Net Worth	100.0	100.0
						INCOME DATA		
	100.0	100.0	100.0	100.0		Net Sales	100.0	100.0
	31.7	25.8	21.4	20.4		Gross Profit	29.0	27.5
	31.1	24.6	19.1	23.7		Operating Expenses	25.1	25.0
	.6	1.1	2.3	-3.3		Operating Profit	3.8	2.6
	.6	.7	1.8	1.2		All Other Expenses (net)	.5	.5
	.0	.4	.5	-4.5		Profit Before Taxes	3.4	2.1

RATIOS

0-500M	500M-2MM	2-10MM	10-50MM	50-100MM	100-250MM		4/1/06-3/31/07 ALL	4/1/07-3/31/08 ALL
	2.7	2.8	4.4	5.0		Current	3.4	2.8
	1.6	1.6	2.1	2.5			2.1	1.7
	1.1	1.0	1.1	1.3			1.2	1.1
	.9	1.2	2.0	2.1		Quick	1.5	1.4
	.7	.5	.9	.8			.9	.6
	.3	.4	.4	.4			.4	.4
	9 41.0	14 26.8	17 21.0	9 38.7		Sales/Receivables	12 29.8	12 29.8
	21 17.2	34 10.9	37 9.9	27 13.3			29 12.4	28 12.8
	50 7.3	52 7.1	41 8.9	41 9.0			42 8.6	40 9.1
	17 21.3	45 8.2	36 10.3	45 8.2		Cost of Sales/Inventory	36 10.3	37 9.9
	49 7.4	69 5.3	51 7.1	58 6.3			54 6.7	53 6.9
	119 3.1	109 3.3	61 6.0	97 3.7			91 4.0	81 4.5
	22 16.5	16 23.0	8 48.6	12 29.3		Cost of Sales/Payables	12 30.9	11 33.6
	32 11.3	26 14.0	24 15.0	17 22.0			20 17.9	20 18.5
	57 6.4	40 9.1	26 14.0	23 15.7			35 10.4	34 10.6
	6.5	4.4	4.4	3.7		Sales/Working Capital	5.3	5.7
	19.6	11.5	7.6	10.1			9.8	12.7
	NM	NM	263.3	15.9			27.5	79.5
	9.7	10.8	38.5	13.7		EBIT/Interest	13.1	10.1
	2.3	(25) .9	(19) 10.7	5.4			(84) 3.2	(79) 2.1
	-3.8	-2.3	1.6	-7.8			1.3	-.1
						Net Profit + Depr., Dep.,	4.4	5.3
						Amort./Cur. Mat. L/T/D	(20) 2.4	(23) .8
							.5	.2
	.2	.1	.2	.3		Fixed/Worth	.2	.2
	.5	.4	.4	.6			.4	.6
	NM	.8	1.6	NM			1.0	1.3
	.9	.8	.3	.4		Debt/Worth	.5	.5
	1.1	1.5	1.0	1.2			1.3	1.9
	NM	5.8	9.1	NM			4.2	6.6
	17.6	19.2	42.3			% Profit Before Taxes/Tangible	37.4	38.5
	(11) 9.7	(23) -.1	(20) 23.3			Net Worth	(86) 19.8	(75) 12.7
	-7.1	-13.0	3.3				4.2	-2.0
	6.7	9.4	17.3	34.1		% Profit Before Taxes/Total	16.2	17.0
	1.6	.0	10.2	6.0		Assets	6.2	5.0
	-6.2	-4.4	1.9	-33.2			1.3	-2.2
	39.6	74.4	24.8	21.4		Sales/Net Fixed Assets	43.9	63.4
	24.1	22.5	14.0	16.8			19.2	19.7
	9.4	8.1	8.6	7.7			10.1	10.0
	4.7	3.7	3.2	4.3		Sales/Total Assets	4.4	4.0
	3.1	2.4	2.7	2.1			2.9	3.0
	2.4	1.8	2.1	1.7			2.2	2.3
	.2	.8	.7			% Depr., Dep., Amort./Sales	.4	.4
	(23) .5	(22) 1.0	.9				(81) 1.0	(75) .8
	1.2	1.8	1.3				1.4	1.4
						% Officers', Directors'	2.3	2.3
						Owners' Comp/Sales	(39) 3.9	(29) 3.4
							6.8	5.9
10035M	62961M	374343M	1341855M	1816190M	944046M	Net Sales ($)	4932490M	5511356M
1121M	16912M	132903M	493809M	690814M	592312M	Total Assets ($)	2048606M	2167492M

M = $ thousand   MM = $ million
See Pages 9 through 22 for Explanation of Ratios and Data

Comparative Historical Data | Current Data Sorted by Sales

4/1/08-3/31/09 ALL	4/1/09-3/31/10 ALL	4/1/10-3/31/11 ALL	Type of Statement	0-1MM	1-3MM	3-5MM	5-10MM	10-25MM	25MM & OVER
18	19	16	Unqualified					1	15
15	12	13	Reviewed		2		3	5	3
10	9	11	Compiled			4	4	3	
10	7	8	Tax Returns	2	3	1	1		1
35	33	34	Other	1	3	1	5	6	18
						12 (4/1-9/30/10)		70 (10/1/10-3/31/11)	
88	**80**	**82**	**NUMBER OF STATEMENTS**	**3**	**8**	**6**	**13**	**15**	**37**
%	%	%	**ASSETS**	%	%	%	%	%	%
7.7	9.5	8.3	Cash & Equivalents				8.1	9.7	9.2
22.9	24.2	23.6	Trade Receivables (net)				16.0	24.3	23.8
37.0	32.3	31.8	Inventory				30.5	36.9	32.5
2.6	2.5	4.8	All Other Current				2.6	1.8	4.3
70.3	68.5	68.6	Total Current				57.1	72.7	69.8
20.6	19.6	19.2	Fixed Assets (net)				19.2	18.5	20.2
2.1	3.4	3.5	Intangibles (net)				.1	5.1	3.7
7.0	8.5	8.7	All Other Non-Current				23.5	3.7	6.3
100.0	100.0	100.0	Total				100.0	100.0	100.0
			LIABILITIES						
17.6	10.8	10.1	Notes Payable-Short Term				27.2	11.1	6.1
2.7	3.3	2.7	Cur. Mat.-L.T.D.				2.2	1.9	1.7
13.6	14.0	16.8	Trade Payables				18.4	12.7	16.2
.1	.3	.5	Income Taxes Payable				.2	.1	.8
13.2	8.0	14.2	All Other Current				17.3	9.8	11.8
47.2	36.5	44.3	Total Current				65.3	35.6	36.6
19.0	19.7	15.4	Long-Term Debt				12.0	5.6	20.5
.3	.3	.4	Deferred Taxes				.9	.3	.4
7.8	5.4	5.3	All Other Non-Current				3.0	3.3	5.9
25.7	38.1	34.6	Net Worth				18.9	55.3	36.6
100.0	100.0	100.0	Total Liabilities & Net Worth				100.0	100.0	100.0
			INCOME DATA						
100.0	100.0	100.0	Net Sales				100.0	100.0	100.0
25.8	26.4	25.2	Gross Profit				20.8	23.8	21.5
25.7	23.9	24.3	Operating Expenses				24.8	21.9	19.3
.1	2.5	.9	Operating Profit				-4.0	1.9	2.2
1.2	.7	1.1	All Other Expenses (net)				1.0	.3	1.6
-1.1	1.8	-.2	Profit Before Taxes				-4.9	1.7	.6
			RATIOS						
4.0	4.1	3.4	Current				1.9	4.3	4.0
1.8	2.2	1.7					1.4	2.0	2.6
1.0	1.2	1.1					.7	1.5	1.3
1.9	2.1	1.5	Quick				.8	2.1	1.7
.8	1.1	.8					.4	1.0	1.0
.4	.5	.4					.3	.5	.5
19 19.3	23 16.1	15 24.3	Sales/Receivables				10 36.8	21 17.1	19 19.1
31 11.8	36 10.2	34 10.9					13 27.3	42 8.8	33 11.2
40 9.1	46 7.9	46 8.0					41 8.9	53 6.9	40 9.1
36 10.1	34 10.6	35 10.5	Cost of Sales/Inventory				10 35.7	44 8.2	42 8.7
60 6.0	51 7.2	56 6.5					68 5.3	67 5.5	54 6.7
102 3.6	91 4.0	96 3.8					97 3.7	105 3.5	70 5.2
10 38.0	10 35.3	15 24.6	Cost of Sales/Payables				5 75.3	10 37.5	14 26.4
17 21.5	22 16.7	24 15.0					32 11.3	20 18.1	23 15.5
31 11.6	35 10.6	39 9.4					50 7.3	29 12.6	28 13.2
5.0	4.8	4.3	Sales/Working Capital				6.7	3.7	4.1
11.3	8.4	9.6					32.3	9.6	8.9
202.1	31.6	45.4					-8.4	15.4	21.0
6.1	11.5	13.7	EBIT/Interest				.6	17.9	38.8
(79) 1.1	(71) 2.5	(75) 2.6					(12) -1.9	(13) 1.4	(34) 10.4
-2.4	-.2	-.5					-4.5	-.2	.7
7.4	4.2	10.4	Net Profit + Depr., Dep., Amort./Cur. Mat. L/T/D						
(21) 2.3	(14) 1.1	(13) 3.9							
-5.6	-.2	-.8							
.2	.2	.2	Fixed/Worth				.1	.3	.2
.5	.4	.4					.5	.4	.4
2.2	1.4	1.2					1.7	.5	1.0
.5	.4	.4	Debt/Worth				1.0	.3	.3
1.5	1.1	1.2					1.7	1.0	1.0
13.9	4.1	9.1					16.8	1.5	5.4
16.0	40.1	37.5	% Profit Before Taxes/Tangible Net Worth				-7.1	34.8	49.8
(71) 5.0	(68) 8.7	(69) 9.7					(11) -13.0	2.2	(32) 20.1
-10.2	-10.0	-4.3					-24.9	-2.0	.3
7.9	14.1	12.6	% Profit Before Taxes/Total Assets				-1.0	18.9	20.7
.7	3.7	3.6					-7.9	1.9	10.2
-11.8	-4.0	-2.7					-9.4	-1.5	-.2
31.8	32.3	43.6	Sales/Net Fixed Assets				50.0	51.6	26.2
18.3	16.4	18.0					24.8	17.6	16.8
10.0	9.4	8.4					8.9	6.1	8.6
4.1	3.7	3.7	Sales/Total Assets				3.5	4.0	3.7
2.9	2.8	2.6					2.5	2.4	2.7
2.2	1.7	1.8					1.0	1.9	2.0
.6	.7	.6	% Depr., Dep., Amort./Sales				.3	.8	.6
(80) .9	(65) 1.1	(73) .9					(11) 1.0	(13) 1.3	(33) .9
1.5	2.0	1.5					1.4	1.9	1.9
1.6	1.4	1.6	% Officers', Directors' Owners' Comp/Sales						
(33) 2.8	(18) 3.0	(20) 3.4							
5.3	3.8	5.6							
4058096M	4166300M	4549430M	Net Sales ($)	1027M	16956M	23659M	93142M	240058M	4174588M
1601647M	1865964M	1927871M	Total Assets ($)	388M	8648M	11693M	62135M	104347M	1740660M

© RMA 2011

M = $ thousand   MM = $ million

See Pages 9 through 22 for Explanation of Ratios and Data

Current Data Sorted by Assets   Comparative Historical Data

Current data date ranges: **5 (4/1-9/30/10)** and **65 (10/1/10-3/31/11)**

0-500M	500M-2MM	2-10MM	10-50MM	50-100MM	100-250MM	Type of Statement	4/1/06-3/31/07 ALL	4/1/07-3/31/08 ALL
		2	1	3	1	Unqualified	20	10
		9	6		1	Reviewed	19	19
	6	1				Compiled	28	15
2	5					Tax Returns	14	14
4	4	8	11	3	3	Other	41	39
6	15	20	18	6	5	**NUMBER OF STATEMENTS**	122	97
%	%	%	%	%	%	**ASSETS**	%	%
	7.5	10.5	5.0			Cash & Equivalents	6.9	8.1
	10.4	19.6	23.1			Trade Receivables (net)	22.1	21.5
	48.6	33.1	36.2			Inventory	35.5	35.9
	6.1	3.2	2.6			All Other Current	3.7	3.9
	72.6	66.4	66.9			Total Current	68.2	69.4
	24.4	22.7	21.0			Fixed Assets (net)	23.7	23.0
	1.5	2.2	5.5			Intangibles (net)	2.9	2.3
	1.4	8.7	6.6			All Other Non-Current	5.3	5.3
	100.0	100.0	100.0			Total	100.0	100.0
						LIABILITIES		
	19.4	9.6	13.5			Notes Payable-Short Term	14.9	15.9
	1.1	3.2	6.7			Cur. Mat.-L.T.D.	2.5	3.4
	15.1	11.7	13.7			Trade Payables	14.0	14.7
	.0	.0	.2			Income Taxes Payable	.2	.2
	12.3	9.2	9.4			All Other Current	17.2	13.1
	47.8	33.7	43.5			Total Current	49.0	47.3
	6.1	21.1	19.1			Long-Term Debt	16.8	19.5
	.2	.0	.0			Deferred Taxes	.4	.1
	17.2	4.1	9.3			All Other Non-Current	5.3	6.5
	28.7	41.1	28.0			Net Worth	28.5	26.7
	100.0	100.0	100.0			Total Liabilities & Net Worth	100.0	100.0
						INCOME DATA		
	100.0	100.0	100.0			Net Sales	100.0	100.0
	44.8	27.8	26.6			Gross Profit	28.3	31.4
	44.6	25.9	25.4			Operating Expenses	25.3	28.7
	.2	1.9	1.3			Operating Profit	3.0	2.7
	.8	-.1	.7			All Other Expenses (net)	1.1	.4
	-.6	2.0	.6			Profit Before Taxes	1.9	2.3
						RATIOS		
	5.1	3.4	3.6			Current	3.0	3.2
	1.4	1.8	1.6				1.6	1.7
	1.2	1.5	1.2				1.1	1.0
	1.3	1.9	1.5			Quick	1.2	1.5
	(14) .5	.8	.7				.7	.6
	.1	.5	.4				.4	.3
	1 368.4	18 20.3	28 13.0			Sales/Receivables	16 22.9	13 27.2
	11 34.2	28 13.2	39 9.5				27 13.3	27 13.3
	13 27.2	44 8.3	48 7.6				43 8.5	41 8.8
	60 6.1	38 9.5	51 7.2			Cost of Sales/Inventory	32 11.6	31 11.8
	109 3.3	81 4.5	87 4.2				62 5.9	65 5.6
	241 1.5	119 3.1	119 3.1				98 3.7	99 3.7
	11 33.6	11 34.6	18 20.1			Cost of Sales/Payables	10 35.6	14 26.8
	27 13.4	18 20.1	31 11.9				20 18.2	22 16.9
	59 6.2	41 8.8	41 9.0				36 10.2	39 9.4
	4.8	4.2	5.0			Sales/Working Capital	6.0	4.7
	10.2	7.9	9.7				10.8	9.7
	26.4	12.5	NM				233.2	303.0
	3.4	14.3	12.2			EBIT/Interest	7.7	7.6
	(13) -1.6	4.1	2.1				(116) 3.4	(86) 2.4
	-3.2	-.5	-1.7				1.0	.0
						Net Profit + Depr., Dep., Amort./Cur. Mat. L/T/D	7.2	7.2
							(32) 4.1	(21) 1.7
							1.6	-.3
	.2	.1	.3			Fixed/Worth	.3	.2
	.6	.4	.4				.6	.5
	16.8	.8	-7.3				2.6	2.2
	.2	.7	.4			Debt/Worth	.9	.8
	3.1	1.4	2.3				1.8	2.1
	38.1	2.2	-23.2				7.2	8.8
	12.9	32.4	49.2			% Profit Before Taxes/Tangible Net Worth	45.3	63.0
	(13) 1.8	(18) 8.0	(13) 11.7				(104) 17.7	(81) 18.2
	-47.3	-7.0	-8.7				2.8	-.1
	7.7	16.8	10.1			% Profit Before Taxes/Total Assets	15.6	14.4
	.6	5.0	1.8				6.9	4.5
	-10.4	-2.9	-5.3				.0	-4.4
	31.6	40.0	26.5			Sales/Net Fixed Assets	31.6	38.1
	11.0	10.5	9.8				15.6	12.7
	8.6	4.3	5.8				6.8	7.0
	3.4	3.0	3.0			Sales/Total Assets	3.6	3.8
	2.5	2.0	2.2				2.5	2.7
	2.2	1.6	1.7				2.0	1.9
	.7	.4	.9			% Depr., Dep., Amort./Sales	.8	.6
	(14) 2.1	(19) 1.3	1.8				(103) 1.4	(80) 1.4
	3.2	3.5	2.9				2.5	2.5
	1.7					% Officers', Directors' Owners' Comp/Sales	1.7	2.2
	(11) 4.2						(49) 3.1	(43) 3.7
	7.2						5.9	6.7
12569M	37025M	253036M	905947M	1098711M	861239M	Net Sales ($)	6772905M	3846608M
2086M	12794M	95303M	386692M	489721M	694238M	Total Assets ($)	2928046M	1903848M

M = $ thousand   MM = $ million
See Pages 9 through 22 for Explanation of Ratios and Data

Comparative Historical Data / Current Data Sorted by Sales

Type of Statement	4/1/08-3/31/09 ALL	4/1/09-3/31/10 ALL	4/1/10-3/31/11 ALL	0-1MM	1-3MM	3-5MM	5-10MM	10-25MM	25MM & OVER
Unqualified	9	9	7				2		5
Reviewed	15	11	16				4	7	5
Compiled	13	7	7		5		2		
Tax Returns	21	17	7		4	3			
Other	44	31	33	2	6	3	1	6	15
					5 (4/1-9/30/10)		65 (10/1/10-3/31/11)		
NUMBER OF STATEMENTS	102	75	70	2	15	6	9	13	25
	%	%	%	%	%	%	%	%	%
ASSETS									
Cash & Equivalents	6.8	6.5	8.5		7.3			7.9	8.6
Trade Receivables (net)	19.8	17.9	18.9		14.3			20.6	23.7
Inventory	41.0	39.5	36.3		46.6			37.0	34.3
All Other Current	2.6	3.4	3.4		6.1			3.7	2.3
Total Current	70.2	67.3	67.1		74.3			69.2	68.8
Fixed Assets (net)	21.8	26.6	22.9		19.2			19.7	19.2
Intangibles (net)	1.8	1.0	2.6		1.6			1.1	4.1
All Other Non-Current	6.2	5.1	7.4		4.8			9.9	7.9
Total	100.0	100.0	100.0		100.0			100.0	100.0
LIABILITIES									
Notes Payable-Short Term	15.4	14.7	13.6		21.7			11.0	13.1
Cur. Mat.-L.T.D.	2.5	4.3	3.8		1.4			1.6	5.0
Trade Payables	13.5	15.0	13.4		16.8			14.3	12.8
Income Taxes Payable	.1	.0	.1		.0			.3	.0
All Other Current	14.2	13.8	10.8		15.0			9.2	9.4
Total Current	45.7	47.8	41.6		54.9			36.4	40.3
Long-Term Debt	15.0	17.3	15.3		9.4			9.7	15.4
Deferred Taxes	.1	.1	.1		.2			.0	.1
All Other Non-Current	6.3	8.9	9.1		6.4			7.0	8.5
Net Worth	32.9	25.9	33.9		29.2			46.9	35.7
Total Liabilities & Net Worth	100.0	100.0	100.0		100.0			100.0	100.0
INCOME DATA									
Net Sales	100.0	100.0	100.0		100.0			100.0	100.0
Gross Profit	29.7	31.7	32.3		41.4			32.5	25.2
Operating Expenses	29.2	33.1	31.2		40.5			30.2	24.4
Operating Profit	.6	-1.4	1.1		.9			2.3	.8
All Other Expenses (net)	.9	.3	.5		1.1			-.3	1.1
Profit Before Taxes	-.3	-1.7	.6		-.1			2.7	-.3
RATIOS									
Current	3.3	3.2	3.5		3.5			3.2	3.2
	1.6	1.7	1.7		1.4			1.6	1.7
	1.1	1.2	1.3		.8			1.5	1.3
Quick	1.5	1.4	1.5		1.3			1.8	1.5
	(100) .6	(69) .6	.7		(14) .5			.6	.9
	.3	.2	.4		.1			.4	.4
Sales/Receivables	10 35.7	9 38.6	11 32.1		1 368.4			21 17.3	26 14.2
	29 12.8	30 12.0	29 12.5		12 31.4			37 9.8	40 9.1
	40 9.2	43 8.5	47 7.8		44 8.3			48 7.6	49 7.5
Cost of Sales/Inventory	46 8.0	47 7.8	43 8.5		44 8.3			64 5.7	47 7.7
	81 4.5	82 4.5	87 4.2		109 3.3			112 3.3	86 4.2
	136 2.7	133 2.8	127 2.9		241 1.5			160 2.3	122 3.0
Cost of Sales/Payables	10 34.8	14 27.0	14 25.9		15 24.0			19 19.6	16 22.2
	21 17.3	26 14.1	25 14.6		27 13.4			30 12.0	26 14.3
	38 9.6	39 9.4	40 9.2		59 6.2			47 7.8	36 10.1
Sales/Working Capital	4.4	4.4	4.2		4.2			3.4	5.1
	9.2	8.4	8.0		9.3			7.9	7.0
	33.9	18.3	26.1		-39.0			11.5	22.4
EBIT/Interest	7.3	3.5	12.1		3.4			18.4	18.4
	(91) 1.9	(70) .4	(66) 2.2		(13) 1.3			2.7	2.2
	-1.9	-4.1	-1.7		-2.9			-.6	-.3
Net Profit + Depr., Dep., Amort./Cur. Mat. L/T/D	6.0	1.9	2.9						
	(19) .7	(12) .8	(13) 1.4						
	-8.0	-3.3	-.2						
Fixed/Worth	.2	.2	.2		.2			.1	.3
	.5	.7	.5		.3			.4	.4
	3.0	-43.6	1.6		16.8			.8	.9
Debt/Worth	.6	.7	.6		1.5			.5	.6
	1.8	1.8	1.4		2.7			1.8	1.1
	9.0	-18.3	5.1		38.1			2.3	5.4
% Profit Before Taxes/Tangible Net Worth	22.6	20.7	28.7		35.0			43.1	37.3
	(83) 7.0	(55) .1	(58) 7.0		(13) 2.9			(12) 12.4	(21) 6.7
	-11.7	-19.8	-7.0		-42.0			-.6	-2.6
% Profit Before Taxes/Total Assets	10.8	5.0	12.0		12.0			16.1	12.3
	1.9	-1.7	3.0		1.1			3.5	2.9
	-6.9	-11.1	-4.2		-10.4			-1.3	-3.6
Sales/Net Fixed Assets	38.7	30.6	32.9		59.0			71.6	26.7
	15.5	11.0	10.7		19.7			7.5	14.2
	6.8	4.7	6.5		9.9			5.5	7.1
Sales/Total Assets	3.5	3.1	3.2		3.4			2.9	3.0
	2.6	2.2	2.2		2.4			1.9	2.3
	1.9	1.5	1.7		2.1			1.4	1.7
% Depr., Dep., Amort./Sales	.9	.8	.8		.7			.7	.8
	(84) 1.6	(65) 2.1	(63) 1.6		(13) 1.2			1.7	(23) 1.6
	2.7	3.2	3.0		4.1			3.5	2.2
% Officers', Directors' Owners' Comp/Sales	2.1	2.2	2.1		1.9				
	(43) 3.6	(32) 4.6	(23) 3.9		(10) 4.3				
	5.4	8.3	5.5		9.1				
Net Sales ($)	3604471M	2819114M	3168527M	1418M	29138M	23852M	68193M	221145M	2824781M
Total Assets ($)	1821421M	1511608M	1680834M	529M	12114M	8039M	33911M	133219M	1493022M

M = $ thousand   MM = $ million
See Pages 9 through 22 for Explanation of Ratios and Data

Current Data Sorted by Assets   Comparative Historical Data

| Type of Statement | | | | | | | | |

0-500M	500M-2MM	2-10MM	10-50MM	50-100MM	100-250MM	Type of Statement	4/1/06-3/31/07 ALL	4/1/07-3/31/08 ALL
1	3	2	7	1	2	Unqualified	31	23
	4	9	6			Reviewed	31	29
1	5	5	1			Compiled	20	18
1	5	3				Tax Returns	19	14
1	9	15	10	5	2	Other	56	61
	15 (4/1-9/30/10)	77 (10/1/10-3/31/11)						
3	21	34	24	6	4	NUMBER OF STATEMENTS	157	145
%	%	%	%	%	%	**ASSETS**	%	%
	5.0	10.7	7.4			Cash & Equivalents	7.1	6.3
	28.8	26.3	24.0			Trade Receivables (net)	29.1	30.4
	28.4	33.3	26.3			Inventory	27.4	25.7
	3.5	1.8	1.9			All Other Current	2.7	3.3
	65.6	72.1	59.5			Total Current	66.2	65.7
	23.5	19.4	27.1			Fixed Assets (net)	22.5	22.6
	4.2	3.5	6.4			Intangibles (net)	4.2	5.6
	6.7	5.1	7.0			All Other Non-Current	7.1	6.1
	100.0	100.0	100.0			Total	100.0	100.0
						LIABILITIES		
	16.9	10.6	6.8			Notes Payable-Short Term	14.8	13.6
	11.3	3.9	3.7			Cur. Mat.-L.T.D.	2.3	2.5
	11.8	13.3	11.3			Trade Payables	15.4	15.4
	.0	.2	.1			Income Taxes Payable	.2	.1
	7.9	14.8	11.5			All Other Current	12.2	14.9
	48.0	42.8	33.5			Total Current	44.8	46.5
	32.7	8.9	18.7			Long-Term Debt	15.8	15.4
	.0	.1	.1			Deferred Taxes	.4	.3
	8.6	6.3	2.2			All Other Non-Current	5.4	5.4
	10.7	41.9	45.6			Net Worth	33.6	32.4
	100.0	100.0	100.0			Total Liabilities & Net Worth	100.0	100.0
						INCOME DATA		
	100.0	100.0	100.0			Net Sales	100.0	100.0
	31.6	32.3	26.5			Gross Profit	28.9	31.2
	30.2	28.7	22.3			Operating Expenses	24.5	25.9
	1.4	3.6	4.2			Operating Profit	4.4	5.3
	1.1	.2	.9			All Other Expenses (net)	1.3	1.3
	.4	3.4	3.3			Profit Before Taxes	3.2	3.9
						RATIOS		
	2.3	2.3	3.0				2.4	2.1
	1.6	1.8	2.0			Current	1.6	1.5
	1.1	1.2	1.2				1.1	1.1
	1.2	1.3	1.6				1.5	1.3
	.8	.9	1.1			Quick	.8	.8
	.4	.5	.5				.5	.5
	22 16.5	25 14.8	27 13.6				29 12.4	27 13.3
	35 10.6	41 8.8	38 9.6			Sales/Receivables	40 9.1	41 8.8
	61 5.9	49 7.4	61 6.0				59 6.2	57 6.4
	26 13.9	37 9.8	32 11.5				30 12.0	33 11.2
	48 7.6	74 4.9	53 6.8			Cost of Sales/Inventory	51 7.2	49 7.5
	97 3.8	94 3.9	96 3.8				87 4.2	86 4.3
	14 26.7	10 35.8	16 22.6				16 22.7	16 23.4
	24 15.4	21 17.3	26 14.1			Cost of Sales/Payables	27 13.7	26 13.9
	38 9.6	45 8.1	36 10.1				41 9.0	43 8.5
	6.0	5.5	4.0				6.0	6.4
	10.6	11.4	7.0			Sales/Working Capital	11.1	12.4
	NM	23.6	28.9				41.5	81.5
	7.8	12.5	15.1				8.3	8.7
	(18) 1.8	(29) 5.3	(22) 4.5			EBIT/Interest	(148) 3.1	(133) 3.8
	-1.6	-.9	1.3				1.1	1.6
						Net Profit + Depr., Dep.,	6.5	8.4
						Amort./Cur. Mat. L/T/D	(40) 2.7 (32) 3.3	
							1.0	1.4
	.2	.2	.4				.3	.3
	.4	.4	.8			Fixed/Worth	.6	.6
	4.5	1.3	1.6				1.7	4.1
	1.0	.7	.5				.9	.9
	2.0	1.3	1.6			Debt/Worth	1.8	2.5
	7.6	3.7	4.3				6.1	10.4
	27.7	52.5	44.5			% Profit Before Taxes/Tangible	41.3	53.3
	(17) 8.4	(31) 25.9	(23) 14.7			Net Worth	(135) 20.9	(121) 27.9
	-22.5	10.7	-1.9				2.9	10.2
	10.2	17.9	12.8			% Profit Before Taxes/Total	15.4	16.4
	3.1	10.3	7.2			Assets	6.8	9.3
	-7.0	.2	-2.0				.4	2.0
	34.3	38.4	14.8				41.6	35.8
	17.4	14.3	8.9			Sales/Net Fixed Assets	11.0	13.0
	5.8	8.5	4.8				6.3	6.5
	3.2	3.0	2.7				3.3	3.3
	2.4	2.4	1.9			Sales/Total Assets	2.4	2.5
	1.8	1.8	1.5				1.8	1.8
	.7	.8	1.2				.6	.7
	(16) 1.8	(26) 1.6	(20) 1.6			% Depr., Dep., Amort./Sales	(138) 1.4	(125) 1.6
	3.5	2.2	2.3				2.4	2.5
	3.4	1.7				% Officers', Directors'	1.8	1.9
	(13) 4.0	(13) 2.8				Owners' Comp/Sales	(56) 3.2	(45) 4.0
	5.9	4.4					5.1	6.3
3521M	69706M	480206M	871262M	651102M	824148M	Net Sales ($)	4242755M	4861713M
963M	24920M	180287M	430444M	374714M	509879M	Total Assets ($)	2242635M	2401610M

M = $ thousand   MM = $ million
See Pages 9 through 22 for Explanation of Ratios and Data

Comparative Historical Data | **Current Data Sorted by Sales**

Type of Statement

	4/1/08-3/31/09 ALL	4/1/09-3/31/10 ALL	4/1/10-3/31/11 ALL	Type of Statement	0-1MM	1-3MM	3-5MM	5-10MM	10-25MM	25MM & OVER
	22	16	12	Unqualified					2	10
	28	24	19	Reviewed	1	1	2	4	7	4
	20	12	10	Compiled	2	2	1	2	2	1
	11	6	9	Tax Returns		3	1	5		
	35	56	42	Other		5	4	6	10	17
					15 (4/1-9/30/10)			77 (10/1/10-3/31/11)		
NUMBER OF STATEMENTS	116	114	92		3	11	8	17	21	32

Main Table

Columns: three comparative historical periods (ALL), then current data sorted by sales (0-1MM, 1-3MM, 3-5MM, 5-10MM, 10-25MM, 25MM & OVER).

08-09 ALL	09-10 ALL	10-11 ALL	Item	0-1MM	1-3MM	3-5MM	5-10MM	10-25MM	25MM & OVER
%	%	%	**ASSETS**	%	%	%	%	%	%
7.5	9.0	7.8	Cash & Equivalents		4.2		10.1	8.3	8.1
28.3	24.6	27.2	Trade Receivables (net)		28.3		23.0	27.3	25.7
25.4	27.1	28.2	Inventory		26.8		32.3	30.5	26.8
2.8	2.5	2.4	All Other Current		4.4		2.8	1.0	2.3
64.1	63.2	65.6	Total Current		63.8		68.2	67.1	62.8
25.7	24.1	22.8	Fixed Assets (net)		24.5		19.2	23.9	22.7
5.2	6.2	5.3	Intangibles (net)		.5		3.5	4.8	8.7
5.1	6.5	6.2	All Other Non-Current		11.2		9.1	4.2	5.8
100.0	100.0	100.0	Total		100.0		100.0	100.0	100.0
			LIABILITIES						
11.1	12.1	10.5	Notes Payable-Short Term		15.2		15.3	9.2	5.5
3.0	3.1	5.2	Cur. Mat.-L.T.D.		4.8		11.4	3.6	2.9
14.3	13.4	13.2	Trade Payables		14.6		10.2	14.1	12.0
.1	.2	.1	Income Taxes Payable		.0		.0	.3	.1
15.4	11.6	12.2	All Other Current		9.0		14.1	15.0	10.9
43.9	40.5	41.2	Total Current		43.6		50.9	42.1	31.4
17.4	18.1	17.5	Long-Term Debt		17.2		33.6	10.8	14.0
.5	.5	.2	Deferred Taxes		.0		.1	.0	.5
4.9	7.0	6.0	All Other Non-Current		7.6		4.1	3.1	6.9
33.4	33.9	35.1	Net Worth		31.5		11.2	44.0	47.2
100.0	100.0	100.0	Total Liabilities & Net Worth		100.0		100.0	100.0	100.0
			INCOME DATA						
100.0	100.0	100.0	Net Sales		100.0		100.0	100.0	100.0
30.2	30.4	29.8	Gross Profit		33.7		29.1	32.3	26.2
25.1	27.8	26.7	Operating Expenses		35.6		26.0	28.1	21.6
5.1	2.6	3.1	Operating Profit		-1.8		3.1	4.2	4.6
1.2	1.4	.7	All Other Expenses (net)		1.0		-.2	.6	1.0
3.9	1.1	2.4	Profit Before Taxes		-2.9		3.3	3.6	3.6
			RATIOS						
2.6	2.7	2.4	Current		2.5		2.9	2.2	2.9
1.6	1.7	1.8			1.6		1.2	1.8	2.2
1.2	1.1	1.2			.9		1.0	1.1	1.7
1.6	1.6	1.3	Quick		1.2		1.4	1.2	1.7
.8	.8	.9			.8		.6	.9	1.1
.5	.5	.5			.4		.4	.4	.8
27 13.6	25 14.4	26 13.8	Sales/Receivables		26 13.8		18 20.2	25 14.8	27 13.5
38 9.6	37 9.8	41 8.8			35 10.6		41 8.8	39 9.3	42 8.8
53 6.9	49 7.4	56 6.5			60 6.1		45 8.1	53 6.9	58 6.3
29 12.5	31 11.7	32 11.5	Cost of Sales/Inventory		16 22.9		36 10.2	37 9.9	32 11.5
50 7.3	49 7.4	57 6.4			58 6.3		81 4.5	65 5.6	52 7.0
92 4.0	102 3.6	92 4.0			128 2.9		94 3.9	87 4.2	96 3.8
14 25.2	14 26.9	14 26.0	Cost of Sales/Payables		15 23.9		10 36.2	11 33.8	15 24.8
25 14.8	24 15.0	25 14.5			23 15.7		19 19.3	28 13.1	25 14.6
39 9.4	40 9.1	40 9.2			47 7.8		35 10.3	45 8.0	35 10.6
6.2	4.6	5.0	Sales/Working Capital		4.8		7.2	5.8	4.3
11.2	10.0	10.2			7.9		15.9	9.3	6.3
40.0	59.2	22.7			-63.2		NM	507.9	11.9
17.1	12.6	11.4	EBIT/Interest				7.9	14.6	24.3
(109) 4.7	(104) 2.7	(81) 4.5					(13) 1.7	(20) 7.9	(30) 4.8
1.4	-.2	.2					-2.4	2.3	1.6
12.9	11.1	8.9	Net Profit + Depr., Dep., Amort./Cur. Mat. L/T/D						9.4
(33) 3.4	(36) 1.6	(19) 2.9							(12) 3.2
1.0	.8	.7							.1
.3	.3	.3	Fixed/Worth		.1		.3	.2	.3
.8	.6	.5			.4		.6	.5	.5
5.0	4.9	1.7			-6.1		1.4	1.9	1.3
.8	.8	.8	Debt/Worth		.8		.7	.8	.4
2.2	2.1	1.6			1.6		2.4	1.1	1.7
13.0	12.0	5.0			-18.1		6.9	3.3	4.3
51.6	48.4	46.2	% Profit Before Taxes/Tangible Net Worth				51.2	43.6	57.2
(94) 22.5	(93) 15.5	(82) 18.0					(15) 13.8	(19) 22.5	(31) 18.6
6.5	-2.5	-.2					-9.4	15.2	10.0
17.9	12.7	12.8	% Profit Before Taxes/Total Assets		6.5		18.8	14.3	13.0
7.0	4.1	7.2			2.9		2.2	10.9	7.6
1.1	-2.7	-2.2			-24.9		-4.5	3.9	.8
29.2	25.8	21.9	Sales/Net Fixed Assets		29.1		65.1	23.2	16.9
9.9	11.3	12.4			10.3		13.9	11.7	9.9
6.4	6.1	6.6			5.3		6.3	6.8	7.3
3.2	2.9	2.9	Sales/Total Assets		2.7		2.9	3.3	2.9
2.4	2.2	2.1			2.1		2.1	2.4	2.0
1.8	1.7	1.7			1.6		1.8	1.7	1.7
.8	.8	1.2	% Depr., Dep., Amort./Sales				.9	1.1	1.1
(102) 1.9	(94) 1.9	(73) 1.7					(12) 2.0	(17) 1.6	(27) 1.8
2.7	3.0	2.7					2.9	2.4	2.4
1.7	1.7	1.8	% Officers', Directors' Owners' Comp/Sales						
(35) 2.9	(34) 3.8	(35) 3.2							
5.4	8.2	5.7							
3786059M	4773864M	2899945M	Net Sales ($)	2165M	21490M	32244M	125268M	356963M	2361815M
1792355M	2521370M	1521207M	Total Assets ($)	1620M	11520M	11756M	63953M	165530M	1266828M

© RMA 2011

M = $ thousand   MM = $ million
See Pages 9 through 22 for Explanation of Ratios and Data

Current Data Sorted by Assets   Comparative Historical Data

0-500M	500M-2MM	2-10MM	10-50MM	50-100MM	100-250MM	Type of Statement	8	6
	4	2	1		1	Unqualified	8	6
	5	8	2			Reviewed	26	14
	2	5	1			Compiled	11	8
1	3	3				Tax Returns	5	10
1	3	7	3	1	1	Other	14	15
	12 (4/1-9/30/10)		39 (10/1/10-3/31/11)				4/1/06-3/31/07 ALL	4/1/07-3/31/08 ALL
0-500M	500M-2MM	2-10MM	10-50MM	50-100MM	100-250MM			
2	14	25	7	1	2	**NUMBER OF STATEMENTS**	64	53

0-500M	500M-2MM	2-10MM	10-50MM	50-100MM	100-250MM		4/1/06-3/31/07 ALL	4/1/07-3/31/08 ALL
%	%	%	%	%	%	**ASSETS**	%	%
	6.2	8.8				Cash & Equivalents	5.9	7.5
	38.7	33.9				Trade Receivables (net)	33.0	36.9
	31.6	21.0				Inventory	21.5	19.0
	1.7	3.3				All Other Current	5.6	3.9
	78.2	67.1				Total Current	66.0	67.3
	18.1	26.7				Fixed Assets (net)	27.0	25.1
	.6	1.3				Intangibles (net)	1.5	1.8
	3.1	4.9				All Other Non-Current	5.5	5.9
	100.0	100.0				Total	100.0	100.0
						LIABILITIES		
	8.7	12.4				Notes Payable-Short Term	12.5	9.5
	2.5	3.3				Cur. Mat.-L.T.D.	3.6	2.8
	17.2	13.0				Trade Payables	15.8	15.1
	.0	.1				Income Taxes Payable	.2	.3
	23.5	8.4				All Other Current	11.2	15.6
	51.9	37.2				Total Current	43.3	43.3
	11.3	14.7				Long-Term Debt	17.1	16.9
	.0	.8				Deferred Taxes	.9	.7
	4.6	2.5				All Other Non-Current	6.1	6.6
	32.2	44.8				Net Worth	32.6	32.5
	100.0	100.0				Total Liabilities & Net Worth	100.0	100.0
						INCOME DATA		
	100.0	100.0				Net Sales	100.0	100.0
	32.8	27.3				Gross Profit	27.4	31.6
	32.7	24.7				Operating Expenses	24.2	27.5
	.1	2.5				Operating Profit	3.2	4.0
	.8	.5				All Other Expenses (net)	1.1	.7
	-.7	2.0				Profit Before Taxes	2.1	3.3
						RATIOS		
	2.7	3.0				Current	2.3	2.6
	1.6	1.9					1.6	1.5
	1.1	1.3					1.1	1.1
	1.6	1.8				Quick	1.3	1.5
	1.0	1.2					.9	1.0
	.3	.6					.6	.6
17	21.0	35 10.5				Sales/Receivables	30 12.0	29 12.4
40	9.2	54 6.8					42 8.8	44 8.3
93	3.9	71 5.2					61 6.0	63 5.8
3	137.9	16 23.4				Cost of Sales/Inventory	15 23.8	5 67.1
35	10.4	41 9.0					38 9.6	33 10.9
129	2.8	86 4.2					62 5.9	68 5.4
20	18.1	16 22.5				Cost of Sales/Payables	16 22.3	14 26.6
35	10.4	23 16.1					22 16.5	23 15.9
48	7.7	38 9.6					37 9.8	37 9.9
	5.2	4.0				Sales/Working Capital	6.1	5.7
	9.4	7.1					12.0	12.8
	NM	12.8					45.4	30.4
	14.1	10.5				EBIT/Interest	9.7	12.9
(13)	1.1	(21) 2.6					(59) 4.2	(48) 4.4
	-11.1	.2					1.4	2.3
						Net Profit + Depr., Dep., Amort./Cur. Mat. L/T/D	7.6	11.2
							(27) 5.4	(16) 6.6
							2.2	2.0
	.1	.3				Fixed/Worth	.4	.3
	.3	.7					.6	.6
	NM	1.3					1.8	2.8
	.5	.6				Debt/Worth	.8	.8
	1.5	1.5					1.8	2.3
	NM	2.9					5.4	6.3
	17.2	29.0				% Profit Before Taxes/Tangible Net Worth	37.9	40.8
(11)	11.3	5.6					(53) 21.5	(43) 22.4
	-7.3	-8.0					4.9	9.8
	7.9	12.2				% Profit Before Taxes/Total Assets	15.1	18.2
	.8	2.6					8.1	8.2
	-4.9	-2.5					1.3	2.8
	35.9	14.3				Sales/Net Fixed Assets	22.1	23.7
	20.2	9.4					13.3	13.7
	15.3	4.8					5.5	6.7
	3.8	3.0				Sales/Total Assets	3.5	3.7
	2.6	2.2					2.6	2.7
	2.0	1.6					2.0	2.2
	.4	1.7				% Depr., Dep., Amort./Sales	.9	.8
(13)	1.0	(24) 2.4					(58) 1.7	(50) 1.5
	1.7	3.2					2.7	2.9
		2.1				% Officers', Directors' Owners' Comp/Sales	2.0	2.3
	(14)	3.4					(25) 4.0	(29) 4.7
		5.0					7.0	8.2
1605M	51123M	218505M	208107M	189945M	394847M	Net Sales ($)	1407239M	897453M
536M	18748M	99292M	115261M	83558M	221449M	Total Assets ($)	646161M	396110M

Comparative Historical Data / Current Data Sorted by Sales

			Type of Statement	0-1MM	1-3MM	3-5MM	5-10MM	10-25MM	25MM & OVER
5	5	4	Unqualified					2	2
14	15	14	Reviewed		3	1	4	5	1
8	8	11	Compiled		2	5	3	1	
5	5	6	Tax Returns	1	1		2	2	
16	14	16	Other	1	1	2	6	3	3
4/1/08-3/31/09 ALL	4/1/09-3/31/10 ALL	4/1/10-3/31/11 ALL			12 (4/1-9/30/10)			39 (10/1/10-3/31/11)	
48	47	51	NUMBER OF STATEMENTS	2	7	8	15	13	6
%	%	%	ASSETS	%	%	%	%	%	%
6.6	5.7	8.4	Cash & Equivalents				5.2	13.1	
35.0	32.9	32.2	Trade Receivables (net)				35.1	30.6	
19.4	21.3	24.4	Inventory				24.2	25.9	
6.6	5.1	2.8	All Other Current				4.4	2.5	
67.6	65.0	67.8	Total Current				69.0	72.1	
27.3	28.0	25.5	Fixed Assets (net)				23.9	22.2	
1.0	1.7	1.2	Intangibles (net)				1.1	1.0	
4.1	5.2	5.5	All Other Non-Current				6.1	4.6	
100.0	100.0	100.0	Total				100.0	100.0	
			LIABILITIES						
8.5	11.2	16.5	Notes Payable-Short Term				16.6	4.5	
3.6	3.6	2.7	Cur. Mat.-L.T.D.				3.0	2.0	
15.5	16.3	14.3	Trade Payables				13.6	11.3	
.1	.1	.1	Income Taxes Payable				.0	.0	
13.0	12.0	14.3	All Other Current				16.8	13.4	
40.8	43.1	47.9	Total Current				50.1	31.2	
19.0	20.4	13.4	Long-Term Debt				14.3	5.0	
.6	.6	.6	Deferred Taxes				.7	.8	
4.2	3.7	3.6	All Other Non-Current				3.4	1.8	
35.5	32.2	34.4	Net Worth				31.5	61.2	
100.0	100.0	100.0	Total Liabilities & Net Worth				100.0	100.0	
			INCOME DATA						
100.0	100.0	100.0	Net Sales				100.0	100.0	
28.4	25.2	29.9	Gross Profit				29.0	28.4	
25.0	23.0	27.1	Operating Expenses				28.7	23.6	
3.5	2.2	2.8	Operating Profit				.4	4.8	
1.0	.8	.6	All Other Expenses (net)				.5	-.4	
2.5	1.4	2.2	Profit Before Taxes				-.1	5.3	
			RATIOS						
2.9	2.3	2.8	Current				2.0	3.7	
1.7	1.6	1.8					1.4	2.4	
1.4	1.2	1.3					1.3	1.7	
1.8	1.3	1.7	Quick				1.5	2.4	
1.1	.9	1.0					.6	1.4	
.7	.6	.5					.5	1.1	
35 10.5	33 11.0	29 12.7	Sales/Receivables				45 8.2	30 12.0	
48 7.6	42 8.6	48 7.6					51 7.2	48 7.6	
71 5.2	61 6.0	65 5.6					65 5.6	64 5.7	
9 39.0	7 51.8	13 29.0	Cost of Sales/Inventory				20 18.2	23 15.7	
23 15.6	35 10.5	41 8.8					28 13.0	55 6.6	
66 5.6	77 4.7	104 3.5					79 4.6	112 3.3	
16 23.4	14 25.9	17 22.1	Cost of Sales/Payables				15 24.4	13 28.9	
23 15.8	22 16.8	25 14.5					22 16.8	22 16.3	
37 9.9	38 9.6	41 8.8					41 8.9	33 11.0	
5.2	6.1	4.0	Sales/Working Capital				5.4	3.4	
9.5	11.4	7.1					9.7	4.6	
16.2	34.9	16.0					29.8	8.9	
10.4	8.5	11.0	EBIT/Interest				11.7		
(47) 3.5	(43) 1.9	(45) 3.4					(14) 1.9		
1.1	.1	-.3					-4.4		
6.6	5.3	6.4	Net Profit + Depr., Dep., Amort./Cur. Mat. L/T/D						
(19) 1.4	(13) 3.6	(12) 2.6							
.3	1.3	.1							
.4	.5	.3	Fixed/Worth				.4	.2	
.7	.8	.5					.8	.3	
1.3	2.0	1.3					1.8	.6	
.9	.8	.5	Debt/Worth				1.1	.3	
1.5	2.2	1.5					2.2	.5	
3.7	6.5	4.6					5.2	1.3	
28.9	21.1	26.2	% Profit Before Taxes/Tangible Net Worth				24.1	38.0	
(43) 15.2	(42) 7.1	(46) 8.1					(14) 5.6	22.4	
3.2	-6.4	-2.8					-30.8	3.5	
11.1	10.1	11.0	% Profit Before Taxes/Total Assets				10.1	20.0	
6.3	2.6	4.3					1.7	7.7	
.3	-1.2	-1.9					-16.2	2.2	
18.3	25.7	21.3	Sales/Net Fixed Assets				21.3	22.3	
10.7	12.2	12.7					10.7	9.5	
4.5	6.2	5.4					6.0	5.7	
3.3	3.3	3.2	Sales/Total Assets				3.2	3.3	
2.4	2.6	2.2					2.7	2.3	
1.9	1.9	1.6					1.6	1.7	
1.2	.7	1.0	% Depr., Dep., Amort./Sales				.8	.8	
(46) 1.8	(42) 1.5	(46) 2.2					1.8	(11) 2.4	
3.1	3.2	3.1					2.7	3.0	
2.0	2.1	1.8	% Officers', Directors' Owners' Comp/Sales						
(23) 5.3	(18) 2.4	(23) 2.8							
7.1	6.4	5.2							
845706M	936923M	1064132M	Net Sales ($)	1605M	15161M	34323M	93950M	198566M	720527M
400058M	448715M	538844M	Total Assets ($)	536M	9833M	14588M	45711M	99037M	369139M

M = $ thousand   MM = $ million

See Pages 9 through 22 for Explanation of Ratios and Data

Current Data Sorted by Assets

Comparative Historical Data

	0-500M	500M-2MM	2-10MM	10-50MM	50-100MM	100-250MM	Type of Statement		4/1/06-3/31/07 ALL	4/1/07-3/31/08 ALL
			1		1		Unqualified		2	
		1	6		1		Reviewed		9	9
		1	4				Compiled		4	5
	4	1	1				Tax Returns		3	3
	1	2	6	2			Other		8	5
		3 (4/1-9/30/10)		29 (10/1/10-3/31/11)						
NUMBER OF STATEMENTS	5	5	18	2	2				26	22
	%	%	%	%	%	%	ASSETS		%	%
			10.8				Cash & Equivalents		7.4	7.9
			33.5			D	Trade Receivables (net)		32.8	42.5
			19.7			A	Inventory		19.8	16.1
			4.4			T	All Other Current		4.7	2.2
			68.5			A	Total Current		64.7	68.7
			26.7				Fixed Assets (net)		30.1	26.5
			.8			N	Intangibles (net)		.2	.4
			4.0			O	All Other Non-Current		5.0	4.3
			100.0			T	Total		100.0	100.0
						A	LIABILITIES			
			14.7			V	Notes Payable-Short Term		14.2	18.2
			2.7			A	Cur. Mat.-L.T.D.		2.8	2.5
			14.3			I	Trade Payables		13.8	14.1
			.0			L	Income Taxes Payable		.3	.2
			11.1			A	All Other Current		19.0	12.2
			42.8			B	Total Current		50.0	47.2
			8.5				Long-Term Debt		17.3	17.0
			.5			E	Deferred Taxes		.2	.2
			4.9				All Other Non-Current		19.1	11.3
			43.4				Net Worth		13.3	24.3
			100.0				Total Liabilties & Net Worth		100.0	100.0
							INCOME DATA			
			100.0				Net Sales		100.0	100.0
			29.4				Gross Profit		30.9	31.0
			28.4				Operating Expenses		27.7	27.4
			1.0				Operating Profit		3.2	3.6
			1.3				All Other Expenses (net)		.1	.9
			-.3				Profit Before Taxes		3.1	2.7
							RATIOS			
			3.7						3.0	2.3
			1.8				Current		1.6	1.5
			1.0						.9	1.0
			2.2						1.7	1.9
			1.0				Quick		.9	1.2
			.7						.4	.7
		34	10.8					37	9.9	33	11.1
		53	6.9				Sales/Receivables	51	7.1	49	7.5
		77	4.7					68	5.4	71	5.1
		17	21.0					15	24.5	8	45.5
		47	7.8				Cost of Sales/Inventory	30	12.3	21	17.4
		75	4.9					89	4.1	37	9.8
		21	17.5					13	29.2	8	45.2
		27	13.3				Cost of Sales/Payables	25	14.3	25	14.3
		46	7.9					43	8.4	38	9.7
			3.9						5.6	6.9
			6.2				Sales/Working Capital		8.8	11.8
			-536.1						-28.1	NM
			16.0						11.5	20.7
		(17)	2.2				EBIT/Interest	(23)	4.2	4.8
			-3.3						-1.1	-.7
							Net Profit + Depr., Dep., Amort./Cur. Mat. L/T/D			
			.3						.5	.4
			.4				Fixed/Worth		1.1	.8
			1.9						-7.6	2.9
			.4						1.5	1.1
			1.6				Debt/Worth		2.8	1.8
			5.2						-16.2	10.8
			36.3						67.4	68.9
			8.4				% Profit Before Taxes/Tangible Net Worth	(19)	20.0	(18)	30.9
			-41.6						1.1	-15.8
			15.0						16.4	18.8
			3.1				% Profit Before Taxes/Total Assets		7.3	7.2
			-10.0						-10.1	-6.4
			23.9						25.0	21.7
			8.8				Sales/Net Fixed Assets		8.6	16.3
			4.3						5.1	7.8
			2.6						3.3	3.8
			2.2				Sales/Total Assets		2.4	2.9
			1.4						1.7	2.3
			1.6						1.2	1.0
		(17)	2.1				% Depr., Dep., Amort./Sales	(23)	1.9	(17)	1.6
			3.2						2.9	2.8
							% Officers', Directors' Owners' Comp/Sales		2.8	2.3
								(12)	3.5	(15)	7.7
									4.8	11.5
Net Sales ($)	3776M	15219M	163723M	71190M	139788M				295344M	242048M
Total Assets ($)	862M	5433M	75983M	27620M	125339M				145678M	94507M

M = $ thousand   MM = $ million
See Pages 9 through 22 for Explanation of Ratios and Data

Comparative Historical Data | Current Data Sorted by Sales

Type of Statement

4/1/08-3/31/09 ALL	4/1/09-3/31/10 ALL	4/1/10-3/31/11 ALL	Type of Statement	0-1MM	1-3MM	3-5MM	5-10MM	10-25MM	25MM & OVER
2	1	2	Unqualified					1	1
8	6	8	Reviewed			2	2	3	1
3	4	5	Compiled		1	1	2	1	
4	5	6	Tax Returns	3	1	1	1	1	
9	12	11	Other	1	2	2	4		2
	3 (4/1-9/30/10)					29 (10/1/10-3/31/11)			
26	28	32	**NUMBER OF STATEMENTS**	4	4	6	8	6	4

ASSETS

4/1/08-3/31/09 %	4/1/09-3/31/10 %	4/1/10-3/31/11 %	ASSETS
7.6	13.4	9.5	Cash & Equivalents
37.9	36.7	33.8	Trade Receivables (net)
16.7	15.7	20.0	Inventory
3.5	6.0	3.5	All Other Current
65.8	71.9	66.9	Total Current
24.8	22.1	24.7	Fixed Assets (net)
5.9	2.1	3.3	Intangibles (net)
3.5	4.0	5.2	All Other Non-Current
100.0	100.0	100.0	Total

LIABILITIES

			LIABILITIES
14.5	14.2	17.4	Notes Payable-Short Term
2.2	4.2	1.7	Cur. Mat.-L.T.D.
14.4	14.2	17.2	Trade Payables
.4	.9	.0	Income Taxes Payable
12.7	20.9	19.5	All Other Current
44.2	54.4	55.8	Total Current
11.4	11.2	12.4	Long-Term Debt
1.2	.3	.3	Deferred Taxes
22.4	13.9	16.0	All Other Non-Current
20.9	20.2	15.6	Net Worth
100.0	100.0	100.0	Total Liabilties & Net Worth

INCOME DATA

			INCOME DATA
100.0	100.0	100.0	Net Sales
25.9	28.8	30.0	Gross Profit
24.8	28.1	30.0	Operating Expenses
1.1	.7	.0	Operating Profit
.9	.0	1.0	All Other Expenses (net)
.2	.7	-1.0	Profit Before Taxes

RATIOS

			RATIOS
2.3	2.9	3.0	Current
1.5	1.5	1.9	
1.1	1.0	1.0	
1.9	2.1	2.2	Quick
1.1	1.1	.9	
.6	.6	.7	
25 14.8	27 13.5	33 10.9	Sales/Receivables
47 7.8	47 7.8	46 8.0	
70 5.2	58 6.3	73 5.0	
9 41.0	7 50.7	13 27.4	Cost of Sales/Inventory
26 13.8	17 21.8	35 10.5	
43 8.5	35 10.5	70 5.2	
11 33.2	12 29.5	20 18.3	Cost of Sales/Payables
20 18.4	18 20.4	28 13.2	
33 11.0	35 10.3	48 7.6	
6.5	4.7	4.6	Sales/Working Capital
10.2	20.4	8.1	
NM	NM	-387.7	
3.8	15.6	14.9	EBIT/Interest
(25) 1.8	(26) 2.4	(30) 1.9	
-1.3	-.5	-1.7	
			Net Profit + Depr., Dep., Amort./Cur. Mat. L/T/D
.4	.2	.3	Fixed/Worth
.8	.8	1.0	
NM	-6.7	13.0	
.7	.6	.6	Debt/Worth
3.3	2.5	1.6	
NM	-20.4	61.2	
36.1	33.0	32.2	% Profit Before Taxes/Tangible Net Worth
(20) 1.8	(19) 10.0	(26) 6.3	
-19.6	-3.3	-28.2	
9.7	18.6	12.7	% Profit Before Taxes/Total Assets
1.9	1.7	1.6	
-6.1	-4.3	-9.9	
22.6	33.3	26.1	Sales/Net Fixed Assets
12.0	10.1	10.5	
7.2	8.7	6.9	
3.5	3.2	3.2	Sales/Total Assets
3.1	2.7	2.5	
2.3	1.9	1.6	
.7	.9	.8	% Depr., Dep., Amort./Sales
(22) 1.7	(24) 1.8	(30) 2.1	
2.7	2.8	3.3	
1.5	2.4	1.9	% Officers', Directors' Owners' Comp/Sales
(13) 3.7	(17) 5.7	(14) 3.9	
8.1	10.4	8.0	

Net Sales / Total Assets

4/1/08-3/31/09	4/1/09-3/31/10	4/1/10-3/31/11		0-1MM	1-3MM	3-5MM	5-10MM	10-25MM	25MM & OVER
441609M	369666M	393696M	Net Sales ($)	2629M	7689M	23870M	58736M	89794M	210978M
163094M	169475M	235237M	Total Assets ($)	682M	3772M	14880M	28523M	34421M	152959M

M = $ thousand   MM = $ million
See Pages 9 through 22 for Explanation of Ratios and Data

Current Data Sorted by Assets   **Comparative Historical Data**

0-500M	500M-2MM	2-10MM	10-50MM	50-100MM	100-250MM	Type of Statement	4/1/06-3/31/07 ALL	4/1/07-3/31/08 ALL
		1	1	3	1	Unqualified	16	12
	1	11	2			Reviewed	18	16
	1	3	1			Compiled	3	6
	1	2				Tax Returns	5	3
1	1	8	10	3	1	Other	27	24
		10 (4/1-9/30/10)	41 (10/1/10-3/31/11)					
1	8	21	13	6	2	**NUMBER OF STATEMENTS**	69	61
%	%	%	%	%	%	**ASSETS**	%	%
		4.6	6.9			Cash & Equivalents	6.4	7.5
		32.9	31.7			Trade Receivables (net)	30.3	36.2
		28.3	18.0			Inventory	24.6	21.2
		6.3	2.6			All Other Current	3.4	3.2
		72.1	59.2			Total Current	64.7	68.1
		17.2	22.3			Fixed Assets (net)	19.3	19.6
		5.3	11.5			Intangibles (net)	10.5	7.6
		5.4	7.0			All Other Non-Current	5.5	4.7
		100.0	100.0			Total	100.0	100.0
						LIABILITIES		
		12.2	4.9			Notes Payable-Short Term	12.4	14.9
		3.0	2.5			Cur. Mat.-L.T.D.	4.5	3.0
		19.7	17.5			Trade Payables	17.5	18.3
		.1	.8			Income Taxes Payable	.2	.3
		12.4	11.1			All Other Current	11.4	12.8
		47.3	36.7			Total Current	45.9	49.3
		11.7	20.0			Long-Term Debt	18.3	18.0
		.0	1.1			Deferred Taxes	.6	.5
		2.9	7.6			All Other Non-Current	7.0	5.2
		38.1	34.5			Net Worth	28.1	27.0
		100.0	100.0			Total Liabilities & Net Worth	100.0	100.0
						INCOME DATA		
		100.0	100.0			Net Sales	100.0	100.0
		33.0	31.0			Gross Profit	32.1	30.4
		29.4	26.0			Operating Expenses	27.3	26.6
		3.6	5.0			Operating Profit	4.8	3.8
		.7	1.2			All Other Expenses (net)	1.2	1.4
		2.9	3.9			Profit Before Taxes	3.6	2.4
						RATIOS		
		2.4	2.3				2.2	2.2
		1.4	1.7			Current	1.4	1.6
		1.1	1.4				1.1	1.1
		.9	1.3				1.3	1.4
		.7	1.1			Quick	.8	.9
		.6	.9				.5	.6
		38 9.6	32 11.5				29 12.5	36 10.0
		43 8.5	58 6.3			Sales/Receivables	42 8.7	48 7.6
		55 6.6	68 5.4				55 6.7	64 5.7
		27 13.6	26 14.0				23 16.0	20 18.0
		53 6.9	39 9.3			Cost of Sales/Inventory	42 8.7	36 10.2
		91 4.0	65 5.6				83 4.4	67 5.4
		18 20.1	23 15.8				14 25.3	20 18.6
		33 11.1	45 8.2			Cost of Sales/Payables	31 11.9	31 11.6
		61 6.0	53 6.8				47 7.8	44 8.3
		7.4	7.1				7.5	7.4
		11.3	11.6			Sales/Working Capital	13.2	12.3
		39.6	20.9				95.7	50.6
		29.4	49.1				8.6	9.1
		(19) 6.1	(10) 4.4			EBIT/Interest	(64) 3.5	(57) 2.9
		1.9	2.2				1.4	1.2
							7.0	11.3
						Net Profit + Depr., Dep., Amort./Cur. Mat. L/T/D	(28) 2.6	(27) 2.5
							1.0	1.8
		.2	.4				.3	.5
		.4	.7			Fixed/Worth	.9	1.0
		3.3	1.5				-9.7	-30.2
		.8	.9				1.0	1.3
		1.9	1.9			Debt/Worth	2.5	3.7
		14.9	8.7				-32.8	-147.3
		40.2	95.3				51.7	39.1
		(18) 21.5	(12) 23.6			% Profit Before Taxes/Tangible Net Worth	(50) 23.9	(45) 17.7
		4.9	12.8				4.9	4.9
		11.6	19.8				15.3	12.5
		7.4	5.5			% Profit Before Taxes/Total Assets	6.6	5.1
		1.8	3.5				1.1	.8
		43.4	42.1				39.4	44.3
		21.2	12.0			Sales/Net Fixed Assets	18.2	14.9
		11.1	5.6				7.6	8.6
		3.2	3.1				3.7	3.6
		2.7	2.2			Sales/Total Assets	2.6	2.6
		2.0	1.5				1.7	1.9
		.8	.8				.5	.8
		(18) 1.3	(12) 1.8			% Depr., Dep., Amort./Sales	(63) 1.4	(51) 1.3
		1.8	3.1				2.4	2.5
							2.0	2.8
						% Officers', Directors' Owners' Comp/Sales	(17) 2.7	(14) 3.4
							7.3	6.1
1057M	33997M	281713M	789464M	800274M	205193M	Net Sales ($)	2988289M	3209410M
312M	9583M	102862M	328404M	389688M	268916M	Total Assets ($)	1561824M	1598090M

M = $ thousand   MM = $ million
See Pages 9 through 22 for Explanation of Ratios and Data

Comparative Historical Data | Current Data Sorted by Sales

						Type of Statement		0-1MM	1-3MM	3-5MM	5-10MM	10-25MM	25MM & OVER
	15		20		7	Unqualified			1			1	5
	12		17		14	Reviewed				1	4	6	3
	2		4		5	Compiled			1	2	1	1	
	2		2		2	Tax Returns			1	1			
	29		24		23	Other			1		3	6	13
	4/1/08-		4/1/09-		4/1/10-				10 (4/1-9/30/10)		41 (10/1/10-3/31/11)		
	3/31/09		3/31/10		3/31/11								
	ALL		ALL		ALL								
	60		67		51	**NUMBER OF STATEMENTS**		4	4	9	13	21	
	%		%		%	**ASSETS**	%	%	%	%	%	%	%
	5.9		8.0		9.2	Cash & Equivalents	D					4.0	6.7
	32.4		29.9		35.1	Trade Receivables (net)	A					32.7	35.0
	24.2		25.9		21.8	Inventory	T					27.2	16.8
	3.1		3.9		3.8	All Other Current	A					7.3	2.8
	65.5		67.6		69.9	Total Current						71.2	61.2
	21.3		20.4		17.4	Fixed Assets (net)						19.0	22.7
	7.3		6.5		7.9	Intangibles (net)	N					4.6	9.3
	5.9		5.5		4.9	All Other Non-Current	O					5.2	6.7
	100.0		100.0		100.0	Total	T					100.0	100.0
						LIABILITIES	A						
	11.6		9.0		8.2	Notes Payable-Short Term	V					9.0	4.8
	2.6		4.1		2.6	Cur. Mat.-L.T.D.	A					2.2	3.1
	15.3		15.5		18.0	Trade Payables	I					17.7	15.6
	.4		.4		.3	Income Taxes Payable	L					.2	.7
	12.4		13.2		11.7	All Other Current	A					13.8	12.2
	42.3		42.2		40.9	Total Current	B					42.8	36.4
	17.2		17.1		14.2	Long-Term Debt						8.4	20.5
	.6		.6		.5	Deferred Taxes	L					.1	1.1
	5.3		8.4		4.3	All Other Non-Current	E					2.2	7.3
	34.5		31.7		40.2	Net Worth						46.5	34.7
	100.0		100.0		100.0	Total Liabilities & Net Worth						100.0	100.0
						INCOME DATA							
	100.0		100.0		100.0	Net Sales						100.0	100.0
	30.3		31.3		30.6	Gross Profit						33.7	27.3
	26.0		27.5		26.7	Operating Expenses						31.3	21.4
	4.3		3.8		4.0	Operating Profit						2.4	5.9
	1.2		1.5		1.0	All Other Expenses (net)						.3	1.5
	3.1		2.3		3.0	Profit Before Taxes						2.1	4.5
						RATIOS							
	2.7		2.4		2.7							2.0	2.4
	1.6		1.7		1.6	Current						1.6	1.7
	1.2		1.3		1.3							1.3	1.5
	1.4		1.5		1.6							1.4	1.6
	.9		.9		1.0	Quick						.8	1.1
	.6		.7		.7							.5	.8
34	10.8	33	11.0	38	9.6						36	10.1 / 38	9.6
42	8.6	41	8.8	49	7.4	Sales/Receivables					39	9.4 / 57	6.4
53	7.0	53	6.8	64	5.7						58	6.2 / 75	4.9
22	16.6	25	14.3	23	15.8						43	8.4 / 19	19.4
40	9.2	49	7.5	46	7.9	Cost of Sales/Inventory					53	6.8 / 38	9.5
73	5.0	84	4.4	73	5.0						72	5.0 / 71	5.2
14	26.9	17	21.8	19	19.4						15	24.6 / 19	19.2
23	15.8	30	12.0	33	11.1	Cost of Sales/Payables					33	11.1 / 34	10.7
42	8.7	45	8.1	56	6.5						53	6.9 / 49	7.4
	6.6		5.7		6.1							7.7	6.3
	11.3		10.0		9.7	Sales/Working Capital						11.3	9.6
	32.3		21.9		15.7							15.1	16.8
	8.0		11.8		23.1							36.9	23.0
(54)	4.1	(62)	3.3	(44)	5.1	EBIT/Interest			(11)	13.1	(18)	6.3
	1.5		1.2		2.1							2.0	2.4
	8.3		5.5		11.2	Net Profit + Depr., Dep.,							12.0
(30)	2.8	(27)	2.3	(18)	3.6	Amort./Cur. Mat. L/T/D					(10)	4.3
	.1		.3		1.4								1.4
	.4		.3		.2							.2	.4
	.7		.7		.5	Fixed/Worth						.4	.7
	2.3		2.0		1.4							.8	3.4
	.9		.8		.8							.9	.9
	2.4		1.8		1.8	Debt/Worth						1.2	1.9
	9.2		11.6		11.3							2.8	9.0
	45.7		43.3		49.3	% Profit Before Taxes/Tangible						33.6	72.5
(48)	21.2	(54)	18.8	(43)	20.2	Net Worth					(12)	11.2 / (18)	25.2
	11.0		1.2		9.8							2.6	13.4
	18.8		13.3		10.9	% Profit Before Taxes/Total						14.6	9.0
	7.4		4.1		5.5	Assets						8.1	5.5
	3.0		-.3		2.2							1.8	3.8
	43.5		32.6		57.0							38.2	29.2
	14.2		14.0		21.2	Sales/Net Fixed Assets						21.2	8.6
	8.5		6.4		8.4							11.1	5.4
	3.9		3.3		3.2							3.3	3.2
	2.6		2.4		2.5	Sales/Total Assets						3.0	2.2
	1.9		1.7		1.8							2.0	1.5
	.8		.7		.6							.5	1.5
(54)	1.4	(58)	1.9	(44)	1.5	% Depr., Dep., Amort./Sales					(12)	1.2 / (18)	2.0
	2.2		2.6		2.3							2.3	4.4
			1.1		2.2								
		(15)	2.8	(14)	3.3	% Officers', Directors'							
			4.4		4.2	Owners' Comp/Sales							
	3030620M		3958712M		2111698M	Net Sales ($)		6502M	15738M	74248M	187665M	1827545M	
	1323590M		1910115M		1099765M	Total Assets ($)		2830M	6483M	35518M	77699M	977235M	

M = $ thousand   MM = $ million
See Pages 9 through 22 for Explanation of Ratios and Data

Current Data Sorted by Assets   Comparative Historical Data

0-500M	500M-2MM	2-10MM	10-50MM	50-100MM	100-250MM	Type of Statement	4/1/06-3/31/07 ALL	4/1/07-3/31/08 ALL
			11	5	1	Unqualified	22	22
	3	19	4			Reviewed	38	42
1	6	5				Compiled	16	27
3	9	4				Tax Returns	12	13
	10	18	12	1		Other	34	47
	21 (4/1-9/30/10)		91 (10/1/10-3/31/11)					
4	28	46	27	6	1	NUMBER OF STATEMENTS	122	151
%	%	%	%	%	%	ASSETS	%	%
	9.1	7.6	10.8			Cash & Equivalents	7.6	8.3
	33.9	32.1	26.3			Trade Receivables (net)	33.5	32.6
	17.1	25.9	22.8			Inventory	23.1	23.2
	1.4	1.5	2.8			All Other Current	2.3	3.2
	61.4	67.0	62.7			Total Current	66.6	67.3
	22.8	24.4	23.6			Fixed Assets (net)	25.4	24.0
	3.8	3.3	8.8			Intangibles (net)	4.5	4.5
	12.0	5.3	4.8			All Other Non-Current	3.5	4.2
	100.0	100.0	100.0			Total	100.0	100.0
						LIABILITIES		
	19.4	15.9	12.6			Notes Payable-Short Term	13.8	16.4
	9.3	2.8	7.0			Cur. Mat.-L.T.D.	3.7	3.8
	20.7	16.7	11.3			Trade Payables	15.1	17.5
	.2	.4	.2			Income Taxes Payable	.3	.5
	7.5	10.8	10.6			All Other Current	11.6	12.7
	57.1	46.6	41.6			Total Current	44.5	51.0
	11.9	14.0	13.8			Long-Term Debt	18.8	18.7
	.0	.2	.8			Deferred Taxes	.4	.2
	20.1	8.7	8.1			All Other Non-Current	3.2	6.3
	10.9	30.4	35.8			Net Worth	33.0	23.7
	100.0	100.0	100.0			Total Liabilities & Net Worth	100.0	100.0
						INCOME DATA		
	100.0	100.0	100.0			Net Sales	100.0	100.0
	35.4	28.3	23.9			Gross Profit	29.4	29.6
	33.7	25.8	21.9			Operating Expenses	24.3	24.6
	1.7	2.6	2.1			Operating Profit	5.1	4.9
	.8	.6	1.7			All Other Expenses (net)	1.1	1.4
	.9	2.0	.4			Profit Before Taxes	4.0	3.6
						RATIOS		
	1.8	2.5	2.3			Current	2.1	2.2
	1.1	1.7	1.5				1.4	1.5
	.7	1.1	1.2				1.1	1.1
	1.2	1.7	1.4			Quick	1.3	1.3
	.7	1.0	.8				.8	.8
	.5	.5	.5				.6	.6
	16 22.6	33 11.0	37 9.9			Sales/Receivables	33 11.1	28 12.9
	37 9.8	47 7.7	44 8.2				45 8.1	44 8.4
	54 6.7	57 6.4	68 5.3				62 5.9	60 6.1
	4 82.4	19 19.7	23 16.1			Cost of Sales/Inventory	21 17.1	20 18.4
	18 19.8	50 7.3	54 6.8				44 8.4	44 8.4
	64 5.7	87 4.2	94 3.9				71 5.1	71 5.1
	13 27.1	16 23.5	12 29.6			Cost of Sales/Payables	17 21.7	15 23.9
	37 9.9	30 12.0	19 19.0				27 13.7	26 14.1
	57 6.5	45 8.1	43 8.5				41 8.8	39 9.4
	8.2	5.8	5.4			Sales/Working Capital	6.6	6.9
	33.5	9.9	10.7				13.8	12.4
	-35.4	52.2	24.7				43.1	66.3
	5.6	8.9	6.1			EBIT/Interest	9.9	9.1
	(26) 1.6	(42) 3.7	(25) 1.5				(114) 3.5	(137) 3.5
	.1	.9	-.9				1.7	1.5
		9.0				Net Profit + Depr., Dep., Amort./Cur. Mat. L/T/D	6.9	6.8
		(10) 5.8					(43) 3.3	(42) 3.5
		2.0					1.1	1.5
	.4	.2	.3			Fixed/Worth	.3	.3
	1.6	.7	1.1				.7	.8
	-1.1	1.6	5.1				1.8	3.0
	1.4	1.0	.7			Debt/Worth	1.0	1.0
	4.0	1.6	2.1				2.1	2.5
	-9.8	3.6	16.9				4.5	10.5
	42.3	26.3	30.8			% Profit Before Taxes/Tangible Net Worth	50.0	64.7
	(18) 11.2	(41) 15.7	(22) 13.2				(110) 18.1	(124) 24.2
	.8	3.2	-1.4				6.5	9.1
	9.2	13.0	5.2			% Profit Before Taxes/Total Assets	17.9	16.7
	2.4	4.5	2.4				6.3	8.7
	-1.7	.2	-1.5				1.8	1.5
	37.1	35.0	15.2			Sales/Net Fixed Assets	28.5	29.6
	22.4	11.1	9.7				11.7	15.0
	10.2	5.4	4.5				6.8	7.1
	5.1	3.1	2.3			Sales/Total Assets	3.3	3.6
	3.4	2.3	1.9				2.7	2.6
	2.0	1.8	1.6				1.9	1.9
	.8	.8	1.5			% Depr., Dep., Amort./Sales	1.0	.9
	(23) 1.3	(43) 2.2	(20) 2.1				(106) 1.6	(129) 1.5
	2.6	3.5	3.7				2.8	2.9
	2.2	2.3				% Officers', Directors' Owners' Comp/Sales	1.9	2.2
	(20) 5.4	(16) 3.7					(48) 3.9	(61) 3.9
	8.3	5.5					6.4	5.9
9229M	105399M	524696M	1177037M	769641M	253295M	Net Sales ($)	3199665M	4027661M
1015M	29962M	213380M	615689M	485259M	186456M	Total Assets ($)	1513065M	1930541M

© RMA 2011

M = $ thousand   MM = $ million
See Pages 9 through 22 for Explanation of Ratios and Data

Comparative Historical Data

Current Data Sorted by Sales

4/1/08-3/31/09 ALL	4/1/09-3/31/10 ALL	4/1/10-3/31/11 ALL	Type of Statement	0-1MM	1-3MM	3-5MM	5-10MM	10-25MM	25MM & OVER
21	15	17	Unqualified					2	15
39	19	26	Reviewed		1	3	7	13	2
20	12	12	Compiled		1	6	3	1	
12	9	16	Tax Returns	1	5	5	5	1	
40	46	41	Other	1	4	6	9	5	16
					21 (4/1-9/30/10)		91 (10/1/10-3/31/11)		
132	101	112	**NUMBER OF STATEMENTS**	2	11	20	24	22	33
%	%	%	**ASSETS**	%	%	%	%	%	%
9.6	7.7	9.9	Cash & Equivalents		14.9	7.0	10.1	9.6	9.4
26.9	27.3	29.9	Trade Receivables (net)		27.4	37.3	28.7	29.9	28.7
23.6	23.7	21.9	Inventory		14.8	21.6	21.5	24.4	23.2
2.4	2.2	2.0	All Other Current		.5	1.4	1.5	.8	3.9
62.5	61.0	63.7	Total Current		57.6	67.3	61.8	64.7	65.1
27.0	26.8	24.0	Fixed Assets (net)		24.7	22.1	24.8	24.8	22.0
5.0	6.8	5.8	Intangibles (net)		4.8	2.8	4.5	6.2	9.0
5.5	5.4	6.5	All Other Non-Current		12.8	7.8	8.9	4.2	3.8
100.0	100.0	100.0	Total		100.0	100.0	100.0	100.0	100.0
			LIABILITIES						
11.1	14.8	16.7	Notes Payable-Short Term		24.4	15.7	17.0	12.6	11.6
3.6	4.1	5.5	Cur. Mat.-L.T.D.		4.7	7.4	6.4	2.6	5.7
14.1	14.1	16.1	Trade Payables		15.9	22.8	17.2	13.2	13.4
.3	.1	.3	Income Taxes Payable		.0	.4	.0	.7	.3
11.5	11.4	9.8	All Other Current		4.6	10.1	10.0	8.9	12.3
40.6	44.6	48.4	Total Current		49.5	56.3	50.6	38.0	43.2
21.7	19.4	13.9	Long-Term Debt		12.7	17.0	11.8	11.3	15.8
.2	.3	.3	Deferred Taxes		.0	.3	.2	.0	.8
5.8	7.8	12.7	All Other Non-Current		9.5	12.6	17.3	8.9	6.5
31.7	27.9	24.8	Net Worth		28.3	13.8	20.2	41.8	33.7
100.0	100.0	100.0	Total Liabilities & Net Worth		100.0	100.0	100.0	100.0	100.0
			INCOME DATA						
100.0	100.0	100.0	Net Sales		100.0	100.0	100.0	100.0	100.0
28.6	26.9	29.4	Gross Profit		40.1	32.9	26.6	28.6	25.9
25.2	26.4	26.9	Operating Expenses		39.6	31.2	24.5	24.9	23.2
3.4	.5	2.5	Operating Profit		.4	1.8	2.1	3.7	2.7
1.4	1.7	1.1	All Other Expenses (net)		.8	1.1	.2	.5	1.7
2.0	-1.3	1.4	Profit Before Taxes		-.4	.7	1.9	3.2	1.0
			RATIOS						
2.4	2.6	2.3	Current		1.9	1.6	2.4	3.0	2.4
1.6	1.6	1.5			1.1	1.2	1.8	1.5	1.5
1.1	1.0	1.1			.8	.9	.8	1.2	1.1
1.6	1.5	1.6	Quick		1.8	1.3	1.9	1.6	1.6
.9	.8	.9			.8	.8	1.1	1.0	.9
.5	.5	.5			.5	.4	.4	.7	.5
27 13.6	30 12.2	30 12.3	Sales/Receivables		0 999.8	19 19.3	22 16.9	33 11.0	37 9.9
38 9.7	40 9.0	45 8.2			39 9.4	46 7.9	40 9.0	44 8.3	47 7.7
51 7.1	60 6.1	60 6.1			51 7.2	70 5.2	54 6.9	53 6.9	69 5.3
17 21.4	22 16.6	14 25.3	Cost of Sales/Inventory		0 UND	12 31.2	6 62.7	24 15.2	23 15.8
49 7.4	50 7.4	45 8.1			18 20.8	20 18.0	44 8.3	48 7.6	56 6.5
77 4.7	85 4.3	80 4.5			119 3.1	80 4.5	65 5.6	77 4.8	84 4.4
14 25.3	14 25.5	15 24.7	Cost of Sales/Payables		13 28.1	20 18.1	15 24.1	13 27.7	13 28.1
27 13.4	25 14.7	26 14.1			23 15.8	41 9.0	29 12.7	19 19.1	21 17.3
37 9.9	39 9.4	44 8.2			88 4.2	47 7.7	52 7.0	39 9.4	44 8.3
6.0	5.4	5.8	Sales/Working Capital		5.4	8.2	5.8	6.5	4.9
10.6	10.2	11.2			49.6	29.5	10.2	12.8	9.1
56.3	550.2	98.2			-181.3	NM	-28.9	30.1	34.5
8.8	7.4	8.2	EBIT/Interest				5.9	10.0	10.9	6.0
(118) 2.2	(95) 1.3	(102) 2.4					1.9	(21) 3.6	(21) 4.8	(29) 2.0
.0	-2.2	.7					.2	.3	1.6	.1
4.4	5.8	6.0	Net Profit + Depr., Dep., Amort./Cur. Mat. L/T/D						
(39) 2.1	(29) 1.7	(28) 2.5							
.7	-.6	1.0							
.4	.3	.3	Fixed/Worth		.3	.2	.2	.3	.4
1.0	1.0	.9			1.7	1.2	.7	.7	.7
4.2	18.4	4.9			27.7	NM	NM	1.1	4.3
.9	.8	1.0	Debt/Worth		1.3	1.7	.8	1.0	.8
2.5	2.9	1.8			2.4	2.9	1.4	1.6	2.5
10.3	54.9	16.6			253.3	NM	NM	1.9	16.4
47.2	28.4	36.3	% Profit Before Taxes/Tangible Net Worth			43.8	22.0	42.5	25.1
(107) 19.1	(78) 5.6	(89) 14.1				(15) 17.7	(18) 8.0	(20) 17.3	(27) 12.5
2.0	-31.0	2.1				.9	2.1	5.0	-1.3
13.8	8.2	11.3	% Profit Before Taxes/Total Assets		7.0	11.9	11.1	16.3	7.6
4.5	1.6	3.6			1.9	2.2	5.0	6.3	3.3
-3.0	-10.2	-.6			-5.9	-1.9	.4	1.6	-1.0
24.8	25.4	30.4	Sales/Net Fixed Assets		30.2	47.8	30.0	28.5	24.0
10.8	10.4	11.4			17.7	29.0	14.2	9.7	9.7
6.4	4.6	5.8			4.1	9.9	5.5	6.1	6.4
3.1	2.9	3.2	Sales/Total Assets		4.0	5.2	3.9	3.6	2.4
2.4	2.1	2.3			1.9	2.7	2.3	2.4	1.9
1.9	1.6	1.7			1.8	1.8	2.0	1.6	1.6
1.1	1.4	1.0	% Depr., Dep., Amort./Sales			.6	.8	.7	1.4
(113) 1.6	(90) 2.2	(97) 2.1				(18) 1.3	(23) 2.3	(20) 2.2	(26) 2.0
3.1	3.8	3.2				3.0	3.3	3.9	3.0
1.9	2.8	2.4	% Officers', Directors' Owners' Comp/Sales			2.2			
(52) 3.2	(34) 4.6	(41) 4.7				(12) 3.8	(12) 3.6		
6.0	7.2	6.2				5.9	8.6		
4005616M	2826805M	2839297M	Net Sales ($)	1085M	21075M	81987M	169629M	343324M	2222197M
1976262M	1483178M	1531761M	Total Assets ($)	852M	11049M	38365M	68526M	158314M	1254655M

© RMA 2011

M = $ thousand   MM = $ million

See Pages 9 through 22 for Explanation of Ratios and Data

Current Data Sorted by Assets							Comparative Historical Data	
						Type of Statement		
		7	1	1	1	Unqualified	13	6
	1	3	1			Reviewed	8	11
	3	1				Compiled	9	7
1	3					Tax Returns	1	2
		11	6	2	2	Other	13	11
4 (4/1-9/30/10)			**40 (10/1/10-3/31/11)**				**4/1/06-3/31/07 ALL**	**4/1/07-3/31/08 ALL**
0-500M	500M-2MM	2-10MM	10-50MM	50-100MM	100-250MM			
1	7	22	8	3	3	**NUMBER OF STATEMENTS**	44	37
%	%	%	%	%	%	**ASSETS**	%	%
		9.3				Cash & Equivalents	10.7	12.2
		28.7				Trade Receivables (net)	25.8	26.8
		26.1				Inventory	22.3	22.1
		2.6				All Other Current	2.7	3.1
		66.8				Total Current	61.5	64.1
		22.5				Fixed Assets (net)	25.9	24.4
		3.8				Intangibles (net)	5.1	4.8
		6.9				All Other Non-Current	7.5	6.6
		100.0				Total	100.0	100.0
						LIABILITIES		
		10.1				Notes Payable-Short Term	7.4	8.1
		1.3				Cur. Mat.-L.T.D.	3.6	3.5
		14.7				Trade Payables	18.9	17.5
		.3				Income Taxes Payable	.2	.2
		5.9				All Other Current	11.0	11.2
		32.4				Total Current	41.0	40.5
		9.3				Long-Term Debt	12.6	14.3
		.6				Deferred Taxes	.8	.6
		7.8				All Other Non-Current	7.6	3.8
		49.9				Net Worth	38.0	40.8
		100.0				Total Liabilities & Net Worth	100.0	100.0
						INCOME DATA		
		100.0				Net Sales	100.0	100.0
		28.7				Gross Profit	34.1	33.4
		23.6				Operating Expenses	30.3	30.5
		5.1				Operating Profit	3.8	2.9
		.3				All Other Expenses (net)	.2	.5
		4.8				Profit Before Taxes	3.6	2.5
						RATIOS		
		4.7					2.7	3.4
		2.0				Current	1.7	1.5
		1.3					1.1	1.1
		2.4					1.7	2.1
		1.1				Quick	.9	.9
		.6					.6	.6
		21 17.3					18 19.8	17 21.6
		32 11.5				Sales/Receivables	32 11.4	30 12.0
		42 8.7					43 8.5	44 8.4
		24 15.4					23 15.9	20 17.9
		46 7.9				Cost of Sales/Inventory	33 10.9	33 11.1
		57 6.4					44 8.4	47 7.8
		15 24.5					16 23.0	16 22.2
		23 16.0				Cost of Sales/Payables	25 14.9	24 15.1
		36 10.3					38 9.6	41 8.8
		5.1					6.7	5.9
		10.6				Sales/Working Capital	13.3	15.8
		20.0					131.3	79.3
		9.1					19.2	14.0
		(14) 2.6				EBIT/Interest	(42) 6.1	(32) 2.4
		.0					1.1	-.8
						Net Profit + Depr., Dep.,	10.6	
						Amort./Cur. Mat. L/T/D	(14) 3.8	
							-.3	
		.1					.4	.3
		.5				Fixed/Worth	.6	.5
		1.4					1.2	2.6
		.2					.7	.4
		.9				Debt/Worth	1.3	1.4
		2.4					5.2	4.3
		36.5					41.9	38.7
		(19) 14.4				% Profit Before Taxes/Tangible Net Worth	(36) 16.7	(32) 18.8
		4.8					2.2	-4.5
		17.8					21.4	18.9
		3.6				% Profit Before Taxes/Total Assets	9.9	7.1
		.3					1.0	-1.8
		46.2					31.2	34.4
		16.1				Sales/Net Fixed Assets	17.0	16.2
		9.2					7.5	7.9
		3.8					4.4	4.9
		2.9				Sales/Total Assets	3.5	3.1
		2.1					2.3	2.1
		.7					1.1	1.1
		(19) 1.2				% Depr., Dep., Amort./Sales	(40) 1.4	(32) 1.5
		2.0					1.8	2.6
							1.5	1.2
						% Officers', Directors' Owners' Comp/Sales	(14) 3.6	(15) 2.2
							4.4	4.1
958M	34936M	263911M	492673M	427401M	1140309M	Net Sales ($)	2011355M	1808364M
178M	8595M	91746M	176580M	218182M	409993M	Total Assets ($)	788643M	578486M

© RMA 2011

M = $ thousand   MM = $ million
See Pages 9 through 22 for Explanation of Ratios and Data

Comparative Historical Data | Current Data Sorted by Sales

			Type of Statement	0-1MM	1-3MM	3-5MM	5-10MM	10-25MM	25MM & OVER
5	3	3	Unqualified						3
11	11	9	Reviewed			1	2	5	1
13	7	7	Compiled	1	2	1	1	1	1
4	2	4	Tax Returns		1	1	1		1
13	20	21	Other				5	6	10
4/1/08-3/31/09 ALL	4/1/09-3/31/10 ALL	4/1/10-3/31/11 ALL		4 (4/1-9/30/10)			40 (10/1/10-3/31/11)		
46	43	44	**NUMBER OF STATEMENTS**	1	3	3	9	13	15
%	%	%	**ASSETS**	%	%	%	%	%	%
8.8	12.3	10.4	Cash & Equivalents					8.4	14.1
24.8	22.2	27.2	Trade Receivables (net)					28.6	24.3
22.3	25.7	27.1	Inventory					25.3	26.6
3.8	3.3	3.0	All Other Current					1.5	3.7
59.7	63.5	67.7	Total Current					63.8	68.7
27.8	26.3	21.8	Fixed Assets (net)					25.1	20.0
3.8	4.9	4.6	Intangibles (net)					5.6	6.1
8.7	5.4	5.8	All Other Non-Current					5.6	5.3
100.0	100.0	100.0	Total					100.0	100.0
			LIABILITIES						
12.7	7.1	8.8	Notes Payable-Short Term					8.1	5.8
2.0	3.4	2.1	Cur. Mat.-L.T.D.					1.1	1.7
17.6	18.9	16.5	Trade Payables					16.0	12.3
.7	.1	.3	Income Taxes Payable					.5	.5
8.5	8.3	10.9	All Other Current					7.3	14.4
41.5	37.9	38.6	Total Current					33.0	34.7
17.0	15.0	10.6	Long-Term Debt					12.9	11.9
.4	.3	.8	Deferred Taxes					1.0	1.5
5.7	6.3	11.4	All Other Non-Current					12.0	13.0
35.4	40.4	38.5	Net Worth					41.1	38.9
100.0	100.0	100.0	Total Liabilties & Net Worth					100.0	100.0
			INCOME DATA						
100.0	100.0	100.0	Net Sales					100.0	100.0
30.3	33.5	30.2	Gross Profit					27.1	32.0
31.3	31.4	26.2	Operating Expenses					24.0	27.1
-1.0	2.1	4.0	Operating Profit					3.2	4.8
.9	.1	.4	All Other Expenses (net)					.2	.6
-1.8	2.0	3.6	Profit Before Taxes					2.9	4.2
			RATIOS						
3.1	3.2	3.2	Current					4.7	3.2
1.4	1.7	1.9						1.7	2.4
1.0	1.0	1.1						1.1	1.1
1.8	2.1	2.0	Quick					2.5	1.9
.7	.8	1.1						1.2	1.3
.5	.4	.5						.5	.7
18 20.1	16 22.9	17 21.0	Sales/Receivables					17 21.5	17 21.2
33 11.2	28 13.2	33 11.0						24 15.5	39 9.3
47 7.8	43 8.6	44 8.2						32 11.5	44 8.2
27 13.7	27 13.3	26 13.8	Cost of Sales/Inventory					21 17.5	26 13.9
38 9.7	42 8.7	44 8.3						35 10.3	44 8.2
52 7.0	79 4.6	61 6.0						50 7.3	69 5.3
14 26.2	16 23.0	16 22.1	Cost of Sales/Payables					15 24.7	16 22.7
24 15.2	27 13.6	23 15.6						19 19.0	20 18.3
46 7.9	49 7.5	38 9.6						29 12.6	34 10.6
5.9	5.2	5.1	Sales/Working Capital					5.8	4.8
18.7	12.7	11.9						15.6	8.4
-174.5	247.8	42.8						NM	23.5
4.0	13.7	9.0	EBIT/Interest						10.7
(40) .1	(36) 3.5	(32) 2.9							(11) 3.7
-6.3	-.4	-.2							-.5
2.9	5.4	6.3	Net Profit + Depr., Dep., Amort./Cur. Mat. L/T/D						
(15) 1.3	(15) 2.2	(10) 2.8							
-10.4	1.5	.3							
.3	.2	.2	Fixed/Worth					.1	.2
.7	.6	.5						.6	.4
2.1	3.7	4.9						-15.4	2.0
.6	.5	.5	Debt/Worth					.2	.6
1.6	1.4	1.4						1.0	.9
7.0	11.6	19.8						-82.1	5.8
16.8	57.7	44.3	% Profit Before Taxes/Tangible Net Worth						46.8
(39) 1.5	(37) 17.5	(34) 14.7						(12)	24.0
-42.9	-2.8	4.5							4.2
6.8	16.0	12.6	% Profit Before Taxes/Total Assets					24.1	12.7
-5.7	6.2	4.8						5.2	6.5
-18.4	-3.1	.3						-3.4	1.5
29.9	29.5	42.3	Sales/Net Fixed Assets					46.7	33.0
12.1	14.3	17.7						19.5	16.3
5.3	6.6	9.7						8.8	11.3
4.0	4.0	4.1	Sales/Total Assets					5.0	3.6
3.1	2.8	2.8						3.6	2.4
2.1	2.0	2.2						2.2	2.2
1.1	1.0	.8	% Depr., Dep., Amort./Sales					.6	.9
(38) 1.4	(37) 1.5	(40) 1.2						(12) 1.0	(14) 1.1
2.6	2.7	1.9						2.9	1.6
1.0	.8	.8	% Officers', Directors' Owners' Comp/Sales						
(13) 3.0	(14) 1.7	(15) 2.9							
5.9	5.8	7.5							
2355476M	1646937M	2360188M	Net Sales ($)	958M	7360M	12488M	64112M	186567M	2088703M
774157M	574351M	905274M	Total Assets ($)	178M	2330M	5015M	25553M	58971M	813227M

© RMA 2011   M = $ thousand   MM = $ million
See Pages 9 through 22 for Explanation of Ratios and Data

Current Data Sorted by Assets   Comparative Historical Data

0-500M	500M-2MM	2-10MM	10-50MM	50-100MM	100-250MM	Type of Statement	4/1/06-3/31/07 ALL	4/1/07-3/31/08 ALL
			2	1	1	Unqualified	8	5
		7	1			Reviewed	5	6
1		1				Compiled	8	3
1	1	1				Tax Returns	2	1
1	4	4	3	1		Other	7	15
		3 (4/1-9/30/10)	27 (10/1/10-3/31/11)					
3	5	13	6	2	1	NUMBER OF STATEMENTS	30	30
%	%	%	%	%	%	**ASSETS**	%	%
		6.5				Cash & Equivalents	9.4	7.4
		27.6				Trade Receivables (net)	28.1	32.1
		44.8				Inventory	34.7	34.3
		.8				All Other Current	2.7	4.0
		79.7				Total Current	75.0	77.9
		13.3				Fixed Assets (net)	15.0	16.2
		2.8				Intangibles (net)	6.1	3.3
		4.2				All Other Non-Current	3.8	2.7
		100.0				Total	100.0	100.0
						LIABILITIES		
		14.4				Notes Payable-Short Term	15.3	17.7
		1.6				Cur. Mat.-L.T.D.	2.8	3.0
		18.6				Trade Payables	16.0	22.1
		.2				Income Taxes Payable	.3	.6
		13.6				All Other Current	12.3	13.8
		48.4				Total Current	46.7	57.2
		10.5				Long-Term Debt	12.9	9.1
		.1				Deferred Taxes	.3	.2
		5.5				All Other Non-Current	14.3	4.8
		35.5				Net Worth	25.9	28.7
		100.0				Total Liabilities & Net Worth	100.0	100.0
						INCOME DATA		
		100.0				Net Sales	100.0	100.0
		32.9				Gross Profit	33.1	31.8
		31.6				Operating Expenses	26.7	28.2
		1.4				Operating Profit	6.4	3.6
		.7				All Other Expenses (net)	1.2	1.6
		.6				Profit Before Taxes	5.2	1.9
						RATIOS		
		2.9					4.1	2.2
		1.6				Current	1.8	1.4
		1.1					1.1	1.1
		1.0					1.9	1.1
		.8				Quick	.9	.8
		.3					.6	.4
		19 19.5					27 13.7	26 13.9
		29 12.5				Sales/Receivables	35 10.5	38 9.5
		52 7.0					42 8.7	49 7.4
		55 6.6					37 9.9	36 10.2
		73 5.0				Cost of Sales/Inventory	55 6.6	61 6.0
		111 3.3					80 4.6	81 4.5
		11 33.3					14 25.2	20 18.2
		35 10.5				Cost of Sales/Payables	27 13.4	31 11.8
		44 8.4					39 9.3	56 6.5
		4.5					4.9	7.2
		10.5				Sales/Working Capital	9.8	15.8
		32.5					66.0	62.4
		9.8					(25) 15.2	(27) 7.6
		(12) 2.2				EBIT/Interest	5.5	3.6
		-8.0					2.6	1.2
						Net Profit + Depr., Dep., Amort./Cur. Mat. L/T/D		
		.1					.1	.3
		.3				Fixed/Worth	.4	.4
		2.0					NM	16.0
		1.0					.3	.8
		2.5				Debt/Worth	2.0	2.8
		5.9					NM	95.2
		17.5				% Profit Before Taxes/Tangible	(23) 36.3	(24) 43.9
		(12) 2.2				Net Worth	17.7	18.1
		-29.4					9.9	1.9
		7.4				% Profit Before Taxes/Total	18.0	13.3
		1.2				Assets	11.0	5.2
		-5.3					5.4	.6
		77.4					57.2	43.0
		31.0				Sales/Net Fixed Assets	31.4	33.0
		19.8					15.2	12.1
		4.4					4.1	4.6
		3.2				Sales/Total Assets	2.8	3.3
		2.1					2.3	2.3
		.7					(22) .4	(23) .7
		(10) 1.1				% Depr., Dep., Amort./Sales	.8	1.1
		1.6					2.4	2.0
						% Officers', Directors'	(11) 1.4	(15) 1.5
						Owners' Comp/Sales	4.1	2.8
							7.2	5.7
11880M	15646M	180407M	379989M	51640M	498072M	Net Sales ($)	1181808M	736946M
1153M	4949M	53120M	153651M	132027M	242014M	Total Assets ($)	493991M	296718M

See Pages 9 through 22 for Explanation of Ratios and Data

Comparative Historical Data **Current Data Sorted by Sales**

			Type of Statement						
4	1	4	Unqualified						4
4	7	8	Reviewed				3	4	1
4	2	2	Compiled		1			1	
1	1	3	Tax Returns		1	1	1		
13	14	13	Other	1	1	2	3	2	4
4/1/08-3/31/09 ALL	4/1/09-3/31/10 ALL	4/1/10-3/31/11 ALL		0-1MM	1-3MM	3 (4/1-9/30/10) 3-5MM	5-10MM	27 (10/1/10-3/31/11) 10-25MM	25MM & OVER
26	25	30	NUMBER OF STATEMENTS	1	3	3	7	7	9
%	%	%	**ASSETS**	%	%	%	%	%	%
5.0	7.1	8.5	Cash & Equivalents						
29.3	25.5	24.1	Trade Receivables (net)						
34.9	35.4	35.9	Inventory						
3.3	3.0	1.8	All Other Current						
72.5	71.0	70.3	Total Current						
17.9	17.1	14.3	Fixed Assets (net)						
4.1	7.0	11.1	Intangibles (net)						
5.5	4.9	4.4	All Other Non-Current						
100.0	100.0	100.0	Total						
			LIABILITIES						
15.8	20.8	21.3	Notes Payable-Short Term						
1.8	2.0	1.5	Cur. Mat.-L.T.D.						
21.0	19.2	17.7	Trade Payables						
.2	.1	.1	Income Taxes Payable						
13.2	12.2	13.1	All Other Current						
51.9	54.4	53.6	Total Current						
16.2	12.5	14.1	Long-Term Debt						
.3	.8	.9	Deferred Taxes						
4.1	5.9	7.1	All Other Non-Current						
27.5	26.5	24.3	Net Worth						
100.0	100.0	100.0	Total Liabilities & Net Worth						
			INCOME DATA						
100.0	100.0	100.0	Net Sales						
31.5	34.0	36.5	Gross Profit						
29.5	32.3	34.5	Operating Expenses						
2.0	1.7	2.0	Operating Profit						
1.5	2.0	3.2	All Other Expenses (net)						
.5	-.4	-1.3	Profit Before Taxes						
			RATIOS						
2.2	2.1	2.5							
1.5	1.5	1.5	Current						
1.1	1.1	1.1							
1.0	1.1	1.2							
.8	.8	.8	Quick						
.4	.3	.4							
26 14.2	25 14.6	18 20.7							
36 10.1	34 10.6	29 12.6	Sales/Receivables						
49 7.4	46 7.9	57 6.4							
47 7.7	55 6.7	53 6.8							
62 5.9	70 5.2	74 5.0	Cost of Sales/Inventory						
89 4.1	87 4.2	99 3.7							
19 18.9	20 18.5	14 26.8							
32 11.3	35 10.5	31 11.7	Cost of Sales/Payables						
43 8.4	42 8.6	42 8.7							
6.6	6.5	4.7							
10.8	12.2	15.3	Sales/Working Capital						
34.4	45.0	34.6							
4.5	9.5	7.9							
(24) 2.2	(23) 2.3	(28) 2.0	EBIT/Interest						
-3.0	-3.5	.1							
			Net Profit + Depr., Dep., Amort./Cur. Mat. L/T/D						
.3	.3	.2							
.5	.4	.7	Fixed/Worth						
NM	-25.5	-1.0							
.9	.9	1.2							
2.4	2.9	3.4	Debt/Worth						
NM	-59.0	-6.2							
28.4	34.8	16.7							
(20) 10.2	(18) 3.6	(21) 6.3	% Profit Before Taxes/Tangible Net Worth						
-12.2	-19.5	-8.6							
8.2	11.3	6.5							
4.2	1.3	1.1	% Profit Before Taxes/Total Assets						
-6.6	-10.6	-3.9							
40.2	48.3	55.3							
23.1	20.8	26.9	Sales/Net Fixed Assets						
11.8	12.0	11.1							
4.0	3.7	4.4							
2.9	2.8	3.0	Sales/Total Assets						
2.2	1.9	1.8							
.6	.8	.8							
(19) 1.2	(19) 1.3	(19) 1.3	% Depr., Dep., Amort./Sales						
2.1	2.5	1.9							
1.5	1.5	2.1							
(10) 3.4	(11) 4.2	(12) 2.8	% Officers', Directors' Owners' Comp/Sales						
4.8	5.6	4.7							
1782762M	983819M	1137634M	Net Sales ($)	991M	7084M	9988M	44712M	103437M	971422M
735327M	437196M	586914M	Total Assets ($)	700M	2652M	4756M	27923M	28651M	522232M

M = $ thousand   MM = $ million
See Pages 9 through 22 for Explanation of Ratios and Data

Current Data Sorted by Assets   Comparative Historical Data

Type of Statement

	0-500M	500M-2MM	2-10MM	10-50MM	50-100MM	100-250MM		4/1/06-3/31/07 ALL	4/1/07-3/31/08 ALL
Unqualified			8	19	11	12		51	47
Reviewed	2	1	18	9				17	18
Compiled	3	5	8	1				12	12
Tax Returns	1	6	6			1		6	6
Other	3	8	25	25	9	9		80	68
	24 (4/1-9/30/10)			166 (10/1/10-3/31/11)					

	0-500M	500M-2MM	2-10MM	10-50MM	50-100MM	100-250MM		4/1/06-3/31/07 ALL	4/1/07-3/31/08 ALL
NUMBER OF STATEMENTS	9	20	65	54	20	22		166	151
ASSETS	%	%	%	%	%	%		%	%
Cash & Equivalents		11.4	10.7	15.0	12.7	13.1		11.1	12.9
Trade Receivables (net)		26.5	25.9	22.5	21.1	14.2		22.6	22.2
Inventory		25.4	23.6	22.0	16.9	10.7		23.2	23.4
All Other Current		1.9	2.5	2.7	4.2	2.2		2.2	2.6
Total Current		65.2	62.8	62.1	55.0	40.2		59.0	61.0
Fixed Assets (net)		13.5	23.2	25.1	16.0	18.4		21.2	22.2
Intangibles (net)		9.0	6.2	8.4	24.1	37.8		14.2	11.9
All Other Non-Current		12.3	7.8	4.4	4.9	3.6		5.5	4.9
Total		100.0	100.0	100.0	100.0	100.0		100.0	100.0
LIABILITIES									
Notes Payable-Short Term		10.6	6.2	6.3	1.8	2.6		5.7	7.6
Cur. Mat.-L.T.D.		1.7	3.7	2.8	3.6	5.2		4.2	3.2
Trade Payables		11.9	14.0	8.9	6.0	4.4		10.6	11.2
Income Taxes Payable		.2	.0	.2	.3	.2		.5	.3
All Other Current		13.0	8.9	11.3	13.9	7.6		9.6	10.2
Total Current		37.4	32.8	29.5	25.6	20.0		30.5	32.5
Long-Term Debt		9.6	12.9	16.5	13.5	15.9		14.1	14.8
Deferred Taxes		.0	.2	.8	1.3	2.6		.6	.7
All Other Non-Current		8.2	6.7	9.0	11.6	11.2		5.6	6.9
Net Worth		44.8	47.4	44.2	48.0	50.3		49.3	45.1
Total Liabilities & Net Worth		100.0	100.0	100.0	100.0	100.0		100.0	100.0
INCOME DATA									
Net Sales		100.0	100.0	100.0	100.0	100.0		100.0	100.0
Gross Profit		45.8	43.8	42.6	52.5	47.9		45.9	45.2
Operating Expenses		43.4	35.0	35.4	43.8	35.0		37.8	37.5
Operating Profit		2.5	8.8	7.2	8.7	12.9		8.1	7.6
All Other Expenses (net)		1.9	.5	1.6	1.9	4.1		1.9	1.6
Profit Before Taxes		.5	8.3	5.6	6.8	8.8		6.2	6.0
RATIOS									
Current		3.0	4.2	3.6	4.8	5.3		3.9	3.5
		1.6	2.2	2.0	2.5	2.0		2.1	2.2
		1.0	1.2	1.5	1.3	1.1		1.3	1.3
Quick		1.7	2.5	2.3	3.1	3.9		2.3	2.1
		1.0	1.3	1.3	1.4	1.4	(165)	1.1	1.2
		.5	.6	.8	.7	.8		.7	.6
Sales/Receivables		27 13.4	36 10.2	39 9.4	39 9.3	37 9.8	38	9.7	37 9.9
		39 9.3	46 7.9	50 7.3	55 6.7	52 7.0	49	7.4	47 7.8
		51 7.1	54 6.8	61 6.0	63 5.8	62 5.9	62	5.9	60 6.1
Cost of Sales/Inventory		9 41.4	42 8.7	60 6.0	59 6.2	43 8.5	59	6.2	60 6.1
		72 5.1	68 5.3	98 3.7	98 3.7	83 4.4	95	3.8	91 4.0
		121 3.0	108 3.4	127 2.9	209 1.8	148 2.5	141	2.6	148 2.5
Cost of Sales/Payables		18 19.8	18 20.4	18 20.4	17 21.9	19 19.5	20	17.9	20 18.4
		29 12.7	34 10.8	29 12.4	32 11.5	32 11.4	35	10.3	33 11.2
		54 6.8	65 5.6	55 6.7	49 7.4	46 8.0	64	5.7	57 6.4
Sales/Working Capital		3.9	3.7	3.2	1.9	2.1		3.4	3.4
		9.1	6.6	5.0	4.4	6.2		5.7	5.4
		224.9	22.6	10.2	13.2	31.1		16.4	13.6
EBIT/Interest		6.8	38.7	16.8	57.9	14.0		16.2	15.8
	(16)	2.9	(56) 11.6	(51) 4.8	8.9	(19) 2.2	(139)	4.9	(124) 4.0
		-8.3	5.2	.2	1.3	.8		1.8	1.4
Net Profit + Depr., Dep., Amort./Cur. Mat. L/T/D			16.3	9.2				15.1	6.8
		(11)	7.5	(21) 2.7			(57)	3.2	(42) 2.5
			1.4	1.1				.8	1.4
Fixed/Worth		.1	.2	.1	.1	.4		.2	.2
		.5	.5	.6	1.1	34.2		.6	.5
		1.0	1.4	2.2	-1.1	-.5		2.6	1.9
Debt/Worth		.5	.3	.6	.5	.2		.4	.4
		1.7	1.3	1.1	2.2	69.7		1.3	1.2
		10.5	2.8	3.7	-9.8	-2.2		6.0	3.9
% Profit Before Taxes/Tangible Net Worth		48.2	62.3	42.0	67.6	32.5		48.8	40.9
	(17)	14.2	(60) 38.1	(44) 18.6	(13) 24.0	(12) 26.8	(134)	26.4	(125) 19.0
		-9.0	18.7	2.7	7.8	-1.8		6.7	6.9
% Profit Before Taxes/Total Assets		18.8	29.4	20.3	14.5	16.9		19.3	20.1
		4.9	13.5	7.1	9.1	4.0		10.5	9.2
		-2.6	6.2	-1.2	1.2	-.3		2.3	1.6
Sales/Net Fixed Assets		64.2	20.8	17.0	18.9	11.0		21.9	21.7
		34.4	11.9	7.0	12.0	5.2		9.2	8.8
		10.4	5.0	3.6	5.7	3.0		4.6	4.0
Sales/Total Assets		3.4	2.5	1.9	1.6	1.2		2.2	2.3
		2.2	2.0	1.5	1.1	.7		1.6	1.6
		1.0	1.5	1.2	.7	.5		1.0	1.0
% Depr., Dep., Amort./Sales		.3	.9	1.5	2.5	2.8		1.5	1.2
	(11)	.8	(57) 2.1	(48) 2.6	(17) 4.0	(16) 4.0	(138)	2.6	(127) 2.9
		2.3	4.6	5.2	7.0	6.2		4.8	4.6
% Officers', Directors' Owners' Comp/Sales		2.6	2.6					2.9	3.2
	(10)	7.1	(24) 4.6				(34)	5.5	(26) 5.4
		13.2	6.9					9.2	11.5
Net Sales ($)	12702M	62648M	694601M	1982525M	1931196M	3068497M		6560031M	5493474M
Total Assets ($)	3247M	27802M	353900M	1309521M	1454667M	2986068M		5465559M	5010160M

M = $ thousand   MM = $ million
See Pages 9 through 22 for Explanation of Ratios and Data

	Comparative Historical Data				Current Data Sorted by Sales					
Type of Statement										
Unqualified	50	54	50				3	10	37	
Reviewed	22	26	30	1	2		9	14	4	
Compiled	15	23	17		7	1	6	3		
Tax Returns	9	14	14	2	2	3	2	4	1	
Other	82	80	79	1	8	5	11	17	37	
	4/1/08-3/31/09 ALL	4/1/09-3/31/10 ALL	4/1/10-3/31/11 ALL	24 (4/1-9/30/10)	166 (10/1/10-3/31/11)					
				0-1MM	1-3MM	3-5MM	5-10MM	10-25MM	25MM & OVER	
NUMBER OF STATEMENTS	178	197	190	4	19	9	31	48	79	
	%	%	%	%	%	%	%	%	%	
ASSETS										
Cash & Equivalents	11.3	12.2	12.8		10.0		14.2	10.6	13.9	
Trade Receivables (net)	23.4	23.7	23.5		26.7		23.8	25.2	21.5	
Inventory	23.8	22.8	20.8		22.7		21.4	22.6	18.7	
All Other Current	2.3	2.9	2.7		2.4		3.8	1.2	3.2	
Total Current	60.7	61.5	59.7		61.9		63.2	59.6	57.3	
Fixed Assets (net)	20.1	20.4	20.9		17.9		21.8	28.8	18.2	
Intangibles (net)	14.1	11.7	13.1		9.5		6.0	6.9	19.9	
All Other Non-Current	5.0	6.4	6.3		10.8		8.9	4.7	4.6	
Total	100.0	100.0	100.0		100.0		100.0	100.0	100.0	
LIABILITIES										
Notes Payable-Short Term	8.2	8.3	6.3		16.6		3.6	9.1	3.5	
Cur. Mat.-L.T.D.	3.6	3.5	3.6		3.3		4.5	3.6	3.3	
Trade Payables	12.2	10.7	11.1		20.2		10.8	13.9	7.6	
Income Taxes Payable	.3	.3	.2		.5		.0	.1	.2	
All Other Current	10.8	10.4	10.3		8.4		12.0	6.6	12.1	
Total Current	35.1	33.3	31.5		49.0		30.9	33.3	26.8	
Long-Term Debt	17.0	13.6	14.2		11.7		12.5	14.0	15.5	
Deferred Taxes	.7	.9	.7		.1		.1	.1	1.5	
All Other Non-Current	7.5	8.1	8.8		6.2		5.8	5.5	10.7	
Net Worth	39.6	44.1	44.8		33.0		50.7	47.1	45.5	
Total Liabilties & Net Worth	100.0	100.0	100.0		100.0		100.0	100.0	100.0	
INCOME DATA										
Net Sales	100.0	100.0	100.0		100.0		100.0	100.0	100.0	
Gross Profit	44.8	46.0	45.2		45.5		47.0	40.6	46.4	
Operating Expenses	36.6	37.4	37.3		42.9		39.3	32.2	37.3	
Operating Profit	8.2	8.6	7.9		2.6		7.7	8.4	9.0	
All Other Expenses (net)	2.1	2.1	1.7		1.6		.1	1.0	2.4	
Profit Before Taxes	6.2	6.5	6.2		1.1		7.6	7.5	6.6	
RATIOS										
Current	3.4 / 1.9 / 1.2	3.9 / 2.1 / 1.2	3.9 / 2.0 / 1.2		1.9 / 1.2 / .8		4.6 / 2.4 / 1.3	4.0 / 2.2 / 1.1	3.9 / 2.1 / 1.5	
Quick	2.2 / 1.1 / .6	2.2 / 1.1 / .6	2.4 / 1.2 / .6		1.1 / .7 / .5		2.8 / 1.3 / .7	2.3 / 1.4 / .6	2.8 / 1.3 / .8	
Sales/Receivables	38 9.7 / 46 7.9 / 58 6.3	34 10.7 / 44 8.2 / 58 6.3	36 10.2 / 47 7.8 / 58 6.3		26 13.9 / 42 8.8 / 56 6.5		34 10.8 / 43 8.5 / 51 7.2	38 9.5 / 47 7.8 / 54 6.8	39 9.4 / 53 6.9 / 63 5.8	
Cost of Sales/Inventory	60 6.1 / 84 4.4 / 131 2.8	50 7.3 / 90 4.1 / 134 2.7	44 8.3 / 77 4.7 / 120 3.0		6 62.5 / 30 12.3 / 115 3.2		34 10.7 / 56 6.5 / 137 2.7	48 7.6 / 67 5.5 / 106 3.4	56 6.5 / 96 3.8 / 130 2.8	
Cost of Sales/Payables	22 16.8 / 35 10.5 / 56 6.5	19 19.4 / 32 11.5 / 49 7.5	18 20.5 / 32 11.4 / 55 6.7		21 17.0 / 33 11.0 / 72 5.1		13 27.7 / 28 12.9 / 47 7.8	20 18.6 / 37 9.9 / 63 5.8	18 20.3 / 30 12.2 / 50 7.3	
Sales/Working Capital	3.5 / 5.8 / 16.2	3.2 / 6.4 / 19.7	3.2 / 6.3 / 16.1		4.1 / 31.5 / -21.8		3.2 / 6.1 / 12.7	3.7 / 8.1 / 72.1	2.6 / 5.3 / 11.0	
EBIT/Interest	14.2 / (153) 4.3 / 1.8	17.6 / (169) 5.7 / 1.7	24.5 / (168) 6.0 / 1.2		16.5 / (17) 2.0 / -1.8		29.8 / (25) 10.0 / 3.7	30.4 / (43) 9.2 / 2.0	20.0 / (73) 5.2 / .9	
Net Profit + Depr., Dep., Amort./Cur. Mat. L/T/D	14.9 / (52) 3.7 / 1.9	6.3 / (67) 3.3 / 1.6	13.6 / (52) 2.7 / 1.3					14.9 / (10) 2.8 / 1.5	14.2 / (33) 2.8 / 1.4	
Fixed/Worth	.2 / .6 / 6.6	.2 / .5 / 2.3	.2 / .6 / 3.0		.4 / 1.0 / -4.2		.1 / .6 / 1.5	.3 / .6 / 1.8	.1 / .6 / -1.3	
Debt/Worth	.5 / 1.6 / 18.3	.4 / 1.5 / 8.9	.5 / 1.4 / 12.3		.5 / 3.2 / -11.5		.2 / 1.3 / 2.7	.5 / 1.3 / 3.4	.5 / 1.4 / -7.8	
% Profit Before Taxes/Tangible Net Worth	46.2 / (138) 26.7 / 12.5	45.1 / (158) 22.2 / 6.5	49.7 / (150) 27.2 / 8.0		32.8 / (13) 15.1 / -1.1		44.8 / (28) 32.7 / 5.7	63.8 / (44) 37.2 / 16.1	39.9 / (55) 24.0 / 5.7	
% Profit Before Taxes/Total Assets	19.4 / 8.2 / 2.5	21.6 / 8.6 / 1.6	20.3 / 9.3 / 1.1		19.7 / 3.2 / -7.3		26.9 / 9.4 / 4.3	21.8 / 15.1 / 2.9	15.9 / 7.2 / .8	
Sales/Net Fixed Assets	23.1 / 10.1 / 4.6	26.4 / 10.8 / 4.6	27.9 / 10.3 / 4.4		58.4 / 22.2 / 5.6		18.1 / 11.5 / 5.0	22.4 / 8.0 / 3.2	19.6 / 8.9 / 4.1	
Sales/Total Assets	2.5 / 1.6 / 1.0	2.3 / 1.7 / 1.1	2.3 / 1.6 / 1.1		4.5 / 2.5 / 1.0		2.5 / 1.9 / 1.3	2.5 / 1.7 / 1.3	1.8 / 1.4 / .8	
% Depr., Dep., Amort./Sales	.9 / (142) 2.3 / 4.2	1.1 / (155) 2.3 / 4.7	1.1 / (153) 2.6 / 4.7		.7 / (10) 2.9 / 4.8		.6 / (28) 2.2 / 3.4	1.2 / (39) 2.8 / 6.6	1.8 / (67) 3.0 / 4.5	
% Officers', Directors' Owners' Comp/Sales	2.9 / (34) 5.6 / 9.2	2.6 / (39) 5.9 / 9.4	2.4 / (49) 4.4 / 8.4					2.7 / (14) 4.8 / 7.2	2.3 / (17) 3.4 / 7.5	
Net Sales ($)	8755231M	7804768M	7752169M	2233M	36430M	37712M	226374M	766839M	6682581M	
Total Assets ($)	6984919M	5993680M	6135205M	3893M	20631M	23687M	158852M	465501M	5462641M	

M = $ thousand   MM = $ million
See Pages 9 through 22 for Explanation of Ratios and Data

Current Data Sorted by Assets   **Comparative Historical Data**

Type of Statement	0-500M	500M-2MM	2-10MM	10-50MM	50-100MM	100-250MM		4/1/06-3/31/07 ALL	4/1/07-3/31/08 ALL
Unqualified		2	2	15	7	3		32	40
Reviewed		1	18	9				21	22
Compiled		9	7	2				22	21
Tax Returns	5	7	4					10	12
Other	3	7	17	24	5	7		50	49
		21 (4/1-9/30/10)		133 (10/1/10-3/31/11)					
NUMBER OF STATEMENTS	8	26	48	50	12	10		135	144
ASSETS	%	%	%	%	%	%		%	%
Cash & Equivalents		11.9	9.1	12.7	10.9	4.8		8.2	11.5
Trade Receivables (net)		31.7	29.2	22.5	17.4	13.5		29.5	26.6
Inventory		27.1	28.1	23.6	20.3	17.8		24.1	22.7
All Other Current		5.8	1.8	3.1	6.2	2.1		3.1	3.4
Total Current		76.6	68.2	61.8	54.8	38.3		65.0	64.3
Fixed Assets (net)		12.9	20.9	21.5	17.1	26.4		20.5	19.7
Intangibles (net)		5.5	7.4	9.2	25.2	28.0		8.5	10.4
All Other Non-Current		5.0	3.6	7.4	2.9	7.3		6.0	5.7
Total		100.0	100.0	100.0	100.0	100.0		100.0	100.0
LIABILITIES									
Notes Payable-Short Term		13.0	8.0	9.0	6.0	5.2		9.5	8.2
Cur. Mat.-L.T.D.		1.3	4.2	3.1	2.0	3.4		3.5	2.2
Trade Payables		14.2	12.4	10.3	7.0	4.3		12.9	13.8
Income Taxes Payable		.0	.1	.1	.0	.0		.1	.3
All Other Current		8.3	9.9	9.3	9.9	11.7		11.0	8.6
Total Current		36.7	34.7	31.7	25.0	24.7		37.0	33.1
Long-Term Debt		14.0	18.7	9.6	9.8	17.6		15.0	14.1
Deferred Taxes		.1	.4	.5	1.4	2.1		.5	.5
All Other Non-Current		11.8	7.3	5.8	7.0	7.2		3.9	4.7
Net Worth		37.4	38.9	52.4	56.7	48.3		43.5	47.6
Total Liabilties & Net Worth		100.0	100.0	100.0	100.0	100.0		100.0	100.0
INCOME DATA									
Net Sales		100.0	100.0	100.0	100.0	100.0		100.0	100.0
Gross Profit		49.0	45.3	43.7	46.7	38.9		40.6	42.1
Operating Expenses		44.1	37.8	33.2	41.2	26.8		34.6	35.7
Operating Profit		4.9	7.5	10.5	5.6	12.1		5.9	6.4
All Other Expenses (net)		.7	.8	1.2	.8	4.3		1.3	1.4
Profit Before Taxes		4.2	6.7	9.2	4.8	7.8		4.6	5.0
RATIOS									
Current		7.5	3.9	3.3	3.1	3.2		3.2	3.5
		1.8	2.9	2.2	2.1	2.1		1.8	2.2
		1.2	1.2	1.3	1.5	.9		1.2	1.4
Quick		6.0	2.5	2.1	1.7	1.9		1.9	2.0
		1.0	1.2	1.2	1.1	1.1		1.0	1.1
		.6	.7	.6	.8	.4		.6	.7
Sales/Receivables		26 14.3	35 10.4	35 10.4	41 8.9	38 9.6		38 9.6	34 10.7
		47 7.8	48 7.6	47 7.8	49 7.4	47 7.8		49 7.4	45 8.1
		70 5.2	61 5.9	57 6.4	58 6.3	55 6.7		64 5.7	59 6.1
Cost of Sales/Inventory		20 18.0	46 7.9	47 7.7	82 4.5	49 7.4		39 9.4	31 11.8
		50 7.2	63 5.8	77 4.7	107 3.4	64 5.7		71 5.1	65 5.6
		117 3.1	115 3.2	131 2.8	143 2.5	121 3.0		118 3.1	121 3.0
Cost of Sales/Payables		8 45.1	13 29.2	25 14.7	25 14.6	17 21.4		17 20.9	18 20.4
		24 15.5	26 14.2	34 10.7	35 10.6	20 18.0		34 10.8	32 11.5
		63 5.8	45 8.2	46 7.9	43 8.5	28 13.2		50 7.3	52 7.0
Sales/Working Capital		4.7	4.3	3.2	3.1	4.1		4.3	4.0
		6.3	6.8	5.2	4.6	5.9		8.1	6.5
		16.9	17.5	18.5	7.7	-25.1		18.2	19.5
EBIT/Interest		15.0	31.3	20.9	28.6			12.5	15.8
		(23) 4.2	(38) 7.5	(42) 8.0	10.7			(122) 3.6	(126) 4.9
		1.2	2.4	2.3	2.1			1.3	2.1
Net Profit + Depr., Dep., Amort./Cur. Mat. L/T/D				25.3				7.2	9.7
			(12) 3.2					(45) 2.2	(51) 4.0
			1.8					1.1	1.7
Fixed/Worth		.1	.1	.2	.4	.6		.2	.2
		.3	.6	.4	.5	1.7		.6	.5
		2.1	NM	.9	NM	-.7		1.6	1.5
Debt/Worth		.7	.4	.5	.7	.6		.6	.5
		2.3	1.3	1.0	1.1	11.3		1.6	1.3
		12.4	NM	3.0	NM	-3.0		4.3	4.0
% Profit Before Taxes/Tangible Net Worth		41.5	71.9	50.6				41.3	50.6
		(22) 9.6	(36) 27.9	(47) 29.3				(119) 19.2	(123) 23.5
		1.8	9.5	10.3				4.1	8.0
% Profit Before Taxes/Total Assets		21.6	24.5	26.3	12.5	10.7		14.7	19.0
		5.1	11.2	10.2	10.0	3.5		8.0	9.3
		.0	3.8	2.3	1.9	1.5		1.2	2.4
Sales/Net Fixed Assets		128.0	37.7	17.7	14.7	6.0		26.1	32.4
		33.4	18.0	9.8	8.7	3.9		11.9	12.6
		10.1	6.9	5.3	5.3	2.6		5.6	6.4
Sales/Total Assets		3.5	2.9	1.9	1.6	1.3		3.0	2.9
		2.4	2.3	1.6	1.4	.9		2.0	2.0
		1.9	1.9	1.4	.8	.7		1.4	1.3
% Depr., Dep., Amort./Sales		.6	.7	1.4	2.0			.9	.9
		(18) 1.1	(39) 1.6	(43) 2.1	(10) 3.7			(112) 1.8	(115) 1.8
		2.1	2.6	3.8	4.4			3.1	3.5
% Officers', Directors' Owners' Comp/Sales		4.2	2.8					3.9	2.5
		(17) 7.0	(14) 5.4					(43) 5.4	(50) 4.3
		10.4	11.8					10.1	8.2
Net Sales ($)	12115M	77714M	510114M	1919934M	1217415M	1565276M		5409810M	5123530M
Total Assets ($)	2221M	28627M	223120M	1122669M	915317M	1556428M		4048330M	3872816M

Comparative Historical Data				Current Data Sorted by Sales					
			Type of Statement						
34	24	29	Unqualified		1	1	1	5	21
32	31	28	Reviewed	1	1	1	7	11	7
26	16	18	Compiled	1	5	2	5	4	1
27	22	16	Tax Returns	1	7	5	2	1	
72	66	63	Other	1	7	4	7	17	27
4/1/08-3/31/09 ALL	4/1/09-3/31/10 ALL	4/1/10-3/31/11 ALL		21 (4/1-9/30/10)			133 (10/1/10-3/31/11)		
				0-1MM	1-3MM	3-5MM	5-10MM	10-25MM	25MM & OVER
191	159	154	**NUMBER OF STATEMENTS**	4	21	13	22	38	56
%	%	%	**ASSETS**	%	%	%	%	%	%
9.3	11.0	10.9	Cash & Equivalents		11.3	12.6	10.3	11.8	9.8
26.2	28.0	26.6	Trade Receivables (net)		31.9	30.2	31.6	27.1	20.6
25.5	24.1	24.6	Inventory		27.2	23.5	25.7	27.7	22.0
3.0	3.0	3.2	All Other Current		1.6	2.2	2.0	1.6	4.0
64.0	66.1	65.3	Total Current		71.9	68.6	69.7	68.2	56.4
21.1	20.5	19.5	Fixed Assets (net)		16.9	13.6	21.7	22.7	19.8
8.9	8.0	10.1	Intangibles (net)		7.9	9.4	4.8	4.5	17.4
5.9	5.3	5.1	All Other Non-Current		3.3	8.4	3.8	4.6	6.3
100.0	100.0	100.0	Total		100.0	100.0	100.0	100.0	100.0
			LIABILITIES						
9.6	8.4	9.6	Notes Payable-Short Term		17.4	10.4	9.5	6.9	8.3
2.6	3.0	3.0	Cur. Mat.-L.T.D.		1.5	2.7	1.4	6.3	2.1
12.7	14.0	11.5	Trade Payables		13.1	22.4	7.7	12.8	9.2
.2	.2	.1	Income Taxes Payable		.0	.0	.0	.1	.1
11.6	11.5	9.7	All Other Current		7.7	9.2	12.5	8.9	9.7
36.6	37.1	33.9	Total Current		39.8	44.7	31.2	35.0	29.5
14.7	12.1	13.7	Long-Term Debt		17.5	18.3	10.2	18.4	10.3
.2	.5	.6	Deferred Taxes		.0	.3	.6	.4	1.0
7.5	6.5	8.3	All Other Non-Current		4.4	9.1	12.0	5.9	7.2
41.0	43.7	43.6	Net Worth		38.3	27.6	46.1	40.3	52.0
100.0	100.0	100.0	Total Liabilties & Net Worth		100.0	100.0	100.0	100.0	100.0
			INCOME DATA						
100.0	100.0	100.0	Net Sales		100.0	100.0	100.0	100.0	100.0
41.3	43.3	44.6	Gross Profit		47.4	44.6	50.2	46.3	40.9
34.6	35.9	36.7	Operating Expenses		42.4	42.5	43.6	35.8	31.6
6.7	7.4	7.9	Operating Profit		4.9	2.1	6.6	10.5	9.4
1.3	1.2	1.1	All Other Expenses (net)		.7	.7	.4	1.7	1.4
5.4	6.2	6.7	Profit Before Taxes		4.3	1.4	6.1	8.8	8.0
			RATIOS						
3.3	3.4	3.9			8.2	2.5	5.2	3.7	2.9
1.9	2.1	2.3	Current		1.8	1.5	3.3	2.6	2.1
1.1	1.3	1.3			1.2	1.1	1.4	1.3	1.3
2.0	2.2	2.3			6.3	1.4	2.9	2.4	1.7
1.0	1.1	1.1	Quick		1.1	.9	1.8	1.2	1.1
.5	.7	.7			.6	.6	.8	.6	.7
30 12.2	**34** 10.6	**35** 10.4			**8** 46.3	**27** 13.3	**23** 15.8	**39** 9.4	**36** 10.1
41 8.9	**45** 8.1	**47** 7.7	Sales/Receivables		**47** 7.8	**45** 8.1	**45** 8.1	**49** 7.5	**46** 7.9
55 6.7	**63** 5.8	**57** 6.4			**81** 4.5	**50** 7.3	**71** 5.1	**59** 6.1	**55** 6.7
30 12.1	**35** 10.4	**44** 8.3			**0** UND	**22** 16.9	**34** 10.8	**55** 6.7	**48** 7.6
64 5.7	**70** 5.2	**73** 5.0	Cost of Sales/Inventory		**43** 8.4	**56** 6.6	**59** 6.1	**85** 4.3	**74** 4.9
121 3.0	**117** 3.1	**116** 3.1			**122** 3.0	**131** 2.8	**127** 2.9	**128** 2.8	**113** 3.2
17 21.4	**18** 20.8	**17** 21.2			**0** UND	**23** 15.9	**9** 38.7	**23** 16.0	**22** 16.6
29 12.6	**31** 11.9	**28** 13.1	Cost of Sales/Payables		**18** 20.1	**26** 13.9	**19** 19.5	**40** 9.2	**30** 12.1
48 7.6	**52** 7.0	**46** 8.0			**52** 7.0	**77** 4.7	**29** 12.7	**65** 5.6	**40** 9.0
4.4	4.0	3.8			4.6	6.5	3.9	3.5	3.3
7.3	6.7	6.1	Sales/Working Capital		7.3	13.0	6.0	5.1	6.1
43.7	18.3	17.6			21.9	162.3	30.0	16.0	17.0
13.3	24.6	21.7			19.0	5.6	53.5	28.4	28.5
(167) 4.0	(134) 6.3	(130) 5.9	EBIT/Interest		(19) 6.0	2.4	(15) 3.4	(34) 8.0	(48) 8.2
1.4	2.0	1.8			1.4	.8	1.4	2.4	1.8
10.5	13.7	14.3							34.1
(45) 4.1	(41) 4.5	(30) 3.6	Net Profit + Depr., Dep., Amort./Cur. Mat. L/T/D						(18) 4.8
1.6	1.5	2.7							2.9
.2	.2	.2			.1	.1	.1	.2	.3
.6	.5	.5	Fixed/Worth		.4	1.4	.6	.6	.5
2.1	1.4	1.9			1.7	-2.0	-10.2	1.4	1.8
.6	.4	.5			1.0	1.6	.2	.5	.6
1.7	1.2	1.4	Debt/Worth		2.3	3.7	1.1	.9	1.2
11.4	4.7	5.4			5.8	-9.1	-39.5	4.1	4.2
51.3	50.1	48.3			42.1		81.3	50.7	48.4
(157) 22.5	(136) 25.0	(126) 26.0	% Profit Before Taxes/Tangible Net Worth		(19) 26.2		(16) 13.3	(34) 29.8	(46) 31.5
6.6	7.3	8.9			3.7		3.7	12.7	14.3
17.2	23.9	22.7			20.5	6.3	40.0	25.0	22.0
8.8	9.8	8.8	% Profit Before Taxes/Total Assets		6.9	1.9	8.9	11.7	9.5
1.1	1.5	1.9			-.4	-1.2	1.9	5.2	2.3
32.6	28.5	30.8			81.6	99.7	57.4	19.2	17.2
12.5	12.3	12.7	Sales/Net Fixed Assets		27.6	33.9	22.1	10.4	9.8
6.0	5.5	5.8			9.9	14.2	4.7	4.4	5.3
3.3	2.9	2.7			4.3	3.3	3.2	2.6	2.0
2.1	2.1	1.9	Sales/Total Assets		2.7	2.4	2.2	1.9	1.6
1.5	1.5	1.4			1.9	1.7	1.9	1.4	1.2
.9	1.0	1.1			.7	.3	.7	1.4	1.4
(159) 1.7	(132) 1.9	(120) 1.9	% Depr., Dep., Amort./Sales		(16) 1.5	(10) 1.1	(17) 1.7	(34) 2.3	(42) 2.0
3.4	3.6	3.5			2.0	2.1	6.0	4.3	3.9
1.9	2.6	3.7			4.1				
(53) 4.8	(51) 4.4	(39) 6.4	% Officers', Directors' Owners' Comp/Sales		(13) 7.0				
9.8	9.9	10.0			11.9				
6469088M	6258573M	5302568M	Net Sales ($)	2229M	44402M	52042M	164852M	610213M	4428830M
4742981M	4374966M	3848382M	Total Assets ($)	1186M	20603M	23857M	74633M	372307M	3355796M

M = $ thousand MM = $ million

See Pages 9 through 22 for Explanation of Ratios and Data

Current Data Sorted by Assets   Comparative Historical Data

Type of Statement

0-500M	500M-2MM	2-10MM	10-50MM	50-100MM	100-250MM	Type of Statement	4/1/06-3/31/07 ALL	4/1/07-3/31/08 ALL
			1	1	3	Unqualified	6	8
	2	4	2			Reviewed	11	4
		4				Compiled	1	2
2	2	4				Tax Returns	7	2
1	6	3	3		7	Other	11	22
	8 (4/1-9/30/10)		37 (10/1/10-3/31/11)					
3	10	15	6	1	10	NUMBER OF STATEMENTS	36	38
%	%	%	%	%	%	**ASSETS**	%	%
	16.5	6.3			3.9	Cash & Equivalents	10.6	12.6
	34.6	26.3			15.2	Trade Receivables (net)	25.1	24.8
	19.7	18.7			18.1	Inventory	18.1	22.5
	2.1	2.2			1.9	All Other Current	2.6	3.2
	73.0	53.5			39.0	Total Current	56.5	63.1
	11.0	33.5			22.9	Fixed Assets (net)	28.5	22.3
	6.4	9.4			36.8	Intangibles (net)	8.7	12.1
	9.6	3.6			1.3	All Other Non-Current	6.3	2.5
	100.0	100.0			100.0	Total	100.0	100.0
						LIABILITIES		
	13.8	6.1			10.3	Notes Payable-Short Term	10.5	13.2
	1.0	4.2			2.0	Cur. Mat.-L.T.D.	5.0	3.0
	17.2	15.1			5.9	Trade Payables	11.7	8.4
	.0	.5			.0	Income Taxes Payable	.1	.2
	9.1	11.0			7.9	All Other Current	10.5	8.9
	41.1	36.9			26.2	Total Current	37.7	33.8
	10.9	20.3			17.8	Long-Term Debt	19.4	13.7
	.0	1.4			3.2	Deferred Taxes	.6	.7
	.8	2.5			4.0	All Other Non-Current	6.2	5.2
	47.3	38.8			48.8	Net Worth	36.1	46.6
	100.0	100.0			100.0	Total Liabilties & Net Worth	100.0	100.0
						INCOME DATA		
	100.0	100.0			100.0	Net Sales	100.0	100.0
	52.6	44.4			43.4	Gross Profit	47.8	44.3
	49.5	37.8			34.6	Operating Expenses	42.2	36.4
	3.1	6.6			8.8	Operating Profit	5.7	7.9
	.2	1.2			3.5	All Other Expenses (net)	1.2	1.5
	2.8	5.4			5.3	Profit Before Taxes	4.4	6.5
						RATIOS		
	3.4	2.4			2.8	Current	2.8	2.7
	2.2	1.4			1.7		1.6	1.8
	1.2	1.2			1.2		1.1	1.3
	2.6	1.6			1.2	Quick	1.5	1.5
	1.8	1.0			.9		1.0	1.1
	.7	.6			.6		.7	.7
37 9.8	26 13.9			40 9.2		Sales/Receivables	33 11.2	34 10.9
38 9.5	44 8.4			45 8.1			43 8.6	47 7.8
43 8.6	52 7.0			49 7.5			54 6.8	53 6.9
6 62.0	20 18.6			67 5.5		Cost of Sales/Inventory	20 18.1	31 11.9
43 8.6	40 9.2			95 3.9			59 6.2	76 4.8
155 2.4	93 3.9			131 2.8			112 3.3	121 3.0
17 21.0	20 18.2			19 19.4		Cost of Sales/Payables	24 15.2	14 26.4
32 11.5	39 9.4			33 11.0			36 10.1	27 13.5
61 6.0	47 7.7			50 7.3			54 6.7	48 7.6
	3.5	7.8			5.2	Sales/Working Capital	5.0	3.8
	11.3	12.7			7.2		11.5	8.3
	28.8	27.6			17.7		80.9	21.3
		23.7			19.7	EBIT/Interest	26.6	12.2
		9.5			4.6		(34) 3.6	(37) 3.9
		2.9			.3		1.6	2.0
						Net Profit + Depr., Dep., Amort./Cur. Mat. L/T/D	3.6	10.9
							(15) 2.0	(14) 3.8
							.9	1.5
	.1	.4			.7	Fixed/Worth	.4	.2
	.3	1.3			1.2		1.0	.7
	.6	2.0			NM		2.2	1.8
	.3	.8			1.0	Debt/Worth	.7	.9
	1.8	1.9			2.0		1.8	1.4
	6.8	5.7			NM		4.9	4.0
	139.1	99.4				% Profit Before Taxes/Tangible Net Worth	68.3	55.1
	49.3	(13) 34.6					(33) 25.5	(34) 24.3
	-5.8	15.5					10.6	10.3
	28.7	23.0			14.5	% Profit Before Taxes/Total Assets	17.0	16.6
	10.9	9.1			4.7		8.1	9.9
	-1.7	3.3			-1.1		1.9	3.7
	88.2	14.4			17.4	Sales/Net Fixed Assets	17.9	21.0
	46.1	8.5			5.3		8.2	10.2
	16.3	4.0			3.0		3.6	5.2
	4.5	2.7			1.9	Sales/Total Assets	2.7	2.8
	3.2	2.3			1.1		1.9	1.9
	2.1	1.6			.6		1.3	1.2
		1.0			1.3	% Depr., Dep., Amort./Sales	1.3	1.2
	(14)	1.9					(34) 1.8	(34) 1.9
		3.6					4.2	4.3
						% Officers', Directors' Owners' Comp/Sales	3.0	2.4
							(17) 5.3	(12) 5.4
							9.9	9.0
1223M	37782M	154338M	248179M	221571M	1807841M	Net Sales ($)	1044834M	2824284M
589M	11298M	71539M	131336M	51199M	1508212M	Total Assets ($)	697398M	1789806M

M = $ thousand   MM = $ million
See Pages 9 through 22 for Explanation of Ratios and Data

Comparative Historical Data & Current Data Sorted by Sales

Type of Statement	4/1/08-3/31/09 ALL	4/1/09-3/31/10 ALL	4/1/10-3/31/11 ALL	0-1MM	1-3MM	3-5MM	5-10MM	10-25MM	25MM & OVER
Unqualified	9	9	5						5
Reviewed	4	6	8		1		1	4	2
Compiled	2	1	4			1		2	
Tax Returns	5	5	8	1		1	1	1	
Other	22	20	20	3	2	2	2	3	9
					8 (4/1-9/30/10)			37 (10/1/10-3/31/11)	
NUMBER OF STATEMENTS	42	41	45	4	3	4	8	10	16
ASSETS	%	%	%	%	%	%	%	%	%
Cash & Equivalents	10.6	6.8	8.6					5.5	5.0
Trade Receivables (net)	24.2	22.0	26.0					28.5	19.2
Inventory	22.9	27.0	18.7					19.2	21.6
All Other Current	2.4	2.7	2.2					2.3	2.0
Total Current	60.1	58.4	55.6					55.5	47.7
Fixed Assets (net)	22.3	20.1	25.4					31.0	23.8
Intangibles (net)	13.0	16.3	14.6					9.6	26.3
All Other Non-Current	4.7	5.3	4.3					3.8	2.1
Total	100.0	100.0	100.0					100.0	100.0
LIABILITIES									
Notes Payable-Short Term	9.2	10.4	10.4					7.8	10.2
Cur. Mat.-L.T.D.	9.4	2.6	3.7					4.7	2.7
Trade Payables	10.8	9.1	13.3					20.5	7.8
Income Taxes Payable	.2	.3	.2					.0	.0
All Other Current	12.1	10.7	9.8					8.9	11.2
Total Current	41.8	33.2	37.5					41.9	31.9
Long-Term Debt	22.0	13.7	18.7					19.9	13.7
Deferred Taxes	.8	.5	1.2					.0	2.2
All Other Non-Current	3.9	2.8	3.2					2.4	5.8
Net Worth	31.4	49.7	39.4					35.8	46.4
Total Liabilities & Net Worth	100.0	100.0	100.0					100.0	100.0
INCOME DATA									
Net Sales	100.0	100.0	100.0					100.0	100.0
Gross Profit	46.0	45.5	44.2					41.0	41.9
Operating Expenses	39.2	40.9	39.9					34.1	37.4
Operating Profit	6.8	4.6	4.3					6.9	4.5
All Other Expenses (net)	2.1	1.4	1.4					1.6	2.0
Profit Before Taxes	4.7	3.2	2.9					5.2	2.6
RATIOS									
Current	3.2	2.7	2.6					1.5	3.1
	1.9	1.7	1.7					1.3	1.7
	1.2	1.4	1.2					1.2	1.2
Quick	1.4	1.4	1.7					1.1	1.2
	1.1	.8	1.0					.9	1.0
	.7	.6	.7					.6	.7
Sales/Receivables	30 12.2	30 12.3	37 9.9					26 13.9	41 8.9
	39 9.4	41 8.9	43 8.4					37 9.9	45 8.1
	45 8.1	50 7.2	49 7.4					50 7.3	49 7.5
Cost of Sales/Inventory	45 8.1	59 6.2	20 18.6					20 18.6	65 5.6
	81 4.5	98 3.7	64 5.7					40 9.2	95 3.9
	151 2.4	142 2.6	118 3.1					72 5.1	140 2.6
Cost of Sales/Payables	16 23.0	16 23.0	17 21.1					34 10.8	16 23.3
	31 11.9	30 12.2	30 12.0					46 8.0	30 12.2
	48 7.7	58 6.3	52 7.0					66 5.6	68 5.3
Sales/Working Capital	4.5	6.2	5.7					11.1	4.7
	8.4	8.1	12.0					18.3	8.6
	24.5	14.3	24.5					29.1	19.3
EBIT/Interest	11.1	11.9	15.7					22.4	12.7
	(41) 3.1	(38) 4.8	(42) 7.2					8.3	6.8
	.8	1.2	1.3					2.5	.7
Net Profit + Depr., Dep., Amort./Cur. Mat. L/T/D	10.7	4.1	7.0						
	(12) 3.8	(14) 2.2	(12) 3.3						
	.9	1.5	.5						
Fixed/Worth	.2	.2	.3					.7	.5
	.7	.6	.9					1.3	1.1
	2.5	1.2	2.0					2.3	2.8
Debt/Worth	.8	.8	.9					1.6	1.0
	1.5	1.2	1.7					3.1	1.4
	NM	3.3	5.5					6.0	5.2
% Profit Before Taxes/Tangible Net Worth	66.7	55.5	74.1						77.3
	(32) 12.2	(37) 24.5	(39) 34.6					(13)	32.0
	.1	5.9	8.7						12.9
% Profit Before Taxes/Total Assets	13.3	17.6	16.8					21.4	14.7
	4.8	7.5	8.4					11.3	9.4
	-.9	.8	-.8					6.6	-.1
Sales/Net Fixed Assets	19.8	26.0	36.1					15.5	29.4
	11.7	11.4	9.5					9.0	5.5
	5.3	5.2	3.9					5.2	3.1
Sales/Total Assets	2.9	2.8	3.2					3.8	2.0
	2.0	1.9	1.9					2.4	1.4
	1.2	1.1	1.4					1.7	.7
% Depr., Dep., Amort./Sales	1.6	.9	1.0						1.1
	(34) 2.1	(33) 2.5	(34) 2.3					(12)	2.6
	3.3	3.9	4.1						4.0
% Officers', Directors' Owners' Comp/Sales	1.5								
	(10) 5.1								
	7.1								
Net Sales ($)	3171281M	2551656M	2470934M	2094M	4681M	16599M	55000M	131945M	2260615M
Total Assets ($)	1609088M	1806568M	1774173M	1241M	2055M	6151M	26397M	63848M	1674481M

M = $ thousand   MM = $ million
See Pages 9 through 22 for Explanation of Ratios and Data

Current Data Sorted by Assets   Comparative Historical Data

0-500M	500M-2MM	2-10MM	10-50MM	50-100MM	100-250MM	Type of Statement	4/1/06-3/31/07 ALL	4/1/07-3/31/08 ALL
			2	2	3	Unqualified	9	9
		4	1			Reviewed	7	5
	2	2				Compiled	6	6
	2					Tax Returns	2	2
	5	2	4	3	2	Other	10	15
	7 (4/1-9/30/10)		27 (10/1/10-3/31/11)					
	9	8	7	5	5	NUMBER OF STATEMENTS	34	37
%	%	%	%	%	%	**ASSETS**	%	%
						Cash & Equivalents	10.8	7.9
						Trade Receivables (net)	22.7	24.3
						Inventory	21.3	25.5
						All Other Current	3.3	3.1
						Total Current	58.1	60.7
						Fixed Assets (net)	20.1	20.4
						Intangibles (net)	10.5	9.7
						All Other Non-Current	11.3	9.3
						Total	100.0	100.0
						LIABILITIES		
						Notes Payable-Short Term	8.7	7.6
						Cur. Mat.-L.T.D.	3.6	3.8
						Trade Payables	15.7	16.6
						Income Taxes Payable	.2	.1
						All Other Current	8.8	11.3
						Total Current	37.0	39.5
						Long-Term Debt	17.7	20.5
						Deferred Taxes	.3	.8
						All Other Non-Current	11.5	2.6
						Net Worth	33.5	36.6
						Total Liabilities & Net Worth	100.0	100.0
						INCOME DATA		
						Net Sales	100.0	100.0
						Gross Profit	44.7	43.8
						Operating Expenses	37.9	36.5
						Operating Profit	6.8	7.3
						All Other Expenses (net)	1.7	1.3
						Profit Before Taxes	5.2	6.0
						RATIOS		
						Current	2.2	2.4
							1.6	1.6
							1.0	1.0
						Quick	1.4	1.1
							.8	.7
							.5	.5
						Sales/Receivables	24 15.1	31 11.7
							43 8.5	44 8.4
							57 6.4	51 7.1
						Cost of Sales/Inventory	27 13.6	32 11.5
							75 4.8	86 4.2
							115 3.2	136 2.7
						Cost of Sales/Payables	25 14.8	26 14.1
							43 8.4	46 8.0
							80 4.5	85 4.3
						Sales/Working Capital	7.2	4.9
							14.4	9.5
							NM	NM
						EBIT/Interest	10.1	9.7
							(32) 4.0	(35) 3.6
							1.5	1.2
						Net Profit + Depr., Dep., Amort./Cur. Mat. L/T/D		38.0
								(13) 3.6
								1.5
						Fixed/Worth	.2	.2
							.5	.8
							2.0	2.9
						Debt/Worth	.7	1.0
							1.9	2.0
							5.8	9.7
						% Profit Before Taxes/Tangible Net Worth	54.1	53.0
							(29) 17.6	(31) 20.1
							5.2	3.5
						% Profit Before Taxes/Total Assets	12.4	16.2
							6.2	6.0
							1.3	1.0
						Sales/Net Fixed Assets	61.2	54.7
							13.8	11.3
							6.1	6.2
						Sales/Total Assets	3.6	3.4
							2.1	2.0
							1.4	1.2
						% Depr., Dep., Amort./Sales	.7	.8
							(29) 2.1	(30) 2.1
							2.9	3.6
						% Officers', Directors' Owners' Comp/Sales		
	34741M	106394M	259745M	396033M	1334714M	Net Sales ($)	1503789M	2063753M
	10393M	43143M	170996M	384631M	804167M	Total Assets ($)	1122330M	1561789M

(Left-side asset columns: DATA NOT AVAILABLE)

© RMA 2011

M = $ thousand   MM = $ million
See Pages 9 through 22 for Explanation of Ratios and Data

Comparative Historical Data				Current Data Sorted by Sales					
			Type of Statement						
11	14	7	Unqualified					1	6
4	3	5	Reviewed				3	2	
3	4	4	Compiled		1		1	2	
2	3	2	Tax Returns		1	1			
11	12	16	Other		3	1	3	1	8
					7 (4/1-9/30/10)		27 (10/1/10-3/31/11)		
4/1/08-3/31/09 ALL	4/1/09-3/31/10 ALL	4/1/10-3/31/11 ALL		0-1MM	1-3MM	3-5MM	5-10MM	10-25MM	25MM & OVER
31	36	34	**NUMBER OF STATEMENTS**		5	2	7	6	14
%	%	%	**ASSETS**	%	%	%	%	%	%
7.6	7.8	7.2	Cash & Equivalents	DATA NOT AVAILABLE					9.1
20.7	23.2	24.2	Trade Receivables (net)						18.7
26.6	21.5	24.0	Inventory						22.2
2.9	3.8	2.7	All Other Current						4.6
57.8	56.3	58.1	Total Current						54.7
22.6	21.6	20.2	Fixed Assets (net)						21.2
9.3	14.0	13.4	Intangibles (net)						17.9
10.3	8.1	8.3	All Other Non-Current						6.2
100.0	100.0	100.0	Total						100.0
			LIABILITIES						
10.7	8.0	6.6	Notes Payable-Short Term						2.3
4.0	3.7	3.4	Cur. Mat.-L.T.D.						3.1
15.8	16.3	18.4	Trade Payables						14.8
.3	.4	.1	Income Taxes Payable						.1
6.3	9.6	8.2	All Other Current						8.2
37.0	38.0	36.6	Total Current						28.6
15.7	14.7	16.7	Long-Term Debt						14.2
.8	.5	.9	Deferred Taxes						1.7
3.0	7.9	4.6	All Other Non-Current						4.8
43.4	38.8	41.2	Net Worth						50.7
100.0	100.0	100.0	Total Liabilties & Net Worth						100.0
			INCOME DATA						
100.0	100.0	100.0	Net Sales						100.0
47.0	44.9	43.0	Gross Profit						39.6
38.6	38.4	34.9	Operating Expenses						31.6
8.3	6.5	8.0	Operating Profit						8.0
1.1	1.3	1.5	All Other Expenses (net)						1.0
7.2	5.1	6.5	Profit Before Taxes						6.9
			RATIOS						
3.0	2.7	2.5							2.7
1.4	1.4	1.6	Current						1.7
1.1	1.1	1.2							1.4
1.3	1.3	1.4							1.3
.7	.8	.8	Quick						.9
.4	.5	.6							.6
26 13.8	**30** 12.1	**33** 11.2							**33** 11.2
40 9.0	**39** 9.5	**43** 8.6	Sales/Receivables						**45** 8.1
49 7.5	**45** 8.1	**49** 7.5							**55** 6.6
27 13.6	**34** 10.8	**31** 11.8							**58** 6.3
97 3.7	**81** 4.5	**76** 4.8	Cost of Sales/Inventory						**94** 3.9
156 2.3	**126** 2.9	**136** 2.7							**144** 2.5
28 13.2	**25** 14.9	**26** 14.0							**34** 10.8
46 7.9	**41** 8.9	**60** 6.1	Cost of Sales/Payables						**65** 5.6
84 4.4	**67** 5.5	**80** 4.5							**91** 4.0
5.9	4.6	4.3							3.4
9.7	12.1	9.6	Sales/Working Capital						4.7
56.9	67.5	26.0							11.7
13.5	15.9	12.9							68.6
(27) 2.2	(35) 2.5	(32) 4.8	EBIT/Interest						12.5
1.1	1.0	1.5							3.5
3.8	8.8	6.7							
(13) 2.2	(13) 3.1	(12) 2.5	Net Profit + Depr., Dep., Amort./Cur. Mat. L/T/D						
.9	.6	1.2							
.2	.3	.3							.3
.7	.7	.6	Fixed/Worth						.6
1.0	4.0	2.9							NM
.8	.7	.6							.6
1.4	1.8	1.5	Debt/Worth						1.2
4.9	16.3	15.9							NM
50.4	38.1	38.8							38.8
(27) 17.6	(29) 10.4	(27) 18.0	% Profit Before Taxes/Tangible Net Worth						(11) 15.6
3.9	-1.0	6.4							8.3
17.4	12.9	11.8							12.6
7.3	4.0	8.0	% Profit Before Taxes/Total Assets						8.8
1.5	.1	2.4							4.5
24.3	34.9	48.0							53.0
9.0	12.7	15.9	Sales/Net Fixed Assets						9.5
4.7	5.1	6.2							4.1
2.4	3.1	2.7							2.3
1.9	1.6	1.9	Sales/Total Assets						1.4
1.4	.9	1.2							1.1
1.3	1.2	.7							.9
(25) 2.1	(28) 2.0	(25) 2.2	% Depr., Dep., Amort./Sales						(10) 2.3
3.9	3.0	3.3							3.1
		3.1							
		(11) 4.9	% Officers', Directors' Owners' Comp/Sales						
		6.3							
1795085M	**1769103M**	**2131627M**	Net Sales ($)		**10312M**	**8186M**	**52419M**	**103949M**	**1956761M**
1246214M	**1339203M**	**1413330M**	Total Assets ($)		**5779M**	**3067M**	**50793M**	**58323M**	**1295368M**

M = $ thousand MM = $ million

See Pages 9 through 22 for Explanation of Ratios and Data

Current Data Sorted by Assets   **Comparative Historical Data**

0-500M	500M-2MM	2-10MM	10-50MM	50-100MM	100-250MM	Type of Statement	4/1/06-3/31/07 ALL	4/1/07-3/31/08 ALL
		1	1	1		Unqualified	3	1
		1	1			Reviewed	9	3
3		1				Compiled	9	6
15	6					Tax Returns	16	9
4	3	1			2	Other	17	14
		7 (4/1-9/30/10)		33 (10/1/10-3/31/11)				
22	9	4	2	1	2	**NUMBER OF STATEMENTS**	54	33
%	%	%	%	%	%	**ASSETS**	%	%
17.6						Cash & Equivalents	13.1	11.1
18.0						Trade Receivables (net)	24.5	25.9
2.3						Inventory	7.8	9.2
3.7						All Other Current	4.8	2.0
41.5						Total Current	50.2	48.2
41.5						Fixed Assets (net)	28.1	34.1
9.2						Intangibles (net)	13.4	3.2
7.7						All Other Non-Current	8.3	14.4
100.0						Total	100.0	100.0
						LIABILITIES		
16.9						Notes Payable-Short Term	7.5	16.3
9.2						Cur. Mat.-L.T.D.	6.5	4.6
14.6						Trade Payables	10.8	9.8
.0						Income Taxes Payable	.2	.5
13.6						All Other Current	7.8	9.1
54.2						Total Current	32.8	40.3
24.6						Long-Term Debt	24.2	17.5
.1						Deferred Taxes	.8	1.3
4.9						All Other Non-Current	5.5	1.6
16.2						Net Worth	36.8	39.2
100.0						Total Liabilities & Net Worth	100.0	100.0
						INCOME DATA		
100.0						Net Sales	100.0	100.0
						Gross Profit		
96.1						Operating Expenses	92.9	92.6
3.9						Operating Profit	7.1	7.4
.7						All Other Expenses (net)	1.4	1.5
3.2						Profit Before Taxes	5.7	5.9
						RATIOS		
2.6							3.0	2.5
.7						Current	1.6	1.6
.2							1.3	.7
2.0							2.5	2.0
.5						Quick	1.4	1.3
.2							.8	.4
0 UND							25 14.4	24 15.1
0 UND						Sales/Receivables	36 10.2	35 10.3
35 10.5							42 8.8	41 9.0
						Cost of Sales/Inventory		
						Cost of Sales/Payables		
36.6							7.8	10.7
-40.4						Sales/Working Capital	16.4	19.8
-9.4							28.0	-14.1
7.9							12.6	11.8
(15) 3.4						EBIT/Interest	(49) 3.5	(31) 6.1
.5							1.4	1.1
							2.7	4.8
						Net Profit + Depr., Dep., Amort./Cur. Mat. L/T/D	(11) 1.8	(10) 2.3
							1.6	1.8
.6							.4	.5
3.0						Fixed/Worth	1.0	.9
-2.5							5.0	1.9
.5							.8	.7
5.8						Debt/Worth	2.5	1.7
-4.1							18.9	5.0
288.8							82.5	74.6
(14) 98.6						% Profit Before Taxes/Tangible Net Worth	(43) 27.5	(30) 30.1
32.0							14.3	7.5
37.0							28.7	27.6
11.5						% Profit Before Taxes/Total Assets	7.8	10.5
-.7							2.1	1.0
44.5							31.8	23.9
22.6						Sales/Net Fixed Assets	12.3	12.4
5.4							6.3	5.9
6.4							4.0	4.0
4.4						Sales/Total Assets	2.7	3.2
3.5							1.3	1.9
1.1							1.4	1.2
(15) 1.8						% Depr., Dep., Amort./Sales	(41) 2.5	(29) 1.8
2.8							3.9	3.4
4.0							5.3	6.6
(16) 5.4						% Officers', Directors' Owners' Comp/Sales	(30) 7.1	(22) 12.6
15.2							12.5	17.2
38632M	34503M	52394M	106330M	221571M	255952M	Net Sales ($)	2107905M	591272M
6570M	9564M	20187M	49489M	51199M	327328M	Total Assets ($)	564854M	377354M

© RMA 2011

M = $ thousand   MM = $ million
See Pages 9 through 22 for Explanation of Ratios and Data

Comparative Historical Data   Current Data Sorted by Sales

			Type of Statement	0-1MM	1-3MM	3-5MM	5-10MM	10-25MM	25MM & OVER
2	2	3	Unqualified					1	2
3	2	2	Reviewed					1	1
10	5	4	Compiled		3			1	
15	17	21	Tax Returns	7	8	3	3	1	
10	19	10	Other	2	3	1	1	1	2
4/1/08-3/31/09 ALL	4/1/09-3/31/10 ALL	4/1/10-3/31/11 ALL		7 (4/1-9/30/10)		33 (10/1/10-3/31/11)			
40	45	40	**NUMBER OF STATEMENTS**	9	14	4	4	4	5
%	%	%	**ASSETS**	%	%	%	%	%	%
18.2	13.7	15.1	Cash & Equivalents		10.3				
21.2	27.0	23.6	Trade Receivables (net)		34.3				
6.3	7.1	4.2	Inventory		4.6				
2.5	3.9	3.1	All Other Current		4.0				
48.2	51.6	46.0	Total Current		53.3				
31.3	29.2	35.2	Fixed Assets (net)		21.1				
8.5	7.5	10.4	Intangibles (net)		9.1				
12.1	11.7	8.4	All Other Non-Current		16.5				
100.0	100.0	100.0	Total		100.0				
			LIABILITIES						
22.6	12.9	12.4	Notes Payable-Short Term		23.7				
3.0	4.8	8.0	Cur. Mat.-L.T.D.		12.2				
8.8	8.7	13.4	Trade Payables		22.8				
.4	.4	.4	Income Taxes Payable		.0				
9.0	10.4	12.1	All Other Current		10.4				
43.9	37.3	46.3	Total Current		69.2				
22.6	27.4	25.1	Long-Term Debt		15.3				
.8	.4	.5	Deferred Taxes		.2				
1.9	3.2	6.0	All Other Non-Current		10.7				
30.9	31.7	22.1	Net Worth		4.7				
100.0	100.0	100.0	Total Liabilities & Net Worth		100.0				
			INCOME DATA						
100.0	100.0	100.0	Net Sales		100.0				
			Gross Profit						
94.9	93.7	95.6	Operating Expenses		96.9				
5.1	6.3	4.4	Operating Profit		3.1				
1.2	.9	1.7	All Other Expenses (net)		.3				
3.9	5.5	2.6	Profit Before Taxes		2.9				
			RATIOS						
2.3	3.4	2.2	Current		1.6				
1.4	1.5	1.1			.8				
1.1	.8	.5			.5				
1.9	2.6	1.7	Quick		1.0				
1.1	1.1	.9			.6				
.8	.6	.5			.5				
0 UND	1 309.9	0 UND	Sales/Receivables		0 UND				
32 11.3	35 10.5	33 10.9			35 10.4				
42 8.8	40 9.0	41 9.0			43 8.5				
			Cost of Sales/Inventory						
			Cost of Sales/Payables						
14.1	8.2	14.1	Sales/Working Capital		20.2				
27.7	31.2	74.5			-43.9				
479.2	-56.3	-12.7			-10.3				
21.9	24.2	9.8	EBIT/Interest		9.1				
(36) 3.6	(37) 5.0	(30) 3.5			(12) 3.3				
.1	1.7	.6			.8				
2.0			Net Profit + Depr., Dep., Amort./Cur. Mat. L/T/D						
(10) 1.1									
.5									
.3	.3	.6	Fixed/Worth		.4				
.7	1.0	3.0			3.3				
4.0	UND	NM			-2.2				
.6	.4	.8	Debt/Worth		2.7				
1.4	3.7	6.7			22.1				
6.5	UND	-5.9			-4.1				
58.8	109.6	172.8	% Profit Before Taxes/Tangible Net Worth						
(35) 24.8	(35) 52.2	(29) 43.1							
2.7	19.7	17.8							
28.8	36.1	30.8	% Profit Before Taxes/Total Assets		21.1				
8.0	12.9	11.5			5.3				
-1.1	3.0	.5			-6.8				
42.0	51.7	40.0	Sales/Net Fixed Assets		55.2				
16.1	18.2	16.7			33.0				
7.6	6.5	6.1			11.5				
6.1	5.5	5.2	Sales/Total Assets		5.7				
3.9	3.6	3.9			4.0				
2.2	2.2	2.5			3.3				
1.3	1.2	1.1	% Depr., Dep., Amort./Sales		.7				
(30) 2.0	(31) 1.8	(29) 2.0			(11) 2.0				
3.3	3.6	3.3			2.8				
6.1	5.0	4.1	% Officers', Directors' Owners' Comp/Sales		4.0				
(23) 8.2	(30) 8.6	(24) 6.5			(11) 5.9				
14.3	13.5	10.3			9.6				
1452494M	421439M	709382M	Net Sales ($)	4974M	27140M	15555M	25466M	52394M	583853M
509397M	270208M	464337M	Total Assets ($)	2798M	6620M	2945M	3771M	20187M	428016M

M = $ thousand   MM = $ million
See Pages 9 through 22 for Explanation of Ratios and Data

Current Data Sorted by Assets   Comparative Historical Data

						Type of Statement		
2	3	2 23	11 6	6	1	Unqualified	32	25
2	6	8				Reviewed	53	46
6	14	8			1	Compiled	12	14
3	10	8 23	8	6	1	Tax Returns	16	17
						Other	36	32
	31 (4/1-9/30/10)		119 (10/1/10-3/31/11)				4/1/06- 3/31/07	4/1/07- 3/31/08
0-500M	500M-2MM	2-10MM	10-50MM	50-100MM	100-250MM		ALL	ALL
13	33	64	25	12	3	NUMBER OF STATEMENTS	149	134
%	%	%	%	%	%	ASSETS	%	%
7.5	10.9	12.3	7.5	4.6		Cash & Equivalents	6.0	5.8
28.7	28.0	25.7	25.4	14.2		Trade Receivables (net)	28.0	27.7
23.7	31.0	35.9	46.3	38.9		Inventory	48.7	47.1
.8	1.6	1.9	1.5	1.2		All Other Current	1.2	1.8
60.7	71.6	75.9	80.6	58.9		Total Current	83.9	82.4
11.3	20.1	17.7	11.1	23.5		Fixed Assets (net)	9.4	10.2
11.9	1.2	1.6	2.0	11.0		Intangibles (net)	2.8	1.9
16.1	7.2	4.9	6.2	6.6		All Other Non-Current	3.9	5.6
100.0	100.0	100.0	100.0	100.0		Total	100.0	100.0
						LIABILITIES		
14.1	11.8	11.5	17.8	16.5		Notes Payable-Short Term	27.5	25.7
.4	3.6	1.9	1.8	2.6		Cur. Mat.-L.T.D.	1.9	2.4
13.7	23.1	16.3	12.0	8.9		Trade Payables	17.9	18.7
.0	.2	.1	.1	1.5		Income Taxes Payable	.3	.5
21.8	8.3	10.2	11.1	14.1		All Other Current	6.3	7.8
50.1	47.0	40.0	42.7	43.6		Total Current	53.8	55.1
13.9	15.3	12.1	7.0	15.1		Long-Term Debt	7.0	5.8
.0	.2	.5	1.0	.3		Deferred Taxes	.4	.3
16.1	5.7	3.7	.6	1.6		All Other Non-Current	3.6	5.2
19.8	31.7	43.8	48.7	39.5		Net Worth	35.2	33.6
100.0	100.0	100.0	100.0	100.0		Total Liabilties & Net Worth	100.0	100.0
						INCOME DATA		
100.0	100.0	100.0	100.0	100.0		Net Sales	100.0	100.0
41.6	45.1	35.1	24.8	29.4		Gross Profit	27.0	27.4
45.1	39.7	30.3	18.8	23.1		Operating Expenses	22.2	23.6
-3.5	5.4	4.8	6.0	6.3		Operating Profit	4.9	3.8
-.1	1.0	.4	.9	4.0		All Other Expenses (net)	1.6	1.2
-3.4	4.3	4.4	5.1	2.3		Profit Before Taxes	3.3	2.6
						RATIOS		
7.8	2.6	3.2	3.7	1.7			2.1	2.0
1.5	1.6	1.9	1.7	1.4	Current	1.4	1.4
.7	1.0	1.3	1.4	1.1		1.2	1.2
3.9	1.9	1.5	1.3	.7		1.0	1.0
1.1	.8	.8	.7	.5	Quick	(148) .6	.6
.6	.4	.6	.4	.2		.4	.3

											Sales/Receivables				
0	UND	21	17.6	31	11.9	35	10.3	17	21.2			29	12.6	24	15.0
19	19.3	31	11.9	50	7.3	54	6.7	47	7.7			55	6.6	48	7.6
43	8.4	61	6.0	75	4.8	78	4.7	75	4.9			78	4.7	82	4.5

											Cost of Sales/Inventory				
0	UND	7	50.8	40	9.1	59	6.2	74	4.9			74	4.9	58	6.3
28	13.1	69	5.3	92	4.0	148	2.5	175	2.1			137	2.7	116	3.1
76	4.8	170	2.1	196	1.9	272	1.3	265	1.4			227	1.6	225	1.6

											Cost of Sales/Payables				
0	UND	22	16.6	16	22.2	8	46.0	24	15.4			12	29.6	11	34.2
6	64.6	39	9.3	37	9.8	26	14.1	40	9.2			39	9.3	40	9.2
32	11.5	118	3.1	84	4.3	48	7.6	70	5.3			81	4.5	81	4.5

0-500M	500M-2MM	2-10MM	10-50MM	50-100MM		Ratio	ALL	ALL
7.5	4.4	3.2	2.0	6.4			3.8	3.8
24.5	10.5	5.7	5.9	8.5	Sales/Working Capital	7.2	7.9
UND	NM	14.2	9.7	15.4		13.8	17.2
	5.6	15.6	18.6	21.6		4.5	4.9
	(28) 3.7	(58) 5.0	(23) 4.7	4.5	EBIT/Interest	(138) 2.0	(123) 1.9
	1.6	1.6	2.1	1.4		1.3	1.1
		5.8				Net Profit + Depr., Dep.,	10.4	14.1
		(16) 2.5			Amort./Cur. Mat. L/T/D	(28) 3.4	(20) 3.6
		-.1				1.5	.8
.0	.1	.1	.1	.2		.1	.1
.2	.5	.3	.2	.8	Fixed/Worth	.2	.2
NM	2.8	.8	.4	1.5		.5	.5
.2	.8	.6	.3	1.2		1.2	1.2
2.2	2.7	1.4	1.8	2.8	Debt/Worth	2.3	2.3
-3.2	8.6	2.9	2.3	5.4		4.7	4.6
	61.1	40.0	36.7	57.7	% Profit Before Taxes/Tangible	31.3	28.7
	(29) 27.8	(60) 13.2	13.5	(11) 19.6	Net Worth	(137) 11.4	(128) 8.7
	6.7	3.9	5.2	6.2		3.1	1.1
32.0	11.3	17.5	12.5	11.3	% Profit Before Taxes/Total	7.9	8.1
-7.7	5.2	4.8	7.7	5.2	Assets	3.2	2.5
-18.0	3.0	1.2	1.4	.7		.7	.3
UND	58.1	55.9	44.1	51.6		122.7	133.7
227.4	23.9	21.3	20.9	7.8	Sales/Net Fixed Assets	34.4	40.8
21.0	7.9	7.5	11.8	3.4		12.3	14.6
6.3	3.6	2.5	2.7	1.5		2.4	2.6
4.8	2.4	1.8	1.4	1.2	Sales/Total Assets	1.6	1.8
2.0	2.0	1.3	.9	.9		1.2	1.2
	.7	.4	.4	1.2		.3	.2
	(26) 1.7	(47) .8	(23) .8	(11) 2.8	% Depr., Dep., Amort./Sales	(130) .8	(111) .7
	3.9	2.7	2.2	9.6		1.3	1.2
	3.5	1.7			% Officers', Directors'	1.3	1.1
	(22) 4.5	(32) 3.1			Owners' Comp/Sales	(79) 2.3	(69) 2.7
	8.6	6.3				5.5	6.4
13357M	89271M	616702M	825501M	1072304M	1025300M	Net Sales ($)	5486358M	5586316M
2696M	35847M	309636M	526010M	833233M	598605M	Total Assets ($)	3659601M	2894524M

M = $ thousand   MM = $ million
See Pages 9 through 22 for Explanation of Ratios and Data

Comparative Historical Data | | | | Current Data Sorted by Sales

			Type of Statement						
28	33	20	Unqualified				1	7	12
36	36	34	Reviewed	1	3	5	8	11	6
15	20	16	Compiled	1	5	6	1	3	
25	43	29	Tax Returns	8	8	6	4	2	1
68	62	51	Other	2	8	11	9	10	11
4/1/08-3/31/09 ALL	4/1/09-3/31/10 ALL	4/1/10-3/31/11 ALL		0-1MM	1-3MM	3-5MM	5-10MM	10-25MM	25MM & OVER
					31 (4/1-9/30/10)			119 (10/1/10-3/31/11)	
172	194	150	NUMBER OF STATEMENTS	12	24	28	23	33	30
%	%	%	ASSETS	%	%	%	%	%	%
7.2	8.8	10.1	Cash & Equivalents	9.2	11.8	12.2	9.5	10.9	6.4
23.9	25.6	25.4	Trade Receivables (net)	29.6	26.8	21.8	26.0	25.7	25.3
43.0	37.9	35.9	Inventory	24.5	32.6	34.6	35.2	40.1	40.2
1.5	1.0	1.6	All Other Current	.8	1.6	1.6	3.3	.9	1.5
75.6	73.3	73.0	Total Current	64.1	72.8	70.2	74.0	77.6	73.4
14.2	18.0	17.1	Fixed Assets (net)	16.2	15.9	19.9	20.0	14.1	17.1
2.5	1.9	3.2	Intangibles (net)	11.9	1.0	2.0	1.6	4.3	2.9
7.7	6.8	6.6	All Other Non-Current	7.8	10.3	7.9	4.4	4.1	6.7
100.0	100.0	100.0	Total	100.0	100.0	100.0	100.0	100.0	100.0
			LIABILITIES						
23.9	18.1	13.5	Notes Payable-Short Term	3.8	16.8	9.4	12.0	16.3	16.5
3.1	3.4	2.2	Cur. Mat.-L.T.D.	.1	2.9	3.0	2.1	2.0	1.9
14.2	16.6	16.1	Trade Payables	14.3	22.5	21.2	14.4	10.7	14.0
.5	.1	.2	Income Taxes Payable	.1	.0	.0	.3	.1	.6
14.0	11.0	11.2	All Other Current	21.3	10.5	8.1	13.4	9.2	10.9
55.6	49.2	43.1	Total Current	39.7	52.6	41.8	42.2	38.3	44.0
10.4	11.4	12.2	Long-Term Debt	18.9	11.3	13.9	13.4	11.8	8.4
.3	.2	.4	Deferred Taxes	.1	.2	.7	.3	.7	.3
3.7	5.0	4.9	All Other Non-Current	14.0	7.9	5.7	4.0	1.0	3.0
30.0	34.1	39.4	Net Worth	27.3	27.9	38.0	40.1	48.2	44.4
100.0	100.0	100.0	Total Liabilities & Net Worth	100.0	100.0	100.0	100.0	100.0	100.0
			INCOME DATA						
100.0	100.0	100.0	Net Sales	100.0	100.0	100.0	100.0	100.0	100.0
33.2	33.2	35.8	Gross Profit	48.8	39.8	42.5	38.1	30.5	24.9
29.2	30.5	31.2	Operating Expenses	50.4	35.8	39.7	32.2	24.5	18.5
3.9	2.7	4.6	Operating Profit	-1.6	4.0	2.8	6.0	6.0	6.4
1.6	1.2	.9	All Other Expenses (net)	.8	.3	.4	.9	1.6	1.0
2.4	1.5	3.7	Profit Before Taxes	-2.4	3.7	2.5	5.1	4.4	5.4
			RATIOS						
2.3	2.9	3.0	Current	7.9	2.5	2.8	2.7	4.5	1.9
1.5	1.6	1.7		2.9	1.5	1.7	2.0	1.8	1.5
1.1	1.1	1.2		1.2	.9	1.1	1.1	1.4	1.3
1.0	1.5	1.4	Quick	4.4	1.4	1.1	1.3	2.3	1.2
.5	.7	.8		1.7	.8	.7	.8	1.0	.7
.4	.4	.5		.6	.4	.4	.6	.5	.4
18 20.5	30 12.2	25 14.5	Sales/Receivables	14 25.8	17 20.9	14 25.5	43 8.5	31 11.7	29 12.6
40 9.1	48 7.5	43 8.5		55 6.7	36 10.1	28 13.2	63 5.8	48 7.6	48 7.7
62 5.9	70 5.2	72 5.1		162 2.3	59 6.2	46 8.0	84 4.3	66 5.5	62 5.9
51 7.1	35 10.3	33 10.9	Cost of Sales/Inventory	0 UND	7 50.3	9 41.4	68 5.4	50 7.3	52 7.0
114 3.2	92 4.0	92 4.0		54 6.8	61 5.9	83 4.4	101 3.6	106 3.5	83 4.4
236 1.5	212 1.7	195 1.9		365 1.0	188 1.9	188 1.9	208 1.8	190 1.9	236 1.5
9 40.8	14 25.6	14 25.4	Cost of Sales/Payables	0 UND	17 21.8	25 14.6	22 16.5	8 47.2	14 26.0
25 14.5	31 11.8	32 11.5		23 16.2	35 10.5	44 8.3	45 8.1	25 14.7	26 14.1
58 6.3	61 6.0	75 4.9		139 2.6	132 2.8	99 3.7	83 4.4	50 7.2	51 7.2
3.9	3.5	3.4	Sales/Working Capital	1.3	3.2	3.8	4.3	2.7	4.4
8.1	6.8	7.7		3.7	8.2	9.4	7.1	6.5	8.2
37.1	27.9	19.1		77.4	UND	46.8	11.2	13.1	14.8
5.4	7.7	11.8	EBIT/Interest		7.1	3.9	18.2	15.6	30.1
(157) 2.2	(170) 2.0	(131) 4.0			(19) 3.6	(25) 3.1	(22) 6.0	(30) 7.1	(29) 5.5
.9	-.2	1.6			1.1	1.3	1.4	2.4	3.7
7.7	5.9	7.9	Net Profit + Depr., Dep., Amort./Cur. Mat. L/T/D						
(31) 2.3	(30) 1.3	(30) 2.4							
.6	.1	.7							
.1	.1	.1	Fixed/Worth	.0	.0	.1	.1	.1	.1
.2	.3	.3		.1	.6	.3	.5	.2	.3
.8	1.1	1.0		.9	-1.2	2.2	1.0	.6	.7
.8	.7	.7	Debt/Worth	.4	.7	.8	.6	.4	1.0
1.9	1.7	1.9		2.0	2.0	2.3	1.8	1.3	1.9
3.8	6.8	3.7		14.3	-16.6	4.4	3.5	3.0	3.0
31.5	32.7	39.7	% Profit Before Taxes/Tangible Net Worth	28.3	78.0	37.7	56.5	38.6	46.9
(158) 8.4	(171) 8.8	(137) 14.3		(10) 2.2	(17) 12.5	(27) 7.5	(22) 17.4	(31) 18.6	18.3
.4	-.4	4.0		-18.4	.5	1.5	3.4	6.7	10.7
10.7	11.5	13.3	% Profit Before Taxes/Total Assets	8.1	18.8	4.6	21.6	17.2	13.9
3.0	2.5	5.1		.8	6.5	2.8	6.0	6.5	8.4
-.1	-3.1	1.2		-15.7	.2	.6	1.1	2.1	3.9
98.5	74.0	61.2	Sales/Net Fixed Assets	UND	221.1	57.1	36.8	46.9	87.3
31.3	21.0	23.2		23.6	45.3	22.0	10.1	19.5	20.2
10.7	7.4	7.7		8.6	8.4	11.0	4.8	8.6	8.5
3.0	2.8	2.8	Sales/Total Assets	2.6	3.5	3.6	2.0	2.9	3.1
1.9	1.8	1.9		1.1	2.3	2.2	1.8	2.3	1.5
1.2	1.2	1.2		.5	.9	1.4	1.3	1.4	1.1
.3	.5	.5	% Depr., Dep., Amort./Sales		.6	.7	.3	.5	.4
(141) 1.0	(165) 1.2	(114) 1.1			(13) 1.8	(23) 1.1	(18) 1.2	(28) 1.0	(26) .8
1.8	2.8	3.0			4.3	3.7	2.6	3.0	2.4
1.7	1.4	1.7	% Officers', Directors' Owners' Comp/Sales		3.3	3.5	.9	1.6	
(82) 3.4	(97) 3.5	(71) 3.8			(16) 6.4	(18) 4.6	(11) 2.9	(16) 2.0	
6.3	5.6	7.8			11.8	5.9	4.5	3.7	
4749716M	3721836M	3642435M	Net Sales ($)	6130M	48816M	110202M	163066M	535709M	2778512M
2658158M	2174498M	2306027M	Total Assets ($)	6069M	31161M	64000M	121238M	390320M	1693239M

M = $ thousand   MM = $ million
See Pages 9 through 22 for Explanation of Ratios and Data

Current Data Sorted by Assets   **Comparative Historical Data**

0-500M	500M-2MM	2-10MM	10-50MM	50-100MM	100-250MM	Type of Statement	4/1/06-3/31/07 ALL	4/1/07-3/31/08 ALL
				1		Unqualified	3	3
		8				Reviewed	9	11
	1					Compiled	2	4
	1					Tax Returns	2	1
1	1	4	6			Other	7	3
		5 (4/1-9/30/10)	18 (10/1/10-3/31/11)					
1	3	12	7			**NUMBER OF STATEMENTS**	23	22
%	%	%	%	%	%	**ASSETS**	%	%
		14.1				Cash & Equivalents	11.1	14.8
		34.3		D	D	Trade Receivables (net)	34.3	33.8
		28.6		A	A	Inventory	24.7	30.0
		4.4		T	T	All Other Current	1.7	1.0
		81.4		A	A	Total Current	71.7	79.6
		11.8				Fixed Assets (net)	16.1	11.7
		1.9		N	N	Intangibles (net)	7.3	4.0
		4.9		O	O	All Other Non-Current	4.9	4.6
		100.0		T	T	Total	100.0	100.0
				A	A	**LIABILITIES**		
		12.7		V	V	Notes Payable-Short Term	12.7	19.0
		1.6		A	A	Cur. Mat.-L.T.D.	2.5	1.4
		16.9		I	I	Trade Payables	18.4	16.6
		.1		L	L	Income Taxes Payable	.2	.0
		11.4		A	A	All Other Current	7.0	9.2
		42.7		B	B	Total Current	40.9	46.2
		7.3		L	L	Long-Term Debt	10.4	4.9
		.2		E	E	Deferred Taxes	.0	.3
		6.5				All Other Non-Current	3.0	30.3
		43.3				Net Worth	45.7	18.2
		100.0				Total Liabilities & Net Worth	100.0	100.0
						INCOME DATA		
		100.0				Net Sales	100.0	100.0
		40.9				Gross Profit	41.6	35.6
		36.3				Operating Expenses	32.9	31.9
		4.5				Operating Profit	8.7	3.6
		-.4				All Other Expenses (net)	.7	.5
		4.9				Profit Before Taxes	7.9	3.1
						RATIOS		
		3.0					3.5	3.1
		2.2				Current	2.2	2.0
		1.4					1.2	1.1
		1.8					2.0	1.9
		1.2				Quick	1.0	.9
		.6					.8	.8
		36 10.1					24 15.2 26 14.0	
		61 6.0				Sales/Receivables	47 7.8 50 7.2	
		81 4.5					72 5.1 71 5.1	
		27 13.4					18 20.2 28 13.0	
		103 3.5				Cost of Sales/Inventory	57 6.4 57 6.4	
		159 2.3					86 4.3 124 2.9	
		32 11.5					12 30.7 16 22.3	
		42 8.7				Cost of Sales/Payables	48 7.6 30 12.1	
		64 5.7					56 6.6 44 8.3	
		3.8					5.1	5.4
		6.5				Sales/Working Capital	7.7	8.4
		11.0					32.0	23.7
							19.6	9.5
						EBIT/Interest	(22) 8.4 (21) 2.7	
							3.8	.3
						Net Profit + Depr., Dep., Amort./Cur. Mat. L/T/D		
		.1					.1	.1
		.2				Fixed/Worth	.4	.2
		.6					.9	.5
		1.0					.4	.5
		1.3				Debt/Worth	1.6	1.6
		2.4					6.4	3.8
		66.3					87.1	94.2
		(11) 19.6				% Profit Before Taxes/Tangible Net Worth	(19) 33.9 (20) 17.6	
		.2					14.8	-3.3
		29.7					32.7	34.0
		8.2				% Profit Before Taxes/Total Assets	17.8	8.6
		-5.0					7.6	-2.2
		36.0					45.3	76.2
		23.2				Sales/Net Fixed Assets	23.0	34.2
		10.6					17.7	14.6
		2.4					3.4	3.8
		2.1				Sales/Total Assets	2.3	2.7
		1.6					1.9	1.9
							.5	.4
						% Depr., Dep., Amort./Sales	(21) .6 (19) .6	
							2.4	1.2
							2.4	2.3
						% Officers', Directors' Owners' Comp/Sales	(11) 4.1 (12) 4.7	
							7.1	8.1
1705M	10624M	124953M	441650M			Net Sales ($)	376280M	450803M
282M	2953M	57087M	196672M			Total Assets ($)	161476M	208636M

Comparative Historical Data | Current Data Sorted by Sales

					Type of Statement		0-1MM	1-3MM	3-5MM	5-10MM	10-25MM	25MM & OVER
	3		3		1	Unqualified						1
	11		6		8	Reviewed				3		5
	5		4		1	Compiled			1			
	2		1		1	Tax Returns		1				
	5		7		12	Other		1	1	3	2	5
	4/1/08-3/31/09 ALL		4/1/09-3/31/10 ALL		4/1/10-3/31/11 ALL			5 (4/1-9/30/10)			18 (10/1/10-3/31/11)		
	26		21		23	NUMBER OF STATEMENTS		2	2	6	8	5
	%		%		%	ASSETS	%	%	%	%	%	%
	9.3		14.5		12.3	Cash & Equivalents						
	30.3		33.1		38.0	Trade Receivables (net)						
	32.3		29.9		24.4	Inventory						
	2.4		4.2		2.9	All Other Current						
	74.2		81.8		77.6	Total Current						
	14.2		9.9		11.1	Fixed Assets (net)						
	3.4		1.7		5.9	Intangibles (net)						
	8.1		6.6		5.4	All Other Non-Current						
	100.0		100.0		100.0	Total						
						LIABILITIES						
	17.0		16.8		14.4	Notes Payable-Short Term						
	4.8		3.0		2.5	Cur. Mat.-L.T.D.						
	18.2		16.9		16.9	Trade Payables						
	.0		.1		.1	Income Taxes Payable						
	9.7		9.6		11.2	All Other Current						
	49.8		46.3		45.0	Total Current						
	12.8		6.6		5.5	Long-Term Debt						
	.3		.0		.1	Deferred Taxes						
	6.5		8.8		7.7	All Other Non-Current						
	30.6		38.3		41.7	Net Worth						
	100.0		100.0		100.0	Total Liabilties & Net Worth						
						INCOME DATA						
	100.0		100.0		100.0	Net Sales						
	38.0		37.7		38.6	Gross Profit						
	34.8		31.8		32.6	Operating Expenses						
	3.2		5.8		6.0	Operating Profit						
	1.2		.2		.6	All Other Expenses (net)						
	2.0		5.7		5.4	Profit Before Taxes						
						RATIOS						
	2.7		3.4		2.8	Current						
	1.7		1.9		1.5							
	1.1		1.2		1.2							
	1.3		2.1		1.6	Quick						
	.7		1.0		1.0							
	.4		.5		.7							
28	12.9	33	11.0	41	9.0	Sales/Receivables						
38	9.6	57	6.4	53	6.8							
57	6.4	70	5.2	78	4.7							
27	13.5	25	14.8	21	17.3	Cost of Sales/Inventory						
57	6.4	66	5.5	61	6.0							
123	3.0	133	2.7	137	2.7							
27	13.7	21	17.7	30	12.0	Cost of Sales/Payables						
37	9.7	31	11.7	41	9.0							
55	6.7	68	5.4	56	6.5							
	5.0		3.1		4.4	Sales/Working Capital						
	8.5		6.0		10.2							
	34.0		19.4		17.4							
	12.5		18.2		13.9	EBIT/Interest						
	2.2	(18)	4.5	(19)	4.9							
	.7		1.3		1.4							
						Net Profit + Depr., Dep., Amort./Cur. Mat. L/T/D						
	.1		.1		.1	Fixed/Worth						
	.3		.2		.3							
	.8		.6		.7							
	.9		.8		1.0	Debt/Worth						
	2.6		1.7		1.4							
	6.6		4.1		3.9							
	77.0		53.6		65.0	% Profit Before Taxes/Tangible Net Worth						
(22)	16.9	(19)	13.2	(19)	31.9							
	3.2		5.8		5.3							
	20.9		24.4		28.8	% Profit Before Taxes/Total Assets						
	4.3		7.3		10.7							
	.1		2.1		1.5							
	102.3		120.9		60.1	Sales/Net Fixed Assets						
	23.8		35.6		35.1							
	13.7		15.2		11.9							
	3.7		3.3		2.7	Sales/Total Assets						
	2.8		2.3		2.2							
	1.9		1.6		1.7							
	.4		.2		.6	% Depr., Dep., Amort./Sales						
(24)	.8	(17)	.9	(17)	1.1							
	2.2		1.5		1.4							
	2.3		1.1		2.2	% Officers', Directors' Owners' Comp/Sales						
(14)	3.3	(12)	4.2	(10)	3.4							
	5.4		6.9		6.6							
	604524M		333210M		578932M	Net Sales ($)		4144M	7062M	42112M	122295M	403319M
	302129M		147855M		256994M	Total Assets ($)		1199M	3801M	21255M	60545M	170194M

M = $ thousand   MM = $ million
See Pages 9 through 22 for Explanation of Ratios and Data

Current Data Sorted by Assets   Comparative Historical Data

0-500M	500M-2MM	2-10MM	10-50MM	50-100MM	100-250MM	Type of Statement	4/1/06-3/31/07 ALL	4/1/07-3/31/08 ALL
		8	25	4	3	Unqualified	45	41
	1	16	8			Reviewed	31	34
2	3	8	3	1		Compiled	24	17
4	7	11				Tax Returns	20	14
5	14	30	19	13	7	Other	63	61
	32 (4/1-9/30/10)		160 (10/1/10-3/31/11)					
11	25	73	55	18	10	NUMBER OF STATEMENTS	183	167
%	%	%	%	%	%	**ASSETS**	%	%
22.5	14.3	6.3	10.0	4.5	5.6	Cash & Equivalents	5.6	6.8
19.5	21.0	22.5	21.1	27.3	13.7	Trade Receivables (net)	25.1	24.1
31.4	39.1	42.3	36.7	27.8	16.5	Inventory	39.6	39.2
.0	3.4	3.8	3.5	4.4	4.2	All Other Current	2.9	3.0
73.3	77.7	74.8	71.4	64.1	40.0	Total Current	73.1	73.1
18.5	15.9	15.3	13.4	8.9	7.2	Fixed Assets (net)	14.9	13.3
5.6	3.5	4.3	9.3	20.4	37.5	Intangibles (net)	5.7	6.7
2.5	2.9	5.6	5.9	6.6	15.3	All Other Non-Current	6.3	6.9
100.0	100.0	100.0	100.0	100.0	100.0	Total	100.0	100.0
						LIABILITIES		
21.4	20.8	14.1	9.6	2.7	1.0	Notes Payable-Short Term	17.6	19.3
8.9	1.4	2.8	5.4	1.2	2.0	Cur. Mat.-L.T.D.	2.4	2.9
21.8	10.1	14.5	11.6	13.0	6.9	Trade Payables	13.4	13.5
.2	.0	.2	.4	.4	.5	Income Taxes Payable	.3	.6
8.9	7.2	11.0	9.8	17.2	6.6	All Other Current	9.4	10.9
61.2	39.6	42.5	36.7	34.5	17.0	Total Current	43.1	47.1
12.4	11.8	9.7	8.6	27.9	24.5	Long-Term Debt	10.3	13.1
.0	.0	.2	.5	1.5	2.7	Deferred Taxes	.3	.3
48.4	24.8	5.7	8.0	7.8	8.1	All Other Non-Current	7.2	7.5
-21.9	23.8	41.8	46.2	28.3	47.7	Net Worth	39.1	32.0
100.0	100.0	100.0	100.0	100.0	100.0	Total Liabilities & Net Worth	100.0	100.0
						INCOME DATA		
100.0	100.0	100.0	100.0	100.0	100.0	Net Sales	100.0	100.0
47.7	46.8	36.1	34.5	34.9	39.8	Gross Profit	35.1	36.5
42.4	38.1	31.3	28.5	30.6	30.9	Operating Expenses	30.1	30.5
5.4	8.7	4.8	6.1	4.3	8.9	Operating Profit	5.0	6.0
1.0	1.6	1.0	.8	6.0	2.5	All Other Expenses (net)	1.4	1.8
4.4	7.1	3.8	5.2	-1.6	6.4	Profit Before Taxes	3.7	4.2
						RATIOS		
9.4	4.2	2.7	4.8	3.8	3.0	Current	2.9	3.0
1.4	2.1	1.8	1.9	1.9	2.2		1.9	1.7
.8	1.4	1.3	1.2	1.4	1.6		1.3	1.1
6.6	2.0	1.2	2.8	1.4	1.3	Quick	1.4	1.4
.6	1.0	.6	.8	1.0	1.1		.8	.6
.2	.5	.4	.4	.5	.7		.4	.4
0 UND	20 18.6	26 13.9	32 11.4	47 7.8	32 11.6	Sales/Receivables	26 14.0	24 15.0
18 20.1	28 12.9	34 10.6	43 8.5	61 6.0	47 7.8		41 8.9	41 8.9
25 14.5	51 7.1	49 7.5	59 6.2	91 4.0	69 5.3		62 5.9	62 5.9
0 UND	58 6.3	79 4.6	88 4.1	78 4.7	68 5.4	Cost of Sales/Inventory	71 5.2	73 5.0
23 15.6	127 2.9	108 3.4	117 3.1	109 3.3	114 3.2		97 3.7	110 3.3
92 4.0	192 1.9	154 2.4	164 2.2	159 2.3	144 2.5		148 2.5	167 2.2
0 UND	13 27.9	15 24.0	15 23.8	23 15.9	24 15.2	Cost of Sales/Payables	18 20.8	13 27.3
7 51.5	28 13.1	30 12.1	27 13.5	42 8.7	37 9.8		29 12.5	28 13.2
44 8.4	50 7.3	50 7.2	41 9.0	75 4.9	58 6.3		45 8.1	52 7.1
6.4	3.7	4.2	2.8	2.7	2.8	Sales/Working Capital	4.0	4.0
32.8	5.0	5.8	4.7	5.3	4.6		6.9	8.1
-19.4	10.1	14.0	17.3	8.8	16.3		14.6	23.3
	23.6	12.1	18.0	23.7	11.8	EBIT/Interest	8.5	8.9
	(21) 6.0	(64) 5.3	(48) 4.6	(16) .9	2.7		(168) 3.1	(149) 3.0
	3.0	1.4	1.8	-.9	1.9		1.0	1.1
		28.3	5.0			Net Profit + Depr., Dep.,	7.3	11.8
		(14) 5.0	(15) 1.7			Amort./Cur. Mat. L/T/D	(46) 2.4	(46) 2.1
		1.8	.3				1.0	.4
.2	.1	.1	.1	.1	.2	Fixed/Worth	.1	.1
.7	.3	.3	.3	NM	.8		.4	.3
-.1	NM	1.1	1.5	-.1	-.2		1.1	1.6
.4	.4	.5	.3	.9	.8	Debt/Worth	.7	.7
6.8	1.8	1.3	1.3	NM	11.2		1.8	2.3
-1.9	-12.3	4.8	9.1	-3.3	-2.4		4.9	10.6
	92.2	32.7	42.9			% Profit Before Taxes/Tangible	40.2	46.6
	(18) 60.3	(65) 17.4	(46) 20.9	(10) 2.1		Net Worth	(161) 14.2	(134) 18.9
	17.8	6.2	10.4				2.4	4.3
36.3	26.3	16.6	12.4	6.5	8.1	% Profit Before Taxes/Total	16.8	15.7
9.4	14.5	7.4	7.9	1.9	6.8	Assets	6.6	6.6
-9.9	4.1	1.4	2.5	-5.2	3.7		.3	.7
86.3	77.9	60.6	43.8	58.3	24.1	Sales/Net Fixed Assets	52.3	55.7
41.3	25.1	21.0	15.2	21.5	12.8		21.0	22.3
7.8	8.2	10.3	7.7	11.7	9.2		8.8	10.0
7.2	2.4	2.6	2.1	1.6	1.3	Sales/Total Assets	2.9	2.8
5.8	2.1	2.1	1.6	1.4	.9		2.1	2.0
3.6	1.7	1.7	1.3	1.2	.7		1.5	1.4
	.4	.6	1.2	1.3		% Depr., Dep., Amort./Sales	.7	.7
	(12) 1.0	(60) 1.3	(47) 2.2	(10) 2.1			(150) 1.4	(132) 1.5
	4.5	2.4	3.4	5.2			2.2	2.6
	4.5	4.5				% Officers', Directors'	2.6	3.1
	(11) 5.6	(28) 4.1				Owners' Comp/Sales	(43) 4.2	(41) 5.6
	7.2	7.6					7.1	10.8
17319M	69800M	792096M	2157971M	1863135M	1974698M	Net Sales ($)	5878327M	5142252M
3471M	29555M	355689M	1301383M	1321840M	1963989M	Total Assets ($)	3512663M	3262106M

© RMA 2011

M = $ thousand   MM = $ million
See Pages 9 through 22 for Explanation of Ratios and Data

Comparative Historical Data   Current Data Sorted by Sales

Type of Statement									
	39	34	40	Unqualified			3	14	23
	29	31	25	Reviewed		1	3	7	10	4
	16	14	17	Compiled		4	2	5	4	2
	22	23	22	Tax Returns	2	6	5	7	2	
	90	94	88	Other	5	11	5	13	18	36

	4/1/08-3/31/09 ALL	4/1/09-3/31/10 ALL	4/1/10-3/31/11 ALL	0-1MM	1-3MM	3-5MM	5-10MM	10-25MM	25MM & OVER
				32 (4/1-9/30/10)	160 (10/1/10-3/31/11)				
NUMBER OF STATEMENTS	196	196	192	7	22	15	35	48	65
ASSETS	%	%	%	%	%	%	%	%	%
Cash & Equivalents	7.6	8.0	9.1		18.9	6.4	6.8	8.2	7.3
Trade Receivables (net)	21.7	21.9	21.7		19.9	17.8	20.1	23.5	23.0
Inventory	40.0	33.4	37.0		33.8	45.4	40.9	41.4	31.4
All Other Current	3.1	3.2	3.5		2.5	1.1	4.2	3.4	4.2
Total Current	72.5	66.5	71.3		75.1	70.6	71.9	76.6	66.0
Fixed Assets (net)	13.9	16.4	14.0		17.2	16.2	16.4	12.8	10.8
Intangibles (net)	7.8	10.5	8.9		4.6	8.3	5.0	5.2	16.4
All Other Non-Current	5.8	6.6	5.8		3.1	4.9	6.8	5.3	6.8
Total	100.0	100.0	100.0		100.0	100.0	100.0	100.0	100.0
LIABILITIES									
Notes Payable-Short Term	17.7	15.6	12.4		21.6	23.9	12.6	11.8	7.0
Cur. Mat.-L.T.D.	2.9	2.7	3.5		4.5	2.2	3.8	2.5	4.1
Trade Payables	13.8	12.0	13.0		16.1	12.1	12.1	13.2	13.4
Income Taxes Payable	.5	.2	.2		.1	.0	.2	.3	.4
All Other Current	10.4	10.3	10.4		11.2	5.7	10.3	10.5	12.1
Total Current	45.4	40.8	39.5		53.5	43.8	39.0	38.4	36.9
Long-Term Debt	13.0	18.2	12.3		15.8	11.7	13.4	7.1	14.5
Deferred Taxes	.3	.4	.5		.0	.1	.2	.3	1.2
All Other Non-Current	9.4	8.9	11.6		20.5	4.3	6.8	4.5	9.5
Net Worth	32.0	31.7	36.1		10.1	40.1	40.6	49.8	37.8
Total Liabilities & Net Worth	100.0	100.0	100.0		100.0	100.0	100.0	100.0	100.0
INCOME DATA									
Net Sales	100.0	100.0	100.0		100.0	100.0	100.0	100.0	100.0
Gross Profit	35.5	38.0	37.8		45.1	38.9	39.9	32.3	35.5
Operating Expenses	32.6	33.9	31.9		36.6	34.4	34.4	27.1	29.7
Operating Profit	2.9	4.1	5.9		8.5	4.4	5.5	5.2	5.7
All Other Expenses (net)	1.9	2.6	1.6		1.9	1.6	1.1	.7	2.4
Profit Before Taxes	1.0	1.4	4.3		6.7	2.9	4.4	4.5	3.3
RATIOS									
Current	3.3 / 1.7 / 1.2	3.3 / 1.7 / 1.2	3.7 / 1.9 / 1.3		3.3 / 1.7 / 1.0	2.4 / 1.7 / 1.3	2.6 / 1.8 / 1.3	4.2 / 2.1 / 1.5	3.6 / 1.9 / 1.2
Quick	1.4 / .7 / .4	1.5 / .8 / .4	1.6 / .8 / .4		2.3 / .8 / .2	1.1 / .4 / .3	1.1 / .6 / .4	1.8 / .8 / .5	1.5 / .9 / .5
Sales/Receivables	22 16.4 / 37 9.9 / 56 6.5	24 15.4 / 41 9.0 / 58 6.3	26 14.1 / 40 9.2 / 57 6.4	7 50.2 / 22 17.0 / 47 7.8	27 13.5 / 32 11.4 / 46 8.0	24 15.4 / 33 11.1 / 50 7.3	25 14.3 / 35 10.5 / 51 7.1	39 9.3 / 48 7.5 / 68 5.4
Cost of Sales/Inventory	75 4.8 / 112 3.3 / 161 2.3	65 5.6 / 98 3.7 / 146 2.5	69 5.3 / 109 3.4 / 156 2.5	25 14.6 / 73 5.0 / 163 2.2	101 3.6 / 157 2.3 / 240 1.5	85 4.3 / 126 2.9 / 161 2.3	66 5.5 / 94 3.9 / 148 2.5	80 4.5 / 107 3.4 / 134 2.7
Cost of Sales/Payables	16 23.0 / 30 12.1 / 50 7.2	14 26.4 / 29 12.5 / 45 8.1	16 22.5 / 29 12.4 / 48 7.6	8 45.6 / 25 14.4 / 45 8.2	20 18.0 / 34 10.8 / 63 5.8	14 25.3 / 29 12.7 / 51 7.2	12 31.6 / 27 13.5 / 40 9.1	22 16.4 / 34 10.6 / 53 6.9
Sales/Working Capital	3.8 / 7.0 / 17.7	3.7 / 6.4 / 21.6	3.4 / 5.7 / 14.3		4.2 / 7.5 / NM	4.3 / 6.6 / 13.8	4.2 / 5.7 / 13.7	3.2 / 5.3 / 13.7	3.3 / 5.5 / 19.3
EBIT/Interest	6.5 / (179) 1.9 / .0	9.6 / (176) 2.3 / -.2	16.4 / (166) 4.6 / 1.4	15.3 / (19) 5.1 / 2.1	7.9 / (13) 2.3 / .3	10.7 / (29) 5.8 / 1.1	24.0 / (42) 7.6 / 2.8	16.0 / (59) 3.1 / 1.5
Net Profit + Depr., Dep., Amort./Cur. Mat. L/T/D	5.9 / (38) 1.7 / .4	3.9 / (38) 1.7 / .0	11.1 / (38) 2.6 / .8					25.2 / (11) 4.2 / 1.7	31.4 / (20) 2.6 / .3
Fixed/Worth	.1 / .4 / 1.7	.1 / .4 / NM	.1 / .3 / 3.6		.1 / .9 / -.5	.2 / .3 / .9	.1 / .3 / 2.0	.1 / .2 / .9	.2 / .4 / -1.7
Debt/Worth	.7 / 1.9 / 11.8	.6 / 1.9 / -63.2	.4 / 1.5 / 17.8		.4 / 8.2 / -2.8	.5 / 1.3 / 5.9	.6 / 1.3 / 5.4	.4 / 1.0 / 2.3	.5 / 4.1 / -9.2
% Profit Before Taxes/Tangible Net Worth	36.7 / (157) 13.0 / -3.7	33.3 / (146) 12.7 / -2.9	43.5 / (151) 20.0 / 8.6	86.3 / (14) 63.6 / 17.8	36.4 / (13) 6.0 / -9.9	31.5 / (30) 17.7 / 5.6	43.7 / (44) 20.3 / 9.6	38.9 / (45) 20.0 / 9.9
% Profit Before Taxes/Total Assets	10.8 / 3.2 / -2.4	11.4 / 3.6 / -3.0	15.7 / 7.4 / 1.7	35.9 / 15.3 / .0	5.6 / 2.0 / -2.6	16.8 / 9.4 / .9	16.4 / 10.0 / 2.5	9.8 / 6.1 / 2.3
Sales/Net Fixed Assets	48.5 / 21.8 / 8.9	49.3 / 15.8 / 7.4	54.3 / 19.3 / 9.0	64.1 / 38.1 / 9.1	46.1 / 10.6 / 6.6	49.7 / 19.8 / 7.5	65.6 / 22.9 / 10.9	54.5 / 16.5 / 9.0
Sales/Total Assets	2.6 / 1.8 / 1.4	2.5 / 1.7 / 1.3	2.4 / 1.9 / 1.3	5.9 / 2.2 / 1.7	2.0 / 1.7 / 1.4	2.6 / 2.1 / 1.6	2.9 / 2.0 / 1.5	2.1 / 1.5 / 1.2
% Depr., Dep., Amort./Sales	.8 / (150) 1.5 / 2.7	1.0 / (138) 2.1 / 3.4	.9 / (142) 1.8 / 3.2	.7 / (12) 1.5 / 3.0	.5 / 1.4 / 3.4	1.1 / (26) 1.8 / 3.2	.9 / (37) 1.3 / 2.6	1.0 / (50) 2.2 / 3.3
% Officers', Directors' Owners' Comp/Sales	1.9 / (48) 4.5 / 8.0	2.3 / (42) 4.5 / 7.7	2.0 / (52) 4.3 / 7.4	3.9 / (11) 5.6 / 9.1			1.5 / (17) 4.2 / 7.2	2.4 / (13) 4.1 / 8.1	
Net Sales ($)	6999057M	7755975M	6875019M	4400M	44858M	61024M	264581M	806815M	5693341M
Total Assets ($)	4317975M	5458449M	4975927M	3386M	21890M	38182M	153457M	454893M	4304119M

M = $ thousand   MM = $ million
See Pages 9 through 22 for Explanation of Ratios and Data

Current Data Sorted by Assets   Comparative Historical Data

0-500M	500M-2MM	2-10MM	10-50MM	50-100MM	100-250MM	Type of Statement	4/1/06-3/31/07 ALL	4/1/07-3/31/08 ALL
		1	5		1	Unqualified	19	15
		16	5			Reviewed	9	8
1	1	2				Compiled	3	2
	3	1				Tax Returns	2	4
2	2	6	9	2	3	Other	15	18
	7 (4/1-9/30/10)		53 (10/1/10-3/31/11)					
3	6	26	19	3	3	NUMBER OF STATEMENTS	48	47
%	%	%	%	%	%	**ASSETS**	%	%
		11.6	7.9			Cash & Equivalents	5.2	12.2
		29.8	27.2			Trade Receivables (net)	32.4	27.0
		34.9	28.0			Inventory	34.8	33.5
		2.2	2.4			All Other Current	1.9	2.9
		78.5	65.6			Total Current	74.4	75.6
		12.6	19.7			Fixed Assets (net)	12.0	13.3
		1.4	8.7			Intangibles (net)	8.8	7.6
		7.5	5.9			All Other Non-Current	4.9	3.5
		100.0	100.0			Total	100.0	100.0
						LIABILITIES		
		12.0	13.0			Notes Payable-Short Term	26.5	16.0
		2.7	1.5			Cur. Mat.-L.T.D.	5.0	6.2
		17.7	16.1			Trade Payables	17.4	14.4
		.0	.2			Income Taxes Payable	.1	.1
		11.2	9.6			All Other Current	9.4	11.0
		43.6	40.5			Total Current	58.5	47.8
		8.7	6.2			Long-Term Debt	11.3	10.1
		.2	.7			Deferred Taxes	.4	.8
		7.5	3.6			All Other Non-Current	5.8	6.7
		40.0	49.1			Net Worth	24.1	34.7
		100.0	100.0			Total Liabilities & Net Worth	100.0	100.0
						INCOME DATA		
		100.0	100.0			Net Sales	100.0	100.0
		37.7	32.2			Gross Profit	36.5	36.4
		33.6	27.3			Operating Expenses	34.1	32.1
		4.1	5.0			Operating Profit	2.3	4.3
		.0	1.1			All Other Expenses (net)	2.2	1.5
		4.0	3.8			Profit Before Taxes	.1	2.8
						RATIOS		
		2.9	2.4			Current	2.1	3.1
		1.7	1.4				1.5	2.0
		1.3	1.1				1.0	1.2
		2.0	1.3			Quick	1.2	1.7
		1.0	.6				.7	.9
		.6	.4				.4	.5
		36 10.2	46 7.9			Sales/Receivables	39 9.3	28 12.8
		52 7.1	64 5.7				65 5.6	49 7.4
		66 5.5	88 4.1				86 4.2	79 4.6
		44 8.2	45 8.1			Cost of Sales/Inventory	59 6.2	58 6.3
		91 4.0	117 3.1				120 3.0	102 3.6
		162 2.2	158 2.3				151 2.4	122 3.0
		20 18.0	22 16.9			Cost of Sales/Payables	23 16.0	13 27.7
		33 11.0	40 9.2				46 8.0	38 9.7
		72 5.1	91 4.0				82 4.4	66 5.5
		4.3	3.1			Sales/Working Capital	4.7	3.8
		6.0	8.9				9.2	6.0
		16.8	63.2				-159.1	18.1
		15.1	10.6			EBIT/Interest	7.4	9.3
		(23) 5.5	(15) 2.3				(45) 2.3	(40) 3.9
		1.3	1.7				.0	.3
						Net Profit + Depr., Dep., Amort./Cur. Mat. L/T/D	10.1	9.3
							(11) 1.6	(11) 2.4
							.9	1.8
		.1	.1			Fixed/Worth	.2	.1
		.3	.4				.5	.4
		1.3	1.1				-5.9	UND
		.5	.4			Debt/Worth	1.0	.5
		1.6	.9				3.5	2.7
		42.8	9.5				-22.9	UND
		38.9	26.6			% Profit Before Taxes/Tangible Net Worth	48.4	56.0
		(22) 17.8	(16) 13.4				(33) 21.3	(37) 17.5
		-.7	.7				7.4	-2.9
		13.9	9.9			% Profit Before Taxes/Total Assets	10.8	16.9
		8.4	3.8				4.1	7.3
		1.5	.4				-6.8	-2.9
		95.9	42.4			Sales/Net Fixed Assets	44.8	57.9
		23.7	15.1				17.7	18.6
		10.0	6.1				9.4	9.4
		2.6	2.0			Sales/Total Assets	2.2	2.7
		2.1	1.4				1.8	2.0
		1.6	1.0				1.3	1.5
		.5	.9			% Depr., Dep., Amort./Sales	.8	.9
		(25) 1.9	(17) 1.9				(44) 1.7	(35) 1.8
		2.7	4.0				3.2	3.3
						% Officers', Directors' Owners' Comp/Sales	.7	2.4
							(14) 1.6	(10) 4.1
							4.5	7.8
717M	23671M	331262M	679205M	273905M	914906M	Net Sales ($)	2228183M	1923559M
206M	7845M	150305M	412488M	229720M	694653M	Total Assets ($)	1220601M	1116828M

M = $ thousand   MM = $ million
See Pages 9 through 22 for Explanation of Ratios and Data

Comparative Historical Data   **Current Data Sorted by Sales**

			Type of Statement	0-1MM	1-3MM	3-5MM	5-10MM	10-25MM	25MM & OVER
15	14	7	Unqualified					2	5
10	11	21	Reviewed		1		8	10	2
3	3	4	Compiled	1	1	1		1	
1	5	4	Tax Returns		1	1			
27	20	24	Other	2	1	2	2	7	11
4/1/08-3/31/09 ALL	4/1/09-3/31/10 ALL	4/1/10-3/31/11 ALL			7 (4/1-9/30/10)		53 (10/1/10-3/31/11)		
56	53	60	**NUMBER OF STATEMENTS**	3	2	5	12	20	18
%	%	%	**ASSETS**	%	%	%	%	%	%
10.1	10.1	9.6	Cash & Equivalents				17.5	7.8	6.2
27.0	26.1	28.1	Trade Receivables (net)				22.8	30.3	29.4
32.8	28.5	31.7	Inventory				27.3	35.2	26.0
2.9	3.7	2.2	All Other Current				.6	3.3	2.9
72.8	68.4	71.5	Total Current				68.3	76.5	64.6
12.8	15.1	15.4	Fixed Assets (net)				20.5	12.0	16.7
7.5	8.0	6.6	Intangibles (net)				.7	6.7	12.2
6.9	8.6	6.4	All Other Non-Current				10.5	4.9	6.6
100.0	100.0	100.0	Total				100.0	100.0	100.0
			LIABILITIES						
15.5	12.5	23.5	Notes Payable-Short Term				16.1	12.3	13.8
1.5	1.9	2.9	Cur. Mat.-L.T.D.				4.7	1.2	2.0
16.1	14.7	17.6	Trade Payables				10.4	23.5	14.3
.1	.3	.1	Income Taxes Payable				.1	.0	.3
19.5	10.5	9.1	All Other Current				4.6	15.2	8.5
52.7	39.9	53.2	Total Current				36.0	52.2	39.1
9.8	9.7	12.0	Long-Term Debt				2.5	11.4	19.6
.5	.4	.5	Deferred Taxes				.2	.0	1.6
8.0	6.3	4.8	All Other Non-Current				1.4	7.8	4.4
29.0	43.9	29.4	Net Worth				60.0	28.6	35.4
100.0	100.0	100.0	Total Liabilities & Net Worth				100.0	100.0	100.0
			INCOME DATA						
100.0	100.0	100.0	Net Sales				100.0	100.0	100.0
34.7	38.7	34.9	Gross Profit				37.0	36.1	30.3
35.0	33.3	31.2	Operating Expenses				33.6	31.3	25.8
-.3	5.3	3.7	Operating Profit				3.4	4.8	4.4
1.2	2.0	1.0	All Other Expenses (net)				-.4	.9	2.0
-1.5	3.4	2.7	Profit Before Taxes				3.8	3.9	2.4
			RATIOS						
2.7	3.2	2.4					3.9	2.1	2.4
1.5	1.9	1.5	Current				1.7	1.6	1.5
1.2	1.2	1.1					.9	1.2	1.1
1.2	1.9	1.3					3.2	1.2	1.4
.7	.9	.7	Quick				.8	.6	.7
.5	.6	.4					.4	.5	.5
31 11.9	28 13.2	35 10.4					33 11.0	39 9.5	40 9.1
51 7.2	51 7.1	52 7.1	Sales/Receivables				49 7.5	53 6.9	53 6.9
73 5.0	66 5.5	68 5.3					65 5.6	81 4.5	76 4.8
61 6.0	51 7.2	46 8.0					56 6.5	40 9.0	37 10.0
100 3.7	92 4.0	93 3.9	Cost of Sales/Inventory				93 3.9	100 3.6	97 3.8
133 2.7	124 2.9	145 2.5					174 2.1	166 2.2	121 3.0
17 21.1	15 24.1	19 19.7					10 37.1	29 12.8	15 23.6
38 9.7	33 10.9	36 10.0	Cost of Sales/Payables				26 13.9	43 8.5	40 9.2
63 5.8	58 6.3	71 5.2					71 5.1	108 3.4	60 6.1
4.2	4.1	4.9					2.7	5.8	6.7
9.2	6.8	9.0	Sales/Working Capital				8.7	7.7	9.0
23.0	16.5	20.5					NM	18.3	19.1
8.7	18.3	10.2						8.8	20.4
(51) 2.4	(48) 6.8	(52) 4.2	EBIT/Interest				(19) 4.3	(15) 5.0
1.0	1.3	.9						1.3	1.7
7.7	13.9								
(15) 3.3	(15) 4.5		Net Profit + Depr., Dep., Amort./Cur. Mat. L/T/D						
1.8	2.4								
.1	.1	.1					.0	.2	.2
.4	.3	.3	Fixed/Worth				.1	.5	.3
1.3	1.1	1.9					.5	NM	-2.6
.8	.6	.6					.3	1.1	.5
2.4	1.5	1.8	Debt/Worth				.7	3.9	3.1
19.3	8.7	122.9					1.5	NM	-9.9
46.1	75.0	40.8					29.0	45.4	34.6
(44) 11.0	(47) 37.5	(47) 18.8	% Profit Before Taxes/Tangible Net Worth				14.5	(15) 16.7	(12) 20.5
.1	2.8	2.1					-.9	1.4	13.2
11.5	24.2	13.6					14.4	13.5	12.8
2.8	11.2	6.5	% Profit Before Taxes/Total Assets				7.1	6.8	7.6
-4.7	.5	.3					-.6	.5	2.0
85.3	69.5	55.5					122.6	84.0	42.5
25.2	25.8	23.3	Sales/Net Fixed Assets				38.3	18.1	19.6
6.8	7.8	8.5					3.7	10.5	6.2
2.6	2.7	2.6					2.1	2.7	2.6
2.0	1.9	1.9	Sales/Total Assets				1.4	2.2	1.5
1.4	1.3	1.4					.7	1.5	1.4
.6	.7	.8					.2	.6	1.0
(46) 1.4	(38) 1.6	(49) 1.9	% Depr., Dep., Amort./Sales				(10) 1.3	(19) 1.2	(14) 1.9
2.8	3.3	3.3					6.7	3.1	3.6
2.1	1.5								
(11) 2.8	(19) 3.3		% Officers', Directors' Owners' Comp/Sales						
5.2	4.9								
2248261M	2537216M	2223666M	Net Sales ($)	717M	4979M	20247M	96954M	311720M	1789049M
1358878M	1599258M	1495217M	Total Assets ($)	206M	3420M	7937M	84893M	166856M	1231905M

© RMA 2011

M = $ thousand   MM = $ million
See Pages 9 through 22 for Explanation of Ratios and Data

Current Data Sorted by Assets   Comparative Historical Data

							Type of Statement		
			5	12	2	2	Unqualified	29	23
	6	33	15				Reviewed	55	42
4	7	15					Compiled	39	36
14	18	5				1	Tax Returns	27	28
11	17	36	15			1	Other	75	75
	36 (4/1-9/30/10)			183 (10/1/10-3/31/11)				4/1/06-3/31/07 ALL	4/1/07-3/31/08 ALL
0-500M	500M-2MM	2-10MM	10-50MM	50-100MM	100-250MM		NUMBER OF STATEMENTS		
29	48	94	42	2	4			225	204
%	%	%	%	%	%		**ASSETS**	%	%
10.8	12.2	10.7	7.2				Cash & Equivalents	7.9	8.8
18.9	31.3	35.0	29.3				Trade Receivables (net)	35.6	34.8
7.9	16.0	19.0	19.9				Inventory	19.9	17.2
2.9	1.8	3.3	7.0				All Other Current	3.0	3.6
40.4	61.5	68.0	63.4				Total Current	66.3	64.3
37.8	22.7	25.3	24.4				Fixed Assets (net)	22.9	25.1
10.4	6.6	1.5	6.3				Intangibles (net)	4.6	4.8
11.5	9.2	5.2	5.9				All Other Non-Current	6.2	5.7
100.0	100.0	100.0	100.0				Total	100.0	100.0
							LIABILITIES		
16.4	16.5	9.4	9.7				Notes Payable-Short Term	13.2	13.5
7.0	4.6	3.2	3.7				Cur. Mat.-L.T.D.	5.8	6.6
15.5	17.7	15.4	14.3				Trade Payables	18.1	15.8
.0	.1	.1	.2				Income Taxes Payable	.3	.6
10.4	11.0	14.5	12.5				All Other Current	14.2	14.8
49.3	49.8	42.6	40.4				Total Current	51.6	51.4
56.5	16.6	13.0	13.0				Long-Term Debt	18.5	21.1
.0	.1	.8	.6				Deferred Taxes	.4	.3
33.2	5.2	5.5	6.7				All Other Non-Current	4.4	7.8
-39.0	28.3	38.0	39.3				Net Worth	25.2	19.4
100.0	100.0	100.0	100.0				Total Liabilities & Net Worth	100.0	100.0
							INCOME DATA		
100.0	100.0	100.0	100.0				Net Sales	100.0	100.0
54.9	46.7	33.6	31.8				Gross Profit	36.9	39.6
48.8	45.5	30.7	24.4				Operating Expenses	33.1	35.0
6.1	1.2	2.9	7.4				Operating Profit	3.7	4.6
1.5	1.1	.4	2.5				All Other Expenses (net)	1.0	1.4
4.6	.1	2.5	4.9				Profit Before Taxes	2.7	3.2
							RATIOS		
1.9	1.8	2.7	2.1					2.1	2.1
.8	1.4	1.7	1.5				Current	1.5	1.4
.6	.9	1.2	1.3					1.1	1.0
1.4	1.4	1.6	1.3					1.5	1.4
.6	.9	1.2	.9				Quick	.9	.9
.2	.4	.8	.6					.6	.6
0 UND	24 15.2	40 9.1	39 9.3					35 10.3	31 11.8
19 18.7	42 8.7	52 7.0	55 6.7				Sales/Receivables	49 7.4	47 7.8
35 10.4	58 6.3	71 5.1	72 5.1					63 5.8	61 6.0
0 UND	10 36.0	17 22.0	23 15.8					17 21.0	16 23.5
10 34.9	36 10.3	39 9.3	49 7.4				Cost of Sales/Inventory	39 9.3	35 10.5
32 11.6	69 5.3	64 5.7	77 4.7					65 5.8	58 6.3
0 UND	15 24.2	17 21.6	25 14.6					20 18.1	17 21.6
21 17.5	32 11.5	28 12.8	35 10.3				Cost of Sales/Payables	33 11.1	31 11.7
60 6.0	62 5.9	51 7.2	48 7.7					54 6.8	49 7.5
12.6	5.7	5.6	5.5					7.1	7.8
-43.6	19.0	8.2	8.1				Sales/Working Capital	13.7	15.1
-17.0	-45.0	24.1	18.5					66.8	NM
5.0	5.8	14.6	17.2					11.3	11.6
(25) 1.5	(41) 1.1	(85) 3.7	(39) 4.0				EBIT/Interest	(213) 3.6	(191) 3.3
-.9	-.8	.7	1.5					1.3	1.0
		6.8	8.0					4.4	9.4
	(32) 2.8	(13) 5.6					Net Profit + Depr., Dep., Amort./Cur. Mat. L/T/D	(52) 2.8	(45) 2.1
	1.1	1.6						1.3	1.4
.8	.2	.2	.3					.3	.3
-20.3	.7	.7	.8				Fixed/Worth	.8	1.0
-.3	2.0	1.6	1.8					2.5	88.5
1.5	.8	.7	.9					1.1	1.2
-23.3	2.3	1.5	1.9				Debt/Worth	2.6	3.2
-1.7	11.9	3.9	4.4					9.8	NM
111.2	28.5	34.5	33.6				% Profit Before Taxes/Tangible Net Worth	54.4	57.6
(13) 22.9	(40) 4.0	(86) 14.5	(36) 18.4					(183) 24.8	(153) 26.0
-28.6	-7.7	.5	7.9					10.1	7.1
34.8	11.0	12.7	16.6				% Profit Before Taxes/Total Assets	15.7	17.1
3.8	.8	6.2	5.9					6.8	6.4
-3.7	-4.0	.0	2.1					1.0	.3
31.1	26.5	24.9	23.4				Sales/Net Fixed Assets	30.2	31.6
11.5	12.8	11.3	10.9					14.8	14.6
7.1	7.8	5.6	4.7					8.0	7.2
4.3	3.3	2.8	2.3				Sales/Total Assets	3.3	3.4
3.4	2.7	2.3	2.0					2.6	2.6
2.5	2.0	1.8	1.5					2.0	1.9
2.0	1.1	1.0	1.0				% Depr., Dep., Amort./Sales	1.0	.9
(21) 3.2	(38) 2.5	(87) 1.8	(36) 1.9					(200) 1.8	(173) 1.6
7.3	4.2	3.1	2.4					2.8	3.1
3.9	2.4	2.1					% Officers', Directors' Owners' Comp/Sales	2.4	3.2
(22) 9.5	(32) 6.0	(33) 3.7						(89) 4.5	(84) 4.8
12.9	8.7	5.2						7.2	8.3
23187M	146518M	1047522M	1623559M	213934M	1338682M		Net Sales ($)	4008176M	4204965M
6867M	52438M	448053M	854791M	127562M	731145M		Total Assets ($)	1881883M	2026325M

M = $ thousand   MM = $ million
See Pages 9 through 22 for Explanation of Ratios and Data

Comparative Historical Data   **Current Data Sorted by Sales**

			Type of Statement	0-1MM	1-3MM	3-5MM	5-10MM	10-25MM	25MM & OVER
23	20	21	Unqualified		2	8	3	6	12
51	42	54	Reviewed	1	10	3	14	20	10
36	31	26	Compiled	12	14	6	9	2	1
40	33	38	Tax Returns	9	10	11	3	1	2
92	85	80	Other				13	27	10
4/1/08-3/31/09 ALL	4/1/09-3/31/10 ALL	4/1/10-3/31/11 ALL		36 (4/1-9/30/10)			183 (10/1/10-3/31/11)		
242	211	219	**NUMBER OF STATEMENTS**	22	36	28	42	56	35
%	%	%	**ASSETS**	%	%	%	%	%	%
9.5	9.7	10.2	Cash & Equivalents	9.8	14.6	8.4	12.0	8.8	7.8
30.7	30.4	30.5	Trade Receivables (net)	14.3	26.6	31.9	35.9	32.7	33.6
18.9	17.2	16.9	Inventory	9.3	12.3	15.8	16.0	22.4	19.4
4.0	3.6	3.6	All Other Current	3.3	1.6	2.4	3.1	5.6	4.2
63.1	60.8	61.2	Total Current	36.6	55.1	58.5	67.0	69.4	65.0
25.7	25.8	26.8	Fixed Assets (net)	38.8	26.6	32.6	25.6	20.5	26.1
4.7	5.6	4.9	Intangibles (net)	14.2	8.2	1.9	1.3	4.7	2.6
6.5	7.8	7.1	All Other Non-Current	10.4	10.1	6.9	6.0	5.4	6.3
100.0	100.0	100.0	Total	100.0	100.0	100.0	100.0	100.0	100.0
			LIABILITIES						
13.1	12.4	11.9	Notes Payable-Short Term	20.3	13.7	14.0	8.8	10.0	10.0
5.7	4.5	4.2	Cur. Mat.-L.T.D.	6.8	6.3	3.3	2.7	3.1	4.6
15.1	13.5	15.6	Trade Payables	14.8	14.8	11.8	16.7	18.0	15.1
.2	.2	.1	Income Taxes Payable	.0	.0	.1	.1	.1	.2
13.5	12.0	12.7	All Other Current	5.6	12.8	13.3	11.9	14.0	15.2
47.6	42.6	44.5	Total Current	47.5	47.6	42.4	40.2	45.1	45.1
20.5	19.8	19.9	Long-Term Debt	59.8	26.9	17.7	14.0	10.0	12.2
.3	.5	.5	Deferred Taxes	.0	.0	1.5	.7	.2	.8
5.3	7.3	9.3	All Other Non-Current	42.4	5.6	5.2	3.0	8.9	4.0
26.3	29.7	25.8	Net Worth	-49.7	19.9	33.3	42.0	35.7	37.8
100.0	100.0	100.0	Total Liabilties & Net Worth	100.0	100.0	100.0	100.0	100.0	100.0
			INCOME DATA						
100.0	100.0	100.0	Net Sales	100.0	100.0	100.0	100.0	100.0	100.0
38.2	40.2	39.0	Gross Profit	61.3	46.2	43.1	33.1	31.5	33.6
34.8	37.7	35.2	Operating Expenses	54.3	44.7	40.9	32.0	25.9	27.8
3.4	2.5	3.8	Operating Profit	6.9	1.5	2.2	1.1	5.6	5.8
1.0	1.2	1.2	All Other Expenses (net)	2.7	.8	.7	.3	1.8	.9
2.4	1.4	2.6	Profit Before Taxes	4.2	.7	1.4	.9	3.8	4.8
			RATIOS						
2.2	2.5	2.2		1.8	1.9	2.1	3.0	2.2	2.3
1.5	1.6	1.5	Current	.7	1.4	1.5	1.6	1.7	1.5
1.1	1.1	1.1		.4	.7	1.1	1.1	1.3	1.2
1.5	1.7	1.4		1.4	1.8	1.4	1.7	1.5	1.3
.9	1.0	1.0	Quick	.4	1.0	1.1	1.2	.9	1.0
.6	.6	.6		.0	.5	.7	.9	.6	.7
26 14.3	27 13.3	31 11.6		0 UND	23 16.0	36 10.2	45 8.2	35 10.3	36 10.0
40 9.2	42 8.6	48 7.6	Sales/Receivables	15 23.6	35 10.4	48 7.6	52 7.0	53 6.8	53 6.9
56 6.5	63 5.8	68 5.3		39 9.4	54 6.7	70 5.2	72 5.1	69 5.3	68 5.3
15 23.8	16 22.6	13 27.4		0 UND	4 88.3	14 26.4	15 24.9	22 16.3	17 21.3
36 10.2	39 9.5	38 9.6	Cost of Sales/Inventory	16 23.2	20 18.6	38 9.5	35 10.5	49 7.4	45 8.1
63 5.8	68 5.4	63 5.8		47 7.7	52 7.0	74 5.0	61 6.0	68 5.4	78 4.7
17 21.3	18 20.1	17 21.7		0 UND	15 24.4	12 29.8	14 25.9	21 17.3	22 16.5
28 13.2	29 12.6	30 12.1	Cost of Sales/Payables	25 14.9	31 11.7	25 14.7	31 11.8	29 12.4	31 11.9
45 8.2	48 7.5	51 7.2		76 4.8	62 5.9	43 8.5	59 6.1	50 7.3	48 7.7
6.9	5.6	5.8		8.2	5.7	4.6	5.0	5.7	6.4
13.9	11.1	11.4	Sales/Working Capital	-39.4	19.6	12.9	7.8	8.4	8.6
106.6	70.6	79.6		-9.1	-19.3	65.3	-57.0	18.0	24.8
9.6	8.5	11.4		5.1	4.6	6.0	5.4	15.5	28.3
(222) 3.1	(187) 2.9	(196) 2.9	EBIT/Interest	(20) 1.6	(30) 1.0	(25) 3.2	(35) 1.2	(53) 4.3	(33) 9.6
.9	-.9	.5		.9	-2.3	.8	-2.7	1.6	2.5
6.4	4.6	7.2					1.7	11.6	8.3
(52) 2.0	(41) 2.0	(58) 3.2	Net Profit + Depr., Dep., Amort./Cur. Mat. L/T/D			(13) 1.0	(19) 4.9	(11) 5.6	
1.0	-.6	1.0					-.3	2.0	1.4
.3	.3	.3		.5	.3	.7	.2	.2	.3
.8	.8	.8	Fixed/Worth	-15.7	1.2	.9	.6	.5	.5
3.1	5.4	2.4		-.3	3.6	2.7	1.4	1.7	1.3
.9	.8	.9		1.5	1.1	.8	.7	.8	.8
2.4	1.9	2.0	Debt/Worth	-5.1	2.7	2.3	1.5	1.9	1.7
9.5	9.8	6.7		-1.4	18.7	5.5	3.6	4.6	2.8
50.3	35.9	34.6			22.7	36.6	30.1	37.8	35.6
(197) 21.9	(167) 12.3	(179) 14.2	% Profit Before Taxes/Tangible Net Worth		(28) 3.7	(26) 9.4	(41) 5.3	(46) 14.5	(30) 27.5
5.7	-1.0	-.3			-30.6	-.6	-12.7	6.4	11.5
15.4	13.7	14.5		33.8	11.1	9.6	9.2	14.4	21.5
6.3	4.0	4.5	% Profit Before Taxes/Total Assets	5.4	.5	2.9	1.8	6.8	11.6
-.5	-4.9	-.9		-.3	-12.3	-.3	-5.4	2.4	2.0
30.7	27.8	24.8		19.2	24.7	13.8	22.2	28.7	21.5
13.7	11.1	11.5	Sales/Net Fixed Assets	10.4	11.6	7.5	10.3	17.6	11.3
6.7	5.6	6.3		6.0	7.0	3.5	5.5	8.5	5.0
3.5	3.1	3.1		3.5	3.6	3.0	2.8	3.1	2.9
2.6	2.3	2.3	Sales/Total Assets	2.8	2.7	2.1	2.2	2.4	2.2
2.0	1.6	1.8		1.5	2.2	1.4	1.8	1.8	1.6
.9	1.1	1.1		2.6	1.5	1.6	1.0	.8	1.1
(209) 2.0	(168) 2.2	(185) 2.1	% Depr., Dep., Amort./Sales	(16) 4.9	(27) 2.8	(24) 2.8	(39) 2.0	(50) 1.3	(29) 1.8
3.0	3.5	3.5		12.6	4.6	5.5	3.2	2.1	2.9
2.7	2.6	2.1		4.3	3.4	3.0	2.2	.8	
(103) 5.2	(78) 4.4	(95) 4.8	% Officers', Directors' Owners' Comp/Sales	(15) 9.7	(26) 7.8	(17) 4.8	(16) 3.9	(14) 2.8	
9.3	7.9	8.0		11.9	9.5	5.7	5.9	4.9	
4548104M	4402482M	4393402M	Net Sales ($)	12192M	67216M	110872M	305397M	933272M	2964453M
2154924M	2495686M	2220856M	Total Assets ($)	5866M	30483M	67342M	143228M	510166M	1463771M

M = $ thousand   MM = $ million
See Pages 9 through 22 for Explanation of Ratios and Data

Current Data Sorted by Assets   Comparative Historical Data

Type of Statement	0-500M	500M-2MM	2-10MM	10-50MM	50-100MM	100-250MM		4/1/06-3/31/07 ALL	4/1/07-3/31/08 ALL
Unqualified			1	3	3	3		11	9
Reviewed		2	12	5				17	21
Compiled		3	5					11	14
Tax Returns	2	5						10	7
Other	2	6	12	11	9	3		20	19
		30 (4/1-9/30/10)		57 (10/1/10-3/31/11)					
NUMBER OF STATEMENTS	4	16	30	19	12	6		69	70
ASSETS	%	%	%	%	%	%		%	%
Cash & Equivalents		7.0	8.3	10.3	10.3			9.5	10.5
Trade Receivables (net)		30.7	26.8	24.7	21.4			28.4	24.4
Inventory		26.9	27.1	24.8	21.3			25.4	25.1
All Other Current		.5	1.8	4.5	6.9			1.4	2.4
Total Current		65.2	63.9	64.3	60.0			64.6	62.5
Fixed Assets (net)		19.0	26.2	19.7	18.5			24.1	24.8
Intangibles (net)		5.3	5.6	9.3	18.6			4.8	6.2
All Other Non-Current		10.4	4.3	6.6	2.9			6.4	6.5
Total		100.0	100.0	100.0	100.0			100.0	100.0
LIABILITIES									
Notes Payable-Short Term		15.3	8.4	9.0	5.7			8.5	11.8
Cur. Mat.-L.T.D.		.7	3.5	2.6	3.5			1.8	3.2
Trade Payables		19.5	12.2	13.0	10.5			14.5	16.0
Income Taxes Payable		.2	.1	1.1	.1			.3	.2
All Other Current		3.1	8.3	12.5	14.7			11.9	7.5
Total Current		38.9	32.5	38.1	34.5			36.9	38.6
Long-Term Debt		14.4	12.8	10.2	13.9			15.1	14.9
Deferred Taxes		.5	1.0	1.2	.8			.7	.6
All Other Non-Current		4.5	1.6	5.8	6.8			6.0	7.2
Net Worth		41.8	52.1	44.7	44.1			41.4	38.7
Total Liabilties & Net Worth		100.0	100.0	100.0	100.0			100.0	100.0
INCOME DATA									
Net Sales		100.0	100.0	100.0	100.0			100.0	100.0
Gross Profit		33.1	32.2	30.0	25.2			34.4	30.1
Operating Expenses		29.4	25.1	20.6	17.6			28.2	25.8
Operating Profit		3.7	7.1	9.5	7.6			6.1	4.3
All Other Expenses (net)		.8	.9	1.9	1.3			.9	1.1
Profit Before Taxes		2.9	6.2	7.6	6.3			5.3	3.3
RATIOS									
Current		3.0	2.7	3.4	2.1			3.4	3.4
		1.7	1.9	1.9	1.9			1.9	1.8
		1.1	1.3	1.2	1.5			1.3	1.2
Quick		1.7	1.4	1.8	1.1			2.2	2.4
		.8	1.0	1.2	.9			1.0	.9
		.6	.8	.6	.7			.7	.6
Sales/Receivables		36 10.2	36 10.0	41 8.9	32 11.4			36 10.1	33 11.0
		40 9.1	46 8.0	53 6.9	49 7.4			42 8.7	42 8.7
		46 7.9	56 6.5	59 6.2	62 5.9			53 6.8	49 7.4
Cost of Sales/Inventory		35 10.6	43 8.5	54 6.7	45 8.0			34 10.9	33 11.1
		49 7.5	69 5.3	74 4.9	69 5.3			60 6.0	54 6.7
		88 4.2	99 3.7	102 3.6	102 3.6			101 3.6	89 4.1
Cost of Sales/Payables		20 18.2	18 19.9	25 14.7	17 21.8			19 19.7	20 18.4
		38 9.6	25 14.4	34 10.9	23 15.5			28 12.9	28 12.9
		54 6.7	40 9.2	51 7.1	43 8.4			45 8.1	41 8.8
Sales/Working Capital		5.8	3.9	3.2	4.4			4.4	4.7
		9.7	7.3	5.4	7.1			9.0	8.9
		26.6	14.2	29.0	9.4			14.2	21.5
EBIT/Interest		20.5	16.3	27.6	23.8			14.5	8.2
		(14) 6.6	(25) 7.7	(18) 10.3	(10) 13.4			(60) 4.7	(63) 4.3
		2.3	4.3	2.8	1.5			1.9	1.2
Net Profit + Depr., Dep., Amort./Cur. Mat. L/T/D								14.9	5.8
								(17) 3.5	(21) 2.2
								1.5	.7
Fixed/Worth		.2	.2	.3	.5			.2	.3
		.8	.5	.5	.8			.6	.6
		NM	.8	1.3	-2.0			1.6	2.6
Debt/Worth		.6	.7	.5	1.1			.5	.6
		1.4	1.0	1.8	1.8			1.5	1.7
		NM	1.9	5.1	-12.5			6.5	5.0
% Profit Before Taxes/Tangible Net Worth		40.1	57.3	74.2				41.6	37.9
		(12) 19.3	(29) 19.6	(17) 38.7				(61) 20.1	(60) 16.0
		1.4	12.3	15.2				8.7	6.5
% Profit Before Taxes/Total Assets		18.5	17.8	23.4	15.0			15.2	14.6
		7.2	10.1	12.0	9.5			8.9	6.2
		1.1	5.5	4.1	3.0			3.1	.8
Sales/Net Fixed Assets		81.2	22.4	17.9	14.1			32.8	28.8
		27.3	9.5	7.6	11.3			9.7	10.3
		4.0	4.5	6.3	6.4			4.6	4.4
Sales/Total Assets		3.3	2.8	2.0	2.4			3.0	2.8
		2.5	1.9	1.7	1.4			2.3	2.1
		1.6	1.6	1.4	1.1			1.5	1.5
% Depr., Dep., Amort./Sales		.9	.3	.6	2.1			.8	.8
		(12) 1.5	(27) 1.6	(17) 1.2	(11) 2.5			(59) 1.5	(62) 1.7
		2.3	3.2	3.3	4.0			3.4	3.0
% Officers', Directors' Owners' Comp/Sales			1.8					2.8	3.0
			(10) 3.9					(25) 5.1	(25) 6.2
			8.2					9.7	9.8
Net Sales ($)	6419M	50511M	336203M	623625M	1310593M	1177262M		1875748M	1641741M
Total Assets ($)	1117M	20036M	158849M	369712M	820798M	977993M		1419161M	1168963M

© RMA 2011

M = $ thousand   MM = $ million
See Pages 9 through 22 for Explanation of Ratios and Data

Comparative Historical Data   Current Data Sorted by Sales

			Type of Statement						
14	11	10	Unqualified				1	2	7
18	19	19	Reviewed		1	1	5	8	4
12	14	8	Compiled		1	2	3	2	
9	6	7	Tax Returns	1	3	3			
27	33	43	Other	1	4	4	6	9	19
4/1/08-3/31/09 ALL	4/1/09-3/31/10 ALL	4/1/10-3/31/11 ALL		0-1MM	1-3MM	3-5MM	5-10MM	10-25MM	25MM & OVER
						30 (4/1-9/30/10)		57 (10/1/10-3/31/11)	
80	83	87	NUMBER OF STATEMENTS	2	9	10	15	21	30
%	%	%	ASSETS	%	%	%	%	%	%
9.6	10.4	9.1	Cash & Equivalents			8.9	6.0	9.6	11.0
25.8	24.4	26.9	Trade Receivables (net)			39.8	24.3	25.9	25.4
23.6	22.8	24.3	Inventory			25.4	26.8	27.5	22.2
2.9	2.9	3.0	All Other Current			.5	2.4	5.9	3.1
61.9	60.5	63.3	Total Current			74.6	59.5	68.9	61.6
21.7	25.2	21.7	Fixed Assets (net)			14.5	22.1	24.5	18.8
10.1	7.8	9.1	Intangibles (net)			1.6	12.8	3.2	13.7
6.3	6.4	5.9	All Other Non-Current			9.4	5.6	3.5	5.9
100.0	100.0	100.0	Total			100.0	100.0	100.0	100.0
			LIABILITIES						
7.2	7.5	8.8	Notes Payable-Short Term			19.9	6.1	10.3	6.3
3.5	4.3	3.5	Cur. Mat.-L.T.D.			.0	3.4	2.7	4.6
12.7	12.4	13.8	Trade Payables			21.1	14.1	13.0	11.3
.2	.2	.4	Income Taxes Payable			.1	.1	.8	.4
6.8	7.3	9.7	All Other Current			7.0	8.7	12.7	11.1
30.4	31.7	36.1	Total Current			48.2	32.5	39.5	33.8
15.2	13.2	12.8	Long-Term Debt			3.0	10.0	10.4	11.3
.7	.9	.9	Deferred Taxes			.1	1.8	.5	1.0
10.4	6.9	4.7	All Other Non-Current			1.3	4.9	3.9	7.2
43.3	47.4	45.5	Net Worth			47.4	50.8	45.7	46.7
100.0	100.0	100.0	Total Liabilities & Net Worth			100.0	100.0	100.0	100.0
			INCOME DATA						
100.0	100.0	100.0	Net Sales			100.0	100.0	100.0	100.0
33.4	30.7	32.2	Gross Profit			29.1	34.2	29.9	30.1
27.8	26.8	24.8	Operating Expenses			23.8	27.4	22.1	20.7
5.6	3.9	7.4	Operating Profit			5.3	6.7	7.8	9.4
1.0	.7	1.2	All Other Expenses (net)			.1	1.9	.8	1.5
4.6	3.2	6.2	Profit Before Taxes			5.2	4.8	7.0	7.9
			RATIOS						
3.8	3.5	2.6	Current			2.9	2.2	2.9	3.0
2.0	2.0	1.8	Current			1.7	1.8	1.7	1.9
1.3	1.3	1.3	Current			1.1	1.5	1.2	1.4
2.1	2.1	1.6	Quick			1.9	1.2	1.6	1.8
1.1	1.2	1.0	Quick			1.1	1.1	.9	1.0
.7	.7	.7	Quick			.7	.8	.6	.8
33 11.1	38 9.7	39 9.5	Sales/Receivables			33 11.2	40 9.2	35 10.5	41 8.9
41 8.9	43 8.5	46 7.9	Sales/Receivables			45 8.1	52 7.1	43 8.5	50 7.2
48 7.7	54 6.8	56 6.5	Sales/Receivables			54 6.8	56 6.5	55 6.6	60 6.1
27 13.3	39 9.3	43 8.4	Cost of Sales/Inventory			26 14.3	44 8.3	44 8.3	46 8.0
52 7.0	61 6.0	69 5.3	Cost of Sales/Inventory			46 7.9	68 5.4	71 5.1	75 4.9
87 4.2	90 4.0	95 3.9	Cost of Sales/Inventory			86 4.3	111 3.3	94 3.9	92 4.0
18 19.8	19 18.8	19 18.9	Cost of Sales/Payables			16 22.9	22 16.9	20 18.6	20 18.3
26 13.9	28 13.0	31 11.7	Cost of Sales/Payables			37 9.8	34 10.8	35 10.5	26 14.0
39 9.4	44 8.4	44 8.4	Cost of Sales/Payables			45 8.0	55 6.6	51 7.1	38 9.5
5.0	3.7	4.3	Sales/Working Capital			6.1	4.7	3.6	4.0
8.8	6.3	7.8	Sales/Working Capital			18.1	7.8	6.8	6.0
16.7	16.9	17.5	Sales/Working Capital			NM	12.5	23.2	12.6
10.9	8.3	17.6	EBIT/Interest				15.8	16.5	35.8
(70) 2.9	(70) 3.6	(74) 8.1	EBIT/Interest				(14) 7.2	(19) 9.7	(25) 13.4
1.6	.9	3.5	EBIT/Interest				2.3	3.6	3.4
2.0	2.8	9.2	Net Profit + Depr., Dep., Amort./Cur. Mat. L/T/D						13.1
(16) 1.2	(20) 1.4	(17) 2.2	Net Profit + Depr., Dep., Amort./Cur. Mat. L/T/D					(11)	3.7
.6	.3	1.1	Net Profit + Depr., Dep., Amort./Cur. Mat. L/T/D						1.0
.2	.3	.3	Fixed/Worth			.0	.4	.4	.3
.7	.6	.6	Fixed/Worth			.3	.5	.6	.5
2.1	1.3	1.3	Fixed/Worth			NM	1.9	1.0	NM
.6	.5	.7	Debt/Worth			.4	.8	.7	.6
1.8	1.4	1.4	Debt/Worth			1.1	1.0	1.3	1.6
6.2	3.0	4.7	Debt/Worth			NM	2.8	4.0	NM
33.0	34.6	57.3	% Profit Before Taxes/Tangible Net Worth				45.1	99.4	51.0
(67) 15.9	(74) 8.5	(73) 27.8	% Profit Before Taxes/Tangible Net Worth				(13) 14.9	55.0	(23) 37.3
6.0	.1	10.8	% Profit Before Taxes/Tangible Net Worth				8.7	10.3	20.7
11.9	11.1	18.4	% Profit Before Taxes/Total Assets			24.3	10.1	22.5	22.8
6.4	3.6	9.7	% Profit Before Taxes/Total Assets			7.2	7.8	16.6	10.7
2.0	.2	4.5	% Profit Before Taxes/Total Assets			1.2	3.5	5.2	5.8
51.0	18.3	25.0	Sales/Net Fixed Assets			UND	15.7	23.7	19.2
11.4	7.9	9.8	Sales/Net Fixed Assets			55.5	10.8	7.6	9.5
5.3	3.9	5.3	Sales/Net Fixed Assets			10.8	6.9	5.3	5.8
3.0	2.4	2.5	Sales/Total Assets			3.6	2.6	2.6	2.2
2.2	1.7	1.8	Sales/Total Assets			3.0	1.7	1.8	1.7
1.6	1.3	1.5	Sales/Total Assets			2.0	1.5	1.6	1.2
.8	1.0	.9	% Depr., Dep., Amort./Sales				.7	.3	1.0
(65) 1.7	(69) 2.6	(74) 2.0	% Depr., Dep., Amort./Sales				(12) 1.9	(18) 1.6	2.5
2.9	4.0	3.1	% Depr., Dep., Amort./Sales				3.2	3.2	3.7
2.9	2.6	2.6	% Officers', Directors' Owners' Comp/Sales						
(29) 4.6	(28) 4.8	(27) 5.5	% Officers', Directors' Owners' Comp/Sales						
7.8	8.2	10.2	% Officers', Directors' Owners' Comp/Sales						
2279084M	2769891M	3504613M	Net Sales ($)	901M	19677M	35436M	108262M	331067M	3009270M
1505367M	2051638M	2348505M	Total Assets ($)	597M	12168M	13531M	73512M	235483M	2013214M

M = $ thousand   MM = $ million
See Pages 9 through 22 for Explanation of Ratios and Data

Current Data Sorted by Assets   Comparative Historical Data

	0-500M	500M-2MM	2-10MM	10-50MM	50-100MM	100-250MM		4/1/06-3/31/07 ALL	4/1/07-3/31/08 ALL
Type of Statement									
Unqualified				5	4	2		11	6
Reviewed				1				5	7
Compiled		1	2					6	7
Tax Returns	1	2	2					3	1
Other	1	2	1	3	1	1		10	10
		7 (4/1-9/30/10)		22 (10/1/10-3/31/11)					
NUMBER OF STATEMENTS	2	5	5	9	5	3		35	31
	%	%	%	%	%	%	**ASSETS**	%	%
							Cash & Equivalents	5.6	5.5
							Trade Receivables (net)	22.6	23.6
							Inventory	36.4	39.2
							All Other Current	1.5	2.5
							Total Current	66.1	70.8
							Fixed Assets (net)	21.6	18.5
							Intangibles (net)	2.9	2.9
							All Other Non-Current	9.4	7.8
							Total	100.0	100.0
							LIABILITIES		
							Notes Payable-Short Term	11.7	25.1
							Cur. Mat.-L.T.D.	2.0	3.4
							Trade Payables	12.5	9.6
							Income Taxes Payable	.3	.2
							All Other Current	12.6	10.7
							Total Current	39.1	48.9
							Long-Term Debt	22.0	16.3
							Deferred Taxes	.2	.3
							All Other Non-Current	7.9	7.8
							Net Worth	30.8	26.7
							Total Liabilities & Net Worth	100.0	100.0
							INCOME DATA		
							Net Sales	100.0	100.0
							Gross Profit	35.8	38.5
							Operating Expenses	31.2	32.3
							Operating Profit	4.7	6.2
							All Other Expenses (net)	2.2	1.7
							Profit Before Taxes	2.5	4.5
							RATIOS		
							Current	3.4 / 1.9 / 1.1	3.2 / 2.2 / 1.5
							Quick	1.1 / .8 / .6	1.3 / .9 / .6
							Sales/Receivables	25 14.5 / 37 9.8 / 58 6.3	31 11.6 / 45 8.1 / 61 6.0
							Cost of Sales/Inventory	83 4.4 / 132 2.8 / 185 2.0	96 3.8 / 136 2.7 / 186 2.0
							Cost of Sales/Payables	14 26.2 / 32 11.3 / 52 7.1	10 35.5 / 26 14.0 / 61 6.0
							Sales/Working Capital	3.0 / 5.1 / 20.9	3.0 / 5.2 / 9.0
							EBIT/Interest	12.0 / (32) 4.0 / .7	11.9 / (28) 2.6 / 1.4
							Net Profit + Depr., Dep., Amort./Cur. Mat. L/T/D	15.4 / (13) 5.7 / 2.0	10.7 / (11) 4.2 / 1.2
							Fixed/Worth	.1 / .4 / -16.0	.2 / .3 / 5.8
							Debt/Worth	.4 / 2.2 / -14.2	.4 / 1.1 / -43.0
							% Profit Before Taxes/Tangible Net Worth	34.8 / (25) 20.2 / 2.3	25.6 / (23) 9.2 / 1.5
							% Profit Before Taxes/Total Assets	13.9 / 7.4 / -.5	14.3 / 4.6 / 1.0
							Sales/Net Fixed Assets	26.0 / 11.3 / 6.7	25.8 / 10.9 / 6.6
							Sales/Total Assets	2.1 / 1.6 / 1.3	1.9 / 1.6 / 1.3
							% Depr., Dep., Amort./Sales	1.0 / (32) 1.7 / 2.6	.9 / (28) 1.9 / 3.1
							% Officers', Directors', Owners' Comp/Sales	2.8 / (10) 6.4 / 12.6	
3380M	11477M	30875M	359352M	539722M	814743M	Net Sales ($)	1839767M	1386547M
601M	4646M	28039M	247179M	386127M	449684M	Total Assets ($)	1180316M	918876M

M = $ thousand MM = $ million
See Pages 9 through 22 for Explanation of Ratios and Data

Comparative Historical Data | Current Data Sorted by Sales

4/1/08-3/31/09 ALL	4/1/09-3/31/10 ALL	4/1/10-3/31/11 ALL	Type of Statement	0-1MM	1-3MM	3-5MM	5-10MM	10-25MM	25MM & OVER
5	9	11	Unqualified					2	9
9	2	2	Reviewed			1			1
4	5	4	Compiled	1	1	1	1		
1	3	2	Tax Returns		1	1			
19	13	10	Other		3			2	5
				7 (4/1-9/30/10)			22 (10/1/10-3/31/11)		
38	32	29	NUMBER OF STATEMENTS	1	5	3	3	2	15
%	%	%	**ASSETS**	%	%	%	%	%	%
8.1	13.9	10.5	Cash & Equivalents						7.6
22.1	16.3	19.5	Trade Receivables (net)						22.2
38.0	34.9	35.6	Inventory						33.1
2.5	3.5	2.5	All Other Current						3.3
70.7	68.6	68.1	Total Current						66.1
19.2	20.6	19.2	Fixed Assets (net)						22.2
1.7	4.1	3.9	Intangibles (net)						5.7
8.3	6.7	8.8	All Other Non-Current						5.9
100.0	100.0	100.0	Total						100.0
			LIABILITIES						
10.9	9.7	11.6	Notes Payable-Short Term						6.3
2.7	1.4	3.3	Cur. Mat.-L.T.D.						4.3
9.1	10.4	10.1	Trade Payables						11.3
.4	.2	.4	Income Taxes Payable						.5
11.7	6.3	8.8	All Other Current						8.5
34.8	28.1	34.3	Total Current						31.0
14.2	16.4	24.4	Long-Term Debt						22.6
.4	.3	.1	Deferred Taxes						.2
7.3	7.3	8.5	All Other Non-Current						4.2
43.3	48.0	32.6	Net Worth						42.0
100.0	100.0	100.0	Total Liabilties & Net Worth						100.0
			INCOME DATA						
100.0	100.0	100.0	Net Sales						100.0
36.6	38.2	41.7	Gross Profit						37.4
30.8	33.2	36.6	Operating Expenses						29.6
5.8	5.0	5.1	Operating Profit						7.9
1.2	1.4	1.6	All Other Expenses (net)						1.6
4.6	3.6	3.6	Profit Before Taxes						6.3
			RATIOS						
3.8	6.3	4.0							3.9
2.1	2.6	2.1	Current						2.3
1.4	1.5	1.2							1.4
1.5	1.8	1.7							1.6
.8	1.1	.8	Quick						1.1
.5	.6	.6							.7
31 11.7	27 13.8	29 12.5							47 7.8
41 9.0	38 9.7	48 7.7	Sales/Receivables						51 7.1
63 5.8	53 6.8	53 6.9							54 6.7
97 3.8	92 4.0	97 3.8							97 3.8
134 2.7	123 3.0	140 2.6	Cost of Sales/Inventory						116 3.1
186 2.0	184 2.0	209 1.7							147 2.5
10 35.1	12 30.2	18 20.3							25 14.9
22 16.3	21 17.7	37 9.8	Cost of Sales/Payables						42 8.7
49 7.4	58 6.3	56 6.5							58 6.3
3.2	2.4	2.5							2.6
4.8	3.6	4.0	Sales/Working Capital						4.0
9.9	7.3	13.8							7.5
8.3	15.2	14.0							21.2
(33) 3.2	(26) 3.4	(26) 2.6	EBIT/Interest					(14)	3.2
1.6	.5	1.2							2.0
12.1		18.4	Net Profit + Depr., Dep.,						
(16) 9.0		(11) 1.8	Amort./Cur. Mat. L/T/D						
2.5		.7							
.2	.1	.2							.2
.3	.4	.8	Fixed/Worth						.4
1.1	1.5	-1.1							-3.8
.4	.2	.4							.4
.8	.8	1.7	Debt/Worth						.9
5.3	3.6	-7.6							-10.6
26.7	19.2	21.5	% Profit Before Taxes/Tangible						32.0
(32) 12.4	(27) 10.8	(18) 8.4	Net Worth					(11)	12.7
2.1	.9	1.9							3.3
16.3	13.4	12.9	% Profit Before Taxes/Total						21.0
6.2	7.3	4.7	Assets						9.7
.8	.1	.7							2.4
25.9	26.1	21.6							13.6
9.6	8.1	8.0	Sales/Net Fixed Assets						7.4
5.6	5.3	5.5							4.9
2.1	1.9	2.1							2.0
1.6	1.6	1.7	Sales/Total Assets						1.7
1.2	1.0	1.1							1.2
.7	.7	.7							1.5
(35) 1.7	(28) 2.0	(26) 1.8	% Depr., Dep., Amort./Sales					(14)	2.4
2.8	3.0	3.2							3.4
			% Officers', Directors' Owners' Comp/Sales						
2308964M	1584082M	1759549M	Net Sales ($)	688M	10185M	11647M	23212M	39132M	1674685M
1365003M	1074835M	1116276M	Total Assets ($)	640M	3435M	10342M	18869M	43311M	1039679M

M = $ thousand   MM = $ million
See Pages 9 through 22 for Explanation of Ratios and Data

Current Data Sorted by Assets   Comparative Historical Data

0-500M	500M-2MM	2-10MM	10-50MM	50-100MM	100-250MM		4/1/06-3/31/07 ALL	4/1/07-3/31/08 ALL
	1	1	1	1		Type of Statement		
	2	2	3			Unqualified	9	4
	2					Reviewed	7	5
						Compiled	5	4
						Tax Returns	3	1
1	4 (4/1-9/30/10)	6	16 (10/1/10-3/31/11)	1		Other	8	7
1	1	11	6	2		**NUMBER OF STATEMENTS**	32	21
%	%	%	%	%	%	**ASSETS**	%	%
		6.9				Cash & Equivalents	4.9	7.0
		27.1				Trade Receivables (net)	22.9	22.6
		36.1				Inventory	34.6	35.7
D		.8			D	All Other Current	1.5	1.1
A		71.1			A	Total Current	63.9	66.5
T		21.9			T	Fixed Assets (net)	23.8	23.0
A		1.7			A	Intangibles (net)	5.8	3.0
		5.3				All Other Non-Current	6.5	7.6
N		100.0			N	Total	100.0	100.0
O					O	**LIABILITIES**		
T		12.0			T	Notes Payable-Short Term	11.3	8.5
		1.9				Cur. Mat.-L.T.D.	5.2	4.6
A		10.7			A	Trade Payables	16.0	14.0
V		.1			V	Income Taxes Payable	.5	.0
A		6.5			A	All Other Current	8.7	9.0
I		31.2			I	Total Current	41.6	36.0
L		15.3			L	Long-Term Debt	16.5	18.6
A		.3			A	Deferred Taxes	.5	.3
B		4.8			B	All Other Non-Current	3.8	1.6
L		48.5			L	Net Worth	37.5	43.5
E		100.0			E	Total Liabilties & Net Worth	100.0	100.0
						INCOME DATA		
		100.0				Net Sales	100.0	100.0
		37.9				Gross Profit	32.4	31.1
		29.3				Operating Expenses	27.3	24.8
		8.6				Operating Profit	5.0	6.4
		1.4				All Other Expenses (net)	.8	1.3
		7.2				Profit Before Taxes	4.2	5.0
						RATIOS		
		10.0					3.1	4.0
		1.7				Current	2.2	2.1
		1.5					1.2	1.4
		3.7					1.4	2.0
		1.0				Quick	.9	.9
		.5					.5	.4
	36	10.0					33 10.9	26 14.1
	46	7.9				Sales/Receivables	40 9.0	33 11.2
	55	6.6					50 7.3	41 8.8
	60	6.0					57 6.4	64 5.7
	114	3.2				Cost of Sales/Inventory	86 4.2	82 4.5
	174	2.1					122 3.0	97 3.7
	8	45.0					17 21.2	15 24.3
	24	15.0				Cost of Sales/Payables	27 13.3	20 17.9
	47	7.7					43 8.6	39 9.4
		3.4					3.9	3.8
		5.3				Sales/Working Capital	6.6	6.4
		11.7					27.6	14.9
							9.3	18.7
						EBIT/Interest	(30) 2.7	(19) 3.6
							.8	1.2
						Net Profit + Depr., Dep., Amort./Cur. Mat. L/T/D		
		.2					.2	.2
		.6				Fixed/Worth	.5	.4
		1.1					2.1	1.7
		.3					.5	.3
		1.2				Debt/Worth	1.8	2.1
		4.1					4.9	3.0
		56.6					30.2	33.0
	(10)	32.0				% Profit Before Taxes/Tangible Net Worth	(26) 16.6	(19) 17.9
		8.3					2.5	2.0
		31.2					19.7	21.2
		8.9				% Profit Before Taxes/Total Assets	5.4	4.4
		1.4					-.9	1.2
		22.1					24.4	35.9
		8.8				Sales/Net Fixed Assets	9.7	11.8
		6.0					5.1	6.2
		2.5					2.6	2.8
		1.9				Sales/Total Assets	1.9	2.0
		1.4					1.5	1.8
		1.7					.9	.8
	(10)	2.9				% Depr., Dep., Amort./Sales	(26) 1.9	(17) 2.3
		3.5					3.2	3.1
						% Officers', Directors' Owners' Comp/Sales		
	3911M	100251M	225275M	180731M		Net Sales ($)	998928M	368382M
	1124M	46282M	115113M	127236M		Total Assets ($)	699693M	241868M

M = $ thousand   MM = $ million
See Pages 9 through 22 for Explanation of Ratios and Data

Comparative Historical Data

Current Data Sorted by Sales

						Type of Statement		0-1MM	1-3MM	3-5MM	5-10MM	10-25MM	25MM & OVER
	2		3		3	Unqualified						1	2
	6		6		5	Reviewed						4	1
	1		4		2	Compiled		1	1				
	1		1			Tax Returns							
	13		7		10	Other		3	1		4		2
	4/1/08-		4/1/09-		4/1/10-								
	3/31/09		3/31/10		3/31/11				4 (4/1-9/30/10)			16 (10/1/10-3/31/11)	
	ALL		ALL		ALL								
	23		21		20	NUMBER OF STATEMENTS		4	2		9		5
	%		%		%	ASSETS		%	%	%	%	%	%
	6.4		8.9		8.4	Cash & Equivalents							
	21.5		24.9		24.2	Trade Receivables (net)		D	D				
	36.1		31.3		37.5	Inventory		A	A				
	2.0		1.2		1.2	All Other Current		T	T				
	66.1		66.4		71.4	Total Current		A	A				
	21.5		20.3		21.3	Fixed Assets (net)							
	6.0		8.1		1.4	Intangibles (net)		N	N				
	6.4		5.2		6.0	All Other Non-Current		O	O				
	100.0		100.0		100.0	Total		T	T				
						LIABILITIES		A	A				
	9.9		8.6		10.8	Notes Payable-Short Term		V	V				
	3.3		5.2		1.7	Cur. Mat.-L.T.D.		A	A				
	13.1		13.8		11.9	Trade Payables		I	I				
	.1		.0		.2	Income Taxes Payable		L	L				
	4.5		7.0		5.5	All Other Current		A	A				
	30.9		34.7		30.1	Total Current		B	B				
	16.5		15.4		13.6	Long-Term Debt		L	L				
	.2		.3		.2	Deferred Taxes		E	E				
	3.2		4.3		4.9	All Other Non-Current							
	49.1		45.3		51.2	Net Worth							
	100.0		100.0		100.0	Total Liabilities & Net Worth							
						INCOME DATA							
	100.0		100.0		100.0	Net Sales							
	27.7		30.4		35.1	Gross Profit							
	25.6		24.8		28.0	Operating Expenses							
	2.2		5.6		7.1	Operating Profit							
	.7		1.4		.9	All Other Expenses (net)							
	1.4		4.2		6.2	Profit Before Taxes							
						RATIOS							
	4.5		3.7		5.3								
	2.5		1.9		3.0	Current							
	1.3		1.4		1.5								
	2.0		1.8		3.0								
	.8		.9		1.4	Quick							
	.4		.6		.5								
30	12.1	34	10.7	35	10.5								
37	9.9	42	8.7	41	8.9	Sales/Receivables							
46	7.9	49	7.5	49	7.4								
68	5.4	58	6.3	70	5.2								
100	3.7	79	4.6	98	3.7	Cost of Sales/Inventory							
113	3.2	132	2.8	142	2.6								
13	27.9	17	21.7	16	22.9								
30	12.3	26	14.0	30	12.3	Cost of Sales/Payables							
39	9.3	46	7.9	45	8.1								
	4.3		4.1		3.4								
	6.4		5.7		4.9	Sales/Working Capital							
	13.3		11.5		10.8								
	8.8		15.5		16.2								
(19)	1.0	(19)	1.5	(16)	3.4	EBIT/Interest							
	-.6		.4		.9								
						Net Profit + Depr., Dep., Amort./Cur. Mat. L/T/D							
	.3		.2		.2								
	.5		.5		.5	Fixed/Worth							
	1.4		4.6		1.0								
	.3		.4		.3								
	1.2		1.7		.8	Debt/Worth							
	2.4		12.0		3.8								
	16.0		31.9		53.3	% Profit Before Taxes/Tangible							
(20)	4.5	(17)	7.8	(19)	20.5	Net Worth							
	-11.5		-1.9		3.9								
	11.3		12.0		26.8	% Profit Before Taxes/Total							
	.3		4.5		10.2	Assets							
	-3.6		-.6		.4								
	25.1		31.4		26.8								
	9.2		12.2		8.9	Sales/Net Fixed Assets							
	5.5		4.7		5.9								
	2.3		2.7		2.5								
	2.1		1.9		1.9	Sales/Total Assets							
	1.8		1.4		1.6								
	1.2		.9		1.1								
(16)	2.8	(17)	2.5	(18)	2.4	% Depr., Dep., Amort./Sales							
	3.7		3.9		3.5								
						% Officers', Directors' Owners' Comp/Sales							
	580915M		690356M		510168M	Net Sales ($)		16572M	12947M		144551M		336098M
	343149M		431093M		289755M	Total Assets ($)		10126M	8591M		65286M		205752M

© RMA 2011

M = $ thousand   MM = $ million
See Pages 9 through 22 for Explanation of Ratios and Data

Current Data Sorted by Assets | Comparative Historical Data

Type of Statement							104	83
Unqualified	2		17	47	7	14	104	83
Reviewed	1	17	58	24	1		96	76
Compiled	4	19	32	7			68	62
Tax Returns	22	50	24				83	71
Other	14	61	85	63	10	11	179	179
		124 (4/1-9/30/10)		466 (10/1/10-3/31/11)			4/1/06-3/31/07 ALL	4/1/07-3/31/08 ALL
	0-500M	500M-2MM	2-10MM	10-50MM	50-100MM	100-250MM		
NUMBER OF STATEMENTS	43	147	216	141	18	25	530	471
ASSETS	%	%	%	%	%	%	%	%
Cash & Equivalents	16.0	14.6	7.7	8.6	6.6	6.0	8.2	9.5
Trade Receivables (net)	21.6	26.7	27.6	24.3	17.3	19.4	27.1	24.8
Inventory	26.4	26.5	31.1	27.3	22.6	19.5	27.2	27.5
All Other Current	2.4	1.6	2.2	2.4	1.9	3.8	2.6	3.1
Total Current	66.4	69.4	68.6	62.5	48.3	48.7	65.0	64.9
Fixed Assets (net)	20.5	20.4	21.7	22.4	25.2	21.5	23.4	23.2
Intangibles (net)	7.5	2.7	4.1	10.1	11.6	22.1	5.9	5.3
All Other Non-Current	5.6	7.5	5.6	4.9	14.8	7.6	5.7	6.6
Total	100.0	100.0	100.0	100.0	100.0	100.0	100.0	100.0
LIABILITIES								
Notes Payable-Short Term	25.0	14.7	12.6	10.5	6.9	4.0	13.5	12.9
Cur. Mat.-L.T.D.	3.4	2.4	3.9	2.4	2.3	2.3	3.2	4.3
Trade Payables	17.6	15.7	16.3	12.8	12.9	9.3	15.9	13.2
Income Taxes Payable	.1	.1	.2	.4	.3	.6	.3	.2
All Other Current	14.7	10.1	9.7	10.2	13.3	11.3	10.5	11.8
Total Current	60.8	42.9	42.7	36.3	35.7	27.5	43.3	42.4
Long-Term Debt	26.8	16.7	14.7	13.2	26.0	14.6	16.0	16.0
Deferred Taxes	.2	.1	.3	.6	.2	2.1	.5	.4
All Other Non-Current	10.8	10.5	4.4	9.4	10.7	7.5	7.4	4.8
Net Worth	1.4	29.7	37.9	40.4	27.3	48.3	32.8	36.4
Total Liabilities & Net Worth	100.0	100.0	100.0	100.0	100.0	100.0	100.0	100.0
INCOME DATA								
Net Sales	100.0	100.0	100.0	100.0	100.0	100.0	100.0	100.0
Gross Profit	44.7	41.1	34.1	29.4	25.8	27.9	33.7	35.1
Operating Expenses	39.8	36.1	28.9	24.0	19.1	21.4	28.5	28.7
Operating Profit	4.9	5.0	5.2	5.5	6.7	6.5	5.2	6.4
All Other Expenses (net)	1.2	1.3	1.0	1.2	2.7	1.8	1.5	1.3
Profit Before Taxes	3.7	3.7	4.2	4.3	4.0	4.7	3.7	5.1
RATIOS								
Current	2.2	4.4	2.6	2.9	2.0	2.5	2.6	2.6
	1.2	1.8	1.7	1.9	1.5	2.1	1.6	1.7
	.8	1.1	1.2	1.3	1.2	1.5	1.1	1.1
Quick	1.4	2.7	1.4	1.5	1.0	1.3	1.4	1.5
	.7	1.1	.9	.9	.6	1.1	.9	.8
	.2	.5	.5	.6	.4	.7	.5	.5
Sales/Receivables	0 UND	16 22.1	30 12.1	36 10.1	21 17.4	44 8.3	29 12.8	26 14.0
	18 19.8	32 11.3	45 8.1	49 7.5	44 8.2	56 6.5	44 8.3	40 9.1
	43 8.5	55 6.7	59 6.2	61 6.0	57 6.4	62 5.9	59 6.2	58 6.2
Cost of Sales/Inventory	8 48.6	10 35.1	41 9.0	47 7.8	41 8.9	57 6.5	37 9.9	36 10.2
	43 8.4	50 7.3	77 4.8	77 4.7	66 5.5	71 5.1	65 5.6	64 5.7
	123 3.0	100 3.6	127 2.9	110 3.3	81 4.5	101 3.6	109 3.3	113 3.2
Cost of Sales/Payables	1 316.0	13 29.1	18 20.0	21 17.6	19 19.6	23 16.2	18 20.0	16 22.4
	20 18.2	29 12.5	34 10.8	32 11.4	31 11.7	38 9.7	33 11.2	29 12.7
	38 9.6	50 7.3	53 6.8	46 7.9	45 8.2	45 8.1	53 6.9	47 7.8
Sales/Working Capital	7.9	4.2	4.6	3.8	5.8	3.9	5.0	4.7
	15.9	10.0	8.1	6.6	11.1	6.1	9.3	8.6
	-23.6	78.9	25.4	15.8	42.3	8.8	42.9	32.5
EBIT/Interest	14.5	11.4	13.9	12.4	7.4	11.5	10.6	10.8
	(32) 5.1	(120) 3.9	(193) 3.8	(129) 4.4	(16) 2.7	(24) 4.5	(480) 3.6	(414) 3.7
	1.5	.8	1.2	1.2	1.1	.5	1.1	1.3
Net Profit + Depr., Dep., Amort./Cur. Mat. L/T/D		3.8	3.8	7.1		4.0	8.3	6.5
		(13) 2.3	(53) 1.8	(51) 3.4		(13) 2.3	(121) 3.0	(121) 2.7
		-10.7	.5	1.5		.0	1.4	.9
Fixed/Worth	.2	.1	.2	.2	.4	.3	.3	.3
	.7	.4	.5	.6	.7	.6	.7	.6
	-1.3	2.4	1.6	2.4	NM	5.1	2.4	1.5
Debt/Worth	1.1	.5	.7	.6	1.2	.6	.8	.8
	4.5	1.6	1.6	1.7	2.8	2.3	2.1	1.7
	-5.7	9.2	5.3	6.9	NM	12.9	9.3	5.5
% Profit Before Taxes/Tangible Net Worth	96.7	62.1	46.0	39.3	55.7	34.8	57.0	58.6
	(25) 36.8	(120) 30.6	(188) 14.4	(118) 19.1	(14) 10.9	(21) 13.6	(437) 24.1	(410) 25.5
	10.8	6.0	1.6	6.0	.4	-3.9	5.5	5.3
% Profit Before Taxes/Total Assets	26.6	23.4	13.2	13.0	14.2	10.6	17.5	19.0
	13.8	6.7	4.9	7.2	3.1	5.1	7.2	7.7
	3.7	-.4	.5	.8	.8	-1.3	.4	1.3
Sales/Net Fixed Assets	102.3	46.7	27.6	25.4	31.9	10.6	30.8	32.5
	36.5	21.1	12.9	11.4	6.7	6.5	11.8	12.2
	12.8	9.1	5.6	4.5	4.1	4.1	5.5	5.5
Sales/Total Assets	5.3	3.9	2.8	2.3	2.1	1.5	2.9	3.0
	2.9	2.6	2.0	1.8	1.8	1.2	2.1	2.1
	1.9	1.6	1.5	1.2	1.0	1.0	1.5	1.4
% Depr., Dep., Amort./Sales	.4	.6	.9	1.0	.8	1.8	.9	.9
	(25) 1.2	(105) 1.5	(189) 1.9	(124) 2.0	(15) 2.1	(20) 2.9	(447) 1.8	(394) 1.9
	3.1	3.3	3.4	3.7	3.4	4.4	3.2	3.3
% Officers', Directors' Owners' Comp/Sales	3.8	2.8	1.7	.9			2.2	2.2
	(20) 6.5	(75) 5.4	(78) 3.3	(21) 2.3			(171) 3.8	(157) 3.9
	10.9	8.8	6.1	3.3			7.2	6.8
Net Sales ($)	62471M	492911M	2353550M	5620609M	2385137M	4801886M	15845763M	12453260M
Total Assets ($)	12969M	168426M	1041047M	3086233M	1312154M	3955673M	9279684M	7296445M

M = $ thousand   MM = $ million
See Pages 9 through 22 for Explanation of Ratios and Data

Comparative Historical Data

Current Data Sorted by Sales

92	97	87	Type of Statement	1	1	1	6	19	59
79	90	101	Reviewed	1	14	7	26	34	19
50	43	62	Compiled	6	3	14	22	13	4
85	100	96	Tax Returns	14	32	21	21	8	
213	257	244	Other	14	40	37	32	52	69
4/1/08-3/31/09 ALL	4/1/09-3/31/10 ALL	4/1/10-3/31/11 ALL		124 (4/1-9/30/10)			466 (10/1/10-3/31/11)		
				0-1MM	1-3MM	3-5MM	5-10MM	10-25MM	25MM & OVER
519	587	590	NUMBER OF STATEMENTS	36	90	80	107	126	151
%	%	%	ASSETS	%	%	%	%	%	%
9.3	9.8	10.1	Cash & Equivalents	14.7	14.7	11.7	9.1	9.3	6.9
23.9	23.4	25.5	Trade Receivables (net)	13.2	24.4	26.4	26.3	29.3	24.7
28.9	26.7	28.0	Inventory	30.0	24.7	28.2	28.3	31.3	26.3
3.0	3.4	2.2	All Other Current	1.7	1.9	1.5	2.1	2.6	2.5
65.1	63.4	65.7	Total Current	59.6	65.7	67.8	65.8	72.5	60.4
21.6	23.8	21.6	Fixed Assets (net)	24.3	22.1	21.2	23.5	19.1	21.5
6.8	6.6	6.4	Intangibles (net)	7.9	5.5	3.9	4.6	4.1	11.3
6.5	6.2	6.3	All Other Non-Current	8.2	6.7	7.1	6.1	4.3	6.8
100.0	100.0	100.0	Total	100.0	100.0	100.0	100.0	100.0	100.0
			LIABILITIES						
13.2	12.4	13.0	Notes Payable-Short Term	23.4	10.0	19.6	12.9	10.6	10.8
3.4	4.1	3.0	Cur. Mat.-L.T.D.	2.3	3.3	2.7	4.0	3.4	2.1
14.3	14.8	15.0	Trade Payables	9.4	11.5	17.0	16.2	18.1	14.0
.3	.2	.3	Income Taxes Payable	.0	.1	.1	.4	.2	.4
11.1	12.5	10.5	All Other Current	16.6	7.6	11.2	10.1	10.2	10.8
42.3	44.1	41.7	Total Current	51.7	32.4	50.6	43.6	42.6	38.0
18.0	17.6	16.1	Long-Term Debt	21.5	23.4	17.1	14.0	12.0	14.8
.3	.4	.4	Deferred Taxes	.3	.0	.3	.3	.6	.6
7.1	8.0	7.9	All Other Non-Current	18.3	8.6	9.8	4.5	5.3	8.6
32.3	30.0	33.9	Net Worth	8.2	35.5	22.3	37.7	39.5	38.0
100.0	100.0	100.0	Total Liabilities & Net Worth	100.0	100.0	100.0	100.0	100.0	100.0
			INCOME DATA						
100.0	100.0	100.0	Net Sales	100.0	100.0	100.0	100.0	100.0	100.0
32.9	34.2	35.0	Gross Profit	45.4	44.8	37.3	34.2	32.5	28.1
27.9	30.4	29.7	Operating Expenses	40.5	40.0	33.3	28.7	26.9	22.1
4.9	3.8	5.3	Operating Profit	4.9	4.9	4.0	5.5	5.6	5.9
1.4	1.8	1.2	All Other Expenses (net)	2.7	1.5	1.2	.8	.8	1.4
3.5	2.0	4.1	Profit Before Taxes	2.2	3.3	2.9	4.8	4.8	4.6
			RATIOS						
2.9	3.1	2.8	Current	3.4	5.7	2.7	2.4	2.8	2.5
1.7	1.7	1.8		1.5	2.1	1.5	1.8	1.8	1.7
1.1	1.1	1.2		.7	1.2	1.0	1.2	1.3	1.3
1.7	1.7	1.6	Quick	1.6	3.7	1.7	1.5	1.4	1.4
.8	.8	.9		.4	1.2	1.0	.8	.9	.8
.5	.5	.5		.1	.6	.4	.5	.6	.5
25 14.5	27 13.3	27 13.4	Sales/Receivables	4 86.8	22 16.3	17 21.9	29 12.7	29 12.8	34 10.8
37 9.7	43 8.6	44 8.3		20 18.7	40 9.1	41 8.9	44 8.3	46 8.0	47 7.8
54 6.8	58 6.3	58 6.3		63 5.8	57 6.4	57 6.5	57 6.4	57 6.4	59 6.2
37 9.9	38 9.7	35 10.4	Cost of Sales/Inventory	4 83.4	22 16.4	30 12.0	34 10.6	36 10.2	45 8.0
73 5.0	76 4.8	70 5.2		110 3.3	66 5.5	60 6.1	63 5.8	73 5.0	71 5.1
109 3.4	123 3.0	113 3.2		289 1.3	154 2.4	116 3.2	112 3.3	125 2.9	93 3.9
15 24.5	17 21.2	18 20.8	Cost of Sales/Payables	8 46.5	11 32.2	16 23.0	17 21.3	21 17.8	21 17.5
27 13.4	30 12.4	30 12.0		23 15.6	30 12.2	31 11.9	32 11.6	30 12.0	32 11.4
48 7.6	52 7.0	49 7.4		77 4.8	54 6.8	50 7.3	47 7.7	53 6.9	45 8.1
4.6	4.1	4.4	Sales/Working Capital	3.4	3.0	4.8	4.8	4.3	4.9
9.0	8.3	8.5		11.4	6.9	9.8	8.4	8.1	8.8
34.3	61.9	28.6		-13.0	38.4	226.4	30.2	22.0	19.6
10.7	9.9	12.3	EBIT/Interest	5.7	9.3	11.2	15.1	16.0	13.7
(455) 3.2	(519) 2.7	(514) 3.9		(26) 1.7	(73) 2.2	(68) 3.6	(95) 4.2	(111) 5.4	(141) 4.4
.8	.0	1.1		-1.2	.5	1.1	1.5	2.1	1.2
6.2	5.7	6.3	Net Profit + Depr., Dep., Amort./Cur. Mat. L/T/D			4.1	3.7	5.1	7.1
(119) 3.0	(129) 2.4	(138) 2.7			(11) 1.9	(28) 1.7	(35) 2.3	(59) 3.4	
1.1	.6	.9				.2	.1	1.4	1.3
.2	.2	.2	Fixed/Worth	.1	.1	.1	.2	.2	.2
.6	.7	.6		.8	.6	.6	.6	.5	.6
2.2	3.3	2.3		-1.8	3.3	4.7	2.3	1.2	2.5
.7	.7	.7	Debt/Worth	.8	.5	.6	.6	.6	.8
1.8	2.0	1.7		5.4	1.7	1.7	1.4	1.4	2.1
8.0	14.8	8.0		-4.3	8.2	28.3	7.4	5.2	9.2
43.6	38.6	52.7	% Profit Before Taxes/Tangible Net Worth	53.6	53.8	51.8	55.0	53.8	51.7
(429) 19.4	(467) 15.9	(486) 18.9		(21) 10.5	(71) 15.9	(64) 15.2	(89) 17.9	(113) 20.6	(128) 19.2
1.7	1.7	3.4		4.8	1.1	.9	5.5	3.7	5.1
16.3	12.1	17.0	% Profit Before Taxes/Total Assets	19.3	19.2	15.2	15.5	17.3	14.0
5.9	4.4	6.4		4.7	5.2	4.1	6.2	9.0	7.1
-.1	-2.5	.6		-1.8	-2.2	-.1	1.7	1.8	.9
34.5	29.7	34.9	Sales/Net Fixed Assets	64.7	35.5	42.6	26.2	39.3	30.1
13.0	10.2	14.2		13.9	17.5	18.6	11.8	15.6	11.9
6.0	4.5	5.4		3.2	5.3	8.3	5.5	6.9	4.7
2.9	2.6	2.9	Sales/Total Assets	2.2	3.0	3.9	3.0	3.0	2.5
2.1	1.9	2.0		1.4	1.9	2.5	2.1	2.2	1.8
1.4	1.2	1.4		.8	1.3	1.6	1.4	1.7	1.3
.8	1.0	.9	% Depr., Dep., Amort./Sales	.6	.7	.6	1.0	.8	.9
(425) 1.8	(465) 2.3	(478) 1.8		(23) 2.2	(67) 1.9	(60) 1.6	(94) 2.1	(104) 1.6	(130) 1.8
3.1	4.4	3.6		7.5	4.3	3.8	3.8	3.0	3.5
1.9	1.6	2.2	% Officers', Directors', Owners' Comp/Sales	3.9	3.0	2.3	2.4	1.4	.7
(156) 3.8	(171) 3.5	(195) 3.8		(15) 8.5	(43) 5.7	(39) 4.4	(44) 3.4	(36) 2.9	(18) 2.3
7.3	6.8	7.1		19.2	8.2	6.7	6.1	3.8	7.2
18464887M	16106926M	15716564M	Net Sales ($)	20940M	170434M	311068M	785395M	2008612M	12420115M
11019501M	10297634M	9576502M	Total Assets ($)	21107M	133707M	162472M	418525M	1025632M	7815059M

M = $ thousand   MM = $ million
See Pages 9 through 22 for Explanation of Ratios and Data

Current Data Sorted by Assets | Comparative Historical Data

Type of Statement

Type of Statement	0-500M	500M-2MM	2-10MM	10-50MM	50-100MM	100-250MM	4/1/06-3/31/07 ALL	4/1/07-3/31/08 ALL
Unqualified		2	7	20	3	9	37	39
Reviewed	3	6	32	32	5	2	58	62
Compiled	4	14	26	8	2		60	50
Tax Returns	18	29	30	2	2		46	57
Other	11	32	50	40	12	8	137	137

Current columns: 50 (4/1-9/30/10) [500M-2MM], 359 (10/1/10-3/31/11) [10-50MM]

	0-500M	500M-2MM	2-10MM	10-50MM	50-100MM	100-250MM	4/1/06-3/31/07 ALL	4/1/07-3/31/08 ALL
NUMBER OF STATEMENTS	36	83	145	102	24	19	338	345
	%	%	%	%	%	%	%	%
ASSETS								
Cash & Equivalents	18.4	12.1	10.7	9.5	7.5	16.1	7.0	8.1
Trade Receivables (net)	12.7	16.9	18.6	17.9	16.3	8.7	19.8	18.0
Inventory	31.0	49.0	43.7	37.1	45.4	38.3	47.5	44.9
All Other Current	8.8	.9	3.4	2.3	2.6	4.3	2.9	3.2
Total Current	71.0	78.9	76.4	66.8	71.8	67.5	77.2	74.2
Fixed Assets (net)	20.3	14.5	16.3	20.2	16.7	21.8	15.5	17.7
Intangibles (net)	2.7	2.8	3.1	5.7	2.8	4.9	2.5	2.9
All Other Non-Current	6.0	3.8	4.2	7.3	8.7	5.9	4.8	5.3
Total	100.0	100.0	100.0	100.0	100.0	100.0	100.0	100.0
LIABILITIES								
Notes Payable-Short Term	17.8	27.2	20.0	27.2	42.2	28.2	33.5	30.6
Cur. Mat.-L.T.D.	1.5	1.4	1.4	4.1	4.9	4.3	2.8	3.3
Trade Payables	15.9	22.8	15.8	11.8	7.8	6.8	10.9	10.4
Income Taxes Payable	.2	.2	.1	.2	.6	.1	.1	.1
All Other Current	23.2	9.8	11.9	10.1	6.8	7.3	10.7	9.3
Total Current	58.6	61.4	49.2	53.5	62.3	46.7	58.1	53.7
Long-Term Debt	22.2	10.8	8.6	10.1	11.5	14.9	12.0	13.2
Deferred Taxes	.0	.0	.3	.8	2.3	1.1	.3	.5
All Other Non-Current	5.9	5.8	7.1	4.1	2.3	2.3	4.3	4.8
Net Worth	13.3	22.0	34.8	31.6	21.6	34.9	25.4	27.9
Total Liabilities & Net Worth	100.0	100.0	100.0	100.0	100.0	100.0	100.0	100.0
INCOME DATA								
Net Sales	100.0	100.0	100.0	100.0	100.0	100.0	100.0	100.0
Gross Profit	36.5	24.4	25.5	24.5	21.7	20.0	23.2	24.3
Operating Expenses	33.5	21.3	22.4	21.1	18.1	16.0	19.6	20.2
Operating Profit	3.0	3.1	3.1	3.4	3.6	4.0	3.6	4.1
All Other Expenses (net)	1.3	.6	.3	.2	.4	.8	.8	.9
Profit Before Taxes	1.7	2.5	2.8	3.2	3.2	3.2	2.9	3.2

RATIOS

	0-500M	500M-2MM	2-10MM	10-50MM	50-100MM	100-250MM	4/1/06-3/31/07 ALL	4/1/07-3/31/08 ALL
Current	4.0	1.9	2.3	1.5	1.4	1.7	1.7	2.0
	1.4	1.3	1.5	1.2	1.3	1.2	1.2	1.3
	.6	.9	1.2	1.0	1.0	1.0	1.0	1.1
Quick	1.5	.8	1.0	.8	.5	.8	.9	1.0
	.5	.3	.5	.5	.3	.3	.4 (344)	.4
	.2	.1	.3	.3	.2	.2	.2	.2
Sales/Receivables	0 UND	0 999.8	9 41.4	11 33.4	11 32.8	11 32.9	6 60.6	5 70.4
	4 82.3	8 47.1	20 18.5	18 20.1	20 18.0	21 17.1	15 23.6	16 23.3
	22 16.9	26 14.0	30 12.0	38 9.6	34 10.6	29 12.4	33 11.0	31 11.8
Cost of Sales/Inventory	2 166.6	30 12.2	36 10.3	35 10.3	63 5.8	54 6.7	33 11.0	35 10.4
	33 11.2	59 6.2	64 5.7	65 5.6	90 4.0	90 4.0	63 5.8	64 5.7
	92 4.0	96 3.8	102 3.6	93 3.9	104 3.5	128 2.8	95 3.8	105 3.5
Cost of Sales/Payables	0 UND	1 355.8	5 71.8	8 43.1	8 44.6	9 42.2	3 128.0	3 125.5
	3 108.5	14 26.0	16 22.5	17 21.9	14 25.9	17 21.3	8 44.0	9 40.1
	33 11.1	55 6.6	41 9.0	32 11.5	18 20.2	27 13.7	24 15.4	23 15.7
Sales/Working Capital	6.8	9.6	6.3	10.0	11.1	5.4	8.8	7.1
	27.7	25.8	11.4	21.9	17.3	14.2	23.2	18.3
	-26.5	-87.4	31.4	85.6	53.0	92.0	99.4	60.8
EBIT/Interest	18.8	9.9	8.2	6.5	6.3	9.1	4.7	5.2
	(25) 3.0	(68) 3.2	(132) 3.7	(95) 3.5	(23) 3.3	(16) 4.1	(290) 2.2	(308) 2.4
	.9	1.5	1.8	1.7	1.5	1.9	1.2	1.3
Net Profit + Depr., Dep., Amort./Cur. Mat. L/T/D			19.9	5.2			4.6	4.1
			(22) 2.2	(28) 1.6			(53) 1.5	(58) 1.5
			1.6	.8			.9	.9
Fixed/Worth	.0	.1	.1	.2	.1	.1	.1	.1
	.5	.4	.3	.6	.4	.7	.4	.5
	-1.2	7.1	1.5	2.2	1.4	1.8	1.6	1.5
Debt/Worth	.7	1.6	1.1	1.6	1.7	1.2	1.5	1.4
	5.2	3.7	1.9	3.3	3.1	2.6	3.9	3.3
	-5.8	101.7	6.2	8.5	9.7	8.0	12.0	8.3
% Profit Before Taxes/Tangible Net Worth	62.9	89.9	35.8	41.6	43.3	29.1	44.3	45.9
	(24) 28.4	(65) 34.8	(132) 16.4	(94) 22.4	(22) 22.8	(18) 22.9	(292) 22.3	(308) 19.7
	2.8	13.1	6.1	8.6	7.3	6.7	6.7	6.7
% Profit Before Taxes/Total Assets	22.5	13.8	10.5	8.4	9.9	8.5	11.4	13.0
	7.3	7.6	5.2	4.1	4.1	3.6	4.4	4.4
	.0	1.4	1.2	1.5	1.1	2.6	.9	1.3
Sales/Net Fixed Assets	726.5	234.4	123.4	55.1	95.6	83.7	154.6	106.9
	108.8	59.3	37.3	18.0	40.2	9.0	46.2	32.7
	13.9	18.9	13.0	6.0	9.0	4.8	12.8	9.9
Sales/Total Assets	7.1	6.4	4.0	3.4	3.2	2.5	4.4	4.2
	4.6	3.9	3.0	2.5	2.2	1.8	3.1	2.9
	2.0	2.3	2.1	1.5	1.6	1.1	1.9	1.9
% Depr., Dep., Amort./Sales	.2	.2	.3	.3	.3	.2	.2	.3
	(20) .7	(59) .8	(124) .6	(93) 1.0	(18) .8	(11) 1.0	(268) .5	(264) .6
	1.8	1.6	1.5	2.9	3.1	2.5	1.6	1.7
% Officers', Directors' Owners' Comp/Sales	1.8	.7	.7	.3			.6	.6
	(17) 4.2	(41) 2.1	(66) 1.5	(23) .6			(135) 1.2	(115) 1.4
	12.4	4.3	1.7				2.7	3.1
Net Sales ($)	60777M	532898M	2433106M	5845398M	5100783M	6098234M	19082781M	19387565M
Total Assets ($)	10908M	90805M	719636M	2320675M	1630628M	3203795M	5850871M	6360001M

Comparative Historical Data   Current Data Sorted by Sales

			Type of Statement						
41	48	41	Unqualified	1			1	7	32
62	57	80	Reviewed	2	1	4	14	23	36
54	51	54	Compiled	2	7	6	16	10	13
70	74	81	Tax Returns	11	13	11	16	19	11
168	148	153	Other	8	21	12	21	31	60
4/1/08-3/31/09 ALL	4/1/09-3/31/10 ALL	4/1/10-3/31/11 ALL		50 (4/1-9/30/10) 0-1MM	1-3MM	3-5MM	359 (10/1/10-3/31/11) 5-10MM	10-25MM	25MM & OVER
395	378	409	NUMBER OF STATEMENTS	24	42	33	68	90	152
%	%	%	ASSETS	%	%	%	%	%	%
8.3	12.2	11.4	Cash & Equivalents	14.2	13.4	13.9	11.1	10.1	10.8
17.0	16.8	17.0	Trade Receivables (net)	8.3	17.3	17.9	15.5	19.3	17.3
45.4	41.5	41.9	Inventory	30.3	36.9	41.0	46.4	42.8	42.7
3.1	3.0	3.1	All Other Current	8.9	4.9	1.4	1.7	2.7	2.9
73.8	73.5	73.3	Total Current	61.8	72.4	74.3	74.8	74.8	73.7
17.1	16.2	17.5	Fixed Assets (net)	28.3	19.5	13.8	17.6	15.4	17.4
2.6	3.5	3.8	Intangibles (net)	1.5	6.0	3.9	3.2	4.3	3.4
6.4	6.8	5.4	All Other Non-Current	8.5	2.1	8.0	4.4	5.5	5.6
100.0	100.0	100.0	Total	100.0	100.0	100.0	100.0	100.0	100.0
			LIABILITIES						
26.4	26.4	24.7	Notes Payable-Short Term	18.1	17.3	20.9	20.2	25.3	30.4
4.1	3.4	2.4	Cur. Mat.-L.T.D.	2.1	1.9	1.4	1.5	1.7	3.7
11.3	12.4	15.3	Trade Payables	17.4	18.4	17.9	16.0	17.3	12.2
.1	.1	.2	Income Taxes Payable	.0	.2	.1	.3	.2	.3
12.4	10.6	11.5	All Other Current	16.1	20.9	9.1	11.6	10.8	9.1
54.4	52.9	54.2	Total Current	53.7	58.8	49.4	49.7	55.2	55.6
15.9	12.3	11.1	Long-Term Debt	37.2	12.1	9.7	12.0	5.5	9.8
.3	.4	.5	Deferred Taxes	.0	.0	.5	.1	.3	1.0
5.9	4.7	5.5	All Other Non-Current	8.5	5.0	2.5	7.9	4.4	5.3
23.5	29.6	28.8	Net Worth	.6	24.0	37.9	30.3	34.6	28.4
100.0	100.0	100.0	Total Liabilities & Net Worth	100.0	100.0	100.0	100.0	100.0	100.0
			INCOME DATA						
100.0	100.0	100.0	Net Sales	100.0	100.0	100.0	100.0	100.0	100.0
23.8	25.3	25.5	Gross Profit	46.7	37.3	31.6	26.1	23.1	18.9
21.4	22.8	22.3	Operating Expenses	40.5	33.5	27.4	22.8	20.6	16.0
2.4	2.5	3.2	Operating Profit	6.2	3.7	4.2	3.3	2.5	2.9
1.1	.8	.5	All Other Expenses (net)	3.9	1.1	.3	.2	.1	.1
1.4	1.7	2.8	Profit Before Taxes	2.3	2.6	3.9	3.1	2.4	2.7
			RATIOS						
1.9	2.1	1.9		4.6	2.4	3.1	2.2	1.7	1.6
1.4	1.4	1.3	Current	1.3	1.5	1.4	1.5	1.3	1.3
1.1	1.1	1.1		.6	.9	1.1	1.1	1.0	1.1
.8	1.0	.8		.8	1.3	1.9	1.0	.8	.8
.4 (377)	.5	.5	Quick	.3	.5	.6	.5	.5	.4
.2	.2	.3		.2	.2	.1	.2	.3	.3
7 52.7	5 66.6	6 59.1		0 UND	1 244.3	2 193.6	5 74.0	7 55.6	9 39.7
15 23.7	16 23.0	16 22.2	Sales/Receivables	3 120.8	21 17.2	13 28.9	18 20.5	20 18.6	16 23.2
29 12.5	32 11.3	30 12.3		33 11.0	39 9.3	36 10.0	32 11.4	32 11.4	27 13.4
34 10.6	31 11.9	32 11.4		0 UND	21 17.4	29 12.6	38 9.6	31 11.7	37 9.9
65 5.6	62 5.9	64 5.7	Cost of Sales/Inventory	60 6.1	73 5.0	54 6.8	68 5.4	58 6.3	63 5.8
102 3.6	107 3.4	99 3.7		227 1.6	109 3.4	96 3.8	129 2.8	89 4.1	92 4.0
4 86.5	3 113.5	5 80.5		0 UND	0 UND	3 126.2	3 109.6	4 91.7	7 52.1
11 33.1	13 27.7	15 24.5	Cost of Sales/Payables	2 195.8	26 13.9	21 17.8	20 18.3	17 21.4	14 26.6
28 13.2	30 12.3	37 9.8		38 9.5	69 5.3	63 5.8	41 9.0	43 8.4	22 16.8
7.9	7.4	8.0		4.1	5.1	4.6	5.3	8.7	11.0
18.2	15.9	17.3	Sales/Working Capital	20.9	13.5	15.0	10.9	17.6	21.4
128.5	89.1	98.3		-17.2	-27.0	86.0	65.7	172.0	54.4
5.5	5.5	8.0		3.0	10.1	16.8	10.7	7.9	7.1
(363) 2.2	(325) 2.2	(359) 3.6	EBIT/Interest	(15) 1.1	(34) 2.7	(27) 4.9	(62) 3.6	(82) 3.4	(139) 3.7
.9	1.1	1.6		.8	1.6	2.6	1.4	1.6	2.0
4.8	4.9	5.8	Net Profit + Depr., Dep.,					25.5	4.6
(66) 1.5	(62) 1.6	(69) 1.7	Amort./Cur. Mat. L/T/D					(13) 1.7	(44) 1.4
.8	.8	1.0						.8	.9
.1	.1	.1		.1	.1	.0	.1	.1	.2
.5	.4	.5	Fixed/Worth	2.9	.8	.3	.5	.3	.5
2.0	1.7	2.0		-.5	-46.7	1.2	3.4	1.5	1.5
1.5	1.1	1.3		2.3	1.1	.6	1.0	1.4	1.5
3.3	2.8	2.9	Debt/Worth	5.5	2.9	2.0	2.3	2.4	3.1
9.6	11.7	9.0		-5.7	-68.2	6.9	21.1	6.4	7.6
40.3	34.9	43.4	% Profit Before Taxes/Tangible	46.7	46.3	49.2	46.9	41.3	43.4
(341) 15.4	(329) 13.8	(355) 21.7	Net Worth	(16) 12.9	(30) 24.0	(28) 22.5	(57) 26.4	(84) 17.4	(140) 23.1
3.7	3.5	7.2		1.4	3.0	9.9	5.8	6.0	7.9
10.2	8.5	10.6	% Profit Before Taxes/Total	14.5	16.0	10.8	11.5	10.4	10.5
3.7	3.0	5.5	Assets	3.0	6.4	8.2	5.6	4.6	4.8
-.3	.4	1.4		.0	1.3	4.7	.7	1.0	2.2
109.0	121.6	111.5		726.5	114.9	329.9	102.2	163.6	84.5
31.1	32.7	35.2	Sales/Net Fixed Assets	15.2	22.8	44.1	33.0	40.1	33.2
10.0	9.4	10.8		3.0	9.9	19.4	12.4	11.3	8.5
4.0	4.3	4.3		4.3	4.1	5.3	4.1	4.7	4.0
2.9	2.8	2.9	Sales/Total Assets	1.5	2.7	3.3	2.8	3.1	2.9
2.0	1.7	1.8		1.1	1.8	1.2	1.9	2.2	1.9
.3	.3	.3		1.7	.5	.3	.2	.3	.3
(310) .7	(285) .9	(325) .7	% Depr., Dep., Amort./Sales	(11) 2.3	(32) 1.0	(27) .8	(59) .6	(72) .5	(124) .7
2.1	2.1	1.9		13.9	2.9	1.5	1.3	2.3	1.7
.8	.8	.7	% Officers', Directors'		1.9	.8	1.0	.7	.3
(152) 1.7	(134) 1.6	(155) 1.7	Owners' Comp/Sales		(23) 4.0	(13) 1.8	(36) 2.0	(39) 1.3	(37) .6
3.3	4.0	4.1			8.9	6.1	4.3	2.2	1.7
15443253M	18952473M	20071196M	Net Sales ($)	14326M	77938M	133846M	496093M	1518921M	17830072M
6447458M	7569302M	7976447M	Total Assets ($)	12280M	36074M	74360M	261575M	669497M	6922661M

Current Data Sorted by Assets   Comparative Historical Data

0-500M	500M-2MM	2-10MM	10-50MM	50-100MM	100-250MM	Type of Statement		
		8	27	11	8	Unqualified	78	65
	9	64	58	1		Reviewed	117	104
6	20	45	6		2	Compiled	101	101
12	33	36	1			Tax Returns	67	58
8	36	70	64	12	9	Other	146	164
	76 (4/1-9/30/10)		470 (10/1/10-3/31/11)				4/1/06-3/31/07 ALL	4/1/07-3/31/08 ALL
26	98	223	156	24	19	NUMBER OF STATEMENTS	509	492
%	%	%	%	%	%	**ASSETS**	%	%
14.6	9.0	6.5	4.2	6.6	8.1	Cash & Equivalents	5.1	6.0
19.6	20.8	25.5	23.9	21.4	18.7	Trade Receivables (net)	24.6	23.9
43.7	51.0	50.1	47.4	40.4	36.0	Inventory	49.6	49.3
1.0	2.4	2.8	3.3	2.0	1.3	All Other Current	1.8	2.1
78.9	83.1	84.9	78.8	70.4	64.1	Total Current	81.1	81.2
12.0	10.1	8.5	11.8	11.6	12.5	Fixed Assets (net)	11.2	11.3
5.2	2.8	2.4	4.1	15.4	18.7	Intangibles (net)	2.8	3.7
4.1	3.9	4.3	5.3	2.7	4.7	All Other Non-Current	4.8	3.8
100.0	100.0	100.0	100.0	100.0	100.0	Total	100.0	100.0
						LIABILITIES		
25.9	14.3	14.2	19.0	18.5	9.8	Notes Payable-Short Term	17.9	17.9
2.3	2.1	2.2	1.9	1.1	1.4	Cur. Mat.-L.T.D.	2.2	2.2
17.0	18.7	21.8	19.7	17.2	17.5	Trade Payables	21.8	21.7
.4	.1	.2	.2	.1	.1	Income Taxes Payable	.2	.2
7.4	5.9	7.0	7.6	6.6	7.2	All Other Current	9.1	6.7
53.0	41.1	45.4	48.4	43.6	36.0	Total Current	51.1	48.7
14.5	11.3	7.6	8.1	15.6	17.0	Long-Term Debt	11.8	11.0
.0	.1	.1	.3	.0	1.2	Deferred Taxes	.3	.2
8.8	9.1	6.0	4.8	5.4	2.8	All Other Non-Current	5.8	6.7
23.6	38.4	40.9	38.4	35.3	42.9	Net Worth	31.0	33.5
100.0	100.0	100.0	100.0	100.0	100.0	Total Liabilities & Net Worth	100.0	100.0
						INCOME DATA		
100.0	100.0	100.0	100.0	100.0	100.0	Net Sales	100.0	100.0
33.3	34.5	30.1	31.1	27.5	33.0	Gross Profit	31.2	30.4
30.1	31.1	26.4	26.3	21.6	26.6	Operating Expenses	27.7	26.5
3.2	3.3	3.6	4.8	5.9	6.4	Operating Profit	3.5	3.9
1.2	.3	.3	.7	1.6	1.1	All Other Expenses (net)	.9	1.0
2.0	3.0	3.3	4.2	4.3	5.3	Profit Before Taxes	2.6	2.9
						RATIOS		
3.2	4.3	3.0	2.3	2.0	2.8		2.6	2.6
1.6	2.3	1.8	1.7	1.4	2.0	Current	1.7	1.6
1.0	1.4	1.4	1.3	1.3	1.1		1.3	1.3
1.2	1.3	1.1	1.0	1.0	1.1		1.0	1.0
.6	.7	.6	(155) .5	.5	.7	Quick	.6	.6
.3	.4	.4	.4	.3	.4		.4	.4
6 57.8	15 24.6	25 14.9	28 13.0	26 14.0	33 11.2		24 15.0	23 15.6
24 15.3	27 13.8	34 10.7	39 9.3	37 9.9	44 8.2	Sales/Receivables	34 10.8	33 11.2
38 9.7	37 9.9	47 7.8	51 7.1	46 8.0	57 6.4		47 7.8	45 8.1
32 11.3	66 5.5	61 6.0	78 4.7	60 6.1	98 3.7		67 5.4	67 5.4
53 6.9	99 3.7	113 3.2	128 2.9	106 3.4	144 2.5	Cost of Sales/Inventory	111 3.3	109 3.4
130 2.8	145 2.5	168 2.2	196 1.9	134 2.7	195 1.9		167 2.3	157 2.3
10 35.3	15 24.8	24 15.2	22 16.5	27 13.4	29 12.8		23 16.2	24 15.3
23 15.6	32 11.4	37 9.8	47 7.8	38 9.5	61 5.9	Cost of Sales/Payables	40 9.1	41 8.9
43 8.4	54 6.7	59 6.2	68 5.4	57 6.4	84 4.3		66 5.5	62 5.8
4.5	3.7	3.8	4.2	6.0	2.4		4.3	4.6
16.0	6.3	5.9	6.9	8.8	6.0	Sales/Working Capital	7.6	7.7
NM	12.2	12.9	12.8	18.9	23.8		18.1	15.1
15.1	18.5	11.9	17.3	8.6	11.2		6.6	6.6
(19) 3.1	(81) 4.0	(197) 4.1	(148) 5.6	(23) 6.0	(17) 4.2	EBIT/Interest	(465) 2.8	(444) 2.6
1.0	1.1	1.8	2.3	2.0	1.9		1.3	1.4
		6.7	7.8				6.6	5.5
	(40) 2.6	(55) 2.4				Net Profit + Depr., Dep., Amort./Cur. Mat. L/T/D	(133) 2.0	(136) 2.5
		.9	1.1				.9	.8
.0	.1	.1	.1	.1	.3		.1	.1
.4	.2	.1	.2	.5	.7	Fixed/Worth	.2	.3
-21.1	.9	.5	.8	-3.6	20.7		.8	.8
.6	.7	.7	.9	1.6	1.1		.9	1.0
3.9	1.8	1.7	1.8	5.8	3.2	Debt/Worth	2.1	2.1
-18.6	4.9	3.9	4.6	-15.1	113.8		5.9	5.5
38.8	40.4	34.4	40.5	50.6	44.8		36.7	39.3
(18) 19.9	(87) 15.0	(213) 13.2	(143) 18.0	(17) 25.3	(15) 22.3	% Profit Before Taxes/Tangible Net Worth	(454) 16.1	(442) 17.4
6.8	2.8	3.9	7.7	15.0	17.6		4.4	5.7
10.9	16.5	12.1	12.4	9.7	9.5		12.0	13.0
6.2	6.1	4.9	6.0	7.7	6.3	% Profit Before Taxes/Total Assets	4.4	5.1
.9	.6	1.3	2.5	3.9	2.1		.8	1.4
UND	107.3	108.1	77.7	63.8	42.6		86.5	86.5
46.0	41.4	50.3	35.6	25.6	17.6	Sales/Net Fixed Assets	37.0	36.9
22.5	22.8	25.4	13.4	17.6	8.4		17.8	17.5
5.3	3.7	3.1	2.5	2.6	1.7		3.1	3.2
3.4	2.8	2.4	2.0	2.2	1.4	Sales/Total Assets	2.4	2.4
2.1	2.1	1.8	1.5	1.5	1.2		1.8	1.8
.3	.3	.4	.4	.6	1.1		.4	.4
(15) 1.0	(66) .7	(178) .7	(139) .7	(21) 1.1	(14) 1.3	% Depr., Dep., Amort./Sales	(437) .8	(422) .8
2.1	1.2	1.2	1.2	1.2	1.5		1.3	1.3
2.3	2.0	1.4	.8				1.7	1.5
(11) 3.9	(48) 3.2	(103) 2.1	(34) 1.2			% Officers', Directors' Owners' Comp/Sales	(192) 2.9	(191) 2.8
11.1	7.1	2.7					5.7	5.1
33600M	354831M	2886013M	6960245M	3510211M	4592150M	Net Sales ($)	14133794M	16845240M
9001M	121307M	1135257M	3352911M	1605476M	2774516M	Total Assets ($)	6768111M	7905636M

M = $ thousand   MM = $ million
See Pages 9 through 22 for Explanation of Ratios and Data

Comparative Historical Data   ## Current Data Sorted by Sales

			Type of Statement						
69	66	54	Unqualified				1	9	44
108	110	132	Reviewed	1	1	8	15	59	48
101	85	79	Compiled	2	9	11	25	26	6
64	63	82	Tax Returns	8	20	18	19	16	1
197	197	199	Other	5	27	17	26	46	78
4/1/08-3/31/09 ALL	4/1/09-3/31/10 ALL	4/1/10-3/31/11 ALL		0-1MM	76 (4/1-9/30/10) 1-3MM	3-5MM	5-10MM	470 (10/1/10-3/31/11) 10-25MM	25MM & OVER
539	521	546	**NUMBER OF STATEMENTS**	16	57	54	86	156	177
%	%	%	**ASSETS**	%	%	%	%	%	%
5.6	7.0	6.7	Cash & Equivalents	14.7	9.6	6.4	7.8	6.3	5.1
22.7	22.9	23.5	Trade Receivables (net)	12.2	19.5	21.5	23.9	25.0	24.8
50.8	47.8	48.3	Inventory	39.2	52.1	51.9	47.8	48.9	46.4
2.6	2.5	2.7	All Other Current	3.1	2.2	4.6	2.5	2.8	2.3
81.7	80.2	81.2	Total Current	69.2	83.3	84.4	82.1	83.0	78.6
10.6	11.6	10.2	Fixed Assets (net)	18.8	8.6	9.9	10.1	9.1	11.0
3.7	4.1	4.2	Intangibles (net)	5.3	3.9	2.1	3.0	2.5	6.9
4.0	4.1	4.4	All Other Non-Current	6.8	4.1	3.6	4.9	5.5	3.5
100.0	100.0	100.0	Total	100.0	100.0	100.0	100.0	100.0	100.0
			LIABILITIES						
19.0	19.4	16.2	Notes Payable-Short Term	23.0	14.7	19.7	11.6	15.4	17.9
2.4	2.3	2.0	Cur. Mat.-L.T.D.	.9	2.4	1.6	2.3	2.4	1.6
19.7	19.6	20.1	Trade Payables	14.4	18.2	14.5	17.6	21.8	22.6
.2	.2	.2	Income Taxes Payable	.2	.1	.2	.1	.3	.1
7.9	6.9	7.0	All Other Current	12.2	3.7	6.8	8.7	6.7	7.0
49.2	48.5	45.5	Total Current	50.6	39.2	42.9	40.3	46.7	49.3
10.0	9.4	9.4	Long-Term Debt	24.2	11.3	7.4	9.2	8.0	9.4
.1	.2	.2	Deferred Taxes	.0	.1	.2	.3	.1	.3
5.1	7.1	6.2	All Other Non-Current	6.4	15.1	5.4	5.1	6.2	4.0
35.5	34.7	38.8	Net Worth	18.6	34.3	44.2	45.2	39.0	37.0
100.0	100.0	100.0	Total Liabilities & Net Worth	100.0	100.0	100.0	100.0	100.0	100.0
			INCOME DATA						
100.0	100.0	100.0	Net Sales	100.0	100.0	100.0	100.0	100.0	100.0
31.0	31.2	31.3	Gross Profit	40.2	35.3	35.0	30.9	30.6	28.9
27.9	28.5	27.2	Operating Expenses	34.1	32.5	31.6	26.6	27.2	23.8
3.0	2.8	4.1	Operating Profit	6.1	2.8	3.4	4.3	3.4	5.1
.8	1.0	.5	All Other Expenses (net)	5.0	.5	-.1	.3	.3	.7
2.2	1.7	3.5	Profit Before Taxes	1.1	2.3	3.5	4.0	3.2	4.3
			RATIOS						
2.6	2.9	2.9	Current	3.9	4.0	5.0	3.7	2.8	2.1
1.7	1.7	1.8		2.1	2.3	2.2	2.0	1.8	1.6
1.2	1.2	1.3		.7	1.4	1.3	1.5	1.4	1.3
.9	1.1	1.1	Quick	1.5	1.1	1.2	1.5	1.0	1.0
.5	.6 (545)	.6		.5	.7	.6	.7	.6 (176)	.6
.3	.4	.4		.1	.4	.4	.5	.4	.4
21 17.0	23 16.0	22 16.3	Sales/Receivables	6 65.2	14 26.1	19 19.3	21 17.5	25 14.7	29 12.7
31 11.8	34 10.8	34 10.7		23 15.6	26 14.0	33 11.1	32 11.2	34 10.8	37 9.9
44 8.4	46 8.0	47 7.7		38 9.6	42 8.6	52 7.1	50 7.3	46 7.9	48 7.6
70 5.2	69 5.3	64 5.7	Cost of Sales/Inventory	34 10.8	70 5.2	76 4.8	54 6.7	63 5.8	67 5.5
114 3.2	109 3.4	112 3.3		100 3.6	115 3.2	129 2.8	102 3.6	121 3.0	108 3.4
179 2.0	178 2.0	170 2.2		241 1.5	183 2.0	182 2.0	157 2.3	175 2.1	151 2.4
20 18.6	21 17.6	22 16.8	Cost of Sales/Payables	11 31.8	18 20.5	15 23.5	18 20.5	25 14.8	24 15.3
34 10.9	36 10.1	38 9.6		36 10.1	36 10.1	33 11.2	31 12.0	40 9.1	42 8.6
56 6.6	61 6.0	61 6.0		59 6.2	59 6.1	52 7.1	59 6.2	61 5.9	65 5.6
4.3	4.0	4.1	Sales/Working Capital	3.0	2.8	3.1	3.6	4.4	4.8
7.6	6.8	6.6		7.2	5.7	5.2	5.8	6.1	8.1
18.6	15.8	13.6		-5.3	12.4	15.5	10.5	11.8	17.1
7.5	8.7	14.1	EBIT/Interest		7.5	19.0	17.5	10.9	15.0
(495) 2.9	(471) 3.3	(485) 4.4		(46) 2.8	(47) 3.7	(76) 4.2	(138) 4.2	(169) 6.0	
1.1	1.1	1.8			-.2	2.0	1.9	1.8	2.3
6.8	7.3	7.7	Net Profit + Depr., Dep., Amort./Cur. Mat. L/T/D			4.6		5.6	12.6
(144) 3.0	(128) 2.7	(121) 2.7			(10) 1.7		(41) 2.7	(61) 4.4	
.9	1.0	1.2				.2		1.2	1.6
.1	.1	.1	Fixed/Worth	.0	.1	.0	.0	.1	.1
.2	.2	.2		.2	.2	.2	.1	.1	.3
.7	.7	.7		NM	1.7	.6	.6	.5	.8
.9	.9	.8	Debt/Worth	.4	.7	.4	.5	.8	1.1
2.0	2.0	1.8		2.5	2.3	1.1	1.4	1.7	2.1
5.6	5.5	4.9		-18.6	18.0	5.1	3.0	4.5	6.7
33.3	28.0	37.9	% Profit Before Taxes/Tangible Net Worth	27.5	34.6	30.7	41.3	35.2	46.2
(480) 14.5	(452) 11.9	(493) 17.0		(11) 7.9	(46) 11.8	(49) 14.1	(83) 16.6	(149) 12.2	(155) 21.8
2.9	2.1	5.2		3.0	1.7	4.1	3.6	4.1	10.3
10.7	9.7	12.4	% Profit Before Taxes/Total Assets	6.9	9.4	13.4	15.5	11.1	13.9
4.6	3.7	5.9		2.5	5.9	5.2	6.5	4.8	6.6
2.9	.3	1.6		.0	-1.1	1.3	1.3	1.2	2.9
92.1	89.3	95.3	Sales/Net Fixed Assets	UND	221.0	88.8	110.2	100.4	79.9
37.1	39.3	42.1		25.7	43.1	38.3	50.1	48.4	36.4
17.3	16.3	19.6		11.1	26.6	17.5	18.5	23.0	15.9
3.2	2.9	3.1	Sales/Total Assets	2.5	3.5	2.9	3.4	3.1	3.0
2.4	2.3	2.3		1.9	2.4	2.2	2.4	2.3	2.3
1.7	1.6	1.7		1.1	1.8	1.7	1.6	1.7	1.7
.4	.4	.4	% Depr., Dep., Amort./Sales		.3	.3	.4	.4	.4
(445) .7	(427) .8	(433) .7		(36) .8	(38) .8	(60) .7	(133) .7	(157) .7	
1.2	1.4	1.2			1.3	1.7	1.5	1.2	1.2
1.4	1.6	1.3	% Officers', Directors' Owners' Comp/Sales		2.2	1.9	1.5	1.2	.6
(206) 2.6	(201) 2.8	(199) 2.3		(30) 4.0	(30) 2.8	(36) 2.0	(63) 2.1	(35) 1.1	
4.7	5.4	4.4			8.3	4.3	3.6	3.6	2.6
21023396M	15288872M	18337050M	Net Sales ($)	10802M	112286M	218440M	605966M	2500801M	14888755M
9561307M	7696110M	8998468M	Total Assets ($)	13077M	49667M	109887M	315146M	1249668M	7261023M

© RMA 2011

M = $ thousand   MM = $ million
See Pages 9 through 22 for Explanation of Ratios and Data

Current Data Sorted by Assets   Comparative Historical Data

0-500M	500M-2MM	2-10MM	10-50MM	50-100MM	100-250MM	Type of Statement	4/1/06-3/31/07 ALL	4/1/07-3/31/08 ALL
		1	11	2	7	Unqualified	17	18
	2	15	18	3	1	Reviewed	38	34
1	9	9	6	1		Compiled	36	41
4	5	7	2			Tax Returns	25	16
2	2	24	12	5	10	Other	57	55
27 (4/1-9/30/10)			131 (10/1/10-3/31/11)					
7	18	56	49	11	17	NUMBER OF STATEMENTS	173	164
%	%	%	%	%	%	**ASSETS**	%	%
	10.0	6.3	5.7	4.9	6.6	Cash & Equivalents	6.0	5.3
	30.0	30.7	29.2	32.5	17.8	Trade Receivables (net)	26.2	27.5
	46.3	43.3	40.4	47.5	41.0	Inventory	39.8	41.4
	.8	3.9	2.3	2.2	1.8	All Other Current	3.1	3.3
	87.2	84.1	77.6	87.1	67.2	Total Current	75.1	77.5
	8.7	10.8	17.0	9.9	20.1	Fixed Assets (net)	19.2	15.5
	.4	1.2	1.7	1.4	6.9	Intangibles (net)	1.8	2.5
	3.7	3.8	3.8	1.6	5.8	All Other Non-Current	3.8	4.5
	100.0	100.0	100.0	100.0	100.0	Total	100.0	100.0
						LIABILITIES		
	10.8	12.4	15.2	13.3	5.7	Notes Payable-Short Term	12.9	13.0
	1.5	2.1	1.5	.7	3.4	Cur. Mat.-L.T.D.	3.0	3.1
	39.6	37.0	30.8	41.1	28.1	Trade Payables	32.7	32.5
	.0	.2	.2	.0	.6	Income Taxes Payable	.2	.1
	13.4	9.6	6.2	8.7	5.0	All Other Current	6.3	6.9
	65.2	61.4	53.9	63.8	42.8	Total Current	55.0	55.5
	14.3	5.6	8.1	8.1	17.9	Long-Term Debt	10.9	10.3
	.0	.1	.4	.1	.4	Deferred Taxes	.3	.3
	6.9	3.9	3.6	2.2	4.1	All Other Non-Current	4.9	4.4
	13.5	28.9	33.9	25.9	34.8	Net Worth	28.9	29.5
	100.0	100.0	100.0	100.0	100.0	Total Liabilities & Net Worth	100.0	100.0
						INCOME DATA		
	100.0	100.0	100.0	100.0	100.0	Net Sales	100.0	100.0
	26.3	21.8	21.2	17.6	23.8	Gross Profit	26.0	24.7
	24.4	19.7	18.3	14.5	19.3	Operating Expenses	24.1	22.4
	1.8	2.1	2.9	3.1	4.5	Operating Profit	1.9	2.3
	-.5	-.1	.1	.3	-.3	All Other Expenses (net)	.3	.3
	2.3	2.2	2.8	2.9	4.8	Profit Before Taxes	1.6	2.0
						RATIOS		
	2.7	1.9	1.8	1.7	2.0		1.8	1.7
	1.7	1.4	1.4	1.3	1.5	Current	1.3	1.4
	1.2	1.1	1.2	1.2	1.2		1.1	1.1
	1.3	.8	.8	.9	.8		.8	.7
	.8	.6	.6	.6	.6	Quick	.5	.5
	.4	.4	.4	.4	.4		.4	.4
20	18.7	19 18.8	27 13.3	39 9.4	11 33.0		20 18.6	23 15.9
27	13.5	30 12.2	36 10.1	41 8.9	24 15.3	Sales/Receivables	31 11.8	33 11.2
58	6.3	46 7.9	51 7.1	49 7.4	44 8.2		42 8.6	43 8.4
36	10.2	36 10.3	54 6.8	54 6.8	66 5.6		46 7.9	49 7.5
66	5.5	64 5.7	68 5.4	64 5.7	74 5.0	Cost of Sales/Inventory	68 5.4	69 5.3
89	4.1	97 3.8	87 4.2	96 3.8	94 3.9		87 4.2	93 3.9
26	14.2	36 10.2	36 10.1	51 7.2	42 8.8		33 11.0	32 11.3
38	9.6	51 7.1	54 6.7	65 5.6	61 5.9	Cost of Sales/Payables	50 7.3	53 6.9
47	7.7	75 4.9	74 4.9	72 5.1	77 4.7		71 5.2	73 5.0
	6.1	8.4	7.7	7.7	6.7		8.6	8.2
	9.3	16.5	11.9	10.3	13.0	Sales/Working Capital	16.8	15.5
	26.6	56.2	32.0	21.0	20.6		50.5	42.0
	16.9	9.2	16.5		24.8		8.0	7.9
	(14) 6.0	(54) 5.1	(45) 6.8		9.7	EBIT/Interest	(160) 3.4	(154) 3.3
	1.6	2.3	3.2		2.5		1.6	1.7
		10.5	26.5				4.8	6.3
		(10) 4.6	(14) 6.7			Net Profit + Depr., Dep., Amort./Cur. Mat. L/T/D	(49) 2.3	(43) 3.1
		1.2	1.2				1.3	1.5
	.1	.1	.1	.2	.1		.2	.2
	.2	.3	.5	.2	1.0	Fixed/Worth	.5	.4
	8.6	.7	.9	1.2	1.8		1.4	1.1
	.8	1.2	1.5	1.4	1.3		1.3	1.3
	3.4	3.0	2.3	3.5	2.3	Debt/Worth	2.6	2.5
	NM	7.3	4.0	5.4	9.0		5.1	4.9
	74.3	43.5	33.8	34.7	61.4	% Profit Before Taxes/Tangible	38.0	34.3
	(14) 14.8	(52) 22.3	(48) 21.7	(10) 31.6	(16) 34.3	Net Worth	(158) 19.0	(151) 16.1
	2.1	7.0	15.4	22.7	17.4		4.4	6.9
	14.3	11.6	11.0	12.9	18.8		9.1	9.4
	8.0	5.2	7.0	7.2	8.4	% Profit Before Taxes/Total Assets	4.5	5.2
	1.2	1.9	3.6	3.1	3.9		.8	1.7
	154.0	123.5	57.6	63.5	62.8		54.8	55.2
	61.3	50.1	26.8	42.7	20.5	Sales/Net Fixed Assets	24.8	29.4
	32.9	20.4	8.3	28.2	7.1		10.8	13.1
	4.8	4.3	3.3	3.6	3.0		3.8	3.8
	3.6	3.3	2.5	2.9	2.3	Sales/Total Assets	3.1	3.0
	2.8	2.5	2.1	2.2	1.8		2.4	2.3
	.3	.2	.5	.3	.7		.5	.5
	(12) .7	(46) .7	(46) .8	(10) .6	(16) 1.1	% Depr., Dep., Amort./Sales	(156) 1.0	(147) .9
	1.3	1.3	1.4	.9	2.0		1.6	1.4
	1.7	.7	.6				.9	.6
	(10) 2.9	(26) 1.6	(14) .8			% Officers', Directors' Owners' Comp/Sales	(62) 2.0	(68) 1.2
	4.9	2.8	1.7					
8042M	82551M	959991M	3423919M	2377158M	7312713M	Net Sales ($)	9605214M	9808360M
1414M	23368M	273114M	1284041M	829496M	2782026M	Total Assets ($)	3475371M	4004875M

Comparative Historical Data | Current Data Sorted by Sales

4/1/08-3/31/09 ALL	4/1/09-3/31/10 ALL	4/1/10-3/31/11 ALL	Type of Statement	0-1MM	1-3MM	3-5MM	5-10MM	10-25MM	25MM & OVER
21	23	21	Unqualified					2	19
35	26	38	Reviewed			2	5	7	24
35	30	26	Compiled			3	7	7	7
11	10	18	Tax Returns	1	6	2	1	6	2
57	49	55	Other	1	1	2	9	11	31
					27 (4/1-9/30/10)			131 (10/1/10-3/31/11)	
159	138	158	NUMBER OF STATEMENTS	3	8	9	22	33	83
%	%	%	ASSETS	%	%	%	%	%	%
5.1	5.9	6.6	Cash & Equivalents				6.7	6.6	6.0
24.7	26.0	28.6	Trade Receivables (net)				25.9	30.9	28.3
44.7	41.4	42.6	Inventory				49.1	43.2	41.4
3.0	2.7	2.6	All Other Current				4.4	2.0	2.7
77.6	76.0	80.4	Total Current				86.0	82.8	78.3
15.7	16.9	13.8	Fixed Assets (net)				9.8	13.2	14.9
1.9	2.9	2.0	Intangibles (net)				.6	1.2	2.8
4.9	4.2	3.7	All Other Non-Current				3.6	2.8	4.0
100.0	100.0	100.0	Total				100.0	100.0	100.0
			LIABILITIES						
14.8	12.6	12.6	Notes Payable-Short Term				9.5	12.5	13.0
2.6	2.5	2.0	Cur. Mat.-L.T.D.				1.6	2.4	1.8
30.9	32.1	35.1	Trade Payables				32.9	39.4	32.4
.1	.3	.2	Income Taxes Payable				.0	.3	.2
7.1	8.1	9.9	All Other Current				7.7	5.9	7.8
55.5	55.5	59.8	Total Current				51.7	60.6	55.2
10.0	11.3	9.0	Long-Term Debt				14.3	6.5	9.2
.2	.2	.2	Deferred Taxes				.1	.2	.3
4.7	3.8	5.0	All Other Non-Current				6.2	4.0	3.6
29.6	29.1	26.0	Net Worth				27.7	28.7	31.6
100.0	100.0	100.0	Total Liabilities & Net Worth				100.0	100.0	100.0
			INCOME DATA						
100.0	100.0	100.0	Net Sales				100.0	100.0	100.0
25.2	24.1	22.8	Gross Profit				25.2	20.9	20.6
23.3	22.6	20.2	Operating Expenses				23.3	18.7	17.5
2.0	1.5	2.7	Operating Profit				1.9	2.2	3.1
.4	.0	.0	All Other Expenses (net)				-.2	-.1	.0
1.6	1.5	2.7	Profit Before Taxes				2.1	2.4	3.1
			RATIOS						
1.9	1.8	1.9	Current				2.2	1.8	1.7
1.4	1.4	1.4					1.8	1.3	1.4
1.1	1.1	1.1					1.2	1.1	1.2
.7	.8	.8	Quick				.9	.9	.8
.5	.6	.6					.6	.6	.6
.3	.4	.4					.4	.4	.5
18 20.7	20 18.0	21 17.5	Sales/Receivables				20 18.4	22 16.6	23 15.9
30 12.1	34 10.7	34 10.9					29 12.6	32 11.3	36 10.2
41 8.8	44 8.3	50 7.4					53 6.9	46 7.9	49 7.4
53 6.8	53 6.9	48 7.6	Cost of Sales/Inventory				55 6.6	42 8.7	52 7.0
73 5.0	71 5.1	68 5.4					86 4.3	61 6.0	68 5.4
97 3.7	96 3.8	93 3.9					118 3.1	88 4.1	85 4.3
29 12.6	32 11.5	36 10.2	Cost of Sales/Payables				37 9.9	38 9.7	37 10.0
51 7.2	52 7.0	52 7.0					48 7.6	65 5.6	54 6.8
69 5.3	71 5.1	74 5.0					76 4.8	77 4.7	71 5.1
7.7	7.2	7.5	Sales/Working Capital				5.9	8.6	7.7
14.6	14.1	12.7					8.2	14.5	12.3
34.3	77.1	41.8					22.2	70.0	23.6
7.6	10.9	11.4	EBIT/Interest				9.8	8.5	14.9
(150) 3.4	(132) 4.1	(144) 5.7				(21) 5.1	(30) 4.3	(78) 7.5	
1.4	1.8	2.5					1.9	2.7	3.2
4.4	9.8	11.1	Net Profit + Depr., Dep., Amort./Cur. Mat. L/T/D						11.1
(48) 2.2	(40) 2.6	(40) 5.8						(31) 6.3	
1.3	.8	1.8							1.8
.2	.2	.1	Fixed/Worth				.1	.1	.1
.5	.5	.4					.3	.4	.4
1.1	1.4	1.1					1.0	1.1	1.0
1.3	1.4	1.3	Debt/Worth				.8	1.3	1.5
2.6	2.5	2.7					2.2	3.3	2.5
5.9	5.8	6.1					8.3	6.7	4.5
31.7	30.4	37.7	% Profit Before Taxes/Tangible Net Worth				34.8	41.7	35.7
(147) 13.2	(127) 13.5	(142) 24.4				(19) 19.4	(31) 22.1	(79) 25.9	
3.8	6.4	10.7					6.3	9.1	16.6
8.3	8.8	11.8	% Profit Before Taxes/Total Assets				13.3	11.5	11.1
4.3	4.1	6.9					4.3	5.5	7.4
.9	1.7	2.1					1.2	1.9	3.6
61.8	62.1	100.6	Sales/Net Fixed Assets				101.0	117.8	71.2
28.1	25.8	39.0					36.8	53.3	34.2
13.2	9.9	15.9					24.0	15.9	11.3
3.6	3.5	3.9	Sales/Total Assets				3.6	4.3	3.8
2.9	2.8	2.9					3.1	3.1	2.7
2.2	2.1	2.2					2.2	2.5	2.2
.5	.5	.4	% Depr., Dep., Amort./Sales				.4	.3	.4
(142) .8	(123) .9	(136) .7				(19) .6	(25) .7	(77) .7	
1.3	1.6	1.3					1.3	1.5	1.4
1.0	.8	.7	% Officers', Directors', Owners' Comp/Sales				1.3	.8	.6
(57) 1.6	(52) 1.4	(57) 1.6				(15) 2.1	(15) 1.2	(19) .7	
3.5	3.2	3.0					3.4	1.6	1.7
13499898M	10654643M	14164374M	Net Sales ($)	1147M	15373M	39617M	158528M	541940M	13407769M
4678550M	4191399M	5193459M	Total Assets ($)	247M	4886M	14456M	61422M	202732M	4909716M

M = $ thousand   MM = $ million
See Pages 9 through 22 for Explanation of Ratios and Data

Current Data Sorted by Assets   **Comparative Historical Data**

Type of Statement

	0-500M	500M-2MM	2-10MM	10-50MM	50-100MM	100-250MM	Type of Statement	4/1/06-3/31/07 ALL	4/1/07-3/31/08 ALL
Unqualified		1	2	1	1	1	Unqualified	5	4
Reviewed		1	5	3			Reviewed	17	14
Compiled	1	3	4	2			Compiled	13	14
Tax Returns	1	7	6				Tax Returns	18	10
Other	2	2	4		1		Other	17	11
		16 (4/1-9/30/10)		32 (10/1/10-3/31/11)					
NUMBER OF STATEMENTS	2	14	19	10	2	1	NUMBER OF STATEMENTS	70	53

ASSETS (%)

	0-500M	500M-2MM	2-10MM	10-50MM	50-100MM	100-250MM		4/1/06-3/31/07 ALL	4/1/07-3/31/08 ALL
Cash & Equivalents		8.5	8.1	2.9			Cash & Equivalents	6.7	4.8
Trade Receivables (net)		17.5	17.0	25.6			Trade Receivables (net)	18.2	17.5
Inventory		40.9	48.9	39.9			Inventory	43.9	45.4
All Other Current		.3	4.1	.6			All Other Current	2.8	3.3
Total Current		67.3	78.1	69.0			Total Current	71.6	71.0
Fixed Assets (net)		16.1	15.1	14.9			Fixed Assets (net)	18.2	19.0
Intangibles (net)		5.1	3.2	4.8			Intangibles (net)	2.0	2.8
All Other Non-Current		11.5	3.6	11.3			All Other Non-Current	8.2	7.1
Total		100.0	100.0	100.0			Total	100.0	100.0

LIABILITIES

	0-500M	500M-2MM	2-10MM	10-50MM	50-100MM	100-250MM		4/1/06-3/31/07 ALL	4/1/07-3/31/08 ALL
Notes Payable-Short Term		12.5	12.0	20.1			Notes Payable-Short Term	11.6	15.7
Cur. Mat.-L.T.D.		3.8	2.1	3.1			Cur. Mat.-L.T.D.	2.2	3.7
Trade Payables		12.1	20.6	9.3			Trade Payables	13.8	10.6
Income Taxes Payable		.8	.3	.3			Income Taxes Payable	.2	.0
All Other Current		5.5	5.3	5.7			All Other Current	11.9	13.4
Total Current		34.7	40.4	38.6			Total Current	39.6	43.5
Long-Term Debt		16.4	4.3	9.0			Long-Term Debt	16.0	12.1
Deferred Taxes		.2	.3	.1			Deferred Taxes	.1	.2
All Other Non-Current		4.8	3.6	.9			All Other Non-Current	5.1	3.8
Net Worth		43.9	51.5	51.4			Net Worth	39.2	40.4
Total Liabilities & Net Worth		100.0	100.0	100.0			Total Liabilties & Net Worth	100.0	100.0

INCOME DATA

	0-500M	500M-2MM	2-10MM	10-50MM	50-100MM	100-250MM		4/1/06-3/31/07 ALL	4/1/07-3/31/08 ALL
Net Sales		100.0	100.0	100.0			Net Sales	100.0	100.0
Gross Profit		42.5	31.6	27.5			Gross Profit	36.9	34.3
Operating Expenses		42.3	26.9	22.1			Operating Expenses	33.1	29.3
Operating Profit		.2	4.7	5.4			Operating Profit	3.8	5.0
All Other Expenses (net)		-.8	.1	.3			All Other Expenses (net)	.4	1.0
Profit Before Taxes		1.1	4.6	5.1			Profit Before Taxes	3.4	4.0

RATIOS

	0-500M	500M-2MM	2-10MM	10-50MM	50-100MM	100-250MM		4/1/06-3/31/07 ALL	4/1/07-3/31/08 ALL
		5.0	3.7	2.6				3.6	2.7
Current		1.9	2.0	1.7			Current	2.2	1.7
		1.3	1.4	1.4				1.5	1.3
		2.0	1.4	1.5				1.3	.8
Quick		.6	.6	.5			Quick	.7	.5
		.4	.2	.4				.3	.3
		2 235.5	3 107.8	23 15.9				8 47.4	9 41.6
Sales/Receivables		19 19.4	13 27.7	42 8.6			Sales/Receivables	23 16.1	23 16.0
		30 12.2	31 11.8	72 5.1				35 10.4	36 10.1
		0 UND	32 11.3	54 6.8				46 7.9	54 6.8
Cost of Sales/Inventory		85 4.3	83 4.4	113 3.2			Cost of Sales/Inventory	88 4.1	97 3.8
		140 2.6	110 3.3	236 1.5				140 2.6	200 1.8
		0 UND	13 28.5	4 98.1				5 75.7	7 54.1
Cost of Sales/Payables		17 20.9	22 16.4	15 24.4			Cost of Sales/Payables	17 20.9	17 21.0
		36 10.3	50 7.4	65 5.6				52 7.0	42 8.8
		3.7	4.5	3.8				4.1	3.9
Sales/Working Capital		9.0	8.5	6.1			Sales/Working Capital	7.7	8.1
		21.7	18.2	13.6				17.4	20.3
		8.2	64.3					8.9	8.0
EBIT/Interest		(17) 2.7	11.2				EBIT/Interest	(60) 3.8	(45) 3.6
		-.9	5.2					1.5	1.5
Net Profit + Depr., Dep.,							Net Profit + Depr., Dep.,	3.2	2.6
Amort./Cur. Mat. L/T/D							Amort./Cur. Mat. L/T/D	(12) 1.7	(12) 1.6
								1.0	.6
		.0	.1	.0				.1	.1
Fixed/Worth		.2	.2	.2			Fixed/Worth	.3	.3
		.5	.5	.7				.9	.8
		.5	.6					.5	.6
Debt/Worth		1.0	1.0	1.1			Debt/Worth	1.5	1.7
		5.9	2.1	2.3				3.0	2.6
% Profit Before Taxes/Tangible		46.8	41.3				% Profit Before Taxes/Tangible	34.3	38.2
Net Worth		(13) 14.1	22.9				Net Worth	(63) 13.6	(52) 14.1
		-9.1	12.5					4.5	4.4
		9.6	15.2	14.4			% Profit Before Taxes/Total	19.2	13.2
% Profit Before Taxes/Total Assets		4.6	11.1	9.1			Assets	7.0	6.2
		-3.9	6.0	4.8				1.1	1.4
		300.4	169.1	58.2				55.9	55.5
Sales/Net Fixed Assets		34.6	53.3	15.3			Sales/Net Fixed Assets	24.3	29.1
		16.9	8.7	8.9				11.0	6.6
		4.1	4.2	2.0				3.8	3.5
Sales/Total Assets		3.0	3.4	1.8			Sales/Total Assets	2.7	2.3
		1.6	2.4	1.4				1.7	1.5
			.5					.6	.7
% Depr., Dep., Amort./Sales			(16) .8				% Depr., Dep., Amort./Sales	(59) 1.0	(45) 1.1
			2.0					2.0	2.2
			2.0				% Officers', Directors'	2.3	2.7
% Officers', Directors' Owners' Comp/Sales			(10) 7.3				Owners' Comp/Sales	(37) 4.3	(19) 4.9
			11.8					9.9	11.0
Net Sales ($)	1527M	49304M	271930M	330619M	592047M	295752M	Net Sales ($)	1182649M	1087990M
Total Assets ($)	590M	15345M	74146M	170078M	188151M	138153M	Total Assets ($)	411615M	487047M

M = $ thousand   MM = $ million
See Pages 9 through 22 for Explanation of Ratios and Data

Comparative Historical Data   Current Data Sorted by Sales

			Type of Statement						
5	7	6	Unqualified		1			2	3
13	15	9	Reviewed				1	6	2
21	12	10	Compiled		1	3	3	2	1
11	12	14	Tax Returns	4	2	1	2	3	2
7	14	9	Other	2			2	3	2
4/1/08-3/31/09 ALL	4/1/09-3/31/10 ALL	4/1/10-3/31/11 ALL		\<--- 16 (4/1-9/30/10) ---\>			\<--- 32 (10/1/10-3/31/11) ---\>		
				0-1MM	1-3MM	3-5MM	5-10MM	10-25MM	25MM & OVER
57	60	48	**NUMBER OF STATEMENTS**	4	6	4	8	16	10
%	%	%	**ASSETS**	%	%	%	%	%	%
6.9	7.2	6.5	Cash & Equivalents					4.2	6.8
20.5	21.9	20.0	Trade Receivables (net)					23.1	27.0
45.2	46.6	44.3	Inventory					48.2	33.6
2.6	3.2	2.1	All Other Current					4.0	1.2
75.1	78.9	72.9	Total Current					79.5	68.7
16.5	13.4	15.4	Fixed Assets (net)					15.2	14.4
1.8	2.9	4.4	Intangibles (net)					1.1	6.0
6.5	4.8	7.4	All Other Non-Current					4.2	10.9
100.0	100.0	100.0	Total					100.0	100.0
			LIABILITIES						
14.6	15.5	13.1	Notes Payable-Short Term					11.9	15.8
3.7	3.6	4.8	Cur. Mat.-L.T.D.					2.8	2.3
14.9	16.0	19.4	Trade Payables					20.4	17.6
.3	.1	.4	Income Taxes Payable					.5	.0
13.1	9.2	5.4	All Other Current					6.0	4.5
46.5	44.5	43.1	Total Current					41.7	40.2
11.2	7.9	11.6	Long-Term Debt					5.0	12.5
.3	.2	.2	Deferred Taxes					.2	.1
4.1	8.7	3.1	All Other Non-Current					1.9	1.9
38.0	38.6	42.0	Net Worth					51.2	45.4
100.0	100.0	100.0	Total Liabilties & Net Worth					100.0	100.0
			INCOME DATA						
100.0	100.0	100.0	Net Sales					100.0	100.0
31.3	35.3	33.3	Gross Profit					31.3	20.3
27.7	32.7	30.1	Operating Expenses					25.4	16.9
3.6	2.6	3.3	Operating Profit					5.9	3.4
.7	.7	.0	All Other Expenses (net)					.4	-.2
2.9	1.9	3.3	Profit Before Taxes					5.5	3.6
			RATIOS						
2.7	2.7	3.1						3.7	2.3
1.7	1.6	1.7	Current					1.7	1.5
1.2	1.3	1.4						1.3	1.4
1.4	1.2	1.3						1.4	1.5
.6	.6	.6	Quick					.5	.7
.3	.3	.4						.3	.6
10 38.0	14 25.7	8 48.4						13 28.7	10 36.2
25 14.5	30 12.1	24 14.9	Sales/Receivables					35 10.5	28 13.0
38 9.6	40 9.0	40 9.1						52 7.0	41 8.9
51 7.1	56 6.5	34 10.6						64 5.7	15 24.1
81 4.5	102 3.6	91 4.0	Cost of Sales/Inventory					98 3.7	44 8.3
131 2.8	164 2.2	137 2.7						140 2.6	101 3.6
7 51.2	7 50.2	9 41.4						14 27.0	0 UND
18 20.2	25 14.5	23 15.7	Cost of Sales/Payables					30 12.2	16 22.2
47 7.8	61 6.0	50 7.2						63 5.8	42 8.7
5.0	3.9	4.4						3.6	5.0
10.1	7.2	9.0	Sales/Working Capital					9.1	14.2
24.9	15.3	18.1						12.5	27.5
9.1	13.8	23.9						41.7	
(50) 3.9	(53) 3.7	(45) 7.2	EBIT/Interest					(14) 11.7	
1.7	2.3	2.4						6.5	
4.1	7.1	11.4	Net Profit + Depr., Dep.,						
(13) 1.3	(18) 2.3	(13) 3.6	Amort./Cur. Mat. L/T/D						
.1	1.1	1.4							
.1	.1	.1						.1	.1
.3	.2	.2	Fixed/Worth					.1	.4
.9	.8	.5						.3	.7
.6	.8	.6						.4	.8
1.8	2.0	1.1	Debt/Worth					1.1	1.8
3.7	3.2	2.5						2.0	3.1
35.7	24.9	43.2	% Profit Before Taxes/Tangible					32.5	
(52) 16.3	(53) 13.4	(45) 21.9	Net Worth					22.5	
5.8	5.3	8.3						13.4	
14.1	11.2	14.4	% Profit Before Taxes/Total					15.2	15.6
5.1	4.7	9.0	Assets					10.8	11.1
1.4	1.9	3.3						6.1	6.5
86.5	93.2	138.6						231.4	147.1
30.3	34.7	37.1	Sales/Net Fixed Assets					46.0	35.7
10.0	11.1	11.4						9.6	11.0
3.9	3.4	3.8						4.2	6.3
2.8	2.5	2.7	Sales/Total Assets					2.8	2.5
1.6	1.8	1.8						1.7	1.9
.3	.4	.5						.3	
(49) 1.0	(51) .9	(38) .9	% Depr., Dep., Amort./Sales					(14) .7	
2.1	2.1	1.9						1.8	
2.4	1.7	1.9	% Officers', Directors'						
(27) 4.2	(28) 5.4	(21) 5.0	Owners' Comp/Sales						
7.9	9.0	10.0							
1655383M	1684532M	1541179M	Net Sales ($)	2783M	10697M	16330M	58308M	267918M	1185143M
638739M	728861M	586463M	Total Assets ($)	2261M	4731M	5669M	21548M	123387M	428867M

M = $ thousand   MM = $ million
See Pages 9 through 22 for Explanation of Ratios and Data

Current Data Sorted by Assets | **Comparative Historical Data**

0-500M	500M-2MM	2-10MM	10-50MM	50-100MM	100-250MM	Type of Statement	ALL	ALL
		9	12		1	Unqualified	45	38
1	14	51	19	2	1	Reviewed	79	59
4	14	21	1		1	Compiled	40	37
10	18	19				Tax Returns	26	28
8	32	49	28	4		Other	89	82
	57 (4/1-9/30/10)		261 (10/1/10-3/31/11)				4/1/06-3/31/07	4/1/07-3/31/08
23	78	149	60	6	2	**NUMBER OF STATEMENTS**	279	244
%	%	%	%	%	%	**ASSETS**	%	%
14.1	14.3	8.4	5.9			Cash & Equivalents	7.7	8.1
16.6	32.5	38.9	38.1			Trade Receivables (net)	38.5	40.4
37.6	32.2	28.6	30.4			Inventory	30.1	29.3
6.5	2.2	4.0	3.1			All Other Current	3.9	3.7
74.7	81.2	79.8	77.5			Total Current	80.2	81.5
12.2	10.2	11.9	10.6			Fixed Assets (net)	11.9	10.2
4.7	2.5	3.0	6.4			Intangibles (net)	2.5	2.8
8.4	6.1	5.4	5.5			All Other Non-Current	5.5	5.4
100.0	100.0	100.0	100.0			Total	100.0	100.0
						LIABILITIES		
31.1	10.9	14.2	16.8			Notes Payable-Short Term	18.5	19.1
2.7	2.6	1.8	1.2			Cur. Mat.-L.T.D.	1.7	2.1
22.6	22.0	20.5	17.7			Trade Payables	20.6	19.2
.1	.3	.3	.2			Income Taxes Payable	.2	.2
26.8	15.9	16.1	12.8			All Other Current	17.1	14.8
83.3	51.7	53.0	48.7			Total Current	58.0	55.4
10.5	5.8	6.5	8.1			Long-Term Debt	7.2	5.6
.0	.2	.1	.1			Deferred Taxes	.1	.1
18.8	9.1	3.7	4.6			All Other Non-Current	5.7	5.2
-12.4	33.2	36.7	38.5			Net Worth	29.0	33.7
100.0	100.0	100.0	100.0			Total Liabilities & Net Worth	100.0	100.0
						INCOME DATA		
100.0	100.0	100.0	100.0			Net Sales	100.0	100.0
32.8	30.5	28.8	27.4			Gross Profit	28.9	28.4
32.2	28.0	25.5	25.5			Operating Expenses	25.8	25.2
.6	2.5	3.3	1.9			Operating Profit	3.1	3.2
-.1	.4	.4	.4			All Other Expenses (net)	.6	.6
.7	2.1	2.9	1.5			Profit Before Taxes	2.5	2.5
						RATIOS		
1.8	3.0	2.0	2.5				2.1	2.2
1.1	1.6	1.5	1.6			Current	1.4	1.5
.7	1.1	1.1	1.2				1.1	1.1
.8	1.7	1.3	1.4				1.2	1.3
.4	1.0	.9	1.0			Quick	.8	.9
.1	.5	.6	.5				.5	.6
0 UND	11 31.9	29 12.7	35 10.5				24 15.2	23 15.5
7 51.1	27 13.3	42 8.6	49 7.5			Sales/Receivables	42 8.7	40 9.1
38 9.6	41 9.0	61 6.0	65 5.6				55 6.6	57 6.4
13 27.2	9 41.8	12 30.5	25 14.6				12 30.4	11 34.7
28 12.9	33 11.1	36 10.1	40 9.0			Cost of Sales/Inventory	38 9.5	33 11.1
58 6.3	91 4.0	117 3.1	107 3.4				94 3.9	90 4.1
5 70.3	9 40.8	15 24.6	13 29.1				15 23.8	12 29.4
16 23.4	22 16.4	27 13.8	28 13.2			Cost of Sales/Payables	26 14.3	24 15.2
31 11.8	44 8.3	49 7.4	44 8.3				42 8.8	37 10.0
14.2	6.1	7.8	6.1				7.9	7.4
55.5	11.4	12.5	10.7			Sales/Working Capital	15.4	14.4
-26.2	67.6	36.2	22.0				75.8	32.3
9.3	15.2	15.8	15.1				9.6	8.1
(16) 3.8	(61) 3.6	(125) 5.3	(57) 2.8			EBIT/Interest	(256) 3.4	(220) 3.7
-1.8	.5	1.9	.7				1.3	1.4
		8.8	31.6				13.4	13.4
	(20) 1.8	(14) 5.2				Net Profit + Depr., Dep., Amort./Cur. Mat. L/T/D	(43) 3.5	(42) 4.0
		-.1	1.0				1.1	1.1
.0	.1	.1	.1				.1	.1
.3	.2	.2	.3			Fixed/Worth	.3	.2
-3.2	.9	.7	1.0				1.2	.7
1.6	.7	1.0	.9				1.1	.9
14.4	1.7	2.2	1.8			Debt/Worth	2.5	2.3
-2.0	5.7	4.7	8.9				11.1	5.9
91.6	51.1	42.5	36.0				53.2	49.2
(14) 46.2	(69) 15.6	(139) 17.5	(54) 16.7			% Profit Before Taxes/Tangible Net Worth	(234) 26.5	(217) 23.5
-11.8	.7	5.7	.1				8.3	5.4
20.3	18.2	15.1	10.0				16.4	14.3
9.5	6.5	5.9	3.8			% Profit Before Taxes/Total Assets	6.2	6.6
-17.1	-.2	1.5	-1.1				1.0	1.3
999.8	292.8	148.2	89.5				112.3	118.9
155.4	50.4	61.8	50.1			Sales/Net Fixed Assets	52.7	56.1
25.2	20.6	26.9	18.8				21.5	26.4
8.8	5.5	4.3	3.6				4.4	4.5
5.3	3.7	3.0	2.7			Sales/Total Assets	3.3	3.4
2.7	2.6	2.0	1.8				2.4	2.5
.1	.2	.3	.3				.3	.3
(12) .3	(51) .6	(118) .5	(54) .6			% Depr., Dep., Amort./Sales	(228) .5	(211) .5
.7	.9	.9	1.0				.9	.9
.7	1.5	1.0	.6				1.6	1.4
(10) 3.8	(37) 3.3	(50) 1.8	(11) 1.1			% Officers', Directors' Owners' Comp/Sales	(101) 2.8	(92) 3.1
9.6	4.6	3.9	2.2				5.2	5.4
35932M	356205M	2349504M	3306248M	632708M	600449M	Net Sales ($)	7906078M	8736602M
6738M	89290M	727451M	1178761M	385102M	326289M	Total Assets ($)	2617757M	2501692M

M = $ thousand　　MM = $ million
See Pages 9 through 22 for Explanation of Ratios and Data

Comparative Historical Data　　　Current Data Sorted by Sales

H1	H2	H3	Type of Statement	0-1MM	1-3MM	3-5MM	5-10MM	10-25MM	25MM & OVER
33	33	22	Unqualified				1	7	14
71	77	88	Reviewed		4	6	20	28	30
43	29	40	Compiled	2	7	8	13	8	2
32	41	47	Tax Returns	3	16	9	9	9	1
106	97	121	Other	3	15	15	21	28	39
4/1/08-3/31/09 ALL	4/1/09-3/31/10 ALL	4/1/10-3/31/11 ALL			57 (4/1-9/30/10)		261 (10/1/10-3/31/11)		
285	277	318	NUMBER OF STATEMENTS	8	42	38	64	80	86
%	%	%	ASSETS	%	%	%	%	%	%
7.6	10.4	9.6	Cash & Equivalents		10.5	12.3	12.9	7.8	6.8
36.7	33.5	35.2	Trade Receivables (net)		22.3	26.1	35.3	39.8	43.6
31.1	30.2	30.5	Inventory		38.5	33.3	31.3	27.6	26.0
4.6	3.6	3.7	All Other Current		6.9	3.4	3.1	3.0	3.5
80.0	77.8	79.0	Total Current		78.2	75.2	82.7	78.3	79.9
11.1	12.2	11.6	Fixed Assets (net)		13.8	13.8	9.3	12.3	10.1
3.6	3.9	3.5	Intangibles (net)		1.9	3.6	2.1	4.5	4.2
5.3	6.1	5.8	All Other Non-Current		6.1	7.4	5.9	4.9	5.9
100.0	100.0	100.0	Total		100.0	100.0	100.0	100.0	100.0
			LIABILITIES						
17.0	16.5	15.1	Notes Payable-Short Term		20.9	9.9	12.6	16.3	15.7
1.6	2.1	2.0	Cur. Mat.-L.T.D.		1.2	4.4	2.2	1.8	1.1
19.8	18.6	20.3	Trade Payables		18.3	20.4	23.3	21.0	19.4
.2	.2	.3	Income Taxes Payable		.1	.5	.3	.4	.2
15.4	13.0	16.1	All Other Current		16.9	13.4	17.8	14.1	14.3
54.1	50.4	53.8	Total Current		57.4	48.5	56.1	53.6	50.8
6.0	8.3	7.1	Long-Term Debt		11.8	8.4	3.6	5.0	7.8
.1	.2	.1	Deferred Taxes		.0	.2	.1	.1	.1
5.4	6.9	6.3	All Other Non-Current		16.5	5.5	5.1	3.1	4.2
34.5	34.2	32.7	Net Worth		14.4	37.4	35.1	38.2	37.1
100.0	100.0	100.0	Total Liabilities & Net Worth		100.0	100.0	100.0	100.0	100.0
			INCOME DATA						
100.0	100.0	100.0	Net Sales		100.0	100.0	100.0	100.0	100.0
28.6	29.0	29.3	Gross Profit		34.4	31.0	30.0	28.4	25.1
26.3	27.9	26.7	Operating Expenses		31.9	27.9	27.8	25.5	22.4
2.3	1.1	2.6	Operating Profit		2.5	3.0	2.1	2.9	2.7
.3	.7	.4	All Other Expenses (net)		1.3	.0	.4	.2	.3
2.0	.4	2.2	Profit Before Taxes		1.2	3.0	1.7	2.7	2.3
			RATIOS						
2.2	2.8	2.3	Current		3.2	2.6	2.6	2.0	2.2
1.5	1.6	1.5			1.5	1.6	1.4	1.5	1.6
1.2	1.1	1.1			1.1	.9	1.1	1.1	1.2
1.3	1.6	1.3	Quick		1.4	1.3	1.3	1.2	1.5
.8	(276) .9	.9			.5	.8	.9	.9	1.0
.5	.5	.5			.2	.4	.5	.6	.6
23 15.8	22 16.6	21 17.2	Sales/Receivables	2 198.2	9 40.1	20 18.1	29 12.6	33 11.2	
35 10.6	36 10.0	39 9.3		21 17.7	27 13.7	38 9.6	40 9.0	46 8.0	
51 7.2	53 6.9	58 6.2		54 6.7	45 8.0	52 7.0	66 5.5	60 6.1	
11 32.6	13 28.9	13 28.4	Cost of Sales/Inventory	21 17.5	9 41.7	15 23.9	12 30.6	12 30.4	
35 10.5	36 10.2	36 10.1		61 6.0	54 6.7	36 10.2	36 10.1	28 13.2	
92 4.0	103 3.5	108 3.4		168 2.2	131 2.8	116 3.1	103 3.5	76 4.8	
12 31.3	12 30.7	12 29.7	Cost of Sales/Payables	6 58.6	15 23.9	14 26.8	13 27.6	13 27.3	
21 17.3	25 16.3	25 14.3		26 14.2	25 14.3	30 12.0	25 14.5	24 15.4	
37 9.8	41 8.9	44 8.2		52 7.0	51 7.1	56 6.5	46 7.9	37 9.8	
7.9	5.5	6.7	Sales/Working Capital		6.1	5.5	7.0	8.4	7.9
14.2	11.5	12.3			13.9	9.5	11.3	14.8	11.8
34.7	43.8	41.8			63.7	-37.6	42.4	40.4	23.4
11.5	9.1	14.7	EBIT/Interest		6.1	12.4	14.5	16.4	16.5
(261) 3.9	(245) 2.4	(265) 3.9			(31) 2.5	(29) 3.6	(53) 2.7	(70) 6.1	(76) 4.5
1.1	-.1	1.3			-1.9	2.1	-.6	1.7	1.6
8.4	6.8	9.1	Net Profit + Depr., Dep., Amort./Cur. Mat. L/T/D					10.7	60.5
(38) 4.1	(42) 2.5	(38) 2.6						(13) 3.1	(15) 5.3
2.2	.3	.2						-.6	2.1
.1	.1	.1	Fixed/Worth		.0	.0	.1	.1	.1
.3	.3	.3			.3	.2	.2	.3	.2
.7	1.1	.8			3.7	2.0	.6	.7	.7
.9	.8	.9	Debt/Worth		1.4	.7	.8	1.0	.8
2.2	2.1	1.9			2.5	1.5	2.4	2.0	1.8
5.1	7.1	7.8			39.7	10.9	4.0	7.2	7.4
42.3	35.3	42.4	% Profit Before Taxes/Tangible Net Worth		56.5	45.1	39.9	42.4	47.3
(263) 19.1	(238) 10.5	(283) 16.9			(34) 12.6	(33) 15.6	(59) 13.4	(75) 23.7	(77) 26.5
2.9	-2.7	2.7			-5.2	1.6	-1.8	5.0	7.5
13.8	10.0	14.4	% Profit Before Taxes/Total Assets		13.5	17.8	16.7	14.8	14.0
5.9	3.2	5.2			2.9	6.3	2.9	5.7	6.1
.5	-1.8	.6			-4.3	1.1	-1.8	1.4	1.1
105.9	114.3	154.5	Sales/Net Fixed Assets		505.9	180.7	175.4	120.2	111.7
52.5	48.3	55.5			31.8	50.3	55.0	53.5	65.3
24.9	20.2	22.0			19.2	17.1	28.7	22.3	29.3
4.8	4.4	4.5	Sales/Total Assets		5.1	4.8	4.5	4.2	4.7
3.4	3.1	3.1			2.7	2.9	3.1	3.1	3.5
2.4	2.2	2.2			1.7	1.8	2.2	2.0	2.5
.3	.3	.3	% Depr., Dep., Amort./Sales		.2	.2	.3	.3	.3
(231) .5	(231) .5	(243) .5			(28) .7	(23) .4	(44) .6	(69) .6	(76) .5
1.0	1.1	.9			1.2	1.3	.8	1.1	.8
1.1	1.4	1.1	% Officers', Directors' Owners' Comp/Sales		2.5	.8	1.4	1.1	.6
(98) 2.6	(100) 2.6	(108) 2.4			(22) 4.1	(15) 2.5	(26) 3.4	(27) 1.7	(17) 1.1
4.8	5.5	4.3			6.9	4.0	4.8	3.4	2.6
8791888M	6983518M	7281046M	Net Sales ($)	4542M	84500M	145895M	466027M	1264952M	5315130M
2709360M	2450873M	2713631M	Total Assets ($)	2686M	44924M	66986M	163522M	552426M	1883087M

M = $ thousand　MM = $ million
See Pages 9 through 22 for Explanation of Ratios and Data

Current Data Sorted by Assets   Comparative Historical Data

Type of Statement	0-500M	500M-2MM	2-10MM	10-50MM	50-100MM	100-250MM	4/1/06-3/31/07 ALL	4/1/07-3/31/08 ALL
Unqualified		2	8	24	4	8	60	56
Reviewed		5	52	32	1	1	70	69
Compiled	1	19	15	2			44	38
Tax Returns	3	19	13	1			50	35
Other	9	17	35	39	7	2	124	129
		47 (4/1-9/30/10)		272 (10/1/10-3/31/11)				
NUMBER OF STATEMENTS	13	62	123	98	12	11	348	327
ASSETS	%	%	%	%	%	%	%	%
Cash & Equivalents	25.6	9.7	7.6	7.2	5.2	8.1	8.1	8.0
Trade Receivables (net)	17.7	24.2	28.3	27.7	23.3	18.3	31.6	28.8
Inventory	24.3	42.7	45.1	39.7	41.7	28.6	39.8	40.3
All Other Current	.3	5.8	2.3	3.8	6.0	7.5	2.3	3.0
Total Current	67.8	82.4	83.3	78.5	76.2	62.6	81.8	80.1
Fixed Assets (net)	12.6	11.6	7.9	10.2	7.8	13.0	9.7	10.3
Intangibles (net)	4.3	.9	3.6	5.3	10.3	18.1	2.6	4.1
All Other Non-Current	15.2	5.1	5.3	6.1	5.7	6.3	5.9	5.5
Total	100.0	100.0	100.0	100.0	100.0	100.0	100.0	100.0
LIABILITIES								
Notes Payable-Short Term	32.0	17.4	19.2	15.1	9.8	4.4	16.8	17.7
Cur. Mat.-L.T.D.	.2	3.7	2.4	2.6	2.5	1.7	1.9	2.5
Trade Payables	14.2	24.2	20.5	15.6	17.0	10.6	19.7	18.5
Income Taxes Payable	.4	.4	.1	.1	.4	.6	.2	.1
All Other Current	4.3	12.1	6.9	11.2	14.9	19.4	11.5	10.0
Total Current	51.0	57.7	49.1	44.7	44.6	36.8	50.2	48.7
Long-Term Debt	13.7	8.1	5.2	10.8	10.2	11.3	7.3	9.3
Deferred Taxes	.0	.0	.1	.3	2.7	.6	.1	.3
All Other Non-Current	7.3	5.8	7.4	3.7	10.1	7.1	6.7	6.3
Net Worth	27.9	28.4	38.2	40.6	32.3	44.2	35.7	35.6
Total Liabilities & Net Worth	100.0	100.0	100.0	100.0	100.0	100.0	100.0	100.0
INCOME DATA								
Net Sales	100.0	100.0	100.0	100.0	100.0	100.0	100.0	100.0
Gross Profit	52.7	34.3	31.1	31.4	33.3	41.0	31.0	32.8
Operating Expenses	51.3	32.1	29.2	26.7	27.9	35.2	26.6	28.8
Operating Profit	1.3	2.2	1.9	4.8	5.4	5.8	4.4	4.1
All Other Expenses (net)	-.6	1.0	.7	1.1	1.6	4.0	1.3	1.3
Profit Before Taxes	1.9	1.2	1.2	3.6	3.8	1.8	3.1	2.8

RATIOS

Ratio	0-500M	500M-2MM	2-10MM	10-50MM	50-100MM	100-250MM	4/1/06-3/31/07 ALL	4/1/07-3/31/08 ALL
Current	12.4	2.7	3.0	2.7	2.9	2.8	2.6	2.8
	2.9	1.6	1.7	1.9	2.2	1.8	1.7	1.6
	.5	1.0	1.3	1.3	1.2	1.3	1.2	1.2
Quick	8.9	1.1	1.1	1.5	1.6	1.1	1.3	1.2
	1.0	.6	.7	.8	.6	.5	.7	.7
	.3	.2	.4	.5	.4	.3	.5	.5
Sales/Receivables	0 UND	8 48.0	26 14.2	31 11.7	29 12.5	5 71.7	28 12.9	27 13.8
	15 24.1	29 12.8	40 9.2	45 8.0	42 8.6	39 9.4	40 9.1	40 9.2
	39 9.3	47 7.8	55 6.6	61 6.0	52 7.0	63 5.8	56 6.5	60 6.1
Cost of Sales/Inventory	0 UND	32 11.4	51 7.2	68 5.4	67 5.4	69 5.3	38 9.5	51 7.1
	63 5.8	73 5.0	87 4.2	93 3.9	119 3.1	98 3.7	79 4.6	85 4.3
	185 2.0	149 2.5	168 2.2	125 2.9	182 2.0	217 1.7	128 2.8	142 2.6
Cost of Sales/Payables	0 UND	13 29.0	17 21.0	16 22.7	25 14.6	34 10.7	15 24.6	16 22.7
	16 23.0	29 12.5	27 13.8	30 12.4	35 10.4	40 9.0	29 12.5	28 12.9
	67 5.5	72 5.1	55 6.7	54 6.8	55 6.6	72 5.1	53 6.9	52 7.0
Sales/Working Capital	2.8	4.3	3.9	4.0	4.0	2.7	5.0	4.6
	10.9	11.0	8.0	7.2	6.7	4.6	9.1	8.5
	-9.9	290.6	18.0	11.8	14.0	9.0	19.9	20.3
EBIT/Interest		8.1	10.9	18.8	8.6	14.9	10.1	6.0
		(47) 2.8	(109) 3.0	(89) 6.1	(11) 5.1	(10) 2.7	(314) 3.4	(286) 2.9
		1.1	1.0	1.9	1.9	.2	1.5	1.3
Net Profit + Depr., Dep., Amort./Cur. Mat. L/T/D			5.1	46.7			17.9	8.7
			(19) 2.2	(25) 4.0			(70) 3.8	(64) 3.1
			.2	1.7			1.1	1.4
Fixed/Worth	.0	.1	.1	.1	.2	.1	.1	.1
	.2	.2	.1	.1	.5	.4	.2	.2
	-1.5	.9	.5	.7	1.9	1.2	.5	.7
Debt/Worth	.2	.9	.7	.7	.6	1.1	.8	.8
	1.7	1.9	1.8	1.7	3.5	1.4	1.9	2.0
	-8.5	9.9	6.6	4.0	82.1	3.3	4.7	4.2
% Profit Before Taxes/Tangible Net Worth		57.4	33.3	39.7	90.0		43.9	37.0
		(51) 11.9	(112) 9.6	(88) 18.1	(10) 39.9		(311) 18.7	(289) 16.2
		1.7	.1	3.4	6.8		5.9	4.2
% Profit Before Taxes/Total Assets	31.5	14.4	8.3	14.1	9.8	4.6	16.2	12.7
	6.1	4.7	3.2	6.6	6.1	.7	5.8	4.9
	-7.6	-1.5	.0	1.2	3.6	-.5	1.2	.9
Sales/Net Fixed Assets	813.9	169.7	115.2	107.1	84.1	54.6	112.8	111.4
	64.4	69.1	53.2	45.8	34.1	24.6	48.6	44.3
	14.1	27.3	23.9	18.5	13.7	5.6	23.1	20.0
Sales/Total Assets	4.5	4.3	3.4	2.6	3.0	1.8	3.8	3.5
	2.8	3.0	2.4	2.2	1.8	1.1	2.8	2.5
	1.5	2.0	1.8	1.7	1.4	.7	1.9	1.8
% Depr., Dep., Amort./Sales		.3	.3	.3			.3	.3
		(42) .5	(100) .6	(86) .6			(291) .6	(271) .6
		.9	1.0	1.2			1.0	1.1
% Officers', Directors' Owners' Comp/Sales		1.7	1.3	.7			1.4	1.6
		(29) 2.5	(57) 2.2	(26) 1.8			(156) 2.4	(121) 2.9
		6.1	5.3	4.7			4.6	6.8
Net Sales ($)	9954M	238463M	1693434M	5024458M	1724052M	2004445M	14491988M	12231275M
Total Assets ($)	3702M	70142M	632558M	2289961M	811248M	1592855M	5396338M	5411266M

M = $ thousand   MM = $ million
See Pages 9 through 22 for Explanation of Ratios and Data

Comparative Historical Data			Type of Statement	Current Data Sorted by Sales					
47	36	46	Unqualified	1	1	1	1	3	39
84	79	91	Reviewed	1	1	5	15	37	32
39	41	37	Compiled	2	12	7	8	6	2
46	41	36	Tax Returns	3	15	4	8	6	
121	106	109	Other	6	10	13	14	18	48
4/1/08-3/31/09	4/1/09-3/31/10	4/1/10-3/31/11				47 (4/1-9/30/10)		272 (10/1/10-3/31/11)	
ALL	ALL	ALL		0-1MM	1-3MM	3-5MM	5-10MM	10-25MM	25MM & OVER
337	303	319	NUMBER OF STATEMENTS	13	39	30	46	70	121
%	%	%	ASSETS	%	%	%	%	%	%
8.4	8.5	8.5	Cash & Equivalents	18.5	10.7	6.3	8.9	9.3	6.8
28.3	28.0	26.4	Trade Receivables (net)	15.2	17.9	29.0	24.3	31.4	27.5
40.9	39.7	41.4	Inventory	31.8	47.9	42.3	42.7	40.8	40.0
3.9	3.6	3.7	All Other Current	6.9	2.0	5.0	3.9	2.7	4.0
81.5	79.7	80.0	Total Current	72.4	78.5	82.6	79.8	84.2	78.4
9.8	9.7	9.7	Fixed Assets (net)	11.7	11.3	7.4	10.6	9.6	9.2
2.5	3.8	4.4	Intangibles (net)	4.4	.9	3.8	4.7	1.5	7.2
6.3	6.8	5.9	All Other Non-Current	11.5	9.3	6.2	4.9	4.7	5.3
100.0	100.0	100.0	Total	100.0	100.0	100.0	100.0	100.0	100.0
			LIABILITIES						
18.1	18.7	17.3	Notes Payable-Short Term	34.0	14.6	26.3	19.0	15.2	14.6
2.8	2.6	2.6	Cur. Mat.-L.T.D.	.4	4.7	3.7	1.7	1.6	2.8
17.8	18.3	19.0	Trade Payables	18.1	18.4	19.5	19.4	22.3	17.2
.2	.3	.2	Income Taxes Payable	.4	.1	.5	.1	.1	.2
10.2	11.2	9.9	All Other Current	6.0	11.1	9.6	7.5	8.2	11.7
49.1	51.1	48.9	Total Current	59.0	49.0	59.7	47.7	47.5	46.5
6.3	8.6	8.2	Long-Term Debt	9.1	6.9	6.6	10.0	6.6	9.2
.1	.2	.2	Deferred Taxes	.0	.1	.0	.0	.1	.5
6.3	6.2	6.0	All Other Non-Current	4.8	11.3	3.7	6.5	4.8	5.5
38.2	34.0	36.6	Net Worth	27.2	32.7	30.1	35.7	41.0	38.2
100.0	100.0	100.0	Total Liabilities & Net Worth	100.0	100.0	100.0	100.0	100.0	100.0
			INCOME DATA						
100.0	100.0	100.0	Net Sales	100.0	100.0	100.0	100.0	100.0	100.0
31.4	31.6	33.1	Gross Profit	50.1	40.8	29.2	33.1	29.6	31.8
28.5	29.2	30.0	Operating Expenses	51.3	39.1	29.0	30.6	25.9	27.3
2.8	2.4	3.1	Operating Profit	-1.2	1.7	.2	2.4	3.7	4.6
.9	1.1	1.0	All Other Expenses (net)	-.3	.6	1.6	.9	.6	1.4
2.0	1.3	2.1	Profit Before Taxes	-1.0	1.1	-1.4	1.6	3.1	3.2
			RATIOS						
2.7	2.5	2.9		4.9	4.0	1.9	3.4	2.9	2.6
1.7	1.7	1.8	Current	1.7	2.0	1.4	2.0	1.7	1.9
1.3	1.2	1.2		.6	1.0	1.0	1.2	1.3	1.3
1.3	1.3	1.3		3.0	1.2	.8	1.9	1.5	1.3
.7	.7	.7	Quick	.4	.6	.5	.7	.8	.7
.5	.4	.4		.3	.3	.3	.3	.6	.4
26 14.1	25 14.4	24 15.3		3 131.2	8 47.8	25 14.7	20 18.6	24 15.1	30 12.2
37 9.9	39 9.4	39 9.4	Sales/Receivables	34 10.8	29 12.4	48 7.5	34 10.7	40 9.2	42 8.6
55 6.7	58 6.3	56 6.5		73 5.0	52 7.0	74 4.9	46 7.9	58 6.3	56 6.6
44 8.3	49 7.4	55 6.6		51 7.2	69 5.3	27 13.4	50 7.3	45 8.1	62 5.9
87 4.2	81 4.5	90 4.0	Cost of Sales/Inventory	118 3.1	146 2.5	103 3.5	86 4.2	81 4.5	90 4.0
142 2.6	147 2.5	147 2.5		356 1.0	298 1.2	227 1.6	163 2.2	119 3.1	126 2.9
13 28.2	15 24.2	16 22.5		12 30.5	6 59.7	12 30.4	13 27.7	18 20.5	19 18.7
26 14.2	29 12.8	30 12.3	Cost of Sales/Payables	65 5.6	22 16.2	24 15.0	26 14.1	27 13.3	34 10.8
47 7.8	58 6.3	57 6.4		101 3.6	81 4.5	73 5.0	53 6.9	61 6.0	53 6.9
4.6	4.4	4.0		2.1	3.2	3.6	3.9	4.3	4.4
8.1	7.4	7.6	Sales/Working Capital	6.0	5.0	11.7	7.0	8.4	7.5
18.3	18.8	17.5		-10.6	-81.1	NM	16.3	16.2	13.2
6.2	7.4	12.1			8.1	6.8	12.3	15.7	16.0
(293) 2.3	(270) 2.8	(274) 3.7	EBIT/Interest		(31) 2.7	(25) 1.6	(40) 5.4	(60) 3.4	(111) 5.3
.3	.8	1.3			-.2	.3	.7	1.7	1.6
6.3	6.1	11.3							55.7
(58) 1.6	(44) 1.8	(56) 3.3	Net Profit + Depr., Dep., Amort./Cur. Mat. L/T/D					(33) 4.0	
-.1	.1	.8							1.7
.1	.1	.1		.0	.0	.0	.1	.1	.1
.2	.2	.2	Fixed/Worth	.1	.2	.3	.1	.1	.2
.5	.7	.7		NM	4.9	.6	1.1	.5	.8
.8	.8	.7		.4	.5	1.0	.4	.7	.8
1.8	1.9	1.7	Debt/Worth	1.7	1.6	3.3	1.6	1.6	1.8
4.6	4.6	6.5		NM	14.5	10.0	7.4	4.2	4.8
31.6	30.9	39.8		40.2	33.9	40.8	47.5	36.8	42.1
(307) 11.1	(258) 8.3	(279) 14.7	% Profit Before Taxes/Tangible Net Worth	(10) 8.3	(31) 6.8	(26) 5.7	(38) 10.7	(69) 20.0	(105) 18.3
.0	1.0	1.7		-8.7	.9	-7.1	2.8	3.0	3.1
11.1	10.5	12.5		20.0	7.6	8.4	9.7	14.5	13.4
2.8	2.8	4.5	% Profit Before Taxes/Total Assets	4.1	1.9	1.2	5.9	5.0	5.1
-1.9	-.2	.4		-7.6	-4.2	-3.6	-2.7	1.0	.8
121.8	104.9	115.3		UND	94.8	159.2	118.7	107.5	109.8
47.4	46.4	52.1	Sales/Net Fixed Assets	66.0	39.6	63.9	63.4	50.7	49.2
20.0	22.1	21.9		20.2	14.0	18.1	26.4	22.4	22.7
3.5	3.4	3.2		2.7	3.2	3.6	3.5	3.7	3.1
2.5	2.3	2.3	Sales/Total Assets	1.5	2.0	2.0	2.4	2.5	2.3
1.8	1.7	1.7		.9	1.3	1.3	2.0	1.9	1.8
.3	.3	.3			.3	.2	.6	.3	.3
(263) .6	(229) .6	(249) .6	% Depr., Dep., Amort./Sales		(26) .7	(23) .4	(36) .8	(58) .6	(101) .6
1.2	1.1	1.1			1.5	.5	1.2	.9	1.2
1.1	1.3	1.1			1.1	1.8	1.1	1.1	.5
(138) 2.4	(141) 2.3	(123) 2.1	% Officers', Directors' Owners' Comp/Sales		(16) 5.3	(17) 2.5	(23) 1.9	(35) 2.2	(26) 1.6
5.5	4.2	5.3			10.2	5.1	2.4	6.1	2.7
13416415M	9285708M	10694806M	Net Sales ($)	7294M	77276M	116621M	360907M	1158904M	8973804M
5697910M	4710449M	5400466M	Total Assets ($)	5419M	52295M	78377M	156990M	511111M	4596274M

© RMA 2011

M = $ thousand   MM = $ million
See Pages 9 through 22 for Explanation of Ratios and Data

Current Data Sorted by Assets   Comparative Historical Data

0-500M	500M-2MM	2-10MM	10-50MM	50-100MM	100-250MM	Type of Statement	ALL	ALL
	1	25	61	17	7	Unqualified	168	139
1	29	140	46	6	1	Reviewed	273	260
7	39	60	11	1		Compiled	160	132
19	42	29	3			Tax Returns	93	90
14	53	107	80	17	2	Other	291	353
	142 (4/1-9/30/10)		676 (10/1/10-3/31/11)				4/1/06-3/31/07	4/1/07-3/31/08
41	164	361	201	41	10	NUMBER OF STATEMENTS	985	974
%	%	%	%	%	%	**ASSETS**	%	%
10.5	6.7	7.0	6.3	4.4	5.2	Cash & Equivalents	6.1	6.6
28.3	35.8	29.3	25.6	26.4	22.4	Trade Receivables (net)	33.4	32.1
38.4	34.1	35.5	35.6	35.6	26.5	Inventory	34.3	34.7
1.9	1.9	2.4	3.3	3.3	1.9	All Other Current	2.5	2.7
79.1	78.6	74.2	70.8	69.6	55.9	Total Current	76.3	76.2
14.0	12.9	17.1	19.7	18.1	27.6	Fixed Assets (net)	15.8	16.1
.6	2.0	2.4	2.5	4.2	11.6	Intangibles (net)	2.2	2.1
6.3	6.5	6.4	7.1	8.1	4.8	All Other Non-Current	5.7	5.7
100.0	100.0	100.0	100.0	100.0	100.0	Total	100.0	100.0
						LIABILITIES		
21.8	18.8	19.8	19.1	15.0	8.2	Notes Payable-Short Term	20.1	20.4
5.1	1.5	2.1	1.9	3.8	2.1	Cur. Mat.-L.T.D.	2.4	2.4
20.9	16.9	13.0	11.0	12.4	18.3	Trade Payables	13.9	13.0
.3	.1	.2	.1	.1	.6	Income Taxes Payable	.2	.1
21.1	12.0	7.8	7.1	7.5	6.0	All Other Current	9.1	9.0
69.2	49.4	42.9	39.1	38.9	35.1	Total Current	45.7	45.0
10.2	11.4	10.0	10.2	10.6	19.4	Long-Term Debt	9.3	9.6
.0	.1	.1	.4	.7	.0	Deferred Taxes	.2	.2
12.6	6.5	6.0	4.3	7.2	5.0	All Other Non-Current	4.3	5.6
8.0	32.5	41.0	46.0	42.6	40.5	Net Worth	40.3	39.6
100.0	100.0	100.0	100.0	100.0	100.0	Total Liabilities & Net Worth	100.0	100.0
						INCOME DATA		
100.0	100.0	100.0	100.0	100.0	100.0	Net Sales	100.0	100.0
26.6	23.4	22.1	20.3	20.0	20.5	Gross Profit	21.5	21.5
25.2	22.7	21.2	19.4	20.2	19.7	Operating Expenses	18.6	19.7
1.4	.7	.8	.9	-.1	.7	Operating Profit	2.9	1.7
.5	.6	.2	.2	1.0	.9	All Other Expenses (net)	.5	.6
.9	.1	.6	.7	-1.1	-.2	Profit Before Taxes	2.4	1.2
						RATIOS		
2.9	2.9	3.2	3.1	2.8	2.5		2.7	2.9
1.4	1.7	1.7	1.8	1.8	1.7	Current	1.6	1.7
.8	1.2	1.2	1.3	1.3	1.1		1.2	1.2
1.6	1.4	1.6	1.3	1.2	1.2		1.5	1.5
.6	.9	.9	.7	.8	.7	Quick	.8	.8
.2	.5	.5	.5	.5	.5		.5	.5
7 48.7	16 22.3	23 15.6	27 13.3	29 12.4	26 14.1		23 16.2	22 16.4
18 20.4	32 11.5	33 11.2	35 10.4	36 10.2	31 11.6	Sales/Receivables	32 11.5	32 11.5
32 11.3	50 7.3	46 8.0	45 8.1	41 8.9	41 8.8		42 8.6	44 8.3
9 42.9	11 32.9	31 11.8	47 7.8	41 9.0	25 14.8		27 13.6	28 12.8
46 7.9	37 9.8	55 6.7	63 5.8	57 6.4	52 7.0	Cost of Sales/Inventory	45 8.1	48 7.6
101 3.6	99 3.7	82 4.5	88 4.1	97 3.8	89 4.1		68 5.4	75 4.8
2 154.9	8 43.9	8 45.4	10 35.9	12 29.9	20 18.2		9 42.1	8 47.1
19 18.9	16 22.6	16 23.1	16 23.0	19 19.0	26 14.0	Cost of Sales/Payables	15 24.5	15 25.0
38 9.6	31 11.8	28 13.1	25 14.5	25 14.9	47 7.8		24 15.4	25 14.7
10.3	6.0	5.6	4.8	4.9	6.5		6.8	6.3
31.1	11.5	10.0	8.7	8.7	10.4	Sales/Working Capital	11.8	11.3
-33.0	41.0	24.6	16.8	20.5	122.0		28.9	25.6
4.3	6.6	5.9	6.3	9.9	3.7		8.6	5.8
(35) 2.8	(144) 1.8	(328) 1.9	(183) 1.8	1.7	1.4	EBIT/Interest	(929) 3.2	(920) 2.1
.2	-1.8	-.7	.1	-1.3	-3.8		1.3	.8
	5.5	5.0	6.2	6.3			9.0	7.2
	(12) 1.5	(69) 1.9	(67) 1.6	(15) 3.1		Net Profit + Depr., Dep., Amort./Cur. Mat. L/T/D	(272) 3.3	(245) 2.7
	-1.0	-1.0	.1	1.3			1.4	.8
.0	.0	.1	.2	.3	.4		.1	.1
.5	.2	.3	.4	.4	.8	Fixed/Worth	.3	.4
-.7	1.2	.9	.8	.6	2.1		.8	.9
.9	.8	.6	.6	.7	.9		.7	.7
4.3	1.7	1.5	1.2	1.6	2.8	Debt/Worth	1.6	1.6
-5.2	7.8	3.7	2.8	3.2	6.2		3.5	3.8
33.2	29.5	18.2	13.6	15.9	29.2		37.7	25.9
(24) 7.4	(137) 3.8	(331) 4.5	(193) 4.7	(39) 2.8	7.6	% Profit Before Taxes/Tangible Net Worth	(928) 17.0	(894) 10.5
-1.8	-8.8	-5.0	-4.9	-9.2	-26.2		4.3	.0
10.2	9.7	6.6	6.2	6.5	5.9		14.1	10.5
3.7	1.7	1.5	1.5	.8	.5	% Profit Before Taxes/Total Assets	6.0	3.7
-1.9	-5.3	-4.0	-2.4	-4.3	-5.1		1.3	-.7
685.2	260.5	78.7	45.7	35.7	27.8		83.7	83.2
86.0	60.3	30.9	16.1	18.5	10.0	Sales/Net Fixed Assets	30.0	29.0
18.4	23.0	9.0	6.9	6.9	5.0		12.9	11.8
6.6	5.3	3.8	3.1	3.3	3.6		4.6	4.2
4.2	3.4	2.8	2.4	2.4	2.0	Sales/Total Assets	3.4	3.2
2.7	2.4	2.0	1.7	1.7	1.8		2.5	2.4
.3	.2	.4	.5	.6	.8		.4	.3
(24) .6	(117) .6	(321) .9	(195) .9	(38) 1.1	1.7	% Depr., Dep., Amort./Sales	(871) .7	(857) .8
1.5	1.2	1.5	1.8	1.9	2.9		1.3	1.4
1.7	1.3	.9	.5				1.2	1.2
(20) 4.2	(87) 2.5	(154) 1.8	(46) 1.0			% Officers', Directors' Owners' Comp/Sales	(352) 2.4	(354) 2.3
7.5	4.8	3.5	2.4				4.2	4.7
64321M	836220M	5502386M	11804135M	7426297M	4431747M	Net Sales ($)	55023383M	46893140M
13640M	206865M	1787082M	4444843M	2807615M	1435005M	Total Assets ($)	15945681M	15218062M

M = $ thousand   MM = $ million
See Pages 9 through 22 for Explanation of Ratios and Data

Comparative Historical Data | Current Data Sorted by Sales

			Type of Statement						
127	110	111	Unqualified		1	3	16	91	
233	216	223	Reviewed		7	12	53	90	61
127	115	118	Compiled	7	14	15	39	30	13
85	98	93	Tax Returns	10	17	22	29	13	2
365	305	273	Other	6	28	26	38	78	97
4/1/08-3/31/09 ALL	4/1/09-3/31/10 ALL	4/1/10-3/31/11 ALL		142 (4/1-9/30/10)			676 (10/1/10-3/31/11)		
				0-1MM	1-3MM	3-5MM	5-10MM	10-25MM	25MM & OVER
937	844	818	NUMBER OF STATEMENTS	23	66	76	162	227	264
%	%	%	ASSETS	%	%	%	%	%	%
6.5	7.7	6.8	Cash & Equivalents	5.3	8.2	9.4	7.8	6.8	5.2
29.4	29.1	29.4	Trade Receivables (net)	14.1	27.0	33.7	29.0	30.6	29.4
35.7	33.3	35.3	Inventory	38.2	37.5	30.3	35.9	34.4	36.3
2.9	3.5	2.5	All Other Current	2.8	2.3	1.7	2.2	2.4	3.1
74.5	73.6	74.0	Total Current	60.4	75.1	75.1	74.9	74.1	74.0
16.8	17.6	16.9	Fixed Assets (net)	28.0	13.5	14.9	18.1	17.3	16.3
2.0	2.2	2.4	Intangibles (net)	1.8	1.5	2.3	2.4	2.0	3.2
6.6	6.7	6.6	All Other Non-Current	9.9	9.9	7.7	4.7	6.7	6.4
100.0	100.0	100.0	Total	100.0	100.0	100.0	100.0	100.0	100.0
			LIABILITIES						
21.9	19.6	19.1	Notes Payable-Short Term	21.9	19.4	19.8	16.7	18.7	20.5
2.8	2.5	2.1	Cur. Mat.-L.T.D.	1.8	3.1	2.5	2.2	1.7	2.2
11.8	12.7	13.7	Trade Payables	11.9	17.1	15.1	14.8	13.0	12.5
.2	.2	.2	Income Taxes Payable	.5	.2	.2	.1	.2	.1
8.1	8.3	9.1	All Other Current	37.5	11.9	9.7	8.1	8.2	7.2
44.8	43.3	44.3	Total Current	73.5	51.6	47.3	41.9	41.9	42.6
9.6	10.4	10.5	Long-Term Debt	19.7	10.3	13.9	8.9	11.0	9.2
.2	.3	.2	Deferred Taxes	.0	.1	.0	.2	.2	.4
5.4	6.5	6.1	All Other Non-Current	9.8	8.9	8.4	6.6	4.4	5.4
40.0	39.5	38.9	Net Worth	-3.1	29.1	30.4	42.3	42.5	42.4
100.0	100.0	100.0	Total Liabilities & Net Worth	100.0	100.0	100.0	100.0	100.0	100.0
			INCOME DATA						
100.0	100.0	100.0	Net Sales	100.0	100.0	100.0	100.0	100.0	100.0
21.2	21.9	22.0	Gross Profit	33.1	28.8	25.6	22.3	21.5	18.6
21.0	22.4	21.2	Operating Expenses	29.0	28.8	25.0	22.4	20.2	17.7
.2	-.5	.8	Operating Profit	4.1	-.1	.6	-.1	1.2	.9
.6	.6	.4	All Other Expenses (net)	.7	.4	.8	.1	.3	.4
-.4	-1.1	.4	Profit Before Taxes	3.4	-.4	-.3	-.1	.9	.5
			RATIOS						
3.1	3.2	3.1		2.0	4.2	3.2	3.2	3.5	2.8
1.7	1.8	1.7	Current	.9	1.8	1.6	1.9	1.8	1.7
1.2	1.2	1.2		.5	1.1	1.0	1.3	1.2	1.3
1.6	1.6	1.4		.9	1.6	1.4	1.6	1.7	1.2
.8	.8	.8	Quick	.3	.9	1.0	.8	.9	.8
.4	.5	.5		.1	.4	.4	.5	.5	.5
20 17.9	23 16.1	23 15.9		0 UND	15 23.9	22 16.4	21 17.7	24 15.1	26 14.2
29 12.5	34 10.8	33 11.1	Sales/Receivables	9 38.6	32 11.3	36 10.2	32 11.3	33 11.1	34 10.8
41 8.8	47 7.7	45 8.1		33 11.0	61 6.0	56 6.5	46 7.9	45 8.1	42 8.6
30 12.2	30 12.3	31 11.9		1 312.5	31 11.9	13 27.9	35 10.6	28 12.8	38 9.6
51 7.2	54 6.8	55 6.6	Cost of Sales/Inventory	55 6.6	74 5.0	42 8.7	55 6.6	50 7.4	57 6.4
78 4.7	84 4.3	88 4.2		160 2.3	125 2.9	111 3.3	91 4.0	82 4.5	73 5.0
6 60.2	9 41.7	9 41.1		0 UND	12 29.4	9 40.5	8 43.5	8 43.1	9 38.7
13 27.6	16 22.7	16 22.2	Cost of Sales/Payables	16 22.2	26 14.1	16 22.6	17 21.7	15 23.8	16 22.8
23 15.9	26 14.0	28 13.1		51 7.2	42 8.7	34 10.8	33 11.2	25 14.4	24 15.0
6.0	5.1	5.6		10.3	4.1	4.9	5.1	5.5	6.2
10.6	9.9	10.1	Sales/Working Capital	-64.9	9.4	10.2	9.3	10.1	10.2
27.7	25.6	24.7		-6.0	68.2	364.2	21.2	24.6	18.7
4.4	3.8	6.0		5.3	6.3	6.0	4.3	6.7	6.3
(871) 1.4	(769) 1.0	(741) 1.9	EBIT/Interest	(21) 2.1	(55) 1.4	(65) 2.3	(145) 1.2	(203) 1.9	(252) 2.2
-.9	-2.7	-.5		.5	-3.8	-2.1	-1.7	-.2	.1
4.7	3.3	5.1					4.0	6.1	6.0
(224) 1.4	(179) .8	(169) 1.9	Net Profit + Depr., Dep., Amort./Cur. Mat. L/T/D			(26) 1.0	(46) 3.2	(87) 2.0	
-.3	-.9	-.1					-6.0	.9	.1
.1	.1	.1		.1	.1	.1	.1	.1	.1
.3	.3	.3	Fixed/Worth	5.3	.2	.3	.3	.3	.3
.9	.9	.9		-.3	1.1	1.6	1.0	.9	.7
.6	.6	.6		.8	.5	.7	.6	.5	.7
1.5	1.4	1.5	Debt/Worth	52.7	1.7	2.4	1.4	1.4	1.5
3.6	4.0	4.0		-3.6	10.4	11.5	3.2	3.6	3.1
17.6	12.6	18.9		33.2	17.2	29.4	11.8	18.9	19.1
(858) 3.5	(764) .8	(734) 4.6	% Profit Before Taxes/Tangible Net Worth	(12) 16.8	(51) 1.2	(62) 5.4	(146) 2.0	(211) 5.1	(252) 6.0
-9.6	-15.1	-5.0		3.9	-14.1	-9.3	-6.7	-3.6	-2.9
7.0	4.7	7.0		6.2	8.7	10.5	5.0	7.3	6.7
1.0	.1	1.6	% Profit Before Taxes/Total Assets	2.0	1.2	2.7	.6	1.6	1.9
-5.0	-7.2	-3.3		-1.9	-8.3	-7.6	-4.7	-2.4	-2.1
79.9	76.4	89.9		152.0	117.7	202.3	83.8	78.5	71.4
28.6	24.8	29.7	Sales/Net Fixed Assets	15.3	42.5	39.8	30.0	27.1	25.7
10.5	8.2	9.2		2.7	13.8	9.1	8.1	8.8	9.9
4.1	3.7	3.9		2.9	4.0	4.1	3.8	4.0	3.9
3.0	2.7	2.8	Sales/Total Assets	2.4	2.4	2.7	2.6	3.0	2.9
2.2	1.9	2.0		1.0	1.7	1.8	2.1	1.9	2.1
.4	.4	.4		.4	.4	.3	.4	.5	.4
(824) .9	(723) .9	(705) .9	% Depr., Dep., Amort./Sales	(12) 2.0	(47) .9	(57) .8	(141) 1.0	(203) 1.0	(245) .7
1.7	1.9	1.6		9.9	1.5	1.3	1.8	1.6	1.4
1.1	1.4	1.0			2.3	1.7	1.3	.9	.5
(352) 2.2	(308) 2.6	(313) 1.9	% Officers', Directors' Owners' Comp/Sales		(28) 4.6	(41) 2.5	(93) 2.4	(90) 1.4	(54) 1.0
4.0	4.8	4.0			5.9	5.1	4.3	2.7	2.1
40857294M	30402572M	30065106M	Net Sales ($)	16120M	129781M	310688M	1171535M	3651858M	24785124M
13386766M	11183799M	10695050M	Total Assets ($)	11937M	58340M	138558M	489318M	1509761M	8487136M

M = $ thousand   MM = $ million
See Pages 9 through 22 for Explanation of Ratios and Data

Current Data Sorted by Assets   Comparative Historical Data

						Type of Statement		
1	3	7	16		3	Unqualified	45	37
	13	31	14	1		Reviewed	78	71
4	10	20	4			Compiled	64	47
3	19	17				Tax Returns	44	48
12	19	47	18	2	3	Other	110	101
	35 (4/1-9/30/10)		232 (10/1/10-3/31/11)				4/1/06-3/31/07	4/1/07-3/31/08
0-500M	500M-2MM	2-10MM	10-50MM	50-100MM	100-250MM		ALL	ALL
20	64	122	52	3	6	**NUMBER OF STATEMENTS**	341	304
%	%	%	%	%	%	**ASSETS**	%	%
16.2	11.1	6.2	6.5			Cash & Equivalents	6.0	6.4
25.6	23.6	24.9	23.0			Trade Receivables (net)	30.6	26.9
20.4	32.7	39.7	28.0			Inventory	33.7	33.5
3.2	2.3	2.1	2.6			All Other Current	2.0	2.9
65.5	69.8	72.9	60.1			Total Current	72.4	69.8
28.7	20.6	19.8	29.1			Fixed Assets (net)	20.0	21.8
2.3	2.0	2.0	4.4			Intangibles (net)	2.3	2.8
3.6	7.6	5.4	6.4			All Other Non-Current	5.3	5.6
100.0	100.0	100.0	100.0			Total	100.0	100.0
						LIABILITIES		
28.3	11.4	15.5	11.7			Notes Payable-Short Term	13.4	12.5
6.0	2.2	2.9	3.4			Cur. Mat.-L.T.D.	3.0	3.7
70.1	27.8	20.6	13.0			Trade Payables	21.4	20.4
.3	.1	.1	.3			Income Taxes Payable	.4	.1
9.2	7.7	11.2	6.6			All Other Current	8.9	9.2
113.8	49.2	50.2	35.1			Total Current	47.1	45.9
11.5	14.4	8.9	13.8			Long-Term Debt	12.7	15.4
.0	.0	.2	1.0			Deferred Taxes	.3	.4
14.1	4.9	6.7	5.0			All Other Non-Current	4.7	5.1
-39.5	31.6	34.1	45.1			Net Worth	35.2	33.2
100.0	100.0	100.0	100.0			Total Liabilities & Net Worth	100.0	100.0
						INCOME DATA		
100.0	100.0	100.0	100.0			Net Sales	100.0	100.0
35.9	31.6	30.3	28.6			Gross Profit	29.8	30.4
37.6	29.0	31.2	27.0			Operating Expenses	25.0	27.3
-1.7	2.6	-.9	1.7			Operating Profit	4.8	3.2
.3	.6	.3	1.1			All Other Expenses (net)	.6	.8
-2.0	2.0	-1.1	.6			Profit Before Taxes	4.2	2.3
						RATIOS		
1.9	2.9	2.4	2.7				2.3	2.4
.9	1.6	1.5	1.6			Current	1.6	1.6
.5	1.0	1.1	1.2				1.2	1.1
1.1	1.5	1.1	1.6				1.2	1.2
.4	.8	.6	.7			Quick	.8	.7
.3	.3	.4	.4				.5	.4

											Sales/Receivables				
12	30.6	15	24.7	26	14.2	33	10.9				Sales/Receivables	27	13.3	25	14.4
26	13.8	31	11.7	38	9.5	43	8.4					38	9.5	37	10.0
56	6.5	45	8.1	52	7.1	67	5.5					52	7.0	52	7.1
0	UND	14	25.2	49	7.5	34	10.6				Cost of Sales/Inventory	31	11.8	33	11.2
36	10.1	58	6.3	88	4.2	67	5.4					55	6.7	65	5.6
67	5.4	91	4.0	179	2.0	153	2.4					100	3.7	122	3.0
19	19.7	20	18.1	24	15.0	19	19.4				Cost of Sales/Payables	20	18.0	18	19.7
69	5.3	40	9.2	42	8.7	34	10.9					33	11.0	32	11.3
110	3.3	69	5.3	71	5.2	68	5.4					60	6.1	60	6.1

											Sales/Working Capital				
	15.2		4.5		4.1		3.4				Sales/Working Capital		6.5		5.9
	-106.4		9.3		7.8		7.5						10.3		10.3
	-5.0		-143.8		34.3		17.3						31.7		39.5
	12.9		6.5		3.0		5.3				EBIT/Interest		13.1		7.2
(14)	-.5	(48)	1.7	(108)	.7	(45)	1.5					(309) 4.7	(284)	2.5
	-9.9		-1.5		-2.2		-.3						1.8		.6
					3.4		11.5				Net Profit + Depr., Dep., Amort./Cur. Mat. L/T/D		8.9		6.8
				(21)	1.4	(12)	1.7					(82) 4.1	(76)	2.5
					-.4		.5						2.0		.8
	.8		.1		.1		.3				Fixed/Worth		.2		.2
	-9.4		.6		.4		.7						.5		.6
	-.4		5.1		1.3		1.5						1.1		1.9
	4.0		.6		.7		.5				Debt/Worth		.9		.8
	-20.3		1.5		1.6		1.5						2.1		2.3
	-2.7		23.1		3.8		3.3						4.7		6.7
			52.4		9.1		14.4				% Profit Before Taxes/Tangible Net Worth		59.5		38.8
		(54)	4.6	(106)	1.2	(48)	3.7					(319) 29.5	(263)	16.7
			-9.3		-11.2		-2.4						8.5		1.8
	20.8		9.9		4.4		5.8				% Profit Before Taxes/Total Assets		17.7		13.5
	-4.1		1.2		.1		1.3						9.3		4.7
	-31.8		-3.2		-5.6		-1.3						2.2		-.8
	387.7		103.3		44.7		17.4				Sales/Net Fixed Assets		53.3		45.0
	10.0		22.5		17.3		6.7						19.8		16.1
	5.0		9.7		5.6		2.6						8.4		6.9
	4.2		3.5		2.8		2.1				Sales/Total Assets		3.5		3.4
	3.1		2.5		1.9		1.5						2.7		2.4
	2.0		1.7		1.3		1.1						1.9		1.6
	1.5		.6		.6		.9				% Depr., Dep., Amort./Sales		.6		.7
(14)	3.2	(44)	1.1	(108)	1.6	(48)	2.2					(284) 1.2	(250)	1.4
	6.3		4.5		3.5		4.3						2.5		2.6
			3.1		1.7		.7				% Officers', Directors' Owners' Comp/Sales		1.7		1.5
		(24)	3.7	(52)	2.9	(12)	1.9					(121) 2.9	(121)	2.8
			4.8		4.3		3.3						5.7		6.3

47399M	212572M	1168573M	1679120M	184543M	1294797M	Net Sales ($)	10674602M	9310961M
6860M	80648M	577068M	1104970M	180800M	828118M	Total Assets ($)	4540653M	4242952M

M = $ thousand   MM = $ million
See Pages 9 through 22 for Explanation of Ratios and Data

Comparative Historical Data | | | Current Data Sorted by Sales

			Type of Statement						
28	23	30	Unqualified	1		2	2	11	14
68	66	59	Reviewed	1	7	7	15	19	10
41	39	38	Compiled	1	6	7	10	10	4
41	62	39	Tax Returns	2	11	11	10	5	
102	104	101	Other	9	22	10	27	21	12
4/1/08-3/31/09 ALL	4/1/09-3/31/10 ALL	4/1/10-3/31/11 ALL		35 (4/1-9/30/10)			232 (10/1/10-3/31/11)		
				0-1MM	1-3MM	3-5MM	5-10MM	10-25MM	25MM & OVER
280	294	267	NUMBER OF STATEMENTS	14	46	37	64	66	40
%	%	%	ASSETS	%	%	%	%	%	%
7.4	6.6	8.0	Cash & Equivalents	7.6	13.4	9.9	6.6	5.7	6.4
25.7	23.4	23.9	Trade Receivables (net)	20.8	21.8	23.1	22.8	26.5	25.5
33.8	35.2	34.0	Inventory	17.7	31.9	36.5	40.7	33.9	29.1
3.2	3.0	2.3	All Other Current	3.0	2.1	2.0	1.7	2.3	3.5
70.2	68.2	68.2	Total Current	49.1	69.2	71.6	71.7	68.3	64.5
22.1	23.0	22.9	Fixed Assets (net)	42.3	20.5	23.6	19.4	22.2	25.0
2.0	2.9	3.0	Intangibles (net)	3.3	1.8	1.8	2.6	2.9	5.8
5.7	6.0	6.0	All Other Non-Current	5.4	8.5	3.0	6.2	6.5	4.8
100.0	100.0	100.0	Total	100.0	100.0	100.0	100.0	100.0	100.0
			LIABILITIES						
13.5	12.6	14.5	Notes Payable-Short Term	30.8	14.1	7.8	18.7	13.3	10.5
3.1	3.3	3.0	Cur. Mat.-L.T.D.	8.8	1.6	3.9	3.5	1.9	3.0
20.2	21.9	24.2	Trade Payables	30.7	26.3	23.1	22.6	19.1	31.1
.3	.1	.1	Income Taxes Payable	.1	.0	.2	.1	.1	.5
9.7	8.5	9.1	All Other Current	8.0	10.2	7.5	9.4	10.3	7.2
46.8	46.5	50.9	Total Current	78.3	52.3	42.5	54.3	44.7	52.2
12.5	18.1	12.0	Long-Term Debt	20.2	12.8	14.2	10.6	8.9	13.5
.4	.4	.3	Deferred Taxes	.0	.0	.3	.2	.5	.5
6.0	7.4	6.7	All Other Non-Current	10.2	9.0	4.5	8.1	3.8	7.4
34.3	27.7	30.1	Net Worth	-8.8	26.0	38.5	26.8	42.1	26.3
100.0	100.0	100.0	Total Liabilties & Net Worth	100.0	100.0	100.0	100.0	100.0	100.0
			INCOME DATA						
100.0	100.0	100.0	Net Sales	100.0	100.0	100.0	100.0	100.0	100.0
30.8	30.9	30.9	Gross Profit	31.0	37.6	29.9	32.1	26.6	29.1
29.4	31.9	30.1	Operating Expenses	34.7	34.3	29.3	32.7	26.6	26.2
1.4	-1.0	.7	Operating Profit	-3.7	3.3	.5	-.6	.1	2.9
.5	.8	.5	All Other Expenses (net)	.1	.8	.4	1.0	-.1	.8
.9	-1.7	.2	Profit Before Taxes	-3.8	2.5	.1	-1.7	.1	2.1
			RATIOS						
2.6	2.7	2.6	Current	1.3	4.1	4.2	2.1	2.4	2.7
1.7	1.6	1.6		.7	1.7	2.0	1.5	1.5	1.7
1.2	1.1	1.0		.5	.8	1.1	1.0	1.2	1.2
1.2	1.3	1.3	Quick	.7	1.5	1.7	.9	1.2	1.6
.7	.6	.6		.3	.8	.8	.6	.7	.6
.4	.4	.4		.2	.3	.4	.4	.5	.4
23 16.0	24 15.1	23 15.5	Sales/Receivables	0 UND	13 28.0	25 14.8	24 15.1	31 11.9	28 13.0
35 10.3	37 9.8	38 9.6		28 12.9	30 12.3	36 10.2	40 9.2	42 8.7	37 9.8
53 6.9	54 6.8	52 7.0		80 4.6	58 6.3	45 8.1	47 7.7	57 6.4	53 6.9
33 10.9	40 9.1	34 10.9	Cost of Sales/Inventory	0 UND	12 31.4	58 6.3	46 7.9	36 10.1	30 12.1
69 5.3	83 4.4	73 5.0		41 8.8	56 6.6	78 4.7	86 4.3	69 5.3	75 4.9
118 3.1	148 2.5	148 2.5		73 5.0	212 1.7	131 2.8	161 2.3	134 2.7	140 2.6
19 19.4	19 19.0	22 16.3	Cost of Sales/Payables	17 21.2	18 20.8	19 19.5	25 14.6	20 17.9	23 16.0
31 11.6	35 10.4	41 8.8		70 5.2	44 8.4	31 11.9	45 8.1	36 10.1	34 10.6
56 6.5	67 5.4	71 5.1		146 2.5	77 4.7	67 5.4	77 4.8	64 5.7	70 5.2
4.9	4.2	4.5	Sales/Working Capital	85.0	3.1	3.6	4.8	4.8	4.6
8.8	8.8	8.9		-11.8	8.9	6.7	8.2	9.5	9.5
28.9	36.6	130.5		-3.5	-12.0	41.4	NM	26.7	16.3
5.6	3.4	4.9	EBIT/Interest	1.1	6.6	4.3	3.9	2.8	10.1
(252) 2.0	(264) .8	(224) 1.3		(10) -1.6	(32) 1.5	(30) .5	(55) 1.1	(60) 1.2	(37) 2.6
-.1	-3.3	-1.8		-5.3	-.1	-1.6	-2.2	-1.5	-.3
6.0	2.6	4.2	Net Profit + Depr., Dep., Amort./Cur. Mat. L/T/D				2.7	3.8	11.5
(64) 2.8	(58) .6	(43) 1.3					(11) 1.2	(13) 1.7	(13) 4.2
.7	-.4	.3					-2.7	.1	.6
.2	.2	.1	Fixed/Worth	1.2	.1	.2	.1	.1	.3
.5	.6	.6		3.7	.6	.6	.4	.4	.7
1.3	2.5	2.2		-.8	NM	2.2	1.7	1.5	2.3
.8	.9	.7	Debt/Worth	1.0	.6	.5	.9	.6	.6
1.8	2.2	1.9		NM	1.9	1.2	2.1	1.5	2.2
4.5	8.1	6.2		-2.8	NM	5.3	5.0	3.7	4.6
23.4	14.6	17.5	% Profit Before Taxes/Tangible Net Worth		64.4	16.3	24.1	7.0	21.0
(248) 8.2	(240) 1.2	(223) 3.2			(35) 7.2	(31) 1.1	(56) 1.6	(60) 1.8	(34) 9.8
-2.8	-13.8	-8.3			.0	-11.8	-14.5	-4.5	-.7
8.2	4.3	6.1	% Profit Before Taxes/Total Assets	5.0	10.1	6.2	5.9	3.2	9.7
2.4	-.3	.7		-6.9	2.4	-.1	.3	.6	2.9
-2.7	-8.5	-4.4		-30.0	-1.6	-5.2	-6.5	-2.3	-2.0
50.7	44.6	43.7	Sales/Net Fixed Assets	23.0	93.5	47.2	40.7	43.4	42.8
16.6	15.4	15.1		4.9	23.5	13.3	14.5	17.3	12.8
6.5	4.8	4.8		1.6	5.1	5.6	6.5	3.9	4.6
3.1	2.8	2.9	Sales/Total Assets	2.6	3.1	2.8	3.3	2.9	2.4
2.4	1.9	1.9		1.9	2.0	2.3	2.0	1.9	1.7
1.6	1.3	1.4		.8	1.2	1.5	1.4	1.4	1.4
.7	.7	.7	% Depr., Dep., Amort./Sales	3.3	.7	.9	.6	.6	.6
(231) 1.6	(239) 1.7	(223) 1.8		(10) 5.3	(34) 1.5	(28) 2.7	(53) 1.7	(63) 1.5	(35) 2.1
3.5	3.6	4.1		7.8	5.9	4.7	3.9	2.7	4.5
1.5	2.0	1.8	% Officers', Directors' Owners' Comp/Sales	3.5	1.8	1.8	1.7		
(117) 2.9	(129) 3.3	(95) 3.2		(15) 4.2	(18) 3.7	(26) 3.1	(25) 2.7		
4.6	5.0	5.0		8.4	4.5	4.9	3.2		
6962194M	4938246M	4587004M	Net Sales ($)	9306M	94153M	152047M	450776M	1002237M	2878485M
3475496M	2742055M	2778464M	Total Assets ($)	5644M	60315M	86866M	284259M	644264M	1697116M

M = $ thousand   MM = $ million
See Pages 9 through 22 for Explanation of Ratios and Data

Current Data Sorted by Assets

Comparative Historical Data

Type of Statement	0-500M	500M-2MM	2-10MM	10-50MM	50-100MM	100-250MM		ALL 4/1/06-3/31/07	ALL 4/1/07-3/31/08
Unqualified			5	7	4	4		29	19
Reviewed		4	22	15	1			38	32
Compiled		14	11	4				33	30
Tax Returns	3	10	8	2				12	13
Other	3	7	23	16	4			41	56
		21 (4/1-9/30/10)		146 (10/1/10-3/31/11)					
NUMBER OF STATEMENTS	6	35	69	44	9	4		153	150
	%	%	%	%	%	%	**ASSETS**	%	%
		8.4	9.5	9.4			Cash & Equivalents	7.0	7.9
		26.5	33.8	34.1			Trade Receivables (net)	38.6	33.5
		37.6	36.3	34.2			Inventory	32.7	33.1
		6.0	2.1	3.2			All Other Current	2.5	3.6
		78.5	81.7	81.0			Total Current	80.7	78.1
		16.8	11.7	13.0			Fixed Assets (net)	14.0	14.2
		.2	1.8	2.5			Intangibles (net)	1.5	2.6
		4.6	4.9	3.6			All Other Non-Current	3.8	5.0
		100.0	100.0	100.0			Total	100.0	100.0
							LIABILITIES		
		14.2	12.1	10.1			Notes Payable-Short Term	13.5	13.7
		3.0	2.1	2.3			Cur. Mat.-L.T.D.	2.5	1.7
		17.9	20.7	23.2			Trade Payables	23.2	19.9
		.1	.1	.2			Income Taxes Payable	.2	.2
		4.8	8.1	8.2			All Other Current	9.4	10.0
		40.1	43.1	44.0			Total Current	48.7	45.4
		14.5	6.0	11.9			Long-Term Debt	10.2	9.6
		.9	.1	.3			Deferred Taxes	.1	.2
		11.1	2.9	4.0			All Other Non-Current	3.6	4.0
		33.4	47.9	39.8			Net Worth	37.3	40.7
		100.0	100.0	100.0			Total Liabilities & Net Worth	100.0	100.0
							INCOME DATA		
		100.0	100.0	100.0			Net Sales	100.0	100.0
		28.1	24.5	24.1			Gross Profit	25.2	24.9
		30.0	21.8	21.3			Operating Expenses	20.8	21.7
		-1.9	2.7	2.9			Operating Profit	4.4	3.2
		-.1	.2	.2			All Other Expenses (net)	.2	.1
		-1.8	2.5	2.7			Profit Before Taxes	4.2	3.1
							RATIOS		
		4.6	2.9	2.6			Current	2.3	2.6
		2.2	2.0	1.7				1.7	1.8
		1.1	1.4	1.4				1.3	1.3
		1.8	1.8	1.5			Quick	1.4	1.5
		(34) 1.0	1.0	1.0				.9	.9
		.5	.7	.7				.6	.6
		18 20.8	27 13.3	28 13.1			Sales/Receivables	30 12.3	26 14.0
		28 12.9	38 9.6	47 7.7				43 8.6	39 9.3
		42 8.7	59 6.2	57 6.4				56 6.5	53 6.8
		43 8.5	34 10.8	46 7.9			Cost of Sales/Inventory	30 12.0	33 11.1
		67 5.5	59 6.2	58 6.3				48 7.5	50 7.4
		104 3.5	82 4.4	72 5.1				71 5.1	75 4.8
		15 23.9	20 18.0	25 14.6			Cost of Sales/Payables	19 19.6	16 23.3
		28 12.9	31 12.0	38 9.6				31 11.6	29 12.5
		51 7.2	45 8.1	55 6.6				50 7.3	44 8.3
		4.2	5.2	4.9			Sales/Working Capital	6.5	6.0
		6.6	7.8	9.2				9.9	8.9
		33.1	15.0	12.7				20.7	18.8
		8.8	10.5	18.9			EBIT/Interest	16.0	11.0
		(34) 2.8	(60) 5.3	(39) 5.8				(146) 5.3	(138) 3.9
		-4.2	1.3	1.8				2.2	1.4
			18.5				Net Profit + Depr., Dep.,	10.8	12.9
			(11) 2.9				Amort./Cur. Mat. L/T/D	(41) 4.4	(38) 3.3
			1.4					1.9	1.5
		.1	.1	.1			Fixed/Worth	.1	.1
		.3	.2	.3				.3	.3
		1.3	.5	.8				.7	.8
		.5	.6	.7			Debt/Worth	.9	.6
		2.5	1.1	1.5				1.8	1.5
		8.2	2.3	3.5				3.8	3.8
		27.6	26.2	30.3			% Profit Before Taxes/Tangible	56.2	48.6
		(30) 9.7	(67) 9.6	(40) 15.6			Net Worth	(145) 31.4	(140) 18.3
		-1.6	1.3	6.8				11.4	4.1
		6.9	9.7	11.9			% Profit Before Taxes/Total	21.9	15.5
		2.8	3.3	6.0			Assets	10.4	8.3
		-10.4	.5	1.3				3.0	1.0
		90.0	93.7	49.5			Sales/Net Fixed Assets	75.7	68.5
		43.6	37.4	32.1				31.8	28.4
		12.9	18.2	18.0				17.6	15.7
		3.6	3.5	3.4			Sales/Total Assets	3.9	3.7
		3.0	3.0	2.7				3.2	3.0
		2.1	2.2	2.2				2.6	2.3
		.4	.5	.5			% Depr., Dep., Amort./Sales	.4	.4
		(27) .9	(57) .7	(42) .7				(136) .7	(134) .9
		2.2	1.3	1.4				1.1	1.4
		2.8	1.0	2.4			% Officers', Directors'	1.8	1.4
		(21) 4.1	(23) 2.8	(11) 3.2			Owners' Comp/Sales	(51) 3.0	(60) 2.4
		6.2	3.8	7.9				4.6	4.1
	9325M	122004M	896154M	2475887M	1338518M	1061502M	Net Sales ($)	7319960M	6781047M
	1993M	42865M	302050M	872121M	584945M	509184M	Total Assets ($)	2234246M	2437540M

M = $ thousand   MM = $ million
See Pages 9 through 22 for Explanation of Ratios and Data

Comparative Historical Data | Current Data Sorted by Sales

	4/1/08-3/31/09 ALL	4/1/09-3/31/10 ALL	4/1/10-3/31/11 ALL	Type of Statement	0-1MM	1-3MM	3-5MM	5-10MM	10-25MM	25MM & OVER
	23	18	20	Unqualified				2	1	17
	33	33	42	Reviewed		1	4	5	14	18
	23	23	29	Compiled		8	7	4	6	4
	16	23	23	Tax Returns	3	4	3	8	3	2
	60	46	53	Other	1	5	6	11	8	22
						21 (4/1-9/30/10)		146 (10/1/10-3/31/11)		
NUMBER OF STATEMENTS	155	143	167		4	18	20	30	32	63
	%	%	%	**ASSETS**	%	%	%	%	%	%
Cash & Equivalents	7.4	9.2	9.4			11.7	11.1	9.7	8.8	9.0
Trade Receivables (net)	31.3	30.0	32.9			32.5	25.5	31.0	34.8	35.1
Inventory	34.9	34.1	34.7			29.3	42.5	38.0	33.9	33.6
All Other Current	2.4	4.3	3.2			6.3	3.1	2.5	3.0	2.9
Total Current	76.0	77.6	80.2			79.8	82.2	81.3	80.6	80.6
Fixed Assets (net)	14.9	13.2	13.0			14.4	14.4	13.8	11.4	11.5
Intangibles (net)	3.8	3.1	2.3			.2	.5	.9	3.6	3.7
All Other Non-Current	5.4	6.1	4.6			5.5	3.0	4.1	4.5	4.3
Total	100.0	100.0	100.0			100.0	100.0	100.0	100.0	100.0
				LIABILITIES						
Notes Payable-Short Term	13.9	13.9	12.0			10.7	14.3	9.8	12.7	12.4
Cur. Mat.-L.T.D.	2.4	2.7	2.2			3.1	1.7	3.1	2.2	1.8
Trade Payables	18.8	19.5	20.6			15.9	16.0	21.3	20.4	22.9
Income Taxes Payable	.2	.1	.1			.1	.0	.1	.0	.2
All Other Current	8.9	7.7	7.5			6.2	6.7	7.6	7.4	8.1
Total Current	44.2	43.9	42.5			35.9	38.7	41.9	42.6	45.4
Long-Term Debt	12.5	12.0	11.0			23.4	10.8	7.2	7.7	9.4
Deferred Taxes	.8	.4	.4			1.8	.1	.1	.1	.5
All Other Non-Current	3.7	5.0	4.9			12.8	5.2	6.1	2.2	3.4
Net Worth	38.8	38.7	41.2			26.1	45.1	44.7	47.4	41.4
Total Liabilities & Net Worth	100.0	100.0	100.0			100.0	100.0	100.0	100.0	100.0
				INCOME DATA						
Net Sales	100.0	100.0	100.0			100.0	100.0	100.0	100.0	100.0
Gross Profit	25.1	26.7	25.5			30.3	29.5	23.4	24.1	24.0
Operating Expenses	22.1	25.0	23.6			32.4	27.4	21.1	21.9	20.9
Operating Profit	3.0	1.6	1.9			-2.1	2.1	2.3	2.2	3.0
All Other Expenses (net)	.5	.2	.2			-.1	-.2	.3	.1	.2
Profit Before Taxes	2.5	1.5	1.7			-2.0	2.3	2.0	2.2	2.8
				RATIOS						
Current	2.9	3.2	3.0			6.9	5.0	3.1	3.0	2.7
	1.8	1.7	1.9			2.0	2.2	2.1	2.1	1.6
	1.3	1.3	1.4			1.2	1.3	1.4	1.3	1.4
Quick	1.4	1.8	1.7			3.7	2.1	1.7	1.9	1.5
	.8	.8	(166) 1.0			1.3	1.0	.9	1.0	1.0
	.5	.5	.7			.5	.5	.6	.7	.7
Sales/Receivables	24 15.1	27 13.4	26 14.3			21 17.3	21 17.6	21 17.8	28 12.8	29 12.6
	38 9.5	36 10.0	41 9.0			35 10.3	30 12.4	37 9.8	36 10.2	47 7.8
	55 6.7	54 6.7	59 6.2			70 5.2	63 5.8	54 6.8	59 6.2	58 6.3
Cost of Sales/Inventory	36 10.1	37 9.9	42 8.6			6 60.6	46 7.9	42 8.7	25 14.7	44 8.3
	54 6.8	58 6.3	59 6.2			69 5.3	72 5.0	59 6.2	56 6.5	56 6.5
	79 4.6	84 4.4	79 4.6			125 2.9	129 2.8	81 4.5	75 4.8	71 5.1
Cost of Sales/Payables	14 25.5	16 22.4	20 18.0			1 273.5	20 18.2	19 19.1	18 20.3	25 14.6
	27 13.4	32 11.5	32 11.4			29 12.5	27 13.3	33 11.1	31 12.0	34 10.7
	45 8.1	50 7.4	49 7.5			52 7.1	38 9.6	44 8.2	46 8.0	51 7.1
Sales/Working Capital	5.9	5.1	4.7			3.7	3.7	4.7	5.7	4.9
	8.8	9.2	7.9			7.3	6.4	6.3	9.3	9.5
	18.1	21.0	17.7			23.8	14.0	17.3	18.8	13.7
EBIT/Interest	11.3	10.7	11.6			5.4	10.6	9.7	10.7	18.1
	(144) 3.7	(133) 3.4	(149) 4.4		(15) 1.2	(18) 3.4	(24) 2.8	(31) 6.1	(57) 5.3	
	1.3	.6	1.2			-14.0	-.9	1.3	1.5	2.3
Net Profit + Depr., Dep., Amort./Cur. Mat. L/T/D	4.1	5.1	6.2							6.0
	(31) 2.4	(23) 2.5	(28) 2.2						(19)	2.9
	1.1	.9	.7							.7
Fixed/Worth	.1	.1	.1			.0	.0	.0	.1	.1
	.3	.3	.2			.2	.1	.2	.2	.3
	.8	.8	.7			NM	.8	.6	.4	.7
Debt/Worth	.7	.7	.6			.7	.2	.6	.6	.7
	1.7	1.8	1.5			2.3	.9	1.3	1.4	1.5
	4.1	4.6	3.8			NM	6.0	2.7	2.5	3.1
% Profit Before Taxes/Tangible Net Worth	40.1	38.9	30.5			67.8	37.2	24.3	35.7	29.1
	(141) 18.0	(133) 13.0	(153) 11.9		(14) 10.0	(19) 5.0	(29) 9.6	(31) 17.4	(58) 13.0	
	5.3	1.4	3.7			-.7	-4.1	1.6	.3	7.3
% Profit Before Taxes/Total Assets	14.9	11.6	10.9			12.6	13.1	10.4	10.0	11.0
	5.9	3.7	3.9			3.0	2.9	2.7	4.3	5.4
	.9	-.3	.5			-11.4	-2.3	.4	.4	1.8
Sales/Net Fixed Assets	71.4	61.8	80.9			422.6	87.8	113.6	79.2	59.9
	30.8	33.9	37.2			47.4	45.4	32.4	40.8	34.2
	12.2	16.4	16.0			13.1	13.7	12.8	21.4	20.4
Sales/Total Assets	3.6	3.6	3.5			4.5	3.5	3.6	3.9	3.4
	2.9	2.7	2.9			2.3	2.6	3.0	3.2	2.8
	2.2	2.1	2.2			1.6	1.8	2.4	2.4	2.3
% Depr., Dep., Amort./Sales	.5	.5	.5			.9	.2	.5	.5	.5
	(132) .9	(117) .8	(141) .7		(11) 1.5	(16) .6	(25) .8	(27) .6	(60) .7	
	1.4	1.4	1.5			2.4	2.0	1.2	1.3	1.4
% Officers', Directors' Owners' Comp/Sales	1.1	1.3	1.2			1.3		1.3	1.0	1.2
	(53) 2.5	(57) 2.9	(61) 3.2		(10) 3.3		(13) 3.4	(15) 1.6	(12) 3.2	
	4.3	4.8	5.2			5.4		6.7	3.4	7.5
Net Sales ($)	6709454M	5643477M	5903390M		3173M	37513M	80635M	214262M	494690M	5073117M
Total Assets ($)	2604509M	2085012M	2313158M		2033M	16657M	35954M	77906M	174522M	2006086M

M = $ thousand   MM = $ million
See Pages 9 through 22 for Explanation of Ratios and Data

Current Data Sorted by Assets   **Comparative Historical Data**

0-500M	500M-2MM	2-10MM	10-50MM	50-100MM	100-250MM	Type of Statement	ALL	ALL
1		8	18	6	3	Unqualified	41	41
	8	42	17	1		Reviewed	82	68
7	16	26	2			Compiled	49	46
10	26	20				Tax Returns	35	45
13	39	39	18	4	1	Other	94	99
	44 (4/1-9/30/10)		281 (10/1/10-3/31/11)				4/1/06-3/31/07	4/1/07-3/31/08
31	89	135	55	11	4	**NUMBER OF STATEMENTS**	301	299
%	%	%	%	%	%	**ASSETS**	%	%
17.9	12.4	8.6	6.9	3.5		Cash & Equivalents	7.3	7.2
30.4	28.9	34.3	27.1	22.5		Trade Receivables (net)	36.3	34.7
33.0	32.9	34.6	33.3	31.0		Inventory	30.0	31.1
3.9	2.9	2.0	3.7	9.3		All Other Current	3.1	2.8
85.3	77.1	79.4	71.0	66.4		Total Current	76.7	75.7
11.2	14.5	13.3	18.6	20.2		Fixed Assets (net)	16.5	15.5
.0	2.9	3.0	4.6	10.1		Intangibles (net)	1.7	3.2
3.6	5.5	4.3	5.8	3.3		All Other Non-Current	5.1	5.6
100.0	100.0	100.0	100.0	100.0		Total	100.0	100.0
						LIABILITIES		
25.4	15.4	16.9	12.7	19.7		Notes Payable-Short Term	15.5	16.8
2.9	2.4	1.7	3.2	1.1		Cur. Mat.-L.T.D.	2.7	3.6
27.8	19.4	18.0	12.3	10.7		Trade Payables	19.3	18.2
.0	.1	.1	.2	.0		Income Taxes Payable	.2	.2
19.0	6.4	6.0	9.2	9.9		All Other Current	10.5	9.1
75.0	43.7	42.8	37.6	41.4		Total Current	48.2	47.9
10.5	10.2	7.6	9.5	8.8		Long-Term Debt	12.7	11.2
.0	.0	.2	.3	.4		Deferred Taxes	.2	.3
13.5	8.3	7.4	2.9	3.4		All Other Non-Current	4.8	4.1
.9	37.7	42.1	49.6	46.0		Net Worth	34.1	36.5
100.0	100.0	100.0	100.0	100.0		Total Liabilities & Net Worth	100.0	100.0
						INCOME DATA		
100.0	100.0	100.0	100.0	100.0		Net Sales	100.0	100.0
36.4	31.2	27.1	24.3	22.0		Gross Profit	27.8	27.5
37.5	28.2	24.5	23.7	23.7		Operating Expenses	23.6	24.1
-1.1	3.0	2.6	.6	-1.8		Operating Profit	4.3	3.4
.5	.4	.3	.2	-.3		All Other Expenses (net)	.6	.4
-1.6	2.6	2.3	.4	-1.4		Profit Before Taxes	3.6	3.0
						RATIOS		
3.2	3.7	3.2	4.1	1.9		Current	2.6	2.8
1.5	1.9	2.0	1.8	1.7			1.6	1.7
1.0	1.3	1.4	1.2	1.3			1.2	1.2
2.2	2.1	1.6	1.9	1.0		Quick	1.6	1.5
.8	1.0	1.1	.8	.6			.9	.9
.4	.6	.7	.6	.4			.6	.6
10 38.0	19 19.0	30 12.2	31 11.9	30 12.3		Sales/Receivables	28 12.8	30 12.3
31 11.7	33 11.0	45 8.1	41 9.0	44 8.2			42 8.8	39 9.4
41 8.9	54 6.7	67 5.5	50 7.4	59 6.2			56 6.5	53 6.9
0 UND	18 20.6	36 10.0	49 7.5	53 6.9		Cost of Sales/Inventory	26 14.0	29 12.7
47 7.8	56 6.5	68 5.4	64 5.7	83 4.4			45 8.2	51 7.2
83 4.4	109 3.4	98 3.7	91 4.0	97 3.8			74 4.9	75 4.9
6 65.9	14 26.3	17 21.9	14 27.0	14 25.6		Cost of Sales/Payables	16 23.1	16 22.9
31 11.9	28 13.2	28 13.1	21 17.5	23 16.0			27 13.5	24 15.5
55 6.7	54 6.7	47 7.8	34 10.8	34 10.7			43 8.5	40 9.1
8.2	4.2	4.5	4.5	6.2		Sales/Working Capital	6.4	6.0
13.6	8.4	7.6	8.2	8.1			10.7	10.4
-89.4	23.5	12.1	23.2	10.2			29.8	22.5
16.3	13.3	11.0	7.8	15.0		EBIT/Interest	11.0	10.6
(25) 2.8	(69) 4.1	(120) 3.7	(53) 3.3	.3			(279) 4.6	(278) 3.5
-2.4	1.1	1.2	-.4	-1.2			1.9	1.5
		9.0	3.0			Net Profit + Depr., Dep., Amort./Cur. Mat. L/T/D	10.8	7.1
	(15) 2.8	(17) 1.4				(77) 3.8	(69) 3.0
		1.0	-.1				1.5	1.1
.1	.0	.1	.1	.2		Fixed/Worth	.1	.1
.3	.2	.2	.3	.4			.3	.3
-.3	.9	.7	.8	1.1			1.0	.9
.7	.6	.7	.4	1.2		Debt/Worth	.8	.8
3.3	1.7	1.4	1.4	1.4			2.0	1.7
-4.2	4.8	3.5	2.7	1.9			4.3	4.3
70.1	34.9	30.4	12.7	15.4		% Profit Before Taxes/Tangible Net Worth	53.3	45.5
(21) 10.1	(78) 17.7	(123) 12.6	(52) 5.1	-2.1			(273) 28.4	(275) 21.3
-22.5	1.2	1.5	-4.4	-9.4			12.2	7.0
22.2	13.1	11.3	7.0	5.6		% Profit Before Taxes/Total Assets	17.2	16.8
.3	5.3	4.3	1.2	-.9			8.7	6.9
-40.9	.2	.2	-3.4	-2.5			3.2	1.7
211.8	144.8	80.3	43.5	31.4		Sales/Net Fixed Assets	65.8	74.1
86.3	38.4	32.1	22.3	10.5			28.4	30.5
32.3	13.8	15.6	9.2	7.1			12.5	13.5
7.7	3.9	3.2	3.0	2.4		Sales/Total Assets	3.9	3.8
3.9	2.8	2.4	2.3	2.1			3.1	2.9
2.7	1.7	1.8	1.7	1.5			2.4	2.2
.6	.3	.5	.6	.9		% Depr., Dep., Amort./Sales	.5	.5
(13) .8	(59) .7	(121) .8	(52) .8	(10) 1.7			(252) .9	(258) .9
1.6	1.5	1.6	2.1	2.7			1.6	1.8
3.4	1.8	1.9				% Officers', Directors' Owners' Comp/Sales	1.4	1.2
(15) 4.5	(44) 3.3	(59) 2.9					(97) 2.6	(105) 2.6
9.1	5.4	5.6					5.0	5.4
35215M	348596M	1651534M	2944306M	1457457M	1292118M	Net Sales ($)	10166947M	10948669M
8225M	103697M	594357M	1144218M	743693M	568679M	Total Assets ($)	3519887M	4219611M

M = $ thousand   MM = $ million
See Pages 9 through 22 for Explanation of Ratios and Data

Comparative Historical Data

Current Data Sorted by Sales

			Type of Statement	0-1MM	1-3MM	3-5MM	5-10MM	10-25MM	25MM & OVER
42	34	36	Unqualified		1	1	3	9	22
73	75	68	Reviewed	1	4	4	20	22	17
55	38	51	Compiled	6	8	5	18	12	2
62	42	56	Tax Returns	8	17	12	12	5	2
108	114	114	Other	9	21	21	18	23	22
4/1/08-3/31/09 ALL	4/1/09-3/31/10 ALL	4/1/10-3/31/11 ALL		44 (4/1-9/30/10)			281 (10/1/10-3/31/11)		
340	303	325	NUMBER OF STATEMENTS	24	51	43	71	71	65
%	%	%	**ASSETS**	%	%	%	%	%	%
8.4	8.9	10.0	Cash & Equivalents	12.6	15.1	11.2	8.5	9.8	6.2
31.0	29.4	30.7	Trade Receivables (net)	29.3	26.1	24.6	37.1	31.8	30.5
32.5	31.6	33.5	Inventory	35.4	31.4	34.6	34.7	34.2	31.4
3.1	2.5	3.0	All Other Current	4.5	2.4	1.6	2.9	2.2	5.0
75.0	72.4	77.2	Total Current	81.9	75.0	72.1	83.1	78.0	73.1
17.2	19.2	14.8	Fixed Assets (net)	13.1	16.8	16.0	11.2	14.5	17.1
3.3	3.0	3.2	Intangibles (net)	2.0	1.6	5.0	2.8	3.2	4.2
4.5	5.3	4.9	All Other Non-Current	3.2	6.6	6.9	2.9	4.3	5.6
100.0	100.0	100.0	Total	100.0	100.0	100.0	100.0	100.0	100.0
			LIABILITIES						
16.6	14.4	16.5	Notes Payable-Short Term	24.4	16.3	15.0	18.8	14.9	13.9
3.4	2.8	2.3	Cur. Mat.-L.T.D.	2.2	3.7	2.2	1.8	1.6	2.5
15.4	15.7	18.2	Trade Payables	13.1	26.1	16.3	19.3	17.0	15.1
.2	.1	.1	Income Taxes Payable	.1	.1	.0	.1	.2	.1
7.9	7.3	8.0	All Other Current	7.1	13.3	6.6	5.7	6.1	10.0
43.6	40.3	45.1	Total Current	47.0	59.6	40.2	45.8	39.8	41.5
12.2	12.5	9.1	Long-Term Debt	13.5	15.1	7.3	7.2	7.5	8.1
.4	.2	.2	Deferred Taxes	.0	.0	.2	.2	.2	.3
4.1	5.9	7.3	All Other Non-Current	15.6	11.0	5.6	7.2	6.4	3.6
39.8	41.0	38.2	Net Worth	24.0	14.3	46.8	39.7	46.1	46.5
100.0	100.0	100.0	Total Liabilities & Net Worth	100.0	100.0	100.0	100.0	100.0	100.0
			INCOME DATA						
100.0	100.0	100.0	Net Sales	100.0	100.0	100.0	100.0	100.0	100.0
27.8	28.2	28.4	Gross Profit	38.3	35.4	30.9	26.1	27.3	21.1
25.3	26.5	26.6	Operating Expenses	38.0	32.1	27.7	25.1	24.6	20.9
2.6	1.7	1.8	Operating Profit	.3	3.2	3.1	1.0	2.7	.2
.6	.5	.3	All Other Expenses (net)	1.3	.5	.1	-.1	.5	.1
2.0	1.2	1.5	Profit Before Taxes	-1.1	2.7	3.0	1.0	2.2	.2
			RATIOS						
3.2	3.2	3.3	Current	7.9	3.3	4.2	3.2	3.1	2.9
1.8	1.9	1.8		2.3	1.9	2.3	1.6	2.0	1.7
1.3	1.3	1.3		1.2	1.0	1.4	1.3	1.3	1.3
1.6	1.7	1.7	Quick	4.1	2.1	2.2	1.6	1.9	1.4
.9	1.0	.9		1.0	.9	1.2	1.0	1.0	.8
.5	.6	.6		.4	.5	.4	.6	.6	.6
24 · 15.1	26 · 14.2	24 · 15.2	Sales/Receivables	22 · 16.4	15 · 23.7	17 · 21.8	30 · 12.2	27 · 13.6	28 · 13.1
37 · 10.0	37 · 9.9	40 · 9.1		37 · 10.0	38 · 9.7	38 · 9.6	45 · 8.1	41 · 8.8	41 · 9.0
51 · 7.1	54 · 6.7	57 · 6.4		72 · 5.1	55 · 6.6	55 · 6.7	73 · 5.0	59 · 6.2	48 · 7.6
28 · 13.3	31 · 11.9	31 · 11.9	Cost of Sales/Inventory	4 · 86.8	4 · 95.5	30 · 12.0	31 · 11.9	37 · 9.9	30 · 12.2
54 · 6.8	57 · 6.4	60 · 6.0		75 · 4.9	59 · 6.1	66 · 5.6	70 · 5.2	59 · 6.2	56 · 6.5
82 · 4.4	91 · 4.0	99 · 3.7		247 · 1.5	115 · 3.2	104 · 3.5	102 · 3.6	80 · 4.6	74 · 5.0
11 · 32.8	13 · 29.2	15 · 24.9	Cost of Sales/Payables	4 · 102.1	19 · 19.0	10 · 35.3	17 · 21.0	17 · 21.9	12 · 30.2
20 · 18.3	24 · 15.5	27 · 13.5		30 · 12.1	42 · 8.7	21 · 17.1	27 · 13.5	30 · 12.4	21 · 17.5
38 · 9.7	38 · 9.5	46 · 7.9		78 · 4.7	68 · 5.4	42 · 8.6	46 · 7.9	47 · 7.8	31 · 11.7
5.3	5.0	4.6	Sales/Working Capital	2.5	5.4	4.0	4.6	4.8	5.2
9.1	8.3	8.6		7.4	7.9	7.9	8.1	8.4	9.3
20.1	16.5	17.1		47.4	359.8	15.5	15.4	14.9	21.3
10.7	7.1	11.3	EBIT/Interest	5.6	15.3	12.8	8.6	13.7	8.9
(306) 3.3	(271) 1.8	(282) 3.4		(19) 1.0	(43) 4.0	(32) 5.4	(63) 2.9	(64) 4.5	(61) 3.3
.9	-.6	.8		-5.4	1.0	2.3	1.0	1.1	-.1
5.9	4.5	5.4	Net Profit + Depr., Dep., Amort./Cur. Mat. L/T/D					7.0	3.2
(70) 2.1	(62) 1.7	(43) 1.8						(13) 2.8	(18) 1.4
.4	.0	.7						1.1	-.3
.1	.1	.1	Fixed/Worth	.1	.1	.1	.1	.1	.1
.3	.4	.3		.3	.4	.3	.2	.2	.4
.9	1.2	.9		-11.9	3.8	1.1	.4	.8	.7
.7	.6	.6	Debt/Worth	1.8	.7	.4	.8	.5	.5
1.7	1.6	1.5		3.2	1.7	1.0	1.6	1.3	1.4
4.7	3.6	3.7		-19.2	40.1	2.7	3.4	3.5	3.5
34.3	23.4	28.8	% Profit Before Taxes/Tangible Net Worth	69.0	44.6	37.9	23.2	32.4	13.7
(311) 15.6	(274) 7.4	(289) 10.7		(17) 1.9	(41) 18.6	(38) 13.5	(64) 11.2	(66) 13.0	(63) 6.0
1.4	-5.9	.6		-20.0	1.1	1.4	.9	1.2	-4.5
14.7	9.4	11.3	% Profit Before Taxes/Total Assets	5.7	13.2	16.2	9.1	12.2	7.2
5.1	2.6	3.9		-.6	4.4	7.7	3.2	4.6	1.7
-.1	-3.0	-1.1		-19.6	-1.2	.8	-.4	.2	-2.3
72.0	55.1	90.4	Sales/Net Fixed Assets	202.2	108.1	93.1	97.4	67.8	46.7
28.8	21.7	32.3		50.1	35.0	34.4	33.5	36.1	24.2
11.3	7.9	12.8		10.3	15.3	10.6	17.2	12.6	9.8
3.7	3.5	3.4	Sales/Total Assets	3.5	3.7	3.6	3.4	3.7	3.3
2.9	2.5	2.6		2.2	2.7	2.5	2.6	2.6	2.5
2.1	1.7	1.8		1.2	1.7	1.7	1.9	1.8	2.0
.5	.5	.5	% Depr., Dep., Amort./Sales	.8	.5	.3	.5	.4	.5
(282) .9	(252) 1.1	(258) .8		(13) 1.3	(29) .8	(30) .9	(62) .8	(65) .8	(59) .8
2.0	2.3	1.7		6.2	1.5	3.4	1.2	1.9	1.8
1.8	2.1	1.9	% Officers', Directors', Owners' Comp/Sales	3.1	1.8	1.8		1.8	
(141) 2.8	(126) 3.6	(127) 3.3		(10) 4.2	(27) 4.5	(18) 4.1	(36) 2.3	(28) 2.4	
4.9	6.5	5.9		7.5	6.9	6.2	4.3	5.8	
13065514M	8156121M	7729226M	Net Sales ($)	16249M	93858M	168345M	520291M	1126838M	5803645M
4337331M	3640964M	3162869M	Total Assets ($)	10324M	44212M	76543M	225344M	471661M	2334785M

© RMA 2011   M = $ thousand   MM = $ million
See Pages 9 through 22 for Explanation of Ratios and Data

Current Data Sorted by Assets   Comparative Historical Data

Columns 50-100MM and 100-250MM: DATA NOT AVAILABLE

Type of Statement	0-500M	500M-2MM	2-10MM	10-50MM	50-100MM	100-250MM		4/1/06-3/31/07 ALL	4/1/07-3/31/08 ALL
Unqualified			2	5				5	5
Reviewed			11	8				13	11
Compiled	1	4	1					3	5
Tax Returns	1	7	4					7	5
Other	3	5	7	4				9	13
	0-500M	500M-2MM	9 (4/1-9/30/10) 2-10MM	54 (10/1/10-3/31/11) 10-50MM	50-100MM	100-250MM			
NUMBER OF STATEMENTS	5	16	25	17				37	39
ASSETS	%	%	%	%	%	%		%	%
Cash & Equivalents		15.9	12.3	5.6				10.6	7.6
Trade Receivables (net)		30.8	27.4	36.6				35.5	35.5
Inventory		21.3	38.6	37.6				34.1	30.4
All Other Current		.0	.9	3.0				3.4	3.4
Total Current		68.1	79.2	82.8				83.6	76.8
Fixed Assets (net)		12.8	13.2	10.3				10.2	13.6
Intangibles (net)		12.0	1.8	4.2				3.1	3.7
All Other Non-Current		7.2	5.8	2.7				3.2	5.9
Total		100.0	100.0	100.0				100.0	100.0
LIABILITIES									
Notes Payable-Short Term		10.0	13.8	16.0				16.5	16.9
Cur. Mat.-L.T.D.		1.6	3.2	1.1				1.6	1.8
Trade Payables		23.9	21.5	29.9				23.6	22.2
Income Taxes Payable		.1	.5	.2				.2	.3
All Other Current		6.5	7.0	10.5				15.9	15.4
Total Current		42.1	45.9	57.7				57.8	56.5
Long-Term Debt		19.6	7.8	2.8				6.5	7.4
Deferred Taxes		.0	.1	.2				.0	.1
All Other Non-Current		2.2	2.4	2.9				6.7	6.0
Net Worth		36.1	43.7	36.4				29.0	30.1
Total Liabilities & Net Worth		100.0	100.0	100.0				100.0	100.0
INCOME DATA									
Net Sales		100.0	100.0	100.0				100.0	100.0
Gross Profit		31.6	30.8	22.4				30.7	27.8
Operating Expenses		23.5	27.1	19.0				25.9	24.2
Operating Profit		8.1	3.8	3.3				4.7	3.6
All Other Expenses (net)		.7	1.0	.1				.8	1.4
Profit Before Taxes		7.5	2.8	3.2				3.9	2.2
RATIOS									
Current		2.6	2.7	2.1				2.3	1.9
		1.5	2.0	1.4				1.5	1.4
		1.0	1.3	1.2				1.2	1.1
Quick		2.4	1.6	.9				1.1	1.0
		1.0	.8	.8				.8	.8
		.7	.6	.6				.6	.6
Sales/Receivables		8 43.8	25 14.6	33 11.0				30 12.3	28 12.9
		25 14.8	33 11.0	45 8.1				42 8.6	41 8.8
		52 7.0	41 8.9	68 5.4				49 7.5	54 6.8
Cost of Sales/Inventory		0 UND	34 10.9	35 10.5				37 10.0	30 12.3
		29 12.5	54 6.8	52 7.0				58 6.3	45 8.1
		87 4.2	89 4.1	102 3.6				110 3.3	88 4.2
Cost of Sales/Payables		12 31.5	14 26.5	30 12.0				23 15.6	18 20.3
		28 12.8	28 12.9	45 8.1				37 10.0	29 12.4
		46 7.9	53 6.9	77 4.8				54 6.8	47 7.8
Sales/Working Capital		6.6	5.6	6.8				6.7	8.7
		39.1	9.0	12.6				10.5	11.4
		848.9	23.2	19.2				34.9	51.6
EBIT/Interest		17.2	56.2	15.2				10.8	11.1
		(12) 8.4	(24) 5.6	(15) 5.4				(35) 4.1	(37) 4.7
		4.0	2.2	2.1				1.2	1.7
Net Profit + Depr., Dep., Amort./Cur. Mat. L/T/D									5.9
								(13) 3.2	3.2
									1.3
Fixed/Worth		.0	.0	.1				.1	.1
		.1	.2	.3				.3	.4
		2.6	.5	.5				1.0	1.5
Debt/Worth		1.4	.6	1.0				.8	1.0
		2.0	1.0	2.5				2.5	2.7
		18.6	2.7	4.9				5.8	9.1
% Profit Before Taxes/Tangible Net Worth		128.9	40.3	56.1				71.5	51.2
		(14) 56.9	(22) 20.5	36.5				(31) 30.3	(33) 23.9
		25.1	7.4	8.8				3.6	5.6
% Profit Before Taxes/Total Assets		23.9	20.4	9.5				17.3	13.0
		20.3	6.0	6.7				7.1	5.6
		6.6	2.3	2.0				.8	1.6
Sales/Net Fixed Assets		UND	134.2	99.1				247.2	183.5
		226.1	46.8	42.3				60.9	43.0
		46.4	23.4	15.0				26.6	14.2
Sales/Total Assets		6.2	4.3	3.5				4.0	3.9
		3.2	3.3	2.7				3.2	3.0
		1.4	2.6	1.9				2.0	2.3
% Depr., Dep., Amort./Sales			.4	.3				.3	.3
			(19) .9	(15) .7				(27) .9	(31) .7
			1.2	1.2				1.5	1.5
% Officers', Directors' Owners' Comp/Sales			.8					1.2	.8
			(11) 1.8					(15) 2.7	(14) 2.7
			3.5					6.2	6.0
Net Sales ($)	3569M	98673M	423648M	849642M				1430825M	1934990M
Total Assets ($)	1430M	18273M	122428M	275458M				582407M	782547M

M = $ thousand   MM = $ million
See Pages 9 through 22 for Explanation of Ratios and Data

Comparative Historical Data | Current Data Sorted by Sales

Type of Statement — current data periods: **9 (4/1-9/30/10)** covers 0-1MM, 1-3MM, 3-5MM; **54 (10/1/10-3/31/11)** covers 5-10MM, 10-25MM, 25MM & OVER.

4/1/08-3/31/09 ALL	4/1/09-3/31/10 ALL	4/1/10-3/31/11 ALL		0-1MM	1-3MM	3-5MM	5-10MM	10-25MM	25MM & OVER
7	8	7	Unqualified				5	2	5
15	18	20	Reviewed		1		3		11
2	5	6	Compiled		3		1	1	
4	14	14	Tax Returns	1	3	1	3	5	
13	11	16	Other	3	1	2	3	5	6
41	56	63	**NUMBER OF STATEMENTS**	7	6	3	12	13	22
%	%	%	**ASSETS**	%	%	%	%	%	%
8.2	13.5	11.8	Cash & Equivalents				8.6	15.1	9.0
31.9	26.6	30.1	Trade Receivables (net)				33.7	27.2	35.7
33.6	33.3	33.6	Inventory				32.4	40.6	37.9
1.6	1.4	1.3	All Other Current				.8	1.5	2.0
75.2	74.9	76.8	Total Current				75.5	84.4	84.6
12.2	13.6	12.7	Fixed Assets (net)				15.6	9.6	8.1
7.4	6.0	5.1	Intangibles (net)				4.2	.9	3.9
5.3	5.6	5.4	All Other Non-Current				4.7	5.1	3.4
100.0	100.0	100.0	Total				100.0	100.0	100.0
			LIABILITIES						
13.2	9.5	12.4	Notes Payable-Short Term				19.4	9.3	17.0
3.2	3.1	2.0	Cur. Mat.-L.T.D.				5.8	.9	.9
17.1	25.2	23.5	Trade Payables				28.5	22.2	28.7
.1	.4	.3	Income Taxes Payable				1.0	.3	.1
13.3	11.2	7.8	All Other Current				9.2	7.5	9.6
46.8	49.4	45.9	Total Current				63.8	40.1	56.3
9.6	7.3	10.9	Long-Term Debt				4.9	5.8	3.4
.0	.1	.1	Deferred Taxes				.2	.0	.2
4.1	4.8	2.3	All Other Non-Current				3.0	4.8	1.2
39.5	38.5	40.9	Net Worth				28.2	49.2	38.9
100.0	100.0	100.0	Total Liabilities & Net Worth				100.0	100.0	100.0
			INCOME DATA						
100.0	100.0	100.0	Net Sales				100.0	100.0	100.0
29.3	29.1	29.2	Gross Profit				38.3	20.0	21.9
26.6	25.8	23.6	Operating Expenses				34.2	17.9	17.9
2.7	3.3	5.6	Operating Profit				4.1	2.1	4.0
.6	.2	.6	All Other Expenses (net)				1.5	.2	.2
2.1	3.1	5.0	Profit Before Taxes				2.6	1.8	3.8
			RATIOS						
2.3	2.4	2.7	Current				2.0	3.0	2.1
1.6	1.6	1.7					1.2	2.7	1.5
1.2	1.1	1.2					.9	1.6	1.3
1.1	1.4	1.5	Quick				1.4	1.6	1.1
.8	.8	.9					.6	.8	.8
.5	.5	.6					.3	.7	.6
27 13.8	16 22.5	19 19.4	Sales/Receivables			31 11.9	7 51.7	25 14.4
36 10.2	32 11.6	34 10.7				35 10.5	28 13.0	42 8.7
56 6.5	46 7.9	50 7.3				41 8.9	36 10.1	57 6.4
30 12.3	25 14.8	29 12.8	Cost of Sales/Inventory			32 11.6	25 14.3	32 11.3
48 7.7	46 7.9	51 7.1				58 6.3	48 7.6	46 7.9
87 4.2	93 3.9	93 3.9				71 5.1	143 2.6	71 5.1
13 27.8	17 21.2	13 27.4	Cost of Sales/Payables			13 28.5	14 26.6	21 17.5
24 15.2	37 9.8	31 11.7				46 8.0	25 14.5	32 11.3
52 7.0	66 5.6	55 6.6				74 4.9	41 9.0	58 6.3
5.8	6.1	5.6	Sales/Working Capital				8.8	3.5	7.5
12.3	14.0	9.9					28.5	9.0	12.6
25.8	106.9	35.5					-54.7	37.1	18.9
11.0	22.8	34.1	EBIT/Interest				18.1	82.0	38.1
(37) 2.3	(51) 7.0	(54) 6.7				(11) 3.7	(11) 6.9	(21) 8.6
.0	2.7	3.4					-6.7	1.7	4.4
	13.4	90.8	Net Profit + Depr., Dep., Amort./Cur. Mat. L/T/D						
	(17) 3.3	(14) 10.9							
	.7	2.8							
.1	.1	.0	Fixed/Worth				.0	.0	.1
.4	.3	.2					.7	.2	.2
.9	.9	1.0					UND	.3	.4
1.0	.7	.7	Debt/Worth				.9	.5	1.0
2.8	2.6	1.5					2.0	.8	2.3
6.6	6.3	4.1					UND	2.6	3.6
41.2	50.4	63.9	% Profit Before Taxes/Tangible Net Worth					35.0	63.3
(35) 17.2	(49) 22.1	(57) 27.7						14.1	41.4
-4.1	11.4	9.3						5.5	14.9
14.8	14.2	23.1	% Profit Before Taxes/Total Assets				23.0	19.0	22.1
4.8	6.1	8.6					7.1	5.2	8.3
-2.3	2.8	2.8					-10.9	2.3	3.0
157.7	184.0	312.4	Sales/Net Fixed Assets				150.8	750.6	116.6
44.9	57.5	63.6					51.7	63.6	47.6
19.3	18.0	23.9					13.3	14.1	36.0
4.2	4.0	4.2	Sales/Total Assets				3.9	8.5	4.7
2.8	2.9	2.9					3.3	3.3	3.3
2.1	2.1	1.8					2.7	1.8	2.6
.5	.2	.4	% Depr., Dep., Amort./Sales						.4
(30) 1.0	(45) .8	(42) .7						(18)	.6
1.6	2.0	1.2							1.0
1.3	.9		% Officers', Directors' Owners' Comp/Sales						
(15) 2.4	(25) 2.7	(25) 1.8							
6.4	4.5	4.1							
1597524M	1440546M	1375532M	Net Sales ($)	3745M	11458M	11792M	83296M	214175M	1051066M
729891M	655047M	417589M	Total Assets ($)	3515M	5838M	5754M	28910M	75237M	298335M

M = $ thousand   MM = $ million
See Pages 9 through 22 for Explanation of Ratios and Data

Current Data Sorted by Assets   **Comparative Historical Data**

0-500M	500M-2MM	2-10MM	10-50MM	50-100MM	100-250MM	Type of Statement	4/1/06-3/31/07 ALL	4/1/07-3/31/08 ALL
		2	13	1	5	Unqualified	36	36
	9	26	11	2		Reviewed	49	46
3	13	11				Compiled	39	25
7	13	12				Tax Returns	23	18
3	16	23	13	3		Other	76	65
	47 (4/1-9/30/10)		139 (10/1/10-3/31/11)					
13	51	74	37	6	5	**NUMBER OF STATEMENTS**	223	190
%	%	%	%	%	%	**ASSETS**	%	%
19.4	9.9	10.5	6.3			Cash & Equivalents	8.2	8.3
29.4	30.9	33.4	30.9			Trade Receivables (net)	32.2	31.8
29.3	32.5	29.5	26.8			Inventory	31.4	29.8
2.2	2.8	4.8	6.0			All Other Current	3.6	5.4
80.2	76.1	78.2	70.0			Total Current	75.5	75.3
10.8	14.2	11.9	17.4			Fixed Assets (net)	14.3	14.5
3.3	3.8	3.7	7.5			Intangibles (net)	3.7	3.9
5.7	5.9	6.2	5.1			All Other Non-Current	6.5	6.3
100.0	100.0	100.0	100.0			Total	100.0	100.0
						LIABILITIES		
7.6	8.8	13.0	11.2			Notes Payable-Short Term	13.6	13.6
2.9	3.1	2.1	4.1			Cur. Mat.-L.T.D.	3.1	3.7
29.6	16.9	17.4	19.1			Trade Payables	19.0	20.2
.0	.1	.0	.8			Income Taxes Payable	.4	.4
10.7	10.0	17.7	13.1			All Other Current	16.2	17.0
50.9	39.0	50.3	48.3			Total Current	52.2	54.9
33.0	9.7	9.2	13.3			Long-Term Debt	11.6	11.4
.0	.1	.4	.3			Deferred Taxes	.3	.3
12.4	7.2	6.4	5.2			All Other Non-Current	6.3	5.8
3.8	44.0	33.7	32.8			Net Worth	29.6	27.6
100.0	100.0	100.0	100.0			Total Liabilities & Net Worth	100.0	100.0
						INCOME DATA		
100.0	100.0	100.0	100.0			Net Sales	100.0	100.0
49.3	42.7	39.0	34.9			Gross Profit	37.8	37.9
45.0	39.0	35.4	30.2			Operating Expenses	34.6	34.1
4.3	3.7	3.6	4.7			Operating Profit	3.2	3.7
.5	-.1	-.1	.5			All Other Expenses (net)	.3	.5
3.8	3.8	3.7	4.2			Profit Before Taxes	2.9	3.2
						RATIOS		
5.0	2.6	2.6	2.1			Current	2.1	2.0
1.8	1.9	1.6	1.4				1.5	1.4
1.1	1.6	1.1	1.2				1.1	1.1
2.5	1.7	1.6	1.1			Quick	1.1	1.1
1.2	1.1	.9	.8				.7	.7
.8	.7	.5	.5				.5	.5
13 27.5	22 16.6	25 14.5	28 12.9			Sales/Receivables	25 14.7	26 13.8
18 19.9	30 12.1	34 10.7	44 8.4				35 10.4	35 10.3
28 13.2	42 8.8	45 8.1	59 6.2				44 8.3	47 7.8
26 14.0	26 14.1	34 10.8	45 8.1			Cost of Sales/Inventory	37 10.0	34 10.8
45 8.2	63 5.8	59 6.2	68 5.4				65 5.6	59 6.1
79 4.6	83 4.4	89 4.1	89 4.1				92 4.0	83 4.4
10 35.5	19 19.6	14 26.4	18 20.0			Cost of Sales/Payables	14 26.6	17 21.6
31 11.8	29 12.4	27 13.5	34 10.7				30 12.3	30 12.0
49 7.4	48 7.5	48 7.6	54 6.8				49 7.4	50 7.3
6.4	7.3	5.7	6.5			Sales/Working Capital	7.7	7.5
14.4	10.5	11.6	11.1				14.7	13.9
147.9	19.6	49.6	40.4				46.8	59.4
	32.3	17.6	25.1			EBIT/Interest	10.9	9.6
(44)	8.4 (66)	6.7 (34)	6.1				(188) 3.9	(160) 3.5
	1.8	2.8	2.1				1.6	1.7
	8.3	30.9				Net Profit + Depr., Dep., Amort./Cur. Mat. L/T/D	6.1	5.9
(12)	1.0 (16)	7.1					(50) 2.1	(46) 1.7
	-.1	1.1					.9	.6
.0	.1	.1	.1			Fixed/Worth	.1	.1
.2	.2	.3	.5				.3	.4
NM	1.0	1.1	3.4				1.5	1.6
.5	.6	.8	1.0			Debt/Worth	1.1	1.0
3.1	1.3	2.4	2.5				2.3	2.2
-3.7	3.3	5.5	10.7				8.0	9.0
	54.1	49.9	42.2			% Profit Before Taxes/Tangible Net Worth	51.5	45.8
(44)	21.4 (66)	22.1 (30)	19.1				(189) 23.8	(156) 19.3
	4.1	8.5	9.9				7.3	6.8
49.1	19.5	15.3	12.9			% Profit Before Taxes/Total Assets	14.3	14.3
3.5	6.6	6.3	7.0				7.1	6.7
-7.9	1.6	2.1	3.1				1.8	1.6
UND	91.4	102.4	90.7			Sales/Net Fixed Assets	82.6	82.3
95.1	43.7	46.1	22.3				33.0	35.2
37.7	17.8	17.4	6.6				15.2	12.6
6.2	4.6	4.1	3.3			Sales/Total Assets	4.3	4.0
4.3	3.6	3.2	2.3				3.1	3.1
2.9	2.4	2.3	1.8				2.3	2.2
	.4	.3	.5			% Depr., Dep., Amort./Sales	.4	.5
(42)	.9 (62)	.7 (33)	1.2				(194) 1.0	(163) .9
	1.7	1.9	3.1				2.2	2.0
	2.9	2.0				% Officers', Directors' Owners' Comp/Sales	2.7	2.4
(25)	6.0 (32)	3.4					(73) 4.3	(56) 4.2
	9.7	6.3					6.1	6.6
19232M	257325M	1176148M	2057877M	595534M	976855M	Net Sales ($)	5283938M	5913624M
3969M	66620M	350298M	790274M	405502M	755700M	Total Assets ($)	2050876M	2237934M

M = $ thousand   MM = $ million
See Pages 9 through 22 for Explanation of Ratios and Data

Comparative Historical Data				Current Data Sorted by Sales					
			Type of Statement						
27	19	21	Unqualified					3	18
40	40	48	Reviewed			2	15	17	14
32	23	27	Compiled	1	4	7	9	6	
24	28	32	Tax Returns	1	13	3	9	4	2
81	70	58	Other	3	4	7	11	10	23
4/1/08-3/31/09 ALL	4/1/09-3/31/10 ALL	4/1/10-3/31/11 ALL		0-1MM	1-3MM	3-5MM	5-10MM	10-25MM	25MM & OVER
					47 (4/1-9/30/10)		139 (10/1/10-3/31/11)		
204	180	186	NUMBER OF STATEMENTS	5	21	19	44	40	57
%	%	%	**ASSETS**	%	%	%	%	%	%
7.9	10.0	10.4	Cash & Equivalents		12.1	11.5	9.9	10.5	8.6
30.8	31.0	31.3	Trade Receivables (net)		31.0	30.3	28.6	36.3	32.3
28.5	26.9	29.3	Inventory		34.9	26.8	35.6	25.6	27.0
4.2	5.4	4.8	All Other Current		2.6	.8	4.6	5.0	6.9
71.3	73.3	75.8	Total Current		80.7	69.4	78.6	77.5	74.8
14.8	12.4	13.1	Fixed Assets (net)		8.5	18.7	11.7	13.3	11.6
5.9	5.7	4.9	Intangibles (net)		2.5	3.8	4.4	3.9	7.2
7.9	8.6	6.2	All Other Non-Current		8.3	8.1	5.3	5.3	6.4
100.0	100.0	100.0	Total		100.0	100.0	100.0	100.0	100.0
			LIABILITIES						
15.7	12.0	10.6	Notes Payable-Short Term		10.9	9.4	10.3	11.9	10.8
3.1	4.0	2.8	Cur. Mat.-L.T.D.		2.2	3.0	3.2	2.6	2.4
16.9	19.9	18.0	Trade Payables		21.9	18.7	16.0	20.0	17.7
.2	.2	.3	Income Taxes Payable		.1	.2	.0	.5	.4
15.4	16.0	14.2	All Other Current		9.5	7.8	14.3	13.0	18.9
51.3	52.1	45.8	Total Current		44.6	39.2	43.8	48.0	50.2
11.7	10.7	12.3	Long-Term Debt		21.2	14.2	8.8	7.9	11.1
.2	.3	.3	Deferred Taxes		.0	.1	.5	.4	.3
5.4	5.7	6.6	All Other Non-Current		12.1	11.0	7.3	5.5	3.5
31.4	31.3	35.0	Net Worth		22.1	35.5	39.5	38.3	34.9
100.0	100.0	100.0	Total Liabilities & Net Worth		100.0	100.0	100.0	100.0	100.0
			INCOME DATA						
100.0	100.0	100.0	Net Sales		100.0	100.0	100.0	100.0	100.0
37.6	39.5	40.0	Gross Profit		46.6	43.3	40.7	39.3	34.0
34.5	35.2	35.7	Operating Expenses		45.3	39.8	37.1	35.6	28.7
3.1	4.3	4.2	Operating Profit		1.3	3.5	3.5	3.7	5.2
.5	.6	.1	All Other Expenses (net)		.4	-.5	-.2	.0	.6
2.6	3.7	4.1	Profit Before Taxes		.9	4.0	3.7	3.7	4.7
			RATIOS						
2.1	2.2	2.4	Current		3.1	2.8	2.7	3.1	2.2
1.4	1.4	1.7			1.8	1.9	1.9	1.5	1.7
1.1	1.1	1.2			1.2	1.3	1.4	1.1	1.2
1.2	1.3	1.5	Quick		1.8	2.1	1.4	1.7	1.3
.8	(179) .8	.9			.9	1.2	.9	1.0	.8
.5	.5	.6			.6	.7	.5	.5	.5
26 14.0	25 14.7	24 15.4	Sales/Receivables		18 20.3	22 16.3	23 15.9	24 15.4	28 13.1
35 10.5	35 10.5	35 10.5			30 12.1	32 11.4	31 11.9	36 10.1	38 9.5
46 7.9	46 8.0	47 7.8			50 7.3	44 8.2	41 8.8	49 7.4	55 6.7
28 13.1	29 12.7	35 10.4	Cost of Sales/Inventory		46 8.0	17 21.2	44 8.3	22 16.5	41 8.8
58 6.2	57 6.4	63 5.8			71 5.2	63 5.8	65 5.7	47 7.7	64 5.7
89 4.1	90 4.1	89 4.1			144 2.5	89 4.1	86 4.3	94 3.9	81 4.5
14 25.5	18 20.3	16 22.5	Cost of Sales/Payables		20 18.6	19 19.6	12 29.4	14 26.9	16 22.6
24 15.1	33 11.1	30 12.2			48 7.5	31 11.8	27 13.4	31 11.8	25 14.8
48 7.7	58 6.3	49 7.5			63 5.8	54 6.8	46 8.0	48 7.6	44 8.4
8.2	6.3	5.7	Sales/Working Capital		4.3	4.7	6.1	6.1	5.5
16.2	12.8	10.5			8.7	8.2	9.1	15.8	10.3
85.4	82.7	27.4			21.9	22.4	15.0	51.0	33.7
8.2	17.4	18.5	EBIT/Interest		7.8	12.6	18.2	29.1	24.3
(178) 3.0	(158) 5.6	(159) 7.4			(17) 1.8	(15) 3.6	(39) 8.9	(35) 7.7	(51) 8.2
1.2	1.8	2.5			.1	1.6	3.2	3.9	
10.2	11.9	16.7	Net Profit + Depr., Dep., Amort./Cur. Mat. L/T/D				27.1		47.7
(44) 2.9	(38) 3.8	(41) 3.2					(10) 3.4		(14) 4.6
.9	1.8	1.0					1.4		2.1
.1	.1	.1	Fixed/Worth		.0	.1	.1	.1	.1
.4	.3	.2			.2	.2	.3	.3	.2
1.5	2.4	1.3			10.4	1.8	1.5	1.0	1.1
1.1	1.0	.8	Debt/Worth		1.2	.6	.8	.5	.9
2.3	2.5	1.9			3.3	1.2	1.7	1.8	2.1
10.2	8.1	5.5			185.3	6.4	4.5	4.7	5.2
40.4	47.2	50.2	% Profit Before Taxes/Tangible Net Worth		32.9	23.5	59.6	62.8	49.8
(166) 19.5	(152) 24.0	(159) 21.6			(17) 7.4	(15) 9.6	(39) 21.7	(35) 22.2	(50) 23.8
5.1	9.3	7.4			-1.5	1.2	8.6	6.0	11.7
12.4	15.0	16.3	% Profit Before Taxes/Total Assets		5.6	22.1	19.3	19.9	14.4
5.4	7.2	6.6			2.5	3.8	7.7	7.2	8.0
.7	1.0	2.1			-1.1	1.1	3.4	2.2	3.9
83.4	90.6	97.5	Sales/Net Fixed Assets		202.3	147.8	70.0	109.1	116.6
35.5	41.7	43.6			60.1	33.3	38.1	47.3	46.8
11.9	16.1	16.7			23.2	7.6	18.3	14.5	16.7
4.1	4.0	4.2	Sales/Total Assets		5.1	3.6	4.3	4.6	3.9
3.0	2.9	3.0			2.7	2.6	3.4	3.6	2.7
2.1	2.2	2.1			2.0	2.1	2.5	2.2	1.7
.5	.5	.4	% Depr., Dep., Amort./Sales		.4	.3	.5	.3	.4
(169) 1.0	(139) 1.0	(149) .8			(14) .8	(15) .6	(37) .9	(36) .7	(46) 1.0
2.4	2.3	2.1			2.5	1.6	1.7	2.0	3.0
1.9	1.4	2.2	% Officers', Directors' Owners' Comp/Sales		4.3	4.6	2.0	1.9	
(71) 3.6	(77) 2.9	(68) 4.2			(14) 7.6	(10) 5.5	(18) 2.9	(17) 2.4	
6.8	7.7	7.0			11.5	6.9	6.8	4.7	
5176938M	4578564M	5082971M	Net Sales ($)	2424M	43138M	72065M	310822M	689293M	3965229M
2158204M	2073318M	2372363M	Total Assets ($)	1322M	18257M	27632M	102314M	235392M	1987446M

M = $ thousand   MM = $ million
See Pages 9 through 22 for Explanation of Ratios and Data

Current Data Sorted by Assets | Comparative Historical Data

						Type of Statement		
		11	27	3	7	Unqualified	51	49
1	9	21	22			Reviewed	44	33
3	7	13	2			Compiled	27	16
10	14	15	1			Tax Returns	21	20
5	33	44	24	5	8	Other	101	111
	37 (4/1-9/30/10)		248 (10/1/10-3/31/11)				4/1/06-3/31/07	4/1/07-3/31/08
0-500M	500M-2MM	2-10MM	10-50MM	50-100MM	100-250MM		ALL	ALL
19	63	104	76	8	15	NUMBER OF STATEMENTS	244	229
%	%	%	%	%	%	ASSETS	%	%
31.2	14.1	13.9	13.2		8.3	Cash & Equivalents	12.1	12.3
27.1	40.3	45.3	42.4		46.5	Trade Receivables (net)	44.4	43.7
16.1	19.4	21.2	21.8		16.9	Inventory	20.3	18.4
1.7	4.5	3.2	2.9		6.1	All Other Current	3.6	4.3
76.1	78.2	83.5	80.3		77.8	Total Current	80.4	78.8
10.6	9.3	9.2	5.7		4.0	Fixed Assets (net)	9.0	8.6
6.5	5.2	2.8	7.9		7.5	Intangibles (net)	5.1	7.1
6.8	7.2	4.5	6.2		10.7	All Other Non-Current	5.5	5.5
100.0	100.0	100.0	100.0		100.0	Total	100.0	100.0
						LIABILITIES		
23.4	12.2	12.4	14.8		10.5	Notes Payable-Short Term	15.0	14.0
3.6	1.7	2.0	1.3		3.4	Cur. Mat.-L.T.D.	1.8	2.0
17.4	27.3	31.2	28.9		30.9	Trade Payables	27.1	25.0
.1	.4	.4	.2		.0	Income Taxes Payable	.4	.4
32.7	12.2	10.4	13.7		17.8	All Other Current	12.8	12.8
77.2	53.8	56.4	58.9		62.6	Total Current	57.0	54.2
14.2	5.8	7.4	3.9		3.3	Long-Term Debt	8.4	7.6
.0	.1	.0	.6		.9	Deferred Taxes	.2	.2
10.7	10.3	5.1	4.7		5.1	All Other Non-Current	6.6	6.8
-2.1	30.0	31.1	32.0		28.1	Net Worth	27.7	31.2
100.0	100.0	100.0	100.0		100.0	Total Liabilities & Net Worth	100.0	100.0
						INCOME DATA		
100.0	100.0	100.0	100.0		100.0	Net Sales	100.0	100.0
52.5	32.0	30.5	22.7		15.9	Gross Profit	32.6	32.4
45.4	30.0	24.6	18.8		13.5	Operating Expenses	28.0	27.5
7.1	2.0	5.8	3.8		2.4	Operating Profit	4.6	4.9
1.1	-.4	.7	.5		.1	All Other Expenses (net)	.7	.6
6.0	2.4	5.2	3.3		2.3	Profit Before Taxes	4.0	4.2
						RATIOS		
2.4	2.4	2.2	1.7		1.9		2.1	2.1
1.1	1.5	1.4	1.3		1.2	Current	1.4	1.4
.8	1.1	1.2	1.1		1.0		1.0	1.1
2.0	1.8	1.5	1.3		1.5		1.5	1.6
1.0	1.2	1.0	1.0		.9	Quick	.9	1.1
.4	.7	.8	.7		.6		.6	.7

												Sales/Receivables				
0	UND	20	18.2	26	13.8	37	10.0			36	10.1		28	12.9	32	11.5
21	17.8	35	10.3	42	8.7	50	7.3			57	6.4		42	8.6	44	8.3
43	8.5	49	7.5	62	5.9	67	5.4			120	3.1		64	5.7	63	5.8

												Cost of Sales/Inventory				
0	UND	2	146.7	3	118.2	7	56.1			0	823.4		3	144.9	2	163.8
21	17.4	19	19.0	21	17.5	24	15.3			13	28.4		24	15.3	21	17.3
58	6.2	39	9.3	55	6.6	57	6.5			31	11.8		44	8.3	50	7.2

												Cost of Sales/Payables				
0	UND	12	31.6	26	14.3	22	16.2			22	16.3		20	17.9	19	19.2
17	22.0	27	13.6	39	9.4	44	8.4			38	9.7		35	10.5	33	11.1
55	6.6	48	7.6	59	6.2	62	5.9			54	6.8		54	6.7	54	6.8

						Sales/Working Capital		
7.9	8.9	6.6	8.2		9.0		8.5	8.2
30.4	17.2	17.8	17.0		28.2	Sales/Working Capital	17.0	13.8
-20.2	151.6	36.2	43.7		-254.5		138.0	44.7

												EBIT/Interest				
	9.7		17.7		28.7		41.8				9.1			18.6		17.2
(15)	4.0	(46)	6.2	(86)	7.4	(65)	9.4			(14)	5.8		(206)	4.6	(193)	5.4
	1.0		2.5		2.8		3.4				2.9			1.7		1.6

												Net Profit + Depr., Dep., Amort./Cur. Mat. L/T/D				
					22.2		84.6							13.0		27.2
				(16)	5.9	(15)	5.1						(47)	4.5	(46)	5.3
					3.3		1.9							1.4		1.4

						Fixed/Worth		
.0	.0	.0	.1		.0		.1	.1
.3	.2	.1	.2		.1	Fixed/Worth	.2	.2
8.2	2.8	.7	.5		1.4		1.1	.8

						Debt/Worth		
.8	.8	1.0	1.2		1.1		1.2	.9
3.9	2.5	2.8	3.1		3.4	Debt/Worth	2.6	2.4
-2.7	59.7	5.7	6.9		-56.2		13.8	7.2

												% Profit Before Taxes/Tangible Net Worth				
	114.3		56.9		79.9		69.1				63.0			63.4		74.7
(13)	48.3	(49)	30.7	(93)	35.1	(66)	29.2			(11)	11.8		(198)	29.2	(193)	34.1
	10.9		1.7		13.5		14.0				3.3			10.4		8.7

						% Profit Before Taxes/Total Assets		
44.1	19.2	20.0	16.1		6.8		19.4	20.7
13.7	7.0	10.1	7.8		3.8	% Profit Before Taxes/Total Assets	8.2	8.8
.0	.6	2.2	3.1		.7		1.9	1.9

						Sales/Net Fixed Assets		
UND	883.2	314.1	222.8		385.2		228.2	193.6
121.1	217.7	103.4	99.1		132.0	Sales/Net Fixed Assets	81.1	71.7
36.5	34.8	36.2	28.7		72.7		31.7	30.6

						Sales/Total Assets		
5.7	5.4	4.7	4.0		4.4		5.0	4.8
3.7	4.6	3.7	3.2		3.1	Sales/Total Assets	3.7	3.5
3.0	2.9	2.5	2.0		1.5		2.6	2.4

												% Depr., Dep., Amort./Sales				
			.2		.1		.1				.1			.2		.2
		(34)	.5	(72)	.4	(61)	.3			(12)	.2		(174)	.4	(171)	.5
			1.0		.8		.7				.8			1.2		1.0

												% Officers', Directors' Owners' Comp/Sales				
	4.1		2.6		.9		.2							1.2		1.1
(11)	7.4	(28)	3.9	(38)	1.8	(15)	.9						(71)	3.4	(59)	2.5
	9.5		6.3		3.2		1.1							6.8		6.8

26437M	389924M	2090478M	5205418M	1616777M	7057884M	Net Sales ($)	13770370M	17426211M
6148M	79162M	523036M	1628440M	591978M	2452916M	Total Assets ($)	4833975M	5657814M

© RMA 2011

M = $ thousand   MM = $ million
See Pages 9 through 22 for Explanation of Ratios and Data

Comparative Historical Data / Current Data Sorted by Sales

						Type of Statement							
	58		54		48	Unqualified			1	3	6	38
	38		42		53	Reviewed	1		1	7	13	31
	21		19		25	Compiled	3	2	2	4	8	6
	31		30		40	Tax Returns	2	13	1	9	10	5
	110		108		119	Other	2	14	14	20	27	42
	4/1/08-3/31/09 ALL		4/1/09-3/31/10 ALL		4/1/10-3/31/11 ALL			37 (4/1-9/30/10)		248 (10/1/10-3/31/11)		
							0-1MM	1-3MM	3-5MM	5-10MM	10-25MM	25MM & OVER
	258		253		285	NUMBER OF STATEMENTS	8	29	19	43	64	122
	%		%		%	ASSETS	%	%	%	%	%	%
	13.4		15.5		14.3	Cash & Equivalents		20.5	15.0	15.1	14.1	11.8
	41.7		41.0		42.3	Trade Receivables (net)		26.3	42.2	41.7	41.3	47.9
	20.3		19.6		20.2	Inventory		13.2	12.3	24.0	22.8	20.9
	3.6		3.8		3.6	All Other Current		4.2	6.0	4.0	3.4	3.2
	79.0		79.9		80.4	Total Current		64.2	75.5	84.9	81.6	83.8
	8.3		8.2		8.0	Fixed Assets (net)		14.9	12.2	7.8	9.4	4.9
	6.2		5.7		5.2	Intangibles (net)		7.1	7.1	.9	4.3	5.8
	6.5		6.2		6.4	All Other Non-Current		13.8	5.3	6.3	4.8	5.5
	100.0		100.0		100.0	Total		100.0	100.0	100.0	100.0	100.0
						LIABILITIES						
	12.1		14.2		13.9	Notes Payable-Short Term		23.5	15.3	10.6	9.9	14.4
	2.3		2.2		1.9	Cur. Mat.-L.T.D.		5.0	1.8	1.5	1.2	1.6
	26.4		27.2		28.9	Trade Payables		18.8	24.1	24.5	29.5	34.5
	.3		.2		.3	Income Taxes Payable		.1	.7	.6	.2	.3
	12.2		12.8		13.6	All Other Current		12.2	12.9	11.7	12.3	13.2
	53.3		56.6		58.7	Total Current		59.6	55.0	48.9	53.2	63.9
	9.4		6.5		6.2	Long-Term Debt		18.7	2.8	6.2	5.6	4.6
	.2		.2		.2	Deferred Taxes		.0	.1	.0	.3	.3
	6.4		7.6		6.4	All Other Non-Current		15.6	14.9	5.7	4.9	4.0
	30.8		29.1		28.5	Net Worth		6.1	27.2	39.3	36.0	27.2
	100.0		100.0		100.0	Total Liabilities & Net Worth		100.0	100.0	100.0	100.0	100.0
						INCOME DATA						
	100.0		100.0		100.0	Net Sales		100.0	100.0	100.0	100.0	100.0
	29.2		28.8		29.1	Gross Profit		45.4	41.2	32.6	33.2	18.3
	25.2		25.7		24.8	Operating Expenses		42.3	37.9	27.9	27.5	15.1
	4.0		3.2		4.3	Operating Profit		3.1	3.4	4.7	5.6	3.2
	.8		.4		.4	All Other Expenses (net)		1.6	-.4	-.4	.5	.3
	3.2		2.7		3.9	Profit Before Taxes		1.4	3.7	5.1	5.1	2.9
						RATIOS						
	2.2		2.1		2.0			2.8	2.4	3.0	2.3	1.7
	1.4		1.4		1.3	Current		1.3	1.5	1.7	1.4	1.3
	1.1		1.1		1.1			.8	1.0	1.2	1.2	1.1
	1.6		1.5		1.4			1.7	2.2	1.8	1.3	1.3
	1.0		1.0		1.0	Quick		1.2	1.1	1.2	1.0	1.0
	.7		.7		.7			.5	.9	.9	.8	.7

27	13.6	25	14.5	26	13.9		21	17.7	21	17.2	21	17.8	25	14.5	30	12.3
41	8.9	42	8.7	42	8.7	Sales/Receivables	40	9.0	37	9.9	42	8.7	41	8.9	44	8.3
58	6.2	63	5.8	63	5.8		55	6.6	57	6.4	72	5.1	61	6.0	67	5.5

2	173.1	2	215.9	3	113.6		0	UND	0	UND	7	51.1	8	45.3	4	90.3
21	17.7	18	20.0	21	17.4	Cost of Sales/Inventory	24	15.3	4	82.6	26	13.9	32	11.5	15	23.6
47	7.8	48	7.5	52	7.1		54	6.7	43	8.5	67	5.5	74	4.9	40	9.0

17	21.3	17	21.2	20	18.5		7	50.2	13	27.2	13	27.3	21	17.3	23	16.2
30	12.2	33	11.0	37	9.9	Cost of Sales/Payables	30	12.2	34	10.7	35	10.4	38	9.5	37	9.9
51	7.1	54	6.8	58	6.3		76	4.8	64	5.7	48	7.6	57	6.4	59	6.2

	8.1		7.5		8.6			6.4	7.0	5.3	6.5	13.3
	16.0		16.9		18.5	Sales/Working Capital		22.8	18.5	10.9	17.4	22.8
	51.3		50.3		53.2			-20.0	468.1	22.2	49.7	48.6

	21.7		22.1		22.6			5.9		-23.0	33.4	39.7	26.8
(216)	4.7	(213)	5.5	(234)	7.4	EBIT/Interest	(24)	3.8	(12)	5.4	(36)	9.7	(50)	7.8	(108)	8.6
	1.7		1.5		2.8			.4		-.3	2.6	2.4	3.9

	28.5		20.0		20.3								18.9
(46)	4.1	(44)	3.2	(43)	5.7	Net Profit + Depr., Dep., Amort./Cur. Mat. L/T/D						(27)	4.6
	1.3		1.2		3.0								2.5

	.1		.1		.0			.1	.0	.0	.1	.0
	.2		.2		.1	Fixed/Worth		.7	.3	.1	.2	.1
	.7		.7		.7			-1.6	2.6	.4	.8	.5

	.9		1.0		1.1			1.3	.7	.6	.7	1.4
	2.2		2.7		3.0	Debt/Worth		7.4	2.8	1.7	2.9	3.4
	6.1		7.7		7.8			-5.4	86.0	4.3	6.6	6.9

	65.1		54.4		67.1			53.9	57.2	52.7	81.4	69.9
(219)	23.0	(218)	21.4	(240)	32.9	% Profit Before Taxes/Tangible Net Worth	(18)	30.9	(15)	34.1	(40)	32.5	(56)	42.2	(106)	24.8
	6.3		4.2		10.3			-1.3	-7.9	9.7	13.1	11.0

	16.2		14.8		18.2			15.6	22.5	19.2	24.9	15.2
	6.4		5.8		8.3	% Profit Before Taxes/Total Assets		6.6	9.8	10.7	9.8	7.5
	1.8		.8		1.7			-3.8	-4.3	1.9	2.5	2.3

	290.7		314.1		366.7			269.5	500.3	792.0	225.4	384.4
	84.1		103.3		106.5	Sales/Net Fixed Assets		52.8	144.9	139.7	61.7	139.7
	33.3		36.6		35.9			14.8	13.3	42.3	26.4	51.7

	5.2		4.9		4.9			3.6	5.6	5.1	4.7	5.0
	3.6		3.3		3.4	Sales/Total Assets		3.0	3.3	3.7	3.7	3.5
	2.3		2.3		2.3			1.5	2.8	2.2	2.5	2.4

	.1		.1		.1			.5	.1	.1	.2	.1
(191)	.4	(182)	.5	(192)	.4	% Depr., Dep., Amort./Sales	(14)	1.2	(11)	.4	(25)	.5	(45)	.5	(95)	.2
	1.0		1.1		.8			1.6	4.0	.7	1.0	.6

	1.0		1.0		.9			3.3		1.9		.8	.2
(68)	2.3	(68)	2.4	(95)	2.4	% Officers', Directors' Owners' Comp/Sales	(18)	6.1	(15)	2.6	(29)	2.0	(25)	.9
	4.7		5.4		4.2			9.5		4.0		3.6	1.6

19252775M		13948886M		16386918M		Net Sales ($)	4110M	56035M	78036M	326076M	1073527M	14849134M
5930116M		4985789M		5281680M		Total Assets ($)	4719M	26491M	24029M	123174M	359888M	4743379M

M = $ thousand   MM = $ million
See Pages 9 through 22 for Explanation of Ratios and Data

Current Data Sorted by Assets   Comparative Historical Data

	0-500M	500M-2MM	2-10MM	10-50MM	50-100MM	100-250MM	Type of Statement		4/1/06-3/31/07 ALL	4/1/07-3/31/08 ALL
		1	4	7	1	6	Unqualified		29	19
		6	38	14	1		Reviewed		47	41
	4	19	13	2			Compiled		36	26
	8	22	11	1			Tax Returns		35	29
	7	17	38	19	4	2	Other		74	89
		38 (4/1-9/30/10)		207 (10/1/10-3/31/11)						
	19	65	104	43	6	8	**NUMBER OF STATEMENTS**		221	204
	%	%	%	%	%	%	**ASSETS**		%	%
	21.4	10.2	7.9	8.3			Cash & Equivalents		8.5	7.6
	35.5	34.5	33.7	25.5			Trade Receivables (net)		34.9	31.9
	19.2	33.6	35.0	29.7			Inventory		32.5	33.6
	.2	.8	3.0	4.4			All Other Current		3.3	3.4
	76.4	79.0	79.4	67.9			Total Current		79.1	76.4
	17.2	12.6	12.5	19.7			Fixed Assets (net)		12.0	15.6
	2.5	3.9	2.1	6.7			Intangibles (net)		4.1	3.1
	3.8	4.5	5.9	5.8			All Other Non-Current		4.7	4.9
	100.0	100.0	100.0	100.0			Total		100.0	100.0
							LIABILITIES			
	15.9	13.7	13.7	12.3			Notes Payable-Short Term		15.1	13.8
	6.7	3.8	2.8	2.1			Cur. Mat.-L.T.D.		2.8	2.9
	20.0	22.8	18.7	17.4			Trade Payables		21.6	20.9
	.2	.0	.0	.0			Income Taxes Payable		.2	.2
	4.9	9.5	12.8	11.7			All Other Current		12.2	13.3
	47.7	49.9	48.0	43.5			Total Current		51.9	51.0
	8.5	10.4	8.1	10.9			Long-Term Debt		9.6	10.2
	.0	.1	.4	.1			Deferred Taxes		.3	.3
	19.9	6.5	4.6	6.0			All Other Non-Current		4.4	4.0
	23.8	33.1	38.8	39.5			Net Worth		33.8	34.5
	100.0	100.0	100.0	100.0			Total Liabilities & Net Worth		100.0	100.0
							INCOME DATA			
	100.0	100.0	100.0	100.0			Net Sales		100.0	100.0
	44.9	32.2	27.6	29.6			Gross Profit		29.3	31.3
	37.9	29.0	24.6	21.7			Operating Expenses		24.8	26.4
	7.1	3.3	3.0	8.0			Operating Profit		4.5	5.0
	.3	.5	.0	1.0			All Other Expenses (net)		.0	.7
	6.8	2.8	3.0	7.0			Profit Before Taxes		4.5	4.2
							RATIOS			
	3.5	2.7	2.5	2.4					2.2	2.2
	1.7	1.6	1.6	1.6			Current		1.5	1.6
	1.1	1.1	1.2	1.2					1.2	1.1
	2.0	1.4	1.4	1.2					1.2	1.2
	1.2	.8	.8	.8			Quick		.8	.9
	.7	.5	.6	.5					.6	.5
11	34.6	20 18.2	29 12.7	30 12.3			Sales/Receivables	26	14.0	24 15.5
19	19.0	34 10.6	42 8.7	40 9.2				41	8.9	37 9.9
52	7.1	53 6.9	58 6.3	52 7.1				56	6.5	52 7.1
0	UND	23 15.9	31 11.7	42 8.7			Cost of Sales/Inventory	25	14.6	28 13.0
32	11.4	57 6.4	61 6.0	72 5.1				53	6.9	59 6.2
100	3.7	107 3.4	101 3.6	106 3.4				86	4.2	93 3.9
6	63.0	12 31.4	16 22.3	21 17.3			Cost of Sales/Payables	15	24.2	15 23.6
20	17.9	29 12.4	26 13.9	34 10.8				31	11.8	28 12.8
46	8.0	52 7.0	48 7.6	54 6.7				52	7.0	48 7.6
	6.6	6.1	5.2	4.6			Sales/Working Capital		6.9	6.3
	11.5	11.0	9.2	9.0					12.2	10.4
	48.2	81.2	25.1	20.6					29.5	37.4
	35.3	15.6	10.4	23.8			EBIT/Interest		12.2	10.5
(14)	6.8	(57) 4.0	(95) 2.7	(38) 6.0				(196)	5.0	(181) 4.4
	1.6	1.9	1.5	3.2					2.3	1.8
			3.9	10.7			Net Profit + Depr., Dep., Amort./Cur. Mat. L/T/D		11.3	18.3
			(18) 2.1	(12) 8.4				(42)	4.5	(40) 4.3
			.7	2.8					1.7	1.2
	.0	.1	.1	.1			Fixed/Worth		.1	.1
	.3	.3	.2	.5					.3	.3
	3.4	2.1	1.0	1.1					.8	1.1
	.6	.7	.7	1.0			Debt/Worth		1.0	.8
	4.0	2.1	1.9	2.2					2.3	2.0
	-6.0	8.7	4.9	4.6					5.9	5.6
	103.1	63.6	30.6	48.9			% Profit Before Taxes/Tangible Net Worth		60.7	51.7
(13)	44.7	(53) 23.2	(98) 15.1	(39) 27.3				(197)	29.2	(177) 25.8
	.0	6.0	3.4	15.7					11.8	9.1
	33.7	16.3	9.8	15.8			% Profit Before Taxes/Total Assets		17.5	15.7
	19.0	5.8	3.8	10.4					7.9	7.7
	.0	1.8	1.1	3.6					2.5	2.4
	UND	192.5	140.4	86.1			Sales/Net Fixed Assets		117.1	123.4
	41.1	61.5	57.3	18.7					47.9	44.2
	13.7	14.7	18.7	4.5					19.0	14.7
	5.8	4.6	3.5	2.8			Sales/Total Assets		4.0	4.1
	3.0	3.3	2.8	2.1					3.1	2.9
	2.4	2.4	2.0	1.5					2.1	2.0
		.3	.3	.5			% Depr., Dep., Amort./Sales		.3	.3
		(44) .7	(80) .6	(38) 1.1				(182)	.6	(167) .7
		1.5	1.2	2.3					1.1	1.4
	1.6	2.7	1.5	1.5			% Officers', Directors' Owners' Comp/Sales		2.0	1.8
(12)	4.3	(37) 3.6	(39) 2.8	(10) 2.0				(77)	3.6	(69) 3.2
	10.6	6.4	5.0	3.3					5.3	6.1
	20304M	269664M	1452897M	1893258M	661357M	2379992M	Net Sales ($)		6840362M	6216107M
	5227M	80825M	510284M	881076M	368135M	1293148M	Total Assets ($)		2745547M	2397226M

Comparative Historical Data | | | Type of Statement | | Current Data Sorted by Sales

			Type of Statement						
23	27	19	Unqualified			1	2	3	13
55	55	59	Reviewed		1	7	17	17	17
35	37	38	Compiled		8	7	13	6	3
29	33	42	Tax Returns	1	11	12	5	6	2
80	80	87	Other	6	9	6	21	21	24
4/1/08-	4/1/09-	4/1/10-		6					
3/31/09	3/31/10	3/31/11			38 (4/1-9/30/10)		207 (10/1/10-3/31/11)		
ALL	ALL	ALL		0-1MM	1-3MM	3-5MM	5-10MM	10-25MM	25MM & OVER
222	232	245	NUMBER OF STATEMENTS	13	29	33	58	53	59
%	%	%	ASSETS	%	%	%	%	%	%
8.9	9.8	9.3	Cash & Equivalents	23.8	9.8	15.7	7.3	6.2	7.1
28.3	30.0	32.0	Trade Receivables (net)	31.2	29.3	31.1	33.8	34.3	30.3
34.0	32.6	31.6	Inventory	21.1	28.9	35.6	34.3	33.6	28.6
3.2	3.6	2.5	All Other Current	.3	.5	.9	1.3	4.7	3.9
74.5	75.9	75.4	Total Current	76.4	68.5	83.4	76.7	78.7	69.9
15.5	14.2	14.4	Fixed Assets (net)	16.3	19.5	10.8	15.0	12.7	14.5
4.0	5.1	4.8	Intangibles (net)	3.7	5.6	1.3	3.3	3.2	9.5
6.1	4.8	5.3	All Other Non-Current	3.5	6.4	4.4	5.0	5.4	6.1
100.0	100.0	100.0	Total	100.0	100.0	100.0	100.0	100.0	100.0
			LIABILITIES						
14.7	13.7	13.6	Notes Payable-Short Term	19.1	11.4	12.3	12.6	15.5	13.4
2.8	2.7	3.3	Cur. Mat.-L.T.D.	4.3	4.0	4.5	3.3	2.4	2.9
17.3	17.3	19.3	Trade Payables	16.6	22.9	17.4	20.5	17.9	19.1
.2	.1	.1	Income Taxes Payable	.0	.2	.0	.0	.0	.2
12.6	11.6	10.9	All Other Current	3.3	9.5	7.2	13.9	11.1	12.1
47.6	45.4	47.1	Total Current	43.4	48.0	41.4	50.4	47.0	47.7
12.5	12.1	10.2	Long-Term Debt	9.1	19.4	9.1	7.5	6.8	12.3
.2	.4	.4	Deferred Taxes	.1	.0	.1	.4	.4	.9
5.5	5.1	6.5	All Other Non-Current	26.2	5.2	11.3	4.2	5.4	3.4
34.2	37.0	35.7	Net Worth	21.3	27.3	38.1	37.5	40.4	35.7
100.0	100.0	100.0	Total Liabilties & Net Worth	100.0	100.0	100.0	100.0	100.0	100.0
			INCOME DATA						
100.0	100.0	100.0	Net Sales	100.0	100.0	100.0	100.0	100.0	100.0
31.3	30.4	30.7	Gross Profit	51.0	36.9	30.3	31.1	28.7	24.8
26.7	27.2	26.3	Operating Expenses	42.0	30.9	28.6	27.7	23.7	20.1
4.6	3.2	4.4	Operating Profit	8.9	6.0	1.7	3.4	4.9	4.7
.6	.7	.4	All Other Expenses (net)	.2	1.4	.2	.2	.0	.7
4.1	2.4	4.0	Profit Before Taxes	8.7	4.6	1.6	3.1	5.0	4.0
			RATIOS						
2.4	3.1	2.5		3.6	2.2	3.4	2.4	2.4	2.3
1.6	1.8	1.6	Current	1.9	1.2	2.3	1.5	1.6	1.6
1.1	1.2	1.2		1.1	.9	1.5	1.2	1.2	1.2
1.3	1.6	1.4		2.5	1.1	2.1	1.3	1.3	1.3
.8	.9	.8	Quick	1.2	.7	1.0	.9	.8	.8
.4	.5	.6		.7	.5	.6	.5	.5	.6

							Sales/Receivables										
24	15.2	24	14.9	26	14.2		8	45.2	16	23.3	19	19.0	30	12.2	29	12.5	30	12.3
34	10.6	37	9.8	39	9.5		14	25.4	30	12.2	33	11.2	41	8.8	44	8.3	40	9.2
46	7.9	54	6.8	55	6.7		61	6.0	48	7.6	58	6.3	64	6.9	64	5.7	54	6.8

						Cost of Sales/Inventory											
30	12.1	30	12.1	28	13.0	0	UND	16	22.3	24	15.1	25	14.9	35	10.5	30	12.0
63	5.8	60	6.1	57	6.4	64	5.7	43	8.4	73	5.0	64	5.7	61	5.9	55	6.6
96	3.8	99	3.7	99	3.7	153	2.4	110	3.3	127	2.9	121	3.0	80	4.6	76	4.8

						Cost of Sales/Payables											
12	29.2	14	26.2	16	23.1	0	UND	16	22.3	9	41.5	17	21.9	16	23.0	19	18.8
25	14.6	28	13.3	27	13.4	27	13.7	38	9.6	20	18.4	29	12.6	27	13.4	27	13.4
46	8.0	46	8.0	50	7.2	71	5.2	55	6.7	40	9.2	55	6.6	47	7.7	49	7.4

			Sales/Working Capital						
6.5	5.1	5.6		5.4	7.5	4.2	5.0	5.2	7.1
10.9	8.7	9.8		7.4	17.2	6.5	11.1	9.8	10.8
35.2	23.8	31.8		25.5	-53.7	11.4	29.1	31.4	29.1

					EBIT/Interest							
	9.8		9.3		13.2			16.2		7.3	10.1	21.1	14.7
(198)	3.3	(198)	2.5	(217)	4.2	(25)	2.7	(29)	2.8	(52) 2.8	(48) 3.9	(54) 4.9
	1.6		.6		1.7		1.0		1.6	1.5	2.2	3.0

					Net Profit + Depr., Dep., Amort./Cur. Mat. L/T/D					
	9.6		6.6		9.4				3.2	9.8
(44)	2.6	(40)	1.9	(43)	2.7		(12)	2.5	(16)	5.7
	.7		1.1		1.1				1.1	1.7

			Fixed/Worth						
.1	.1	.1		.0	.1	.0	.1	.0	.1
.3	.2	.3		.2	.7	.1	.3	.2	.5
1.2	1.1	1.1		NM	NM	1.1	1.0	1.0	1.3

			Debt/Worth						
.8	.6	.7		.5	.9	.5	.7	.7	1.3
2.1	1.8	2.1		4.0	3.4	1.8	2.3	1.5	2.7
5.3	5.4	6.6		-5.7	-37.1	6.0	4.9	4.5	9.0

					% Profit Before Taxes/Tangible Net Worth							
	55.2		40.9		48.9			69.3	31.7	33.1	47.3	48.8
(191)	21.2	(201)	12.7	(211)	19.2	(21)	34.2	(29)	8.4	(53) 13.1	(48) 23.6	(51) 25.6
	5.7		1.1		4.7		17.9		3.4	1.5	5.4	11.9

			% Profit Before Taxes/Total Assets						
16.4	12.6	14.7		32.9	17.7	11.9	10.6	17.9	13.3
5.8	3.6	5.6		18.2	5.7	3.1	4.0	5.1	6.7
1.4	-.8	1.4		.0	.9	1.2	.7	1.4	3.7

			Sales/Net Fixed Assets						
102.4	105.9	144.3		UND	192.5	294.3	101.5	159.8	82.5
34.2	34.5	49.3		41.1	26.6	64.8	43.8	71.3	49.6
13.7	13.2	12.7		13.3	8.1	19.2	12.2	19.9	10.6

			Sales/Total Assets						
3.8	3.7	3.7		3.0	3.9	4.9	3.8	3.6	3.6
2.9	2.8	2.8		2.6	2.6	2.8	2.9	2.8	2.7
2.0	1.9	1.9		2.1	1.7	2.2	2.0	2.0	1.7

					% Depr., Dep., Amort./Sales							
	.3		.4		.4			.5	.3	.4	.3	.4
(187)	.7	(187)	.8	(179)	.8	(14)	1.1	(25)	.6	(45) .8	(41) .6	(47) .7
	1.6		1.5		1.6		4.3		1.1	1.9	1.3	1.4

					% Officers', Directors' Owners' Comp/Sales							
	1.8		1.6		1.8			2.4	2.3	2.0	2.0	.8
(80)	3.4	(91)	3.5	(99)	3.0	(15)	3.8	(21)	3.1	(20) 3.4	(19) 3.0	(16) 1.7
	6.4		6.7		6.0		6.1		7.1	5.9	6.4	2.5

			Net Sales ($)						
7768600M	7168031M	6677472M		8126M	63671M	132026M	432556M	875357M	5165736M
3011899M	3330617M	3138695M	Total Assets ($)	3320M	49407M	53928M	214533M	388438M	2429069M

M = $ thousand   MM = $ million
See Pages 9 through 22 for Explanation of Ratios and Data

Current Data Sorted by Assets | Comparative Historical Data

Type of Statement	0-500M	500M-2MM	2-10MM	10-50MM	50-100MM	100-250MM		4/1/06-3/31/07 ALL	4/1/07-3/31/08 ALL
Unqualified		1	9	29	10	9		56	53
Reviewed		6	37	16	2	1		53	49
Compiled	3	27	30	2	1			50	45
Tax Returns	22	28	23					45	53
Other	14	43	68	33	8	10		139	122
		62 (4/1-9/30/10)		370 (10/1/10-3/31/11)				343	322
NUMBER OF STATEMENTS	39	105	167	80	21	20		343	322
ASSETS	%	%	%	%	%	%		%	%
Cash & Equivalents	19.8	11.9	8.7	9.7	5.0	5.9		8.0	9.2
Trade Receivables (net)	27.2	29.8	37.1	29.9	24.3	27.8		35.6	33.1
Inventory	18.3	26.5	28.3	26.4	24.1	22.3		27.5	29.2
All Other Current	3.1	3.1	2.8	3.0	3.8	2.1		2.0	2.0
Total Current	68.5	71.4	76.9	68.9	57.2	58.2		73.1	73.6
Fixed Assets (net)	12.2	15.2	13.6	12.8	18.5	15.3		14.8	13.7
Intangibles (net)	7.0	5.2	4.9	14.0	14.8	23.5		6.6	7.1
All Other Non-Current	12.4	8.1	4.6	4.3	9.4	3.1		5.4	5.6
Total	100.0	100.0	100.0	100.0	100.0	100.0		100.0	100.0
LIABILITIES									
Notes Payable-Short Term	24.0	15.7	12.0	11.5	11.6	7.3		15.4	13.8
Cur. Mat.-L.T.D.	2.2	4.3	3.1	2.3	2.7	1.5		3.9	3.2
Trade Payables	19.8	22.3	24.2	17.2	12.8	14.0		21.8	21.7
Income Taxes Payable	.0	.0	.2	.7	.0	.2		.3	.2
All Other Current	20.1	10.9	8.1	10.0	8.1	14.1		10.1	10.3
Total Current	66.1	53.2	47.5	41.7	35.2	37.0		51.6	49.1
Long-Term Debt	16.6	15.3	10.4	8.6	16.5	14.8		11.8	12.0
Deferred Taxes	.0	.2	.2	.5	1.7	1.8		.2	.2
All Other Non-Current	9.3	4.1	5.7	4.8	2.8	3.8		4.3	5.8
Net Worth	7.9	27.1	36.2	44.4	43.8	42.6		32.2	32.9
Total Liabilities & Net Worth	100.0	100.0	100.0	100.0	100.0	100.0		100.0	100.0
INCOME DATA									
Net Sales	100.0	100.0	100.0	100.0	100.0	100.0		100.0	100.0
Gross Profit	48.6	47.2	37.0	40.2	37.5	37.5		41.8	40.1
Operating Expenses	40.3	41.9	31.7	32.3	32.3	27.8		36.3	34.2
Operating Profit	8.3	5.3	5.3	7.8	5.2	9.7		5.5	5.9
All Other Expenses (net)	1.5	.7	.3	1.4	1.2	2.0		1.2	1.5
Profit Before Taxes	6.7	4.6	4.9	6.5	3.9	7.7		4.3	4.4
RATIOS									
Current	2.0	2.7	2.8	2.3	2.9	2.3		2.3	2.4
	1.0	1.4	1.6	1.7	1.5	1.7		1.4	1.5
	.7	.9	1.2	1.2	1.1	1.2		1.1	1.1
Quick	1.6	1.5	1.6	1.6	1.6	1.4		1.4	1.4
	.8	.8	.9	1.0	.7	1.0		.8	.9
	.3	.5	.6	.6	.6	.5		.6	.6
Sales/Receivables	0 UND	19 18.9	33 11.1	35 10.5	35 10.5	35 10.6		33 11.0	32 11.5
	26 14.2	35 10.5	42 8.7	44 8.2	45 8.1	49 7.4		46 8.0	42 8.7
	46 8.0	51 7.2	55 6.6	60 6.1	61 6.0	57 6.4		60 6.1	58 6.2
Cost of Sales/Inventory	0 UND	18 19.9	31 11.8	36 10.1	34 10.7	40 9.1		31 11.9	32 11.3
	29 12.5	56 6.5	50 7.3	55 6.7	68 5.4	50 7.4		54 6.7	60 6.1
	73 5.0	101 3.6	95 3.8	109 3.4	108 3.4	123 3.0		105 3.5	105 3.5
Cost of Sales/Payables	0 UND	14 26.6	25 14.7	24 15.4	21 17.3	19 19.6		22 16.6	24 15.4
	31 11.9	38 9.6	40 9.1	36 10.1	37 9.8	35 10.3		38 9.5	39 9.3
	73 5.0	67 5.5	61 5.9	68 5.4	64 5.7	48 7.5		63 5.8	66 5.5
Sales/Working Capital	9.9	7.2	5.2	5.2	5.4	4.3		6.4	6.0
	299.1	17.7	11.2	9.3	8.4	9.0		14.3	11.9
	-17.5	-55.1	27.1	22.1	37.4	33.2		49.1	37.2
EBIT/Interest	29.1	21.1	29.9	48.9	44.6	28.8		12.6	12.3
	(25) 7.7	(94) 4.2	(143) 5.4	(73) 11.5	(20) 3.1	(18) 4.6		(311) 3.8	(286) 4.1
	1.1	1.3	2.3	3.1	.8	2.3		1.4	1.7
Net Profit + Depr., Dep., Amort./Cur. Mat. L/T/D		12.2	19.1	56.7				8.4	8.5
		(11) 2.1	(27) 5.1	(19) 10.0				(62) 2.9	(55) 3.4
		1.2	1.7	2.6				1.3	1.5
Fixed/Worth	.1	.1	.1	.1	.2	.3		.1	.1
	2.0	.3	.3	.4	.6	1.1		.4	.4
	-.3	1.8	1.3	1.3	3.9	NM		2.0	1.6
Debt/Worth	.9	1.0	.8	.8	1.1	1.1		1.0	.9
	17.9	2.5	2.1	1.5	2.1	5.6		2.6	2.3
	-4.1	16.2	6.6	4.6	14.2	NM		8.8	9.3
% Profit Before Taxes/Tangible Net Worth	182.9	94.8	62.4	69.8	28.4	43.3		65.3	61.7
	(26) 69.0	(86) 27.6	(149) 27.2	(69) 34.7	(18) 21.0	(15) 31.3		(284) 23.8	(265) 27.9
	-.8	3.1	10.4	19.4	3.3	20.1		6.7	8.9
% Profit Before Taxes/Total Assets	58.8	21.6	20.2	24.5	13.0	15.3		21.2	19.2
	15.2	6.7	8.8	10.5	4.6	5.0		6.7	7.8
	.0	.5	2.8	4.7	.0	4.1		1.0	1.9
Sales/Net Fixed Assets	549.3	174.1	158.1	87.1	50.6	18.9		108.2	133.1
	80.0	37.8	41.5	25.0	10.4	14.2		32.6	34.9
	23.6	22.0	12.9	9.7	5.3	5.3		12.2	12.1
Sales/Total Assets	7.5	4.2	4.0	3.4	2.8	3.0		3.8	3.8
	4.0	3.0	2.9	2.1	1.6	1.4		2.9	2.8
	2.4	2.0	1.9	1.4	1.2	.9		1.8	1.7
% Depr., Dep., Amort./Sales	.8	.3	.3	.3	.4	1.1		.3	.3
	(14) 1.2	(68) .6	(132) .7	(66) .7	(14) 1.6	(18) 1.9		(268) .8	(240) .8
	5.0	1.3	1.7	2.0	3.9	3.6		2.3	2.0
% Officers', Directors' Owners' Comp/Sales	2.0	3.1	1.4	1.2				2.0	2.5
	(15) 4.6	(58) 4.8	(65) 2.3	(13) 2.0				(129) 4.1	(109) 4.2
	12.4	9.8	4.1	4.9				8.0	7.6
Net Sales ($)	71844M	438733M	2401369M	4162119M	3047859M	5399544M		10515648M	10781124M
Total Assets ($)	10694M	128512M	799798M	1841942M	1547040M	3005168M		4089966M	4431483M

M = $ thousand   MM = $ million
See Pages 9 through 22 for Explanation of Ratios and Data

Comparative Historical Data | Current Data Sorted by Sales

	52 / 54 / 58	63 / 63 / 62	55 / 53 / 63	Type of Statement	0-1MM	1-3MM	3-5MM	5-10MM	10-25MM	25MM & OVER
	52	54	58	Unqualified		1	1	1	11	44
	63	63	62	Reviewed		2	5	7	31	17
	55	53	63	Compiled	4	11	13	14	18	3
	65	64	73	Tax Returns	11	19	12	9	20	2
	168	165	176	Other	8	21	27	25	41	54
	4/1/08-3/31/09 ALL	4/1/09-3/31/10 ALL	4/1/10-3/31/11 ALL			62 (4/1-9/30/10)			370 (10/1/10-3/31/11)	
NUMBER OF STATEMENTS	403	399	432		23	54	58	56	121	120
	%	%	%	**ASSETS**	%	%	%	%	%	%
	8.7	10.4	10.4	Cash & Equivalents	12.7	15.1	12.9	13.1	7.8	7.9
	33.7	32.8	32.1	Trade Receivables (net)	24.9	29.4	30.2	30.5	35.1	33.2
	28.7	27.6	26.1	Inventory	21.2	18.1	28.8	29.0	28.2	25.9
	3.2	2.8	2.9	All Other Current	4.4	1.5	4.9	3.1	2.3	3.0
	74.3	73.6	71.5	Total Current	63.2	64.2	76.8	75.7	73.3	70.0
	14.0	14.8	14.0	Fixed Assets (net)	19.7	15.0	13.4	14.4	13.1	13.5
	6.1	7.0	8.2	Intangibles (net)	8.1	7.0	5.1	5.6	8.2	11.5
	5.6	4.7	6.3	All Other Non-Current	9.0	13.9	4.6	4.3	5.4	5.0
	100.0	100.0	100.0	Total	100.0	100.0	100.0	100.0	100.0	100.0
				LIABILITIES						
	15.2	14.4	13.6	Notes Payable-Short Term	24.1	17.6	15.8	10.7	12.9	11.0
	4.1	3.2	3.1	Cur. Mat.-L.T.D.	4.3	1.4	6.2	4.8	2.5	1.8
	21.4	21.2	21.0	Trade Payables	16.6	20.0	20.6	20.6	24.8	18.9
	.2	.2	.2	Income Taxes Payable	.0	.0	.1	.1	.3	.4
	9.6	9.7	10.5	All Other Current	27.4	7.5	13.1	7.1	8.7	10.7
	50.5	48.6	48.4	Total Current	72.3	46.5	55.7	43.2	49.2	42.8
	12.0	12.1	12.3	Long-Term Debt	20.9	15.1	14.3	13.5	10.3	10.0
	.2	.2	.4	Deferred Taxes	.0	.3	.2	.1	.2	.8
	4.8	5.5	5.3	All Other Non-Current	4.3	9.7	4.8	5.1	4.6	4.3
	32.5	33.5	33.6	Net Worth	2.4	28.4	24.9	38.0	35.6	42.1
	100.0	100.0	100.0	Total Liabilities & Net Worth	100.0	100.0	100.0	100.0	100.0	100.0
				INCOME DATA						
	100.0	100.0	100.0	Net Sales	100.0	100.0	100.0	100.0	100.0	100.0
	40.2	39.9	41.2	Gross Profit	56.6	52.0	47.3	41.2	36.0	35.5
	34.5	34.1	34.9	Operating Expenses	44.7	46.2	43.3	35.6	30.1	28.5
	5.7	5.9	6.2	Operating Profit	11.8	5.8	4.0	5.6	5.9	7.0
	.9	.7	.8	All Other Expenses (net)	1.8	1.1	.6	.7	.6	1.0
	4.7	5.1	5.4	Profit Before Taxes	10.0	4.7	3.4	4.9	5.3	6.0
				RATIOS						
	2.4	2.4	2.6	Current	2.5	3.4	2.4	3.3	2.2	2.5
	1.5	1.5	1.6		1.0	1.6	1.4	1.8	1.5	1.7
	1.1	1.2	1.1		.4	.8	1.0	1.2	1.1	1.2
	1.5	1.5	1.5	Quick	1.5	1.9	1.7	2.1	1.2	1.5
	.8	.9	.9		.5	1.0	.7	.9	.9	1.0
	.5	.6	.5		.2	.5	.5	.5	.6	.6
	30 / 12.1	30 / 12.4	28 / 13.1	Sales/Receivables	1 / 287.3	20 / 18.3	25 / 14.4	22 / 16.7	31 / 12.0	34 / 10.8
	42 / 8.6	42 / 8.7	41 / 8.9		30 / 12.3	38 / 9.7	41 / 8.9	37 / 9.8	41 / 9.0	44 / 8.2
	59 / 6.2	57 / 6.4	56 / 6.6		73 / 5.0	62 / 5.9	59 / 6.2	57 / 6.4	51 / 7.1	59 / 6.2
	29 / 12.4	28 / 13.1	30 / 12.3	Cost of Sales/Inventory	30 / 12.1	0 / UND	31 / 11.6	29 / 10.2	29 / 12.7	33 / 10.9
	54 / 6.7	52 / 7.0	51 / 7.1		58 / 6.2	48 / 7.7	70 / 5.2	59 / 6.2	48 / 7.6	49 / 7.4
	101 / 3.6	96 / 3.8	99 / 3.7		190 / 1.9	88 / 4.1	123 / 3.0	107 / 3.4	75 / 4.9	91 / 4.0
	21 / 17.1	20 / 18.5	21 / 17.1	Cost of Sales/Payables	8 / 44.6	13 / 27.0	19 / 19.3	18 / 19.8	23 / 16.2	22 / 16.3
	38 / 9.6	40 / 9.2	38 / 9.7		53 / 6.9	41 / 9.0	43 / 8.5	40 / 9.1	37 / 9.8	36 / 10.3
	67 / 5.5	67 / 5.5	63 / 5.8		106 / 3.4	86 / 4.2	65 / 5.6	67 / 5.4	57 / 6.4	56 / 6.6
	6.0	6.0	5.8	Sales/Working Capital	6.0	6.3	4.9	3.8	6.7	5.7
	12.3	11.3	12.4		-83.0	13.6	11.9	9.8	14.9	9.3
	48.1	33.9	54.9		-4.0	-16.5	205.9	26.5	42.8	30.7
	14.9	21.6	30.7	EBIT/Interest	58.6	13.8	15.1	21.0	29.9	57.3
	(346) 4.5	(348) 6.1	(373) 5.6		(12) 8.7	(45) 3.4	(52) 3.1	(49) 5.6	(107) 5.3	(108) 10.6
	1.6	2.0	2.0		2.1	-.1	.0	2.5	2.1	3.0
	10.4	12.2	12.6	Net Profit + Depr., Dep., Amort./Cur. Mat. L/T/D					15.9	14.2
	(70) 3.0	(72) 4.2	(72) 4.8						(22) 3.7	(32) 7.4
	1.0	1.8	1.8						1.2	3.2
	.1	.1	.1	Fixed/Worth	.1	.0	.1	.0	.1	.1
	.4	.3	.4		2.3	.3	.6	.3	.3	.4
	1.7	1.5	1.7		-2.3	5.4	1.7	1.5	1.5	1.3
	.9	.9	.8	Debt/Worth	.6	.8	.9	.7	.8	.8
	2.6	2.1	2.2		20.4	1.9	2.9	1.8	2.1	2.0
	10.3	8.2	13.7		-4.0	90.3	12.2	8.7	10.6	6.0
	61.1	65.1	68.8	% Profit Before Taxes/Tangible Net Worth	999.8	93.6	45.5	51.0	84.0	58.5
	(333) 27.4	(332) 30.7	(363) 29.9		(15) 69.3	(42) 39.4	(48) 21.6	(48) 26.4	(104) 29.5	(106) 31.1
	9.2	11.2	11.4		.0	4.0	-6.3	11.7	11.6	19.2
	18.2	20.6	21.5	% Profit Before Taxes/Total Assets	52.0	27.2	15.1	17.8	26.6	21.0
	6.9	9.6	9.0		9.7	9.6	4.6	9.6	8.1	9.7
	1.8	2.6	2.0		.0	-.7	-1.9	4.3	2.7	4.3
	130.4	134.2	146.0	Sales/Net Fixed Assets	172.0	257.9	106.9	268.9	142.2	104.2
	36.9	33.0	35.0		31.7	39.9	28.6	42.5	44.0	23.3
	14.0	11.0	12.0		10.9	19.7	11.2	17.4	13.7	9.5
	3.9	3.8	3.9	Sales/Total Assets	4.0	3.8	3.7	4.0	4.3	3.7
	2.7	2.7	2.8		2.5	2.3	2.4	2.9	3.1	2.7
	1.8	1.8	1.8		1.1	1.8	1.8	1.8	2.1	1.4
	.3	.3	.3	% Depr., Dep., Amort./Sales		.4	.5	.2	.3	.3
	(299) .7	(298) .8	(312) .8			(30) 1.1	(42) 1.0	(39) .6	(95) .7	(97) .7
	1.9	1.8	1.9			1.4	3.4	1.5	1.6	2.0
	2.0	1.9	1.7	% Officers', Directors' Owners' Comp/Sales		3.8	2.8	1.5	.7	
	(146) 3.6	(144) 3.6	(153) 3.4			(22) 5.3	(31) 4.1	(26) 3.5	(51) 2.6	(17) 1.3
	7.4	6.9	6.0			12.3	10.7	7.8	4.4	2.5
	21124280M	15516500M	15521468M	Net Sales ($)	12962M	107109M	228947M	401765M	1921437M	12849248M
	6455148M	6612639M	7333154M	Total Assets ($)	8640M	49879M	107748M	164380M	786912M	6215595M

M = $ thousand   MM = $ million
See Pages 9 through 22 for Explanation of Ratios and Data

Current Data Sorted by Assets   Comparative Historical Data

Type of Statement

0-500M	500M-2MM	2-10MM	10-50MM	50-100MM	100-250MM	Type of Statement	4/1/06-3/31/07 ALL	4/1/07-3/31/08 ALL
		3	3		1	Unqualified	9	4
	1	4	3			Reviewed	7	3
	4	5				Compiled	6	4
	3	1				Tax Returns	1	2
1		7	4		1	Other	6	9
			10 (4/1-9/30/10)	31 (10/1/10-3/31/11)				
1	8	20	10		2	NUMBER OF STATEMENTS	29	22

0-500M %	500M-2MM %	2-10MM %	10-50MM %	50-100MM %	100-250MM %		ALL %	ALL %
						ASSETS		
		8.9	4.4	D		Cash & Equivalents	7.2	8.2
		37.4	29.3	A		Trade Receivables (net)	27.9	31.6
		31.7	39.9	T		Inventory	39.7	35.7
		2.5	2.3	A		All Other Current	2.3	3.2
		80.5	75.8			Total Current	77.2	78.7
		7.5	7.1	N		Fixed Assets (net)	11.0	10.1
		7.7	12.2	O		Intangibles (net)	5.6	7.6
		4.4	4.9	T		All Other Non-Current	6.3	3.5
		100.0	100.0			Total	100.0	100.0
				A		**LIABILITIES**		
		13.0	15.1	V		Notes Payable-Short Term	11.2	13.3
		1.9	2.2	A		Cur. Mat.-L.T.D.	2.5	.7
		35.1	20.4	I		Trade Payables	26.0	25.8
		.1	.3	L		Income Taxes Payable	.1	.2
		7.5	8.0	A		All Other Current	12.6	21.5
		57.7	46.0	B		Total Current	52.4	61.5
		8.4	8.9	L		Long-Term Debt	8.0	6.1
		.0	.0	E		Deferred Taxes	.0	.2
		.8	1.1			All Other Non-Current	2.0	3.4
		33.1	44.0			Net Worth	37.6	28.8
		100.0	100.0			Total Liabilities & Net Worth	100.0	100.0
						INCOME DATA		
		100.0	100.0			Net Sales	100.0	100.0
		39.7	38.0			Gross Profit	37.4	37.3
		35.5	33.6			Operating Expenses	33.9	33.7
		4.3	4.4			Operating Profit	3.5	3.6
		.4	1.3			All Other Expenses (net)	.9	1.0
		3.9	3.1			Profit Before Taxes	2.6	2.6
						RATIOS		
		1.9	2.7			Current	2.1	1.8
		1.4	1.5				1.6	1.3
		1.0	1.1				1.1	1.1
		1.0	1.4			Quick	1.1	1.0
		.9	.6				(28) .8	.7
		.6	.4				.5	.4
		32 11.3	34 10.7			Sales/Receivables	28 13.0	28 13.0
		39 9.5	39 9.4				35 10.5	40 9.2
		64 5.7	52 7.1				44 8.4	60 6.1
		29 12.7	50 7.3			Cost of Sales/Inventory	44 8.3	48 7.5
		85 4.3	126 2.9				99 3.7	68 5.3
		165 2.2	180 2.0				150 2.4	136 2.7
		36 10.0	30 12.2			Cost of Sales/Payables	32 11.5	23 16.0
		49 7.4	51 7.2				38 9.7	44 8.3
		69 5.3	78 4.7				83 4.4	87 4.2
		5.6	7.6			Sales/Working Capital	5.5	7.4
		12.5	11.5				14.3	14.7
		NM	22.3				51.1	55.2
		18.4	26.0			EBIT/Interest	18.3	12.1
		(17) 9.7	9.9				(28) 4.0	(20) 3.9
		2.8	2.9				1.6	1.3
						Net Profit + Depr., Dep., Amort./Cur. Mat. L/T/D		
		.1	.1			Fixed/Worth	.1	.1
		.2	.2				.2	.2
		.4	.5				.6	1.8
		1.3	1.4			Debt/Worth	.9	1.5
		2.3	2.0				1.7	2.8
		13.3	3.6				4.0	7.8
		56.7	52.8			% Profit Before Taxes/Tangible Net Worth	57.6	118.5
		(18) 41.1	36.9				(26) 31.5	(19) 21.8
		21.6	9.8				9.3	8.1
		16.6	16.9			% Profit Before Taxes/Total Assets	15.6	15.1
		9.3	7.8				10.8	4.5
		1.8	3.2				1.3	1.7
		254.4	64.3			Sales/Net Fixed Assets	163.7	211.6
		99.9	45.3				37.4	47.9
		22.0	17.1				13.0	23.3
		4.1	3.7			Sales/Total Assets	4.0	3.8
		2.5	2.4				2.9	2.8
		1.8	1.5				1.8	2.0
		.1	.4			% Depr., Dep., Amort./Sales	.3	.1
		(17) .3	.8				(20) .7	(16) .3
		.8	2.9				1.9	.7
						% Officers', Directors' Owners' Comp/Sales	2.1	
							(10) 4.1	
							10.8	
1602M	30188M	358910M	574112M		621210M	Net Sales ($)	1094723M	541467M
279M	9608M	111402M	199524M		394929M	Total Assets ($)	541407M	311171M

Comparative Historical Data | Current Data Sorted by Sales

	4/1/08-3/31/09 ALL	4/1/09-3/31/10 ALL	4/1/10-3/31/11 ALL	0-1MM	1-3MM	3-5MM	5-10MM	10-25MM	25MM & OVER
Type of Statement									
Unqualified	5	2	7	1			1	2	4
Reviewed	6	5	8				1	5	1
Compiled	4	5	9			3	2	3	1
Tax Returns	3	3	5		2	1	1		1
Other	10	12	12			1		6	5
				10 (4/1-9/30/10)			31 (10/1/10-3/31/11)		
NUMBER OF STATEMENTS	28	27	41	1	2	5	5	16	12
	%	%	%	%	%	%	%	%	%
ASSETS									
Cash & Equivalents	6.6	3.4	9.6					7.1	7.1
Trade Receivables (net)	28.9	30.9	33.0					31.2	40.5
Inventory	37.6	37.5	34.5					40.8	26.1
All Other Current	3.2	3.8	2.4					1.5	3.2
Total Current	76.3	75.7	79.4					80.6	76.8
Fixed Assets (net)	7.5	6.3	7.3					7.8	5.6
Intangibles (net)	5.2	11.8	8.8					7.8	13.6
All Other Non-Current	11.0	6.2	4.5					3.9	4.0
Total	100.0	100.0	100.0					100.0	100.0
LIABILITIES									
Notes Payable-Short Term	19.0	17.6	13.8					18.7	6.8
Cur. Mat.-L.T.D.	.9	1.5	1.7					1.7	2.1
Trade Payables	31.1	28.0	31.3					24.1	35.8
Income Taxes Payable	.3	.1	.1					.3	.0
All Other Current	11.2	7.8	6.5					6.9	9.5
Total Current	62.5	55.0	53.3					51.7	54.3
Long-Term Debt	7.3	6.7	9.2					10.4	10.9
Deferred Taxes	.0	.5	.0					.0	.0
All Other Non-Current	1.7	4.1	3.4					1.2	5.8
Net Worth	28.5	33.7	34.1					36.7	28.9
Total Liabilities & Net Worth	100.0	100.0	100.0					100.0	100.0
INCOME DATA									
Net Sales	100.0	100.0	100.0					100.0	100.0
Gross Profit	40.4	40.2	38.0					42.2	30.8
Operating Expenses	35.4	37.4	33.9					39.2	26.0
Operating Profit	5.0	2.8	4.2					2.9	4.8
All Other Expenses (net)	.6	1.1	1.0					.2	2.2
Profit Before Taxes	4.4	1.7	3.2					2.7	2.6
RATIOS									
Current	1.9	1.9	2.0					2.1	1.7
	1.2	1.3	1.5					1.5	1.4
	.9	1.1	1.1					1.1	1.1
Quick	.9	.9	1.0					1.0	1.4
	.6	.6	.8					.8	.7
	.4	.4	.5					.5	.6
Sales/Receivables	33 11.0	32 11.3	33 11.2					37 9.9	32 11.4
	41 8.8	41 8.9	39 9.4					39 9.5	37 9.7
	59 6.2	49 7.4	57 6.5					50 7.3	48 7.7
Cost of Sales/Inventory	54 6.8	50 7.3	44 8.3					73 5.0	9 41.8
	107 3.4	90 4.1	83 4.4					123 3.0	55 6.6
	193 1.9	175 2.1	158 2.3					184 2.0	133 2.8
Cost of Sales/Payables	31 11.9	40 9.1	36 10.3					35 10.4	37 10.0
	59 6.2	56 6.5	50 7.3					48 7.7	53 6.8
	107 3.4	80 4.5	72 5.0					69 5.3	72 5.1
Sales/Working Capital	6.4	8.1	5.6					5.6	9.1
	16.2	12.8	12.7					9.2	13.3
	-82.2	50.3	30.6					24.9	30.0
EBIT/Interest	10.5	15.3	18.7					13.8	41.3
	(25) 4.9	7.6	(35) 8.4					(14) 9.6	16.5
	1.2	1.0	2.7					5.5	.8
Net Profit + Depr., Dep., Amort./Cur. Mat. L/T/D			8.3						
			(16) 3.9						
			1.9						
Fixed/Worth	.1	.1	.1					.0	.1
	.2	.2	.2					.2	.2
	.6	.7	.4					.3	1.0
Debt/Worth	1.8	1.8	1.2					1.5	1.8
	2.7	2.7	2.2					2.2	2.6
	5.5	12.6	8.3					5.5	16.0
% Profit Before Taxes/Tangible Net Worth	61.9	73.9	53.8					44.3	116.5
	(26) 29.4	(22) 25.9	(36) 36.9					37.7	(10) 45.5
	6.2	2.5	10.3					16.3	-2.4
% Profit Before Taxes/Total Assets	15.1	14.5	15.9					12.4	17.1
	5.8	5.8	7.0					7.8	9.0
	.9	.1	2.4					3.2	-.4
Sales/Net Fixed Assets	162.5	148.1	197.4					179.7	230.8
	42.6	63.8	54.7					70.5	56.0
	20.2	22.5	21.3					21.2	29.6
Sales/Total Assets	3.3	3.8	3.9					3.2	5.1
	2.3	2.5	2.6					2.4	3.1
	1.6	1.4	1.8					1.8	1.7
% Depr., Dep., Amort./Sales	.2	.3	.3					.3	.1
	(24) .5	(19) .6	(35) .7					(13) .7	.7
	1.2	1.2	1.0					1.5	1.7
% Officers', Directors' Owners' Comp/Sales	2.7	1.6	.9						
	(13) 3.9	(11) 4.0	(16) 2.1						
	6.4	5.4	3.2						
Net Sales ($)	472084M	1163852M	1586022M	949M	3792M	20986M	34445M	246293M	1279557M
Total Assets ($)	202685M	601041M	715742M	590M	1408M	8101M	19634M	105084M	580925M

© RMA 2011

M = $ thousand   MM = $ million
See Pages 9 through 22 for Explanation of Ratios and Data

Current Data Sorted by Assets   Comparative Historical Data

	0-500M	500M-2MM	2-10MM	10-50MM	50-100MM	100-250MM	Type of Statement	4/1/06-3/31/07 ALL	4/1/07-3/31/08 ALL
			2	8	1	1	Unqualified	11	13
	4	20	3				Reviewed	26	26
1	3	6					Compiled	17	17
5	9	4					Tax Returns	10	12
3	10	13	14	1	1		Other	23	29
	14 (4/1-9/30/10)			95 (10/1/10-3/31/11)					
9	26	45	25	2	2		NUMBER OF STATEMENTS	87	97
%	%	%	%	%	%		**ASSETS**	%	%
	12.7	10.9	8.6				Cash & Equivalents	7.1	9.3
	34.8	37.8	33.0				Trade Receivables (net)	34.9	29.2
	26.7	30.0	25.8				Inventory	31.2	31.8
	2.0	3.7	3.3				All Other Current	3.2	2.4
	76.1	82.4	70.6				Total Current	76.4	72.8
	14.2	6.2	14.4				Fixed Assets (net)	13.3	13.9
	4.9	5.0	10.4				Intangibles (net)	4.9	8.6
	4.8	6.5	4.6				All Other Non-Current	5.4	4.6
	100.0	100.0	100.0				Total	100.0	100.0
							LIABILITIES		
	11.4	13.8	13.5				Notes Payable-Short Term	11.6	14.3
	1.4	.9	2.0				Cur. Mat.-L.T.D.	3.2	2.7
	19.4	21.9	18.8				Trade Payables	21.7	22.8
	.0	.2	.4				Income Taxes Payable	.1	.3
	8.1	11.0	9.5				All Other Current	12.1	11.3
	40.3	47.8	44.3				Total Current	48.8	51.4
	10.5	4.1	11.1				Long-Term Debt	11.8	10.6
	.1	.1	.4				Deferred Taxes	.0	.1
	7.3	9.0	13.9				All Other Non-Current	4.2	7.1
	41.8	39.0	30.3				Net Worth	35.2	30.7
	100.0	100.0	100.0				Total Liabilities & Net Worth	100.0	100.0
							INCOME DATA		
	100.0	100.0	100.0				Net Sales	100.0	100.0
	37.3	32.4	31.9				Gross Profit	35.3	36.0
	32.0	27.1	30.1				Operating Expenses	30.3	32.3
	5.2	5.3	1.9				Operating Profit	5.1	3.7
	.4	.1	1.1				All Other Expenses (net)	1.5	1.3
	4.8	5.1	.8				Profit Before Taxes	3.6	2.4
							RATIOS		
	3.4	2.5	2.4					2.6	2.2
	2.0	1.6	1.5				Current	1.6	1.6
	1.4	1.4	1.2					1.2	1.1
	2.3	1.4	1.5					1.2	1.1
	1.4	1.0	.9				Quick	(86) .9	.8
	.6	.6	.6					.6	.5
	10 36.7	29 12.8	36 10.2					28 13.1	28 13.1
	35 10.4	45 8.2	47 7.8				Sales/Receivables	41 8.9	40 9.2
	52 7.0	67 5.4	57 6.4					53 6.9	52 7.0
	9 39.2	22 16.2	35 10.4					31 11.7	35 10.4
	39 9.4	59 6.2	63 5.8				Cost of Sales/Inventory	64 5.7	70 5.2
	99 3.7	90 4.0	100 3.7					103 3.5	111 3.3
	3 115.2	17 21.1	25 14.4					21 17.1	24 15.2
	30 12.0	34 10.7	45 8.1				Cost of Sales/Payables	33 10.9	36 10.2
	54 6.8	60 6.1	65 5.6					58 6.3	70 5.2
	5.2	5.9	4.8					5.6	6.5
	10.0	8.5	8.3				Sales/Working Capital	9.6	11.6
	24.5	17.1	17.4					35.3	59.2
	41.4	34.7	20.3					11.1	9.9
	(24) 6.3	(40) 6.8	(24) 7.7				EBIT/Interest	(82) 4.5	(88) 3.7
	2.8	2.4	1.3					1.6	1.3
							Net Profit + Depr., Dep.,	27.5	11.5
							Amort./Cur. Mat. L/T/D	(19) 7.8	(18) 3.4
								2.0	1.8
	.1	.0	.3					.1	.1
	.2	.1	.5				Fixed/Worth	.3	.4
	.7	.3	NM					.9	3.9
	.7	.7	1.5					.9	1.1
	1.3	1.7	2.6				Debt/Worth	2.1	2.7
	4.0	3.7	NM					7.3	95.3
	81.9	59.5	55.1					60.3	43.9
	(24) 19.1	(43) 24.0	(19) 23.0				% Profit Before Taxes/Tangible Net Worth	(77) 26.5	(78) 18.3
	8.2	6.7	11.1					7.7	5.4
	25.5	18.6	13.5					16.6	13.9
	8.6	6.4	5.6				% Profit Before Taxes/Total Assets	6.1	6.6
	2.6	2.1	.1					1.6	.7
	103.4	274.6	63.0					137.2	82.6
	61.8	61.0	29.8				Sales/Net Fixed Assets	45.4	33.9
	25.7	25.2	9.0					12.3	11.3
	5.3	3.4	3.0					3.9	3.5
	3.3	3.0	2.0				Sales/Total Assets	2.8	2.6
	2.9	2.1	1.6					2.0	1.9
	.2	.1	.2					.3	.5
	(18) .4	(37) .4	(23) 1.3				% Depr., Dep., Amort./Sales	(74) .8	(74) 1.1
	1.1	.7	2.1					2.1	2.8
	2.5	1.0						2.1	2.4
	(14) 3.5	(20) 2.3					% Officers', Directors' Owners' Comp/Sales	(36) 3.1	(37) 3.9
	4.7	4.1						4.8	5.2
9769M	133192M	643568M	1211753M	409461M	622224M		Net Sales ($)	1642442M	1860265M
2089M	33792M	215744M	586676M	128375M	304030M		Total Assets ($)	830656M	930534M

Comparative Historical Data   Current Data Sorted by Sales

Type of Statement

Type of Statement	4/1/08-3/31/09 ALL	4/1/09-3/31/10 ALL	4/1/10-3/31/11 ALL	0-1MM	1-3MM	3-5MM	5-10MM	10-25MM	25MM & OVER
Unqualified	12	12	12	1	1	3	8	4	8
Reviewed	23	19	27		2	1	4	12	2
Compiled	11	17	10			1		3	
Tax Returns	15	21	18	3	5	2	2	2	1
Other	34	45	42	1	3	5	10	8	17
					14 (4/1-9/30/10)		95 (10/1/10-3/31/11)		
NUMBER OF STATEMENTS	95	114	109	5	11	12	24	29	28

Assets / Liabilities / Income Data (%)

	4/1/08-3/31/09 ALL	4/1/09-3/31/10 ALL	4/1/10-3/31/11 ALL	0-1MM	1-3MM	3-5MM	5-10MM	10-25MM	25MM & OVER
	%	%	%	%	%	%	%	%	%
ASSETS									
Cash & Equivalents	7.4	7.1	10.4		5.5	20.4	11.0	11.7	6.2
Trade Receivables (net)	28.5	32.9	35.0		31.5	29.7	38.2	37.6	34.5
Inventory	35.9	31.1	28.4		30.7	32.9	25.7	29.7	27.0
All Other Current	3.8	3.5	3.1		2.1	.3	4.9	3.0	3.7
Total Current	75.7	74.7	76.8		69.8	83.2	79.8	82.0	71.5
Fixed Assets (net)	12.5	13.0	10.7		19.6	12.0	9.7	6.6	12.4
Intangibles (net)	7.4	6.0	6.6		9.3	1.4	7.3	4.8	10.1
All Other Non-Current	4.4	6.3	5.9		1.3	3.4	3.3	6.6	6.0
Total	100.0	100.0	100.0		100.0	100.0	100.0	100.0	100.0
LIABILITIES									
Notes Payable-Short Term	21.1	17.2	13.8		6.0	11.2	15.7	12.4	13.9
Cur. Mat.-L.T.D.	2.0	2.4	1.6		2.8	1.5	.7	1.0	1.6
Trade Payables	19.5	20.2	21.2		26.7	15.9	16.9	26.0	20.7
Income Taxes Payable	.2	.1	.2		.0	.0	.1	.5	.2
All Other Current	10.1	9.3	10.4		13.0	4.1	8.1	12.9	11.2
Total Current	52.9	49.2	47.1		48.5	32.6	41.5	52.8	47.6
Long-Term Debt	11.4	10.9	8.7		24.1	8.3	5.9	3.4	11.1
Deferred Taxes	.2	.1	.2		.0	.0	.1	.1	.6
All Other Non-Current	6.4	6.3	10.0		13.4	7.6	4.4	2.6	11.9
Net Worth	29.2	33.4	34.0		14.0	51.4	48.1	41.1	28.8
Total Liabilties & Net Worth	100.0	100.0	100.0		100.0	100.0	100.0	100.0	100.0
INCOME DATA									
Net Sales	100.0	100.0	100.0		100.0	100.0	100.0	100.0	100.0
Gross Profit	33.5	33.7	34.2		44.8	42.4	35.6	30.5	29.1
Operating Expenses	30.5	29.9	29.9		41.3	38.1	28.9	27.1	25.7
Operating Profit	2.9	3.8	4.3		3.6	4.4	6.7	3.4	3.4
All Other Expenses (net)	1.5	.6	.5		.6	-.2	.3	.3	.9
Profit Before Taxes	1.5	3.2	3.8		3.0	4.6	6.4	3.2	2.5

Ratios

	4/1/08-3/31/09 ALL	4/1/09-3/31/10 ALL	4/1/10-3/31/11 ALL	0-1MM	1-3MM	3-5MM	5-10MM	10-25MM	25MM & OVER
Current	2.0	2.6	2.6		2.7	4.1	3.2	1.9	2.4
	1.5	1.5	1.6		2.1	2.6	1.7	1.5	1.5
	1.1	1.2	1.2		1.1	1.7	1.5	1.3	1.2
Quick	1.1	1.3	1.5		1.2	2.5	2.4	1.2	1.3
	.7	.8	.9		.8	1.5	1.2	.9	.7
	.5	.5	.6		.5	.6	1.2	.9	.6
Sales/Receivables	25 14.4	30 12.3	26 14.1	17 21.3	0 UND	28 13.2	30 12.1	28 13.3	
	37 9.8	42 8.8	39 9.3	38 9.7	33 11.2	36 10.1	46 7.9	44 8.3	
	50 7.3	58 6.2	56 6.5	51 7.1	60 6.0	51 7.1	67 5.4	56 6.5	
Cost of Sales/Inventory	34 10.7	21 17.2	22 16.2	26 13.8	28 13.2	11 34.0	22 16.2	32 11.5	
	66 5.5	61 6.0	58 6.3	48 7.6	69 5.3	36 10.2	61 6.0	52 7.0	
	122 3.0	118 3.1	95 3.8	115 3.2	175 2.1	91 4.0	82 4.4	92 4.0	
Cost of Sales/Payables	18 20.3	18 20.5	20 18.5	21 17.5	0 UND	7 53.6	23 15.9	23 15.6	
	32 11.5	32 11.2	36 10.3	52 7.0	36 10.3	28 13.2	36 10.3	39 9.3	
	56 6.6	57 6.4	58 6.3	64 5.7	49 7.4	43 8.4	65 5.6	63 5.8	
Sales/Working Capital	6.1	5.6	5.7		5.8	2.8	4.3	7.1	5.6
	12.6	11.6	9.1		10.4	5.3	9.1	11.2	10.4
	34.5	25.3	23.1		50.6	11.0	17.3	17.9	32.5
EBIT/Interest	7.9	12.3	24.2			12.6	72.3	54.4	20.3
	(83) 4.3	(100) 4.4	(98) 6.5			(10) 4.4	(23) 10.0	(26) 8.4	8.5
	1.8	1.2	2.4			2.3	2.7	2.3	2.0
Net Profit + Depr., Dep., Amort./Cur. Mat. L/T/D	8.0	7.2	8.1						
	(20) 3.2	(25) 3.5	(19) 3.2						
	1.2	.4	2.4						
Fixed/Worth	.1	.1	.1		.2	.0	.1	.0	.1
	.3	.3	.3		1.6	.1	.1	.1	.6
	1.1	1.3	.8		-.6	.3	.4	.4	-3.1
Debt/Worth	1.4	1.2	.8		.8	.5	.5	.8	1.6
	2.6	2.3	1.9		3.6	.7	1.4	1.9	2.7
	11.0	12.5	8.2		-2.7	2.6	4.1	3.8	-53.2
% Profit Before Taxes/Tangible Net Worth	42.6	49.9	58.6			37.3	112.8	61.9	38.0
	(82) 21.9	(95) 23.0	(91) 23.5			10.6	(23) 32.5	28.9	(20) 20.7
	7.7	5.6	8.9			1.5	8.7	9.5	11.2
% Profit Before Taxes/Total Assets	10.9	14.9	16.8		15.4	21.6	36.1	19.6	13.7
	5.8	6.8	6.7		6.7	3.4	8.5	6.4	9.4
	1.7	1.0	2.1		4.2	.9	2.9	2.3	2.0
Sales/Net Fixed Assets	93.2	120.6	131.6		98.3	142.1	262.7	261.7	70.5
	38.6	38.3	51.1		30.0	75.5	56.1	59.6	45.1
	15.4	15.3	21.4		14.5	24.1	28.0	22.0	17.3
Sales/Total Assets	3.8	3.6	3.7		6.4	3.3	5.1	3.4	3.2
	2.7	2.6	2.9		2.9	3.0	3.2	3.0	2.2
	1.9	1.9	2.0		2.1	1.4	2.3	2.1	1.8
% Depr., Dep., Amort./Sales	.3	.3	.2				.1	.1	.2
	(78) .6	(91) .6	(85) .5			(16) .5	(26) .4	(25) .6	
	1.3	1.7	1.3				.7	.7	2.0
% Officers', Directors', Owners' Comp/Sales	2.5	1.3	1.4				2.5	.9	
	(31) 4.0	(52) 3.1	(45) 3.4			(13) 3.2	(10) 1.8		
	6.5	5.0	5.0				4.2	3.4	
Net Sales ($)	2914159M	3049980M	3029967M	2357M	20595M	49573M	172919M	508807M	2275716M
Total Assets ($)	1397772M	1434509M	1270706M	2698M	7734M	24338M	58952M	198655M	978329M

© RMA 2011

M = $ thousand   MM = $ million
See Pages 9 through 22 for Explanation of Ratios and Data

Current Data Sorted by Assets   Comparative Historical Data

0-500M	500M-2MM	2-10MM	10-50MM	50-100MM	100-250MM	Type of Statement	140 / 177 / 104 / 49 / 207	130 / 168 / 108 / 56 / 211
1	3	16	72	24	12	Unqualified	140	130
1	10	82	67	5	3	Reviewed	177	168
6	24	54	11			Compiled	104	108
14	31	30	5			Tax Returns	49	56
3	31	92	76	29	19	Other	207	211
118 (4/1-9/30/10)			603 (10/1/10-3/31/11)				4/1/06-3/31/07 ALL	4/1/07-3/31/08 ALL
25	99	274	231	58	34	NUMBER OF STATEMENTS	677	673
%	%	%	%	%	%	**ASSETS**	%	%
29.7	12.2	7.1	6.2	4.8	6.5	Cash & Equivalents	6.0	6.2
21.7	35.8	32.7	27.3	26.7	22.1	Trade Receivables (net)	34.1	33.4
16.7	32.0	40.8	43.1	46.3	41.2	Inventory	40.4	39.8
2.0	1.9	1.7	2.9	1.6	5.1	All Other Current	2.0	2.0
70.1	81.9	82.3	79.5	79.5	75.0	Total Current	82.5	81.4
16.6	11.9	11.4	13.9	11.5	13.0	Fixed Assets (net)	11.9	12.0
2.6	1.3	2.2	2.6	3.8	8.0	Intangibles (net)	1.8	2.3
10.7	4.9	4.1	4.0	5.2	4.0	All Other Non-Current	3.8	4.3
100.0	100.0	100.0	100.0	100.0	100.0	Total	100.0	100.0
						LIABILITIES		
41.2	16.9	17.8	18.2	18.3	11.6	Notes Payable-Short Term	20.1	20.1
1.3	3.0	1.9	2.9	1.7	1.6	Cur. Mat.-L.T.D.	1.5	2.0
19.2	24.3	24.8	17.6	17.2	13.9	Trade Payables	22.4	21.5
.1	.3	.2	.1	.4	.5	Income Taxes Payable	.4	.2
4.9	5.7	6.0	5.9	4.7	7.6	All Other Current	7.7	7.6
66.7	50.1	50.7	44.8	42.3	35.2	Total Current	52.2	51.4
22.4	7.6	7.0	6.8	12.2	13.7	Long-Term Debt	8.8	8.4
.0	.2	.2	.3	.2	1.1	Deferred Taxes	.3	.3
13.4	5.0	6.0	5.2	5.4	4.7	All Other Non-Current	3.9	3.8
-2.5	37.0	36.0	42.9	39.9	45.4	Net Worth	34.8	36.0
100.0	100.0	100.0	100.0	100.0	100.0	Total Liabilities & Net Worth	100.0	100.0
						INCOME DATA		
100.0	100.0	100.0	100.0	100.0	100.0	Net Sales	100.0	100.0
29.5	21.6	20.6	17.4	16.7	17.5	Gross Profit	19.9	19.3
29.5	18.2	17.3	13.4	11.5	10.7	Operating Expenses	14.6	14.5
.0	3.5	3.3	4.0	5.2	6.9	Operating Profit	5.3	4.9
.9	.7	.5	.7	.9	2.5	All Other Expenses (net)	.7	.9
-.9	2.7	2.7	3.4	4.2	4.3	Profit Before Taxes	4.5	3.9
						RATIOS		
3.0	2.9	2.5	3.5	3.0	3.9	Current	2.5	2.4
1.1	1.5	1.6	1.7	2.0	2.5		1.6	1.5
.7	1.3	1.2	1.3	1.4	1.5		1.2	1.2
1.6	1.9	1.3	1.3	1.2	1.5	Quick	1.2	1.3
.9	1.0	.7	.7	.7	.8		.8	.7
.5	.6	.5	.5	.5	.6		.5	.5
0 UND	22 16.3	31 11.8	33 11.1	36 10.0	36 10.1	Sales/Receivables	30 12.0	30 12.0
15 23.7	38 9.5	42 8.7	42 8.6	44 8.2	44 8.3		40 9.2	39 9.4
27 13.3	52 7.0	53 6.9	51 7.1	54 6.8	51 7.2		50 7.3	49 7.4
0 UND	5 71.8	41 9.0	53 6.9	66 5.6	51 7.2	Cost of Sales/Inventory	33 11.1	35 10.5
6 64.9	45 8.1	68 5.4	87 4.2	88 4.2	88 4.1		65 5.6	62 5.9
26 14.3	101 3.6	117 3.1	126 2.9	138 2.6	133 2.7		99 3.7	102 3.6
0 UND	14 26.9	21 17.4	16 22.5	20 18.3	15 24.3	Cost of Sales/Payables	17 21.9	17 21.7
7 53.0	30 12.1	35 10.3	29 12.6	33 11.2	27 13.6		29 12.4	30 12.3
25 14.8	53 6.9	58 6.3	42 8.7	45 8.1	47 7.7		47 7.8	44 8.4
11.6	6.0	4.6	3.6	3.6	3.1	Sales/Working Capital	5.8	5.7
129.7	10.4	11.2	6.9	5.1	4.4		11.0	10.5
-51.6	22.5	24.4	16.9	11.5	11.7		24.7	25.7
24.7	14.3	11.5	12.8	12.1	36.7	EBIT/Interest	13.0	10.7
(20) 5.6	(83) 3.8	(253) 4.0	(209) 5.2	(56) 5.3	(31) 4.8		(622) 5.1	(617) 4.0
.6	1.1	1.5	2.3	3.4	2.1		1.9	1.7
		4.6	10.9	35.0	40.4	Net Profit + Depr., Dep., Amort./Cur. Mat. L/T/D	16.0	10.2
	(51) 1.7	(60) 3.8	(21) 11.0	(15) 3.0			(157) 6.0	(174) 4.0
	.8	1.6	2.5	.7			2.5	1.7
.0	.0	.0	.1	.1	.1	Fixed/Worth	.1	.1
.3	.2	.2	.2	.3	.3		.2	.2
NM	.6	.6	.7	.8	1.0		.7	.6
1.1	.6	.8	.7	.7	.7	Debt/Worth	1.0	.9
5.4	1.8	2.1	1.7	1.8	1.2		2.3	2.2
-7.3	5.4	5.4	3.6	3.6	3.9		5.2	5.1
88.7	57.7	41.6	33.7	39.6	48.6	% Profit Before Taxes/Tangible Net Worth	60.2	51.0
(15) 23.3	(88) 15.3	(253) 15.4	(214) 15.8	(53) 21.0	(30) 24.4		(632) 30.6	(634) 27.7
2.8	1.5	3.6	6.8	9.5	10.0		12.9	11.2
41.8	12.7	11.2	11.7	11.8	17.1	% Profit Before Taxes/Total Assets	18.9	17.4
7.8	5.2	4.9	5.9	6.7	9.4		9.6	8.8
-1.0	.2	1.0	2.3	4.0	2.4		2.7	2.3
UND	999.8	264.6	143.6	111.5	83.5	Sales/Net Fixed Assets	184.8	200.7
156.0	78.1	50.5	24.0	29.7	17.5		42.4	38.1
9.8	17.1	14.7	9.6	10.8	10.6		15.8	14.7
16.0	5.1	3.5	2.9	2.8	2.4	Sales/Total Assets	3.8	3.9
6.1	3.1	2.6	2.2	2.1	1.9		2.9	2.8
2.4	2.1	1.8	1.6	1.6	1.6		2.2	2.1
	.2	.3	.3	.3	.2	% Depr., Dep., Amort./Sales	.3	.2
	(60) .6	(222) .7	(200) .8	(52) .8	(33) 1.1		(549) .6	(568) .6
	1.8	1.4	1.5	1.8	1.9		1.1	1.2
1.7	1.7	1.2	.6	.3		% Officers', Directors' Owners' Comp/Sales	1.2	1.1
(12) 7.5	(55) 3.1	(124) 2.2	(63) 1.3	(10) .9			(236) 2.2	(256) 2.3
26.2	6.2	4.1	2.8	2.6			4.2	3.9
64904M	522371M	4447152M	13321975M	9255660M	11688815M	Net Sales ($)	46285245M	41914843M
6431M	133833M	1481519M	5698500M	4038013M	5714560M	Total Assets ($)	16122295M	15379804M

Comparative Historical Data | | Current Data Sorted by Sales

H1	H2	H3	Type of Statement	0-1MM	1-3MM	3-5MM	5-10MM	10-25MM	25MM & OVER
116	119	128	Unqualified	1	2	1	5	9	111
172	148	168	Reviewed	4	10	3	20	64	76
101	100	95	Compiled	7	12	12	22	33	11
55	59	80	Tax Returns	4	12	18	24	37	10
269	266	250	Other	2	12	14	37	12	124
4/1/08-3/31/09 ALL	4/1/09-3/31/10 ALL	4/1/10-3/31/11 ALL		118 (4/1-9/30/10)			603 (10/1/10-3/31/11)		
713	692	721	NUMBER OF STATEMENTS	14	40	48	108	179	332
%	%	%	ASSETS	%	%	%	%	%	%
8.0	8.9	8.1	Cash & Equivalents	14.3	17.1	15.0	10.1	7.0	5.7
29.8	28.4	30.0	Trade Receivables (net)	13.7	25.9	27.4	30.4	32.6	30.1
40.7	38.1	39.9	Inventory	21.7	32.4	41.5	36.2	41.2	41.9
2.7	2.5	2.3	All Other Current	.1	3.5	.9	1.5	2.0	2.9
81.2	77.9	80.3	Total Current	50.0	78.9	84.8	78.1	82.7	80.6
12.7	15.1	12.5	Fixed Assets (net)	34.3	12.3	12.1	13.9	10.4	12.4
2.2	2.6	2.6	Intangibles (net)	5.8	.7	1.4	2.6	1.9	3.3
3.9	4.5	4.5	All Other Non-Current	9.9	8.1	1.8	5.4	4.9	3.7
100.0	100.0	100.0	Total	100.0	100.0	100.0	100.0	100.0	100.0
			LIABILITIES						
20.6	18.2	18.4	Notes Payable-Short Term	37.3	21.7	19.2	15.0	18.9	17.8
2.1	3.1	2.3	Cur. Mat.-L.T.D.	.8	1.2	5.1	1.5	2.2	2.4
18.9	18.4	21.1	Trade Payables	8.3	22.3	21.5	21.8	24.1	19.6
.2	.2	.2	Income Taxes Payable	.2	.5	.0	.3	.1	.2
8.0	6.4	5.9	All Other Current	2.0	6.0	5.0	4.6	6.0	6.5
49.8	46.3	47.9	Total Current	48.6	51.7	50.8	43.2	51.4	46.6
8.8	9.8	8.3	Long-Term Debt	33.5	9.8	7.9	9.5	6.5	7.7
.2	.4	.3	Deferred Taxes	.1	.1	.0	.4	.2	.4
5.2	5.5	5.8	All Other Non-Current	13.8	7.9	8.1	5.2	6.5	4.6
36.1	38.0	37.8	Net Worth	4.0	30.6	33.3	41.7	35.4	40.7
100.0	100.0	100.0	Total Liabilities & Net Worth	100.0	100.0	100.0	100.0	100.0	100.0
			INCOME DATA						
100.0	100.0	100.0	Net Sales	100.0	100.0	100.0	100.0	100.0	100.0
19.5	19.6	19.5	Gross Profit	43.3	26.2	23.1	23.4	19.0	16.2
14.7	18.1	15.8	Operating Expenses	41.4	23.5	20.6	20.1	15.5	11.9
4.9	1.5	3.7	Operating Profit	1.9	2.8	2.5	3.3	3.5	4.4
.9	.8	.7	All Other Expenses (net)	3.6	.3	.8	.5	.7	.8
3.9	.7	3.0	Profit Before Taxes	-1.8	2.5	1.7	2.8	2.8	3.6
			RATIOS						
2.8	3.1	2.9	Current	4.5	4.2	3.4	3.5	2.7	2.8
1.7	1.7	1.7		1.6	1.5	1.8	1.8	1.5	1.7
1.2	1.2	1.2		.8	1.1	1.3	1.3	1.2	1.3
1.4	1.4	1.3	Quick	2.2	2.2	1.7	1.5	1.2	1.3
(712) .7	.8	.8		.6	.8	.9	1.0	.7	.8
.5	.5	.5		.3	.5	.4	.6	.5	.5
22 16.5	31 11.9	31 11.7	Sales/Receivables	0 UND	23 15.7	19 19.4	31 11.7	32 11.4	32 11.3
32 11.6	39 9.3	42 8.7		18 20.8	44 8.4	39 9.4	43 8.5	42 8.8	42 8.7
43 8.4	52 7.0	52 7.1		38 9.7	61 6.0	56 6.5	54 6.7	53 6.9	50 7.3
30 12.3	39 9.5	40 9.1	Cost of Sales/Inventory	6 56.7	0 770.3	22 16.3	28 12.8	42 8.6	44 8.2
58 6.3	70 5.2	74 4.9		24 15.3	79 4.6	93 3.9	63 5.8	73 5.0	77 4.7
99 3.7	113 3.2	121 3.0		118 3.1	152 2.4	138 2.6	129 2.8	117 3.1	114 3.2
10 37.6	15 24.2	18 20.3	Cost of Sales/Payables	0 UND	16 22.8	22 16.8	15 25.1	20 17.8	18 20.4
21 17.1	27 13.4	31 11.8		9 41.5	33 11.0	35 10.4	35 10.4	37 9.9	26 13.8
39 9.4	44 8.3	49 7.5		38 9.6	56 6.6	60 6.1	63 5.8	50 7.3	42 8.7
5.3	4.0	4.2	Sales/Working Capital	4.7	3.5	4.0	3.7	4.5	3.9
10.9	8.3	8.5		9.4	9.5	8.9	7.5	10.0	8.0
29.2	21.0	21.4		-26.2	34.9	19.5	18.1	23.2	20.9
13.2	8.8	12.9	EBIT/Interest	10.3	8.4	9.1	13.4	14.3	14.0
(656) 5.1	(629) 2.3	(652) 4.7		(10) .1	(30) 2.3	(43) 2.9	(99) 4.3	(167) 3.9	(303) 5.5
1.6	-.7	1.8		-3.8	1.2	1.1	1.4	1.5	2.8
13.2	6.3	10.3	Net Profit + Depr., Dep., Amort./Cur. Mat. L/T/D				3.1	4.2	15.6
(153) 4.3	(161) 1.9	(154) 3.2					(21) 1.6	(32) 1.7	(96) 5.6
1.6	.3	1.2					1.0	.4	1.9
.1	.1	.0	Fixed/Worth	.1	.0	.0	.0	.0	.1
.2	.3	.2		.6	.2	.2	.2	.2	.2
.7	.8	.7		NM	1.6	1.1	.7	.6	.7
.8	.7	.7	Debt/Worth	.1	.8	.5	.6	.9	.7
1.9	1.7	1.9		2.4	3.0	1.9	1.3	2.4	1.7
5.0	4.6	4.3		-26.5	12.9	5.3	4.2	5.5	3.7
57.5	28.1	39.6	% Profit Before Taxes/Tangible Net Worth	18.8	64.5	49.2	30.7	39.2	42.3
(649) 27.1	(627) 8.7	(653) 16.7		(10) 2.1	(34) 13.1	(39) 8.7	(98) 12.4	(164) 17.3	(308) 20.3
8.0	-5.3	5.4		-10.8	2.8	.2	2.3	2.8	9.1
19.9	10.0	12.0	% Profit Before Taxes/Total Assets	10.5	9.4	12.7	10.6	11.9	12.6
8.5	2.8	5.8		2.1	4.0	4.0	5.1	5.4	6.4
1.9	-3.3	1.5		-5.7	.7	.2	.6	.7	3.1
228.3	142.7	209.9	Sales/Net Fixed Assets	63.1	472.6	307.9	232.8	306.6	178.9
42.6	28.4	40.2		7.9	53.0	63.2	47.6	54.1	31.0
16.6	9.0	11.6		3.8	14.8	18.0	11.4	14.0	11.1
4.4	3.2	3.3	Sales/Total Assets	2.8	3.0	3.5	3.5	3.4	3.3
3.1	2.4	2.4		1.8	2.0	2.4	2.4	2.5	2.4
2.2	1.7	1.8		.7	1.6	1.6	1.7	1.9	1.8
.2	.3	.3	% Depr., Dep., Amort./Sales		.3	.2	.4	.3	.2
(577) .6	(575) .9	(575) .8			(24) .5	(34) .6	(79) .9	(138) .8	(292) .7
1.1	1.8	1.5			1.8	1.3	1.8	1.5	1.3
1.0	1.3	1.1	% Officers', Directors' Owners' Comp/Sales		2.5	1.6	1.7	1.1	.5
(269) 2.2	(249) 2.3	(267) 2.1			(18) 6.0	(23) 3.5	(59) 3.1	(79) 1.9	(82) 1.1
4.7	4.7	4.3			10.8	5.4	5.2	3.3	2.2
53073352M	38713803M	39300877M	Net Sales ($)	6549M	88804M	188575M	786998M	2931673M	35298278M
17351241M	16272173M	17072856M	Total Assets ($)	6419M	48077M	82685M	391133M	1295050M	15249492M

M = $ thousand   MM = $ million
See Pages 9 through 22 for Explanation of Ratios and Data

Current Data Sorted by Assets | Comparative Historical Data

						Type of Statement		
		1	3	2	1	Unqualified	10	12
		6	5			Reviewed	12	9
1	3	3				Compiled	11	10
		4				Tax Returns	3	4
2	4	5	10	12		Other	14	15
	8 (4/1-9/30/10)		54 (10/1/10-3/31/11)				4/1/06-3/31/07	4/1/07-3/31/08
0-500M	500M-2MM	2-10MM	10-50MM	50-100MM	100-250MM		ALL	ALL
3	7	19	18	14	1	NUMBER OF STATEMENTS	50	50
%	%	%	%	%	%	ASSETS	%	%
		19.2	7.0	6.9		Cash & Equivalents	8.3	12.4
		32.5	29.5	28.0		Trade Receivables (net)	40.7	31.6
		17.2	25.5	33.1		Inventory	22.1	23.8
		1.8	2.9	3.2		All Other Current	1.9	2.6
		70.6	64.9	71.2		Total Current	73.0	70.4
		14.2	25.6	22.5		Fixed Assets (net)	16.2	22.6
		.3	.9	3.0		Intangibles (net)	2.2	1.8
		14.8	8.7	3.3		All Other Non-Current	8.5	5.3
		100.0	100.0	100.0		Total	100.0	100.0
						LIABILITIES		
		11.9	10.4	9.1		Notes Payable-Short Term	12.1	12.9
		5.3	8.6	.9		Cur. Mat.-L.T.D.	5.1	2.2
		22.7	17.6	15.3		Trade Payables	24.8	20.1
		.0	.0	.4		Income Taxes Payable	.2	.1
		9.8	6.5	5.9		All Other Current	10.9	10.6
		49.7	43.1	31.7		Total Current	53.1	45.9
		5.0	11.6	8.3		Long-Term Debt	11.1	13.2
		.0	.7	.0		Deferred Taxes	.1	.0
		1.6	8.3	4.8		All Other Non-Current	5.3	4.9
		43.7	36.2	55.2		Net Worth	30.3	35.9
		100.0	100.0	100.0		Total Liabilties & Net Worth	100.0	100.0
						INCOME DATA		
		100.0	100.0	100.0		Net Sales	100.0	100.0
		20.9	17.0	19.1		Gross Profit	18.0	21.8
		18.0	13.7	8.9		Operating Expenses	13.7	16.9
		2.8	3.4	10.3		Operating Profit	4.3	4.9
		.1	.2	1.0		All Other Expenses (net)	.4	.9
		2.7	3.2	9.2		Profit Before Taxes	3.9	4.1
						RATIOS		
		3.5	2.9	3.3			2.1	2.5
		1.7	1.8	2.5		Current	1.2	1.5
		.8	1.3	1.4			1.0	1.0
		2.9	1.6	1.6			1.3	1.7
		1.0	1.0	1.2		Quick	.9	.9
		.7	.5	.8			.5	.5
		22 16.2	26 14.1	38 9.5			22 16.3	21 17.7
		35 10.4	34 10.6	43 8.5		Sales/Receivables	32 11.5	33 11.1
		53 6.9	43 8.5	50 7.3			45 8.1	44 8.3
		0 UND	4 85.7	31 11.9			0 UND	0 UND
		11 33.5	39 9.3	54 6.7		Cost of Sales/Inventory	29 12.8	28 12.8
		60 6.1	72 5.0	97 3.8			61 6.0	52 7.0
		19 19.3	13 27.3	21 17.4			10 37.5	11 32.6
		29 12.5	19 19.1	25 14.7		Cost of Sales/Payables	22 16.5	22 16.6
		50 7.3	30 12.2	42 8.7			40 9.1	39 9.3
		6.0	6.2	3.8			8.0	7.4
		15.0	11.2	5.4		Sales/Working Capital	45.8	18.2
		-48.1	NM	8.9			-536.0	NM
		26.5	19.4	116.4			13.4	35.9
		(15) 2.7	(17) 8.2	(13) 13.3		EBIT/Interest	(47) 4.3	(49) 6.5
		.8	.5	7.8			1.7	1.9
						Net Profit + Depr., Dep., Amort./Cur. Mat. L/T/D	5.4	
							(12) 3.0	
							.9	
		.0	.0	.1			.1	.0
		.3	.5	.1		Fixed/Worth	.3	.3
		1.1	1.1	.8			1.7	.8
		.4	.6	.3			1.0	.7
		1.4	1.1	.8		Debt/Worth	2.9	2.0
		17.9	12.4	2.3			11.0	4.5
		46.5	53.4	50.4			55.7	50.3
		(17) 24.6	(17) 21.6	22.9		% Profit Before Taxes/Tangible Net Worth	(45) 29.8	(47) 25.7
		1.4	2.8	14.0			14.6	15.1
		21.1	19.0	20.7			17.3	16.8
		11.1	10.9	11.9		% Profit Before Taxes/Total Assets	7.2	9.1
		-.3	-.3	8.9			2.5	3.3
		770.8	999.8	75.4			336.9	765.3
		237.1	21.8	35.4		Sales/Net Fixed Assets	67.4	50.8
		7.2	4.2	4.6			11.8	5.7
		4.3	5.0	2.7			7.0	5.0
		3.2	2.5	2.3		Sales/Total Assets	3.7	3.4
		1.3	1.0	1.5			2.1	1.7
		.1	1.1	.4			.1	.1
		(16) .2	(12) 2.4	(12) .8		% Depr., Dep., Amort./Sales	(40) .4	(39) .8
		3.0	7.9	1.6			1.7	5.1
							.6	1.0
						% Officers', Directors' Owners' Comp/Sales	(10) 1.4	(11) 1.6
							3.0	4.1
7501M	38352M	281628M	1145445M	2371696M	108841M	Net Sales ($)	3272445M	4610038M
785M	8392M	89323M	430310M	1060947M	153480M	Total Assets ($)	947670M	1153000M

© RMA 2011

M = $ thousand   MM = $ million
See Pages 9 through 22 for Explanation of Ratios and Data

Comparative Historical Data | Current Data Sorted by Sales

	4/1/08-3/31/09 ALL	4/1/09-3/31/10 ALL	4/1/10-3/31/11 ALL	0-1MM	1-3MM	3-5MM	5-10MM	10-25MM	25MM & OVER
Type of Statement									
Unqualified	9	10	7		1		1	1	6
Reviewed	13	14	11		2		2	3	6
Compiled	5	5	7		1			2	
Tax Returns	3	7	4		3	1	1	2	
Other	20	20	33	1		2	3	5	19
					8 (4/1-9/30/10)		54 (10/1/10-3/31/11)		
NUMBER OF STATEMENTS	50	56	62	1	7	3	7	13	31
	%	%	%	%	%	%	%	%	%
ASSETS									
Cash & Equivalents	9.2	14.5	12.7					8.5	8.9
Trade Receivables (net)	33.1	29.2	30.5					25.0	36.2
Inventory	23.6	24.0	22.5					17.3	26.9
All Other Current	7.4	5.7	3.5					7.8	3.1
Total Current	73.3	73.4	69.3					58.6	75.1
Fixed Assets (net)	17.4	16.5	19.6					29.0	18.0
Intangibles (net)	2.5	2.5	2.1					.4	2.2
All Other Non-Current	6.8	7.6	9.0					12.0	4.8
Total	100.0	100.0	100.0					100.0	100.0
LIABILITIES									
Notes Payable-Short Term	13.7	14.5	12.4					15.4	9.2
Cur. Mat.-L.T.D.	1.5	3.5	4.9					10.1	2.1
Trade Payables	25.2	16.0	19.3					21.5	20.5
Income Taxes Payable	.3	.5	.1					.0	.2
All Other Current	14.1	11.3	8.6					18.7	5.9
Total Current	54.9	45.8	45.4					65.7	37.8
Long-Term Debt	7.3	14.9	11.2					9.0	9.3
Deferred Taxes	.1	.0	.2					.0	.4
All Other Non-Current	4.3	3.5	4.3					1.1	5.9
Net Worth	33.3	35.7	39.0					24.2	46.5
Total Liabilities & Net Worth	100.0	100.0	100.0					100.0	100.0
INCOME DATA									
Net Sales	100.0	100.0	100.0					100.0	100.0
Gross Profit	12.4	18.6	21.7					23.6	13.1
Operating Expenses	8.2	13.0	17.1					20.3	7.7
Operating Profit	4.2	5.6	4.6					3.3	5.5
All Other Expenses (net)	.6	1.7	.5					.4	.5
Profit Before Taxes	3.6	3.9	4.2					2.9	5.0
RATIOS									
	2.4	3.0	3.2					1.8	3.2
Current	1.3	1.7	1.7					1.0	1.9
	1.0	1.1	1.0					.5	1.5
	1.3	1.7	1.6					1.3	1.6
Quick	1.0	1.0	1.0					.7	1.3
	.4	.6	.6					.2	.8
	18 20.4	19 18.8	23 15.9					11 33.5	33 11.1
Sales/Receivables	26 14.1	33 11.1	36 10.1					32 11.3	39 9.3
	43 8.5	46 8.0	47 7.7					45 8.1	47 7.7
	0 UND	0 UND	0 UND					0 UND	4 81.6
Cost of Sales/Inventory	15 24.4	35 10.5	35 10.3					26 13.9	46 8.0
	56 6.6	72 5.0	72 5.1					56 6.5	71 5.1
	10 36.3	8 44.1	15 23.7					11 34.0	18 19.8
Cost of Sales/Payables	23 16.1	22 16.8	24 15.0					29 12.5	23 15.7
	39 9.2	35 10.3	42 8.8					53 6.9	38 9.7
	7.6	4.9	5.7					6.5	5.9
Sales/Working Capital	23.6	10.8	9.6					999.8	7.8
	926.7	43.0	313.8					-8.7	17.3
	28.5	20.8	25.1					13.3	34.5
EBIT/Interest	(47) 6.8	(52) 6.4	(53) 8.2					(12) 1.9	(28) 13.3
	1.4	1.6	1.0					-.4	3.2
		10.0	17.0						
Net Profit + Depr., Dep., Amort./Cur. Mat. L/T/D		(13) 2.3	(13) 3.1						
		-.7	.3						
	.0	.0	.0					.1	.0
Fixed/Worth	.3	.3	.2					1.1	.1
	1.5	1.4	1.1					NM	.8
	.9	.7	.4					.4	.6
Debt/Worth	2.9	1.9	1.4					4.5	.9
	6.4	8.3	5.6					NM	2.6
	61.2	37.9	43.3					52.7	43.6
% Profit Before Taxes/Tangible Net Worth	(47) 28.5	(48) 19.2	(56) 22.2					(10) 28.6	29.3
	4.0	4.3	5.1					3.3	14.9
	21.3	15.6	20.0					21.2	19.8
% Profit Before Taxes/Total Assets	6.8	7.0	11.1					3.1	12.4
	.7	1.4	.1					-1.6	9.5
	986.7	543.9	477.5					999.8	434.5
Sales/Net Fixed Assets	45.8	45.0	39.6					28.2	39.6
	9.8	9.4	6.5					3.1	6.7
	6.4	4.7	4.2					4.9	4.1
Sales/Total Assets	3.6	2.9	2.8					3.2	2.6
	2.4	1.6	1.4					1.1	1.7
	.1	.1	.1					.1	.1
% Depr., Dep., Amort./Sales	(39) .7	(40) .9	(46) .8					(10) .8	(24) .8
	1.7	4.3	2.7					14.2	2.2
	.3	.8	1.1						
% Officers', Directors' Owners' Comp/Sales	(12) 1.1	(17) 1.5	(15) 3.5						
	2.4	3.1	5.5						
Net Sales ($)	5939018M	3936119M	3953463M	549M	13163M	13653M	53340M	208995M	3663763M
Total Assets ($)	1312159M	1533598M	1743237M	58M	12387M	2906M	49879M	193804M	1484203M

M = $ thousand   MM = $ million
See Pages 9 through 22 for Explanation of Ratios and Data

Current Data Sorted by Assets   Comparative Historical Data

						Type of Statement		
1		10	34	15	10	Unqualified	88	69
1	14	87	36	3	3	Reviewed	154	129
3	31	43	11	1	1	Compiled	109	104
18	47	40	5			Tax Returns	52	62
14	41	83	63	24	7	Other	184	170
	104 (4/1-9/30/10)		542 (10/1/10-3/31/11)				4/1/06-3/31/07 ALL	4/1/07-3/31/08 ALL
0-500M	500M-2MM	2-10MM	10-50MM	50-100MM	100-250MM	NUMBER OF STATEMENTS	587	534
37	133	263	149	43	21			
%	%	%	%	%	%	ASSETS	%	%
19.9	10.5	8.2	7.3	6.5	6.3	Cash & Equivalents	7.0	7.4
26.6	35.6	38.6	36.9	34.6	35.5	Trade Receivables (net)	39.6	37.4
26.7	34.2	32.9	34.6	27.7	30.4	Inventory	33.1	33.5
4.0	2.7	2.2	2.7	3.6	4.4	All Other Current	2.1	2.2
77.2	83.0	81.9	81.5	72.3	76.6	Total Current	81.7	80.6
10.7	8.7	10.4	9.2	15.6	12.0	Fixed Assets (net)	10.5	11.8
3.7	2.6	2.6	3.8	4.8	7.4	Intangibles (net)	3.0	3.2
8.4	5.7	5.1	5.5	7.2	4.0	All Other Non-Current	4.8	4.5
100.0	100.0	100.0	100.0	100.0	100.0	Total	100.0	100.0
						LIABILITIES		
17.1	11.6	13.9	14.8	9.3	10.8	Notes Payable-Short Term	15.8	14.2
2.6	1.2	2.1	1.3	1.3	1.7	Cur. Mat.-L.T.D.	2.4	2.4
16.0	23.9	23.0	21.5	15.4	21.8	Trade Payables	24.1	23.6
.0	.2	.3	.1	.1	.5	Income Taxes Payable	.3	.4
11.1	7.6	9.1	7.4	9.8	10.2	All Other Current	9.8	9.1
46.9	44.5	48.4	45.1	35.9	45.0	Total Current	52.4	49.6
8.9	10.1	7.5	5.2	10.2	10.0	Long-Term Debt	8.4	10.0
.0	.1	.3	.2	.1	.6	Deferred Taxes	.1	.1
11.3	4.6	4.2	4.1	3.6	4.7	All Other Non-Current	4.4	5.5
32.9	40.7	39.7	45.4	50.2	39.8	Net Worth	34.7	34.9
100.0	100.0	100.0	100.0	100.0	100.0	Total Liabilities & Net Worth	100.0	100.0
						INCOME DATA		
100.0	100.0	100.0	100.0	100.0	100.0	Net Sales	100.0	100.0
40.7	31.9	29.6	24.7	24.3	22.7	Gross Profit	28.2	28.9
36.4	28.4	25.9	20.8	19.5	19.3	Operating Expenses	23.5	24.2
4.2	3.5	3.7	3.9	4.7	3.4	Operating Profit	4.7	4.7
.5	.3	.5	.3	.4	.8	All Other Expenses (net)	.5	.5
3.7	3.2	3.2	3.7	4.4	2.6	Profit Before Taxes	4.3	4.2
						RATIOS		
5.6	3.1	2.6	2.7	3.6	2.6		2.3	2.5
2.0	1.9	1.8	1.8	2.1	1.8	Current	1.6	1.7
1.0	1.4	1.3	1.4	1.6	1.3		1.2	1.3
3.6	1.7	1.6	1.5	1.9	1.7		1.3	1.4
1.2	1.0	1.0	.9	1.1	.9	Quick	.9	.9
.6	.7	.6	.7	.9	.6		.6	.6

											Sales/Receivables				
4	92.4	30	12.3	38	9.6	43	8.5	44	8.3	46	8.0		37	9.8	34	10.7
24	15.4	39	9.5	49	7.5	52	7.0	52	7.0	50	7.3	Sales/Receivables	48	7.6	46	7.9
51	7.2	56	6.6	61	6.0	63	5.8	64	5.7	61	6.0		58	6.2	59	6.2
0	UND	25	14.8	31	11.8	44	8.3	37	9.9	40	9.2		32	11.3	34	10.9
16	23.0	59	6.1	58	6.3	63	5.8	57	6.4	61	6.0	Cost of Sales/Inventory	52	7.0	55	6.6
80	4.6	111	3.3	96	3.8	99	3.7	92	4.0	84	4.3		85	4.3	92	4.0
1	415.5	20	18.2	23	15.9	29	12.4	21	17.1	29	12.7		24	14.9	24	14.9
23	15.7	36	10.3	37	9.8	39	9.4	32	11.4	36	10.1	Cost of Sales/Payables	36	10.1	36	10.0
39	9.4	52	7.0	58	6.3	51	7.2	42	8.7	59	6.2		49	7.4	53	6.9

									Ratio		
5.1		4.7		4.9		4.8		3.8		4.9	
7.4		8.1		8.2		7.5		6.9		9.0	Sales/Working Capital
NM		15.8		17.5		12.0		10.3		15.8	

												Ratio			
	8.1		18.6		17.9		24.8		53.9		15.5		15.1		13.9
(24)	1.1	(106)	4.5	(233)	5.5	(134)	7.7	(38)	11.4	(19)	6.7	EBIT/Interest	(523)	5.2	(481)	5.1
	-2.8		1.3		2.0		3.1		2.9		4.1		2.2		1.8

												Ratio			
			5.2		6.1		17.2		38.2				14.5		14.3
		(12)	3.4	(52)	3.0	(43)	4.6	(14)	13.5			Net Profit + Depr., Dep., Amort./Cur. Mat. L/T/D	(155)	5.4	(156)	4.7
			.3		1.0		2.1		1.7				1.9		1.8

						Ratio		
.0	.0	.1	.1	.1	.1		.1	.1
.1	.1	.2	.2	.3	.4	Fixed/Worth	.2	.2
NM	.4	.5	.4	.6	.5		.6	.6
.5	.7	.8	.7	.4	.9		.9	.9
2.0	1.3	1.6	1.4	1.3	1.7	Debt/Worth	1.9	1.8
-31.0	4.5	3.6	2.7	2.2	7.4		5.1	4.3

												Ratio			
	81.8		52.6		36.7		31.4		26.8		57.5		54.1		48.2
(27)	16.5	(121)	19.7	(244)	18.0	(143)	14.1	(40)	16.2	(19)	23.7	% Profit Before Taxes/Tangible Net Worth	(527)	30.9	(486)	26.1
	-8.9		2.4		3.4		5.6		8.5		9.7		13.7		8.9

						% Profit Before Taxes/Total Assets		
24.4	16.5	14.3	11.9	11.3	12.6		18.9	17.1
3.8	5.0	5.9	6.3	8.0	5.8	% Profit Before Taxes/Total Assets	9.5	9.0
-4.4	1.0	1.5	2.4	3.7	3.6		3.4	2.3

						Sales/Net Fixed Assets		
UND	583.5	140.6	79.6	52.4	117.5		117.0	95.1
76.8	78.2	51.7	40.3	17.7	49.3	Sales/Net Fixed Assets	46.8	41.1
27.0	29.6	21.9	17.9	8.7	8.9		21.1	19.0

						Sales/Total Assets		
6.2	4.1	3.4	3.1	3.0	3.2		3.7	3.6
3.6	3.1	2.7	2.7	2.3	2.4	Sales/Total Assets	3.0	2.9
2.5	2.2	2.1	2.0	1.7	1.8		2.3	2.2

												Ratio			
	.5		.2		.2		.3		.5		.3		.3		.3
(16)	1.0	(77)	.5	(213)	.5	(136)	.5	(39)	.8	(18)	.5	% Depr., Dep., Amort./Sales	(493)	.5	(437)	.6
	1.4		1.2		1.1		.9		2.0		1.4		1.0		1.1

											Ratio			
	3.6		2.1		1.7		.8					1.7		1.7
(24)	5.9	(80)	4.2	(114)	3.2	(36)	1.3				% Officers', Directors' Owners' Comp/Sales	(213)	3.2	(216)	3.5
	12.0		8.0		5.9		2.8					6.2		6.0

43254M	581841M	3858318M	8086802M	7665597M	8415230M	Net Sales ($)	25229382M	26241237M
10281M	163119M	1369059M	3282452M	3194928M	3310072M	Total Assets ($)	8711042M	9225007M

Comparative Historical Data				Current Data Sorted by Sales					
			Type of Statement						
75	61	70	Unqualified	1			1	10	58
135	147	144	Reviewed	1	5	10	18	60	50
100	90	90	Compiled	4	14	14	17	30	11
83	86	110	Tax Returns	8	30	19	29	17	7
203	219	232	Other	7	27	16	29	58	95
4/1/08-3/31/09 ALL	**4/1/09-3/31/10 ALL**	**4/1/10-3/31/11 ALL**		**104 (4/1-9/30/10)**			**542 (10/1/10-3/31/11)**		
				0-1MM	**1-3MM**	**3-5MM**	**5-10MM**	**10-25MM**	**25MM & OVER**
596	603	646	**NUMBER OF STATEMENTS**	21	76	59	94	175	221
%	%	%	**ASSETS**	%	%	%	%	%	%
8.3	9.1	9.0	Cash & Equivalents	19.2	12.1	9.9	10.1	8.5	6.6
35.2	34.9	36.5	Trade Receivables (net)	23.5	28.6	33.1	38.1	39.4	38.4
34.7	33.7	32.8	Inventory	32.2	34.7	33.6	31.1	32.5	32.9
2.3	2.5	2.7	All Other Current	5.1	3.3	1.1	2.3	2.4	3.1
80.5	80.2	80.9	Total Current	80.0	78.7	77.7	81.5	82.9	80.9
11.0	11.2	10.2	Fixed Assets (net)	12.5	9.7	11.3	9.8	9.7	10.4
2.9	3.3	3.2	Intangibles (net)	3.1	3.6	4.9	3.1	1.7	3.9
5.6	5.3	5.6	All Other Non-Current	4.4	8.0	6.1	5.5	5.7	4.8
100.0	100.0	100.0	Total	100.0	100.0	100.0	100.0	100.0	100.0
			LIABILITIES						
14.9	14.3	13.4	Notes Payable-Short Term	16.8	13.3	12.9	11.6	14.1	13.5
2.1	2.4	1.7	Cur. Mat.-L.T.D.	4.8	2.0	1.9	1.6	1.5	1.4
21.6	21.1	21.9	Trade Payables	10.2	20.6	18.6	21.9	25.1	21.8
.1	.1	.2	Income Taxes Payable	.1	.3	.2	.2	.3	.1
8.9	8.4	8.6	All Other Current	5.2	10.5	7.2	9.5	8.2	8.5
47.7	46.2	45.8	Total Current	37.0	46.7	40.8	44.7	49.3	45.4
9.7	7.9	7.8	Long-Term Debt	15.1	9.4	10.9	9.5	6.3	6.3
.2	.2	.2	Deferred Taxes	.0	.1	.0	.1	.3	.2
4.2	5.1	4.6	All Other Non-Current	4.1	9.5	3.5	2.7	4.7	4.1
38.2	40.7	41.5	Net Worth	43.7	34.4	44.8	42.9	39.4	44.0
100.0	100.0	100.0	Total Liabilties & Net Worth	100.0	100.0	100.0	100.0	100.0	100.0
			INCOME DATA						
100.0	100.0	100.0	Net Sales	100.0	100.0	100.0	100.0	100.0	100.0
28.9	29.5	29.0	Gross Profit	43.1	37.2	32.0	31.3	28.3	23.6
25.1	26.6	25.2	Operating Expenses	37.2	33.8	28.9	27.6	24.8	19.5
3.8	2.9	3.8	Operating Profit	5.9	3.4	3.1	3.7	3.6	4.1
.4	.4	.4	All Other Expenses (net)	1.8	.6	-.1	.4	.3	.4
3.3	2.5	3.4	Profit Before Taxes	4.2	2.8	3.3	3.3	3.3	3.7
			RATIOS						
2.6	2.8	2.8		7.2	3.7	2.9	3.4	2.4	2.6
1.7	1.8	1.8	Current	2.9	2.0	1.9	1.8	1.7	1.8
1.3	1.3	1.3		1.3	1.2	1.4	1.3	1.3	1.4
1.4	1.6	1.7		4.9	2.2	1.8	1.8	1.5	1.6
.9	.9	1.0	Quick	1.3	1.0	1.1	1.0	1.0	1.0
.6	.6	.7		.6	.5	.7	.7	.7	.7
32 11.3	**35** 10.3	**36** 10.1		**13** 27.4	**23** 15.6	**36** 10.2	**34** 10.7	**38** 9.5	**42** 8.7
40 9.0	**47** 7.8	**48** 7.5	Sales/Receivables	**37** 9.8	**39** 9.3	**42** 8.7	**45** 8.1	**49** 7.4	**51** 7.2
53 6.8	**59** 6.1	**61** 6.0		**71** 5.2	**58** 6.3	**58** 6.3	**59** 6.2	**61** 6.0	**62** 5.9
32 11.3	**36** 10.2	**31** 11.7		**0** UND	**20** 18.3	**17** 21.0	**25** 14.8	**33** 11.1	**41** 8.8
57 6.5	**60** 6.1	**59** 6.2	Cost of Sales/Inventory	**73** 5.0	**86** 4.3	**64** 5.7	**52** 7.0	**58** 6.3	**57** 6.4
90 4.0	**105** 3.5	**97** 3.8		**230** 1.6	**127** 2.9	**116** 3.1	**92** 4.0	**91** 4.0	**81** 4.5
20 18.3	**23** 15.7	**23** 15.6		**13** 28.6	**16** 22.4	**19** 19.3	**20** 18.6	**24** 15.1	**28** 12.8
31 11.7	**36** 10.2	**37** 10.0	Cost of Sales/Payables	**29** 12.4	**41** 9.0	**34** 10.8	**35** 10.5	**38** 9.7	**37** 9.9
47 7.7	**50** 7.3	**52** 7.0		**39** 9.4	**71** 5.2	**47** 7.7	**51** 7.2	**61** 6.0	**47** 7.7
5.5	4.9	4.8		2.4	3.7	4.8	4.9	4.9	5.1
9.1	7.8	7.9	Sales/Working Capital	5.7	6.9	7.0	9.1	8.2	8.0
18.4	16.0	14.8		10.7	23.3	12.6	15.9	17.9	12.4
16.3	12.9	19.9		6.5	14.8	26.8	13.9	17.3	32.5
(531) 5.4	(536) 3.7	(554) 6.0	EBIT/Interest	(16) .3	(55) 4.2	(54) 5.4	(72) 4.8	(157) 5.7	(200) 8.3
1.7	1.0	2.0		-3.8	.6	.5	1.8	2.3	3.3
12.6	6.4	10.2				4.6	3.0	6.6	19.4
(154) 4.2	(128) 2.5	(129) 3.8	Net Profit + Depr., Dep., Amort./Cur. Mat. L/T/D			(11) 2.9	(12) 1.7	(39) 4.0	(64) 5.3
1.9	.9	1.6				.5	.7	1.8	2.0
.1	.1	.1		.0	.0	.0	.0	.1	.1
.2	.2	.2	Fixed/Worth	.1	.1	.1	.2	.2	.2
.6	.5	.5		11.1	.5	.6	.5	.5	.5
.7	.6	.7		.2	.6	.6	.6	.8	.7
1.6	1.6	1.5	Debt/Worth	1.0	1.9	1.2	1.5	1.5	1.5
4.1	3.6	3.5		23.6	9.2	3.2	4.1	3.3	2.9
43.8	30.8	39.4		76.4	49.8	42.4	42.1	36.6	34.0
(544) 23.0	(556) 10.5	(594) 16.7	% Profit Before Taxes/Tangible Net Worth	(17) 14.6	(62) 17.7	(54) 16.9	(86) 16.4	(165) 19.1	(210) 16.2
6.9	.7	4.0		-11.0	1.7	-1.4	4.6	3.2	7.3
16.0	11.2	14.0		14.1	17.2	15.4	15.7	13.7	12.4
7.5	3.7	5.9	% Profit Before Taxes/Total Assets	3.7	4.9	4.3	5.5	6.1	6.8
1.6	.1	1.6		-5.2	-1.6	.0	1.6	1.7	2.8
115.3	114.0	148.5		UND	724.0	177.8	208.1	137.3	86.4
47.0	43.4	50.4	Sales/Net Fixed Assets	64.2	80.5	49.9	52.6	50.8	42.8
20.2	17.7	19.1		11.3	32.3	20.9	23.2	20.5	16.7
3.8	3.5	3.4		3.0	3.9	3.4	3.7	3.4	3.3
3.0	2.7	2.7	Sales/Total Assets	1.9	2.5	2.6	2.9	2.8	2.7
2.3	2.0	2.1		1.1	2.0	2.0	2.1	2.1	2.1
.3	.4	.3		.7	.3	.2	.2	.3	.3
(476) .6	(485) .6	(499) .6	% Depr., Dep., Amort./Sales	(10) 1.3	(41) .6	(40) .5	(68) .7	(141) .6	(199) .6
1.0	1.2	1.1		4.1	1.2	1.1	1.3	1.0	1.0
1.7	1.8	1.6		7.0	2.6	2.6	1.8	1.4	.7
(224) 3.4	(239) 3.5	(264) 3.3	% Officers', Directors' Owners' Comp/Sales	(11) 12.5	(49) 5.1	(36) 4.6	(49) 3.3	(73) 2.4	(46) 1.5
6.9	7.4	6.3		24.5	8.8	7.4	5.6	4.8	3.1
29206552M	**27561436M**	**28651042M**	Net Sales ($)	**11858M**	**150074M**	**239289M**	**663902M**	**2861056M**	**24724863M**
10307329M	**10855210M**	**11329911M**	Total Assets ($)	**8435M**	**67548M**	**99991M**	**261228M**	**1136555M**	**9756154M**

M = $ thousand MM = $ million

See Pages 9 through 22 for Explanation of Ratios and Data

Current Data Sorted by Assets / Comparative Historical Data

0-500M	500M-2MM	2-10MM	10-50MM	50-100MM	100-250MM	Type of Statement	4/1/06-3/31/07 ALL	4/1/07-3/31/08 ALL
		2	11	5	3	Unqualified	27	22
	4	21	9		1	Reviewed	27	26
1	7	9	1		1	Compiled	20	16
1	11	7	1			Tax Returns	11	12
1	9	21	19	7	2	Other	50	51
	27 (4/1-9/30/10)		126 (10/1/10-3/31/11)				135	127
3	31	60	41	13	5	**NUMBER OF STATEMENTS**	135	127
%	%	%	%	%	%	**ASSETS**	%	%
	8.9	10.9	10.2	4.9		Cash & Equivalents	8.2	6.5
	26.6	30.8	22.5	34.0		Trade Receivables (net)	34.7	32.0
	47.8	40.6	45.8	36.2		Inventory	40.5	44.1
	1.6	2.7	3.0	3.4		All Other Current	1.9	1.9
	84.9	84.9	81.5	78.4		Total Current	85.4	84.4
	10.2	8.2	10.0	7.3		Fixed Assets (net)	7.7	8.1
	.9	2.2	2.9	8.5		Intangibles (net)	2.6	4.7
	4.0	4.6	5.6	5.8		All Other Non-Current	4.3	2.8
	100.0	100.0	100.0	100.0		Total	100.0	100.0
						LIABILITIES		
	22.1	15.6	9.1	11.8		Notes Payable-Short Term	17.9	17.0
	1.9	2.0	1.0	3.2		Cur. Mat.-L.T.D.	1.7	1.4
	24.6	24.0	20.8	24.4		Trade Payables	24.4	24.9
	.1	.1	.2	.1		Income Taxes Payable	.2	.3
	9.0	10.1	11.0	8.9		All Other Current	10.9	10.4
	57.6	51.6	42.1	48.3		Total Current	55.0	53.9
	11.7	4.1	4.9	9.7		Long-Term Debt	5.6	6.3
	.1	.1	.1	.3		Deferred Taxes	.1	.1
	4.0	6.5	6.9	7.9		All Other Non-Current	2.9	3.6
	26.7	37.6	46.0	33.8		Net Worth	36.3	36.0
	100.0	100.0	100.0	100.0		Total Liabilities & Net Worth	100.0	100.0
						INCOME DATA		
	100.0	100.0	100.0	100.0		Net Sales	100.0	100.0
	29.5	24.1	22.6	16.9		Gross Profit	23.6	25.4
	27.8	22.5	19.5	13.5		Operating Expenses	20.6	22.0
	1.7	1.6	3.1	3.3		Operating Profit	3.0	3.4
	.8	.1	-.1	.5		All Other Expenses (net)	.4	1.0
	.9	1.5	3.2	2.9		Profit Before Taxes	2.6	2.4
						RATIOS		
	2.3	2.3	2.9	2.2		Current	2.2	2.2
	1.7	1.6	2.0	1.6			1.5	1.6
	1.1	1.2	1.5	1.4			1.2	1.2
	1.0	1.6	1.2	1.2		Quick	1.2	1.1
	.7	.8	.8	.8			.7	.7
	.4	.4	.4	.5			.5	.5
	13 27.3	20 18.2	18 20.1	28 13.1		Sales/Receivables	28 12.8	26 14.3
	22 16.6	30 12.3	30 12.4	36 10.2			37 9.9	34 10.6
	45 8.0	45 8.1	36 10.0	59 6.2			47 7.8	47 7.8
	35 10.5	31 11.7	60 6.0	28 12.9		Cost of Sales/Inventory	40 9.1	46 7.9
	75 4.9	66 5.5	74 5.0	55 6.7			62 5.9	69 5.3
	105 3.5	101 3.6	102 3.6	72 5.1			91 4.0	102 3.6
	12 30.7	17 22.1	16 23.4	22 16.4		Cost of Sales/Payables	19 18.8	19 19.7
	35 10.5	29 12.5	27 13.6	32 11.5			32 11.5	32 11.3
	59 6.2	47 7.7	45 8.0	44 8.4			48 7.6	50 7.3
	5.8	4.9	5.3	6.6		Sales/Working Capital	6.5	6.6
	11.6	11.7	8.4	10.8			10.6	10.5
	113.0	22.1	13.2	16.4			22.1	22.4
	7.6	17.9	23.6	21.7		EBIT/Interest	10.7	8.0
	(26) 1.5	(54) 3.2	(38) 6.9	(12) 13.3			(121) 3.4	(111) 3.7
	-1.2	1.6	1.2	2.1			1.6	1.3
			45.6			Net Profit + Depr., Dep., Amort./Cur. Mat. L/T/D	9.7	14.1
			(10) 14.4				(29) 4.3	(23) 7.0
			1.0				1.1	1.1
	.0	.1	.1	.2		Fixed/Worth	.1	.1
	.1	.1	.1	.3			.2	.2
	1.0	.4	.3	.5			.4	.5
	.8	.8	.5	1.8		Debt/Worth	.9	.9
	1.5	1.7	.9	2.4			2.0	2.3
	13.6	3.9	2.8	3.9			4.7	5.0
	31.4	29.0	31.8	39.4		% Profit Before Taxes/Tangible Net Worth	53.6	49.7
	(25) 18.7	(56) 14.5	(39) 21.1	(11) 28.5			(128) 18.3	(115) 23.0
	-1.1	4.1	1.2	16.7			7.9	6.9
	9.2	13.1	16.6	10.7		% Profit Before Taxes/Total Assets	15.0	13.7
	2.0	4.2	8.5	6.3			5.8	7.2
	-7.7	1.4	.2	5.3			2.0	1.2
	435.6	152.2	98.3	116.2		Sales/Net Fixed Assets	171.8	178.3
	121.7	63.0	44.6	58.5			60.3	63.8
	29.5	27.0	22.9	17.3			29.7	25.7
	5.1	3.9	3.7	4.0		Sales/Total Assets	4.0	4.0
	3.8	3.2	3.1	2.8			3.1	3.0
	2.8	2.5	2.4	2.2			2.5	2.3
	.1	.2	.3	.2		% Depr., Dep., Amort./Sales	.2	.2
	(21) .4	(51) .4	(38) .5	(10) .2			(115) .4	(105) .4
	1.1	.9	1.1	.6			.8	.9
	1.6	.9	.6			% Officers', Directors' Owners' Comp/Sales	1.4	1.3
	(18) 3.0	(23) 1.8	(10) 1.0				(45) 2.2	(41) 2.6
	6.1	2.9	2.8				4.4	4.1
3745M	166057M	1178558M	3061281M	2944940M	3051715M	Net Sales ($)	7616253M	6973602M
775M	40575M	343918M	911561M	937664M	710159M	Total Assets ($)	2493762M	2711124M

M = $ thousand   MM = $ million
See Pages 9 through 22 for Explanation of Ratios and Data

Comparative Historical Data | | | | Current Data Sorted by Sales

			Type of Statement	0-1MM	1-3MM	3-5MM	5-10MM	10-25MM	25MM & OVER
26	19	21	Unqualified				1	2	19
31	25	34	Reviewed			3	4	15	15
20	18	19	Compiled	1	2	3	8	8	1
20	22	20	Tax Returns	1	4	1	8	3	1
44	61	59	Other	1	5	2	9	9	33
4/1/08-3/31/09 ALL	4/1/09-3/31/10 ALL	4/1/10-3/31/11 ALL			27 (4/1-9/30/10)		126 (10/1/10-3/31/11)		
141	145	153	**NUMBER OF STATEMENTS**	3	11	9	22	37	71
%	%	%	**ASSETS**	%	%	%	%	%	%
7.4	9.9	9.4	Cash & Equivalents		8.9		6.4	11.4	9.2
29.4	31.4	27.7	Trade Receivables (net)		24.9		25.2	29.6	28.8
42.4	40.6	43.5	Inventory		46.1		42.5	44.1	41.6
3.0	2.4	2.5	All Other Current		1.1		1.4	2.2	3.3
82.1	84.2	83.1	Total Current		81.0		75.5	87.3	82.9
10.0	8.9	9.1	Fixed Assets (net)		3.9		13.6	8.5	9.3
3.8	3.0	2.9	Intangibles (net)		.1		5.1	.6	3.6
4.1	3.9	4.8	All Other Non-Current		15.0		5.8	3.6	4.2
100.0	100.0	100.0	Total		100.0		100.0	100.0	100.0
			LIABILITIES						
18.2	16.5	14.8	Notes Payable-Short Term		32.9		16.5	16.2	10.0
2.4	2.0	1.8	Cur. Mat.-L.T.D.		2.2		1.2	1.2	2.4
23.1	23.4	24.3	Trade Payables		28.3		21.8	23.9	24.8
.2	.2	.1	Income Taxes Payable		.0		.1	.0	.2
10.1	9.4	11.4	All Other Current		8.8		13.1	7.4	11.0
54.0	51.6	52.4	Total Current		72.2		52.8	48.7	48.4
7.8	6.1	7.3	Long-Term Debt		13.4		5.7	5.2	6.0
.2	.0	.1	Deferred Taxes		.2		.1	.2	.1
3.1	6.7	6.1	All Other Non-Current		4.4		9.7	6.8	5.3
34.9	35.6	34.1	Net Worth		9.8		31.7	39.2	40.3
100.0	100.0	100.0	Total Liabilities & Net Worth		100.0		100.0	100.0	100.0
			INCOME DATA						
100.0	100.0	100.0	Net Sales		100.0		100.0	100.0	100.0
23.8	23.5	24.5	Gross Profit		29.8		29.6	25.1	20.8
22.1	21.6	22.1	Operating Expenses		29.5		28.6	23.1	17.5
1.7	1.9	2.3	Operating Profit		.3		.9	2.0	3.2
.9	.4	.2	All Other Expenses (net)		-.3		1.0	.3	.1
.8	1.5	2.1	Profit Before Taxes		.7		-.1	1.7	3.1
			RATIOS						
2.6	2.6	2.5			2.3		1.8	2.8	2.5
1.6	1.6	1.7	Current		1.5		1.5	1.7	1.8
1.2	1.2	1.3			.8		1.1	1.3	1.4
1.1	1.5	1.2			1.0		.9	1.7	1.2
.7	.8	.8	Quick		.5		.7	.8	.8
.4	.6	.4			.3		.3		.5
21 17.2	23 15.9	20 18.6			13 27.3		17 21.1	20 17.9	21 17.7
32 11.6	31 11.9	30 12.4	Sales/Receivables		31 11.8		22 16.3	34 10.9	30 12.2
47 7.8	49 7.5	45 8.1			52 7.0		37 10.0	46 7.9	43 8.4
41 8.9	39 9.3	41 9.0			35 10.4		34 10.6	40 9.2	35 10.6
60 6.1	62 5.9	67 5.4	Cost of Sales/Inventory		82 4.5		70 5.2	71 5.2	62 5.9
106 3.4	96 3.8	102 3.6			141 2.6		116 3.1	103 3.5	80 4.6
18 20.8	17 21.9	16 22.4			12 29.4	8 44.5	20 18.0	16 22.4	
30 11.6	31 11.7	30 12.2	Cost of Sales/Payables		41 8.9	23 15.9	32 11.3	29 12.6	
46 8.0	46 7.9	50 7.4			64 5.7	45 7.2	51 7.2	41 9.0	
5.7	5.5	5.4			3.6		6.8	4.6	6.5
11.4	9.7	10.7	Sales/Working Capital		10.8		14.4	8.1	10.6
27.8	20.7	21.2			-21.9		71.5	18.2	17.8
13.8	14.1	17.3			10.9		6.7	7.5	28.4
(129) 3.6	(133) 4.0	(136) 4.3	EBIT/Interest	(10) 1.9		(20) 3.0	(35) 3.2	(63) 9.2	
1.0	.5	1.2			-1.6		.9	1.3	2.2
19.9	54.2	37.8	Net Profit + Depr., Dep.,						54.9
(24) 6.0	(22) 2.8	(26) 6.2	Amort./Cur. Mat. L/T/D					(15) 23.8	
.8	.0	1.1							1.2
.1	.0	.1			.0		.1	.0	.1
.2	.2	.2	Fixed/Worth		.1		.1	.1	.2
.5	.4	.4			2.8		1.0	.3	.4
.8	.8	.8			.4		1.2	.8	.7
2.1	1.9	1.7	Debt/Worth		2.3		2.1	1.4	1.7
5.6	5.0	4.1			-4.5		5.5	3.2	3.3
31.6	31.1	31.8					32.3	25.9	40.3
(124) 13.4	(129) 11.6	(135) 20.0	% Profit Before Taxes/Tangible Net Worth		(20) 13.8		(35) 12.3	(65) 26.6	
1.9	2.2	5.0			-2.8		3.5	12.9	
8.5	10.0	13.5			15.3		7.6	13.2	15.8
4.3	3.7	5.9	% Profit Before Taxes/Total Assets		1.8		4.0	3.6	8.5
.0	-.8	.9			-10.6		-1.9	.9	3.2
168.0	223.7	164.7			UND		192.3	160.7	135.0
62.0	68.7	61.3	Sales/Net Fixed Assets		119.1		49.4	62.4	58.5
22.9	29.9	26.9			35.7		19.6	27.9	21.8
4.3	4.3	4.1			3.8		4.3	3.8	4.6
3.1	2.9	3.1	Sales/Total Assets		2.4		3.3	3.0	3.3
2.0	2.2	2.5			1.9		2.1	2.6	2.6
.2	.2	.2					.1	.2	.2
(116) .4	(103) .4	(125) .4	% Depr., Dep., Amort./Sales		(19) .3	(31) .4	(62) .4		
.8	.8	.9					1.3	.7	.8
1.2	1.0	.8					1.3	.9	.6
(49) 1.8	(47) 2.0	(54) 1.7	% Officers', Directors' Owners' Comp/Sales		(13) 1.8	(15) 1.3	(16) .8		
4.0	3.6	3.6					6.2	2.9	2.0
7797522M	8335990M	10406296M	Net Sales ($)	1966M	25048M	37202M	163512M	603074M	9575494M
2817052M	2608827M	2944652M	Total Assets ($)	7288M	13739M	11986M	60623M	240228M	2610788M

© RMA 2011

M = $ thousand   MM = $ million
See Pages 9 through 22 for Explanation of Ratios and Data

Current Data Sorted by Assets   **Comparative Historical Data**

						Type of Statement		
		16	25	16	7	Unqualified	72	63
1	8	68	19		1	Reviewed	90	78
2	16	26	6	1		Compiled	55	46
4	23	24	1			Tax Returns	28	34
4	22	55	55	10	8	Other	117	105
	78 (4/1-9/30/10)		340 (10/1/10-3/31/11)				4/1/06-3/31/07	4/1/07-3/31/08
0-500M	500M-2MM	2-10MM	10-50MM	50-100MM	100-250MM		ALL	ALL
11	69	189	106	27	16	NUMBER OF STATEMENTS	362	326
%	%	%	%	%	%	**ASSETS**	%	%
15.4	11.8	10.2	9.9	5.4	7.7	Cash & Equivalents	7.8	8.9
21.2	36.3	35.3	33.2	38.1	39.1	Trade Receivables (net)	36.5	37.9
42.2	31.7	35.6	33.5	34.0	29.0	Inventory	34.7	33.7
.7	3.4	2.2	4.1	3.8	2.7	All Other Current	2.7	2.8
79.4	83.1	83.4	80.7	81.3	78.4	Total Current	81.8	83.2
9.2	8.4	8.1	8.5	8.0	7.3	Fixed Assets (net)	8.8	8.8
8.9	3.2	2.5	7.3	5.5	11.4	Intangibles (net)	4.0	3.3
2.5	5.2	6.1	3.4	5.2	2.9	All Other Non-Current	5.4	4.7
100.0	100.0	100.0	100.0	100.0	100.0	Total	100.0	100.0
						LIABILITIES		
27.3	12.8	12.2	14.7	13.6	11.6	Notes Payable-Short Term	14.6	15.2
1.5	1.8	1.4	1.8	1.1	.8	Cur. Mat.-L.T.D.	1.8	1.5
17.3	28.9	25.1	20.0	24.9	28.4	Trade Payables	23.8	23.9
.1	.3	.2	.2	.8	.4	Income Taxes Payable	.3	.3
53.3	8.0	8.3	9.7	10.7	11.5	All Other Current	10.4	10.3
99.4	51.8	47.1	46.4	51.2	52.6	Total Current	51.0	51.3
39.8	10.4	4.9	7.9	6.6	11.6	Long-Term Debt	8.1	7.6
.0	.1	.1	.3	.3	.3	Deferred Taxes	.2	.2
3.5	10.1	4.8	5.4	2.4	1.5	All Other Non-Current	3.8	4.2
-42.8	27.6	43.0	39.9	39.6	34.0	Net Worth	37.0	36.8
100.0	100.0	100.0	100.0	100.0	100.0	Total Liabilities & Net Worth	100.0	100.0
						INCOME DATA		
100.0	100.0	100.0	100.0	100.0	100.0	Net Sales	100.0	100.0
37.3	33.4	28.7	25.2	22.5	21.6	Gross Profit	28.9	28.6
37.5	30.2	24.8	19.6	16.2	16.3	Operating Expenses	25.1	24.9
-.2	3.2	3.9	5.6	6.3	5.2	Operating Profit	3.8	3.7
.3	.5	.2	.6	.5	1.1	All Other Expenses (net)	.5	.5
-.5	2.7	3.7	5.1	5.8	4.1	Profit Before Taxes	3.3	3.1
						RATIOS		
2.9	2.6	2.8	2.5	2.0	2.2		2.3	2.4
1.6	1.7	1.7	1.8	1.5	1.3	Current	1.6	1.6
1.2	1.1	1.3	1.3	1.3	1.1		1.2	1.2
1.9	1.5	1.6	1.5	1.2	1.0		1.3	1.4
(10) 1.1	1.0	.9	.9	.8	.9	Quick	.9	.9
.3	.6	.6	.6	.6	.6		.6	.6
0 UND	26 13.8	32 11.3	37 10.0	38 9.6	40 9.2		33 11.0	34 10.8
4 81.7	41 8.9	45 8.2	47 7.8	49 7.4	49 7.5	Sales/Receivables	45 8.1	44 8.3
34 10.8	50 7.3	57 6.5	58 6.3	63 5.8	60 6.1		57 6.4	58 6.3
15 24.9	17 21.1	36 10.1	40 9.1	36 10.3	22 16.5		35 10.4	31 11.9
23 16.0	43 8.5	61 6.0	63 5.8	61 6.0	40 9.0	Cost of Sales/Inventory	63 5.8	56 6.6
108 3.4	92 3.9	98 3.7	98 3.7	83 4.4	64 5.7		98 3.7	90 4.1
0 UND	20 18.5	23 16.0	23 16.1	24 15.4	34 10.7		21 17.2	20 18.5
14 26.5	40 9.0	37 10.0	35 10.4	37 9.8	47 7.8	Cost of Sales/Payables	38 9.7	36 10.1
23 15.7	69 5.3	57 6.4	51 7.1	60 6.1	60 6.0		59 6.2	53 6.9
11.1	5.5	4.8	4.6	5.2	7.6		5.6	5.5
19.0	12.0	8.9	8.0	11.4	17.3	Sales/Working Capital	10.1	10.1
75.0	45.8	18.2	16.5	17.5	29.3		22.1	20.7
	23.0	18.2	25.4	108.9	39.3		13.1	17.0
(57) 4.0	(154) 5.9	(96) 7.8	(26) 14.6	(14) 7.4		EBIT/Interest	(326) 4.2	(289) 4.2
.5	2.0	2.6	7.0	1.6			1.7	1.4
		20.8	13.2	59.0		Net Profit + Depr., Dep.,	10.6	18.6
	(32) 2.7	(21) 5.9	(14) 15.9			Amort./Cur. Mat. L/T/D	(83) 3.5	(64) 4.9
	.9	1.7	4.0				1.1	1.9
.0	.0	.0	.1	.1	.1		.1	.1
.2	.2	.1	.1	.2	.3	Fixed/Worth	.2	.2
-.6	2.3	.3	.8	.5	.8		.6	.5
1.1	1.0	.6	.8	.9	1.3		.8	.8
4.3	2.3	1.6	2.0	1.9	4.2	Debt/Worth	2.0	1.9
-1.6	19.7	3.8	4.1	4.6	11.9		4.8	4.7
	66.9	40.8	51.3	76.2	64.7	% Profit Before Taxes/Tangible	46.5	45.1
(55) 26.3	(180) 16.9	(92) 24.5	(25) 30.2	(13) 27.9		Net Worth	(327) 20.8	(296) 22.1
4.7	4.7	10.8	20.7	20.3			6.9	7.2
20.6	19.6	14.7	18.9	17.4	14.9	% Profit Before Taxes/Total	17.1	15.7
.0	6.4	6.2	9.2	11.1	8.1	Assets	6.9	6.8
-38.2	.3	1.8	3.2	4.4	3.2		1.5	1.3
UND	351.5	307.0	141.4	98.5	146.0		133.1	156.8
511.5	93.8	69.1	56.4	50.9	37.0	Sales/Net Fixed Assets	51.4	55.5
34.8	40.1	26.2	26.7	13.5	26.3		22.0	21.7
12.9	4.4	3.7	3.2	3.6	3.7		3.8	3.8
7.0	3.4	2.8	2.6	2.6	3.1	Sales/Total Assets	2.8	3.0
2.9	2.2	2.2	1.8	1.9	2.0		2.2	2.2
	.1	.2	.3	.3	.2		.3	.2
(44) .4	(148) .4	(95) .4	(24) .5	(14) .4		% Depr., Dep., Amort./Sales	(308) .5	(267) .4
1.4	.9	.8	.6	.7			1.1	1.0
	2.5	1.4	.6				1.7	1.2
(42) 4.3	(76) 2.6	(22) 1.0				% Officers', Directors' Owners' Comp/Sales	(127) 3.0	(111) 2.6
8.7	4.5	2.2					6.2	5.7
26279M	311620M	2924966M	5782515M	5158265M	7040005M	Net Sales ($)	15244374M	14538678M
2817M	83119M	1003076M	2237921M	1893002M	2406845M	Total Assets ($)	6056800M	5306933M

M = $ thousand   MM = $ million
See Pages 9 through 22 for Explanation of Ratios and Data

Comparative Historical Data   Current Data Sorted by Sales

Type of Statement

4/1/08-3/31/09 ALL	4/1/09-3/31/10 ALL	4/1/10-3/31/11 ALL	Type of Statement	0-1MM	1-3MM	3-5MM	5-10MM	10-25MM	25MM & OVER
80	59	64	Unqualified	2		1	5	9	49
84	92	97	Reviewed			2	15	51	27
42	47	51	Compiled		5	7	12	21	6
44	40	52	Tax Returns	2	14	11	11	11	3
142	175	154	Other	4	9	7	26	36	72
					78 (4/1-9/30/10)			**340 (10/1/10-3/31/11)**	
392	**413**	**418**	**NUMBER OF STATEMENTS**	**8**	**28**	**28**	**69**	**128**	**157**
%	%	%	**ASSETS**	%	%	%	%	%	%
9.9	10.5	10.1	Cash & Equivalents		10.1	21.6	11.6	9.5	8.2
35.0	33.2	34.9	Trade Receivables (net)		25.4	32.9	35.0	35.5	36.6
33.6	34.1	34.3	Inventory		42.6	26.1	31.4	36.6	33.8
2.5	3.3	3.0	All Other Current		2.7	2.1	3.0	1.9	3.7
81.1	81.0	82.2	Total Current		80.8	82.7	81.0	83.4	82.4
8.9	8.2	8.2	Fixed Assets (net)		7.1	9.9	10.0	7.0	8.0
3.9	5.1	4.5	Intangibles (net)		4.6	2.9	2.1	4.4	5.8
6.1	5.6	5.0	All Other Non-Current		7.4	4.5	6.9	5.2	3.9
100.0	100.0	100.0	Total		100.0	100.0	100.0	100.0	100.0
			LIABILITIES						
14.4	14.6	13.4	Notes Payable-Short Term		16.2	11.3	10.2	12.6	14.9
1.8	1.9	1.5	Cur. Mat.-L.T.D.		2.6	.6	1.3	1.8	1.5
22.8	24.1	24.3	Trade Payables		24.6	19.1	28.2	24.0	24.0
.2	.2	.2	Income Taxes Payable		.3	.4	.2	.2	.3
9.3	9.0	10.1	All Other Current		10.1	11.4	8.7	7.7	10.0
48.6	49.7	49.6	Total Current		53.9	42.7	48.6	46.3	50.8
7.7	7.8	7.9	Long-Term Debt		7.2	18.4	5.6	7.9	6.9
.1	.2	.2	Deferred Taxes		.1	.0	.2	.2	.2
4.3	6.2	5.5	All Other Non-Current		10.2	4.4	2.7	5.8	4.1
39.3	36.1	36.9	Net Worth		28.6	34.4	42.9	39.9	38.0
100.0	100.0	100.0	Total Liabilities & Net Worth		100.0	100.0	100.0	100.0	100.0
			INCOME DATA						
100.0	100.0	100.0	Net Sales		100.0	100.0	100.0	100.0	100.0
28.6	28.3	28.2	Gross Profit		36.3	39.8	30.4	27.4	23.4
25.3	25.9	23.8	Operating Expenses		35.2	35.1	26.1	23.0	18.4
3.4	2.4	4.3	Operating Profit		1.1	4.7	4.3	4.5	4.9
.4	.5	.4	All Other Expenses (net)		.6	-.1	.2	.3	.6
3.0	1.9	3.9	Profit Before Taxes		.5	4.8	4.1	4.2	4.4
			RATIOS						
2.6 / 1.7 / 1.2	2.6 / 1.6 / 1.2	2.6 / 1.7 / 1.2	Current		2.7 / 1.5 / 1.0	3.3 / 2.5 / 1.4	2.5 / 1.7 / 1.2	2.9 / 1.9 / 1.3	2.2 / 1.5 / 1.2
1.5 / .9 / .6	1.5 / .8 / .5	1.5 / .9 (417) / .6	Quick		(27) 1.6 / .7 / .4	2.3 / 1.6 / .8	1.4 / .9 / .6	1.6 / 1.0 / .6	1.2 / .8 / .6
31 11.9 / 42 8.7 / 54 6.7	31 12.0 / 43 8.6 / 60 6.1	34 10.8 / 45 8.2 / 56 6.5	Sales/Receivables	25 14.6 / 39 9.3 / 50 7.4	22 16.7 / 42 8.7 / 64 5.7	32 11.4 / 42 8.7 / 53 6.9	31 11.6 / 46 7.9 / 59 6.2	36 10.0 / 46 7.9 / 56 6.5	
30 12.2 / 54 6.7 / 96 3.8	28 12.8 / 55 6.7 / 104 3.5	34 10.8 / 57 6.4 / 94 3.9	Cost of Sales/Inventory		44 8.3 / 88 4.1 / 138 2.6	15 24.6 / 35 10.4 / 155 2.4	34 10.8 / 58 6.3 / 85 4.3	30 12.1 / 62 5.9 / 109 3.4	35 10.4 / 52 7.0 / 83 4.4
20 18.7 / 32 11.5 / 52 7.0	22 16.6 / 38 9.6 / 59 6.2	22 16.4 / 36 10.1 / 58 6.3	Cost of Sales/Payables		22 16.6 / 41 8.9 / 100 3.7	14 25.8 / 41 9.0 / 63 5.8	27 13.5 / 50 7.4 / 74 4.9	21 17.5 / 35 10.5 / 58 6.3	23 16.1 / 35 10.3 / 50 7.3
5.3 / 9.5 / 23.2	5.0 / 10.4 / 24.5	5.0 / 9.6 / 21.0	Sales/Working Capital		4.5 / 12.2 / 65.6	3.8 / 5.9 / 16.2	5.1 / 9.4 / 23.9	4.8 / 8.0 / 18.3	6.0 / 11.0 / 22.2
(322) 14.0 / 4.2 / 1.5	(360) 16.5 / 3.7 / 1.2	(355) 22.8 / 6.3 / 2.1	EBIT/Interest		(23) 3.4 / 1.6 / -1.3	(21) 41.8 / 6.2 / 1.0	(56) 15.5 / 6.4 / 3.2	(105) 24.4 / 5.8 / 1.7	(144) 28.3 / 9.5 / 2.9
(83) 13.7 / 4.4 / 1.2	(79) 14.5 / 2.3 / .8	(76) 23.5 / 5.3 / 1.3	Net Profit + Depr., Dep., Amort./Cur. Mat. L/T/D				(11) 2.7 / 1.2 / .8	(22) 28.1 / 3.7 / 1.0	(41) 25.0 / 7.5 / 3.5
.1 / .2 / .5	.0 / .2 / .6	.0 / .1 / .6	Fixed/Worth		.0 / .2 / UND	.0 / .1 / 2.2	.1 / .1 / .6	.0 / .1 / .3	.1 / .2 / .5
.7 / 1.8 / 4.3	.9 / 2.2 / 5.4	.8 / 1.8 / 4.5	Debt/Worth		1.0 / 2.7 / UND	.5 / 1.2 / 5.5	.7 / 1.4 / 2.9	.7 / 1.7 / 4.3	.9 / 2.3 / 4.6
(347) 38.7 / 17.6 / 3.8	(359) 35.1 / 15.3 / 1.9	(372) 50.7 / 21.7 / 6.5	% Profit Before Taxes/Tangible Net Worth		(22) 31.5 / 4.4 / -4.6	(23) 51.0 / 22.9 / 3.0	(66) 48.8 / 15.9 / 5.5	(117) 43.5 / 20.5 / 5.0	(140) 56.0 / 26.3 / 14.1
15.4 / 5.4 / .9	12.8 / 4.2 / .3	16.3 / 7.2 / 1.9	% Profit Before Taxes/Total Assets		9.0 / 1.1 / -3.5	27.1 / 10.2 / -.8	13.8 / 6.2 / 2.7	17.2 / 6.4 / 2.0	17.8 / 8.9 / 3.4
149.7 / 51.9 / 24.9	176.8 / 62.6 / 24.2	242.4 / 65.2 / 26.8	Sales/Net Fixed Assets		605.9 / 68.7 / 19.6	915.7 / 154.4 / 30.9	134.7 / 56.4 / 18.4	294.7 / 81.0 / 26.7	144.7 / 55.6 / 28.4
4.0 / 3.0 / 2.1	3.7 / 2.8 / 1.9	3.8 / 2.8 / 2.1	Sales/Total Assets		4.1 / 2.9 / 1.7	3.6 / 2.8 / 2.1	3.8 / 2.7 / 2.1	3.9 / 2.7 / 2.1	3.7 / 2.9 / 2.2
(319) .2 / .5 / 1.1	(306) .2 / .5 / 1.1	(330) .2 / .4 / .9	% Depr., Dep., Amort./Sales		(17) .2 / .6 / 1.6	(17) .1 / .4 / 1.2	(54) .1 / .6 / .9	(99) .2 / .4 / .9	(141) .2 / .4 / .7
(130) 1.4 / 3.2 / 6.0	(120) 1.8 / 3.0 / 6.0	(145) 1.3 / 2.7 / 5.1	% Officers', Directors' Owners' Comp/Sales		(17) 2.6 / 5.8 / 9.7	(17) 2.0 / 4.4 / 6.4	(34) 2.1 / 3.5 / 5.1	(48) 1.3 / 2.5 / 3.5	(27) .6 / 1.0 / 1.9
21097761M	19489850M	21243650M	Net Sales ($)	3965M	58750M	110062M	536840M	2080631M	18453402M
7304452M	7508373M	7626780M	Total Assets ($)	3471M	25657M	41354M	211321M	829841M	6515136M

M = $ thousand   MM = $ million
See Pages 9 through 22 for Explanation of Ratios and Data

Current Data Sorted by Assets   Comparative Historical Data

	0-500M	500M-2MM	2-10MM	10-50MM	50-100MM	100-250MM		4/1/06-3/31/07 ALL	4/1/07-3/31/08 ALL
Type of Statement									
Unqualified		1	4	20	3	1		30	33
Reviewed		10	57	18	1			75	61
Compiled	4	11	29	4				47	39
Tax Returns	5	25	23	2				37	37
Other	6	23	49	34	5	1		72	86
	61 (4/1-9/30/10)			275 (10/1/10-3/31/11)					
NUMBER OF STATEMENTS	15	70	162	78	9	2		261	256
	%	%	%	%	%	%		%	%
ASSETS									
Cash & Equivalents	8.3	9.4	8.0	6.9				7.6	7.0
Trade Receivables (net)	25.2	30.5	29.9	27.3				30.5	28.9
Inventory	47.5	40.6	45.2	41.9				42.6	43.9
All Other Current	.9	2.5	1.9	2.1				1.2	1.9
Total Current	81.9	82.9	85.0	78.2				81.9	81.6
Fixed Assets (net)	9.8	10.5	9.3	11.4				11.9	11.2
Intangibles (net)	1.0	.6	2.0	5.1				1.8	2.4
All Other Non-Current	7.2	6.0	3.7	5.2				4.4	4.8
Total	100.0	100.0	100.0	100.0				100.0	100.0
LIABILITIES									
Notes Payable-Short Term	29.9	15.3	17.6	12.8				15.1	17.9
Cur. Mat.-L.T.D.	.0	2.7	2.2	1.6				1.9	5.2
Trade Payables	32.5	21.1	16.2	18.1				19.9	19.4
Income Taxes Payable	.0	.1	.1	.1				.3	.2
All Other Current	4.8	8.6	6.7	6.4				7.7	7.2
Total Current	67.3	47.8	42.8	39.0				44.9	49.9
Long-Term Debt	11.3	9.1	9.0	8.2				10.9	10.3
Deferred Taxes	.0	.0	.1	.5				.2	.2
All Other Non-Current	32.4	3.6	5.4	3.6				3.4	5.2
Net Worth	-10.9	39.5	42.7	48.7				40.7	34.4
Total Liabilities & Net Worth	100.0	100.0	100.0	100.0				100.0	100.0
INCOME DATA									
Net Sales	100.0	100.0	100.0	100.0				100.0	100.0
Gross Profit	33.5	34.3	32.1	30.2				31.2	31.7
Operating Expenses	34.2	31.8	28.7	26.4				26.5	27.4
Operating Profit	-.7	2.5	3.4	3.8				4.7	4.2
All Other Expenses (net)	.8	.7	.5	.4				.6	.7
Profit Before Taxes	-1.5	1.9	3.0	3.4				4.1	3.6
RATIOS									
Current	3.7	3.4	3.5	3.8				3.2	2.9
	1.0	2.0	2.0	2.3				1.9	1.8
	.9	1.2	1.4	1.4				1.4	1.3
Quick	1.1	1.6	1.6	1.6				1.4	1.3
	.5	.8	.8	1.0				.8	.7
	.2	.5	.5	.5				.5	.5
Sales/Receivables	14 26.9	28 12.8	30 12.0	34 10.8				30 12.4	30 12.2
	24 15.1	37 9.8	41 8.8	42 8.7				38 9.7	38 9.6
	36 10.1	54 6.8	56 6.6	53 6.9				48 7.7	51 7.2
Cost of Sales/Inventory	24 15.3	41 8.9	57 6.4	67 5.5				48 7.6	61 6.0
	71 5.2	79 4.6	104 3.5	96 3.8				86 4.3	97 3.8
	124 2.9	131 2.8	166 2.2	136 2.7				121 3.0	128 2.8
Cost of Sales/Payables	12 30.2	20 18.1	17 21.2	23 16.2				20 18.5	20 18.2
	31 11.8	37 9.8	32 11.4	36 10.1				31 11.6	34 10.7
	115 3.2	49 7.5	48 7.6	54 6.8				47 7.8	50 7.3
Sales/Working Capital	5.8	4.5	3.9	3.5				5.0	5.0
	114.4	7.1	5.6	6.0				7.8	7.8
	-18.9	20.5	10.4	10.1				13.8	14.7
EBIT/Interest	6.5	16.2	11.3	15.8				11.4	10.7
	(10) -1.4	(60) 4.6	(142) 3.1	(68) 4.5				(231) 4.2	(227) 3.3
	-5.3	.8	1.3	1.9				1.8	1.5
Net Profit + Depr., Dep., Amort./Cur. Mat. L/T/D			6.3	5.0				10.2	6.7
			(33) 2.0	(24) 2.0				(65) 4.3	(63) 3.2
			.4	.5				2.0	.9
Fixed/Worth	.0	.1	.1	.1				.1	.1
	.3	.2	.1	.2				.2	.2
	-.3	.6	.5	.7				.6	.6
Debt/Worth	.7	.5	.7	.4				.7	.7
	5.4	1.5	1.4	1.0				1.5	1.7
	-3.0	4.1	3.2	3.4				3.4	3.8
% Profit Before Taxes/Tangible Net Worth	73.0	41.3	28.9	24.5				40.3	37.5
	(10) 44.7	(61) 12.4	(153) 10.7	(70) 11.5				(242) 20.3	(235) 16.0
	-77.1	-2.9	1.8	3.9				7.1	4.4
% Profit Before Taxes/Total Assets	29.1	14.6	10.8	11.1				17.5	14.5
	1.7	5.2	3.5	4.1				7.8	6.3
	-43.0	-1.5	.4	1.6				2.7	1.2
Sales/Net Fixed Assets	UND	99.8	105.2	73.1				86.7	92.8
	64.5	46.7	42.1	32.9				38.9	41.3
	17.6	24.7	18.9	16.1				18.7	18.7
Sales/Total Assets	4.3	3.5	3.0	2.9				3.6	3.3
	3.3	2.9	2.4	2.2				2.8	2.6
	2.5	1.9	1.8	1.7				2.1	2.1
% Depr., Dep., Amort./Sales		.3	.3	.4				.4	.3
		(60) .7	(148) .5	(70) .7				(219) .7	(216) .6
		1.2	.9	1.1				1.1	1.1
% Officers', Directors' Owners' Comp/Sales		2.5	1.7	1.0				2.2	2.1
		(40) 4.8	(88) 3.1	(20) 2.5				(124) 3.5	(116) 3.5
		7.6	4.9	6.5				7.5	7.3
Net Sales ($)	13731M	240619M	1890373M	3507537M	1195848M	746930M		6777157M	7640239M
Total Assets ($)	4145M	86900M	769306M	1544401M	568820M	324604M		2633625M	3232255M

M = $ thousand   MM = $ million
See Pages 9 through 22 for Explanation of Ratios and Data

Comparative Historical Data   Current Data Sorted by Sales

			Type of Statement						
41	43	29	Unqualified	1	1		2	6	20
81	80	86	Reviewed		2	5	25	33	20
38	44	48	Compiled		10	6	17	13	2
47	61	55	Tax Returns	5	14	13	11	10	2
107	117	118	Other	4	13	15	19	32	35
4/1/08-3/31/09	4/1/09-3/31/10	4/1/10-3/31/11		61 (4/1-9/30/10)			275 (10/1/10-3/31/11)		
ALL	ALL	ALL		0-1MM	1-3MM	3-5MM	5-10MM	10-25MM	25MM & OVER
314	345	336	NUMBER OF STATEMENTS	10	40	39	74	94	79
%	%	%	**ASSETS**	%	%	%	%	%	%
6.8	7.9	7.9	Cash & Equivalents	15.9	11.8	9.1	7.9	6.0	6.8
28.5	27.1	29.1	Trade Receivables (net)	23.8	24.9	29.9	28.9	31.3	29.0
44.9	42.9	43.5	Inventory	38.4	45.1	39.2	46.0	44.3	42.2
2.2	3.0	2.1	All Other Current	.0	2.7	2.6	1.6	2.0	2.3
82.4	80.8	82.6	Total Current	78.1	84.5	80.9	84.4	83.6	80.4
10.7	11.4	10.3	Fixed Assets (net)	14.5	8.4	11.4	10.1	10.5	10.0
3.0	2.9	2.4	Intangibles (net)	.0	1.8	1.1	2.4	1.8	4.3
3.9	4.9	4.7	All Other Non-Current	7.3	5.3	6.7	3.2	4.1	5.3
100.0	100.0	100.0	Total	100.0	100.0	100.0	100.0	100.0	100.0
			LIABILITIES						
19.2	17.2	16.7	Notes Payable-Short Term	13.2	19.3	13.4	19.4	17.5	14.0
2.2	2.8	2.1	Cur. Mat.-L.T.D.	.0	1.8	2.2	2.7	2.4	1.5
16.7	17.4	18.6	Trade Payables	32.9	15.5	24.2	16.9	16.0	20.3
.3	.2	.1	Income Taxes Payable	.0	.2	.2	.1	.1	.1
7.8	7.6	6.9	All Other Current	4.2	6.3	9.3	7.9	5.3	7.4
46.3	45.1	44.4	Total Current	50.3	43.2	49.3	46.9	41.2	43.3
9.0	9.2	8.8	Long-Term Debt	16.8	9.5	9.0	10.0	8.5	6.6
.2	.2	.2	Deferred Taxes	.0	.0	.1	.1	.2	.5
4.2	5.0	5.8	All Other Non-Current	14.2	12.8	3.5	5.9	4.7	3.3
40.4	40.6	40.8	Net Worth	18.8	34.5	38.0	37.1	45.4	46.4
100.0	100.0	100.0	Total Liabilities & Net Worth	100.0	100.0	100.0	100.0	100.0	100.0
			INCOME DATA						
100.0	100.0	100.0	Net Sales	100.0	100.0	100.0	100.0	100.0	100.0
31.4	31.2	31.9	Gross Profit	40.6	34.9	33.2	33.8	30.5	28.7
28.0	29.2	28.9	Operating Expenses	46.0	32.5	29.7	30.2	27.0	25.5
3.5	2.1	3.0	Operating Profit	-5.3	2.4	3.5	3.6	3.5	3.1
.6	.4	.5	All Other Expenses (net)	1.0	.9	.5	.7	.2	.4
2.9	1.7	2.5	Profit Before Taxes	-6.4	1.5	3.0	2.9	3.3	2.8
			RATIOS						
3.1	3.3	3.5	Current	4.3	6.4	3.1	3.1	3.8	3.2
1.8	2.0	2.0		1.7	2.3	2.0	1.8	2.0	2.1
1.3	1.3	1.3		1.0	1.3	1.1	1.3	1.5	1.3
1.3	1.5	1.6	Quick	1.4	2.5	1.2	1.6	1.6	1.5
.8 (344)	.7	.8		1.0	.8	.8	.8	.8	.9
.4	.5	.5		.4	.5	.4	.5	.5	.5
28 13.2	29 12.8	30 12.0	Sales/Receivables	10 37.8	25 14.9	28 12.8	31 11.7	30 12.0	35 10.4
37 9.9	38 9.5	40 9.1		30 12.3	37 9.9	37 9.9	41 8.9	42 8.6	41 8.8
48 7.6	50 7.2	54 6.8		57 6.4	53 6.9	56 6.6	53 6.8	57 6.4	51 7.2
55 6.7	55 6.7	54 6.8	Cost of Sales/Inventory	0 UND	64 5.7	31 11.7	58 6.3	56 6.5	54 6.8
95 3.9	95 3.8	96 3.8		45 8.2	120 3.0	99 3.7	113 3.2	95 3.8	92 4.0
144 2.5	142 2.6	148 2.5		159 2.3	183 2.0	132 2.8	175 2.1	136 2.7	123 3.0
16 23.0	18 20.0	20 17.9	Cost of Sales/Payables	19 19.4	11 32.8	28 13.1	20 18.4	16 22.1	27 13.7
30 12.2	32 11.3	34 10.8		137 2.7	37 10.0	38 9.5	36 10.0	28 12.8	38 9.7
45 8.1	48 7.6	50 7.3		268 1.4	49 7.4	65 5.6	48 7.6	42 8.7	56 6.6
4.8	4.3	4.1	Sales/Working Capital	3.8	2.8	4.5	4.1	4.3	4.2
7.6	6.4	6.5		12.6	5.0	7.2	6.8	5.6	7.2
15.0	14.3	12.6		NM	12.9	42.1	12.3	10.9	13.8
9.4	9.6	11.9	EBIT/Interest		14.2	12.8	9.4	17.4	11.1
(271) 3.0	(303) 2.8	(290) 3.4		(32) 3.1	(32) 3.7	(67) 2.5	(87) 4.2	(68) 3.0	
1.5	.9	1.2			-1.0	1.0	1.1	1.8	1.1
7.5	6.7	4.3	Net Profit + Depr., Dep., Amort./Cur. Mat. L/T/D				6.2	5.5	4.3
(76) 4.0	(82) 2.6	(72) 1.8				(13) 1.3	(24) 2.5	(28) 1.8	
.8	.7	.4					.3	.5	.3
.1	.1	.1	Fixed/Worth	.0	.0	.1	.1	.1	.1
.2	.2	.2		.3	.1	.2	.2	.2	.2
.5	.6	.6		-.3	.6	1.0	.7	.5	.6
.6	.6	.5	Debt/Worth	.5	.4	.5	.9	.6	.4
1.8	1.4	1.5		.9	1.6	2.1	1.9	1.3	1.3
4.1	4.0	3.7		-12.8	5.2	4.9	4.5	2.7	3.5
35.2	25.5	30.9	% Profit Before Taxes/Tangible Net Worth		58.3	28.9	37.6	32.0	23.5
(289) 14.6	(316) 8.2	(305) 11.1		(34) 10.0	(35) 9.5	(66) 9.6	(92) 11.7	(71) 11.1	
3.2	-.2	1.8		-12.8	-.3	.8	3.5	2.5	
12.9	11.2	11.9	% Profit Before Taxes/Total Assets	24.6	14.5	8.6	10.8	12.3	9.9
4.3	3.3	3.8		-1.8	2.2	4.5	2.3	4.3	3.2
.9	-.4	.2		-22.5	-10.6	-.1	.3	1.1	.5
96.0	84.2	94.8	Sales/Net Fixed Assets	UND	201.5	88.4	104.0	85.2	78.8
38.6	36.4	40.7		46.7	46.4	40.5	37.8	42.1	37.4
16.6	16.7	18.2		7.9	22.6	25.2	19.0	16.8	20.5
3.3	3.2	3.1	Sales/Total Assets	3.4	3.1	3.5	3.1	3.1	3.0
2.6	2.4	2.4		1.8	2.1	2.9	2.4	2.5	2.4
2.0	1.8	1.8		1.4	1.4	1.7	1.7	2.1	2.0
.4	.4	.3	% Depr., Dep., Amort./Sales		.2	.2	.3	.3	.4
(264) .6	(292) .7	(295) .6		(30) .9	(34) .5	(69) .7	(88) .5	(71) .6	
1.1	1.3	1.1		1.7	1.1	1.2	.9	1.1	
2.1	2.0	1.8	% Officers', Directors' Owners' Comp/Sales		3.1	2.3	2.1	1.2	1.0
(122) 3.8	(152) 3.9	(156) 3.6		(22) 4.9	(25) 4.4	(44) 3.6	(44) 2.4	(17) 3.1	
7.0	6.8	6.5		7.1	8.7	5.0	4.4	9.0	
10309827M	9170963M	7595038M	Net Sales ($)	4548M	75111M	160127M	543346M	1482237M	5329669M
4578978M	4230835M	3298176M	Total Assets ($)	3623M	45142M	68699M	248565M	643388M	2288759M

M = $ thousand   MM = $ million
See Pages 9 through 22 for Explanation of Ratios and Data

Current Data Sorted by Assets   Comparative Historical Data

Type of Statement

Type of Statement	0-500M	500M-2MM	2-10MM	10-50MM	50-100MM	100-250MM	ALL 4/1/06-3/31/07	ALL 4/1/07-3/31/08
Unqualified			3	18	7	1	47	38
Reviewed	2	7	70	26	1		116	101
Compiled	3	23	31	3			89	85
Tax Returns	12	33	18	1			41	37
Other	3	14	38	54	4	5	95	100
	54 (4/1-9/30/10)			323 (10/1/10-3/31/11)				
NUMBER OF STATEMENTS	20	77	160	102	12	6	388	361

	0-500M %	500M-2MM %	2-10MM %	10-50MM %	50-100MM %	100-250MM %	ALL %	ALL %
ASSETS								
Cash & Equivalents	18.1	9.4	6.9	5.6	5.7		6.1	7.0
Trade Receivables (net)	31.8	30.4	32.2	32.2	27.4		34.1	33.2
Inventory	22.4	37.8	40.8	40.2	33.3		40.5	39.7
All Other Current	.2	2.2	1.9	2.5	5.3		2.2	2.7
Total Current	72.5	79.8	81.9	80.5	71.7		82.9	82.7
Fixed Assets (net)	16.2	12.0	11.0	12.2	16.1		9.8	11.2
Intangibles (net)	1.8	3.3	1.2	2.5	2.0		2.0	1.8
All Other Non-Current	9.5	4.9	5.9	4.8	10.2		5.3	4.4
Total	100.0	100.0	100.0	100.0	100.0		100.0	100.0
LIABILITIES								
Notes Payable-Short Term	14.3	12.5	15.4	18.1	9.3		16.6	16.9
Cur. Mat.-L.T.D.	2.7	2.1	2.1	2.2	1.2		2.5	2.2
Trade Payables	21.0	18.3	20.0	19.0	12.5		19.9	20.3
Income Taxes Payable	.1	.2	.1	.2	.1		.3	.3
All Other Current	20.8	7.4	6.7	7.5	10.0		8.4	7.8
Total Current	58.8	40.6	44.4	47.1	33.1		47.8	47.3
Long-Term Debt	23.1	12.5	6.8	7.1	11.3		8.1	8.1
Deferred Taxes	.0	.1	.2	.3	.4		.2	.2
All Other Non-Current	17.0	6.6	5.3	5.5	5.5		3.5	4.3
Net Worth	1.1	40.2	43.3	40.0	49.7		40.5	40.1
Total Liabilties & Net Worth	100.0	100.0	100.0	100.0	100.0		100.0	100.0
INCOME DATA								
Net Sales	100.0	100.0	100.0	100.0	100.0		100.0	100.0
Gross Profit	44.3	34.8	29.7	26.0	27.1		28.4	29.2
Operating Expenses	41.1	33.4	26.8	24.5	25.2		24.6	25.6
Operating Profit	3.2	1.4	2.9	1.5	1.9		3.8	3.6
All Other Expenses (net)	.2	.3	.1	.3	-.4		.2	.2
Profit Before Taxes	3.0	1.1	2.8	1.2	2.3		3.7	3.4

RATIOS

Ratio	0-500M	500M-2MM	2-10MM	10-50MM	50-100MM	100-250MM	ALL 4/1/06-3/31/07	ALL 4/1/07-3/31/08
Current	3.5	2.9	2.7	2.5	3.5		2.7	2.7
	1.9	2.2	1.8	1.7	2.6		1.7	1.8
	1.2	1.5	1.4	1.3	1.6		1.4	1.4
Quick	2.6	1.7	1.3	1.3	1.5		1.3	1.4
	1.3	1.0	.8	.8	1.2		.8	.8
	.7	.6	.5	.5	.7		.6	.5
Sales/Receivables	11 32.7	22 16.4	36 10.1	38 9.5	39 9.4		33 11.1	32 11.4
	27 13.8	38 9.7	44 8.3	48 7.7	46 8.0		42 8.7	40 9.0
	39 9.4	47 7.8	56 6.5	60 6.1	58 6.3		51 7.1	51 7.2
Cost of Sales/Inventory	0 UND	34 10.6	53 6.9	59 6.1	61 6.0		46 8.0	51 7.2
	31 11.8	72 5.1	86 4.3	87 4.2	82 4.5		74 4.9	73 5.0
	79 4.6	123 3.0	117 3.1	113 3.2	93 3.9		102 3.6	102 3.6
Cost of Sales/Payables	3 120.7	18 20.8	24 15.2	28 13.0	14 25.8		21 17.5	21 17.1
	32 11.3	30 12.2	34 10.6	33 11.2	31 11.8		31 11.9	33 11.1
	63 5.8	53 6.9	55 6.6	44 8.3	40 9.1		44 8.3	46 7.9
Sales/Working Capital	5.9	4.6	4.4	4.7	4.0		5.3	5.0
	10.8	8.2	6.9	7.1	5.1		8.8	8.2
	42.6	12.9	12.0	13.6	8.6		15.2	15.3
EBIT/Interest	9.1	14.8	11.5	8.2	11.3		12.4	10.9
	(14) 2.5	(64) 2.8	(146) 3.9	(94) 3.4	5.1		(355) 4.8	(328) 4.0
	1.4	.8	1.4	1.2	1.3		2.1	1.6
Net Profit + Depr., Dep., Amort./Cur. Mat. L/T/D			9.6	7.4			7.8	7.4
			(48) 2.4	(27) 3.9			(101) 3.2	(114) 3.5
			1.0	.6			1.7	1.6
Fixed/Worth	.1	.1	.1	.1	.2		.1	.1
	.7	.2	.2	.2	.3		.2	.2
	-.7	1.0	.5	.5	.4		.4	.5
Debt/Worth	.7	.6	.6	.8	.7		.8	.7
	2.1	1.4	1.3	1.5	1.3		1.6	1.4
	-6.6	4.2	2.7	3.4	1.9		3.4	3.3
% Profit Before Taxes/Tangible Net Worth	57.4	22.2	23.9	16.7	19.9		42.8	34.2
	(13) 22.5	(66) 10.0	(151) 9.9	(92) 7.7	11.7		(368) 22.6	(336) 20.8
	3.8	1.7	2.3	1.5	.6		8.8	6.6
% Profit Before Taxes/Total Assets	18.9	11.5	10.6	6.4	7.9		16.8	14.8
	4.0	3.2	3.9	2.5	5.2		8.0	7.4
	2.1	-.4	.8	.6	.3		2.9	2.1
Sales/Net Fixed Assets	116.0	98.9	89.6	54.7	31.5		83.6	65.6
	42.1	49.9	37.3	27.9	14.1		40.6	36.3
	16.7	19.9	16.5	14.1	12.0		22.1	19.8
Sales/Total Assets	5.2	4.1	3.2	2.8	2.6		3.7	3.5
	3.3	2.9	2.5	2.3	2.4		2.9	2.8
	2.7	2.1	1.9	1.9	1.6		2.3	2.2
% Depr., Dep., Amort./Sales	.2	.3	.4	.4	.6		.3	.4
	(12) .9	(65) .7	(144) .6	(91) .7	(11) 1.3		(330) .6	(315) .7
	3.5	1.5	1.0	1.0	1.6		.9	1.0
% Officers', Directors' Owners' Comp/Sales	3.9	2.5	1.8				1.3	1.5
	(12) 6.9	(46) 4.8	(72) 3.0	(27) 1.2			(165) 2.8	(152) 2.6
	13.0	7.1	5.2	2.0			6.1	5.5
Net Sales ($)	31993M	308301M	2102280M	5417166M	1761421M	1918581M	13587240M	11999810M
Total Assets ($)	5756M	99406M	823526M	2221562M	791987M	861536M	4677584M	4461018M

M = $ thousand   MM = $ million
See Pages 9 through 22 for Explanation of Ratios and Data

Comparative Historical Data | | | | Current Data Sorted by Sales

4/1/08-3/31/09 ALL	4/1/09-3/31/10 ALL	4/1/10-3/31/11 ALL	Type of Statement	0-1MM	1-3MM	3-5MM	5-10MM	10-25MM	25MM & OVER
36	42	29	Unqualified	1	3	3	30	45	26
123	102	106	Reviewed	2	16	9	11	19	24
74	59	60	Compiled	6	16	17	19	5	3
50	60	64	Tax Returns	3	6	6	13	30	1
104	137	118	Other					3	60
				54 (4/1-9/30/10)			323 (10/1/10-3/31/11)		
387	400	377	**NUMBER OF STATEMENTS**	12	41	35	73	102	114
%	%	%	**ASSETS**	%	%	%	%	%	%
7.2	7.6	7.6	Cash & Equivalents	19.5	12.3	8.5	8.0	6.0	5.7
31.3	30.3	31.6	Trade Receivables (net)	21.4	26.6	26.1	32.6	33.6	33.7
40.4	40.5	38.7	Inventory	23.7	35.1	43.2	39.7	39.5	39.0
2.5	2.7	2.2	All Other Current	.1	2.3	1.7	1.3	2.4	2.9
81.3	81.1	80.2	Total Current	64.6	76.3	79.5	81.7	81.5	81.3
11.1	11.5	12.1	Fixed Assets (net)	19.2	14.0	12.2	10.7	12.1	11.5
2.1	1.8	2.1	Intangibles (net)	8.0	3.5	2.3	1.1	1.4	2.2
5.5	5.6	5.7	All Other Non-Current	8.2	6.2	6.0	6.6	5.1	5.0
100.0	100.0	100.0	Total	100.0	100.0	100.0	100.0	100.0	100.0
			LIABILITIES						
17.0	17.4	15.2	Notes Payable-Short Term	5.6	21.0	13.0	11.3	16.1	16.4
2.6	2.1	2.1	Cur. Mat.-L.T.D.	1.7	1.9	3.3	2.8	1.5	2.0
18.9	19.1	19.1	Trade Payables	16.6	15.4	17.3	20.0	20.4	19.7
.2	.2	.2	Income Taxes Payable	.0	.3	.2	.1	.2	.2
8.8	8.6	7.9	All Other Current	12.9	13.2	5.3	6.3	7.9	7.2
47.5	47.3	44.5	Total Current	36.7	51.8	39.1	40.5	46.1	45.5
9.0	8.4	9.1	Long-Term Debt	30.4	14.5	15.8	6.9	6.9	6.3
.4	.3	.3	Deferred Taxes	.0	.0	.4	.2	.2	.4
4.2	5.0	6.2	All Other Non-Current	10.5	12.0	7.4	5.9	4.2	5.2
38.8	39.0	40.0	Net Worth	22.4	21.7	37.2	46.6	42.7	42.6
100.0	100.0	100.0	Total Liabilities & Net Worth	100.0	100.0	100.0	100.0	100.0	100.0
			INCOME DATA						
100.0	100.0	100.0	Net Sales	100.0	100.0	100.0	100.0	100.0	100.0
28.8	30.2	30.4	Gross Profit	41.3	39.8	37.2	29.3	29.7	25.0
26.4	29.1	28.2	Operating Expenses	40.1	37.5	34.3	27.0	27.3	23.1
2.5	1.1	2.2	Operating Profit	1.3	2.4	2.9	2.3	2.3	1.9
.3	.4	.2	All Other Expenses (net)	1.2	.5	.4	-.1	.1	.2
2.1	.7	2.0	Profit Before Taxes	.1	1.8	2.6	2.4	2.2	1.6
			RATIOS						
2.6	2.6	2.8	Current	3.8	2.7	4.3	2.9	2.5	3.0
1.7	1.8	1.9		2.6	1.9	2.2	2.0	1.8	1.8
1.3	1.3	1.4		1.5	1.2	1.5	1.5	1.4	1.3
1.3	1.4	1.5	Quick	2.6	1.6	2.4	1.6	1.2	1.4
.8	.8	.9		1.3	.8	.9	1.0	.8	.8
.5	.5	.6		.5	.4	.4	.6	.6	.6
29 12.4	31 11.6	34 10.8	Sales/Receivables	3 132.1	21 17.5	29 12.6	35 10.5	35 10.5	39 9.4
38 9.7	41 8.9	43 8.6		26 14.1	34 10.7	39 9.4	40 9.0	44 8.2	45 8.1
48 7.6	52 7.0	54 6.8		48 7.6	47 7.8	47 7.8	53 6.9	57 6.5	57 6.4
46 8.0	52 7.0	50 7.2	Cost of Sales/Inventory	16 23.1	42 8.8	41 8.9	48 7.6	49 7.4	53 6.9
76 4.8	81 4.5	81 4.5		60 6.1	85 4.3	109 3.3	72 5.1	86 4.2	78 4.7
103 3.0	121 3.0	114 3.2		124 2.9	138 2.6	162 2.3	111 3.3	117 3.1	100 3.6
19 19.5	22 16.6	24 15.3	Cost of Sales/Payables	12 29.9	19 18.9	17 22.1	21 17.4	25 14.4	26 13.9
27 13.3	32 11.4	33 11.1		38 9.7	30 12.2	35 10.4	30 12.1	37 9.8	32 11.2
44 8.2	46 7.9	51 7.2		71 5.2	55 6.7	77 4.7	54 6.8	54 6.8	41 9.0
5.1	4.8	4.5	Sales/Working Capital	3.9	4.4	3.2	4.3	4.8	4.6
9.6	7.9	7.3		7.1	6.9	7.4	6.9	7.9	7.1
15.8	16.7	12.7		23.6	20.6	10.8	13.1	12.8	11.8
9.8	9.8	11.0	EBIT/Interest		10.7	5.7	17.2	11.0	9.9
(350) 3.4	(361) 2.4	(335) 3.5		(36) 2.5	(30) 2.4	(61) 4.7	(94) 3.6	(106) 3.8	
1.2	-.3	1.2			.8	.9	1.1	1.6	1.2
6.0	7.0	8.1	Net Profit + Depr., Dep., Amort./Cur. Mat. L/T/D				7.8	4.1	17.8
(104) 2.5	(98) 2.2	(94) 2.8				(19) 1.4	(31) 2.5	(35) 4.5	
1.2	.4	.9					.5	1.4	1.3
.1	.1	.1	Fixed/Worth	.0	.1	.1	.1	.1	.1
.2	.2	.2		1.7	.3	.2	.2	.2	.2
.5	.6	.5		-.7	2.6	1.1	.3	.6	.4
.8	.7	.6	Debt/Worth	.8	.5	.7	.5	.6	.7
1.5	1.5	1.4		3.5	1.8	1.6	1.1	1.3	1.4
3.2	3.4	3.0		-4.6	NM	6.8	1.8	2.8	2.9
27.4	19.3	21.1	% Profit Before Taxes/Tangible Net Worth		19.4	19.6	26.3	23.6	16.9
(353) 15.1	(360) 6.4	(340) 9.0		(31) 7.5	(31) 8.9	(68) 9.8	(98) 9.2	(105) 7.9	
2.4	-4.1	2.0			-1.7	1.6	1.1	2.9	1.4
11.8	8.4	8.9	% Profit Before Taxes/Total Assets	15.5	8.6	9.9	12.0	8.5	7.6
5.2	2.4	3.8		5.9	3.8	3.0	4.1	3.7	4.1
.5	-3.2	.7		.1	-.6	.2	.3	1.2	.8
74.4	70.9	74.8	Sales/Net Fixed Assets	UND	90.4	81.6	95.7	81.4	55.8
38.8	37.0	34.0		15.0	35.3	35.2	50.0	36.5	27.2
19.2	16.1	15.1		3.9	13.7	14.2	19.1	16.2	14.2
3.6	3.3	3.2	Sales/Total Assets	3.2	3.5	3.5	3.7	3.3	2.9
2.9	2.6	2.5		2.6	2.4	2.4	2.7	2.5	2.5
2.2	2.0	2.0		.8	1.7	2.0	1.9	2.0	2.2
.4	.4	.4	% Depr., Dep., Amort./Sales		.3	.3	.3	.4	.5
(330) .6	(339) .7	(329) .7		(32) .8	(31) .8	(64) .5	(91) .6	(104) .7	
1.0	1.2	1.0			2.6	1.5	1.1	1.0	1.0
1.5	1.5	1.5	% Officers', Directors' Owners' Comp/Sales		3.9	2.1	1.8	1.5	.9
(164) 2.8	(162) 3.1	(157) 3.4		(23) 6.9	(27) 3.7	(47) 3.5	(30) 2.6	(25) 1.3	
5.6	6.3	6.4			13.3	6.2	5.2	4.3	2.3
14160590M	11497174M	11539742M	Net Sales ($)	7691M	81490M	136632M	547187M	1682613M	9084129M
5326975M	4840325M	4803773M	Total Assets ($)	8188M	38646M	70152M	228098M	715699M	3742990M

© RMA 2011

M = $ thousand   MM = $ million
See Pages 9 through 22 for Explanation of Ratios and Data

Current Data Sorted by Assets | Comparative Historical Data

Type of Statement	0-500M	500M-2MM	2-10MM	10-50MM	50-100MM	100-250MM		4/1/06-3/31/07 ALL	4/1/07-3/31/08 ALL
Unqualified			4	20	8	3		38	36
Reviewed		6	47	26				72	64
Compiled	1	16	22	3				39	39
Tax Returns	6	18	7					33	25
Other	5	6	31	26	5	6		61	70
		44 (4/1-9/30/10)		222 (10/1/10-3/31/11)					
NUMBER OF STATEMENTS	12	46	111	75	13	9		243	234

ASSETS	%	%	%	%	%	%		%	%
Cash & Equivalents	8.1	11.9	7.8	4.4	7.0			6.6	5.9
Trade Receivables (net)	55.5	37.6	37.6	34.9	31.4			39.7	37.7
Inventory	17.1	28.2	36.5	42.3	39.6			37.2	38.1
All Other Current	1.3	1.6	2.1	3.4	2.5			1.9	2.9
Total Current	82.0	79.3	84.0	85.0	80.5			85.3	84.6
Fixed Assets (net)	7.5	9.3	8.4	8.0	13.1			9.1	9.7
Intangibles (net)	3.3	4.6	2.2	2.9	2.0			1.2	1.6
All Other Non-Current	7.2	6.9	5.3	4.1	4.4			4.4	4.1
Total	100.0	100.0	100.0	100.0	100.0			100.0	100.0

LIABILITIES									
Notes Payable-Short Term	30.2	10.6	11.5	21.1	15.3			19.0	17.9
Cur. Mat.-L.T.D.	2.2	2.2	1.5	1.1	2.2			2.0	1.6
Trade Payables	31.6	25.0	25.8	16.5	13.9			23.3	22.2
Income Taxes Payable	.0	.3	.5	.1	.0			.3	.2
All Other Current	24.9	12.2	11.0	9.7	7.3			10.4	9.9
Total Current	88.8	50.2	50.4	48.6	38.8			55.0	51.8
Long-Term Debt	13.6	8.9	5.5	4.0	9.6			6.8	7.6
Deferred Taxes	.0	.1	.4	.2	.0			.1	.2
All Other Non-Current	7.8	3.4	3.6	5.2	2.0			5.3	4.0
Net Worth	-10.3	37.4	40.1	42.0	49.6			32.7	36.4
Total Liabilities & Net Worth	100.0	100.0	100.0	100.0	100.0			100.0	100.0

INCOME DATA									
Net Sales	100.0	100.0	100.0	100.0	100.0			100.0	100.0
Gross Profit	28.1	30.4	28.4	25.0	24.9			27.2	27.9
Operating Expenses	27.0	29.2	26.2	22.0	19.6			23.4	24.2
Operating Profit	1.2	1.2	2.2	3.0	5.4			3.8	3.6
All Other Expenses (net)	.0	.1	-.1	.3	1.2			.3	.3
Profit Before Taxes	1.1	1.1	2.3	2.8	4.1			3.5	3.3

RATIOS									
Current	2.4	2.7	2.4	2.5	5.1			2.1	2.2
	1.0	1.8	1.7	1.7	2.6			1.5	1.6
	.9	1.2	1.3	1.3	1.2			1.2	1.3
Quick	1.4	1.7	1.3	1.3	2.4			1.2	1.2
	.9	1.0	.9	.8	1.1			.8	.8
	.7	.7	.6	.5	.6			.5	.6
Sales/Receivables	48 7.6	29 12.6	34 10.6	34 10.7	39 9.3			34 10.9	33 11.1
	55 6.6	43 8.6	46 7.9	45 8.2	49 7.4			44 8.4	42 8.7
	88 4.1	55 6.6	62 5.9	53 6.9	55 6.6			58 6.3	55 6.7
Cost of Sales/Inventory	0 UND	16 22.6	32 11.5	60 6.1	59 6.2			27 13.5	33 11.0
	10 36.4	49 7.5	73 5.0	80 4.6	84 4.3			70 5.2	70 5.2
	37 9.8	91 4.0	103 3.5	102 3.6	105 3.5			99 3.7	100 3.6
Cost of Sales/Payables	33 11.2	25 14.7	28 13.1	16 22.4	16 22.1			17 21.6	19 19.1
	47 7.8	38 9.6	44 8.3	23 15.6	21 17.5			32 11.3	31 11.9
	83 4.4	56 6.5	63 5.8	39 9.2	39 9.4			54 6.7	48 7.7
Sales/Working Capital	11.8	5.3	5.6	4.9	3.1			6.2	6.2
	NM	12.6	8.6	7.6	5.1			10.0	8.7
	-30.3	30.6	15.6	13.1	18.2			20.4	17.6
EBIT/Interest	6.6	27.6	16.8	15.6				10.0	13.3
	(11) 3.5	(40) 3.6	(100) 4.8	(73) 5.6				(221) 3.8	(221) 4.6
	1.1	.2	1.5	2.6				2.0	2.1
Net Profit + Depr., Dep., Amort./Cur. Mat. L/T/D			11.6	10.2				10.6	14.8
		(28) 4.0	(27) 3.3					(60) 3.3	(66) 4.1
			2.0	2.0				1.7	2.0
Fixed/Worth	.1	.1	.1	.1	.1			.1	.1
	19.6	.2	.2	.2	.3			.2	.2
	-.3	1.6	.4	.4	.6			.5	.5
Debt/Worth	2.5	.7	.7	.7	.3			1.0	.9
	173.4	2.2	1.4	1.6	1.5			2.2	1.8
	-7.7	14.2	3.9	3.1	3.5			4.3	3.9
% Profit Before Taxes/Tangible Net Worth		44.1	26.7	30.5	28.4			41.2	46.3
		(40) 20.7	(101) 10.4	(70) 19.0	20.0			(226) 25.0	(217) 22.8
		-5.9	1.4	7.8	11.4			10.0	10.6
% Profit Before Taxes/Total Assets	11.1	18.2	11.3	11.7	14.9			15.4	16.1
	4.0	6.9	4.0	6.7	7.8			7.4	7.7
	.5	-1.2	.7	2.3	3.7			2.6	3.6
Sales/Net Fixed Assets	365.3	242.4	127.0	119.9	65.2			124.6	128.3
	77.0	55.1	50.5	56.3	26.8			56.1	51.7
	24.8	28.0	24.0	31.8	14.4			24.8	23.8
Sales/Total Assets	4.8	4.0	3.4	3.1	3.0			3.6	3.6
	3.2	2.8	2.8	2.7	2.6			3.0	2.9
	1.8	2.4	2.2	2.2	1.6			2.5	2.5
% Depr., Dep., Amort./Sales		.2	.3	.3	.5			.3	.3
		(35) .8	(94) .5	(71) .5	(12) .7			(213) .5	(194) .5
		1.3	1.1	.6	1.2			.9	.9
% Officers', Directors' Owners' Comp/Sales		3.3	1.3	1.0				1.6	1.3
		(27) 5.3	(47) 2.5	(14) 1.6				(96) 3.3	(91) 2.8
		6.7	4.8	2.7				6.2	5.1
Net Sales ($)	19212M	181358M	1558798M	3975356M	2153272M	3509323M		9472276M	10222574M
Total Assets ($)	4241M	55465M	549616M	1476718M	908182M	1750116M		3206660M	3687623M

M = $ thousand   MM = $ million
See Pages 9 through 22 for Explanation of Ratios and Data

Comparative Historical Data | Current Data Sorted by Sales

4/1/08-3/31/09 ALL	4/1/09-3/31/10 ALL	4/1/10-3/31/11 ALL	Type of Statement	0-1MM	1-3MM	3-5MM	5-10MM	10-25MM	25MM & OVER
37	38	35	Unqualified				3	33	32
80	77	79	Reviewed		3	4	13	33	26
36	39	42	Compiled		8	4	14	12	4
41	31	31	Tax Returns	2	10	9	6	4	
82	77	79	Other	3	4	3	9	26	34
					44 (4/1-9/30/10)		222 (10/1/10-3/31/11)		
276	262	266	NUMBER OF STATEMENTS	5	25	20	42	78	96
%	%	%	**ASSETS**	%	%	%	%	%	%
6.6	7.3	7.4	Cash & Equivalents		11.7	13.5	6.8	6.6	5.7
37.1	36.5	37.1	Trade Receivables (net)		35.0	38.2	35.3	39.9	35.2
37.1	36.9	35.7	Inventory		27.6	28.1	38.0	36.6	38.6
2.7	2.6	2.4	All Other Current		1.2	2.1	1.4	2.8	3.0
83.4	83.4	82.5	Total Current		75.6	82.0	81.5	86.0	82.6
9.3	9.6	8.7	Fixed Assets (net)		12.4	8.5	8.5	8.5	8.4
2.0	2.3	3.4	Intangibles (net)		3.0	2.8	4.2	1.3	4.9
5.4	4.7	5.3	All Other Non-Current		9.0	6.7	5.8	4.3	4.2
100.0	100.0	100.0	Total		100.0	100.0	100.0	100.0	100.0
			LIABILITIES						
20.1	15.5	15.0	Notes Payable-Short Term		13.1	11.8	11.6	13.1	18.2
2.0	1.9	1.7	Cur. Mat.-L.T.D.		3.2	1.1	3.0	.9	1.7
21.4	22.6	22.7	Trade Payables		20.6	23.9	25.8	26.1	18.5
.3	.2	.3	Income Taxes Payable		.4	.3	.3	.4	.2
11.8	11.4	11.2	All Other Current		19.9	14.0	10.2	11.1	9.2
55.6	51.6	51.0	Total Current		57.1	51.2	50.9	51.5	47.8
7.2	5.7	6.4	Long-Term Debt		10.0	7.8	6.7	5.4	5.1
.2	.2	.3	Deferred Taxes		1.2	.1	.1	.1	.4
3.9	5.2	4.1	All Other Non-Current		2.6	4.5	1.6	5.0	4.1
33.0	37.3	38.2	Net Worth		29.1	36.4	40.6	38.0	42.6
100.0	100.0	100.0	Total Liabilities & Net Worth		100.0	100.0	100.0	100.0	100.0
			INCOME DATA						
100.0	100.0	100.0	Net Sales		100.0	100.0	100.0	100.0	100.0
27.0	27.4	27.4	Gross Profit		34.0	27.8	29.5	26.6	25.3
24.3	25.3	24.9	Operating Expenses		34.0	27.7	28.1	23.7	21.6
2.6	2.0	2.5	Operating Profit		.0	.1	1.4	2.8	3.6
.1	.0	.2	All Other Expenses (net)		.0	-.2	.0	.0	.5
2.5	2.0	2.3	Profit Before Taxes		.0	.3	1.4	2.8	3.1
			RATIOS						
2.2 / 1.5 / 1.2	2.4 / 1.6 / 1.2	2.5 / 1.6 / 1.3	Current		2.8 / 1.5 / .9	2.7 / 1.7 / 1.2	2.5 / 1.8 / 1.3	2.4 / 1.7 / 1.3	2.6 / 1.7 / 1.3
1.2 / .7 / .5	1.3 / .8 / .5	1.3 / .9 / .6	Quick		1.7 / .8 / .5	1.9 / 1.1 / .7	1.1 / .9 / .6	1.3 / .9 / .6	1.3 / .9 / .6
31 11.8 / 41 8.9 / 55 6.7	33 11.0 / 43 8.5 / 57 6.5	34 10.7 / 46 7.9 / 58 6.3	Sales/Receivables		30 12.0 / 48 7.6 / 59 6.2	24 15.5 / 45 8.1 / 71 5.2	33 10.9 / 41 8.9 / 53 6.8	34 10.7 / 46 7.9 / 59 5.9	37 9.9 / 47 7.8 / 56 6.5
27 13.4 / 67 5.4 / 100 3.7	30 12.2 / 77 4.8 / 109 3.3	32 11.5 / 70 5.2 / 102 3.6	Cost of Sales/Inventory		15 24.9 / 64 5.7 / 101 3.6	11 32.8 / 38 9.6 / 82 4.4	22 16.4 / 76 4.8 / 110 3.3	30 12.1 / 73 5.0 / 103 3.6	52 7.0 / 74 5.0 / 100 3.6
18 20.7 / 29 12.4 / 49 7.4	20 18.2 / 33 11.0 / 55 6.6	21 17.1 / 37 9.9 / 58 6.3	Cost of Sales/Payables		16 22.9 / 37 9.9 / 56 6.6	26 14.0 / 39 9.4 / 58 6.3	28 13.2 / 42 8.7 / 59 6.2	26 14.2 / 44 8.3 / 63 5.8	18 20.7 / 30 12.3 / 42 8.7
6.1 / 10.1 / 24.3	5.4 / 8.8 / 18.5	5.0 / 8.7 / 17.3	Sales/Working Capital		5.0 / 16.5 / -128.7	4.6 / 11.1 / 23.9	5.7 / 11.4 / 17.6	5.3 / 7.6 / 15.0	4.9 / 8.4 / 14.1
11.1 / (257) 4.2 / 1.5	13.3 / (241) 4.3 / 1.1	16.5 / (241) 4.3 / 1.9	EBIT/Interest		8.4 / (22) 2.6 / -7.0	17.3 / (17) 4.0 / .9	15.4 / (39) 4.5 / -.2	17.6 / (70) 5.0 / 2.0	17.4 / (89) 5.6 / 2.5
12.5 / (62) 4.8 / 2.1	9.0 / (60) 2.9 / .4	11.6 / (72) 3.4 / 1.5	Net Profit + Depr., Dep., Amort./Cur. Mat. L/T/D					(21) 3.6	7.6 / 3.6 / 1.5	24.2 / (37) 3.3 / 1.2
.1 / .2 / .5	.1 / .2 / .6	.1 / .2 / .6	Fixed/Worth		.1 / .6 / 5.4	.1 / .2 / 1.3	.1 / .2 / .4	.1 / .2 / .5	.1 / .2 / .4
1.0 / 2.1 / 5.1	.8 / 1.7 / 4.3	.7 / 1.7 / 4.9	Debt/Worth		.7 / 3.1 / 18.1	.9 / 1.8 / 14.5	.7 / 1.4 / 3.7	.7 / 1.7 / 5.4	.7 / 1.7 / 4.0
38.5 / (249) 16.4 / 4.8	28.4 / (242) 12.1 / 2.9	34.4 / (238) 15.1 / 3.6	% Profit Before Taxes/Tangible Net Worth		55.6 / (21) 14.3 / -8.6	34.3 / (17) 19.1 / -.8	36.4 / (37) 9.4 / -1.4	27.6 / (72) 12.2 / 3.7	34.7 / (88) 19.6 / 9.6
12.6 / 5.5 / .9	9.8 / 4.0 / .3	12.2 / 5.4 / 1.0	% Profit Before Taxes/Total Assets		12.2 / 5.2 / -4.1	17.2 / 3.8 / -.2	12.2 / 3.1 / -1.3	10.4 / 4.5 / 1.2	12.7 / 7.6 / 2.4
118.8 / 49.3 / 25.2	121.8 / 49.1 / 22.6	128.7 / 51.3 / 23.9	Sales/Net Fixed Assets		103.2 / 25.0 / 15.4	221.0 / 47.4 / 29.0	119.4 / 52.7 / 26.0	154.2 / 55.0 / 24.0	114.0 / 53.4 / 22.5
3.7 / 3.0 / 2.4	3.5 / 2.7 / 2.2	3.3 / 2.7 / 2.2	Sales/Total Assets		3.6 / 2.5 / 2.1	3.9 / 2.6 / 2.1	3.8 / 2.8 / 2.2	3.5 / 2.7 / 2.3	3.2 / 2.8 / 2.2
.3 / (237) .5 / .8	.3 / (232) .6 / .9	.3 / (226) .5 / 1.0	% Depr., Dep., Amort./Sales		.8 / (17) 1.2 / 1.8	.2 / (16) .8 / 1.4	.2 / (35) .5 / 1.0	.3 / (66) .5 / .9	.3 / (89) .5 / .7
1.4 / (99) 2.9 / 5.1	1.5 / (83) 2.9 / 5.9	1.3 / (96) 3.0 / 5.8	% Officers', Directors' Owners' Comp/Sales		4.6 / (14) 6.3 / 8.7	1.2 / (15) 3.6 / 8.5	1.6 / (16) 4.0 / 6.4	(34) 2.1 / 3.3	1.0 / (15) 1.8 / 3.7
10890428M	9568577M	11397319M	Net Sales ($)	2610M	48480M	79143M	317498M	1281491M	9668097M
3948396M	3642777M	4744338M	Total Assets ($)	1393M	20515M	32505M	117122M	475467M	4097336M

© RMA 2011

M = $ thousand   MM = $ million
See Pages 9 through 22 for Explanation of Ratios and Data

Current Data Sorted by Assets

Comparative Historical Data

		2	6	1		Type of Statement		13	7
		11	5			Unqualified		13	15
1	6	2	1			Reviewed		13	14
1	3	2	1			Compiled		11	2
2	5	8	7			Tax Returns		18	18
	10 (4/1-9/30/10)		54 (10/1/10-3/31/11)			Other		4/1/06- 3/31/07	4/1/07- 3/31/08
0-500M	500M-2MM	2-10MM	10-50MM	50-100MM	100-250MM			ALL	ALL
4	14	25	20	1		NUMBER OF STATEMENTS		68	56
%	%	%	%	%	%	ASSETS		%	%
	14.3	11.3	8.5			Cash & Equivalents		7.0	10.1
	34.2	25.2	24.7		D	Trade Receivables (net)		28.6	27.2
	28.3	36.4	44.2		A	Inventory		41.0	37.0
	2.7	3.7	4.0		T	All Other Current		1.9	3.5
	79.5	76.6	81.3		A	Total Current		78.5	77.9
	8.7	10.3	10.2			Fixed Assets (net)		13.5	13.3
	3.7	8.6	.7		N	Intangibles (net)		4.5	4.4
	8.1	4.5	7.8		O	All Other Non-Current		3.5	4.5
	100.0	100.0	100.0		T	Total		100.0	100.0
					A	LIABILITIES			
	12.1	9.9	12.3		V	Notes Payable-Short Term		18.2	17.3
	3.7	3.6	1.7		A	Cur. Mat.-L.T.D.		2.2	2.0
	19.0	20.0	18.1		I	Trade Payables		20.3	16.7
	.2	.1	.3		L	Income Taxes Payable		.3	.4
	7.4	9.8	8.8		A	All Other Current		8.3	8.7
	42.4	43.4	41.2		B	Total Current		49.4	45.0
	12.4	7.8	2.8		L	Long-Term Debt		10.1	8.9
	.0	.2	.3		E	Deferred Taxes		.3	.1
	3.1	2.8	12.2			All Other Non-Current		5.8	6.1
	42.1	45.8	43.5			Net Worth		34.4	39.8
	100.0	100.0	100.0			Total Liabilities & Net Worth		100.0	100.0
						INCOME DATA			
	100.0	100.0	100.0			Net Sales		100.0	100.0
	32.7	29.8	24.0			Gross Profit		29.0	32.0
	31.0	26.2	18.9			Operating Expenses		23.6	25.1
	1.7	3.6	5.2			Operating Profit		5.4	6.9
	-.4	.7	.1			All Other Expenses (net)		1.4	.9
	2.1	2.9	5.1			Profit Before Taxes		4.0	6.0
						RATIOS			
	3.2	3.0	4.0					2.6	2.6
	1.7	1.7	2.1			Current		1.7	1.8
	1.4	1.2	1.5					1.2	1.4
	1.4	1.2	1.3					1.3	1.3
	1.1	.9	.8			Quick		.6	.8
	.7	.6	.4					.4	.4

20	18.6	25	14.7	22	16.3		25	14.8	24	15.4
26	13.8	32	11.5	33	11.0	Sales/Receivables	34	10.7	35	10.6
42	8.7	41	8.9	38	9.5		47	7.7	45	8.2
3	111.9	56	6.5	33	11.0		40	9.2	31	11.8
26	14.1	79	4.6	80	4.5	Cost of Sales/Inventory	73	5.0	76	4.8
93	3.9	120	3.0	123	3.0		125	2.9	127	2.9
12	30.8	17	21.3	16	23.0		20	18.0	14	26.4
31	11.8	33	11.2	31	11.9	Cost of Sales/Payables	32	11.3	28	13.1
56	6.5	46	7.9	40	9.2		51	7.1	46	7.9

					Ratio					
	5.1		5.3		3.9			5.8		4.8
	10.5		8.4		6.8	Sales/Working Capital		9.8		8.7
	25.9		19.4		16.9			23.0		12.5
	34.0		10.6		39.1			9.2		9.7
(12)	7.8	(19)	5.0	(19)	16.5	EBIT/Interest	(62)	3.1	(53)	4.0
	2.0		2.9		6.7			1.8		2.4
						Net Profit + Depr., Dep.,		40.7		31.4
						Amort./Cur. Mat. L/T/D	(13)	8.3	(18)	10.7
								1.8		1.4
	.1		.1		.1			.2		.2
	.3		.2		.2	Fixed/Worth		.3		.3
	.8		.9		.4			.7		.8
	.5		.5		.5			1.0		.9
	1.1		1.3		1.0	Debt/Worth		2.2		1.7
	8.2		4.0		2.3			5.9		3.4
	75.0		45.5		41.0	% Profit Before Taxes/Tangible		42.2		56.7
(13)	16.8	(22)	15.0	(18)	18.9	Net Worth	(62)	24.6	(50)	24.8
	.5		6.0		14.4			9.3		8.8
	15.9		11.9		21.7	% Profit Before Taxes/Total		14.5		16.4
	9.5		5.6		10.6	Assets		7.6		8.4
	.4		2.5		7.4			2.6		3.1
	89.4		131.8		103.3			75.5		63.4
	44.2		33.7		40.0	Sales/Net Fixed Assets		38.9		32.2
	24.8		18.1		18.9			12.3		12.8
	4.7		3.0		3.6			3.4		3.4
	3.3		2.5		2.8	Sales/Total Assets		2.7		2.7
	2.4		2.1		2.0			2.2		2.0
	.4		.2		.3			.3		.4
(10)	1.2	(21)	.6	(19)	.7	% Depr., Dep., Amort./Sales	(57)	.8	(49)	.8
	1.8		1.0		.9			1.1		1.2
						% Officers', Directors'		2.6		1.8
						Owners' Comp/Sales	(27)	3.7	(24)	3.8
								7.8		5.9

4523M	59150M	347930M	1178022M	98930M		Net Sales ($)		1859369M	1537966M
1186M	16580M	134734M	435957M	78920M		Total Assets ($)		778296M	622284M

M = $ thousand   MM = $ million
See Pages 9 through 22 for Explanation of Ratios and Data

Comparative Historical Data

Current Data Sorted by Sales

4/1/08-3/31/09 ALL	4/1/09-3/31/10 ALL	4/1/10-3/31/11 ALL	Type of Statement	0-1MM	1-3MM	3-5MM	5-10MM	10-25MM	25MM & OVER
8	11	9	Unqualified				2	2	7
20	18	16	Reviewed		4		2	9	5
12	12	10	Compiled				2	2	1
17	5	7	Tax Returns	1	2	2	3	1	
23	26	22	Other	1	2	1	5	6	7
					10 (4/1-9/30/10)		54 (10/1/10-3/31/11)		
80	72	64	**NUMBER OF STATEMENTS**	2	6	4	12	20	20
%	%	%	**ASSETS**	%	%	%	%	%	%
10.6	11.7	11.5	Cash & Equivalents				12.7	10.1	10.7
24.6	26.4	27.3	Trade Receivables (net)				34.8	24.0	24.3
38.0	38.5	36.0	Inventory				24.4	40.3	40.9
3.0	3.4	3.8	All Other Current				4.9	3.0	4.2
76.2	80.0	78.6	Total Current				76.7	77.5	80.1
12.9	11.2	10.2	Fixed Assets (net)				8.2	9.8	10.9
6.0	4.7	5.0	Intangibles (net)				7.4	8.7	.7
5.0	4.1	6.2	All Other Non-Current				7.8	4.1	8.3
100.0	100.0	100.0	Total				100.0	100.0	100.0
			LIABILITIES						
20.0	13.3	10.5	Notes Payable-Short Term				6.9	12.7	10.5
2.4	2.2	3.0	Cur. Mat.-L.T.D.				7.0	2.1	1.9
17.2	18.5	18.7	Trade Payables				21.0	19.5	17.8
.2	.1	.4	Income Taxes Payable				.1	.1	.3
9.0	8.4	8.6	All Other Current				11.4	8.0	9.1
48.8	42.5	41.3	Total Current				46.5	42.3	39.6
11.8	7.8	8.2	Long-Term Debt				13.2	5.8	3.3
.2	.2	.2	Deferred Taxes				.0	.3	.3
5.5	6.7	5.6	All Other Non-Current				5.0	7.4	7.4
33.7	42.7	44.8	Net Worth				35.3	44.2	49.4
100.0	100.0	100.0	Total Liabilties & Net Worth				100.0	100.0	100.0
			INCOME DATA						
100.0	100.0	100.0	Net Sales				100.0	100.0	100.0
28.6	28.7	30.0	Gross Profit				29.4	31.5	24.1
25.1	25.0	25.9	Operating Expenses				27.3	27.0	18.7
3.5	3.7	4.1	Operating Profit				2.1	4.5	5.4
.3	.3	.2	All Other Expenses (net)				.5	.8	-.1
3.2	3.4	3.8	Profit Before Taxes				1.7	3.7	5.4
			RATIOS						
2.8	3.1	3.3	Current				2.8	3.1	4.5
1.7	2.0	1.8					1.5	1.7	2.1
1.2	1.4	1.4					1.2	1.3	1.5
1.1	1.4	1.4	Quick				1.3	1.2	1.8
.7	.9	1.0					.9	.9	.9
.4	.6	.6					.6	.5	.6
21 17.8	24 15.1	23 16.0	Sales/Receivables				26 14.3	23 15.6	22 16.3
27 13.5	34 10.8	31 11.7					35 10.3	29 12.7	32 11.6
39 9.4	40 9.0	40 9.1					44 8.2	36 10.2	38 9.5
34 10.8	44 8.2	26 14.2	Cost of Sales/Inventory				6 56.2	59 6.2	33 11.0
59 6.1	75 4.8	75 4.9					26 14.1	85 4.3	72 5.1
123 3.0	124 2.9	123 3.0					83 4.4	138 2.6	123 3.0
11 34.5	17 21.8	17 21.5	Cost of Sales/Payables				15 23.6	17 21.0	16 23.5
26 13.8	31 11.8	32 11.6					26 14.1	32 11.4	26 14.0
36 10.1	48 7.6	44 8.3					44 8.4	46 7.9	40 9.2
4.6	4.3	4.8	Sales/Working Capital				6.5	3.7	3.9
10.8	6.7	7.7					17.8	8.0	6.8
36.4	11.8	17.1					39.0	14.5	16.9
9.8	12.6	31.6	EBIT/Interest				51.2	12.1	103.7
(73) 3.5	(64) 5.5	(54) 9.0		(10) 4.2		(16) 6.2		(19) 19.8	
1.6	2.7	3.8					1.9	3.0	7.9
42.1	6.6	6.5	Net Profit + Depr., Dep., Amort./Cur. Mat. L/T/D						
(19) 5.6	(16) 5.2	(17) 2.8							
2.0	2.8	1.7							
.1	.1	.1	Fixed/Worth				.1	.1	.1
.3	.2	.2					.4	.2	.2
1.4	.5	.6					2.6	1.0	.3
.7	.5	.5	Debt/Worth				.8	.4	.5
1.6	1.2	1.2					5.5	1.4	.9
7.0	3.2	3.3					21.8	2.9	1.7
38.3	26.9	38.7	% Profit Before Taxes/Tangible Net Worth				69.5	47.4	40.9
(66) 16.5	(64) 13.9	(57) 16.9		(10) 12.3		(17) 16.2		(19) 18.5	
7.1	4.7	9.6					2.8	10.8	14.7
12.9	11.4	14.8	% Profit Before Taxes/Total Assets				16.1	12.6	21.7
5.8	5.8	8.6					2.9	6.9	11.6
2.1	2.1	3.8					.8	4.0	7.6
93.3	73.0	106.1	Sales/Net Fixed Assets				129.2	132.6	47.0
43.7	38.2	36.6					77.2	42.1	35.2
18.4	16.6	20.1					27.2	20.2	15.1
3.9	3.3	3.5	Sales/Total Assets				4.3	2.9	3.6
2.9	2.6	2.6					3.4	2.5	2.8
2.1	1.9	2.2					2.5	2.1	2.0
.4	.5	.4	% Depr., Dep., Amort./Sales					.1	.5
(66) .7	(58) .8	(53) .8					(18)	.6	(19) .7
1.0	1.3	1.1						.9	.9
2.1	1.6	2.4	% Officers', Directors' Owners' Comp/Sales						
(35) 4.5	(14) 2.5	(20) 3.4							
6.8	4.4	5.1							
2273007M	2200014M	1688555M	Net Sales ($)	894M	11090M	13803M	84092M	325658M	1253018M
993486M	939613M	667377M	Total Assets ($)	400M	4713M	4044M	26273M	131290M	500657M

M = $ thousand   MM = $ million
See Pages 9 through 22 for Explanation of Ratios and Data

Current Data Sorted by Assets | Comparative Historical Data

Type of Statement

	0-500M	500M-2MM	2-10MM	10-50MM	50-100MM	100-250MM	Type of Statement	ALL	ALL
	1	14	17	48	18	30	Unqualified	115	120
	3	12	75	45	5	2	Reviewed	108	118
	13	32	38	8	2		Compiled	48	70
	6	28	24	24			Tax Returns	44	45
			81	52	19	29	Other	115	177
	82 (4/1-9/30/10)			518 (10/1/10-3/31/11)				4/1/06-3/31/07	4/1/07-3/31/08
NUMBER OF STATEMENTS	23	86	235	153	44	59		430	530

ASSETS

	0-500M %	500M-2MM %	2-10MM %	10-50MM %	50-100MM %	100-250MM %	ALL %	ALL %
Cash & Equivalents	14.6	12.9	8.3	5.8	2.7	2.7	5.3	5.6
Trade Receivables (net)	16.2	26.3	18.9	15.1	15.7	16.1	20.0	16.9
Inventory	37.1	42.6	47.5	50.4	52.3	46.9	46.0	49.5
All Other Current	2.8	1.5	1.6	1.8	2.1	1.9	1.8	2.0
Total Current	70.7	83.2	76.3	73.1	72.9	67.6	73.1	74.0
Fixed Assets (net)	14.4	11.0	17.1	20.1	22.6	24.1	22.2	21.3
Intangibles (net)	5.0	1.8	2.7	1.4	1.9	1.3	1.4	1.4
All Other Non-Current	9.8	4.0	3.9	5.4	2.6	7.0	3.3	3.3
Total	100.0	100.0	100.0	100.0	100.0	100.0	100.0	100.0

LIABILITIES

	0-500M	500M-2MM	2-10MM	10-50MM	50-100MM	100-250MM	ALL	ALL
Notes Payable-Short Term	25.7	20.3	24.3	26.7	26.3	19.3	25.6	27.8
Cur. Mat.-L.T.D.	8.5	2.6	4.3	5.1	4.2	2.5	4.0	5.2
Trade Payables	12.9	18.7	13.3	9.6	8.4	11.1	14.0	12.7
Income Taxes Payable	.0	.2	.2	.6	1.0	.4	.3	.3
All Other Current	20.3	9.0	7.0	6.1	7.0	7.8	8.3	7.5
Total Current	67.4	50.7	49.1	48.1	46.9	41.1	52.1	53.6
Long-Term Debt	18.2	10.8	9.4	10.9	11.4	15.0	12.5	14.0
Deferred Taxes	.0	.2	.7	1.0	1.4	1.0	.5	.5
All Other Non-Current	19.1	5.3	4.0	3.2	3.8	3.8	5.1	3.8
Net Worth	-4.6	33.0	36.8	36.8	36.6	39.1	29.9	28.2
Total Liabilities & Net Worth	100.0	100.0	100.0	100.0	100.0	100.0	100.0	100.0

INCOME DATA

	0-500M	500M-2MM	2-10MM	10-50MM	50-100MM	100-250MM	ALL	ALL
Net Sales	100.0	100.0	100.0	100.0	100.0	100.0	100.0	100.0
Gross Profit	41.5	28.9	28.2	25.6	23.3	25.2	26.5	26.0
Operating Expenses	37.6	26.1	25.3	21.8	19.6	20.1	20.6	20.7
Operating Profit	3.9	2.8	3.0	3.8	3.7	5.1	5.9	5.3
All Other Expenses (net)	.5	.7	1.1	.8	.8	1.0	1.2	1.3
Profit Before Taxes	3.4	2.2	1.9	3.0	2.8	4.2	4.7	3.9

RATIOS

Ratio	0-500M	500M-2MM	2-10MM	10-50MM	50-100MM	100-250MM	ALL	ALL
Current	2.2	2.5	2.2	2.0	2.2	2.1	1.9	1.8
	1.3	1.6	1.6	1.4	1.4	1.6	1.4	1.3
	.6	1.2	1.2	1.2	1.2	1.3	1.1	1.1
Quick	1.3	1.3	.9	.7	.7	.7	.9	.7
	.6	.8	.5	.4	.3	.5	(429) .4	.4
	.1	.4	.3	.2	.2	.3	.2	.2
Sales/Receivables	0 UND	11 32.1	20 17.9	24 15.5	30 12.3	33 11.1	20 18.0	17 21.1
	15 23.7	34 10.7	33 11.0	38 9.5	41 8.8	43 8.4	33 11.0	30 12.4
	38 9.5	52 7.0	51 7.2	53 6.9	49 7.4	52 7.0	47 7.8	45 8.1
Cost of Sales/Inventory	3 107.8	23 16.2	58 6.3	102 3.6	83 4.4	108 3.4	50 7.2	59 6.2
	61 6.0	78 4.7	134 2.7	153 2.4	189 1.9	158 2.3	112 3.2	124 2.9
	124 3.0	129 2.8	222 1.6	245 1.5	283 1.3	228 1.6	187 2.0	207 1.8
Cost of Sales/Payables	0 UND	9 38.8	12 29.8	11 34.3	13 27.2	23 15.9	10 38.2	11 34.2
	12 29.6	24 15.4	23 15.6	21 17.3	26 14.2	37 9.7	23 15.9	22 16.8
	44 8.3	47 7.7	50 7.4	44 8.2	35 10.4	52 7.0	48 7.7	47 7.8
Sales/Working Capital	5.0	5.1	3.8	3.6	3.6	3.4	5.7	5.2
	25.5	9.9	6.8	6.6	6.6	5.7	10.2	9.8
	-34.7	29.0	17.1	12.1	15.5	8.7	28.9	27.8
EBIT/Interest	7.2	11.1	8.6	8.3	6.5	7.0	6.0	4.9
	(18) 3.8	(73) 2.4	(220) 2.4	(152) 2.9	3.8	(58) 4.0	(407) 2.8	(509) 2.4
	-1.1	.8	1.0	1.3	1.7	2.4	1.6	1.3
Net Profit + Depr., Dep., Amort./Cur. Mat. L/T/D			7.3	8.1	22.7		8.6	7.0
		(59) 3.0	(42) 3.4	(11) 3.6			(114) 3.5	(137) 2.0
			.8	1.2	.3		1.0	.7
Fixed/Worth	.1	.0	.1	.1	.1	.3	.2	.1
	.5	.2	.3	.4	.3	.6	.5	.4
	-.4	1.1	1.2	1.0	1.2	.9	1.4	1.5
Debt/Worth	1.3	.9	.9	.9	1.5	1.1	1.4	1.6
	6.5	2.3	1.7	2.0	2.0	1.6	3.0	3.0
	-4.0	9.9	4.1	3.7	3.5	2.6	5.0	5.9
% Profit Before Taxes/Tangible Net Worth	103.3	57.9	23.9	20.2	16.5	17.3	41.0	39.1
	(14) 23.9	(74) 16.3	(213) 7.8	(146) 9.1	10.7	(58) 13.1	(412) 23.2	(498) 18.8
	3.3	-2.3	1.3	3.4	7.0	8.3	10.5	6.5
% Profit Before Taxes/Total Assets	21.0	16.0	8.3	6.9	5.4	7.6	11.5	9.6
	7.6	3.9	2.4	3.2	3.6	4.8	5.6	4.5
	-2.6	-.5	.1	.8	.6	3.4	2.4	1.1
Sales/Net Fixed Assets	202.0	157.9	46.8	36.1	41.1	16.1	46.5	51.9
	58.1	53.7	21.9	17.7	17.6	7.5	18.1	19.4
	13.6	21.3	9.1	4.9	3.8	3.7	5.5	5.4
Sales/Total Assets	4.2	3.9	2.5	1.7	1.7	1.6	2.6	2.5
	3.2	2.8	1.7	1.4	1.3	1.3	1.9	1.8
	2.1	1.8	1.2	1.0	1.1	1.1	1.4	1.3
% Depr., Dep., Amort./Sales	.5	.3	.7	.7	.9	.8	.6	.6
	(11) 2.3	(57) .7	(181) 1.3	(109) 1.6	(25) 1.5	(22) 1.0	(341) 1.1	(405) 1.1
	4.9	2.0		6.5	7.4	3.4	3.9	4.8
% Officers', Directors' Owners' Comp/Sales	4.8	2.0	1.3	1.0			1.3	1.0
	(13) 6.5	(43) 2.9	(81) 2.3	(24) 2.3			(120) 2.2	(121) 2.2
	9.9	5.0	4.2	3.2			5.1	4.9
Net Sales ($)	21838M	328337M	2180597M	5377999M	4295860M	12528447M	22652797M	26164916M
Total Assets ($)	5623M	107494M	1170303M	3692863M	2993110M	9364977M	13652684M	15861361M

M = $ thousand   MM = $ million
See Pages 9 through 22 for Explanation of Ratios and Data

Comparative Historical Data | | | Type of Statement | | Current Data Sorted by Sales

Comparative Historical Data						Type of Statement	0-1MM	1-3MM	3-5MM	5-10MM	10-25MM	25MM & OVER
	145		124		113	Unqualified		1	2	6	22	82
	128		127		140	Reviewed	2	9	16	31	53	29
	63		75		63	Compiled	2	9	8	20	20	4
	49		59		69	Tax Returns	10	17	11	20	11	
	222		227		215	Other	7	27	31	27	41	82
	4/1/08-		4/1/09-		4/1/10-			82 (4/1-9/30/10)		518 (10/1/10-3/31/11)		
	3/31/09		3/31/10		3/31/11							
	ALL		ALL		ALL							
	607		612		600	**NUMBER OF STATEMENTS**	21	63	68	104	147	197
	%		%		%	**ASSETS**	%	%	%	%	%	%
	5.4		7.3		7.6	Cash & Equivalents	11.2	10.6	10.6	6.8	10.2	3.7
	16.0		17.0		18.4	Trade Receivables (net)	13.7	18.4	22.2	19.1	19.4	16.3
	49.9		46.9		47.4	Inventory	45.1	39.9	45.4	49.4	44.5	51.8
	2.1		1.9		1.8	All Other Current	2.5	2.2	1.3	1.1	2.0	1.9
	73.5		73.2		75.2	Total Current	72.5	71.1	79.5	76.4	76.1	73.8
	20.9		20.0		18.0	Fixed Assets (net)	19.1	18.9	14.7	17.6	17.0	19.7
	1.5		1.9		2.1	Intangibles (net)	2.7	3.7	3.3	2.6	1.3	1.6
	4.2		4.9		4.7	All Other Non-Current	5.8	6.3	2.5	3.4	5.7	4.8
	100.0		100.0		100.0	Total	100.0	100.0	100.0	100.0	100.0	100.0
						LIABILITIES						
	29.5		23.8		24.0	Notes Payable-Short Term	18.5	26.5	25.7	22.6	21.6	25.9
	4.4		4.5		4.2	Cur. Mat.-L.T.D.	10.2	3.5	4.9	4.6	4.3	3.3
	11.2		11.0		12.5	Trade Payables	9.4	13.4	12.8	13.9	13.7	10.9
	.3		.3		.4	Income Taxes Payable	.0	.0	.2	.3	.3	.7
	7.8		9.0		7.6	All Other Current	21.9	7.6	6.0	6.3	7.8	7.3
	53.1		48.6		48.8	Total Current	59.9	51.0	49.6	47.7	47.8	48.1
	13.1		13.1		11.0	Long-Term Debt	30.5	14.4	9.6	9.8	8.7	10.9
	.6		.7		.7	Deferred Taxes	.0	.7	.7	.5	.7	1.0
	3.0		3.6		4.5	All Other Non-Current	17.5	9.7	3.7	4.2	2.8	3.1
	30.2		34.0		34.9	Net Worth	-8.0	24.2	36.5	37.8	40.0	36.9
	100.0		100.0		100.0	Total Liabilities & Net Worth	100.0	100.0	100.0	100.0	100.0	100.0
						INCOME DATA						
	100.0		100.0		100.0	Net Sales	100.0	100.0	100.0	100.0	100.0	100.0
	26.0		28.3		27.5	Gross Profit	43.6	37.4	29.2	27.5	25.7	23.4
	21.9		26.5		24.1	Operating Expenses	41.9	33.5	25.8	24.0	22.9	19.4
	4.1		1.9		3.5	Operating Profit	1.7	3.9	3.4	3.5	2.9	4.0
	1.1		1.1		.9	All Other Expenses (net)	2.7	1.9	1.2	.9	.3	.8
	3.0		.7		2.6	Profit Before Taxes	-1.0	2.0	2.2	2.6	2.6	3.2
						RATIOS						
	2.0		2.3		2.1		2.8	2.1	2.6	2.4	2.3	2.0
	1.3		1.5		1.5	Current	1.4	1.3	1.6	1.6	1.6	1.5
	1.1		1.2		1.2		.8	1.0	1.2	1.2	1.2	1.2
	.7		.9		.9		1.1	1.0	1.2	.8	1.2	.7
(606)	.3		.4		.5	Quick	.5	.5	.6	.5	.6	.4
	.2		.2		.3		.1	.2	.3	.3	.3	.2
17	21.2	20	18.3	22	16.8		0 UND	11 32.6	20 18.6	20 18.3	23 16.2	27 13.7
28	13.0	33	11.0	36	10.2	Sales/Receivables	24 15.0	37 9.8	37 9.9	35 10.5	35 10.5	38 9.5
43	8.5	48	7.6	51	7.2		68 5.4	66 5.5	52 7.0	51 7.1	50 7.3	50 7.3
69	5.3	67	5.5	64	5.7		39 9.3	23 15.6	40 9.2	55 6.6	53 6.9	93 3.9
136	2.7	156	2.3	134	2.7	Cost of Sales/Inventory	124 3.0	119 3.1	118 3.1	128 2.9	120 3.0	155 2.4
219	1.7	253	1.4	224	1.6		390 .9	269 1.4	217 1.7	222 1.6	208 1.8	230 1.6
9	42.1	10	35.9	12	31.1		0 UND	12 31.7	12 29.8	11 33.9	11 33.7	15 23.9
19	19.4	20	18.0	24	15.1	Cost of Sales/Payables	12 29.6	30 12.4	20 18.2	24 15.0	22 16.8	28 13.2
42	8.7	41	8.9	46	8.0		36 10.2	80 4.6	47 7.8	40 9.1	46 7.9	44 8.3
	4.9		3.5		3.8		1.3	3.8	4.0	3.7	4.0	3.7
	9.3		6.8		6.9	Sales/Working Capital	8.9	9.8	6.6	6.8	7.2	6.7
	24.9		17.8		17.1		-9.9	-79.9	18.3	17.2	17.1	12.0
	5.2		4.1		7.9		3.3	4.4	6.8	9.4	10.0	8.0
(578)	2.3	(567)	1.7	(565)	2.9	EBIT/Interest	(17) 1.2	(58) 1.6	(60) 2.0	(96) 3.0	(139) 3.0	(195) 3.9
	1.2		1.3		1.3		-6.5	.2	.7	1.1	1.4	1.8
	6.5		5.1		8.0					7.1	9.0	10.2
(144)	1.9	(119)	1.7	(123)	3.1	Net Profit + Depr., Dep., Amort./Cur. Mat. L/T/D			(29) 3.1	(37) 3.8	(43) 3.7
	.5		.5		1.0					.7	1.3	1.2
	.2		.1		.1		.0	.1	.1	.1	.1	.1
	.5		.4		.3	Fixed/Worth	2.0	.4	.3	.2	.4	.4
	1.4		1.2		1.1		-.4	8.0	.8	1.3	.8	1.0
	1.4		1.0		1.0		1.1	1.2	1.0	.8	.8	1.2
	2.8		2.1		1.9	Debt/Worth	21.4	3.5	2.0	1.7	1.6	1.9
	5.6		4.4		3.9		-3.4	23.4	4.3	4.2	2.9	3.3
	28.8		17.8		24.0	% Profit Before Taxes/Tangible Net Worth	83.7	30.4	31.7	29.7	25.1	19.9
(572)	13.7	(568)	5.6	(549)	9.5		(12) 16.1	(49) 3.1	(61) 6.8	(92) 8.1	(141) 9.4	(194) 11.5
	3.6		-3.6		2.5		-11.8	-6.2	-1.7	1.4	2.6	6.4
	8.8		5.6		8.2	% Profit Before Taxes/Total Assets	10.9	10.7	9.4	12.5	8.2	7.6
	3.3		1.6		3.5		1.4	.8	2.0	3.1	3.3	4.4
	.4		-1.7		.6		-12.6	-2.7	-1.2	.3	.7	2.1
	41.0		39.8		49.7	Sales/Net Fixed Assets	88.0	86.9	92.4	52.4	45.7	35.4
	16.8		16.5		20.9		16.7	26.1	32.8	22.9	21.1	16.4
	5.1		5.2		6.4		5.0	8.0	10.3	8.7	7.9	4.7
	2.4		2.2		2.4	Sales/Total Assets	2.9	2.6	3.2	2.9	2.5	1.8
	1.7		1.4		1.6		1.4	1.4	1.4	1.8	1.8	1.5
	1.2		1.0		1.1		.8	.9	1.1	1.3	1.2	1.1
	.7		.7		.7	% Depr., Dep., Amort./Sales	1.4	.5	.5	.6	.7	.7
(443)	1.3	(421)	1.5	(405)	1.3		(12) 4.1	(47) 2.1	(38) 1.5	(80) 1.1	(115) 1.3	(113) 1.1
	4.4		4.7		4.7		21.2	10.6	5.6	4.9	4.0	3.4
	1.3		1.5		1.5	% Officers', Directors' Owners' Comp/Sales		2.9	2.0	1.8	1.3	1.8
(155)	2.1	(183)	2.9	(168)	2.6			(27) 5.0	(23) 2.9	(48) 2.3	(44) 2.0	(17) 1.9
	4.2		5.8		4.5			6.6	4.0	4.2	3.0	3.1
32829823M		23930316M		24733078M		Net Sales ($)	11863M	131797M	279532M	758534M	2294000M	21257352M
20495425M		18153636M		17334370M		Total Assets ($)	14590M	111350M	194359M	466709M	1585674M	14961688M

M = $ thousand   MM = $ million
See Pages 9 through 22 for Explanation of Ratios and Data

Current Data Sorted by Assets

Comparative Historical Data

0-500M	500M-2MM	2-10MM	10-50MM	50-100MM	100-250MM	Type of Statement	4/1/06-3/31/07 ALL	4/1/07-3/31/08 ALL
		5	23	7	4	Unqualified	42	36
	2	35	37	7	7	Reviewed	81	69
1	13	34	13	1		Compiled	84	94
3	9	23	6			Tax Returns	55	43
4	13	37	40	8	1	Other	94	105
	55 (4/1-9/30/10)		271 (10/1/10-3/31/11)					
8	37	134	119	23	5	**NUMBER OF STATEMENTS**	356	347
%	%	%	%	%	%	**ASSETS**	%	%
	11.4	7.8	5.3	3.6		Cash & Equivalents	5.7	5.7
	20.2	14.3	13.6	8.6		Trade Receivables (net)	15.5	15.0
	47.9	60.4	62.6	66.7		Inventory	59.3	58.3
	2.4	2.0	2.4	2.3		All Other Current	1.9	2.4
	82.0	84.5	83.9	81.2		Total Current	82.3	81.5
	13.9	10.7	10.8	13.6		Fixed Assets (net)	11.3	12.3
	.5	1.0	1.7	1.5		Intangibles (net)	1.7	1.6
	3.6	3.9	3.5	3.8		All Other Non-Current	4.7	4.6
	100.0	100.0	100.0	100.0		Total	100.0	100.0
						LIABILITIES		
	16.5	25.2	29.2	20.4		Notes Payable-Short Term	25.3	24.2
	2.8	2.0	1.4	1.3		Cur. Mat.-L.T.D.	2.3	2.5
	15.1	15.7	16.9	16.4		Trade Payables	19.1	18.5
	.1	.1	.2	.6		Income Taxes Payable	.2	.1
	6.1	9.0	9.7	13.7		All Other Current	9.0	9.9
	40.5	52.0	57.4	52.3		Total Current	55.9	55.2
	11.3	6.8	6.7	10.0		Long-Term Debt	8.6	8.7
	.0	.2	.3	.3		Deferred Taxes	.1	.2
	5.0	3.1	4.0	1.3		All Other Non-Current	3.4	4.0
	43.1	37.8	31.6	36.2		Net Worth	31.9	31.8
	100.0	100.0	100.0	100.0		Total Liabilities & Net Worth	100.0	100.0
						INCOME DATA		
	100.0	100.0	100.0	100.0		Net Sales	100.0	100.0
	35.8	24.5	19.5	17.7		Gross Profit	21.7	22.9
	33.6	21.8	16.4	13.2		Operating Expenses	19.1	20.0
	2.2	2.7	3.1	4.4		Operating Profit	2.7	2.9
	.7	.1	.0	.3		All Other Expenses (net)	.6	.6
	1.5	2.6	3.0	4.1		Profit Before Taxes	2.1	2.3
						RATIOS		
	3.3	2.3	1.8	1.9		Current	2.0	1.9
	2.0	1.6	1.4	1.4			1.4	1.5
	1.4	1.3	1.2	1.3			1.2	1.2
	1.7	.8	.6	.5		Quick	.7	.7
	.7	.4	.3	.2			.3	.3
	.3	.2	.1	.1			.1	.1
	11 32.9	8 43.2	7 52.9	3 117.9		Sales/Receivables	7 53.9	7 52.8
	24 15.1	19 19.4	13 27.2	10 37.6			17 21.5	17 20.9
	41 8.9	33 11.0	39 9.4	32 11.6			34 10.8	35 10.4
	57 6.4	89 4.1	89 4.1	98 3.7		Cost of Sales/Inventory	73 5.0	80 4.6
	95 3.8	128 2.8	130 2.8	119 3.1			114 3.2	116 3.1
	249 1.5	176 2.1	165 2.2	211 1.7			177 2.1	168 2.2
	4 96.7	8 47.9	7 52.1	5 71.1		Cost of Sales/Payables	9 41.6	9 40.0
	23 15.6	23 15.9	23 15.7	20 17.8			25 14.3	26 14.1
	41 8.8	48 7.6	49 7.5	52 7.1			52 7.0	54 6.8
	3.3	4.2	6.3	4.1		Sales/Working Capital	5.7	5.5
	5.7	7.8	9.0	8.9			9.8	9.6
	12.9	14.1	14.1	14.3			20.0	17.3
	6.8	9.1	11.1	19.3		EBIT/Interest	5.4	5.7
	(35) 2.7	(128) 3.4	(115) 4.2	10.1			(345) 2.5	(337) 2.6
	1.0	1.4	2.2	3.0			1.3	1.4
		5.0	11.9			Net Profit + Depr., Dep., Amort./Cur. Mat. L/T/D	4.1	5.1
		(30) 2.5	(40) 4.2				(89) 2.6	(100) 2.6
		1.4	2.1				1.0	1.2
	.0	.1	.1	.2		Fixed/Worth	.1	.1
	.1	.2	.3	.3			.3	.3
	.5	.5	.6	.5			.7	.7
	.6	.9	1.4	1.1		Debt/Worth	1.1	1.1
	1.1	1.8	2.5	2.4			2.4	2.6
	3.8	3.8	4.1	3.1			5.9	4.5
	39.3	28.4	32.4	38.4		% Profit Before Taxes/Tangible Net Worth	28.4	28.7
	7.4	(127) 10.8	(114) 20.0	21.0			(323) 14.5	(323) 13.9
	-1.0	2.7	9.8	9.9			4.4	4.9
	9.5	10.1	9.6	11.8		% Profit Before Taxes/Total Assets	8.9	9.6
	3.6	3.0	4.8	7.5			4.0	3.8
	-.4	.8	2.6	3.6			1.0	1.2
	208.0	83.4	59.0	61.9		Sales/Net Fixed Assets	70.6	72.3
	30.1	38.5	34.1	21.4			33.1	31.9
	11.4	15.5	15.8	10.1			16.3	14.4
	3.6	2.9	2.7	3.0		Sales/Total Assets	3.1	2.9
	2.9	2.3	2.2	2.1			2.3	2.3
	1.0	1.8	1.7	1.4			1.8	1.8
	.3	.4	.4	.3		% Depr., Dep., Amort./Sales	.4	.4
	(24) 1.0	(111) .7	(102) .7	(19) .6			(308) .7	(293) .8
	3.0	1.3	1.3	.8			1.2	1.4
	2.6	.9	.8			% Officers', Directors' Owners' Comp/Sales	1.0	1.0
	(23) 3.7	(73) 1.6	(36) 1.4				(166) 2.0	(148) 1.8
	9.7	3.3	2.1				3.9	3.5
11643M	106012M	1483000M	6192180M	3273321M	1775463M	Net Sales ($)	8726333M	11011927M
3110M	40749M	640303M	2696895M	1530755M	893340M	Total Assets ($)	3608731M	4713147M

© RMA 2011

M = $ thousand   MM = $ million
See Pages 9 through 22 for Explanation of Ratios and Data

Comparative Historical Data			Type of Statement	Current Data Sorted by Sales					
39	43	39	Unqualified		1	3	1	7	31
75	72	81	Reviewed				14	25	38
74	51	62	Compiled	5	6	4	17	19	11
49	43	41	Tax Returns	4	6	2	17	7	5
91	93	103	Other	1	11	8	19	23	41
4/1/08-3/31/09 ALL	4/1/09-3/31/10 ALL	4/1/10-3/31/11 ALL		0-1MM	1-3MM 55 (4/1-9/30/10)	3-5MM	5-10MM	10-25MM 271 (10/1/10-3/31/11)	25MM & OVER
328	302	326	NUMBER OF STATEMENTS	10	24	17	68	81	126
%	%	%	**ASSETS**	%	%	%	%	%	%
6.7	6.5	7.0	Cash & Equivalents	14.7	10.9	4.9	8.1	7.7	5.0
14.0	14.3	14.1	Trade Receivables (net)	5.6	14.3	20.7	14.1	16.0	12.6
60.2	57.9	60.4	Inventory	51.5	60.3	53.8	58.8	59.0	63.9
2.4	2.0	2.3	All Other Current	3.5	1.0	1.0	3.2	1.9	2.3
83.3	80.7	83.8	Total Current	75.3	86.6	80.5	84.2	84.7	83.7
11.3	12.9	11.3	Fixed Assets (net)	23.0	9.3	13.3	12.0	9.9	11.0
1.1	1.7	1.3	Intangibles (net)	.0	.8	.2	.3	1.9	1.7
4.2	4.7	3.7	All Other Non-Current	1.7	3.4	6.1	3.6	3.5	3.6
100.0	100.0	100.0	Total	100.0	100.0	100.0	100.0	100.0	100.0
			LIABILITIES						
25.2	26.8	25.6	Notes Payable-Short Term	20.0	21.9	26.5	26.4	24.7	26.8
2.7	2.1	1.8	Cur. Mat.-L.T.D.	4.2	2.3	2.5	2.5	1.3	1.4
18.5	17.0	16.4	Trade Payables	3.8	19.7	14.9	13.6	17.0	18.0
.3	.2	.1	Income Taxes Payable	.0	.0	.0	.1	.1	.3
9.2	7.1	9.2	All Other Current	1.1	6.2	4.1	6.6	11.1	11.4
55.9	53.3	53.2	Total Current	29.0	50.1	47.9	49.1	54.2	57.9
7.2	8.2	7.6	Long-Term Debt	11.7	10.5	16.6	7.2	6.1	6.6
.1	.4	.2	Deferred Taxes	.0	.0	.1	.3	.3	.2
4.0	4.2	3.8	All Other Non-Current	7.4	7.2	5.3	3.2	3.5	3.3
32.8	34.0	35.2	Net Worth	51.8	32.2	30.1	40.2	35.8	32.0
100.0	100.0	100.0	Total Liabilities & Net Worth	100.0	100.0	100.0	100.0	100.0	100.0
			INCOME DATA						
100.0	100.0	100.0	Net Sales	100.0	100.0	100.0	100.0	100.0	100.0
22.3	22.7	23.6	Gross Profit	47.7	34.4	29.2	25.0	23.0	18.6
19.0	20.2	20.6	Operating Expenses	43.5	32.4	26.3	21.7	20.7	15.2
3.3	2.5	3.0	Operating Profit	4.2	2.0	3.0	3.3	2.3	3.4
.3	.4	.3	All Other Expenses (net)	1.4	2.1	.6	.3	-.1	.0
3.0	2.1	2.7	Profit Before Taxes	2.8	-.1	2.4	3.1	2.4	3.4
			RATIOS						
2.0	2.2	2.1	Current	13.4	3.3	2.2	3.0	2.0	1.7
1.5	1.5	1.5		2.1	2.0	1.8	1.9	1.5	1.4
1.2	1.2	1.3		1.3	1.2	1.3	1.3	1.3	1.2
.6	.8	.7	Quick	3.8	1.0	1.2	1.0	.8	.5
.3	.3	.3		.3	.5	.5	.4	.4	.2
.1	.1	.1		.2	.1	.2	.2	.2	.1
6 64.1	7 50.9	7 52.3	Sales/Receivables	0 UND	5 76.5	9 38.9	11 33.5	8 47.3	5 71.9
15 24.6	16 22.9	16 23.4		6 60.7	19 19.3	29 12.4	20 17.8	16 22.6	11 32.4
31 11.9	35 10.4	36 10.2		38 9.6	37 9.8	53 6.9	34 10.7		33 11.2
76 4.8	78 4.7	86 4.2	Cost of Sales/Inventory	189 1.9	68 5.4	84 4.3	69 5.3	89 4.1	87 4.2
117 3.1	119 3.1	125 2.9		491 .7	138 2.6	172 2.1	128 2.8	119 3.1	116 3.1
168 2.2	184 2.0	176 2.1		835 .4	251 1.5	248 1.5	185 2.0	162 2.2	160 2.3
7 48.9	9 39.1	7 52.9	Cost of Sales/Payables	0 UND	10 37.7	15 25.1	6 63.9	8 48.0	7 55.5
22 16.3	24 14.9	23 15.7		0 UND	32 11.5	33 11.1	21 17.3	23 15.7	25 14.4
53 6.8	53 6.9	47 7.8		49 7.4	50 7.3	51 7.1	39 9.2	55 6.6	52 7.0
5.8	5.0	4.9	Sales/Working Capital	1.0	3.7	4.6	3.5	5.6	6.5
10.1	8.5	8.2		2.3	6.4	6.7	6.0	8.2	10.4
19.3	15.3	14.3		4.8	12.3	11.6	17.3	13.6	16.0
8.6	8.1	11.0	EBIT/Interest		9.8	7.1	12.4	6.2	14.2
(317) 4.0	(287) 3.0	(313) 3.8		(23) 3.7	1.9	(64) 3.2	(78) 3.1	(123) 6.4	
1.7	1.1	1.7		1.0	1.0	1.2	1.4	2.9	
5.1	6.1	7.1	Net Profit + Depr., Dep., Amort./Cur. Mat. L/T/D					4.8	18.8
(84) 2.9	(86) 3.4	(75) 3.4					(28) 2.5	(35) 4.9	
1.5	1.1	1.6					1.4	2.4	
.1	.1	.1	Fixed/Worth	.0	.0	.1	.1	.1	.2
.3	.2	.2		.5	.1	.4	.2	.2	.3
.6	.6	.5		1.5	.5	1.1	.5	.5	.5
1.1	1.0	1.0	Debt/Worth	.1	.6	1.2	.7	1.1	1.5
2.1	2.1	2.2		.7	1.9	1.6	1.3	2.0	2.5
4.4	4.6	3.9		3.3	17.2	5.0	3.9	3.8	3.9
35.4	28.5	30.5	% Profit Before Taxes/Tangible Net Worth		16.2	39.9	34.7	19.6	36.7
(309) 18.2	(285) 13.5	(310) 14.6		(20) 7.4	(16) 13.8	(65) 12.1	(78) 9.9	(122) 23.0	
6.4	1.7	5.7		1.8	1.2	2.3	3.8	12.8	
12.0	9.2	10.0	% Profit Before Taxes/Total Assets	8.3	6.4	13.6	12.8	7.1	11.2
5.1	3.7	4.1		-.3	3.0	2.6	3.1	2.8	6.2
1.9	.3	1.5		-4.8	-.6	-.4	.7	1.0	3.2
74.8	66.6	76.4	Sales/Net Fixed Assets	123.1	771.0	53.5	107.4	69.9	65.3
38.0	31.2	35.0		10.2	82.5	29.7	36.1	41.0	32.7
16.5	13.4	14.6		.8	15.1	10.2	13.7	15.8	17.2
3.2	2.9	3.0	Sales/Total Assets	1.1	3.7	3.4	3.2	2.8	3.0
2.5	2.2	2.3		.7	2.7	1.8	2.3	2.3	2.3
1.8	1.6	1.7		.4	1.5	1.5	1.8	1.8	1.8
.4	.4	.4	% Depr., Dep., Amort./Sales		.2	.4	.4	.4	.3
(273) .7	(253) .8	(261) .7		(12) .9	(15) 1.1	(52) .7	(70) .7	(105) .6	
1.3	1.6	1.3		2.2	1.8	1.3	1.4	1.0	
.9	.9	1.0	% Officers', Directors' Owners' Comp/Sales		2.8	1.2	1.2	1.2	.6
(129) 1.8	(115) 1.9	(140) 1.8		(11) 3.7	(12) 2.0	(39) 2.2	(42) 1.7	(30) 1.2	
3.4	4.0	3.5		9.1	3.4	4.9	3.1	1.7	
12846978M	11774119M	12841619M	Net Sales ($)	5222M	46990M	66320M	490321M	1324734M	10908032M
5195260M	5588385M	5805152M	Total Assets ($)	9029M	24493M	41203M	248471M	656556M	4825400M

Current Data Sorted by Assets

Comparative Historical Data

Type of Statement								
		5	33	82	23	21	208	205	Unqualified
3	31	176	91	6			342	284	Reviewed
13	83	94	20				238	208	Compiled
31	88	62	6				104	118	Tax Returns
19	97	195	124	29	17		349	416	Other

	0-500M	500M-2MM 264 (4/1-9/30/10)	2-10MM	10-50MM 1,085 (10/1/10-3/31/11)	50-100MM	100-250MM		4/1/06-3/31/07 ALL	4/1/07-3/31/08 ALL
NUMBER OF STATEMENTS	66	304	560	323	58	38		1241	1231
ASSETS	%	%	%	%	%	%		%	%
Cash & Equivalents	14.2	9.6	9.7	8.9	4.0	8.1		6.9	7.6
Trade Receivables (net)	33.5	33.5	31.6	28.2	23.9	21.1		32.0	31.1
Inventory	25.2	34.3	35.0	33.6	37.0	32.8		35.8	35.7
All Other Current	3.3	2.1	2.2	2.9	4.0	3.1		2.5	2.7
Total Current	76.3	79.5	78.4	73.7	68.9	65.2		77.3	77.2
Fixed Assets (net)	15.1	12.1	14.1	17.0	19.1	22.9		14.7	15.2
Intangibles (net)	2.2	2.1	2.6	3.8	5.3	6.3		2.5	2.6
All Other Non-Current	6.4	6.2	5.0	5.5	6.7	5.6		5.5	5.1
Total	100.0	100.0	100.0	100.0	100.0	100.0		100.0	100.0
LIABILITIES									
Notes Payable-Short Term	26.3	15.4	14.6	13.7	19.9	12.7		16.4	17.1
Cur. Mat.-L.T.D.	2.3	2.4	3.0	3.3	2.4	2.4		3.0	3.3
Trade Payables	23.8	23.3	18.7	16.2	15.0	11.8		19.9	19.0
Income Taxes Payable	.0	.1	.2	.2	.3	.4		.3	.3
All Other Current	16.7	10.8	9.6	11.2	10.4	11.2		11.0	10.8
Total Current	69.1	52.0	46.1	44.7	48.0	38.4		50.7	50.4
Long-Term Debt	12.9	10.9	8.2	9.4	13.4	15.2		10.7	9.9
Deferred Taxes	.0	.1	.3	.7	.9	1.4		.4	.3
All Other Non-Current	11.8	5.3	4.5	3.8	2.4	2.7		3.6	4.0
Net Worth	6.3	31.8	40.9	41.4	35.3	42.3		34.7	35.4
Total Liabilties & Net Worth	100.0	100.0	100.0	100.0	100.0	100.0		100.0	100.0
INCOME DATA									
Net Sales	100.0	100.0	100.0	100.0	100.0	100.0		100.0	100.0
Gross Profit	39.6	33.4	31.0	28.3	27.1	28.5		30.0	29.7
Operating Expenses	34.9	31.3	27.4	23.8	22.6	22.4		25.4	25.1
Operating Profit	4.7	2.1	3.6	4.4	4.5	6.0		4.5	4.6
All Other Expenses (net)	.4	.3	.3	.6	.8	.6		.7	.7
Profit Before Taxes	4.4	1.8	3.2	3.9	3.7	5.4		3.9	3.9
RATIOS									
Current	2.9	2.7	2.7	2.5	2.0	2.8		2.3	2.2
	1.5	1.6	1.7	1.6	1.4	1.5		1.6	1.6
	.8	1.1	1.3	1.2	1.1	1.2		1.2	1.2
Quick	1.7	1.4	1.5	1.3	.9	1.2		1.2	1.2
	.8	.9	.9	.8	.6	.8	(1240)	.8	.8
	.4	.5	.5	.5	.3	.3		.5	.5
Sales/Receivables	11 31.8	27 13.3	33 11.0	38 9.6	33 11.2	37 9.9		32 11.5	30 12.2
	37 9.9	41 9.0	43 8.5	47 7.8	45 8.1	48 7.6		42 8.6	40 9.2
	49 7.4	57 6.4	54 6.8	59 6.1	55 6.6	59 6.1		53 6.9	51 7.1
Cost of Sales/Inventory	3 126.1	26 13.8	38 9.6	49 7.4	52 7.0	68 5.3		37 10.0	35 10.4
	30 12.1	60 6.1	69 5.3	81 4.5	90 4.1	98 3.7		62 5.8	63 5.8
	99 3.7	110 3.3	121 3.0	127 2.9	146 2.5	210 1.7		108 3.4	107 3.4
Cost of Sales/Payables	10 36.3	20 18.4	19 19.7	20 18.4	25 14.8	21 17.3		19 19.3	18 20.7
	36 10.2	37 10.0	32 11.3	31 11.6	32 11.5	34 10.9		32 11.4	31 11.9
	61 6.0	61 6.0	50 7.2	47 7.8	60 6.0	48 7.6		50 7.4	47 7.8
Sales/Working Capital	6.1	4.8	4.7	4.4	5.1	3.7		6.0	5.9
	26.0	9.6	8.4	7.9	9.2	6.5		10.2	10.2
	-26.5	56.9	16.9	17.8	25.1	17.3		25.3	25.9
EBIT/Interest	16.7	13.7	18.7	18.2	13.4	22.2		11.0	10.1
	(47) 5.5	(257) 3.9	(505) 4.9	(292) 6.4	(57) 4.3	(37) 5.7	(1125)	4.3	(1109) 3.8
	-.9	1.1	1.8	2.3	2.0	3.2		1.9	1.7
Net Profit + Depr., Dep., Amort./Cur. Mat. L/T/D		5.5	5.9	16.8	21.5			7.6	6.8
		(43) 2.2	(123) 2.4	(91) 4.6	(22) 4.6		(357)	3.2	(329) 2.8
		.7	1.1	1.6	2.5			1.5	1.3
Fixed/Worth	.0	.1	.1	.1	.2	.2		.1	.1
	.2	.2	.2	.3	.6	.6		.3	.3
	NM	1.1	.7	1.1	1.3	1.2		1.0	1.0
Debt/Worth	.7	.8	.7	.9	1.1	1.2		.9	.9
	2.4	2.1	1.5	1.7	2.7	1.7		2.0	1.9
	-21.0	7.3	3.4	3.5	5.3	4.1		4.9	4.8
% Profit Before Taxes/Tangible Net Worth	91.2	37.8	37.7	32.8	39.0	47.6		45.3	44.2
	(46) 43.6	(253) 11.9	(533) 15.8	(305) 18.0	(56) 22.0	17.2	(1144)	23.7	(1130) 21.1
	1.6	1.2	4.7	6.7	6.6	6.4		9.0	7.4
% Profit Before Taxes/Total Assets	35.7	11.9	13.5	12.4	9.7	13.2		15.0	14.7
	13.2	4.7	5.6	5.9	5.4	5.7		6.8	6.7
	-1.2	.1	1.6	2.2	2.3	2.4		2.3	2.0
Sales/Net Fixed Assets	603.4	152.3	89.1	50.0	33.1	25.5		80.5	75.1
	79.2	49.4	31.7	19.0	16.3	8.0		33.5	32.8
	22.2	19.5	11.7	7.1	6.7	3.2		11.7	11.7
Sales/Total Assets	5.8	3.9	3.3	2.6	2.3	2.0		3.6	3.6
	3.2	2.8	2.5	2.0	1.8	1.3		2.7	2.7
	2.2	1.9	1.8	1.4	1.3	.9		1.9	1.9
% Depr., Dep., Amort./Sales	.2	.3	.3	.6	.6	1.0		.4	.4
	(38) .5	(208) .7	(460) .8	(281) 1.1	(49) 1.5	(24) 2.0	(1054)	.8	(1023) .7
	2.2	1.8	2.1	3.0	5.1	2.6		1.8	1.8
% Officers', Directors' Owners' Comp/Sales	4.7	3.1	1.6	.7				1.9	1.8
	(37) 8.3	(168) 5.2	(223) 3.1	(61) 2.1			(438)	3.8	(438) 3.9
	12.2	7.6	5.2	3.9				6.4	6.7
Net Sales ($)	85957M	1073482M	6919020M	13940316M	7339690M	7933616M		39004288M	41247601M
Total Assets ($)	19979M	366921M	2731626M	6903653M	3803644M	5496147M		17786929M	19071611M

© RMA 2011

M = $ thousand   MM = $ million
See Pages 9 through 22 for Explanation of Ratios and Data

Comparative Historical Data   Current Data Sorted by Sales

			Type of Statement						
206	175	164	Unqualified		3	2	11	34	114
317	284	307	Reviewed	3	18	19	60	122	85
224	204	210	Compiled	8	41	42	57	53	9
159	145	187	Tax Returns	17	57	34	51	22	6
533	436	481	Other	22	57	44	90	113	155
4/1/08-3/31/09 ALL	4/1/09-3/31/10 ALL	4/1/10-3/31/11 ALL		264 (4/1-9/30/10)			1,085 (10/1/10-3/31/11)		
				0-1MM	1-3MM	3-5MM	5-10MM	10-25MM	25MM & OVER
1439	1244	1349	NUMBER OF STATEMENTS	50	176	141	269	344	369
%	%	%	ASSETS	%	%	%	%	%	%
8.0	8.4	9.4	Cash & Equivalents	11.9	11.2	8.6	10.0	9.6	7.9
29.6	27.8	30.7	Trade Receivables (net)	27.2	27.1	32.8	31.6	32.7	29.5
35.7	34.9	34.0	Inventory	23.1	35.7	35.3	35.8	33.1	33.9
3.0	3.2	2.5	All Other Current	5.1	2.5	1.4	2.1	2.5	3.0
76.3	74.4	76.6	Total Current	67.4	76.5	78.1	79.4	77.8	74.3
15.4	16.8	14.9	Fixed Assets (net)	22.7	13.3	14.8	12.7	14.4	16.5
3.0	3.2	3.0	Intangibles (net)	1.9	2.9	1.5	2.6	2.9	4.0
5.3	5.5	5.5	All Other Non-Current	8.0	7.3	5.6	5.3	4.8	5.2
100.0	100.0	100.0	Total	100.0	100.0	100.0	100.0	100.0	100.0
			LIABILITIES						
17.5	15.9	15.3	Notes Payable-Short Term	28.1	14.9	14.6	16.1	13.8	14.9
3.2	3.3	2.9	Cur. Mat.-L.T.D.	2.7	2.6	2.7	2.8	3.4	2.7
18.7	16.8	19.0	Trade Payables	19.3	19.1	23.7	20.3	18.2	17.1
.2	.2	.2	Income Taxes Payable	.0	.1	.1	.2	.1	.2
10.4	9.4	10.7	All Other Current	18.9	11.0	8.2	10.1	10.2	11.3
50.0	45.6	48.1	Total Current	68.9	47.8	49.3	49.6	45.6	46.1
10.1	10.7	9.7	Long-Term Debt	20.6	13.0	10.8	7.8	6.9	10.2
.3	.4	.4	Deferred Taxes	.0	.1	.1	.2	.6	.7
4.5	4.6	4.7	All Other Non-Current	14.1	6.8	4.7	4.2	4.6	3.0
35.1	38.6	37.1	Net Worth	-3.6	32.4	35.0	38.2	42.2	39.9
100.0	100.0	100.0	Total Liabilities & Net Worth	100.0	100.0	100.0	100.0	100.0	100.0
			INCOME DATA						
100.0	100.0	100.0	Net Sales	100.0	100.0	100.0	100.0	100.0	100.0
29.7	31.0	31.1	Gross Profit	47.2	36.8	33.0	30.6	29.5	27.2
26.0	28.8	27.5	Operating Expenses	42.3	34.7	30.0	27.4	25.7	22.6
3.6	2.2	3.6	Operating Profit	4.9	2.1	3.0	3.2	3.7	4.6
.6	.7	.4	All Other Expenses (net)	.8	.5	.7	.2	.3	.5
3.0	1.5	3.2	Profit Before Taxes	4.1	1.6	2.3	3.0	3.4	4.1
			RATIOS						
2.3	2.7	2.6	Current	3.2	3.3	2.6	2.6	2.6	2.4
1.5	1.7	1.6		1.3	1.8	1.5	1.7	1.6	1.5
1.2	1.2	1.2		.7	1.1	1.1	1.2	1.2	1.2
1.2	1.4	1.4	Quick	1.8	1.5	1.3	1.5	1.5	1.2
(1438) .8	.8	.9		.6	.8	.9	.9	.9	.8
.5	.5	.5		.2	.4	.5	.5	.6	.5
27 13.7	29 12.6	33 11.1	Sales/Receivables	14 25.4	23 16.0	29 12.6	31 11.8	36 10.1	36 10.2
38 9.7	40 9.1	43 8.4		44 8.4	40 9.0	42 8.8	41 8.8	45 8.1	45 8.1
51 7.2	53 6.9	56 6.5		73 5.0	60 6.0	60 6.1	53 6.9	57 6.4	56 6.6
33 11.1	37 9.8	39 9.4	Cost of Sales/Inventory	0 UND	28 13.3	35 10.6	36 10.3	39 9.3	46 8.0
64 5.7	72 5.1	71 5.2		73 5.0	86 4.3	70 5.2	68 5.4	63 5.8	71 5.1
114 3.2	135 2.7	121 3.0		165 2.2	191 1.9	122 3.0	122 3.0	109 3.3	108 3.4
16 23.0	16 22.5	19 18.9	Cost of Sales/Payables	14 26.7	17 22.0	21 17.0	19 19.2	18 19.8	20 18.3
28 13.2	30 12.3	33 11.2		44 8.3	34 10.6	41 9.0	34 10.7	30 12.3	32 11.6
47 7.8	47 7.7	51 7.1		101 3.6	63 5.7	67 5.5	51 7.2	46 8.0	46 7.9
5.7	4.5	4.7	Sales/Working Capital	2.6	3.4	4.7	4.9	4.9	5.2
10.6	8.2	8.6		38.6	6.9	9.3	8.9	8.2	9.0
25.8	22.7	22.4		-5.6	66.1	25.5	20.7	18.4	20.2
12.0	9.2	17.3	EBIT/Interest	14.4	7.4	11.9	15.9	22.3	23.5
(1296) 3.5	(1125) 2.3	(1195) 4.8		(39) 3.2	(141) 2.4	(122) 3.2	(236) 3.9	(314) 6.2	(343) 6.6
1.4	.3	1.8		-1.2	-.7	1.3	1.4	2.3	2.6
8.7	8.7	8.3	Net Profit + Depr., Dep., Amort./Cur. Mat. L/T/D		4.5	5.4	5.1	7.7	17.4
(342) 3.1	(304) 2.3	(291) 3.0			(20) 1.3	(24) 1.2	(58) 2.4	(76) 2.9	(113) 4.6
1.1	.7	1.2			.1	.8	.8	1.2	1.9
.1	.1	.1	Fixed/Worth	.0	.1	.1	.1	.1	.1
.3	.3	.3		.4	.3	.3	.2	.2	.3
1.0	1.0	.9		NM	2.0	1.1	.6	.7	1.0
.9	.7	.8	Debt/Worth	.8	.7	.9	.7	.7	1.0
2.1	1.7	1.8		5.0	2.1	2.1	1.7	1.6	1.8
4.8	4.3	4.1		-7.0	19.1	4.7	4.0	3.1	3.8
40.2	25.0	38.2	% Profit Before Taxes/Tangible Net Worth	95.1	34.3	33.9	37.3	38.1	40.5
(1317) 16.6	(1139) 7.9	(1231) 16.5		(32) 31.4	(140) 7.6	(128) 11.2	(246) 14.8	(328) 16.5	(357) 20.1
4.1	-1.7	4.8		-.6	-4.6	2.2	4.0	6.1	8.4
13.3	9.3	13.4	% Profit Before Taxes/Total Assets	23.4	12.5	10.3	14.0	12.6	13.7
5.2	2.6	5.7		9.4	2.7	3.7	5.1	5.8	7.0
1.1	-1.2	1.4		-3.9	-1.8	.7	1.0	2.1	2.7
81.4	67.9	86.5	Sales/Net Fixed Assets	UND	127.6	123.8	99.5	90.0	54.8
32.1	26.0	30.2		27.5	35.1	37.0	37.4	30.2	22.3
11.9	8.6	10.9		4.1	11.1	11.8	13.9	11.1	8.2
3.6	3.3	3.2	Sales/Total Assets	2.8	3.1	3.4	3.5	3.3	3.0
2.7	2.3	2.4		1.8	2.1	2.5	2.6	2.5	2.2
1.9	1.5	1.6		.8	1.4	1.8	1.8	1.7	1.7
.4	.5	.4	% Depr., Dep., Amort./Sales	.4	.4	.3	.3	.4	.5
(1151) .8	(997) 1.0	(1060) .9		(25) 3.0	(117) .9	(104) .8	(220) .8	(281) .8	(313) 1.0
1.9	2.6	2.4		15.9	2.8	1.9	1.9	2.5	2.6
1.8	1.8	2.0	% Officers', Directors' Owners' Comp/Sales	6.3	3.6	2.8	1.9	1.5	.5
(475) 3.4	(429) 3.7	(491) 3.9		(23) 10.8	(88) 5.7	(82) 5.0	(136) 3.6	(119) 3.0	(43) 1.7
6.1	6.5	6.1		18.7	8.5	7.0	5.8	5.0	3.4
50340857M	34660009M	37292081M	Net Sales ($)	30393M	359797M	558399M	1978861M	5628999M	28735632M
23402505M	19367366M	19321970M	Total Assets ($)	26319M	205651M	292342M	899817M	2764266M	15133575M

© RMA 2011

M = $ thousand   MM = $ million
See Pages 9 through 22 for Explanation of Ratios and Data

Current Data Sorted by Assets   Comparative Historical Data

	0-500M	500M-2MM	2-10MM	10-50MM	50-100MM	100-250MM	Type of Statement	4/1/06-3/31/07 ALL	4/1/07-3/31/08 ALL
	4	2	15	26			Unqualified	72	70
	14	13	94	54			Reviewed	164	141
	11	25	56	9			Compiled	115	91
		31	22	1			Tax Returns	47	51
		35	89	68	5	5	Other	161	151
		114 (4/1-9/30/10)			476 (10/1/10-3/31/11)				
	29	106	276	158	11	10	NUMBER OF STATEMENTS	559	504
	%	%	%	%	%	%	**ASSETS**	%	%
	10.3	7.4	8.4	6.7	4.5	1.1	Cash & Equivalents	5.5	6.4
	35.2	36.0	33.2	30.7	32.8	27.9	Trade Receivables (net)	34.4	32.9
	35.6	39.2	36.4	34.2	35.5	24.9	Inventory	37.9	37.9
	2.1	1.4	1.8	2.7	4.4	4.8	All Other Current	2.0	2.2
	83.2	84.1	79.9	74.3	77.2	58.7	Total Current	79.8	79.5
	10.2	9.6	11.7	12.9	15.3	7.2	Fixed Assets (net)	12.1	12.6
	1.7	1.8	3.5	5.4	3.4	31.2	Intangibles (net)	3.4	2.8
	4.9	4.5	4.9	7.4	4.2	2.9	All Other Non-Current	4.7	5.2
	100.0	100.0	100.0	100.0	100.0	100.0	Total	100.0	100.0
							LIABILITIES		
	13.3	14.1	14.4	15.0	17.5	1.3	Notes Payable-Short Term	16.7	16.1
	4.7	2.4	2.7	2.1	1.1	1.1	Cur. Mat.-L.T.D.	2.1	2.4
	44.5	27.5	20.0	16.8	15.8	13.3	Trade Payables	21.8	21.1
	.0	.1	.3	.4	.1	.5	Income Taxes Payable	.3	.2
	13.1	10.7	7.1	7.9	7.2	6.4	All Other Current	7.9	7.2
	75.6	54.8	44.5	42.1	41.7	22.7	Total Current	48.8	46.9
	10.4	10.1	6.2	9.9	11.5	28.2	Long-Term Debt	9.8	9.7
	.0	.1	.2	.4	1.0	1.9	Deferred Taxes	.3	.3
	8.6	4.6	4.7	4.0	4.7	2.9	All Other Non-Current	4.1	4.3
	5.4	30.4	44.5	43.6	41.2	44.4	Net Worth	37.0	38.8
	100.0	100.0	100.0	100.0	100.0	100.0	Total Liabilities & Net Worth	100.0	100.0
							INCOME DATA		
	100.0	100.0	100.0	100.0	100.0	100.0	Net Sales	100.0	100.0
	35.9	32.3	30.4	31.3	28.4	24.9	Gross Profit	29.9	29.8
	31.8	29.3	26.1	26.3	25.6	18.7	Operating Expenses	24.9	25.0
	4.1	3.0	4.3	5.0	2.8	6.2	Operating Profit	5.0	4.8
	.4	.7	.3	.7	1.5	1.5	All Other Expenses (net)	.7	.6
	3.7	2.3	3.9	4.3	1.3	4.7	Profit Before Taxes	4.3	4.2
							RATIOS		
	1.9	2.3	3.1	2.8	3.1	3.0		2.6	2.8
	1.1	1.6	1.9	1.8	2.1	2.4	Current	1.7	1.7
	.8	1.2	1.3	1.3	1.5	1.6		1.2	1.3
	1.2	1.4	1.7	1.5	1.7	1.5		1.3	1.4
	.7	.8	.9	.9	.8	1.1	Quick	.8	.9
	.4	.5	.6	.6	.6	1.0		.5	.6
	20 18.3	30 12.0	33 10.9	38 9.5	44 8.2	45 8.2		35 10.4	33 10.9
	41 8.9	40 9.1	42 8.6	47 7.8	57 6.4	53 6.8	Sales/Receivables	42 8.7	41 9.0
	55 6.7	49 7.4	51 7.2	54 6.7	67 5.5	66 5.6		50 7.3	50 7.4
	8 46.1	34 10.8	38 9.6	44 8.3	53 6.9	47 7.8		39 9.3	42 8.8
	53 6.9	65 5.6	64 5.7	75 4.9	80 4.6	62 5.9	Cost of Sales/Inventory	64 5.7	68 5.4
	118 3.1	121 3.0	108 3.4	127 2.9	130 2.8	76 4.8		101 3.6	101 3.6
	33 10.9	22 16.4	20 18.5	25 14.6	29 12.6	24 15.5		23 16.2	21 17.2
	59 6.2	39 9.3	32 11.5	33 10.9	34 10.6	35 10.4	Cost of Sales/Payables	35 10.4	33 11.0
	121 3.0	60 6.1	50 7.3	50 7.3	51 7.2	45 8.1		49 7.4	47 7.7
	8.2	6.4	4.9	4.9	3.4	4.5		5.9	5.3
	65.2	11.3	8.4	7.7	6.6	6.1	Sales/Working Capital	9.5	8.8
	-12.6	24.1	16.5	13.2	9.2	7.8		22.1	19.7
	11.2	13.8	19.9	22.2	20.0	37.8		11.9	11.5
	(23) 3.2	(92) 5.0	(249) 5.5	(150) 8.7	4.1	13.1	EBIT/Interest	(521) 4.6	(458) 4.4
	-1.5	1.8	2.0	2.4	.5	2.0		1.9	1.9
		5.0	8.2	12.1			Net Profit + Depr., Dep.,	10.7	10.8
		(14) 2.2	(63) 3.4	(52) 4.4			Amort./Cur. Mat. L/T/D	(153) 4.1	(128) 3.4
		.8	1.5	1.7				1.3	1.6
	.0	.1	.1	.1	.1	.1		.1	.1
	.3	.2	.2	.3	.3	.6	Fixed/Worth	.3	.2
	UND	.7	.6	.7	.6	-.3		.8	.7
	2.2	1.0	.6	.7	.5	1.4		.8	.7
	28.5	1.8	1.4	1.5	1.4	3.5	Debt/Worth	1.8	1.7
	-7.4	6.6	3.3	3.1	1.9	-3.4		4.8	4.0
	999.8	56.3	39.4	36.9	11.4		% Profit Before Taxes/Tangible	48.1	42.0
	(19) 92.9	(91) 26.7	(255) 20.6	(142) 19.5	(10) 5.9		Net Worth	(499) 26.1	(458) 22.8
	24.4	7.9	7.4	10.0	-3.8			9.1	9.8
	31.9	19.4	15.9	13.6	4.8	14.3	% Profit Before Taxes/Total	16.3	15.7
	7.3	7.0	8.0	8.6	2.1	10.4	Assets	8.3	7.9
	-3.1	1.0	2.4	4.2	-2.0	3.3		2.4	2.8
	UND	172.4	78.2	56.5	38.7	175.2		102.8	90.8
	98.6	60.1	34.2	24.8	18.1	91.5	Sales/Net Fixed Assets	40.4	40.3
	19.9	22.3	15.9	10.1	8.7	11.5		17.3	17.0
	5.5	4.2	3.6	3.0	2.2	2.6		3.7	3.7
	3.7	3.1	2.8	2.1	2.1	2.0	Sales/Total Assets	2.9	2.8
	1.9	2.3	2.1	1.7	1.7	1.3		2.1	2.1
	.6	.3	.4	.5	.6			.4	.4
	(12) 1.1	(70) .8	(223) .7	(151) .8	(10) 1.4		% Depr., Dep., Amort./Sales	(478) .7	(430) .6
	3.3	1.5	1.2	1.8	2.0			1.2	1.1
	2.8	2.7	1.7	.6				1.8	1.9
	(13) 6.6	(56) 5.3	(112) 2.9	(26) 1.7			% Officers', Directors' Owners' Comp/Sales	(198) 3.2	(194) 3.4
	14.1	7.9	5.7	5.9				5.6	6.0
	31691M	437797M	3592244M	7511954M	1699303M	2833713M	Net Sales ($)	16934650M	15481090M
	8239M	136187M	1291530M	3261655M	813710M	1463968M	Total Assets ($)	6523371M	5892633M

M = $ thousand   MM = $ million
See Pages 9 through 22 for Explanation of Ratios and Data

Comparative Historical Data | | | ## Current Data Sorted by Sales

4/1/08-3/31/09 ALL	4/1/09-3/31/10 ALL	4/1/10-3/31/11 ALL	Type of Statement	0-1MM	1-3MM	3-5MM	5-10MM	10-25MM	25MM & OVER
73	72	54	Unqualified		1		8	10	35
157	132	161	Reviewed		4	12	35	57	53
102	99	94	Compiled	2	11	12	31	30	8
70	56	68	Tax Returns	12	14	15	15	12	
183	194	213	Other	7	16	15	41	59	75
				114 (4/1-9/30/10)			476 (10/1/10-3/31/11)		
585	553	590	NUMBER OF STATEMENTS	21	46	54	130	168	171
%	%	%	ASSETS	%	%	%	%	%	%
6.8	8.2	7.7	Cash & Equivalents	13.6	9.0	7.6	8.2	9.0	4.8
32.2	30.4	33.1	Trade Receivables (net)	36.5	28.4	30.3	32.9	32.8	35.1
38.4	37.1	36.1	Inventory	30.3	44.4	37.0	37.4	35.5	33.9
2.1	2.5	2.1	All Other Current	.2	2.6	1.3	2.1	1.6	3.0
79.4	78.2	78.9	Total Current	80.5	84.3	76.3	80.6	78.9	76.8
11.7	12.4	11.6	Fixed Assets (net)	11.5	11.1	10.6	11.4	12.6	11.2
3.6	4.0	4.1	Intangibles (net)	3.1	.3	5.4	2.4	3.9	6.3
5.3	5.5	5.4	All Other Non-Current	4.9	4.3	7.8	5.6	4.6	5.8
100.0	100.0	100.0	Total	100.0	100.0	100.0	100.0	100.0	100.0
			LIABILITIES						
17.5	16.0	14.3	Notes Payable-Short Term	17.0	11.0	12.9	15.1	14.1	14.9
2.2	2.8	2.5	Cur. Mat.-L.T.D.	3.2	2.7	2.5	2.8	2.8	1.9
19.7	18.3	21.5	Trade Payables	40.5	26.4	21.6	23.6	19.7	18.0
.2	.2	.3	Income Taxes Payable	.0	.0	.1	.3	.3	.3
7.7	7.1	8.2	All Other Current	7.7	17.5	7.9	6.7	6.8	8.5
47.3	44.4	46.8	Total Current	68.4	57.7	44.9	48.5	43.7	43.6
8.2	9.2	8.6	Long-Term Debt	9.0	11.6	12.3	5.1	8.5	9.2
.2	.2	.3	Deferred Taxes	.0	.1	.1	.2	.2	.5
5.2	4.7	4.7	All Other Non-Current	7.0	4.3	8.3	4.7	3.9	4.0
39.2	41.5	39.7	Net Worth	15.6	26.3	34.4	41.6	43.7	42.7
100.0	100.0	100.0	Total Liabilities & Net Worth	100.0	100.0	100.0	100.0	100.0	100.0
			INCOME DATA						
100.0	100.0	100.0	Net Sales	100.0	100.0	100.0	100.0	100.0	100.0
29.6	31.1	31.1	Gross Profit	37.5	36.6	34.8	29.8	31.1	28.7
25.0	27.8	26.9	Operating Expenses	34.1	32.6	31.2	26.7	25.6	24.5
4.6	3.3	4.2	Operating Profit	3.4	4.0	3.6	3.1	5.5	4.2
.6	.6	.5	All Other Expenses (net)	.9	1.5	.4	.2	.6	.6
4.0	2.7	3.7	Profit Before Taxes	2.5	2.5	3.2	3.0	4.9	3.6
			RATIOS						
2.7	3.2	2.8	Current	1.9	2.9	2.8	2.8	2.9	2.7
1.7	1.8	1.7		1.3	1.7	1.7	1.7	1.8	1.8
1.2	1.3	1.3		.8	1.1	1.3	1.2	1.3	1.3
1.3	1.6	1.5	Quick	1.2	1.4	1.7	1.6	1.8	1.5
.9	.9	.9		.8	.8	.8	.8	.9	.9
.5	.5	.6		.4	.4	.5	.5	.6	.6
30 · 12.2	31 · 11.7	35 · 10.6	Sales/Receivables	41 · 9.0	27 · 13.5	30 · 12.1	33 · 10.9	34 · 10.7	39 · 9.4
38 · 9.5	40 · 9.2	44 · 8.4		54 · 6.7	38 · 9.6	37 · 10.0	42 · 8.7	42 · 8.6	48 · 7.7
48 · 7.6	50 · 7.3	52 · 7.0		68 · 5.4	50 · 7.2	50 · 7.3	49 · 7.4	50 · 7.3	55 · 6.6
37 · 9.8	37 · 10.0	38 · 9.5	Cost of Sales/Inventory	0 · UND	47 · 7.7	44 · 8.2	38 · 9.5	37 · 10.0	39 · 9.4
63 · 5.8	67 · 5.4	67 · 5.5		69 · 5.3	102 · 3.6	86 · 4.3	63 · 5.8	64 · 5.7	61 · 5.9
110 · 3.3	121 · 3.0	116 · 3.1		322 · 1.1	158 · 2.3	126 · 2.9	104 · 3.5	113 · 3.2	106 · 3.4
19 · 19.6	19 · 19.2	23 · 16.0	Cost of Sales/Payables	35 · 10.4	27 · 13.6	20 · 18.0	22 · 16.8	20 · 18.0	24 · 15.1
30 · 12.3	30 · 12.1	34 · 10.6		83 · 4.4	39 · 9.3	43 · 8.5	36 · 10.3	31 · 11.8	32 · 11.4
45 · 8.1	46 · 7.9	54 · 6.8		162 · 2.3	65 · 5.6	59 · 6.2	54 · 6.8	51 · 7.2	44 · 8.3
5.5	4.4	4.9	Sales/Working Capital	3.2	3.6	5.1	4.7	4.5	5.5
9.6	8.1	8.6		26.0	9.8	9.2	8.5	8.6	8.1
21.8	18.2	18.4		-11.2	58.0	15.9	20.7	16.4	14.8
14.5	13.0	19.0	EBIT/Interest	6.8	15.5	10.3	16.0	22.3	22.6
(535) 4.8	(504) 3.7	(535) 6.3		(16) 1.8	(36) 6.0	(47) 3.0	(116) 5.1	(156) 7.1	(164) 8.6
1.7	1.2	2.1		-7.1	-.6	1.2	1.8	3.3	2.3
11.4	8.2	10.9	Net Profit + Depr., Dep., Amort./Cur. Mat. L/T/D				7.7	8.1	13.4
(142) 3.3	(138) 2.9	(138) 3.4					(26) 3.4	(51) 3.3	(53) 7.4
1.4	1.0	1.5					1.7	1.4	2.2
.1	.1	.1	Fixed/Worth	.0	.0	.1	.1	.1	.1
.3	.3	.2		.1	.3	.2	.2	.3	.3
.7	.7	.7		UND	2.4	.8	.5	.8	.6
.7	.6	.6	Debt/Worth	1.5	.7	.8	.5	.6	.7
1.7	1.6	1.6		10.5	2.3	1.9	1.6	1.4	1.5
4.5	4.0	4.2		-7.4	37.5	6.5	3.9	3.3	4.1
46.0	30.2	43.2	% Profit Before Taxes/Tangible Net Worth	128.0	110.4	46.1	36.8	48.8	38.6
(517) 24.7	(491) 13.9	(523) 21.6		(14) 28.8	(38) 36.5	(47) 23.4	(118) 16.3	(154) 21.6	(152) 23.2
6.9	2.8	8.0		-5.6	.8	4.0	4.9	9.8	9.4
17.1	11.8	15.2	% Profit Before Taxes/Total Assets	15.1	27.1	14.6	12.8	16.3	14.0
7.6	5.2	8.1		2.7	7.8	7.0	5.3	9.2	8.7
1.6	.5	2.3		-6.0	-1.6	.6	1.4	3.8	2.7
108.7	93.6	92.7	Sales/Net Fixed Assets	UND	139.0	151.1	110.3	75.8	71.8
43.5	36.1	34.6		46.6	36.6	56.0	40.8	27.8	33.8
18.2	15.3	15.5		11.1	18.6	17.0	17.2	12.1	16.1
3.8	3.4	3.5	Sales/Total Assets	3.4	3.7	4.0	3.5	3.7	3.4
2.9	2.6	2.6		1.7	2.5	2.5	2.8	2.7	2.6
2.1	1.8	1.9		.9	1.8	1.7	2.1	2.0	1.9
.3	.4	.4	% Depr., Dep., Amort./Sales	1.1	.5	.3	.3	.5	.5
(493) .6	(445) .8	(475) .8		(10) 2.1	(28) .7	(37) .8	(103) .7	(135) .8	(162) .7
1.2	1.5	1.4		6.2	1.1	1.9	1.3	1.4	1.5
1.6	1.9	1.7	% Officers', Directors' Owners' Comp/Sales		3.1	1.9	2.1	1.4	.7
(233) 3.0	(198) 3.4	(208) 3.3			(25)	(24) 4.1	(55) 3.3	(72) 2.8	(23) 1.9
6.2	6.6	6.7			10.5	7.2	6.6	5.9	5.9
22410395M	15164013M	16106702M	Net Sales ($)	11597M	94967M	214460M	979043M	2593330M	12213305M
7872875M	6270446M	6975289M	Total Assets ($)	7515M	48678M	94156M	410917M	1105895M	5308128M

M = $ thousand   MM = $ million
See Pages 9 through 22 for Explanation of Ratios and Data

Current Data Sorted by Assets | Comparative Historical Data

Type of Statement	0-500M	500M-2MM	2-10MM	10-50MM	50-100MM	100-250MM	4/1/06-3/31/07 ALL	4/1/07-3/31/08 ALL
Unqualified			2	7	3	1	10	14
Reviewed		9	24	8			43	44
Compiled	2	16	16	4			39	25
Tax Returns	9	15	9				28	15
Other	7	18	27	9	1	1	36	54
		37 (4/1-9/30/10)		151 (10/1/10-3/31/11)				
NUMBER OF STATEMENTS	18	58	78	28	4	2	156	152
ASSETS	%	%	%	%	%	%	%	%
Cash & Equivalents	11.0	10.9	6.3	8.4			7.0	7.2
Trade Receivables (net)	19.0	32.9	33.4	27.9			32.9	33.1
Inventory	30.9	29.7	34.1	32.4			34.6	34.2
All Other Current	3.3	4.4	2.4	4.4			3.5	3.9
Total Current	64.2	78.0	76.1	73.2			78.0	78.5
Fixed Assets (net)	17.5	11.3	10.9	12.1			13.0	11.4
Intangibles (net)	8.7	5.9	4.4	7.1			3.9	5.7
All Other Non-Current	9.5	4.8	8.5	7.6			5.1	4.4
Total	100.0	100.0	100.0	100.0			100.0	100.0
LIABILITIES								
Notes Payable-Short Term	18.6	8.9	16.4	19.7			11.6	14.8
Cur. Mat.-L.T.D.	4.0	2.4	1.8	1.5			2.9	2.6
Trade Payables	24.4	24.5	19.5	16.1			21.4	22.7
Income Taxes Payable	.5	.2	.1	.6			.3	.2
All Other Current	11.9	17.7	11.1	7.0			11.4	12.6
Total Current	59.5	53.7	48.9	44.9			47.6	52.8
Long-Term Debt	11.9	12.9	7.9	6.3			10.9	9.5
Deferred Taxes	.0	.0	.1	.2			.2	.2
All Other Non-Current	10.1	8.2	4.8	9.1			7.3	5.4
Net Worth	18.5	25.3	38.3	39.5			34.0	32.0
Total Liabilities & Net Worth	100.0	100.0	100.0	100.0			100.0	100.0
INCOME DATA								
Net Sales	100.0	100.0	100.0	100.0			100.0	100.0
Gross Profit	51.4	32.0	31.4	29.0			32.0	30.2
Operating Expenses	44.7	30.7	28.8	25.6			28.7	27.3
Operating Profit	6.6	1.4	2.7	3.4			3.3	2.8
All Other Expenses (net)	.6	-.2	.1	.3			.2	.4
Profit Before Taxes	6.0	1.6	2.6	3.1			3.1	2.4
RATIOS								
Current	2.6	2.4	2.4	2.6			2.5	2.0
	1.0	1.5	1.5	1.6			1.7	1.5
	.7	1.0	1.2	1.2			1.2	1.1
Quick	.9	1.6	1.3	1.5			1.3	1.1
	.5	.8	.8	.7			.8	.7
	.4	.5	.5				.5	.5
Sales/Receivables	0 UND	19 19.0	32 11.4	26 14.2			26 14.2	25 14.4
	21 17.0	30 12.0	39 9.4	38 9.6			36 10.2	38 9.7
	31 11.8	44 8.3	56 6.5	45 8.1			47 7.8	49 7.5
Cost of Sales/Inventory	14 25.3	20 17.9	37 9.9	37 9.9			33 11.2	33 11.0
	56 6.5	35 10.6	56 6.6	54 6.8			54 6.8	49 7.4
	94 3.9	82 4.5	91 4.0	97 3.7			84 4.3	80 4.6
Cost of Sales/Payables	0 UND	14 26.5	17 22.0	17 21.4			21 17.1	18 19.8
	26 13.9	32 11.6	33 11.0	23 16.2			33 11.2	29 12.7
	52 7.0	49 7.4	53 6.9	36 10.2			44 8.3	48 7.6
Sales/Working Capital	11.2	6.3	6.2	4.8			6.7	7.3
	NM	14.7	11.3	10.5			11.2	12.9
	-21.8	229.9	32.3	50.7			23.5	44.7
EBIT/Interest	12.5	10.3	11.7	10.5			8.0	7.4
	(12) 6.1	(52) 4.1	(75) 2.7	(24) 3.0			(138) 3.8	(136) 3.0
	1.4	1.2	1.0	2.0			1.8	1.3
Net Profit + Depr., Dep., Amort./Cur. Mat. L/T/D			7.2				6.4	5.0
			(13) 2.3				(54) 2.4	(47) 2.4
			-.3				1.1	.9
Fixed/Worth	.1	.1	.1	.1			.1	.1
	UND	.4	.2	.3			.4	.3
	-1.7	-10.4	.7	1.6			1.7	1.2
Debt/Worth	.8	1.2	.8	.8			.9	1.2
	UND	3.4	1.8	2.6			2.5	2.6
	-4.9	-26.3	4.3	7.6			6.0	8.1
% Profit Before Taxes/Tangible Net Worth		45.6	23.4	34.0			38.5	44.2
		(43) 14.4	(69) 10.1	(26) 21.1			(139) 19.9	(129) 18.3
		5.7	1.5	9.4			6.9	5.8
% Profit Before Taxes/Total Assets	32.7	11.8	8.5	10.5			12.5	12.0
	20.5	5.8	3.4	6.0			5.8	5.0
	4.0	.5	.1	2.3			2.3	1.3
Sales/Net Fixed Assets	106.2	187.7	76.1	71.4			73.1	86.6
	41.8	55.0	42.2	28.2			35.8	43.8
	17.1	22.8	23.2	15.0			19.9	20.9
Sales/Total Assets	6.1	5.0	3.5	3.6			4.2	4.2
	4.7	3.5	3.0	3.0			3.2	3.2
	2.6	2.5	2.2	1.9			2.4	2.4
% Depr., Dep., Amort./Sales	.3	.4	.4	.5			.4	.4
	(11) .8	(44) .7	(68) .6	(25) .8			(131) .7	(125) .7
	1.3	1.1	1.2	1.8			1.1	1.1
% Officers', Directors' Owners' Comp/Sales	1.8	2.6	2.3				1.8	1.6
	(13) 9.5	(37) 4.7	(42) 3.5				(79) 3.2	(60) 3.4
	14.8	7.3	5.7				5.7	6.0
Net Sales ($)	27578M	282888M	993647M	2026710M	573759M	1025374M	6104866M	5524602M
Total Assets ($)	5142M	74269M	361519M	623812M	291820M	304428M	1701982M	1734646M

© RMA 2011

M = $ thousand   MM = $ million
See Pages 9 through 22 for Explanation of Ratios and Data

Comparative Historical Data | Current Data Sorted by Sales

4/1/08-3/31/09 ALL	4/1/09-3/31/10 ALL	4/1/10-3/31/11 ALL	Type of Statement	0-1MM	1-3MM	3-5MM	5-10MM	10-25MM	25MM & OVER
15	17	13	Unqualified		1	2		3	10
43	45	41	Reviewed				13	13	12
30	41	38	Compiled	2	3	7	7	15	4
33	26	33	Tax Returns	5	10	3	10	5	
56	62	63	Other	3	12	9	14	13	12
					37 (4/1-9/30/10)			151 (10/1/10-3/31/11)	
177	191	188	**NUMBER OF STATEMENTS**	10	26	21	44	49	38
%	%	%	**ASSETS**	%	%	%	%	%	%
7.4	6.9	8.3	Cash & Equivalents	3.9	10.5	12.1	8.8	7.7	6.1
31.7	30.9	30.7	Trade Receivables (net)	11.1	28.2	27.6	38.8	31.8	28.6
32.5	33.3	31.7	Inventory	30.9	29.6	24.6	32.5	37.3	29.0
3.7	3.7	3.5	All Other Current	6.3	4.9	2.7	3.3	2.0	4.5
75.2	74.9	74.2	Total Current	52.2	73.3	67.0	83.4	78.7	68.2
12.1	13.3	12.1	Fixed Assets (net)	21.2	10.9	14.9	9.7	10.8	13.5
5.5	5.0	6.4	Intangibles (net)	17.3	8.7	5.7	1.4	4.0	11.1
7.1	6.8	7.3	All Other Non-Current	9.3	7.1	12.3	5.5	6.5	7.2
100.0	100.0	100.0	Total	100.0	100.0	100.0	100.0	100.0	100.0
			LIABILITIES						
16.0	15.3	14.3	Notes Payable-Short Term	9.3	16.5	12.5	15.9	11.7	16.7
2.6	2.7	2.2	Cur. Mat.-L.T.D.	8.4	1.8	2.6	2.0	1.5	1.7
18.2	20.2	20.9	Trade Payables	8.2	23.5	19.5	25.7	21.3	17.0
.2	.2	.3	Income Taxes Payable	.1	.0	.3	.3	.2	.5
12.0	13.1	12.6	All Other Current	10.3	13.5	20.9	13.8	11.7	7.5
49.0	51.5	50.2	Total Current	36.4	55.2	55.7	57.6	46.4	43.5
9.2	13.5	10.0	Long-Term Debt	16.1	13.5	9.6	11.4	6.8	8.9
.2	.2	.1	Deferred Taxes	.0	.0	.0	.1	.0	.4
5.1	6.1	6.9	All Other Non-Current	10.3	8.5	11.3	4.6	4.9	7.8
36.6	28.7	32.8	Net Worth	37.0	22.9	23.4	26.3	41.9	39.4
100.0	100.0	100.0	Total Liabilities & Net Worth	100.0	100.0	100.0	100.0	100.0	100.0
			INCOME DATA						
100.0	100.0	100.0	Net Sales	100.0	100.0	100.0	100.0	100.0	100.0
32.7	31.6	33.1	Gross Profit	55.0	39.9	34.6	29.9	31.9	27.2
29.5	29.7	30.3	Operating Expenses	51.9	34.7	31.9	28.5	29.3	24.1
3.2	1.9	2.8	Operating Profit	3.2	5.2	2.7	1.4	2.6	3.1
.5	.4	.1	All Other Expenses (net)	1.7	.1	-.7	.1	.1	.2
2.7	1.5	2.7	Profit Before Taxes	1.5	5.1	3.4	1.3	2.5	2.9
			RATIOS						
2.3	2.6	2.3	Current	7.0	3.5	2.0	2.1	2.6	2.4
1.5	1.5	1.5		1.7	1.2	1.4	1.5	1.7	1.7
1.1	1.1	1.1		.5	.9	.7	1.1	1.2	1.1
1.3	1.2	1.3	Quick	1.6	1.3	1.2	1.3	1.3	1.4
.8	.8	.8		.4	.7	.6	.8	.8	.7
.5	.5	.5		.1	.5	.4	.5	.6	.5
22 16.4	23 15.9	23 15.6	Sales/Receivables	0 UND	20 17.9	18 20.5	25 14.4	30 12.1	26 14.1
35 10.4	34 10.9	35 10.4		13 27.2	31 11.7	32 11.5	39 9.4	36 10.2	36 10.1
45 8.1	46 8.0	47 7.7		34 10.7	51 7.2	46 7.9	58 6.3	48 7.6	43 8.4
27 13.6	31 11.6	29 12.8	Cost of Sales/Inventory	0 UND	23 15.7	15 24.1	25 14.6	36 10.0	31 11.7
50 7.3	52 7.0	51 7.2		75 4.9	68 5.4	33 11.2	43 8.4	58 6.3	44 8.2
85 4.3	79 4.6	89 4.1		175 2.1	97 3.8	79 4.6	79 4.6	93 3.9	66 5.6
14 26.8	16 23.1	16 23.1	Cost of Sales/Payables	0 UND	16 23.5	14 26.6	16 23.0	20 17.9	16 22.3
23 15.9	28 13.3	30 12.3		8 47.0	34 10.8	35 10.5	35 10.4	30 12.0	25 14.6
39 9.4	43 8.4	50 7.3		31 11.7	70 5.2	55 6.7	55 6.6	50 7.3	37 9.9
7.4	6.6	6.5	Sales/Working Capital	6.8	5.0	6.6	7.3	6.1	7.1
13.7	14.3	12.8		27.6	21.8	18.0	13.6	10.6	12.7
53.5	73.3	54.0		-5.5	-30.8	-20.7	38.6	26.2	54.6
12.8	9.1	10.5	EBIT/Interest		22.8	10.0	7.4	16.8	11.6
(156) 4.1	(170) 2.9	(169) 3.1			(20) 6.9	(20) 3.3	(41) 2.8	(46) 3.1	(35) 3.7
1.4	.9	1.3			1.6	.9	.1	1.5	2.1
10.1	7.3	8.0	Net Profit + Depr., Dep., Amort./Cur. Mat. L/T/D						9.3
(48) 3.5	(41) 2.1	(28) 2.2						(11)	2.3
1.0	1.2	1.1							1.6
.1	.1	.1	Fixed/Worth	.1	.1	.1	.1	.1	.2
.3	.4	.3		NM	.4	.4	.3	.2	.5
.9	2.4	2.0		-.8	-1.4	NM	1.0	.6	2.0
.8	.9	1.0	Debt/Worth	.2	1.1	1.2	1.5	.6	.8
2.1	2.6	2.5		NM	10.5	3.0	3.0	1.5	2.3
6.7	23.6	14.9		-3.0	-10.0	NM	8.3	4.3	14.1
36.8	32.3	29.6	% Profit Before Taxes/Tangible Net Worth		83.7	51.5	35.1	23.9	28.4
(151) 17.9	(151) 17.8	(151) 12.8			(16) 12.7	(16) 9.9	(38) 13.0	(44) 11.7	(32) 21.1
6.3	3.3	3.0			-.1	-3.4	1.0	3.9	7.7
13.2	10.7	11.9	% Profit Before Taxes/Total Assets	32.5	20.4	15.8	8.4	12.3	9.9
6.4	4.8	4.9		5.3	8.4	5.5	3.7	3.5	6.2
1.1	-.4	.8		-10.0	2.8	-.2	-1.2	.8	2.0
107.6	106.0	95.7	Sales/Net Fixed Assets	UND	89.5	139.5	183.3	95.3	52.0
47.0	46.1	41.3		11.9	38.0	31.0	62.9	49.3	27.2
20.7	19.5	19.1		4.8	17.0	21.5	31.5	22.8	13.9
4.2	4.2	4.1	Sales/Total Assets	4.3	4.6	3.4	4.7	4.0	3.6
3.2	3.2	3.1		2.1	3.3	2.9	3.5	3.3	3.2
2.5	2.4	2.2		1.1	2.0	2.1	2.7	2.2	2.2
.4	.3	.4	% Depr., Dep., Amort./Sales		.4	.7	.3	.3	.5
(139) .7	(160) .7	(154) .7			(19) .6	(15) 1.1	(38) .5	(42) .6	(34) .8
1.2	1.4	1.3			1.2	1.9	1.1	1.3	1.5
1.8	1.8	2.3	% Officers', Directors' Owners' Comp/Sales		1.6	1.9	2.4	2.5	
(84) 3.3	(86) 4.1	(98) 4.5			(16) 4.6	(11)	(30) 4.8	(27) 4.1	
6.1	7.1	7.8			9.5	10.5	7.6	5.3	
6960256M	6607243M	4929956M	Net Sales ($)	6020M	52902M	82289M	303894M	693571M	3791280M
2090554M	2039301M	1660990M	Total Assets ($)	4651M	28300M	34848M	94231M	255983M	1242977M

© RMA 2011

M = $ thousand   MM = $ million
See Pages 9 through 22 for Explanation of Ratios and Data

Current Data Sorted by Assets / Comparative Historical Data

0-500M	500M-2MM	2-10MM	10-50MM	50-100MM	100-250MM	Type of Statement	4/1/06-3/31/07 ALL	4/1/07-3/31/08 ALL
1	2	8	12	7	4	Unqualified	32	32
	2	27	15	1		Reviewed	41	48
4	8	17	4			Compiled	32	29
7	11	9				Tax Returns	24	14
2	15	21	25	1	1	Other	68	89
	39 (4/1-9/30/10)		165 (10/1/10-3/31/11)					
14	38	82	56	9	5	NUMBER OF STATEMENTS	197	212
%	%	%	%	%	%	ASSETS	%	%
14.2	13.5	8.2	8.1			Cash & Equivalents	9.8	6.3
26.9	22.6	22.3	21.8			Trade Receivables (net)	24.6	22.0
40.8	43.1	42.7	41.9			Inventory	42.0	44.2
2.8	3.1	3.3	6.3			All Other Current	3.8	2.8
84.6	82.3	76.5	78.1			Total Current	80.3	75.3
8.5	11.3	15.7	13.1			Fixed Assets (net)	12.6	16.1
4.8	.7	2.8	4.5			Intangibles (net)	1.7	2.3
2.1	5.7	5.0	4.3			All Other Non-Current	5.5	6.3
100.0	100.0	100.0	100.0			Total	100.0	100.0
						LIABILITIES		
15.2	12.1	16.7	11.9			Notes Payable-Short Term	20.7	22.3
.8	3.2	3.5	4.2			Cur. Mat.-L.T.D.	2.8	3.5
15.8	18.2	14.7	13.9			Trade Payables	18.7	15.3
.0	.1	.2	.2			Income Taxes Payable	.3	.2
42.2	7.5	10.3	9.0			All Other Current	9.0	9.3
73.9	41.2	45.3	39.2			Total Current	51.5	50.6
15.0	4.5	9.1	8.0			Long-Term Debt	9.2	11.0
.2	.1	.1	.4			Deferred Taxes	.2	.2
12.9	7.1	6.3	4.2			All Other Non-Current	4.5	5.1
-2.0	47.0	39.2	48.3			Net Worth	34.5	33.1
100.0	100.0	100.0	100.0			Total Liabilities & Net Worth	100.0	100.0
						INCOME DATA		
100.0	100.0	100.0	100.0			Net Sales	100.0	100.0
42.8	35.4	27.5	29.3			Gross Profit	28.0	29.0
38.7	31.5	23.7	20.7			Operating Expenses	22.7	22.6
4.1	3.9	3.8	8.6			Operating Profit	5.4	6.4
.7	.5	.4	1.6			All Other Expenses (net)	.9	1.3
3.4	3.4	3.4	7.0			Profit Before Taxes	4.4	5.1
						RATIOS		
2.6	3.5	3.2	3.1			Current	2.4	2.4
1.8	2.1	1.8	2.0				1.5	1.5
.9	1.3	1.2	1.3				1.2	1.1
2.2	1.4	1.2	1.1			Quick	1.2	.9
.9	.9	.6	.7				(196) .6	(211) .6
.3	.3	.3	.3				.3	.3
0 UND	11 32.0	16 23.2	24 15.4			Sales/Receivables	12 29.4	14 26.1
16 22.5	27 13.5	31 11.9	42 8.7				31 11.8	32 11.3
52 7.0	50 7.3	45 8.1	57 6.5				54 6.8	47 7.8
0 UND	34 10.8	42 8.7	41 9.0			Cost of Sales/Inventory	24 15.5	41 8.9
49 7.5	71 5.1	72 5.1	114 3.2				73 5.0	80 4.6
126 2.9	161 2.3	142 2.6	256 1.4				151 2.4	158 2.3
0 UND	17 21.4	18 20.6	20 18.5			Cost of Sales/Payables	13 28.7	10 34.8
16 22.2	28 13.0	28 13.2	35 10.5				25 14.3	23 15.8
42 8.8	49 7.4	43 8.4	58 6.3				50 7.4	42 8.6
7.7	4.5	4.4	2.4			Sales/Working Capital	4.4	5.0
14.6	6.3	8.2	4.3				11.2	11.1
-52.8	15.9	22.5	13.4				32.5	42.8
	37.2	19.6	22.5			EBIT/Interest	10.8	9.4
	(29) 8.5	(79) 5.1	(49) 6.5				(169) 3.7	(194) 3.3
	2.0	1.9	1.7				1.6	1.8
		7.2	35.4			Net Profit + Depr., Dep., Amort./Cur. Mat. L/T/D	9.8	8.0
		(22) 3.9	(13) 5.4				(44) 2.0	(41) 2.3
		.9	1.2				1.3	1.2
.0	.0	.1	.0			Fixed/Worth	.1	.1
.0	.1	.3	.2				.2	.3
NM	.7	.7	.6				.7	1.0
1.7	.4	.6	.5			Debt/Worth	.8	.9
14.1	1.0	1.5	1.2				2.2	2.1
-4.2	2.1	4.2	3.2				5.5	5.1
	38.6	37.6	42.1			% Profit Before Taxes/Tangible Net Worth	54.4	46.4
	(34) 14.3	(77) 18.1	18.8				(183) 24.9	(196) 25.4
	6.8	3.6	6.5				9.1	9.2
53.9	19.9	13.4	15.6			% Profit Before Taxes/Total Assets	17.1	15.7
7.2	8.3	6.6	8.4				6.9	6.7
.0	2.0	1.2	2.4				2.7	2.2
UND	419.1	102.3	88.9			Sales/Net Fixed Assets	143.3	113.3
488.1	89.3	27.7	28.3				48.3	33.4
41.6	13.9	9.6	8.7				15.7	10.5
13.7	4.1	3.3	2.4			Sales/Total Assets	3.7	3.6
4.8	3.0	2.5	1.7				2.5	2.3
2.7	2.3	1.7	1.1				1.6	1.6
	.3	.3	.3			% Depr., Dep., Amort./Sales	.3	.3
	(23) .4	(68) .7	(52) .6				(154) .6	(169) .7
	2.3	2.0	1.4				1.2	1.6
	4.1	1.2				% Officers', Directors' Owners' Comp/Sales	1.7	1.0
	(20) 6.9	(26) 3.3					(73) 4.1	(68) 2.3
	9.9	6.0					6.8	4.8
17473M	152372M	1124737M	2141394M	1274444M	776379M	Net Sales ($)	5348387M	6892841M
2828M	43859M	433859M	1175207M	636911M	622129M	Total Assets ($)	2450687M	3239597M

M = $ thousand   MM = $ million
See Pages 9 through 22 for Explanation of Ratios and Data

Comparative Historical Data | Current Data Sorted by Sales

Hist 1	Hist 2	Hist 3	Type of Statement	0-1MM	1-3MM	3-5MM	5-10MM	10-25MM	25MM & OVER
37	31	34	Unqualified	1		1		10	22
53	27	45	Reviewed		2	4	10	13	16
28	21	33	Compiled	2	5	5	11	8	2
24	20	27	Tax Returns	5	8	3	8	3	
89	92	65	Other	2	8	5	13	19	18
4/1/08-3/31/09 ALL	4/1/09-3/31/10 ALL	4/1/10-3/31/11 ALL		39 (4/1-9/30/10)			165 (10/1/10-3/31/11)		
231	191	204	**NUMBER OF STATEMENTS**	10	23	18	42	53	58
%	%	%	**ASSETS**	%	%	%	%	%	%
8.2	7.8	9.3	Cash & Equivalents	7.2	7.9	17.0	7.7	8.0	10.1
22.6	22.2	22.4	Trade Receivables (net)	16.1	25.8	18.9	22.5	22.2	23.3
43.9	42.6	42.9	Inventory	53.9	47.8	30.2	40.9	45.3	42.4
2.4	3.0	4.0	All Other Current	1.1	2.3	2.2	6.3	3.1	4.9
77.1	75.6	78.6	Total Current	78.2	83.9	68.3	77.3	78.7	80.7
15.0	15.4	13.5	Fixed Assets (net)	7.1	10.5	20.5	16.2	14.7	10.8
1.9	2.6	3.1	Intangibles (net)	4.4	2.2	3.1	1.2	3.2	4.6
6.0	6.4	4.7	All Other Non-Current	10.4	3.4	8.1	5.3	3.5	3.9
100.0	100.0	100.0	Total	100.0	100.0	100.0	100.0	100.0	100.0
			LIABILITIES						
19.5	19.7	15.1	Notes Payable-Short Term	16.6	11.1	19.0	14.6	17.8	13.1
3.3	3.2	3.4	Cur. Mat.-L.T.D.	4.9	3.6	1.8	2.1	5.6	2.3
15.6	15.8	14.9	Trade Payables	5.6	18.4	12.2	13.9	15.9	15.8
.2	.1	.1	Income Taxes Payable	.0	.1	.1	.2	.1	.1
11.5	11.0	11.4	All Other Current	54.2	9.2	5.9	8.0	10.2	10.1
50.1	49.9	44.9	Total Current	81.3	42.5	39.1	38.9	49.6	41.4
10.9	9.2	8.3	Long-Term Debt	9.4	8.6	1.8	7.4	12.5	6.7
.3	.1	.2	Deferred Taxes	.0	.1	.3	.1	.3	.3
4.6	5.9	6.8	All Other Non-Current	17.5	13.3	7.2	5.7	3.6	6.0
34.2	34.9	39.8	Net Worth	-8.1	35.5	51.6	47.9	34.1	45.6
100.0	100.0	100.0	Total Liabilities & Net Worth	100.0	100.0	100.0	100.0	100.0	100.0
			INCOME DATA						
100.0	100.0	100.0	Net Sales	100.0	100.0	100.0	100.0	100.0	100.0
28.4	29.2	30.5	Gross Profit	49.0	38.4	34.0	33.1	27.3	24.0
23.4	25.3	24.9	Operating Expenses	45.2	34.3	30.1	26.6	22.0	17.4
5.0	3.9	5.6	Operating Profit	3.8	4.1	4.0	6.5	5.3	6.6
1.1	.9	1.1	All Other Expenses (net)	2.9	.8	-.2	1.1	.9	1.4
3.9	3.0	4.5	Profit Before Taxes	.9	3.3	4.2	5.4	4.4	5.1
			RATIOS						
2.4	2.7	3.2	Current	3.2	3.2	3.1	3.3	2.5	3.2
1.5	1.5	1.9		1.2	1.9	1.8	2.5	1.8	2.0
1.2	1.2	1.2		.9	1.5	1.3	1.4	1.2	1.2
1.1	1.0	1.2	Quick	1.2	1.2	2.8	1.4	1.1	1.3
.6	.6	.7		.4	.8	.8	.8	.5	.7
.3	.3	.3		.3	.4	.4	.4	.2	.4
14 26.5	20 18.6	16 23.1	Sales/Receivables	0 UND	14 26.8	7 49.8	20 17.9	18 20.1	19 19.1
32 11.3	34 10.8	32 11.3		15 24.6	32 11.3	27 13.5	31 11.7	32 11.3	38 9.7
48 7.6	55 6.6	52 7.0		46 7.9	53 6.9	39 9.3	50 7.3	55 6.6	51 7.1
37 9.8	43 8.5	40 9.0	Cost of Sales/Inventory	61 5.9	34 10.6	1 381.2	45 8.2	43 8.5	37 9.8
95 3.8	99 3.7	88 4.1		124 2.9	105 3.5	65 5.6	86 4.2	97 3.8	78 4.7
175 2.1	199 1.8	174 2.1		181 2.0	276 1.3	168 2.2	146 2.5	229 1.6	139 2.6
11 32.6	16 23.5	18 20.8	Cost of Sales/Payables	0 UND	24 15.2	10 37.9	16 23.4	18 20.1	19 19.7
27 13.6	30 12.0	29 12.7		10 35.0	31 11.8	30 12.4	28 13.2	29 12.5	32 11.4
49 7.4	50 7.3	46 8.0		42 8.8	77 4.8	47 7.7	47 7.8	53 6.9	43 8.5
4.5	4.2	3.7	Sales/Working Capital	5.4	3.1	5.1	3.2	3.5	3.6
9.4	7.5	6.5		12.8	6.1	7.4	6.3	6.4	6.4
30.7	40.3	18.9		-49.2	11.3	21.8	18.1	26.7	17.9
10.5	10.2	20.7	EBIT/Interest		16.7	31.3	25.1	17.3	21.6
(209) 3.0	(171) 3.2	(179) 5.7		(17) 5.2	(13) 7.6	(41) 6.4	(51) 4.7	(50) 6.1	
1.3	1.1	1.5			.7	1.2	1.5	1.9	2.0
13.2	7.4	13.1	Net Profit + Depr., Dep., Amort./Cur. Mat. L/T/D				6.0	8.6	36.7
(50) 2.8	(33) 2.8	(42) 4.5				(11) 4.1	(11) 4.4	(14) 8.1	
.9	1.3	.9					2.6	.9	.5
.1	.1	.0	Fixed/Worth	.0	.0	.0	.1	.1	.0
.3	.3	.2		.1	.1	.4	.2	.3	.1
.8	1.0	.7		NM	1.0	.6	.6	1.0	.5
1.0	.8	.6	Debt/Worth	2.7	.7	.4	.4	.9	.6
2.2	2.0	1.5		15.6	1.9	.9	1.1	1.9	1.5
4.9	4.1	4.0		-10.9	7.8	1.6	3.0	4.5	3.2
45.9	33.1	42.6	% Profit Before Taxes/Tangible Net Worth		57.9	48.7	36.5	38.7	49.2
(213) 22.8	(167) 14.7	(189) 18.6		(20) 12.0	(17) 12.8	(39) 15.2	(49) 19.2	(57) 25.7	
3.4	3.4	5.2			1.0	1.7	5.0	3.6	8.3
13.9	12.7	15.6	% Profit Before Taxes/Total Assets	46.3	12.8	24.3	14.6	14.3	18.0
5.3	3.7	7.5		4.4	4.4	8.2	5.2	7.5	8.3
.9	.3	1.9		-10.3	.0	1.5	1.2	1.5	3.1
123.0	113.9	122.0	Sales/Net Fixed Assets	UND	674.7	315.2	99.6	135.3	102.7
39.9	30.1	37.7		47.9	90.1	14.7	41.1	26.1	45.5
11.0	9.9	11.7		12.4	14.0	8.1	7.2	7.1	17.3
3.4	3.2	3.2	Sales/Total Assets	11.0	3.6	3.7	3.2	3.4	3.2
2.3	2.1	2.3		2.7	2.7	2.3	2.2	2.1	2.2
1.5	1.3	1.4		.8	1.7	1.9	1.1	1.3	1.6
.3	.3	.3	% Depr., Dep., Amort./Sales		.3	.7	.3	.3	.2
(175) .7	(154) .7	(161) .7		(12) .5	(13) 1.1	(33) .6	(43) .5	(55) .7	
1.7	1.4	1.7			2.8	2.8	3.8	1.7	1.2
1.3	1.9	2.1	% Officers', Directors' Owners' Comp/Sales			5.2	2.6	1.4	1.0
(89) 4.0	(56) 3.3	(60) 4.4		(11) 7.0	(16) 4.3	(12) 2.8	(10) 1.9		
7.9	7.5	7.1			13.4	6.9	4.6	4.6	
7049465M	5394444M	5486799M	Net Sales ($)	4826M	46580M	69034M	304313M	830794M	4231252M
3563493M	3235022M	2914793M	Total Assets ($)	4901M	28650M	30215M	207882M	533937M	2109208M

See Pages 9 through 22 for Explanation of Ratios and Data

Current Data Sorted by Assets　　　　　　Comparative Historical Data

Type of Statement	0-500M	500M-2MM	2-10MM	10-50MM	50-100MM	100-250MM	4/1/06-3/31/07 ALL	4/1/07-3/31/08 ALL
Unqualified			8	19	8	6	44	43
Reviewed	1	12	44	17	3	1	71	80
Compiled	4	15	23	4			47	40
Tax Returns	10	36	33	1			51	40
Other	14	41	52	41	11	10	126	133
		76 (4/1-9/30/10)		338 (10/1/10-3/31/11)				
NUMBER OF STATEMENTS	29	104	160	82	22	17	339	336
ASSETS	%	%	%	%	%	%	%	%
Cash & Equivalents	16.8	10.5	10.0	7.4	5.4	5.2	7.3	8.3
Trade Receivables (net)	24.0	25.2	24.9	27.9	35.3	24.0	27.0	26.6
Inventory	30.9	42.4	44.3	42.9	33.6	34.3	44.8	42.9
All Other Current	2.6	2.0	1.8	2.6	3.1	3.0	2.4	3.0
Total Current	74.2	80.1	81.0	80.8	77.4	66.5	81.5	80.8
Fixed Assets (net)	7.9	9.9	9.2	9.2	8.9	9.0	9.5	8.6
Intangibles (net)	6.2	4.4	4.7	4.9	5.2	18.1	4.2	5.3
All Other Non-Current	11.7	5.6	5.2	5.1	8.5	6.3	4.8	5.3
Total	100.0	100.0	100.0	100.0	100.0	100.0	100.0	100.0
LIABILITIES								
Notes Payable-Short Term	17.2	16.7	14.3	18.7	16.3	12.1	17.8	18.0
Cur. Mat.-L.T.D.	.6	2.6	1.8	2.3	1.5	1.4	2.1	2.0
Trade Payables	22.4	20.6	21.6	16.2	21.3	16.3	19.7	20.7
Income Taxes Payable	.0	.1	.1	.6	.1	.3	.2	.2
All Other Current	16.1	11.2	9.4	11.5	12.0	16.8	10.5	8.4
Total Current	56.4	51.2	47.2	49.3	51.3	47.0	50.2	49.2
Long-Term Debt	12.5	10.2	6.6	7.5	9.4	4.9	9.1	7.6
Deferred Taxes	.2	.1	.1	.2	.2	1.8	.2	.2
All Other Non-Current	17.0	5.1	6.8	5.1	3.8	11.8	8.4	6.3
Net Worth	13.9	33.5	39.2	37.8	35.4	34.6	32.0	36.7
Total Liabilities & Net Worth	100.0	100.0	100.0	100.0	100.0	100.0	100.0	100.0
INCOME DATA								
Net Sales	100.0	100.0	100.0	100.0	100.0	100.0	100.0	100.0
Gross Profit	37.9	35.4	30.9	28.9	26.3	28.4	32.3	31.7
Operating Expenses	34.6	31.5	27.3	23.7	19.7	21.6	28.2	27.2
Operating Profit	3.3	3.8	3.6	5.2	6.6	6.8	4.1	4.5
All Other Expenses (net)	.4	.4	.5	.7	1.1	1.1	1.0	1.2
Profit Before Taxes	2.9	3.5	3.1	4.6	5.5	5.7	3.1	3.4
RATIOS								
Current	2.5	3.0	3.1	2.9	2.6	2.5	2.9	2.6
	1.3	1.8	1.7	1.7	1.3	1.4	1.5	1.7
	1.0	1.2	1.3	1.2	1.1	1.1	1.2	1.2
Quick	1.2	1.3	1.5	1.1	1.3	1.4	1.2	1.2
	.7	.7	.7	.6	.8	.7	.6 (335)	.7
	.2	.4	.4	.4	.5	.4	.4	.4
Sales/Receivables	0 UND	12　30.3	19　18.9	29　12.6	33　11.2	40　9.1	16　23.0	19　19.4
	11　33.3	27　13.5	33　11.1	53　6.9	50　7.3	71　5.2	37　9.9	36　10.2
	35　10.3	43　8.5	52　7.0	74　5.0	92　4.0	85　4.3	60　6.1	54　6.7
Cost of Sales/Inventory	0 UND	44　8.4	53　6.8	68　5.4	66　5.6	99　3.7	63　5.8	53　6.9
	14　26.3	90　4.1	98　3.7	130　2.8	83　4.4	104　3.5	101　3.6	101　3.6
	106　3.4	173　2.1	152　2.4	172　2.1	95　3.8	159　2.3	150　2.4	147　2.5
Cost of Sales/Payables	0 UND	12　29.4	18　19.9	15　23.8	15　24.4	34　10.8	14　26.5	15　24.8
	11　32.0	27　13.8	37　10.0	37　10.0	39　9.3	53　6.8	32　11.5	32　11.3
	59　6.1	52　7.0	67　5.4	59　6.2	66　5.5	62　5.9	55　6.6	56　6.5
Sales/Working Capital	8.9	4.9	4.4	3.6	3.9	3.1	4.3	4.5
	20.5	9.3	8.0	7.0	11.0	9.8	8.4	8.5
	UND	34.5	18.1	11.5	33.6	21.7	20.8	20.0
EBIT/Interest	17.8	10.7	12.0	20.0	25.4	11.6	7.9	9.7
	(19)　10.5	(87)　3.5	(145)　3.9	(78)　4.4	5.7	7.1	(307)　2.9	(303)　2.9
	.3	1.3	1.4	1.6	3.5	1.7	1.1	1.3
Net Profit + Depr., Dep., Amort./Cur. Mat. L/T/D				9.1	39.4		11.4	9.3
			(20)　2.2	(24)　4.8			(69)　3.2	(59)　2.8
			1.0	1.1			.7	.9
Fixed/Worth	.0	.0	.0	.1	.1	.1	.1	.1
	.1	.2	.1	.2	.2	.5	.2	.2
	NM	.7	.6	.6	1.8	NM	.9	.7
Debt/Worth	.9	.6	.7	.8	1.1	1.0	.8	.8
	2.6	2.1	1.7	2.3	2.2	3.0	2.2	1.8
	-3.7	7.1	4.2	5.3	10.9	NM	9.4	6.2
% Profit Before Taxes/Tangible Net Worth	89.2	49.0	41.5	47.4	60.5	64.0	38.2	43.5
	(21)　54.4	(87)　16.4	(147)　14.5	(74)　26.0	(20)　29.5	(13)　24.0	(284)　15.3	(292)　20.7
	17.9	3.4	3.5	9.9	10.2	.5	3.6	5.1
% Profit Before Taxes/Total Assets	36.4	15.5	13.2	14.5	24.8	12.2	12.5	15.6
	14.0	5.9	4.8	7.0	7.9	6.3	4.6	6.6
	.6	.9	.8	1.9	3.6	1.5	.5	1.0
Sales/Net Fixed Assets	UND	177.5	137.6	100.0	231.8	45.5	130.1	157.3
	194.9	57.8	55.1	42.4	55.2	29.6	47.7	52.7
	34.7	22.1	20.5	15.3	18.2	9.4	21.3	22.6
Sales/Total Assets	7.2	3.9	3.3	2.3	3.2	2.1	3.3	3.4
	4.7	3.0	2.5	1.8	2.0	1.5	2.4	2.5
	2.5	2.0	1.7	1.5	1.5	1.1	1.7	1.7
% Depr., Dep., Amort./Sales	.4	.3	.3	.3	.4	.5	.3	.3
	(12)　.9	(67)　.6	(124)　.7	(70)　.6	(15)　.6	(15)　.7	(255)　.7	(254)　.6
	1.6	1.3	1.1	1.4	.8	3.1	1.1	1.1
% Officers', Directors' Owners' Comp/Sales	3.1	2.5	1.1	1.4			1.7	1.4
	(15)　6.8	(60)　4.4	(72)　2.4	(15)　2.5			(140)　3.8	(143)　3.0
	10.6	7.2	4.0	4.9			5.7	5.7
Net Sales ($)	39026M	404594M	2200205M	4055935M	3489026M	5287992M	10252247M	12932831M
Total Assets ($)	7535M	126202M	786379M	1948342M	1504871M	2897537M	4469077M	5776951M

© RMA 2011

M = $ thousand　　MM = $ million
See Pages 9 through 22 for Explanation of Ratios and Data

	Comparative Historical Data				Current Data Sorted by Sales					
Type of Statement										
Unqualified	60	62	41				2	5	34
Reviewed	82	92	78		7	7	14	30	20
Compiled	54	42	46	2	7	8	15	10	4
Tax Returns	60	71	80	7	22	20	18	11	2
Other	138	155	169	10	23	19	25	30	62
	4/1/08-3/31/09 ALL	4/1/09-3/31/10 ALL	4/1/10-3/31/11 ALL	76 (4/1-9/30/10)			338 (10/1/10-3/31/11)		
				0-1MM	1-3MM	3-5MM	5-10MM	10-25MM	25MM & OVER
NUMBER OF STATEMENTS	394	422	414	19	59	54	74	86	122
ASSETS	%	%	%	%	%	%	%	%	%
Cash & Equivalents	8.1	9.4	9.6	17.1	10.3	10.4	12.5	8.3	7.0
Trade Receivables (net)	24.0	26.9	26.0	15.9	21.9	24.5	25.3	27.8	29.5
Inventory	45.3	40.8	41.6	32.6	45.2	40.7	43.8	42.0	40.2
All Other Current	2.7	2.3	2.2	.4	1.9	1.0	1.9	3.2	2.6
Total Current	80.0	79.4	79.5	66.0	79.4	76.5	83.5	81.3	79.3
Fixed Assets (net)	9.6	10.0	9.2	16.6	6.2	11.9	9.5	9.1	8.3
Intangibles (net)	5.8	5.4	5.3	4.9	8.3	5.6	1.6	4.3	6.9
All Other Non-Current	4.6	5.1	5.9	12.5	6.1	6.0	5.4	5.3	5.5
Total	100.0	100.0	100.0	100.0	100.0	100.0	100.0	100.0	100.0
LIABILITIES									
Notes Payable-Short Term	18.4	18.7	16.0	13.8	20.8	13.4	13.3	16.2	16.6
Cur. Mat.-L.T.D.	2.3	2.2	2.0	5.0	1.8	2.0	1.3	1.6	2.3
Trade Payables	19.2	20.3	20.1	10.2	18.5	21.4	20.6	23.1	19.4
Income Taxes Payable	.1	.2	.2	.0	.1	.1	.1	.1	.4
All Other Current	9.1	9.7	11.2	32.2	8.1	10.1	8.9	9.9	12.2
Total Current	49.1	51.1	49.5	61.2	49.3	47.0	44.2	50.9	51.0
Long-Term Debt	8.4	10.3	8.2	11.7	11.9	11.3	6.3	6.5	6.8
Deferred Taxes	.2	.2	.2	.3	.0	.2	.1	.3	.3
All Other Non-Current	6.0	7.1	6.8	26.0	4.1	6.2	3.5	4.4	9.0
Net Worth	36.3	31.3	35.3	.8	34.7	35.3	45.9	37.8	32.9
Total Liabilties & Net Worth	100.0	100.0	100.0	100.0	100.0	100.0	100.0	100.0	100.0
INCOME DATA									
Net Sales	100.0	100.0	100.0	100.0	100.0	100.0	100.0	100.0	100.0
Gross Profit	31.6	31.9	31.8	43.5	38.3	37.3	31.1	28.9	26.8
Operating Expenses	28.0	28.3	27.5	39.4	34.9	32.2	28.4	25.1	21.2
Operating Profit	3.6	3.7	4.2	4.2	3.4	5.1	2.7	3.8	5.6
All Other Expenses (net)	.8	1.0	.5	.4	.8	.7	-.3	.5	.9
Profit Before Taxes	2.8	2.7	3.7	3.8	2.7	4.4	3.0	3.2	4.7
RATIOS									
Current	2.7	2.8	2.8	2.7	3.0	3.3	3.8	2.4	2.8
	1.7	1.6	1.6	1.1	1.6	1.9	1.8	1.5	1.5
	1.2	1.2	1.2	.5	1.2	1.2	1.4	1.2	1.2
Quick	1.2	1.3	1.2	2.2	1.1	2.0	2.1	1.1	1.1
	.6	.7	.7	.4	.6	.7	.8	.6	.7
	.4	.4	.4	.2	.4	.4	.4	.4	.4
Sales/Receivables	19 19.1	19 19.1	19 19.0	13 29.1	5 73.3	19 19.5	16 23.4	24 15.2	27 13.3
	36 10.2	37 9.8	33 10.9	22 16.5	22 16.5	31 11.7	32 11.4	36 10.2	45 8.0
	53 6.9	59 6.2	59 6.2	58 6.3	47 7.8	50 7.3	50 7.4	55 6.6	70 5.2
Cost of Sales/Inventory	58 6.3	52 7.0	51 7.1	0 UND	43 8.6	56 6.6	49 7.5	47 7.7	55 6.6
	100 3.6	89 4.1	100 3.7	160 2.3	114 3.2	106 3.4	89 4.1	99 3.7	99 3.7
	159 2.3	142 2.6	153 2.4	327 1.1	177 2.1	162 2.3	148 2.5	139 2.6	148 2.5
Cost of Sales/Payables	14 27.0	14 26.2	15 24.5	6 64.0	5 71.1	16 22.8	15 23.9	23 15.9	15 23.7
	31 11.9	31 11.8	35 10.3	19 18.8	26 14.3	39 9.3	32 11.5	40 9.2	37 9.8
	55 6.6	55 6.7	59 6.2	63 5.8	56 6.5	69 5.3	52 7.0	66 5.5	59 6.2
Sales/Working Capital	4.7	4.3	4.4	2.2	3.7	3.6	4.3	5.1	4.4
	7.9	8.7	8.4	59.8	10.3	8.3	7.4	9.0	7.9
	19.9	33.1	22.2	-5.4	32.7	22.9	14.5	22.6	19.1
EBIT/Interest	9.4	12.6	15.1	8.8	10.9	11.0	19.4	14.0	21.5
	(357) 3.0	(386) 3.3	(368) 4.2	(10) 1.4	(53) 3.6	(47) 4.2	(60) 4.0	(81) 4.2	(117) 5.1
	1.1	1.2	1.5	-.8	1.1	1.4	1.4	1.7	2.1
Net Profit + Depr., Dep., Amort./Cur. Mat. L/T/D	8.9	9.4	13.2					16.3	13.5
	(76) 3.6	(72) 2.9	(62) 3.3					(19) 5.4	(29) 3.3
	1.1	.7	1.2					1.6	1.0
Fixed/Worth	.1	.0	.0	.0	.0	.0	.0	.1	.1
	.2	.2	.2	.8	.1	.2	.1	.1	.2
	.9	.9	.7	-.5	.4	2.3	.4	.6	.7
Debt/Worth	.8	.7	.7	.6	.5	.6	.4	1.0	.8
	1.9	2.2	2.2	6.6	2.1	1.4	1.5	2.4	2.6
	7.4	8.9	6.0	-2.5	9.8	7.5	2.8	4.4	7.9
% Profit Before Taxes/Tangible Net Worth	41.4	48.1	48.7	56.3	71.7	48.3	22.8	48.6	55.9
	(340) 14.1	(359) 19.7	(362) 20.2	(12) 20.1	(48) 10.3	(44) 20.1	(70) 11.5	(79) 26.4	(109) 27.1
	3.3	4.1	5.1	-1.3	.4	5.0	2.9	6.5	10.8
% Profit Before Taxes/Total Assets	13.1	15.5	14.8	13.7	19.8	14.8	14.0	13.8	15.8
	4.5	5.5	6.3	4.3	8.0	4.8	5.0	7.2	7.0
	.3	.6	1.1	-1.8	.4	1.3	.8	1.6	2.5
Sales/Net Fixed Assets	134.3	173.5	139.2	272.0	213.9	194.7	150.2	118.5	118.5
	53.2	56.9	50.6	21.5	77.5	45.6	48.1	48.1	51.1
	19.9	18.4	20.6	9.6	31.5	14.2	17.5	20.7	19.7
Sales/Total Assets	3.4	3.3	3.4	2.4	4.1	3.4	3.7	3.2	3.1
	2.3	2.3	2.3	1.3	2.6	2.3	2.8	2.6	2.0
	1.7	1.7	1.6	.8	1.7	1.7	1.7	1.9	1.6
% Depr., Dep., Amort./Sales	.3	.3	.3	.9	.4	.1	.3	.4	.3
	(294) .6	(305) .6	(303) .6	(13) 1.6	(31) .7	(37) .6	(50) .6	(72) .7	(100) .5
	1.1	1.3	1.2	2.6	1.1	1.3	1.1	1.2	1.0
% Officers', Directors' Owners' Comp/Sales	1.4	1.6	1.6		3.7	2.3	1.6	1.0	.6
	(154) 3.1	(158) 3.4	(168) 3.2		(38) 6.8	(31) 3.4	(33) 3.2	(35) 1.8	(23) 1.7
	6.0	5.9	5.6		8.5	5.5	5.3	3.2	4.0
Net Sales ($)	14160930M	19238299M	15476778M	10864M	115529M	206300M	550525M	1349892M	13243668M
Total Assets ($)	6490458M	7647073M	7270866M	9601M	53017M	100282M	243776M	620531M	6243659M

M = $ thousand   MM = $ million
See Pages 9 through 22 for Explanation of Ratios and Data

Current Data Sorted by Assets							Comparative Historical Data	
						Type of Statement		
	1	1	10	5	6	Unqualified	20	21
	3	20	9			Reviewed	24	22
	8	15	4	1		Compiled	17	7
6	17	6				Tax Returns	23	19
3	14	16	14	2	4	Other	42	60
	34 (4/1-9/30/10)		131 (10/1/10-3/31/11)				4/1/06-3/31/07	4/1/07-3/31/08
0-500M	**500M-2MM**	**2-10MM**	**10-50MM**	**50-100MM**	**100-250MM**		**ALL**	**ALL**
9	43	58	37	8	10	**NUMBER OF STATEMENTS**	126	129
%	%	%	%	%	%	**ASSETS**	%	%
	10.9	7.5	9.6		5.0	Cash & Equivalents	8.3	8.8
	28.8	26.3	25.8		25.2	Trade Receivables (net)	27.2	25.7
	42.1	42.0	35.7		30.8	Inventory	40.3	40.3
	3.3	4.2	4.3		7.2	All Other Current	2.9	5.0
	85.2	80.1	75.5		68.2	Total Current	78.7	79.7
	7.5	9.9	11.8		19.8	Fixed Assets (net)	12.3	12.0
	3.0	2.4	7.0		9.8	Intangibles (net)	3.8	3.0
	4.3	7.6	5.7		2.2	All Other Non-Current	5.2	5.2
	100.0	100.0	100.0		100.0	Total	100.0	100.0
						LIABILITIES		
	17.4	18.0	17.5		11.2	Notes Payable-Short Term	21.8	20.4
	.6	2.3	1.9		7.9	Cur. Mat.-L.T.D.	2.0	2.2
	19.7	18.4	13.7		21.5	Trade Payables	19.0	17.8
	.2	.1	.3		.0	Income Taxes Payable	.2	.7
	6.6	10.2	11.8		5.4	All Other Current	7.4	8.2
	44.4	48.8	45.2		46.0	Total Current	50.4	49.2
	4.8	6.3	6.5		25.4	Long-Term Debt	12.7	10.3
	.0	.1	.1		.0	Deferred Taxes	.1	.1
	15.6	6.1	8.4		4.6	All Other Non-Current	8.1	7.5
	35.1	38.6	39.9		24.0	Net Worth	28.6	32.9
	100.0	100.0	100.0		100.0	Total Liabilties & Net Worth	100.0	100.0
						INCOME DATA		
	100.0	100.0	100.0		100.0	Net Sales	100.0	100.0
	31.0	36.5	30.9		43.1	Gross Profit	34.4	35.6
	27.4	32.1	25.2		36.1	Operating Expenses	30.3	31.7
	3.6	4.4	5.7		7.0	Operating Profit	4.2	3.9
	.5	.7	1.0		1.5	All Other Expenses (net)	1.4	1.4
	3.1	3.7	4.7		5.5	Profit Before Taxes	2.8	2.5
						RATIOS		
	5.1	2.6	3.5		2.6		2.7	2.8
	2.1	1.9	1.6		1.6	Current	1.7	1.7
	1.3	1.2	1.2		1.0		1.2	1.2
	2.0	1.1	1.4		1.3		1.4	1.1
	1.0	.7	.9		.6	Quick	.7	.6
	.5	.3	.4		.3		.3	.4
	11 34.3	**17** 20.9	**29** 12.5		**13** 28.5		**18** 20.5	**21** 17.2
	23 15.8	**36** 10.0	**37** 9.8		**34** 10.8	Sales/Receivables	**33** 11.2	**34** 10.6
	48 7.6	**53** 6.9	**66** 5.6		**87** 4.2		**61** 6.0	**55** 6.7
	15 24.3	**48** 7.7	**61** 6.0		**95** 3.8		**46** 7.9	**48** 7.7
	55 6.7	**107** 3.4	**128** 2.8		**139** 2.6	Cost of Sales/Inventory	**96** 3.8	**109** 3.4
	152 2.4	**172** 2.1	**164** 2.2		**173** 2.1		**136** 2.7	**163** 2.2
	5 68.3	**16** 23.1	**20** 18.3		**58** 6.3		**14** 25.4	**19** 19.3
	25 14.7	**30** 12.2	**29** 12.4		**72** 5.1	Cost of Sales/Payables	**32** 11.5	**32** 11.5
	44 8.3	**70** 5.2	**42** 8.7		**84** 4.4		**54** 6.7	**67** 5.5
	3.6	4.1	3.6		3.1		4.6	4.5
	8.2	8.8	5.6		8.6	Sales/Working Capital	8.5	7.6
	34.2	17.1	17.6		NM		23.2	21.9
	22.3	8.9	30.3				9.1	6.4
	(34) 5.9	(51) 3.3	(34) 5.9			EBIT/Interest	(112) 2.8	(115) 2.1
	1.4	2.1	2.4				1.5	1.0
							14.0	18.3
						Net Profit + Depr., Dep., Amort./Cur. Mat. L/T/D	(21) 3.8	(22) 3.0
							-.4	.6
	.0	.0	.0		.2		.0	.0
	.1	.2	.2		.5	Fixed/Worth	.3	.2
	.9	.5	.8		NM		1.2	1.2
	.5	.9	.7		1.5		.8	.8
	2.3	1.9	1.5		2.9	Debt/Worth	2.0	1.9
	17.2	3.1	4.4		NM		8.5	6.7
	60.1	39.8	50.1				52.9	41.6
	(35) 21.9	(54) 14.8	(31) 22.3			% Profit Before Taxes/Tangible Net Worth	(108) 14.8	(110) 14.2
	6.7	2.2	9.1				4.9	1.7
	19.1	16.1	18.2		12.0		12.5	13.4
	6.5	4.5	6.7		6.9	% Profit Before Taxes/Total Assets	5.5	3.6
	2.1	1.3	2.3		4.4		1.3	.2
	508.3	175.0	161.6		35.0		114.4	126.7
	99.8	53.5	33.8		13.7	Sales/Net Fixed Assets	39.9	40.1
	33.4	14.4	8.8		9.8		13.4	14.2
	5.1	3.3	2.4		2.5		3.6	3.1
	2.8	2.4	1.6		1.6	Sales/Total Assets	2.6	2.2
	1.9	1.5	1.2		1.0		1.6	1.6
	.2	.3	.3				.3	.3
	(28) .3	(39) .6	(31) .7			% Depr., Dep., Amort./Sales	(102) .7	(99) .8
	.8	1.3	1.9				1.5	1.9
	1.6	1.8	.4				1.4	1.7
	(24) 3.6	(24) 2.8	(10) .5			% Officers', Directors' Owners' Comp/Sales	(49) 3.2	(50) 4.0
	7.5	4.5	1.5				5.9	7.4
20588M	**226769M**	**642558M**	**1835559M**	**1339218M**	**2393003M**	Net Sales ($)	**3875225M**	**4843369M**
2632M	**52579M**	**268288M**	**862859M**	**596248M**	**1493038M**	Total Assets ($)	**1716334M**	**2383819M**

M = $ thousand MM = $ million

See Pages 9 through 22 for Explanation of Ratios and Data

Comparative Historical Data | Current Data Sorted by Sales

4/1/08-3/31/09 ALL	4/1/09-3/31/10 ALL	4/1/10-3/31/11 ALL	Type of Statement	0-1MM	1-3MM	3-5MM	5-10MM	10-25MM	25MM & OVER
23	14	23	Unqualified		1		1	3	18
26	23	32	Reviewed		2	4	7	15	4
15	15	28	Compiled		5	2	10	4	7
24	26	29	Tax Returns	3	10	8	4	4	
61	60	53	Other	1	7	8	11	7	19
					34 (4/1-9/30/10)		131 (10/1/10-3/31/11)		
149	138	165	**NUMBER OF STATEMENTS**	4	25	22	33	33	48
%	%	%	**ASSETS**	%	%	%	%	%	%
9.3	9.5	8.7	Cash & Equivalents		10.7	6.3	9.4	7.6	9.1
25.4	26.2	27.8	Trade Receivables (net)		22.9	26.0	21.6	32.0	31.3
40.4	39.7	38.8	Inventory		42.5	40.1	44.5	38.9	33.6
4.3	3.0	4.2	All Other Current		6.8	3.0	3.4	2.6	4.6
79.5	78.4	79.5	Total Current		82.9	75.4	78.8	81.2	78.5
12.5	12.0	10.1	Fixed Assets (net)		6.9	13.9	7.5	9.7	11.6
3.5	3.2	4.1	Intangibles (net)		1.3	4.2	3.2	5.8	5.5
4.5	6.5	6.3	All Other Non-Current		8.9	6.6	10.5	3.4	4.4
100.0	100.0	100.0	Total		100.0	100.0	100.0	100.0	100.0
			LIABILITIES						
18.2	16.1	17.1	Notes Payable-Short Term		18.9	18.6	19.5	18.0	14.6
3.1	2.6	2.3	Cur. Mat.-L.T.D.		.2	3.4	1.7	1.0	3.0
20.0	16.8	19.0	Trade Payables		18.1	18.4	18.9	17.5	21.4
.1	.3	.1	Income Taxes Payable		.3	.1	.0	.2	.2
6.9	6.9	9.4	All Other Current		6.6	6.3	10.2	14.8	6.6
48.2	42.7	47.9	Total Current		44.1	46.7	50.2	51.4	45.8
9.2	7.9	7.4	Long-Term Debt		4.2	10.9	3.6	5.3	11.7
.1	.1	.1	Deferred Taxes		.0	.0	.1	.1	.0
9.0	7.6	9.2	All Other Non-Current		19.3	7.7	5.7	8.4	7.5
33.6	41.7	35.4	Net Worth		32.3	34.7	40.4	34.8	35.0
100.0	100.0	100.0	Total Liabilities & Net Worth		100.0	100.0	100.0	100.0	100.0
			INCOME DATA						
100.0	100.0	100.0	Net Sales		100.0	100.0	100.0	100.0	100.0
33.1	34.7	33.6	Gross Profit		34.5	38.7	35.4	32.5	30.4
30.9	30.7	28.9	Operating Expenses		30.9	34.2	30.1	28.5	25.0
2.2	4.0	4.7	Operating Profit		3.6	4.5	5.3	4.0	5.3
1.2	.6	.7	All Other Expenses (net)		.4	1.2	1.1	.1	.8
1.0	3.5	4.0	Profit Before Taxes		3.2	3.3	4.2	3.9	4.6
			RATIOS						
2.9	3.0	3.1			6.8	3.2	3.0	2.5	3.1
1.8	1.9	1.7	Current		2.3	1.8	1.5	1.6	1.6
1.2	1.3	1.2			1.1	1.0	1.1	1.3	1.2
1.3	1.5	1.3			1.5	1.2	1.8	1.2	1.4
.7	.9	.8	Quick		.7	.7	.7	.9	.9
.4	.4	.4			.2	.2	.3	.4	.4
20 18.7	18 20.5	14 26.7			4 101.1	16 22.2	11 34.4	27 13.5	24 15.3
36 10.2	36 10.0	35 10.6	Sales/Receivables		20 18.0	32 11.5	25 14.7	40 9.2	35 10.5
56 6.5	57 6.4	54 6.8			51 7.2	43 8.5	49 7.4	59 6.2	68 5.4
43 8.5	44 8.3	40 9.1			20 18.7	48 7.6	42 8.6	42 8.8	44 8.3
108 3.4	101 3.6	97 3.8	Cost of Sales/Inventory		107 3.4	83 4.4	123 3.0	97 3.8	84 4.4
168 2.2	168 2.2	161 2.3			237 1.5	169 2.2	193 1.9	143 2.5	159 2.3
16 22.2	16 23.0	13 28.5			1 674.7	5 66.7	12 31.4	22 16.6	21 17.5
32 11.2	31 11.8	31 11.6	Cost of Sales/Payables		21 17.5	33 11.2	26 13.9	31 11.6	37 9.8
60 6.1	51 7.2	64 5.7			78 4.7	71 5.1	49 7.4	53 6.8	68 5.3
4.6	4.0	4.0			2.2	3.9	4.5	5.5	3.7
8.2	6.9	8.7	Sales/Working Capital		4.6	8.3	10.5	8.7	8.6
22.8	14.7	24.8			32.0	NM	95.2	14.7	19.4
6.9	18.7	16.4			24.6	5.9	12.7	13.2	22.6
(127) 2.1	(122) 5.3	(139) 4.8	EBIT/Interest		(18) 4.4	(20) 2.6	(27) 2.8	(30) 6.2	(42) 7.6
.8	1.7	2.1			.9	1.1	2.1	2.3	2.7
6.2	3.7	6.8							13.4
(20) 2.2	(16) 1.8	(23) 3.5	Net Profit + Depr., Dep., Amort./Cur. Mat. L/T/D						(11) 5.7
1.0	1.4	1.2							3.3
.0	.0	.0			.0	.1	.0	.1	.0
.2	.1	.2	Fixed/Worth		.1	.4	.2	.2	.2
.8	.6	.7			.5	1.4	1.0	.7	.8
.7	.7	.9			.5	1.1	.5	1.0	1.0
1.9	1.3	2.0	Debt/Worth		3.1	1.8	1.9	2.6	1.9
4.3	3.4	6.6			13.6	6.4	4.5	5.1	4.9
32.1	43.8	60.2			82.7	53.6	60.4	39.8	64.5
(135) 9.0	(127) 22.7	(142) 22.6	% Profit Before Taxes/Tangible Net Worth		(22) 19.3	(18) 13.7	(27) 12.2	(30) 27.3	(42) 35.6
.2	3.7	7.4			4.5	1.5	5.5	6.8	13.4
10.8	16.7	17.6			17.6	29.7	11.4	16.4	20.0
2.6	7.6	6.5	% Profit Before Taxes/Total Assets		6.5	4.3	4.5	6.6	9.5
-1.2	1.1	2.3			.5	.3	2.4	2.1	4.4
287.1	229.2	247.2			528.9	111.2	247.2	185.3	208.7
49.6	47.1	55.8	Sales/Net Fixed Assets		99.8	31.7	74.7	66.7	33.0
11.7	14.6	15.1			26.0	12.3	14.7	20.9	13.7
3.6	3.2	3.5			2.6	4.4	3.8	3.6	2.9
2.2	2.2	2.3	Sales/Total Assets		1.9	2.6	2.2	2.5	2.2
1.5	1.4	1.5			1.2	1.4	1.5	1.7	1.3
.3	.4	.2			.2	.3	.1	.4	.2
(109) .7	(88) .9	(115) .6	% Depr., Dep., Amort./Sales		(15) .5	(15) 1.3	(20) .4	(23) .6	(41) .9
2.0	1.6	1.5			1.0	3.4	.8	2.1	1.5
1.8	1.9	1.4			3.1	2.8	1.3	1.5	.5
(60) 3.7	(56) 3.9	(65) 2.7	% Officers', Directors' Owners' Comp/Sales		(14) 4.0	(13) 3.5	(14) 2.6	(10) 2.1	(13) .7
6.1	7.5	5.2			7.1	8.5	5.6	3.0	1.6
5719380M	5319086M	6457695M	Net Sales ($)	2852M	49848M	89399M	261072M	530542M	5523982M
2740491M	2607094M	3275644M	Total Assets ($)	960M	31376M	52953M	126958M	242223M	2821174M

M = $ thousand   MM = $ million
See Pages 9 through 22 for Explanation of Ratios and Data

Current Data Sorted by Assets   Comparative Historical Data

Type of Statement	0-500M	500M-2MM	2-10MM	10-50MM	50-100MM	100-250MM		4/1/06-3/31/07 ALL	4/1/07-3/31/08 ALL
Unqualified		2	5	19	8	8		33	39
Reviewed	1	4	42	42	4			83	85
Compiled	16	22	31	9	3	1		56	61
Tax Returns	11	33	32	5		1		54	65
Other		28	78	67	13	10		121	156
	69 (4/1-9/30/10)		426 (10/1/10-3/31/11)						
NUMBER OF STATEMENTS	28	89	188	142	28	20		347	406
	%	%	%	%	%	%		%	%
ASSETS									
Cash & Equivalents	17.4	13.7	9.7	6.2	7.1	4.6		10.3	11.1
Trade Receivables (net)	15.1	22.1	25.3	29.1	24.7	28.0		30.3	29.6
Inventory	16.6	19.4	21.1	22.3	24.8	19.1		19.3	18.5
All Other Current	6.0	1.5	2.1	3.2	3.3	4.7		3.0	2.5
Total Current	55.1	56.6	58.2	60.7	59.8	56.3		62.8	61.7
Fixed Assets (net)	29.9	32.9	32.3	28.3	25.1	26.3		29.4	28.4
Intangibles (net)	3.0	3.2	3.1	4.2	5.5	12.5		2.2	3.1
All Other Non-Current	12.0	7.4	6.5	6.8	9.6	4.9		5.5	6.7
Total	100.0	100.0	100.0	100.0	100.0	100.0		100.0	100.0
LIABILITIES									
Notes Payable-Short Term	16.1	9.9	10.0	12.6	14.4	9.0		11.0	11.0
Cur. Mat.-L.T.D.	3.7	4.4	4.8	3.5	3.2	3.4		4.0	4.0
Trade Payables	25.2	14.5	16.3	17.0	14.6	16.1		18.2	17.9
Income Taxes Payable	.0	.3	.1	.3	.4	.1		.4	.3
All Other Current	18.0	6.9	9.2	7.2	10.2	7.1		8.4	8.5
Total Current	63.0	35.9	40.4	40.6	42.8	35.6		42.0	41.6
Long-Term Debt	16.2	22.0	15.2	13.9	10.7	16.8		17.4	15.1
Deferred Taxes	.0	.1	.5	.3	.9	1.1		.3	.3
All Other Non-Current	12.7	8.7	6.1	4.8	4.7	16.0		3.8	4.7
Net Worth	8.1	33.2	37.8	40.4	40.9	30.5		36.4	38.2
Total Liabilities & Net Worth	100.0	100.0	100.0	100.0	100.0	100.0		100.0	100.0
INCOME DATA									
Net Sales	100.0	100.0	100.0	100.0	100.0	100.0		100.0	100.0
Gross Profit	33.4	34.2	25.0	18.7	12.5	11.2		25.7	24.4
Operating Expenses	28.6	28.8	20.4	14.5	8.0	9.1		19.2	18.0
Operating Profit	4.8	5.4	4.6	4.2	4.5	2.1		6.5	6.4
All Other Expenses (net)	.4	-.2	.5	.2	-.1	1.5		.5	.5
Profit Before Taxes	4.4	5.6	4.2	4.0	4.6	.6		6.0	5.8
RATIOS									
Current	2.2	4.6	2.7	2.2	2.2	2.1		2.7	2.6
	1.0	1.8	1.5	1.5	1.5	1.4		1.6	1.5
	.6	.9	.9	1.1	1.1	1.2		1.1	1.1
Quick	1.5	2.0	1.7	1.3	1.4	1.6		1.7	1.8
	.4	1.0	.9	.8	.8	1.0		(346) 1.0	(405) 1.1
	.1	.5	.5	.5	.5	.6		.6	.6
Sales/Receivables	0 UND	3 113.8	10 35.7	23 16.0	23 15.7	27 13.5		16 22.2	15 24.3
	1 531.9	16 23.1	26 14.0	34 10.7	33 10.9	35 10.3		31 11.9	29 12.5
	22 16.6	31 11.9	40 9.0	43 8.5	38 9.5	43 8.6		43 8.5	41 8.8
Cost of Sales/Inventory	0 UND	2 171.3	7 54.0	11 32.8	17 21.0	11 32.6		6 60.8	5 79.0
	1 256.0	11 32.4	21 17.2	26 14.0	29 12.6	16 22.2		17 20.9	14 26.1
	14 26.2	44 8.3	43 8.6	43 8.5	50 7.3	35 10.5		40 9.1	34 10.7
Cost of Sales/Payables	0 UND	1 356.5	6 56.5	12 31.1	11 34.7	15 25.1		8 44.2	7 50.3
	3 113.1	11 33.5	16 23.2	22 16.8	20 17.9	20 18.4		21 17.2	19 19.1
	25 14.6	29 12.5	34 10.8	37 9.8	27 13.5	29 12.5		35 10.4	35 10.3
Sales/Working Capital	15.4	7.7	9.2	8.7	7.0	9.1		8.9	9.1
	NM	26.7	19.3	21.2	15.1	20.3		17.5	21.4
	-22.2	-168.8	-100.6	83.8	48.8	33.4		70.8	86.8
EBIT/Interest	25.8	24.6	22.7	15.8	31.2	15.7		25.3	24.3
	(19) 4.3	(74) 8.7	(171) 7.1	(131) 7.3	(27) 15.0	(19) 4.0		(319) 8.2	(379) 8.3
	2.0	3.0	2.5	2.7	6.3	2.1		2.9	2.8
Net Profit + Depr., Dep., Amort./Cur. Mat. L/T/D		4.1	6.5	9.0				11.1	10.9
		(12) 2.2	(28) 2.2	(27) 2.8				(68) 3.8	(87) 4.0
		1.3	.6	1.2				1.7	1.4
Fixed/Worth	.0	.2	.3	.3	.4	.3		.3	.2
	1.2	.9	.8	.7	.7	1.0		.7	.6
	NM	2.6	2.4	1.8	1.7	3.8		1.7	1.7
Debt/Worth	.6	.6	.7	.7	.7	.7		.7	.7
	3.8	1.4	1.7	1.7	1.5	2.0		1.7	1.7
	-19.1	9.0	6.6	4.4	3.1	7.7		4.9	4.4
% Profit Before Taxes/Tangible Net Worth	134.5	86.2	53.6	49.7	55.2	41.4		80.1	78.8
	(19) 79.6	(74) 34.5	(163) 25.1	(132) 23.1	(24) 31.6	(16) 20.0		(317) 47.8	(377) 43.8
	27.5	12.0	9.4	10.6	19.6	10.5		22.0	21.6
% Profit Before Taxes/Total Assets	66.0	28.1	20.9	15.0	16.2	8.5		33.5	31.2
	20.8	14.9	9.4	8.8	11.9	6.0		15.6	15.4
	3.1	3.8	2.8	3.5	4.4	2.9		5.0	5.4
Sales/Net Fixed Assets	224.0	71.8	31.9	30.6	24.3	21.8		44.6	41.1
	39.1	18.6	13.8	11.4	11.8	11.9		14.9	16.9
	13.4	6.2	5.2	5.6	7.0	5.0		7.1	7.0
Sales/Total Assets	12.2	7.5	5.0	4.4	3.8	3.7		5.3	5.3
	6.1	4.1	3.3	3.0	3.0	2.7		3.5	3.7
	4.3	2.4	2.1	1.9	2.4	1.8		2.5	2.4
% Depr., Dep., Amort./Sales	.5	.3	.9	.7	1.0	.5		.7	.6
	(14) 1.5	(64) 1.5	(153) 2.0	(135) 1.6	(14) 1.4	1.6		(302) 1.5	(362) 1.6
	3.7	4.0	3.6	2.8	2.0	2.5		3.0	2.9
% Officers', Directors' Owners' Comp/Sales	1.2	.3	1.3	.6	.6			.8	.9
	(17)	(44) 3.4	(83) 1.7	(39) 1.0				(148) 2.6	(169) 2.0
	10.5	5.5	3.4	1.9				5.5	4.8
Net Sales ($)	81301M	604623M	3572477M	10664147M	5759238M	10245645M		18292630M	26482551M
Total Assets ($)	8919M	105586M	967497M	3195434M	1908968M	3054121M		5086591M	7369954M

© RMA 2011

M = $ thousand   MM = $ million
See Pages 9 through 22 for Explanation of Ratios and Data

Comparative Historical Data / Current Data Sorted by Sales

			Type of Statement	0-1MM	1-3MM	3-5MM	5-10MM	10-25MM	25MM & OVER
41	39	42	Unqualified		1		1	4	36
86	81	92	Reviewed		1	1	9	23	57
56	51	67	Compiled	1	9	3	10	24	20
60	75	87	Tax Returns	6	14	11	20	27	9
184	173	207	Other	3	18	15	22	46	103
4/1/08-3/31/09 ALL	4/1/09-3/31/10 ALL	4/1/10-3/31/11 ALL		69 (4/1-9/30/10)			426 (10/1/10-3/31/11)		
427	419	495	**NUMBER OF STATEMENTS**	10	43	31	62	124	225
%	%	%	**ASSETS**	%	%	%	%	%	%
13.2	10.9	9.5	Cash & Equivalents	12.0	11.9	14.7	13.5	11.7	5.9
22.8	24.0	25.3	Trade Receivables (net)	8.7	21.8	11.1	22.5	22.2	31.1
15.8	17.7	21.0	Inventory	18.9	17.8	15.8	18.3	20.0	23.7
3.6	3.8	2.7	All Other Current	4.3	1.4	4.1	1.1	2.7	3.2
55.4	56.3	58.5	Total Current	44.0	52.9	45.7	55.3	56.6	63.8
31.8	33.7	30.5	Fixed Assets (net)	35.7	33.4	39.5	32.6	33.4	26.3
4.0	3.4	3.9	Intangibles (net)	14.9	3.0	7.8	2.9	2.8	4.0
8.8	6.6	7.1	All Other Non-Current	5.4	10.6	7.1	9.2	7.3	6.0
100.0	100.0	100.0	Total	100.0	100.0	100.0	100.0	100.0	100.0
			LIABILITIES						
12.3	11.3	11.3	Notes Payable-Short Term	17.0	7.5	9.9	12.8	8.6	13.0
3.8	4.2	4.1	Cur. Mat.-L.T.D.	2.4	3.9	5.9	4.7	4.3	3.8
15.6	14.8	16.6	Trade Payables	5.8	12.5	22.5	14.4	16.0	17.9
.3	.3	.2	Income Taxes Payable	.1	.3	.0	.1	.2	.2
7.3	7.5	8.7	All Other Current	4.3	9.5	16.9	4.7	9.4	8.3
39.3	38.1	40.9	Total Current	29.6	33.8	55.2	36.7	38.6	43.2
17.4	16.4	15.9	Long-Term Debt	20.7	27.0	22.0	16.6	15.4	12.8
.3	.4	.4	Deferred Taxes	.0	.1	.4	.3	.5	.4
5.3	6.2	6.9	All Other Non-Current	11.0	12.7	7.9	9.2	5.7	5.5
37.6	38.9	35.9	Net Worth	38.6	26.4	14.6	37.1	39.8	38.2
100.0	100.0	100.0	Total Liabilities & Net Worth	100.0	100.0	100.0	100.0	100.0	100.0
			INCOME DATA						
100.0	100.0	100.0	Net Sales	100.0	100.0	100.0	100.0	100.0	100.0
20.7	24.7	24.1	Gross Profit	47.8	45.3	38.3	31.0	24.5	14.9
16.6	22.7	19.5	Operating Expenses	45.9	36.1	33.2	26.7	19.7	11.2
4.1	2.1	4.6	Operating Profit	2.0	9.2	5.2	4.3	4.8	3.7
.4	.6	.3	All Other Expenses (net)	-1.6	.3	.3	.4	.5	.2
3.7	1.5	4.3	Profit Before Taxes	3.5	8.9	4.9	3.8	4.3	3.4
			RATIOS						
2.6	3.0	2.7	Current	12.4	3.6	4.8	3.0	3.2	2.2
1.5	1.6	1.5		1.0	1.7	1.1	1.7	1.6	1.5
.9	1.0	1.0		.7	.8	.6	.7	.9	1.1
1.8	2.0	1.6	Quick	.9	2.2	1.8	1.9	1.7	1.4
.9	(418) .9	.9		.6	.9	.7	.9	.9	.9
.3	.5	.5		.3	.4	.4	.5	.4	.5
6 62.0	16 23.1	11 34.5	Sales/Receivables	0 UND	8 46.3	0 UND	6 61.8	9 40.5	19 19.0
16 23.4	32 11.3	27 13.5		8 45.5	26 14.0	16 23.1	26 13.9	23 15.8	30 12.0
28 13.2	48 7.6	40 9.0		35 10.5	45 8.0	31 11.7	38 9.5	38 9.6	41 8.8
3 114.6	8 -43.5	7 54.9	Cost of Sales/Inventory	0 UND	0 UND	2 172.4	3 145.2	6 60.4	11 32.9
10 35.6	26 14.1	21 17.8		0 UND	13 27.1	11 33.8	16 22.6	20 17.8	25 14.5
22 16.4	53 6.9	42 8.6		355 1.0	64 5.7	69 5.3	44 8.3	42 8.7	40 9.1
4 90.2	10 36.8	7 53.0	Cost of Sales/Payables	0 UND	1 307.0	0 999.8	3 134.3	5 75.0	10 37.4
11 33.3	22 16.9	18 20.7		24 15.0	16 23.3	26 14.2	14 26.2	16 22.5	18 20.1
24 15.1	41 9.0	32 11.4		61 6.0	43 8.4	55 6.6	37 10.0	33 11.1	29 12.4
12.1	6.7	8.8	Sales/Working Capital	4.8	7.0	6.0	7.1	9.6	9.6
33.0	14.4	21.8		NM	16.2	247.3	18.7	19.7	21.8
-131.0	999.8	999.8		-10.8	-51.9	-12.9	-57.0	-114.3	68.0
19.8	11.9	21.1	EBIT/Interest		14.7	11.2	18.5	27.3	23.7
(393) 6.0	(376) 3.4	(441) 7.3			(31) 7.6	(25) 4.5	(56) 4.3	(110) 8.7	(213) 8.2
1.8	-.3	2.7			1.6	1.0	1.3	2.9	3.1
12.0	2.9	8.9	Net Profit + Depr., Dep., Amort./Cur. Mat. L/T/D					3.7	12.8
(87) 4.2	(62) 1.2	(84) 2.7						(23) 2.1	(44) 3.7
1.7	-.1	1.0						1.1	1.3
.3	.3	.3	Fixed/Worth	.1	.1	.6	.2	.2	.3
.9	.8	.8		1.4	1.0	2.0	1.0	.8	.7
2.6	2.5	2.1		2.6	93.5	-116.7	2.6	2.2	1.7
.7	.5	.7	Debt/Worth	.6	.4	.7	.6	.4	.8
1.8	1.6	1.6		3.4	1.3	3.3	1.9	1.4	1.8
4.9	4.7	6.0		10.9	152.0	-150.2	4.3	5.6	4.7
71.6	32.5	56.3	% Profit Before Taxes/Tangible Net Worth		73.3	68.7	71.9	53.0	56.4
(372) 36.8	(367) 12.1	(428) 28.3			(33) 32.0	(22) 23.5	(53) 20.9	(107) 29.4	(204) 28.3
9.9	-3.8	10.9			9.9	-4.2	4.0	9.4	13.9
27.0	12.3	20.2	% Profit Before Taxes/Total Assets	16.6	27.4	23.7	22.7	22.4	16.5
12.7	4.2	10.0		3.6	15.8	5.5	7.2	11.3	9.6
1.9	-2.8	3.3		.3	3.9	-1.6	1.1	3.4	4.0
46.1	24.6	37.9	Sales/Net Fixed Assets	UND	56.6	20.1	42.5	33.5	38.5
17.9	9.0	13.5		3.5	11.6	6.0	16.8	12.4	15.7
7.9	3.8	5.8		2.3	4.6	3.8	6.8	5.4	7.3
6.8	3.6	5.1	Sales/Total Assets	2.8	4.6	3.7	5.6	5.6	5.1
4.5	2.4	3.3		1.2	2.7	2.4	3.5	3.3	3.6
2.6	1.6	2.2		.7	1.6	1.6	2.1	2.1	2.5
.8	1.1	.8	% Depr., Dep., Amort./Sales		.5	2.0	.7	1.0	.6
(357) 1.5	(357) 2.8	(408) 1.7			(31) 2.6	(24) 3.4	(46) 1.9	(103) 2.3	(198) 1.3
3.0	5.1	3.3			5.4	7.4	3.7	3.5	2.4
1.0	1.2	.7	% Officers', Directors' Owners' Comp/Sales		3.3	2.1	1.5	.7	.4
(162) 2.3	(163) 2.7	(185) 1.8			(17) 4.1	(12) 4.1	(40) 3.2	(56) 1.3	(55) .8
4.1	4.6	3.6			11.3	7.0	3.8	2.8	1.4
33145394M	15348257M	30927431M	Net Sales ($)	6380M	85151M	122673M	470111M	1984249M	28258867M
7846744M	6942041M	9240525M	Total Assets ($)	6405M	38371M	57494M	178794M	712603M	8246858M

M = $ thousand   MM = $ million
See Pages 9 through 22 for Explanation of Ratios and Data

Current Data Sorted by Assets   Comparative Historical Data

Date ranges: **36 (4/1-9/30/10)**   **157 (10/1/10-3/31/11)**   Historical: **4/1/06-3/31/07 ALL**   **4/1/07-3/31/08 ALL**

Type of Statement

Type of Statement	0-500M	500M-2MM	2-10MM	10-50MM	50-100MM	100-250MM	4/1/06-3/31/07 ALL	4/1/07-3/31/08 ALL
Unqualified				6	3	3	23	24
Reviewed		3	30	10	1		64	62
Compiled	3	7	17	3			37	33
Tax Returns	4	24	21	2			36	31
Other	2	14	22	13	2	3	64	45
NUMBER OF STATEMENTS	9	48	90	34	6	6	224	195

Common-Size and Ratio Data

	0-500M %	500M-2MM %	2-10MM %	10-50MM %	50-100MM %	100-250MM %		ALL %	ALL %
ASSETS									
Cash & Equivalents		16.3	8.6	6.7				7.5	7.1
Trade Receivables (net)		20.9	28.5	34.2				27.3	28.6
Inventory		45.0	51.1	43.1				50.3	49.7
All Other Current		1.3	2.4	2.5				2.0	2.7
Total Current		83.5	90.6	86.6				87.1	88.1
Fixed Assets (net)		8.7	4.1	7.5				6.7	6.2
Intangibles (net)		1.3	1.3	1.5				2.0	1.8
All Other Non-Current		6.5	4.0	4.5				4.1	3.8
Total		100.0	100.0	100.0				100.0	100.0
LIABILITIES									
Notes Payable-Short Term		13.2	13.1	20.7				19.3	20.2
Cur. Mat.-L.T.D.		1.1	1.0	3.3				2.3	1.9
Trade Payables		21.7	30.5	26.8				21.7	22.6
Income Taxes Payable		.0	.3	.2				.3	.2
All Other Current		8.7	7.6	7.4				10.3	9.1
Total Current		44.7	52.5	58.5				53.8	54.0
Long-Term Debt		7.3	4.2	4.1				6.0	7.1
Deferred Taxes		.0	.0	.3				.1	.1
All Other Non-Current		9.8	5.6	3.2				4.9	4.9
Net Worth		38.2	37.7	33.9				35.2	33.8
Total Liabilities & Net Worth		100.0	100.0	100.0				100.0	100.0
INCOME DATA									
Net Sales		100.0	100.0	100.0				100.0	100.0
Gross Profit		34.2	22.7	24.9				28.9	25.0
Operating Expenses		31.9	19.4	20.5				25.1	20.8
Operating Profit		2.3	3.2	4.4				3.8	4.3
All Other Expenses (net)		.7	.5	.6				1.1	1.2
Profit Before Taxes		1.6	2.7	3.8				2.7	3.1
RATIOS									
Current		4.0	2.9	2.0				2.4	2.4
		2.6	1.7	1.5				1.5	1.6
		1.2	1.3	1.2				1.2	1.2
Quick		2.0	1.4	1.0				1.1	1.0
		.8	.7	.7				(223) .6	(193) .6
		.4	.4	.4				.3	.4
Sales/Receivables		2 175.8	17 21.3	10 35.8				15 24.1	20 18.3
		19 19.7	35 10.5	59 6.2				48 7.6	49 7.4
		52 7.0	75 4.9	84 4.4				83 4.4	84 4.3
Cost of Sales/Inventory		22 16.9	44 8.2	47 7.8				60 6.1	56 6.6
		89 4.1	106 3.4	87 4.2				129 2.8	114 3.2
		174 2.1	202 1.8	154 2.4				278 1.3	196 1.9
Cost of Sales/Payables		6 61.2	14 25.5	25 14.5				12 29.6	14 26.4
		27 13.7	38 9.5	57 6.4				47 7.8	43 8.5
		61 6.0	109 3.4	78 4.7				99 3.7	91 4.0
Sales/Working Capital		3.4	3.6	4.2				3.3	3.8
		6.1	7.0	6.9				6.2	7.0
		47.6	23.4	39.9				12.7	15.3
EBIT/Interest		28.9	23.5	15.2				6.3	6.1
		(32) 5.1	(75) 6.0	(33) 7.1				(194) 2.2	(178) 2.3
		.9	2.1	2.2				1.3	1.2
Net Profit + Depr., Dep., Amort./Cur. Mat. L/T/D								9.8	5.0
								(25) 2.2	(20) 2.2
								.5	.4
Fixed/Worth		.0	.0	.0				.0	.0
		.1	.1	.1				.1	.1
		.4	.2	.3				.4	.4
Debt/Worth		.4	.8	1.2				.9	1.0
		1.3	1.8	2.0				2.2	2.2
		8.3	5.7	3.4				4.3	4.5
% Profit Before Taxes/Tangible Net Worth		54.4	62.0	43.7				31.9	27.9
		(41) 15.9	(84) 17.2	(33) 24.6				(205) 10.3	(176) 14.0
		.3	5.4	7.4				2.6	3.6
% Profit Before Taxes/Total Assets		18.7	14.1	15.5				10.1	10.3
		6.2	5.0	5.9				3.3	3.5
		-1.4	1.2	1.4				.7	.8
Sales/Net Fixed Assets		999.8	999.8	367.5				382.5	539.5
		106.5	325.0	83.5				65.4	113.5
		35.2	45.1	31.8				22.2	28.5
Sales/Total Assets		4.6	3.8	2.8				2.8	3.1
		3.0	2.4	1.9				1.8	2.0
		1.8	1.3	1.5				1.2	1.3
% Depr., Dep., Amort./Sales		.2	.1	.2				.1	.1
		(25) .6	(52) .3	(30) .4				(180) .4	(146) .2
		1.1	.8	.7				.9	.7
% Officers', Directors', Owners' Comp/Sales		2.3	1.3	.7				1.1	.8
		(28) 5.0	(55) 2.5	(18) 1.5				(121) 2.8	(114) 2.1
		7.4	3.8	5.8				5.5	4.6
Net Sales ($)	29115M	346240M	2231735M	4536091M	645816M	12651341M		10549097M	11996294M
Total Assets ($)	2744M	54434M	418686M	662276M	424432M	1001423M		3569170M	4168621M

M = $ thousand   MM = $ million
See Pages 9 through 22 for Explanation of Ratios and Data

Comparative Historical Data   ## Current Data Sorted by Sales

4/1/08-3/31/09 ALL	4/1/09-3/31/10 ALL	4/1/10-3/31/11 ALL	Type of Statement	0-1MM	1-3MM	3-5MM	5-10MM	10-25MM	25MM & OVER
22	16	12	Unqualified		1	3	10	2	10
68	57	44	Reviewed					20	10
25	30	30	Compiled	2	3	7	7	6	5
32	48	51	Tax Returns	5	8	13	10	9	6
76	62	56	Other	1	12	4	9	13	17
					36 (4/1-9/30/10)		157 (10/1/10-3/31/11)		
223	213	193	**NUMBER OF STATEMENTS**	8	24	27	36	50	48
%	%	%	**ASSETS**	%	%	%	%	%	%
5.8	9.7	11.1	Cash & Equivalents		8.7	11.9	11.8	9.2	12.4
25.3	28.4	26.2	Trade Receivables (net)		25.8	21.1	28.0	35.9	21.1
53.8	47.5	47.6	Inventory		52.4	52.5	47.6	44.0	46.9
2.7	1.6	2.0	All Other Current		2.3	1.3	1.2	1.3	4.1
87.7	87.2	87.0	Total Current		89.1	86.7	88.6	90.5	84.5
6.1	5.5	5.9	Fixed Assets (net)		4.6	3.2	4.9	5.2	6.2
1.4	1.5	2.1	Intangibles (net)		1.7	1.4	1.3	1.8	4.1
4.8	5.8	5.0	All Other Non-Current		4.6	8.7	5.3	2.5	5.2
100.0	100.0	100.0	Total		100.0	100.0	100.0	100.0	100.0
			LIABILITIES						
20.1	17.2	14.0	Notes Payable-Short Term		11.2	16.9	10.6	17.6	12.6
1.9	1.5	1.4	Cur. Mat.-L.T.D.		.6	.1	2.2	1.1	2.2
22.1	25.7	26.1	Trade Payables		25.7	29.0	29.7	28.0	23.1
.1	.2	.2	Income Taxes Payable		.0	.0	.2	.3	.4
11.3	8.4	8.6	All Other Current		6.6	4.1	10.7	9.0	8.8
55.4	52.9	50.3	Total Current		44.2	50.2	53.4	56.0	47.2
6.5	5.7	5.2	Long-Term Debt		5.8	4.6	6.9	2.4	2.9
.1	.1	.2	Deferred Taxes		.0	.0	.0	.1	.8
5.4	7.7	6.3	All Other Non-Current		8.1	5.4	7.2	3.8	6.6
32.6	33.7	37.9	Net Worth		41.9	39.9	32.5	37.8	42.5
100.0	100.0	100.0	Total Liabilities & Net Worth		100.0	100.0	100.0	100.0	100.0
			INCOME DATA						
100.0	100.0	100.0	Net Sales		100.0	100.0	100.0	100.0	100.0
26.4	25.3	27.2	Gross Profit		42.1	26.6	31.7	19.5	23.1
24.0	22.3	23.8	Operating Expenses		37.3	23.9	29.5	16.1	19.0
2.4	3.0	3.4	Operating Profit		4.8	2.7	2.2	3.5	4.2
1.2	.9	.6	All Other Expenses (net)		.7	.0	.7	.3	.4
1.2	2.1	2.8	Profit Before Taxes		4.1	2.8	1.6	3.2	3.7
			RATIOS						
2.2	2.5	3.0	Current		3.5	4.4	2.5	2.6	3.1
1.5	1.6	1.8			2.7	1.9	1.7	1.6	1.8
1.3	1.3	1.2			1.5	1.1	1.3	1.2	1.3
.9	1.1	1.4	Quick		1.9	2.0	1.3	1.3	1.2
.5	.7	.7			.8	.7	.7	.8	.7
.3	.4	.4			.5	.2	.3	.6	.3
18 20.7	11 34.3	8 45.2	Sales/Receivables	27 13.5	7 56.1	10 37.5	25 14.8	2 211.3	
42 8.7	48 7.7	33 11.1		51 7.2	28 13.3	36 10.2	44 8.4	14 26.7	
68 5.4	77 4.7	64 5.7		85 4.3	44 8.3	78 4.7	80 4.5	43 8.5	
65 5.6	45 8.1	37 9.8	Cost of Sales/Inventory	129 2.8	47 7.8	69 5.3	32 11.2	8 46.5	
133 2.7	108 3.4	92 4.0		182 2.0	108 3.4	109 3.4	74 4.9	52 7.0	
247 1.5	213 1.7	173 2.1		307 1.2	218 1.7	225 1.6	130 2.8	142 2.6	
14 26.4	13 28.6	12 29.4	Cost of Sales/Payables	20 18.2	17 21.6	17 22.0	17 21.9	3 130.7	
43 8.5	45 8.2	38 9.6		71 5.2	38 9.7	59 6.2	38 9.6	25 14.8	
90 4.1	89 4.1	83 4.4		153 2.4	113 3.2	123 3.0	74 4.9	56 6.6	
3.7	3.0	3.9	Sales/Working Capital		2.4	3.5	3.5	4.2	5.0
6.2	6.3	6.9			3.9	6.8	6.1	8.9	13.6
17.3	18.0	29.1			9.6	23.5	13.6	32.3	82.1
5.2	9.2	19.5	EBIT/Interest		78.0	8.3	7.4	18.4	41.4
(201) 2.1	(175) 2.9	(153) 5.5			(19) 7.1	(16) 4.5	(27) 3.0	(47) 7.1	(38) 10.4
1.0	1.3	1.8			1.1	1.0	1.0	2.7	2.4
20.5	52.7	17.3	Net Profit + Depr., Dep.,						
(18) 1.6	(14) 6.4	(15) 8.3	Amort./Cur. Mat. L/T/D						
.1	.1	.8							
.0	.0	.0	Fixed/Worth		.0	.0	.0	.0	.0
.1	.1	.1			.0	.0	.1	.1	.1
.3	.2	.2			.3	.1	.1	.2	.3
1.1	.9	.7	Debt/Worth		.5	.6	.8	.8	.7
2.3	2.1	1.7			1.0	1.7	2.0	2.0	1.5
4.4	5.4	5.5			5.9	5.2	8.5	8.8	2.7
26.8	36.0	48.9	% Profit Before Taxes/Tangible		39.5	53.4	35.5	79.0	68.7
(204) 6.6	(196) 11.5	(176) 17.6	Net Worth		(21) 5.4	(25) 22.9	(33) 11.9	(48) 21.3	(44) 25.6
.4	2.3	4.0			.5	5.7	2.0	8.2	4.6
7.9	11.5	15.9	% Profit Before Taxes/Total		15.9	14.8	9.3	11.9	29.8
2.1	2.9	5.2	Assets		3.8	5.2	2.7	4.5	12.8
.1	.6	1.0			.0	.3	.5	1.9	1.5
462.4	721.5	999.8	Sales/Net Fixed Assets		309.2	UND	999.8	999.8	999.8
120.4	126.9	134.1			101.8	140.2	256.2	162.2	189.0
30.3	36.4	38.8			32.1	53.7	37.3	38.6	37.5
3.0	3.2	4.0	Sales/Total Assets		2.1	4.0	3.2	3.9	20.9
1.9	2.0	2.4			1.8	2.6	2.2	2.7	3.2
1.2	1.2	1.5			.9	1.3	1.2	1.6	1.7
.1	.1	.1	% Depr., Dep., Amort./Sales		.4	.2	.1	.1	.0
(174) .3	(159) .2	(118) .4			(10) .7	(12) .6	(23) .2	(33) .4	(34) .3
.7	.7	.9			1.0	1.5	.8	.6	.7
1.1	1.4	1.3	% Officers', Directors'		3.2	2.3	2.6	1.3	.4
(127) 2.4	(127) 2.8	(109) 2.8	Owners' Comp/Sales		(12) 5.8	(16) 3.0	(24) 3.6	(32) 1.8	(20) .9
5.1	5.1	5.7			8.2	5.7	7.3	3.0	3.5
16616821M	21525980M	20440338M	Net Sales ($)	4316M	49109M	105514M	253437M	796554M	19231408M
4933873M	3793394M	2563995M	Total Assets ($)	4374M	36489M	52710M	141958M	332310M	1996154M

© RMA 2011

M = $ thousand   MM = $ million

See Pages 9 through 22 for Explanation of Ratios and Data

Current Data Sorted by Assets   Comparative Historical Data

0-500M	500M-2MM	2-10MM	10-50MM	50-100MM	100-250MM	Type of Statement	4/1/06-3/31/07 ALL	4/1/07-3/31/08 ALL
1	1	8	31	6	5	Unqualified	49	50
1	16	70	23			Reviewed	107	109
11	39	42	6			Compiled	114	90
57	102	58	5			Tax Returns	129	143
19	84	106	47	15	4	Other	187	209
115 (4/1-9/30/10)			642 (10/1/10-3/31/11)					
89	242	284	112	21	9	NUMBER OF STATEMENTS	586	601
%	%	%	%	%	%	**ASSETS**	%	%
24.0	12.5	10.6	6.7	7.0		Cash & Equivalents	8.3	8.6
23.5	31.0	29.8	29.7	29.0		Trade Receivables (net)	32.9	30.4
28.2	33.9	37.2	35.7	30.7		Inventory	35.8	37.1
1.2	2.4	2.3	3.8	4.7		All Other Current	2.7	2.5
76.9	79.7	79.9	75.9	71.4		Total Current	79.6	78.6
12.8	10.7	10.8	12.7	9.3		Fixed Assets (net)	12.2	11.2
2.5	4.1	4.2	5.6	15.7		Intangibles (net)	2.7	4.3
7.8	5.4	5.1	5.8	3.7		All Other Non-Current	5.4	5.9
100.0	100.0	100.0	100.0	100.0		Total	100.0	100.0
						LIABILITIES		
15.5	15.5	13.8	16.6	17.4		Notes Payable-Short Term	17.4	17.2
1.4	2.5	1.7	1.3	2.1		Cur. Mat.-L.T.D.	2.9	3.1
27.9	22.1	20.4	18.6	23.0		Trade Payables	22.4	22.6
.0	.2	.2	.2	.6		Income Taxes Payable	.2	.1
12.6	6.3	9.1	7.7	8.5		All Other Current	9.9	10.4
57.4	46.7	45.1	44.3	51.6		Total Current	52.9	53.4
17.6	10.7	9.4	6.9	12.4		Long-Term Debt	11.1	10.0
.0	.0	.2	.2	.1		Deferred Taxes	.2	.1
14.0	8.3	5.2	5.2	4.9		All Other Non-Current	6.0	6.9
11.0	34.3	40.1	43.5	31.0		Net Worth	29.8	29.6
100.0	100.0	100.0	100.0	100.0		Total Liabilities & Net Worth	100.0	100.0
						INCOME DATA		
100.0	100.0	100.0	100.0	100.0		Net Sales	100.0	100.0
39.1	34.2	32.1	26.5	29.6		Gross Profit	31.2	33.0
35.3	30.5	27.5	21.4	22.8		Operating Expenses	26.4	28.3
3.9	3.7	4.6	5.1	6.7		Operating Profit	4.8	4.7
.2	.6	.4	.8	1.1		All Other Expenses (net)	.8	.9
3.6	3.0	4.1	4.3	5.6		Profit Before Taxes	4.0	3.7
						RATIOS		
3.6	3.4	3.0	2.8	2.0			2.6	2.4
2.0	1.8	1.7	1.7	1.3		Current	1.5	1.5
1.1	1.3	1.3	1.2	1.0			1.1	1.1
2.5	2.0	1.5	1.3	1.1			1.4	1.3
1.1	1.0	.8	.8	.7		Quick (585)	.8	.8
.4	.5	.5	.5	.4			.5	.5
0 UND	18 20.0	27 13.4	28 12.9	29 12.5			24 15.4	24 15.5
17 21.9	35 10.4	41 8.9	45 8.1	37 9.8		Sales/Receivables	37 9.8	37 10.0
37 9.9	49 7.4	56 6.5	67 5.4	59 6.2			53 6.8	52 7.0
0 UND	24 15.4	36 10.2	45 8.1	19 19.7			25 14.5	30 12.1
27 13.5	51 7.1	73 5.0	76 4.8	71 5.1		Cost of Sales/Inventory	58 6.3	67 5.4
84 4.4	102 3.6	137 2.7	133 2.8	142 2.6			115 3.2	117 3.1
2 155.4	13 27.2	19 19.3	15 24.6	23 15.8			15 24.0	16 22.6
23 15.9	29 12.6	33 11.0	32 11.3	34 10.8		Cost of Sales/Payables	31 11.8	33 11.1
51 7.2	55 6.7	62 5.9	51 7.2	61 6.0			54 6.8	56 6.6
6.7	5.1	4.1	4.1	5.9			5.7	5.6
11.9	9.2	8.4	7.1	15.4		Sales/Working Capital	10.5	11.4
189.2	27.0	21.4	21.4	NM			46.2	49.2
17.0	17.0	17.1	24.0	16.5			11.3	11.1
(64) 5.0	(199) 4.6	(252) 4.9	(103) 6.6	(19) 4.8		EBIT/Interest (525)	3.8	(533) 3.8
1.0	1.6	1.7	2.0	1.3			1.5	1.5
	13.8	10.7	23.2	23.3			7.4	8.2
	(10) 4.3	(40) 3.3	(26) 7.4	(11) 4.4		Net Profit + Depr., Dep., Amort./Cur. Mat. L/T/D (84)	2.2	(75) 2.7
	1.0	1.2	2.9	1.1			.9	.6
.0	.0	.0	.1	.1			.1	.1
.2	.2	.1	.2	.4		Fixed/Worth	.2	.2
-.8	.8	.6	.7	NM			1.1	1.3
.4	.7	.8	.6	1.4			1.0	1.1
2.0	1.8	1.7	1.6	3.8		Debt/Worth	2.4	2.5
-5.4	7.6	4.6	4.6	NM			8.2	9.5
89.7	60.4	44.8	48.5	44.9			64.8	62.8
(59) 47.1	(202) 23.6	(252) 21.0	(103) 21.2	(16) 32.5		% Profit Before Taxes/Tangible Net Worth (505)	31.4	(502) 28.7
6.7	7.2	6.3	7.5	14.4			8.1	9.2
39.9	20.3	15.6	14.1	16.8			18.2	18.1
12.9	7.1	6.7	8.8	5.9		% Profit Before Taxes/Total Assets	8.0	6.9
.4	1.0	1.4	2.1	.7			1.5	1.6
583.6	432.2	204.3	91.0	83.0			153.4	159.2
126.9	66.9	61.5	35.3	40.4		Sales/Net Fixed Assets	52.8	50.0
21.5	23.7	18.8	10.9	17.1			19.6	20.7
7.3	4.5	3.5	3.2	3.3			4.1	3.9
4.2	3.2	2.4	2.2	2.1		Sales/Total Assets	3.0	2.9
2.2	2.3	1.7	1.5	1.3			2.1	2.1
.2	.2	.2	.3	.3			.3	.2
(49) .5	(140) .7	(217) .5	(94) .7	(16) 1.1		% Depr., Dep., Amort./Sales (443)	.6	(452) .6
1.7	1.4	1.1	1.2	1.8			1.3	1.4
2.0	2.0	1.4	.5				1.6	2.0
(52) 4.6	(131) 3.6	(143) 3.1	(28) 1.2			% Officers', Directors' Owners' Comp/Sales (264)	3.4	(282) 3.7
9.3	6.0	5.5	2.9				6.3	7.0
149637M	1041044M	3721317M	5936030M	3763341M	2477397M	Net Sales ($)	12822273M	14313178M
25333M	281936M	1326118M	2364310M	1428613M	1436109M	Total Assets ($)	4682018M	5106697M

Comparative Historical Data | Current Data Sorted by Sales

Type of Statement									
	54	63	52	Unqualified	1	1	1	1	13	36
	118	102	110	Reviewed	1	5	13	21	46	24
	114	97	98	Compiled	10	17	17	20	27	7
	188	212	222	Tax Returns	35	61	50	42	26	8
	257	251	275	Other	14	48	40	57	53	63
	4/1/08-3/31/09 ALL	4/1/09-3/31/10 ALL	4/1/10-3/31/11 ALL		115 (4/1-9/30/10)		642 (10/1/10-3/31/11)			
					0-1MM	1-3MM	3-5MM	5-10MM	10-25MM	25MM & OVER
NUMBER OF STATEMENTS	731	725	757		60	132	121	141	165	138
	%	%	%	**ASSETS**	%	%	%	%	%	%
	9.3	11.1	12.1	Cash & Equivalents	19.3	14.0	11.4	12.4	11.2	8.4
	28.8	30.9	29.4	Trade Receivables (net)	18.4	25.6	30.0	31.6	30.6	33.5
	38.1	34.7	34.7	Inventory	33.9	33.0	37.6	33.3	36.4	33.4
	2.7	2.9	2.5	All Other Current	1.9	2.0	1.4	2.2	3.1	3.5
	78.9	79.6	78.6	Total Current	73.6	74.7	80.4	79.5	81.4	78.8
	12.1	10.9	11.2	Fixed Assets (net)	14.9	12.8	10.8	9.5	11.0	10.1
	3.8	4.1	4.6	Intangibles (net)	4.9	6.1	3.3	3.7	3.8	5.9
	5.2	5.4	5.6	All Other Non-Current	6.6	6.4	5.5	7.2	3.8	5.2
	100.0	100.0	100.0	Total	100.0	100.0	100.0	100.0	100.0	100.0
				LIABILITIES						
	18.3	16.4	15.0	Notes Payable-Short Term	18.3	13.1	16.0	14.8	12.9	17.3
	2.9	2.5	1.9	Cur. Mat.-L.T.D.	2.0	2.1	2.0	2.1	1.7	1.4
	21.0	22.0	21.6	Trade Payables	14.5	20.9	21.8	22.2	23.4	22.3
	.1	.1	.2	Income Taxes Payable	.1	.2	.2	.1	.2	.3
	9.7	9.9	8.3	All Other Current	14.7	5.0	7.0	8.2	9.5	8.6
	52.0	51.0	47.0	Total Current	49.6	41.3	47.1	47.4	47.8	49.9
	10.5	10.3	10.6	Long-Term Debt	25.0	13.6	11.1	7.3	8.1	7.1
	.1	.1	.1	Deferred Taxes	.0	.0	.2	.2	.2	.2
	5.9	6.6	7.3	All Other Non-Current	22.7	10.4	4.3	5.6	4.5	5.0
	31.4	32.0	35.0	Net Worth	2.6	34.6	37.3	39.5	39.4	37.8
	100.0	100.0	100.0	Total Liabilities & Net Worth	100.0	100.0	100.0	100.0	100.0	100.0
				INCOME DATA						
	100.0	100.0	100.0	Net Sales	100.0	100.0	100.0	100.0	100.0	100.0
	31.9	32.0	32.7	Gross Profit	46.3	39.8	33.7	30.4	30.1	24.6
	27.8	28.5	28.3	Operating Expenses	42.7	35.7	29.8	26.2	25.1	19.7
	4.1	3.5	4.4	Operating Profit	3.6	4.0	3.9	4.1	5.1	4.9
	.8	.7	.6	All Other Expenses (net)	1.1	.6	.7	.2	.5	.6
	3.3	2.8	3.8	Profit Before Taxes	2.5	3.5	3.2	3.9	4.5	4.3
				RATIOS						
	2.5	2.8	3.1	Current	5.1	3.8	3.9	3.0	3.1	2.4
	1.6	1.7	1.7		1.9	2.1	1.8	1.7	1.8	1.6
	1.1	1.1	1.2		1.2	1.2	1.2	1.2	1.3	1.2
	1.3	1.4	1.6	Quick	2.4	2.2	1.9	1.6	1.6	1.3
	.7	.8	.9		.9	1.0	.9	.9	.9	.8
	.4	.5	.5		.5	.5	.5	.5	.5	.5
	20 18.7	23 15.8	22 16.9	Sales/Receivables	0 UND	15 24.5	20 18.4	27 13.4	24 15.2	27 13.7
	34 10.9	37 9.9	37 9.7		23 16.0	33 11.0	35 10.4	39 9.4	38 9.6	42 8.8
	48 7.6	54 6.8	54 6.7		51 7.2	50 7.3	56 6.5	53 6.8	55 6.7	56 6.5
	29 12.4	26 14.0	27 13.7	Cost of Sales/Inventory	0 UND	26 13.8	28 13.2	24 15.5	34 10.6	26 14.1
	66 5.5	64 5.7	62 5.9		92 4.0	60 6.0	68 5.4	53 6.9	66 5.5	57 6.3
	129 2.8	119 3.1	123 3.0		299 1.2	109 3.4	131 2.8	122 3.0	119 3.1	101 3.6
	13 28.1	15 25.0	15 24.7	Cost of Sales/Payables	4 103.0	19 19.5	10 36.3	13 27.1	18 20.3	17 21.7
	28 13.2	31 11.8	31 11.9		22 16.8	38 9.5	32 11.6	28 12.9	28 13.0	31 11.8
	52 7.0	54 6.8	55 6.6		82 4.5	63 5.8	69 5.3	53 6.9	51 7.2	48 7.7
	5.2	5.1	4.8	Sales/Working Capital	2.5	4.4	4.7	5.2	4.2	5.5
	10.2	9.9	8.8		5.6	7.6	9.2	10.0	8.5	10.4
	46.1	34.9	26.6		55.6	25.4	32.4	27.4	14.7	31.8
	9.9	12.8	17.3	EBIT/Interest	10.7	16.2	14.5	15.3	23.7	27.0
	(651) 3.5	(638) 4.3	(646) 4.9		(43) 1.4	(106) 3.9	(100) 4.0	(124) 4.6	(147) 7.0	(126) 6.7
	1.2	1.2	1.7		-.9	1.2	1.5	1.7	2.7	2.3
	6.6	6.5	15.1	Net Profit + Depr., Dep., Amort./Cur. Mat. L/T/D			8.3	6.4	19.3	22.6
	(102) 2.9	(98) 2.9	(92) 4.8				(10) 2.1	(12) 3.0	(30) 6.0	(36) 5.6
	.9	.7	1.5				.6	.8	2.6	2.2
	.1	.0	.0	Fixed/Worth	.0	.0	.0	.0	.0	.1
	.2	.2	.2		.3	.2	.2	.1	.2	.2
	1.1	1.1	.8		-1.4	2.6	1.1	.5	.6	.7
	.9	.8	.7	Debt/Worth	.7	.7	.5	.8	.7	.8
	2.4	2.1	1.8		3.8	1.7	1.8	1.6	1.7	1.9
	9.7	8.9	7.1		-5.7	294.2	7.2	5.4	3.7	6.1
	53.6	54.2	54.8	% Profit Before Taxes/Tangible Net Worth	69.3	64.5	44.9	58.2	47.5	60.2
	(612) 23.0	(609) 19.3	(640) 23.8		(39) 23.8	(100) 29.5	(102) 22.6	(125) 21.7	(153) 21.2	(121) 29.0
	4.0	2.9	7.1		-.9	4.2	7.2	6.6	7.2	11.5
	16.3	15.5	18.4	% Profit Before Taxes/Total Assets	24.7	23.9	17.2	18.4	17.4	16.9
	5.3	5.5	7.6		2.8	7.0	6.0	6.7	9.0	8.9
	.6	.4	1.4		-5.1	.5	1.0	1.5	1.8	3.5
	200.6	233.1	251.7	Sales/Net Fixed Assets	386.4	324.3	376.6	307.1	195.1	143.4
	53.9	61.4	58.6		36.4	52.5	71.9	67.1	61.8	49.1
	18.0	18.5	19.2		10.1	16.5	18.3	24.5	17.7	19.9
	4.1	4.0	4.0	Sales/Total Assets	3.4	3.9	4.0	4.3	3.9	3.8
	2.9	2.7	2.7		2.0	2.7	2.8	2.9	2.7	2.8
	1.9	1.9	1.8		.9	1.7	1.8	2.0	1.9	2.0
	.3	.2	.2	% Depr., Dep., Amort./Sales	.3	.3	.2	.2	.2	.2
	(542) .7	(522) .6	(525) .6		(29) 1.6	(77) .8	(79) .7	(94) .5	(133) .6	(113) .6
	1.4	1.3	1.3		5.3	1.7	1.6	1.3	1.0	1.0
	1.9	2.0	1.6	% Officers', Directors' Owners' Comp/Sales	3.6	2.3	2.5	1.6	1.1	.5
	(309) 3.4	(329) 3.3	(358) 3.3		(28) 8.2	(71) 4.0	(71) 4.1	(76) 3.2	(78) 2.0	(34) 1.1
	6.6	6.7	5.8		12.7	6.3	7.3	5.3	3.7	2.3
	15047492M	16563935M	17088766M	Net Sales ($)	35845M	258772M	479125M	1011050M	2587643M	12716331M
	6243671M	6687697M	6862419M	Total Assets ($)	32494M	121896M	204724M	423657M	1176101M	4903547M

M = $ thousand   MM = $ million
See Pages 9 through 22 for Explanation of Ratios and Data

Current Data Sorted by Assets

Comparative Historical Data

	0-500M	500M-2MM	2-10MM	10-50MM	50-100MM	100-250MM	Type of Statement	4/1/06-3/31/07 ALL	4/1/07-3/31/08 ALL
		1	4	6	3	4	Unqualified	28	22
		2	15	6	1		Reviewed	21	22
	1	5	6				Compiled	20	9
	4	3	5	2			Tax Returns	11	11
	3	9	10	9	3	4	Other	46	35
		16 (4/1-9/30/10)		90 (10/1/10-3/31/11)					
NUMBER OF STATEMENTS	8	20	40	23	7	8		126	99
	%	%	%	%	%	%	**ASSETS**	%	%
		7.1	6.9	6.1			Cash & Equivalents	4.6	5.5
		37.6	44.3	42.7			Trade Receivables (net)	39.6	40.7
		28.4	29.8	25.7			Inventory	25.7	29.5
		2.5	2.2	1.9			All Other Current	2.5	2.2
		75.6	83.1	76.4			Total Current	72.4	77.9
		11.1	9.2	15.1			Fixed Assets (net)	14.6	11.9
		3.0	2.5	2.2			Intangibles (net)	3.1	4.1
		10.2	5.1	6.3			All Other Non-Current	9.8	6.2
		100.0	100.0	100.0			Total	100.0	100.0
							LIABILITIES		
		16.5	19.4	18.2			Notes Payable-Short Term	19.5	18.3
		2.1	2.0	2.4			Cur. Mat.-L.T.D.	3.2	1.7
		30.3	24.1	24.8			Trade Payables	25.1	25.4
		.0	.1	.0			Income Taxes Payable	.1	.1
		9.5	8.1	6.3			All Other Current	8.3	8.0
		58.3	53.8	51.8			Total Current	56.1	53.5
		7.6	8.8	9.6			Long-Term Debt	14.0	9.4
		.0	.1	.0			Deferred Taxes	.2	.2
		10.4	2.8	6.1			All Other Non-Current	4.7	3.1
		23.6	34.5	32.5			Net Worth	25.0	33.9
		100.0	100.0	100.0			Total Liabilities & Net Worth	100.0	100.0
							INCOME DATA		
		100.0	100.0	100.0			Net Sales	100.0	100.0
		22.7	21.5	16.5			Gross Profit	23.5	22.0
		20.3	19.3	14.9			Operating Expenses	21.2	20.2
		2.4	2.2	1.6			Operating Profit	2.3	1.8
		.2	.3	.2			All Other Expenses (net)	.5	.4
		2.2	2.0	1.4			Profit Before Taxes	1.8	1.4
							RATIOS		
		2.9	2.3	2.1			Current	2.0	1.9
		1.5	1.5	1.3				1.3	1.4
		.8	1.3	1.1				1.0	1.2
		1.3	1.2	1.3			Quick	1.1	1.2
		.8	1.0	.8				.7	.9
		.6	.6	.7				.6	.6
	25 14.4	30 12.3	34 10.7				Sales/Receivables	30 12.1	30 12.1
	37 9.9	40 9.2	38 9.6					39 9.3	40 9.2
	47 7.8	48 7.5	53 6.9					49 7.5	49 7.4
	14 25.8	13 29.1	18 20.5				Cost of Sales/Inventory	13 28.4	17 21.2
	21 17.1	34 10.8	34 10.7					32 11.4	36 10.1
	61 6.0	82 4.5	43 8.6					52 7.1	60 6.1
	12 29.7	15 24.4	16 22.9				Cost of Sales/Payables	17 22.1	18 20.7
	26 14.0	26 14.1	23 15.6					26 13.9	28 13.0
	39 9.3	40 9.2	36 10.2					44 8.2	40 9.1
	6.0	7.4	9.4				Sales/Working Capital	9.2	9.0
	21.3	14.9	15.4					23.2	16.6
	-26.7	28.8	55.2					-999.8	48.5
	8.2	11.5	33.6				EBIT/Interest	5.7	9.0
	(18) 3.8	(37) 3.7	(21) 5.6					(118) 2.3	(91) 2.5
	1.2	1.1	1.7					1.1	1.2
							Net Profit + Depr., Dep., Amort./Cur. Mat. L/T/D	3.5	6.2
								(20) 1.2	(23) 1.4
								.4	.6
	.0	.0	.0				Fixed/Worth	.1	.1
	.6	.1	.3					.4	.3
	NM	.5	1.0					2.0	.8
	.9	1.2	1.5				Debt/Worth	1.3	1.1
	3.7	2.3	3.0					3.0	2.3
	NM	5.1	5.8					12.1	6.0
	68.8	43.1	28.2				% Profit Before Taxes/Tangible Net Worth	38.2	32.8
	(15) 32.6	(39) 15.4	(22) 19.7					(106) 19.2	(92) 14.1
	6.4	2.6	10.4					5.5	3.1
	17.2	11.0	10.4				% Profit Before Taxes/Total Assets	11.3	9.6
	3.5	4.4	4.6					3.9	3.6
	-.5	.7	2.2					.6	.5
	639.6	433.4	322.3				Sales/Net Fixed Assets	210.4	183.4
	80.8	109.6	58.7					56.1	57.9
	26.4	33.4	12.3					15.8	18.6
	5.7	5.1	4.7				Sales/Total Assets	4.7	4.9
	3.7	3.7	3.4					3.6	3.9
	3.1	2.8	3.0					2.6	2.8
	.1	.1	.2				% Depr., Dep., Amort./Sales	.2	.1
	(15) .3	(32) .4	(22) .3					(93) .4	(83) .5
	.8	.8	.7					1.4	.9
	1.4	1.2					% Officers', Directors' Owners' Comp/Sales	.8	.9
	(10) 3.8	(18) 2.3						(40) 2.3	(39) 2.8
	7.5	3.7						4.2	5.2
11512M	116699M	941235M	1973613M	1843922M	3469648M		Net Sales ($)	10792844M	8427830M
2128M	22847M	219069M	515738M	481737M	1275112M		Total Assets ($)	2979746M	2172061M

© RMA 2011

M = $ thousand   MM = $ million
See Pages 9 through 22 for Explanation of Ratios and Data

Comparative Historical Data | Current Data Sorted by Sales

			Type of Statement						
26	17	18	Unqualified				1	3	14
30	24	24	Reviewed				4	8	12
11	18	12	Compiled		3	2	1	4	2
27	28	14	Tax Returns	2	3	1	3	3	2
31	39	38	Other	1	2	6	4	3	22
4/1/08-3/31/09	4/1/09-3/31/10	4/1/10-3/31/11		16 (4/1-9/30/10)			90 (10/1/10-3/31/11)		
ALL	ALL	ALL		0-1MM	1-3MM	3-5MM	5-10MM	10-25MM	25MM & OVER
125	126	106	**NUMBER OF STATEMENTS**	3	9	9	12	21	52
%	%	%	**ASSETS**	%	%	%	%	%	%
6.3	7.7	7.8	Cash & Equivalents				6.9	5.3	7.2
37.3	39.9	41.1	Trade Receivables (net)				34.2	41.6	47.2
27.7	27.3	26.5	Inventory				29.7	31.8	25.0
3.1	2.3	3.4	All Other Current				2.6	1.1	1.9
74.4	77.1	78.9	Total Current				73.5	79.8	81.3
13.7	12.9	11.9	Fixed Assets (net)				22.0	12.2	9.2
3.4	3.7	3.0	Intangibles (net)				2.2	1.4	2.8
8.6	6.3	6.2	All Other Non-Current				2.3	6.6	6.7
100.0	100.0	100.0	Total				100.0	100.0	100.0
			LIABILITIES						
23.7	18.1	20.3	Notes Payable-Short Term				11.7	22.9	18.8
3.3	2.2	1.9	Cur. Mat.-L.T.D.				5.4	2.7	.8
20.4	23.5	25.3	Trade Payables				17.9	24.6	29.1
.2	.1	.1	Income Taxes Payable				.1	.2	.1
9.3	9.0	9.8	All Other Current				14.6	5.4	8.6
56.9	52.8	57.4	Total Current				49.6	55.9	57.4
11.9	13.6	9.5	Long-Term Debt				15.8	12.2	5.5
.2	.1	.1	Deferred Taxes				.0	.1	.2
4.0	6.3	9.3	All Other Non-Current				4.8	2.3	3.8
27.1	27.2	23.7	Net Worth				29.7	29.6	33.1
100.0	100.0	100.0	Total Liabilities & Net Worth				100.0	100.0	100.0
			INCOME DATA						
100.0	100.0	100.0	Net Sales				100.0	100.0	100.0
21.5	21.8	20.9	Gross Profit				32.0	21.2	14.5
19.4	19.9	18.7	Operating Expenses				28.2	19.6	12.5
2.1	2.0	2.2	Operating Profit				3.8	1.6	2.0
.6	.5	.3	All Other Expenses (net)				.2	.6	.2
1.4	1.4	1.9	Profit Before Taxes				3.6	1.0	1.8
			RATIOS						
2.2	2.7	2.3	Current				2.4	2.3	2.1
1.4	1.6	1.4					1.5	1.5	1.3
1.0	1.1	1.1					1.2	1.1	1.1
1.3	1.5	1.3	Quick				1.0	1.3	1.3
.8	1.0	.9					.9	.9	1.0
.6	.6	.6					.9	.5	.7
27 13.6	29 12.6	29 12.4	Sales/Receivables				35 10.4	32 11.3	31 11.8
34 10.6	40 9.2	39 9.4					39 9.4	40 9.1	39 9.3
43 8.5	52 7.0	48 7.7					42 8.6	48 7.6	53 6.9
16 23.5	15 23.9	13 27.1	Cost of Sales/Inventory				20 18.3	20 18.0	12 29.4
32 11.4	35 10.4	32 11.3					29 12.7	41 8.8	33 11.1
53 6.9	58 6.3	53 6.9					99 3.7	83 4.4	42 8.6
13 27.2	15 24.4	16 23.0	Cost of Sales/Payables				13 27.8	16 22.9	16 22.6
22 16.4	26 14.3	25 14.4					29 12.6	31 11.8	24 15.1
37 10.0	43 8.5	39 9.4					46 7.9	42 8.7	37 10.0
8.4	6.8	7.7	Sales/Working Capital				5.8	7.9	8.7
18.1	12.0	15.4					10.6	14.1	18.2
151.6	45.1	82.5					32.9	43.7	60.0
8.1	11.6	11.0	EBIT/Interest				7.9	6.5	23.7
(120) 2.3	(113) 3.0	(95) 3.9					(11) 4.7	(20) 1.8	(46) 5.5
1.1	1.1	1.5					1.1	.7	2.3
4.0	4.0	6.9	Net Profit + Depr., Dep.,						
(24) 1.1	(20) 1.9	(15) 3.4	Amort./Cur. Mat. L/T/D						
.0	-.2	1.9							
.1	.1	.0	Fixed/Worth				.1	.0	.1
.4	.2	.2					.7	.2	.2
1.2	1.3	.8					3.2	.7	.5
1.1	.8	1.1	Debt/Worth				1.4	1.1	1.2
2.7	2.3	2.8					3.0	2.9	2.5
14.1	8.9	9.7					8.2	13.0	5.7
31.3	35.1	35.4	% Profit Before Taxes/Tangible				68.6	33.7	34.7
(104) 15.9	(110) 14.6	(92) 18.3	Net Worth				(11) 32.6	(19) 7.6	(49) 18.9
4.4	1.5	6.4					5.4	-.3	11.3
8.8	11.5	11.2	% Profit Before Taxes/Total				15.7	7.5	11.6
3.3	3.4	4.2	Assets				5.5	1.9	4.8
.2	.4	1.4					.7	-.7	2.4
203.6	288.6	398.3	Sales/Net Fixed Assets				52.2	362.5	433.4
69.4	77.2	82.3					19.9	137.2	103.5
15.7	14.9	22.6					9.3	23.7	27.2
4.7	4.7	5.1	Sales/Total Assets				4.6	4.2	5.3
3.9	3.3	3.6					3.1	3.5	4.1
2.7	2.6	2.8					1.6	2.7	3.0
.2	.2	.1	% Depr., Dep., Amort./Sales				.5	.1	.1
(99) .4	(98) .4	(88) .3					(10) 1.2	(17) .5	(47) .3
1.1	.9	.8					3.5	1.2	.4
1.1	1.3	1.0	% Officers', Directors'					1.2	.7
(52) 2.7	(56) 2.5	(44) 1.9	Owners' Comp/Sales					(12) 1.9	(14) 1.0
4.7	5.3	6.2						3.2	1.8
8392298M	7797035M	8356629M	Net Sales ($)	1893M	15930M	34103M	95802M	358784M	7850117M
2415288M	2260557M	2516631M	Total Assets ($)	1351M	4575M	8418M	42510M	113556M	2346221M

M = $ thousand   MM = $ million
See Pages 9 through 22 for Explanation of Ratios and Data

Current Data Sorted by Assets　　　　　　　　　**Comparative Historical Data**

0-500M	500M-2MM	2-10MM	10-50MM	50-100MM	100-250MM	Type of Statement	4/1/06-3/31/07 ALL	4/1/07-3/31/08 ALL
	1	1	4	2	1	Unqualified	10	12
1	4	26	9			Reviewed	40	33
3	11	12	1			Compiled	26	18
3	9	3				Tax Returns	16	13
1	14	14	14	1	4	Other	40	38
	27 (4/1-9/30/10)		112 (10/1/10-3/31/11)					
8	39	56	28	3	5	**NUMBER OF STATEMENTS**	132	114
%	%	%	%	%	%	**ASSETS**	%	%
	10.1	8.7	4.6			Cash & Equivalents	6.2	6.8
	36.8	36.1	36.9			Trade Receivables (net)	42.2	38.4
	25.0	27.5	28.0			Inventory	28.2	29.0
	3.1	4.8	5.0			All Other Current	2.0	3.0
	75.0	77.0	74.6			Total Current	78.5	77.1
	12.2	11.1	14.5			Fixed Assets (net)	12.0	11.1
	6.2	4.2	7.8			Intangibles (net)	4.7	6.2
	6.6	7.6	3.1			All Other Non-Current	4.8	5.6
	100.0	100.0	100.0			Total	100.0	100.0
						LIABILITIES		
	12.2	14.5	28.4			Notes Payable-Short Term	16.2	20.6
	3.8	1.8	3.6			Cur. Mat.-L.T.D.	2.5	2.7
	26.9	24.6	22.6			Trade Payables	26.6	23.5
	.1	.2	.2			Income Taxes Payable	.3	.2
	12.4	10.6	14.5			All Other Current	10.1	11.4
	55.4	51.7	69.3			Total Current	55.7	58.3
	6.9	8.4	6.4			Long-Term Debt	11.2	11.0
	.2	.4	.2			Deferred Taxes	.3	.2
	8.3	7.6	14.5			All Other Non-Current	6.1	5.8
	29.2	32.0	9.5			Net Worth	26.6	24.6
	100.0	100.0	100.0			Total Liabilities & Net Worth	100.0	100.0
						INCOME DATA		
	100.0	100.0	100.0			Net Sales	100.0	100.0
	33.8	31.1	31.9			Gross Profit	31.6	31.3
	32.0	29.6	28.2			Operating Expenses	28.0	28.6
	1.8	1.5	3.7			Operating Profit	3.6	2.7
	-.1	.6	.8			All Other Expenses (net)	.9	.9
	2.0	.9	2.9			Profit Before Taxes	2.6	1.8
						RATIOS		
	2.5	2.4	2.2				2.0	2.2
	1.8	1.4	1.4			Current	1.4	1.4
	.8	1.2	.9				1.1	1.1
	1.6	1.4	1.3				1.3	1.4
	.9	.9	.7			Quick	.9	.8
	.6	.6	.4				.6	.6
23 16.2	29 12.5	29 12.8					30 12.3	28 13.2
32 11.3	41 9.0	41 8.9				Sales/Receivables	38 9.6	39 9.5
43 8.4	54 6.8	49 7.4					51 7.2	49 7.5
9 41.5	23 15.9	17 21.3					15 24.9	20 18.4
32 11.3	39 9.4	48 7.6				Cost of Sales/Inventory	33 11.2	39 9.4
72 5.1	86 4.2	97 3.8					76 4.8	80 4.6
19 19.4	23 15.8	24 15.2					19 19.3	18 19.9
28 13.1	35 10.4	35 10.3				Cost of Sales/Payables	30 12.1	28 12.9
51 7.2	51 7.1	46 7.9					46 8.0	44 8.4
	7.3	8.5	7.0				8.9	8.5
	15.2	13.7	32.5			Sales/Working Capital	16.9	16.3
	-32.1	35.1	-73.5				55.6	120.3
	15.0	5.8	20.6				6.2	7.4
(36)	3.9	(51) 2.8	(27) 4.5			EBIT/Interest	(115) 2.9	(104) 2.4
	.5	.9	2.1				1.1	1.1
		11.9	7.1				11.6	6.5
	(15)	1.9	(10) 5.1			Net Profit + Depr., Dep., Amort./Cur. Mat. L/T/D	(34) 3.3	(30) 2.6
		1.2	1.2				1.1	1.3
	.1	.1	.2				.1	.1
	.5	.2	.6			Fixed/Worth	.4	.4
	.9	.8	NM				1.5	1.3
	1.1	1.2	1.1				1.4	1.2
	2.4	2.6	3.3			Debt/Worth	2.6	2.9
	10.7	5.8	NM				7.2	15.8
	50.2	24.3	87.3				46.7	45.2
(32)	18.7	(49) 11.5	(21) 24.7			% Profit Before Taxes/Tangible Net Worth	(111) 21.5	(91) 23.6
	1.9	1.1	6.3				6.0	7.7
	13.4	5.1	17.4				12.8	13.4
	4.5	2.1	7.7			% Profit Before Taxes/Total Assets	5.6	4.2
	-.6	.2	3.1				.3	.4
	471.0	172.6	98.5				123.9	139.3
	50.9	74.4	44.6			Sales/Net Fixed Assets	56.9	53.5
	20.1	17.1	12.9				19.8	21.8
	5.5	4.0	4.8				5.4	4.8
	4.0	3.1	3.5			Sales/Total Assets	3.8	3.9
	2.8	2.1	2.2				2.7	2.5
	.2	.2	.6				.4	.3
(29)	.4	(48) .6	(26) .7			% Depr., Dep., Amort./Sales	(105) .7	(88) .7
	1.0	1.3	1.1				1.3	1.5
	3.1	1.2					1.4	1.6
(20)	4.4	(32) 1.8				% Officers', Directors' Owners' Comp/Sales	(59) 3.4	(51) 3.4
	6.4	3.5					6.7	6.2
14117M	333205M	874940M	1722841M	801984M	2656719M	Net Sales ($)	5714360M	5511059M
2518M	48054M	282647M	525107M	213626M	907818M	Total Assets ($)	1677941M	1673556M

© RMA 2011

M = $ thousand　　MM = $ million
See Pages 9 through 22 for Explanation of Ratios and Data

Comparative Historical Data | | Current Data Sorted by Sales

4/1/08-3/31/09 ALL	4/1/09-3/31/10 ALL	4/1/10-3/31/11 ALL	Type of Statement	0-1MM	1-3MM	3-5MM	5-10MM	10-25MM	25MM & OVER
12	9	9	Unqualified			3	7	21	9
44	47	40	Reviewed	1	2	5	8	8	9
22	22	27	Compiled	2	4	4	4	1	3
22	12	15	Tax Returns	4	3	4	3		
45	47	48	Other	4	3	7		11	20
					27 (4/1-9/30/10)		112 (10/1/10-3/31/11)		
145	137	139	**NUMBER OF STATEMENTS**	7	9	19	22	41	41
%	%	%	**ASSETS**	%	%	%	%	%	%
6.6	7.4	8.6	Cash & Equivalents			8.5	7.9	10.1	6.2
39.7	37.2	36.6	Trade Receivables (net)			38.7	34.6	40.2	40.1
29.6	28.7	26.0	Inventory			22.0	28.3	25.6	25.1
2.5	3.9	4.4	All Other Current			1.6	4.6	5.7	5.1
78.3	77.1	75.6	Total Current			70.8	75.3	81.6	76.5
12.0	11.6	11.8	Fixed Assets (net)			17.6	11.1	9.6	11.9
5.1	6.4	6.1	Intangibles (net)			4.8	6.6	4.6	6.2
4.6	4.9	6.5	All Other Non-Current			6.8	7.0	4.2	5.4
100.0	100.0	100.0	Total			100.0	100.0	100.0	100.0
			LIABILITIES						
19.1	17.8	16.0	Notes Payable-Short Term			11.0	11.8	16.3	22.3
3.7	3.5	3.0	Cur. Mat.-L.T.D.			3.9	2.1	2.2	3.7
23.3	26.5	25.8	Trade Payables			30.6	25.6	26.5	28.8
.3	.2	.1	Income Taxes Payable			.0	.3	.2	.2
8.8	9.7	11.7	All Other Current			10.5	17.1	11.6	11.8
55.1	57.6	56.6	Total Current			56.0	56.8	56.8	66.8
10.5	9.9	8.4	Long-Term Debt			8.0	13.3	4.4	7.5
.3	.3	.3	Deferred Taxes			.3	.4	.3	.2
8.0	5.9	8.6	All Other Non-Current			11.3	3.0	8.0	9.3
26.1	26.3	26.2	Net Worth			24.3	26.4	30.5	16.2
100.0	100.0	100.0	Total Liabilties & Net Worth			100.0	100.0	100.0	100.0
			INCOME DATA						
100.0	100.0	100.0	Net Sales			100.0	100.0	100.0	100.0
30.3	32.6	32.0	Gross Profit			33.9	32.6	31.3	27.0
27.9	31.0	30.0	Operating Expenses			32.4	31.5	29.0	23.8
2.5	1.6	2.0	Operating Profit			1.5	1.1	2.3	3.2
.9	.6	.5	All Other Expenses (net)			.4	.6	.4	.3
1.6	1.0	1.5	Profit Before Taxes			1.1	.5	1.9	2.8
			RATIOS						
2.0	2.0	2.4				3.3	2.1	2.0	2.0
1.4	1.5	1.5	Current			1.4	1.7	1.4	1.3
1.1	1.0	1.0				.7	1.0	1.1	1.0
1.3	1.2	1.5				2.8	1.4	1.4	1.3
.8	.7	.9	Quick			.9	1.1	.9	.8
.6	.6	.5				.5	.5	.6	.5
28 12.9	27 13.7	28 13.2				21 17.1	25 14.4	30 12.3	29 12.7
38 9.5	38 9.5	37 9.8	Sales/Receivables			36 10.2	33 11.0	43 8.5	39 9.4
48 7.6	47 7.8	48 7.6				46 8.0	42 8.8	58 6.3	49 7.5
18 20.8	16 22.6	16 22.4				8 46.3	12 31.6	22 16.6	16 22.9
35 10.5	33 8.5	33 10.9	Cost of Sales/Inventory			35 10.5	31 11.7	33 10.9	31 11.6
84 4.4	83 4.4	79 4.6				67 5.4	98 3.7	82 4.4	58 6.3
18 20.3	20 18.5	22 16.2				14 26.7	22 16.7	23 15.7	26 14.3
29 12.8	34 10.9	35 10.5	Cost of Sales/Payables			33 11.1	29 12.4	35 10.5	36 10.0
45 8.2	49 7.4	51 7.2				56 6.5	45 8.0	58 6.3	46 8.0
8.9	7.4	7.4				6.3	9.0	10.6	7.7
15.5	14.2	13.9	Sales/Working Capital			25.8	14.4	13.9	23.5
48.9	251.0	207.3				-19.3	NM	40.8	-109.1
6.0	5.6	9.4				12.9	6.8	6.1	18.9
(134) 2.7	(121) 2.7	(130) 3.3	EBIT/Interest			(18) 3.6	(21) 1.4	(35) 3.3	4.6
1.0	-.2	.9				.8	.4	1.1	2.7
6.0	3.7	5.3	Net Profit + Depr., Dep.,					17.8	6.1
(33) 2.4	(41) 2.0	(35) 1.9	Amort./Cur. Mat. L/T/D				(12) 2.4	(14) 4.2	
1.1	.6	.9						1.5	1.1
.1	.1	.1				.2	.0	.1	.2
.4	.4	.3	Fixed/Worth			.5	.3	.2	.3
1.7	2.4	.9				-2.5	.8	.7	1.3
1.3	1.1	1.1				.7	1.2	1.3	1.5
3.0	2.8	2.6	Debt/Worth			2.7	2.1	2.8	3.1
18.3	23.5	13.2				-27.5	15.0	8.9	32.8
42.6	31.4	35.6	% Profit Before Taxes/Tangible Net Worth			32.3	23.5	41.2	82.9
(119) 14.5	(106) 11.4	(112) 15.4				(14) 12.4	(18) 6.7	(36) 15.8	(32) 24.7
1.9	-.1	1.5				2.2	1.0	1.8	7.7
12.1	10.0	9.9	% Profit Before Taxes/Total Assets			11.7	5.6	7.9	17.4
3.7	2.7	3.6				2.7	1.8	4.0	7.9
.3	-1.8	.1				-.3	-.8	.2	3.1
97.0	165.6	152.9				80.1	349.3	155.4	127.0
44.3	43.4	56.0	Sales/Net Fixed Assets			38.5	104.6	82.6	54.7
20.9	18.1	18.5				14.4	18.8	19.6	18.5
5.0	4.8	4.8				4.9	5.1	4.5	4.9
3.7	3.4	3.5	Sales/Total Assets			3.7	4.0	3.4	3.9
2.5	2.3	2.2				3.3	1.8	2.3	2.4
.3	.4	.3				.3	.1	.2	.4
(117) .6	(106) .7	(114) .6	% Depr., Dep., Amort./Sales			(17) .5	(19) .3	(34) .6	(36) .7
1.3	1.3	1.1				1.0	1.0	1.3	1.1
1.4	1.3	1.4				3.2	2.3	1.1	
(59) 3.2	(61) 3.3	(64) 3.1	% Officers', Directors' Owners' Comp/Sales			(14) 4.4	(13) 3.6	(22) 1.5	
6.9	6.3	5.2				5.6	4.9	2.6	
5843959M	4692606M	6403806M	Net Sales ($)	4626M	17885M	77988M	155288M	659382M	5488637M
1851895M	1515748M	1979770M	Total Assets ($)	3494M	10927M	26547M	55800M	228783M	1654219M

© RMA 2011

M = $ thousand   MM = $ million
See Pages 9 through 22 for Explanation of Ratios and Data

Current Data Sorted by Assets — Comparative Historical Data

0-500M	500M-2MM	2-10MM	10-50MM	50-100MM	100-250MM	Type of Statement	4/1/06-3/31/07 ALL	4/1/07-3/31/08 ALL
	3	3	12	5	3	Unqualified	24	24
	6	43	20			Reviewed	57	60
2	8	23	2			Compiled	35	26
2	15	6	1			Tax Returns	16	20
2	10	25	11	2	3	Other	71	75
	46 (4/1-9/30/10)			161 (10/1/10-3/31/11)				
6	42	100	46	7	6	NUMBER OF STATEMENTS	203	205
%	%	%	%	%	%	**ASSETS**	%	%
	7.5	6.4	5.4			Cash & Equivalents	4.9	5.6
	40.1	35.7	39.5			Trade Receivables (net)	41.8	40.8
	35.9	34.9	29.9			Inventory	30.2	29.9
	2.1	2.4	4.3			All Other Current	2.4	2.3
	85.6	79.4	79.2			Total Current	79.3	78.7
	7.9	12.8	13.3			Fixed Assets (net)	12.4	13.6
	2.1	2.5	2.4			Intangibles (net)	3.0	2.5
	4.4	5.3	5.1			All Other Non-Current	5.3	5.2
	100.0	100.0	100.0			Total	100.0	100.0
						LIABILITIES		
	14.0	14.4	21.0			Notes Payable-Short Term	17.9	18.3
	2.4	1.7	1.6			Cur. Mat.-L.T.D.	2.1	2.7
	26.9	25.2	21.8			Trade Payables	28.3	28.7
	.2	.2	.1			Income Taxes Payable	.4	.2
	6.5	6.0	9.5			All Other Current	7.4	8.1
	50.0	47.6	54.1			Total Current	56.1	58.0
	6.8	7.7	6.9			Long-Term Debt	9.5	11.3
	.2	.3	.4			Deferred Taxes	.1	.2
	6.6	4.9	3.1			All Other Non-Current	4.3	3.3
	36.4	39.5	35.6			Net Worth	30.0	27.2
	100.0	100.0	100.0			Total Liabilities & Net Worth	100.0	100.0
						INCOME DATA		
	100.0	100.0	100.0			Net Sales	100.0	100.0
	24.5	23.6	22.7			Gross Profit	22.7	23.3
	22.0	21.5	20.5			Operating Expenses	19.8	20.8
	2.5	2.1	2.3			Operating Profit	2.9	2.6
	.3	.2	.4			All Other Expenses (net)	.7	.5
	2.2	1.9	1.8			Profit Before Taxes	2.3	2.0
						RATIOS		
	2.9	2.6	2.2			Current	2.1	2.0
	1.8	1.7	1.5				1.4	1.4
	1.2	1.3	1.1				1.1	1.1
	1.6	1.3	1.3			Quick	1.3	1.3
	.9	.9	.8				.8	.8
	.6	.6	.6				.6	.6
25 14.8	26 13.8	34 10.7				Sales/Receivables	31 11.7	29 12.5
34 10.7	33 11.0	39 9.3					38 9.6	37 9.9
40 9.1	41 8.8	50 7.2					46 7.9	47 7.8
27 13.5	32 11.3	31 11.8				Cost of Sales/Inventory	25 14.8	25 14.9
38 9.5	44 8.4	39 9.2					40 9.1	39 9.3
49 7.4	66 5.6	57 6.4					55 6.6	57 6.4
10 35.3	18 20.7	16 22.2				Cost of Sales/Payables	19 19.5	20 18.3
31 11.6	30 12.1	23 15.9					30 12.1	30 12.1
52 7.0	43 8.4	44 8.2					46 8.0	44 8.3
	7.7	6.9	7.5			Sales/Working Capital	8.3	9.1
	12.1	12.9	13.0				17.4	18.2
	34.5	29.1	41.8				59.6	61.8
	10.0	14.1	12.5			EBIT/Interest	10.0	6.9
(35) 2.5	(90) 4.3	(43) 4.1					(190) 3.1	(198) 2.3
	.4	1.6	2.0				1.4	1.2
		6.6	7.8			Net Profit + Depr., Dep., Amort./Cur. Mat. L/T/D	6.2	3.9
	(24) 3.2	(20) 3.6					(45) 2.8	(54) 2.5
	1.1	1.2					.8	1.2
	.0	.1	.1			Fixed/Worth	.1	.1
	.1	.2	.3				.4	.4
	.6	.8	.6				1.2	1.0
	.7	.7	1.0			Debt/Worth	1.2	1.2
	2.1	1.7	2.0				2.8	3.0
	8.4	3.8	4.0				8.5	7.4
	58.0	33.8	26.7			% Profit Before Taxes/Tangible Net Worth	48.0	36.8
(39) 6.0	(90) 14.0	(43) 15.7					(178) 21.1	(182) 17.8
	-3.0	2.8	5.9				7.1	4.6
	14.2	9.8	7.9			% Profit Before Taxes/Total Assets	13.6	11.7
	3.7	5.4	3.7				5.7	4.0
	-1.6	.8	2.4				1.2	.7
	470.9	163.5	95.1			Sales/Net Fixed Assets	147.6	142.0
	146.2	53.6	40.9				58.8	51.1
	34.8	16.7	14.4				18.6	21.4
	5.9	4.4	4.3			Sales/Total Assets	4.7	5.0
	4.3	3.5	3.4				3.7	3.9
	3.1	2.9	2.7				2.9	2.7
	.1	.2	.3			% Depr., Dep., Amort./Sales	.2	.2
(28) .3	(80) .6	(43) .5					(169) .5	(180) .5
	1.0	1.1	1.0				.9	1.0
	2.0	1.1	1.8			% Officers', Directors' Owners' Comp/Sales	1.2	1.3
(26) 3.8	(48) 1.8	(10) 2.3					(84) 2.7	(91) 2.5
	6.2	4.1	3.0				4.8	4.8
7732M	244556M	1812815M	3301914M	1531304M	3401654M	Net Sales ($)	12404359M	14037694M
2054M	51474M	495609M	968940M	510657M	897994M	Total Assets ($)	3057303M	3802187M

M = $ thousand   MM = $ million
See Pages 9 through 22 for Explanation of Ratios and Data

Comparative Historical Data / Current Data Sorted by Sales

Current data periods: **46 (4/1-9/30/10)** covers 0-1MM / 1-3MM / 3-5MM — **161 (10/1/10-3/31/11)** covers 5-10MM / 10-25MM / 25MM & Over.

Item	4/1/08-3/31/09 ALL	4/1/09-3/31/10 ALL	4/1/10-3/31/11 ALL	0-1MM	1-3MM	3-5MM	5-10MM	10-25MM	25MM & OVER
Type of Statement									
Unqualified	23	25	26		1	2		4	19
Reviewed	66	65	69			3	9	29	28
Compiled	31	35	35	1	2		8	20	4
Tax Returns	24	28	24	2	2	3	11	5	1
Other	84	67	53		5	3	7	15	23
NUMBER OF STATEMENTS	228	220	207	3	10	11	35	73	75
ASSETS (%)	%	%	%	%	%	%	%	%	%
Cash & Equivalents	4.7	7.0	6.5		13.3	10.5	5.6	7.1	4.9
Trade Receivables (net)	39.4	36.1	37.7		37.9	29.9	38.8	37.9	38.5
Inventory	30.8	30.0	33.4		21.2	40.5	37.2	34.1	30.9
All Other Current	2.9	3.4	2.8		6.3	.8	1.2	2.4	4.0
Total Current	77.8	76.6	80.4		78.8	81.7	82.8	81.5	78.3
Fixed Assets (net)	13.9	14.4	12.0		9.5	12.2	11.3	10.9	14.0
Intangibles (net)	3.2	3.9	2.7		6.3	1.3	1.2	2.3	3.2
All Other Non-Current	5.0	5.2	4.8		5.5	4.9	4.7	5.4	4.5
Total	100.0	100.0	100.0		100.0	100.0	100.0	100.0	100.0
LIABILITIES									
Notes Payable-Short Term	19.3	16.5	16.7		20.1	11.7	13.2	15.1	17.6
Cur. Mat.-L.T.D.	3.0	2.4	1.7		.1	6.2	1.7	1.7	1.5
Trade Payables	25.2	24.4	24.1		17.0	24.9	25.0	26.1	22.9
Income Taxes Payable	.1	.2	.2		.3	.3	.0	.3	.2
All Other Current	7.3	7.8	7.1		2.0	6.1	8.1	5.5	9.2
Total Current	54.9	51.3	49.7		39.5	49.1	48.0	48.6	51.3
Long-Term Debt	11.5	10.0	8.0		.2	16.5	8.6	6.7	9.0
Deferred Taxes	.3	.3	.3		.9	.0	.2	.2	.4
All Other Non-Current	5.8	5.0	4.8		3.8	12.6	4.6	5.0	3.6
Net Worth	27.5	33.5	37.1		55.6	21.9	38.6	39.4	35.7
Total Liabilities & Net Worth	100.0	100.0	100.0		100.0	100.0	100.0	100.0	100.0
INCOME DATA									
Net Sales	100.0	100.0	100.0		100.0	100.0	100.0	100.0	100.0
Gross Profit	23.7	23.9	23.5		22.5	25.1	27.6	22.5	22.0
Operating Expenses	21.3	21.7	21.1		18.3	24.0	24.8	20.4	19.6
Operating Profit	2.4	2.2	2.5		4.2	1.1	2.9	2.2	2.4
All Other Expenses (net)	.5	.5	.3		.2	.7	.2	.2	.5
Profit Before Taxes	2.0	1.6	2.1		4.0	.3	2.7	2.0	1.9
RATIOS									
Current	2.0	2.3	2.6		5.1	2.4	2.9	2.7	2.3
	1.4	1.5	1.6		2.1	1.8	1.8	1.7	1.6
	1.1	1.1	1.2		1.3	1.3	1.1	1.3	1.2
Quick	1.2	1.4	1.4		2.9	1.7	1.4	1.4	1.3
	.8	.8	.9		1.3	.9	.9	.9	.9
	.5	.6	.6		.9	.5	.6	.9	.6
Sales/Receivables	28 13.0	28 13.2	29 12.8		34 10.8	25 14.8	25 14.6	28 13.2	30 12.3
	34 10.6	35 10.4	35 10.4		37 9.9	33 10.9	34 10.8	35 10.5	38 9.6
	42 8.7	45 8.2	44 8.4		50 7.3	39 9.3	40 9.1	45 8.2	46 7.9
Cost of Sales/Inventory	24 15.2	26 14.2	32 11.4		8 46.5	34 10.7	34 10.7	31 11.7	32 11.3
	39 9.4	39 9.5	41 8.8		33 10.9	49 7.4	43 8.6	41 8.9	40 9.2
	55 6.6	61 6.0	61 6.0		50 7.3	93 3.9	63 5.8	59 6.2	57 6.4
Cost of Sales/Payables	17 22.0	17 21.5	17 22.0		5 77.3	26 13.9	11 33.2	18 20.7	17 22.0
	27 13.5	28 13.2	28 12.9		20 17.9	32 11.5	28 13.0	33 11.2	24 15.3
	40 9.1	46 7.9	44 8.3		56 6.6	42 8.7	52 7.0	43 8.5	39 9.3
Sales/Working Capital	8.8	8.0	7.2		4.9	5.8	7.2	7.3	7.4
	17.9	13.9	12.8		8.2	9.8	13.6	11.4	14.2
	49.1	47.0	31.7		15.6	20.2	58.0	28.8	35.3
EBIT/Interest	7.2	10.1	11.4			3.5	14.2	13.3	12.5
	(212) 3.1	(203) 3.3	(185) 4.1			(10) .5	(31) 5.2	(64) 3.9	(71) 4.1
	1.3	1.2	1.6			-3.4	1.6	1.6	2.0
Net Profit + Depr., Dep., Amort./Cur. Mat. L/T/D	4.7	5.2	7.6					6.9	9.9
	(55) 2.1	(55) 1.9	(53) 3.3					(16) 3.2	(27) 3.8
	1.0	.3	1.0					.8	1.6
Fixed/Worth	.1	.1	.1		.0	.2	.0	.1	.1
	.4	.3	.2		.0	.7	.2	.2	.3
	1.2	1.0	.8		.3	2.2	.6	.7	.8
Debt/Worth	1.2	1.0	.8		.3	1.9	.5	.6	1.0
	2.8	2.2	1.9		.6	3.6	1.9	1.7	2.0
	8.0	5.9	4.2		3.5	19.3	6.9	3.9	3.9
% Profit Before Taxes/Tangible Net Worth	32.6	32.9	34.0		67.9	86.8	38.4	37.8	29.0
	(195) 16.4	(196) 14.7	(188) 15.2		11.7	(10) -1.2	(32) 16.5	(65) 13.5	(70) 16.8
	4.8	3.1	3.5		-8.9	-32.6	4.6	1.4	6.6
% Profit Before Taxes/Total Assets	10.4	10.1	9.5		19.6	4.6	11.9	10.6	8.7
	4.5	3.5	4.8		4.3	-1.2	5.5	4.8	5.2
	.8	.4	1.1		-6.7	-7.7	1.8	.7	2.5
Sales/Net Fixed Assets	180.5	143.2	173.9		UND	67.3	350.9	188.0	100.5
	52.4	47.2	58.5		193.6	34.0	118.7	61.0	42.4
	17.7	16.3	17.0		90.4	14.8	21.2	22.0	14.5
Sales/Total Assets	5.2	4.5	4.5		4.0	4.3	5.9	4.8	4.3
	3.8	3.5	3.5		3.0	3.6	4.3	3.6	3.4
	2.8	2.5	2.7		1.9	2.5	2.9	3.0	2.7
% Depr., Dep., Amort./Sales	.2	.3	.3				.2	.2	.3
	(179) .6	(182) .6	(165) .6				(26) .4	(58) .5	(67) .6
	1.1	1.3	1.0				1.3	.9	1.0
% Officers', Directors', Owners' Comp/Sales	1.2	1.2	1.3				2.0	1.1	.6
	(87) 2.5	(98) 2.5	(92) 2.3				(22) 3.6	(35) 2.0	(23) 1.4
	3.9	4.0	4.6				6.8	4.1	2.6
Net Sales ($)	14529538M	12497523M	10299975M	1874M	18482M	43432M	249420M	1190817M	8795950M
Total Assets ($)	3458210M	3641056M	2926728M	943M	6487M	13531M	67612M	337034M	2501121M

M = $ thousand   MM = $ million
See Pages 9 through 22 for Explanation of Ratios and Data

Current Data Sorted by Assets — Comparative Historical Data

Type of Statement	0-500M	500M-2MM	2-10MM	10-50MM	50-100MM	100-250MM		4/1/06-3/31/07 ALL	4/1/07-3/31/08 ALL
Unqualified		1	9	29	8	11		43	27
Reviewed			27	16		1		33	37
Compiled	4	7	8	1				27	22
Tax Returns	5	18	12	1				25	28
Other	4	14	40	32	8	8		82	108
		28 (4/1-9/30/10)		236 (10/1/10-3/31/11)					
NUMBER OF STATEMENTS	13	40	96	79	16	20		210	222
	%	%	%	%	%	%	ASSETS	%	%
	6.4	13.5	10.8	10.5	10.7	11.0	Cash & Equivalents	10.1	9.0
	23.0	34.4	30.5	32.8	24.1	25.9	Trade Receivables (net)	35.3	30.8
	47.3	30.5	34.6	31.4	20.5	25.0	Inventory	30.4	32.8
	6.0	2.4	2.2	3.0	2.0	4.8	All Other Current	3.5	3.2
	82.8	80.8	78.1	77.8	57.3	66.7	Total Current	79.3	75.9
	9.2	8.0	10.7	10.5	11.2	8.0	Fixed Assets (net)	9.7	11.0
	3.7	5.7	7.1	8.2	26.0	21.0	Intangibles (net)	6.4	7.5
	4.3	5.4	4.1	3.6	5.6	4.4	All Other Non-Current	4.5	5.6
	100.0	100.0	100.0	100.0	100.0	100.0	Total	100.0	100.0
							LIABILITIES		
	9.0	15.7	14.2	12.2	4.7	7.9	Notes Payable-Short Term	14.9	15.6
	.6	.9	1.8	2.3	.8	1.0	Cur. Mat.-L.T.D.	2.6	2.1
	33.7	28.3	24.3	27.0	21.8	19.0	Trade Payables	25.6	24.2
	.0	.1	.2	.3	.1	.1	Income Taxes Payable	.3	.2
	9.0	6.9	8.2	8.6	13.8	13.4	All Other Current	9.2	9.1
	52.1	51.8	48.7	50.4	41.2	41.3	Total Current	52.7	51.1
	3.7	6.6	8.9	5.6	10.4	14.5	Long-Term Debt	11.2	11.5
	.0	.0	.1	.3	1.3	1.2	Deferred Taxes	.1	.2
	11.1	6.6	7.5	3.8	7.3	7.3	All Other Non-Current	4.3	5.0
	33.1	35.0	34.8	39.9	39.7	35.7	Net Worth	31.7	32.2
	100.0	100.0	100.0	100.0	100.0	100.0	Total Liabilities & Net Worth	100.0	100.0
							INCOME DATA		
	100.0	100.0	100.0	100.0	100.0	100.0	Net Sales	100.0	100.0
	36.9	33.0	31.5	28.7	41.1	32.4	Gross Profit	32.4	33.3
	32.8	28.0	26.6	22.9	34.9	23.5	Operating Expenses	26.0	27.4
	4.0	5.0	4.8	5.8	6.1	8.9	Operating Profit	6.3	5.9
	.7	.5	.7	.7	1.6	4.2	All Other Expenses (net)	.6	.8
	3.3	4.5	4.2	5.1	4.5	4.7	Profit Before Taxes	5.7	5.1
							RATIOS		
	3.5	2.8	2.7	2.1	3.0	2.3		2.4	2.3
	1.4	1.6	1.7	1.4	1.6	1.7	Current	1.5	1.5
	1.0	1.1	1.3	1.2	1.0	1.2		1.2	1.2
	.9	1.6	1.4	1.2	1.6	1.5		1.4	1.2
	.6	.8	.8	.8	.9	.9	Quick	.8	.7
	.3	.5	.5	.6	.3	.5		.6	.6
	2 209.7	15 24.2	28 12.9	30 12.2	38 9.6	30 12.0		26 14.1	22 16.4
	9 40.2	26 14.1	37 9.7	41 8.9	52 7.1	38 9.6	Sales/Receivables	38 9.7	35 10.4
	43 8.5	47 7.8	52 7.0	54 6.7	72 5.1	51 7.2		56 6.5	49 7.4
	25 14.6	8 48.1	35 10.5	27 13.3	18 20.0	25 14.8		22 16.3	27 13.5
	85 4.3	37 9.8	63 5.8	66 5.6	47 7.7	65 5.6	Cost of Sales/Inventory	49 7.4	53 6.9
	137 2.7	62 5.9	95 3.8	112 3.3	146 2.5	163 2.2		91 4.0	104 3.5
	14 26.6	17 21.0	19 19.7	27 13.3	16 23.5	27 13.5		18 20.0	20 18.3
	40 9.2	26 14.2	38 9.5	41 8.9	34 10.9	37 9.9	Cost of Sales/Payables	36 10.0	39 9.4
	129 2.8	43 8.5	62 5.9	62 5.8	80 4.5	46 8.0		58 6.3	58 6.3
	8.3	6.8	5.7	5.8	3.5	4.4		6.4	6.4
	16.4	13.1	10.5	11.1	9.1	8.5	Sales/Working Capital	14.1	13.5
	UND	51.6	22.1	29.2	267.5	31.8		35.5	34.1
		13.3	30.5	34.7	18.2	9.5		17.6	13.9
	(29) 3.8	(79) 6.3	(68) 8.6	(13) 5.5	(17) 4.1		EBIT/Interest	(177) 4.8	(194) 4.6
		1.2	2.6	2.7	.1	.9		2.0	2.0
			25.5	15.2				6.9	14.8
		(16) 2.6	(19) 3.9				Net Profit + Depr., Dep., Amort./Cur. Mat. L/T/D	(30) 3.6	(43) 5.0
			.9	1.4				1.6	1.7
	.0	.0	.1	.0	.2	.0		.1	.1
	.1	.2	.1	.2	.1	.1	Fixed/Worth	.2	.3
	UND	.4	1.2	.8	NM	2.8		1.0	1.2
	.9	1.2	.8	.8	1.1	1.2		1.0	1.1
	2.5	2.0	1.7	2.1	5.1	4.9	Debt/Worth	2.8	2.5
	UND	6.2	6.4	4.8	NM	NM		9.1	10.3
	103.4	87.6	66.8	50.8	57.3	45.4		83.8	76.6
	(10) 60.9	(34) 24.5	(80) 27.1	(71) 24.5	(12) 27.3	(15) 20.5	% Profit Before Taxes/Tangible Net Worth	(183) 35.2	(188) 36.4
	2.1	9.1	12.7	9.4	7.3	9.1		13.7	11.3
	37.8	26.5	19.4	19.6	14.2	8.9		22.2	25.0
	12.0	8.3	7.9	6.9	4.8	5.4	% Profit Before Taxes/Total Assets	8.9	9.6
	.4	2.4	2.6	2.2	-1.8	1.1		3.2	2.6
	UND	892.7	174.4	205.5	72.2	176.8		236.7	204.5
	392.8	105.6	72.6	61.1	21.7	126.4	Sales/Net Fixed Assets	69.0	54.9
	68.6	45.5	29.6	18.2	9.8	12.8		26.7	22.4
	9.1	7.1	4.0	3.7	2.8	4.1		4.8	4.4
	4.9	4.3	3.0	3.0	1.6	2.1	Sales/Total Assets	3.4	3.2
	2.3	2.9	1.8	1.9	.6	.8		2.0	1.9
		.2	.2	.1	.2	.1		.1	.2
		(22) .4	(75) .5	(67) .4	(10) 1.3	(14) .3	% Depr., Dep., Amort./Sales	(164) .4	(166) .6
		.6	.9	1.0	1.9	1.1		1.1	1.1
		2.3	1.1	.2				1.3	1.0
		(21) 3.3	(44) 2.6	(23) 1.0			% Officers', Directors' Owners' Comp/Sales	(67) 2.2	(78) 2.4
		5.4	3.6	1.8				5.4	6.3
	17274M	258291M	1633889M	5041533M	1981819M	7440658M	Net Sales ($)	17793121M	13324737M
	3496M	44271M	519415M	1738351M	1060262M	3161730M	Total Assets ($)	5177806M	5057294M

© RMA 2011

M = $ thousand   MM = $ million
See Pages 9 through 22 for Explanation of Ratios and Data

Comparative Historical Data | | | Current Data Sorted by Sales

			Type of Statement						
53	55	58	Unqualified			3	7	48	
47	56	44	Reviewed		1	8	18	17	
21	19	20	Compiled		3	5	5	2	
37	38	36	Tax Returns	2	6	10	10	1	
101	97	106	Other	2	7	13	23	51	
4/1/08-	4/1/09-	4/1/10-		5	8				
3/31/09	3/31/10	3/31/11		28 (4/1-9/30/10)		236 (10/1/10-3/31/11)			
ALL	ALL	ALL		0-1MM	1-3MM	3-5MM	5-10MM	10-25MM	25MM & OVER
259	265	264	**NUMBER OF STATEMENTS**	9	16	18	39	63	119
%	%	%	**ASSETS**	%	%	%	%	%	%
10.1	10.6	10.9	Cash & Equivalents		9.7	9.4	13.0	10.3	11.1
30.6	29.4	30.7	Trade Receivables (net)		26.2	32.7	27.7	29.3	32.9
31.8	32.1	32.1	Inventory		43.3	29.7	34.3	34.7	29.5
3.7	3.6	2.8	All Other Current		2.6	2.1	2.3	2.4	3.0
76.2	75.7	76.5	Total Current		81.8	73.9	77.2	76.7	76.5
9.7	10.0	10.0	Fixed Assets (net)		6.6	16.5	8.1	10.1	9.3
8.2	8.5	9.3	Intangibles (net)		6.7	2.6	10.7	9.1	10.5
5.9	5.8	4.2	All Other Non-Current		4.9	7.0	4.0	4.1	3.7
100.0	100.0	100.0	Total		100.0	100.0	100.0	100.0	100.0
			LIABILITIES						
15.5	13.3	12.5	Notes Payable-Short Term		11.8	16.3	14.3	15.0	10.8
2.4	2.4	1.6	Cur. Mat.-L.T.D.		1.2	1.0	1.8	1.6	1.8
24.3	22.8	25.6	Trade Payables		20.7	26.8	22.0	24.7	27.2
.2	.2	.2	Income Taxes Payable		.0	.3	.1	.3	.2
8.6	10.4	8.9	All Other Current		8.2	7.0	6.5	6.7	10.7
50.9	49.1	48.8	Total Current		42.0	51.3	44.7	48.3	50.7
12.3	8.3	7.8	Long-Term Debt		5.9	16.9	12.7	5.2	6.9
.5	.3	.3	Deferred Taxes		.0	.0	.0	.2	.6
5.0	7.5	6.4	All Other Non-Current		11.2	9.4	9.9	7.1	3.6
31.4	34.8	36.6	Net Worth		40.9	22.3	32.7	39.3	38.3
100.0	100.0	100.0	Total Liabilities & Net Worth		100.0	100.0	100.0	100.0	100.0
			INCOME DATA						
100.0	100.0	100.0	Net Sales		100.0	100.0	100.0	100.0	100.0
31.3	31.7	31.8	Gross Profit		46.8	30.1	36.6	29.8	28.7
26.0	26.8	26.3	Operating Expenses		41.1	27.7	31.8	25.5	22.1
5.2	5.0	5.5	Operating Profit		5.7	2.3	4.8	4.2	6.7
1.0	.8	1.0	All Other Expenses (net)		.4	1.3	.8	.5	1.3
4.2	4.1	4.5	Profit Before Taxes		5.3	1.0	4.0	3.7	5.4
			RATIOS						
2.3	2.3	2.3			4.7	2.2	3.7	2.5	2.1
1.5	1.5	1.6	Current		2.3	1.5	1.8	1.7	1.5
1.1	1.2	1.2			1.5	1.0	1.2	1.3	1.2
1.3	1.2	1.4			1.7	1.6	1.5	1.4	1.3
.8	.8	.8	Quick		.7	.9	1.0	.7	.9
.5	.5	.5			.5	.4	.5	.5	.6

							Sales/Receivables										
25	14.7	25	14.7	26	14.0			8	45.7	20	17.8	22	16.9	24	15.5	31	11.6
38	9.5	38	9.6	37	9.9	Sales/Receivables		32	11.3	40	9.1	35	10.3	31	11.8	40	9.2
50	7.3	51	7.2	53	6.9			61	5.9	66	5.6	51	7.1	44	8.4	52	7.0
23	16.0	28	13.3	27	13.3			28	13.0	12	30.2	35	10.4	30	12.4	20	18.7
52	7.1	61	6.0	58	6.3	Cost of Sales/Inventory		79	4.6	54	6.8	62	5.9	62	5.9	49	7.4
112	3.2	119	3.1	107	3.4			174	2.1	92	4.0	137	2.7	100	3.7	100	3.7
21	17.3	20	18.2	22	16.9			14	26.7	17	22.0	22	16.6	16	22.1	26	14.2
37	9.9	34	10.6	36	10.0	Cost of Sales/Payables		25	14.6	34	10.8	45	8.2	27	13.4	38	9.7
57	6.4	59	6.2	60	6.1			66	5.5	99	3.7	60	6.1	52	7.0	58	6.3

						Sales/Working Capital						
	5.7		6.1		6.1			3.4	9.4	4.9	5.8	6.6
	12.6		11.6		11.0	Sales/Working Capital		7.6	14.0	12.0	10.3	11.6
	41.8		26.5		29.4			18.6	NM	33.4	29.0	29.2

						EBIT/Interest									
	22.1		18.6		26.0				31.2		4.7		22.3	35.0	26.0
(236)	6.0	(227)	5.8	(214)	6.2	EBIT/Interest	(13)	5.6	(12)	2.9	(33)	5.0	(54)	6.8	(98) 9.1
	2.3		2.2		2.3				2.4		.5		1.5	2.5	2.8

						Net Profit + Depr., Dep., Amort./Cur. Mat. L/T/D								
	11.1		11.3		16.4								29.0	15.2
(40)	1.5	(49)	3.5	(42)	2.6	Net Profit + Depr., Dep., Amort./Cur. Mat. L/T/D					(13)	3.1	(23) 3.9
	.2		1.0		1.1								1.1	1.4

						Fixed/Worth						
	.0		.0		.0			.0	.0	.0	.1	.0
	.3		.2		.2	Fixed/Worth		.1	.2	.1	.2	.2
	1.0		.9		.9			.6	1.6	-5.9	.8	.8

						Debt/Worth						
	1.1		1.0		.9			.4	1.6	1.0	.8	.9
	2.9		2.3		2.1	Debt/Worth		2.0	2.7	2.0	1.7	2.2
	12.1		5.4		7.7			UND	5.8	-24.3	6.4	7.5

						% Profit Before Taxes/Tangible Net Worth								
	78.9		62.5		61.2				76.5		80.2	68.7	59.8	56.6
(213)	35.4	(233)	27.3	(222)	26.8	% Profit Before Taxes/Tangible Net Worth	(13)	53.0	(17)	19.5	(29)	21.7	(52) 27.6	(104) 27.3
	10.4		11.1		10.2				6.8		9.8	5.3	10.5	10.4

						% Profit Before Taxes/Total Assets						
	18.1		16.4		19.1			28.3	18.0	23.2	18.6	19.5
	7.5		6.8		7.4	% Profit Before Taxes/Total Assets		8.3	6.7	6.0	8.1	7.8
	1.9		2.5		2.2			2.3	1.1	2.3	2.1	2.8

						Sales/Net Fixed Assets						
	245.5		275.0		236.5			355.9	UND	571.1	186.0	183.9
	68.8		66.5		80.9	Sales/Net Fixed Assets		129.6	87.9	85.5	66.5	76.2
	23.1		19.4		23.8			21.6	8.7	32.0	24.2	19.7

						Sales/Total Assets						
	4.3		4.0		4.2			6.5	5.0	4.0	4.5	4.0
	3.0		2.8		3.0	Sales/Total Assets		3.0	3.2	3.0	3.1	3.0
	1.8		1.9		1.8			2.1	1.3	1.6	2.1	1.9

						% Depr., Dep., Amort./Sales								
	.2		.2		.2				.2		.1	.1	.1	
(187)	.5	(176)	.5	(192)	.4	% Depr., Dep., Amort./Sales		(12)	.6	(26)	.3	(49) .4	(94) .4
	1.4		1.5		1.0				4.0		.8	.9	1.0	

						% Officers', Directors' Owners' Comp/Sales								
	1.1		1.0		1.0				3.5		1.7	.7	.3	
(88)	2.1	(95)	2.2	(99)	2.1	% Officers', Directors' Owners' Comp/Sales	(10)	4.3		(24) 3.3	(26) 1.8	(28) 1.2	
	4.4		4.3		3.7				6.5		5.7	3.4	1.9	

16340606M		17515127M		16373464M		Net Sales ($)		4416M	34673M	68980M	298247M	1118194M	14848954M
6330924M		6158936M		6527525M		Total Assets ($)		3156M	15432M	35976M	136447M	493552M	5842962M

© RMA 2011

M = $ thousand   MM = $ million

See Pages 9 through 22 for Explanation of Ratios and Data

Current Data Sorted by Assets | Comparative Historical Data

Date-range groupings for current data: **39 (4/1-9/30/10)** · **169 (10/1/10-3/31/11)**

Type of Statement	0-500M	500M-2MM	2-10MM	10-50MM	50-100MM	100-250MM	4/1/06-3/31/07 ALL	4/1/07-3/31/08 ALL
Unqualified	1	9	1	8	4		25	15
Reviewed			36	15			48	51
Compiled	1	10	16	3			26	30
Tax Returns	14	10	11	3			20	26
Other	4	18	23	18	3		46	46
NUMBER OF STATEMENTS	20	47	87	47	7		165	168

M = $ thousand   MM = $ million

	0-500M %	500M-2MM %	2-10MM %	10-50MM %	50-100MM %	100-250MM %	ALL %	ALL %
ASSETS								
Cash & Equivalents	20.9	12.6	6.2	6.2			8.3	7.9
Trade Receivables (net)	21.0	31.6	29.3	25.9			30.7	30.5
Inventory	33.2	34.1	43.2	45.6			37.2	39.7
All Other Current	2.7	7.9	1.9	4.5			3.8	3.0
Total Current	77.8	86.1	80.6	82.1			80.0	81.2
Fixed Assets (net)	14.1	3.7	8.9	9.1			10.3	8.6
Intangibles (net)	5.9	4.0	3.9	3.6			3.1	3.1
All Other Non-Current	2.2	6.2	6.7	5.2			6.6	7.1
Total	100.0	100.0	100.0	100.0			100.0	100.0
LIABILITIES								
Notes Payable-Short Term	11.3	15.9	14.5	19.9			16.7	17.1
Cur. Mat.-L.T.D.	6.6	3.4	2.3	1.9			1.9	1.6
Trade Payables	21.0	24.5	22.1	17.4			21.6	19.3
Income Taxes Payable	.1	.2	.1	.1			.3	.1
All Other Current	10.0	7.6	5.0	8.2			8.7	7.0
Total Current	49.0	51.5	44.1	47.5			49.2	45.1
Long-Term Debt	17.3	10.1	7.4	6.2			7.5	6.4
Deferred Taxes	.0	.0	.1	.4			.1	.2
All Other Non-Current	6.3	7.9	10.5	3.0			5.3	7.2
Net Worth	27.4	30.5	37.9	43.0			37.9	41.1
Total Liabilities & Net Worth	100.0	100.0	100.0	100.0			100.0	100.0
INCOME DATA								
Net Sales	100.0	100.0	100.0	100.0			100.0	100.0
Gross Profit	40.2	35.1	28.8	27.8			30.4	30.4
Operating Expenses	34.4	30.7	25.0	23.0			26.0	26.6
Operating Profit	5.8	4.3	3.9	4.8			4.3	3.8
All Other Expenses (net)	.8	.3	.4	.5			1.0	.9
Profit Before Taxes	5.0	4.0	3.5	4.2			3.4	2.8

(Column 50-100MM and 100-250MM: **DATA NOT AVAILABLE**)

RATIOS

Ratio	0-500M	500M-2MM	2-10MM	10-50MM	ALL	ALL
Current	3.7	3.3	3.6	2.4	2.7	2.9
	1.4	1.8	1.8	1.6	1.7	1.6
	.9	1.1	1.3	1.3	1.2	1.3
Quick	2.2	1.8	1.5	1.3	1.3	1.3
	1.0	.8	.7	.6	.8	.9
	.3	.5	.4	.4	.5	.5
Sales/Receivables	0 UND	16 23.2	23 16.1	26 14.1	22 16.3	26 14.0
	13 28.1	38 9.5	44 8.4	38 9.5	42 8.6	41 8.8
	30 12.3	62 5.9	66 5.5	56 6.5	64 5.7	57 6.4
Cost of Sales/Inventory	2 198.1	20 18.0	50 7.3	62 5.9	38 9.6	42 8.6
	22 16.5	53 6.9	97 3.8	113 3.2	80 4.5	86 4.2
	97 3.8	136 2.7	147 2.5	138 2.7	144 2.5	149 2.4
Cost of Sales/Payables	4 91.5	14 27.0	19 19.5	17 20.9	15 23.8	16 22.7
	16 22.6	29 12.4	41 9.0	32 11.4	37 9.9	33 11.0
	58 6.3	60 6.1	64 5.7	48 7.6	64 5.7	55 6.6
Sales/Working Capital	6.6	3.8	3.6	4.6	4.5	4.0
	34.7	7.9	6.7	7.3	8.4	7.1
	NM	100.9	16.8	13.0	21.8	18.3
EBIT/Interest	16.3	12.2	22.8	22.2	9.3	7.0
	(15) 2.9	(36) 5.0	(80) 5.2	6.1	(147) 3.5	(145) 2.8
	1.6	1.7	1.7	2.8	1.2	1.2
Net Profit + Depr., Dep., Amort./Cur. Mat. L/T/D				10.2	13.8	21.2
				(12) 2.4	(20) 4.4	(17) 3.0
				1.0	.6	2.1
Fixed/Worth	.0	.0	.0	.0	.0	.0
	.1	.1	.1	.2	.1	.1
	7.6	.3	.5	.4	.5	.4
Debt/Worth	.6	1.0	.7	.9	.8	.5
	2.9	1.9	1.7	1.8	1.8	1.7
	NM	9.4	4.9	2.8	4.1	4.5
% Profit Before Taxes/Tangible Net Worth	91.9	51.4	43.1	45.6	40.8	33.7
	(15) 38.5	(38) 28.3	(77) 22.2	(46) 20.7	(150) 15.6	(153) 14.1
	21.8	10.5	10.4	8.7	4.9	2.2
% Profit Before Taxes/Total Assets	29.1	18.0	13.8	17.4	14.9	13.1
	14.6	7.7	7.5	6.7	5.4	5.0
	4.1	2.9	1.9	2.2	.9	.9
Sales/Net Fixed Assets	UND	860.5	347.1	170.0	241.0	302.7
	160.3	242.0	105.4	43.7	69.9	68.8
	28.6	45.6	34.2	20.6	20.2	23.2
Sales/Total Assets	5.9	4.1	3.2	3.0	3.2	3.3
	4.7	3.0	2.3	2.2	2.4	2.4
	2.9	1.9	1.9	1.7	1.8	1.7
% Depr., Dep., Amort./Sales		.1	.1	.1	.2	.2
		(25) .3	(60) .3	(38) .6	(130) .4	(116) .4
		.7	1.0	.9	1.2	1.1
% Officers', Directors' Owners' Comp/Sales	2.9	1.7	.9	1.0	1.8	2.2
	(10) 6.9	(24) 3.8	(42) 2.4	(19) 1.7	(89) 3.3	(90) 4.0
	11.0	6.6	5.3	8.1	5.2	6.5

	0-500M	500M-2MM	2-10MM	10-50MM	50-100MM		ALL	ALL
Net Sales ($)	26354M	185805M	1131284M	2645881M	976566M		4115955M	6295508M
Total Assets ($)	5656M	56630M	446033M	981955M	503962M		1868694M	2559889M

Comparative Historical Data | Current Data Sorted by Sales

	Hist 1	Hist 2	Hist 3	Type of Statement	0-1MM	1-3MM	3-5MM	5-10MM	10-25MM	25MM & OVER
	18	22	13	Unqualified		1	5	13	2	11
	55	44	61	Reviewed		7	6	10	28	14
	30	24	30	Compiled		15	2	5	5	2
	25	37	38	Tax Returns	5	6	7	3		
	52	48	66	Other	3	11	2	9	12	22
	4/1/08-3/31/09 ALL	4/1/09-3/31/10 ALL	4/1/10-3/31/11 ALL		__ 39 (4/1-9/30/10) __			__ 169 (10/1/10-3/31/11) __		
	180	175	208	NUMBER OF STATEMENTS	8	34	22	38	54	52
	%	%	%	ASSETS	%	%	%	%	%	%
	10.0	9.9	8.9	Cash & Equivalents		15.2	9.5	6.4	7.2	6.2
	27.1	29.8	28.3	Trade Receivables (net)		29.2	28.5	28.2	27.5	31.7
	42.7	41.2	40.2	Inventory		30.9	37.2	41.0	45.9	42.8
	3.3	3.5	4.3	All Other Current		4.1	2.7	3.7	3.3	4.3
	83.2	84.4	81.7	Total Current		79.4	78.0	79.2	83.9	84.9
	8.4	6.6	8.4	Fixed Assets (net)		6.3	13.2	8.4	7.0	7.6
	2.4	3.4	4.3	Intangibles (net)		8.2	5.2	3.5	3.0	3.7
	6.0	5.6	5.7	All Other Non-Current		6.0	3.6	8.9	6.1	3.7
	100.0	100.0	100.0	Total		100.0	100.0	100.0	100.0	100.0
				LIABILITIES						
	18.9	17.6	15.6	Notes Payable-Short Term		15.2	9.4	16.5	17.4	16.1
	2.2	3.1	2.8	Cur. Mat.-L.T.D.		7.4	1.6	2.4	1.7	1.9
	17.2	20.1	21.3	Trade Payables		19.3	22.5	21.1	20.5	24.9
	.1	.1	.2	Income Taxes Payable		.2	.1	.3	.1	.1
	9.2	9.3	7.4	All Other Current		9.5	4.0	6.0	7.5	7.2
	47.7	50.2	47.3	Total Current		51.6	37.7	46.4	47.2	50.2
	7.8	7.6	8.7	Long-Term Debt		17.3	13.0	5.9	3.1	7.7
	.1	.2	.1	Deferred Taxes		.0	.0	.0	.3	.3
	5.6	8.8	7.5	All Other Non-Current		9.4	9.2	12.0	7.0	2.9
	38.9	33.2	36.3	Net Worth		21.7	40.1	35.6	42.4	39.0
	100.0	100.0	100.0	Total Liabilities & Net Worth		100.0	100.0	100.0	100.0	100.0
				INCOME DATA						
	100.0	100.0	100.0	Net Sales		100.0	100.0	100.0	100.0	100.0
	32.0	31.7	31.1	Gross Profit		40.8	36.7	28.3	28.7	25.2
	28.9	27.9	26.7	Operating Expenses		36.4	31.5	25.2	24.0	20.9
	3.2	3.8	4.4	Operating Profit		4.3	5.3	3.1	4.7	4.3
	.9	.7	.5	All Other Expenses (net)		.3	1.4	-.3	.7	.4
	2.3	3.0	3.9	Profit Before Taxes		4.1	3.8	3.5	4.0	3.9
				RATIOS						
	2.8	3.0	3.2	Current		3.7	4.4	3.2	3.3	2.3
	1.7	1.7	1.7			1.5	2.4	1.6	1.8	1.6
	1.3	1.2	1.2			.9	1.6	1.1	1.3	1.3
	1.2	1.4	1.4	Quick		2.4	2.3	1.4	1.4	1.3
	.7	.8	.7			.9	.9	.6	.7	.8
	.4	.4	.4			.4	.5	.4	.4	.4
	22 16.6	26 14.2	19 18.8	Sales/Receivables	12 30.3	18 20.7	18 20.5	28 12.9	25 14.6	
	40 9.2	40 9.1	37 9.9		31 11.7	37 9.9	42 8.7	42 8.8	37 10.0	
	59 6.2	62 5.9	58 6.3		51 7.1	63 5.8	63 5.8	62 5.9	56 6.5	
	47 7.8	48 7.5	37 9.8	Cost of Sales/Inventory	15 24.1	41 9.0	31 11.9	55 6.6	45 8.1	
	101 3.6	94 3.9	86 4.2		67 5.5	137 2.7	84 4.3	101 3.6	76 4.8	
	157 2.3	147 2.5	135 2.7		116 3.1	185 2.0	144 2.5	138 2.6	123 3.0	
	15 25.0	18 20.8	16 22.6	Cost of Sales/Payables	7 55.8	12 29.4	17 21.3	15 24.8	22 16.6	
	29 12.6	34 10.9	31 11.8		26 14.2	37 9.8	28 12.8	29 12.7	36 10.1	
	51 7.2	53 6.9	57 6.4		53 6.9	65 5.6	49 7.4	49 7.4	59 6.2	
	3.8	3.9	4.2	Sales/Working Capital		3.7	3.0	4.2	4.3	5.0
	7.3	7.1	7.9			10.0	5.7	8.2	7.2	8.5
	15.5	16.5	24.6			-55.2	-12.4	37.0	18.1	17.5
	6.3	13.4	19.7	EBIT/Interest		13.0	11.8	14.6	32.8	21.4
	(153) 2.8	(151) 2.8	(184) 5.0			(26) 2.6	(18) 4.3	(33) 4.4	(50) 7.4	(50) 7.9
	.6	1.3	1.9			1.2	1.8	1.7	1.8	3.2
	7.3	2.6	14.0	Net Profit + Depr., Dep., Amort./Cur. Mat. L/T/D						46.0
	(22) 2.5	(19) 1.7	(22) 3.0						(11)	2.5
	.4	-.3	1.0							1.0
	.0	.0	.0	Fixed/Worth		.0	.0	.0	.0	.0
	.1	.1	.1			.1	.1	.1	.1	.1
	.4	.4	.5			-.4	1.0	.4	.3	.4
	.8	.8	.9	Debt/Worth		.7	.6	1.0	.7	1.0
	1.8	2.0	1.9			4.2	2.0	1.9	1.6	1.7
	3.6	4.7	4.7			-5.3	9.8	5.0	3.1	3.1
	33.3	39.8	47.3	% Profit Before Taxes/Tangible Net Worth		50.1	51.9	48.0	39.3	49.4
	(165) 13.5	(153) 15.3	(181) 22.3			(22) 23.2	(19) 30.8	(33) 20.8	(51) 19.6	(49) 24.2
	1.6	2.3	10.2			13.3	4.3	6.4	10.1	12.6
	10.5	13.5	17.3	% Profit Before Taxes/Total Assets		18.2	16.4	13.5	16.5	17.4
	4.4	4.3	7.7			8.6	5.0	7.5	7.4	8.7
	.3	.8	2.2			2.4	1.4	1.5	1.8	3.5
	365.5	440.0	433.3	Sales/Net Fixed Assets		587.2	999.8	565.3	174.0	274.8
	74.3	76.9	108.4			134.3	243.5	163.2	80.4	64.8
	20.4	32.0	29.3			32.0	8.0	41.7	35.3	24.2
	3.1	3.2	3.5	Sales/Total Assets		5.0	3.3	3.2	3.2	4.1
	2.3	2.2	2.4			2.9	2.0	2.3	2.3	2.4
	1.6	1.7	1.8			1.9	1.2	1.9	1.9	2.0
	.2	.2	.1	% Depr., Dep., Amort./Sales		.2	.2	.1	.1	.1
	(133) .4	(129) .4	(136) .4			(19) .3	(13) .6	(25) .3	(39) .4	(39) .4
	.9	1.0	.8			.8	3.0	.6	.8	.9
	1.7	1.6	1.3	% Officers', Directors' Owners' Comp/Sales		2.4	1.5	1.6	.7	.7
	(93) 3.4	(89) 3.4	(97) 2.5			(16) 5.4	(15) 4.1	(24) 3.4	(21) 1.2	(19) 2.0
	6.9	7.0	6.3			8.1	4.7	5.2	3.4	8.1
	4951055M	4640146M	4965890M	Net Sales ($)	4667M	65882M	85514M	260173M	854090M	3695564M
	1976343M	1971063M	1994236M	Total Assets ($)	3002M	25602M	48669M	116336M	458880M	1341747M

M = $ thousand   MM = $ million
See Pages 9 through 22 for Explanation of Ratios and Data

Current Data Sorted by Assets   Comparative Historical Data

1	1	5	19	4	3	Type of Statement		
	8	25	13		1	Unqualified	23	26
2	4	7	2			Reviewed	39	36
4	7	9	1			Compiled	18	9
1	9	21	28	3	3	Tax Returns	11	8
						Other	35	42
	20 (4/1-9/30/10)		161 (10/1/10-3/31/11)				4/1/06-3/31/07	4/1/07-3/31/08
0-500M	500M-2MM	2-10MM	10-50MM	50-100MM	100-250MM		ALL	ALL
8	29	67	63	8	6	NUMBER OF STATEMENTS	126	121
%	%	%	%	%	%	ASSETS	%	%
	8.9	8.9	5.4			Cash & Equivalents	7.1	8.5
	33.5	30.2	33.7			Trade Receivables (net)	31.3	32.7
	34.7	41.0	41.0			Inventory	41.2	39.6
	6.1	5.6	4.0			All Other Current	2.9	4.4
	83.3	85.7	84.2			Total Current	82.6	85.2
	8.1	7.3	7.7			Fixed Assets (net)	10.1	7.1
	3.5	2.3	4.5			Intangibles (net)	2.5	2.8
	5.1	4.7	3.6			All Other Non-Current	4.7	4.9
	100.0	100.0	100.0			Total	100.0	100.0
						LIABILITIES		
	14.7	13.9	21.6			Notes Payable-Short Term	20.6	20.7
	5.2	1.4	1.8			Cur. Mat.-L.T.D.	1.2	2.1
	21.7	17.1	16.7			Trade Payables	17.3	17.1
	.0	.2	.4			Income Taxes Payable	.2	.2
	16.2	16.9	10.5			All Other Current	7.2	7.6
	57.8	49.5	51.0			Total Current	46.5	47.6
	5.4	5.2	4.3			Long-Term Debt	5.8	5.4
	.0	.0	.1			Deferred Taxes	.1	.1
	16.7	9.4	4.6			All Other Non-Current	7.0	6.2
	20.1	35.9	40.0			Net Worth	40.6	40.7
	100.0	100.0	100.0			Total Liabilities & Net Worth	100.0	100.0
						INCOME DATA		
	100.0	100.0	100.0			Net Sales	100.0	100.0
	34.4	30.1	31.9			Gross Profit	32.4	30.0
	31.7	26.8	25.3			Operating Expenses	28.2	26.3
	2.8	3.3	6.6			Operating Profit	4.2	3.8
	1.0	.8	.5			All Other Expenses (net)	.9	1.0
	1.7	2.5	6.2			Profit Before Taxes	3.3	2.8
						RATIOS		
	5.7	3.3	2.1				2.9	3.2
	1.7	2.2	1.6			Current	1.8	1.8
	1.1	1.4	1.3				1.2	1.3
	2.1	1.5	1.0				1.4	1.5
	1.0	.9	.7			Quick	.8	.9
	.4	.5	.6				.4	.5
	25 14.7	29 12.7	28 13.0				29 12.6	30 12.1
	42 8.8	43 8.5	53 6.9			Sales/Receivables	47 7.8	39 9.3
	48 7.6	60 6.1	76 4.8				64 5.7	68 5.4
	22 16.4	48 7.7	67 5.5				48 7.6	44 8.2
	61 6.0	88 4.2	125 2.9			Cost of Sales/Inventory	96 3.8	97 3.7
	147 2.5	151 2.4	166 2.2				150 2.4	146 2.5
	5 80.2	10 37.9	19 19.5				16 23.0	11 32.9
	25 14.4	22 16.8	34 10.7			Cost of Sales/Payables	31 11.8	23 16.2
	59 6.2	54 6.7	59 6.2				51 7.2	53 6.9
	5.0	3.4	4.3				3.9	3.8
	9.6	6.0	7.5			Sales/Working Capital	6.6	7.2
	34.0	12.7	11.4				18.6	13.2
	9.2	23.5	19.3				10.4	6.3
	(19) 3.4	(60) 4.6	(53) 10.2			EBIT/Interest	(111) 3.1	(110) 2.5
	.1	1.6	4.1				1.4	1.3
			85.5			Net Profit + Depr., Dep.,	16.0	12.5
		(16) 16.8				Amort./Cur. Mat. L/T/D	(25) 4.9	(19) 8.5
			5.6				2.6	1.4
	.0	.0	.0				.0	.0
	.1	.0	.1			Fixed/Worth	.1	.1
	.5	.2	.5				.4	.4
	.2	.5	.8				.5	.5
	1.5	1.3	1.6			Debt/Worth	1.5	1.5
	6.4	4.4	3.6				4.2	4.1
	48.9	43.2	59.1			% Profit Before Taxes/Tangible	37.9	34.1
	(23) 16.9	(61) 20.2	(59) 33.9			Net Worth	(116) 15.8	(109) 13.6
	2.1	2.5	8.6				3.9	1.5
	18.2	16.6	21.0			% Profit Before Taxes/Total	13.2	14.2
	6.4	5.0	12.4			Assets	6.3	5.4
	-2.1	1.2	3.0				1.3	.4
	UND	536.7	204.0				159.7	167.6
	71.3	100.1	78.3			Sales/Net Fixed Assets	56.2	88.9
	30.2	29.2	18.1				20.1	28.0
	4.2	3.2	2.9				3.1	3.1
	2.7	2.4	2.1			Sales/Total Assets	2.4	2.3
	1.7	1.6	1.7				1.7	1.8
	.4	.1	.2				.3	.2
	(17) 1.1	(45) .3	(50) .4			% Depr., Dep., Amort./Sales	(103) .5	(98) .4
	1.6	.8	1.5				.9	.8
	1.9	1.6	.5				1.5	1.6
	(12) 3.2	(24) 2.9	(16) 1.8			% Officers', Directors' Owners' Comp/Sales	(57) 3.2	(54) 3.1
	7.6	4.5	2.6				6.3	5.1
5524M	123334M	769095M	3272981M	1188009M	1329709M	Net Sales ($)	4639333M	6052756M
1855M	34742M	312280M	1438416M	587901M	765972M	Total Assets ($)	2390595M	2790167M

Comparative Historical Data			Type of Statement	Current Data Sorted by Sales					
32	34	33	Unqualified		2		3	2	26
51	52	47	Reviewed		3	5	15	16	8
16	11	15	Compiled	2	5	2		5	1
15	17	21	Tax Returns	6	3	3	3	4	2
50	46	65	Other	2	3	6	8	17	29
4/1/08-3/31/09 ALL	4/1/09-3/31/10 ALL	4/1/10-3/31/11 ALL		20 (4/1-9/30/10)			161 (10/1/10-3/31/11)		
				0-1MM	1-3MM	3-5MM	5-10MM	10-25MM	25MM & OVER
164	160	181	NUMBER OF STATEMENTS	10	16	16	29	44	66
%	%	%	ASSETS	%	%	%	%	%	%
8.6	11.3	7.9	Cash & Equivalents	13.5	9.4	5.2	11.3	7.6	5.9
30.0	29.8	31.3	Trade Receivables (net)	18.8	23.6	31.5	26.0	36.3	34.0
43.2	36.3	39.4	Inventory	46.0	40.2	36.6	41.9	36.8	39.5
3.1	4.4	5.0	All Other Current	.0	10.9	5.5	8.5	3.2	4.0
84.9	81.8	83.6	Total Current	78.4	84.1	78.7	87.7	83.8	83.4
7.2	8.9	7.6	Fixed Assets (net)	10.8	7.2	16.3	4.2	6.6	7.4
2.7	3.0	4.2	Intangibles (net)	9.5	.2	2.4	3.1	4.0	5.4
5.2	6.3	4.6	All Other Non-Current	1.3	8.5	2.6	5.0	5.5	3.8
100.0	100.0	100.0	Total	100.0	100.0	100.0	100.0	100.0	100.0
			LIABILITIES						
18.7	16.7	16.6	Notes Payable-Short Term	18.0	13.5	10.4	13.1	19.9	18.1
2.2	1.8	2.1	Cur. Mat.-L.T.D.	2.1	6.7	4.2	1.6	.5	1.9
17.0	16.7	17.5	Trade Payables	15.7	20.3	12.4	15.2	18.9	18.5
.1	.1	.4	Income Taxes Payable	.5	.8	.0	.0	.4	.4
8.4	10.8	14.9	All Other Current	29.4	4.9	29.0	14.6	16.7	10.5
46.4	46.2	51.5	Total Current	65.7	46.1	56.1	44.6	56.4	49.3
4.9	5.4	4.4	Long-Term Debt	4.0	.8	11.8	3.4	4.4	4.1
.2	.1	.2	Deferred Taxes	.0	.0	.0	.0	.2	.3
6.1	6.6	12.2	All Other Non-Current	72.0	4.9	20.6	8.7	9.8	6.0
42.4	41.6	31.7	Net Worth	-41.7	48.3	11.5	43.3	29.2	40.4
100.0	100.0	100.0	Total Liabilties & Net Worth	100.0	100.0	100.0	100.0	100.0	100.0
			INCOME DATA						
100.0	100.0	100.0	Net Sales	100.0	100.0	100.0	100.0	100.0	100.0
30.6	33.5	31.8	Gross Profit	43.6	39.3	29.1	32.5	27.6	31.4
27.2	29.2	27.0	Operating Expenses	32.6	36.6	32.4	28.2	23.8	24.2
3.5	4.3	4.8	Operating Profit	11.0	2.7	-3.3	4.3	3.8	7.2
.5	.6	.8	All Other Expenses (net)	3.5	.5	.2	1.0	.6	.6
3.0	3.7	4.0	Profit Before Taxes	7.5	2.2	-3.5	3.3	3.2	6.6
			RATIOS						
3.5	4.3	3.2		14.4	6.6	6.0	4.0	2.4	2.8
1.9	1.9	1.8	Current	1.3	1.9	2.5	2.2	1.8	1.7
1.4	1.3	1.3		.8	1.2	1.1	1.4	1.2	1.3
1.5	1.8	1.5		2.2	2.3	3.2	1.7	1.5	1.4
.8	.9	.8	Quick	.8	.6	1.0	.9	.8	.8
.5	.4	.5		.0	.4	.3	.4	.6	.5
24	15.1	25	14.6	25	14.5		0	UND	35	10.5	27	13.6	27	13.7	34	10.8	24	15.5
41	8.9	43	8.5	45	8.1	Sales/Receivables	3	141.6	45	8.1	50	7.4	38	9.7	53	6.8	47	7.7
61	6.0	63	5.8	65	5.6		56	6.5	51	7.1	90	4.1	50	7.3	76	4.8	67	5.5
51	7.1	41	8.9	43	8.5		3	132.7	50	7.3	35	10.5	64	5.7	33	11.0	48	7.7
102	3.6	88	4.2	104	3.5	Cost of Sales/Inventory	126	2.9	132	2.8	111	3.3	89	4.1	84	4.4	105	3.5
160	2.3	138	2.6	156	2.3		324	1.1	296	1.2	152	2.4	171	2.1	136	2.7	153	2.4
10	35.8	12	31.0	11	32.7		0	UND	1	463.6	5	69.6	7	53.1	11	32.9	17	22.1
23	15.6	26	14.0	29	12.4	Cost of Sales/Payables	5	77.3	27	13.5	29	12.4	21	17.1	26	14.3	33	11.0
46	7.9	54	6.8	55	6.6		59	6.1	101	3.6	66	5.6	49	7.5	48	7.6	58	6.3
3.3	3.8	3.7		3.4	2.4	2.6	3.4	4.1	4.6
7.0	6.9	7.1	Sales/Working Capital	69.8	5.2	5.5	4.4	8.0	7.7
14.2	14.9	18.3		-7.5	25.0	753.1	8.1	26.4	12.8
8.9	18.3	18.3			3.6	5.9	24.8	19.6	28.4
(142) 4.0	(137) 5.8	(147) 6.4	EBIT/Interest	(11) 3.1	(12) 2.9	(23) 4.5	(39) 4.8	(57) 10.2
1.3	1.6	1.9		.1	-4.2	2.8	1.5	5.3
26.4	17.5	33.4							25.8
(24) 8.7	(19) 7.0	(26) 7.0	Net Profit + Depr., Dep., Amort./Cur. Mat. L/T/D					(19)	7.2
2.5	1.7	4.2							4.2
.0	.0	.0		.0	.0	.0	.0	.0	.0
.1	.1	.1	Fixed/Worth	2.4	.1	.1	.0	.1	.1
.3	.3	.4		-.1	.3	NM	.1	.5	.5
.6	.4	.6		3.1	.2	.3	.4	.7	.7
1.5	1.1	1.5	Debt/Worth	UND	1.4	1.2	1.3	1.4	1.5
3.6	3.5	5.2		-1.7	4.3	NM	5.6	5.4	3.7
41.8	37.9	54.2			21.4	19.5	43.2	48.8	59.0
(151) 15.5	(146) 15.5	(158) 25.3	% Profit Before Taxes/Tangible Net Worth	(15) 10.7	(12) 7.2	(26) 22.3	(40) 27.3	(60) 33.7
2.8	3.0	7.3		-.9	1.5	3.9	7.8	14.0
13.6	16.5	18.9		59.4	14.7	6.3	20.2	18.7	21.9
5.1	6.6	8.7	% Profit Before Taxes/Total Assets	18.0	4.6	1.6	7.3	6.3	12.5
.8	1.1	1.7		1.8	-2.3	-10.0	2.1	1.4	5.5
225.6	200.2	313.0		UND	UND	314.1	768.3	750.4	205.9
70.0	61.0	91.2	Sales/Net Fixed Assets	UND	38.7	42.1	89.7	107.2	93.8
25.7	23.4	27.6		27.9	16.1	4.2	42.2	22.1	26.3
3.4	3.2	3.2		6.5	2.7	2.8	3.1	3.7	3.1
2.3	2.4	2.2	Sales/Total Assets	2.3	2.0	1.8	2.2	2.4	2.2
1.6	1.7	1.7		1.1	1.2	1.2	1.5	1.9	1.8
.2	.3	.2			.6	.1	.2	.1	.2
(128) .4	(124) .5	(126) .4	% Depr., Dep., Amort./Sales	(10) 1.4	(13) .5	(19) .3	(25) .4	(55) .4
1.0	1.0	1.3		1.8	1.5	.8	.9	1.9
1.7	1.5	1.2						1.2	.2
(69) 3.0	(61) 3.3	(54) 2.5	% Officers', Directors' Owners' Comp/Sales			(15)	2.1	(12) 1.3
5.0	6.6	4.8						3.1	3.3
6184835M	6017797M	6688652M	Net Sales ($)	6177M	34040M	63008M	225669M	742062M	5617696M
2668616M	2782683M	3141166M	Total Assets ($)	3648M	27414M	39015M	114250M	397342M	2559497M

M = $ thousand   MM = $ million
See Pages 9 through 22 for Explanation of Ratios and Data

Current Data Sorted by Assets   Comparative Historical Data

	0-500M	500M-2MM	2-10MM	10-50MM	50-100MM	100-250MM	Type of Statement	4/1/06-3/31/07 ALL	4/1/07-3/31/08 ALL
		3	7	27	9	3	Unqualified	29	26
		16	29	19	1		Reviewed	44	31
		10	4	3			Compiled	10	13
	3	11	11				Tax Returns	21	31
	10	13	30	27	17	7	Other	43	68
		43 (4/1-9/30/10)			217 (10/1/10-3/31/11)				
NUMBER OF STATEMENTS	13	53	81	76	27	10		147	169
ASSETS	%	%	%	%	%	%		%	%
Cash & Equivalents	26.9	12.7	11.9	8.9	4.8	3.1		13.0	9.5
Trade Receivables (net)	17.0	26.1	35.1	31.1	31.7	25.4		30.4	32.6
Inventory	36.4	37.0	33.4	36.4	35.4	27.0		36.0	37.4
All Other Current	1.7	6.6	7.1	5.6	4.2	1.2		4.1	4.5
Total Current	81.9	82.4	87.5	82.0	76.1	56.8		83.6	84.0
Fixed Assets (net)	5.0	9.9	6.0	7.7	6.9	10.3		7.1	8.0
Intangibles (net)	1.1	.5	.9	3.8	11.2	28.7		1.8	2.3
All Other Non-Current	11.8	7.3	5.7	6.6	5.7	4.2		7.5	5.6
Total	100.0	100.0	100.0	100.0	100.0	100.0		100.0	100.0
LIABILITIES									
Notes Payable-Short Term	32.8	17.8	18.1	21.8	23.6	20.0		18.5	22.9
Cur. Mat.-L.T.D.	4.1	1.1	1.0	1.5	10.2	3.5		1.5	1.0
Trade Payables	6.2	23.2	27.3	21.1	17.4	8.3		19.1	18.7
Income Taxes Payable	.0	.0	.6	.1	.1	.0		.3	.2
All Other Current	6.7	15.2	12.0	8.6	12.4	5.6		8.1	8.6
Total Current	49.8	57.2	59.1	53.1	63.8	37.5		47.5	51.4
Long-Term Debt	7.1	5.6	5.5	7.1	4.2	11.1		4.8	7.4
Deferred Taxes	.0	.0	.0	.3	.8	.9		.1	.1
All Other Non-Current	23.6	13.5	3.8	9.7	9.7	7.2		4.8	5.1
Net Worth	19.4	23.7	31.7	29.8	21.5	43.3		42.8	36.0
Total Liabilities & Net Worth	100.0	100.0	100.0	100.0	100.0	100.0		100.0	100.0
INCOME DATA									
Net Sales	100.0	100.0	100.0	100.0	100.0	100.0		100.0	100.0
Gross Profit	49.2	34.7	29.0	30.8	31.1	33.0		33.7	34.0
Operating Expenses	38.1	32.5	24.7	25.3	25.2	23.7		28.8	28.5
Operating Profit	11.1	2.2	4.3	5.5	5.9	9.3		4.9	5.5
All Other Expenses (net)	.6	.5	1.0	.9	1.4	1.6		.6	1.3
Profit Before Taxes	10.5	1.7	3.3	4.6	4.5	7.7		4.3	4.1
RATIOS									
	5.4	3.3	2.3	2.5	1.5	2.1		2.8	3.0
Current	2.7	1.7	1.5	1.4	1.3	1.6		1.8	1.8
	.9	1.2	1.2	1.1	1.1	1.2		1.3	1.3
	2.3	1.5	1.4	1.4	1.0	1.1		1.5	1.4
Quick	1.1	.7	.8	(75) .7	.5	.8		.9	.9
	.2	.4	.4	.5	.4	.6		.5	.5
	0 UND	13 27.6	18 19.8	23 16.0	35 10.5	52 7.0		22 16.3	24 15.5
Sales/Receivables	18 20.2	31 11.8	37 9.9	43 8.5	57 6.4	65 5.6		43 8.4	46 7.9
	32 11.4	48 7.7	56 6.5	63 5.8	75 4.9	75 4.9		63 5.8	68 5.4
	0 UND	34 10.8	23 16.2	39 9.4	56 6.5	70 5.2		39 9.2	46 7.9
Cost of Sales/Inventory	54 6.7	67 5.5	49 7.4	68 5.3	85 4.3	88 4.1		75 4.9	81 4.5
	199 1.8	112 3.3	87 4.2	112 3.3	134 2.7	129 2.8		129 2.8	140 2.6
	0 UND	14 25.8	20 18.3	15 24.0	20 18.0	21 17.3		14 25.8	16 23.2
Cost of Sales/Payables	0 UND	27 13.7	33 11.2	35 10.5	43 8.5	30 12.3		28 13.1	32 11.3
	35 10.6	66 5.6	54 6.8	56 6.5	64 5.7	43 8.6		56 6.5	50 7.3
	2.9	4.7	6.7	5.4	7.9	4.9		3.8	4.3
Sales/Working Capital	7.3	9.7	10.7	9.4	12.1	7.1		7.8	6.9
	NM	24.4	33.0	40.1	37.1	14.7		15.8	16.2
		7.8	18.1	17.3	10.8	14.6		9.0	9.3
EBIT/Interest		(41) 3.1	(63) 5.1	(68) 4.2	(26) 3.3	5.1		(125) 4.4	(148) 3.7
		1.6	1.7	2.0	1.5	4.0		1.9	1.5
				43.7				27.0	60.6
Net Profit + Depr., Dep., Amort./Cur. Mat. L/T/D				(14) 8.2				(22) 5.4	(25) 9.5
				.6				2.8	1.0
	.0	.0	.0	.1	.1	.2		.0	.0
Fixed/Worth	.1	.1	.1	.2	.3	.6		.1	.1
	NM	.5	.5	.7	-.6	NM		.3	.3
	.6	.7	.8	.8	2.1	2.0		.6	.7
Debt/Worth	4.4	1.8	2.1	2.5	3.5	4.2		1.3	1.6
	-5.5	5.4	6.0	10.1	-6.8	NM		3.2	5.3
		36.8	52.0	67.3	96.4			51.8	57.4
% Profit Before Taxes/Tangible Net Worth		(45) 17.3	(70) 25.0	(66) 30.9	(18) 39.9			(139) 19.4	(152) 23.2
		4.8	8.4	9.9	10.6			5.8	5.7
	54.7	12.4	20.4	23.8	22.3	15.0		18.2	18.6
% Profit Before Taxes/Total Assets	31.9	3.0	7.7	8.6	5.0	9.9		8.0	6.4
	2.3	1.4	2.1	1.6	1.5	6.0		2.5	1.3
	UND	824.6	714.4	157.0	112.5	72.1		286.4	269.6
Sales/Net Fixed Assets	75.0	83.7	163.9	68.7	61.1	22.0		91.7	85.5
	41.8	25.2	50.1	36.7	26.8	9.4		29.3	29.0
	4.2	4.2	4.5	3.6	2.6	1.9		3.4	3.2
Sales/Total Assets	2.3	3.0	3.0	2.7	2.0	1.5		2.5	2.4
	1.7	2.1	2.1	2.0	1.5	1.1		1.8	1.7
		.2	.1	.2	.2			.1	.2
% Depr., Dep., Amort./Sales		(29) .3	(48) .4	(61) .4	(18) .4			(109) .4	(127) .4
		.9	.8	.7	.8			.9	.8
		1.6	1.3	.8	.5			1.5	1.8
% Officers', Directors' Owners' Comp/Sales		(19) 2.2	(30) 2.7	(19) 2.4	(10) 1.3			(68) 2.9	(82) 3.0
		5.9	4.3	3.6	2.9			6.2	5.0
Net Sales ($)	15149M	214819M	1445757M	4581371M	3842031M	2661135M		5789653M	7515694M
Total Assets ($)	3115M	65481M	424669M	1642106M	1897767M	1820294M		2680493M	3452492M

M = $ thousand   MM = $ million
See Pages 9 through 22 for Explanation of Ratios and Data

	Comparative Historical Data			Current Data Sorted by Sales					
Type of Statement									
Unqualified	28	47	49		1		4	6	38
Reviewed	31	57	65	1	3	6	12	18	25
Compiled	14	11	17		2	5	3	3	4
Tax Returns	19	43	25	4	3	4	6	4	4
Other	69	60	104	9	8	3	15	16	53
	4/1/08-3/31/09 ALL	4/1/09-3/31/10 ALL	4/1/10-3/31/11 ALL	43 (4/1-9/30/10) 0-1MM	1-3MM	3-5MM	217 (10/1/10-3/31/11) 5-10MM	10-25MM	25MM & OVER
NUMBER OF STATEMENTS	161	218	260	14	17	18	40	47	124
ASSETS	%	%	%	%	%	%	%	%	%
Cash & Equivalents	10.6	12.2	10.8	19.5	16.1	8.6	15.7	12.2	7.4
Trade Receivables (net)	30.2	33.3	30.5	16.7	27.3	23.1	29.8	33.4	32.6
Inventory	36.8	33.0	35.1	28.9	39.8	38.1	35.3	34.0	35.2
All Other Current	4.1	5.1	5.8	1.5	4.4	10.3	7.0	8.6	4.3
Total Current	81.7	83.6	82.2	66.7	87.7	80.1	87.8	88.1	79.5
Fixed Assets (net)	7.0	7.2	7.5	18.1	7.4	12.3	4.2	4.6	7.8
Intangibles (net)	4.0	3.7	3.8	.1	2.1	.1	.8	1.5	6.8
All Other Non-Current	7.2	5.5	6.5	14.9	2.8	7.6	7.1	5.8	6.0
Total	100.0	100.0	100.0	100.0	100.0	100.0	100.0	100.0	100.0
LIABILITIES									
Notes Payable-Short Term	20.7	20.6	20.5	34.7	17.9	11.5	18.6	23.7	19.9
Cur. Mat.-L.T.D.	1.4	2.0	2.4	4.4	.0	2.4	1.2	.6	3.5
Trade Payables	18.6	22.0	21.8	7.1	24.9	16.2	26.2	24.6	21.4
Income Taxes Payable	.1	.1	.2	.0	.0	.0	.0	1.0	.1
All Other Current	9.6	8.9	11.2	6.0	30.0	10.7	10.8	10.5	9.7
Total Current	50.4	53.6	56.1	52.2	72.8	40.8	56.8	60.4	54.7
Long-Term Debt	6.9	5.0	6.1	11.6	3.3	8.1	4.3	6.3	6.2
Deferred Taxes	.2	.2	.2	.0	.0	.0	.0	.0	.5
All Other Non-Current	7.6	10.1	9.2	18.7	16.3	5.9	11.3	6.5	8.0
Net Worth	34.9	31.1	28.3	17.6	7.6	45.2	27.6	26.8	30.6
Total Liabilities & Net Worth	100.0	100.0	100.0	100.0	100.0	100.0	100.0	100.0	100.0
INCOME DATA									
Net Sales	100.0	100.0	100.0	100.0	100.0	100.0	100.0	100.0	100.0
Gross Profit	32.7	31.7	32.1	53.5	38.8	39.8	28.2	27.8	30.5
Operating Expenses	28.6	27.0	27.2	38.5	37.3	36.0	26.0	24.8	24.5
Operating Profit	4.1	4.7	4.9	15.0	1.4	3.8	2.3	3.0	6.0
All Other Expenses (net)	1.3	1.2	.9	3.2	.3	.7	.6	.9	.9
Profit Before Taxes	2.7	3.5	4.0	11.8	1.1	3.1	1.6	2.1	5.1
RATIOS									
Current	2.6	2.8	2.6	3.6	4.3	3.9	3.0	2.3	2.2
	1.7	1.7	1.5	1.0	1.9	2.0	1.6	1.4	1.4
	1.2	1.2	1.2	.5	1.0	1.5	1.2	1.1	1.2
Quick	1.6	1.6	1.2	1.3	1.8	1.6	1.9	1.4	1.2
	.8	.8	(259) .7	.7	.6	.8	.7	(123) .7	.7
	.5	.6	.5	.3	.3	.3	.4	.4	.5
Sales/Receivables	24　15.3	22　16.2	19　19.3	0　UND	14　25.6	18　19.8	11　32.4	24　15.2	23　15.9
	41　9.0	41　8.8	41　8.8	25　14.7	34　10.7	31　11.8	32　11.5	48　7.7	45　8.1
	56　6.5	63　5.8	60　6.1	60　6.1	60　6.1	46　8.0	47　7.8	72　5.1	65　5.6
Cost of Sales/Inventory	38　9.6	30　12.1	33　11.1	0　UND	39　9.3	49　7.4	15　24.6	30　12.0	36　10.0
	75　4.8	57　6.4	65　5.6	32　11.5	108　3.4	82　4.5	46　8.0	63　5.8	65　5.6
	131　2.8	91　4.0	111　3.3	338　1.1	171　2.1	114　3.2	93　3.9	107　3.4	102　3.6
Cost of Sales/Payables	13　28.9	15　24.4	18　20.6	0　UND	12　31.2	6　60.7	16　23.3	27　13.5	19　19.2
	30　12.2	31　11.9	33　11.2	0　UND	51　7.2	23　15.7	27　13.4	40　9.2	34　10.9
	55　6.6	57　6.4	56　6.5	51　7.1	103　3.5	59　6.2	56　6.5	55　6.6	54　6.7
Sales/Working Capital	4.9	5.2	5.7	2.8	3.6	4.7	6.5	6.4	5.7
	8.2	8.9	9.8	UND	7.3	7.7	11.5	8.4	10.9
	18.9	24.4	31.9	-5.8	NM	10.4	25.6	25.4	36.0
EBIT/Interest	8.1	15.2	14.9			4.4	8.8	17.3	17.6
	(141) 2.8	(188) 4.4	(213) 4.2			(15) 2.2	(30) 4.5	(40) 3.2	(112) 5.2
	.9	1.8	1.7			1.6	1.6	1.1	2.9
Net Profit + Depr., Dep., Amort./Cur. Mat. L/T/D	6.5	22.4	19.4						18.9
	(21) 1.7	(28) 2.7	(36) 3.5						(24) 5.4
	.0	.3	.7						1.7
Fixed/Worth	.0	.0	.0	.0	.0	.0	.0	.0	.1
	.1	.1	.1	.2	.2	.1	.1	.1	.2
	.4	.4	.6	NM	.5	.7	.2	.7	.8
Debt/Worth	.6	.7	.9	1.4	.6	.5	1.0	.9	1.0
	1.7	1.9	2.4	3.8	2.3	1.6	1.7	3.1	2.6
	5.0	5.7	8.1	-6.3	-4.3	4.5	7.1	20.9	7.7
% Profit Before Taxes/Tangible Net Worth	52.1	62.8	61.1	60.3	55.0	33.3	46.2	44.2	82.2
	(142) 18.4	(191) 27.0	(215) 29.2	(10) 29.5	(12) 16.6	(35) 9.4	(37) 23.7	(103) 18.5	43.0
	1.3	8.4	7.7	15.0	4.9	3.0	6.6	3.7	17.1
% Profit Before Taxes/Total Assets	16.9	20.4	19.1	36.0	13.4	6.1	15.4	16.4	24.4
	5.2	7.8	7.0	5.5	2.5	3.7	6.1	4.7	10.1
	-.2	1.7	1.9	2.4	-7.9	1.8	1.6	.3	3.4
Sales/Net Fixed Assets	191.4	438.7	279.8	UND	360.2	270.7	999.8	645.8	182.1
	73.1	114.8	85.8	50.7	62.8	47.5	212.8	94.5	75.7
	30.2	40.9	34.1	7.5	32.2	14.5	59.2	45.3	34.3
Sales/Total Assets	3.8	3.9	3.8	2.2	3.1	3.4	4.5	4.1	4.1
	2.6	2.8	2.7	1.5	2.7	3.0	3.4	2.7	2.7
	1.8	1.9	1.9	1.1	1.6	2.2	2.1	1.8	1.9
% Depr., Dep., Amort./Sales	.2	.2	.2			.2	.1	.3	.2
	(111) .4	(143) .4	(165) .4			(12) .7	(22) .3	(30) .5	(89) .4
	1.0	.8	.8			1.0	.6	.8	.8
% Officers', Directors' Owners' Comp/Sales	1.4	1.0	1.2				1.8	1.3	.6
	(65) 3.1	(107) 2.5	(85) 2.4				(14) 2.8	(17) 2.9	(35) 1.4
	5.4	5.0	4.0				5.3	4.0	3.3
Net Sales ($)	7810144M	9115726M	12760262M	7609M	31691M	72245M	281306M	793083M	11574328M
Total Assets ($)	3518063M	3625124M	5853432M	8530M	14464M	27495M	99956M	342988M	5359999M

WHOLESALE—Footwear Merchant Wholesalers NAICS 424340

Current Data Sorted by Assets **Comparative Historical Data**

0-500M	500M-2MM	2-10MM	10-50MM	50-100MM	100-250MM	Type of Statement	4/1/06-3/31/07 ALL	4/1/07-3/31/08 ALL
		1		10	5	Unqualified	13	10
1	1	3	21	10		Reviewed	21	27
		2	7	1	1	Compiled	5	9
1	1	5	4			Tax Returns	8	6
1	1	1	15	13	7	Other	30	41
	25 (4/1-9/30/10)			85 (10/1/10-3/31/11)				
3	12	47	34	13	1	**NUMBER OF STATEMENTS**	77	93
%	%	%	%	%	%	**ASSETS**	%	%
	12.0	8.2	9.5	18.5		Cash & Equivalents	11.1	7.3
	21.3	31.6	29.2	22.2		Trade Receivables (net)	33.4	33.0
	53.4	45.0	41.3	33.5		Inventory	39.5	39.4
	2.0	3.4	6.4	6.3		All Other Current	2.8	2.9
	88.6	88.2	86.4	80.6		Total Current	86.9	82.6
	5.3	5.5	7.3	7.7		Fixed Assets (net)	5.4	7.1
	.5	2.2	1.4	5.6		Intangibles (net)	3.0	4.1
	5.6	4.1	4.9	6.2		All Other Non-Current	4.8	6.1
	100.0	100.0	100.0	100.0		Total	100.0	100.0
						LIABILITIES		
	17.3	16.5	23.7	5.7		Notes Payable-Short Term	17.1	20.0
	.0	2.3	.5	.2		Cur. Mat.-L.T.D.	.4	1.0
	15.3	23.7	21.5	25.9		Trade Payables	21.2	15.9
	.0	.3	.3	.1		Income Taxes Payable		.2
	5.7	6.8	12.5	9.7		All Other Current	10.7	8.6
	38.4	49.6	58.6	41.6		Total Current	49.5	45.7
	12.2	2.1	8.7	3.9		Long-Term Debt	3.3	4.5
	.0	.0	.1	1.5		Deferred Taxes	.1	.1
	.4	7.7	5.3	6.8		All Other Non-Current	5.7	4.2
	49.0	40.6	27.4	46.1		Net Worth	41.3	45.6
	100.0	100.0	100.0	100.0		Total Liabilities & Net Worth	100.0	100.0
						INCOME DATA		
	100.0	100.0	100.0	100.0		Net Sales	100.0	100.0
	32.7	33.5	31.4	37.5		Gross Profit	31.9	34.1
	34.1	28.4	26.1	32.4		Operating Expenses	28.7	29.6
	-1.4	5.1	5.3	5.1		Operating Profit	3.2	4.5
	.5	.6	.8	-.1		All Other Expenses (net)	.7	1.0
	-1.9	4.4	4.5	5.2		Profit Before Taxes	2.4	3.5
						RATIOS		
	17.3	3.0	2.0	4.2			3.0	2.8
	2.4	2.0	1.4	2.1		Current	1.9	1.8
	1.5	1.2	1.2	1.4			1.3	1.3
	1.9	1.6	1.1	2.4			1.5	1.5
	.6	.8	.7	1.2		Quick	.9	.9
	.2	.4	.4	.5			.6	.6
	4 83.0	30 12.1	23 15.6	21 17.1			35 10.3	38 9.6
	16 23.2	48 7.6	48 7.7	42 8.6		Sales/Receivables	52 7.1	53 6.9
	50 7.3	73 5.0	63 5.8	53 6.9			72 5.1	75 4.9
	69 5.3	74 4.9	51 7.2	57 6.5			56 6.5	59 6.2
	85 4.3	117 3.1	77 4.7	91 4.0		Cost of Sales/Inventory	88 4.1	95 3.9
	217 1.7	159 2.3	153 2.4	130 2.8			126 2.9	157 2.3
	2 189.4	17 21.6	18 20.1	26 14.3			12 29.4	13 29.0
	13 28.6	47 7.8	36 10.1	85 4.3		Cost of Sales/Payables	27 13.6	34 10.8
	38 9.6	81 4.5	60 6.1	100 3.7			71 5.2	58 6.3
		2.7	3.5	5.1	3.0		3.7	3.8
		9.6	6.0	9.3	5.4	Sales/Working Capital	6.1	6.3
		14.1	19.1	16.5	8.5		12.0	10.9
			9.8	15.8	62.9		5.7	7.4
		(43) 6.6	(32) 4.6	(10) 19.9		EBIT/Interest	(64) 2.3	(85) 3.0
		1.6	2.3	10.0			.7	1.3
						Net Profit + Depr., Dep., Amort./Cur. Mat. L/T/D		75.5
								(14) 8.1
								2.2
	.0	.0	.1	.1			.0	.0
	.1	.1	.1	.2		Fixed/Worth	.1	.1
	.2	.2	.5	.3			.2	.3
	.1	.6	1.2	.5			.4	.5
	1.0	1.3	2.4	1.0		Debt/Worth	1.4	1.3
	6.3	4.5	4.7	2.5			4.1	3.0
	32.8	44.0	74.2	28.8			32.8	36.7
	(10) 6.3	(45) 20.7	(32) 24.3	(11) 16.3		% Profit Before Taxes/Tangible Net Worth	(70) 12.3	(89) 12.9
	-7.8	5.7	9.5	7.7			1.3	4.1
	11.4	17.0	20.2	15.8			14.5	14.1
	1.6	7.6	7.5	10.6		% Profit Before Taxes/Total Assets	4.2	5.3
	-2.7	1.1	2.1	5.2			.2	.9
	UND	424.7	110.7	43.0			265.5	181.4
	115.5	63.0	66.8	34.3		Sales/Net Fixed Assets	86.9	63.8
	42.8	28.4	25.3	20.2			34.8	25.4
	4.2	3.2	3.5	2.7			3.2	3.1
	2.6	2.2	2.5	2.4		Sales/Total Assets	2.3	2.1
	2.1	1.8	1.8	1.6			1.8	1.6
		.2	.3	.7			.2	.2
		(34) .5	(27) .5	(10) 1.1		% Depr., Dep., Amort./Sales	(59) .5	(69) .5
		1.1	.8	1.4			.8	1.1
		1.5					1.7	1.1
		(20) 2.2				% Officers', Directors' Owners' Comp/Sales	(26) 3.9	(38) 2.6
		5.5					12.7	6.8
6737M	39637M	613436M	1810648M	2038703M	229231M	Net Sales ($)	2620222M	3731593M
618M	13526M	239591M	700117M	973740M	223435M	Total Assets ($)	1323369M	2056942M

© RMA 2011

M = $ thousand   MM = $ million

See Pages 9 through 22 for Explanation of Ratios and Data

Comparative Historical Data / Current Data Sorted by Sales

Hist 4/1/08-3/31/09 ALL	Hist 4/1/09-3/31/10 ALL	Hist 4/1/10-3/31/11 ALL	Type of Statement	0-1MM	1-3MM	3-5MM	5-10MM	10-25MM	25MM & OVER
11	18	17	Unqualified			1		1	15
17	31	35	Reviewed		2	3	9	12	9
7	11	11	Compiled			3	4	2	2
11	7	10	Tax Returns		1	1	1	3	2
52	35	37	Other	2	3	3	5	9	20
				25 (4/1-9/30/10)			85 (10/1/10-3/31/11)		
98	102	110	NUMBER OF STATEMENTS	2	6	10	19	27	46
%	%	%	**ASSETS**	%	%	%	%	%	%
7.7	11.9	10.1	Cash & Equivalents			8.6	4.7	6.5	14.2
28.7	32.7	29.0	Trade Receivables (net)			40.9	24.2	32.1	26.9
43.3	35.9	43.0	Inventory			41.5	52.4	44.7	36.5
4.1	4.1	4.5	All Other Current			1.6	1.6	5.6	6.5
83.8	84.5	86.7	Total Current			92.5	83.0	88.8	84.0
7.1	6.6	6.2	Fixed Assets (net)			4.0	5.8	7.2	7.2
4.7	4.2	2.2	Intangibles (net)			.2	2.8	1.9	2.7
4.4	4.7	4.9	All Other Non-Current			3.3	8.4	2.2	6.0
100.0	100.0	100.0	Total			100.0	100.0	100.0	100.0
			LIABILITIES						
18.7	16.4	17.1	Notes Payable-Short Term			8.1	14.3	19.9	17.2
1.6	1.6	1.2	Cur. Mat.-L.T.D.			.0	3.6	1.5	.4
17.1	17.5	22.0	Trade Payables			20.4	19.6	26.4	23.2
.1	.3	.2	Income Taxes Payable			.0	.2	.4	.2
7.8	11.8	8.8	All Other Current			4.0	5.2	8.6	12.2
45.3	47.7	49.3	Total Current			32.4	42.9	56.8	53.2
5.5	5.3	5.5	Long-Term Debt			.0	2.1	3.0	7.1
.2	.2	.2	Deferred Taxes			.0	.0	.0	.5
10.5	5.6	6.4	All Other Non-Current			7.3	6.3	7.3	5.5
38.5	41.1	38.6	Net Worth			60.3	48.7	32.9	33.7
100.0	100.0	100.0	Total Liabilities & Net Worth			100.0	100.0	100.0	100.0
			INCOME DATA						
100.0	100.0	100.0	Net Sales			100.0	100.0	100.0	100.0
32.8	31.6	32.8	Gross Profit			26.6	34.3	33.7	32.9
30.1	27.8	28.3	Operating Expenses			24.1	31.9	27.1	27.5
2.7	3.8	4.4	Operating Profit			2.5	2.5	6.7	5.4
1.0	.4	.6	All Other Expenses (net)			-.2	.4	.9	.6
1.7	3.4	3.9	Profit Before Taxes			2.7	2.0	5.7	4.8
			RATIOS						
3.2	2.9	3.1	Current			13.1	2.9	2.6	2.3
1.9	1.8	1.8				4.6	2.0	1.7	1.7
1.4	1.4	1.3				1.6	1.5	1.1	1.3
1.4	1.8	1.4	Quick			6.2	1.0	1.0	1.3
.8	1.0	.8				1.7	.6	.6	.8
.6	.5	.4				.8	.4	.4	.5
30 12.2	33 11.0	22 16.8	Sales/Receivables		39 9.2	26 14.0	29 12.5	21 17.3	
50 7.3	50 7.3	44 8.3			57 6.3	44 8.3	48 7.6	42 8.7	
65 5.6	69 5.3	61 6.0			77 4.7	62 5.9	60 6.1	56 6.5	
71 5.2	44 8.3	58 6.3	Cost of Sales/Inventory		66 5.5	83 4.4	58 6.3	48 7.6	
103 3.6	91 4.0	92 4.0			103 3.6	137 2.7	103 3.5	77 4.7	
167 2.2	142 2.6	153 2.4			154 2.4	203 1.8	153 2.4	131 2.8	
10 36.7	11 31.9	16 22.7	Cost of Sales/Payables		8 47.0	17 21.9	22 16.7	26 14.3	
28 12.8	30 12.4	38 9.6			17 21.8	39 9.3	52 7.0	41 8.8	
57 6.4	55 6.7	74 4.9			83 4.4	57 6.4	81 4.5	77 4.8	
3.6	3.8	3.8	Sales/Working Capital			2.4	3.8	4.2	4.6
6.0	6.2	7.4				3.0	6.0	6.7	8.7
10.8	15.1	16.1				12.5	12.2	35.9	16.5
7.1	11.2	17.0	EBIT/Interest				6.3	11.9	23.8
(85) 2.6	(88) 4.1	(96) 6.2				(16) 3.4	(26) 7.4	(41) 10.0	
1.5	1.5	1.8					1.2	1.7	2.6
11.7	12.2	21.8	Net Profit + Depr., Dep., Amort./Cur. Mat. L/T/D						
(18) 4.1	(20) 5.3	(18) 5.7							
1.6	2.3	1.5							
.1	.0	.0	Fixed/Worth			.0	.0	.0	.1
.1	.1	.1				.0	.1	.1	.1
.5	.4	.2				.2	.2	.6	.3
.7	.6	.7	Debt/Worth			.2	.3	.9	.9
1.9	1.4	1.5				.6	1.2	2.0	1.6
4.5	4.2	4.5				1.6	3.0	11.2	3.7
34.2	32.5	53.1	% Profit Before Taxes/Tangible Net Worth			22.9	20.7	93.5	53.8
(87) 14.4	(92) 16.6	(102) 19.8				5.7	10.2	(25) 32.1	(42) 22.7
3.6	4.1	6.2				-1.6	.9	10.0	9.9
10.6	14.3	17.1	% Profit Before Taxes/Total Assets			20.8	7.6	22.4	19.2
4.0	5.0	7.6				4.3	4.9	10.5	9.4
.4	.6	1.8				-.6	.2	2.0	3.3
100.6	209.5	199.3	Sales/Net Fixed Assets			UND	87.1	264.1	110.7
47.9	63.9	60.6				80.8	44.7	37.9	54.6
26.7	29.1	27.0				26.9	22.6	27.1	21.1
3.1	3.1	3.3	Sales/Total Assets			2.4	2.7	3.6	3.4
2.2	2.3	2.4				2.2	1.9	2.5	2.6
1.6	1.7	1.9				1.9	1.6	1.9	2.0
.3	.2	.3	% Depr., Dep., Amort./Sales				.1	.4	.3
(78) .5	(81) .5	(78) .6					(14) .5	(21) .5	(35) .7
.9	1.1	1.0					1.0	.8	1.0
.8	1.3	1.9	% Officers', Directors' Owners' Comp/Sales					1.4	
(37) 2.1	(34) 2.4	(31) 2.1						(13) 2.1	
4.8	5.3	5.9						5.1	
4485191M	4569900M	4738392M	Net Sales ($)	1164M	11192M	44070M	136492M	459864M	4085610M
2223321M	2469810M	2151027M	Total Assets ($)	675M	3705M	19661M	72477M	202580M	1851929M

M = $ thousand   MM = $ million
See Pages 9 through 22 for Explanation of Ratios and Data

Current Data Sorted by Assets   Comparative Historical Data

	0-500M	500M-2MM	2-10MM	10-50MM	50-100MM	100-250MM	Type of Statement	4/1/06-3/31/07 ALL	4/1/07-3/31/08 ALL
	1	2	4	37	16	19	Unqualified	81	79
	1	6	31	40			Reviewed	89	71
	5	20	28	10	1		Compiled	83	56
	9	47	35	3			Tax Returns	53	50
	8	20	67	49	10	14	Other	122	128
	103 (4/1-9/30/10)			380 (10/1/10-3/31/11)					
	24	95	165	139	27	33	NUMBER OF STATEMENTS	428	384
	%	%	%	%	%	%	**ASSETS**	%	%
	12.8	9.9	8.9	6.7	6.2	6.5	Cash & Equivalents	7.7	7.7
	18.6	28.5	32.6	30.3	27.6	26.1	Trade Receivables (net)	30.5	29.9
	32.7	32.1	34.2	31.9	25.8	30.6	Inventory	30.8	31.0
	1.0	4.7	2.5	3.8	5.0	3.7	All Other Current	2.7	3.8
	65.1	75.2	78.2	72.7	64.6	66.9	Total Current	71.6	72.5
	25.9	13.9	14.6	18.7	26.2	24.7	Fixed Assets (net)	19.3	18.8
	1.2	5.0	1.8	2.7	2.1	3.2	Intangibles (net)	2.3	2.9
	7.8	5.9	5.4	5.9	7.1	5.1	All Other Non-Current	6.8	5.8
	100.0	100.0	100.0	100.0	100.0	100.0	Total	100.0	100.0
							LIABILITIES		
	14.6	8.2	12.4	16.7	12.4	9.4	Notes Payable-Short Term	14.0	15.0
	1.0	2.6	1.8	1.5	3.8	1.3	Cur. Mat.-L.T.D.	2.9	2.9
	21.2	30.8	24.2	20.6	24.4	23.2	Trade Payables	25.5	23.8
	.1	.0	.2	.1	.6	.3	Income Taxes Payable	.3	.3
	9.9	9.6	9.3	9.6	10.1	10.3	All Other Current	8.9	8.3
	46.9	51.3	47.9	48.5	51.3	44.6	Total Current	51.6	50.4
	27.3	11.8	8.3	10.6	15.4	18.3	Long-Term Debt	13.9	13.0
	.0	.1	.2	.3	.7	.9	Deferred Taxes	.3	.2
	6.0	6.1	7.6	4.4	4.5	4.2	All Other Non-Current	5.4	5.6
	19.9	30.8	36.1	36.2	28.1	32.1	Net Worth	28.8	30.8
	100.0	100.0	100.0	100.0	100.0	100.0	Total Liabilities & Net Worth	100.0	100.0
							INCOME DATA		
	100.0	100.0	100.0	100.0	100.0	100.0	Net Sales	100.0	100.0
	29.5	22.1	17.7	17.4	14.8	12.3	Gross Profit	18.7	18.6
	26.9	20.4	15.6	15.3	13.3	10.2	Operating Expenses	16.6	16.5
	2.6	1.7	2.1	2.1	1.5	2.1	Operating Profit	2.1	2.0
	.7	-.1	.2	.5	.2	.6	All Other Expenses (net)	.4	.4
	1.9	1.8	1.9	1.6	1.3	1.6	Profit Before Taxes	1.8	1.7
							RATIOS		
	3.4	2.7	2.6	2.2	1.5	2.1	Current	2.0	2.2
	1.6	1.5	1.7	1.4	1.2	1.4		1.4	1.4
	.8	1.2	1.2	1.2	1.0	1.2		1.1	1.1
	1.4	1.3	1.5	1.3	.9	1.1	Quick	1.1	1.1
	.7	(94) .8	.8	.7	.5	.7		.7	.7
	.2	.5	.6	.5	.5	.5		.5	.5
	0 UND	2 146.4	15 23.8	15 24.5	10 38.4	9 38.7	Sales/Receivables	12 31.3	13 27.6
	5 73.7	18 20.1	25 14.5	26 14.3	19 19.5	15 25.1		22 16.7	23 16.1
	24 14.9	35 10.5	36 10.1	34 10.9	26 14.0	26 13.9		34 10.6	33 11.0
	9 41.7	12 29.8	17 21.7	18 20.4	16 22.8	15 25.1	Cost of Sales/Inventory	15 25.0	16 22.9
	25 14.7	25 14.5	28 13.2	29 12.8	21 17.5	22 16.9		25 14.4	27 13.5
	47 7.7	45 8.2	49 7.4	48 7.6	26 14.1	29 12.5		40 9.1	43 8.5
	2 235.2	9 38.5	10 34.9	11 34.8	12 30.3	12 29.8	Cost of Sales/Payables	10 35.1	10 35.3
	9 38.9	21 17.1	20 18.2	19 19.7	16 22.6	17 21.1		18 19.8	19 19.2
	41 8.8	44 8.2	30 12.1	31 11.6	31 11.8	22 16.5		35 10.5	34 10.7
	14.0	9.7	8.8	10.3	37.7	15.8	Sales/Working Capital	12.3	11.6
	38.4	21.8	17.3	20.2	54.2	29.4		26.6	25.7
	-46.7	75.8	42.8	57.6	205.4	64.6		87.6	62.4
	9.7	16.6	13.8	12.2	8.5	6.8	EBIT/Interest	9.2	8.5
	(14) 1.4	(73) 4.1	(143) 3.3	(126) 4.5	(26) 4.4	(32) 3.4		(380) 3.0	(346) 2.9
	-1.3	.6	1.4	1.9	2.5	2.0		1.5	1.4
			7.8	11.2	6.5	14.9	Net Profit + Depr., Dep., Amort./Cur. Mat. L/T/D	5.0	7.6
			(29) 2.0	(44) 5.6	(18) 2.7	(13) 3.6		(108) 3.0	(100) 2.4
			1.0	2.5	1.7	2.5		1.3	.9
	.2	.0	.1	.2	.4	.2	Fixed/Worth	.1	.1
	1.2	.3	.3	.5	1.3	.9		.5	.5
	-1.2	1.5	.9	1.3	1.9	1.8		1.4	1.6
	.5	1.0	.9	1.0	1.3	1.4	Debt/Worth	1.1	1.1
	3.8	2.3	1.9	2.6	3.6	2.7		2.4	2.7
	-5.2	11.2	4.3	4.7	6.5	6.6		5.4	6.7
	69.2	47.5	28.5	39.1	38.7	31.0	% Profit Before Taxes/Tangible Net Worth	40.4	41.1
	(16) 31.1	(77) 22.0	(152) 13.2	(135) 21.3	(25) 22.4	(32) 21.0		(384) 18.2	(344) 18.5
	8.0	4.1	3.0	8.3	7.1	8.0		6.7	6.3
	28.3	17.3	10.7	11.3	8.4	8.9	% Profit Before Taxes/Total Assets	11.9	11.0
	8.0	5.2	4.5	6.2	5.2	4.6		4.9	5.2
	-.8	.1	.9	2.4	2.4	2.4		1.5	1.1
	152.1	449.1	227.0	107.3	50.7	95.6	Sales/Net Fixed Assets	128.9	113.6
	56.6	75.7	62.9	31.0	28.7	25.9		42.8	39.5
	13.3	27.8	22.3	14.9	11.7	11.4		14.3	13.7
	11.2	7.8	7.1	6.6	7.1	7.9	Sales/Total Assets	6.9	6.7
	6.2	5.5	4.8	4.5	5.3	5.2		5.1	4.7
	4.0	3.6	2.8	2.7	4.6	4.2		3.5	3.1
	.1	.2	.2	.2	.3	.3	% Depr., Dep., Amort./Sales	.2	.2
	(19) .5	(65) .4	(131) .5	(132) .5	(26) .5	(26) .5		(353) .6	(329) .5
	1.4	1.4	.8	.9	1.2	.7		1.1	1.0
		.8	.6				% Officers', Directors' Owners' Comp/Sales	.5	.6
		(53) 1.5	(80) 1.2	(45) .8				(174) 1.5	(134) 1.5
		3.7	2.2	1.6				2.9	2.8
	51524M	696566M	4038999M	15775556M	11098825M	31801872M	Net Sales ($)	43168750M	44906671M
	6627M	114199M	781172M	2979039M	1904072M	5497398M	Total Assets ($)	8671036M	9537092M

M = $ thousand   MM = $ million
See Pages 9 through 22 for Explanation of Ratios and Data

Comparative Historical Data

Current Data Sorted by Sales

				Type of Statement						
82	82	79		Unqualified	1	1			4	73
90	86	78		Reviewed		2	2	3	15	56
44	67	64		Compiled	1	9	10	12	10	22
73	85	94		Tax Returns	3	8	13	24	36	10
132	136	168		Other	3	6	11	15	34	99
4/1/08- 3/31/09 ALL	4/1/09- 3/31/10 ALL	4/1/10- 3/31/11 ALL				103 (4/1-9/30/10)			380 (10/1/10-3/31/11)	
					0-1MM	1-3MM	3-5MM	5-10MM	10-25MM	25MM & OVER
421	456	483		NUMBER OF STATEMENTS	8	26	36	54	99	260
%	%	%		ASSETS	%	%	%	%	%	%
7.1	8.9	8.3		Cash & Equivalents	7.3	11.3	11.1	9.5	6.8	
31.9	30.1	29.7		Trade Receivables (net)	26.5	24.0	26.2	30.8	31.4	
32.6	30.5	32.3		Inventory	33.2	31.3	33.2	31.0	32.5	
3.2	3.4	3.5		All Other Current	3.6	1.3	4.1	3.5	3.7	
74.8	72.9	73.8		Total Current	70.6	67.9	74.7	74.9	74.4	
17.4	18.7	17.5		Fixed Assets (net)	21.1	19.5	15.5	15.9	17.8	
2.8	3.1	2.8		Intangibles (net)	1.0	4.0	3.4	2.9	2.6	
5.1	5.3	5.9		All Other Non-Current	7.2	8.6	6.4	6.3	5.2	
100.0	100.0	100.0		Total	100.0	100.0	100.0	100.0	100.0	
				LIABILITIES						
15.1	13.6	12.7		Notes Payable-Short Term	5.7	13.8	9.0	9.1	15.5	
2.7	3.0	1.9		Cur. Mat.-L.T.D.	2.2	2.8	3.2	1.3	1.8	
24.0	24.0	24.3		Trade Payables	26.9	24.1	26.0	27.9	22.7	
.2	.3	.2		Income Taxes Payable	.1	.1	.1	.1	.2	
9.1	9.6	9.6		All Other Current	12.0	9.6	6.7	11.2	9.3	
51.1	50.4	48.6		Total Current	47.0	50.4	44.9	49.6	49.6	
12.7	12.7	11.6		Long-Term Debt	25.6	14.9	9.5	9.8	10.5	
.3	.3	.3		Deferred Taxes	.0	.0	.3	.1	.4	
4.4	4.9	5.9		All Other Non-Current	2.8	9.3	11.1	5.2	4.8	
31.4	31.7	33.6		Net Worth	24.5	25.5	34.2	35.3	34.7	
100.0	100.0	100.0		Total Liabilities & Net Worth	100.0	100.0	100.0	100.0	100.0	
				INCOME DATA						
100.0	100.0	100.0		Net Sales	100.0	100.0	100.0	100.0	100.0	
17.4	19.0	18.5		Gross Profit	28.5	26.8	22.4	18.4	15.1	
15.5	17.0	16.5		Operating Expenses	26.2	24.3	20.6	16.1	13.4	
1.9	2.0	2.0		Operating Profit	2.3	2.5	1.8	2.3	1.8	
.3	.3	.3		All Other Expenses (net)	.9	.0	.1	.2	.4	
1.5	1.7	1.7		Profit Before Taxes	1.4	2.5	1.7	2.1	1.4	
				RATIOS						
2.1	2.3	2.4			3.5	2.7	3.1	2.6	2.1	
1.4	1.5	1.5		Current	1.8	1.3	1.7	1.6	1.4	
1.1	1.1	1.2			1.0	1.0	1.2	1.1	1.2	
1.1	1.3	1.3			1.3	1.5	1.4	1.7	1.2	
.7	.8 (482)	.8		Quick	.9	.7 (53)	.8	.9	.7	
.5	.5	.5			.4	.4	.5	.6	.5	

15	24.0	12	30.2	11	31.8			0	UND	3	129.1	7	51.4	15	24.1	12	29.3

Sales/Receivables:

15	24.0	12	30.2	11	31.8		0	UND	3	129.1	7	51.4	15	24.1	12	29.3
24	15.2	23	15.7	23	15.9	Sales/Receivables	26	14.0	23	15.9	22	16.8	26	13.9	22	16.6
35	10.4	34	10.7	33	10.9		57	6.4	46	8.0	38	9.6	36	10.3	29	12.5
16	23.3	15	24.5	15	23.7		27	13.6	6	57.8	15	24.6	14	26.9	16	23.0
27	13.6	26	14.1	26	13.8	Cost of Sales/Inventory	48	7.7	35	10.6	30	12.3	28	13.1	25	14.7
44	8.3	44	8.4	44	8.2		84	4.3	68	5.4	51	7.2	53	6.9	33	11.0
10	37.2	10	35.6	10	36.0		8	47.4	10	37.3	10	36.3	11	33.0	10	36.3
19	19.7	18	19.8	19	19.4	Cost of Sales/Payables	35	10.4	22	16.6	23	16.2	21	17.1	17	21.9
30	12.2	32	11.5	31	11.7		60	6.0	57	6.3	43	8.5	33	10.9	26	14.2

11.0	10.0	10.2		Sales/Working Capital	5.8	8.0	7.2	8.7	12.9	
25.1	22.4	22.1			14.3	20.5	16.9	17.9	27.1	
80.8	72.9	65.0			NM	NM	40.4	72.9	64.7	

	9.0		12.8		12.5			10.2	13.8	16.2	22.6	11.1
(380)	3.6	(400)	4.6	(414)	4.1	EBIT/Interest	(17)	1.5	(27) 1.5	(46) 3.7	(85) 4.7	(235) 4.2
	1.7		1.9		1.6			.1	-1.8	1.7	1.4	1.9

	7.0		8.9		10.6						5.0	10.6
(95)	3.7	(98)	3.2	(107)	3.9	Net Profit + Depr., Dep., Amort./Cur. Mat. L/T/D				(17)	2.7	(81) 4.0
	1.5		1.5		1.9						1.2	2.0

.1	.1	.1		Fixed/Worth	.0	.1	.1	.1	.1	
.4	.4	.4			.3	.5	.4	.3	.5	
1.4	1.5	1.4			NM	NM	1.1	1.1	1.4	
1.3	1.1	.9		Debt/Worth	.4	.8	1.0	.9	1.1	
2.7	2.4	2.4			2.9	2.1	2.4	2.2	2.5	
6.1	6.0	5.2			NM	-30.6	5.5	4.6	5.2	

	42.3		42.2		36.6			43.8	46.9	36.1	36.0	35.1
(378)	19.3	(407)	22.0	(437)	19.2	% Profit Before Taxes/Tangible Net Worth	(20)	23.0	(26) 22.8	(49) 13.2	(89) 14.8	(247) 21.4
	7.2		8.3		5.8			1.5	3.2	4.5	2.7	7.3

11.3	13.4	11.4		% Profit Before Taxes/Total Assets	11.9	18.0	12.5	11.6	10.6	
5.8	6.1	5.3			4.5	3.8	5.0	5.2	5.4	
1.6	2.0	1.5			-4.6	-2.4	1.4	.8	2.2	
152.2	153.8	171.9		Sales/Net Fixed Assets	177.1	131.0	199.3	224.6	166.4	
50.5	47.5	51.0			28.6	32.5	54.3	54.5	49.8	
16.7	14.8	17.0			12.2	13.6	19.2	16.8	18.3	
6.9	6.9	7.2		Sales/Total Assets	4.9	6.0	6.7	7.3	7.8	
5.0	4.7	5.1			3.0	4.3	4.2	4.8	5.4	
3.2	3.0	3.1			1.9	2.3	2.9	2.7	4.0	

	.2		.2		.2			.3	.3	.3	.1	.2
(348)	.5	(371)	.5	(399)	.5	% Depr., Dep., Amort./Sales	(20)	1.1	(26) .7	(43) .6	(77) .5	(227) .4
	.9		1.0		.9			1.7	2.5	1.3	.9	.8

	.8		.6		.6			1.4	.8	.8	.4	.4
(144)	1.6	(169)	1.4	(190)	1.1	% Officers', Directors' Owners' Comp/Sales	(11)	2.6	(19) 1.3	(26) 1.7	(54) 1.2	(79) .8
	2.8		3.2		2.6			4.0	4.3	4.1	2.3	1.6

47154033M	49142349M	63463342M		Net Sales ($)	5246M	49057M	143080M	413730M	1573279M	61278950M
9534459M	10066495M	11282507M		Total Assets ($)	1506M	21328M	48202M	118838M	464513M	10628120M

© RMA 2011

M = $ thousand   MM = $ million
See Pages 9 through 22 for Explanation of Ratios and Data

Current Data Sorted by Assets   Comparative Historical Data

Type of Statement

Type of Statement	0-500M	500M-2MM	2-10MM	10-50MM	50-100MM	100-250MM		4/1/06-3/31/07 ALL	4/1/07-3/31/08 ALL
Unqualified			5	17	6	5		27	30
Reviewed	1		16	8				26	20
Compiled		6	6	3				11	12
Tax Returns	4	9	9	1				9	11
Other		7	19	20	7	2		51	53
	33 (4/1-9/30/10)			118 (10/1/10-3/31/11)					
NUMBER OF STATEMENTS	5	22	55	49	13	7		124	126

Main Data

	0-500M %	500M-2MM %	2-10MM %	10-50MM %	50-100MM %	100-250MM %		4/1/06-3/31/07 ALL %	4/1/07-3/31/08 ALL %
ASSETS									
Cash & Equivalents		11.9	8.2	3.6	1.3			6.4	6.7
Trade Receivables (net)		34.0	34.2	30.8	24.0			32.6	34.5
Inventory		31.1	31.5	35.7	36.9			32.2	30.4
All Other Current		2.5	2.0	3.5	1.7			2.5	2.9
Total Current		79.5	75.9	73.7	63.9			73.7	74.6
Fixed Assets (net)		10.6	15.9	15.1	23.7			16.5	17.9
Intangibles (net)		5.9	3.6	8.4	8.9			4.0	2.1
All Other Non-Current		4.0	4.6	2.9	3.5			5.7	5.4
Total		100.0	100.0	100.0	100.0			100.0	100.0
LIABILITIES									
Notes Payable-Short Term		19.6	16.8	21.7	18.9			20.0	20.6
Cur. Mat.-L.T.D.		1.4	2.5	2.8	5.2			2.8	2.1
Trade Payables		35.4	26.7	20.1	13.6			22.0	24.4
Income Taxes Payable		.1	.1	.3	.0			.3	.1
All Other Current		5.3	6.8	6.9	7.5			7.4	8.7
Total Current		61.6	53.0	51.9	45.2			52.4	56.0
Long-Term Debt		6.9	6.8	9.9	22.8			12.1	12.9
Deferred Taxes		.0	.2	.2	.2			.5	.2
All Other Non-Current		2.2	6.9	6.6	2.4			3.7	8.4
Net Worth		29.2	33.1	31.4	29.3			31.3	22.5
Total Liabilities & Net Worth		100.0	100.0	100.0	100.0			100.0	100.0
INCOME DATA									
Net Sales		100.0	100.0	100.0	100.0			100.0	100.0
Gross Profit		22.2	20.0	16.0	13.0			19.4	19.5
Operating Expenses		19.4	18.0	14.5	10.2			16.7	16.3
Operating Profit		2.8	2.1	1.5	2.9			2.6	3.2
All Other Expenses (net)		-.1	.3	.4	1.0			.4	.8
Profit Before Taxes		2.9	1.8	1.2	1.8			2.2	2.4
RATIOS									
Current		2.6	2.0	1.9	1.9			2.4	2.1
		1.5	1.5	1.3	1.3			1.4	1.3
		1.2	1.0	1.1	1.2			1.1	1.0
Quick		1.7	1.4	.9	.7			1.5	1.2
		.8	.7	.6	.5			.7	.7
		.5	.5	.4	.3			.5	.4
Sales/Receivables		4 85.5	22 16.9	19 19.0	15 24.0			18 20.3	19 18.8
		19 19.0	30 12.3	29 12.7	24 15.5			24 15.5	27 13.6
		36 10.2	38 9.6	37 10.0	35 10.5			36 10.0	40 9.1
Cost of Sales/Inventory		14 26.0	20 18.7	21 17.1	26 14.3			18 20.8	16 22.4
		24 15.3	34 10.7	34 10.7	43 8.4			30 12.3	29 12.5
		48 7.6	56 6.5	72 5.1	66 5.5			54 6.8	53 6.9
Cost of Sales/Payables		3 143.3	14 26.4	12 29.6	10 36.3			12 30.0	14 25.2
		15 25.0	22 16.8	22 16.7	18 20.5			20 18.6	22 16.5
		41 8.8	43 8.5	31 11.9	29 12.8			32 11.4	37 9.8
Sales/Working Capital		8.8	7.4	11.2	12.3			9.3	11.3
		26.8	22.4	21.4	16.9			18.8	27.1
		86.0	-762.6	54.6	44.8			98.4	106.6
EBIT/Interest		32.7	12.0	7.7	4.6			8.2	7.2
		(18) 3.4	(50) 4.6	(48) 3.1	2.5			(113) 3.3	(118) 2.7
		2.6	1.4	1.7	1.6			1.4	1.3
Net Profit + Depr., Dep., Amort./Cur. Mat. L/T/D			3.9	7.9				10.4	10.7
			(10) 1.9	(18) 2.5				(42) 5.4	(32) 3.6
			-1.1	.7				1.7	1.3
Fixed/Worth		.0	.1	-.1	.3			.1	.1
		.1	.4	.5	.9			.5	.5
		.6	2.1	2.0	4.0			1.1	1.5
Debt/Worth		.7	.9	1.8	1.8			.8	1.5
		2.9	3.0	3.2	3.0			2.9	3.2
		16.0	9.6	8.8	12.6			8.1	7.0
% Profit Before Taxes/Tangible Net Worth		50.0	36.5	34.7	23.2			37.8	50.1
		(19) 29.4	(47) 25.9	(40) 15.5	(11) 19.5			(109) 21.5	(109) 22.1
		16.3	7.9	6.6	15.0			7.0	8.6
% Profit Before Taxes/Total Assets		14.6	11.1	9.9	8.9			14.3	12.2
		6.2	5.3	3.9	3.8			5.6	4.1
		4.1	1.2	1.4	2.0			1.5	1.5
Sales/Net Fixed Assets		UND	158.7	359.3	48.3			126.0	146.2
		194.2	43.0	41.4	17.3			38.1	35.4
		21.3	17.5	11.0	5.5			15.5	14.7
Sales/Total Assets		8.9	5.6	5.7	6.1			6.1	5.7
		4.6	4.0	3.6	2.4			4.1	4.1
		3.2	2.7	2.5	2.1			2.7	2.6
% Depr., Dep., Amort./Sales		.2	.2	.1	.3			.2	.3
		(14) .3	(46) .7	(41) .5	.6			(104) .5	(97) .5
		.8	1.2	1.5	1.6			1.0	1.1
% Officers', Directors' Owners' Comp/Sales		.9	.7	.4				.7	1.1
		(11) 1.6	(26) 1.7	(14) 1.0				(41) 1.4	(39) 1.8
		3.3	3.2	4.8				2.7	3.2
Net Sales ($)	12046M	165204M	1125623M	4736452M	3387463M	5183794M		13551278M	13864858M
Total Assets ($)	779M	25478M	268990M	1088168M	945379M	1177988M		2991634M	3550459M

Comparative Historical Data | Current Data Sorted by Sales

Type of Statement (Current side grouped: 33 (4/1-9/30/10) over 0-1MM / 1-3MM / 3-5MM; 118 (10/1/10-3/31/11) over 5-10MM / 10-25MM / 25MM & OVER)

ALL 4/1/08-3/31/09	ALL 4/1/09-3/31/10	ALL 4/1/10-3/31/11	Type of Statement	0-1MM	1-3MM	3-5MM	5-10MM	10-25MM	25MM & OVER
45	29	33	Unqualified					5	28
30	27	25	Reviewed			1		9	12
18	21	15	Compiled		3	1	3	3	5
20	19	23	Tax Returns	1	5	4	7	4	2
50	59	55	Other		1		5	16	33
163	155	151	NUMBER OF STATEMENTS	1	9	6	18	37	80
%	%	%	**ASSETS**	%	%	%	%	%	%
7.0	6.9	7.1	Cash & Equivalents				15.2	7.2	4.0
32.3	33.4	32.2	Trade Receivables (net)				29.2	36.5	31.1
32.1	30.5	32.6	Inventory				32.2	30.1	35.6
3.1	2.9	2.5	All Other Current				.6	3.2	2.7
74.5	73.7	74.5	Total Current				77.1	77.0	73.4
16.4	17.1	16.0	Fixed Assets (net)				11.6	16.6	16.4
2.6	4.7	5.7	Intangibles (net)				5.1	2.8	6.8
6.5	4.5	3.8	All Other Non-Current				6.2	3.7	3.4
100.0	100.0	100.0	Total				100.0	100.0	100.0
			LIABILITIES						
21.5	17.1	18.2	Notes Payable-Short Term				11.7	21.1	19.5
2.4	2.3	2.6	Cur. Mat.-L.T.D.				1.8	2.6	3.0
22.8	22.2	25.2	Trade Payables				21.1	35.5	21.0
.1	.2	.1	Income Taxes Payable				.1	.1	.2
7.9	7.6	6.8	All Other Current				4.5	6.0	7.6
54.7	49.4	52.8	Total Current				39.2	65.2	51.3
10.1	12.6	10.3	Long-Term Debt				5.3	8.3	13.0
.3	.2	.2	Deferred Taxes				.1	.2	.3
4.5	4.5	5.8	All Other Non-Current				9.9	5.5	4.7
30.4	33.3	30.8	Net Worth				45.5	20.8	30.8
100.0	100.0	100.0	Total Liabilities & Net Worth				100.0	100.0	100.0
			INCOME DATA						
100.0	100.0	100.0	Net Sales				100.0	100.0	100.0
17.2	18.3	18.3	Gross Profit				22.2	19.9	15.4
14.6	15.5	16.1	Operating Expenses				19.0	18.3	13.5
2.6	2.8	2.1	Operating Profit				3.2	1.6	1.9
.5	.6	.3	All Other Expenses (net)				.5	-.4	.7
2.2	2.2	1.8	Profit Before Taxes				2.7	2.0	1.2
			RATIOS						
1.8	2.1	2.0	Current				4.1	1.6	1.9
1.3	1.4	1.4					1.9	1.3	1.3
1.1	1.2	1.1					1.5	1.1	1.1
1.1	1.2	1.2	Quick				3.1	1.1	1.0
.6	.7	.7					1.0	.7	.6
.4	.5	.4					.5	.4	.4
17 21.5	18 19.8	17 21.1	Sales/Receivables				24 14.9	17 21.1	21 17.7
27 13.7	27 13.4	27 13.7					33 11.0	30 12.3	26 13.9
36 10.2	36 10.1	36 10.2					37 9.9	40 9.2	35 10.4
18 20.6	19 18.8	19 19.1	Cost of Sales/Inventory				28 13.2	16 23.5	21 17.2
29 12.4	29 12.4	31 11.6					49 7.5	24 15.3	32 11.6
53 6.9	54 6.8	64 5.7					77 4.8	51 7.1	62 5.9
13 29.0	11 31.9	12 30.6	Cost of Sales/Payables				13 27.9	16 22.6	13 29.0
20 18.0	21 17.7	20 18.0					20 18.3	28 12.9	20 18.1
30 12.1	30 12.0	34 10.6					41 8.8	44 8.2	29 12.6
11.7	9.6	9.4	Sales/Working Capital				5.0	11.1	11.5
25.3	19.1	21.4					8.2	27.0	22.6
112.2	65.0	63.2					16.6	77.2	54.9
7.9	8.4	9.3	EBIT/Interest				12.6	12.0	8.1
(155) 2.8	(144) 3.7	(140) 3.2					(14) 2.7	(34) 3.1	(79) 3.1
1.4	1.8	1.9					1.6	1.9	1.7
5.3	8.2	6.7	Net Profit + Depr., Dep., Amort./Cur. Mat. L/T/D						7.2
(45) 2.2	(35) 2.6	(37) 2.3							(28) 2.9
1.0	1.7	1.1							1.1
.1	.1	.1	Fixed/Worth				.1	.1	.1
.4	.5	.5					.4	.3	.6
1.2	1.6	2.0					.9	3.1	2.1
1.5	1.0	1.5	Debt/Worth				.4	1.9	1.7
3.0	2.9	3.2					1.3	4.4	3.3
7.1	5.7	9.9					10.0	11.3	8.4
50.3	52.0	36.6	% Profit Before Taxes/Tangible Net Worth				33.5	47.5	32.6
(149) 18.1	(138) 22.1	(127) 23.4					(15) 16.3	(31) 28.9	(68) 19.5
7.1	6.5	10.3					9.4	15.1	9.8
11.2	12.7	10.8	% Profit Before Taxes/Total Assets				9.8	10.9	11.2
4.3	6.0	4.7					4.4	5.3	4.5
1.4	1.9	1.9					2.7	1.5	1.5
252.4	184.7	280.0	Sales/Net Fixed Assets				146.1	392.7	220.5
45.3	34.3	42.9					40.8	54.7	35.8
16.9	15.1	16.2					17.7	9.9	16.8
6.3	6.3	5.8	Sales/Total Assets				4.4	6.3	5.8
4.6	4.2	3.9					3.4	4.6	4.5
2.4	2.4	2.5					2.2	2.4	2.6
.2	.2	.2	% Depr., Dep., Amort./Sales				.3	.1	.2
(139) .5	(126) .6	(123) .5					(16) .8	(28) .4	(70) .5
.9	1.1	1.1					1.3	1.5	1.0
.8	1.2	.6	% Officers', Directors' Owners' Comp/Sales				1.7	.5	.4
(52) 1.6	(48) 1.9	(54) 1.6					(11) 3.3	(15) 1.3	(24)
2.4	2.9	3.3					6.6	2.9	3.1
18021918M	16552126M	14610582M	Net Sales ($)	245M	16478M	24126M	135880M	628919M	13804934M
3751837M	3614234M	3506782M	Total Assets ($)	70M	7479M	4884M	49338M	185840M	3259171M

M = $ thousand   MM = $ million
See Pages 9 through 22 for Explanation of Ratios and Data

WHOLESALE—Dairy Product (except Dried or Canned) Merchant Wholesalers NAICS 424430

Current Data Sorted by Assets							Comparative Historical Data	
		3	9	2	6	**Type of Statement**		
		16	5			Unqualified	16	17
1	5	4	2			Reviewed	18	27
3	2	5				Compiled	21	12
2	2	11	11	1	3	Tax Returns	10	7
	21 (4/1-9/30/10)		72 (10/1/10-3/31/11)			Other	33	31
0-500M	500M-2MM	2-10MM	10-50MM	50-100MM	100-250MM		4/1/06-3/31/07 ALL	4/1/07-3/31/08 ALL
6	9	39	27	3	9	**NUMBER OF STATEMENTS**	98	94
%	%	%	%	%	%	**ASSETS**	%	%
		10.3	8.5			Cash & Equivalents	9.1	8.1
		32.8	37.0			Trade Receivables (net)	36.6	37.6
		24.4	21.3			Inventory	21.5	20.8
		3.5	4.1			All Other Current	2.6	2.0
		71.0	70.9			Total Current	69.8	68.5
		22.9	17.2			Fixed Assets (net)	19.9	22.2
		1.9	7.4			Intangibles (net)	4.8	3.6
		4.1	4.5			All Other Non-Current	5.4	5.7
		100.0	100.0			Total	100.0	100.0
						LIABILITIES		
		11.8	8.3			Notes Payable-Short Term	11.3	11.0
		2.9	4.7			Cur. Mat.-L.T.D.	2.1	3.5
		28.0	41.3			Trade Payables	32.9	37.8
		.1	.1			Income Taxes Payable	.1	.1
		9.7	9.4			All Other Current	8.2	9.1
		52.4	63.7			Total Current	54.7	61.5
		7.9	8.6			Long-Term Debt	11.8	11.4
		.2	.2			Deferred Taxes	.2	.5
		3.5	2.9			All Other Non-Current	3.3	3.5
		36.0	24.5			Net Worth	29.9	23.0
		100.0	100.0			Total Liabilities & Net Worth	100.0	100.0
						INCOME DATA		
		100.0	100.0			Net Sales	100.0	100.0
		20.6	18.6			Gross Profit	17.9	15.9
		18.6	15.5			Operating Expenses	15.5	14.3
		1.9	3.1			Operating Profit	2.4	1.6
		.4	.3			All Other Expenses (net)	.3	.3
		1.5	2.7			Profit Before Taxes	2.1	1.2
						RATIOS		
		1.7	1.4				1.7	1.5
		1.4	1.1			Current	1.3	1.1
		1.0	.9				.9	.9
		1.1	.9				1.2	1.0
		.8	.8			Quick	.8	.7
		.6	.6				.5	.5
		17 22.0	23 15.8				19 18.8	18 19.9
		25 14.4	27 13.4			Sales/Receivables	25 14.5	27 13.7
		34 10.8	32 11.3				37 9.8	37 9.8
		11 33.0	9 39.0				7 51.4	7 48.8
		19 19.7	16 22.3			Cost of Sales/Inventory	19 18.9	16 22.6
		37 9.9	31 11.9				32 11.4	34 10.6
		13 28.9	23 15.7				18 20.6	21 17.8
		26 14.0	30 12.0			Cost of Sales/Payables	26 14.2	29 12.6
		34 10.8	53 6.9				41 8.9	44 8.4
		14.4	19.9				14.7	17.5
		23.7	87.9			Sales/Working Capital	30.9	121.6
		-357.9	-65.1				-104.6	-90.3
		8.9	24.0				16.3	8.8
		(32) 3.5	(25) 10.5			EBIT/Interest	(85) 3.8	(85) 3.2
		.1	2.2				1.7	1.3
			10.6				10.1	3.6
		(14)	3.5			Net Profit + Depr., Dep., Amort./Cur. Mat. L/T/D	(18) 2.2	(23) 2.0
			1.5				1.2	.7
		.0	.5				.1	.2
		.7	1.1			Fixed/Worth	.7	1.0
		1.6	3.7				1.9	5.0
		.9	1.9				1.2	1.7
		2.0	4.8			Debt/Worth	3.6	4.6
		4.4	28.3				8.4	13.0
		33.2	67.7				49.8	49.2
		(37) 9.4	(22) 36.3			% Profit Before Taxes/Tangible Net Worth	(86) 22.5	(80) 22.0
		.8	15.3				6.9	6.0
		8.7	16.6				14.0	10.2
		4.9	9.3			% Profit Before Taxes/Total Assets	5.9	4.2
		-.2	1.3				2.0	.7
		783.4	70.5				316.1	222.4
		23.4	29.9			Sales/Net Fixed Assets	31.6	30.0
		10.4	15.1				11.7	9.7
		6.9	6.8				6.2	6.4
		4.2	5.0			Sales/Total Assets	4.9	4.7
		2.9	3.2				2.6	2.7
		.5	.4				.2	.3
		(30) 1.1	(26) .8			% Depr., Dep., Amort./Sales	(77) .8	(79) .8
		2.5	1.6				1.6	1.6
		.6					.6	.7
		(20) 1.6				% Officers', Directors' Owners' Comp/Sales	(37) 2.0	(32) 1.2
		2.1					3.4	2.6
11810M	75278M	979266M	3046105M	1776613M	4200987M	Net Sales ($)	9416886M	11461123M
1130M	11444M	207861M	579972M	257221M	1376096M	Total Assets ($)	2360896M	2643801M

© RMA 2011

M = $ thousand   MM = $ million
See Pages 9 through 22 for Explanation of Ratios and Data

Comparative Historical Data / Current Data Sorted by Sales

				Type of Statement		21 (4/1-9/30/10)		72 (10/1/10-3/31/11)		
					0-1MM	1-3MM	3-5MM	5-10MM	10-25MM	25MM & OVER
16	24	20	Unqualified							20
32	23	21	Reviewed				1	1	7	12
14	15	12	Compiled		1			4	3	4
13	7	10	Tax Returns			2	1	1	2	4
24	30	30	Other		2		1	5	5	17
4/1/08-3/31/09 ALL	4/1/09-3/31/10 ALL	4/1/10-3/31/11 ALL								
99	99	93	**NUMBER OF STATEMENTS**		3	2	3	11	17	57
%	%	%	**ASSETS**		%	%	%	%	%	%
12.3	9.0	10.0	Cash & Equivalents					7.8	6.8	9.6
35.3	35.0	34.0	Trade Receivables (net)					30.8	42.4	34.7
21.0	24.0	23.8	Inventory					31.8	21.4	21.8
2.7	3.1	3.5	All Other Current					.8	6.9	3.1
71.3	71.1	71.3	Total Current					71.2	77.5	69.2
20.6	20.3	20.9	Fixed Assets (net)					23.0	16.7	22.0
3.8	3.0	3.5	Intangibles (net)					.2	1.9	4.9
4.3	5.6	4.3	All Other Non-Current					5.5	3.9	4.0
100.0	100.0	100.0	Total					100.0	100.0	100.0
			LIABILITIES							
16.1	15.7	15.4	Notes Payable-Short Term					10.9	6.4	10.3
2.3	2.7	3.7	Cur. Mat.-L.T.D.					9.1	2.8	3.3
29.7	30.2	31.0	Trade Payables					34.6	33.0	32.1
.1	.2	.1	Income Taxes Payable					.0	.2	.1
9.0	8.5	10.5	All Other Current					10.8	8.3	11.0
57.2	57.3	60.6	Total Current					65.4	50.7	56.9
10.0	10.9	11.8	Long-Term Debt					30.7	2.9	9.8
.3	.3	.3	Deferred Taxes					.0	.1	.4
4.1	5.1	4.9	All Other Non-Current					11.3	2.0	2.5
28.4	26.4	22.5	Net Worth					-7.5	44.3	30.4
100.0	100.0	100.0	Total Liabilities & Net Worth					100.0	100.0	100.0
			INCOME DATA							
100.0	100.0	100.0	Net Sales					100.0	100.0	100.0
17.1	19.8	19.7	Gross Profit					22.3	18.5	17.1
15.7	16.8	16.7	Operating Expenses					17.7	16.4	14.9
1.4	3.0	3.0	Operating Profit					4.7	2.1	2.2
.4	.5	.4	All Other Expenses (net)					1.9	-.4	.2
1.0	2.6	2.6	Profit Before Taxes					2.8	2.4	2.0
			RATIOS							
1.9	1.7	1.7						1.9	2.1	1.5
1.3	1.3	1.3	Current					1.2	1.6	1.2
1.0	1.1	1.0						.6	1.2	1.0
1.3	1.1	1.1						.9	1.5	1.1
.8	.8	.8	Quick					.6	1.0	.8
.6	.6	.5						.3	.6	.6
16 22.6	18 20.3	19 19.6						14 26.3	18 20.6	19 19.0
22 16.3	27 13.6	25 14.6	Sales/Receivables					24 15.0	28 13.0	25 14.4
30 12.0	37 9.9	33 11.2						42 8.6	33 11.1	32 11.3
8 46.0	9 41.9	9 39.4						18 20.3	8 48.4	10 37.4
15 23.8	15 23.7	21 17.7	Cost of Sales/Inventory					37 9.9	15 24.0	18 20.6
28 13.0	48 7.6	35 10.3						85 4.3	36 10.0	30 12.0
14 26.9	14 26.6	15 23.6						17 22.0	11 31.9	16 22.7
19 19.6	25 14.7	25 14.7	Cost of Sales/Payables					21 17.4	22 16.3	26 14.0
29 12.7	37 9.9	35 10.4						80 4.5	32 11.5	37 9.9
13.8	12.6	15.3						12.3	14.9	18.0
39.0	29.7	34.8	Sales/Working Capital					24.4	18.7	39.7
966.6	236.7	-353.9						-26.2	48.5	-660.1
12.5	15.0	22.7							36.0	23.9
(88) 4.9	(89) 6.0	(80) 5.6	EBIT/Interest						(15) 4.6	(51) 8.3
1.6	2.2	1.5							-.4	2.2
3.6	8.0	5.0								10.1
(19) 2.4	(26) 3.5	(25) 3.0	Net Profit + Depr., Dep., Amort./Cur. Mat. L/T/D							(19) 3.6
1.4	2.0	1.6								1.8
.1	.0	.1						.0	.0	.3
.6	.7	.8	Fixed/Worth					.3	.2	.9
2.0	2.1	1.9						3.8	.8	1.9
1.0	1.0	1.2						1.7	.6	1.2
2.4	2.7	2.7	Debt/Worth					4.8	1.6	3.0
6.4	6.4	6.8						999.8	3.3	6.4
44.8	50.6	48.6							29.9	45.2
(85) 19.7	(85) 24.5	(80) 21.2	% Profit Before Taxes/Tangible Net Worth						(16) 13.8	(50) 25.4
7.0	8.5	8.4							-.4	10.2
12.2	13.8	14.9						19.0	14.5	12.8
6.3	7.4	7.0	% Profit Before Taxes/Total Assets					8.3	3.4	7.2
1.9	1.9	1.4						-.2	-1.6	2.6
270.8	377.3	225.9						999.8	799.9	66.5
31.7	29.1	29.9	Sales/Net Fixed Assets					182.3	83.0	22.5
12.4	11.5	12.8						4.6	11.7	12.8
7.2	6.1	7.0						8.3	8.1	6.8
5.3	4.3	4.4	Sales/Total Assets					3.1	5.2	4.9
3.4	2.8	3.0						2.1	3.0	3.2
.2	.4	.4							.3	.4
(80) .6	(78) .8	(72) .9	% Depr., Dep., Amort./Sales						(13) .9	(51) .9
1.7	2.0	2.0							2.4	1.7
1.1	.9	.6								.6
(47) 1.7	(34) 2.1	(34) 1.6	% Officers', Directors' Owners' Comp/Sales							(21) 1.6
3.0	4.6	2.3								2.4
9245984M	11366407M	10090059M	Net Sales ($)		1094M	2824M	10656M	83910M	285656M	9705919M
2162218M	2453572M	2433724M	Total Assets ($)		362M	360M	4333M	27348M	67254M	2334067M

Current Data Sorted by Assets   Comparative Historical Data

0-500M	500M-2MM	2-10MM	10-50MM	50-100MM	100-250MM	Type of Statement	4/1/06-3/31/07 ALL	4/1/07-3/31/08 ALL
		2	7	2	3	Unqualified	12	12
	2	3	6			Reviewed	15	9
	4	4				Compiled	6	9
2	3	3	1			Tax Returns	4	2
	6	7	9	4	2	Other	12	17
	15 (4/1-9/30/10)		55 (10/1/10-3/31/11)					
2	15	19	23	6	5	NUMBER OF STATEMENTS	49	49
%	%	%	%	%	%	ASSETS	%	%
	13.5	6.8	4.8			Cash & Equivalents	6.4	5.9
	44.8	41.4	38.1			Trade Receivables (net)	43.6	43.2
	23.3	24.4	19.0			Inventory	18.7	20.4
	.8	.9	5.0			All Other Current	4.7	3.1
	82.4	73.5	66.9			Total Current	73.4	72.6
	13.1	16.6	20.2			Fixed Assets (net)	18.2	19.7
	1.6	1.3	5.6			Intangibles (net)	2.5	2.6
	2.8	8.6	7.3			All Other Non-Current	5.9	5.0
	100.0	100.0	100.0			Total	100.0	100.0
						LIABILITIES		
	27.9	21.1	11.6			Notes Payable-Short Term	14.9	15.1
	2.5	10.5	1.9			Cur. Mat.-L.T.D.	4.0	3.4
	22.7	30.7	29.8			Trade Payables	25.3	24.8
	.0	.0	.0			Income Taxes Payable	.1	.1
	7.8	9.0	7.1			All Other Current	8.3	6.5
	60.9	71.4	50.4			Total Current	52.6	49.9
	7.3	10.0	9.0			Long-Term Debt	8.5	11.1
	.0	.0	.4			Deferred Taxes	.0	.0
	8.5	.3	3.3			All Other Non-Current	2.2	2.7
	23.3	18.3	36.8			Net Worth	36.7	36.3
	100.0	100.0	100.0			Total Liabilities & Net Worth	100.0	100.0
						INCOME DATA		
	100.0	100.0	100.0			Net Sales	100.0	100.0
	18.5	17.5	11.6			Gross Profit	16.9	15.8
	17.7	15.3	10.6			Operating Expenses	14.1	13.0
	.8	2.3	1.0			Operating Profit	2.8	2.8
	.1	1.3	-.1			All Other Expenses (net)	.3	.2
	.7	.9	1.1			Profit Before Taxes	2.5	2.6
						RATIOS		
	2.0	1.9	1.7				2.2	1.9
	1.4	1.4	1.2			Current	1.5	1.4
	1.1	1.1	.9				1.1	1.1
	1.4	1.6	1.1				1.5	1.5
	1.0	.9	.7			Quick	1.0	1.0
	.5	.5	.5				.6	.7
	12 29.8	20 18.3	14 26.5				16 22.9	15 24.0
	19 19.4	29 12.8	23 15.9			Sales/Receivables	22 16.7	21 17.3
	23 16.0	34 10.7	36 10.1				29 12.6	29 12.5
	1 296.4	5 66.9	7 51.8				6 63.9	6 65.5
	11 34.5	13 27.7	13 28.4			Cost of Sales/Inventory	10 35.4	10 35.2
	14 27.0	30 12.3	18 19.8				24 15.4	23 15.8
	1 581.0	10 36.4	10 35.2				8 45.7	9 42.4
	5 69.1	16 22.6	17 21.0			Cost of Sales/Payables	15 24.8	13 27.4
	26 14.3	34 10.7	35 10.5				25 14.9	21 17.4
	22.1	13.6	19.4				16.4	21.5
	43.5	31.3	60.8			Sales/Working Capital	31.6	35.7
	139.3	201.3	-91.2				93.2	97.2
	10.1	15.4	26.1				7.3	9.5
	(14) 1.4	(15) 2.7	(22) 5.1			EBIT/Interest	(46) 2.4	(46) 3.8
	-.5	-.8	1.2				1.2	1.7
						Net Profit + Depr., Dep., Amort./Cur. Mat. L/T/D		
	.0	.0	.2				.0	.1
	.5	.4	.7			Fixed/Worth	.2	.3
	2.0	1.2	2.6				1.3	1.6
	1.5	1.0	1.1				.8	1.1
	4.9	1.2	2.9			Debt/Worth	1.9	2.1
	15.8	4.6	4.5				5.0	4.2
	90.0	31.3	44.8				37.5	55.2
	(13) 9.4	(16) 13.0	(21) 19.8			% Profit Before Taxes/Tangible Net Worth	(45) 15.7	(47) 24.1
	-29.3	-1.2	2.0				1.9	8.9
	18.2	10.3	14.9				17.5	18.1
	.7	6.0	8.2			% Profit Before Taxes/Total Assets	4.5	8.2
	-3.4	-.7	1.0				.7	2.9
	999.8	589.2	83.2				999.8	690.3
	129.5	58.4	30.6			Sales/Net Fixed Assets	66.8	66.7
	45.2	12.7	14.7				14.0	12.3
	12.9	7.1	8.4				10.2	10.0
	9.6	4.4	6.6			Sales/Total Assets	7.0	6.9
	6.9	2.8	3.6				4.0	4.6
	.2	.4	.2				.1	.1
	(10) .3	(15) .6	(22) .5			% Depr., Dep., Amort./Sales	(38) .4	(34) .5
	.4	1.2	1.0				1.7	1.7
							.5	.3
						% Officers', Directors' Owners' Comp/Sales	(18) 1.2	(15) 1.4
							3.2	2.8
5458M	168542M	463668M	3144770M	2181919M	1321307M	Net Sales ($)	3555839M	4143212M
641M	17342M	86712M	469968M	446293M	823935M	Total Assets ($)	1021766M	990984M

M = $ thousand   MM = $ million
See Pages 9 through 22 for Explanation of Ratios and Data

Comparative Historical Data — Current Data Sorted by Sales

Current Data period groupings: **15 (4/1-9/30/10)** covers 0-1MM, 1-3MM, 3-5MM; **55 (10/1/10-3/31/11)** covers 5-10MM, 10-25MM, 25MM & OVER.
Note: For the 0-1MM, 1-3MM, and 3-5MM columns the percentage and ratio data are marked "DATA NOT AVAILABLE".

4/1/08-3/31/09 ALL	4/1/09-3/31/10 ALL	4/1/10-3/31/11 ALL		0-1MM	1-3MM	3-5MM	5-10MM	10-25MM	25MM & OVER
			Type of Statement						
13	9	14	Unqualified				1		13
14	13	11	Reviewed				2	3	6
9	7	8	Compiled				2	5	1
2	7	9	Tax Returns	1		2	1	2	3
19	20	28	Other			1	5	7	16
57	56	70	**NUMBER OF STATEMENTS**	1		3	10	17	39
%	%	%	**ASSETS**	%	%	%	%	%	%
7.7	6.5	7.6	Cash & Equivalents				9.8	9.1	5.6
40.3	39.9	36.8	Trade Receivables (net)				32.4	40.5	38.2
22.5	20.2	23.2	Inventory				30.2	20.9	23.4
3.6	4.9	2.7	All Other Current				1.2	5.7	2.1
74.2	71.5	70.3	Total Current				73.6	76.2	69.3
18.9	18.1	20.6	Fixed Assets (net)				10.8	15.1	22.1
2.3	2.0	3.0	Intangibles (net)				4.3	.2	4.1
4.6	8.5	6.1	All Other Non-Current				11.2	8.5	4.4
100.0	100.0	100.0	Total				100.0	100.0	100.0
			LIABILITIES						
21.1	16.3	17.3	Notes Payable-Short Term				17.5	29.0	11.4
2.4	2.9	4.7	Cur. Mat.-L.T.D.				4.8	11.0	1.8
24.7	26.7	26.0	Trade Payables				25.8	24.9	26.6
.4	.2	.1	Income Taxes Payable				.0	.0	.2
6.2	8.3	7.9	All Other Current				3.3	13.3	6.7
54.8	54.4	56.0	Total Current				51.4	78.2	46.6
10.2	10.4	12.5	Long-Term Debt				14.2	8.1	9.0
.1	.3	.4	Deferred Taxes				.1	.0	.6
1.8	3.8	3.8	All Other Non-Current				9.8	4.3	2.3
33.1	31.1	27.3	Net Worth				24.6	9.4	41.3
100.0	100.0	100.0	Total Liabilties & Net Worth				100.0	100.0	100.0
			INCOME DATA						
100.0	100.0	100.0	Net Sales				100.0	100.0	100.0
13.3	13.9	16.6	Gross Profit				25.5	13.1	13.9
11.3	11.8	14.6	Operating Expenses				25.0	11.7	11.1
2.0	2.1	2.1	Operating Profit				.5	1.4	2.8
.2	.2	.6	All Other Expenses (net)				.0	1.4	.3
1.8	1.9	1.5	Profit Before Taxes				.6	.0	2.6
			RATIOS						
2.0	2.2	2.1	Current				2.0	2.3	2.4
1.2	1.3	1.4					1.5	1.4	1.5
1.0	1.0	1.0					1.1	1.0	1.1
1.3	1.3	1.3	Quick				1.3	1.4	1.4
.8	.8	.8					.8	1.0	.7
.7	.5	.5					.4	.5	.6
15 23.6	13 29.0	15 23.7	Sales/Receivables				16 22.4	15 23.9	15 23.7
21 17.4	20 18.2	23 16.0					20 17.9	23 15.9	23 15.9
29 12.6	29 12.7	30 12.2					23 15.9	35 10.4	31 11.7
6 62.3	5 71.8	7 51.9	Cost of Sales/Inventory				7 53.3	1 244.6	8 44.3
14 26.4	10 37.0	13 28.0					13 27.3	12 30.0	13 27.6
22 16.4	25 14.8	32 11.3					36 10.0	26 14.0	37 9.9
8 45.9	10 35.0	10 38.3	Cost of Sales/Payables				10 38.3	1 370.5	11 33.7
13 28.1	14 25.9	16 22.4					21 17.1	14 25.3	15 23.6
19 18.9	24 15.4	30 12.0					28 12.9	42 8.8	27 13.3
21.3	14.5	13.6	Sales/Working Capital				12.9	26.7	11.5
36.6	37.0	32.2					28.1	43.5	23.3
254.3	271.7	247.8					150.0	NM	201.3
8.3	22.6	14.6	EBIT/Interest				3.8	12.8	34.7
(53) 4.9	(49) 6.3	(63) 2.8					.2	(15) 2.7	(35) 8.0
1.8	1.2	.6					-1.8	1.0	1.6
24.3			Net Profit + Depr., Dep.,						
(12) 9.4			Amort./Cur. Mat. L/T/D						
3.9									
.1	.0	.1	Fixed/Worth				.1	.0	.1
.4	.4	.5					.5	.4	.5
1.4	1.8	1.8					1.7	NM	1.6
1.1	.9	1.0	Debt/Worth				1.1	1.0	.6
2.3	3.1	2.7					5.8	1.5	2.6
4.6	6.8	6.8					16.6	NM	3.8
43.3	57.6	38.2	% Profit Before Taxes/Tangible					59.8	38.2
(51) 24.7	(49) 33.6	(61) 16.4	Net Worth				(13) 9.9	(37) 19.7	
8.3	10.8	.0						.8	9.1
15.4	19.3	14.3	% Profit Before Taxes/Total				7.9	12.8	15.7
5.9	9.0	5.5	Assets				-1.7	4.1	8.6
1.2	1.3	-.9					-3.2	-1.2	2.7
668.2	736.2	352.7	Sales/Net Fixed Assets				318.2	999.8	332.4
61.7	64.0	48.5					63.2	115.6	30.8
18.8	16.4	12.2					24.2	21.5	10.2
9.7	10.5	9.1	Sales/Total Assets				8.1	11.9	8.4
7.2	7.0	6.2					6.2	6.0	6.6
5.0	4.7	2.9					2.9	2.8	3.0
.1	.0	.2	% Depr., Dep., Amort./Sales					.2	.1
(45) .3	(44) .2	(54) .5					(13) .4	(30) .5	
.7	1.1	1.2						1.2	1.1
.4	.3	.4	% Officers', Directors'						
(14) .9	(18) 1.1	(11) 1.9	Owners' Comp/Sales						
1.9	3.2	3.3							
6232383M	6366833M	7285664M	Net Sales ($)	811M		13516M	80406M	264427M	6926504M
1228841M	1358847M	1844891M	Total Assets ($)	208M		4028M	18791M	76041M	1745823M

M = $ thousand   MM = $ million
See Pages 9 through 22 for Explanation of Ratios and Data

Current Data Sorted by Assets   Comparative Historical Data

Period columns: **26 (4/1-9/30/10)** and **52 (10/1/10-3/31/11)**

0-500M	500M-2MM	2-10MM	10-50MM	50-100MM	100-250MM	Type of Statement	4/1/06-3/31/07 ALL	4/1/07-3/31/08 ALL
		1	6			Unqualified	3	7
	1	15	8			Reviewed	15	18
	2	7	1			Compiled	18	15
	7	4	1			Tax Returns	15	12
1	4	9	8	1	2	Other	20	21
1	14	36	24	1	2	NUMBER OF STATEMENTS	71	73
%	%	%	%	%	%	**ASSETS**	%	%
	11.4	5.7	5.2			Cash & Equivalents	8.0	7.4
	26.3	29.4	30.4			Trade Receivables (net)	25.3	27.3
	33.8	33.0	36.7			Inventory	37.4	37.3
	.4	2.7	2.7			All Other Current	2.1	3.0
	71.9	70.8	75.0			Total Current	72.8	75.0
	24.2	22.4	16.4			Fixed Assets (net)	19.5	18.2
	2.9	2.2	3.1			Intangibles (net)	2.8	2.3
	1.0	4.6	5.4			All Other Non-Current	4.8	4.5
	100.0	100.0	100.0			Total	100.0	100.0
						LIABILITIES		
	12.2	13.6	16.6			Notes Payable-Short Term	18.7	15.7
	2.5	2.1	1.3			Cur. Mat.-L.T.D.	2.1	3.4
	19.8	22.6	21.9			Trade Payables	19.4	18.3
	.1	.3	.0			Income Taxes Payable	.2	.1
	5.8	6.1	8.8			All Other Current	10.1	12.8
	40.4	44.8	48.6			Total Current	50.4	50.1
	20.2	16.3	6.8			Long-Term Debt	13.4	13.0
	.0	.0	.1			Deferred Taxes	.2	.4
	3.8	5.7	6.6			All Other Non-Current	7.0	12.1
	35.6	33.2	38.0			Net Worth	29.0	24.4
	100.0	100.0	100.0			Total Liabilities & Net Worth	100.0	100.0
						INCOME DATA		
	100.0	100.0	100.0			Net Sales	100.0	100.0
	32.9	22.4	23.7			Gross Profit	24.7	27.1
	32.2	19.6	20.7			Operating Expenses	22.6	24.4
	.7	2.8	3.0			Operating Profit	2.1	2.7
	.3	.8	1.0			All Other Expenses (net)	.6	.6
	.4	2.0	1.9			Profit Before Taxes	1.4	2.2
						RATIOS		
	3.9	2.2	2.1			Current	2.6	3.1
	1.6	1.6	1.4				1.4	1.5
	1.3	1.3	1.2				1.1	1.1
	1.7	1.0	1.1			Quick	1.0	1.1
	.9	.8	.7				.6	.6
	.6	.5	.5				.5	.4
	9 40.4	18 20.1	20 18.6			Sales/Receivables	13 27.4	16 22.5
	19 19.2	25 14.8	31 11.6				26 14.0	25 14.3
	35 10.4	38 9.5	43 8.5				37 9.8	36 10.1
	24 15.1	20 17.9	30 12.1			Cost of Sales/Inventory	25 14.3	29 12.8
	46 8.0	49 7.5	44 8.3				51 7.1	53 6.9
	61 6.0	70 5.2	63 5.8				82 4.5	73 5.0
	10 37.0	13 28.3	14 26.4			Cost of Sales/Payables	9 39.8	9 38.6
	19 19.0	25 14.6	20 18.0				22 16.3	22 16.8
	41 8.9	48 7.6	50 7.2				35 10.4	41 9.0
	7.4	9.5	9.1			Sales/Working Capital	8.6	8.3
	21.7	17.1	14.1				16.8	15.4
	33.6	28.0	50.0				72.2	36.0
	7.3	8.3	46.0			EBIT/Interest	7.2	9.2
	2.7	(35) 3.4	(23) 6.6				(67) 2.5	(68) 2.6
	-.2	1.5	2.2				.3	1.2
		6.6				Net Profit + Depr., Dep., Amort./Cur. Mat. L/T/D	9.8	4.0
		(12) 2.7					(16) 3.2	(17) 2.0
		1.3					1.0	1.2
	.2	.2	.1			Fixed/Worth	.2	.1
	.5	.5	.3				.4	.4
	1.3	1.6	.9				1.3	2.0
	1.2	.8	1.0			Debt/Worth	.7	.8
	2.0	2.0	1.8				2.4	2.2
	3.3	6.5	4.1				5.7	9.8
	35.1	37.3	46.2			% Profit Before Taxes/Tangible Net Worth	49.8	40.7
	(13) 15.3	(31) 18.8	(21) 20.4				(64) 17.6	(60) 14.0
	-3.3	3.7	10.0				-.1	5.3
	10.9	10.2	15.8			% Profit Before Taxes/Total Assets	10.1	14.2
	2.2	4.8	9.5				4.5	4.1
	-3.4	1.4	1.9				-2.4	.6
	103.2	63.4	153.1			Sales/Net Fixed Assets	72.3	93.9
	32.7	23.9	38.2				26.5	46.1
	8.3	7.8	14.0				10.9	10.8
	6.4	4.8	4.4			Sales/Total Assets	5.3	5.2
	3.9	3.5	3.7				3.4	3.5
	3.1	2.4	2.7				2.4	2.4
	.3	.4	.1			% Depr., Dep., Amort./Sales	.3	.3
	(10) 1.8	(33) .7	(23) .5				(65) .9	(62) .6
	3.4	2.0	1.6				2.1	2.0
		.8				% Officers', Directors' Owners' Comp/Sales	.8	1.4
		(20) 1.3					(38) 2.1	(33) 2.4
		3.2					4.2	4.8
4015M	106267M	771880M	1765589M	113000M	521800M	Net Sales ($)	1714281M	2147674M
111M	18246M	185884M	438379M	52010M	247372M	Total Assets ($)	514728M	661605M

Comparative Historical Data   Current Data Sorted by Sales

	4/1/08-3/31/09 ALL		4/1/09-3/31/10 ALL		4/1/10-3/31/11 ALL	Type of Statement	0-1MM	1-3MM	3-5MM	5-10MM	10-25MM	25MM & OVER
	8		11		7	Unqualified					1	6
	16		20		24	Reviewed	1			2	8	13
	17		17		10	Compiled			2	1	6	1
	9		13		12	Tax Returns			3	2	4	3
	27		16		25	Other		1	4	2	6	12
								26 (4/1-9/30/10)			52 (10/1/10-3/31/11)	
	77		77		78	**NUMBER OF STATEMENTS**	1	1	9	7	25	35
	%		%		%	**ASSETS**	%	%	%	%	%	%
	6.7		6.6		6.9	Cash & Equivalents					6.7	4.5
	29.8		27.3		28.3	Trade Receivables (net)					28.9	32.4
	36.4		33.7		34.0	Inventory					37.0	33.9
	3.4		3.0		2.2	All Other Current					1.6	1.6
	76.3		70.7		71.4	Total Current					74.2	72.3
	16.3		21.2		21.2	Fixed Assets (net)					20.0	18.7
	3.2		3.2		2.5	Intangibles (net)					2.7	2.2
	4.2		4.9		4.8	All Other Non-Current					3.2	6.7
	100.0		100.0		100.0	Total					100.0	100.0
						LIABILITIES						
	16.9		18.2		14.1	Notes Payable-Short Term					14.7	15.8
	1.2		2.0		1.8	Cur. Mat.-L.T.D.					1.6	1.7
	19.9		18.8		21.4	Trade Payables					23.9	23.2
	.1		.2		.2	Income Taxes Payable					.1	.4
	10.2		8.8		6.9	All Other Current					9.0	7.3
	48.3		47.9		44.5	Total Current					49.2	48.4
	9.5		12.5		13.9	Long-Term Debt					15.2	9.0
	.2		.2		.0	Deferred Taxes					.0	.1
	3.1		6.5		5.5	All Other Non-Current					6.4	6.4
	38.9		32.8		36.0	Net Worth					29.2	36.1
	100.0		100.0		100.0	Total Liabilities & Net Worth					100.0	100.0
						INCOME DATA						
	100.0		100.0		100.0	Net Sales					100.0	100.0
	22.2		23.1		24.6	Gross Profit					25.0	20.8
	19.3		20.8		21.9	Operating Expenses					22.3	17.8
	3.0		2.3		2.7	Operating Profit					2.7	3.0
	.3		.5		.8	All Other Expenses (net)					.6	1.0
	2.7		1.8		1.9	Profit Before Taxes					2.1	2.0
						RATIOS						
	2.7		2.6		2.1						1.9	2.0
	1.5		1.6		1.5	Current					1.5	1.4
	1.2		1.2		1.2						1.2	1.2
	1.2		1.2		1.1						1.0	1.1
	.7		.8		.8	Quick					.8	.7
	.5		.5		.5						.5	.5
18	19.9	17	21.3	18	20.6						17 21.7	19 19.1
27	13.7	27	13.7	26	13.8	Sales/Receivables					24 15.3	30 12.4
34	10.8	37	9.9	38	9.5						39 9.4	38 9.5
27	13.7	25	14.8	25	14.4						28 13.1	18 20.1
48	7.7	46	7.9	47	7.8	Cost of Sales/Inventory					48 7.6	42 8.7
70	5.2	66	5.5	65	5.6						65 5.6	63 5.8
9	42.5	10	36.8	13	28.2						13 28.1	13 28.1
19	19.7	22	16.9	24	15.5	Cost of Sales/Payables					25 14.7	23 16.1
36	10.0	37	9.8	48	7.6						42 8.8	47 7.8
	8.3		8.4		9.5						10.2	11.7
	15.0		16.7		18.3	Sales/Working Capital					17.5	21.7
	31.2		41.7		29.5						31.8	30.6
	9.0		9.6		9.5						9.5	13.8
(72)	3.8	(74)	4.0	(76)	4.0	EBIT/Interest					3.2	(33) 5.0
	1.5		1.3		1.5						1.8	2.2
	2.9		15.1		5.4							6.0
(15)	2.0	(17)	3.2	(18)	2.6	Net Profit + Depr., Dep., Amort./Cur. Mat. L/T/D						(10) 3.9
	.5		1.0		1.4							2.1
	.1		.1		.2						.3	.1
	.4		.4		.5	Fixed/Worth					.6	.4
	.8		1.3		1.3						1.9	.9
	.7		.9		.9						1.0	1.1
	1.8		1.9		1.7	Debt/Worth					3.0	1.5
	4.7		4.9		3.9						10.1	3.7
	43.3		34.8		38.1						42.6	35.2
(71)	15.3	(68)	17.5	(69)	19.0	% Profit Before Taxes/Tangible Net Worth					(21) 21.5	(31) 19.3
	5.0		5.7		5.4						3.9	9.9
	14.8		12.1		13.5						11.6	15.3
	6.5		6.3		5.4	% Profit Before Taxes/Total Assets					4.5	9.2
	1.0		.9		1.3						1.7	2.9
	165.8		106.9		88.7						99.1	79.9
	40.6		30.1		29.7	Sales/Net Fixed Assets					43.4	29.1
	13.0		9.3		8.2						10.5	12.8
	5.0		4.6		4.5						5.6	5.0
	3.7		3.3		3.6	Sales/Total Assets					3.8	3.7
	2.5		2.4		2.4						2.7	2.8
	.2		.2		.3						.3	.2
(69)	.6	(67)	.6	(69)	.9	% Depr., Dep., Amort./Sales					(23) .7	(34) .5
	1.3		1.6		2.0						2.2	1.7
	1.0		1.1		.8						.9	.6
(31)	2.2	(45)	2.2	(37)	1.5	% Officers', Directors' Owners' Comp/Sales					(16) 1.5	(14) .8
	4.2		4.8		2.8						3.2	2.1
	3159738M		2902395M		3282551M	Net Sales ($)	958M	1450M	35926M	55580M	394053M	2794584M
	998253M		894387M		942002M	Total Assets ($)	571M	633M	10321M	26637M	112426M	791414M

© RMA 2011

M = $ thousand   MM = $ million
See Pages 9 through 22 for Explanation of Ratios and Data

Current Data Sorted by Assets   Comparative Historical Data

0-500M	500M-2MM	2-10MM	10-50MM	50-100MM	100-250MM	Type of Statement	4/1/06-3/31/07 ALL	4/1/07-3/31/08 ALL
1		3	14	12	2	Unqualified	42	40
1	3	40	19	1		Reviewed	55	47
3	7	12	1			Compiled	34	30
3	20	14				Tax Returns	26	21
3	8	28	33	11	5	Other	82	104
	51 (4/1-9/30/10)		193 (10/1/10-3/31/11)					
11	38	97	67	24	7	NUMBER OF STATEMENTS	239	242
%	%	%	%	%	%	ASSETS	%	%
10.0	14.4	7.9	3.7	4.2		Cash & Equivalents	5.6	6.2
29.2	38.3	39.3	30.8	27.6		Trade Receivables (net)	37.2	36.3
11.8	20.5	30.8	41.4	41.1		Inventory	34.8	35.7
.9	3.5	1.6	3.4	2.8		All Other Current	2.5	2.8
51.9	76.7	79.6	79.4	75.7		Total Current	80.0	81.1
35.9	14.7	13.1	12.5	16.8		Fixed Assets (net)	13.4	13.1
.6	.9	2.8	5.2	1.9		Intangibles (net)	2.1	2.2
11.6	7.6	4.5	2.9	5.6		All Other Non-Current	4.5	3.6
100.0	100.0	100.0	100.0	100.0		Total	100.0	100.0
						LIABILITIES		
23.9	8.2	18.4	27.8	28.4		Notes Payable-Short Term	26.9	24.3
2.8	2.3	1.7	1.2	1.5		Cur. Mat.-L.T.D.	2.1	2.8
30.1	29.0	26.6	23.4	17.7		Trade Payables	23.8	25.1
.0	.1	.3	.1	.0		Income Taxes Payable	.1	.1
22.8	7.4	5.4	6.9	6.0		All Other Current	8.0	8.0
79.8	47.0	52.4	59.4	53.6		Total Current	60.8	60.3
8.2	8.1	6.9	8.3	7.9		Long-Term Debt	6.7	7.2
.3	.0	.2	.2	.0		Deferred Taxes	.3	.3
6.2	9.1	5.8	5.3	1.4		All Other Non-Current	6.1	5.8
5.4	35.8	34.9	26.8	37.2		Net Worth	26.1	26.4
100.0	100.0	100.0	100.0	100.0		Total Liabilities & Net Worth	100.0	100.0
						INCOME DATA		
100.0	100.0	100.0	100.0	100.0		Net Sales	100.0	100.0
19.0	15.9	15.1	12.1	15.0		Gross Profit	14.3	14.6
17.2	14.4	13.6	9.6	12.1		Operating Expenses	12.0	12.4
1.8	1.4	1.5	2.5	2.9		Operating Profit	2.4	2.2
.2	.1	.4	.5	.7		All Other Expenses (net)	.8	.8
1.6	1.3	1.1	2.0	2.2		Profit Before Taxes	1.6	1.4
						RATIOS		
1.7	2.4	2.1	1.7	1.8			1.7	1.8
.9	1.6	1.4	1.3	1.4	Current	1.3	1.3
.6	1.2	1.1	1.1	1.1		1.1	1.1
1.2	1.3	1.4	.9	.8		1.0	1.0
.6	1.0	.8	.6	.6	Quick	.7	.6
.2	.7	.6	.4	.4		.5	.5
0 999.8	13 27.2	22 16.8	26 14.0	27 13.7			24 15.3	23 16.0
7 49.2	25 14.4	34 10.7	29 12.4	35 10.4		Sales/Receivables	34 10.9	31 11.6
24 15.0	37 9.8	40 9.1	40 9.1	41 8.9			42 8.7	40 9.1
0 UND	2 240.1	10 36.7	25 14.4	40 9.2			16 22.5	14 25.3
4 89.7	11 32.0	31 11.9	46 7.9	63 5.8		Cost of Sales/Inventory	38 9.6	37 9.8
7 53.0	37 9.9	52 7.0	75 4.9	84 4.3			68 5.4	66 5.5
0 UND	5 66.8	13 27.7	15 24.8	18 20.2			11 32.7	13 29.1
4 85.2	17 21.5	23 16.2	25 14.7	28 13.3		Cost of Sales/Payables	24 15.3	23 15.7
28 13.0	34 10.8	34 10.7	35 10.5	35 10.4			37 9.8	36 10.0
58.9	11.6	9.2	9.2	6.5			10.5	10.7
-621.2	21.7	16.8	20.2	17.0		Sales/Working Capital	21.9	21.2
-30.9	89.9	57.3	49.0	122.0			81.3	70.0
	19.5	11.7	8.8	8.3			5.0	5.6
	(33) 4.3	(88) 5.2	(61) 3.7	(22) 2.8		EBIT/Interest	(228) 2.4	(228) 2.6
	1.0	2.2	2.1	1.3			1.1	1.4
		8.6	13.4	17.7			11.9	8.5
		(14) 4.4	(23) 4.4	(12) 6.1		Net Profit + Depr., Dep., Amort./Cur. Mat. L/T/D	(61) 4.3	(57) 4.9
		1.7	1.7	2.7			1.5	1.6
1.2	.1	.0	.0	.1			.1	.1
1.4	.4	.2	.2	.2	Fixed/Worth	.3	.3
-12.8	.7	.7	1.1	.8		.9	.9
.9	.9	1.1	2.0	1.2			1.5	1.5
1.6	1.8	2.5	3.6	2.3	Debt/Worth	3.3	3.4
-42.6	4.4	5.8	7.0	3.4		8.0	7.7
	43.0	47.5	41.4	28.3			35.8	35.5
	(34) 23.2	(87) 23.1	(62) 22.7	(23) 9.7		% Profit Before Taxes/Tangible Net Worth	(216) 18.1	(218) 19.4
	5.9	9.3	8.5	4.1			4.0	7.6
34.1	13.7	11.8	11.8	7.5			9.4	10.1
5.8	6.2	4.6	4.2	2.8	% Profit Before Taxes/Total Assets	4.7	4.1
.0	1.5	1.7	1.9	1.3		.7	1.4
112.3	172.9	350.1	999.8	272.0			351.4	339.4
49.2	84.8	102.9	141.3	25.8		Sales/Net Fixed Assets	79.0	74.7
18.5	17.8	19.8	22.7	10.3			22.4	24.6
27.4	8.7	5.5	4.9	3.5			5.6	5.6
15.0	5.7	4.0	3.6	3.0		Sales/Total Assets	3.9	4.0
6.7	3.7	2.9	2.6	2.2		2.7	2.9
	.3	.1	.1	.1			.1	.1
	(28) .5	(74) .4	(57) .3	(22) .4		% Depr., Dep., Amort./Sales	(197) .4	(203) .3
	1.1	1.0	.9	1.5			.9	.8
	1.2	.8	.7				.7	.7
	(27) 1.8	(52) 1.4	(15) .7			% Officers', Directors' Owners' Comp/Sales	(97) 1.6	(89) 1.5
	3.3	2.5	2.1				3.1	3.9
45627M	284749M	2163605M	6066298M	4774339M	3042569M	Net Sales ($)	12728433M	12960161M
2982M	45744M	492238M	1576267M	1692327M	1154766M	Total Assets ($)	4429787M	3992636M

M = $ thousand   MM = $ million

See Pages 9 through 22 for Explanation of Ratios and Data

Comparative Historical Data | Current Data Sorted by Sales

4/1/08-3/31/09 ALL	4/1/09-3/31/10 ALL	4/1/10-3/31/11 ALL	Type of Statement	0-1MM	1-3MM	3-5MM	5-10MM	10-25MM	25MM & OVER
42	35	32	Unqualified		2			1	29
59	62	64	Reviewed			1	5	24	34
31	30	23	Compiled	1	3	3	2	10	4
33	35	37	Tax Returns		5	8	10	10	4
112	95	88	Other		2		16	14	56
					51 (4/1-9/30/10)		193 (10/1/10-3/31/11)		
277	257	244	NUMBER OF STATEMENTS	1	12	12	33	59	127
%	%	%	ASSETS	%	%	%	%	%	%
8.0	6.2	7.4	Cash & Equivalents		10.4	7.8	17.5	8.4	4.1
32.8	35.3	34.8	Trade Receivables (net)		20.4	18.8	34.3	41.5	34.3
34.4	35.0	32.7	Inventory		21.8	27.3	22.3	26.6	40.1
2.4	2.0	2.6	All Other Current		1.6	.8	1.8	3.0	2.9
77.6	78.5	77.6	Total Current		54.3	54.7	75.9	79.5	81.4
15.3	14.0	14.5	Fixed Assets (net)		20.6	33.1	17.8	13.8	11.7
2.7	2.9	2.9	Intangibles (net)		.4	.6	4.7	2.5	3.2
4.4	4.6	5.0	All Other Non-Current		24.8	11.6	1.7	4.2	3.8
100.0	100.0	100.0	Total		100.0	100.0	100.0	100.0	100.0
			LIABILITIES						
24.0	22.1	21.2	Notes Payable-Short Term		23.4	12.2	6.3	17.9	27.4
2.0	3.1	1.7	Cur. Mat.-L.T.D.		2.4	4.3	2.6	1.9	1.1
23.0	23.7	25.1	Trade Payables		22.8	13.5	24.4	28.2	24.6
.1	.1	.2	Income Taxes Payable		.2	.2	.1	.4	.1
8.4	6.2	7.0	All Other Current		17.8	7.8	7.7	5.2	6.7
57.5	55.1	55.2	Total Current		66.6	38.0	41.1	53.6	59.8
9.1	9.8	7.5	Long-Term Debt		6.5	23.7	7.0	7.3	6.4
.2	.2	.2	Deferred Taxes		.0	.0	.5	.1	.1
4.5	5.5	5.6	All Other Non-Current		19.6	5.9	7.8	4.6	4.3
28.7	29.4	31.5	Net Worth		7.3	32.2	43.6	34.4	29.5
100.0	100.0	100.0	Total Liabilities & Net Worth		100.0	100.0	100.0	100.0	100.0
			INCOME DATA						
100.0	100.0	100.0	Net Sales		100.0	100.0	100.0	100.0	100.0
15.2	14.5	14.4	Gross Profit		25.7	16.8	18.5	14.7	12.0
13.1	12.5	12.5	Operating Expenses		27.4	16.8	16.0	12.6	9.7
2.1	2.0	2.0	Operating Profit		-1.7	.0	2.5	2.1	2.3
.6	.5	.4	All Other Expenses (net)		.3	1.3	.1	.4	.5
1.5	1.5	1.5	Profit Before Taxes		-2.1	-1.3	2.4	1.7	1.9
			RATIOS						
1.8	1.8	1.9	Current		2.5	2.2	3.3	2.0	1.7
1.4	1.4	1.4			1.1	1.4	1.9	1.4	1.3
1.1	1.1	1.1			.8	1.0	1.3	1.2	1.1
1.0	1.1	1.1	Quick		1.1	1.0	2.2	1.2	.9
.7	.7	.7			.6	.7	1.2	.9	.6
.5	.5	.5			.4	.3	.7	.7	.4
22 16.9	23 15.8	21 17.0	Sales/Receivables	8 43.4	5 72.9	16 23.1	25 14.8	24 15.4	
29 12.8	29 12.4	30 12.0		16 23.4	15 24.5	31 11.9	34 10.7	30 12.0	
37 9.7	39 9.4	39 9.3		32 11.6	40 9.0	40 9.2	41 8.8	39 9.3	
14 25.3	16 22.7	12 31.3	Cost of Sales/Inventory	2 148.8	5 73.4	3 104.8	7 52.4	23 15.7	
35 10.5	39 9.5	34 10.8		16 22.5	18 20.0	16 22.8	29 12.4	43 8.5	
59 6.2	58 6.3	65 5.6		82 4.5	55 6.6	37 9.8	44 8.3	75 4.9	
12 29.5	13 27.8	12 29.6	Cost of Sales/Payables	5 80.3	0 UND	11 33.0	13 28.4	15 24.8	
22 17.0	22 16.3	23 16.1		16 22.9	6 63.3	27 13.7	22 16.3	24 15.1	
31 11.9	33 11.0	34 10.7		52 7.0	19 19.1	37 9.8	34 10.9	35 10.6	
10.6	10.3	10.3	Sales/Working Capital		5.5	12.1	5.8	10.9	11.0
18.9	17.5	19.2			218.4	33.2	11.7	17.7	20.3
57.0	56.4	70.0			-28.0	NM	65.8	45.7	56.4
	6.4		7.8		10.2	EBIT/Interest		41.0	8.5	15.1	10.4	9.7
(257) 2.5	(243) 3.1	(219) 4.4	EBIT/Interest	(11) 1.9	(11) 3.1	(27) 4.5	(54) 5.0	(116) 3.7	
1.2	1.3	1.8			-5.7	-.5	.8	2.3	2.2
12.4	7.5	10.2	Net Profit + Depr., Dep., Amort./Cur. Mat. L/T/D					8.5	13.4
(70) 2.9	(64) 3.9	(53) 4.3						(11) 2.5	(38) 4.8
1.5	1.0	1.7						1.7	1.8
.1	.0	.0	Fixed/Worth		.1	.3	.0	.0	.0
.3	.3	.3			.4	.9	.3	.2	.2
1.1	1.0	1.0			15.9	1.8	1.4	.6	.9
1.3	1.4	1.2	Debt/Worth		.9	.7	.5	1.3	1.5
2.7	2.9	2.6			2.2	1.9	1.3	2.8	3.0
7.5	7.7	6.0			NM	6.4	3.6	5.4	6.2
38.8	39.3	44.8	% Profit Before Taxes/Tangible Net Worth			35.4	49.4	54.7	41.6
(250) 14.9	(232) 15.3	(221) 21.6				(10) 19.5	(28) 21.4	(56) 23.0	(117) 20.7
5.0	4.5	7.5				6.5	2.6	7.9	8.5
10.2	10.4	11.6	% Profit Before Taxes/Total Assets		26.1	10.0	18.8	11.4	10.8
3.9	3.8	4.3			2.5	4.3	5.9	5.4	4.2
1.1	.9	1.7			-10.7	-7.6	.1	1.7	2.1
315.4	385.6	422.9	Sales/Net Fixed Assets		117.0	31.2	194.6	349.9	768.0
64.3	79.9	88.1			26.9	14.8	72.4	120.7	154.5
18.2	20.8	17.7			10.4	11.7	12.9	29.5	23.8
5.5	5.3	5.6	Sales/Total Assets		6.4	5.8	7.1	6.4	5.1
3.9	4.1	3.9			3.4	3.9	3.5	4.6	3.6
2.8	2.7	2.8			1.5	2.0	2.9	3.0	2.8
.1	.1	.1	% Depr., Dep., Amort./Sales			.7	.3	.1	.1
(231) .4	(212) .4	(191) .4			(11) 1.2	(24) .7	(43) .2	(105) .3	
1.0	.9	1.0			2.2	1.2	1.1	.8	
.8	.8	.8	% Officers', Directors' Owners' Comp/Sales				1.7	.8	.4
(108) 1.5	(110) 1.3	(105) 1.5				(20) 2.3	(35) 1.3	(37) .8	
2.9	2.4	2.7							
16806383M	15630556M	16377187M	Net Sales ($)	15M	25037M	47297M	240880M	1008255M	15055703M
5148197M	5174124M	4964324M	Total Assets ($)	1M	11387M	21379M	67886M	251320M	4612351M

Current Data Sorted by Assets | **Comparative Historical Data**

Type of Statement

0-500M	500M-2MM	2-10MM	10-50MM	50-100MM	100-250MM	Type of Statement	4/1/06-3/31/07 ALL	4/1/07-3/31/08 ALL
		5	16	8	3	Unqualified	27	25
	3	30	16			Reviewed	56	52
2	14	22	8			Compiled	38	29
3	17	5	2			Tax Returns	14	18
3	12	23	19	9	7	Other	60	52
	35 (4/1-9/30/10)		192 (10/1/10-3/31/11)					
8	46	85	61	17	10	**NUMBER OF STATEMENTS**	195	176

Assets (%)

0-500M	500M-2MM	2-10MM	10-50MM	50-100MM	100-250MM	ASSETS	4/1/06-3/31/07	4/1/07-3/31/08
	10.1	6.6	6.4	2.9	6.3	Cash & Equivalents	8.3	6.9
	35.5	42.9	36.3	28.9	30.4	Trade Receivables (net)	37.4	37.5
	24.0	28.3	26.7	31.2	31.7	Inventory	24.8	25.7
	1.9	1.4	4.4	2.9	2.6	All Other Current	1.7	2.4
	71.6	79.2	73.8	65.8	70.9	Total Current	72.4	72.6
	18.7	14.1	17.2	21.3	20.5	Fixed Assets (net)	19.1	18.0
	4.6	2.1	4.3	10.8	6.9	Intangibles (net)	3.6	5.0
	5.1	4.5	4.7	2.1	1.7	All Other Non-Current	5.0	4.4
	100.0	100.0	100.0	100.0	100.0	Total	100.0	100.0

Liabilities

0-500M	500M-2MM	2-10MM	10-50MM	50-100MM	100-250MM	LIABILITIES	4/1/06-3/31/07	4/1/07-3/31/08
	13.9	17.3	17.6	16.6	6.2	Notes Payable-Short Term	16.9	18.6
	4.7	2.2	2.7	1.7	1.0	Cur. Mat.-L.T.D.	2.5	2.6
	25.2	21.1	17.6	17.3	22.5	Trade Payables	22.2	21.4
	.2	.1	.1	.1	.0	Income Taxes Payable	.2	.1
	5.8	5.5	10.7	5.8	12.6	All Other Current	8.3	7.5
	49.8	46.3	48.7	41.5	42.3	Total Current	50.2	50.1
	15.5	5.7	10.2	14.4	20.3	Long-Term Debt	12.2	12.5
	.0	.1	.2	.3	.4	Deferred Taxes	.1	.1
	13.2	5.6	5.0	2.1	2.2	All Other Non-Current	4.1	5.2
	21.4	42.3	35.9	41.7	34.8	Net Worth	33.4	32.2
	100.0	100.0	100.0	100.0	100.0	Total Liabilities & Net Worth	100.0	100.0

Income Data

0-500M	500M-2MM	2-10MM	10-50MM	50-100MM	100-250MM	INCOME DATA	4/1/06-3/31/07	4/1/07-3/31/08
	100.0	100.0	100.0	100.0	100.0	Net Sales	100.0	100.0
	16.5	13.1	15.0	13.0	12.1	Gross Profit	15.1	14.0
	15.4	11.3	12.2	9.8	10.0	Operating Expenses	13.3	11.7
	1.1	1.9	2.9	3.2	2.1	Operating Profit	1.8	2.3
	.3	.3	.5	.5	.4	All Other Expenses (net)	.2	.7
	.7	1.6	2.4	2.7	1.8	Profit Before Taxes	1.6	1.6

Ratios

0-500M	500M-2MM	2-10MM	10-50MM	50-100MM	100-250MM	RATIOS	4/1/06-3/31/07	4/1/07-3/31/08
	2.2	3.0	2.5	2.5	2.9	Current	2.2	2.1
	1.5	1.6	1.4	1.7	1.5		1.4	1.4
	1.0	1.3	1.2	1.2	1.2		1.1	1.1
	1.5	1.8	1.4	1.2	1.5	Quick	1.4	1.3
	.9	1.1	.9	.8	.8		.9	.9
	.6	.5	.5	.6	.6		.6	.6
10 35.0		17 21.7	16 23.0	19 19.2	13 27.9	Sales/Receivables	15 23.7	15 24.0
15 25.1		23 16.0	22 16.8	22 16.4	20 18.2		22 16.8	20 18.5
25 14.8		31 11.6	27 13.7	31 11.6	26 14.2		31 11.8	27 13.7
5 71.4		9 42.6	10 36.0	19 19.7	19 19.5	Cost of Sales/Inventory	8 48.5	8 45.1
12 30.8		17 21.3	19 19.4	32 11.6	26 14.0		17 21.3	16 22.9
21 17.2		31 11.8	33 11.2	52 7.0	30 12.3		31 11.9	28 12.9
6 64.1		7 51.9	6 56.3	12 31.0	13 28.3	Cost of Sales/Payables	7 49.3	8 48.3
14 26.3		12 31.0	13 27.8	15 24.2	16 22.3		13 27.4	13 28.3
22 16.4		18 20.8	20 18.7	18 20.1	23 15.6		21 17.5	18 19.8
	20.4	11.3	11.6	8.4	13.2	Sales/Working Capital	14.1	15.9
	39.1	19.1	21.2	14.1	21.3		30.0	28.0
	870.1	44.2	54.7	39.5	49.3		82.1	100.8
	29.2	16.8	12.7	10.6		EBIT/Interest	6.2	6.4
	(38) 5.9	(74) 3.9	(56) 5.6	4.3			(164) 2.8	(158) 2.7
	.9	1.3	2.0	2.6			1.5	1.4
		9.4	16.2			Net Profit + Depr., Dep., Amort./Cur. Mat. L/T/D	9.1	15.5
		(12) 2.6	(19) 8.3				(39) 6.1	(35) 3.9
		.5	2.6				1.4	1.2
	.1	.1	.1	.4	.2	Fixed/Worth	.1	.1
	.8	.3	.4	.6	.8		.5	.4
	4.1	.6	1.2	1.3	1.2		1.6	1.4
	1.3	.7	.8	.9	1.6	Debt/Worth	1.0	1.2
	3.1	1.7	2.3	2.7	3.4		2.5	2.8
	39.1	3.0	5.3	5.4	7.5		6.2	5.4
	98.0	36.5	41.4	34.2	42.2	% Profit Before Taxes/Tangible Net Worth	47.2	41.3
	(38) 38.1	(80) 15.7	(54) 21.8	(15) 22.7	27.4		(174) 22.0	(160) 20.1
	7.2	3.3	9.9	15.2	21.8		6.0	7.0
	23.7	15.2	13.8	11.6	9.5	% Profit Before Taxes/Total Assets	13.3	10.5
	7.8	4.8	7.5	5.8	7.8		6.0	5.0
	-.3	1.0	2.0	4.6	4.4		1.2	1.4
	380.5	349.1	383.1	75.9	238.5	Sales/Net Fixed Assets	238.1	238.8
	66.5	83.2	57.2	39.5	24.6		57.5	64.1
	21.1	23.1	12.1	7.0	14.3		14.4	18.9
	11.6	9.0	7.5	7.3	6.8	Sales/Total Assets	8.3	8.4
	7.2	5.8	5.3	3.7	5.6		5.8	6.0
	4.6	4.4	3.1	1.8	4.5		3.7	3.9
	.2	.1	.2	.3		% Depr., Dep., Amort./Sales	.1	.1
	(29) .5	(71) .3	(51) .8	(15) .8			(167) .4	(148) .4
	1.3	.8	1.1				.9	.8
	.6	.5	.4			% Officers', Directors' Owners' Comp/Sales	.5	.5
	(29) 1.1	(43) 1.0	(16) 1.1				(82) 1.2	(74) 1.2
	2.6	2.4	2.2				2.3	2.2
32277M	501625M	2761640M	7109083M	5798756M	6869888M	Net Sales ($)	13119561M	16572918M
1981M	59808M	402752M	1270351M	1187850M	1256140M	Total Assets ($)	2486896M	3163148M

M = $ thousand   MM = $ million
See Pages 9 through 22 for Explanation of Ratios and Data

Comparative Historical Data				Current Data Sorted by Sales					
			Type of Statement				1	5	26
32	32	32	Unqualified			1		15	33
53	52	49	Reviewed	1	3	2	8	15	17
35	45	46	Compiled		1	2	11	9	4
27	20	27	Tax Returns		1	4	5	17	46
60	69	73	Other						
4/1/08-3/31/09 ALL	4/1/09-3/31/10 ALL	4/1/10-3/31/11 ALL		0-1MM	1-3MM	3-5MM	5-10MM	10-25MM	25MM & OVER
					35 (4/1-9/30/10)		192 (10/1/10-3/31/11)		
207	218	227	NUMBER OF STATEMENTS	1	5	9	25	61	126
%	%	%	ASSETS	%	%	%	%	%	%
7.7	8.4	7.3	Cash & Equivalents				4.8	8.3	5.7
38.1	37.0	37.8	Trade Receivables (net)				28.7	38.6	40.5
26.8	25.7	27.1	Inventory				26.6	27.8	28.0
2.4	2.8	2.4	All Other Current				1.6	2.5	2.6
75.0	73.9	74.5	Total Current				61.7	77.1	76.8
16.7	17.3	16.9	Fixed Assets (net)				25.1	14.5	15.3
3.5	4.9	4.2	Intangibles (net)				7.7	2.9	4.4
4.9	4.0	4.4	All Other Non-Current				5.6	5.4	3.5
100.0	100.0	100.0	Total				100.0	100.0	100.0
			LIABILITIES						
18.0	17.4	15.9	Notes Payable-Short Term				9.8	15.8	17.7
1.9	1.8	2.9	Cur. Mat.-L.T.D.				6.4	2.1	2.4
21.1	18.7	21.0	Trade Payables				18.4	21.9	21.1
.1	.2	.1	Income Taxes Payable				.1	.1	.2
7.5	7.6	7.3	All Other Current				3.6	6.5	9.0
48.7	45.7	47.3	Total Current				38.1	46.4	50.4
10.3	11.7	10.3	Long-Term Debt				23.7	5.2	9.3
.1	.1	.2	Deferred Taxes				.1	.1	.2
6.0	9.8	6.8	All Other Non-Current				12.5	8.6	4.7
34.9	32.7	35.5	Net Worth				25.6	39.7	35.3
100.0	100.0	100.0	Total Liabilities & Net Worth				100.0	100.0	100.0
			INCOME DATA						
100.0	100.0	100.0	Net Sales				100.0	100.0	100.0
14.6	16.5	14.5	Gross Profit				17.5	14.4	12.4
12.4	13.9	12.5	Operating Expenses				16.9	12.0	10.1
2.2	2.6	2.1	Operating Profit				.6	2.4	2.2
.4	.3	.4	All Other Expenses (net)				.8	.2	.4
1.8	2.3	1.7	Profit Before Taxes				-.1	2.2	1.9
			RATIOS						
2.3	2.8	2.4					6.2	2.7	2.2
1.5	1.6	1.6	Current				1.9	1.6	1.4
1.2	1.2	1.2					1.0	1.3	1.2
1.5	1.6	1.6					1.9	1.8	1.4
.9	.9	.9	Quick				.9	.9	.9
.6	.6	.6					.4	.6	.7
14 26.4	15 24.8	15 25.0					11 34.6	14 25.8	16 22.7
19 19.0	21 17.5	21 17.5	Sales/Receivables				16 23.5	22 16.7	21 17.3
27 13.6	29 12.8	28 12.8					29 12.5	29 12.7	27 13.5
8 48.0	8 43.6	8 43.7					6 65.2	9 41.1	9 42.6
16 22.4	18 20.4	18 19.9	Cost of Sales/Inventory				17 21.6	19 19.3	18 19.8
30 12.3	31 11.6	31 11.9					44 8.3	31 11.8	31 11.9
7 53.3	7 49.4	7 51.7					5 74.3	6 60.7	8 45.5
12 31.4	12 31.0	13 28.0	Cost of Sales/Payables				13 28.4	13 29.0	13 28.4
20 18.4	18 20.0	20 18.4					22 16.8	19 19.5	19 18.8
15.0	11.2	11.6					7.5	11.3	14.1
30.1	23.2	23.3	Sales/Working Capital				28.8	20.5	24.2
74.8	68.2	57.6					-340.9	54.3	50.2
9.3	16.5	15.7					15.7	22.3	12.7
(185) 3.7	(195) 5.2	(199) 5.0	EBIT/Interest		(23) 2.8	(49) 3.6		(115) 5.7	
1.5	2.0	1.9					1.0	1.3	2.4
5.9	15.5	14.4							14.5
(35) 2.8	(39) 4.7	(39) 5.1	Net Profit + Depr., Dep., Amort./Cur. Mat. L/T/D						(31) 8.1
1.0	1.5	1.4							2.6
.1	.1	.1					.4	.1	.1
.4	.4	.4	Fixed/Worth				.9	.3	.4
1.0	1.7	1.0					3.7	.9	1.0
1.0	.8	1.0					1.2	.7	1.2
2.2	2.2	2.1	Debt/Worth				2.9	1.5	2.4
4.5	7.1	4.6					16.8	3.1	4.8
47.2	55.1	43.3					105.8	51.7	40.2
(191) 23.4	(188) 27.9	(203) 23.3	% Profit Before Taxes/Tangible Net Worth		(20) 10.0	(56) 24.0		(114) 25.5	
7.1	12.3	7.1					1.0	3.8	13.3
14.2	18.2	15.3					16.3	23.4	12.8
6.2	8.2	6.9	% Profit Before Taxes/Total Assets				3.7	5.9	7.0
2.1	2.5	2.0					-.4		2.9
316.7	234.6	315.3					255.3	301.5	378.2
81.0	67.9	70.4	Sales/Net Fixed Assets				42.4	75.6	80.7
21.8	15.6	16.3					8.9	20.0	19.2
9.4	8.1	8.7					6.6	10.3	9.0
6.2	5.6	5.8	Sales/Total Assets				5.1	5.8	6.3
4.2	3.7	4.0					3.1	4.1	4.1
.1	.1	.1					.2	.2	.1
(167) .4	(176) .4	(180) .5	% Depr., Dep., Amort./Sales		(18) 1.0	(45) .5		(108) .3	
.9	.8	1.0					1.8	1.0	.8
.5	.7	.5					.6	.6	.4
(93) 1.0	(86) 1.6	(94) 1.1	% Officers', Directors', Owners' Comp/Sales		(18) 1.9	(30) 1.1		(38) .8	
.9	3.0	2.5					3.2	2.5	1.5
19013536M	20612883M	23073269M	Net Sales ($)	202M	9433M	35104M	190564M	1065125M	21772841M
3607430M	3994373M	4178882M	Total Assets ($)	97M	2440M	8061M	49614M	217395M	3901275M

© RMA 2011

M = $ thousand   MM = $ million
See Pages 9 through 22 for Explanation of Ratios and Data

Current Data Sorted by Assets   Comparative Historical Data

0-500M	500M-2MM	2-10MM	10-50MM	50-100MM	100-250MM	Type of Statement	4/1/06-3/31/07 ALL	4/1/07-3/31/08 ALL
1	1	7	16	10	5	Unqualified	41	36
	4	38	27	2	1	Reviewed	75	70
1	17	26	19			Compiled	70	75
3	15	20	1			Tax Returns	24	22
3	5	53	34	9	2	Other	64	85
	90 (4/1-9/30/10)		230 (10/1/10-3/31/11)					
8	42	144	97	21	8	NUMBER OF STATEMENTS	274	288
%	%	%	%	%	%	**ASSETS**	%	%
	15.8	10.0	10.5	6.2		Cash & Equivalents	8.9	10.1
	41.1	47.0	33.5	26.2		Trade Receivables (net)	41.7	41.6
	11.1	10.9	12.0	15.6		Inventory	9.6	8.1
	6.4	5.0	3.0	5.0		All Other Current	3.7	5.9
	74.4	73.0	59.0	53.0		Total Current	63.9	65.7
	16.0	18.4	31.8	31.3		Fixed Assets (net)	25.0	23.8
	2.4	2.3	3.5	9.5		Intangibles (net)	3.1	3.0
	7.2	6.3	5.7	6.1		All Other Non-Current	8.0	7.6
	100.0	100.0	100.0	100.0		Total	100.0	100.0
						LIABILITIES		
	7.8	8.4	5.9	6.7		Notes Payable-Short Term	9.9	10.3
	2.0	1.9	2.6	4.1		Cur. Mat.-L.T.D.	2.6	2.4
	28.9	36.6	27.3	19.2		Trade Payables	32.5	31.2
	.4	.1	.3	.2		Income Taxes Payable	.1	.2
	9.2	9.9	9.2	8.3		All Other Current	9.7	9.0
	48.3	56.9	45.2	38.5		Total Current	54.8	53.1
	6.5	7.7	16.7	24.2		Long-Term Debt	12.7	12.0
	.1	.2	.4	1.9		Deferred Taxes	.6	.4
	2.4	4.4	4.3	2.3		All Other Non-Current	3.7	3.2
	42.8	30.9	33.4	33.1		Net Worth	28.3	31.4
	100.0	100.0	100.0	100.0		Total Liabilities & Net Worth	100.0	100.0
						INCOME DATA		
	100.0	100.0	100.0	100.0		Net Sales	100.0	100.0
	18.7	20.1	21.1	19.3		Gross Profit	20.3	20.0
	17.3	16.4	16.4	14.6		Operating Expenses	17.5	16.3
	1.4	3.7	4.7	4.7		Operating Profit	2.8	3.7
	-.6	.5	.1	-.1		All Other Expenses (net)	.9	.3
	2.1	3.1	4.6	4.8		Profit Before Taxes	1.9	3.4
						RATIOS		
	2.7	1.7	1.9	1.7			1.7	1.7
	1.6	1.2	1.3	1.4		Current	1.2	1.2
	1.0	1.0	1.0	1.2			1.0	1.0
	2.0	1.4	1.5	1.2			1.3	1.3
	1.2	1.0	1.0	.9		Quick	.9	.9
	.7	.8	.7	.5			.7	.7
	8 43.6	23 15.9	23 16.2	27 13.7			21 17.4	20 18.2
	25 14.4	30 12.2	28 13.0	29 12.5		Sales/Receivables	28 12.9	28 13.1
	34 10.8	39 9.5	36 10.1	37 9.8			37 9.9	39 9.4
	0 UND	2 146.1	4 89.4	6 61.7			2 176.5	1 506.6
	2 148.0	6 61.6	8 47.6	7 52.7		Cost of Sales/Inventory	6 60.0	5 76.4
	11 32.7	12 30.4	22 16.7	65 5.6			12 30.9	10 37.3
	5 75.2	17 21.1	19 19.2	17 21.0			16 22.9	15 23.7
	18 20.1	29 12.5	29 12.7	24 15.4		Cost of Sales/Payables	24 14.9	25 14.7
	31 11.8	41 9.0	42 8.7	47 7.8			37 9.8	36 10.2
	9.7	15.4	11.5	10.6			18.7	18.8
	22.2	47.8	28.4	24.6		Sales/Working Capital	53.9	53.8
	NM	295.0	163.3	43.7			-255.9	-999.8
	19.7	28.7	21.4	13.3			12.3	14.2
	(33) 3.4	(128) 8.0	(89) 7.9	(19) 6.6		EBIT/Interest	(251) 3.8	(258) 5.0
	-.5	2.7	2.8	3.8			1.3	1.8
		9.0	8.2	6.9		Net Profit + Depr., Dep.,	8.2	10.5
		(33) 3.1	(34) 3.8	(11) 2.9		Amort./Cur. Mat. L/T/D	(72) 4.1	(70) 3.4
		1.4	2.6	2.5			1.5	1.7
	.0	.1	.4	.8			.3	.2
	.2	.5	.9	1.4		Fixed/Worth	.7	.6
	.5	1.2	2.0	3.0			1.8	2.0
	.6	1.2	1.3	1.2			1.2	1.3
	1.5	2.6	2.3	2.8		Debt/Worth	2.4	2.4
	4.3	6.4	4.5	6.8			5.3	5.0
	58.6	57.3	47.6	59.1		% Profit Before Taxes/Tangible	43.6	50.7
	(38) 18.5	(133) 27.5	(90) 25.8	(18) 27.1		Net Worth	(247) 17.8	(257) 20.0
	3.9	7.1	11.0	19.9			4.8	8.2
	17.1	15.9	13.4	14.1		% Profit Before Taxes/Total	12.5	16.0
	4.3	6.4	6.7	9.1		Assets	5.4	6.0
	1.1	1.8	2.7	5.5			.7	1.4
	576.7	201.8	45.8	18.1			103.2	119.4
	79.4	47.6	11.5	11.7		Sales/Net Fixed Assets	26.5	29.7
	28.0	16.6	5.0	6.7			10.1	10.6
	9.4	7.9	6.0	4.9			7.8	7.9
	6.3	6.1	3.7	3.4		Sales/Total Assets	5.4	5.2
	3.3	3.9	2.0	1.6			3.2	2.7
	.2	.2	.5	1.0			.3	.2
	(35) .3	(118) .5	(88) 1.1	(19) 1.4		% Depr., Dep., Amort./Sales	(247) .7	(255) .7
	.9	.9	2.3	3.0			1.4	1.4
	1.3	.7	.4			% Officers', Directors'	.9	.6
	(25) 2.0	(66) 1.5	(25) .6			Owners' Comp/Sales	(113) 1.7	(110) 1.7
	3.1	2.7	1.4				2.5	2.6
27371M	360920M	4261843M	7876414M	4645463M	2596427M	Net Sales ($)	15638859M	20524342M
2229M	50106M	726811M	2065633M	1444881M	1232790M	Total Assets ($)	3771877M	4886626M

© RMA 2011

M = $ thousand   MM = $ million
See Pages 9 through 22 for Explanation of Ratios and Data

Comparative Historical Data | | | | Current Data Sorted by Sales

			Type of Statement						
38	42	40	Unqualified		1		1	7	31
73	76	72	Reviewed		1		3	15	52
67	76	63	Compiled		5	4	9	17	28
40	43	39	Tax Returns		2	3	14	14	6
93	101	106	Other	1	3	1	9	25	67
4/1/08-3/31/09	4/1/09-3/31/10	4/1/10-3/31/11			90 (4/1-9/30/10)		230 (10/1/10-3/31/11)		
ALL	ALL	ALL		0-1MM	1-3MM	3-5MM	5-10MM	10-25MM	25MM & OVER
311	338	320	NUMBER OF STATEMENTS	1	12	9	36	78	184
%	%	%	ASSETS	%	%	%	%	%	%
9.7	11.3	10.7	Cash & Equivalents		17.9		15.9	10.1	9.1
40.6	41.2	40.0	Trade Receivables (net)		24.1		36.0	40.1	41.7
10.0	9.5	11.6	Inventory		8.1		11.2	12.3	11.1
5.7	5.3	4.4	All Other Current		10.2		6.7	2.9	4.3
66.0	67.3	66.8	Total Current		60.4		69.9	65.5	66.3
22.7	22.0	23.9	Fixed Assets (net)		28.1		20.9	26.0	24.0
3.0	2.7	3.2	Intangibles (net)		.7		3.0	1.9	4.1
8.3	8.0	6.1	All Other Non-Current		10.8		6.3	6.7	5.7
100.0	100.0	100.0	Total		100.0		100.0	100.0	100.0
			LIABILITIES						
9.6	9.3	8.0	Notes Payable-Short Term		4.1		16.5	8.0	6.3
2.2	2.5	2.3	Cur. Mat.-L.T.D.		2.5		2.1	2.8	2.1
32.7	31.8	31.3	Trade Payables		25.4		25.4	29.6	33.5
.2	.2	.2	Income Taxes Payable		.1		.1	.2	.1
9.3	8.9	9.3	All Other Current		7.2		12.0	6.7	10.3
53.9	52.5	51.1	Total Current		39.3		56.0	47.4	52.4
12.8	12.6	12.2	Long-Term Debt		27.6		10.7	9.4	13.0
.4	.3	.4	Deferred Taxes		.2		.0	.2	.6
5.4	3.8	3.8	All Other Non-Current		1.7		3.1	5.9	3.2
27.5	30.8	32.5	Net Worth		31.1		30.2	37.1	30.8
100.0	100.0	100.0	Total Liabilities & Net Worth		100.0		100.0	100.0	100.0
			INCOME DATA						
100.0	100.0	100.0	Net Sales		100.0		100.0	100.0	100.0
20.0	19.1	20.3	Gross Profit		36.8		28.6	21.8	16.7
17.1	16.3	16.2	Operating Expenses		30.3		22.5	17.4	13.2
2.9	2.9	4.1	Operating Profit		6.5		6.1	4.3	3.5
.4	.2	.3	All Other Expenses (net)		.0		1.5	.0	.2
2.6	2.7	3.8	Profit Before Taxes		6.5		4.6	4.3	3.3
			RATIOS						
1.6	1.9	1.8	Current		2.9		2.0	2.3	1.7
1.2	1.3	1.3			1.8		1.4	1.3	1.3
1.0	1.0	1.0			.8		.9	1.0	1.1
1.3	1.4	1.4	Quick		2.2		1.4	1.8	1.3
.9	1.0	1.0			1.0		1.0	1.1	1.0
.7	.7	.7			.7		.7	.6	.7
20 18.0	21 17.7	23 16.2	Sales/Receivables	0 UND			22 16.4	22 16.3	23 16.0
28 13.2	29 12.6	29 12.7		25 14.4			31 11.9	31 11.8	28 12.9
37 9.9	37 9.7	37 9.8		28 13.1			61 6.0	42 8.7	35 10.5
2 214.3	2 199.3	3 138.3	Cost of Sales/Inventory	0 UND			1 619.3	3 106.3	3 125.2
6 66.3	6 61.8	6 56.9		1 347.6			7 50.5	8 45.7	6 57.2
12 31.6	11 34.3	15 24.5		10 36.1			23 15.7	21 17.1	12 30.7
15 24.7	15 24.3	17 21.6	Cost of Sales/Payables	3 106.5			11 32.8	17 21.3	18 20.1
25 14.7	25 14.8	27 13.3		17 21.4			26 13.9	29 12.5	27 13.8
36 10.1	37 9.8	41 9.0		62 5.9			44 8.2	44 8.2	38 9.5
19.9	14.7	13.7	Sales/Working Capital		3.5		10.4	13.4	16.2
43.2	35.3	34.8			11.6		21.1	27.8	39.4
999.8	725.5	228.6			-38.1		NM	384.9	164.4
14.3	16.2	21.6	EBIT/Interest				11.5	20.9	21.6
(283) 4.4	(298) 6.1	(282) 6.9					(30) 3.3	(70) 7.9	(165) 7.0
1.8	1.7	2.7					-2.3	1.9	3.0
6.6	8.8	7.7	Net Profit + Depr., Dep., Amort./Cur. Mat. L/T/D					6.7	8.1
(76) 2.8	(82) 3.0	(86) 3.4						(16) 2.3	(62) 3.4
1.5	1.4	2.2						1.1	2.5
.2	.2	.2	Fixed/Worth		.0		.2	.1	.2
.6	.6	.7			.6		.4	.7	.8
1.8	1.8	1.6			7.2		1.5	1.3	1.7
1.3	1.0	1.1	Debt/Worth		.4		.7	.9	1.3
2.7	2.4	2.3			1.9		1.8	2.0	2.6
7.1	6.0	5.2			14.5		7.1	3.8	6.2
50.7	50.1	52.3	% Profit Before Taxes/Tangible Net Worth		137.3		69.7	51.0	51.5
(274) 20.0	(303) 20.3	(292) 26.6		(10) 35.6		(32) 26.4	(72) 25.5	(169) 26.6	
4.9	5.1	8.1			3.7		-2.2	6.6	11.4
13.5	15.2	14.9	% Profit Before Taxes/Total Assets		22.1		15.8	16.2	13.8
5.5	5.0	6.8			6.3		6.2	7.6	6.6
1.0	1.4	1.9			-1.2		-2.5	1.6	2.3
120.4	161.0	119.1	Sales/Net Fixed Assets		459.5		94.1	67.9	126.6
35.3	34.9	28.4			15.8		29.1	23.8	32.9
12.0	10.2	9.1			4.0		9.1	7.4	9.8
7.7	7.5	7.3	Sales/Total Assets		5.0		6.8	7.1	7.9
5.6	5.3	5.3			2.9		3.5	4.5	5.5
3.0	3.0	2.6			1.3		1.8	2.6	3.0
.2	.2	.3	% Depr., Dep., Amort./Sales				.2	.4	.3
(263) .6	(278) .7	(269) .6				(32) .6	(66) .7	(159) .6	
1.4	1.6	1.7					1.8	2.2	1.5
.6	.8	.7	% Officers', Directors' Owners' Comp/Sales				.8	.7	.5
(118) 1.5	(125) 1.7	(121) 1.4				(18) 2.3	(40) 1.6	(54) .9	
2.6	3.1	2.6					2.7	3.0	1.7
19652929M	21831021M	19768438M	Net Sales ($)	381M	25724M	36300M	252615M	1328530M	18124888M
5352042M	5676819M	5522450M	Total Assets ($)	11M	40968M	14556M	134728M	436440M	4895747M

M = $ thousand   MM = $ million
See Pages 9 through 22 for Explanation of Ratios and Data

Current Data Sorted by Assets | Comparative Historical Data

Type of Statement	0-500M	500M-2MM	2-10MM	10-50MM	50-100MM	100-250MM		4/1/06-3/31/07 ALL	4/1/07-3/31/08 ALL
Unqualified		4	16	34	18	8		76	78
Reviewed		9	52	43	2	1		71	65
Compiled	3	22	31	6	1	1		58	51
Tax Returns	8	29	27	4	1			43	47
Other	7	19	59	60	14	6		115	115
	108 (4/1-9/30/10)			376 (10/1/10-3/31/11)					
NUMBER OF STATEMENTS	18	83	185	147	36	15		363	356
ASSETS	%	%	%	%	%	%		%	%
Cash & Equivalents	9.6	12.2	7.3	7.0	6.6	7.2		8.4	7.9
Trade Receivables (net)	22.2	33.8	32.8	29.1	28.2	24.6		28.7	28.3
Inventory	32.5	26.5	34.0	32.6	28.8	32.1		29.7	29.9
All Other Current	4.7	4.5	2.1	3.6	4.7	2.0		2.6	3.5
Total Current	69.0	77.0	76.1	72.2	68.4	65.9		69.5	69.6
Fixed Assets (net)	16.2	14.1	15.1	18.3	20.2	15.9		19.8	19.4
Intangibles (net)	11.2	4.0	3.2	4.9	6.5	13.0		4.8	4.4
All Other Non-Current	3.5	4.8	5.6	4.6	5.0	5.2		6.0	6.6
Total	100.0	100.0	100.0	100.0	100.0	100.0		100.0	100.0
LIABILITIES									
Notes Payable-Short Term	29.4	12.8	14.8	16.0	19.2	13.3		17.1	17.0
Cur. Mat.-L.T.D.	2.2	2.6	1.8	2.4	2.0	2.0		2.7	2.5
Trade Payables	15.5	26.1	29.6	23.3	18.4	25.3		22.5	22.2
Income Taxes Payable	.0	.0	.3	.2	.4	.8		.2	.2
All Other Current	5.8	8.0	7.5	7.7	12.0	14.5		9.1	8.9
Total Current	53.0	49.5	54.0	49.6	51.9	55.9		51.7	50.9
Long-Term Debt	20.1	12.5	9.1	9.9	15.8	7.9		13.9	15.7
Deferred Taxes	.0	.0	.4	.2	.4	.4		.4	.4
All Other Non-Current	3.3	5.3	5.0	3.8	2.2	3.4		4.6	4.8
Net Worth	23.6	32.7	31.5	36.5	29.6	32.4		29.3	28.4
Total Liabilities & Net Worth	100.0	100.0	100.0	100.0	100.0	100.0		100.0	100.0
INCOME DATA									
Net Sales	100.0	100.0	100.0	100.0	100.0	100.0		100.0	100.0
Gross Profit	33.9	24.9	23.3	19.3	18.6	22.5		25.7	24.6
Operating Expenses	26.5	22.2	20.4	15.4	14.5	14.4		22.3	21.4
Operating Profit	7.4	2.6	2.9	3.9	4.2	8.1		3.3	3.2
All Other Expenses (net)	.7	.2	.4	.3	.5	.4		.7	.7
Profit Before Taxes	6.6	2.4	2.5	3.6	3.7	7.7		2.6	2.5
RATIOS									
Current	2.8	2.4	2.0	2.1	2.0	1.3		2.0	2.2
	1.7	1.5	1.4	1.4	1.3	1.2		1.4	1.4
	1.1	1.2	1.1	1.1	1.1	1.0		1.1	1.1
Quick	1.1	1.4	1.1	1.1	1.0	.9		1.2	1.3
	.7	.9	.7	.7	.7	.5		.7 (355)	.7
	.4	.6	.5	.5	.5	.4		.4	.4
Sales/Receivables	0 UND	18 20.4	22 16.7	21 17.3	19 19.5	13 28.3		18 20.2	18 20.7
	18 19.9	25 14.6	30 12.0	29 12.7	26 13.9	28 13.0		28 12.9	26 13.9
	40 9.1	33 11.2	41 9.0	38 9.6	40 9.2	46 7.9		39 9.5	37 9.8
Cost of Sales/Inventory	7 51.0	7 52.6	21 17.5	20 18.2	22 16.8	17 21.3		18 19.8	18 20.5
	39 9.3	26 14.3	42 8.6	38 9.6	36 10.0	54 6.8		36 10.2	34 10.8
	121 3.0	51 7.1	72 5.1	74 4.9	60 6.1	95 3.8		67 5.5	62 5.9
Cost of Sales/Payables	0 UND	13 27.6	18 20.8	15 24.7	11 34.0	20 17.9		15 24.8	13 28.7
	13 29.2	25 14.6	31 11.6	24 15.0	23 16.0	23 15.8		26 14.2	25 14.5
	40 9.2	43 8.6	51 7.2	43 8.5	30 12.0	46 8.0		38 9.5	37 10.0
Sales/Working Capital	7.8	9.3	9.2	7.6	10.2	17.8		9.9	9.7
	13.4	18.0	17.7	16.0	24.4	34.2		22.0	19.8
	NM	72.9	55.1	79.2	109.4	260.7		101.8	79.7
EBIT/Interest	56.6	18.0	12.4	21.7	15.7	40.9		10.2	10.7
	(12) 5.5	(74) 4.1	(162) 5.0	(135) 7.3	(34) 4.5	(14) 5.5		(330) 3.1	(320) 3.2
	1.9	1.1	1.8	2.8	3.6	4.3		1.3	1.4
Net Profit + Depr., Dep., Amort./Cur. Mat. L/T/D			8.0	8.4	16.4			10.4	17.6
			(40) 3.3	(43) 2.6	(14) 5.3			(96) 4.3	(85) 6.0
			2.1	1.2	2.3			1.5	2.0
Fixed/Worth	.0	.0	.1	.1	.2	.4		.1	.1
	.2	.3	.3	.4	.9	.8		.5	.5
	1.2	1.3	1.1	1.8	2.2	1.3		1.9	1.7
Debt/Worth	.5	1.0	1.1	1.1	1.5	1.9		1.1	1.1
	1.6	2.7	2.6	2.1	3.1	4.1		2.7	2.4
	-8.3	7.3	6.4	6.6	10.1	5.2		7.9	8.1
% Profit Before Taxes/Tangible Net Worth	92.6	52.5	50.1	50.7	53.6	56.4		47.0	45.1
	(13) 29.9	(70) 16.4	(172) 20.4	(134) 25.0	(31) 35.2	(14) 41.7		(305) 19.6	(308) 21.6
	3.8	2.8	6.5	15.9	20.8	23.0		7.4	7.8
% Profit Before Taxes/Total Assets	38.5	17.3	13.0	16.3	14.4	10.7		14.3	14.0
	11.5	4.6	5.6	7.9	8.2	7.7		6.3	6.2
	3.9	.8	1.6	4.0	6.5	4.8		1.4	1.3
Sales/Net Fixed Assets	UND	999.8	165.4	210.0	84.2	150.6		134.9	140.7
	71.0	62.5	49.0	38.8	25.8	21.3		32.4	34.6
	24.2	22.9	16.6	9.5	11.0	7.2		10.5	11.7
Sales/Total Assets	6.8	6.1	5.3	4.8	5.6	4.3		5.5	5.3
	3.4	4.4	3.6	3.0	3.3	2.5		3.4	3.5
	2.0	3.2	2.4	2.1	1.8	1.4		2.4	2.6
% Depr., Dep., Amort./Sales		.2	.2	.2	.2	.3		.3	.3
		(53) .7	(144) .5	(124) .6	(31) .6	(12) 1.0		(303) .7	(288) .7
		1.6	1.3	1.7	1.5	1.8		2.0	1.5
% Officers', Directors' Owners' Comp/Sales		1.2	1.1	.5				.9	.9
		(47) 2.8	(83) 1.9	(38) 1.3				(126) 2.3	(137) 1.8
		4.1	3.2	3.2				4.0	4.4
Net Sales ($)	29942M	524233M	3747212M	12417564M	10025822M	7181111M		24191539M	25557364M
Total Assets ($)	5434M	101749M	907612M	3260114M	2373214M	2300816M		7185386M	7713201M

© RMA 2011

M = $ thousand   MM = $ million
See Pages 9 through 22 for Explanation of Ratios and Data

Comparative Historical Data — Current Data Sorted by Sales

	4/1/08-3/31/09 ALL	4/1/09-3/31/10 ALL	4/1/10-3/31/11 ALL	Type of Statement	108 (4/1-9/30/10) 0-1MM	1-3MM	376 (10/1/10-3/31/11) 3-5MM	5-10MM	10-25MM	25MM & OVER
	63	80	80	Unqualified		2	2	2	9	67
	90	100	107	Reviewed	2	1		9	34	61
	51	49	63	Compiled	1	8	7	18	19	10
	54	66	69	Tax Returns	4	11	5	27	17	5
	150	157	165	Other	3	8	6	22	39	87
	408	452	484	**NUMBER OF STATEMENTS**	10	27	21	78	118	230
	%	%	%	**ASSETS**	%	%	%	%	%	%
	7.1	7.9	8.1	Cash & Equivalents	12.3	11.5	15.5	8.1	7.5	7.0
	29.2	30.2	30.9	Trade Receivables (net)	23.6	21.2	21.4	32.3	32.1	32.1
	31.5	30.9	31.8	Inventory	33.9	19.8	34.0	36.8	30.2	32.0
	4.0	3.1	3.2	All Other Current	3.2	8.1	4.4	1.4	2.7	3.4
	71.8	72.0	73.9	Total Current	73.1	60.5	75.3	78.7	72.5	74.5
	18.0	17.8	16.4	Fixed Assets (net)	20.1	24.5	15.9	12.3	17.0	16.3
	4.2	4.8	4.7	Intangibles (net)	4.4	8.9	3.4	3.0	5.4	4.6
	6.1	5.4	5.0	All Other Non-Current	2.1	6.0	5.4	6.1	5.1	4.6
	100.0	100.0	100.0	Total	100.0	100.0	100.0	100.0	100.0	100.0
				LIABILITIES						
	17.4	15.8	15.7	Notes Payable-Short Term	16.0	23.1	15.5	13.1	15.1	16.0
	2.9	2.8	2.2	Cur. Mat.-L.T.D.	5.0	2.7	2.7	2.1	2.2	2.0
	21.9	22.8	25.6	Trade Payables	12.6	18.8	22.5	31.0	25.3	25.6
	.2	.3	.2	Income Taxes Payable	.0	.0	.0	.2	.3	.3
	9.0	9.0	8.1	All Other Current	3.9	9.5	5.1	8.2	6.8	9.0
	51.3	50.7	51.8	Total Current	37.5	54.1	45.7	54.6	49.6	52.8
	12.5	12.3	10.8	Long-Term Debt	11.7	24.4	15.5	10.3	9.0	9.8
	.3	.3	.3	Deferred Taxes	.0	.0	.0	.0	.5	.3
	4.0	4.5	4.4	All Other Non-Current	8.0	4.2	2.6	4.8	5.5	3.7
	31.9	32.2	32.8	Net Worth	42.8	17.3	36.2	30.3	35.4	33.4
	100.0	100.0	100.0	Total Liabilities & Net Worth	100.0	100.0	100.0	100.0	100.0	100.0
				INCOME DATA						
	100.0	100.0	100.0	Net Sales	100.0	100.0	100.0	100.0	100.0	100.0
	22.9	23.5	22.4	Gross Profit	38.9	37.1	26.7	24.7	23.5	18.2
	20.1	19.9	18.8	Operating Expenses	31.5	32.4	23.8	22.5	19.9	14.4
	2.8	3.6	3.6	Operating Profit	7.4	4.7	2.9	2.2	3.5	3.8
	.7	.4	.3	All Other Expenses (net)	.8	.7	.7	.3	.4	.2
	2.1	3.2	3.2	Profit Before Taxes	6.6	4.1	2.2	1.9	3.1	3.6
				RATIOS						
	2.2	2.1	2.1	Current	5.1	2.1	3.0	2.4	2.0	2.0
	1.4	1.5	1.4		1.8	1.6	2.2	1.4	1.4	1.4
	1.1	1.1	1.1		1.1	1.0	1.1	1.1	1.2	1.1
	1.2	1.1	1.1	Quick	3.2	1.0	2.0	1.1	1.2	1.1
	.7	.8	.7		1.0	.7	1.0	.7	.8	.7
	.5	.5	.5		.6	.3	.4	.4	.5	.5
	18 20.0	19 19.1	20 18.3	Sales/Receivables	0 UND	14 26.3	15 24.1	22 16.4	22 16.4	19 18.9
	27 13.5	27 13.3	28 13.0		36 10.2	26 14.2	23 16.0	32 11.3	30 12.2	27 13.4
	37 9.8	38 9.6	38 9.5		100 3.7	35 10.3	30 12.3	43 8.5	39 9.4	38 9.7
	19 19.5	19 19.5	19 19.4	Cost of Sales/Inventory	0 UND	8 45.0	16 22.9	25 14.3	20 18.2	18 19.9
	33 11.2	37 9.9	36 10.2		97 3.7	28 13.1	44 8.4	54 6.8	29 12.4	34 10.7
	63 5.8	62 5.9	68 5.3		242 1.5	63 5.8	77 4.8	91 4.0	65 5.6	63 5.8
	14 26.7	15 24.7	14 25.5	Cost of Sales/Payables	3 107.8	12 31.7	11 33.5	16 23.0	14 25.3	14 25.6
	23 15.9	24 15.2	26 14.1		43 8.5	26 13.9	30 12.0	39 9.5	27 13.7	23 16.0
	36 10.2	38 9.7	45 8.1		76 4.8	57 6.4	45 8.1	66 5.5	47 7.8	36 10.1
	9.0	8.9	8.9	Sales/Working Capital	2.4	8.9	8.0	7.4	9.6	9.8
	18.9	17.6	17.8		5.7	12.5	11.0	15.0	19.6	20.5
	65.2	69.6	64.6		NM	-999.8	81.3	62.1	73.1	65.5
	11.5	16.4	14.8	EBIT/Interest		7.6	12.3	9.4	14.0	21.7
	(376) 3.6	(416) 5.2	(431) 5.6			(25) 3.7	(14) 4.1	(66) 2.8	(109) 6.3	(211) 6.5
	1.4	2.0	2.3			1.1	-1.0	1.3	2.2	3.0
	11.7	9.6	9.5	Net Profit + Depr., Dep., Amort./Cur. Mat. L/T/D					7.8	11.7
	(91) 5.0	(112) 4.0	(111) 3.3						(35) 3.1	(69) 3.6
	1.7	1.8	1.8						1.6	1.8
	.1	.1	.1	Fixed/Worth	.0	.0	.0	.1	.1	.1
	.4	.4	.4		.0	.7	.3	.3	.3	.4
	1.5	1.7	1.5		1.0	-4.9	1.7	1.6	1.2	1.6
	1.0	1.0	1.0	Debt/Worth	.4	.8	.5	1.0	1.0	1.2
	2.5	2.4	2.6		1.4	3.9	1.0	2.9	3.0	2.5
	6.9	6.4	6.8		NM	-5.9	3.0	7.6	6.0	6.8
	41.2	45.3	51.9	% Profit Before Taxes/Tangible Net Worth		89.9	37.2	37.0	55.8	53.6
	(352) 19.7	(397) 25.1	(434) 23.8			(18) 27.2	(18) 16.7	(71) 14.8	(110) 23.1	(209) 28.9
	6.6	11.1	9.8			-7.4	1.6	3.2	6.6	17.0
	13.0	14.9	15.2	% Profit Before Taxes/Total Assets	17.6	15.1	25.5	8.6	15.2	16.0
	6.1	7.2	6.8		6.8	5.9	5.3	3.5	5.3	8.0
	1.1	2.5	2.6		1.9		-1.5	.5	2.0	4.6
	188.5	162.0	232.2	Sales/Net Fixed Assets	UND	999.8	UND	235.4	150.7	268.2
	41.0	39.5	47.7		UND	21.9	36.4	51.4	53.1	46.6
	11.6	11.6	13.8		2.3	6.9	16.9	24.1	12.8	13.7
	5.1	5.4	5.4	Sales/Total Assets	2.3	3.8	4.9	4.9	5.6	5.7
	3.5	3.5	3.5		1.4	3.0	3.7	3.4	3.7	3.7
	2.5	2.4	2.4		1.2	1.8	2.6	2.3	2.4	2.5
	.2	.2	.2	% Depr., Dep., Amort./Sales		.9	.5	.2	.2	.1
	(324) .6	(364) .7	(371) .6			(16) 2.3	(13) .9	(55) .4	(93) .6	(191) .5
	1.5	1.6	1.5			4.2	1.6	1.1	1.7	1.4
	.9	.8	1.1	% Officers', Directors' Owners' Comp/Sales		2.5	2.6	1.1	1.0	.5
	(145) 1.5	(170) 1.8	(182) 2.0			(12) 3.9	(12) 3.1	(44) 2.0	(48) 1.8	(64) 1.4
	3.2	3.7	3.5			8.9	5.6	3.1	3.0	
	32108238M	34063970M	33925884M	Net Sales ($)	5690M	50485M	84337M	582641M	1905277M	31297454M
	8755269M	9107496M	8948939M	Total Assets ($)	4680M	19757M	26425M	193118M	631641M	8073318M

M = $ thousand   MM = $ million
See Pages 9 through 22 for Explanation of Ratios and Data

Current Data Sorted by Assets   Comparative Historical Data

0-500M	500M-2MM	2-10MM	10-50MM	50-100MM	100-250MM	Type of Statement	4/1/06-3/31/07 ALL	4/1/07-3/31/08 ALL
1	1	46	85	25	27	Unqualified	197	220
	7	44	18			Reviewed	89	92
	6	7	4		1	Compiled	18	17
3	4	17	1		1	Tax Returns	9	11
1	9	21	26	10	7	Other	57	79
	196 (4/1-9/30/10)			176 (10/1/10-3/31/11)				
5	27	135	134	35	36	**NUMBER OF STATEMENTS**	370	419
%	%	%	%	%	%	**ASSETS**	%	%
	16.7	12.3	9.1	5.4	4.1	Cash & Equivalents	7.0	7.3
	29.0	22.2	15.0	16.2	16.1	Trade Receivables (net)	17.6	17.8
	24.8	30.1	39.2	39.8	43.6	Inventory	36.2	38.9
	3.5	5.5	8.6	9.2	8.7	All Other Current	7.6	8.1
	74.0	70.1	71.9	70.6	72.4	Total Current	68.5	72.2
	17.2	22.6	22.6	21.6	19.9	Fixed Assets (net)	24.8	21.2
	.3	.9	1.1	.6	.6	Intangibles (net)	.7	.4
	8.6	6.4	4.5	7.2	7.2	All Other Non-Current	6.0	6.1
	100.0	100.0	100.0	100.0	100.0	Total	100.0	100.0
						LIABILITIES		
	18.2	12.9	20.0	17.6	21.9	Notes Payable-Short Term	20.5	27.1
	.9	1.7	2.2	1.2	2.8	Cur. Mat.-L.T.D.	1.7	1.6
	21.7	21.1	17.8	17.8	16.4	Trade Payables	16.7	16.2
	.1	.4	.2	.2	.2	Income Taxes Payable	.3	.3
	8.1	12.5	12.7	12.0	12.2	All Other Current	10.6	10.0
	49.0	48.6	53.0	48.8	53.9	Total Current	49.8	55.4
	10.0	8.8	9.2	11.4	11.9	Long-Term Debt	10.0	9.1
	.1	1.5	1.4	1.0	.9	Deferred Taxes	1.1	1.1
	3.3	6.2	1.7	2.0	1.5	All Other Non-Current	2.1	1.2
	37.6	35.0	34.7	36.8	31.9	Net Worth	36.9	33.2
	100.0	100.0	100.0	100.0	100.0	Total Liabilities & Net Worth	100.0	100.0
						INCOME DATA		
	100.0	100.0	100.0	100.0	100.0	Net Sales	100.0	100.0
	16.0	12.8	11.1	11.8	9.2	Gross Profit	11.4	10.9
	14.6	10.2	7.1	7.5	6.3	Operating Expenses	9.1	7.9
	1.4	2.7	4.0	4.3	2.9	Operating Profit	2.4	3.0
	.0	-.2	.1	.2	.1	All Other Expenses (net)	.5	.6
	1.4	2.9	3.9	4.1	2.9	Profit Before Taxes	1.9	2.5
						RATIOS		
	2.3	2.2	1.6	1.7	1.7	Current	1.7	1.6
	1.4	1.4	1.3	1.4	1.3		1.3	1.2
	1.1	1.1	1.1	1.1	1.1		1.1	1.1
	1.7	1.2	.7	.8	.6	Quick	.8	.8
	.8	.6	(133) .4	.2	.4		.4	.4
	.5	.4	.2	.1	.2		.2	.2
	10 35.7	7 52.3	6 64.4	7 48.7	11 34.1	Sales/Receivables	4 91.7	7 51.1
	26 14.1	17 21.7	15 24.9	15 23.9	18 19.9		17 22.1	17 21.5
	42 8.8	33 11.0	30 12.1	30 12.2	32 11.6		31 11.9	33 11.2
	1 279.1	13 27.0	25 14.5	33 11.1	44 8.4	Cost of Sales/Inventory	24 15.0	29 12.4
	26 13.9	35 10.3	56 6.5	55 6.7	66 5.6		49 7.4	55 6.6
	50 7.3	67 5.4	109 3.3	102 3.6	116 3.2		90 4.0	92 4.0
	3 123.8	6 60.6	6 62.2	11 34.4	12 29.4	Cost of Sales/Payables	6 58.7	7 54.6
	17 22.1	15 23.8	20 18.4	18 19.9	19 19.2		15 24.9	16 23.5
	33 11.1	37 9.9	39 9.3	39 9.4	39 9.3		37 10.0	34 10.9
	10.6	8.4	9.9	8.1	9.5	Sales/Working Capital	10.5	12.2
	18.7	16.2	17.1	15.9	13.6		20.3	20.7
	106.5	47.2	25.8	25.7	27.1		41.3	37.8
	44.0	17.0	17.9	18.2	12.4	EBIT/Interest	5.3	3.9
(21)	3.7	(127) 6.5	(130) 7.8	5.6	(33) 4.6		(351) 2.7	(400) 2.4
	1.9	2.6	3.8	4.2	1.7		1.5	1.5
		9.8	11.2	6.6	6.8	Net Profit + Depr., Dep., Amort./Cur. Mat. L/T/D	8.9	6.7
	(42)	4.8	(56) 4.8	(13) 5.4	(17) 3.5		(131) 3.9	(148) 4.2
		2.7	2.3	4.0	.6		2.3	2.4
	.1	.2	.4	.4	.3	Fixed/Worth	.4	.4
	.3	.5	.7	.6	.6		.7	.7
	1.1	.9	1.0	.8	.9		1.1	1.1
	.7	.9	1.1	1.1	1.3	Debt/Worth	1.0	1.2
	1.9	1.6	2.2	2.1	2.2		1.8	2.3
	3.9	3.4	3.8	3.3	5.3		4.0	5.0
	88.7	26.7	33.0	26.8	33.6	% Profit Before Taxes/Tangible Net Worth	21.4	25.1
(24)	21.1	(131) 17.3	(132) 24.4	21.7	22.9		(360) 11.7	(411) 14.8
	4.4	9.3	14.8	15.3	7.2		4.8	7.6
	18.9	11.5	13.1	11.9	11.3	% Profit Before Taxes/Total Assets	8.1	7.1
	6.7	6.6	7.6	7.6	5.3		4.0	4.1
	2.1	2.3	3.5	3.9	1.8		1.3	1.8
	197.4	49.5	23.8	24.0	26.2	Sales/Net Fixed Assets	27.3	28.2
	24.5	15.7	13.4	11.9	14.8		11.8	14.1
	7.7	9.0	7.8	7.3	8.4		7.2	9.2
	7.4	4.8	3.9	3.2	3.3	Sales/Total Assets	4.0	3.9
	4.0	3.3	2.6	2.7	2.6		2.8	2.7
	2.1	2.1	1.7	1.8	1.8		2.0	1.9
	.4	.5	.5	.6	.4	% Depr., Dep., Amort./Sales	.7	.6
(19)	1.2	(117) .9	(129) .9	(33) 1.0	(34) 1.0		(344) 1.2	(394) 1.0
	2.1	1.3	1.3	1.4	1.3		1.7	1.4
	1.2	.6	.3			% Officers', Directors' Owners' Comp/Sales	.6	.5
(11)	2.1	(29) 1.4	(18) .9				(59) 1.3	(57) 1.4
	4.1	2.6	2.2				2.8	3.1
11781M	139364M	2737634M	9301971M	10040769M	15563762M	Net Sales ($)	30036924M	28552463M
1020M	31054M	740642M	3065209M	2581485M	5908654M	Total Assets ($)	7562133M	11187017M

M = $ thousand   MM = $ million
See Pages 9 through 22 for Explanation of Ratios and Data

Comparative Historical Data | | Current Data Sorted by Sales

			Type of Statement						
174	171	185	Unqualified	1	1	1	10	33	139
73	65	69	Reviewed	1	3	4	7	35	19
17	11	18	Compiled	1	2	1	1	7	6
18	19	26	Tax Returns	1	1	3	7	10	4
76	50	74	Other	1	2	5	8	14	44
4/1/08-3/31/09 ALL	4/1/09-3/31/10 ALL	4/1/10-3/31/11 ALL			196 (4/1-9/30/10)			176 (10/1/10-3/31/11)	
				0-1MM	1-3MM	3-5MM	5-10MM	10-25MM	25MM & OVER
358	316	372	NUMBER OF STATEMENTS	5	9	14	33	99	212
%	%	%	ASSETS	%	%	%	%	%	%
8.1	10.1	10.1	Cash & Equivalents			5.1	17.8	11.2	8.1
19.0	19.2	19.0	Trade Receivables (net)			34.6	20.1	18.8	17.8
39.1	34.4	35.2	Inventory			35.6	26.4	33.5	38.0
9.8	4.9	7.1	All Other Current			.8	5.1	5.9	8.5
76.1	68.7	71.4	Total Current			76.0	69.5	69.4	72.4
17.8	23.8	21.7	Fixed Assets (net)			15.3	22.2	23.5	21.2
.5	.4	.8	Intangibles (net)			2.0	1.9	.7	.7
5.6	7.1	6.1	All Other Non-Current			6.7	6.5	6.3	5.7
100.0	100.0	100.0	Total			100.0	100.0	100.0	100.0
			LIABILITIES						
26.0	13.6	17.2	Notes Payable-Short Term			19.0	14.0	15.9	18.6
2.2	2.2	1.9	Cur. Mat.-L.T.D.			1.8	1.5	2.4	1.8
17.6	19.2	19.2	Trade Payables			19.9	22.7	20.5	18.3
.4	.4	.3	Income Taxes Payable			.0	.2	.4	.3
12.5	11.8	12.2	All Other Current			11.1	16.3	10.2	12.6
58.6	47.2	50.8	Total Current			51.8	54.7	49.4	51.6
7.9	11.6	9.5	Long-Term Debt			15.1	7.9	8.6	9.6
.8	1.3	1.2	Deferred Taxes			.0	.7	1.6	1.3
1.6	2.1	3.7	All Other Non-Current			4.3	3.1	2.3	2.2
31.0	37.8	34.8	Net Worth			28.8	33.4	38.1	35.3
100.0	100.0	100.0	Total Liabilities & Net Worth			100.0	100.0	100.0	100.0
			INCOME DATA						
100.0	100.0	100.0	Net Sales			100.0	100.0	100.0	100.0
10.1	10.6	12.0	Gross Profit			25.3	14.6	13.8	9.6
7.1	7.7	8.8	Operating Expenses			15.7	12.5	10.1	6.5
3.1	3.0	3.2	Operating Profit			9.6	2.1	3.7	3.1
.4	-.1	-.1	All Other Expenses (net)			.5	-.9	.0	.0
2.6	3.1	3.2	Profit Before Taxes			9.1	3.0	3.7	3.0
			RATIOS						
1.6	1.9	1.8				1.9	2.1	2.1	1.8
1.2	1.4	1.3	Current			1.5	1.3	1.3	1.4
1.1	1.2	1.1				1.2	1.1	1.1	1.1
.8	1.0	1.0				.9	1.1	1.1	.8
.4 (315)	.6 (371)	.5	Quick			.7	.7 (98)	.6	.4
.2	.3	.2				.6	.5	.2	.2
6 57.4	6 60.6	7 48.7		21 17.6	8 45.1	6 62.8	7 49.1		
15 24.0	13 27.3	17 22.0	Sales/Receivables	37 9.9	16 23.5	17 21.7	15 23.6		
31 11.8	28 13.1	31 11.6		70 5.2	36 10.2	33 11.0	28 12.9		
24 15.3	16 22.4	22 16.7		27 13.7	13 28.9	15 24.5	23 15.6		
49 7.4	37 9.9	44 8.2	Cost of Sales/Inventory	47 7.7	42 8.8	40 9.1	48 7.6		
87 4.2	67 5.5	87 4.2		100 3.7	91 4.0	90 4.1	83 4.4		
5 74.5	6 60.6	7 54.7		4 87.9	6 65.2	6 63.5	8 45.2		
13 28.8	16 22.4	18 20.5	Cost of Sales/Payables	20 18.5	17 21.3	18 20.3	18 20.1		
31 11.9	30 12.3	37 9.8		55 6.6	75 4.8	42 8.7	34 10.7		
12.7	10.5	9.5				6.4	7.0	8.2	10.7
23.1	19.4	16.4	Sales/Working Capital			13.9	16.9	15.7	17.1
51.4	37.4	32.1				23.2	223.1	36.9	29.0
6.4	13.6	16.9				30.9	26.6	12.3	18.1
2.7 (343)	5.5 (349)	6.6	EBIT/Interest			3.8 (28)	6.6 (95)	6.3 (203)	7.1
1.6	2.7	2.9				2.2	1.8	3.0	3.4
9.6	9.9	8.8						11.4	8.7
4.4 (144)	5.9 (107)	4.8 (133)	Net Profit + Depr., Dep., Amort./Cur. Mat. L/T/D				(28)	4.9 (94)	4.8
2.5	2.8	2.5						2.4	2.8
.3	.3	.3				.1	.2	.3	.3
.6	.6	.6	Fixed/Worth			.4	.6	.6	.6
1.0	1.0	.9				3.8	1.3	.9	.9
1.5	1.0	1.1				1.4	.9	.9	1.2
2.7	1.7	2.0	Debt/Worth			2.5	2.2	1.7	2.0
5.1	3.4	3.7				8.3	4.5	3.4	3.7
34.4	37.1	31.8				163.1	28.9	26.8	32.6
21.0 (349)	23.2 (309)	22.1 (362)	% Profit Before Taxes/Tangible Net Worth	(12)	27.8 (30)	18.8 (98)	17.3 (210)	23.5	
9.1	10.1	11.3				3.8	8.8	9.8	14.3
10.3	14.4	12.3				25.2	9.6	11.7	12.7
5.3	7.8	7.0	% Profit Before Taxes/Total Assets			8.1	5.7	6.5	7.9
2.0	3.3	3.2				.5	2.1	2.9	3.6
45.8	32.3	35.7				155.0	42.8	36.8	32.7
18.2	15.6	14.9	Sales/Net Fixed Assets			33.2	13.5	14.7	15.2
10.9	9.3	8.3				9.7	6.7	7.2	9.3
4.5	4.9	4.3				4.4	4.6	4.1	4.3
3.1	3.4	2.9	Sales/Total Assets			2.7	2.6	2.8	3.1
2.1	2.5	1.9				1.8	1.6	1.8	2.1
.4	.4	.5				.4	.7	.5	.4
.7 (326)	.8 (294)	.9 (334)	% Depr., Dep., Amort./Sales	(10)	1.2 (27)	1.2 (88)	.9 (199)	.9	
1.0	1.2	1.3				1.9	1.6	1.6	1.3
.3	.3	.7						.6	.5
1.0 (60)	.8 (55)	1.4 (63)	% Officers', Directors' Owners' Comp/Sales				(23)	1.4 (26)	1.2
1.7	2.4	2.4						2.5	2.2
49371391M	39026495M	37795281M	Net Sales ($)	2721M	18478M	55266M	257645M	1697717M	35763454M
12476073M	10341080M	12328064M	Total Assets ($)	1705M	14371M	28944M	124455M	839265M	11319324M

M = $ thousand   MM = $ million
See Pages 9 through 22 for Explanation of Ratios and Data

Current Data Sorted by Assets | Comparative Historical Data

Type of Statement	0-500M	500M-2MM	2-10MM	10-50MM	50-100MM	100-250MM	4/1/06-3/31/07 ALL	4/1/07-3/31/08 ALL
Unqualified	1		4	3		2	5	3
Reviewed		2	2	2			2	3
Compiled	2	2	1	1			7	2
Tax Returns		1	3	2			8	9
Other							17	17
		5 (4/1-9/30/10)		23 (10/1/10-3/31/11)				
NUMBER OF STATEMENTS	3	5	10	8		2	39	34
ASSETS	%	%	%	%	%	%	%	%
Cash & Equivalents			1.6				9.9	13.1
Trade Receivables (net)			19.6				25.8	23.7
Inventory			32.5				21.7	20.1
All Other Current			8.8				6.6	7.3
Total Current			62.5				64.1	64.2
Fixed Assets (net)			27.8				24.5	23.8
Intangibles (net)			1.0				2.2	.2
All Other Non-Current			8.7				9.2	11.7
Total			100.0				100.0	100.0
LIABILITIES								
Notes Payable-Short Term			25.9				20.0	23.8
Cur. Mat.-L.T.D.			5.6				2.4	2.1
Trade Payables			8.8				15.9	11.5
Income Taxes Payable			.1				.1	.1
All Other Current			16.2				17.8	12.8
Total Current			56.6				56.2	50.2
Long-Term Debt			20.9				20.4	21.2
Deferred Taxes			.4				.1	.1
All Other Non-Current			1.5				.9	1.2
Net Worth			20.7				22.3	27.3
Total Liabilities & Net Worth			100.0				100.0	100.0
INCOME DATA								
Net Sales			100.0				100.0	100.0
Gross Profit			20.9				18.8	19.2
Operating Expenses			20.1				17.4	19.5
Operating Profit			.8				1.4	-.3
All Other Expenses (net)			1.7				.6	-.5
Profit Before Taxes			-.9				.9	.2
RATIOS								
Current			1.8				1.8	2.2
			1.3				1.1	1.1
			.9				.9	.9
Quick			1.2				1.1	1.7
			.3				.8	.9
			.2				.5	.3
Sales/Receivables		7	49.9				5 73.2	0 UND
		15	25.0				13 27.5	6 58.6
		26	13.8				24 15.2	18 20.7
Cost of Sales/Inventory		1	277.2				2 194.8	1 459.4
		31	11.9				6 57.9	4 87.2
		99	3.7				25 14.4	28 12.9
Cost of Sales/Payables		3	141.6				0 974.6	0 UND
		6	65.0				4 81.5	3 126.5
		22	16.6				14 25.8	14 26.5
Sales/Working Capital			7.0				26.7	22.3
			89.9				178.7	127.3
			-88.1				-202.0	-130.1
EBIT/Interest			3.4				8.8	11.2
			1.5				(37) 2.7	(30) 2.2
			-4.9				.6	1.0
Net Profit + Depr., Dep., Amort./Cur. Mat. L/T/D								
Fixed/Worth			.5				.2	.3
			1.0				.7	.9
			4.8				1.9	1.8
Debt/Worth			1.0				1.6	1.0
			7.2				4.4	3.8
			NM				8.7	12.0
% Profit Before Taxes/Tangible Net Worth							63.4	64.9
							(35) 15.7	(30) 20.7
							-4.2	-.1
% Profit Before Taxes/Total Assets			3.8				17.4	14.0
			1.5				5.1	2.5
			-3.2				-1.1	-.2
Sales/Net Fixed Assets			100.0				285.9	175.6
			29.4				39.1	35.5
			8.1				13.3	14.9
Sales/Total Assets			8.8				14.9	15.3
			4.7				8.1	7.2
			2.0				3.0	3.9
% Depr., Dep., Amort./Sales							.2	.2
							(35) .5	(32) .5
							1.2	.8
% Officers', Directors' Owners' Comp/Sales							.4	.3
							(14) 1.2	(13) 1.1
							1.9	2.2
Net Sales ($)	4255M	68457M	234798M	1174049M		972671M	3521343M	906105M
Total Assets ($)	1020M	6345M	50505M	250631M		313733M	422192M	146092M

(Balance sheet / income columns for 10-50MM and 50-100MM: **DATA NOT AVAILABLE**)

M = $ thousand   MM = $ million
See Pages 9 through 22 for Explanation of Ratios and Data

Comparative Historical Data | Current Data Sorted by Sales

						Type of Statement						
	9		4		5	Unqualified						5
	3		4		7	Reviewed		1		1	3	2
	4		4		5	Compiled		3				2
	5		11		5	Tax Returns	1	1			2	1
	8		7		6	Other	1	1			1	4
	4/1/08- 3/31/09 ALL		4/1/09- 3/31/10 ALL		4/1/10- 3/31/11 ALL			5 (4/1-9/30/10)			23 (10/1/10-3/31/11)	
							0-1MM	1-3MM	3-5MM	5-10MM	10-25MM	25MM & OVER
	29		30		28	NUMBER OF STATEMENTS	1	6		1	6	14
	%		%		%	ASSETS	%	%	%	%	%	%
	10.2		12.4		6.2	Cash & Equivalents						7.5
	24.0		27.0		22.4	Trade Receivables (net)			D			24.0
	25.7		24.9		28.0	Inventory			A			24.2
	4.4		3.6		5.2	All Other Current			T			7.4
	64.3		67.9		61.9	Total Current			A			63.1
	24.4		21.6		27.4	Fixed Assets (net)						25.8
	3.2		1.4		2.0	Intangibles (net)			N			3.8
	8.1		9.1		8.7	All Other Non-Current			O			7.4
	100.0		100.0		100.0	Total			T			100.0
						LIABILITIES			A			
	24.6		16.5		16.7	Notes Payable-Short Term			V			11.7
	2.7		4.3		4.8	Cur. Mat.-L.T.D.			A			5.6
	9.6		13.0		17.5	Trade Payables			I			17.8
	.9		.2		.1	Income Taxes Payable			L			.1
	16.7		21.5		11.4	All Other Current			A			16.2
	54.4		55.5		50.5	Total Current			B			51.5
	12.3		15.5		21.9	Long-Term Debt			L			17.6
	.0		.0		.1	Deferred Taxes			E			.0
	3.6		2.4		8.2	All Other Non-Current						4.6
	29.7		26.6		19.3	Net Worth						26.3
	100.0		100.0		100.0	Total Liabilties & Net Worth						100.0
						INCOME DATA						
	100.0		100.0		100.0	Net Sales						100.0
	23.6		26.5		23.6	Gross Profit						12.8
	21.5		25.3		21.5	Operating Expenses						10.8
	2.1		1.3		2.1	Operating Profit						2.0
	-.2		-.5		1.0	All Other Expenses (net)						.2
	2.4		1.7		1.1	Profit Before Taxes						1.8
						RATIOS						
	2.1		2.1		2.0							1.7
	1.3		1.4		1.4	Current						1.4
	.9		1.0		1.0							1.0
	1.2		1.0		1.4							1.2
	.6		.8		.7	Quick						.7
	.3		.5		.3							.4
1	486.4	4	88.7	10	36.0						8	44.4
9	40.0	15	23.6	16	23.0	Sales/Receivables					16	23.0
21	17.3	23	15.9	29	12.5						25	14.5
2	156.3	3	140.7	3	138.6						2	241.6
19	19.1	18	20.4	30	12.2	Cost of Sales/Inventory					9	39.3
46	7.9	62	5.9	80	4.6						58	6.3
1	505.2	0	UND	1	254.1						2	201.0
4	103.0	9	42.3	9	42.4	Cost of Sales/Payables					9	39.5
21	17.5	19	18.9	46	7.9						40	9.2
	18.3		13.7		13.0							13.8
	63.6		35.7		24.0	Sales/Working Capital						26.5
	NM		-573.5		NM							NM
	12.6		13.1		7.4							15.4
(23)	1.9	(26)	3.5	(26)	2.6	EBIT/Interest					(13)	3.2
	.8		1.3		1.2							1.4
						Net Profit + Depr., Dep., Amort./Cur. Mat. L/T/D						
	.3		.1		.4							.4
	.8		.8		1.0	Fixed/Worth						.8
	3.1		2.5		3.7							2.9
	.7		1.1		1.0							1.0
	3.2		3.9		4.6	Debt/Worth						4.6
	11.9		18.9		11.3							25.5
	51.6		57.6		55.4							94.9
(24)	22.4	(27)	17.0	(25)	24.9	% Profit Before Taxes/Tangible Net Worth					(12)	40.3
	2.7		7.1		3.8							18.5
	28.4		13.0		11.6							15.4
	4.9		4.8		4.8	% Profit Before Taxes/Total Assets						9.3
	.5		.9		.5							1.6
	173.8		249.0		57.2							165.8
	35.6		28.1		18.2	Sales/Net Fixed Assets						25.9
	17.8		11.8		8.0							9.3
	12.4		11.7		8.2							9.1
	6.5		5.2		4.0	Sales/Total Assets						4.7
	3.9		3.3		2.1							3.1
	.3		.2		.3							.2
(26)	.5	(26)	.7	(24)	1.1	% Depr., Dep., Amort./Sales					(13)	.5
	1.7		2.5		3.1							1.7
			.3		.4							
		(12)	1.1	(11)	2.8	% Officers', Directors' Owners' Comp/Sales						
			5.4		4.1							
	1094056M		3650854M		2454230M	Net Sales ($)	966M	12729M		6004M	127140M	2307391M
	201868M		345547M		622234M	Total Assets ($)	478M	6739M		7291M	47522M	560204M

© RMA 2011

M = $ thousand   MM = $ million

See Pages 9 through 22 for Explanation of Ratios and Data

Current Data Sorted by Assets   **Comparative Historical Data**

Type of Statement

0-500M	500M-2MM	2-10MM	10-50MM	50-100MM	100-250MM	Type of Statement	4/1/06-3/31/07 ALL	4/1/07-3/31/08 ALL
		6	8	4	7	Unqualified	32	29
		11	7	2	2	Reviewed	25	21
	4	15	2	2		Compiled	11	16
	5	8	4			Tax Returns	15	11
	4	9	9	5	2	Other	32	51
	46 (4/1-9/30/10)		68 (10/1/10-3/31/11)					
	13	49	30	13	9	NUMBER OF STATEMENTS	115	128

Assets / Liabilities / Income Data

(0-500M and 100-250MM columns: DATA NOT AVAILABLE)

500M-2MM	2-10MM	10-50MM	50-100MM		4/1/06-3/31/07 ALL	4/1/07-3/31/08 ALL
%	%	%	%	**ASSETS**	%	%
36.1	12.3	7.1	9.5	Cash & Equivalents	7.3	7.4
18.5	43.7	32.0	23.1	Trade Receivables (net)	33.7	34.6
31.9	22.6	28.6	34.4	Inventory	31.7	32.5
5.2	5.5	8.5	5.0	All Other Current	6.1	5.9
91.7	84.1	76.1	72.0	Total Current	78.8	80.4
3.4	12.2	18.5	12.0	Fixed Assets (net)	14.5	14.2
.1	1.3	.8	10.1	Intangibles (net)	1.2	1.3
4.9	2.4	4.7	5.9	All Other Non-Current	5.6	4.2
100.0	100.0	100.0	100.0	Total	100.0	100.0
				LIABILITIES		
10.3	11.0	14.0	16.8	Notes Payable-Short Term	21.5	23.5
1.6	2.1	1.6	1.4	Cur. Mat.-L.T.D.	1.3	1.3
12.5	33.9	26.1	19.5	Trade Payables	21.3	20.5
.0	.1	.1	.6	Income Taxes Payable	.2	.1
17.4	11.7	10.3	18.6	All Other Current	11.4	11.5
41.8	58.8	52.0	56.8	Total Current	55.6	56.9
.7	4.5	7.7	8.1	Long-Term Debt	7.9	7.4
.1	.1	.3	.3	Deferred Taxes	.2	.2
8.4	4.7	5.3	4.5	All Other Non-Current	3.1	4.4
49.1	31.8	34.7	30.3	Net Worth	33.1	31.2
100.0	100.0	100.0	100.0	Total Liabilities & Net Worth	100.0	100.0
				INCOME DATA		
100.0	100.0	100.0	100.0	Net Sales	100.0	100.0
23.0	18.6	13.5	15.5	Gross Profit	17.3	16.5
23.0	13.3	9.9	10.6	Operating Expenses	14.9	12.5
.1	5.3	3.6	4.9	Operating Profit	2.4	3.9
.2	2.3	.3	.3	All Other Expenses (net)	.8	1.1
-.2	3.0	3.3	4.7	Profit Before Taxes	1.7	2.8

Ratios

0-500M	500M-2MM	2-10MM	10-50MM	50-100MM	100-250MM	RATIOS	4/1/06-3/31/07 ALL	4/1/07-3/31/08 ALL
	4.9	1.9	2.0	2.0		Current	2.3	1.9
	2.8	1.3	1.5	1.2			1.3	1.3
	1.4	1.1	1.1	1.0			1.1	1.1
	2.5	1.5	1.1	1.2		Quick	1.1	1.1
	1.2	1.0	.8	.5			(114) .6	.8
	.3	.5	.5	.3			.4	.5
0 UND	13 28.4	26 14.2	25 14.6			Sales/Receivables	19 19.3	17 21.2
13 28.8	33 11.0	41 8.9	42 8.7				30 12.0	34 10.8
18 20.7	44 8.2	63 5.8	57 6.4				48 7.6	45 8.0
0 UND	0 UND	21 17.8	27 13.8			Cost of Sales/Inventory	10 36.8	9 40.7
1 244.8	12 30.6	46 7.9	77 4.8				45 8.2	42 8.7
132 2.8	92 4.0	87 4.2	138 2.6				85 4.3	90 4.0
0 814.8	12 30.6	12 30.2	15 24.8			Cost of Sales/Payables	9 40.6	9 41.3
3 143.5	30 12.2	24 15.0	17 21.0				20 18.0	21 17.5
23 16.0	66 5.5	82 4.4	32 11.4				38 9.6	42 8.7
	4.6	9.2	4.9	6.9		Sales/Working Capital	8.1	10.2
	7.5	16.1	13.6	16.2			20.0	18.9
	12.2	104.3	28.1	NM			54.5	37.7
	22.9	43.6	12.9	30.2		EBIT/Interest	5.4	7.3
(10)	5.9	(46) 5.4	(29) 7.7	6.5			(109) 2.4	(122) 2.8
	1.4	1.3	1.8	2.2			1.2	1.6
						Net Profit + Depr., Dep., Amort./Cur. Mat. L/T/D	8.5	16.0
							(18) 4.7	(27) 5.4
							2.8	2.1
	.0	.0	.1	.1		Fixed/Worth	.0	.0
	.0	.2	.5	.5			.2	.2
	.1	.9	.9	2.6			.9	.7
	.3	1.2	1.0	1.5		Debt/Worth	1.1	1.3
	1.2	2.9	2.5	4.6			2.5	2.7
	3.5	8.4	4.3	14.0			5.2	5.2
	27.6	78.0	50.9	62.0		% Profit Before Taxes/Tangible Net Worth	39.8	37.8
	15.6	(46) 13.0	(29) 21.0	(11) 30.7			(109) 14.4	(122) 16.8
	1.8	2.6	6.2	18.0			2.9	6.2
	12.2	12.9	13.4	14.6		% Profit Before Taxes/Total Assets	10.1	10.4
	6.9	4.2	8.9	9.0			4.0	4.4
	.5	.7	1.6	2.3			.8	1.7
	999.8	999.8	62.5	114.3		Sales/Net Fixed Assets	379.7	410.3
	471.3	95.2	13.0	15.0			46.0	46.6
	41.2	10.7	9.5	6.9			11.1	11.1
	5.8	9.1	3.8	3.0		Sales/Total Assets	5.0	4.8
	3.3	4.1	2.5	1.8			3.4	3.3
	2.7	2.0	1.8	1.4			2.3	2.1
		.0	.3	.1		% Depr., Dep., Amort./Sales	.1	.1
	(37)	.4	(27) .7	(12) .6			(90) .5	(103) .5
		1.5	1.3	3.0			1.8	1.5
		.7				% Officers', Directors' Owners' Comp/Sales	.6	.6
	(14)	1.8					(29) 1.4	(36) 1.4
		3.2					3.5	3.3

500M-2MM	2-10MM	10-50MM	50-100MM	100-250MM		4/1/06-3/31/07 ALL	4/1/07-3/31/08 ALL
74174M	1398864M	2122351M	1922766M	3309668M	Net Sales ($)	9101429M	9391871M
14171M	249961M	750371M	890853M	1405330M	Total Assets ($)	2429252M	3135412M

M = $ thousand   MM = $ million
See Pages 9 through 22 for Explanation of Ratios and Data

Comparative Historical Data   Current Data Sorted by Sales

4/1/08-3/31/09 ALL	4/1/09-3/31/10 ALL	4/1/10-3/31/11 ALL	Type of Statement	0-1MM	1-3MM	3-5MM	5-10MM	10-25MM	25MM & OVER
25	22	25	Unqualified		1		1	1	22
26	27	20	Reviewed				4	3	13
19	14	23	Compiled		2	2	3	12	4
21	15	17	Tax Returns	1	1	1	3	3	8
45	33	29	Other		2		1	8	18
				46 (4/1-9/30/10)			**68 (10/1/10-3/31/11)**		
136	111	114	**NUMBER OF STATEMENTS**	1	6	3	12	27	65
%	%	%	**ASSETS**	%	%	%	%	%	%
8.7	9.7	12.6	Cash & Equivalents				17.1	12.4	8.6
34.5	37.5	34.1	Trade Receivables (net)				31.0	36.5	38.0
30.5	29.7	27.8	Inventory				35.5	21.4	26.3
5.6	5.0	6.1	All Other Current				2.1	7.6	7.0
79.4	81.8	80.6	Total Current				85.8	78.0	79.9
14.2	12.9	13.4	Fixed Assets (net)				11.2	17.7	12.9
1.5	.8	2.2	Intangibles (net)				.1	1.1	3.4
4.8	4.6	3.8	All Other Non-Current				3.0	3.2	3.9
100.0	100.0	100.0	Total				100.0	100.0	100.0
			LIABILITIES						
24.2	19.8	13.4	Notes Payable-Short Term				12.2	10.6	14.9
1.6	1.0	1.8	Cur. Mat.-L.T.D.				1.0	3.4	1.2
23.4	22.6	26.3	Trade Payables				25.6	28.6	28.9
.2	.2	.1	Income Taxes Payable				.1	.0	.2
8.8	13.1	12.4	All Other Current				13.6	13.7	11.8
58.1	56.7	54.1	Total Current				52.4	56.3	56.9
6.7	6.8	5.9	Long-Term Debt				4.0	5.0	7.4
.1	.2	.2	Deferred Taxes				.2	.1	.3
2.8	2.8	5.1	All Other Non-Current				2.1	4.3	3.8
32.2	33.4	34.7	Net Worth				41.3	34.2	31.6
100.0	100.0	100.0	Total Liabilities & Net Worth				100.0	100.0	100.0
			INCOME DATA						
100.0	100.0	100.0	Net Sales				100.0	100.0	100.0
16.2	16.4	17.1	Gross Profit				18.3	21.1	12.5
13.0	12.4	13.0	Operating Expenses				16.0	16.3	8.5
3.2	4.0	4.0	Operating Profit				2.2	4.8	4.0
.9	.8	1.2	All Other Expenses (net)				-.1	1.8	1.1
2.4	3.2	2.9	Profit Before Taxes				2.3	3.0	2.9
			RATIOS						
1.9 / 1.3 / 1.1	1.9 / 1.3 / 1.1	2.0 / 1.5 / 1.1	Current				2.1 / 1.6 / 1.2	2.4 / 1.3 / 1.0	1.7 / 1.4 / 1.2
1.2 / .8 / .4	1.2 / .8 / .5	1.3 / .8 / .4	Quick				1.5 / .9 / .5	2.1 / 1.0 / .4	1.2 / .8 / .8
19 19.2 / 30 12.1 / 47 7.8	23 15.8 / 37 9.9 / 59 6.2	17 21.9 / 35 10.5 / 50 7.3	Sales/Receivables				20 18.7 / 44 8.3 / 100 3.6	13 28.8 / 32 11.3 / 54 6.8	20 18.4 / 35 10.3 / 51 7.2
8 48.2 / 34 10.6 / 86 4.2	3 140.5 / 33 11.2 / 86 4.2	3 117.3 / 39 9.2 / 93 3.9	Cost of Sales/Inventory				2 185.0 / 101 3.6 / 132 2.8	0 UND / 30 12.3 / 87 4.2	8 46.5 / 33 11.2 / 80 4.6
9 39.7 / 23 15.8 / 51 7.1	9 40.8 / 27 13.5 / 49 7.5	12 29.8 / 24 15.1 / 55 6.7	Cost of Sales/Payables				8 45.0 / 46 8.0 / 104 3.5	8 43.7 / 30 12.2 / 80 4.6	13 27.9 / 22 16.4 / 36 10.3
10.1 / 21.2 / 44.4	7.8 / 16.1 / 37.9	7.0 / 13.2 / 34.0	Sales/Working Capital				3.2 / 7.3 / 19.3	8.8 / 14.6 / 999.8	8.7 / 16.2 / 39.2
7.8 / (129) 3.5 / 1.3	24.8 / (105) 6.2 / 1.7	18.3 / (107) 6.5 / 1.7	EBIT/Interest				67.3 / (11) 2.6 / 1.0	39.4 / 4.9 / 1.1	17.9 / (61) 8.3 / 2.9
7.9 / (22) 4.0 / 2.2	9.5 / (19) 4.5 / 1.8	16.5 / (16) 3.5 / .2	Net Profit + Depr., Dep., Amort./Cur. Mat. L/T/D						17.3 / (10) 5.5 / .9
.1 / .3 / 1.0	.0 / .2 / .8	.0 / .3 / .9	Fixed/Worth				.0 / .1 / .7	.0 / .4 / 1.0	.1 / .4 / .9
1.1 / 2.6 / 5.6	1.2 / 2.4 / 4.9	1.0 / 2.6 / 5.4	Debt/Worth				.9 / 1.7 / 3.0	.6 / 2.8 / 8.6	1.4 / 3.0 / 5.8
39.1 / (127) 18.1 / 2.6	60.7 / (104) 25.1 / 7.6	51.2 / (108) 19.2 / 4.6	% Profit Before Taxes/Tangible Net Worth				25.9 / 6.2 / .3	84.9 / (26) 23.7 / 3.3	51.2 / (60) 23.9 / 10.2
11.5 / 5.0 / .5	15.2 / 7.8 / 1.5	12.3 / 6.4 / 1.3	% Profit Before Taxes/Total Assets				9.1 / 2.6 / .1	20.9 / 3.6 / .4	12.8 / 7.3 / 1.9
286.1 / 47.6 / 11.2	574.0 / 38.6 / 11.5	341.8 / 32.8 / 10.6	Sales/Net Fixed Assets				179.9 / 83.8 / 10.6	999.8 / 23.1 / 8.6	371.5 / 31.7 / 11.5
5.3 / 3.3 / 2.0	4.6 / 3.0 / 1.9	4.5 / 2.9 / 1.8	Sales/Total Assets				2.7 / 2.0 / 1.3	4.8 / 3.3 / 2.1	6.1 / 3.0 / 1.8
.2 / (106) .6 / 1.9	.3 / (82) .8 / 1.6	.1 / (91) .7 / 1.4	% Depr., Dep., Amort./Sales					.4 / (18) 1.0 / 2.3	.0 / (57) .5 / 1.1
.4 / (40) .9 / 3.1	.6 / (31) 1.5 / 2.4	.7 / (29) 1.7 / 3.5	% Officers', Directors' Owners' Comp/Sales						.5 / (18) 1.0 / 3.0
9129058M	6705988M	8827823M	Net Sales ($)	253M	11741M	12181M	91473M	424179M	8287996M
2867251M	2501937M	3310686M	Total Assets ($)	924M	13157M	3498M	55863M	142920M	3094324M

M = $ thousand   MM = $ million
See Pages 9 through 22 for Explanation of Ratios and Data

Current Data Sorted by Assets   Comparative Historical Data

						Type of Statement		
	2	4	12	6	2	Unqualified	16	20
1	4	15	14			Reviewed	46	35
5	7	13	1			Compiled	28	25
4	6	9	2			Tax Returns	16	18
	13	24	15	2	4	Other	62	62
	26 (4/1-9/30/10)		139 (10/1/10-3/31/11)				4/1/06-3/31/07 ALL	4/1/07-3/31/08 ALL
0-500M	500M-2MM	2-10MM	10-50MM	50-100MM	100-250MM	NUMBER OF STATEMENTS	168	160
10	32	65	44	8	6			
%	%	%	%	%	%	ASSETS	%	%
14.0	14.2	8.0	8.8			Cash & Equivalents	7.0	6.4
24.1	44.2	40.0	40.3			Trade Receivables (net)	39.5	40.1
38.9	23.0	31.8	27.7			Inventory	30.5	30.4
1.4	1.9	1.4	2.1			All Other Current	1.8	2.5
78.5	83.3	81.1	78.8			Total Current	78.8	79.5
10.8	9.3	11.6	14.1			Fixed Assets (net)	12.5	11.7
.0	1.4	2.3	3.1			Intangibles (net)	2.4	2.4
10.7	6.0	5.0	4.0			All Other Non-Current	6.3	6.4
100.0	100.0	100.0	100.0			Total	100.0	100.0
						LIABILITIES		
20.8	16.2	12.6	17.9			Notes Payable-Short Term	17.7	17.2
1.1	.9	1.7	1.0			Cur. Mat.-L.T.D.	2.0	2.4
29.2	31.2	26.4	27.8			Trade Payables	24.7	27.8
.0	.1	.2	.4			Income Taxes Payable	.3	.1
30.8	6.9	6.1	7.9			All Other Current	8.2	9.2
81.9	55.4	47.1	55.0			Total Current	52.9	56.7
8.4	6.3	7.4	6.2			Long-Term Debt	7.4	8.6
.0	.0	.2	.1			Deferred Taxes	.1	.2
4.9	7.0	5.5	1.5			All Other Non-Current	4.7	4.6
4.7	31.3	39.8	37.3			Net Worth	34.9	29.8
100.0	100.0	100.0	100.0			Total Liabilities & Net Worth	100.0	100.0
						INCOME DATA		
100.0	100.0	100.0	100.0			Net Sales	100.0	100.0
34.2	26.5	24.1	20.4			Gross Profit	24.6	23.0
34.0	20.6	21.0	15.7			Operating Expenses	19.9	19.0
.2	5.9	3.1	4.7			Operating Profit	4.7	4.0
.3	.5	.4	.2			All Other Expenses (net)	.7	.8
.0	5.4	2.7	4.5			Profit Before Taxes	3.9	3.1
						RATIOS		
1.9	2.7	2.9	2.1			Current	2.2	2.0
.9	1.7	1.6	1.4				1.4	1.4
.6	1.0	1.3	1.1				1.2	1.1
1.4	1.8	1.7	1.1			Quick	1.2	1.2
.4	1.1	.9	.9				.8	.8
.1	.8	.6	.6				.6	.6
5 73.3	25 14.8	35 10.5	38 9.7			Sales/Receivables	35 10.5	33 11.2
19 19.5	40 9.0	45 8.2	46 8.0				45 8.2	43 8.4
30 12.2	57 6.4	55 6.7	67 5.5				55 6.6	56 6.6
0 UND	6 64.0	16 23.1	26 13.9			Cost of Sales/Inventory	22 16.7	23 16.1
56 6.6	35 10.6	46 7.6	48 7.6				48 7.5	48 7.6
98 3.7	69 5.3	91 4.0	66 5.5				74 4.9	85 4.3
0 UND	10 36.2	24 15.2	27 13.5			Cost of Sales/Payables	22 16.9	25 14.4
38 9.7	31 11.7	36 10.3	44 8.2				35 10.4	39 9.4
45 8.2	53 6.8	52 7.0	57 6.4				48 7.6	55 6.6
11.0	6.3	5.6	6.7			Sales/Working Capital	7.4	7.9
-107.0	13.3	8.9	13.7				12.2	12.8
-16.7	140.6	26.4	31.3				27.6	34.6
	33.4	15.8	35.3			EBIT/Interest	17.2	9.7
	(28) 5.7	(54) 6.1	(40) 8.3				(155) 4.5	(143) 2.9
	1.9	3.1	2.6				2.1	1.6
			15.4			Net Profit + Depr., Dep., Amort./Cur. Mat. L/T/D	13.0	7.3
		(13) 8.1					(36) 6.5	(30) 4.0
			2.4				3.0	1.6
.0	.0	.0	.0			Fixed/Worth	.1	.0
NM	.1	.1	.2				.2	.2
-.3	1.1	.4	.6				.7	.9
1.2	.6	.8	.8			Debt/Worth	.9	1.1
NM	1.4	1.8	2.4				2.0	2.8
-3.6	19.7	3.4	4.9				5.6	7.6
	55.4	46.6	47.6			% Profit Before Taxes/Tangible Net Worth	47.0	42.7
	(27) 29.1	(63) 20.1	(43) 25.3				(153) 25.2	(139) 25.5
	8.0	9.3	11.8				11.6	9.4
35.3	26.7	14.4	16.4			% Profit Before Taxes/Total Assets	19.6	14.7
-.3	9.2	6.6	8.3				8.4	6.0
-10.1	2.5	3.0	3.5				3.1	2.2
317.6	999.8	331.9	541.9			Sales/Net Fixed Assets	296.2	298.8
114.3	177.1	45.1	54.2				64.9	68.8
24.9	20.6	13.6	11.0				15.2	14.7
7.3	6.1	4.2	3.3			Sales/Total Assets	3.9	3.9
5.6	3.7	2.7	2.7				3.1	3.0
3.2	2.7	2.0	2.2				2.4	2.3
	.1	.3	.1			% Depr., Dep., Amort./Sales	.2	.2
	(18) .5	(47) .8	(37) .5				(138) .6	(123) .6
	1.9	1.5	1.5				1.1	1.3
	2.0	.7	.5			% Officers', Directors' Owners' Comp/Sales	1.3	.9
	(22) 3.9	(27) 1.3	(18) 1.0				(77) 2.7	(73) 2.6
	6.3	3.4	2.4				6.2	5.4
17407M	169518M	1114106M	2604772M	2020695M	2374428M	Net Sales ($)	5927417M	6421253M
2343M	37861M	339797M	941080M	560152M	895072M	Total Assets ($)	1792775M	2296577M

Comparative Historical Data / Current Data Sorted by Sales

Current date ranges: 26 (4/1-9/30/10) and 139 (10/1/10-3/31/11)

4/1/08-3/31/09 ALL	4/1/09-3/31/10 ALL	4/1/10-3/31/11 ALL		0-1MM	1-3MM	3-5MM	5-10MM	10-25MM	25MM & OVER
			Type of Statement						
25	26	26	Unqualified				2	4	20
31	33	33	Reviewed		1	2	4	13	13
10	16	22	Compiled	1	3	5	6	4	3
17	26	22	Tax Returns	3	1	4	4	7	3
49	63	62	Other	2	7	5	7	15	26
132	164	165	**NUMBER OF STATEMENTS**	6	12	16	23	43	65
%	%	%	**ASSETS**	%	%	%	%	%	%
7.6	8.3	9.3	Cash & Equivalents		11.7	14.9	8.5	8.5	8.2
40.1	40.2	39.9	Trade Receivables (net)		33.8	37.4	37.2	40.5	43.6
30.0	28.4	29.7	Inventory		27.9	28.6	30.9	30.2	28.4
2.3	1.9	1.8	All Other Current		1.9	1.4	1.3	1.7	2.2
80.0	78.8	80.7	Total Current		75.4	82.3	77.8	80.9	82.4
11.4	11.1	11.7	Fixed Assets (net)		11.0	10.2	13.8	11.0	11.5
2.3	3.2	2.6	Intangibles (net)		.2	.8	.6	3.6	3.7
6.4	6.9	5.0	All Other Non-Current		13.5	6.8	7.8	4.4	2.4
100.0	100.0	100.0	Total		100.0	100.0	100.0	100.0	100.0
			LIABILITIES						
21.4	17.4	15.2	Notes Payable-Short Term		13.9	14.7	17.6	13.0	16.0
1.9	1.6	1.4	Cur. Mat.-L.T.D.		.8	1.4	1.1	2.0	1.3
24.7	28.0	28.0	Trade Payables		26.9	34.0	21.6	29.2	29.1
.1	.2	.2	Income Taxes Payable		.3	.0	.2	.5	.1
7.9	6.4	8.2	All Other Current		15.6	7.4	5.7	6.3	6.9
56.0	53.6	53.0	Total Current		57.4	57.6	46.2	51.0	53.4
8.5	9.3	7.4	Long-Term Debt		4.6	9.3	7.3	6.4	7.5
.1	.3	.2	Deferred Taxes		.1	.0	.2	.3	.2
6.8	6.3	4.2	All Other Non-Current		9.8	7.9	7.2	3.5	2.1
28.6	30.5	35.1	Net Worth		28.1	25.2	39.0	38.9	36.8
100.0	100.0	100.0	Total Liabilities & Net Worth		100.0	100.0	100.0	100.0	100.0
			INCOME DATA						
100.0	100.0	100.0	Net Sales		100.0	100.0	100.0	100.0	100.0
22.0	21.5	23.3	Gross Profit		37.9	32.3	23.5	22.1	17.3
20.1	18.1	19.4	Operating Expenses		34.2	26.7	19.6	18.4	13.4
1.9	3.4	3.8	Operating Profit		3.7	5.6	3.9	3.7	4.0
.8	.6	.4	All Other Expenses (net)		-.2	.5	.7	.4	.2
1.1	2.8	3.5	Profit Before Taxes		3.9	5.0	3.2	3.2	3.7
			RATIOS						
2.1	2.4	2.5			2.0	2.6	2.9	3.0	2.4
1.4	1.5	1.5	Current		1.3	1.7	1.6	1.5	1.5
1.1	1.1	1.1			.9	.9	1.4	1.2	1.1
1.2	1.4	1.5			1.4	1.5	1.7	1.8	1.4
.8	.9	.9	Quick		.9	1.0	.9	.9	.9
.5	.6	.6			.4	.7	.5	.9	.6
31 11.8 / 35 10.6 / 31 11.6					9 40.5	25 14.7	25 14.7	35 10.5	37 9.8
37 9.8 / 44 8.3 / 44 8.3		Sales/Receivables			39 9.4	44 8.4	41 8.8	45 8.2	44 8.2
51 7.2 / 58 6.3 / 56 6.5					51 7.1	66 5.5	59 6.2	52 7.0	60 6.1
16 23.4 / 17 21.4 / 22 16.6					6 57.3	31 11.9	14 25.8	10 37.3	27 13.4
40 9.1 / 47 7.8 / 45 8.2		Cost of Sales/Inventory			40 9.2	40 9.2	44 8.4	47 7.8	44 8.3
77 4.7 / 75 4.9 / 76 4.8					100 3.6	104 3.5	107 3.4	82 4.4	61 6.0
17 21.6 / 21 17.6 / 23 15.6					22 16.8	21 17.3	9 39.4	19 19.1	27 13.3
31 11.7 / 37 9.8 / 36 10.0		Cost of Sales/Payables			38 9.7	38 9.7	31 11.7	36 10.3	41 8.9
41 8.8 / 55 6.7 / 51 7.1					53 6.8	75 4.9	54 6.7	49 7.5	50 7.3
8.2	6.2	5.9			7.2	5.7	5.6	5.9	6.4
15.0	12.7	11.9	Sales/Working Capital		24.0	7.1	11.5	12.1	11.9
67.3	40.6	35.4			-91.6	-41.0	15.8	31.5	28.3
7.9	16.1	26.8					47.2	15.4	20.0	30.0
(119) 3.3	(146) 6.0	(143) 6.4	EBIT/Interest				(14) 4.3	(20) 5.7	(37) 5.9	(59) 7.0
1.1	1.6	2.6					1.5	2.2	3.1	3.0
9.0	5.3	13.1								15.0
(26) 3.2	(32) 2.5	(31) 4.4	Net Profit + Depr., Dep., Amort./Cur. Mat. L/T/D						(18) 8.2
1.4	1.1	2.1								1.7
.0	.0	.0			.1	.0	.0	.0	.0
.2	.2	.1	Fixed/Worth		.4	.1	.3	.1	.1
1.0	1.0	.6			NM	2.0	.6	.4	.5
1.2	1.1	.8			.8	.7	.7	.7	.9
2.7	2.6	2.0	Debt/Worth		1.9	2.8	1.4	1.8	2.5
7.0	7.3	5.6			NM	22.9	2.2	5.8	5.0
39.5	53.6	47.3					45.8	45.2	46.6	55.2
(115) 19.0	(146) 27.4	(151) 23.2	% Profit Before Taxes/Tangible Net Worth				(13) 26.1	(21) 20.1	(41) 23.2	(63) 23.6
4.9	5.8	9.3					1.0	4.3	9.6	12.8
11.0	15.3	16.3			34.8	25.1	18.6	14.7	15.0
5.5	6.0	6.9	% Profit Before Taxes/Total Assets		12.5	5.4	8.7	6.6	7.3
.7	1.2	3.0			-5.8	.9	1.4	4.0	3.3
517.3	548.2	499.0			245.1	871.7	408.8	329.3	973.1
82.0	85.4	62.3	Sales/Net Fixed Assets		50.8	86.8	35.6	59.0	110.0
18.5	14.5	14.9			9.1	20.7	11.2	18.7	12.7
4.4	3.9	4.2			5.9	4.2	4.3	4.5	3.5
3.4	2.9	3.0	Sales/Total Assets		2.8	3.2	3.2	3.1	2.9
2.6	2.2	2.3			2.1	2.0	2.0	2.3	2.4
.1	.1	.2					.1	.2	.4	.1
(105) .5	(111) .7	(120) .7	% Depr., Dep., Amort./Sales				(10) .6	(17) 1.1	(29) .7	(52) .4
1.3	2.0	1.7					2.0	1.8	.9	1.3
1.0	.6	.8					1.4	.9	.5	.5
(60) 2.6	(67) 1.7	(72) 2.2	% Officers', Directors' Owners" Comp/Sales				(10) 4.9	(14) 2.8	(15) 2.2	(22) .8
5.3	4.5	4.3					9.3	4.4	2.5	1.9
8024058M	6745514M	8300926M	Net Sales ($)	4133M	23566M	67406M	166358M	724508M	7314955M
2233752M	2361354M	2776305M	Total Assets ($)	1817M	9659M	24654M	58181M	241086M	2440908M

M = $ thousand   MM = $ million
See Pages 9 through 22 for Explanation of Ratios and Data

Current Data Sorted by Assets   Comparative Historical Data

Type of Statement

Type of Statement	0-500M	500M-2MM	2-10MM	10-50MM	50-100MM	100-250MM		4/1/06-3/31/07 ALL	4/1/07-3/31/08 ALL
Unqualified			12	32	12	6		68	69
Reviewed		5	43	32	2			93	84
Compiled	5	14	33	3		2		54	48
Tax Returns	4	32	25	2				33	37
Other	10	33	64	53	12	1		112	110
	77 (4/1-9/30/10)		360 (10/1/10-3/31/11)						
NUMBER OF STATEMENTS	19	84	177	122	26	9		360	348

ASSETS

%	%	%	%	%	%	ASSETS	%	%
11.2	10.6	7.3	7.0	4.3		Cash & Equivalents	7.3	8.2
31.5	39.3	37.4	35.6	27.8		Trade Receivables (net)	38.1	37.2
27.7	25.9	33.9	31.4	22.2		Inventory	27.5	27.8
8.7	2.3	2.0	2.4	2.6		All Other Current	1.9	2.3
79.0	78.1	80.5	76.5	56.9		Total Current	74.9	75.4
13.7	10.3	12.0	14.1	28.1		Fixed Assets (net)	16.0	16.1
3.8	4.4	2.8	5.1	11.3		Intangibles (net)	2.5	3.0
3.5	7.2	4.7	4.3	3.7		All Other Non-Current	6.6	5.5
100.0	100.0	100.0	100.0	100.0		Total	100.0	100.0

LIABILITIES

						LIABILITIES		
20.4	10.2	14.3	14.6	11.5		Notes Payable-Short Term	16.2	16.9
.7	2.1	2.0	1.9	2.6		Cur. Mat.-L.T.D.	2.3	3.2
31.4	24.2	26.2	23.0	17.8		Trade Payables	25.7	25.2
.4	.1	.2	.2	.1		Income Taxes Payable	.3	.2
2.9	7.1	6.4	7.8	7.3		All Other Current	9.7	8.7
55.8	43.8	49.2	47.5	39.2		Total Current	54.2	54.3
3.2	15.3	7.7	7.3	15.1		Long-Term Debt	9.8	10.3
.0	.0	.3	.6	1.8		Deferred Taxes	.4	.3
5.5	8.1	3.5	2.9	2.8		All Other Non-Current	4.0	3.8
35.6	32.8	39.3	41.7	41.1		Net Worth	31.6	31.4
100.0	100.0	100.0	100.0	100.0		Total Liabilities & Net Worth	100.0	100.0

INCOME DATA

						INCOME DATA		
100.0	100.0	100.0	100.0	100.0		Net Sales	100.0	100.0
34.1	33.4	25.4	20.4	26.3		Gross Profit	25.0	25.4
26.7	30.4	21.4	15.4	20.3		Operating Expenses	21.4	20.9
7.4	3.0	4.0	5.0	6.0		Operating Profit	3.6	4.4
-.3	.8	.2	.4	.8		All Other Expenses (net)	.5	.6
7.7	2.3	3.8	4.6	5.2		Profit Before Taxes	3.2	3.9

RATIOS

0-500M	500M-2MM	2-10MM	10-50MM	50-100MM	100-250MM	RATIOS	Hist1	Hist2
3.2	3.3	2.3	2.2	2.2		Current	1.9	2.0
1.5	1.9	1.6	1.6	1.5			1.4	1.4
1.0	1.4	1.3	1.3	1.0			1.1	1.1
1.8	2.1	1.3	1.3	1.5		Quick	1.2	1.2
.8	1.1	.9	.9	.8			.8 (347)	.8
.4	.7	.6	.6	.6			.6	.6
14 26.8	31 11.7	32 11.4	37 9.9	37 9.9		Sales/Receivables	34 10.9	33 11.0
29 12.7	38 9.5	39 9.5	45 8.2	46 7.9			43 8.6	43 8.5
49 7.5	53 6.8	49 7.4	57 6.4	53 6.9			53 6.9	52 7.0
3 142.0	12 31.0	33 11.1	32 11.5	29 12.5		Cost of Sales/Inventory	22 16.3	24 15.3
24 15.4	37 9.8	48 7.5	51 7.1	51 7.2			43 8.4	45 8.2
94 3.9	70 5.3	83 4.4	76 4.8	64 5.7			61 5.9	65 5.6
15 23.6	16 22.6	23 15.7	25 14.7	25 14.8		Cost of Sales/Payables	22 16.6	24 15.5
27 13.5	33 11.1	35 10.3	37 9.8	39 9.5			36 10.2	36 10.2
69 5.3	49 7.5	50 7.3	51 7.1	47 7.8			53 6.8	54 6.8
6.6	6.2	7.0	6.4	5.6		Sales/Working Capital	8.2	8.3
15.4	9.8	11.1	10.1	19.0			15.7	15.2
-179.8	18.2	19.7	20.4	112.1			54.2	41.9
20.0	19.3	31.0	23.8	15.5		EBIT/Interest	9.5	9.3
(11) 7.3	(66) 6.2	(162) 8.9	(109) 9.3	(25) 5.1			(327) 3.7	(313) 3.8
1.0	1.4	2.9	4.1	2.5			1.8	2.0
		10.6	12.7	13.8		Net Profit + Depr., Dep., Amort./Cur. Mat. L/T/D	8.2	7.1
		(36) 3.9	(38) 5.4	(11) 4.0			(96) 4.0	(97) 3.2
		2.4	3.5	1.4			1.7	1.2
.0	.0	.0	.0	.3		Fixed/Worth	.1	.1
.0	.2	.2	.2	.9			.3	.3
.9	.6	.5	.7	2.4			1.3	1.1
.3	.8	.8	.9	1.0		Debt/Worth	1.0	1.1
2.0	2.1	1.7	1.7	1.9			2.4	2.5
20.4	7.9	3.6	3.5	13.3			6.7	6.9
168.6	55.6	46.6	48.3	34.6		% Profit Before Taxes/Tangible Net Worth	50.8	53.6
(17) 51.8	(70) 24.9	(168) 24.2	(116) 25.9	(21) 23.9			(328) 26.4	(312) 28.5
6.4	7.5	8.9	16.2	10.3			10.4	10.3
66.7	17.7	18.6	15.6	14.7		% Profit Before Taxes/Total Assets	15.0	15.4
14.1	5.9	9.1	8.8	8.0			6.7	8.6
.0	1.0	2.6	4.7	3.1			2.4	2.9
UND	316.5	252.6	306.4	61.0		Sales/Net Fixed Assets	150.4	138.4
999.8	71.7	55.6	34.2	10.5			38.1	39.1
22.3	27.0	16.4	10.3	3.5			11.7	11.1
6.5	4.6	4.2	3.7	2.9		Sales/Total Assets	4.2	4.0
4.4	3.4	3.1	2.7	2.0			3.2	3.1
2.0	2.5	2.4	1.7	1.2			2.2	2.1
	.3	.2	.1	1.0		% Depr., Dep., Amort./Sales	.3	.3
	(50) .6	(142) .6	(106) .6	(23) 2.1			(302) .7	(291) .7
	1.3	1.2	1.9	4.4			1.7	1.8
	2.0	1.5	.6			% Officers', Directors' Owners' Comp/Sales	1.4	1.5
	(45) 4.3	(77) 2.4	(29) 1.4				(123) 3.0	(119) 2.9
	7.9	4.0	3.2				5.8	5.7
23541M	375930M	2960675M	7763324M	4301252M	4269621M	Net Sales ($)	17665194M	17186747M
5518M	104867M	869894M	2892410M	1835957M	1419283M	Total Assets ($)	6597703M	6129167M

M = $ thousand   MM = $ million

See Pages 9 through 22 for Explanation of Ratios and Data

Comparative Historical Data — Current Data Sorted by Sales

	71 (4/1/08-3/31/09) ALL	73 (4/1/09-3/31/10) ALL	62 (4/1/10-3/31/11) ALL	Type of Statement	0-1MM	1-3MM	3-5MM	5-10MM	10-25MM	25MM & OVER
	71	73	62	Unqualified		1	2	13	26	53
	84	89	82	Reviewed		3	5	19	7	40
	47	47	57	Compiled	5	10	14	19	19	6
	52	53	63	Tax Returns	3			16	15	5
	156	152	173	Other	6	14	16	27	34	76
	4/1/08-3/31/09 ALL	4/1/09-3/31/10 ALL	4/1/10-3/31/11 ALL		77 (4/1-9/30/10) →			360 (10/1/10-3/31/11) →		
	410	414	437	**NUMBER OF STATEMENTS**	14	28	37	77	101	180
	%	%	%	**ASSETS**	%	%	%	%	%	%
	7.8	10.2	7.8	Cash & Equivalents	10.0	7.5	10.2	9.4	8.6	6.1
	37.5	34.0	36.3	Trade Receivables (net)	11.8	32.0	43.9	35.6	36.7	37.3
	31.4	29.1	30.4	Inventory	22.4	31.7	24.1	28.5	35.4	30.2
	2.3	2.8	2.5	All Other Current	10.7	2.5	1.4	2.7	1.8	2.4
	78.9	76.0	77.1	Total Current	54.9	73.7	79.6	76.3	82.6	76.0
	13.6	15.1	13.5	Fixed Assets (net)	28.6	12.3	8.0	15.1	10.3	14.7
	2.7	3.9	4.5	Intangibles (net)	8.6	5.9	4.6	3.2	2.8	5.5
	4.8	5.0	4.9	All Other Non-Current	7.9	8.1	7.8	5.4	4.3	3.8
	100.0	100.0	100.0	Total	100.0	100.0	100.0	100.0	100.0	100.0
				LIABILITIES						
	17.6	14.1	13.6	Notes Payable-Short Term	17.6	16.3	8.6	11.5	15.5	13.8
	2.2	2.2	2.0	Cur. Mat.-L.T.D.	1.5	1.0	3.1	1.5	2.6	1.8
	24.4	22.3	24.5	Trade Payables	15.5	24.9	27.1	25.6	24.7	23.9
	.2	.3	.2	Income Taxes Payable	.0	.3	.2	.1	.2	.2
	8.3	8.5	6.9	All Other Current	1.3	4.5	5.1	7.9	6.1	8.2
	52.7	47.3	47.2	Total Current	35.8	46.9	44.1	46.6	49.1	47.9
	8.8	9.6	9.3	Long-Term Debt	26.7	10.3	14.1	10.4	7.2	7.6
	.3	.4	.4	Deferred Taxes	.0	.0	.0	.2	.2	.9
	3.7	3.0	4.3	All Other Non-Current	8.4	1.7	11.1	6.7	2.3	3.0
	34.5	39.7	38.8	Net Worth	29.0	41.1	30.7	36.1	41.2	40.6
	100.0	100.0	100.0	Total Liabilities & Net Worth	100.0	100.0	100.0	100.0	100.0	100.0
				INCOME DATA						
	100.0	100.0	100.0	Net Sales	100.0	100.0	100.0	100.0	100.0	100.0
	24.1	26.4	26.1	Gross Profit	49.8	33.2	34.2	28.9	25.4	20.6
	19.4	21.9	21.7	Operating Expenses	41.8	30.8	31.5	25.3	20.5	15.8
	4.7	4.4	4.4	Operating Profit	8.1	2.4	2.7	3.6	4.9	4.8
	.5	.4	.4	All Other Expenses (net)	5.6	.3	-.6	.3	.1	.4
	4.2	4.1	4.0	Profit Before Taxes	2.5	2.1	3.4	3.3	4.7	4.4
				RATIOS						
	2.1	2.5	2.5	Current	4.0	4.1	2.9	3.1	2.3	2.2
	1.5	1.6	1.7		1.3	1.9	1.9	1.6	1.7	1.6
	1.2	1.2	1.3		.8	1.0	1.4	1.2	1.4	1.2
	1.3	1.6	1.4	Quick	1.3	2.2	2.0	1.6	1.4	1.3
	.8	1.0	.9		.7	.8	1.2	1.0	.9	.9
	.6	.6	.6		.1	.5	.9	.7	.6	.6
	30 12.1	32 11.4	32 11.3	Sales/Receivables	0 UND	21 17.3	33 11.1	32 11.4	33 11.1	36 10.2
	39 9.3	41 8.8	41 8.9		17 22.0	37 9.8	46 8.0	39 9.4	38 9.6	43 8.4
	50 7.2	53 6.9	52 7.0		55 6.6	48 7.6	67 5.4	49 7.4	49 7.5	53 6.9
	22 16.4	26 14.0	26 13.9	Cost of Sales/Inventory	0 UND	22 16.8	17 21.7	24 15.0	36 10.0	26 13.9
	47 7.8	48 7.6	48 7.6		65 5.6	45 8.2	43 8.5	47 7.8	53 6.9	47 7.8
	76 4.8	82 4.4	77 4.7		215 1.7	113 3.2	77 4.7	82 4.4	84 4.3	68 5.4
	18 20.4	23 16.1	23 15.8	Cost of Sales/Payables	0 UND	19 19.1	24 15.1	25 14.6	23 16.2	24 15.4
	28 12.8	33 11.0	35 10.5		26 14.0	31 11.7	41 8.9	37 9.9	36 10.2	34 10.7
	47 7.8	48 7.6	49 7.4		53 6.8	64 5.7	57 6.4	56 6.5	49 7.4	45 8.0
	7.4	6.1	6.5	Sales/Working Capital	3.0	5.4	5.2	5.7	6.9	7.0
	12.6	10.5	10.5		14.9	11.9	9.2	9.7	10.1	11.5
	31.9	21.3	21.3		-62.9	230.2	13.2	24.8	15.0	24.5
	13.3	16.3	23.8	EBIT/Interest		40.4	14.4	13.1	31.3	26.7
	(363) 5.7	(369) 4.8	(381) 7.9		(21) 5.0	(32) 5.1	(65) 3.9	(96) 10.8	(161) 9.3	
	2.0	2.1	2.6			-.8	2.3	1.7	3.8	4.3
	12.6	9.0	12.5	Net Profit + Depr., Dep., Amort./Cur. Mat. L/T/D				4.1	15.9	13.6
	(93) 4.1	(95) 3.2	(96) 4.7				(14) 1.9	(23) 6.2	(56) 5.6	
	1.7	1.4	2.5					1.0	3.4	3.1
	.0	.0	.0	Fixed/Worth	.0	.0	.0	.0	.0	.0
	.2	.2	.2		.5	.2	.2	.3	.1	.2
	.8	.9	.7		UND	1.0	.6	.8	.5	.8
	.9	.8	.8	Debt/Worth	1.3	.3	1.2	.7	.8	.9
	2.4	1.8	1.8		2.7	1.2	2.1	1.7	1.6	1.7
	5.0	3.9	4.2		UND	16.6	6.0	5.3	3.2	4.0
	55.0	49.2	48.5	% Profit Before Taxes/Tangible Net Worth	202.0	49.0	61.2	40.2	50.5	46.8
	(375) 28.7	(387) 24.7	(400) 25.2		(11) 8.1	(22) 28.1	(33) 20.8	(70) 19.4	(97) 24.8	(167) 28.2
	9.3	8.4	11.3		-.9	2.6	9.2	3.8	12.4	16.3
	17.3	17.1	16.7	% Profit Before Taxes/Total Assets	30.0	26.1	15.7	14.1	18.9	15.9
	8.7	7.2	8.5		.3	4.4	5.7	4.8	10.9	9.6
	2.5	2.3	2.9		-.4	.0	3.1	1.2	3.8	4.9
	284.7	189.2	286.2	Sales/Net Fixed Assets	UND	264.5	174.6	281.2	269.8	380.6
	50.7	40.7	50.5		19.8	70.3	58.0	37.2	62.8	46.6
	14.7	11.7	13.7		2.8	23.2	20.6	12.3	23.0	9.7
	4.4	3.8	4.0	Sales/Total Assets	2.8	3.9	4.0	3.9	4.2	4.0
	3.3	2.8	3.0		1.2	3.1	3.2	3.0	3.1	3.0
	2.3	2.1	2.2		.3	2.3	2.2	2.2	2.5	1.9
	.2	.3	.2	% Depr., Dep., Amort./Sales		.4	.4	.3	.2	.1
	(333) .5	(323) .8	(333) .6			(13) .5	(23) .9	(53) .9	(85) .5	(153) .6
	1.4	2.0	1.6			1.3	1.6	1.6	1.0	2.1
	1.2	1.6	1.4	% Officers', Directors' Owners' Comp/Sales			1.8	1.9	1.4	.6
	(149) 3.0	(148) 3.3	(161) 2.6				(22)	(36) 3.2	(46) 2.2	(43) 1.8
	5.6	6.0	5.2				8.0	5.7	4.5	2.6
	25017181M	21351752M	19694343M	Net Sales ($)	6022M	53989M	144910M	561861M	1649666M	17277895M
	7669498M	7775832M	7127929M	Total Assets ($)	8778M	19623M	54293M	209656M	584847M	6250732M

M = $ thousand   MM = $ million
See Pages 9 through 22 for Explanation of Ratios and Data

Current Data Sorted by Assets   Comparative Historical Data

Type of Statement	0-500M	500M-2MM	2-10MM	10-50MM	50-100MM	100-250MM		4/1/06-3/31/07 ALL	4/1/07-3/31/08 ALL
Unqualified	2	2	11	30	11	11		36	57
Reviewed	2	2	47	52	3			88	68
Compiled	5	13	36	13	2			83	83
Tax Returns	11	15	19	3		1		30	26
Other	3	11	36	41	8	5		60	86
		111 (4/1-9/30/10)			282 (10/1/10-3/31/11)				
NUMBER OF STATEMENTS	21	43	149	139	24	17		297	320
ASSETS	%	%	%	%	%	%		%	%
Cash & Equivalents	12.7	12.6	11.6	7.7	6.8	3.2		9.2	8.2
Trade Receivables (net)	20.1	33.3	35.4	28.0	29.6	21.9		35.4	35.3
Inventory	17.4	16.3	15.5	11.8	10.3	22.6		14.3	14.5
All Other Current	3.7	4.1	3.0	4.0	1.8	3.0		3.2	2.9
Total Current	53.9	66.3	65.4	51.5	48.4	50.7		62.1	60.9
Fixed Assets (net)	20.2	24.1	25.0	36.5	41.2	34.8		28.3	30.3
Intangibles (net)	7.6	2.4	3.5	3.4	2.9	8.3		3.2	3.2
All Other Non-Current	18.0	7.2	6.1	8.6	7.4	6.2		6.4	5.6
Total	100.0	100.0	100.0	100.0	100.0	100.0		100.0	100.0
LIABILITIES									
Notes Payable-Short Term	11.5	13.0	8.8	11.2	9.5	9.5		12.0	12.9
Cur. Mat.-L.T.D.	4.9	2.5	3.0	3.7	3.0	2.0		3.4	3.8
Trade Payables	25.0	33.0	28.7	22.3	21.6	19.9		28.8	27.4
Income Taxes Payable	1.1	.1	.3	.1	.0	.9		.2	.1
All Other Current	24.4	8.1	9.3	7.4	8.5	7.3		7.6	6.1
Total Current	66.9	56.7	50.1	44.6	42.6	39.6		52.0	50.3
Long-Term Debt	11.4	20.1	12.6	16.9	19.1	27.3		16.5	17.1
Deferred Taxes	.0	.3	.4	.9	1.1	.2		.9	.8
All Other Non-Current	8.0	4.8	3.5	3.2	3.8	3.6		3.1	3.3
Net Worth	14.0	18.2	33.3	34.3	33.4	29.2		27.6	28.5
Total Liabilties & Net Worth	100.0	100.0	100.0	100.0	100.0	100.0		100.0	100.0
INCOME DATA									
Net Sales	100.0	100.0	100.0	100.0	100.0	100.0		100.0	100.0
Gross Profit	13.2	14.1	9.8	13.5	9.3	11.3		10.7	10.7
Operating Expenses	13.9	13.0	9.3	10.4	8.7	8.8		9.5	9.6
Operating Profit	-.8	1.1	.5	3.2	.6	2.5		1.2	1.1
All Other Expenses (net)	-.2	-.6	-.1	.2	.1	.7		.0	.1
Profit Before Taxes	-.6	1.7	.5	2.9	.5	1.9		1.1	1.0
RATIOS									
Current	1.8	2.9	1.7	1.5	1.6	1.8		1.6	1.6
	1.2	1.2	1.3	1.1	1.1	1.2		1.2	1.2
	.4	.9	1.0	.9	.8	.8		1.0	1.0
Quick	1.1	2.0	1.2	1.1	1.3	.7		1.1	1.1
	.6	.8	.9	.8	.8	.6		.9	.9
	.2	.5	.7	.6	.6	.4		.6	.7
Sales/Receivables	0 999.8	3 105.8	11 33.8	8 48.3	7 49.5	7 54.8		.9 38.4	11 33.2
	8 47.1	19 18.8	16 23.2	15 24.3	15 24.8	12 29.9		16 23.3	18 20.5
	18 20.7	29 12.6	26 14.0	26 13.9	27 13.7	20 18.4		26 14.1	28 13.0
Cost of Sales/Inventory	0 UND	3 124.9	3 133.4	3 107.0	4 101.3	3 104.9		3 126.5	3 116.1
	3 106.0	10 36.1	7 50.7	6 59.8	8 46.8	8 43.3		7 55.7	7 53.9
	12 30.5	17 21.2	19 19.6	13 27.1	11 34.3	19 19.5		11 32.3	13 27.8
Cost of Sales/Payables	1 503.2	5 77.8	9 38.9	10 37.2	10 37.6	8 44.1		10 38.0	11 34.1
	9 40.6	12 31.2	14 26.9	13 27.4	13 28.7	12 30.3		13 27.3	14 26.5
	26 14.2	20 18.2	20 18.4	17 21.4	16 22.7	19 18.8		18 20.2	20 18.5
Sales/Working Capital	23.4	16.0	20.7	31.8	30.9	18.1		32.8	27.2
	158.9	46.3	52.4	101.0	154.5	58.6		76.5	82.1
	-33.8	-259.1	999.8	-123.1	-88.2	-88.3		-619.0	-999.8
EBIT/Interest	3.0	12.1	9.9	8.7	10.0	7.0		6.5	5.0
	(12) 1.7	(38) 2.7	(131) 2.8	(129) 3.1	3.2	4.2		(282) 2.8	(302) 2.5
	-1.1	1.0	1.3	1.7	1.3	1.9		1.4	1.3
Net Profit + Depr., Dep., Amort./Cur. Mat. L/T/D			5.6	3.7				3.9	4.3
			(41) 2.5	(55) 1.9				(119) 2.3	(109) 1.9
			1.3	1.2				1.3	1.0
Fixed/Worth	.0	.4	.3	.6	.8	.2		.5	.5
	1.7	1.1	.7	1.1	1.2	1.9		1.0	1.2
	-19.7	-5.5	1.7	2.1	2.7	2.5		2.0	2.3
Debt/Worth	1.8	.9	1.3	1.1	1.4	2.5		1.5	1.5
	6.4	4.5	2.5	2.2	2.5	4.1		2.9	3.3
	-42.2	-268.0	4.6	4.5	4.2	10.1		6.8	6.4
% Profit Before Taxes/Tangible Net Worth	68.4	52.7	29.4	30.6	20.0	30.3		35.1	33.0
	(15) 16.9	(32) 18.4	(139) 11.4	(134) 15.2	(23) 12.0	(15) 18.3		(269) 16.2	(291) 13.7
	-2.1	.0	3.7	7.3	3.6	4.3		5.2	4.3
% Profit Before Taxes/Total Assets	9.7	15.9	7.3	8.3	5.9	5.7		8.7	8.0
	3.1	3.6	3.1	4.2	3.0	4.4		4.5	3.2
	-5.7	-.1	1.0	1.7	.5	2.1		1.1	.9
Sales/Net Fixed Assets	UND	358.3	105.1	47.3	23.2	500.5		69.9	63.2
	119.4	34.2	39.8	20.5	15.0	13.6		31.4	27.8
	26.9	14.8	15.5	8.8	8.8	5.7		14.5	12.4
Sales/Total Assets	19.6	12.1	11.1	9.0	7.6	10.7		11.0	9.8
	9.8	6.1	6.6	6.4	6.2	5.3		7.5	6.8
	5.2	4.3	4.8	3.9	4.7	2.5		5.0	4.5
% Depr., Dep., Amort./Sales	.3	.3	.3	.4	.6	.1		.3	.4
	(13) .7	(31) .7	(130) .6	(134) .7	.8	(13) .9		(279) .6	(291) .6
	1.1	2.1	1.0	1.3	1.1	1.8		1.0	1.2
% Officers', Directors' Owners' Comp/Sales	.3	.5	.3	.4				.2	.2
	(12) .9	(27) 1.3	(53) .4	(39) .3				(104) .5	(112) .6
	2.0	2.2	.7	.7				1.2	1.2
Net Sales ($)	74880M	504583M	7058320M	20294415M	10930749M	23496176M		43541526M	58700713M
Total Assets ($)	5568M	53876M	862066M	3039282M	1666422M	3137826M		5002308M	7566895M

M = $ thousand   MM = $ million
See Pages 9 through 22 for Explanation of Ratios and Data

Comparative Historical Data | | | | Current Data Sorted by Sales

Hist 1	Hist 2	Hist 3	Type of Statement	0-1MM	1-3MM	3-5MM	5-10MM	10-25MM	25MM & OVER
41	56	67	Unqualified	1	1	1	4	7	53
87	96	104	Reviewed		1		3	12	88
48	63	69	Compiled	1	3	4	9	11	41
28	38	49	Tax Returns		6	4	8	11	20
97	98	104	Other	1	5	3	5	16	74
4/1/08-3/31/09 ALL	4/1/09-3/31/10 ALL	4/1/10-3/31/11 ALL		111 (4/1-9/30/10)			282 (10/1/10-3/31/11)		
301	351	393	**NUMBER OF STATEMENTS**	3	16	12	29	57	276
%	%	%	**ASSETS**	%	%	%	%	%	%
10.2	10.8	9.7	Cash & Equivalents		7.9	6.0	18.6	8.7	9.0
30.2	28.6	30.8	Trade Receivables (net)		26.1	26.9	16.2	31.4	32.7
14.1	14.0	14.4	Inventory		16.2	10.9	16.1	19.2	13.3
3.4	2.6	3.4	All Other Current		2.9	4.9	4.1	3.0	3.4
57.8	56.1	58.3	Total Current		53.1	48.8	55.0	62.3	58.4
33.3	32.0	30.1	Fixed Assets (net)		38.0	41.3	23.6	24.9	31.1
3.2	4.1	3.7	Intangibles (net)		4.1	2.9	7.3	5.2	3.1
5.8	7.9	7.8	All Other Non-Current		4.6	7.0	14.1	7.6	7.4
100.0	100.0	100.0	Total		100.0	100.0	100.0	100.0	100.0
			LIABILITIES						
10.5	9.0	10.3	Notes Payable-Short Term		7.1	8.2	16.0	10.7	10.0
3.9	3.8	3.3	Cur. Mat.-L.T.D.		5.7	3.6	1.6	3.9	3.1
23.1	24.0	25.9	Trade Payables		16.4	16.2	15.2	28.3	27.2
.2	.2	.3	Income Taxes Payable		.2	.0	.5	.2	.3
7.3	9.6	9.1	All Other Current		27.6	6.1	16.2	9.2	7.5
44.9	46.6	48.9	Total Current		56.9	34.1	49.4	52.3	48.1
17.0	19.1	15.9	Long-Term Debt		28.7	23.6	15.3	12.8	15.5
.6	.6	.6	Deferred Taxes		.0	1.2	.1	.5	.7
3.0	2.8	3.8	All Other Non-Current		9.0	9.9	1.0	2.2	3.8
34.5	30.8	30.8	Net Worth		5.5	31.2	34.3	32.2	31.9
100.0	100.0	100.0	Total Liabilities & Net Worth		100.0	100.0	100.0	100.0	100.0
			INCOME DATA						
100.0	100.0	100.0	Net Sales		100.0	100.0	100.0	100.0	100.0
9.2	12.2	11.8	Gross Profit		24.3	26.6	22.4	17.4	8.1
8.0	10.8	10.3	Operating Expenses		27.0	18.4	17.4	14.9	7.2
1.2	1.4	1.5	Operating Profit		-2.7	8.3	5.0	2.5	.9
.1	.0	.0	All Other Expenses (net)		.1	2.9	.1	-.2	-.1
1.1	1.4	1.5	Profit Before Taxes		-2.8	5.4	4.9	2.7	1.0
			RATIOS						
1.7	1.7	1.6	Current		1.7	3.5	2.9	1.7	1.5
1.3	1.2	1.2			1.2	1.2	1.4	1.3	1.2
1.0	.9	.9			.5	.8	.8	1.0	.9
1.3	1.2	1.2	Quick		1.1	3.0	2.0	1.3	1.1
.8	.8	.8			.7	.8	.9	.8	.8
.6	.6	.6			.4	.6	.4	.6	.6
6 63.1	8 45.3	8 45.3	Sales/Receivables	9 42.3	13 28.6	0 999.8	18 20.1	8 45.5	
11 33.1	15 24.2	15 24.0		19 19.0	24 15.1	10 36.9	25 14.5	14 25.9	
20 18.1	25 14.7	26 14.0		27 13.7	36 10.1	22 16.4	32 11.3	22 16.8	
2 152.9	3 113.4	3 120.9	Cost of Sales/Inventory	8 45.4	4 93.5	3 130.7	7 54.3	3 139.9	
5 72.0	7 51.7	7 50.7		16 22.4	12 29.3	10 38.2	17 21.9	6 62.4	
10 37.9	15 23.6	15 23.8		26 13.9	22 16.7	27 13.4	34 10.8	10 35.4	
6 61.3	10 36.5	9 39.7	Cost of Sales/Payables	4 86.1	5 72.8	2 243.1	10 35.9	9 38.6	
9 40.9	13 27.4	13 27.6		13 28.0	11 34.2	11 32.9	19 18.9	13 28.1	
14 26.5	20 18.3	18 20.4		27 13.7	29 12.4	23 16.2	31 11.9	16 22.7	
32.1	24.3	24.5	Sales/Working Capital		21.7	8.0	12.4	14.7	31.6
81.1	70.6	73.4			42.0	81.0	74.9	34.8	94.4
-999.8	-172.6	-257.7			-13.2	-46.4	-63.6	221.2	-275.1
7.1	8.0	8.4	EBIT/Interest		2.8	8.5	12.0	9.1	8.3
(290) 3.3	(329) 3.0	(351) 2.9		(13) 1.7	(11) 2.6	(23) 5.2	(50) 2.6	(253) 3.0	
1.6	1.5	1.5			.9	1.0	2.7	1.0	1.6
5.1	5.5	4.1	Net Profit + Depr., Dep., Amort./Cur. Mat. L/T/D				5.0	4.1	
(107) 2.5	(108) 2.4	(112) 2.1					(12) 2.5	(94) 2.0	
1.4	1.4	1.2					1.6	1.2	
.5	.5	.5	Fixed/Worth		.6	.5	.2	.3	.5
1.0	1.2	1.0			2.0	2.3	1.0	.7	1.0
2.0	2.7	2.3			-4.6	4.3	50.0	1.7	2.2
1.1	1.3	1.3	Debt/Worth		2.2	.8	.6	.9	1.4
2.5	2.6	2.5			7.0	3.6	2.4	1.7	2.6
4.8	6.9	5.9			-9.6	14.6	611.4	5.2	4.9
36.7	37.7	30.7	% Profit Before Taxes/Tangible Net Worth		23.5	59.3	68.4	35.4	26.6
(281) 19.4	(317) 16.6	(358) 13.9		(10) 14.5	(11) 28.0	(23) 25.2	(50) 10.8	(262) 13.6	
5.9	4.6	4.4			-7.2	-.8	11.4	2.2	5.1
11.3	8.7	7.9	% Profit Before Taxes/Total Assets		3.4	18.6	19.6	10.9	7.0
4.7	4.2	3.5			1.0	4.1	11.3	2.3	3.2
1.5	1.1	1.1			-9.9	.3	3.1	.0	1.2
77.2	58.6	81.8	Sales/Net Fixed Assets		104.1	32.5	469.2	85.1	79.2
31.1	24.4	29.2			13.3	22.8	52.1	33.7	29.8
13.5	9.8	11.1			3.9	4.3	14.5	9.4	12.7
12.7	9.0	9.9	Sales/Total Assets		5.8	10.2	12.5	6.9	10.7
8.7	6.1	6.5			4.8	5.2	4.7	5.0	7.4
5.6	3.6	4.3			2.0	2.2	3.0	2.4	5.1
.3	.5	.4	% Depr., Dep., Amort./Sales		.5	.5	.8	.4	.3
(280) .5	(318) .8	(345) .7		(14) 2.1	(11) 1.1	(16) 1.1	(47) .7	(256) .6	
1.0	1.4	1.1			5.6	3.5	2.6	2.5	1.0
.2	.3	.3	% Officers', Directors' Owners' Comp/Sales				.4	.5	.2
(98) .4	(114) .6	(133) .4				(14) 1.1	(20) .8	(86) .3	
.9	1.3	1.0					1.8	1.5	.6
66936986M	43368505M	62359123M	Net Sales ($)	1622M	32330M	47651M	214692M	948829M	61113999M
6682355M	7795804M	8765040M	Total Assets ($)	400M	19517M	47395M	72471M	301669M	8323588M

M = $ thousand   MM = $ million
See Pages 9 through 22 for Explanation of Ratios and Data

Current Data Sorted by Assets / Comparative Historical Data

Type of Statement

Type of Statement	0-500M	500M-2MM	2-10MM	10-50MM	50-100MM	100-250MM	4/1/06-3/31/07 ALL	4/1/07-3/31/08 ALL
Unqualified		3	6	44	22	23	109	95
Reviewed	1	7	75	82	5	1	185	180
Compiled	3	17	64	27			135	127
Tax Returns	4	24	22	5			39	44
Other	4	22	74	103	20	19	166	198
		181 (4/1-9/30/10)		496 (10/1/10-3/31/11)				
NUMBER OF STATEMENTS	12	73	241	261	47	43	634	644

Common Size / Ratios

	0-500M %	500M-2MM %	2-10MM %	10-50MM %	50-100MM %	100-250MM %		4/1/06-3/31/07 ALL %	4/1/07-3/31/08 ALL %
							ASSETS		
	17.0	16.6	13.1	8.4	6.7	5.0	Cash & Equivalents	9.2	8.4
	19.9	37.1	36.1	32.1	31.1	23.2	Trade Receivables (net)	36.4	37.9
	21.9	14.1	15.3	14.1	17.6	20.0	Inventory	14.2	13.9
	3.2	2.2	3.4	3.6	2.8	4.8	All Other Current	3.5	3.2
	62.0	70.0	67.9	58.3	58.3	52.9	Total Current	63.3	63.4
	23.7	20.7	21.0	28.2	32.0	36.7	Fixed Assets (net)	26.2	26.5
	5.4	1.2	3.5	3.8	4.7	5.1	Intangibles (net)	3.2	2.7
	8.9	8.1	7.6	9.8	5.1	5.3	All Other Non-Current	7.3	7.3
	100.0	100.0	100.0	100.0	100.0	100.0	Total	100.0	100.0
							LIABILITIES		
	61.0	11.0	10.1	12.1	11.4	10.7	Notes Payable-Short Term	11.1	12.8
	2.4	1.7	2.2	3.3	2.3	2.3	Cur. Mat.-L.T.D.	3.1	3.1
	28.5	27.6	31.4	27.0	25.5	20.5	Trade Payables	31.1	29.5
	.1	.0	.1	.3	.4	.1	Income Taxes Payable	.3	.3
	2.7	8.4	8.2	6.8	5.6	6.1	All Other Current	7.6	7.3
	94.6	48.7	52.0	49.4	45.1	39.7	Total Current	53.3	52.9
	18.5	10.5	11.4	13.9	18.7	23.3	Long-Term Debt	15.3	15.6
	.8	.4	.5	.8	.9	.4	Deferred Taxes	.7	.6
	8.4	4.5	2.8	3.6	5.3	3.9	All Other Non-Current	4.0	3.7
	-22.3	35.8	33.3	32.3	30.1	32.7	Net Worth	26.8	27.2
	100.0	100.0	100.0	100.0	100.0	100.0	Total Liabilities & Net Worth	100.0	100.0
							INCOME DATA		
	100.0	100.0	100.0	100.0	100.0	100.0	Net Sales	100.0	100.0
	19.1	16.4	11.1	9.3	8.6	6.7	Gross Profit	10.5	9.7
	17.4	15.7	10.0	8.2	7.4	4.8	Operating Expenses	9.2	8.6
	1.7	.7	1.1	1.1	1.3	1.9	Operating Profit	1.3	1.1
	.8	-.1	.0	.0	.1	.4	All Other Expenses (net)	.1	.1
	.9	.8	1.1	1.1	1.2	1.5	Profit Before Taxes	1.2	1.0
							RATIOS		
	2.0	2.1	1.7	1.4	2.0	1.5	Current	1.5	1.5
	1.4	1.4	1.3	1.1	1.2	1.3		1.2	1.2
	.7	1.2	1.0	.9	.9	1.0		.9	1.0
	1.0	1.5	1.2	1.1	1.3	1.0	Quick	1.2	1.1
	.8	1.1	.9	.8	.8	.7		.9 (643)	.9
	.3	.8	.6	.6	.5	.4		.6	.6
	0 UND	8 43.9	9 40.7	9 42.3	10 35.2	5 76.2	Sales/Receivables	10 36.3	10 36.3
	8 46.3	20 18.5	17 22.0	16 22.7	18 20.2	11 34.4		18 20.3	18 20.0
	24 15.3	32 11.5	29 12.5	29 12.7	28 13.1	26 14.1		29 12.6	30 12.1
	2 176.8	0 999.8	3 143.9	2 157.7	4 89.5	3 118.1	Cost of Sales/Inventory	2 162.6	2 167.7
	10 35.4	7 49.7	6 57.8	6 61.1	8 46.2	9 41.7		6 61.6	6 61.3
	18 20.6	21 17.3	15 23.8	14 26.4	17 21.4	20 18.5		14 26.0	12 29.4
	1 543.5	7 53.8	10 35.4	10 35.3	10 38.2	9 42.5	Cost of Sales/Payables	10 34.9	10 36.6
	15 24.2	14 26.4	13 27.4	13 27.4	15 24.0	12 30.3		14 25.5	14 26.9
	38 9.6	24 14.9	22 16.7	18 20.1	20 18.7	16 22.5		23 15.6	21 17.5
	20.5	12.7	18.9	26.4	22.2	21.1	Sales/Working Capital	26.8	29.9
	51.3	28.4	63.6	83.8	69.5	45.5		82.6	86.4
	-156.1	132.7	-897.8	-164.3	-192.9	-633.3		-241.7	-306.4
		13.3	14.5	10.4	11.7	5.1	EBIT/Interest	6.9	5.8
		(56) 3.3	(213) 3.6	(249) 4.2	(46) 4.3	(41) 3.6		(596) 3.1	(606) 2.6
		-.8	1.6	1.9	2.5	1.7		1.6	1.4
		11.2	4.5	7.1	18.5	4.5	Net Profit + Depr., Dep., Amort./Cur. Mat. L/T/D	5.1	4.5
		(12) 2.7	(52) 2.0	(92) 2.9	(15) 5.2	(13) 2.4		(212) 2.4	(208) 2.4
		.4	1.3	1.6	3.4	1.1		1.3	1.3
	.6	.1	.2	.4	.5	.3	Fixed/Worth	.4	.4
	.8	.4	.6	1.0	1.3	1.1		1.0	1.0
	-.8	1.1	1.3	1.9	3.4	2.9		2.4	2.2
	1.0	.9	1.2	1.4	1.7	1.7	Debt/Worth	1.6	1.7
	3.7	1.9	2.2	2.5	3.4	2.9		3.3	3.4
	-3.3	4.6	5.1	5.6	8.5	5.8		7.1	6.6
		48.4	30.1	34.4	28.3	31.7	% Profit Before Taxes/Tangible Net Worth	40.1	34.8
		(66) 10.2	(217) 15.5	(249) 15.9	(43) 19.1	(42) 18.7		(571) 20.3	(582) 17.4
		1.7	5.1	8.1	10.3	9.3		8.9	6.1
	15.8	10.7	8.6	8.1	8.4	9.2	% Profit Before Taxes/Total Assets	9.5	8.2
	1.9	3.6	3.9	4.2	5.3	4.9		4.8	3.9
	-5.2	.1	1.1	1.9	2.4	1.8		1.8	1.2
	155.4	227.1	154.7	63.4	39.7	232.7	Sales/Net Fixed Assets	81.7	85.2
	38.8	51.4	48.3	29.1	18.8	10.4		36.3	35.2
	23.0	17.4	18.8	12.9	11.3	6.2		14.9	14.9
	12.5	11.5	11.5	9.6	8.2	10.2	Sales/Total Assets	10.0	10.5
	8.2	6.5	7.2	6.4	6.5	4.5		7.0	7.0
	5.5	3.0	4.5	4.1	4.2	2.7		4.4	4.6
	.2	.3	.2	.4	.4	.2	% Depr., Dep., Amort./Sales	.3	.3
	(10) 1.1	(51) .7	(207) .5	(242) .6	.7	(36) .9		(569) .6	(573) .5
	1.5	1.2	1.0	1.2	1.2	1.5		1.0	.9
		.5	.2	.2			% Officers', Directors' Owners' Comp/Sales	.3	.2
		(32) 1.1	(81) .4	(67) .5				(201) .6	(216) .5
		2.9	.9	.8				1.3	1.0
	28649M	815456M	11330418M	40365425M	21999323M	42386286M	Net Sales ($)	100603833M	126804496M
	3751M	92889M	1327269M	5673177M	3280566M	6603351M	Total Assets ($)	13991713M	16476615M

M = $ thousand   MM = $ million
See Pages 9 through 22 for Explanation of Ratios and Data

Comparative Historical Data

Current Data Sorted by Sales

			Type of Statement	0-1MM	1-3MM	3-5MM	5-10MM	10-25MM	25MM & OVER
109	107	98	Unqualified		1	1	1	2	93
197	184	171	Reviewed		1	3	7	18	142
112	107	111	Compiled	1	5	3	6	31	65
50	59	55	Tax Returns	3	6	8	7	7	24
232	250	242	Other		9	3	17	30	183
4/1/08-3/31/09 ALL	4/1/09-3/31/10 ALL	4/1/10-3/31/11 ALL			181 (4/1-9/30/10)			496 (10/1/10-3/31/11)	
700	707	677	NUMBER OF STATEMENTS	4	22	18	38	88	507
%	%	%	ASSETS	%	%	%	%	%	%
11.3	11.5	10.8	Cash & Equivalents		15.4	13.5	13.3	12.5	9.9
33.0	31.8	33.2	Trade Receivables (net)		17.9	24.7	33.0	34.0	34.2
13.5	13.9	15.3	Inventory		19.4	17.3	20.1	16.0	14.5
3.5	3.7	3.4	All Other Current		1.7	1.1	1.2	2.9	3.8
61.4	60.8	62.7	Total Current		54.5	56.6	67.6	65.3	62.4
27.1	27.8	25.5	Fixed Assets (net)		29.2	34.3	22.4	21.1	26.1
3.6	3.8	3.6	Intangibles (net)		3.4	1.7	1.5	3.5	3.9
7.9	7.6	8.2	All Other Non-Current		12.9	7.4	8.5	10.1	7.6
100.0	100.0	100.0	Total		100.0	100.0	100.0	100.0	100.0
			LIABILITIES						
11.2	9.4	12.0	Notes Payable-Short Term		34.6	11.5	9.7	11.2	11.2
3.5	3.0	2.6	Cur. Mat.-L.T.D.		1.5	3.8	2.4	2.3	2.7
26.4	27.0	28.1	Trade Payables		18.6	16.1	26.2	26.8	29.5
.2	.2	.2	Income Taxes Payable		.0	.0	.0	.1	.2
8.3	8.0	7.2	All Other Current		10.9	6.5	6.8	7.2	7.2
49.7	47.7	50.2	Total Current		65.6	38.0	45.1	47.7	50.7
16.0	16.7	13.6	Long-Term Debt		21.4	14.5	17.4	13.5	13.0
.6	.5	.6	Deferred Taxes		.6	.2	.4	.9	.6
3.5	3.4	3.6	All Other Non-Current		1.4	12.2	1.7	4.2	3.4
30.3	31.7	31.9	Net Worth		10.9	35.1	35.4	33.7	32.2
100.0	100.0	100.0	Total Liabilities & Net Worth		100.0	100.0	100.0	100.0	100.0
			INCOME DATA						
100.0	100.0	100.0	Net Sales		100.0	100.0	100.0	100.0	100.0
9.1	11.5	10.6	Gross Profit		25.1	31.7	20.5	14.2	7.7
8.0	10.2	9.5	Operating Expenses		22.8	29.8	18.7	12.7	6.8
1.2	1.3	1.1	Operating Profit		2.2	1.9	1.8	1.5	.9
.0	-.1	.0	All Other Expenses (net)		.1	.3	-.2	.3	-.1
1.2	1.4	1.1	Profit Before Taxes		2.1	1.6	2.0	1.2	1.0
			RATIOS						
1.6	1.6	1.6	Current		2.4	2.1	2.0	1.8	1.5
1.2	1.2	1.2			1.5	1.4	1.5	1.3	1.2
1.0	1.0	1.0			.9	1.1	1.1	1.0	1.0
1.2	1.2	1.2	Quick		1.4	1.6	1.5	1.3	1.2
.9	.9	.9			.9	.9	1.0	.9	.8
.6	.6	.6			.4	.6	.5	.5	.6
5 66.5	9 42.9	8 43.9	Sales/Receivables		6 64.3	6 59.3	17 22.1	11 33.9	8 45.6
12 30.4	16 23.1	16 22.4			21 17.0	23 15.7	29 12.7	21 17.3	15 24.4
23 16.0	28 13.1	29 12.7			33 11.0	36 10.2	44 8.3	32 11.3	26 14.1
1 246.7	2 165.3	2 148.5	Cost of Sales/Inventory		9 40.0	2 172.6	5 76.9	3 123.6	2 159.2
4 85.1	6 56.9	7 54.4			19 18.8	14 26.4	11 33.8	9 39.9	5 68.4
10 36.9	15 25.2	16 23.4			56 6.5	42 8.6	86 4.3	29 12.5	12 30.5
6 59.8	10 36.8	10 36.9	Cost of Sales/Payables		1 272.6	4 83.5	12 30.4	11 32.9	10 37.0
9 39.5	14 26.5	13 27.3			15 23.6	16 22.5	22 16.7	17 22.0	13 28.5
16 23.0	21 17.6	20 18.0			41 8.9	31 12.0	48 7.7	34 10.8	17 21.1
32.2	22.5	21.8	Sales/Working Capital		5.5	11.3	10.0	17.2	31.0
107.6	67.8	63.6			22.0	25.9	16.1	41.4	77.6
-421.8	-999.8	-415.1			-68.6	70.8	110.5	-187.8	-375.7
7.2	9.8	10.4	EBIT/Interest		14.6	8.8	10.2	9.5	11.0
(666) 3.4	(657) 3.5	(614) 3.8			(16) 2.1	(13) 3.0	(32) 2.5	(78) 3.6	(472) 4.1
1.7	1.7	1.7			-2.2	.2	.9	1.4	1.9
5.9	5.9	6.5	Net Profit + Depr., Dep., Amort./Cur. Mat. L/T/D					4.5	6.8
(225) 2.6	(208) 2.5	(185) 2.7						(22) 2.0	(149) 2.8
1.6	1.3	1.5						.7	1.5
.4	.3	.3	Fixed/Worth		.1	.3	.1	.2	.3
1.0	.9	.8			1.0	1.0	.5	.6	.8
2.3	2.3	1.8			NM	2.0	.9	1.4	1.9
1.4	1.3	1.2	Debt/Worth		.7	.9	.9	1.0	1.5
3.0	2.5	2.5			1.4	1.7	1.9	1.8	2.7
6.4	6.3	5.6			NM	7.5	4.5	6.9	5.4
41.4	37.4	31.9	% Profit Before Taxes/Tangible Net Worth		63.6	58.0	30.7	31.0	31.8
(640) 21.3	(645) 17.3	(625) 15.8			(17) 11.4	(16) 6.8	(35) 13.5	(76) 15.8	(477) 16.6
8.3	5.3	6.4			-11.2	2.1	1.7	5.7	7.5
11.0	10.0	8.5	% Profit Before Taxes/Total Assets		19.2	9.9	8.8	8.6	8.5
5.4	4.5	4.2			2.9	3.8	2.6	4.2	4.4
1.6	1.3	1.4			-7.1	.6	-.1	1.3	1.7
117.1	85.7	94.6	Sales/Net Fixed Assets		66.4	99.2	64.1	137.3	93.6
42.5	29.9	35.8			25.2	20.5	23.0	39.9	38.4
16.2	11.9	14.0			5.8	5.8	10.1	10.9	15.0
13.9	9.7	10.2	Sales/Total Assets		6.8	6.9	5.2	7.9	11.0
8.8	6.1	6.7			2.6	4.7	3.5	4.9	7.5
5.0	3.9	4.1			1.7	2.4	2.5	2.9	4.8
.2	.3	.3	% Depr., Dep., Amort./Sales		.1	.6	.6	.3	.3
(627) .5	(620) .7	(593) .6			(18) 1.5	(15) 1.1	(33) .9	(72) .8	(453) .5
.9	1.2	1.1			3.2	3.6	2.2	1.7	1.0
.2	.2	.2	% Officers', Directors' Owners' Comp/Sales				.6	.5	.2
(200) .5	(222) .5	(186) .5					(16) 1.2	(29) .9	(126) .4
1.2	1.4	1.1					2.0	1.9	.7
182793373M	123954917M	116925557M	Net Sales ($)	1914M	45872M	71077M	281873M	1474376M	115050445M
18605472M	18554210M	16981003M	Total Assets ($)	5208M	19005M	27273M	103544M	432913M	16393060M

© RMA 2011

M = $ thousand   MM = $ million

See Pages 9 through 22 for Explanation of Ratios and Data

Current Data Sorted by Assets   Comparative Historical Data

Type of Statement

0-500M	500M-2MM	2-10MM	10-50MM	50-100MM	100-250MM	Type of Statement	4/1/06-3/31/07 ALL	4/1/07-3/31/08 ALL
		13	49	23	8	Unqualified	114	108
	10	48	57	3	1	Reviewed	109	110
2	7	25	10	1	1	Compiled	66	56
	13	9	6	1		Tax Returns	18	18
3	8	51	78	26	26	Other	146	157
	62 (4/1-9/30/10)		416 (10/1/10-3/31/11)					
5	38	146	200	54	35	**NUMBER OF STATEMENTS**	453	449
%	%	%	%	%	%	**ASSETS**	%	%
	13.3	13.6	8.6	3.6	4.0	Cash & Equivalents	12.1	10.8
	9.5	8.8	10.0	5.8	6.4	Trade Receivables (net)	10.1	9.7
	41.1	26.7	17.9	11.6	13.8	Inventory	19.8	20.3
	1.7	2.7	1.8	2.1	1.8	All Other Current	2.5	3.1
	65.5	51.7	38.2	23.2	26.1	Total Current	44.5	43.8
	15.8	19.6	18.7	20.8	14.6	Fixed Assets (net)	23.0	21.7
	9.3	19.2	33.4	51.2	50.6	Intangibles (net)	24.2	25.8
	9.3	9.5	9.7	4.8	8.7	All Other Non-Current	8.3	8.7
	100.0	100.0	100.0	100.0	100.0	Total	100.0	100.0
						LIABILITIES		
	7.7	6.9	6.3	4.3	2.2	Notes Payable-Short Term	7.4	7.0
	2.9	3.6	4.7	3.7	1.6	Cur. Mat.-L.T.D.	3.4	3.6
	19.4	11.5	8.7	5.8	6.8	Trade Payables	11.5	10.7
	.2	.1	.1	.1	.0	Income Taxes Payable	.1	.1
	8.8	8.4	6.9	6.0	4.9	All Other Current	7.6	7.2
	39.0	30.3	26.7	20.0	15.4	Total Current	30.0	28.6
	12.1	15.4	24.9	35.3	36.0	Long-Term Debt	24.0	24.9
	.2	.4	.5	.5	.1	Deferred Taxes	.4	.4
	4.9	5.9	5.3	4.1	4.7	All Other Non-Current	3.0	4.6
	43.7	48.0	42.6	40.2	43.7	Net Worth	42.7	41.5
	100.0	100.0	100.0	100.0	100.0	Total Liabilties & Net Worth	100.0	100.0
						INCOME DATA		
	100.0	100.0	100.0	100.0	100.0	Net Sales	100.0	100.0
	23.6	25.6	26.1	25.7	26.2	Gross Profit	25.1	25.3
	21.2	21.4	21.0	19.7	20.5	Operating Expenses	21.6	21.3
	2.5	4.2	5.1	6.0	5.7	Operating Profit	3.5	4.1
	.1	.3	.8	1.2	1.0	All Other Expenses (net)	.4	.2
	2.4	3.9	4.3	4.8	4.6	Profit Before Taxes	3.1	3.8
						RATIOS		
	3.1	3.3	2.6	1.8	2.3		2.5	2.5
	1.9	1.8	1.6	1.3	1.7	Current	1.6	1.4
	1.1	1.1	1.0	1.0	1.3		1.0	1.0
	1.4	1.6	1.2	.7	1.0		1.3	1.3
	.7	.7	.7	.5	.6	Quick	.7	.6
	.3	.3	.3	.2	.3		.3	.3
0 UND	1 333.4	2 160.7	2 193.2	3 109.6			2 235.5	2 209.5
2 200.1	3 104.6	6 63.7	5 70.7	6 61.1		Sales/Receivables	5 79.2	5 71.5
12 30.8	14 25.6	22 17.0	14 25.5	15 23.8			18 19.8	18 20.5
23 15.6	20 18.1	22 16.2	23 16.1	24 15.4			13 28.0	16 22.7
27 13.6	25 14.8	26 13.8	26 14.3	28 12.9		Cost of Sales/Inventory	23 16.1	24 15.1
36 10.1	31 11.6	33 11.0	32 11.6	31 11.6			31 11.9	32 11.4
4 103.3	5 72.7	8 45.5	8 46.8	8 46.9			7 52.0	7 54.4
10 37.3	11 33.1	12 29.5	12 29.5	14 25.3		Cost of Sales/Payables	13 28.9	13 29.1
19 18.8	17 21.9	18 20.5	17 20.9	21 17.0			19 19.0	19 19.3
	14.0	11.7	12.7	20.9	10.0		13.3	12.5
	25.2	21.8	23.8	50.7	23.7	Sales/Working Capital	26.4	27.7
	62.0	163.4	-334.6	-606.6	36.5		999.8	562.1
	16.9	26.3	15.3	9.4	8.4		11.0	10.9
(32) 6.0	(130) 7.7	(186) 6.7	4.8	5.0		EBIT/Interest	(410) 4.6	(404) 4.7
	1.9	3.4	3.5	3.3	3.4		2.0	2.3
		4.4	8.2	10.4			5.4	6.6
	(22) 2.4	(48) 3.3	(15) 3.3			Net Profit + Depr., Dep., Amort./Cur. Mat. L/T/D	(84) 2.3	(100) 3.0
		1.2	1.5	2.0			1.2	2.0
	.1	.2	.4	1.9	.9		.4	.4
	.4	.6	1.8	-1.6	-4.8	Fixed/Worth	1.1	1.2
	1.1	10.8	-.6	-.3	-.3		-2.0	-1.5
	.6	.4	1.0	3.7	2.6		.7	.9
	1.3	1.4	5.7	-4.1	-10.5	Debt/Worth	2.7	3.0
	7.6	61.5	-3.3	-1.8	-2.5		-9.0	-6.0
	56.7	55.9	65.2	66.9	234.4		57.6	65.3
	(33) 33.0	(112) 32.6	(120) 38.0	(17) 51.6	(15) 61.0	% Profit Before Taxes/Tangible Net Worth	(312) 26.2	(302) 33.9
	4.6	13.5	21.9	21.7	50.8		11.8	18.5
	25.7	20.8	16.4	12.6	11.7		16.5	18.1
	11.8	12.9	10.7	9.2	8.6	% Profit Before Taxes/Total Assets	9.3	10.5
	.3	5.4	5.9	6.4	4.8		3.9	5.5
	157.6	61.9	47.5	40.8	39.1		42.0	44.0
	62.4	29.3	24.1	15.0	15.9	Sales/Net Fixed Assets	21.4	20.9
	23.7	15.8	9.6	6.5	10.1		10.2	10.4
	8.7	5.8	3.6	2.6	2.6		4.9	4.6
	6.3	4.2	2.8	2.2	2.2	Sales/Total Assets	3.5	3.3
	3.9	3.0	2.1	1.6	1.8		2.5	2.5
	.3	.5	.7	.8	.6		.7	.7
	(28) .7	(120) 1.0	(172) 1.0	(53) 1.3	(29) 1.1	% Depr., Dep., Amort./Sales	(413) 1.1	(399) 1.1
	1.2	1.5	1.3	1.7	1.4		1.6	1.6
	1.4	1.1	.6				1.1	.8
	(23) 2.1	(59) 1.8	(45) .9			% Officers', Directors' Owners' Comp/Sales	(160) 1.8	(140) 1.5
	2.9	3.9	2.0				3.0	2.9
8610M	302997M	3409068M	13067121M	7561380M	11846367M	Net Sales ($)	27454232M	30407156M
1452M	48704M	778624M	4690253M	3645588M	5362168M	Total Assets ($)	8925421M	10654488M

© RMA 2011

M = $ thousand   MM = $ million
See Pages 9 through 22 for Explanation of Ratios and Data

Comparative Historical Data   Current Data Sorted by Sales

Type of Statement groups (right side): 62 (4/1-9/30/10) | 416 (10/1/10-3/31/11)

4/1/08-3/31/09 ALL	4/1/09-3/31/10 ALL	4/1/10-3/31/11 ALL	Type of Statement	0-1MM	1-3MM	3-5MM	5-10MM	10-25MM	25MM & OVER
100	118	93	Unqualified					10	83
129	106	119	Reviewed		1	2	7	37	72
64	52	45	Compiled	1	1	1	5	17	20
22	22	29	Tax Returns	1	1	2	5	8	10
185	195	192	Other	3	1	5	8	24	151
500	493	478	**NUMBER OF STATEMENTS**	4	5	12	25	96	336
%	%	%	**ASSETS**	%	%	%	%	%	%
10.4	10.1	9.7	Cash & Equivalents			12.8	12.4	14.1	7.9
9.3	8.5	8.9	Trade Receivables (net)			10.8	9.5	8.0	9.0
19.2	19.9	21.8	Inventory			40.4	37.4	23.4	19.3
2.6	2.3	2.1	All Other Current			2.5	2.0	2.7	1.9
41.5	40.8	42.5	Total Current			66.5	61.3	48.2	38.2
20.7	19.9	18.6	Fixed Assets (net)			16.7	19.4	17.0	19.0
29.1	29.3	30.1	Intangibles (net)			7.5	12.0	24.7	34.5
8.8	10.0	8.9	All Other Non-Current			9.3	7.4	10.1	8.4
100.0	100.0	100.0	Total			100.0	100.0	100.0	100.0
			LIABILITIES						
6.8	6.1	6.2	Notes Payable-Short Term			10.1	7.1	6.9	5.7
3.6	3.4	3.8	Cur. Mat.-L.T.D.			2.0	1.6	4.7	3.9
9.5	8.9	10.0	Trade Payables			24.9	15.3	10.6	8.8
.1	.1	.1	Income Taxes Payable			.1	.0	.1	.1
6.2	7.0	7.3	All Other Current			6.7	7.5	7.2	7.2
26.2	25.5	27.5	Total Current			43.7	31.6	29.5	25.7
26.8	25.6	22.8	Long-Term Debt			18.1	11.9	20.9	24.7
.4	.4	.4	Deferred Taxes			.0	.7	.3	.4
3.9	5.6	5.4	All Other Non-Current			7.8	4.4	2.9	5.9
42.8	42.8	43.9	Net Worth			30.4	51.4	46.4	43.2
100.0	100.0	100.0	Total Liabilities & Net Worth			100.0	100.0	100.0	100.0
			INCOME DATA						
100.0	100.0	100.0	Net Sales			100.0	100.0	100.0	100.0
25.3	25.1	25.6	Gross Profit			24.1	23.8	25.6	25.5
21.1	20.5	20.9	Operating Expenses			21.6	20.7	21.5	20.7
4.2	4.7	4.7	Operating Profit			2.5	3.1	4.1	4.8
.4	.4	.6	All Other Expenses (net)			.7	.3	.2	.7
3.8	4.3	4.1	Profit Before Taxes			1.8	2.8	3.9	4.1
			RATIOS						
2.5	2.8	2.7	Current			3.3	4.8	3.1	2.4
1.6	1.6	1.6				1.6	2.2	1.7	1.6
1.1	1.1	1.0				1.1	1.2	1.1	1.0
1.3	1.2	1.2	Quick			1.0	2.1	1.4	1.1
.7	.7	.6				.6	.7	.7	.6
.3	.3	.3				.3	.5	.3	.3
2 222.8	1 273.0	2 196.7	Sales/Receivables			1 303.8	0 999.8	1 466.2	2 170.7
5 79.3	4 101.5	5 76.5				4 92.5	5 80.5	3 112.0	5 70.7
18 20.8	17 21.3	17 21.4				13 27.1	21 17.1	14 25.5	17 21.2
18 20.6	19 19.0	22 16.6	Cost of Sales/Inventory			21 17.4	24 15.3	21 17.5	22 16.6
24 15.0	23 15.8	26 13.8				37 9.8	29 12.6	25 14.6	26 13.8
32 11.5	31 11.6	33 11.1				69 5.3	49 7.5	30 12.1	32 11.5
7 51.9	6 62.1	6 58.0	Cost of Sales/Payables			7 53.3	5 78.3	5 70.6	7 51.2
12 30.4	11 32.8	12 30.2				16 23.5	14 26.5	10 35.5	12 29.5
18 20.7	16 22.7	18 20.4				59 6.2	20 17.9	16 22.9	17 20.9
12.9	13.1	12.9	Sales/Working Capital			11.3	12.3	12.3	13.9
24.1	25.1	24.8				26.3	24.0	23.7	25.3
116.9	181.1	224.2				65.5	70.5	205.9	NM
12.2	14.1	16.4	EBIT/Interest			12.5	20.6	27.1	14.2
(457) 4.8	(445) 6.3	(440) 6.6				(10) 3.5	(24) 5.9	(85) 7.5	(316) 6.5
2.5	3.3	3.4				-.1	2.1	3.2	3.5
7.9	8.7	8.5	Net Profit + Depr., Dep., Amort./Cur. Mat. L/T/D					3.9	9.8
(115) 2.6	(94) 3.3	(95) 3.3						(13) 3.0	(76) 3.4
1.6	1.9	1.5						1.1	1.6
.3	.3	.3	Fixed/Worth			.0	.2	.2	.5
1.4	1.4	1.4				.6	.4	.8	2.5
-1.1	-1.1	-.8				80.0	1.2	-2.5	-.5
.8	.8	.8	Debt/Worth			1.0	.4	.6	1.0
3.1	3.1	4.1				3.4	1.4	1.9	5.9
-4.0	-4.3	-4.0				219.8	3.0	-12.7	-3.1
67.6	67.7	61.3	% Profit Before Taxes/Tangible Net Worth			250.1	49.3	61.3	65.8
(325) 32.5	(312) 38.7	(300) 35.2				(10) 16.0	(23) 32.8	(68) 35.2	(192) 36.5
13.9	20.9	20.2				-20.5	2.6	22.1	21.3
16.4	17.6	16.8	% Profit Before Taxes/Total Assets			15.4	19.9	21.6	15.7
9.5	11.7	10.2				4.6	9.8	13.5	10.0
4.6	6.6	5.6				-5.1	.6	6.0	5.8
43.3	51.1	55.7	Sales/Net Fixed Assets			UND	77.3	70.7	48.0
21.5	22.5	25.7				51.2	32.3	36.0	23.1
10.1	10.4	11.2				11.5	14.3	19.1	10.1
4.5	4.5	4.5	Sales/Total Assets			6.5	7.7	5.7	3.9
3.1	3.0	3.0				3.8	4.8	3.9	2.8
2.3	2.2	2.2				2.7	2.2	2.4	2.1
.7	.7	.6	% Depr., Dep., Amort./Sales				.4	.5	.7
(437) 1.1	(423) 1.0	(405) 1.0					(18) 1.0	(76) .9	(297) 1.0
1.6	1.4	1.4					1.7	1.4	1.4
.9	.8	.7	% Officers', Directors' Owners' Comp/Sales				1.4	1.2	.6
(132) 1.6	(135) 1.6	(134) 1.6					(17) 2.1	(38) 1.8	(69) 1.1
3.0	2.9	2.8					3.0	3.5	2.1
32256216M	36717361M	36195543M	Net Sales ($)	1642M	9995M	49232M	187932M	1641403M	34305339M
12604666M	14725305M	14526789M	Total Assets ($)	9488M	36444M	12720M	55519M	570883M	13841735M

M = $ thousand   MM = $ million
See Pages 9 through 22 for Explanation of Ratios and Data

Current Data Sorted by Assets   Comparative Historical Data

0-500M	500M-2MM	2-10MM	10-50MM	50-100MM	100-250MM	Type of Statement	4/1/06-3/31/07 ALL	4/1/07-3/31/08 ALL
1		2	19	13	14	Unqualified	46	46
		9	9	2	1	Reviewed	22	18
2	1	11	1	1	1	Compiled	14	17
6	9	10	4	1		Tax Returns	11	25
1	13	18	18	8	21	Other	50	63
	39 (4/1-9/30/10)		156 (10/1/10-3/31/11)					
10	23	50	51	24	37	NUMBER OF STATEMENTS	143	169
%	%	%	%	%	%	**ASSETS**	%	%
3.2	3.7	6.1	7.4	4.9	3.6	Cash & Equivalents	5.5	6.5
20.7	27.4	26.1	24.6	18.9	20.5	Trade Receivables (net)	22.0	22.0
50.3	54.8	49.4	35.2	40.7	32.9	Inventory	42.3	42.5
.6	1.8	2.4	2.8	3.8	3.2	All Other Current	2.7	3.4
74.8	87.6	84.0	70.0	68.3	60.3	Total Current	72.5	74.5
12.3	8.9	8.8	11.0	9.8	10.8	Fixed Assets (net)	11.0	9.9
4.4	1.8	4.0	9.7	19.4	16.0	Intangibles (net)	9.9	9.9
8.4	1.7	3.3	9.2	2.4	12.9	All Other Non-Current	6.6	5.8
100.0	100.0	100.0	100.0	100.0	100.0	Total	100.0	100.0
						LIABILITIES		
20.0	20.0	10.9	12.7	19.5	9.5	Notes Payable-Short Term	14.3	13.7
8.1	4.7	1.8	1.4	2.2	3.0	Cur. Mat.-L.T.D.	1.8	1.7
21.5	38.8	31.6	21.0	17.1	22.3	Trade Payables	23.7	24.4
.1	.0	.1	.1	.5	.0	Income Taxes Payable	.2	.1
32.3	6.7	6.9	10.7	8.8	9.0	All Other Current	11.4	9.9
81.9	70.2	51.2	45.9	48.0	43.8	Total Current	51.4	49.8
11.5	8.9	8.5	12.0	13.1	21.4	Long-Term Debt	12.2	11.7
.0	.2	.1	.1	.4	.2	Deferred Taxes	.2	.4
8.2	4.5	4.8	4.0	3.6	3.7	All Other Non-Current	4.4	5.9
-1.6	16.1	35.4	38.0	34.9	30.8	Net Worth	31.8	32.1
100.0	100.0	100.0	100.0	100.0	100.0	Total Liabilities & Net Worth	100.0	100.0
						INCOME DATA		
100.0	100.0	100.0	100.0	100.0	100.0	Net Sales	100.0	100.0
33.2	30.8	29.2	27.1	23.2	24.5	Gross Profit	25.9	26.8
33.2	28.4	25.1	22.5	19.9	20.4	Operating Expenses	22.2	22.6
.0	2.3	4.1	4.6	3.3	4.2	Operating Profit	3.7	4.1
.8	.6	.2	.6	.8	.8	All Other Expenses (net)	.6	.5
-.8	1.7	3.9	4.0	2.5	3.4	Profit Before Taxes	3.1	3.6
						RATIOS		
3.2	1.8	2.2	2.2	1.8	2.2	Current	1.9	2.1
1.1	1.3	1.6	1.4	1.4	1.5		1.3	1.5
.7	.9	1.3	1.1	1.1	1.2		1.1	1.2
1.5	.6	.9	.9	.7	.9	Quick	.8	.9
.3	(22) .5	.6	.6	.5	.6		.5	.6
.0	.3	.4	.4	.2	.4		.4	.4
0 UND	9 42.8	11 34.7	21 17.4	7 50.9	14 25.7	Sales/Receivables	8 44.1	9 40.0
0 UND	30 12.3	38 9.6	32 11.2	27 13.7	29 12.5		30 12.2	31 11.7
50 7.3	56 6.5	54 6.7	47 7.8	44 8.2	43 8.6		48 7.6	45 8.1
35 10.3	58 6.3	53 6.9	41 8.9	46 7.9	39 9.4	Cost of Sales/Inventory	44 8.3	41 9.0
90 4.1	100 3.7	84 4.3	59 6.1	65 5.6	51 7.1		62 5.9	60 6.1
246 1.5	121 3.0	135 2.7	87 4.2	83 4.4	71 5.1		93 3.9	101 3.6
0 UND	39 9.5	30 12.3	19 19.1	18 20.2	22 16.9	Cost of Sales/Payables	23 16.2	21 17.0
25 14.5	68 5.4	51 7.1	35 10.4	33 11.1	32 11.5		32 11.3	35 10.5
105 3.5	119 3.1	71 5.2	56 6.6	41 8.8	42 8.6		53 6.8	66 5.6
4.6	7.5	4.6	6.0	5.7	8.7	Sales/Working Capital	7.5	6.8
21.2	14.1	8.9	13.4	15.1	14.6		13.5	13.5
-18.5	-103.4	17.4	44.5	36.8	39.6		86.7	36.3
	15.6	19.6	21.0	12.6	22.7	EBIT/Interest	13.0	15.0
(22)	6.6	(44) 5.9	(49) 6.5	6.5	6.7		(134) 4.5	(158) 4.9
	2.6	2.2	2.4	3.8	3.0		1.6	2.0
	12.6	16.0			15.4	Net Profit + Depr., Dep., Amort./Cur. Mat. L/T/D	24.4	10.9
	(11) 6.2	(12) 6.4		(11)	9.1		(22) 6.6	(33) 4.5
	2.6	1.0			4.7		2.3	1.7
.0	.1	.0	.1	.2	.1	Fixed/Worth	.1	.1
1.3	.3	.1	.2	1.4	.8		.3	.3
-.3	57.5	.7	1.3	-1.7	-3.5		1.8	1.8
1.5	2.1	.8	.9	1.5	1.3	Debt/Worth	1.4	1.4
7.5	4.0	2.3	2.0	14.6	3.8		2.6	2.9
-5.6	534.0	7.6	3.6	-15.2	-35.9		56.6	15.4
	62.1	47.6	44.7	66.8	56.9	% Profit Before Taxes/Tangible Net Worth	46.4	82.5
(18)	32.2	(45) 24.3	(42) 23.8	(15) 33.0	(27) 36.6		(110) 18.9	(141) 28.9
	11.8	12.7	3.6	10.1	16.2		5.7	10.3
16.2	14.0	14.2	16.2	11.8	13.0	% Profit Before Taxes/Total Assets	16.4	15.5
5.4	4.7	7.3	7.0	6.9	8.1		7.0	8.5
-6.3	2.2	2.7	1.8	3.7	4.7		1.3	2.7
UND	444.3	325.9	196.6	110.9	101.5	Sales/Net Fixed Assets	151.9	171.3
191.6	74.8	140.9	76.0	48.9	31.1		52.9	57.0
8.3	21.7	36.7	21.0	21.8	12.6		22.8	22.3
3.6	4.2	3.7	3.7	3.6	3.5	Sales/Total Assets	4.1	4.1
2.4	3.0	2.8	2.8	3.2	2.6		2.9	2.9
1.8	2.0	1.9	1.9	1.7	1.8		2.0	2.1
	.2	.2	.2	.4	.4	% Depr., Dep., Amort./Sales	.3	.3
(15)	.5	(40) .3	(43) .4	(20) .8	(31) .8		(114) .5	(130) .5
	1.8	1.0	1.0	1.2	1.4		.9	1.0
	2.3	2.7	1.0			% Officers', Directors', Owners' Comp/Sales	1.8	1.5
(14)	4.1	(20) 4.0	(15) 2.6				(36) 3.4	(45) 2.7
	6.2	6.1	5.2				7.7	4.4
10340M	88838M	721954M	3439516M	4675660M	15779987M	Net Sales ($)	14844663M	16833017M
3074M	24584M	242631M	1190680M	1690723M	5820259M	Total Assets ($)	5859229M	6474514M

© RMA 2011

M = $ thousand   MM = $ million

See Pages 9 through 22 for Explanation of Ratios and Data

Comparative Historical Data | Current Data Sorted by Sales

4/1/08-3/31/09 ALL	4/1/09-3/31/10 ALL	4/1/10-3/31/11 ALL	Type of Statement	0-1MM	1-3MM	3-5MM	5-10MM	10-25MM	25MM & OVER
54	51	49	Unqualified	1			1		47
24	35	21	Reviewed				1	6	14
24	18	17	Compiled	1	2	1	4	6	3
22	17	29	Tax Returns	4	4	8	7	3	3
68	67	79	Other	4	6	3	10	9	47
				39 (4/1-9/30/10)			*156 (10/1/10-3/31/11)*		
192	188	195	**NUMBER OF STATEMENTS**	10	12	12	23	24	114
%	%	%	**ASSETS**	%	%	%	%	%	%
6.8	6.5	5.4	Cash & Equivalents	6.2	3.2	2.1	6.4	7.2	5.3
21.2	21.7	23.7	Trade Receivables (net)	22.2	26.0	26.4	19.9	30.9	22.5
41.8	41.5	42.2	Inventory	54.0	48.0	49.1	56.9	40.9	37.1
2.9	2.7	2.7	All Other Current	1.4	.6	4.9	3.0	2.3	2.8
72.8	72.4	73.9	Total Current	83.8	77.7	82.5	86.3	81.3	67.6
11.3	11.2	10.1	Fixed Assets (net)	13.0	14.1	8.9	6.5	9.7	10.3
10.9	9.9	9.4	Intangibles (net)	.5	3.6	3.3	3.5	5.7	13.5
5.1	6.5	6.6	All Other Non-Current	2.7	4.7	5.3	3.7	3.3	8.6
100.0	100.0	100.0	Total	100.0	100.0	100.0	100.0	100.0	100.0
			LIABILITIES						
15.4	13.8	13.7	Notes Payable-Short Term	26.0	17.2	15.0	12.9	11.2	12.8
2.0	1.6	2.6	Cur. Mat.-L.T.D.	1.9	9.1	4.5	1.9	2.2	2.1
23.5	23.1	25.6	Trade Payables	25.3	32.7	35.3	29.8	32.6	21.6
.2	.1	.1	Income Taxes Payable	.1	.0	.0	.0	.1	.1
9.4	9.5	9.8	All Other Current	32.8	7.1	5.2	6.6	7.8	9.6
50.6	48.2	51.9	Total Current	86.1	66.0	60.0	51.3	53.9	46.2
11.8	14.5	12.6	Long-Term Debt	10.9	12.4	6.6	7.5	11.9	14.6
.3	.3	.2	Deferred Taxes	.0	.0	.0	.4	.0	.2
4.0	4.0	4.4	All Other Non-Current	9.0	10.8	4.3	6.3	1.4	3.6
33.2	33.1	31.0	Net Worth	-6.0	10.8	29.1	34.6	32.8	35.4
100.0	100.0	100.0	Total Liabilties & Net Worth	100.0	100.0	100.0	100.0	100.0	100.0
			INCOME DATA						
100.0	100.0	100.0	Net Sales	100.0	100.0	100.0	100.0	100.0	100.0
27.1	26.6	27.4	Gross Profit	34.9	31.6	31.8	27.9	31.4	24.9
24.1	23.2	23.7	Operating Expenses	36.3	28.3	28.5	24.2	26.1	21.0
3.0	3.4	3.7	Operating Profit	-1.4	3.2	3.4	3.7	5.3	3.9
.5	.5	.6	All Other Expenses (net)	1.6	.0	.4	.3	.7	.6
2.6	2.9	3.1	Profit Before Taxes	-3.0	3.3	2.9	3.4	4.6	3.3
			RATIOS						
2.2	2.1	2.2	Current	3.2	1.7	1.7	2.4	2.2	2.2
1.5	1.5	1.5		1.8	1.2	1.4	1.5	1.6	1.5
1.1	1.2	1.2		.7	.8	1.2	1.3	1.2	1.2
.9	.9	.9	Quick	1.5	.7	.6	.8	.8	.9
.6	.6 (194)	.6		.4	.4	.4	.5 (22)	.7	.6
.4	.4	.4		.1	.1	.3	.2	.4	.4
10 37.2	10 35.2	13 28.2	Sales/Receivables	0 UND	5 67.0	21 17.8	4 89.4	22 16.6	14 26.4
31 11.8	30 12.4	31 11.7		13 28.2	33 11.2	47 7.7	27 13.4	40 9.2	29 12.4
43 8.6	44 8.3	47 7.8		50 7.3	86 4.2	72 5.0	51 7.1	62 5.9	42 8.6
41 8.9	39 9.4	45 8.1	Cost of Sales/Inventory	72 5.1	53 6.8	51 7.1	76 4.8	46 7.9	41 8.9
67 5.5	67 5.5	67 5.5		247 1.5	105 3.5	109 3.3	102 3.6	72 5.0	58 6.3
100 3.6	102 3.6	110 3.3		516 .7	132 2.8	208 1.8	145 2.5	120 3.0	77 4.8
21 17.4	18 20.3	23 16.1	Cost of Sales/Payables	0 UND	40 9.2	29 12.5	39 9.5	29 12.7	20 18.2
34 10.9	32 11.3	38 9.5		52 7.0	58 6.3	72 5.1	51 7.1	59 6.2	33 11.2
60 6.1	56 6.5	62 5.9		124 2.9	138 2.6	141 2.6	69 5.3	82 4.5	47 7.7
7.0	6.5	6.6	Sales/Working Capital	2.5	7.2	4.4	4.3	5.2	8.0
12.7	11.3	12.7		5.0	18.6	10.7	8.9	9.1	14.5
49.4	32.3	30.9		-6.1	-23.2	22.5	16.8	25.2	38.8
9.3	18.9	18.8	EBIT/Interest		7.7	10.4	28.1	18.5	19.1
(169) 3.7	(164) 5.9	(185) 6.4			(11) 6.4	(11) 6.3	(21) 5.7	(22) 5.6	(111) 6.7
1.2	1.8	2.6			2.2	2.7	2.2	2.2	3.0
8.1	7.5	11.4	Net Profit + Depr., Dep., Amort./Cur. Mat. L/T/D						10.9
(42) 3.5	(41) 2.9	(42) 6.2						(29)	5.8
1.1	1.3	2.7							2.5
.1	.1	.1	Fixed/Worth	.0	-.1	.0	.0	.0	.1
.3	.3	.3		.8	.9	.1	.1	.2	.4
2.6	1.9	2.1		-.2	-1.5	1.1	.4	1.4	NM
1.2	1.0	1.2	Debt/Worth	1.5	3.4	1.3	.7	.9	1.1
3.4	2.3	3.2		6.1	8.0	3.9	3.4	2.3	2.8
23.0	20.2	29.3		-3.4	-26.1	17.6	8.1	8.1	NM
45.6	51.2	50.3	% Profit Before Taxes/Tangible Net Worth			61.9	65.6	43.6	49.0
(149) 22.0	(148) 22.6	(153) 29.8			(10) 19.2	(22) 31.7	(20) 19.7		(86) 31.4
5.2	5.5	10.7				11.3	22.5	6.6	12.1
13.4	15.3	14.3	% Profit Before Taxes/Total Assets	14.7	12.1	8.9	17.8	13.4	14.6
6.1	7.5	6.9		-.1	3.5	4.5	6.1	7.3	8.0
.8	2.0	3.0		-7.6	1.9	2.8	3.0	3.1	3.8
116.6	154.2	196.6	Sales/Net Fixed Assets	UND	241.6	UND	692.6	198.1	135.3
55.0	58.6	72.9		67.1	59.9	94.8	148.5	125.1	54.9
19.5	22.6	20.8		7.3	10.7	19.2	58.5	23.2	15.0
3.7	3.8	3.7	Sales/Total Assets	2.2	3.5	3.5	3.4	3.7	3.8
2.9	3.0	2.8		1.7	2.9	2.1	2.6	2.8	3.1
2.0	1.9	1.9		.8	2.1	1.4	2.0	1.8	2.0
.3	.3	.2	% Depr., Dep., Amort./Sales				.1	.2	.3
(154) .6	(151) .6	(154) .5				(17) .3	(19) .3	(97) .6	
1.3	1.3	1.2					.9	1.0	1.2
1.3	1.2	2.3	% Officers', Directors' Owners' Comp/Sales				2.5	2.3	.7
(42) 2.6	(47) 2.1	(59) 3.5				(10) 4.8	(11) 4.1	(16) 2.1	
4.7	4.6	6.2				6.7	8.0	3.9	
22478097M	22779131M	24716295M	Net Sales ($)	5893M	23331M	43603M	174462M	394565M	24074441M
8649454M	8700126M	8971951M	Total Assets ($)	4427M	17059M	21632M	77163M	183082M	8668588M

M = $ thousand   MM = $ million
See Pages 9 through 22 for Explanation of Ratios and Data

Current Data Sorted by Assets / Comparative Historical Data

Type of Statement	0-500M	500M-2MM	2-10MM	10-50MM	50-100MM	100-250MM		4/1/06-3/31/07 ALL	4/1/07-3/31/08 ALL
Unqualified		19	171	240	68	41		608	587
Reviewed		9	54	16	1			78	74
Compiled	3	11	25	8				49	65
Tax Returns	6	22	9	1				34	44
Other	4	16	47	42	14	10		118	120
		377 (4/1-9/30/10)		460 (10/1/10-3/31/11)					
NUMBER OF STATEMENTS	13	77	306	307	83	51		887	890
	%	%	%	%	%	%		%	%
ASSETS									
Cash & Equivalents	7.1	12.9	8.7	5.2	3.5	3.8		5.8	6.9
Trade Receivables (net)	24.9	20.6	21.3	20.9	17.0	19.4		18.3	22.2
Inventory	37.2	31.2	30.5	31.4	36.3	33.7		30.8	32.3
All Other Current	8.0	2.6	4.3	7.3	9.3	10.7		8.6	5.9
Total Current	77.2	67.3	64.8	64.7	66.1	67.5		63.5	67.3
Fixed Assets (net)	19.5	21.8	20.9	21.3	20.3	20.3		22.5	19.8
Intangibles (net)	1.2	1.0	.8	1.2	1.4	.6		.8	.7
All Other Non-Current	2.3	9.9	13.5	12.8	12.3	11.6		13.2	12.3
Total	100.0	100.0	100.0	100.0	100.0	100.0		100.0	100.0
LIABILITIES									
Notes Payable-Short Term	26.3	10.1	12.4	17.6	19.9	20.1		17.9	20.6
Cur. Mat.-L.T.D.	5.0	3.3	2.0	2.1	1.6	1.5		1.8	1.9
Trade Payables	29.3	14.6	19.3	20.6	19.9	20.1		17.5	17.7
Income Taxes Payable	.0	.2	.3	.4	.4	.4		.4	.6
All Other Current	15.3	7.0	7.8	7.6	8.8	7.8		7.0	7.9
Total Current	75.9	35.2	41.8	48.2	50.6	49.9		45.1	48.7
Long-Term Debt	13.9	11.7	7.3	7.9	9.9	8.4		8.1	8.0
Deferred Taxes	.0	.2	.3	.6	.4	.6		.4	.3
All Other Non-Current	2.2	3.5	1.0	2.0	3.0	3.9		1.8	2.0
Net Worth	7.8	49.4	49.6	41.2	36.1	37.2		44.6	41.0
Total Liabilities & Net Worth	100.0	100.0	100.0	100.0	100.0	100.0		100.0	100.0
INCOME DATA									
Net Sales	100.0	100.0	100.0	100.0	100.0	100.0		100.0	100.0
Gross Profit	28.6	25.3	16.8	13.7	12.7	12.9		16.1	15.6
Operating Expenses	24.7	23.8	14.8	11.1	10.2	10.0		14.2	13.3
Operating Profit	4.0	1.5	2.0	2.7	2.6	2.9		1.8	2.3
All Other Expenses (net)	.8	-.4	-.9	-.8	-.8	-.3		-.6	-.6
Profit Before Taxes	3.1	2.0	2.9	3.5	3.4	3.2		2.4	2.9
RATIOS									
Current	1.8	3.1	2.1	1.6	1.6	1.7		1.8	1.7
	1.3	1.9	1.6	1.3	1.3	1.3		1.3	1.3
	.7	1.4	1.2	1.2	1.1	1.2		1.2	1.1
Quick	.8	1.6	1.1	.8	.6	.8		.8	.9
	.2	1.0	.7	.5	.4	.5		.5	.6
	.1	.5	.5	.3	.2	.3		.3	.4
Sales/Receivables	0 UND	10 36.2	18 20.5	18 20.4	14 26.0	17 21.6		13 27.9	19 19.5
	13 28.2	22 16.5	27 13.5	29 12.6	28 12.9	30 12.0		23 15.6	30 12.2
	27 13.7	39 9.3	40 9.2	46 7.9	42 8.7	45 8.1		35 10.3	45 8.2
Cost of Sales/Inventory	4 100.7	26 13.8	31 11.7	37 9.8	43 8.6	36 10.3		34 10.8	36 10.1
	25 14.5	53 7.0	57 6.4	57 6.4	63 5.8	53 6.8		53 6.9	58 6.3
	60 6.0	84 4.4	84 4.3	91 4.0	127 2.9	89 4.1		81 4.5	85 4.3
Cost of Sales/Payables	6 58.8	7 49.1	16 22.5	19 18.8	22 16.6	20 18.6		15 23.7	15 23.9
	20 18.4	19 19.7	28 13.2	31 11.7	34 10.6	35 10.4		26 13.9	28 13.0
	57 6.4	43 8.4	46 8.0	63 5.8	64 5.7	56 6.5		44 8.3	47 7.8
Sales/Working Capital	14.6	5.4	6.2	9.7	10.5	10.1		8.9	8.5
	40.7	9.1	11.1	14.2	15.5	13.9		16.1	15.1
	-21.8	-21.5	22.7	22.2	20.3	19.6		28.0	28.4
EBIT/Interest	13.0	14.3	22.0	15.5	11.3	12.6		5.7	6.4
	(12) 5.2	(65) 5.0	(285) 6.8	(297) 7.8	(81) 7.2	7.1		(830) 3.1	(833) 3.4
	1.4	1.0	2.4	3.7	4.5	4.4		1.8	2.1
Net Profit + Depr., Dep., Amort./Cur. Mat. L/T/D		11.1	9.6	10.9	14.5	12.7		7.0	9.9
		(10) 3.0	(98) 5.3	(186) 6.1	(54) 6.0	(31) 5.6		(401) 4.5	(427) 5.8
		2.0	2.5	3.5	4.0	4.1		2.7	3.5
Fixed/Worth	.0	.1	.2	.3	.4	.5		.3	.3
	.5	.4	.4	.5	.5	.6		.5	.5
	-2.3	.7	.7	.7	.7	.7		.7	.7
Debt/Worth	1.5	.4	.5	.9	1.2	1.1		.6	.8
	4.6	1.0	.9	1.5	1.9	1.4		1.3	1.5
	-14.6	2.3	2.0	2.6	3.7	3.7		2.4	2.9
% Profit Before Taxes/Tangible Net Worth		29.4	20.8	24.6	26.0	24.9		18.2	23.9
		(71) 8.8	(299) 11.5	(300) 17.5	(82) 19.2	21.0		(868) 11.2	(868) 15.3
		1.3	5.1	10.6	14.5	15.0		5.4	8.7
% Profit Before Taxes/Total Assets	24.8	12.0	10.0	10.1	8.5	10.6		8.2	9.6
	7.3	5.1	5.7	6.6	6.4	6.9		4.7	5.9
	2.5	2.4	2.4	3.8	4.1	4.6		2.2	3.3
Sales/Net Fixed Assets	402.0	40.3	23.3	16.3	14.9	17.5		17.8	21.1
	65.2	14.1	12.5	10.9	10.9	10.9		11.0	13.0
	14.4	7.9	7.7	7.5	7.2	8.4		7.5	8.4
Sales/Total Assets	8.5	4.2	3.2	2.9	2.6	2.8		3.0	2.9
	5.2	2.9	2.2	2.1	1.9	2.2		2.2	2.2
	3.9	1.8	1.7	1.6	1.4	1.5		1.8	1.7
% Depr., Dep., Amort./Sales		.7	.8	.9	1.0	.8		1.0	.8
		(61) 1.4	(284) 1.3	(295) 1.3	(82) 1.3	(48) 1.2		(852) 1.4	(844) 1.2
		2.5	1.8	1.7	1.7	1.5		2.0	1.7
% Officers', Directors' Owners' Comp/Sales		1.9	1.3	.4				1.1	1.1
		(31) 3.2	(44) 2.1	(18) 1.4				(91) 2.0	(107) 2.2
		5.6	3.4	5.0				4.6	4.8
Net Sales ($)	23665M	302563M	4408649M	16356603M	12698455M	17239076M		37554454M	46797126M
Total Assets ($)	4042M	94421M	1658111M	6957878M	5927675M	7483320M		15683424M	20583502M

M = $ thousand   MM = $ million
See Pages 9 through 22 for Explanation of Ratios and Data

Comparative Historical Data / Current Data Sorted by Sales

			Type of Statement						
519	526	539	Unqualified	1	10	19	60	129	320
81	88	80	Reviewed		10	6	17	27	20
71	60	47	Compiled	1	6	4	15	14	7
33	30	38	Tax Returns	3	15	7	3	8	2
148	142	133	Other	2	10	11	19	30	61
4/1/08- 3/31/09 ALL	4/1/09- 3/31/10 ALL	4/1/10- 3/31/11 ALL			377 (4/1-9/30/10)		460 (10/1/10-3/31/11)		
				0-1MM	1-3MM	3-5MM	5-10MM	10-25MM	25MM & OVER
852	846	837	NUMBER OF STATEMENTS	7	51	47	114	208	410
%	%	%	ASSETS	%	%	%	%	%	%
6.6	7.7	6.9	Cash & Equivalents		12.8	9.9	9.7	7.6	4.7
21.6	21.7	20.6	Trade Receivables (net)		21.0	16.4	17.9	21.1	21.7
34.4	30.9	31.8	Inventory		29.3	31.6	31.4	32.5	31.8
7.0	5.0	6.2	All Other Current		2.3	5.1	4.6	5.1	7.7
69.6	65.4	65.5	Total Current		65.5	63.0	63.6	66.3	65.9
18.8	20.8	21.0	Fixed Assets (net)		22.7	21.2	21.6	19.9	21.0
.8	.9	1.0	Intangibles (net)		1.5	1.6	.7	1.0	1.0
10.8	12.9	12.5	All Other Non-Current		10.3	14.2	14.2	12.7	12.2
100.0	100.0	100.0	Total		100.0	100.0	100.0	100.0	100.0
			LIABILITIES						
18.5	14.8	15.5	Notes Payable-Short Term		10.4	15.0	12.8	13.8	17.9
1.9	1.7	2.1	Cur. Mat.-L.T.D.		4.3	2.0	2.0	1.7	2.0
20.0	19.9	19.6	Trade Payables		15.1	11.7	16.3	21.0	21.1
.5	.3	.3	Income Taxes Payable		.1	.1	.2	.3	.4
9.1	7.9	7.9	All Other Current		8.2	8.2	6.4	8.6	7.6
50.0	44.6	45.4	Total Current		38.0	37.0	37.7	45.4	49.0
7.9	7.8	8.4	Long-Term Debt		13.0	6.2	7.7	7.3	8.3
.3	.4	.4	Deferred Taxes		.1	.2	.3	.4	.6
1.7	2.2	2.0	All Other Non-Current		3.6	2.6	.8	1.2	2.4
40.1	44.9	43.8	Net Worth		45.3	54.0	53.6	45.8	39.7
100.0	100.0	100.0	Total Liabilities & Net Worth		100.0	100.0	100.0	100.0	100.0
			INCOME DATA						
100.0	100.0	100.0	Net Sales		100.0	100.0	100.0	100.0	100.0
15.5	15.1	16.0	Gross Profit		26.6	22.3	18.9	16.0	12.7
12.4	13.2	13.7	Operating Expenses		24.1	20.4	17.1	13.5	10.3
3.1	1.9	2.3	Operating Profit		2.5	1.9	1.8	2.5	2.5
-.6	-.9	-.8	All Other Expenses (net)		-.3	-1.2	-1.3	-.8	-.7
3.7	2.8	3.1	Profit Before Taxes		2.8	3.1	3.1	3.3	3.1
			RATIOS						
1.7	1.9	1.8			3.5	2.4	2.4	1.8	1.6
1.3	1.4	1.4	Current		1.9	1.7	1.7	1.4	1.3
1.2	1.2	1.2			1.3	1.4	1.3	1.2	1.2
.9	1.0	.9			1.4	1.3	1.2	.9	.8
(851) .5	.6	.6	Quick		1.0	.8	.8	.6	.5
.3	.4	.4			.5	.4	.4	.4	.3
16 23.0	17 21.3	17 22.0		10 37.3	11 32.0	17 21.1	17 21.7	17 21.3	
26 14.2	26 13.9	27 13.5	Sales/Receivables	25 14.6	24 15.4	27 13.7	29 12.8	27 13.4	
39 9.4	40 9.2	42 8.7		42 8.7	47 7.8	41 8.8	46 8.0	42 8.8	
34 10.8	29 12.7	34 10.7		25 14.5	40 9.2	39 9.3	34 10.7	32 11.3	
57 6.5	49 7.5	57 6.4	Cost of Sales/Inventory	65 5.6	69 5.3	71 5.2	59 6.2	50 7.3	
85 4.3	81 4.5	90 4.1		96 3.8	98 3.7	91 4.0	94 3.9	86 4.3	
15 23.7	15 24.0	17 21.3		12 29.9	8 47.0	16 23.2	18 20.6	19 19.1	
28 13.1	26 14.0	29 12.4	Cost of Sales/Payables	22 16.5	21 17.5	27 13.6	31 11.7	29 12.4	
46 8.0	47 7.8	51 7.1		50 7.3	42 8.7	49 7.5	57 6.4	52 7.1	
9.5	8.1	7.9			4.6	5.7	5.2	7.7	10.6
16.3	13.7	13.5	Sales/Working Capital		7.2	7.2	8.4	12.7	15.5
27.7	24.8	22.5			24.0	18.1	18.6	20.0	23.9
10.1	13.5	15.9			9.8	19.0	19.2	20.9	13.9
(794) 5.1	(793) 6.0	(791) 7.1	EBIT/Interest	(45) 5.2	(42) 3.5	(101) 5.5	(198) 7.4	(399) 7.5	
2.8	2.4	3.0			1.7	1.7	2.1	2.7	4.1
12.7	10.9	10.7					6.7	8.9	12.1
(383) 6.6	(384) 6.0	(379) 5.6	Net Profit + Depr., Dep., Amort./Cur. Mat. L/T/D			(28) 4.3	(86) 5.5	(250) 6.3	
3.8	3.0	3.4					2.0	3.4	3.7
.3	.3	.3			.1	.2	.2	.3	.4
.4	.4	.5	Fixed/Worth		.3	.4	.3	.4	.5
.7	.7	.7			.9	.9	.7	.7	.7
.8	.6	.7			.4	.4	.4	.6	.9
1.7	1.2	1.3	Debt/Worth		1.0	.6	.9	1.1	1.5
3.0	2.3	2.6			2.3	2.3	1.6	2.3	2.8
34.3	25.9	24.2			31.9	20.5	20.0	21.8	25.4
(834) 22.0	(818) 16.4	(812) 16.1	% Profit Before Taxes/Tangible Net Worth	(46) 10.1	(46) 8.6	(113) 9.2	(200) 14.5	(404) 18.5	
12.0	6.6	8.1			1.2	3.8	3.6	6.8	11.2
12.5	11.5	10.1			11.9	9.4	10.1	10.7	9.9
7.8	6.9	6.3	% Profit Before Taxes/Total Assets		5.4	5.1	4.8	6.3	6.7
4.5	2.5	3.2			.6	1.7	1.9	2.9	4.2
27.0	22.8	19.3			42.7	16.4	23.3	21.0	17.9
15.6	13.2	11.8	Sales/Net Fixed Assets		14.1	11.8	10.9	11.5	11.8
10.2	8.7	7.6			6.7	6.3	6.2	7.5	8.2
3.4	3.3	3.0			3.4	2.4	2.5	3.1	3.1
2.5	2.5	2.2	Sales/Total Assets		2.4	1.8	2.0	2.2	2.4
1.9	1.9	1.6			1.4	1.5	1.5	1.6	1.8
.7	.8	.8			.8	.9	.9	.8	.8
(803) 1.0	(800) 1.1	(778) 1.3	% Depr., Dep., Amort./Sales	(40) 1.6	(41) 1.6	(105) 1.4	(192) 1.2	(394) 1.2	
1.5	1.7	1.8			3.7	2.8	1.9	1.9	1.6
1.0	1.0	.9			3.0	1.0	.8	.9	.4
(105) 2.1	(100) 2.0	(105) 2.1	% Officers', Directors' Owners' Comp/Sales	(20) 4.0	(13) 2.0	(19) 2.0	(25) 2.1	(26) 1.4	
4.0	4.6	4.6			7.0	6.0	2.8	3.2	2.7
62130173M	54874862M	51029011M	Net Sales ($)	4054M	109806M	189794M	881946M	3546120M	46297291M
22981696M	20463262M	22125447M	Total Assets ($)	3846M	54525M	109231M	476066M	1771041M	19710738M

M = $ thousand   MM = $ million
See Pages 9 through 22 for Explanation of Ratios and Data

Current Data Sorted by Assets | **Comparative Historical Data**

0-500M	500M-2MM	2-10MM	10-50MM	50-100MM	100-250MM	Type of Statement	4/1/06-3/31/07 ALL	4/1/07-3/31/08 ALL
		1	7			Unqualified	14	9
	3	5	3			Reviewed	9	9
	2	4	1			Compiled	9	6
2	1	1	2			Tax Returns	6	8
2	3	11	7	2		Other	16	22
	13 (4/1-9/30/10)		44 (10/1/10-3/31/11)					
4	9	22	20	2		NUMBER OF STATEMENTS	54	54
%	%	%	%	%	%	**ASSETS**	%	%
		6.0	10.6		DATA NOT AVAILABLE	Cash & Equivalents	11.2	8.7
		29.3	22.2			Trade Receivables (net)	26.4	28.9
		29.4	38.7			Inventory	33.1	32.4
		2.8	4.0			All Other Current	3.7	4.1
		67.5	75.4			Total Current	74.5	74.0
		14.4	13.1			Fixed Assets (net)	15.0	12.1
		6.1	3.4			Intangibles (net)	3.3	3.7
		12.0	8.1			All Other Non-Current	7.2	10.1
		100.0	100.0			Total	100.0	100.0
						LIABILITIES		
		10.4	10.1			Notes Payable-Short Term	9.1	15.2
		1.7	1.7			Cur. Mat.-L.T.D.	.9	1.7
		25.8	29.0			Trade Payables	27.5	33.2
		.0	.1			Income Taxes Payable	.3	.3
		10.0	9.4			All Other Current	9.1	11.8
		48.0	50.4			Total Current	47.0	62.2
		16.6	7.6			Long-Term Debt	10.7	8.6
		.2	.0			Deferred Taxes	.1	.0
		3.6	1.0			All Other Non-Current	5.3	3.8
		31.6	41.1			Net Worth	36.9	25.4
		100.0	100.0			Total Liabilties & Net Worth	100.0	100.0
						INCOME DATA		
		100.0	100.0			Net Sales	100.0	100.0
		36.9	34.3			Gross Profit	35.4	33.6
		30.4	31.8			Operating Expenses	31.8	31.2
		6.5	2.4			Operating Profit	3.6	2.4
		2.3	.4			All Other Expenses (net)	.5	.6
		4.1	2.1			Profit Before Taxes	3.1	1.8
						RATIOS		
		2.7	2.6				3.4	2.0
		1.7	1.4			Current	1.6	1.2
		1.1	1.1				1.0	1.0
		1.5	1.0				1.4	1.0
		.7	.8			Quick	.8	.6
		.4	.4				.5	.4
		22 16.9	**19** 18.9				**16** 23.4	**21** 17.6
		38 9.6	**31** 11.6			Sales/Receivables	**34** 10.8	**43** 8.6
		71 5.1	**49** 7.5				**61** 6.0	**62** 5.9
		32 11.4	**60** 6.1				**31** 11.6	**34** 10.9
		68 5.4	**89** 4.1			Cost of Sales/Inventory	**62** 5.9	**59** 6.1
		118 3.1	**153** 2.4				**156** 2.3	**152** 2.4
		17 21.9	**25** 14.7				**23** 15.8	**25** 14.5
		35 10.3	**55** 6.6			Cost of Sales/Payables	**58** 6.3	**60** 6.0
		68 5.4	**99** 3.7				**97** 3.8	**104** 3.5
		5.9	3.4				4.0	6.4
		12.2	11.9			Sales/Working Capital	10.0	20.6
		NM	71.1				NM	-98.8
		19.3	54.5				14.2	11.8
		(21) 3.5	(18) 11.5			EBIT/Interest	(43) 5.4	(47) 3.7
		1.2	1.8				1.9	1.1
							24.1	35.8
						Net Profit + Depr., Dep., Amort./Cur. Mat. L/T/D	(10) 5.0	(10) 7.2
							1.0	1.3
		.2	.1				.1	.2
		.6	.4			Fixed/Worth	.4	.4
		2.5	.6				1.3	2.1
		.8	1.0				.6	1.1
		2.0	2.0			Debt/Worth	2.4	4.0
		20.2	3.4				6.6	17.6
		53.1	47.9				42.3	54.0
		(18) 31.2	10.4			% Profit Before Taxes/Tangible Net Worth	(49) 17.9	(44) 14.1
		6.5	4.4				4.4	3.7
		19.1	14.6				12.2	11.1
		8.3	4.6			% Profit Before Taxes/Total Assets	5.9	3.4
		1.1	1.2				1.6	.2
		63.5	50.7				51.5	175.2
		33.3	23.3			Sales/Net Fixed Assets	23.5	30.7
		13.3	8.9				11.0	15.1
		3.6	2.9				4.6	4.1
		2.9	2.2			Sales/Total Assets	2.2	2.4
		1.9	1.6				1.4	1.5
		.5	.4				.5	.4
		(20) 1.1	(19) .9			% Depr., Dep., Amort./Sales	(46) .9	(40) .9
		2.4	1.6				1.5	1.6
							2.2	1.3
						% Officers', Directors' Owners' Comp/Sales	(12) 4.2	(16) 2.6
							10.6	6.2
6760M	39761M	324253M	1276526M	273152M		Net Sales ($)	2888461M	2418762M
1228M	10791M	104760M	515213M	129664M		Total Assets ($)	1567954M	1199469M

M = $ thousand MM = $ million

See Pages 9 through 22 for Explanation of Ratios and Data

Comparative Historical Data   Current Data Sorted by Sales

						Type of Statement		0-1MM	1-3MM	3-5MM	5-10MM	10-25MM	25MM & OVER
	9		7		8	Unqualified					1		7
	7		11		11	Reviewed			1		1	6	2
	8		9		7	Compiled		1	2		2	1	2
	13		13		6	Tax Returns			1	1	1	2	
	23		28		25	Other	1	2	3	3	4	11
	4/1/08-3/31/09		4/1/09-3/31/10		4/1/10-3/31/11				13 (4/1-9/30/10)			44 (10/1/10-3/31/11)	
	ALL		ALL		ALL								
	60		68		57	NUMBER OF STATEMENTS	3	6	5	8	13	22
	%		%		%	ASSETS	%	%	%	%	%	%
	10.3		10.0		7.8	Cash & Equivalents					9.1	8.9
	28.5		26.5		26.0	Trade Receivables (net)					18.7	30.8
	31.3		33.1		34.1	Inventory					37.6	30.5
	4.7		4.2		2.8	All Other Current					1.1	5.8
	74.8		73.7		70.7	Total Current					66.5	76.0
	15.0		14.0		14.9	Fixed Assets (net)					13.6	11.3
	4.1		4.0		5.6	Intangibles (net)					8.1	5.2
	6.1		8.3		8.8	All Other Non-Current					11.8	7.6
	100.0		100.0		100.0	Total					100.0	100.0
						LIABILITIES						
	13.9		9.5		10.1	Notes Payable-Short Term					9.9	8.1
	3.2		4.6		2.3	Cur. Mat.-L.T.D.					2.0	1.1
	32.8		28.7		28.9	Trade Payables					16.2	34.6
	.2		.1		.1	Income Taxes Payable					.1	.1
	14.1		12.5		8.5	All Other Current					4.1	11.1
	64.3		55.5		49.8	Total Current					32.2	55.1
	9.8		11.6		12.4	Long-Term Debt					18.1	4.3
	.0		.1		.1	Deferred Taxes					.3	.0
	5.7		4.6		4.5	All Other Non-Current					3.8	3.1
	20.2		28.3		33.2	Net Worth					45.6	37.5
	100.0		100.0		100.0	Total Liabilties & Net Worth					100.0	100.0
						INCOME DATA						
	100.0		100.0		100.0	Net Sales					100.0	100.0
	36.7		36.0		35.0	Gross Profit					35.7	31.3
	34.1		32.3		31.4	Operating Expenses					33.1	27.3
	2.6		3.7		3.6	Operating Profit					2.6	4.0
	.2		.5		1.2	All Other Expenses (net)					.6	.5
	2.4		3.2		2.4	Profit Before Taxes					1.9	3.5
						RATIOS						
	1.8		2.3		2.4						5.0	2.0
	1.2		1.3		1.5	Current					2.7	1.3
	1.0		1.0		1.1						1.5	1.1
	.9		1.1		1.2						2.8	1.0
(59)	.6		.6		.7	Quick					1.0	.8
	.4		.3		.4						.3	.4
18	19.9	17	21.7	20	18.2					11	32.5	21	17.6
37	9.9	34	10.6	35	10.5	Sales/Receivables				31	11.8	39	9.4
65	5.6	59	6.2	61	6.0					40	9.2	62	5.9
19	19.4	18	20.1	32	11.5					38	9.6	23	16.2
56	6.5	74	4.9	69	5.3	Cost of Sales/Inventory				89	4.1	65	5.6
127	2.9	152	2.4	122	3.0					181	2.0	91	4.0
19	19.4	28	13.0	21	17.6					16	23.0	30	12.0
67	5.5	53	6.8	45	8.1	Cost of Sales/Payables				29	12.6	73	5.0
103	3.5	88	4.1	90	4.0					53	6.9	101	3.6
	6.6		3.9		5.6						3.0	7.3
	23.8		13.0		13.4	Sales/Working Capital					6.4	13.9
	-162.8		NM		114.8						20.1	94.0
	11.2		19.6		25.4						9.0	56.1
(49)	4.2	(54)	3.7	(52)	3.5	EBIT/Interest				(12)	3.4	(20)	13.3
	.8		1.2		1.3						2.0	2.3
						Net Profit + Depr., Dep., Amort./Cur. Mat. L/T/D						
	.1		.1		.2						.1	.2
	.5		.5		.4	Fixed/Worth					.3	.4
	3.5		2.3		1.8						1.7	.8
	1.3		1.5		.9						.7	1.0
	3.3		3.1		2.4	Debt/Worth					1.5	2.7
	28.3		17.1		7.1						18.4	5.2
	48.8		44.9		43.4	% Profit Before Taxes/Tangible Net Worth					31.7	61.4
(47)	15.7	(56)	20.3	(48)	17.3					(11)	13.1	(21)	19.7
	1.3		2.7		2.4						1.7	5.0
	13.1		14.2		11.8	% Profit Before Taxes/Total Assets					14.0	18.8
	4.4		3.5		4.6						5.7	4.8
	-.8		.0		-.1						2.3	1.4
	95.0		102.0		83.3						54.0	81.8
	39.2		31.8		31.3	Sales/Net Fixed Assets					20.7	33.4
	15.9		14.4		11.4						7.6	16.1
	4.1		3.8		3.6						3.5	3.6
	2.5		2.4		2.6	Sales/Total Assets					2.4	2.6
	1.6		1.6		1.7						1.4	2.0
	.5		.6		.4						.5	.4
(44)	.9	(52)	1.1	(49)	1.0	% Depr., Dep., Amort./Sales				(12)	1.2	(20)	.7
	1.4		1.7		1.7						2.5	1.3
	1.8		1.8		2.3	% Officers', Directors' Owners' Comp/Sales						
(21)	2.4	(21)	2.6	(14)	3.9							
	3.6		4.4		7.4							
	2138924M		1771196M		1920452M	Net Sales ($)	1533M	12890M	21583M	60252M	191521M	1632673M
	1069132M		710370M		761656M	Total Assets ($)	3416M	8510M	6966M	21193M	110426M	611145M

M = $ thousand   MM = $ million
See Pages 9 through 22 for Explanation of Ratios and Data

Current Data Sorted by Assets | | | **Comparative Historical Data**

The 50-100MM and 100-250MM columns of the Assets/Liabilities/Income section are marked vertically "DATA NOT AVAILABLE".

Type of Statement	0-500M	500M-2MM	2-10MM	10-50MM	50-100MM	100-250MM	4/1/06-3/31/07 ALL	4/1/07-3/31/08 ALL
Unqualified			3	6			19	13
Reviewed		6	20	7			26	34
Compiled	4	6	13	2			41	31
Tax Returns	9	14	13				25	16
Other	5	11	10	9	1		33	40
	44 (4/1-9/30/10)			95 (10/1/10-3/31/11)				
NUMBER OF STATEMENTS	18	37	59	24	1		144	134
ASSETS	%	%	%	%	%	%	%	%
Cash & Equivalents	8.1	7.8	8.2	6.3			9.4	7.9
Trade Receivables (net)	14.5	25.2	24.8	32.4			25.1	25.1
Inventory	32.1	24.9	26.6	22.4			28.6	28.2
All Other Current	2.9	3.1	4.4	6.1			3.1	4.0
Total Current	57.5	61.1	64.0	67.2			66.1	65.1
Fixed Assets (net)	26.3	25.6	27.6	18.5			23.5	21.9
Intangibles (net)	4.2	3.3	2.2	4.4			3.5	4.7
All Other Non-Current	12.0	10.0	6.1	9.9			6.9	8.2
Total	100.0	100.0	100.0	100.0			100.0	100.0
LIABILITIES								
Notes Payable-Short Term	28.9	16.2	10.7	13.1			21.3	14.4
Cur. Mat.-L.T.D.	4.7	2.6	3.9	4.0			3.9	3.6
Trade Payables	24.8	20.7	19.8	19.3			18.3	17.0
Income Taxes Payable	.2	.1	.3	.5			.4	.6
All Other Current	16.8	8.7	6.6	7.5			9.4	7.4
Total Current	75.5	48.3	41.2	44.3			53.4	43.0
Long-Term Debt	30.5	20.6	18.6	7.3			15.1	12.3
Deferred Taxes	.0	.1	.9	.9			.5	.4
All Other Non-Current	26.3	10.6	12.9	4.1			7.9	7.6
Net Worth	-32.2	20.4	26.5	43.4			23.1	36.6
Total Liabilities & Net Worth	100.0	100.0	100.0	100.0			100.0	100.0
INCOME DATA								
Net Sales	100.0	100.0	100.0	100.0			100.0	100.0
Gross Profit	46.3	37.2	34.1	26.4			34.4	33.6
Operating Expenses	49.7	36.1	31.5	25.7			32.6	30.4
Operating Profit	-3.4	1.1	2.5	.7			1.8	3.2
All Other Expenses (net)	1.7	1.2	.4	.2			.7	1.0
Profit Before Taxes	-5.1	.0	2.1	.4			1.0	2.2
RATIOS								
	3.0	2.9	2.3	2.3			2.1	3.1
Current	1.2	1.5	1.5	1.6			1.4	1.6
	.5	1.1	.9	1.2			.9	1.1
	1.1	1.9	1.3	1.3			1.1	1.3
Quick	.6	.9	.8	.9			(143) .7	.8
	.1	.3	.4	.4			.3	.4
	0 UND	3 145.0	13 27.3	20 18.5			12 29.4	13 27.2
Sales/Receivables	6 62.4	20 18.6	30 12.0	39 9.3			29 12.8	27 13.5
	26 14.0	46 7.9	41 8.9	68 5.3			42 8.8	43 8.4
	0 UND	1 257.8	4 89.7	9 40.2			14 25.4	15 25.0
Cost of Sales/Inventory	48 7.6	49 7.5	49 7.4	33 11.0			44 8.2	47 7.8
	111 3.3	113 3.2	130 2.8	129 2.8			118 3.1	108 3.4
	0 UND	2 146.5	13 28.9	20 18.3			10 37.1	12 29.2
Cost of Sales/Payables	31 11.9	27 13.7	33 11.2	30 12.0			29 12.7	26 14.2
	64 5.7	57 6.5	55 6.6	35 10.6			53 6.9	46 8.0
	6.4	9.2	4.6	6.1			6.4	4.6
Sales/Working Capital	33.6	14.1	17.6	8.9			17.0	13.1
	-8.9	67.3	-45.5	37.6			-62.7	75.2
	1.8	3.6	20.7	7.6			7.9	7.5
EBIT/Interest	(17) .9	(36) 1.7	(55) 3.2	1.5			(135) 2.2	(124) 2.0
	-8.9	.2	1.1	-.9			.3	1.0
Net Profit + Depr., Dep.,				6.5			5.7	5.1
Amort./Cur. Mat. L/T/D				(11) 2.4			(30) 3.8	(33) 2.9
				.4			1.5	1.0
	.2	.3	.1	.2			.2	.2
Fixed/Worth	8.2	.6	.9	.4			.9	.6
	-.9	-11.5	8.6	.8			3.6	1.9
	2.0	.7	.7	.8			1.0	.8
Debt/Worth	-7.8	2.9	1.5	1.3			2.6	1.8
	-2.4	-31.9	46.4	2.5			13.6	6.9
% Profit Before Taxes/Tangible		24.1	40.5	19.7			41.1	32.1
Net Worth		(26) 4.1	(46) 12.5	(21) 3.9			(112) 15.0	(115) 11.1
		-2.6	3.2	-3.2			3.9	1.6
% Profit Before Taxes/Total	5.9	7.0	9.8	5.5			13.1	10.6
Assets	-4.8	1.5	4.0	.7			3.6	3.7
	-18.7	-2.4	.3	-3.0			-2.6	-.2
	77.1	46.2	61.8	79.4			47.1	48.8
Sales/Net Fixed Assets	30.9	19.4	14.7	14.5			19.8	22.5
	7.7	5.5	4.9	9.1			7.8	6.1
	7.7	4.1	4.0	3.6			4.2	3.9
Sales/Total Assets	3.7	2.9	2.6	2.6			3.0	2.7
	2.3	1.9	1.5	1.6			2.0	1.7
	.7	.9	.5	.6			.6	.5
% Depr., Dep., Amort./Sales	(15) 1.7	(30) 1.9	(56) 1.3	(22) 1.0			(134) 1.2	(123) 1.1
	3.6	3.1	2.9	2.0			2.1	2.2
	2.2	2.4					1.8	2.1
% Officers', Directors' Owners' Comp/Sales	(10) 4.4	(22) 4.2	(32) 2.5				(68) 2.9	(51) 3.5
	7.1	6.1	4.6				6.3	5.6
Net Sales ($)	24928M	172592M	757089M	1270456M	49490M		2553893M	2508432M
Total Assets ($)	5891M	47428M	250405M	485987M	63933M		1044025M	1091134M

M = $ thousand   MM = $ million
See Pages 9 through 22 for Explanation of Ratios and Data

Comparative Historical Data | | | | Current Data Sorted by Sales

4/1/08-3/31/09 ALL	4/1/09-3/31/10 ALL	4/1/10-3/31/11 ALL	Type of Statement	0-1MM	1-3MM	3-5MM	5-10MM	10-25MM	25MM & OVER
					44 (4/1-9/30/10)			95 (10/1/10-3/31/11)	
9	14	9	Unqualified			1		2	6
34	26	33	Reviewed		1	5	11	10	6
28	27	25	Compiled		6	2	5	10	2
23	29	36	Tax Returns	6	9	11	3	6	1
50	47	36	Other	2	9	4	6	6	9
144	143	139	**NUMBER OF STATEMENTS**	8	25	23	25	34	24
%	%	%	**ASSETS**	%	%	%	%	%	%
6.0	8.7	7.7	Cash & Equivalents		6.4	7.4	5.6	12.4	6.6
26.4	24.1	25.0	Trade Receivables (net)		14.3	18.2	20.1	31.4	42.8
27.5	29.2	26.1	Inventory		30.5	26.6	33.3	24.6	12.6
4.5	3.1	4.1	All Other Current		3.2	2.2	3.1	6.6	5.7
64.4	65.1	62.9	Total Current		54.3	54.5	62.0	75.0	67.7
24.8	24.5	25.2	Fixed Assets (net)		28.4	31.8	27.0	18.9	18.2
3.4	3.7	3.4	Intangibles (net)		3.5	1.7	4.3	1.1	6.2
7.5	6.7	8.5	All Other Non-Current		13.7	12.0	6.6	5.0	7.9
100.0	100.0	100.0	Total		100.0	100.0	100.0	100.0	100.0
			LIABILITIES						
15.7	12.6	15.0	Notes Payable-Short Term		25.3	7.6	12.9	13.6	11.7
3.7	3.7	3.6	Cur. Mat.-L.T.D.		2.9	6.5	5.0	2.4	2.4
16.4	16.2	20.6	Trade Payables		17.7	16.3	13.6	25.2	22.3
.3	.3	.3	Income Taxes Payable		.0	.1	.3	.3	.5
7.4	5.8	8.6	All Other Current		16.4	1.6	3.5	7.9	7.7
43.4	38.7	48.1	Total Current		62.3	32.1	35.3	49.2	44.5
14.8	18.1	18.7	Long-Term Debt		21.6	36.8	18.6	6.0	6.9
.2	.1	.6	Deferred Taxes		.0	.3	1.6	.9	.2
8.4	9.5	12.5	All Other Non-Current		27.3	4.1	11.5	3.3	23.3
33.3	33.6	20.2	Net Worth		-11.2	26.7	33.0	40.6	25.1
100.0	100.0	100.0	Total Liabilties & Net Worth		100.0	100.0	100.0	100.0	100.0
			INCOME DATA						
100.0	100.0	100.0	Net Sales		100.0	100.0	100.0	100.0	100.0
36.8	36.2	35.1	Gross Profit		44.6	38.2	34.9	30.0	23.3
35.1	34.8	34.0	Operating Expenses		45.9	36.3	31.6	28.0	23.0
1.8	1.5	1.0	Operating Profit		-1.3	1.8	3.4	2.0	.3
.9	1.4	.8	All Other Expenses (net)		1.5	1.4	1.2	-.2	-.7
.9	.1	.3	Profit Before Taxes		-2.9	.4	2.2	2.3	1.0
			RATIOS						
2.9	3.4	2.5	Current		2.1	3.8	2.6	2.3	2.2
1.5	1.9	1.5			1.1	1.9	2.0	1.5	1.6
1.0	1.1	1.0			.4	1.2	.8	1.0	1.2
1.4	1.5	1.4	Quick		.8	2.1	1.2	1.6	1.7
.8	.9	.8			.4	.9	.6	.9	1.0
.4	.4	.4			.1	.3	.3	.5	.8
17 21.6	12 30.4	9 42.6	Sales/Receivables		0 UND	3 143.7	12 29.4	13 27.9	25 14.3
29 12.8	29 12.4	26 13.9			16 22.5	19 19.5	26 14.1	27 13.5	40 9.2
44 8.3	40 9.0	46 7.9			49 7.4	38 9.5	47 7.7	37 9.7	69 5.3
13 29.0	12 31.4	6 59.0	Cost of Sales/Inventory		0 UND	11 33.4	16 23.5	0 UND	2 178.9
43 8.5	48 7.6	48 7.7			60 6.1	62 5.9	69 5.3	31 11.9	11 32.2
127 2.9	156 2.3	121 3.0			152 2.4	175 2.1	203 1.8	91 4.0	46 8.0
11 33.8	10 38.1	13 29.0	Cost of Sales/Payables		0 UND	7 55.4	9 38.5	14 26.7	21 17.7
24 15.3	23 15.6	31 11.8			40 9.1	30 12.0	30 12.3	30 12.0	30 12.0
41 8.9	45 8.1	56 6.5			60 6.0	80 4.6	61 6.0	49 7.5	35 10.6
5.0	5.0	6.1	Sales/Working Capital		7.7	3.8	3.2	6.5	8.4
15.8	10.2	17.1			36.8	13.2	9.4	22.2	17.6
146.9	32.8	999.8			-6.5	58.8	-31.0	NM	40.3
6.0	7.1	8.1	EBIT/Interest		2.3	2.8	9.9	37.2	13.0
(132) 1.7	(131) 1.8	(133) 1.8			.9	1.2	1.8	(30) 11.7	(23) 3.1
-.4	.2	.2			-7.6	.3	1.2	.7	-1.0
4.1	4.2	5.6	Net Profit + Depr., Dep., Amort./Cur. Mat. L/T/D						
(38) 1.9	(35) 1.7	(25) 2.2							
.7	.9	.6							
.2	.2	.2	Fixed/Worth		.4	.3	.1	.1	.2
.6	.6	.6			-19.0	1.3	.6	.4	.4
3.0	3.3	-19.0			-.7	-4.6	NM	1.1	1.2
.8	.7	.9	Debt/Worth		1.4	.5	.5	.7	.9
1.9	1.6	2.0			-42.6	2.6	1.2	1.3	1.6
9.2	7.5	-28.0			-2.5	-8.4	NM	6.0	2.7
25.9	27.4	31.6	% Profit Before Taxes/Tangible Net Worth		7.4	9.7	18.6	53.0	31.8
(117) 7.8	(116) 8.8	(101) 8.7			(11) .3	(17) 1.7	(19) 8.0	(30) 29.1	(20) 9.1
-1.6	-.9	.2			-20.5	-7.5	2.1	8.6	-.9
7.9	10.1	7.6	% Profit Before Taxes/Total Assets		5.3	4.0	7.1	25.1	10.2
2.0	2.6	1.7			-.5	.6	2.4	8.6	2.3
-3.5	-2.4	-1.8			-18.9	-1.4	.7	.0	-3.0
50.3	56.4	63.1	Sales/Net Fixed Assets		51.2	36.3	41.6	189.5	79.4
17.5	15.6	19.1			20.9	16.6	14.7	45.8	23.3
7.0	5.2	6.3			4.6	3.4	5.3	9.7	11.0
4.1	4.2	4.1	Sales/Total Assets		3.7	3.6	3.1	5.9	5.1
2.8	2.5	2.7			2.3	2.1	1.9	3.8	2.9
1.9	1.7	1.8			1.7	1.3	1.6	2.6	2.3
.6	.7	.7	% Depr., Dep., Amort./Sales		1.1	.9	.8	.2	.6
(127) 1.2	(126) 1.4	(124) 1.4			(23) 2.3	(20) 2.1	(21) 1.6	(30) .8	(23) .8
2.6	3.5	2.9			4.4	4.9	2.9	2.2	1.3
2.2	1.8	1.9	% Officers', Directors' Owners' Comp/Sales		4.5	1.9	1.9	1.3	
(55) 3.2	(59) 2.9	(70) 2.9			(13) 5.0	(17) 2.6	(11) 2.5	(19) 2.4	
6.9	6.4	4.8			6.8	4.4	4.8	3.8	
2974366M	2864066M	2274555M	Net Sales ($)	4853M	47686M	87576M	181933M	543275M	1409232M
1236129M	1374721M	853644M	Total Assets ($)	3147M	24210M	49192M	90488M	190952M	495655M

M = $ thousand   MM = $ million
See Pages 9 through 22 for Explanation of Ratios and Data

Current Data Sorted by Assets   Comparative Historical Data

Type of Statement

						Type of Statement	25	27
		6	8	6	1	Unqualified		
	1	25	9			Reviewed	42	36
1	3	12	1		1	Compiled	19	9
7	3	10	1		1	Tax Returns	14	10
2	3	10	17	1	3	Other	29	26
	19 (4/1-9/30/10)		**111 (10/1/10-3/31/11)**				**4/1/06-3/31/07 ALL**	**4/1/07-3/31/08 ALL**
0-500M	**500M-2MM**	**2-10MM**	**10-50MM**	**50-100MM**	**100-250MM**	**NUMBER OF STATEMENTS**	**129**	**108**
10	10	63	36	7	4			

0-500M	500M-2MM	2-10MM	10-50MM	50-100MM	100-250MM		ALL	ALL
%	%	%	%	%	%	**ASSETS**	%	%
33.8	11.0	12.3	8.9			Cash & Equivalents	8.7	8.2
11.1	13.7	32.0	30.0			Trade Receivables (net)	34.2	31.5
38.4	51.6	36.0	35.2			Inventory	35.8	36.9
.1	1.1	2.0	3.7			All Other Current	2.5	2.9
83.4	77.3	82.3	77.9			Total Current	81.3	79.4
12.5	15.4	9.4	14.0			Fixed Assets (net)	10.5	11.1
3.7	.1	1.3	3.3			Intangibles (net)	1.3	1.6
.4	7.1	7.0	4.8			All Other Non-Current	6.9	7.9
100.0	100.0	100.0	100.0			Total	100.0	100.0
						LIABILITIES		
2.8	7.1	15.9	19.5			Notes Payable-Short Term	25.0	23.5
1.7	4.2	1.1	1.2			Cur. Mat.-L.T.D.	2.0	1.8
25.8	22.3	18.5	18.9			Trade Payables	19.2	17.5
.0	.0	.2	.5			Income Taxes Payable	.1	.2
4.4	8.1	8.6	6.4			All Other Current	6.9	6.6
34.6	41.7	44.3	46.5			Total Current	53.1	49.5
13.4	17.6	7.2	7.0			Long-Term Debt	9.1	9.6
.0	.0	.3	.1			Deferred Taxes	.2	.2
9.3	3.8	3.8	4.5			All Other Non-Current	4.1	3.5
42.7	36.8	44.5	41.8			Net Worth	33.5	37.2
100.0	100.0	100.0	100.0			Total Liabilties & Net Worth	100.0	100.0
						INCOME DATA		
100.0	100.0	100.0	100.0			Net Sales	100.0	100.0
13.2	13.7	8.6	11.5			Gross Profit	9.6	9.6
10.6	11.5	7.8	10.1			Operating Expenses	8.2	7.9
2.6	2.2	.9	1.5			Operating Profit	1.4	1.7
.4	.0	.0	.3			All Other Expenses (net)	.1	-.1
2.1	2.2	.8	1.2			Profit Before Taxes	1.3	1.8
						RATIOS		
5.9	4.7	2.5	2.7			Current	2.5	2.5
3.2	1.8	1.9	1.4				1.4	1.5
1.2	1.2	1.4	1.2				1.1	1.1
2.9		1.6	1.4			Quick	1.4	1.3
1.9		.9	.8				.8	.7
.5		.7	.5				.5	.5
0 UND	0 997.5	7 51.3	11 34.2			Sales/Receivables	11 34.7	9 42.2
0 UND	2 216.0	12 29.9	16 23.3				16 23.5	15 24.6
10 38.2	11 32.8	18 20.8	21 17.5				22 16.6	21 17.4
5 66.9	19 18.8	9 39.0	11 32.1			Cost of Sales/Inventory	11 33.9	11 33.1
13 27.9	30 12.3	17 22.1	16 22.1				17 21.3	18 20.3
21 17.3	34 10.7	25 14.4	31 11.7				33 11.2	27 13.3
0 UND	2 211.6	2 217.7	4 91.0			Cost of Sales/Payables	4 98.4	4 102.9
8 46.8	10 36.7	6 60.7	9 41.8				7 51.0	8 45.1
16 22.1	35 10.4	15 25.0	14 26.6				16 23.3	15 23.7
11.2	20.9	14.9	14.3			Sales/Working Capital	14.2	14.4
36.0	28.3	24.6	33.1				33.2	32.3
NM	59.1	40.7	58.1				78.7	92.9
		9.6	16.3			EBIT/Interest	9.7	6.5
		(50) 2.8	(32) 5.8				(120) 2.2	(102) 2.5
		1.9	2.0				1.1	1.5
		7.2				Net Profit + Depr., Dep., Amort./Cur. Mat. L/T/D	5.8	5.8
		(14) 3.4					(38) 2.7	(35) 2.9
		2.0					1.0	1.4
.0	.1	.0	.1			Fixed/Worth	.1	.1
.0	.2	.2	.2				.3	.2
1.7	.6	.4	.6				.8	.8
.3	.4	.7	.5			Debt/Worth	.8	.8
1.0	3.3	1.4	1.9				2.2	2.4
8.6	5.2	3.4	6.0				6.9	4.9
	151.9	26.4	31.4			% Profit Before Taxes/Tangible Net Worth	30.4	26.2
	31.5	12.5	(34) 25.3				(119) 12.0	(102) 12.4
	9.3	5.3	11.9				4.1	4.3
69.8	24.8	9.9	15.3			% Profit Before Taxes/Total Assets	9.8	7.7
25.3	9.4	4.4	5.7				4.3	3.9
-2.7	4.6	2.5	2.9				.4	1.6
UND	378.8	402.3	266.2			Sales/Net Fixed Assets	332.2	229.6
UND	153.0	116.8	83.7				105.4	120.7
30.1	43.8	57.5	23.2				47.7	47.3
16.4	12.1	11.5	12.1			Sales/Total Assets	10.2	9.5
9.6	7.2	8.6	7.4				7.7	7.9
8.0	4.5	6.1	2.8				4.9	5.4
		.1	.1			% Depr., Dep., Amort./Sales	.1	.1
	(52)	.2	(34) .3				(106) .2	(100) .2
		.3	.6				.4	.4
		.3				% Officers', Directors' Owners' Comp/Sales	.3	.3
	(36)	.7					(48) .7	(37) .6
		1.1					1.9	1.8
33290M	103184M	3019598M	5950639M	4907721M	3944240M	Net Sales ($)	13221136M	19840027M
2615M	12760M	320414M	823489M	514533M	523506M	Total Assets ($)	2046171M	2550502M

© RMA 2011

M = $ thousand   MM = $ million
See Pages 9 through 22 for Explanation of Ratios and Data

Comparative Historical Data   Current Data Sorted by Sales

Hist 1	Hist 2	Hist 3	Type of Statement	0-1MM	1-3MM	3-5MM	5-10MM	10-25MM	25MM & OVER
25	27	21	Unqualified					1	20
35	45	35	Reviewed			1	1	7	26
14	22	17	Compiled			1	1	5	10
17	20	21	Tax Returns		6		4	1	10
29	37	36	Other		2		3	6	25
4/1/08-3/31/09 ALL	4/1/09-3/31/10 ALL	4/1/10-3/31/11 ALL			19 (4/1-9/30/10)			111 (10/1/10-3/31/11)	
120	151	130	**NUMBER OF STATEMENTS**		8	2	9	20	91
%	%	%	**ASSETS**	%	%	%	%	%	%
8.4	9.0	12.2	Cash & Equivalents					10.3	10.3
31.1	32.0	29.0	Trade Receivables (net)					17.1	35.1
37.3	37.7	36.8	Inventory					46.5	34.1
2.8	2.7	2.3	All Other Current					1.3	2.6
79.5	81.5	80.3	Total Current					75.2	82.2
12.8	10.3	11.7	Fixed Assets (net)					15.6	10.1
1.4	1.6	2.1	Intangibles (net)					2.1	2.0
6.3	6.6	5.9	All Other Non-Current					7.1	5.7
100.0	100.0	100.0	Total					100.0	100.0
			LIABILITIES						
20.2	18.4	15.5	Notes Payable-Short Term					17.5	17.7
2.5	2.0	1.4	Cur. Mat.-L.T.D.					1.6	1.1
20.2	19.2	19.9	Trade Payables					18.5	19.8
.1	.4	.3	Income Taxes Payable					.0	.5
7.3	8.4	7.4	All Other Current					3.9	7.9
50.5	48.4	44.5	Total Current					41.5	47.0
11.1	7.2	8.8	Long-Term Debt					11.7	7.1
.1	.1	.2	Deferred Taxes					.0	.3
3.5	4.6	4.3	All Other Non-Current					9.3	2.5
34.9	39.7	42.2	Net Worth					37.5	43.1
100.0	100.0	100.0	Total Liabilities & Net Worth					100.0	100.0
			INCOME DATA						
100.0	100.0	100.0	Net Sales					100.0	100.0
11.1	10.3	10.1	Gross Profit					12.6	8.3
10.2	8.2	8.8	Operating Expenses					12.2	7.2
.9	2.1	1.3	Operating Profit					.5	1.1
.4	.0	.1	All Other Expenses (net)					.9	-.1
.5	2.1	1.2	Profit Before Taxes					-.5	1.2
			RATIOS						
2.7	2.6	2.7	Current					3.9	2.4
1.6	1.7	1.8						1.7	1.8
1.2	1.2	1.2						1.1	1.2
1.4	1.5	1.6	Quick					1.5	1.4
.8	.8	(129) .9						.5	.9
.5	.5	.6						.3	.7
(9) 40.8	(8) 44.3	(7) 51.6	Sales/Receivables					(7) 55.7	(9) 40.3
(15) 25.0	(14) 25.7	(12) 29.3						(16) 23.0	(13) 27.8
(22) 16.5	(19) 19.0	(18) 20.7						(23) 15.9	(18) 20.4
(11) 34.3	(11) 32.6	(10) 35.3	Cost of Sales/Inventory					(26) 14.1	(9) 39.0
(16) 23.5	(17) 21.3	(16) 22.2						(35) 10.3	(14) 25.8
(30) 12.0	(29) 12.7	(29) 12.8						(46) 7.9	(21) 17.6
(4) 84.4	(3) 126.1	(3) 113.7	Cost of Sales/Payables					(6) 63.7	(3) 130.6
(9) 42.3	(8) 47.2	(8) 47.5						(11) 33.5	(6) 56.4
(16) 22.7	(14) 26.2	(14) 25.8						(25) 14.7	(12) 29.6
14.6	14.6	16.1	Sales/Working Capital					6.0	18.3
32.2	28.5	28.2						20.9	28.5
99.1	64.2	53.2						114.8	53.9
7.0	17.9	12.1	EBIT/Interest					10.2	12.5
(110) 2.6	(136) 5.9	(106) 4.7						(18) 2.5	(76) 5.3
1.4	2.6	2.0						.3	2.2
6.0	15.8	15.8	Net Profit + Depr., Dep., Amort./Cur. Mat. L/T/D						16.8
(28) 2.0	(35) 6.7	(29) 8.1							(26) 8.1
.3	2.9	2.6							2.2
.1	.1	.1	Fixed/Worth					.1	.1
.3	.2	.2						.3	.2
.8	.6	.5						.7	.5
.8	.7	.6	Debt/Worth					.7	.7
2.2	1.8	1.8						3.3	1.8
4.8	4.3	3.9						6.0	3.5
25.8	44.5	35.4	% Profit Before Taxes/Tangible Net Worth					76.3	29.7
(111) 14.2	(145) 20.2	(127) 18.5						(19) 6.2	(90) 18.3
3.8	9.3	7.5						-.4	9.6
9.1	14.3	13.9	% Profit Before Taxes/Total Assets					8.2	12.0
3.4	7.2	6.4						3.3	6.2
1.1	3.3	2.5						-.8	3.1
243.1	386.3	370.3	Sales/Net Fixed Assets					180.7	388.1
95.5	130.4	113.0						63.3	124.1
41.5	55.2	46.3						19.0	55.0
10.3	11.5	11.6	Sales/Total Assets					7.5	12.2
8.3	8.4	8.6						5.0	9.9
5.4	5.7	5.6						2.8	6.5
.1	.1	.1	% Depr., Dep., Amort./Sales					.1	.1
(105) .2	(125) .2	(108) .2						(18) .3	(79) .2
.4	.4	.4						.6	.4
.4	.3	.3	% Officers', Directors' Owners' Comp/Sales						.2
(51) .8	(68) .6	(55) .8							(37) .6
1.4	1.3	1.3							.9
14055654M	19811176M	17958672M	Net Sales ($)		15887M	7590M	71722M	348191M	17515282M
1868636M	2973422M	2197317M	Total Assets ($)		2562M	2468M	12702M	148751M	2030834M

(For the Current Data size columns 0-1MM, 1-3MM, 3-5MM, and 5-10MM the balance-sheet and most ratio data are marked "DATA NOT AVAILABLE".)

© RMA 2011   M = $ thousand   MM = $ million
See Pages 9 through 22 for Explanation of Ratios and Data

Current Data Sorted by Assets | Comparative Historical Data

© RMA 2011

M = $ thousand   MM = $ million
See Pages 9 through 22 for Explanation of Ratios and Data

	0-500M		500M-2MM		2-10MM		10-50MM	50-100MM	100-250MM	Type of Statement		4/1/06-3/31/07		4/1/07-3/31/08
			1				4			Unqualified			11		9
			1		6		2			Reviewed			17		9
	1		3		2		1			Compiled			8		5
	3		5		1					Tax Returns			14		14
	1		6		8		4		1	Other			13		17
			5 (4/1-9/30/10)				45 (10/1/10-3/31/11)						ALL		ALL
	5		16		17		11		1	NUMBER OF STATEMENTS			63		54
	%		%		%		%	%	%	ASSETS			%		%
			5.4		7.6		2.8			Cash & Equivalents			6.4		5.8
			34.3		36.4		26.5			Trade Receivables (net)			31.8		30.9
			38.4		32.5		39.8			Inventory			36.8		38.4
			4.5		1.7		4.6			All Other Current			2.5		4.1
			82.6		78.1		73.7			Total Current			77.5		79.2
			8.0		11.6		12.9			Fixed Assets (net)			13.6		10.9
			8.6		2.1		6.7			Intangibles (net)			3.6		3.1
			.9		8.2		6.7			All Other Non-Current			5.3		6.8
			100.0		100.0		100.0			Total			100.0		100.0
										LIABILITIES					
			18.0		13.2		13.7			Notes Payable-Short Term			13.4		14.3
			2.7		1.2		3.0			Cur. Mat.-L.T.D.			1.9		2.3
			43.0		20.5		22.5			Trade Payables			25.5		28.1
			.1		.6		.1			Income Taxes Payable			.3		.2
			3.3		5.4		6.8			All Other Current			7.8		9.9
			67.0		41.0		46.1			Total Current			48.9		54.9
			10.5		9.8		20.2			Long-Term Debt			10.5		11.6
			.0		.1		.5			Deferred Taxes			.2		.3
			6.1		7.2		16.3			All Other Non-Current			3.5		5.6
			16.4		41.9		17.0			Net Worth			36.9		27.6
			100.0		100.0		100.0			Total Liabilties & Net Worth			100.0		100.0
										INCOME DATA					
			100.0		100.0		100.0			Net Sales			100.0		100.0
			30.5		32.8		30.2			Gross Profit			30.6		30.2
			29.5		28.4		28.3			Operating Expenses			26.8		27.2
			1.0		4.4		1.9			Operating Profit			3.7		3.1
			-.5		.6		1.5			All Other Expenses (net)			-.2		.3
			1.5		3.7		.4			Profit Before Taxes			3.9		2.8
										RATIOS					
			1.8		3.0		2.6						2.5		2.0
			1.3		2.1		1.5			Current			1.6		1.4
			.9		1.5		1.3						1.2		1.1
			1.1		2.0		.8						1.3		.9
			.7		1.1		.7			Quick			.8		.6
			.4		.6		.5						.5		.4
	28	13.2	31	11.7	39	9.4					31	11.7	28	13.0
	41	8.9	47	7.8	43	8.4			Sales/Receivables		39	9.3	36	10.0
	55	6.6	70	5.2	57	6.4					49	7.5	49	7.4
	34	10.9	35	10.3	74	5.0					44	8.2	51	7.1
	85	4.3	70	5.2	79	4.6			Cost of Sales/Inventory		73	5.0	66	5.5
	104	3.5	85	4.3	188	1.9					101	3.6	111	3.3
	31	11.8	22	16.9	28	12.9					25	14.9	26	14.1
	72	5.0	40	9.1	55	6.7			Cost of Sales/Payables		44	8.4	39	9.5
	105	3.5	57	6.4	83	4.4					64	5.7	76	4.8
		7.3		4.8		3.6						6.4		6.9
		17.9		5.9		10.7			Sales/Working Capital			9.9		12.3
		-41.4		19.6		18.0						17.5		29.9
		6.8		23.1		4.7						10.3		9.6
	(15)	1.9	(14)	6.2		3.1			EBIT/Interest	(58)	5.7	(52)	3.3
		1.0		.6		1.3						1.9		1.5
													15.2		13.6
									Net Profit + Depr., Dep., Amort./Cur. Mat. L/T/D	(17)	5.9	(15)	3.9
													2.0		1.7
		.2		.1		.2						.1		.1
		.8		.2		-15.7			Fixed/Worth			.3		.3
		-.5		.9		-.4						.9		1.8
		2.2		.5		1.5						.7		1.2
		7.1		1.2		-112.4			Debt/Worth			1.8		3.0
		-9.3		4.3		-7.9						6.3		11.5
		60.1		35.3								38.7		38.3
	(10)	14.0	(16)	20.5					% Profit Before Taxes/Tangible Net Worth	(55)	22.8	(44)	23.1
		4.1		-.6								11.8		11.0
		7.3		16.7		7.5						14.5		12.2
		2.9		9.5		2.1			% Profit Before Taxes/Total Assets			8.8		5.5
		.2		.1		1.4						3.6		1.4
		115.3		83.3		49.4						88.8		117.9
		51.3		23.4		27.4			Sales/Net Fixed Assets			36.6		41.8
		21.4		12.6		11.8						16.1		17.9
		3.9		3.5		2.6						3.6		3.4
		2.7		2.9		2.2			Sales/Total Assets			2.9		2.9
		2.2		2.0		1.6						2.2		2.3
		.3		.5								.4		.4
	(12)	.7	(12)	.7					% Depr., Dep., Amort./Sales	(51)	.7	(48)	.6
		1.5		1.7								1.3		1.0
		1.8		1.2								1.8		1.7
	(11)	2.7	(10)	3.0					% Officers', Directors' Owners' Comp/Sales	(29)	3.0	(25)	3.4
		4.4		5.8								3.9		5.7
	7655M		58494M		175693M		610984M		176337M	Net Sales ($)			1832196M		2141153M
	1675M		18518M		64617M		295760M		174179M	Total Assets ($)			666079M		847571M

Comparative Historical Data | Current Data Sorted by Sales

			Type of Statement	0-1MM	1-3MM	3-5MM	5-10MM	10-25MM	25MM & OVER
7	5	5	Unqualified				1		4
10	11	9	Reviewed				4	3	2
9	13	7	Compiled		2	1	1	2	1
12	6	9	Tax Returns	1	3	2	3		
19	22	20	Other	1	4	3	2	7	3
4/1/08-3/31/09 ALL	4/1/09-3/31/10 ALL	4/1/10-3/31/11 ALL		5 (4/1-9/30/10)			45 (10/1/10-3/31/11)		
57	57	50	**NUMBER OF STATEMENTS**	2	9	7	10	12	10
%	%	%	**ASSETS**	%	%	%	%	%	%
4.5	6.1	7.3	Cash & Equivalents				8.7	8.2	1.8
30.6	31.4	31.3	Trade Receivables (net)				40.7	35.6	27.1
40.4	39.5	36.8	Inventory				35.1	30.0	38.0
3.6	3.9	3.6	All Other Current				2.2	3.0	3.5
79.1	80.9	79.0	Total Current				86.7	76.8	70.4
11.0	10.0	11.0	Fixed Assets (net)				9.9	8.3	16.1
4.2	4.5	5.3	Intangibles (net)				2.0	2.5	7.7
5.6	4.6	4.7	All Other Non-Current				1.4	12.4	5.8
100.0	100.0	100.0	Total				100.0	100.0	100.0
			LIABILITIES						
16.8	15.5	14.9	Notes Payable-Short Term				15.4	9.7	15.1
2.8	2.2	2.1	Cur. Mat.-L.T.D.				2.9	1.6	2.6
27.0	28.6	28.7	Trade Payables				36.0	20.0	21.2
.1	.1	.3	Income Taxes Payable				.1	.2	.3
7.0	4.4	5.6	All Other Current				3.0	7.5	6.0
53.7	50.8	51.6	Total Current				57.3	39.0	45.2
11.6	14.8	13.0	Long-Term Debt				10.6	14.3	15.5
.2	.3	.3	Deferred Taxes				.0	.2	1.3
7.0	5.3	8.2	All Other Non-Current				13.2	5.0	15.0
27.5	28.8	26.8	Net Worth				18.9	41.5	23.0
100.0	100.0	100.0	Total Liabilities & Net Worth				100.0	100.0	100.0
			INCOME DATA						
100.0	100.0	100.0	Net Sales				100.0	100.0	100.0
31.4	31.8	32.2	Gross Profit				27.3	35.3	28.4
29.3	29.7	28.9	Operating Expenses				25.2	32.0	24.4
2.1	2.1	3.4	Operating Profit				2.2	3.3	4.0
.7	.0	.5	All Other Expenses (net)				.6	.8	1.2
1.4	2.1	2.9	Profit Before Taxes				1.6	2.5	2.8
			RATIOS						
2.2	2.5	2.6					2.3	3.4	3.1
1.4	1.6	1.7	Current				1.8	2.5	1.4
1.2	1.2	1.2					1.0	1.3	1.2
.9	1.4	1.3					1.3	2.1	1.1
.6	.7	.7	Quick				.8	1.2	.6
.5	.5	.5					.6	.7	.5
32 11.4	32 11.6	33 10.9					24 15.4	35 10.3	37 9.7
41 8.9	39 9.5	43 8.5	Sales/Receivables				40 9.1	42 8.7	50 7.3
51 7.1	52 7.1	59 6.2					65 5.6	60 6.1	59 6.2
54 6.8	60 6.1	48 7.6					25 14.8	35 10.5	70 5.2
85 4.3	80 4.6	80 4.5	Cost of Sales/Inventory				61 6.0	67 5.5	78 4.7
114 3.2	127 2.9	112 3.2					79 4.6	90 4.0	161 2.3
27 13.5	28 13.0	28 13.2					33 11.0	16 23.1	24 15.0
44 8.2	57 6.4	52 7.1	Cost of Sales/Payables				44 8.3	35 10.4	32 11.4
76 4.8	78 4.7	83 4.4					75 4.9	76 4.8	65 5.6
6.6	5.8	5.1					5.4	5.2	3.5
11.2	8.5	10.6	Sales/Working Capital				11.2	5.7	11.5
24.8	19.3	33.3					-346.4	22.6	NM
6.6	10.9	10.3					13.9		5.6
(53) 1.6	(49) 2.6	(46) 3.1	EBIT/Interest				2.5		3.5
-.3	.6	1.2					1.3		2.1
7.1		25.6							
(15) 2.3		(10) 1.9	Net Profit + Depr., Dep., Amort./Cur. Mat. L/T/D						
1.3		.9							
.2	.1	.2					.1	.1	.2
.4	.3	.5	Fixed/Worth				.3	.2	NM
1.3	1.2	-3.7					-.2	.7	-.8
1.5	1.4	1.0					1.0	.4	1.2
3.4	3.4	3.7	Debt/Worth				1.9	2.2	NM
13.6	10.2	-46.0					-6.2	4.4	-12.6
44.0	49.8	34.6						39.3	
(47) 14.0	(49) 14.9	(36) 12.9	% Profit Before Taxes/Tangible Net Worth					(11) 21.3	
.7	-.7	3.7						2.2	
11.4	10.2	10.4					10.4	23.6	8.1
2.6	4.0	5.1	% Profit Before Taxes/Total Assets				5.6	9.2	4.5
-3.3	-1.6	.5					.4	-.1	1.8
65.2	78.8	82.2					144.7	125.2	51.0
31.5	29.9	29.4	Sales/Net Fixed Assets				36.4	37.5	23.0
19.3	16.1	17.0					22.0	18.2	7.5
3.5	3.6	3.2					4.5	4.1	2.6
2.5	2.3	2.5	Sales/Total Assets				3.5	3.1	2.3
2.0	1.9	1.9					2.6	1.8	1.6
.5	.5	.4					.4		
(52) 1.0	(44) .9	(37) .7	% Depr., Dep., Amort./Sales				.5		
1.4	1.7	1.6					.9		
1.7	2.4	1.2							
(25) 3.0	(23) 3.3	(25) 2.7	% Officers', Directors' Owners' Comp/Sales						
3.7	5.2	4.5							
1486125M	1414806M	1029163M	Net Sales ($)	1336M	14563M	27560M	66931M	170009M	748764M
609115M	713208M	554749M	Total Assets ($)	1177M	6540M	10275M	22111M	69974M	444672M

M = $ thousand   MM = $ million
See Pages 9 through 22 for Explanation of Ratios and Data

Current Data Sorted by Assets | Comparative Historical Data

	0-500M	500M-2MM	2-10MM	10-50MM	50-100MM	100-250MM	Type of Statement	ALL 4/1/06-3/31/07	ALL 4/1/07-3/31/08
		1	12	28	5	7	Unqualified	81	80
	1	8	88	38	1		Reviewed	117	116
	7	27	64	7			Compiled	93	107
	38	82	70	4			Tax Returns	138	138
	22	64	106	45	13	9	Other	177	224
		125 (4/1-9/30/10)		622 (10/1/10-3/31/11)					
	68	182	340	122	19	16	NUMBER OF STATEMENTS	606	665
	%	%	%	%	%	%	**ASSETS**	%	%
	20.4	11.6	8.2	7.5	20.0	13.7	Cash & Equivalents	9.1	9.7
	22.0	27.1	33.5	27.9	18.9	13.1	Trade Receivables (net)	32.9	30.9
	31.2	35.6	37.9	35.2	26.6	25.9	Inventory	32.7	33.8
	3.0	2.9	2.2	3.7	2.0	5.2	All Other Current	2.7	2.8
	76.5	77.3	81.8	74.4	67.5	57.9	Total Current	77.3	77.1
	12.6	12.9	9.2	13.9	17.3	10.3	Fixed Assets (net)	13.4	13.1
	4.9	3.4	3.4	6.9	13.2	29.2	Intangibles (net)	3.7	4.0
	6.0	6.3	5.5	4.9	1.9	2.6	All Other Non-Current	5.7	5.8
	100.0	100.0	100.0	100.0	100.0	100.0	Total	100.0	100.0
							LIABILITIES		
	21.1	15.7	15.7	15.6	6.3	9.2	Notes Payable-Short Term	17.4	16.5
	5.4	2.3	1.9	2.2	1.3	2.0	Cur. Mat.-L.T.D.	2.8	2.5
	20.7	24.2	25.0	18.2	13.7	9.1	Trade Payables	21.2	21.4
	.1	.1	.1	.1	.0	.3	Income Taxes Payable	.2	.3
	16.0	7.8	6.8	8.7	12.9	8.4	All Other Current	10.3	9.1
	63.2	50.1	49.4	44.8	34.2	29.1	Total Current	52.0	49.9
	19.5	13.9	7.7	10.2	6.3	16.9	Long-Term Debt	11.1	10.7
	.0	.0	.2	.5	.7	1.2	Deferred Taxes	.1	.1
	7.5	11.4	3.9	6.4	5.8	6.6	All Other Non-Current	6.3	6.0
	9.8	24.7	38.8	38.1	53.0	46.1	Net Worth	30.5	33.3
	100.0	100.0	100.0	100.0	100.0	100.0	Total Liabilities & Net Worth	100.0	100.0
							INCOME DATA		
	100.0	100.0	100.0	100.0	100.0	100.0	Net Sales	100.0	100.0
	42.7	34.0	29.5	33.4	29.3	39.4	Gross Profit	32.4	32.5
	38.6	30.7	25.5	27.6	21.1	28.5	Operating Expenses	27.9	28.7
	4.1	3.3	4.0	5.7	8.2	10.9	Operating Profit	4.5	3.9
	.4	.6	.5	.8	.1	2.1	All Other Expenses (net)	1.1	.9
	3.7	2.8	3.5	4.9	8.1	8.8	Profit Before Taxes	3.3	2.9
							RATIOS		
	4.1	3.2	2.6	2.4	3.0	3.7	Current	2.5	2.7
	1.6	1.5	1.6	1.5	1.9	1.7		1.5	1.5
	.8	1.0	1.3	1.3	1.3	1.3		1.2	1.2
	2.8	1.6	1.4	1.2	2.5	2.5	Quick	1.4	1.4
	.7	.8	.9	.8	1.0	1.0		(605) .8	.8
	.3	.4	.5	.5	.5	.4		.5	.5
	0 UND	13 27.9	27 13.8	29 12.5	19 18.7	0 814.5	Sales/Receivables	24 15.1	22 16.5
	16 23.1	28 12.9	38 9.7	43 8.6	34 10.7	17 21.3		38 9.7	37 9.9
	43 8.5	43 8.5	53 6.9	57 6.4	54 6.7	60 6.1		54 6.8	53 6.9
	9 41.0	23 15.6	31 11.9	44 8.2	22 16.7	42 8.6	Cost of Sales/Inventory	26 13.9	27 13.3
	43 8.5	49 7.4	69 5.3	76 4.8	84 4.3	72 5.1		56 6.5	58 6.3
	76 4.8	111 3.3	116 3.2	140 2.6	131 2.8	158 2.3		107 3.4	115 3.2
	0 UND	12 30.3	19 19.6	22 16.3	15 23.7	19 18.8	Cost of Sales/Payables	15 23.7	15 24.6
	12 31.0	28 13.2	35 10.5	38 9.7	36 10.0	22 16.4		31 11.7	30 12.0
	43 8.4	56 6.5	60 6.0	52 7.0	43 8.6	58 6.3		53 6.9	53 6.8
	6.4	5.4	4.9	4.6	3.1	4.2	Sales/Working Capital	5.5	5.4
	17.8	15.1	9.7	9.6	8.6	9.3		11.6	11.6
	-55.6	183.3	22.4	18.6	13.2	18.7		32.5	34.9
	16.6	12.6	15.5	18.9	126.9	103.3	EBIT/Interest	10.7	8.3
	(48) 4.7	(154) 4.4	(298) 5.9	(109) 5.5	(17) 18.8	(15) 5.0		(539) 3.4	(577) 3.0
	.4	1.7	2.2	2.2	6.2	1.9		1.3	1.3
		5.9	6.9	15.4			Net Profit + Depr., Dep., Amort./Cur. Mat. L/T/D	11.7	8.5
		(11) 1.8	(49) 3.0	(40) 6.2				(94) 3.0	(103) 3.4
		.7	1.2	1.9				1.0	.9
	.0	.0	.0	.1	.1	.1	Fixed/Worth	.1	.1
	.2	.2	.1	.3	.3	.9		.3	.2
	-1.6	2.0	.6	1.2	.8	-.1		1.1	.9
	.5	1.0	.8	1.0	.4	.6	Debt/Worth	.9	.9
	4.1	2.9	1.9	1.9	1.4	6.9		2.3	2.3
	-6.5	-14.6	4.5	4.1	3.9	-3.9		7.1	6.7
	104.9	53.3	48.0	46.6	64.9		% Profit Before Taxes/Tangible Net Worth	54.7	46.3
	(42) 53.7	(144) 25.3	(315) 19.1	(107) 20.8	(18) 33.1			(517) 23.0	(575) 18.0
	10.6	7.5	7.0	8.7				7.2	4.4
	32.2	16.4	15.5	15.4	17.0	19.2	% Profit Before Taxes/Total Assets	16.1	14.6
	10.8	5.4	6.2	7.3	12.8	8.6		7.1	5.5
	.2	1.3	2.1	2.5	7.2	4.0		1.6	.9
	928.8	259.3	335.2	89.7	71.2	350.1	Sales/Net Fixed Assets	151.7	142.9
	72.4	71.4	77.2	39.4	23.5	50.6		48.1	51.1
	21.9	18.7	25.0	11.3	10.1	11.9		16.9	16.5
	6.2	4.6	4.0	3.3	2.5	2.8	Sales/Total Assets	4.0	4.0
	4.0	3.2	2.9	2.2	1.8	1.6		2.8	2.8
	2.6	2.2	1.9	1.6	1.2	.9		2.0	1.9
	.4	.2	.2	.3	.5	.2	% Depr., Dep., Amort./Sales	.3	.3
	(31) 1.4	(123) .5	(247) .5	(110) .8	(16) 1.0	(10) 1.3		(477) .7	(516) .6
	2.3	1.3	1.1	1.7	2.4	2.6		1.4	1.4
	2.4	2.3	1.5	.8			% Officers', Directors' Owners' Comp/Sales	1.6	1.6
	(33) 5.2	(113) 3.6	(171) 2.7	(38) 1.4				(285) 3.2	(313) 3.0
	9.3	6.1	4.4	4.1				5.7	5.8
	93189M	831099M	5078597M	6386864M	3167742M	6375295M	Net Sales ($)	19252812M	19693554M
	18779M	204705M	1562365M	2586603M	1356432M	2621161M	Total Assets ($)	7017098M	7432726M

M = $ thousand   MM = $ million
See Pages 9 through 22 for Explanation of Ratios and Data

Comparative Historical Data   ## Current Data Sorted by Sales

55	55	53	Type of Statement — Unqualified		1	1	3	7	41
138	156	136	Reviewed	1	1	13	21	60	40
103	102	105	Compiled	3	18	8	28	35	13
162	199	194	Tax Returns	25	52	33	45	25	14
233	269	259	Other	11	35	33	47	64	69
4/1/08-3/31/09 ALL	4/1/09-3/31/10 ALL	4/1/10-3/31/11 ALL		125 (4/1-9/30/10)			622 (10/1/10-3/31/11)		
				0-1MM	1-3MM	3-5MM	5-10MM	10-25MM	25MM & OVER
691	781	747	**NUMBER OF STATEMENTS**	40	107	88	144	191	177
%	%	%	**ASSETS**	%	%	%	%	%	%
9.1	10.2	10.5	Cash & Equivalents	19.3	13.5	11.6	7.9	8.8	10.0
29.8	30.8	29.2	Trade Receivables (net)	18.1	22.1	25.7	31.8	34.8	29.5
36.3	32.1	35.8	Inventory	28.1	36.4	36.9	39.0	36.4	33.2
3.2	3.2	2.7	All Other Current	4.2	2.5	1.4	2.2	2.3	4.1
78.3	76.2	78.2	Total Current	69.8	74.5	75.7	80.9	82.3	76.9
12.1	12.6	11.4	Fixed Assets (net)	13.9	15.7	12.4	9.3	9.6	11.5
4.2	4.8	4.9	Intangibles (net)	10.3	3.1	4.6	3.3	3.5	7.8
5.4	6.4	5.5	All Other Non-Current	6.0	6.7	7.3	6.5	4.6	3.9
100.0	100.0	100.0	Total	100.0	100.0	100.0	100.0	100.0	100.0
			LIABILITIES						
18.2	15.5	15.8	Notes Payable-Short Term	19.8	16.8	18.2	16.2	15.8	12.7
2.7	2.8	2.4	Cur. Mat.-L.T.D.	6.7	2.9	2.6	2.0	1.9	1.8
21.0	22.5	22.7	Trade Payables	21.6	17.6	20.5	24.3	24.9	23.3
.2	.2	.1	Income Taxes Payable	.0	.0	.0	.1	.1	.2
9.6	8.2	8.4	All Other Current	20.3	8.1	6.5	7.2	7.0	9.1
51.7	49.2	49.3	Total Current	68.4	45.4	47.8	49.7	49.8	47.1
9.4	10.9	10.9	Long-Term Debt	20.5	20.3	13.3	8.6	7.2	7.5
.2	.2	.2	Deferred Taxes	.0	.0	.1	.1	.2	.5
6.9	6.8	6.6	All Other Non-Current	8.8	11.9	8.6	4.5	4.5	5.7
31.9	32.9	33.1	Net Worth	2.3	22.3	30.3	37.1	38.3	39.2
100.0	100.0	100.0	Total Liabilties & Net Worth	100.0	100.0	100.0	100.0	100.0	100.0
			INCOME DATA						
100.0	100.0	100.0	Net Sales	100.0	100.0	100.0	100.0	100.0	100.0
30.7	31.6	32.7	Gross Profit	47.2	40.4	35.6	32.3	27.6	28.9
27.5	27.5	28.3	Operating Expenses	43.6	36.4	32.6	28.6	23.2	23.0
3.3	4.1	4.4	Operating Profit	3.6	4.0	3.0	3.7	4.4	6.0
.8	.8	.6	All Other Expenses (net)	1.2	.9	.6	.4	.3	.7
2.4	3.3	3.8	Profit Before Taxes	2.5	3.1	2.4	3.3	4.1	5.3
			RATIOS						
2.5	2.6	2.8	Current	4.2	4.3	3.1	2.8	2.4	2.5
1.5	1.5	1.6		1.3	1.9	1.5	1.7	1.6	1.5
1.2	1.2	1.2		.7	1.0	1.1	1.3	1.2	1.2
1.3	1.4	1.5	Quick	2.3	2.0	1.6	1.3	1.4	1.3
.7	.8	.8		.5	.8	.7	.8	.9	.8
.5	.5	.5		.2	.4	.4	.5	.5	.5
20 17.9	22 16.7	21 17.5	Sales/Receivables	0 UND	10 38.0	20 17.9	26 14.1	27 13.6	20 18.2
33 10.9	36 10.0	36 10.2		22 16.3	24 15.0	34 10.6	37 9.8	38 9.6	33 10.9
48 7.6	53 6.9	51 7.2		48 7.6	44 8.3	61 6.0	51 7.2	53 6.9	50 7.4
25 14.7	24 15.2	28 13.0	Cost of Sales/Inventory	4 101.9	28 12.8	34 10.7	36 10.2	25 14.7	25 14.5
63 5.8	56 6.5	63 5.8		62 5.9	63 5.8	82 4.5	70 5.2	59 6.2	62 5.9
119 3.1	108 3.4	116 3.1		132 2.8	134 2.7	169 2.2	114 3.2	111 3.3	97 3.8
13 27.8	15 24.6	15 24.8	Cost of Sales/Payables	0 UND	11 34.7	9 40.6	19 19.2	19 18.9	18 20.3
28 12.9	31 11.8	33 11.1		13 27.4	26 14.1	33 11.0	36 10.1	34 10.6	33 11.2
51 7.2	56 6.6	57 6.4		69 5.3	61 6.0	75 4.9	60 6.1	53 6.9	47 7.8
5.8	5.4	5.1	Sales/Working Capital	4.0	4.3	4.6	5.2	5.0	5.9
11.8	11.6	11.0		14.3	9.8	10.6	8.6	11.7	12.1
32.3	38.4	30.4		-11.7	999.8	46.9	22.7	23.2	25.4
9.4	14.4	16.6	EBIT/Interest	7.6	11.8	11.7	12.9	20.1	26.0
(603) 3.0	(677) 4.3	(641) 5.4		(29) 2.0	(91) 4.3	(72) 2.8	(124) 5.0	(170) 6.5	(155) 8.2
1.2	1.4	2.0		-.7	1.1	1.0	1.8	2.9	2.6
6.1	7.3	9.2	Net Profit + Depr., Dep., Amort./Cur. Mat. L/T/D				8.2	8.0	22.0
(109) 2.8	(125) 2.6	(106) 3.3				(15) 2.2	(36) 3.6	(44) 4.5
1.3	.8	1.4					1.2	1.2	2.0
.1	.1	.0	Fixed/Worth	.0	.0	.1	.0	.0	.1
.2	.3	.2		1.2	.2	.3	.1	.1	.2
1.0	1.2	1.0		-.5	3.8	2.4	.7	.5	1.1
1.0	.8	.8	Debt/Worth	1.6	.6	.8	.7	.8	.9
2.2	2.2	2.1		14.5	1.9	2.4	2.0	1.9	2.1
6.4	7.4	7.8		-5.8	-70.3	11.6	5.4	4.3	5.6
41.7	50.0	53.6	% Profit Before Taxes/Tangible Net Worth	100.0	58.8	37.1	38.7	50.7	61.6
(595) 16.8	(666) 20.0	(635) 21.8		(23) 28.5	(80) 22.6	(71) 16.5	(131) 14.6	(175) 20.8	(155) 29.4
2.8	5.1	8.1		7.4	6.2	3.3	3.3	8.5	13.2
12.6	16.2	16.8	% Profit Before Taxes/Total Assets	22.0	20.7	13.7	15.0	17.5	17.8
4.7	5.9	6.8		4.1	6.2	4.8	4.5	7.1	9.4
.5	1.1	2.1		-11.3	1.2	.3	.9	2.9	3.9
198.8	177.8	257.7	Sales/Net Fixed Assets	801.8	287.4	150.0	349.4	344.7	190.7
58.1	53.7	63.4		57.6	44.7	49.1	75.2	82.5	59.8
18.8	16.7	19.8		13.6	14.0	16.1	22.9	26.5	17.8
4.3	4.2	4.1	Sales/Total Assets	3.6	4.0	3.7	4.0	4.4	4.4
2.9	2.8	2.8		1.8	2.7	2.4	3.0	3.0	3.0
2.0	1.9	1.8		1.1	1.8	1.6	2.1	2.0	1.9
.2	.3	.2	% Depr., Dep., Amort./Sales	.5	.4	.2	.2	.2	.2
(527) .6	(568) .6	(537) .5		(20) 1.8	(65) 1.0	(63) .6	(94) .5	(145) .5	(150) .5
1.4	1.5	1.4		2.5	2.0	1.6	1.2	1.1	1.5
1.3	1.3	1.6	% Officers', Directors' Owners' Comp/Sales	3.4	2.6	1.6	2.0	1.3	.7
(322) 2.8	(350) 2.9	(361) 2.9		(14) 7.1	(59) 4.7	(56) 3.2	(82) 3.1	(96) 2.2	(54) 1.4
5.3	5.2	5.2		11.2	8.6	5.6	5.1	3.5	3.2
22453908M	21871028M	21932786M	Net Sales ($)	22318M	207371M	350773M	1072028M	2992334M	17287962M
7840976M	8281865M	8350045M	Total Assets ($)	13341M	92656M	173859M	435880M	1141573M	6492736M

M = $ thousand   MM = $ million
See Pages 9 through 22 for Explanation of Ratios and Data

Current Data Sorted by Assets						Type of Statement	Comparative Historical Data	
			1		1	Unqualified	5	6
	2	3				Reviewed	8	13
	1	2				Compiled	7	2
4	6	1	1			Tax Returns	4	6
1	6	7	5			Other	11	20
	5 (4/1-9/30/10)		36 (10/1/10-3/31/11)				4/1/06-3/31/07	4/1/07-3/31/08
0-500M	500M-2MM	2-10MM	10-50MM	50-100MM	100-250MM		ALL	ALL
5	15	13	7		1	NUMBER OF STATEMENTS	35	47
%	%	%	%	%	%	ASSETS	%	%
	25.2	15.7				Cash & Equivalents	10.9	14.3
	26.1	37.3				Trade Receivables (net)	32.9	43.2
	21.8	25.1				Inventory	34.3	17.9
	5.9	3.5				All Other Current	1.4	6.4
	79.0	81.6				Total Current	79.5	81.9
	9.8	10.9				Fixed Assets (net)	13.3	9.4
	8.1	3.3				Intangibles (net)	4.9	5.3
	3.1	4.2				All Other Non-Current	2.3	3.5
	100.0	100.0				Total	100.0	100.0
						LIABILITIES		
	9.0	11.3				Notes Payable-Short Term	13.9	9.9
	7.9	3.1				Cur. Mat.-L.T.D.	3.4	1.7
	31.6	21.0				Trade Payables	23.3	28.7
	.2	.1				Income Taxes Payable	.2	.2
	9.9	8.7				All Other Current	9.5	16.6
	58.7	44.2				Total Current	50.3	57.0
	10.3	3.2				Long-Term Debt	11.0	4.6
	.0	.0				Deferred Taxes	.0	.1
	1.5	5.6				All Other Non-Current	4.7	3.6
	29.5	47.0				Net Worth	33.9	34.6
	100.0	100.0				Total Liabilties & Net Worth	100.0	100.0
						INCOME DATA		
	100.0	100.0				Net Sales	100.0	100.0
	41.9	31.1				Gross Profit	30.7	32.4
	37.0	25.8				Operating Expenses	28.0	29.4
	4.8	5.2				Operating Profit	2.7	2.9
	.6	3.0				All Other Expenses (net)	.4	.3
	4.3	2.3				Profit Before Taxes	2.3	2.6
						RATIOS		
	4.5	2.9					2.3	2.0
	2.4	1.6				Current	1.6	1.7
	.9	1.4					1.2	1.1
	4.0	2.4					1.3	1.6
	1.2	1.0				Quick	.9	1.1
	.6	.7					.6	.8
3	141.4	24 15.4					18 20.7	26 14.3
26	14.0	54 6.8				Sales/Receivables	42 8.7	49 7.5
48	7.5	64 5.7					54 6.8	65 5.6
0	999.8	7 51.8					18 20.6	4 96.8
18	20.2	52 7.1				Cost of Sales/Inventory	50 7.3	24 15.2
84	4.3	125 2.9					74 5.0	58 6.3
10	35.7	18 20.4					15 24.1	15 24.9
20	17.8	28 12.8				Cost of Sales/Payables	38 9.7	38 9.6
33	11.0	64 5.7					69 5.3	67 5.5
	5.4	4.7					6.7	5.9
	9.3	9.1				Sales/Working Capital	12.7	10.1
	-42.7	15.9					33.7	33.3
	9.0	42.2					7.1	15.8
(10)	2.5	(12) 6.9				EBIT/Interest	(31) 2.6	(40) 7.0
	-.7	2.2					1.4	2.4
								6.6
						Net Profit + Depr., Dep., Amort./Cur. Mat. L/T/D	(11)	3.6
								1.5
	.1	.1					.2	.1
	.2	.2				Fixed/Worth	.3	.3
	.9	.3					1.2	.6
	.5	.8					1.0	1.0
	1.7	1.2				Debt/Worth	2.2	2.0
	9.0	1.9					11.1	6.7
	92.2	36.7				% Profit Before Taxes/Tangible Net Worth	51.5	44.3
(13)	44.6	23.9					(30) 15.2	(42) 22.4
	7.8	7.1					4.0	7.1
	49.8	21.5				% Profit Before Taxes/Total Assets	17.6	18.5
	11.3	6.0					4.0	8.9
	.5	2.9					.7	3.7
	298.0	82.2					112.6	93.8
	44.7	41.8				Sales/Net Fixed Assets	34.0	57.3
	25.4	18.0					16.9	19.7
	6.7	4.2					4.5	4.3
	4.6	2.5				Sales/Total Assets	3.3	3.3
	2.6	2.0					2.3	2.5
	.2	.6					.4	.2
(10)	.9	(10) .9				% Depr., Dep., Amort./Sales	(27) .9	(38) .7
	1.2	1.3					1.4	1.2
							1.7	2.9
			(12)			% Officers', Directors' Owners' Comp/Sales	5.7	(13) 6.4
							8.0	11.1
13159M	79955M	224805M	383796M		666711M	Net Sales ($)	1091543M	2020937M
1408M	13468M	69544M	135639M		203844M	Total Assets ($)	311113M	677858M

Note: Columns 10-50MM, 50-100MM, and 100-250MM marked "DATA NOT AVAILABLE."

M = $ thousand   MM = $ million
See Pages 9 through 22 for Explanation of Ratios and Data

Comparative Historical Data / Current Data Sorted by Sales

Type of Statement	4/1/08-3/31/09 ALL	4/1/09-3/31/10 ALL	4/1/10-3/31/11 ALL	0-1MM	1-3MM	3-5MM	5-10MM	10-25MM	25MM & OVER
					5 (4/1-9/30/10)		36 (10/1/10-3/31/11)		
Unqualified	5	3	2						2
Reviewed	3	3	5		1	1	1		2
Compiled	4	3	3			1	1	1	
Tax Returns	2	6	12	2	3	3	2		2
Other	17	14	19	1	2	2	5	3	6
NUMBER OF STATEMENTS	31	29	41	3	6	7	9	4	12
	%	%	%	%	%	%	%	%	%
ASSETS									
Cash & Equivalents	12.0	15.5	16.9						13.1
Trade Receivables (net)	29.5	33.1	34.1						45.5
Inventory	29.4	28.8	25.3						17.4
All Other Current	5.9	3.5	4.8						11.8
Total Current	76.8	80.9	81.1						87.8
Fixed Assets (net)	12.7	9.6	10.0						5.9
Intangibles (net)	5.6	4.9	5.4						4.4
All Other Non-Current	5.0	4.6	3.5						1.8
Total	100.0	100.0	100.0						100.0
LIABILITIES									
Notes Payable-Short Term	23.6	11.8	10.2						2.3
Cur. Mat.-L.T.D.	1.1	3.4	7.0						.3
Trade Payables	24.9	23.6	25.3						43.7
Income Taxes Payable	.3	.4	.3						.5
All Other Current	8.4	11.5	14.6						18.7
Total Current	58.3	50.6	57.4						65.4
Long-Term Debt	7.0	2.7	13.4						9.0
Deferred Taxes	.3	.0	.0						.0
All Other Non-Current	3.1	5.4	2.8						1.5
Net Worth	31.2	41.2	26.3						24.0
Total Liabilties & Net Worth	100.0	100.0	100.0						100.0
INCOME DATA									
Net Sales	100.0	100.0	100.0						100.0
Gross Profit	33.2	33.2	36.2						21.6
Operating Expenses	32.2	30.5	31.0						18.9
Operating Profit	1.0	2.7	5.3						2.6
All Other Expenses (net)	.5	.7	1.4						.3
Profit Before Taxes	.5	2.0	3.8						2.3
RATIOS									
Current	2.1	3.0	3.5						2.5
	1.4	1.5	1.6						1.8
	1.1	1.2	1.0						1.3
Quick	1.2	1.6	2.3						2.3
	.7	.8	1.0						1.3
	.4	.5	.5						.9
Sales/Receivables	18 20.3	20 18.4	17 21.6						32 11.4
	37 9.8	35 10.5	45 8.1						48 7.6
	50 7.3	49 7.5	56 6.5						62 5.9
Cost of Sales/Inventory	16 22.9	12 31.6	5 68.8						5 70.7
	54 6.8	56 6.5	36 10.0						16 22.4
	89 4.1	144 2.5	90 4.0						46 8.0
Cost of Sales/Payables	11 34.3	11 32.8	14 26.3						19 19.3
	37 10.0	31 11.9	28 12.8						30 12.2
	76 4.8	49 7.4	48 7.6						43 8.4
Sales/Working Capital	6.0	4.8	5.2						5.9
	15.4	11.2	10.7						10.0
	81.5	68.2	58.8						22.6
EBIT/Interest	18.4	34.2	16.8						16.3
	(28) 4.3	(24) 5.2	(34) 5.2					(11)	6.1
	1.8	-1.2	1.4						4.9
Net Profit + Depr., Dep., Amort./Cur. Mat. L/T/D									
Fixed/Worth	.1	.1	.1						.0
	.4	.2	.2						.2
	1.3	.7	.8						.2
Debt/Worth	1.1	.7	.7						.9
	3.2	1.9	1.4						1.3
	9.6	5.2	6.6						4.7
% Profit Before Taxes/Tangible Net Worth	70.0	47.0	79.1						46.3
	(26) 11.3	(25) 6.1	(37) 30.1					(11)	28.3
	3.9	-7.0	7.1						11.7
% Profit Before Taxes/Total Assets	18.5	14.2	30.7						20.8
	4.4	3.6	9.4						8.5
	1.4	-2.7	1.9						5.4
Sales/Net Fixed Assets	85.9	211.3	243.5						999.8
	34.7	47.2	44.7						76.1
	18.6	20.1	24.1						37.2
Sales/Total Assets	4.3	5.2	5.5						5.1
	3.0	3.2	3.2						4.2
	1.9	2.2	2.4						2.5
% Depr., Dep., Amort./Sales	.2	.4	.5						.2
	(23) .6	(18) 1.3	(29) .9					(10)	.6
	1.7	2.0	1.3						.7
% Officers', Directors' Owners' Comp/Sales		.6	1.4						
		(11) 4.2	(19) 3.0						
		5.3	6.5						
Net Sales ($)	1001021M	601557M	1368426M	2437M	12288M	27141M	64217M	63045M	1199298M
Total Assets ($)	343230M	179131M	423903M	1107M	4180M	7328M	19407M	33723M	358158M

© RMA 2011

M = $ thousand   MM = $ million
See Pages 9 through 22 for Explanation of Ratios and Data

Current Data Sorted by Assets   Comparative Historical Data

Type of Statement	0-500M	500M-2MM	2-10MM	10-50MM	50-100MM	100-250MM		4/1/06-3/31/07 ALL	4/1/07-3/31/08 ALL
Unqualified		1	1	7	3	2		30	17
Reviewed		1	17	6				33	31
Compiled		10	14	1				22	27
Tax Returns	23	23	19					38	30
Other	15	17	22	13		2		67	55
		34 (4/1-9/30/10)		163 (10/1/10-3/31/11)					
NUMBER OF STATEMENTS	38	52	73	27	3	4		190	160
	%	%	%	%	%	%		%	%
ASSETS									
Cash & Equivalents	30.0	14.9	9.2	13.3				9.8	9.0
Trade Receivables (net)	20.5	36.9	37.7	34.8				37.0	37.3
Inventory	21.5	25.9	28.6	20.4				26.9	28.8
All Other Current	1.3	2.5	4.2	4.1				3.1	3.4
Total Current	73.3	80.2	79.6	72.7				76.8	78.5
Fixed Assets (net)	10.0	6.4	12.0	16.5				12.3	12.8
Intangibles (net)	4.1	5.6	2.1	3.0				3.9	2.6
All Other Non-Current	12.5	7.8	6.2	7.8				7.0	6.2
Total	100.0	100.0	100.0	100.0				100.0	100.0
LIABILITIES									
Notes Payable-Short Term	24.8	13.9	15.2	13.9				21.4	19.1
Cur. Mat.-L.T.D.	4.5	2.2	2.3	1.5				2.3	1.8
Trade Payables	24.2	21.1	24.9	17.6				22.1	22.5
Income Taxes Payable	.1	.1	.0	.1				.3	.1
All Other Current	14.0	12.7	11.0	10.2				8.8	8.4
Total Current	67.6	49.9	53.4	43.3				55.0	51.9
Long-Term Debt	11.0	8.5	8.7	8.2				11.0	11.4
Deferred Taxes	.0	.0	.3	.2				.2	.1
All Other Non-Current	12.4	7.2	7.2	4.4				5.7	4.4
Net Worth	9.0	34.4	30.4	43.8				28.2	32.2
Total Liabilities & Net Worth	100.0	100.0	100.0	100.0				100.0	100.0
INCOME DATA									
Net Sales	100.0	100.0	100.0	100.0				100.0	100.0
Gross Profit	33.9	26.2	23.8	27.1				25.2	24.2
Operating Expenses	27.4	21.8	20.4	22.2				21.0	19.8
Operating Profit	6.5	4.4	3.4	4.9				4.1	4.4
All Other Expenses (net)	.4	.6	.4	-.1				.5	1.0
Profit Before Taxes	6.1	3.8	3.0	5.0				3.6	3.4
RATIOS									
Current	3.3	2.8	2.2	2.4				2.3	2.3
	1.9	1.6	1.5	1.8				1.4	1.5
	.5	1.2	1.1	1.2				1.1	1.2
Quick	2.0	1.6	1.3	2.4				1.5	1.5
	1.0	1.1	.9	1.2				.9	.9
	.3	.5	.5	.6				.5	.5
Sales/Receivables	0 UND	10 36.4	24 15.0	27 13.3				19 19.3	18 20.7
	6 62.5	30 12.0	37 10.0	54 6.8				34 10.7	34 10.8
	37 9.8	50 7.4	50 7.3	83 4.4				49 7.5	51 7.2
Cost of Sales/Inventory	0 UND	1 285.2	3 128.0	6 61.3				4 86.1	7 50.4
	7 54.9	24 15.4	35 10.4	36 10.0				29 12.7	31 11.8
	66 5.5	78 4.7	90 4.6	61 6.0				77 4.8	76 4.8
Cost of Sales/Payables	0 UND	9 40.9	10 35.0	11 34.7				8 44.6	8 44.7
	6 62.5	21 17.2	32 11.3	28 13.1				25 14.7	24 15.0
	33 11.0	32 11.4	51 7.1	65 5.6				47 7.8	46 7.9
Sales/Working Capital	6.5	5.5	6.9	6.0				6.9	7.5
	14.7	15.2	16.0	10.3				15.5	16.3
	-14.7	69.6	67.0	28.3				77.2	49.7
EBIT/Interest	16.8	19.3	13.3	29.0				14.0	10.2
	(22) 7.6	(40) 5.8	(67) 3.0	(24) 10.2				(162) 3.7	(140) 3.7
	3.7	3.5	1.4	2.5				1.7	1.5
Net Profit + Depr., Dep., Amort./Cur. Mat. L/T/D			2.0					5.7	9.5
		(10) .8						(36) 3.4	(30) 3.7
			.2					1.4	1.3
Fixed/Worth	.0	.0	.0	.0				.1	.1
	.1	.1	.2	.3				.2	.2
	-1.8	.5	1.2	.7				1.0	.8
Debt/Worth	.5	.8	1.0	1.0				1.0	1.0
	1.8	2.0	3.3	1.5				2.8	2.6
	-5.9	24.9	9.4	2.6				8.0	7.2
% Profit Before Taxes/Tangible Net Worth	100.0	94.3	66.5	67.0				61.3	62.9
	(25) 84.7	(42) 33.3	(64) 26.4	(26) 21.3				(163) 25.8	(141) 24.2
	48.7	15.6	5.7	13.4				7.3	6.6
% Profit Before Taxes/Total Assets	51.8	25.8	15.3	13.6				18.9	19.3
	35.0	10.0	4.5	8.3				6.7	7.6
	6.3	3.1	1.3	4.2				2.1	1.7
Sales/Net Fixed Assets	UND	884.9	450.2	269.7				309.4	290.5
	362.8	129.6	67.7	33.1				57.1	66.2
	49.5	42.6	22.2	6.1				23.1	20.6
Sales/Total Assets	9.2	6.6	5.8	4.1				5.6	6.2
	5.2	3.6	3.5	2.7				3.5	3.6
	2.4	2.3	2.0	.9				2.0	2.4
% Depr., Dep., Amort./Sales	.1	.1	.1	.1				.2	.1
	(15) .4	(31) .3	(51) .4	(24) .7				(131) .6	(121) .4
	.6	1.2	1.1	2.0				1.2	1.1
% Officers', Directors' Owners' Comp/Sales	1.8	1.1	.9					1.0	1.0
	(18) 4.5	(30) 2.6	(46) 1.9					(75) 2.6	(71) 2.4
	8.2	4.9	4.0					6.2	3.6
Net Sales ($)	82395M	345025M	1205184M	1711862M	576728M	2242828M		11566708M	11016257M
Total Assets ($)	10244M	61354M	292802M	559051M	217981M	742369M		2864403M	2604440M

M = $ thousand   MM = $ million
See Pages 9 through 22 for Explanation of Ratios and Data

Comparative Historical Data

Current Data Sorted by Sales

			Type of Statement	0-1MM	1-3MM	3-5MM	5-10MM	10-25MM	25MM & OVER
15	19	14	Unqualified				5	2	12
36	23	24	Reviewed		4	1	5	11	7
24	29	25	Compiled			2	7	7	5
47	40	65	Tax Returns	8	19	10	14	9	5
57	64	69	Other	8	14	7	11	15	14
4/1/08-3/31/09 ALL	4/1/09-3/31/10 ALL	4/1/10-3/31/11 ALL			34 (4/1-9/30/10)		163 (10/1/10-3/31/11)		
179	175	197	**NUMBER OF STATEMENTS**	16	37	20	37	44	43

%	%	%		%	%	%	%	%	%
			ASSETS						
12.0	12.2	15.1	Cash & Equivalents	19.5	20.9	17.7	15.1	11.6	10.7
38.1	36.0	34.0	Trade Receivables (net)	25.3	22.2	24.4	28.9	41.3	48.5
24.2	25.2	25.4	Inventory	24.9	27.6	28.8	29.7	23.4	20.4
4.4	5.1	3.3	All Other Current	.5	2.8	.2	.5	6.9	4.8
78.8	78.5	77.7	Total Current	70.2	73.4	71.2	74.1	83.3	84.4
10.8	10.7	10.8	Fixed Assets (net)	14.0	13.0	8.0	11.9	10.7	8.2
2.6	2.3	3.5	Intangibles (net)	5.0	4.4	6.5	4.8	1.5	1.9
7.9	8.5	8.0	All Other Non-Current	10.8	9.1	14.3	9.2	4.6	5.4
100.0	100.0	100.0	Total	100.0	100.0	100.0	100.0	100.0	100.0
			LIABILITIES						
17.8	16.7	16.9	Notes Payable-Short Term	16.3	23.9	13.7	15.6	12.4	18.3
3.9	3.8	2.6	Cur. Mat.-L.T.D.	.0	5.4	1.2	3.6	2.8	.7
24.4	24.5	22.8	Trade Payables	16.0	21.7	23.0	20.1	27.7	23.6
.1	.1	.1	Income Taxes Payable	.0	.1	.1	.1	.1	.1
11.2	10.5	11.8	All Other Current	15.4	12.9	17.4	9.0	10.9	10.0
57.4	55.6	54.1	Total Current	47.8	63.9	55.4	48.4	53.8	52.8
7.9	8.8	8.9	Long-Term Debt	16.3	13.6	7.7	10.9	5.3	4.8
.1	.1	.1	Deferred Taxes	.0	.0	.1	.2	.2	.2
3.5	4.6	7.6	All Other Non-Current	27.4	6.0	5.7	10.5	3.3	4.5
31.1	31.0	29.2	Net Worth	8.5	16.5	31.2	30.0	37.4	37.7
100.0	100.0	100.0	Total Liabilities & Net Worth	100.0	100.0	100.0	100.0	100.0	100.0
			INCOME DATA						
100.0	100.0	100.0	Net Sales	100.0	100.0	100.0	100.0	100.0	100.0
23.3	26.4	26.5	Gross Profit	30.6	41.7	21.3	29.9	24.7	13.2
20.1	22.7	22.2	Operating Expenses	24.3	36.0	18.4	23.9	20.3	11.5
3.2	3.8	4.4	Operating Profit	6.3	5.6	2.9	6.0	4.4	1.7
.4	.6	.4	All Other Expenses (net)	.8	1.1	.2	.5	-.4	.3
2.8	3.2	4.0	Profit Before Taxes	5.5	4.5	2.7	5.5	4.8	1.4
			RATIOS						
2.2	2.3	2.5	Current	2.8	3.9	2.4	2.6	2.2	2.1
1.4	1.5	1.6		2.3	1.5	1.6	1.7	1.5	1.6
1.1	1.1	1.1		.6	.5	1.1	1.1	1.1	1.2
1.4	1.6	1.6	Quick	1.9	1.5	1.6	1.7	1.5	1.7
.9	.9	1.0		1.1	.6	1.1	.8	.9	1.2
.6	.6	.5		.4	.3	.3	.4	.6	.7
18 20.4	14 25.3	11 32.4	Sales/Receivables	0 UND	0 UND	8 46.0	17 20.9	21 17.5	20 18.6
33 11.0	35 10.5	32 11.3		40 9.1	22 16.9	23 16.1	44 8.4	37 9.9	30 12.2
52 7.0	59 6.2	54 6.8		105 3.5	58 6.2	41 8.8	52 7.0	54 6.8	56 6.5
0 999.8	2 240.2	1 343.6	Cost of Sales/Inventory	0 UND	0 UND	0 UND	3 111.2	3 128.9	1 435.9
18 19.8	28 13.2	27 13.3		37 9.8	45 8.1	45 8.1	38 9.6	25 14.6	18 20.7
64 5.7	69 5.3	78 4.7		136 2.7	88 4.1	89 4.1	104 3.5	59 6.1	37 9.8
10 36.5	9 39.4	7 53.7	Cost of Sales/Payables	0 UND	1 672.2	8 44.9	11 34.2	11 33.9	7 55.8
24 15.0	25 14.5	24 15.4		24 15.1	19 18.8	24 15.0	32 11.5	28 13.3	23 15.6
44 8.3	51 7.1	49 7.4		82 4.5	79 4.6	31 11.6	54 6.7	52 7.0	39 9.3
8.4	6.5	6.1	Sales/Working Capital	5.0	5.4	6.4	5.0	7.4	8.0
19.1	15.0	14.7		5.9	14.2	14.5	12.2	19.0	19.6
97.7	77.8	71.9		-11.7	-12.7	67.2	41.4	72.0	40.1
16.5	13.5	16.4	EBIT/Interest		15.5	8.1	19.0	32.7	11.9
(148) 4.5	(145) 4.3	(159) 5.4			(30) 4.7	(12) 4.8	(33) 5.3	(37) 7.2	(38) 7.3
1.6	1.8	2.0			-.9	2.0	1.9	2.1	2.3
8.3	4.3	10.1	Net Profit + Depr., Dep., Amort./Cur. Mat. L/T/D						35.5
(24) 2.9	(20) 1.7	(24) 2.5						(10)	11.5
1.7	.7	.6							3.0
.0	.0	.0	Fixed/Worth	.0	.1	.0	.0	.0	.0
.2	.2	.2		.0	.7	.0	.2	.2	.1
.6	.9	1.0		NM	-1.2	.2	1.2	.5	.5
.9	.9	1.0	Debt/Worth	.8	1.0	.9	.9	.8	1.0
2.2	2.4	2.3		3.4	4.7	1.6	3.2	2.5	2.0
6.7	6.2	8.5		-4.6	-7.5	3.5	41.7	4.6	3.8
58.4	56.1	80.3	% Profit Before Taxes/Tangible Net Worth	99.1	110.4	76.2	73.2	71.7	62.9
(154) 20.0	(157) 18.9	(164) 33.0		(11) 56.1	(23) 84.7	(17) 19.6	(29) 29.3	(43) 33.4	(41) 26.0
8.9	4.6	10.4		18.4	15.6	5.0	6.6	13.0	10.6
16.0	14.9	24.6	% Profit Before Taxes/Total Assets	42.7	40.0	19.9	23.9	30.9	15.2
6.7	6.7	8.4		8.7	10.7	6.9	12.8	8.5	8.1
1.4	1.8	2.0		-.7	-4.8	1.9	1.8	3.0	3.3
759.5	420.0	706.1	Sales/Net Fixed Assets	UND	311.6	925.3	999.8	528.2	642.4
74.9	75.8	97.9		UND	63.5	250.2	121.2	60.3	176.0
22.1	18.5	27.0		15.9	25.0	36.1	17.0	23.3	33.1
5.9	6.1	6.5	Sales/Total Assets	2.6	7.0	8.1	4.7	7.2	8.9
3.6	3.3	3.4		1.6	3.2	3.4	2.7	4.2	4.7
2.3	2.0	2.1		1.1	1.8	2.4	1.9	2.5	2.8
.2	.1	.1	% Depr., Dep., Amort./Sales		.2	.2	.2	.1	.0
(121) .4	(125) .5	(127) .4			(22) .6	(11) .6	(24) .6	(31) .6	(35) .1
1.0	1.1	1.1			3.2	1.0	1.9	1.1	.7
1.0	1.2	1.1	% Officers', Directors' Owners' Comp/Sales		2.6	1.1	1.2	1.0	.5
(90) 3.1	(78) 2.4	(102) 2.2			(24) 4.7	(11) 2.0	(21) 1.7	(23) 2.2	(20) .9
6.0	5.1	4.7			8.2	5.0	3.5	4.5	1.7
9055793M	12675131M	6164022M	Net Sales ($)	7030M	69388M	81582M	260774M	722363M	5022885M
2169101M	1977019M	1883801M	Total Assets ($)	6989M	33243M	27071M	132178M	252394M	1431926M

M = $ thousand   MM = $ million
See Pages 9 through 22 for Explanation of Ratios and Data

Current Data Sorted by Assets

Comparative Historical Data

0-500M	500M-2MM	2-10MM	10-50MM	50-100MM	100-250MM		ALL 4/1/06-3/31/07	ALL 4/1/07-3/31/08
1	8	20 / 161	39 / 143	16 / 12	11 / 4	**Type of Statement**	169	91
	12	70	24	1	2	Unqualified	404	337
3	24	195	65	3		Reviewed	142	118
9	74	887	657	29	15	Compiled	277	230
	109 (4/1-9/30/10)		2,376 (10/1/10-3/31/11)			Tax Returns	2049	1699
						Other		
13	118	1333	928	61	32	**NUMBER OF STATEMENTS**	3041	2475
%	%	%	%	%	%	**ASSETS**	%	%
9.2	9.3	11.4	13.7	13.6	10.3	Cash & Equivalents	10.1	9.9
11.0	6.7	7.0	7.7	8.6	8.0	Trade Receivables (net)	7.2	7.0
33.7	62.5	62.6	52.0	42.8	39.5	Inventory	62.8	62.8
7.2	3.7	2.3	2.4	2.9	2.4	All Other Current	2.5	2.4
61.2	82.2	83.4	75.8	67.9	60.2	Total Current	82.5	82.1
8.4	10.8	8.3	12.6	18.7	22.2	Fixed Assets (net)	9.5	9.6
7.1	1.2	3.0	3.8	4.8	7.3	Intangibles (net)	2.3	2.7
22.7	5.7	5.3	7.7	8.6	10.3	All Other Non-Current	5.7	5.6
100.0	100.0	100.0	100.0	100.0	100.0	Total	100.0	100.0
						LIABILITIES		
15.4	42.5	51.6	47.4	37.9	31.4	Notes Payable-Short Term	52.3	50.9
1.1	1.8	1.9	1.3	2.2	3.8	Cur. Mat.-L.T.D.	1.7	2.3
39.2	6.9	5.1	4.1	4.4	5.1	Trade Payables	4.3	4.5
.0	.0	.1	.1	.1	.0	Income Taxes Payable	.1	.1
25.7	14.7	9.7	9.3	10.5	12.1	All Other Current	12.6	13.0
81.4	66.0	68.4	62.2	55.1	52.3	Total Current	70.9	70.7
48.6	9.2	6.8	8.2	11.1	19.0	Long-Term Debt	7.2	7.6
.3	.1	.1	.2	.2	.2	Deferred Taxes	.1	.1
8.2	8.8	4.7	3.6	3.8	1.7	All Other Non-Current	3.8	3.6
-38.6	15.9	20.0	25.9	29.6	26.8	Net Worth	18.0	18.0
100.0	100.0	100.0	100.0	100.0	100.0	Total Liabilities & Net Worth	100.0	100.0
						INCOME DATA		
100.0	100.0	100.0	100.0	100.0	100.0	Net Sales	100.0	100.0
29.7	17.3	12.8	12.8	14.0	14.7	Gross Profit	12.8	13.1
25.7	18.0	13.0	12.0	12.0	12.0	Operating Expenses	12.6	12.9
4.0	-.6	-.2	.8	2.0	2.7	Operating Profit	.2	.2
.3	-.5	-1.1	-1.1	-.2	-.2	All Other Expenses (net)	-.3	-.4
3.8	-.1	.9	1.9	2.2	2.9	Profit Before Taxes	.5	.6
						RATIOS		
1.8	1.8	1.4	1.4	1.4	1.2		1.3	1.3
1.0	1.3	1.2	1.2	1.2	1.1	Current	1.1	1.1
.5	1.0	1.1	1.1	1.1	1.0		1.0	1.0
.5	.4	.4	.5	.5	.4		.3	.3
.2	(113) .2	(1331) .2	.3	.4	.3	Quick	(3034) .2	(2472) .2
.0	.1	.2	.2	.2	.2		.1	.1
0 UND	2 226.0	3 129.4	4 95.3	5 77.1	5 74.5		3 120.4	3 131.4
2 181.3	4 83.8	5 71.2	6 58.6	9 41.8	11 33.6	Sales/Receivables	5 66.6	5 70.3
16 23.1	9 40.7	9 40.1	10 36.3	12 29.5	15 24.2		9 38.5	9 39.5
2 222.5	48 7.6	57 6.5	51 7.1	52 7.0	53 6.9		55 6.7	57 6.4
42 8.6	69 5.3	72 5.1	64 5.7	62 5.9	62 5.9	Cost of Sales/Inventory	71 5.1	73 5.0
70 5.3	104 3.5	92 4.0	79 4.6	73 5.0	67 5.4		94 3.9	93 3.9
0 UND	2 240.5	2 169.1	2 155.8	3 119.4	4 94.0		2 207.3	2 205.0
18 20.2	4 89.8	4 95.4	4 95.1	4 81.4	5 72.4	Cost of Sales/Payables	3 113.5	3 111.0
56 6.5	8 44.1	6 59.5	6 61.2	8 43.5	7 51.9		6 66.1	6 66.2
20.2	8.7	14.7	15.1	15.4	23.2		18.3	18.1
999.8	18.7	25.8	28.7	24.7	50.2	Sales/Working Capital	34.7	34.2
-7.9	430.1	63.8	70.3	85.1	NM		132.9	129.1
	4.3	7.7	13.1	15.8	30.9		4.0	3.7
(87) 1.5	(869) 2.9	(612) 4.6	(48) 6.7	(27) 9.7		EBIT/Interest	(2307) 1.7	(1933) 1.7
	-1.1	1.2	2.2	2.7	2.3		.6	.8
		10.3	8.1	10.4	6.7	Net Profit + Depr., Dep.,	5.1	5.9
	(53) 3.0	(75) 3.0	(13) 2.8	(10) 3.7		Amort./Cur. Mat. L/T/D	(199) 2.1	(166) 2.0
		.7	1.5	1.1	1.2		.8	.6
.0	.1	.1	.1	.3	.5		.2	.2
.4	.4	.3	.4	.7	1.1	Fixed/Worth	.5	.5
-1.4	UND	1.2	1.1	1.6	2.2		1.7	1.7
1.8	1.6	2.3	2.0	1.8	2.7		2.8	2.8
-27.3	5.0	4.5	3.9	3.7	3.9	Debt/Worth	5.6	5.6
-2.6	-56.2	12.4	8.3	6.6	9.2		14.9	16.9
	33.2	39.8	48.5	41.4	85.4	% Profit Before Taxes/Tangible	36.3	36.2
	(88) 8.4	(1137) 18.0	(854) 27.1	(58) 23.1	(31) 39.1	Net Worth	(2596) 15.3	(2116) 15.7
	-9.8	4.0	12.6	11.7	20.3		.4	1.5
18.0	5.1	7.3	9.2	7.8	11.6	% Profit Before Taxes/Total	6.3	6.0
4.6	.8	3.4	5.4	5.1	6.8	Assets	2.1	2.1
-32.7	-4.5	.4	2.5	3.0	3.9		-1.0	-.7
UND	188.5	189.3	128.0	44.3	42.7		144.5	142.4
57.2	76.2	83.2	51.2	17.9	11.3	Sales/Net Fixed Assets	67.3	67.7
20.7	28.5	36.1	19.2	8.7	7.2		29.6	28.9
10.9	5.1	4.5	4.2	3.6	3.4		4.5	4.5
4.0	3.9	3.7	3.3	2.8	2.8	Sales/Total Assets	3.6	3.6
2.0	2.7	2.9	2.6	2.1	2.2		2.8	2.8
	.2	.1	.1	.3	.4		.1	.1
	(83) .3	(1091) .2	(836) .3	(58) .5	(27) .6	% Depr., Dep., Amort./Sales	(2637) .2	(2150) .2
	.6	.4	.5	.8	.9		.4	.4
	.6	.4	.2	.1		% Officers', Directors'	.3	.3
	(59) 1.1	(805) .7	(564) .4	(26) .3		Owners' Comp/Sales	(1793) .5	(1514) .5
	2.3	1.2	.9	1.0			1.0	1.0
18342M	637811M	28224607M	56806039M	11916550M	14406687M	Net Sales ($)	150864002M	126662900M
3379M	156264M	7651250M	17055730M	4189286M	5129250M	Total Assets ($)	42067557M	35620298M

© RMA 2011

M = $ thousand   MM = $ million
See Pages 9 through 22 for Explanation of Ratios and Data

Comparative Historical Data   Current Data Sorted by Sales

			Type of Statement	0-1MM	1-3MM	3-5MM	5-10MM	10-25MM	25MM & OVER
86	115	87	Unqualified		2		4	13	68
322	380	328	Reviewed		2	1	17	93	215
126	113	109	Compiled		5	5	9	45	45
265	335	290	Tax Returns	4	10	6	30	130	110
1860	1747	1671	Other	10	26	38	151	492	954
4/1/08-3/31/09 ALL	4/1/09-3/31/10 ALL	4/1/10-3/31/11 ALL		109 (4/1-9/30/10)			2,376 (10/1/10-3/31/11)		
2659	2690	2485	**NUMBER OF STATEMENTS**	14	45	50	211	773	1392
%	%	%	**ASSETS**	%	%	%	%	%	%
9.9	12.3	12.2	Cash & Equivalents	6.5	11.0	11.1	9.9	10.5	13.6
6.6	7.7	7.3	Trade Receivables (net)	8.9	12.8	5.7	6.4	6.7	7.6
61.7	54.7	57.7	Inventory	28.8	50.6	57.7	63.5	61.9	55.0
2.2	2.4	2.5	All Other Current	10.4	1.2	3.5	2.6	2.2	2.5
80.3	77.1	79.7	Total Current	54.6	75.6	77.9	82.5	81.3	78.8
10.4	11.5	10.5	Fixed Assets (net)	24.4	12.4	11.6	9.8	9.6	10.8
3.1	3.9	3.3	Intangibles (net)	2.9	3.9	3.2	2.7	3.5	3.4
6.2	7.4	6.5	All Other Non-Current	17.5	8.1	7.3	5.0	5.6	7.0
100.0	100.0	100.0	Total	100.0	100.0	100.0	100.0	100.0	100.0
			LIABILITIES						
51.7	46.0	48.8	Notes Payable-Short Term	25.9	42.3	37.6	46.9	50.5	49.0
1.9	1.8	1.7	Cur. Mat.-L.T.D.	3.4	.7	1.1	2.1	2.1	1.5
4.2	5.1	5.0	Trade Payables	5.8	11.8	11.0	4.6	5.3	4.5
.1	.1	.1	Income Taxes Payable	.0	.0	.3	.0	.0	.1
11.8	11.0	9.9	All Other Current	10.9	14.7	10.6	10.2	9.7	9.8
69.8	63.9	65.5	Total Current	46.0	69.5	60.6	63.9	67.6	64.8
8.1	9.3	7.9	Long-Term Debt	24.2	22.7	14.2	8.3	7.9	7.0
.1	.1	.1	Deferred Taxes	.9	.1	.0	.2	.1	.1
4.1	4.8	4.5	All Other Non-Current	6.8	3.7	-14.3	6.6	4.7	3.6
18.0	21.9	22.0	Net Worth	22.1	4.1	10.8	21.1	19.7	24.4
100.0	100.0	100.0	Total Liabilities & Net Worth	100.0	100.0	100.0	100.0	100.0	100.0
			INCOME DATA						
100.0	100.0	100.0	Net Sales	100.0	100.0	100.0	100.0	100.0	100.0
13.4	14.0	13.1	Gross Profit	36.8	22.1	17.6	14.1	12.9	12.4
14.2	14.3	12.9	Operating Expenses	31.0	21.0	20.0	14.9	13.2	11.7
-.8	-.3	.3	Operating Profit	5.9	1.0	-2.3	-.7	-.3	.8
-.6	-.9	-1.0	All Other Expenses (net)	1.7	.1	-1.2	-.9	-1.2	-1.0
-.2	.6	1.3	Profit Before Taxes	4.2	.9	-1.1	.1	.9	1.8
			RATIOS						
1.3	1.4	1.4		2.2	1.7	1.7	1.6	1.4	1.4
1.1	1.2	1.2	Current	1.2	1.3	1.3	1.3	1.2	1.2
1.0	1.1	1.1		.4	1.0	1.0	1.1	1.1	1.1
.3	.4	.4		.5	.6	.4	.4	.4	.5
(2657) .2	(2688) .3	(2478) .3	Quick	.2	.2	(46) .2	(210) .2	(772) .2	(1391) .3
.1	.2	.2		.0	.1	.1	.1	.2	.2
3 131.5	3 114.4	3 118.5		0 UND	2 209.5	2 164.7	2 154.4	3 132.2	4 104.2
5 68.1	6 63.5	6 64.4	Sales/Receivables	6 56.8	12 30.4	5 68.5	5 76.3	5 71.2	6 61.2
9 38.7	10 36.1	10 37.4		14 25.9	31 11.7	11 31.8	9 39.2	9 39.7	10 37.5
60 6.0	51 7.2	54 6.8		0 UND	64 5.7	73 5.0	67 5.4	60 6.1	50 7.3
77 4.7	66 5.6	68 5.4	Cost of Sales/Inventory	54 6.8	106 3.4	105 3.5	92 4.0	76 4.8	62 5.9
99 3.7	85 4.3	87 4.2		732 .5	219 1.7	140 2.6	122 3.0	95 3.9	75 4.9
2 201.8	2 165.4	2 163.2		4 86.7	1 395.4	2 156.1	2 198.8	2 169.6	2 159.6
3 113.9	4 95.6	4 94.1	Cost of Sales/Payables	34 10.9	9 42.2	6 60.1	4 89.6	4 91.3	4 98.8
6 66.1	7 56.0	6 57.6		101 3.6	28 13.1	17 21.6	8 44.5	7 54.9	6 64.1
17.4	14.0	14.7		.9	5.1	6.9	9.3	14.8	16.6
34.7	26.8	26.9	Sales/Working Capital	15.5	13.4	13.1	16.6	25.2	29.6
230.1	99.1	69.5		-1.3	206.7	552.3	65.6	61.5	73.9
3.2	6.3	9.8			10.9	2.6	3.5	5.9	14.8
(1975) 1.2	(1830) 2.3	(1650) 3.4	EBIT/Interest	(32) 1.5	(31) .7	(150) 1.7	(528) 2.6	(902) 4.9	
-.4	.8	1.5		-2.6	-2.7	.3	1.1	2.2	
3.7	4.3	8.6						9.0	8.6
(145) 1.6	(157) 1.8	(154) 3.0	Net Profit + Depr., Dep., Amort./Cur. Mat. L/T/D				(38) 2.5	(107) 3.1	
.4	.5	1.2						1.2	1.3
.2	.1	.1		.1	.0	.2	.1	.1	.1
.5	.4	.4	Fixed/Worth	.6	.7	.7	.3	.4	.4
2.2	1.8	1.2		NM	4.5	-2.2	2.0	1.5	1.0
2.8	2.1	2.2		2.2	2.1	1.9	1.8	2.4	2.1
5.4	4.3	4.2	Debt/Worth	3.2	6.2	5.7	3.8	4.7	4.0
18.4	12.6	10.7		NM	UND	-20.7	24.6	14.4	8.7
24.6	34.5	43.7	% Profit Before Taxes/Tangible Net Worth	26.7	50.8	21.7	19.2	34.7	50.7
(2203) 6.2	(2283) 14.3	(2174) 22.1		(11) 2.7	(34) 7.4	(35) 2.1	(170) 7.4	(649) 16.1	(1275) 28.3
-9.3	1.0	7.0		-3.1	-11.4	-11.5	-3.3	2.9	13.5
4.0	6.9	8.2	% Profit Before Taxes/Total Assets	6.6	5.3	2.6	4.4	6.0	9.6
.5	2.7	4.2		.6	.1	-.7	1.1	3.0	5.6
-3.2	-.4	1.1		-1.1	-5.0	-6.6	-1.9	.1	2.6
129.0	130.2	158.9		47.1	227.9	129.5	183.1	163.5	154.3
60.4	57.4	65.1	Sales/Net Fixed Assets	13.3	23.0	54.9	72.3	72.1	63.2
25.4	23.2	26.4		.9	9.3	16.8	30.0	27.9	27.2
4.1	4.3	4.3		1.4	3.0	3.0	3.9	4.2	4.5
3.3	3.4	3.5	Sales/Total Assets	.7	1.8	2.4	3.0	3.4	3.7
2.6	2.6	2.7		.2	.8	1.7	2.2	2.7	3.0
.2	.2	.1			.2	.2	.1	.1	.1
(2297) .3	(2319) .3	(2099) .3	% Depr., Dep., Amort./Sales		(24) .5	(34) .4	(159) .3	(638) .3	(1236) .3
.5	.6	.5			1.0	.8	.5	.5	.5
.3	.3	.3			.8	.5	.5	.4	.3
(1558) .5	(1541) .6	(1468) .6	% Officers', Directors' Owners' Comp/Sales		(20) 1.9	(21) 1.5	(114) .9	(491) .7	(819) .5
1.0	1.2	1.2			3.5	2.3	1.6	1.2	.9
118960218M	107537821M	112010036M	Net Sales ($)	7472M	94185M	196124M	1663377M	13509307M	96539571M
36681715M	34551873M	34185159M	Total Assets ($)	40054M	98507M	110454M	687567M	4401475M	28847102M

M = $ thousand   MM = $ million
See Pages 9 through 22 for Explanation of Ratios and Data

Current Data Sorted by Assets   Comparative Historical Data

Type of Statement	0-500M	500M-2MM	2-10MM	10-50MM	50-100MM	100-250MM	4/1/06-3/31/07 ALL	4/1/07-3/31/08 ALL
Unqualified			6	5	2	1	17	20
Reviewed	1	6	21	5	1		43	25
Compiled	19	54	28	4		1	119	102
Tax Returns	71	120	42	2			256	212
Other	17	61	66	11	2		188	189
	46 (4/1-9/30/10)			500 (10/1/10-3/31/11)				
NUMBER OF STATEMENTS	108	241	163	27	5	2	623	548
ASSETS	%	%	%	%	%	%	%	%
Cash & Equivalents	13.0	7.5	5.6	4.5			7.8	7.5
Trade Receivables (net)	4.7	10.4	17.0	42.2			13.9	13.1
Inventory	64.0	64.7	55.8	26.0			59.9	59.1
All Other Current	1.1	1.7	3.2	5.0			2.1	3.8
Total Current	82.8	84.2	81.6	77.8			83.7	83.5
Fixed Assets (net)	11.5	9.7	11.3	11.0			11.1	10.6
Intangibles (net)	1.4	.9	.9	1.0			1.0	.8
All Other Non-Current	4.3	5.1	6.2	10.2			4.1	5.1
Total	100.0	100.0	100.0	100.0			100.0	100.0
LIABILITIES								
Notes Payable-Short Term	39.6	31.8	36.7	40.1			38.7	37.7
Cur. Mat.-L.T.D.	6.3	3.5	1.8	1.9			3.2	3.2
Trade Payables	6.2	6.9	5.7	3.3			5.3	5.6
Income Taxes Payable	.1	.1	.2	.0			.2	.1
All Other Current	9.0	14.2	12.7	8.1			10.3	10.8
Total Current	61.2	56.5	57.1	53.4			57.7	57.4
Long-Term Debt	14.2	11.0	11.7	11.5			11.4	11.7
Deferred Taxes	.0	.0	.0	.0			.1	.0
All Other Non-Current	11.6	15.8	7.7	4.8			8.3	8.2
Net Worth	13.0	16.6	23.5	30.3			22.4	22.7
Total Liabilities & Net Worth	100.0	100.0	100.0	100.0			100.0	100.0
INCOME DATA								
Net Sales	100.0	100.0	100.0	100.0			100.0	100.0
Gross Profit	21.6	18.4	20.0	30.9			19.2	19.6
Operating Expenses	20.4	16.5	17.0	25.9			17.0	17.4
Operating Profit	1.2	1.9	3.0	5.0			2.2	2.2
All Other Expenses (net)	.1	.7	.5	.6			.7	.8
Profit Before Taxes	1.1	1.2	2.5	4.5			1.5	1.4
RATIOS								
Current	3.3	2.9	1.9	2.0			2.4	2.3
	1.5	1.6	1.4	1.3			1.3	1.4
	1.0	1.1	1.1	1.1			1.1	1.1
Quick	.6	.7	.7	1.3			.8	.7
	(106) .2	(236) .2	(162) .2	.8		(620)	.2	(546) .2
	.1	.1	.1	.2			.1	.1
Sales/Receivables	0 UND	0 UND	1 266.0	5 72.4			0 UND	0 UND
	0 UND	2 148.5	5 76.4	89 4.1			3 111.9	3 117.3
	3 130.6	8 47.0	15 23.8	322 1.1			12 29.4	15 24.8
Cost of Sales/Inventory	35 10.5	45 8.1	46 7.9	41 8.9			40 9.2	41 8.9
	55 6.7	64 5.7	68 5.4	61 6.0			62 5.9	65 5.6
	95 3.8	100 3.6	103 3.6	80 4.5			93 3.9	97 3.8
Cost of Sales/Payables	0 UND	0 999.8	1 298.6	2 183.4			0 UND	0 UND
	0 UND	2 158.8	3 115.6	7 53.5			2 174.3	2 172.2
	5 74.2	7 54.0	11 34.0	15 25.2			7 55.3	7 49.2
Sales/Working Capital	8.4	8.2	6.9	2.8			7.9	6.9
	19.6	16.0	15.7	7.0			18.9	18.9
	-336.8	63.9	41.9	38.1			87.2	77.1
EBIT/Interest	8.1	6.1	5.3	4.5			3.8	4.5
	(88) 2.5	(210) 2.2	(145) 2.9	2.7			(542) 1.8	(485) 1.9
	.0	.9	1.5	1.7			1.0	1.0
Net Profit + Depr., Dep., Amort./Cur. Mat. L/T/D							5.0	11.8
							(24) 1.7	(16) 2.0
							.8	1.0
Fixed/Worth	.0	.0	.0	.1			.0	.0
	.5	.2	.2	.3			.3	.2
	-1.1	2.4	.9	.9			1.7	1.4
Debt/Worth	.9	1.3	1.5	1.6			1.4	1.5
	8.7	4.0	3.5	2.8			4.2	3.9
	-6.0	64.9	8.1	5.6			18.2	16.0
% Profit Before Taxes/Tangible Net Worth	100.0	53.1	45.5	34.0			56.6	48.1
	(70) 29.3	(186) 20.7	(141) 20.8	(25) 26.0			(525) 21.2	(461) 20.2
	-.2	3.0	9.0	15.9			3.7	3.8
% Profit Before Taxes/Total Assets	19.4	12.7	9.8	10.1			10.8	12.2
	6.5	4.3	4.4	6.1			4.2	3.9
	-4.8	-.1	1.4	2.9			.1	.1
Sales/Net Fixed Assets	999.8	605.4	340.4	94.3			461.7	526.3
	143.9	122.1	79.1	36.5			94.7	97.5
	31.9	38.7	22.7	15.0			26.1	25.1
Sales/Total Assets	7.9	6.2	4.8	3.3			6.3	5.9
	5.1	4.3	3.3	1.1			4.2	3.8
	3.1	2.7	1.8	.8			2.5	2.4
% Depr., Dep., Amort./Sales	.1	.1	.1	.2			.1	.1
	(60) .3	(167) .2	(107) .3	(23) .3			(440) .2	(367) .3
	.6	.5	.6	.7			.5	.5
% Officers', Directors' Owners' Comp/Sales	1.4	1.0	.6				.8	.8
	(56) 2.8	(135) 1.7	(94) 1.3				(344) 1.5	(301) 1.6
	3.9	2.7	2.8				3.0	3.0
Net Sales ($)	181629M	1275728M	2277612M	1248267M	591128M	1802454M	9367490M	7942528M
Total Assets ($)	28750M	263492M	649384M	638456M	371639M	399811M	2910959M	2621151M

M = $ thousand   MM = $ million
See Pages 9 through 22 for Explanation of Ratios and Data

Comparative Historical Data | | | | Current Data Sorted by Sales

			Type of Statement						
17	25	14	Unqualified				1	4	9
27	35	34	Reviewed		3	3	9	14	5
108	99	105	Compiled	6	23	30	27	16	3
224	235	236	Tax Returns	34	77	35	48	36	6
192	147	157	Other	9	26	31	30	38	23
4/1/08-3/31/09 ALL	4/1/09-3/31/10 ALL	4/1/10-3/31/11 ALL		0-1MM	1-3MM 46 (4/1-9/30/10)	3-5MM	5-10MM 500 (10/1/10-3/31/11)	10-25MM	25MM & OVER
568	541	546	**NUMBER OF STATEMENTS**	49	129	99	115	108	46
%	%	%	**ASSETS**	%	%	%	%	%	%
7.7	8.3	7.8	Cash & Equivalents	11.9	8.6	5.2	8.5	7.0	7.1
14.3	15.1	13.3	Trade Receivables (net)	8.5	13.4	15.3	10.5	12.1	23.1
56.8	57.5	59.4	Inventory	51.7	59.2	63.8	65.7	57.2	48.5
2.6	2.6	2.2	All Other Current	.8	1.7	1.2	2.3	3.9	2.7
81.5	83.6	82.7	Total Current	72.9	83.0	85.5	87.0	80.4	81.3
11.8	10.2	10.7	Fixed Assets (net)	18.1	9.9	10.2	8.8	11.1	10.1
1.1	1.2	1.1	Intangibles (net)	1.8	1.8	.7	.5	.6	1.2
5.7	5.0	5.5	All Other Non-Current	7.2	5.4	3.5	3.7	7.9	7.3
100.0	100.0	100.0	Total	100.0	100.0	100.0	100.0	100.0	100.0
			LIABILITIES						
42.3	39.8	35.4	Notes Payable-Short Term	25.3	37.1	31.0	40.1	35.5	38.5
2.2	3.6	3.4	Cur. Mat.-L.T.D.	1.7	5.6	5.0	2.1	2.5	1.4
5.0	5.2	6.2	Trade Payables	6.3	4.4	7.6	6.6	6.6	6.2
.1	.1	.1	Income Taxes Payable	.2	.1	.2	.1	.1	.0
12.3	12.7	12.3	All Other Current	7.7	7.7	17.7	13.6	15.0	9.2
61.9	61.3	57.5	Total Current	41.3	55.0	61.5	62.5	59.7	55.3
11.7	11.8	12.0	Long-Term Debt	21.1	15.0	9.5	9.2	8.6	14.1
.0	.1	.0	Deferred Taxes	.0	.0	.0	.0	.0	.0
8.5	11.3	11.8	All Other Non-Current	19.9	12.9	13.9	10.0	10.3	4.0
17.9	15.6	18.7	Net Worth	17.7	17.0	15.1	18.3	21.4	26.6
100.0	100.0	100.0	Total Liabilties & Net Worth	100.0	100.0	100.0	100.0	100.0	100.0
			INCOME DATA						
100.0	100.0	100.0	Net Sales	100.0	100.0	100.0	100.0	100.0	100.0
20.2	20.2	20.4	Gross Profit	30.0	22.3	20.0	17.8	16.9	20.3
18.5	18.6	18.1	Operating Expenses	29.9	19.3	17.5	15.4	15.2	16.6
1.7	1.6	2.3	Operating Profit	.1	3.1	2.5	2.4	1.7	3.7
.9	.8	.5	All Other Expenses (net)	.1	.8	1.0	.5	-.1	.7
.8	.8	1.8	Profit Before Taxes	.0	2.3	1.5	1.9	1.8	2.9
			RATIOS						
2.1	2.4	2.5	Current	6.1	3.7	2.7	2.0	1.7	1.8
1.3	1.4	1.4		2.2	1.6	1.5	1.4	1.3	1.4
1.0	1.1	1.1		1.2	1.0	1.1	1.1	1.1	1.2
.8	.7	.8	Quick	1.8	1.5	.7	.5	.4	1.2
(566) .2	(538) .3	(538) .3		.4 (128)	.3 (95)	.2 (114)	.2 (106)	.2	.4
.1	.1	.1		.1	.1	.1	.1	.1	.2
0 UND	0 UND	0 UND	Sales/Receivables	0 UND	0 UND	0 999.8	0 999.8	0 999.8	2 179.6
3 138.4	3 119.8	3 127.4		0 UND	2 239.5	4 97.7	2 170.0	4 100.0	8 46.8
14 26.5	15 25.1	11 34.5		12 29.6	10 35.7	13 28.6	8 47.2	8 44.9	19 19.2
40 9.0	43 8.5	43 8.4	Cost of Sales/Inventory	46 7.9	47 7.8	45 8.2	44 8.3	38 9.5	33 11.1
65 5.6	65 5.6	63 5.8		102 3.6	75 4.9	67 5.4	62 5.9	58 6.3	51 7.2
101 3.6	100 3.6	97 3.8		171 2.1	109 3.4	109 3.4	92 4.0	74 5.0	66 5.5
0 UND	0 UND	0 UND	Cost of Sales/Payables	0 UND	0 UND	0 999.8	1 604.7	1 467.2	2 199.0
2 167.9	2 181.9	2 154.2		0 UND	1 252.8	3 110.5	3 111.2	2 157.1	5 67.6
7 53.2	7 52.0	7 49.5		7 54.0	5 70.4	13 27.2	7 51.6	7 53.8	12 30.7
7.1	6.7	7.3	Sales/Working Capital	3.0	4.5	7.9	8.7	13.3	6.7
19.6	15.9	15.9		8.0	12.7	15.7	15.4	26.7	16.9
214.4	102.0	58.2		19.2	UND	59.9	65.1	58.1	49.6
4.0	4.9	5.6	EBIT/Interest	8.1	5.2	7.5	5.2	5.6	10.5
(491) 1.5	(472) 2.1	(476) 2.6		(37) 1.3	(110) 2.3	(88) 2.1	(105) 2.4	(93) 2.8	(43) 3.9
.1	.7	1.1		-3.8	.8	.7	1.3	1.5	1.9
14.1	6.4	9.9	Net Profit + Depr., Dep., Amort./Cur. Mat. L/T/D						
(16) 3.1	(21) 3.4	(16) 2.8							
.9	.5	.5							
.0	.0	.0	Fixed/Worth	.0	.0	.1	.0	.1	.0
.3	.3	.2		.4	.2	.3	.3	.3	.2
3.8	4.0	2.2		-3.9	10.1	2.9	1.4	1.0	.7
1.6	1.4	1.4	Debt/Worth	.8	1.3	1.3	1.6	1.5	1.6
4.3	4.1	3.9		4.0	4.1	4.1	3.8	4.2	3.3
33.7	189.5	40.4		-5.1	796.4	-288.5	37.8	10.6	6.6
39.9	39.4	52.4	% Profit Before Taxes/Tangible Net Worth	47.2	56.5	47.4	47.6	51.6	54.9
(445) 13.9	(414) 17.7	(428) 23.0		(32) 25.6	(98) 17.1	(74) 19.3	(91) 23.0	(92) 24.3	(41) 29.1
-5.3	2.8	6.3		-9.3	1.1	5.3	6.5	9.6	17.6
8.9	9.1	12.3	% Profit Before Taxes/Total Assets	14.1	12.8	11.6	12.7	10.8	15.2
2.2	3.9	4.8		.0	5.2	3.3	4.4	5.2	7.3
-4.0	-.8	.2		-9.3	-.1	-.3	1.3	1.3	2.7
408.0	463.8	462.2	Sales/Net Fixed Assets	UND	999.8	541.3	366.4	355.7	394.0
79.5	90.7	96.9		44.3	127.5	88.2	106.6	96.8	76.5
23.7	26.1	27.2		6.1	28.6	27.5	38.6	26.8	21.7
5.5	5.3	5.8	Sales/Total Assets	4.0	5.2	5.9	6.2	6.5	7.1
3.5	3.6	4.0		1.9	3.7	3.7	4.5	4.5	4.5
2.2	2.1	2.3		1.1	2.2	2.4	2.7	3.1	1.7
.1	.1	.1	% Depr., Dep., Amort./Sales	.5	.1	.1	.1	.1	.1
(383) .3	(372) .3	(362) .3		(26) 1.1	(82) .3	(68) .3	(79) .2	(73) .2	(34) .3
.6	.7	.6		2.9	.5	.6	.5	.5	.7
.8	.9	.8	% Officers', Directors' Owners' Comp/Sales	2.7	1.3	.8	1.1	.6	.3
(295) 1.7	(294) 1.8	(292) 1.7		(16) 6.1	(82) 2.6	(45) 1.5	(67) 1.7	(61) 1.0	(21) .5
3.5	3.2	3.2		14.1	3.5	3.5	2.5		2.6
6177684M	9299312M	7376818M	Net Sales ($)	23632M	253893M	386047M	821193M	1640421M	4251632M
2311390M	2945039M	2351532M	Total Assets ($)	16584M	100275M	132630M	240009M	512869M	1349165M

M = $ thousand   MM = $ million
See Pages 9 through 22 for Explanation of Ratios and Data

Current Data Sorted by Assets   Comparative Historical Data

0-500M	500M-2MM	2-10MM	10-50MM	50-100MM	100-250MM	Type of Statement	6 4/1/06-3/31/07 ALL	9 4/1/07-3/31/08 ALL
	6	3 34	6 14		1	Unqualified	6	9
2	34	48	6			Reviewed	45	52
12	41	46	6			Compiled	89	96
5	21	53	18	3		Tax Returns	78	74
	42 (4/1-9/30/10)		317 (10/1/10-3/31/11)			Other	123	123
19	102	184	50	3	1	**NUMBER OF STATEMENTS**	341	354
%	%	%	%	%	%	**ASSETS**	%	%
9.6	8.2	7.7	10.5			Cash & Equivalents	7.2	6.0
8.1	1.9	2.9	4.8			Trade Receivables (net)	2.7	2.8
58.7	75.6	73.6	65.8			Inventory	76.2	77.4
.8	.5	.5	.5			All Other Current	.8	.8
77.2	86.3	84.8	81.6			Total Current	86.9	87.0
19.4	9.7	9.9	11.5			Fixed Assets (net)	9.7	8.9
.9	1.7	3.2	4.6			Intangibles (net)	1.9	2.5
2.5	2.3	2.1	2.4			All Other Non-Current	1.5	1.6
100.0	100.0	100.0	100.0			Total	100.0	100.0
						LIABILITIES		
21.2	47.0	49.7	43.4			Notes Payable-Short Term	51.9	55.9
3.6	3.4	2.1	1.5			Cur. Mat.-L.T.D.	2.5	1.8
8.3	7.5	5.4	8.6			Trade Payables	6.4	6.5
.0	.1	.1	.1			Income Taxes Payable	.1	.1
24.9	7.1	7.7	6.9			All Other Current	7.7	5.9
58.0	65.0	65.0	60.5			Total Current	68.6	70.2
23.6	8.2	7.1	6.8			Long-Term Debt	6.4	6.9
.0	.0	.0	.0			Deferred Taxes	.0	.0
19.9	7.7	5.0	3.6			All Other Non-Current	3.5	3.0
-1.5	19.1	22.9	29.1			Net Worth	21.5	20.0
100.0	100.0	100.0	100.0			Total Liabilities & Net Worth	100.0	100.0
						INCOME DATA		
100.0	100.0	100.0	100.0			Net Sales	100.0	100.0
27.1	21.5	20.3	18.7			Gross Profit	20.8	20.1
25.0	20.6	17.6	16.0			Operating Expenses	18.3	17.5
2.2	.9	2.6	2.6			Operating Profit	2.5	2.6
.8	1.2	.9	.4			All Other Expenses (net)	1.5	1.9
1.4	-.3	1.7	2.2			Profit Before Taxes	.9	.8
						RATIOS		
1.9	1.8	1.6	1.5				1.4	1.3
1.3	1.3	1.3	1.3			Current	1.2	1.2
1.0	1.1	1.1	1.2				1.1	1.1
.5	.2	.2	.3				.2	.2
.2	.1	.1	.2			Quick	.1	.1
.1	.0	.1	.1				.0	.0
0 UND	0 UND	1 610.9	1 314.7				0 999.8	1 711.0
5 79.9	1 471.6	3 141.6	4 83.4			Sales/Receivables	2 211.6	2 172.3
5 67.3	3 104.5	6 65.3	10 37.6				4 85.1	5 73.8
31 11.9	115 3.2	103 3.6	109 3.4				110 3.3	117 3.1
86 4.3	153 2.4	141 2.6	131 2.8			Cost of Sales/Inventory	147 2.5	152 2.4
123 3.0	196 1.9	179 2.0	171 2.1				203 1.8	195 1.9
0 UND	0 999.8	1 245.7	3 112.1				1 410.4	1 359.6
2 206.0	2 153.3	4 103.1	8 47.0			Cost of Sales/Payables	3 114.9	4 102.9
12 29.9	9 41.7	8 44.4	16 22.7				9 41.3	8 43.3
13.5	5.4	7.7	8.0				8.5	10.7
34.8	12.8	13.2	11.7			Sales/Working Capital	17.0	20.0
-127.9	41.8	31.2	18.2				36.9	43.9
3.3	2.8	4.1	4.9				2.4	1.9
(18) 1.4	(98) 1.5	(175) 2.0	(48) 2.3			EBIT/Interest	(317) 1.4	(339) 1.3
-1.0	.4	1.1	1.3				.9	.9
						Net Profit + Depr., Dep.,	17.9	8.1
						Amort./Cur. Mat. L/T/D	(28) 6.0	(34) 2.2
							2.9	.1
.6	.1	.1	.1				.1	.1
-7.4	.3	.3	.3			Fixed/Worth	.3	.3
-.3	3.6	1.2	.9				1.1	1.1
1.8	1.6	1.9	2.1				2.5	3.0
-10.8	3.7	3.9	3.4			Debt/Worth	5.2	5.4
-6.4	85.7	9.3	5.4				11.5	13.3
	22.4	39.8	48.6			% Profit Before Taxes/Tangible	30.9	28.9
(79) 8.8	(158) 18.5	(48) 15.3				Net Worth	(307) 11.0	(318) 8.8
	-4.7	2.8	4.2				.0	-1.4
9.0	6.0	7.7	8.1			% Profit Before Taxes/Total	5.7	4.2
3.2	1.5	3.2	3.6			Assets	2.1	1.5
-6.6	-2.1	.5	1.6				-.4	-.7
132.5	106.9	184.5	96.5				142.4	137.0
43.9	48.7	58.7	40.5			Sales/Net Fixed Assets	52.8	56.3
8.3	23.5	20.3	15.6				20.6	21.4
5.5	3.0	3.1	2.6				3.0	2.9
4.4	2.4	2.4	2.3			Sales/Total Assets	2.3	2.4
2.2	1.9	1.9	1.9				1.7	1.8
.5	.2	.2	.3				.2	.2
(15) 1.3	(75) .5	(148) .4	(46) .4			% Depr., Dep., Amort./Sales	(269) .4	(281) .4
1.8	.9	.8	.9				.8	.7
1.3	1.4	.8	.6				.9	.9
(11) 1.9	(66) 2.8	(113) 1.3	(22) 1.1			% Officers', Directors' Owners' Comp/Sales	(190) 1.9	(197) 1.7
3.6	2.8	2.0	1.6				3.3	3.0
21737M	318931M	2148934M	2111947M	317008M	453276M	Net Sales ($)	8876393M	7492176M
5765M	124949M	840870M	944431M	201656M	157569M	Total Assets ($)	2568536M	3193218M

M = $ thousand   MM = $ million
See Pages 9 through 22 for Explanation of Ratios and Data

Comparative Historical Data | Current Data Sorted by Sales

11	12	10	Type of Statement						
52	42	54	Unqualified				1	2	7
106	108	90	Reviewed		3	3	12	24	12
96	81	105	Compiled	2	25	10	21	25	7
158	154	100	Tax Returns	9	22	20	28	20	6
4/1/08-3/31/09	4/1/09-3/31/10	4/1/10-3/31/11	Other	5	13	15	20	25	22
ALL	ALL	ALL		0-1MM	42 (4/1-9/30/10) 1-3MM	3-5MM	317 (10/1/10-3/31/11) 5-10MM	10-25MM	25MM & OVER
423	397	359	**NUMBER OF STATEMENTS**	16	63	48	82	96	54
%	%	%	**ASSETS**	%	%	%	%	%	%
6.3	9.0	8.3	Cash & Equivalents	13.4	9.5	6.5	6.7	8.0	10.2
2.7	2.9	3.2	Trade Receivables (net)	5.9	2.4	1.9	2.8	2.3	6.4
75.8	71.3	72.0	Inventory	54.2	73.1	74.4	74.8	74.7	64.8
.5	.7	.5	All Other Current	.0	.6	.7	.4	.6	.5
85.4	84.0	84.0	Total Current	73.5	85.6	83.5	84.7	85.6	81.9
10.0	10.8	10.8	Fixed Assets (net)	18.2	12.5	9.8	9.8	10.1	10.3
3.1	3.1	3.0	Intangibles (net)	1.4	1.0	3.1	4.1	1.9	5.7
1.6	2.1	2.2	All Other Non-Current	6.9	.9	3.6	1.4	2.3	2.0
100.0	100.0	100.0	Total	100.0	100.0	100.0	100.0	100.0	100.0
			LIABILITIES						
53.9	45.8	46.4	Notes Payable-Short Term	17.2	41.5	43.9	51.1	52.8	44.1
2.0	3.2	2.5	Cur. Mat.-L.T.D.	3.8	3.1	2.1	3.2	1.9	1.5
4.9	6.3	6.6	Trade Payables	9.8	7.0	7.2	7.0	4.9	6.9
.1	.1	.1	Income Taxes Payable	.0	.0	.0	.1	.1	.1
7.9	8.0	8.3	All Other Current	13.4	7.4	11.3	8.1	7.2	7.6
68.8	63.4	63.8	Total Current	44.3	59.0	64.5	69.5	66.9	60.3
9.2	9.7	8.3	Long-Term Debt	17.4	14.7	8.2	6.5	5.4	5.8
.0	.0	.0	Deferred Taxes	.0	.0	.0	.0	.1	.0
2.9	4.5	6.3	All Other Non-Current	7.3	12.7	5.4	4.3	5.4	4.4
19.0	22.3	21.6	Net Worth	31.0	13.5	21.8	19.8	22.2	29.4
100.0	100.0	100.0	Total Liabilities & Net Worth	100.0	100.0	100.0	100.0	100.0	100.0
			INCOME DATA						
100.0	100.0	100.0	Net Sales	100.0	100.0	100.0	100.0	100.0	100.0
21.2	21.4	20.8	Gross Profit	29.3	22.5	19.6	21.1	20.0	18.3
20.7	20.9	18.7	Operating Expenses	28.2	21.6	18.7	18.2	17.2	15.5
.5	.4	2.1	Operating Profit	1.1	.9	.8	2.8	2.8	2.7
1.7	1.3	.9	All Other Expenses (net)	.9	1.2	1.4	1.0	.8	.5
-1.2	-.8	1.2	Profit Before Taxes	.1	-.4	-.5	1.9	2.0	2.2
			RATIOS						
1.4 / 1.2 / 1.1	1.6 / 1.3 / 1.1	1.6 / 1.3 / 1.1	Current	4.1 / 1.5 / 1.1	2.0 / 1.4 / 1.1	1.8 / 1.3 / 1.0	1.5 / 1.2 / 1.1	1.5 / 1.2 / 1.1	1.5 / 1.3 / 1.2
.2 / (421) .1 / .0	.3 / .1 / .1	.3 / .1 / .1	Quick	.9 / .4 / .1	.3 / .1 / .1	.2 / .1 / .0	.2 / .1 / .1	.2 / .1 / .1	.3 / .2 / .1
0 929.6 / 2 164.1 / 6 61.1	0 999.8 / 2 172.9 / 6 64.8	0 999.8 / 2 185.6 / 5 67.1	Sales/Receivables	0 UND / 1 574.0 / 5 69.1	0 UND / 1 406.0 / 5 78.4	0 999.8 / 1 252.4 / 6 66.0	0 999.8 / 1 249.4 / 5 77.3	1 473.5 / 2 171.0 / 5 69.1	1 259.2 / 4 88.4 / 10 37.6
121 3.0 / 173 2.1 / 236 1.5	109 3.4 / 148 2.5 / 210 1.7	104 3.5 / 140 2.6 / 181 2.0	Cost of Sales/Inventory	106 3.4 / 173 2.1 / 292 1.3	117 3.1 / 168 2.2 / 217 1.7	115 3.2 / 153 2.4 / 193 1.9	100 3.6 / 141 2.6 / 188 1.9	99 3.7 / 136 2.7 / 160 2.3	95 3.8 / 125 2.9 / 151 2.4
1 429.6 / 3 125.1 / 8 46.9	1 319.8 / 4 100.8 / 11 34.1	1 262.5 / 4 95.9 / 10 35.8	Cost of Sales/Payables	0 UND / 2 184.2 / 22 16.6	0 999.8 / 2 154.0 / 8 46.1	1 293.2 / 4 85.8 / 15 24.5	1 361.1 / 3 122.5 / 7 49.1	2 234.3 / 4 95.8 / 10 36.0	3 123.1 / 7 55.7 / 11 33.2
8.1 / 15.6 / 48.1	6.3 / 12.5 / 30.0	7.3 / 13.2 / 32.9	Sales/Working Capital	2.0 / 11.8 / 39.8	4.6 / 10.0 / 26.1	5.4 / 12.0 / 109.1	7.7 / 13.5 / 87.8	9.7 / 15.1 / 32.9	9.5 / 12.6 / 20.2
1.9 / (398) 1.1 / -.1	2.7 / (377) 1.1 / .1	3.5 / (343) 1.8 / 1.0	EBIT/Interest	2.7 / (13) 1.5 / -.6	2.8 / (59) 1.4 / .0	2.0 / (79) 1.1 / .4	3.7 / (90) 1.9 / 1.2	5.4 / 2.2 / 1.2	6.0 / 3.0 / 1.5
8.7 / (27) 1.7 / .0	4.8 / (19) 1.4 / .0	3.7 / (19) 1.2 / -8.5	Net Profit + Depr., Dep., Amort./Cur. Mat. L/T/D						
.1 / .3 / 1.6	.1 / .3 / 1.5	.1 / .3 / 1.5	Fixed/Worth	.1 / .6 / -2.5	.1 / .5 / 91.7	.1 / .4 / -4.0	.1 / .3 / 1.8	.1 / .2 / .8	.1 / .3 / .7
2.6 / 5.2 / 15.5	1.9 / 3.8 / 11.3	1.8 / 3.8 / 12.3	Debt/Worth	.9 / 2.0 / -12.9	1.7 / 3.7 / -97.3	1.4 / 3.5 / -69.6	2.2 / 3.9 / 9.1	2.2 / 4.3 / 9.1	2.0 / 3.4 / 5.4
18.4 / (358) 3.2 / -16.4	23.2 / (332) 5.0 / -9.9	35.3 / (297) 13.8 / 1.6	% Profit Before Taxes/Tangible Net Worth	39.8 / (11) 14.6 / -4.7	18.6 / (47) 6.0 / -4.6	11.4 / (33) .0 / -9.0	34.6 / (68) 16.4 / 5.0	49.8 / (86) 18.6 / 3.9	50.6 / (52) 22.3 / 4.7
3.1 / .2 / -4.5	4.5 / .4 / -9.9	7.1 / 3.0 / 1.6	% Profit Before Taxes/Total Assets	5.8 / 1.6 / -2.7	5.9 / 1.9 / -3.7	4.3 / .4 / -2.0	6.9 / 2.9 / .9	10.2 / 4.5 / .9	10.8 / 4.1 / 1.0
142.5 / 52.5 / 16.9	132.9 / 42.3 / 13.6	138.3 / 49.5 / 20.0	Sales/Net Fixed Assets	48.7 / 17.2 / 4.7	132.5 / 43.7 / 13.0	108.0 / 46.8 / 18.1	113.7 / 50.1 / 24.2	216.0 / 67.5 / 19.5	150.7 / 54.8 / 31.3
2.7 / 2.1 / 1.5	2.9 / 2.2 / 1.6	3.0 / 2.4 / 1.9	Sales/Total Assets	3.1 / 1.8 / .9	2.7 / 2.2 / 1.5	2.7 / 2.3 / 1.7	3.1 / 2.4 / 1.9	3.3 / 2.6 / 2.1	3.0 / 2.5 / 2.1
.2 / (323) .5 / .9	.3 / (300) .5 / 1.2	.2 / (288) .4 / 1.0	% Depr., Dep., Amort./Sales	.5 / (13) 1.4 / 2.7	.3 / (44) .7 / 1.0	.2 / (36) .5 / 1.0	.2 / (66) .4 / .8	.2 / (79) .3 / .7	.2 / (50) .4 / .7
.8 / (233) 1.6 / 2.8	.9 / (228) 1.8 / 3.2	.9 / (213) 1.6 / 2.9	% Officers', Directors' Owners' Comp/Sales		1.5 / (42) 3.1 / 4.7	1.2 / (31) 2.0 /	.8 / (52) 1.8 /	.7 / (56) 1.1 /	.5 / (25) 1.0 / 1.6
7551120M	5583622M	5371833M	Net Sales ($)	10471M	127819M	185080M	574582M	1500765M	2973116M
3637674M	2440040M	2275240M	Total Assets ($)	8398M	67248M	94049M	246953M	606305M	1252287M

© RMA 2011
M = $ thousand   MM = $ million
See Pages 9 through 22 for Explanation of Ratios and Data

Current Data Sorted by Assets | **Comparative Historical Data**

0-500M	500M-2MM	2-10MM	10-50MM	50-100MM	100-250MM	Type of Statement	4/1/06-3/31/07 ALL	4/1/07-3/31/08 ALL
	2	4	2	1		Unqualified	13	10
	13	30	8			Reviewed	45	43
7	33	46	6			Compiled	78	57
3	16	42	1			Tax Returns	68	86
		76	12	1	1	Other	143	127
	28 (4/1-9/30/10)		275 (10/1/10-3/31/11)					
10	64	198	29	2		NUMBER OF STATEMENTS	347	323
%	%	%	%	%	%	**ASSETS**	%	%
7.1	6.6	8.1	11.1			Cash & Equivalents	6.4	6.2
8.6	4.0	4.0	2.9			Trade Receivables (net)	3.5	3.8
56.2	73.3	58.3	32.7			Inventory	66.6	64.8
.8	.8	1.7	1.5			All Other Current	1.3	1.5
72.7	84.7	72.0	48.1			Total Current	77.8	76.3
21.1	8.1	14.4	29.2			Fixed Assets (net)	13.8	13.8
5.2	4.4	8.9	17.9	D		Intangibles (net)	6.1	7.1
.8	2.8	4.6	4.8	A		All Other Non-Current	2.3	2.8
100.0	100.0	100.0	100.0	T		Total	100.0	100.0
				A		**LIABILITIES**		
41.0	40.2	29.7	17.5			Notes Payable-Short Term	34.2	33.6
5.9	3.2	3.9	1.7	N		Cur. Mat.-L.T.D.	3.4	3.6
17.1	15.3	9.4	5.5	O		Trade Payables	11.1	11.7
.0	.1	.0	.9	T		Income Taxes Payable	.1	.1
20.7	9.0	11.3	5.6			All Other Current	9.3	9.7
84.6	67.8	54.3	31.2	A		Total Current	58.0	58.7
16.7	15.6	9.6	17.4	V		Long-Term Debt	11.8	13.7
.0	.0	.0	.3	A		Deferred Taxes	.1	.0
4.9	8.8	5.9	2.7	I		All Other Non-Current	4.8	4.2
-6.3	7.9	30.2	48.5	L		Net Worth	25.3	23.4
100.0	100.0	100.0	100.0	A		Total Liabilities & Net Worth	100.0	100.0
				B		**INCOME DATA**		
100.0	100.0	100.0	100.0	L		Net Sales	100.0	100.0
31.6	21.8	24.3	27.8	E		Gross Profit	22.2	23.1
32.5	22.8	23.3	24.6			Operating Expenses	19.6	21.0
-.9	-1.0	.9	3.2			Operating Profit	2.6	2.1
.1	.2	.4	.7			All Other Expenses (net)	.6	.5
-.9	-1.2	.5	2.5			Profit Before Taxes	2.1	1.6
						RATIOS		
3.1	1.5	1.8	2.2				1.6	1.6
1.1	1.3	1.3	1.7			Current	1.3	1.3
.6	1.0	1.0	1.2				1.1	1.1
	.2	.3	.7				.3	.3
	.1	.1	.4			Quick	(345) .1	(322) .1
	.1	.1	.1				.1	.1
0 UND	1 521.1	1 287.0	1 481.0				1 289.0	2 213.4
1 628.2	3 109.3	4 91.1	5 75.0			Sales/Receivables	4 99.1	4 95.4
4 91.4	9 41.8	7 49.8	9 40.8				6 56.4	7 51.6
11 33.9	110 3.3	88 4.2	75 4.9				99 3.7	94 3.9
138 2.6	153 2.4	117 3.1	104 3.5			Cost of Sales/Inventory	130 2.8	124 2.9
194 1.9	203 1.8	167 2.2	118 3.1				170 2.1	159 2.3
0 895.7	3 142.9	5 66.4	5 75.4				4 85.4	4 82.6
16 22.8	9 41.0	10 36.5	7 48.8			Cost of Sales/Payables	9 40.6	9 41.9
65 5.6	27 13.3	23 16.0	19 19.4				21 17.2	19 19.3
10.1	6.4	7.3	5.0				8.7	8.5
NM	14.7	13.7	9.0			Sales/Working Capital	14.5	15.0
-4.4	NM	65.8	27.6				29.5	44.8
	2.2	4.6	9.1				5.2	4.5
	(58) 1.0	(184) 1.5	(27) 2.6			EBIT/Interest	(321) 2.1	(293) 1.6
	-.7	.2	1.3				1.0	.8
		2.9				Net Profit + Depr., Dep.,	4.7	11.1
	(12) 1.6					Amort./Cur. Mat. L/T/D	(24) 2.5	(20) 1.5
	.3						.8	.2
.2	.1	.1	.5				.2	.2
NM	.9	.6	1.3			Fixed/Worth	.5	.6
-.3	-.2	2.5	5.1				3.5	4.0
1.2	2.4	1.3	.5				1.8	2.0
-4.8	9.6	3.7	2.3			Debt/Worth	4.2	4.5
-2.5	-7.3	12.7	8.1				22.9	21.6
	16.5	26.8	23.2			% Profit Before Taxes/Tangible	49.4	44.2
	(36) 4.5	(165) 7.1	(23) 10.5			Net Worth	(286) 21.6	(257) 15.7
	-13.7	-5.6	3.1				3.5	1.2
15.6	4.2	5.3	7.7			% Profit Before Taxes/Total	10.7	10.1
-5.6	.1	1.7	3.4			Assets	4.5	2.7
-14.9	-8.5	-1.9	.1				-.1	-.6
280.0	150.6	68.6	42.4				81.5	74.5
29.1	66.4	25.9	13.8			Sales/Net Fixed Assets	29.3	29.5
7.1	28.6	11.9	2.2				13.5	13.1
7.8	3.1	3.1	2.1				3.1	3.2
3.4	2.3	2.1	1.4			Sales/Total Assets	2.3	2.5
1.8	1.6	1.6	1.1				1.8	1.7
	.2	.5	.6				.4	.4
	(44) .3	(165) .7	(26) 1.3			% Depr., Dep., Amort./Sales	(275) .7	(271) .7
	1.0	1.2	3.2				1.2	1.3
	1.4	1.0	1.1				.9	.8
	(37) 2.5	(97) 1.6	(12) 1.4			% Officers', Directors' Owners' Comp/Sales	(176) 1.4	(158) 1.4
	3.9	2.8	2.0				2.8	2.9
18081M	216242M	2045231M	789263M	261258M		Net Sales ($)	4993151M	4427901M
2647M	87161M	916168M	502277M	146062M		Total Assets ($)	2271006M	2021485M

(Columns 50-100MM and 100-250MM: DATA NOT AVAILABLE)

M = $ thousand   MM = $ million
See Pages 9 through 22 for Explanation of Ratios and Data

Comparative Historical Data

Current Data Sorted by Sales

				Type of Statement						
	9	6	7	Unqualified		1	1	2	3	
	35	51	40	Reviewed		2	12	20	6	
	79	90	65	Compiled		6	10	26	21	2
	100	68	83	Tax Returns	3	20	22	23	15	
	132	110	108	Other	4	11	10	40	36	7
	4/1/08-3/31/09 ALL	4/1/09-3/31/10 ALL	4/1/10-3/31/11 ALL			28 (4/1-9/30/10)		275 (10/1/10-3/31/11)		
					0-1MM	1-3MM	3-5MM	5-10MM	10-25MM	25MM & OVER
	355	325	303	NUMBER OF STATEMENTS	7	37	45	102	94	18
	%	%	%	ASSETS	%	%	%	%	%	%
	6.8	7.3	8.0	Cash & Equivalents		6.5	6.9	7.8	9.2	10.3
	4.4	3.7	4.0	Trade Receivables (net)		4.7	4.0	3.6	3.9	7.1
	63.4	61.2	58.9	Inventory		70.3	70.2	57.0	54.2	40.8
	1.3	1.7	1.5	All Other Current		1.0	.7	1.5	2.0	2.2
	75.8	73.9	72.4	Total Current		82.5	81.8	69.9	69.3	60.3
	14.9	14.9	14.7	Fixed Assets (net)		10.8	11.3	15.5	14.5	23.2
	6.0	6.9	8.8	Intangibles (net)		5.3	3.5	8.8	12.0	13.0
	3.2	4.3	4.1	All Other Non-Current		1.5	3.4	5.7	4.2	3.4
	100.0	100.0	100.0	Total		100.0	100.0	100.0	100.0	100.0
				LIABILITIES						
	31.3	32.1	31.1	Notes Payable-Short Term		33.8	44.9	30.1	25.4	23.1
	3.7	4.7	3.6	Cur. Mat.-L.T.D.		4.4	4.9	3.6	2.6	2.8
	12.0	9.4	10.6	Trade Payables		14.7	9.3	9.8	10.5	8.3
	.1	.0	.1	Income Taxes Payable		.0	.0	.3	.0	.0
	11.8	11.1	10.6	All Other Current		11.6	8.5	9.2	11.7	9.6
	58.8	57.3	56.0	Total Current		64.6	67.7	53.0	50.2	43.9
	11.5	13.5	11.8	Long-Term Debt		21.8	11.0	11.3	7.0	18.0
	.0	.0	.1	Deferred Taxes		.0	.0	.0	.1	.3
	3.8	5.2	6.1	All Other Non-Current		9.0	6.7	5.8	6.2	1.9
	25.8	24.0	26.1	Net Worth		4.6	14.6	29.9	36.5	36.9
	100.0	100.0	100.0	Total Liabilties & Net Worth		100.0	100.0	100.0	100.0	100.0
				INCOME DATA						
	100.0	100.0	100.0	Net Sales		100.0	100.0	100.0	100.0	100.0
	23.1	23.8	24.4	Gross Profit		23.1	21.8	24.1	24.9	25.5
	21.7	24.3	23.7	Operating Expenses		23.0	23.7	23.4	22.9	23.4
	1.4	-.5	.7	Operating Profit		.1	-1.9	.8	2.1	2.1
	.4	.7	.4	All Other Expenses (net)		1.0	.0	.8	-.1	.3
	1.0	-1.2	.3	Profit Before Taxes		-.9	-1.9	-.1	2.2	1.8
				RATIOS						
	1.7	1.8	1.8			1.6	1.4	1.8	2.0	2.1
	1.3	1.2	1.3	Current		1.3	1.1	1.3	1.4	1.4
	1.0	1.0	1.0			1.1	1.0	1.0	1.1	1.0
	.3	.3	.4			.2	.2	.3	.5	.6
(354)	.1	(324) .1	(302) .1	Quick		.1	.1	.1	.2	.3
	.1	.1	.1			.1	.1	.1	.1	.1
1	282.9	1 360.7	1 327.0		0 936.6	1 326.6	1 341.9	2 214.5	1 250.7	
4	97.9	3 119.2	4 96.5	Sales/Receivables	3 118.2	5 76.9	3 111.7	4 97.7	7 53.4	
8	44.7	7 50.8	4 46.0		12 29.5	9 41.8	6 57.5	8 46.0	12 31.3	
94	3.9	92 4.0	88 4.1		135 2.7	123 3.0	97 3.8	78 4.7	59 6.2	
120	3.0	127 2.9	120 3.0	Cost of Sales/Inventory	183 2.0	167 2.2	121 3.0	95 3.8	87 4.2	
163	2.2	186 2.0	175 2.1		257 1.4	209 1.7	164 2.2	117 3.1	111 3.3	
5	76.5	5 79.7	5 70.6		0 951.2	5 74.3	5 72.5	6 63.6	5 76.3	
9	40.2	9 39.1	10 37.8	Cost of Sales/Payables	7 50.7	12 29.6	10 37.7	9 38.9	9 40.9	
22	16.8	19 19.2	23 16.0		48 7.6	22 16.7	22 16.4	22 16.2	21 17.2	
	8.1	6.8	7.3			5.5	7.7	6.6	7.8	8.3
	16.5	15.2	13.7	Sales/Working Capital		11.0	19.4	14.0	13.3	13.1
	78.5	502.6	81.8			49.7	-403.2	82.8	58.3	703.9
	4.9	2.6	3.8			2.1	1.9	2.7	9.1	9.4
(328)	1.5	(295) .6	(278) 1.4	EBIT/Interest	(34) 1.0	(38) .7	(94) 1.2	(89) 3.2	(17) 2.6	
	.4	-1.0	.0			-.3	-1.3	.0	1.3	.1
	8.7	.5	2.4	Net Profit + Depr., Dep.,						
(27)	1.6	(21) .0	(19) 1.5	Amort./Cur. Mat. L/T/D						
	.7	-1.0	.2							
	.2	.2	.2			.2	.1	.2	.1	.1
	.5	.6	.8	Fixed/Worth		1.0	.5	.8	.6	1.2
	3.6	5.2	8.7			-.3	-4.7	2.2	3.0	2.7
	1.5	1.5	1.4			2.1	2.9	1.3	1.1	1.3
	3.8	4.3	4.2	Debt/Worth		7.7	8.6	4.2	2.2	3.0
	20.2	89.2	162.8			-6.4	-74.7	10.0	22.1	10.2
	31.8	15.9	23.0	% Profit Before Taxes/Tangible		21.9	10.8	15.3	43.1	42.5
(286)	9.9	(249) -.2	(230) 6.4	Net Worth	(21) 11.9	(32) 1.2	(86) 3.8	(73) 14.5	(16) 16.4	
	-2.1	-19.5	-5.2			.1	-32.7	-14.3	3.8	-12.0
	7.6	3.8	5.3	% Profit Before Taxes/Total		4.4	3.3	4.2	9.2	12.7
	1.8	-.9	1.4	Assets		.1	.0	.9	3.8	4.3
	-2.1	-5.8	-3.1			-8.5	-8.3	-3.2	.7	-1.6
	88.1	77.7	82.0			149.9	110.1	61.3	77.3	61.1
	33.1	28.8	30.2	Sales/Net Fixed Assets		38.0	54.1	22.5	33.6	19.7
	13.7	10.0	12.2			14.1	21.5	11.5	13.6	3.2
	3.1	2.9	3.0			2.4	2.5	3.0	3.5	3.1
	2.4	2.2	2.1	Sales/Total Assets		1.6	2.0	2.0	2.6	2.2
	1.8	1.5	1.6			1.3	1.5	1.5	1.9	1.4
	.4	.4	.4			.3	.2	.5	.4	.8
(278)	.7	(266) .8	(243) .7	% Depr., Dep., Amort./Sales	(22) .8	(37) .4	(89) .8	(77) .7	(14) 1.2	
	1.2	1.5	1.4			1.5	.9	1.2	1.3	3.0
	1.0	1.1	1.1			2.8	1.3	1.1	.9	
(193)	1.7	(153) 2.0	(150) 1.7	% Officers', Directors' Owners' Comp/Sales	(19) 3.4	(25) 2.1	(51) 1.9	(46) 1.3		
	2.8	3.9	3.1			5.2	2.7	3.6	2.2	
	5538136M	4140936M	3330075M	Net Sales ($)	3502M	75722M	183412M	769486M	1380028M	917925M
	2578095M	1942958M	1654315M	Total Assets ($)	2105M	46341M	104049M	441035M	602748M	458037M

M = $ thousand   MM = $ million
See Pages 9 through 22 for Explanation of Ratios and Data

Current Data Sorted by Assets   Comparative Historical Data

0-500M	500M-2MM	2-10MM	10-50MM	50-100MM	100-250MM	Type of Statement	3 / 4/1/06-3/31/07 ALL	8 / 4/1/07-3/31/08 ALL
	4	23	6			Unqualified	3	8
3	23	15	3			Reviewed	41	41
7	25	19				Compiled	77	63
9	20	43	14			Tax Returns	61	55
33 (4/1-9/30/10)			181 (10/1/10-3/31/11)			Other	83	94
19	72	100	23			**NUMBER OF STATEMENTS**	265	261
%	%	%	%	%	%	**ASSETS**	%	%
17.6	8.3	8.3	10.3			Cash & Equivalents	6.9	6.4
8.9	4.4	4.8	4.5			Trade Receivables (net)	3.3	4.3
49.7	63.6	62.4	44.3			Inventory	73.0	71.9
2.0	.7	1.5	4.6			All Other Current	1.5	2.1
78.2	77.0	77.0	63.8			Total Current	84.7	84.8
19.3	17.0	17.5	25.5			Fixed Assets (net)	11.2	10.9
.3	1.5	3.0	6.8	DATA NOT AVAILABLE	DATA NOT AVAILABLE	Intangibles (net)	1.7	1.9
2.3	4.6	2.5	4.0			All Other Non-Current	2.3	2.3
100.0	100.0	100.0	100.0			Total	100.0	100.0
						LIABILITIES		
19.9	31.5	43.4	34.6			Notes Payable-Short Term	45.9	42.9
2.4	3.7	1.9	1.0			Cur. Mat.-L.T.D.	2.5	5.0
12.4	7.5	5.4	2.8			Trade Payables	6.6	7.7
.0	.0	.4	.0			Income Taxes Payable	.1	.1
11.0	11.3	9.9	8.3			All Other Current	10.1	10.2
45.7	54.0	61.0	46.7			Total Current	65.2	65.9
25.1	20.1	13.2	12.5			Long-Term Debt	11.7	11.0
.0	.0	.1	.2			Deferred Taxes	.1	.1
12.8	6.1	5.5	7.8			All Other Non-Current	4.0	4.6
16.3	19.9	20.2	32.8			Net Worth	19.0	18.4
100.0	100.0	100.0	100.0			Total Liabilites & Net Worth	100.0	100.0
						INCOME DATA		
100.0	100.0	100.0	100.0			Net Sales	100.0	100.0
39.0	29.8	26.1	25.2			Gross Profit	23.6	22.7
36.8	27.2	23.2	21.2			Operating Expenses	20.5	20.2
2.2	2.6	2.9	4.1			Operating Profit	3.2	2.5
.3	1.3	1.6	1.7			All Other Expenses (net)	1.8	1.7
1.9	1.3	1.3	2.4			Profit Before Taxes	1.4	.8
						RATIOS		
4.1	2.0	1.7	1.5			Current	1.6	1.5
2.4	1.4	1.3	1.2				1.2	1.2
1.2	1.1	1.0	1.1				1.1	1.0
1.0	.5	.4	.5			Quick	.3	.3
.4	.1	.2	.3				(264) .1 / (260) .1	
.1	.1	.1	.1				.0	.0
1 329.0	0 983.8	1 562.7	5 77.1			Sales/Receivables	1 394.9	1 488.3
4 104.3	4 91.5	5 72.3	9 38.5				3 109.8	4 95.8
10 34.8	11 32.3	13 27.2	17 22.0				8 47.7	10 37.1
27 13.4	113 3.2	133 2.7	118 3.1			Cost of Sales/Inventory	132 2.8	133 2.7
105 3.5	167 2.2	168 2.2	188 1.9				196 1.9	188 1.9
166 2.2	247 1.5	236 1.5	237 1.5				259 1.4	253 1.4
0 UND	0 961.8	3 145.8	2 146.3			Cost of Sales/Payables	1 411.8	1 383.6
1 353.9	4 89.5	8 47.9	8 47.3				4 99.8	4 91.2
10 35.7	19 18.9	23 16.0	13 28.6				11 32.1	15 24.8
4.6	4.7	5.7	5.2			Sales/Working Capital	6.7	6.5
11.7	8.5	10.2	9.4				13.1	14.2
49.4	24.8	-446.7	19.2				49.3	48.6
6.0	4.1	4.3	3.5			EBIT/Interest	3.0	2.5
(15) 2.2	(68) 1.6	(98) 1.5	(20) 2.0				(253) 1.5	(252) 1.3
1.1	.5	.8	1.1				1.0	.7
		3.2				Net Profit + Depr., Dep., Amort./Cur. Mat. L/T/D	5.1	4.4
	(12) 1.4						(30) 1.8	(33) 2.3
		1.1					.7	.4
.1	.1	.1	.3			Fixed/Worth	.2	.1
.7	.5	.7	.8				.4	.5
-1.1	11.6	3.8	1.4				2.1	2.4
.6	1.3	1.9	1.7			Debt/Worth	2.6	2.4
2.4	3.5	4.2	3.8				6.3	5.4
-4.0	28.4	33.7	7.0				28.8	24.8
40.3	36.0	32.7	33.8			% Profit Before Taxes/Tangible Net Worth	38.8	29.5
(14) 14.7	(56) 11.6	(81) 13.4	(22) 13.3				(224) 19.5	(221) 9.6
-27.9	-.7	2.1	1.8				1.1	-3.0
15.6	7.7	6.0	7.4			% Profit Before Taxes/Total Assets	7.1	5.2
5.7	2.8	1.5	3.0				2.0	1.4
-9.5	-2.8	-.9	.5				-.2	-1.6
82.4	73.4	104.0	20.0			Sales/Net Fixed Assets	94.0	95.6
30.0	24.8	27.1	6.9				35.8	36.3
8.9	8.4	5.4	2.3				12.9	12.3
5.5	2.7	2.3	1.5			Sales/Total Assets	2.5	2.5
3.3	1.9	1.8	1.1				1.8	1.8
2.3	1.4	1.2	1.0				1.4	1.4
.6	.4	.4	.6			% Depr., Dep., Amort./Sales	.3	.3
(11) .7	(48) .8	(82) .8	(20) 1.2				(219) .6	(212) .5
2.8	1.5	1.7	3.4				1.0	1.0
	1.6	.9				% Officers', Directors' Owners' Comp/Sales	1.0	1.1
	(38) 3.3	(52) 1.8					(148) 1.8	(119) 1.9
	6.1	2.9					3.5	4.0
24655M	166000M	738912M	525033M			Net Sales ($)	6116936M	4211309M
5818M	81188M	421769M	403023M			Total Assets ($)	1977268M	2278530M

M = $ thousand   MM = $ million
See Pages 9 through 22 for Explanation of Ratios and Data

	Comparative Historical Data			Type of Statement	Current Data Sorted by Sales					
				Unqualified						
	6	6		Reviewed		8	7	7	10	1
	25	30	33	Compiled	4	14	11	7	8	
	73	53	44	Tax Returns	5	23	11	5	7	
	54	53	51	Other	8	23	14	19	15	7
	97	91	86			33 (4/1-9/30/10)		181 (10/1/10-3/31/11)		
	4/1/08-3/31/09 ALL	4/1/09-3/31/10 ALL	4/1/10-3/31/11 ALL		0-1MM	1-3MM	3-5MM	5-10MM	10-25MM	25MM & OVER
	255	233	214	NUMBER OF STATEMENTS	17	68	43	38	40	8
	%	%	%	ASSETS	%	%	%	%	%	%
	6.0	8.5	9.3	Cash & Equivalents	4.2	9.0	14.2	7.1	8.8	
	4.3	5.0	5.0	Trade Receivables (net)	4.7	5.0	5.1	5.1	5.0	
	72.2	62.5	59.7	Inventory	59.6	58.7	58.5	67.3	57.8	
	.7	1.4	1.6	All Other Current	1.0	1.2	1.0	2.9	2.1	
	83.3	77.4	75.7	Total Current	69.4	73.9	78.8	82.4	73.8	
	12.3	16.8	18.4	Fixed Assets (net)	27.2	18.9	16.8	12.3	20.7	
	1.9	2.9	2.6	Intangibles (net)	3.4	1.0	2.2	3.6	2.5	
	2.5	2.8	3.4	All Other Non-Current	.1	6.2	2.2	1.6	3.0	
	100.0	100.0	100.0	Total	100.0	100.0	100.0	100.0	100.0	
				LIABILITIES						
	47.3	39.0	36.3	Notes Payable-Short Term	26.5	31.4	36.3	46.2	39.6	
	3.1	3.0	2.5	Cur. Mat.-L.T.D.	1.5	4.4	1.3	2.4	1.4	
	6.8	5.9	6.5	Trade Payables	12.8	8.4	4.0	5.5	4.7	
	.1	.2	.2	Income Taxes Payable	.0	.0	.1	.4	.5	
	9.0	11.1	10.3	All Other Current	9.2	10.2	10.1	11.0	10.4	
	66.3	59.3	55.7	Total Current	50.1	54.4	51.7	65.4	56.6	
	13.0	16.2	16.5	Long-Term Debt	44.0	19.9	13.7	8.7	10.6	
	.0	.1	.1	Deferred Taxes	.0	.0	.1	.0	.3	
	3.5	5.0	6.6	All Other Non-Current	8.0	8.4	7.1	5.7	4.1	
	17.1	19.4	21.1	Net Worth	-2.1	17.3	27.4	20.1	28.3	
	100.0	100.0	100.0	Total Liabilities & Net Worth	100.0	100.0	100.0	100.0	100.0	
				INCOME DATA						
	100.0	100.0	100.0	Net Sales	100.0	100.0	100.0	100.0	100.0	
	24.2	26.2	28.4	Gross Profit	40.6	31.5	27.2	25.9	23.4	
	23.4	25.2	25.5	Operating Expenses	38.2	28.9	24.4	22.5	19.8	
	.8	1.0	2.9	Operating Profit	2.4	2.5	2.8	3.4	3.6	
	1.8	2.2	1.4	All Other Expenses (net)	1.9	1.8	1.0	1.2	1.1	
	-.9	-1.2	1.5	Profit Before Taxes	.5	.7	1.8	2.2	2.5	
				RATIOS						
	1.5	1.7	1.9		3.2	2.0	1.9	1.6	1.7	
	1.2	1.3	1.3	Current	2.0	1.4	1.4	1.3	1.3	
	1.0	1.0	1.1		.8	1.0	1.2	1.1	1.1	
	.3	.4	.5		.5	.6	.6	.4	.4	
(254)	.1	.2	.2	Quick	.2	.1	.3	.1	.2	
	.0	.1	.1		.1	.1	.1	.1	.1	
	1 · 465.5	1 · 415.0	1 · 526.1	Sales/Receivables	2 · 217.0	0 · 999.8	0 · UND	1 · 317.9	2 · 191.6	
	4 · 91.0	5 · 73.8	5 · 70.5		8 · 43.2	4 · 99.6	7 · 52.5	4 · 81.2	5 · 68.0	
	11 · 32.8	12 · 29.8	13 · 28.1		14 · 26.4	10 · 35.9	13 · 28.5	10 · 38.0	15 · 23.9	
	146 · 2.5	103 · 3.5	116 · 3.1	Cost of Sales/Inventory	123 · 3.0	113 · 3.2	104 · 3.5	118 · 3.1	119 · 3.1	
	219 · 1.7	189 · 1.9	167 · 2.2		201 · 1.8	172 · 2.1	184 · 2.0	162 · 2.2	149 · 2.4	
	312 · 1.2	300 · 1.2	236 · 1.5		376 · 1.0	254 · 1.4	275 · 1.3	205 · 1.8	187 · 1.9	
	1 · 371.9	1 · 440.8	1 · 312.8	Cost of Sales/Payables	0 · UND	1 · 521.8	1 · 312.7	1 · 244.4	3 · 145.8	
	4 · 93.6	5 · 71.4	7 · 56.0		0 · UND	6 · 62.4	6 · 57.9	7 · 48.8	7 · 50.4	
	12 · 29.3	15 · 24.5	19 · 19.2		28 · 13.0	42 · 8.7	19 · 19.4	18 · 20.6	12 · 29.8	
	5.8	4.8	5.2	Sales/Working Capital	3.7	5.2	4.4	5.9	6.3	
	12.7	9.4	9.7		4.7	9.0	8.5	11.6	10.2	
	56.8	77.4	50.6		-21.4	259.0	54.4	-932.9	26.1	
	1.7	2.2	4.1	EBIT/Interest	5.0	3.1	5.0	4.1	6.7	
(239)	1.0	(221) 1.0	(201) 1.6		(16) 1.3	(60) 1.4	1.6	(36) 1.6	(38) 2.6	
	-.1	-.3	.8		-1.9	-.3	.8	1.1	1.2	
	2.3	1.6	3.4	Net Profit + Depr., Dep., Amort./Cur. Mat. L/T/D						
(20)	1.3	(30) .4	(20) 1.5							
	.2	-1.0	.8							
	.1	.2	.1	Fixed/Worth	.6	.1	.1	.1	.2	
	.6	.8	.6		21.7	.7	.5	.3	.6	
	3.5	5.9	3.9		-.7	NM	1.5	4.2	1.8	
	2.6	1.7	1.5	Debt/Worth	2.0	1.1	1.4	2.5	1.4	
	5.3	4.8	3.8		32.0	3.9	3.6	4.6	3.7	
	30.3	36.4	22.3		-3.7	-22.6	14.8	41.4	7.7	
	16.7	18.5	33.8	% Profit Before Taxes/Tangible Net Worth		33.0	43.1	34.8	35.4	
(206)	3.1	(186) 3.7	(173) 13.3		(50) 10.8	(39) 12.7	(32) 16.4	(35) 24.2		
	-13.5	-16.1	1.1		-4.6	-.7	5.3	4.2		
	2.9	4.3	7.5	% Profit Before Taxes/Total Assets	8.4	6.8	7.6	8.0	9.8	
	.3	.2	2.5		1.6	1.6	2.0	2.5	3.6	
	-3.9	-4.9	-1.0		-10.5	-3.2	-1.0	.7	.7	
	78.9	69.4	75.6	Sales/Net Fixed Assets	31.5	67.4	166.6	131.8	61.0	
	29.8	20.9	22.2		8.9	20.9	23.4	38.5	15.1	
	11.0	6.4	6.0		3.1	6.3	6.1	16.7	4.9	
	2.3	2.5	2.5	Sales/Total Assets	2.7	2.7	2.3	2.5	2.5	
	1.6	1.7	1.8		1.4	1.7	1.7	2.0	2.0	
	1.1	1.1	1.2		.9	1.2	1.2	1.7	1.3	
	.4	.5	.5	% Depr., Dep., Amort./Sales	.6	.6	.3	.4	.5	
(205)	.8	(189) .9	(161) .8		(10) .9	(49) 1.0	(33) .7	(26) .6	(35) .8	
	1.3	1.7	1.8		3.9	1.8	1.8	1.8	2.2	
	1.3	1.4	1.1	% Officers', Directors' Owners' Comp/Sales		2.0	.9	.9	.7	
(130)	2.4	(115) 2.6	(108) 2.3		(36) 3.1	(21) 1.6	(19) 2.4	(21) 1.2		
	4.8	4.7	1.9			6.0	3.7	3.2	1.9	
	2783410M	1955981M	1454600M	Net Sales ($)	11712M	131386M	170130M	260024M	567662M	313686M
	1804974M	1288789M	911798M	Total Assets ($)	9283M	98930M	119922M	141445M	350103M	192115M

© RMA 2011

M = $ thousand   MM = $ million
See Pages 9 through 22 for Explanation of Ratios and Data

Current Data Sorted by Assets | Comparative Historical Data

Type of Statement

Type of Statement	0-500M	500M-2MM	2-10MM	10-50MM	50-100MM	100-250MM		4/1/06-3/31/07 ALL	4/1/07-3/31/08 ALL
Unqualified	1		7	21	7	5		42	42
Reviewed		3	36	25	3	3		50	44
Compiled	6	12	25	6	1			59	53
Tax Returns	14	42	21	4				67	71
Other	7	26	41	33	4	5		103	120
		57 (4/1-9/30/10)		301 (10/1/10-3/31/11)					
NUMBER OF STATEMENTS	28	83	130	89	15	13		321	330

ASSETS (%)

	0-500M	500M-2MM	2-10MM	10-50MM	50-100MM	100-250MM		4/1/06-3/31/07	4/1/07-3/31/08
Cash & Equivalents	18.1	8.7	9.7	8.9	5.1	5.6		9.0	7.9
Trade Receivables (net)	11.3	11.4	12.8	16.0	10.6	9.9		10.9	11.5
Inventory	43.5	59.4	55.1	42.5	43.2	31.4		55.0	52.2
All Other Current	1.9	1.2	1.8	2.1	4.3	5.1		2.4	3.0
Total Current	74.8	80.7	79.5	69.5	63.2	52.1		77.4	74.7
Fixed Assets (net)	16.1	13.6	13.6	21.1	19.2	32.6		16.3	17.7
Intangibles (net)	.5	1.3	1.8	1.7	3.4	2.6		1.1	1.5
All Other Non-Current	8.9	4.3	5.1	7.7	14.2	12.6		5.2	6.0
Total	100.0	100.0	100.0	100.0	100.0	100.0		100.0	100.0

LIABILITIES

	0-500M	500M-2MM	2-10MM	10-50MM	50-100MM	100-250MM		4/1/06-3/31/07	4/1/07-3/31/08
Notes Payable-Short Term	37.0	31.1	30.9	31.7	31.4	25.1		38.8	31.4
Cur. Mat.-L.T.D.	6.4	2.9	3.8	5.2	5.3	9.3		3.5	4.7
Trade Payables	20.0	14.5	12.2	9.8	8.1	5.6		9.6	10.4
Income Taxes Payable	.1	.0	.1	.1	.2	.3		.1	.1
All Other Current	29.5	7.6	7.1	6.6	6.1	5.4		9.8	10.4
Total Current	93.0	56.1	54.1	53.5	51.1	45.7		61.8	57.0
Long-Term Debt	4.7	12.6	8.5	13.9	13.6	23.0		13.5	14.1
Deferred Taxes	.0	.0	.1	.9	2.5	1.3		.2	.3
All Other Non-Current	28.4	12.0	4.7	2.1	4.5	6.2		2.9	3.5
Net Worth	-26.4	19.4	32.5	29.6	28.2	23.8		21.7	25.1
Total Liabilities & Net Worth	100.0	100.0	100.0	100.0	100.0	100.0		100.0	100.0

INCOME DATA

	0-500M	500M-2MM	2-10MM	10-50MM	50-100MM	100-250MM		4/1/06-3/31/07	4/1/07-3/31/08
Net Sales	100.0	100.0	100.0	100.0	100.0	100.0		100.0	100.0
Gross Profit	32.5	24.7	21.1	23.0	16.2	22.4		21.0	22.0
Operating Expenses	29.4	22.5	19.6	20.6	13.7	18.6		18.2	19.5
Operating Profit	3.1	2.2	1.6	2.4	2.5	3.8		2.8	2.5
All Other Expenses (net)	.9	1.0	.2	.2	.3	1.3		.7	.7
Profit Before Taxes	2.1	1.3	1.4	2.2	2.3	2.5		2.1	1.8

RATIOS

Ratio	0-500M	500M-2MM	2-10MM	10-50MM	50-100MM	100-250MM		4/1/06-3/31/07	4/1/07-3/31/08
Current	4.0	2.4	1.9	1.5	1.5	1.3		1.6	1.8
	1.2	1.4	1.5	1.2	1.2	1.1		1.2	1.3
	.6	1.1	1.2	1.0	1.1	1.0		1.0	1.1
Quick	1.8	.8	.7	.6	.5	.4		.5	.6
	.5	.3	.4	.4	.3	.3		.3 (327)	.3
	.0	.1	.2	.2	.1	.2		.1	.1
Sales/Receivables	0 UND	1 532.8	5 67.2	10 37.8	7 50.8	11 33.2		4 97.9	4 104.2
	1 707.9	7 52.4	14 26.4	18 20.5	13 27.6	25 14.4		10 38.0	11 32.7
	17 22.1	21 17.6	23 15.7	28 13.1	27 13.7	33 11.1		19 18.9	22 17.0
Cost of Sales/Inventory	10 36.1	53 6.9	53 6.9	47 7.8	58 6.3	56 6.6		49 7.5	50 7.3
	30 12.2	89 4.1	88 4.2	65 5.7	82 4.4	91 4.0		87 4.2	79 4.6
	208 1.8	204 1.8	131 2.8	110 3.3	90 4.1	134 2.7		133 2.7	124 2.9
Cost of Sales/Payables	0 UND	0 UND	6 59.1	7 49.2	6 56.3	6 62.6		2 164.8	3 145.3
	1 453.8	9 41.3	14 26.7	14 26.7	14 25.5	17 21.8		8 45.3	8 44.6
	37 9.9	37 9.9	24 15.3	22 16.3	28 12.9	38 9.6		19 19.2	19 19.2
Sales/Working Capital	10.4	5.3	6.5	10.5	12.5	12.2		10.0	8.4
	178.9	15.9	10.5	21.0	19.0	40.2		22.5	18.5
	-17.9	63.2	26.9	134.2	74.9	108.1		151.2	80.3
EBIT/Interest	34.3	5.1	8.1	6.8	4.5	2.8		4.7	4.6
	(20) 2.7	(74) 2.7	(120) 2.4	(86) 3.0	(14) 2.8	(12) 2.2		(295) 2.2	(302) 2.1
	.3	1.0	1.0	1.7	2.0	1.2		1.3	1.2
Net Profit + Depr., Dep., Amort./Cur. Mat. L/T/D			7.3	3.2				6.1	7.0
		(20) 2.5		(21) 1.4				(49) 2.4	(48) 1.4
			1.1	.8				1.1	.8
Fixed/Worth	.1	.1	.1	.2	.4	1.3		.2	.2
	.7	.3	.3	.6	.9	1.9		.5	.5
	-.4	3.2	1.0	2.0	1.6	2.2		1.7	1.6
Debt/Worth	.7	1.5	1.1	1.8	2.0	2.1		1.8	1.5
	6.6	4.6	2.1	3.4	3.0	4.0		4.8	3.4
	-2.5	12.4	4.9	5.7	3.9	10.4		10.7	8.7
% Profit Before Taxes/Tangible Net Worth	98.7	60.7	28.0	32.9	36.1	19.0		48.0	40.0
	(16) 35.1	(65) 19.8	(115) 14.9	(86) 17.4	16.1	17.1		(284) 25.0	(294) 18.7
	20.0	2.6	1.4	7.4	6.8	6.2		8.5	5.1
% Profit Before Taxes/Total Assets	32.7	12.4	9.5	8.5	8.2	3.7		9.1	9.8
	5.8	5.8	3.9	3.7	3.9	3.3		4.6	4.1
	-1.5	.0	.2	1.6	2.1	1.3		.9	.5
Sales/Net Fixed Assets	297.8	163.3	91.8	60.2	30.7	13.3		111.9	84.4
	57.2	45.0	43.8	18.6	10.7	7.5		35.6	27.8
	19.4	12.4	14.3	4.6	7.1	2.4		12.1	9.6
Sales/Total Assets	8.0	4.8	3.9	3.6	2.6	2.6		3.8	3.6
	3.9	2.7	2.9	2.3	2.3	1.4		2.8	2.7
	2.2	1.6	2.0	1.6	1.8	1.3		1.9	2.0
% Depr., Dep., Amort./Sales	.2	.3	.3	.4	.4			.2	.3
	(16) .9	(57) .7	(107) .5	(85) 1.0	.9			(269) .6	(275) .7
	1.8	2.4	1.2	4.3	2.8			1.8	2.0
% Officers', Directors' Owners' Comp/Sales	2.3	1.8	.7	1.0				.5	.7
	(13) 5.2	(45) 2.2	(69) 1.6	(21) 1.4				(125) 1.3	(120) 1.6
	10.0	4.2	2.9	4.3				2.7	4.1
Net Sales ($)	33624M	315786M	2068634M	5044843M	2505272M	3280782M		12560940M	11361900M
Total Assets ($)	6495M	90487M	696615M	1923694M	1040203M	1953265M		4511508M	4631918M

© RMA 2011

M = $ thousand   MM = $ million
See Pages 9 through 22 for Explanation of Ratios and Data

Comparative Historical Data   Current Data Sorted by Sales

			Type of Statement	0-1MM	1-3MM	3-5MM	5-10MM	10-25MM	25MM & OVER
37	34	41	Unqualified	1				3	37
52	66	70	Reviewed	1	1	1	13	23	31
46	43	50	Compiled	5	6	6	10	18	5
56	77	81	Tax Returns	11	24	15	12	15	4
117	104	116	Other	10	12	4	18	28	44
4/1/08-3/31/09 ALL	4/1/09-3/31/10 ALL	4/1/10-3/31/11 ALL		57 (4/1-9/30/10)			301 (10/1/10-3/31/11)		
308	324	358	NUMBER OF STATEMENTS	28	43	26	53	87	121
%	%	%	ASSETS	%	%	%	%	%	%
7.8	8.3	9.6	Cash & Equivalents	11.9	9.4	9.2	8.8	11.1	8.5
11.2	12.4	13.0	Trade Receivables (net)	5.8	15.6	11.1	9.2	14.6	14.6
52.5	51.7	50.7	Inventory	52.8	52.4	55.5	60.3	51.4	43.8
2.1	2.4	2.0	All Other Current	2.5	.4	2.0	2.0	1.5	2.7
73.5	74.8	75.2	Total Current	73.0	77.7	77.8	80.3	78.7	69.6
18.0	17.3	16.6	Fixed Assets (net)	17.3	16.4	15.3	13.2	14.3	19.9
2.1	2.0	1.7	Intangibles (net)	.3	1.9	3.1	.8	1.4	2.1
6.4	5.9	6.5	All Other Non-Current	9.6	4.0	3.8	5.6	5.5	8.4
100.0	100.0	100.0	Total	100.0	100.0	100.0	100.0	100.0	100.0
			LIABILITIES						
32.2	34.0	31.4	Notes Payable-Short Term	46.6	26.5	30.1	31.8	25.2	34.3
4.4	4.2	4.4	Cur. Mat.-L.T.D.	7.6	1.8	3.8	4.1	2.9	5.9
8.6	10.1	12.3	Trade Payables	16.0	13.9	8.7	12.4	15.0	9.7
.1	.0	.1	Income Taxes Payable	.1	.1	.0	.1	.2	.1
9.4	9.8	8.7	All Other Current	29.6	6.0	6.9	5.9	7.6	7.4
54.7	58.2	57.0	Total Current	99.8	48.4	49.5	54.3	50.9	57.4
15.4	13.5	11.2	Long-Term Debt	6.6	13.7	16.1	11.4	9.4	11.6
.3	.2	.4	Deferred Taxes	.0	.0	.0	.1	.1	1.1
5.0	8.8	7.7	All Other Non-Current	29.5	19.1	4.5	4.8	3.0	3.8
24.5	19.3	23.6	Net Worth	-36.1	18.8	29.9	29.5	36.5	26.1
100.0	100.0	100.0	Total Liabilties & Net Worth	100.0	100.0	100.0	100.0	100.0	100.0
			INCOME DATA						
100.0	100.0	100.0	Net Sales	100.0	100.0	100.0	100.0	100.0	100.0
22.2	23.4	23.2	Gross Profit	34.2	30.4	21.8	22.7	22.1	19.3
20.8	22.3	21.0	Operating Expenses	32.4	27.5	18.1	21.7	20.1	17.0
1.4	1.1	2.2	Operating Profit	1.7	2.9	3.7	1.0	2.0	2.3
.7	.8	.5	All Other Expenses (net)	2.1	.9	.3	.6	-.1	.3
.7	.3	1.7	Profit Before Taxes	-.4	2.0	3.4	.4	2.1	2.0
			RATIOS						
1.7 / 1.3 / 1.0	1.8 / 1.3 / 1.1	1.9 / 1.3 / 1.1	Current	2.1 / 1.1 / .6	4.5 / 1.7 / 1.0	2.4 / 1.5 / 1.2	2.0 / 1.5 / 1.2	2.1 / 1.5 / 1.2	1.4 / 1.2 / 1.0
.6 / .3 / .1	.7 / .3 / .1	.7 / .4 / .2	Quick	.6 / .1 / .0	1.7 / .6 / .1	1.0 / .3 / .1	.6 / .4 / .1	.8 / .4 / .2	.6 / .3 / .2
5 / 79.3 12 / 29.8 25 / 14.6	5 / 77.5 14 / 25.4 27 / 13.8	4 / 82.7 14 / 26.4 25 / 14.5	Sales/Receivables	0 / UND 0 / UND 20 / 18.3	3 / 132.5 14 / 25.5 29 / 12.6	0 / UND 9 / 42.0 21 / 17.0	3 / 124.6 9 / 38.6 23 / 16.0	6 / 59.8 14 / 26.4 24 / 15.2	9 / 42.8 17 / 21.7 26 / 14.1
53 / 6.8 82 / 4.4 135 / 2.7	51 / 7.2 86 / 4.3 145 / 2.5	49 / 7.5 82 / 4.5 131 / 2.8	Cost of Sales/Inventory	50 / 7.2 242 / 1.5 360 / 1.0	51 / 7.2 98 / 3.7 216 / 1.7	50 / 7.3 79 / 4.6 123 / 3.0	63 / 5.8 104 / 3.5 171 / 2.1	48 / 7.7 80 / 4.6 117 / 3.1	46 / 7.9 65 / 5.7 95 / 3.9
3 / 125.6 9 / 41.3 19 / 18.9	4 / 85.4 12 / 30.3 24 / 15.3	4 / 84.8 13 / 27.2 25 / 14.6	Cost of Sales/Payables	0 / UND 0 / UND 44 / 8.3	4 / 97.4 18 / 20.6 43 / 8.4	0 / UND 7 / 50.4 15 / 24.9	3 / 128.7 14 / 26.4 26 / 14.3	6 / 60.3 15 / 24.8 24 / 15.0	7 / 55.9 13 / 27.1 21 / 17.4
8.5 / 18.6 / 128.3	7.1 / 17.2 / 88.1	7.4 / 16.1 / 78.3	Sales/Working Capital	4.5 / 175.4 / -3.9	4.3 / 11.2 / 256.4	6.9 / 13.9 / 26.1	5.1 / 12.2 / 26.2	6.4 / 10.1 / 36.7	12.5 / 25.0 / 115.8
3.7 / (277) 1.7 / .9	3.8 / (286) 1.7 / .4	7.1 / (326) 2.7 / 1.2	EBIT/Interest	5.6 / (20) 1.3 / -.8	3.5 / (37) 1.4 / .1	8.3 / (25) 3.1 / 1.3	6.1 / (50) 1.9 / .9	11.4 / (81) 2.8 / 1.0	6.5 / (113) 3.0 / 1.9
3.9 / (47) 1.5 / .8	3.5 / (47) 1.2 / .7	3.0 / (56) 1.4 / .9	Net Profit + Depr., Dep., Amort./Cur. Mat. L/T/D					5.7 / (13) 2.5 / 1.2	2.7 / (36) 1.3 / .9
.2 / .6 / 2.5	.1 / .5 / 2.1	.1 / .4 / 2.0	Fixed/Worth	.0 / 3.6 / -.3	.1 / .4 / -66.0	.1 / .3 / 1.7	.1 / .3 / 1.0	.1 / .3 / .9	.2 / .7 / 1.9
1.7 / 3.7 / 11.9	1.6 / 3.2 / 10.9	1.3 / 3.0 / 7.1	Debt/Worth	2.0 / UND / -2.4	1.3 / 2.8 / -48.8	1.4 / 2.5 / 7.0	1.1 / 2.8 / 8.6	1.0 / 2.0 / 4.7	1.9 / 3.5 / 6.1
31.0 / (272) 11.0 / .0	27.0 / (278) 9.6 / -5.0	34.5 / (310) 17.1 / 4.3	% Profit Before Taxes/Tangible Net Worth	70.3 / (14) 19.3 / -21.3	34.3 / (31) 16.3 / 2.2	112.0 / (23) 26.8 / 4.1	21.9 / (47) 12.3 / -.7	29.9 / (81) 13.5 / .9	34.6 / (114) 19.0 / 8.8
7.8 / 2.0 / -.6	6.5 / 2.0 / -1.8	10.0 / 3.8 / .6	% Profit Before Taxes/Total Assets	13.0 / 2.1 / -6.1	12.6 / 1.6 / -.6	17.3 / 11.0 / 4.1	6.7 / 2.5 / -.4	10.8 / 4.7 / .1	8.4 / 3.7 / 2.3
67.1 / 28.6 / 8.4	79.8 / 27.3 / 8.1	86.1 / 34.7 / 10.4	Sales/Net Fixed Assets	254.1 / 30.7 / 9.1	118.4 / 36.1 / 13.6	144.5 / 37.7 / 11.5	126.9 / 45.0 / 12.8	99.8 / 42.4 / 12.6	61.0 / 19.3 / 7.3
3.5 / 2.5 / 1.7	3.6 / 2.5 / 1.6	3.9 / 2.6 / 1.7	Sales/Total Assets	2.4 / 1.6 / 1.0	3.6 / 2.1 / 1.6	5.3 / 3.4 / 2.0	3.9 / 2.6 / 1.6	4.1 / 2.9 / 2.1	3.9 / 2.9 / 1.8
.4 / (251) .9 / 2.6	.4 / (267) .8 / 2.7	.3 / (288) .8 / 2.2	% Depr., Dep., Amort./Sales	.5 / (15) 1.1 / 2.5	.3 / (30) .8 / 2.3	.4 / (23) 1.7 / 3.0	.4 / (38) 1.0 / 2.5	.3 / (72) .5 / 1.2	.3 / (110) .7 / 2.5
1.0 / (124) 1.8 / 3.7	1.0 / (138) 2.1 / 3.9	1.0 / (149) 1.9 / 3.4	% Officers', Directors', Owners' Comp/Sales		1.9 / (25) 3.0 / 5.0	1.3 / (17) 2.3 / 4.2	1.1 / (29) 1.9 / 2.8	.7 / (44) 1.4 / 2.3	.7 / (25) 1.2 / 3.2
9663951M	8485708M	13248941M	Net Sales ($)	15749M	78888M	96987M	405360M	1434867M	11217090M
4272693M	3771432M	5710759M	Total Assets ($)	11635M	41575M	33186M	206967M	571369M	4846027M

Current Data Sorted by Assets

Comparative Historical Data

						Type of Statement		
	1	6	5	2	4	Unqualified	23	15
	9	31	12	1		Reviewed	59	29
18	27	28	5			Compiled	95	74
63	70	35	4		1	Tax Returns	114	113
23	45	46	19	6	5	Other	95	106
	64 (4/1-9/30/10)		402 (10/1/10-3/31/11)				4/1/06-3/31/07	4/1/07-3/31/08
0-500M	500M-2MM	2-10MM	10-50MM	50-100MM	100-250MM		ALL	ALL
104	152	146	45	9	10	NUMBER OF STATEMENTS	386	337
%	%	%	%	%	%	ASSETS	%	%
13.2	9.0	6.5	5.7		10.6	Cash & Equivalents	6.8	6.8
12.0	14.4	16.4	12.7		18.9	Trade Receivables (net)	17.0	15.4
49.5	48.2	49.2	40.3		35.1	Inventory	47.3	48.2
1.7	1.2	1.4	2.7		3.9	All Other Current	2.5	2.7
76.4	72.9	73.4	61.4		68.4	Total Current	73.6	73.1
15.3	16.8	15.9	26.0		14.2	Fixed Assets (net)	17.6	17.7
3.4	4.0	3.5	5.2		11.2	Intangibles (net)	3.4	3.3
4.8	6.3	7.2	7.4		6.2	All Other Non-Current	5.4	5.9
100.0	100.0	100.0	100.0		100.0	Total	100.0	100.0
						LIABILITIES		
11.8	8.6	10.0	9.1		3.1	Notes Payable-Short-Term	12.8	10.4
3.2	2.4	3.2	2.8		.8	Cur. Mat.-L.T.D.	4.5	4.2
23.0	19.0	20.8	18.1		19.7	Trade Payables	20.7	18.8
.1	.1	.0	.3		.2	Income Taxes Payable	.2	.1
15.0	8.7	8.4	8.0		15.4	All Other Current	7.9	8.6
53.1	38.9	42.5	38.2		39.2	Total Current	46.1	42.1
22.9	18.7	15.6	19.2		17.7	Long-Term Debt	21.0	21.5
.0	.0	.1	.6		.9	Deferred Taxes	.1	.1
15.3	8.8	6.5	4.4		13.4	All Other Non-Current	5.2	7.0
8.7	33.6	35.3	37.6		28.8	Net Worth	27.6	29.3
100.0	100.0	100.0	100.0		100.0	Total Liabilties & Net Worth	100.0	100.0
						INCOME DATA		
100.0	100.0	100.0	100.0		100.0	Net Sales	100.0	100.0
40.3	37.2	36.1	39.4		43.1	Gross Profit	37.4	37.0
35.7	34.5	32.3	34.6		34.8	Operating Expenses	33.8	34.1
4.6	2.7	3.9	4.8		8.3	Operating Profit	3.6	2.9
.8	.5	1.0	.8		5.0	All Other Expenses (net)	.6	.6
3.8	2.3	2.9	3.9		3.3	Profit Before Taxes	3.0	2.3
						RATIOS		
4.3	3.8	2.7	2.9		3.5		3.0	3.1
2.1	2.1	1.7	1.6		1.9	Current	1.7	1.9
1.2	1.3	1.2	1.0		1.2		1.2	1.2
1.4	1.0	.8	.9		1.1		.9	1.0
.6	.6	.5	.5		.8	Quick	.5	.5
.2	.3	.3	.3		.4		.3	.3
0 UND	6 65.5	10 36.8	10 37.5		10 38.3		8 48.0	8 48.5
6 57.5	20 18.5	24 15.3	22 16.3		39 9.5	Sales/Receivables	22 16.9	22 16.8
20 17.9	31 11.8	32 11.4	39 9.2		62 5.9		33 11.0	32 11.3
37 9.7	44 8.4	60 6.0	60 6.1		29 12.6		55 6.7	62 5.9
71 5.2	105 3.5	98 3.7	129 2.8		95 3.8	Cost of Sales/Inventory	95 3.8	104 3.5
133 2.7	190 1.9	179 2.0	182 2.0		179 2.0		161 2.3	168 2.2
6 65.9	17 21.5	25 14.8	25 14.6		34 10.8		19 19.7	17 21.5
22 16.6	32 11.5	39 9.4	51 7.1		61 6.0	Cost of Sales/Payables	36 10.0	34 10.6
37 9.9	58 6.3	61 6.0	67 5.5		74 4.9		60 6.1	61 6.0
5.0	3.9	4.2	3.5		2.9		4.9	4.0
11.1	7.0	8.9	9.1		9.8	Sales/Working Capital	9.5	8.3
60.1	26.1	34.5	NM		20.2		33.3	25.6
11.0	15.6	8.3	12.4				7.4	5.8
(79) 3.8	(132) 3.4	(132) 3.7	(44) 4.0			EBIT/Interest	(343) 2.6	(300) 2.3
1.1	1.1	1.6	1.4				1.3	1.1
	4.3	5.9	4.6			Net Profit + Depr., Dep.,	7.2	4.4
	(13) 2.1	(31) 2.7	(20) 2.4			Amort./Cur. Mat. L/T/D	(61) 2.3	(55) 1.5
	.6	.8	1.3				1.3	.5
.1	.1	.1	.2		.3		.1	.1
.4	.3	.3	.8		.4	Fixed/Worth	.4	.4
-1.9	1.7	1.0	1.9		NM		1.5	1.7
.5	.8	.9	.7		1.5		.9	.9
1.9	1.6	2.1	2.1		3.9	Debt/Worth	2.0	2.2
-7.0	9.4	4.9	6.8		NM		6.9	8.8
82.7	35.9	32.7	21.8			% Profit Before Taxes/Tangible	41.2	42.2
(72) 30.5	(125) 14.1	(133) 14.8	(40) 11.1			Net Worth	(327) 16.0	(285) 15.5
11.3	2.2	4.8	4.0				4.6	4.4
35.7	13.2	11.6	6.0		15.8	% Profit Before Taxes/Total	14.0	11.6
10.3	5.1	4.7	3.0		10.2	Assets	4.8	4.3
1.8	-.3	1.2	1.0		1.6		1.0	.6
204.4	89.8	53.3	38.7		66.0		62.3	60.2
59.2	37.8	28.5	14.0		24.7	Sales/Net Fixed Assets	25.8	24.8
21.2	14.1	12.8	3.5		7.7		11.8	11.7
5.9	3.7	3.4	2.3		3.0		3.9	3.6
4.0	2.5	2.5	1.7		1.8	Sales/Total Assets	2.8	2.5
2.7	1.8	1.8	1.1		1.1		1.9	1.8
.4	.4	.5	.8				.5	.5
(59) .8	(112) .9	(123) 1.1	(41) 1.3			% Depr., Dep., Amort./Sales	(306) 1.1	(272) 1.0
1.6	1.9	1.7	2.0				1.7	1.7
3.0	2.2	1.3	1.2			% Officers', Directors'	2.0	1.5
(50) 4.3	(93) 3.9	(76) 2.1	(19) 1.6			Owners' Comp/Sales	(187) 3.2	(185) 3.3
6.8	5.6	3.8	3.1				5.4	5.9
119043M	478812M	1551680M	1899893M	1514316M	3039010M	Net Sales ($)	8783395M	6929065M
26986M	158229M	596325M	1084425M	726862M	1574996M	Total Assets ($)	3195924M	3011706M

© RMA 2011

M = $ thousand   MM = $ million
See Pages 9 through 22 for Explanation of Ratios and Data

Comparative Historical Data | Current Data Sorted by Sales

						Type of Statement						
	20		20		18	Unqualified			1	2	4	11
	45		55		53	Reviewed		7	3	10	20	13
	80		77		78	Compiled	10	23	11	19	12	3
	133		158		173	Tax Returns	43	61	27	26	11	5
	98		116		144	Other	17	36	17	26	23	25
	4/1/08-3/31/09		4/1/09-3/31/10		4/1/10-3/31/11			64 (4/1-9/30/10)		402 (10/1/10-3/31/11)		
	ALL		ALL		ALL		0-1MM	1-3MM	3-5MM	5-10MM	10-25MM	25MM & OVER
	376		426		466	NUMBER OF STATEMENTS	70	127	59	83	70	57
	%		%		%	ASSETS	%	%	%	%	%	%
	6.7		7.5		8.8	Cash & Equivalents	10.6	9.0	9.7	7.8	8.4	7.3
	16.7		14.1		14.5	Trade Receivables (net)	10.9	12.7	18.1	16.4	14.6	16.1
	48.2		46.2		47.4	Inventory	46.6	49.7	48.6	51.3	44.3	40.5
	1.8		1.9		1.6	All Other Current	2.0	1.2	.7	1.2	1.9	3.0
	73.4		69.7		72.3	Total Current	70.1	72.7	77.2	76.8	69.2	66.9
	17.8		19.6		17.1	Fixed Assets (net)	21.2	17.4	12.8	12.6	18.6	20.8
	3.0		4.6		4.2	Intangibles (net)	3.9	3.5	5.0	4.1	2.7	7.3
	5.8		6.1		6.3	All Other Non-Current	4.8	6.5	5.0	6.5	9.5	5.0
	100.0		100.0		100.0	Total	100.0	100.0	100.0	100.0	100.0	100.0
						LIABILITIES						
	11.2		12.1		9.7	Notes Payable-Short Term	11.6	10.3	7.1	10.3	9.5	7.8
	3.2		3.0		2.8	Cur. Mat.-L.T.D.	3.0	3.0	3.4	2.6	2.5	2.4
	20.8		20.1		20.3	Trade Payables	16.1	17.8	26.5	21.4	22.5	20.6
	.1		.1		.1	Income Taxes Payable	.0	.1	.1	.0	.1	.3
	10.5		8.9		10.2	All Other Current	12.7	9.3	11.6	8.1	11.0	9.5
	45.8		44.2		43.1	Total Current	43.4	40.4	48.7	42.5	45.6	40.5
	19.9		21.6		18.8	Long-Term Debt	23.4	24.1	18.1	11.8	13.9	18.4
	.2		.1		.1	Deferred Taxes	.0	.0	.0	.1	.2	.6
	5.4		7.1		9.2	All Other Non-Current	21.6	6.9	8.4	9.4	3.6	6.5
	28.6		27.0		28.8	Net Worth	11.6	28.5	24.8	36.2	36.7	34.0
	100.0		100.0		100.0	Total Liabilties & Net Worth	100.0	100.0	100.0	100.0	100.0	100.0
						INCOME DATA						
	100.0		100.0		100.0	Net Sales	100.0	100.0	100.0	100.0	100.0	100.0
	36.5		37.3		37.7	Gross Profit	41.6	41.3	34.1	34.8	34.3	37.0
	33.8		34.9		33.9	Operating Expenses	36.6	37.2	30.6	32.1	31.1	32.7
	2.6		2.4		3.8	Operating Profit	5.0	4.1	3.5	2.7	3.2	4.3
	.9		.8		.9	All Other Expenses (net)	1.7	1.0	.3	.4	.2	1.5
	1.8		1.6		2.9	Profit Before Taxes	3.2	3.2	3.1	2.3	3.0	2.8
						RATIOS						
	3.1		3.3		3.4		5.8	3.8	4.0	3.0	2.2	2.8
	1.8		1.7		1.8	Current	2.6	2.1	2.1	2.0	1.6	1.6
	1.2		1.1		1.2		1.0	1.3	1.2	1.3	1.1	1.1
	1.0		1.0		1.0		1.3	1.0	1.1	1.0	.7	.9
	.5		.5		.5	Quick	.6	.6	.6	.5	.4	.5
	.3		.3		.3		.2	.2	.3	.3	.3	.3

8	48.0	6	60.4	5	68.7	Sales/Receivables	0	UND	3	105.4	10	38.3	9	39.1	7	50.4	8	43.7
21	17.2	20	18.2	19	18.9		9	40.2	16	22.8	23	15.6	24	15.4	17	21.1	29	12.7
33	11.1	33	11.2	31	11.8		25	14.5	29	12.6	32	11.4	32	11.4	30	12.3	46	7.9
53	6.9	55	6.7	52	7.0	Cost of Sales/Inventory	44	8.3	53	6.9	44	8.4	53	6.9	50	7.3	57	6.4
97	3.8	104	3.5	98	3.7		117	3.1	104	3.5	101	3.6	98	3.7	76	4.8	97	3.8
172	2.1	187	2.0	172	2.1		219	1.7	191	1.9	191	1.9	169	2.2	130	2.8	153	2.4
19	19.4	21	17.2	18	20.5	Cost of Sales/Payables	0	UND	14	26.5	25	14.5	22	16.5	20	18.1	29	12.5
35	10.4	37	9.7	35	10.5		20	18.0	30	12.1	32	11.4	37	9.9	38	9.7	51	7.1
57	6.4	59	6.2	59	6.2		45	8.1	47	7.8	75	4.9	59	6.2	55	6.6	65	5.6
	4.2		4.2		4.2	Sales/Working Capital		3.2		4.0		3.7		3.9		5.7		5.2
	9.1		8.0		8.4			6.3		8.0		6.8		8.7		11.2		10.8
	31.4		39.4		37.0			-218.3		31.9		34.4		26.6		48.9		136.8
	7.7		6.1		11.8	EBIT/Interest		9.7		10.3		13.9		18.7		11.8		14.6
(339)	2.9	(381)	2.6	(403)	3.7		(53)	2.8	(109)	3.0	(52)	3.8	(74)	4.5	(63)	4.0	(52)	3.8
	1.0		1.0		1.2			.4		1.0		1.1		1.9		1.5		1.4
	5.2		4.8		4.7	Net Profit + Depr., Dep., Amort./Cur. Mat. L/T/D				2.2				6.5		21.6		4.3
(64)	2.0	(62)	2.1	(72)	2.5				(12)	1.9			(14)	2.7	(17)	3.6	(23)	2.3
	.8		.6		.8					.4				.6		2.5		.9
	.1		.1		.1	Fixed/Worth		.1		.1		.1		.1		.1		.2
	.4		.4		.3			.4		.3		.3		.3		.3		.5
	1.7		3.3		1.9			-5.5		2.0		5.0		.7		1.1		5.4
	.9		1.0		.8	Debt/Worth		.6		.6		.9		.8		1.0		1.0
	2.3		2.3		1.8			2.6		1.6		1.9		1.6		1.8		2.7
	8.2		13.8		9.0			-12.6		15.5		104.5		5.0		4.1		15.4
	34.5		30.8		39.8	% Profit Before Taxes/Tangible Net Worth		75.5		40.7		38.2		38.6		31.5		40.1
(312)	13.9	(343)	11.4	(383)	17.2		(49)	19.7	(100)	18.0	(45)	12.0	(78)	15.8	(65)	15.2	(46)	19.6
	2.3		.4		4.4			6.7		3.5		1.5		5.8		4.1		7.0
	11.0		9.9		13.2	% Profit Before Taxes/Total Assets		23.6		13.0		16.4		12.3		12.1		10.9
	4.2		3.5		5.4			6.6		6.6		4.3		5.2		4.9		4.2
	.0		-.2		.6			-1.5		.1		.4		2.0		.7		1.0
	67.2		65.1		81.6	Sales/Net Fixed Assets		161.9		106.1		84.3		63.6		66.6		41.2
	26.9		23.6		32.7			32.4		38.4		39.4		36.4		30.8		20.9
	12.3		8.9		12.3			8.4		12.3		20.6		17.4		10.6		7.1
	3.8		3.4		3.9	Sales/Total Assets		4.2		4.0		4.2		3.8		4.0		3.2
	2.6		2.4		2.6			2.6		2.6		2.5		2.8		3.1		2.2
	1.9		1.7		1.8			1.5		1.8		1.8		2.0		1.9		1.5
	.5		.6		.5	% Depr., Dep., Amort./Sales		.6		.4		.4		.6		.5		.7
(307)	1.0	(342)	1.1	(350)	1.0		(45)	1.4	(86)	.9	(47)	.8	(65)	1.0	(58)	1.1	(49)	1.2
	1.9		1.8		1.8			3.7		2.0		1.4		1.7		1.7		1.9
	1.6		1.8		1.8	% Officers', Directors' Owners' Comp/Sales		3.3		2.7		1.8		1.4		1.1		1.2
(183)	3.1	(222)	3.2	(240)	3.3		(37)	5.2	(66)	4.1	(36)	2.8	(48)	1.9	(36)	2.0	(17)	2.2
	5.6		6.2		5.3			7.3		5.9		4.2		3.4		4.3		6.9
	9273020M		7950722M		8602754M	Net Sales ($)		43087M	233303M	220824M	587039M	1087687M	6430814M
	3884791M		3851618M		4167823M	Total Assets ($)		26883M	128151M	94758M	236850M	502641M	3178540M

M = $ thousand   MM = $ million
See Pages 9 through 22 for Explanation of Ratios and Data

Current Data Sorted by Assets   Comparative Historical Data

							Type of Statement		
1	6	1 27	6 12	4	4		Unqualified	13	15
11	10	15	5				Reviewed	29	40
24	14	10	2				Compiled	37	42
13	19	13	15	1	4		Tax Returns	36	42
	38 (4/1-9/30/10)		179 (10/1/10-3/31/11)				Other	25	33
0-500M	500M-2MM	2-10MM	10-50MM	50-100MM	100-250MM			4/1/06- 3/31/07 ALL	4/1/07- 3/31/08 ALL
49	49	66	40	5	8		NUMBER OF STATEMENTS	140	172
%	%	%	%	%	%		ASSETS	%	%
20.6	11.1	9.6	5.4				Cash & Equivalents	6.4	7.9
9.8	19.0	18.5	18.1				Trade Receivables (net)	20.5	20.4
33.6	35.0	40.7	39.7				Inventory	40.5	38.0
2.5	1.6	4.0	1.4				All Other Current	2.4	2.5
66.5	66.7	72.9	64.6				Total Current	69.9	68.8
19.7	20.5	19.5	29.0				Fixed Assets (net)	21.8	23.9
7.5	7.2	2.0	1.6				Intangibles (net)	1.9	.9
6.3	5.6	5.6	4.9				All Other Non-Current	6.4	6.5
100.0	100.0	100.0	100.0				Total	100.0	100.0
							LIABILITIES		
9.6	6.7	9.9	5.4				Notes Payable-Short Term	10.9	9.2
4.2	2.7	3.2	2.4				Cur. Mat.-L.T.D.	2.9	4.0
28.8	28.8	31.0	30.0				Trade Payables	30.9	33.2
.0	.2	.0	.1				Income Taxes Payable	.2	.2
23.3	7.7	7.0	8.3				All Other Current	7.3	8.3
65.9	46.0	51.2	46.1				Total Current	52.1	54.9
28.6	21.9	6.7	12.0				Long-Term Debt	15.1	17.9
.0	.1	.1	.3				Deferred Taxes	.2	.2
5.5	3.7	1.9	3.1				All Other Non-Current	5.0	5.9
.0	28.3	40.0	38.5				Net Worth	27.6	20.9
100.0	100.0	100.0	100.0				Total Liabilities & Net Worth	100.0	100.0
							INCOME DATA		
100.0	100.0	100.0	100.0				Net Sales	100.0	100.0
44.4	40.0	32.6	30.8				Gross Profit	34.4	34.5
41.2	36.5	29.4	28.1				Operating Expenses	31.7	31.6
3.1	3.5	3.2	2.7				Operating Profit	2.8	2.9
.8	.9	-.2	-.1				All Other Expenses (net)	.1	.3
2.4	2.6	3.4	2.8				Profit Before Taxes	2.7	2.7
							RATIOS		
2.0	2.6	1.9	1.8					2.0	2.0
1.4	1.5	1.4	1.4				Current	1.4	1.4
.8	1.0	1.1	1.2					1.0	1.0
1.0	1.2	1.0	.7					.8	.8
.4	(48) .7	.5	.5				Quick	.5	.5
.2	.4	.3	.4					.3	.3
0 UND	8 46.2	9 38.4	8 43.2					11 33.7	9 38.7
5 74.7	19 19.5	21 17.6	28 13.0				Sales/Receivables	22 16.9	20 18.2
9 38.8	37 9.8	36 10.1	36 10.2					36 10.0	34 10.8
21 17.4	39 9.5	52 7.0	58 6.3					50 7.3	43 8.5
37 9.9	67 5.4	71 5.2	73 5.0				Cost of Sales/Inventory	70 5.2	65 5.6
63 5.8	92 4.0	96 3.8	103 3.6					98 3.7	90 4.1
8 47.1	33 11.1	36 10.0	41 8.8					33 11.0	32 11.4
25 14.6	46 8.0	52 7.0	56 6.6				Cost of Sales/Payables	49 7.4	49 7.4
48 7.7	79 4.6	69 5.3	75 4.9					74 4.9	69 5.3
14.1	6.2	7.6	8.0					7.5	8.4
41.6	16.3	14.9	15.0				Sales/Working Capital	16.6	19.4
-51.1	300.9	41.9	45.5					-582.0	75.8
4.1	9.5	14.8	15.6					7.8	8.3
(39) 1.9	(43) 3.1	(60) 5.6	(36) 6.5				EBIT/Interest	(129) 3.5	(153) 3.5
-2.2	1.6	2.4	2.3					1.8	1.9
		9.2	8.8					5.5	9.4
	(14) 3.4	(16) 5.1					Net Profit + Depr., Dep., Amort./Cur. Mat. L/T/D	(40) 2.6	(34) 4.1
	2.6	2.7						1.0	2.2
.1	.2	.1	.4					.3	.2
3.3	.7	.5	.6				Fixed/Worth	.7	.7
-.5	21.3	.9	1.1					1.8	2.0
1.7	1.0	.8	.9					1.0	1.0
-52.3	3.9	1.5	1.9				Debt/Worth	2.8	2.1
-3.7	NM	3.5	3.6					7.6	7.2
119.5	42.4	29.1	33.7					38.7	37.3
(23) 34.3	(37) 11.0	(63) 21.0	18.1				% Profit Before Taxes/Tangible Net Worth	(120) 21.1	(146) 20.9
2.0	2.7	8.4	4.6					6.8	8.7
22.4	12.9	13.2	11.8					12.6	13.0
9.0	3.9	6.6	6.3				% Profit Before Taxes/Total Assets	5.3	5.5
-7.1	.3	2.0	1.8					1.7	2.2
137.6	61.4	50.1	21.7					47.8	46.9
33.8	29.4	21.7	12.8				Sales/Net Fixed Assets	17.9	19.3
16.2	11.0	11.5	5.5					9.0	9.7
9.4	4.1	3.9	3.4					3.8	4.4
6.1	3.3	3.1	2.4				Sales/Total Assets	3.1	3.3
3.4	2.0	2.1	2.0					2.4	2.4
.6	.9	.8	.9					.6	.7
(31) 1.1	(40) 1.2	(61) 1.3	1.4				% Depr., Dep., Amort./Sales	(128) 1.3	(155) 1.2
1.8	1.7	1.7	1.9					1.8	1.9
2.4	2.2	.9	.6					1.3	1.2
(27) 4.4	(21) 5.0	(18) 1.6	(10) 1.1				% Officers', Directors' Owners' Comp/Sales	(76) 3.0	(94) 3.1
7.0	6.2	2.5	2.9					5.7	5.9
61607M	162693M	1108271M	2434646M	1118193M	2384478M		Net Sales ($)	5316430M	6816057M
11763M	51585M	357758M	908669M	345857M	1149912M		Total Assets ($)	1730625M	2124796M

© RMA 2011

M = $ thousand   MM = $ million
See Pages 9 through 22 for Explanation of Ratios and Data

Comparative Historical Data | Current Data Sorted by Sales

			Type of Statement						
16	17	15	Unqualified					2	13
46	33	46	Reviewed		4	2	10	13	17
37	32	41	Compiled	5	10	3	4	12	7
32	49	50	Tax Returns	11	21	3	9	4	2
44	39	65	Other	8	17	4	4	9	23
4/1/08-3/31/09 ALL	4/1/09-3/31/10 ALL	4/1/10-3/31/11 ALL			38 (4/1-9/30/10)		179 (10/1/10-3/31/11)		
				0-1MM	1-3MM	3-5MM	5-10MM	10-25MM	25MM & OVER
175	170	217	**NUMBER OF STATEMENTS**	24	52	12	27	40	62
%	%	%	**ASSETS**	%	%	%	%	%	%
7.2	9.1	11.5	Cash & Equivalents	17.3	17.2	11.8	12.4	7.3	6.9
19.4	18.7	16.3	Trade Receivables (net)	12.1	13.4	15.1	18.4	20.3	17.1
42.0	38.7	37.3	Inventory	34.1	30.9	43.5	35.3	42.2	40.5
3.1	2.7	2.5	All Other Current	3.7	1.9	.8	5.1	3.0	1.5
71.7	69.3	67.7	Total Current	67.1	63.4	71.2	71.3	72.8	66.0
20.3	20.4	22.1	Fixed Assets (net)	20.9	21.8	17.7	18.8	20.4	26.0
2.2	4.2	4.4	Intangibles (net)	3.5	10.0	6.3	3.0	1.5	2.3
5.8	6.0	5.8	All Other Non-Current	8.6	4.8	4.8	6.9	5.3	5.7
100.0	100.0	100.0	Total	100.0	100.0	100.0	100.0	100.0	100.0
			LIABILITIES						
10.4	9.8	8.2	Notes Payable-Short Term	7.2	8.9	10.8	3.6	12.2	6.8
3.3	3.1	3.2	Cur. Mat.-L.T.D.	2.7	4.2	3.5	2.2	3.4	2.9
30.0	32.2	29.7	Trade Payables	23.7	27.0	37.7	29.2	32.2	31.2
.1	.1	.1	Income Taxes Payable	.1	.2	.0	.0	.0	.1
8.9	7.2	11.0	All Other Current	29.2	11.3	9.1	11.1	6.1	7.2
52.7	52.3	52.1	Total Current	62.8	51.6	61.1	46.1	53.8	48.2
11.3	17.4	16.5	Long-Term Debt	27.1	28.9	13.3	12.5	6.4	10.7
.3	.2	.1	Deferred Taxes	.0	.0	.0	.2	.1	.3
6.9	3.0	3.3	All Other Non-Current	7.5	4.3	3.0	.4	3.2	2.3
28.8	27.1	28.0	Net Worth	2.6	15.1	22.7	40.9	36.4	38.5
100.0	100.0	100.0	Total Liabilties & Net Worth	100.0	100.0	100.0	100.0	100.0	100.0
			INCOME DATA						
100.0	100.0	100.0	Net Sales	100.0	100.0	100.0	100.0	100.0	100.0
33.5	34.9	36.4	Gross Profit	45.8	43.7	34.8	32.9	34.2	29.8
31.0	32.4	33.2	Operating Expenses	42.3	39.8	33.6	28.1	32.1	26.9
2.5	2.5	3.2	Operating Profit	3.4	4.0	1.2	4.8	2.1	2.9
.0	.2	.3	All Other Expenses (net)	1.5	1.0	-.1	-.1	-.4	-.2
2.4	2.3	2.9	Profit Before Taxes	1.9	2.9	1.3	4.9	2.5	3.1
			RATIOS						
2.1	1.9	1.9		2.2	2.4	2.4	2.3	1.9	1.8
1.4	1.4	1.4	Current	1.4	1.4	1.4	1.7	1.3	1.3
1.1	1.0	1.0		.8	1.0	.7	1.1	1.1	1.1
.7	.9	.9		1.0	1.4	.8	1.1	.9	.7
.5 (169)	.5 (216)	.5	Quick	.5 (51)	.6	.4	.6	.5	.5
.3	.3	.3		.3	.3	.2	.4	.3	.3
10 37.8	7 51.5	6 66.3		0 UND	3 139.9	6 63.9	12 29.8	11 32.9	7 54.9
19 18.8	18 20.8	15 24.7	Sales/Receivables	10 35.6	7 55.4	9 39.1	27 13.3	22 16.3	21 17.6
33 11.1	33 11.1	32 11.4		22 16.5	25 14.8	20 18.7	37 9.9	37 9.9	33 10.9
48 7.6	45 8.1	44 8.4		33 10.9	24 15.3	33 10.9	50 7.3	56 6.5	53 6.9
68 5.4	65 5.6	64 5.7	Cost of Sales/Inventory	61 6.0	43 8.5	48 7.6	67 5.4	71 5.1	72 5.1
100 3.6	94 3.9	93 3.9		123 3.0	75 4.9	72 5.6	104 3.5	101 3.6	91 4.0
33 11.1	35 10.4	29 12.4		15 24.9	16 23.2	24 14.9	35 10.4	37 10.0	40 9.1
49 7.5	49 7.4	48 7.6	Cost of Sales/Payables	37 9.9	33 11.1	36 10.1	46 8.0	55 6.7	56 6.5
66 5.5	66 5.5	67 5.4		53 6.9	67 5.4	65 5.6	78 4.7	70 5.2	69 5.3
8.5	9.3	8.2		6.9	11.8	7.7	5.5	8.6	8.6
16.7	15.6	18.4	Sales/Working Capital	19.0	24.5	22.4	10.9	16.1	18.8
77.8	221.5	273.2		-86.1	UND	-28.7	54.3	47.9	62.0
10.2	10.7	13.5		3.0	5.8	14.8	18.3	13.3	17.5
(157) 4.7	(147) 4.1	(191) 4.6	EBIT/Interest	(19) 1.6	(43) 2.6	(11) 5.4	(23) 6.5	(37) 5.4	(58) 7.0
1.8	1.4	1.6		-.5	-.1	-.9	2.7	1.8	2.8
7.6	5.0	9.1	Net Profit + Depr., Dep.,						8.8
(42) 2.8	(37) 2.8	(37) 4.7	Amort./Cur. Mat. L/T/D						(24) 4.6
1.3	1.8	2.8							2.7
.2	.2	.2		.2	.1	.1	.1	.2	.3
.6	.6	.7	Fixed/Worth	3.0	1.2	1.0	.4	.6	.6
1.5	1.5	2.8		-.6	-2.0	NM	1.0	.9	1.2
1.1	1.0	1.0		1.3	1.3	.8	.7	.8	1.0
2.2	2.1	2.4	Debt/Worth	-191.2	6.1	2.8	1.4	1.7	1.9
5.2	5.3	9.8		-4.2	-4.8	NM	4.1	5.6	3.8
33.0	35.8	34.1	% Profit Before Taxes/Tangible	80.3	74.1		30.9	28.7	33.3
(150) 16.1	(144) 15.5	(176) 20.3	Net Worth	(11) 20.7	(32) 21.1		(25) 21.5	(37) 16.2	24.6
4.8	6.1	5.3		2.0	3.3		4.4	6.8	6.2
12.2	11.8	13.4	% Profit Before Taxes/Total	14.2	19.2	18.9	17.8	12.0	11.7
5.3	5.1	6.0	Assets	.9	9.0	5.0	8.4	5.4	6.6
1.5	.6	1.3		-6.9	.1	-5.8	1.8	1.7	2.1
44.2	56.6	54.7		101.5	76.1	88.9	47.4	47.6	28.7
20.6	20.3	22.2	Sales/Net Fixed Assets	32.7	28.1	43.7	27.6	19.5	16.4
11.8	10.2	9.7		7.1	11.0	16.2	12.8	10.3	7.2
4.2	4.2	4.5		6.4	6.9	5.4	3.3	3.9	3.8
3.2	3.2	3.2	Sales/Total Assets	3.1	4.1	4.1	2.6	3.2	2.8
2.5	2.2	2.1		1.7	2.5	3.7	1.9	2.1	2.1
.7	.7	.8		1.0	.8	.9	.5	.9	.7
(157) 1.2	(143) 1.2	(185) 1.3	% Depr., Dep., Amort./Sales	(14) 1.5	(38) 1.2	(10) 1.2	(25) 1.1	(36) 1.4	1.3
1.8	1.8	1.8		2.2	2.1	1.5	1.5	2.0	1.8
.7	1.2	1.6	% Officers', Directors'	6.0	2.5		1.7		.5
(67) 1.7	(79) 3.0	(81) 2.8	Owners' Comp/Sales	(11) 6.7	(25) 4.3		(14) 2.1		(15) 1.2
5.3	6.3	5.6		10.2	5.4		3.7		1.7
7102577M	6316932M	7269888M	Net Sales ($)	16658M	92656M	49461M	196472M	636393M	6278248M
2255184M	2256498M	2825544M	Total Assets ($)	7882M	28609M	11352M	85782M	231626M	2460293M

© RMA 2011

M = $ thousand   MM = $ million
See Pages 9 through 22 for Explanation of Ratios and Data

Current Data Sorted by Assets

Comparative Historical Data

	0-500M	500M-2MM	2-10MM	10-50MM	50-100MM	100-250MM	Type of Statement	4/1/06-3/31/07 ALL	4/1/07-3/31/08 ALL
	1	1	5	20	11	9	Unqualified	52	52
	2	15	36	25		1	Reviewed	97	90
	10	45	49	6		1	Compiled	168	132
	51	70	33	2		1	Tax Returns	149	164
	17	65	70	42	10	11	Other	225	198
		122 (4/1-9/30/10)		487 (10/1/10-3/31/11)					
NUMBER OF STATEMENTS	81	196	193	95	21	23		691	636
ASSETS	%	%	%	%	%	%		%	%
Cash & Equivalents	14.2	9.2	10.5	6.8	10.9	11.1		8.9	9.2
Trade Receivables (net)	10.0	12.3	11.7	14.5	11.0	17.4		12.7	12.5
Inventory	53.0	49.4	47.5	38.5	33.0	20.5		48.9	47.5
All Other Current	1.9	1.5	2.4	2.3	1.9	1.3		2.5	2.7
Total Current	79.0	72.5	72.1	62.1	56.8	50.3		73.0	71.8
Fixed Assets (net)	12.6	19.2	19.0	29.2	28.3	41.4		19.5	20.3
Intangibles (net)	1.7	1.1	2.6	1.3	8.6	3.9		2.2	1.9
All Other Non-Current	6.6	7.2	6.3	7.4	6.3	4.5		5.2	5.9
Total	100.0	100.0	100.0	100.0	100.0	100.0		100.0	100.0
LIABILITIES									
Notes Payable-Short Term	16.9	12.4	9.7	7.4	3.5	7.1		11.9	11.7
Cur. Mat.-L.T.D.	2.9	2.0	2.2	2.2	3.8	2.1		2.6	2.5
Trade Payables	19.0	18.6	19.1	15.2	14.2	8.5		19.1	18.3
Income Taxes Payable	.7	.1	.1	.1	.3	.4		.2	.2
All Other Current	24.9	17.8	19.1	19.1	15.4	9.7		17.9	18.7
Total Current	64.4	51.0	50.2	44.0	37.3	27.9		51.7	51.4
Long-Term Debt	16.4	16.8	13.2	15.8	23.5	21.2		14.3	14.5
Deferred Taxes	.0	.1	.0	.1	.8	1.3		.1	.0
All Other Non-Current	15.4	10.7	5.6	8.6	10.2	3.0		5.4	6.7
Net Worth	3.8	21.4	31.0	31.4	28.2	46.6		28.5	27.3
Total Liabilities & Net Worth	100.0	100.0	100.0	100.0	100.0	100.0		100.0	100.0
INCOME DATA									
Net Sales	100.0	100.0	100.0	100.0	100.0	100.0		100.0	100.0
Gross Profit	44.3	42.4	42.0	40.6	43.1	46.5		41.7	42.5
Operating Expenses	41.5	40.3	39.8	38.1	42.9	41.8		39.6	40.4
Operating Profit	2.8	2.2	2.2	2.5	.2	4.7		2.1	2.1
All Other Expenses (net)	.7	.5	.2	.6	-.3	.5		.5	.5
Profit Before Taxes	2.1	1.7	2.0	1.9	.5	4.2		1.6	1.7
RATIOS									
Current	3.1	2.8	2.2	2.0	2.9	3.2		2.4	2.3
	1.5	1.7	1.6	1.4	1.3	1.4		1.4	1.4
	.9	1.1	1.1	1.1	1.1	1.0		1.1	1.0
Quick	.9	.9	.8	.9	1.2	2.0		.8	.9
	(80) .3	.3	.3	.4	.5	.9		(684) .3	(632) .3
	.2	.1	.1	.1	.2	.1		.1	.1
Sales/Receivables	0 UND	0 UND	0 999.8	1 402.0	1 326.1	1 380.4		0 999.8	0 999.8
	0 UND	4 88.8	3 129.3	3 106.2	2 153.3	17 21.2		4 86.2	4 99.5
	15 24.5	20 18.5	19 19.0	26 14.1	18 20.4	89 4.1		23 15.9	19 19.1
Cost of Sales/Inventory	47 7.8	55 6.6	72 5.1	63 5.8	64 5.7	66 5.5		67 5.4	65 5.6
	92 4.0	117 3.1	114 3.2	98 3.7	111 3.3	88 4.2		111 3.3	104 3.5
	165 2.2	196 1.9	194 1.9	126 2.9	136 2.7	108 3.4		160 2.3	156 2.3
Cost of Sales/Payables	0 UND	15 24.6	20 17.9	20 18.4	22 16.3	21 17.6		19 19.0	17 22.1
	22 16.9	30 12.1	34 10.6	33 11.2	43 8.6	36 10.2		34 10.7	32 11.3
	54 6.8	49 7.5	58 6.3	49 7.4	58 6.3	59 6.2		54 6.7	51 7.2
Sales/Working Capital	5.7	5.1	5.2	9.3	5.2	4.2		6.1	5.9
	13.0	12.9	11.2	15.2	22.1	6.3		13.8	16.0
	-50.8	71.3	57.1	47.4	55.6	57.6		95.2	-446.3
EBIT/Interest	14.3	11.6	17.8	15.7	10.8	11.2		7.2	6.4
	(55) 3.5	(159) 1.7	(162) 2.5	(82) 3.1	(20) 2.3	(21) 3.6		(586) 2.3	(524) 2.4
	.2	-.1	.9	1.0	.7	.9		.7	.3
Net Profit + Depr., Dep., Amort./Cur. Mat. L/T/D		7.0	8.4	8.6				9.1	8.1
		(11) .3	(26) 3.0	(23) 2.7				(106) 1.9	(87) 2.6
		-4.1	.2	1.2				.5	-.4
Fixed/Worth	.0	.1	.1	.2	.6	.5		.2	.2
	.3	.5	.4	.7	.8	.7		.6	.7
	-14.4	6.3	1.9	2.6	NM	1.9		2.6	3.4
Debt/Worth	.8	.8	.8	.8	.8	.6		1.0	1.0
	3.3	2.7	2.2	1.8	3.7	1.4		2.5	2.7
	-4.6	34.4	6.4	4.9	NM	2.3		9.8	12.5
% Profit Before Taxes/Tangible Net Worth	76.9	56.2	33.7	35.8	48.1	33.0		37.9	40.7
	(56) 28.8	(154) 13.4	(165) 12.9	(84) 14.6	(16) 13.2	(22) 9.4		(580) 12.5	(516) 14.1
	3.3	-4.7	2.6	3.7	3.9	.9		.6	1.3
% Profit Before Taxes/Total Assets	21.3	14.8	10.8	11.6	14.1	11.8		11.9	12.2
	7.3	2.6	3.6	4.4	3.6	5.5		3.5	4.0
	-2.2	-2.4	.1	.5	-.2	-.4		-1.0	-1.6
Sales/Net Fixed Assets	216.9	80.7	53.2	40.4	14.3	5.3		59.6	60.1
	68.1	27.0	24.9	11.6	8.9	3.3		22.7	22.4
	22.0	11.0	8.3	5.4	5.0	2.1		9.7	9.1
Sales/Total Assets	5.5	4.0	3.5	3.9	3.2	1.9		3.9	4.0
	3.9	2.7	2.5	2.7	1.9	1.4		2.8	2.9
	2.0	1.8	1.6	1.4	1.3	.8		1.9	1.9
% Depr., Dep., Amort./Sales	.2	.4	.4	.6	1.8	1.5		.4	.4
	(52) .6	(156) .7	(161) .8	(85) 1.3	(20) 2.3	(19) 2.3		(558) .8	(505) .8
	1.4	1.3	1.3	2.1	2.9	2.9		1.3	1.5
% Officers', Directors' Owners' Comp/Sales	2.8	1.7	1.3	.6				1.4	1.6
	(48) 4.8	(103) 3.1	(89) 2.6	(21) 1.5				(317) 3.2	(280) 3.5
	6.6	5.5	3.7	3.0				6.0	5.9
Net Sales ($)	92215M	744277M	2440312M	5299682M	3349537M	5625614M		20241115M	21887143M
Total Assets ($)	23668M	225440M	886799M	1982389M	1585294M	3728888M		8663545M	8771758M

M = $ thousand   MM = $ million
See Pages 9 through 22 for Explanation of Ratios and Data

Comparative Historical Data			Type of Statement	Current Data Sorted by Sales					
46	70	47	Unqualified	1	1		2	7	36
83	105	79	Reviewed		6	7	13	17	36
126	148	111	Compiled	11	35	16	20	20	9
163	176	157	Tax Returns	31	59	26	30	6	5
238	230	215	Other	16	32	21	41	42	63
4/1/08-3/31/09 ALL	4/1/09-3/31/10 ALL	4/1/10-3/31/11 ALL		122 (4/1-9/30/10)		487 (10/1/10-3/31/11)			
				0-1MM	1-3MM	3-5MM	5-10MM	10-25MM	25MM & OVER
656	729	609	NUMBER OF STATEMENTS	59	133	70	106	92	149
%	%	%	ASSETS	%	%	%	%	%	%
9.3	9.6	10.0	Cash & Equivalents	11.8	8.4	8.7	11.7	13.5	8.1
12.4	11.8	12.3	Trade Receivables (net)	8.2	9.2	10.4	15.2	13.4	14.9
45.0	45.1	45.9	Inventory	50.4	51.6	51.2	48.1	39.8	38.9
2.8	2.2	2.0	All Other Current	1.1	1.9	1.8	1.4	2.2	2.7
69.5	68.7	70.2	Total Current	71.4	71.1	72.1	76.3	68.8	64.6
22.1	22.2	21.0	Fixed Assets (net)	20.6	19.4	20.5	15.3	21.0	26.6
3.1	3.1	2.1	Intangibles (net)	1.5	1.6	.7	1.9	2.8	2.9
5.3	6.0	6.7	All Other Non-Current	6.4	7.9	6.6	6.4	7.4	5.8
100.0	100.0	100.0	Total	100.0	100.0	100.0	100.0	100.0	100.0
			LIABILITIES						
13.8	11.2	10.9	Notes Payable-Short Term	18.9	14.8	9.6	9.5	7.7	7.6
3.3	2.7	2.3	Cur. Mat.-L.T.D.	3.1	2.1	2.4	2.9	1.6	2.0
16.3	18.4	17.7	Trade Payables	11.3	16.6	18.1	19.4	19.7	18.7
.2	.2	.2	Income Taxes Payable	.1	.4	.1	.2	.2	.3
16.7	19.8	19.0	All Other Current	22.8	16.7	18.8	21.6	18.1	18.4
50.4	52.2	50.1	Total Current	56.2	50.6	49.0	53.5	47.3	47.0
17.1	15.0	15.8	Long-Term Debt	22.3	22.5	16.2	9.8	11.8	14.0
.1	.1	.1	Deferred Taxes	.0	.0	.1	.1	.0	.4
7.0	7.1	9.1	All Other Non-Current	13.8	15.5	8.1	4.3	5.0	8.0
25.5	25.6	24.9	Net Worth	7.7	11.4	26.6	32.4	36.0	30.6
100.0	100.0	100.0	Total Liabilities & Net Worth	100.0	100.0	100.0	100.0	100.0	100.0
			INCOME DATA						
100.0	100.0	100.0	Net Sales	100.0	100.0	100.0	100.0	100.0	100.0
42.4	42.1	42.4	Gross Profit	49.1	43.6	44.3	40.3	39.6	41.1
41.3	41.0	40.1	Operating Expenses	44.8	42.5	41.7	37.7	37.1	38.9
1.1	1.1	2.3	Operating Profit	4.4	1.1	2.6	2.6	2.5	2.2
.6	.5	.4	All Other Expenses (net)	2.6	.1	.1	.4	.1	.2
.5	.6	1.9	Profit Before Taxes	1.8	1.0	2.5	2.2	2.4	2.0
			RATIOS						
2.4	2.3	2.5		4.3	2.9	2.7	2.2	2.2	2.2
1.4	1.4	1.5	Current	2.0	1.8	1.5	1.6	1.5	1.4
1.0	1.0	1.1		1.1	1.0	1.1	1.1	1.1	1.1
.8	.8	.9		.9	.8	.9	.9	1.0	1.0
(654) .3	(724) .3	(608) .3	Quick	(58) .3	.2	.3	.4	.4	.4
.1	.1	.1		.2	.1	.1	.2	.2	.1
0 999.8	0 UND	0 999.8		0 UND	0 UND	0 UND	1 451.0	0 999.8	1 419.1
3 110.6	3 118.6	3 113.2	Sales/Receivables	2 153.8	3 106.4	2 238.1	6 66.0	3 136.8	4 86.5
19 19.6	20 18.4	20 18.4		21 17.3	17 20.9	10 35.1	27 13.4	21 17.5	28 13.2
56 6.5	59 6.2	62 5.9		89 4.1	77 4.7	78 4.7	38 9.5	51 7.1	62 5.9
101 3.6	102 3.6	108 3.4	Cost of Sales/Inventory	174 2.1	136 2.7	137 2.7	107 3.4	91 4.0	92 4.0
154 2.4	150 2.4	173 2.1		342 1.1	211 1.7	187 2.0	171 2.1	123 3.0	120 3.0
14 26.0	17 21.1	16 22.7		0 UND	10 35.5	20 18.3	17 22.1	20 18.6	20 18.0
28 13.0	33 11.2	32 11.5	Cost of Sales/Payables	22 16.9	29 12.4	36 10.1	30 12.1	34 10.7	34 10.7
49 7.5	53 6.9	51 7.1		45 8.1	59 6.1	59 6.2	46 7.9	52 7.0	51 7.2
6.4	6.6	5.4		2.8	4.4	4.5	6.0	7.4	7.7
15.7	16.5	12.5	Sales/Working Capital	5.9	9.2	9.3	12.1	13.8	18.6
114.4	UND	66.6		45.2	496.2	68.6	74.8	79.6	55.6
5.8	7.1	13.4		4.7	6.3	15.6	13.8	18.8	22.4
(560) 1.6	(611) 2.1	(499) 2.5	EBIT/Interest	(42) 1.6	(111) 1.5	(59) 2.5	(85) 2.3	(73) 3.4	(129) 4.1
-.5	-.5	.6		-.7	.2	.4	-.1	1.1	1.0
5.0	5.6	7.2	Net Profit + Depr., Dep.,				5.9	15.2	7.4
(86) 2.0	(104) 2.1	(74) 2.7	Amort./Cur. Mat. L/T/D			(13) 1.9	(13) 3.5	(36) 2.9	
.2	.4	.4				-.9	1.1	1.4	
.2	.2	.2		.1	.1	.2	.1	.2	.2
.8	.8	.5	Fixed/Worth	.5	.5	.5	.3	.5	.7
5.2	5.5	2.9		98.1	-27.1	2.8	2.0	1.8	2.2
1.0	1.0	.8		.7	.9	.8	.8	.8	.9
2.9	2.6	2.3	Debt/Worth	3.6	2.9	3.3	2.0	1.7	1.9
17.0	21.3	10.1		-10.6	-36.1	10.1	6.8	6.0	4.4
31.8	32.7	42.1	% Profit Before Taxes/Tangible	55.9	41.4	47.6	44.0	40.8	43.1
(522) 7.3	(572) 10.6	(497) 14.3	Net Worth	(43) 15.3	(96) 9.8	(58) 17.2	(91) 16.2	(80) 13.1	(129) 19.0
-5.0	-.8	.7		-7.3	-4.3	1.5	1.5	2.7	3.4
9.0	9.4	13.3	% Profit Before Taxes/Total	14.0	10.6	14.3	14.6	12.1	13.7
1.6	2.7	4.1	Assets	4.0	1.7	3.8	4.5	4.3	5.8
-4.2	-4.0	-.7		-4.2	-3.1	-.7	-.3	.5	.3
57.0	58.7	64.4		137.3	77.7	57.3	107.7	56.1	46.9
20.9	22.4	24.1	Sales/Net Fixed Assets	24.1	22.3	25.6	35.6	27.7	12.7
8.4	8.0	8.2		9.1	9.5	8.7	15.1	7.1	5.4
4.3	4.3	3.9		3.6	3.9	3.4	4.3	4.5	4.0
2.8	2.8	2.6	Sales/Total Assets	1.6	2.3	2.5	3.0	2.8	2.9
1.8	1.7	1.6		1.2	1.6	1.7	2.2	2.0	1.6
.4	.5	.4		.5	.4	.4	.3	.3	.7
(520) 1.0	(594) 1.0	(493) .9	% Depr., Dep., Amort./Sales	(43) 1.3	(107) .7	(55) .8	(79) .7	(80) .8	(129) 1.5
1.6	1.7	1.6		2.3	1.3	1.3	1.2	1.4	2.3
1.6	1.6	1.5		2.8	2.7	1.6	1.2	1.1	.5
(292) 3.1	(308) 3.0	(265) 3.0	% Officers', Directors' Owners' Comp/Sales	(36) 5.6	(70) 4.2	(37) 3.1	(55) 2.5	(37) 1.5	(30) 1.6
5.5	5.4	5.3		7.4	6.2	4.6	3.6	2.7	3.1
21661544M	24075403M	17551637M	Net Sales ($)	33449M	253246M	273558M	749450M	1409555M	14832379M
9445744M	10598271M	8432478M	Total Assets ($)	26041M	125522M	147880M	291417M	584540M	7257078M

M = $ thousand   MM = $ million
See Pages 9 through 22 for Explanation of Ratios and Data

Current Data Sorted by Assets | Comparative Historical Data

0-500M	500M-2MM	2-10MM	10-50MM	50-100MM	100-250MM	Type of Statement	4/1/06-3/31/07 ALL	4/1/07-3/31/08 ALL
1	1	3	2	2	1	Unqualified	17	13
1	10	34	4			Reviewed	49	52
6	28	12	1			Compiled	91	70
42	50	12	2		1	Tax Returns	92	88
18	41	40	11	1		Other	109	114
	59 (4/1-9/30/10)		265 (10/1/10-3/31/11)					
68	130	101	20	3	2	NUMBER OF STATEMENTS	358	337
%	%	%	%	%	%	**ASSETS**	%	%
14.9	10.1	9.7	8.1			Cash & Equivalents	8.5	9.4
16.2	25.3	25.3	22.0			Trade Receivables (net)	31.1	28.7
39.9	34.8	30.4	33.7			Inventory	32.2	31.9
2.7	2.5	2.6	3.9			All Other Current	2.8	4.0
73.7	72.6	68.1	67.6			Total Current	74.6	73.9
18.5	15.8	20.9	20.1			Fixed Assets (net)	16.4	16.9
2.7	3.4	2.2	6.5			Intangibles (net)	2.6	2.4
5.1	8.1	8.8	5.8			All Other Non-Current	6.4	6.8
100.0	100.0	100.0	100.0			Total	100.0	100.0
						LIABILITIES		
20.6	18.2	11.5	9.0			Notes Payable-Short Term	13.9	14.4
10.5	2.1	2.2	2.8			Cur. Mat.-L.T.D.	2.8	3.0
24.9	19.2	17.6	19.6			Trade Payables	19.8	19.4
.0	.3	.1	.0			Income Taxes Payable	.2	.3
22.5	23.9	18.0	12.8			All Other Current	15.7	14.7
78.5	63.7	49.5	44.3			Total Current	52.3	51.8
16.5	8.8	10.8	7.9			Long-Term Debt	12.0	14.5
.0	.0	.1	.5			Deferred Taxes	.1	.1
11.2	7.0	7.3	5.6			All Other Non-Current	4.6	5.3
-6.3	20.5	32.3	41.7			Net Worth	31.0	28.3
100.0	100.0	100.0	100.0			Total Liabilities & Net Worth	100.0	100.0
						INCOME DATA		
100.0	100.0	100.0	100.0			Net Sales	100.0	100.0
39.7	36.4	33.2	34.0			Gross Profit	33.9	35.3
37.6	35.3	31.1	32.9			Operating Expenses	30.7	32.7
2.2	1.1	2.0	1.1			Operating Profit	3.1	2.6
1.7	.3	.3	-.4			All Other Expenses (net)	.4	.4
.5	.8	1.7	1.5			Profit Before Taxes	2.7	2.2
						RATIOS		
2.1	2.4	2.5	2.7			Current	2.4	2.5
1.2	1.3	1.5	1.9				1.5	1.5
.7	.8	1.0	1.2				1.1	1.1
.9	1.1	1.6	1.2			Quick	1.4	1.3
.5	.7	.6	.7				.7	.7
.2	.3	.3	.4				.4	.4
2　224.0	7　53.2	14　26.2	10　35.6			Sales/Receivables	12　30.8	11　33.1
11　32.6	22　16.3	28　12.9	21　17.3				26　13.9	25　14.4
20　17.9	40　9.2	46　8.0	37　10.0				43　8.5	43　8.5
19　19.5	21　17.7	29　12.7	29　12.6			Cost of Sales/Inventory	20　18.5	19　19.3
46　7.9	46　8.0	53　6.9	63　5.8				38　9.5	41　8.9
89　4.1	99　3.7	91　4.0	96　3.8				77　4.8	76　4.8
11　33.9	14　25.2	17　21.3	20　18.5			Cost of Sales/Payables	13　27.9	13　27.3
24　15.5	24　15.1	30　12.1	23　16.0				24　15.0	24　15.4
51　7.1	43　8.5	44　8.3	40　9.2				40　9.2	43　8.5
9.8	6.2	6.8	4.9			Sales/Working Capital	7.7	7.5
47.2	19.9	14.3	8.2				14.3	14.4
-29.3	-37.5	95.4	45.8				71.5	109.4
9.1	8.1	7.1	11.8			EBIT/Interest	14.9	11.0
(54)　1.6	(110)　1.9	(90)　2.6	(16)　4.1				(320)　4.2	(293)　3.3
-4.1	.0	.5	-1.6				1.4	1.2
		2.9				Net Profit + Depr., Dep., Amort./Cur. Mat. L/T/D	5.0	4.4
	(13)　1.7						(49)　2.9	(41)　1.8
		-.1					1.0	.6
.2	.1	.1	.3			Fixed/Worth	.1	.1
1.9	.5	.4	.6				.4	.4
-.6	16.8	1.2	1.1				1.6	1.4
1.5	.8	.8	.5			Debt/Worth	.9	1.0
10.6	2.2	2.1	1.3				2.1	2.3
-3.5	-43.9	3.6	2.7				6.1	7.2
65.7	41.3	30.1	28.3			% Profit Before Taxes/Tangible Net Worth	59.9	52.2
(37)　11.6	(96)　11.2	(91)　9.7	(17)　5.9				(318)　25.2	(288)　21.5
-10.5	-.2	-.9	1.0				7.2	4.4
19.8	9.5	9.4	8.4			% Profit Before Taxes/Total Assets	19.2	16.3
2.1	2.4	3.1	2.6				7.7	5.8
-15.1	-2.5	-.2	-2.3				1.8	.6
89.1	76.7	56.0	46.8			Sales/Net Fixed Assets	89.6	86.5
33.3	31.7	24.3	14.1				37.4	33.1
16.9	12.8	7.9	8.3				17.3	15.3
6.8	4.7	3.5	4.2			Sales/Total Assets	5.1	4.8
4.6	3.2	2.8	3.1				3.8	3.7
3.2	2.0	2.1	1.7				2.8	2.5
.3	.4	.4	.6			% Depr., Dep., Amort./Sales	.3	.4
(49)　.6	(100)　.7	(91)　.7	(16)　.8				(293)　.7	(274)　.7
1.2	1.3	1.5	1.2				1.2	1.2
3.5	1.9	1.0				% Officers', Directors' Owners' Comp/Sales	1.7	1.9
(46)　6.9	(80)　3.5	(58)　2.0					(221)　3.3	(202)　3.6
10.6	5.3	3.9					5.9	6.6
71353M	472093M	1312716M	1568322M	1195068M	442560M	Net Sales ($)	5433190M	5731901M
16381M	140705M	451248M	373601M	245800M	316159M	Total Assets ($)	1528665M	1653845M

M = $ thousand　　MM = $ million
See Pages 9 through 22 for Explanation of Ratios and Data

Comparative Historical Data / Current Data Sorted by Sales

11	9	10	Type of Statement	1		1		3	5
49	52	49	Reviewed	1	4	3	18	16	7
78	53	47	Compiled	5	15	9	9	7	2
110	121	107	Tax Returns	25	42	17	12	8	3
118	124	111	Other	11	30	14	24	15	17
4/1/08-3/31/09 ALL	4/1/09-3/31/10 ALL	4/1/10-3/31/11 ALL		59 (4/1-9/30/10)			265 (10/1/10-3/31/11)		
				0-1MM	1-3MM	3-5MM	5-10MM	10-25MM	25MM & OVER
366	359	324	NUMBER OF STATEMENTS	43	91	44	63	49	34
%	%	%	ASSETS	%	%	%	%	%	%
8.3	10.3	10.8	Cash & Equivalents	13.9	12.1	8.5	10.5	10.6	7.6
25.2	21.1	22.8	Trade Receivables (net)	12.4	21.5	22.2	27.3	28.7	24.0
34.4	33.7	34.4	Inventory	42.5	35.5	34.5	28.9	30.3	37.6
2.8	3.6	2.8	All Other Current	2.4	2.6	2.3	3.0	2.5	4.2
70.7	68.8	70.9	Total Current	71.2	71.7	67.5	69.6	72.0	73.4
17.6	18.3	18.4	Fixed Assets (net)	18.6	18.9	18.3	17.5	20.0	16.8
3.9	4.2	3.2	Intangibles (net)	4.1	2.6	4.7	1.1	2.9	6.5
7.8	8.8	7.5	All Other Non-Current	6.1	6.9	9.5	11.8	5.0	3.4
100.0	100.0	100.0	Total	100.0	100.0	100.0	100.0	100.0	100.0
			LIABILITIES						
15.6	15.2	15.8	Notes Payable-Short Term	22.0	17.8	12.4	17.9	10.4	11.0
4.7	4.1	4.0	Cur. Mat.-L.T.D.	12.2	4.4	2.4	1.1	1.8	3.1
19.4	19.4	19.9	Trade Payables	17.7	20.5	22.1	18.0	19.7	21.8
.1	.3	.1	Income Taxes Payable	.0	.0	.7	.0	.1	.0
17.3	17.7	21.2	All Other Current	12.9	24.7	24.3	19.5	13.1	32.7
57.1	56.7	61.0	Total Current	64.7	67.5	62.0	56.6	45.1	68.6
13.0	14.7	11.5	Long-Term Debt	14.1	15.3	12.1	5.5	10.1	10.7
.1	.1	.1	Deferred Taxes	.0	.0	.0	.0	.2	.3
6.8	9.5	8.2	All Other Non-Current	13.7	8.0	3.4	7.8	5.4	12.4
23.0	19.0	19.2	Net Worth	7.5	9.1	22.6	30.0	39.1	8.0
100.0	100.0	100.0	Total Liabilities & Net Worth	100.0	100.0	100.0	100.0	100.0	100.0
			INCOME DATA						
100.0	100.0	100.0	Net Sales	100.0	100.0	100.0	100.0	100.0	100.0
34.7	37.5	36.1	Gross Profit	45.1	37.6	34.8	33.8	31.3	33.8
34.0	37.6	34.5	Operating Expenses	44.8	34.8	33.5	32.8	29.1	32.6
.8	-.1	1.6	Operating Profit	.3	2.8	1.3	1.0	2.3	1.1
.4	.6	.6	All Other Expenses (net)	.8	1.4	.3	.1	-.1	.7
.4	-.7	1.0	Profit Before Taxes	-.5	1.4	1.0	.8	2.4	.4
			RATIOS						
2.2	2.4	2.5	Current	5.2	2.5	1.6	2.2	2.4	2.8
1.4	1.4	1.3		1.3	1.3	1.2	1.5	1.6	1.3
1.0	.9	.9		.6	.8	.8	1.0	1.0	1.0
1.2	1.2	1.2	Quick	1.2	1.1	.9	1.5	1.6	.9
(365) .6	(358) .6	.6		.5	.6	.6	.7	.7	.5
.3	.2	.3		.1	.3	.2	.4	.4	.3
8 48.4	6 57.0	6 56.7	Sales/Receivables	2 158.2	5 69.4	8 48.3	14 26.7	16 22.5	7 56.0
23 15.6	20 18.5	21 17.5		9 40.1	16 22.7	16 22.1	26 14.2	29 12.5	21 17.4
39 9.4	32 11.3	39 9.4		34 10.7	33 11.1	36 10.2	40 9.2	47 7.8	30 12.2
22 16.8	24 15.4	23 16.2	Cost of Sales/Inventory	20 17.8	21 17.8	22 16.6	26 14.0	24 15.3	26 13.8
45 8.1	49 7.4	51 7.2		85 4.3	56 6.5	47 7.8	41 9.0	46 8.0	57 6.4
94 3.9	92 4.0	97 3.8		287 3.5	105 3.5	94 3.9	70 5.3	88 4.1	83 4.4
13 27.8	14 26.9	15 24.8	Cost of Sales/Payables	7 51.7	13 29.0	21 17.8	17 21.3	18 19.8	16 22.3
23 15.9	25 14.8	25 14.5		23 15.9	23 15.6	28 13.1	27 13.7	27 13.5	23 16.0
40 9.0	43 8.5	45 8.2		71 5.2	45 8.2	46 7.9	38 9.6	46 8.0	37 10.0
8.4	6.7	6.7	Sales/Working Capital	3.2	5.5	10.6	7.1	7.0	6.2
18.5	17.2	19.5		27.6	15.6	32.5	19.9	12.6	19.6
-230.7	-50.2	-93.4		-13.8	-39.4	-27.1	117.2	72.2	-233.6
6.4	5.3	7.8	EBIT/Interest	5.8	8.9	5.5	7.5	10.9	8.5
(315) 1.8	(299) 1.0	(275) 2.1		(30) 1.6	(76) 1.6	(41) 2.1	(54) 2.4	(45) 3.4	(29) 2.1
-.7	-4.1	-.5		-1.5	-2.1	-.6	-.5	1.9	-3.1
4.7	3.9	3.2	Net Profit + Depr., Dep., Amort./Cur. Mat. L/T/D						
(44) 1.5	(37) 1.7	(25) 2.0							
-.2	-.2	.7							
.2	.2	.1	Fixed/Worth	.1	.2	.2	.1	.1	.3
.5	.6	.6		.6	.9	.5	.4	.4	.6
6.3	165.0	4.8		-1.0	-3.3	4.5	1.5	1.2	15.3
.9	.8	.8	Debt/Worth	.7	.9	1.1	.7	.9	.6
2.5	2.4	2.3		8.2	3.4	3.7	1.8	1.7	2.1
26.5	-70.7	UND		-3.6	-8.1	134.2	5.0	2.8	NM
36.5	26.1	39.2	% Profit Before Taxes/Tangible Net Worth	41.1	48.6	51.9	33.6	32.0	38.0
(292) 12.2	(268) 5.6	(243) 9.7		(23) 5.2	(62) 11.2	(35) 8.1	(52) 7.5	(45) 12.9	(26) 11.4
-5.6	-12.7	-.9		-5.7	-3.9	-3.3	-4.1	5.5	-4.1
9.2	8.6	10.6	% Profit Before Taxes/Total Assets	14.1	13.7	7.7	9.7	12.2	12.4
2.3	.9	2.7		1.6	1.6	1.5	2.4	5.1	2.9
-4.2	-9.3	-2.9		-4.0	-10.1	-2.1	-2.9	1.6	-5.6
76.8	65.7	72.3	Sales/Net Fixed Assets	137.0	81.3	103.4	61.2	57.2	57.3
32.4	28.1	29.9		20.8	30.2	43.3	33.7	26.8	44.0
15.4	12.0	11.4		7.6	12.4	11.5	13.3	8.6	11.5
5.1	4.7	4.7	Sales/Total Assets	4.9	5.0	4.3	4.8	3.9	5.2
3.6	3.3	3.2		2.2	3.3	3.4	3.3	3.1	4.0
2.3	2.1	2.1		1.2	1.8	2.6	2.6	2.6	2.4
.4	.4	.4	% Depr., Dep., Amort./Sales	.3	.5	.4	.3	.4	.5
(288) .7	(280) .9	(258) .7		(28) .7	(71) .9	(36) .6	(53) .8	(44) .6	(26) .8
1.2	1.6	1.3		2.0	1.2	1.2	1.5	1.2	1.1
1.7	2.1	1.6	% Officers', Directors' Owners' Comp/Sales	4.5	2.9	1.6	1.2	.7	
(210) 3.3	(193) 3.9	(191) 3.5		(24) 7.1	(62) 4.7	(28) 3.7	(40) 2.2	(29) 1.2	
6.3	7.2	6.6		15.3	7.5	5.2	3.8	3.2	
5396098M	7966895M	5062112M	Net Sales ($)	27393M	165983M	162785M	449521M	711643M	3544787M
1749744M	2342391M	1543894M	Total Assets ($)	19717M	71944M	58667M	155641M	261041M	976884M

M = $ thousand   MM = $ million
See Pages 9 through 22 for Explanation of Ratios and Data

Current Data Sorted by Assets   Comparative Historical Data

Type of Statement	0-500M	500M-2MM	2-10MM	10-50MM	50-100MM	100-250MM		4/1/06-3/31/07 ALL	4/1/07-3/31/08 ALL
Unqualified				7	3	4		9	12
Reviewed		1	7	2				15	14
Compiled	4	9	9	2				30	24
Tax Returns	28	20	7	2	1			60	69
Other	18	18	9	8	3	4		52	49
		25 (4/1-9/30/10)		141 (10/1/10-3/31/11)					
NUMBER OF STATEMENTS	50	48	32	21	7	8		166	168
	%	%	%	%	%	%		%	%
ASSETS									
Cash & Equivalents	15.8	10.6	7.8	12.0				10.2	8.7
Trade Receivables (net)	14.3	11.5	12.2	13.2				12.1	9.2
Inventory	37.1	49.9	46.9	40.8				49.9	53.6
All Other Current	4.5	1.2	2.2	2.9				2.6	1.9
Total Current	71.8	73.1	69.0	68.9				74.8	73.3
Fixed Assets (net)	13.6	14.3	19.9	18.8				16.9	19.1
Intangibles (net)	4.4	4.0	2.5	3.8				3.4	3.1
All Other Non-Current	10.2	8.6	8.7	8.4				4.8	4.6
Total	100.0	100.0	100.0	100.0				100.0	100.0
LIABILITIES									
Notes Payable-Short Term	21.0	11.2	9.2	7.8				13.4	14.0
Cur. Mat.-L.T.D.	2.0	1.6	3.1	2.1				4.0	4.4
Trade Payables	18.5	19.8	18.2	18.6				18.5	20.0
Income Taxes Payable	.1	.0	.4	.1				.2	.3
All Other Current	19.2	11.5	17.2	12.1				14.0	16.3
Total Current	60.9	44.1	48.1	40.7				50.2	55.1
Long-Term Debt	16.1	15.5	11.5	13.6				17.2	15.1
Deferred Taxes	.0	.0	.0	.1				.0	.1
All Other Non-Current	11.0	6.4	2.8	3.7				6.4	9.1
Net Worth	12.1	34.0	37.6	41.9				26.3	20.8
Total Liabilities & Net Worth	100.0	100.0	100.0	100.0				100.0	100.0
INCOME DATA									
Net Sales	100.0	100.0	100.0	100.0				100.0	100.0
Gross Profit	45.3	41.8	46.2	41.3				44.7	44.7
Operating Expenses	42.6	40.4	42.8	39.5				41.5	41.4
Operating Profit	2.7	1.4	3.3	1.8				3.2	3.3
All Other Expenses (net)	.6	-.1	.3	2.6				1.1	1.1
Profit Before Taxes	2.2	1.5	3.0	-.8				2.1	2.2
RATIOS									
Current	3.1	3.2	2.2	2.6				2.4	2.3
	1.4	1.6	1.4	2.0				1.6	1.4
	.8	1.1	.9	1.0				1.1	.9
Quick	1.2	1.1	.7	1.3				.7	.6
	.4 (47)	.5	.3	.5				(165) .4 (166)	.3
	.1	.2	.1	.2				.2	.1
Sales/Receivables	0 UND	0 UND	0 999.8	3 123.4				0 UND	0 UND
	5 68.1	10 35.4	7 55.1	11 33.0				8 45.4	4 103.2
	22 16.6	26 14.2	25 14.4	37 9.9				27 13.6	19 19.5
Cost of Sales/Inventory	10 35.0	71 5.2	69 5.3	65 5.6				68 5.4	70 5.2
	62 5.9	148 2.5	131 2.8	109 3.3				117 3.1	111 3.3
	168 2.2	219 1.7	206 1.8	202 1.8				192 1.9	171 2.1
Cost of Sales/Payables	0 UND	19 19.2	24 14.9	21 17.7				17 21.2	20 17.9
	24 15.1	40 9.2	45 8.1	43 8.4				41 8.8	40 9.1
	50 7.2	87 4.2	62 5.9	83 4.4				64 5.7	63 5.8
Sales/Working Capital	5.7	3.8	4.8	4.2				5.0	6.5
	32.1	8.0	13.9	6.1				10.3	15.3
	-14.8	33.8	-124.7	NM				56.0	-87.4
EBIT/Interest	6.1	7.7	9.1	13.8				10.0	6.8
	(30) 2.8	(37) 2.7	(29) 3.5	(18) 6.0				(150) 2.9	(146) 2.6
	-.2	.4	1.8	1.2				.9	.8
Net Profit + Depr., Dep., Amort./Cur. Mat. L/T/D								12.5	43.8
								(14) 3.3	(18) 6.1
								.9	1.8
Fixed/Worth	.1	.1	.2	.2				.1	.2
	.5	.3	.8	.4				.4	.6
	-1.3	1.4	1.2	1.5				4.5	10.3
Debt/Worth	.5	.7	.9	.6				1.1	1.3
	4.8	2.6	1.8	1.5				2.4	2.7
	-9.1	9.8	5.1	3.9				20.4	31.0
% Profit Before Taxes/Tangible Net Worth	58.6	35.2	57.7	22.5				59.2	57.9
	(32) 19.4	(39) 10.2	(30) 10.5	(19) 13.7				(133) 18.5	(130) 18.0
	.2	.0	2.3	2.6				3.7	1.5
% Profit Before Taxes/Total Assets	16.4	7.8	14.7	12.4				14.7	17.2
	5.4	2.0	3.7	7.2				4.9	4.7
	-4.4	-.7	1.0	.0				-.1	-.8
Sales/Net Fixed Assets	301.2	98.3	51.5	37.4				62.6	63.1
	53.6	30.0	14.7	15.3				24.4	25.0
	19.1	13.9	6.7	7.0				12.0	12.5
Sales/Total Assets	5.0	3.1	3.3	3.1				3.7	4.1
	3.8	2.3	2.5	2.1				2.7	2.9
	2.2	1.6	1.9	1.6				1.9	2.0
% Depr., Dep., Amort./Sales	.3	.4	.3	.6				.4	.4
	(26) .8	(33) .9	(28) 1.0	(19) .9				(123) 1.0	(130) .9
	1.8	1.2	2.3	2.3				1.6	1.6
% Officers', Directors' Owners' Comp/Sales	2.8	2.2	1.4					2.6	2.2
	(31) 5.8	(30) 4.5	(21) 2.9					(92) 4.1	(80) 4.0
	7.2	8.7	7.3					8.0	6.4
Net Sales ($)	57085M	127502M	378213M	1165388M	1374621M	2466720M		3614861M	4483701M
Total Assets ($)	13787M	55954M	140374M	473029M	522043M	1215478M		1408024M	1645637M

© RMA 2011

M = $ thousand   MM = $ million
See Pages 9 through 22 for Explanation of Ratios and Data

Comparative Historical Data / Current Data Sorted by Sales

4/1/08-3/31/09 ALL	4/1/09-3/31/10 ALL	4/1/10-3/31/11 ALL	Type of Statement	0-1MM	1-3MM	3-5MM	5-10MM	10-25MM	25MM & OVER
7	12	14	Unqualified		1	1	2	1	13
15	14	10	Reviewed					4	2
32	28	24	Compiled	2	8	5	3	4	2
65	63	58	Tax Returns	19	18	9	5	5	2
67	69	60	Other	11	25	2	2	5	15
						25 (4/1-9/30/10)		141 (10/1/10-3/31/11)	
186	186	166	**NUMBER OF STATEMENTS**	32	52	17	12	19	34
%	%	%	**ASSETS**	%	%	%	%	%	%
9.2	13.0	12.7	Cash & Equivalents	13.5	11.4	11.0	12.4	12.7	14.8
11.7	11.1	11.8	Trade Receivables (net)	13.6	13.5	10.9	13.4	8.7	9.2
49.6	44.5	43.4	Inventory	36.0	46.4	46.8	50.7	43.7	41.2
3.5	3.0	2.9	All Other Current	5.5	1.9	.8	1.8	2.4	3.5
73.9	71.6	70.7	Total Current	68.5	73.2	69.5	78.4	67.6	68.7
17.7	16.7	16.7	Fixed Assets (net)	15.3	14.3	18.8	12.6	21.1	19.7
3.5	3.6	3.9	Intangibles (net)	5.8	3.3	3.8	.4	2.4	5.4
4.9	8.2	8.6	All Other Non-Current	10.4	9.2	7.8	8.7	8.9	6.2
100.0	100.0	100.0	Total	100.0	100.0	100.0	100.0	100.0	100.0
			LIABILITIES						
13.1	13.9	13.0	Notes Payable-Short Term	16.3	17.6	6.4	9.9	12.6	7.3
3.2	2.9	2.0	Cur. Mat.-L.T.D.	2.5	1.7	1.8	3.4	2.1	1.4
21.1	17.7	18.7	Trade Payables	17.6	18.2	23.0	16.9	17.8	19.4
.1	.2	.2	Income Taxes Payable	.1	.0	.1	.2	.1	.6
15.9	16.8	15.2	All Other Current	14.1	16.9	13.8	23.9	10.5	13.8
53.3	51.4	49.0	Total Current	50.7	54.5	45.0	54.4	43.1	42.5
19.7	17.1	13.9	Long-Term Debt	14.1	21.6	9.9	5.6	8.0	10.1
.1	.2	.1	Deferred Taxes	.0	.0	.0	.0	.0	.3
12.4	8.9	6.6	All Other Non-Current	10.1	8.7	6.5	3.8	2.1	3.5
14.6	22.4	30.4	Net Worth	25.2	15.1	38.6	36.2	46.8	43.5
100.0	100.0	100.0	Total Liabilities & Net Worth	100.0	100.0	100.0	100.0	100.0	100.0
			INCOME DATA						
100.0	100.0	100.0	Net Sales	100.0	100.0	100.0	100.0	100.0	100.0
43.2	44.0	43.9	Gross Profit	48.8	42.5	46.6	40.3	43.3	41.9
41.7	41.5	41.2	Operating Expenses	45.0	41.1	44.9	39.9	38.5	37.7
1.5	2.6	2.7	Operating Profit	3.8	1.3	1.6	.5	4.8	4.1
.5	.6	.5	All Other Expenses (net)	1.0	.3	-.2	-.7	.3	1.5
1.0	1.9	2.2	Profit Before Taxes	2.8	1.1	1.9	1.2	4.5	2.6
			RATIOS						
2.6	2.8	2.9	Current	3.5	3.2	2.3	2.8	2.6	2.5
1.5	1.6	1.6		1.4	1.7	1.4	1.6	1.7	1.9
1.0	1.0	1.0		.8	.9	1.1	1.0	1.1	1.1
.9	1.1	1.1	Quick	1.1	1.3	.7	1.3	1.1	1.0
(184) .4	.4	(165) .4		.5	(51) .5	.4	.3	.3	.4
.1	.1	.2		.1	.1	.2	.1	.1	.2
0 UND	0 UND	0 UND	Sales/Receivables	0 UND	0 UND	3 141.3	0 UND	0 UND	0 785.0
5 80.9	6 58.9	7 56.1		8 46.7	7 50.6	11 34.0	8 46.9	3 113.8	3 105.6
21 17.7	23 15.7	22 16.4		32 11.5	23 15.6	20 18.6	26 14.1	20 18.5	16 23.5
54 6.8	63 5.8	49 7.5	Cost of Sales/Inventory	11 31.8	35 10.5	86 4.2	31 11.9	75 4.9	61 6.0
114 3.2	119 3.1	110 3.3		93 3.9	104 3.5	167 2.2	125 2.9	124 2.9	100 3.7
193 1.9	188 1.9	189 1.9		245 1.5	206 1.9	193 1.9	241 1.5	169 2.2	178 2.0
16 22.7	17 21.5	18 20.8	Cost of Sales/Payables	0 UND	11 34.4	27 13.3	9 40.3	26 13.8	24 15.5
34 10.7	34 10.8	36 10.3		32 11.4	33 11.2	60 6.1	27 13.5	41 8.9	41 8.9
64 5.7	61 6.0	63 5.8		62 5.9	55 6.6	108 3.4	52 7.0	60 6.1	77 4.7
5.2	5.0	4.7	Sales/Working Capital	4.7	4.5	5.0	4.8	4.9	4.8
11.4	11.4	10.1		11.8	11.9	17.6	25.4	6.8	7.0
-104.1	-119.1	NM		-19.3	NM	104.6	NM	-306.2	98.9
7.5	7.6	10.1	EBIT/Interest	6.7	5.8	12.8		34.7	30.4
(158) 2.5	(149) 2.8	(127) 4.1		(18) 2.8	(39) 1.7	(15) 3.8		(18) 7.7	(29) 10.3
-.7	.3	1.1		-.2	.2	1.7		3.4	2.2
6.7	17.3	32.2	Net Profit + Depr., Dep., Amort./Cur. Mat. L/T/D						
(14) 1.2	(21) 2.1	(19) 2.7							
-.3	.0	.8							
.2	.1	.1	Fixed/Worth	.0	.1	.2	.1	.1	.2
.7	.6	.4		.5	.3	.8	.5	.6	.6
11.3	UND	1.8		UND	-10.5	10.2	1.1	1.1	1.1
1.1	.9	.7	Debt/Worth	.4	1.1	.6	.4	.5	.6
2.9	2.4	2.3		4.1	4.0	1.4	3.0	1.5	1.3
NM	-52.2	10.5		-11.7	-29.6	29.9	6.5	2.6	3.6
45.9	46.1	45.1	% Profit Before Taxes/Tangible Net Worth	52.8	41.0	34.9	35.2	53.7	53.9
(140) 12.1	(138) 14.7	(134) 15.9		(22) 6.9	(38) 16.0	(14) 4.4	(11) 9.4	(18) 20.6	(31) 18.6
-.5	1.2	2.3		-1.9	-.1	-4.1	-9.0	2.5	11.4
11.6	15.4	13.4	% Profit Before Taxes/Total Assets	15.7	7.8	14.2	10.4	19.1	16.1
2.8	4.0	4.9		3.5	2.2	2.1	2.1	7.6	7.5
-5.2	-2.6	.0		-4.3	-1.7	.6	-1.9	1.1	4.6
67.7	69.2	89.1	Sales/Net Fixed Assets	254.1	140.6	44.7	212.7	94.2	32.5
26.9	24.4	24.6		31.8	49.9	20.0	22.2	14.2	12.9
9.7	8.3	9.8		14.3	13.5	11.6	11.3	5.6	6.4
3.9	3.7	3.7	Sales/Total Assets	4.0	4.5	3.1	4.0	3.3	3.1
2.7	2.5	2.6		2.3	2.5	2.6	2.6	2.6	2.5
1.9	1.8	1.8		1.4	1.6	2.0	2.1	1.6	1.8
.5	.5	.5	% Depr., Dep., Amort./Sales	.5	.4	.4	.2	.4	.6
(132) 1.1	(137) 1.0	(117) 1.0		(17) 1.2	(30) .9	(16) .9	(10) 1.2	(16) 1.0	(28) 1.0
1.8	2.0	1.8		2.6	1.5	1.3	2.7	1.3	2.4
1.8	2.0	2.0	% Officers', Directors' Owners' Comp/Sales	4.4	2.1	3.9	2.0	.8	
(87) 3.7	(96) 4.6	(91) 4.1		(18) 6.2	(33) 4.1	(11) 8.5	(11) 2.7	(11) 2.9	
7.3	7.4	7.6		9.8	6.5	10.2	4.3	8.2	
5787317M	5084226M	5569529M	Net Sales ($)	17811M	98673M	61938M	92266M	293245M	5005596M
2293305M	2198927M	2420665M	Total Assets ($)	8800M	47004M	27899M	31835M	132440M	2172687M

M = $ thousand   MM = $ million
See Pages 9 through 22 for Explanation of Ratios and Data

Current Data Sorted by Assets | Comparative Historical Data

						Type of Statement		
		2	3		1	Unqualified		
		5	4	1		Reviewed	8	6
4	12	14	1			Compiled	13	13
13	12	7				Tax Returns	29	29
4	11	12	9	1	4	Other	35	29
	22 (4/1-9/30/10)		98 (10/1/10-3/31/11)				38	41
							4/1/06-	4/1/07-
							3/31/07	3/31/08
0-500M	500M-2MM	2-10MM	10-50MM	50-100MM	100-250MM		ALL	ALL
21	35	40	17	2	5	NUMBER OF STATEMENTS	123	118
%	%	%	%	%	%	ASSETS	%	%
15.6	9.3	9.4	13.0			Cash & Equivalents	10.8	12.6
10.6	13.8	13.9	9.5			Trade Receivables (net)	15.8	17.9
47.8	50.5	51.7	48.2			Inventory	47.7	44.6
2.0	1.6	3.1	2.7			All Other Current	2.9	2.4
76.0	75.2	78.0	73.4			Total Current	77.2	77.5
22.6	16.6	17.8	22.1			Fixed Assets (net)	15.9	14.1
.0	5.5	.5	2.4			Intangibles (net)	1.8	3.0
1.3	2.7	3.7	2.0			All Other Non-Current	5.2	5.5
100.0	100.0	100.0	100.0			Total	100.0	100.0
						LIABILITIES		
23.5	20.3	10.7	14.7			Notes Payable-Short Term	12.3	13.4
3.1	2.7	3.6	3.1			Cur. Mat.-L.T.D.	2.7	3.1
29.8	21.8	16.2	19.3			Trade Payables	22.1	19.6
.0	.0	.1	.6			Income Taxes Payable	.1	.1
21.8	13.7	15.1	17.8			All Other Current	17.2	14.2
78.2	58.5	45.7	55.5			Total Current	54.4	50.5
13.5	14.9	9.4	5.3			Long-Term Debt	12.1	13.7
.0	.1	.0	.1			Deferred Taxes	.1	.0
8.1	7.5	7.7	3.7			All Other Non-Current	7.8	6.4
.1	19.0	37.2	35.4			Net Worth	25.6	29.3
100.0	100.0	100.0	100.0			Total Liabilities & Net Worth	100.0	100.0
						INCOME DATA		
100.0	100.0	100.0	100.0			Net Sales	100.0	100.0
36.2	31.6	29.7	32.8			Gross Profit	34.3	32.9
36.0	30.7	28.6	31.0			Operating Expenses	31.3	29.6
.2	1.0	1.1	1.8			Operating Profit	3.0	3.2
.0	.8	-.1	-.6			All Other Expenses (net)	.3	.5
.3	.1	1.2	2.4			Profit Before Taxes	2.7	2.7
						RATIOS		
2.1	2.5	2.8	1.6				2.3	2.5
1.0	1.4	1.9	1.3			Current	1.5	1.4
.5	1.0	1.1	1.1				1.1	1.1
.7	1.0	.9	.6				.9	1.1
(20) .4	(34) .4	.5	.3			Quick	.4	.6
.2	.2	.2	.2				.2	.2
0 UND	2 171.5	6 56.9	6 58.4				5 69.6	5 72.5
5 80.3	8 43.2	12 31.6	10 36.5			Sales/Receivables	12 30.4	14 25.2
14 26.7	24 15.3	20 17.8	18 20.2				23 15.7	31 11.9
24 15.1	48 7.7	62 5.8	75 4.8				49 7.5	45 8.1
76 4.8	76 4.8	94 3.9	85 4.3			Cost of Sales/Inventory	75 4.9	69 5.3
109 3.4	116 3.1	113 3.2	115 3.2				118 3.1	105 3.5
8 44.9	14 25.9	11 33.1	15 24.5				16 22.2	12 29.9
38 9.5	32 11.3	19 19.1	19 19.4			Cost of Sales/Payables	33 11.1	27 13.6
65 5.7	54 6.7	39 9.4	51 7.2				57 6.4	49 7.4
9.2	8.2	5.0	10.2				7.5	6.6
-105.4	14.5	12.5	19.2			Sales/Working Capital	15.1	13.8
-11.8	165.1	36.0	61.5				84.3	67.7
3.4	13.7	13.0	27.5				9.7	7.0
(14) .4	(31) 2.2	(33) 2.0	(16) 3.5			EBIT/Interest	(100) 3.5	(99) 3.2
-5.7	.9	1.0	2.1				1.2	1.5
						Net Profit + Depr., Dep.,	25.1	5.7
						Amort./Cur. Mat. L/T/D	(13) 4.8	(16) 2.5
							2.1	.4
.1	.2	.2	.2				.2	.1
4.3	.5	.3	.9			Fixed/Worth	.5	.4
-.4	2.4	.8	1.2				4.0	1.5
2.0	.9	.9	1.1				1.4	.9
6.8	3.0	1.5	1.8			Debt/Worth	3.1	2.3
-3.3	22.4	4.6	3.3				16.0	12.0
92.7	35.9	24.6	26.2			% Profit Before Taxes/Tangible	55.8	48.1
(12) 11.7	(29) 15.5	(38) 6.2	(16) 13.6			Net Worth	(99) 22.2	(96) 26.5
-19.6	4.4	.3	4.9				8.1	8.5
9.7	8.5	8.2	6.7			% Profit Before Taxes/Total	14.7	16.1
-.3	3.8	1.8	3.7			Assets	5.5	6.9
-11.5	-.7	-.2	.7				1.0	1.7
136.3	94.9	46.2	33.4				102.7	87.9
38.9	34.8	23.1	14.9			Sales/Net Fixed Assets	38.0	34.9
17.5	13.5	15.3	9.5				14.1	15.3
6.3	4.9	3.8	3.4				4.5	4.7
3.7	3.6	2.9	2.8			Sales/Total Assets	3.4	3.5
3.1	2.2	2.2	2.4				2.4	2.4
.2	.5	.3	.6				.4	.3
(15) .4	(26) .9	(35) .6	.8			% Depr., Dep., Amort./Sales	(98) .8	(91) .7
.8	1.8	1.1	1.4				1.6	1.2
1.8	1.7	1.0				% Officers', Directors'	1.3	1.6
(11) 4.8	(22) 2.8	(14) 2.3				Owners' Comp/Sales	(60) 2.7	(56) 2.8
8.2	4.1	3.3					6.1	4.2
20786M	143214M	698449M	835970M	235810M	1406857M	Net Sales ($)	2108692M	2348291M
4996M	39496M	191658M	341447M	109599M	562348M	Total Assets ($)	676697M	738055M

M = $ thousand   MM = $ million
See Pages 9 through 22 for Explanation of Ratios and Data

Comparative Historical Data   Current Data Sorted by Sales

			Type of Statement						
6	5	6	Unqualified				1	1	4
18	17	10	Reviewed					4	6
29	23	31	Compiled	3	6	4	6	10	2
40	45	32	Tax Returns	7	14	5	4	1	1
39	42	41	Other	4	6	2	7	4	18
4/1/08-3/31/09	4/1/09-3/31/10	4/1/10-3/31/11		22 (4/1-9/30/10)			98 (10/1/10-3/31/11)		
ALL	ALL	ALL		0-1MM	1-3MM	3-5MM	5-10MM	10-25MM	25MM & OVER
132	132	120	NUMBER OF STATEMENTS	14	26	11	18	20	31
%	%	%	**ASSETS**	%	%	%	%	%	%
10.5	10.9	10.7	Cash & Equivalents	17.0	6.4	6.2	14.4	10.5	11.0
13.7	13.4	13.3	Trade Receivables (net)	5.5	15.4	16.7	11.1	12.6	15.6
48.2	45.1	49.2	Inventory	45.6	47.4	60.3	48.9	52.6	46.2
2.3	2.3	2.7	All Other Current	2.1	1.4	.4	1.7	6.4	3.2
74.6	71.7	75.9	Total Current	70.2	70.7	83.6	76.0	82.2	75.9
18.0	18.7	18.6	Fixed Assets (net)	28.6	21.0	11.7	19.2	12.7	17.9
2.2	3.6	2.7	Intangibles (net)	.1	7.0	.5	.6	1.9	2.9
5.1	6.0	2.8	All Other Non-Current	1.0	1.3	4.3	4.2	3.2	3.3
100.0	100.0	100.0	Total	100.0	100.0	100.0	100.0	100.0	100.0
			LIABILITIES						
15.1	15.3	17.5	Notes Payable-Short Term	20.5	26.5	17.9	6.7	13.2	17.3
4.3	4.1	3.0	Cur. Mat.-L.T.D.	.1	4.4	1.2	5.0	3.8	2.0
18.9	21.1	20.3	Trade Payables	22.4	24.8	18.9	21.4	11.2	21.4
.1	.1	.1	Income Taxes Payable	.0	.0	.1	.0	.3	.3
14.9	16.8	15.9	All Other Current	22.3	14.8	12.0	10.6	15.3	18.7
53.3	57.3	56.8	Total Current	65.3	70.5	50.0	43.7	43.8	59.7
15.8	16.0	11.1	Long-Term Debt	14.7	19.5	10.8	10.1	8.0	5.0
.0	.1	.2	Deferred Taxes	.0	.0	.0	.1	.1	.5
4.1	8.2	6.8	All Other Non-Current	10.1	5.5	2.1	12.3	6.4	5.1
26.9	18.4	25.2	Net Worth	9.8	4.4	37.1	33.7	41.8	29.7
100.0	100.0	100.0	Total Liabilities & Net Worth	100.0	100.0	100.0	100.0	100.0	100.0
			INCOME DATA						
100.0	100.0	100.0	Net Sales	100.0	100.0	100.0	100.0	100.0	100.0
35.0	33.5	32.1	Gross Profit	37.5	35.4	30.7	30.1	29.3	30.3
33.2	32.1	30.9	Operating Expenses	36.1	35.6	30.4	28.4	27.2	28.6
1.8	1.4	1.2	Operating Profit	1.4	-.2	.3	1.7	2.1	1.7
.2	.4	.2	All Other Expenses (net)	.5	.9	.1	-.5	.2	-.1
1.6	1.0	1.0	Profit Before Taxes	.9	-1.1	.2	2.2	1.9	1.8
			RATIOS						
2.6	2.0	2.5	Current	6.2	1.8	2.5	3.9	2.8	1.6
1.5	1.4	1.4		1.1	1.2	1.7	2.1	2.1	1.2
1.1	1.0	1.0		.5	.7	1.2	1.1	1.4	1.1
.9	.8	.9	Quick	1.1	.8	.7	1.2	.8	.8
.4	.4	(118) .5		.4	(24) .3	.5	.9	.5	.3
.2	.2	.2		.1	.2	.1	.2	.2	.2
3 107.9	4 85.4	4 86.5	Sales/Receivables	0 UND	2 170.5	4 93.0	3 108.9	6 59.0	7 55.5
9 39.8	10 35.5	10 37.7		2 153.5	10 34.8	15 24.9	8 47.8	13 29.0	11 32.6
22 16.4	20 17.9	20 17.8		8 43.5	32 11.3	28 13.0	19 18.8	21 17.6	18 20.0
53 6.9	46 8.0	55 6.6	Cost of Sales/Inventory	21 17.5	68 5.4	55 6.7	34 10.7	56 6.5	65 5.6
76 4.8	76 4.8	81 4.5		75 4.9	85 4.3	149 2.4	70 5.2	94 3.9	77 4.7
114 3.2	111 3.3	114 3.2		148 2.5	126 2.9	206 1.8	105 3.5	108 3.4	104 3.5
14 27.0	16 23.5	13 28.3	Cost of Sales/Payables	0 UND	13 28.0	14 25.9	12 30.9	11 32.1	14 26.9
28 13.2	30 12.0	23 15.8		29 12.8	40 12.0	22 16.6	32 11.5	18 19.8	21 17.7
44 8.3	55 6.6	53 6.9		59 6.2	71 5.1	57 6.4	49 7.5	28 13.0	49 7.5
7.3	7.4	6.7	Sales/Working Capital	3.9	8.0	3.7	6.1	5.6	10.3
12.6	18.2	14.2		NM	23.7	10.9	11.3	9.5	27.9
89.8	810.3	105.9		-9.4	-23.1	17.1	64.6	14.3	104.0
9.0	8.9	9.2	EBIT/Interest		7.4		93.7	9.2	21.3
(109) 2.6	(117) 2.5	(100) 2.3			(21) 2.2		(16) 8.5	(19) 2.0	(26) 3.4
.7	.4	.9			.2		-.1	1.2	1.9
3.2	12.2	17.9	Net Profit + Depr., Dep., Amort./Cur. Mat. L/T/D						
(15) 1.1	(25) 3.1	(20) 2.7							
.4	1.1	.8							
.2	.2	.2	Fixed/Worth	.1	.2	.1	.2	.1	.3
.5	.6	.5		4.2	1.7	.3	.4	.3	.5
4.4	5.0	1.6		-.6	-.7	.7	1.5	.7	1.1
.8	1.3	1.0	Debt/Worth	1.1	2.0	.8	.9	.8	1.6
2.0	3.0	2.5		5.4	5.5	1.1	1.5	1.3	2.6
26.2	48.3	7.6		-3.5	-6.5	5.6	8.8	4.2	4.6
36.6	37.2	27.1	% Profit Before Taxes/Tangible Net Worth		35.9	29.2	44.9	16.7	34.8
(106) 16.4	(101) 13.5	(101) 9.7		(17) 9.3		3.0	(16) 18.6	7.1	(28) 13.7
5.8	1.8	1.8			-8.4	-1.5	-1.2	2.1	4.2
13.3	10.5	8.1	% Profit Before Taxes/Total Assets	6.5	9.0	4.3	23.2	5.6	8.0
4.4	2.6	2.6		1.0	2.8	1.6	4.4	2.6	3.7
-.5	-1.1	-.6		-25.6	-2.5	-.3	-3.4	.9	1.2
68.9	73.9	62.4	Sales/Net Fixed Assets	126.0	79.1	85.1	64.4	52.5	52.8
25.8	27.1	28.3		42.6	29.3	19.3	29.2	27.7	20.7
12.3	11.8	12.9		8.0	12.2	10.3	13.1	18.9	12.2
4.5	4.3	4.3	Sales/Total Assets	6.1	4.4	4.3	4.9	4.0	4.3
3.3	3.1	3.1		3.4	3.3	2.4	3.1	3.0	3.1
2.3	2.3	2.2		.9	2.0	1.9	2.6	2.6	2.4
.4	.4	.3	% Depr., Dep., Amort./Sales		.3		.2	.3	.6
(107) .6	(102) .8	(99) .7			(20) .9		(16) .6	(19) .5	(27) .8
1.2	1.3	1.2			1.6		.9	.9	1.5
1.5	1.4	1.6	% Officers', Directors' Owners' Comp/Sales		1.8		.9		
(74) 3.1	(61) 2.8	(49) 2.6			(16) 3.1		(10) 2.6		
5.3	4.9	4.3			5.0		3.7		
3979457M	2669531M	3341086M	Net Sales ($)	7471M	48345M	46517M	130459M	295386M	2812908M
1060507M	939433M	1249544M	Total Assets ($)	3424M	19756M	19509M	40898M	113878M	1052079M

Current Data Sorted by Assets   Comparative Historical Data

	0-500M	500M-2MM	2-10MM	10-50MM	50-100MM	100-250MM	Type of Statement	ALL 4/1/06-3/31/07	ALL 4/1/07-3/31/08
			5	1	3	5	Unqualified	18	20
		3	10	3			Reviewed	14	20
	1	8	6				Compiled	22	18
	24	19	9			1	Tax Returns	30	30
	5	21	14	14	4	3	Other	53	53
		29 (4/1-9/30/10)		130 (10/1/10-3/31/11)					
NUMBER OF STATEMENTS	30	51	44	18	7	9		137	141
	%	%	%	%	%	%	**ASSETS**	%	%
	18.9	16.4	10.3	12.3			Cash & Equivalents	12.3	12.4
	12.7	22.4	22.8	25.6			Trade Receivables (net)	24.8	23.9
	40.3	30.4	34.6	27.1			Inventory	36.4	36.6
	5.2	5.2	3.9	4.3			All Other Current	3.5	3.7
	77.1	74.3	71.7	69.3			Total Current	77.0	76.6
	9.1	13.0	19.0	12.9			Fixed Assets (net)	15.7	14.8
	7.0	4.2	3.1	9.8			Intangibles (net)	1.7	3.4
	6.8	8.5	6.1	8.0			All Other Non-Current	5.6	5.3
	100.0	100.0	100.0	100.0			Total	100.0	100.0
							LIABILITIES		
	13.2	7.7	5.5	6.6			Notes Payable-Short Term	12.0	14.2
	1.0	1.6	1.4	1.9			Cur. Mat.-L.T.D.	1.7	1.4
	17.6	29.8	24.5	23.9			Trade Payables	26.5	25.1
	.2	.4	.0	.1			Income Taxes Payable	.2	.1
	11.9	10.7	12.7	12.1			All Other Current	16.0	14.9
	43.9	50.2	44.2	44.6			Total Current	56.5	55.7
	20.3	9.5	5.9	9.9			Long-Term Debt	9.8	9.7
	.0	.1	.2	.6			Deferred Taxes	.1	.1
	9.9	4.3	4.2	5.6			All Other Non-Current	6.5	7.9
	25.8	36.0	45.5	39.3			Net Worth	27.1	26.6
	100.0	100.0	100.0	100.0			Total Liabilities & Net Worth	100.0	100.0
							INCOME DATA		
	100.0	100.0	100.0	100.0			Net Sales	100.0	100.0
	44.1	37.3	33.3	34.0			Gross Profit	36.9	34.9
	36.7	32.1	30.5	29.2			Operating Expenses	33.2	32.5
	7.4	5.2	2.8	4.8			Operating Profit	3.8	2.3
	.1	.0	.0	1.3			All Other Expenses (net)	.4	.6
	7.3	5.2	2.8	3.5			Profit Before Taxes	3.3	1.8
							RATIOS		
	5.6	2.6	2.6	2.1			Current	2.0	2.4
	2.0	1.6	1.7	1.6				1.4	1.4
	1.0	1.2	1.2	1.1				1.1	1.0
	1.8	1.1	1.3	1.4			Quick	1.2	1.3
	.7	.8	.7	.8				(136) .7	.7
	.3	.5	.4	.5				.3	.3
	0 UND	7 53.3	3 106.1	20 18.6			Sales/Receivables	6 56.2	6 57.9
	3 128.3	16 22.1	25 14.8	29 12.6				18 20.2	22 16.9
	10 36.3	35 10.3	43 8.6	60 6.1				35 10.6	40 9.1
	24 15.2	12 31.2	27 13.7	16 23.5			Cost of Sales/Inventory	21 17.0	27 13.8
	46 8.0	38 9.7	47 7.7	42 8.6				47 7.8	48 7.6
	89 4.1	101 3.6	79 4.6	87 4.2				90 4.0	94 3.9
	0 UND	21 17.6	17 21.9	24 15.3			Cost of Sales/Payables	18 20.1	17 21.4
	11 34.6	35 10.3	38 9.7	43 8.5				38 9.7	32 11.5
	39 9.5	56 6.5	56 6.6	64 5.7				65 5.6	61 6.0
	5.6	5.5	6.2	7.0			Sales/Working Capital	8.3	7.0
	14.9	15.7	15.5	11.7				17.4	20.1
	468.7	113.9	39.7	42.6				122.3	204.6
	12.6	10.3	36.9	22.5			EBIT/Interest	16.5	10.3
	(18) 5.4	(35) 4.2	(38) 9.5	(15) 10.4				(111) 3.7	(109) 3.5
	2.2	1.6	1.0	1.3				1.4	1.4
							Net Profit + Depr., Dep., Amort./Cur. Mat. L/T/D	14.3	12.9
								(16) 4.9	(19) 7.6
								1.3	1.8
	.0	.1	.2	.1			Fixed/Worth	.2	.2
	.1	.3	.5	.2				.5	.5
	3.6	2.2	.9	1.6				1.5	2.1
	.5	.7	.6	.9			Debt/Worth	1.0	1.0
	2.5	2.8	1.1	1.7				2.7	2.7
	-8.5	8.1	2.9	7.2				8.9	13.9
	144.4	72.1	56.1	94.3			% Profit Before Taxes/Tangible Net Worth	75.8	57.8
	(22) 47.9	(42) 33.0	(42) 24.5	(16) 41.9				(117) 30.2	(111) 26.7
	26.4	3.5	.1	15.2				6.8	6.1
	40.5	29.7	18.9	20.3			% Profit Before Taxes/Total Assets	22.1	16.1
	15.8	9.0	8.8	12.0				8.5	5.7
	6.3	1.3	.0	4.0				1.4	.5
	UND	124.3	133.0	59.0			Sales/Net Fixed Assets	70.6	89.9
	117.1	55.1	25.2	33.5				32.4	34.1
	32.3	14.6	11.3	15.5				15.6	17.3
	6.3	5.9	4.8	3.9			Sales/Total Assets	5.0	4.9
	4.8	3.4	3.1	3.4				3.7	3.4
	3.4	2.2	2.6	1.8				2.8	2.6
	.3	.3	.2	.2			% Depr., Dep., Amort./Sales	.4	.4
	(11) .6	(31) .6	(32) .7	(15) .8				(112) .7	(116) .6
	.9	1.5	2.1	1.6				1.3	1.4
	3.3	1.5	.8				% Officers', Directors' Owners' Comp/Sales	1.6	1.5
	(22) 6.0	(29) 3.6	(14) 1.6					(62) 3.4	(60) 3.8
	8.1	6.3	4.1					7.2	6.7
	43461M	229792M	939416M	1355929M	1476869M	5411205M	Net Sales ($)	4754800M	6068803M
	7970M	54576M	212986M	414000M	509768M	1449457M	Total Assets ($)	1268527M	1752022M

© RMA 2011

M = $ thousand   MM = $ million

See Pages 9 through 22 for Explanation of Ratios and Data

Comparative Historical Data / Current Data Sorted by Sales

Hist 1	Hist 2	Hist 3	Type of Statement	0-1MM	1-3MM	3-5MM	5-10MM	10-25MM	25MM & OVER
13	15	14	Unqualified					4	10
29	20	16	Reviewed	1	2		1	7	5
21	25	15	Compiled	1	4	2	3	4	1
33	39	53	Tax Returns	10	24	6	7	4	2
59	59	61	Other	4	7	5	14	10	21
4/1/08-3/31/09 ALL	4/1/09-3/31/10 ALL	4/1/10-3/31/11 ALL		\<29 (4/1-9/30/10)\>			\<130 (10/1/10-3/31/11)\>		
155	158	159	**NUMBER OF STATEMENTS**	16	37	13	25	29	39
%	%	%	**ASSETS**	%	%	%	%	%	%
12.2	13.7	14.1	Cash & Equivalents	16.4	16.3	9.8	19.1	11.2	11.3
20.7	21.0	20.8	Trade Receivables (net)	12.0	18.0	17.2	27.0	20.4	24.4
37.3	36.3	34.2	Inventory	33.1	38.2	28.5	24.7	38.1	35.8
3.9	2.9	4.4	All Other Current	9.1	2.7	7.2	2.2	4.9	4.1
74.1	73.9	73.4	Total Current	70.6	75.2	62.7	73.1	74.6	75.6
15.4	16.8	14.7	Fixed Assets (net)	12.6	14.1	19.4	14.0	12.4	16.8
3.5	3.2	5.2	Intangibles (net)	14.3	1.3	5.3	6.0	7.1	3.1
6.9	6.1	6.8	All Other Non-Current	2.5	9.4	12.6	6.9	5.9	4.6
100.0	100.0	100.0	Total	100.0	100.0	100.0	100.0	100.0	100.0
			LIABILITIES						
11.9	13.7	8.3	Notes Payable-Short Term	2.7	14.1	9.1	4.0	7.7	8.1
2.4	3.1	1.5	Cur. Mat.-L.T.D.	.7	1.0	1.3	2.4	1.7	1.4
27.6	24.9	25.7	Trade Payables	8.6	16.7	28.1	42.3	24.3	30.6
.1	.3	.2	Income Taxes Payable	.1	.7	.0	.0	.0	.0
14.2	15.1	11.5	All Other Current	13.8	11.5	9.6	13.2	12.1	9.5
56.1	57.2	47.1	Total Current	26.0	44.2	47.8	61.9	45.8	49.7
9.4	15.9	10.7	Long-Term Debt	27.0	13.0	5.8	10.2	7.3	6.2
.1	.1	.1	Deferred Taxes	.0	.1	.2	.5	.1	.0
7.7	6.2	5.6	All Other Non-Current	9.1	6.0	1.8	6.2	5.3	5.0
26.6	20.7	36.5	Net Worth	38.0	36.7	44.3	21.2	41.5	39.1
100.0	100.0	100.0	Total Liabilities & Net Worth	100.0	100.0	100.0	100.0	100.0	100.0
			INCOME DATA						
100.0	100.0	100.0	Net Sales	100.0	100.0	100.0	100.0	100.0	100.0
36.3	35.7	36.1	Gross Profit	52.7	44.5	34.0	34.8	29.1	27.9
33.7	32.5	31.6	Operating Expenses	38.8	39.1	31.4	30.7	27.7	24.9
2.7	3.3	4.5	Operating Profit	13.9	5.3	2.6	4.1	1.4	3.0
.6	.2	.2	All Other Expenses (net)	1.2	.6	-1.2	-.1	.0	.2
2.1	3.1	4.3	Profit Before Taxes	12.6	4.7	3.9	4.2	1.4	2.8
			RATIOS						
1.9	2.3	2.7	Current	15.5	3.3	2.1	1.7	2.0	2.1
1.4	1.4	1.6		3.3	2.0	1.1	1.2	1.7	1.5
1.0	1.0	1.1		1.8	1.2	.8	.9	1.2	1.1
1.0	1.1	1.2	Quick	7.2	2.0	.8	1.0	1.1	1.2
.6	.6	.7		1.1	.8	.5	.9	.7	.7
.3	.2	.4		.4	.5	.2	.5	.3	.4
6 59.0	5 72.3	3 107.2	Sales/Receivables	0 UND	2 178.4	1 720.4	15 25.2	2 201.1	6 60.5
16 22.2	20 18.2	16 22.1		4 99.5	15 24.1	16 22.1	24 15.4	11 33.9	23 16.2
34 10.6	37 9.8	37 10.0		31 11.9	45 8.1	32 11.6	29 12.5	47 7.8	33 10.9
26 13.9	25 14.4	22 16.6	Cost of Sales/Inventory	22 16.3	31 11.8	6 61.1	13 29.0	27 13.4	23 16.0
61 6.0	56 6.5	44 8.3		60 6.0	86 4.2	37 10.0	25 14.6	49 7.5	41 8.9
93 3.9	98 3.7	90 4.0		138 2.7	150 2.4	88 4.1	44 8.4	102 3.6	86 4.2
20 18.6	19 18.8	15 24.3	Cost of Sales/Payables	0 UND	10 37.9	10 35.4	36 10.1	14 26.5	21 17.7
37 9.9	34 10.8	33 10.9		2 237.4	28 12.8	37 10.0	47 7.8	30 12.2	36 10.2
61 6.0	57 6.4	56 6.5		30 12.1	59 6.2	62 5.9	61 6.0	55 6.6	63 5.8
8.8	7.2	6.1	Sales/Working Capital	3.3	4.8	7.5	13.5	6.9	8.6
20.0	17.7	15.1		5.6	8.8	89.9	59.6	18.2	15.3
-284.6	-158.6	68.5		14.4	22.8	-35.0	NM	35.6	64.1
10.8	14.6	18.2	EBIT/Interest		9.5		24.4	22.9	54.5
(123) 3.7	(129) 4.8	(121) 6.0			(29) 2.4		(19) 8.9	(24) 5.6	(33) 13.0
.9	1.2	1.3			1.2		3.1	-1.5	2.4
10.2	9.7	12.5	Net Profit + Depr., Dep., Amort./Cur. Mat. L/T/D						14.0
(27) 2.4	(23) 2.4	(18) 2.4							(11) 5.5
1.0	1.0	.7							-.4
.1	.1	.1	Fixed/Worth	.0	.0	.1	.3	.1	.1
.5	.5	.3		.1	.2	.2	.7	.4	.3
2.0	2.5	1.1		2.7	1.1	.8	-2.8	1.0	1.1
1.2	1.1	.8	Debt/Worth	.2	.5	.5	1.7	.8	1.0
3.5	2.7	1.8		2.5	1.6	1.3	3.9	1.8	1.7
10.8	27.9	7.7		NM	4.2	17.4	-36.4	6.6	7.2
70.0	94.4	73.8	% Profit Before Taxes/Tangible Net Worth	162.8	64.8	117.6	143.2	47.0	89.1
(124) 21.5	(127) 27.8	(136) 31.5		(12) 43.6	(33) 15.7	(11) 22.8	(18) 52.8	(26) 22.2	(36) 33.8
3.5	4.5	3.8		27.4	-.5	3.1	26.5	-2.4	6.8
17.6	19.6	22.8	% Profit Before Taxes/Total Assets	41.6	19.3	27.7	28.6	19.5	19.4
5.6	8.0	10.3		23.9	5.2	5.1	17.1	7.9	11.4
-.6	.6	1.0		8.1	-.3	-.3	6.5	-1.8	1.2
97.5	89.7	139.2	Sales/Net Fixed Assets	UND	237.8	74.8	127.2	207.8	78.7
37.3	27.2	40.9		67.1	34.3	38.7	65.4	51.8	30.1
16.9	13.2	14.0		15.0	13.6	8.2	13.7	12.2	15.0
5.0	4.5	5.2	Sales/Total Assets	4.8	4.5	5.3	7.3	5.3	4.7
3.5	3.3	3.5		2.8	3.0	3.2	4.6	3.2	3.8
2.6	2.4	2.4		1.1	1.8	2.2	3.1	2.6	2.8
.4	.4	.3	% Depr., Dep., Amort./Sales			.4	.1	.4	.3
(116) .7	(117) .8	(102) .7			(21) .8		(18) .5	(17) .8	(32) .7
1.3	1.4	1.5			3.0		1.2	1.8	1.3
1.1	1.4	1.4	% Officers', Directors' Owners' Comp/Sales	5.4	2.8		1.1	.7	.5
(64) 2.6	(64) 3.0	(74) 3.6		(11) 6.5	(23) 5.1		(12) 1.6	(11) .9	(10) 1.3
5.4	6.5	6.5		8.8	10.2		4.5	2.8	4.1
7083331M	7755080M	9456672M	Net Sales ($)	7952M	69292M	48456M	175170M	493516M	8662286M
1918894M	2214872M	2648757M	Total Assets ($)	5832M	29656M	16694M	50655M	161962M	2383958M

Current Data Sorted by Assets   Comparative Historical Data

0-500M	500M-2MM	2-10MM	10-50MM	50-100MM	100-250MM	Type of Statement	4/1/06-3/31/07 ALL	4/1/07-3/31/08 ALL
		6	4		1	Unqualified	11	10
	4	5	5			Reviewed	14	8
2	5	6	1			Compiled	17	5
11	12	8				Tax Returns	33	24
12	13	13	9		1	Other	36	43
	12 (4/1-9/30/10)		106 (10/1/10-3/31/11)					
25	34	38	19		2	NUMBER OF STATEMENTS	111	90
%	%	%	%	%	%	**ASSETS**	%	%
22.8	12.8	16.7	15.0			Cash & Equivalents	10.3	14.0
29.1	29.4	38.7	32.6			Trade Receivables (net)	37.3	36.0
18.7	23.6	17.7	16.3			Inventory	21.6	18.2
4.3	2.5	2.2	3.9			All Other Current	2.1	3.4
75.0	68.2	75.2	67.8			Total Current	71.4	71.6
16.1	14.1	8.7	15.5			Fixed Assets (net)	13.2	13.6
3.3	4.7	9.3	9.9			Intangibles (net)	9.2	8.5
5.6	13.0	6.8	6.7			All Other Non-Current	6.1	6.3
100.0	100.0	100.0	100.0			Total	100.0	100.0
						LIABILITIES		
37.4	13.3	8.5	10.0			Notes Payable-Short Term	16.7	13.0
4.1	1.6	2.2	1.2			Cur. Mat.-L.T.D.	2.3	3.6
26.0	20.0	24.6	27.9			Trade Payables	26.6	27.0
.0	.0	.4	.0			Income Taxes Payable	.3	.2
34.7	14.7	18.0	16.1			All Other Current	18.1	19.0
102.2	49.7	53.7	55.2			Total Current	64.0	62.8
12.4	14.9	9.5	10.0			Long-Term Debt	14.3	11.3
.0	.1	.2	.5			Deferred Taxes	.2	.3
7.8	3.8	7.9	4.8			All Other Non-Current	8.5	4.2
-22.4	31.5	28.7	29.5			Net Worth	12.9	21.5
100.0	100.0	100.0	100.0			Total Liabilities & Net Worth	100.0	100.0
						INCOME DATA		
100.0	100.0	100.0	100.0			Net Sales	100.0	100.0
48.5	43.2	36.3	31.7			Gross Profit	36.6	39.2
47.8	40.1	30.5	27.5			Operating Expenses	32.7	35.6
.6	3.1	5.8	4.2			Operating Profit	3.9	3.7
.7	.4	.2	.5			All Other Expenses (net)	1.0	.8
.0	2.7	5.5	3.7			Profit Before Taxes	3.0	2.9
						RATIOS		
3.3	3.5	2.5	1.4				1.8	2.0
1.1	1.6	1.4	1.1			Current	1.2	1.2
.6	1.1	1.1	1.0				.9	.9
1.7	2.2	1.8	1.2				1.4	1.3
.9	1.1	1.0	.8			Quick	.8	.9
.3	.5	.6	.7				.5	.5
2 175.3	18 19.9	21 17.6	11 32.4				15 24.0	19 19.3
24 15.2	31 11.9	42 8.6	56 6.5			Sales/Receivables	38 9.7	37 9.8
33 11.0	40 9.1	62 5.9	65 5.6				60 6.1	58 6.3
0 UND	5 77.1	1 248.4	0 UND				6 63.1	0 964.7
16 22.2	25 14.9	13 28.0	16 22.6			Cost of Sales/Inventory	26 14.0	18 20.7
47 7.8	74 4.9	46 8.0	50 7.3				53 6.9	47 7.8
7 51.0	11 31.8	17 21.8	19 18.9				23 15.5	21 17.5
34 10.7	29 12.7	37 10.0	37 9.9			Cost of Sales/Payables	36 10.2	37 10.0
53 6.9	45 8.1	53 6.8	63 5.8				52 7.0	57 6.4
8.2	7.2	7.0	13.0				11.6	8.8
101.0	16.9	20.8	27.6			Sales/Working Capital	32.3	24.5
-15.5	162.9	NM	-42.1				-42.7	-55.1
8.2	24.7	52.4	33.1				9.2	10.1
(19) 2.5	(29) 3.4	(33) 17.3	(15) 8.4			EBIT/Interest	(95) 3.5	(75) 3.6
.3	.8	1.7	1.8				1.0	1.8
						Net Profit + Depr., Dep.,	8.4	3.1
						Amort./Cur. Mat. L/T/D	(15) 4.7	(12) 1.6
							2.1	.8
.0	.1	.1	.1				.1	.2
.4	.3	.2	.8			Fixed/Worth	.8	.5
-.7	NM	.9	2.1				-1.2	3.1
1.5	.7	.9	.9				1.6	1.3
-19.1	3.1	2.4	4.2			Debt/Worth	4.9	4.1
-3.3	NM	6.9	22.1				-10.1	NM
95.3	62.7	85.5	74.7			% Profit Before Taxes/Tangible	73.8	81.8
(12) 36.1	(26) 35.1	(32) 45.0	(15) 39.6			Net Worth	(76) 34.8	(68) 34.4
1.6	5.7	6.8	17.6				9.7	13.6
32.2	29.0	26.4	24.4			% Profit Before Taxes/Total	18.3	18.0
9.1	4.7	10.0	9.1			Assets	7.0	7.9
-3.0	.4	1.2	1.5				.5	1.9
660.5	121.9	270.9	70.6				123.7	106.0
61.3	52.2	93.5	46.6			Sales/Net Fixed Assets	41.1	39.8
28.4	25.3	28.1	20.4				17.3	16.5
7.5	4.9	4.7	4.0				5.3	5.1
5.5	3.5	3.4	3.3			Sales/Total Assets	3.6	3.6
3.0	2.5	2.2	1.6				2.3	2.0
.5	.3	.3	.4				.3	.4
(11) .8	(24) .7	(25) .8	(13) .6			% Depr., Dep., Amort./Sales	(88) .7	(61) .7
2.2	1.6	1.9	.9				1.3	1.8
3.4	2.5	1.1				% Officers', Directors'	1.6	1.6
(16) 6.6	(23) 5.8	(16) 2.6				Owners' Comp/Sales	(57) 3.6	(39) 4.0
10.2	9.1	8.7					7.3	9.2
38391M	134637M	690027M	1166433M		1422016M	Net Sales ($)	7129277M	2568355M
6756M	36563M	178278M	397826M		370814M	Total Assets ($)	1557083M	1153130M

(Columns 50-100MM and 100-250MM: DATA NOT AVAILABLE)

© RMA 2011

M = $ thousand   MM = $ million
See Pages 9 through 22 for Explanation of Ratios and Data

Comparative Historical Data   Current Data Sorted by Sales

Type of Statement	4/1/08-3/31/09	4/1/09-3/31/10	4/1/10-3/31/11	0-1MM	1-3MM	3-5MM	5-10MM	10-25MM	25MM & OVER
Unqualified	8	11	11			2	3	1	5
Reviewed	12	14	14			2	2	3	7
Compiled	14	11	14	1	4	2	3	2	2
Tax Returns	35	36	31	5	9	6	8	3	2
Other	48	52	48	5	14	3	7	9	10
	ALL	ALL	ALL	12 (4/1-9/30/10)			106 (10/1/10-3/31/11)		
NUMBER OF STATEMENTS	117	124	118	11	27	15	23	18	24
	%	%	%	%	%	%	%	%	%
ASSETS									
Cash & Equivalents	13.8	15.8	16.4	22.9	11.4	18.9	16.1	20.0	14.8
Trade Receivables (net)	35.8	35.5	32.9	18.1	31.3	37.0	34.3	33.7	37.0
Inventory	18.0	20.3	19.7	16.5	21.0	18.7	18.1	17.5	23.6
All Other Current	2.6	2.8	3.1	.9	5.1	1.5	3.4	1.9	3.3
Total Current	70.2	74.4	72.0	58.4	68.8	76.1	71.9	73.2	78.7
Fixed Assets (net)	17.0	12.5	12.9	26.3	16.6	7.1	14.2	6.7	9.6
Intangibles (net)	6.2	5.6	6.8	6.9	3.0	9.7	6.2	13.0	4.8
All Other Non-Current	6.6	7.5	8.3	8.5	11.6	7.1	7.7	7.0	6.8
Total	100.0	100.0	100.0	100.0	100.0	100.0	100.0	100.0	100.0
LIABILITIES									
Notes Payable-Short Term	13.8	9.7	16.3	37.2	30.5	3.2	11.0	7.1	11.0
Cur. Mat.-L.T.D.	2.9	3.1	2.3	1.8	4.0	1.2	2.6	2.2	.9
Trade Payables	27.3	28.3	24.5	11.0	25.4	23.1	17.0	26.0	36.5
Income Taxes Payable	.9	.5	.2	.0	.0	.0	.0	.9	.0
All Other Current	13.8	14.3	20.2	52.0	13.6	24.1	20.2	16.6	13.5
Total Current	58.7	55.8	63.4	102.0	73.6	51.6	50.8	52.7	61.8
Long-Term Debt	10.3	10.9	11.6	25.4	12.9	9.4	4.8	6.6	15.4
Deferred Taxes	.4	.1	.2	.0	.1	.1	.2	.6	.1
All Other Non-Current	7.1	7.4	6.1	7.5	6.1	6.9	5.6	10.5	2.3
Net Worth	23.6	25.8	18.7	-34.9	7.3	32.0	38.6	29.6	20.4
Total Liabilities & Net Worth	100.0	100.0	100.0	100.0	100.0	100.0	100.0	100.0	100.0
INCOME DATA									
Net Sales	100.0	100.0	100.0	100.0	100.0	100.0	100.0	100.0	100.0
Gross Profit	38.4	36.4	39.8	62.5	43.5	43.9	44.9	36.0	20.4
Operating Expenses	35.6	31.9	36.2	67.8	40.0	34.6	40.4	30.9	18.4
Operating Profit	2.8	4.5	3.6	-5.3	3.5	9.3	4.6	5.1	2.1
All Other Expenses (net)	1.2	.7	.4	2.3	.7	.4	-.4	.3	.2
Profit Before Taxes	1.6	3.8	3.1	-7.6	2.8	8.9	5.0	4.8	1.8
RATIOS									
Current	2.0	2.1	2.5	6.2	2.8	3.5	2.0	2.7	1.7
	1.3	1.2	1.4	2.6	1.1	1.7	1.3	1.3	1.2
	.9	1.0	.9	.6	.7	.9	1.1	1.0	1.0
Quick	1.3	1.5	1.5	5.2	1.6	1.7	2.0	1.7	1.2
	.8	.9	1.0	1.4	.6	1.1	1.0	1.1	.8
	.6	.5	.5	.2	.4	.8	.5	.5	.7
Sales/Receivables	12 31.0	11 32.4	15 24.8	12 30.0	19 19.5	27 13.6	12 31.6	12 30.0	10 36.5
	27 13.3	34 10.8	32 11.6	26 14.1	26 14.0	32 11.2	40 9.2	41 9.0	38 9.7
	48 7.7	55 6.6	52 7.0	38 9.7	47 7.8	54 6.8	57 6.4	50 7.4	59 6.2
Cost of Sales/Inventory	1 585.8	0 848.8	2 207.6	0 UND	3 142.5	0 UND	2 167.9	0 UND	0 UND
	15 24.1	18 20.1	17 21.2	47 7.8	21 17.7	21 17.5	13 28.6	9 41.4	16 22.4
	44 8.2	55 6.7	53 6.8	136 2.7	61 6.0	67 5.4	51 7.2	42 8.6	51 7.2
Cost of Sales/Payables	15 25.0	18 20.6	14 26.0	13 28.7	8 47.5	14 26.0	10 34.9	18 19.9	21 17.2
	32 11.4	38 9.6	34 10.8	53 11.4	64 10.7	33 11.0	28 13.1	31 11.9	36 10.1
	55 6.6	57 6.4	53 6.9	185 2.0	49 7.4	42 8.7	47 7.7	59 6.2	53 6.1
Sales/Working Capital	12.0	8.4	8.1	4.8	8.1	5.3	7.1	8.0	13.3
	32.0	25.1	23.0	10.1	57.3	17.6	17.5	27.3	40.0
	-62.2	442.9	-80.8	-7.3	-16.6	-47.9	101.0	NM	NM
EBIT/Interest	13.1	27.9	30.8		9.9	107.0	40.3	54.5	42.4
	(99) 4.2	(102) 6.0	(98) 5.2	(24) 2.8	(11) 5.9	(21) 17.4	(15) 15.5	(20) 12.5	
	.8	2.0	1.1		1.1	2.6	2.3	1.1	1.8
Net Profit + Depr., Dep., Amort./Cur. Mat. L/T/D	3.7		13.5						
	(11) 1.8		(17) 3.0						
	.4		.9						
Fixed/Worth	.1	.1	.1	.0	.2	.1	.1	.1	.1
	.4	.4	.3	.2	.7	.3	.1	.1	.3
	2.3	2.7	NM	-.9	-.7	-1.0	1.0	NM	1.0
Debt/Worth	1.4	1.2	1.0	.4	1.4	1.4	.7	.7	1.1
	3.4	3.6	3.4	-5.9	4.6	5.8	2.9	2.4	3.3
	14.9	25.1	-22.8	-1.9	-6.9	-23.2	5.5	NM	14.1
% Profit Before Taxes/Tangible Net Worth	74.8	63.5	72.2		63.6	163.9	70.5	88.8	73.8
	(93) 27.8	(97) 31.4	(86) 38.9	(18) 24.7	(10) 63.1	(19) 38.1	(14) 43.0	(20) 47.8	
	2.2	11.4	8.0		5.7	28.4	4.4	5.3	24.9
% Profit Before Taxes/Total Assets	14.9	17.6	28.1	2.0	29.7	36.8	24.2	44.9	23.7
	6.2	7.9	8.6	-3.9	4.8	25.2	10.8	6.4	8.6
	-1.2	1.4	.4	-21.9	.9	2.6	2.5	.7	1.6
Sales/Net Fixed Assets	174.8	226.1	188.7	568.0	96.4	124.6	207.5	305.6	251.1
	47.1	66.7	52.6	28.7	45.9	62.5	45.0	122.1	62.9
	16.8	18.4	22.7	4.4	17.5	22.4	17.4	32.5	23.3
Sales/Total Assets	6.0	5.2	5.2	4.0	6.6	5.4	4.5	4.8	5.0
	4.1	3.6	3.6	2.7	3.6	4.3	3.4	3.9	3.9
	2.8	2.6	2.5	1.6	2.8	1.9	2.0	2.9	2.8
% Depr., Dep., Amort./Sales	.3	.2	.5		.6		.6	.3	.1
	(84) .7	(76) .6	(74) .8	(18) 1.1		(13) 1.1	(10) .7	(18) .5	
	1.5	1.3	1.6		2.3		1.9	2.4	.7
% Officers', Directors' Owners' Comp/Sales	2.8	2.4	2.2		3.5	1.7	2.4		
	(49) 4.2	(50) 4.2	(58) 4.9	(18) 5.9	(12) 3.9	(10) 3.6			
	7.0	7.8	9.2		9.2	5.8	9.0		
Net Sales ($)	3206435M	4059757M	3451504M	7205M	51037M	63353M	176983M	282514M	2870412M
Total Assets ($)	1037608M	1300659M	990237M	4678M	15554M	24098M	83865M	96664M	765378M

© RMA 2011   M = $ thousand   MM = $ million

See Pages 9 through 22 for Explanation of Ratios and Data

Current Data Sorted by Assets   Comparative Historical Data

Type of Statement	4/1/06-3/31/07 ALL	4/1/07-3/31/08 ALL
Unqualified		
Reviewed	7	3
Compiled	4	3
Tax Returns	6	6
Other	2	13

Current data statement counts:
- 0-500M: (Reviewed 1, Compiled 2, Tax Returns 1, Other 1) 4 (4/1-9/30/10)
- 500M-2MM / 2-10MM: (Reviewed 5, Compiled 6, Tax Returns 1, Other 3) 19 (10/1/10-3/31/11); 10-50MM: 3

	0-500M	500M-2MM	2-10MM	10-50MM	50-100MM	100-250MM		4/1/06-3/31/07 ALL	4/1/07-3/31/08 ALL
NUMBER OF STATEMENTS		5	15	3				19	26
	%	%	%	%	%	%	ASSETS	%	%
Cash & Equivalents	D		8.6		D	D	Cash & Equivalents	12.5	12.0
Trade Receivables (net)	A		13.7		A	A	Trade Receivables (net)	11.8	5.5
Inventory	T		48.4		T	T	Inventory	46.2	46.4
All Other Current	A		1.1		A	A	All Other Current	1.6	1.6
Total Current			71.9				Total Current	72.1	65.5
Fixed Assets (net)	N		20.0		N	N	Fixed Assets (net)	22.7	22.9
Intangibles (net)	O		3.2		O	O	Intangibles (net)	.5	5.5
All Other Non-Current	T		5.0		T	T	All Other Non-Current	4.7	6.0
Total			100.0				Total	100.0	100.0
	A				A	A	LIABILITIES		
Notes Payable-Short Term	V		7.0		V	V	Notes Payable-Short Term	11.5	10.7
Cur. Mat.-L.T.D.	A		3.2		A	A	Cur. Mat.-L.T.D.	2.1	3.4
Trade Payables	I		23.0		I	I	Trade Payables	31.5	25.6
Income Taxes Payable	L		.9		L	L	Income Taxes Payable	1.4	.4
All Other Current	A		10.3		A	A	All Other Current	5.4	12.3
Total Current	B		44.4		B	B	Total Current	51.9	52.3
Long-Term Debt	L		4.9		L	L	Long-Term Debt	25.7	25.3
Deferred Taxes	E		.0		E	E	Deferred Taxes	.0	.0
All Other Non-Current			2.2				All Other Non-Current	6.3	3.7
Net Worth			48.5				Net Worth	16.1	18.7
Total Liabilities & Net Worth			100.0				Total Liabilities & Net Worth	100.0	100.0
							INCOME DATA		
Net Sales			100.0				Net Sales	100.0	100.0
Gross Profit			30.5				Gross Profit	37.6	37.6
Operating Expenses			29.4				Operating Expenses	36.9	36.0
Operating Profit			1.1				Operating Profit	.8	1.6
All Other Expenses (net)			-.4				All Other Expenses (net)	1.0	1.2
Profit Before Taxes			1.5				Profit Before Taxes	-.3	.5
							RATIOS		
Current			2.2 / 1.4 / 1.2				Current	2.7 / 1.2 / 1.0	2.5 / 1.3 / .9
Quick			.7 / .5 / .3				Quick	.8 / .4 / .2	.7 / (25) .2 / .1
Sales/Receivables			2 211.2 / 6 65.8 / 28 13.2				Sales/Receivables	1 665.7 / 6 56.7 / 13 28.9	0 UND / 3 140.8 / 6 59.2
Cost of Sales/Inventory			39 9.3 / 48 7.7 / 85 4.3				Cost of Sales/Inventory	36 10.2 / 72 5.1 / 85 4.3	53 6.9 / 73 5.0 / 113 3.2
Cost of Sales/Payables			16 23.1 / 32 11.3 / 41 8.9				Cost of Sales/Payables	27 13.7 / 33 11.1 / 58 6.3	9 39.7 / 30 12.0 / 51 7.2
Sales/Working Capital			10.4 / 14.9 / 42.2				Sales/Working Capital	6.5 / 26.7 / 891.5	9.1 / 26.5 / -98.8
EBIT/Interest			82.1 / 8.9 / -.6				EBIT/Interest	26.3 / (16) 4.7 / 1.6	9.7 / (22) 5.6 / .3
Net Profit + Depr., Dep., Amort./Cur. Mat. L/T/D							Net Profit + Depr., Dep., Amort./Cur. Mat. L/T/D		
Fixed/Worth			.1 / .2 / 1.2				Fixed/Worth	.1 / .6 / 1.1	.2 / .5 / 3.7
Debt/Worth			.6 / 1.0 / 2.4				Debt/Worth	1.1 / 3.1 / 5.6	.9 / 3.6 / NM
% Profit Before Taxes/Tangible Net Worth			35.4 / 20.5 / -7.8				% Profit Before Taxes/Tangible Net Worth	39.8 / (16) 14.3 / 6.5	41.1 / (20) 17.0 / -13.8
% Profit Before Taxes/Total Assets			18.0 / 10.2 / -6.1				% Profit Before Taxes/Total Assets	15.1 / 3.9 / 1.3	13.4 / 4.7 / -3.5
Sales/Net Fixed Assets			58.0 / 40.4 / 13.4				Sales/Net Fixed Assets	68.5 / 31.9 / 5.7	55.7 / 25.8 / 6.5
Sales/Total Assets			6.5 / 4.7 / 3.0				Sales/Total Assets	4.7 / 4.2 / 2.3	4.9 / 3.6 / 2.2
% Depr., Dep., Amort./Sales			.4 / (12) .9 / 2.6				% Depr., Dep., Amort./Sales	.4 / .8 / 3.3	.5 / (22) 1.3 / 3.2
% Officers', Directors' Owners' Comp/Sales							% Officers', Directors' Owners' Comp/Sales	.5 / (10) 2.9 / 8.4	.7 / (12) 2.6 / 4.7
Net Sales ($)		24067M	340249M	189145M			Net Sales ($)	556268M	598290M
Total Assets ($)		6387M	67067M	82628M			Total Assets ($)	120147M	132632M

© RMA 2011

M = $ thousand   MM = $ million
See Pages 9 through 22 for Explanation of Ratios and Data

Comparative Historical Data / Current Data Sorted by Sales

4/1/08-3/31/09 ALL	4/1/09-3/31/10 ALL	4/1/10-3/31/11 ALL	Type of Statement	0-1MM	1-3MM	3-5MM	5-10MM	10-25MM	25MM & OVER
1	1		Unqualified						
7	5	6	Reviewed			1	3	2	
2	5	8	Compiled				3	3	2
9	2	2	Tax Returns			1		1	
17	6	7	Other		1		1		5
					4 (4/1-9/30/10)		19 (10/1/10-3/31/11)		
36	19	23	NUMBER OF STATEMENTS		1	2	7	6	7
%	%	%	ASSETS	%	%	%	%	%	%
11.4	7.7	9.4	Cash & Equivalents	DATA NOT AVAILABLE					
12.1	15.0	13.8	Trade Receivables (net)						
38.6	43.9	49.9	Inventory						
4.2	3.7	1.3	All Other Current						
66.3	70.3	74.3	Total Current						
22.4	20.2	16.2	Fixed Assets (net)						
4.1	3.2	2.6	Intangibles (net)						
7.2	6.3	6.9	All Other Non-Current						
100.0	100.0	100.0	Total						
			LIABILITIES						
13.0	30.1	7.3	Notes Payable-Short Term						
4.2	4.2	4.1	Cur. Mat.-L.T.D.						
19.4	19.3	21.0	Trade Payables						
.2	1.0	.6	Income Taxes Payable						
6.7	11.6	9.0	All Other Current						
43.6	66.2	42.0	Total Current						
21.8	19.8	5.6	Long-Term Debt						
.0	.0	.0	Deferred Taxes						
7.2	4.1	4.5	All Other Non-Current						
27.4	9.8	47.8	Net Worth						
100.0	100.0	100.0	Total Liabilties & Net Worth						
			INCOME DATA						
100.0	100.0	100.0	Net Sales						
40.0	38.0	30.7	Gross Profit						
37.1	35.3	28.7	Operating Expenses						
3.0	2.7	2.0	Operating Profit						
.7	.6	-.4	All Other Expenses (net)						
2.3	2.1	2.3	Profit Before Taxes						
			RATIOS						
2.6	2.9	2.4	Current						
1.6	1.6	1.6							
1.1	1.1	1.2							
.9	.9	.7	Quick						
.4	.4	.5							
.2	.2	.3							
2 148.3	**5** 79.3	**2** 211.2	Sales/Receivables						
5 67.2	**9** 40.3	**7** 53.0							
16 22.3	**24** 15.1	**28** 13.2							
26 13.9	**45** 8.1	**41** 8.8	Cost of Sales/Inventory						
65 5.6	**68** 5.4	**58** 6.3							
81 4.5	**92** 4.0	**89** 4.1							
9 40.5	**7** 50.6	**14** 26.5	Cost of Sales/Payables						
26 14.1	**24** 15.4	**28** 13.2							
50 7.3	**62** 5.9	**42** 8.7							
8.4	8.8	6.3	Sales/Working Capital						
15.3	13.9	14.9							
96.5	97.3	34.4							
7.7	13.7	82.1	EBIT/Interest						
(31) 2.3	5.0	8.1							
.0	1.3	1.5							
			Net Profit + Depr., Dep., Amort./Cur. Mat. L/T/D						
.2	.2	.1	Fixed/Worth						
.6	.6	.2							
2.4	.9	.9							
.9	.5	.6	Debt/Worth						
2.3	1.7	1.0							
8.1	5.8	3.1							
27.2	35.3	40.9	% Profit Before Taxes/Tangible Net Worth						
(32) 10.5	(17) 21.4	20.5							
-3.9	.9	1.6							
18.2	15.9	18.0	% Profit Before Taxes/Total Assets						
4.5	6.8	8.9							
-2.1	.5	1.1							
62.9	48.0	60.3	Sales/Net Fixed Assets						
22.0	24.4	37.7							
10.6	8.5	16.4							
4.6	6.0	6.0	Sales/Total Assets						
4.0	3.9	3.7							
2.5	2.8	2.8							
.6	.6	.5	% Depr., Dep., Amort./Sales						
(30) 1.5	(15) 1.2	(19) 1.0							
3.9	3.2	2.5							
1.0			% Officers', Directors' Owners' Comp/Sales						
(16) 4.2									
6.4									
1393874M	249969M	553461M	Net Sales ($)		1030M	9805M	54813M	105017M	382796M
455637M	75568M	156082M	Total Assets ($)		946M	2093M	18567M	24043M	110433M

M = $ thousand MM = $ million

See Pages 9 through 22 for Explanation of Ratios and Data

Current Data Sorted by Assets | Comparative Historical Data

						Type of Statement		
	1	15	18	5	1	Unqualified	66	56
1	13	50	15	1	1	Reviewed	137	118
4	31	31	9	1		Compiled	123	92
5	21	15	1		1	Tax Returns	64	49
10	18	42	40	4	1	Other	127	117
	36 (4/1-9/30/10)		319 (10/1/10-3/31/11)				4/1/06-3/31/07 ALL	4/1/07-3/31/08 ALL
0-500M	500M-2MM	2-10MM	10-50MM	50-100MM	100-250MM			
20	84	153	83	11	4	NUMBER OF STATEMENTS	517	432

%	%	%	%	%	%	ASSETS	%	%
11.6	10.7	7.5	6.5	9.2		Cash & Equivalents	7.0	7.1
25.4	21.6	22.4	17.3	17.7		Trade Receivables (net)	28.4	27.0
37.5	41.2	37.6	30.9	34.1		Inventory	33.3	33.6
.6	1.7	1.8	4.5	2.1		All Other Current	2.3	2.6
75.1	75.1	69.2	59.2	63.0		Total Current	71.0	70.3
20.0	15.9	21.4	27.1	24.2		Fixed Assets (net)	19.7	21.1
1.3	1.3	1.8	4.9	6.1		Intangibles (net)	2.7	1.9
3.6	7.7	7.5	8.8	6.8		All Other Non-Current	6.7	6.7
100.0	100.0	100.0	100.0	100.0		Total	100.0	100.0

						LIABILITIES		
27.3	15.2	17.4	18.3	8.9		Notes Payable-Short Term	14.7	12.9
1.1	2.0	3.3	3.4	3.3		Cur. Mat.-L.T.D.	2.7	3.5
17.7	15.4	11.4	8.5	11.4		Trade Payables	15.1	13.9
.0	.0	.2	.0	.0		Income Taxes Payable	.1	.1
12.1	9.2	7.4	5.9	7.4		All Other Current	8.4	7.0
58.3	41.9	39.7	36.1	31.0		Total Current	41.1	37.4
30.9	14.2	10.6	14.7	14.7		Long-Term Debt	15.2	14.2
.0	.1	.3	.5	.6		Deferred Taxes	.2	.2
2.8	6.0	5.0	6.1	5.1		All Other Non-Current	4.2	4.4
8.0	37.8	44.4	42.5	48.7		Net Worth	39.3	43.9
100.0	100.0	100.0	100.0	100.0		Total Liabilities & Net Worth	100.0	100.0

						INCOME DATA		
100.0	100.0	100.0	100.0	100.0		Net Sales	100.0	100.0
36.8	27.7	24.8	24.8	24.8		Gross Profit	27.5	27.4
34.9	27.3	25.3	24.5	24.5		Operating Expenses	24.5	25.5
1.8	.4	-.4	.3	.3		Operating Profit	3.0	1.9
.4	-.1	-.3	.3	.4		All Other Expenses (net)	.3	.1
1.4	.5	-.1	.1	-.1		Profit Before Taxes	2.7	1.7

						RATIOS		
4.2	3.5	3.6	2.7	3.6			3.2	3.4
1.9	1.9	2.0	1.5	2.0		Current	1.8	2.0
.8	1.2	1.2	1.1	1.4			1.3	1.4
1.8	1.6	1.7	1.2	1.9			1.5	1.7
.7	.7	.9	.5	.6		Quick	.9	.9
.4	.4	.4	.4	.4			.6	.5
7 54.4	16 22.7	20 17.9	12 31.0	20 18.5			25 14.8	24 15.5
15 23.9	27 13.6	32 11.4	30 12.1	28 12.9		Sales/Receivables	33 11.0	33 10.9
32 11.5	38 9.5	46 7.9	47 7.8	38 9.7			46 8.0	46 7.9
14 25.4	44 8.3	51 7.2	49 7.5	57 6.5			34 10.7	39 9.3
48 7.6	73 5.0	70 5.2	61 6.0	72 5.1		Cost of Sales/Inventory	54 6.8	58 6.3
108 3.4	105 3.5	93 3.9	92 4.0	103 3.5			81 4.5	84 4.5
1 390.8	14 26.7	11 34.6	10 36.1	16 23.2			14 26.3	13 28.1
17 21.7	23 15.7	19 19.2	20 18.6	23 15.5		Cost of Sales/Payables	21 17.6	20 18.3
32 11.3	36 10.2	29 12.5	29 12.7	36 10.2			33 11.0	31 11.9
5.0	4.8	4.9	5.2	4.6			5.7	5.3
15.2	8.5	7.5	11.0	8.0		Sales/Working Capital	9.8	8.3
NM	27.6	21.1	39.0	16.3			20.3	15.7
16.0	4.3	5.0	3.9	13.2			9.4	6.5
(18) 4.9	(73) 1.7	(134) 1.5	(68) 1.1	(10) 1.6		EBIT/Interest	(489) 3.0	(404) 2.2
-.5	.2	-.7	-1.2	-3.4			1.4	.8
	2.8	4.0	2.4			Net Profit + Depr., Dep.,	7.2	7.7
	(12) .9	(44) 2.3	(19) 1.5			Amort./Cur. Mat. L/T/D	(147) 3.3	(121) 2.0
	-.1	.0	.2				1.2	.9
.0	.2	.2	.3	.2			.2	.2
.7	.4	.4	.6	.4		Fixed/Worth	.4	.4
-14.0	1.4	.9	1.6	1.9			1.0	1.1
1.8	.6	.5	.6	.4			.7	.6
3.6	1.9	1.1	1.7	1.5		Debt/Worth	1.5	1.3
-23.9	8.4	3.6	4.8	2.5			3.5	2.7
123.0	23.4	12.3	12.7	11.2		% Profit Before Taxes/Tangible	36.4	24.4
(14) 34.2	(73) 6.3	(142) 3.4	(74) 2.6	(10) 5.5		Net Worth	(471) 15.1	(398) 9.4
-.9	-1.9	-4.8	-11.0	-14.0			3.8	-.3
27.6	8.4	5.6	5.1	6.2		% Profit Before Taxes/Total	14.3	9.7
5.8	1.6	1.3	.9	3.5		Assets	5.0	3.1
-.9	-1.7	-3.2	-2.7	-8.6			1.2	-.6
242.1	80.1	34.3	22.4	39.9			36.9	31.9
32.2	24.1	14.5	8.8	12.9		Sales/Net Fixed Assets	18.0	14.7
16.4	9.9	6.3	4.7	3.6			9.3	7.5
5.8	3.7	3.2	2.7	2.8			3.7	3.5
3.8	2.8	2.5	2.0	2.5		Sales/Total Assets	2.9	2.7
2.5	2.1	1.8	1.5	1.4			2.2	2.0
1.1	.4	.6	.7				.6	.7
(11) 1.5	(69) .8	(142) 1.2	(78) 1.4			% Depr., Dep., Amort./Sales	(466) 1.0	(398) 1.2
2.8	1.5	2.0	2.4				1.6	1.8
3.3	1.8	.8	.3				1.1	1.3
(14) 5.7	(46) 2.8	(79) 1.8	(35) .7			% Officers', Directors' Owners' Comp/Sales	(218) 2.2	(174) 2.3
8.9	6.1	3.2	1.6				4.1	4.3
34255M	322039M	1929198M	4055542M	1933177M	1274426M	Net Sales ($)	18296483M	14652606M
6222M	106335M	745102M	1911721M	850861M	546650M	Total Assets ($)	6780137M	5602496M

© RMA 2011

M = $ thousand   MM = $ million
See Pages 9 through 22 for Explanation of Ratios and Data

Comparative Historical Data | Current Data Sorted by Sales

			Type of Statement						
39	33	40	Unqualified			2	2	16	20
114	102	81	Reviewed	1	7	7	22	28	16
69	75	76	Compiled	1	16	19	20	12	8
44	45	43	Tax Returns	1	19	5	9	8	1
102	102	115	Other	4	12	9	16	30	44
4/1/08-3/31/09 ALL	4/1/09-3/31/10 ALL	4/1/10-3/31/11 ALL		36 (4/1-9/30/10)			319 (10/1/10-3/31/11)		
				0-1MM	1-3MM	3-5MM	5-10MM	10-25MM	25MM & OVER
368	357	355	NUMBER OF STATEMENTS	7	54	42	69	94	89
%	%	%	**ASSETS**	%	%	%	%	%	%
7.3	7.6	8.3	Cash & Equivalents		7.5	6.1	9.7	8.9	7.4
23.9	21.8	20.9	Trade Receivables (net)		22.3	20.5	24.4	19.8	18.5
33.7	33.3	36.9	Inventory		38.4	42.6	34.6	35.7	36.1
2.4	2.3	2.3	All Other Current		1.3	2.2	1.4	2.2	4.0
67.4	65.1	68.4	Total Current		69.6	71.4	70.1	66.6	66.0
21.8	22.8	21.5	Fixed Assets (net)		20.5	21.2	22.0	20.6	23.2
2.3	2.2	2.5	Intangibles (net)		1.8	1.2	1.3	3.4	3.7
8.6	10.0	7.6	All Other Non-Current		8.1	6.2	6.7	9.4	7.1
100.0	100.0	100.0	Total		100.0	100.0	100.0	100.0	100.0
			LIABILITIES						
14.7	12.6	17.2	Notes Payable-Short Term		16.3	13.2	14.6	17.4	20.2
3.4	3.2	2.9	Cur. Mat.-L.T.D.		2.3	1.9	4.8	1.9	3.5
12.3	12.7	11.9	Trade Payables		15.1	13.0	12.5	11.6	9.2
.1	.1	.1	Income Taxes Payable		.1	.1	.1	.2	.0
7.0	6.0	7.7	All Other Current		10.2	9.0	6.3	6.4	7.4
37.5	34.6	39.8	Total Current		43.9	37.2	38.3	37.5	40.3
14.8	16.0	14.0	Long-Term Debt		22.5	14.1	11.9	11.2	12.5
.3	.3	.3	Deferred Taxes		.1	.1	.4	.4	.4
6.1	5.8	5.7	All Other Non-Current		3.5	7.8	6.7	4.6	6.5
41.3	43.3	40.1	Net Worth		30.0	40.8	42.7	46.4	40.3
100.0	100.0	100.0	Total Liabilities & Net Worth		100.0	100.0	100.0	100.0	100.0
			INCOME DATA						
100.0	100.0	100.0	Net Sales		100.0	100.0	100.0	100.0	100.0
27.7	28.5	26.2	Gross Profit		29.8	28.9	27.5	25.1	22.2
27.7	29.5	26.2	Operating Expenses		29.6	29.5	27.8	25.1	21.8
.1	-1.0	.0	Operating Profit		.2	-.5	-.3	.0	.4
.2	.0	.0	All Other Expenses (net)		-.3	.1	.4	-.4	.0
-.2	-1.1	.1	Profit Before Taxes		.4	-.7	-.7	.4	.3
			RATIOS						
3.5	3.5	3.5	Current		3.7	3.3	3.6	4.1	2.7
2.0	2.1	1.9			1.9	1.8	2.3	1.9	1.5
1.3	1.3	1.2			1.0	1.4	1.2	1.2	1.1
1.6	1.6	1.6	Quick		1.8	1.3	1.8	1.8	1.1
.8	.9	.7			.7	.6	1.0	.7	.5
.5	.5	.4			.4	.4	.5	.4	.3
21 17.5	23 15.8	16 22.9	Sales/Receivables		15 23.8	19 18.9	21 17.1	16 23.3	8 46.9
31 11.8	34 10.8	30 12.2			30 12.3	31 11.7	32 11.3	29 12.4	30 12.2
44 8.2	47 7.8	43 8.5			39 9.3	42 8.7	51 7.1	39 9.4	44 8.3
42 8.7	49 7.4	47 7.8	Cost of Sales/Inventory		46 7.9	62 5.9	47 7.8	46 8.0	48 7.6
64 5.7	70 5.3	68 5.4			75 4.9	91 4.0	66 5.5	66 5.5	61 6.0
91 4.0	101 3.6	97 3.8			120 3.1	124 2.9	91 4.0	89 4.1	82 4.4
11 34.6	14 25.9	11 34.7	Cost of Sales/Payables		11 33.3	14 26.8	11 33.1	11 34.4	7 51.6
17 21.2	22 16.6	20 17.9			23 16.2	22 16.5	22 16.5	19 19.3	18 19.8
30 12.1	35 10.5	31 11.8			38 9.6	35 10.4	36 10.0	29 12.6	27 13.8
4.9	4.5	4.8	Sales/Working Capital		3.8	4.3	5.4	5.0	6.0
8.1	7.0	8.6			9.0	7.4	7.1	9.0	11.6
18.5	16.4	28.0			NM	12.9	18.4	23.8	38.0
4.0	3.0	4.7	EBIT/Interest		4.7	4.0	4.8	6.2	4.4
(347) 1.5	(323) .8	(307) 1.4			(46) 1.5	(39) 1.0	(67) 1.2	(82) 1.9	(68) 1.3
-.9	-2.8	-.7			-.3	-.8	-1.4	-.5	-.8
3.4	3.2	3.2	Net Profit + Depr., Dep., Amort./Cur. Mat. L/T/D			2.7	3.2	4.9	2.3
(101) 1.7	(85) 1.2	(79) 1.4				(10) .7	(19) 1.4	(25) 2.5	(21) .4
.3	-.4	.0				-1.9	-.9	.1	-.2
.2	.2	.2	Fixed/Worth			.2	.2	.2	.2
.5	.5	.5				.8	.5	.4	.4	.5
1.1	1.2	1.2				NM	1.2	1.0	.9	1.4
.5	.4	.6	Debt/Worth			.6	.7	.5	.4	.6
1.4	1.2	1.5				2.7	1.4	1.1	1.0	1.7
3.4	3.6	4.9				NM	4.2	4.0	3.6	4.4
12.3	7.0	17.1	% Profit Before Taxes/Tangible Net Worth		36.0	14.4	6.8	13.4	17.9
(328) 3.0	(319) -.7	(316) 3.7			(41) 8.8	(38) 3.8	(65) 1.7	(86) 3.4	(81) 4.4
-8.3	-13.3	-5.2			-3.2	-4.5	-15.5	-4.8	-5.7
5.6	3.1	5.8	% Profit Before Taxes/Total Assets		9.8	5.0	4.2	6.8	6.0
1.1	-.5	1.4			1.7	.6	.5	1.5	1.9
-4.9	-6.9	-2.7			-2.9	-3.4	-6.3	-1.1	-1.6
28.7	24.9	38.4	Sales/Net Fixed Assets		44.3	34.4	33.9	38.0	39.8
14.3	11.0	15.1			22.0	14.7	16.2	14.5	11.5
7.5	6.0	6.7			7.3	6.6	6.1	6.9	5.8
3.3	2.9	3.2	Sales/Total Assets		3.4	3.1	3.2	3.3	3.1
2.5	2.2	2.5			2.4	2.2	2.6	2.6	2.5
1.9	1.6	1.8			1.6	1.6	1.8	1.9	1.9
.8	1.0	.6	% Depr., Dep., Amort./Sales		.4	.4	.8	.8	.4
(329) 1.4	(318) 1.5	(310) 1.2			(44) 1.0	(38) 1.1	(61) 1.1	(82) 1.2	(81) 1.0
2.1	2.4	2.0			1.9	2.3	2.2	1.9	1.9
1.4	1.5	.8	% Officers', Directors' Owners' Comp/Sales		2.0	2.2	1.2	.7	.2
(156) 2.3	(156) 2.8	(176) 2.0			(33) 3.7	(21) 3.4	(40) 2.3	(42) 1.2	(35) .6
4.5	4.4	4.2			7.9	4.9	4.4	2.2	1.2
11505635M	8133858M	9548637M	Net Sales ($)	4582M	112222M	160505M	494605M	1551521M	7225202M
4524109M	3971953M	4166891M	Total Assets ($)	1718M	54087M	77822M	226737M	715850M	3090677M

M = $ thousand   MM = $ million
See Pages 9 through 22 for Explanation of Ratios and Data

Current Data Sorted by Assets | Comparative Historical Data

0-500M	500M-2MM	2-10MM	10-50MM	50-100MM	100-250MM	Type of Statement	4/1/06-3/31/07 ALL	4/1/07-3/31/08 ALL
			1			Unqualified	2	4
1	1	1				Reviewed	13	8
		4				Compiled	11	7
7	8	1	1			Tax Returns	21	15
1	3	2				Other	3	9
	3 (4/1-9/30/10)		28 (10/1/10-3/31/11)					
9	12	8	2			**NUMBER OF STATEMENTS**	50	43
%	%	%	%	%	%	**ASSETS**	%	%
	13.8			D	D	Cash & Equivalents	7.1	8.7
	29.6			A	A	Trade Receivables (net)	24.1	26.9
	31.8			T	T	Inventory	41.3	38.2
	1.8			A	A	All Other Current	.8	1.0
	77.0					Total Current	73.2	74.8
	14.4			N	N	Fixed Assets (net)	13.6	17.9
	3.7			O	O	Intangibles (net)	2.3	1.6
	4.9			T	T	All Other Non-Current	10.9	5.7
	100.0					Total	100.0	100.0
				A	A	**LIABILITIES**		
	3.9			V	V	Notes Payable-Short Term	12.1	12.4
	1.4			A	A	Cur. Mat.-L.T.D.	3.4	2.8
	21.7			I	I	Trade Payables	19.9	19.7
	.0			L	L	Income Taxes Payable	.3	.0
	6.1			A	A	All Other Current	11.9	9.0
	33.1			B	B	Total Current	47.6	43.9
	18.4			L	L	Long-Term Debt	14.9	19.5
	.0			E	E	Deferred Taxes	.3	.0
	10.1					All Other Non-Current	9.0	7.8
	38.4					Net Worth	28.2	28.8
	100.0					Total Liabilities & Net Worth	100.0	100.0
						INCOME DATA		
	100.0					Net Sales	100.0	100.0
	40.6					Gross Profit	35.7	34.7
	37.1					Operating Expenses	34.5	31.9
	3.6					Operating Profit	1.2	2.8
	1.8					All Other Expenses (net)	.4	-.4
	1.8					Profit Before Taxes	.8	3.3
						RATIOS		
	3.3						2.5	3.1
	2.3					Current	1.7	1.7
	1.8						1.1	1.2
	1.9						1.4	1.2
	1.3					Quick	.6	.7
	.8						.4	.4
16	22.3						20 17.9	17 21.9
34	10.8					Sales/Receivables	34 10.8	25 14.3
69	5.3						50 7.3	42 8.6
20	17.9						58 6.3	36 10.1
51	7.1					Cost of Sales/Inventory	80 4.6	60 6.0
118	3.1						130 2.8	102 3.6
30	12.1						17 21.6	17 21.8
44	8.4					Cost of Sales/Payables	37 9.7	33 10.9
66	5.5						63 5.8	49 7.5
	4.4						6.0	6.3
	5.5					Sales/Working Capital	9.3	10.4
	10.5						28.7	32.2
	57.6						8.9	18.1
(10)	4.3					EBIT/Interest	(48) 2.3	(39) 4.7
	.5						.6	.9
						Net Profit + Depr., Dep.,	7.2	12.6
						Amort./Cur. Mat. L/T/D	(10) 1.6	(10) 2.3
							-.6	-.6
	.0						.2	.1
	.3					Fixed/Worth	.6	.4
	3.4						NM	1.8
	.7						.9	.8
	1.9					Debt/Worth	2.6	2.4
	4.6						NM	5.4
	53.4					% Profit Before Taxes/Tangible	27.5	83.5
(11)	12.4					Net Worth	(38) 10.3	(37) 30.9
	-.2						1.2	2.9
	12.2					% Profit Before Taxes/Total	7.4	22.3
	2.0					Assets	2.8	6.8
	-1.9						-1.9	-.9
	298.0						63.4	86.2
	35.6					Sales/Net Fixed Assets	24.8	19.6
	15.0						12.3	11.8
	3.4						3.3	3.8
	3.0					Sales/Total Assets	2.7	3.2
	1.9						1.8	2.7
							.7	.4
						% Depr., Dep., Amort./Sales	(37) 1.0	(35) 1.0
							1.5	1.4
							2.4	.8
						% Officers', Directors'	(27) 3.6	(20) 2.9
						Owners' Comp/Sales	8.0	5.3
7363M	30882M	75670M	66688M			Net Sales ($)	368017M	1170240M
1799M	11296M	31749M	38278M			Total Assets ($)	230624M	329700M

(Columns 50-100MM and 100-250MM display "DATA NOT AVAILABLE")

M = $ thousand   MM = $ million
See Pages 9 through 22 for Explanation of Ratios and Data

Comparative Historical Data / Current Data Sorted by Sales

			Type of Statement	0-1MM	1-3MM	3-5MM	5-10MM	10-25MM	25MM & OVER
3	4	1	Unqualified					1	
11	5	1	Reviewed					1	
6	9	6	Compiled			2		3	
11	10	16	Tax Returns	4	8	3	1		
6	6	7	Other	2	1		2		1
4/1/08-3/31/09 ALL	4/1/09-3/31/10 ALL	4/1/10-3/31/11 ALL			3 (4/1-9/30/10)		28 (10/1/10-3/31/11)		
37	34	31	NUMBER OF STATEMENTS	7	9	6	3	5	1
%	%	%	ASSETS	%	%	%	%	%	%
10.0	7.7	8.6	Cash & Equivalents						
26.3	21.2	27.8	Trade Receivables (net)						
37.2	38.8	37.6	Inventory						
2.0	2.9	1.1	All Other Current						
75.4	70.6	75.1	Total Current						
16.9	18.1	17.1	Fixed Assets (net)						
3.1	5.1	3.0	Intangibles (net)						
4.6	6.2	4.7	All Other Non-Current						
100.0	100.0	100.0	Total						
			LIABILITIES						
11.2	12.7	11.6	Notes Payable-Short Term						
1.2	3.9	3.5	Cur. Mat.-L.T.D.						
18.5	17.0	29.1	Trade Payables						
.0	.2	.0	Income Taxes Payable						
6.8	8.5	9.1	All Other Current						
37.7	42.3	53.4	Total Current						
14.6	27.9	24.9	Long-Term Debt						
.1	.3	.1	Deferred Taxes						
9.6	3.0	9.9	All Other Non-Current						
38.0	26.6	11.7	Net Worth						
100.0	100.0	100.0	Total Liabilties & Net Worth						
			INCOME DATA						
100.0	100.0	100.0	Net Sales						
38.1	34.4	35.7	Gross Profit						
36.9	36.6	34.1	Operating Expenses						
1.2	-2.2	1.7	Operating Profit						
.0	.3	1.4	All Other Expenses (net)						
1.2	-2.5	.2	Profit Before Taxes						
			RATIOS						
3.9	2.4	2.9	Current						
2.4	1.8	1.9							
1.4	1.3	1.1							
2.0	1.1	1.7	Quick						
1.0	.7	1.0							
.5	.3	.4							
12 29.7	15 24.3	16 22.5	Sales/Receivables						
25 14.6	26 14.2	34 10.8							
44 8.4	44 8.3	53 6.9							
36 10.1	53 6.9	35 10.4	Cost of Sales/Inventory						
62 5.9	79 4.6	56 6.5							
112 3.3	122 3.0	116 3.1							
16 22.7	17 21.3	30 12.4	Cost of Sales/Payables						
22 16.8	33 11.1	41 9.0							
57 6.4	57 6.4	59 6.2							
5.7	4.9	4.7	Sales/Working Capital						
7.4	9.2	8.1							
17.7	21.2	35.9							
7.1	4.1	6.0	EBIT/Interest						
(32) 3.0	(32) .8	(28) 1.6							
1.0	-4.0	-1.8							
			Net Profit + Depr., Dep., Amort./Cur. Mat. L/T/D						
.1	.1	.1	Fixed/Worth						
.3	.4	.4							
1.7	3.4	UND							
.5	.8	1.2	Debt/Worth						
1.9	2.0	2.5							
5.3	7.1	UND							
36.3	13.6	23.2	% Profit Before Taxes/Tangible Net Worth						
(31) 12.0	(27) .6	(24) 2.5							
-.5	-14.2	-14.7							
11.8	2.2	7.2	% Profit Before Taxes/Total Assets						
2.8	-.6	1.2							
-.3	-12.1	-8.1							
50.5	72.6	73.6	Sales/Net Fixed Assets						
23.6	22.4	25.7							
15.1	9.9	14.1							
3.8	3.4	3.5	Sales/Total Assets						
3.3	2.5	2.7							
2.9	1.9	2.1							
.6	.8	.6	% Depr., Dep., Amort./Sales						
(32) 1.0	(30) 1.4	(25) 1.3							
1.5	2.2	2.0							
1.7	1.8	.7	% Officers', Directors', Owners' Comp/Sales						
(19) 3.5	(20) 2.9	(22) 2.3							
7.6	5.9	6.8							
335637M	263109M	180603M	Net Sales ($)	3527M	15158M	23261M	19881M	70654M	48122M
132593M	120147M	83122M	Total Assets ($)	1648M	5610M	8717M	10758M	40946M	15443M

© RMA 2011

M = $ thousand   MM = $ million
See Pages 9 through 22 for Explanation of Ratios and Data

Current Data Sorted by Assets   Comparative Historical Data

0-500M	500M-2MM	2-10MM	10-50MM	50-100MM	100-250MM	Type of Statement	4/1/06-3/31/07 ALL	4/1/07-3/31/08 ALL
	1		7		2	Unqualified	10	10
	5	21	7			Reviewed	50	47
9	46	30	3			Compiled	94	90
33	76	25				Tax Returns	77	69
16	54	24	10			Other	95	89
43 (4/1-9/30/10)			326 (10/1/10-3/31/11)					
58	182	100	27		2	NUMBER OF STATEMENTS	326	305

0-500M	500M-2MM	2-10MM	10-50MM	50-100MM	100-250MM	ASSETS	%	%
%	%	%	%	%	%			
7.9	7.2	6.3	4.0			Cash & Equivalents	6.0	6.4
8.3	7.8	9.2	11.6			Trade Receivables (net)	12.6	12.8
57.8	53.2	51.4	49.1			Inventory	52.2	51.0
1.5	2.4	1.4	3.2			All Other Current	2.0	2.2
75.4	70.5	68.2	67.9			Total Current	72.9	72.4
10.0	14.3	17.6	19.8			Fixed Assets (net)	16.1	16.3
1.9	2.4	3.7	3.1			Intangibles (net)	2.0	1.8
12.6	12.8	10.4	9.2			All Other Non-Current	8.9	9.6
100.0	100.0	100.0	100.0			Total	100.0	100.0

(Columns 50-100MM and 100-250MM: DATA NOT AVAILABLE)

0-500M	500M-2MM	2-10MM	10-50MM	LIABILITIES	Hist 1	Hist 2
10.8	6.6	8.9	13.9	Notes Payable-Short Term	9.9	10.3
2.9	2.7	2.9	3.0	Cur. Mat.-L.T.D.	3.2	3.4
14.8	11.9	13.0	15.8	Trade Payables	13.7	13.8
.2	.1	.1	.0	Income Taxes Payable	.2	.2
6.9	7.3	6.6	5.5	All Other Current	6.9	7.5
35.6	28.6	31.6	38.0	Total Current	33.8	35.2
25.4	23.1	17.2	12.5	Long-Term Debt	20.3	21.0
.0	.0	.1	.2	Deferred Taxes	.1	.1
22.2	10.4	8.6	6.5	All Other Non-Current	7.6	6.6
16.7	37.8	42.5	42.9	Net Worth	38.2	37.1
100.0	100.0	100.0	100.0	Total Liabilities & Net Worth	100.0	100.0

0-500M	500M-2MM	2-10MM	10-50MM	INCOME DATA	Hist 1	Hist 2
100.0	100.0	100.0	100.0	Net Sales	100.0	100.0
39.0	39.0	36.9	34.0	Gross Profit	36.7	36.7
40.6	36.7	34.9	31.5	Operating Expenses	34.2	34.4
-1.7	2.2	1.9	2.5	Operating Profit	2.5	2.3
-.8	-.1	-.1	.3	All Other Expenses (net)	.2	.2
-.8	2.4	2.0	2.2	Profit Before Taxes	2.3	2.0

RATIOS

0-500M	500M-2MM	2-10MM	10-50MM	Ratio	Hist 1	Hist 2
4.2	4.9	4.3	3.4		3.9	4.1
2.4	3.4	2.5	1.8	Current	2.5	2.4
1.5	1.9	1.5	1.3		1.6	1.5
1.1	1.0	1.0	.9		1.1	1.1
.4	.6	.4	.3	Quick	.5 (304)	.5
.1	.2	.2	.2		.2	.3
3 129.3	3 107.1	4 88.6	5 76.6		7 50.5	6 56.4
8 43.0	7 49.8	9 42.5	16 22.3	Sales/Receivables	13 28.6	12 29.3
16 23.3	15 24.1	24 15.5	34 10.6		25 14.6	29 12.6
83 4.4	102 3.6	99 3.7	104 3.5		92 4.0	85 4.3
141 2.6	144 2.5	136 2.7	132 2.8	Cost of Sales/Inventory	136 2.7	126 2.9
231 1.6	191 1.9	184 2.0	169 2.2		187 2.0	173 2.1
9 41.6	15 25.1	15 23.8	24 15.1		15 24.5	15 24.3
29 12.4	25 14.8	25 14.8	35 10.4	Cost of Sales/Payables	27 13.7	26 14.3
76 4.8	40 9.2	46 8.0	44 8.3		43 8.6	42 8.6
3.7	3.6	3.8	4.3		3.9	4.2
6.0	4.9	6.0	7.0	Sales/Working Capital	5.5	5.9
10.1	8.2	11.5	18.0		9.7	11.7
5.6	6.7	6.5	10.1		7.2	5.2
(51) 1.4	(163) 3.6	(94) 2.6	(26) 3.7	EBIT/Interest	(304) 3.0	(281) 2.4
-1.5	1.2	1.4	.9		1.3	1.0
	10.0	5.4			2.9	4.3
	(17) 1.6	(15) 1.8		Net Profit + Depr., Dep., Amort./Cur. Mat. L/T/D	(63) 1.5	(61) 1.9
	.7	.9			.8	.7
.1	.1	.1	.1		.1	.1
.3	.3	.4	.3	Fixed/Worth	.3	.4
-.9	1.1	.9	1.0		1.0	1.0
.6	.5	.6	.7		.7	.7
3.2	1.4	1.5	1.6	Debt/Worth	1.5	1.6
-16.8	10.1	3.6	3.0		3.8	4.7
20.2	30.6	22.7	16.2		32.3	25.1
(39) 9.0	(150) 12.7	(94) 9.4	(26) 8.9	% Profit Before Taxes/Tangible Net Worth	(287) 12.3	(269) 9.7
-.5	2.7	2.9	.9		4.3	1.6
9.1	11.2	8.3	8.6		11.1	9.0
2.5	4.9	3.5	3.0	% Profit Before Taxes/Total Assets	4.8	3.5
-4.3	.2	1.0	.0		1.0	.3
121.9	64.7	32.2	37.8		52.0	53.3
63.3	27.8	16.1	17.8	Sales/Net Fixed Assets	20.3	23.1
16.7	9.8	7.9	5.4		9.8	10.2
3.1	2.9	2.6	2.8		2.8	2.9
2.3	2.4	2.2	2.1	Sales/Total Assets	2.4	2.4
1.8	1.7	1.6	1.4		1.7	1.8
.6	.6	.8	.7		.7	.5
(37) 1.2	(131) 1.1	(89) 1.2	(25) 1.3	% Depr., Dep., Amort./Sales	(274) 1.2	(256) 1.2
2.6	2.3	1.8	2.0		2.0	1.8
3.5	1.9	1.1			1.8	2.3
(39) 5.6	(115) 3.6	(60) 2.0		% Officers', Directors' Owners' Comp/Sales	(193) 3.2	(172) 4.0
9.2	5.4	4.0			5.3	6.4
50554M	487478M	886323M	1111398M	738876M (100-250MM) — Net Sales ($)	4969626M	4482123M
20126M	201674M	389845M	543722M	309182M (100-250MM) — Total Assets ($)	1977145M	1909677M

M = $ thousand   MM = $ million
See Pages 9 through 22 for Explanation of Ratios and Data

Comparative Historical Data / Current Data Sorted by Sales

4/1/08-3/31/09 ALL	4/1/09-3/31/10 ALL	4/1/10-3/31/11 ALL	Type of Statement	0-1MM	1-3MM	3-5MM	5-10MM	10-25MM	25MM & OVER
12	6	10	Unqualified				1	2	7
33	48	33	Reviewed		4		5	16	5
83	64	88	Compiled	6	37	14	20	7	4
106	121	134	Tax Returns	29	63	15	25	2	4
103	98	104	Other	14	39	22	12	9	8
				43 (4/1-9/30/10)			326 (10/1/10-3/31/11)		
337	337	369	NUMBER OF STATEMENTS	49	143	54	63	36	24
%	%	%	ASSETS	%	%	%	%	%	%
6.4	7.2	6.8	Cash & Equivalents	7.0	7.1	6.7	7.3	6.5	3.4
10.3	10.0	8.5	Trade Receivables (net)	7.3	6.6	9.6	10.1	11.8	11.1
53.7	51.0	53.1	Inventory	55.7	55.3	47.6	52.8	48.2	54.7
2.6	1.7	2.1	All Other Current	1.2	2.1	3.0	1.6	2.5	2.2
73.0	69.9	70.4	Total Current	71.1	71.1	67.0	71.8	69.0	71.3
14.4	15.3	15.0	Fixed Assets (net)	12.9	13.7	17.4	15.1	15.9	20.0
2.3	3.9	2.7	Intangibles (net)	1.6	3.0	2.4	2.9	3.1	3.5
10.2	10.9	11.8	All Other Non-Current	14.3	12.2	13.2	10.3	12.0	5.2
100.0	100.0	100.0	Total	100.0	100.0	100.0	100.0	100.0	100.0
			LIABILITIES						
12.1	8.9	8.4	Notes Payable-Short Term	6.4	8.6	8.5	6.4	9.9	14.7
3.0	3.5	2.8	Cur. Mat.-L.T.D.	3.0	2.8	3.1	2.4	2.6	2.9
13.2	12.0	12.9	Trade Payables	13.4	11.2	13.2	14.8	11.9	18.6
.1	.2	.1	Income Taxes Payable	.2	.1	.1	.1	.3	.0
7.0	6.5	6.9	All Other Current	6.5	7.2	7.1	7.2	5.3	7.6
35.4	30.9	31.2	Total Current	29.5	29.9	31.9	31.0	30.0	43.8
19.8	22.7	21.0	Long-Term Debt	33.8	23.1	20.3	15.3	13.2	11.4
.1	.1	.1	Deferred Taxes	.0	.0	.1	.1	.3	.3
7.8	9.5	11.5	All Other Non-Current	27.4	12.5	4.0	7.5	8.1	5.3
36.9	36.7	36.1	Net Worth	9.2	34.5	43.6	46.2	48.4	39.2
100.0	100.0	100.0	Total Liabilties & Net Worth	100.0	100.0	100.0	100.0	100.0	100.0
			INCOME DATA						
100.0	100.0	100.0	Net Sales	100.0	100.0	100.0	100.0	100.0	100.0
36.4	38.9	38.0	Gross Profit	41.4	38.7	39.7	34.7	36.3	34.2
34.7	37.2	36.4	Operating Expenses	42.8	37.0	37.2	32.4	34.5	32.2
1.7	1.7	1.6	Operating Profit	-1.4	1.7	2.6	2.3	1.8	2.0
.0	.0	-.2	All Other Expenses (net)	-.7	-.1	-.2	-.3	-.2	.6
1.7	1.8	1.8	Profit Before Taxes	-.7	1.8	2.7	2.7	2.1	1.4
			RATIOS						
4.2	4.9	4.5	Current	5.4	5.0	4.5	4.3	4.4	2.5
2.6	2.8	2.8		2.4	3.5	2.7	2.6	2.9	1.6
1.6	1.6	1.6		1.6	1.8	1.6	1.8	1.5	1.4
1.0	1.1	1.0	Quick	1.2	1.0	1.0	1.2	1.2	.5
.5	.5	.5		.5	.5	.4	.6	.6	.2
.2	.2	.2		.1	.2	.3	.2	.3	.1
4 81.5	5 78.7	4 98.1	Sales/Receivables	2 146.6	3 114.4	5 80.2	4 99.2	5 79.6	4 85.4
9 39.4	10 36.7	8 45.6		10 35.8	7 50.4	8 43.7	9 41.8	9 39.3	13 27.8
22 16.4	20 18.0	18 19.9		17 21.8	13 28.3	23 15.7	27 13.5	24 15.5	20 18.7
94 3.9	95 3.8	100 3.6	Cost of Sales/Inventory	116 3.2	110 3.3	94 3.9	87 4.2	66 5.5	90 4.1
138 2.7	141 2.6	141 2.6		191 1.9	160 2.3	121 3.0	123 3.0	118 3.1	134 2.7
185 2.0	200 1.8	187 1.9		297 1.2	207 1.8	169 2.2	153 2.4	172 2.1	168 2.2
14 26.4	14 26.6	15 24.2	Cost of Sales/Payables	10 35.4	12 30.5	16 23.1	16 23.3	15 24.0	26 13.8
24 15.0	24 15.4	26 13.9		33 11.1	22 16.4	26 13.8	26 14.3	23 15.9	37 9.9
38 9.5	37 9.8	43 8.4		88 4.2	37 9.8	45 8.1	44 8.3	36 10.1	47 7.7
3.8	3.7	3.7	Sales/Working Capital	3.1	3.5	4.0	4.4	4.1	6.7
5.6	5.5	5.4		4.2	4.5	6.2	6.1	6.0	8.5
10.5	9.2	10.1		9.4	8.6	10.0	11.6	12.5	17.4
6.5	6.7	6.6	EBIT/Interest	5.1	6.0	10.2	7.2	7.1	7.8
(306) 2.4	(295) 2.6	(336) 3.0		(44) 1.6	(127) 3.0	(49) 3.8	(58) 3.3	(34) 3.2	2.2
.9	.5	1.0		-1.4	.7	1.2	1.7	1.9	.7
4.1	4.2	5.5	Net Profit + Depr., Dep., Amort./Cur. Mat. L/T/D		4.7				
(54) 1.7	(50) 1.6	(44) 1.6			(11) 1.4				
.4	.5	.4			.9				
.1	.1	.1	Fixed/Worth	.1	.1	.1	.1	.1	.2
.3	.3	.3		.6	.3	.3	.2	.2	.4
1.1	1.6	1.1		-.8	3.3	.7	.6	.7	1.0
.6	.6	.6	Debt/Worth	.9	.5	.4	.6	.6	1.0
1.6	1.7	1.7		5.9	1.5	1.3	1.0	1.2	1.8
4.6	7.3	5.6		-14.5	32.4	3.0	3.2	2.4	3.5
25.4	26.9	23.9	% Profit Before Taxes/Tangible Net Worth	20.9	21.1	42.3	34.7	16.1	15.6
(289) 12.2	(280) 11.0	(311) 11.2		(30) 9.4	(112) 11.2	(50) 13.2	(61) 12.5	(35) 8.4	(23) 12.6
1.5	1.9	2.1		.4	.8	2.2	3.5	3.1	-.1
9.8	9.9	9.9	% Profit Before Taxes/Total Assets	9.5	9.0	13.3	12.2	6.8	8.1
4.2	4.1	4.1		2.8	4.4	6.1	4.8	3.5	2.4
-.2	-.5	.0		-3.9	-1.1	.3	1.3	1.1	-.9
73.0	56.5	64.1	Sales/Net Fixed Assets	79.7	68.6	61.1	49.3	33.5	37.2
26.0	24.4	25.3		31.4	26.1	17.7	25.3	23.1	21.6
10.2	9.7	9.8		9.8	9.5	8.7	12.4	10.2	9.2
3.0	2.9	2.8	Sales/Total Assets	2.4	2.8	3.0	3.0	3.0	2.8
2.4	2.2	2.3		1.9	2.3	2.3	2.3	2.3	2.6
1.8	1.7	1.7		1.3	1.7	1.7	2.0	1.9	1.7
.6	.6	.7	% Depr., Dep., Amort./Sales	.8	.7	.7	.5	.8	.7
(269) 1.2	(270) 1.3	(283) 1.2		(32) 1.9	(103) 1.2	(40) 1.2	(57) 1.0	(29) 1.0	(22) 1.4
2.0	2.2	2.1		3.7	2.4	2.0	1.5	1.4	1.9
1.7	1.9	1.6	% Officers', Directors' Owners' Comp/Sales	4.0	1.8	1.7	1.5	1.2	
(197) 3.1	(201) 3.5	(220) 3.4		(26) 6.8	(90) 3.9	(36) 3.3	(46) 2.3	(15) 2.0	
5.4	5.6	5.6		9.7	5.7	4.3	5.0	3.2	
5286386M	3234499M	3274629M	Net Sales ($)	31281M	275677M	205299M	428265M	553714M	1780393M
2072674M	1496318M	1464549M	Total Assets ($)	18939M	134776M	101186M	176737M	257734M	775177M

M = $ thousand   MM = $ million
See Pages 9 through 22 for Explanation of Ratios and Data

Current Data Sorted by Assets   Comparative Historical Data

0-500M	500M-2MM	2-10MM	10-50MM	50-100MM	100-250MM	Type of Statement	4/1/06-3/31/07 ALL	4/1/07-3/31/08 ALL
		1	17	9	1	Unqualified	34	30
4	20	46	18		1	Reviewed	99	87
12	26	24	3		1	Compiled	90	80
53	63	35	2			Tax Returns	128	133
21	37	45	19	10	2	Other	121	144
	56 (4/1-9/30/10)		423 (10/1/10-3/31/11)					
90	147	160	59	19	4	NUMBER OF STATEMENTS	472	474
%	%	%	%	%	%	ASSETS	%	%
11.3	9.2	8.2	6.1	3.8		Cash & Equivalents	7.2	7.8
26.3	25.4	26.6	21.6	21.6		Trade Receivables (net)	30.2	27.6
28.6	37.7	34.8	33.7	27.2		Inventory	32.8	32.1
1.8	3.1	1.9	1.9	2.7		All Other Current	2.4	3.0
68.0	75.4	71.5	63.2	55.2		Total Current	72.6	70.4
18.9	15.6	18.5	25.6	30.9		Fixed Assets (net)	18.4	19.3
6.1	2.0	2.0	1.8	7.6		Intangibles (net)	2.8	3.4
6.9	7.1	8.0	9.5	6.3		All Other Non-Current	6.3	6.9
100.0	100.0	100.0	100.0	100.0		Total	100.0	100.0
						LIABILITIES		
15.7	14.8	11.7	10.7	12.1		Notes Payable-Short Term	13.7	12.3
5.8	3.0	2.7	3.1	2.0		Cur. Mat.-L.T.D.	3.6	4.1
26.7	20.5	15.5	12.6	10.7		Trade Payables	17.8	17.5
.2	.0	.1	.1	.3		Income Taxes Payable	.3	.1
22.4	9.2	8.1	8.1	6.6		All Other Current	10.7	10.8
70.8	47.6	38.1	34.5	31.7		Total Current	46.0	44.9
22.3	13.7	13.1	14.4	22.1		Long-Term Debt	15.3	16.2
.0	.0	.2	.5	1.1		Deferred Taxes	.2	.2
18.5	7.9	6.8	4.6	3.5		All Other Non-Current	7.8	8.1
-11.6	30.7	41.9	45.9	41.6		Net Worth	30.6	30.6
100.0	100.0	100.0	100.0	100.0		Total Liabilities & Net Worth	100.0	100.0
						INCOME DATA		
100.0	100.0	100.0	100.0	100.0		Net Sales	100.0	100.0
36.4	31.0	30.1	27.9	22.4		Gross Profit	30.1	31.1
36.9	30.2	29.6	27.8	22.5		Operating Expenses	27.0	28.5
-.5	.8	.5	.1	-.1		Operating Profit	3.1	2.6
.6	.1	-.2	.3	.4		All Other Expenses (net)	.4	.7
-1.1	.6	.7	-.2	-.5		Profit Before Taxes	2.7	2.0
						RATIOS		
2.6	2.9	3.2	3.2	3.2		Current	2.5	2.9
1.1	1.7	2.0	1.9	1.9			1.7	1.7
.6	1.1	1.4	1.3	1.2			1.2	1.1
1.3	1.4	1.6	1.5	1.3		Quick	1.4	1.5
.6	.7	.9	.8	.7			.8	.8
.2	.4	.5	.5	.4			.5	.5
5 75.3	17 21.7	26 13.8	23 15.9	32 11.5		Sales/Receivables	22 16.7	21 17.2
19 19.4	29 12.7	34 10.6	35 10.5	42 8.7			34 10.9	31 11.7
35 10.3	44 8.3	48 7.6	53 6.9	49 7.5			47 7.7	46 7.9
4 91.1	30 12.0	41 8.9	55 6.7	54 6.8		Cost of Sales/Inventory	27 13.7	26 14.3
28 13.2	64 5.7	70 5.2	75 4.9	65 5.6			54 6.7	53 6.8
76 4.8	103 3.5	112 3.3	108 3.4	91 4.0			85 4.3	86 4.2
5 70.4	14 25.5	16 23.3	14 25.3	13 27.6		Cost of Sales/Payables	14 26.1	14 26.6
22 16.6	32 11.3	28 13.2	25 14.7	25 14.7			24 15.5	25 14.6
58 6.3	49 7.4	41 8.9	43 8.5	34 10.7			40 9.1	42 8.7
9.1	5.2	4.6	4.6	4.1		Sales/Working Capital	6.6	5.9
152.5	9.0	6.8	8.1	7.9			10.8	10.3
-17.0	72.1	14.2	17.5	18.2			29.6	43.5
3.8	6.1	6.6	6.6	3.3		EBIT/Interest	8.1	7.3
(64) 1.6	(131) 1.7	(151) 2.2	(55) 1.6	1.1			(418) 3.3	(431) 2.5
-1.8	-1.0	-.1	-.5	-.7			1.2	.4
	3.0	5.1	5.5			Net Profit + Depr., Dep., Amort./Cur. Mat. L/T/D	9.2	4.4
	(15) 1.8	(30) 2.3	(21) 2.6				(91) 3.0	(78) 1.5
	.5	.7	.4				.9	.3
.0	.1	.2	.2	.4		Fixed/Worth	.2	.2
.8	.3	.4	.6	.9			.5	.5
-.6	2.5	1.1	1.0	1.7			1.5	1.9
1.2	.7	.6	.6	1.1		Debt/Worth	.8	.9
29.8	2.1	1.4	1.0	1.7			2.0	1.9
-2.6	17.4	3.3	2.7	2.9			6.0	8.4
95.8	23.5	17.5	11.2	15.4		% Profit Before Taxes/Tangible Net Worth	49.7	36.4
(47) 16.8	(121) 5.0	(149) 4.6	(57) 3.3	(17) .6			(406) 19.1	(388) 13.9
-4.4	-9.0	-2.1	-5.4	-10.7			6.5	.7
25.8	8.3	6.9	5.0	4.3		% Profit Before Taxes/Total Assets	14.8	12.4
3.0	1.5	2.0	1.2	.2			6.4	4.5
-16.4	-3.3	-1.8	-3.4	-7.3			.9	-1.7
869.6	84.8	45.8	29.5	17.3		Sales/Net Fixed Assets	57.5	52.7
47.4	32.2	20.1	9.7	5.8			25.6	21.9
14.7	14.5	8.9	4.6	3.3			10.7	9.6
6.2	3.9	3.1	2.8	2.6		Sales/Total Assets	4.1	4.0
4.3	3.0	2.5	2.1	1.5			3.1	2.8
2.9	2.1	1.8	1.5	1.0			2.3	2.1
.4	.4	.6	.9	1.0		% Depr., Dep., Amort./Sales	.5	.6
(45) .9	(108) .9	(140) 1.2	(54) 1.5	(15) 2.1			(405) 1.0	(395) 1.1
2.3	1.8	2.0	2.5	3.4			1.5	2.0
4.2	2.1	1.4	.8			% Officers', Directors' Owners' Comp/Sales	1.5	1.8
(46) 7.9	(79) 3.9	(89) 2.3	(21) 2.1				(210) 3.1	(238) 3.2
11.8	5.8	4.4	3.1				5.2	5.7
118539M	533620M	1733120M	2855655M	2559698M	1457119M	Net Sales ($)	10116751M	9650983M
24059M	168162M	697741M	1350090M	1361818M	777677M	Total Assets ($)	3861566M	3663549M

M = $ thousand   MM = $ million
See Pages 9 through 22 for Explanation of Ratios and Data

Comparative Historical Data

Current Data Sorted by Sales

			Type of Statement	0-1MM	1-3MM	3-5MM	5-10MM	10-25MM	25MM & OVER
38	37	38	Unqualified		1	1	5	6	25
110	94	89	Reviewed	2	6	14	21	27	19
66	74	65	Compiled	5	16	18	14	10	2
130	135	153	Tax Returns	37	47	28	27	13	1
147	143	134	Other	16	25	13	25	28	27
4/1/08-3/31/09	4/1/09-3/31/10	4/1/10-3/31/11		56 (4/1-9/30/10)			423 (10/1/10-3/31/11)		
ALL	ALL	ALL							
491	483	479	NUMBER OF STATEMENTS	60	95	74	92	84	74
%	%	%	ASSETS	%	%	%	%	%	%
8.2	8.9	8.7	Cash & Equivalents	14.4	9.0	7.7	7.4	8.5	6.6
26.0	25.1	25.2	Trade Receivables (net)	19.3	25.2	25.6	28.8	26.9	23.4
34.5	33.0	34.0	Inventory	28.2	34.4	34.4	36.7	36.9	31.3
2.3	2.4	2.3	All Other Current	1.8	2.7	2.9	1.5	2.5	2.4
70.9	69.5	70.2	Total Current	63.6	71.3	70.6	74.3	74.9	63.6
19.1	19.0	19.1	Fixed Assets (net)	20.0	17.5	20.8	15.8	17.0	25.3
2.3	3.4	3.1	Intangibles (net)	8.3	2.8	1.4	2.2	1.3	3.8
7.7	8.1	7.6	All Other Non-Current	8.1	8.4	7.1	7.7	6.8	7.3
100.0	100.0	100.0	Total	100.0	100.0	100.0	100.0	100.0	100.0
			LIABILITIES						
18.0	14.1	13.2	Notes Payable-Short Term	10.7	18.1	10.2	14.7	13.1	9.9
3.6	3.5	3.4	Cur. Mat.-L.T.D.	5.6	2.8	4.8	3.0	2.9	1.9
15.9	17.6	18.5	Trade Payables	22.0	24.0	16.9	18.1	17.1	12.5
.2	.1	.1	Income Taxes Payable	.1	.1	.2	.1	.1	.2
10.4	11.3	11.1	All Other Current	27.7	12.0	8.1	7.2	7.4	8.7
48.2	46.6	46.3	Total Current	66.0	56.9	40.2	43.0	40.5	33.1
17.2	17.2	15.6	Long-Term Debt	28.8	15.1	14.4	12.5	10.4	16.2
.3	.3	.2	Deferred Taxes	.0	.0	.1	.1	.2	.7
5.9	8.7	8.9	All Other Non-Current	29.2	8.0	5.3	7.2	4.8	3.7
28.4	27.3	29.1	Net Worth	-24.1	19.9	40.0	37.2	44.0	46.2
100.0	100.0	100.0	Total Liabilities & Net Worth	100.0	100.0	100.0	100.0	100.0	100.0
			INCOME DATA						
100.0	100.0	100.0	Net Sales	100.0	100.0	100.0	100.0	100.0	100.0
30.0	30.7	31.0	Gross Profit	39.5	33.7	32.0	29.1	27.6	25.8
29.2	30.6	30.6	Operating Expenses	41.1	33.0	30.9	29.0	26.3	25.5
.8	.1	.4	Operating Profit	-1.6	.7	1.1	.0	1.3	.3
.5	.4	.2	All Other Expenses (net)	.9	.1	.0	.0	.0	.3
.3	-.3	.2	Profit Before Taxes	-2.5	.6	1.1	.1	1.3	.0
			RATIOS						
2.9	3.1	3.1	Current	2.8	2.7	3.1	3.2	3.0	3.3
1.8	1.7	1.8		1.6	1.3	2.0	2.0	1.8	2.1
1.1	1.1	1.2		.6	.8	1.4	1.3	1.3	1.3
1.5	1.5	1.4	Quick	1.3	1.1	1.5	1.6	1.3	1.5
.8 (482)	.8	.8		.6	.6	.9	.9	.9	.9
.4	.4	.4		.3	.3	.5	.5	.4	.5
16 22.5	19 19.5	19 19.5	Sales/Receivables	4 93.9	13 28.2	19 19.6	24 15.2	23 16.0	25 14.7
30 12.2	31 11.8	31 11.7		16 22.3	26 14.3	35 10.5	36 10.2	33 11.0	35 10.5
44 8.3	44 8.3	45 8.1		40 9.2	38 9.6	44 8.3	50 7.3	47 7.8	47 7.8
30 12.3	32 11.2	32 11.4	Cost of Sales/Inventory	7 50.3	17 21.2	28 13.0	41 8.9	32 11.3	52 7.0
56 6.5	61 6.0	64 5.7		50 7.3	60 6.1	72 5.1	69 5.3	64 5.7	65 5.6
92 4.0	101 3.6	102 3.6		111 3.3	103 3.5	107 3.4	105 3.5	105 3.5	92 4.0
11 34.0	15 25.2	14 26.3	Cost of Sales/Payables	5 74.8	13 28.2	14 27.0	16 23.2	15 24.2	14 26.7
21 17.5	25 14.4	28 13.2		26 14.1	37 10.0	24 15.3	31 12.0	25 14.4	23 15.7
37 9.8	42 8.6	47 7.8		51 7.2	74 4.9	44 8.4	46 8.0	41 8.9	37 9.8
5.9	4.9	5.1	Sales/Working Capital	3.7	6.2	4.9	5.2	5.1	4.7
10.8	9.5	8.7		45.2	19.5	8.3	7.2	8.9	7.1
69.4	39.5	43.6		-14.1	-32.6	24.9	16.2	17.3	17.5
6.6	5.9	6.4	EBIT/Interest	3.4	5.8	5.5	5.2	8.2	10.3
(443) 2.0	(415) 1.6	(424) 1.8		(42) 1.1	(77) 1.2	(68) 1.9	(86) 1.4	(81) 3.2	(70) 1.7
-.5	-1.6	-.6		-5.0	-1.8	.8	-.7	1.4	-.5
5.7	3.1	4.8	Net Profit + Depr., Dep., Amort./Cur. Mat. L/T/D				2.9	4.0	6.7
(83) 1.7	(73) 1.7	(74) 2.0					(15) 1.2	(19) 2.6	(23) 2.9
.2	.0	.4					.1	.8	.3
.2	.1	.1	Fixed/Worth	.0	.1	.1	.2	.1	.2
.5	.4	.5		1.5	.7	.5	.4	.3	.6
1.7	2.0	1.8		-.3	-1.9	1.6	1.2	.7	1.2
.7	.7	.7	Debt/Worth	1.1	1.0	.7	.7	.7	.4
2.0	1.9	1.7		NM	4.1	1.4	1.5	1.3	1.5
8.4	13.9	8.6		-2.1	-9.3	3.2	7.8	3.1	2.8
27.2	23.9	18.2	% Profit Before Taxes/Tangible Net Worth	43.9	38.4	16.6	22.5	22.9	13.7
(402) 7.9	(388) 4.7	(394) 4.9		(30) 7.1	(63) 4.2	(68) 4.5	(82) 2.9	(82) 8.4	(69) 3.3
-4.2	-8.7	-4.7		-7.0	-8.5	-.7	-3.7	1.3	-5.9
10.5	7.7	7.7	% Profit Before Taxes/Total Assets	11.6	12.1	7.1	5.2	7.6	6.2
2.6	1.4	1.6		.5	1.2	1.7	1.0	3.4	.9
-4.3	-7.1	-3.2		-23.3	-5.0	-.4	-2.4	.6	-3.4
55.6	56.9	64.8	Sales/Net Fixed Assets	898.8	86.4	52.3	48.9	67.0	30.1
24.0	23.1	22.3		36.4	31.7	20.6	23.0	26.0	11.7
10.1	9.7	9.1		9.6	11.5	6.2	11.9	9.2	5.0
4.0	3.7	3.8	Sales/Total Assets	5.0	4.5	3.7	3.4	3.7	2.9
2.9	2.7	2.7		2.8	3.0	2.7	2.7	2.7	2.5
2.1	1.8	1.8		1.5	2.1	1.9	2.2	1.9	1.5
.6	.6	.6	% Depr., Dep., Amort./Sales	.5	.5	.6	.5	.5	.9
(395) 1.1	(399) 1.2	(366) 1.1		(30) 1.1	(65) .9	(59) 1.4	(78) 1.0	(70) .9	(64) 1.5
2.1	2.2	2.1		3.3	3.2	2.1	1.9	1.8	2.4
1.7	1.9	1.8	% Officers', Directors', Owners' Comp/Sales	6.3	2.8	2.7	1.6	1.3	.6
(225) 3.2	(224) 3.2	(237) 3.2		(28) 8.7	(53) 4.8	(40) 3.9	(53) 2.3	(40) 1.9	(23) 1.4
5.8	6.1	6.0		14.0	6.0	6.1	4.2	2.4	3.3
10117302M	8998197M	9257751M	Net Sales ($)	37313M	181471M	288407M	645883M	1289867M	6814810M
4200071M	4110696M	4379547M	Total Assets ($)	16355M	69345M	120268M	279682M	550909M	3342988M

© RMA 2011

M = $ thousand   MM = $ million
See Pages 9 through 22 for Explanation of Ratios and Data

Current Data Sorted by Assets   Comparative Historical Data

	0-500M	500M-2MM	2-10MM	10-50MM	50-100MM	100-250MM		4/1/06-3/31/07 ALL	4/1/07-3/31/08 ALL
		17 (4/1-9/30/10)		91 (10/1/10-3/31/11)			**Type of Statement**		
			1	1	1	1	Unqualified	1	1
	10	10	3				Reviewed	16	6
2	10	7	2				Compiled	26	22
10	15	8	4				Tax Returns	20	22
1	10	14	7	1			Other	27	29
13	35	40	17	2	1		**NUMBER OF STATEMENTS**	90	80
%	%	%	%	%	%		**ASSETS**	%	%
14.2	9.9	6.6	6.8				Cash & Equivalents	6.2	5.3
5.7	12.5	11.3	14.2				Trade Receivables (net)	12.7	10.3
65.9	51.7	58.2	59.9				Inventory	59.4	61.7
.0	2.1	1.1	2.6				All Other Current	1.8	1.3
85.8	76.2	77.2	83.5				Total Current	80.1	78.6
9.5	18.6	14.8	10.6				Fixed Assets (net)	15.3	17.2
1.8	2.1	3.2	2.2				Intangibles (net)	1.8	1.7
2.8	3.0	4.8	3.7				All Other Non-Current	2.8	2.6
100.0	100.0	100.0	100.0				Total	100.0	100.0
							LIABILITIES		
28.0	22.2	27.2	18.5				Notes Payable-Short Term	23.0	19.8
.3	2.7	2.3	1.7				Cur. Mat.-L.T.D.	3.0	4.8
23.4	19.4	17.8	29.0				Trade Payables	24.0	24.3
.0	.0	.1	.1				Income Taxes Payable	.3	.1
17.1	14.1	10.2	5.4				All Other Current	8.3	11.3
68.9	58.5	57.7	54.8				Total Current	58.6	60.4
25.9	13.5	9.8	3.6				Long-Term Debt	13.3	16.1
.0	.1	.5	.0				Deferred Taxes	.2	.4
3.5	10.1	4.2	2.0				All Other Non-Current	5.4	4.7
1.7	17.8	27.9	39.6				Net Worth	22.5	18.5
100.0	100.0	100.0	100.0				Total Liabilities & Net Worth	100.0	100.0
							INCOME DATA		
100.0	100.0	100.0	100.0				Net Sales	100.0	100.0
33.1	32.7	25.2	20.6				Gross Profit	27.7	28.3
30.9	31.3	24.1	20.0				Operating Expenses	25.8	26.5
2.2	1.3	1.0	.6				Operating Profit	1.8	1.8
.5	.8	.1	-.6				All Other Expenses (net)	.8	.9
1.8	.6	1.0	1.1				Profit Before Taxes	1.0	.9
							RATIOS		
2.2	2.0	1.8	2.1					1.8	1.6
1.7	1.3	1.4	1.4				Current	1.4	1.3
1.1	1.0	1.2	1.3					1.1	1.1
.9	.8	.5	.7					.5	.4
.2	.3	.3	.4				Quick	.3 (79)	.2
.0	.1	.2	.1					.1	.1
0 UND	3 109.7	6 57.3	7 52.8					3 106.7	3 138.1
3 138.0	9 41.3	15 23.8	13 27.4				Sales/Receivables	11 33.9	9 42.4
9 38.6	21 17.2	33 11.2	35 10.4					24 15.5	21 17.4
38 9.5	43 8.5	94 3.9	65 5.6					76 4.8	78 4.7
97 3.8	95 3.8	142 2.6	121 3.0				Cost of Sales/Inventory	120 3.0	118 3.1
190 1.9	189 1.9	208 1.8	137 2.7					178 2.1	203 1.8
2 195.2	6 60.5	12 30.5	23 16.1					9 39.7	12 30.0
47 7.8	34 10.8	21 17.4	54 6.7				Cost of Sales/Payables	34 10.6	29 12.7
85 4.3	72 5.1	53 6.9	72 5.0					76 4.8	72 5.1
5.3	7.8	5.9	7.0					6.2	8.4
9.9	15.8	9.2	11.6				Sales/Working Capital	10.6	14.5
36.5	75.8	29.4	16.4					193.7	80.7
10.0	5.3	7.5	14.9					4.7	5.1
(12) 3.7	(33) 2.1	(35) 3.1	(14) 5.6				EBIT/Interest	(87) 1.9	(78) 1.6
.8	.3	1.1	1.4					.9	.9
							Net Profit + Depr., Dep.,	8.0	8.0
							Amort./Cur. Mat. L/T/D	(15) 3.5	(14) 1.8
								1.5	1.2
.0	.2	.1	.2					.1	.2
.2	.9	.3	.2				Fixed/Worth	.3	.5
-1.5	4.4	1.1	.5					2.0	3.4
1.0	1.4	1.4	.8					1.6	1.9
UND	3.4	2.8	2.7				Debt/Worth	3.1	3.7
-3.2	43.8	7.1	3.8					14.7	13.8
	35.7	19.2	28.0				% Profit Before Taxes/Tangible	28.0	34.7
	(28) 13.3	(36) 11.2	15.6				Net Worth	(77) 14.6	(67) 10.5
	-.9	4.0	1.4					1.4	1.8
20.5	8.3	7.8	8.1					7.5	6.9
6.2	2.7	2.6	2.7				% Profit Before Taxes/Total Assets	2.9	1.6
-2.9	-2.1	.6	.6					-.4	-.7
UND	100.9	82.7	53.4					71.7	77.7
60.1	19.4	29.2	41.7				Sales/Net Fixed Assets	30.0	27.4
20.4	9.4	8.2	15.4					12.7	10.7
4.1	3.8	2.8	3.2					3.4	3.8
2.8	2.4	1.9	2.6				Sales/Total Assets	2.5	2.5
2.6	1.9	1.5	2.1					1.6	1.7
	.6	.4	.3					.5	.5
	(26) 1.6	(26) 1.1	(13) .5				% Depr., Dep., Amort./Sales	(67) 1.2	(65) 1.0
	3.1	2.3	1.6					1.8	1.7
	2.0	.7					% Officers', Directors'	1.1	1.0
	(16) 3.1	(19) 1.6					Owners' Comp/Sales	(46) 2.1	(46) 2.4
	5.5	4.1						3.5	3.6
11298M	100329M	452120M	1069373M	409260M	212076M		Net Sales ($)	767047M	1033121M
3681M	36388M	190232M	388724M	133323M	130438M		Total Assets ($)	319605M	419118M

© RMA 2011

M = $ thousand   MM = $ million
See Pages 9 through 22 for Explanation of Ratios and Data

Comparative Historical Data | Current Data Sorted by Sales

			Type of Statement						
			Unqualified					1	3
3	3	4	Reviewed				5	4	4
10	17	13	Compiled	2	6	5	2	4	2
21	26	21	Tax Returns	8	13	7	2	3	4
24	35	37	Other		5	6	10	4	8
25	22	33							
4/1/08-3/31/09 ALL	4/1/09-3/31/10 ALL	4/1/10-3/31/11 ALL		0-1MM	1-3MM	3-5MM	5-10MM	10-25MM	25MM & OVER
					17 (4/1-9/30/10)		91 (10/1/10-3/31/11)		
83	103	108	**NUMBER OF STATEMENTS**	10	24	18	19	16	21
%	%	%	**ASSETS**	%	%	%	%	%	%
6.4	6.9	8.5	Cash & Equivalents	13.3	11.7	6.7	4.0	10.6	6.3
10.6	12.0	11.5	Trade Receivables (net)	5.9	6.8	17.1	12.1	11.2	14.2
61.6	59.2	57.4	Inventory	71.6	57.7	42.2	58.9	58.7	61.3
.6	1.0	1.5	All Other Current	.0	.2	3.3	1.7	1.9	1.7
79.2	79.1	78.9	Total Current	90.8	76.3	69.3	76.7	82.5	83.5
14.4	14.8	14.9	Fixed Assets (net)	6.6	17.6	19.6	17.3	12.8	11.2
1.5	1.5	2.5	Intangibles (net)	2.3	2.4	7.2	.8	.1	1.9
4.9	4.6	3.7	All Other Non-Current	.3	3.6	3.9	5.2	4.6	3.4
100.0	100.0	100.0	Total	100.0	100.0	100.0	100.0	100.0	100.0
			LIABILITIES						
23.6	19.0	23.7	Notes Payable-Short Term	25.0	20.1	29.1	32.6	22.2	15.9
2.4	3.5	2.1	Cur. Mat.-L.T.D.	.1	2.9	1.8	2.5	2.6	1.4
19.5	21.9	21.4	Trade Payables	22.2	18.9	17.8	19.1	17.1	32.1
.3	.1	.1	Income Taxes Payable	.1	.0	.1	.0	.1	.1
10.5	11.1	11.5	All Other Current	19.4	24.7	4.7	4.5	9.8	6.1
56.3	55.6	58.7	Total Current	66.8	66.7	53.5	58.7	51.7	55.6
12.9	13.3	11.8	Long-Term Debt	29.9	16.1	10.7	10.3	7.5	3.8
.2	.1	.2	Deferred Taxes	.0	.0	.2	.9	.2	.0
3.4	5.9	5.5	All Other Non-Current	4.6	11.6	5.2	4.3	2.0	3.1
27.2	25.1	23.7	Net Worth	-1.3	5.6	30.4	25.7	38.7	37.5
100.0	100.0	100.0	Total Liabilities & Net Worth	100.0	100.0	100.0	100.0	100.0	100.0
			INCOME DATA						
100.0	100.0	100.0	Net Sales	100.0	100.0	100.0	100.0	100.0	100.0
28.6	28.6	27.6	Gross Profit	35.4	33.0	28.9	27.8	24.2	19.1
26.5	28.3	26.3	Operating Expenses	34.4	32.4	26.5	27.3	23.5	16.8
2.0	.4	1.3	Operating Profit	1.0	.6	2.5	.5	.8	2.3
1.2	.7	.3	All Other Expenses (net)	2.2	.3	.5	-.1	-.7	.1
.8	-.3	1.0	Profit Before Taxes	-1.2	.3	2.0	.6	1.5	2.2
			RATIOS						
2.2	2.3	1.9		2.3	2.0	1.9	1.5	2.4	1.5
1.5	1.5	1.4	Current	1.7	1.3	1.3	1.3	1.6	1.4
1.1	1.1	1.1		1.0	1.0	.9	1.2	1.2	1.3
.6	.5	.6		1.0	.7	.5	.5	.8	.7
(82) .2	.2	.3	Quick	.1	.2	.3	.3	.4	.4
.1	.1	.1		.1	.1	.1	.2	.2	.1
4 95.9	5 77.3	5 78.7		0 UND	2 160.6	3 122.6	9 42.3	4 88.5	6 59.3
10 37.9	11 32.7	11 32.0	Sales/Receivables	4 84.0	7 48.7	11 32.2	16 22.5	13 28.6	12 29.5
23 16.0	26 14.3	25 14.5		18 20.4	17 21.8	26 14.1	40 9.1	32 11.3	31 11.8
81 4.5	79 4.6	63 5.8		52 7.0	72 5.1	25 14.7	96 3.8	69 5.3	60 6.1
129 2.8	126 2.9	121 3.0	Cost of Sales/Inventory	137 2.7	147 2.5	74 5.0	160 2.3	128 2.9	117 3.1
213 1.7	201 1.8	179 2.0		413 1.7	195 1.9	117 3.1	221 1.6	154 2.4	137 2.7
8 48.4	12 29.3	12 31.7		3 124.0	2 193.4	6 62.0	17 21.3	12 29.5	23 16.1
23 15.5	38 9.5	33 10.9	Cost of Sales/Payables	48 7.7	40 9.2	20 18.0	28 13.2	23 15.6	54 6.7
63 5.8	70 5.2	65 5.6		110 3.3	71 5.1	40 9.2	53 6.8	61 5.9	72 5.0
5.5	5.8	6.0		3.7	5.3	11.5	6.2	4.4	9.0
10.6	10.1	11.7	Sales/Working Capital	7.6	12.9	19.0	9.0	8.3	11.8
20.9	18.5	28.6		NM	74.8	-51.9	21.9	-21.5	18.3
4.5	4.4	8.2			5.4	6.1	6.7	19.1	14.9
(74) 2.0	(98) 2.1	(97) 3.0	EBIT/Interest		(22) 2.2	(17) 3.3	(18) 1.5	(13) 6.5	(18) 7.9
.9	1.1	1.0			.6	.8	.5	1.7	1.6
16.1	5.5	5.3	Net Profit + Depr., Dep.,						
(13) 6.5	(15) 2.9	(17) 2.8	Amort./Cur. Mat. L/T/D						
2.5	1.1	1.0							
.1	.1	.1		.0	.0	.2	.1	.1	.1
.3	.4	.3	Fixed/Worth	.6	.7	1.0	.4	.3	.2
1.7	1.8	1.3		-.5	-.9	1.6	1.4	.6	.6
1.3	1.3	1.3		1.2	1.3	1.6	1.4	.8	1.3
2.5	2.9	2.9	Debt/Worth	UND	6.9	3.0	2.9	1.9	2.5
9.5	12.0	10.0		-3.3	-5.4	12.6	10.2	5.1	3.3
34.4	21.4	31.2	% Profit Before Taxes/Tangible		47.2	38.0	16.8	18.6	33.3
(73) 10.2	(86) 9.7	(91) 14.2	Net Worth	(15) 12.5	(16) 17.7	(18) 10.0	11.0	25.2	
2.1	2.2	2.7			.7	-8.4	1.9	4.6	6.0
6.6	4.9	8.8	% Profit Before Taxes/Total	9.4	8.0	10.4	4.4	9.2	11.8
2.8	2.4	2.8	Assets	1.2	2.3	4.3	1.4	3.0	5.5
.0	.1	.0		-4.7	-1.7	-.3	-.4	1.6	1.6
89.2	78.6	68.6		UND	453.9	50.2	87.8	105.1	58.2
35.6	33.3	29.4	Sales/Net Fixed Assets	42.6	22.9	23.2	44.0	24.1	45.0
11.4	11.6	11.9		6.8	9.3	12.2	5.7	13.2	23.7
3.3	3.2	3.3		5.1	2.8	5.2	2.2	3.3	3.5
2.3	2.3	2.4	Sales/Total Assets	2.6	2.2	3.1	1.7	2.4	2.7
1.6	1.6	1.7		1.1	1.8	1.8	1.5	1.9	2.2
.5	.5	.4			.3	.5	.4	.7	.3
(60) .9	(87) .9	(74) 1.1	% Depr., Dep., Amort./Sales	(14) 1.4	(14) 1.2	(13) 1.1	(10) 1.2	(17) .4	
2.1	1.9	2.2			3.7	2.1	4.5	1.7	1.1
1.3	1.2	.9	% Officers', Directors'		2.4				
(46) 2.4	(53) 2.3	(45) 2.5	Owners' Comp/Sales	(10) 3.3					
5.6	5.6	5.4			5.4				
1400995M	1505132M	2254456M	Net Sales ($)	6789M	47637M	68830M	136354M	237266M	1757580M
597394M	734842M	882786M	Total Assets ($)	3521M	22296M	27397M	77549M	101583M	650440M

© RMA 2011

M = $ thousand   MM = $ million
See Pages 9 through 22 for Explanation of Ratios and Data

Current Data Sorted by Assets   Comparative Historical Data

0-500M	500M-2MM	2-10MM	10-50MM	50-100MM	100-250MM	Type of Statement	4/1/06-3/31/07 ALL	4/1/07-3/31/08 ALL
	1	3	6		1	Unqualified	9	19
1	11	14	9			Reviewed	41	37
9	34	14	1	1		Compiled	79	69
34	35	7	1	1		Tax Returns	52	49
4	20	21	16	3	1	Other	63	70
	35 (4/1-9/30/10)			212 (10/1/10-3/31/11)				
48	101	59	33	4	2	**NUMBER OF STATEMENTS**	244	244
%	%	%	%	%	%	**ASSETS**	%	%
15.4	7.4	5.6	3.9			Cash & Equivalents	7.4	8.0
7.2	12.3	13.3	11.2			Trade Receivables (net)	12.7	14.7
39.1	39.5	34.7	42.8			Inventory	35.0	35.9
.4	1.9	2.4	1.1			All Other Current	2.8	2.3
62.1	61.2	56.1	59.0			Total Current	57.9	60.9
27.8	28.0	34.9	29.4			Fixed Assets (net)	31.8	30.2
3.1	4.4	1.3	5.8			Intangibles (net)	2.9	2.7
6.9	6.3	7.7	5.8			All Other Non-Current	7.4	6.2
100.0	100.0	100.0	100.0			Total	100.0	100.0
						LIABILITIES		
19.4	15.2	12.6	14.6			Notes Payable-Short Term	13.9	15.3
3.2	4.8	4.5	2.0			Cur. Mat.-L.T.D.	5.1	5.0
17.5	13.8	13.0	18.6			Trade Payables	16.8	14.1
.0	.4	.1	.8			Income Taxes Payable	.2	.2
26.2	10.3	10.2	8.4			All Other Current	11.6	7.9
66.4	44.5	40.5	44.3			Total Current	47.6	42.6
31.2	24.7	18.1	15.5			Long-Term Debt	22.9	21.7
.0	.2	.7	1.1			Deferred Taxes	.4	.4
8.1	9.2	3.1	4.3			All Other Non-Current	7.8	6.0
-5.6	21.4	37.7	34.8			Net Worth	21.3	29.2
100.0	100.0	100.0	100.0			Total Liabilities & Net Worth	100.0	100.0
						INCOME DATA		
100.0	100.0	100.0	100.0			Net Sales	100.0	100.0
46.4	39.8	40.6	31.6			Gross Profit	37.6	38.0
45.0	37.8	36.1	29.5			Operating Expenses	34.8	35.1
1.4	2.0	4.5	2.1			Operating Profit	2.9	3.0
1.1	.9	1.0	.5			All Other Expenses (net)	1.0	.9
.3	1.1	3.5	1.5			Profit Before Taxes	1.8	2.0
						RATIOS		
4.4	2.6	2.5	2.1				2.2	2.6
1.3	1.5	1.4	1.2			Current	1.3	1.4
.7	.9	.9	.9				.8	1.0
1.5	1.1	.8	.6				.9	1.1
.3	.4	.5	.2			Quick	.3	.4
.1	.1	.1	.1				.1	.2
0 UND	2 203.8	5 66.8	2 196.2				2 180.2	3 104.9
3 105.4	10 36.0	19 19.5	12 30.9			Sales/Receivables	9 40.3	13 28.4
14 25.4	25 14.7	42 8.8	38 9.7				24 15.4	30 12.1
17 21.6	45 8.1	50 7.3	67 5.4				33 11.0	39 9.3
69 5.3	77 4.8	94 3.9	125 2.9			Cost of Sales/Inventory	70 5.2	75 4.9
143 2.6	158 2.3	163 2.2	159 2.3				118 3.1	136 2.7
0 UND	10 37.6	11 34.1	25 14.8				9 42.3	9 39.7
10 38.0	24 15.4	30 12.1	45 8.1			Cost of Sales/Payables	28 13.3	26 14.3
41 8.8	48 7.6	56 6.5	58 6.3				47 7.8	49 7.4
6.4	5.7	4.6	6.3				8.2	6.1
25.6	14.7	16.7	18.6			Sales/Working Capital	20.4	14.5
-16.9	-110.2	-27.0	-133.0				-31.8	999.8
10.0	4.7	5.0	5.5				5.6	5.8
(43) 1.4	(92) 1.7	(55) 3.0	(29) 1.4			EBIT/Interest	(233) 2.1	(228) 2.0
-1.1	.2	.7	-.3				.8	.9
	11.4	3.6	16.1				3.4	3.7
	(13) 3.4	(13) 2.5	(14) 4.4			Net Profit + Depr., Dep., Amort./Cur. Mat. L/T/D	(46) 2.3	(37) 2.1
	1.0	.2	1.6				1.2	1.0
.2	.2	.4	.4				.4	.3
1.6	1.1	.8	1.3			Fixed/Worth	1.0	.9
-.4	19.9	3.1	3.5				3.9	3.2
.6	1.2	.8	1.4				.9	.9
5.3	3.4	2.0	3.5			Debt/Worth	2.6	2.7
-2.5	NM	5.4	7.1				9.8	7.4
37.4	48.7	32.0	37.9				36.8	34.8
(29) 7.1	(76) 11.4	(55) 13.4	(30) 18.7			% Profit Before Taxes/Tangible Net Worth	(198) 14.2	(206) 12.7
-6.5	-.9	.0	-6.3				.9	.7
15.1	10.7	9.7	7.9				11.6	10.5
1.7	2.4	3.6	1.8			% Profit Before Taxes/Total Assets	3.6	3.1
-5.1	-2.1	-.2	-2.7				-.3	-.4
43.7	42.8	14.4	19.7				25.4	27.6
20.0	12.6	6.2	8.4			Sales/Net Fixed Assets	10.8	10.6
7.6	5.2	3.0	3.2				4.9	4.8
5.6	3.5	3.0	2.9				4.0	3.6
2.9	2.6	1.9	1.8			Sales/Total Assets	2.8	2.5
2.0	1.6	1.2	1.2				1.9	1.6
1.0	1.0	.9	.9				.9	.9
(38) 1.4	(76) 1.7	(52) 1.9	(31) 2.1			% Depr., Dep., Amort./Sales	(216) 1.5	(212) 1.6
3.1	3.8	3.8	4.0				2.6	3.1
4.3	2.6	1.2					1.7	1.6
(29) 5.8	(61) 4.0	(24) 1.9				% Officers', Directors' Owners' Comp/Sales	(129) 3.7	(116) 3.4
9.4	6.6	6.0					6.2	5.7
51568M	307154M	557386M	1276765M	959291M	677725M	Net Sales ($)	4216116M	2626085M
13959M	111896M	267721M	628993M	294390M	251803M	Total Assets ($)	1587781M	1140757M

© RMA 2011

M = $ thousand   MM = $ million
See Pages 9 through 22 for Explanation of Ratios and Data

Comparative Historical Data

Current Data Sorted by Sales

			Type of Statement						
16	17	11	Unqualified			1	1	3	6
46	33	35	Reviewed		3	6	11	12	3
60	48	59	Compiled	8	28	10	5	6	2
54	60	77	Tax Returns	26	30	12	5	3	1
62	64	65	Other	3	21	7	4	16	14
4/1/08-3/31/09	4/1/09-3/31/10	4/1/10-3/31/11			35 (4/1-9/30/10)		212 (10/1/10-3/31/11)		
ALL	ALL	ALL		0-1MM	1-3MM	3-5MM	5-10MM	10-25MM	25MM & OVER
238	222	247	**NUMBER OF STATEMENTS**	37	82	36	26	40	26
%	%	%	**ASSETS**	%	%	%	%	%	%
8.1	7.7	7.9	Cash & Equivalents	14.4	7.5	6.6	7.0	6.6	5.2
12.5	11.3	11.5	Trade Receivables (net)	5.4	9.4	13.1	17.9	16.2	10.5
36.7	37.9	38.9	Inventory	41.5	36.4	37.2	42.3	36.8	44.8
1.9	1.8	1.7	All Other Current	.6	1.4	2.1	3.2	2.1	2.1
59.3	58.7	60.0	Total Current	61.9	54.7	58.9	70.4	61.7	62.7
31.9	32.4	29.6	Fixed Assets (net)	30.0	32.8	32.0	22.0	27.2	27.1
2.0	2.9	3.7	Intangibles (net)	3.7	4.7	2.8	.6	2.9	6.4
6.9	6.1	6.6	All Other Non-Current	4.4	7.8	6.3	7.0	8.3	3.7
100.0	100.0	100.0	Total	100.0	100.0	100.0	100.0	100.0	100.0
			LIABILITIES						
14.7	14.5	15.2	Notes Payable-Short Term	18.1	15.3	13.9	12.2	18.4	10.4
4.8	4.7	4.2	Cur. Mat.-L.T.D.	3.1	4.9	3.5	5.7	3.3	4.7
15.2	16.6	15.2	Trade Payables	17.8	11.5	14.3	15.5	16.5	21.7
.4	.1	.3	Income Taxes Payable	.4	.3	.2	.1	.2	.7
9.2	14.8	13.0	All Other Current	24.8	9.4	16.2	13.0	10.3	7.8
44.3	50.8	47.9	Total Current	64.2	41.4	48.1	46.6	48.7	45.4
22.8	21.3	23.7	Long-Term Debt	41.3	26.7	20.8	10.7	13.4	22.0
.4	.4	.4	Deferred Taxes	.0	.5	.1	.4	.6	.8
6.0	7.3	7.0	All Other Non-Current	8.9	11.1	4.2	3.1	2.2	6.5
26.5	20.2	21.0	Net Worth	-14.4	20.2	26.8	39.3	35.1	25.3
100.0	100.0	100.0	Total Liabilities & Net Worth	100.0	100.0	100.0	100.0	100.0	100.0
			INCOME DATA						
100.0	100.0	100.0	Net Sales	100.0	100.0	100.0	100.0	100.0	100.0
37.6	37.8	39.9	Gross Profit	47.9	44.1	39.7	31.0	35.3	31.5
35.9	36.8	37.4	Operating Expenses	47.3	40.7	36.1	29.7	33.2	28.6
1.7	.9	2.5	Operating Profit	.6	3.4	3.6	1.3	2.1	2.9
.9	.7	1.0	All Other Expenses (net)	1.8	1.8	.4	-.1	-.2	1.0
.8	.2	1.6	Profit Before Taxes	-1.3	1.6	3.2	1.4	2.4	1.9
			RATIOS						
2.3	2.3	2.7		4.1	3.8	2.5	2.4	2.1	2.3
1.4	1.4	1.4	Current	1.5	1.4	1.5	1.5	1.3	1.3
1.0	.9	.9		.7	.8	1.0	1.1	.9	.9
.9	.8	.9		1.2	1.0	1.2	.8	.9	.6
(237) .4	.4	.4	Quick	.1	.4	.5	.6	.3	.2
.1	.1	.1		.1	.1	.2	.2	.1	.1
2 150.6	2 166.8	2 222.0		0 UND	2 206.7	3 130.7	3 108.3	2 176.8	1 296.2
10 36.8	9 41.7	10 35.6	Sales/Receivables	6 66.0	10 37.7	12 31.1	18 20.0	19 18.8	8 46.2
25 14.5	24 15.0	28 13.2		19 19.6	27 13.5	25 14.8	43 8.5	43 8.6	22 16.3
39 9.4	44 8.4	43 8.4		36 10.0	46 8.0	37 9.9	39 9.3	49 7.5	54 6.7
75 4.9	72 5.1	83 4.4	Cost of Sales/Inventory	134 2.7	81 4.5	66 5.6	69 5.3	97 3.8	97 3.8
138 2.6	128 2.6	150 2.4		289 1.3	175 2.1	110 3.3	131 2.4	153 2.4	143 2.6
10 36.5	9 41.3	9 42.5		0 UND	6 59.1	7 51.3	11 34.5	13 27.1	25 14.3
24 15.1	23 15.8	27 13.8	Cost of Sales/Payables	25 14.6	23 16.1	23 15.8	22 16.6	36 10.2	46 7.9
50 7.3	51 7.2	53 6.9		59 6.2	52 7.0	38 9.6	45 8.1	56 6.5	60 6.1
7.5	7.1	5.9		3.4	5.2	7.8	7.1	7.8	6.3
17.1	15.6	17.1	Sales/Working Capital	9.1	19.2	16.6	11.6	19.8	18.7
-901.5	-64.6	-45.0		-9.1	-17.6	NM	80.6	-32.5	-188.7
5.6	5.7	5.2		3.8	3.6	10.3	14.2	3.7	7.4
(220) 1.9	(206) 1.8	(225) 1.8	EBIT/Interest	(33) 1.1	(74) 1.6	(35) 3.9	(25) 3.3	(36) 1.5	(22) 2.5
.3	.1	.0		-1.6	-.4	.4	.4	.1	.1
4.6	5.7	6.8						4.4	25.0
(54) 1.8	(37) 2.9	(42) 2.8	Net Profit + Depr., Dep., Amort./Cur. Mat. L/T/D					(11) 2.6	(12) 4.4
.4	.4	.9						.5	2.0
.4	.4	.3		.3	.4	.3	.1	.4	.3
1.0	1.2	1.0	Fixed/Worth	2.5	1.6	1.2	.4	.7	.9
3.2	14.9	7.4		-.5	NM	3.6	1.3	3.4	2.7
1.0	.9	.9		.9	1.1	.9	.9	.8	1.5
2.7	2.2	2.9	Debt/Worth	46.9	4.2	2.3	1.6	2.1	3.5
6.9	38.0	43.2		-2.3	-62.9	8.2	3.2	9.2	6.7
28.2	25.2	37.5	% Profit Before Taxes/Tangible Net Worth	27.4	39.1	54.6	52.7	32.6	48.5
(197) 9.5	(173) 8.4	(194) 11.5		(19) 6.8	(61) 9.4	(32) 17.9	(24) 14.9	(35) 7.1	(23) 20.2
-4.8	-4.1	-3.7		-5.3	-5.4	-3.3	-.8	-2.4	-3.5
7.8	8.3	10.7	% Profit Before Taxes/Total Assets	7.9	9.0	11.5	13.1	10.3	11.7
2.5	1.6	2.5		.4	2.1	4.7	4.1	1.5	4.5
-2.8	-2.2	-2.9		-9.1	-4.6	-1.5	-2.0	-.9	-1.6
26.0	25.0	31.4	Sales/Net Fixed Assets	38.9	32.5	34.0	68.2	25.3	22.5
9.9	10.1	11.1		9.3	10.5	12.5	23.1	8.9	12.7
4.6	4.7	4.5		4.3	3.2	4.3	6.5	4.6	6.0
3.7	3.6	3.5	Sales/Total Assets	2.7	3.5	4.4	3.8	3.5	3.2
2.6	2.4	2.3		2.0	2.3	2.7	3.0	2.1	2.6
1.8	1.7	1.6		1.4	1.2	1.9	2.1	1.4	2.0
.8	1.0	1.0	% Depr., Dep., Amort./Sales	1.2	1.0	.8	.8	.8	.8
(206) 1.5	(195) 1.8	(202) 1.7		(29) 2.9	(60) 1.8	(32) 1.6	(18) 1.7	1.4	(23) 1.1
3.6	3.6	3.4		3.9	3.9	4.3	2.6	3.5	2.1
1.9	1.5	2.4	% Officers', Directors' Owners' Comp/Sales	4.4	3.6	2.0	1.4	.7	
(116) 3.5	(114) 3.3	(120) 4.2		(21) 6.8	(45) 4.8	(25) 3.7	(14) 2.4	(14) 1.6	
6.9	6.2	7.1		9.4	6.6	6.0	7.1	3.2	
4104721M	3348207M	3829889M	Net Sales ($)	22562M	158730M	138377M	180688M	656562M	2672970M
1832240M	1429329M	1568762M	Total Assets ($)	13701M	96720M	57248M	71027M	349568M	980498M

M = $ thousand   MM = $ million
See Pages 9 through 22 for Explanation of Ratios and Data

Current Data Sorted by Assets

Comparative Historical Data

0-500M	500M-2MM	2-10MM	10-50MM	50-100MM	100-250MM	Type of Statement	ALL	ALL
1		7	28	21	28	Unqualified	82	78
1	10	30	23	4	1	Reviewed	95	93
20	55	61	12	1	1	Compiled	159	161
43	124	61	4			Tax Returns	192	185
11	69	92	63	15	20	Other	223	284
	171 (4/1-9/30/10)		635 (10/1/10-3/31/11)				4/1/06-3/31/07 ALL	4/1/07-3/31/08 ALL
76	258	251	130	41	50	NUMBER OF STATEMENTS	751	801
%	%	%	%	%	%	ASSETS	%	%
16.6	12.6	14.1	10.4	11.1	9.4	Cash & Equivalents	12.5	13.8
3.4	3.5	4.0	5.2	3.5	5.7	Trade Receivables (net)	4.5	4.1
43.5	37.9	24.9	24.7	22.0	21.1	Inventory	30.3	30.6
9.0	3.1	3.2	2.6	3.0	3.8	All Other Current	2.6	3.2
72.4	57.1	46.2	42.9	39.6	40.0	Total Current	49.8	51.7
19.1	27.8	34.1	40.8	46.3	44.0	Fixed Assets (net)	36.0	35.5
3.1	5.0	7.7	5.6	7.6	7.8	Intangibles (net)	5.3	4.9
5.4	10.1	12.0	10.7	6.4	8.3	All Other Non-Current	8.8	7.8
100.0	100.0	100.0	100.0	100.0	100.0	Total	100.0	100.0
						LIABILITIES		
10.1	5.3	3.1	4.1	2.6	4.1	Notes Payable-Short Term	4.6	4.0
4.4	5.0	4.2	4.1	3.7	2.9	Cur. Mat.-L.T.D.	4.1	3.7
18.6	19.0	17.1	18.8	18.8	16.5	Trade Payables	18.1	18.8
.1	.0	.1	.1	.1	.3	Income Taxes Payable	.2	.2
12.3	12.1	9.1	8.9	11.4	12.1	All Other Current	11.1	10.2
45.6	41.4	33.7	36.0	36.7	35.8	Total Current	38.1	36.9
15.1	26.8	25.9	22.0	19.2	18.5	Long-Term Debt	26.1	24.4
.0	.0	.1	.5	1.2	.6	Deferred Taxes	.2	.2
18.7	10.3	7.3	5.9	7.7	8.8	All Other Non-Current	7.2	8.4
20.5	21.5	33.0	35.6	35.2	36.3	Net Worth	28.4	30.1
100.0	100.0	100.0	100.0	100.0	100.0	Total Liabilities & Net Worth	100.0	100.0
						INCOME DATA		
100.0	100.0	100.0	100.0	100.0	100.0	Net Sales	100.0	100.0
28.1	25.6	27.3	24.4	26.6	27.0	Gross Profit	25.2	25.3
26.4	24.6	25.5	23.3	24.8	25.0	Operating Expenses	23.9	24.0
1.7	1.0	1.7	1.1	1.8	2.0	Operating Profit	1.3	1.3
-.4	-.4	-.2	-.1	.3	.3	All Other Expenses (net)	-.3	-.2
2.1	1.4	2.0	1.1	1.6	1.7	Profit Before Taxes	1.5	1.5
						RATIOS		
4.5	2.8	2.5	1.6	1.5	1.5	Current	2.4	2.5
2.3	1.7	1.6	1.2	1.2	1.1		1.4	1.4
1.2	1.0	1.0	.9	.8	.8		1.0	1.0
1.1	.9	1.0	.7	.6	.7	Quick	.9	.9
.4	(255) .3	.5	.4	.3	.3		(749) .4	(799) .4
.1	.1	.2	.2	.1	.2		.2	.2
0 UND	0 UND	0 999.8	1 317.2	1 518.1	3 127.3	Sales/Receivables	0 999.8	0 UND
0 UND	1 667.9	1 318.1	2 159.6	2 201.5	4 82.9		1 243.4	1 326.2
2 232.5	2 202.6	3 115.8	5 76.1	5 72.9	6 62.8		3 107.3	3 128.8
12 30.8	18 19.9	18 20.7	17 21.1	19 19.2	18 20.3	Cost of Sales/Inventory	17 22.1	17 22.1
26 14.3	26 13.9	24 15.1	25 14.5	23 15.7	25 14.3		24 15.2	24 15.4
41 9.0	37 9.8	33 11.0	33 11.0	30 12.2	32 11.5		33 11.1	33 11.1
0 877.1	6 66.1	8 43.1	12 30.2	15 24.4	15 24.7	Cost of Sales/Payables	7 49.1	7 53.2
7 49.3	10 36.7	14 26.9	18 19.7	21 17.5	18 20.2		14 26.0	14 25.8
14 26.8	18 20.2	23 16.2	25 14.7	28 13.0	26 14.0		21 17.2	22 16.9
13.3	15.2	16.1	25.4	29.7	25.5	Sales/Working Capital	17.8	17.1
26.5	32.8	36.7	61.3	59.5	220.1		42.9	40.1
86.8	848.9	-452.1	-102.6	-45.8	-61.3		-478.2	-436.9
12.1	13.8	11.9	9.5	18.1	12.4	EBIT/Interest	8.6	9.8
(43) 3.3	(211) 2.9	(216) 4.0	(125) 3.3	6.3	(48) 4.7		(647) 3.5	(663) 3.7
-.2	.6	1.4	1.0	2.3	1.7		1.3	1.1
	3.0	6.3	4.6	11.0	7.9	Net Profit + Depr., Dep., Amort./Cur. Mat. L/T/D	6.8	4.9
	(15) 1.9	(45) 2.8	(37) 1.8	(14) 3.5	(13) 2.5		(131) 2.6	(119) 2.3
	.2	1.2	.9	1.5	1.9		1.2	1.4
.1	.3	.4	.9	.9	.8	Fixed/Worth	.5	.5
.4	1.1	1.1	1.3	1.8	1.6		1.4	1.3
-4.1	-3.5	12.7	3.6	9.5	5.3		7.2	9.4
.5	.8	.7	.9	1.0	1.3	Debt/Worth	1.0	.8
2.5	3.1	2.0	2.3	2.1	2.7		2.4	2.3
-10.2	-10.5	25.3	5.2	17.3	7.4		15.7	19.5
80.6	62.4	57.0	26.3	34.8	35.9	% Profit Before Taxes/Tangible Net Worth	48.4	44.9
(50) 31.7	(180) 26.7	(198) 20.8	(112) 14.7	(35) 18.6	(43) 21.0		(588) 21.7	(625) 21.2
6.8	5.9	3.7	4.6	7.8	10.0		7.0	6.7
31.3	17.5	14.2	8.9	11.5	10.5	% Profit Before Taxes/Total Assets	15.2	15.7
8.1	5.8	6.1	4.1	5.7	4.6		6.4	6.7
.1	-1.5	.9	.4	2.7	2.7		.9	.6
252.1	86.0	40.8	19.1	15.4	14.3	Sales/Net Fixed Assets	40.1	47.8
69.0	32.0	17.2	11.9	8.8	8.8		16.7	17.8
27.6	13.9	7.8	7.5	6.5	7.1		8.5	8.5
12.6	8.9	6.5	5.7	5.5	4.7	Sales/Total Assets	7.6	7.8
8.9	6.6	4.5	4.5	4.7	4.2		5.3	5.3
4.8	4.4	3.0	3.3	3.5	3.3		3.7	3.6
.3	.4	.5	.8	1.2	.9	% Depr., Dep., Amort./Sales	.6	.6
(46) .7	(217) .7	(230) 1.0	(127) 1.1	(38) 1.6	(25) 1.2		(656) 1.0	(683) 1.0
1.2	1.5	1.8	1.7	2.0	1.7		1.7	1.6
1.2	.8	.5	.3			% Officers', Directors' Owners' Comp/Sales	.7	.8
(40) 2.7	(135) 1.2	(85) .9	(25) 1.0				(282) 1.3	(313) 1.4
4.4	2.2	1.6	3.0				2.6	2.4
214084M	1989088M	5649579M	15245626M	12334250M	33335853M	Net Sales ($)	67025180M	71166362M
22294M	289104M	1161141M	3131130M	2820629M	7857045M	Total Assets ($)	13939925M	15402235M

M = $ thousand　　MM = $ million
See Pages 9 through 22 for Explanation of Ratios and Data

Comparative Historical Data | Current Data Sorted by Sales

77	75	85	Type of Statement	1		1	2	3	78
93	93	69	Unqualified						
136	161	150	Reviewed	1	1	2	12	10	43
254	242	232	Compiled	1	13	19	29	50	38
279	287	270	Tax Returns	12	41	37	64	62	16
4/1/08-3/31/09	4/1/09-3/31/10	4/1/10-3/31/11	Other	4	10	20	55	55	126
ALL	ALL	ALL		**171 (4/1-9/30/10)**			**635 (10/1/10-3/31/11)**		
				0-1MM	1-3MM	3-5MM	5-10MM	10-25MM	25MM & OVER
839	858	806	**NUMBER OF STATEMENTS**	19	65	79	162	180	301
%	%	%	**ASSETS**	%	%	%	%	%	%
13.9	14.0	12.8	Cash & Equivalents	21.1	11.1	14.7	11.1	14.4	12.1
4.2	3.8	4.0	Trade Receivables (net)	3.1	1.7	3.8	3.8	4.4	4.6
29.8	30.9	30.4	Inventory	29.0	37.8	36.5	32.3	32.0	25.3
3.2	2.9	3.7	All Other Current	6.4	6.0	5.2	3.8	3.2	2.7
51.1	51.6	50.9	Total Current	59.5	56.7	60.2	51.0	53.9	44.8
34.0	33.5	33.0	Fixed Assets (net)	24.0	31.5	28.3	29.7	29.8	38.8
4.9	5.6	6.1	Intangibles (net)	12.4	4.2	3.8	7.3	5.4	6.4
10.0	9.3	10.0	All Other Non-Current	4.1	7.6	7.7	12.0	10.9	10.0
100.0	100.0	100.0	Total	100.0	100.0	100.0	100.0	100.0	100.0
			LIABILITIES						
4.9	5.0	4.6	Notes Payable-Short Term	25.0	6.1	6.4	2.8	4.8	3.5
3.1	3.9	4.4	Cur. Mat.-L.T.D.	5.9	5.9	3.3	3.9	5.1	4.1
18.1	19.2	18.2	Trade Payables	7.0	13.2	16.3	15.7	22.4	19.3
.1	.1	.1	Income Taxes Payable	.2	.0	.1	.1	.0	.2
11.2	10.4	10.6	All Other Current	11.4	9.0	8.4	12.7	10.8	10.3
37.4	38.6	37.9	Total Current	49.5	34.2	34.5	35.2	43.1	37.3
24.0	24.3	23.7	Long-Term Debt	20.4	29.1	29.3	25.7	21.8	21.4
.2	.2	.2	Deferred Taxes	.0	.0	.0	.1	.1	.5
8.3	8.3	9.2	All Other Non-Current	12.0	20.1	5.3	11.2	9.5	6.5
30.2	28.5	28.9	Net Worth	18.1	16.6	30.9	27.8	25.5	34.3
100.0	100.0	100.0	Total Liabilities & Net Worth	100.0	100.0	100.0	100.0	100.0	100.0
			INCOME DATA						
100.0	100.0	100.0	Net Sales	100.0	100.0	100.0	100.0	100.0	100.0
25.4	26.6	26.3	Gross Profit	35.6	29.1	24.2	26.7	26.1	25.5
24.2	24.9	24.9	Operating Expenses	31.1	28.5	22.9	25.3	24.9	24.0
1.2	1.7	1.4	Operating Profit	4.6	.6	1.3	1.4	1.2	1.5
-.3	-.3	-.2	All Other Expenses (net)	-.8	-.4	-.1	-.2	-.4	.0
1.5	2.0	1.6	Profit Before Taxes	5.4	.9	1.4	1.7	1.7	1.5
			RATIOS						
2.4	2.6	2.5		10.7	5.1	3.8	2.7	2.5	1.7
1.4	1.4	1.4	Current	2.5	2.3	1.9	1.7	1.4	1.2
.9	.9	.9		.5	1.1	1.1	1.1	.9	.9
.9	1.0	.9		6.0	1.0	1.3	.8	1.0	.7
(837) .4	(855) .4	(803) .4	Quick	.2	.5	.4	(159) .3	.4	.4
.2	.2	.2		.0	.1	.2	.1	.2	.2
0 999.8	0 999.8	0 999.8		0 UND	0 UND	0 UND	0 999.8	0 999.8	1 427.6
1 344.0	1 307.2	1 310.3	Sales/Receivables	0 UND	0 UND	0 978.8	1 507.9	1 428.4	2 161.2
3 117.2	3 122.0	3 106.9		0 UND	1 375.6	3 127.2	2 160.0	2 147.1	5 79.9
17 21.2	17 20.9	18 20.7		0 UND	20 18.4	18 20.1	21 17.8	17 21.0	17 21.1
24 15.2	24 15.0	25 14.5	Cost of Sales/Inventory	42 8.6	40 9.1	26 13.8	27 13.8	23 16.2	24 15.5
34 10.8	34 10.8	35 10.6		86 4.3	58 6.3	38 9.5	36 10.2	31 11.6	30 12.0
7 52.5	7 50.5	8 48.2		0 UND	0 UND	4 84.0	6 58.2	9 41.8	11 33.4
14 26.1	14 26.5	14 27.0	Cost of Sales/Payables	0 UND	7 49.7	9 40.5	12 31.0	14 26.9	18 20.7
22 16.9	22 16.5	22 16.9		10 37.8	16 22.3	16 22.4	19 18.8	22 16.9	25 14.8
16.9	16.7	16.6		5.9	9.0	13.6	18.2	16.4	26.3
41.9	40.8	40.7	Sales/Working Capital	15.4	14.5	24.3	31.2	53.3	62.1
-293.1	-204.5	-243.4		-28.4	77.8	184.1	124.2	-240.4	-109.2
10.7	12.9	12.1		7.0	6.6	12.1	14.7	12.0	13.2
(691) 3.6	(717) 4.6	(684) 3.5	EBIT/Interest	(11) 3.8	(47) 2.0	(63) 2.5	(133) 3.9	(142) 2.7	(288) 4.3
1.3	1.6	1.2		3.3	.3	.6	.6	.9	1.7
4.7	6.8	5.7					2.9	6.8	5.9
(123) 2.4	(150) 2.8	(125) 2.1	Net Profit + Depr., Dep., Amort./Cur. Mat. L/T/D				(14) 2.2	(25) 1.9	(79) 2.1
1.3	1.3	1.1					.7	.8	1.3
.5	.4	.4		.0	.3	.2	.3	.4	.7
1.3	1.3	1.2	Fixed/Worth	.3	1.2	.7	1.1	1.2	1.3
5.9	15.3	15.2		-29.5	-2.6	-41.6	-14.6	-3.3	3.8
.8	.8	.8		.3	.9	.5	.7	.7	.9
2.4	2.3	2.3	Debt/Worth	2.4	4.4	1.7	2.5	2.3	2.0
14.7	64.9	48.9		-4.1	-8.3	-35.9	-20.8	-13.5	5.8
55.2	55.2	51.9		90.0	49.2	49.7	62.0	66.4	36.9
(669) 24.8	(657) 23.1	(618) 20.0	% Profit Before Taxes/Tangible Net Worth	(13) 13.8	(43) 8.0	(57) 16.7	(118) 25.1	(131) 27.4	(256) 18.8
7.6	9.0	5.8		7.7	-2.8	5.6	5.4	3.4	8.3
16.0	16.9	13.9		14.5	13.4	14.1	17.4	17.5	11.9
6.4	7.6	5.5	% Profit Before Taxes/Total Assets	12.5	2.4	6.1	6.6	5.4	5.8
1.0	2.0	.6		4.0	-2.0	-1.6	-1.0	.5	2.1
47.1	47.2	47.0		UND	49.2	89.4	74.8	70.3	23.3
17.3	19.5	18.8	Sales/Net Fixed Assets	26.5	21.7	39.9	23.4	26.3	13.2
8.1	8.6	8.5		4.2	6.7	11.2	8.8	10.7	7.8
7.8	7.7	7.4		5.3	7.2	8.9	7.7	8.9	6.3
5.1	5.5	5.0	Sales/Total Assets	2.6	4.1	5.9	5.5	5.7	4.8
3.7	3.7	3.6		1.1	2.6	3.6	3.4	4.0	3.7
.6	.6	.6			.7	.3	.4	.4	.8
(719) 1.0	(727) 1.0	(683) 1.0	% Depr., Dep., Amort./Sales		(51) 1.2	(61) .8	(131) .9	(166) .8	(265) 1.2
1.6	1.5	1.6			1.9	1.4	1.8	1.3	1.7
.7	.6	.7		3.1	1.2	1.0	.8	.6	.3
(331) 1.3	(322) 1.2	(292) 1.1	% Officers', Directors' Owners' Comp/Sales	(10) 5.7	(32) 2.9	(38) 1.5	(81) 1.2	(74) .9	(57) .7
2.7	2.5	2.3		6.7	4.4	2.1	2.1	1.8	1.8
74780490M	70072922M	68768480M	Net Sales ($)	13254M	131369M	318085M	1181720M	2827869M	64296183M
16330138M	15304591M	15281343M	Total Assets ($)	6670M	40513M	76425M	349960M	555817M	14251958M

M = $ thousand   MM = $ million
See Pages 9 through 22 for Explanation of Ratios and Data

Current Data Sorted by Assets | Comparative Historical Data

0-500M	500M-2MM	2-10MM	10-50MM	50-100MM	100-250MM	Type of Statement	20	19
	1	1	3	1	2	Unqualified	20	19
	1	5	4			Reviewed	10	11
7	13	9	2			Compiled	26	27
87	49	10	4		1	Tax Returns	109	122
23	36	17	6	3	2	Other	51	56
	26 (4/1-9/30/10)		261 (10/1/10-3/31/11)				4/1/06-3/31/07 ALL	4/1/07-3/31/08 ALL
117	100	42	19	4	5	NUMBER OF STATEMENTS	216	235
%	%	%	%	%	%	**ASSETS**	%	%
16.0	11.8	9.3	11.0			Cash & Equivalents	12.1	12.4
2.4	2.6	9.9	5.3			Trade Receivables (net)	4.8	4.0
39.2	17.0	19.8	12.4			Inventory	28.2	27.9
1.8	1.2	.9	1.9			All Other Current	1.8	1.8
59.4	32.5	39.9	30.6			Total Current	47.0	46.1
23.0	54.3	46.6	61.0			Fixed Assets (net)	40.6	39.1
11.0	5.7	4.3	4.4			Intangibles (net)	7.6	8.9
6.6	7.5	9.2	4.0			All Other Non-Current	4.8	6.0
100.0	100.0	100.0	100.0			Total	100.0	100.0
						LIABILITIES		
5.7	5.8	3.3	1.8			Notes Payable-Short Term	3.3	4.8
2.3	2.8	2.7	3.5			Cur. Mat.-L.T.D.	3.4	3.0
9.8	8.3	16.3	13.3			Trade Payables	12.9	12.2
.0	.0	.3	.2			Income Taxes Payable	.1	.1
16.5	9.1	10.4	5.4			All Other Current	13.7	12.5
34.4	26.0	33.0	24.2			Total Current	33.4	32.7
17.9	50.0	36.0	36.1			Long-Term Debt	31.9	31.9
.0	.1	.4	1.4			Deferred Taxes	.2	.2
17.8	7.0	6.2	8.2			All Other Non-Current	10.0	11.1
29.9	16.9	24.4	30.1			Net Worth	24.6	24.2
100.0	100.0	100.0	100.0			Total Liabilities & Net Worth	100.0	100.0
						INCOME DATA		
100.0	100.0	100.0	100.0			Net Sales	100.0	100.0
25.1	20.7	17.8	14.4			Gross Profit	19.2	19.4
23.6	18.6	16.5	13.8			Operating Expenses	17.2	17.3
1.5	2.1	1.2	.7			Operating Profit	2.0	2.1
-.9	.4	-.8	-.1			All Other Expenses (net)	.2	-.2
2.4	1.7	2.0	.8			Profit Before Taxes	1.8	2.3
						RATIOS		
11.7	4.0	2.4	1.8			Current	3.3	4.0
3.7	1.7	1.4	1.3				1.4	1.6
1.4	.8	.8	.8				.8	.8
2.5	1.7	1.2	1.1			Quick	1.4	1.4
(116) .8	(99) .6	.5	.6				(213) .5	(232) .5
.1	.1	.2	.4				.2	.2
0 UND	0 UND	0 999.8	1 435.1			Sales/Receivables	0 UND	0 UND
0 UND	0 UND	2 210.3	3 128.4				0 999.8	0 999.8
0 UND	1 358.8	5 80.4	5 70.4				3 127.4	3 117.4
12 30.7	8 44.5	9 41.7	9 42.0			Cost of Sales/Inventory	9 41.9	9 39.1
22 16.9	13 27.5	12 30.3	11 34.5				13 27.3	15 24.1
46 8.0	25 14.5	19 19.3	14 26.7				31 11.8	34 10.8
0 UND	0 UND	1 457.6	7 56.1			Cost of Sales/Payables	0 UND	0 UND
0 UND	2 148.7	6 59.1	9 40.7				4 87.0	4 101.9
4 89.7	9 38.5	13 27.8	14 26.9				14 26.2	12 29.8
10.7	19.4	22.1	35.0			Sales/Working Capital	20.8	13.7
21.3	41.7	109.8	97.4				65.3	48.3
92.1	-109.8	-115.1	-189.1				-100.3	-106.6
12.5	5.8	4.9	4.3			EBIT/Interest	6.0	5.1
(65) 5.4	(85) 2.3	(40) 2.8	(18) 2.5				(158) 2.4	(170) 2.4
.7	1.1	.9	1.1				.7	1.0
						Net Profit + Depr., Dep., Amort./Cur. Mat. L/T/D	3.0	4.3
							(17) 2.1	(20) 2.4
							1.0	1.4
.0	.9	1.4	1.2			Fixed/Worth	.4	.3
.5	4.6	2.3	3.0				2.5	2.3
7.6	-10.8	10.6	11.7				-179.0	-22.7
.3	1.5	2.1	.8			Debt/Worth	1.3	1.0
1.5	6.6	4.6	3.4				4.1	3.9
-7.6	-14.6	14.8	14.5				-65.1	-24.1
73.9	53.9	52.3	21.3			% Profit Before Taxes/Tangible Net Worth	67.4	67.7
(81) 32.7	(68) 31.7	(35) 22.8	(16) 10.2				(157) 28.8	(166) 33.7
10.3	7.3	4.5	-.4				8.0	11.3
29.6	12.9	8.1	5.0			% Profit Before Taxes/Total Assets	17.3	16.7
13.2	6.0	4.3	3.3				5.5	7.4
1.0	.4	-.1	.2				.2	.7
602.6	22.7	40.1	13.8			Sales/Net Fixed Assets	90.2	64.1
70.5	7.7	9.7	7.7				17.0	16.0
18.2	3.4	3.5	5.2				5.3	6.3
14.2	6.4	8.8	6.1			Sales/Total Assets	9.4	10.1
7.3	3.9	4.4	4.9				5.4	4.9
3.4	2.4	2.2	3.3				3.1	2.5
.2	.6	.6	.9			% Depr., Dep., Amort./Sales	.6	.5
(66) .7	(82) 1.3	(38) 1.1	(17) 1.1				(170) 1.1	(173) 1.0
1.9	2.3	1.8	1.7				1.7	1.7
1.3	.8	.3				% Officers', Directors' Owners' Comp/Sales	.9	1.0
(60) 2.8	(49) 1.5	(13) .7					(80) 1.7	(95) 2.0
5.1	2.7	1.6					3.6	4.7
213187M	498272M	1287653M	2529202M	1337289M	4689678M	Net Sales ($)	24526929M	20740848M
26265M	102401M	203321M	440625M	326734M	866655M	Total Assets ($)	2851434M	2501821M

M = $ thousand   MM = $ million
See Pages 9 through 22 for Explanation of Ratios and Data

Comparative Historical Data

Current Data Sorted by Sales

			Type of Statement						
16	9	8	Unqualified			1	2	1	7
20	15	10	Reviewed						7
20	30	31	Compiled	2	5	6	7	6	5
152	184	151	Tax Returns	49	45	26	19	2	10
57	70	87	Other	10	27	13	11	10	16
4/1/08-3/31/09	4/1/09-3/31/10	4/1/10-3/31/11		26 (4/1-9/30/10)			261 (10/1/10-3/31/11)		
ALL	ALL	ALL		0-1MM	1-3MM	3-5MM	5-10MM	10-25MM	25MM & OVER
265	308	287	NUMBER OF STATEMENTS	61	77	46	39	19	45
%	%	%	ASSETS	%	%	%	%	%	%
12.8	11.7	12.9	Cash & Equivalents	15.0	12.4	12.8	14.4	12.7	9.7
3.8	2.8	3.8	Trade Receivables (net)	.8	2.5	4.3	1.8	7.8	9.5
26.4	29.2	26.0	Inventory	34.0	25.4	26.2	21.9	26.6	19.2
1.6	1.5	1.5	All Other Current	1.5	2.0	.8	1.5	.5	1.7
44.6	45.2	44.2	Total Current	51.4	42.3	44.2	39.7	47.6	40.1
39.4	40.1	41.2	Fixed Assets (net)	28.4	43.5	41.4	46.5	38.6	50.8
10.4	8.2	7.6	Intangibles (net)	14.6	6.7	6.5	5.6	2.4	4.9
5.7	6.5	7.0	All Other Non-Current	5.7	7.5	7.9	8.2	11.4	4.2
100.0	100.0	100.0	Total	100.0	100.0	100.0	100.0	100.0	100.0
			LIABILITIES						
2.9	6.5	5.0	Notes Payable-Short Term	5.3	6.0	5.6	3.2	8.2	2.7
2.8	2.5	2.7	Cur. Mat.-L.T.D.	1.7	3.2	2.0	2.8	3.1	3.6
10.5	11.0	10.7	Trade Payables	1.9	10.7	9.2	8.9	22.5	20.6
.0	.1	.1	Income Taxes Payable	.0	.0	.0	.0	.5	.2
11.4	12.2	12.0	All Other Current	19.7	9.8	9.5	13.0	9.0	8.1
27.5	32.3	30.4	Total Current	28.6	29.8	26.3	27.9	43.2	35.1
36.3	35.8	33.5	Long-Term Debt	23.4	34.9	44.0	39.8	30.0	29.8
.2	.2	.3	Deferred Taxes	.0	.0	.2	.2	.0	1.3
12.1	9.5	11.3	All Other Non-Current	19.7	11.7	10.8	9.0	1.8	5.6
23.8	22.2	24.6	Net Worth	28.3	23.6	18.7	23.1	25.1	28.3
100.0	100.0	100.0	Total Liabilities & Net Worth	100.0	100.0	100.0	100.0	100.0	100.0
			INCOME DATA						
100.0	100.0	100.0	Net Sales	100.0	100.0	100.0	100.0	100.0	100.0
19.0	20.2	21.4	Gross Profit	37.1	21.0	16.2	15.2	17.8	13.3
17.8	18.6	19.8	Operating Expenses	34.5	19.5	13.9	14.4	17.5	12.3
1.2	1.6	1.6	Operating Profit	2.6	1.5	2.2	.9	.3	.9
-.3	-.5	-.3	All Other Expenses (net)	-.7	-.2	.1	-.3	-1.5	.0
1.5	2.2	1.9	Profit Before Taxes	3.4	1.7	2.2	1.2	1.8	.9
			RATIOS						
4.9	4.9	5.3		16.3	6.9	3.8	4.3	1.8	1.5
1.9	1.7	1.8	Current	5.3	2.5	2.4	2.1	1.2	1.1
.9	.9	.9		1.4	.9	1.1	1.0	.7	.8
1.7	1.8	1.9		3.2	2.0	1.8	2.0	1.2	.9
(261) .6	(307) .5	(285) .6	Quick	(60) .8	.5	(45) 1.1	.6	.5	.4
.2	.2	.2		.1	.1	.3	.2	.1	.3
0 UND	0 UND	0 UND		0 UND	0 UND	0 UND	0 UND	0 UND	1 275.4
0 UND	0 UND	0 UND	Sales/Receivables	0 UND	0 UND	0 UND	0 999.8	1 583.9	3 126.9
2 212.7	2 230.3	2 180.1		0 UND	0 999.8	2 211.9	1 269.0	5 78.0	5 67.6
7 50.6	10 37.2	9 40.0		24 15.1	10 37.3	8 43.9	6 58.6	10 35.6	9 41.7
13 27.3	18 20.1	16 23.4	Cost of Sales/Inventory	46 8.0	19 19.7	13 27.4	11 34.6	15 23.9	12 31.3
34 10.8	35 10.3	28 13.1		75 4.9	23 15.6	21 17.2	13 27.6	25 14.6	14 26.2
0 UND	0 UND	0 UND		0 UND	0 UND	0 UND	0 999.8	1 368.0	7 54.2
3 119.5	4 103.2	2 180.3	Cost of Sales/Payables	0 UND	0 UND	1 489.8	4 98.9	10 34.8	11 33.1
10 38.3	13 29.0	10 37.4		2 165.1	6 60.3	7 53.7	8 48.1	17 21.0	18 20.1
15.5	14.5	15.2		6.2	12.5	18.2	22.1	17.9	51.2
45.1	42.6	38.0	Sales/Working Capital	16.6	30.4	27.7	51.3	296.4	240.0
-418.2	-256.6	-240.1		71.4	-150.8	294.3	566.1	-89.5	-55.1
6.0	6.6	7.1		8.0	10.2	7.1	9.0	5.7	4.8
(191) 2.4	(233) 2.7	(217) 2.7	EBIT/Interest	(33) 3.4	(58) 2.3	(38) 2.4	(29) 4.3	(16) 2.3	(43) 3.1
1.1	1.1	1.1		.7	1.0	1.2	.8	-.7	1.2
5.4	4.2	3.7							3.5
(17) 2.4	(20) 2.0	(19) 2.2	Net Profit + Depr., Dep., Amort./Cur. Mat. L/T/D					(13)	2.0
1.3	1.4	1.1							.9
.4	.3	.4		.0	.5	.3	.7	.4	1.2
2.5	2.1	1.8	Fixed/Worth	.6	1.9	3.1	3.4	1.5	2.8
-50.9	195.4	46.0		-47.1	-12.4	-2.9	30.4	4.3	10.0
1.0	1.1	.9		.3	.5	1.1	.9	1.6	1.5
4.3	3.9	3.9	Debt/Worth	3.4	4.8	4.2	4.3	4.1	3.4
-42.0	-66.7	-27.0		-8.7	-14.9	-5.8	79.7	8.0	14.2
73.6	75.3	54.0		72.4	58.3	51.0	53.8	59.5	30.4
(194) 31.4	(224) 29.8	(208) 25.8	% Profit Before Taxes/Tangible Net Worth	(40) 37.2	(56) 27.0	(27) 32.6	(30) 24.4	(18) 23.0	(37) 15.8
8.8	11.3	5.7		14.3	8.9	7.0	-.3	-2.0	3.9
16.5	15.2	16.6		24.9	22.8	18.0	19.2	12.7	7.0
6.8	6.4	6.1	% Profit Before Taxes/Total Assets	9.7	5.6	6.2	8.5	3.8	3.9
1.0	.7	.4		.5	.9	.4	-.3	-.8	.6
86.0	71.1	93.8		UND	65.2	126.1	62.0	73.3	28.7
17.0	15.3	16.0	Sales/Net Fixed Assets	50.9	12.1	12.4	17.3	28.0	9.8
5.9	4.8	5.1		3.4	3.4	4.7	7.8	9.6	7.2
9.5	9.1	9.6		6.9	9.5	9.6	12.3	10.2	10.5
5.1	4.4	4.8	Sales/Total Assets	2.7	4.1	4.9	7.6	7.7	5.8
2.8	2.4	2.7		1.5	2.4	3.1	3.2	4.3	4.1
.4	.5	.5		.5	.7	.3	.4	.3	.7
(195) .9	(223) 1.1	(208) 1.1	% Depr., Dep., Amort./Sales	(33) 2.6	(57) 1.6	(30) .9	(33) 1.1	(18) .5	(37) 1.0
1.9	2.0	1.9		4.6	2.6	1.7	1.6	1.2	1.3
.7	.8	.7		2.5	1.0	.8	.6		.1
(111) 1.6	(149) 1.7	(130) 1.7	% Officers', Directors' Owners' Comp/Sales	(36) 4.3	(31) 2.0	(25) 1.4	(19) .9	(12)	.3
3.0	3.6	3.5		6.7	3.2	1.9	2.1		.7
14585502M	14852356M	10555281M	Net Sales ($)	35837M	141869M	174812M	283862M	303431M	9615470M
2680062M	3010621M	1966001M	Total Assets ($)	18114M	49075M	38263M	74574M	59933M	1726042M

M = $ thousand   MM = $ million
See Pages 9 through 22 for Explanation of Ratios and Data

Current Data Sorted by Assets   Comparative Historical Data

	0-500M	500M-2MM	2-10MM	10-50MM	50-100MM	100-250MM	Type of Statement	4/1/06-3/31/07 ALL	4/1/07-3/31/08 ALL
				1			Unqualified	4	4
	1		2				Reviewed	6	3
	2	1	4				Compiled	10	5
	13	6					Tax Returns	13	24
	4	6	7	1			Other	6	20
	\ 9 (4/1-9/30/10)			39 (10/1/10-3/31/11)					
NUMBER OF STATEMENTS	20	13	13	2				39	56
	%	%	%	%	%	%	**ASSETS**	%	%
	21.4	19.2	14.0		D	D	Cash & Equivalents	13.4	12.4
	6.3	5.4	9.4		A	A	Trade Receivables (net)	17.9	7.8
	16.6	20.6	15.5		T	T	Inventory	23.8	25.1
	.3	1.5	.8		A	A	All Other Current	1.8	1.0
	44.6	46.7	39.6				Total Current	56.9	46.3
	41.3	30.6	46.9		N	N	Fixed Assets (net)	26.2	37.9
	3.4	9.9	2.2		O	O	Intangibles (net)	9.2	9.5
	10.7	12.7	11.2		T	T	All Other Non-Current	7.7	6.3
	100.0	100.0	100.0				Total	100.0	100.0
					A	A	**LIABILITIES**		
	19.0	3.0	4.7		V	V	Notes Payable-Short Term	9.9	5.4
	9.0	3.8	2.9		A	A	Cur. Mat.-L.T.D.	1.8	3.8
	15.8	10.6	12.8		I	I	Trade Payables	18.1	12.3
	.1	.0	.4		L	L	Income Taxes Payable	.0	.1
	7.3	5.1	2.6		A	A	All Other Current	8.7	13.6
	51.2	22.6	23.4		B	B	Total Current	38.6	35.2
	39.2	31.1	38.1		L	L	Long-Term Debt	22.8	26.9
	.0	.0	.0		E	E	Deferred Taxes	.1	.1
	18.2	3.0	7.5				All Other Non-Current	2.5	11.6
	-8.7	43.4	31.0				Net Worth	35.9	26.2
	100.0	100.0	100.0				Total Liabilities & Net Worth	100.0	100.0
							INCOME DATA		
	100.0	100.0	100.0				Net Sales	100.0	100.0
	39.2	37.6	36.0				Gross Profit	32.2	36.1
	35.1	33.3	31.2				Operating Expenses	28.9	35.5
	4.0	4.4	4.8				Operating Profit	3.3	.6
	.7	.9	1.5				All Other Expenses (net)	.7	1.1
	3.3	3.5	3.3				Profit Before Taxes	2.6	-.5
							RATIOS		
	4.3	5.8	2.2					3.4	3.5
	1.3	2.3	1.5				Current	1.6	1.7
	.5	.9	1.1					1.0	.6
	3.7	3.4	2.0					2.1	1.7
	.5	1.7	1.0				Quick	(38) .8	(55) .5
	.2	.3	.4					.3	.1
	0 UND	0 UND	2 221.3					0 999.8	0 UND
	0 UND	4 99.2	5 76.1				Sales/Receivables	8 44.0	2 189.0
	3 141.4	8 44.7	21 17.6					25 14.5	8 43.7
	5 67.9	6 57.4	3 141.8					11 32.2	14 26.6
	13 29.1	28 13.1	9 39.2				Cost of Sales/Inventory	23 15.7	20 18.6
	23 15.7	40 9.1	59 6.2					61 6.0	44 8.4
	0 UND	0 UND	7 49.2					8 47.4	3 107.0
	5 66.5	6 59.4	10 38.1				Cost of Sales/Payables	18 19.8	14 26.3
	22 16.8	31 11.7	16 23.2					31 11.6	24 15.4
	31.8	10.2	10.0					9.3	11.7
	76.7	23.3	34.2				Sales/Working Capital	33.0	55.7
	-29.4	NM	194.5					-424.8	-22.7
	12.1	19.7						11.8	6.9
	(14) 2.6	(11) 9.1					EBIT/Interest	(34) 3.5	(42) 1.4
	1.1	1.6						1.1	-.9
							Net Profit + Depr., Dep., Amort./Cur. Mat. L/T/D		
	.5	.2	.8					.2	.2
	4.1	1.4	2.0				Fixed/Worth	1.1	1.3
	-.9	3.2	4.6					3.2	-5.3
	1.2	.5	1.0					.8	.7
	4.8	2.4	1.6				Debt/Worth	2.2	2.5
	-3.1	5.0	6.2					21.7	-7.7
	246.8	91.5	22.6					32.5	42.8
	(12) 54.9	(11) 45.1	(11) 7.7				% Profit Before Taxes/Tangible Net Worth	(31) 18.1	(39) 14.3
	37.6	6.8	5.6					8.7	-2.4
	32.1	21.5	9.5					13.8	19.7
	17.9	6.3	3.1				% Profit Before Taxes/Total Assets	6.3	2.3
	1.5	1.5	-.4					.6	-4.6
	63.2	139.8	12.4					141.0	73.1
	14.8	24.1	5.4				Sales/Net Fixed Assets	15.2	16.0
	8.2	3.1	1.9					7.9	4.0
	11.9	7.4	4.0					6.8	6.8
	6.3	4.0	2.8				Sales/Total Assets	3.5	4.9
	3.3	1.6	1.4					2.2	2.3
	.4	.5	1.2					.4	.6
	(17) 1.6	(10) 2.1	(10) 2.6				% Depr., Dep., Amort./Sales	(30) 1.0	(42) 1.8
	2.3	3.5	4.6					3.0	4.4
	.7							1.1	1.4
	(12) 3.4						% Officers', Directors' Owners' Comp/Sales	(19) 2.0	(30) 3.3
	8.0							5.6	5.7
	27087M	61289M	151352M	284714M			Net Sales ($)	1037739M	1098310M
	4350M	12293M	44635M	63488M			Total Assets ($)	311661M	457387M

© RMA 2011

M = $ thousand   MM = $ million
See Pages 9 through 22 for Explanation of Ratios and Data

Comparative Historical Data

Current Data Sorted by Sales

			Type of Statement						
4	1	1	Unqualified						1
4	4	3	Reviewed			1	1	1	
9	11	7	Compiled	2	1	1	1	1	1
17	23	19	Tax Returns	7	8	1	3		1
20	27	18	Other	4	5	2		5	2
4/1/08-3/31/09 ALL	4/1/09-3/31/10 ALL	4/1/10-3/31/11 ALL		0-1MM	9 (4/1-9/30/10) 1-3MM	3-5MM	39 (10/1/10-3/31/11) 5-10MM	10-25MM	25MM & OVER
54	66	48	**NUMBER OF STATEMENTS**	13	14	5	5	7	4
%	%	%	**ASSETS**	%	%	%	%	%	%
12.8	11.9	18.1	Cash & Equivalents	23.8	16.4				
9.6	7.4	7.3	Trade Receivables (net)	1.7	8.3				
21.2	21.8	18.1	Inventory	15.7	12.0				
3.1	1.6	1.2	All Other Current	.3	.5				
46.7	42.8	44.6	Total Current	41.5	37.1				
36.8	38.7	39.1	Fixed Assets (net)	44.4	40.1				
10.4	11.0	5.2	Intangibles (net)	6.3	4.2				
6.0	7.5	11.1	All Other Non-Current	7.8	18.7				
100.0	100.0	100.0	Total	100.0	100.0				
			LIABILITIES						
10.4	7.5	10.7	Notes Payable-Short Term	22.9	8.7				
4.8	3.0	5.7	Cur. Mat.-L.T.D.	10.4	6.3				
14.0	16.6	13.2	Trade Payables	4.5	13.7				
.0	.1	.1	Income Taxes Payable	.0	.1				
9.1	14.0	6.1	All Other Current	6.3	4.2				
38.5	41.2	35.9	Total Current	44.0	32.9				
20.2	29.3	35.1	Long-Term Debt	35.3	51.6				
.1	.0	.0	Deferred Taxes	.0	.0				
9.1	15.9	10.8	All Other Non-Current	22.2	6.4				
32.2	13.6	18.1	Net Worth	-1.6	9.1				
100.0	100.0	100.0	Total Liabilities & Net Worth	100.0	100.0				
			INCOME DATA						
100.0	100.0	100.0	Net Sales	100.0	100.0				
33.4	35.2	37.6	Gross Profit	45.9	37.6				
30.7	31.9	33.3	Operating Expenses	41.5	31.4				
2.7	3.3	4.3	Operating Profit	4.4	6.2				
.5	.6	.9	All Other Expenses (net)	1.4	.7				
2.2	2.7	3.4	Profit Before Taxes	3.0	5.5				
			RATIOS						
2.6	2.4	3.6		4.9	6.0				
1.5	1.3	1.6	Current	1.2	2.1				
.7	.7	.7		.4	.6				
1.4	1.1	2.6		4.1	3.7				
.5	(65) .5	.6	Quick	.4	1.4				
.2	.1	.3		.2	.4				
0 UND	0 UND	0 UND		0 UND	0 UND				
1 666.9	1 382.9	2 158.0	Sales/Receivables	0 UND	0 UND				
15 24.1	8 47.7	10 37.4		2 149.6	12 30.7				
8 47.6	6 59.7	5 71.2		4 86.2	2 211.4				
20 18.0	20 18.2	14 25.3	Cost of Sales/Inventory	28 13.1	9 40.0				
40 9.1	32 11.5	34 10.9		53 6.8	16 22.5				
1 605.1	2 187.7	0 UND		0 UND	0 UND				
10 36.4	16 23.5	9 40.0	Cost of Sales/Payables	5 80.8	7 53.0				
30 12.0	28 13.0	22 16.8		17 21.1	25 14.8				
14.5	16.8	15.1		28.0	10.1				
48.7	69.6	38.9	Sales/Working Capital	91.7	36.6				
-34.1	-48.5	-40.3		-6.6	-32.0				
10.1	8.5	13.2		6.2	13.8				
(45) 3.7	(52) 3.1	(36) 3.5	EBIT/Interest	(10) 1.8	(11) 6.8				
.3	.2	1.4		.9	2.0				
			Net Profit + Depr., Dep., Amort./Cur. Mat. L/T/D						
.3	.5	.4		1.1	.5				
1.6	1.8	1.9	Fixed/Worth	2.9	1.7				
UND	-3.2	NM		-1.3	NM				
.8	1.2	1.0		2.7	1.0				
3.0	4.5	2.9	Debt/Worth	4.7	3.0				
-34.0	-5.0	NM		-2.5	NM				
42.2	82.7	74.9			63.6				
(39) 9.2	(45) 21.0	(36) 32.6	% Profit Before Taxes/Tangible Net Worth		(11) 37.5				
-3.7	-6.0	7.8			19.9				
19.5	19.0	21.3		36.3	22.9				
4.9	7.5	9.5	% Profit Before Taxes/Total Assets	9.9	17.0				
-1.9	-3.3	1.5		-.6	8.5				
64.6	61.1	75.6		54.0	32.8				
16.1	16.3	12.4	Sales/Net Fixed Assets	7.9	14.8				
5.3	5.2	3.7		2.8	3.6				
7.5	8.8	7.7		7.6	7.4				
5.0	4.6	4.0	Sales/Total Assets	3.4	3.9				
1.9	2.3	2.3		1.8	2.0				
.5	.6	.7		.7	.8				
(42) 1.2	(50) 1.6	(39) 2.0	% Depr., Dep., Amort./Sales	(11) 2.4	(10) 1.9				
2.9	3.3	3.0		3.7	2.7				
1.0	1.3	.8							
(26) 2.7	(36) 3.2	(26) 3.3	% Officers', Directors' Owners' Comp/Sales						
5.5	6.9	5.8							
998220M	1144166M	524442M	Net Sales ($)	9268M	22653M	19577M	34355M	91217M	347372M
401978M	342653M	124766M	Total Assets ($)	3627M	9629M	6901M	9036M	26123M	69450M

© RMA 2011

M = $ thousand   MM = $ million
See Pages 9 through 22 for Explanation of Ratios and Data

Current Data Sorted by Assets   Comparative Historical Data

Columns 10-50MM, 50-100MM, and 100-250MM for the Asset / Liability / Income Data sections are marked **DATA NOT AVAILABLE**.

0-500M	500M-2MM	2-10MM	10-50MM	50-100MM	100-250MM	Type of Statement	4/1/06-3/31/07 ALL	4/1/07-3/31/08 ALL
	1	1	1			Unqualified	1	1
		1	2			Reviewed	2	1
1	4	7				Compiled	7	13
	4	1	1	1	1	Tax Returns	10	13
	2	1				Other	5	5
	8 (4/1-9/30/10)	20 (10/1/10-3/31/11)						
1	11	11	4	1	1	**NUMBER OF STATEMENTS**	25	33
%	%	%	%	%	%	**ASSETS**	%	%
	20.3	15.6				Cash & Equivalents	17.0	14.5
	5.8	23.4				Trade Receivables (net)	19.2	11.8
	16.8	12.3				Inventory	20.7	21.5
	2.0	1.9				All Other Current	2.3	2.5
	44.9	53.2				Total Current	59.3	50.3
	23.2	33.6				Fixed Assets (net)	25.2	36.3
	15.6	2.4				Intangibles (net)	3.0	8.1
	16.2	10.8				All Other Non-Current	12.5	5.3
	100.0	100.0				Total	100.0	100.0
						LIABILITIES		
	1.7	16.0				Notes Payable-Short Term	9.4	8.6
	8.6	3.0				Cur. Mat.-L.T.D.	.3	2.1
	25.3	34.6				Trade Payables	30.5	29.8
	.1	.3				Income Taxes Payable	.6	.7
	12.5	7.8				All Other Current	21.6	16.2
	48.2	61.6				Total Current	62.4	57.4
	8.6	29.5				Long-Term Debt	11.0	20.2
	.2	.0				Deferred Taxes	.0	.0
	1.3	3.7				All Other Non-Current	3.6	2.6
	41.6	5.1				Net Worth	23.0	19.7
	100.0	100.0				Total Liabilties & Net Worth	100.0	100.0
						INCOME DATA		
	100.0	100.0				Net Sales	100.0	100.0
	29.4	28.5				Gross Profit	26.2	29.4
	27.7	26.4				Operating Expenses	24.9	28.0
	1.8	2.0				Operating Profit	1.3	1.4
	.2	.3				All Other Expenses (net)	-.6	.6
	1.6	1.7				Profit Before Taxes	2.0	.9
						RATIOS		
	1.4	1.2					1.7	1.9
	1.1	.9				Current	1.1	1.1
	.3	.7					.7	.5
	1.1	1.1					1.1	1.2
	.4	.7				Quick	.7 (32)	.5
	.2	.2					.1	.1
0 UND	0 999.8						0 UND	0 UND
0 UND	23 15.7					Sales/Receivables	2 187.0	0 999.8
1 490.8	31 11.7						24 14.9	9 41.0
7 52.8	2 161.1						4 82.2	5 66.8
10 35.9	6 58.6					Cost of Sales/Inventory	8 46.8	9 42.4
14 26.6	20 17.9						19 18.9	22 16.6
3 116.3	15 24.2						0 UND	3 125.6
19 18.9	31 11.7					Cost of Sales/Payables	13 28.4	23 16.0
47 7.8	35 10.4						36 10.3	41 9.0
	45.7	80.4					43.0	28.9
	92.2	-129.9				Sales/Working Capital	114.8	116.9
	-15.8	-27.3					-40.5	-23.4
							22.5	26.2
						EBIT/Interest	(17) 4.4	(26) 5.5
							-1.7	.2
						Net Profit + Depr., Dep., Amort./Cur. Mat. L/T/D		
	.1	.3					.3	.4
	.4	2.8				Fixed/Worth	1.1	1.0
	1.2	-8.9					UND	-.9
	.8	3.1					1.3	.6
	1.9	5.2				Debt/Worth	4.4	3.6
	5.3	-16.5					UND	-16.5
							109.7	47.8
						% Profit Before Taxes/Tangible Net Worth	(19) 34.9	(23) 23.7
							6.7	10.2
	24.0	20.1					23.2	19.9
	5.1	5.6				% Profit Before Taxes/Total Assets	11.9	9.5
	3.0	1.9					-2.2	-.6
	541.6	110.2					117.1	66.9
	53.4	17.1				Sales/Net Fixed Assets	33.1	22.3
	15.6	5.2					15.0	8.3
	9.2	7.8					9.2	9.7
	6.6	6.2				Sales/Total Assets	7.0	5.7
	3.0	2.6					5.0	3.8
		.3					.3	.3
		1.2				% Depr., Dep., Amort./Sales	(22) .5	(26) 1.2
		2.4					1.2	3.2
							1.0	1.3
						% Officers', Directors' Owners' Comp/Sales	(10) 2.5	(15) 2.0
							5.8	5.9
1301M	89590M	315742M	164363M	304472M		Net Sales ($)	473860M	560644M
109M	14704M	48479M	82377M	83641M		Total Assets ($)	73483M	93666M

M = $ thousand   MM = $ million
See Pages 9 through 22 for Explanation of Ratios and Data

Comparative Historical Data   Current Data Sorted by Sales

				Type of Statement						
2	2	3		Unqualified					1	2
2	4	3		Reviewed						3
9	12	12		Compiled	1	1	4	4	2
8	16	5		Tax Returns	1	1	3		
4	10	5		Other			1	2	2
4/1/08-3/31/09 ALL	4/1/09-3/31/10 ALL	4/1/10-3/31/11 ALL			0-1MM	8 (4/1-9/30/10) 1-3MM	3-5MM	5-10MM	20 (10/1/10-3/31/11) 10-25MM	25MM & OVER
25	44	28		NUMBER OF STATEMENTS		2	2	8	7	9
%	%	%		ASSETS	%	%	%	%	%	%
11.3	17.0	16.6		Cash & Equivalents						
15.8	19.0	13.7		Trade Receivables (net)	D					
17.1	17.2	14.4		Inventory	A					
1.5	.9	2.1		All Other Current	T					
45.7	54.0	46.8		Total Current	A					
30.8	34.0	33.5		Fixed Assets (net)						
12.6	5.3	8.5		Intangibles (net)	N					
10.9	6.7	11.2		All Other Non-Current	O					
100.0	100.0	100.0		Total	T					
				LIABILITIES	A					
7.2	6.1	7.8		Notes Payable-Short Term	V					
4.9	5.7	6.4		Cur. Mat.-L.T.D.	A					
24.8	29.5	27.3		Trade Payables	I					
.1	.6	.1		Income Taxes Payable	L					
28.2	11.9	8.8		All Other Current	A					
65.1	53.8	50.4		Total Current	B					
21.1	16.4	32.0		Long-Term Debt	L					
.0	.0	.1		Deferred Taxes	E					
4.2	6.9	3.8		All Other Non-Current						
9.5	22.8	13.6		Net Worth						
100.0	100.0	100.0		Total Liabilties & Net Worth						
				INCOME DATA						
100.0	100.0	100.0		Net Sales						
30.2	29.2	26.7		Gross Profit						
28.9	26.9	23.9		Operating Expenses						
1.3	2.3	2.8		Operating Profit						
.1	.2	.4		All Other Expenses (net)						
1.2	2.1	2.3		Profit Before Taxes						
				RATIOS						
1.6	2.2	1.4								
.8	1.1	.9		Current						
.3	.6	.7								
1.0	2.0	1.1								
.4	(43) .9	.5		Quick						
.1	.3	.2								
0 UND	0 UND	0 UND								
6 64.5	3 135.5	1 653.3		Sales/Receivables						
20 17.9	27 13.3	29 12.7								
5 77.6	4 83.7	3 112.1								
9 40.5	8 44.9	10 37.0		Cost of Sales/Inventory						
20 18.6	22 16.9	17 21.3								
0 UND	3 106.8	9 40.6								
17 21.4	18 20.4	25 14.8		Cost of Sales/Payables						
38 9.5	40 9.1	43 8.5								
46.6	17.4	49.9								
-57.1	127.2	-207.6		Sales/Working Capital						
-7.6	-24.0	-25.7								
14.5	5.7	15.5								
(19) 1.6	(29) 3.4	(23) 4.4		EBIT/Interest						
-.2	.7	2.1								
				Net Profit + Depr., Dep., Amort./Cur. Mat. L/T/D						
.5	.3	.2								
1.4	1.4	1.2		Fixed/Worth						
-2.4	15.6	3.1								
1.6	.8	1.2								
7.8	2.6	4.1		Debt/Worth						
-5.8	NM	36.2								
37.2	92.4	59.4		% Profit Before Taxes/Tangible						
(16) 9.1	(33) 29.5	(22) 28.1		Net Worth						
-28.4	11.7	11.0								
23.3	15.5	21.3		% Profit Before Taxes/Total						
7.2	8.8	6.1		Assets						
-1.9	3.3	2.8								
74.3	76.9	84.6								
28.3	26.6	19.4		Sales/Net Fixed Assets						
8.6	6.3	5.7								
10.8	9.3	7.9								
5.2	4.5	4.6		Sales/Total Assets						
3.5	2.6	2.6								
.5	.5	.3								
(21) .9	(39) 1.1	(24) 1.1		% Depr., Dep., Amort./Sales						
2.7	2.5	2.0								
1.7	1.2	1.6								
(14) 2.5	(21) 2.1	(13) 2.7		% Officers', Directors' Owners' Comp/Sales						
3.7	4.1	4.2								
421864M	1145425M	875468M		Net Sales ($)		3615M	9128M	60900M	113833M	687992M
76698M	299020M	229310M		Total Assets ($)		1077M	4836M	12292M	21638M	189467M

© RMA 2011

M = $ thousand   MM = $ million

See Pages 9 through 22 for Explanation of Ratios and Data

Current Data Sorted by Assets							Comparative Historical Data	
						Type of Statement		
		1				Unqualified	1	1
						Reviewed	1	
		2				Compiled		4
15	7					Tax Returns	20	18
6	2	1	1			Other	2	7
	2 (4/1-9/30/10)		33 (10/1/10-3/31/11)				**4/1/06-3/31/07 ALL**	**4/1/07-3/31/08 ALL**
0-500M	**500M-2MM**	**2-10MM**	**10-50MM**	**50-100MM**	**100-250MM**			
21	9	4	1			**NUMBER OF STATEMENTS**	24	30
%	%	%	%	%	%	**ASSETS**	%	%
14.2				DATA NOT AVAILABLE	DATA NOT AVAILABLE	Cash & Equivalents	13.9	9.0
.2						Trade Receivables (net)	9.6	3.7
5.5						Inventory	5.4	5.1
11.1						All Other Current	.6	3.7
30.9						Total Current	29.6	21.5
45.4						Fixed Assets (net)	42.0	55.3
13.0						Intangibles (net)	10.1	13.2
10.7						All Other Non-Current	18.4	10.0
100.0						Total	100.0	100.0
						LIABILITIES		
4.5						Notes Payable-Short Term	3.7	2.8
1.9						Cur. Mat.-L.T.D.	4.6	4.6
6.3						Trade Payables	10.7	5.6
.0						Income Taxes Payable	.0	.1
36.7						All Other Current	41.6	11.1
49.4						Total Current	60.6	24.2
42.7						Long-Term Debt	39.1	57.8
.0						Deferred Taxes	.3	.2
16.0						All Other Non-Current	2.5	13.5
-8.0						Net Worth	-2.5	4.3
100.0						Total Liabilties & Net Worth	100.0	100.0
						INCOME DATA		
100.0						Net Sales	100.0	100.0
55.5						Gross Profit	61.6	54.5
52.5						Operating Expenses	54.2	52.1
3.1						Operating Profit	7.4	2.4
1.2						All Other Expenses (net)	2.8	2.6
1.9						Profit Before Taxes	4.6	-.2
						RATIOS		
2.0							2.2	2.6
.3						Current	.5	.5
.2							.1	.3
1.1							1.5	1.7
.2						Quick	.4	.4
.0							.0	.2
0 UND							**0** UND	**0** UND
0 UND						Sales/Receivables	**0** UND	**0** UND
0 UND							**2** 174.5	**0** UND
1 535.8							**3** 115.8	**3** 128.8
5 76.0						Cost of Sales/Inventory	**6** 63.6	**7** 48.8
11 33.8							**10** 38.3	**15** 23.6
0 UND							**9** 41.2	**0** UND
8 45.7						Cost of Sales/Payables	**23** 15.7	**17** 21.7
25 14.8							**39** 9.5	**34** 10.6
27.3							17.6	33.2
-30.9						Sales/Working Capital	-41.8	-29.0
-9.4							-8.4	-11.0
10.4							9.8	4.2
(12) 2.1						EBIT/Interest	(19) 6.2	(28) 2.1
-.9							.2	.3
						Net Profit + Depr., Dep., Amort./Cur. Mat. L/T/D		
1.3							.7	2.5
-7.1						Fixed/Worth	4.8	NM
-.4							-1.1	-2.1
1.6							1.1	2.5
-21.8						Debt/Worth	11.1	NM
-1.8							-3.4	-3.6
817.8							137.8	151.1
(10) 72.1						% Profit Before Taxes/Tangible Net Worth	(14) 57.2	(15) 47.8
-41.4							24.2	2.4
53.6							34.9	14.7
10.1						% Profit Before Taxes/Total Assets	14.9	2.8
-14.6							-4.9	-8.2
55.3							26.4	7.4
10.8						Sales/Net Fixed Assets	9.1	3.7
4.4							4.2	2.0
8.7							4.3	3.5
4.3						Sales/Total Assets	3.1	1.9
2.6							2.4	1.1
.6							1.4	2.3
(18) 3.8						% Depr., Dep., Amort./Sales	(21) 3.4	(29) 5.2
7.2							4.7	7.8
							2.9	1.5
						% Officers', Directors' Owners' Comp/Sales	(11) 4.8	(10) 3.7
							12.5	5.0
21031M	**25068M**	**55532M**	**19641M**			Net Sales ($)	**57839M**	**125132M**
4615M	**8507M**	**22126M**	**10310M**			Total Assets ($)	**18268M**	**43793M**

M = $ thousand MM = $ million

See Pages 9 through 22 for Explanation of Ratios and Data

Comparative Historical Data   Current Data Sorted by Sales

			Type of Statement						
		1	Unqualified				1		
2	2	1	Reviewed						
11	2	2	Compiled				2	1	
23	36	22	Tax Returns	10	10	1	1	1	
9	9	10	Other	3	4			2	
4/1/08-	4/1/09-	4/1/10-				2 (4/1/9-9/30/10)		33 (10/1/10-3/31/11)	
3/31/09	3/31/10	3/31/11							
ALL	ALL	ALL		0-1MM	1-3MM	3-5MM	5-10MM	10-25MM	25MM & OVER
45	49	35	NUMBER OF STATEMENTS	13	14	1	4	3	
%	%	%	ASSETS	%	%	%	%	%	%
6.7	7.9	11.4	Cash & Equivalents	14.2	8.5				D
6.6	5.7	1.7	Trade Receivables (net)	.0	1.2				A
3.9	5.2	4.4	Inventory	4.0	4.9				T
5.7	1.6	13.5	All Other Current	9.5	20.2				A
22.9	20.4	31.1	Total Current	27.7	34.7				
50.5	41.2	44.9	Fixed Assets (net)	55.0	39.0				N
11.9	22.0	12.6	Intangibles (net)	6.5	15.3				O
14.8	16.4	11.5	All Other Non-Current	10.8	11.0				T
100.0	100.0	100.0	Total	100.0	100.0				
			LIABILITIES						A
3.7	2.7	5.6	Notes Payable-Short Term	3.6	2.8				V
3.6	2.8	3.7	Cur. Mat.-L.T.D.	.8	4.4				A
7.9	10.1	7.3	Trade Payables	2.5	10.5				I
.0	.1	.0	Income Taxes Payable	.0	.0				L
21.0	28.5	25.9	All Other Current	49.5	15.7				A
36.3	44.3	42.5	Total Current	56.4	33.5				B
39.5	50.9	44.0	Long-Term Debt	34.2	58.1				L
.1	.1	.0	Deferred Taxes	.0	.0				E
14.9	24.3	10.7	All Other Non-Current	21.8	3.5				
9.2	-19.6	2.8	Net Worth	-12.3	4.9				
100.0	100.0	100.0	Total Liabilties & Net Worth	100.0	100.0				
			INCOME DATA						
100.0	100.0	100.0	Net Sales	100.0	100.0				
53.7	57.7	57.0	Gross Profit	57.8	58.7				
49.6	54.4	52.1	Operating Expenses	56.3	52.1				
4.1	3.3	4.9	Operating Profit	1.5	6.6				
3.2	2.0	1.3	All Other Expenses (net)	1.2	.9				
.8	1.4	3.6	Profit Before Taxes	.3	5.7				
			RATIOS						
1.3	1.1	2.1		2.0	2.6				
.6	.5	.6	Current	.3	1.2				
.2	.2	.3		.2	.3				
.7	.7	.8		1.0	.7				
.4	.3	.3	Quick	.2	.2				
.1	.1	.1		.0	.0				
0 UND	0 UND	0 UND		0 UND	0 UND				
0 UND	0 UND	0 UND	Sales/Receivables	0 UND	0 UND				
4 83.2	3 129.4	0 UND		0 UND	0 UND				
3 124.2	3 123.8	2 149.4		0 UND	4 85.3				
5 71.8	6 63.7	5 70.2	Cost of Sales/Inventory	5 76.0	5 70.7				
10 38.0	10 34.9	10 37.0		11 34.5	8 48.4				
0 UND	0 UND	3 110.4		0 UND	14 26.4				
12 29.4	15 23.8	22 16.8	Cost of Sales/Payables	4 99.5	23 15.9				
36 10.0	33 10.9	26 13.9		23 15.7	28 13.2				
64.7	137.2	20.3		33.2	15.6				
-41.3	-31.0	-41.2	Sales/Working Capital	-25.9	79.5				
-15.3	-7.6	-14.2		-3.7	-14.6				
4.4	4.8	10.2			10.4				
(36) 2.1	(40) 1.7	(25) 3.4	EBIT/Interest		(12) 4.7				
.6	.8	1.4			2.1				
			Net Profit + Depr., Dep., Amort./Cur. Mat. L/T/D						
1.5	1.0	.9		1.3	.7				
8.8	-4.1	UND	Fixed/Worth	-7.1	4.5				
-2.3	-.3	-.8		-.6	-.7				
2.1	6.0	1.8		1.6	1.7				
269.0	-5.0	UND	Debt/Worth	-9.7	5.1				
-3.5	-1.6	-2.3		-2.1	-1.9				
73.8	87.3	146.7							
(23) 42.0	(15) 28.7	(18) 45.7	% Profit Before Taxes/Tangible Net Worth						
6.1	2.6	10.8							
15.0	28.8	31.4		34.7	46.3				
5.0	5.6	10.1	% Profit Before Taxes/Total Assets	7.9	17.7				
-1.9	-.7	3.8		-19.1	7.2				
9.3	18.2	24.4		42.4	25.1				
4.9	7.9	6.7	Sales/Net Fixed Assets	6.2	7.8				
3.0	4.1	4.5		2.8	5.4				
4.0	4.2	6.1		5.5	7.1				
2.1	2.5	3.3	Sales/Total Assets	3.9	3.7				
1.6	1.6	1.9		2.0	1.6				
1.8	1.5	1.3		1.6	1.1				
(44) 3.2	(37) 5.0	(30) 2.9	% Depr., Dep., Amort./Sales	(11) 5.1	(13) 1.6				
5.1	7.9	5.1		8.6	4.0				
3.1	2.7	3.4							
(14) 4.7	(14) 4.2	(13) 6.8	% Officers', Directors' Owners' Comp/Sales						
8.1	6.4	13.4							
1635888M	3176672M	121272M	Net Sales ($)	7502M	20872M	4042M	28899M	59957M	
361438M	457986M	45558M	Total Assets ($)	2573M	7534M	368M	14014M	21069M	

© RMA 2011

M = $ thousand   MM = $ million

See Pages 9 through 22 for Explanation of Ratios and Data

Current Data Sorted by Assets

Comparative Historical Data

Type of Statement		4	3
Unqualified		4	3
Reviewed		1	4
Compiled		5	7
Tax Returns		13	9
Other		8	5

							4/1/06-3/31/07 ALL	4/1/07-3/31/08 ALL
		1	2	1	1			
5	4	2	1					
6	3	2						
4	3	3		1				
	8 (4/1-9/30/10)		31 (10/1/10-3/31/11)					
0-500M	500M-2MM	2-10MM	10-50MM	50-100MM	100-250MM			
15	10	8	3	2	1	**NUMBER OF STATEMENTS**	31	28
%	%	%	%	%	%	**ASSETS**	%	%
25.3	12.3					Cash & Equivalents	19.7	15.3
1.0	7.6					Trade Receivables (net)	8.4	6.8
19.9	28.5					Inventory	17.0	25.8
1.8	.3					All Other Current	2.2	1.9
47.9	48.7					Total Current	47.4	49.8
30.9	33.8					Fixed Assets (net)	39.2	34.5
6.2	4.3					Intangibles (net)	7.2	9.6
15.0	13.2					All Other Non-Current	6.2	6.1
100.0	100.0					Total	100.0	100.0
						LIABILITIES		
12.9	7.5					Notes Payable-Short Term	10.1	19.0
2.2	1.7					Cur. Mat.-L.T.D.	4.0	8.2
8.3	15.4					Trade Payables	11.7	11.3
.0	.3					Income Taxes Payable	.1	.4
15.5	7.8					All Other Current	11.1	12.5
38.8	32.8					Total Current	37.0	51.5
28.1	23.3					Long-Term Debt	29.9	23.8
.0	.0					Deferred Taxes	.0	.1
1.3	17.1					All Other Non-Current	.6	1.6
31.9	26.9					Net Worth	32.6	23.0
100.0	100.0					Total Liabilities & Net Worth	100.0	100.0
						INCOME DATA		
100.0	100.0					Net Sales	100.0	100.0
64.5	55.3					Gross Profit	49.0	47.4
60.3	52.0					Operating Expenses	40.0	42.2
4.2	3.3					Operating Profit	8.9	5.2
.6	-.3					All Other Expenses (net)	1.2	1.9
3.6	3.6					Profit Before Taxes	7.8	3.3
						RATIOS		
8.5	2.5						3.3	2.9
2.5	1.7					Current	1.4	1.1
.3	1.0						.9	.5
4.1	2.0						1.8	1.4
.7	.4					Quick	.7	.4
.1	.1						.3	.2
0 UND	0 UND						0 UND	0 UND
0 UND	2 218.6					Sales/Receivables	0 UND	0 999.8
0 UND	18 19.8						9 39.3	11 33.6
9 40.5	48 7.5						8 47.2	33 11.0
23 16.2	95 3.8					Cost of Sales/Inventory	35 10.5	71 5.1
37 9.9	157 2.3						59 6.2	114 3.2
0 UND	19 19.5						0 UND	4 103.5
0 UND	49 7.4					Cost of Sales/Payables	9 39.7	16 22.5
21 17.3	87 4.2						39 9.4	56 6.5
10.8	5.8						7.7	7.5
33.4	10.8					Sales/Working Capital	44.4	143.8
-6.2	NM						-56.2	-11.7
18.4							13.4	10.6
(10) 3.9						EBIT/Interest	(26) 3.1	(26) 2.6
-1.1							1.4	.8
						Net Profit + Depr., Dep., Amort./Cur. Mat. L/T/D		
.2	.5						.3	.5
.5	1.3					Fixed/Worth	1.1	1.6
-2.4	-1.7						25.1	-.8
.2	.9						.4	.3
1.6	1.4					Debt/Worth	1.5	3.4
-3.5	-9.3						92.0	-4.0
67.0							84.5	30.3
(11) 40.3						% Profit Before Taxes/Tangible Net Worth	(24) 38.4	(20) 24.0
-3.2							2.4	1.3
28.3	26.6						39.7	18.5
17.3	7.2					% Profit Before Taxes/Total Assets	10.7	5.5
-.5	-2.5						1.0	-1.1
120.3	12.1						56.9	25.5
18.5	8.5					Sales/Net Fixed Assets	5.9	8.6
5.3	4.4						2.8	3.1
8.0	3.3						4.4	3.7
3.9	2.1					Sales/Total Assets	2.3	2.3
2.5	1.3						1.6	1.5
	.7						.8	1.3
	1.9					% Depr., Dep., Amort./Sales	(23) 2.0	(22) 1.9
	3.1						4.3	3.6
							2.3	2.4
						% Officers', Directors' Owners' Comp/Sales	(11) 4.0	(12) 3.8
							8.2	9.0
18012M	24831M	107786M	174694M	396054M	435636M	Net Sales ($)	962281M	529913M
3934M	11793M	37289M	88483M	111817M	130971M	Total Assets ($)	373117M	252936M

M = $ thousand   MM = $ million
See Pages 9 through 22 for Explanation of Ratios and Data

Comparative Historical Data

Current Data Sorted by Sales

			Type of Statement						
2	6	3	Unqualified						3
4		2	Reviewed						2
7	13	12	Compiled	2	6	1	1	1	1
17	21	11	Tax Returns	6	2		2	2	
8	6	11	Other	2	3	2	2	1	1
4/1/08-3/31/09 ALL	4/1/09-3/31/10 ALL	4/1/10-3/31/11 ALL		0-1MM	8 (4/1-9/30/10) 1-3MM	3-5MM	31 (10/1/10-3/31/11) 5-10MM	10-25MM	25MM & OVER
38	46	39	NUMBER OF STATEMENTS	10	11	4	3	4	7
%	%	%	ASSETS	%	%	%	%	%	%
10.9	17.6	15.2	Cash & Equivalents	27.3	14.4				
7.1	9.2	7.7	Trade Receivables (net)	.1	8.0				
23.9	16.4	24.1	Inventory	8.6	30.6				
3.4	2.3	1.5	All Other Current	1.9	.6				
45.3	45.4	48.6	Total Current	37.9	53.7				
38.0	36.5	35.1	Fixed Assets (net)	34.9	28.8				
9.1	4.1	3.9	Intangibles (net)	7.6	3.9				
7.6	13.9	12.4	All Other Non-Current	19.6	13.7				
100.0	100.0	100.0	Total	100.0	100.0				
			LIABILITIES						
6.4	3.4	10.1	Notes Payable-Short Term	16.4	7.1				
4.4	3.0	2.3	Cur. Mat.-L.T.D.	2.1	1.5				
13.2	9.5	10.3	Trade Payables	1.8	18.8				
.1	.4	.1	Income Taxes Payable	.0	.0				
14.0	16.7	11.2	All Other Current	17.7	8.8				
38.1	33.1	34.1	Total Current	38.0	36.1				
32.1	36.4	24.8	Long-Term Debt	39.2	21.1				
.1	.1	.1	Deferred Taxes	.0	.0				
22.1	13.2	8.0	All Other Non-Current	.4	15.9				
7.6	17.2	33.1	Net Worth	22.6	26.8				
100.0	100.0	100.0	Total Liabilties & Net Worth	100.0	100.0				
			INCOME DATA						
100.0	100.0	100.0	Net Sales	100.0	100.0				
55.0	54.5	50.8	Gross Profit	66.8	57.4				
52.1	49.1	46.7	Operating Expenses	61.9	54.8				
3.0	5.4	4.1	Operating Profit	4.9	2.6				
1.6	1.7	.5	All Other Expenses (net)	.7	-.2				
1.4	3.8	3.7	Profit Before Taxes	4.1	2.8				
			RATIOS						
2.7	4.3	3.0		17.6	3.0				
1.3	1.6	1.5	Current	1.5	1.9				
.7	.6	1.2		.2	.3				
1.1	2.3	1.6		8.7	2.3				
.5	.7	.7	Quick	1.1	.4				
.1	.2	.2		.1	.1				
0 UND	0 UND	0 UND		0 UND	0 UND				
1 370.1	1 595.6	0 999.8	Sales/Receivables	0 UND	1 244.8				
17 21.0	12 30.4	18 20.8		0 UND	16 23.2				
13 27.6	9 40.3	22 16.4		0 UND	37 9.9				
44 8.3	35 10.5	49 7.4	Cost of Sales/Inventory	19 19.7	82 4.5				
76 4.8	68 5.4	88 4.1		34 10.6	131 2.8				
0 UND	0 UND	1 464.7		0 UND	12 30.8				
10 35.0	13 27.6	14 26.7	Cost of Sales/Payables	0 UND	24 15.3				
42 8.6	31 11.9	31 11.6		8 47.4	137 2.7				
13.2	5.9	9.5		9.5	6.4				
25.6	18.6	16.2	Sales/Working Capital	44.8	12.0				
-23.7	-17.1	56.0		-4.5	-10.0				
6.1	8.9	11.8							
(32) 2.2	(35) 3.8	(32) 3.2	EBIT/Interest						
-1.5	1.3	.8							
			Net Profit + Depr., Dep., Amort./Cur. Mat. L/T/D						
.6	.3	.4		.1	.3				
2.0	.9	1.0	Fixed/Worth	1.9	1.7				
-2.5	-2.9	4.4		-1.3	-1.8				
1.7	.6	.6		.1	.7				
4.9	2.4	1.6	Debt/Worth	2.6	4.2				
-5.2	-5.3	7.7		-3.2	-10.7				
75.7	47.9	54.9	% Profit Before Taxes/Tangible Net Worth						
(25) 20.4	(30) 26.6	(31) 25.4							
-2.5	2.8	-1.0							
18.0	20.4	25.7	% Profit Before Taxes/Total Assets	41.9	18.9				
3.0	7.7	8.4		15.0	9.0				
-6.3	.7	-.5		-9.9	3.2				
27.5	17.8	19.7	Sales/Net Fixed Assets	UND	39.0				
7.0	5.8	8.3		13.2	9.7				
3.4	3.9	4.6		4.3	4.6				
4.2	3.9	4.9	Sales/Total Assets	6.4	6.3				
2.3	2.5	2.7		2.7	2.1				
1.5	1.6	1.9		2.2	1.4				
1.1	1.1	.5	% Depr., Dep., Amort./Sales						
(32) 2.2	(35) 2.0	(31) 1.8							
4.6	4.8	4.3							
2.7	3.0	1.5	% Officers', Directors' Owners' Comp/Sales						
(17) 4.3	(18) 5.2	(19) 2.8							
11.3	7.3	6.2							
300326M	714404M	1157013M	Net Sales ($)	6779M	19875M	16189M	24655M	51256M	1038259M
119602M	358976M	384287M	Total Assets ($)	2372M	9432M	3923M	10717M	21713M	336130M

M = $ thousand   MM = $ million
See Pages 9 through 22 for Explanation of Ratios and Data

Current Data Sorted by Assets   Comparative Historical Data

Type of Statement

	0-500M	500M-2MM	2-10MM	10-50MM	50-100MM	100-250MM		ALL 4/1/06-3/31/07	ALL 4/1/07-3/31/08
Unqualified		1	3		3	3		12	14
Reviewed		2	5	1				18	15
Compiled	7	10	6					24	20
Tax Returns	61	23	8	1				113	107
Other	34	18	26	5		3		56	55
		21 (4/1-9/30/10)		204 (10/1/10-3/31/11)		3			
NUMBER OF STATEMENTS	102	54	48	11	4	6		223	211

ASSETS	%	%	%	%	%	%		%	%
Cash & Equivalents	14.9	11.9	14.5	15.7				12.8	11.1
Trade Receivables (net)	5.4	9.9	13.0	11.9				6.1	7.6
Inventory	15.7	14.1	20.7	15.7				16.0	16.2
All Other Current	3.2	1.7	2.1	1.1				3.5	3.4
Total Current	39.2	37.6	50.3	44.4				38.4	38.3
Fixed Assets (net)	39.7	46.2	29.2	39.4				39.8	39.3
Intangibles (net)	13.1	11.0	11.2	9.9				13.8	13.1
All Other Non-Current	8.0	5.2	9.3	6.3				8.0	9.3
Total	100.0	100.0	100.0	100.0				100.0	100.0

LIABILITIES									
Notes Payable-Short Term	9.2	5.2	6.7	9.9				7.5	7.0
Cur. Mat.-L.T.D.	4.0	4.0	4.4	2.4				5.4	4.9
Trade Payables	10.3	10.4	19.0	16.3				13.3	12.2
Income Taxes Payable	.1	.2	.4	.4				.2	.1
All Other Current	23.8	6.3	11.5	12.2				14.9	12.8
Total Current	47.3	26.1	42.0	41.1				41.4	37.0
Long-Term Debt	30.8	32.7	16.7	35.8				29.8	28.8
Deferred Taxes	.0	.0	.3	.1				.2	.1
All Other Non-Current	17.0	11.9	5.9	4.4				13.0	10.0
Net Worth	4.9	29.4	35.1	18.5				15.5	24.1
Total Liabilities & Net Worth	100.0	100.0	100.0	100.0				100.0	100.0

INCOME DATA									
Net Sales	100.0	100.0	100.0	100.0				100.0	100.0
Gross Profit	54.8	47.4	41.5	37.0				51.3	48.7
Operating Expenses	50.4	42.8	34.7	33.0				47.8	45.1
Operating Profit	4.3	4.6	6.8	4.0				3.5	3.6
All Other Expenses (net)	.9	1.2	.4	1.3				1.2	1.1
Profit Before Taxes	3.4	3.4	6.3	2.6				2.3	2.4

RATIOS									
Current	4.4	3.2	1.9	1.6				2.0	2.4
	1.2	1.5	1.2	1.3				1.2	1.2
	.4	.6	.6	.9				.4	.6
Quick	2.1	1.8	1.0	1.0				1.2	1.5
	.6	.9	.6	.7			(220)	.5	(210) .4
	.1	.3	.3	.5				.1	.2
Sales/Receivables	0 UND	0 UND	0 999.8	3 114.2				0 UND	0 UND
	0 UND	2 186.3	4 102.2	6 61.8				0 UND	0 UND
	0 UND	13 27.6	31 11.7	38 9.7				5 70.2	8 45.8
Cost of Sales/Inventory	5 74.0	7 54.9	11 33.3	13 28.0				7 49.7	7 52.5
	12 31.4	15 23.8	25 14.6	20 18.3				16 23.2	14 25.5
	32 11.6	33 11.2	73 5.0	36 10.2				45 8.1	43 8.6
Cost of Sales/Payables	0 UND	1 385.7	13 27.1	8 43.6				0 UND	0 UND
	5 67.2	14 26.5	25 14.4	30 12.2				13 27.3	14 25.2
	25 14.8	30 12.1	44 8.2	36 10.1				35 10.4	35 10.5
Sales/Working Capital	16.2	11.4	10.5	16.1				15.9	15.4
	214.0	30.6	28.4	62.9				126.8	82.2
	-20.2	-29.8	-41.9	-46.8				-15.8	-27.0
EBIT/Interest	13.6	15.5	19.4	8.4				8.3	5.6
	(70) 3.7	(49) 5.1	(43) 8.3	(10) 4.1			(177)	2.8	(161) 2.1
	.5	2.2	4.7	1.9				.6	.8
Net Profit + Depr., Dep., Amort./Cur. Mat. L/T/D								3.0	6.1
							(14)	1.9	(20) 4.0
								1.2	1.2
Fixed/Worth	.6	.5	.3	.8				.6	.7
	14.8	2.0	1.0	1.7				3.9	1.9
	-.7	-9.6	3.1	-5.2				-1.9	-3.4
Debt/Worth	.8	.6	.9	1.6				1.2	1.1
	31.3	3.3	2.4	3.6				7.2	3.5
	-2.4	-12.4	11.5	-10.9				-3.8	-8.8
% Profit Before Taxes/Tangible Net Worth	246.8	71.8	67.4					117.6	95.4
	(60) 109.5	(38) 24.8	(38) 36.0				(135)	34.7	(143) 25.5
	40.4	8.8	20.2					9.8	.7
% Profit Before Taxes/Total Assets	39.9	19.5	25.0	10.2				23.4	21.9
	15.0	6.2	13.3	5.9				6.7	5.1
	.4	1.5	5.9	1.7				-1.8	-1.3
Sales/Net Fixed Assets	38.9	28.6	43.9	21.1				27.7	30.8
	16.6	9.1	11.7	8.8				11.2	14.4
	6.3	3.8	5.9	3.1				3.9	4.5
Sales/Total Assets	8.5	5.0	4.1	3.1				5.1	6.5
	4.3	3.5	2.8	2.7				3.2	3.7
	2.6	2.2	2.2	1.6				1.8	1.8
% Depr., Dep., Amort./Sales	.6	1.1	.8	.8				1.2	.9
	(73) 1.7	(42) 2.3	(38) 1.6	(10) 1.7			(175)	2.1	(177) 1.8
	4.2	4.7	2.5	4.7				4.1	3.4
% Officers', Directors' Owners' Comp/Sales	2.3	1.7	1.4					1.3	1.6
	(57) 5.0	(34) 2.8	(13) 2.5				(94)	3.0	(85) 2.7
	8.0	5.3	10.2					8.2	5.6
Net Sales ($)	106878M	196490M	690673M	523054M	838700M	1751109M		2575641M	5016147M
Total Assets ($)	22465M	52481M	210529M	192772M	234113M	907711M		1015132M	1769575M

M = $ thousand   MM = $ million
See Pages 9 through 22 for Explanation of Ratios and Data

Comparative Historical Data | Current Data Sorted by Sales

			Type of Statement						
20	20	14	Unqualified	1				3	10
20	26	9	Reviewed			2	1	5	1
26	22	23	Compiled	6	4	6	4	3	
120	124	93	Tax Returns	41	29	8	8	6	1
56	63	86	Other	23	23	4	11	13	12
4/1/08-3/31/09 ALL	4/1/09-3/31/10 ALL	4/1/10-3/31/11 ALL		21 (4/1-9/30/10)		204 (10/1/10-3/31/11)			
				0-1MM	1-3MM	3-5MM	5-10MM	10-25MM	25MM & OVER
242	255	225	NUMBER OF STATEMENTS	71	56	20	24	30	24
%	%	%	ASSETS	%	%	%	%	%	%
12.2	15.5	14.4	Cash & Equivalents	11.3	18.2	11.0	16.1	14.5	15.2
7.7	7.2	8.6	Trade Receivables (net)	4.3	4.4	15.7	15.7	11.7	14.3
16.6	18.4	16.0	Inventory	13.8	14.6	17.0	20.2	20.3	15.9
3.2	2.5	2.5	All Other Current	2.6	3.1	.7	2.5	2.6	2.5
39.6	43.6	41.5	Total Current	32.0	40.2	44.5	54.5	49.1	47.9
40.6	36.5	38.9	Fixed Assets (net)	47.5	39.0	34.7	31.3	29.5	36.0
13.5	12.2	12.3	Intangibles (net)	15.7	11.9	12.7	3.8	12.5	10.8
6.3	7.7	7.3	All Other Non-Current	4.9	8.9	8.2	10.4	8.9	5.3
100.0	100.0	100.0	Total	100.0	100.0	100.0	100.0	100.0	100.0
			LIABILITIES						
9.0	7.6	7.4	Notes Payable-Short Term	7.9	9.0	5.3	8.4	4.7	6.2
3.5	4.8	3.9	Cur. Mat.-L.T.D.	4.5	2.6	5.2	4.2	5.4	1.9
12.9	11.7	12.4	Trade Payables	7.0	10.4	13.8	21.2	19.3	14.5
.1	.1	.2	Income Taxes-Payable	.0	.0	.1	.9	.3	.0
13.0	15.2	15.9	All Other Current	25.6	13.0	7.1	12.4	8.7	14.2
38.5	39.4	39.8	Total Current	45.0	34.9	31.6	47.2	38.4	36.9
32.4	29.1	28.3	Long-Term Debt	42.3	22.4	22.9	17.7	19.8	26.7
.1	.1	.1	Deferred Taxes	.0	.0	.0	.1	.2	.5
9.4	8.3	12.5	All Other Non-Current	23.4	5.9	11.8	10.8	3.8	9.5
19.6	23.2	19.2	Net Worth	-10.7	36.9	33.8	24.2	37.8	26.4
100.0	100.0	100.0	Total Liabilities & Net Worth	100.0	100.0	100.0	100.0	100.0	100.0
			INCOME DATA						
100.0	100.0	100.0	Net Sales	100.0	100.0	100.0	100.0	100.0	100.0
47.5	46.6	48.4	Gross Profit	59.1	51.4	40.2	41.8	40.1	33.4
43.5	42.8	43.6	Operating Expenses	55.6	44.2	35.7	37.9	33.9	30.5
4.1	3.8	4.8	Operating Profit	3.4	7.2	4.5	4.0	6.1	2.8
1.4	.8	1.0	All Other Expenses (net)	1.5	.8	.6	-.3	.6	2.0
2.6	3.0	3.8	Profit Before Taxes	1.9	6.4	3.9	4.3	5.5	.9
			RATIOS						
2.4	2.7	3.0		5.1	4.1	2.6	2.3	1.6	2.0
1.2	1.3	1.3	Current	1.1	1.4	1.3	1.4	1.3	1.5
.5	.7	.6		.4	.5	.6	.5	.7	.9
1.2	1.7	1.7		2.0	2.4	1.2	1.5	1.0	1.3
.5	.6	.7	Quick	.6	.8	.9	.7	.5	1.0
.2	.2	.2		.1	.1	.5	.2	.3	.5
0 UND	0 UND	0 UND		0 UND	0 UND	0 UND	0 867.4	0 819.9	2 159.8
0 999.8	0 UND	0 999.8	Sales/Receivables	0 UND	0 UND	2 151.0	5 69.9	6 59.2	5 71.4
10 36.0	6 58.1	9 39.0		0 UND	4 103.4	23 16.0	35 10.4	30 12.2	31 11.9
7 53.9	7 51.4	7 54.9		6 61.5	5 79.0	4 93.3	9 39.0	11 34.4	11 32.4
16 23.5	17 20.9	15 23.8	Cost of Sales/Inventory	12 31.2	12 30.1	14 26.4	18 19.8	22 16.6	17 21.0
37 9.7	47 7.7	39 9.5		34 10.6	33 11.0	31 11.8	63 5.8	66 5.6	38 9.6
1 597.1	0 UND	0 UND		0 UND	0 UND	0 UND	14 26.0	15 24.3	10 35.1
18 20.4	15 24.3	14 26.3	Cost of Sales/Payables	4 92.0	11 32.8	14 27.0	23 15.8	30 12.3	23 15.7
38 9.7	32 11.4	31 11.9		19 19.6	29 12.4	31 11.7	47 7.7	42 8.8	34 10.6
14.3	12.8	12.7		11.8	15.0	14.7	9.5	16.5	10.9
70.6	32.9	54.4	Sales/Working Capital	213.3	86.7	67.6	41.8	27.3	33.9
-29.6	-38.7	-31.0		-10.7	-32.5	-32.2	-24.1	-46.5	-114.2
8.5	13.9	13.2		7.4	19.3	24.1	29.0	21.1	8.0
(186) 2.4	(200) 3.7	(182) 5.1	EBIT/Interest	(52) 2.1	(40) 6.7	(18) 6.6	(22) 6.9	(27) 10.7	(23) 3.0
.7	1.1	1.8		.3	2.3	2.4	2.9	4.8	1.0
9.2	5.0	4.3							5.5
(22) 2.5	(33) 1.6	(22) 2.8	Net Profit + Depr., Dep., Amort./Cur. Mat. L/T/D					(12) 2.5	
1.8	.8	1.8							1.6
.6	.5	.6		1.7	.5	.3	.3	.4	.5
2.3	1.4	1.9	Fixed/Worth	-9.1	1.3	.9	1.0	.9	1.5
-3.4	-4.6	-2.7		-.6	UND	2.7	NM	3.5	5.0
1.1	.8	.9		2.4	.5	.6	.8	.9	1.4
4.5	2.8	4.1	Debt/Worth	-11.5	1.5	2.5	3.8	2.4	1.8
-5.1	-5.1	-5.1		-2.0	UND	NM	NM	6.6	5.2
84.7	75.3	124.4		175.0	282.1	59.3	112.7	82.0	34.4
(154) 27.1	(171) 30.0	(152) 41.1	% Profit Before Taxes/Tangible Net Worth	(31) 56.1	(44) 71.6	(15) 24.0	(18) 33.6	(25) 32.5	(19) 16.8
6.7	10.5	14.9		17.2	23.0	9.5	8.9	13.4	5.4
20.7	24.4	27.5		29.2	47.8	22.7	23.8	23.8	9.6
6.9	9.0	10.1	% Profit Before Taxes/Total Assets	7.1	16.7	8.7	9.3	12.2	5.6
-.9	.7	2.6		-2.6	4.5	4.4	2.1	5.8	.8
32.3	32.8	33.6		22.0	35.2	43.0	49.2	47.8	20.6
10.5	11.9	11.5	Sales/Net Fixed Assets	8.8	15.5	11.3	13.3	16.5	8.2
4.3	5.0	5.1		2.3	6.2	6.1	7.8	5.8	4.2
5.5	5.5	5.8		4.8	9.0	5.8	6.4	4.3	5.2
2.9	3.4	3.3	Sales/Total Assets	2.8	4.6	3.9	3.1	3.3	2.8
1.8	2.0	2.3		1.7	2.5	2.9	2.6	2.4	1.9
1.2	.9	.9		1.4	.7	.8	.8	.8	1.2
(197) 2.5	(208) 1.8	(172) 1.8	% Depr., Dep., Amort./Sales	(50) 3.1	(44) 1.4	(16) 2.3	(16) 1.0	(25) 1.7	(21) 2.0
4.5	3.5	3.9		5.8	3.5	4.0	3.0	2.3	3.1
1.6	.9	1.9		2.6	1.7	1.5	1.6		
(106) 2.9	(116) 3.3	(106) 3.3	% Officers', Directors' Owners' Comp/Sales	(36) 5.4	(32) 3.6	(14) 2.5	(14) 2.6		
6.1	5.7	6.8		8.8	6.5	5.6	4.1		
5038173M	8919875M	4106904M	Net Sales ($)	42058M	106820M	73498M	171336M	440678M	3272514M
1505936M	2455672M	1620071M	Total Assets ($)	16996M	31518M	21477M	57112M	153924M	1339044M

© RMA 2011

M = $ thousand   MM = $ million

See Pages 9 through 22 for Explanation of Ratios and Data

Current Data Sorted by Assets   Comparative Historical Data

0-500M	500M-2MM	2-10MM	10-50MM	50-100MM	100-250MM	Type of Statement	4/1/06-3/31/07 ALL	4/1/07-3/31/08 ALL
1	1	3	3	2	1	Unqualified	14	12
	5	15	4			Reviewed	19	25
13	19	13	3			Compiled	55	69
109	72	26	1		3	Tax Returns	158	194
22	19	18	8	1	2	Other	52	59
	37 (4/1-9/30/10)		327 (10/1/10-3/31/11)					
145	116	75	19	3	6	**NUMBER OF STATEMENTS**	298	359
%	%	%	%	%	%	**ASSETS**	%	%
13.7	12.4	11.7	9.4			Cash & Equivalents	11.7	11.4
1.2	1.4	1.9	4.0			Trade Receivables (net)	2.5	2.3
52.3	43.5	44.9	35.7			Inventory	46.8	45.5
1.6	2.6	2.1	5.5			All Other Current	2.0	2.4
68.8	59.9	60.6	54.7			Total Current	63.0	61.6
14.9	19.1	20.2	22.3			Fixed Assets (net)	17.1	19.1
12.2	15.2	12.6	17.4			Intangibles (net)	13.5	13.8
4.0	5.8	6.6	5.6			All Other Non-Current	6.3	5.6
100.0	100.0	100.0	100.0			Total	100.0	100.0
						LIABILITIES		
6.3	5.6	12.1	9.7			Notes Payable-Short Term	7.7	6.7
4.3	2.1	1.3	1.5			Cur. Mat.-L.T.D.	3.3	2.0
11.2	19.7	19.5	16.4			Trade Payables	18.5	15.5
.1	.1	.0	.0			Income Taxes Payable	.2	.1
9.8	9.1	9.4	8.9			All Other Current	12.0	9.8
31.7	36.6	42.3	36.6			Total Current	41.8	34.1
22.5	26.0	19.0	20.9			Long-Term Debt	21.6	23.0
.0	.0	.0	.0			Deferred Taxes	.2	.0
19.0	13.7	8.2	13.4			All Other Non-Current	6.7	14.0
26.8	23.7	30.4	29.2			Net Worth	29.8	28.9
100.0	100.0	100.0	100.0			Total Liabilities & Net Worth	100.0	100.0
						INCOME DATA		
100.0	100.0	100.0	100.0			Net Sales	100.0	100.0
24.0	23.6	25.1	24.0			Gross Profit	23.8	23.5
23.0	21.5	22.1	21.7			Operating Expenses	21.4	21.6
1.0	2.1	2.9	2.4			Operating Profit	2.4	1.9
-.8	.2	.6	.5			All Other Expenses (net)	.1	-.6
1.8	1.9	2.3	1.8			Profit Before Taxes	2.3	2.5
						RATIOS		
10.0	3.9	2.4	2.7			Current	3.4	5.5
3.1	2.1	1.4	1.5				1.6	2.2
1.5	1.3	1.0	1.0				1.1	1.2
1.8	.9	.7	.7			Quick	.8	.9
(142) .6	(115) .3	.2	.3				(296) .3	(354) .4
.1	.1	.1	.1				.1	.1
0 UND	0 UND	0 UND	0 UND			Sales/Receivables	0 UND	0 UND
0 UND	0 UND	0 UND	1 667.7				0 UND	0 UND
0 UND	1 597.9	2 218.7	6 65.0				1 335.1	1 547.4
33 10.9	40 9.2	45 8.1	22 16.9			Cost of Sales/Inventory	40 9.0	37 10.0
52 7.0	63 5.8	72 5.1	50 7.2				59 6.1	60 6.1
81 4.5	89 4.1	129 2.8	97 3.7				82 4.4	86 4.3
0 UND	0 UND	14 25.5	12 29.4			Cost of Sales/Payables	1 350.6	0 UND
2 151.5	21 17.2	29 12.4	21 17.0				21 17.7	15 25.2
22 16.9	39 9.4	53 6.8	34 10.9				39 9.3	34 10.7
6.2	6.0	7.4	7.7			Sales/Working Capital	8.4	6.6
11.2	11.7	18.7	21.0				16.3	12.7
24.7	50.3	628.4	-246.1				106.3	43.5
8.6	9.8	10.8	6.5			EBIT/Interest	8.0	7.5
(94) 2.9	(89) 2.6	(67) 3.9	(17) 4.4				(240) 3.5	(284) 3.4
.7	.9	1.4	1.8				1.0	1.5
						Net Profit + Depr., Dep., Amort./Cur. Mat. L/T/D	11.4	13.9
							(19) 3.7	(20) 6.8
							1.0	1.8
.0	.2	.2	.5			Fixed/Worth	.2	.2
.5	2.1	.8	1.0				.7	.9
-.7	-.8	-20.1	-1.9				-2.0	-1.8
.5	1.2	1.4	1.1			Debt/Worth	.9	.9
2.8	8.1	3.2	6.1				3.1	4.3
-4.5	-4.1	-15.3	-4.6				-7.0	-6.4
49.5	42.0	55.9	46.0			% Profit Before Taxes/Tangible Net Worth	46.7	60.9
(94) 25.2	(65) 25.7	(53) 15.0	(13) 23.4				(203) 18.6	(243) 28.4
5.5	12.3	6.6	10.8				5.9	10.2
18.0	12.6	10.7	12.2			% Profit Before Taxes/Total Assets	14.2	14.0
7.8	5.6	4.2	6.9				6.3	7.0
-.5	.3	1.1	2.5				.2	2.1
389.1	110.6	83.6	43.5			Sales/Net Fixed Assets	115.3	108.7
70.3	32.7	29.7	24.4				36.1	35.8
24.6	10.9	7.4	8.8				13.9	11.5
6.4	4.8	3.5	3.8			Sales/Total Assets	5.0	5.0
4.1	2.9	2.6	2.9				3.5	3.4
2.9	1.9	1.8	2.4				2.5	2.2
.3	.2	.3	.4			% Depr., Dep., Amort./Sales	.3	.3
(79) .8	(92) .7	(59) .7	(18) .8				(230) .8	(273) .8
2.1	2.0	1.2	1.3				1.6	1.7
1.9	1.3	1.1				% Officers', Directors' Owners' Comp/Sales	1.5	1.5
(84) 3.0	(73) 2.5	(33) 2.0					(162) 2.8	(208) 2.7
5.0	4.0	3.6					4.2	4.3
184886M	530030M	846496M	1523719M	526706M	5853999M	Net Sales ($)	4992693M	6588970M
40817M	118767M	295508M	478512M	268882M	960871M	Total Assets ($)	1604254M	1912616M

M = $ thousand   MM = $ million
See Pages 9 through 22 for Explanation of Ratios and Data

Comparative Historical Data | | | | ## Current Data Sorted by Sales

			Type of Statement	0-1MM	1-3MM	3-5MM	5-10MM	10-25MM	25MM & OVER
17	15	11	Unqualified				1	3	7
29	20	24	Reviewed			2	7	8	7
49	60	48	Compiled	5	13	6	10	10	4
171	224	211	Tax Returns	53	102	20	21	11	4
63	57	70	Other	12	23	6	12	8	9
4/1/08-3/31/09 ALL	4/1/09-3/31/10 ALL	4/1/10-3/31/11 ALL		37 (4/1-9/30/10)			327 (10/1/10-3/31/11)		
329	376	364	**NUMBER OF STATEMENTS**	70	138	34	51	40	31
%	%	%	**ASSETS**	%	%	%	%	%	%
11.0	11.4	12.5	Cash & Equivalents	13.4	11.0	13.1	14.3	13.3	11.8
1.0	1.7	1.6	Trade Receivables (net)	1.9	.9	3.6	.5	1.5	3.7
45.8	46.8	47.1	Inventory	38.8	49.8	52.3	50.3	50.1	38.9
1.5	2.0	2.2	All Other Current	3.5	.8	2.3	2.8	2.7	3.7
59.3	61.9	63.4	Total Current	57.6	62.6	71.3	67.9	67.6	58.2
18.2	17.6	18.0	Fixed Assets (net)	22.6	16.5	11.8	15.3	21.5	21.1
15.4	15.0	13.4	Intangibles (net)	15.0	16.0	10.2	10.9	6.1	15.8
7.0	5.5	5.2	All Other Non-Current	4.7	4.9	6.8	6.0	4.8	4.9
100.0	100.0	100.0	Total	100.0	100.0	100.0	100.0	100.0	100.0
			LIABILITIES						
8.5	6.6	7.6	Notes Payable-Short Term	6.6	4.5	11.5	12.9	7.0	11.6
4.4	3.0	2.8	Cur. Mat.-L.T.D.	5.5	3.0	.8	.8	2.0	2.5
12.7	14.6	16.1	Trade Payables	6.3	13.5	21.4	25.6	24.5	18.2
.0	.1	.1	Income Taxes Payable	.1	.1	.0	.0	.0	.0
10.9	10.3	9.4	All Other Current	8.3	8.6	12.1	12.2	7.7	10.2
36.5	34.6	36.1	Total Current	26.8	29.8	45.9	51.5	41.1	42.4
25.2	23.6	22.6	Long-Term Debt	32.2	26.2	14.5	15.5	14.1	17.0
.0	.0	.0	Deferred Taxes	.0	.0	.0	.0	.1	.0
11.7	12.5	14.6	All Other Non-Current	16.9	21.1	10.8	3.2	8.3	11.1
26.5	29.3	26.7	Net Worth	24.1	22.9	28.8	29.8	36.3	29.5
100.0	100.0	100.0	Total Liabilities & Net Worth	100.0	100.0	100.0	100.0	100.0	100.0
			INCOME DATA						
100.0	100.0	100.0	Net Sales	100.0	100.0	100.0	100.0	100.0	100.0
23.9	23.0	24.0	Gross Profit	27.9	22.6	22.9	22.8	25.0	23.3
21.8	21.2	22.2	Operating Expenses	27.2	21.0	20.1	20.6	22.0	21.3
2.1	1.9	1.9	Operating Profit	.8	1.7	2.9	2.1	3.0	2.1
-.2	-.5	-.1	All Other Expenses (net)	.0	-.5	.0	.2	.5	.2
2.2	2.3	2.0	Profit Before Taxes	.8	2.2	2.9	1.9	2.5	1.9
			RATIOS						
6.0	5.3	4.7		15.7	7.1	3.6	2.2	2.4	2.0
2.0	2.1	2.0	Current	4.3	2.8	1.8	1.3	1.5	1.4
1.1	1.2	1.2		1.2	1.5	1.1	1.0	1.1	.9
1.2	1.2	1.0		2.8	1.5	.9	.4	.7	.7
(325) .3	(370) .4	(360) .3	Quick	.8	(135) .5	.3	(50) .3	.2	.2
.1	.1	.1		.1	.1	.1	.1	.1	.1
0 UND	0 UND	0 UND		0 UND	0 UND	0 UND	0 UND	0 UND	0 999.9
0 UND	0 UND	0 UND	Sales/Receivables	0 UND	0 UND	0 UND	0 UND	0 999.8	1 285.8
0 759.0	1 552.4	0 999.8		0 UND	0 UND	3 122.3	0 999.8	1 425.0	5 79.6
38 9.7	40 9.2	37 10.0		34 10.6	40 9.1	52 7.1	34 10.8	35 10.5	21 17.2
62 5.9	63 5.8	61 6.0	Cost of Sales/Inventory	64 5.7	62 5.9	75 4.8	57 6.4	55 6.6	52 7.0
93 3.9	88 4.1	93 3.9		97 3.8	88 4.1	104 3.5	99 3.7	80 4.6	92 4.0
0 UND	0 UND	0 UND		0 UND	0 UND	17 21.6	11 32.6	18 19.8	9 38.4
11 32.2	12 30.1	17 21.0	Cost of Sales/Payables	2 169.2	8 44.3	30 12.1	27 13.4	31 11.9	21 17.0
28 13.0	33 11.0	34 10.7		15 21.9	28 12.9	50 7.3	44 8.3	50 7.2	30 12.0
6.4	5.8	6.5		4.8	6.1	6.0	12.3	7.4	15.1
14.6	12.1	12.6	Sales/Working Capital	8.5	10.5	11.2	24.6	16.9	26.3
106.0	32.9	48.1		35.1	21.5	110.0	-999.8	73.5	-107.9
8.6	8.0	9.3		4.1	8.2	14.6	11.7	14.9	7.8
(264) 3.6	(276) 3.2	(275) 3.2	EBIT/Interest	(43) 1.5	(100) 2.9	(26) 2.9	(43) 5.5	(36) 4.8	(27) 5.4
1.1	1.1	1.1		-.3	.9	1.1	1.5	2.0	1.9
5.7	7.5	5.1	Net Profit + Depr., Dep.,						
(19) 1.4	(21) 2.2	(14) 1.7	Amort./Cur. Mat. L/T/D						
.1	1.0	.4							
.1	.1	.1		.0	.1	.1	.2	.2	.3
.9	.9	.9	Fixed/Worth	1.5	1.0	.7	.5	.7	1.1
-1.3	-1.7	-1.2		-1.0	-.4	-2.0	-1.4	1.6	-3.6
.9	.8	.9		.7	.7	.8	1.0	1.1	1.5
4.7	3.8	4.3	Debt/Worth	8.8	6.2	5.0	2.5	2.3	5.2
-4.7	-7.4	-5.6		-4.0	-3.2	-10.6	-25.0	6.9	-6.1
57.1	63.5	50.2	% Profit Before Taxes/Tangible	47.2	44.5	61.1	72.2	64.8	84.0
(215) 25.5	(249) 22.7	(233) 23.1	Net Worth	(39) 25.6	(78) 16.8	(22) 28.5	(35) 29.7	(38) 18.4	(21) 23.4
9.8	9.3	7.9		5.9	6.0	10.8	6.3	7.0	17.5
15.5	14.1	13.3	% Profit Before Taxes/Total	13.0	13.1	17.8	11.3	13.9	15.7
6.7	6.1	5.9	Assets	4.9	5.9	6.5	5.3	5.9	7.0
.4	.8	.6		-2.1	.1	1.8	.8	1.9	4.0
126.0	127.8	150.9		388.1	162.7	265.2	240.3	76.3	50.2
33.0	37.1	39.7	Sales/Net Fixed Assets	27.5	50.7	68.9	52.8	27.8	25.4
10.6	11.6	11.9		4.9	12.1	15.7	23.3	12.0	8.8
4.8	4.8	5.3		4.2	5.5	4.9	5.6	5.2	4.9
3.4	3.1	3.3	Sales/Total Assets	2.7	3.4	2.7	3.5	3.5	3.6
2.1	2.1	2.3		1.6	2.4	1.7	2.6	2.6	2.4
.4	.4	.3		.7	.4	.2	.1	.3	.4
(223) .9	(261) .8	(255) .7	% Depr., Dep., Amort./Sales	(36) 2.2	(93) .9	(25) .4	(39) .4	(36) .6	(26) .8
1.9	1.9	1.7		3.8	2.0	2.3	.6	.9	1.1
1.5	1.3	1.5		1.8	1.8	1.2	1.1	.9	
(175) 2.9	(199) 2.5	(197) 2.7	% Officers', Directors' Owners' Comp/Sales	(35) 3.5	(92) 3.5	(19) 1.7	(25) 2.1	(18) 1.3	
5.0	4.1	4.6		7.2	4.7	2.9	4.3	2.4	
6774982M	4940075M	9465836M	Net Sales ($)	44710M	231634M	128850M	355620M	602342M	8102680M
1957276M	1589747M	2163357M	Total Assets ($)	21555M	79857M	53672M	103578M	206679M	1698016M

M = $ thousand   MM = $ million
See Pages 9 through 22 for Explanation of Ratios and Data

Current Data Sorted by Assets   **Comparative Historical Data**

	0-500M	500M-2MM	2-10MM	10-50MM	50-100MM	100-250MM		4/1/06-3/31/07 ALL	4/1/07-3/31/08 ALL
		60 (4/1-9/30/10)		337 (10/1/10-3/31/11)			**Type of Statement**		
	1		8	14	5	1	Unqualified	12	21
	1	10	21	3			Reviewed	27	30
	14	34	18	3			Compiled	73	59
	35	93	18				Tax Returns	135	116
	20	34	34	17	4	9	Other	84	91
	71	171	99	37	9	10	**NUMBER OF STATEMENTS**	331	317
	%	%	%	%	%	%	**ASSETS**	%	%
	17.4	10.4	7.9	6.8		11.5	Cash & Equivalents	11.3	10.9
	14.1	26.2	29.9	30.1		15.1	Trade Receivables (net)	26.2	24.8
	45.9	36.5	26.4	25.0		30.5	Inventory	34.6	34.1
	.9	1.9	3.0	2.9		.7	All Other Current	2.6	2.0
	78.3	74.9	67.2	64.8		57.8	Total Current	74.7	71.8
	11.9	10.1	15.7	16.1		17.5	Fixed Assets (net)	12.8	14.5
	2.6	7.6	9.9	12.0		19.5	Intangibles (net)	6.1	7.1
	7.1	7.4	7.2	7.1		5.2	All Other Non-Current	6.4	6.6
	100.0	100.0	100.0	100.0		100.0	Total	100.0	100.0
							LIABILITIES		
	12.0	7.2	12.6	7.8		2.0	Notes Payable-Short Term	9.4	12.1
	4.9	3.5	3.9	4.5		1.6	Cur. Mat.-L.T.D.	3.7	4.4
	21.0	27.3	25.1	21.2		21.7	Trade Payables	25.5	23.4
	.0	.0	.3	.3		.1	Income Taxes Payable	.2	.1
	15.9	7.7	7.0	9.7		13.6	All Other Current	7.0	8.3
	53.9	45.7	49.0	43.5		38.9	Total Current	45.8	48.2
	13.8	16.6	15.4	14.2		13.4	Long-Term Debt	15.9	16.4
	.0	.1	.1	.1		.2	Deferred Taxes	.1	.1
	8.6	4.8	4.6	7.0		7.3	All Other Non-Current	6.2	6.2
	23.6	32.8	30.9	35.3		40.1	Net Worth	32.0	29.0
	100.0	100.0	100.0	100.0		100.0	Total Liabilities & Net Worth	100.0	100.0
							INCOME DATA		
	100.0	100.0	100.0	100.0		100.0	Net Sales	100.0	100.0
	27.7	23.8	27.8	27.7		26.0	Gross Profit	24.9	26.0
	25.2	21.7	24.9	25.0		23.9	Operating Expenses	22.6	23.9
	2.5	2.2	2.9	2.7		2.1	Operating Profit	2.4	2.1
	.0	.0	.3	.4		2.3	All Other Expenses (net)	.1	.3
	2.5	2.1	2.6	2.3		-.2	Profit Before Taxes	2.2	1.7
							RATIOS		
	4.4	2.7	1.8	2.4		2.8	Current	2.7	2.5
	1.8	1.8	1.4	1.4		1.5		1.8	1.6
	1.0	1.2	1.0	1.2		1.2		1.2	1.1
	2.9	1.4	1.1	1.3		1.2	Quick	1.4	1.2
	(69) .7	.8	.7	.8		.9		.9 (316)	.8
	.3	.5	.5	.6		.3		.5	.5
	0 UND	9 40.6	16 22.8	20 18.5		9 41.5	Sales/Receivables	10 38.0	11 34.0
	4 86.9	18 20.5	24 15.5	30 12.1		12 31.6		19 19.6	19 18.8
	16 22.6	26 13.8	36 10.1	50 7.3		34 10.8		28 13.2	28 13.0
	17 20.9	22 16.4	21 17.0	23 16.0		18 20.6	Cost of Sales/Inventory	22 16.5	22 16.2
	30 12.2	33 11.2	33 11.2	31 11.7		50 7.3		32 11.5	33 11.1
	50 7.3	46 8.0	44 8.3	57 6.4		69 5.3		44 8.2	47 7.7
	0 UND	12 30.8	17 21.1	21 17.5		20 18.6	Cost of Sales/Payables	13 27.4	14 26.1
	12 31.1	20 18.2	30 12.1	34 10.8		37 9.8		21 17.0	21 17.5
	25 14.9	33 11.1	37 9.8	41 8.8		51 7.1		36 10.3	35 10.3
	10.2	9.9	11.3	8.4		10.8	Sales/Working Capital	10.1	11.0
	25.7	16.4	20.7	21.2		15.4		16.3	19.4
	-999.8	53.8	-999.8	38.5		25.4		44.0	93.3
	39.3	24.6	10.8	18.6			EBIT/Interest	12.2	9.9
	(39) 7.0	(136) 3.9	(89) 4.5	(35) 4.5				(261) 3.9	(269) 3.5
	-.1	1.0	2.0	1.8				1.3	1.1
			3.1	6.6			Net Profit + Depr., Dep., Amort./Cur. Mat. L/T/D	4.1	6.2
		(21) 1.3	(10) 2.4					(43) 1.4	(48) 1.8
			.4	.0				.8	.5
	.1	.1	.3	.3		.3	Fixed/Worth	.1	.2
	.2	.3	.5	.6		.7		.4	.5
	7.1	1.7	3.0	1.6		-.4		2.4	3.4
	.3	.8	1.2	1.4		.4	Debt/Worth	.9	.9
	1.9	2.4	3.1	3.2		3.1		2.3	2.4
	-12.0	26.0	16.3	7.1		-4.2		25.1	22.9
	128.0	78.3	78.1	61.8			% Profit Before Taxes/Tangible Net Worth	73.4	57.1
	(51) 55.2	(137) 24.1	(81) 27.2	(30) 26.9				(265) 21.4	(252) 22.4
	18.5	2.9	6.5	.3				6.8	5.9
	47.4	20.6	15.5	12.5		4.3	% Profit Before Taxes/Total Assets	16.7	18.2
	15.9	8.2	6.9	6.8		.3		7.2	5.6
	.8	.1	2.1	-.2		-2.4		1.0	.7
	347.7	366.4	83.3	76.2		22.7	Sales/Net Fixed Assets	136.4	121.7
	113.2	91.1	35.4	29.5		16.1		51.4	48.6
	29.5	38.7	19.4	12.3		10.5		24.4	21.0
	11.7	7.3	5.0	3.9		4.4	Sales/Total Assets	6.6	6.4
	7.0	5.3	4.1	3.2		3.2		4.7	4.7
	4.6	3.8	3.0	2.5		2.0		3.5	3.3
	.1	.2	.4	.4			% Depr., Dep., Amort./Sales	.3	.3
	(43) .3	(108) .4	(75) .7	(33) .8				(263) .5	(261) .6
	1.2	.8	1.0	1.0				.9	1.2
	2.5	1.8	1.3				% Officers', Directors' Owners' Comp/Sales	1.7	1.6
	(33) 5.7	(112) 3.2	(40) 2.1					(181) 3.0	(162) 3.0
	8.1	5.6	3.7					4.9	5.1
	173559M	1111923M	1866920M	2685509M	2257022M	4966102M	Net Sales ($)	8264219M	9487431M
	20265M	188373M	453952M	840994M	670238M	1738994M	Total Assets ($)	2117197M	2354203M

Comparative Historical Data | Current Data Sorted by Sales

			Type of Statement						
22	19	29	Unqualified		1		1	6	21
27	32	35	Reviewed	1	4	2	4	14	10
78	73	69	Compiled	2	17	11	17	18	4
165	160	146	Tax Returns	9	28	38	43	26	2
97	114	118	Other	5	15	6	29	19	44
4/1/08-3/31/09 ALL	4/1/09-3/31/10 ALL	4/1/10-3/31/11 ALL		60 (4/1-9/30/10)			337 (10/1/10-3/31/11)		
				0-1MM	1-3MM	3-5MM	5-10MM	10-25MM	25MM & OVER
389	398	397	NUMBER OF STATEMENTS	17	65	57	94	83	81
%	%	%	ASSETS	%	%	%	%	%	%
12.1	11.9	10.6	Cash & Equivalents	21.1	11.7	12.7	9.9	11.0	6.3
25.0	24.8	25.0	Trade Receivables (net)	12.2	19.3	22.9	24.7	29.2	29.8
33.3	32.6	34.1	Inventory	35.1	42.2	36.0	37.4	29.9	26.7
2.1	1.4	2.0	All Other Current	2.1	1.0	1.7	1.9	3.1	2.2
72.5	70.7	71.8	Total Current	70.4	74.3	73.4	73.8	73.3	65.0
12.9	12.4	12.7	Fixed Assets (net)	23.0	10.4	10.1	12.4	12.2	15.1
7.5	7.6	8.3	Intangibles (net)	1.3	8.5	9.0	6.4	6.3	13.3
7.2	9.4	7.2	All Other Non-Current	5.3	6.8	7.5	7.4	8.2	6.6
100.0	100.0	100.0	Total	100.0	100.0	100.0	100.0	100.0	100.0
			LIABILITIES						
9.8	11.2	9.4	Notes Payable-Short Term	17.7	10.9	5.9	7.4	10.2	10.2
4.5	3.4	4.0	Cur. Mat.-L.T.D.	4.6	4.3	5.2	3.6	3.1	4.1
25.3	27.0	24.8	Trade Payables	18.7	21.2	22.1	25.2	30.2	24.9
.1	.1	.1	Income Taxes Payable	.0	.0	.1	.1	.4	.2
9.5	9.1	9.4	All Other Current	38.4	6.6	8.8	8.0	7.0	9.0
49.2	50.9	47.7	Total Current	79.4	43.0	42.1	45.2	50.8	48.3
16.7	15.1	15.3	Long-Term Debt	17.2	16.7	21.5	16.5	10.8	12.7
.1	.1	.1	Deferred Taxes	.0	.0	.2	.0	.1	.3
4.5	5.7	5.6	All Other Non-Current	12.2	8.9	2.8	4.2	5.8	5.1
29.6	28.2	31.3	Net Worth	-8.9	31.3	33.4	34.1	32.5	33.5
100.0	100.0	100.0	Total Liabilities & Net Worth	100.0	100.0	100.0	100.0	100.0	100.0
			INCOME DATA						
100.0	100.0	100.0	Net Sales	100.0	100.0	100.0	100.0	100.0	100.0
25.2	26.8	26.0	Gross Profit	40.1	28.3	23.8	24.0	24.8	26.2
22.7	23.7	23.5	Operating Expenses	39.8	24.9	22.3	21.3	22.1	24.0
2.4	3.1	2.4	Operating Profit	.3	3.4	1.5	2.7	2.7	2.3
.2	.2	.2	All Other Expenses (net)	.9	.1	-.2	.3	-.1	.6
2.2	2.9	2.2	Profit Before Taxes	-.6	3.3	1.8	2.4	2.7	1.7
			RATIOS						
2.7	2.6	2.6	Current	4.4	3.6	4.3	2.5	2.1	2.1
1.6	1.6	1.6		1.5	1.9	1.8	1.8	1.5	1.4
1.1	1.1	1.1		.6	1.2	1.3	1.2	1.0	1.1
1.5	1.4	1.3	Quick	3.0	2.0	1.9	1.1	1.3	1.1
.8	(395) .8	.8		(16) .9	(64) .7	.9	.7	.7	.8
.5	.5	.5		.1	.3	.5	.5	.5	.5
9 40.7	8 46.2	9 42.2	Sales/Receivables	0 UND	1 271.9	8 44.8	7 53.7	9 39.9	18 20.8
19 18.9	19 18.7	19 19.3		1 272.3	16 22.6	17 21.4	17 22.0	18 19.8	26 13.9
27 13.4	28 12.8	29 12.8		35 10.6	28 13.2	25 14.8	27 13.3	28 13.0	42 8.8
21 17.5	20 18.0	21 17.5	Cost of Sales/Inventory	38 9.5	27 13.3	23 16.0	19 19.1	16 23.5	21 17.1
31 11.9	31 11.9	32 11.3		71 5.2	39 9.3	33 11.2	30 12.1	26 14.3	33 11.2
42 8.7	45 8.1	47 7.8		98 3.7	54 6.8	43 8.6	46 8.0	36 10.1	51 7.2
14 25.9	13 27.1	13 28.7	Cost of Sales/Payables	3 120.3	5 77.3	6 65.4	11 32.5	15 24.1	20 18.1
21 17.4	23 15.6	23 16.0		27 13.7	18 20.8	16 22.6	22 16.8	25 14.4	29 12.4
35 10.5	41 8.9	36 10.1		73 5.0	26 13.9	34 10.6	32 11.5	37 9.8	41 9.0
10.2	10.3	10.2	Sales/Working Capital	6.1	8.3	9.7	10.2	13.3	11.2
20.0	20.8	18.6		14.8	16.5	14.9	16.3	30.9	21.2
71.6	111.4	82.7		-4.4	53.2	32.8	70.5	-729.3	53.0
13.2	18.5	17.3	EBIT/Interest		13.2	15.9	21.8	23.0	10.8
(317) 4.3	(319) 4.9	(317) 4.3		(45) 4.5	(45) 2.9	(74) 5.4	(68) 4.7	(76) 4.0	
1.1	1.4	1.3			1.3	.2	1.3	1.7	1.7
4.8	4.6	4.3	Net Profit + Depr., Dep., Amort./Cur. Mat. L/T/D					4.3	5.0
(44) 1.4	(45) 1.4	(48) 1.3						(10) 1.9	(25) 2.3
.4	.7	.3						.8	.2
.1	.1	.1	Fixed/Worth	.2	.1	.0	.1	.1	.3
.5	.4	.4		7.1	.3	.2	.3	.4	.6
6.0	3.9	3.0		-.5	NM	63.5	1.0	1.5	6.7
.9	.9	.9	Debt/Worth	.2	.5	.5	.8	1.0	1.5
2.5	2.8	2.7		29.6	2.1	2.1	1.9	3.1	3.2
257.1	44.6	27.5		-2.7	-24.6	-122.5	9.0	11.3	30.2
64.8	88.1	82.8	% Profit Before Taxes/Tangible Net Worth		99.5	50.9	81.2	100.2	67.8
(296) 27.0	(305) 33.5	(314) 27.1		(48) 46.6	(42) 21.5	(78) 26.7	(72) 27.4	(65) 22.7	
7.8	10.6	4.2			17.4	.0	3.3	5.9	1.9
19.9	22.6	19.9	% Profit Before Taxes/Total Assets	37.0	26.0	18.0	25.0	18.4	12.0
7.6	9.3	7.8		9.0	14.4	5.5	9.5	7.3	6.0
.9	1.3	.5		-36.4	3.0	-1.3	.7	1.6	.3
149.5	180.2	200.1	Sales/Net Fixed Assets	55.3	299.1	397.9	366.8	185.4	67.7
59.4	58.0	59.5		16.0	89.8	114.8	80.9	59.8	29.5
27.4	25.3	23.9		4.6	29.4	40.0	29.1	27.7	15.3
6.7	6.5	6.8	Sales/Total Assets	4.2	7.0	6.9	7.7	7.4	4.6
4.8	4.6	4.6		2.2	4.6	5.6	5.5	5.2	3.8
3.4	3.5	3.4		1.6	3.1	4.2	3.9	3.8	2.7
.3	.2	.2	% Depr., Dep., Amort./Sales	.6	.1	.1	.2	.2	.5
(297) .6	(288) .6	(275) .5		(13) 1.2	(44) .3	(35) .3	(55) .5	(56) .5	(72) .8
1.1	1.1	1.0		3.8	1.0	.9	.8	.8	1.1
1.7	1.5	1.7	% Officers', Directors' Owners' Comp/Sales		3.2	1.8	1.7	1.4	
(210) 3.1	(218) 2.8	(188) 3.1		(34) 5.7	(35) 3.1	(63) 2.9	(45) 2.7		
5.3	4.3	5.7			8.0	5.2	5.6	4.0	
10579641M	8741307M	13061035M	Net Sales ($)	9169M	134342M	223502M	656333M	1266040M	10771649M
2839091M	2596477M	3912816M	Total Assets ($)	4797M	32722M	49214M	141020M	264136M	3420927M

M = $ thousand   MM = $ million
See Pages 9 through 22 for Explanation of Ratios and Data

Current Data Sorted by Assets   Comparative Historical Data

Type of Statement	0-500M	500M-2MM	2-10MM	10-50MM	50-100MM	100-250MM		4/1/06-3/31/07 ALL	4/1/07-3/31/08 ALL
Unqualified				5	2			6	7
Reviewed			3	1				2	8
Compiled	1	2	2					4	6
Tax Returns	9	11	4	1				20	12
Other	3	7	7	7	4			7	16
		9 (4/1-9/30/10)		60 (10/1/10-3/31/11)					
NUMBER OF STATEMENTS	13	20	16	14	6			39	49

0-500M	500M-2MM	2-10MM	10-50MM	50-100MM	100-250MM		4/1/06-3/31/07	4/1/07-3/31/08
%	%	%	%	%	%	**ASSETS**	%	%
29.5	7.6	10.5	18.8			Cash & Equivalents	8.1	11.0
4.7	15.6	12.8	9.6			Trade Receivables (net)	17.5	16.8
46.6	45.3	49.2	31.2			Inventory	45.3	46.9
3.3	.3	1.7	4.5	D		All Other Current	4.0	2.6
84.1	68.7	74.2	64.1	A		Total Current	74.8	77.3
9.4	19.0	12.6	22.4	T		Fixed Assets (net)	14.0	10.7
3.2	7.2	10.1	10.4	A		Intangibles (net)	3.9	4.0
3.2	5.1	3.1	3.0			All Other Non-Current	7.4	8.0
100.0	100.0	100.0	100.0	N		Total	100.0	100.0
				O		**LIABILITIES**		
12.7	17.3	7.4	11.4	T		Notes Payable-Short Term	19.8	14.3
4.1	2.4	4.2	4.3			Cur. Mat.-L.T.D.	3.3	1.2
26.7	21.7	22.5	14.0	A		Trade Payables	20.8	20.4
.1	.2	.1	.1	V		Income Taxes Payable	.4	.1
3.0	11.0	5.3	8.7	A		All Other Current	9.9	16.4
46.5	52.7	39.4	38.4	I		Total Current	54.3	52.3
2.6	18.8	5.5	26.9	L		Long-Term Debt	13.9	11.7
.0	.0	.0	.0	A		Deferred Taxes	.0	.3
9.8	2.7	8.2	7.1	B		All Other Non-Current	10.4	8.0
41.1	25.7	46.9	27.5	L		Net Worth	21.4	27.8
100.0	100.0	100.0	100.0	E		Total Liabilities & Net Worth	100.0	100.0
						INCOME DATA		
100.0	100.0	100.0	100.0			Net Sales	100.0	100.0
47.7	43.5	46.5	49.7			Gross Profit	42.6	45.3
42.9	35.3	39.5	45.8			Operating Expenses	39.5	40.1
4.8	8.3	7.0	3.9			Operating Profit	3.2	5.2
.4	1.5	.8	1.1			All Other Expenses (net)	1.1	.6
4.4	6.8	6.2	2.8			Profit Before Taxes	2.1	4.6
						RATIOS		
10.0	2.6	4.5	2.7				3.1	3.5
2.4	1.4	2.5	1.5			Current	1.5	1.8
1.2	1.0	1.1	1.0				1.0	1.0
2.7	.9	1.5	1.5				.9	1.6
.3	.3	.6	.5			Quick	(38) .5	.5
.0	.1	.2	.2				.2	.3
0 UND	0 UND	3 115.1	3 111.8				0 UND	2 241.7
0 UND	13 27.2	18 20.1	11 33.9			Sales/Receivables	10 35.3	21 17.7
10 37.6	33 10.9	32 11.5	45 8.1				32 11.3	47 7.8
55 6.6	56 6.5	84 4.3	81 4.5				46 8.0	78 4.7
113 3.2	82 4.5	123 3.0	113 3.2			Cost of Sales/Inventory	89 4.1	134 2.7
179 2.0	150 2.4	162 2.2	190 1.9				194 1.9	201 1.8
18 20.4	4 90.2	22 16.5	23 16.1				9 42.8	22 16.3
42 8.8	19 19.6	33 11.0	39 9.4			Cost of Sales/Payables	37 10.0	46 7.9
66 5.5	67 5.5	67 5.4	81 4.5				83 4.4	79 4.6
3.3	5.0	4.3	3.2				4.5	4.2
7.6	17.4	7.4	11.3			Sales/Working Capital	15.3	7.1
43.6	NM	29.2	-343.0				89.0	289.9
	12.8	78.6	31.2				5.7	19.7
	(13) 5.2	(11) 1.8	(12) 1.8			EBIT/Interest	(30) 3.3	(43) 6.0
	1.6	-1.3	-.5				1.2	1.7
						Net Profit + Depr., Dep., Amort./Cur. Mat. L/T/D		
.0	.0	.0	.2				.0	.1
.2	.1	.2	3.2			Fixed/Worth	.3	.3
NM	2.3	1.1	-2.5				5.4	1.0
.2	.7	.5	.9				.8	.7
.8	3.2	1.1	15.8			Debt/Worth	3.0	2.5
NM	21.4	7.2	-13.1				-7.5	39.4
125.7	190.9	80.8					46.8	57.7
(10) 22.9	(16) 42.7	(14) 32.0				% Profit Before Taxes/Tangible Net Worth	(28) 26.4	(38) 31.0
4.4	9.5	8.3					13.9	14.3
61.7	23.9	28.2	13.4				14.6	22.2
7.5	9.8	11.9	1.6			% Profit Before Taxes/Total Assets	5.0	9.8
.4	.9	-2.3	-2.8				.4	1.1
999.8	UND	279.0	32.5				192.0	120.6
148.4	66.1	43.2	13.2			Sales/Net Fixed Assets	73.3	43.4
19.4	11.6	11.4	6.4				16.1	13.7
4.5	4.1	3.4	3.3				5.1	3.2
3.6	3.1	2.7	1.7			Sales/Total Assets	2.6	2.5
2.0	1.7	1.9	1.3				1.7	1.6
		.2	.6				.3	.3
	(11) 1.4	(13) 1.9				% Depr., Dep., Amort./Sales	(27) .8	(39) .8
		2.1	4.5				1.7	1.4
							1.5	1.8
						% Officers', Directors' Owners' Comp/Sales	(19) 1.9	(21) 2.7
							5.1	8.4
12610M	65000M	203463M	665345M	717159M		Net Sales ($)	1832206M	1216371M
3641M	20936M	79065M	328299M	500798M		Total Assets ($)	791503M	605558M

(Columns 50-100MM and 100-250MM: "DATA NOT AVAILABLE" for Assets, Liabilities, Income Data and Ratios.)

Comparative Historical Data / Current Data Sorted by Sales

					Type of Statement						
7		10		7	Unqualified					4	7
6		5		4	Reviewed						
12		12		5	Compiled	2	1		2		
19		20		25	Tax Returns	6	7	5	3	3	1
24		25		28	Other	2	6	2	2	8	8
							9 (4/1-9/30/10)		60 (10/1/10-3/31/11)		
4/1/08- 3/31/09 ALL		4/1/09- 3/31/10 ALL		4/1/10- 3/31/11 ALL		0-1MM	1-3MM	3-5MM	5-10MM	10-25MM	25MM & OVER
68		72		69	**NUMBER OF STATEMENTS**	10	14	7	7	15	16
%		%		%	**ASSETS**	%	%	%	%	%	%
11.5		12.6		14.4	Cash & Equivalents	21.1	18.2			15.7	9.9
13.4		13.1		11.5	Trade Receivables (net)	4.3	7.1			13.4	10.6
44.6		44.4		41.4	Inventory	40.3	45.6			41.5	28.5
2.8		3.4		3.0	All Other Current	2.4	1.6			1.3	8.1
72.4		73.5		70.4	Total Current	68.1	72.5			71.8	57.2
16.6		16.9		16.7	Fixed Assets (net)	24.3	15.3			10.2	26.4
6.5		3.8		9.0	Intangibles (net)	3.5	8.3			15.5	12.7
4.5		5.8		3.9	All Other Non-Current	4.1	3.9			2.5	3.7
100.0		100.0		100.0	Total	100.0	100.0			100.0	100.0
					LIABILITIES						
16.6		11.0		11.5	Notes Payable-Short Term	13.6	8.6			6.0	7.1
1.5		2.2		3.5	Cur. Mat.-L.T.D.	3.6	4.2			2.9	4.8
18.3		19.9		20.2	Trade Payables	15.4	21.3			16.7	14.9
.0		.1		.2	Income Taxes Payable	.1	.1			.1	.2
10.1		12.4		7.5	All Other Current	12.5	6.0			5.5	9.8
46.6		45.7		42.9	Total Current	45.3	40.1			31.3	36.8
19.3		14.3		14.0	Long-Term Debt	16.8	11.7			4.4	28.2
.2		.2		.1	Deferred Taxes	.0	.0			.0	.5
16.0		8.1		6.4	All Other Non-Current	10.7	5.1			8.2	7.4
17.7		31.7		36.5	Net Worth	27.1	43.1			56.1	27.2
100.0		100.0		100.0	Total Liabilties & Net Worth	100.0	100.0			100.0	100.0
					INCOME DATA						
100.0		100.0		100.0	Net Sales	100.0	100.0			100.0	100.0
43.7		47.7		47.7	Gross Profit	47.0	48.8			46.4	51.7
38.5		43.5		41.0	Operating Expenses	44.8	38.4			38.8	46.7
5.2		4.1		6.7	Operating Profit	2.1	10.4			7.7	5.0
1.4		.8		1.0	All Other Expenses (net)	2.0	.7			.2	1.1
3.8		3.3		5.7	Profit Before Taxes	.2	9.8			7.5	4.0
					RATIOS						
3.6		4.1		3.4		15.2	2.8			4.7	2.6
1.8		1.7		1.9	Current	2.8	2.1			2.5	1.5
1.1		1.1		1.1		.9	1.2			1.5	1.0
1.3		1.3		1.2		2.0	1.4			1.7	.8
.4		.6		.5	Quick	.1	.2			.7	.5
.2		.2		.2		.0	.0			.3	.2
2 153.9	0	UND	1	391.1		0 UND	0 UND			9 40.2	3 107.6
12 31.0	7	54.1	10	35.3	Sales/Receivables	0 UND	0 UND			26 14.1	8 43.7
28 13.1	32	11.3	30	12.1		12 31.2	17 22.1			43 8.4	32 11.4
63 5.8	68	5.3	69	5.3		64 5.7	53 6.8			86 4.3	61 6.0
117 3.1	112	3.3	112	3.3	Cost of Sales/Inventory	141 2.6	118 3.1			124 2.9	84 4.4
202 1.8	165	2.2	176	2.1		300 1.2	248 1.5			186 2.0	180 2.0
15 24.7	26	14.2	15	24.1		0 UND	0 UND			18 19.8	25 14.3
34 10.6	34	10.7	32	11.5	Cost of Sales/Payables	22 16.8	28 13.0			34 10.6	40 9.2
61 6.0	56	6.5	68	5.3		51 7.2	116 3.1			70 5.2	79 4.6
4.0		4.0		4.5		2.9	4.4			4.1	4.5
7.0		9.9		9.8	Sales/Working Capital	11.5	7.7			5.8	11.5
41.3		56.0		77.3		-44.5	55.4			9.4	NM
6.7		10.9		20.1						42.9	37.8
(55) 2.3	(53)	3.2	(48)	4.8	EBIT/Interest				(12)	11.8	(13) 2.4
-1.6		-.4		.6						-1.2	.2
				24.4	Net Profit + Depr., Dep.,						
		(10)		5.2	Amort./Cur. Mat. L/T/D						
				1.9							
.0		.0		.0		.0	.0			.0	.4
.3		.3		.3	Fixed/Worth	.4	.3			.2	1.5
3.1		1.3		3.5		-9.1	6.6			.8	-1.6
.8		.6		.5		.3	.4			.3	1.0
2.1		1.6		1.8	Debt/Worth	2.5	1.9			1.0	4.1
19.5		8.2		25.6		-32.6	12.8			5.5	-8.2
39.5		54.3		87.3			298.1			70.2	
(53) 13.6	(57)	16.7	(53)	29.6	% Profit Before Taxes/Tangible Net Worth		(12) 82.6			(13) 29.6	
-1.6		.5		7.7			12.1			7.1	
14.5		19.9		24.2		10.4	83.8			27.5	10.6
4.9		5.3		7.5	% Profit Before Taxes/Total Assets	2.4	15.7			12.2	3.1
-4.8		-4.2		.4		-2.1	6.6			-3.3	-1.6
150.3		179.8		273.2		UND	999.8			213.7	19.8
39.3		44.0		31.9	Sales/Net Fixed Assets	67.3	66.1			31.3	12.2
10.6		7.0		9.0		2.9	20.2			15.4	5.1
3.7		3.5		3.6		3.7	4.5			2.8	3.3
2.4		2.7		2.5	Sales/Total Assets	1.8	2.9			2.0	2.1
1.6		1.9		1.5		.8	1.7			1.3	1.3
.3		.2		.3						.2	1.5
(50) 1.1	(46)	1.3	(45)	1.5	% Depr., Dep., Amort./Sales					(12) 1.1	2.5
2.1		3.2		3.0						2.1	4.7
1.5		1.3		1.3							
(30) 2.9	(26)	3.4	(28)	2.4	% Officers', Directors' Owners' Comp/Sales						
5.7		7.7		5.1							
1431678M		1714207M		1663577M	Net Sales ($)	5506M	25386M	29469M	44154M	246859M	1312203M
751535M		765714M		932739M	Total Assets ($)	4034M	9860M	8180M	15308M	146572M	748785M

M = $ thousand   MM = $ million
See Pages 9 through 22 for Explanation of Ratios and Data

Current Data Sorted by Assets

Comparative Historical Data

							Type of Statement		
							Unqualified		
			3				Reviewed	4	
1		1	1				Compiled	5	3
1	1	2					Tax Returns	10	7
16	7	2			2	1	Other	18	20
5		2						9	13
	3 (4/1-9/30/10)		42 (10/1/10-3/31/11)					4/1/06-3/31/07	4/1/07-3/31/08
0-500M	500M-2MM	2-10MM	10-50MM	50-100MM	100-250MM			ALL	ALL
23	8	7	4	2	1	NUMBER OF STATEMENTS		46	43
%	%	%	%	%	%		ASSETS	%	%
20.9							Cash & Equivalents	13.8	11.9
10.0							Trade Receivables (net)	11.9	14.4
29.8							Inventory	29.7	25.3
2.3							All Other Current	2.0	3.1
63.1							Total Current	57.4	54.6
23.7							Fixed Assets (net)	23.6	25.4
9.6							Intangibles (net)	11.3	11.0
3.7							All Other Non-Current	7.8	8.9
100.0							Total	100.0	100.0
							LIABILITIES		
11.6							Notes Payable-Short Term	6.9	13.1
4.9							Cur. Mat.-L.T.D.	4.8	5.5
12.7							Trade Payables	20.3	25.6
.5							Income Taxes Payable	.0	.0
12.4							All Other Current	15.0	13.9
42.0							Total Current	47.0	58.2
24.7							Long-Term Debt	34.1	22.4
.0							Deferred Taxes	.1	.0
16.8							All Other Non-Current	8.3	9.1
16.6							Net Worth	10.6	10.3
100.0							Total Liabilties & Net Worth	100.0	100.0
							INCOME DATA		
100.0							Net Sales	100.0	100.0
62.1							Gross Profit	57.1	58.9
56.6							Operating Expenses	50.1	52.8
5.4							Operating Profit	7.1	6.1
.6							All Other Expenses (net)	1.5	1.3
4.8							Profit Before Taxes	5.5	4.8
							RATIOS		
3.0								2.6	2.2
1.9							Current	1.5	1.1
1.2								.8	.6
1.7								1.4	1.3
.8							Quick	(44) .8	.6
.4								.3	.1
0 UND								0 UND	0 UND
5 70.0							Sales/Receivables	9 41.3	9 39.6
18 20.0								22 16.7	21 17.5
54 6.8								41 8.9	22 16.6
74 4.9							Cost of Sales/Inventory	64 5.7	63 5.8
96 3.8								99 3.7	107 3.4
22 16.9								19 19.3	15 24.7
29 12.5							Cost of Sales/Payables	31 11.7	36 10.0
43 8.5								77 4.7	70 5.3
7.4								8.9	12.7
21.0							Sales/Working Capital	27.3	82.0
56.0								-18.4	-22.0
38.0								13.5	11.5
(14) 6.1							EBIT/Interest	(37) 2.5	(33) 3.3
-8.7								.5	1.0
							Net Profit + Depr., Dep., Amort./Cur. Mat. L/T/D		
.2								.2	.3
.4							Fixed/Worth	1.2	1.4
19.8								-1.1	-.8
.5								1.0	1.1
1.6							Debt/Worth	5.9	3.4
-22.4								-4.2	-3.0
520.8							% Profit Before Taxes/Tangible Net Worth	115.4	72.6
(17) 72.2								(29) 49.4	(28) 24.8
12.8								9.5	2.0
58.5							% Profit Before Taxes/Total Assets	26.1	33.3
15.4								7.3	9.5
-9.4								-.4	.0
114.7							Sales/Net Fixed Assets	93.3	101.4
17.5								25.5	21.8
8.0								7.5	8.8
5.4							Sales/Total Assets	5.3	6.1
3.4								3.2	3.6
2.9								2.2	2.4
.3							% Depr., Dep., Amort./Sales	.8	.4
(18) 1.2								(32) 1.6	(29) 1.3
2.5								2.5	2.4
							% Officers', Directors' Owners' Comp/Sales	2.2	1.9
								(22) 7.0	(21) 4.5
								15.8	7.0
23344M	33980M	70794M	360418M	195016M	242074M	Net Sales ($)		915311M	747487M
5136M	7772M	23659M	88644M	116052M	126473M	Total Assets ($)		551932M	406937M

M = $ thousand   MM = $ million
See Pages 9 through 22 for Explanation of Ratios and Data

Comparative Historical Data / Current Data Sorted by Sales

	Hist 1	Hist 2	Hist 3	Type of Statement	0-1MM	1-3MM	3-5MM	5-10MM	10-25MM	25MM & OVER
	.1	2	3	Unqualified						3
	5	2	3	Reviewed		1		1	1	
	3	5	4	Compiled		1		1	1	
	12	22	25	Tax Returns	11	8	1	3	2	
	15	21	10	Other	3	2	1	1	1	3
	4/1/08-3/31/09 ALL	4/1/09-3/31/10 ALL	4/1/10-3/31/11 ALL		| 3 (4/1-9/30/10)			42 (10/1/10-3/31/11)		
	36	52	45	NUMBER OF STATEMENTS	14	12	2	6	5	6
	%	%	%	**ASSETS**	%	%	%	%	%	%
	13.2	13.4	14.4	Cash & Equivalents	17.3	16.1				
	15.5	9.1	12.9	Trade Receivables (net)	11.0	9.9				
	26.1	26.3	28.1	Inventory	29.7	28.7				
	2.5	2.5	1.8	All Other Current	1.0	3.8				
	57.3	51.3	57.2	Total Current	59.0	58.6				
	25.9	25.7	25.0	Fixed Assets (net)	23.3	22.7				
	8.4	10.3	11.9	Intangibles (net)	13.7	13.8				
	8.4	12.6	5.9	All Other Non-Current	4.0	5.0				
	100.0	100.0	100.0	Total	100.0	100.0				
				LIABILITIES						
	8.5	5.8	8.5	Notes Payable-Short Term	18.4	3.8				
	6.1	7.1	5.5	Cur. Mat.-L.T.D.	5.6	4.8				
	15.2	19.9	18.0	Trade Payables	11.7	15.1				
	.2	.0	.2	Income Taxes Payable	.0	.9				
	19.1	21.8	11.9	All Other Current	16.3	5.9				
	49.1	54.7	44.1	Total Current	52.0	30.5				
	21.9	17.3	24.1	Long-Term Debt	25.1	30.3				
	.0	.1	.0	Deferred Taxes	.0	.0				
	10.6	8.6	9.8	All Other Non-Current	21.0	8.6				
	18.4	19.3	22.0	Net Worth	1.9	30.6				
	100.0	100.0	100.0	Total Liabilities & Net Worth	100.0	100.0				
				INCOME DATA						
	100.0	100.0	100.0	Net Sales	100.0	100.0				
	56.1	58.5	61.2	Gross Profit	59.3	62.4				
	49.3	52.9	54.9	Operating Expenses	56.6	54.0				
	6.8	5.6	6.3	Operating Profit	2.7	8.4				
	1.7	.5	.6	All Other Expenses (net)	.7	.7				
	5.1	5.1	5.7	Profit Before Taxes	2.1	7.7				
				RATIOS						
	2.7	2.2	2.4	Current	2.7	2.4				
	1.2	1.3	1.4		1.4	1.9				
	.8	.9	.9		.8	1.5				
	1.1	.8	1.1	Quick	1.9	1.1				
	.6	.4	.6		.6	.8				
	.2	.1	.3		.2	.6				
	1 495.8	0 UND	0 UND	Sales/Receivables	0 UND	0 UND				
	12 31.4	1 404.6	10 35.1		7 49.7	2 186.2				
	22 16.9	16 23.2	20 18.3		22 16.5	17 21.5				
	32 11.3	35 10.5	52 7.1	Cost of Sales/Inventory	55 6.6	36 10.0				
	76 4.8	90 4.0	80 4.6		72 5.1	81 4.5				
	128 2.9	183 2.0	117 3.1		107 3.4	104 3.5				
	2 189.7	21 17.4	22 16.7	Cost of Sales/Payables	14 26.2	21 17.5				
	28 13.2	46 8.0	41 9.0		29 12.7	32 11.3				
	46 7.9	122 3.0	61 6.0		47 7.8	47 7.8				
	11.6	12.6	12.4	Sales/Working Capital	7.3	7.4				
	31.3	30.3	22.3		24.8	18.6				
	-27.8	-38.8	-50.9		-30.5	27.8				
	12.1	27.6	20.7	EBIT/Interest						
	(28) 3.4	(36) 4.4	(35) 6.8							
	1.5	2.3	2.5							
				Net Profit + Depr., Dep., Amort./Cur. Mat. L/T/D						
	.3	.3	.3	Fixed/Worth	.0	.4				
	.9	.8	.7		.6	1.0				
	-1.7	NM	-2.6		-2.6	NM				
	.7	.8	.7	Debt/Worth	.5	.6				
	6.4	3.3	2.3		2.9	3.3				
	-5.2	-11.6	-7.5		-4.6	NM				
	77.8	145.1	110.9	% Profit Before Taxes/Tangible Net Worth						
	(23) 47.6	(38) 66.4	(32) 56.7							
	7.3	30.5	19.7							
	31.4	30.0	36.6	% Profit Before Taxes/Total Assets	54.0	55.7				
	10.2	9.3	13.0		9.8	13.3				
	2.7	1.6	4.5		-12.1	4.9				
	70.3	69.5	43.8	Sales/Net Fixed Assets	UND	27.2				
	16.7	13.2	17.0		12.1	18.0				
	6.8	5.5	8.4		7.8	14.5				
	5.6	3.8	5.0	Sales/Total Assets	4.3	5.4				
	2.6	2.5	3.4		3.3	3.6				
	1.8	1.7	2.4		2.4	2.7				
	.5	.5	.6	% Depr., Dep., Amort./Sales	.6	.4				
	(25) 1.9	(30) 1.2	(39) 1.6		(10) 2.0	(10) 1.2				
	5.1	2.7	3.1		4.3	3.5				
	7.0	2.7	2.1	% Officers', Directors' Owners' Comp/Sales						
	(13) 9.6	(23) 6.9	(18) 6.0							
	12.4	12.3	11.1							
	629321M	727408M	925626M	Net Sales ($)	7179M	17688M	6719M	42035M	63089M	788916M
	285235M	248819M	367736M	Total Assets ($)	2486M	4967M	3534M	18655M	17110M	320984M

M = $ thousand   MM = $ million
See Pages 9 through 22 for Explanation of Ratios and Data

Current Data Sorted by Assets   Comparative Historical Data

		2 1 3 1 5			3	Type of Statement	4	3 2 1 6 4
1 5 5	2 4 3					Unqualified		
						Reviewed		
						Compiled	1	
						Tax Returns	4	
						Other	4	
0-500M	500M-2MM	2-10MM	10-50MM	50-100MM	100-250MM		4/1/06-3/31/07 ALL	4/1/07-3/31/08 ALL
		3 (4/1-9/30/10)	35 (10/1/10-3/31/11)					
11	9	12	2	1	3	NUMBER OF STATEMENTS	13	16
%	%	%	%	%	%	**ASSETS**	%	%
15.5		13.5				Cash & Equivalents	7.0	10.8
8.3		17.3				Trade Receivables (net)	17.5	10.1
30.3		34.5				Inventory	39.5	33.6
1.5		11.1				All Other Current	5.3	6.1
55.6		76.3				Total Current	69.3	60.6
22.8		12.8				Fixed Assets (net)	21.3	19.9
15.4		7.0				Intangibles (net)	5.2	6.7
6.2		3.9				All Other Non-Current	4.2	12.8
100.0		100.0				Total	100.0	100.0
						LIABILITIES		
5.6		9.6				Notes Payable-Short Term	15.0	12.6
8.3		.9				Cur. Mat.-L.T.D.	2.7	.9
12.1		30.6				Trade Payables	22.5	17.3
.0		.0				Income Taxes Payable	.8	.2
4.0		25.9				All Other Current	8.7	9.8
30.0		67.0				Total Current	49.7	40.8
79.5		5.8				Long-Term Debt	29.0	25.4
.0		.3				Deferred Taxes	.4	.0
23.8		4.8				All Other Non-Current	5.7	26.1
-33.4		22.1				Net Worth	15.3	7.7
100.0		100.0				Total Liabilities & Net Worth	100.0	100.0
						INCOME DATA		
100.0		100.0				Net Sales	100.0	100.0
56.0		46.6				Gross Profit	44.4	51.3
54.3		41.7				Operating Expenses	38.7	50.5
1.8		5.0				Operating Profit	5.7	.8
1.1		-.1				All Other Expenses (net)	1.5	1.7
.6		5.0				Profit Before Taxes	4.2	-.9
						RATIOS		
2.8		2.5					1.9	3.1
2.2		1.4				Current	1.4	1.5
1.1		.8					1.0	1.0
1.7		1.0					.9	1.0
(10) .7		.5				Quick	.4	.3
.2		.1					.2	.1
0 UND		0 824.1					1 357.4	0 UND
0 UND		4 99.8				Sales/Receivables	14 26.6	2 165.7
14 27.0		44 8.3					37 9.9	19 18.8
23 16.0		26 13.9					39 9.3	25 14.4
50 7.3		40 9.0				Cost of Sales/Inventory	65 5.6	73 5.0
91 4.0		64 5.7					156 2.3	153 2.4
0 UND		15 23.6					17 21.1	21 17.0
11 33.1		27 13.7				Cost of Sales/Payables	39 9.3	34 10.6
49 7.4		71 5.1					82 4.5	60 6.1
5.9		5.9					8.6	5.4
11.8		34.2				Sales/Working Capital	22.0	19.5
165.5		NM					177.9	NM
							7.5	7.3
						EBIT/Interest	(11) 2.2	(14) 1.6
							-3.1	-9.6
						Net Profit + Depr., Dep., Amort./Cur. Mat. L/T/D		
.5		.1					.3	.2
-.4		.4				Fixed/Worth	2.2	.4
-.2		NM					-1.4	NM
4.2		.6					1.5	1.0
-3.2		2.0				Debt/Worth	8.5	4.0
-1.8		NM					-6.2	NM
								248.7
						% Profit Before Taxes/Tangible Net Worth		(12) 31.0
								-7.4
34.4		26.9					26.5	21.4
28.2		8.0				% Profit Before Taxes/Total Assets	11.5	3.6
6.1		-5.3					-6.7	-10.9
78.1		68.9					73.5	73.3
16.2		44.3				Sales/Net Fixed Assets	12.7	24.8
6.4		31.9					10.6	6.6
5.3		7.5					4.3	4.9
2.9		4.5				Sales/Total Assets	3.3	2.6
2.4		3.3					2.3	1.2
		.4					.3	.3
		(11) 1.0				% Depr., Dep., Amort./Sales	1.1	(12) 1.1
		1.2					1.7	2.9
						% Officers', Directors' Owners' Comp/Sales		
9662M	35025M	358279M	87585M	69314M	1021204M	Net Sales ($)	640153M	710699M
2380M	9176M	58562M	34971M	61919M	374400M	Total Assets ($)	203043M	341564M

M = $ thousand   MM = $ million
See Pages 9 through 22 for Explanation of Ratios and Data

Comparative Historical Data — Current Data Sorted by Sales

H: 5 / 2 / 2 / 3 / 10	H: 5 / 2 / 3 / 14 / 16	H: 5 / 1 / 6 / 10 / 16	Type of Statement	0-1MM	1-3MM	3-5MM	5-10MM	10-25MM	25MM & OVER
			Unqualified					1	4
			Reviewed						1
			Compiled	1	1	1	2	1	
			Tax Returns	4	2	2	1	1	
			Other	5	1	1	1	3	5
4/1/08-3/31/09 ALL	4/1/09-3/31/10 ALL	4/1/10-3/31/11 ALL		| 3 (4/1-9/30/10) |			| 35 (10/1/10-3/31/11) |		
22	40	38	**NUMBER OF STATEMENTS**	10	4	4	4	6	10
%	%	%	**ASSETS**	%	%	%	%	%	%
11.9	13.3	17.5	Cash & Equivalents	15.1					32.2
13.8	12.5	12.2	Trade Receivables (net)	10.7					6.4
31.5	27.5	27.1	Inventory	26.6					23.1
12.3	7.0	5.6	All Other Current	1.6					6.1
69.6	60.3	62.4	Total Current	53.9					67.8
21.7	20.7	19.2	Fixed Assets (net)	27.9					23.2
5.6	9.2	9.8	Intangibles (net)	11.9					2.3
3.1	9.8	8.6	All Other Non-Current	6.2					6.7
100.0	100.0	100.0	Total	100.0					100.0
			LIABILITIES						
11.4	9.2	8.8	Notes Payable-Short Term	4.5					4.8
3.1	5.5	3.8	Cur. Mat.-L.T.D.	2.6					1.1
18.0	23.7	17.7	Trade Payables	9.2					22.1
.8	.0	.1	Income Taxes Payable	.0					.5
18.8	15.8	13.2	All Other Current	3.5					15.4
52.1	54.3	43.6	Total Current	19.8					43.8
35.7	21.1	34.1	Long-Term Debt	64.6					15.4
.3	.0	.2	Deferred Taxes	.0					.4
15.8	17.3	11.1	All Other Non-Current	27.6					4.4
-3.8	7.3	11.1	Net Worth	-12.0					36.0
100.0	100.0	100.0	Total Liabilties & Net Worth	100.0					100.0
			INCOME DATA						
100.0	100.0	100.0	Net Sales	100.0					100.0
48.5	54.7	52.1	Gross Profit	65.0					61.3
41.1	48.7	47.6	Operating Expenses	61.3					56.0
7.4	6.1	4.6	Operating Profit	3.7					5.3
1.3	1.2	.2	All Other Expenses (net)	1.3					-.4
6.1	4.9	4.4	Profit Before Taxes	2.3					5.7
			RATIOS						
2.2	3.0	2.9		8.9					3.6
1.4	1.5	1.8	Current	2.2					1.9
.9	.9	1.0		1.6					1.1
1.2	1.5	1.8							2.8
.4	.5 (37)	.7	Quick						1.1
.1	.1	.1							.2
1 561.1	0 UND	0 999.8		0 UND					2 186.8
8 45.1	3 136.8	5 70.7	Sales/Receivables	0 UND					6 60.3
47 7.8	17 21.0	23 15.8		40 9.1					10 37.3
47 7.7	26 13.9	26 14.2		36 10.1					33 11.0
81 4.5	59 6.2	51 7.1	Cost of Sales/Inventory	76 4.8					61 6.0
101 3.6	104 3.5	84 4.4		134 2.7					92 4.0
11 32.6	4 103.1	10 35.0		0 UND					15 23.8
32 11.4	24 15.2	31 11.7	Cost of Sales/Payables	30 12.2					41 8.9
62 5.9	60 6.1	52 7.0		121 3.0					98 3.7
6.2	11.2	5.7		3.4					4.1
18.0	27.2	14.2	Sales/Working Capital	8.5					11.7
-70.3	-48.1	NM		52.9					NM
19.1	20.0	9.4							
(15) 4.8	(30) 3.6	(29) 3.3	EBIT/Interest						
.6	1.2	1.5							
			Net Profit + Depr., Dep., Amort./Cur. Mat. L/T/D						
.2	.2	.2		.5					.2
1.3	1.0	.7	Fixed/Worth	-1.6					.4
-.8	-.5	-.3		-.3					NM
1.3	.9	.5		.8					.3
1.7	2.5	3.2	Debt/Worth	-5.1					.5
-4.7	-2.3	-2.7		-1.7					NM
112.8	105.3	89.1	% Profit Before Taxes/Tangible Net Worth						
(13) 50.7	(25) 45.0	(23) 27.0							
21.8	18.7	8.4							
39.4	32.7	35.0	% Profit Before Taxes/Total Assets	37.6					39.0
17.2	16.8	11.5		10.6					23.3
1.7	.6	1.6		-7.3					-3.1
95.1	104.0	74.5	Sales/Net Fixed Assets	20.5					90.1
13.3	25.9	21.7		9.9					14.9
7.9	10.5	12.9		6.0					9.2
5.1	7.1	5.5	Sales/Total Assets	3.2					8.1
3.2	4.0	3.8		2.5					3.2
2.3	2.4	2.2		1.7					2.1
.4	.5	.6	% Depr., Dep., Amort./Sales						
(16) 1.0	(26) 1.0	(26) 1.2							
2.5	2.3	1.7							
	2.7	2.7	% Officers', Directors' Owners' Comp/Sales						
	(14) 9.8	(14) 9.3							
	14.6	19.5							
2716142M	1355877M	1581069M	Net Sales ($)	5914M	7207M	15131M	30320M	100811M	1421686M
963324M	444400M	541408M	Total Assets ($)	2719M	2337M	3914M	6882M	27210M	498346M

	Current Data Sorted by Assets						Type of Statement	Comparative Historical Data	
			1	1		1	Unqualified	4	2
			4				Reviewed		1
1	3		4				Compiled	3	6
9	4		4				Tax Returns	3	2
7	7		4	3	2	2	Other	5	11
	8 (4/1-9/30/10)			45 (10/1/10-3/31/11)				4/1/06-3/31/07	4/1/07-3/31/08
0-500M	500M-2MM		2-10MM	10-50MM	50-100MM	100-250MM		ALL	ALL
17	14		13	4	2	3	NUMBER OF STATEMENTS	15	22
%	%		%	%	%	%	ASSETS	%	%
29.9	11.3		4.9				Cash & Equivalents	11.6	7.5
17.7	16.5		30.0				Trade Receivables (net)	41.0	33.5
27.0	21.8		24.8				Inventory	23.8	20.5
1.7	4.2		1.8				All Other Current	1.0	2.7
76.3	53.8		61.6				Total Current	77.4	64.2
14.1	29.4		25.8				Fixed Assets (net)	12.4	18.9
6.3	8.6		10.5				Intangibles (net)	2.9	9.6
3.3	8.1		2.2				All Other Non-Current	7.2	7.3
100.0	100.0		100.0				Total	100.0	100.0
							LIABILITIES		
28.7	6.6		17.7				Notes Payable-Short Term	11.5	25.7
5.8	2.0		3.1				Cur. Mat.-L.T.D.	6.0	4.1
16.9	24.7		18.8				Trade Payables	17.3	20.3
.3	3.8		.0				Income Taxes Payable	1.3	1.1
16.8	20.1		8.5				All Other Current	8.4	9.5
68.4	57.1		48.1				Total Current	44.5	60.7
32.7	17.0		13.4				Long-Term Debt	9.4	12.1
.0	.0		.3				Deferred Taxes	.2	.4
7.8	.4		.0				All Other Non-Current	6.8	5.2
-8.9	25.5		38.3				Net Worth	39.1	21.6
100.0	100.0		100.0				Total Liabilties & Net Worth	100.0	100.0
							INCOME DATA		
100.0	100.0		100.0				Net Sales	100.0	100.0
53.5	53.0		51.1				Gross Profit	50.4	53.9
50.6	47.3		44.7				Operating Expenses	45.0	50.4
2.9	5.8		6.4				Operating Profit	5.5	3.5
.5	1.1		1.4				All Other Expenses (net)	-.1	1.5
2.4	4.7		5.0				Profit Before Taxes	5.5	1.9
							RATIOS		
8.3	3.6		1.9					3.7	2.4
2.5	1.4		1.2				Current	1.4	1.1
.7	.5		1.1					1.2	.9
3.6	1.0		1.0					3.1	1.3
1.5	.6		.8				Quick	1.1	.9
.5	.2		.6					.7	.4
0 UND	0 UND	29	12.8					30 12.1	22 16.8
1 592.0	15 23.8	37	9.7				Sales/Receivables	44 8.3	37 9.9
29 12.5	27 13.5	54	6.8					78 4.7	71 5.1
0 UND	17 21.4	28	12.8					23 16.2	26 13.8
40 9.2	30 12.2	42	8.8				Cost of Sales/Inventory	46 7.9	37 9.7
82 4.5	58 6.3	78	4.7					110 3.3	81 4.5
0 UND	21 17.8	21	17.3					12 31.0	24 14.9
6 61.2	43 8.4	45	8.1				Cost of Sales/Payables	28 13.1	57 6.5
32 11.4	69 5.3	79	4.6					67 5.5	107 3.4
6.2	11.2		10.7					6.1	8.1
11.2	64.4		20.8				Sales/Working Capital	9.7	68.6
-45.7	-15.6		NM					27.4	-76.5
10.9	28.9		23.4					17.2	22.6
(12) 5.6	(11) 1.6		11.0				EBIT/Interest	(13) 5.9	(21) 4.8
.2	.7		2.2					3.9	-.5
							Net Profit + Depr., Dep., Amort./Cur. Mat. L/T/D		
.1	.1		.2					.1	.3
.5	1.2		.5				Fixed/Worth	.2	.8
-.1	18.7		1.5					.7	NM
.7	.7		.9					.7	1.1
2.1	2.3		1.7				Debt/Worth	2.5	3.0
-2.3	NM		4.9					6.1	NM
95.5	92.9		86.5					46.6	57.2
(11) 21.8	(11) 27.5	(12)	27.1				% Profit Before Taxes/Tangible Net Worth	(14) 27.1	(17) 40.8
1.1	-6.0		6.8					9.4	-8.9
43.9	22.1		27.5					23.4	20.5
14.7	3.0		8.5				% Profit Before Taxes/Total Assets	12.4	5.2
-24.0	-2.1		2.7					5.5	-5.6
250.0	118.6		66.3					106.0	52.0
66.2	27.8		14.4				Sales/Net Fixed Assets	38.4	18.3
18.9	6.6		6.9					12.8	9.0
7.8	5.7		4.4					4.8	4.0
5.1	3.2		2.7				Sales/Total Assets	3.2	2.9
3.8	2.1		1.4					2.1	2.0
			.5					.4	.7
			1.7				% Depr., Dep., Amort./Sales	(10) 1.3	(19) 1.5
			5.4					3.3	4.0
4.8									
(12) 8.5							% Officers', Directors' Owners' Comp/Sales		
17.0									
21986M	59857M		149537M	311838M	138991M	403545M	Net Sales ($)	320112M	331576M
4099M	15905M		55384M	106625M	133938M	450685M	Total Assets ($)	141629M	171495M

M = $ thousand   MM = $ million
See Pages 9 through 22 for Explanation of Ratios and Data

Comparative Historical Data					Type of Statement	Current Data Sorted by Sales					
	6		4		3	Unqualified				1		2
	1		2		4	Reviewed		1		1	1	1
	5		5		8	Compiled		1		4	2	
	8		9		13	Tax Returns	1	1	1	1		
	12		11		25	Other	5	6	1	1		
	4/1/08-		4/1/09-		4/1/10-		3	6	2	4	4	6
	3/31/09		3/31/10		3/31/11			8 (4/1-9/30/10)		45 (10/1/10-3/31/11)		
	ALL		ALL		ALL		0-1MM	1-3MM	3-5MM	5-10MM	10-25MM	25MM & OVER
	32		31		53	NUMBER OF STATEMENTS	9	14	3	11	7	9
	%		%		%	ASSETS	%	%	%	%	%	%
	7.7		8.6		15.8	Cash & Equivalents		20.4		9.2		
	28.8		32.5		20.6	Trade Receivables (net)		17.0		29.6		
	17.9		22.8		22.8	Inventory		15.0		24.8		
	4.6		6.2		2.8	All Other Current		4.4		2.3		
	59.0		70.1		61.9	Total Current		56.8		65.9		
	16.8		18.8		20.9	Fixed Assets (net)		22.1		23.5		
	17.0		5.2		13.2	Intangibles (net)		14.4		5.0		
	7.2		5.9		4.0	All Other Non-Current		6.7		5.6		
	100.0		100.0		100.0	Total		100.0		100.0		
						LIABILITIES						
	13.0		7.9		15.8	Notes Payable-Short Term		6.3		13.4		
	3.4		3.9		4.2	Cur. Mat.-L.T.D.		2.2		1.9		
	21.0		29.2		19.1	Trade Payables		10.1		33.7		
	1.0		1.5		1.3	Income Taxes Payable		.1		4.8		
	9.2		17.4		14.7	All Other Current		20.9		19.3		
	47.5		59.8		55.1	Total Current		39.5		73.0		
	11.2		17.1		20.2	Long-Term Debt		25.3		19.4		
	.6		.3		.7	Deferred Taxes		.0		.3		
	3.5		6.0		3.7	All Other Non-Current		3.0		.4		
	37.1		16.8		20.3	Net Worth		32.1		6.9		
	100.0		100.0		100.0	Total Liabilties & Net Worth		100.0		100.0		
						INCOME DATA						
	100.0		100.0		100.0	Net Sales		100.0		100.0		
	54.9		52.9		52.6	Gross Profit		55.6		52.3		
	49.2		47.6		47.2	Operating Expenses		51.2		46.5		
	5.7		5.2		5.4	Operating Profit		4.4		5.8		
	1.0		1.6		1.5	All Other Expenses (net)		.5		1.3		
	4.7		3.7		3.9	Profit Before Taxes		3.9		4.5		
						RATIOS						
	1.7		2.3		2.5			7.9		2.1		
	1.2		1.4		1.5	Current		2.6		1.5		
	.9		1.0		.8			.7		.7		
	1.3		1.2		1.5			5.2		.9		
	.9	(30)	.8		.9	Quick		1.4		.8		
	.5		.5		.4			.5		.6		
12	30.2	15	24.3	0	UND		0	UND	6	61.0		
42	8.7	52	7.0	24	15.0	Sales/Receivables	15	23.8	30	12.4		
56	6.5	61	5.9	45	8.1		33	11.1	44	8.2		
20	18.3	14	26.6	19	19.5		3	108.8	27	13.7		
40	9.0	43	8.5	40	9.2	Cost of Sales/Inventory	29	12.5	42	8.8		
55	6.7	63	5.8	80	4.6		77	4.7	49	7.5		
27	13.6	26	14.1	12	30.9		0	UND	34	10.8		
60	6.1	50	7.3	37	9.9	Cost of Sales/Payables	15	23.6	45	8.1		
81	4.5	99	3.7	68	5.3		51	7.2	70	5.2		
	9.1		7.9		6.5			6.0		10.9		
	24.0		17.4		20.0	Sales/Working Capital		10.8		15.3		
	-48.0		-135.8		-39.0			-45.7		-17.2		
	34.0		14.9		13.6			22.6		24.6		
(27)	5.9	(25)	4.1	(43)	4.5	EBIT/Interest	(10)	4.3	(10)	6.8		
	2.1		1.7		.9			1.2		2.5		
						Net Profit + Depr., Dep., Amort./Cur. Mat. L/T/D						
	.3		.2		.2			.1		.2		
	.8		.9		.8	Fixed/Worth		.7		.5		
	-.9		-3.0		NM			NM		17.4		
	1.0		1.3		.9			.4		.8		
	2.6		4.3		2.1	Debt/Worth		1.9		1.7		
	-11.7		-13.8		-4.2			-2.6		49.1		
	90.6		95.8		76.1	% Profit Before Taxes/Tangible Net Worth		39.8				
(23)	28.7	(21)	36.5	(38)	24.6		(10)	4.5				
	15.6		13.4		.6			-8.4				
	24.7		23.3		26.4	% Profit Before Taxes/Total Assets		27.0		20.1		
	7.7		8.9		7.4			2.7		6.6		
	2.6		.4		-.9			-4.6		.4		
	97.9		82.3		113.6			139.4		114.7		
	26.3		26.6		24.4	Sales/Net Fixed Assets		46.0		38.9		
	9.3		13.3		8.4			7.5		8.2		
	3.8		4.5		5.7			4.8		5.8		
	2.7		3.4		3.5	Sales/Total Assets		3.3		3.4		
	2.0		2.0		1.8			2.3		1.7		
	.7		.6		.6					.3		
(21)	1.1	(23)	1.2	(37)	1.5	% Depr., Dep., Amort./Sales			(10)	1.1		
	4.3		5.8		3.3					4.3		
	2.3		3.7		3.0			4.2				
(16)	7.0	(16)	5.7	(25)	5.0	% Officers', Directors' Owners' Comp/Sales	(10)	6.9				
	18.8		11.9		10.6			21.2				
	1014568M		1066570M		1085754M	Net Sales ($)	4968M	24835M	11676M	76784M	105798M	861693M
	422442M		405311M		766636M	Total Assets ($)	2526M	11141M	3017M	30260M	41638M	678054M

M = $ thousand   MM = $ million
See Pages 9 through 22 for Explanation of Ratios and Data

Current Data Sorted by Assets   **Comparative Historical Data**

Type of Statement	0-500M	500M-2MM	2-10MM	10-50MM	50-100MM	100-250MM		4/1/06-3/31/07 ALL	4/1/07-3/31/08 ALL
Unqualified		1	7	43	24	18		93	72
Reviewed	3	12	35	51	8			107	75
Compiled	43	67	71	19	1			179	170
Tax Returns	232	175	96	9		1		376	366
Other	75	112	99	61	24	19		254	286
	149 (4/1-9/30/10)			**1,157 (10/1/10-3/31/11)**					
NUMBER OF STATEMENTS	353	367	308	183	57	38		1009	969
ASSETS	%	%	%	%	%	%		%	%
Cash & Equivalents	17.8	10.3	8.2	10.5	9.0	7.4		11.7	11.1
Trade Receivables (net)	4.9	3.9	7.4	8.8	8.2	4.8		7.4	7.1
Inventory	39.7	14.7	12.0	12.6	9.3	11.2		18.9	19.8
All Other Current	1.8	1.5	1.9	2.1	2.5	2.1		2.7	2.0
Total Current	64.2	30.4	29.6	34.0	29.1	25.5		40.7	40.0
Fixed Assets (net)	19.8	53.1	57.9	53.0	58.8	59.3		47.0	47.0
Intangibles (net)	8.2	9.0	5.0	4.6	5.2	8.8		7.2	6.5
All Other Non-Current	7.8	7.6	7.5	8.4	6.9	6.4		5.2	6.5
Total	100.0	100.0	100.0	100.0	100.0	100.0		100.0	100.0
LIABILITIES									
Notes Payable-Short Term	5.3	2.7	3.9	3.8	2.1	1.9		4.6	4.7
Cur. Mat.-L.T.D.	3.6	3.5	4.1	3.8	5.2	3.4		3.0	3.2
Trade Payables	19.6	11.0	14.4	19.6	16.5	15.7		17.7	18.2
Income Taxes Payable	.1	.1	.1	.1	.1	.3		.2	.2
All Other Current	13.4	9.1	6.8	7.9	8.3	6.0		10.9	8.8
Total Current	41.9	26.4	29.3	35.2	32.3	27.2		36.3	35.1
Long-Term Debt	19.6	49.9	46.6	30.1	31.0	35.9		36.8	38.0
Deferred Taxes	.0	.0	.1	.7	1.1	.6		.2	.2
All Other Non-Current	19.7	9.5	5.0	3.8	3.4	6.2		9.0	11.0
Net Worth	18.8	14.2	19.1	30.1	32.2	30.1		17.7	15.6
Total Liabilities & Net Worth	100.0	100.0	100.0	100.0	100.0	100.0		100.0	100.0
INCOME DATA									
Net Sales	100.0	100.0	100.0	100.0	100.0	100.0		100.0	100.0
Gross Profit	13.6	13.1	12.9	11.3	10.8	10.3		12.5	12.7
Operating Expenses	12.9	11.8	11.5	10.5	9.2	8.8		11.7	11.8
Operating Profit	.7	1.3	1.5	.9	1.6	1.5		.7	.9
All Other Expenses (net)	-.4	.3	.5	.0	.1	.2		.1	.3
Profit Before Taxes	1.1	1.0	.9	.9	1.5	1.3		.6	.6
RATIOS									
Current	4.3	3.3	2.2	1.3	1.2	1.1		2.1	2.2
	2.1	1.5	1.2	1.0	.9	.9		1.2	1.2
	1.0	.8	.7	.7	.7	.6		.7	.8
Quick	1.6	1.3	1.1	.8	.7	.6		1.0	1.0
	(349) .6	.5	(307) .5	.5	(182) .5	.5	.4	(1004) .5	(967) .5
	.2	.2	.2	.3	.3	.2		.2	.2
Sales/Receivables	0 UND	0 UND	0 UND	2 213.9	2 166.0	2 189.6		0 UND	0 UND
	0 UND	0 999.8	2 230.6	4 101.8	4 101.4	3 111.2		2 223.1	1 299.5
	1 327.6	2 205.3	4 87.0	7 52.1	6 62.6	4 88.3		5 76.7	5 80.1
Cost of Sales/Inventory	6 58.2	6 64.3	5 75.7	5 71.5	4 92.0	4 89.7		5 75.5	5 69.2
	9 38.9	9 40.9	8 44.5	8 44.6	7 49.3	8 48.3		8 47.1	8 45.1
	14 25.3	14 26.7	12 30.7	12 31.6	10 37.3	11 32.6		12 30.8	12 29.3
Cost of Sales/Payables	0 UND	0 UND	2 211.4	9 40.6	10 36.0	10 35.3		2 168.0	2 227.7
	2 157.3	4 103.3	7 49.1	13 29.0	12 30.1	12 29.9		7 49.9	7 49.8
	8 48.4	9 42.4	13 28.3	15 24.0	14 25.8	15 24.8		13 28.8	13 28.6
Sales/Working Capital	28.9	27.4	38.3	65.2	121.3	164.3		37.6	40.1
	55.0	72.9	210.2	-999.8	-154.1	-159.1		163.6	154.4
	-999.8	-112.6	-53.5	-60.7	-50.2	-52.6		-85.0	-83.3
EBIT/Interest	13.0	4.2	4.3	6.6	7.3	8.2		4.0	3.6
	(151) 3.1	(316) 1.9	(290) 2.0	(172) 2.4	3.2	(37) 4.1		(809) 1.7	(776) 1.7
	.9	.9	.8	1.3	1.8	2.2		.7	.7
Net Profit + Depr., Dep., Amort./Cur. Mat. L/T/D		2.6	3.9	3.6	4.2	4.5		5.3	5.3
		(17) 1.2	(41) 1.7	(48) 1.9	(25) 2.1	(11) 3.6		(107) 3.0	(118) 2.6
		.7	1.3	1.1	1.3	2.4		1.7	1.3
Fixed/Worth	.0	1.3	1.6	1.1	1.5	1.6		.9	.9
	.5	5.8	3.9	2.2	2.6	2.6		3.2	3.4
	-4.0	-5.0	-24.9	5.4	3.8	5.5		-14.5	-14.1
Debt/Worth	.7	1.9	2.0	1.4	1.5	1.7		1.6	1.7
	2.7	9.4	4.8	3.0	2.8	2.5		5.6	5.5
	-10.8	-7.6	-41.8	8.1	5.1	7.6		-16.0	-18.6
% Profit Before Taxes/Tangible Net Worth	100.0	54.2	39.9	24.6	31.2	34.0		44.8	44.2
	(239) 36.5	(235) 23.1	(225) 16.5	(153) 12.6	(52) 17.3	(33) 23.1		(707) 19.2	(678) 18.7
	11.9	3.7	2.9	5.4	7.4	7.9		3.6	4.7
% Profit Before Taxes/Total Assets	27.1	10.3	8.0	7.5	9.4	8.8		9.4	9.1
	9.9	4.2	3.1	3.1	5.3	4.6		3.3	3.0
	.2	-.2	-.5	1.3	1.9	2.5		-1.3	-.9
Sales/Net Fixed Assets	999.8	42.9	23.9	18.4	13.1	10.6		68.9	70.6
	165.7	9.4	6.2	10.9	7.6	7.5		14.6	13.8
	45.8	3.9	2.9	6.0	5.5	5.9		5.3	5.5
Sales/Total Assets	24.5	9.2	8.8	8.2	6.5	6.1		12.8	12.3
	15.4	4.8	4.0	5.7	5.5	5.0		6.3	6.4
	8.7	2.9	2.3	3.7	3.4	4.0		3.5	3.5
% Depr., Dep., Amort./Sales	.1	.5	.6	.6	.7	.7		.5	.5
	(198) .5	(306) 1.1	(280) 1.1	(176) 1.0	(55) 1.1	(26) 1.0		(832) .9	(801) .9
	1.1	1.9	2.0	1.3	1.4	1.1		1.5	1.5
% Officers', Directors' Owners' Comp/Sales	.6	.5	.2	.2				.4	.3
	(169) .9	(166) .9	(128) .5	(52) .3				(398) .8	(389) .7
	1.6	1.6	1.1	.6				1.7	1.6
Net Sales ($)	1300720M	2702348M	9162007M	26230309M	22430867M	33402421M		82182727M	67922918M
Total Assets ($)	86589M	408461M	1384217M	4199119M	3981221M	6045455M		12523505M	11583578M

M = $ thousand   MM = $ million
See Pages 9 through 22 for Explanation of Ratios and Data

Comparative Historical Data

Current Data Sorted by Sales

			Type of Statement			149 (4/1-9/30/10)		1,157 (10/1/10-3/31/11)		
108	93	93	Unqualified			1		2	90	
130	122	109	Reviewed	1		5	5	11	87	
189	175	201	Compiled	3	28	32	52	31	55	
433	603	513	Tax Returns	20	148	147	122	46	30	
362	322	390	Other	12	56	46	82	47	147	

4/1/08-3/31/09 ALL	4/1/09-3/31/10 ALL	4/1/10-3/31/11 ALL		0-1MM	1-3MM	3-5MM	5-10MM	10-25MM	25MM & OVER
1222	1315	1306	**NUMBER OF STATEMENTS**	36	232	231	261	137	409
%	%	%	**ASSETS**	%	%	%	%	%	%
12.6	12.0	11.7	Cash & Equivalents	4.8	11.5	12.7	14.2	11.2	10.5
6.5	5.4	5.9	Trade Receivables (net)	4.0	3.0	3.4	4.2	5.8	10.3
17.4	20.8	20.2	Inventory	23.1	28.3	24.1	18.8	14.7	15.8
2.4	2.0	1.8	All Other Current	.1	1.4	1.6	1.5	2.3	2.5
38.9	40.3	39.6	Total Current	32.0	44.2	41.8	38.6	34.0	39.0
47.2	44.6	45.6	Fixed Assets (net)	47.9	40.8	43.1	45.4	50.8	48.0
6.7	7.4	7.1	Intangibles (net)	14.6	8.7	6.9	8.1	7.1	4.8
7.2	7.7	7.7	All Other Non-Current	5.4	6.3	8.1	7.8	8.1	8.2
100.0	100.0	100.0	Total	100.0	100.0	100.0	100.0	100.0	100.0
			LIABILITIES						
4.4	4.4	3.8	Notes Payable-Short Term	10.1	4.5	2.6	2.0	4.3	4.5
3.3	2.9	3.8	Cur. Mat.-L.T.D.	4.2	4.2	4.2	3.2	4.2	3.7
14.7	15.8	15.7	Trade Payables	9.3	11.8	11.3	13.2	14.9	22.9
.1	.1	.1	Income Taxes Payable	.0	.1	.0	.0	.1	.1
10.2	10.8	9.4	All Other Current	23.3	9.7	8.8	10.1	7.2	8.7
32.8	34.0	32.8	Total Current	46.9	29.9	26.9	28.5	30.7	39.9
37.4	35.9	36.9	Long-Term Debt	34.9	38.6	40.5	42.2	41.7	29.1
.2	.3	.2	Deferred Taxes	.0	.0	.0	.0	.0	.6
9.0	10.9	10.0	All Other Non-Current	34.0	14.5	13.8	9.0	8.8	4.3
20.7	18.9	20.1	Net Worth	-15.7	17.0	18.8	20.3	18.7	26.0
100.0	100.0	100.0	Total Liabilities & Net Worth	100.0	100.0	100.0	100.0	100.0	100.0
			INCOME DATA						
100.0	100.0	100.0	Net Sales	100.0	100.0	100.0	100.0	100.0	100.0
12.3	13.5	12.8	Gross Profit	30.5	15.7	12.5	12.0	12.6	10.3
10.8	12.7	11.7	Operating Expenses	28.4	14.6	11.4	10.4	11.4	9.5
1.4	.8	1.1	Operating Profit	2.1	1.1	1.1	1.6	1.2	.8
.4	.1	.1	All Other Expenses (net)	.1	-.1	.2	.3	.3	.0
1.1	.8	1.0	Profit Before Taxes	2.0	1.2	.9	1.3	.8	.8
			RATIOS						
2.5	2.5	2.8	Current	1.8	5.0	4.0	3.5	2.1	1.4
1.2	1.3	1.3		1.0	2.2	1.8	1.5	1.2	1.0
.8	.8	.8		.3	.9	.8	.9	.7	.7
1.2	1.1	1.1	Quick	.8	1.5	1.6	1.6	1.1	.8
(1219) .6	(1313) .5	(1300) .5		(35) .3	(229) .6	(230) .6	.6	.6	(408) .5
.2	.2	.2		.2	.2	.2	.2	.3	.3
0 UND	0 UND	0 UND	Sales/Receivables	0 UND	0 UND	0 UND	0 UND	0 UND	2 222.6
1 371.5	1 478.2	1 420.9		0 UND	0 UND	0 UND	0 999.8	1 312.8	3 109.8
3 107.8	3 105.5	4 101.1		4 87.0	1 485.5	2 234.5	2 190.3	4 100.7	6 57.4
4 89.8	6 65.3	5 67.4	Cost of Sales/Inventory	10 37.6	9 40.1	7 55.5	5 75.0	4 86.2	5 77.7
7 56.1	9 40.0	9 42.6		34 10.6	13 27.3	9 40.6	7 49.0	6 58.2	8 48.2
10 35.7	14 26.1	13 28.9		44 8.3	19 19.1	12 30.5	10 35.1	10 36.3	11 34.4
1 308.5	1 406.0	1 488.7	Cost of Sales/Payables	0 UND	0 UND	0 UND	0 639.5	2 180.5	8 44.0
5 71.9	6 59.1	6 61.2		1 530.0	1 343.2	2 160.9	1 99.9	6 58.2	12 30.5
9 38.9	12 29.3	12 30.2		19 19.3	8 45.6	7 51.5	8 46.5	11 32.5	15 24.9
40.2	32.2	34.8	Sales/Working Capital	19.8	21.1	28.2	34.1	50.0	69.0
150.3	109.2	115.6		UND	42.7	57.1	80.7	220.2	-999.9
-100.9	-77.9	-81.6		-5.8	-317.7	-155.2	-205.6	-67.0	-60.7
5.7	4.7	5.3	EBIT/Interest	3.7	3.7	5.0	4.4	5.0	7.4
(999) 2.4	(1006) 2.0	(1023) 2.2		(18) 1.5	(145) 1.7	(165) 1.8	(188) 2.1	(122) 1.9	(385) 3.0
1.1	.9	1.0		.5	.6	.9	1.0		1.4
4.3	3.4	3.9	Net Profit + Depr., Dep., Amort./Cur. Mat. L/T/D					3.3	4.2
(151) 2.4	(150) 2.0	(144) 1.9						(20) 1.6	(106) 2.2
1.3	1.3	1.2						1.0	1.2
.8	.7	.7	Fixed/Worth	1.8	.2	.3	.5	1.1	1.1
2.6	2.7	2.9		18.5	3.4	4.0	3.1	3.6	2.2
UND	-15.3	-21.8		-1.3	-8.8	-6.1	-9.2	-3.8	6.7
1.4	1.3	1.4	Debt/Worth	2.4	1.6	1.2	1.3	1.8	1.5
3.9	4.1	4.2		354.9	5.7	5.9	4.5	4.6	3.1
-80.2	-19.4	-28.6		-2.4	-12.3	-17.9	-12.5	-9.5	13.0
56.5	47.8	47.4	% Profit Before Taxes/Tangible Net Worth	97.8	73.0	66.7	53.9	51.3	30.6
(903) 23.8	(943) 20.9	(937) 20.6		(20) 5.3	(157) 26.7	(155) 27.3	(177) 28.3	(90) 18.4	(338) 15.6
7.3	4.9	5.6		-13.0	6.4	6.1	7.3	1.4	5.9
13.2	10.9	11.4	% Profit Before Taxes/Total Assets	10.0	13.2	14.0	13.7	11.0	8.7
5.1	3.9	4.6		2.0	5.3	5.5	5.8	3.4	3.8
.3	.1	.2		-2.8	-1.1	.0	.9	-1.1	1.3
65.9	84.6	81.0	Sales/Net Fixed Assets	172.0	233.1	201.2	133.4	44.5	33.1
15.6	13.6	14.2		7.8	21.1	19.8	13.1	11.5	13.9
6.2	4.9	5.1		1.1	3.4	3.8	4.5	4.6	7.4
13.0	12.2	12.7	Sales/Total Assets	5.7	13.6	16.5	13.4	13.1	10.7
7.2	5.9	6.2		1.6	5.4	7.2	5.9	6.5	6.5
3.9	3.1	3.4		.8	2.7	2.9	3.3	3.4	4.6
.4	.5	.5	% Depr., Dep., Amort./Sales	1.0	.6	.4	.4	.4	.5
(981) .8	(1037) 1.0	(1041) 1.0		(22) 4.0	(160) 1.2	(160) 1.0	(200) 1.1	(121) 1.1	(378) .8
1.4	1.8	1.6		13.3	2.4	1.8	1.8	1.8	1.1
.3	.4	.4	% Officers', Directors' Owners' Comp/Sales	2.4	.7	.6	.4	.3	.2
(467) .6	(572) .8	(531) .7		(10) 4.3	(103) 1.2	(108) .9	(134) .7	(60) .7	(116) .3
1.3	1.6	1.4		5.7	2.2	1.5	1.1	1.2	.6
125639612M	84856215M	95228672M	Net Sales ($)	22252M	474314M	921300M	1852308M	2125313M	89833185M
17069698M	15791819M	16105062M	Total Assets ($)	18160M	146785M	214032M	440112M	466198M	14819775M

© RMA 2011

M = $ thousand   MM = $ million
See Pages 9 through 22 for Explanation of Ratios and Data

Current Data Sorted by Assets   Comparative Historical Data

0-500M	500M-2MM	2-10MM	10-50MM	50-100MM	100-250MM	Type of Statement	4/1/06-3/31/07 ALL	4/1/07-3/31/08 ALL
		1	8	7	6	Unqualified	46	39
	2	8	13	2	2	Reviewed	54	56
7	13	17	6	1	,	Compiled	49	47
20	21	10				Tax Returns	106	83
16	16	31	21	8	9	Other	86	82
	39 (4/1-9/30/10)		206 (10/1/10-3/31/11)					
43	52	67	48	18	17	NUMBER OF STATEMENTS	341	307
%	%	%	%	%	%	ASSETS	%	%
16.3	8.9	9.4	10.5	12.3	5.4	Cash & Equivalents	11.1	10.2
8.7	9.6	12.5	10.6	14.5	7.4	Trade Receivables (net)	9.9	12.4
30.5	16.9	8.3	10.5	9.2	7.2	Inventory	14.6	14.6
8.3	6.2	3.3	4.0	3.2	2.2	All Other Current	1.9	2.2
63.8	41.6	33.5	35.6	39.2	22.2	Total Current	37.5	39.4
23.7	47.4	50.0	52.2	52.2	62.8	Fixed Assets (net)	48.3	47.8
8.5	6.7	5.0	2.8	4.8	5.2	Intangibles (net)	6.3	5.7
4.0	4.4	11.5	9.5	3.7	9.8	All Other Non-Current	7.8	7.1
100.0	100.0	100.0	100.0	100.0	100.0	Total	100.0	100.0
						LIABILITIES		
6.6	3.8	4.5	2.3	2.5	.8	Notes Payable-Short Term	4.4	4.2
2.2	3.4	3.3	3.5	3.7	3.5	Cur. Mat.-L.T.D.	4.2	3.5
21.8	21.5	13.1	17.7	16.3	16.4	Trade Payables	18.3	17.7
.2	.0	.0	.5	.1	.1	Income Taxes Payable	.1	.1
18.3	7.7	5.0	6.2	6.4	5.2	All Other Current	8.8	8.3
49.2	36.4	25.9	30.1	29.0	26.0	Total Current	35.9	33.9
16.1	46.5	42.7	28.4	23.3	32.2	Long-Term Debt	34.5	33.7
.0	.0	.2	.7	.3	.7	Deferred Taxes	.3	.2
17.3	3.0	4.0	4.6	3.1	6.7	All Other Non-Current	7.1	5.7
17.3	14.1	27.1	36.1	44.2	34.4	Net Worth	22.2	26.6
100.0	100.0	100.0	100.0	100.0	100.0	Total Liabilities & Net Worth	100.0	100.0
						INCOME DATA		
100.0	100.0	100.0	100.0	100.0	100.0	Net Sales	100.0	100.0
15.7	13.2	12.8	11.9	9.2	9.3	Gross Profit	12.9	12.2
15.2	12.0	10.6	9.6	7.9	7.7	Operating Expenses	11.5	10.6
.5	1.3	2.2	2.3	1.3	1.6	Operating Profit	1.5	1.5
-.2	.6	.4	1.1	-.2	.2	All Other Expenses (net)	.3	.3
.7	.7	1.9	1.2	1.5	1.4	Profit Before Taxes	1.2	1.3
						RATIOS		
3.0	3.3	2.8	1.6	1.9	1.1		1.8	1.9
1.5	2.0	1.5	1.1	1.3	.9	Current	1.0	1.1
.9	1.0	.9	.9	.9	.6		.7	.8
1.2	1.5	1.5	.9	1.6	.7		1.0	1.0
.7	.8	(65) .9	.6	.8	.5	Quick	(306) .6	.6
.3	.3	.3	.4	.5	.3		.3	.3
0 UND	0 UND	0 999.8	2 204.4	3 131.2	3 118.7		0 999.8	0 999.8
0 UND	2 176.3	3 123.8	4 86.5	6 63.7	4 85.2	Sales/Receivables	3 120.2	3 104.3
3 122.5	7 55.4	10 38.3	9 41.9	12 30.0	7 48.7		7 53.9	9 39.3
4 85.3	6 57.0	3 112.0	3 128.0	4 90.7	3 125.4		4 89.3	4 91.5
8 44.5	9 42.3	6 57.7	6 65.5	7 48.8	4 96.8	Cost of Sales/Inventory	7 52.5	7 53.3
13 28.8	14 26.3	11 33.2	10 36.7	9 39.5	9 42.3		11 32.9	10 35.4
0 UND	0 UND	2 188.3	6 64.5	6 60.7	11 34.0		4 99.6	4 98.7
3 144.1	7 52.2	7 49.0	11 33.9	11 32.0	13 29.1	Cost of Sales/Payables	9 39.9	9 38.9
10 37.9	14 26.2	13 28.4	14 26.5	16 23.0	15 23.6		14 25.4	14 26.0
34.9	23.2	29.4	39.1	17.6	381.5		48.6	47.0
61.8	55.8	68.8	264.7	53.8	-169.2	Sales/Working Capital	580.0	205.4
-999.8	NM	-173.0	-146.3	-192.8	-47.7		-67.7	-82.2
19.0	4.4	5.0	10.8	19.8	10.4		4.7	4.9
(23) 3.2	(43) 1.8	(65) 2.4	(43) 2.6	3.9	4.1	EBIT/Interest	(292) 2.1	(263) 2.1
1.8	.8	1.6	1.2	2.1	2.0		1.0	1.2
		4.6	3.7				4.6	4.4
	(11) 1.1	(13) 1.8				Net Profit + Depr., Dep., Amort./Cur. Mat. L/T/D	(57) 2.3	(53) 2.0
		.9	1.2				1.6	.9
.1	.8	.7	.9	.9	1.6		1.0	.9
.7	3.4	2.2	1.5	1.4	2.4	Fixed/Worth	2.5	2.2
9.5	-20.9	11.1	3.2	2.5	6.8		UND	12.2
.4	1.5	1.4	1.0	.7	1.4		1.7	1.4
2.9	7.7	2.9	2.2	1.7	2.2	Debt/Worth	4.1	3.4
-8.6	-8.5	15.0	4.1	2.9	9.3		-252.0	26.6
46.0	38.9	39.6	17.5	26.6	41.2		45.8	39.7
(30) 31.4	(36) 12.1	(55) 19.7	(45) 12.4	20.0	(16) 25.9	% Profit Before Taxes/Tangible Net Worth	(254) 20.1	(244) 17.7
13.8	-5.9	6.4	2.7	7.9	18.0		5.8	6.0
20.5	7.2	8.4	7.3	10.5	10.6		10.5	10.1
10.6	3.4	4.7	3.3	5.5	6.9	% Profit Before Taxes/Total Assets	4.3	4.6
.7	-1.8	1.9	.5	3.0	3.0		.2	.7
343.5	46.3	31.0	22.8	16.9	12.3		41.2	44.3
91.6	10.0	8.3	10.3	12.4	8.5	Sales/Net Fixed Assets	13.0	12.2
38.0	4.8	3.4	6.2	6.9	4.8		5.7	5.3
24.4	10.2	7.7	9.9	7.5	6.7		11.2	11.0
13.9	5.3	4.4	6.1	5.6	4.8	Sales/Total Assets	6.0	6.4
9.6	3.4	2.3	3.5	3.6	3.5		3.6	3.7
.1	.4	.4	.6	.6			.6	.4
(24) .4	(44) .9	(52) .8	(46) .9	(17) 1.0		% Depr., Dep., Amort./Sales	(300) .9	(265) .9
.8	1.8	1.7	1.2	1.4			1.4	1.3
.5	.2	.3					.3	.3
(24) 1.1	(21) .6	(29) .6				% Officers', Directors' Owners' Comp/Sales	(142) .8	(116) .7
3.1	.9	1.1					1.8	1.2
152973M	465279M	1933738M	7666023M	7225154M	15230305M	Net Sales ($)	29704678M	36904497M
10741M	62768M	325533M	1020175M	1242203M	2978163M	Total Assets ($)	4859743M	5883973M

© RMA 2011

M = $ thousand   MM = $ million
See Pages 9 through 22 for Explanation of Ratios and Data

Comparative Historical Data / Current Data Sorted by Sales

H1	H2	H3	Type of Statement	0-1MM	1-3MM	3-5MM	5-10MM	10-25MM	25MM & OVER
13	25	22	Unqualified		1			1	20
10	31	27	Reviewed		1		1	3	22
20	44	44	Compiled		4	8	11	4	17
61	67	51	Tax Returns	4	11	11	11	9	5
38	107	101	Other	1	9	12	23	9	47
4/1/08-3/31/09 ALL	4/1/09-3/31/10 ALL	4/1/10-3/31/11 ALL		39 (4/1-9/30/10)			206 (10/1/10-3/31/11)		
142	274	245	NUMBER OF STATEMENTS	5	26	31	46	26	111
%	%	%	**ASSETS**	%	%	%	%	%	%
12.1	11.5	10.7	Cash & Equivalents		10.9	10.5	10.9	5.7	11.3
10.1	9.8	10.6	Trade Receivables (net)		9.4	2.9	9.7	7.6	14.4
17.9	14.2	14.4	Inventory		24.3	17.6	16.4	10.6	11.2
2.3	2.9	4.8	All Other Current		7.6	3.2	5.5	4.5	4.2
42.4	38.4	40.6	Total Current		52.1	34.2	42.6	28.5	41.2
43.3	46.3	46.3	Fixed Assets (net)		35.2	51.3	45.4	51.1	46.9
5.0	6.8	5.5	Intangibles (net)		8.8	8.2	5.6	8.2	3.6
9.3	8.5	7.6	All Other Non-Current		3.9	6.3	6.4	12.2	8.3
100.0	100.0	100.0	Total		100.0	100.0	100.0	100.0	100.0
			LIABILITIES						
6.6	4.3	3.9	Notes Payable-Short Term		6.9	1.5	5.8	1.9	3.6
3.8	4.0	3.2	Cur. Mat.-L.T.D.		2.7	2.5	2.6	5.1	3.4
15.3	14.3	17.8	Trade Payables		18.6	11.7	12.1	10.0	23.9
.1	.1	.1	Income Taxes Payable		.0	.3	.0	.0	.2
12.5	9.7	8.3	All Other Current		11.1	11.0	7.2	10.3	6.3
38.1	32.3	33.3	Total Current		39.3	27.1	27.7	27.3	37.5
35.3	35.5	33.9	Long-Term Debt		42.1	44.2	41.0	42.1	24.9
.1	.7	.3	Deferred Taxes		.0	.0	.1	.3	.5
9.2	7.1	6.4	All Other Non-Current		7.4	9.0	4.9	1.7	4.3
17.2	24.3	26.2	Net Worth		11.2	19.7	26.2	28.6	32.7
100.0	100.0	100.0	Total Liabilties & Net Worth		100.0	100.0	100.0	100.0	100.0
			INCOME DATA						
100.0	100.0	100.0	Net Sales		100.0	100.0	100.0	100.0	100.0
12.8	14.1	12.7	Gross Profit		17.2	14.6	16.3	10.9	8.8
11.7	12.4	11.1	Operating Expenses		16.3	13.0	12.4	9.6	7.9
1.1	1.7	1.6	Operating Profit		.9	1.6	3.9	1.3	.9
.3	.3	.4	All Other Expenses (net)		1.8	.0	.9	.0	.0
.7	1.3	1.2	Profit Before Taxes		-.9	1.6	3.0	1.3	.9
			RATIOS						
2.5	2.2	2.4	Current		5.9	5.5	3.4	2.9	1.5
1.2	1.2	1.3			2.1	1.6	2.0	1.3	1.1
.8	.7	.9			.8	1.0	1.2	.7	.8
1.4	1.3	1.2	Quick		1.6	1.7	1.7	1.3	1.0
.6	.6 (243)	.7			.7 (30)	.8 (45)	.9	.6	.6
.3	.3	.4			.3	.2	.4	.3	.4
0 UND	0 734.2	0 UND	Sales/Receivables		0 UND	0 UND	0 UND	0 UND	2 154.7
2 216.7	3 137.8	3 123.8			0 UND	2 193.4	3 143.3	4 85.7	
6 60.4	7 51.6	7 51.9			5 74.9	2 182.4	7 63.6	6 63.6	10 38.3
4 99.4	5 75.6	4 95.6	Cost of Sales/Inventory		5 78.0	7 53.4	5 67.1	3 119.2	3 121.1
6 65.3	8 46.7	7 51.3			10 36.9	10 37.9	8 48.3	6 56.5	5 67.7
10 35.6	12 29.8	11 33.0			17 20.9	13 27.1	11 33.5	10 35.8	9 40.8
1 320.9	2 198.4	2 186.4	Cost of Sales/Payables		0 UND	0 UND	0 UND	1 278.5	7 48.8
5 76.4	9 41.6	9 39.4			5 74.9	2 212.7	4 93.1	4 84.5	11 32.5
10 38.2	14 26.4	13 27.1			14 26.9	8 46.8	13 27.8	11 32.0	15 24.5
39.9	30.4	30.2	Sales/Working Capital		16.2	26.9	18.9	44.5	40.0
145.6	132.1	93.5			30.9	57.6	51.2	146.8	316.0
-125.7	-73.6	-171.3			-64.7	999.8	127.6	-81.4	-107.6
7.0	5.8	7.3	EBIT/Interest		4.3	3.5	5.3	4.3	13.2
(121) 2.3	(243) 2.6	(209) 2.6			(16) 2.0	(23) 2.4	(38) 2.1	(25) 2.4	(104) 3.9
1.2	1.1	1.5			1.0	1.5	1.5	.7	1.7
12.6	3.6	4.8	Net Profit + Depr., Dep., Amort./Cur. Mat. L/T/D						5.3
(18) 5.6	(39) 2.2	(37) 3.1						(26)	3.6
2.3	1.5	1.2							1.3
.6	.9	.7	Fixed/Worth		.1	.7	.7	1.0	.8
1.9	2.1	1.7			2.4	3.0	3.0	1.7	1.5
36.1	21.9	7.6			-4.4	15.0	-13.3	10.5	3.3
1.1	1.4	1.3	Debt/Worth		1.1	2.0	1.3	1.3	1.2
4.1	3.0	2.6			11.7	5.4	7.2	2.3	2.2
291.7	34.6	12.7			-4.5	-150.8	-17.4	22.8	4.3
54.3	39.6	34.1	% Profit Before Taxes/Tangible Net Worth		42.7	55.0	43.5	38.9	26.5
(109) 21.6	(217) 16.0	(200) 17.9			(16) 29.7	(23) 32.1	(33) 21.9	(21) 10.7	(103) 16.4
7.9	4.3	5.9			12.2	18.7	.5	1.7	6.4
13.2	8.7	9.6	% Profit Before Taxes/Total Assets		13.1	11.9	11.7	12.0	8.3
5.2	3.9	4.6			4.5	6.0	5.7	4.5	3.6
.9	.0	1.3			-1.4	2.2	1.0	.1	1.9
87.4	40.3	44.5	Sales/Net Fixed Assets		258.8	69.7	63.1	24.5	30.7
21.2	10.9	13.0			53.3	5.8	9.2	8.6	14.1
6.9	5.7	5.5			4.4	3.0	4.3	5.4	8.0
15.4	9.5	10.4	Sales/Total Assets		16.1	12.8	10.3	7.8	9.9
7.5	5.4	6.0			6.4	3.9	4.7	4.8	6.8
4.3	3.1	3.3			2.2	2.1	2.6	3.1	4.6
.4	.6	.4	% Depr., Dep., Amort./Sales		.3	.4	.4	.7	.4
(120) .7	(218) 1.0	(191) .8			(17) .7	(21) 1.3	(32) .9	(21) 1.2	(97) .7
1.3	1.6	1.4			1.4	1.9	1.9	2.1	1.1
.3	.4	.3	% Officers', Directors' Owners' Comp/Sales		.6	.3	.3	.3	.2
(55) .6	(99) .8	(88) .6			(12) .8	(12) .7	(22) .6	(11) .9	(28) .4
1.0	2.0	1.2			1.5	1.6	1.4	2.1	.5
17696951M	27193363M	32673472M	Net Sales ($)	3608M	53773M	120017M	333555M	415511M	31747008M
2383327M	5501208M	5639583M	Total Assets ($)	875M	29408M	40540M	111756M	108645M	5348359M

M = $ thousand   MM = $ million
See Pages 9 through 22 for Explanation of Ratios and Data

Current Data Sorted by Assets   Comparative Historical Data

Type of Statement

Type of Statement	0-500M	500M-2MM	2-10MM	10-50MM	50-100MM	100-250MM		4/1/06-3/31/07 ALL	4/1/07-3/31/08 ALL
Unqualified		2	4	3		2		6	6
Reviewed	7	3	2	1	1			13	12
Compiled	5	4	1		1			13	10
Tax Returns	1	14	6	2				16	11
Other				2				27	18
	15 (4/1-9/30/10)			44 (10/1/10-3/31/11)					
NUMBER OF STATEMENTS	13	23	13	6	2	2		75	57

	%	%	%	%	%	%		%	%
ASSETS									
Cash & Equivalents	7.5	17.7	8.6					10.6	12.0
Trade Receivables (net)	6.3	5.1	12.1					10.0	6.8
Inventory	60.7	43.3	43.2					50.1	53.2
All Other Current	.5	1.2	5.4					1.7	2.8
Total Current	75.0	67.3	69.3					72.4	74.7
Fixed Assets (net)	14.3	16.3	8.2					19.1	18.7
Intangibles (net)	2.3	.1	5.9					2.2	1.4
All Other Non-Current	8.3	16.3	16.7					6.3	5.2
Total	100.0	100.0	100.0					100.0	100.0
LIABILITIES									
Notes Payable-Short Term	18.1	7.1	9.2					13.9	10.5
Cur. Mat.-L.T.D.	.7	1.3	5.0					2.9	2.4
Trade Payables	24.9	26.0	16.3					23.1	26.1
Income Taxes Payable	.0	.1	.1					.1	1.2
All Other Current	36.5	6.1	11.6					8.7	10.1
Total Current	80.2	40.6	42.2					48.6	50.4
Long-Term Debt	1.7	12.0	2.5					18.4	16.7
Deferred Taxes	.0	.0	.0					.1	.1
All Other Non-Current	1.7	3.1	14.4					7.4	9.3
Net Worth	16.4	44.3	40.8					25.4	23.6
Total Liabilities & Net Worth	100.0	100.0	100.0					100.0	100.0
INCOME DATA									
Net Sales	100.0	100.0	100.0					100.0	100.0
Gross Profit	46.8	55.8	46.7					45.7	46.0
Operating Expenses	46.8	45.9	43.9					42.3	44.0
Operating Profit	.0	9.8	2.8					3.4	2.0
All Other Expenses (net)	.1	.5	.9					.5	1.1
Profit Before Taxes	-.1	9.3	1.9					2.8	.9
RATIOS									
Current	2.9	3.0	3.7					3.2	2.2
	1.4	2.0	1.9					1.8	1.5
	.6	1.2	1.1					1.2	1.1
Quick	.7	1.3	1.5					1.1	.6
	.2	.5	.3					.3	.2
	.0	.2	.1					.1	.1
Sales/Receivables	0 UND	0 UND	0 UND					0 UND	0 UND
	1 262.0	1 593.3	6 62.3					5 68.6	2 186.3
	9 39.3	12 29.2	40 9.2					22 16.5	16 22.4
Cost of Sales/Inventory	88 4.2	133 2.7	129 2.8					84 4.4	96 3.8
	128 2.8	154 2.4	170 2.2					148 2.5	137 2.7
	178 2.0	207 1.8	311 1.2					209 1.7	196 1.9
Cost of Sales/Payables	10 37.7	39 9.3	41 9.0					33 11.2	40 9.2
	52 7.0	77 4.8	57 6.4					50 7.3	61 6.0
	95 3.8	187 1.9	110 3.3					89 4.1	97 3.8
Sales/Working Capital	6.9	4.4	2.1					4.7	6.1
	28.6	6.1	4.0					7.5	11.2
	-7.8	43.9	53.0					26.3	125.9
EBIT/Interest		38.7	5.9					11.5	4.9
		(15) 6.1	(11) 1.1					(65) 2.7	(45) 2.0
		3.4	-4.8					.8	.0
Net Profit + Depr., Dep., Amort./Cur. Mat. L/T/D									
Fixed/Worth	.1	.1	.0					.1	.1
	.5	.4	.2					.4	.5
	-4.9	1.1	NM					1.4	2.2
Debt/Worth	.5	.4	.4					.7	1.1
	1.7	.9	.6					1.8	1.6
	-27.7	2.4	NM					5.6	20.3
% Profit Before Taxes/Tangible Net Worth		88.6	21.3					33.3	25.5
		(20) 16.5	(10) 3.6					(63) 13.1	(44) 9.4
		8.5	-16.4					2.4	.5
% Profit Before Taxes/Total Assets	18.6	32.4	10.9					14.5	12.0
	1.2	8.5	.8					5.3	3.1
	-8.4	4.6	-15.7					-.1	-.3
Sales/Net Fixed Assets	100.8	60.3	172.8					71.3	72.0
	42.4	27.6	30.3					16.6	19.9
	16.2	6.9	11.9					8.0	7.9
Sales/Total Assets	3.9	2.7	2.7					3.2	3.8
	3.5	2.0	1.1					2.4	2.6
	2.6	1.7	.9					1.8	2.0
% Depr., Dep., Amort./Sales		.2						.4	.3
		(17) .7						(61) 1.1	(42) 1.0
		1.5						1.6	1.6
% Officers', Directors' Owners' Comp/Sales								2.6	1.6
								(46) 6.5	(25) 5.4
								11.4	7.9
Net Sales ($)	13049M	54431M	76367M	164252M	174757M	751529M		2053029M	3671737M
Total Assets ($)	3800M	25752M	47534M	115624M	132412M	316208M		783013M	1204920M

© RMA 2011

M = $ thousand   MM = $ million
See Pages 9 through 22 for Explanation of Ratios and Data

Comparative Historical Data | Current Data Sorted by Sales

4/1/08-3/31/09 ALL	4/1/09-3/31/10 ALL	4/1/10-3/31/11 ALL	Type of Statement	0-1MM	1-3MM	3-5MM	5-10MM	10-25MM	25MM & OVER
10	4	2	Unqualified						2
9	7	9	Reviewed		1	3		3	2
10	10	13	Compiled	5	5	1	2		
16	15	11	Tax Returns	5	4	1			1
21	18	24	Other	1	14	2	4	1	2
				| 15 (4/1-9/30/10) |		| 44 (10/1/10-3/31/11) |			
66	54	59	**NUMBER OF STATEMENTS**	11	24	7	6	4	7
%	%	%	**ASSETS**	%	%	%	%	%	%
11.1	12.4	13.5	Cash & Equivalents	6.4	16.7				
7.1	6.4	7.6	Trade Receivables (net)	6.4	4.9				
47.2	50.1	45.1	Inventory	53.0	45.6				
2.6	2.6	1.9	All Other Current	.0	.8				
68.0	71.5	68.1	Total Current	65.9	67.9				
19.5	17.4	15.7	Fixed Assets (net)	24.2	10.2				
3.7	3.0	3.0	Intangibles (net)	2.8	.1				
8.8	8.1	13.2	All Other Non-Current	7.1	21.8				
100.0	100.0	100.0	Total	100.0	100.0				
			LIABILITIES						
8.7	8.4	9.1	Notes Payable-Short Term	23.5	6.7				
2.3	3.0	2.0	Cur. Mat.-L.T.D.	.3	1.5				
24.2	23.6	22.0	Trade Payables	19.5	26.8				
.2	.2	.1	Income Taxes Payable	.0	.0				
10.8	13.8	15.1	All Other Current	13.5	18.5				
46.2	49.0	48.3	Total Current	56.7	53.6				
20.2	15.1	9.3	Long-Term Debt	8.6	5.3				
.0	.1	.0	Deferred Taxes	.0	.0				
6.0	2.9	5.5	All Other Non-Current	5.2	2.2				
27.6	32.8	37.0	Net Worth	29.5	38.9				
100.0	100.0	100.0	Total Liabilities & Net Worth	100.0	100.0				
			INCOME DATA						
100.0	100.0	100.0	Net Sales	100.0	100.0				
48.2	44.6	51.0	Gross Profit	49.0	53.4				
45.5	42.6	45.0	Operating Expenses	47.7	44.9				
2.7	1.9	6.0	Operating Profit	1.3	8.5				
.7	.5	.5	All Other Expenses (net)	.7	-.2				
2.0	1.4	5.5	Profit Before Taxes	.7	8.7				
			RATIOS						
2.5	3.0	3.0	Current	2.2	3.0				
1.8	1.7	1.9		1.2	2.1				
1.1	1.1	1.1		.6	1.2				
.8	.8	1.2	Quick	1.2	.9				
.3	.3	.3		.1	.5				
.1	.1	.1		.1	.2				
0 UND	0 UND	0 UND	Sales/Receivables	0 UND	0 UND				
1 250.7	3 118.0	1 262.0		4 94.3	0 796.5				
12 30.1	12 30.0	15 24.9		18 20.3	5 80.7				
85 4.3	83 4.4	114 3.2	Cost of Sales/Inventory	84 4.3	133 2.8				
138 2.6	143 2.5	148 2.5		146 2.5	152 2.4				
204 1.8	229 1.6	225 1.6		294 1.2	183 2.0				
33 11.0	32 11.2	34 10.6	Cost of Sales/Payables	24 15.1	44 8.3				
59 6.2	49 7.5	60 6.1		51 7.2	71 5.1				
103 3.5	89 4.1	147 2.5		136 2.7	183 2.0				
4.5	4.3	4.2	Sales/Working Capital	5.7	4.0				
9.4	9.0	7.2		28.6	6.4				
24.2	35.6	43.9		-9.2	40.2				
5.7	6.1	21.6	EBIT/Interest		38.7				
(55) 2.1	(45) 3.0	(42) 4.9			(15) 6.1				
-.5	-.6	.7			.8				
			Net Profit + Depr., Dep., Amort./Cur. Mat. L/T/D						
.1	.1	.1	Fixed/Worth	.2	.1				
.6	.5	.4		.6	.1				
2.6	UND	2.2		-7.0	.8				
.8	.7	.4	Debt/Worth	.7	.4				
2.0	1.4	1.0		4.6	.7				
30.3	UND	14.8		-46.8	2.0				
33.6	24.5	59.0	% Profit Before Taxes/Tangible Net Worth		85.8				
(51) 12.0	(41) 13.0	(47) 15.9			(21) 13.9				
-2.2	.6	5.9			3.8				
10.1	9.8	15.2	% Profit Before Taxes/Total Assets	17.6	29.1				
4.5	4.4	6.1		4.6	8.0				
-4.5	-4.6	.8		-7.9	.5				
44.6	53.3	64.0	Sales/Net Fixed Assets	49.7	78.8				
14.7	17.8	27.6		18.5	34.7				
7.7	7.4	10.1		2.6	15.5				
3.0	3.2	3.1	Sales/Total Assets	3.5	3.2				
2.2	2.3	2.0		2.1	2.0				
1.7	1.5	1.3		.7	1.7				
.4	.4	.3	% Depr., Dep., Amort./Sales		.2				
(58) 1.0	(43) .7	(43) .9			(19) .4				
1.9	1.9	1.6			.9				
3.0	1.9	3.4	% Officers', Directors', Owners' Comp/Sales						
(25) 6.3	(21) 5.0	(23) 6.6							
12.7	7.7	11.3							
4100298M	2597531M	1234385M	Net Sales ($)	7382M	47294M	25927M	44296M	52324M	1057162M
1725007M	1084817M	641330M	Total Assets ($)	5226M	28001M	15812M	42649M	23494M	526148M

M = $ thousand   MM = $ million
See Pages 9 through 22 for Explanation of Ratios and Data

Current Data Sorted by Assets | Comparative Historical Data

C1	C2	C3	C4	C5	C6	Type of Statement	4/1/06-3/31/07 ALL	4/1/07-3/31/08 ALL
		2	8	3	1	Unqualified	17	15
		5	5	1		Reviewed	11	12
4	5	5				Compiled	10	12
13	8	4				Tax Returns	27	14
13	3	4	6	1	8	Other	33	31
15 (4/1-9/30/10)			84 (10/1/10-3/31/11)					
0-500M	500M-2MM	2-10MM	10-50MM	50-100MM	100-250MM		ALL	ALL
30	16	20	19	5	9	NUMBER OF STATEMENTS	98	84

0-500M	500M-2MM	2-10MM	10-50MM	50-100MM	100-250MM		ALL	ALL
%	%	%	%	%	%	**ASSETS**	%	%
21.9	11.3	16.2	14.0			Cash & Equivalents	14.4	12.8
4.1	17.3	11.4	11.9			Trade Receivables (net)	8.5	6.5
47.7	35.2	42.2	29.2			Inventory	49.6	51.2
4.3	7.3	2.3	9.6			All Other Current	2.5	3.4
78.0	71.1	72.0	64.7			Total Current	75.1	73.9
12.1	18.0	20.0	22.9			Fixed Assets (net)	17.4	17.9
5.9	1.5	2.9	1.1			Intangibles (net)	1.8	2.9
4.1	9.4	5.1	11.3			All Other Non-Current	5.6	5.3
100.0	100.0	100.0	100.0			Total	100.0	100.0
						LIABILITIES		
24.1	18.9	7.7	2.1			Notes Payable-Short Term	10.7	12.4
9.6	1.5	1.3	1.0			Cur. Mat.-L.T.D.	4.8	6.4
7.9	20.9	31.1	23.4			Trade Payables	17.1	19.6
.2	.0	.9	.0			Income Taxes Payable	.3	.4
18.8	5.7	9.3	15.2			All Other Current	10.0	12.4
60.7	47.1	50.3	41.8			Total Current	42.8	51.3
16.9	18.4	2.7	5.4			Long-Term Debt	10.7	14.0
.0	.0	.0	1.1			Deferred Taxes	.2	.1
13.6	4.4	7.5	6.7			All Other Non-Current	4.1	7.9
8.8	30.0	39.5	45.1			Net Worth	42.1	26.7
100.0	100.0	100.0	100.0			Total Liabilities & Net Worth	100.0	100.0
						INCOME DATA		
100.0	100.0	100.0	100.0			Net Sales	100.0	100.0
51.8	44.9	43.7	42.7			Gross Profit	43.1	44.3
44.6	39.3	41.8	39.9			Operating Expenses	39.5	41.8
7.2	5.6	1.9	2.8			Operating Profit	3.5	2.5
1.4	1.4	.1	.4			All Other Expenses (net)	1.2	.9
5.8	4.2	1.8	2.3			Profit Before Taxes	2.3	1.6
						RATIOS		
5.6	3.2	2.8	2.5			Current	5.3	2.5
2.1	2.2	1.5	1.5				1.9	1.5
1.0	.8	1.1	1.4				1.1	1.2
2.8	1.7	1.1	1.1			Quick	1.5	.8
(29) .5	.4	.8	.5				(97) .4	.3
.1	.1	.1	.2				.1	.1
0 UND	0 UND	0 UND	0 UND			Sales/Receivables	0 UND	0 UND
0 UND	2 243.0	2 209.2	3 134.9				2 235.2	2 199.9
1 399.0	42 8.6	16 23.0	30 12.1				16 23.3	8 47.4
52 7.0	24 14.9	50 7.4	28 13.1			Cost of Sales/Inventory	66 5.5	76 4.8
113 3.2	160 2.3	89 4.1	54 6.7				100 3.6	112 3.3
215 1.7	221 1.7	112 3.3	100 3.6				155 2.3	184 2.0
0 UND	10 36.8	38 9.6	23 15.9			Cost of Sales/Payables	9 41.9	21 17.1
6 64.1	41 8.8	48 7.7	40 9.2				30 12.3	36 10.0
28 13.0	92 4.0	78 4.7	59 6.1				60 6.0	69 5.3
4.2	3.7	7.0	7.2			Sales/Working Capital	4.6	6.0
10.3	8.4	14.6	14.3				9.3	13.7
NM	-12.4	47.1	42.7				75.6	32.5
9.6	14.7	17.9	33.3			EBIT/Interest	23.4	7.7
(21) 3.5	(15) 2.3	(16) 3.2	(17) 12.6				(80) 4.3	(73) 1.8
1.1	.4	.0	1.3				-.5	-1.2
						Net Profit + Depr., Dep., Amort./Cur. Mat. L/T/D	8.4	19.4
							(13) 2.4	(12) 2.6
							.1	1.6
.0	.1	.1	.1			Fixed/Worth	.1	.2
.3	.8	.3	.4				.3	.6
NM	NM	.9	1.2				.9	1.6
.4	.5	.7	.5			Debt/Worth	.5	.9
4.9	2.1	1.5	1.2				1.3	2.0
-11.4	NM	5.3	1.8				3.2	10.8
124.2	60.5	39.8	40.0			% Profit Before Taxes/Tangible Net Worth	45.5	47.3
(21) 35.5	(12) 38.7	(18) 14.6	(18) 15.0				(86) 19.3	(67) 16.0
12.9	6.6	1.0	4.3				-.2	-.6
48.6	13.2	19.7	22.2			% Profit Before Taxes/Total Assets	21.9	19.0
13.9	9.0	7.9	6.7				7.1	3.5
4.1	-1.0	.3	.9				-4.2	-3.6
UND	226.7	83.5	60.9			Sales/Net Fixed Assets	88.2	51.0
36.6	11.5	25.5	21.0				26.1	21.0
15.9	7.6	8.1	8.0				7.8	9.4
4.7	2.7	4.4	5.1			Sales/Total Assets	4.3	4.2
3.2	2.3	3.8	3.3				3.1	2.7
2.3	1.6	2.6	2.6				2.0	2.0
.4	.6	.3	.8			% Depr., Dep., Amort./Sales	.4	.5
(17) .7	(11) 1.6	(18) 1.3	(18) 2.0				(72) .9	(58) 1.2
.9	2.6	1.9	3.2				2.0	2.1
4.5		.5				% Officers', Directors', Owners' Comp/Sales	1.9	1.7
(13) 6.8		(13) 2.8					(45) 4.7	(30) 3.6
11.6		3.9					7.5	5.4
19991M	40662M	321629M	1588047M	1075380M	3768466M	Net Sales ($)	4718795M	4032536M
6191M	17428M	85430M	423258M	384564M	1486942M	Total Assets ($)	1754615M	1531599M

© RMA 2011

M = $ thousand   MM = $ million
See Pages 9 through 22 for Explanation of Ratios and Data

Comparative Historical Data | Current Data Sorted by Sales

			Type of Statement	0-1MM	1-3MM	3-5MM	5-10MM	10-25MM	25MM & OVER
19	16	14	Unqualified					2	12
15	11	11	Reviewed		1	1		3	6
15	9	14	Compiled	5	3	1	1	3	1
23	38	25	Tax Returns	10	8	2	2	3	
31	35	35	Other	10	6	1		3	16
4/1/08-3/31/09 ALL	4/1/09-3/31/10 ALL	4/1/10-3/31/11 ALL		15 (4/1-9/30/10)			84 (10/1/10-3/31/11)		
103	109	99	NUMBER OF STATEMENTS	25	18	5	3	13	35
%	%	%	**ASSETS**	%	%	%	%	%	%
11.7	14.5	16.5	Cash & Equivalents	19.2	18.0			14.2	14.4
8.2	4.9	8.9	Trade Receivables (net)	4.8	6.3			13.1	8.1
42.0	41.3	38.8	Inventory	49.4	40.7			39.3	31.6
4.1	5.5	5.3	All Other Current	7.3	2.4			3.5	6.8
66.1	66.3	69.5	Total Current	80.6	67.5			70.1	60.9
21.7	23.9	19.0	Fixed Assets (net)	12.8	19.4			17.1	25.4
3.4	3.9	4.2	Intangibles (net)	3.8	5.7			2.3	5.3
8.8	5.9	7.3	All Other Non-Current	2.8	7.5			10.5	8.4
100.0	100.0	100.0	Total	100.0	100.0			100.0	100.0
			LIABILITIES						
13.0	8.8	12.6	Notes Payable-Short Term	32.9	10.8			10.3	1.7
3.6	4.8	4.2	Cur. Mat.-L.T.D.	9.2	4.8			.7	2.3
15.5	13.7	18.9	Trade Payables	7.3	16.0			36.5	21.6
.4	.1	.3	Income Taxes Payable	.3	.4			.0	.0
12.0	15.1	13.4	All Other Current	17.8	11.9			10.2	14.4
44.6	42.6	49.3	Total Current	67.5	43.8			57.7	40.0
13.3	15.9	12.1	Long-Term Debt	19.5	16.3			1.4	10.1
.3	.5	.3	Deferred Taxes	.0	.0			.0	.8
6.2	8.0	8.8	All Other Non-Current	16.4	1.0			12.2	6.5
35.6	33.0	29.5	Net Worth	-3.3	38.9			28.6	42.6
100.0	100.0	100.0	Total Liabilties & Net Worth	100.0	100.0			100.0	100.0
			INCOME DATA						
100.0	100.0	100.0	Net Sales	100.0	100.0			100.0	100.0
46.7	46.4	46.4	Gross Profit	51.2	49.1			40.7	43.4
44.5	44.8	41.5	Operating Expenses	44.7	42.5			40.2	39.1
2.2	1.6	4.9	Operating Profit	6.6	6.6			.5	4.3
.8	.9	1.0	All Other Expenses (net)	1.6	1.4			.0	1.0
1.4	.7	3.9	Profit Before Taxes	5.0	5.2			.6	3.3
			RATIOS						
3.3	3.6	3.0		6.0	3.6			2.3	2.2
1.7	1.7	1.7	Current	1.8	2.0			1.3	1.6
1.0	1.1	1.0		.8	.9			1.0	1.1
1.0	1.0	1.2		2.1	1.2			1.0	1.0
(101) .4	.4	(98) .5	Quick	(24) .3	.4			.5	.5
.1	.2	.1		.1	.2			.1	.2
0 UND	0 UND	0 UND		0 UND	0 UND			0 UND	0 999.8
1 479.8	0 999.8	1 446.5	Sales/Receivables	0 UND	0 UND			0 UND	2 213.8
15 24.3	4 94.9	9 39.4		1 627.5	10 37.8			10 35.6	7 55.0
56 6.5	50 7.2	49 7.5		67 5.5	49 7.4			39 9.3	42 8.7
98 3.7	84 4.3	86 4.3	Cost of Sales/Inventory	117 3.1	127 2.9			85 4.3	61 6.0
173 2.1	148 2.5	141 2.6		220 1.7	217 1.7			103 3.5	112 3.3
9 38.7	8 43.6	16 22.9		0 UND	7 49.2			38 9.7	24 15.2
31 11.8	22 17.0	36 10.0	Cost of Sales/Payables	2 156.0	26 14.2			52 7.0	38 9.7
53 6.9	53 6.9	61 6.0		34 10.9	74 4.9			83 4.4	59 6.1
5.4	5.6	5.5		4.1	4.1			7.7	7.3
13.1	12.4	13.1	Sales/Working Capital	10.5	12.1			20.4	13.4
304.4	58.2	136.1		-12.7	-35.4			NM	112.4
4.9	8.8	18.6		10.1	4.8			31.9	28.6
(78) 1.2	(81) 1.4	(81) 4.4	EBIT/Interest	(19) 3.3	(14) 2.3		(11) 1.2	(30) 12.5	
-1.1	-5.1	1.2		1.0	.3			-3.0	3.1
6.2	22.3	12.7							
(15) 1.4	(14) 1.9	(13) 4.1	Net Profit + Depr., Dep., Amort./Cur. Mat. L/T/D						
.8	-.3	1.3							
.1	.2	.1		.0	.1			.1	.3
.6	.6	.5	Fixed/Worth	.5	.3			.2	.6
2.5	2.0	1.6		-.4	3.5			1.2	1.6
.5	.5	.5		.5	.5			1.5	.7
1.2	1.5	1.6	Debt/Worth	12.8	1.8			1.7	1.2
10.3	8.0	14.2		-3.2	NM			6.0	4.0
29.3	33.5	69.2		129.1	71.5			43.3	69.9
(80) 8.5	(90) 12.0	(79) 25.0	% Profit Before Taxes/Tangible Net Worth	(16) 27.8	(14) 33.4		(11) 1.0	(30) 21.1	
-4.8	-7.2	4.8		7.8	2.8			-80.4	6.3
14.2	13.8	22.0		51.9	18.5			18.4	20.7
1.7	3.2	11.3	% Profit Before Taxes/Total Assets	12.4	7.4			.3	11.5
-4.5	-6.9	.9		.1	1.4			-14.9	2.6
42.0	44.9	82.4		UND	44.3			171.9	27.6
16.0	15.1	16.7	Sales/Net Fixed Assets	24.9	14.3			54.1	14.6
7.4	7.3	9.1		11.4	8.2			11.4	8.0
4.1	3.9	4.2		4.4	3.3			4.3	4.8
2.8	2.8	2.9	Sales/Total Assets	2.7	2.3			3.8	3.0
1.8	2.1	2.2		2.0	1.6			2.9	2.4
.4	.6	.5		.4	.6			.1	1.1
(74) 1.1	(80) 1.5	(72) 1.3	% Depr., Dep., Amort./Sales	(16) .7	(11) 1.1		(12) 1.4	(27) 2.0	
2.0	2.6	2.5		1.6	2.5			2.2	3.2
2.0	1.8	1.8		5.3					
(43) 3.0	(43) 4.0	(38) 3.6	% Officers', Directors' Owners' Comp/Sales	(11) 6.8					
5.2	6.1	7.1		11.5					
5455843M	8363772M	6814175M	Net Sales ($)	12358M	30678M	19650M	23757M	201841M	6525891M
2384260M	3128948M	2403813M	Total Assets ($)	4755M	15920M	8514M	6561M	63273M	2304790M

© RMA 2011

M = $ thousand   MM = $ million
See Pages 9 through 22 for Explanation of Ratios and Data

Current Data Sorted by Assets   Comparative Historical Data

						Type of Statement	7	9
			4	5	1	Unqualified	7	9
		6	2	1		Reviewed	16	10
2	4	7	7			Compiled	11	6
8	15	2				Tax Returns	19	16
3	7	10	7	2	6	Other	19	31
	13 (4/1-9/30/10)		79 (10/1/10-3/31/11)				4/1/06-3/31/07	4/1/07-3/31/08
0-500M	500M-2MM	2-10MM	10-50MM	50-100MM	100-250MM		ALL	ALL
13	26	25	13	8	7	NUMBER OF STATEMENTS	72	72
%	%	%	%	%	%	**ASSETS**	%	%
12.6	10.3	10.4	9.8			Cash & Equivalents	11.6	10.6
3.2	2.7	16.4	6.5			Trade Receivables (net)	5.1	7.1
74.4	60.6	51.4	42.8			Inventory	55.8	49.2
2.4	2.0	2.0	3.9			All Other Current	1.5	2.5
92.6	75.6	80.1	62.9			Total Current	74.0	69.3
5.3	18.8	13.5	24.6			Fixed Assets (net)	18.1	20.8
1.1	.8	.8	6.2			Intangibles (net)	2.2	3.0
1.0	4.8	5.6	6.3			All Other Non-Current	5.7	6.9
100.0	100.0	100.0	100.0			Total	100.0	100.0
						LIABILITIES		
24.7	5.8	8.7	7.0			Notes Payable-Short Term	8.7	8.5
2.7	5.8	4.3	.6			Cur. Mat.-L.T.D.	3.0	3.0
22.3	15.2	30.3	15.2			Trade Payables	16.5	17.2
.0	.1	.6	.0			Income Taxes Payable	.3	.3
5.3	4.1	12.6	16.4			All Other Current	12.2	12.3
54.9	31.0	56.4	39.3			Total Current	40.8	41.2
5.9	19.2	2.3	11.9			Long-Term Debt	14.0	15.5
.0	.0	.0	.1			Deferred Taxes	.0	.4
3.6	7.6	6.7	8.3			All Other Non-Current	5.6	7.2
35.6	42.3	34.6	40.5			Net Worth	39.6	35.8
100.0	100.0	100.0	100.0			Total Liabilities & Net Worth	100.0	100.0
						INCOME DATA		
100.0	100.0	100.0	100.0			Net Sales	100.0	100.0
45.0	41.5	39.2	44.5			Gross Profit	41.1	43.5
40.6	36.7	37.1	40.6			Operating Expenses	39.2	40.2
4.4	4.8	2.1	3.8			Operating Profit	2.0	3.3
.4	.8	-.9	.3			All Other Expenses (net)	.4	.8
4.0	3.9	3.0	3.6			Profit Before Taxes	1.6	2.4
						RATIOS		
8.6	3.9	2.5	3.0				3.8	3.0
3.7	2.4	1.4	1.6			Current	1.8	1.7
1.4	1.8	.9	1.2				1.3	1.3
1.2	.7	1.5	1.2				.9	.9
.1	.3	.3	.2			Quick	.3	.3
.0	.1	.1	.1				.2	.1
0 UND	0 UND	0 UND	0 UND				0 UND	0 UND
0 UND	0 UND	3 119.7	2 148.5			Sales/Receivables	1 277.1	1 271.7
3 132.8	5 72.7	20 17.8	7 53.9				8 43.4	10 35.3
73 5.0	95 3.8	60 6.1	53 6.9				75 4.8	64 5.7
123 3.0	191 1.9	115 3.2	95 3.8			Cost of Sales/Inventory	115 3.2	114 3.2
242 1.5	333 1.1	159 2.3	171 2.1				187 1.9	154 2.4
7 51.8	14 25.2	18 20.1	11 33.7				10 35.4	14 25.6
26 14.2	33 11.1	53 6.9	31 11.8			Cost of Sales/Payables	24 15.1	36 10.2
56 6.5	69 5.3	80 4.6	48 7.7				59 6.2	66 5.5
3.7	2.4	7.3	6.3				5.0	6.0
5.7	5.3	12.9	14.0			Sales/Working Capital	8.8	10.6
17.5	10.2	-119.9	65.0				22.9	26.7
	14.4	41.0					11.9	4.7
	(18) 2.8	(22) 2.9				EBIT/Interest	(58) 3.0	(60) 1.8
	1.0	.8					.3	.4
						Net Profit + Depr., Dep.,	3.9	2.5
						Amort./Cur. Mat. L/T/D	(19) 2.6	(15) .2
							1.2	-1.3
.0	.1	.0	.2				.2	.3
.1	.2	.4	.5			Fixed/Worth	.5	.5
1.2	1.2	2.5	3.0				1.4	1.9
.1	.5	.7	.6				.6	.8
1.0	1.7	1.9	2.9			Debt/Worth	1.3	1.7
14.6	5.0	29.9	8.5				4.2	7.2
58.9	30.7	52.7	80.6				41.1	32.9
(11) 18.1	(24) 14.1	(21) 33.3	(12) 32.5			% Profit Before Taxes/Tangible Net Worth	(63) 12.1	(62) 7.9
1.3	1.5	1.4	7.6				-3.2	1.0
36.0	15.2	22.8	19.0				14.1	9.6
24.0	6.3	3.2	6.5			% Profit Before Taxes/Total Assets	4.9	2.8
.9	.4	-.1	4.3				-1.8	-3.0
217.3	85.2	587.0	37.1				46.4	31.8
109.6	20.4	27.2	18.3			Sales/Net Fixed Assets	17.1	15.3
36.0	9.2	12.9	6.9				9.9	8.7
5.8	3.3	5.0	4.9				3.9	3.9
4.5	1.8	3.2	2.8			Sales/Total Assets	2.7	2.7
2.2	1.4	2.3	1.7				2.1	2.0
	.7	.3	.4				.5	.6
	(17) .8	(19) .6	(10) 1.1			% Depr., Dep., Amort./Sales	(61) .8	(60) 1.0
	1.9	.9	1.7				1.3	2.0
	1.4	.8					2.0	2.2
	(13) 3.0	(11) 1.6				% Officers', Directors' Owners' Comp/Sales	(30) 3.8	(26) 3.3
	8.7	2.1					8.3	6.4
12523M	72985M	395147M	1071135M	1888922M	2547117M	Net Sales ($)	3614967M	5269706M
3632M	28993M	105385M	312032M	655164M	1033771M	Total Assets ($)	1410220M	1986777M

© RMA 2011

M = $ thousand   MM = $ million
See Pages 9 through 22 for Explanation of Ratios and Data

Comparative Historical Data | Current Data Sorted by Sales

Type of Statement

4/1/08-3/31/09 ALL	4/1/09-3/31/10 ALL	4/1/10-3/31/11 ALL	Type of Statement	0-1MM	1-3MM	3-5MM	5-10MM	10-25MM	25MM & OVER
10	11	10	Unqualified						10
10	20	9	Reviewed			1	1	2	5
11	13	13	Compiled	1	4	1	3	2	2
27	24	25	Tax Returns	6	13	3	1	2	
35	30	35	Other	5	2	3	6	3	16
					13 (4/1-9/30/10)		79 (10/1/10-3/31/11)		
93	98	92	NUMBER OF STATEMENTS	12	19	8	11	9	33

ASSETS

4/1/08-3/31/09	4/1/09-3/31/10	4/1/10-3/31/11		0-1MM	1-3MM	3-5MM	5-10MM	10-25MM	25MM & OVER
%	%	%		%	%	%	%	%	%
11.0	14.8	11.9	Cash & Equivalents	5.1	10.9		16.9		13.9
9.0	8.2	7.3	Trade Receivables (net)	.4	4.9		12.7		8.3
46.0	46.5	54.1	Inventory	72.7	60.6		41.5		43.9
3.0	2.4	2.4	All Other Current	2.6	2.6		2.4		3.0
69.0	71.9	75.7	Total Current	80.7	79.0		73.5		69.1
20.3	17.2	17.1	Fixed Assets (net)	18.1	13.9		21.6		19.9
1.9	3.3	2.3	Intangibles (net)	.4	1.4		1.2		4.9
8.8	7.6	4.9	All Other Non-Current	.8	5.7		3.8		6.0
100.0	100.0	100.0	Total	100.0	100.0		100.0		100.0

LIABILITIES

4/1/08-3/31/09	4/1/09-3/31/10	4/1/10-3/31/11		0-1MM	1-3MM	3-5MM	5-10MM	10-25MM	25MM & OVER
7.9	7.4	8.8	Notes Payable-Short Term	9.3	17.0		14.5		4.2
2.5	2.9	3.5	Cur. Mat.-L.T.D.	2.5	6.2		.7		.9
19.0	16.3	22.0	Trade Payables	7.0	22.0		22.7		24.8
.2	.3	.3	Income Taxes Payable	.0	.0		1.2		.1
13.0	13.4	9.2	All Other Current	3.9	4.8		7.0		12.6
42.6	40.3	43.6	Total Current	22.8	50.1		46.1		42.7
12.6	14.3	10.8	Long-Term Debt	11.6	17.4		11.1		8.5
.0	.1	.1	Deferred Taxes	.0	.0		.0		.2
6.9	6.2	6.4	All Other Non-Current	6.3	6.2		8.0		5.3
37.9	39.2	39.1	Net Worth	59.3	26.3		34.8		43.2
100.0	100.0	100.0	Total Liabilities & Net Worth	100.0	100.0		100.0		100.0

INCOME DATA

4/1/08-3/31/09	4/1/09-3/31/10	4/1/10-3/31/11		0-1MM	1-3MM	3-5MM	5-10MM	10-25MM	25MM & OVER
100.0	100.0	100.0	Net Sales	100.0	100.0		100.0		100.0
44.3	44.0	42.3	Gross Profit	43.1	44.1		43.0		42.8
41.1	40.9	38.3	Operating Expenses	35.0	40.7		41.6		38.4
3.2	3.1	4.0	Operating Profit	8.1	3.4		1.4		4.4
.7	.2	.2	All Other Expenses (net)	.9	.8		-2.5		.4
2.6	2.8	3.8	Profit Before Taxes	7.2	2.6		3.9		4.0

RATIOS

4/1/08-3/31/09	4/1/09-3/31/10	4/1/10-3/31/11		0-1MM	1-3MM	3-5MM	5-10MM	10-25MM	25MM & OVER
3.2	4.3	3.2	Current	8.6	5.6		3.3		2.5
1.8	2.0	2.0		3.6	2.2		2.0		1.6
1.1	1.2	1.3		2.4	1.3		1.4		1.2
1.0	1.2	1.1	Quick	1.1	.6		1.6		1.0
.5	.6	.3		.1	.3		1.0		.4
.1	.2	.1		.0	.1		.1		.1
0 UND	0 UND	0 UND	Sales/Receivables	0 UND	0 UND		0 UND		0 999.8
1 280.9	0 973.0	1 325.1		0 UND	0 UND		3 128.5		2 183.7
12 29.7	13 28.1	6 58.7		1 298.1	15 24.4		68 5.4		12 30.4
60 6.0	73 5.0	72 5.1	Cost of Sales/Inventory	180 2.0	74 5.0		63 5.8		61 6.0
105 3.5	109 3.4	120 3.1		278 1.3	121 3.0		93 3.9		97 3.7
164 2.2	179 2.0	210 1.7		525 .7	230 1.6		188 1.9		136 2.7
21 17.4	11 32.7	17 22.0	Cost of Sales/Payables	7 53.8	19 19.6		12 30.7		20 17.9
38 9.7	34 10.8	41 9.0		19 19.2	36 10.1		50 7.2		43 8.4
62 5.9	53 6.9	69 5.3		66 5.5	70 5.2		66 5.5		70 5.2
6.0	4.3	4.0	Sales/Working Capital	1.8	3.7		7.1		6.7
12.4	9.0	8.9		3.3	6.1		9.9		13.0
45.2	29.8	30.8		5.3	18.8		14.0		46.8
12.4	12.7	20.2	EBIT/Interest		10.7				23.4
(75) 3.3	(73) 4.0	(71) 6.0			(13) 4.3				(28) 12.3
.6	1.2	1.4			1.2				3.4
14.1	8.3	10.4	Net Profit + Depr., Dep., Amort./Cur. Mat. L/T/D						
(10) 2.3	(12) 1.5	(13) 2.2							
-1.0	-3.9	.3							
.1	.1	.1	Fixed/Worth	.0	.1		.2		.2
.4	.4	.3		.1	.4		.5		.5
1.0	1.1	1.4		.2	2.2		4.7		1.0
.7	.5	.5	Debt/Worth	.2	.2		.5		.6
1.4	1.2	1.5		.8	2.8		1.7		1.4
2.6	5.4	5.2		1.6	26.5		16.5		4.1
53.2	58.0	50.6	% Profit Before Taxes/Tangible Net Worth	40.8	31.2		55.8		50.7
(83) 13.5	(84) 15.2	(82) 22.5		9.2	(15) 16.8		(10) 7.0		(31) 30.7
1.1	4.0	3.7		2.3	.0		-48.6		12.8
18.7	16.7	19.4	% Profit Before Taxes/Total Assets	29.3	22.3		20.2		15.4
5.8	5.4	7.5		5.7	5.2		2.9		8.9
-.3	.7	1.2		1.4	.0		-.6		5.3
55.5	114.0	92.8	Sales/Net Fixed Assets	130.6	112.4		38.9		30.9
18.3	21.1	24.9		56.3	22.6		27.2		17.8
9.0	10.5	10.2		12.2	15.3		6.6		9.1
4.1	4.2	4.4	Sales/Total Assets	2.7	4.9		3.1		4.8
2.6	2.8	2.6		1.6	2.2		2.4		3.3
2.0	1.7	1.7		.9	1.5		1.6		1.8
.6	.5	.4	% Depr., Dep., Amort./Sales		.6				.5
(66) 1.2	(68) 1.1	(67) .7			(14) .9				(26) .9
2.2	1.6	1.5			1.7				2.0
2.1	1.3	1.1	% Officers', Directors', Owners' Comp/Sales		2.2				
(40) 4.1	(37) 3.8	(30) 2.6			(11) 3.5				
7.7	6.7	5.6			5.2				
5043540M	3894911M	5987829M	Net Sales ($)	7954M	33875M	31246M	84329M	141766M	5688659M
1671505M	1358963M	2138977M	Total Assets ($)	6936M	15294M	13270M	46544M	31031M	2025902M

M = $ thousand   MM = $ million
See Pages 9 through 22 for Explanation of Ratios and Data

Current Data Sorted by Assets　　　　　　　　　　　Comparative Historical Data

						Type of Statement		
		1	1	2	1	Unqualified	2	11
	2	6				Reviewed	8	7
2	4	3				Compiled	16	7
10	7	8				Tax Returns	18	18
7	8	5				Other	21	9
	6 (4/1-9/30/10)		67 (10/1/10-3/31/11)				4/1/06-3/31/07 ALL	4/1/07-3/31/08 ALL
0-500M	500M-2MM	2-10MM	10-50MM	50-100MM	100-250MM	NUMBER OF STATEMENTS	65	52
19	21	23	3	5	2			

0-500M	500M-2MM	2-10MM	10-50MM	50-100MM	100-250MM		4/1/06-3/31/07 ALL	4/1/07-3/31/08 ALL
%	%	%	%	%	%	**ASSETS**	%	%
7.6	12.8	15.7				Cash & Equivalents	15.4	13.4
11.2	15.6	15.1				Trade Receivables (net)	12.6	14.3
59.8	42.9	41.4				Inventory	42.7	44.1
.9	.6	.9				All Other Current	2.3	1.9
79.6	71.9	73.1				Total Current	73.0	73.7
12.5	20.6	12.7				Fixed Assets (net)	13.1	14.3
3.0	1.7	2.2				Intangibles (net)	4.2	5.9
5.0	5.7	12.0				All Other Non-Current	9.6	6.2
100.0	100.0	100.0				Total	100.0	100.0
						LIABILITIES		
11.8	9.1	1.1				Notes Payable-Short Term	9.9	9.5
5.3	3.1	1.4				Cur. Mat.-L.T.D.	.8	2.2
15.9	11.6	28.8				Trade Payables	20.8	22.2
.0	.1	.4				Income Taxes Payable	.2	.5
8.3	8.5	7.3				All Other Current	12.3	10.0
41.3	32.2	39.0				Total Current	44.1	44.4
27.9	20.3	16.5				Long-Term Debt	10.6	10.6
.0	.0	.0				Deferred Taxes	.1	.3
14.1	15.1	5.6				All Other Non-Current	7.4	7.0
16.7	32.3	38.9				Net Worth	37.8	37.7
100.0	100.0	100.0				Total Liabilities & Net Worth	100.0	100.0
						INCOME DATA		
100.0	100.0	100.0				Net Sales	100.0	100.0
48.6	49.5	40.3				Gross Profit	45.1	45.7
44.0	45.0	35.9				Operating Expenses	41.7	40.7
4.6	4.5	4.4				Operating Profit	3.5	5.1
1.3	1.7	.0				All Other Expenses (net)	.6	1.0
3.2	2.9	4.4				Profit Before Taxes	2.9	4.1
						RATIOS		
6.7	8.6	3.5					2.9	2.8
2.7	2.1	1.9				Current	2.0	1.9
.7	1.6	1.1					1.3	1.2
.7	1.8	1.6					1.3	1.2
.4	.8	.9				Quick	.6	.5
.3	.3	.2					.2	.2
0 UND	0 UND	0 999.8					0 UND	0 UND
0 UND	5 79.8	8 48.3				Sales/Receivables	3 109.2	7 49.3
15 25.0	42 8.6	32 11.4					36 10.2	32 11.5
58 6.3	92 4.0	42 8.8					58 6.3	74 5.0
111 3.3	133 2.8	102 3.6				Cost of Sales/Inventory	107 3.4	110 3.3
243 1.5	213 1.7	142 2.6					215 1.7	190 1.9
0 UND	8 44.3	31 11.9					21 17.7	17 21.7
16 22.3	32 11.6	63 5.8				Cost of Sales/Payables	50 7.3	54 6.8
45 8.1	62 5.9	76 4.8					75 4.9	69 5.3
4.8	4.1	4.1					5.1	4.7
7.5	6.4	7.9				Sales/Working Capital	7.4	9.2
-35.0	9.2	32.7					24.1	19.6
26.5	9.2	22.8					22.0	13.9
(14) 5.0	(15) 2.5	(15) 9.2				EBIT/Interest	(56) 4.1	(44) 4.1
-.7	.2	2.5					.7	1.5
						Net Profit + Depr., Dep., Amort./Cur. Mat. L/T/D		
.1	.2	.1					.1	.1
.3	.4	.2				Fixed/Worth	.2	.3
-.3	NM	.8					1.4	2.4
.3	.7	.7					.7	.5
1.5	1.7	2.2				Debt/Worth	1.4	1.8
-4.5	NM	4.0					7.4	10.6
59.6	45.5	48.0					66.3	57.3
(11) 43.1	(16) 19.1	(22) 22.8				% Profit Before Taxes/Tangible Net Worth	(56) 18.3	(44) 17.5
18.8	5.1	8.7					4.3	5.6
38.0	18.0	19.1					23.5	22.9
8.5	9.3	9.6				% Profit Before Taxes/Total Assets	6.1	6.6
-7.5	-.8	1.9					-.1	1.3
203.0	69.6	130.2					107.8	72.8
46.7	18.4	31.4				Sales/Net Fixed Assets	26.8	26.0
18.6	6.3	13.5					14.8	12.2
6.7	2.9	3.6					3.9	3.7
3.8	2.2	2.9				Sales/Total Assets	2.6	2.6
1.9	1.7	1.9					1.6	1.8
.3	.2	.2					.4	.6
(11) 1.2	(15) 1.1	(18) .5				% Depr., Dep., Amort./Sales	(50) .9	(39) .9
2.1	1.4	1.9					1.5	2.1
3.0	2.0	2.0					2.2	2.2
(10) 5.3	(11) 5.7	(10) 2.8				% Officers', Directors' Owners' Comp/Sales	(33) 4.4	(17) 3.1
7.6	7.6	3.6					9.2	7.6
18405M	60718M	283905M	154268M	539205M	352238M	Net Sales ($)	1518311M	1541693M
4358M	22963M	96375M	51804M	347398M	311760M	Total Assets ($)	725533M	740768M

© RMA 2011

M = $ thousand　　MM = $ million
See Pages 9 through 22 for Explanation of Ratios and Data

Comparative Historical Data | Current Data Sorted by Sales

			Type of Statement						
5	4	5	Unqualified		1		1	1	4
7	6	8	Reviewed					4	2
7	3	9	Compiled		3	2	3		1
17	35	25	Tax Returns	7	8	3	5	2	
20	22	26	Other	6	7	1	5	1	6
4/1/08-3/31/09 ALL	4/1/09-3/31/10 ALL	4/1/10-3/31/11 ALL		0-1MM	6 (4/1-9/30/10) 1-3MM	3-5MM	67 (10/1/10-3/31/11) 5-10MM	10-25MM	25MM & OVER
56	70	73	NUMBER OF STATEMENTS	13	19	6	14	8	13
%	%	%	ASSETS	%	%	%	%	%	%
12.9	12.0	11.3	Cash & Equivalents	8.7	11.3		12.8		5.4
10.7	11.0	12.7	Trade Receivables (net)	1.4	18.2		17.3		4.8
42.3	48.1	45.2	Inventory	61.2	44.9		49.4		38.5
3.7	2.4	1.7	All Other Current	.2	1.4		.2		6.1
69.6	73.4	71.0	Total Current	71.5	75.8		79.8		54.8
17.4	14.7	17.8	Fixed Assets (net)	22.7	15.2		9.5		27.5
3.7	4.3	3.5	Intangibles (net)	1.9	2.3		3.3		8.7
9.4	7.6	7.8	All Other Non-Current	4.0	6.7		7.4		9.1
100.0	100.0	100.0	Total	100.0	100.0		100.0		100.0
			LIABILITIES						
8.7	14.1	6.4	Notes Payable-Short Term	11.1	11.2		1.6		3.3
2.2	2.6	3.1	Cur. Mat.-L.T.D.	8.9	.3		2.7		2.1
16.3	24.3	18.2	Trade Payables	6.0	18.1		24.6		19.2
.1	.3	.4	Income Taxes Payable	.0	.1		.3		1.7
9.6	8.7	9.3	All Other Current	7.4	8.1		5.9		17.2
36.9	50.1	37.5	Total Current	33.4	37.8		35.0		43.4
12.9	13.3	22.1	Long-Term Debt	43.0	15.3		15.9		21.8
.2	.3	.3	Deferred Taxes	.0	.0		.0		1.7
8.1	10.5	12.1	All Other Non-Current	15.6	18.9		8.8		12.9
42.0	25.8	28.1	Net Worth	7.9	28.0		40.2		20.2
100.0	100.0	100.0	Total Liabilities & Net Worth	100.0	100.0		100.0		100.0
			INCOME DATA						
100.0	100.0	100.0	Net Sales	100.0	100.0		100.0		100.0
48.9	48.0	46.8	Gross Profit	54.6	45.7		39.8		48.6
47.1	45.7	42.4	Operating Expenses	48.7	42.2		35.9		43.9
1.7	2.4	4.4	Operating Profit	6.0	3.5		3.9		4.6
.5	.7	.9	All Other Expenses (net)	2.1	1.5		-.5		.6
1.3	1.6	3.5	Profit Before Taxes	3.9	1.9		4.4		4.0
			RATIOS						
4.4	3.4	4.7		7.2	12.9		3.8		2.1
2.3	1.7	1.9	Current	2.3	3.8		2.3		1.2
1.2	.9	1.2		1.7	1.2		1.8		.9
1.0	.9	1.3		.5	3.1		2.5		.5
.5 (69)	.4	.5	Quick	.3	.7		1.1		.2
.2	.1	.2		.2	.4		.3		.1
0 UND	0 UND	0 UND		0 UND	0 UND		1 520.9		0 999.8
4 85.5	2 152.9	3 104.7	Sales/Receivables	0 UND	8 45.7		9 42.7		6 62.4
28 13.2	20 18.6	23 15.6		0 UND	45 8.1		41 9.0		12 29.3
80 4.6	61 6.0	72 5.1		108 3.4	66 5.5		69 5.3		75 4.9
119 3.1	124 2.9	114 3.2	Cost of Sales/Inventory	235 1.6	110 3.3		106 3.4		114 3.2
197 1.9	268 1.4	182 2.0		404 .9	147 2.5		140 2.6		172 2.1
7 54.5	11 33.0	8 44.3		0 UND	2 220.8		29 12.5		35 10.5
24 15.3	38 9.5	41 9.0	Cost of Sales/Payables	16 22.3	18 20.8		49 7.4		44 8.4
55 6.7	76 4.8	67 5.5		43 8.6	75 4.8		67 5.5		67 5.5
4.4	3.6	4.3		3.7	4.2		3.9		6.7
6.9	8.5	7.6	Sales/Working Capital	7.1	5.8		7.5		17.5
50.1	-82.0	27.3		13.7	36.3		8.3		-139.9
17.4	10.1	16.3			9.6		354.8		17.5
(43) 2.1	(53) 3.1	(54) 5.4	EBIT/Interest	(14) 1.6		(10) 9.9		(12) 10.4
-2.1	-.6	.3			-2.0		2.2		-.3
			Net Profit + Depr., Dep., Amort./Cur. Mat. L/T/D						
.1	.1	.1		.1	.1		.1		.4
.4	.4	.5	Fixed/Worth	1.9	.4		.2		1.1
1.0	NM	NM		-.2	-.5		.7		-4.8
.4	.5	.6		1.0	.3		.4		2.4
1.0	2.2	2.4	Debt/Worth	6.6	1.5		1.7		3.8
12.9	NM	NM		-4.9	-5.3		4.4		-9.6
47.5	57.2	47.3	% Profit Before Taxes/Tangible Net Worth		49.6		57.8		
(47) 22.2	(53) 20.0	(55) 23.0		(13) 19.9		(13) 21.9		
-13.3	-4.7	9.2			7.5		6.9		
26.1	24.6	19.4	% Profit Before Taxes/Total Assets	25.7	24.1		17.8		18.8
3.6	6.5	7.8		8.5	6.8		8.6		4.6
-7.7	-3.6	.0		-7.5	-7.5		1.7		-1.7
60.8	103.1	89.9		106.3	178.6		169.6		19.7
17.6	30.9	22.7	Sales/Net Fixed Assets	25.9	27.4		47.2		7.6
9.1	11.8	8.1		3.5	14.7		13.6		5.1
3.7	4.1	3.8		4.6	4.1		3.7		3.5
2.4	2.4	2.5	Sales/Total Assets	1.9	2.5		3.0		2.3
1.7	1.7	1.7		1.2	1.9		2.0		1.2
.3	.4	.3			.2		.2		
(42) 1.5	(52) .7	(52) 1.2	% Depr., Dep., Amort./Sales	(10) 1.1		(13) .3		
2.9	1.9	2.3			1.4		1.5		
2.0	1.9	2.3							
(22) 3.5	(30) 5.0	(31) 3.4	% Officers', Directors' Owners' Comp/Sales						
5.5	10.3	6.8							
1746798M	916192M	1408739M	Net Sales ($)	6539M	31270M	22372M	94997M	125041M	1128520M
1001515M	526226M	834658M	Total Assets ($)	3585M	11710M	12386M	37248M	40555M	729174M

© RMA 2011

M = $ thousand   MM = $ million
See Pages 9 through 22 for Explanation of Ratios and Data

Current Data Sorted by Assets   Comparative Historical Data

0-500M	500M-2MM	2-10MM	10-50MM	50-100MM	100-250MM	Type of Statement	4/1/06-3/31/07 ALL	4/1/07-3/31/08 ALL
1		2	3	1	2	Unqualified	12	11
1	4	16	4			Reviewed	21	17
2	11	2	2			Compiled	24	20
15	19	17	1			Tax Returns	56	45
12	15	18	6	5		Other	44	56
	30 (4/1-9/30/10)		129 (10/1/10-3/31/11)					
31	**49**	**55**	**16**	**6**	**2**	**NUMBER OF STATEMENTS**	**157**	**149**
%	%	%	%	%	%	**ASSETS**	%	%
9.6	12.3	10.5	6.7			Cash & Equivalents	9.5	8.7
11.0	10.4	11.6	13.6			Trade Receivables (net)	9.4	10.3
54.9	48.9	44.3	46.3			Inventory	51.9	48.7
2.1	1.1	3.6	1.0			All Other Current	2.2	2.8
77.6	72.8	70.0	67.6			Total Current	73.0	70.5
9.7	16.6	20.2	17.8			Fixed Assets (net)	18.1	18.8
7.0	2.5	4.2	9.0			Intangibles (net)	3.1	4.8
5.7	8.1	5.6	5.7			All Other Non-Current	5.8	6.0
100.0	100.0	100.0	100.0			Total	100.0	100.0
						LIABILITIES		
22.4	11.4	8.7	7.5			Notes Payable-Short Term	14.7	14.6
2.5	1.7	3.0	6.2			Cur. Mat.-L.T.D.	2.7	3.5
20.6	23.6	21.1	20.3			Trade Payables	18.8	16.7
.2	.1	.1	.0			Income Taxes Payable	.3	.1
7.0	8.4	9.1	8.5			All Other Current	11.1	11.9
52.7	45.2	42.1	42.5			Total Current	47.7	46.8
9.2	13.9	9.0	16.8			Long-Term Debt	12.2	16.3
.0	.0	.1	.2			Deferred Taxes	.1	.3
10.9	8.2	7.3	11.1			All Other Non-Current	4.0	8.7
27.2	32.6	41.5	29.4			Net Worth	35.9	27.9
100.0	100.0	100.0	100.0			Total Liabilties & Net Worth	100.0	100.0
						INCOME DATA		
100.0	100.0	100.0	100.0			Net Sales	100.0	100.0
51.4	43.7	48.5	49.0			Gross Profit	46.2	45.7
44.3	38.7	45.8	43.2			Operating Expenses	41.4	42.1
7.1	5.0	2.7	5.8			Operating Profit	4.7	3.6
.9	1.2	.4	.9			All Other Expenses (net)	.8	1.4
6.2	3.8	2.2	4.9			Profit Before Taxes	3.9	2.2
						RATIOS		
3.3	3.0	2.4	3.3			Current	3.0	3.0
2.1	1.7	1.7	1.9				1.6	1.7
.9	1.1	1.2	1.1				1.1	1.1
1.0	1.1	1.0	.9			Quick	.7	.8
.4	.4	.3	.4				(156) .3	(148) .3
.1	.1	.2	.0				.1	.1
0 UND	0 UND	0 UND	3 138.2			Sales/Receivables	0 UND	0 UND
0 UND	3 134.0	3 104.7	10 37.2				2 196.0	2 155.9
18 20.1	20 18.6	32 11.3	53 6.9				25 14.8	28 13.2
62 5.9	67 5.4	73 5.0	152 2.4			Cost of Sales/Inventory	74 4.9	81 4.5
118 3.1	129 2.8	126 2.9	181 2.0				125 2.9	139 2.6
179 2.0	187 2.0	218 1.7	238 1.5				191 1.9	222 1.6
6 65.6	21 17.1	28 12.9	27 13.4			Cost of Sales/Payables	14 25.8	14 26.4
24 15.0	49 7.5	47 7.8	64 5.7				37 10.0	36 10.1
69 5.3	77 4.7	93 3.9	100 3.7				59 6.2	68 5.4
5.3	4.2	5.2	4.0			Sales/Working Capital	4.9	4.9
10.4	9.8	8.7	6.1				10.1	10.0
-45.6	95.8	22.4	83.7				56.7	65.7
19.4	20.5	8.4	7.0			EBIT/Interest	11.6	8.0
(22) 6.2	(39) 4.5	(47) 2.5	(15) 2.7				(136) 3.8	(132) 2.4
1.0	1.0	.5	1.8				1.4	.8
						Net Profit + Depr., Dep., Amort./Cur. Mat. L/T/D	6.3	10.9
							(19) 3.7	(24) 2.4
							1.1	1.2
.0	.0	.1	.1			Fixed/Worth	.1	.2
.3	.2	.5	.3				.4	.6
62.0	2.0	1.5	2.5				1.6	10.5
.5	.7	.6	.9			Debt/Worth	.6	.8
2.4	2.0	1.3	1.6				1.8	3.1
-21.4	45.8	6.3	8.0				6.0	59.1
100.8	71.5	24.7	34.1			% Profit Before Taxes/Tangible Net Worth	69.3	54.1
(23) 71.8	(40) 20.9	(48) 9.6	(14) 20.5				(134) 27.2	(118) 21.0
8.0	5.5	1.2	8.7				4.0	3.1
30.8	17.8	8.4	8.9			% Profit Before Taxes/Total Assets	19.4	15.7
13.9	5.3	2.2	5.2				6.8	6.5
.8	.5	-.5	2.0				.9	-.7
284.0	192.8	51.9	37.4			Sales/Net Fixed Assets	65.6	44.6
52.7	31.0	17.1	20.8				25.4	19.7
17.9	12.7	8.8	10.4				10.3	8.7
4.8	4.0	3.1	2.8			Sales/Total Assets	3.7	3.5
3.5	2.8	2.4	2.0				2.8	2.5
2.4	1.7	1.7	.9				1.8	1.7
.6	.2	.6	.8			% Depr., Dep., Amort./Sales	.4	.5
(15) .7	(29) .7	(48) 1.0	(14) 1.2				(125) 1.0	(115) 1.0
2.2	1.7	2.3	2.7				1.9	1.8
2.5	2.4	2.0				% Officers', Directors' Owners' Comp/Sales	2.2	2.3
(19) 4.5	(26) 4.5	(29) 3.4					(79) 4.5	(78) 4.0
6.6	6.3	5.4					6.5	6.7
32588M	169666M	602457M	641382M	933895M	608069M	Net Sales ($)	1693187M	3091418M
9512M	57265M	247056M	323100M	496961M	271897M	Total Assets ($)	701886M	1344396M

© RMA 2011

M = $ thousand   MM = $ million
See Pages 9 through 22 for Explanation of Ratios and Data

Comparative Historical Data				Current Data Sorted by Sales					

			Type of Statement						
16	19	9	Unqualified		1			2	6
21	19	25	Reviewed		5	2	5	9	4
17	22	17	Compiled	3	5	1	6	1	1
34	54	52	Tax Returns	9	21	4	15	2	1
42	55	56	Other	9	7	11	9	11	9
4/1/08-3/31/09 ALL	4/1/09-3/31/10 ALL	4/1/10-3/31/11 ALL		0-1MM	30 (4/1-9/30/10) 1-3MM	3-5MM	129 (10/1/10-3/31/11) 5-10MM	10-25MM	25MM & OVER
130	169	159	NUMBER OF STATEMENTS	21	39	18	35	25	21
%	%	%	ASSETS	%	%	%	%	%	%
8.4	11.1	10.4	Cash & Equivalents	6.0	10.3	12.0	14.2	8.3	9.9
12.7	10.9	10.9	Trade Receivables (net)	10.4	11.5	5.9	12.0	12.8	10.4
46.4	44.2	47.7	Inventory	49.4	53.4	46.3	42.7	46.6	46.4
2.4	2.0	2.3	All Other Current	1.7	1.0	1.5	4.2	2.5	2.6
69.9	68.2	71.3	Total Current	67.5	76.1	65.7	73.1	70.2	69.4
19.3	19.9	17.3	Fixed Assets (net)	16.9	12.8	22.5	17.6	20.1	18.0
4.6	5.0	5.1	Intangibles (net)	7.9	3.8	4.5	2.4	4.8	10.0
6.2	6.8	6.2	All Other Non-Current	7.7	7.2	7.3	6.9	4.9	2.7
100.0	100.0	100.0	Total	100.0	100.0	100.0	100.0	100.0	100.0
			LIABILITIES						
13.6	13.6	11.7	Notes Payable-Short Term	20.1	13.6	18.2	7.4	8.9	4.9
3.6	3.5	2.7	Cur. Mat.-L.T.D.	3.8	1.7	1.0	3.2	4.9	1.8
21.5	19.1	21.3	Trade Payables	16.9	21.6	18.2	26.2	21.2	19.8
.1	.1	.1	Income Taxes Payable	.0	.2	.3	.1	.1	.2
11.8	9.4	8.7	All Other Current	5.4	9.1	7.9	7.8	9.6	12.4
50.6	45.7	44.6	Total Current	46.2	46.0	45.6	44.7	44.6	39.2
14.3	17.8	12.4	Long-Term Debt	16.2	15.6	3.8	6.8	8.2	24.0
.1	.1	.1	Deferred Taxes	.0	.0	.0	.1	.1	.1
7.5	12.7	8.8	All Other Non-Current	14.9	9.0	5.0	5.8	9.8	9.2
27.5	23.6	34.2	Net Worth	22.7	29.4	45.5	42.5	37.3	27.4
100.0	100.0	100.0	Total Liabilities & Net Worth	100.0	100.0	100.0	100.0	100.0	100.0
			INCOME DATA						
100.0	100.0	100.0	Net Sales	100.0	100.0	100.0	100.0	100.0	100.0
45.0	46.2	47.7	Gross Profit	50.8	44.0	58.2	43.2	49.1	48.0
42.4	42.7	42.9	Operating Expenses	42.6	40.3	52.0	39.0	46.6	42.1
2.6	3.6	4.8	Operating Profit	8.2	3.8	6.2	4.2	2.5	5.8
1.5	1.2	.9	All Other Expenses (net)	2.0	.5	.8	.8	.5	1.4
1.1	2.4	3.9	Profit Before Taxes	6.2	3.3	5.4	3.4	2.0	4.5
			RATIOS						
2.5	2.5	2.9		6.1	2.8	3.0	2.9	2.3	2.8
1.5	1.7	1.8	Current	2.4	1.9	1.7	1.7	1.6	2.1
1.0	1.1	1.1		.8	1.2	1.0	1.0	1.3	1.2
.8	1.1	1.0		1.0	1.1	.7	1.2	.9	.9
.3	(168) .4	.4	Quick	.4	.4	.3	.4	.3	.5
.1	.1	.1		.1	.1	.1	.1	.2	.1
0 UND	0 UND	0 UND		0 UND	0 UND	1 639.7	0 UND	0 999.8	1 314.5
5 66.9	4 94.4	3 128.3	Sales/Receivables	0 UND	2 191.4	3 118.6	2 151.5	5 81.0	5 74.5
32 11.5	29 12.8	26 14.2		26 13.8	26 14.2	14 25.5	19 19.1	32 11.3	39 9.3
77 4.7	74 4.9	73 5.0		57 6.4	76 4.8	96 3.8	60 6.1	73 5.0	116 3.1
113 3.2	120 3.0	132 2.8	Cost of Sales/Inventory	145 2.5	132 2.8	164 2.2	103 3.5	115 3.2	163 2.2
215 1.7	200 1.8	204 1.8		259 1.4	189 1.9	273 1.3	153 2.4	223 1.6	197 1.8
20 18.0	17 21.5	20 18.5		6 64.4	14 26.0	11 33.3	33 10.9	27 13.4	22 16.3
42 8.6	42 8.8	44 8.3	Cost of Sales/Payables	30 12.3	50 7.4	46 8.0	54 6.8	42 8.8	41 8.8
77 4.7	75 4.9	85 4.3		64 5.7	89 4.1	117 3.1	89 4.1	73 5.0	83 4.4
5.8	4.7	5.0		3.1	3.8	5.0	5.3	6.4	4.2
11.7	10.1	8.6	Sales/Working Capital	9.2	7.6	9.8	7.2	10.2	7.3
140.6	64.2	43.5		-18.3	26.1	NM	266.1	23.3	60.2
6.7	8.9	13.7		5.4	19.0	53.3	20.5	4.9	35.0
(108) 2.2	(136) 3.3	(131) 3.3	EBIT/Interest	(13) 1.5	(34) 5.1	(15) 3.1	(27) 4.5	(22) 2.5	(20) 2.6
-.4	.6	1.0		.9	.6	.0	1.4	.4	1.2
6.2	11.2	16.8	Net Profit + Depr., Dep.,						
(14) 2.8	(19) 2.7	(14) 4.0	Amort./Cur. Mat. L/T/D						
.7	1.1	1.3							
.1	.1	.1		.0	.1	.1	.0	.2	.2
.6	.5	.4	Fixed/Worth	.3	.4	.4	.2	.5	.8
3.4	9.9	1.9		NM	1.5	1.2	1.5	2.0	NM
1.0	.7	.7		.5	.8	.5	.6	.8	.7
2.5	2.3	2.0	Debt/Worth	3.0	2.6	1.2	1.6	1.3	3.3
11.8	45.9	10.8		-17.3	73.3	5.0	4.1	5.6	NM
43.1	45.7	53.9	% Profit Before Taxes/Tangible	122.1	81.8	34.0	38.4	27.7	40.5
(105) 14.1	(130) 15.5	(131) 18.6	Net Worth	(15) 13.9	(31) 26.6	(16) 17.1	(32) 9.6	(21) 16.1	(16) 24.2
.2	1.2	4.4		4.3	3.4	1.3	2.6	6.0	10.2
14.8	16.5	15.4	% Profit Before Taxes/Total	23.8	28.5	19.1	13.2	12.3	15.4
3.4	5.5	4.6	Assets	5.3	4.6	2.7	3.6	4.1	5.9
-3.9	-1.3	.6		.7	.2	-1.7	.8	.1	1.1
60.4	86.9	81.5		UND	103.1	40.4	366.6	34.9	37.2
19.6	21.7	21.5	Sales/Net Fixed Assets	23.1	33.1	18.1	28.3	16.7	20.6
8.6	8.0	9.9		6.0	15.1	6.2	10.3	9.8	8.0
3.6	3.5	3.6		4.3	3.9	3.1	4.1	4.1	3.1
2.4	2.4	2.6	Sales/Total Assets	2.3	2.9	2.2	2.8	2.6	2.3
1.7	1.6	1.7		1.5	1.5	1.7	1.7	2.0	1.8
.6	.4	.5			.4	.4	.3	.6	.8
(101) 1.2	(122) 1.0	(111) 1.0	% Depr., Dep., Amort./Sales	(25) .7	(12) 2.6	(25) .9	(23) .9	(18) 1.3	
2.1	2.1	2.3		1.3	5.4	2.7	2.2	2.9	
2.0	2.4	2.1		2.4	1.9		2.3		
(63) 3.7	(90) 4.0	(80) 3.7	% Officers', Directors' Owners' Comp/Sales	(11) 4.6	(23) 3.4		(22) 3.7		
6.2	6.5	5.8		6.7	5.9		5.9		
3048118M	3789332M	2988057M	Net Sales ($)	12373M	74961M	68061M	260525M	398254M	2173883M
1584245M	1544098M	1405791M	Total Assets ($)	7801M	33519M	38872M	133794M	164907M	1026898M

© RMA 2011   M = $ thousand   MM = $ million

See Pages 9 through 22 for Explanation of Ratios and Data

Current Data Sorted by Assets   Comparative Historical Data

Type of Statement								
	2	8	5 / 5	1	2	Unqualified	10	6
1	3	3	2			Reviewed	7	12
13	16	6	1	1		Compiled	12	16
6	4	8	6	2		Tax Returns	18	22
						Other	32	29
	15 (4/1-9/30/10)		80 (10/1/10-3/31/11)				4/1/06-3/31/07	4/1/07-3/31/08
0-500M	500M-2MM	2-10MM	10-50MM	50-100MM	100-250MM		ALL	ALL
20	25	25	19	4	2	NUMBER OF STATEMENTS	79	85
%	%	%	%	%	%	ASSETS	%	%
6.1	7.1	10.9	16.7			Cash & Equivalents	9.8	9.3
2.5	3.4	4.0	7.0			Trade Receivables (net)	5.9	5.3
72.6	64.5	59.1	44.5			Inventory	65.5	61.1
4.0	.4	.4	1.2			All Other Current	1.6	2.4
85.2	75.4	74.4	69.5			Total Current	82.8	78.1
5.8	14.9	14.7	21.3			Fixed Assets (net)	11.3	14.7
3.0	1.1	1.1	1.7			Intangibles (net)	2.6	1.3
6.1	8.6	9.8	7.6			All Other Non-Current	3.4	5.9
100.0	100.0	100.0	100.0			Total	100.0	100.0
						LIABILITIES		
11.2	8.1	7.2	14.0			Notes Payable-Short Term	14.0	9.9
1.4	1.8	1.5	.4			Cur. Mat.-L.T.D.	2.9	3.7
13.3	28.5	23.6	18.6			Trade Payables	22.8	23.0
.0	.0	.1	.0			Income Taxes Payable	.1	.0
9.9	4.9	7.6	11.7			All Other Current	10.1	10.4
35.9	43.3	40.0	44.6			Total Current	49.8	47.0
14.0	20.3	7.1	6.6			Long-Term Debt	15.2	7.0
.0	.1	.1	.1			Deferred Taxes	.0	.0
22.9	8.1	8.7	5.1			All Other Non-Current	4.3	5.7
27.3	28.2	44.0	43.7			Net Worth	30.6	40.2
100.0	100.0	100.0	100.0			Total Liabilities & Net Worth	100.0	100.0
						INCOME DATA		
100.0	100.0	100.0	100.0			Net Sales	100.0	100.0
38.6	47.0	39.2	42.0			Gross Profit	42.2	43.1
35.0	45.1	33.5	36.4			Operating Expenses	38.7	39.6
3.6	1.9	5.7	5.6			Operating Profit	3.5	3.4
.9	.7	-.4	.5			All Other Expenses (net)	.9	.8
2.8	1.2	6.1	5.0			Profit Before Taxes	2.6	2.7
						RATIOS		
4.0	2.7	3.3	3.8				2.9	3.5
2.6	2.1	1.9	1.6			Current	2.0	1.7
1.9	1.5	1.4	1.0				1.3	1.2
.5	.5	.8	1.4				.8	.7
.1	.2	.3	.5			Quick	.1	.3
.0	.0	.1	.3				.1	.1
0 UND	0 UND	0 999.8	1 496.3				0 UND	0 UND
0 UND	0 UND	1 544.2	4 104.0			Sales/Receivables	1 558.5	0 389.0
0 UND	1 257.5	8 47.6	20 18.6				4 92.5	6 60.2
87 4.2	107 3.4	108 3.4	72 5.1				109 3.3	98 3.7
164 2.2	181 2.0	126 2.9	122 3.0			Cost of Sales/Inventory	184 2.0	167 2.2
286 1.3	267 1.4	188 1.9	188 1.9				232 1.6	219 1.7
0 UND	35 10.5	34 10.9	22 16.4				26 13.9	22 16.7
22 16.5	55 6.7	51 7.2	40 9.2			Cost of Sales/Payables	44 8.2	42 8.6
36 10.1	74 4.9	59 6.1	61 6.0				73 5.0	82 4.4
3.6	3.8	4.3	3.9				3.7	4.0
5.2	7.6	8.3	8.8			Sales/Working Capital	6.3	7.2
14.6	18.4	16.3	200.7				20.0	21.2
3.6	6.2	26.1	75.8				7.6	9.6
(14) 2.6	(21) 1.9	(20) 8.2	(16) 9.4			EBIT/Interest	(73) 2.5	(66) 2.9
1.3	1.0	2.4	1.7				.4	.8
						Net Profit + Depr., Dep.,	13.4	2.5
						Amort./Cur. Mat. L/T/D	(14) 3.0	(14) .7
							1.4	-22.3
.0	.1	.1	.3				.1	.1
.1	.2	.2	.4			Fixed/Worth	.3	.3
UND	2.8	.5	2.0				.9	.9
.6	1.1	.6	.2				.8	.6
1.9	1.7	1.3	1.3			Debt/Worth	1.9	1.5
UND	11.9	3.2	13.8				5.1	5.2
41.2	25.6	55.1	24.1				33.0	39.1
(15) 28.5	(21) 14.1	29.4	(17) 20.0			% Profit Before Taxes/Tangible Net Worth	(68) 14.4	(78) 17.5
11.7	1.9	7.6	8.7				.7	.7
20.0	9.2	27.8	20.0				11.5	14.5
5.9	2.5	9.1	7.6			% Profit Before Taxes/Total Assets	3.8	5.2
3.6	.0	4.4	2.2				-1.0	-1.1
UND	69.5	75.6	20.8				107.0	79.5
81.3	34.2	25.4	12.9			Sales/Net Fixed Assets	34.5	25.6
37.2	14.6	12.6	8.4				14.2	11.8
4.8	3.5	3.2	2.9				3.5	3.6
3.0	2.4	2.7	2.1			Sales/Total Assets	2.4	2.5
2.0	1.6	2.2	1.8				1.8	1.9
.3	.5	.4	.8				.5	.5
(11) .6	(21) .9	(23) .8	(16) 1.0			% Depr., Dep., Amort./Sales	(60) .7	(68) .9
1.0	1.8	1.2	2.5				1.3	1.8
1.9	2.6	1.6					1.9	1.6
(16) 5.4	(19) 3.9	(11) 2.4				% Officers', Directors' Owners' Comp/Sales	(45) 4.7	(39) 3.4
8.2	7.1	5.0					9.0	7.3
19424M	75154M	309527M	1100685M	504571M	301883M	Net Sales ($)	3391706M	4221032M
5917M	27514M	106850M	434947M	316355M	347320M	Total Assets ($)	1562172M	1726681M

M = $ thousand   MM = $ million
See Pages 9 through 22 for Explanation of Ratios and Data

Comparative Historical Data | Current Data Sorted by Sales

4/1/08-3/31/09 ALL	4/1/09-3/31/10 ALL	4/1/10-3/31/11 ALL	Type of Statement	0-1MM	1-3MM	3-5MM	5-10MM	10-25MM	25MM & OVER
7	4	8	Unqualified						8
9	8	15	Reviewed		1	1	3	4	6
14	17	9	Compiled	1		1	4	2	1
29	31	37	Tax Returns	10	11	9	4	1	2
31	38	26	Other	4	4	2	2	7	7
				15 (4/1-9/30/10)			80 (10/1/10-3/31/11)		
90	98	95	**NUMBER OF STATEMENTS**	15	16	13	13	14	24
%	%	%	**ASSETS**	%	%	%	%	%	%
13.3	11.0	10.0	Cash & Equivalents	6.4	5.8	6.8	12.5	13.2	13.5
4.3	5.3	4.1	Trade Receivables (net)	1.5	4.4	4.6	2.4	4.5	6.2
58.0	58.7	58.4	Inventory	72.9	65.7	58.1	57.5	58.3	45.0
2.2	2.3	1.8	All Other Current	.9	4.3	.6	.2	.6	3.1
77.9	77.3	74.3	Total Current	81.7	80.1	70.1	72.6	76.5	67.8
14.5	13.1	14.7	Fixed Assets (net)	11.2	9.6	18.9	9.3	15.0	20.8
2.8	3.5	3.1	Intangibles (net)	4.0	1.3	.2	2.0	.6	7.5
4.8	6.2	7.8	All Other Non-Current	3.2	9.0	10.9	16.1	7.8	3.9
100.0	100.0	100.0	Total	100.0	100.0	100.0	100.0	100.0	100.0
			LIABILITIES						
11.5	10.1	9.2	Notes Payable-Short Term	13.2	8.0	8.6	2.9	14.9	7.9
3.3	3.9	1.3	Cur. Mat.-L.T.D.	.4	3.2	1.7	.5	1.8	.6
22.7	18.6	20.8	Trade Payables	6.4	24.6	20.0	35.2	24.0	18.0
.1	.2	.0	Income Taxes Payable	.0	.0	.0	.1	.0	.0
9.4	21.5	8.2	All Other Current	11.3	4.8	5.8	6.0	8.1	11.1
47.0	54.3	39.6	Total Current	31.3	40.7	36.2	44.8	48.9	37.6
14.5	12.1	13.1	Long-Term Debt	13.6	30.3	13.6	5.0	8.4	8.2
.0	.0	.1	Deferred Taxes	.0	.0	.4	.0	.0	.2
6.0	2.5	11.0	All Other Non-Current	18.2	18.6	8.6	5.7	6.8	8.3
32.4	31.0	36.2	Net Worth	37.1	10.4	41.2	44.5	35.9	45.7
100.0	100.0	100.0	Total Liabilities & Net Worth	100.0	100.0	100.0	100.0	100.0	100.0
			INCOME DATA						
100.0	100.0	100.0	Net Sales	100.0	100.0	100.0	100.0	100.0	100.0
41.9	45.0	42.3	Gross Profit	39.0	48.5	39.9	45.9	36.4	42.9
39.2	41.9	38.0	Operating Expenses	34.9	46.4	34.4	41.4	32.0	38.0
2.7	3.1	4.3	Operating Profit	4.2	2.2	5.5	4.5	4.4	5.0
.8	1.5	.6	All Other Expenses (net)	1.5	.8	-.9	-.2	.3	1.2
1.9	1.6	3.7	Profit Before Taxes	2.7	1.3	6.4	4.6	4.1	3.8
			RATIOS						
3.2	3.0	3.4	Current	3.4	4.9	2.4	3.3	2.9	3.7
1.7	1.8	2.1		2.6	2.6	1.9	2.1	1.6	2.1
1.2	1.2	1.5		1.9	1.5	1.4	1.4	1.1	1.2
.9	.8	.7	Quick	.4	.8	.5	.7	.9	1.4
.2	.2	.3		.0	.2	.2	.3	.3	.5
.1	.0	.0		.0	.0	.1	.1	.1	.2
0 UND	0 UND	0 UND	Sales/Receivables	0 UND	0 UND	0 UND	0 UND	0 UND	0 874.0
0 UND	0 999.8	1 544.2		0 UND	0 UND	1 444.6	1 544.2	1 366.7	2 194.0
4 95.0	6 56.5	5 76.8		3 142.0	1 453.1	11 31.9	5 71.0	8 45.2	10 38.3
81 4.5	88 4.2	95 3.8	Cost of Sales/Inventory	105 3.5	148 2.5	71 5.2	106 3.4	101 3.6	77 4.7
159 2.3	163 2.2	144 2.5		197 1.9	194 1.9	122 3.0	150 2.4	114 3.2	126 2.9
232 1.6	255 1.4	213 1.7		373 1.0	276 1.3	214 1.7	204 1.8	147 2.5	147 2.5
22 17.0	15 24.6	27 13.4	Cost of Sales/Payables	0 UND	22 16.4	31 11.8	42 8.6	35 10.3	23 15.7
40 9.0	40 9.2	42 8.8		27 13.5	53 6.8	51 7.2	54 6.7	51 7.2	33 10.9
76 4.8	75 4.9	59 6.1		36 10.0	91 4.0	62 5.9	100 3.6	58 6.2	55 6.7
3.9	3.6	3.9	Sales/Working Capital	3.0	3.7	5.2	3.9	5.4	4.0
7.6	8.3	7.4		4.1	4.9	8.9	7.6	11.7	6.3
41.0	24.2	18.4		12.2	8.8	19.0	12.8	110.8	36.8
11.6	23.3	12.8	EBIT/Interest	3.9	5.5	10.8		22.9	75.8
(76) 3.0	(76) 4.2	(77) 2.9		(12) 2.8	(13) 1.9	(10) 5.2		(13) 5.5	(20) 2.4
.2	.6	1.3		1.2	1.1	1.4		2.2	1.3
1.9	3.9	9.4	Net Profit + Depr., Dep., Amort./Cur. Mat. L/T/D						
(14) 1.4	(13) 2.1	(13) 2.7							
.0	1.2	.8							
.1	.1	.1	Fixed/Worth	.0	.1	.1	.1	.1	.2
.3	.3	.3		.1	.9	.2	.2	.2	.7
1.7	1.2	2.0		.6	-.3	.9	.3	1.5	2.1
.6	.5	.7	Debt/Worth	.6	1.2	.8	.5	.6	.3
1.7	1.6	1.7		1.9	11.2	1.3	1.1	2.4	1.6
8.1	6.9	5.6		3.2	-4.3	2.6	1.7	3.7	13.1
46.0	36.8	36.7	% Profit Before Taxes/Tangible Net Worth	37.9		66.1	49.7	37.2	25.0
(74) 15.5	(79) 16.7	(82) 20.7		(14) 21.5		21.1	(12) 20.2	(13) 28.7	(21) 17.1
2.0	.2	7.3		7.1		4.1	6.5	9.9	5.6
13.6	17.6	17.6	% Profit Before Taxes/Total Assets	17.6	8.7	31.2	20.2	13.2	19.7
4.1	5.5	6.7		5.5	3.1	9.2	6.8	8.3	6.2
-2.3	-1.6	2.1		2.5	.8	1.4	2.3	3.3	1.5
71.7	93.7	71.4	Sales/Net Fixed Assets	UND	67.6	81.8	206.0	75.2	20.7
26.9	25.6	29.4		61.6	43.5	34.2	25.4	32.4	13.4
11.4	11.6	11.3		13.5	18.2	10.7	21.9	12.1	8.4
3.5	3.4	3.5	Sales/Total Assets	3.5	3.8	3.7	3.4	3.2	3.4
2.4	2.4	2.4		2.1	2.4	3.2	2.6	2.8	2.2
1.8	1.7	1.9		1.0	1.6	2.1	2.0	2.3	1.8
.5	.4	.6	% Depr., Dep., Amort./Sales		.4	.7	.2	.4	.8
(71) .9	(73) .7	(76) .9			(13) .6	(11) 1.0	(11) .6	.8	(19) 1.8
1.9	1.5	1.8			1.5	1.6	1.2	1.0	2.5
1.7	2.1	2.1	% Officers', Directors' Owners' Comp/Sales	1.9	3.1		2.3		
(47) 4.3	(56) 4.1	(51) 3.6		(11) 5.2	(12) 4.7		(11) 3.3		
7.4	7.9	6.6		8.7	7.7		5.8		
1950471M	2235573M	2311244M	Net Sales ($)	8987M	25193M	46257M	92768M	213618M	1924421M
951869M	1011578M	1238903M	Total Assets ($)	5344M	10911M	20394M	46411M	87715M	1068128M

© RMA 2011

M = $ thousand   MM = $ million
See Pages 9 through 22 for Explanation of Ratios and Data

Current Data Sorted by Assets   Comparative Historical Data

0-500M	500M-2MM	2-10MM	10-50MM	50-100MM	100-250MM	Type of Statement	4/1/06-3/31/07 ALL	4/1/07-3/31/08 ALL
		1	11	1	2	Unqualified	12	14
	1	23	10			Reviewed	45	45
3	23	32	6			Compiled	66	55
18	38	24	1			Tax Returns	79	73
3	26	25	12	3	5	Other	70	89
	71 (4/1-9/30/10)		197 (10/1/10-3/31/11)					
24	88	105	40	4	7	**NUMBER OF STATEMENTS**	272	276
%	%	%	%	%	%	**ASSETS**	%	%
12.4	9.7	7.2	4.3			Cash & Equivalents	6.8	5.8
.6	4.6	6.9	12.8			Trade Receivables (net)	8.1	8.1
68.6	69.8	66.4	61.9			Inventory	68.5	68.7
.5	1.2	2.5	.9			All Other Current	1.2	1.5
82.1	85.3	83.0	79.8			Total Current	84.5	84.1
9.9	8.2	11.0	13.3			Fixed Assets (net)	10.3	10.2
4.4	1.7	.9	2.7			Intangibles (net)	1.3	1.6
3.6	4.8	5.1	4.3			All Other Non-Current	3.8	4.1
100.0	100.0	100.0	100.0			Total	100.0	100.0
						LIABILITIES		
38.9	11.6	11.8	16.2			Notes Payable-Short Term	14.2	15.1
3.7	2.4	1.6	3.8			Cur. Mat.-L.T.D.	2.3	2.3
15.8	18.6	18.9	16.5			Trade Payables	22.9	20.9
.0	.3	.2	.0			Income Taxes Payable	.1	.1
22.8	9.5	7.2	9.9			All Other Current	9.4	9.1
81.2	42.4	39.6	46.4			Total Current	48.9	47.4
12.6	13.9	8.1	9.0			Long-Term Debt	9.5	13.5
.0	.0	.0	.1			Deferred Taxes	.0	.1
29.1	7.0	7.8	6.7			All Other Non-Current	5.6	7.9
-22.8	36.7	44.5	37.8			Net Worth	36.0	31.1
100.0	100.0	100.0	100.0			Total Liabilties & Net Worth	100.0	100.0
						INCOME DATA		
100.0	100.0	100.0	100.0			Net Sales	100.0	100.0
53.9	45.8	41.0	40.0			Gross Profit	42.7	43.1
48.4	40.2	36.6	36.3			Operating Expenses	38.1	39.0
5.5	5.6	4.4	3.7			Operating Profit	4.6	4.1
2.3	1.1	1.0	1.7			All Other Expenses (net)	1.3	1.9
3.3	4.5	3.4	2.0			Profit Before Taxes	3.3	2.2
						RATIOS		
2.6	4.2	3.9	2.2			Current	2.6	2.9
1.7	2.3	1.9	1.7				1.7	1.9
1.1	1.5	1.5	1.5				1.3	1.3
.4	.9	.7	.7			Quick	.6	.6
.2	.3	.2	.3				.2	.2
.0	.1	.1	.1				.1	.1
0 UND	0 UND	0 758.1	3 115.1			Sales/Receivables	0 UND	0 UND
0 UND	3 108.9	5 70.2	14 25.7				5 67.7	6 60.5
2 191.0	13 29.1	20 18.6	58 6.3				22 16.8	20 18.2
140 2.6	204 1.8	186 2.0	151 2.4			Cost of Sales/Inventory	189 1.9	189 1.9
269 1.4	302 1.2	295 1.2	293 1.2				290 1.3	304 1.2
371 1.0	514 .7	445 .8	428 .9				374 1.0	438 .8
5 74.6	23 16.1	37 10.0	33 11.1			Cost of Sales/Payables	40 9.1	30 12.2
30 12.1	51 7.1	67 5.4	62 5.9				77 4.7	68 5.4
75 4.9	129 2.8	110 3.3	87 4.2				132 2.8	126 2.9
3.8	2.2	2.1	2.5			Sales/Working Capital	2.6	2.5
8.7	3.7	3.6	3.9				4.8	4.4
21.1	6.7	7.9	7.0				8.1	7.6
4.1	8.5	10.0	6.5			EBIT/Interest	6.4	5.3
(21) 2.6	(82) 4.0	(98) 2.6	(38) 3.0				(243) 2.6	(258) 2.1
-.3	1.3	.9	1.3				1.1	1.0
		2.8	9.1			Net Profit + Depr., Dep., Amort./Cur. Mat. L/T/D	3.3	4.7
	(17) .8	(12) 2.7					(43) 1.3	(50) 1.7
		.3	1.0				.6	.4
.0	.1	.1	.1			Fixed/Worth	.1	.1
.2	.2	.2	.3				.2	.2
-.8	.6	.5	.6				.6	.7
1.5	.6	.7	.7			Debt/Worth	.9	.9
3.0	1.7	1.4	1.4				1.8	2.0
-5.3	6.8	2.8	3.6				3.7	5.9
71.4	33.2	24.4	17.3			% Profit Before Taxes/Tangible Net Worth	29.5	26.2
(15) 19.4	(75) 13.9	(102) 8.2	(36) 8.8				(244) 11.2	(237) 9.2
7.5	3.9	.1	.7				3.0	1.2
16.0	11.4	9.0	7.1			% Profit Before Taxes/Total Assets	10.7	8.4
5.5	5.3	3.1	2.3				4.4	2.9
-2.8	1.0	-.1	.5				.5	-.2
825.5	94.8	54.1	46.4			Sales/Net Fixed Assets	71.8	79.9
41.7	30.9	20.1	15.5				24.6	23.7
14.3	11.5	9.1	7.0				10.7	10.4
3.5	2.2	2.1	1.8			Sales/Total Assets	2.1	2.0
2.0	1.5	1.4	1.4				1.6	1.5
1.3	1.0	.9	1.0				1.2	1.2
.4	.4	.3	.4			% Depr., Dep., Amort./Sales	.4	.4
(15) .9	(59) .8	(92) .8	(36) 1.2				(224) .8	(217) .9
2.7	1.7	1.6	2.4				1.6	1.7
3.8	4.6	2.3	1.6			% Officers', Directors' Owners' Comp/Sales	3.1	2.9
(17) 8.4	(56) 7.7	(52) 3.6	(15) 2.5				(152) 5.3	(147) 5.2
12.3	9.9	5.7	3.8				8.3	8.5
12727M	165887M	829361M	1479726M	770123M	1661229M	Net Sales ($)	4775457M	7046532M
6349M	95128M	507275M	926486M	260373M	1141040M	Total Assets ($)	3206450M	3982732M

© RMA 2011

M = $ thousand   MM = $ million
See Pages 9 through 22 for Explanation of Ratios and Data

Comparative Historical Data | | | | Current Data Sorted by Sales

			Type of Statement						
12	16	15	Unqualified				1	3	11
36	31	34	Reviewed	1	3	4	7	11	8
73	56	64	Compiled	5	22	11	15	10	1
68	92	81	Tax Returns	28	28	11	10	4	
90	81	74	Other	10	19	7	7	16	15
4/1/08-3/31/09	4/1/09-3/31/10	4/1/10-3/31/11		71 (4/1-9/30/10)			197 (10/1/10-3/31/11)		
ALL	ALL	ALL		0-1MM	1-3MM	3-5MM	5-10MM	10-25MM	25MM & OVER
279	276	268	NUMBER OF STATEMENTS	44	72	33	40	44	35
%	%	%	ASSETS	%	%	%	%	%	%
5.6	7.8	8.0	Cash & Equivalents	9.2	8.5	8.6	6.8	8.6	5.8
7.3	7.4	6.3	Trade Receivables (net)	1.7	5.3	5.1	4.7	9.2	13.8
68.6	65.5	66.9	Inventory	71.4	68.4	68.1	70.1	63.3	57.5
1.5	1.7	1.7	All Other Current	1.6	1.0	1.5	2.5	1.9	2.1
83.0	82.4	82.9	Total Current	83.8	83.2	83.3	84.1	83.0	79.2
10.1	10.5	10.5	Fixed Assets (net)	9.1	9.9	10.3	9.5	12.0	13.2
2.0	2.3	1.9	Intangibles (net)	2.9	1.9	1.6	.5	.9	4.1
4.9	4.9	4.6	All Other Non-Current	4.2	5.0	4.8	6.0	4.1	3.5
100.0	100.0	100.0	Total	100.0	100.0	100.0	100.0	100.0	100.0
			LIABILITIES						
15.1	14.5	14.8	Notes Payable-Short Term	28.1	10.5	11.3	13.0	12.5	15.1
3.7	2.4	2.4	Cur. Mat.-L.T.D.	2.3	3.0	1.6	2.4	1.3	3.3
19.1	17.7	18.0	Trade Payables	13.8	18.3	20.1	19.7	18.1	18.6
.1	.2	.2	Income Taxes Payable	.0	.4	.1	.3	.1	.1
8.8	9.0	9.9	All Other Current	17.1	7.2	11.0	6.9	8.0	10.9
46.8	43.8	45.2	Total Current	61.2	39.4	44.0	42.3	40.0	48.0
12.8	12.4	11.5	Long-Term Debt	14.3	14.3	12.7	4.9	5.9	15.8
.1	.1	.2	Deferred Taxes	.0	.0	.1	.0	.1	1.0
8.7	8.3	9.4	All Other Non-Current	20.5	8.9	5.5	4.9	6.4	8.7
31.6	35.4	33.8	Net Worth	3.9	37.4	37.7	47.8	47.6	26.5
100.0	100.0	100.0	Total Liabilities & Net Worth	100.0	100.0	100.0	100.0	100.0	100.0
			INCOME DATA						
100.0	100.0	100.0	Net Sales	100.0	100.0	100.0	100.0	100.0	100.0
43.6	42.7	43.8	Gross Profit	52.3	45.3	43.4	37.6	40.4	41.5
40.7	39.4	39.1	Operating Expenses	47.1	40.0	39.3	33.9	35.5	37.5
3.0	3.3	4.7	Operating Profit	5.3	5.3	4.1	3.7	4.9	4.0
1.5	1.3	1.3	All Other Expenses (net)	1.7	1.7	1.4	.5	.3	2.3
1.5	2.1	3.3	Profit Before Taxes	3.6	3.6	2.8	3.1	4.6	1.7
			RATIOS						
3.1	3.4	3.7	Current	4.6	4.2	3.4	3.3	3.8	2.3
1.9	2.0	2.0		2.3	2.3	1.9	1.9	2.0	1.7
1.4	1.4	1.4		1.2	1.6	1.5	1.4	1.6	1.3
.5	.6	.7	Quick	.6	.9	.4	.5	.9	.6
(277) .2	.3	.2		.2	.2	.2	.2	.5	.3
.1	.1	.1		.0	.1	.1	.1	.2	.1
0 UND	0 UND	0 UND	Sales/Receivables	0 UND	0 UND	0 UND	0 UND	1 248.1	2 165.6
5 68.4	5 68.2	4 102.0		2 199.0	2 169.8	7 55.0	3 106.3	11 31.9	10 36.5
18 20.2	18 20.2	15 24.2		8 45.5	13 29.2	14 25.6	13 27.7	34 10.6	34 10.7
193 1.9	185 2.0	183 2.0	Cost of Sales/Inventory	268 1.4	226 1.6	176 2.1	180 2.0	147 2.5	149 2.5
312 1.2	308 1.2	291 1.3		483 .8	317 1.2	368 1.0	239 1.5	248 1.5	204 1.8
479 .8	496 .7	456 .8		838 .4	468 .8	568 .6	358 1.0	336 1.1	322 1.1
28 12.8	24 14.9	28 13.2	Cost of Sales/Payables	14 26.2	24 15.0	46 7.9	31 11.7	27 13.5	32 11.3
58 6.3	54 6.7	56 6.5		45 8.2	60 6.1	74 4.9	61 6.0	59 6.2	54 6.7
118 3.1	102 3.6	104 3.5		98 3.7	132 2.8	150 2.4	100 3.7	91 4.0	73 5.0
2.5	2.0	2.3	Sales/Working Capital	1.3	2.3	2.1	2.7	2.4	4.3
4.4	3.9	4.0		3.2	3.6	3.1	4.2	3.6	5.7
8.7	8.4	8.3		14.7	6.0	7.4	6.2	10.0	10.2
5.9	8.1	7.7	EBIT/Interest	4.2	6.3	10.2	11.8	17.7	7.1
(261) 1.7	(249) 2.8	(249) 3.1		(40) 2.7	(66) 2.8	(31) 2.0	(39) 4.2	(41) 5.3	(32) 2.3
.5	1.0	.6		1.0	.8	.7	1.4	2.3	.6
1.9	6.8	4.2	Net Profit + Depr., Dep., Amort./Cur. Mat. L/T/D					7.9	9.4
(47) .7	(36) 1.4	(39) 1.6						(11) 2.9	(12) 2.2
.0	.7	.2						.0	-.1
.1	.0	.1	Fixed/Worth	.0	.1	.1	.1	.1	.1
.2	.2	.2		.1	.2	.2	.2	.2	.4
.7	.6	.6		3.8	.7	.7	.3	.5	2.3
.8	.7	.7	Debt/Worth	.9	.7	.9	.8	.4	1.1
1.9	1.8	1.6		2.3	1.7	1.7	1.4	1.1	2.1
5.6	5.9	3.9		-7.9	5.2	4.8	2.0	2.9	15.9
22.1	20.7	25.9	% Profit Before Taxes/Tangible Net Worth	26.0	28.4	27.8	20.3	31.0	20.1
(243) 7.6	(237) 8.2	(235) 10.0		(31) 12.7	(63) 7.9	(32) 8.2	7.7	(42) 15.3	(27) 10.0
-.7	1.7	1.4		2.6	-.5	-.9	1.1	2.6	1.2
7.2	8.1	9.6	% Profit Before Taxes/Total Assets	7.9	11.4	10.3	8.9	12.7	7.8
1.9	2.8	3.6		3.7	2.9	2.5	3.7	5.7	3.5
-1.6	-.2	.1		.3	-.5	-.3	.5	1.3	.5
80.4	68.2	63.6	Sales/Net Fixed Assets	556.9	67.8	84.9	70.9	49.8	54.0
25.4	21.2	23.5		34.9	24.5	31.3	18.7	18.1	16.5
10.1	8.5	10.5		10.9	10.6	7.8	9.8	10.3	9.9
2.1	2.0	2.2	Sales/Total Assets	2.0	2.1	2.0	2.2	2.6	2.4
1.5	1.4	1.5		1.2	1.5	1.3	1.6	1.5	1.8
1.1	1.0	1.0		.8	.9	.9	1.2	1.1	1.3
.3	.5	.4	% Depr., Dep., Amort./Sales	.4	.4	.3	.3	.5	.6
(212) .9	(207) 1.1	(213) .9		(27) 1.1	(53) .9	(28) .6	(35) .6	(40) .8	(30) 1.8
1.9	2.0	1.9		2.0	1.9	1.9	1.0	1.5	2.7
3.1	2.8	2.6	% Officers', Directors' Owners' Comp/Sales	5.2	4.6	2.9	2.3	1.9	
(138) 5.5	(124) 5.3	(140) 4.9		(26) 8.3	(44) 7.1	(21) 4.0	(23) 3.1	(19) 2.5	
9.7	9.3	8.4		12.3	9.6	7.0	6.0	4.9	
5279892M	4469390M	4919053M	Net Sales ($)	25450M	133002M	129611M	300664M	652327M	3677999M
3232773M	2776435M	2936651M	Total Assets ($)	25748M	110881M	113401M	203296M	437408M	2045917M

M = $ thousand   MM = $ million
See Pages 9 through 22 for Explanation of Ratios and Data

Current Data Sorted by Assets | Comparative Historical Data

	1	2	10	4	2	Type of Statement	13	14
	7	17	6	1		Unqualified	40	34
4	20	23	4			Reviewed	73	65
46	58	17			1	Compiled	96	101
18	48	41	14	2	6	Tax Returns	109	94
						Other		

	65 (4/1-9/30/10)		287 (10/1/10-3/31/11)				4/1/06-3/31/07 ALL	4/1/07-3/31/08 ALL
0-500M	500M-2MM	2-10MM	10-50MM	50-100MM	100-250MM			
68	134	100	34	7	9	NUMBER OF STATEMENTS	331	308
%	%	%	%	%	%	ASSETS	%	%
13.1	9.5	8.7	8.3			Cash & Equivalents	9.0	9.8
5.2	6.9	4.6	7.2			Trade Receivables (net)	7.3	6.2
59.7	55.1	58.9	50.0			Inventory	57.8	57.3
1.3	1.3	1.8	4.6			All Other Current	1.6	2.0
79.4	72.9	73.9	70.2			Total Current	75.7	75.3
10.9	17.1	18.0	19.6			Fixed Assets (net)	15.9	16.3
4.1	4.9	2.2	5.9			Intangibles (net)	3.2	3.5
5.6	5.2	5.9	4.3			All Other Non-Current	5.2	4.9
100.0	100.0	100.0	100.0			Total	100.0	100.0
						LIABILITIES		
14.3	13.3	10.6	12.1			Notes Payable-Short Term	14.0	13.7
4.7	2.3	3.2	1.6			Cur. Mat.-L.T.D.	2.5	2.0
24.1	23.0	25.5	20.7			Trade Payables	24.3	23.7
.0	.1	.0	.2			Income Taxes Payable	.2	.1
10.9	11.4	7.7	9.2			All Other Current	8.6	12.1
54.1	50.1	47.2	43.7			Total Current	49.6	51.6
18.9	20.1	11.7	15.6			Long-Term Debt	14.9	15.4
.0	.0	.1	.1			Deferred Taxes	.2	.0
10.8	10.3	5.0	5.1			All Other Non-Current	8.2	9.3
16.1	19.5	36.1	35.4			Net Worth	27.1	23.7
100.0	100.0	100.0	100.0			Total Liabilties & Net Worth	100.0	100.0
						INCOME DATA		
100.0	100.0	100.0	100.0			Net Sales	100.0	100.0
37.7	39.1	37.1	33.1			Gross Profit	37.3	38.5
35.1	36.0	33.4	28.6			Operating Expenses	34.4	35.7
2.5	3.0	3.7	4.5			Operating Profit	2.8	2.9
1.0	1.6	.7	.8			All Other Expenses (net)	1.4	1.4
1.5	1.5	3.0	3.8			Profit Before Taxes	1.4	1.5
						RATIOS		
4.0	2.5	2.5	2.1			Current	2.4	2.3
1.6	1.5	1.6	1.6				1.6	1.6
.9	1.1	1.2	1.3				1.1	1.1
1.0	.8	.4	.6			Quick	.6	.6
.3	.2	.2	.3				(328) .2	(305) .2
.1	.1	.0	.1				.1	.1
0 UND	0 UND	0 UND	0 950.8			Sales/Receivables	0 UND	0 UND
0 UND	2 232.2	1 372.0	3 128.9				2 174.1	2 222.5
5 69.4	11 34.7	7 51.9	8 47.6				14 25.3	11 34.5
62 5.9	96 3.8	101 3.6	86 4.2			Cost of Sales/Inventory	90 4.1	87 4.2
123 3.0	139 2.6	152 2.4	135 2.7				134 2.7	146 2.5
189 1.9	202 1.8	218 1.7	195 1.9				199 1.8	205 1.8
1 244.6	21 17.0	34 10.8	28 13.2			Cost of Sales/Payables	25 14.7	27 13.5
37 9.8	45 8.0	49 7.4	44 8.3				50 7.3	50 7.3
91 4.0	89 4.1	90 4.0	70 5.2				84 4.3	79 4.6
5.6	5.5	4.7	4.2			Sales/Working Capital	4.9	5.6
10.6	9.9	8.5	9.7				9.6	9.3
-188.7	74.3	24.2	21.2				35.5	44.7
8.4	9.0	11.0	12.4			EBIT/Interest	6.4	5.6
(51) 1.7	(114) 2.4	(90) 4.5	(31) 5.5				(287) 2.4	(267) 2.2
-1.9	.1	1.8	2.3				1.0	.7
		6.5				Net Profit + Depr., Dep.,	6.0	7.7
	(17)	3.5				Amort./Cur. Mat. L/T/D	(43) 2.5	(36) 1.9
		.9					1.0	.6
.1	.1	.2	.1			Fixed/Worth	.1	.1
.5	.4	.3	.5				.4	.4
-.8	-36.2	1.3	2.9				1.6	4.1
1.0	1.1	1.0	1.2			Debt/Worth	1.0	1.1
4.6	2.8	2.3	2.2				2.3	2.8
-5.9	-47.4	3.7	4.2				10.3	20.0
63.7	46.4	41.7	32.4			% Profit Before Taxes/Tangible	41.1	40.9
(44) 17.7	(96) 22.1	(92) 18.9	(31) 20.2			Net Worth	(271) 14.7	(247) 16.1
-6.6	4.0	6.1	16.2				2.3	.8
14.1	12.1	13.4	11.8			% Profit Before Taxes/Total	11.4	9.5
4.0	4.4	5.6	7.3			Assets	4.0	3.4
-5.1	-1.8	1.7	3.4				-.2	-1.5
244.1	94.8	63.8	85.0			Sales/Net Fixed Assets	75.2	86.1
48.0	32.8	20.7	32.2				27.8	29.4
19.3	10.3	10.4	5.7				11.2	10.7
4.7	3.3	3.1	3.3			Sales/Total Assets	3.4	3.3
3.0	2.3	2.3	2.0				2.4	2.4
2.3	1.6	1.6	1.5				1.7	1.7
.4	.3	.4	.2			% Depr., Dep., Amort./Sales	.4	.5
(39) .7	(86) .7	(83) .7	(31) .8				(267) .9	(218) .9
1.4	1.7	1.6	2.5				1.6	2.0
3.4	2.2	1.0				% Officers', Directors'	2.0	2.1
(41) 4.4	(75) 3.8	(45) 1.7				Owners' Comp/Sales	(175) 3.5	(144) 4.1
7.4	6.9	3.5					6.5	6.9
73031M	373200M	1002789M	1583423M	980917M	2869245M	Net Sales ($)	6035112M	6858998M
20221M	151108M	412986M	680195M	446845M	1249746M	Total Assets ($)	2809946M	3188658M

© RMA 2011

M = $ thousand   MM = $ million
See Pages 9 through 22 for Explanation of Ratios and Data

Comparative Historical Data | Current Data Sorted by Sales

			Type of Statement						
23	20	19	Unqualified			1	1	1	16
24	34	31	Reviewed	1	3	4	7	12	4
59	65	51	Compiled	1	14	9	13	12	2
106	101	122	Tax Returns	33	52	19	12	5	1
111	125	129	Other	20	31	24	11	22	21
4/1/08-3/31/09 ALL	4/1/09-3/31/10 ALL	4/1/10-3/31/11 ALL		65 (4/1-9/30/10) 0-1MM	1-3MM	3-5MM	287 (10/1/10-3/31/11) 5-10MM	10-25MM	25MM & OVER
323	345	352	NUMBER OF STATEMENTS	55	100	57	44	52	44
%	%	%	ASSETS	%	%	%	%	%	%
8.8	9.6	9.6	Cash & Equivalents	10.2	9.6	10.4	12.4	7.9	6.7
6.2	5.5	5.8	Trade Receivables (net)	4.1	6.3	4.8	6.4	6.4	6.8
59.5	58.0	56.7	Inventory	53.1	57.0	57.6	58.5	59.5	54.5
1.8	2.1	1.8	All Other Current	2.1	1.2	.6	2.3	2.2	3.5
76.3	75.2	73.9	Total Current	69.6	74.0	73.4	79.6	76.0	71.5
15.3	16.0	16.4	Fixed Assets (net)	20.4	14.5	17.3	14.1	16.6	16.4
3.3	4.5	4.4	Intangibles (net)	3.5	5.3	2.5	3.5	3.0	8.7
5.1	4.3	5.3	All Other Non-Current	6.5	6.2	6.8	2.8	4.4	3.4
100.0	100.0	100.0	Total	100.0	100.0	100.0	100.0	100.0	100.0
			LIABILITIES						
14.5	12.8	12.1	Notes Payable-Short Term	15.3	14.8	9.5	8.2	12.4	8.9
2.5	3.8	3.1	Cur. Mat.-L.T.D.	3.8	3.8	1.6	2.1	3.6	2.7
24.4	25.4	23.7	Trade Payables	21.5	21.2	28.5	20.8	28.2	23.2
.2	.2	.1	Income Taxes Payable	.0	.1	.1	.1	.0	.2
11.2	12.3	10.0	All Other Current	13.0	10.0	9.3	8.4	9.1	10.2
52.8	54.6	49.0	Total Current	53.6	50.0	49.0	39.6	53.4	45.2
15.9	14.4	17.1	Long-Term Debt	25.7	23.1	11.9	9.4	10.3	15.4
.0	.1	.1	Deferred Taxes	.0	.0	.0	.0	.2	.3
6.3	6.2	8.6	All Other Non-Current	12.6	11.3	7.2	5.2	4.6	7.4
25.0	24.8	25.2	Net Worth	8.1	15.7	31.9	45.8	31.6	31.7
100.0	100.0	100.0	Total Liabilities & Net Worth	100.0	100.0	100.0	100.0	100.0	100.0
			INCOME DATA						
100.0	100.0	100.0	Net Sales	100.0	100.0	100.0	100.0	100.0	100.0
37.6	36.9	37.6	Gross Profit	44.7	36.8	36.2	37.1	36.0	35.0
35.7	34.8	34.5	Operating Expenses	40.2	34.9	32.9	33.3	32.3	32.1
1.9	2.1	3.2	Operating Profit	4.5	1.9	3.4	3.8	3.6	2.9
1.1	.8	1.2	All Other Expenses (net)	2.4	1.2	1.0	.4	.7	.9
.8	1.2	2.0	Profit Before Taxes	2.1	.7	2.4	3.4	2.9	2.1
			RATIOS						
2.4	2.6	2.5	Current	2.2	3.9	2.3	3.3	2.0	2.4
1.6	1.5	1.6		1.4	1.6	1.6	2.1	1.4	1.6
1.0	1.1	1.1		.9	1.0	1.2	1.4	1.2	1.2
.6	.6	.7	Quick	.8	.8	.7	1.2	.5	.4
(320) .2	(343) .2	.2		.2	.3	.2	.4	.2	.2
.1	.1	.1		.1	.1	.1	.1	.1	.1
0 UND	0 UND	0 UND	Sales/Receivables	0 UND	0 UND	0 UND	0 UND	0 UND	0 974.0
1 309.4	2 219.6	1 302.5		0 UND	2 208.0	0 999.8	1 462.5	3 137.7	2 147.5
9 39.3	8 43.6	7 50.2		4 87.4	8 47.6	7 53.6	10 37.4	10 35.6	7 49.7
91 4.0	91 4.0	93 3.9	Cost of Sales/Inventory	118 3.1	90 4.1	100 3.7	95 3.9	87 4.2	84 4.3
136 2.7	144 2.5	140 2.6		180 2.0	144 2.5	142 2.6	136 2.7	118 3.1	140 2.6
199 1.8	209 1.7	201 1.8		282 1.3	195 1.9	208 1.8	180 2.0	163 2.2	187 2.0
23 16.1	25 14.8	23 15.6	Cost of Sales/Payables	12 29.6	12 30.6	30 12.3	22 16.3	36 10.2	32 11.3
46 7.9	48 7.5	47 7.8		57 7.9	40 9.0	58 6.3	39 9.4	49 7.4	49 7.4
79 4.6	84 4.4	87 4.2		119 3.1	89 4.1	102 3.6	56 6.5	74 4.9	71 5.2
5.6	4.9	5.3	Sales/Working Capital	5.5	4.3	5.9	4.4	6.6	5.7
11.0	10.1	9.4		11.4	9.2	11.0	6.6	12.4	9.4
154.8	51.1	45.4		-33.7	274.5	40.8	12.7	26.4	25.7
6.7	7.1	10.1	EBIT/Interest	5.3	6.6	10.3	29.7	15.7	10.5
(275) 2.2	(301) 2.1	(301) 3.2		(45) 1.5	(82) 1.9	(47) 2.4	(40) 5.5	(48) 6.9	(39) 4.4
-.3	.1	.7		-1.6	-.6	.3	1.7	2.3	1.1
10.0	8.1	6.6	Net Profit + Depr., Dep., Amort./Cur. Mat. L/T/D					6.9	15.1
(38) 2.0	(47) 1.6	(42) 2.5						(10) 5.5	(14) 2.7
.5	.3	.3						2.1	.3
.1	.1	.1	Fixed/Worth	.3	.1	.1	.1	.2	.2
.5	.4	.4		2.0	.5	.3	.2	.4	.5
3.6	6.3	2.9		-.8	-4.8	1.8	.4	.9	3.2
1.1	1.0	1.1	Debt/Worth	1.6	1.1	.9	.6	1.2	1.4
3.2	2.9	2.7		18.2	4.0	2.1	1.1	2.5	2.6
21.4	26.3	24.8		-5.9	-9.2	5.2	2.8	5.0	6.1
36.7	31.3	44.9	% Profit Before Taxes/Tangible Net Worth	51.3	57.2	28.9	34.0	54.4	32.8
(259) 13.8	(264) 12.7	(273) 19.0		(32) 14.4	(67) 22.6	(48) 13.4	(41) 16.4	(50) 28.0	(35) 20.2
-3.8	-.3	4.3		-5.2	3.3	1.1	3.3	11.5	13.7
10.8	9.3	12.6	% Profit Before Taxes/Total Assets	10.6	12.6	9.9	15.4	13.6	12.5
3.0	3.4	5.0		2.3	3.6	4.5	6.8	6.4	6.6
-3.2	-2.3	-.3		-5.1	-3.6	-.2	1.7	3.2	.9
85.7	80.3	88.8	Sales/Net Fixed Assets	79.6	161.8	97.0	105.2	67.3	50.9
29.5	27.2	28.7		19.0	32.6	41.8	33.5	24.9	20.9
12.2	10.8	11.0		5.3	11.8	7.9	14.9	12.0	10.7
3.4	3.2	3.3	Sales/Total Assets	2.5	3.3	3.5	3.7	3.6	3.2
2.5	2.3	2.4		1.6	2.2	2.4	2.6	2.8	2.5
1.8	1.7	1.6		1.1	1.6	1.7	2.0	2.2	1.9
.4	.4	.4	% Depr., Dep., Amort./Sales	.6	.4	.2	.4	.3	.4
(232) .8	(256) .8	(253) .8		(34) 1.0	(60) .7	(38) .7	(36) .7	(45) .7	(40) 1.3
1.5	1.7	1.7		2.0	1.9	1.4	1.4	1.4	2.5
2.0	1.8	1.6	% Officers', Directors' Owners' Comp/Sales	3.7		1.4	.7	1.1	
(141) 3.5	(166) 3.3	(168) 3.5		(29) 6.6	(56) 4.1	(35) 2.8	(25) 1.8	(17) 1.6	
6.1	6.2	6.5		9.1	6.6	4.1	3.4	3.5	
8895047M	9031200M	6882605M	Net Sales ($)	35035M	179766M	216196M	302100M	769035M	5380473M
3554149M	3416877M	2961101M	Total Assets ($)	27655M	92639M	102072M	134015M	327718M	2277002M

© RMA 2011

M = $ thousand   MM = $ million
See Pages 9 through 22 for Explanation of Ratios and Data

Current Data Sorted by Assets   Comparative Historical Data

0-500M	500M-2MM	2-10MM	10-50MM	50-100MM	100-250MM		4/1/06-3/31/07 ALL	4/1/07-3/31/08 ALL
	1	2	1	2	2	Type of Statement — Unqualified	4	4
		1	1			Reviewed	7	4
3	3	1				Compiled	8	10
8	9	2				Tax Returns	18	23
10	5	7				Other	21	18
	9 (4/1-9/30/10)			53 (10/1/10-3/31/11)				
21	18	13	4	2	4	**NUMBER OF STATEMENTS**	58	59
%	%	%	%	%	%	**ASSETS**	%	%
13.7	13.3	12.6				Cash & Equivalents	10.3	11.4
8.6	3.8	9.9				Trade Receivables (net)	7.9	5.8
57.7	58.5	48.0				Inventory	55.6	54.2
1.6	1.2	3.2				All Other Current	2.0	3.0
81.6	76.9	73.6				Total Current	75.8	74.3
11.3	12.8	15.2				Fixed Assets (net)	16.0	16.6
4.0	4.9	3.5				Intangibles (net)	3.6	2.3
3.2	5.4	7.7				All Other Non-Current	4.5	6.8
100.0	100.0	100.0				Total	100.0	100.0
						LIABILITIES		
25.2	10.7	8.2				Notes Payable-Short Term	10.1	13.3
3.5	.5	2.0				Cur. Mat.-L.T.D.	3.7	4.1
13.9	19.1	20.6				Trade Payables	21.1	17.5
.0	.2	.1				Income Taxes Payable	.8	.2
13.7	14.3	12.3				All Other Current	6.3	10.4
56.3	44.7	43.2				Total Current	41.9	45.5
26.5	25.7	18.8				Long-Term Debt	26.0	18.2
.0	.0	.6				Deferred Taxes	.3	.2
16.2	7.4	6.4				All Other Non-Current	6.9	6.0
1.0	22.2	31.0				Net Worth	25.0	30.1
100.0	100.0	100.0				Total Liabilities & Net Worth	100.0	100.0
						INCOME DATA		
100.0	100.0	100.0				Net Sales	100.0	100.0
47.1	38.7	42.6				Gross Profit	44.0	41.4
44.2	35.3	37.1				Operating Expenses	41.3	37.6
2.8	3.3	5.5				Operating Profit	2.6	3.8
2.8	1.1	1.1				All Other Expenses (net)	1.6	1.7
.0	2.3	4.3				Profit Before Taxes	1.1	2.1
						RATIOS		
2.8	3.3	2.8				Current	3.7	3.6
1.7	1.8	1.6					2.0	1.8
1.1	1.4	1.3					1.2	1.1
.9	1.0	.9				Quick	1.0	.6
.3	.4	.6					(57) .4	.3
.1	.1	.2					.1	.1
0 UND	0 UND	1 414.8				Sales/Receivables	0 UND	0 UND
1 700.5	0 881.7	8 46.6					1 297.1	0 910.5
5 78.0	8 44.9	29 12.8					14 25.8	7 53.9
53 6.9	63 5.8	78 4.7				Cost of Sales/Inventory	74 5.0	90 4.1
96 3.8	113 3.2	90 4.0					131 2.8	126 2.9
287 1.3	165 2.2	173 2.1					215 1.7	180 2.0
0 UND	12 30.3	24 15.3				Cost of Sales/Payables	14 25.9	14 25.4
16 23.1	32 11.2	56 6.6					40 9.1	32 11.6
39 9.4	55 6.7	74 5.0					70 5.2	52 7.0
5.7	5.0	5.1				Sales/Working Capital	4.6	4.6
9.4	9.1	9.6					7.4	10.3
87.7	21.4	19.3					31.0	82.2
5.1	14.8	19.8				EBIT/Interest	4.1	7.0
(17) 1.8	(15) 2.2	6.2					(52) 2.1	(45) 2.4
-3.6	.2	1.4					1.0	.7
						Net Profit + Depr., Dep., Amort./Cur. Mat. L/T/D		
.0	.1	.1				Fixed/Worth	.1	.1
-1.5	.4	.4					.4	.3
-.3	-1.5	1.2					3.0	3.5
1.5	1.0	1.0				Debt/Worth	1.0	.6
-7.5	1.7	3.2					3.2	2.0
-2.9	-11.5	6.2					81.4	15.2
	70.2	87.4				% Profit Before Taxes/Tangible Net Worth	68.1	45.7
	(13) 25.0	48.2					(45) 23.5	(50) 15.2
	-3.2	4.8					6.7	-4.8
22.3	17.6	11.3				% Profit Before Taxes/Total Assets	10.4	15.4
5.3	8.7	3.9					5.1	4.6
-3.9	-3.2	1.2					.0	-1.1
281.7	103.9	105.8				Sales/Net Fixed Assets	88.4	111.0
68.8	32.2	26.5					36.5	48.0
24.0	13.7	5.7					10.0	11.5
5.8	4.7	4.4				Sales/Total Assets	3.9	4.2
4.3	2.7	2.2					2.5	2.7
1.5	2.1	1.4					1.5	1.6
.4	.4	.4				% Depr., Dep., Amort./Sales	.5	.4
(10) .8	(13) 1.2	(11) .5					(40) .9	(42) .8
1.8	2.1	2.6					1.7	2.5
		1.5				% Officers', Directors' Owners' Comp/Sales	1.9	2.3
	(12)	3.3					(27) 3.1	(33) 3.7
		6.0					6.7	5.8
21094M	73917M	165391M	194355M	308552M	1612547M	Net Sales ($)	1792483M	505075M
5031M	19576M	68907M	95133M	143287M	652680M	Total Assets ($)	921054M	246125M

Comparative Historical Data | Current Data Sorted by Sales

Type of Statement

4		6		8	Unqualified			1	2	5
6		4		2	Reviewed				1	1
6		4		7	Compiled	2	3	1	1	1
18		27		19	Tax Returns	7	4	3	1	4
8		19		26	Other	9	6	1	1	6	3
4/1/08-		4/1/09-		4/1/10-			9 (4/1-9/30/10)		53 (10/1/10-3/31/11)	
3/31/09		3/31/10		3/31/11						
ALL		ALL		ALL		0-1MM	1-3MM	3-5MM	5-10MM	10-25MM	25MM & OVER
42		60		62	**NUMBER OF STATEMENTS**	18	13	6	4	12	9

%		%		%	ASSETS	%	%	%	%	%	%
8.8		9.0		12.5	Cash & Equivalents	12.1	13.0			13.2	
6.3		6.7		7.9	Trade Receivables (net)	9.0	4.7			7.4	
62.3		57.9		53.8	Inventory	60.0	51.2			56.6	
1.4		2.1		1.9	All Other Current	.9	2.7			2.7	
78.8		75.7		76.1	Total Current	82.0	71.7			79.9	
11.4		14.0		13.6	Fixed Assets (net)	10.9	14.3			7.7	
4.0		6.3		5.3	Intangibles (net)	4.1	5.4			8.7	
5.8		4.0		5.0	All Other Non-Current	3.0	8.6			3.8	
100.0		100.0		100.0	Total	100.0	100.0			100.0	

					LIABILITIES						
13.5		8.9		14.3	Notes Payable-Short Term	27.5	11.7			11.3	
2.1		2.0		1.9	Cur. Mat.-L.T.D.	1.4	4.2			1.2	
15.8		15.4		16.9	Trade Payables	10.6	19.4			19.8	
.0		.1		.1	Income Taxes Payable	.0	.1			.2	
11.7		11.9		14.8	All Other Current	13.2	14.8			14.9	
43.1		38.2		48.0	Total Current	52.7	50.3			47.3	
24.7		26.1		21.9	Long-Term Debt	18.3	26.6			11.6	
.3		.1		.2	Deferred Taxes	.0	.0			.0	
7.1		5.0		10.8	All Other Non-Current	18.7	11.1			4.5	
24.8		30.6		19.1	Net Worth	10.2	12.0			36.6	
100.0		100.0		100.0	Total Liabilities & Net Worth	100.0	100.0			100.0	

					INCOME DATA						
100.0		100.0		100.0	Net Sales	100.0	100.0			100.0	
42.4		45.3		42.7	Gross Profit	50.6	41.6			36.8	
39.9		41.8		39.6	Operating Expenses	46.4	40.1			32.3	
2.5		3.5		3.1	Operating Profit	4.2	1.5			4.5	
1.5		1.3		1.7	All Other Expenses (net)	3.2	.7			.7	
1.0		2.2		1.4	Profit Before Taxes	1.0	.8			3.9	

					RATIOS						
3.9		4.3		2.6		3.0	3.5			2.5	
2.3		2.2		1.8	Current	2.0	1.4			1.7	
1.3		1.4		1.3		1.3	1.1			1.3	

.8		1.1		.9		.9	1.1			.8	
.3	(59)	.3		.4	Quick	.3	.4			.5	
.1		.2		.1		.0	.1			.1	

0	UND	0	UND	0	UND		0	UND	0	UND			0	924.5	
1	388.9	2	216.8	1	245.2	Sales/Receivables	1	373.5	0	763.5			2	156.8	
17	22.1	15	23.9	13	29.1		14	26.7	8	46.9			13	27.3	

88	4.2	96	3.8	75	4.9		81	4.5	53	6.9			71	5.2	
164	2.2	168	2.2	107	3.4	Cost of Sales/Inventory	193	1.9	103	3.6			79	4.6	
229	1.6	243	1.5	199	1.8		477	.8	141	2.6			99	3.7	

14	25.7	23	15.9	15	24.0		0	UND	8	45.5			20	18.5	
25	14.5	37	9.8	35	10.5	Cost of Sales/Payables	24	15.1	26	13.8			31	11.9	
45	8.2	57	6.5	56	6.5		39	9.4	59	6.2			59	6.1	

4.2		3.1		6.3		4.3	5.7			8.0	
5.8		5.9		9.2	Sales/Working Capital	7.2	10.0			13.4	
21.8		16.4		25.9		26.7	87.7			24.8	

	7.3		10.0		9.0			4.1		6.0			116.3	
(40)	2.5	(53)	3.2	(55)	2.4	EBIT/Interest	(15)	1.8	(10)	1.8			13.5	
	-.5		-.1		-.3			-2.7		-5.6			1.3	

					Net Profit + Depr., Dep., Amort./Cur. Mat. L/T/D						

.1		.1		.1		.0	.3			.1	
.2		.3		.5	Fixed/Worth	UND	.7			.3	
4.8		2.0		-1.0		-.4	-.3			.9	

.7		.6		1.1		.6	1.3			.9	
2.4		2.3		3.9	Debt/Worth	UND	5.8			3.1	
-16.8		10.4		-6.2		-3.0	-4.4			6.9	

	40.1		71.2		69.9	% Profit Before Taxes/Tangible Net Worth							119.6	
(31)	12.5	(50)	17.5	(42)	23.3						(11)	59.8	
	-6.7		-5.2		3.5							7.9	

14.1		12.2		14.2	% Profit Before Taxes/Total Assets	23.8	10.4			27.5	
3.4		6.3		4.0		5.2	2.0			9.2	
-5.2		-3.8		-2.4		-1.7	-12.2			1.1	

119.7		112.9		124.3	Sales/Net Fixed Assets	251.9	79.2			147.3	
40.9		31.7		32.2		65.0	32.3			105.8	
21.2		9.7		11.0		21.7	14.0			27.1	

3.1		3.0		4.7	Sales/Total Assets	5.2	4.6			5.7	
2.3		2.1		2.5		2.3	3.3			3.7	
2.0		1.5		1.9		1.2	2.0			2.2	

	.5		.5		.4	% Depr., Dep., Amort./Sales								
(29)	.9	(42)	.8	(42)	.9									
	1.6		2.7		2.1									

	2.0		1.3		2.4	% Officers', Directors' Owners' Comp/Sales								
(20)	2.8	(31)	3.1	(26)	5.1									
	5.3		6.5		8.9									

789892M		1343624M		2375856M	Net Sales ($)	10589M	28374M	20868M	26946M	194745M	2094334M
351167M		779602M		984614M	Total Assets ($)	4453M	11598M	16268M	12493M	63982M	875820M

M = $ thousand   MM = $ million
See Pages 9 through 22 for Explanation of Ratios and Data

Current Data Sorted by Assets   Comparative Historical Data

0-500M	500M-2MM	2-10MM	10-50MM	50-100MM	100-250MM	Type of Statement	4/1/06-3/31/07 ALL	4/1/07-3/31/08 ALL
	1					Unqualified	2	
	3	6				Reviewed	19	13
2	9	10	1	1	1	Compiled	20	22
13	9	5				Tax Returns	21	16
4	8	16	4	2		Other	20	23
	22 (4/1-9/30/10)		73 (10/1/10-3/31/11)					
19	30	37	5	3	1	NUMBER OF STATEMENTS	82	74
%	%	%	%	%	%	ASSETS	%	%
10.1	5.0	5.3				Cash & Equivalents	5.3	6.7
5.9	11.5	10.8				Trade Receivables (net)	13.7	13.0
59.7	61.7	59.8				Inventory	58.2	55.7
1.6	1.1	3.3				All Other Current	2.7	1.8
77.3	79.3	79.2				Total Current	79.9	77.2
11.8	13.4	12.9				Fixed Assets (net)	13.1	14.4
3.5	3.0	1.6				Intangibles (net)	2.0	2.1
7.5	4.3	6.3				All Other Non-Current	5.1	6.3
100.0	100.0	100.0				Total	100.0	100.0
						LIABILITIES		
15.1	17.6	16.0				Notes Payable-Short Term	22.6	19.4
1.6	3.7	2.3				Cur. Mat.-L.T.D.	4.7	4.1
11.8	19.0	16.1				Trade Payables	13.6	17.2
.0	.0	.1				Income Taxes Payable	.2	.3
12.6	10.8	9.9				All Other Current	7.4	7.3
41.3	51.1	44.5				Total Current	48.5	48.2
19.6	16.4	9.9				Long-Term Debt	12.5	17.4
.0	.0	.2				Deferred Taxes	.2	.1
12.9	7.8	6.9				All Other Non-Current	5.0	5.6
26.3	24.6	38.4				Net Worth	33.8	28.7
100.0	100.0	100.0				Total Liabilities & Net Worth	100.0	100.0
						INCOME DATA		
100.0	100.0	100.0				Net Sales	100.0	100.0
51.1	41.0	41.2				Gross Profit	42.5	41.8
47.5	37.7	37.3				Operating Expenses	39.8	37.9
3.7	3.3	3.9				Operating Profit	2.7	3.9
1.7	1.6	2.4				All Other Expenses (net)	2.0	1.6
2.0	1.8	1.5				Profit Before Taxes	.7	2.4
						RATIOS		
9.0	2.6	3.6					2.3	2.0
2.0	1.4	1.7				Current	1.7	1.6
1.2	1.1	1.2					1.3	1.2
1.0	.5	.6					.8	.7
.5	.2	.4				Quick	(81) .3	.3
.1	.1	.1					.1	.1
0 UND	0 999.8	4 87.7					5 71.5	2 146.4
4 91.2	6 59.6	10 35.0				Sales/Receivables	13 29.1	11 32.4
10 37.3	22 16.8	32 11.4					34 10.6	31 11.9
110 3.3	121 3.0	131 2.8					134 2.7	105 3.5
271 1.3	191 1.9	215 1.7				Cost of Sales/Inventory	192 1.9	181 2.0
449 .8	368 1.0	347 1.1					277 1.3	270 1.4
0 UND	28 13.1	26 14.0					19 18.8	16 23.0
15 24.0	43 8.4	49 7.5				Cost of Sales/Payables	36 10.1	37 9.8
59 6.2	81 4.5	71 5.2					76 4.8	85 4.3
2.9	4.1	2.8					3.6	3.6
4.3	7.8	5.3				Sales/Working Capital	6.1	8.8
18.4	36.8	16.2					11.5	22.8
7.6	5.2	4.3					2.6	3.1
(14) 1.6	(28) 1.8	(33) 2.1				EBIT/Interest	(77) 1.4	(69) 1.8
.9	1.2	.9					.4	1.2
						Net Profit + Depr., Dep.,	2.1	13.9
						Amort./Cur. Mat. L/T/D	(20) .4	(15) 3.3
							-.3	1.6
.1	.1	.0					.1	.1
.3	.3	.2				Fixed/Worth	.3	.3
-1.5	2.4	1.4					.8	1.7
.9	1.4	.7					1.0	1.1
3.4	3.9	2.1				Debt/Worth	2.1	2.3
-12.5	16.7	5.6					4.6	7.8
92.2	34.3	23.3				% Profit Before Taxes/Tangible	16.5	30.6
(14) 33.8	(27) 10.6	(34) 9.0				Net Worth	(76) 5.3	(62) 8.6
2.2	-.1	-.7					-8.5	1.2
14.9	7.6	6.8				% Profit Before Taxes/Total	5.7	8.3
4.0	2.3	2.8				Assets	1.8	2.9
.0	.1	-1.6					-2.4	.5
189.0	108.9	94.1					50.3	57.4
31.0	39.2	26.7				Sales/Net Fixed Assets	21.8	24.6
10.8	9.1	7.5					11.3	10.6
3.2	3.0	2.5					2.6	3.0
1.8	2.0	1.7				Sales/Total Assets	1.8	1.9
1.3	1.3	1.4					1.3	1.4
.3	.4	.4					.5	.4
(10) 1.0	(20) .8	(25) .8				% Depr., Dep., Amort./Sales	(65) 1.0	(60) .9
2.8	1.3	5.1					2.0	1.9
3.8	2.1	1.0					2.0	2.0
(12) 7.3	(18) 4.5	(12) 2.0				% Officers', Directors' Owners' Comp/Sales	(40) 3.2	(38) 4.5
9.1	7.3	3.4					6.1	6.2
13531M	77893M	341374M	140371M	224542M	306927M	Net Sales ($)	657976M	604247M
6532M	34893M	174663M	76954M	228847M	119007M	Total Assets ($)	441559M	377513M

Comparative Historical Data | Current Data Sorted by Sales

Type of Statement

			Type of Statement	0-1MM	1-3MM	3-5MM	5-10MM	10-25MM	25MM & OVER
2	6	4	Unqualified	1	4	1	1	1	3
13	12	9	Reviewed	2	5	2	7	2	
19	20	21	Compiled	12	8	5	3	2	
21	25	27	Tax Returns	5	4	2	8	9	4
22	12	34	Other			4			
4/1/08-3/31/09 ALL	4/1/09-3/31/10 ALL	4/1/10-3/31/11 ALL		22 (4/1-9/30/10)			73 (10/1/10-3/31/11)		

Data

4/1/08-3/31/09 ALL	4/1/09-3/31/10 ALL	4/1/10-3/31/11 ALL		0-1MM	1-3MM	3-5MM	5-10MM	10-25MM	25MM & OVER
77	75	95	NUMBER OF STATEMENTS	20	21	14	19	14	7
%	%	%	**ASSETS**	%	%	%	%	%	%
7.5	6.3	6.0	Cash & Equivalents	7.4	5.8	4.5	5.7	7.2	
12.0	10.9	12.7	Trade Receivables (net)	6.4	5.1	12.8	10.6	21.4	
60.7	62.2	57.9	Inventory	59.1	58.5	65.5	64.1	54.1	
1.7	2.4	2.4	All Other Current	1.9	2.4	3.9	1.3	2.1	
81.9	81.8	79.0	Total Current	74.8	71.8	86.7	81.7	84.8	
13.5	12.3	12.7	Fixed Assets (net)	15.0	17.3	7.9	11.9	6.4	
.9	1.9	2.4	Intangibles (net)	3.2	4.5	.3	1.2	2.1	
3.7	4.0	5.8	All Other Non-Current	7.0	6.4	5.1	5.2	6.7	
100.0	100.0	100.0	Total	100.0	100.0	100.0	100.0	100.0	
			LIABILITIES						
17.0	17.2	16.7	Notes Payable-Short Term	21.5	14.6	17.9	18.1	11.7	
3.7	2.8	2.4	Cur. Mat.-L.T.D.	2.0	3.6	2.1	2.9	2.1	
18.6	14.8	16.0	Trade Payables	7.9	16.5	20.9	17.3	20.6	
.5	.1	.1	Income Taxes Payable	.0	.0	.0	.0	.3	
8.7	7.5	10.9	All Other Current	8.4	12.7	11.4	11.2	12.6	
48.4	42.4	46.0	Total Current	39.8	47.4	52.4	49.5	47.4	
14.4	12.0	14.8	Long-Term Debt	20.0	17.0	14.4	8.6	3.6	
.1	.1	.1	Deferred Taxes	.0	.0	.0	.2	.1	
4.0	9.3	8.0	All Other Non-Current	15.2	8.8	12.4	3.5	1.3	
33.1	36.1	31.1	Net Worth	25.1	26.8	20.8	38.1	47.5	
100.0	100.0	100.0	Total Liabilities & Net Worth	100.0	100.0	100.0	100.0	100.0	
			INCOME DATA						
100.0	100.0	100.0	Net Sales	100.0	100.0	100.0	100.0	100.0	
41.9	43.5	43.8	Gross Profit	49.2	45.9	43.9	41.8	34.9	
39.8	42.0	40.2	Operating Expenses	44.8	42.0	41.6	36.8	33.8	
2.1	1.5	3.6	Operating Profit	4.4	3.9	2.3	4.9	1.1	
1.0	.5	1.9	All Other Expenses (net)	3.0	1.6	.5	3.3	.5	
1.1	1.0	1.7	Profit Before Taxes	1.4	2.3	1.8	1.7	.6	
			RATIOS						
2.7	3.5	3.0		4.7	2.9	2.3	5.0	3.0	
1.8	1.9	1.7	Current	1.9	1.6	1.6	1.5	1.8	
1.3	1.3	1.2		1.3	1.0	1.3	1.1	1.6	
.8	.7	.6		.9	.4	.6	.6	1.6	
.3	.3	.3	Quick	.3	.2	.2	.4	.5	
.1	.1	.1		.1	.1	.1	.1	.2	
1 282.8	2 147.7	2 174.0		0 UND	0 UND	0 999.8	4 88.4	10 35.4	
11 32.6	11 32.2	10 37.9	Sales/Receivables	6 60.5	4 91.2	6 58.8	14 26.2	28 13.0	
26 14.0	24 15.5	29 12.4		12 29.5	13 28.0	42 8.6	25 14.3	45 8.1	
119 3.1	142 2.6	124 2.9		172 2.1	127 2.9	125 2.9	157 2.3	85 4.3	
190 1.9	227 1.6	196 1.9	Cost of Sales/Inventory	311 1.2	196 1.9	233 1.6	215 1.7	127 2.9	
310 1.2	321 1.1	348 1.0		460 .8	327 1.1	356 1.0	347 1.1	152 2.4	
15 23.7	16 22.8	22 16.4		0 UND	27 13.5	28 13.0	25 14.8	22 16.9	
40 9.1	36 10.2	39 9.2	Cost of Sales/Payables	24 15.5	42 8.7	53 6.9	47 7.8	43 8.5	
76 4.8	55 6.7	68 5.3		72 5.0	95 3.9	83 4.4	88 4.2	61 6.0	
4.0	2.8	3.0		2.5	4.0	2.8	3.4	4.4	
6.8	5.0	5.3	Sales/Working Capital	3.8	7.5	5.8	8.8	6.6	
14.4	11.1	22.1		11.2	NM	18.0	33.0	10.3	
5.1	5.3	5.2		2.6	3.0	4.1	9.7	7.3	
(69) 2.0	(70) 1.5	(84) 2.1	EBIT/Interest	(16) 1.4	(19) 1.7	(13) 2.1	(18) 3.7	(12) 3.2	
.4	.6	1.1		.6	1.1	1.1	1.1	-.6	
17.7	29.6	5.3							
(19) 4.0	(15) 5.5	(11) 1.7	Net Profit + Depr., Dep., Amort./Cur. Mat. L/T/D						
.5	.4	.7							
.1	.1	.1		.1	.2	.0	.0	.0	
.2	.2	.3	Fixed/Worth	.6	1.2	.1	.3	.1	
.8	1.1	1.7		16.5	2.9	1.0	1.6	.2	
.8	.9	1.0		1.2	1.5	1.4	.4	.4	
1.8	2.1	2.6	Debt/Worth	3.5	3.9	2.6	2.0	1.2	
4.5	4.2	9.1		81.9	11.1	9.5	14.4	2.3	
18.3	19.2	34.3		90.3	35.2	36.6	35.4	27.0	
(70) 4.8	(68) 4.4	(83) 10.6	% Profit Before Taxes/Tangible Net Worth	(16) 21.3	(18) 8.2	(13) 3.7	(17) 12.5	(13) 12.3	
-4.1	-3.6	.7		-5.4	-.2	.9	3.5	-4.4	
6.6	5.8	8.8		11.8	11.5	4.8	9.4	10.6	
2.1	1.3	2.5	% Profit Before Taxes/Total Assets	2.5	2.2	2.2	4.7	4.2	
-1.9	-1.7	.0		-1.7	.1	.3	.3	-4.0	
73.5	87.6	96.7		152.9	65.4	999.8	124.3	105.3	
26.3	26.1	26.7	Sales/Net Fixed Assets	27.5	17.5	81.0	48.2	55.9	
10.1	12.1	9.6		6.2	7.8	18.7	7.0	23.1	
2.9	2.7	2.6		2.0	2.8	2.8	2.8	2.7	
2.1	1.8	1.7	Sales/Total Assets	1.4	1.8	1.9	1.7	2.4	
1.4	1.3	1.3		1.0	1.2	1.3	1.5	2.0	
.6	.5	.4		.5	.4		.4	.2	
(62) 1.1	(63) 1.0	(64) .9	% Depr., Dep., Amort./Sales	(11) 1.1	(15) 1.0		(11) .8	(12) .5	
2.1	2.1	2.1		1.8	4.0		7.3	.9	
2.5	2.2	2.2		5.1	2.3				
(35) 3.7	(38) 4.5	(44) 3.9	% Officers', Directors' Owners' Comp/Sales	(11) 8.8	(15) 3.7				
6.4	8.2	7.5		9.2	6.6				
1043948M	1215551M	1104638M	Net Sales ($)	11716M	37946M	54794M	125624M	218802M	655756M
543393M	613180M	640896M	Total Assets ($)	9064M	24023M	30515M	75031M	101130M	401133M

© RMA 2011

M = $ thousand   MM = $ million

See Pages 9 through 22 for Explanation of Ratios and Data

Current Data Sorted by Assets   Comparative Historical Data

						Type of Statement		
		2	6	3		Unqualified	10	14
	4	4	4			Reviewed	9	4
1	4	4	1			Compiled	11	9
7	4	6				Tax Returns	14	13
11	5	4	7		1	Other	19	17
	25 (4/1-9/30/10)		49 (10/1/10-3/31/11)				4/1/06-3/31/07 ALL	4/1/07-3/31/08 ALL
0-500M	500M-2MM	2-10MM	10-50MM	50-100MM	100-250MM	NUMBER OF STATEMENTS	63	57
19	13	20	18	3	1			
%	%	%	%	%	%	**ASSETS**	%	%
9.8	7.7	12.4	11.3			Cash & Equivalents	12.6	14.5
2.6	14.9	14.0	8.6			Trade Receivables (net)	7.9	6.4
63.4	43.4	42.6	37.1			Inventory	47.1	50.6
1.1	.5	5.2	3.3			All Other Current	2.0	1.7
76.9	66.4	74.3	60.3			Total Current	69.5	73.2
7.6	17.5	16.0	29.7			Fixed Assets (net)	22.8	19.5
2.3	3.9	2.7	5.0			Intangibles (net)	2.3	2.7
13.2	12.1	7.0	5.0			All Other Non-Current	5.3	4.6
100.0	100.0	100.0	100.0			Total	100.0	100.0
						LIABILITIES		
41.0	17.6	11.3	7.2			Notes Payable-Short Term	13.9	15.8
2.9	.1	1.2	1.6			Cur. Mat.-L.T.D.	2.1	2.3
18.8	38.5	26.0	14.0			Trade Payables	21.8	28.6
1.5	.0	.5	.0			Income Taxes Payable	.3	2.1
13.5	9.9	15.4	9.5			All Other Current	12.4	14.4
77.8	66.1	54.5	32.4			Total Current	50.4	63.1
15.4	4.9	10.4	14.6			Long-Term Debt	9.0	10.6
.0	.0	.1	.3			Deferred Taxes	.3	.2
14.9	.2	.8	4.7			All Other Non-Current	6.7	4.9
-8.1	28.7	34.1	48.1			Net Worth	33.5	21.2
100.0	100.0	100.0	100.0			Total Liabilities & Net Worth	100.0	100.0
						INCOME DATA		
100.0	100.0	100.0	100.0			Net Sales	100.0	100.0
39.4	32.6	39.7	44.5			Gross Profit	40.5	37.6
39.9	31.0	36.2	41.4			Operating Expenses	39.1	36.2
-.5	1.6	3.5	3.1			Operating Profit	1.3	1.4
1.2	-.1	.4	1.1			All Other Expenses (net)	1.0	1.1
-1.8	1.6	3.1	2.0			Profit Before Taxes	.4	.4
						RATIOS		
2.6	1.4	2.3	3.8				2.8	2.6
1.6	.9	1.5	2.3			Current	1.6	1.5
.7	.6	1.2	1.3				1.0	.8
.7	.7	1.0	1.0				.7	.8
(18) .2	.2	.6	.6			Quick	.3	.3
.0	.1	.2	.3				.1	.1
0 UND	1 269.9	1 263.9	2 194.7				1 311.1	1 477.1
0 UND	4 94.9	7 49.2	8 47.6			Sales/Receivables	3 107.2	3 107.2
0 UND	22 16.3	24 15.5	33 11.0				13 27.3	14 25.2
55 6.6	61 6.0	51 7.1	88 4.1				69 5.3	77 4.7
154 2.4	92 4.0	90 4.1	141 2.6			Cost of Sales/Inventory	103 3.5	115 3.2
250 1.5	133 2.8	149 2.4	208 1.8				162 2.2	146 2.5
9 40.5	43 8.4	28 13.0	22 16.6				15 23.6	27 13.4
41 8.9	57 6.4	63 5.8	42 8.6			Cost of Sales/Payables	46 8.0	44 8.2
84 4.3	102 3.6	70 5.2	79 4.6				82 4.4	78 4.7
4.3	13.0	7.2	3.6				5.9	6.5
8.7	-38.9	12.4	6.7			Sales/Working Capital	10.3	14.4
-22.7	-12.0	21.3	16.2				-191.6	-22.3
9.1	11.7	52.4	10.8				11.3	10.3
(12) -1.0	(10) 4.8	(19) 8.6	(15) 5.1			EBIT/Interest	(53) 3.0	(48) 1.8
-5.9	-2.3	1.1	-.7				1.0	.5
						Net Profit + Depr., Dep.,	9.4	
						Amort./Cur. Mat. L/T/D	(11) 3.8	
							1.7	
.0	.0	.1	.3				.2	.2
.1	.6	.3	.5			Fixed/Worth	.6	.6
.4	1.7	1.0	1.3				4.7	-1.0
.6	1.0	.7	.5				.5	.5
2.8	7.0	1.3	1.4			Debt/Worth	1.6	3.3
-3.2	11.2	3.3	2.6				100.8	-5.4
79.1	54.4	53.4	22.6				24.3	14.4
(12) 4.7	(11) 36.2	(17) 17.2	(17) 7.6			% Profit Before Taxes/Tangible Net Worth	(51) 8.8	(40) 5.7
-4.6	8.7	4.2	-3.1				1.2	-1.3
28.3	14.3	16.4	6.7				9.2	7.9
-1.9	5.2	7.4	3.8			% Profit Before Taxes/Total Assets	3.6	1.7
-24.1	.2	.5	-2.4				-1.3	-2.1
UND	439.5	92.8	37.5				47.5	55.2
90.2	38.6	24.8	6.3			Sales/Net Fixed Assets	16.7	15.2
19.7	9.2	9.6	2.8				6.0	7.6
3.5	3.9	3.3	2.1				3.6	3.6
3.0	2.7	2.8	1.7			Sales/Total Assets	2.4	2.6
1.9	2.3	2.4	1.3				1.9	1.7
		.6	1.4				.9	.8
	(18) 1.1	(16) 1.8				% Depr., Dep., Amort./Sales	(54) 1.3	(46) 1.4
	1.9	2.8					2.3	1.9
							1.9	2.2
						% Officers', Directors' Owners' Comp/Sales	(23) 4.0	(12) 4.2
							6.4	8.1
14380M	36866M	249162M	710106M	452369M	227388M	Net Sales ($)	1246712M	2483349M
4268M	13665M	90076M	391667M	225499M	106228M	Total Assets ($)	544870M	948334M

M = $ thousand   MM = $ million
See Pages 9 through 22 for Explanation of Ratios and Data

Comparative Historical Data | | | | ## Current Data Sorted by Sales

			Type of Statement					5	6
13	8	11	Unqualified					5	6
3	4	8	Reviewed				2	4	2
10	7	10	Compiled		3	3	2	1	1
16	22	17	Tax Returns	5	5		3	4	
17	18	28	Other	9	6	1	1	4	7
4/1/08- 3/31/09 ALL	4/1/09- 3/31/10 ALL	4/1/10- 3/31/11 ALL		0-1MM	1-3MM	3-5MM	5-10MM	10-25MM	25MM & OVER
				25 (4/1-9/30/10)			49 (10/1/10-3/31/11)		
59	59	74	NUMBER OF STATEMENTS	14	14	4	8	18	16
%	%	%	**ASSETS**	%	%	%	%	%	%
13.3	14.0	10.6	Cash & Equivalents	11.4	5.1			13.2	10.8
6.7	5.0	9.9	Trade Receivables (net)	3.6	6.6			12.7	9.0
44.9	50.7	46.0	Inventory	64.3	48.2			41.4	38.8
2.4	2.2	2.7	All Other Current	.4	1.1			6.7	3.0
67.2	71.9	69.1	Total Current	79.6	61.0			74.0	61.5
23.3	17.6	18.4	Fixed Assets (net)	12.6	13.5			20.7	27.1
1.7	2.8	3.4	Intangibles (net)	1.6	7.8			1.0	5.3
7.8	7.7	9.1	All Other Non-Current	6.1	17.7			4.3	6.1
100.0	100.0	100.0	Total	100.0	100.0			100.0	100.0
			LIABILITIES						
9.7	14.8	18.7	Notes Payable-Short Term	24.8	38.2			15.1	6.5
1.8	2.9	1.6	Cur. Mat.-L.T.D.	3.9	.2			1.2	1.2
28.6	22.0	23.5	Trade Payables	20.9	25.6			21.5	21.1
.7	.6	.6	Income Taxes Payable	2.1	.0			.6	.1
21.2	14.7	12.0	All Other Current	11.1	15.3			7.0	8.9
62.1	55.1	56.4	Total Current	62.8	79.4			45.4	37.7
11.1	17.6	12.2	Long-Term Debt	19.0	9.4			9.4	10.2
.1	.3	.1	Deferred Taxes	.0	.0			.2	.3
11.0	3.9	7.5	All Other Non-Current	7.0	14.4			1.6	14.3
15.6	23.1	23.7	Net Worth	11.3	-3.2			43.3	37.5
100.0	100.0	100.0	Total Liabilties & Net Worth	100.0	100.0			100.0	100.0
			INCOME DATA						
100.0	100.0	100.0	Net Sales	100.0	100.0			100.0	100.0
43.5	41.3	40.1	Gross Profit	43.2	33.7			39.5	44.4
40.9	37.9	38.2	Operating Expenses	43.9	33.5			36.6	41.8
2.6	3.4	1.9	Operating Profit	-.7	.3			2.9	2.6
.9	.9	.8	All Other Expenses (net)	1.5	.4			.1	.9
1.7	2.6	1.1	Profit Before Taxes	-2.2	-.2			2.8	1.7
			RATIOS						
2.4	2.8	2.5	Current	4.1	1.9			3.0	2.9
1.5	1.8	1.5		1.6	1.3			1.6	1.9
.9	1.0	1.0		.7	.8			1.3	1.2
.9	1.0	.9	Quick	.7	.6			1.0	.8
.4	.4	(73) .4		(13) .2	.2			.7	.5
.1	.2	.1		.1	.0			.3	.2
0 754.0	0 UND	1 679.0	Sales/Receivables	0 UND	0 UND			2 174.2	2 189.0
2 166.8	3 142.9	3 111.5		0 UND	3 133.3			9 39.8	5 80.9
11 32.6	17 21.2	20 18.3		4 93.9	9 38.7			22 16.7	25 14.5
70 5.2	92 4.0	67 5.4	Cost of Sales/Inventory	110 3.3	48 7.6			56 6.5	81 4.5
113 3.2	123 3.0	112 3.2		196 1.9	93 3.9			94 3.9	122 3.0
153 2.4	161 2.3	168 2.2		319 1.1	135 2.7			163 2.2	160 2.3
26 14.1	21 17.5	24 15.3	Cost of Sales/Payables	19 19.2	1 280.4			11 34.6	28 13.2
53 6.9	47 7.8	57 6.5		64 5.7	62 5.9			42 8.7	48 7.6
98 3.7	79 4.6	82 4.4		87 4.2	95 3.8			67 5.5	89 4.1
6.4	4.8	5.3	Sales/Working Capital	3.2	9.3			5.2	5.4
12.0	9.0	12.4		9.2	23.4			9.1	9.2
-23.1	474.7	120.9		-5.8	-26.6			15.3	21.8
12.7	15.7	14.2	EBIT/Interest	9.3	7.3			35.8	22.1
(51) 3.2	(46) 3.9	(59) 5.1		(10) -2.6	(10) 4.8			7.3	(12) 3.4
-.1	.7	-.8		-6.8	-2.3			1.7	-.4
			Net Profit + Depr., Dep., Amort./Cur. Mat. L/T/D						
.2	.1	.1	Fixed/Worth	.0	.0			.1	.3
.5	.4	.4		.1	.3			.4	.5
-5.7	1.8	1.4		NM	1.0			1.0	NM
.6	.5	.7	Debt/Worth	.6	.7			.7	.5
2.1	1.7	2.0		4.0	3.5			1.3	1.5
-12.5	64.1	11.0		-5.7	-8.5			2.3	NM
38.7	38.9	46.9	% Profit Before Taxes/Tangible Net Worth		57.3			47.2	28.7
(42) 13.2	(46) 9.3	(58) 14.7			(10) 15.8		(17)	11.4	(12) 11.6
1.0	.8	.8			-6.0			2.4	.6
13.1	14.9	14.3	% Profit Before Taxes/Total Assets	28.3	12.0			15.6	8.6
6.8	3.2	4.2		-.7	2.2			6.4	2.5
-2.3	.2	-2.7		-26.5	-4.4			2.0	-2.7
51.5	139.7	110.0	Sales/Net Fixed Assets	UND	UND			97.9	34.1
13.0	20.8	24.8		64.0	51.1			19.8	10.1
7.7	8.7	7.6		10.8	8.6			7.5	4.1
3.3	3.3	3.3	Sales/Total Assets	3.1	3.6			3.3	2.5
2.6	2.5	2.5		2.1	3.0			2.7	2.0
2.2	1.7	1.7		1.5	2.4			1.6	1.5
.7	.7	.8	% Depr., Dep., Amort./Sales					.7	1.3
(47) 1.1	(39) 1.3	(55) 1.4					(17)	1.1	(14) 1.5
1.9	2.2	2.1						1.8	2.7
1.8	2.8	1.8	% Officers', Directors' Owners' Comp/Sales						
(22) 3.0	(22) 4.6	(18) 3.5							
3.8	8.2	6.2							
1265366M	1644900M	1690271M	Net Sales ($)	6705M	24068M	16376M	60659M	291763M	1290700M
538209M	739325M	831403M	Total Assets ($)	3984M	9946M	4553M	41962M	141716M	629242M

© RMA 2011

M = $ thousand   MM = $ million
See Pages 9 through 22 for Explanation of Ratios and Data

Current Data Sorted by Assets   **Comparative Historical Data**

						Type of Statement		
			4		3	Unqualified	7	6
		3	4			Reviewed	6	4
	3	2				Compiled	8	3
1	3	1				Tax Returns	6	9
	1	2	2	1	1	Other	14	17
	4 (4/1-9/30/10)		27 (10/1/10-3/31/11)				4/1/06-3/31/07	4/1/07-3/31/08
0-500M	500M-2MM	2-10MM	10-50MM	50-100MM	100-250MM		ALL	ALL
1	7	8	10	1	4	NUMBER OF STATEMENTS	41	39
%	%	%	%	%	%	ASSETS	%	%
			21.7			Cash & Equivalents	9.9	7.1
			2.2			Trade Receivables (net)	11.8	9.5
			41.3			Inventory	46.0	48.2
			3.0			All Other Current	1.6	2.7
			68.2			Total Current	69.3	67.6
			24.7			Fixed Assets (net)	21.1	21.7
			2.3			Intangibles (net)	3.8	3.3
			4.8			All Other Non-Current	5.7	7.4
			100.0			Total	100.0	100.0
						LIABILITIES		
			2.5			Notes Payable-Short Term	10.0	7.1
			3.1			Cur. Mat.-L.T.D.	1.9	2.1
			14.4			Trade Payables	18.9	16.5
			.0			Income Taxes Payable	.5	.1
			9.0			All Other Current	8.5	8.8
			29.1			Total Current	39.9	34.6
			15.1			Long-Term Debt	22.3	16.3
			.9			Deferred Taxes	.4	.4
			6.3			All Other Non-Current	4.5	5.2
			48.7			Net Worth	33.0	43.5
			100.0			Total Liabilities & Net Worth	100.0	100.0
						INCOME DATA		
			100.0			Net Sales	100.0	100.0
			37.1			Gross Profit	37.4	40.1
			27.0			Operating Expenses	35.7	36.5
			10.0			Operating Profit	1.7	3.6
			-.7			All Other Expenses (net)	.6	.7
			10.7			Profit Before Taxes	1.1	2.9
						RATIOS		
			4.6				3.7	3.5
			2.6			Current	2.0	2.4
			1.5				1.3	1.5
			2.9				1.1	1.3
			1.0			Quick	.4	.4
			.5				.1	.1
		0 UND					0 UND	0 UND
		1 607.6				Sales/Receivables	4 86.3	4 93.2
		7 50.8					21 17.2	18 20.2
		36 10.1					52 7.1	56 6.6
		107 3.4				Cost of Sales/Inventory	118 3.1	118 3.1
		136 2.7					197 1.9	200 1.8
		8 45.8					18 20.4	14 25.4
		31 11.9				Cost of Sales/Payables	42 8.7	29 12.8
		42 8.6					62 5.9	53 6.8
			2.9				4.0	3.6
			6.6			Sales/Working Capital	6.6	6.3
			18.2				39.2	14.3
			5.4				5.4	8.3
						EBIT/Interest	(34) 2.8	(34) 3.1
			1.4				1.4	1.3
							6.3	3.5
						Net Profit + Depr., Dep., Amort./Cur. Mat. L/T/D	(10) 3.3	(10) 1.9
							.9	.6
			.2				.2	.1
			.6			Fixed/Worth	.5	.4
			1.3				3.6	1.1
			.4				.7	.4
			1.4			Debt/Worth	1.7	1.2
			3.9				13.0	2.9
			38.7				33.0	15.2
			14.3			% Profit Before Taxes/Tangible Net Worth	(35) 11.3	(34) 5.5
			5.9				4.2	1.0
			18.1				10.4	8.8
			4.6			% Profit Before Taxes/Total Assets	4.4	3.1
			3.0				1.6	.3
			88.4				75.4	71.8
			13.6			Sales/Net Fixed Assets	18.3	16.4
			3.5				7.1	5.8
			3.7				4.0	3.6
			2.3			Sales/Total Assets	2.2	2.3
			1.3				1.6	1.5
							.4	.4
						% Depr., Dep., Amort./Sales	(33) .9	(30) 1.2
							2.2	3.4
							3.7	1.4
						% Officers', Directors' Owners' Comp/Sales	(14) 4.5	(10) 2.8
							7.7	8.5
1080M	29256M	180996M	685676M	56259M	1548179M	Net Sales ($)	3123374M	3396186M
284M	9426M	42598M	228210M	50357M	544132M	Total Assets ($)	1030968M	1426787M

© RMA 2011

M = $ thousand   MM = $ million
See Pages 9 through 22 for Explanation of Ratios and Data

Comparative Historical Data				**Current Data Sorted by Sales**					
			Type of Statement						
13	10	7	Unqualified					1	6
4	9	7	Reviewed		1			2	4
4	9	5	Compiled		1	1	1		2
8	9	5	Tax Returns		2		2		
6	16	7	Other	1			2	1	4
4/1/08- 3/31/09 ALL	4/1/09- 3/31/10 ALL	4/1/10- 3/31/11 ALL			4 (4/1-9/30/10)		27 (10/1/10-3/31/11)		
				0-1MM	1-3MM	3-5MM	5-10MM	10-25MM	25MM & OVER
35	53	31	**NUMBER OF STATEMENTS**	1	4	1	5	4	16
%	%	%	**ASSETS**	%	%	%	%	%	%
9.8	15.0	14.2	Cash & Equivalents						15.5
5.4	9.2	9.9	Trade Receivables (net)						9.5
50.4	45.0	47.9	Inventory						46.2
1.1	1.7	1.8	All Other Current						3.3
66.7	71.0	73.8	Total Current						74.5
24.5	21.6	17.1	Fixed Assets (net)						16.7
2.5	2.4	1.7	Intangibles (net)						3.0
6.4	5.0	7.4	All Other Non-Current						5.8
100.0	100.0	100.0	Total						100.0
			LIABILITIES						
9.7	10.3	9.3	Notes Payable-Short Term						6.7
1.7	2.1	1.9	Cur. Mat.-L.T.D.						2.1
13.8	16.4	18.8	Trade Payables						22.7
.1	.5	.1	Income Taxes Payable						.3
9.9	7.9	8.7	All Other Current						9.6
35.3	37.2	38.8	Total Current						41.4
17.7	14.5	12.2	Long-Term Debt						8.1
.5	.5	.3	Deferred Taxes						.0
8.2	9.3	6.0	All Other Non-Current						4.5
38.3	38.6	42.6	Net Worth						45.9
100.0	100.0	100.0	Total Liabilities & Net Worth						100.0
			INCOME DATA						
100.0	100.0	100.0	Net Sales						100.0
42.7	41.1	39.4	Gross Profit						38.6
38.1	35.9	34.0	Operating Expenses						34.7
4.6	5.2	5.4	Operating Profit						3.9
1.7	2.5	.1	All Other Expenses (net)						.5
3.0	2.7	5.3	Profit Before Taxes						3.4
			RATIOS						
3.8	3.1	2.9	Current						3.4
2.1	2.1	1.9							1.6
1.3	1.3	1.3							1.3
1.2	1.2	1.2	Quick						1.3
.3	.8	.6							.6
.1	.2	.2							.2
0 UND	0 UND	0 999.8	Sales/Receivables					0 UND	
2 228.1	2 216.7	2 167.5						1 275.7	
15 24.8	15 24.1	15 24.3						11 32.7	
94 3.9	54 6.8	54 6.8	Cost of Sales/Inventory					53 6.9	
124 2.9	104 3.5	106 3.4						101 3.6	
215 1.7	155 2.4	136 2.7						139 2.6	
12 30.9	8 43.0	14 26.9	Cost of Sales/Payables					27 13.4	
29 12.7	26 14.2	36 10.1						43 8.5	
54 6.8	42 8.7	50 7.3						61 6.0	
3.9	5.4	3.8	Sales/Working Capital						3.7
6.2	7.7	8.1							12.6
18.3	19.3	17.7							21.9
8.7	25.9	28.6	EBIT/Interest						55.8
(34) 1.9	(44) 5.3	(28) 4.3						(15) 10.3	
-.2	1.8	1.4							1.6
		8.9	Net Profit + Depr., Dep., Amort./Cur. Mat. L/T/D						
	(18) 3.4								
		.1							
.2	.1	.1	Fixed/Worth						.2
.5	.4	.4							.4
1.7	1.2	.8							.7
.7	.5	.6	Debt/Worth						.6
2.0	1.6	1.5							1.5
3.7	6.3	2.7							3.0
34.2	41.6	46.1	% Profit Before Taxes/Tangible Net Worth						50.2
(32) 7.8	(46) 17.5	(29) 17.4							25.5
-7.4	5.7	4.3							4.6
9.1	16.6	20.2	% Profit Before Taxes/Total Assets						24.3
3.5	8.0	4.7							5.4
-2.4	1.7	.9							1.3
37.8	88.3	149.3	Sales/Net Fixed Assets						45.5
12.9	24.3	28.7							27.3
5.0	7.9	11.6							12.0
3.1	4.2	4.2	Sales/Total Assets						4.6
2.3	2.7	2.9							3.2
1.5	1.8	1.8							1.9
.6	.3	.5	% Depr., Dep., Amort./Sales						.4
(27) 1.5	(46) .9	(24) .7						(14) 1.0	
2.3	2.0	1.5							1.3
1.1	1.8	.8	% Officers', Directors' Owners' Comp/Sales						
(11) 4.1	(24) 3.3	(10) 2.1							
7.3	5.5	5.7							
2906528M	3072976M	2501446M	Net Sales ($)	933M	7120M	4501M	38248M	65844M	2384800M
1277213M	1193591M	875007M	Total Assets ($)	1426M	13940M	1347M	10779M	28015M	819500M

Current Data Sorted by Assets

Comparative Historical Data

Type of Statement	0-500M	500M-2MM	2-10MM	10-50MM	50-100MM	100-250MM	12 4/1/06-3/31/07 ALL	10 4/1/07-3/31/08 ALL
Unqualified			1	3	6	5	12	10
Reviewed		1	8	9	1		23	18
Compiled	5	14	9	1			23	25
Tax Returns	21	28	3				44	42
Other	7	10	15	13	2	2	45	44
	22 (4/1-9/30/10)			141 (10/1/10-3/31/11)				
NUMBER OF STATEMENTS	33	53	36	26	8	7	147	139
ASSETS	%	%	%	%	%	%	%	%
Cash & Equivalents	17.1	11.4	9.5	6.7			12.9	10.9
Trade Receivables (net)	4.0	8.4	10.4	3.6			7.3	9.5
Inventory	52.0	47.9	46.6	52.4			43.6	43.9
All Other Current	.9	1.6	3.1	4.8			2.5	3.2
Total Current	74.0	69.2	69.6	67.6			66.4	67.4
Fixed Assets (net)	15.6	16.6	16.0	27.3			24.4	21.4
Intangibles (net)	1.7	6.5	6.6	2.2			3.4	4.8
All Other Non-Current	8.7	7.7	7.9	3.0			5.8	6.3
Total	100.0	100.0	100.0	100.0			100.0	100.0
LIABILITIES								
Notes Payable-Short Term	13.6	7.9	8.4	9.8			9.4	8.6
Cur. Mat.-L.T.D.	6.3	2.3	1.7	1.5			2.7	2.4
Trade Payables	16.4	17.0	15.1	16.4			19.1	16.7
Income Taxes Payable	.0	.2	.0	.1			.1	.2
All Other Current	6.3	8.8	9.4	12.6			12.3	8.0
Total Current	42.6	36.2	34.7	40.5			43.6	35.9
Long-Term Debt	22.9	25.4	14.7	13.7			19.6	20.7
Deferred Taxes	.0	.1	.3	.2			.1	.1
All Other Non-Current	16.4	10.3	7.7	2.4			9.4	9.5
Net Worth	18.1	27.9	42.6	43.1			27.3	33.9
Total Liabilities & Net Worth	100.0	100.0	100.0	100.0			100.0	100.0
INCOME DATA								
Net Sales	100.0	100.0	100.0	100.0			100.0	100.0
Gross Profit	42.0	37.4	35.9	30.7			40.3	41.5
Operating Expenses	36.6	33.5	31.6	26.8			36.6	37.7
Operating Profit	5.4	3.9	4.3	3.9			3.7	3.8
All Other Expenses (net)	.6	.7	.1	.8			.8	.9
Profit Before Taxes	4.8	3.2	4.3	3.1			2.9	2.8
RATIOS								
Current	4.1	4.7	6.1	2.5			2.9	3.6
	2.0	2.3	2.0	1.5			1.7	2.0
	1.1	1.2	1.2	1.2			1.2	1.3
Quick	1.4	1.1	1.2	.6			1.1	1.2
	.5	(52) .4	.4	(25) .1			.4	.4
	.2	.2	.2	.0			.1	.1
Sales/Receivables	0 UND	0 UND	0 999.8	1 559.4			0 UND	0 UND
	0 UND	3 110.1	2 151.4	2 211.9			1 324.0	2 178.4
	5 71.1	19 19.6	19 18.8	3 115.3			10 36.5	17 21.0
Cost of Sales/Inventory	47 7.8	48 7.7	47 7.8	59 6.2			40 9.2	41 9.0
	108 3.4	94 3.9	104 3.5	138 2.6			89 4.1	103 3.6
	161 2.3	175 2.1	160 2.3	169 2.2			168 2.2	167 2.2
Cost of Sales/Payables	0 UND	7 52.1	10 37.6	17 20.9			8 43.6	9 41.0
	13 28.5	21 17.0	22 16.9	34 10.6			23 15.8	27 13.3
	47 7.8	42 8.8	44 8.4	56 6.6			51 7.1	52 7.1
Sales/Working Capital	4.0	4.0	3.7	5.0			5.5	4.2
	14.1	8.9	8.9	8.8			9.7	9.2
	131.2	28.4	23.7	25.2			45.4	28.3
EBIT/Interest	4.6	6.0	7.7	26.9			6.7	8.0
	(23) 2.8	(47) 2.1	(28) 4.3	(24) 9.5			(129) 2.7	(119) 2.5
	-2.8	1.0	1.5	3.1			1.1	1.2
Net Profit + Depr., Dep., Amort./Cur. Mat. L/T/D							10.0	18.9
							(19) 2.9	(23) 3.1
							1.6	1.2
Fixed/Worth	.0	.1	.1	.3			.2	.2
	.6	.6	.4	.6			.7	.7
	-1.1	35.0	1.3	1.1			3.9	8.4
Debt/Worth	.4	.6	.7	.6			.7	.6
	4.6	4.4	2.1	1.4			2.0	2.0
	-12.3	NM	4.6	3.9			21.5	17.4
% Profit Before Taxes/Tangible Net Worth	102.3	59.4	40.3	41.1			38.2	38.1
	(20) 61.1	(40) 18.6	(31) 13.8	(25) 26.4			(116) 18.7	(107) 14.5
	9.0	2.8	4.2	5.9			4.8	3.8
% Profit Before Taxes/Total Assets	37.4	14.2	12.0	17.1			15.6	13.3
	9.9	4.8	4.0	7.7			4.8	4.3
	-2.3	-.2	1.3	2.2			.0	.8
Sales/Net Fixed Assets	216.0	285.2	64.5	30.2			46.3	45.7
	36.8	47.7	24.2	15.8			20.1	21.4
	9.7	10.0	9.9	6.7			7.3	7.5
Sales/Total Assets	5.8	4.1	3.2	3.2			4.2	3.8
	3.2	2.6	2.5	2.4			2.6	2.4
	2.3	1.8	1.6	1.8			1.9	1.4
% Depr., Dep., Amort./Sales	.3	.3	.5	.7			.5	.6
	(21) .7	(37) 1.0	(28) .8	(25) .9			(123) 1.0	(110) 1.2
	1.6	2.2	1.3	1.3			1.7	2.0
% Officers', Directors' Owners' Comp/Sales	3.1	2.2	1.4				1.7	2.0
	(15) 4.5	(30) 3.9	(13) 1.9				(61) 3.9	(64) 3.6
	11.2	7.4	5.2				8.3	9.5
Net Sales ($)	46160M	187256M	460828M	1625195M	977969M	4026325M	5002651M	5651576M
Total Assets ($)	8455M	56794M	174271M	624429M	534628M	1344830M	1797338M	2374406M

M = $ thousand   MM = $ million
See Pages 9 through 22 for Explanation of Ratios and Data

Comparative Historical Data — Current Data Sorted by Sales

Type of Statement									
Unqualified	12	20	15		1		3	1	14
Reviewed	17	19	18					6	8
Compiled	15	15	29	5	9	2	6	5	2
Tax Returns	49	61	52	17	19	8	4	4	
Other	45	62	49	7	8	4	6	8	16
	4/1/08-3/31/09 ALL	4/1/09-3/31/10 ALL	4/1/10-3/31/11 ALL	22 (4/1-9/30/10)			141 (10/1/10-3/31/11)		
				0-1MM	1-3MM	3-5MM	5-10MM	10-25MM	25MM & OVER
NUMBER OF STATEMENTS	138	177	163	29	37	14	19	24	40
	%	%	%	%	%	%	%	%	%
ASSETS									
Cash & Equivalents	11.0	12.3	11.1	13.4	12.9	14.3	10.3	10.0	7.7
Trade Receivables (net)	8.7	8.8	7.2	3.9	5.1	15.6	15.2	5.6	5.8
Inventory	47.9	43.9	48.4	45.9	52.5	39.4	44.4	53.5	48.4
All Other Current	5.1	2.8	2.3	.9	1.8	1.1	2.2	3.1	3.8
Total Current	72.6	67.8	69.0	64.1	72.3	70.4	72.1	72.3	65.7
Fixed Assets (net)	16.2	20.0	19.1	21.4	16.4	10.9	16.1	18.7	24.4
Intangibles (net)	4.3	6.1	5.0	4.1	4.1	11.9	5.8	3.2	4.8
All Other Non-Current	6.9	6.1	6.9	10.4	7.3	6.8	6.0	5.8	5.1
Total	100.0	100.0	100.0	100.0	100.0	100.0	100.0	100.0	100.0
LIABILITIES									
Notes Payable-Short Term	10.9	9.9	9.3	12.6	10.1	8.6	4.5	8.9	8.7
Cur. Mat.-L.T.D.	3.5	2.6	2.9	5.5	2.8	5.2	1.8	1.1	1.8
Trade Payables	15.2	14.9	16.4	13.5	14.3	22.5	18.2	15.0	18.3
Income Taxes Payable	.1	.1	.1	.0	.0	.0	.3	.1	.1
All Other Current	11.3	10.6	9.2	8.4	4.6	5.3	11.9	15.9	9.9
Total Current	40.9	38.2	37.8	40.1	31.7	41.6	36.8	41.1	38.8
Long-Term Debt	16.1	20.0	20.3	31.7	21.7	19.8	20.9	14.9	14.1
Deferred Taxes	.1	.1	.2	.0	.0	.0	.3	.4	.3
All Other Non-Current	10.2	11.1	9.0	18.4	10.7	9.3	5.2	8.3	2.8
Net Worth	32.7	30.5	32.7	9.8	35.9	29.4	36.8	35.3	43.9
Total Liabilities & Net Worth	100.0	100.0	100.0	100.0	100.0	100.0	100.0	100.0	100.0
INCOME DATA									
Net Sales	100.0	100.0	100.0	100.0	100.0	100.0	100.0	100.0	100.0
Gross Profit	39.4	40.1	36.7	46.9	38.8	36.3	27.1	37.6	31.7
Operating Expenses	35.3	37.0	32.4	40.5	35.3	31.4	23.4	34.1	27.2
Operating Profit	4.1	3.1	4.4	6.4	3.4	5.0	3.7	3.5	4.5
All Other Expenses (net)	1.2	.8	.8	2.3	-.1	.4	.3	.4	1.0
Profit Before Taxes	2.8	2.3	3.6	4.1	3.5	4.5	3.4	3.1	3.5
RATIOS									
Current	4.0	4.1	3.8	4.2	4.9	4.2	5.0	6.7	2.4
	2.0	2.1	1.8	2.0	2.5	2.0	2.4	1.7	1.6
	1.3	1.2	1.2	.9	1.3	1.2	1.3	1.1	1.3
Quick	1.1	1.2	1.0	1.6	1.1	1.9	1.3	.7	.6
	(137) .4	(176) .4	(161) .4	.3	(36) .4	.6	.8	.3	(39) .3
	.1	.1	.2	.1	.2	.3	.3	.1	.0
Sales/Receivables	0 UND	0 UND	0 UND	0 UND	0 UND	1 345.3	0 999.8	0 UND	1 665.5
	2 183.7	2 184.8	2 153.7	0 UND	3 122.7	8 45.0	3 141.4	1 625.3	2 147.5
	18 20.5	12 29.4	13 27.1	9 38.7	12 30.8	31 11.6	44 8.3	12 31.3	7 52.2
Cost of Sales/Inventory	47 7.7	36 10.2	51 7.2	80 4.6	48 7.7	22 16.3	13 28.5	51 7.1	49 7.4
	96 3.8	99 3.7	110 3.3	149 2.5	112 3.3	60 6.1	66 5.5	110 3.3	116 3.1
	166 2.2	181 2.0	164 2.2	323 1.1	163 2.2	126 2.9	104 3.5	184 2.0	161 2.3
Cost of Sales/Payables	4 94.5	6 56.4	7 48.8	0 UND	5 76.7	12 31.5	4 94.3	6 62.6	27 13.4
	22 16.8	23 15.7	27 13.5	21 17.0	25 14.8	22 16.8	11 32.3	17 21.1	34 10.6
	42 8.7	48 7.7	48 7.6	60 6.1	39 9.5	75 4.8	47 7.7	38 9.5	54 6.8
Sales/Working Capital	4.4	4.5	4.1	3.1	3.7	5.6	4.2	5.6	5.3
	8.6	8.0	10.3	10.3	6.2	12.6	12.5	12.0	10.2
	28.7	31.1	35.0	NM	15.2	20.1	35.0	76.5	20.2
EBIT/Interest	12.9	15.9	10.7	4.5	5.1	16.8	6.5	6.2	21.4
	(118) 3.7	(144) 3.9	(136) 3.0	(20) 2.1	(30) 2.2	(11) 5.4	(16) 1.8	(21) 3.2	(38) 8.7
	.7	.6	1.2	-1.8	.8	1.1	1.4	1.7	2.7
Net Profit + Depr., Dep., Amort./Cur. Mat. L/T/D	16.9	9.0	12.9						14.9
	(18) 3.0	(25) 3.7	(17) 4.8						(11) 7.2
	1.5	2.2	2.4						4.2
Fixed/Worth	.1	.1	.1	.3	.1	.0	.1	.2	.3
	.4	.5	.6	7.7	.2	.6	.4	.7	.6
	1.9	2.7	4.5	-.8	5.3	2.2	-2.6	2.2	1.0
Debt/Worth	.7	.7	.7	1.4	.5	.6	.3	.9	.8
	1.6	2.1	2.3	26.7	1.7	6.0	2.6	2.6	1.6
	7.3	8.5	26.7	-5.8	6.8	NM	-102.2	20.3	3.3
% Profit Before Taxes/Tangible Net Worth	48.9	50.9	58.2	94.3	65.4	60.0	66.2	56.8	37.3
	(115) 13.7	(143) 19.5	(130) 19.7	(16) 46.8	(31) 13.1	(11) 27.0	(14) 21.6	(19) 7.9	(39) 19.4
	2.0	4.4	4.1	14.2	1.5	15.7	3.7	3.2	3.9
% Profit Before Taxes/Total Assets	18.7	16.3	15.0	23.4	14.2	18.5	12.1	10.8	16.6
	4.5	6.1	5.2	8.4	4.4	6.3	4.1	3.5	6.9
	-.8	-.9	.6	-.6	-.2	1.1	.7	1.0	1.7
Sales/Net Fixed Assets	71.6	56.2	83.2	78.0	148.5	UND	273.7	64.5	28.8
	29.6	21.4	21.6	18.9	41.5	45.9	56.9	21.4	15.3
	12.4	8.6	8.8	4.8	11.1	16.3	20.3	8.9	7.7
Sales/Total Assets	4.4	3.8	3.8	3.0	3.9	3.2	6.6	5.0	3.3
	2.8	2.5	2.6	1.9	2.7	2.7	2.9	2.8	2.5
	2.0	1.8	1.8	1.0	1.8	2.3	1.9	2.2	2.0
% Depr., Dep., Amort./Sales	.4	.7	.6	.8	.2		.3	.5	.8
	(101) .9	(133) 1.2	(123) .9	(19) 2.1	(24) .9		(15) .6	(21) .8	(35) 1.0
	1.6	2.0	1.9	4.4	2.4		.9	1.5	1.5
% Officers', Directors' Owners' Comp/Sales	1.9	1.8	1.8	2.4	2.4				
	(59) 4.0	(70) 3.9	(61) 3.8	(11) 12.1	(21) 4.9				
	8.9	6.9	6.8	17.6	7.3				
Net Sales ($)	5301191M	8503183M	7323733M	16991M	76098M	56647M	126587M	389473M	6657937M
Total Assets ($)	1992501M	3142103M	2743407M	30792M	33670M	22275M	43546M	137560M	2475564M

© RMA 2011

M = $ thousand   MM = $ million
See Pages 9 through 22 for Explanation of Ratios and Data

Current Data Sorted by Assets   Comparative Historical Data

	0-500M	500M-2MM	2-10MM	10-50MM	50-100MM	100-250MM	Type of Statement	4/1/06-3/31/07 ALL	4/1/07-3/31/08 ALL
							Unqualified		2
				1			Reviewed	8	3
	1	1	2				Compiled	13	13
	4	4	3				Tax Returns	33	31
	15	6	2			1	Other	15	22
	5	1	5	1	1				
		15 (4/1-9/30/10)		38 (10/1/10-3/31/11)					
NUMBER OF STATEMENTS	25	12	12	2	1	1		69	71
	%	%	%	%	%	%	**ASSETS**	%	%
	21.8	5.2	15.9				Cash & Equivalents	10.8	10.2
	12.0	14.2	12.8				Trade Receivables (net)	13.0	15.8
	29.2	26.9	30.7				Inventory	20.9	23.2
	2.4	3.1	2.4				All Other Current	2.2	2.6
	65.4	49.3	61.8				Total Current	46.9	51.8
	21.8	44.4	12.5				Fixed Assets (net)	37.9	34.7
	3.3	3.9	18.5				Intangibles (net)	7.9	6.8
	9.6	2.4	7.3				All Other Non-Current	7.2	6.7
	100.0	100.0	100.0				Total	100.0	100.0
							LIABILITIES		
	9.8	13.8	7.1				Notes Payable-Short Term	8.2	17.4
	6.2	4.9	3.0				Cur. Mat.-L.T.D.	4.9	5.3
	18.3	25.9	14.0				Trade Payables	14.5	19.5
	.1	.0	.0				Income Taxes Payable	.0	.1
	10.8	13.0	11.0				All Other Current	14.4	11.7
	45.2	57.6	35.0				Total Current	42.1	53.9
	25.4	20.8	14.3				Long-Term Debt	35.4	42.9
	.0	.0	.0				Deferred Taxes	.3	.1
	20.5	20.4	11.3				All Other Non-Current	12.0	12.8
	8.8	1.1	39.4				Net Worth	10.3	-9.8
	100.0	100.0	100.0				Total Liabilities & Net Worth	100.0	100.0
							INCOME DATA		
	100.0	100.0	100.0				Net Sales	100.0	100.0
	55.9	60.1	51.0				Gross Profit	53.3	53.7
	53.5	62.1	51.2				Operating Expenses	52.1	52.3
	2.4	-2.0	-.3				Operating Profit	1.2	1.4
	-.8	.8	-.8				All Other Expenses (net)	1.6	1.2
	3.2	-2.8	.5				Profit Before Taxes	-.3	.2
							RATIOS		
	5.1	1.2	3.8				Current	2.6	2.6
	1.4	.9	2.0					1.7	1.3
	.7	.7	1.1					.7	.8
	3.6	.6	2.1				Quick	1.4	1.3
	.8	.4	1.1					.6	.6
	.3	.2	.5					.2	.2
	0 UND	9 42.2	3 135.1				Sales/Receivables	6 60.9	5 77.2
	6 59.5	13 29.1	20 18.3					11 33.7	13 28.8
	14 26.8	23 15.9	32 11.3					24 15.2	26 14.2
	21 17.3	47 7.8	41 8.9				Cost of Sales/Inventory	20 18.3	21 17.1
	45 8.0	71 5.1	96 3.8					56 6.5	53 6.9
	67 5.4	132 2.8	118 3.1					105 3.5	90 4.0
	0 UND	20 18.7	25 14.7				Cost of Sales/Payables	2 197.8	8 47.8
	32 11.3	62 5.9	38 9.7					29 12.4	34 10.9
	54 6.7	154 2.4	51 7.2					59 6.2	58 6.3
	7.3	38.7	3.6				Sales/Working Capital	8.8	9.7
	33.6	NM	10.2					22.1	34.6
	-51.4	-13.0	468.9					-24.7	-22.6
	10.4	3.9					EBIT/Interest	4.9	5.8
	(13) .6	(11) .0						(61) 1.5	(58) 1.5
	-2.4	-15.1						.3	.0
							Net Profit + Depr., Dep., Amort./Cur. Mat. L/T/D		
	.1	1.0	.0				Fixed/Worth	.7	.4
	.6	2.2	.4					1.8	2.0
	-.5	-2.1	4.5					-1.1	-.8
	.3	1.5	.3				Debt/Worth	.9	.8
	2.6	3.3	1.5					2.9	4.0
	-3.4	-3.5	13.1					-3.2	-2.9
	91.9		18.0				% Profit Before Taxes/Tangible Net Worth	36.3	58.9
	(14) 5.2		(10) -.4					(40) 10.3	(41) 22.9
	-15.9		-6.7					.1	1.1
	48.2	2.1	3.6				% Profit Before Taxes/Total Assets	12.6	13.1
	2.6	-5.0	1.0					3.5	1.7
	-5.1	-18.6	-2.5					-3.6	-3.8
	106.2	14.0	200.7				Sales/Net Fixed Assets	18.1	31.8
	35.0	6.8	28.8					8.9	10.1
	9.2	4.7	12.6					4.0	5.5
	7.4	3.5	3.2				Sales/Total Assets	4.5	4.9
	5.4	2.8	2.5					2.5	3.0
	3.4	2.3	2.0					1.7	1.8
	.5	1.3	.3				% Depr., Dep., Amort./Sales	1.3	1.1
	(19) .7	(11) 2.1	(11) 1.4					(61) 2.1	(55) 2.0
	2.9	2.7	2.2					3.3	3.4
	3.7						% Officers', Directors' Owners' Comp/Sales	3.1	3.5
	(15) 6.6							(36) 5.3	(46) 6.0
	10.0							9.4	10.3
	21769M	34111M	109543M	30639M	22592M	846690M	Net Sales ($)	1858561M	449284M
	5062M	11423M	43631M	30434M	66712M	147000M	Total Assets ($)	370771M	195675M

M = $ thousand   MM = $ million
See Pages 9 through 22 for Explanation of Ratios and Data

Comparative Historical Data | | | Type of Statement | Current Data Sorted by Sales

			Type of Statement					
1	2	1	Unqualified				1	
4	3	4	Reviewed	1	1	1	1	
18	7	11	Compiled	3	3	3	1	1	
30	25	25	Tax Returns	12	8	1	2	1	1
8	15	12	Other	5	1	3	1	2	
4/1/08- 3/31/09 ALL	4/1/09- 3/31/10 ALL	4/1/10- 3/31/11 ALL		15 (4/1-9/30/10)			38 (10/1/10-3/31/11)		
				0-1MM	1-3MM	3-5MM	5-10MM	10-25MM	25MM & OVER
61	52	53	NUMBER OF STATEMENTS	20	13	8	5	6	1
%	%	%	ASSETS	%	%	%	%	%	%
7.7	11.7	15.1	Cash & Equivalents	20.2	14.3				
13.5	14.9	12.1	Trade Receivables (net)	11.7	11.4				
23.0	20.6	27.6	Inventory	30.4	28.4				
2.0	3.6	2.8	All Other Current	2.4	2.1				
46.3	50.8	57.7	Total Current	64.8	56.2				
32.9	36.2	27.0	Fixed Assets (net)	21.6	37.2				
13.4	6.8	6.6	Intangibles (net)	4.1	1.4				
7.5	6.2	8.8	All Other Non-Current	9.6	5.2				
100.0	100.0	100.0	Total	100.0	100.0				
			LIABILITIES						
12.3	10.8	10.2	Notes Payable-Short Term	11.9	9.2				
4.7	4.7	4.8	Cur. Mat.-L.T.D.	7.6	3.4				
13.6	27.9	18.5	Trade Payables	18.1	25.0				
.0	.1	.1	Income Taxes Payable	.2	.0				
11.2	17.9	11.7	All Other Current	10.4	12.6				
41.8	61.3	45.4	Total Current	48.1	50.2				
34.6	40.8	22.4	Long-Term Debt	31.2	15.7				
.2	.0	.0	Deferred Taxes	.0	.0				
9.8	14.6	16.9	All Other Non-Current	25.6	18.7				
13.6	-16.6	15.3	Net Worth	-4.9	15.4				
100.0	100.0	100.0	Total Liabilities & Net Worth	100.0	100.0				
			INCOME DATA						
100.0	100.0	100.0	Net Sales	100.0	100.0				
53.4	54.4	55.5	Gross Profit	56.4	57.5				
52.4	53.3	54.8	Operating Expenses	53.2	59.4				
1.0	1.1	.6	Operating Profit	3.2	-1.8				
.4	.4	-.1	All Other Expenses (net)	-.3	-.4				
.6	.7	.8	Profit Before Taxes	3.5	-1.5				
			RATIOS						
2.1	1.8	3.5		5.1	2.2				
1.2	1.2	1.1	Current	1.1	1.1				
.7	.8	.7		.7	.7				
1.0	.9	1.4		4.0	1.2				
.6	.5	.6	Quick	.7	.4				
.2	.3	.3		.3	.2				
4 88.3	7 49.4	2 161.6		0 UND	3 106.4				
12 30.7	13 27.6	10 37.6	Sales/Receivables	7 55.6	9 42.9				
20 18.6	22 16.6	22 16.6		15 25.1	13 29.1				
19 19.5	22 16.2	24 15.2		21 17.6	33 10.9				
36 10.2	38 9.6	59 6.2	Cost of Sales/Inventory	45 8.1	65 5.6				
93 3.9	104 3.5	112 3.3		73 5.0	128 2.9				
10 35.8	9 39.7	16 22.8		0 UND	16 22.8				
34 10.8	42 8.7	41 8.9	Cost of Sales/Payables	33 11.1	42 8.7				
53 6.8	66 5.5	78 4.7		59 6.2	155 2.3				
10.1	11.0	8.4		7.6	11.4				
66.8	50.6	44.3	Sales/Working Capital	202.0	76.4				
-33.5	-25.7	-25.6		-38.4	-14.6				
4.6	5.6	3.7		15.4					
(57) 1.8	(45) 1.4	(37) .8	EBIT/Interest	(11) 1.0					
-.1	-.4	-3.3		.3					
			Net Profit + Depr., Dep., Amort./Cur. Mat. L/T/D						
.5	.6	.2		.1	.1				
1.9	7.2	1.4	Fixed/Worth	-2.4	1.4				
-1.3	-1.7	-1.5		-.3	-2.4				
1.6	3.1	.5		.4	.7				
6.6	15.3	3.0	Debt/Worth	-10.7	2.1				
-3.7	-3.5	-5.0		-3.1	-3.9				
46.9	135.2	25.2							
(38) 9.6	(31) 28.9	(35) -1.6	% Profit Before Taxes/Tangible Net Worth						
-5.2	2.6	-12.8							
9.1	16.7	6.1		49.6	2.8				
3.0	1.6	.0	% Profit Before Taxes/Total Assets	3.8	-7.0				
-4.7	-7.2	-6.2		-3.2	-12.3				
64.0	29.7	98.2		98.8	76.2				
12.9	13.2	15.5	Sales/Net Fixed Assets	38.2	9.5				
5.1	3.3	6.5		9.2	4.7				
4.9	4.7	5.6		8.1	4.5				
2.8	2.7	3.4	Sales/Total Assets	5.6	2.9				
1.9	1.7	2.3		3.4	2.4				
1.1	1.2	.5		.6	.4				
(52) 1.9	(40) 2.2	(45) 1.6	% Depr., Dep., Amort./Sales	(14) .7	(12) 1.7				
3.2	3.8	2.7		4.1	2.4				
3.0	2.4	3.1		3.7					
(35) 5.3	(30) 5.4	(27) 6.0	% Officers', Directors' Owners' Comp/Sales	(11) 7.0					
8.6	7.2	9.2		15.4					
798579M	157394M	1065344M	Net Sales ($)	11664M	25130M	34872M	36249M	110739M	846690M
169612M	69580M	304262M	Total Assets ($)	2940M	8055M	21033M	11271M	113963M	147000M

© RMA 2011

M = $ thousand   MM = $ million

See Pages 9 through 22 for Explanation of Ratios and Data

Current Data Sorted by Assets   Comparative Historical Data

0-500M	500M-2MM	2-10MM	10-50MM	50-100MM	100-250MM	Type of Statement	4/1/06-3/31/07 ALL	4/1/07-3/31/08 ALL
		2	3	1		Unqualified	11	7
	3	12	3			Reviewed	23	15
3	10	4				Compiled	23	28
8	9	6				Tax Returns	42	20
5	18	11	7	1		Other	31	37
	19 (4/1-9/30/10)		87 (10/1/10-3/31/11)					
16	40	35	13	2		**NUMBER OF STATEMENTS**	130	107
%	%	%	%	%	%	**ASSETS**	%	%
15.9	9.6	10.6	11.2			Cash & Equivalents	8.8	9.8
9.3	24.5	31.8	38.5			Trade Receivables (net)	32.6	29.8
27.1	31.4	22.0	21.6			Inventory	27.8	32.1
6.3	3.2	5.1	1.7			All Other Current	2.6	2.5
58.5	68.6	69.5	73.1			Total Current	71.8	74.2
9.5	10.6	19.7	11.1			Fixed Assets (net)	16.4	13.4
17.5	8.8	4.5	11.4			Intangibles (net)	4.0	6.0
14.4	12.0	6.3	4.4			All Other Non-Current	7.8	6.4
100.0	100.0	100.0	100.0			Total	100.0	100.0
11.2	15.7	11.4	16.1			**LIABILITIES** Notes Payable-Short Term	12.8	13.2
6.3	1.6	7.0	3.1			Cur. Mat.-L.T.D.	6.8	4.9
19.2	27.3	19.0	22.5			Trade Payables	23.3	27.2
.4	.5	.2	.0			Income Taxes Payable	.2	.1
4.8	10.2	14.0	14.8			All Other Current	12.3	13.9
41.8	55.3	51.5	56.6			Total Current	55.4	59.3
26.4	12.5	15.1	5.3			Long-Term Debt	11.3	16.3
.0	.0	.2	.0			Deferred Taxes	.2	.1
16.2	4.9	5.1	6.5			All Other Non-Current	5.8	6.0
15.6	27.4	28.1	31.6			Net Worth	27.2	18.4
100.0	100.0	100.0	100.0			Total Liabilties & Net Worth	100.0	100.0
100.0	100.0	100.0	100.0			**INCOME DATA** Net Sales	100.0	100.0
47.4	38.3	37.5	30.8			Gross Profit	37.4	37.7
43.8	37.0	34.9	27.9			Operating Expenses	35.5	35.8
3.6	1.2	2.5	2.9			Operating Profit	2.0	1.9
1.2	.3	.5	.4			All Other Expenses (net)	.4	.4
2.3	.9	2.0	2.5			Profit Before Taxes	1.6	1.5
4.3	1.9	2.2	1.5			**RATIOS** Current	2.3	2.1
2.0	1.2	1.3	1.4			Current	1.5	1.5
.9	.7	1.0	1.1				1.1	1.0
2.0	1.3	1.3	1.1			Quick	1.3	1.2
.5	.6	1.0	.8			Quick	.9	.7
.1	.4	.5	.7				.5	.4
0 UND	16 22.9	22 16.9	35 10.4			Sales/Receivables	23 16.1	11 32.1
7 52.4	29 12.6	32 11.5	44 8.2			Sales/Receivables	33 11.0	28 12.9
19 19.4	34 10.7	37 9.9	58 6.3				48 7.6	37 9.7
4 83.2	23 15.9	12 30.6	17 21.9			Cost of Sales/Inventory	21 17.8	24 14.9
28 12.8	52 7.0	32 11.4	37 10.0			Cost of Sales/Inventory	46 8.0	50 7.3
113 3.2	88 4.1	68 5.4	48 7.6				90 4.0	95 3.8
0 UND	21 17.7	18 20.4	26 14.1			Cost of Sales/Payables	18 20.2	19 18.7
14 26.3	31 11.8	26 14.0	33 11.1			Cost of Sales/Payables	31 11.8	30 12.2
47 7.8	60 6.1	44 8.3	43 8.5				52 7.0	53 6.9
9.0	9.6	8.4	10.2			Sales/Working Capital	7.7	9.2
20.9	29.0	20.7	14.2			Sales/Working Capital	14.6	16.2
-63.0	-25.1	643.3	NM				97.7	200.6
18.6	5.6	9.9	15.2			EBIT/Interest	8.2	6.9
(13) 2.5	(36) 1.7	(34) 3.4	(12) 5.0			EBIT/Interest	(112) 2.5	(97) 2.3
-.1	.1	1.3	2.2				.9	.7
						Net Profit + Depr., Dep., Amort./Cur. Mat. L/T/D	3.2	6.3
						Net Profit + Depr., Dep., Amort./Cur. Mat. L/T/D	(22) 1.5 (18) 2.9	
							1.0	1.6
.1	.1	.1	.2			Fixed/Worth	.1	.1
.5	.5	.6	.7			Fixed/Worth	.4	.4
-.5	-.9	2.6	1.1				2.9	-4.0
.7	1.4	1.0	2.2			Debt/Worth	.8	.8
5.0	2.5	2.5	2.6			Debt/Worth	2.0	2.4
-2.5	-11.0	7.2	10.5				8.6	-22.6
	25.1	49.5	55.4			% Profit Before Taxes/Tangible Net Worth	37.0	32.0
	(27) 8.4	(32) 11.9	(11) 23.2			% Profit Before Taxes/Tangible Net Worth	(105) 11.8	(76) 13.2
	-2.7	.6	6.8				1.9	2.4
30.5	9.9	9.4	11.7			% Profit Before Taxes/Total Assets	10.8	13.0
7.0	2.4	3.6	4.1			% Profit Before Taxes/Total Assets	3.3	3.4
-5.4	-2.2	.2	2.0				.0	-.3
185.8	160.2	84.1	87.8			Sales/Net Fixed Assets	75.7	90.6
40.7	48.1	32.8	37.8			Sales/Net Fixed Assets	35.6	40.4
19.1	17.4	11.0	21.0				13.6	18.5
6.2	4.9	4.6	4.2			Sales/Total Assets	4.7	5.3
3.4	3.8	3.4	3.1			Sales/Total Assets	3.3	3.4
1.6	2.5	2.7	2.2				2.3	2.5
	.4	.6	.5			% Depr., Dep., Amort./Sales	.5	.4
	(29) 1.0	(29) 1.0	(12) 1.1			% Depr., Dep., Amort./Sales	(104) 1.0	(82) .7
	1.4	1.4	1.9				1.9	1.6
	2.4	.7				% Officers', Directors' Owners' Comp/Sales	2.2	2.0
	(21) 4.7	(14) 2.1				% Officers', Directors' Owners' Comp/Sales	(73) 4.2	(47) 3.3
	6.2	4.1					7.1	6.4
19184M	173826M	563696M	632598M	256335M		Net Sales ($)	1763714M	1449974M
4071M	46177M	159059M	206959M	101551M		Total Assets ($)	540121M	569719M

Note: Columns 50-100MM and 100-250MM in the upper sections are marked **DATA NOT AVAILABLE**.

M = $ thousand   MM = $ million
See Pages 9 through 22 for Explanation of Ratios and Data

Comparative Historical Data | | | Current Data Sorted by Sales

			Type of Statement						
3	7	6	Unqualified		1	2	3	3 / 8	3 / 4
14	12	18	Reviewed	3	3	5	2	2	2
30	24	17	Compiled	6	6	4	2	1	2
29	33	23	Tax Returns	3	6	4	9	6	11
40	37	42	Other	2	10	4	9		
4/1/08-3/31/09 ALL	4/1/09-3/31/10 ALL	4/1/10-3/31/11 ALL		0-1MM	1-3MM	3-5MM	5-10MM	10-25MM	25MM & OVER
					19 (4/1-9/30/10)		87 (10/1/10-3/31/11)		
116	113	106	NUMBER OF STATEMENTS	11	20	15	20	20	20
%	%	%	ASSETS	%	%	%	%	%	%
10.0	8.7	11.0	Cash & Equivalents	7.8	13.9	9.4	13.5	9.5	9.9
29.4	29.2	25.9	Trade Receivables (net)	7.3	14.6	31.0	26.5	31.6	37.1
29.2	27.8	26.5	Inventory	25.9	28.3	26.0	33.2	22.2	22.9
1.5	3.1	4.2	All Other Current	.6	5.0	5.1	6.1	4.5	2.4
70.2	68.8	67.5	Total Current	41.6	61.8	71.5	79.4	67.9	72.3
17.6	17.4	13.7	Fixed Assets (net)	12.5	16.6	12.5	10.1	15.7	14.2
4.9	5.8	9.3	Intangibles (net)	29.8	5.5	7.9	5.3	6.6	9.7
7.3	8.0	9.4	All Other Non-Current	16.1	16.1	8.1	5.3	9.8	3.8
100.0	100.0	100.0	Total	100.0	100.0	100.0	100.0	100.0	100.0
			LIABILITIES						
17.3	16.0	13.5	Notes Payable-Short Term	10.1	14.9	18.0	11.9	12.7	13.0
5.1	3.4	4.2	Cur. Mat.-L.T.D.	1.2	5.5	2.1	1.9	10.7	2.0
26.0	22.4	22.7	Trade Payables	13.5	20.1	26.6	29.1	19.3	24.3
.2	.1	.3	Income Taxes Payable	.5	.0	.6	.4	.1	.3
12.1	10.5	11.3	All Other Current	5.4	5.4	9.6	13.7	18.1	12.5
60.7	52.4	52.0	Total Current	30.7	46.0	56.9	57.0	60.9	52.1
15.2	14.2	14.6	Long-Term Debt	42.4	18.1	6.5	16.6	8.5	6.0
.1	.1	.1	Deferred Taxes	.0	.0	.0	.0	.3	.4
3.8	5.2	6.8	All Other Non-Current	3.6	14.3	7.0	3.9	4.7	6.1
20.3	28.0	26.4	Net Worth	23.3	21.6	29.5	22.6	25.6	35.5
100.0	100.0	100.0	Total Liabilities & Net Worth	100.0	100.0	100.0	100.0	100.0	100.0
			INCOME DATA						
100.0	100.0	100.0	Net Sales	100.0	100.0	100.0	100.0	100.0	100.0
38.7	38.7	38.9	Gross Profit	46.9	44.8	36.3	40.0	34.6	34.0
37.1	37.3	36.7	Operating Expenses	42.9	43.5	34.4	37.8	31.7	32.3
1.7	1.3	2.2	Operating Profit	4.1	1.3	1.8	2.3	2.9	1.7
.4	.3	.5	All Other Expenses (net)	3.0	.5	1.1	-.6	.6	-.2
1.2	1.0	1.7	Profit Before Taxes	1.1	.8	.7	2.8	2.3	1.9
			RATIOS						
1.9	2.0	2.1	Current	3.7	4.1	1.9	1.9	2.0	1.8
1.2	1.3	1.3		1.2	1.5	1.2	1.4	1.3	1.4
.8	1.0	1.0		.9	.7	.7	1.0	.8	1.2
1.1	1.2	1.3	Quick	2.2	1.4	1.2	1.2	1.3	1.2
.7	.8	.8		.4	.5	.7	.8	.8	.9
.4	.4	.4		.2	.3	.5	.4	.5	.7
15 24.1	21 17.6	12 30.6	Sales/Receivables	0 UND	0 UND	29 12.4	10 38.0	22 16.5	23 15.5
28 12.9	29 12.4	29 12.7		10 35.9	16 22.5	33 11.1	26 14.3	31 11.8	39 9.4
39 9.3	40 9.1	36 10.1		20 18.3	31 11.6	38 9.7	31 11.7	39 9.9	49 7.4
19 18.7	16 23.0	18 20.1	Cost of Sales/Inventory	7 55.3	18 20.3	23 15.9	23 15.9	11 32.2	16 22.7
40 9.1	39 9.4	40 9.2		50 7.3	55 6.6	50 7.2	49 7.4	32 11.4	35 10.4
106 3.4	93 3.9	74 4.9		135 2.7	115 3.2	74 4.9	76 4.8	47 7.7	49 7.5
18 20.7	20 18.7	18 19.8	Cost of Sales/Payables	7 53.0	6 61.9	22 16.8	22 16.9	14 25.8	21 17.7
34 10.7	34 10.8	28 13.1		26 14.1	30 12.3	27 13.8	34 10.7	26 14.0	29 12.5
54 6.7	49 7.4	49 7.4		67 5.4	65 5.6	52 7.0	50 7.4	43 8.5	43 8.5
12.0	9.7	9.1	Sales/Working Capital	7.2	5.6	11.0	7.4	10.2	9.3
40.8	22.4	21.0		56.8	15.4	28.4	21.4	30.9	15.6
-26.3	-165.8	-122.3		-56.2	-19.3	-14.9	NM	-40.1	46.9
5.8	7.6	9.7	EBIT/Interest	2.6	18.6	3.9	11.3	6.7	15.4
(107) 1.8	(104) 1.9	(97) 2.9		(10) 1.7	(17) 1.6	(14) 1.3	(19) 4.2	(18) 2.9	(19) 9.7
-.6	.0	1.0		.2	-4.5	.0	1.8	.8	2.5
5.0	5.7	6.2	Net Profit + Depr., Dep., Amort./Cur. Mat. L/T/D						
(15) 2.1	(18) 2.4	(15) 2.5							
1.7	-.6	1.3							
.2	.2	.1	Fixed/Worth	.0	.1	.2	.1	.1	.2
.8	.7	.6		1.3	.5	.6	.5	.9	.5
-8.9	4.8	4.8		-.3	NM	-.9	NM	3.1	1.5
1.3	1.0	1.3	Debt/Worth	1.5	.6	1.1	1.1	1.0	1.4
3.5	2.6	2.6		6.3	3.6	2.5	2.8	2.8	2.5
-13.4	33.1	NM		-2.0	-82.6	-22.7	NM	16.5	5.6
43.1	35.7	38.3	% Profit Before Taxes/Tangible Net Worth		28.7	32.9	42.0	56.1	52.0
(84) 14.3	(87) 5.8	(80) 10.2			(14) 4.1	(11) 2.2	(15) 21.0	(17) 5.9	(17) 14.7
-6.2	-1.7	.3			-6.3	-11.3	8.4	-.7	7.2
13.3	11.6	10.8	% Profit Before Taxes/Total Assets	7.1	22.1	6.4	25.1	13.5	9.2
1.9	2.3	3.5		2.2	.6	.5	7.4	4.5	4.2
-3.9	-1.8	-.2		-.7	-10.6	-3.3	1.9	.1	2.0
71.5	75.4	100.8	Sales/Net Fixed Assets	93.8	70.1	167.1	160.2	95.9	79.7
34.7	35.2	35.7		23.0	29.1	38.3	52.0	35.1	34.8
13.0	10.7	17.1		18.6	15.5	13.3	31.0	12.8	16.2
5.2	4.8	4.9	Sales/Total Assets	3.0	5.7	4.4	5.7	5.1	4.9
3.4	3.4	3.4		1.5	3.0	3.7	3.9	3.4	3.5
2.3	2.2	2.2		.9	1.8	2.6	3.4	2.5	2.8
.4	.5	.5	% Depr., Dep., Amort./Sales		.5	.4	.4	.5	.7
(96) .8	(91) 1.1	(79) 1.0			(11) 1.1	(12) .7	(16) 1.0	(15) 1.0	(18) 1.1
1.7	2.2	1.5			3.9	1.1	1.3	1.5	1.8
1.7	1.8	1.4	% Officers', Directors', Owners' Comp/Sales					1.8	
(52) 2.9	(54) 3.3	(45) 4.1						(11) 3.3	
8.3	6.5	6.9						6.3	
2184617M	2282500M	1645639M	Net Sales ($)	5453M	42058M	59436M	143285M	320184M	1075223M
689537M	721321M	517817M	Total Assets ($)	5722M	15643M	17643M	37990M	102452M	338367M

M = $ thousand   MM = $ million
See Pages 9 through 22 for Explanation of Ratios and Data

Current Data Sorted by Assets   Comparative Historical Data

						Type of Statement		
		2	2	3	2	2	Unqualified	8	8
		15	6			Reviewed	13	20
17	11	11	1			Compiled	33	29
49	34	12	3			Tax Returns	71	77
25	16	23	10	2	1	Other	53	57
	34 (4/1-9/30/10)		213 (10/1/10-3/31/11)				4/1/06-3/31/07	4/1/07-3/31/08
0-500M	500M-2MM	2-10MM	10-50MM	50-100MM	100-250MM		ALL	ALL
91	63	63	23	4	3	NUMBER OF STATEMENTS	178	191
%	%	%	%	%	%	ASSETS	%	%
15.7	14.4	12.1	13.0			Cash & Equivalents	12.7	14.4
3.5	4.4	11.5	8.6			Trade Receivables (net)	8.4	6.5
54.9	44.9	41.5	29.6			Inventory	45.7	46.3
.8	2.6	4.0	3.3			All Other Current	2.5	3.4
74.8	66.3	69.0	54.5			Total Current	69.3	70.6
15.6	23.4	21.0	34.6			Fixed Assets (net)	19.5	21.2
4.3	2.9	1.7	3.0			Intangibles (net)	3.6	2.8
5.2	7.4	8.3	7.8			All Other Non-Current	7.5	5.4
100.0	100.0	100.0	100.0			Total	100.0	100.0
						LIABILITIES		
11.8	9.4	10.5	5.8			Notes Payable-Short Term	9.5	9.3
4.9	3.3	2.5	3.5			Cur. Mat.-L.T.D.	2.5	2.5
31.6	16.7	16.8	14.8			Trade Payables	16.1	18.1
.0	.1	.1	.2			Income Taxes Payable	.2	.2
19.3	8.9	8.0	6.8			All Other Current	12.2	9.7
67.5	38.3	37.9	31.1			Total Current	40.4	39.8
21.1	24.7	14.5	21.4			Long-Term Debt	18.1	21.6
.0	.3	.1	.0			Deferred Taxes	.0	.0
13.6	6.8	8.3	1.6			All Other Non-Current	9.6	9.1
-2.2	29.9	39.3	45.8			Net Worth	31.8	29.5
100.0	100.0	100.0	100.0			Total Liabilities & Net Worth	100.0	100.0
						INCOME DATA		
100.0	100.0	100.0	100.0			Net Sales	100.0	100.0
48.7	50.4	46.7	48.1			Gross Profit	49.1	48.6
45.4	44.9	42.6	39.7			Operating Expenses	44.9	43.7
3.3	5.5	4.1	8.4			Operating Profit	4.3	4.9
1.5	2.0	1.1	2.0			All Other Expenses (net)	.7	1.3
1.8	3.5	3.0	6.4			Profit Before Taxes	3.5	3.6
						RATIOS		
5.9	3.9	3.2	3.4				4.0	3.6
1.7	1.8	1.9	1.8			Current	2.0	1.8
.9	1.1	1.3	.9				1.3	1.2
1.2	1.5	1.2	1.4				1.2	1.1
(90) .3	(62) .3	(62) .4	(22) .6			Quick	(177) .4	(188) .5
.1	.1	.2	.2				.1	.2
0 UND	0 UND	0 UND	0 999.8				0 UND	0 UND
0 UND	1 606.5	1 293.7	2 174.1			Sales/Receivables	0 UND	0 UND
1 266.5	4 82.0	28 12.9	16 22.7				10 35.0	5 74.1
53 6.9	61 6.0	58 6.3	45 8.1				57 6.4	66 5.5
130 2.8	113 3.2	131 2.8	67 5.5			Cost of Sales/Inventory	122 3.0	126 2.9
207 1.8	205 1.8	242 1.5	111 3.3				209 1.7	201 1.8
0 UND	5 72.5	19 19.7	22 16.7				8 43.8	5 72.4
26 13.9	24 15.0	35 10.3	34 10.7			Cost of Sales/Payables	36 10.0	31 11.8
114 3.2	77 4.8	66 5.6	47 7.8				71 5.1	67 5.5
4.7	5.4	4.3	5.0				4.1	4.7
16.6	10.5	7.6	12.2			Sales/Working Capital	8.2	8.4
-37.2	153.0	26.3	-80.1				27.5	26.0
6.2	13.7	9.6	6.1				10.1	10.6
(64) 2.4	(55) 2.5	(55) 3.3	(17) 2.5			EBIT/Interest	(152) 2.8	(151) 3.1
-.2	.1	1.1	-1.5				.9	.8
		9.0				Net Profit + Depr., Dep.,	7.7	8.8
		(11) 2.2				Amort./Cur. Mat. L/T/D	(19) 1.6	(17) 3.6
		1.2					.4	.7
.1	.1	.1	.3				.1	.1
.4	.3	.5	.6			Fixed/Worth	.4	.5
-2.7	8.3	1.7	2.0				2.4	2.3
.4	.7	.8	.5				.6	.8
5.4	2.6	1.7	1.3			Debt/Worth	1.7	2.0
-5.2	28.0	4.0	3.1				9.2	9.3
65.6 *	67.6	41.6	45.5			% Profit Before Taxes/Tangible	45.3	50.4
(57) 14.7	(51) 27.7	(58) 15.6	(22) 24.7			Net Worth	(145) 18.5	(156) 26.8
-.1	2.5	1.4	8.7				1.4	1.9
18.3	22.2	12.5	21.9				19.8	19.9
5.4	4.7	3.9	8.7			% Profit Before Taxes/Total	6.4	7.3
-5.1	-2.0	.4	1.5			Assets	.2	-.3
180.3	168.0	70.7	28.0				66.7	65.5
33.1	27.4	22.4	13.0			Sales/Net Fixed Assets	24.3	21.1
12.3	7.1	6.2	3.1				9.7	8.7
4.8	4.3	3.1	4.4				3.6	3.7
2.9	2.6	2.0	2.3			Sales/Total Assets	2.6	2.5
2.0	1.4	1.4	1.0				1.8	1.7
.4	.4	.7	1.5				.6	.6
(51) .8	(44) .9	(55) 1.3	(20) 2.6			% Depr., Dep., Amort./Sales	(131) 1.1	(147) 1.1
2.2	2.6	2.9	3.1				1.9	2.1
2.7	2.1	.9					2.8	2.5
(46) 6.2	(37) 4.0	(26) 2.5				% Officers', Directors'	(88) 5.7	(95) 4.8
8.6	6.2	4.2				Owners' Comp/Sales	8.4	7.1
75904M	230612M	783349M	1822217M	562225M	1321734M	Net Sales ($)	3938594M	4223496M
22897M	65360M	323304M	453384M	317462M	669167M	Total Assets ($)	1294092M	1770342M

M = $ thousand   MM = $ million
See Pages 9 through 22 for Explanation of Ratios and Data

Comparative Historical Data   Current Data Sorted by Sales

4/1/08-3/31/09 ALL	4/1/09-3/31/10 ALL	4/1/10-3/31/11 ALL	Type of Statement	0-1MM	1-3MM	3-5MM	5-10MM	10-25MM	25MM & OVER
11	11	9	Unqualified					2	7
21	8	23	Reviewed			1	9	7	6
30	37	40	Compiled	16	8	3	5	6	2
83	100	98	Tax Returns	44	30	12	6	4	2
49	81	77	Other	21	16	7	6	15	12
				34 (4/1-9/30/10)		213 (10/1/10-3/31/11)			
194	237	247	**NUMBER OF STATEMENTS**	81	54	23	26	34	29
%	%	%	**ASSETS**	%	%	%	%	%	%
12.3	14.2	14.1	Cash & Equivalents	14.4	15.8	15.5	9.3	13.7	13.9
5.8	5.8	6.3	Trade Receivables (net)	3.3	2.9	7.2	7.4	14.1	10.4
47.8	45.1	45.8	Inventory	48.0	53.5	41.3	49.2	36.5	36.7
2.9	3.9	2.4	All Other Current	.6	1.1	4.0	3.9	5.8	3.4
68.8	68.9	68.6	Total Current	66.2	73.3	67.9	69.9	70.1	64.5
22.6	21.7	21.2	Fixed Assets (net)	24.1	15.7	22.9	23.5	19.0	22.8
2.7	2.9	3.4	Intangibles (net)	4.9	3.4	1.4	1.4	1.1	5.1
5.9	6.4	6.7	All Other Non-Current	4.8	7.6	7.7	5.1	9.8	7.6
100.0	100.0	100.0	Total	100.0	100.0	100.0	100.0	100.0	100.0
			LIABILITIES						
9.9	17.2	10.2	Notes Payable-Short Term	11.4	9.2	8.4	10.9	11.4	8.0
3.6	3.0	3.7	Cur. Mat.-L.T.D.	6.2	2.2	2.5	4.2	1.3	2.6
17.1	17.4	22.0	Trade Payables	26.8	26.9	13.4	15.3	15.2	20.2
.1	.1	.1	Income Taxes Payable	.0	.1	.0	.0	.2	.3
8.8	11.7	12.3	All Other Current	18.0	9.1	9.9	8.9	11.2	8.9
39.4	49.5	48.2	Total Current	62.3	47.4	34.1	39.4	39.2	40.0
18.4	18.5	20.7	Long-Term Debt	30.5	17.6	15.2	15.5	15.5	14.6
.1	.1	.1	Deferred Taxes	.0	.2	.5	.0	.1	.3
10.5	12.7	9.2	All Other Non-Current	16.2	7.3	5.0	10.3	2.4	4.0
31.7	19.3	21.7	Net Worth	-8.9	27.5	45.2	34.7	42.9	41.1
100.0	100.0	100.0	Total Liabilties & Net Worth	100.0	100.0	100.0	100.0	100.0	100.0
			INCOME DATA						
100.0	100.0	100.0	Net Sales	100.0	100.0	100.0	100.0	100.0	100.0
47.9	49.3	48.6	Gross Profit	50.7	49.5	47.9	53.2	41.4	46.4
45.1	45.8	44.1	Operating Expenses	46.7	44.7	41.7	48.6	37.7	41.1
2.8	3.5	4.6	Operating Profit	3.9	4.8	6.3	4.6	3.7	5.4
1.5	1.1	1.6	All Other Expenses (net)	2.5	1.4	1.2	1.8	.5	1.2
1.3	2.5	2.9	Profit Before Taxes	1.4	3.5	5.1	2.8	3.1	4.2
			RATIOS						
3.9	3.2	3.8		6.7	3.6	4.6	3.9	2.6	2.7
1.9	1.7	1.8	Current	1.5	2.0	2.0	2.4	1.8	1.5
1.2	1.0	1.0		.9	1.2	1.3	1.0	1.3	1.1
1.0	.9	1.2		1.5	1.1	2.9	2.2	1.2	1.1
(192) .4	.4	(243) .4	Quick	(80) .3	.2	(22) .4	(25) .4	.6	(28) .5
.1	.1	.1		.1	.1	.1	.2	.4	.2
0 UND	0 UND	0 UND		0 UND	0 UND	0 999.8	0 UND	0 UND	0 846.8
0 999.8	0 999.8	0 999.8	Sales/Receivables	0 UND	0 999.8	1 606.5	1 255.2	1 425.6	3 143.3
8 47.1	4 99.7	5 74.3		1 289.8	3 138.1	16 22.3	11 33.5	38 9.7	17 21.8
61 6.0	70 5.2	55 6.7		83 4.4	50 7.2	51 7.1	86 4.3	37 9.9	33 11.0
130 2.8	136 2.7	116 3.1	Cost of Sales/Inventory	159 2.3	107 3.4	112 3.3	131 2.8	80 4.6	60 6.1
211 1.7	217 1.7	198 1.8		275 1.3	218 1.7	156 1.4	265 1.4	143 2.6	123 3.0
7 51.8	9 39.0	8 45.8		0 UND	6 56.2	4 81.8	11 33.8	17 21.0	28 13.2
28 12.9	35 10.4	31 11.7	Cost of Sales/Payables	24 15.2	31 11.7	23 15.7	30 12.0	31 12.0	42 8.8
63 5.8	74 4.9	80 4.6		118 3.1	104 3.5	56 6.5	86 4.3	57 6.4	58 6.3
4.8	5.0	5.0		3.5	5.2	5.4	4.1	5.7	6.6
8.9	10.6	10.5	Sales/Working Capital	10.7	14.9	9.2	7.2	9.4	15.9
38.1	NM	153.0		-23.4	98.4	19.8	112.2	24.8	49.6
8.3	10.4	9.2		4.4	13.4	15.9	5.2	11.8	20.5
(158) 2.5	(185) 3.2	(198) 2.6	EBIT/Interest	(60) 1.9	(45) 3.1	(18) 2.1	(25) 2.6	(27) 6.0	(23) 4.9
-.1	.4	.4		-.2	.8	-1.7	-2.0	1.5	2.0
6.0	3.8	16.1	Net Profit + Depr., Dep.,						
(15) 2.5	(19) 2.2	(17) 2.2	Amort./Cur. Mat. L/T/D						
.9	-.2	1.0							
.2	.1	.1		.2	.0	.1	.1	.1	.3
.5	.6	.5	Fixed/Worth	1.6	.3	.3	.5	.3	.5
2.3	23.2	4.7		-2.1	163.8	1.3	2.1	.7	1.8
.6	.8	.6		.9	.5	.5	1.0	.8	.6
2.5	2.3	2.4	Debt/Worth	10.0	2.5	1.2	2.2	1.4	1.4
6.9	UND	60.9		-6.6	-91.9	3.1	7.3	2.9	4.3
40.4	50.3	53.0	% Profit Before Taxes/Tangible	70.0	64.5	56.4	51.1	48.9	46.0
(166) 20.0	(178) 22.7	(192) 19.1	Net Worth	(50) 16.6	(39) 24.9	(22) 15.1	(23) 11.9	(33) 17.8	(25) 32.1
.1	2.4	2.9		-1.3	9.7	-.9	-4.1	5.4	16.3
15.9	19.2	16.8	% Profit Before Taxes/Total	13.2	25.2	35.3	12.3	16.8	26.4
4.4	5.1	5.1	Assets	3.4	6.4	6.4	2.9	6.9	8.8
-3.4	-1.1	-1.1		-5.2	-.1	-1.0	-4.5	1.4	4.5
49.4	76.3	96.7		64.6	297.0	97.9	54.9	173.3	42.6
17.7	22.1	24.8	Sales/Net Fixed Assets	19.0	33.9	21.5	24.7	34.4	13.5
7.4	8.1	8.0		5.6	11.1	7.1	6.1	8.6	8.8
3.8	3.7	3.9		3.0	5.0	4.0	3.3	3.5	4.6
2.6	2.4	2.5	Sales/Total Assets	2.2	3.2	2.6	1.9	2.5	2.9
1.6	1.6	1.5		1.1	2.0	1.7	1.4	1.9	1.9
.7	.5	.5		.5	.4	.3	.7	.4	1.2
(156) 1.2	(186) 1.3	(173) 1.2	% Depr., Dep., Amort./Sales	(48) 1.7	(33) 1.0	(21) .9	(23) 1.0	(27) 1.2	(21) 1.9
2.5	2.4	2.7		3.4	2.4	2.4	2.5	2.9	2.9
2.1	2.1	2.1		3.7	2.4	1.0	1.4	.8	
(88) 3.9	(101) 3.8	(117) 4.0	% Officers', Directors' Owners' Comp/Sales	(41) 4.9	(29) 4.2	(14) 2.4	(13) 3.7	(12) 1.6	
7.0	6.9	6.9		8.5	7.1	4.1	8.3	4.0	
3462194M	3921186M	4796041M	Net Sales ($)	43739M	103053M	88911M	200686M	500133M	3859519M
1400336M	1793172M	1851574M	Total Assets ($)	29579M	48260M	48387M	117955M	215017M	1392376M

M = $ thousand   MM = $ million
See Pages 9 through 22 for Explanation of Ratios and Data

Current Data Sorted by Assets

Comparative Historical Data

Type of Statement	0-500M	500M-2MM	2-10MM	10-50MM	50-100MM	100-250MM		4/1/06-3/31/07 ALL	4/1/07-3/31/08 ALL
Unqualified		3	2	5				8	10
Reviewed		4	8	2				6	3
Compiled	5	14	1	1				17	11
Tax Returns	18	8	5	1				29	34
Other	5		11	3				23	31
	24 (4/1-9/30/10)			72 (10/1/10-3/31/11)					
NUMBER OF STATEMENTS	28	29	27	12				83	89
ASSETS	%	%	%	%	%	%		%	%
Cash & Equivalents	25.6	11.6	12.2	12.6				11.1	11.9
Trade Receivables (net)	8.3	18.8	24.6	11.1				13.8	13.4
Inventory	27.9	32.0	29.1	24.2				35.6	40.0
All Other Current	5.7	8.5	4.7	1.2				3.2	3.3
Total Current	67.6	70.8	70.6	49.1				63.7	68.6
Fixed Assets (net)	17.9	19.0	19.0	42.1				21.9	21.9
Intangibles (net)	6.9	4.3	3.9	4.9				5.4	3.5
All Other Non-Current	7.7	5.8	6.4	3.9				9.0	6.0
Total	100.0	100.0	100.0	100.0				100.0	100.0
LIABILITIES									
Notes Payable-Short Term	31.7	12.1	6.0	5.8				12.1	13.3
Cur. Mat.-L.T.D.	9.3	2.9	.7	1.8				3.2	3.3
Trade Payables	6.2	7.4	6.3	4.5				8.7	9.3
Income Taxes Payable	.6	.3	.5	.0				.3	.1
All Other Current	22.2	13.7	16.0	6.4				28.7	7.9
Total Current	70.0	36.5	29.5	18.5				52.9	33.9
Long-Term Debt	13.9	6.5	8.1	18.3				16.4	17.0
Deferred Taxes	.0	.0	.1	.1				.1	.1
All Other Non-Current	5.7	5.3	5.1	4.9				7.2	13.5
Net Worth	10.4	51.7	57.3	58.2				23.4	35.5
Total Liabilities & Net Worth	100.0	100.0	100.0	100.0				100.0	100.0
INCOME DATA									
Net Sales	100.0	100.0	100.0	100.0				100.0	100.0
Gross Profit	64.2	59.6	57.1	54.9				55.8	52.3
Operating Expenses	59.5	53.6	48.3	46.5				50.4	47.6
Operating Profit	4.7	6.1	8.8	8.4				5.4	4.7
All Other Expenses (net)	.8	.4	1.1	.5				1.6	1.0
Profit Before Taxes	3.9	5.7	7.7	7.8				3.8	3.7
RATIOS									
Current	7.5	7.4	7.0	5.5				4.2	6.0
	2.3	2.1	2.7	2.9				2.0	2.5
	1.5	1.2	1.4	1.7				.9	1.2
Quick	3.8	3.0	2.3	2.9				1.4	1.8
	1.6	.8	1.2	1.5				.5 (88)	.8
	.2	.4	.6	.7				.1	.2
Sales/Receivables	0 UND	0 UND	0 999.8	1 432.4				0 UND	0 UND
	0 UND	2 183.2	9 41.6	8 43.6				6 63.3	7 52.9
	3 116.5	47 7.8	140 2.6	44 8.2				56 6.5	58 6.3
Cost of Sales/Inventory	13 28.4	27 13.5	38 9.7	20 18.3				50 7.3	34 10.7
	66 5.6	101 3.6	137 2.7	116 3.1				116 3.1	119 3.1
	133 2.7	197 1.9	193 1.9	350 1.0				261 1.4	314 1.2
Cost of Sales/Payables	0 UND	3 128.9	4 84.4	7 51.1				3 127.8	0 UND
	2 147.2	14 25.3	13 27.1	20 17.8				17 22.1	9 40.3
	23 16.1	35 10.3	40 9.0	53 6.9				48 7.6	42 8.7
Sales/Working Capital	4.5	4.2	1.7	2.9				3.2	2.4
	9.8	11.6	7.2	4.8				6.3	6.3
	64.0	23.7	20.7	13.1				-96.5	37.8
EBIT/Interest	27.3	127.8	54.9	102.8				9.2	10.5
	(20) 7.6	(20) 4.6	(22) 12.2	(10) 10.5				(71) 2.0	(77) 3.7
	-.4	1.0	4.2	2.0				-.2	.7
Net Profit + Depr., Dep., Amort./Cur. Mat. L/T/D									
Fixed/Worth	.0	.1	.0	.2				.1	.0
	.3	.3	.2	.9				.4	.4
	1.2	.9	.6	1.5				6.1	2.6
Debt/Worth	.3	.1	.4	.2				.5	.5
	.7	1.0	.8	.6				1.4	1.2
	8.2	4.5	1.4	4.4				UND	9.7
% Profit Before Taxes/Tangible Net Worth	149.0	52.8	49.3	31.9				47.0	52.7
	(22) 42.1	(25) 36.1	22.2	(11) 23.3				(63) 25.6	(72) 19.4
	7.5	7.5	9.8	7.6				8.0	3.2
% Profit Before Taxes/Total Assets	58.9	36.9	25.0	22.0				17.8	21.4
	19.0	10.7	10.4	9.7				7.0	6.8
	-6.7	3.1	4.1	2.4				-1.1	-.5
Sales/Net Fixed Assets	UND	123.5	81.5	14.5				49.6	95.3
	73.6	25.6	29.0	6.2				19.3	23.3
	17.2	13.0	11.4	1.7				8.7	6.1
Sales/Total Assets	10.3	5.6	4.1	2.3				3.5	3.7
	5.3	2.4	1.8	1.2				1.9	1.8
	2.1	1.4	1.2	1.1				1.2	1.1
% Depr., Dep., Amort./Sales	.4	.3	.4	1.3				.3	.4
	(18) .8	(24) .7	(21) 1.0	(11) 2.0				(67) 1.0	(58) 1.1
	1.3	1.6	1.6	2.7				2.3	2.0
% Officers', Directors' Owners' Comp/Sales	1.5	.7						2.7	2.4
	(13) 6.3	(18) 1.6						(40) 4.6	(47) 4.2
	7.6	4.8						9.8	11.1
Net Sales ($)	36636M	130763M	365901M	361951M				1072961M	1750442M
Total Assets ($)	6588M	32508M	125323M	232838M				530198M	653642M

Note: Columns 50-100MM and 100-250MM marked "DATA NOT AVAILABLE"

M = $ thousand   MM = $ million
See Pages 9 through 22 for Explanation of Ratios and Data

Comparative Historical Data | Current Data Sorted by Sales

			Type of Statement						
9	10	7	Unqualified					1	6
6	10	13	Reviewed		5	3	2	2	1
8	10	11	Compiled	6	1		2	1	1
39	33	38	Tax Returns	11	13	7	6	1	
24	20	27	Other	5	3	2	7	4	6
4/1/08-3/31/09 ALL	4/1/09-3/31/10 ALL	4/1/10-3/31/11 ALL		24 (4/1-9/30/10)			72 (10/1/10-3/31/11)		
				0-1MM	1-3MM	3-5MM	5-10MM	10-25MM	25MM & OVER
86	83	96	NUMBER OF STATEMENTS	22	22	12	17	9	14
%	%	%	ASSETS	%	%	%	%	%	%
14.5	14.5	16.0	Cash & Equivalents	21.1	16.1	10.7	13.2		15.4
11.2	13.2	16.4	Trade Receivables (net)	4.7	28.3	23.3	20.1		4.2
34.4	35.4	29.0	Inventory	34.1	27.1	30.2	25.1		24.6
5.5	5.4	5.7	All Other Current	6.6	8.0	4.9	5.5		2.9
65.5	68.5	67.1	Total Current	66.5	79.5	69.1	63.9		47.1
23.0	21.3	21.6	Fixed Assets (net)	23.6	9.0	23.3	19.8		43.4
3.8	3.0	5.0	Intangibles (net)	6.8	5.2	3.2	6.0		.4
7.7	7.2	6.3	All Other Non-Current	3.1	6.2	4.5	10.3		9.0
100.0	100.0	100.0	Total	100.0	100.0	100.0	100.0		100.0
			LIABILITIES						
13.3	15.4	15.3	Notes Payable-Short Term	15.7	11.5	9.7	35.9		3.4
3.0	4.9	4.0	Cur. Mat.-L.T.D.	1.4	.8	20.6	3.4		1.4
11.8	6.7	6.4	Trade Payables	6.3	2.5	5.8	8.0		9.1
.1	.1	.4	Income Taxes Payable	.0	1.3	.0	.6		.0
14.1	13.4	15.9	All Other Current	8.4	18.7	36.5	10.4		14.2
42.3	40.4	42.0	Total Current	31.7	34.7	72.5	58.3		28.0
16.6	12.1	10.6	Long-Term Debt	17.0	7.0	7.3	6.7		16.2
.0	.0	.0	Deferred Taxes	.0	.0	.0	.0		.1
10.6	5.4	5.3	All Other Non-Current	4.0	5.7	7.0	8.3		1.1
30.5	42.1	42.0	Net Worth	47.2	52.6	13.2	26.7		54.5
100.0	100.0	100.0	Total Liabilities & Net Worth	100.0	100.0	100.0	100.0		100.0
			INCOME DATA						
100.0	100.0	100.0	Net Sales	100.0	100.0	100.0	100.0		100.0
56.2	58.7	59.6	Gross Profit	63.1	60.2	57.4	64.5		58.1
51.5	52.7	52.9	Operating Expenses	58.5	52.1	46.6	59.4		52.3
4.7	6.0	6.7	Operating Profit	4.6	8.1	10.8	5.2		5.8
.8	.6	.7	All Other Expenses (net)	1.3	.4	.4	1.0		-.1
3.9	5.3	6.0	Profit Before Taxes	3.3	7.7	10.4	4.1		5.9
			RATIOS						
8.8	5.7	6.4		14.8	19.0	3.6	6.2		2.8
2.3	2.1	2.4	Current	2.3	2.5	2.6	3.0		2.1
1.2	1.4	1.4		2.0	1.3	.5	1.4		1.2
2.4	2.2	3.0		4.6	6.4	2.2	3.1		1.8
.7	.8	1.2	Quick	1.2	1.8	1.0	1.6		.8
.2	.3	.5		.4	.5	.2	.5		.3
0 UND	0 UND	0 UND		0 UND	0 UND	1 379.3	0 999.8		0 UND
1 333.5	3 113.7	2 190.1	Sales/Receivables	0 UND	46 8.0	3 110.6	7 55.3		2 159.6
35 10.5	45 8.1	68 5.4		8 46.6	144 2.5	147 2.5	59 6.1		9 42.1
26 14.3	46 8.0	27 13.3		72 5.1	32 11.4	27 13.4	16 23.2		24 15.1
97 3.8	124 2.9	95 3.9	Cost of Sales/Inventory	131 2.8	105 3.5	65 5.6	113 3.2		38 9.5
225 1.6	254 1.4	179 2.0		359 1.0	216 1.7	155 2.4	154 2.4		133 2.8
0 UND	0 UND	2 178.7		0 UND	0 UND	4 91.9	8 46.3		13 28.3
8 43.0	14 25.9	13 27.1	Cost of Sales/Payables	4 102.7	5 70.4	11 31.9	40 9.1		26 13.8
30 12.2	36 10.1	34 10.7		67 5.4	21 17.7	20 18.0	68 5.4		46 8.0
3.2	2.6	3.1		3.3	2.1	2.4	2.7		10.2
9.3	6.2	8.7	Sales/Working Capital	5.7	7.2	8.5	8.4		14.4
59.2	22.6	23.4		12.5	38.9	-36.8	13.0		NM
15.2	31.8	41.3		27.3	35.0	166.3	89.9		68.6
(71) 4.8	(64) 6.0	(72) 8.2	EBIT/Interest	(16) 2.9	(15) 7.0	(11) 9.9	(12) 12.2		(13) 10.8
1.1	1.2	1.4		-1.0	1.6	4.3	-.5		1.8
			Net Profit + Depr., Dep., Amort./Cur. Mat. L/T/D						
.1	.0	.1		.0	.0	.0	.0		.3
.3	.2	.3	Fixed/Worth	.3	.2	.3	.4		.7
2.4	1.0	.9		.7	.8	NM	.7		1.3
.4	.3	.3		.3	.1	.3	.2		.4
1.0	.9	.8	Debt/Worth	.7	.6	.9	.8		.8
15.4	2.7	3.0		3.0	10.0	NM	2.8		1.3
48.6	49.3	54.8		53.8	101.4		38.0		55.7
(68) 17.1	(72) 20.1	(85) 30.1	% Profit Before Taxes/Tangible Net Worth	(20) 14.7	(19) 43.4		(16) 17.2		19.8
-1.3	4.6	8.7		-14.1	14.0		1.7		8.5
23.5	28.6	31.6		26.7	40.2	50.4	24.0		33.1
5.4	9.5	11.6	% Profit Before Taxes/Total Assets	8.5	15.8	21.5	8.4		10.5
-4.1	1.8	2.8		-8.0	4.1	9.5	-2.6		3.4
96.8	118.6	110.8		UND	132.3	212.1	221.1		22.9
22.0	24.4	29.1	Sales/Net Fixed Assets	26.4	49.2	46.4	29.0		12.6
9.8	10.4	10.9		5.0	14.1	18.7	12.7		3.1
5.0	4.5	5.5		4.9	5.2	9.6	5.3		5.4
2.6	2.0	2.4	Sales/Total Assets	1.9	1.6	2.1	2.4		3.7
1.5	1.2	1.4		.5	1.4	1.4	1.1		1.4
.5	.3	.4		.4	.3	.2	.3		1.0
(62) 1.2	(64) 1.0	(74) 1.0	% Depr., Dep., Amort./Sales	(14) 1.0	(17) .5	(11) .8	(14) 1.0		(11) 1.3
2.6	2.0	1.8		4.4	1.6	1.4	2.8		2.6
2.0	1.2	1.2		1.5	.7				
(41) 3.2	(43) 3.4	(42) 2.6	% Officers', Directors' Owners' Comp/Sales	(11) 6.3	(11) 3.8				
8.4	7.0	6.0		7.6	6.2				
1199473M	813923M	895251M	Net Sales ($)	11038M	40873M	47856M	117527M	131496M	546461M
565723M	471343M	397257M	Total Assets ($)	9621M	22198M	19971M	66364M	55682M	223421M

© RMA 2011

M = $ thousand   MM = $ million
See Pages 9 through 22 for Explanation of Ratios and Data

Current Data Sorted by Assets						Type of Statement	Comparative Historical Data	
			3	1		Unqualified	2	3
		3				Reviewed	3	4
3	1	4	1			Compiled	4	6
20	2	5				Tax Returns	17	10
8	1	9	1	1	1	Other	6	12
	12 (4/1-9/30/10)		52 (10/1/10-3/31/11)				4/1/06-3/31/07	4/1/07-3/31/08
0-500M	500M-2MM	2-10MM	10-50MM	50-100MM	100-250MM		ALL	ALL
31	4	21	5	2	1	NUMBER OF STATEMENTS	32	35
%	%	%	%	%	%	ASSETS	%	%
8.6		6.2				Cash & Equivalents	12.8	9.4
.7		12.3				Trade Receivables (net)	9.0	14.6
50.0		41.4				Inventory	51.2	45.2
4.8		1.8				All Other Current	1.1	4.2
64.1		61.8				Total Current	74.0	73.4
22.3		28.0				Fixed Assets (net)	17.3	17.4
6.7		5.3				Intangibles (net)	2.7	4.1
6.9		4.9				All Other Non-Current	6.0	5.2
100.0		100.0				Total	100.0	100.0
						LIABILITIES		
24.8		11.2				Notes Payable-Short Term	10.6	19.8
11.3		2.6				Cur. Mat.-L.T.D.	.9	2.2
19.0		18.5				Trade Payables	19.8	19.2
.1		.2				Income Taxes Payable	.0	.0
14.0		7.0				All Other Current	11.6	11.2
69.3		39.4				Total Current	42.9	52.3
16.0		15.3				Long-Term Debt	19.9	15.9
.0		.3				Deferred Taxes	.0	.0
18.2		5.3				All Other Non-Current	24.7	7.7
-3.5		39.7				Net Worth	12.5	24.1
100.0		100.0				Total Liabilties & Net Worth	100.0	100.0
						INCOME DATA		
100.0		100.0				Net Sales	100.0	100.0
47.1		39.0				Gross Profit	37.3	37.0
43.9		34.0				Operating Expenses	35.2	34.0
3.2		5.0				Operating Profit	2.0	3.0
.9		.0				All Other Expenses (net)	.8	.8
2.3		5.0				Profit Before Taxes	1.2	2.3
						RATIOS		
3.1		2.7					3.7	2.7
1.7		1.6				Current	2.4	1.7
.8		1.0					1.2	1.2
.7		.8					.9	.9
.1		.4				Quick	.4	.4
.0		.2					.1	.2
0 UND		0 999.8					0 UND	0 999.8
0 UND		4 92.5				Sales/Receivables	0 UND	4 102.6
0 UND		22 16.7					6 61.5	24 15.2
39 9.3		42 8.7					50 7.4	37 9.9
60 6.0		59 6.2				Cost of Sales/Inventory	65 5.6	56 6.6
114 3.2		76 4.8					82 4.4	102 3.6
0 UND		14 25.9					13 27.3	4 103.6
22 16.8		26 14.0				Cost of Sales/Payables	23 16.2	23 15.7
36 10.3		45 8.2					41 8.9	46 8.0
10.7		13.7					8.5	8.5
20.5		17.9				Sales/Working Capital	12.8	12.8
-24.7		NM					63.2	62.0
12.0		31.1					7.4	13.9
(25) 7.5		(18) 4.5				EBIT/Interest	(26) 3.4	(27) 2.5
.3		1.6					1.0	1.1
						Net Profit + Depr., Dep., Amort./Cur. Mat. L/T/D		
.3		.2					.1	.1
4.5		.7				Fixed/Worth	.6	.6
-.2		1.9					NM	1.3
.9		1.2					.6	1.0
44.3		1.8				Debt/Worth	2.6	2.8
-3.0		4.3					-131.4	8.0
81.5		65.7				% Profit Before Taxes/Tangible Net Worth	49.4	48.3
(16) 43.6		25.3					(23) 20.0	(28) 20.8
15.9		5.7					4.3	2.7
27.2		22.1				% Profit Before Taxes/Total Assets	16.7	18.1
8.6		6.7					7.0	3.7
-2.5		1.5					-1.1	.2
132.9		53.5				Sales/Net Fixed Assets	103.6	112.3
35.9		19.4					37.3	35.9
12.6		6.9					22.2	12.7
7.0		5.5				Sales/Total Assets	5.9	5.4
4.3		3.5					4.8	3.7
2.9		1.7					2.9	2.6
.6		.5				% Depr., Dep., Amort./Sales	.5	.4
(19) 1.0		(18) .7					(25) .9	(26) .9
2.0		1.1					1.3	1.7
2.7		1.0				% Officers', Directors' Owners' Comp/Sales	1.4	2.3
(14) 4.4		(10) 2.4					(10) 2.9	(17) 3.4
10.7		4.2					10.5	5.7
39610M	23134M	379233M	261653M	365156M	306800M	Net Sales ($)	366346M	608088M
8599M	4342M	96711M	96254M	136507M	202500M	Total Assets ($)	91423M	170063M

M = $ thousand   MM = $ million
See Pages 9 through 22 for Explanation of Ratios and Data

Comparative Historical Data

Current Data Sorted by Sales

			Type of Statement						
3	6	4	Unqualified			1	1	1	4
6	8	3	Reviewed						
5	10	9	Compiled	1	2	2	2	2	2
14	28	27	Tax Returns	10	11	1	1	2	1
12	19	21	Other	7	1	2		4	7
4/1/08- 3/31/09 ALL	4/1/09- 3/31/10 ALL	4/1/10- 3/31/11 ALL		0-1MM	12 (4/1-9/30/10) 1-3MM	3-5MM	52 (10/1/10-3/31/11) 5-10MM	10-25MM	25MM & OVER
40	71	64	**NUMBER OF STATEMENTS**	18	14	5	4	9	14
%	%	%	**ASSETS**	%	%	%	%	%	%
11.1	9.7	7.6	Cash & Equivalents	8.4	8.8				9.5
9.9	7.7	6.2	Trade Receivables (net)	.9	2.0				8.8
47.1	46.5	46.3	Inventory	46.4	55.6				43.5
1.6	2.2	3.4	All Other Current	.5	7.8				2.5
69.7	66.2	63.5	Total Current	56.2	74.2				64.3
22.4	23.7	24.8	Fixed Assets (net)	29.4	13.5				26.7
2.9	4.8	6.2	Intangibles (net)	10.7	1.0				6.1
5.0	5.4	5.4	All Other Non-Current	3.7	11.2				3.0
100.0	100.0	100.0	Total	100.0	100.0				100.0
			LIABILITIES						
12.2	13.3	17.5	Notes Payable-Short Term	38.7	5.7				11.1
1.9	1.5	6.7	Cur. Mat.-L.T.D.	1.1	23.9				2.4
17.3	17.2	17.4	Trade Payables	9.7	27.9				19.0
.1	.1	.1	Income Taxes Payable	.2	.0				.2
7.4	9.3	10.3	All Other Current	14.9	11.6				8.1
38.8	41.4	52.0	Total Current	64.7	69.1				40.9
20.3	24.3	16.2	Long-Term Debt	22.8	11.9				10.5
.1	.1	.1	Deferred Taxes	.0	.0				.4
9.1	6.9	11.7	All Other Non-Current	29.1	5.0				8.1
31.7	27.3	19.9	Net Worth	-16.6	14.0				40.1
100.0	100.0	100.0	Total Liabilties & Net Worth	100.0	100.0				100.0
			INCOME DATA						
100.0	100.0	100.0	Net Sales	100.0	100.0				100.0
38.3	36.7	42.5	Gross Profit	53.4	37.8				36.5
33.9	34.2	38.7	Operating Expenses	50.9	34.2				33.3
4.3	2.5	3.8	Operating Profit	2.5	3.7				3.2
.6	.7	.5	All Other Expenses (net)	1.3	.1				.6
3.8	1.9	3.3	Profit Before Taxes	1.3	3.6				2.7
			RATIOS						
2.7	2.9	3.1		5.5	3.6				2.2
1.9	1.6	1.7	Current	2.1	1.6				1.6
1.3	1.1	.9		.9	.6				1.3
1.1	.8	.7		.9	.7				.6
.4	(70) .4	.3	Quick	.2	.1				.5
.1	.1	.0		.0	.0				.2
0 UND	0 UND	0 UND		0 UND	0 UND			0	833.8
3 138.1	1 601.5	0 UND	Sales/Receivables	0 UND	0 UND			5	76.4
19 19.2	8 46.9	7 52.1		0 UND	0 UND			12	30.0
49 7.5	48 7.6	44 8.3		22 16.4	43 8.5			50	7.3
67 5.4	62 5.9	61 6.0	Cost of Sales/Inventory	98 3.7	51 7.1			63	5.8
106 3.4	95 3.8	109 3.3		158 2.3	65 5.6			110	3.3
12 29.6	12 30.8	7 52.5		0 UND	16 22.9			14	25.5
21 17.2	24 14.9	23 15.8	Cost of Sales/Payables	8 44.6	31 11.6			31	11.7
39 9.4	41 8.9	36 10.2		26 13.9	36 10.2			45	8.1
5.6	8.6	10.0		6.5	11.0				9.0
13.7	15.6	16.8	Sales/Working Capital	17.8	19.7				14.5
24.7	125.8	-180.0		-291.3	-15.7				NM
11.6	16.2	13.3		10.3	13.0				36.3
(34) 2.8	(65) 4.0	(55) 7.0	EBIT/Interest	(14) .9	(12) 8.1			(13)	8.2
.7	.9	1.2		.1	1.9				5.2
			Net Profit + Depr., Dep., Amort./Cur. Mat. L/T/D						
.2	.2	.3		.6	.2				.3
.7	.8	1.0	Fixed/Worth	-3.6	.6				.8
2.5	4.0	NM		-.6	-.1				1.7
1.0	1.1	1.1		1.9	.9				1.3
2.6	2.9	2.1	Debt/Worth	-40.8	1.4				1.4
6.2	10.9	NM		-3.7	-3.0				4.0
70.2	61.4	65.8							55.2
(37) 27.8	(58) 33.5	(48) 32.7	% Profit Before Taxes/Tangible Net Worth					(13)	37.8
1.1	9.1	12.0							13.7
17.5	18.8	20.7		14.5	53.2				18.1
8.7	9.6	8.7	% Profit Before Taxes/Total Assets	2.2	12.6				10.4
.1	-.1	.9		-4.1	7.3				5.2
44.9	66.6	58.0		44.3	147.6				37.6
29.9	26.3	28.6	Sales/Net Fixed Assets	22.2	68.9				21.2
10.0	8.1	9.0		11.6	29.8				6.1
5.6	5.1	6.3		5.7	8.0				5.2
3.9	3.5	4.1	Sales/Total Assets	3.5	5.8				3.4
2.3	2.3	2.2		2.0	3.8				2.3
.5	.4	.5		1.2					.6
(31) 1.0	(52) 1.0	(46) 1.0	% Depr., Dep., Amort./Sales	(10) 1.8				(13)	1.0
2.0	1.7	1.8		3.0					2.0
1.3	2.3	2.1							
(18) 3.0	(31) 3.6	(26) 3.3	% Officers', Directors' Owners' Comp/Sales						
5.4	6.4	6.6							
981931M	1951133M	1375586M	Net Sales ($)	11136M	29924M	19153M	29154M	144817M	1141402M
314951M	689655M	544913M	Total Assets ($)	4041M	6081M	10344M	13355M	35880M	475212M

M = $ thousand   MM = $ million
See Pages 9 through 22 for Explanation of Ratios and Data

Current Data Sorted by Assets | Comparative Historical Data

Type of Statement

						Type of Statement		
			2	1	2	Unqualified	3	2
		2	4			Reviewed	9	7
		2	1			Compiled	2	4
8	8	2	4			Tax Returns	4	10
4	4	5	4			Other	6	10
	8 (4/1-9/30/10)		39 (10/1/10-3/31/11)				4/1/06-3/31/07	4/1/07-3/31/08
0-500M	500M-2MM	2-10MM	10-50MM	50-100MM	100-250MM		ALL	ALL
12	12	9	11	1	2	NUMBER OF STATEMENTS	24	33

0-500M	500M-2MM	2-10MM	10-50MM	50-100MM	100-250MM		4/1/06-3/31/07 ALL	4/1/07-3/31/08 ALL
%	%	%	%	%	%	**ASSETS**	%	%
14.1	16.0		11.1			Cash & Equivalents	6.2	14.4
8.1	17.8		4.6			Trade Receivables (net)	11.7	10.4
35.3	41.8		69.6			Inventory	66.6	53.4
.5	.7		2.5			All Other Current	2.4	3.9
58.0	76.3		87.7			Total Current	86.9	82.0
25.9	19.7		3.5			Fixed Assets (net)	5.7	9.9
6.6	.4		.0			Intangibles (net)	.9	2.4
9.5	3.5		8.8			All Other Non-Current	6.5	5.7
100.0	100.0		100.0			Total	100.0	100.0
						LIABILITIES		
15.1	10.1		36.8			Notes Payable-Short Term	18.5	12.3
6.3	.2		.0			Cur. Mat.-L.T.D.	1.8	5.2
17.9	26.6		15.5			Trade Payables	12.4	17.9
.0	.0		.0			Income Taxes Payable	.3	.0
22.4	7.0		15.5			All Other Current	8.9	7.8
61.7	43.9		67.9			Total Current	41.8	43.2
5.6	9.5		.4			Long-Term Debt	9.6	13.7
.0	.0		.0			Deferred Taxes	.0	.0
12.6	8.4		12.6			All Other Non-Current	17.2	7.8
19.9	38.2		19.1			Net Worth	31.3	35.2
100.0	100.0		100.0			Total Liabilities & Net Worth	100.0	100.0
						INCOME DATA		
100.0	100.0		100.0			Net Sales	100.0	100.0
56.1	47.9		37.2			Gross Profit	37.3	45.0
53.6	48.6		25.3			Operating Expenses	30.7	37.0
2.5	-.7		11.9			Operating Profit	6.6	7.9
.9	.7		9.4			All Other Expenses (net)	1.2	-.3
1.6	-1.4		2.4			Profit Before Taxes	5.3	8.2
						RATIOS		
1.9	20.2		2.3				5.0	3.5
1.1	1.8		1.0			Current	1.8	2.3
.6	1.1		.8				1.2	1.2
.9	5.3		.6				1.3	1.1
.3	.8		.2			Quick	.4	.6
.1	.2		.0				.1	.2
0　UND	0　UND		0　UND				1　629.0	0　UND
0　UND	10　34.8		15　23.8			Sales/Receivables	11　32.2	15　24.2
8　43.0	93　3.9		36　10.1				36　10.0	36　10.2
25　14.7	29　12.5		374　1.0				150　2.4	69　5.3
69　5.3	203　1.8		524　.7			Cost of Sales/Inventory	259　1.4	170　2.2
138　2.6	377　1.0		1170　.3				550　.7	607　.6
0　UND	0　752.4		3　126.7				7　48.7	1　402.6
16　22.7	54　6.7		9　42.6			Cost of Sales/Payables	43　8.6	58　6.3
69　5.3	163　2.2		119　3.1				84　4.4	99　3.7
9.6	2.7		1.0				1.2	1.9
NM	6.0		-15.8			Sales/Working Capital	4.5	5.0
-13.5	72.5		-7.9				15.6	21.9
	18.7						8.3	6.1
	(10)　3.6					EBIT/Interest	(19)　4.2	(21)　3.7
	-.6						.7	1.5
						Net Profit + Depr., Dep., Amort./Cur. Mat. L/T/D		
.3	.0		.1				.0	.0
1.0	.5		.2			Fixed/Worth	.1	.1
-1.6	6.0		4.7				.5	UND
1.1	.2		1.5				.7	.6
18.1	2.2		10.4			Debt/Worth	1.6	1.6
-9.8	35.2		65.5				10.0	UND
	118.3					% Profit Before Taxes/Tangible	46.0	45.2
	(10)　18.4					Net Worth	(21)　27.5	(26)　26.1
	-1.0						3.9	6.0
72.4	19.3		15.6			% Profit Before Taxes/Total	17.1	21.5
22.8	4.2		.6			Assets	5.6	10.3
-12.1	-4.4		-2.0				.9	2.9
58.2	77.5		133.8				124.8	289.7
24.1	29.9		19.5			Sales/Net Fixed Assets	66.1	48.0
6.5	2.8		12.5				29.2	14.5
7.3	4.8		1.0				2.3	3.0
4.7	1.4		.8			Sales/Total Assets	1.5	1.8
2.6	.4		.5				.8	.9
.4							.2	.3
(10)　.9						% Depr., Dep., Amort./Sales	(20)　.5	(23)　.6
1.7							.9	1.4
							.9	2.1
						% Officers', Directors' Owners' Comp/Sales	(13)　2.9	(20)　4.9
							11.8	12.4
13037M	28265M	27203M	170449M	145306M	173546M	Net Sales ($)	737161M	944104M
2317M	12233M	28558M	231826M	79779M	333117M	Total Assets ($)	665893M	744445M

© RMA 2011

M = $ thousand　　MM = $ million
See Pages 9 through 22 for Explanation of Ratios and Data

Comparative Historical Data   Current Data Sorted by Sales

			Type of Statement						
4	4	2	Unqualified						
6	7	9	Reviewed		2		2	1	4
3	6	1	Compiled				2	1	
11	12	18	Tax Returns	8	5	2	3		
16	16	17	Other	5	4	3	1	4	
4/1/08- 3/31/09	4/1/09- 3/31/10	4/1/10- 3/31/11		8 (4/1-9/30/10)			39 (10/1/10-3/31/11)		
ALL	ALL	ALL		0-1MM	1-3MM	3-5MM	5-10MM	10-25MM	25MM & OVER
40	45	47	**NUMBER OF STATEMENTS**	13	11	5	8	6	4
%	%	%	**ASSETS**	%	%	%	%	%	%
6.4	16.3	12.1	Cash & Equivalents	9.2	9.5				
10.7	8.8	9.0	Trade Receivables (net)	8.0	8.0				
47.2	49.2	53.2	Inventory	33.8	63.4				
.8	1.2	1.6	All Other Current	1.1	1.0				
65.1	75.5	76.0	Total Current	52.1	82.0				
22.1	14.1	15.6	Fixed Assets (net)	39.1	6.9				
3.3	2.3	2.3	Intangibles (net)	1.1	7.0				
9.4	8.1	6.1	All Other Non-Current	7.8	4.1				
100.0	100.0	100.0	Total	100.0	100.0				
			LIABILITIES						
9.7	13.5	16.6	Notes Payable-Short Term	9.8	13.0				
2.2	.9	1.9	Cur. Mat.-L.T.D.	4.4	2.2				
20.3	9.3	17.7	Trade Payables	15.5	21.5				
.0	.3	.0	Income Taxes Payable	.0	.0				
11.5	9.8	13.5	All Other Current	17.6	7.3				
43.6	33.7	49.6	Total Current	47.3	44.0				
17.3	12.8	5.9	Long-Term Debt	11.3	9.7				
.0	.0	.0	Deferred Taxes	.0	.0				
20.0	9.5	9.7	All Other Non-Current	15.8	4.9				
19.0	43.9	34.7	Net Worth	25.5	41.4				
100.0	100.0	100.0	Total Liabilities & Net Worth	100.0	100.0				
			INCOME DATA						
100.0	100.0	100.0	Net Sales	100.0	100.0				
45.8	42.1	46.5	Gross Profit	61.3	54.2				
40.0	36.1	39.8	Operating Expenses	63.0	46.7				
5.8	6.0	6.7	Operating Profit	-1.7	7.5				
3.2	1.6	2.7	All Other Expenses (net)	1.2	1.0				
2.6	4.4	4.0	Profit Before Taxes	-2.8	6.5				
			RATIOS						
4.5	5.0	5.2		5.1	5.2				
2.1	2.4	1.6	Current	1.4	2.1				
1.0	1.4	.9		.7	1.4				
1.4	2.1	1.1		1.2	.8				
.4	.6	.4	Quick	.5	.3				
.1	.2	.1		.1	.1				
0 UND	0 UND	0 UND		0 UND	0 UND				
12 31.1	13 27.6	6 58.4	Sales/Receivables	4 95.6	2 150.4				
52 7.1	49 7.4	40 9.0		114 3.2	50 7.3				
96 3.8	69 5.3	80 4.5		69 5.3	80 4.5				
222 1.6	247 1.5	209 1.7	Cost of Sales/Inventory	190 1.9	328 1.1				
443 .8	655 .6	795 .5		367 1.0	1221 .3				
5 75.8	2 167.1	8 48.2		0 UND	38 9.7				
31 11.9	25 14.5	42 8.6	Cost of Sales/Payables	20 18.5	78 4.7				
79 4.6	77 4.8	105 3.5		133 2.7	99 3.7				
2.2	1.5	1.1		2.5	.6				
3.4	4.3	6.4	Sales/Working Capital	9.6	3.6				
313.3	20.0	-15.9		-8.2	14.4				
9.0	14.2	15.7			16.2				
(31) 3.4	(35) 4.1	(37) 4.0	EBIT/Interest		6.9				
1.2	1.6	.8			2.3				
			Net Profit + Depr., Dep., Amort./Cur. Mat. L/T/D						
.1	.0	.1		.5	.0				
1.2	.2	.4	Fixed/Worth	2.3	.2				
12.0	2.0	4.7		-2.3	1.1				
.5	.4	.4		.2	.4				
2.2	1.6	2.3	Debt/Worth	2.7	1.2				
79.2	6.8	49.5		-7.5	45.8				
31.3	49.2	77.0	% Profit Before Taxes/Tangible Net Worth		214.5				
(31) 8.9	(41) 14.7	(39) 17.4			(10) 13.2				
2.0	4.6	.5			1.3				
10.3	11.0	19.7	% Profit Before Taxes/Total Assets	18.3	20.2				
3.3	5.8	6.4		-.9	6.9				
-1.5	.6	-.3		-24.9	.7				
47.2	98.0	84.2		22.8	UND				
16.1	22.0	24.2	Sales/Net Fixed Assets	6.3	51.5				
4.1	9.5	7.8		.8	8.8				
2.5	2.5	4.5		4.6	4.8				
1.5	1.6	1.2	Sales/Total Assets	1.2	1.5				
.8	.5	.5		.3	.4				
.5	.2	.3		.8					
(30) 1.2	(28) 1.2	(33) .7	% Depr., Dep., Amort./Sales	(10) 1.2					
2.1	1.9	1.6		3.5					
2.8	2.0	2.6	% Officers', Directors' Owners' Comp/Sales						
(18) 4.7	(25) 3.2	(29) 6.0							
8.0	7.5	10.1							
662825M	870265M	557806M	Net Sales ($)	5385M	17615M	18926M	57481M	89073M	369326M
744966M	689616M	687830M	Total Assets ($)	8570M	20317M	9181M	92737M	103907M	453118M

M = $ thousand   MM = $ million
See Pages 9 through 22 for Explanation of Ratios and Data

Current Data Sorted by Assets

Comparative Historical Data

						Type of Statement		
	1	1	3			Unqualified	4	4
	4	3	2		1	Reviewed	9	4
3	16	13	1		1	Compiled	53	44
9	11	2	1		1	Tax Returns	31	39
2	16	10	3	1		Other	27	24
	18 (4/1-9/30/10)		87 (10/1/10-3/31/11)				4/1/06-3/31/07	4/1/07-3/31/08
0-500M	500M-2MM	2-10MM	10-50MM	50-100MM	100-250MM		ALL	ALL
14	48	29	10	1	3	NUMBER OF STATEMENTS	124	115
%	%	%	%	%	%	ASSETS	%	%
11.0	15.0	14.9	9.6			Cash & Equivalents	9.8	7.6
19.8	8.1	11.9	10.9			Trade Receivables (net)	8.2	8.4
37.1	44.4	41.0	36.5			Inventory	59.8	56.5
.1	4.7	4.9	1.1			All Other Current	2.9	4.2
68.0	72.2	72.6	58.1			Total Current	80.7	76.8
14.0	20.0	13.9	25.9			Fixed Assets (net)	14.1	14.7
.1	1.4	1.2	1.4			Intangibles (net)	.8	1.3
17.9	6.4	12.3	14.6			All Other Non-Current	4.4	7.2
100.0	100.0	100.0	100.0			Total	100.0	100.0
						LIABILITIES		
65.1	27.5	21.8	18.8			Notes Payable-Short Term	41.2	36.4
17.3	3.1	2.7	1.2			Cur. Mat.-L.T.D.	3.5	3.0
8.0	3.9	5.7	6.6			Trade Payables	6.2	8.7
.0	.3	.2	.1			Income Taxes Payable	.1	.0
.8	13.8	14.0	12.2			All Other Current	13.2	11.9
91.2	48.7	44.4	38.8			Total Current	64.2	60.1
22.8	11.6	8.6	14.9			Long-Term Debt	7.7	9.9
.0	.0	.0	.0			Deferred Taxes	.0	.0
34.7	8.3	9.3	7.8			All Other Non-Current	2.9	5.1
-48.8	31.4	37.6	38.5			Net Worth	25.1	24.9
100.0	100.0	100.0	100.0			Total Liabilties & Net Worth	100.0	100.0
						INCOME DATA		
100.0	100.0	100.0	100.0			Net Sales	100.0	100.0
26.6	31.4	27.7	26.4			Gross Profit	24.0	22.9
23.2	28.0	26.1	25.1			Operating Expenses	20.4	21.0
3.4	3.4	1.7	1.3			Operating Profit	3.6	1.8
1.4	.3	-.1	-1.3			All Other Expenses (net)	1.0	1.1
2.0	3.0	1.8	2.6			Profit Before Taxes	2.7	.7
						RATIOS		
4.2	2.4	3.3	3.3				1.7	2.0
1.9	1.6	1.5	1.8			Current	1.2	1.2
.4	1.1	1.1	.9				1.0	1.0
2.0	1.2	.9	1.9				.5	.6
.2	.4	.6	.4		(123)	Quick	.2	(113) .2
.1	.2	.2	.2				.1	.1
0 UND	0 UND	1 663.7	1 340.2				0 UND	0 999.8
3 136.7	4 103.9	6 60.2	9 40.1			Sales/Receivables	4 100.2	6 58.5
46 8.0	26 13.8	28 13.0	38 9.5				22 16.8	19 19.4
0 UND	75 4.9	62 5.9	15 24.9				85 4.3	96 3.8
59 6.1	137 2.7	111 3.3	122 3.0			Cost of Sales/Inventory	142 2.6	141 2.6
143 2.5	177 2.1	316 1.2	156 2.3				201 1.8	201 1.8
0 UND	0 UND	1 301.6	5 79.8				0 UND	1 633.3
7 54.8	5 67.1	13 28.2	9 40.0			Cost of Sales/Payables	4 100.4	4 81.3
21 17.1	19 18.9	30 12.0	31 11.8				11 34.4	15 24.2
4.8	4.0	2.0	3.3				5.7	4.8
15.6	6.8	5.6	9.3			Sales/Working Capital	13.5	11.8
-7.5	47.6	37.8	-18.0				121.9	UND
6.4	7.1	11.3	9.6				5.1	3.8
(10) 1.2	(45) 2.1	3.4	4.6			EBIT/Interest	(117) 2.1	(109) 1.4
-.7	.8	1.1	2.0				.8	.6
						Net Profit + Depr., Dep., Amort./Cur. Mat. L/T/D		
.0	.1	.1	.4				.1	.1
.1	.5	.3	.6			Fixed/Worth	.4	.5
-.6	2.3	.7	1.3				1.6	3.4
.1	.8	.8	.6				1.4	1.2
15.6	3.2	1.7	2.0			Debt/Worth	3.5	3.7
-1.7	7.4	6.4	3.8				16.7	44.0
	28.3	17.9					50.3	36.8
(40)	17.1	(27) 8.8				% Profit Before Taxes/Tangible Net Worth	(107) 18.1	(94) 12.3
	1.6	1.0					1.3	-2.5
19.8	9.7	8.1	11.3				12.0	8.8
-2.6	3.5	2.8	4.8			% Profit Before Taxes/Total Assets	4.1	2.3
-14.7	-.5	.2	1.7				-.7	-2.9
UND	27.9	47.2	17.3				111.6	67.7
56.4	15.0	16.9	6.5			Sales/Net Fixed Assets	32.8	24.4
4.9	6.8	4.4	3.7				9.7	9.2
4.0	2.5	2.4	2.3				2.7	2.9
2.3	1.9	1.3	1.9			Sales/Total Assets	2.0	2.1
1.3	1.2	.8	.9				1.6	1.4
	.4	.4					.3	.4
(36)	.8	(23) .6				% Depr., Dep., Amort./Sales	(96) .5	(94) .7
	1.9	1.5					1.0	1.4
	2.0	.3					1.2	1.4
(26)	2.8	(11) 4.1				% Officers', Directors' Owners' Comp/Sales	(59) 2.5	(52) 2.6
	5.2	6.9					3.5	3.8
9720M	103994M	188097M	365818M	284217M	1227331M	Net Sales ($)	779721M	891560M
3948M	55855M	125990M	197832M	89942M	516502M	Total Assets ($)	482506M	448878M

M = $ thousand   MM = $ million
See Pages 9 through 22 for Explanation of Ratios and Data

Comparative Historical Data | Current Data Sorted by Sales

	4/1/08-3/31/09 ALL	4/1/09-3/31/10 ALL	4/1/10-3/31/11 ALL	Type of Statement	0-1MM	1-3MM	3-5MM	5-10MM	10-25MM	25MM & OVER
	9	6	5	Unqualified		1		2		2
	16	15	10	Reviewed		1	3	1	3	2
	33	26	34	Compiled	7	14	4	5	2	2
	45	28	24	Tax Returns	8	11	3		1	1
	36	31	32	Other	6	10	10	1	3	2
					18 (4/1-9/30/10)			87 (10/1/10-3/31/11)		
	139	106	105	NUMBER OF STATEMENTS	21	37	20	9	9	9
	%	%	%	**ASSETS**	%	%	%	%	%	%
	9.8	8.9	13.9	Cash & Equivalents	9.3	14.6	17.5			
	7.8	8.6	11.1	Trade Receivables (net)	9.7	12.8	5.3			
	53.9	49.7	40.6	Inventory	31.6	46.0	47.0			
	3.4	4.9	3.6	All Other Current	8.8	1.5	4.6			
	74.9	72.1	69.2	Total Current	59.4	74.9	74.4			
	16.7	18.1	18.8	Fixed Assets (net)	24.9	16.7	14.9			
	1.6	1.3	1.3	Intangibles (net)	.3	.6	3.8			
	6.8	8.5	10.7	All Other Non-Current	15.4	7.8	7.0			
	100.0	100.0	100.0	Total	100.0	100.0	100.0			
				LIABILITIES						
	33.6	37.6	29.3	Notes Payable-Short Term	47.3	28.0	24.5			
	4.8	3.9	4.6	Cur. Mat.-L.T.D.	2.1	9.6	1.3			
	5.1	5.3	5.6	Trade Payables	4.6	4.2	3.8			
	.1	.1	.2	Income Taxes Payable	.0	.4	.0			
	13.6	13.2	11.5	All Other Current	7.0	14.8	11.7			
	57.1	60.1	51.3	Total Current	61.0	56.9	41.4			
	14.8	16.4	13.5	Long-Term Debt	18.7	12.7	11.2			
	.0	.0	.0	Deferred Taxes	.0	.0	.0			
	5.8	9.0	13.8	All Other Non-Current	36.3	4.3	8.3			
	22.3	14.4	21.4	Net Worth	-15.9	26.0	39.1			
	100.0	100.0	100.0	Total Liabilities & Net Worth	100.0	100.0	100.0			
				INCOME DATA						
	100.0	100.0	100.0	Net Sales	100.0	100.0	100.0			
	25.3	27.7	28.5	Gross Profit	39.7	27.4	25.7			
	22.7	26.4	25.8	Operating Expenses	36.7	25.5	22.4			
	2.6	1.2	2.7	Operating Profit	2.9	2.0	3.3			
	1.2	1.2	.2	All Other Expenses (net)	.0	.5	.1			
	1.4	.1	2.5	Profit Before Taxes	2.9	1.4	3.2			
				RATIOS						
	2.4	2.2	2.5	Current	7.0	2.1	4.5			
	1.3	1.3	1.6		2.1	1.4	1.9			
	1.0	.9	1.0		.5	.9	1.1			
	.7	.6	1.1	Quick	1.4	1.3	1.4			
	.3	(105) .2	.5		.2	.5	.6			
	.1	.1	.2		.1	.2	.2			
0	UND	0 UND	0 UND	Sales/Receivables	0 UND	0 UND	0 UND			
5	78.6	5 79.4	6 60.6		0 UND	7 50.3	6 65.0			
22	16.6	20 18.5	29 12.8		18 20.2	37 10.0	14 26.3			
83	4.4	73 5.0	60 6.1	Cost of Sales/Inventory	13 27.2	66 5.6	90 4.0			
141	2.6	159 2.3	117 3.1		167 2.2	135 2.7	119 3.1			
226	1.6	271 1.3	176 2.1		465 .8	176 2.1	202 1.8			
0	UND	0 UND	0 UND	Cost of Sales/Payables	0 UND	0 UND	1 309.5			
4	82.9	6 64.8	8 45.7		11 32.5	3 112.9	8 48.3			
15	24.3	18 20.4	21 17.6		28 13.2	20 18.3	18 20.6			
	3.9	4.1	3.5	Sales/Working Capital	1.1	4.5	3.1			
	13.2	17.1	8.1		6.0	7.3	5.6			
	-73.6	-32.7	-595.5		-10.4	-37.4	36.6			
	3.5	3.8	8.7	EBIT/Interest	6.9	4.8	18.9			
(132)	1.4	(104) 1.3	(98) 2.7		(16) 2.3	(35) 1.7	1.9			
	.0	-.5	.9		.2	.1	.9			
	6.3	6.2		Net Profit + Depr., Dep., Amort./Cur. Mat. L/T/D						
(18)	2.5	(11) 3.5								
	.0	-3.2								
	.1	.2	.1	Fixed/Worth	.1	.1	.1			
	.5	.7	.4		1.4	.4	.3			
	2.6	-4.4	1.6		-1.6	1.2	.7			
	1.2	1.8	.8	Debt/Worth	.2	.7	.8			
	3.9	4.4	2.4		4.7	2.6	1.7			
	17.4	-23.2	8.4		-4.1	20.1	7.5			
	25.9	34.3	24.7	% Profit Before Taxes/Tangible Net Worth	54.1	25.7	24.7			
(112)	8.9	(76) 10.0	(87) 11.4		(13) 3.5	(30) 6.7	(19) 16.3			
	-5.8	-7.9	1.0		-10.1	-.5	-.8			
	7.3	7.0	8.8	% Profit Before Taxes/Total Assets	20.6	7.2	9.1			
	1.5	1.4	3.6		1.4	2.3	4.3			
	-4.1	-5.4	-.5		-6.0	-1.8	-.3			
	76.0	46.8	42.7	Sales/Net Fixed Assets	55.7	52.7	54.7			
	27.3	14.3	14.6		3.5	16.9	23.2			
	7.1	5.1	5.1		1.7	9.2	7.9			
	2.9	2.3	2.5	Sales/Total Assets	1.9	2.5	2.7			
	1.8	1.7	1.8		1.1	1.8	1.8			
	1.1	1.1	1.0		.4	1.0	.8			
	.3	.6	.6	% Depr., Dep., Amort./Sales	2.0	.5	.3			
(110)	.7	(80) .9	(78) .9		(13) 2.3	(26) .8	(15) .6			
	1.7	1.9	2.0		6.8	1.5	1.1			
	1.5	1.3	1.7	% Officers', Directors' Owners' Comp/Sales		2.1	.9			
(65)	2.4	(43) 2.5	(42) 2.8			(19) 2.9	(11) 2.7			
	4.1	4.3	5.5			5.7	3.3			
1751751M		1333561M	2179177M	Net Sales ($)	11840M	69843M	72461M	66888M	152256M	1805889M
873106M		682865M	990069M	Total Assets ($)	19066M	62166M	49199M	41702M	74481M	743455M

M = $ thousand   MM = $ million
See Pages 9 through 22 for Explanation of Ratios and Data

Current Data Sorted by Assets   Comparative Historical Data

						Type of Statement		
		5	1		2	Unqualified	1	1
	2	2		1	1	Reviewed	2	2
16	7	7				Compiled	10	4
	7	5				Tax Returns	5	3
	9 (4/1-9/30/10)		48 (10/1/10-3/31/11)			Other	1	6
							4/1/06- 3/31/07	4/1/07- 3/31/08
0-500M	500M-2MM	2-10MM	10-50MM	50-100MM	100-250MM		ALL	ALL
16	16	19	2	1	3	NUMBER OF STATEMENTS	19	16
%	%	%	%	%	%	ASSETS	%	%
19.5	6.2	7.5				Cash & Equivalents	13.8	16.7
11.7	22.2	10.3				Trade Receivables (net)	9.0	7.2
30.0	39.2	44.6				Inventory	39.9	44.9
.3	.2	4.3				All Other Current	4.7	6.1
61.5	67.8	66.7				Total Current	67.4	74.7
23.6	20.5	18.0				Fixed Assets (net)	24.5	14.2
2.1	2.5	8.5				Intangibles (net)	3.4	5.0
12.8	9.2	6.8				All Other Non-Current	4.7	6.0
100.0	100.0	100.0				Total	100.0	100.0
						LIABILITIES		
10.7	15.9	12.3				Notes Payable-Short Term	12.1	6.7
3.4	1.8	1.7				Cur. Mat.-L.T.D.	2.9	1.3
18.3	24.0	16.5				Trade Payables	12.4	18.8
.9	.0	.3				Income Taxes Payable	.3	.1
25.2	6.6	12.5				All Other Current	8.9	9.9
58.3	48.3	43.3				Total Current	36.7	36.8
20.7	17.9	21.3				Long-Term Debt	12.3	5.6
.0	.0	.0				Deferred Taxes	.0	.0
35.0	10.5	11.9				All Other Non-Current	5.2	3.4
-14.0	23.4	23.5				Net Worth	45.8	54.2
100.0	100.0	100.0				Total Liabilties & Net Worth	100.0	100.0
						INCOME DATA		
100.0	100.0	100.0				Net Sales	100.0	100.0
49.1	39.9	26.2				Gross Profit	13.8	15.9
45.0	37.3	25.1				Operating Expenses	11.4	13.1
4.0	2.6	1.2				Operating Profit	2.4	2.9
1.3	.9	.9				All Other Expenses (net)	.3	.0
2.7	1.7	.2				Profit Before Taxes	2.2	2.8
						RATIOS		
2.8	2.2	2.7					4.4	7.5
1.0	1.5	1.7				Current	2.4	2.8
.5	1.0	1.0					1.0	1.2
2.0	.8	1.0					2.0	2.3
.4	.3	.2				Quick	.9	.8
.2	.2	.1					.1	.1
0 UND	0 UND	0 UND					1 363.1	0 UND
1 256.8	5 78.2	3 135.7				Sales/Receivables	2 157.1	1 250.9
22 16.9	42 8.7	21 17.5					6 57.9	4 94.8
1 264.1	10 34.8	22 16.5					13 27.7	16 23.2
25 14.3	98 3.7	46 7.9				Cost of Sales/Inventory	20 18.2	26 14.3
61 6.0	142 2.6	101 3.6					32 11.5	43 8.4
0 UND	3 134.2	5 80.1					0 UND	2 240.8
0 UND	37 9.8	12 29.4				Cost of Sales/Payables	8 44.9	11 32.2
49 7.4	82 4.5	53 6.9					14 25.6	21 17.0
7.6	7.3	7.1					11.7	10.4
UND	21.7	30.3				Sales/Working Capital	22.2	23.4
-15.8	NM	948.5					-278.2	70.5
14.8	12.3	11.9					8.7	73.1
(10) 3.8	(13) 6.2	(15) 2.1				EBIT/Interest	(16) 3.0	(12) 4.4
.8	1.3	-.2					1.2	.8
						Net Profit + Depr., Dep., Amort./Cur. Mat. L/T/D		
.0	.1	.1					.1	.0
2.5	.5	.7				Fixed/Worth	.5	.2
-1.0	NM	5.4					2.7	.6
4.1	1.0	1.5					.3	.1
-16.2	2.2	3.5				Debt/Worth	2.2	.9
-3.4	NM	21.8					5.7	5.3
	40.0	42.9				% Profit Before Taxes/Tangible Net Worth	47.3	53.3
	(12) 28.1	(15) 20.0					(18) 23.4	(13) 36.6
	10.2	-2.5					4.2	4.2
48.7	19.4	10.9				% Profit Before Taxes/Total Assets	22.8	32.5
5.3	5.5	4.7					9.3	17.0
-9.0	1.1	-.7					.9	-.2
860.9	493.5	292.0				Sales/Net Fixed Assets	153.8	333.5
42.3	14.7	38.9					35.4	94.6
11.0	12.2	13.5					19.8	26.7
11.5	4.0	6.7				Sales/Total Assets	9.6	9.9
5.9	3.0	3.5					7.3	7.1
1.5	2.3	1.5					5.7	5.7
.8	.7	.3					.2	.1
(11) 1.4	(14) 1.4	(14) .8				% Depr., Dep., Amort./Sales	(18) .4	(12) .3
3.3	2.7	2.4					.7	.6
						% Officers', Directors' Owners' Comp/Sales		
22696M	71437M	282564M	183203M	593224M	1564601M	Net Sales ($)	739801M	644183M
4286M	15746M	69004M	30516M	67460M	435399M	Total Assets ($)	160480M	163413M

M = $ thousand   MM = $ million
See Pages 9 through 22 for Explanation of Ratios and Data

Comparative Historical Data | Current Data Sorted by Sales

Type of Statement	4/1/08-3/31/09 ALL	4/1/09-3/31/10 ALL	4/1/10-3/31/11 ALL		0-1MM	1-3MM	3-5MM	5-10MM	10-25MM	25MM & OVER
Unqualified		1	3							3
Reviewed	3	7	7					1	2	5
Compiled	9	4	4				1	4	1	1
Tax Returns	3	33	30		11	8	2	2	3	2
Other	7	23	13		1	7	2			1
					9 (4/1-9/30/10)			48 (10/1/10-3/31/11)		
NUMBER OF STATEMENTS	22	68	57		12	15	5	7	6	12
ASSETS	%	%	%		%	%	%	%	%	%
Cash & Equivalents	12.8	10.0	10.0		19.2	8.5				5.1
Trade Receivables (net)	9.8	10.9	15.0		6.5	22.7				12.6
Inventory	45.3	39.7	38.8		27.1	40.8				49.7
All Other Current	5.0	2.6	2.4		.3	.0				4.6
Total Current	72.9	63.2	66.1		53.1	72.1				72.0
Fixed Assets (net)	15.6	21.7	20.1		28.9	14.7				16.2
Intangibles (net)	2.5	5.2	4.2		.9	6.7				1.4
All Other Non-Current	9.0	9.8	9.6		17.2	6.5				10.4
Total	100.0	100.0	100.0		100.0	100.0				100.0
LIABILITIES										
Notes Payable-Short Term	23.2	12.1	12.8		9.9	16.3				14.5
Cur. Mat.-L.T.D.	1.1	2.5	3.0		3.3	1.9				5.6
Trade Payables	15.0	18.3	19.0		9.2	24.2				16.9
Income Taxes Payable	.0	.1	.4		.0	.9				.3
All Other Current	6.6	10.1	14.0		28.0	3.9				10.7
Total Current	46.0	43.0	49.2		50.4	47.1				48.0
Long-Term Debt	11.8	19.7	18.8		31.1	11.7				7.8
Deferred Taxes	.0	.0	.0		.0	.0				.0
All Other Non-Current	3.7	17.4	17.1		38.1	18.7				6.2
Net Worth	38.6	19.9	14.9		-19.5	22.5				38.0
Total Liabilities & Net Worth	100.0	100.0	100.0		100.0	100.0				100.0
INCOME DATA										
Net Sales	100.0	100.0	100.0		100.0	100.0				100.0
Gross Profit	17.5	35.5	35.8		53.6	41.7				17.1
Operating Expenses	16.1	35.6	33.3		49.5	39.1				14.9
Operating Profit	1.4	-.1	2.5		4.1	2.6				2.2
All Other Expenses (net)	.2	.5	.9		1.9	2.3				-.4
Profit Before Taxes	1.3	-.6	1.6		2.2	.2				2.6
RATIOS										
Current	3.0	2.9	2.2		2.5	3.0				1.9
	1.6	1.4	1.4		1.0	1.4				1.6
	1.1	1.1	1.0		.5	1.0				1.1
Quick	.8	1.0	.9		1.8	1.6				.7
	(21) .5	.3	.4		.2	.7				.4
	.2	.1	.2		.2	.2				.1
Sales/Receivables	1 535.2	0 823.1	0 UND		0 UND	0 UND				2 170.3
	4 87.3	3 122.2	3 130.4		0 UND	15 24.7				3 118.5
	8 45.7	21 17.2	24 15.2		8 44.6	46 7.9				10 35.3
Cost of Sales/Inventory	21 17.5	16 23.0	11 33.8		0 UND	25 14.4				24 14.9
	28 13.1	42 8.8	40 9.2		25 14.7	40 9.1				33 11.0
	55 6.6	134 2.7	117 3.1		190 1.9	148 2.5				58 6.3
Cost of Sales/Payables	3 118.1	8 47.1	0 UND		0 UND	0 UND				9 42.9
	11 34.0	21 17.5	19 19.3		0 UND	40 9.0				11 31.9
	17 22.0	57 6.3	53 6.9		68 5.4	96 3.8				16 23.3
Sales/Working Capital	18.0	6.7	7.1		3.9	5.5				11.3
	27.5	19.1	30.3		UND	17.8				31.3
	115.4	106.9	-248.8		-10.8	-120.1				114.2
EBIT/Interest	13.2	13.3	13.7							17.0
	(18) 2.0	(50) 3.3	(44) 4.2							11.1
	.0	.2	1.2							1.9
Net Profit + Depr., Dep., Amort./Cur. Mat. L/T/D										
Fixed/Worth	.1	.2	.1		.0	.0				.1
	.3	.7	.7		NM	.4				.6
	.8	14.5	-7.1		-1.0	-10.1				1.2
Debt/Worth	.5	1.2	1.1		3.1	1.0				1.3
	2.6	3.0	4.1		-6.8	4.7				1.9
	8.6	UND	-13.3		-3.4	-22.3				4.0
% Profit Before Taxes/Tangible Net Worth	35.8	71.5	57.5			55.1				59.1
	(19) 16.4	(52) 25.4	(40) 24.5		(10) 28.1					20.7
	4.2	2.1	6.9			6.1				13.1
% Profit Before Taxes/Total Assets	18.2	20.4	16.5		25.3	17.5				18.1
	2.9	3.2	5.4		4.4	1.8				11.1
	-2.4	-4.8	.0		-8.5	-7.7				2.2
Sales/Net Fixed Assets	152.1	101.4	245.6		UND	635.3				100.2
	70.9	30.0	36.5		23.3	41.2				49.8
	23.2	9.5	12.8		5.5	10.0				22.1
Sales/Total Assets	7.5	5.4	7.0		7.4	3.6				8.4
	5.6	2.9	3.3		1.8	2.7				6.5
	4.9	1.9	1.8		1.4	1.6				3.2
% Depr., Dep., Amort./Sales	.1	.3	.4			.6				.3
	(18) .3	(51) 1.0	(44) 1.1			(11) 1.6			(11)	.4
	.5	3.1	2.7			3.3				.7
% Officers', Directors' Owners' Comp/Sales		1.7	1.2							
		(26) 3.8	(25) 4.5							
		7.2	6.9							
Net Sales ($)	235669M	2697543M	2717725M		7278M	31415M	19444M	47965M	89329M	2522294M
Total Assets ($)	43994M	748514M	622411M		3194M	20023M	8040M	12498M	15945M	562711M

M = $ thousand   MM = $ million
See Pages 9 through 22 for Explanation of Ratios and Data

Current Data Sorted by Assets   Comparative Historical Data

							Type of Statement		36	42
		1	4	16	8	6	Unqualified		36	42
13	10	21	10	1	1		Reviewed		52	51
76	29	34	5	1			Compiled		89	76
33	56	29	3				Tax Returns		152	128
	61	49	25	6	8		Other		159	179
	79 (4/1-9/30/10)			426 (10/1/10-3/31/11)					4/1/06-3/31/07 ALL	4/1/07-3/31/08 ALL
0-500M	500M-2MM	2-10MM	10-50MM	50-100MM	100-250MM					
122	157	137	59	16	14		NUMBER OF STATEMENTS		488	476

0-500M	500M-2MM	2-10MM	10-50MM	50-100MM	100-250MM			488	476
%	%	%	%	%	%		**ASSETS**	%	%
12.9	10.5	10.2	8.9	15.3	17.9		Cash & Equivalents	10.9	9.7
9.1	14.1	18.9	14.6	16.1	14.3		Trade Receivables (net)	18.1	18.6
43.3	38.1	36.4	37.2	25.7	27.1		Inventory	37.8	37.9
2.6	2.2	2.9	4.3	6.8	6.0		All Other Current	2.6	3.5
67.9	64.9	68.4	65.0	63.9	65.3		Total Current	69.4	69.8
20.1	21.7	22.0	23.4	22.7	22.0		Fixed Assets (net)	20.6	19.1
4.1	5.0	5.0	6.3	6.9	2.2		Intangibles (net)	4.6	5.1
7.8	8.3	4.7	5.3	6.4	10.5		All Other Non-Current	5.5	6.0
100.0	100.0	100.0	100.0	100.0	100.0		Total	100.0	100.0
							LIABILITIES		
25.4	10.9	10.2	11.5	11.7	6.8		Notes Payable-Short Term	14.0	13.8
3.7	3.3	3.5	2.8	1.8	1.0		Cur. Mat.-L.T.D.	2.7	3.5
15.4	16.5	20.6	16.8	19.1	13.9		Trade Payables	18.7	21.5
.1	.0	.1	.2	.0	.0		Income Taxes Payable	.4	.4
25.2	12.6	12.3	12.0	11.4	15.8		All Other Current	12.9	12.1
69.7	43.4	46.8	43.4	43.9	37.6		Total Current	48.8	51.3
16.1	18.0	13.1	14.3	13.5	32.9		Long-Term Debt	17.7	17.4
.0	.1	.2	.3	.3	.2		Deferred Taxes	.2	.2
14.3	9.0	7.0	6.7	10.4	11.3		All Other Non-Current	8.7	8.5
-.1	29.6	32.8	35.2	31.9	18.0		Net Worth	24.6	22.6
100.0	100.0	100.0	100.0	100.0	100.0		Total Liabilities & Net Worth	100.0	100.0
							INCOME DATA		
100.0	100.0	100.0	100.0	100.0	100.0		Net Sales	100.0	100.0
47.1	42.1	39.0	36.4	36.6	34.3		Gross Profit	39.4	37.5
44.8	39.6	34.3	30.9	32.0	27.9		Operating Expenses	35.9	33.8
2.3	2.5	4.8	5.5	4.6	6.4		Operating Profit	3.5	3.7
.9	1.1	1.4	1.2	1.9	1.1		All Other Expenses (net)	1.0	1.0
1.4	1.4	3.4	4.3	2.7	5.2		Profit Before Taxes	2.5	2.7
							RATIOS		
3.5	3.4	2.2	2.5	2.0	2.6			2.4	2.3
1.4	1.6	1.5	1.4	1.4	1.5	Current		1.5	1.5
.7	.9	1.0	1.0	1.1	1.3			1.0	1.0
.9	1.3	1.0	.9	1.0	1.4			1.1	1.1
.4	.5	.6	.5	.7	1.0	Quick		(487) .6	(474) .6
.1	.2	.3	.2	.2	.4			.2	.2
0 UND	1 686.9	3 109.5	5 80.0	9 38.6	4 95.2			2 199.1	2 206.1
0 UND	9 40.7	18 20.9	18 20.4	27 13.6	13 28.4	Sales/Receivables		16 23.1	15 23.8
11 33.7	30 12.2	42 8.7	43 8.4	51 7.2	71 5.1			39 9.3	39 9.4
20 18.7	29 12.4	28 13.0	48 7.6	38 9.6	32 11.5			29 12.5	24 15.0
59 6.2	69 5.3	67 5.5	108 3.4	63 5.8	80 4.6	Cost of Sales/Inventory		70 5.2	70 5.2
133 2.7	126 2.9	139 2.6	144 2.5	117 3.1	162 2.2			137 2.7	137 2.7
0 UND	7 53.0	17 21.6	19 19.4	25 14.5	18 19.9			11 34.2	16 23.4
12 30.5	27 13.5	39 9.4	29 12.4	47 7.7	29 12.5	Cost of Sales/Payables		31 11.8	34 10.6
43 8.5	48 7.6	68 5.4	52 7.0	81 4.5	45 8.1			57 6.4	60 6.0
6.6	5.6	6.4	6.0	4.3	3.2			5.5	6.2
28.8	13.0	12.9	14.0	9.1	10.0	Sales/Working Capital		13.5	13.9
-25.6	-124.8	69.7	73.4	50.6	24.0			195.3	106.1
7.8	7.8	11.4	13.8	25.5	24.8			8.3	11.0
(87) 2.6	(120) 2.1	(127) 4.2	(54) 3.3	(15) 1.3	(11) 5.2	EBIT/Interest		(426) 2.6	(414) 3.1
.0	-.3	1.5	1.5	.3	1.9			.9	1.0
		4.9	3.3				Net Profit + Depr., Dep.,	10.1	10.8
	(22) 2.1	(19) 1.3					Amort./Cur. Mat. L/T/D	(54) 3.4	(90) 2.9
	.4	.2						1.3	1.1
.1	.1	.1	.2	.4	.2			.2	.2
.6	.6	.6	.7	.8	.6	Fixed/Worth		.6	.5
-1.1	5.4	2.1	2.0	1.5	1.7			2.9	2.5
.5	.7	1.2	.9	1.4	.6			1.0	1.1
4.5	2.0	2.5	1.9	1.8	2.3	Debt/Worth		2.7	2.9
-4.8	16.3	7.3	4.8	4.1	9.2			12.1	11.9
97.6	38.7	51.5	36.7	32.1	48.2			46.8	50.7
(81) 29.2	(124) 14.1	(121) 20.8	(50) 20.6	(14) 16.6	(13) 15.6	% Profit Before Taxes/Tangible Net Worth		(391) 18.8	(394) 22.2
4.2	-1.5	5.4	10.6	-4.6	9.1			2.5	4.1
20.1	15.5	13.5	15.3	15.3	21.8			15.2	15.7
8.0	4.0	5.6	5.9	2.5	6.2	% Profit Before Taxes/Total Assets		4.6	5.3
-1.3	-2.5	1.2	1.5	-1.1	3.5			-.2	-.1
184.0	116.4	89.7	44.1	21.7	42.5			67.2	73.5
37.3	31.3	22.7	21.6	11.4	13.2	Sales/Net Fixed Assets		24.6	26.4
12.0	10.3	7.5	5.6	5.3	6.1			8.8	9.5
6.4	4.1	3.5	3.1	2.8	3.9			4.2	4.2
4.1	2.8	2.5	1.9	1.6	2.5	Sales/Total Assets		2.7	2.7
2.4	1.8	1.7	1.1	1.2	1.3			1.8	1.9
.5	.3	.5	.4	.4	1.4			.5	.4
(77) 1.0	(108) .8	(114) 1.1	(52) 1.4	(15) 2.2	2.2	% Depr., Dep., Amort./Sales		(378) 1.1	(361) 1.1
2.4	2.2	1.8	2.9	3.2				2.5	2.3
4.1	1.9	1.0						1.9	1.7
(75) 7.0	(84) 4.2	(63) 2.1				% Officers', Directors' Owners' Comp/Sales		(214) 3.8	(188) 3.7
10.6	7.0	3.7						8.0	6.7
161796M	614487M	1850155M	3200273M	2329965M	6160985M		Net Sales ($)	14042309M	16083622M
30538M	178136M	623070M	1241907M	1152642M	2209588M		Total Assets ($)	6187560M	7452913M

M = $ thousand   MM = $ million
See Pages 9 through 22 for Explanation of Ratios and Data

Comparative Historical Data | Current Data Sorted by Sales

Hist 1	Hist 2	Hist 3	Type of Statement	0-1MM	1-3MM	3-5MM	5-10MM	10-25MM	25MM & OVER
51	45	35	Unqualified			2	2	3	28
72	69	42	Reviewed		4	5	8	17	8
66	82	82	Compiled	8	17	16	17	13	11
184	187	164	Tax Returns	47	56	22	23	11	5
215	205	182	Other	33	32	27	20	36	34
4/1/08-3/31/09 ALL	4/1/09-3/31/10 ALL	4/1/10-3/31/11 ALL		79 (4/1-9/30/10)			426 (10/1/10-3/31/11)		
588	588	505	**NUMBER OF STATEMENTS**	88	109	72	70	80	86
%	%	%	**ASSETS**	%	%	%	%	%	%
10.2	11.7	11.2	Cash & Equivalents	12.0	10.4	9.7	11.8	10.0	12.9
17.0	14.9	14.3	Trade Receivables (net)	9.1	11.3	13.6	17.5	18.8	17.5
38.5	37.3	38.1	Inventory	37.7	40.2	39.0	37.7	40.3	33.2
3.1	2.7	3.0	All Other Current	2.3	2.4	2.1	1.7	4.1	5.1
68.7	66.6	66.6	Total Current	61.1	64.3	64.4	68.9	73.3	68.7
20.8	20.2	21.7	Fixed Assets (net)	25.5	22.4	22.3	19.0	18.9	21.0
4.9	5.8	4.9	Intangibles (net)	6.9	5.2	4.8	4.2	2.8	5.1
5.6	7.3	6.9	All Other Non-Current	6.4	8.1	8.5	8.0	5.0	5.2
100.0	100.0	100.0	Total	100.0	100.0	100.0	100.0	100.0	100.0
			LIABILITIES						
17.3	13.0	14.2	Notes Payable-Short Term	22.8	12.4	11.1	19.9	9.3	10.2
3.7	3.7	3.3	Cur. Mat.-L.T.D.	3.1	3.6	5.1	2.9	3.2	2.1
17.8	18.6	17.4	Trade Payables	11.4	14.9	16.8	21.1	23.2	18.7
.2	.2	.1	Income Taxes Payable	.1	.0	.0	.0	.2	.2
11.6	14.3	15.5	All Other Current	18.5	22.9	9.8	12.1	12.2	14.0
50.5	49.9	50.5	Total Current	56.0	53.8	42.9	55.9	48.2	45.1
18.4	17.9	16.1	Long-Term Debt	21.8	17.1	17.3	13.4	9.2	16.5
.3	.3	.1	Deferred Taxes	.0	.0	.1	.3	.2	.3
7.8	9.3	9.6	All Other Non-Current	20.8	6.3	7.7	7.9	6.7	7.8
23.0	22.5	23.7	Net Worth	1.4	22.7	32.1	22.5	35.8	30.4
100.0	100.0	100.0	Total Liabilities & Net Worth	100.0	100.0	100.0	100.0	100.0	100.0
			INCOME DATA						
100.0	100.0	100.0	Net Sales	100.0	100.0	100.0	100.0	100.0	100.0
38.8	39.6	41.4	Gross Profit	52.5	45.6	41.5	38.0	37.8	30.9
35.1	36.4	37.8	Operating Expenses	51.0	41.4	38.8	33.2	33.2	27.2
3.7	3.2	3.6	Operating Profit	1.5	4.2	2.7	4.8	4.7	3.6
1.0	.9	1.2	All Other Expenses (net)	3.1	1.0	.5	.4	1.1	.7
2.7	2.2	2.4	Profit Before Taxes	-1.6	3.2	2.2	4.4	3.6	3.0
			RATIOS						
2.6	2.6	2.7		3.3	4.9	2.6	2.7	2.5	2.2
1.5	1.5	1.5	Current	1.2	1.5	1.5	1.6	1.5	1.4
1.1	1.0	1.0		.6	.8	1.0	1.0	1.1	1.2
1.1	1.1	1.0		.9	1.4	.8	1.2	1.0	1.1
(587) .5	(587) .5	.5	Quick	.4	.5	.4	.6	.6	.7
.2	.2	.2		.1	.1	.2	.2	.2	.3
2 228.6	1 507.0	0 999.8		0 UND	0 UND	2 205.9	1 243.9	2 225.8	5 80.9
14 26.9	10 35.7	10 36.4	Sales/Receivables	0 UND	4 102.3	11 33.0	15 24.0	16 23.0	17 21.4
35 10.5	36 10.1	33 11.2		18 20.2	22 16.5	32 11.4	40 9.2	44 8.3	41 8.9
26 14.2	28 13.0	30 12.0		27 13.8	31 11.7	35 10.3	25 14.3	35 10.4	25 14.3
75 4.9	70 5.2	69 5.3	Cost of Sales/Inventory	106 3.4	73 5.0	68 5.3	59 6.2	68 5.4	63 5.8
150 2.4	139 2.6	137 2.7		216 1.7	126 2.9	145 2.5	111 3.3	124 2.9	116 3.2
9 39.8	12 31.7	8 43.5		0 UND	3 104.8	13 28.3	8 43.8	20 18.2	16 22.6
30 12.0	29 12.4	28 13.1	Cost of Sales/Payables	10 36.9	22 16.3	33 10.9	35 10.0	34 10.7	28 12.9
56 6.5	57 6.5	56 6.6		45 8.0	55 6.7	62 5.9	60 6.1	58 6.3	51 7.1
6.0	6.2	6.0		4.4	5.7	7.2	6.2	6.1	7.1
14.1	14.5	15.0	Sales/Working Capital	18.0	15.9	18.7	15.2	12.8	14.5
96.5	-155.8	-168.1		-14.6	-33.5	-367.2	-626.8	55.9	39.2
7.1	9.5	10.1		4.0	8.6	8.3	13.6	14.8	21.9
(510) 2.8	(507) 2.8	(414) 3.2	EBIT/Interest	(64) 1.2	(80) 2.5	(62) 2.6	(58) 4.1	(73) 4.5	(77) 5.2
.7	.6	.7		-.4	.3	-.9	.6	1.9	1.1
7.2	5.7	6.3						9.7	5.5
(89) 2.5	(108) 2.3	(60) 2.1	Net Profit + Depr., Dep., Amort./Cur. Mat. L/T/D				(14) 2.4	(30) 2.0	
1.2	.6	.7						.9	.9
.2	.2	.1		.1	.1	.1	.1	.1	.2
.6	.7	.6	Fixed/Worth	1.7	.6	.4	.4	.3	.7
4.1	13.4	3.6		-.8	6.5	3.1	2.7	1.4	1.8
1.0	.9	.9		.9	.5	1.0	.8	.8	1.2
2.8	2.8	2.4	Debt/Worth	9.6	2.4	2.3	2.3	1.8	2.0
24.8	100.8	19.6		-3.1	32.7	8.9	11.6	5.2	6.3
49.5	53.3	50.1		53.6	57.9	38.6	67.5	46.6	56.8
(464) 18.9	(452) 16.5	(403) 19.0	% Profit Before Taxes/Tangible Net Worth	(53) 11.4	(87) 17.6	(61) 14.8	(56) 25.2	(73) 18.8	(73) 19.6
2.0	1.9	3.4		-.7	1.0	-16.3	4.5	10.0	6.7
14.8	14.0	15.6		11.3	16.9	12.2	19.0	15.3	18.0
4.6	4.8	5.5	% Profit Before Taxes/Total Assets	1.0	5.5	6.2	5.6	6.8	6.0
-.5	-.7	-.4		-8.2	-.5	-2.0	.4	2.5	.6
77.3	80.1	106.3		148.1	108.5	99.7	112.2	110.6	56.5
22.2	21.9	26.4	Sales/Net Fixed Assets	22.8	26.4	28.5	37.5	29.0	22.9
7.5	7.1	7.9		4.6	10.1	11.2	11.5	8.0	7.8
4.2	4.0	4.2		3.8	4.5	3.8	4.6	4.1	4.4
2.6	2.7	2.7	Sales/Total Assets	2.2	3.0	2.8	3.0	2.7	3.0
1.7	1.7	1.8		1.2	1.8	1.8	2.1	1.8	1.8
.5	.5	.4		.7	.4	.4	.4	.4	.4
(452) 1.1	(447) 1.1	(374) 1.1	% Depr., Dep., Amort./Sales	(54) 1.6	(73) 1.4	(49) 1.2	(57) .9	(71) .7	(70) 1.2
2.4	2.4	2.4		3.6	2.6	2.1	1.6	1.7	2.6
1.8	1.8	1.6		5.3	3.5	1.9	1.0	1.0	.5
(222) 3.4	(238) 3.8	(232) 4.2	% Officers', Directors' Owners' Comp/Sales	(50) 8.4	(62) 5.3	(38) 2.9	(34) 3.0	(36) 1.4	(12) 1.1
5.9	6.5	7.9		13.0	7.8	5.3	6.4	2.4	1.1
18080077M	14869721M	14317661M	Net Sales ($)	47712M	199791M	279637M	487405M	1204054M	12099062M
8120300M	7178099M	5435881M	Total Assets ($)	33815M	91225M	138128M	214515M	588938M	4369260M

M = $ thousand   MM = $ million
See Pages 9 through 22 for Explanation of Ratios and Data

Current Data Sorted by Assets   Comparative Historical Data

Type of Statement	0-500M	500M-2MM	2-10MM	10-50MM	50-100MM	100-250MM	4/1/06-3/31/07 ALL	4/1/07-3/31/08 ALL
Unqualified			2	8	7	3	8	8
Reviewed		4	7	4			4	4
Compiled	2	11	2				3	5
Tax Returns	4	11	11	1			8	11
Other	5	9	13	10	5	7	22	30
			15 (4/1-9/30/10)		100 (10/1/10-3/31/11)			
NUMBER OF STATEMENTS	11	24	35	23	12	10	45	58
ASSETS	%	%	%	%	%	%	%	%
Cash & Equivalents	19.0	25.5	14.9	26.9	15.5	15.5	13.5	19.2
Trade Receivables (net)	10.0	10.5	11.7	8.9	5.4	18.2	13.4	13.3
Inventory	24.5	39.9	47.8	26.4	40.8	18.1	40.7	39.4
All Other Current	10.4	3.7	3.8	6.5	4.2	3.2	5.5	5.4
Total Current	64.0	79.6	78.2	68.7	65.9	55.0	73.1	77.3
Fixed Assets (net)	15.4	10.0	10.0	18.7	13.6	8.9	13.4	13.0
Intangibles (net)	2.5	3.7	6.5	7.5	18.7	30.2	8.5	5.9
All Other Non-Current	18.1	6.7	5.3	5.2	1.8	5.8	5.0	3.8
Total	100.0	100.0	100.0	100.0	100.0	100.0	100.0	100.0
LIABILITIES								
Notes Payable-Short Term	9.5	17.4	10.7	2.5	9.2	3.9	11.8	15.6
Cur. Mat.-L.T.D.	.6	1.0	1.9	1.4	4.2	.9	1.8	2.9
Trade Payables	33.3	23.1	32.9	17.4	19.2	18.8	21.7	22.5
Income Taxes Payable	1.8	.0	.1	.3	.3	.0	.3	.1
All Other Current	15.7	4.8	8.9	11.9	17.0	13.4	14.4	16.4
Total Current	60.9	46.3	54.5	33.5	50.0	37.1	50.0	57.5
Long-Term Debt	2.4	7.9	11.1	13.9	8.5	7.7	13.0	9.5
Deferred Taxes	.0	.0	.1	.3	1.1	2.1	.2	.3
All Other Non-Current	.6	3.3	3.1	2.4	1.4	6.2	3.4	10.1
Net Worth	36.1	42.5	31.2	50.0	38.9	46.8	33.4	22.7
Total Liabilities & Net Worth	100.0	100.0	100.0	100.0	100.0	100.0	100.0	100.0
INCOME DATA								
Net Sales	100.0	100.0	100.0	100.0	100.0	100.0	100.0	100.0
Gross Profit	40.2	36.2	38.7	39.1	36.0	33.6	39.6	38.6
Operating Expenses	32.2	31.4	34.3	37.6	37.2	33.5	36.0	33.4
Operating Profit	8.0	4.8	4.4	1.5	-1.3	.1	3.6	5.2
All Other Expenses (net)	-.3	.6	.2	.1	1.4	.7	.8	.6
Profit Before Taxes	8.3	4.3	4.2	1.5	-2.7	-.6	2.9	4.6
RATIOS								
Current	3.4	3.6	2.4	3.1	1.5	1.8	2.2	2.2
	1.2	1.7	1.4	1.9	1.4	1.4	1.5	1.6
	.8	1.3	.9	1.3	1.1	1.2	1.0	1.0
Quick	1.7	1.8	.9	1.6	.7	1.2	1.0	1.1
	.6	.6	.4	.8	.4	.9	.5	.5
	.1	.3	.1	.4	.1	.3	.2	.2
Sales/Receivables	0 UND	0 UND	0 794.7	0 999.8	1 314.1	1 500.0	1 279.4	2 234.3
	0 UND	3 116.0	5 67.6	2 212.1	3 128.3	4 91.5	6 65.2	6 62.9
	9 40.8	13 29.2	20 18.1	11 32.8	14 25.3	67 5.4	22 16.6	14 25.2
Cost of Sales/Inventory	0 999.8	13 28.8	46 7.9	15 25.1	39 9.3	14 26.3	42 8.7	31 12.0
	6 57.3	41 8.9	78 4.7	73 5.0	93 3.9	43 8.5	89 4.1	71 5.2
	31 11.7	100 3.6	108 3.4	131 2.8	131 2.8	79 4.6	130 2.8	123 3.0
Cost of Sales/Payables	0 UND	3 126.5	24 14.9	23 15.6	20 18.2	33 11.1	25 14.8	17 21.4
	21 17.7	20 18.2	43 8.5	35 10.5	39 9.4	48 7.7	40 9.1	25 14.3
	45 8.2	54 6.7	68 5.4	42 8.6	65 5.6	54 6.8	62 5.9	53 6.9
Sales/Working Capital	13.2	7.4	7.2	5.3	11.0	6.8	7.2	7.4
	103.5	17.5	15.9	8.7	19.6	14.7	14.2	13.6
	-75.9	44.3	-77.0	20.7	68.9	24.3	586.1	207.5
EBIT/Interest		64.0	57.1	19.6	9.4	14.3	10.6	14.5
	(19) 4.7	(31) 11.3	(17) 5.6	2.3	4.8		(38) 3.4	(47) 4.7
		1.2	4.6	-4.4	-12.4	-2.9	-2.2	1.6
Net Profit + Depr., Dep., Amort./Cur. Mat. L/T/D							39.2	44.5
							(13) 7.4	(11) 9.2
							4.1	1.6
Fixed/Worth	.0	.0	.0	.1	.3	.2	.2	.1
	.5	.1	.3	.5	.8	.7	.4	.5
	UND	1.4	1.8	1.2	NM	NM	1.4	2.3
Debt/Worth	.1	.6	1.1	.6	1.2	1.5	1.2	1.1
	4.0	1.3	3.7	1.3	3.4	5.1	2.2	2.4
	-46.3	7.0	9.7	1.9	NM	NM	5.7	8.5
% Profit Before Taxes/Tangible Net Worth		94.9	98.9	48.4			51.6	71.1
	(21) 54.5	(29) 54.9	(21) 28.6				(40) 18.2	(50) 38.7
		14.0	25.7	7.8			-9.4	-.2
% Profit Before Taxes/Total Assets	160.5	45.6	30.4	17.4	7.1	8.3	21.7	21.0
	61.5	18.1	9.9	10.2	2.6	6.6	6.3	11.1
	15.1	1.0	5.9	1.2	-17.1	-6.4	-4.4	-.1
Sales/Net Fixed Assets	UND	UND	298.0	42.4	49.0	36.2	92.9	144.9
	270.9	148.2	68.0	23.8	19.6	20.9	33.8	40.9
	37.9	50.7	37.6	12.3	10.6	16.3	16.7	15.2
Sales/Total Assets	18.7	7.3	5.1	3.3	4.0	3.7	4.9	4.9
	8.1	4.3	3.8	2.9	2.3	1.7	2.7	3.6
	5.4	3.0	2.7	1.7	1.6	1.2	2.0	2.5
% Depr., Dep., Amort./Sales		.3	.2	.5	.7		.5	.3
	(12) .5	(26) .6	(21) 1.1	(10) 2.0			(39) .7	(40) .8
		1.1	1.5	2.9	3.5		1.5	1.9
% Officers', Directors' Owners' Comp/Sales		1.4	1.0				2.1	.6
	(13) 1.8	(15) 2.2					(15) 4.2	(18) 3.3
		5.6	3.8				6.1	7.6
Net Sales ($)	25530M	164751M	688365M	1444897M	2706514M	4445748M	4985701M	6637379M
Total Assets ($)	2159M	24600M	177368M	519554M	904886M	1810640M	2070103M	2219788M

M = $ thousand   MM = $ million
See Pages 9 through 22 for Explanation of Ratios and Data

Comparative Historical Data | Current Data Sorted by Sales

				Type of Statement						
15		13		20	Unqualified					2	18
5		4		11	Reviewed					4	7
6		4		8	Compiled	1		3		2	
14		15		27	Tax Returns		5	7	5	8	2
40		46		49	Other	3	2	4	5	9	26
4/1/08-		4/1/09-		4/1/10-			15 (4/1-9/30/10)		100 (10/1/10-3/31/11)		
3/31/09		3/31/10		3/31/11		0-1MM	1-3MM	3-5MM	5-10MM	10-25MM	25MM & OVER
ALL		ALL		ALL							
80		82		115	**NUMBER OF STATEMENTS**	4	9	14	10	25	53
%		%		%	**ASSETS**	%	%	%	%	%	%
15.0		16.9		20.0	Cash & Equivalents			26.9	21.9	23.0	17.4
10.6		10.5		10.6	Trade Receivables (net)			6.1	5.5	15.9	9.4
37.7		36.3		36.3	Inventory			41.0	46.5	35.8	35.3
7.4		4.9		4.9	All Other Current			3.2	3.7	5.4	5.0
70.8		68.6		71.9	Total Current			77.1	77.7	80.1	67.0
14.4		15.4		12.5	Fixed Assets (net)			9.5	7.9	10.7	14.0
8.6		10.3		9.1	Intangibles (net)			6.8	2.4	5.0	13.7
6.2		5.7		6.5	All Other Non-Current			6.6	12.0	4.2	5.3
100.0		100.0		100.0	Total			100.0	100.0	100.0	100.0
					LIABILITIES						
16.2		9.4		9.6	Notes Payable-Short Term			11.0	21.2	9.7	5.9
2.4		2.0		1.7	Cur. Mat.-L.T.D.			2.0	.8	1.9	1.8
25.6		22.1		25.1	Trade Payables			19.4	26.3	24.9	26.0
.4		.4		.3	Income Taxes Payable			.0	.0	.1	.2
15.0		13.6		10.5	All Other Current			5.5	11.0	9.1	13.9
59.7		47.5		47.2	Total Current			37.9	59.3	45.7	47.9
11.2		11.8		9.6	Long-Term Debt			9.6	6.8	11.5	9.2
.2		.4		.4	Deferred Taxes			.0	.0	.1	.8
6.6		5.0		2.8	All Other Non-Current			1.6	3.0	1.7	3.0
22.4		35.3		40.0	Net Worth			50.9	30.8	41.0	39.1
100.0		100.0		100.0	Total Liabilities & Net Worth			100.0	100.0	100.0	100.0
					INCOME DATA						
100.0		100.0		100.0	Net Sales			100.0	100.0	100.0	100.0
40.6		39.2		37.7	Gross Profit			38.0	31.7	38.4	37.0
37.5		34.8		34.4	Operating Expenses			32.2	34.0	33.2	35.3
3.1		4.5		3.3	Operating Profit			5.8	-2.2	5.1	1.7
1.5		.8		.4	All Other Expenses (net)			.3	.8	.1	.4
1.6		3.6		2.9	Profit Before Taxes			5.4	-3.1	5.1	1.3
					RATIOS						
2.1		2.3		2.5				7.7	2.8	2.6	1.9
1.5		1.5		1.5	Current			2.3	1.3	1.9	1.4
1.0		1.1		1.1				1.2	.7	1.2	1.0
1.0		1.1		1.1				6.7	1.3	1.1	1.0
.4		.6		.5	Quick			.5	.3	.8	.5
.1		.2		.3				.3	.1	.5	.2

1	592.4	0	999.8	0	999.8		0	UND	0	UND	1	391.8	0	765.4		
4	83.5	3	117.9	3	134.8	Sales/Receivables	0	UND	1	386.8	6	62.9	2	187.8		
13	27.3	14	25.7	14	26.4		10	35.6	11	34.2	25	14.7	12	29.8		
24	15.2	30	12.3	17	21.5		1	262.1	18	19.9	13	27.3	32	11.4		
68	5.4	61	6.0	59	6.2	Cost of Sales/Inventory	31	11.6	94	3.9	52	7.0	73	5.0		
132	2.8	107	3.4	102	3.6		111	3.3	124	2.9	95	3.8	100	3.6		
16	22.8	20	18.0	20	18.7		0	UND	0	UND	12	30.5	28	13.1		
32	11.3	34	10.7	35	10.3	Cost of Sales/Payables	22	16.3	40	9.1	35	10.6	39	9.5		
56	6.5	53	6.9	56	6.5		43	8.5	61	6.0	61	6.0	56	6.5		

8.4		7.7		7.2	Sales/Working Capital			8.4	5.8	6.9	7.0
18.9		17.3		15.9				14.8	29.7	15.4	17.1
193.4		158.1		143.0				NM	-35.6	40.2	171.4

	13.5		56.2		23.5						51.2		20.6
(61)	3.8	(65)	9.3	(93)	7.6	EBIT/Interest				(22)	8.3	(46)	5.9
	-.5		1.7		1.5						4.3		1.1

			146.8		17.1								20.6
		(13)	25.1	(15)	8.3	Net Profit + Depr., Dep., Amort./Cur. Mat. L/T/D						(12)	8.9
			2.8		2.9								1.9

.2		.1		.1				.0	.0	.0	.2
.4		.4		.3	Fixed/Worth			.1	.1	.2	.6
UND		2.1		1.5				NM	NM	.6	1.7
.8		.8		.9				.1	.6	.6	1.1
2.7		1.9		2.2	Debt/Worth			1.2	4.8	1.9	2.8
UND		7.9		8.1				NM	-43.6	4.9	8.6

	65.4		76.4		75.7			119.9			98.7		49.0
(60)	34.7	(70)	39.9	(96)	40.5	% Profit Before Taxes/Tangible Net Worth	(11)	47.2	(22)	64.0	(44)	27.8
	7.7		15.6		11.8			14.4			40.8		4.1

21.5		27.2		30.4	% Profit Before Taxes/Total Assets			90.5	32.1	38.3	15.3
7.5		11.8		9.7				25.5	1.7	17.9	7.8
-3.5		2.1		1.2				5.6	-9.0	6.9	.7
98.5		110.0		241.0	Sales/Net Fixed Assets			UND	UND	276.9	50.9
32.6		31.3		45.4				315.4	164.3	80.5	25.9
14.7		16.3		20.0				39.3	33.8	42.0	16.7
4.9		5.5		5.4	Sales/Total Assets			9.6	5.2	5.2	4.4
3.2		3.4		3.4				5.1	3.9	4.1	3.0
2.2		2.4		2.2				2.8	2.1	2.7	2.0

	.4		.5		.4						.2		.6
(50)	.7	(53)	1.2	(77)	.9	% Depr., Dep., Amort./Sales			(18)	.4	(45)	1.2
	1.9		2.5		2.1						1.1		2.8

	1.3		1.0		1.0	% Officers', Directors' Owners' Comp/Sales					.5
(15)	5.7	(21)	2.6	(35)	2.0					(12)	1.0
	9.4		7.6		4.6						3.6

7315087M		6007468M		9475805M	Net Sales ($)	1895M	16309M	57309M	66881M	390535M	8942876M
2432713M		2497632M		3439207M	Total Assets ($)	865M	5304M	13825M	35469M	117209M	3266535M

M = $ thousand   MM = $ million
See Pages 9 through 22 for Explanation of Ratios and Data

Current Data Sorted by Assets

Comparative Historical Data

	0-500M	500M-2MM	2-10MM	10-50MM	50-100MM	100-250MM			4/1/06-3/31/07 ALL		4/1/07-3/31/08 ALL

Type of Statement

								Type of Statement			
			2	15	6	8		Unqualified	34		34
		1	6	2	1			Reviewed	20		19
		4	4	2				Compiled	16		16
	1	5	1	2				Tax Returns	22		24
	5	8	20	17	8	2		Other	53		53
		21 (4/1-9/30/10)		99 (10/1/10-3/31/11)							
	6	18	33	38	15	10		**NUMBER OF STATEMENTS**	145		146
	%	%	%	%	%	%		**ASSETS**	%		%
	25.1	14.1	11.9	17.7	20.6			Cash & Equivalents	12.2		16.1
	11.5	12.7	9.6	9.2	13.7			Trade Receivables (net)	12.5		11.1
	39.7	44.2	37.4	32.5	29.7			Inventory	39.9		38.0
	.1	4.0	6.5	5.3	5.0			All Other Current	4.7		4.8
	76.4	74.9	65.4	64.7	69.1			Total Current	69.1		69.9
	14.6	15.4	12.1	16.4	14.3			Fixed Assets (net)	14.4		12.8
	5.5	2.4	15.9	12.8	12.5			Intangibles (net)	7.7		9.5
	3.5	7.3	6.6	6.1	4.1			All Other Non-Current	8.8		7.8
	100.0	100.0	100.0	100.0	100.0			Total	100.0		100.0
								LIABILITIES			
	12.6	10.6	7.0	4.7	5.3			Notes Payable-Short Term	11.6		11.6
	1.0	1.4	3.2	1.6	3.5			Cur. Mat.-L.T.D.	2.3		3.1
	10.1	24.2	20.6	17.6	23.6			Trade Payables	27.2		22.5
	.0	.4	.4	.4	.2			Income Taxes Payable	.3		.3
	5.6	9.2	13.1	11.9	15.7			All Other Current	15.1		12.7
	29.3	45.8	44.2	36.2	48.3			Total Current	56.5		50.2
	11.7	7.4	9.1	8.5	7.1			Long-Term Debt	11.3		11.8
	.0	.0	1.7	.5	.0			Deferred Taxes	.4		.6
	9.5	10.4	7.8	5.5	1.9			All Other Non-Current	7.0		6.9
	49.5	36.4	37.1	49.2	42.7			Net Worth	24.8		30.6
	100.0	100.0	100.0	100.0	100.0			Total Liabilities & Net Worth	100.0		100.0
								INCOME DATA			
	100.0	100.0	100.0	100.0	100.0			Net Sales	100.0		100.0
	38.8	43.8	47.3	49.2	33.2			Gross Profit	43.5		43.1
	36.4	39.9	39.4	46.0	29.0			Operating Expenses	41.2		39.5
	2.4	3.8	7.9	3.2	4.2			Operating Profit	2.4		3.7
	1.5	.4	1.0	1.1	.6			All Other Expenses (net)	.7		.8
	.9	3.5	6.9	2.1	3.6			Profit Before Taxes	1.7		2.9
								RATIOS			
	7.5	2.7	2.2	3.5	2.0				2.2		2.8
	5.0	1.7	1.5	1.5	1.4			Current	1.3		1.5
	1.2	1.1	1.0	1.1	1.2				1.0		1.1
	6.0	1.1	.8	1.8	1.1				.8		1.2
	1.8	.4	.5	.8	.8			Quick	(144) .3		.4
	.2	.1	.5	.5	.3				.1		.1
	1 296.7	2 187.6	2 241.9	3 143.4	2 165.5				1 438.6	1	445.0
	7 53.9	5 73.4	3 132.7	8 46.3	5 71.5			Sales/Receivables	5 71.3	5	67.6
	19 19.6	21 17.0	15 23.7	32 11.6	48 7.6				14 25.3	15	24.4
	21 17.4	40 9.1	60 6.1	59 6.2	14 26.3				44 8.4	39	9.3
	59 6.2	90 4.0	80 4.6	91 4.0	80 4.5			Cost of Sales/Inventory	78 4.7	78	4.7
	114 3.2	145 2.5	133 2.7	137 2.7	108 3.4				121 3.0	116	3.1
	4 81.5	21 17.3	23 15.6	34 10.6	33 10.9				20 18.2	18	19.9
	16 23.5	36 10.2	35 10.4	45 8.0	53 6.9			Cost of Sales/Payables	42 8.6	34	10.6
	31 11.8	54 6.7	62 5.9	90 4.1	67 5.5				61 5.9	63	5.8
	4.7	5.9	7.8	5.3	6.8				7.6		6.8
	6.6	12.2	13.6	11.3	17.6			Sales/Working Capital	21.8		13.7
	50.4	201.7	NM	41.2	39.1				-132.0		54.0
	70.7	17.0	65.8	28.3					17.2		15.9
	(13) 8.9	(27) 5.5	(32) 13.9	(13) 7.3				EBIT/Interest	(122) 5.1	(114)	3.9
	-1.3	1.1	4.6	3.0					1.0		1.4
			25.9						15.9		21.2
			(10) 5.3					Net Profit + Depr., Dep., Amort./Cur. Mat. L/T/D	(21) 6.9	(21)	3.8
			1.5						2.4		2.3
	.0	.1	.2	.1	.2				.1		.1
	.2	.3	.4	.5	.5			Fixed/Worth	.5		.3
	4.0	1.7	2.1	-3.1	1.3				2.7		2.0
	.2	.6	1.0	.3	.9				.9		.7
	.6	1.5	3.1	1.8	2.5			Debt/Worth	2.9		1.7
	14.7	2.8	14.2	-14.1	6.0				42.6		19.5
	90.6	50.7	152.7	25.5				% Profit Before Taxes/Tangible Net Worth	62.0		60.9
	(15) 39.3	(28) 13.3	(31) 52.3	(11) 15.7					(110) 27.9	(115)	31.1
	3.4	2.1	25.5	1.0					6.3		9.4
	38.4	19.9	23.7	10.8	12.1			% Profit Before Taxes/Total Assets	17.5		20.5
	13.2	6.9	13.6	4.5	9.1				7.9		8.1
	-6.8	1.7	5.6	.6	3.8				-.4		1.1
	493.9	107.3	97.1	50.5	65.6				95.7		121.9
	65.6	41.2	28.2	20.3	27.7			Sales/Net Fixed Assets	37.4		37.6
	19.3	17.6	13.3	9.2	8.9				17.2		14.9
	4.2	5.8	3.9	2.8	4.6				5.3		4.5
	3.6	3.4	2.7	2.3	2.1			Sales/Total Assets	3.5		3.2
	2.5	2.8	1.8	1.7	1.7				2.6		2.2
	.2	.4	.5	.9					.5		.4
	(10) .5	(25) .9	(28) 1.0	(14) 1.2				% Depr., Dep., Amort./Sales	(109) .8	(103)	.8
	1.1	1.2	1.4	2.1					1.5		1.6
									1.8		1.2
								% Officers', Directors' Owners' Comp/Sales	(34) 3.2	(37)	3.0
									6.3		7.4
	6170M	88107M	697026M	3005595M	2484189M	5078620M		Net Sales ($)	11479835M		12385152M
	1604M	24529M	173286M	984814M	1102410M	1605435M		Total Assets ($)	3830512M		5015679M

M = $ thousand　　MM = $ million
See Pages 9 through 22 for Explanation of Ratios and Data

Comparative Historical Data				Current Data Sorted by Sales					
			Type of Statement						
30	31	31	Unqualified					2	29
11	13	10	Reviewed				1	4	5
15	10	10	Compiled		2		3	4	1
19	12	9	Tax Returns	1	1	1	3	1	2
62	58	60	Other	2	6	2	4	14	32
4/1/08-3/31/09 ALL	4/1/09-3/31/10 ALL	4/1/10-3/31/11 ALL		21 (4/1-9/30/10)			99 (10/1/10-3/31/11)		
				0-1MM	1-3MM	3-5MM	5-10MM	10-25MM	25MM & OVER
137	124	120	NUMBER OF STATEMENTS	3	9	3	11	25	69
%	%	%	ASSETS	%	%	%	%	%	%
11.6	13.3	16.5	Cash & Equivalents				24.3	16.6	15.2
11.4	12.8	11.1	Trade Receivables (net)				12.9	14.8	9.4
40.8	37.0	38.1	Inventory				40.2	42.7	36.3
4.4	4.4	4.3	All Other Current				6.1	4.2	4.9
68.1	67.5	70.1	Total Current				83.4	78.3	65.7
16.3	16.4	14.5	Fixed Assets (net)				8.0	15.2	13.8
8.0	8.4	9.5	Intangibles (net)				5.5	1.9	13.3
7.7	7.7	5.9	All Other Non-Current				3.1	4.6	7.2
100.0	100.0	100.0	Total				100.0	100.0	100.0
			LIABILITIES						
15.4	10.0	10.4	Notes Payable-Short Term				10.4	10.1	6.6
3.0	2.0	2.1	Cur. Mat.-L.T.D.				.3	1.8	2.6
21.5	21.2	19.6	Trade Payables				9.2	18.5	22.7
.3	.3	.3	Income Taxes Payable				.0	.0	.5
12.5	10.6	10.4	All Other Current				7.7	12.0	12.0
52.6	44.1	42.8	Total Current				27.5	42.4	44.3
11.8	11.8	10.1	Long-Term Debt				5.2	5.8	9.4
.4	.8	.6	Deferred Taxes				.0	.0	.6
8.4	15.0	7.9	All Other Non-Current				.0	4.9	9.0
26.7	28.3	38.7	Net Worth				67.3	46.9	36.3
100.0	100.0	100.0	Total Liabilties & Net Worth				100.0	100.0	100.0
			INCOME DATA						
100.0	100.0	100.0	Net Sales				100.0	100.0	100.0
44.2	43.4	44.1	Gross Profit				38.4	41.8	46.3
41.9	39.3	39.1	Operating Expenses				29.8	37.1	40.8
2.4	4.1	5.0	Operating Profit				8.6	4.7	5.5
.9	1.0	.9	All Other Expenses (net)				.7	.3	.9
1.5	3.1	4.1	Profit Before Taxes				7.9	4.3	4.6
			RATIOS						
2.4	2.8	2.9					8.7	3.1	2.2
1.5	1.7	1.6	Current				5.7	1.7	1.4
.9	1.1	1.1					1.6	1.1	1.1
1.0	1.2	1.1					6.0	1.3	1.0
.4	.6	.6	Quick				1.2	.8	.5
.1	.2	.2					.6	.2	.2
2 201.3	2 171.4	2 182.1					2 236.8	2 185.3	2 181.0
6 59.6	7 55.9	5 78.3	Sales/Receivables				5 76.5	8 46.8	4 99.6
19 19.3	21 17.4	20 18.1					15 24.9	28 13.1	17 22.0
35 10.4	45 8.0	46 7.9					22 16.6	40 9.1	56 6.6
79 4.6	82 4.5	81 4.5	Cost of Sales/Inventory				53 6.8	104 3.5	82 4.4
140 2.6	124 2.9	128 2.8					97 3.8	145 2.5	131 2.8
20 18.4	19 19.4	20 18.6					5 78.0	12 30.0	26 14.1
37 9.9	35 10.3	35 10.4	Cost of Sales/Payables				13 28.2	29 12.4	39 9.3
60 6.1	53 6.9	59 6.2					30 12.0	51 7.1	62 5.9
7.0	5.8	6.1					5.0	5.4	7.6
14.9	11.6	12.1	Sales/Working Capital				6.3	8.8	15.7
-77.9	76.7	75.3					12.8	53.3	110.7
10.0	20.5	23.8						17.2	42.9
(118) 3.5	(102) 5.1	(99) 7.6	EBIT/Interest					(21) 3.4	(60) 11.4
-1.3	1.1	2.3						-.7	3.7
21.4	20.4	24.4							25.4
(27) 6.2	(26) 3.6	(23) 5.4	Net Profit + Depr., Dep., Amort./Cur. Mat. L/T/D						(21) 6.6
1.5	.9	1.7							1.8
.2	.1	.1					.0	.1	.1
.5	.4	.4	Fixed/Worth				.1	.3	.5
3.7	1.9	1.7					.3	.6	3.0
.9	.6	.5					.1	.5	.9
2.2	1.7	2.0	Debt/Worth				.2	1.5	2.8
27.6	7.5	9.0					1.4	2.2	16.2
71.6	55.8	66.0					90.6	37.9	68.6
(107) 20.5	(98) 24.6	(97) 29.0	% Profit Before Taxes/Tangible Net Worth				61.0	(23) 12.7	(54) 33.1
2.8	10.3	7.2					9.4	-6.8	15.1
13.6	17.4	16.1					52.9	25.3	14.8
6.5	9.1	10.2	% Profit Before Taxes/Total Assets				25.2	7.3	10.2
-2.2	1.3	2.5					3.9	-.5	3.6
84.5	69.0	109.5					517.5	68.4	84.3
30.9	28.6	31.7	Sales/Net Fixed Assets				73.2	35.2	29.7
11.3	13.3	13.5					24.8	17.3	12.6
4.4	4.8	4.1					4.7	4.6	4.1
3.1	3.1	3.1	Sales/Total Assets				3.9	3.1	2.8
2.2	1.9	2.1					2.7	2.4	1.8
.6	.5	.4						.2	.5
(102) 1.0	(90) .8	(88) 1.0	% Depr., Dep., Amort./Sales					(21) .9	(54) 1.0
1.7	1.6	1.5						1.2	1.6
1.9	1.1	2.0							
(35) 2.7	(21) 3.0	(26) 3.2	% Officers', Directors' Owners' Comp/Sales						
6.2	5.6	7.8							
11992022M	11333065M	11359707M	Net Sales ($)	1850M	15053M	13011M	71314M	416366M	10842113M
3847815M	4602199M	3892078M	Total Assets ($)	1274M	6700M	7702M	26065M	131412M	3718925M

M = $ thousand   MM = $ million
See Pages 9 through 22 for Explanation of Ratios and Data

RETAIL—Vending Machine Operators   NAICS 454210

Current Data Sorted by Assets							Comparative Historical Data		

	0-500M	500M-2MM	2-10MM	10-50MM	50-100MM	100-250MM	Type of Statement	4/1/06-3/31/07 ALL	4/1/07-3/31/08 ALL
			2	4	2		Unqualified	8	4
		1	11	5			Reviewed	24	17
	4	6	7				Compiled	27	17
	9	7	4				Tax Returns	27	17
	4	9	10	8		1	Other	27	31
	20 (4/1-9/30/10)			74 (10/1/10-3/31/11)					
NUMBER OF STATEMENTS	17	23	34	17	2	1		113	86
	%	%	%	%	%	%	ASSETS	%	%
Cash & Equivalents	14.5	19.1	13.5	13.7				9.4	9.5
Trade Receivables (net)	2.2	6.9	7.6	12.9				6.5	6.5
Inventory	19.9	13.7	14.7	17.1				16.2	15.6
All Other Current	5.4	2.7	2.7	3.4				2.1	2.7
Total Current	42.0	42.3	38.4	47.1				34.3	34.4
Fixed Assets (net)	43.5	40.1	45.2	40.0				50.8	51.9
Intangibles (net)	2.5	11.5	9.1	8.3				7.8	8.3
All Other Non-Current	11.9	6.0	7.2	4.6				7.2	5.4
Total	100.0	100.0	100.0	100.0				100.0	100.0
							LIABILITIES		
Notes Payable-Short Term	20.2	6.6	4.6	7.5				7.4	8.2
Cur. Mat.-L.T.D.	5.7	5.5	8.0	5.5				9.5	7.3
Trade Payables	22.7	18.3	9.9	16.2				13.2	14.1
Income Taxes Payable	.0	.0	.0	.5				.1	.1
All Other Current	7.4	9.6	8.4	11.8				7.7	8.8
Total Current	56.0	40.1	30.8	41.4				37.9	38.5
Long-Term Debt	51.7	15.5	27.8	19.0				31.7	29.4
Deferred Taxes	.0	.0	.4	.8				.3	.4
All Other Non-Current	1.1	5.8	10.2	13.5				9.3	10.5
Net Worth	-8.9	38.5	30.7	25.3				20.9	21.1
Total Liabilities & Net Worth	100.0	100.0	100.0	100.0				100.0	100.0
							INCOME DATA		
Net Sales	100.0	100.0	100.0	100.0				100.0	100.0
Gross Profit	42.2	48.2	48.3	39.0				46.7	46.8
Operating Expenses	38.3	42.0	46.8	35.6				43.0	45.0
Operating Profit	3.9	6.2	1.6	3.3				3.8	1.8
All Other Expenses (net)	.4	-.5	-.2	1.1				1.3	1.1
Profit Before Taxes	3.5	6.7	1.8	2.2				2.4	.7
							RATIOS		
Current	3.3	1.5	2.3	1.4				1.5	1.3
	.9	1.1	1.2	1.1				.8	.9
	.4	.7	.8	.7				.5	.6
Quick	1.4	.9	1.5	.9				.7	.6
	.4	.6	.5	.6				.4	.4
	.1	.4	.4	.3				.2	.2
Sales/Receivables	0 UND	0 UND	2 215.2	3 114.9				0 768.5	1 391.2
	0 UND	2 210.2	9 42.9	13 27.4				5 71.0	5 79.9
	4 86.8	6 65.5	13 27.5	23 15.7				14 26.6	11 32.1
Cost of Sales/Inventory	11 32.0	6 58.3	23 16.0	25 14.3				19 19.1	22 16.5
	22 16.6	30 12.2	39 9.3	34 10.8				31 11.7	32 11.3
	42 8.8	49 7.5	52 7.0	43 8.5				46 8.0	43 8.5
Cost of Sales/Payables	0 UND	10 35.4	9 39.9	21 17.1				9 42.0	13 27.1
	8 46.5	30 12.4	21 17.5	38 9.5				26 14.1	29 12.7
	22 16.3	67 5.4	38 9.6	46 7.9				42 8.8	44 8.2
Sales/Working Capital	16.4	27.0	11.7	25.6				23.6	36.4
	-338.5	154.4	70.9	68.2				-105.9	-73.1
	-15.0	-26.1	-42.5	-23.7				-16.5	-18.9
EBIT/Interest	5.2	20.5	5.1	8.8				3.9	4.1
	(12) 1.7	(21) 4.2	(32) 2.1	(16) 3.0				(107) 1.9	(82) 1.6
	-7.4	2.0	.6	-.5				.7	.5
Net Profit + Depr., Dep., Amort./Cur. Mat. L/T/D								2.6	3.5
								(13) 2.2	(12) 1.9
								1.1	1.3
Fixed/Worth	.6	.8	.7	.8				1.3	1.2
	1.4	1.4	2.2	2.9				3.0	2.9
	-.9	3.4	-6.6	NM				-13.9	-63.5
Debt/Worth	.3	.7	.5	1.6				1.3	1.5
	3.6	2.2	3.5	3.5				3.3	4.3
	-2.4	5.4	-9.8	NM				-27.6	-90.8
% Profit Before Taxes/Tangible Net Worth	30.8	86.3	30.8	65.0				36.4	37.0
	(10) 6.1	(19) 29.2	(25) 10.4	(13) 42.4				(82) 12.6	(64) 16.8
	-.1	8.7	.7	.6				-6.6	-1.9
% Profit Before Taxes/Total Assets	28.1	23.8	9.7	11.7				10.6	9.6
	5.9	8.1	3.3	6.4				4.3	2.2
	-3.5	.9	-.3	-4.3				-1.4	-1.5
Sales/Net Fixed Assets	23.8	13.6	12.4	14.8				9.6	8.9
	13.8	9.6	5.3	7.0				6.5	6.1
	5.6	5.8	3.1	5.2				4.3	3.6
Sales/Total Assets	9.5	5.2	3.5	3.8				4.1	3.9
	3.8	2.9	2.4	3.3				3.0	2.9
	2.6	2.2	1.6	2.3				2.2	2.1
% Depr., Dep., Amort./Sales	2.0	1.4	3.9	2.1				3.1	3.3
	(12) 4.5	(16) 3.3	(29) 4.7	3.3				(104) 4.3	(79) 4.3
	6.4	6.1	6.8	5.9				6.7	6.5
% Officers', Directors' Owners' Comp/Sales			.6					1.5	1.3
			(12) 1.5					(46) 3.2	(34) 2.8
			3.5					5.2	6.2
Net Sales ($)	16219M	100564M	361505M	791354M	167603M	136208M		1519696M	1703879M
Total Assets ($)	3673M	21671M	137696M	261377M	124049M	119540M		535289M	677679M

M = $ thousand   MM = $ million
See Pages 9 through 22 for Explanation of Ratios and Data

Comparative Historical Data | Current Data Sorted by Sales

Hist 1	Hist 2	Hist 3	Type of Statement	0-1MM	1-3MM	3-5MM	5-10MM	10-25MM	25MM & OVER
6	6	8	Unqualified				1		7
24	14	17	Reviewed		1		5	5	6
23	15	17	Compiled	2	4	4	3	3	1
17	17	20	Tax Returns	6	7	3	4		
32	39	32	Other	6	7	1	4	8	6
4/1/08-3/31/09 ALL	4/1/09-3/31/10 ALL	4/1/10-3/31/11 ALL		20 (4/1-9/30/10)			74 (10/1/10-3/31/11)		
102	91	94	**NUMBER OF STATEMENTS**	14	19	8	17	16	20
%	%	%	**ASSETS**	%	%	%	%	%	%
9.1	12.8	15.0	Cash & Equivalents	15.9	20.6		9.8	13.0	17.3
8.6	9.0	7.6	Trade Receivables (net)	1.3	5.0		5.7	8.8	14.1
17.7	14.9	15.6	Inventory	15.5	14.9		13.2	19.8	15.2
2.4	1.9	3.8	All Other Current	5.3	2.9		.7	4.0	5.9
37.9	38.6	41.9	Total Current	37.9	43.3		29.5	45.7	52.4
47.8	45.3	42.1	Fixed Assets (net)	40.9	41.7		52.5	41.0	32.9
6.7	10.1	8.2	Intangibles (net)	7.1	9.0		8.9	7.2	8.3
7.6	6.0	7.7	All Other Non-Current	14.1	6.1		9.2	6.1	6.4
100.0	100.0	100.0	Total	100.0	100.0		100.0	100.0	100.0
			LIABILITIES						
7.9	7.2	8.7	Notes Payable-Short Term	18.9	6.2		3.3	5.2	9.3
8.3	8.5	6.3	Cur. Mat.-L.T.D.	3.1	5.8		13.5	5.2	4.9
15.5	11.5	15.4	Trade Payables	23.9	11.4		11.4	13.8	17.0
.1	.1	.1	Income Taxes Payable	.0	.0		.0	.6	.0
10.2	7.4	9.5	All Other Current	3.9	10.1		6.6	9.2	13.2
42.1	34.7	40.0	Total Current	49.8	33.5		34.9	33.8	44.4
30.0	29.7	27.1	Long-Term Debt	57.0	18.0		39.2	21.9	11.6
.5	.3	.3	Deferred Taxes	.0	.0		.2	.7	.7
8.9	10.6	9.0	All Other Non-Current	1.4	1.3		11.4	12.7	17.1
18.6	24.7	23.6	Net Worth	-8.3	47.2		14.4	30.9	26.2
100.0	100.0	100.0	Total Liabilities & Net Worth	100.0	100.0		100.0	100.0	100.0
			INCOME DATA						
100.0	100.0	100.0	Net Sales	100.0	100.0		100.0	100.0	100.0
43.0	45.4	44.8	Gross Profit	49.9	47.8		53.2	42.3	34.6
41.5	41.4	41.2	Operating Expenses	40.3	43.5		50.7	41.6	31.8
1.5	4.0	3.6	Operating Profit	9.6	4.4		2.5	.7	2.7
.7	.8	.2	All Other Expenses (net)	.8	-.6		.7	-.4	.8
.8	3.2	3.4	Profit Before Taxes	8.8	4.9		1.9	1.2	1.9
			RATIOS						
1.5	1.8	2.0	Current	4.3	2.5		1.2	2.3	1.4
1.0	1.1	1.1		.9	1.2		.9	1.4	1.1
.6	.6	.7		.4	.9		.5	.8	.7
.8	1.2	1.1	Quick	2.1	1.9		.6	1.4	1.0
.4	(90) .5	.5		.4	.6		.4	.5	.6
.2	.2	.3		.1	.2		.2	.2	.3
2 231.5	0 999.8	0 867.5	Sales/Receivables	0 UND	0 UND		1 322.0	3 111.5	3 106.4
6 62.1	3 106.3	4 86.5		0 UND	2 199.7		6 65.5	7 53.6	13 27.9
14 26.4	12 30.0	13 28.5		1 276.2	7 52.0		14 25.9	17 21.8	23 15.9
17 21.7	14 25.9	15 23.9	Cost of Sales/Inventory	6 59.5	8 44.2		14 25.7	30 12.2	16 22.6
31 11.6	32 11.3	34 10.8		16 22.9	41 9.0		39 9.5	42 8.7	30 12.2
45 8.0	47 7.8	49 7.5		33 11.0	54 6.8		59 6.2	56 6.5	39 9.4
11 33.5	7 53.7	10 37.4	Cost of Sales/Payables	0 UND	8 47.7		19 18.9	12 29.2	11 32.0
24 15.1	17 21.3	27 13.7		8 46.8	22 16.8		31 11.8	26 14.3	34 10.9
42 8.6	37 9.9	42 8.6		31 11.7	59 6.2		41 9.0	48 7.5	44 8.3
26.8	16.5	18.4	Sales/Working Capital	15.4	8.8		64.5	7.9	25.0
-139.7	133.0	81.5		-206.9	45.5		-61.7	31.5	60.1
-15.3	-20.7	-25.1		-11.1	-66.9		-13.4	-46.9	-28.1
3.6	6.1	7.3	EBIT/Interest	8.7	25.5		2.9	5.1	9.4
(99) 1.6	(84) 2.3	(83) 2.5		(10) 3.8	(16) 4.0		(16) 2.2	2.0	(17) 4.1
.5	.8	.9		-1.2	-.7		1.0	.0	.4
5.2	2.7	5.6	Net Profit + Depr., Dep., Amort./Cur. Mat. L/T/D						
(18) 2.0	(13) 2.1	(16) 2.9							
1.2	1.4	1.2							
1.3	1.0	.7	Fixed/Worth	.5	.6		1.6	.6	.5
2.6	2.8	1.9		1.3	.9		7.2	2.1	1.8
-11.3	-13.3	-8.9		-.8	2.0		-2.1	3.4	NM
1.5	1.3	.7	Debt/Worth	.3	.5		2.1	1.0	1.1
4.4	4.4	3.4		1.7	.7		10.3	3.6	3.5
-15.9	-24.2	-19.1		-1.9	3.8		-4.3	7.0	NM
32.9	71.5	49.8	% Profit Before Taxes/Tangible Net Worth		45.0		40.0	46.4	89.9
(70) 16.4	(66) 19.0	(69) 19.7		(17) 15.9		(10) 8.4	(13) 8.9	(15) 49.1	
-4.7	.9	1.4			-3.4		-1.5	.3	19.7
8.5	11.9	11.9	% Profit Before Taxes/Total Assets	33.7	18.5		8.8	6.8	11.8
2.7	3.6	5.4		16.1	5.1		4.7	2.4	8.8
-3.0	-.8	-.1		3.2	-3.9		.0	-3.7	-2.4
13.5	12.4	15.7	Sales/Net Fixed Assets	23.8	13.6		7.1	13.3	18.6
6.9	6.4	7.3		11.9	7.3		5.0	6.3	8.7
5.0	3.6	4.1		3.5	4.0		2.9	4.1	5.7
5.0	4.1	4.0	Sales/Total Assets	8.1	3.4		3.7	3.6	4.8
3.3	2.8	2.9		2.9	2.8		2.4	2.8	3.4
2.4	1.7	2.0		1.1	1.9		1.8	2.1	2.4
2.9	3.0	2.3	% Depr., Dep., Amort./Sales		2.0		4.2	1.1	1.8
(92) 4.3	(68) 5.0	(76) 4.1		(13) 5.1		(14) 5.2	4.0	(18) 2.8	
5.7	6.6	6.3			10.1		12.6	6.1	4.7
1.2	1.5	.9	% Officers', Directors', Owners' Comp/Sales						
(43) 2.6	(31) 3.2	(30) 3.0							
4.1	5.8	4.6							
1921358M	1389197M	1573453M	Net Sales ($)	6782M	40514M	29203M	129402M	223833M	1143719M
668637M	493798M	668006M	Total Assets ($)	3140M	18756M	9874M	64449M	88124M	483663M

M = $ thousand   MM = $ million
See Pages 9 through 22 for Explanation of Ratios and Data

Current Data Sorted by Assets   Comparative Historical Data

Type of Statement								
Unqualified	1		7	14	3	1	30	29
Reviewed	1	10	53	14	1		106	117
Compiled	12	22	23	2		1	70	73
Tax Returns	6	22	5			1	36	37
Other	4	10	15	12	8	6	52	58
	135 (4/1-9/30/10)			119 (10/1/10-3/31/11)			4/1/06-3/31/07	4/1/07-3/31/08
	0-500M	500M-2MM	2-10MM	10-50MM	50-100MM	100-250MM	ALL	ALL
NUMBER OF STATEMENTS	24	64	103	42	12	9	294	314
	%	%	%	%	%	%	%	%
ASSETS								
Cash & Equivalents	31.7	13.8	14.0	12.5	11.9		14.9	13.9
Trade Receivables (net)	21.4	33.1	31.6	27.4	23.0		27.3	31.1
Inventory	13.3	13.9	10.2	11.4	11.1		12.4	11.3
All Other Current	2.0	2.0	2.3	3.1	3.7		2.2	2.6
Total Current	68.4	62.8	58.1	54.4	49.7		56.8	58.9
Fixed Assets (net)	20.9	22.4	23.5	28.0	39.0		25.7	25.8
Intangibles (net)	2.9	5.9	9.1	6.9	3.8		10.3	8.0
All Other Non-Current	7.7	9.0	9.3	10.7	7.5		7.2	7.3
Total	100.0	100.0	100.0	100.0	100.0		100.0	100.0
LIABILITIES								
Notes Payable-Short Term	17.6	14.4	11.6	9.0	3.6		9.8	13.2
Cur. Mat.-L.T.D.	2.5	3.1	2.8	2.7	2.2		4.6	4.0
Trade Payables	20.1	19.2	18.0	19.5	14.5		18.2	19.0
Income Taxes Payable	.1	.0	.2	.3	.0		.2	.2
All Other Current	19.3	14.2	16.1	14.5	21.9		22.8	20.7
Total Current	59.5	50.9	48.7	46.0	42.1		55.6	57.1
Long-Term Debt	15.6	18.0	11.8	16.6	23.9		17.0	15.6
Deferred Taxes	.1	.0	.6	.9	.3		.4	.4
All Other Non-Current	16.4	7.5	6.0	3.5	7.0		5.5	5.1
Net Worth	8.5	23.5	32.9	33.0	26.8		21.6	21.8
Total Liabilities & Net Worth	100.0	100.0	100.0	100.0	100.0		100.0	100.0
INCOME DATA								
Net Sales	100.0	100.0	100.0	100.0	100.0		100.0	100.0
Gross Profit	21.1	21.9	18.6	13.4	15.7		17.1	16.5
Operating Expenses	19.7	19.6	17.3	12.6	14.2		15.7	15.4
Operating Profit	1.3	2.2	1.3	.8	1.5		1.4	1.1
All Other Expenses (net)	.2	.3	.2	.0	-.5		.2	.2
Profit Before Taxes	1.1	1.9	1.1	.8	2.1		1.1	.9
RATIOS								
Current	3.3	1.9	1.8	1.6	1.3		1.4	1.4
	1.2	1.3	1.1	1.1	1.2		1.0	1.0
	.7	.9	.9	.9	.9		.8	.8
Quick	2.7	1.6	1.4	1.3	1.1		1.1	1.1
	.8	.9	.9	.8	.8		.7	.8
	.6	.7	.6	.6	.6		.5	.5
Sales/Receivables	3 130.7	13 29.2	14 27.0	9 42.0	11 32.3		10 35.4	11 31.7
	9 40.8	23 15.5	22 16.3	18 19.9	16 22.9		19 19.4	20 18.2
	19 19.6	33 11.1	35 10.5	26 13.8	31 11.8		28 13.0	33 11.0
Cost of Sales/Inventory	1 539.6	4 103.7	4 94.3	5 76.5	7 52.9		4 88.4	4 103.0
	6 61.3	8 47.1	10 36.9	9 41.2	10 36.9		8 44.0	8 42.5
	18 20.3	16 22.6	19 19.6	18 20.3	14 25.4		15 24.4	14 25.6
Cost of Sales/Payables	8 46.3	10 38.0	10 38.1	9 39.3	7 49.5		8 47.7	9 42.0
	12 31.6	17 21.7	15 24.5	13 29.0	16 23.1		13 27.4	14 26.7
	19 19.1	26 13.8	23 15.9	19 19.5	23 16.2		19 19.0	21 17.4
Sales/Working Capital	12.0	13.9	18.0	17.7	12.2		26.9	22.8
	78.5	35.1	78.2	166.7	67.6		564.1	214.7
	-27.0	-93.0	-56.0	-67.0	NM		-35.8	-38.6
EBIT/Interest	14.4	9.6	7.5	12.3	14.3		5.2	5.1
	(18) 3.9	(56) 2.4	(90) 2.8	(41) 3.4	5.9		(280) 2.1	(292) 2.2
	-.4	1.1	1.3	1.7	1.4		.8	.9
Net Profit + Depr., Dep., Amort./Cur. Mat. L/T/D			3.7	10.2			3.7	3.2
			(31) 2.2	(23) 2.0			(80) 2.0	(99) 2.0
			1.3	1.0			1.2	1.2
Fixed/Worth	.2	.4	.3	.5	.8		.5	.6
	1.2	.8	.9	1.2	2.9		1.9	1.5
	-2.0	142.2	10.8	3.6	4.1		-7.0	-7.1
Debt/Worth	1.7	1.2	1.0	1.4	1.3		1.8	1.6
	6.7	4.8	2.8	2.6	3.9		5.3	4.6
	-5.1	755.8	25.5	8.5	9.3		-19.9	-27.2
% Profit Before Taxes/Tangible Net Worth	40.9	76.3	37.0	28.1	28.6		35.2	31.2
	(16) 11.9	(49) 17.4	(82) 14.1	(36) 16.4	(11) 14.4		(204) 13.7	(226) 14.6
	-11.0	1.2	3.1	4.2	4.1		2.3	2.6
% Profit Before Taxes/Total Assets	20.4	12.5	8.4	7.4	9.9		7.6	7.8
	5.1	4.9	4.3	4.1	5.5		2.9	3.2
	-2.8	.4	.6	.7	1.2		-.3	.0
Sales/Net Fixed Assets	70.1	59.9	58.9	45.7	21.7		51.0	52.5
	37.9	34.6	19.7	23.3	13.5		26.0	22.5
	19.1	15.9	11.1	11.7	4.8		11.6	12.2
Sales/Total Assets	10.5	6.3	6.2	7.8	6.6		6.9	6.8
	6.5	5.0	4.1	4.5	5.1		4.8	4.7
	3.6	3.4	3.1	3.3	2.3		3.3	3.4
% Depr., Dep., Amort./Sales	.5	.5	.7	.6	.5		.6	.6
	(18) .6	(55) .9	(95) 1.2	(40) .8	(11) 1.1		(254) 1.1	(281) 1.1
	1.6	1.5	1.9	1.5	3.0		1.8	1.7
% Officers', Directors' Owners' Comp/Sales	1.8	1.3	.9	.4			.7	.9
	(13) 4.4	(48) 2.4	(58) 1.5	(18) .8			(146) 1.7	(154) 1.7
	6.6	3.9	3.2	1.8			3.1	3.0
Net Sales ($)	59079M	380386M	2345471M	5153223M	4138703M	7793568M	15926861M	19437758M
Total Assets ($)	8629M	73815M	480087M	897804M	847367M	1389918M	3203639M	3997671M

© RMA 2011

M = $ thousand   MM = $ million

See Pages 9 through 22 for Explanation of Ratios and Data

Comparative Historical Data | Current Data Sorted by Sales

			Type of Statement	0-1MM	1-3MM	3-5MM	5-10MM	10-25MM	25MM & OVER
28	26	26	Unqualified		1			4	21
93	97	79	Reviewed		5	3	8	35	28
63	60	60	Compiled	1	11	11	16	11	10
31	36	34	Tax Returns	1	4	11	10	4	4
46	54	55	Other	2	6	4	7	7	29
4/1/08-3/31/09 ALL	4/1/09-3/31/10 ALL	4/1/10-3/31/11 ALL			135 (4/1-9/30/10)			119 (10/1/10-3/31/11)	
261	273	254	NUMBER OF STATEMENTS	4	27	29	41	61	92
%	%	%	**ASSETS**	%	%	%	%	%	%
18.0	18.0	14.9	Cash & Equivalents		24.0	16.5	12.7	12.7	13.4
27.8	24.8	29.8	Trade Receivables (net)		16.8	27.1	33.9	33.1	29.9
10.3	10.9	11.9	Inventory		16.8	13.4	11.7	10.4	11.2
2.8	3.6	2.4	All Other Current		.7	3.6	.3	2.8	3.0
58.8	57.3	59.0	Total Current		58.4	60.5	58.7	59.0	57.6
24.4	25.6	24.9	Fixed Assets (net)		24.6	21.7	24.6	23.5	27.6
8.4	7.8	7.1	Intangibles (net)		4.4	6.3	8.0	8.7	7.0
8.4	9.2	9.0	All Other Non-Current		12.6	11.4	8.7	8.8	7.8
100.0	100.0	100.0	Total		100.0	100.0	100.0	100.0	100.0
			LIABILITIES						
13.3	9.8	12.1	Notes Payable-Short Term		12.6	18.9	17.1	10.7	9.1
3.4	4.2	2.9	Cur. Mat.-L.T.D.		3.9	3.0	2.6	3.4	2.4
16.9	17.8	18.2	Trade Payables		14.0	18.4	19.2	17.6	19.8
.3	.2	.1	Income Taxes Payable		.1	.0	.0	.2	.1
17.5	20.2	15.8	All Other Current		12.8	23.6	15.7	16.9	14.3
51.4	52.3	49.2	Total Current		43.5	63.9	54.5	48.8	45.6
15.3	15.1	15.3	Long-Term Debt		22.6	14.9	19.5	11.3	14.6
.4	.5	.5	Deferred Taxes		.1	.0	.1	.6	.8
7.9	6.9	6.9	All Other Non-Current		15.7	6.6	6.9	6.6	3.4
24.9	25.2	28.1	Net Worth		18.2	14.6	19.0	32.6	35.4
100.0	100.0	100.0	Total Liabilities & Net Worth		100.0	100.0	100.0	100.0	100.0
			INCOME DATA						
100.0	100.0	100.0	Net Sales		100.0	100.0	100.0	100.0	100.0
14.1	19.8	18.4	Gross Profit		29.3	21.2	21.1	18.6	12.8
13.2	17.8	17.0	Operating Expenses		26.4	19.9	19.6	17.4	11.7
.9	2.1	1.5	Operating Profit		2.9	1.3	1.5	1.1	1.1
.0	.1	.1	All Other Expenses (net)		.7	.2	.3	.2	-.1
.9	2.0	1.3	Profit Before Taxes		2.2	1.2	1.2	.9	1.2
			RATIOS						
1.6	1.7	1.8	Current		2.3	1.5	1.5	1.8	1.7
1.1	1.1	1.2			1.6	1.0	1.2	1.2	1.2
.8	.8	.9			.9	.6	.8	.9	.9
1.3	1.3	1.4	Quick		1.7	1.3	1.3	1.4	1.4
.9	.8	.9			.8	.7	.9	.9	.9
.6	.5	.6			.6	.4	.5	.7	.6
9 39.5	8 43.4	11 33.6	Sales/Receivables		7 51.6	10 37.1	12 29.6	14 25.7	9 40.9
16 22.6	16 23.0	21 17.8			19 19.2	20 18.6	26 14.0	23 16.1	17 21.2
26 13.9	28 12.9	32 11.5			26 14.0	30 12.0	39 9.4	35 10.6	28 13.1
2 161.4	4 102.2	4 97.2	Cost of Sales/Inventory		3 108.9	3 91.1	4	5 79.2	3 120.5
6 60.4	8 43.1	9 42.0			10 37.0	7 51.3	8 47.1	10 35.5	8 47.3
12 29.4	16 23.3	19 19.7			52 7.0	18 20.2	14 25.5	19 19.7	15 23.8
7 52.3	8 43.0	9 39.3	Cost of Sales/Payables		9 38.9	7 52.5	10 36.8	10 37.2	9 42.2
11 34.4	14 26.2	14 25.4			15 24.6	17 21.2	17 22.1	15 24.3	13 28.7
16 23.4	24 15.3	23 16.1			26 13.9	30 12.2	27 13.6	23 16.0	18 20.6
22.4	19.7	14.5	Sales/Working Capital		9.0	16.9	21.5	21.4	15.3
124.6	72.1	73.3			18.2	-180.4	67.4	47.0	90.4
-63.6	-59.1	-66.5			-82.3	-26.4	-23.9	-74.7	-199.6
5.7	12.3	9.5	EBIT/Interest		10.4	6.6	7.4	10.4	9.6
(246) 2.2	(247) 3.9	(224) 2.9			(21) 3.0	(27) 2.2	(36) 2.7	(56) 2.3	(84) 3.5
1.1	1.5	1.2			-.2	.2	-.6	1.1	2.0
3.8	6.8	4.1	Net Profit + Depr., Dep., Amort./Cur. Mat. L/T/D					3.6	5.4
(85) 2.1	(82) 2.8	(73) 2.1						(21) 2.1	(39) 2.1
1.1	1.3	1.3						.6	1.4
.5	.4	.4	Fixed/Worth		.2	.4	.5	.3	.4
1.2	1.1	1.0			1.1	2.2	1.1	1.1	.9
9.5	17.4	9.1			10.8	-1.1	-12.3	3.7	3.8
1.4	1.2	1.1	Debt/Worth		1.1	1.7	1.3	.9	1.0
3.8	3.2	3.2			3.8	9.5	5.6	3.0	2.5
48.5	324.7	19.1			39.7	-5.9	-26.5	11.4	9.3
37.7	55.3	38.6	% Profit Before Taxes/Tangible Net Worth		81.4	72.9	64.5	30.6	31.3
(199) 16.8	(206) 21.7	(201) 15.6			(21) 15.6	(17) 1.9	(29) 17.4	(51) 14.5	(79) 17.4
4.1	8.2	2.5			-8.6	-8.7	2.1	1.7	6.0
8.3	13.8	9.5	% Profit Before Taxes/Total Assets		15.3	10.2	9.4	7.7	8.9
3.3	5.9	4.4			6.1	5.2	3.4	3.9	4.5
.5	1.5	.5			-2.6	-1.5	-1.6	.1	2.0
62.8	54.7	54.3	Sales/Net Fixed Assets		47.4	56.3	42.4	40.6	69.7
27.3	19.9	23.5			27.3	29.1	27.1	19.7	22.1
15.3	11.7	12.4			9.0	17.4	11.3	12.2	12.3
7.9	6.5	6.7	Sales/Total Assets		4.8	7.0	5.9	6.3	7.6
5.4	4.3	4.4			3.4	5.3	4.0	4.4	4.8
3.8	3.2	3.2			2.3	3.7	2.9	3.2	3.5
.5	.6	.6	% Depr., Dep., Amort./Sales		.7	.5	.6	.7	.5
(233) .9	(234) 1.2	(227) .9		(25) 1.2	(25) .7	(37) .9	(57) 1.1	(83) .8	
1.5	1.9	1.8			3.0	1.7	1.9	1.9	1.5
.7	1.2	.9	% Officers', Directors', Owners' Comp/Sales		2.4	1.3	1.2	.8	.4
(139) 1.3	(145) 2.0	(141) 1.7		(19) 4.1	(18) 2.7	(28) 1.9	(38) 1.5	(37) 1.0	
2.7	4.0	3.4			8.8	5.1	3.4	2.5	2.1
19228617M	17798414M	19870430M	Net Sales ($)	1382M	58144M	118133M	317168M	964147M	18411456M
3468379M	3552805M	3697620M	Total Assets ($)	1145M	21811M	27300M	82451M	247250M	3317663M

M = $ thousand   MM = $ million
See Pages 9 through 22 for Explanation of Ratios and Data

Current Data Sorted by Assets   Comparative Historical Data

0-500M	500M-2MM	2-10MM	10-50MM	50-100MM	100-250MM	Type of Statement	4/1/06-3/31/07 ALL	4/1/07-3/31/08 ALL
	1	3	6	4		Unqualified	18	18
	3	8	4			Reviewed	26	17
2	8	8				Compiled	24	18
5	5	7	1			Tax Returns	23	18
	5	7	4	5	1	Other	18	35
	29 (4/1-9/30/10)		58 (10/1/10-3/31/11)					
7	22	33	15	9	1	**NUMBER OF STATEMENTS**	109	106
%	%	%	%	%	%	**ASSETS**	%	%
	9.8	11.3	6.1			Cash & Equivalents	9.0	8.1
	29.5	23.1	16.8			Trade Receivables (net)	23.5	24.5
	12.1	14.5	8.7			Inventory	12.5	12.0
	2.5	2.9	4.5			All Other Current	2.9	3.6
	54.0	51.7	36.2			Total Current	47.9	48.2
	33.6	37.3	47.0			Fixed Assets (net)	41.2	40.2
	1.7	4.7	10.8			Intangibles (net)	5.3	4.2
	10.7	6.3	6.0			All Other Non-Current	5.7	7.4
	100.0	100.0	100.0			Total	100.0	100.0
						LIABILITIES		
	8.8	4.6	4.2			Notes Payable-Short Term	8.7	7.9
	7.3	4.0	4.5			Cur. Mat.-L.T.D.	5.0	4.7
	23.7	15.4	12.0			Trade Payables	18.5	18.4
	.0	.9	.0			Income Taxes Payable	.3	.4
	10.7	12.9	14.3			All Other Current	8.9	12.2
	50.5	37.7	35.0			Total Current	41.3	43.6
	19.2	13.4	19.4			Long-Term Debt	24.6	26.2
	.0	.2	2.5			Deferred Taxes	.9	1.2
	5.8	4.2	3.1			All Other Non-Current	5.4	5.5
	24.5	44.4	40.0			Net Worth	27.8	23.5
	100.0	100.0	100.0			Total Liabilities & Net Worth	100.0	100.0
						INCOME DATA		
	100.0	100.0	100.0			Net Sales	100.0	100.0
	22.6	30.1	31.7			Gross Profit	28.8	27.4
	21.7	25.5	26.2			Operating Expenses	26.0	24.9
	.9	4.6	5.4			Operating Profit	2.8	2.5
	.0	.2	1.2			All Other Expenses (net)	.8	1.0
	.9	4.3	4.2			Profit Before Taxes	2.0	1.5
						RATIOS		
	2.0	2.2	3.0				2.0	1.8
	1.0	1.4	1.1			Current	1.3	1.2
	.7	.9	.5				.8	.8
	1.8	1.7	1.7				1.4	1.3
	.7	.8	.7			Quick	.9	.8
	.5	.5	.3				.6	.5
21 17.1	16 22.7	18 20.4					16 22.4	18 19.8
34 10.6	29 12.7	26 13.9				Sales/Receivables	26 14.3	30 12.4
41 8.8	39 9.4	45 8.1					41 8.9	38 9.6
6 59.7	11 33.1	10 36.8					7 51.2	8 47.0
12 30.2	21 17.2	20 18.2				Cost of Sales/Inventory	16 23.1	16 22.4
22 16.9	30 12.0	42 8.8					31 11.9	29 12.6
7 52.0	15 24.1	15 24.8					12 31.5	14 25.9
30 12.2	20 18.1	22 16.9				Cost of Sales/Payables	25 14.8	23 16.1
54 6.8	29 12.5	33 11.0					42 8.7	36 10.2
	11.4	8.6	7.1				10.1	14.8
	NM	22.0	80.6			Sales/Working Capital	43.4	45.5
	-22.1	-100.4	-6.6				-49.6	-34.4
	7.7	24.2	28.7				7.1	5.9
	1.5	(30) 4.6	12.0			EBIT/Interest	(104) 2.5	(100) 2.4
	-3.1	1.7	.5				.9	1.1
							6.0	6.0
						Net Profit + Depr., Dep., Amort./Cur. Mat. L/T/D	(24) 1.9	(33) 2.0
							1.0	1.3
	.5	.5	.7				.7	.6
	1.5	1.1	1.5			Fixed/Worth	1.9	1.7
	-5.2	1.5	7.5				6.5	35.1
	.8	.6	.6				1.1	1.2
	2.9	1.5	1.5			Debt/Worth	2.6	2.7
	-12.8	2.7	11.2				12.8	110.3
	37.2	35.6	46.4				32.2	33.4
	(16) 5.8	(31) 22.0	(12) 31.1			% Profit Before Taxes/Tangible Net Worth	(88) 16.0	(81) 17.2
	-18.3	6.3	18.1				2.4	4.1
	9.4	17.3	15.6				11.5	10.3
	1.6	3.8	10.8			% Profit Before Taxes/Total Assets	3.4	4.9
	-7.0	1.9	-2.5				-.9	.3
	28.3	16.9	7.0				20.0	15.7
	9.2	8.0	4.9			Sales/Net Fixed Assets	5.8	7.3
	6.7	3.8	2.5				3.2	3.3
	5.1	3.9	3.0				4.1	4.7
	3.4	2.7	2.4			Sales/Total Assets	2.5	2.6
	2.3	2.1	1.1				1.7	1.9
	1.0	1.9	2.4				1.6	1.6
	(18) 2.2	(31) 3.4	3.9			% Depr., Dep., Amort./Sales	(99) 3.2	(96) 3.2
	4.2	4.5	5.2				4.6	4.6
		1.5					1.3	1.6
		(16) 1.9				% Officers', Directors' Owners' Comp/Sales	(45) 2.8	(46) 3.1
		3.6					4.4	6.1
13671M	93160M	560717M	726462M	1605424M	177148M	Net Sales ($)	3747511M	4180002M
2511M	23983M	160932M	316958M	597028M	109781M	Total Assets ($)	1602474M	1492095M

M = $ thousand   MM = $ million
See Pages 9 through 22 for Explanation of Ratios and Data

Comparative Historical Data | Current Data Sorted by Sales

Current data periods: 29 (4/1-9/30/10) covers 0-1MM, 1-3MM, 3-5MM; 58 (10/1/10-3/31/11) covers 5-10MM, 10-25MM, 25MM & OVER

4/1/08-3/31/09 ALL	4/1/09-3/31/10 ALL	4/1/10-3/31/11 ALL		0-1MM	1-3MM	3-5MM	5-10MM	10-25MM	25MM & OVER
			Type of Statement						
22	15	14	Unqualified		2			3	9
17	18	15	Reviewed		1		5	6	3
22	13	18	Compiled		4	5	3	4	2
22	27	18	Tax Returns	1	8		3	3	3
23	31	22	Other		2	3	2	7	8
106	104	87	**NUMBER OF STATEMENTS**	1	17	8	13	23	25
%	%	%	**ASSETS**	%	%	%	%	%	%
11.0	11.6	10.1	Cash & Equivalents		12.9		12.3	8.5	8.4
23.1	20.4	22.8	Trade Receivables (net)		23.0		24.0	22.0	23.5
10.2	10.7	12.7	Inventory		13.8		13.5	12.3	11.6
3.7	3.8	3.0	All Other Current		5.5		2.1	3.3	2.0
48.0	46.5	48.6	Total Current		55.2		52.0	46.1	45.5
38.7	40.3	38.8	Fixed Assets (net)		34.1		38.7	38.0	43.4
5.7	6.9	5.4	Intangibles (net)		2.5		2.6	7.3	5.7
7.5	6.2	7.1	All Other Non-Current		8.2		6.8	8.6	5.3
100.0	100.0	100.0	Total		100.0		100.0	100.0	100.0
			LIABILITIES						
5.3	6.6	5.4	Notes Payable-Short Term		5.7		7.8	4.1	3.8
7.1	6.9	4.8	Cur. Mat.-L.T.D.		4.0		6.9	3.1	3.9
16.5	13.3	17.0	Trade Payables		27.8		10.7	17.1	13.1
.1	.2	.4	Income Taxes Payable		.0		1.9	.1	.2
12.2	11.8	12.2	All Other Current		15.0		16.8	13.7	9.0
41.3	38.7	39.8	Total Current		52.6		44.2	38.1	30.0
24.4	24.7	20.6	Long-Term Debt		34.2		12.5	16.6	19.7
1.0	1.4	1.3	Deferred Taxes		.0		.4	.0	4.2
5.4	3.0	4.1	All Other Non-Current		1.3		7.8	3.6	3.2
28.0	32.3	34.1	Net Worth		11.9		35.1	41.7	43.0
100.0	100.0	100.0	Total Liabilties & Net Worth		100.0		100.0	100.0	100.0
			INCOME DATA						
100.0	100.0	100.0	Net Sales		100.0		100.0	100.0	100.0
25.6	33.2	28.9	Gross Profit		31.0		31.4	30.9	27.5
23.0	28.4	25.5	Operating Expenses		30.3		28.0	25.4	23.6
2.6	4.9	3.4	Operating Profit		.7		3.5	5.5	3.8
.7	.4	.4	All Other Expenses (net)		.4		-.1	.9	.2
1.8	4.4	3.0	Profit Before Taxes		.3		3.6	4.6	3.6
			RATIOS						
2.0	2.2	2.4			1.9		1.9	2.5	2.8
1.2	1.3	1.2	Current		1.0		1.2	1.4	1.5
.7	.8	.8			.6		.7	.6	1.1
1.4	1.9	1.7			1.7		1.7	1.9	1.7
.8	.9	.8	Quick		.6		.8	.8	1.0
.5	.4	.5			.5		.5	.3	.7
14 25.6	15 25.1	16 23.3			14 25.4		13 27.1	16 22.9	17 21.5
27 13.7	26 14.2	29 12.6	Sales/Receivables		34 10.7		28 12.9	31 11.7	28 13.1
35 10.4	35 10.4	40 9.2			42 8.6		51 7.2	44 8.4	37 9.8
6 61.0	9 40.8	10 37.4			10 37.5		10 36.8	13 28.4	10 37.7
14 27.0	18 20.0	18 20.3	Cost of Sales/Inventory		18 19.8		21 17.6	21 17.2	18 20.3
30 12.3	37 9.8	35 10.4			31 11.9		35 10.4	31 12.0	39 9.3
9 41.2	10 38.4	14 25.8			16 23.2		8 44.5	16 23.4	14 25.8
17 21.0	19 19.5	22 16.9	Cost of Sales/Payables		36 10.2		25 14.5	20 18.1	20 18.4
30 12.0	34 10.8	36 10.2			61 6.0		33 11.1	34 10.6	24 15.0
12.6	8.6	8.8			8.3		10.0	12.4	7.1
58.4	31.0	33.5	Sales/Working Capital		-179.8		29.2	22.0	22.0
-28.9	-33.4	-29.7			-16.2		-23.7	-14.5	305.3
9.3	17.7	16.5			10.3		22.4	25.8	27.5
(100) 3.0	(95) 3.5	(82) 2.7	EBIT/Interest	(16) .8		(12) 3.6	(21) 4.1	3.2
1.1	1.4	.7			-2.0		1.8	.5	2.3
5.3	21.7	15.7	Net Profit + Depr., Dep.,						20.7
(23) 3.1	(22) 3.8	(17) 3.0	Amort./Cur. Mat. L/T/D					(12) 1.7	
1.1	1.5	1.3							1.3
.6	.6	.6			.3		.6	.6	.6
1.8	1.3	1.3	Fixed/Worth		1.4		1.4	1.1	1.4
5.9	3.4	3.1			-5.2		NM	1.5	2.5
1.0	.8	.7			.7		.6	.6	.7
2.6	2.0	1.8	Debt/Worth		5.2		1.5	1.7	2.0
13.3	6.0	7.7			-11.2		NM	2.4	3.7
46.4	56.6	37.1	% Profit Before Taxes/Tangible		38.0		30.0	62.9	40.2
(87) 23.1	(85) 23.1	(73) 18.5	Net Worth	(12) 5.8		(10) 22.2	(20) 17.0	21.1
6.9	5.1	5.0			-2.2		10.5	2.2	10.8
13.9	17.0	14.2	% Profit Before Taxes/Total		9.2		13.9	18.7	14.5
4.6	6.3	4.1	Assets		.1		3.8	4.6	4.6
1.4	1.2	-.1			-10.7		3.2	-.4	2.7
18.7	18.3	18.1			24.8		13.1	19.8	13.0
8.3	6.8	7.2	Sales/Net Fixed Assets		11.8		7.9	7.2	6.7
3.6	3.4	3.7			3.4		3.4	3.1	3.9
4.7	3.8	3.9			4.9		3.5	3.9	3.9
2.9	2.6	2.7	Sales/Total Assets		2.9		2.7	2.3	2.7
1.8	1.7	1.9			1.8		1.9	2.0	1.9
1.4	2.1	1.9			1.7		3.1	1.9	2.0
(97) 3.0	(85) 3.2	(79) 3.4	% Depr., Dep., Amort./Sales	(15) 3.0		(10) 4.6	3.4	(24) 2.7
4.7	5.9	4.7			4.1		6.0	5.0	4.1
1.0	1.5	1.6	% Officers', Directors'						
(40) 2.1	(30) 3.0	(29) 2.6	Owners' Comp/Sales						
4.3	6.5	4.9							
5726298M	4043586M	3176582M	Net Sales ($)	861M	35786M	32609M	91647M	345047M	2670632M
1900396M	1324791M	1211193M	Total Assets ($)	425M	14597M	8996M	40557M	164452M	982166M

M = $ thousand   MM = $ million
See Pages 9 through 22 for Explanation of Ratios and Data

Current Data Sorted by Assets   Comparative Historical Data

Type of Statement

Type of Statement	0-500M	500M-2MM	2-10MM	10-50MM	50-100MM	100-250MM	4/1/06-3/31/07 ALL	4/1/07-3/31/08 ALL
Unqualified	1		4	9	6	8	15	12
Reviewed		1	7	2			13	10
Compiled	5	16	10	1			31	23
Tax Returns	35	52	7				82	80
Other	24	32	27	12	6	4	65	75
	26 (4/1-9/30/10)			243 (10/1/10-3/31/11)				
NUMBER OF STATEMENTS	65	101	55	24	12	12	206	200

ASSETS

	0-500M %	500M-2MM %	2-10MM %	10-50MM %	50-100MM %	100-250MM %	Hist %	Hist %
Cash & Equivalents	21.5	14.2	11.6	27.1	16.6	17.1	14.1	16.5
Trade Receivables (net)	14.1	23.2	23.3	19.1	15.8	11.2	24.0	21.9
Inventory	24.8	34.4	29.5	18.1	30.1	20.2	24.6	28.2
All Other Current	2.2	1.7	4.9	4.5	7.1	5.3	3.3	3.5
Total Current	62.5	73.4	69.3	68.8	69.7	53.8	66.0	70.1
Fixed Assets (net)	17.5	12.5	19.0	13.3	23.9	13.0	19.8	17.8
Intangibles (net)	9.9	6.0	3.0	8.2	3.3	21.2	4.9	5.0
All Other Non-Current	10.2	8.0	8.7	9.8	3.2	12.0	9.3	7.2
Total	100.0	100.0	100.0	100.0	100.0	100.0	100.0	100.0

LIABILITIES

	0-500M	500M-2MM	2-10MM	10-50MM	50-100MM	100-250MM	Hist	Hist
Notes Payable-Short Term	16.8	12.9	12.2	5.5	8.6	.0	15.2	13.3
Cur. Mat.-L.T.D.	4.7	3.9	4.9	2.3	1.4	1.2	2.8	4.0
Trade Payables	22.9	21.2	20.7	13.8	16.4	10.5	17.9	20.0
Income Taxes Payable	.1	.1	.4	.3	1.6	.6	.3	.3
All Other Current	35.6	16.4	15.7	19.1	22.8	14.1	12.6	16.3
Total Current	80.3	54.5	53.9	41.1	50.7	26.4	48.8	54.0
Long-Term Debt	16.0	15.9	11.8	7.8	5.3	25.1	18.1	21.3
Deferred Taxes	.3	.1	.3	.1	.4	2.4	.1	.2
All Other Non-Current	17.0	7.6	4.2	6.4	10.8	3.4	6.2	5.7
Net Worth	-13.4	21.8	29.8	44.7	32.8	42.7	26.9	18.8
Total Liabilities & Net Worth	100.0	100.0	100.0	100.0	100.0	100.0	100.0	100.0

INCOME DATA

	0-500M	500M-2MM	2-10MM	10-50MM	50-100MM	100-250MM	Hist	Hist
Net Sales	100.0	100.0	100.0	100.0	100.0	100.0	100.0	100.0
Gross Profit	42.5	43.6	40.0	47.7	47.4	52.9	43.5	42.6
Operating Expenses	41.2	38.8	35.7	40.9	40.4	39.8	37.2	36.0
Operating Profit	1.3	4.8	4.3	6.8	7.0	13.2	6.2	6.6
All Other Expenses (net)	.6	.6	.6	1.1	.8	1.4	.7	.9
Profit Before Taxes	.7	4.2	3.7	5.7	6.2	11.8	5.6	5.7

RATIOS

	0-500M	500M-2MM	2-10MM	10-50MM	50-100MM	100-250MM	Hist	Hist
Current	2.1	2.3	1.7	2.7	2.2	2.6	2.5	3.0
	.9	1.6	1.2	1.8	1.6	1.8	1.4	1.5
	.5	.9	.8	1.0	.8	1.4	.9	1.0
Quick	1.1	1.5	.9	2.3	.9	1.3	1.4	1.6
	.5	.8	.6	1.1	.4	.9	(205) .8	.8
	.2	.4	.3	.8	.2	.6	.3	.3
Sales/Receivables	0 UND	1 348.2	3 123.0	3 114.4	1 508.1	2 179.4	1 306.8	1 374.3
	2 191.0	19 19.3	22 17.0	18 20.4	5 68.2	19 19.1	19 19.7	18 20.2
	30 12.2	39 9.5	60 6.1	52 7.0	40 9.1	29 12.5	46 7.9	41 8.9
Cost of Sales/Inventory	0 UND	12 29.9	6 62.2	18 20.8	21 17.6	32 11.3	6 58.0	5 66.6
	18 20.0	60 6.1	47 7.7	42 8.6	83 4.4	78 4.7	34 10.6	38 9.6
	79 4.6	126 2.9	111 3.3	79 4.6	163 2.2	126 2.9	71 5.2	89 4.1
Cost of Sales/Payables	0 UND	12 30.9	11 32.0	19 19.5	16 22.2	19 18.9	4 94.6	8 46.7
	17 22.0	32 11.5	37 9.9	29 12.7	35 10.4	28 13.2	27 13.3	26 14.1
	59 6.2	64 5.7	57 6.4	58 6.3	49 7.5	50 7.3	56 6.5	52 7.0
Sales/Working Capital	11.1	6.8	7.2	4.3	4.3	5.4	8.0	6.7
	-733.0	13.2	17.5	9.0	11.5	11.9	18.7	13.7
	-11.0	-68.1	-77.7	-404.7	-42.2	20.9	-118.1	NM
EBIT/Interest	16.4	12.0	30.5	18.9	69.2	660.3	15.1	14.9
	(43) 2.6	(81) 3.6	(48) 4.9	(18) 9.0	(11) 10.8	(11) 24.4	(170) 5.2	(168) 5.2
	-1.0	1.1	1.3	1.4	2.1	3.1	1.5	1.5
Net Profit + Depr., Dep., Amort./Cur. Mat. L/T/D			8.3				4.5	10.5
			(11) 1.3				(21) 2.1	(19) 2.3
			1.0				1.4	.9
Fixed/Worth	.0	.0	.2	.1	.2	.1	.1	.1
	.6	.3	.4	.3	.6	.5	.7	.6
	-.8	UND	4.3	1.5	5.2	-.2	11.9	UND
Debt/Worth	1.7	.9	1.1	.5	1.0	.6	1.0	1.0
	30.5	2.9	3.0	1.3	2.8	1.0	2.7	4.0
	-2.4	-51.7	10.9	13.1	7.2	-1.9	122.3	UND
% Profit Before Taxes/Tangible Net Worth	151.0	89.9	95.4	53.2	100.0		114.2	107.3
	(34) 36.1	(75) 41.8	(46) 30.0	(22) 29.0	(11) 59.4		(162) 49.2	(150) 45.9
	-9.3	11.6	4.7	7.6	8.8		12.0	18.6
% Profit Before Taxes/Total Assets	23.5	26.0	24.1	21.7	21.0	45.7	30.3	29.7
	7.9	9.2	7.9	10.6	13.4	26.0	11.2	11.5
	-6.5	1.3	.6	3.4	4.6	8.7	2.0	2.2
Sales/Net Fixed Assets	UND	274.6	100.4	118.3	50.8	36.1	156.2	126.1
	71.4	63.6	30.3	28.0	17.1	21.8	33.4	38.4
	22.4	17.4	13.0	15.1	7.7	9.3	10.6	14.2
Sales/Total Assets	9.0	4.7	4.9	3.1	4.7	2.8	5.9	5.1
	4.3	3.6	2.7	2.2	2.9	2.2	3.4	3.2
	2.6	2.2	2.0	1.5	1.8	1.2	2.2	2.0
% Depr., Dep., Amort./Sales	.3	.4	.3	.4	.5	1.0	.4	.4
	(33) 1.0	(60) .9	(44) .9	(17) 1.8	(11) .8	(10) 1.8	(139) .9	(140) .9
	2.1	1.5	2.1	4.6	2.2	2.1	2.3	1.8
% Officers', Directors' Owners' Comp/Sales	3.6	1.6	1.5				1.7	2.4
	(31) 8.0	(62) 3.3	(19) 2.8				(100) 4.4	(98) 4.5
	14.6	6.5	5.1				7.9	7.9
Net Sales ($)	83070M	387638M	836490M	1380635M	2678918M	4853155M	5804759M	6204997M
Total Assets ($)	14263M	105410M	246674M	501714M	811726M	2202480M	2115109M	2412357M

M = $ thousand   MM = $ million
See Pages 9 through 22 for Explanation of Ratios and Data

Comparative Historical Data / Current Data Sorted by Sales

Type of Statement	H (4/1/08-3/31/09)	H (4/1/09-3/31/10)	H (4/1/10-3/31/11)		0-1MM	1-3MM	3-5MM	5-10MM	10-25MM	25MM & OVER
Unqualified	18	23	28		1		1	1	2	23
Reviewed	11	23	10			1	1	1	5	2
Compiled	24	23	32		2	4	7	12	4	3
Tax Returns	86	92	94		25	28	20	18	2	1
Other	88	92	105		20	21	15	10	17	22
	ALL	ALL	ALL		26 (4/1-9/30/10)			243 (10/1/10-3/31/11)		
NUMBER OF STATEMENTS	227	253	269		48	54	44	42	30	51
ASSETS	%	%	%		%	%	%	%	%	%
Cash & Equivalents	11.8	15.0	16.8		20.6	16.0	14.1	12.3	11.1	23.4
Trade Receivables (net)	22.8	21.6	19.8		14.3	19.8	24.9	21.3	23.9	16.8
Inventory	30.3	27.9	28.8		28.0	30.2	32.8	32.4	25.2	23.6
All Other Current	2.7	3.2	3.1		2.1	1.0	.8	3.0	8.3	5.4
Total Current	67.6	67.7	68.5		65.1	67.1	72.6	68.9	68.5	69.2
Fixed Assets (net)	18.5	17.8	15.7		15.1	18.2	11.9	15.5	18.3	15.3
Intangibles (net)	5.7	6.9	7.1		9.6	8.4	5.0	5.5	4.7	7.8
All Other Non-Current	8.1	7.6	8.8		10.4	6.3	10.5	10.1	8.5	7.6
Total	100.0	100.0	100.0		100.0	100.0	100.0	100.0	100.0	100.0
LIABILITIES										
Notes Payable-Short Term	17.2	14.2	12.3		14.9	11.4	22.4	9.0	11.8	5.0
Cur. Mat.-L.T.D.	4.0	3.4	3.9		6.0	1.9	4.0	6.7	3.8	1.9
Trade Payables	17.7	17.2	20.2		15.5	20.9	28.8	18.8	20.8	17.1
Income Taxes Payable	.2	.2	.3		.0	.2	.2	.3	.2	.7
All Other Current	17.3	16.0	21.3		46.5	16.4	10.8	14.0	18.6	19.5
Total Current	56.5	51.0	58.0		83.0	50.7	66.3	48.8	55.1	44.2
Long-Term Debt	22.3	19.2	14.3		15.0	22.7	12.0	12.7	7.9	11.9
Deferred Taxes	.2	.1	.3		.0	.0	.2	.8	.2	.7
All Other Non-Current	8.9	6.1	9.0		23.0	7.6	4.5	5.2	5.2	6.8
Net Worth	12.2	23.6	18.4		-20.7	19.0	17.1	32.5	31.6	36.4
Total Liabilties & Net Worth	100.0	100.0	100.0		100.0	100.0	100.0	100.0	100.0	100.0
INCOME DATA										
Net Sales	100.0	100.0	100.0		100.0	100.0	100.0	100.0	100.0	100.0
Gross Profit	40.1	42.0	43.5		47.7	44.4	40.4	38.3	43.2	46.0
Operating Expenses	35.6	36.9	39.1		46.5	40.5	36.0	33.8	36.7	38.9
Operating Profit	4.6	5.1	4.5		1.2	3.9	4.4	4.5	6.5	7.1
All Other Expenses (net)	1.3	1.0	.7		.9	.6	.4	.9	.2	1.0
Profit Before Taxes	3.3	4.1	3.8		.4	3.3	4.0	3.5	6.3	6.1
RATIOS										
Current	2.0	2.7	2.2		2.2	2.3	1.8	2.3	2.0	2.3
	1.2	1.5	1.5		.9	1.6	1.2	1.6	1.2	1.7
	.8	1.0	.8		.6	.9	.7	.9	.9	1.0
Quick	1.1	1.6	1.3		1.4	1.5	1.2	1.5	1.0	1.5
	(226) .6	(251) .8	.7		.6	.7	.7	.7	.7	.9
	.3	.3	.4		.2	.4	.3	.3	.4	.5
Sales/Receivables	3 127.8	1 343.1	1 636.6		0 UND	0 UND	1 282.7	1 317.7	1 575.9	2 165.7
	22 16.6	15 24.8	14 26.3		2 212.5	18 20.1	20 17.9	19 19.2	18 20.7	13 28.8
	39 9.4	39 9.4	40 9.1		46 8.0	37 9.8	39 9.5	50 7.3	55 6.7	30 12.2
Cost of Sales/Inventory	11 34.5	8 45.4	9 41.2		0 UND	7 51.3	1 315.4	16 23.5	0 UND	17 21.5
	43 8.4	40 9.1	47 7.7		62 5.9	46 7.9	31 11.9	49 7.4	46 8.0	49 7.5
	102 3.6	92 4.0	109 3.3		248 1.5	108 3.4	81 4.5	96 3.8	91 4.0	96 3.8
Cost of Sales/Payables	9 38.8	6 58.2	10 38.2		0 UND	0 UND	16 22.4	2 147.2	13 29.0	18 19.7
	24 15.4	24 15.5	29 12.6		23 16.0	33 11.2	26 13.9	28 12.9	30 12.2	31 11.9
	45 8.1	49 7.5	57 6.4		99 3.7	63 5.8	69 5.3	47 7.8	47 7.8	50 7.3
Sales/Working Capital	8.6	6.7	7.3		5.5	8.3	7.2	7.4	8.7	6.6
	23.8	21.2	17.5		-474.5	13.6	30.4	12.8	21.3	10.9
	-43.6	-150.5	-63.5		-6.4	-76.7	-22.8	-132.7	-77.7	-206.4
EBIT/Interest	13.4	18.5	21.4		4.7	10.1	16.3	50.2	21.1	62.5
	(190) 3.5	(201) 4.3	(212) 4.3		(33) 1.1	(37) 3.0	(38) 6.8	(38) 4.5	(22) 5.3	(44) 14.2
	1.2	1.2	1.1		-1.5	-.6	2.4	1.3	1.6	3.1
Net Profit + Depr., Dep., Amort./Cur. Mat. L/T/D	5.6	13.9	11.9							39.1
	(23) 1.3	(21) 3.2	(26) 2.9						(16)	6.1
	.7	1.2	1.0							1.7
Fixed/Worth	.1	.1	.1		.0	.1	.0	.1	.1	.1
	.9	.6	.5		.3	.8	.3	.2	.4	.5
	-4.2	44.8	14.9		-.4	-3.2	88.3	1.2	5.4	6.0
Debt/Worth	1.4	.8	1.0		1.5	1.4	1.5	.7	.8	.7
	5.5	3.8	3.5		UND	8.7	4.4	2.0	2.8	1.7
	-11.8	UND	-25.5		-2.2	-4.3	-36.2	6.4	15.7	18.2
% Profit Before Taxes/Tangible Net Worth	92.3	102.9	97.0		112.6	126.1	89.7	89.2	106.1	100.4
	(160) 29.3	(190) 31.2	(196) 36.4		(24) 11.2	(36) 37.2	(32) 42.9	(36) 29.4	(26) 65.3	(42) 36.9
	5.7	9.5	8.9		-16.4	8.4	17.1	7.9	5.5	18.4
% Profit Before Taxes/Total Assets	23.6	28.1	24.7		18.8	24.9	26.5	38.0	28.9	27.3
	7.2	9.4	9.2		.0	8.5	10.2	7.6	9.9	11.8
	.1	.9	.2		-9.9	-3.1	4.6	2.1	2.6	7.8
Sales/Net Fixed Assets	109.2	115.5	187.7		UND	131.5	316.7	166.2	105.1	100.9
	31.6	33.3	44.5		44.9	31.2	79.9	65.3	28.8	25.0
	12.5	11.6	15.6		12.7	15.1	22.0	13.6	12.9	14.0
Sales/Total Assets	5.2	5.5	5.0		4.7	5.4	5.7	4.7	5.5	4.9
	3.2	3.1	3.2		2.5	3.5	4.1	3.5	3.1	2.7
	2.0	2.0	2.0		1.3	2.1	2.7	2.2	2.4	1.9
% Depr., Dep., Amort./Sales	.5	.4	.4		.8	.4	.3	.4	.2	.4
	(145) 1.1	(162) 1.3	(175) 1.0		(20) 1.5	(35) 1.1	(28) .8	(27) .7	(25) .9	(40) 1.1
	2.3	2.4	2.0		3.1	2.0	1.2	1.6	2.3	2.2
% Officers', Directors' Owners' Comp/Sales	1.6	1.8	1.8		5.6	3.3	1.2	1.6	1.3	
	(94) 3.3	(103) 3.7	(116) 3.6		(19) 10.9	(30) 4.5	(25) 2.8	(25) 2.6	(10) 2.7	
	7.4	7.5	9.2		17.4	12.6	6.9	5.1	11.6	
Net Sales ($)	9205659M	11173401M	10219906M		24889M	104188M	175175M	286995M	456578M	9172081M
Total Assets ($)	3162562M	4100067M	3882267M		14785M	35170M	55662M	108605M	164936M	3503109M

© RMA 2011

M = $ thousand   MM = $ million

See Pages 9 through 22 for Explanation of Ratios and Data

TRANSPORTATION AND
WAREHOUSING

Current Data Sorted by Assets   Comparative Historical Data

Type of Statement

Type of Statement	0-500M	500M-2MM	2-10MM	10-50MM	50-100MM	100-250MM		4/1/06-3/31/07 ALL	4/1/07-3/31/08 ALL
Unqualified			1	5	2	3		11	12
Reviewed		3	3	3				4	2
Compiled		4	1	1				3	1
Tax Returns	1	3	4	12				6	8
Other	3	3	12	12	3	6		34	28
	11 (4/1-9/30/10)		59 (10/1/10-3/31/11)						
NUMBER OF STATEMENTS	4	10	21	21	5	9		58	51

Financial Data

Item	0-500M %	500M-2MM %	2-10MM %	10-50MM %	50-100MM %	100-250MM %		ALL %	ALL %
ASSETS									
Cash & Equivalents		10.3	13.8	9.7				14.0	17.6
Trade Receivables (net)		13.0	23.2	18.9				16.3	16.4
Inventory		2.4	8.4	7.6				4.9	6.5
All Other Current		6.4	3.6	2.3				5.1	3.3
Total Current		32.2	49.0	38.6				40.4	43.8
Fixed Assets (net)		46.5	37.2	41.8				44.4	42.9
Intangibles (net)		.1	4.5	4.6				5.0	4.1
All Other Non-Current		21.3	9.2	15.0				10.3	9.2
Total		100.0	100.0	100.0				100.0	100.0
LIABILITIES									
Notes Payable-Short Term		4.4	6.7	1.6				4.1	7.0
Cur. Mat.-L.T.D.		7.7	3.5	3.5				4.8	5.6
Trade Payables		5.6	19.0	10.7				14.1	13.7
Income Taxes Payable		.0	.1	.3				.2	.1
All Other Current		4.7	20.8	12.1				16.3	15.0
Total Current		22.4	50.0	28.0				39.5	41.4
Long-Term Debt		67.5	25.3	18.7				39.7	31.2
Deferred Taxes		.0	.2	1.8				.1	.5
All Other Non-Current		5.4	1.1	7.9				5.0	13.8
Net Worth		4.7	23.4	43.6				15.8	13.2
Total Liabilities & Net Worth		100.0	100.0	100.0				100.0	100.0
INCOME DATA									
Net Sales		100.0	100.0	100.0				100.0	100.0
Gross Profit									
Operating Expenses		84.5	96.3	91.3				95.3	92.3
Operating Profit		15.5	3.7	8.7				4.7	7.7
All Other Expenses (net)		8.8	2.0	.9				3.3	1.6
Profit Before Taxes		6.7	1.7	7.8				1.4	6.1
RATIOS									
Current		4.1	1.9	2.6				1.5	2.0
		.9	1.2	1.4				1.0	1.3
		.5	.7	.9				.7	.8
Quick		2.1	1.8	1.8				1.0	1.5
		.8	.7	.9				.7	.8
		.4	.4	.5				.5	.5
Sales/Receivables		0 UND	4 90.6	12 30.0				12 30.3	10 36.9
		26 14.0	23 15.6	25 14.9				21 17.5	23 15.9
		28 13.0	61 6.0	41 8.9				34 10.6	39 9.3
Cost of Sales/Inventory									
Cost of Sales/Payables									
Sales/Working Capital		4.1	7.4	6.6				15.8	10.2
		NM	40.9	19.6				-571.5	27.9
		-35.8	-14.2	NM				-14.9	-19.0
EBIT/Interest			17.2	26.8				5.0	5.1
			(18) 2.5	(20) 7.8				(48) 2.3	(43) 3.1
			.6	2.9				.8	1.4
Net Profit + Depr., Dep., Amort./Cur. Mat. L/T/D								3.4	6.3
								(14) .5	(13) 1.7
								-2.1	.6
Fixed/Worth		.1	.3	.7				.9	1.1
		1.5	2.9	1.1				2.5	2.5
		NM	NM	1.8				-14.1	30.3
Debt/Worth		.5	1.4	.7				1.7	1.4
		3.4	4.8	.9				4.4	4.3
		-10.4	NM	3.3				-29.2	47.7
% Profit Before Taxes/Tangible Net Worth			44.6	40.3				60.9	56.2
			(16) 10.0	(18) 29.4				(40) 32.5	(40) 31.2
			1.5	22.1				1.3	8.7
% Profit Before Taxes/Total Assets		23.0	11.2	22.5				14.6	18.8
		5.1	2.2	14.8				4.8	7.5
		-7.8	-.2	3.4				-.9	1.7
Sales/Net Fixed Assets		36.5	115.2	16.0				16.6	16.3
		4.2	4.5	4.5				3.9	5.6
		.6	1.5	1.8				1.7	2.4
Sales/Total Assets		2.6	3.5	3.3				3.3	3.4
		1.8	1.7	1.6				1.9	2.5
		.6	1.0	1.0				1.1	1.4
% Depr., Dep., Amort./Sales			.7	1.2				1.6	1.5
			(17) 2.9	(19) 3.7				(50) 4.2	(46) 3.7
			10.0	6.9				6.8	6.6
% Officers', Directors' Owners' Comp/Sales								2.2	1.0
								(15) 3.0	(15) 1.4
								7.5	11.6
Net Sales ($)	6348M	19908M	269785M	1008816M	558363M	1856969M		4674435M	3787906M
Total Assets ($)	1369M	12823M	107467M	472910M	337647M	1294385M		2092881M	1701582M

M = $ thousand   MM = $ million
See Pages 9 through 22 for Explanation of Ratios and Data

Comparative Historical Data | **Current Data Sorted by Sales**

			Type of Statement	0-1MM	1-3MM	3-5MM	5-10MM	10-25MM	25MM & OVER
11	13	11	Unqualified					3	8
2	6	6	Reviewed					2	4
5	1	5	Compiled					1	
5	15	9	Tax Returns	2	2	2	1		1
30	31	39	Other	5	3	2	4	7	18
4/1/08-3/31/09 ALL	4/1/09-3/31/10 ALL	4/1/10-3/31/11 ALL		11 (4/1-9/30/10)			59 (10/1/10-3/31/11)		
53	66	70	NUMBER OF STATEMENTS	7	8	6	5	13	31
%	%	%	ASSETS	%	%	%	%	%	%
13.1	12.5	12.5	Cash & Equivalents					11.5	13.0
18.2	16.7	18.1	Trade Receivables (net)					19.8	21.8
6.1	6.4	5.6	Inventory					10.7	3.9
5.6	4.6	4.6	All Other Current					2.1	5.5
43.0	40.3	40.8	Total Current					44.1	44.2
40.2	41.4	41.7	Fixed Assets (net)					47.4	34.7
3.7	5.0	3.5	Intangibles (net)					4.2	3.5
13.0	13.2	14.0	All Other Non-Current					4.3	17.5
100.0	100.0	100.0	Total					100.0	100.0
			LIABILITIES						
8.0	7.9	4.3	Notes Payable-Short Term					1.4	4.1
3.8	4.9	4.6	Cur. Mat.-L.T.D.					3.5	4.6
11.1	12.4	13.7	Trade Payables					13.3	15.4
.2	.1	.1	Income Taxes Payable					.1	.3
20.3	14.5	13.7	All Other Current					9.6	20.4
43.3	39.8	36.5	Total Current					27.9	44.7
37.9	27.7	29.5	Long-Term Debt					26.2	15.4
.1	.9	.7	Deferred Taxes					.7	1.2
4.6	5.3	4.2	All Other Non-Current					7.4	4.6
14.1	26.4	29.0	Net Worth					37.8	34.0
100.0	100.0	100.0	Total Liabilities & Net Worth					100.0	100.0
			INCOME DATA						
100.0	100.0	100.0	Net Sales					100.0	100.0
			Gross Profit						
95.6	94.6	91.5	Operating Expenses					93.0	91.2
4.4	5.4	8.5	Operating Profit					7.0	8.8
3.2	1.8	2.7	All Other Expenses (net)					1.5	1.3
1.3	3.6	5.8	Profit Before Taxes					5.5	7.5
			RATIOS						
1.9	2.5	2.5						2.9	1.7
1.1	1.3	1.3	Current					1.7	1.1
.7	.7	.6						1.1	.5
1.4	1.7	1.8						2.3	1.4
.7	.8	.8	Quick					1.6	.8
.5	.5	.4						.6	.3
8 45.2	10 35.7	9 38.6						23 15.7	13 28.7
24 15.5	23 15.7	24 15.5	Sales/Receivables					36 10.2	25 14.9
34 10.8	44 8.2	40 9.0						61 6.0	40 9.2
			Cost of Sales/Inventory						
			Cost of Sales/Payables						
9.8	6.0	6.9						4.9	13.6
46.1	22.0	24.5	Sales/Working Capital					6.5	75.0
-20.2	-17.1	-15.3						53.9	-7.7
7.2	8.0	16.9						7.8	57.6
(44) 1.8	(56) 3.3	(58) 3.9	EBIT/Interest					3.0	(25) 16.4
.1	.4	1.3						1.5	3.0
	4.3	4.3	Net Profit + Depr., Dep.,						
	(13) 2.0	(14) 1.7	Amort./Cur. Mat. L/T/D						
	.9	.9							
.7	.9	.4						1.0	.2
1.6	1.4	1.5	Fixed/Worth					1.5	1.1
NM	6.0	4.2						3.3	3.6
1.4	.9	.7						.8	.6
4.0	3.1	2.5	Debt/Worth					2.0	1.9
-42.8	9.4	9.3						5.1	7.0
48.5	45.1	44.8	% Profit Before Taxes/Tangible					29.4	50.3
(39) 22.4	(54) 23.7	(56) 26.5	Net Worth					(11) 8.1	(26) 39.9
-3.0	5.0	4.7						4.4	24.5
11.9	13.3	19.0	% Profit Before Taxes/Total					16.8	26.1
2.7	5.2	8.7	Assets					3.4	13.6
-3.8	-1.2	.5						1.4	3.8
45.1	19.7	23.6						9.2	35.7
6.0	4.2	4.5	Sales/Net Fixed Assets					2.6	11.3
1.9	1.8	1.6						1.4	1.9
4.3	2.8	3.1						2.0	3.8
2.2	1.8	1.7	Sales/Total Assets					1.5	2.2
1.0	1.0	.9						.8	1.1
1.1	1.2	1.2						2.1	.4
(44) 4.0	(58) 4.1	(58) 3.6	% Depr., Dep., Amort./Sales					(12) 5.0	(24) 1.9
7.7	9.0	7.7						7.8	5.3
1.2	1.5	1.4	% Officers', Directors'						
(15) 1.6	(12) 3.7	(12) 2.0	Owners' Comp/Sales						
6.5	9.3	4.7							
5109112M	2422050M	3720189M	Net Sales ($)	4355M	14911M	22308M	31734M	207561M	3439320M
2144300M	1443375M	2226601M	Total Assets ($)	15163M	13448M	8179M	23733M	283717M	1882361M

M = $ thousand   MM = $ million
See Pages 9 through 22 for Explanation of Ratios and Data

Current Data Sorted by Assets   Comparative Historical Data

0-500M	500M-2MM	2-10MM	10-50MM	50-100MM	100-250MM	Type of Statement	4/1/06-3/31/07 ALL	4/1/07-3/31/08 ALL
		7	3		3	Unqualified	18	22
		7	6	1		Reviewed	11	6
	3	5	1			Compiled	13	12
3	1	6	1			Tax Returns	12	12
2	10	15	13	4	3	Other	54	50
	12 (4/1-9/30/10)		82 (10/1/10-3/31/11)					
5	14	40	24	5	6	NUMBER OF STATEMENTS	108	102
%	%	%	%	%	%	**ASSETS**	%	%
	12.1	9.8	11.2			Cash & Equivalents	11.3	9.7
	12.0	16.4	13.3			Trade Receivables (net)	17.2	22.3
	1.7	7.8	8.1			Inventory	9.7	7.6
	6.6	5.3	5.0			All Other Current	4.8	5.3
	32.4	39.3	37.6			Total Current	43.0	44.9
	45.3	47.1	53.1			Fixed Assets (net)	42.7	43.7
	5.2	4.5	2.4			Intangibles (net)	3.7	2.4
	17.1	9.1	6.8			All Other Non-Current	10.6	9.0
	100.0	100.0	100.0			Total	100.0	100.0
						LIABILITIES		
	4.2	6.7	5.0			Notes Payable-Short Term	8.6	7.6
	1.1	5.5	8.1			Cur. Mat.-L.T.D.	6.7	4.7
	6.2	12.0	9.0			Trade Payables	11.0	16.0
	.0	.6	.4			Income Taxes Payable	.4	.7
	14.1	9.3	12.1			All Other Current	8.3	11.8
	25.7	34.1	34.6			Total Current	34.9	40.8
	51.6	38.6	33.6			Long-Term Debt	40.5	44.3
	.0	.4	1.3			Deferred Taxes	.7	.4
	6.9	11.8	3.2			All Other Non-Current	6.3	6.4
	15.8	15.1	27.2			Net Worth	17.6	8.1
	100.0	100.0	100.0			Total Liabilities & Net Worth	100.0	100.0
						INCOME DATA		
	100.0	100.0	100.0			Net Sales	100.0	100.0
						Gross Profit		
	87.5	95.1	92.1			Operating Expenses	94.0	95.2
	12.5	4.9	7.9			Operating Profit	6.0	4.8
	7.2	3.5	3.9			All Other Expenses (net)	2.8	3.3
	5.3	1.4	3.9			Profit Before Taxes	3.2	1.5
						RATIOS		
	3.7	1.7	1.5				2.3	1.9
	.9	1.2	1.0			Current	1.2	1.1
	.4	.8	.5				.8	.8
	2.3	1.4	1.2				1.5	1.3
	.7	.8	.8			Quick	.8	.7
	.3	.3	.3				.4	.3
0 UND		14 25.5	6 63.0				12 30.0	16 22.3
21 17.2		25 14.5	24 15.3			Sales/Receivables	28 12.9	27 13.4
32 11.2		41 8.8	39 9.3				43 8.6	48 7.6
						Cost of Sales/Inventory		
						Cost of Sales/Payables		
	4.1	9.2	12.8				8.2	10.8
	-65.8	32.4	NM			Sales/Working Capital	36.7	58.4
	-9.9	-28.7	-3.4				-25.3	-13.5
	17.3	3.5	5.6				5.6	7.5
	(13) 3.4	(39) 2.7	(19) 3.7			EBIT/Interest	(93) 2.8	(90) 3.1
	1.4	-.5	1.4				.6	.5
						Net Profit + Depr., Dep., Amort./Cur. Mat. L/T/D	3.6	3.8
							(15) 1.7	(18) 1.4
							1.1	.9
	.2	1.2	1.1				.7	.6
	1.7	3.3	1.7			Fixed/Worth	1.7	2.5
	-1.5	-40.7	NM				26.5	-4.8
	.6	1.3	.9				1.2	1.7
	1.7	4.7	2.6			Debt/Worth	3.0	4.9
	-3.9	-257.4	NM				40.6	-11.7
		35.8	45.1				45.4	55.6
	(29)	11.4	(18) 19.5			% Profit Before Taxes/Tangible Net Worth	(83) 22.6	(71) 30.1
		-10.3	12.1				1.2	10.1
	15.5	10.0	14.0				14.2	12.7
	3.9	2.7	5.6			% Profit Before Taxes/Total Assets	6.1	6.0
	1.1	-4.0	.0				-1.3	-2.2
	29.9	14.6	4.8				19.4	15.9
	3.9	2.9	2.9			Sales/Net Fixed Assets	4.6	4.2
	.9	1.6	1.1				1.8	1.7
	3.1	2.4	1.9				3.1	3.1
	1.1	1.4	1.2			Sales/Total Assets	1.8	1.7
	.5	1.0	.7				1.0	1.0
		2.4	3.3				1.2	1.2
	(31)	6.3	(21) 5.9			% Depr., Dep., Amort./Sales	(78) 3.8	(80) 3.9
		10.8	13.1				10.4	9.0
		1.8					2.0	1.5
	(12)	2.9				% Officers', Directors' Owners' Comp/Sales	(26) 3.7	(19) 3.4
		5.0					5.2	6.6
8120M	30874M	338912M	677673M	466692M	1144861M	Net Sales ($)	2462377M	3023799M
1404M	16090M	197746M	529154M	369508M	909090M	Total Assets ($)	1623201M	2430649M

© RMA 2011

M = $ thousand   MM = $ million
See Pages 9 through 22 for Explanation of Ratios and Data

Comparative Historical Data / Current Data Sorted by Sales

	4/1/08-3/31/09 ALL	4/1/09-3/31/10 ALL	4/1/10-3/31/11 ALL	Type of Statement	0-1MM	1-3MM	3-5MM	5-10MM	10-25MM	25MM & OVER
	11	16	13	Unqualified		1	1	3	3	7
	6	12	14	Reviewed				2	8	2
	12	11	9	Compiled	2	1	1	3		1
	9	7	11	Tax Returns	3	4	1	3		
	46	45	47	Other	6	6	2	11	9	13
					12 (4/1-9/30/10)			82 (10/1/10-3/31/11)		
	84	91	94	NUMBER OF STATEMENTS	11	12	6	22	20	23
	%	%	%	**ASSETS**	%	%	%	%	%	%
	11.0	9.9	10.8	Cash & Equivalents	10.7	14.6		12.8	8.4	9.1
	15.0	15.1	16.0	Trade Receivables (net)	12.7	12.5		16.4	18.9	18.1
	8.2	8.5	7.0	Inventory	2.4	1.3		5.9	7.6	10.9
	5.2	5.1	6.0	All Other Current	8.5	2.7		6.3	7.5	6.2
	39.4	38.6	39.8	Total Current	34.3	31.1		41.4	42.4	44.4
	46.0	45.7	45.8	Fixed Assets (net)	53.9	57.8		42.1	46.7	35.1
	4.4	4.6	4.8	Intangibles (net)	2.1	.3		6.7	3.4	8.6
	10.2	11.1	9.6	All Other Non-Current	9.8	10.7		9.9	7.5	12.0
	100.0	100.0	100.0	Total	100.0	100.0		100.0	100.0	100.0
				LIABILITIES						
	11.1	11.4	6.5	Notes Payable-Short Term	6.3	7.6		8.1	4.6	4.6
	5.4	6.2	5.8	Cur. Mat.-L.T.D.	.5	5.1		6.0	8.7	6.7
	10.0	13.6	10.5	Trade Payables	9.7	2.6		11.8	12.8	12.8
	.5	.2	.4	Income Taxes Payable	.0	.1		1.1	.2	.5
	10.5	12.5	14.1	All Other Current	4.7	17.1		10.4	11.6	22.6
	37.5	43.9	37.3	Total Current	21.2	32.5		37.5	37.9	47.1
	44.6	38.5	41.2	Long-Term Debt	58.1	97.7		36.8	28.1	19.1
	.7	.9	.9	Deferred Taxes	.0	.7		.4	1.6	1.6
	5.7	7.1	15.1	All Other Non-Current	14.2	48.0		10.9	7.9	10.5
	11.5	9.5	5.5	Net Worth	6.5	-78.9		14.4	24.5	21.6
	100.0	100.0	100.0	Total Liabilities & Net Worth	100.0	100.0		100.0	100.0	100.0
				INCOME DATA						
	100.0	100.0	100.0	Net Sales	100.0	100.0		100.0	100.0	100.0
				Gross Profit						
	98.3	98.7	93.3	Operating Expenses	81.2	92.6		93.4	94.9	96.7
	1.7	1.3	6.7	Operating Profit	18.8	7.4		6.6	5.1	3.3
	2.9	2.8	4.0	All Other Expenses (net)	11.3	7.6		1.3	2.7	1.9
	-1.2	-1.5	2.6	Profit Before Taxes	7.5	-.2		5.4	2.4	1.4
				RATIOS						
	1.8	1.7	1.7	Current	5.9	4.2		1.6	1.7	1.5
	1.1	1.0	1.1		1.9	1.0		1.2	1.0	1.0
	.7	.5	.6		.5	.5		.9	.5	.6
	1.4	1.1	1.3	Quick	4.8	2.6		1.2	1.2	1.1
	.6	.6	.7		.8	1.0		.9	.6	.5
	.3	.2	.3		.3	.2		.4	.3	.4
	5 69.7	13 27.4	14 26.4	Sales/Receivables	3 118.6	0 UND		10 34.9	15 24.5	21 17.3
	19 19.5	25 14.4	26 14.3		24 15.1	9 39.8		26 14.3	28 13.0	32 11.4
	37 9.9	43 8.5	42 8.7		99 3.7	34 10.6		57 6.4	46 7.9	49 7.4
				Cost of Sales/Inventory						
				Cost of Sales/Payables						
	12.1	10.8	9.3	Sales/Working Capital	3.2	4.6		9.3	7.7	14.4
	83.9	256.1	118.0		13.0	NM		33.5	NM	-181.1
	-18.1	-7.4	-11.5		-5.4	-11.0		-44.7	-15.7	-7.5
	4.6	4.5	6.1	EBIT/Interest		7.6		9.0	4.4	9.3
	(75) 1.4	(79) .7	(86) 2.7			(10) 2.8		(21) 2.7	2.9	(20) 2.5
	-1.2	-.1	.2			-.8		-.2	.6	-.3
	8.8	2.6	1.5	Net Profit + Depr., Dep., Amort./Cur. Mat. L/T/D						
	(22) 2.7	(22) 1.2	(17) .6							
	.9	.4	.0							
	.9	.9	1.2	Fixed/Worth	1.6	1.3		1.2	.6	1.2
	3.1	3.3	2.5		1.9	-4.7		3.3	1.4	2.5
	-4.5	-3.8	-2.7		-.8	-.6		-5.9	NM	-1.4
	1.2	1.3	1.1	Debt/Worth	.6	.8		2.0	1.0	1.4
	4.4	6.4	4.3		1.0	-5.7		4.2	1.7	5.2
	-9.6	-9.2	-5.5		-2.1	-2.3		-8.6	NM	-6.1
	42.9	30.3	40.2	% Profit Before Taxes/Tangible Net Worth				36.0	41.3	45.2
	(58) 15.1	(59) 5.3	(63) 13.3					(16) 8.8	(15) 13.8	(16) 24.5
	-3.9	-8.3	.6					-14.1	-1.0	9.2
	9.7	7.2	11.8	% Profit Before Taxes/Total Assets	8.1	27.8		11.3	10.9	16.1
	1.7	-.9	3.2		4.6	6.9		2.0	3.2	3.9
	-7.5	-5.8	-2.9		1.4	-5.5		-2.9	-.2	-5.7
	17.6	9.1	12.4	Sales/Net Fixed Assets	12.4	12.4		12.9	14.5	19.6
	4.3	3.1	3.7		1.0	1.9		5.3	3.7	5.0
	1.8	1.5	1.4		.3	.9		1.7	1.3	3.1
	3.6	2.2	2.4	Sales/Total Assets	1.3	3.3		2.5	2.3	2.7
	2.0	1.4	1.4		.5	1.1		1.5	1.5	1.8
	1.0	.9	.8		.3	.6		1.1	.9	1.1
	1.8	2.1	2.5	% Depr., Dep., Amort./Sales				2.8	1.9	2.5
	(69) 3.9	(68) 5.2	(70) 5.3					(17) 6.3	(18) 5.6	(19) 4.0
	9.4	10.3	10.7					9.6	11.3	5.3
	1.6	1.8	1.8	% Officers', Directors' Owners' Comp/Sales						
	(16) 3.8	(16) 2.9	(20) 2.9							
	7.6	5.8	6.1							
	2609380M	2667953M	2667132M	Net Sales ($)	5906M	24122M	24780M	151576M	299349M	2161399M
	1932324M	2309377M	2022992M	Total Assets ($)	12243M	37803M	28482M	173063M	254988M	1516413M

M = $ thousand   MM = $ million
See Pages 9 through 22 for Explanation of Ratios and Data

Current Data Sorted by Assets

Comparative Historical Data

						Type of Statement		
		1	7	2	1	Unqualified	12	12
		2	2			Reviewed	12	11
1	1	1	2			Compiled	7	4
1	3	3				Tax Returns	5	7
4	5	7	4	1	4	Other	20	21
	6 (4/1-9/30/10)		46 (10/1/10-3/31/11)				4/1/06-3/31/07	4/1/07-3/31/08
0-500M	500M-2MM	2-10MM	10-50MM	50-100MM	100-250MM		ALL	ALL
6	9	14	15	3	5	NUMBER OF STATEMENTS	56	55
%	%	%	%	%	%	ASSETS	%	%
		5.5	15.6			Cash & Equivalents	6.4	7.8
		8.5	12.7			Trade Receivables (net)	14.5	17.6
		11.3	2.5			Inventory	10.5	8.3
		3.2	2.3			All Other Current	4.5	1.6
		28.5	33.2			Total Current	35.9	35.3
		52.7	52.4			Fixed Assets (net)	52.1	47.7
		3.4	6.0			Intangibles (net)	2.1	1.9
		15.3	8.4			All Other Non-Current	9.9	15.1
		100.0	100.0			Total	100.0	100.0
						LIABILITIES		
		6.5	2.0			Notes Payable-Short Term	7.4	8.8
		2.7	10.7			Cur. Mat.-L.T.D.	4.4	5.5
		4.0	6.6			Trade Payables	13.8	10.5
		.0	.0			Income Taxes Payable	.2	.2
		7.0	5.7			All Other Current	15.5	17.3
		20.2	25.0			Total Current	41.3	42.3
		43.9	18.7			Long-Term Debt	36.1	39.4
		1.3	1.8			Deferred Taxes	.3	.2
		4.6	7.5			All Other Non-Current	9.9	16.2
		30.1	47.0			Net Worth	12.4	2.0
		100.0	100.0			Total Liabilities & Net Worth	100.0	100.0
						INCOME DATA		
		100.0	100.0			Net Sales	100.0	100.0
						Gross Profit		
		82.8	92.5			Operating Expenses	97.2	89.1
		17.2	7.5			Operating Profit	2.8	10.9
		18.0	1.5			All Other Expenses (net)	4.2	3.1
		-.8	6.0			Profit Before Taxes	-1.4	7.8
						RATIOS		
		4.4	3.6				1.8	1.6
		1.2	1.5			Current	.9	1.0
		.8	.9				.5	.4
		2.9	3.4				.9	1.1
		1.0	1.4			Quick	.5	.5
		.4	.7				.2	.2
		0 UND	9 42.4				6 62.8	9 42.6
		36 10.1	26 14.1			Sales/Receivables	19 19.5	22 16.6
		45 8.1	39 9.3				38 9.6	35 10.5
						Cost of Sales/Inventory		
						Cost of Sales/Payables		
		6.4	4.2				12.9	16.1
		16.8	12.2			Sales/Working Capital	-60.1	-298.1
		-16.5	-42.1				-6.6	-7.6
			19.3				6.2	8.8
			(14) 5.3			EBIT/Interest	(51) .7	(46) 2.2
			1.1				-1.0	.1
						Net Profit + Depr., Dep.,	7.9	
						Amort./Cur. Mat. L/T/D	(13) 1.0	
							-1.2	
		.5	.5				.7	.5
		1.3	1.1			Fixed/Worth	2.5	2.1
		7.5	12.9				20.0	-224.1
		.9	.3				1.2	1.1
		2.1	.7			Debt/Worth	3.1	4.6
		12.7	15.1				UND	-311.0
		8.1	32.1			% Profit Before Taxes/Tangible	32.2	40.8
		(12) .8	(12) 10.6			Net Worth	(43) 8.2	(41) 21.8
		-22.1	6.0				-6.8	7.8
		3.4	16.1			% Profit Before Taxes/Total	8.5	13.5
		-.2	7.8			Assets	-1.2	6.5
		-5.1	-.1				-8.6	-.6
		14.5	6.8				13.4	15.4
		1.2	2.8			Sales/Net Fixed Assets	2.6	3.2
		.2	1.5				.9	1.7
		1.2	1.9				2.6	2.6
		.7	1.4			Sales/Total Assets	1.4	1.4
		.1	1.0				.6	1.1
		1.6	2.6				1.5	2.1
		(11) 9.0	4.9			% Depr., Dep., Amort./Sales	(47) 5.5	(44) 4.7
		37.6	8.7				12.1	10.3
						% Officers', Directors'	1.7	1.9
						Owners' Comp/Sales	(13) 3.4	(13) 4.5
							8.1	8.2
5958M	28566M	80943M	449691M	83378M	846051M	Net Sales ($)	1182014M	1494790M
937M	9028M	83198M	292758M	184660M	835851M	Total Assets ($)	767397M	811656M

© RMA 2011

M = $ thousand   MM = $ million
See Pages 9 through 22 for Explanation of Ratios and Data

Comparative Historical Data				Current Data Sorted by Sales					
			Type of Statement						
10	12	11	Unqualified					5	6
3	5	4	Reviewed			1	1	2	
5	5	5	Compiled		3		1		1
5	4	7	Tax Returns	5	1		1		
27	25	25	Other	6	4	2	4	4	5
4/1/08-3/31/09 ALL	4/1/09-3/31/10 ALL	4/1/10-3/31/11 ALL		6 (4/1-9/30/10)			46 (10/1/10-3/31/11)		
				0-1MM	1-3MM	3-5MM	5-10MM	10-25MM	25MM & OVER
50	51	52	**NUMBER OF STATEMENTS**	11	8	3	7	11	12
%	%	%	**ASSETS**	%	%	%	%	%	%
10.3	8.3	10.7	Cash & Equivalents	8.0				13.8	12.5
17.9	13.2	12.7	Trade Receivables (net)	2.6				18.3	12.2
5.2	6.3	6.3	Inventory	1.4				2.9	5.8
3.4	3.6	3.0	All Other Current	3.1				3.2	2.8
36.7	31.4	32.7	Total Current	15.1				38.2	33.4
47.9	51.1	54.2	Fixed Assets (net)	73.9				49.0	61.0
5.7	5.9	3.0	Intangibles (net)	.5				6.2	.7
9.7	11.6	10.0	All Other Non-Current	10.5				6.6	5.0
100.0	100.0	100.0	Total	100.0				100.0	100.0
			LIABILITIES						
7.0	8.3	10.7	Notes Payable-Short Term	17.9				2.2	.6
7.8	4.7	6.0	Cur. Mat.-L.T.D.	3.6				12.6	3.5
9.3	12.4	5.9	Trade Payables	3.2				8.3	6.3
.1	.2	.0	Income Taxes Payable	.0				.0	.0
11.4	14.1	6.2	All Other Current	5.6				9.1	7.4
35.6	39.7	28.9	Total Current	30.3				32.2	17.9
43.4	40.1	40.7	Long-Term Debt	81.7				16.7	35.6
.6	.8	1.2	Deferred Taxes	.0				1.9	1.4
6.1	5.2	4.1	All Other Non-Current	6.8				4.9	5.9
14.3	14.2	25.2	Net Worth	-18.9				44.3	39.2
100.0	100.0	100.0	Total Liabilities & Net Worth	100.0				100.0	100.0
			INCOME DATA						
100.0	100.0	100.0	Net Sales	100.0				100.0	100.0
			Gross Profit						
88.9	87.8	87.9	Operating Expenses	72.4				85.9	96.6
11.1	12.2	12.1	Operating Profit	27.6				14.1	3.4
7.4	7.1	7.1	All Other Expenses (net)	21.3				.4	2.0
3.8	5.1	5.0	Profit Before Taxes	6.3				13.7	1.5
			RATIOS						
2.2	1.6	3.2		.6				3.5	3.0
1.1	.9	1.2	Current	.4				1.5	1.3
.5	.5	.4		.1				1.1	.6
1.7	1.0	2.3		.4				3.2	2.2
.7	.6	.8	Quick	.2				1.2	.8
.3	.3	.3		.1				.7	.4
7 49.7	0 999.8	0 UND		0 UND				4 96.9	18 20.1
26 13.9	25 14.7	23 16.0	Sales/Receivables	0 UND				26 14.1	27 13.7
43 8.6	44 8.3	40 9.1		15 24.8				41 8.9	39 9.3
			Cost of Sales/Inventory						
			Cost of Sales/Payables						
9.8	12.6	8.6		-17.0				4.9	8.2
133.0	-56.8	20.1	Sales/Working Capital	-8.6				12.2	18.2
-7.4	-6.6	-11.1		-2.3				34.1	-24.0
9.2	4.7	14.2							27.9
(37) 2.7	(39) 2.0	(41) 4.3	EBIT/Interest						(11) 4.5
.5	-.3	.0							1.1
2.6	12.5	9.5	Net Profit + Depr., Dep.,						
(11) 1.6	(10) 2.7	(11) 2.8	Amort./Cur. Mat. L/T/D						
.1	.4	2.2							
.5	.8	.6		8.7				.6	.6
1.9	2.3	1.6	Fixed/Worth	-37.7				1.1	1.4
-6.4	-6.5	19.2		-1.5				-30.0	15.5
1.0	1.3	.7		7.8				.4	.5
4.3	3.6	2.1	Debt/Worth	-38.7				.7	1.2
-9.7	-7.3	NM		-3.3				-31.4	19.1
75.5	26.1	56.7	% Profit Before Taxes/Tangible						46.0
(35) 24.7	(35) 8.9	(39) 9.5	Net Worth						(10) 12.0
-3.0	-4.8	1.8							8.1
15.2	7.8	16.0	% Profit Before Taxes/Total	25.5				24.2	14.7
5.6	3.3	3.5	Assets	.4				8.3	3.5
-1.5	-3.0	-3.3		-14.5				3.9	-1.9
28.8	12.4	8.7		5.9				8.6	6.2
3.4	1.6	2.3	Sales/Net Fixed Assets	.7				3.4	1.7
1.0	.9	.9		.1				1.3	.9
2.7	1.9	2.1		2.6				2.1	2.0
1.4	1.0	1.1	Sales/Total Assets	.6				1.3	1.3
.8	.5	.6		.1				1.0	.6
1.1	3.2	2.9						1.6	2.4
(43) 6.5	(42) 7.1	(41) 6.6	% Depr., Dep., Amort./Sales					4.9	(11) 5.2
14.4	12.3	18.5						11.2	8.2
		1.0	% Officers', Directors'						
	(12)	1.8	Owners' Comp/Sales						
		8.9							
1627505M	1194015M	1494587M	Net Sales ($)	4547M	15531M	12610M	55113M	207393M	1199393M
1056612M	936038M	1406432M	Total Assets ($)	19302M	15131M	12382M	150772M	208523M	1000322M

M = $ thousand   MM = $ million
See Pages 9 through 22 for Explanation of Ratios and Data

Current Data Sorted by Assets | Comparative Historical Data

© RMA 2011

0-500M	500M-2MM	2-10MM	10-50MM	50-100MM	100-250MM	Type of Statement	4/1/06-3/31/07 ALL	4/1/07-3/31/08 ALL
		4	9	2	6	Unqualified	20	20
		3	3		1	Reviewed	4	14
1	2	3				Compiled	6	4
1	2	1			1	Tax Returns	2	5
2	3	10	14	1	5	Other	29	28
		16 (4/1-9/30/10)		**58 (10/1/10-3/31/11)**				
4	7	21	26	3	13	**NUMBER OF STATEMENTS**	61	71
%	%	%	%	%	%	**ASSETS**	%	%
		11.8	11.7		9.5	Cash & Equivalents	9.0	9.6
		14.8	15.7		7.0	Trade Receivables (net)	17.8	15.8
		5.2	2.8		.9	Inventory	1.3	3.9
		2.8	2.4		4.9	All Other Current	5.3	4.9
		34.6	32.7		22.4	Total Current	33.4	34.2
		48.4	57.1		69.0	Fixed Assets (net)	54.5	54.2
		3.8	.6		3.3	Intangibles (net)	3.6	1.6
		13.3	9.6		5.3	All Other Non-Current	8.5	10.0
		100.0	100.0		100.0	Total	100.0	100.0
						LIABILITIES		
		5.8	2.9		3.9	Notes Payable-Short Term	5.8	3.2
		4.6	4.9		2.0	Cur. Mat.-L.T.D.	3.4	3.6
		8.0	8.0		2.9	Trade Payables	10.6	11.1
		.4	.3		.1	Income Taxes Payable	.5	.2
		9.0	7.4		9.1	All Other Current	9.2	7.8
		27.8	23.6		18.0	Total Current	29.5	25.9
		26.6	22.2		18.8	Long-Term Debt	28.4	26.3
		.8	3.8		10.2	Deferred Taxes	2.6	1.7
		5.3	10.7		6.6	All Other Non-Current	6.2	4.1
		39.5	39.7		46.3	Net Worth	33.3	42.2
		100.0	100.0		100.0	Total Liabilities & Net Worth	100.0	100.0
						INCOME DATA		
		100.0	100.0		100.0	Net Sales	100.0	100.0
						Gross Profit		
		87.5	85.6		87.1	Operating Expenses	84.8	80.9
		12.5	14.4		12.9	Operating Profit	15.2	19.1
		2.6	.0		-.5	All Other Expenses (net)	1.2	1.5
		10.0	14.4		13.4	Profit Before Taxes	14.0	17.6
						RATIOS		
		2.9	2.1		2.0	Current	1.7	2.4
		1.5	1.5		1.3		1.0	1.4
		.7	.9		.8		.7	.9
		2.8	1.5		1.6	Quick	1.4	1.7
		1.1	1.1		1.1		.9	1.0
		.4	.7		.6		.5	.5
		22 16.3	32 11.4		26 13.8	Sales/Receivables	31 11.6	26 14.3
		33 11.0	47 7.7		49 7.5		45 8.2	44 8.3
		51 7.2	68 5.4		60 6.1		64 5.7	58 6.3
						Cost of Sales/Inventory		
						Cost of Sales/Payables		
		3.9	4.6		5.2	Sales/Working Capital	10.6	5.1
		11.1	11.7		20.5		486.8	12.4
		-10.7	-74.7		-14.4		-12.2	-30.4
		10.3	15.8		16.7	EBIT/Interest	12.9	17.2
		(17) 3.0	(25) 5.4		(11) 7.7		(55) 3.8	(60) 7.5
		1.4	2.8		2.6		2.1	3.8
			4.4			Net Profit + Depr., Dep.,	8.8	14.7
			(11) 1.8			Amort./Cur. Mat. L/T/D	(24) 2.4	(23) 2.4
			.7				1.4	1.7
		.4	.9		1.1	Fixed/Worth	.8	.8
		1.2	1.9		1.6		1.9	1.3
		4.9	3.1		3.2		5.5	3.2
		.6	.6		.8	Debt/Worth	.7	.6
		2.1	2.2		1.0		3.0	1.4
		6.7	4.1		3.0		6.3	3.3
		50.3	47.5		27.2	% Profit Before Taxes/Tangible	51.9	56.7
		(19) 10.9	(25) 20.9		(11) 12.2	Net Worth	(56) 27.2	(66) 30.3
		-.5	10.1		8.7		8.5	13.0
		9.5	14.4		11.4	% Profit Before Taxes/Total	15.8	19.4
		5.4	9.4		5.6	Assets	8.8	11.3
		.9	3.4		4.4		3.1	5.5
		16.6	3.2		1.1	Sales/Net Fixed Assets	4.4	5.1
		3.1	1.1		.7		1.4	1.5
		.3	.6		.5		.7	.7
		1.9	1.6		.8	Sales/Total Assets	1.8	1.8
		1.0	.7		.5		.8	.8
		.3	.5		.4		.4	.5
		1.7	4.0			% Depr., Dep., Amort./Sales	3.7	2.9
		(19) 6.8	(23) 8.0				(57) 7.3	(63) 6.2
		16.0	10.9				11.1	9.6
						% Officers', Directors' Owners' Comp/Sales		
4495M	20934M	166481M	783882M	687718M	2758353M	Net Sales ($)	1945841M	2088264M
1317M	8404M	123380M	589818M	204811M	2051105M	Total Assets ($)	2097061M	2039450M

M = $ thousand   MM = $ million
See Pages 9 through 22 for Explanation of Ratios and Data

Comparative Historical Data | Current Data Sorted by Sales

Type of Statement

	4/1/08-3/31/09 ALL	4/1/09-3/31/10 ALL	4/1/10-3/31/11 ALL	0-1MM	1-3MM	3-5MM	5-10MM	10-25MM	25MM & OVER
Unqualified	19	22	21		1	1	1	9	9
Reviewed	12	8	7	1	2			1	3
Compiled	9	6	6		3		1	2	
Tax Returns	5	8	5	1	2				2
Other	33	33	35	3	7	2	5	7	11
					16 (4/1-9/30/10)		58 (10/1/10-3/31/11)		
NUMBER OF STATEMENTS	78	77	74	5	15	3	7	19	25

ASSETS

	%	%	%	%	%	%	%	%	%
Cash & Equivalents	7.2	9.5	12.2		14.3			13.0	13.9
Trade Receivables (net)	16.4	16.0	15.9		14.3			17.8	18.8
Inventory	2.1	2.0	2.8		.6			7.1	1.3
All Other Current	3.5	3.5	3.4		1.1			1.7	3.1
Total Current	29.2	30.9	34.2		30.4			39.6	37.2
Fixed Assets (net)	56.2	52.3	53.9		52.1			51.4	50.3
Intangibles (net)	2.2	2.9	2.0		3.7			1.4	2.0
All Other Non-Current	12.4	13.9	9.9		13.8			7.6	10.5
Total	100.0	100.0	100.0		100.0			100.0	100.0

LIABILITIES

Notes Payable-Short Term	5.7	2.6	4.0		2.4			3.6	6.2
Cur. Mat.-L.T.D.	4.8	6.0	5.1		8.3			4.2	3.8
Trade Payables	8.6	9.0	8.5		9.0			11.2	7.8
Income Taxes Payable	1.0	.4	.2		.0			.4	.4
All Other Current	12.4	27.1	9.5		10.4			6.5	12.7
Total Current	32.5	45.0	27.3		30.0			25.9	30.9
Long-Term Debt	27.4	29.4	22.5		22.5			26.8	17.2
Deferred Taxes	1.9	2.3	3.5		.0			2.4	6.2
All Other Non-Current	4.1	3.2	6.7		4.6			5.3	6.4
Net Worth	34.1	20.2	39.9		42.9			39.7	39.2
Total Liabilities & Net Worth	100.0	100.0	100.0		100.0			100.0	100.0

INCOME DATA

Net Sales	100.0	100.0	100.0		100.0			100.0	100.0
Gross Profit									
Operating Expenses	82.9	88.9	86.1		82.9			87.0	91.3
Operating Profit	17.1	11.1	13.9		17.1			13.0	8.7
All Other Expenses (net)	1.7	2.0	1.0		1.1			-.3	.0
Profit Before Taxes	15.4	9.1	12.9		16.1			13.4	8.7

RATIOS

Current	1.9	2.3	2.1		2.8			1.7	1.7
	1.1	1.1	1.4		1.5			1.5	1.1
	.6	.6	.7		.6			.9	.9
Quick	1.7	1.8	1.8		2.8			1.4	1.5
	.7	.8	1.1		1.1			1.0	1.1
	.4	.4	.6		.6			.7	.7
Sales/Receivables	18 20.7	15 24.9	23 16.2		15 24.3			23 15.5	27 13.7
	36 10.2	38 9.5	40 9.2		37 9.9			37 9.8	45 8.1
	55 6.6	57 6.4	58 6.3		64 5.7			55 6.6	56 6.6
Cost of Sales/Inventory									
Cost of Sales/Payables									
Sales/Working Capital	7.6	6.2	5.4		5.4			5.9	6.8
	67.1	74.0	22.2		16.1			11.1	44.0
	-10.9	-8.4	-23.1		-5.1			-86.0	-68.8
EBIT/Interest	10.1	8.7	14.9		10.8			16.8	15.3
	(68) 3.8	(69) 2.8	(63) 4.8	(10) 5.0			(18) 5.6		(22) 4.4
	2.1	1.2	2.6		.5			3.6	1.2
Net Profit + Depr., Dep., Amort./Cur. Mat. L/T/D	9.2	5.6	5.5						11.9
	(24) 3.9	(28) 1.9	(23) 1.8					(12)	2.0
	1.3	1.4	.7						.8
Fixed/Worth	.9	.8	.6		.5			.5	.4
	1.7	1.5	1.6		.9			1.8	1.6
	3.9	4.7	3.1		6.1			3.1	2.7
Debt/Worth	.7	.6	.8		.3			.7	.9
	2.1	1.8	1.8		1.1			2.1	1.8
	6.2	7.2	4.1		5.2			4.1	4.1
% Profit Before Taxes/Tangible Net Worth	64.3	32.0	50.3		62.5			59.7	40.0
	(71) 30.3	(66) 15.2	(70) 21.5	(13) 33.6				27.8	12.2
	10.1	3.6	6.3		12.3			19.1	4.1
% Profit Before Taxes/Total Assets	14.6	12.8	14.5		21.6			16.5	12.2
	7.6	6.3	7.9		9.5			10.7	5.6
	2.9	.8	3.4		2.7			6.4	1.1
Sales/Net Fixed Assets	7.3	7.1	5.7		4.4			16.8	30.2
	1.7	1.7	1.4		1.6			1.4	2.6
	.6	.7	.6		.3			.8	.6
Sales/Total Assets	2.3	2.4	2.0		3.0			1.9	2.9
	.9	.9	.8		.5			1.0	1.4
	.5	.4	.4		.3			.6	.5
% Depr., Dep., Amort./Sales	2.2	3.8	2.5		2.0			2.1	.8
	(69) 6.7	(70) 8.8	(63) 7.4	(14) 6.6			(16) 7.7		(20) 5.6
	9.1	11.6	11.4		16.1			11.3	9.2
% Officers', Directors' Owners' Comp/Sales									
Net Sales ($)	2528706M	2172616M	4421863M	2441M	27367M	12780M	51690M	305046M	4022539M
Total Assets ($)	2882789M	2766320M	2978835M	7692M	64760M	31165M	90590M	344948M	2439680M

M = $ thousand   MM = $ million
See Pages 9 through 22 for Explanation of Ratios and Data

Current Data Sorted by Assets							Comparative Historical Data	
			1	2 2 2	3	3	**Type of Statement** Unqualified Reviewed Compiled Tax Returns Other	7 2 1 5
			1					5 2 1 1 5
1	0 (4/1-9/30/10)			3	1	2		4/1/06- 3/31/07
0-500M	500M-2MM	2-10MM	10-50MM	21 (10/1/10-3/31/11) 50-100MM	100-250MM			4/1/07- 3/31/08
1		2	9	4	5		**NUMBER OF STATEMENTS**	15 ALL	13 ALL
%	%	%	%	%	%			%	%
							ASSETS		
							Cash & Equivalents	11.5	12.2
							Trade Receivables (net)	13.7	12.6
							Inventory	.5	.2
							All Other Current	4.1	4.8
							Total Current	29.8	29.8
							Fixed Assets (net)	57.9	58.5
							Intangibles (net)	2.3	5.0
							All Other Non-Current	10.0	6.7
							Total	100.0	100.0
							LIABILITIES		
							Notes Payable-Short Term	1.3	2.2
							Cur. Mat.-L.T.D.	4.0	3.8
							Trade Payables	4.4	6.6
							Income Taxes Payable	.7	.7
							All Other Current	9.9	10.0
							Total Current	20.3	23.3
							Long-Term Debt	33.8	37.3
							Deferred Taxes	1.6	2.2
							All Other Non-Current	7.8	1.9
							Net Worth	36.4	35.3
							Total Liabilties & Net Worth	100.0	100.0
							INCOME DATA		
							Net Sales	100.0	100.0
							Gross Profit		
							Operating Expenses	81.6	82.5
							Operating Profit	18.4	17.5
							All Other Expenses (net)	7.7	2.9
							Profit Before Taxes	10.8	14.6
							RATIOS		
							Current	2.4 1.6 .6	3.5 1.1 .4
							Quick	2.0 1.1 .5	2.3 1.0 .3
							Sales/Receivables	20 18.7 36 10.2 79 4.6	14 26.6 30 12.3 61 6.0
							Cost of Sales/Inventory		
							Cost of Sales/Payables		
							Sales/Working Capital	7.2 12.3 -16.9	5.1 39.8 -4.5
							EBIT/Interest	7.5 (13) 4.0 2.5	12.0 3.8 2.3
							Net Profit + Depr., Dep., Amort./Cur. Mat. L/T/D		
							Fixed/Worth	.4 1.9 2.9	.6 1.4 NM
							Debt/Worth	.9 1.9 3.7	.8 1.1 NM
							% Profit Before Taxes/Tangible Net Worth	43.6 (13) 28.2 8.6	36.8 (10) 26.5 10.5
							% Profit Before Taxes/Total Assets	18.3 9.2 2.8	15.6 9.4 5.5
							Sales/Net Fixed Assets	6.5 1.3 .5	3.9 1.1 .6
							Sales/Total Assets	2.0 .8 .4	1.6 .6 .4
							% Depr., Dep., Amort./Sales	3.3 (14) 5.8 8.0	3.6 (11) 4.7 8.3
							% Officers', Directors' Owners' Comp/Sales		
3091M 454M	34909M 15520M	165755M 263912M	165460M 350548M	551987M 733710M			Net Sales ($) Total Assets ($)	618380M 898421M	826546M 1170225M

M = $ thousand   MM = $ million
See Pages 9 through 22 for Explanation of Ratios and Data

Comparative Historical Data | Current Data Sorted by Sales

				Type of Statement						
7		13	9	Unqualified				1		8
		3	2	Reviewed			1	1		
1		1	2	Compiled				1	1	1
		2	1	Tax Returns						
5		12	7	Other	2		1			4

4/1/08-3/31/09 ALL		4/1/09-3/31/10 ALL	4/1/10-3/31/11 ALL		0-1MM	0 (4/1-9/30/10) 1-3MM	3-5MM	21 (10/1/10-3/31/11) 5-10MM	10-25MM	25MM & OVER
13		31	21	**NUMBER OF STATEMENTS**	2		2	4	2	13
%		%	%	**ASSETS**	%	%	%	%	%	%
6.6		12.6	12.1	Cash & Equivalents						10.0
10.7		12.9	11.7	Trade Receivables (net)	D	D				9.9
.2		1.9	.8	Inventory	A	A				1.3
5.9		5.6	3.4	All Other Current	T	T				5.3
23.4		33.0	28.0	Total Current	A	A				26.5
63.5		55.0	64.6	Fixed Assets (net)						67.1
3.5		2.5	2.7	Intangibles (net)	N	N				2.8
9.7		9.5	4.7	All Other Non-Current	O	O				3.5
100.0		100.0	100.0	Total	T	T				100.0
				LIABILITIES	A	A				
1.1		5.8	6.4	Notes Payable-Short Term	V	V				4.1
2.7		6.3	3.8	Cur. Mat.-L.T.D.	A	A				2.5
3.7		7.4	5.1	Trade Payables	I	I				4.7
.0		.1	1.0	Income Taxes Payable	L	L				1.6
7.0		7.4	8.5	All Other Current	A	A				13.1
14.6		27.0	24.8	Total Current	B	B				26.1
30.5		28.2	36.0	Long-Term Debt	L	L				32.8
1.1		2.3	.0	Deferred Taxes	E	E				.1
10.1		5.2	7.6	All Other Non-Current						8.7
43.7		37.3	31.5	Net Worth						32.4
100.0		100.0	100.0	Total Liabilities & Net Worth						100.0
				INCOME DATA						
100.0		100.0	100.0	Net Sales						100.0
				Gross Profit						
79.3		86.8	85.8	Operating Expenses						88.6
20.7		13.2	14.2	Operating Profit						11.4
6.2		1.9	5.4	All Other Expenses (net)						5.6
14.5		11.3	8.7	Profit Before Taxes						5.8
				RATIOS						
3.3		2.2	2.0							2.6
1.1		1.2	1.1	Current						1.2
.9		.7	.6							.6
1.9		1.8	1.8							2.1
1.0		1.0	1.0	Quick						1.0
.9		.2	.4							.3
23 16.1	14 25.6	32 11.6						34	10.8
30 12.0	38 9.7	39 9.3	Sales/Receivables					51	7.2
81 4.5	55 6.7	54 6.7						57	6.4
				Cost of Sales/Inventory						
				Cost of Sales/Payables						
4.3		7.0	5.2							4.6
29.0		38.2	58.3	Sales/Working Capital						29.3
-91.3		-9.2	-8.7							-8.7
6.4		5.1	13.5							6.8
(11) 4.0	(27) 1.8	(20) 3.0	EBIT/Interest						2.9
2.6		1.2	.4							.2
				Net Profit + Depr., Dep., Amort./Cur. Mat. L/T/D						
.7		1.1	1.2							1.2
2.0		1.6	2.0	Fixed/Worth						2.0
2.6		4.4	7.5							5.7
.5		.7	1.0							1.2
1.6		2.1	2.9	Debt/Worth						2.9
2.1		6.2	8.7							7.0
32.2		47.3	70.8	% Profit Before Taxes/Tangible						57.4
(12) 21.8	(29) 15.3	(18) 20.5	Net Worth					(12)	20.5
9.1		2.1	-2.6							-4.5
12.8		9.1	14.2	% Profit Before Taxes/Total						12.3
9.5		3.4	4.8	Assets						4.3
4.9		1.6	-1.2							-1.2
2.2		10.5	2.1							2.1
.9		1.1	.7	Sales/Net Fixed Assets						.7
.6		.5	.4							.4
1.1		2.5	1.2							1.2
.6		.5	.5	Sales/Total Assets						.5
.4		.3	.3							.3
3.2		2.2	2.8							1.9
(10) 4.4	(24) 5.5	(17) 9.3	% Depr., Dep., Amort./Sales					(11)	5.7
6.7		11.5	17.1							10.6
				% Officers', Directors' Owners' Comp/Sales						
904061M		1469650M	921202M	Net Sales ($)			7648M	28747M	37123M	847684M
1439483M		1993348M	1364144M	Total Assets ($)			25852M	103487M	46312M	1188493M

M = $ thousand   MM = $ million
See Pages 9 through 22 for Explanation of Ratios and Data

Current Data Sorted by Assets | Comparative Historical Data

		2	3	3	10	Type of Statement		30	26
		6	5	3		Unqualified			
			2			Reviewed		7	3
2	4	6				Compiled		9	8
4	6	3				Tax Returns		5	7
	9	20	15	3	12	Other		43	39
	11 (4/1-9/30/10)		101 (10/1/10-3/31/11)					4/1/06-3/31/07	4/1/07-3/31/08
0-500M	500M-2MM	2-10MM	10-50MM	50-100MM	100-250MM			ALL	ALL
6	19	31	25	9	22	NUMBER OF STATEMENTS		94	83
%	%	%	%	%	%	ASSETS		%	%
	26.5	19.2	7.9		6.8	Cash & Equivalents		8.2	10.5
	18.2	20.9	8.7		8.6	Trade Receivables (net)		14.8	12.1
	.8	.4	1.8		3.1	Inventory		1.5	1.2
	4.5	6.8	4.3		2.6	All Other Current		2.5	4.5
	49.9	47.3	22.8		21.1	Total Current		27.0	28.3
	40.5	46.8	71.1		67.1	Fixed Assets (net)		62.9	64.9
	.4	1.9	1.3		3.0	Intangibles (net)		2.4	1.6
	9.3	4.0	4.8		8.9	All Other Non-Current		7.7	5.3
	100.0	100.0	100.0		100.0	Total		100.0	100.0
						LIABILITIES			
	2.9	5.1	2.8		1.9	Notes Payable-Short Term		5.1	3.5
	2.3	5.7	5.4		6.8	Cur. Mat.-L.T.D.		4.5	4.0
	10.1	11.0	5.6		6.1	Trade Payables		7.4	4.7
	.0	.0	.3		.2	Income Taxes Payable		.3	.4
	13.1	10.2	7.0		8.1	All Other Current		6.3	6.6
	28.4	32.1	21.1		23.1	Total Current		23.7	19.1
	27.1	34.4	37.8		33.4	Long-Term Debt		34.4	37.3
	.0	.0	2.3		4.0	Deferred Taxes		2.5	2.5
	11.3	6.7	.8		2.2	All Other Non-Current		2.8	2.6
	33.3	26.8	38.1		37.3	Net Worth		36.6	38.4
	100.0	100.0	100.0		100.0	Total Liabilities & Net Worth		100.0	100.0
						INCOME DATA			
	100.0	100.0	100.0		100.0	Net Sales		100.0	100.0
						Gross Profit			
	83.8	87.8	78.3		89.5	Operating Expenses		80.8	80.0
	16.2	12.2	21.7		10.5	Operating Profit		19.2	20.0
	4.4	3.6	5.5		2.5	All Other Expenses (net)		4.2	5.5
	11.8	8.6	16.2		8.0	Profit Before Taxes		15.0	14.5
						RATIOS			
	9.4	3.0	2.5		1.6			2.1	3.2
	2.6	1.5	1.3		1.1	Current		1.1	1.3
	1.0	.8	.4		.6			.5	.8
	9.4	2.3	2.4		1.2			1.8	2.8
	2.6	1.2	.9		.7	Quick		.9	1.1
	.9	.7	.2		.4			.5	.6

0	UND	12	30.4	22	16.3		23	15.5	Sales/Receivables	18	20.5	23	16.2
18	20.1	27	13.7	40	9.0		36	10.3		39	9.2	38	9.5
44	8.3	43	8.5	49	7.4		48	7.6		63	5.8	55	6.6

						Cost of Sales/Inventory			

						Cost of Sales/Payables			

	4.1	5.6	4.9		12.0	Sales/Working Capital		7.2	4.0
	15.4	10.3	25.4		65.3			38.1	20.7
	-622.9	-38.7	-7.2		-11.4			-11.3	-28.7

	66.2		17.7	14.9		5.6	EBIT/Interest		16.7		13.9
(11)	20.1	(24)	7.3	(23) 6.4		3.9		(83)	5.1	(67)	4.6
	1.7		1.9	2.9		2.8			2.3		2.4

							Net Profit + Depr., Dep.,		4.5		3.3
		(23)					Amort./Cur. Mat. L/T/D	(23)	2.2	(18)	2.3
									1.2		1.5

	.1	.4	.9		1.1	Fixed/Worth		1.0	.9
	.8	2.1	2.3		1.8			1.9	1.9
	6.2	6.4	5.0		3.7			5.1	4.7
	.2	.7	.7		1.1	Debt/Worth		.9	.7
	.7	2.8	1.7		1.6			2.0	2.0
	8.5	20.0	4.8		3.4			5.0	4.9

	47.5		111.3	48.5		25.2	% Profit Before Taxes/Tangible		51.8		46.9
(16)	33.6	(25)	30.7	(23) 26.1	(20)	16.2	Net Worth	(85)	33.7	(78)	27.3
	19.3		11.7	15.6		8.9			16.9		15.8

	37.2	30.5	17.7		7.9	% Profit Before Taxes/Total Assets		20.6	18.4
	12.7	7.7	7.9		6.0			9.8	9.5
	4.6	2.2	3.6		3.7			4.4	4.5
	94.7	16.0	2.0		2.5	Sales/Net Fixed Assets		3.3	2.6
	9.5	3.2	1.0		1.0			1.6	1.0
	1.6	1.2	.5		.7			.8	.6
	7.3	2.9	1.4		1.4	Sales/Total Assets		1.5	1.5
	2.6	2.0	.6		.8			.9	.7
	1.2	.8	.5		.5			.6	.5

	1.8		1.2	3.8		2.4	% Depr., Dep., Amort./Sales		2.7		3.1
(12)	6.3	(26)	4.6	7.5	(13)	5.8		(81)	5.4	(69)	6.0
	27.4		9.4	16.6		10.3			10.3		10.4

							% Officers', Directors'		.8		.6
							Owners' Comp/Sales	(23)	2.8	(17)	2.2
									10.0		8.4

4604M	93446M	335808M	511433M	382130M	3319236M	Net Sales ($)		4013975M	3859157M
1720M	23996M	143509M	678949M	652756M	3259272M	Total Assets ($)		4505600M	4651107M

© RMA 2011

M = $ thousand   MM = $ million
See Pages 9 through 22 for Explanation of Ratios and Data

Comparative Historical Data / Current Data Sorted by Sales

		Comparative Historical Data		Type of Statement		11 (4/1-9/30/10)		101 (10/1/10-3/31/11)		
	23	23	18	Unqualified				1	2	15
	9	11	8	Reviewed				1	4	3
	8	11	14	Compiled	2	5	2	4	6	1
	11	12	13	Tax Returns	4	1	1	1	6	
	59	70	59	Other	3	7	10	7	11	21
	4/1/08-3/31/09 ALL	4/1/09-3/31/10 ALL	4/1/10-3/31/11 ALL		0-1MM	1-3MM	3-5MM	5-10MM	10-25MM	25MM & OVER
	110	127	112	**NUMBER OF STATEMENTS**	9	13	13	14	23	40
	%	%	%	**ASSETS**	%	%	%	%	%	%
	10.1	12.3	15.3	Cash & Equivalents		10.0	19.5	17.1	17.4	9.1
	12.8	12.1	14.7	Trade Receivables (net)		17.3	10.7	20.4	15.5	14.5
	4.0	.9	1.4	Inventory		.0	.5	.5	1.8	1.9
	4.2	3.8	4.4	All Other Current		8.0	1.4	5.3	2.4	5.7
	31.2	29.1	35.8	Total Current		35.2	32.2	43.3	37.2	31.1
	58.1	61.4	56.6	Fixed Assets (net)		58.4	52.1	48.3	59.1	60.6
	3.7	2.5	1.6	Intangibles (net)		1.7	1.1	2.4	.8	2.0
	7.0	7.0	5.9	All Other Non-Current		4.7	14.6	6.1	2.9	6.3
	100.0	100.0	100.0	Total		100.0	100.0	100.0	100.0	100.0
				LIABILITIES						
	3.1	3.0	3.4	Notes Payable-Short Term		6.3	.9	7.3	4.1	1.7
	4.5	6.2	5.0	Cur. Mat.-L.T.D.		5.6	5.9	2.1	6.0	5.3
	7.8	6.0	8.6	Trade Payables		5.4	.8	7.5	12.6	9.8
	.2	.2	.1	Income Taxes Payable		.0	.0	.0	.3	.1
	7.9	10.3	9.5	All Other Current		8.4	8.1	7.2	12.9	10.5
	23.6	25.6	26.6	Total Current		25.7	15.7	24.1	35.9	27.4
	36.0	37.3	33.8	Long-Term Debt		62.3	30.0	24.5	33.4	27.2
	1.7	1.3	1.5	Deferred Taxes		.0	.3	.0	1.8	2.9
	3.3	4.5	4.7	All Other Non-Current		3.4	12.3	8.0	4.7	2.2
	35.3	31.3	33.4	Net Worth		8.6	41.7	43.4	24.1	40.3
	100.0	100.0	100.0	Total Liabilities & Net Worth		100.0	100.0	100.0	100.0	100.0
				INCOME DATA						
	100.0	100.0	100.0	Net Sales		100.0	100.0	100.0	100.0	100.0
				Gross Profit						
	84.2	87.8	85.5	Operating Expenses		83.5	90.7	79.5	88.0	86.1
	15.8	12.2	14.5	Operating Profit		16.5	9.3	20.5	12.0	13.9
	3.4	5.1	4.0	All Other Expenses (net)		8.1	5.5	4.0	2.6	2.1
	12.4	7.0	10.5	Profit Before Taxes		8.5	3.9	16.5	9.4	11.8
				RATIOS						
	2.3	2.5	3.1			2.7	13.4	3.9	2.1	2.2
	1.5	1.4	1.4	Current		1.7	2.3	2.0	1.1	1.3
	.9	.6	.7			.7	.8	.7	.5	.7
	1.8	2.1	2.5			2.1	13.3	3.7	1.6	2.1
	1.2	1.0	1.1	Quick		1.2	1.2	1.6	.9	1.0
	.4	.4	.5			.5	.7	.7	.4	.4
	16 23.1	5 66.7	12 30.4			0 UND	0 UND	0 UND	13 28.3	25 14.6
	34 10.9	30 12.2	31 11.9	Sales/Receivables		31 11.8	27 13.7	18 19.9	32 11.4	39 9.3
	47 7.8	47 7.7	47 7.8			64 5.7	33 11.1	52 7.0	42 8.7	57 6.4
				Cost of Sales/Inventory						
				Cost of Sales/Payables						
	5.8	5.6	5.4			4.2	5.4	4.0	5.5	6.8
	14.9	24.2	17.8	Sales/Working Capital		13.9	9.6	9.5	106.6	28.2
	-165.4	-9.5	-22.8			-28.1	-30.7	-27.0	-9.5	-13.1
	11.1	7.9	14.7			10.2	32.2	10.2		32.3
	(94) 4.6	(102) 2.9	(93) 5.1	EBIT/Interest		(10) 2.2	(10) 14.8	(18) 4.2		(39) 4.5
	2.0	.4	2.2			1.2	5.2	2.5		2.8
	11.8	4.6	3.9							
	(25) 3.9	(16) 3.3	(13) 1.3	Net Profit + Depr., Dep., Amort./Cur. Mat. L/T/D						
	2.4	1.1	1.0							
	.9	1.0	.7			.6	.4	.3	1.0	.8
	2.0	2.4	1.7	Fixed/Worth		2.5	2.8	1.2	2.3	1.6
	5.0	10.6	5.0			NM	NM	5.3	4.6	3.1
	.8	.8	.7			1.9	.2	.4	1.6	.8
	2.1	2.1	2.2	Debt/Worth		3.0	2.5	.8	2.4	1.6
	6.0	12.9	5.7			NM	NM	5.3	7.6	2.9
	49.4	49.0	46.8			44.8	43.2	94.3	49.0	46.8
	(95) 28.5	(105) 16.4	(98) 23.3	% Profit Before Taxes/Tangible Net Worth		(10) 26.2	(10) 14.1	(12) 44.1	(20) 27.5	(38) 20.4
	10.2	-1.6	11.8			12.2	-3.2	23.0	14.9	11.0
	16.9	11.1	15.2			12.9	21.6	38.1	16.2	17.0
	8.7	4.8	7.4	% Profit Before Taxes/Total Assets		5.9	4.4	11.2	7.4	7.0
	3.2	-2.2	3.1			2.7	-1.4	6.9	3.1	3.8
	3.7	3.6	7.5			7.3	33.5	17.6	16.0	3.0
	1.4	1.2	1.7	Sales/Net Fixed Assets		1.2	1.9	6.9	2.0	1.4
	.7	.6	.8			.7	1.1	.8	.7	.8
	1.8	1.6	2.3			1.4	2.6	3.4	3.7	1.7
	.9	.9	1.1	Sales/Total Assets		.9	1.1	2.4	1.4	.9
	.5	.5	.6			.6	.6	.5	.8	.6
	2.9	4.0	2.6			3.8	4.7	2.4	2.8	2.1
	(86) 5.9	(97) 8.7	(88) 6.9	% Depr., Dep., Amort./Sales		(10) 10.7	(11) 9.2	(10) 3.6	(20) 5.8	(30) 5.1
	8.9	18.4	12.8			29.6	15.1	15.5	12.1	9.1
	.9	1.3	1.2							
	(23) 1.3	(17) 2.3	(21) 2.6	% Officers', Directors' Owners' Comp/Sales						
	3.2	12.2	5.1							
	5518590M	4402210M	4646657M	Net Sales ($)	3028M	25687M	55840M	105888M	372153M	4084061M
	5969113M	5381805M	4760202M	Total Assets ($)	9881M	31595M	123973M	194015M	380973M	4019765M

M = $ thousand   MM = $ million
See Pages 9 through 22 for Explanation of Ratios and Data

Current Data Sorted by Assets   Comparative Historical Data

Type of Statement

	0-500M	500M-2MM	2-10MM	10-50MM	50-100MM	100-250MM		4/1/06-3/31/07 ALL	4/1/07-3/31/08 ALL
Unqualified	2	2	9	24	13	10		81	63
Reviewed	2	21	91	38		1		191	195
Compiled	48	56	82	14	2			237	231
Tax Returns	124	90	46	5		2		214	245
Other	62	104	123	63	18	10		337	347
		132 (4/1-9/30/10)			928 (10/1/10-3/31/11)				
NUMBER OF STATEMENTS	236	273	351	144	33	23		1060	1081

ASSETS

	%	%	%	%	%	%		%	%
Cash & Equivalents	18.5	12.3	9.2	9.5	7.9	7.4		10.4	10.6
Trade Receivables (net)	22.3	31.9	31.3	26.1	23.0	17.3		26.8	26.7
Inventory	1.2	1.6	1.8	2.9	.8	.4		1.6	1.4
All Other Current	3.9	4.8	4.1	2.8	4.1	3.9		3.9	4.0
Total Current	45.8	50.6	46.4	41.3	35.8	29.1		42.7	42.7
Fixed Assets (net)	40.1	37.3	40.5	47.3	49.6	50.3		45.6	45.9
Intangibles (net)	3.9	2.0	2.5	3.7	6.7	14.3		2.8	3.2
All Other Non-Current	10.2	10.1	10.7	7.6	7.9	6.4		8.9	8.2
Total	100.0	100.0	100.0	100.0	100.0	100.0		100.0	100.0

LIABILITIES

Notes Payable-Short Term	16.7	10.0	8.5	7.8	2.8	3.6		8.9	8.8
Cur. Mat.-L.T.D.	11.1	7.0	7.5	8.5	8.4	6.8		8.5	9.2
Trade Payables	10.3	11.8	11.5	10.0	6.9	7.1		11.2	11.1
Income Taxes Payable	.1	.0	.2	.2	.1	.3		.3	.3
All Other Current	17.5	10.9	8.0	8.7	10.4	7.2		11.0	9.5
Total Current	55.8	39.7	35.7	35.3	28.7	25.0		39.9	38.9
Long-Term Debt	42.6	25.9	22.9	24.6	33.5	23.9		30.8	31.8
Deferred Taxes	.0	.4	.9	2.2	3.1	3.1		.9	.8
All Other Non-Current	11.5	5.9	4.9	3.5	4.0	4.4		4.5	5.1
Net Worth	-9.9	28.2	35.7	34.4	30.6	43.5		23.8	23.4
Total Liabilities & Net Worth	100.0	100.0	100.0	100.0	100.0	100.0		100.0	100.0

INCOME DATA

Net Sales	100.0	100.0	100.0	100.0	100.0	100.0		100.0	100.0
Gross Profit									
Operating Expenses	96.5	95.9	95.2	95.5	94.3	94.6		95.0	95.5
Operating Profit	3.5	4.1	4.8	4.5	5.7	5.4		5.0	4.5
All Other Expenses (net)	.8	.7	.8	1.4	1.5	2.5		1.1	1.2
Profit Before Taxes	2.7	3.4	4.1	3.1	4.2	2.9		3.8	3.2

RATIOS

	0-500M	500M-2MM	2-10MM	10-50MM	50-100MM	100-250MM		Hist. 1	Hist. 2
Current	2.7	2.9	2.3	1.7	1.5	1.6		2.1	2.0
	1.0	1.3	1.3	1.2	1.2	1.2		1.1	1.1
	.3	.7	.9	.8	.9	.6		.7	.7
Quick	2.3	2.4	2.1	1.5	1.2	1.5		1.9	1.7
	.8	(272) 1.2	1.1	1.1	1.0	1.0		(1058) 1.0	(1080) 1.0
	.3	.6	.7	.6	.7	.5		.6	.6
Sales/Receivables	0 UND	10 34.9	23 15.5	29 12.5	36 10.3	33 11.1		16 23.5	14 25.3
	2 165.5	27 13.3	36 10.1	39 9.3	43 8.6	43 8.6		31 11.7	31 11.7
	29 12.6	45 8.2	50 7.3	53 6.9	53 6.9	56 6.5		43 8.4	45 8.1
Cost of Sales/Inventory									
Cost of Sales/Payables									
Sales/Working Capital	19.2	9.3	9.0	13.0	15.0	16.0		13.2	13.3
	UND	37.6	27.8	35.0	31.5	53.2		75.6	76.2
	-15.2	-26.9	-48.5	-35.0	-30.7	-11.6		-22.0	-24.9
EBIT/Interest	10.3	9.8	9.8	7.2	5.7	6.9		7.5	5.7
	(182) 2.7	(237) 3.2	(321) 3.5	(134) 2.8	(32) 3.4	(21) 3.5		(936) 3.0	(961) 2.1
	.2	1.0	1.2	1.2	1.5	1.2		1.1	.7
Net Profit + Depr., Dep., Amort./Cur. Mat. L/T/D		3.4	2.4	2.5	2.2			3.2	2.6
		(28) 2.0	(79) 1.8	(51) 1.5	(10) 1.6			(217) 1.7	(212) 1.5
		1.0	1.2	1.0	1.2			1.1	1.0
Fixed/Worth	.3	.2	.5	.8	1.4	.9		.7	.7
	2.1	1.0	1.2	1.5	1.8	1.5		1.8	1.8
	-1.0	7.8	2.8	3.0	3.1	-63.9		6.6	11.3
Debt/Worth	.9	.7	.8	1.1	1.5	.8		1.0	1.1
	5.7	1.9	1.7	2.4	2.2	2.1		2.7	2.9
	-3.2	23.2	5.0	6.3	3.8	-96.4		13.7	23.9
% Profit Before Taxes/Tangible Net Worth	124.2	55.1	43.0	32.9	36.1	26.8		53.6	47.6
	(144) 35.7	(215) 18.8	(318) 18.4	(130) 17.2	(30) 18.0	(17) 11.6		(855) 23.5	(855) 17.5
	2.4	.8	2.6	3.4	7.8	5.3		5.3	1.6
% Profit Before Taxes/Total Assets	32.1	19.7	14.2	11.3	14.0	8.0		16.2	14.0
	8.9	6.3	6.3	4.6	5.2	6.1		6.6	4.6
	-3.7	-.1	.5	.6	1.2	1.5		.6	-1.0
Sales/Net Fixed Assets	58.5	45.1	18.8	8.4	4.7	4.9		18.2	20.0
	18.9	12.2	6.8	4.1	3.3	2.5		6.6	6.4
	7.2	4.3	3.4	2.4	2.5	2.0		3.2	3.1
Sales/Total Assets	9.0	5.4	4.1	2.8	2.1	2.0		4.6	4.5
	5.2	3.6	2.6	2.0	1.7	1.5		2.8	2.8
	2.8	2.1	1.8	1.4	1.4	1.2		1.8	1.7
% Depr., Dep., Amort./Sales	1.4	.9	1.8	2.6	3.6			2.0	1.9
	(143) 3.9	(199) 3.4	(313) 3.9	(135) 4.6	(23) 5.4			(907) 4.4	(910) 4.6
	7.3	7.8	7.1	7.9	8.4			7.7	8.7
% Officers', Directors' Owners' Comp/Sales	2.6	1.9	1.1	.8				1.6	1.3
	(100) 4.2	(126) 3.1	(138) 2.2	(25) 2.3				(411) 3.0	(396) 2.8
	6.8	5.4	4.2	2.9				6.2	5.9
Net Sales ($)	385779M	1336449M	4610440M	7721986M	4190219M	12957524M		26170393M	22125752M
Total Assets ($)	58959M	311883M	1560598M	3166592M	2221640M	3668765M		9074639M	9801992M

M = $ thousand   MM = $ million
See Pages 9 through 22 for Explanation of Ratios and Data

Comparative Historical Data | Current Data Sorted by Sales

			Type of Statement						
56	63	58	Unqualified			2		7	49
180	173	153	Reviewed	1	7	17	27	59	42
195	191	202	Compiled	23	45	25	44	52	13
233	274	267	Tax Returns	63	91	41	38	27	7
331	349	380	Other	48	64	39	64	73	92
4/1/08-3/31/09 ALL	4/1/09-3/31/10 ALL	4/1/10-3/31/11 ALL		132 (4/1-9/30/10)			928 (10/1/10-3/31/11)		
				0-1MM	1-3MM	3-5MM	5-10MM	10-25MM	25MM & OVER
995	1050	1060	NUMBER OF STATEMENTS	135	207	124	173	218	203
%	%	%	ASSETS	%	%	%	%	%	%
11.5	11.1	12.0	Cash & Equivalents	16.2	14.2	12.2	12.3	9.8	9.1
25.4	25.3	28.2	Trade Receivables (net)	17.1	25.3	27.0	29.6	35.6	30.0
1.8	2.1	1.7	Inventory	1.3	1.2	1.9	1.7	2.2	1.7
4.0	4.4	4.1	All Other Current	2.9	4.6	4.2	3.7	5.2	3.4
42.6	42.8	46.0	Total Current	37.6	45.2	45.3	47.3	52.8	44.2
44.9	43.5	41.0	Fixed Assets (net)	46.6	43.7	37.3	39.9	35.9	43.2
3.0	4.0	3.2	Intangibles (net)	3.2	2.6	3.9	2.7	2.4	4.6
9.4	9.7	9.8	All Other Non-Current	12.6	8.4	13.6	10.0	8.9	7.9
100.0	100.0	100.0	Total	100.0	100.0	100.0	100.0	100.0	100.0
			LIABILITIES						
10.8	11.0	10.3	Notes Payable-Short Term	13.4	13.7	8.4	8.7	10.8	6.8
9.0	9.5	8.3	Cur. Mat.-L.T.D.	8.3	10.2	7.6	8.2	7.8	7.6
10.5	10.5	10.9	Trade Payables	7.0	10.3	11.2	9.7	13.8	11.7
.3	.2	.2	Income Taxes Payable	.0	.2	.1	.1	.2	.2
11.0	10.6	11.0	All Other Current	18.2	12.9	8.1	9.2	8.7	10.2
41.6	41.8	40.7	Total Current	46.8	47.3	35.3	35.9	41.3	36.6
31.1	30.2	28.6	Long-Term Debt	35.5	36.4	32.4	25.6	22.7	22.6
.7	.9	.8	Deferred Taxes	.0	.2	.8	.7	.8	2.2
5.9	7.1	6.4	All Other Non-Current	11.1	8.2	9.8	3.5	4.6	3.7
20.6	20.1	23.4	Net Worth	6.4	8.0	21.6	34.2	30.5	34.9
100.0	100.0	100.0	Total Liabilities & Net Worth	100.0	100.0	100.0	100.0	100.0	100.0
			INCOME DATA						
100.0	100.0	100.0	Net Sales	100.0	100.0	100.0	100.0	100.0	100.0
			Gross Profit						
95.7	96.7	95.7	Operating Expenses	91.3	95.4	96.5	97.0	96.9	95.9
4.3	3.3	4.3	Operating Profit	8.7	4.6	3.5	3.0	3.1	4.1
1.5	1.6	.9	All Other Expenses (net)	2.9	.8	.7	.1	.6	.9
2.9	1.6	3.4	Profit Before Taxes	5.8	3.9	2.9	3.0	2.5	3.2
			RATIOS						
2.0	2.1	2.2	Current	2.2	3.2	2.8	2.7	2.1	1.7
1.1	1.1	1.2		.9	1.1	1.2	1.4	1.4	1.2
.6	.6	.7		.2	.5	.7	.8	.9	.9
1.7	1.8	2.0	Quick	2.2	2.9	2.6	2.4	1.8	1.5
1.0	.9 (1059)	1.1		.7	1.0 (123)	1.0	1.2	1.1	1.1
.5	.5	.6		.1	.4	.6	.7	.7	.8
9 41.7	11 31.8	12 29.3	Sales/Receivables	0 UND	0 UND	2 182.2	20 18.7	23 15.9	29 12.6
27 13.3	32 11.6	32 11.5		0 UND	24 15.1	30 12.1	32 11.5	35 10.3	39 9.5
42 8.7	46 8.0	47 7.7		44 8.3	47 7.8	47 7.8	47 7.8	48 7.6	49 7.4
			Cost of Sales/Inventory						
			Cost of Sales/Payables						
13.7	11.3	11.2	Sales/Working Capital	12.5	8.6	9.1	9.4	11.1	15.5
92.0	82.4	46.3		-93.7	72.7	47.4	33.1	29.3	35.2
-17.8	-16.6	-27.4		-4.9	-17.2	-24.4	-46.0	-51.8	-66.3
6.6	6.3	9.2	EBIT/Interest	10.0	8.6	9.0	11.1	9.1	8.5
(877) 2.3	(927) 1.9	(927) 3.2		(86) 2.9	(176) 2.7	(112) 2.4	(160) 4.0	(204) 3.1	(189) 3.9
.5	-.4	1.0		-.5	.8	.6	1.1	1.2	1.4
2.4	2.3	2.5	Net Profit + Depr., Dep., Amort./Cur. Mat. L/T/D		2.7	2.3	2.4	2.6	2.7
(199) 1.5	(188) 1.2	(177) 1.7		(12) 1.4	(20) 1.6	(23) 1.7	(55) 1.8	(64) 1.7	
1.0	.7	1.1		.7	.9	1.3	1.1	1.2	
.6	.6	.5	Fixed/Worth	.2	.5	.3	.5	.4	.7
1.7	1.7	1.3		2.2	1.5	1.1	1.2	1.2	1.3
13.8	25.5	6.6		-5.7	-5.7	20.9	3.4	3.3	2.7
1.0	.9	.8	Debt/Worth	.6	.8	.6	.7	1.0	1.1
2.8	2.7	2.2		3.3	3.3	1.9	1.7	2.2	2.1
28.8	UND	14.2		-6.9	-11.6	42.1	8.0	8.9	5.0
47.1	33.8	46.5	% Profit Before Taxes/Tangible Net Worth	70.4	70.9	47.9	44.8	44.4	37.4
(778) 19.4	(790) 10.6	(854) 18.9		(91) 15.5	(147) 27.0	(96) 12.1	(151) 22.5	(188) 17.5	(181) 18.8
2.7	-5.5	2.5		-1.3	5.0	.0	1.7	3.2	5.5
14.1	11.4	16.7	% Profit Before Taxes/Total Assets	16.8	24.6	16.3	16.7	15.6	13.6
4.7	2.7	6.1		5.2	7.9	4.3	7.3	5.9	5.8
-1.4	-5.8	.0		-5.0	-.2	-.7	.2	.8	1.4
21.5	22.3	28.8	Sales/Net Fixed Assets	30.9	26.7	35.3	26.8	35.5	18.8
7.2	7.7	8.2		7.4	8.4	12.0	8.1	10.5	4.9
3.3	3.0	3.6		2.0	3.9	4.3	3.9	4.3	2.9
5.0	4.8	5.0	Sales/Total Assets	4.6	6.0	5.4	5.0	5.0	4.0
3.0	2.7	2.9		2.1	3.3	3.4	3.2	3.3	2.4
1.8	1.6	1.8		.8	2.0	1.8	2.0	2.2	1.6
1.9	1.8	1.7	% Depr., Dep., Amort./Sales	3.2	1.8	1.2	2.0	1.3	1.4
(811) 4.6	(804) 5.0	(821) 3.9		(84) 8.6	(152) 5.0	(92) 3.8	(140) 3.7	(188) 3.2	(165) 3.5
7.9	8.9	7.6		16.7	9.7	6.8	6.7	5.9	7.1
1.5	1.6	1.5	% Officers', Directors' Owners' Comp/Sales	3.8	2.8	1.9	1.3	1.1	.7
(338) 2.7	(389) 3.4	(395) 3.0		(32) 5.9	(96) 4.2	(59) 2.7	(79) 2.1	(91) 2.3	(38) 1.8
5.7	6.2	5.4		12.5	6.2	5.6	3.8	4.1	3.1
20491156M	24314987M	31202397M	Net Sales ($)	69595M	379881M	490509M	1247479M	3376444M	25638489M
8263007M	11173569M	10988437M	Total Assets ($)	70767M	172514M	253064M	474945M	1318591M	8698556M

M = $ thousand   MM = $ million
See Pages 9 through 22 for Explanation of Ratios and Data

Current Data Sorted by Assets | Comparative Historical Data

0-500M	500M-2MM	2-10MM	10-50MM	50-100MM	100-250MM	Type of Statement	4/1/06-3/31/07 ALL	4/1/07-3/31/08 ALL
	3	10	47	30	32	Unqualified	176	137
6	23	116	101	5		Reviewed	281	251
18	74	126	24	2	1	Compiled	303	268
74	70	48	3	1	1	Tax Returns	170	147
38	108	154	150	42	41	Other	464	477
187 (4/1-9/30/10)			1,161 (10/1/10-3/31/11)					
136	278	454	325	80	75	**NUMBER OF STATEMENTS**	1394	1280
%	%	%	%	%	%	**ASSETS**	%	%
19.4	10.8	8.9	7.2	6.2	4.2	Cash & Equivalents	8.6	8.1
28.6	37.2	30.4	25.0	22.5	19.3	Trade Receivables (net)	27.6	28.1
.9	1.4	1.0	1.9	1.4	1.4	Inventory	1.2	1.5
6.7	5.5	4.9	4.4	4.6	5.4	All Other Current	4.3	4.7
55.6	54.9	45.3	38.5	34.7	30.2	Total Current	41.7	42.3
29.3	30.5	43.1	51.3	54.3	56.4	Fixed Assets (net)	48.1	46.7
1.2	3.0	1.9	3.0	4.0	8.3	Intangibles (net)	1.8	2.3
13.9	11.6	9.7	7.2	6.9	5.1	All Other Non-Current	8.4	8.6
100.0	100.0	100.0	100.0	100.0	100.0	Total	100.0	100.0
						LIABILITIES		
19.4	9.7	8.0	7.5	5.0	2.4	Notes Payable-Short Term	8.0	8.4
9.0	6.6	9.0	11.0	9.4	8.5	Cur. Mat.-L.T.D.	9.8	9.8
21.6	12.8	9.9	7.9	7.5	7.2	Trade Payables	9.5	9.5
.0	.1	.5	.2	.1	.1	Income Taxes Payable	.3	.2
17.1	13.0	10.0	7.2	9.0	9.0	All Other Current	10.5	9.7
67.1	42.2	37.3	33.7	31.0	27.2	Total Current	38.1	37.6
33.8	22.9	24.9	24.2	29.1	30.4	Long-Term Debt	31.2	30.2
.0	.3	.9	2.2	3.1	4.7	Deferred Taxes	1.4	1.4
8.6	9.6	3.1	3.6	4.0	4.5	All Other Non-Current	3.8	3.7
-9.5	25.1	33.9	36.3	32.7	33.3	Net Worth	25.6	27.1
100.0	100.0	100.0	100.0	100.0	100.0	Total Liabilities & Net Worth	100.0	100.0
						INCOME DATA		
100.0	100.0	100.0	100.0	100.0	100.0	Net Sales	100.0	100.0
						Gross Profit		
96.3	95.6	93.6	94.6	95.7	96.7	Operating Expenses	95.1	96.2
3.7	4.4	6.4	5.4	4.3	3.3	Operating Profit	4.9	3.8
.6	.7	1.7	1.1	1.4	1.9	All Other Expenses (net)	1.2	1.1
3.2	3.6	4.7	4.2	2.9	1.4	Profit Before Taxes	3.7	2.7
						RATIOS		
2.4	2.5	2.0	1.6	1.7	1.5		1.7	1.7
1.0	1.4	1.2	1.1	1.2	1.1	Current	1.1	1.1
.5	.9	.7	.8	.8	.8		.7	.7
2.2	2.2	1.7	1.4	1.4	1.2		1.5	1.5
(135) .9	1.2	1.1	.9	1.0	.9	Quick	.9	.9
.4	.7	.6	.6	.6	.6		.6	.6
0 UND	15 24.3	23 15.9	30 12.1	34 10.8	36 10.2		23 16.1	23 16.0
8 48.3	29 12.4	33 11.0	38 9.5	41 8.9	39 9.3	Sales/Receivables	32 11.2	33 11.0
28 13.0	44 8.3	42 8.6	46 7.9	51 7.1	43 8.4		42 8.7	44 8.4
						Cost of Sales/Inventory		
						Cost of Sales/Payables		
28.9	10.8	13.0	14.5	13.4	18.0		18.1	16.4
617.2	33.3	44.4	67.8	38.5	50.8	Sales/Working Capital	124.0	70.1
-16.4	-70.2	-28.5	-26.1	-27.6	-29.7		-24.5	-23.1
7.5	11.5	7.9	7.3	4.7	4.7		6.0	4.5
(92) 2.1	(232) 3.2	(409) 3.4	(310) 3.3	(74) 2.5	(74) 2.1	EBIT/Interest	(1285) 2.6	(1173) 2.0
-.7	.8	1.5	1.7	1.1	.4		1.3	.7
	3.3	2.9	2.3	2.5		Net Profit + Depr., Dep.,	2.3	2.3
	(30) 1.7	(99) 1.7	(132) 1.4	(27) 1.4		Amort./Cur. Mat. L/T/D	(379) 1.5	(336) 1.3
	1.0	1.1	1.0	.8			1.0	.9
.1	.2	.6	1.0	1.1	1.2		.8	.7
1.0	.9	1.3	1.6	1.8	2.2	Fixed/Worth	1.9	1.8
-2.5	6.9	3.2	2.9	3.4	4.8		4.8	4.3
.8	.9	.9	.9	.9	1.1		1.3	1.2
8.5	2.6	1.9	2.1	2.2	2.4	Debt/Worth	2.8	2.7
-3.1	111.6	5.2	4.6	4.3	6.9		7.8	7.4
107.0	64.9	40.3	29.6	23.0	28.4	% Profit Before Taxes/Tangible	46.5	33.3
(87) 37.7	(212) 22.1	(404) 20.1	(304) 16.8	(72) 9.2	(66) 11.6	Net Worth	(1210) 22.5	(1108) 12.9
-2.2	2.3	4.6	6.5	2.5	-.3		7.2	.0
28.7	18.5	13.5	9.6	6.8	7.1	% Profit Before Taxes/Total	13.4	10.3
5.4	7.6	6.8	5.4	3.9	2.7	Assets	5.5	3.5
-7.0	.2	1.5	2.3	.6	-1.6		1.1	-1.0
999.8	105.8	22.1	7.1	5.6	4.7		16.2	17.5
56.4	17.5	6.8	3.9	3.3	3.0	Sales/Net Fixed Assets	5.3	5.7
11.4	6.4	3.5	2.5	2.3	2.2		2.7	2.8
12.3	6.1	4.3	2.7	2.5	2.2		4.4	4.4
7.2	4.3	3.0	2.1	1.8	1.7	Sales/Total Assets	2.7	2.7
4.2	2.6	2.0	1.5	1.4	1.4		1.7	1.7
.5	.7	1.6	3.5	3.9	2.2		1.9	1.9
(67) 3.1	(185) 2.9	(396) 4.4	(306) 6.4	(56) 5.8	(11) 2.8	% Depr., Dep., Amort./Sales	(1157) 4.9	(1069) 4.9
6.8	6.7	7.7	9.5	7.8	5.6		8.2	8.3
1.8	1.4	.9	.4	1.1		% Officers', Directors'	1.1	1.2
(57) 3.9	(115) 2.8	(151) 1.8	(74) 1.3	(11) 1.4		Owners' Comp/Sales	(468) 2.3	(392) 2.5
7.0	5.2	3.3	4.3	6.0			4.8	5.4
288089M	1519388M	7300254M	18182770M	11146149M	26151593M	Net Sales ($)	59769526M	55675103M
31637M	323404M	2282483M	7845403M	5347869M	11520109M	Total Assets ($)	25756691M	25058200M

© RMA 2011

M = $ thousand   MM = $ million
See Pages 9 through 22 for Explanation of Ratios and Data

Comparative Historical Data

Current Data Sorted by Sales

			Type of Statement						
142	140	122	Unqualified		3	1	1	10	107
237	231	251	Reviewed	5	9	13	25	82	117
255	214	245	Compiled	16	29	29	59	68	44
166	161	197	Tax Returns	32	56	33	37	31	8
490	463	533	Other	28	55	47	66	112	225
4/1/08-	4/1/09-	4/1/10-			187 (4/1-9/30/10)		1,161 (10/1/10-3/31/11)		
3/31/09	3/31/10	3/31/11							
ALL	ALL	ALL		0-1MM	1-3MM	3-5MM	5-10MM	10-25MM	25MM & OVER
1290	1209	1348	NUMBER OF STATEMENTS	81	152	123	188	303	501
%	%	%	ASSETS	%	%	%	%	%	%
9.7	9.6	9.5	Cash & Equivalents	14.5	14.4	12.6	8.4	8.9	7.3
26.8	26.8	29.2	Trade Receivables (net)	13.3	27.0	29.8	33.4	31.4	29.5
1.4	1.4	1.3	Inventory	.5	.9	.8	2.0	1.1	1.7
5.0	5.5	5.1	All Other Current	9.0	4.5	6.1	5.3	4.6	4.7
42.9	43.3	45.2	Total Current	37.3	46.7	49.3	49.1	45.8	43.1
46.0	45.7	42.5	Fixed Assets (net)	51.1	38.0	37.4	36.8	42.0	46.2
2.2	2.8	2.8	Intangibles (net)	1.8	3.7	1.5	2.1	2.5	3.5
8.9	8.2	9.5	All Other Non-Current	9.9	11.6	11.8	12.0	9.8	7.2
100.0	100.0	100.0	Total	100.0	100.0	100.0	100.0	100.0	100.0
			LIABILITIES						
8.4	10.5	8.9	Notes Payable-Short Term	12.7	7.9	12.4	11.5	8.3	7.1
10.2	10.2	9.0	Cur. Mat.-L.T.D.	8.9	7.4	9.4	7.1	9.8	9.5
9.6	9.7	10.9	Trade Payables	14.0	11.9	10.9	11.9	11.7	9.3
.2	.1	.2	Income Taxes Payable	.0	.0	.1	.2	.5	.2
10.7	11.2	10.5	All Other Current	11.5	12.9	9.7	12.3	9.6	9.8
39.1	41.8	39.5	Total Current	47.1	40.2	42.4	43.1	39.8	35.9
28.6	26.8	25.8	Long-Term Debt	37.0	25.5	34.0	25.2	24.3	23.1
1.3	1.5	1.3	Deferred Taxes	.1	.3	.4	.7	1.1	2.4
4.6	5.1	5.2	All Other Non-Current	3.0	10.2	12.9	5.0	3.0	3.7
26.3	24.9	28.2	Net Worth	12.9	23.8	10.4	26.0	31.8	34.9
100.0	100.0	100.0	Total Liabilties & Net Worth	100.0	100.0	100.0	100.0	100.0	100.0
			INCOME DATA						
100.0	100.0	100.0	Net Sales	100.0	100.0	100.0	100.0	100.0	100.0
			Gross Profit						
95.9	96.6	94.8	Operating Expenses	73.5	93.7	96.2	96.5	96.5	96.7
4.1	3.4	5.2	Operating Profit	26.5	6.3	3.8	3.5	3.5	3.3
1.3	1.5	1.2	All Other Expenses (net)	8.4	1.1	1.1	.6	.6	.8
2.8	1.9	3.9	Profit Before Taxes	18.1	5.2	2.8	2.9	2.9	2.5
			RATIOS						
1.8	1.9	1.9		2.6	2.8	2.6	2.1	1.8	1.7
1.1	1.1	1.2	Current	1.0	1.3	1.3	1.2	1.2	1.2
.7	.7	.8		.3	.6	.7	.7	.8	.8
1.5	1.6	1.6		2.0	2.3	2.4	1.7	1.6	1.5
.9 (1207)	.9 (1347)	1.0	Quick	.6 (151)	1.1	1.1	1.0	1.0	1.0
.6	.5	.6		.5	.5	.7	.7	.7	.7
18 19.8	21 17.4	21 17.2		0 UND	1 585.1	5 80.9	19 19.5	24 15.1	32 11.4
28 13.0	34 10.8	34 10.7	Sales/Receivables	0 UND	22 16.7	30 12.3	29 12.4	33 11.1	39 9.4
38 9.7	44 8.4	44 8.3		32 11.3	44 8.3	40 9.0	40 9.0	42 8.6	45 8.1
			Cost of Sales/Inventory						
			Cost of Sales/Payables						
16.0	13.5	14.1		7.1	10.1	12.0	15.7	14.5	15.1
72.4	82.4	50.6	Sales/Working Capital	-115.5	44.6	38.3	68.2	66.8	42.7
-26.7	-17.4	-29.1		-3.1	-19.2	-37.2	-30.5	-31.7	-44.0
4.9	4.9	7.8		8.1	9.5	8.4	7.2	7.6	7.7
(1173) 2.0	(1078) 1.7 (1191)	3.1	EBIT/Interest	(48) 4.0	(113) 2.6	(108) 2.6	(170) 2.6	(276) 3.4	(476) 3.2
.7	-.3	1.3		1.0	-.5	.3	.8	1.5	1.6
2.2	2.0	2.7			3.4	2.0	3.2	3.0	2.5
(302) 1.3	(273) 1.2 (295)	1.5	Net Profit + Depr., Dep.,	(13) 2.0	(15) 1.5	(27) 1.4	(68) 1.5	(171) 1.4
.9	.8	1.0	Amort./Cur. Mat. L/T/D		.3	1.0	1.0	1.1	1.0
.7	.7	.6		.4	.2	.3	.2	.6	.8
1.8	1.7	1.5	Fixed/Worth	2.0	1.3	1.6	1.2	1.3	1.5
4.8	4.6	3.6		15.4	6.7	-11.7	5.4	3.1	2.9
1.1	1.0	.9		.7	.7	.9	.9	1.0	1.0
2.5	2.5	2.2	Debt/Worth	3.1	2.1	3.4	2.7	1.9	2.0
7.6	8.8	7.2		UND	69.4	-11.7	13.0	5.2	4.9
32.9	28.7	40.0	% Profit Before Taxes/Tangible	77.6	60.0	50.5	55.5	41.8	32.5
(1088) 13.4	(1004) 8.5 (1145)	17.9	Net Worth	(61) 25.6	(117) 20.5	(88) 19.4	(149) 15.8	(266) 20.3	(464) 16.7
1.3	-6.3	4.4		3.5	1.2	.1	1.0	6.2	5.2
10.1	8.7	13.0	% Profit Before Taxes/Total	19.1	17.6	17.3	16.7	13.4	10.1
3.5	2.2	5.7	Assets	5.7	5.5	5.6	6.5	6.6	5.2
-.8	-4.1	.8		.0	-2.0	-1.8	-.4	1.8	1.5
20.2	19.8	24.8		21.4	67.9	44.3	78.0	24.1	12.0
5.9	5.7	6.4	Sales/Net Fixed Assets	3.3	11.0	12.7	11.6	7.3	4.6
3.1	2.7	3.2		.3	3.6	4.5	4.6	3.5	2.9
4.6	4.3	4.6		4.3	5.9	6.5	5.7	4.6	3.7
2.8	2.6	2.8	Sales/Total Assets	.9	3.1	3.9	4.0	2.9	2.3
1.8	1.6	1.8		.2	1.6	2.3	2.4	2.0	1.7
2.0	2.1	1.8		4.7	1.9	2.1	.8	1.6	2.1
(1009) 5.0	(942) 5.7 (1021)	4.9	% Depr., Dep., Amort./Sales	(55) 15.4	(94) 6.3	(83) 4.0	(144) 4.0	(266) 4.5	(379) 4.9
8.1	9.8	8.0		29.6	14.3	9.8	7.1	7.4	7.5
1.2	1.5	1.1		3.2	1.8	1.6	1.4	.9	.6
(395) 2.6	(353) 2.8 (417)	2.3	% Officers', Directors'	(16) 5.4	(57) 3.8	(54) 3.1	(75) 2.3	(109) 1.6	(106) 1.4
5.4	6.0	4.5	Owners' Comp/Sales	18.8	8.9	5.3	3.8	2.8	3.8
65282580M	49389067M	64588243M	Net Sales ($)	35414M	310610M	494082M	1381943M	4887711M	57478483M
27427207M	24328149M	27350905M	Total Assets ($)	91849M	225096M	253329M	627918M	2030370M	24122343M

M = $ thousand   MM = $ million
See Pages 9 through 22 for Explanation of Ratios and Data

Current Data Sorted by Assets   Comparative Historical Data

Type of Statement

0-500M	500M-2MM	2-10MM	10-50MM	50-100MM	100-250MM	Type of Statement	4/1/06-3/31/07 ALL	4/1/07-3/31/08 ALL
		3	5	4	7	Unqualified	26	22
3	1	9	9	1	2	Reviewed	21	20
2	7	4	6			Compiled	26	27
3	4	3				Tax Returns	11	11
4	9	12	13	3	9	Other	44	44
	17 (4/1-9/30/10)		106 (10/1/10-3/31/11)					
12	21	31	33	8	18	**NUMBER OF STATEMENTS**	128	124
%	%	%	%	%	%	**ASSETS**	%	%
20.2	11.8	6.8	9.3		4.8	Cash & Equivalents	8.3	7.4
35.6	36.6	35.9	21.2		21.6	Trade Receivables (net)	27.5	26.4
.1	.5	1.5	2.7		1.9	Inventory	1.7	2.1
10.1	6.2	2.5	5.0		4.0	All Other Current	3.1	5.7
66.0	55.1	46.7	38.2		32.3	Total Current	40.6	41.5
22.9	36.6	45.2	53.5		58.1	Fixed Assets (net)	47.8	47.8
1.7	1.9	1.8	1.9		2.7	Intangibles (net)	4.2	2.9
9.4	6.3	6.3	6.4		7.0	All Other Non-Current	7.5	7.8
100.0	100.0	100.0	100.0		100.0	Total	100.0	100.0
						LIABILITIES		
10.2	10.6	7.0	4.5		1.4	Notes Payable-Short Term	5.6	7.0
8.9	8.8	10.6	11.2		6.6	Cur. Mat.-L.T.D.	10.1	10.1
15.4	16.9	10.7	9.4		7.4	Trade Payables	8.9	11.5
.3	.0	.3	.2		.1	Income Taxes Payable	.1	.2
10.8	12.9	8.7	7.3		12.1	All Other Current	10.9	10.8
45.6	49.3	37.3	32.5		27.5	Total Current	35.5	39.6
50.4	21.0	22.0	28.8		25.7	Long-Term Debt	30.8	30.4
.0	.7	1.0	2.9		1.2	Deferred Taxes	1.8	1.0
1.2	9.5	6.0	1.1		8.6	All Other Non-Current	2.0	4.3
2.7	19.6	33.7	34.6		37.0	Net Worth	29.9	24.7
100.0	100.0	100.0	100.0		100.0	Total Liabilities & Net Worth	100.0	100.0
						INCOME DATA		
100.0	100.0	100.0	100.0		100.0	Net Sales	100.0	100.0
						Gross Profit		
101.0	99.7	93.7	93.1		97.3	Operating Expenses	95.7	94.8
-1.0	.3	6.3	6.9		2.7	Operating Profit	4.3	5.2
.9	-.6	3.9	2.0		1.3	All Other Expenses (net)	1.3	2.0
-1.9	.9	2.3	5.0		1.4	Profit Before Taxes	3.1	3.3
						RATIOS		
5.5	3.7	2.2	1.9		1.4	Current	1.7	1.5
1.6	1.2	1.2	1.3		1.3		1.2	1.0
.7	.5	.7	.8		.9		.8	.7
4.3	3.5	2.2	1.7		1.3	Quick	1.6	1.2
1.2	1.1	1.1	1.0		1.1		1.0 (123)	.9
.7	.4	.7	.5		.7		.7	.6
2 229.0	10 36.5	26 14.3	28 13.2		39 9.4	Sales/Receivables	26 14.3	24 15.4
18 20.4	30 12.1	36 10.0	39 9.5		40 9.1		35 10.4	34 10.7
47 7.8	37 9.8	48 7.6	42 8.7		44 8.3		42 8.7	43 8.6
						Cost of Sales/Inventory		
						Cost of Sales/Payables		
7.2	11.6	14.6	9.2		17.9	Sales/Working Capital	15.9	21.8
33.4	54.9	49.7	38.1		39.5		48.1	512.1
NM	-13.2	-20.3	-25.0		-71.0		-48.8	-20.9
	8.9	16.8	6.3		4.3	EBIT/Interest	5.6	6.4
	(20) 2.2	(27) 3.5	(32) 2.5		1.7		(111) 3.0	(112) 2.0
	-.2	1.1	1.3		-.2		1.7	.6
			2.6			Net Profit + Depr., Dep., Amort./Cur. Mat. L/T/D	2.1	2.1
			(13) 1.4				(45) 1.4	(31) 1.3
			1.1				.9	.9
.0	.4	.4	.8		1.0	Fixed/Worth	.9	.9
.2	1.7	1.5	1.8		1.6		1.9	1.9
NM	-4.9	7.3	4.1		2.7		4.5	5.3
.3	.8	.9	.7		.8	Debt/Worth	1.1	1.2
.9	3.1	1.6	2.1		1.4		2.4	2.7
-4.1	-7.9	15.3	6.2		2.7		8.8	8.3
	98.6	33.9	23.2		16.6	% Profit Before Taxes/Tangible Net Worth	43.7	43.0
	(15) 23.0	(25) 17.9	(30) 12.7		(15) 6.8		(107) 23.6	(105) 15.6
	.0	2.4	2.1		-4.8		10.1	.7
10.4	18.4	14.2	7.8		6.9	% Profit Before Taxes/Total Assets	13.1	9.8
2.0	5.1	5.4	3.4		1.3		6.0	3.8
-11.6	-3.5	.4	.6		-3.0		2.9	-1.1
UND	49.5	18.4	6.3		5.0	Sales/Net Fixed Assets	16.3	13.3
43.7	29.9	8.9	3.6		3.4		5.1	5.0
8.4	6.6	3.5	2.7		1.8		2.6	2.7
9.8	6.9	4.4	3.1		2.3	Sales/Total Assets	4.1	3.5
4.1	5.3	3.9	1.8		2.0		2.6	2.6
2.1	3.4	2.0	1.6		1.3		1.6	1.7
	.6	.9	2.6			% Depr., Dep., Amort./Sales	1.7	2.2
	(17) 3.1	(27) 3.7	(32) 5.7				(98) 4.6	(99) 5.3
	7.3	6.8	8.6				7.0	8.3
						% Officers', Directors' Owners' Comp/Sales	1.5	1.4
							(36) 3.6	(32) 2.6
							5.3	4.9
21883M	117093M	535585M	1696749M	1347043M	5503920M	Net Sales ($)	9800860M	8216990M
2919M	22680M	154663M	817757M	540740M	2946733M	Total Assets ($)	4670421M	3550159M

M = $ thousand   MM = $ million

See Pages 9 through 22 for Explanation of Ratios and Data

Comparative Historical Data | Current Data Sorted by Sales

			Type of Statement	0-1MM	1-3MM	3-5MM	5-10MM	10-25MM	25MM & OVER
25	19	19	Unqualified					4	15
19	16	25	Reviewed	4		1		6	14
19	16	19	Compiled	2	1	3	3	5	5
7	13	10	Tax Returns	3	1		4	2	5
49	36	50	Other	2	4	4	7	7	26
4/1/08-3/31/09 ALL	4/1/09-3/31/10 ALL	4/1/10-3/31/11 ALL		17 (4/1-9/30/10)			106 (10/1/10-3/31/11)		
119	100	123	**NUMBER OF STATEMENTS**	11	6	8	14	24	60
%	%	%	**ASSETS**	%	%	%	%	%	%
8.0	8.2	9.1	Cash & Equivalents	6.6			18.4	9.2	6.6
27.5	28.9	29.3	Trade Receivables (net)	30.8			30.0	39.7	24.6
2.1	1.6	1.6	Inventory	.0			2.5	.5	2.2
4.3	3.5	5.3	All Other Current	10.2			2.5	4.3	5.1
42.0	42.2	45.2	Total Current	47.7			53.4	53.7	38.4
45.6	47.6	46.0	Fixed Assets (net)	41.6			39.3	38.4	52.8
3.6	2.4	1.9	Intangibles (net)	1.9			3.2	1.6	1.9
8.7	7.8	6.9	All Other Non-Current	8.8			4.0	6.3	6.9
100.0	100.0	100.0	Total	100.0			100.0	100.0	100.0
			LIABILITIES						
5.2	6.1	6.3	Notes Payable-Short Term	3.7			6.6	4.7	5.5
8.8	9.3	9.5	Cur. Mat.-L.T.D.	4.7			9.7	9.6	10.2
8.8	8.4	11.4	Trade Payables	13.2			9.9	16.6	9.6
.2	.1	.2	Income Taxes Payable	.0			.0	.3	.2
11.5	11.9	10.4	All Other Current	11.3			11.4	8.7	11.0
34.4	35.8	37.8	Total Current	32.8			37.5	39.8	36.5
28.0	26.6	27.2	Long-Term Debt	42.6			39.5	16.7	25.5
1.3	1.5	1.5	Deferred Taxes	.0			1.0	.8	2.5
3.5	3.4	5.4	All Other Non-Current	3.6			.3	6.1	4.7
32.8	32.7	28.2	Net Worth	21.0			21.7	36.7	30.7
100.0	100.0	100.0	Total Liabilities & Net Worth	100.0			100.0	100.0	100.0
			INCOME DATA						
100.0	100.0	100.0	Net Sales	100.0			100.0	100.0	100.0
			Gross Profit						
93.0	96.0	96.2	Operating Expenses	91.8			89.3	97.5	97.4
7.0	4.0	3.8	Operating Profit	8.2			10.7	2.5	2.6
2.8	2.8	1.8	All Other Expenses (net)	10.9			1.0	.6	1.1
4.2	1.2	2.1	Profit Before Taxes	-2.6			9.8	1.9	1.5
			RATIOS						
1.7	1.9	2.1		6.7			3.5	2.2	1.5
1.2	1.2	1.2	Current	1.2			1.5	1.7	1.2
.7	.8	.7		.3			.9	.7	.8
1.5	1.7	1.7		5.0			3.4	2.2	1.3
1.0	1.0	1.1	Quick	1.2			1.1	1.4	1.0
.6	.6	.6		.3			.4	.7	.6
22 16.6	31 11.7	26 14.3		0 UND			0 UND	32 11.5	31 11.9
30 12.3	37 9.9	38 9.6	Sales/Receivables	24 15.0			25 14.4	39 9.3	39 9.4
39 9.3	47 7.7	44 8.3		52 7.1			46 7.9	48 7.7	43 8.5
			Cost of Sales/Inventory						
			Cost of Sales/Payables						
16.9	14.2	11.8		6.9			8.1	11.9	16.5
49.6	37.1	46.4	Sales/Working Capital	46.4			27.0	17.3	50.9
-23.1	-25.1	-20.3		-3.3			-755.0	-21.6	-22.6
6.8	3.6	7.0					44.8	23.6	4.2
(100) 2.7	(89) 1.4	(109) 2.3	EBIT/Interest	(13) 9.3			(21) 3.5	(59) 1.9	
.9	-.2	.3					2.5	1.6	-.1
2.7	2.2	2.1							2.5
(33) 1.2	(29) 1.3	(30) 1.3	Net Profit + Depr., Dep., Amort./Cur. Mat. L/T/D					(19) 1.2	
.9	.8	.7							.7
.6	.6	.5		.0			.4	.3	.9
1.8	1.6	1.8	Fixed/Worth	.5			1.1	1.2	1.7
8.3	3.1	6.6		6.6			NM	3.4	4.4
1.1	1.0	.8		.4			.5	.9	1.0
2.0	1.9	1.9	Debt/Worth	.8			1.7	1.2	1.9
18.7	5.4	9.8		7.3			NM	4.6	6.2
41.2	19.7	25.0					79.5	34.5	20.5
(98) 16.7	(86) 6.4	(100) 13.0	% Profit Before Taxes/Tangible Net Worth				(11) 22.5	(21) 18.8	(51) 12.2
3.1	-3.3	.7					15.5	3.2	.1
11.0	6.7	10.5		8.1			41.0	17.0	6.7
4.8	1.1	2.9	% Profit Before Taxes/Total Assets	.4			10.5	7.0	1.8
-.3	-2.7	-2.4		-18.0			4.2	1.3	-2.9
22.3	14.5	16.6		UND			60.8	34.9	8.2
5.3	5.5	5.7	Sales/Net Fixed Assets	12.8			14.8	9.7	4.3
2.6	2.4	3.1		.5			5.1	3.2	2.7
4.5	3.9	4.4		3.7			6.3	5.6	3.2
2.5	2.2	2.7	Sales/Total Assets	1.8			4.9	3.9	2.2
1.7	1.5	1.8		.5			2.3	1.9	1.6
1.8	2.5	2.1					.5	.6	3.0
(91) 4.4	(73) 5.0	(91) 4.3	% Depr., Dep., Amort./Sales				(11) 3.1	(21) 2.7	(44) 4.5
7.5	8.3	7.4					8.0	6.1	6.7
1.4	1.2	1.0							.9
(29) 2.2	(30) 2.5	(27) 2.2	% Officers', Directors' Owners' Comp/Sales					(10) 1.1	
2.9	6.2	4.4							9.5
8616177M	5623594M	9222273M	Net Sales ($)	5385M	11417M	29330M	98687M	397862M	8679592M
3827601M	2974051M	4485492M	Total Assets ($)	8781M	2953M	7519M	99916M	141857M	4224466M

Current Data Sorted by Assets   Comparative Historical Data

						Type of Statement		
1		4	7		2	Unqualified	10	7
2	7	25	8			Reviewed	33	32
8	23	8	3			Compiled	24	18
24	16	8			1	Tax Returns	27	15
9	24	20	9	1	3	Other	47	36
	17 (4/1-9/30/10)		**196 (10/1/10-3/31/11)**				**4/1/06-3/31/07**	**4/1/07-3/31/08**
0-500M	**500M-2MM**	**2-10MM**	**10-50MM**	**50-100MM**	**100-250MM**		**ALL**	**ALL**
44	70	65	27	1	6	NUMBER OF STATEMENTS	141	108
%	%	%	%	%	%	ASSETS	%	%
21.4	13.0	12.1	9.7			Cash & Equivalents	9.0	9.8
24.3	30.1	30.7	32.9			Trade Receivables (net)	29.5	28.0
2.1	1.1	1.8	1.1			Inventory	.7	1.7
3.9	3.9	5.1	5.0			All Other Current	5.6	6.7
51.8	48.1	49.6	48.7			Total Current	44.9	46.1
34.0	31.9	37.3	34.5			Fixed Assets (net)	38.9	38.4
2.8	5.1	2.0	4.7			Intangibles (net)	2.9	3.6
11.4	14.9	11.1	12.1			All Other Non-Current	13.3	11.9
100.0	100.0	100.0	100.0			Total	100.0	100.0
						LIABILITIES		
15.9	7.8	5.6	6.0			Notes Payable-Short Term	8.1	8.5
5.7	8.9	6.2	5.5			Cur. Mat.-L.T.D.	6.7	8.3
10.9	9.0	10.3	13.4			Trade Payables	9.7	9.6
.1	.4	.1	.1			Income Taxes Payable	.3	.1
28.9	12.0	10.7	11.1			All Other Current	9.2	11.2
61.5	38.2	33.0	36.2			Total Current	33.9	37.7
30.3	23.5	22.9	20.5			Long-Term Debt	27.7	27.7
.2	.7	1.1	.8			Deferred Taxes	.8	.9
19.1	11.1	3.8	4.4			All Other Non-Current	8.9	10.1
-11.1	26.6	39.3	38.1			Net Worth	28.7	23.6
100.0	100.0	100.0	100.0			Total Liabilties & Net Worth	100.0	100.0
						INCOME DATA		
100.0	100.0	100.0	100.0			Net Sales	100.0	100.0
						Gross Profit		
93.6	90.8	91.2	94.1			Operating Expenses	95.6	98.1
6.4	9.2	8.8	5.9			Operating Profit	4.4	1.9
.7	2.9	3.7	.3			All Other Expenses (net)	1.8	.9
5.7	6.4	5.1	5.6			Profit Before Taxes	2.6	1.0
						RATIOS		
3.6	3.1	2.4	1.8				2.2	2.0
1.2	1.5	1.6	1.5			Current	1.3	1.3
.6	.7	1.0	1.1				1.0	.8
3.3	2.8	2.0	1.6				1.9	1.6
.8	1.4	1.3	1.3			Quick	1.1	1.1
.4	.5	.9	.8				.8	.6
0 UND	14 26.1	26 14.2	39 9.4				20 18.2	21 17.3
16 23.2	29 12.4	37 9.7	50 7.2			Sales/Receivables	34 10.6	38 9.6
34 10.8	49 7.4	57 6.4	63 5.8				55 6.6	52 7.1
						Cost of Sales/Inventory		
						Cost of Sales/Payables		
12.5	8.2	9.1	8.2				11.1	10.7
93.6	29.6	17.4	14.0			Sales/Working Capital	34.6	26.7
-19.4	-18.2	NM	39.5				-339.2	-40.4
14.0	17.0	19.5	12.5				5.8	4.0
(34) 1.7	(62) 3.5	(52) 3.4	(23) 2.9			EBIT/Interest	(125) 2.4	(98) 2.1
-.1	1.0	1.7	1.8				1.2	.4
	3.8	3.3	12.8				3.3	4.1
(11)	1.2 (25)	1.5 (16)	3.6			Net Profit + Depr., Dep., Amort./Cur. Mat. L/T/D	1.6 (27)	1.8
	1.1	.7	1.4				1.1	.9
.5	.3	.3	.5				.5	.6
3.6	.8	1.0	.7			Fixed/Worth	1.2	1.2
-.9	5.9	3.4	2.1				3.7	5.1
.8	.5	.7	.7				1.0	1.0
16.4	1.7	1.4	2.2			Debt/Worth	2.1	2.2
-2.8	15.8	6.2	4.0				7.2	10.0
145.7	41.5	43.9	51.4				42.8	36.0
(26) 62.0	(56) 18.3	(59) 14.4	(26) 16.9			% Profit Before Taxes/Tangible Net Worth	(122) 15.4	(89) 9.1
-1.2	.4	1.4	6.2				2.5	-1.6
43.3	23.2	12.1	18.1				11.9	9.8
6.9	5.1	6.3	3.8			% Profit Before Taxes/Total Assets	4.7	3.6
-2.8	-.1	1.8	2.0				.7	-3.0
53.7	38.4	30.5	21.2				21.2	16.7
20.1	14.0	9.3	7.3			Sales/Net Fixed Assets	8.5	8.3
6.0	5.9	3.3	2.4				4.3	3.6
7.6	4.6	3.8	3.1				3.8	3.7
4.4	2.9	2.6	2.1			Sales/Total Assets	2.7	2.6
3.1	2.2	1.5	1.1				1.9	1.7
1.4	1.4	1.4	1.7				1.7	1.6
(28) 2.6	(58) 2.7	(57) 2.6	(25) 2.8			% Depr., Dep., Amort./Sales	(118) 3.2	(94) 2.8
5.4	4.1	5.9	4.3				5.4	4.4
4.0	2.8	1.6					2.3	1.5
(19) 11.3	(33) 5.0	(15) 2.0				% Officers', Directors' Owners' Comp/Sales	(54) 4.4	(32) 4.3
14.2	7.3	5.1					8.8	9.3
56167M	249066M	773373M	1231733M	72813M	2724180M	Net Sales ($)	2657587M	2639031M
11127M	76444M	289511M	550202M	68131M	968415M	Total Assets ($)	1217296M	1289952M

© RMA 2011

M = $ thousand   MM = $ million
See Pages 9 through 22 for Explanation of Ratios and Data

Comparative Historical Data				Current Data Sorted by Sales					
			Type of Statement						
9	8	14	Unqualified	1	1		1	2	9
29	43	42	Reviewed		5	3	12	15	7
31	39	42	Compiled	6	12	11	8	4	1
34	34	49	Tax Returns	21	10	8	6	3	1
43	64	66	Other	12	14	10	6	13	11
4/1/08-3/31/09 ALL	4/1/09-3/31/10 ALL	4/1/10-3/31/11 ALL		17 (4/1-9/30/10)			196 (10/1/10-3/31/11)		
				0-1MM	1-3MM	3-5MM	5-10MM	10-25MM	25MM & OVER
146	188	213	**NUMBER OF STATEMENTS**	40	42	32	33	37	29
%	%	%	**ASSETS**	%	%	%	%	%	%
12.4	12.5	13.8	Cash & Equivalents	12.5	18.4	9.7	18.9	12.0	9.9
31.1	30.0	29.8	Trade Receivables (net)	13.2	31.2	31.8	29.5	34.6	42.8
1.0	.5	1.5	Inventory	2.2	.8	1.3	2.0	1.5	1.3
5.4	5.5	4.4	All Other Current	2.2	4.1	4.7	4.1	6.3	5.6
50.0	48.5	49.5	Total Current	30.1	54.5	47.5	54.5	54.4	59.6
31.5	33.9	34.4	Fixed Assets (net)	53.9	30.9	29.1	33.0	29.1	26.8
3.5	4.3	3.6	Intangibles (net)	3.3	4.1	5.4	1.5	3.2	4.0
15.0	13.4	12.5	All Other Non-Current	12.7	10.5	18.0	11.0	13.3	9.6
100.0	100.0	100.0	Total	100.0	100.0	100.0	100.0	100.0	100.0
			LIABILITIES						
8.1	8.4	8.9	Notes Payable-Short Term	10.3	12.6	10.4	4.4	6.8	8.1
8.7	8.4	6.8	Cur. Mat.-L.T.D.	4.2	9.3	6.6	10.5	5.7	4.1
10.2	10.3	10.6	Trade Payables	3.0	11.5	11.5	9.7	11.8	18.3
.1	.3	.2	Income Taxes Payable	.1	.2	.6	.3	.1	.0
12.5	16.7	14.9	All Other Current	16.0	23.6	8.9	15.5	10.7	12.1
39.6	44.1	41.4	Total Current	33.6	57.1	38.0	40.4	35.0	42.7
26.1	26.0	24.3	Long-Term Debt	37.7	28.5	21.8	20.2	17.1	16.0
.9	.3	.8	Deferred Taxes	.4	.4	.7	1.8	.7	.8
13.9	8.1	9.8	All Other Non-Current	8.7	16.6	18.5	4.3	2.6	7.0
19.4	21.4	23.8	Net Worth	19.7	-2.7	21.0	33.2	44.6	33.6
100.0	100.0	100.0	Total Liabilities & Net Worth	100.0	100.0	100.0	100.0	100.0	100.0
			INCOME DATA						
100.0	100.0	100.0	Net Sales	100.0	100.0	100.0	100.0	100.0	100.0
			Gross Profit						
97.7	97.2	92.1	Operating Expenses	75.7	93.2	96.4	98.1	96.0	96.8
2.3	2.8	7.9	Operating Profit	24.3	6.8	3.6	1.9	4.0	3.2
1.3	2.0	2.3	All Other Expenses (net)	9.9	2.2	.1	-.1	-.2	.3
1.0	.7	5.6	Profit Before Taxes	14.4	4.5	3.5	2.0	4.2	2.9
			RATIOS						
2.3	2.9	2.5		3.7	4.3	2.6	2.3	2.4	1.8
1.3	1.4	1.5	Current	1.2	1.4	1.2	1.5	1.6	1.6
1.0	.7	.7		.4	.6	.8	.8	1.2	1.2
2.0	2.4	2.3		3.1	3.8	2.2	1.9	2.2	1.6
1.1	1.2	1.2	Quick	.8	1.2	1.2	1.1	1.3	1.3
.7	.6	.7		.2	.5	.7	.7	.9	1.2
16 23.1	19 19.7	17 21.7		0 UND	11 34.4	20 18.4	22 16.9	33 11.0	39 9.4
33 11.1	38 9.7	35 10.3	Sales/Receivables	10 36.6	33 11.1	35 10.5	35 10.6	38 9.6	50 7.2
49 7.5	57 6.4	53 6.9		29 12.5	55 6.7	55 6.6	49 7.5	64 5.7	62 5.9
			Cost of Sales/Inventory						
			Cost of Sales/Payables						
11.9	9.0	9.8		11.4	8.2	9.7	9.8	7.3	12.2
31.0	26.1	21.2	Sales/Working Capital	55.8	31.6	58.0	22.3	13.7	14.5
-434.9	-23.3	-28.8		-5.4	-13.6	-32.2	-25.3	43.5	32.1
4.5	7.8	13.8		19.5	17.5	20.7	6.7	19.5	10.4
(129) 2.1	(158) 1.8	(178) 3.3	EBIT/Interest	(23) 1.6	(35) 5.5	3.6	(30) 2.2	(32) 3.5	(26) 3.0
-.4	-2.0	1.1		.9	-.8	1.1	1.1	2.0	1.8
3.5	3.7	3.8	Net Profit + Depr., Dep., Amort./Cur. Mat. L/T/D				3.7	13.9	3.8
(44) 1.6	(44) 1.7	(56) 1.7				(16) 1.3	(13) 1.2	(16) 2.8	
.6	.1	1.0					.6	.8	1.5
.5	.4	.4		.5	.4	.4	.3	.3	.5
1.0	.9	1.0	Fixed/Worth	2.5	2.2	.8	1.1	.7	.6
3.1	4.0	5.1		44.8	-.7	NM	3.4	1.8	1.4
.8	.7	.7		.6	.5	.6	1.0	.6	1.1
2.0	1.7	2.1	Debt/Worth	6.2	3.7	2.0	2.0	1.4	2.1
6.8	10.1	9.9		-207.1	-3.3	NM	7.6	3.3	4.6
34.7	30.3	50.2	% Profit Before Taxes/Tangible Net Worth	118.3	91.9	28.8	39.2	45.7	40.1
(121) 8.5	(151) 7.0	(173) 17.6		(29) 33.4	(29) 38.6	(24) 15.6	(31) 11.0	(32) 13.7	(28) 20.7
-1.2	-6.4	2.5		.0	-10.5	2.1	2.4	5.2	7.7
9.8	10.1	17.8	% Profit Before Taxes/Total Assets	24.0	36.5	15.6	10.2	13.5	17.8
2.6	1.7	5.2		7.2	6.5	5.9	3.2	5.7	4.8
-2.0	-5.3	.4		.0	-5.1	.3	.4	2.2	2.5
31.7	28.2	32.4		21.1	37.7	20.4	45.8	33.1	28.1
14.4	12.0	12.8	Sales/Net Fixed Assets	4.4	19.4	12.6	14.0	11.6	17.5
5.3	4.1	4.3		.3	6.0	7.3	3.8	4.7	5.7
5.0	4.3	4.5		3.6	5.3	4.4	4.8	4.3	4.5
3.4	2.8	3.0	Sales/Total Assets	1.8	3.3	2.9	3.1	2.7	3.0
2.1	1.7	1.7		.2	2.5	2.3	1.7	1.6	1.9
1.1	1.6	1.5		2.9	1.4	1.4	1.3	1.5	1.2
(123) 2.5	(151) 2.9	(174) 2.7	% Depr., Dep., Amort./Sales	(30) 12.3	(30) 2.8	(26) 2.3	(29) 2.5	(32) 2.5	(27) 2.1
4.0	4.8	4.5		16.8	4.4	3.6	4.1	4.1	3.2
2.3	2.2	2.2		11.2	3.2	2.6	1.9		
(52) 3.2	(62) 4.9	(71) 4.7	% Officers', Directors' Owners' Comp/Sales	(10) 13.8	(19) 4.8	(17) 4.6	(13) 4.5		
6.8	9.0	9.3		16.2	9.3	6.0	8.6		
4316329M	3010282M	5107332M	Net Sales ($)	23697M	85936M	124977M	242439M	574026M	4056257M
1633344M	1258368M	1963830M	Total Assets ($)	37574M	29710M	43710M	107233M	275786M	1469817M

M = $ thousand   MM = $ million
See Pages 9 through 22 for Explanation of Ratios and Data

Current Data Sorted by Assets   **Comparative Historical Data**

Type of Statement	0-500M	500M-2MM	2-10MM	10-50MM	50-100MM	100-250MM	4/1/06-3/31/07 ALL	4/1/07-3/31/08 ALL
Unqualified			6	3	1	2	11	12
Reviewed	6	11	31	20	1		32	28
Compiled	10	15	17	1	1	2	30	36
Tax Returns	29	28	9	1			45	54
Other	11	31	34	13	4	1	53	73
	47 (4/1-9/30/10)		241 (10/1/10-3/31/11)					
NUMBER OF STATEMENTS	56	85	97	38	7	5	171	203
	%	%	%	%	%	%	%	%
ASSETS								
Cash & Equivalents	21.0	14.2	10.8	6.6			12.1	9.9
Trade Receivables (net)	16.9	29.1	25.4	26.2			22.1	26.2
Inventory	1.3	1.1	1.3	2.2			2.6	2.4
All Other Current	4.9	4.6	4.6	5.4			5.2	5.9
Total Current	44.1	49.1	42.1	40.4			42.0	44.4
Fixed Assets (net)	36.4	37.9	48.1	51.7			47.9	43.2
Intangibles (net)	5.0	5.3	2.4	2.1			2.6	2.7
All Other Non-Current	14.5	7.7	7.3	5.7			7.5	9.7
Total	100.0	100.0	100.0	100.0			100.0	100.0
LIABILITIES								
Notes Payable-Short Term	21.8	9.5	6.5	5.5			8.7	11.1
Cur. Mat.-L.T.D.	10.4	7.9	8.7	9.7			7.8	6.8
Trade Payables	14.6	9.5	9.9	11.1			10.3	14.1
Income Taxes Payable	.1	.2	.3	.1			.4	.7
All Other Current	11.5	13.8	8.6	6.8			7.4	8.5
Total Current	58.4	40.9	34.0	33.2			34.6	40.7
Long-Term Debt	46.4	24.6	24.9	23.1			29.2	28.8
Deferred Taxes	.1	.1	.8	1.2			.5	.6
All Other Non-Current	12.2	5.4	1.8	.7			4.0	3.2
Net Worth	-17.0	28.9	38.4	41.8			31.6	26.7
Total Liabilities & Net Worth	100.0	100.0	100.0	100.0			100.0	100.0
INCOME DATA								
Net Sales	100.0	100.0	100.0	100.0			100.0	100.0
Gross Profit								
Operating Expenses	91.1	94.8	95.6	95.5			94.0	96.2
Operating Profit	8.9	5.2	4.4	4.5			6.0	3.8
All Other Expenses (net)	1.8	.0	.5	.8			1.0	.5
Profit Before Taxes	7.1	5.1	3.9	3.7			5.0	3.3
RATIOS								
Current	3.0	3.0	2.2	2.0			2.2	2.0
	1.1	1.7	1.3	1.2			1.3	1.2
	.3	.7	.7	.7			.7	.6
Quick	2.1	2.7	2.0	1.6			1.7	1.6
	1.1	1.6	1.0	.9			1.1	.9
	.2	.5	.6	.6			.6	.4
Sales/Receivables	0 UND	5 72.9	21 17.0	26 14.0			11 34.1	10 36.2
	6 61.5	30 12.0	35 10.4	37 10.0			27 13.3	28 13.2
	33 11.0	43 8.4	49 7.5	48 7.6			41 8.9	42 8.7
Cost of Sales/Inventory								
Cost of Sales/Payables								
Sales/Working Capital	15.3	10.4	10.7	8.6			12.4	12.7
	93.4	21.0	39.5	43.3			39.0	48.9
	-10.7	-38.3	-22.3	-23.3			-25.1	-22.7
EBIT/Interest	9.1	17.7	9.9	11.7			8.3	7.7
	(43) 2.8	(72) 4.7	(91) 2.9	(37) 4.7			(153) 3.3	(179) 2.7
	-.6	1.0	.6	2.1			1.5	1.1
Net Profit + Depr., Dep., Amort./Cur. Mat. L/T/D			2.9	3.7			3.4	6.0
			(26) 1.5	(14) 2.2			(41) 2.0	(46) 1.7
			.4	1.7			1.2	1.1
Fixed/Worth	.5	.2	.7	.7			.7	.6
	5.2	1.0	1.6	1.3			1.6	1.5
	-1.5	8.1	2.5	2.3			5.1	6.0
Debt/Worth	1.8	.6	.7	.7			.9	1.0
	29.2	1.8	1.9	1.6			2.3	3.0
	-3.2	18.1	3.1	3.1			7.8	11.3
% Profit Before Taxes/Tangible Net Worth	394.3	91.0	43.3	27.4			67.7	59.0
	(31) 37.5	(66) 35.2	(90) 12.5	(37) 15.7			(146) 29.2	(167) 21.8
	-3.6	10.6	-4.6	9.5			9.6	7.4
% Profit Before Taxes/Total Assets	44.2	28.5	14.5	12.2			20.2	15.5
	6.9	12.7	6.2	7.8			7.4	7.5
	-3.9	1.7	-1.4	2.9			1.8	.4
Sales/Net Fixed Assets	120.4	45.4	12.0	8.3			13.7	20.8
	18.9	11.2	4.7	4.3			6.0	7.6
	3.9	4.2	2.6	2.6			2.7	3.7
Sales/Total Assets	9.4	5.6	3.6	2.8			4.2	4.6
	3.7	3.4	2.2	2.1			2.6	2.9
	1.9	2.2	1.5	1.8			1.7	2.0
% Depr., Dep., Amort./Sales	2.6	2.1	2.0	2.9			2.3	1.8
	(31) 6.8	(55) 6.1	(86) 5.8	5.4			(138) 5.7	(168) 4.9
	13.0	9.7	9.9	8.3			9.0	8.4
% Officers', Directors', Owners' Comp/Sales	3.1	1.8	1.3				1.1	1.1
	(22) 5.9	(37) 4.4	(27) 2.3				(69) 3.0	(81) 2.8
	8.2	6.5	4.9				5.4	6.4
Net Sales ($)	62128M	344547M	1297801M	1812789M	605597M	1477556M	2700331M	7040280M
Total Assets ($)	13099M	90700M	487782M	718576M	389275M	866262M	1166443M	1289395M

M = $ thousand   MM = $ million
See Pages 9 through 22 for Explanation of Ratios and Data

Comparative Historical Data

Current Data Sorted by Sales

				Type of Statement						
11		7	12	Unqualified		1		2	1	8
48		49	69	Reviewed	2	12	6	6	24	19
46		39	46	Compiled	5	10	10	9	6	6
45		60	67	Tax Returns	22	19	9	12	4	1
86		94	94	Other	9	18	12	18	21	16
4/1/08-3/31/09 ALL		4/1/09-3/31/10 ALL	4/1/10-3/31/11 ALL			47 (4/1-9/30/10)			241 (10/1/10-3/31/11)	
					0-1MM	1-3MM	3-5MM	5-10MM	10-25MM	25MM & OVER
236		249	288	NUMBER OF STATEMENTS	38	60	37	47	56	50
%		%	%	ASSETS	%	%	%	%	%	%
10.8		12.0	13.2	Cash & Equivalents	15.1	16.8	13.9	11.4	11.5	10.3
23.7		23.1	24.6	Trade Receivables (net)	13.8	21.7	20.0	32.4	29.5	27.1
1.7		1.8	1.3	Inventory	.1	2.2	.3	1.1	1.5	2.0
6.0		4.5	5.0	All Other Current	5.3	3.4	5.3	4.6	6.7	4.6
42.2		41.3	44.1	Total Current	34.3	44.2	39.6	49.5	49.2	44.0
46.1		45.8	43.4	Fixed Assets (net)	42.5	43.2	43.6	40.9	42.8	47.1
2.1		2.7	4.1	Intangibles (net)	8.5	4.1	7.7	.7	2.2	3.5
9.6		10.0	8.4	All Other Non-Current	14.6	8.6	9.1	8.9	5.8	5.4
100.0		100.0	100.0	Total	100.0	100.0	100.0	100.0	100.0	100.0
				LIABILITIES						
11.7		6.9	10.1	Notes Payable-Short Term	12.5	16.6	4.0	14.7	6.0	5.2
9.0		9.6	8.9	Cur. Mat.-L.T.D.	11.2	7.1	12.1	7.4	8.8	8.4
11.0		10.7	10.6	Trade Payables	13.2	9.3	5.9	13.6	9.0	12.8
.3		.3	.2	Income Taxes Payable	.0	.4	.1	.0	.4	.1
10.2		7.7	10.3	All Other Current	8.1	17.6	10.4	9.7	6.7	7.9
42.3		35.3	40.2	Total Current	45.1	51.0	32.5	45.3	31.1	34.5
29.2		33.8	29.6	Long-Term Debt	45.0	35.9	32.6	20.5	22.4	24.4
.9		.5	.5	Deferred Taxes	.1	.2	.2	.6	.8	1.0
5.5		4.7	5.0	All Other Non-Current	15.8	4.2	2.6	5.2	3.8	.6
22.2		25.7	24.8	Net Worth	-5.9	8.6	32.1	28.3	42.0	39.5
100.0		100.0	100.0	Total Liabilities & Net Worth	100.0	100.0	100.0	100.0	100.0	100.0
				INCOME DATA						
100.0		100.0	100.0	Net Sales	100.0	100.0	100.0	100.0	100.0	100.0
				Gross Profit						
95.3		95.8	94.1	Operating Expenses	84.1	95.2	95.0	96.9	97.0	94.0
4.7		4.2	5.9	Operating Profit	15.9	4.8	5.0	3.1	3.0	6.0
1.3		1.2	.7	All Other Expenses (net)	3.7	.6	.0	-.5	.3	.5
3.4		3.0	5.2	Profit Before Taxes	12.1	4.2	5.0	3.5	2.7	5.5
				RATIOS						
2.0		2.3	2.4		3.4	2.5	2.2	2.0	2.9	2.1
1.2		1.2	1.3	Current	1.1	1.5	1.5	1.1	1.5	1.3
.7		.6	.7		.3	.5	.6	.6	.8	.7
1.7		2.0	2.1		3.2	2.1	2.0	2.0	2.4	1.8
.9		1.0	1.2	Quick	1.1	1.2	1.5	1.0	1.3	1.1
.5		.5	.5		.2	.3	.5	.5	.7	.6
10 37.8	11	32.5	14 26.7		0 UND	0 UND	8 47.2	15 24.7	20 18.2	27 13.7
25 14.5	26	13.9	32 11.5	Sales/Receivables	13 27.7	27 13.7	28 13.1	34 10.7	33 11.2	35 10.3
39 9.4	43	8.5	47 7.8		40 9.2	52 7.1	39 9.3	44 8.4	48 7.7	48 7.6
				Cost of Sales/Inventory						
				Cost of Sales/Payables						
13.7		12.4	11.2		11.7	10.1	10.2	17.4	8.4	12.4
65.2		82.4	38.1	Sales/Working Capital	92.3	34.1	21.6	117.9	23.7	40.7
-21.6		-21.9	-22.6		-5.7	-21.3	-22.5	-12.9	-29.7	-34.1
7.8		7.8	11.0		8.8	10.4	30.5	8.4	11.4	12.3
(207) 2.8	(218)	2.8	(253) 3.8	EBIT/Interest	(29) 3.3	(51) 2.8	(33) 3.6	(43) 4.5	(49) 3.2	(48) 5.6
.9		.1	.9		-.1	-.1	1.2	.9	.5	2.3
5.3		2.4	3.0						3.0	3.3
(51) 1.9	(52)	1.6	(53) 1.9	Net Profit + Depr., Dep., Amort./Cur. Mat. L/T/D				(21) 1.6	(16) 2.0
1.0		.8	.9						.4	1.6
.6		.6	.6		1.2	.5	.6	.6	.4	.7
1.5		1.4	1.6	Fixed/Worth	9.2	1.8	1.2	1.3	1.0	1.3
6.1		8.0	5.4		-1.7	10.7	7.9	2.9	2.2	2.6
.8		.8	.7		1.8	.6	.5	.9	.8	.6
2.4		2.3	2.2	Debt/Worth	43.1	3.4	1.8	2.2	1.5	1.9
9.5		20.8	13.8		-3.3	-19.5	9.4	4.7	2.8	4.3
51.8		45.0	60.8		346.7	44.8	85.0	61.5	52.3	44.6
(195) 20.1	(195)	15.9	(232) 21.8	% Profit Before Taxes/Tangible Net Worth	(20) 40.2	(44) 24.0	(29) 34.5	(39) 25.2	(54) 13.1	(46) 18.5
4.6		.0	2.3		-2.8	-7.2	6.2	4.4	-4.6	9.9
15.6		17.6	23.0		36.8	24.3	30.0	19.0	15.5	16.1
5.8		5.6	8.2	% Profit Before Taxes/Total Assets	8.1	9.2	12.6	8.8	6.0	8.6
-.7		-2.3	.1		-2.3	-2.2	.2	-.1	-1.8	3.6
18.4		18.1	25.1		43.5	47.4	21.0	31.4	26.5	11.8
6.3		6.1	6.2	Sales/Net Fixed Assets	4.4	6.3	6.6	7.1	6.5	4.9
3.3		2.8	3.0		2.5	3.2	3.3	3.2	3.0	2.8
4.6		4.5	4.4		3.2	4.5	5.1	6.0	4.1	3.9
2.6		2.5	2.6	Sales/Total Assets	1.9	2.7	2.9	3.7	2.7	2.4
1.9		1.7	1.7		.7	1.7	1.6	1.8	1.9	1.8
1.6		2.1	2.6		8.1	2.6	3.5	1.6	2.0	2.4
(199) 4.3	(196)	5.1	(216) 5.8	% Depr., Dep., Amort./Sales	(20) 14.4	(45) 6.8	(24) 6.0	(36) 4.8	(46) 5.8	(45) 4.0
8.5		10.3	9.9		26.4	10.1	11.4	9.2	9.4	6.9
1.3		1.3	1.5		5.4	2.6	1.8	1.0	1.3	
(89) 3.3	(85)	3.1	(96) 3.4	% Officers', Directors' Owners' Comp/Sales	(11) 7.8	(27) 4.7	(11) 3.3	(21) 3.0	(17) 2.3	
6.9		6.3	6.5		10.4	7.8	5.6	4.9	5.5	
5836992M		3796516M	5600418M	Net Sales ($)	16168M	117210M	148519M	336906M	903732M	4077883M
2303670M		1646024M	2565694M	Total Assets ($)	16310M	61187M	76901M	135009M	392645M	1883642M

M = $ thousand   MM = $ million
See Pages 9 through 22 for Explanation of Ratios and Data

Current Data Sorted by Assets / Comparative Historical Data

	0-500M	500M-2MM	2-10MM	10-50MM	50-100MM	100-250MM	Type of Statement	4/1/06-3/31/07 ALL	4/1/07-3/31/08 ALL
		1	2	25	5	13	Unqualified	29	38
	2	3	29	23	6	1	Reviewed	38	38
	1	10	13	6	1	1	Compiled	24	21
	7	13	5		1		Tax Returns	9	13
	2	12	26	25	11	10	Other	56	53
		29 (4/1-9/30/10)		218 (10/1/10-3/31/11)					
	12	39	75	79	19	23	NUMBER OF STATEMENTS	156	163
	%	%	%	%	%	%	ASSETS	%	%
	24.5	16.1	9.4	7.6	8.1	2.7	Cash & Equivalents	9.3	8.0
	29.9	28.0	31.7	24.9	20.9	18.4	Trade Receivables (net)	25.4	29.0
	.0	1.5	1.5	1.7	.8	1.5	Inventory	1.1	1.3
	4.4	4.4	3.5	4.6	2.3	4.0	All Other Current	3.7	3.9
	58.8	50.1	46.1	38.8	32.1	26.6	Total Current	39.5	42.2
	28.7	36.3	43.8	48.2	56.2	56.1	Fixed Assets (net)	50.1	47.8
	1.2	2.8	2.0	4.5	4.7	13.6	Intangibles (net)	2.0	2.5
	11.4	10.9	8.1	8.5	7.1	3.6	All Other Non-Current	8.5	7.6
	100.0	100.0	100.0	100.0	100.0	100.0	Total	100.0	100.0
							LIABILITIES		
	21.1	9.6	8.0	7.2	2.4	3.7	Notes Payable-Short Term	6.3	7.8
	7.5	9.0	8.3	10.4	9.9	7.3	Cur. Mat.-L.T.D.	11.0	9.4
	14.1	11.7	11.9	8.0	5.8	5.7	Trade Payables	8.1	9.9
	.0	.0	.2	.4	.2	.0	Income Taxes Payable	.2	.3
	16.6	10.7	7.2	8.1	8.3	7.5	All Other Current	9.3	9.2
	59.3	41.1	35.6	34.1	26.6	24.3	Total Current	35.0	36.7
	52.9	26.5	19.3	23.6	36.8	36.6	Long-Term Debt	27.9	27.9
	.0	.3	1.3	2.8	3.9	4.1	Deferred Taxes	2.4	1.7
	3.2	9.3	3.1	3.9	9.2	6.4	All Other Non-Current	4.1	2.5
	-15.5	22.8	40.6	35.5	23.5	28.7	Net Worth	30.6	31.2
	100.0	100.0	100.0	100.0	100.0	100.0	Total Liabilities & Net Worth	100.0	100.0
							INCOME DATA		
	100.0	100.0	100.0	100.0	100.0	100.0	Net Sales	100.0	100.0
							Gross Profit		
	101.0	94.0	96.3	95.2	94.6	95.2	Operating Expenses	95.0	95.8
	-1.0	6.0	3.7	4.8	5.4	4.8	Operating Profit	5.0	4.2
	-.7	1.1	.6	1.1	.1	2.3	All Other Expenses (net)	.5	1.0
	-.4	4.9	3.2	3.7	5.3	2.5	Profit Before Taxes	4.5	3.3
							RATIOS		
	2.3	3.5	2.6	1.6	1.8	1.5	Current	1.7	1.7
	.8	1.2	1.2	1.2	1.3	1.3		1.1	1.1
	.3	.8	.8	.8	.7	.7		.8	.8
	2.3	3.0	2.3	1.4	1.6	1.2	Quick	1.4	1.5
	.7	1.1	1.1	1.0	1.2	1.0		.9	1.0
	.3	.6	.7	.6	.6	.5		.6	.6
	0 UND	0 UND	24 15.1	29 12.5	36 10.3	37 9.8	Sales/Receivables	23 15.7	26 14.0
	14 25.3	26 14.0	33 11.0	38 9.6	42 8.8	41 8.8		34 10.8	34 10.7
	35 10.4	34 10.7	47 7.8	50 7.4	54 6.7	48 7.6		43 8.6	45 8.1
							Cost of Sales/Inventory		
							Cost of Sales/Payables		
	16.5	12.5	10.4	13.9	11.9	15.0	Sales/Working Capital	17.2	14.4
	-114.2	69.8	40.7	50.5	27.0	25.3		93.4	82.5
	-22.4	-37.9	-42.9	-20.2	-14.7	-18.6		-37.5	-26.2
		13.4	9.2	7.4	9.8	5.2	EBIT/Interest	7.5	5.6
		(35) 5.6	(69) 4.3	(78) 3.5	3.9	(22) 2.5		(143) 3.1	(156) 2.6
		1.7	1.5	1.3	1.4	.2		1.7	1.0
			3.1	2.6			Net Profit + Depr., Dep., Amort./Cur. Mat. L/T/D	2.2	2.0
			(24) 1.5	(44) 1.4				(50) 1.4	(60) 1.4
			1.0	1.0				1.0	.9
	.0	.3	.5	.7	1.6	1.8	Fixed/Worth	1.0	.7
	2.1	1.3	1.2	1.7	2.4	2.9		1.9	1.8
	-2.1	78.3	2.7	3.9	3.4	198.9		3.5	3.6
	1.3	1.2	.5	.9	1.9	1.4	Debt/Worth	1.2	1.1
	5.9	3.5	1.5	2.2	2.5	3.3		2.6	2.6
	-3.7	877.0	4.3	6.8	4.3	275.6		5.1	4.8
		194.2	44.5	28.5	37.6	85.6	% Profit Before Taxes/Tangible Net Worth	50.6	38.4
		(30) 37.2	(69) 19.8	(69) 15.6	(17) 11.9	(18) 33.0		(146) 26.4	(152) 17.4
		13.7	3.5	5.8	7.9	3.3		11.2	2.4
	24.4	26.1	15.5	10.9	14.3	7.5	% Profit Before Taxes/Total Assets	15.5	14.7
	20.6	13.9	7.3	4.6	5.9	3.3		6.7	5.0
	-.8	2.0	.8	.8	1.5	-3.0		2.5	.4
	UND	69.5	17.5	9.7	4.7	4.1	Sales/Net Fixed Assets	9.0	12.7
	66.8	21.0	7.3	4.0	2.9	2.8		4.3	4.7
	21.7	4.9	3.6	2.9	2.1	1.6		2.5	2.6
	20.5	8.6	4.4	2.7	2.3	1.8	Sales/Total Assets	3.4	3.8
	5.5	4.7	3.0	2.0	1.6	1.5		2.3	2.5
	4.5	2.9	2.1	1.6	1.4	1.1		1.6	1.6
		.9	1.5	2.3	2.8		% Depr., Dep., Amort./Sales	2.7	2.4
		(26) 3.3	(67) 3.4	(76) 5.5	(12) 5.8			(133) 5.1	(132) 5.2
		6.6	6.6	9.4	6.6			8.2	7.8
		1.1	1.0	.5			% Officers', Directors' Owners' Comp/Sales	1.1	1.1
		(17) 1.6	(34) 1.9	(15) 1.0				(43) 3.0	(52) 2.5
		5.1	4.9	2.0				4.5	5.8
	25688M	276320M	1136225M	4419931M	2468630M	5361730M	Net Sales ($)	6529744M	7476195M
	2599M	48466M	347804M	1875369M	1308557M	3563027M	Total Assets ($)	3302879M	3783342M

Comparative Historical Data | Current Data Sorted by Sales

			Type of Statement						
48	43	46	Unqualified	2	1	2	8	6	40
45	44	58	Reviewed	1	1	6	9	17	28
26	28	31	Compiled	1	1	6	9	8	6
20	22	26	Tax Returns	4	4	5	8	3	2
75	85	86	Other	1	6	3	9	25	42
4/1/08-3/31/09 ALL	4/1/09-3/31/10 ALL	4/1/10-3/31/11 ALL		0-1MM	29 (4/1-9/30/10) 1-3MM	3-5MM	218 (10/1/10-3/31/11) 5-10MM	10-25MM	25MM & OVER
214	222	247	NUMBER OF STATEMENTS	8	12	16	34	59	118
%	%	%	**ASSETS**	%	%	%	%	%	%
9.7	10.3	9.9	Cash & Equivalents		10.8	13.7	14.4	10.2	7.5
27.4	23.5	26.8	Trade Receivables (net)		28.8	20.2	28.7	30.3	25.9
1.4	1.9	1.4	Inventory		.0	4.0	.9	1.4	1.5
4.2	4.6	4.0	All Other Current		1.0	2.2	3.6	3.9	4.7
42.7	40.2	42.1	Total Current		40.6	40.1	47.6	45.9	39.5
45.7	47.2	45.4	Fixed Assets (net)		43.8	55.7	40.2	43.0	47.4
3.8	4.1	4.2	Intangibles (net)		3.4	.0	1.6	2.2	6.2
7.8	8.4	8.3	All Other Non-Current		12.2	4.2	10.6	8.9	6.9
100.0	100.0	100.0	Total		100.0	100.0	100.0	100.0	100.0
			LIABILITIES						
8.1	12.0	7.8	Notes Payable-Short Term		8.3	8.2	10.1	7.1	6.3
8.7	9.8	9.1	Cur. Mat.-L.T.D.		7.3	9.6	11.1	8.8	9.2
9.5	8.2	9.7	Trade Payables		15.1	10.7	11.2	11.6	8.0
.1	.3	.2	Income Taxes Payable		.0	.0	.1	.2	.3
10.6	10.9	8.6	All Other Current		17.6	8.1	6.1	6.7	9.3
37.0	41.2	35.4	Total Current		48.3	36.7	38.6	34.4	33.1
28.3	27.1	26.4	Long-Term Debt		22.1	29.8	27.4	17.3	27.8
1.8	1.8	2.0	Deferred Taxes		.9	.0	1.4	1.3	3.1
4.6	4.6	5.1	All Other Non-Current		7.2	11.5	2.0	3.2	4.9
28.3	25.3	31.0	Net Worth		21.5	22.0	30.5	43.7	31.1
100.0	100.0	100.0	Total Liabilities & Net Worth		100.0	100.0	100.0	100.0	100.0
			INCOME DATA						
100.0	100.0	100.0	Net Sales		100.0	100.0	100.0	100.0	100.0
			Gross Profit						
95.4	97.5	95.6	Operating Expenses		91.1	92.7	97.5	96.8	95.8
4.6	2.5	4.4	Operating Profit		8.9	7.3	2.5	3.2	4.2
.8	1.0	.9	All Other Expenses (net)		.7	2.4	.1	.2	1.0
3.8	1.5	3.5	Profit Before Taxes		8.2	4.9	2.3	3.0	3.2
			RATIOS						
1.8	1.8	2.1	Current		1.6	3.0	2.9	3.2	1.7
1.1	1.1	1.2			.9	1.0	1.1	1.3	1.3
.8	.7	.7			.3	.6	.8	.8	.8
1.6	1.6	1.8	Quick		1.6	2.3	2.7	2.3	1.4
1.0	.9	1.1			.8	.7	1.1	1.2	1.0
.5	.5	.6			.3	.4	.6	.7	.6
20 17.9	20 18.6	26 14.3	Sales/Receivables	0 UND	1 334.3	17 21.2	22 16.5	31 11.7	
30 12.0	34 10.7	36 10.2		30 12.2	27 13.6	32 11.4	33 11.1	40 9.2	
40 9.2	44 8.4	47 7.8		49 7.5	37 9.7	45 8.2	47 7.8	48 7.6	
			Cost of Sales/Inventory						
			Cost of Sales/Payables						
15.7	15.9	12.5	Sales/Working Capital		19.7	9.5	11.3	10.4	15.0
74.6	98.7	48.2			-58.5	NM	102.0	31.4	32.9
-37.1	-16.9	-26.4			-7.4	-18.1	-48.5	-42.9	-33.3
6.8	5.9	9.5	EBIT/Interest		10.4	20.9	9.3	15.0	8.1
(199) 2.6	(205) 2.3	(231) 3.9		(10) 7.6	5.2	(32) 2.6	(55) 4.3	(115) 3.5	
1.3	.4	1.4			4.0	.2	.3	1.7	1.4
3.0	2.5	3.0	Net Profit + Depr., Dep., Amort./Cur. Mat. L/T/D				3.9	3.1	3.7
(68) 1.5	(74) 1.3	(85) 1.5				(10) 1.5	(19) 1.7	(51) 1.6	
1.0	.9	1.0					1.0	1.1	1.1
.7	.7	.6	Fixed/Worth		.6	1.3	.4	.5	.9
1.7	1.8	1.6			1.9	2.8	1.3	1.1	2.0
3.9	3.9	6.0			NM	96.1	4.2	2.8	3.9
1.1	1.1	1.0	Debt/Worth		1.3	1.1	.9	.4	1.3
2.6	2.6	2.4			5.9	5.4	2.3	1.1	2.5
8.4	7.4	11.5			NM	686.1	23.9	4.3	8.1
37.6	34.2	47.0	% Profit Before Taxes/Tangible Net Worth		219.1	56.4	47.2	37.6	
(182) 20.4	(189) 13.5	(210) 21.4			(13) 42.9	(29) 24.4	(51) 21.0	(103) 16.6	
4.7	-.4	6.2			-.4	-1.7	3.8	7.5	
12.7	10.1	16.4	% Profit Before Taxes/Total Assets		23.4	24.1	18.4	17.0	11.0
5.0	3.6	6.4			14.4	14.5	7.4	8.4	4.5
1.2	-1.9	1.3			3.4	-3.1	-3.0	2.4	.8
17.5	15.3	16.2	Sales/Net Fixed Assets		173.0	19.6	29.7	19.4	9.8
6.1	5.5	5.4			6.2	5.4	12.2	7.1	4.1
3.1	2.6	2.9			3.6	2.4	3.8	3.6	2.8
4.6	4.1	4.2	Sales/Total Assets		4.5	4.8	5.8	4.7	2.9
2.6	2.5	2.5			3.0	3.1	3.5	3.0	2.0
1.8	1.5	1.7			2.2	1.5	1.9	2.1	1.5
2.2	2.3	1.9	% Depr., Dep., Amort./Sales			.6	2.3	1.4	2.0
(163) 4.7	(180) 5.2	(188) 4.0			(11) 4.5	(26) 4.1	(54) 3.3	(89) 4.5	
7.1	8.7	7.4				6.4	9.1	7.0	6.8
1.0	1.0	.9	% Officers', Directors' Owners' Comp/Sales			1.0	.7	.5	
(63) 2.2	(68) 2.2	(78)			(18) 1.5	(23) 1.6	(22) 1.2		
5.1	5.0	4.9				4.3	4.8	3.6	
12059235M	13484310M	13688524M	Net Sales ($)	3785M	21630M	60026M	260055M	945660M	12397368M
5474850M	6123903M	7145822M	Total Assets ($)	6128M	12579M	37021M	88732M	364236M	6637126M

© RMA 2011

M = $ thousand   MM = $ million
See Pages 9 through 22 for Explanation of Ratios and Data

Current Data Sorted by Assets   Comparative Historical Data

						Type of Statement		
			6			Unqualified	4	2
		3	1	2		Reviewed	8	3
5		1				Compiled	10	13
12	6	3				Tax Returns	7	9
9	8	10				Other	20	21
	7 (4/1-9/30/10)		60 (10/1/10-3/31/11)				4/1/06-3/31/07	4/1/07-3/31/08
0-500M	500M-2MM	2-10MM	10-50MM	50-100MM	100-250MM		ALL	ALL
26	14	17	8	2		NUMBER OF STATEMENTS	49	48
%	%	%	%	%	%	ASSETS	%	%
16.4	5.1	18.7			D	Cash & Equivalents	9.4	13.4
13.8	17.2	13.8			A	Trade Receivables (net)	16.9	17.8
.2	.4	.4			T	Inventory	.6	.5
3.4	23.3	8.1			A	All Other Current	2.0	5.2
33.8	46.0	41.0				Total Current	29.0	36.9
32.9	34.2	36.6			N	Fixed Assets (net)	39.0	34.7
11.5	6.2	7.7			O	Intangibles (net)	12.3	16.3
22.1	13.5	14.7			T	All Other Non-Current	19.7	12.0
100.0	100.0	100.0				Total	100.0	100.0
					A	LIABILITIES		
20.4	8.9	10.5			V	Notes Payable-Short Term	15.7	6.9
3.5	11.7	1.6			A	Cur. Mat.-L.T.D.	5.0	4.2
19.9	3.6	5.1			I	Trade Payables	7.7	6.1
.1	.1	.4			L	Income Taxes Payable	.5	.2
26.5	18.2	17.7			A	All Other Current	13.2	12.3
70.4	42.4	35.3			B	Total Current	42.0	29.6
20.1	29.7	18.2			L	Long-Term Debt	26.3	35.5
.0	.0	.1			E	Deferred Taxes	1.0	.4
31.3	22.3	7.0				All Other Non-Current	3.9	9.5
-22.0	5.6	39.4				Net Worth	26.8	25.0
100.0	100.0	100.0				Total Liabilties & Net Worth	100.0	100.0
						INCOME DATA		
100.0	100.0	100.0				Net Sales	100.0	100.0
						Gross Profit		
98.4	86.5	85.5				Operating Expenses	91.3	89.0
1.6	13.5	14.5				Operating Profit	8.7	11.0
.2	5.6	7.0				All Other Expenses (net)	3.8	3.7
1.5	7.9	7.6				Profit Before Taxes	4.9	7.3
						RATIOS		
1.1	7.8	3.4					1.4	3.0
.6	1.0	1.2				Current	.9	.9
.1	.2	.7					.3	.5
1.1	2.3	2.5					1.3	2.2
.5	.3	1.1				Quick	.7	.9
.1	.1	.5					.3	.4
0 UND	0 UND	1 320.3					1 505.1	2 237.4
0 UND	9 38.8	28 12.8				Sales/Receivables	26 13.9	16 22.7
25 14.5	33 11.2	38 9.5					51 7.2	50 7.3
						Cost of Sales/Inventory		
						Cost of Sales/Payables		
103.1	3.7	4.1					15.6	8.1
-24.0	NM	34.6				Sales/Working Capital	-33.3	-109.1
-9.4	-3.1	-14.7					-9.7	-16.4
7.2	20.6	22.3					9.5	12.8
(13) 2.4	(12) 3.8	(14) 5.2				EBIT/Interest	(41) 3.1	(36) 6.1
-5.9	.3	1.8					.6	.6
						Net Profit + Depr., Dep.,	2.8	6.3
						Amort./Cur. Mat. L/T/D	(14) 1.7	(10) 2.4
							.7	1.6
.2	.5	.4					.7	.2
NM	2.2	1.0				Fixed/Worth	2.1	1.7
-.7	-3.5	6.8					-5.4	-4.7
3.4	1.7	.6					1.0	.6
-10.9	42.0	2.0				Debt/Worth	2.8	2.0
-2.0	-6.3	12.9					-9.5	-4.4
25.7		96.1				% Profit Before Taxes/Tangible	57.3	60.4
(11) -38.0		(15) 29.1				Net Worth	(34) 19.4	(31) 31.9
-200.0		10.3					3.2	1.6
16.1	16.5	28.3				% Profit Before Taxes/Total	15.9	31.8
1.3	5.4	7.7				Assets	5.1	10.7
-19.4	-5.3	1.8					-1.8	-1.2
310.5	28.3	27.2					17.9	84.9
37.0	10.5	7.1				Sales/Net Fixed Assets	4.9	8.1
12.5	5.0	1.8					2.9	3.6
10.0	3.2	3.8					3.5	3.9
4.1	2.2	1.8				Sales/Total Assets	1.8	2.3
2.0	1.5	.9					1.1	1.2
.6		3.0					2.2	2.7
(10) 3.4		(15) 7.0				% Depr., Dep., Amort./Sales	(37) 5.4	(27) 4.8
7.5		12.9					10.2	7.8
						% Officers', Directors'	2.3	2.6
						Owners' Comp/Sales	(15) 4.2	(12) 4.5
							13.0	9.1
35855M	40093M	226786M	350931M	109833M		Net Sales ($)	821639M	1886509M
5795M	15407M	95301M	200182M	178545M		Total Assets ($)	543953M	786526M

M = $ thousand   MM = $ million
See Pages 9 through 22 for Explanation of Ratios and Data

Comparative Historical Data | Current Data Sorted by Sales

Type of Statement

	4/1/08-3/31/09 ALL	4/1/09-3/31/10 ALL	4/1/10-3/31/11 ALL			7 (4/1-9/30/10)		60 (10/1/10-3/31/11)	
				0-1MM	1-3MM	3-5MM	5-10MM	10-25MM	25MM & OVER
Unqualified	10	8	6				1	3	6
Reviewed	4	6	6				1		2
Compiled	10	7	6	2	2		1		1
Tax Returns	10	9	21	7	6	5	2	1	
Other	19	22	28	9	7	5		4	2
NUMBER OF STATEMENTS	53	52	67	18	15	10	5	8	11

ASSETS (%)

	%	%	%	%	%	%	%	%	%
Cash & Equivalents	15.3	20.9	16.1	11.3	12.3	21.8			24.3
Trade Receivables (net)	13.5	16.3	13.2	8.2	17.2	17.8			14.1
Inventory	1.0	.6	.3	.3	.1	.2			.5
All Other Current	4.9	11.3	9.0	2.6	20.6	11.7			4.2
Total Current	34.7	49.2	38.6	22.3	50.3	51.5			43.2
Fixed Assets (net)	35.9	31.3	35.2	33.4	36.4	21.1			38.5
Intangibles (net)	13.1	8.0	9.4	13.6	3.0	9.9			8.8
All Other Non-Current	16.4	11.5	16.9	31.0	10.3	17.6			9.5
Total	100.0	100.0	100.0	100.0	100.0	100.0			100.0

LIABILITIES

Notes Payable-Short Term	6.3	10.0	12.9	7.2	14.6	31.7			9.6
Cur. Mat.-L.T.D.	6.3	6.2	4.9	3.8	6.3	1.9			3.6
Trade Payables	8.1	12.2	10.2	12.5	21.1	1.6			7.7
Income Taxes Payable	.0	.1	.2	.4	.0	.3			.0
All Other Current	15.0	23.2	21.4	25.1	12.5	35.1			16.5
Total Current	35.7	51.6	49.6	49.1	54.4	70.6			37.4
Long-Term Debt	27.7	19.4	21.8	25.3	28.6	14.3			13.1
Deferred Taxes	1.0	1.1	.3	.0	.1	.0			1.9
All Other Non-Current	14.8	9.0	19.2	40.2	15.9	19.7			1.0
Net Worth	20.8	18.8	9.1	-14.8	1.0	-4.6			46.6
Total Liabilities & Net Worth	100.0	100.0	100.0	100.0	100.0	100.0			100.0

INCOME DATA

Net Sales	100.0	100.0	100.0	100.0	100.0	100.0			100.0
Gross Profit									
Operating Expenses	93.5	88.8	89.2	85.6	94.7	88.0			90.3
Operating Profit	6.5	11.2	10.8	14.4	5.3	12.0			9.7
All Other Expenses (net)	1.1	3.9	4.4	9.5	.7	6.6			.5
Profit Before Taxes	5.4	7.3	6.4	4.9	4.6	5.3			9.2

RATIOS

Current	2.5	1.9	2.3	1.9	15.3	8.5			1.6
	1.2	1.1	.8	.5	.7	1.2			1.1
	.3	.5	.3	.1	.4	.2			.7
Quick	2.2	1.6	1.6	1.6	2.1	3.5			1.6
	(52) .9	.7	.6	.2	.6	.9			1.1
	.3	.3	.2	.0	.1	.2			.5
Sales/Receivables	0 999.8	0 744.1	0 UND	0 UND	0 UND	0 UND			1 279.1
	10 36.1	14 26.7	9 38.8	0 UND	11 33.6	12 30.7			13 27.8
	31 11.8	32 11.3	29 12.5	30 12.0	27 13.8	33 11.2			17 21.8
Cost of Sales/Inventory									
Cost of Sales/Payables									
Sales/Working Capital	16.7	11.3	8.3	17.3	3.0	4.6			17.2
	129.0	76.4	-84.8	-11.6	-320.6	UND			43.1
	-12.1	-13.0	-10.6	-2.2	-14.9	-11.1			-24.2
EBIT/Interest	10.1	18.3	13.5		12.1				
	(38) 5.1	(37) 5.9	(47) 5.8		(12) 2.4				
	1.0	.8	1.2		-.8				
Net Profit + Depr., Dep., Amort./Cur. Mat. L/T/D	16.2	6.9							
	(10) 2.5	(10) 3.4							
	1.3	1.8							
Fixed/Worth	.2	.2	.5	.0	.5	.5			.4
	1.7	1.5	2.3	2.7	2.6	NM			1.5
	-2.0	-6.2	-3.0	-1.7	-2.1	-.1			1.7
Debt/Worth	.6	1.3	1.4	3.6	2.0	.7			.9
	2.2	4.8	6.0	43.0	80.4	NM			1.8
	-5.4	-14.7	-5.7	-2.0	-5.2	-2.0			2.6
% Profit Before Taxes/Tangible Net Worth	68.7	86.8	71.0	29.5					102.3
	(37) 26.9	(36) 50.4	(43) 18.8	(10) 10.0				(10)	50.2
	3.1	15.5	7.2	-80.0					17.0
% Profit Before Taxes/Total Assets	21.4	30.0	17.5	12.0	15.1	15.2			41.1
	6.9	9.0	6.5	1.3	1.2	3.9			18.8
	.7	1.4	-1.8	-13.2	-11.9	-6.7			9.3
Sales/Net Fixed Assets	42.2	78.5	63.6	UND	44.2	159.0			31.1
	7.7	11.1	11.9	21.6	14.0	46.7			6.6
	4.0	5.3	4.4	1.8	5.2	6.8			3.4
Sales/Total Assets	4.2	4.5	4.9	3.9	7.2	13.5			5.9
	2.6	2.5	2.3	1.9	2.9	2.7			2.6
	1.4	1.7	1.5	.2	1.5	1.4			1.9
% Depr., Dep., Amort./Sales	2.4	3.1	3.2						3.4
	(36) 6.3	(29) 5.9	(42) 5.9					(10)	7.6
	10.0	7.8	9.2						8.0
% Officers', Directors' Owners' Comp/Sales	1.7	1.0	1.8						
	(17) 4.3	(12) 4.0	(19) 4.2						
	9.3	8.6	6.6						
Net Sales ($)	840527M	1251672M	763498M	6886M	27926M	36914M	35663M	128622M	527487M
Total Assets ($)	529154M	885993M	495230M	11084M	13944M	58513M	15696M	156186M	239807M

M = $ thousand   MM = $ million
See Pages 9 through 22 for Explanation of Ratios and Data

TRANSPORTATION—Limousine Service NAICS 485320

Current Data Sorted by Assets | **Comparative Historical Data**

0-500M	500M-2MM	2-10MM	10-50MM	50-100MM	100-250MM	Type of Statement	4/1/06-3/31/07 ALL	4/1/07-3/31/08 ALL
						Unqualified	4	5
	1	1	1			Reviewed	2	1
2	7	5				Compiled	2	6
15	4	3				Tax Returns	8	20
1	7	5			1	Other	16	22
18	19	14	1		1	**NUMBER OF STATEMENTS**	32	54

Left periods: 5 (4/1-9/30/10); 48 (10/1/10-3/31/11)

0-500M	500M-2MM	2-10MM	10-50MM	50-100MM	100-250MM		4/1/06-3/31/07 ALL	4/1/07-3/31/08 ALL
%	%	%	%	%	%	**ASSETS**	%	%
17.8	13.4	6.6		D		Cash & Equivalents	10.1	10.0
18.5	12.2	20.2		A		Trade Receivables (net)	18.7	15.8
4.7	2.7	.0		T		Inventory	1.8	1.3
12.2	2.6	2.3		A		All Other Current	2.9	5.5
53.3	30.9	29.1				Total Current	33.4	32.7
44.3	56.5	58.6		N		Fixed Assets (net)	53.2	54.4
1.3	6.8	3.9		O		Intangibles (net)	6.0	5.9
1.1	5.8	8.4		T		All Other Non-Current	7.3	7.0
100.0	100.0	100.0				Total	100.0	100.0
				A		**LIABILITIES**		
12.4	7.8	2.8		V		Notes Payable-Short Term	9.3	7.9
10.9	12.5	14.9		A		Cur. Mat.-L.T.D.	11.5	8.2
32.0	2.2	10.3		I		Trade Payables	6.9	6.8
.0	.8	.1		L		Income Taxes Payable	.3	.0
15.2	3.7	5.4		A		All Other Current	8.8	13.8
70.5	27.0	33.5		B		Total Current	36.8	36.7
60.3	52.7	30.3		L		Long-Term Debt	64.2	39.9
.0	.0	1.2		E		Deferred Taxes	1.2	.5
4.6	9.0	5.7				All Other Non-Current	4.1	6.0
-35.5	11.3	29.3				Net Worth	-6.2	16.9
100.0	100.0	100.0				Total Liabilities & Net Worth	100.0	100.0
						INCOME DATA		
100.0	100.0	100.0				Net Sales	100.0	100.0
						Gross Profit		
99.8	93.5	95.3				Operating Expenses	94.8	94.4
.2	6.5	4.7				Operating Profit	5.2	5.6
.8	1.5	1.3				All Other Expenses (net)	1.7	2.3
-.5	5.0	3.3				Profit Before Taxes	3.5	3.2

(Middle columns 10-50MM / 50-100MM / 100-250MM for the ASSETS and LIABILITIES sections marked "DATA NOT AVAILABLE")

0-500M	500M-2MM	2-10MM	10-50MM	50-100MM	100-250MM	RATIOS	4/1/06-3/31/07 ALL	4/1/07-3/31/08 ALL
1.5	4.1	1.9				Current	1.7	1.7
.9	1.3	1.6					1.1	1.0
.4	.2	.3					.4	.6
1.2	4.1	1.9				Quick	1.6	1.2
.5	.8	1.4					.8	.8
.1	.2	.3					.4	.4
0 UND	0 UND	7 50.4				Sales/Receivables	0 UND	0 UND
0 UND	5 71.2	21 17.4					21 17.7	13 27.3
12 31.0	21 17.6	39 9.3					35 10.3	37 9.9
						Cost of Sales/Inventory		
						Cost of Sales/Payables		
46.9	9.1	14.3				Sales/Working Capital	15.6	22.9
NM	48.0	24.3					NM	412.7
-16.3	-11.8	-10.4					-12.5	-27.8
10.3	9.3	5.0				EBIT/Interest	6.4	4.7
(13) 2.0	3.3	2.9					(30) 2.5	(46) 2.1
.3	1.0	1.5					1.8	.6
						Net Profit + Depr., Dep., Amort./Cur. Mat. L/T/D		
.0	1.3	.8				Fixed/Worth	1.1	1.1
3.9	10.7	1.9					5.5	3.9
-2.3	-1.9	NM					-2.2	-117.5
4.0	2.4	.8				Debt/Worth	1.4	1.5
-192.9	9.8	3.0					7.5	5.2
-2.5	-10.4	NM					-5.9	-131.7
	80.5	20.1				% Profit Before Taxes/Tangible Net Worth	80.4	79.5
	(12) 48.8	(11) 14.3					(21) 37.2	(40) 28.2
	-8.4	-2.1					15.3	-.3
23.7	39.8	16.4				% Profit Before Taxes/Total Assets	15.7	18.8
3.1	10.2	5.6					8.8	6.9
-3.7	-.1	.9					2.6	-1.0
UND	11.0	7.1				Sales/Net Fixed Assets	18.3	9.9
11.7	4.1	3.8					4.3	5.6
4.8	3.4	2.9					2.1	3.1
13.8	4.9	3.5				Sales/Total Assets	5.1	4.6
6.0	3.1	2.5					2.2	2.8
3.9	2.2	1.7					1.5	1.8
5.3	3.3	4.6				% Depr., Dep., Amort./Sales	2.3	3.4
(11) 6.2	(16) 7.8	6.9					(27) 7.3	(51) 7.1
13.4	11.9	9.4					10.8	10.3
						% Officers', Directors' Owners' Comp/Sales	2.1	2.9
							(15) 4.4	(24) 4.3
							13.3	8.6
15167M	78352M	160318M	116533M		182610M	Net Sales ($)	617259M	845007M
2376M	19924M	57237M	27453M		128604M	Total Assets ($)	282448M	407383M

M = $ thousand   MM = $ million
See Pages 9 through 22 for Explanation of Ratios and Data

Comparative Historical Data | | Current Data Sorted by Sales

			Type of Statement						
3	3	3	Unqualified				1	1	1
4	1	5	Reviewed				3	2	
5	10	12	Compiled	4	2	1	2	3	
13	14	19	Tax Returns	9	9		1		
17	14	14	Other		5		5	3	1
4/1/08- 3/31/09 ALL	4/1/09- 3/31/10 ALL	4/1/10- 3/31/11 ALL		5 (4/1-9/30/10) 0-1MM	1-3MM	3-5MM	48 (10/1/10-3/31/11) 5-10MM	10-25MM	25MM & OVER
42	42	53	**NUMBER OF STATEMENTS**	13	16	1	12	9	2
%	%	%	**ASSETS**	%	%	%	%	%	%
13.0	9.9	12.8	Cash & Equivalents	19.1	13.6		11.9		
11.9	13.3	17.2	Trade Receivables (net)	19.7	8.0		16.3		
.8	1.8	2.6	Inventory	.0	5.3		4.2		
4.5	1.8	5.8	All Other Current	3.7	12.8		2.7		
30.1	26.7	38.3	Total Current	42.6	39.8		35.1		
52.4	47.3	51.1	Fixed Assets (net)	56.4	48.9		55.3		
8.0	14.1	5.3	Intangibles (net)	1.0	4.1		4.0		
9.5	12.0	5.2	All Other Non-Current	.0	7.3		5.7		
100.0	100.0	100.0	Total	100.0	100.0		100.0		
			LIABILITIES						
15.6	6.6	8.1	Notes Payable-Short Term	6.1	11.2		6.2		
9.9	10.1	12.2	Cur. Mat.-L.T.D.	9.4	15.4		12.5		
4.8	8.7	15.7	Trade Payables	23.3	17.9		2.8		
.0	.0	.3	Income Taxes Payable	.4	.0		.1		
22.7	9.1	8.0	All Other Current	12.0	8.9		3.5		
52.9	34.6	44.3	Total Current	51.2	53.4		25.1		
44.7	42.3	50.6	Long-Term Debt	61.2	59.4		40.6		
.4	.3	.4	Deferred Taxes	.0			.4		
5.5	8.7	6.6	All Other Non-Current	1.6	8.0		9.5		
-3.4	14.2	-1.9	Net Worth	-14.0	-20.9		24.4		
100.0	100.0	100.0	Total Liabilities & Net Worth	100.0	100.0		100.0		
			INCOME DATA						
100.0	100.0	100.0	Net Sales	100.0	100.0		100.0		
			Gross Profit						
96.9	97.3	96.3	Operating Expenses	97.5	95.3		95.2		
3.1	2.7	3.7	Operating Profit	2.5	4.7		4.8		
1.9	1.7	1.4	All Other Expenses (net)	1.6	1.8		.6		
1.2	1.0	2.2	Profit Before Taxes	.9	2.9		4.1		
			RATIOS						
1.8	2.2	2.0		2.0	2.5		2.3		
1.0	.8	1.2	Current	1.1	1.0		1.6		
.5	.3	.3		.3	.2		.5		
1.3	2.2	1.8		2.0	1.3		1.9		
.9	.7	.8	Quick	.9	.4		1.4		
.5	.2	.3		.3	.1		.3		
0 UND	0 UND	0 UND		0 UND	0 UND		0 UND		
4 97.0	12 31.1	8 48.3	Sales/Receivables	0 UND	1 323.5		12 30.0		
29 12.4	36 10.2	25 14.6		16 23.0	11 33.5		38 9.6		
			Cost of Sales/Inventory						
			Cost of Sales/Payables						
20.0	23.8	17.0		36.2	9.4		16.7		
452.3	-65.6	145.9	Sales/Working Capital	314.0	NM		27.8		
-18.0	-9.7	-11.6		-10.1	-12.2		-19.8		
5.5	4.8	8.5		(10) 10.3	(14) 5.5		16.0		
(35) 1.6	(37) 1.5	(48) 2.8	EBIT/Interest	1.5	1.9		2.8		
-.3	.0	.9		-.7	.9		1.4		
			Net Profit + Depr., Dep., Amort./Cur. Mat. L/T/D						
1.1	1.3	.9		.6	.8		.9		
2.4	UND	3.6	Fixed/Worth	4.9	7.4		1.9		
-2.8	-1.6	-4.4		-164.1	-1.7		NM		
1.0	1.8	3.0		4.0	3.4		1.0		
4.6	UND	7.9	Debt/Worth	9.8	NM		3.2		
-2.9	-3.3	-4.6		-3.7	-2.9		NM		
63.4	66.8	80.5							
(25) 43.3	(22) 13.8	(32) 28.1	% Profit Before Taxes/Tangible Net Worth						
-3.3	-4.3	2.1							
17.1	10.9	19.6		36.4	17.2		36.5		
5.0	1.5	6.6	% Profit Before Taxes/Total Assets	2.1	4.4		8.4		
-7.7	-3.8	-.2		-2.1	-1.7		1.2		
9.3	18.1	24.0		UND	402.5		17.9		
5.2	5.8	6.0	Sales/Net Fixed Assets	7.8	5.5		5.6		
3.2	2.7	3.3		2.0	3.3		3.8		
4.5	3.9	7.0		12.3	8.4		4.8		
2.4	2.1	3.5	Sales/Total Assets	5.2	3.1		3.6		
1.7	1.3	2.2		1.4	2.3		2.7		
3.6	2.3	4.2		4.9			3.4		
(29) 9.6	(36) 7.6	(43) 6.8	% Depr., Dep., Amort./Sales	(10) 6.9			7.0		
12.9	13.0	11.2		18.7			9.0		
2.5	3.1	3.5							
(14) 3.4	(20) 5.5	(27) 4.5	% Officers', Directors' Owners' Comp/Sales						
4.7	7.3	8.1							
1076300M	389918M	552980M	Net Sales ($)	6897M	27051M	3918M	73816M	142155M	299143M
506764M	163926M	235594M	Total Assets ($)	2454M	11843M	1495M	23809M	39936M	156057M

M = $ thousand   MM = $ million
See Pages 9 through 22 for Explanation of Ratios and Data

Current Data Sorted by Assets   Comparative Historical Data

Type of Statement	0-500M	500M-2MM	2-10MM	10-50MM	50-100MM	100-250MM		4/1/06-3/31/07 ALL	4/1/07-3/31/08 ALL
Unqualified		1	4	8	3	1		16	22
Reviewed	1	4	26	11	2	1		50	48
Compiled	3	15	13	5		1		36	32
Tax Returns	8	18	8	1		1		8	16
Other	1	7	8	7	1	1		31	29
	66 (4/1-9/30/10)			93 (10/1/10-3/31/11)					
NUMBER OF STATEMENTS	13	45	59	32	6	4		141	147
ASSETS	%	%	%	%	%	%		%	%
Cash & Equivalents	19.5	13.7	11.0	13.9				12.7	12.0
Trade Receivables (net)	8.1	9.2	11.3	12.7				11.2	11.0
Inventory	6.9	2.5	3.6	1.2				2.7	2.3
All Other Current	4.3	3.2	2.4	3.0				4.0	3.7
Total Current	38.9	28.6	28.3	30.8				30.6	29.0
Fixed Assets (net)	50.2	58.2	58.0	60.6				58.2	59.3
Intangibles (net)	.2	3.8	2.4	3.7				1.9	2.8
All Other Non-Current	10.8	9.3	11.2	5.0				9.3	8.9
Total	100.0	100.0	100.0	100.0				100.0	100.0
LIABILITIES									
Notes Payable-Short Term	11.2	6.3	4.3	4.6				5.0	5.9
Cur. Mat.-L.T.D.	11.1	12.2	13.6	10.3				12.2	12.7
Trade Payables	4.0	4.4	5.6	3.0				3.8	3.4
Income Taxes Payable	.0	.0	.5	.1				.3	.3
All Other Current	2.1	3.9	4.7	6.7				7.0	5.9
Total Current	28.4	26.8	28.7	24.8				28.3	28.2
Long-Term Debt	36.8	37.5	27.2	25.6				29.7	35.0
Deferred Taxes	.4	.6	2.0	2.2				1.4	1.4
All Other Non-Current	3.1	5.2	4.2	4.2				4.5	3.8
Net Worth	31.2	30.0	37.9	43.2				36.0	31.5
Total Liabilties & Net Worth	100.0	100.0	100.0	100.0				100.0	100.0
INCOME DATA									
Net Sales	100.0	100.0	100.0	100.0				100.0	100.0
Gross Profit									
Operating Expenses	92.0	93.2	92.8	90.9				93.1	91.7
Operating Profit	8.0	6.8	7.2	9.1				6.9	8.3
All Other Expenses (net)	1.7	2.6	.8	1.2				1.6	2.3
Profit Before Taxes	6.3	4.3	6.4	7.9				5.3	6.0
RATIOS									
Current	6.2	2.4	1.6	3.3				1.7	1.9
	1.7	1.2	.9	1.1				1.0	1.1
	.3	.5	.5	.6				.5	.5
Quick	2.4	1.9	1.5	3.0				1.4	1.7
	1.1	.9	.7	1.0				.8	(146) .9
	.3	.3	.4	.4				.4	.3
Sales/Receivables	0 UND	0 UND	6 65.1	16 22.2				6 63.5	3 138.6
	0 UND	4 86.4	17 20.9	27 13.5				18 20.1	20 18.7
	2 187.7	28 13.0	37 9.9	43 8.5				32 11.4	33 11.1
Cost of Sales/Inventory									
Cost of Sales/Payables									
Sales/Working Capital	8.4	10.0	13.4	6.1				12.1	9.9
	22.2	58.2	-66.4	69.6				-339.4	90.4
	-13.1	-11.5	-10.8	-10.2				-10.8	-11.0
EBIT/Interest	13.9	5.3	6.7	12.8				6.6	6.3
	(10) 3.1	(40) 2.9	(54) 3.1	8.1				(135) 2.9	(144) 3.0
	.2	1.6	1.3	3.0				1.5	1.3
Net Profit + Depr., Dep., Amort./Cur. Mat. L/T/D			2.2	3.5				2.1	1.9
			(21) 1.5	(14) 1.9				(50) 1.5	(53) 1.5
			1.0	1.3				1.2	1.0
Fixed/Worth	.0	.9	.8	.9				1.0	.9
	1.0	1.9	1.6	1.4				1.7	1.9
	NM	91.7	3.5	3.3				3.2	4.9
Debt/Worth	.4	.6	.8	.7				.8	.9
	1.1	4.1	1.8	1.4				1.7	1.9
	NM	96.0	5.0	3.3				4.1	5.2
% Profit Before Taxes/Tangible Net Worth	100.3	60.7	38.0	39.3				41.2	43.4
	(10) 39.9	(35) 28.3	(56) 18.6	(31) 23.8				(129) 17.7	(130) 22.5
	-1.7	5.0	10.5	17.9				5.5	7.2
% Profit Before Taxes/Total Assets	59.6	16.7	13.7	14.9				12.3	13.7
	11.0	7.1	5.9	9.3				6.0	7.4
	-3.2	1.1	1.5	5.9				1.7	1.2
Sales/Net Fixed Assets	415.4	6.8	5.3	3.9				4.7	4.8
	4.6	3.4	2.5	2.4				2.9	2.7
	2.9	1.9	1.7	1.4				1.6	1.6
Sales/Total Assets	3.9	2.8	2.4	1.8				2.2	2.3
	2.9	1.9	1.5	1.4				1.7	1.6
	2.2	1.4	1.2	1.1				1.2	1.1
% Depr., Dep., Amort./Sales	4.2	6.4	7.0	4.5				7.2	6.5
	(11) 8.2	(40) 12.0	(53) 9.9	(30) 8.2				(132) 9.9	(141) 9.9
	14.1	16.7	15.6	12.6				14.0	13.4
% Officers', Directors' Owners' Comp/Sales		2.9	2.7	.5				1.2	2.1
		(27) 6.2	(27) 4.4	(15) .9				(71) 3.3	(71) 3.7
		8.3	6.2	2.5				7.0	7.5
Net Sales ($)	15587M	123551M	559095M	1275380M	529027M	1341654M		1770317M	1834974M
Total Assets ($)	3931M	54274M	304714M	789802M	405472M	634309M		1103233M	1196549M

© RMA 2011

M = $ thousand   MM = $ million
See Pages 9 through 22 for Explanation of Ratios and Data

Comparative Historical Data   Current Data Sorted by Sales

			Type of Statement						
14	15	17	Unqualified		1	1	1	6	8
36	40	45	Reviewed	2	5	2	13	15	8
32	31	36	Compiled	5	8	8	9	3	3
28	31	36	Tax Returns	10	9	5	8	1	3
31	31	25	Other	1	4	1	6	5	8
4/1/08- 3/31/09 ALL	4/1/09- 3/31/10 ALL	4/1/10- 3/31/11 ALL		0-1MM	66 (4/1-9/30/10) 1-3MM	3-5MM	93 (10/1/10-3/31/11) 5-10MM	10-25MM	25MM & OVER
141	148	159	NUMBER OF STATEMENTS	18	27	17	37	30	30
%	%	%	ASSETS	%	%	%	%	%	%
13.8	14.1	13.0	Cash & Equivalents	15.4	15.9	13.1	10.5	13.4	11.7
10.5	10.4	10.8	Trade Receivables (net)	6.5	8.0	10.4	9.9	13.8	14.4
2.2	1.7	3.0	Inventory	2.4	.7	1.5	5.9	3.9	2.0
3.8	2.1	3.0	All Other Current	3.5	3.3	3.5	1.9	2.9	3.6
30.3	28.3	29.9	Total Current	27.9	27.9	28.6	28.1	34.1	31.6
56.4	59.5	57.6	Fixed Assets (net)	66.3	56.8	59.3	58.1	55.7	53.6
3.5	4.3	3.5	Intangibles (net)	.0	5.3	2.7	1.1	4.4	6.7
9.8	8.0	9.0	All Other Non-Current	5.8	10.0	9.4	12.7	5.8	8.1
100.0	100.0	100.0	Total	100.0	100.0	100.0	100.0	100.0	100.0
			LIABILITIES						
7.5	5.7	5.4	Notes Payable-Short Term	8.4	2.5	4.7	6.7	6.2	4.4
10.7	12.1	12.4	Cur. Mat.-L.T.D.	16.4	13.3	9.7	12.8	10.6	11.9
3.5	2.9	4.5	Trade Payables	1.8	3.6	4.5	4.6	7.6	3.7
.3	.4	.2	Income Taxes Payable	.0	.1	.0	.0	.9	.1
6.8	6.1	4.8	All Other Current	1.6	1.9	5.1	6.7	6.0	5.6
28.8	27.1	27.3	Total Current	28.2	21.4	24.0	30.8	31.4	25.6
33.4	33.9	31.0	Long-Term Debt	42.8	34.3	40.5	26.6	24.1	28.0
1.1	1.7	1.6	Deferred Taxes	.3	.9	.6	2.4	1.9	2.1
4.6	4.3	4.3	All Other Non-Current	6.7	3.9	3.4	5.0	3.1	3.9
32.1	32.9	35.8	Net Worth	22.0	39.5	31.4	35.3	39.5	40.4
100.0	100.0	100.0	Total Liabilties & Net Worth	100.0	100.0	100.0	100.0	100.0	100.0
			INCOME DATA						
100.0	100.0	100.0	Net Sales	100.0	100.0	100.0	100.0	100.0	100.0
			Gross Profit						
91.8	91.8	92.5	Operating Expenses	89.8	89.6	94.4	94.3	93.4	92.7
8.2	8.2	7.5	Operating Profit	10.2	10.4	5.6	5.7	6.6	7.3
1.6	1.7	1.5	All Other Expenses (net)	4.6	2.2	-.1	1.0	.8	1.4
6.6	6.5	5.9	Profit Before Taxes	5.5	8.2	5.6	4.7	5.8	5.9
			RATIOS						
2.1	2.1	2.1		4.1	3.3	2.1	1.9	2.5	2.3
1.1	1.0	1.1	Current	.9	1.3	1.3	.9	1.0	1.2
.5	.5	.5		.3	.5	.7	.4	.5	.8
1.8	1.9	1.8		2.1	2.1	1.4	1.8	2.2	1.9
.8	.9	.9	Quick	.7	1.0	1.0	.7	.9	1.0
.4	.4	.4		.2	.3	.6	.4	.4	.5

1	255.6	3	106.1	2	184.0		0	UND	1	655.5	0	UND	3	114.9	9	38.6	20	18.1
16	22.2	18	20.1	15	23.7	Sales/Receivables	0	UND	6	65.1	15	24.1	14	25.5	23	15.7	30	12.1
31	11.8	34	10.8	35	10.3		2	172.1	29	12.7	31	11.9	35	10.4	37	9.8	44	8.4

			Cost of Sales/Inventory						

			Cost of Sales/Payables						

	10.2		10.0		9.4			7.5		8.3		14.4		22.3		8.6		7.3
	183.2		853.4		107.0	Sales/Working Capital		NM		25.6		22.1		-47.9		195.3		48.6
	-12.6		-10.1		-10.8			-8.8		-10.7		-80.3		-10.2		-10.6		-28.1
	7.6		7.6		8.3			11.4		7.4		5.3		6.8		8.7		11.1
(132)	2.8	(141)	3.7	(146)	3.4	EBIT/Interest	(14)	2.7	(26)	3.4		4.1	(32)	1.8	(27)	3.1		5.0
	1.3		2.0		1.4			.1		1.6		1.9		1.3		1.9		2.9
	2.3		2.5		2.4									2.0		2.2		3.3
(40)	1.6	(57)	1.9	(46)	1.7	Net Profit + Depr., Dep., Amort./Cur. Mat. L/T/D					(14)	1.2	(11)	1.5	(12)	2.1
	1.2		1.2		1.1									.9		.9		1.5
	1.1		1.1		.9			.8		.8		1.2		.9		.6		.9
	1.8		2.0		1.6	Fixed/Worth		1.7		1.6		2.4		1.7		1.7		1.4
	6.6		5.7		4.6			-8.4		-17.7		5.6		4.4		4.4		3.1
	.9		1.0		.8			.9		.4		.9		.8		.7		.8
	1.8		2.1		1.8	Debt/Worth		2.1		1.3		2.6		1.8		1.9		1.7
	8.2		7.2		6.9			-10.2		-26.1		13.7		6.0		5.9		4.4
	43.3		50.4		46.5	% Profit Before Taxes/Tangible Net Worth		39.9		51.9		63.4		55.0		45.8		30.8
(118)	22.3	(123)	26.8	(139)	22.7		(13)	18.8	(20)	25.3	(16)	31.5	(35)	23.1	(29)	18.4	(26)	21.4
	5.4		13.0		12.4			-3.4		5.7		13.8		5.7		14.5		16.1
	15.7		13.9		15.4	% Profit Before Taxes/Total Assets		17.4		19.3		15.5		14.9		14.7		14.5
	6.7		8.1		7.5			.1		9.7		8.9		5.3		7.5		8.2
	1.3		2.7		1.5			-3.9		1.2		3.3		1.4		3.6		5.0
	5.5		4.9		5.4			4.9		4.4		8.5		5.4		7.0		5.2
	3.0		2.7		3.0	Sales/Net Fixed Assets		2.7		2.6		2.8		3.2		3.0		3.4
	1.8		1.6		1.8			1.0		1.8		1.5		1.9		1.7		1.8
	2.5		2.4		2.5			2.9		2.0		2.7		2.4		2.8		2.5
	1.8		1.6		1.6	Sales/Total Assets		2.2		1.5		1.8		1.6		1.7		1.6
	1.2		1.1		1.2			.9		1.3		1.1		1.3		1.2		1.2
	6.1		6.3		5.9			8.2		8.3		7.5		6.8		4.2		4.1
(126)	9.4	(134)	9.8	(142)	9.8	% Depr., Dep., Amort./Sales	(17)	12.6	(24)	14.5	(15)	9.9	(35)	9.9	(25)	8.0	(26)	6.7
	13.5		13.3		14.6			23.5		18.0		15.3		15.6		11.9		9.8
	1.2		2.1		1.3					4.2		3.3		2.6		.9		.4
(77)	3.5	(76)	3.9	(82)	4.3	% Officers', Directors' Owners' Comp/Sales		(17)	5.7	(10)	5.5	(19)	3.7	(15)	1.7	(12)	2.2
	5.9		6.3		7.0				8.5		8.0		6.2		6.2		2.2
2046608M		2983604M		3844294M		Net Sales ($)	12436M		51449M		65380M		267328M		491096M		2956605M
1471929M		1872455M		2192502M		Total Assets ($)	11690M		35001M		39663M		162314M		308997M		1634837M

M = $ thousand   MM = $ million
See Pages 9 through 22 for Explanation of Ratios and Data

Current Data Sorted by Assets   Comparative Historical Data

0-500M	500M-2MM	2-10MM	10-50MM	50-100MM	100-250MM	Type of Statement	4/1/06-3/31/07 ALL	4/1/07-3/31/08 ALL
	2	2	5	1	1	Unqualified	7	8
	2	19	6			Reviewed	24	25
	6	6	5			Compiled	21	29
4	13	17				Tax Returns	21	34
5	17	29	14	1	2	Other	45	42
	31 (4/1-9/30/10)		126 (10/1/10-3/31/11)					
9	40	73	30	2	3	**NUMBER OF STATEMENTS**	118	138
%	%	%	%	%	%	**ASSETS**	%	%
	10.7	5.9	11.9			Cash & Equivalents	6.9	10.2
	9.8	9.1	6.3			Trade Receivables (net)	9.4	7.8
	1.6	1.7	1.6			Inventory	1.9	1.8
	5.1	3.4	3.1			All Other Current	3.4	3.3
	27.2	20.0	22.9			Total Current	21.7	23.2
	57.3	69.2	69.7			Fixed Assets (net)	69.1	68.5
	4.2	2.5	.8			Intangibles (net)	1.5	1.2
	11.3	8.3	6.6			All Other Non-Current	7.8	7.1
	100.0	100.0	100.0			Total	100.0	100.0
						LIABILITIES		
	7.7	2.7	1.3			Notes Payable-Short Term	3.6	3.1
	12.1	13.4	9.7			Cur. Mat.-L.T.D.	11.8	12.1
	6.3	4.7	3.3			Trade Payables	4.8	5.3
	.3	.3	.4			Income Taxes Payable	.5	.6
	9.7	7.0	6.2			All Other Current	8.5	6.9
	36.1	28.1	20.8			Total Current	29.2	28.0
	53.7	47.2	34.0			Long-Term Debt	55.7	51.7
	.0	2.8	3.9			Deferred Taxes	1.6	1.7
	10.6	3.2	6.8			All Other Non-Current	4.1	8.0
	-.4	18.7	34.5			Net Worth	9.4	10.5
	100.0	100.0	100.0			Total Liabilities & Net Worth	100.0	100.0
						INCOME DATA		
	100.0	100.0	100.0			Net Sales	100.0	100.0
						Gross Profit		
	91.9	94.2	92.0			Operating Expenses	93.6	93.0
	8.1	5.8	8.0			Operating Profit	6.4	7.0
	2.0	2.3	2.8			All Other Expenses (net)	3.0	2.9
	6.1	3.6	5.1			Profit Before Taxes	3.4	4.1
						RATIOS		
	1.8	1.1	2.2				1.4	1.3
	.8	.6	1.3			Current	.7	.8
	.3	.3	.8				.4	.5
	1.1	.8	1.7				1.1	1.0
	.5	.4	.9			Quick	(114) .6	(137) .6
	.2	.3	.4				.3	.3
1 392.6	5 67.0	15 24.9					7 53.0	5 79.1
10 35.6	16 22.7	21 17.4				Sales/Receivables	13 27.6	12 29.8
21 17.8	25 14.7	28 12.9					33 11.2	30 12.2
						Cost of Sales/Inventory		
						Cost of Sales/Payables		
	18.6	90.5	8.5				24.2	40.4
	-52.9	-14.0	20.7			Sales/Working Capital	-27.1	-39.1
	-7.6	-6.4	-23.2				-7.5	-10.3
	12.8	3.9	5.1				4.7	3.1
(37) 3.4	(71) 1.6	(28) 2.5				EBIT/Interest	(105) 2.2	(128) 1.9
	1.1	.9	1.2				1.1	1.0
		1.5	2.9			Net Profit + Depr., Dep.,	2.0	1.9
	(27) 1.1	(17) 1.3				Amort./Cur. Mat. L/T/D	(34) 1.3	(35) 1.5
		.9	1.0				1.1	1.0
	1.8	1.9	1.4				1.8	1.7
	7.9	3.1	2.4			Fixed/Worth	4.0	5.4
	-2.5	NM	3.9				-11.2	-11.1
	2.0	1.5	1.3				1.8	1.8
	20.2	3.2	2.1			Debt/Worth	5.6	5.9
	-4.8	NM	4.1				-13.5	-14.9
	120.2	23.3	22.6			% Profit Before Taxes/Tangible	35.5	33.2
(23) 48.3	(55) 10.7	(29) 12.5				Net Worth	(84) 16.8	(94) 16.5
	2.0	-1.7	5.7				5.8	5.3
	33.9	7.1	9.0			% Profit Before Taxes/Total	9.9	9.8
	8.7	3.2	4.0			Assets	5.1	4.2
	-.3	-.3	1.3				.6	.1
	8.0	3.0	1.9				3.1	4.3
	4.3	1.8	1.3			Sales/Net Fixed Assets	1.9	2.2
	2.7	1.2	1.1				1.2	1.1
	3.4	1.8	1.3				2.2	2.5
	2.6	1.4	1.0			Sales/Total Assets	1.3	1.5
	1.9	1.0	.7				.8	.9
	4.1	7.0	6.9				6.1	6.8
(30) 8.1	(64) 11.3	(29) 9.2				% Depr., Dep., Amort./Sales	(108) 9.5	(125) 10.5
	15.1	15.2	11.9				14.9	14.5
	2.1	1.4				% Officers', Directors'	1.4	2.0
(20) 2.9	(24) 2.7					Owners' Comp/Sales	(45) 3.0	(49) 3.2
	5.5	4.0					6.8	5.7
12616M	158485M	559965M	571114M	151339M	391197M	Net Sales ($)	1285015M	1391293M
2240M	50641M	394001M	583210M	140455M	468106M	Total Assets ($)	1094715M	1124561M

M = $ thousand   MM = $ million
See Pages 9 through 22 for Explanation of Ratios and Data

Comparative Historical Data   Current Data Sorted by Sales

				Type of Statement						
7	5	11		Unqualified		1	1	1	4	4
20	21	27		Reviewed		1	4	11	9	2
26	24	17		Compiled		2	5	4	6	
16	22	34		Tax Returns	4	8	9	11	2	
45	50	68		Other	2	18	9	19	14	6
4/1/08-3/31/09 ALL	4/1/09-3/31/10 ALL	4/1/10-3/31/11 ALL				31 (4/1-9/30/10)		126 (10/1/10-3/31/11)		
					0-1MM	1-3MM	3-5MM	5-10MM	10-25MM	25MM & OVER
114	122	157		NUMBER OF STATEMENTS	6	30	28	46	35	12
%	%	%		ASSETS	%	%	%	%	%	%
8.9	10.7	9.3		Cash & Equivalents		6.9	7.4	9.5	11.2	12.2
9.4	8.4	8.7		Trade Receivables (net)		7.2	5.6	9.6	9.9	10.7
1.8	2.0	1.5		Inventory		.7	2.3	1.8	1.4	1.5
3.6	4.3	4.1		All Other Current		5.8	2.6	3.2	4.9	6.0
23.8	25.4	23.6		Total Current		20.6	17.9	24.0	27.5	30.4
64.9	64.7	64.8		Fixed Assets (net)		61.5	73.4	63.8	63.2	57.8
2.6	2.4	2.8		Intangibles (net)		3.6	4.0	2.9	.6	5.5
8.8	7.5	8.9		All Other Non-Current		14.3	4.7	9.3	8.7	6.2
100.0	100.0	100.0		Total		100.0	100.0	100.0	100.0	100.0
				LIABILITIES						
4.1	4.9	6.5		Notes Payable-Short Term		18.8	7.0	3.4	1.7	3.3
12.1	12.4	11.8		Cur. Mat.-L.T.D.		10.1	14.4	14.7	10.4	6.4
4.5	5.1	5.1		Trade Payables		4.4	4.7	3.3	7.1	5.0
.3	.2	.3		Income Taxes Payable		.1	.3	.5	.1	.8
11.0	8.5	7.8		All Other Current		11.6	5.4	7.0	8.4	7.6
31.9	31.3	31.5		Total Current		45.0	31.8	28.9	27.6	23.1
45.4	49.2	47.7		Long-Term Debt		61.5	57.7	47.1	35.0	25.0
1.1	1.4	2.1		Deferred Taxes		.5	1.4	3.4	2.6	2.7
4.9	7.1	7.1		All Other Non-Current		7.8	4.3	6.3	6.4	8.5
16.6	11.0	11.6		Net Worth		-14.8	4.8	14.4	28.4	40.7
100.0	100.0	100.0		Total Liabilities & Net Worth		100.0	100.0	100.0	100.0	100.0
				INCOME DATA						
100.0	100.0	100.0		Net Sales		100.0	100.0	100.0	100.0	100.0
				Gross Profit						
93.2	94.4	93.5		Operating Expenses		91.4	94.6	95.3	93.7	96.2
6.8	5.6	6.5		Operating Profit		8.6	5.4	4.7	6.3	3.8
2.3	1.9	2.2		All Other Expenses (net)		2.7	2.1	1.3	1.9	1.3
4.5	3.7	4.3		Profit Before Taxes		6.0	3.3	3.5	4.4	2.5
				RATIOS						
1.3	1.6	1.5				.9	1.3	1.6	1.6	2.1
.7	.8	.7		Current		.5	.5	.7	1.1	1.2
.4	.4	.4				.3	.3	.4	.7	.8
.9	1.2	1.0				.6	.8	1.0	1.3	1.5
.5	.6	.5		Quick		.4	.4	.5	.8	.9
.3	.3	.3				.2	.2	.3	.4	.5
5 74.0	5 75.8	5 69.2			0 UND	3 145.8	4 101.3	11 34.3	21 17.5	
13 27.3	13 27.7	16 22.7		Sales/Receivables	8 44.5	12 31.5	17 21.4	19 19.2	26 14.3	
24 15.5	27 13.4	25 14.3			16 23.1	21 17.5	26 13.9	30 12.1	29 12.5	
				Cost of Sales/Inventory						
				Cost of Sales/Payables						
30.7	15.8	17.7			-74.1	NM	22.1	12.2	6.7	
-25.0	-41.0	-28.6		Sales/Working Capital	-18.2	-9.0	-16.8	131.1	29.5	
-10.5	-9.1	-7.4			-6.3	-5.8	-8.0	-18.6	-26.8	
4.3	4.1	4.7			12.4	3.4	4.2	5.3	7.4	
(105) 2.5	(114) 2.5	(147) 2.2		EBIT/Interest	(27) 1.6	1.6	(44) 2.1	(33) 2.2	(11) 2.0	
1.2	1.1	.9			.6	1.0	1.1	.8	.0	
2.0	2.2	1.8					1.4	2.6		
(39) 1.5	(34) 1.5	(48) 1.3		Net Profit + Depr., Dep., Amort./Cur. Mat. L/T/D		(17) 1.1	(19) 1.3		
1.0	1.3	1.0					.8	1.0		
1.6	1.5	1.6			1.9	3.1	1.7	1.5	1.1	
3.0	3.2	3.1		Fixed/Worth	7.5	9.1	3.1	2.4	1.5	
UND	-5.0	-32.8			-1.6	-2.9	NM	5.1	2.3	
1.5	1.5	1.5			1.6	2.7	1.4	1.3	1.2	
3.4	4.4	3.3		Debt/Worth	9.6	10.4	3.4	2.4	1.9	
UND	-7.2	-44.8			-2.9	-5.1	NM	7.0	2.8	
37.6	34.3	32.8			135.9	68.2	27.1	27.6	22.1	
(86) 18.9	(84) 18.6	(115) 13.8		% Profit Before Taxes/Tangible Net Worth	(18) 22.1	(16) 17.0	(35) 14.5	(31) 11.8	(11) 12.9	
7.3	5.7	.4			-.6	-2.5	2.5	-1.4	-2.6	
10.8	10.6	10.8			24.3	9.9	8.7	10.7	11.2	
5.3	5.0	3.9		% Profit Before Taxes/Total Assets	4.5	3.3	4.8	3.9	3.7	
.7	.7	-.3			-1.3	-.2	.3	-.6	-3.1	
5.1	4.3	4.1			8.3	3.4	4.7	3.4	2.6	
2.3	2.2	2.1		Sales/Net Fixed Assets	3.6	1.8	1.8	2.0	1.9	
1.2	1.3	1.4			2.1	1.2	1.3	1.3	1.7	
2.7	2.4	2.4			3.2	2.1	2.9	2.1	1.5	
1.5	1.4	1.5		Sales/Total Assets	2.0	1.4	1.5	1.4	1.2	
1.0	1.0	1.0			1.2	1.0	.9	1.0	.9	
6.4	5.7	6.7			4.6	6.5	8.1	6.1	4.4	
(101) 9.2	(108) 10.3	(131) 9.4		% Depr., Dep., Amort./Sales	(21) 8.3	(26) 12.0	(39) 11.0	(31) 7.1	(10) 7.6	
13.5	15.1	14.0			15.9	15.0	14.2	11.4	10.0	
1.3	1.5	1.5			1.5	2.5	1.7	.8		
(40) 2.5	(48) 2.8	(59) 2.7		% Officers', Directors' Owners' Comp/Sales	(17) 4.6	(11) 3.1	(13) 2.2	(14) 1.8		
4.9	4.8	4.6			7.2	4.8	3.5	3.0		
2040455M	1383072M	1844716M		Net Sales ($)	4134M	60433M	111404M	342688M	533061M	792996M
1235336M	1157546M	1638653M		Total Assets ($)	6712M	38449M	89934M	291298M	414766M	797494M

Current Data Sorted by Assets   **Comparative Historical Data**

						Type of Statement		
1		5				Unqualified		
	1		1			Reviewed	1	1
1	5	1				Compiled	4	
4	1	1				Tax Returns	2	3
3	5	5	2			Other	1	1
0-500M	6 (4/1-9/30/10) 500M-2MM	2-10MM	30 (10/1/10-3/31/11) 10-50MM	50-100MM	100-250MM		4/1/06-3/31/07 ALL	4/1/07-3/31/08 ALL
9	12	12	3			NUMBER OF STATEMENTS	8	6
%	%	%	%	%	%	ASSETS	%	%
	6.6	16.6				Cash & Equivalents		
	29.3	26.3				Trade Receivables (net)		
	4.0	.4	D	D		Inventory		
	.4	3.9	A	A		All Other Current		
	40.5	47.3	T	T		Total Current		
	43.9	43.4	A	A		Fixed Assets (net)		
	9.1	.8				Intangibles (net)		
	6.5	8.5	N	N		All Other Non-Current		
	100.0	100.0	O	O		Total		
			T	T		LIABILITIES		
	12.7	7.3				Notes Payable-Short Term		
	4.6	6.1	A	A		Cur. Mat.-L.T.D.		
	4.9	13.2	V	V		Trade Payables		
	.6	1.2	A	A		Income Taxes Payable		
	12.2	9.4	I	I		All Other Current		
	35.0	37.2	L	L		Total Current		
	20.2	16.5	A	A		Long-Term Debt		
	.5	2.9	B	B		Deferred Taxes		
	5.4	1.9	L	L		All Other Non-Current		
	38.9	41.5	E	E		Net Worth		
	100.0	100.0				Total Liabilities & Net Worth		
						INCOME DATA		
	100.0	100.0				Net Sales		
						Gross Profit		
	88.9	88.1				Operating Expenses		
	11.1	11.9				Operating Profit		
	.2	5.0				All Other Expenses (net)		
	10.9	6.9				Profit Before Taxes		
						RATIOS		
	3.5	5.0						
	1.7	1.9				Current		
	.4	.8						
	3.5	4.2						
	1.6	1.7				Quick		
	.3	.6						
0	UND	19	19.6					
35	10.3	42	8.8			Sales/Receivables		
67	5.5	47	7.7					
						Cost of Sales/Inventory		
						Cost of Sales/Payables		
	9.5	6.1						
	22.9	13.7				Sales/Working Capital		
	-11.1	-255.2						
	23.5	14.9						
(11)	10.5	(10) 7.1				EBIT/Interest		
	9.3	.7						
						Net Profit + Depr., Dep., Amort./Cur. Mat. L/T/D		
	.4	.5						
	1.7	.8				Fixed/Worth		
	-24.9	3.8						
	.2	.6						
	2.0	1.7				Debt/Worth		
	-32.8	6.1						
		55.8						
		23.2				% Profit Before Taxes/Tangible Net Worth		
		3.0						
	46.6	12.0						
	23.3	6.3				% Profit Before Taxes/Total Assets		
	13.9	1.0						
	24.4	25.2						
	6.7	7.4				Sales/Net Fixed Assets		
	3.5	2.8						
	3.8	3.4						
	3.0	2.8				Sales/Total Assets		
	2.2	1.7						
		1.3						
	(10)	3.4				% Depr., Dep., Amort./Sales		
		9.1						
						% Officers', Directors' Owners' Comp/Sales		
12382M	41013M	116178M	271797M			Net Sales ($)	136963M	123170M
2405M	14120M	49046M	77844M			Total Assets ($)	51947M	64210M

M = $ thousand   MM = $ million
See Pages 9 through 22 for Explanation of Ratios and Data

Comparative Historical Data | Current Data Sorted by Sales

			Type of Statement						
4	4	6	Unqualified	1	1	1		3	
	2	2	Reviewed			1			
2	4	7	Compiled	1	1	2	2	1	1
7	7	6	Tax Returns	2	2	1	1		
6	11	15	Other	3	4	2	2	2	2
4/1/08-3/31/09 ALL	4/1/09-3/31/10 ALL	4/1/10-3/31/11 ALL		6 (4/1-9/30/10) 0-1MM	1-3MM	3-5MM	30 (10/1/10-3/31/11) 5-10MM	10-25MM	25MM & OVER
12	28	36	NUMBER OF STATEMENTS	7	8	7	5	6	3
%	%	%	ASSETS	%	%	%	%	%	%
9.7	14.6	15.9	Cash & Equivalents						
25.6	30.0	27.7	Trade Receivables (net)						
1.5	1.4	1.5	Inventory						
7.9	4.3	1.8	All Other Current						
44.7	50.3	46.9	Total Current						
38.4	43.8	38.8	Fixed Assets (net)						
4.9	1.2	3.6	Intangibles (net)						
12.1	4.7	10.8	All Other Non-Current						
100.0	100.0	100.0	Total						
			LIABILITIES						
4.9	7.5	9.3	Notes Payable-Short Term						
6.1	14.1	6.1	Cur. Mat.-L.T.D.						
20.3	8.6	10.6	Trade Payables						
.0	.9	.7	Income Taxes Payable						
15.9	11.3	14.1	All Other Current						
47.2	42.5	40.9	Total Current						
18.5	36.0	19.9	Long-Term Debt						
.0	.3	1.1	Deferred Taxes						
6.0	2.8	2.5	All Other Non-Current						
28.3	18.4	35.6	Net Worth						
100.0	100.0	100.0	Total Liabilties & Net Worth						
			INCOME DATA						
100.0	100.0	100.0	Net Sales						
			Gross Profit						
92.4	92.7	89.6	Operating Expenses						
7.6	7.3	10.4	Operating Profit						
.6	1.9	2.0	All Other Expenses (net)						
7.0	5.4	8.4	Profit Before Taxes						
			RATIOS						
2.7	4.8	3.3	Current						
1.1	2.1	1.7							
.3	.6	.6							
2.1	4.7	3.3	Quick						
.8	1.4	1.6							
.2	.4	.5							
0 UND	0 UND	0 UND	Sales/Receivables						
25 14.7	32 11.3	38 9.6							
48 7.6	48 7.5	47 7.8							
			Cost of Sales/Inventory						
			Cost of Sales/Payables						
7.1	5.9	8.1	Sales/Working Capital						
NM	13.4	24.3							
-12.0	-13.8	-14.5							
12.8	13.4	17.9	EBIT/Interest						
(11) 7.1	(22) 4.4	(28) 9.8							
2.4	1.2	1.4							
			Net Profit + Depr., Dep., Amort./Cur. Mat. L/T/D						
.7	.3	.4	Fixed/Worth						
1.8	1.6	.8							
NM	-260.2	8.5							
.7	.5	.6	Debt/Worth						
1.3	1.3	2.0							
NM	-294.6	19.6							
	84.9	84.3	% Profit Before Taxes/Tangible Net Worth						
(20)	53.6 (30)	26.5							
	16.5	7.2							
25.0	53.7	32.9	% Profit Before Taxes/Total Assets						
7.2	14.7	14.0							
5.6	.0	4.5							
28.5	28.4	27.8	Sales/Net Fixed Assets						
7.4	8.9	8.9							
4.0	4.1	4.2							
3.8	4.9	4.2	Sales/Total Assets						
3.2	3.5	3.1							
2.2	1.8	2.2							
	1.4	1.4	% Depr., Dep., Amort./Sales						
(24)	4.4 (28)	3.0							
	11.1	7.8							
	1.5	3.2	% Officers', Directors' Owners' Comp/Sales						
(16)	4.1 (13)	4.7							
	6.4	7.9							
971029M	332268M	441370M	Net Sales ($)	4137M	18025M	25291M	37120M	85000M	271797M
283295M	114373M	143415M	Total Assets ($)	8000M	8807M	10068M	12033M	26663M	77844M

M = $ thousand   MM = $ million
See Pages 9 through 22 for Explanation of Ratios and Data

Current Data Sorted by Assets   Comparative Historical Data

0-500M	500M-2MM	2-10MM	10-50MM	50-100MM	100-250MM	Type of Statement	24	21
1	1	6	4	2	2	Unqualified	24	21
	5	11	5			Reviewed	14	15
4	10	3			1	Compiled	13	9
6	11	5				Tax Returns	22	16
7	11	13	5	1	1	Other	31	26
	21 (4/1-9/30/10)		94 (10/1/10-3/31/11)				4/1/06-3/31/07 ALL	4/1/07-3/31/08 ALL
18	38	38	14	3	4	NUMBER OF STATEMENTS	104	87
%	%	%	%	%	%	**ASSETS**	%	%
13.1	18.3	10.0	6.7			Cash & Equivalents	13.8	10.8
19.4	21.4	21.5	31.2			Trade Receivables (net)	23.4	22.7
.3	.4	1.3	.4			Inventory	.8	.6
9.9	3.2	5.1	3.8			All Other Current	5.2	4.7
42.7	43.2	37.9	42.0			Total Current	43.2	38.8
40.6	41.0	44.5	35.2			Fixed Assets (net)	41.3	43.3
5.4	8.9	7.7	10.2			Intangibles (net)	5.7	9.1
11.3	6.9	9.8	12.5			All Other Non-Current	9.8	8.9
100.0	100.0	100.0	100.0			Total	100.0	100.0
						LIABILITIES		
12.2	8.7	6.3	7.9			Notes Payable-Short Term	7.8	9.2
19.7	10.7	8.1	9.0			Cur. Mat.-L.T.D.	10.2	11.3
5.0	7.4	8.0	9.4			Trade Payables	11.5	10.9
.1	.2	.4	.9			Income Taxes Payable	.2	.1
24.5	10.8	7.8	13.7			All Other Current	13.0	10.6
61.4	38.0	30.7	40.9			Total Current	42.7	42.1
23.7	31.4	25.6	21.0			Long-Term Debt	23.6	30.0
.0	.1	.2	.0			Deferred Taxes	.5	.4
5.8	3.3	4.8	7.0			All Other Non-Current	8.8	6.6
9.0	27.3	38.8	31.1			Net Worth	24.4	20.9
100.0	100.0	100.0	100.0			Total Liabilties & Net Worth	100.0	100.0
						INCOME DATA		
100.0	100.0	100.0	100.0			Net Sales	100.0	100.0
						Gross Profit		
96.0	92.3	95.5	95.1			Operating Expenses	94.8	95.2
4.0	7.7	4.5	4.9			Operating Profit	5.2	4.8
.2	1.4	.8	.1			All Other Expenses (net)	1.2	2.5
3.7	6.3	3.8	4.9			Profit Before Taxes	3.9	2.3
						RATIOS		
2.2	2.7	1.7	1.9			Current	2.4	2.3
.7	1.3	1.1	.9				1.2	.9
.2	.4	.7	.6				.6	.5
2.2	2.5	1.5	1.5			Quick	2.2	1.9
.4	1.2	.9	.9				1.0	.8
.1	.4	.5	.5				.5	.3
0 UND	0 UND	10 35.9	27 13.5			Sales/Receivables	6 65.2	11 33.6
0 UND	19 18.9	22 16.9	44 8.3				27 13.4	30 12.2
44 8.3	37 9.8	39 9.3	55 6.6				48 7.6	57 6.4
						Cost of Sales/Inventory		
						Cost of Sales/Payables		
37.2	9.7	16.2	8.8			Sales/Working Capital	10.7	8.5
-71.3	34.7	139.8	-290.0				38.6	-106.6
-9.0	-9.6	-24.7	-14.0				-19.6	-12.7
56.0	10.4	10.2	14.6			EBIT/Interest	11.8	4.5
(11) 7.0	(32) 4.4	(35) 5.6	(12) 5.7				(90) 4.2	(74) 2.0
1.0	1.1	2.6	1.9				1.2	.7
						Net Profit + Depr., Dep., Amort./Cur. Mat. L/T/D	3.2	2.0
							(17) 2.1	(20) 1.1
							.8	.4
.3	.5	.8	.4			Fixed/Worth	.5	.7
9.3	1.6	1.4	3.8				1.3	3.4
-3.1	-3.0	5.6	-20.2				74.5	-2.4
.5	.9	1.0	1.1			Debt/Worth	.6	1.5
64.4	2.8	2.2	9.1				2.4	4.9
-7.0	-9.4	7.6	-39.6				173.2	-5.7
150.1	107.2	73.3	67.4			% Profit Before Taxes/Tangible Net Worth	76.9	60.6
(10) 54.9	(27) 50.6	(32) 38.0	(10) 26.5				(79) 31.0	(58) 20.8
9.9	2.9	9.5	1.0				7.7	5.8
65.8	30.7	21.1	21.4			% Profit Before Taxes/Total Assets	24.4	12.2
9.8	7.5	7.9	9.3				8.7	4.4
-.2	.2	3.4	.6				.2	-1.3
180.6	31.5	13.7	44.3			Sales/Net Fixed Assets	18.5	15.5
19.2	10.2	6.7	7.5				9.8	6.3
7.9	3.7	2.1	2.9				3.8	2.9
9.7	4.5	4.3	3.5			Sales/Total Assets	4.5	3.2
5.4	3.5	2.1	2.3				2.9	2.2
3.5	2.2	1.4	1.7				1.9	1.4
	2.7	1.8	2.5			% Depr., Dep., Amort./Sales	1.9	2.5
	(26) 4.8	(33) 4.6	(10) 4.3				(86) 4.2	(77) 4.3
	9.4	10.1	7.2				6.6	7.7
	3.4	.9				% Officers', Directors' Owners' Comp/Sales	1.3	2.1
	(14) 5.1	(13) 2.9					(30) 3.8	(25) 3.6
	8.8	4.9					8.2	12.7
31097M	164300M	559846M	675352M	354891M	1214373M	Net Sales ($)	2196328M	1728676M
4692M	45351M	172218M	251454M	207819M	807905M	Total Assets ($)	1073857M	1193951M

M = $ thousand   MM = $ million
See Pages 9 through 22 for Explanation of Ratios and Data

Comparative Historical Data | Current Data Sorted by Sales

Type of Statement	4/1/08-3/31/09 ALL	4/1/09-3/31/10 ALL	4/1/10-3/31/11 ALL		0-1MM	1-3MM	3-5MM	5-10MM	10-25MM	25MM & OVER
Unqualified	21	19	15			2			3	10
Reviewed	14	18	22			2	5	4	6	5
Compiled	12	23	18		1	4	4	7	1	1
Tax Returns	16	14	22		4	4	6	5	3	
Other	41	36	38		4	10	6	7	5	6
					21 (4/1-9/30/10)			94 (10/1/10-3/31/11)		
NUMBER OF STATEMENTS	104	110	115		9	22	21	23	18	22
ASSETS	%	%	%		%	%	%	%	%	%
Cash & Equivalents	10.4	12.7	12.6			11.0	14.5	18.7	8.3	8.9
Trade Receivables (net)	22.2	21.7	22.2			17.6	22.3	23.6	25.0	29.5
Inventory	.6	.7	.9			.3	.5	.8	.6	2.4
All Other Current	4.2	4.0	5.1			8.5	5.6	2.8	5.5	4.9
Total Current	37.4	39.1	40.7			37.4	43.0	45.9	39.4	45.7
Fixed Assets (net)	44.3	40.7	40.4			47.4	43.9	35.3	35.7	26.9
Intangibles (net)	9.7	7.1	9.3			8.0	4.9	7.8	15.2	13.4
All Other Non-Current	8.7	13.1	9.6			7.2	8.2	11.0	9.7	14.0
Total	100.0	100.0	100.0			100.0	100.0	100.0	100.0	100.0
LIABILITIES										
Notes Payable-Short Term	8.8	7.6	8.3			12.9	4.2	4.7	9.8	8.5
Cur. Mat.-L.T.D.	7.3	9.0	10.6			14.7	9.8	13.2	6.2	6.9
Trade Payables	6.3	8.5	7.5			2.6	6.7	8.6	6.7	15.2
Income Taxes Payable	.3	.2	.4			.1	.0	.5	.3	.6
All Other Current	12.5	10.6	12.3			7.0	9.4	13.1	14.0	11.1
Total Current	35.2	35.9	39.1			37.2	30.1	40.2	37.0	42.4
Long-Term Debt	25.9	26.8	27.4			33.7	29.4	36.4	23.2	21.9
Deferred Taxes	.7	.5	.2			.0	.1	.0	.3	.6
All Other Non-Current	7.1	4.2	6.4			5.9	5.9	4.2	4.9	13.8
Net Worth	31.1	32.6	26.9			23.2	34.6	19.2	34.5	21.4
Total Liabilities & Net Worth	100.0	100.0	100.0			100.0	100.0	100.0	100.0	100.0
INCOME DATA										
Net Sales	100.0	100.0	100.0			100.0	100.0	100.0	100.0	100.0
Gross Profit										
Operating Expenses	93.9	94.9	94.5			94.0	98.8	90.7	95.7	95.9
Operating Profit	6.1	5.1	5.5			6.0	1.2	9.3	4.3	4.1
All Other Expenses (net)	2.0	1.3	1.2			.5	.5	.8	.8	2.2
Profit Before Taxes	4.1	3.8	4.3			5.5	.7	8.4	3.5	2.0
RATIOS										
Current	2.6	2.2	2.1			4.1	2.9	2.1	2.3	1.3
	1.3	1.1	1.1			1.0	1.3	1.3	1.4	1.0
	.7	.5	.5			.3	.7	.8	.4	.8
Quick	2.3	2.1	1.9			4.0	2.5	2.0	2.1	1.1
	1.1	.9	1.0			.6	1.3	1.1	1.2	.9
	.6	.4	.4			.1	.6	.7	.4	.6
Sales/Receivables	4 86.1	4 93.6	2 158.2		0 UND	14 25.4	3 127.2	16 22.3	12 31.3	
	27 13.6	26 13.9	22 16.3		3 112.7	22 16.3	20 18.3	33 11.2	36 10.2	
	57 6.4	52 7.0	44 8.3		40 9.1	43 8.6	35 10.5	47 7.8	44 8.3	
Cost of Sales/Inventory										
Cost of Sales/Payables										
Sales/Working Capital	8.3	8.9	12.4			8.4	9.1	12.4	7.9	27.0
	45.1	74.3	178.4			NM	30.2	37.2	30.0	NM
	-20.6	-16.1	-15.6			-7.9	-34.3	-37.4	-10.9	-31.2
EBIT/Interest	10.8	11.9	11.8			13.5	8.8	13.7	15.6	13.7
	(91) 3.6	(99) 3.4	(97) 4.9		(16) 2.1	(18) 3.4	(22) 7.5	(16) 5.1	(21) 6.3	
	.9	1.3	1.1			1.0	.2	4.0	2.1	.9
Net Profit + Depr., Dep., Amort./Cur. Mat. L/T/D	3.1	2.3	3.4							
	(19) 1.5	(24) 1.7	(16) 2.0							
	.4	1.2	.7							
Fixed/Worth	.7	.5	.6			.5	.4	.6	.5	.9
	1.7	1.7	1.8			9.3	3.0	1.4	3.7	1.8
	NM	12.4	-7.6			-3.1	6.5	4.8	-2.5	-1.1
Debt/Worth	.8	.8	1.1			.5	.4	1.2	1.3	2.1
	2.2	2.6	2.8			39.6	3.6	2.0	7.6	7.0
	NM	157.5	-19.0			-5.5	9.0	6.7	-7.1	-15.0
% Profit Before Taxes/Tangible Net Worth	69.1	58.7	84.4			132.1	62.3	133.8	84.2	71.2
	(78) 30.7	(84) 27.0	(81) 41.6		(12) 41.4	(18) 13.6	(18) 73.0	(11) 47.9	(15) 51.7	
	3.7	4.5	5.1			-.3	-5.2	20.9	10.0	15.2
% Profit Before Taxes/Total Assets	20.5	19.0	26.0			48.1	11.4	44.8	18.4	20.5
	6.5	6.9	7.8			4.6	3.7	22.3	7.9	7.9
	-.3	1.1	.1			-.7	-4.0	7.3	2.9	-.3
Sales/Net Fixed Assets	16.1	16.8	30.8			23.4	25.8	30.8	16.3	40.4
	6.9	8.4	9.6			9.7	5.9	10.7	10.9	13.1
	2.9	3.1	3.5			2.4	2.5	4.8	3.9	5.3
Sales/Total Assets	3.6	3.5	4.7			5.3	3.9	5.6	4.8	4.3
	2.3	2.4	2.9			3.5	2.5	3.6	2.4	3.2
	1.5	1.6	1.7			2.0	1.6	2.1	1.9	1.5
% Depr., Dep., Amort./Sales	2.6	2.3	2.1			1.7	3.2	2.0	.7	1.3
	(80) 4.2	(90) 4.7	(81) 4.6		(11) 5.6	(16) 6.8	(17) 4.8	(16) 2.9	(15) 3.1	
	7.2	9.1	7.8			16.8	16.0	7.9	5.4	5.6
% Officers', Directors' Owners' Comp/Sales	1.6	1.7	2.5							
	(38) 3.5	(36) 4.8	(37) 3.5							
	8.7	12.4	6.3							
Net Sales ($)	3340932M	3163278M	2999859M		3006M	39947M	84484M	153683M	276069M	2442670M
Total Assets ($)	1695713M	1712174M	1489439M		5824M	16930M	40206M	57713M	122142M	1246624M

© RMA 2011

M = $ thousand   MM = $ million
See Pages 9 through 22 for Explanation of Ratios and Data

Current Data Sorted by Assets | Comparative Historical Data

						Type of Statement		
	1	1	1		1	Unqualified	5	1
		2	2			Reviewed	4	4
		4				Compiled	1	3
1	2	2				Tax Returns	2	4
4	3	2	3		1	Other	14	10
	1 (4/1-9/30/10)		29 (10/1/10-3/31/11)				4/1/06-3/31/07	4/1/07-3/31/08
0-500M	500M-2MM	2-10MM	10-50MM	50-100MM	100-250MM		ALL	ALL
5	6	11	6		2	NUMBER OF STATEMENTS	26	22
%	%	%	%	%	%	ASSETS	%	%
		12.6				Cash & Equivalents	14.2	20.5
		11.9				Trade Receivables (net)	6.2	12.4
		1.3				Inventory	1.7	5.4
		.2				All Other Current	4.0	2.0
		26.0				Total Current	26.1	40.2
		43.6				Fixed Assets (net)	52.6	46.6
		17.6				Intangibles (net)	4.5	.8
		12.8				All Other Non-Current	16.8	12.4
		100.0				Total	100.0	100.0
						LIABILITIES		
		1.4				Notes Payable-Short Term	.9	9.5
		2.3				Cur. Mat.-L.T.D.	4.8	5.6
		7.3				Trade Payables	8.3	14.0
		.0				Income Taxes Payable	.0	2.2
		5.5				All Other Current	7.4	14.7
		16.4				Total Current	21.3	46.0
		49.5				Long-Term Debt	45.8	51.1
		.0				Deferred Taxes	.3	.2
		5.4				All Other Non-Current	13.8	8.6
		28.6				Net Worth	18.8	-5.9
		100.0				Total Liabilities & Net Worth	100.0	100.0
						INCOME DATA		
		100.0				Net Sales	100.0	100.0
						Gross Profit		
		86.3				Operating Expenses	90.0	92.0
		13.7				Operating Profit	10.0	8.0
		3.5				All Other Expenses (net)	2.4	2.2
		10.1				Profit Before Taxes	7.5	5.8
						RATIOS		
		2.2					1.8	1.8
		1.8				Current	1.0	1.0
		1.1					.5	.6
		2.0					1.1	1.5
		1.6				Quick	.6	.7
		1.0					.4	.4
	0	UND					1 285.3	0 872.0
	3	105.9				Sales/Receivables	7 54.9	11 33.5
	22	16.5					15 25.1	23 16.2
						Cost of Sales/Inventory		
						Cost of Sales/Payables		
		5.4					28.8	10.2
		12.7				Sales/Working Capital	NM	NM
		73.3					-13.2	-18.0
							5.3	6.5
						EBIT/Interest	(24) 2.4	(18) 2.2
							1.2	.9
						Net Profit + Depr., Dep., Amort./Cur. Mat. L/T/D		
		.5					1.1	.8
		3.3				Fixed/Worth	3.0	2.0
		-5.6					-7.7	NM
		1.4					1.7	1.4
		3.4				Debt/Worth	3.4	3.8
		-9.2					-9.8	NM
							58.7	60.5
						% Profit Before Taxes/Tangible Net Worth	(17) 20.6	(17) 8.0
							7.8	2.5
		21.2					19.2	23.0
		4.7				% Profit Before Taxes/Total Assets	7.2	4.3
		2.0					.5	-.1
		6.6					7.2	13.7
		2.2				Sales/Net Fixed Assets	2.7	7.5
		1.5					1.3	1.4
		1.4					2.5	3.7
		.9				Sales/Total Assets	1.5	2.2
		.6					.9	1.0
		2.5					3.3	1.3
	(10)	5.4				% Depr., Dep., Amort./Sales	6.1	(21) 4.7
		10.4					9.1	6.6
						% Officers', Directors' Owners' Comp/Sales		
3441M	8518M	84245M	148371M		214206M	Net Sales ($)	519503M	381173M
1326M	7688M	53082M	107231M		235056M	Total Assets ($)	452803M	243836M

(Column spanning assets 2-10MM through 100-250MM marked "DATA NOT AVAILABLE")

M = $ thousand   MM = $ million
See Pages 9 through 22 for Explanation of Ratios and Data

Comparative Historical Data				Current Data Sorted by Sales					
			Type of Statement						
4	5	4	Unqualified		1			1	2
5	1	4	Reviewed		1		1	1	
5	3	4	Compiled		2	1	1		
4	3	5	Tax Returns	2	2	1	1		
13	15	13	Other	3	4	1		2	3
4/1/08-3/31/09	4/1/09-3/31/10	4/1/10-3/31/11		1 (4/1-9/30/10)		29 (10/1/10-3/31/11)			
ALL	ALL	ALL		0-1MM	1-3MM	3-5MM	5-10MM	10-25MM	25MM & OVER
31	27	30	**NUMBER OF STATEMENTS**	5	10	2	3	4	6
%	%	%	**ASSETS**	%	%	%	%	%	%
15.6	13.6	15.4	Cash & Equivalents		12.9				
5.7	6.6	8.2	Trade Receivables (net)		16.8				
2.6	1.8	3.4	Inventory		5.8				
1.9	2.0	3.2	All Other Current		.9				
25.8	24.1	30.1	Total Current		36.4				
53.2	56.5	50.7	Fixed Assets (net)		35.9				
10.4	8.6	10.1	Intangibles (net)		12.3				
10.5	10.8	9.2	All Other Non-Current		15.4				
100.0	100.0	100.0	Total		100.0				
			LIABILITIES						
5.9	4.6	9.5	Notes Payable-Short Term		20.2				
7.3	5.6	4.1	Cur. Mat.-L.T.D.		2.1				
6.3	4.1	5.4	Trade Payables		7.6				
.0	.0	.0	Income Taxes Payable		.1				
18.3	23.9	9.8	All Other Current		5.1				
37.8	38.2	29.0	Total Current		35.0				
50.4	55.2	44.7	Long-Term Debt		43.8				
.4	.5	.3	Deferred Taxes		.0				
9.6	19.8	4.9	All Other Non-Current		4.7				
1.8	-13.7	21.1	Net Worth		16.4				
100.0	100.0	100.0	Total Liabilties & Net Worth		100.0				
			INCOME DATA						
100.0	100.0	100.0	Net Sales		100.0				
			Gross Profit						
90.9	89.7	85.9	Operating Expenses		87.2				
9.1	10.3	14.1	Operating Profit		12.8				
3.2	5.1	2.9	All Other Expenses (net)		2.6				
5.8	5.2	11.2	Profit Before Taxes		10.2				
			RATIOS						
2.4	2.4	2.0			1.8				
1.2	.8	1.1	Current		1.1				
.4	.3	.7			.6				
2.2	1.7	1.9			1.8				
.9	.5	.9	Quick		.9				
.2	.2	.3			.2				
0 UND	0 UND	0 UND		0 UND					
4 93.5	1 305.1	4 97.6	Sales/Receivables	0 UND					
15 24.1	12 31.0	17 20.9		25 14.5					
			Cost of Sales/Inventory						
			Cost of Sales/Payables						
9.3	12.5	9.4			9.7				
45.0	-48.2	293.4	Sales/Working Capital		NM				
-8.2	-6.2	-12.5			-6.5				
4.2	4.3	8.1			14.9				
(28) 2.3	(22) 2.5	(27) 3.6	EBIT/Interest		2.2				
1.0	.4	1.5			1.0				
			Net Profit + Depr., Dep., Amort./Cur. Mat. L/T/D						
1.4	1.7	1.5			.5				
5.5	7.4	3.5	Fixed/Worth		2.4				
-3.0	-1.3	-4.5			-2.5				
1.0	1.9	1.7			.8				
5.7	11.9	3.9	Debt/Worth		4.6				
-4.6	-3.2	-9.1			-4.8				
60.2	37.2	77.3							
(19) 27.8	(14) 10.4	(19) 24.6	% Profit Before Taxes/Tangible Net Worth						
10.6	-20.6	12.2							
12.0	14.6	21.1			33.7				
7.7	3.5	7.1	% Profit Before Taxes/Total Assets		5.8				
1.5	-2.1	2.6			-.3				
5.8	5.0	5.8			8.0				
2.1	2.2	2.0	Sales/Net Fixed Assets		5.9				
1.4	1.2	1.4			1.6				
1.9	2.1	1.7			1.9				
1.2	1.0	1.0	Sales/Total Assets		1.0				
.9	.7	.8			.5				
3.6	4.0	3.9							
(26) 6.1	(24) 6.3	(27) 6.2	% Depr., Dep., Amort./Sales						
9.9	11.6	9.6							
			% Officers', Directors' Owners' Comp/Sales						
459023M	339159M	458781M	Net Sales ($)	2102M	18288M	7338M	18149M	62352M	350552M
386319M	340968M	404383M	Total Assets ($)	2394M	20906M	9875M	16654M	48687M	305867M

M = $ thousand   MM = $ million
See Pages 9 through 22 for Explanation of Ratios and Data

Current Data Sorted by Assets   Comparative Historical Data

Type of Statement (number of statements)

Type of Statement	0-500M	500M-2MM	2-10MM	10-50MM	50-100MM	100-250MM	4/1/06-3/31/07 ALL	4/1/07-3/31/08 ALL
Unqualified			1				16	21
Reviewed		1	6	6	7	7	10	12
Compiled	1	2	3	2	1		10	10
Tax Returns	2	5	3				11	11
Other	4	13	15	9	1	1	43	35
		17 (4/1-9/30/10)		73 (10/1/10-3/31/11)				
NUMBER OF STATEMENTS	7	21	28	17	9	8	90	89

Data Table

0-500M	500M-2MM	2-10MM	10-50MM	50-100MM	100-250MM		4/1/06-3/31/07 ALL	4/1/07-3/31/08 ALL
%	%	%	%	%	%	**ASSETS**	%	%
	9.7	9.7	8.9			Cash & Equivalents	14.4	10.0
	14.7	19.2	24.3			Trade Receivables (net)	18.6	15.3
	12.1	7.3	7.9			Inventory	12.4	10.2
	4.6	4.6	3.9			All Other Current	3.9	3.6
	41.2	40.7	44.9			Total Current	49.3	39.1
	44.5	46.4	43.8			Fixed Assets (net)	36.3	46.6
	4.5	4.7	2.9			Intangibles (net)	4.6	4.4
	9.8	8.2	8.4			All Other Non-Current	9.8	9.9
	100.0	100.0	100.0			Total	100.0	100.0
						LIABILITIES		
	10.9	4.1	6.5			Notes Payable-Short Term	5.9	8.0
	3.4	2.2	7.6			Cur. Mat.-L.T.D.	3.6	4.4
	5.3	9.1	11.4			Trade Payables	12.6	10.9
	.3	.0	.2			Income Taxes Payable	.4	.5
	9.0	12.6	7.8			All Other Current	13.8	14.3
	29.0	27.9	33.4			Total Current	36.4	38.1
	34.9	23.5	28.1			Long-Term Debt	28.2	30.7
	.9	.2	.1			Deferred Taxes	.5	.3
	25.5	5.1	4.7			All Other Non-Current	6.9	5.5
	9.6	43.3	33.7			Net Worth	27.9	25.4
	100.0	100.0	100.0			Total Liabilities & Net Worth	100.0	100.0
						INCOME DATA		
	100.0	100.0	100.0			Net Sales	100.0	100.0
						Gross Profit		
	93.8	90.9	93.3			Operating Expenses	94.7	91.4
	6.2	9.1	6.7			Operating Profit	5.3	8.6
	4.0	1.8	3.0			All Other Expenses (net)	1.7	4.0
	2.3	7.3	3.8			Profit Before Taxes	3.6	4.6
						RATIOS		
	2.2	2.3	2.4			Current	2.1	2.0
	1.5	1.3	1.5				1.3	1.2
	.8	.9	.8				.9	.6
	1.6	1.8	1.8			Quick	1.3	1.3
	.6	.9	1.2				.9	.8
	.2	.6	.5				.5	.3
	0 UND	10 37.9	16 22.9			Sales/Receivables	10 37.7	10 35.9
	5 80.4	22 16.5	37 10.0				26 14.0	26 14.3
	42 8.7	44 8.4	47 7.7				50 7.3	42 8.6
						Cost of Sales/Inventory		
						Cost of Sales/Payables		
	7.0	4.5	7.0			Sales/Working Capital	8.9	10.1
	16.6	29.7	19.0				23.2	36.8
	-15.1	-125.0	-31.1				-100.8	-15.0
	10.1	7.2	12.6			EBIT/Interest	7.8	4.7
	(17) 3.4	(20) 3.5	(15) 4.9				(74) 2.4	(70) 2.1
	-3.4	.7	1.9				.7	.9
						Net Profit + Depr., Dep., Amort./Cur. Mat. L/T/D	3.8	7.7
							(16) 2.0	(15) 1.7
							1.3	1.1
	.3	.6	.4			Fixed/Worth	.4	1.0
	1.3	1.5	1.5				1.4	2.1
	8.2	2.6	3.6				UND	11.4
	.6	.7	1.2			Debt/Worth	.9	1.0
	1.7	1.7	2.0				3.3	3.1
	10.8	4.0	4.9				UND	27.8
	82.5	29.0	46.3			% Profit Before Taxes/Tangible Net Worth	55.5	50.4
	(17) 27.6	(25) 13.2	(15) 23.9				(69) 22.7	(69) 20.4
	-.1	2.9	14.7				4.3	2.0
	23.7	10.8	14.8			% Profit Before Taxes/Total Assets	14.4	11.6
	3.1	5.4	8.1				4.2	4.3
	-5.8	.4	.9				-.1	-.3
	21.8	21.9	16.6			Sales/Net Fixed Assets	31.3	19.2
	2.4	3.0	4.5				6.0	4.3
	1.1	1.3	1.6				3.3	1.2
	3.6	2.2	2.9			Sales/Total Assets	3.3	3.1
	1.4	1.5	2.0				2.3	1.7
	.6	.8	1.1				1.4	.6
	2.8	1.1	1.3			% Depr., Dep., Amort./Sales	1.1	1.0
	(15) 11.7	(26) 2.6	(14) 2.6				(71) 2.4	(77) 3.3
	22.5	5.6	6.9				5.3	8.0
		.8				% Officers', Directors' Owners' Comp/Sales	1.5	1.9
		(12) 1.7					(21) 2.5	(21) 3.2
		2.1					5.7	7.1
12876M	56335M	292834M	667303M	469323M	1043914M	Net Sales ($)	2664869M	3079264M
1802M	27979M	142470M	330193M	631337M	1252353M	Total Assets ($)	2113459M	2465041M

Comparative Historical Data / Current Data Sorted by Sales

			Type of Statement						
25	28	21	Unqualified		3	2	1	3	12
15	16	10	Reviewed			2	2	2	4
9	7	6	Compiled	3	1	1	1		1
13	12	10	Tax Returns	3	1	1	4	1	
38	55	43	Other	7	10	5	8	4	9
4/1/08-3/31/09 ALL	4/1/09-3/31/10 ALL	4/1/10-3/31/11 ALL		17 (4/1-9/30/10)			73 (10/1/10-3/31/11)		
				0-1MM	1-3MM	3-5MM	5-10MM	10-25MM	25MM & OVER
100	118	90	**NUMBER OF STATEMENTS**	13	15	10	16	10	26
%	%	%	**ASSETS**	%	%	%	%	%	%
12.9	10.9	10.7	Cash & Equivalents	18.1	8.4	12.9	8.2	6.7	10.5
17.5	15.1	16.5	Trade Receivables (net)	6.3	12.7	6.9	18.5	19.5	25.2
9.5	7.7	7.3	Inventory	8.1	9.6	6.3	7.8	12.1	3.7
3.3	4.6	6.5	All Other Current	5.1	2.8	6.4	12.9	2.9	6.9
43.1	38.3	41.0	Total Current	37.6	33.5	32.5	47.3	41.1	46.4
42.8	47.3	46.6	Fixed Assets (net)	53.0	51.0	54.9	43.1	50.6	38.1
5.6	7.0	4.7	Intangibles (net)	3.7	1.7	9.1	3.4	.7	7.7
8.4	7.4	7.7	All Other Non-Current	5.7	13.9	3.5	6.2	7.6	7.8
100.0	100.0	100.0	Total	100.0	100.0	100.0	100.0	100.0	100.0
			LIABILITIES						
7.7	10.7	7.6	Notes Payable-Short Term	20.6	3.9	.0	11.7	7.6	3.5
3.7	3.4	3.6	Cur. Mat.-L.T.D.	1.9	3.9	1.4	2.8	3.0	5.7
11.8	9.5	7.7	Trade Payables	.2	2.1	5.9	9.9	12.2	12.4
.1	.2	.1	Income Taxes Payable	.0	.0	.7	.0	.0	.2
13.6	11.7	13.6	All Other Current	12.5	10.3	12.7	19.9	12.0	13.1
37.0	35.5	32.6	Total Current	35.3	20.1	20.7	44.3	34.7	34.9
31.8	33.0	25.7	Long-Term Debt	27.4	32.4	8.1	32.4	24.4	24.1
.3	.4	.3	Deferred Taxes	.0	1.3	.4	.0	.0	.2
7.7	8.9	10.6	All Other Non-Current	12.4	4.8	.5	35.7	3.9	3.9
23.1	22.2	30.8	Net Worth	24.9	41.3	70.3	-12.5	36.9	36.9
100.0	100.0	100.0	Total Liabilities & Net Worth	100.0	100.0	100.0	100.0	100.0	100.0
			INCOME DATA						
100.0	100.0	100.0	Net Sales	100.0	100.0	100.0	100.0	100.0	100.0
			Gross Profit						
95.1	95.4	93.7	Operating Expenses	88.1	85.7	100.2	95.2	101.1	95.0
4.9	4.6	6.3	Operating Profit	11.9	14.3	-.2	4.8	-1.1	5.0
2.3	3.3	2.2	All Other Expenses (net)	4.8	5.8	-1.2	1.0	1.0	1.4
2.6	1.3	4.1	Profit Before Taxes	7.2	8.5	1.0	3.8	-2.1	3.6
			RATIOS						
2.1	2.0	2.4		14.3	2.4	4.5	3.4	2.4	2.3
1.2	1.2	1.4	Current	1.6	1.4	1.5	1.5	1.2	1.5
.7	.6	.9		.2	1.0	1.0	.7	1.1	.9
1.3	1.3	1.8		13.6	2.0	3.3	2.3	1.5	1.6
.9	.7	1.0	Quick	.5	.9	1.0	1.0	1.0	1.1
.4	.4	.5		.0	.3	.5	.6	.5	.6
9 42.2	9 39.1	9 39.6		0 UND	0 UND	5 73.7	10 37.7	17 21.0	21 17.7
19 19.3	22 16.9	24 15.4	Sales/Receivables	0 UND	13 29.2	15 24.1	25 14.8	28 13.1	44 8.4
44 8.4	39 9.3	53 6.9		70 5.2	23 15.6	41 9.0	72 5.1	39 9.4	57 6.4
			Cost of Sales/Inventory						
			Cost of Sales/Payables						
8.9	8.3	5.8		1.0	4.2	8.0	4.5	16.0	7.3
32.6	30.3	16.4	Sales/Working Capital	3.5	16.6	12.8	16.7	24.7	15.0
-28.0	-16.1	-84.1		-8.9	291.4	NM	-26.9	NM	-83.8
8.7	7.8	9.4			7.4		14.8		13.2
(86) 2.5	(101) 2.1	(70) 3.5	EBIT/Interest		(12) 2.9		(14) .8		(23) 4.9
.6	-.8	.6			1.0		-1.6		1.2
25.6	8.7	29.4	Net Profit + Depr., Dep.,						
(15) 4.9	(20) 2.4	(10) 2.5	Amort./Cur. Mat. L/T/D						
1.3	.5	1.2							
.8	.8	.6		.5	.7	.5	.2	.9	.6
1.5	1.7	1.3	Fixed/Worth	.8	1.2	.8	3.5	1.4	1.5
-18.4	-9.5	3.8		NM	2.4	1.5	-2.6	3.9	3.8
.7	.9	.7		.1	.7	.0	.8	.6	1.3
2.8	2.7	1.6	Debt/Worth	1.2	1.7	.8	4.9	2.7	2.0
-28.0	-16.2	5.6		NM	3.7	1.4	-4.1	5.7	6.1
55.2	46.8	35.4	% Profit Before Taxes/Tangible	14.2	52.4	41.6	73.5		38.1
(71) 13.1	(84) 14.1	(74) 14.5	Net Worth	(10) 5.9	(14) 5.4	5.6	(10) 26.1		(21) 21.4
.0	-1.6	.5		-5.2	1.9	-.7	-6.4		8.5
12.0	10.3	13.0	% Profit Before Taxes/Total	10.1	24.4	29.0	23.4	8.6	9.4
3.2	2.5	5.3	Assets	3.1	1.5	2.2	7.8	4.0	8.2
-1.0	-4.1	-.7		-15.4	-.1	-.2	-5.0	-1.8	.6
45.0	13.1	12.6		8.4	2.9	13.4	33.4	21.4	9.3
5.3	3.7	3.2	Sales/Net Fixed Assets	1.3	1.7	2.3	10.1	3.0	5.3
1.6	1.3	1.1		.6	.3	.8	1.7	1.8	2.2
3.4	2.9	2.4		1.4	1.4	3.3	4.3	2.8	2.8
2.0	1.5	1.4	Sales/Total Assets	.4	1.1	.9	2.1	1.8	1.6
1.0	.7	.7		.2	.3	.6	1.1	1.1	1.1
.7	1.6	1.5			5.5		.9	1.4	1.3
(82) 1.9	(99) 3.9	(73) 4.7	% Depr., Dep., Amort./Sales		(12) 16.3		(13) 2.9	2.7	(21) 3.6
5.8	7.3	11.3			29.2		5.3	18.1	7.3
1.7	1.6	1.5	% Officers', Directors'				1.3		
(30) 2.9	(25) 2.7	(24) 2.1	Owners' Comp/Sales				(10) 1.7		
6.5	9.7	6.8					2.5		
4574897M	4543989M	2542585M	Net Sales ($)	5084M	32100M	38616M	114649M	166381M	2185755M
2619653M	3542363M	2386134M	Total Assets ($)	11456M	110497M	197834M	172665M	320873M	1572809M

© RMA 2011

M = $ thousand   MM = $ million
See Pages 9 through 22 for Explanation of Ratios and Data

Current Data Sorted by Assets   Comparative Historical Data

0-500M	500M-2MM	2-10MM	10-50MM	50-100MM	100-250MM	Type of Statement	4/1/06-3/31/07 ALL	4/1/07-3/31/08 ALL
1	3	6	8	2	3	Unqualified	11	19
1	3	12	4	1		Reviewed	7	8
1	3	2	1			Compiled	11	4
4	3	3				Tax Returns	3	7
2	6	19	7	4	3	Other	20	28
	16 (4/1-9/30/10)		82 (10/1/10-3/31/11)					
8	15	42	20	7	6	**NUMBER OF STATEMENTS**	52	66
%	%	%	%	%	%	**ASSETS**	%	%
	15.9	12.2	8.5			Cash & Equivalents	13.3	9.9
	15.0	29.3	15.0			Trade Receivables (net)	19.4	19.7
	20.6	20.9	14.7			Inventory	17.5	13.7
	.4	3.2	5.7			All Other Current	4.1	4.9
	52.0	65.6	43.9			Total Current	54.3	48.1
	38.2	24.8	44.0			Fixed Assets (net)	35.3	36.4
	5.4	1.6	5.2			Intangibles (net)	3.4	4.4
	4.5	8.0	6.9			All Other Non-Current	7.0	11.1
	100.0	100.0	100.0			Total	100.0	100.0
						LIABILITIES		
	11.8	5.7	6.0			Notes Payable-Short Term	13.1	7.4
	3.5	3.1	5.7			Cur. Mat.-L.T.D.	6.1	6.1
	10.8	17.0	8.5			Trade Payables	16.4	12.6
	.3	.4	.0			Income Taxes Payable	.3	.6
	8.8	11.7	10.0			All Other Current	17.5	11.5
	35.2	37.9	30.2			Total Current	53.4	38.2
	23.8	16.7	25.0			Long-Term Debt	34.0	27.3
	.2	.3	.6			Deferred Taxes	.4	.3
	.5	6.9	5.7			All Other Non-Current	7.3	10.8
	40.4	38.3	38.5			Net Worth	4.9	23.5
	100.0	100.0	100.0			Total Liabilities & Net Worth	100.0	100.0
						INCOME DATA		
	100.0	100.0	100.0			Net Sales	100.0	100.0
						Gross Profit		
	90.7	92.2	93.3			Operating Expenses	95.2	94.8
	9.3	7.8	6.7			Operating Profit	4.8	5.2
	4.5	2.8	.5			All Other Expenses (net)	2.4	1.4
	4.8	5.0	6.2			Profit Before Taxes	2.4	3.8
						RATIOS		
	3.7	2.4	2.1			Current	1.7	2.2
	2.4	1.6	1.4				1.1	1.3
	.7	1.3	1.1				.6	.8
	2.4	1.6	1.2			Quick	1.5	1.5
	.9	1.1	.8				.7	.7
	.5	.8	.5				.3	.4
	6 58.2	19 19.1	15 24.9			Sales/Receivables	11 33.5	15 24.5
	31 11.6	38 9.6	28 12.9				21 17.1	25 14.7
	41 8.9	60 6.1	48 7.7				43 8.5	51 7.2
						Cost of Sales/Inventory		
						Cost of Sales/Payables		
	4.8	5.2	6.2			Sales/Working Capital	8.2	6.1
	8.1	9.3	17.9				26.1	28.1
	-30.1	20.9	104.4				-15.0	-23.1
	10.1	26.2	25.3			EBIT/Interest	10.4	8.6
	(13) 3.6	(35) 3.6	(18) 6.2				(46) 3.2	(60) 2.8
	1.5	2.1	2.8				1.0	1.4
		6.2				Net Profit + Depr., Dep., Amort./Cur. Mat. L/T/D	21.2	10.9
		(15) 3.3					(13) 5.4	(20) 2.9
		1.8					1.8	1.7
	.2	.2	.7			Fixed/Worth	.6	.4
	.6	.5	1.3				1.4	1.6
	7.3	1.3	2.1				-11.5	NM
	.6	.9	1.1			Debt/Worth	1.4	1.2
	.8	1.7	1.6				3.2	2.4
	6.9	3.2	3.1				-21.3	NM
	26.8	52.4	50.9			% Profit Before Taxes/Tangible Net Worth	43.4	56.1
	(12) 10.2	(38) 25.3	(19) 39.9				(38) 23.2	(50) 28.0
	-3.3	5.0	6.5				9.2	10.9
	13.9	23.1	15.9			% Profit Before Taxes/Total Assets	12.7	21.1
	6.3	3.9	11.7				5.7	6.5
	.3	1.7	4.2				-1.1	-.5
	21.4	55.9	9.1			Sales/Net Fixed Assets	32.1	15.7
	16.0	18.5	4.9				10.3	6.6
	2.7	4.5	1.7				3.4	3.0
	3.2	3.4	2.8			Sales/Total Assets	3.5	3.1
	2.6	2.3	1.4				2.5	1.9
	1.2	1.7	1.0				1.4	1.2
	1.0	.9	.9			% Depr., Dep., Amort./Sales	.9	1.4
	(11) 1.8	(31) 1.6	(18) 2.0				(44) 2.3	(57) 2.8
	4.7	2.9	7.2				4.0	3.9
		1.9				% Officers', Directors' Owners' Comp/Sales	3.8	4.3
		(13) 4.3					(11) 5.7	(13) 6.2
		8.3					20.6	16.5
4212M	67035M	572313M	613214M	690861M	1074630M	Net Sales ($)	1463927M	2809757M
1329M	20842M	222588M	326882M	487082M	1049394M	Total Assets ($)	964805M	2000009M

M = $ thousand   MM = $ million
See Pages 9 through 22 for Explanation of Ratios and Data

Comparative Historical Data | **Current Data Sorted by Sales**

			Type of Statement	0-1MM	1-3MM	3-5MM	5-10MM	10-25MM	25MM & OVER
20	15	19	Unqualified				2	7	10
16	12	21	Reviewed		4		5	9	3
5	8	7	Compiled	2		1	2	1	1
6	11	10	Tax Returns	5	3		1	1	
32	37	41	Other	5	2	3	5	14	12
4/1/08-3/31/09 ALL	4/1/09-3/31/10 ALL	4/1/10-3/31/11 ALL		16 (4/1-9/30/10)			82 (10/1/10-3/31/11)		
79	83	98	**NUMBER OF STATEMENTS**	12	9	4	15	32	26
%	%	%	**ASSETS**	%	%	%	%	%	%
10.7	14.3	12.4	Cash & Equivalents	17.0			16.7	13.2	7.3
17.2	18.0	22.1	Trade Receivables (net)	12.2			24.4	23.2	26.7
17.2	15.8	19.2	Inventory	11.0			22.6	23.8	14.1
7.0	4.3	3.7	All Other Current	.6			6.3	2.8	5.8
52.0	52.4	57.4	Total Current	40.9			70.0	63.0	53.9
35.4	36.6	31.3	Fixed Assets (net)	57.9			21.7	27.0	29.7
3.0	4.9	3.7	Intangibles (net)	.3			.6	3.7	5.9
9.6	6.0	7.6	All Other Non-Current	1.0			7.6	6.3	10.5
100.0	100.0	100.0	Total	100.0			100.0	100.0	100.0
			LIABILITIES						
9.3	7.3	7.7	Notes Payable-Short Term	8.0			3.3	8.2	9.5
4.3	4.1	3.8	Cur. Mat.-L.T.D.	1.4			3.5	3.6	4.6
10.8	9.3	12.8	Trade Payables	6.6			10.8	15.2	13.3
.2	.1	.4	Income Taxes Payable	.0			.4	.4	.5
12.7	11.3	12.4	All Other Current	12.1			8.5	12.3	15.1
37.3	32.2	37.0	Total Current	28.0			26.4	39.7	43.0
22.9	31.1	19.4	Long-Term Debt	32.4			10.8	19.6	16.9
.1	.1	.4	Deferred Taxes	.0			.5	.5	.5
8.0	7.1	5.7	All Other Non-Current	7.6			6.0	6.5	6.5
31.7	29.4	37.5	Net Worth	32.0			56.3	33.6	33.0
100.0	100.0	100.0	Total Liabilties & Net Worth	100.0			100.0	100.0	100.0
			INCOME DATA						
100.0	100.0	100.0	Net Sales	100.0			100.0	100.0	100.0
			Gross Profit						
93.7	92.7	92.3	Operating Expenses	77.0			92.9	94.8	94.4
6.3	7.3	7.7	Operating Profit	23.0			7.1	5.2	5.6
1.7	1.9	2.4	All Other Expenses (net)	10.1			.4	1.4	1.5
4.6	5.3	5.3	Profit Before Taxes	13.0			6.7	3.8	4.1
			RATIOS						
2.5	2.6	2.5		3.9			3.6	2.1	1.9
1.4	1.7	1.6	Current	1.5			2.8	1.5	1.5
.8	1.0	1.2		.4			2.3	1.2	1.0
1.6	1.6	1.5		2.8			2.4	1.3	1.4
.7	1.0	1.0	Quick	1.2			1.4	1.0	.9
.4	.6	.5		.3			1.0	.6	.5
8 43.3	13 28.9	16 22.7		0 UND			20 18.6	15 25.0	20 17.9
23 16.0	24 15.2	36 10.1	Sales/Receivables	1 398.9			41 8.9	36 10.2	40 9.0
50 7.3	48 7.6	55 6.6		43 8.6			61 6.0	53 6.9	60 6.1
			Cost of Sales/Inventory						
			Cost of Sales/Payables						
7.0	6.1	5.0		3.2			3.3	5.5	6.1
23.4	13.8	10.1	Sales/Working Capital	9.3			5.0	13.0	19.3
-29.4	-297.7	37.2		-10.7			7.2	34.6	NM
10.2	10.2	19.2					26.5	18.2	25.3
(71) 3.4	(73) 3.6	(82) 3.6	EBIT/Interest			(14) 5.3	(28) 3.6	(24) 5.8	
1.2	1.8	1.8					2.2	2.5	.5
6.6	12.2	4.6						5.2	
(19) 1.3	(14) 3.2	(28) 2.3	Net Profit + Depr., Dep., Amort./Cur. Mat. L/T/D				(14) 2.5		
-.2	2.0	.8						1.8	
.3	.4	.3		.4			.0	.3	.5
1.2	1.3	.7	Fixed/Worth	2.2			.3	.6	.8
8.0	9.6	2.1		6.8			.6	2.5	2.0
.7	.8	.8		1.1			.3	1.0	1.1
2.3	2.4	1.7	Debt/Worth	3.3			.5	1.9	1.8
20.4	32.9	4.2		6.8			1.6	5.8	4.6
58.8	52.6	49.8	% Profit Before Taxes/Tangible Net Worth	102.3			43.5	53.9	47.1
(63) 21.6	(69) 24.3	(87) 17.8		18.6		(14) 15.4	(29) 27.9	(21) 16.4	
2.0	3.6	4.3		-10.2			4.2	10.0	.5
16.8	15.9	17.5	% Profit Before Taxes/Total Assets	29.4			22.8	15.8	20.0
6.7	5.4	6.6		4.9			10.8	6.8	7.0
.2	1.0	1.1		-1.0			1.7	2.0	-.6
21.3	24.9	26.0	Sales/Net Fixed Assets	14.3			147.9	48.6	19.1
6.5	6.3	8.9		2.4			16.0	16.1	6.9
2.8	1.8	3.8		.2			3.9	4.0	4.2
2.8	3.3	2.9	Sales/Total Assets	2.6			2.6	3.3	3.8
1.9	1.7	2.0		1.7			2.1	2.3	1.7
1.2	1.1	1.2		.1			1.6	1.4	1.1
.9	1.2	.9	% Depr., Dep., Amort./Sales				.7	.9	.6
(70) 2.5	(68) 2.3	(75) 1.8				(10) 2.2	(25) 1.6	(22) 1.2	
4.1	5.0	4.6					3.5	3.3	2.3
.9	2.1	1.6	% Officers', Directors' Owners' Comp/Sales				2.3		
(17) 3.4	(26) 4.1	(24) 4.4				(11) 5.7			
7.0	11.6	8.3					11.3		
3916291M	3003771M	3022265M	Net Sales ($)	5805M	18199M	15506M	110648M	524968M	2347139M
2533158M	2034493M	2108117M	Total Assets ($)	19960M	9831M	11949M	67739M	320863M	1677775M

M = $ thousand   MM = $ million
See Pages 9 through 22 for Explanation of Ratios and Data

Current Data Sorted by Assets   **Comparative Historical Data**

Period headers: 16 (4/1-9/30/10) | 81 (10/1/10-3/31/11) | 4/1/06-3/31/07 ALL | 4/1/07-3/31/08 ALL

	0-500M	500M-2MM	2-10MM	10-50MM	50-100MM	100-250MM	Type of Statement	4/1/06-3/31/07 ALL	4/1/07-3/31/08 ALL
			6	9	3	3	Unqualified	26	34
			4	8	2		Reviewed	13	9
		1	2				Compiled	8	8
		1	3	2			Tax Returns	2	2
	1	9	15	15	7	6	Other	33	30
NUMBER OF STATEMENTS	1	11	30	34	12	9		82	83
	%	%	%	%	%	%	**ASSETS**	%	%
Cash & Equivalents		19.4	13.5	15.3	11.2			11.6	11.0
Trade Receivables (net)		32.1	26.6	17.2	15.8			24.1	22.6
Inventory		1.3	.5	3.0	2.0			2.0	1.8
All Other Current		3.7	5.6	5.6	9.7			3.7	6.6
Total Current		56.5	46.2	41.0	38.7			41.4	42.0
Fixed Assets (net)		26.1	36.7	42.1	53.1			44.4	44.6
Intangibles (net)		5.5	3.1	8.8	5.3			2.7	3.8
All Other Non-Current		11.9	14.0	8.0	2.9			11.5	9.7
Total		100.0	100.0	100.0	100.0			100.0	100.0
							LIABILITIES		
Notes Payable-Short Term		10.3	8.2	3.5	6.7			5.4	4.5
Cur. Mat.-L.T.D.		6.3	3.5	3.6	3.9			4.8	4.8
Trade Payables		31.8	11.9	7.8	5.6			10.4	11.0
Income Taxes Payable		1.0	.1	.2	.0			.4	.7
All Other Current		15.5	11.2	8.8	5.0			10.6	9.1
Total Current		65.0	35.0	24.0	21.3			31.6	30.2
Long-Term Debt		37.1	25.5	22.0	20.4			22.8	31.9
Deferred Taxes		.0	.0	1.6	1.4			1.4	1.1
All Other Non-Current		.0	2.8	3.9	10.2			4.9	5.0
Net Worth		-2.1	36.7	48.5	46.8			39.2	31.8
Total Liabilties & Net Worth		100.0	100.0	100.0	100.0			100.0	100.0
							INCOME DATA		
Net Sales		100.0	100.0	100.0	100.0			100.0	100.0
Gross Profit									
Operating Expenses		96.4	85.8	85.4	87.4			85.7	90.0
Operating Profit		3.6	14.2	14.6	12.6			14.3	10.0
All Other Expenses (net)		1.9	6.8	1.5	3.8			2.1	1.8
Profit Before Taxes		1.7	7.4	13.0	8.8			12.2	8.3
							RATIOS		
Current		4.9	1.9	3.2	3.7			2.3	2.3
		1.1	1.0	2.1	1.8			1.3	1.4
		.5	.8	1.1	.9			.9	.8
Quick		4.6	1.6	2.9	2.9			2.0	2.0
		1.0	.9	1.7	1.7			1.1	1.0
		.5	.7	.7	.7			.6	.6
Sales/Receivables		13 27.4	26 13.9	27 13.7	36 10.1			30 12.1	28 13.1
		37 10.0	44 8.3	38 9.6	40 9.1			39 9.3	43 8.5
		59 6.2	76 4.8	56 6.5	45 8.1			59 6.2	59 6.2
Cost of Sales/Inventory									
Cost of Sales/Payables									
Sales/Working Capital		7.3	9.4	2.9	5.0			6.8	6.1
		89.3	287.1	6.4	13.1			24.0	15.3
		-4.4	-15.9	59.4	NM			-68.0	-28.8
EBIT/Interest			16.6	21.6	30.6			11.0	15.2
		(18) 4.6	(30) 9.0	(10) 9.1				(68) 7.3	(71) 4.1
			.9	3.1	2.7			3.6	2.0
Net Profit + Depr., Dep., Amort./Cur. Mat. L/T/D				14.0				7.9	5.6
			(14) 4.8					(21) 3.3	(22) 2.9
				2.9				2.6	1.6
Fixed/Worth		.2	.4	.5	.7			.5	.6
		.3	.9	1.2	1.2			1.1	1.3
		5.0	2.0	2.5	2.4			2.5	2.6
Debt/Worth		.2	.5	.6	.5			.7	.8
		1.8	2.6	1.4	1.0			1.5	1.7
		6.2	6.6	3.1	2.9			3.8	4.8
% Profit Before Taxes/Tangible Net Worth			72.6	41.3	49.7			63.5	46.9
		(28) 18.6	(29) 21.2	(11) 34.9				(73) 36.7	(70) 29.1
			-4.8	7.1	5.3			19.7	13.8
% Profit Before Taxes/Total Assets		31.1	23.9	17.6	19.4			22.3	17.4
		8.9	5.7	9.2	11.5			12.6	8.6
		-16.6	-.5	4.2	-.1			7.8	2.8
Sales/Net Fixed Assets		102.2	19.7	13.1	5.0			12.8	10.4
		11.9	6.2	2.2	2.0			3.4	3.4
		5.2	1.5	1.1	.9			1.3	1.5
Sales/Total Assets		6.0	3.2	2.1	2.3			2.3	2.2
		3.5	1.9	.9	1.2			1.6	1.3
		1.4	.7	.5	.7			.7	.8
% Depr., Dep., Amort./Sales			3.1	2.6	3.9			2.1	2.1
		(22) 4.9	(32) 6.8	(11) 8.4				(70) 4.3	(71) 4.8
			11.8	11.1	10.2			7.0	7.4
% Officers', Directors', Owners' Comp/Sales									.5
								(10) 3.6	
									9.1
Net Sales ($)	1504M	51930M	398186M	1001171M	1302513M	1420594M		4641255M	5102525M
Total Assets ($)	318M	13031M	183771M	791380M	917757M	1271351M		2695661M	3113007M

M = $ thousand   MM = $ million
See Pages 9 through 22 for Explanation of Ratios and Data

Comparative Historical Data | Current Data Sorted by Sales

4/1/08-3/31/09 ALL	4/1/09-3/31/10 ALL	4/1/10-3/31/11 ALL	Type of Statement	0-1MM	1-3MM	3-5MM	5-10MM	10-25MM	25MM & OVER
37	28	21	Unqualified		2	1	2	5	11
10	11	14	Reviewed			4	1	3	6
3	6	3	Compiled				1	2	
2	10	6	Tax Returns	1	1		1	3	
33	45	53	Other	2	9	3	7	7	25
					16 (4/1-9/30/10)		81 (10/1/10-3/31/11)		
85	100	97	**NUMBER OF STATEMENTS**	3	12	8	12	20	42
%	%	%	**ASSETS**	%	%	%	%	%	%
10.7	10.9	14.1	Cash & Equivalents		10.8		13.1	18.6	12.4
21.9	18.9	20.9	Trade Receivables (net)		13.7		19.8	23.2	23.2
1.7	1.5	1.7	Inventory		1.2		.3	1.3	2.7
6.1	5.7	6.1	All Other Current		3.9		6.4	6.2	8.1
40.5	36.9	42.8	Total Current		29.7		39.6	49.2	46.5
46.2	47.1	42.3	Fixed Assets (net)		46.8		52.6	29.5	43.6
2.5	5.1	5.4	Intangibles (net)		5.2		1.9	14.8	2.2
10.9	10.9	9.5	All Other Non-Current		18.3		5.9	6.5	7.7
100.0	100.0	100.0	Total		100.0		100.0	100.0	100.0
			LIABILITIES						
7.2	4.9	5.8	Notes Payable-Short Term		4.1		9.0	6.2	5.0
5.5	8.0	4.0	Cur. Mat.-L.T.D.		7.8		3.8	4.0	3.2
11.0	9.7	11.1	Trade Payables		23.1		8.2	10.7	10.0
.2	.2	.6	Income Taxes Payable		3.6		.0	.1	.2
9.1	11.4	9.6	All Other Current		13.9		8.0	9.5	9.1
32.9	34.2	31.2	Total Current		52.4		29.0	30.5	27.5
33.3	30.5	25.8	Long-Term Debt		51.7		30.1	11.0	20.5
.8	.7	.7	Deferred Taxes		.0		.0	.5	1.5
5.9	10.2	3.7	All Other Non-Current		.4		2.2	9.0	3.3
27.0	24.3	38.6	Net Worth		-4.6		38.7	48.9	47.2
100.0	100.0	100.0	Total Liabilities & Net Worth		100.0		100.0	100.0	100.0
			INCOME DATA						
100.0	100.0	100.0	Net Sales		100.0		100.0	100.0	100.0
			Gross Profit						
87.9	88.0	87.2	Operating Expenses		83.7		94.9	89.9	88.8
12.1	12.0	12.8	Operating Profit		16.3		5.1	10.1	11.2
1.2	2.7	3.7	All Other Expenses (net)		6.9		1.3	2.0	1.5
10.9	9.3	9.1	Profit Before Taxes		9.3		3.8	8.1	9.7
			RATIOS						
2.5	2.2	3.1	Current		1.3		2.1	3.6	3.4
1.4	1.2	1.4			.8		1.5	1.5	1.7
.9	.7	.8			.2		1.0	1.0	1.0
2.1	1.8	2.6	Quick		1.1		2.0	2.8	2.7
1.0	.9	1.1			.8		1.0	1.3	1.4
.6	.5	.7			.2		.8	.9	.7
24 / 15.2	25 / 14.9	27 / 13.6	Sales/Receivables	0 / UND	21 / 17.6		31 / 11.9	35 / 10.5	
38 / 9.6	39 / 9.3	41 / 8.8		16 / 22.9	40 / 9.0		42 / 8.7	41 / 8.8	
60 / 6.0	57 / 6.4	58 / 6.3		66 / 5.6	74 / 4.9		58 / 6.3	48 / 7.6	
			Cost of Sales/Inventory						
			Cost of Sales/Payables						
6.6	6.5	5.0	Sales/Working Capital		18.2		3.8	3.2	5.0
14.1	31.5	15.6			-17.7		10.0	12.5	14.1
-52.1	-10.6	-30.2			-3.4		NM	-188.7	NM
10.3	11.2	23.9	EBIT/Interest		17.0		19.4	119.3	28.2
(77) 4.9	(87) 3.7	(74) 6.3			(10) 2.8	(10) 9.0	(15) 8.6	(35) 5.8	
2.3	.8	1.9			-3.8		-.1	1.1	2.4
8.9	6.2	13.3	Net Profit + Depr., Dep., Amort./Cur. Mat. L/T/D						14.0
(25) 3.7	(27) 3.2	(23) 4.9						(14) 6.6	
2.0	2.4	2.6							2.8
.7	.8	.5	Fixed/Worth		.5		.8	.5	.4
1.4	1.5	1.1			1.9		1.2	.9	1.0
2.8	2.7	2.4			NM		3.2	2.5	2.3
.8	.7	.5	Debt/Worth		.6		.7	.6	.5
2.2	1.8	1.6			2.4		1.9	1.8	1.4
4.0	4.6	4.3			NM		4.6	6.2	2.8
55.2	47.4	47.2	% Profit Before Taxes/Tangible Net Worth				29.8	74.1	45.0
(77) 28.7	(83) 17.1	(86) 25.0					(11) 25.0	(16) 22.8	(40) 31.6
13.8	3.2	4.9					-31.6	1.8	9.3
17.3	14.0	21.0	% Profit Before Taxes/Total Assets		11.3		14.9	20.1	24.1
9.0	5.3	8.8			7.9		6.4	11.0	9.5
3.4	.2	1.8			-12.8		-5.0	.7	3.6
9.5	10.0	12.7	Sales/Net Fixed Assets		10.8		5.6	47.3	13.6
3.3	2.7	3.5			2.5		1.5	7.5	4.2
1.3	1.0	1.1			.5		.8	1.7	1.7
2.4	2.0	2.6	Sales/Total Assets		2.0		1.8	2.7	2.9
1.6	1.3	1.3			.7		.8	2.0	1.7
.8	.6	.6			.4		.5	.4	.8
2.0	3.1	3.1	% Depr., Dep., Amort./Sales				4.0	1.5	2.6
(72) 4.0	(85) 5.8	(79) 6.6					(11) 5.7	(19) 4.2	(32) 4.4
8.4	10.4	10.2					17.8	6.9	9.4
			% Officers', Directors' Owners' Comp/Sales						
5756588M	4875476M	4175898M	Net Sales ($)	1409M	24026M	34098M	82270M	329280M	3704815M
3167574M	3954039M	3177608M	Total Assets ($)	14377M	41012M	77512M	117723M	437054M	2489930M

M = $ thousand   MM = $ million
See Pages 9 through 22 for Explanation of Ratios and Data

Current Data Sorted by Assets | Comparative Historical Data

0-500M	500M-2MM	2-10MM	10-50MM	50-100MM	100-250MM	Type of Statement		
		1	1		4	Unqualified	10	9
	2	4	6	1	1	Reviewed	11	12
	2	6	2			Compiled	18	8
1	2	1				Tax Returns	4	6
		12	5	5	7	Other	28	21
	16 (4/1-9/30/10)		47 (10/1/10-3/31/11)				4/1/06-3/31/07 ALL	4/1/07-3/31/08 ALL
1	6	24	14	6	12	**NUMBER OF STATEMENTS**	71	56
%	%	%	%	%	%	**ASSETS**	%	%
		12.2	10.5		4.2	Cash & Equivalents	14.8	15.8
		24.1	12.4		7.0	Trade Receivables (net)	18.0	14.4
		.4	2.4		2.1	Inventory	1.9	3.5
		2.5	5.3		4.5	All Other Current	4.9	3.7
		39.1	30.6		17.8	Total Current	39.6	37.4
		45.9	60.8		77.5	Fixed Assets (net)	51.8	46.7
		1.7	2.3		1.2	Intangibles (net)	1.6	4.1
		13.3	6.3		3.5	All Other Non-Current	6.9	11.8
		100.0	100.0		100.0	Total	100.0	100.0
						LIABILITIES		
		4.7	3.3		1.8	Notes Payable-Short Term	3.5	6.0
		3.5	2.9		3.9	Cur. Mat.-L.T.D.	4.6	4.7
		8.0	5.9		3.9	Trade Payables	8.4	6.6
		.1	.5		.0	Income Taxes Payable	.6	.4
		6.1	5.0		5.7	All Other Current	7.0	6.3
		22.4	17.6		15.3	Total Current	24.1	24.0
		24.0	40.5		35.2	Long-Term Debt	27.4	28.4
		.3	4.5		2.5	Deferred Taxes	1.2	1.3
		2.9	1.1		2.2	All Other Non-Current	5.8	4.2
		50.4	36.4		44.9	Net Worth	41.5	42.1
		100.0	100.0		100.0	Total Liabilities & Net Worth	100.0	100.0
						INCOME DATA		
		100.0	100.0		100.0	Net Sales	100.0	100.0
						Gross Profit		
		82.5	92.1		93.0	Operating Expenses	83.2	81.5
		17.5	7.9		7.0	Operating Profit	16.8	18.5
		2.1	1.6		3.0	All Other Expenses (net)	2.1	1.7
		15.4	6.3		4.0	Profit Before Taxes	14.7	16.8
						RATIOS		
		5.6	2.6		2.3		2.4	3.4
		1.5	2.2		1.3	Current	1.7	1.7
		.8	1.1		.8		1.0	.7
		5.6	2.1		1.7		2.1	3.2
		1.4	1.4		.9	Quick	1.3	1.3
		.8	.8		.5		.8	.5
		11 31.9	37 9.9		25 14.9		20 18.1	5 74.0
		49 7.5	44 8.2		39 9.3	Sales/Receivables	41 8.9	37 10.0
		70 5.2	55 6.7		52 7.0		58 6.3	52 7.0
						Cost of Sales/Inventory		
						Cost of Sales/Payables		
		5.2	4.7		4.3		6.6	5.2
		17.3	8.0		14.7	Sales/Working Capital	13.0	15.6
		-44.3	40.0		-21.6		-846.0	-18.8
		11.2	6.5		3.3		9.7	16.8
		(20) 6.1	2.8		2.0	EBIT/Interest	(65) 6.3	(49) 6.0
		1.3	1.0		.9		2.9	2.2
							5.9	9.4
						Net Profit + Depr., Dep., Amort./Cur. Mat. L/T/D	(24) 3.1	(16) 2.9
							1.9	1.6
		.3	.7		1.1		.7	.6
		1.1	1.5		2.0	Fixed/Worth	1.3	1.3
		2.9	5.6		3.2		2.5	3.2
		.3	.6		.7		.6	.7
		.9	1.4		1.5	Debt/Worth	1.6	1.9
		2.9	5.4		2.8		3.2	4.5
		51.2	35.5		20.7		63.8	64.3
		(22) 19.3	(13) 24.2		7.6	% Profit Before Taxes/Tangible Net Worth	(69) 34.4	(52) 34.2
		3.9	.5		-1.3		16.0	17.8
		20.2	14.9		5.3		23.3	28.5
		11.5	4.7		2.8	% Profit Before Taxes/Total Assets	11.1	12.5
		1.1	.0		-.5		4.8	4.7
		10.4	3.7		1.3		6.4	8.9
		4.0	1.5		.7	Sales/Net Fixed Assets	2.3	2.8
		1.1	1.0		.5		1.2	1.1
		2.4	1.5		.9		2.1	2.3
		1.5	1.0		.6	Sales/Total Assets	1.3	1.1
		.7	.8		.4		.8	.7
		2.5	2.9				2.5	1.7
		(23) 5.8	7.2			% Depr., Dep., Amort./Sales	(63) 5.7	(49) 6.0
		8.2	18.8				8.2	10.7
							1.4	3.9
						% Officers', Directors' Owners' Comp/Sales	(13) 4.6	(15) 11.3
							9.4	15.2
1463M	22744M	213705M	401391M	456535M	1032616M	Net Sales ($)	2053663M	1611756M
366M	8106M	125425M	382816M	502880M	1659202M	Total Assets ($)	2053737M	1814615M

M = $ thousand   MM = $ million
See Pages 9 through 22 for Explanation of Ratios and Data

Comparative Historical Data | Current Data Sorted by Sales

Hist 1	Hist 2	Hist 3	Type of Statement	0-1MM	1-3MM	3-5MM	5-10MM	10-25MM	25MM & OVER
10	12	7	Unqualified					1	6
8	7	11	Reviewed		1			5	3
16	13	10	Compiled		3	2	1	2	1
5	2	4	Tax Returns	1			1	1	
22	30	31	Other	2	1	1	4	9	14
4/1/08-3/31/09 ALL	4/1/09-3/31/10 ALL	4/1/10-3/31/11 ALL			16 (4/1-9/30/10)		47 (10/1/10-3/31/11)		
61	64	63	**NUMBER OF STATEMENTS**	4	6	4	7	18	24
%	%	%	**ASSETS**	%	%	%	%	%	%
12.0	12.3	12.1	Cash & Equivalents					10.1	7.4
16.5	16.4	16.5	Trade Receivables (net)					23.8	9.8
1.4	1.9	1.5	Inventory					2.4	2.0
3.2	1.7	3.5	All Other Current					4.0	4.9
33.1	32.3	33.6	Total Current					40.3	24.1
56.1	54.1	56.2	Fixed Assets (net)					51.9	68.6
2.2	2.1	2.1	Intangibles (net)					.1	2.0
8.7	11.5	8.1	All Other Non-Current					7.7	5.4
100.0	100.0	100.0	Total					100.0	100.0
			LIABILITIES						
2.4	3.2	3.5	Notes Payable-Short Term					8.8	1.5
5.2	5.1	4.0	Cur. Mat.-L.T.D.					3.3	3.0
5.8	5.7	5.8	Trade Payables					10.6	4.8
.3	.1	.1	Income Taxes Payable					.1	.3
5.4	8.6	5.8	All Other Current					5.1	5.7
19.1	22.7	19.2	Total Current					27.9	15.2
31.5	37.0	31.1	Long-Term Debt					40.1	31.8
1.7	1.1	1.6	Deferred Taxes					1.8	2.7
4.2	3.0	2.2	All Other Non-Current					2.1	2.0
43.6	36.2	45.9	Net Worth					28.1	48.3
100.0	100.0	100.0	Total Liabilities & Net Worth					100.0	100.0
			INCOME DATA						
100.0	100.0	100.0	Net Sales					100.0	100.0
			Gross Profit						
81.7	84.4	86.0	Operating Expenses					88.2	90.8
18.3	15.6	14.0	Operating Profit					11.8	9.2
3.5	3.0	2.6	All Other Expenses (net)					2.2	2.1
14.8	12.6	11.4	Profit Before Taxes					9.6	7.1
			RATIOS						
2.4	2.8	2.9	Current					2.4	2.6
1.4	1.4	1.5						1.5	1.6
.8	.9	1.0						.9	1.1
2.1	1.9	2.3	Quick					1.9	2.1
1.3	1.3	1.2						1.2	1.1
.6	.8	.8						.8	.6
15 24.8	21 17.5	22 17.0	Sales/Receivables					25 14.6	25 14.9
36 10.2	38 9.5	44 8.4						44 8.4	38 9.5
45 8.2	55 6.6	58 6.3						55 6.7	52 7.0
			Cost of Sales/Inventory						
			Cost of Sales/Payables						
7.6	6.3	4.8	Sales/Working Capital					5.5	5.0
20.5	22.0	13.3						20.6	12.0
-33.4	-51.0	-142.6						-123.6	38.3
18.6	9.8	9.6	EBIT/Interest					10.1	10.3
(53) 5.9	(54) 3.7	(57) 2.8						3.5	2.7
2.3	1.8	1.3						.4	1.5
8.4	3.9	9.2	Net Profit + Depr., Dep., Amort./Cur. Mat. L/T/D						
(17) 2.7	(12) 2.1	(13) 2.3							
1.3	1.8	1.5							
.6	.7	.6	Fixed/Worth					.5	.9
1.5	1.5	1.3						1.9	1.4
2.5	3.4	3.3						5.6	2.8
.7	.8	.5	Debt/Worth					.9	.5
1.5	1.6	1.0						2.7	1.1
2.8	4.8	3.2						7.3	2.7
50.5	55.1	34.9	% Profit Before Taxes/Tangible Net Worth					59.9	25.8
(57) 28.2	(57) 12.8	(59) 19.1						(16) 20.9	17.3
10.0	3.1	2.1						-.8	1.5
20.7	15.0	15.2	% Profit Before Taxes/Total Assets					18.5	11.6
11.3	7.5	5.1						4.7	4.1
4.2	1.7	.8						-.1	.8
7.8	6.4	5.8	Sales/Net Fixed Assets					16.1	1.8
2.0	1.6	1.7						2.2	1.1
.9	.9	.9						1.2	.5
2.5	1.7	1.8	Sales/Total Assets					2.8	1.1
1.2	.9	1.0						1.5	.8
.6	.6	.7						.9	.5
2.7	2.2	3.5	% Depr., Dep., Amort./Sales					3.3	4.3
(50) 6.4	(51) 5.8	(56) 7.1						(17) 6.0	(20) 7.9
11.4	10.2	10.6						17.0	10.4
	1.6	1.4	% Officers', Directors' Owners' Comp/Sales						
	(16) 8.1	(11) 3.3							
	17.8	14.1							
2045891M	2437926M	2128454M	Net Sales ($)	2539M	12051M	14586M	52228M	289885M	1757165M
2175498M	2924423M	2678795M	Total Assets ($)	4969M	21215M	10978M	37556M	242702M	2361375M

M = $ thousand   MM = $ million
See Pages 9 through 22 for Explanation of Ratios and Data

Current Data Sorted by Assets   Comparative Historical Data

	0-500M	500M-2MM	2-10MM	10-50MM	50-100MM	100-250MM		4/1/06-3/31/07 ALL	4/1/07-3/31/08 ALL
Type of Statement									
Unqualified			1	2	2	3		11	21
Reviewed			3	4				9	3
Compiled		3	1	1				7	7
Tax Returns		2		2				6	6
Other		3	10	5	2	3		26	20
		4 (4/1-9/30/10)		43 (10/1/10-3/31/11)					
NUMBER OF STATEMENTS		8	15	14		6		59	57
	%	%	%	%	%	%		%	%
ASSETS									
Cash & Equivalents			11.3	10.6				11.6	12.4
Trade Receivables (net)			27.2	15.4				22.7	19.0
Inventory			2.0	5.9				3.8	5.0
All Other Current			1.2	6.4				5.0	4.9
Total Current			41.7	38.3				43.1	41.4
Fixed Assets (net)			52.4	51.9				47.3	49.7
Intangibles (net)			1.2	2.2				3.1	1.4
All Other Non-Current			4.7	7.6				6.5	7.5
Total			100.0	100.0				100.0	100.0
LIABILITIES									
Notes Payable-Short Term			5.3	4.6				5.1	6.9
Cur. Mat.-L.T.D.			3.9	4.0				5.5	5.7
Trade Payables			17.7	7.7				12.2	9.0
Income Taxes Payable			.1	.3				.2	.1
All Other Current			10.2	10.1				14.2	13.4
Total Current			37.2	26.6				37.3	35.0
Long-Term Debt			40.8	31.5				25.9	29.7
Deferred Taxes			.0	.0				1.2	.9
All Other Non-Current			7.1	13.6				1.7	3.4
Net Worth			15.0	28.3				34.0	31.0
Total Liabilties & Net Worth			100.0	100.0				100.0	100.0
INCOME DATA									
Net Sales			100.0	100.0				100.0	100.0
Gross Profit									
Operating Expenses			85.4	86.4				83.6	81.7
Operating Profit			14.6	13.6				16.4	18.3
All Other Expenses (net)			4.2	4.0				1.9	4.2
Profit Before Taxes			10.3	9.6				14.5	14.1
RATIOS									
Current			3.1	2.2				1.9	2.6
			1.8	1.5				1.3	1.4
			.5	1.3				.6	.9
Quick			2.9	1.9				1.6	2.3
			1.7	1.3				.9	1.0
			.4	.6				.4	.5
Sales/Receivables			25 14.4	0 UND				8 45.9	5 70.9
			53 6.9	32 11.4				45 8.2	48 7.6
			62 5.9	48 7.6				75 4.9	65 5.6
Cost of Sales/Inventory									
Cost of Sales/Payables									
Sales/Working Capital			5.9	3.0				7.0	5.4
			11.3	9.6				27.3	19.1
			-7.5	17.6				-9.8	-50.2
EBIT/Interest			28.8	7.6				18.4	13.2
			(13) 2.5	(11) 1.9				(52) 4.4	(46) 4.2
			1.8	.9				1.2	1.4
Net Profit + Depr., Dep., Amort./Cur. Mat. L/T/D								3.5	5.3
								(11) 2.3	(13) 2.6
								1.6	1.7
Fixed/Worth			.5	1.2				.6	.6
			1.8	1.7				1.5	1.7
			-5.0	4.3				10.5	4.2
Debt/Worth			.7	1.0				.8	1.0
			2.6	1.9				1.8	2.1
			-7.5	3.7				13.4	5.4
% Profit Before Taxes/Tangible Net Worth			51.9	19.2				74.3	64.1
			(11) 30.8	(12) 12.3				(50) 41.4	(48) 29.0
			12.0	.2				16.3	16.8
% Profit Before Taxes/Total Assets			28.9	8.8				31.7	21.9
			6.0	3.7				9.4	9.0
			1.8	-.1				1.6	1.0
Sales/Net Fixed Assets			7.1	5.4				12.1	10.4
			2.0	1.5				3.2	2.8
			.7	1.0				1.3	.8
Sales/Total Assets			3.1	1.4				2.3	2.3
			1.6	.9				1.5	1.2
			.7	.4				.9	.6
% Depr., Dep., Amort./Sales			2.8	2.2				1.6	2.3
			(13) 5.1	(12) 5.1				(55) 4.4	(46) 4.6
			13.7	17.5				7.3	9.3
% Officers', Directors' Owners' Comp/Sales								1.5	1.4
								(13) 4.4	(17) 2.8
								8.2	8.6
Net Sales ($)		28787M	121821M	307935M	371443M	1146351M		1995740M	2737819M
Total Assets ($)		10949M	66487M	329203M	310245M	1026481M		1540375M	2711292M

(The left "0-500M" column and rows in this size category are marked "DATA NOT AVAILABLE".)

Comparative Historical Data | Current Data Sorted by Sales

11 6 6 5 20 4/1/08- 3/31/09 ALL	8 4 6 4 27 4/1/09- 3/31/10 ALL	8 7 5 4 23 4/1/10- 3/31/11 ALL	Type of Statement Unqualified Reviewed Compiled Tax Returns Other	0-1MM	1-3MM	4 (4/1-9/30/10) 3-5MM	5-10MM	43 (10/1/10-3/31/11) 10-25MM	25MM & OVER
			Unqualified	1				1	6
			Reviewed		1		1	4	1
			Compiled	1	1	2		1	
			Tax Returns		3	1			
			Other		3	4	3	6	7
48	49	47	NUMBER OF STATEMENTS	2	8	7	4	12	14
%	%	%	**ASSETS**	%	%	%	%	%	%
11.1	12.2	9.1	Cash & Equivalents					12.1	9.6
18.9	17.9	21.2	Trade Receivables (net)					25.1	19.1
3.9	2.4	4.0	Inventory					1.9	3.0
6.0	6.0	4.8	All Other Current					6.3	7.9
39.9	38.5	39.1	Total Current					45.3	39.7
50.3	48.9	50.2	Fixed Assets (net)					46.4	41.0
2.6	3.2	4.2	Intangibles (net)					.7	10.5
7.2	9.4	6.6	All Other Non-Current					7.7	8.8
100.0	100.0	100.0	Total					100.0	100.0
			LIABILITIES						
5.0	4.6	5.5	Notes Payable-Short Term					6.2	.3
4.6	3.9	4.4	Cur. Mat.-L.T.D.					3.9	3.3
9.4	10.3	11.7	Trade Payables					13.6	7.8
.0	.3	.3	Income Taxes Payable					.4	.7
11.0	9.7	8.4	All Other Current					10.5	9.7
30.0	28.7	30.4	Total Current					34.6	21.7
30.0	27.2	31.4	Long-Term Debt					26.2	22.9
1.1	1.4	.6	Deferred Taxes					.0	2.0
8.6	5.1	14.4	All Other Non-Current					10.6	11.0
30.3	37.6	23.2	Net Worth					28.6	42.5
100.0	100.0	100.0	Total Liabilities & Net Worth					100.0	100.0
			INCOME DATA						
100.0	100.0	100.0	Net Sales					100.0	100.0
			Gross Profit						
87.7	89.5	89.9	Operating Expenses					92.6	89.6
12.3	10.5	10.1	Operating Profit					7.4	10.4
4.1	4.7	3.4	All Other Expenses (net)					1.1	2.9
8.2	5.9	6.8	Profit Before Taxes					6.3	7.5
			RATIOS						
2.4	2.8	2.5	Current					1.9	2.6
1.4	1.4	1.6						1.4	1.8
.9	.8	.8						.7	1.2
1.5	2.3	1.9	Quick					1.6	1.5
1.0	1.0	1.0						1.1	1.1
.5	.4	.6						.4	.8
12 31.5	23 15.7	16 23.5	Sales/Receivables					32 11.5	12 31.4
37 9.8	38 9.6	35 10.4						44 8.3	31 11.9
58 6.3	63 5.8	61 6.0						61 6.0	63 5.8
			Cost of Sales/Inventory						
			Cost of Sales/Payables						
5.6	4.7	5.9	Sales/Working Capital					6.9	6.4
13.0	11.4	10.2						9.6	10.2
-123.2	-26.2	-26.7						-12.3	NM
13.7	25.6	9.7	EBIT/Interest						12.8
(40) 4.3	(35) 2.9	(40) 2.2						(13)	4.0
1.6	1.5	.8							1.7
3.1	5.9	6.1	Net Profit + Depr., Dep.,						
(12) 1.9	(10) 3.6	(11) 1.7	Amort./Cur. Mat. L/T/D						
1.6	1.5	.9							
.6	.3	.9	Fixed/Worth					.4	.5
1.8	1.5	2.1						1.4	1.6
5.5	5.3	-18.8						4.0	NM
1.1	.8	1.0	Debt/Worth					.8	1.0
2.2	1.9	2.8						1.7	2.2
8.9	9.9	-41.2						4.4	NM
63.0	42.4	43.7	% Profit Before Taxes/Tangible					24.3	56.2
(41) 27.3	(41) 21.5	(34) 14.9	Net Worth				(10)	11.5	(11) 14.7
4.1	1.4	1.4						.0	7.6
20.8	19.8	19.0	% Profit Before Taxes/Total					10.5	15.2
7.5	4.8	3.9	Assets					4.1	5.5
.5	.1	-.1						.3	2.8
13.1	13.3	5.8	Sales/Net Fixed Assets					6.1	64.0
3.1	2.4	2.6						3.2	4.6
1.1	.9	1.2						1.2	1.3
2.3	1.9	2.1	Sales/Total Assets					1.9	2.4
1.4	.9	1.2						1.2	1.3
.7	.5	.7						.7	.9
2.2	2.5	2.3	% Depr., Dep., Amort./Sales					1.4	
(42) 5.7	(39) 5.5	(38) 5.0						(11) 3.3	
10.8	16.0	15.3						10.3	
1.8	.9		% Officers', Directors'						
(11) 2.6	(12) 2.8		Owners' Comp/Sales						
8.4	5.9								
1968024M	1732681M	1976337M	Net Sales ($)	1294M	18311M	28126M	31169M	186039M	1711398M
1510684M	1677439M	1743365M	Total Assets ($)	4447M	49275M	25686M	47649M	198214M	1418094M

M = $ thousand   MM = $ million
See Pages 9 through 22 for Explanation of Ratios and Data

Current Data Sorted by Assets | Comparative Historical Data

						Type of Statement		
		3	3	1	1	Unqualified	6	4
7	5	1				Reviewed	1	5
39	30	2				Compiled	23	22
9	13	11	6	3		Tax Returns	51	45
						Other	52	37
	24 (4/1-9/30/10)		110 (10/1/10-3/31/11)				4/1/06-3/31/07	4/1/07-3/31/08
0-500M	500M-2MM	2-10MM	10-50MM	50-100MM	100-250MM		ALL	ALL
55	48	17	9	4	1	**NUMBER OF STATEMENTS**	133	113
%	%	%	%	%	%	**ASSETS**	%	%
14.8	13.2	7.9				Cash & Equivalents	13.1	14.9
10.8	13.3	9.4				Trade Receivables (net)	11.9	12.2
5.9	6.1	8.7				Inventory	11.0	10.4
6.2	1.6	6.2				All Other Current	3.7	3.5
37.8	34.3	32.2				Total Current	39.7	41.0
45.1	49.4	50.1				Fixed Assets (net)	46.5	44.3
11.6	7.5	10.4				Intangibles (net)	6.1	7.7
5.4	8.8	7.3				All Other Non-Current	7.8	7.1
100.0	100.0	100.0				Total	100.0	100.0
						LIABILITIES		
13.9	6.2	6.1				Notes Payable-Short Term	7.6	9.7
14.5	10.8	5.7				Cur. Mat.-L.T.D.	6.6	8.6
7.1	5.0	9.2				Trade Payables	9.0	9.6
.1	.1	.0				Income Taxes Payable	.1	.5
10.7	3.5	7.5				All Other Current	12.5	6.8
46.3	25.5	28.4				Total Current	35.8	35.2
47.7	41.6	27.9				Long-Term Debt	39.6	39.4
.1	.2	.5				Deferred Taxes	.1	.2
23.6	2.2	7.6				All Other Non-Current	7.0	7.5
-17.8	30.6	35.5				Net Worth	17.5	17.7
100.0	100.0	100.0				Total Liabilties & Net Worth	100.0	100.0
						INCOME DATA		
100.0	100.0	100.0				Net Sales	100.0	100.0
						Gross Profit		
95.6	92.3	93.3				Operating Expenses	93.7	92.7
4.4	7.7	6.7				Operating Profit	6.3	7.3
.5	1.8	.7				All Other Expenses (net)	1.5	2.4
3.9	5.9	6.0				Profit Before Taxes	4.8	5.0
						RATIOS		
1.7	2.8	1.5					2.6	2.5
.8	1.7	1.0				Current	1.3	1.2
.4	.7	.6					.6	.7
1.0	2.5	1.0					1.8	1.6
.5	1.0	.6				Quick	.7	.8
.3	.4	.2					.3	.3
0 UND	0 UND	2 206.6					1 382.4	0 999.8
4 88.2	12 29.9	11 32.7				Sales/Receivables	10 38.3	11 32.4
15 24.9	28 13.1	23 15.7					22 16.4	26 13.9
						Cost of Sales/Inventory		
						Cost of Sales/Payables		
25.8	7.7	15.0					11.6	10.6
-142.3	24.2	UND				Sales/Working Capital	76.4	77.5
-11.6	-28.0	-31.5					-21.8	-20.2
7.0	10.2	9.2					7.7	5.8
(43) 3.1	(43) 3.8	(14) 3.5				EBIT/Interest	(115) 3.5	(100) 2.4
1.2	1.4	2.1					1.3	1.1
								14.2
						Net Profit + Depr., Dep., Amort./Cur. Mat. L/T/D	(15)	1.7
								1.0
1.2	.7	.8					.6	.6
-14.6	1.6	1.8				Fixed/Worth	2.4	2.5
-.5	-4.9	10.8					-9.4	-14.2
1.9	.6	1.2					1.2	1.1
-10.3	1.8	2.9				Debt/Worth	3.6	4.5
-2.4	-14.3	14.7					-11.0	-11.9
81.8	60.4	84.9					74.9	82.6
(24) 30.4	(33) 24.6	(14) 41.4				% Profit Before Taxes/Tangible Net Worth	(90) 39.7	(78) 23.6
.9	3.0	13.4					13.9	7.8
39.8	25.9	23.0					21.2	18.0
13.3	7.2	6.2				% Profit Before Taxes/Total Assets	8.5	6.4
.0	1.1	4.4					1.1	1.9
32.0	16.1	16.1					21.2	29.5
11.3	5.0	3.4				Sales/Net Fixed Assets	6.2	6.6
5.2	3.0	2.8					3.1	3.4
5.5	3.9	2.6					4.8	3.8
4.4	2.6	2.0				Sales/Total Assets	2.8	2.7
3.0	1.9	1.7					1.6	1.7
2.0	4.6	2.4					1.7	1.9
(36) 4.1	(30) 8.2	(13) 5.3				% Depr., Dep., Amort./Sales	(100) 4.7	(93) 4.6
7.9	10.9	8.1					8.7	7.9
2.9	3.0						2.5	2.4
(32) 5.5	(34) 4.0					% Officers', Directors' Owners' Comp/Sales	(66) 3.9	(59) 4.1
10.3	6.8						7.7	9.0
64371M	132937M	162044M	283277M	555025M	75260M	Net Sales ($)	1170065M	1320074M
13872M	47798M	72792M	173844M	287392M	100101M	Total Assets ($)	770175M	626677M

M = $ thousand   MM = $ million
See Pages 9 through 22 for Explanation of Ratios and Data

Comparative Historical Data   Current Data Sorted by Sales

			Type of Statement						
3	6	5	Unqualified					1	4
1	6	3	Reviewed						
11	15	13	Compiled				1	2	
48	60	71	Tax Returns	4	5	3	1		
21	31	42	Other	23	35	9	4		
4/1/08-3/31/09	4/1/09-3/31/10	4/1/10-3/31/11		8	9	8	3	7	7
ALL	ALL	ALL		24 (4/1-9/30/10)			110 (10/1/10-3/31/11)		
				0-1MM	1-3MM	3-5MM	5-10MM	10-25MM	25MM & OVER
84	118	134	NUMBER OF STATEMENTS	35	49	20	9	10	11
%	%	%	ASSETS	%	%	%	%	%	%
13.2	12.6	13.2	Cash & Equivalents	13.3	15.2	11.0		9.4	16.0
11.6	10.9	11.5	Trade Receivables (net)	12.4	10.4	9.4		8.7	11.3
10.3	7.0	6.8	Inventory	6.4	4.9	8.5		17.7	8.0
3.7	2.9	4.4	All Other Current	5.7	4.4	1.6		7.8	3.1
38.7	33.4	35.8	Total Current	37.8	35.0	30.5		43.6	38.4
49.3	47.5	46.7	Fixed Assets (net)	42.5	48.6	53.3		36.9	37.6
4.2	10.7	10.3	Intangibles (net)	13.7	7.4	12.2		8.4	18.7
7.8	8.4	7.1	All Other Non-Current	5.9	9.0	4.0		11.0	5.4
100.0	100.0	100.0	Total	100.0	100.0	100.0		100.0	100.0
			LIABILITIES						
18.5	12.4	9.3	Notes Payable-Short Term	19.0	6.2	5.1		6.9	5.9
11.2	9.7	11.3	Cur. Mat.-L.T.D.	8.3	13.2	16.5		8.3	3.8
9.3	7.6	6.7	Trade Payables	4.7	6.9	4.8		13.0	8.2
.3	.3	.2	Income Taxes Payable	.1	.1	.1		.1	2.0
7.9	10.4	7.9	All Other Current	9.5	4.8	9.9		9.4	15.9
47.3	40.5	35.4	Total Current	41.5	31.2	36.3		37.7	35.7
41.7	51.3	41.7	Long-Term Debt	34.9	52.2	40.9		25.9	34.7
.2	.3	.2	Deferred Taxes	.2	.0	.4		.0	.3
4.8	12.5	11.8	All Other Non-Current	23.3	9.4	9.7		2.3	3.6
6.0	-4.6	10.9	Net Worth	.1	7.2	12.7		34.1	25.6
100.0	100.0	100.0	Total Liabilities & Net Worth	100.0	100.0	100.0		100.0	100.0
			INCOME DATA						
100.0	100.0	100.0	Net Sales	100.0	100.0	100.0		100.0	100.0
			Gross Profit						
95.5	93.1	93.8	Operating Expenses	92.8	94.0	94.7		92.5	91.9
4.5	6.9	6.2	Operating Profit	7.2	6.0	5.3		7.5	8.1
1.4	3.1	1.1	All Other Expenses (net)	1.4	.7	1.2		-.3	2.4
3.1	3.8	5.1	Profit Before Taxes	5.7	5.3	4.1		7.8	5.7
			RATIOS						
2.8	1.9	2.0		2.4	2.3	2.1		1.4	1.6
1.1	1.0	1.0	Current	1.0	1.1	.8		1.0	1.0
.5	.3	.5		.4	.6	.4		.5	.7
1.4	1.7	1.6		1.7	2.1	.9		.9	1.6
.7	.6	.6	Quick	.5	.8	.5		.2	.6
.2	.2	.3		.2	.4	.1		.1	.3
0 UND	0 UND	0 UND		0 UND	0 UND	0 UND		1 294.1	7 51.9
8 42.9	8 48.3	8 43.5	Sales/Receivables	3 142.0	7 51.0	2 169.6		6 61.5	12 30.4
24 15.5	25 14.9	24 15.3		24 15.3	18 20.7	23 15.9		17 21.0	33 11.0
			Cost of Sales/Inventory						
			Cost of Sales/Payables						
13.1	17.1	11.7		8.3	11.1	12.2		15.4	13.6
110.4	-807.8	UND	Sales/Working Capital	UND	114.5	-99.8		UND	-618.5
-12.4	-9.6	-24.1		-8.2	-28.1	-16.7		-168.0	-23.1
7.1	5.6	7.5		7.0	10.0	16.6			
(72) 1.6	(103) 1.7	(111) 3.3	EBIT/Interest	(27) 3.1	(43) 3.4	(16) 4.2			
-.2	.3	1.2		1.4	1.0	2.3			
	16.7								
	(13) 1.7		Net Profit + Depr., Dep., Amort./Cur. Mat. L/T/D						
	1.0								
.7	1.0	.9		.7	.8	1.5		.5	.4
3.2	4.8	2.8	Fixed/Worth	5.3	4.4	2.4		1.3	5.8
-5.8	-1.1	-1.6		-1.6	-.7	-1.9		NM	-1.1
1.4	1.7	1.1		1.7	.8	1.1		1.5	1.2
5.0	9.9	5.2	Debt/Worth	-34.6	8.9	3.8		2.8	6.1
-10.2	-2.9	-4.0		-3.0	-2.9	-3.0		NM	-2.8
63.7	100.0	73.2		62.2	65.9	96.4			
(52) 22.9	(71) 18.1	(81) 25.1	% Profit Before Taxes/Tangible Net Worth	(16) 16.3	(30) 29.5	(13) 37.1			
.1	-4.3	3.0		1.9	2.5	4.5			
24.6	19.2	27.8		29.3	38.3	27.2		36.6	22.6
5.1	4.6	7.2	% Profit Before Taxes/Total Assets	6.1	10.4	8.6		9.2	2.3
-4.6	-2.4	.5		.6	.0	2.0		4.6	-6.2
16.2	19.3	19.6		20.9	20.2	17.3		32.6	29.6
6.3	6.0	6.3	Sales/Net Fixed Assets	7.9	8.6	5.4		11.7	4.2
3.3	3.0	3.4		2.9	3.9	3.2		3.2	3.2
4.5	4.2	4.6		4.6	4.9	5.8		4.6	2.9
3.0	2.4	2.9	Sales/Total Assets	3.0	3.4	3.5		2.0	1.8
1.8	1.5	1.9		1.4	2.2	2.2		1.6	.9
2.1	2.9	2.2		3.1	2.0	2.7			
(69) 5.1	(87) 5.4	(91) 5.4	% Depr., Dep., Amort./Sales	(20) 6.1	(35) 5.2	(13) 6.2			
10.2	12.5	9.5		11.3	9.9	9.3			
2.5	2.6	2.9		4.8	3.0	1.5			
(43) 4.2	(57) 5.4	(74) 4.5	% Officers', Directors' Owners' Comp/Sales	(15) 8.2	(39) 4.3	(10) 3.7			
7.6	9.4	7.9		16.2	6.9	5.5			
629495M	879655M	1272914M	Net Sales ($)	20630M	94144M	80189M	61022M	142775M	874154M
339352M	534418M	695799M	Total Assets ($)	11203M	31045M	28703M	33014M	87664M	504170M

© RMA 2011

M = $ thousand   MM = $ million
See Pages 9 through 22 for Explanation of Ratios and Data

Current Data Sorted by Assets   Comparative Historical Data

Type of Statement	0-500M	500M-2MM	2-10MM	10-50MM	50-100MM	100-250MM		4/1/06-3/31/07 ALL	4/1/07-3/31/08 ALL
Unqualified			5	2				10	5
Reviewed	3	2	6	4	1	2		15	16
Compiled	1	2	7	1				4	9
Tax Returns	4	6	4	1				15	20
Other	3	13	9	3	2	1		22	27
	12 (4/1-9/30/10)			70 (10/1/10-3/31/11)					
NUMBER OF STATEMENTS	11	23	31	11	3	3		66	77
ASSETS	%	%	%	%	%	%		%	%
Cash & Equivalents	9.3	11.6	18.0	6.7				9.6	12.3
Trade Receivables (net)	19.4	19.6	20.6	13.6				24.0	23.5
Inventory	5.7	6.3	6.3	7.8				8.7	7.4
All Other Current	19.9	6.3	1.4	2.8				3.9	5.2
Total Current	54.4	43.8	46.3	31.0				46.3	48.3
Fixed Assets (net)	31.9	39.8	32.9	58.1				42.0	39.2
Intangibles (net)	.0	7.2	10.1	6.7				5.0	4.5
All Other Non-Current	13.7	9.2	10.7	4.2				6.7	8.1
Total	100.0	100.0	100.0	100.0				100.0	100.0
LIABILITIES									
Notes Payable-Short Term	65.9	4.5	3.7	6.6				9.1	9.9
Cur. Mat.-L.T.D.	2.5	2.5	3.2	7.2				7.5	7.7
Trade Payables	17.4	7.9	9.4	6.9				15.5	8.8
Income Taxes Payable	.0	.0	.0	.0				.1	.2
All Other Current	36.5	14.0	8.7	7.0				10.0	11.2
Total Current	122.3	29.0	25.0	27.6				42.2	37.8
Long-Term Debt	8.1	34.7	17.2	28.8				23.0	26.0
Deferred Taxes	.0	.0	.4	.0				.5	.6
All Other Non-Current	4.4	6.4	10.4	.4				4.7	12.0
Net Worth	-34.8	29.9	47.0	43.3				29.5	23.5
Total Liabilties & Net Worth	100.0	100.0	100.0	100.0				100.0	100.0
INCOME DATA									
Net Sales	100.0	100.0	100.0	100.0				100.0	100.0
Gross Profit									
Operating Expenses	98.7	87.7	87.0	84.3				91.0	89.3
Operating Profit	1.3	12.3	13.0	15.7				9.0	10.7
All Other Expenses (net)	-.3	2.9	2.1	6.6				3.1	2.5
Profit Before Taxes	1.5	9.4	10.9	9.1				5.9	8.3
RATIOS									
Current	11.4	2.9	4.5	1.9				1.9	2.8
	1.0	1.2	2.3	1.0				1.1	1.4
	.5	.7	.9	.6				.7	.7
Quick	1.8	1.9	3.6	1.0				1.5	1.8
	.8	.9	1.9	.7				.8	1.0
	.4	.5	.7	.3				.4	.4
Sales/Receivables	0 UND	0 UND	7 53.8	15 24.4				0 UND	0 UND
	18 20.2	19 19.2	31 11.7	27 13.3				26 13.9	28 13.2
	38 9.7	50 7.3	44 8.2	36 10.1				48 7.6	48 7.5
Cost of Sales/Inventory									
Cost of Sales/Payables									
Sales/Working Capital	4.1	8.2	4.2	5.8				11.0	6.9
	-999.8	20.0	10.9	-237.2				96.5	26.0
	-12.0	-19.0	-104.4	-7.7				-17.8	-15.5
EBIT/Interest		8.4	11.3					9.0	12.0
		(17) 4.6	(23) 6.0					(51) 3.5	(60) 3.4
		.9	1.9					1.2	1.0
Net Profit + Depr., Dep., Amort./Cur. Mat. L/T/D								6.3	12.0
								(14) 2.1	(11) 2.6
								1.2	1.8
Fixed/Worth	.0	.3	.1	1.3				.4	.2
	.4	1.3	.7	2.1				1.5	1.5
	8.5	31.6	2.7	3.5				4.4	7.7
Debt/Worth	.2	1.1	.4	1.2				1.1	.9
	3.1	1.9	1.5	2.1				2.3	2.4
	-94.0	108.0	4.2	3.4				10.2	15.1
% Profit Before Taxes/Tangible Net Worth		96.8	48.1	38.5				55.9	65.9
	(19) 30.8	(26) 21.9	20.7					(54) 25.2	(62) 26.1
	15.0	7.3	11.2					8.8	2.9
% Profit Before Taxes/Total Assets	59.8	20.3	19.0	21.1				18.5	19.7
	25.5	8.1	6.1	5.4				6.0	8.8
	-18.0	2.8	3.9	3.6				1.5	-.2
Sales/Net Fixed Assets	UND	28.8	90.2	6.3				38.0	57.1
	34.4	6.8	8.8	3.5				8.0	11.1
	6.4	1.8	2.2	.7				2.2	2.2
Sales/Total Assets	32.3	3.4	4.0	2.5				4.2	4.5
	3.0	2.6	1.8	1.3				2.3	2.5
	1.2	1.0	.7	.7				.9	.9
% Depr., Dep., Amort./Sales		1.0	1.2	2.5				.7	.8
		(14) 2.6	(26) 2.6	6.6				(56) 3.3	(61) 3.8
		15.2	9.7	14.0				10.1	10.9
% Officers', Directors' Owners' Comp/Sales								1.6	2.0
								(21) 3.5	(26) 3.3
								5.0	6.6
Net Sales ($)	27029M	65487M	314624M	329989M	140863M	565568M		2453096M	856170M
Total Assets ($)	2785M	26145M	141050M	180421M	223210M	382420M		995234M	491334M

Comparative Historical Data

Current Data Sorted by Sales

4/1/08-3/31/09 ALL	4/1/09-3/31/10 ALL	4/1/10-3/31/11 ALL	Type of Statement	0-1MM	1-3MM	3-5MM	5-10MM	10-25MM	25MM & OVER
7	5	10	Unqualified		1	1	1	1	6
6	15	15	Reviewed	4		3	3	4	
7	12	11	Compiled	1	5	1	1	3	1
16	23	15	Tax Returns	6	2	3	1	3	
27	32	31	Other	4	7	3	6	6	5
				12 (4/1-9/30/10)			70 (10/1/10-3/31/11)		
63	87	82	**NUMBER OF STATEMENTS**	15	15	11	12	17	12
%	%	%	**ASSETS**	%	%	%	%	%	%
12.6	18.0	13.0	Cash & Equivalents	12.8	9.8	10.9	23.8	9.9	12.8
18.0	18.3	18.5	Trade Receivables (net)	4.9	23.5	9.5	19.6	28.2	22.3
5.6	5.5	6.0	Inventory	.4	8.6	11.0	2.3	6.8	7.5
6.2	5.1	5.5	All Other Current	16.6	6.4	1.2	2.2	2.2	2.3
42.4	46.8	42.9	Total Current	34.7	48.3	32.6	47.9	47.1	44.9
43.3	36.0	38.8	Fixed Assets (net)	58.3	33.8	40.5	41.0	24.5	37.6
7.0	8.2	8.4	Intangibles (net)	4.0	5.5	8.2	6.8	11.5	15.0
7.3	8.9	9.8	All Other Non-Current	3.0	12.3	18.7	4.3	16.9	2.5
100.0	100.0	100.0	Total	100.0	100.0	100.0	100.0	100.0	100.0
			LIABILITIES						
9.9	6.0	12.5	Notes Payable-Short Term	1.7	6.3	35.8	27.9	6.8	4.8
7.0	7.9	3.5	Cur. Mat.-L.T.D.	4.8	1.8	4.9	1.6	2.9	5.3
8.4	8.5	9.3	Trade Payables	5.5	6.5	7.9	5.8	17.7	10.1
.2	.0	.0	Income Taxes Payable	.0	.0	.0	.0	.0	.1
11.8	9.0	13.6	All Other Current	8.7	10.5	16.0	27.6	10.2	12.0
37.4	31.5	38.8	Total Current	20.7	25.2	64.6	63.0	37.5	32.3
27.5	26.1	22.5	Long-Term Debt	40.7	20.3	20.7	22.8	15.3	14.3
.3	.1	.2	Deferred Taxes	.0	.0	.1	.4	.6	.2
4.9	9.3	6.8	All Other Non-Current	11.9	8.6	11.8	5.0	1.5	2.7
29.9	33.0	31.7	Net Worth	26.7	46.0	2.8	8.8	45.0	50.6
100.0	100.0	100.0	Total Liabilities & Net Worth	100.0	100.0	100.0	100.0	100.0	100.0
			INCOME DATA						
100.0	100.0	100.0	Net Sales	100.0	100.0	100.0	100.0	100.0	100.0
			Gross Profit						
91.7	87.8	89.0	Operating Expenses	77.9	85.4	93.0	92.6	93.4	93.8
8.3	12.2	11.0	Operating Profit	22.1	14.6	7.0	7.4	6.6	6.2
3.2	3.2	2.5	All Other Expenses (net)	7.7	3.1	.4	.6	.4	2.1
5.2	9.0	8.5	Profit Before Taxes	14.3	11.5	6.6	6.8	6.2	4.1
			RATIOS						
2.2	2.8	3.3	Current	8.8	7.4	2.3	4.0	2.2	2.1
1.0	1.5	1.4		1.1	2.3	1.0	3.0	1.0	1.3
.5	.8	.7		.5	.9	.7	1.2	.6	1.0
2.0	2.4	2.5	Quick	1.8	3.8	1.3	3.5	2.1	1.9
.8	1.2	1.0		.8	1.8	.7	2.6	.8	1.1
.4	.6	.6		.4	.7	.3	1.1	.6	.8
7 55.7	1 293.0	5 74.4	Sales/Receivables	0 UND	5 70.0	0 UND	7 49.4	8 46.5	21 17.5
29 12.7	22 16.7	26 14.1		0 UND	47 7.8	5 66.4	27 13.7	30 12.2	31 11.8
41 8.9	41 8.9	44 8.4		34 10.6	60 6.0	36 10.2	38 9.6	45 8.1	44 8.3
			Cost of Sales/Inventory						
			Cost of Sales/Payables						
8.7	5.9	5.3	Sales/Working Capital	2.4	4.7	7.1	5.0	10.2	7.0
243.9	24.4	19.4		30.1	13.5	-180.1	11.5	-999.8	32.4
-15.0	-37.4	-19.4		-12.0	-55.3	-10.9	NM	-16.0	NM
9.0	15.3	16.5	EBIT/Interest		21.4			22.7	17.1
(48) 4.1	(67) 3.6	(63) 5.1			(11) 5.0		(15) 4.4	(11) 5.3
.0	1.2	2.1			2.2			2.5	2.1
		2.8	Net Profit + Depr., Dep., Amort./Cur. Mat. L/T/D						
	(13)	1.7							
		1.3							
.5	.1	.3	Fixed/Worth	1.0	.0	.3	.3	.0	.5
1.6	1.0	1.2		2.7	.7	1.4	.9	.4	1.2
4.0	3.3	3.6		31.6	2.5	-.8	2.0	2.9	NM
1.1	.5	.6	Debt/Worth	1.1	.2	.9	.4	.9	.4
2.2	1.6	1.7		3.1	1.6	1.7	.9	1.8	1.4
8.7	8.8	5.3		32.0	2.5	-12.9	1.5	4.0	NM
43.4	58.3	51.6	% Profit Before Taxes/Tangible Net Worth	73.6	62.4		50.2	51.9	
(53) 17.0	(69) 27.0	(68) 23.4		(13) 31.3	(14) 29.8		(10) 22.4	(14) 28.2	
-5.6	4.7	8.0		5.9	7.4		7.1	6.3	
16.1	22.5	20.4	% Profit Before Taxes/Total Assets	8.1	38.2	23.4	19.8	21.5	20.2
5.5	7.4	6.4		4.3	10.7	11.2	10.8	5.4	6.3
-3.1	.5	2.9		-7.9	2.3	4.0	1.9	4.2	3.6
41.1	82.3	48.1	Sales/Net Fixed Assets	4.7	144.8	34.4	34.6	285.1	29.6
5.9	8.7	5.7		1.1	10.4	8.8	11.2	52.9	3.7
1.1	2.0	2.0		.2	2.5	2.8	3.2	2.4	2.6
3.6	3.0	3.4	Sales/Total Assets	1.2	3.3	3.4	4.5	6.6	3.8
2.3	1.8	1.8		.7	2.3	3.0	2.3	2.9	1.9
.7	.9	.7		.1	.6	.7	1.6	1.3	1.0
1.2	1.0	1.5	% Depr., Dep., Amort./Sales	6.7			1.1	.8	1.3
(49) 3.7	(61) 4.1	(61) 3.3		(12) 20.3		(11) 1.8	(12) 2.6	(10) 4.4
11.0	12.4	13.8		21.1			3.9	6.0	7.7
2.5	1.7	1.7	% Officers', Directors' Owners' Comp/Sales						
(17) 4.0	(25) 2.8	(21) 3.7							
9.5	7.1	6.2							
1791648M	1293595M	1443560M	Net Sales ($)	6763M	27616M	43293M	90134M	265595M	1010159M
1264312M	841924M	956031M	Total Assets ($)	19246M	30956M	28928M	46440M	183768M	646693M

M = $ thousand   MM = $ million
See Pages 9 through 22 for Explanation of Ratios and Data

Current Data Sorted by Assets   Comparative Historical Data

						Type of Statement		
1	1	9	29	13	6	Unqualified	58	48
5	7	41	23	2		Reviewed	83	92
6	24	25	7			Compiled	66	69
24	40	24	1		1	Tax Returns	47	73
16	46	62	57	12	13	Other	131	154
	63 (4/1-9/30/10)		432 (10/1/10-3/31/11)				4/1/06-3/31/07 ALL	4/1/07-3/31/08 ALL
0-500M	500M-2MM	2-10MM	10-50MM	50-100MM	100-250MM	**NUMBER OF STATEMENTS**		
52	118	161	117	27	20		385	436
%	%	%	%	%	%	**ASSETS**	%	%
27.8	15.7	13.9	9.2	8.3	9.3	Cash & Equivalents	12.8	12.4
26.8	52.8	54.7	49.0	40.1	37.8	Trade Receivables (net)	49.2	51.0
1.6	.5	.6	1.2	.5	1.2	Inventory	1.4	.7
5.2	4.0	4.1	7.2	9.0	8.6	All Other Current	6.1	5.5
61.4	73.1	73.3	66.6	57.8	56.9	Total Current	69.5	69.6
18.9	12.9	16.7	19.8	19.2	23.6	Fixed Assets (net)	18.6	19.1
2.1	1.6	3.3	6.2	13.3	15.2	Intangibles (net)	4.0	4.0
17.6	12.4	6.7	7.4	9.7	4.3	All Other Non-Current	7.8	7.3
100.0	100.0	100.0	100.0	100.0	100.0	Total	100.0	100.0
						LIABILITIES		
30.9	8.8	9.0	9.4	8.4	8.4	Notes Payable-Short Term	11.0	10.8
6.4	2.7	2.7	3.1	2.6	3.0	Cur. Mat.-L.T.D.	3.0	3.9
19.9	31.1	31.1	26.7	20.4	18.7	Trade Payables	28.1	29.2
.3	.0	.3	.3	.4	.4	Income Taxes Payable	.2	.3
22.2	11.2	11.1	15.4	16.6	11.0	All Other Current	14.1	10.0
79.7	53.9	54.2	54.9	48.4	41.5	Total Current	56.4	54.1
18.5	11.6	7.0	12.4	14.3	11.8	Long-Term Debt	11.8	14.2
.0	.0	.1	.7	1.1	2.0	Deferred Taxes	.4	.3
13.2	3.4	5.1	3.9	4.2	4.7	All Other Non-Current	3.7	4.5
-11.4	31.1	33.7	28.1	32.0	40.0	Net Worth	27.7	26.9
100.0	100.0	100.0	100.0	100.0	100.0	Total Liabilities & Net Worth	100.0	100.0
						INCOME DATA		
100.0	100.0	100.0	100.0	100.0	100.0	Net Sales	100.0	100.0
						Gross Profit		
96.1	94.3	94.7	94.3	95.1	94.2	Operating Expenses	94.5	94.9
3.9	5.7	5.3	5.7	4.9	5.8	Operating Profit	5.5	5.1
-.3	1.4	1.0	.6	1.1	2.5	All Other Expenses (net)	.7	1.1
4.2	4.2	4.3	5.1	3.8	3.3	Profit Before Taxes	4.7	4.0
						RATIOS		
3.8	2.1	2.0	1.6	1.8	2.1		1.8	1.8
.9	1.4	1.4	1.2	1.2	1.4	Current	1.2	1.3
.3	.9	1.0	1.0	.9	1.0		1.0	1.0
3.3	1.9	1.9	1.4	1.6	1.9		1.7	1.6
.8	1.3	1.3	1.2	1.1	1.2	Quick	1.2	1.2
.2	.9	.9	.8	.7	.7		.9	.9
0 UND	22 16.3	30 12.3	34 10.7	39 9.4	38 9.7		27 13.3	28 12.9
0 UND	34 10.8	40 9.1	47 7.8	51 7.2	44 8.3	Sales/Receivables	39 9.4	41 8.9
29 12.7	52 7.0	53 6.8	61 6.0	66 5.5	69 5.3		56 6.5	57 6.4
						Cost of Sales/Inventory		
						Cost of Sales/Payables		
16.1	10.2	10.4	13.4	10.6	9.5		12.3	12.0
-157.3	29.2	23.3	33.0	34.1	11.7	Sales/Working Capital	32.3	30.0
-35.8	-221.6	NM	-932.4	-49.4	NM		-409.6	-459.8
21.6	20.6	36.3	35.2	23.5	17.0		22.0	15.8
(30) 10.3	(81) 7.9	(120) 8.2	(106) 9.6	(23) 6.7	(18) 3.2	EBIT/Interest	(311) 6.0	(348) 4.9
1.9	1.7	2.4	2.7	1.2	.8		1.9	1.5
		21.8	8.2	7.6		Net Profit + Depr., Dep.,	10.4	7.0
		(26) 7.0	(40) 3.2	(11) 3.7		Amort./Cur. Mat. L/T/D	(86) 3.7	(79) 2.6
		2.0	.8	.8			1.6	.8
.0	.0	.1	.1	.3	.2		.1	.1
1.0	.2	.3	.6	.7	1.4	Fixed/Worth	.4	.4
-1.1	1.3	1.6	2.1	3.0	2.1		2.1	2.1
1.6	.8	1.0	1.3	1.4	.9		1.2	1.1
17.6	2.1	2.5	2.9	2.9	2.0	Debt/Worth	3.1	2.8
-3.5	25.3	6.3	9.7	8.0	9.9		9.8	11.2
318.4	72.1	75.3	79.7	41.6	27.3	% Profit Before Taxes/Tangible	75.1	69.6
(31) 89.9	(102) 38.0	(143) 36.6	(103) 32.1	(22) 10.6	(17) 18.8	Net Worth	(329) 33.1	(371) 29.1
34.2	8.4	12.1	13.0	2.7	5.3		11.6	9.2
61.1	25.6	19.9	15.6	7.8	7.8	% Profit Before Taxes/Total	18.6	18.5
21.3	9.3	9.4	8.9	2.5	2.9	Assets	8.4	6.8
.4	1.6	2.3	2.7	.5	.1		2.2	1.5
999.8	657.2	314.3	157.0	74.1	64.1		257.6	299.4
181.8	141.7	55.1	37.7	28.5	23.5	Sales/Net Fixed Assets	52.3	61.9
30.2	31.6	14.8	8.3	8.5	4.3		10.1	11.1
16.1	8.3	7.0	5.1	4.8	4.3		6.5	6.5
8.6	5.5	4.9	3.6	2.4	2.0	Sales/Total Assets	4.3	4.3
4.5	3.0	2.8	2.0	.9	1.0		1.9	2.3
.1	.1	.2	.3	.5	.3		.2	.2
(29) .3	(75) .4	(120) .5	(93) .8	(24) 1.3	(11) .6	% Depr., Dep., Amort./Sales	(294) .5	(307) .6
1.4	1.1	1.4	2.2	4.0	1.6		2.1	2.5
2.4	1.9	.9	1.1			% Officers', Directors'	1.0	1.3
(21) 4.9	(56) 3.2	(54) 2.1	(19) 1.5			Owners' Comp/Sales	(104) 2.0	(146) 2.5
8.5	5.8	6.0	4.3				3.7	5.3
119101M	765873M	3694593M	10317110M	5568049M	8461188M	Net Sales ($)	18386786M	19105539M
12174M	136038M	731774M	2602262M	1909310M	3213349M	Total Assets ($)	6472929M	6186957M

M = $ thousand   MM = $ million
See Pages 9 through 22 for Explanation of Ratios and Data

Comparative Historical Data | | | | Current Data Sorted by Sales

Hist 1	Hist 2	Hist 3	Type of Statement	0-1MM	1-3MM	3-5MM	5-10MM	10-25MM	25MM & OVER
41	43	59	Unqualified	1		1	2	8	47
77	70	78	Reviewed	3	3	2	8	22	40
62	50	62	Compiled	4	13	4	9	19	13
67	56	90	Tax Returns	11	15	18	25	13	8
196	194	206	Other	10	19	16	20	44	97
4/1/08-3/31/09 ALL	4/1/09-3/31/10 ALL	4/1/10-3/31/11 ALL		63 (4/1-9/30/10)			432 (10/1/10-3/31/11)		
443	413	495	**NUMBER OF STATEMENTS**	29	50	41	64	106	205
%	%	%	**ASSETS**	%	%	%	%	%	%
13.8	13.5	14.2	Cash & Equivalents	25.5	15.7	21.9	16.2	14.6	9.8
48.2	48.1	48.5	Trade Receivables (net)	21.3	37.3	43.2	50.9	46.5	56.4
.6	.7	.8	Inventory	.0	2.6	1.0	.0	.5	.9
5.9	7.1	5.4	All Other Current	4.8	2.7	1.8	5.7	7.2	5.8
68.6	69.4	68.9	Total Current	51.6	58.3	67.9	72.7	68.9	72.9
18.3	17.4	17.2	Fixed Assets (net)	30.9	20.5	15.6	15.7	19.3	14.1
4.5	4.4	4.5	Intangibles (net)	1.4	3.5	3.8	1.8	3.3	6.8
8.6	8.8	9.5	All Other Non-Current	16.1	17.8	12.7	9.7	8.5	6.2
100.0	100.0	100.0	Total	100.0	100.0	100.0	100.0	100.0	100.0
			LIABILITIES						
12.6	11.9	11.3	Notes Payable-Short Term	15.5	15.9	12.7	12.0	9.5	10.0
3.8	3.2	3.2	Cur. Mat.-L.T.D.	1.6	6.0	2.1	3.5	3.3	2.8
29.3	27.1	27.8	Trade Payables	7.0	21.0	25.8	34.9	26.8	31.1
.2	.1	.3	Income Taxes Payable	.1	.3	.3	.1	.4	.3
12.8	11.5	13.6	All Other Current	19.0	19.7	8.0	12.6	10.1	14.6
58.8	53.8	56.1	Total Current	43.2	62.8	48.9	63.0	50.1	58.8
10.7	11.6	11.2	Long-Term Debt	20.2	18.6	12.2	11.7	9.8	8.4
.4	.4	.3	Deferred Taxes	.0	.0	.2	.0	.2	.7
4.0	4.3	5.2	All Other Non-Current	13.2	9.4	3.9	2.5	4.4	4.6
26.1	29.9	27.2	Net Worth	23.3	9.2	34.7	22.8	35.6	27.6
100.0	100.0	100.0	Total Liabilities & Net Worth	100.0	100.0	100.0	100.0	100.0	100.0
			INCOME DATA						
100.0	100.0	100.0	Net Sales	100.0	100.0	100.0	100.0	100.0	100.0
			Gross Profit						
95.2	96.4	94.7	Operating Expenses	83.1	90.9	93.2	95.0	95.9	96.8
4.8	3.6	5.3	Operating Profit	16.9	9.1	6.8	5.0	4.1	3.2
.8	1.4	.9	All Other Expenses (net)	9.5	.3	.5	.5	.3	.4
4.0	2.1	4.4	Profit Before Taxes	7.4	8.8	6.3	4.5	3.9	2.8
			RATIOS						
1.7	2.1	1.9	Current	6.3	2.5	3.0	2.0	1.9	1.7
1.3	1.3	1.3		1.2	1.2	1.5	1.3	1.4	1.2
.9	1.0	.9		.5	.6	.9	.9	1.0	1.0
1.6	1.8	1.7	Quick	6.3	2.4	3.0	1.8	1.8	1.5
1.1	1.2	1.2		1.1	1.2	1.4	1.2	1.3	1.2
.8	.8	.8		.3	.5	.8	.8	.9	.9
23 16.2	28 12.8	25 14.5	Sales/Receivables	0 UND	6 58.6	12 30.0	22 16.3	27 13.4	31 11.6
35 10.5	40 9.1	40 9.2		1 534.0	38 9.6	33 11.0	36 10.2	38 9.6	44 8.3
52 7.0	61 6.0	56 6.5		68 5.3	94 3.9	56 6.5	49 7.4	48 7.6	56 6.5
			Cost of Sales/Inventory						
			Cost of Sales/Payables						
14.8	9.9	11.1	Sales/Working Capital	3.9	7.0	7.0	11.4	12.1	14.8
36.3	26.7	29.6		31.1	21.3	24.0	37.4	21.8	34.3
-107.9	-261.6	-133.4		-13.5	-19.2	-83.2	-70.5	-999.8	-999.8
19.0	17.0	25.8	EBIT/Interest	18.8	30.5	57.2	21.0	23.4	32.1
(360) 6.0	(321) 4.1	(378) 8.2		(12) 9.0	(36) 9.8	(28) 6.6	(42) 8.0	(87) 6.1	(173) 9.1
1.6	.5	2.2		5.4	1.5	1.9	1.0	2.2	2.6
12.1	19.5	10.1	Net Profit + Depr., Dep., Amort./Cur. Mat. L/T/D					10.5	11.8
(89) 4.0	(65) 3.5	(87) 3.4						(20) 2.7	(56) 5.9
1.4	.9	1.1						1.2	1.3
.1	.1	.1	Fixed/Worth	.0	.1	.0	.0	.1	.1
.4	.3	.4		1.3	.4	.2	.3	.4	.5
1.7	1.8	2.1		UND	3.1	2.7	5.6	1.5	2.0
1.1	1.0	1.1	Debt/Worth	.5	.6	.6	1.3	.9	1.4
2.7	2.6	2.8		5.0	2.4	2.4	2.6	2.0	3.3
10.1	8.3	10.7		-35.4	UND	310.3	26.0	5.2	8.6
68.0	52.4	76.9	% Profit Before Taxes/Tangible Net Worth	78.3	100.0	155.0	67.7	61.0	83.2
(376) 25.7	(347) 18.1	(418) 33.9		(21) 22.1	(39) 43.3	(32) 58.1	(55) 35.0	(94) 28.5	(177) 32.4
9.3	2.0	10.0		-.2	11.5	12.8	6.0	8.8	12.9
17.3	15.8	21.2	% Profit Before Taxes/Total Assets	29.5	43.1	38.9	21.5	18.1	19.2
6.9	4.9	8.9		5.1	16.4	14.0	5.2	9.3	7.9
1.9	-1.3	1.8		-1.4	2.4	3.5	.8	2.1	2.0
287.3	253.9	305.7	Sales/Net Fixed Assets	467.5	630.0	474.2	451.0	294.5	222.6
62.3	50.8	63.8		35.2	36.2	71.4	107.8	45.3	70.4
15.0	12.2	14.6		.4	8.3	19.7	26.9	13.5	18.6
7.5	6.3	7.1	Sales/Total Assets	6.1	5.6	8.5	8.6	7.1	6.8
4.9	3.9	4.7		2.6	2.8	5.2	5.8	4.6	4.8
2.6	2.0	2.5		.2	1.3	1.8	3.5	2.8	2.8
.2	.3	.2	% Depr., Dep., Amort./Sales	.3	.3	.3	.1	.2	.2
(314) .6	(283) .8	(352) .5		(19) 1.5	(27) 1.1	(25) .7	(45) .3	(85) .6	(151) .5
2.0	2.4	1.7		20.5	3.6	3.2	1.3	1.8	1.3
1.3	1.3	1.4	% Officers', Directors' Owners' Comp/Sales		4.2	2.1	1.5	1.3	.8
(133) 2.7	(125) 3.3	(155) 2.8		(20) 7.2	(23) 4.7	(28) 2.9	(35) 2.0	(42) 1.5	
6.3	7.9	5.9			11.5	8.6	4.4	4.0	2.7
21198825M	23691187M	28925914M	Net Sales ($)	12438M	101423M	156147M	452610M	1716396M	26486900M
6494826M	6538872M	8604907M	Total Assets ($)	22958M	50267M	82681M	251422M	686348M	7511231M

M = $ thousand   MM = $ million
See Pages 9 through 22 for Explanation of Ratios and Data

Current Data Sorted by Assets   Comparative Historical Data

						Type of Statement		
1			5	1	1	Unqualified	11	11
	3	4	2			Reviewed	7	12
1	3	6				Compiled	8	6
2	3	5				Tax Returns	6	3
5	6	6	2	2		Other	22	30
							4/1/06-3/31/07	4/1/07-3/31/08
0-500M	500M-2MM	2-10MM	10-50MM	50-100MM	100-250MM		ALL	ALL
9	15	21	9	3	1	NUMBER OF STATEMENTS	54	62
%	%	%	%	%	%		%	%
						ASSETS		
	15.5	9.9				Cash & Equivalents	9.1	7.9
	34.0	32.6				Trade Receivables (net)	37.6	37.6
	9.1	3.5				Inventory	9.6	10.1
	7.2	1.6				All Other Current	4.6	4.4
	65.8	47.6				Total Current	60.9	59.9
	17.3	31.5				Fixed Assets (net)	24.1	24.9
	9.8	.7				Intangibles (net)	3.9	6.3
	7.1	20.2				All Other Non-Current	11.1	8.8
	100.0	100.0				Total	100.0	100.0
						LIABILITIES		
	11.8	6.1				Notes Payable-Short Term	13.1	9.1
	.8	3.3				Cur. Mat.-L.T.D.	5.6	2.9
	15.3	8.9				Trade Payables	24.2	21.5
	.0	.0				Income Taxes Payable	.4	.3
	14.3	13.7				All Other Current	18.8	9.3
	42.3	32.0				Total Current	62.1	43.1
	11.7	19.6				Long-Term Debt	14.5	18.2
	.8	1.8				Deferred Taxes	.1	.2
	8.7	3.8				All Other Non-Current	7.7	4.5
	36.5	42.8				Net Worth	15.5	33.9
	100.0	100.0				Total Liabilities & Net Worth	100.0	100.0
						INCOME DATA		
	100.0	100.0				Net Sales	100.0	100.0
						Gross Profit		
	93.9	87.2				Operating Expenses	94.8	92.9
	6.1	12.8				Operating Profit	5.2	7.1
	1.0	3.8				All Other Expenses (net)	1.1	.8
	5.1	8.9				Profit Before Taxes	4.1	6.2
						RATIOS		
	4.6	3.3				Current	2.0	2.3
	2.2	1.7					1.2	1.4
	.9	.9					.8	1.0
	4.4	2.8				Quick	1.4	1.9
	2.2	1.5					.9	1.0
	.6	.9					.5	.7
24	15.2	29 12.4				Sales/Receivables	33 11.0	34 10.8
33	11.0	45 8.1					52 7.1	50 7.4
52	7.0	63 5.8					68 5.4	63 5.8
						Cost of Sales/Inventory		
						Cost of Sales/Payables		
	8.5	7.2				Sales/Working Capital	7.8	6.3
	17.4	12.5					31.0	15.6
	-48.3	NM					-41.0	NM
	19.3	41.2				EBIT/Interest	10.0	8.0
(12)	5.1	(15) 9.1					(48) 4.5	(48) 5.5
	.0	1.2					1.3	2.9
						Net Profit + Depr., Dep., Amort./Cur. Mat. L/T/D	10.3	7.7
							(10) 3.4	(10) 4.2
							2.1	2.6
	.1	.2				Fixed/Worth	.2	.2
	.7	.6					.7	.7
	1.9	2.6					2.4	2.6
	.5	.3				Debt/Worth	1.1	.7
	2.2	1.8					2.9	2.3
	-7.4	4.8					31.0	9.0
	73.9	51.9				% Profit Before Taxes/Tangible Net Worth	67.1	77.0
(11)	11.6	(20) 21.1					(42) 26.4	(53) 28.1
	-12.1	5.3					11.2	17.1
	35.7	24.8				% Profit Before Taxes/Total Assets	16.9	20.9
	7.7	9.3					8.7	12.0
	-1.6	2.2					1.6	4.5
	43.2	38.8				Sales/Net Fixed Assets	40.9	65.4
	19.8	8.3					16.1	14.9
	9.7	3.9					5.6	5.6
	3.7	3.8				Sales/Total Assets	3.4	3.4
	3.2	2.4					2.5	2.7
	2.3	1.2					1.7	1.9
	.4	1.0				% Depr., Dep., Amort./Sales	.8	.5
(10)	1.4	(19) 2.2					(44) 1.8	(52) 1.0
	2.4	7.8					4.7	2.8
						% Officers', Directors' Owners' Comp/Sales	1.6	1.5
							(20) 4.5	(24) 2.8
							11.7	5.4
12153M	91565M	197052M	498743M	634115M	61666M	Net Sales ($)	1539815M	3308363M
2065M	19630M	80624M	194839M	216666M	115834M	Total Assets ($)	749625M	1367162M

M = $ thousand   MM = $ million
See Pages 9 through 22 for Explanation of Ratios and Data

Comparative Historical Data | Current Data Sorted by Sales

4/1/08-3/31/09 ALL	4/1/09-3/31/10 ALL	4/1/10-3/31/11 ALL	Type of Statement	0-1MM	1-3MM	3-5MM	5-10MM	10-25MM	25MM & OVER
8	4	8	Unqualified	1			1		6
15	15	9	Reviewed			2	3	3	1
15	11	10	Compiled	1	2	1	5	1	
7	13	10	Tax Returns	1	4	1	2		1
10	33	21	Other	4	3	3	3	4	4
			7 (4/1-9/30/10)				51 (10/1/10-3/31/11)		
55	76	58	**NUMBER OF STATEMENTS**	7	9	7	14	9	12
%	%	%	**ASSETS**	%	%	%	%	%	%
14.1	12.4	12.2	Cash & Equivalents				9.8		17.9
31.3	29.7	32.0	Trade Receivables (net)				38.7		33.3
9.7	11.4	8.4	Inventory				4.2		16.0
5.0	2.6	4.3	All Other Current				2.2		4.8
60.0	56.1	56.8	Total Current				54.8		72.0
24.1	28.5	24.2	Fixed Assets (net)				26.9		12.6
3.9	4.8	7.4	Intangibles (net)				6.0		8.9
11.9	10.6	11.6	All Other Non-Current				12.3		6.4
100.0	100.0	100.0	Total				100.0		100.0
			LIABILITIES						
9.6	16.9	8.8	Notes Payable-Short Term				10.0		6.9
2.1	4.3	2.3	Cur. Mat.-L.T.D.				3.4		2.9
20.1	14.8	12.8	Trade Payables				15.1		21.9
.6	.1	.1	Income Taxes Payable				.0		.2
9.5	13.7	13.5	All Other Current				7.2		14.3
41.9	49.8	37.3	Total Current				35.8		46.3
14.1	14.9	17.4	Long-Term Debt				17.7		13.8
.3	.3	1.0	Deferred Taxes				.2		.3
3.5	2.9	8.0	All Other Non-Current				7.2		1.7
40.1	32.2	36.2	Net Worth				39.1		37.9
100.0	100.0	100.0	Total Liabilities & Net Worth				100.0		100.0
			INCOME DATA						
100.0	100.0	100.0	Net Sales				100.0		100.0
			Gross Profit						
92.7	90.6	91.1	Operating Expenses				95.2		93.0
7.3	9.4	8.9	Operating Profit				4.8		7.0
.8	2.4	2.0	All Other Expenses (net)				1.5		.4
6.5	7.0	6.9	Profit Before Taxes				3.4		6.5
			RATIOS						
2.6	2.6	3.9	Current				5.5		3.6
1.6	1.4	1.7					1.8		1.6
1.1	.9	1.0					.9		1.2
2.1	2.4	2.6	Quick				4.6		1.7
1.3	1.3	1.3					1.6		1.2
.8	.6	.5					.8		.6
23 15.9	29 12.7	24 14.9	Sales/Receivables				33 11.2		13 27.8
38 9.6	45 8.0	45 8.1					50 7.4		50 7.3
55 6.6	61 6.0	62 5.9					69 5.3		59 6.2
			Cost of Sales/Inventory						
			Cost of Sales/Payables						
6.1	6.3	6.9	Sales/Working Capital				7.7		6.0
12.6	15.5	14.5					12.7		17.9
249.1	-51.0	NM					-40.7		47.6
23.4	21.0	19.4	EBIT/Interest				18.5		85.8
(43) 5.6	(59) 5.0	(42) 5.2					(13) 4.3		(11) 7.7
1.7	1.3	.1					.4		3.1
8.4	4.2		Net Profit + Depr., Dep., Amort./Cur. Mat. L/T/D						
(11) 3.9	(12) 1.9								
1.8	1.1								
.1	.3	.1	Fixed/Worth				.4		.0
.5	.8	.7					1.3		.2
1.4	2.4	3.4					NM		1.0
.6	.7	.8	Debt/Worth				.8		.9
1.0	1.9	1.9					2.0		1.9
2.7	8.1	7.4					NM		4.1
66.4	56.6	65.6	% Profit Before Taxes/Tangible Net Worth				71.3		85.6
(48) 30.5	(64) 27.5	(46) 19.2					(11) 29.0		(10) 19.8
4.7	7.8	3.4					10.1		12.0
30.8	19.4	24.9	% Profit Before Taxes/Total Assets				21.4		18.5
11.4	8.0	6.5					10.5		5.3
2.1	2.2	.4					.1		3.9
72.8	31.7	48.4	Sales/Net Fixed Assets				19.1		112.4
16.9	12.1	19.7					11.0		45.5
7.9	5.1	7.9					6.6		12.3
4.7	3.5	3.9	Sales/Total Assets				3.4		4.3
2.9	2.5	2.8					2.7		3.1
2.0	1.3	1.7					1.7		2.0
.6	.9	.6	% Depr., Dep., Amort./Sales				1.2		
(44) 1.2	(58) 2.1	(42) 1.6					(12) 1.7		
2.6	3.8	3.0					3.4		
1.9	1.8	1.8	% Officers', Directors' Owners' Comp/Sales						
(26) 4.3	(25) 4.6	(18) 3.9							
8.3	7.2	6.4							
2140662M	1577275M	1495294M	Net Sales ($)	2268M	20314M	27868M	101961M	121914M	1220969M
1009503M	674622M	629658M	Total Assets ($)	8310M	5952M	14198M	51524M	47604M	502070M

© RMA 2011
M = $ thousand   MM = $ million
See Pages 9 through 22 for Explanation of Ratios and Data

Current Data Sorted by Assets   **Comparative Historical Data**

						Type of Statement		
		3	7	2	3	Unqualified	29	14
	3	10	3			Reviewed	20	15
3	6	4				Compiled	22	11
12	7	3				Tax Returns	20	10
6	20	21	9	5	1	Other	43	45
	21 (4/1-9/30/10)		107 (10/1/10-3/31/11)				4/1/06-3/31/07	4/1/07-3/31/08
0-500M	500M-2MM	2-10MM	10-50MM	50-100MM	100-250MM	NUMBER OF STATEMENTS	ALL	ALL
21	36	41	19	7	4		134	95
%	%	%	%	%	%	**ASSETS**	%	%
28.7	12.2	12.1	16.6			Cash & Equivalents	11.5	11.3
17.8	32.8	33.6	20.3			Trade Receivables (net)	30.1	29.5
5.4	4.3	3.7	3.8			Inventory	5.7	7.2
1.3	2.1	5.1	6.6			All Other Current	4.3	3.6
53.2	51.5	54.5	47.3			Total Current	51.6	51.5
21.1	31.0	38.4	47.4			Fixed Assets (net)	37.3	35.0
6.7	11.4	.8	1.4			Intangibles (net)	4.3	6.7
19.0	6.1	6.3	3.9			All Other Non-Current	6.8	6.8
100.0	100.0	100.0	100.0			Total	100.0	100.0
						LIABILITIES		
13.0	10.3	8.2	3.2			Notes Payable-Short Term	7.6	8.5
8.4	3.8	3.2	4.5			Cur. Mat.-L.T.D.	5.9	6.0
10.6	9.3	13.6	7.9			Trade Payables	11.4	14.0
1.0	.1	.4	.1			Income Taxes Payable	.2	.1
15.5	8.1	9.0	17.4			All Other Current	15.4	10.7
48.4	31.5	34.4	33.1			Total Current	40.5	39.3
25.4	31.8	15.9	20.3			Long-Term Debt	20.5	21.3
.0	.3	.6	.4			Deferred Taxes	.7	.9
9.0	11.4	3.5	7.7			All Other Non-Current	5.5	5.2
17.2	25.0	45.6	38.6			Net Worth	32.8	33.4
100.0	100.0	100.0	100.0			Total Liabilties & Net Worth	100.0	100.0
						INCOME DATA		
100.0	100.0	100.0	100.0			Net Sales	100.0	100.0
						Gross Profit		
89.3	93.8	86.3	91.8			Operating Expenses	91.7	91.7
10.7	6.2	13.7	8.2			Operating Profit	8.3	8.3
1.2	1.1	3.8	.9			All Other Expenses (net)	1.6	1.5
9.5	5.1	9.9	7.3			Profit Before Taxes	6.7	6.7
						RATIOS		
4.3	3.5	2.4	2.9				2.3	2.1
1.0	1.7	1.4	1.4			Current	1.3	1.2
.5	1.0	1.0	1.0				.8	.9
4.3	2.9	2.1	2.4				1.7	1.7
.9	1.4	1.4	1.0			Quick	1.0	1.0
.4	.9	.8	.6				.6	.7
0 UND	10 34.8	3 138.1	5 72.7				14 26.7	16 22.7
0 UND	34 10.8	44 8.3	28 12.9			Sales/Receivables	32 11.3	34 10.7
38 9.6	68 5.4	66 5.6	43 8.6				53 6.9	48 7.5
						Cost of Sales/Inventory		
						Cost of Sales/Payables		
22.4	6.5	7.0	7.3				9.9	10.3
204.7	23.0	13.2	19.7			Sales/Working Capital	36.8	49.0
-23.0	393.3	-587.8	-58.7				-34.7	-56.5
14.9	21.5	26.1	25.5				12.5	14.1
(13) 5.9	(28) 4.5	(35) 8.4	(16) 3.9			EBIT/Interest	(96) 3.7	(79) 4.1
1.5	-1.3	1.6	2.1				1.4	1.7
						Net Profit + Depr., Dep.,	4.5	5.4
						Amort./Cur. Mat. L/T/D	(25) 2.1	(22) 2.1
							1.0	1.5
.0	.2	.2	.3				.2	.3
.5	1.0	.7	1.6			Fixed/Worth	1.0	1.2
NM	-112.0	1.3	3.3				3.4	5.9
.3	.7	.7	.7				.9	.8
1.6	5.1	1.4	1.9			Debt/Worth	2.2	2.5
-2.2	-126.8	2.6	3.8				7.2	19.6
113.8	72.6	64.6	40.2			% Profit Before Taxes/Tangible	62.0	58.6
(14) 27.4	(26) 29.0	(39) 25.2	(18) 20.2			Net Worth	(113) 29.7	(76) 32.0
-.3	4.2	3.5	5.0				10.6	10.9
37.2	20.2	25.1	14.1			% Profit Before Taxes/Total	21.4	19.4
14.3	9.1	11.9	5.4			Assets	9.2	9.0
.6	-4.2	-.1	3.3				2.2	2.0
UND	64.3	40.9	18.8				76.3	72.3
87.5	16.0	10.0	3.7			Sales/Net Fixed Assets	8.5	8.5
8.4	4.1	3.3	1.8				3.7	3.6
6.9	4.9	4.4	2.3				4.5	4.7
4.3	2.8	2.6	1.7			Sales/Total Assets	2.6	2.4
1.5	1.1	1.3	1.0				1.4	1.6
	.7	.7	1.7				.7	.7
	(23) 1.8	(29) 3.4	(16) 5.4			% Depr., Dep., Amort./Sales	(101) 2.9	(77) 2.9
	9.0	8.1	14.1				6.1	6.1
	1.9	1.2					1.5	2.3
	(14) 3.1	(17) 4.3				% Officers', Directors'	(32) 3.0	(22) 3.4
	6.2	8.4				Owners' Comp/Sales	9.7	5.8
33985M	136353M	701992M	722322M	1038674M	1161410M	Net Sales ($)	7064537M	4052955M
5118M	40784M	188822M	411660M	509790M	715115M	Total Assets ($)	3130752M	1875802M

M = $ thousand   MM = $ million
See Pages 9 through 22 for Explanation of Ratios and Data

Comparative Historical Data | Current Data Sorted by Sales

4/1/08-3/31/09 ALL	4/1/09-3/31/10 ALL	4/1/10-3/31/11 ALL	Type of Statement	0-1MM	1-3MM	3-5MM	5-10MM	10-25MM	25MM & OVER
28	23	15	Unqualified			1	1	1	12
20	17	16	Reviewed		1	2	2	5	6
16	15	13	Compiled	5	3	1	1	3	
28	27	22	Tax Returns	6	5	5	5	1	
53	48	62	Other	12	12	5	11	9	13
				21 (4/1-9/30/10)			**107 (10/1/10-3/31/11)**		
145	130	128	**NUMBER OF STATEMENTS**	23	21	14	20	19	31
%	%	%	**ASSETS**	%	%	%	%	%	%
15.2	16.0	15.3	Cash & Equivalents	15.1	19.1	7.5	16.5	16.4	15.1
26.8	29.3	28.2	Trade Receivables (net)	13.4	22.5	45.6	33.0	35.1	28.0
5.2	5.6	3.9	Inventory	5.3	1.1	8.2	2.7	3.6	3.7
3.5	5.0	3.7	All Other Current	.7	2.3	1.7	5.4	3.9	6.7
50.7	56.0	51.2	Total Current	34.5	45.1	63.0	57.7	59.0	53.4
35.5	30.2	34.2	Fixed Assets (net)	45.6	37.6	32.0	23.2	32.4	32.5
6.8	6.4	6.9	Intangibles (net)	6.5	10.6	2.0	5.1	5.0	9.1
6.9	7.5	7.8	All Other Non-Current	13.3	6.8	2.9	14.0	3.6	5.0
100.0	100.0	100.0	Total	100.0	100.0	100.0	100.0	100.0	100.0
			LIABILITIES						
12.9	6.5	8.2	Notes Payable-Short Term	10.6	6.7	7.2	16.6	4.4	4.7
6.3	4.9	4.8	Cur. Mat.-L.T.D.	4.3	7.3	1.3	6.6	4.1	4.2
11.9	14.8	10.4	Trade Payables	6.7	8.4	13.5	9.6	13.1	12.0
.4	.2	.4	Income Taxes Payable	.2	.8	.1	.2	.6	.4
14.6	12.4	11.8	All Other Current	11.7	6.6	12.3	6.8	15.7	15.9
46.1	38.7	35.5	Total Current	33.5	29.7	34.3	39.7	37.9	37.2
25.7	23.1	23.5	Long-Term Debt	37.8	34.3	21.0	17.9	13.1	16.7
.2	.4	.4	Deferred Taxes	.0	.2	.4	.9	.5	.6
3.8	7.7	8.2	All Other Non-Current	7.5	9.3	8.7	12.3	1.1	9.4
24.1	30.1	32.4	Net Worth	21.2	26.4	35.6	29.2	47.3	36.2
100.0	100.0	100.0	Total Liabilities & Net Worth	100.0	100.0	100.0	100.0	100.0	100.0
			INCOME DATA						
100.0	100.0	100.0	Net Sales	100.0	100.0	100.0	100.0	100.0	100.0
			Gross Profit						
94.6	92.0	90.1	Operating Expenses	84.5	85.1	93.0	93.4	94.8	91.5
5.4	8.0	9.9	Operating Profit	15.5	14.9	7.0	6.6	5.2	8.5
1.8	1.6	2.1	All Other Expenses (net)	8.0	.8	.4	1.3	-.4	1.2
3.6	6.4	7.8	Profit Before Taxes	7.4	14.1	6.7	5.2	5.6	7.3
			RATIOS						
1.9	2.7	2.5	Current	2.0	3.6	3.6	2.3	2.5	2.3
1.2	1.4	1.4		1.0	1.9	1.6	1.3	1.5	1.3
.8	.9	.9		.4	.8	1.1	.7	1.0	1.1
1.7	2.3	2.1	Quick	2.0	3.3	2.6	2.1	2.5	2.0
.9	1.2	1.2		.6	1.8	1.4	1.1	1.4	1.2
.6	.7	.6		.4	.5	.9	.7	.9	.6
9 42.3	16 23.1	5 78.8	Sales/Receivables	0 UND	0 UND	23 15.6	16 23.5	26 13.9	22 17.0
29 12.6	33 11.2	34 10.7		0 UND	34 10.8	51 7.1	29 12.8	56 6.5	34 10.7
47 7.8	53 6.9	60 6.1		53 6.9	49 7.5	73 5.0	65 5.6	76 4.8	46 7.9
			Cost of Sales/Inventory						
			Cost of Sales/Payables						
13.3	7.8	7.2	Sales/Working Capital	5.1	10.1	6.5	6.9	4.1	11.4
43.2	18.8	26.4		48.8	30.2	9.4	37.4	11.7	27.3
-41.2	-74.3	-161.5		-2.6	-84.1	NM	-72.7	-999.8	184.3
13.1	17.0	22.4	EBIT/Interest	8.6	32.9	23.9	23.9	21.4	28.7
(114) 3.3	(94) 4.8	(102) 5.2		(14) 3.5	(15) 17.4	(12) 5.1	(17) 3.1	(17) 6.4	(27) 5.1
1.2	1.6	1.7		.2	3.8	-1.6	-2.0	2.1	2.2
7.5	7.7	7.7	Net Profit + Depr., Dep., Amort./Cur. Mat. L/T/D						
(21) 2.1	(18) 3.2	(11) 3.8							
1.4	1.4	1.3							
.4	.2	.2	Fixed/Worth	.0	.1	.3	.0	.2	.3
1.5	.9	1.0		1.4	1.3	.9	.5	.8	1.0
UND	3.6	5.9		-416.0	-3.3	2.8	1.3	1.8	3.3
1.1	.6	.7	Debt/Worth	.5	.3	.6	.4	.7	1.3
2.9	1.9	2.1		8.3	2.2	1.5	2.2	1.2	2.3
UND	42.1	17.6		-11.4	-5.6	5.9	8.4	2.7	4.5
61.8	67.7	62.6	% Profit Before Taxes/Tangible Net Worth	96.1	258.2	60.6	94.4	50.2	51.6
(109) 20.1	(101) 23.1	(102) 23.7		(16) 15.2	(13) 23.9	(12) 36.3	(17) 25.5	20.0	(25) 24.7
5.1	7.1	4.3		-11.7	6.9	7.3	-5.5	3.7	5.4
14.4	17.9	20.7	% Profit Before Taxes/Total Assets	20.4	36.0	19.7	38.4	16.2	20.7
5.9	8.7	9.5		3.8	17.3	5.5	11.7	4.2	8.3
.7	1.7	.9		-2.1	4.5	-8.2	-5.0	1.1	3.3
77.3	66.5	64.3	Sales/Net Fixed Assets	125.5	71.4	38.7	UND	46.3	48.9
12.3	13.9	11.2		3.0	9.0	12.2	20.8	10.0	8.3
3.4	3.7	3.3		.3	2.0	5.2	9.6	3.6	3.4
5.8	4.8	4.3	Sales/Total Assets	2.0	4.9	4.2	5.7	2.7	6.5
2.6	2.5	2.4		.9	2.4	3.1	3.2	2.2	2.7
1.5	1.4	1.3		.2	1.0	1.9	2.6	1.7	1.5
.9	.8	.8	% Depr., Dep., Amort./Sales	9.1	.8	.8	.2	1.1	.7
(109) 2.7	(91) 2.2	(86) 2.9		(12) 18.4	(11) 3.5	(13) 2.0	(10) 1.3	(16) 2.8	(24) 2.6
7.4	5.9	8.5		46.0	16.5	6.6	6.8	5.5	5.6
2.0	1.9	1.6	% Officers', Directors' Owners' Comp/Sales					2.2	
(33) 3.9	(38) 4.0	(43) 3.3						(12) 4.1	
7.2	6.7	7.8						8.2	
5323990M	4528771M	3794736M	Net Sales ($)	11076M	36763M	56874M	147522M	303991M	3238510M
2327227M	2196723M	1871289M	Total Assets ($)	26075M	37465M	40994M	44747M	218750M	1503258M

M = $ thousand   MM = $ million
See Pages 9 through 22 for Explanation of Ratios and Data

Current Data Sorted by Assets | Comparative Historical Data

Type of Statement	0-500M	500M-2MM	2-10MM	10-50MM	50-100MM	100-250MM		4/1/06-3/31/07 ALL	4/1/07-3/31/08 ALL
Unqualified			2	8	4	2		9	11
Reviewed	1	6	7	3				13	12
Compiled	1	4	6					15	16
Tax Returns	10	4	2					19	16
Other	11	10	17	10		1		33	35
	7 (4/1-9/30/10)			102 (10/1/10-3/31/11)					
NUMBER OF STATEMENTS	23	24	34	21	4	3		89	90
	%	%	%	%	%	%		%	%
ASSETS									
Cash & Equivalents	17.1	10.8	9.5	12.4				11.2	9.9
Trade Receivables (net)	21.2	42.3	46.2	31.7				31.6	32.5
Inventory	.0	.8	1.3	1.2				1.6	2.8
All Other Current	3.1	5.0	9.5	3.4				6.0	4.6
Total Current	41.3	58.9	66.5	48.7				50.4	49.8
Fixed Assets (net)	31.3	20.3	22.4	24.2				29.3	28.1
Intangibles (net)	12.8	10.9	6.9	19.5				9.5	11.5
All Other Non-Current	14.6	9.9	4.2	7.7				10.8	10.6
Total	100.0	100.0	100.0	100.0				100.0	100.0
LIABILITIES									
Notes Payable-Short Term	22.5	14.9	14.3	8.1				14.8	16.4
Cur. Mat.-L.T.D.	9.2	6.0	5.1	4.6				11.9	6.4
Trade Payables	14.1	9.8	11.9	14.9				8.2	15.8
Income Taxes Payable	.5	.0	.3	.2				.2	.2
All Other Current	11.8	9.8	11.8	9.5				14.0	14.1
Total Current	58.1	40.6	43.4	37.3				49.1	53.0
Long-Term Debt	33.9	32.2	12.1	17.3				25.3	20.3
Deferred Taxes	.0	.2	.1	2.0				.4	.8
All Other Non-Current	5.2	1.7	4.9	5.9				8.3	4.3
Net Worth	2.8	25.4	39.5	37.5				16.9	21.6
Total Liabilities & Net Worth	100.0	100.0	100.0	100.0				100.0	100.0
INCOME DATA									
Net Sales	100.0	100.0	100.0	100.0				100.0	100.0
Gross Profit									
Operating Expenses	94.9	97.0	94.2	97.0				94.7	95.6
Operating Profit	5.1	3.0	5.8	3.0				5.3	4.4
All Other Expenses (net)	1.5	.3	3.5	1.7				1.4	.7
Profit Before Taxes	3.7	2.8	2.3	1.3				3.9	3.8
RATIOS									
Current	2.7	2.7	2.1	1.7				2.2	1.7
	.7	1.7	1.4	1.3				1.2	1.1
	.3	1.0	1.0	.8				.7	.7
Quick	2.3	2.6	1.8	1.5				2.0	1.4
	.7	1.6	1.1	1.2				1.0	.9
	.3	.9	.8	.6				.5	.5
Sales/Receivables	0 UND	16 23.3	27 13.3	30 12.2				5 75.0	14 25.9
	0 UND	27 13.4	39 9.4	39 9.4				27 13.5	32 11.5
	21 17.0	38 9.6	44 8.4	54 6.8				38 9.5	42 8.8
Cost of Sales/Inventory									
Cost of Sales/Payables									
Sales/Working Capital	54.4	13.3	8.7	12.8				11.6	16.9
	-141.8	41.8	25.7	21.0				67.3	196.2
	-18.3	NM	700.4	-26.6				-35.3	-27.6
EBIT/Interest	19.3	13.4	19.8	8.2				14.5	12.7
	(17) 2.6	(21) 4.1	(30) 9.1	(17) .9				(79) 5.0	(84) 4.9
	-1.5	2.4	3.9	-1.8				1.3	1.7
Net Profit + Depr., Dep., Amort./Cur. Mat. L/T/D				4.0				6.5	5.1
			(10) .6					(14) 2.1	(17) 2.7
				-.4				.9	.7
Fixed/Worth	.6	.3	.1	.5				.3	.3
	6.3	1.0	.5	2.1				1.1	1.4
	-.7	-2.0	1.5	-.7				-2.4	22.8
Debt/Worth	1.5	.8	1.0	1.2				1.0	1.2
	52.4	6.4	1.8	1.9				2.9	3.5
	-2.5	-6.1	4.8	-5.7				-5.9	NM
% Profit Before Taxes/Tangible Net Worth	307.5	122.8	73.4	36.3				78.7	91.5
	(12) 26.8	(17) 26.1	(31) 25.4	(14) 16.7				(62) 36.2	(68) 40.2
	8.1	9.4	12.3	3.0				10.3	15.8
% Profit Before Taxes/Total Assets	36.5	21.5	23.1	11.0				27.8	21.7
	7.0	10.3	8.0	3.5				9.1	12.5
	-6.8	3.0	5.8	-7.5				-.4	2.5
Sales/Net Fixed Assets	113.8	113.7	113.2	31.2				89.7	103.8
	49.4	43.2	44.5	11.0				27.8	39.4
	19.2	15.0	9.6	6.5				5.8	6.3
Sales/Total Assets	16.9	7.0	6.6	4.2				6.9	7.1
	6.3	6.2	4.8	1.8				4.5	4.7
	4.9	4.5	3.0	1.3				2.4	2.2
% Depr., Dep., Amort./Sales	.3	.3	.3	1.1				.7	.6
	(13) 1.0	(18) 1.1	(27) .7	(19) 1.6				(69) 1.7	(65) 1.3
	3.9	2.3	2.7	5.4				4.8	3.5
% Officers', Directors' Owners' Comp/Sales	4.9			1.5				2.4	1.2
	(14) 7.2		(11) 2.6					(40) 3.8	(35) 3.5
	15.4		4.1					6.4	7.4
Net Sales ($)	55196M	174366M	657583M	1382159M	530671M	977848M		1773656M	2387107M
Total Assets ($)	5923M	26691M	138807M	545503M	272056M	597242M		417481M	678283M

M = $ thousand   MM = $ million
See Pages 9 through 22 for Explanation of Ratios and Data

Comparative Historical Data | Current Data Sorted by Sales

			Type of Statement						
9	12	16	Unqualified					3	13
12	15	17	Reviewed		1		4	5	7
11	14	11	Compiled		2	1	3	3	2
16	21	16	Tax Returns	7	4		2	3	
20	53	49	Other	3	6	7	7	12	14
4/1/08-3/31/09	**4/1/09-3/31/10**	**4/1/10-3/31/11**			7 (4/1-9/30/10)		102 (10/1/10-3/31/11)		
ALL	**ALL**	**ALL**		**0-1MM**	**1-3MM**	**3-5MM**	**5-10MM**	**10-25MM**	**25MM & OVER**
68	115	109	**NUMBER OF STATEMENTS**	10	13	8	16	26	36
%	%	%	**ASSETS**	%	%	%	%	%	%
8.7	12.9	11.9	Cash & Equivalents	12.5	11.7		14.2	13.4	9.8
33.3	34.3	35.7	Trade Receivables (net)	5.3	25.6		42.9	40.3	40.4
1.5	.7	1.3	Inventory	.0	.0		1.7	1.7	1.7
6.3	5.1	5.7	All Other Current	.7	2.4		5.8	7.5	3.6
49.9	53.0	54.6	Total Current	18.5	39.7		64.6	62.9	55.5
29.6	26.9	24.1	Fixed Assets (net)	47.7	22.7		22.8	22.9	20.3
9.9	11.0	13.1	Intangibles (net)	25.3	18.4		3.8	7.2	18.6
10.7	9.1	8.2	All Other Non-Current	8.4	19.2		8.8	7.0	5.6
100.0	100.0	100.0	Total	100.0	100.0		100.0	100.0	100.0
			LIABILITIES						
16.7	15.9	14.5	Notes Payable-Short Term	.9	21.4		16.0	17.6	12.7
5.0	5.3	5.9	Cur. Mat.-L.T.D.	1.1	13.0		6.0	6.7	4.9
9.8	11.5	12.3	Trade Payables	7.6	17.6		13.4	9.4	14.7
.1	.2	.3	Income Taxes Payable	.0	.9		.0	.3	.3
13.8	14.5	11.0	All Other Current	10.9	8.0		12.8	8.5	11.8
45.4	47.5	44.0	Total Current	20.5	61.0		48.2	42.5	44.3
18.2	21.2	23.1	Long-Term Debt	46.7	36.9		23.4	16.1	16.3
.4	.6	.5	Deferred Taxes	.0	.0		.2	.1	1.2
5.5	5.6	5.7	All Other Non-Current	7.9	2.1		2.4	4.7	8.8
30.6	25.1	26.6	Net Worth	24.9	.0		25.8	36.7	29.3
100.0	100.0	100.0	Total Liabilties & Net Worth	100.0	100.0		100.0	100.0	100.0
			INCOME DATA						
100.0	100.0	100.0	Net Sales	100.0	100.0		100.0	100.0	100.0
			Gross Profit						
95.2	94.7	95.6	Operating Expenses	82.9	97.4		97.3	96.7	96.5
4.8	5.3	4.4	Operating Profit	17.1	2.6		2.7	3.3	3.5
1.8	2.8	2.2	All Other Expenses (net)	13.1	.3		.6	.8	2.2
3.0	2.6	2.2	Profit Before Taxes	4.0	2.3		2.1	2.5	1.3
			RATIOS						
1.8	2.0	2.1		4.2	4.2		2.2	2.4	1.8
1.1	1.3	1.3	Current	1.8	.6		1.8	1.2	1.3
.8	.8	.8		.2	.3		1.0	1.0	.9
1.5	1.7	1.9		4.1	3.9		1.8	1.9	1.7
.9	1.0	1.2	Quick	1.8	.6		1.4	1.1	1.1
.6	.7	.6		.2	.3		.9	.8	.7
14 25.7	14 25.8	16 22.6		0 UND	0 UND		20 17.8	21 17.6	30 12.3
31 11.7	31 11.8	32 11.3	Sales/Receivables	0 UND	8 48.2		28 12.9	34 10.6	39 9.4
40 9.2	42 8.8	43 8.5		0 UND	41 8.8		42 8.7	43 8.4	48 7.7
			Cost of Sales/Inventory						
			Cost of Sales/Payables						
16.4	15.7	13.7		27.0	37.1		11.3	11.1	14.5
264.1	51.8	49.8	Sales/Working Capital	114.6	-259.4		18.6	46.4	26.7
-39.0	-47.8	-50.9		-10.2	-21.8		NM	-764.1	-293.4
10.0	11.4	14.3			11.5		15.2	22.6	11.8
(57) 3.7	(99) 4.5	(91) 4.3	EBIT/Interest	(11) 2.4		(14) 4.8	(24) 5.9	(30) 4.2	
1.5	1.4	.9			-1.0		2.6	2.0	-.5
3.9	7.1	4.2	Net Profit + Depr., Dep.,						4.5
(12) 2.5	(17) 2.8	(20) 1.1	Amort./Cur. Mat. L/T/D					(14) .9	
1.7	1.4	.0							-.2
.6	.3	.3		.6	.5		.4	.1	.4
1.4	1.2	1.1	Fixed/Worth	4.1	-2.8		1.4	.7	1.1
UND	16.2	-3.3		-.2	-.5		114.1	2.8	-1.8
.9	1.2	1.0		.1	4.3		.7	.7	1.1
3.1	3.3	3.3	Debt/Worth	6.3	-7.1		8.3	1.6	2.0
UND	-57.6	-6.7		-1.7	-2.6		256.4	6.9	-7.8
96.1	70.3	81.7	% Profit Before Taxes/Tangible				133.2	53.6	87.5
(52) 31.0	(84) 28.7	(78) 20.1	Net Worth			(13) 21.1	(21) 17.2	(26) 31.6	
3.0	5.3	9.0					12.4	11.1	8.8
19.3	17.4	18.2	% Profit Before Taxes/Total	27.9	26.0		13.1	19.4	13.9
7.4	9.1	7.1	Assets	5.3	5.3		8.8	7.1	7.5
.0	1.4	.3		-3.2	-7.2		6.9	2.0	-4.5
84.9	110.2	78.8		55.1	105.0		98.1	122.4	66.0
22.8	28.5	34.3	Sales/Net Fixed Assets	17.2	38.9		35.6	43.7	24.4
5.3	7.5	9.8		1.3	23.8		13.8	10.1	8.7
6.6	7.0	6.8		6.3	13.4		7.7	6.3	6.2
4.7	4.5	4.8	Sales/Total Assets	4.5	5.2		6.3	4.8	3.6
2.5	2.2	2.4		1.0	3.3		3.4	3.1	1.7
.6	.7	.5					.4	.2	.8
(48) 2.1	(78) 1.7	(82) 1.2	% Depr., Dep., Amort./Sales			(13) 1.4	(23) .8	(29) 1.4	
4.0	3.8	2.7					2.7	2.5	4.0
2.5	2.8	1.7							1.2
(23) 4.9	(44) 4.3	(40) 3.5	% Officers', Directors' Owners' Comp/Sales				(13) 1.8	
12.1	9.2	6.6						3.8	
2402521M	5504625M	3777823M	Net Sales ($)	4340M	28100M	34253M	114748M	393465M	3202917M
638763M	1354402M	1586222M	Total Assets ($)	3868M	5635M	9605M	22864M	128325M	1415925M

© RMA 2011

M = $ thousand   MM = $ million
See Pages 9 through 22 for Explanation of Ratios and Data

Current Data Sorted by Assets   Comparative Historical Data

						Type of Statement		
2	1	6	12	7	4	Unqualified	39	31
1	7	28	21		2	Reviewed	48	45
10	16	22	6	1		Compiled	67	67
15	49	23	3			Tax Returns	67	86
16	55	57	30	3	3	Other	108	117
	38 (4/1-9/30/10)		362 (10/1/10-3/31/11)				4/1/06-3/31/07	4/1/07-3/31/08
0-500M	500M-2MM	2-10MM	10-50MM	50-100MM	100-250MM		ALL	ALL
44	128	136	72	11	9	NUMBER OF STATEMENTS	329	346
%	%	%	%	%	%	ASSETS	%	%
24.5	10.3	11.0	10.3	15.0		Cash & Equivalents	8.7	12.1
28.2	19.9	17.1	17.7	15.7		Trade Receivables (net)	20.6	18.4
.7	1.6	1.1	2.5	.0		Inventory	3.0	2.6
3.0	1.9	3.9	3.9	1.7		All Other Current	3.3	3.6
56.3	33.7	33.1	34.5	32.5		Total Current	35.6	36.7
24.4	52.9	53.8	50.1	41.8		Fixed Assets (net)	49.6	49.5
3.3	4.8	4.2	5.9	20.7		Intangibles (net)	4.4	3.3
16.0	8.6	8.9	9.6	5.0		All Other Non-Current	10.5	10.4
100.0	100.0	100.0	100.0	100.0		Total	100.0	100.0
						LIABILITIES		
20.5	7.1	4.5	6.4	.7		Notes Payable-Short Term	8.0	7.6
3.9	3.4	4.7	4.1	3.9		Cur. Mat.-L.T.D.	3.9	4.4
11.7	8.3	6.5	7.4	9.3		Trade Payables	10.0	8.5
.1	.0	.1	.0	.0		Income Taxes Payable	.2	.2
43.6	12.3	8.3	9.6	7.2		All Other Current	9.2	10.1
79.7	31.1	24.1	27.4	21.2		Total Current	31.4	30.7
19.0	41.3	40.9	31.3	24.1		Long-Term Debt	33.0	35.4
.0	.0	.2	.5	.8		Deferred Taxes	.4	.3
12.5	4.7	5.0	7.2	15.0		All Other Non-Current	4.5	6.9
-11.2	22.9	29.7	33.6	39.0		Net Worth	30.7	26.7
100.0	100.0	100.0	100.0	100.0		Total Liabilities & Net Worth	100.0	100.0
						INCOME DATA		
100.0	100.0	100.0	100.0	100.0		Net Sales	100.0	100.0
						Gross Profit		
93.8	80.9	82.2	86.4	93.3		Operating Expenses	84.8	84.9
6.2	19.1	17.8	13.6	6.7		Operating Profit	15.2	15.1
1.1	10.0	9.1	6.6	4.1		All Other Expenses (net)	6.1	6.8
5.1	9.1	8.7	7.0	2.6		Profit Before Taxes	9.1	8.3
						RATIOS		
6.6	3.0	2.7	2.3	2.7			2.2	2.3
1.5	1.1	1.2	1.3	1.7		Current	1.2	1.3
.4	.4	.6	.9	1.1			.6	.7
6.0	2.7	2.3	1.9	2.6			2.0	2.1
1.2	1.1	1.0	1.1	1.5		Quick	.9	1.1
.4	.4	.4	.6	1.1			.4	.5
0 UND	0 UND	3 118.9	13 27.9	15 23.7			9 41.5	0 940.0
15 24.4	24 15.0	30 12.1	37 9.8	37 9.8		Sales/Receivables	31 11.9	29 12.4
42 8.7	42 8.6	47 7.8	50 7.3	47 7.8			49 7.4	51 7.1
						Cost of Sales/Inventory		
						Cost of Sales/Payables		
9.3	8.8	6.2	5.7	3.8			7.9	7.3
71.2	74.8	33.9	28.4	12.4		Sales/Working Capital	38.8	25.3
-9.0	-10.3	-10.0	-74.0	76.5			-13.4	-15.7
11.6	13.7	11.0	10.1	36.8			10.8	8.9
(22) 4.5	(82) 3.8	(101) 3.4	(61) 3.7	(10) 2.9		EBIT/Interest	(252) 3.5	(268) 2.7
.6	.5	1.5	2.0	-.5			1.5	1.2
			11.1	4.0			4.9	5.0
		(22) 4.2	(28) 2.0			Net Profit + Depr., Dep., Amort./Cur. Mat. L/T/D	(64) 2.0	(52) 2.0
		2.0	1.3				.9	.8
.0	.6	.6	.7	.7			.5	.6
.6	2.3	2.1	1.4	3.7		Fixed/Worth	1.6	1.8
6.2	-45.5	25.1	6.1	-.9			4.7	6.1
.3	.8	.8	.9	.4			.9	1.1
3.8	2.9	2.1	2.2	3.9		Debt/Worth	2.3	2.6
-4.7	-48.7	26.6	7.6	-2.1			7.3	10.8
67.8	68.3	43.8	37.2			% Profit Before Taxes/Tangible Net Worth	47.6	48.4
(29) 23.6	(92) 27.3	(109) 15.2	(58) 16.3				(279) 19.0	(288) 20.1
-6.4	6.8	2.6	8.4				5.3	4.6
23.5	17.7	12.8	12.2	11.1		% Profit Before Taxes/Total Assets	14.1	13.8
8.3	5.8	4.9	4.9	9.1			6.2	4.8
-5.1	-.9	.6	1.6	-7.0			.9	.1
204.7	22.7	11.2	15.0	23.6		Sales/Net Fixed Assets	14.5	14.1
34.9	3.1	1.5	3.1	2.0			3.8	4.1
6.7	.3	.3	.5	.9			.6	.6
8.4	3.1	2.4	2.4	2.3		Sales/Total Assets	3.0	3.0
4.0	1.3	.8	1.1	1.0			1.4	1.4
2.1	.3	.3	.4	.4			.4	.5
.7	2.1	2.5	2.1	1.9		% Depr., Dep., Amort./Sales	2.0	2.0
(19) 1.9	(99) 5.8	(113) 5.1	(69) 5.7	(10) 7.0			(284) 4.3	(299) 4.2
4.1	13.0	14.1	12.1	14.2			9.8	10.5
3.5	3.4	1.5	1.7			% Officers', Directors' Owners' Comp/Sales	2.2	2.3
(14) 6.4	(38) 6.0	(34) 3.5	(13) 4.8				(70) 4.8	(92) 5.2
12.5	11.3	5.3	7.6				12.4	10.0
71951M	298933M	894495M	2443594M	1102250M	2977744M	Net Sales ($)	6522171M	8755211M
11328M	149480M	620738M	1543029M	793772M	1366921M	Total Assets ($)	3955567M	4760011M

M = $ thousand   MM = $ million
See Pages 9 through 22 for Explanation of Ratios and Data

Comparative Historical Data   ## Current Data Sorted by Sales

			Type of Statement						
32	33	32	Unqualified		3	1	6	5	17
62	59	59	Reviewed	2	13	6	12	15	11
56	47	55	Compiled	18	19	3	7	6	2
90	111	90	Tax Returns	41	23	13	8	4	1
133	132	164	Other	43	39	20	14	20	28
4/1/08-3/31/09 ALL	4/1/09-3/31/10 ALL	4/1/10-3/31/11 ALL		38 (4/1-9/30/10)	362 (10/1/10-3/31/11)				
				0-1MM	1-3MM	3-5MM	5-10MM	10-25MM	25MM & OVER
373	382	400	NUMBER OF STATEMENTS	104	97	43	47	50	59
%	%	%	ASSETS	%	%	%	%	%	%
10.1	10.8	12.2	Cash & Equivalents	7.5	12.8	18.6	14.1	14.7	11.1
16.8	18.1	19.5	Trade Receivables (net)	5.4	17.1	24.2	26.4	31.8	29.2
3.4	2.5	1.9	Inventory	.2	1.4	2.2	.6	1.9	6.4
3.9	3.5	3.1	All Other Current	1.9	4.2	1.5	2.8	4.2	3.6
34.2	34.9	36.7	Total Current	15.0	35.4	46.5	43.9	52.6	50.3
52.6	51.5	48.9	Fixed Assets (net)	74.7	48.1	42.6	36.1	36.6	30.1
4.6	4.4	5.0	Intangibles (net)	2.4	5.5	3.2	6.9	2.4	10.5
8.5	9.1	9.5	All Other Non-Current	7.9	11.0	7.8	13.1	8.3	9.0
100.0	100.0	100.0	Total	100.0	100.0	100.0	100.0	100.0	100.0
			LIABILITIES						
6.3	8.4	7.6	Notes Payable-Short Term	9.4	8.8	3.3	3.8	7.0	9.2
4.2	5.7	4.0	Cur. Mat.-L.T.D.	3.9	4.6	3.4	2.3	5.9	3.6
6.7	7.4	8.0	Trade Payables	1.8	7.7	9.2	12.0	10.5	13.3
.1	.2	.1	Income Taxes Payable	.0	.0	.1	.1	.0	.2
9.5	9.1	13.7	All Other Current	13.5	17.6	13.7	10.8	11.7	12.1
26.9	30.8	33.5	Total Current	28.7	38.6	29.7	29.0	35.1	38.3
43.5	38.4	35.9	Long-Term Debt	53.3	41.8	32.5	27.5	21.5	16.8
.2	.2	.2	Deferred Taxes	.1	.1	.0	.5	.6	.3
6.7	6.8	6.4	All Other Non-Current	5.7	4.2	5.4	10.9	5.6	9.1
22.7	23.9	24.0	Net Worth	12.1	15.3	32.3	32.1	37.2	35.6
100.0	100.0	100.0	Total Liabilities & Net Worth	100.0	100.0	100.0	100.0	100.0	100.0
			INCOME DATA						
100.0	100.0	100.0	Net Sales	100.0	100.0	100.0	100.0	100.0	100.0
			Gross Profit						
83.1	85.1	84.4	Operating Expenses	67.8	86.0	86.6	93.6	91.9	95.7
16.9	14.9	15.6	Operating Profit	32.2	14.0	13.4	6.4	8.1	4.3
8.0	7.7	7.7	All Other Expenses (net)	19.5	6.7	5.0	1.5	1.3	1.2
8.9	7.3	7.9	Profit Before Taxes	12.7	7.3	8.4	4.9	6.8	3.1
			RATIOS						
2.4	2.4	2.7		2.6	2.7	3.9	2.8	3.0	2.2
1.3	1.2	1.2	Current	.7	1.1	1.6	1.7	1.4	1.3
.6	.6	.6		.2	.4	1.0	1.0	.9	1.0
1.8	2.0	2.5		1.9	2.2	3.7	2.5	2.7	2.1
.9	1.0	1.1	Quick	.5	.8	1.4	1.5	1.3	1.1
.4	.5	.4		.1	.3	.9	.9	.7	.8
0 UND	0 UND	3 118.9		0 UND	7 53.0	12 30.2	14 26.0	33 11.1	34 10.6
27 13.7	28 13.0	30 12.2	Sales/Receivables	0 UND	30 12.1	39 9.5	29 12.5	43 8.5	44 8.3
42 8.7	45 8.1	46 7.9		15 23.8	44 8.3	49 7.4	44 8.4	51 7.2	55 6.7
			Cost of Sales/Inventory						
			Cost of Sales/Payables						
8.4	7.5	6.8		10.0	6.7	5.5	7.2	5.8	6.5
33.1	41.4	36.4	Sales/Working Capital	-17.3	82.5	14.4	17.7	22.7	23.7
-13.3	-12.9	-12.7		-3.5	-5.9	320.3	-815.1	-80.9	999.8
	9.4		8.3		10.9		4.9		9.5	36.5	14.9	14.9	10.4
(266) 3.2	(285) 2.9	(285) 3.5	EBIT/Interest	(40) 3.1	(71) 2.3	(35) 3.9	(34) 4.6	(47) 5.9	(58) 3.8
1.2	1.0	1.4		.9	.5	2.0	1.5	3.1	1.7
4.7	3.5	7.8	Net Profit + Depr., Dep.,			13.0	4.6	9.0	
(59) 2.4	(67) 2.0	(62) 3.3	Amort./Cur. Mat. L/T/D			(10) 5.8	(16) 2.8	(25) 4.3	
1.0	1.2	1.6				1.7	1.9	1.9	
.7	.7	.6		1.6	.5	.4	.3	.4	.6
2.2	2.1	1.7	Fixed/Worth	3.9	1.7	1.3	1.0	1.1	1.0
28.2	23.1	34.2		-23.2	-18.0	27.4	9.4	3.4	2.6
1.0	1.0	.8		1.1	.8	.3	.7	.7	.9
3.2	2.9	2.5	Debt/Worth	3.6	2.2	2.5	1.9	1.6	2.1
43.4	278.2	115.5		-20.6	-18.5	70.2	27.3	5.8	9.5
49.4	42.5	51.3	% Profit Before Taxes/Tangible	35.3	53.3	61.2	52.1	55.2	44.1
(286) 17.3	(288) 16.3	(303) 17.5	Net Worth	(73) 13.1	(67) 14.1	(33) 32.3	(37) 20.8	(45) 27.1	(48) 16.8
4.1	5.3	5.8		-.5	-.4	12.0	6.9	14.9	6.8
12.7	11.2	13.9	% Profit Before Taxes/Total	10.7	13.7	21.3	16.3	15.9	13.2
4.6	4.7	5.4	Assets	2.8	4.7	9.2	5.4	9.3	6.1
.4	-.1	.5		-.9	-1.6	1.4	.9	5.6	1.6
16.6	15.1	21.7		1.0	25.1	16.5	55.8	24.8	24.1
2.7	2.7	3.7	Sales/Net Fixed Assets	.3	3.7	5.6	14.6	9.5	10.5
.5	.5	.5		.2	.7	.8	1.4	2.4	3.9
3.3	2.8	3.1		.6	2.9	3.1	4.9	4.2	3.5
1.2	1.1	1.3	Sales/Total Assets	.2	1.3	1.8	2.4	2.4	2.1
.3	.3	.4		.1	.5	.5	.8	1.1	1.3
1.9	2.0	2.1		7.8	3.1	1.6	.9	1.6	1.1
(328) 5.8	(319) 5.1	(317) 5.1	% Depr., Dep., Amort./Sales	(80) 14.0	(69) 6.1	(34) 3.9	(39) 2.9	(42) 3.4	(53) 2.1
14.1	12.2	12.7		21.5	14.7	8.9	5.1	6.6	4.1
2.0	2.6	2.0	% Officers', Directors'	4.6	3.6	3.4	1.6	.9	
(91) 4.3	(99) 5.0	(101) 4.7	Owners' Comp/Sales	(12) 6.9	(29) 5.9	(18) 5.0	(18) 3.4	(15) 2.0	
7.6	9.6	9.7		14.2	11.4	11.1	8.9	4.8	
9295829M	7699245M	7788967M	Net Sales ($)	46463M	182756M	170943M	333032M	733035M	6322738M
4980000M	4929404M	4485268M	Total Assets ($)	182960M	290984M	223631M	278739M	509109M	2999845M

M = $ thousand   MM = $ million
See Pages 9 through 22 for Explanation of Ratios and Data

Current Data Sorted by Assets | Comparative Historical Data

	0-500M	500M-2MM	2-10MM	10-50MM	50-100MM	100-250MM	Type of Statement	4/1/06-3/31/07 ALL	4/1/07-3/31/08 ALL
		1	7	11	4	3	Unqualified	21	25
		3	5	7	1		Reviewed	13	15
	2	4	13	5		1	Compiled	25	17
	3	8	9	1			Tax Returns	4	9
	3	10	19	17	7	2	Other	41	43
		21 (4/1-9/30/10)		125 (10/1/10-3/31/11)					
NUMBER OF STATEMENTS	8	26	53	41	12	6		104	109
	%	%	%	%	%	%	ASSETS	%	%
		8.6	7.7	9.1	8.3		Cash & Equivalents	10.6	7.8
		20.0	13.1	9.8	6.1		Trade Receivables (net)	18.1	15.1
		.7	5.5	7.2	1.9		Inventory	2.8	5.4
		2.2	2.0	2.5	.6		All Other Current	2.7	2.9
		31.5	28.3	28.6	16.9		Total Current	34.3	31.2
		56.7	63.1	67.4	71.4		Fixed Assets (net)	57.2	57.6
		1.5	2.3	1.9	.3		Intangibles (net)	2.5	3.7
		10.3	6.3	2.2	11.4		All Other Non-Current	6.0	7.4
		100.0	100.0	100.0	100.0		Total	100.0	100.0
							LIABILITIES		
		6.0	5.4	6.9	.2		Notes Payable-Short Term	5.8	13.6
		5.3	3.6	3.1	3.5		Cur. Mat.-L.T.D.	4.7	7.0
		9.3	4.7	3.5	3.0		Trade Payables	6.5	5.5
		.0	.2	.8	.0		Income Taxes Payable	.2	.1
		9.6	6.8	5.5	4.3		All Other Current	14.1	7.6
		30.1	20.7	19.8	11.0		Total Current	31.2	33.8
		37.1	45.5	40.4	31.6		Long-Term Debt	32.3	32.4
		1.6	.1	1.3	.1		Deferred Taxes	.7	.7
		23.5	5.7	5.9	9.1		All Other Non-Current	4.4	6.8
		7.6	27.9	32.6	48.2		Net Worth	31.4	26.3
		100.0	100.0	100.0	100.0		Total Liabilities & Net Worth	100.0	100.0
							INCOME DATA		
		100.0	100.0	100.0	100.0		Net Sales	100.0	100.0
							Gross Profit		
		85.3	81.4	86.1	69.7		Operating Expenses	87.0	86.7
		14.7	18.6	13.9	30.3		Operating Profit	13.0	13.3
		7.6	7.7	5.2	8.3		All Other Expenses (net)	5.7	6.0
		7.1	10.9	8.7	22.0		Profit Before Taxes	7.3	7.3
							RATIOS		
		2.9	2.7	2.4	3.5			2.2	2.2
		1.2	1.4	1.5	1.1		Current	1.4	1.2
		.5	.5	.8	.4			.9	.7
		2.6	2.3	2.0	1.6			2.0	1.9
		1.1	1.1	1.1	1.0		Quick	1.1	.9
		.5	.5	.5	.3			.6	.5
	0 UND	0 UND	22 16.3	29 12.7				23 15.6	22 16.3
	30 12.2	28 13.2	37 10.0	38 9.5			Sales/Receivables	38 9.5	36 10.0
	44 8.4	43 8.5	47 7.8	51 7.2				52 7.1	48 7.6
							Cost of Sales/Inventory		
							Cost of Sales/Payables		
		10.9	5.6	4.4	3.1			7.3	9.0
		98.8	26.3	11.4	61.2		Sales/Working Capital	20.0	28.0
		-12.4	-32.1	-25.6	-7.4			-35.4	-16.2
		12.4	15.7	6.3	6.0			8.2	4.8
	(18)	2.6 (43)	4.5 (33)	2.6 (10)	4.6		EBIT/Interest	(88) 2.4	(91) 2.5
		1.2	1.6	1.2	2.6			1.1	1.2
				3.6				4.2	7.8
			(15)	2.2			Net Profit + Depr., Dep., Amort./Cur. Mat. L/T/D	(20) 1.6	(32) 3.4
				1.9				1.0	1.5
		1.0	.9	1.1	1.2			.8	.9
		3.6	2.7	2.4	1.8		Fixed/Worth	1.7	2.1
		-8.8	23.9	5.4	2.2			4.0	7.0
		2.3	.7	.8	.8			1.0	1.0
		4.9	4.1	2.6	1.1		Debt/Worth	1.8	2.2
		-11.4	30.1	9.7	1.7			5.7	11.5
		100.4	54.3	26.4	23.3			30.8	39.4
	(17)	40.4 (45)	26.5 (36)	14.2	18.6		% Profit Before Taxes/Tangible Net Worth	(96) 15.2	(93) 17.5
		17.4	12.4	3.1	11.2			4.9	6.2
		18.1	15.3	10.8	11.5			11.8	11.5
		5.2	7.9	4.3	7.6		% Profit Before Taxes/Total Assets	5.0	5.2
		.8	.9	.4	3.8			.5	.9
		17.9	6.0	1.7	.9			7.1	6.7
		3.4	1.6	.7	.6		Sales/Net Fixed Assets	1.3	1.5
		.9	.4	.6	.3			.6	.7
		3.9	2.1	1.0	.7			2.6	2.6
		2.0	.9	.5	.4		Sales/Total Assets	.8	1.0
		.6	.3	.3	.2			.4	.5
		3.2	3.2	5.0	8.7			3.0	3.0
	(19)	4.9 (52)	5.5 (40)	9.2	10.8		% Depr., Dep., Amort./Sales	(90) 8.3	(99) 7.5
		7.0	15.3	13.6	17.0			11.8	10.7
								2.4	1.8
							% Officers', Directors' Owners' Comp/Sales	(30) 5.4	(32) 4.9
								9.3	8.2
	5924M	69249M	351225M	774155M	358448M	792708M	Net Sales ($)	3626877M	4079182M
	1577M	29182M	264982M	933492M	818721M	891280M	Total Assets ($)	2693867M	3254726M

M = $ thousand   MM = $ million
See Pages 9 through 22 for Explanation of Ratios and Data

Comparative Historical Data			Type of Statement	Current Data Sorted by Sales					
18	29	26	Unqualified		1	7	4	6	8
11	10	16	Reviewed		2	5	7	1	1
20	19	25	Compiled	2	3	5	8	4	3
18	11	21	Tax Returns	13	3	1	1	3	
49	45	58	Other	9	10	4	11	12	12
4/1/08-3/31/09 ALL	4/1/09-3/31/10 ALL	4/1/10-3/31/11 ALL		21 (4/1-9/30/10)			125 (10/1/10-3/31/11)		
				0-1MM	1-3MM	3-5MM	5-10MM	10-25MM	25MM & OVER
116	114	146	**NUMBER OF STATEMENTS**	24	19	22	31	26	24
%	%	%	**ASSETS**	%	%	%	%	%	%
9.0	10.2	9.4	Cash & Equivalents	6.2	14.5	9.3	6.7	8.2	13.6
13.2	12.2	13.4	Trade Receivables (net)	8.3	9.1	16.1	12.7	19.8	13.5
4.7	4.3	4.8	Inventory	5.3	.8	5.2	5.3	6.0	4.9
3.4	2.2	2.4	All Other Current	3.2	1.7	1.5	3.4	1.1	2.7
30.3	28.8	29.9	Total Current	23.0	26.2	32.1	28.1	35.1	34.6
57.4	60.6	61.5	Fixed Assets (net)	63.4	70.8	56.5	66.8	56.2	56.1
4.4	4.3	2.4	Intangibles (net)	1.8	.6	.4	.9	4.5	6.2
7.9	6.3	6.1	All Other Non-Current	11.8	2.5	10.9	4.2	4.2	3.2
100.0	100.0	100.0	Total	100.0	100.0	100.0	100.0	100.0	100.0
			LIABILITIES						
10.6	6.6	5.1	Notes Payable-Short Term	5.4	6.1	6.3	5.7	5.0	2.6
4.5	5.8	3.5	Cur. Mat.-L.T.D.	2.3	6.3	3.4	2.9	4.5	2.3
5.8	4.6	5.0	Trade Payables	2.1	1.5	9.4	3.9	8.0	5.0
.1	.2	.3	Income Taxes Payable	.0	.0	.2	.0	.2	1.4
6.3	12.1	8.7	All Other Current	5.3	22.0	8.0	5.3	9.3	6.2
27.3	29.4	22.7	Total Current	15.0	35.9	27.4	17.8	26.9	17.5
32.4	36.9	39.1	Long-Term Debt	56.1	38.2	34.8	41.4	34.2	29.2
1.1	.8	.9	Deferred Taxes	1.8	.0	.3	.2	1.0	1.9
6.6	7.2	9.1	All Other Non-Current	8.2	14.2	13.4	7.3	5.4	8.0
32.6	25.8	28.2	Net Worth	18.9	11.6	24.1	33.3	32.5	43.4
100.0	100.0	100.0	Total Liabilities & Net Worth	100.0	100.0	100.0	100.0	100.0	100.0
			INCOME DATA						
100.0	100.0	100.0	Net Sales	100.0	100.0	100.0	100.0	100.0	100.0
			Gross Profit						
88.0	86.4	83.4	Operating Expenses	65.5	81.5	83.4	86.9	92.2	88.9
12.0	13.6	16.6	Operating Profit	34.5	18.5	16.6	13.1	7.8	11.1
4.2	5.3	6.5	All Other Expenses (net)	17.9	9.4	4.2	3.6	3.6	2.1
7.9	8.3	10.0	Profit Before Taxes	16.6	9.2	12.4	9.5	4.2	9.0
			RATIOS						
2.4	2.5	2.7	Current	3.0	3.6	2.5	2.5	2.3	3.7
1.2	1.1	1.4		.9	1.0	1.4	1.6	1.3	1.5
.7	.5	.7		.3	.3	.8	.9	.5	1.1
2.0	2.1	2.3	Quick	3.0	3.6	1.9	2.3	1.7	2.1
.9	.9	1.1		.6	.8	1.2	1.0	.8	1.4
.5	.4	.5		.1	.2	.6	.5	.5	1.0
17 21.7	17 21.8	14 25.8	Sales/Receivables	0 UND	0 UND	0 UND	27 13.5	27 13.4	32 11.5
32 11.3	29 12.5	32 11.5		0 UND	20 18.1	39 9.4	37 9.8	33 11.1	40 9.1
43 8.5	41 9.0	46 8.0		30 12.0	25 14.7	50 7.3	48 7.7	43 8.6	50 7.3
			Cost of Sales/Inventory						
			Cost of Sales/Payables						
8.0	9.1	6.2	Sales/Working Capital	4.9	5.6	7.8	5.6	7.5	4.8
34.2	40.7	26.5		NM	502.0	21.0	13.5	26.0	14.2
-16.6	-9.6	-18.4		-5.0	-5.8	-29.2	-92.8	-11.6	63.3
7.0	7.1	11.0	EBIT/Interest	13.1	4.4	12.1	12.4	11.4	7.2
(98) 2.9	(96) 2.9	(114) 3.0		(10) 2.7	(12) 1.4	(19) 2.8	(28) 3.2	(24) 3.1	(21) 4.6
1.2	1.2	1.5		2.0	1.1	1.5	1.2	1.7	2.1
5.7	6.3	5.5	Net Profit + Depr., Dep., Amort./Cur. Mat. L/T/D					4.3	12.7
(26) 1.9	(32) 2.1	(30) 2.8						(12) 2.7	(12) 4.2
1.0	1.4	2.0						1.9	2.0
.9	1.0	.9	Fixed/Worth	.8	1.0	1.0	1.2	.8	.7
2.1	2.3	2.3		7.2	3.3	2.2	1.9	2.2	1.9
4.6	8.1	17.4		64.6	-98.6	10.6	5.0	6.2	3.1
.8	.9	.8	Debt/Worth	1.4	.6	1.0	.9	1.0	.8
1.8	2.2	2.9		12.1	31.0	3.1	1.8	2.5	1.7
7.2	11.0	22.9		118.8	-7.9	12.7	4.8	6.3	4.8
37.4	37.8	39.7	% Profit Before Taxes/Tangible Net Worth	119.1	90.1	44.0	31.4	30.0	25.7
(103) 19.7	(98) 16.7	(121) 20.0		(19) 40.0	(12) 31.2	(18) 27.9	(28) 17.8	(22) 17.1	(22) 16.9
5.7	6.2	9.7		4.9	4.0	12.3	7.1	2.7	10.3
14.6	12.6	12.2	% Profit Before Taxes/Total Assets	8.6	18.1	17.3	13.4	10.9	13.1
6.2	5.9	6.1		4.2	1.3	5.9	7.1	6.8	7.3
1.1	.6	.9		.9	-1.6	2.5	.7	.9	1.9
5.0	6.0	5.9	Sales/Net Fixed Assets	2.3	2.6	6.8	3.4	13.5	5.7
1.6	1.3	1.2		.4	1.2	1.1	1.4	3.0	1.3
.7	.6	.6		.2	.4	.6	.6	.6	.8
2.0	2.4	2.0	Sales/Total Assets	.6	2.0	3.0	1.7	3.3	1.5
1.0	.8	.8		.3	1.1	.8	.8	1.4	.9
.5	.5	.4		.2	.3	.4	.5	.5	.6
3.4	3.4	3.5	% Depr., Dep., Amort./Sales	9.0	7.0	3.6	3.5	2.9	3.1
(99) 7.4	(101) 7.9	(132) 7.6		(18) 22.2	(16) 12.2	(21) 6.7	(30) 6.7	(25) 5.1	(22) 6.6
10.5	11.0	13.6		30.8	22.4	10.2	13.3	10.1	9.4
1.5	2.2	1.4	% Officers', Directors' Owners' Comp/Sales						
(33) 4.8	(20) 4.8	(27) 3.2							
11.0	7.0	9.3							
3142074M	2512483M	2351709M	Net Sales ($)	12713M	36361M	88440M	224485M	414277M	1575433M
2686390M	3024988M	2939234M	Total Assets ($)	55685M	74760M	196447M	363975M	497273M	1751094M

M = $ thousand   MM = $ million
See Pages 9 through 22 for Explanation of Ratios and Data

Current Data Sorted by Assets

Comparative Historical Data

						Type of Statement		
1	2	12	11	2	2	Unqualified	32	35
	4	12	11	1		Reviewed	33	35
		5	1			Compiled	12	14
	6	5				Tax Returns	8	5
2	2	6	9			Other	14	18
	54 (4/1-9/30/10)		40 (10/1/10-3/31/11)				4/1/06-3/31/07	4/1/07-3/31/08
0-500M	500M-2MM	2-10MM	10-50MM	50-100MM	100-250MM		ALL	ALL
3	14	40	32	3	2	NUMBER OF STATEMENTS	99	107
%	%	%	%	%	%	ASSETS	%	%
	10.0	8.9	8.2			Cash & Equivalents	9.4	9.0
	21.8	12.8	13.6			Trade Receivables (net)	17.8	16.1
	15.9	27.4	23.7			Inventory	22.6	27.2
	5.6	5.8	9.3			All Other Current	5.8	7.3
	53.3	54.9	54.9			Total Current	55.7	59.5
	37.6	37.0	34.5			Fixed Assets (net)	37.8	34.0
	.0	1.1	.2			Intangibles (net)	.4	.6
	9.0	7.0	10.4			All Other Non-Current	6.1	5.8
	100.0	100.0	100.0			Total	100.0	100.0
						LIABILITIES		
	11.8	13.4	10.0			Notes Payable-Short Term	24.5	21.5
	2.8	2.9	4.9			Cur. Mat.-L.T.D.	3.4	3.7
	11.3	11.7	14.0			Trade Payables	9.5	10.9
	.1	.1	.2			Income Taxes Payable	.2	.4
	10.8	10.8	9.7			All Other Current	10.9	10.6
	36.8	38.9	38.8			Total Current	48.4	47.1
	24.1	12.6	20.1			Long-Term Debt	15.4	15.4
	1.0	1.7	.7			Deferred Taxes	1.1	.8
	6.8	1.1	3.6			All Other Non-Current	2.0	1.8
	31.3	45.7	36.8			Net Worth	33.1	35.0
	100.0	100.0	100.0			Total Liabilties & Net Worth	100.0	100.0
						INCOME DATA		
	100.0	100.0	100.0			Net Sales	100.0	100.0
						Gross Profit		
	96.7	94.1	95.9			Operating Expenses	91.0	90.7
	3.3	5.9	4.1			Operating Profit	9.0	9.3
	.9	.6	.7			All Other Expenses (net)	1.6	2.5
	2.4	5.3	3.4			Profit Before Taxes	7.4	6.8
						RATIOS		
	2.0	2.1	2.6				1.9	1.7
	1.7	1.4	1.4			Current	1.2	1.2
	.8	1.1	1.2				1.1	1.0
	1.8	1.4	1.2				1.1	1.1
	.8	.6	.5			Quick	.5	.5
	.3	.3	.3				.2	.2
10	35.7	8	46.9	8	47.8		9	39.7	6	58.4
28	12.9	14	25.3	21	17.7	Sales/Receivables	23	16.1	18	19.8
43	8.4	34	10.7	54	6.8		45	8.0	41	8.9
						Cost of Sales/Inventory		
						Cost of Sales/Payables		
	7.5	7.8	7.2				8.5	8.7
	14.0	17.0	21.0			Sales/Working Capital	20.6	26.4
	-82.8	50.3	29.8				116.1	252.7
	14.4	10.3	8.4				8.8	6.1
(12)	2.2	(39)	4.6	4.4		EBIT/Interest	(92)	2.9	(102)	2.3
	1.1	1.8	1.8				1.7	1.4
		8.0	10.6				12.0	6.2
		(14)	2.5	(15)	3.9	Net Profit + Depr., Dep., Amort./Cur. Mat. L/T/D	(36)	3.4	(31)	3.6
		1.6	1.4				1.7	1.2
	.4	.5	.5				.5	.5
	.8	.9	.8			Fixed/Worth	1.0	1.0
	3.6	1.1	1.7				1.8	1.7
	.4	.6	1.0				.7	.9
	1.4	1.2	1.6			Debt/Worth	2.0	2.3
	13.3	2.3	4.4				4.5	4.9
	24.1	21.7	24.3			% Profit Before Taxes/Tangible Net Worth	35.1	34.5
(12)	12.2	(38)	13.7	(31)	17.2		(92)	16.9	(102)	17.1
	6.0	5.8	8.6				7.6	7.5
	12.9	10.6	8.7			% Profit Before Taxes/Total Assets	11.1	9.4
	4.9	4.3	4.6				5.0	5.1
	.5	1.0	1.9				2.2	1.7
	28.7	21.9	17.2				15.5	20.8
	14.9	11.0	10.6			Sales/Net Fixed Assets	7.6	8.2
	3.0	1.6	3.4				3.0	2.7
	5.5	3.5	3.3				3.7	3.2
	2.6	1.9	2.3			Sales/Total Assets	2.1	2.1
	1.5	.9	.8				1.0	1.1
	.9	.6	.6				.8	.8
(13)	1.2	(38)	1.2	1.3		% Depr., Dep., Amort./Sales	(94)	1.8	(96)	1.6
	4.4	4.6	2.9				3.4	2.8
						% Officers', Directors' Owners' Comp/Sales	.9	.8
							(19)	2.0	(23)	2.1
							4.9	3.1
12555M	62836M	489671M	1951678M	755380M	226357M	Net Sales ($)	3271539M	3484657M
715M	16321M	197053M	695330M	209851M	261108M	Total Assets ($)	1197133M	1809747M

M = $ thousand   MM = $ million
See Pages 9 through 22 for Explanation of Ratios and Data

Comparative Historical Data

Current Data Sorted by Sales

			Type of Statement						
32	25	30	Unqualified	1	3	2	4	6	14
37	38	28	Reviewed	1	2	2	6	8	9
4	6	6	Compiled		1	2	2	1	
6	9	11	Tax Returns	1	2		5	2	1
15	15	19	Other	1	5			6	7
4/1/08-3/31/09 ALL	4/1/09-3/31/10 ALL	4/1/10-3/31/11 ALL		0-1MM	54 (4/1-9/30/10) 1-3MM	3-5MM	40 (10/1/10-3/31/11) 5-10MM	10-25MM	25MM & OVER
94	93	94	**NUMBER OF STATEMENTS**	4	13	6	17	23	31
%	%	%	**ASSETS**	%	%	%	%	%	%
10.7	10.2	9.1	Cash & Equivalents		7.0		8.7	11.4	8.5
16.3	13.5	16.0	Trade Receivables (net)		18.3		15.9	16.0	16.8
23.3	23.4	24.4	Inventory		4.9		24.2	29.3	31.0
10.4	6.1	7.2	All Other Current		11.2		5.3	4.9	9.4
60.8	53.3	56.7	Total Current		41.4		54.1	61.5	65.8
32.9	37.2	34.4	Fixed Assets (net)		51.5		34.0	30.1	25.7
.8	.7	.6	Intangibles (net)		.0		2.1	.4	.2
5.5	8.8	8.4	All Other Non-Current		7.1		9.8	8.0	8.3
100.0	100.0	100.0	Total		100.0		100.0	100.0	100.0
			LIABILITIES						
18.3	12.1	12.8	Notes Payable-Short Term		5.7		12.7	12.6	16.3
3.7	3.1	3.3	Cur. Mat.-L.T.D.		3.6		4.2	5.2	1.8
10.3	11.1	14.2	Trade Payables		18.3		11.1	14.5	16.6
.4	.4	.1	Income Taxes Payable		.1		.3	.1	.2
11.5	10.1	11.1	All Other Current		8.6		12.9	11.5	12.3
44.2	36.8	41.6	Total Current		36.4		41.1	44.0	47.2
13.1	15.4	16.8	Long-Term Debt		30.2		18.5	11.0	12.7
.7	1.1	1.2	Deferred Taxes		1.0		.6	1.6	1.2
1.5	1.8	3.6	All Other Non-Current		7.0		8.8	1.5	1.9
40.6	44.9	36.8	Net Worth		25.5		31.0	41.9	37.0
100.0	100.0	100.0	Total Liabilties & Net Worth		100.0		100.0	100.0	100.0
			INCOME DATA						
100.0	100.0	100.0	Net Sales		100.0		100.0	100.0	100.0
			Gross Profit						
89.5	90.6	94.8	Operating Expenses		86.9		96.7	95.3	97.3
10.5	9.4	5.2	Operating Profit		13.1		3.3	4.7	2.7
1.5	1.2	.7	All Other Expenses (net)		1.9		1.2	-.2	.0
9.0	8.3	4.5	Profit Before Taxes		11.2		2.1	4.8	2.8
			RATIOS						
2.1	2.3	2.1			3.6		2.1	2.2	1.8
1.3	1.4	1.5	Current		1.7		1.4	1.5	1.3
1.0	1.0	1.1			.9		.9	1.1	1.1
1.1	1.1	1.3			2.5		1.4	1.3	.8
.5	.6	.7	Quick		1.1		.7	.8	.5
.2	.3	.3			.3		.1	.3	.2
5 78.0	4 85.4	9 42.1		12 30.0		1 538.1	9 40.3		7 55.5
14 26.5	17 22.0	20 18.3	Sales/Receivables	29 12.6		14 25.7	15 23.7		16 23.2
38 9.6	33 11.0	42 8.8		48 7.6		64 5.7	60 6.1		26 14.0
			Cost of Sales/Inventory						
			Cost of Sales/Payables						
6.0	8.0	7.8			6.1		6.8	7.6	13.5
20.2	18.7	17.4	Sales/Working Capital		9.8		17.5	15.0	21.2
54.2	151.9	42.4			NM		-80.0	41.6	31.0
13.5	11.4	10.9		17.5		7.5	9.9		12.1
(90) 3.4	(87) 5.0	(89) 4.0	EBIT/Interest	(12) 4.2		(14) 1.7	(22) 6.4		5.3
2.0	2.5	1.8		-1.0		1.2	2.5		2.4
9.7	24.4	7.5	Net Profit + Depr., Dep., Amort./Cur. Mat. L/T/D						8.3
(31) 4.7	(29) 6.0	(32) 3.5						(14)	4.2
2.2	3.1	1.4							1.6
.4	.4	.4			.9		.5	.4	.4
.7	.8	.8	Fixed/Worth		1.1		.8	.6	.7
1.2	1.3	1.3			10.1		4.1	1.4	1.0
.7	.6	.7			.3		.9	.7	1.0
1.9	1.4	1.5	Debt/Worth		.7		2.4	1.4	1.6
4.3	3.1	4.1			25.1		8.4	2.4	4.7
40.4	34.7	24.3	% Profit Before Taxes/Tangible Net Worth	33.9		29.7	18.5		29.4
(91) 22.8	(91) 21.1	(88) 15.7		(11) 15.9		(15) 15.1	(21) 13.6		18.9
9.2	10.2	6.5		6.9		3.4	7.4		12.1
14.6	15.5	10.8	% Profit Before Taxes/Total Assets		20.5		10.2	10.1	11.2
7.1	6.8	4.6			10.6		3.0	4.9	5.4
3.4	2.9	1.6			-2.0		.4	3.7	2.9
28.3	21.4	23.2	Sales/Net Fixed Assets		28.1		19.9	25.7	23.0
11.6	9.6	10.7			1.3		9.9	11.1	16.6
2.1	1.5	3.1			.8		2.2	3.3	10.5
3.7	3.7	3.6	Sales/Total Assets		3.1		3.9	3.7	4.7
2.0	1.8	2.3			.9		1.6	2.2	3.0
.9	.8	1.0			.5		.7	1.3	2.1
.6	.7	.6	% Depr., Dep., Amort./Sales		1.3		1.2	.7	.4
(87) 1.4	(85) 1.6	(89) 1.2		(11) 4.7		(15) 1.8	(22) 1.2		.7
3.8	4.3	3.3			8.9		5.9	2.6	1.3
.3	.6	.4	% Officers', Directors' Owners' Comp/Sales						
(16) 1.2	(21) 2.0	(23) 1.5							
2.6	2.6	3.8							
4662486M	2226041M	3498477M	Net Sales ($)	2906M	27261M	22073M	129108M	368300M	2948829M
1784822M	1168421M	1380378M	Total Assets ($)	6511M	32721M	19079M	108242M	327741M	886084M

M = $ thousand   MM = $ million
See Pages 9 through 22 for Explanation of Ratios and Data

Current Data Sorted by Assets   **Comparative Historical Data**

Type of Statement	0-500M	500M-2MM	2-10MM	10-50MM	50-100MM	100-250MM		ALL 4/1/06-3/31/07	ALL 4/1/07-3/31/08
Unqualified				5		1		8	9
Reviewed	1	2	14	6				14	20
Compiled	3	7	3					13	12
Tax Returns	5	9	9					14	13
Other	5	14	13	16	2	3		25	39
		10 (4/1-9/30/10)		108 (10/1/10-3/31/11)					
NUMBER OF STATEMENTS	14	32	39	27	2	4		74	93
	%	%	%	%	%	%	**ASSETS**	%	%
Cash & Equivalents	12.6	12.1	8.9	12.2				10.3	12.6
Trade Receivables (net)	19.8	19.5	18.9	20.3				16.8	20.9
Inventory	1.5	5.2	4.6	10.0				6.0	3.2
All Other Current	6.4	3.1	2.9	4.1				3.0	2.8
Total Current	40.2	39.9	35.3	46.6				36.1	39.5
Fixed Assets (net)	52.5	48.9	54.1	36.3				52.7	45.7
Intangibles (net)	6.2	1.6	5.8	7.5				4.6	8.1
All Other Non-Current	1.0	9.6	4.8	9.6				6.6	6.8
Total	100.0	100.0	100.0	100.0				100.0	100.0
							LIABILITIES		
Notes Payable-Short Term	6.9	7.4	5.2	1.8				9.6	6.7
Cur. Mat.-L.T.D.	2.5	3.4	4.6	2.5				3.5	4.3
Trade Payables	8.1	6.0	7.2	11.1				7.5	14.2
Income Taxes Payable	.0	.1	.0	.0				.5	.2
All Other Current	5.0	9.8	5.8	6.2				8.6	7.8
Total Current	22.5	26.7	22.9	21.6				29.8	33.1
Long-Term Debt	73.9	39.9	39.3	25.0				34.5	33.9
Deferred Taxes	.1	.0	.1	.0				.6	.2
All Other Non-Current	2.2	4.8	7.8	1.6				3.6	5.2
Net Worth	1.3	28.6	29.9	51.7				31.6	27.5
Total Liabilities & Net Worth	100.0	100.0	100.0	100.0				100.0	100.0
							INCOME DATA		
Net Sales	100.0	100.0	100.0	100.0				100.0	100.0
Gross Profit									
Operating Expenses	85.3	82.2	79.6	83.7				79.2	83.3
Operating Profit	14.7	17.8	20.4	16.3				20.8	16.7
All Other Expenses (net)	7.8	8.6	10.1	2.7				7.4	5.0
Profit Before Taxes	6.9	9.2	10.3	13.6				13.4	11.7
							RATIOS		
Current	4.3	2.8	2.5	2.8				2.8	3.1
	1.9	1.3	1.4	1.9				1.3	1.5
	1.0	.9	.8	1.0				.6	.9
Quick	2.6	2.5	2.1	1.9				2.1	2.5
	1.2	1.2	.9	1.0				1.1	1.2
	.3	.5	.6	.8				.4	.7
Sales/Receivables	0 UND	0 UND	0 UND	22 16.3				0 UND	7 55.4
	4 96.0	34 10.8	25 14.6	39 9.5				27 13.3	36 10.2
	35 10.5	60 6.1	45 8.1	57 6.4				50 7.3	54 6.7
Cost of Sales/Inventory									
Cost of Sales/Payables									
Sales/Working Capital	7.6	5.7	7.6	4.2				8.6	5.8
	17.5	20.8	17.6	11.8				18.6	17.5
	NM	-23.2	-24.5	915.6				-13.0	-68.6
EBIT/Interest		14.8	13.2	23.2				24.8	9.3
		(22) 4.6	(28) 5.1	(22) 3.6				(56) 6.0	(73) 4.9
		.6	1.9	.6				2.3	2.0
Net Profit + Depr., Dep., Amort./Cur. Mat. L/T/D				31.2				9.0	7.0
				(13) 2.4				(14) 4.6	(21) 2.5
				2.0				1.4	.8
Fixed/Worth	.6	.7	.8	.2				.6	.6
	NM	1.8	2.2	.9				1.5	1.7
	-.7	18.9	8.6	1.6				NM	9.5
Debt/Worth	.6	.9	.8	.4				.7	.7
	NM	2.3	2.6	1.3				1.9	2.3
	-2.5	31.0	14.8	3.2				NM	48.4
% Profit Before Taxes/Tangible Net Worth		79.2	41.9	45.6				53.1	47.5
		(27) 20.3	(32) 14.3	(26) 22.5				(56) 25.6	(71) 29.1
		2.8	5.8	-4.1				12.8	10.9
% Profit Before Taxes/Total Assets	27.7	18.7	13.3	24.9				21.5	15.8
	8.8	2.5	6.6	8.2				8.6	7.9
	-1.5	-1.2	1.9	-1.1				1.7	2.6
Sales/Net Fixed Assets	35.2	21.8	8.5	43.6				15.1	11.8
	4.8	2.7	3.5	4.6				3.1	4.3
	.5	.3	.3	1.9				.5	.8
Sales/Total Assets	5.0	2.9	2.5	2.7				3.1	2.7
	1.9	1.5	1.2	1.3				1.3	1.7
	.4	.2	.2	.5				.3	.5
% Depr., Dep., Amort./Sales		1.9	2.2	1.2				1.9	1.9
		(22) 6.6	(32) 8.0	(24) 3.0				(69) 4.2	(78) 4.4
		14.4	16.7	5.8				11.6	9.3
% Officers', Directors' Owners' Comp/Sales		1.9	1.5					3.2	3.3
		(11) 4.7	(10) 4.8					(16) 6.4	(20) 4.7
		7.4	8.3					12.6	13.4
Net Sales ($)	15172M	62580M	518685M	1442653M	95224M	334342M		826148M	1923904M
Total Assets ($)	4051M	37073M	224317M	668330M	104168M	624173M		653290M	1317907M

M = $ thousand   MM = $ million
See Pages 9 through 22 for Explanation of Ratios and Data

Comparative Historical Data / Current Data Sorted by Sales

8	7	6	Type of Statement						
22	25	23						3	3
10	13	13						9	4
19	18	23		2	2	2	4	1	
42	44	53		2	8		2	1	
4/1/08-3/31/09	4/1/09-3/31/10	4/1/10-3/31/11	Unqualified / Reviewed / Compiled / Tax Returns / Other	14	2	2	4	7	14
ALL	ALL	ALL		11	11	2	8		
				10 (4/1-9/30/10)			**108 (10/1/10-3/31/11)**		
				0-1MM	1-3MM	3-5MM	5-10MM	10-25MM	25MM & OVER
101	107	118	NUMBER OF STATEMENTS	29	23	6	18	21	21
%	%	%	**ASSETS**	%	%	%	%	%	%
12.4	9.8	10.5	Cash & Equivalents	5.6	14.2		11.4	14.2	7.6
20.9	18.3	18.9	Trade Receivables (net)	2.5	21.7		24.7	24.1	26.7
3.5	3.7	6.8	Inventory	.8	4.2		3.3	4.4	22.0
4.1	3.5	3.9	All Other Current	5.0	2.4		2.6	3.0	6.4
40.9	35.2	40.1	Total Current	14.0	42.5		42.0	45.7	62.6
47.2	49.3	47.6	Fixed Assets (net)	78.7	44.1		40.7	38.4	26.3
5.1	6.5	5.4	Intangibles (net)	4.7	2.6		7.9	8.1	5.7
6.7	8.9	6.9	All Other Non-Current	2.7	10.7		9.5	7.7	5.4
100.0	100.0	100.0	Total	100.0	100.0		100.0	100.0	100.0
			LIABILITIES						
11.9	6.1	5.5	Notes Payable-Short Term	1.7	7.2		7.2	5.0	5.2
6.6	4.5	3.4	Cur. Mat.-L.T.D.	3.3	4.5		4.0	2.6	2.2
8.2	6.1	7.9	Trade Payables	.9	7.6		5.6	6.7	19.8
.2	.1	.0	Income Taxes Payable	.0	.1		.0	.0	.0
9.9	6.3	7.0	All Other Current	2.6	9.5		9.0	8.2	8.2
36.8	23.1	23.9	Total Current	8.5	28.8		25.9	22.5	35.4
33.5	41.6	39.5	Long-Term Debt	61.7	63.1		25.2	14.3	21.3
.2	.2	.1	Deferred Taxes	.0	.0		.1	.0	.4
4.6	8.0	5.1	All Other Non-Current	7.5	2.9		5.4	4.8	4.6
25.0	27.1	31.4	Net Worth	22.3	5.2		43.4	58.4	38.4
100.0	100.0	100.0	Total Liabilities & Net Worth	100.0	100.0		100.0	100.0	100.0
			INCOME DATA						
100.0	100.0	100.0	Net Sales	100.0	100.0		100.0	100.0	100.0
			Gross Profit						
86.1	83.4	82.2	Operating Expenses	62.2	86.6		90.5	85.0	93.4
13.9	16.6	17.8	Operating Profit	37.8	13.4		9.5	15.0	6.6
7.6	7.1	7.5	All Other Expenses (net)	21.8	4.8		2.1	1.4	2.3
6.2	9.5	10.3	Profit Before Taxes	16.0	8.7		7.4	13.6	4.2
			RATIOS						
3.5	2.3	2.8	Current	2.8	3.0		5.5	4.0	2.6
1.4	1.5	1.5		1.3	1.4		1.2	1.9	1.9
.9	.8	.9		.3	.9		.7	1.1	1.3
2.8	2.1	2.4	Quick	1.7	3.0		5.3	3.8	1.3
1.2	1.1	1.0		.9	1.2		.9	1.5	1.0
.7	.6	.6		.2	.7		.7	.9	.8
10 38.3	5 76.6	0 UND	Sales/Receivables	0 UND	0 UND		30 12.1	25 14.6	23 15.7
33 11.1	38 9.7	32 11.4		0 UND	36 10.2		41 9.0	39 9.3	39 9.5
45 8.1	52 7.1	50 7.3		10 37.1	60 6.1		59 6.2	57 6.5	50 7.2
			Cost of Sales/Inventory						
			Cost of Sales/Payables						
6.7	7.2	5.6	Sales/Working Capital	4.4	6.5		4.7	6.0	4.2
18.8	17.6	13.5		17.9	17.1		56.1	10.4	12.3
-46.9	-33.0	-70.5		-4.5	-25.2		-20.1	468.5	24.6
8.1	15.2	13.1	EBIT/Interest	6.0	14.8		7.9	31.2	17.3
(76) 3.9	(79) 3.6	(83) 4.4		(10) 1.8	(18) 4.3		(12) 3.5	(19) 13.1	(19) 2.0
1.5	1.1	1.3		1.3	.6		1.6	3.7	.6
10.7	9.4	13.0	Net Profit + Depr., Dep., Amort./Cur. Mat. L/T/D						14.2
(15) 3.5	(27) 5.1	(24) 3.5							(11) 2.4
1.2	1.6	1.9							2.1
.5	.6	.5	Fixed/Worth	1.8	.8		.4	.3	.2
1.6	1.6	1.4		5.1	2.5		1.2	.8	.7
7.6	12.2	8.9		40.5	-1.1		5.3	1.6	1.3
.8	.8	.7	Debt/Worth	1.3	.8		.8	.3	1.0
3.2	2.4	2.2		4.9	3.2		1.3	.5	2.3
15.4	31.1	15.1		44.7	-6.4		5.4	2.5	5.3
54.4	59.6	45.3	% Profit Before Taxes/Tangible Net Worth	49.7	63.7		34.1	72.2	39.0
(84) 22.5	(82) 25.5	(97) 16.9		(23) 6.7	(13) 35.9		(16) 14.6	(20) 31.7	(20) 14.6
1.7	8.0	3.3		-2.6	3.2		3.3	12.3	-5.0
12.9	16.0	15.8	% Profit Before Taxes/Total Assets	8.8	23.0		14.6	26.4	15.6
5.1	5.1	5.7		3.0	10.0		5.3	12.0	3.3
-.2	.4	.6		.6	-1.9		1.2	7.4	-1.2
16.0	11.4	17.7	Sales/Net Fixed Assets	.5	37.9		67.8	21.7	66.2
4.7	3.3	3.2		.2	7.2		4.9	5.5	8.4
.8	.5	.5		.1	.7		1.3	2.6	2.9
3.3	2.7	2.7	Sales/Total Assets	.4	3.0		3.1	3.5	3.6
1.6	1.3	1.3		.2	1.5		1.3	1.9	2.4
.5	.4	.3		.1	.7		.9	.8	1.3
2.1	2.6	1.9	% Depr., Dep., Amort./Sales	9.6	1.8		1.9	1.8	.7
(84) 5.0	(96) 5.3	(92) 4.2		(24) 15.6	(13) 6.6		(14) 3.8	(17) 3.4	(20) 1.8
9.2	10.5	12.0		23.3	19.0		10.7	6.4	4.1
2.4		1.9	% Officers', Directors' Owners' Comp/Sales						
(25) 5.2	(18) 4.6	(27) 4.6							
8.0	9.0	7.4							
1458707M	2312895M	2468656M	Net Sales ($)	10753M	41444M	24978M	138685M	334841M	1917955M
1001471M	2118779M	1662112M	Total Assets ($)	57498M	51611M	36409M	122591M	310098M	1083905M

© RMA 2011

M = $ thousand   MM = $ million
See Pages 9 through 22 for Explanation of Ratios and Data

INFORMATION

Current Data Sorted by Assets   Comparative Historical Data

0-500M	500M-2MM	2-10MM	10-50MM	50-100MM	100-250MM		4/1/06-3/31/07 ALL	4/1/07-3/31/08 ALL
			5	4	2	Type of Statement		
	1	8				Unqualified	23	20
1	2	1	1			Reviewed	20	13
7	3	3	1			Compiled	5	4
3	2	14	14	5	4	Tax Returns	13	13
						Other	35	31
	25 (4/1-9/30/10)		56 (10/1/10-3/31/11)					
11	8	26	21	9	6	**NUMBER OF STATEMENTS**	96	81
%	%	%	%	%	%	**ASSETS**	%	%
8.4		13.2	16.0			Cash & Equivalents	14.5	10.9
32.6		23.0	16.8			Trade Receivables (net)	23.8	24.8
2.3		3.4	5.7			Inventory	3.9	4.3
2.5		2.0	2.9			All Other Current	2.6	3.9
45.8		41.6	41.4			Total Current	44.7	43.9
29.7		30.0	31.3			Fixed Assets (net)	26.4	25.4
16.6		13.6	20.4			Intangibles (net)	18.8	19.7
7.9		14.8	6.8			All Other Non-Current	10.1	11.0
100.0		100.0	100.0			Total	100.0	100.0
						LIABILITIES		
18.5		5.7	3.9			Notes Payable-Short Term	4.2	3.1
2.9		3.4	7.3			Cur. Mat.-L.T.D.	4.0	3.9
13.6		10.7	6.4			Trade Payables	8.3	8.3
.0		.2	.0			Income Taxes Payable	.1	.1
15.0		6.7	14.5			All Other Current	13.5	12.7
50.0		26.7	32.0			Total Current	30.1	28.1
23.9		18.3	19.7			Long-Term Debt	26.0	22.1
.0		.0	.5			Deferred Taxes	.8	.5
.6		3.0	11.3			All Other Non-Current	13.0	13.9
25.6		52.1	36.5			Net Worth	30.2	35.3
100.0		100.0	100.0			Total Liabilities & Net Worth	100.0	100.0
						INCOME DATA		
100.0		100.0	100.0			Net Sales	100.0	100.0
64.2		48.8	58.8			Gross Profit	51.5	47.6
61.5		41.0	52.3			Operating Expenses	44.3	39.9
2.7		7.9	6.5			Operating Profit	7.2	7.7
1.1		1.0	1.9			All Other Expenses (net)	1.6	1.5
1.5		6.9	4.6			Profit Before Taxes	5.6	6.2
						RATIOS		
3.3		3.0	3.8				2.4	2.6
.9		1.6	1.2			Current	1.5	1.8
.6		1.0	.7				1.0	1.1
1.9		2.9	2.9				2.1	2.2
.9		1.4	.8			Quick	1.2	1.4
.4		.8	.5				.8	.8
0 UND		35 10.3	29 12.5				32 11.4	35 10.4
22 16.4		41 8.9	35 10.3			Sales/Receivables	37 9.8	39 9.3
43 8.4		57 6.4	37 9.7				47 7.7	49 7.5
0 UND		0 UND	8 45.5				0 796.7	0 UND
0 UND		8 45.6	28 12.8			Cost of Sales/Inventory	9 42.3	6 63.0
0 UND		13 28.5	52 7.0				22 16.7	18 20.5
0 UND		15 24.6	7 54.5				14 26.9	12 30.9
19 18.8		24 15.4	39 9.3			Cost of Sales/Payables	22 16.3	23 15.9
56 6.5		69 5.3	49 7.5				42 8.7	42 8.7
44.5		7.1	4.3				8.6	6.6
-78.0		15.7	53.0			Sales/Working Capital	16.4	13.2
-14.8		437.3	-21.5				-300.0	67.4
		18.4	6.9				10.9	12.5
		(21) 4.7	(17) 2.9			EBIT/Interest	(81) 3.8	(67) 4.5
		2.2	.8				1.9	1.4
							3.6	8.3
						Net Profit + Depr., Dep., Amort./Cur. Mat. L/T/D	(25) 1.8	(12) 2.5
							1.0	1.0
.2		.2	.6				.3	.3
1.0		.7	3.5			Fixed/Worth	1.3	1.2
80.0		3.2	-2.5				-4.5	-1.5
1.1		.3	.9				.7	.7
16.3		1.8	20.1			Debt/Worth	2.4	2.6
-4.5		2.9	-4.7				-8.9	-4.4
		56.9	16.4				46.6	52.5
		(23) 19.2	(11) 4.4			% Profit Before Taxes/Tangible Net Worth	(67) 20.4	(53) 20.9
		8.2	-8.2				4.2	9.9
7.5		14.7	14.0				17.2	14.9
3.5		8.0	3.2			% Profit Before Taxes/Total Assets	7.3	7.8
-5.0		3.7	.4				2.1	1.7
205.1		27.7	10.3				33.1	36.6
40.9		8.9	3.9			Sales/Net Fixed Assets	8.7	8.3
4.6		4.2	2.5				3.7	3.5
8.2		2.1	2.0				2.7	2.7
3.8		1.7	1.4			Sales/Total Assets	1.9	1.6
2.4		1.2	.8				1.3	1.1
		1.0	2.6				1.5	1.2
		(24) 2.5	(18) 3.8			% Depr., Dep., Amort./Sales	(83) 3.0	(67) 2.7
		4.4	5.9				4.8	4.8
							4.1	1.6
						% Officers', Directors' Owners' Comp/Sales	(22) 7.7	(19) 3.8
							12.5	5.4
15927M	28118M	267392M	696468M	529667M	719208M	Net Sales ($)	3986837M	2943685M
3184M	8150M	140676M	435948M	617601M	982185M	Total Assets ($)	3065974M	2751466M

M = $ thousand   MM = $ million
See Pages 9 through 22 for Explanation of Ratios and Data

Comparative Historical Data

Current Data Sorted by Sales

			Type of Statement	0-1MM	1-3MM	3-5MM	5-10MM	10-25MM	25MM & OVER
12	20	11	Unqualified					1	10
11	6	9	Reviewed		1	1	4	3	
3	1	5	Compiled		2	2		1	
12	17	14	Tax Returns	4	6	1	2		1
36	27	42	Other	1	2	1	10	12	16
4/1/08-3/31/09 ALL	4/1/09-3/31/10 ALL	4/1/10-3/31/11 ALL			25 (4/1-9/30/10)		56 (10/1/10-3/31/11)		
74	71	81	NUMBER OF STATEMENTS	5	11	5	16	17	27
%	%	%	ASSETS	%	%	%	%	%	%
11.5	11.6	12.7	Cash & Equivalents		6.9		12.5	16.1	12.9
26.6	23.0	21.9	Trade Receivables (net)		37.8		23.8	20.3	15.6
3.0	3.3	4.0	Inventory		6.4		1.0	4.9	4.9
2.4	2.8	3.1	All Other Current		4.2		3.0	1.7	3.8
43.4	40.7	41.8	Total Current		55.4		40.3	43.1	37.2
25.5	28.1	29.2	Fixed Assets (net)		16.0		27.0	33.3	31.2
19.2	19.8	18.4	Intangibles (net)		7.5		19.3	17.8	22.7
12.0	11.4	10.6	All Other Non-Current		21.1		13.4	5.9	8.9
100.0	100.0	100.0	Total		100.0		100.0	100.0	100.0
			LIABILITIES						
7.4	6.8	6.7	Notes Payable-Short Term		21.3		6.2	4.7	2.6
4.3	4.3	4.3	Cur. Mat.-L.T.D.		4.7		1.8	4.5	6.0
13.4	9.6	8.8	Trade Payables		12.6		10.1	8.2	5.9
.3	.2	.1	Income Taxes Payable		.0		.1	.2	.0
11.5	15.1	10.8	All Other Current		10.5		3.7	11.9	14.1
37.0	36.0	30.8	Total Current		49.0		21.9	29.5	28.6
25.3	24.4	24.3	Long-Term Debt		25.1		13.3	15.5	35.1
.6	.4	.4	Deferred Taxes		.0		.0	.1	1.1
12.0	17.6	6.8	All Other Non-Current		9.2		2.9	3.9	11.5
25.2	21.6	37.7	Net Worth		16.7		61.9	51.0	23.8
100.0	100.0	100.0	Total Liabilties & Net Worth		100.0		100.0	100.0	100.0
			INCOME DATA						
100.0	100.0	100.0	Net Sales		100.0		100.0	100.0	100.0
53.6	50.0	55.6	Gross Profit		63.7		55.6	52.5	49.9
49.7	46.9	49.7	Operating Expenses		61.6		46.5	48.1	43.9
3.9	3.1	5.9	Operating Profit		2.1		9.1	4.4	6.0
2.4	2.0	2.4	All Other Expenses (net)		1.3		1.0	1.8	4.6
1.5	1.1	3.5	Profit Before Taxes		.8		8.1	2.7	1.4
			RATIOS						
2.6	2.5	2.9			4.0		3.6	4.2	1.9
1.3	1.4	1.4	Current		1.8		1.5	1.6	1.2
.8	.8	.9			.9		1.0	.7	.9
2.3	1.9	2.3			3.7		3.4	3.4	1.4
1.1	1.1	1.0	Quick		1.0		1.4	.9	.9
.7	.7	.7			.8		.8	.6	.6
31 11.9	33 11.2	30 12.3			27 13.8		36 10.2	34 10.8	30 12.2
38 9.7	39 9.5	37 9.9	Sales/Receivables		46 7.9		42 8.7	37 9.9	36 10.2
47 7.7	50 7.2	52 7.1			64 5.7		61 6.0	58 6.3	40 9.0
0 UND	0 UND	0 UND			0 UND		0 UND	8 47.7	7 51.4
7 53.2	6 66.3	9 42.7	Cost of Sales/Inventory		5 78.1		0 UND	15 24.7	15 25.1
24 15.1	16 22.9	26 14.2			41 8.8		9 42.0	42 8.6	33 10.9
13 29.1	10 37.0	11 33.2			11 31.8		15 24.2	6 64.1	8 46.1
28 13.0	17 20.9	24 15.3	Cost of Sales/Payables		19 18.8		28 13.1	37 9.8	23 15.7
53 6.9	44 8.4	55 6.6			34 10.7		75 4.8	55 6.6	51 7.2
7.0	7.7	7.1			7.4		5.8	3.2	6.0
15.2	31.5	22.4	Sales/Working Capital		10.2		16.7	18.1	27.2
-26.2	-24.2	-35.4			-57.9		NM	-20.0	-52.8
7.7	4.4	6.4			3.2		34.9	25.4	5.6
(61) 1.6	(57) 1.0	(66) 2.9	EBIT/Interest		-3.9	(11) 4.0	(16) 4.0	(22) 1.7
-.6	-.9	-.1			-8.8		1.7	1.1	-.1
3.3		4.2							
(15) 1.1		(17) 2.0	Net Profit + Depr., Dep., Amort./Cur. Mat. L/T/D						
.3		.5							
.3	.5	.3			.4		.1	.4	.7
1.3	2.9	1.2	Fixed/Worth		1.6		.3	1.1	7.4
-2.2	-1.2	-4.9			-.3		2.6	NM	-.6
.7	.6	.5			.5		.3	.4	1.0
3.5	8.3	2.4	Debt/Worth		17.5		1.5	1.4	-15.0
-4.4	-2.8	-6.7			-3.0		2.7	NM	-3.6
27.0	25.6	49.2					74.1	24.8	25.2
(50) 7.8	(40) 9.3	(55) 13.6	% Profit Before Taxes/Tangible Net Worth			(15) 25.4	(13) 13.6	(13) 8.4
-5.5	-7.6	-5.1					1.6	-1.9	-8.3
10.9	8.1	12.3			7.3		21.2	14.0	9.3
3.6	1.9	5.0	% Profit Before Taxes/Total Assets		-4.0		9.8	5.4	1.9
-4.2	-5.0	-2.5			-26.8		1.3	.7	-2.7
30.3	30.8	27.4			74.5		32.0	9.7	14.3
8.2	7.4	6.7	Sales/Net Fixed Assets		22.1		13.6	4.2	4.3
4.1	2.9	2.5			9.8		1.7	2.5	2.3
2.5	2.6	2.6			4.0		1.9	2.1	1.9
1.6	1.4	1.7	Sales/Total Assets		3.5		1.6	1.7	1.3
1.1	1.0	.9			1.5		1.1	.8	.7
1.0	1.0	1.1			.3		1.1	2.1	2.6
(58) 2.7	(57) 3.2	(65) 3.0	% Depr., Dep., Amort./Sales		.8	(13) 2.0	(16) 4.0	(18) 3.8
4.3	4.8	5.3			3.3		3.7	11.6	5.2
1.1	2.1	2.3							
(20) 3.3	(13) 3.3	(19) 7.3	% Officers', Directors' Owners' Comp/Sales						
6.1	15.7	9.2							
1826852M	2236585M	2256780M	Net Sales ($)	2075M	24204M	19233M	112887M	265293M	1833088M
1537891M	2043962M	2187744M	Total Assets ($)	1131M	14897M	4282M	89423M	276061M	1801950M

© RMA 2011
M = $ thousand   MM = $ million
See Pages 9 through 22 for Explanation of Ratios and Data

Current Data Sorted by Assets　　　　　Comparative Historical Data

Type of Statement	0-500M	500M-2MM	2-10MM	10-50MM	50-100MM	100-250MM	4/1/06-3/31/07 ALL	4/1/07-3/31/08 ALL
Unqualified			8	10	3		25	25
Reviewed		3	3	2			19	15
Compiled	2	6	6	2			9	9
Tax Returns	4	2	3				13	13
Other	6	8	12	15	6	7	34	37
	19 (4/1-9/30/10)			89 (10/1/10-3/31/11)				
NUMBER OF STATEMENTS	12	19	32	29	9	7	100	99

	0-500M	500M-2MM	2-10MM	10-50MM	50-100MM	100-250MM	4/1/06-3/31/07 ALL	4/1/07-3/31/08 ALL
	%	%	%	%	%	%	%	%
ASSETS								
Cash & Equivalents	14.5	20.0	18.4	15.5			15.7	13.8
Trade Receivables (net)	33.6	42.6	28.8	19.1			26.3	27.2
Inventory	7.2	4.3	7.8	5.3			6.8	6.0
All Other Current	6.5	5.8	2.3	3.5			4.5	4.4
Total Current	61.8	72.7	57.3	43.4			53.3	51.5
Fixed Assets (net)	20.2	10.6	17.0	15.2			13.7	18.5
Intangibles (net)	14.2	3.4	13.2	35.0			21.6	17.0
All Other Non-Current	3.8	13.3	12.5	6.4			11.4	13.0
Total	100.0	100.0	100.0	100.0			100.0	100.0
LIABILITIES								
Notes Payable-Short Term	42.0	31.9	9.0	1.4			9.7	7.7
Cur. Mat.-L.T.D.	7.5	5.4	3.1	3.0			4.8	4.2
Trade Payables	8.9	16.5	10.5	6.8			13.1	12.5
Income Taxes Payable	.0	.0	.0	.6			.4	.2
All Other Current	15.3	19.4	17.8	24.5			19.5	21.9
Total Current	73.7	73.1	40.4	36.3			47.5	46.5
Long-Term Debt	51.9	17.3	20.2	24.5			26.6	24.0
Deferred Taxes	.0	.0	.0	.2			.4	.2
All Other Non-Current	2.6	10.3	17.1	22.0			12.3	19.5
Net Worth	-28.2	-.7	22.3	17.0			13.2	9.8
Total Liabilities & Net Worth	100.0	100.0	100.0	100.0			100.0	100.0
INCOME DATA								
Net Sales	100.0	100.0	100.0	100.0			100.0	100.0
Gross Profit	64.4	51.4	55.1	49.7			51.7	48.2
Operating Expenses	56.1	52.7	50.4	43.3			44.4	41.5
Operating Profit	8.3	-1.3	4.8	6.4			7.2	6.8
All Other Expenses (net)	2.1	1.7	1.2	2.4			2.2	1.5
Profit Before Taxes	6.2	-3.0	3.6	4.0			5.0	5.2
RATIOS								
Current	2.8	2.3	2.5	2.1			1.8	2.1
	.7	1.3	1.8	1.2			1.2	1.4
	.4	.6	.7	.8			.7	.8
Quick	1.0	2.0	2.1	1.6			1.3	1.6
	.5	1.2	1.3	1.0			1.0 (98)	1.1
	.3	.5	.6	.6			.6	.6
Sales/Receivables	0 UND	32 11.5	28 13.1	27 13.3			30 12.3	30 12.0
	29 12.7	46 7.9	42 8.7	37 10.0			41 8.9	41 8.9
	55 6.7	59 6.2	59 6.2	59 6.1			62 5.9	61 6.0
Cost of Sales/Inventory	0 UND	0 UND	0 UND	0 UND			0 UND	0 UND
	0 UND	0 UND	4 82.9	6 57.6			8 44.6	5 68.1
	0 UND	0 UND	29 12.6	33 11.1			29 12.7	29 12.6
Cost of Sales/Payables	0 UND	7 49.0	23 15.8	11 32.3			15 25.0	18 20.8
	6 59.2	23 15.8	40 9.1	25 14.6			30 12.0	29 12.6
	34 10.7	45 8.0	76 4.8	37 9.8			69 5.3	58 6.3
Sales/Working Capital	9.8	6.8	4.8	7.0			8.7	7.0
	-19.3	14.6	13.6	33.7			24.7	18.2
	-6.1	-11.0	-18.3	-31.6			-13.7	-29.8
EBIT/Interest	10.9	4.1	33.8	17.2			13.6	9.2
	(10) 3.2	(17) 1.7	(29) 5.2	(21) 4.6			(85) 4.4	(84) 3.4
	.6	-1.0	1.6	.3			.9	.8
Net Profit + Depr., Dep., Amort./Cur. Mat. L/T/D							15.5	24.8
							(24) 3.2	(22) 3.3
							1.1	.4
Fixed/Worth	.1	.0	.3	.4			.2	.3
	3.7	.3	1.7	-2.5			1.4	1.8
	-.1	-.4	-.3	-.1			-.1	-.4
Debt/Worth	1.2	.8	1.1	1.1			1.3	1.3
	-8.2	4.4	24.5	-7.9			8.2	5.9
	-1.8	-2.8	-5.7	-1.7			-2.2	-3.5
% Profit Before Taxes/Tangible Net Worth		34.6	70.7	83.1			78.5	65.3
		(10) 7.9	(17) 23.0	(12) 11.9			(55) 35.6	(62) 29.7
		-3.4	8.0	4.3			13.8	1.2
% Profit Before Taxes/Total Assets	48.4	11.7	16.6	15.3			20.7	16.9
	20.1	2.8	6.1	6.5			8.0	7.8
	-1.4	-9.7	1.4	-2.5			-.1	-.9
Sales/Net Fixed Assets	130.8	233.1	73.9	49.4			63.4	45.5
	49.2	44.6	28.7	11.9			29.7	18.4
	15.8	22.1	9.2	6.8			11.1	8.2
Sales/Total Assets	5.5	4.9	2.9	1.9			3.4	3.0
	4.6	3.2	2.1	1.5			2.0	2.0
	2.3	2.5	1.4	1.1			1.3	1.2
% Depr., Dep., Amort./Sales			.7	1.8			.7	.6
		(25) 1.3	(18) 2.4				(72) 1.4	(76) 1.4
		1.9	4.5				3.2	3.1
% Officers', Directors' Owners' Comp/Sales			2.1				3.0	2.8
		(10) 3.0					(28) 4.3	(29) 4.3
		4.9					11.7	6.4
Net Sales ($)	14376M	71892M	307332M	1126688M	1665331M	1333260M	2362486M	2763068M
Total Assets ($)	3921M	20094M	145466M	745564M	753108M	1165422M	2179697M	2196962M

© RMA 2011

M = $ thousand　　MM = $ million
See Pages 9 through 22 for Explanation of Ratios and Data

Comparative Historical Data — Current Data Sorted by Sales

	4/1/08-3/31/09 ALL		4/1/09-3/31/10 ALL		4/1/10-3/31/11 ALL	Type of Statement	0-1MM	1-3MM	3-5MM	5-10MM	10-25MM	25MM & OVER
	24		17		21	Unqualified				3	7	11
	10		11		8	Reviewed		1	1	3	2	1
	8		9		16	Compiled	1	4	4	3	4	
	13		10		9	Tax Returns	3	2	1	3		
	53		58		54	Other	2	10	3	6	11	22
							19 (4/1-9/30/10)			89 (10/1/10-3/31/11)		
	108		105		108	**NUMBER OF STATEMENTS**	6	17	9	18	24	34
	%		%		%	**ASSETS**	%	%	%	%	%	%
	13.9		14.2		16.8	Cash & Equivalents		13.5		16.7	18.5	14.9
	26.8		25.6		26.4	Trade Receivables (net)		31.4		36.9	26.6	15.8
	5.2		5.9		5.6	Inventory		8.9		6.6	5.6	4.6
	4.7		4.6		4.3	All Other Current		4.7		3.8	3.4	4.6
	50.6		50.3		53.1	Total Current		58.5		64.0	54.0	39.9
	14.0		14.8		15.2	Fixed Assets (net)		17.7		18.1	15.4	15.1
	22.0		25.8		22.5	Intangibles (net)		12.7		10.2	21.6	37.5
	13.4		9.1		9.2	All Other Non-Current		11.2		7.7	8.9	7.5
	100.0		100.0		100.0	Total		100.0		100.0	100.0	100.0
						LIABILITIES						
	6.7		8.2		13.9	Notes Payable-Short Term		28.1		12.1	6.5	2.7
	3.6		6.8		4.9	Cur. Mat.-L.T.D.		5.6		2.1	4.5	5.6
	14.0		12.9		10.2	Trade Payables		13.2		10.8	9.4	8.7
	.8		.3		.2	Income Taxes Payable		.0		.0	.6	.3
	17.7		21.8		20.0	All Other Current		21.3		13.1	17.6	25.9
	42.8		50.0		49.2	Total Current		68.2		38.1	38.5	43.3
	26.4		26.1		24.8	Long-Term Debt		64.9		10.8	20.0	17.3
	.2		.5		.1	Deferred Taxes		.2		.0	.0	.3
	20.0		19.1		15.1	All Other Non-Current		4.0		21.9	14.0	21.2
	10.5		4.4		10.7	Net Worth		-37.3		29.2	27.4	17.9
	100.0		100.0		100.0	Total Liabilities & Net Worth		100.0		100.0	100.0	100.0
						INCOME DATA						
	100.0		100.0		100.0	Net Sales		100.0		100.0	100.0	100.0
	51.8		47.9		54.0	Gross Profit		61.2		60.9	46.4	52.4
	47.1		44.4		48.9	Operating Expenses		55.7		55.5	40.6	45.1
	4.7		3.5		5.1	Operating Profit		5.5		5.3	5.8	7.3
	2.1		3.4		2.0	All Other Expenses (net)		4.4		.2	2.3	1.5
	2.6		.0		3.1	Profit Before Taxes		1.2		5.1	3.6	5.9
						RATIOS						
	2.3		2.0		2.3	Current		1.8		2.7	2.3	2.0
	1.3		1.0		1.2			1.0		1.9	1.6	1.1
	.7		.6		.7			.4		1.3	.9	.6
	2.0		1.5		1.9	Quick		1.1		2.7	2.0	1.6
	.9		.8		1.0			.6		1.8	1.1	.8
	.5		.4		.5			.3		.7	.7	.5
23	15.9	28	13.2	27	13.5	Sales/Receivables		25 14.8		26 13.9	32 11.3	25 14.7
37	10.0	39	9.4	41	8.8			42 8.6		40 9.0	42 8.7	35 10.6
56	6.5	60	6.0	58	6.3			55 6.7		61 6.8	68 5.4	66 6.5
0	UND	0	UND	0	UND	Cost of Sales/Inventory		0 UND		0 UND	0 UND	0 UND
5	74.5	5	67.7	3	143.8			0 UND		0 UND	0 UND	15 24.9
25	14.4	23	15.6	23	15.5			12 29.7		39 9.3	19 19.7	30 12.0
15	23.8	15	24.6	12	29.5	Cost of Sales/Payables		17 22.0		12 31.2	15 23.7	10 37.7
32	11.5	33	11.0	29	12.6			33 11.2		40 9.2	27 13.3	31 11.8
66	5.6	84	4.3	54	6.7			90 4.0		67 5.4	43 8.5	71 5.1
	6.6		8.3		6.4	Sales/Working Capital		8.4		4.5	5.5	6.2
	25.4		183.6		22.6			-225.0		11.9	16.3	66.5
	-15.0		-8.1		-11.4			-6.5		67.9	-43.0	-7.2
	20.6		7.0		13.0	EBIT/Interest		12.3		56.1	27.8	14.9
(89)	3.0	(89)	1.6	(89)	3.6		(14) 2.1		(15) 6.1	(22) 4.2	(25) 4.2
	.1		-.9		.6			-.4		3.6	1.3	.5
	5.1		2.3		2.5	Net Profit + Depr., Dep., Amort./Cur. Mat. L/T/D						
(23)	2.0	(18)	.6	(12)	2.1							
	.3		-3.8		.6							
	.3		.3		.2	Fixed/Worth		.0		.2	.4	.6
	-2.1		49.0		NM			2.2		.5	-2.6	-1.7
	-.2		-.1		-.2			-.3		-.3	-.3	-.1
	1.5		1.8		1.3	Debt/Worth		2.0		.7	.8	2.6
	-14.2		-8.0		-15.7			-14.0		2.1	-16.3	-6.8
	-2.8		-1.8		-2.1			-1.7		-3.3	-4.3	-1.7
	77.2		55.7		70.9	% Profit Before Taxes/Tangible Net Worth				37.3	98.2	83.1
(48)	33.3	(47)	10.1	(48)	18.8					(13) 23.0	(11) 21.1	(12) 19.2
	2.5		-18.5		4.7					4.9	7.6	4.9
	16.7		9.7		16.0	% Profit Before Taxes/Total Assets		30.4		21.8	16.4	12.0
	4.7		2.0		6.0			5.3		13.0	7.8	6.6
	-3.6		-8.1		-1.6			-5.3		2.9	-.6	-.9
	60.8		66.0		71.6	Sales/Net Fixed Assets		164.2		76.8	62.5	44.1
	28.2		20.8		25.2			26.6		30.9	25.2	14.1
	10.5		10.2		9.9			13.3		8.9	9.7	8.0
	3.5		3.0		3.0	Sales/Total Assets		4.7		3.8	2.6	1.9
	2.0		2.0		2.0			2.5		2.7	2.0	1.4
	1.2		1.0		1.3			1.7		1.4	1.4	.8
	.8		.8		.8	% Depr., Dep., Amort./Sales				.8	.6	1.8
(64)	1.5	(64)	1.4	(64)	1.6					(15) 1.1	(17) 1.7	(18) 2.3
	3.8		2.2		2.8					1.7	3.5	4.5
	2.5		2.6		2.5	% Officers', Directors' Owners' Comp/Sales						
(26)	4.3	(29)	5.2	(27)	5.3							
	7.0		10.5		9.5							
	3011835M		3000648M		4518879M	Net Sales ($)	3499M	34033M	33436M	132665M	363302M	3951944M
	2852811M		3007780M		2833575M	Total Assets ($)	2545M	53727M	13140M	61411M	208111M	2494641M

© RMA 2011

M = $ thousand   MM = $ million
See Pages 9 through 22 for Explanation of Ratios and Data

Current Data Sorted by Assets   Comparative Historical Data

0-500M	500M-2MM	2-10MM	10-50MM	50-100MM	100-250MM	Type of Statement	4/1/06-3/31/07 ALL	4/1/07-3/31/08 ALL
	1	6	6	5	2	Unqualified	30	25
		8	8		1	Reviewed	25	26
1	1	3	2			Compiled	9	5
2	3	4			1	Tax Returns	10	7
3	5	10	10	9	3	Other	36	40
	24 (4/1-9/30/10)		69 (10/1/10-3/31/11)					
6	10	31	26	14	6	**NUMBER OF STATEMENTS**	110	103
%	%	%	%	%	%	**ASSETS**	%	%
	10.3	10.8	17.0	12.6		Cash & Equivalents	12.0	9.9
	15.5	27.3	18.1	22.6		Trade Receivables (net)	24.0	27.7
	49.1	34.1	19.8	15.9		Inventory	29.2	29.4
	5.5	7.7	5.9	5.3		All Other Current	3.5	3.6
	80.4	79.9	60.7	56.4		Total Current	68.7	70.5
	6.8	8.0	17.6	11.4		Fixed Assets (net)	10.5	12.1
	1.1	2.9	13.1	26.8		Intangibles (net)	10.8	8.7
	11.7	9.2	8.6	5.4		All Other Non-Current	10.0	8.7
	100.0	100.0	100.0	100.0		Total	100.0	100.0
						LIABILITIES		
	7.2	7.4	4.0	4.7		Notes Payable-Short Term	10.3	8.4
	1.7	2.2	2.8	3.6		Cur. Mat.-L.T.D.	2.3	2.6
	17.8	16.0	11.1	8.5		Trade Payables	14.9	13.5
	.3	.1	.5	.9		Income Taxes Payable	.3	.3
	7.5	15.3	15.0	18.3		All Other Current	11.5	15.1
	34.5	40.9	33.5	35.9		Total Current	39.3	40.0
	1.8	8.7	10.2	9.9		Long-Term Debt	9.2	11.9
	.0	.3	.6	1.2		Deferred Taxes	.5	.2
	25.5	13.8	11.7	2.7		All Other Non-Current	6.2	9.5
	38.2	36.3	44.1	50.3		Net Worth	44.8	38.4
	100.0	100.0	100.0	100.0		Total Liabilities & Net Worth	100.0	100.0
						INCOME DATA		
	100.0	100.0	100.0	100.0		Net Sales	100.0	100.0
	54.6	48.7	55.5	56.0		Gross Profit	54.5	48.5
	58.6	46.5	49.7	45.8		Operating Expenses	49.0	42.3
	-4.0	2.1	5.8	10.2		Operating Profit	5.5	6.2
	.4	1.2	-.8	2.0		All Other Expenses (net)	.9	1.6
	-4.4	.9	6.7	8.2		Profit Before Taxes	4.6	4.6
						RATIOS		
	4.5	4.0	3.1	2.9			3.0	2.9
	2.5	2.1	2.1	2.1		Current	1.9	2.0
	1.6	1.6	1.3	.9			1.2	1.3
	1.4	1.5	1.7	1.9			1.8	1.6
	.7	1.0	1.1	1.4		Quick	1.0	1.0
	.5	.7	.5	.5			.5	.6
	(13) 29.2	(28) 13.1	(22) 16.4	(42) 8.6			(31) 11.6	(36) 10.0
	(20) 18.5	(49) 7.4	(43) 8.4	(75) 4.8		Sales/Receivables	(54) 6.8	(57) 6.4
	(34) 10.7	(95) 3.8	(70) 5.2	(104) 3.5			(74) 4.9	(91) 4.0
	(85) 4.3	(81) 4.5	(50) 7.3	(67) 5.4			(75) 4.9	(62) 5.9
	(273) 1.3	(164) 2.2	(105) 3.5	(113) 3.2		Cost of Sales/Inventory	(161) 2.3	(151) 2.4
	(466) .8	(264) 1.4	(217) 1.7	(179) 2.0			(266) 1.4	(276) 1.3
	(22) 16.5	(22) 16.4	(28) 12.9	(31) 11.7			(30) 12.3	(24) 15.1
	(45) 8.2	(44) 8.3	(51) 7.2	(42) 8.8		Cost of Sales/Payables	(55) 6.6	(48) 7.7
	(87) 4.2	(74) 4.9	(71) 5.1	(66) 5.6			(119) 3.1	(98) 3.7
	2.5	2.5	2.3	2.5			2.7	2.6
	5.5	4.2	3.9	3.6		Sales/Working Capital	5.8	4.0
	8.5	7.9	12.1	-22.1			15.5	13.4
		10.0	18.2	12.9			7.0	10.2
		(26) 3.6	(21) 6.7	(11) 6.0		EBIT/Interest	(91) 3.2	(84) 3.6
		-2.4	2.4	2.5			1.4	.7
						Net Profit + Depr., Dep.,	5.1	8.9
						Amort./Cur. Mat. L/T/D	(20) 2.5	(20) 2.5
							1.7	1.2
	.0	.0	.1	.2			.1	.1
	.1	.1	.4	.3		Fixed/Worth	.2	.2
	.5	1.3	1.1	-2.8			1.1	1.1
	.3	.4	.7	.6			.6	.6
	1.0	1.0	1.4	1.9		Debt/Worth	1.3	1.4
	4.6	4.6	4.2	-12.2			7.7	7.7
		34.8	43.7			% Profit Before Taxes/Tangible	34.0	35.8
		(26) 8.5	(22) 10.0			Net Worth	(93) 13.5	(87) 12.3
		-3.1	3.7				2.2	1.9
	4.4	10.3	10.4	11.5		% Profit Before Taxes/Total	12.1	12.7
	-1.7	2.8	4.8	7.0		Assets	5.0	4.9
	-18.9	-3.0	2.2	.7			1.2	-.9
	UND	177.8	50.2	26.0			76.1	79.1
	69.2	34.9	18.1	16.3		Sales/Net Fixed Assets	26.4	22.3
	17.6	16.5	3.2	7.2			12.0	7.9
	3.4	2.3	1.8	1.5			2.0	2.0
	2.0	1.7	1.5	1.1		Sales/Total Assets	1.5	1.4
	1.1	1.1	1.0	.8			1.0	1.0
		.4	.6				.7	.7
		(22) 1.0	(20) 2.0			% Depr., Dep., Amort./Sales	(75) 1.5	(69) 1.7
		1.5	4.8				2.8	2.7
		1.4					2.1	2.0
		(11) 2.7				% Officers', Directors' Owners' Comp/Sales	(29) 5.3	(21) 3.6
		5.3					13.1	9.1
2814M	28743M	264770M	788939M	1180137M	647687M	Net Sales ($)	3055349M	3283561M
1495M	13686M	153043M	546223M	961895M	904589M	Total Assets ($)	2594843M	3081407M

M = $ thousand   MM = $ million
See Pages 9 through 22 for Explanation of Ratios and Data

Comparative Historical Data | Current Data Sorted by Sales

Comp 1	Comp 2	Comp 3	Type of Statement	0-1MM	1-3MM	3-5MM	5-10MM	10-25MM	25MM & OVER
23	22	20	Unqualified			1	4	2	13
21	22	17	Reviewed		1	2	4	7	3
3	2	7	Compiled	1	1			5	
11	12	9	Tax Returns	2	3	1	1	2	
34	41	40	Other	4	2	4	7	7	16
4/1/08-3/31/09 ALL	4/1/09-3/31/10 ALL	4/1/10-3/31/11 ALL		24 (4/1-9/30/10)			69 (10/1/10-3/31/11)		
92	99	93	**NUMBER OF STATEMENTS**	7	7	8	16	23	32
%	%	%	**ASSETS**	%	%	%	%	%	%
11.0	12.5	14.1	Cash & Equivalents				11.4	13.0	18.0
22.9	22.2	21.8	Trade Receivables (net)				27.4	24.0	19.7
29.3	26.3	26.9	Inventory				34.0	25.7	14.4
4.9	6.5	6.6	All Other Current				2.5	8.6	7.0
68.2	67.6	69.4	Total Current				75.3	71.3	59.2
12.4	11.6	10.9	Fixed Assets (net)				9.6	17.7	9.7
12.0	13.6	11.2	Intangibles (net)				7.3	5.3	24.1
7.4	7.2	8.5	All Other Non-Current				7.8	5.7	7.0
100.0	100.0	100.0	Total				100.0	100.0	100.0
			LIABILITIES						
9.2	8.2	6.1	Notes Payable-Short Term				7.9	3.8	4.0
1.7	2.6	4.1	Cur. Mat.-L.T.D.				1.6	1.8	8.1
11.4	10.6	13.0	Trade Payables				14.4	15.6	9.8
.2	.4	.4	Income Taxes Payable				.2	.1	.9
11.8	13.4	14.8	All Other Current				13.4	13.3	18.8
34.3	35.1	38.3	Total Current				37.7	34.6	41.6
12.3	16.0	9.9	Long-Term Debt				4.3	9.2	13.0
.3	.4	.6	Deferred Taxes				1.1	.2	1.0
14.8	12.6	17.8	All Other Non-Current				6.2	12.9	13.0
38.4	35.9	33.4	Net Worth				50.7	43.1	31.4
100.0	100.0	100.0	Total Liabilities & Net Worth				100.0	100.0	100.0
			INCOME DATA						
100.0	100.0	100.0	Net Sales				100.0	100.0	100.0
53.0	53.0	53.2	Gross Profit				45.0	53.7	55.9
49.4	50.2	49.6	Operating Expenses				43.6	49.1	48.3
3.6	2.8	3.7	Operating Profit				1.4	4.7	7.6
2.0	2.1	1.9	All Other Expenses (net)				.7	-.4	3.8
1.6	.7	1.7	Profit Before Taxes				.8	5.1	3.8
			RATIOS						
3.5	3.2	3.4	Current				4.2	4.0	2.9
2.2	2.1	2.2					2.4	2.1	2.0
1.4	1.3	1.3					1.8	1.5	.9
1.6	1.8	1.7	Quick				1.6	1.7	1.7
.9	.9	1.1					1.1	1.1	1.3
.5	.5	.5					.7	.7	.4
31 11.6	28 13.2	23 15.7	Sales/Receivables	42 8.8	28 13.2	24 15.3			
51 7.1	49 7.4	50 7.3		58 6.3	50 7.3	58 6.3			
71 5.2	83 4.4	88 4.2		86 4.2	73 5.0	93 3.9			
50 7.3	63 5.8	58 6.3	Cost of Sales/Inventory	87 4.2	90 4.1	25 14.4			
174 2.1	140 2.6	116 3.1		152 2.4	109 3.4	79 4.6			
247 1.5	246 1.5	237 1.5		248 1.5	210 1.7	135 2.7			
24 15.1	23 15.6	26 14.0	Cost of Sales/Payables	14 27.0	24 15.0	32 11.5			
51 7.2	47 7.7	47 7.8		44 8.2	47 7.8	50 7.3			
75 4.8	87 4.2	81 4.5		72 5.1	65 5.6	85 4.3			
2.7	2.6	2.3	Sales/Working Capital				2.4	2.5	2.4
5.2	4.3	4.0					4.0	6.2	4.7
10.2	11.6	10.1					7.4	9.3	NM
6.3	8.1	11.6	EBIT/Interest				9.9	19.3	17.1
(78) 2.3	(86) 2.8	(72) 4.0					(14) 4.0	(20) 6.4	(22) 6.3
.4	-1.0	.4					-3.6	1.6	2.5
6.7	15.3	13.5	Net Profit + Depr., Dep., Amort./Cur. Mat. L/T/D						
(21) 1.7	(20) 1.8	(14) 1.5							
.7	.6	-.3							
.1	.1	.1	Fixed/Worth				.0	.1	.1
.3	.3	.3					.1	.4	.3
1.0	1.6	1.3					.5	.9	-1.8
.5	.5	.6	Debt/Worth				.5	.3	.6
1.5	1.7	1.4					1.0	1.4	2.1
6.7	34.6	24.6					1.7	3.6	-4.4
19.3	24.5	35.5	% Profit Before Taxes/Tangible Net Worth				25.8	44.0	37.7
(75) 5.1	(76) 6.2	(73) 9.4					(15) 4.0	(22) 19.3	(20) 12.4
-2.6	-3.7	.0					-4.0	2.7	7.2
7.7	9.4	9.1	% Profit Before Taxes/Total Assets				8.3	25.1	9.2
2.3	2.4	3.5					2.1	4.9	4.8
-2.2	-3.4	-2.5					-3.7	2.4	1.3
37.9	55.2	75.9	Sales/Net Fixed Assets				880.5	53.7	36.9
22.7	24.6	24.1					41.9	16.5	21.7
7.4	8.2	10.0					14.2	3.5	8.8
2.2	1.8	2.1	Sales/Total Assets				2.4	2.2	1.7
1.5	1.4	1.5					1.8	1.7	1.2
1.0	1.0	.9					1.1	1.2	.8
1.0	.6	.6	% Depr., Dep., Amort./Sales					.4	1.4
(67) 1.7	(71) 1.8	(63) 1.5						(21) 1.0	(21) 2.1
3.0	2.9	2.5						4.7	2.7
3.2	3.8	1.4	% Officers', Directors' Owners' Comp/Sales						
(18) 6.3	(19) 5.0	(17) 2.9							
10.9	11.8	14.7							
2874421M	3031102M	2913090M	Net Sales ($)	3258M	13758M	32219M	115863M	377972M	2370020M
2702938M	2670146M	2580931M	Total Assets ($)	2759M	15733M	23482M	86020M	253176M	2199761M

M = $ thousand   MM = $ million
See Pages 9 through 22 for Explanation of Ratios and Data

Current Data Sorted by Assets | Comparative Historical Data

0-500M	500M-2MM	2-10MM	10-50MM	50-100MM	100-250MM	Type of Statement	4/1/06-3/31/07 ALL	4/1/07-3/31/08 ALL
		1		2		Unqualified	4	5
	2	3				Reviewed	7	4
	1	1				Compiled	2	2
	3					Tax Returns	5	6
2	8	10	2			Other	9	16
	3 (4/1-9/30/10)		32 (10/1/10-3/31/11)					
2	14	15	2	2		NUMBER OF STATEMENTS	27	33
%	%	%	%	%	%	**ASSETS**	%	%
	7.5	8.8			DATA NOT AVAILABLE	Cash & Equivalents	6.4	9.5
	56.0	41.1				Trade Receivables (net)	40.1	33.4
	.6	5.3				Inventory	3.3	7.1
	1.0	1.1				All Other Current	5.2	6.1
	65.1	56.3				Total Current	54.9	56.0
	5.4	21.0				Fixed Assets (net)	31.5	21.3
	8.4	8.9				Intangibles (net)	6.9	13.6
	21.0	13.8				All Other Non-Current	6.8	9.0
	100.0	100.0				Total	100.0	100.0
						LIABILITIES		
	4.1	7.7				Notes Payable-Short Term	8.2	21.6
	.5	4.1				Cur. Mat.-L.T.D.	2.2	3.1
	14.7	15.2				Trade Payables	15.4	13.2
	.0	.0				Income Taxes Payable	.0	.0
	65.0	26.0				All Other Current	21.4	17.4
	84.3	52.9				Total Current	47.2	55.5
	8.3	9.5				Long-Term Debt	26.1	25.9
	.0	.1				Deferred Taxes	.1	.1
	89.2	11.8				All Other Non-Current	10.8	8.8
	-81.8	25.6				Net Worth	15.7	9.8
	100.0	100.0				Total Liabilties & Net Worth	100.0	100.0
						INCOME DATA		
	100.0	100.0				Net Sales	100.0	100.0
						Gross Profit		
	95.1	88.2				Operating Expenses	98.6	94.2
	4.9	11.8				Operating Profit	1.4	5.8
	.9	2.5				All Other Expenses (net)	2.5	1.5
	4.0	9.3				Profit Before Taxes	-1.1	4.3
						RATIOS		
	1.8	2.0					1.9	1.8
	.8	1.0				Current	1.4	1.1
	.4	.7					.7	.7
	1.8	1.5					1.7	1.5
	.8	.8				Quick	1.2	.8
	.4	.6					.6	.5
	54 6.7	49 7.4					20 17.9	14 25.3
	138 2.6	60 6.1				Sales/Receivables	53 6.9	41 9.0
	241 1.5	171 2.1					71 5.2	63 5.8
						Cost of Sales/Inventory		
						Cost of Sales/Payables		
	7.2	8.8					11.3	9.3
	-7.1	-140.6				Sales/Working Capital	34.8	80.9
	-1.6	-8.1					-40.2	-23.2
		21.4					16.9	13.1
		(11) 7.1				EBIT/Interest	(22) 4.5	(30) 4.7
		1.1					-.2	.4
						Net Profit + Depr., Dep., Amort./Cur. Mat. L/T/D		
	.0	.1					.5	.3
	.0	1.1				Fixed/Worth	1.5	1.6
	NM	7.2					-2.5	-.9
	2.7	1.0					.7	1.7
	-3.8	4.1				Debt/Worth	4.5	6.9
	-1.3	37.2					-4.8	-4.9
		128.6					30.1	67.9
		(13) 39.4				% Profit Before Taxes/Tangible Net Worth	(18) 19.0	(18) 47.6
		8.7					-1.2	15.6
	25.1	15.8					17.0	24.3
	.5	7.2				% Profit Before Taxes/Total Assets	3.2	12.2
	-17.6	.2					-13.7	-1.3
	UND	162.7					32.4	43.3
	UND	15.7				Sales/Net Fixed Assets	15.4	17.6
	38.2	4.5					5.0	10.3
	2.5	3.3					5.9	5.4
	1.4	2.0				Sales/Total Assets	3.4	3.0
	.7	.9					1.9	1.5
		.8					1.0	1.2
		(11) 1.7				% Depr., Dep., Amort./Sales	(21) 1.8	(24) 1.9
		2.6					4.3	3.9
							1.4	
						% Officers', Directors' Owners' Comp/Sales	(11) 8.5	
							9.8	
1487M	36104M	126101M	138430M	245005M		Net Sales ($)	1480752M	1398945M
343M	17116M	69770M	52631M	177707M		Total Assets ($)	552469M	871888M

M = $ thousand MM = $ million

See Pages 9 through 22 for Explanation of Ratios and Data

Comparative Historical Data

Current Data Sorted by Sales

									Type of Statement												
	4		4		3				Unqualified										1		2
	4		5		5				Reviewed										3		
	5		2		2				Compiled			1			1						
	8		3		3				Tax Returns			1			1				1		
	16		11		22				Other	1	1								1		1
	4/1/08-		4/1/09-		4/1/10-					6	7	1			3				4		1
	3/31/09		3/31/10		3/31/11							3 (4/1-9/30/10)				32 (10/1/10-3/31/11)					
	ALL		ALL		ALL					0-1MM	1-3MM	3-5MM			5-10MM		10-25MM			25MM & OVER	
	37		25		35				NUMBER OF STATEMENTS	7	8	3			5		9			3	
	%		%		%				ASSETS	%	%	%			%		%			%	
	13.3		11.6		8.5				Cash & Equivalents												
	29.3		31.6		45.1				Trade Receivables (net)												
	6.4		6.6		2.5				Inventory												
	2.8		2.5		1.8				All Other Current												
	51.8		52.2		57.8				Total Current												
	24.2		23.2		15.7				Fixed Assets (net)												
	13.6		12.7		9.1				Intangibles (net)												
	10.3		11.8		17.4				All Other Non-Current												
	100.0		100.0		100.0				Total												
									LIABILITIES												
	4.4		8.1		6.8				Notes Payable-Short Term												
	4.2		5.6		3.5				Cur. Mat.-L.T.D.												
	12.5		11.9		15.2				Trade Payables												
	.0		.0		.0				Income Taxes Payable												
	19.3		21.3		42.0				All Other Current												
	40.4		46.9		67.5				Total Current												
	20.9		21.9		15.2				Long-Term Debt												
	.1		.2		.1				Deferred Taxes												
	10.6		10.6		44.7				All Other Non-Current												
	28.0		20.4		-27.5				Net Worth												
	100.0		100.0		100.0				Total Liabilties & Net Worth												
									INCOME DATA												
	100.0		100.0		100.0				Net Sales												
									Gross Profit												
	93.3		97.4		92.7				Operating Expenses												
	6.7		2.6		7.3				Operating Profit												
	2.0		1.6		1.6				All Other Expenses (net)												
	4.7		.9		5.7				Profit Before Taxes												
									RATIOS												
	2.0		1.9		1.8																
	1.4		1.1		.9				Current												
	.9		.7		.6																
	1.5		1.5		1.5																
	1.2		.9		.8				Quick												
	.8		.6		.5																
22	16.4	26	14.2	37	9.8																
42	8.6	46	7.9	67	5.5				Sales/Receivables												
57	6.4	85	4.3	212	1.7																
									Cost of Sales/Inventory												
									Cost of Sales/Payables												
	8.8		8.1		8.8																
	23.0		49.7		-40.1				Sales/Working Capital												
	-65.1		-10.7		-4.2																
	9.4		16.0		20.5																
(32)	2.1	(20)	3.5	(20)	4.2				EBIT/Interest												
	-7.2		.1		.0																
									Net Profit + Depr., Dep., Amort./Cur. Mat. L/T/D												
	.2		.5		.0																
	1.2		4.4		1.0				Fixed/Worth												
	NM		-.8		42.4																
	.8		1.0		2.6																
	2.9		7.9		53.1				Debt/Worth												
	NM		-10.3		-2.5																
	112.1		79.5		100.7				% Profit Before Taxes/Tangible Net Worth												
(28)	20.7	(17)	25.2	(19)	38.0																
	-10.7		-68.5		-4.6																
	28.4		13.1		23.7				% Profit Before Taxes/Total Assets												
	3.5		5.2		3.3																
	-5.7		-2.6		-9.3																
	59.0		36.7		UND				Sales/Net Fixed Assets												
	14.9		14.6		38.1																
	5.9		5.1		8.5																
	4.1		4.2		3.3				Sales/Total Assets												
	2.8		2.7		1.7																
	1.4		1.2		.9																
	.7		.9		.4				% Depr., Dep., Amort./Sales												
(24)	2.4	(18)	2.4	(18)	1.7																
	4.6		5.3		2.8																
									% Officers', Directors' Owners' Comp/Sales												
	1129280M		721265M		547127M				Net Sales ($)	4565M	14796M	11052M			32707M		116575M			367432M	
	717157M		656929M		317567M				Total Assets ($)	5252M	20117M	12059M			15636M		68612M			195891M	

© RMA 2011   **M = $ thousand   MM = $ million**
See Pages 9 through 22 for Explanation of Ratios and Data

Current Data Sorted by Assets   Comparative Historical Data

Type of Statement

0-500M	500M-2MM	2-10MM	10-50MM	50-100MM	100-250MM		4/1/06-3/31/07 ALL	4/1/07-3/31/08 ALL
	1	4	4	3	5	Unqualified	20	10
	2	7	2			Reviewed	15	14
1	1	1				Compiled	6	4
2	3	1				Tax Returns	7	5
3	3	5	5	5	2	Other	26	30
	10 (4/1-9/30/10)		50 (10/1/10-3/31/11)				4/1/06-3/31/07 ALL	4/1/07-3/31/08 ALL
6	10	18	11	8	7	**NUMBER OF STATEMENTS**	74	63
%	%	%	%	%	%	**ASSETS**	%	%
	12.2	13.9	28.3			Cash & Equivalents	13.5	12.0
	46.6	25.9	17.0			Trade Receivables (net)	29.8	26.9
	24.4	11.3	9.5			Inventory	13.0	15.3
	2.0	4.8	5.7			All Other Current	4.2	4.9
	85.2	55.9	60.5			Total Current	60.6	59.1
	4.0	22.3	8.6			Fixed Assets (net)	18.6	16.3
	5.7	16.3	27.6			Intangibles (net)	11.0	11.5
	5.1	5.5	3.3			All Other Non-Current	9.8	13.1
	100.0	100.0	100.0			Total	100.0	100.0
						LIABILITIES		
	15.2	7.8	2.5			Notes Payable-Short Term	10.8	10.3
	.8	2.4	3.5			Cur. Mat.-L.T.D.	4.9	2.7
	21.1	10.8	13.7			Trade Payables	14.6	11.2
	.1	.4	3.2			Income Taxes Payable	.2	.6
	8.8	10.7	17.7			All Other Current	18.9	17.6
	46.1	32.1	40.6			Total Current	49.3	42.4
	10.0	9.6	11.2			Long-Term Debt	17.3	17.0
	.0	.6	.5			Deferred Taxes	.6	.5
	20.3	10.9	9.1			All Other Non-Current	12.6	13.4
	23.7	46.8	38.7			Net Worth	20.2	26.7
	100.0	100.0	100.0			Total Liabilties & Net Worth	100.0	100.0
						INCOME DATA		
	100.0	100.0	100.0			Net Sales	100.0	100.0
	51.3	51.9	60.7			Gross Profit	52.1	49.2
	44.8	45.7	50.7			Operating Expenses	45.7	42.1
	6.5	6.3	10.0			Operating Profit	6.4	7.1
	.6	1.7	4.2			All Other Expenses (net)	1.4	1.1
	5.9	4.6	5.9			Profit Before Taxes	5.0	6.1
						RATIOS		
	2.9	4.0	3.2				2.4	2.5
	1.9	1.5	1.4			Current	1.5	1.3
	1.2	1.1	.9				.9	1.1
	2.8	3.6	1.7				1.8	1.5
	1.2	1.2	1.3			Quick	.9	1.0
	.6	.8	.5				.6	.6
27 13.3		32 11.5	21 17.2				29 12.4	29 12.5
49 7.5		53 6.9	34 10.9			Sales/Receivables	47 7.7	46 8.0
69 5.3		90 4.1	38 9.6				66 5.5	62 5.8
0 UND		0 UND	0 UND				3 134.1	2 169.1
24 15.0		11 34.7	7 49.8			Cost of Sales/Inventory	27 13.7	32 11.2
65 5.6		90 4.0	68 5.3				72 5.0	105 3.5
16 23.3		14 25.8	16 22.2				21 17.7	17 21.6
42 8.8		29 12.8	65 5.6			Cost of Sales/Payables	43 8.6	37 9.9
211 1.7		84 4.4	99 3.7				75 4.9	53 6.9
	4.4	3.2	4.2				5.1	5.9
	12.2	8.3	15.1			Sales/Working Capital	14.0	18.1
	27.8	140.4	-93.7				-44.6	110.4
	35.9	31.3					7.3	12.5
	9.6	(15) 6.3				EBIT/Interest	(61) 3.3	(51) 4.7
	3.5	.9					1.1	1.2
						Net Profit + Depr., Dep.,	14.3	4.0
						Amort./Cur. Mat. L/T/D	(14) 2.6	(14) 2.3
							1.4	.6
	.0	.1	.2				.2	.1
	.2	.8	1.0			Fixed/Worth	.8	.6
	.5	NM	-.1				-1.9	-3.1
	2.6	.6	.5				1.0	.7
	4.4	1.7	7.2			Debt/Worth	3.1	2.3
	NM	NM	-1.9				-13.1	-69.0
		69.8				% Profit Before Taxes/Tangible	79.1	73.6
		(14) 23.1				Net Worth	(51) 42.8	(47) 35.2
		1.3					8.3	7.9
	42.3	13.6	33.0			% Profit Before Taxes/Total	18.5	27.1
	18.3	6.6	3.2			Assets	7.8	8.4
	2.5	.6	-.2				.4	1.9
	388.9	103.3	65.9				91.2	49.9
	142.9	14.4	42.0			Sales/Net Fixed Assets	15.4	21.0
	39.4	5.2	17.3				7.7	6.9
	4.7	2.2	2.2				2.8	3.1
	3.7	1.7	1.9			Sales/Total Assets	2.1	2.1
	2.3	1.2	1.0				1.3	1.3
		.6					1.3	.7
		(12) 1.1				% Depr., Dep., Amort./Sales	(48) 2.5	(52) 1.7
		2.7					4.6	3.4
							4.1	2.0
						% Officers', Directors' Owners' Comp/Sales	(15) 6.2	(15) 5.2
							12.7	8.4
9004M	44802M	168433M	449663M	773643M	886116M	Net Sales ($)	2770868M	2019283M
1463M	11624M	99013M	236678M	581913M	1056107M	Total Assets ($)	1776051M	1452575M

M = $ thousand   MM = $ million
See Pages 9 through 22 for Explanation of Ratios and Data

Comparative Historical Data | Current Data Sorted by Sales

			Type of Statement	1	2	2	2		10
13	17	17	Unqualified		1	2	2	2	10
8	9	11	Reviewed	1		1	5	2	2
5	2	3	Compiled	1	1			1	
8	3	6	Tax Returns		2	2	2		
28	29	23	Other		5	1	1	5	11
4/1/08-3/31/09 ALL	4/1/09-3/31/10 ALL	4/1/10-3/31/11 ALL		10 (4/1-9/30/10)			50 (10/1/10-3/31/11)		
				0-1MM	1-3MM	3-5MM	5-10MM	10-25MM	25MM & OVER
62	60	60	NUMBER OF STATEMENTS	2	9	6	10	10	23
%	%	%	ASSETS	%	%	%	%	%	%
13.0	13.7	17.8	Cash & Equivalents				9.3	22.8	20.8
26.5	25.2	25.5	Trade Receivables (net)				29.1	30.0	17.8
14.6	12.1	13.4	Inventory				9.1	17.6	11.2
4.8	5.2	5.7	All Other Current				1.9	7.7	6.3
59.0	56.2	62.3	Total Current				49.5	78.1	56.2
16.8	16.4	13.3	Fixed Assets (net)				17.3	11.8	10.9
13.7	19.7	17.2	Intangibles (net)				27.0	3.2	24.7
10.6	7.7	7.2	All Other Non-Current				6.2	7.0	8.1
100.0	100.0	100.0	Total				100.0	100.0	100.0
			LIABILITIES						
9.7	7.2	9.0	Notes Payable-Short Term				11.8	5.4	3.5
3.9	2.7	2.2	Cur. Mat.-L.T.D.				4.1	.5	3.1
14.5	15.0	14.7	Trade Payables				10.6	12.3	11.8
.9	.2	.8	Income Taxes Payable				.1	.2	1.7
15.7	15.9	16.0	All Other Current				7.1	14.5	19.9
44.7	40.9	42.8	Total Current				33.7	32.9	40.0
16.8	13.7	11.2	Long-Term Debt				12.0	7.7	13.2
.9	.8	.4	Deferred Taxes				.5	.0	.5
11.2	17.2	13.6	All Other Non-Current				14.3	.2	9.6
26.4	27.5	32.0	Net Worth				39.5	59.2	36.6
100.0	100.0	100.0	Total Liabilities & Net Worth				100.0	100.0	100.0
			INCOME DATA						
100.0	100.0	100.0	Net Sales				100.0	100.0	100.0
50.9	52.0	55.5	Gross Profit				46.0	58.7	56.6
46.2	47.0	47.9	Operating Expenses				40.2	51.0	46.6
4.6	5.0	7.6	Operating Profit				5.8	7.7	10.0
1.8	3.0	2.5	All Other Expenses (net)				1.4	1.1	4.2
2.8	2.0	5.1	Profit Before Taxes				4.4	6.6	5.7
			RATIOS						
2.4	2.1	2.5					2.1	7.3	1.7
1.4	1.4	1.4	Current				1.5	2.9	1.4
.9	1.0	1.0					1.0	1.3	1.0
1.4	1.5	1.6					2.0	4.8	1.4
.9	1.0	1.0	Quick				1.1	1.5	.8
.5	.6	.6					.8	.9	.4
26 13.9	32 11.3	26 14.0					27 13.5	24 15.2	34 10.9
48 7.5	44 8.2	41 8.8	Sales/Receivables				46 8.0	41 9.0	42 8.7
65 5.6	64 5.7	65 5.6					66 5.6	61 6.0	68 5.4
0 UND	0 UND	0 UND					0 UND	0 UND	0 UND
31 11.8	15 25.1	20 18.2	Cost of Sales/Inventory				18 19.9	15 24.3	34 10.7
128 2.9	77 4.7	88 4.1					29 12.4	297 1.2	85 4.3
18 20.5	17 22.1	16 22.8					15 24.3	20 18.2	20 18.1
30 12.1	42 8.6	45 8.1	Cost of Sales/Payables				26 13.8	44 8.2	55 6.6
89 4.1	82 4.5	91 4.0					52 7.0	97 3.8	99 3.7
4.9	5.6	4.3					5.1	2.5	5.0
15.1	16.6	15.8	Sales/Working Capital				16.4	4.8	15.1
-36.0	-78.4	201.2					NM	71.9	-421.5
6.1	8.9	22.1							14.5
(48) 3.2	(53) 3.2	(49) 5.1	EBIT/Interest					(19)	3.8
.3		.9							.4
5.8	6.8	5.4	Net Profit + Depr., Dep.,						
(16) 1.0	(12) 4.1	(14) 2.0	Amort./Cur. Mat. L/T/D						
.1	1.1	.5							
.2	.2	.1					.5	.0	.3
1.1	1.6	.6	Fixed/Worth				1.1	.1	1.2
-1.0	-.7	NM					-.4	.7	-.3
1.0	1.3	1.0					1.8	.2	1.5
5.0	6.5	6.3	Debt/Worth				3.2	.5	7.2
-8.2	-4.0	-9.3					-10.8	2.7	-4.9
111.8	80.8	110.5	% Profit Before Taxes/Tangible					108.9	132.6
(42) 23.9	(37) 18.0	(41) 24.7	Net Worth					23.1	(15) 64.3
1.3	-6.5	3.4						5.4	4.6
15.9	15.2	19.6					13.3	20.3	27.1
5.7	5.2	6.8	% Profit Before Taxes/Total Assets				5.8	7.9	7.0
-2.3	-6.4	.3					2.2	2.9	-2.3
72.0	61.3	107.3					115.0	104.3	44.7
16.2	19.9	27.7	Sales/Net Fixed Assets				26.8	36.7	20.2
6.9	6.4	6.4					5.5	6.6	6.3
3.1	2.7	2.9					3.6	2.8	2.1
1.8	1.9	1.8	Sales/Total Assets				1.9	1.9	1.4
1.3	1.1	1.0					1.1	1.2	.9
.8	.7	.7							1.7
(44) 2.3	(41) 1.9	(37) 1.5	% Depr., Dep., Amort./Sales					(14)	3.2
3.5	3.5	3.3							6.3
2.6		2.6							
(16) 3.8	(16)	3.6	% Officers', Directors' Owners' Comp/Sales						
9.7		10.1							
2466502M	1988380M	2331661M	Net Sales ($)	912M	17826M	23296M	79054M	143492M	2067081M
1420493M	1673610M	1986798M	Total Assets ($)	649M	7859M	13955M	52280M	115795M	1796260M

© RMA 2011

M = $ thousand   MM = $ million
See Pages 9 through 22 for Explanation of Ratios and Data

Current Data Sorted by Assets — **Comparative Historical Data**

0-500M	500M-2MM	2-10MM	10-50MM	50-100MM	100-250MM	Type of Statement	4/1/06-3/31/07 ALL	4/1/07-3/31/08 ALL
		14	26	17	32	Unqualified	46	71
	4	5	4	1		Reviewed	12	17
2	4	4	1			Compiled	12	17
7	10	4				Tax Returns	9	15
4	18	29	40	19	27	Other	82	97
	52 (4/1-9/30/10)		220 (10/1/10-3/31/11)					
13	36	56	71	37	59	NUMBER OF STATEMENTS	161	217
%	%	%	%	%	%	ASSETS	%	%
38.3	23.1	23.1	31.0	23.3	14.6	Cash & Equivalents	22.2	24.9
29.3	32.4	36.7	24.3	17.3	13.8	Trade Receivables (net)	32.9	28.7
3.0	2.4	1.2	2.6	2.7	.6	Inventory	2.2	1.8
1.2	7.5	8.9	6.7	8.1	5.4	All Other Current	4.8	4.3
71.9	65.6	70.0	64.7	51.3	34.4	Total Current	62.1	59.7
6.9	17.2	10.4	9.4	7.6	5.0	Fixed Assets (net)	11.4	10.2
8.1	6.8	11.8	18.0	34.9	51.8	Intangibles (net)	19.7	22.5
12.9	10.5	7.8	7.9	6.2	8.8	All Other Non-Current	6.8	7.6
100.0	100.0	100.0	100.0	100.0	100.0	Total	100.0	100.0
						LIABILITIES		
31.9	10.7	6.2	3.0	.2	.5	Notes Payable-Short Term	6.2	5.4
.0	6.0	10.0	2.7	4.4	2.0	Cur. Mat.-L.T.D.	3.2	2.8
15.5	11.9	14.1	8.9	5.1	5.4	Trade Payables	10.6	9.2
.0	.1	1.6	1.8	.4	.5	Income Taxes Payable	.7	.7
8.7	25.5	37.4	38.3	29.9	23.5	All Other Current	26.5	25.0
56.2	54.2	69.3	54.7	40.0	31.9	Total Current	47.1	43.0
18.8	16.5	5.2	17.2	20.7	24.6	Long-Term Debt	9.3	16.8
.2	.3	.2	.9	1.1	3.4	Deferred Taxes	.3	.6
2.0	9.4	8.9	11.3	14.1	15.1	All Other Non-Current	17.4	13.5
22.8	19.6	16.4	16.0	24.1	25.0	Net Worth	25.8	26.1
100.0	100.0	100.0	100.0	100.0	100.0	Total Liabilties & Net Worth	100.0	100.0
						INCOME DATA		
100.0	100.0	100.0	100.0	100.0	100.0	Net Sales	100.0	100.0
						Gross Profit		
88.0	92.4	94.4	94.6	89.3	93.1	Operating Expenses	95.7	94.1
12.0	7.6	5.6	5.4	10.7	6.9	Operating Profit	4.3	5.9
2.7	3.2	.4	2.9	6.4	6.5	All Other Expenses (net)	1.2	2.1
9.3	4.4	5.2	2.5	4.4	.4	Profit Before Taxes	3.2	3.8
						RATIOS		
8.4	3.0	2.2	1.9	1.8	1.5	Current	2.9	2.2
1.3	1.6	1.2	1.2	1.2	1.1		1.5	1.4
1.1	.8	.8	.8	.9	.8		1.0	.9
8.4	2.5	1.9	1.7	1.5	1.2	Quick	2.4	2.1
1.3	1.4	1.0	1.0	1.0	.9		1.3	1.2
1.0	.6	.6	.6	.6	.6		.8	.7
0 UND	12 31.7	36 10.1	36 10.0	45 8.1	47 7.7	Sales/Receivables	42 8.6	41 9.0
27 13.6	45 8.1	58 6.3	56 6.5	61 6.0	62 5.9		67 5.4	68 5.4
40 9.0	70 5.2	82 4.5	73 5.0	97 3.8	82 4.5		86 4.3	90 4.1
						Cost of Sales/Inventory		
						Cost of Sales/Payables		
7.2	5.5	5.2	5.4	3.0	6.7	Sales/Working Capital	3.9	3.4
45.9	12.1	28.7	14.9	13.2	30.2		8.6	9.3
UND	-44.3	-15.3	-11.5	-15.6	-8.2		-110.3	-19.7
	21.2	48.9	13.3	7.0	2.7	EBIT/Interest	15.8	13.5
	(23) 8.8	(36) 4.1	(54) 3.5	(31) 2.3	(49) .9		(112) 3.3	(153) 3.2
	-1.1	-1.2	-4.2	-.9	-1.8		-1.8	-.9
			4.6	2.8		Net Profit + Depr., Dep., Amort./Cur. Mat. L/T/D	7.8	10.1
		(18) 1.4	(14) 1.3				(23) .9	(37) 4.3
		.4	.2				-2.4	1.0
.0	.1	.1	.2	.4	.3	Fixed/Worth	.1	.1
.0	.4	.4	1.0	-.4	-.1		.4	.6
.0	NM	-6.3	-.1	-.1	.0		-.8	-.4
.1	.7	1.0	1.4	2.6	4.0	Debt/Worth	.9	.9
1.7	1.7	3.9	8.4	-7.4	-2.0		2.6	4.6
NM	NM	-15.0	-3.4	-1.8	-1.4		-6.0	-3.9
968.7	82.1	146.1	73.2	111.4	33.1	% Profit Before Taxes/Tangible Net Worth	57.5	56.7
(10) 99.1	(27) 44.1	(39) 33.1	(42) 18.7	(17) 22.7	(19) 5.1		(112) 21.9	(135) 26.5
-24.0	3.0	17.9	-16.4	.7	-8.5		-2.3	-1.1
92.0	32.9	19.0	17.0	12.4	5.5	% Profit Before Taxes/Total Assets	19.5	19.2
22.6	10.6	10.7	6.2	4.9	-.3		5.5	6.2
-29.3	-1.2	-.6	-5.6	-4.1	-7.5		-4.7	-3.8
UND	103.7	85.8	53.7	34.5	37.2	Sales/Net Fixed Assets	50.2	47.5
999.8	39.8	31.4	26.8	16.4	22.7		25.4	21.2
108.0	15.7	15.1	11.4	9.3	12.5		12.9	12.3
14.9	4.3	3.1	2.1	1.1	1.0	Sales/Total Assets	2.8	2.3
4.6	3.1	2.0	1.5	.8	.6		1.6	1.4
3.1	2.2	1.4	1.1	.6	.4		.9	.8
	.5	.4	1.1	1.9	2.7	% Depr., Dep., Amort./Sales	.9	.8
	(19) 1.5	(33) 1.3	(48) 2.7	(23) 4.3	(13) 3.6		(105) 2.0	(124) 2.1
	5.1	2.7	5.7	7.2	4.2		4.1	4.4
	2.9	3.5				% Officers', Directors' Owners' Comp/Sales	3.5	5.5
	(15) 6.3	(11) 7.6					(22) 12.7	(30) 9.7
	10.7	11.4					24.2	18.9
23241M	135220M	642386M	3114515M	2548082M	6738043M	Net Sales ($)	6142797M	9940731M
3159M	42463M	290756M	1898208M	2604550M	9439953M	Total Assets ($)	6005632M	10928344M

© RMA 2011

M = $ thousand   MM = $ million

See Pages 9 through 22 for Explanation of Ratios and Data

Comparative Historical Data | Current Data Sorted by Sales

Hist 4/1/08-3/31/09 ALL	Hist 4/1/09-3/31/10 ALL	Hist 4/1/10-3/31/11 ALL	Type of Statement	0-1MM	1-3MM	3-5MM	5-10MM	10-25MM	25MM & OVER
76	86	89	Unqualified		4	1	5	18	65
14	17	14	Reviewed		2		2	4	4
8	6	11	Compiled	2	1	2	4		2
17	15	21	Tax Returns	4	6	5	3	3	
122	135	137	Other	2	10	9	22	19	75
				52 (4/1-9/30/10)		220 (10/1/10-3/31/11)			
237	259	272	**NUMBER OF STATEMENTS**	8	21	17	36	44	146
%	%	%	**ASSETS**	%	%	%	%	%	%
25.9	26.2	24.1	Cash & Equivalents		22.2	26.1	27.3	24.6	23.0
25.7	24.2	24.9	Trade Receivables (net)		33.8	27.0	31.8	32.3	20.0
1.6	1.7	1.9	Inventory		.6	2.4	2.8	1.3	1.9
5.2	5.8	6.9	All Other Current		6.1	12.7	6.0	7.0	6.9
58.4	57.8	57.8	Total Current		62.7	68.2	67.9	65.3	51.8
10.0	10.7	9.3	Fixed Assets (net)		14.3	9.0	12.3	9.1	7.2
23.8	22.1	24.4	Intangibles (net)		9.1	20.2	8.5	16.1	34.1
7.8	9.4	8.4	All Other Non-Current		13.9	2.6	11.4	9.6	6.9
100.0	100.0	100.0	Total		100.0	100.0	100.0	100.0	100.0
			LIABILITIES						
7.3	6.5	5.1	Notes Payable-Short Term		25.0	9.8	5.1	3.9	1.9
2.6	4.0	4.6	Cur. Mat.-L.T.D.		1.1	10.1	2.9	11.9	2.9
7.2	5.9	9.4	Trade Payables		13.1	17.3	8.5	11.9	7.8
.6	.7	1.0	Income Taxes Payable		.1	.8	1.8	.9	1.0
27.2	31.8	30.6	All Other Current		19.1	35.6	37.2	34.6	30.3
44.8	49.0	50.7	Total Current		58.4	73.5	55.4	63.3	43.9
15.8	16.8	16.8	Long-Term Debt		18.8	6.3	3.8	8.3	21.7
1.1	1.1	1.2	Deferred Taxes		.6	.0	.5	.4	2.0
10.6	9.5	11.3	All Other Non-Current		4.4	13.3	7.7	12.3	12.5
27.7	23.7	19.9	Net Worth		17.8	6.9	32.6	15.8	19.9
100.0	100.0	100.0	Total Liabilities & Net Worth		100.0	100.0	100.0	100.0	100.0
			INCOME DATA						
100.0	100.0	100.0	Net Sales		100.0	100.0	100.0	100.0	100.0
			Gross Profit						
94.8	92.9	92.9	Operating Expenses		98.5	95.7	90.5	95.9	92.1
5.2	7.1	7.1	Operating Profit		1.5	4.3	9.5	4.1	7.9
2.7	3.8	3.7	All Other Expenses (net)		.4	.1	1.6	2.3	5.0
2.5	3.4	3.4	Profit Before Taxes		1.1	4.3	7.9	1.7	2.9
			RATIOS						
2.6	2.4	2.0	Current		2.8	2.3	2.3	2.1	1.8
1.3	1.3	1.2			1.4	1.5	1.3	1.1	1.2
.9	.8	.8			.9	.6	.7	.8	.8
2.1	2.1	1.6	Quick		2.8	2.1	1.9	1.9	1.4
1.2	1.0	1.0			1.2	.8	1.3	.9	1.0
.7	.6	.6			.7	.5	.6	.6	.6
40 9.0	39 9.5	36 10.1	Sales/Receivables	33 11.1	13 27.3	17 21.7	47 7.8	42 8.6	
61 6.0	59 6.2	56 6.5		61 6.0	36 10.1	52 7.0	61 6.0	58 6.3	
81 4.5	80 4.6	77 4.7		95 3.9	60 6.1	69 5.3	83 4.4	77 4.7	
			Cost of Sales/Inventory						
			Cost of Sales/Payables						
4.0	4.5	5.5	Sales/Working Capital		5.1	4.2	7.2	4.4	5.5
12.5	15.1	18.5			11.7	13.5	20.8	27.2	18.1
-15.5	-12.4	-17.3			-42.0	-6.6	-36.2	-18.2	-12.7
15.6	12.3	11.4	EBIT/Interest		16.6	55.7	24.1	14.0	6.9
(165) 2.3	(190) 3.1	(201) 2.3		(13) 6.8	(15) 10.9	(21) 7.4	(31) 2.7	(118) 1.4	
-1.7	-1.6	-1.3		-6.9	.6	-.3	-4.6	-1.2	
44.4	8.0	4.1	Net Profit + Depr., Dep., Amort./Cur. Mat. L/T/D					18.9	3.8
(30) 3.1	(35) 2.8	(51) 1.3					(10) 2.3	(34) 1.5	
1.6	-.3	.0						.3	.2
.2	.2	.1	Fixed/Worth		.1	.1	.1	.1	.2
.9	.7	1.0			.6	.3	.4	1.0	-2.6
-.1	-.2	-.1			-.2	-.3	1.7	-.1	-.1
.9	.9	1.3	Debt/Worth		.8	1.3	.5	1.4	1.9
5.7	5.2	8.7			1.8	12.2	1.7	7.8	-8.0
-2.6	-2.7	-2.2			-3.9	-7.5	13.3	-3.3	-1.7
56.9	74.3	97.5	% Profit Before Taxes/Tangible Net Worth		46.8	121.6	147.9	133.4	71.0
(138) 22.1	(162) 21.2	(154) 25.9		(13) 20.2	(11) 46.8	(28) 41.9	(28) 21.9	(68) 22.0	
-.2	.9	2.5		-15.2	3.0	21.8	4.4	-6.3	
18.6	16.3	16.0	% Profit Before Taxes/Total Assets		22.2	22.4	41.9	14.8	10.3
4.1	4.7	4.9			3.0	10.1	12.2	7.1	1.9
-3.2	-6.2	-4.8			-14.7	-.5	.8	-7.2	-5.2
42.2	48.2	53.7	Sales/Net Fixed Assets		310.0	190.2	84.0	53.7	42.0
22.1	19.7	27.5			25.5	50.3	28.1	30.4	22.5
12.4	11.3	14.0			10.9	40.9	14.6	16.7	11.6
2.4	2.2	2.4	Sales/Total Assets		3.4	4.2	4.0	2.5	1.8
1.3	1.2	1.4			2.2	2.7	2.6	1.4	1.0
.8	.8	.7			1.1	1.1	1.6	1.1	.6
.9	1.2	1.1	% Depr., Dep., Amort./Sales		1.1		.5	1.0	1.5
(124) 2.2	(142) 2.5	(139) 2.5			(10) 3.3	(17) 2.1	(31) 2.4	(70) 3.1	
4.1	4.7	4.6			7.4		3.6	4.2	6.1
3.8	4.2	3.2	% Officers', Directors' Owners' Comp/Sales						
(29) 8.7	(28) 9.5	(37) 7.6							
18.9	15.1	12.6							
11215388M	12382776M	13201487M	Net Sales ($)	2486M	39629M	67015M	264492M	728430M	12099435M
12148508M	14052707M	14279089M	Total Assets ($)	3174M	24326M	36727M	148516M	551806M	13514540M

M = $ thousand   MM = $ million
See Pages 9 through 22 for Explanation of Ratios and Data

Current Data Sorted by Assets   **Comparative Historical Data**

Type of Statement	0-500M	500M-2MM	2-10MM	10-50MM	50-100MM	100-250MM		137 4/1/06-3/31/07 ALL	127 4/1/07-3/31/08 ALL
Unqualified			2	6	6	3		13	17
Reviewed		7	17	5	1			23	19
Compiled	3	6	5	4				25	13
Tax Returns	16	10	8					22	26
Other	11	14	19	9	3	3		54	52
	20 (4/1-9/30/10)			**138 (10/1/10-3/31/11)**					
NUMBER OF STATEMENTS	30	37	51	24	10	6		137	127
	%	%	%	%	%	%	**ASSETS**	%	%
Cash & Equivalents	28.5	16.8	18.7	18.3	12.2			14.9	14.6
Trade Receivables (net)	22.0	21.5	28.0	16.0	9.5			26.2	26.3
Inventory	1.2	2.8	2.5	1.8	2.8			2.9	3.6
All Other Current	2.2	3.2	6.7	6.2	3.7			4.6	5.2
Total Current	53.8	44.4	56.0	42.3	28.2			48.6	49.7
Fixed Assets (net)	27.7	38.0	30.2	40.9	41.2			35.5	34.7
Intangibles (net)	6.0	7.4	6.9	8.4	18.3			6.8	5.4
All Other Non-Current	12.5	10.3	7.0	8.4	12.2			9.1	10.2
Total	100.0	100.0	100.0	100.0	100.0			100.0	100.0
							LIABILITIES		
Notes Payable-Short Term	30.5	12.4	5.6	1.6	5.3			16.3	9.9
Cur. Mat.-L.T.D.	6.6	5.7	5.2	5.3	1.6			6.7	5.1
Trade Payables	7.9	9.3	10.1	6.4	4.1			11.5	18.3
Income Taxes Payable	.2	.5	.3	.3	.0			.6	.3
All Other Current	35.4	15.5	17.6	13.1	12.8			16.8	17.6
Total Current	80.6	43.4	38.9	26.8	23.8			51.9	51.1
Long-Term Debt	41.4	19.0	17.4	23.6	34.3			22.0	23.8
Deferred Taxes	.0	.5	.3	.5	1.3			.7	.7
All Other Non-Current	6.4	10.2	3.0	15.3	34.8			15.3	13.8
Net Worth	-28.4	26.9	40.4	33.9	5.9			10.0	10.7
Total Liabilities & Net Worth	100.0	100.0	100.0	100.0	100.0			100.0	100.0
							INCOME DATA		
Net Sales	100.0	100.0	100.0	100.0	100.0			100.0	100.0
Gross Profit									
Operating Expenses	92.1	91.9	93.1	84.9	79.3			92.0	91.4
Operating Profit	7.9	8.1	6.9	15.1	20.7			8.0	8.6
All Other Expenses (net)	.4	1.0	.8	4.5	17.1			2.4	1.5
Profit Before Taxes	7.5	7.1	6.1	10.6	3.6			5.6	7.2
							RATIOS		
Current	2.3	2.7	3.6	2.8	2.8			1.9	2.4
	.9	1.0	1.8	1.4	1.5			1.1	1.3
	.3	.6	.9	.7	.6			.7	.8
Quick	2.3	1.9	2.9	2.3	2.6			1.8	2.1
	.8	.9	1.2	1.2	.9			.9	1.1
	.3	.4	.8	.5	.3			.5	.6
Sales/Receivables	0 UND	0 UND	17 21.2	23 15.9	20 18.2			15 24.8	17 21.9
	0 UND	20 18.3	38 9.6	51 7.1	23 16.2			42 8.7	47 7.7
	37 9.8	43 8.6	66 5.5	69 5.3	57 6.4			65 5.6	68 5.4
Cost of Sales/Inventory									
Cost of Sales/Payables									
Sales/Working Capital	19.7	10.4	5.0	2.7	3.5			8.1	7.5
	-86.1	594.6	10.4	5.0	17.2			76.6	22.6
	-6.3	-14.4	-77.2	-22.4	-11.7			-17.0	-30.5
EBIT/Interest	30.3	11.3	16.0	16.1				10.3	13.7
	(23) 10.1	(22) 3.3	(43) 4.5	(20) 6.1				(118) 2.9	(107) 5.1
	1.5	.7	.6	1.7				.7	1.4
Net Profit + Depr., Dep., Amort./Cur. Mat. L/T/D			9.6					5.3	3.9
			(11) 3.8					(26) 2.1	(18) 2.3
			2.9					1.1	1.4
Fixed/Worth	.1	.3	.3	.1	2.3			.4	.4
	1.2	1.8	.7	1.5	NM			1.5	1.6
	-.7	NM	3.2	31.0	-.2			28.2	8.3
Debt/Worth	1.1	.5	.5	.9	1.7			1.1	.9
	4.4	3.3	1.2	2.1	NM			3.0	3.0
	-2.4	NM	6.0	32.0	-2.7			-15.5	-115.2
% Profit Before Taxes/Tangible Net Worth	229.7	98.0	58.1	39.1				91.5	94.1
	(17) 100.0	(28) 25.3	(44) 20.3	(20) 25.1				(101) 36.1	(94) 43.3
	17.6	2.4	3.7	6.7				3.9	12.4
% Profit Before Taxes/Total Assets	58.7	22.7	18.1	21.2	9.5			26.1	31.1
	28.0	10.5	8.1	7.2	1.9			8.4	10.9
	1.5	-.2	.4	1.1	-.2			-1.3	.7
Sales/Net Fixed Assets	792.0	24.2	21.1	23.0	119.8			29.4	19.5
	39.0	9.7	9.6	2.6	1.4			8.5	9.0
	13.1	5.4	4.0	.9	1.1			3.3	3.4
Sales/Total Assets	9.9	4.0	3.0	1.4	1.6			3.6	3.2
	4.7	3.1	2.0	.9	.8			2.3	2.1
	3.2	1.8	1.4	.5	.4			1.4	1.2
% Depr., Dep., Amort./Sales	.4	1.6	1.7	4.9				2.1	1.8
	(14) .8	(27) 3.7	(45) 3.9	(16) 8.2				(95) 4.4	(89) 3.7
	4.5	7.5	7.1	21.6				8.4	7.5
% Officers', Directors' Owners' Comp/Sales	6.2	3.7	1.9					4.1	4.4
	(18) 14.3	(22) 7.1	(19) 5.2					(53) 8.7	(44) 7.0
	17.7	10.8	10.1					14.9	12.0
Net Sales ($)	43952M	116064M	576743M	536900M	701846M	874017M		2681369M	2614474M
Total Assets ($)	7025M	36725M	245788M	545729M	710749M	989633M		1969125M	2079897M

M = $ thousand   MM = $ million
See Pages 9 through 22 for Explanation of Ratios and Data

Comparative Historical Data

Current Data Sorted by Sales

Comparative Historical Data			Type of Statement	0-1MM	1-3MM	3-5MM	5-10MM	10-25MM	25MM & OVER
15	16	17	Unqualified		1		1	5	10
21	19	30	Reviewed		3	4	12	9	2
15	12	18	Compiled	2	5	1	6	3	1
23	32	34	Tax Returns	9	10	7	7	1	
52	62	59	Other	4	16	7	8	12	12
4/1/08-3/31/09 ALL	4/1/09-3/31/10 ALL	4/1/10-3/31/11 ALL		20 (4/1-9/30/10)			138 (10/1/10-3/31/11)		
126	141	158	NUMBER OF STATEMENTS	15	35	19	34	30	25
%	%	%	ASSETS	%	%	%	%	%	%
16.9	16.9	19.1	Cash & Equivalents	31.6	18.6	22.3	17.7	16.0	15.7
21.5	23.0	21.9	Trade Receivables (net)	18.9	23.9	16.6	22.5	26.2	19.2
4.1	3.7	2.8	Inventory	.0	1.0	2.1	4.2	1.8	6.8
6.0	6.7	4.8	All Other Current	4.1	.8	1.4	7.5	7.2	7.0
48.4	50.3	48.7	Total Current	54.5	44.4	42.4	51.9	51.2	48.6
36.0	36.0	33.6	Fixed Assets (net)	28.7	34.1	45.4	30.0	37.0	27.4
4.7	4.8	8.4	Intangibles (net)	11.8	7.7	3.8	7.7	5.7	15.2
10.9	8.9	9.3	All Other Non-Current	5.0	13.8	8.3	10.4	6.2	8.8
100.0	100.0	100.0	Total	100.0	100.0	100.0	100.0	100.0	100.0
			LIABILITIES						
9.9	10.3	12.4	Notes Payable-Short Term	19.9	25.4	9.3	6.0	2.1	13.1
5.5	4.9	5.2	Cur. Mat.-L.T.D.	9.9	3.8	3.4	4.6	8.8	2.2
10.9	9.3	8.8	Trade Payables	6.6	8.2	6.1	10.1	8.9	10.9
.2	.4	.3	Income Taxes Payable	.4	.2	.5	.0	.6	.1
13.1	17.0	19.3	All Other Current	19.4	19.5	33.5	15.6	17.9	14.9
39.7	41.9	45.9	Total Current	56.3	57.1	52.7	36.3	38.4	41.3
24.8	21.6	25.8	Long-Term Debt	50.9	27.4	27.2	13.7	19.9	30.8
.7	.4	.4	Deferred Taxes	.0	.4	.3	.4	.4	.5
8.9	8.0	9.6	All Other Non-Current	4.7	10.8	1.7	12.1	11.6	10.8
25.9	28.1	18.3	Net Worth	-11.8	4.4	18.1	37.4	29.7	16.6
100.0	100.0	100.0	Total Liabilities & Net Worth	100.0	100.0	100.0	100.0	100.0	100.0
			INCOME DATA						
100.0	100.0	100.0	Net Sales	100.0	100.0	100.0	100.0	100.0	100.0
			Gross Profit						
91.1	91.1	90.5	Operating Expenses	85.4	91.7	91.2	95.3	87.3	88.3
8.9	8.9	9.5	Operating Profit	14.6	8.3	8.8	4.7	12.7	11.7
3.5	2.2	3.3	All Other Expenses (net)	.5	1.6	3.7	.5	3.2	10.8
5.4	6.7	6.3	Profit Before Taxes	14.2	6.7	5.2	4.2	9.5	.8
			RATIOS						
2.3	2.9	2.7		2.9	2.1	2.6	3.7	2.5	2.7
1.3	1.3	1.2	Current	.8	.9	1.2	1.8	1.6	1.2
.7	.8	.7		.4	.4	.6	1.0	.7	.8
1.8	2.4	2.4		2.9	2.1	2.4	3.2	2.1	2.1
1.0	.9	1.0	Quick	.7	.9	1.2	1.3	1.0	.9
.4	.5	.5		.4	.3	.5	.5	.6	.5
8 44.8	7 50.4	5 69.1		0 UND	0 UND	0 UND	6 64.7	23 16.0	21 17.4
36 10.2	37 9.8	33 11.1	Sales/Receivables	0 UND	29 12.6	24 15.0	32 11.5	44 8.3	47 7.8
62 5.9	64 5.7	58 6.3		53 7.0	44 8.3	55 6.6	66 5.5	63 5.8	62 5.9
			Cost of Sales/Inventory						
			Cost of Sales/Payables						
5.9	5.9	5.4		6.8	11.9	6.1	4.3	4.9	4.4
22.1	25.1	28.0	Sales/Working Capital	-26.9	-174.4	31.7	11.3	12.1	17.2
-19.7	-16.7	-16.5		-4.5	-8.3	-16.8	NM	-32.3	-30.4
					15.7	6.8	23.0	16.0	9.3
(107) 4.2	(110) 4.3	(120) 4.5	EBIT/Interest		(25) 4.0	(14) 3.9	(27) 3.6	(25) 7.9	(20) 2.0
.9	-.1	1.0			.5	.5	.0	3.0	1.0
4.9	4.5	5.3						6.5	
(20) 2.9	(21) 2.0	(21) 3.0	Net Profit + Depr., Dep., Amort./Cur. Mat. L/T/D					(11) 3.8	
1.4	.9	1.5						2.3	
.3	.3	.2		.0	.3	.5	.2	.4	.0
1.3	.9	1.2	Fixed/Worth	.2	5.3	2.4	.7	1.1	2.2
17.2	5.7	47.2		2.1	-1.0	8.6	2.5	3.2	-3.2
.8	.6	.7		.4	1.1	1.0	.4	.6	1.7
2.7	2.0	2.9	Debt/Worth	1.9	9.8	3.3	1.1	1.2	12.9
NM	19.9	-61.8		-1.6	-3.8	33.9	9.5	6.0	-4.0
99.9	67.9	70.3			589.2	124.5	41.9	61.4	71.7
(95) 26.8	(113) 21.1	(116) 26.3	% Profit Before Taxes/Tangible Net Worth		(21) 41.9	(17) 18.3	(29) 12.4	(25) 29.4	(15) 49.0
7.6	2.2	4.4			-.1	5.8	-4.7	18.7	15.8
17.9	21.3	22.9		41.7	37.5	18.6	12.9	23.5	12.9
6.3	6.7	9.1	% Profit Before Taxes/Total Assets	13.3	20.6	7.0	3.9	12.9	4.4
-2.7	-1.5	.0		.0	.0	.2	-1.6	5.7	-.4
25.2	23.8	38.7		UND	48.3	16.5	30.0	15.6	225.7
7.9	7.2	10.5	Sales/Net Fixed Assets	15.9	14.5	9.6	13.4	7.0	41.9
2.8	2.6	3.3		3.5	6.3	2.3	3.9	2.5	1.7
3.1	3.3	3.7		4.4	4.7	3.6	3.5	3.1	2.5
1.9	1.9	2.1	Sales/Total Assets	2.4	3.2	2.3	1.9	1.8	1.4
1.0	1.1	1.2		.8	2.0	.8	1.2	1.1	.7
1.7	2.1	1.1			.7	1.2	1.5	1.8	
(85) 3.7	(90) 4.7	(108) 3.9	% Depr., Dep., Amort./Sales		(20) 2.2	(18) 3.8	(25) 5.9	(29) 4.9	
8.5	10.1	7.6			7.4	6.6	8.3	8.4	
5.1	5.0	4.0			5.7	4.1	1.9		
(48) 6.5	(50) 8.3	(64) 7.1	% Officers', Directors' Owners' Comp/Sales		(22) 10.5	(10) 8.3	(17) 6.2		
10.3	12.7	13.8			15.8	16.4	13.1		
2641816M	2440448M	2849522M	Net Sales ($)	7104M	65016M	72315M	242484M	467443M	1995160M
2289836M	1998862M	2535649M	Total Assets ($)	6103M	25515M	89060M	194483M	422100M	1798388M

M = $ thousand   MM = $ million
See Pages 9 through 22 for Explanation of Ratios and Data

Current Data Sorted by Assets   Comparative Historical Data

0-500M	500M-2MM	2-10MM	10-50MM	50-100MM	100-250MM	Type of Statement	4/1/06-3/31/07 ALL	4/1/07-3/31/08 ALL
		2	9	5	1	Unqualified	19	14
		2	3			Reviewed	12	11
3	7	8	4			Compiled	18	10
10	15	5	2			Tax Returns	18	15
3	6	11	16	7		Other	43	37
	6 (4/1-9/30/10)		113 (10/1/10-3/31/11)					
16	28	28	34	12	1	NUMBER OF STATEMENTS	110	87
%	%	%	%	%	%	**ASSETS**	%	%
30.4	17.8	9.1	7.1	4.4		Cash & Equivalents	11.9	11.2
7.4	.2	3.7	1.5	1.3		Trade Receivables (net)	1.5	.4
5.8	.5	1.0	.7	.4		Inventory	.8	.9
2.2	.5	1.6	.9	1.3		All Other Current	1.5	1.7
45.8	18.9	15.4	10.3	7.5		Total Current	15.7	14.3
39.2	74.9	78.6	80.0	80.3		Fixed Assets (net)	69.7	75.2
6.4	2.5	1.6	3.7	5.9		Intangibles (net)	4.7	3.0
8.4	3.7	4.3	6.1	6.3		All Other Non-Current	9.9	7.5
100.0	100.0	100.0	100.0	100.0		Total	100.0	100.0
						LIABILITIES		
28.4	2.2	10.9	2.1	2.0		Notes Payable-Short Term	4.9	1.8
1.0	8.7	3.8	4.9	3.8		Cur. Mat.-L.T.D.	3.7	3.7
19.3	6.2	7.1	4.6	4.0		Trade Payables	6.9	7.0
.0	.0	.0	.0	.2		Income Taxes Payable	.1	.1
28.8	5.9	3.2	7.8	5.6		All Other Current	10.5	8.9
77.4	23.0	25.1	19.4	15.6		Total Current	26.0	21.4
45.1	39.7	63.8	50.6	40.5		Long-Term Debt	44.6	44.8
.0	.1	.0	.0	.0		Deferred Taxes	.1	.1
22.0	3.1	5.0	4.6	18.5		All Other Non-Current	12.5	17.4
-44.5	34.1	6.1	25.4	25.4		Net Worth	16.9	16.3
100.0	100.0	100.0	100.0	100.0		Total Liabilities & Net Worth	100.0	100.0
						INCOME DATA		
100.0	100.0	100.0	100.0	100.0		Net Sales	100.0	100.0
						Gross Profit		
93.6	89.8	84.2	87.3	92.9		Operating Expenses	87.4	93.0
6.4	10.2	15.8	12.7	7.1		Operating Profit	12.6	7.0
3.4	3.6	6.7	9.7	4.6		All Other Expenses (net)	6.6	6.8
3.0	6.6	9.1	3.0	2.5		Profit Before Taxes	6.1	.2
						RATIOS		
1.5	1.3	2.0	.8	1.1			1.3	1.3
1.0	.9	.8	.5	.5		Current	.7	.5
.3	.3	.3	.3	.3			.2	.3
1.5	1.3	1.9	.7	.8			1.1	.7
.9	.8	.6	.4	.4		Quick	.5	.4
.1	.2	.2	.2	.2			.2	.2
0 UND	0 UND	0 UND	0 UND	1 327.5			0 UND	0 UND
0 UND	0 UND	0 UND	1 279.3	4 95.3		Sales/Receivables	0 UND	0 UND
1 311.3	0 UND	0 859.3	5 77.9	5 75.2			2 200.8	2 182.4
						Cost of Sales/Inventory		
						Cost of Sales/Payables		
63.5	32.3	10.7	-32.5	42.0			28.7	123.0
-431.4	-106.0	-31.6	-12.7	-18.6		Sales/Working Capital	-29.1	-14.2
-16.9	-11.8	-11.9	-5.0	-5.4			-7.1	-6.4
	21.0	3.5	3.1	2.8			3.1	2.4
	(21) 4.8	(27) 2.3	(27) 1.7	1.9		EBIT/Interest	(84) 1.8	(69) 1.3
	.6	1.0	.6	.4			.9	.3
							2.8	4.7
						Net Profit + Depr., Dep., Amort./Cur. Mat. L/T/D	(14) 1.9 (14) 1.7	
							1.2	.7
.6	1.0	2.0	2.0	2.8			1.7	2.1
UND	3.0	3.0	4.2	9.0		Fixed/Worth	3.8	5.0
-.5	8.8	NM	10.4	44.9			-17.2	155.3
2.8	.8	1.6	1.7	1.9			1.6	1.5
-14.1	2.7	4.6	3.5	9.1		Debt/Worth	3.8	4.4
-1.7	9.6	NM	10.0	47.4			-16.7	159.6
	87.5	41.0	24.6	39.8			40.7	32.9
	(24) 34.4	(21) 16.6	(30) 9.7	(10) 3.6		% Profit Before Taxes/Tangible Net Worth	(80) 12.3	(67) 5.2
	-5.4	6.8	-3.8	-30.2			-.9	-19.6
77.2	23.5	7.3	4.5	-6.3			8.5	7.8
5.3	7.7	4.7	2.3	2.4		% Profit Before Taxes/Total Assets	3.1	1.4
-9.1	-1.2	.0	-1.0	-1.7			-.6	-4.0
227.8	5.2	1.2	1.8	1.5			3.3	2.8
41.2	1.6	.7	.9	.9		Sales/Net Fixed Assets	1.1	.9
6.5	.7	.5	.5	.5			.6	.5
15.6	2.9	1.1	1.3	1.2			2.0	1.6
4.7	1.4	.6	.8	.8		Sales/Total Assets	.8	.8
3.9	.7	.5	.3	.4			.5	.4
.5	2.9	6.3	6.2	6.1			3.9	4.2
(10) 2.3	(26) 5.4	(27) 8.8	(33) 8.9	7.1		% Depr., Dep., Amort./Sales	(96) 6.5	(83) 6.7
5.2	9.9	13.2	12.8	7.5			10.6	10.5
	1.5						2.4	1.8
	(14) 3.1					% Officers', Directors' Owners' Comp/Sales	(24) 3.6	(22) 3.7
	4.5						7.2	7.7
37136M	63087M	215716M	800859M	691270M	76368M	Net Sales ($)	2422932M	1959478M
3941M	33207M	157613M	837861M	842789M	185866M	Total Assets ($)	2489647M	2124375M

M = $ thousand   MM = $ million
See Pages 9 through 22 for Explanation of Ratios and Data

Comparative Historical Data / Current Data Sorted by Sales

Type of Statement	4/1/08-3/31/09 ALL	4/1/09-3/31/10 ALL	4/1/10-3/31/11 ALL		0-1MM	1-3MM	3-5MM	5-10MM	10-25MM	25MM & OVER
Unqualified	18	14	17					3	3	11
Reviewed	12	14	5			2		1	1	1
Compiled	16	18	22			11	4	5	2	
Tax Returns	13	21	32		12	10	6	2	1	1
Other	50	54	43		4	11	4	2	1	12
					6 (4/1-9/30/10)			113 (10/1/10-3/31/11)		
NUMBER OF STATEMENTS	109	121	119		16	34	14	13	17	25
ASSETS	%	%	%		%	%	%	%	%	%
Cash & Equivalents	7.4	9.8	13.0		11.7	9.2	31.3	18.2	6.3	10.5
Trade Receivables (net)	.9	.8	2.5		6.4	.6	.0	6.7	2.1	2.0
Inventory	1.3	1.2	1.4		.3	2.7	.4	.3	.9	1.6
All Other Current	2.4	1.8	1.2		1.1	.8	1.5	.1	1.4	1.9
Total Current	12.0	13.6	18.0		19.6	13.3	33.2	25.2	10.7	16.1
Fixed Assets (net)	77.7	75.9	73.0		73.2	78.3	61.1	56.5	84.8	72.8
Intangibles (net)	5.1	4.9	3.5		2.9	3.9	2.8	1.6	1.4	6.0
All Other Non-Current	5.1	5.5	5.5		4.1	4.5	2.8	16.7	3.0	5.0
Total	100.0	100.0	100.0		100.0	100.0	100.0	100.0	100.0	100.0
LIABILITIES										
Notes Payable-Short Term	2.5	2.7	7.7		29.4	2.0	.0	1.4	1.6	13.3
Cur. Mat.-L.T.D.	6.3	6.6	5.0		6.4	2.8	7.4	5.4	6.0	4.6
Trade Payables	5.5	8.0	7.5		.8	4.0	10.3	12.3	8.7	11.5
Income Taxes Payable	.0	.2	.0		.0	.0	.0	.0	.0	.1
All Other Current	8.8	9.9	8.8		10.5	9.3	2.3	5.1	11.5	11.0
Total Current	23.1	27.3	29.0		47.0	18.1	20.1	24.2	27.8	40.4
Long-Term Debt	46.3	42.0	49.3		68.1	50.7	44.9	38.9	57.3	37.7
Deferred Taxes	.2	.1	.0		.0	.0	.2	.0	.0	.0
All Other Non-Current	11.6	12.6	8.1		17.2	3.4	4.1	8.4	1.2	15.2
Net Worth	18.9	17.9	13.7		-32.3	27.7	30.7	28.5	13.7	6.6
Total Liabilties & Net Worth	100.0	100.0	100.0		100.0	100.0	100.0	100.0	100.0	100.0
INCOME DATA										
Net Sales	100.0	100.0	100.0		100.0	100.0	100.0	100.0	100.0	100.0
Gross Profit										
Operating Expenses	89.7	86.6	88.6		81.5	86.9	83.6	91.3	90.4	95.6
Operating Profit	10.3	13.4	11.4		18.5	13.1	16.4	8.7	9.6	4.4
All Other Expenses (net)	7.5	7.2	6.2		11.0	9.4	4.5	1.7	5.4	2.6
Profit Before Taxes	2.8	6.3	5.2		7.5	3.7	11.9	7.0	4.2	1.8
RATIOS										
Current	1.0	1.0	1.3		1.4	1.2	2.1	2.0	.8	.9
	.3	.5	.7		.5	.6	1.2	1.2	.5	.5
	.1	.2	.3		.1	.3	.7	.6	.3	.2
Quick	.8	.8	1.1		1.4	1.0	1.9	2.0	.7	.7
	(108) .2	.4	.5		.3	.5	1.1	1.2	.4	.3
	.1	.1	.2		.1	.2	.6	.6	.3	.2
Sales/Receivables	0 UND	0 UND	0 UND		0 UND	0 UND	0 UND	0 UND	0 UND	0 UND
	0 UND	0 UND	0 UND		0 UND	0 UND	0 UND	0 823.7	2 165.0	1 255.8
	1 380.8	3 129.9	3 123.3		0 UND	0 953.0	0 UND	53 6.9	5 76.6	5 77.8
Cost of Sales/Inventory										
Cost of Sales/Payables										
Sales/Working Capital	-207.4	UND	52.1		92.5	82.5	15.3	5.9	-43.7	-104.4
	-13.7	-17.3	-25.9		-41.5	-24.3	119.6	44.0	-16.4	-15.9
	-4.8	-5.6	-7.3		-2.1	-9.0	-26.1	-23.0	-5.5	-5.3
EBIT/Interest	3.3	4.0	4.7			5.3	32.2	23.0	3.1	3.5
	(83) 1.5	(93) 2.1	(97) 2.1		(25) 2.2	(11) 2.5	(12) 2.6	(16) 1.8	(24) 1.9	
	.4	1.4	.8			.7	1.5	1.9	1.1	.3
Net Profit + Depr., Dep., Amort./Cur. Mat. L/T/D	5.6	15.5	9.6							
	(12) 2.0	(17) 3.1	(12) 2.3							
	.9	1.4	1.0							
Fixed/Worth	2.3	2.0	1.7		1.2	1.7	.6	.9	2.6	1.9
	5.1	4.0	3.7		8.4	3.5	2.3	2.3	6.2	3.9
	-13.3	-28.3	68.4		-3.8	NM	24.0	UND	29.0	45.3
Debt/Worth	1.8	1.5	1.5		1.6	.8	1.3	1.1	1.9	1.4
	5.0	3.5	3.5		13.7	2.8	2.3	2.7	6.1	3.7
	-17.9	-30.0	133.0		-2.5	NM	40.0	UND	29.4	53.6
% Profit Before Taxes/Tangible Net Worth	33.8	46.7	51.4			40.5	124.7	52.4	50.5	56.5
	(74) 10.8	(89) 18.5	(93) 15.3		(26) 8.1	(12) 40.0	(11) 16.8	(15) 18.1	(20) 7.2	
	-2.5	6.8	-1.3			-6.8	19.2	5.9	-1.4	-4.4
% Profit Before Taxes/Total Assets	7.7	10.5	8.2		4.8	11.2	40.3	20.2	10.1	5.8
	1.5	3.6	2.9		.5	2.1	8.3	2.6	3.8	2.9
	-3.5	1.2	-.7		-11.0	-1.4	2.4	.5	-.2	-1.0
Sales/Net Fixed Assets	2.8	2.8	3.4		8.7	2.8	41.8	13.2	1.4	3.3
	1.0	1.1	1.1		.7	.9	2.7	.9	.9	2.1
	.6	.6	.6		.3	.4	.7	.5	.7	1.0
Sales/Total Assets	1.8	2.1	2.1		4.4	1.7	3.7	2.6	1.1	2.0
	.9	1.0	.9		.7	.7	2.2	.7	.8	1.4
	.5	.5	.5		.3	.4	.6	.3	.6	.8
% Depr., Dep., Amort./Sales	4.4	4.3	4.4		5.7	4.0	1.4	4.0	6.3	5.1
	(94) 7.0	(115) 6.5	(108) 7.3		(13) 9.0	(32) 9.3	(12) 4.6	(11) 5.7	(16) 9.4	(24) 6.6
	11.2	10.1	10.9		29.7	13.9	8.8	8.8	11.3	7.3
% Officers', Directors' Owners' Comp/Sales	1.9	1.4	1.6			2.5				
	(21) 4.9	(20) 2.9	(27) 3.6			(10) 3.6				
	9.9	5.4	6.7			8.0				
Net Sales ($)	2143388M	2637099M	1884436M		7326M	59248M	54503M	89983M	273442M	1399934M
Total Assets ($)	2263197M	2579884M	2061277M		14630M	143987M	57035M	224826M	372233M	1248566M

M = $ thousand   MM = $ million
See Pages 9 through 22 for Explanation of Ratios and Data

Current Data Sorted by Assets | Comparative Historical Data

	0-500M	500M-2MM	2-10MM	10-50MM	50-100MM	100-250MM	Type of Statement	4/1/06-3/31/07 ALL	4/1/07-3/31/08 ALL
			2				Unqualified	2	2
			1	1			Reviewed	1	3
			4				Compiled	3	1
	5		6	2			Tax Returns	1	
	2	3					Other	5	8
	0-500M	5 (4/1-9/30/10) 500M-2MM	2-10MM	21 (10/1/10-3/31/11) 10-50MM	50-100MM	100-250MM			
NUMBER OF STATEMENTS	7	3	13	3				12	14
	%	%	%	%	%	%	ASSETS	%	%
Cash & Equivalents			16.8		D	D		11.7	9.7
Trade Receivables (net)			21.9		A	A		23.9	26.8
Inventory			4.7		T	T		3.2	5.5
All Other Current			1.7		A	A		2.4	2.1
Total Current			45.1					41.2	44.1
Fixed Assets (net)			36.6		N	N		41.2	36.6
Intangibles (net)			8.8		O	O		9.8	10.9
All Other Non-Current			9.6		T	T		7.7	8.5
Total			100.0					100.0	100.0
					A	A	LIABILITIES		
Notes Payable-Short Term			8.2		V	V		5.3	4.9
Cur. Mat.-L.T.D.			3.2		A	A		5.3	19.8
Trade Payables			7.4		I	I		9.0	11.0
Income Taxes Payable			.3		L	L		.0	.4
All Other Current			9.7		A	A		13.7	9.5
Total Current			28.8		B	B		33.3	45.5
Long-Term Debt			23.2		L	L		14.3	18.3
Deferred Taxes			.0		E	E		1.1	.4
All Other Non-Current			3.8					4.1	21.4
Net Worth			44.2					47.3	14.4
Total Liabilties & Net Worth			100.0					100.0	100.0
							INCOME DATA		
Net Sales			100.0					100.0	100.0
Gross Profit									
Operating Expenses			88.8					98.0	98.4
Operating Profit			11.2					2.0	1.6
All Other Expenses (net)			2.3					.7	2.2
Profit Before Taxes			9.0					1.3	-.6
							RATIOS		
Current			3.5					1.9	1.7
			1.2					1.2	1.3
			.9					.9	.8
Quick			3.5					1.5	1.4
			1.1					.9	1.2
			.7					.9	.6
Sales/Receivables		6	58.0					36 10.0	26 13.8
		44	8.2					55 6.7	56 6.5
		73	5.0					92 4.0	71 5.1
Cost of Sales/Inventory									
Cost of Sales/Payables									
Sales/Working Capital			3.9					5.9	9.9
			23.4					24.6	24.6
			-39.3					-51.7	-11.3
EBIT/Interest			38.7					11.1	9.9
		(11)	22.1					(11) 2.4	(11) 2.3
			2.5					1.3	.4
Net Profit + Depr., Dep., Amort./Cur. Mat. L/T/D									
Fixed/Worth			.4					.6	.6
			1.8					1.3	1.5
			3.8					2.0	NM
Debt/Worth			.5					.6	.8
			1.8					1.2	2.8
			6.9					2.6	NM
% Profit Before Taxes/Tangible Net Worth			86.3					27.4	29.0
		(12)	34.3					(10) 4.2	(11) 16.9
			3.4					2.6	7.3
% Profit Before Taxes/Total Assets			20.3					9.4	7.5
			9.1					2.6	4.7
			-4.8					.6	-3.4
Sales/Net Fixed Assets			19.8					7.0	29.7
			3.9					4.1	7.7
			2.4					2.2	1.9
Sales/Total Assets			2.6					2.0	3.3
			1.5					1.5	1.4
			1.2					1.0	1.0
% Depr., Dep., Amort./Sales			2.8					5.5	.7
		(10)	6.3					(10) 8.8	(12) 6.2
			7.7					12.2	13.4
% Officers', Directors' Owners' Comp/Sales									
Net Sales ($)	11819M	11253M	104963M	74461M				361408M	292599M
Total Assets ($)	1546M	4633M	63715M	59735M				432111M	230210M

M = $ thousand   MM = $ million
See Pages 9 through 22 for Explanation of Ratios and Data

Comparative Historical Data

Current Data Sorted by Sales

			Type of Statement						
4		2	Unqualified				1	1	1
7	3	2	Reviewed					2	
6	2		Compiled				2	1	
3		9	Tax Returns	2	3	1	5	2	
15	13	13	Other		4	1			
4/1/08-3/31/09 ALL	4/1/09-3/31/10 ALL	4/1/10-3/31/11 ALL		0-1MM	1-3MM	3-5MM	5-10MM	10-25MM	25MM & OVER
					5 (4/1-9/30/10)		21 (10/1/10-3/31/11)		
35	18	26	NUMBER OF STATEMENTS	2	7	2	8	6	1
%	%	%	**ASSETS**	%	%	%	%	%	%
13.8	13.5	23.4	Cash & Equivalents						
27.4	24.1	20.7	Trade Receivables (net)						
1.1	.6	2.4	Inventory						
4.2	3.4	1.5	All Other Current						
46.5	41.6	48.0	Total Current						
37.2	38.1	30.4	Fixed Assets (net)						
6.8	6.2	9.7	Intangibles (net)						
9.5	14.1	12.0	All Other Non-Current						
100.0	100.0	100.0	Total						
			LIABILITIES						
15.3	16.0	10.6	Notes Payable-Short Term						
5.0	5.9	3.0	Cur. Mat.-L.T.D.						
10.6	12.8	6.1	Trade Payables						
.4	.2	.2	Income Taxes Payable						
11.9	12.6	13.4	All Other Current						
43.1	47.5	33.4	Total Current						
22.3	23.8	24.1	Long-Term Debt						
.5	.7	.0	Deferred Taxes						
3.3	20.9	14.3	All Other Non-Current						
30.8	7.1	28.3	Net Worth						
100.0	100.0	100.0	Total Liabilities & Net Worth						
			INCOME DATA						
100.0	100.0	100.0	Net Sales						
			Gross Profit						
93.5	99.0	90.0	Operating Expenses						
6.5	1.0	10.0	Operating Profit						
1.1	2.6	3.0	All Other Expenses (net)						
5.4	-1.6	7.0	Profit Before Taxes						
			RATIOS						
2.6	1.6	4.4	Current						
1.5	1.2	1.2							
.8	.7	.7							
2.3	1.5	4.2	Quick						
1.4	.9	1.1							
.7	.6	.7							
28 13.0	27 13.6	0 UND	Sales/Receivables						
43 8.4	41 8.9	44 8.4							
62 5.8	74 4.9	72 5.1							
			Cost of Sales/Inventory						
			Cost of Sales/Payables						
6.7	6.7	4.0	Sales/Working Capital						
16.7	32.3	25.1							
-23.1	-17.9	-44.7							
8.7	5.0	41.8	EBIT/Interest						
(31) 2.2	(16) 1.1	(22) 11.6							
-1.2	-13.5	1.6							
			Net Profit + Depr., Dep., Amort./Cur. Mat. L/T/D						
.5	.8	.2	Fixed/Worth						
1.3	1.5	1.2							
5.1	NM	3.1							
.6	1.0	.5	Debt/Worth						
2.2	2.1	1.9							
12.8	NM	15.9							
68.7	47.0	178.2	% Profit Before Taxes/Tangible Net Worth						
(30) 19.5	(14) -17.2	(22) 45.6							
-9.3	-47.5	7.9							
14.8	13.2	29.1	% Profit Before Taxes/Total Assets						
8.4	.8	9.3							
-2.9	-24.7	1.1							
18.5	27.5	72.8	Sales/Net Fixed Assets						
5.8	4.9	10.0							
3.5	3.4	2.8							
3.2	3.2	3.0	Sales/Total Assets						
2.0	1.9	2.0							
1.5	1.3	1.2							
4.2	2.5	3.5	% Depr., Dep., Amort./Sales						
(25) 5.3	(13) 4.4	(15) 6.1							
9.3	12.7	8.7							
1.7			% Officers', Directors' Owners' Comp/Sales						
(12) 10.7									
24.8									
1523206M	437719M	202496M	Net Sales ($)	784M	9615M	7716M	56606M	88040M	39735M
438427M	315694M	129629M	Total Assets ($)	4098M	4075M	6007M	33777M	50528M	31144M

M = $ thousand   MM = $ million
See Pages 9 through 22 for Explanation of Ratios and Data

Current Data Sorted by Assets   **Comparative Historical Data**

Type of Statement

	0-500M	500M-2MM	2-10MM	10-50MM	50-100MM	100-250MM	Type of Statement	4/1/06-3/31/07 ALL	4/1/07-3/31/08 ALL
		1	4	2	1		Unqualified	4	3
		1	1	1	1		Reviewed	3	4
	1	1	3	1			Compiled	3	2
2	1	6	3	1		1	Tax Returns	7	7
2	1		24 (10/1/10-3/31/11)				Other	14	17
0-500M	500M-2MM	2-10MM	10-50MM	50-100MM	100-250MM	NUMBER OF STATEMENTS	31	33
4	3	14	7	2				

6 (4/1-9/30/10) 24 (10/1/10-3/31/11)

0-500M %	500M-2MM %	2-10MM %	10-50MM %	50-100MM %	100-250MM %		ALL %	ALL %
						ASSETS		
		7.7				Cash & Equivalents	19.9	15.5
		30.7				Trade Receivables (net)	28.9	26.1
		1.6				Inventory	3.3	2.6
		3.2				All Other Current	2.0	1.9
		43.2				Total Current	54.1	46.0
		43.7				Fixed Assets (net)	31.7	34.3
		1.6				Intangibles (net)	6.6	7.8
		11.4				All Other Non-Current	7.5	11.9
		100.0				Total	100.0	100.0
						LIABILITIES		
		10.0				Notes Payable-Short Term	12.4	8.7
		11.7				Cur. Mat.-L.T.D.	3.9	3.8
		12.9				Trade Payables	12.0	8.3
		1.2				Income Taxes Payable	.4	.8
		5.1				All Other Current	9.6	18.6
		40.9				Total Current	38.3	40.1
		22.1				Long-Term Debt	8.2	15.7
		.0				Deferred Taxes	.0	.1
		6.1				All Other Non-Current	13.1	6.1
		30.9				Net Worth	40.3	37.9
		100.0				Total Liabilities & Net Worth	100.0	100.0
						INCOME DATA		
		100.0				Net Sales	100.0	100.0
						Gross Profit		
		96.0				Operating Expenses	95.4	95.1
		4.0				Operating Profit	4.6	4.9
		1.5				All Other Expenses (net)	.4	1.0
		2.5				Profit Before Taxes	4.2	3.9

(Columns 0-500M, 500M-2MM, 10-50MM, 50-100MM and 100-250MM marked "DATA NOT AVAILABLE")

RATIOS

2-10MM		Ratio	4/1/06-3/31/07 ALL	4/1/07-3/31/08 ALL
	2.0	Current	3.0	2.6
	1.2		1.3	1.6
	.6		.8	.5
	1.6	Quick	2.9	2.5
	.9		1.1	1.4
	.6		.7	.5
36	10.2	Sales/Receivables	30 12.1	22 16.9
51	7.1		43 8.4	44 8.3
63	5.8		63 5.8	63 5.8
		Cost of Sales/Inventory		
		Cost of Sales/Payables		
	14.7	Sales/Working Capital	7.5	6.0
	46.8		22.5	13.0
	-8.6		-70.5	-13.5
	30.8	EBIT/Interest	16.2	38.3
	2.3		(25) 8.1	(30) 2.3
	-.1		1.3	.4
		Net Profit + Depr., Dep., Amort./Cur. Mat. L/T/D		
	.6	Fixed/Worth	.2	.2
	4.3		.7	.8
	NM		3.4	5.5
	.5	Debt/Worth	.6	.4
	9.6		1.5	1.6
	NM		6.6	NM
	86.2	% Profit Before Taxes/Tangible Net Worth	60.5	51.4
	(11) 27.0		(27) 39.1	(25) 14.6
	7.7		6.3	-1.2
	23.0	% Profit Before Taxes/Total Assets	23.5	16.4
	4.8		13.9	2.9
	-4.1		2.3	-2.5
	10.9	Sales/Net Fixed Assets	38.6	21.9
	4.7		9.0	6.3
	3.1		4.6	3.2
	2.6	Sales/Total Assets	3.9	4.1
	2.1		2.6	1.8
	1.6		1.5	1.0
	2.1	% Depr., Dep., Amort./Sales	(23) 2.7	(27) 2.2
	(13) 6.1		5.6	5.6
	9.2		7.4	9.4
		% Officers', Directors' Owners' Comp/Sales	2.2	2.6
			(14) 5.9	(13) 7.7
			17.7	14.9

0-500M	500M-2MM	2-10MM	10-50MM	50-100MM		4/1/06-3/31/07 ALL	4/1/07-3/31/08 ALL
9788M	4839M	139550M	302537M	126872M	Net Sales ($)	430089M	586661M
1119M	2258M	58327M	197549M	132259M	Total Assets ($)	445800M	492300M

M = $ thousand   MM = $ million
See Pages 9 through 22 for Explanation of Ratios and Data

Comparative Historical Data   Current Data Sorted by Sales

			Type of Statement						
2	1	2	Unqualified						2
1	4	7	Reviewed		1	1	1	1	3
5	6	2	Compiled					1	1
1	5	6	Tax Returns		3		3		
16	12	13	Other	1	2	1	4	3	2
4/1/08-3/31/09	4/1/09-3/31/10	4/1/10-3/31/11			6 (4/1-9/30/10)		24 (10/1/10-3/31/11)		
ALL	ALL	ALL		0-1MM	1-3MM	3-5MM	5-10MM	10-25MM	25MM & OVER
25	28	30	**NUMBER OF STATEMENTS**	1	6	2	8	5	8
%	%	%	**ASSETS**	%	%	%	%	%	%
11.4	15.7	17.1	Cash & Equivalents						
21.4	25.5	29.3	Trade Receivables (net)						
3.4	5.8	3.2	Inventory						
2.4	4.3	4.2	All Other Current						
38.7	51.3	53.9	Total Current						
42.5	35.2	32.4	Fixed Assets (net)						
6.7	2.5	6.8	Intangibles (net)						
12.1	10.9	6.9	All Other Non-Current						
100.0	100.0	100.0	Total						
			LIABILITIES						
4.9	13.7	9.7	Notes Payable-Short Term						
9.9	6.3	8.3	Cur. Mat.-L.T.D.						
10.0	10.3	13.5	Trade Payables						
.1	.4	.6	Income Taxes Payable						
10.1	9.2	12.0	All Other Current						
35.1	40.0	44.1	Total Current						
32.9	18.4	16.2	Long-Term Debt						
.3	.7	.2	Deferred Taxes						
6.0	11.3	5.4	All Other Non-Current						
25.9	29.6	34.1	Net Worth						
100.0	100.0	100.0	Total Liabilities & Net Worth						
			INCOME DATA						
100.0	100.0	100.0	Net Sales						
			Gross Profit						
98.7	94.8	95.7	Operating Expenses						
1.3	5.2	4.3	Operating Profit						
1.2	1.2	.7	All Other Expenses (net)						
.1	4.0	3.6	Profit Before Taxes						
			RATIOS						
2.9	3.2	2.0							
1.5	1.3	1.2	Current						
.6	.8	.7							
2.3	2.5	1.6							
1.2	1.2	1.0	Quick						
.5	.6	.6							
(24) 15.1	(28) 13.1	(36) 10.2							
(51) 7.2	(39) 9.3	(54) 6.7	Sales/Receivables						
(66) 5.5	(60) 6.1	(71) 5.1							
			Cost of Sales/Inventory						
			Cost of Sales/Payables						
5.4	7.1	5.9							
16.2	14.1	32.1	Sales/Working Capital						
-28.0	-18.0	-9.1							
18.6	8.3	19.7							
(21) 2.2	(27) 2.8	(26) 4.0	EBIT/Interest						
-.9	.8	-.7							
			Net Profit + Depr., Dep., Amort./Cur. Mat. L/T/D						
.5	.5	.4							
2.0	1.3	.9	Fixed/Worth						
-179.0	3.7	11.1							
.4	.5	.6							
3.3	2.2	3.9	Debt/Worth						
-262.8	17.3	61.5							
35.1	56.5	73.3							
(18) 13.9	(24) 8.1	(24) 24.3	% Profit Before Taxes/Tangible Net Worth						
-26.2	-.7	1.3							
12.0	7.5	22.9							
4.4	4.1	6.3	% Profit Before Taxes/Total Assets						
-10.7	-.4	-2.0							
11.5	30.8	24.5							
5.3	5.6	6.0	Sales/Net Fixed Assets						
2.2	2.7	3.1							
2.8	3.0	2.6							
1.3	2.2	1.9	Sales/Total Assets						
1.0	1.2	1.4							
3.8	1.9	2.1							
(20) 8.4	(21) 4.3	(23) 5.8	% Depr., Dep., Amort./Sales						
10.5	10.9	10.1							
3.7	2.2	6.0							
(12) 10.0	(13) 4.7	(11) 6.7	% Officers', Directors' Owners' Comp/Sales						
16.8	12.5	15.9							
402404M	717648M	583586M	Net Sales ($)	98M	10199M	6781M	62275M	78833M	425400M
346614M	520012M	391512M	Total Assets ($)	137M	5107M	5180M	46094M	41964M	293030M

© RMA 2011

M = $ thousand   MM = $ million
See Pages 9 through 22 for Explanation of Ratios and Data

Current Data Sorted by Assets

Comparative Historical Data

0-500M	500M-2MM	2-10MM	10-50MM	50-100MM	100-250MM		4/1/06-3/31/07 ALL	4/1/07-3/31/08 ALL
						Type of Statement		
		8	13	6	4	Unqualified	35	39
		6	3			Reviewed	11	5
	1	2	2			Compiled	12	8
4	5	6				Tax Returns	7	12
8	11	21	17	3	4	Other	33	46
	23 (4/1-9/30/10)		101 (10/1/10-3/31/11)					
12	17	43	35	9	8	**NUMBER OF STATEMENTS**	98	110
%	%	%	%	%	%	**ASSETS**	%	%
31.5	16.5	7.8	6.5			Cash & Equivalents	16.4	10.9
8.1	9.3	10.9	6.9			Trade Receivables (net)	12.9	10.5
.0	.0	.1	.0			Inventory	.3	.4
1.9	3.1	3.4	3.0			All Other Current	2.8	2.8
41.5	28.9	22.2	16.5			Total Current	32.4	24.6
33.5	25.2	31.0	21.0			Fixed Assets (net)	23.6	25.3
19.5	36.7	35.0	48.2			Intangibles (net)	32.4	38.3
5.8	9.2	11.9	14.4			All Other Non-Current	11.7	11.8
100.0	100.0	100.0	100.0			Total	100.0	100.0
						LIABILITIES		
1.5	5.0	1.8	4.0			Notes Payable-Short Term	3.3	4.1
11.1	9.8	4.9	10.2			Cur. Mat.-L.T.D.	2.9	4.2
5.7	3.2	2.5	1.1			Trade Payables	3.5	2.2
.0	.3	.1	.0			Income Taxes Payable	.1	.0
12.1	27.1	10.7	6.3			All Other Current	4.6	5.8
30.4	45.4	19.9	21.7			Total Current	14.4	16.3
89.8	38.0	47.8	29.3			Long-Term Debt	38.0	40.5
.0	.0	.1	.0			Deferred Taxes	.8	.7
7.6	22.4	18.4	17.9			All Other Non-Current	8.9	7.8
-27.5	-5.8	13.7	31.1			Net Worth	37.9	34.7
100.0	100.0	100.0	100.0			Total Liabilities & Net Worth	100.0	100.0
						INCOME DATA		
100.0	100.0	100.0	100.0			Net Sales	100.0	100.0
						Gross Profit		
79.0	96.4	90.5	87.0			Operating Expenses	86.2	88.8
21.0	3.6	9.5	13.0			Operating Profit	13.8	11.2
6.2	7.7	4.9	7.5			All Other Expenses (net)	4.8	7.9
14.8	-4.1	4.5	5.4			Profit Before Taxes	9.0	3.3
						RATIOS		
5.2	7.6	3.0	2.2				6.6	4.1
1.6	.7	1.5	1.2			Current	2.5	1.9
.4	.2	.7	.3				1.2	.9
5.1	7.3	2.7	1.9				5.3	3.8
.8	.7	1.4	1.0			Quick	2.1	1.6
.3	.2	.6	.7				1.1	.7
0 UND	0 UND	23 15.7	37 9.8				30 12.1	34 10.8
0 UND	14 26.4	45 8.1	48 7.7			Sales/Receivables	48 7.5	51 7.2
43 8.5	38 9.5	59 6.2	58 6.3				64 5.7	61 6.0
						Cost of Sales/Inventory		
						Cost of Sales/Payables		
7.1	13.4	5.1	6.5				3.0	4.3
38.5	-22.0	15.8	21.9			Sales/Working Capital	6.5	8.7
-5.7	-2.5	-11.4	-2.4				23.6	-55.4
	2.1	2.9	4.6				7.0	8.1
(11) .7		(37) .9	(25) 2.7			EBIT/Interest	(73) 2.7	(85) 2.1
	-.7	-.7	1.1				.5	.4
							5.8	8.7
						Net Profit + Depr., Dep., Amort./Cur. Mat. L/T/D	(16) 2.4	(18) 1.7
							1.4	1.0
.2	.7	1.1	1.2				.4	.7
5.3	-.5	-.9	-4.3			Fixed/Worth	2.4	NM
-.5	-.1	-.3	-.2				-.5	-.3
.4	.8	.8	1.9				.6	1.0
16.8	-1.9	-4.7	-7.1			Debt/Worth	11.0	NM
-1.6	-1.5	-1.5	-1.6				-1.9	-1.8
		36.5	37.9				93.2	80.8
	(18) 10.1		(14) 14.2			% Profit Before Taxes/Tangible Net Worth	(55) 29.3	(55) 28.4
		-1.0	1.8				7.2	8.7
65.1	2.2	7.2	8.6				17.8	11.5
27.6	-1.4	.8	2.2			% Profit Before Taxes/Total Assets	6.0	2.3
10.1	-5.7	-2.2	-.8				-1.9	-3.8
207.5	54.6	7.6	6.7				8.3	8.8
5.4	7.3	3.1	3.0			Sales/Net Fixed Assets	4.3	3.7
4.3	1.1	1.3	1.5				2.4	2.1
2.4	1.4	1.0	.6				1.4	1.2
2.0	.7	.6	.4			Sales/Total Assets	.8	.7
1.2	.5	.5	.3				.5	.4
		2.7	3.2				2.7	3.0
	(35) 6.1		(32) 5.7			% Depr., Dep., Amort./Sales	(82) 5.0	(92) 5.8
		9.6	8.6				8.7	8.5
		3.7					2.9	2.9
	(10) 6.9					% Officers', Directors' Owners' Comp/Sales	(16) 5.2	(21) 5.1
		11.0					7.7	7.7
5461M	18989M	183982M	424603M	596177M	487953M	Net Sales ($)	1365714M	1740783M
2852M	18243M	238882M	838381M	618929M	1274472M	Total Assets ($)	2087407M	3381785M

M = $ thousand   MM = $ million
See Pages 9 through 22 for Explanation of Ratios and Data

Comparative Historical Data   Current Data Sorted by Sales

Type of Statement	4/1/08-3/31/09 ALL	4/1/09-3/31/10 ALL	4/1/10-3/31/11 ALL	0-1MM	1-3MM	3-5MM	5-10MM	10-25MM	25MM & OVER
Unqualified	26	25	31		4	2	6	9	10
Reviewed	9	5	9		2	1	2	4	
Compiled	10	8	5		3	2			
Tax Returns	18	12	15	9	4	2			
Other	53	63	64	15	15	10	6	13	5
				23 (4/1-9/30/10)		101 (10/1/10-3/31/11)			
NUMBER OF STATEMENTS	116	113	124	24	28	17	14	26	15
	%	%	%	%	%	%	%	%	%
ASSETS									
Cash & Equivalents	10.3	7.8	10.5	23.8	7.6	8.3	5.0	7.8	7.0
Trade Receivables (net)	10.2	12.4	9.4	2.5	9.0	12.2	10.5	11.9	12.7
Inventory	.2	.2	.0	.0	.0	.0	.0	.1	.0
All Other Current	2.6	2.8	3.4	3.2	3.7	1.9	.7	4.6	5.5
Total Current	23.4	23.1	23.3	29.4	20.3	22.4	16.2	24.4	25.2
Fixed Assets (net)	27.0	23.1	25.1	32.2	31.5	25.9	20.1	20.3	14.1
Intangibles (net)	37.4	42.4	40.8	30.9	41.0	30.3	51.9	43.8	52.9
All Other Non-Current	12.3	11.3	10.8	7.7	7.2	21.5	11.8	11.6	7.8
Total	100.0	100.0	100.0	100.0	100.0	100.0	100.0	100.0	100.0
LIABILITIES									
Notes Payable-Short Term	4.5	7.9	2.7	1.7	4.2	6.6	3.1	.4	.7
Cur. Mat.-L.T.D.	5.0	6.9	9.9	8.4	9.0	7.8	7.8	6.7	24.1
Trade Payables	3.3	4.1	2.8	2.2	3.2	2.9	2.1	2.0	4.6
Income Taxes Payable	.2	.0	.3	.0	.2	.1	.0	.1	2.0
All Other Current	6.7	17.1	11.0	10.6	10.3	26.4	6.0	8.0	5.3
Total Current	19.6	36.0	26.7	22.9	26.9	43.8	18.9	17.1	36.6
Long-Term Debt	44.9	40.0	44.2	46.3	75.4	27.1	34.8	32.3	31.9
Deferred Taxes	.8	.6	.3	.0	.0	.0	.3	.1	2.4
All Other Non-Current	10.9	15.9	15.9	18.8	18.9	9.2	40.9	7.0	5.3
Net Worth	23.9	7.4	12.9	12.2	-21.2	19.9	5.1	43.6	23.8
Total Liabilities & Net Worth	100.0	100.0	100.0	100.0	100.0	100.0	100.0	100.0	100.0
INCOME DATA									
Net Sales	100.0	100.0	100.0	100.0	100.0	100.0	100.0	100.0	100.0
Gross Profit									
Operating Expenses	90.4	91.5	88.5	90.0	87.7	92.3	86.5	90.0	82.3
Operating Profit	9.6	8.5	11.5	10.0	12.3	7.7	13.5	10.0	17.7
All Other Expenses (net)	9.4	10.9	7.4	8.4	7.7	4.4	7.6	4.7	13.3
Profit Before Taxes	.2	-2.4	4.1	1.6	4.6	3.3	5.9	5.3	4.4
RATIOS									
Current	3.0	2.4	2.7	5.2	2.5	2.7	2.1	5.7	2.0
	1.5	1.3	1.2	.9	.7	.6	1.3	2.0	1.2
	.6	.5	.5	.4	.3	.2	.5	1.1	.5
Quick	2.6	2.2	2.3	5.1	2.0	2.1	2.0	3.3	1.4
	1.2	1.1	1.0	.8	.7	.6	1.2	1.3	1.1
	.5	.5	.4	.2	.2	.2	.5	.9	.5
Sales/Receivables	29 12.7	39 9.4	23 15.7	0 UND	0 731.4	27 13.5	40 9.0	37 9.8	50 7.3
	48 7.6	55 6.6	45 8.1	0 UND	43 8.4	54 6.8	49 7.5	47 7.8	62 5.9
	57 6.4	67 5.5	59 6.2	21 17.7	52 7.0	61 6.0	60 6.0	60 6.0	70 5.2
Cost of Sales/Inventory									
Cost of Sales/Payables									
Sales/Working Capital	4.5	5.6	6.3	7.5	5.9	4.4	8.7	5.4	7.1
	13.0	15.9	23.9	NM	-15.0	-5.7	21.5	7.8	23.5
	-12.4	-5.3	-4.8	-9.4	-3.1	-1.2	-6.0	NM	-3.1
EBIT/Interest	3.9	3.0	3.6	3.2	2.6	3.4	9.7	4.6	8.9
	(85) 1.3	(88) 1.0	(94) 1.5	(14) .8	(23) 1.1	(14) 1.2	(13) 1.5	(20) 2.7	(10) 2.1
	-.4	-.6	.4	-.6	-.7	.1	.8	.7	1.4
Net Profit + Depr., Dep., Amort./Cur. Mat. L/T/D	3.3	2.8	3.5						
	(22) .8	(20) 1.0	(16) 1.1						
	-.9	.1	.6						
Fixed/Worth	.8	1.5	1.1	.2	-6.5	.8	2.8	1.0	1.1
	-3.1	-.8	-1.2	5.8	-.4	-2.4	-.4	6.6	-.2
	-.3	-.2	-.2	-.5	-.1	-.4	-.1	-.4	-.1
Debt/Worth	1.4	5.5	1.6	.6	-7.8	.9	5.5	1.1	3.3
	-5.5	-2.9	-3.3	NM	-1.8	-5.5	-1.7	20.2	-2.1
	-1.7	-1.5	-1.5	-1.6	-1.3	-2.4	-1.3	-2.1	-1.2
% Profit Before Taxes/Tangible Net Worth	43.2	45.5	72.0	259.5				65.9	
	(51) 14.9	(37) 5.9	(48) 14.3	(12) 30.5				(14) 12.9	
	-1.2	-1.0	.2	-.2				-12.1	
% Profit Before Taxes/Total Assets	6.8	3.9	8.9	17.7	7.0	7.9	8.8	9.6	12.8
	.7	-.3	1.7	.1	.6	.5	1.7	3.6	2.7
	-4.7	-7.2	-1.7	-5.0	-2.2	-1.4	-1.6	-1.3	1.3
Sales/Net Fixed Assets	7.4	8.4	8.6	15.3	8.6	5.9	7.8	6.9	11.4
	3.4	3.2	3.7	4.9	3.4	1.9	5.6	3.5	4.5
	1.8	1.8	1.8	1.3	1.3	1.3	2.7	2.1	2.3
Sales/Total Assets	1.2	1.0	1.0	1.5	.9	.9	1.1	1.1	.6
	.6	.5	.6	.8	.6	.5	.6	.6	.5
	.4	.4	.4	.4	.4	.3	.4	.4	.3
% Depr., Dep., Amort./Sales	3.1	3.4	3.3	4.2	3.5	4.0	2.7	3.2	3.1
	(107) 5.6	(97) 6.3	(98) 6.1	(12) 10.4	(22) 7.6	(15) 7.2	(13) 3.3	(23) 4.9	(13) 5.6
	10.3	10.0	10.1	12.7	10.9	10.1	8.0	8.2	11.5
% Officers', Directors' Owners' Comp/Sales	4.3	3.3	5.2	5.1					
	(19) 6.5	(20) 5.9	(25) 6.4	(10) 7.2					
	10.7	8.4	9.6	11.0					
Net Sales ($)	2057681M	1852322M	1717165M	12014M	55268M	70986M	99959M	417588M	1061350M
Total Assets ($)	3651609M	3626548M	2991759M	28561M	113708M	167446M	172283M	747550M	1762211M

M = $ thousand   MM = $ million
See Pages 9 through 22 for Explanation of Ratios and Data

Current Data Sorted by Assets   Comparative Historical Data

0-500M	500M-2MM	2-10MM	10-50MM	50-100MM	100-250MM	Type of Statement	4/1/06-3/31/07 ALL	4/1/07-3/31/08 ALL
1	2	12	18	6	8	Unqualified	39	42
		2	2			Reviewed	7	3
		1	1		1	Compiled	5	3
		1				Tax Returns	5	3
1	6	2	15	4	4	Other	33	34
	35 (4/1-9/30/10)		52 (10/1/10-3/31/11)					
2	8	18	36	10	13	**NUMBER OF STATEMENTS**	89	85
%	%	%	%	%	%	**ASSETS**	%	%
		8.9	8.5	10.5	8.6	Cash & Equivalents	10.8	9.7
		4.5	8.9	16.5	10.4	Trade Receivables (net)	11.4	12.4
		.1	.3	.1	.1	Inventory	.6	.3
		5.5	4.3	3.9	3.3	All Other Current	3.0	5.6
		19.0	22.0	31.0	22.4	Total Current	25.8	27.9
		66.6	39.8	37.2	24.4	Fixed Assets (net)	45.9	40.7
		5.9	20.1	14.0	41.6	Intangibles (net)	12.1	17.3
		8.6	18.0	17.7	11.6	All Other Non-Current	16.2	14.1
		100.0	100.0	100.0	100.0	Total	100.0	100.0
						LIABILITIES		
		.7	2.0	1.0	.9	Notes Payable-Short Term	4.1	4.0
		3.1	4.7	3.9	2.1	Cur. Mat.-L.T.D.	2.4	4.7
		4.7	5.1	4.3	2.6	Trade Payables	4.0	5.1
		.3	.0	.0	.0	Income Taxes Payable	.1	.4
		4.8	7.0	5.2	3.8	All Other Current	11.8	12.7
		13.7	18.8	14.5	9.4	Total Current	22.4	26.8
		20.3	23.7	90.1	33.9	Long-Term Debt	24.4	28.5
		.4	1.3	.0	.8	Deferred Taxes	.7	.8
		2.5	7.9	7.4	2.9	All Other Non-Current	10.6	13.3
		63.2	48.2	-12.1	53.0	Net Worth	41.9	30.6
		100.0	100.0	100.0	100.0	Total Liabilities & Net Worth	100.0	100.0
						INCOME DATA		
		100.0	100.0	100.0	100.0	Net Sales	100.0	100.0
						Gross Profit		
		93.6	94.9	79.8	86.4	Operating Expenses	91.1	92.7
		6.4	5.1	20.2	13.6	Operating Profit	8.9	7.3
		2.7	2.7	3.8	5.4	All Other Expenses (net)	2.5	4.3
		3.7	2.5	16.4	8.2	Profit Before Taxes	6.4	3.0
						RATIOS		
		2.2	2.8	3.9	2.5		3.4	2.6
		1.4	1.1	1.5	1.8	Current	1.6	1.7
		.9	.8	1.0	1.3		.8	.9
		1.8	2.1	3.4	2.2		2.6	2.0
		1.2	1.0	1.3	1.2	Quick	1.2	1.4
		.8	.5	1.0	.9		.6	.7
		5 81.0	24 15.5	44 8.4	45 8.1		25 14.4	17 21.7
		13 29.2	49 7.4	62 5.9	58 6.3	Sales/Receivables	47 7.7	46 7.9
		29 12.5	65 5.7	67 5.5	71 5.2		66 5.5	72 5.1
						Cost of Sales/Inventory		
						Cost of Sales/Payables		
		9.6	3.6	4.6	3.8		3.5	4.9
		23.5	39.5	9.3	6.6	Sales/Working Capital	10.5	8.7
		-35.7	-19.3	-758.3	28.5		-29.9	-43.5
		6.9	8.2		6.6		9.2	8.9
		(16) -.1	(28) 3.3		(12) 3.9	EBIT/Interest	(72) 3.0	(68) 2.2
		-13.6	-.8		2.4		-.2	.1
						Net Profit + Depr., Dep.,	23.3	8.2
						Amort./Cur. Mat. L/T/D	(14) 2.2	(10) 3.9
							.7	-1.0
		.9	.7	.4	.3		.6	.7
		1.1	1.0	2.9	-2.5	Fixed/Worth	1.1	1.8
		1.8	-9.0	-1.9	-1.0		5.3	-1.8
		.2	.4	1.2	.4		.2	.3
		.3	.9	4.6	-5.7	Debt/Worth	1.2	2.9
		.9	-15.4	-4.5	-2.7		18.0	-4.0
		10.3	17.4			% Profit Before Taxes/Tangible	28.0	26.5
		(15) -.2	(25) 4.7			Net Worth	(69) 9.6	(56) 8.0
		-9.4	-6.1				.3	-1.9
		8.2	9.6	24.9	7.8	% Profit Before Taxes/Total	10.1	10.2
		-2.4	3.8	7.3	5.1	Assets	4.1	2.5
		-8.1	-3.9	2.9	-.3		-.7	-2.3
		2.3	2.8	9.1	4.1		3.6	4.1
		1.1	1.8	2.3	2.2	Sales/Net Fixed Assets	1.6	2.0
		.8	1.1	1.2	1.9		.9	1.1
		1.1	.8	1.5	.7		1.1	1.0
		.7	.6	.7	.5	Sales/Total Assets	.7	.7
		.5	.4	.4	.4		.4	.5
		6.7	5.9				5.3	4.3
		(17) 14.7	(34) 9.1			% Depr., Dep., Amort./Sales	(86) 9.4	(75) 6.6
		21.8	15.3				13.1	11.4
						% Officers', Directors' Owners' Comp/Sales		
1362M	15100M	97080M	616952M	711826M	1037083M	Net Sales ($)	1886885M	2301767M
490M	9327M	114011M	991112M	697189M	1977004M	Total Assets ($)	2660652M	3370153M

M = $ thousand   MM = $ million
See Pages 9 through 22 for Explanation of Ratios and Data

Comparative Historical Data / Current Data Sorted by Sales

	4/1/08-3/31/09 ALL	4/1/09-3/31/10 ALL	4/1/10-3/31/11 ALL	Type of Statement	0-1MM	1-3MM	3-5MM	5-10MM	10-25MM	25MM & OVER
	40	40	47	Unqualified	1	6	1	11	11	17
	5	2	4	Reviewed			1		3	
	8	5	3	Compiled		1			1	1
	1	2	2	Tax Returns	1	1				
	42	32	31	Other	2	4	2	5	9	9
						35 (4/1-9/30/10)			52 (10/1/10-3/31/11)	
NUMBER OF STATEMENTS	96	81	87		4	12	4	16	24	27
	%	%	%	**ASSETS**	%	%	%	%	%	%
Cash & Equivalents	10.3	8.4	11.3			10.0		7.0	12.4	8.7
Trade Receivables (net)	12.0	8.8	10.9			10.1		6.6	7.7	14.0
Inventory	.8	.2	.5			1.2		.1	.1	.4
All Other Current	5.9	5.1	4.9			6.7		4.1	4.4	4.1
Total Current	29.0	22.6	27.5			28.1		17.8	24.5	27.2
Fixed Assets (net)	38.5	41.2	41.0			51.4		53.1	43.1	29.3
Intangibles (net)	19.2	20.7	17.4			12.9		13.4	14.9	29.1
All Other Non-Current	13.3	15.5	14.2			7.7		15.8	17.5	14.4
Total	100.0	100.0	100.0			100.0		100.0	100.0	100.0
				LIABILITIES						
Notes Payable-Short Term	6.3	3.9	2.2			.7		.8	2.6	1.2
Cur. Mat.-L.T.D.	7.4	5.2	3.5			2.6		3.0	5.3	2.9
Trade Payables	4.7	4.3	4.8			5.0		4.5	5.3	4.4
Income Taxes Payable	.2	.1	.1			.0		.0	.3	.0
All Other Current	7.6	7.1	6.7			13.5		3.4	8.6	5.1
Total Current	26.1	20.5	17.3			21.7		11.6	22.0	13.6
Long-Term Debt	28.2	35.1	31.2			25.7		22.6	21.8	50.7
Deferred Taxes	.8	.6	.8			2.5		.1	.5	.8
All Other Non-Current	14.9	11.5	5.6			.6		4.0	8.5	6.1
Net Worth	30.1	32.3	45.2			49.5		61.7	47.2	28.8
Total Liabilities & Net Worth	100.0	100.0	100.0			100.0		100.0	100.0	100.0
				INCOME DATA						
Net Sales	100.0	100.0	100.0			100.0		100.0	100.0	100.0
Gross Profit										
Operating Expenses	94.6	98.0	92.6			94.5		91.5	95.6	86.9
Operating Profit	5.4	2.0	7.4			5.5		8.5	4.4	13.1
All Other Expenses (net)	6.3	4.6	3.3			10.4		1.0	.3	4.5
Profit Before Taxes	-.9	-2.6	4.1			-4.9		7.5	4.1	8.6
				RATIOS						
Current	3.0	2.7	2.6			5.2		4.2	2.5	2.5
	1.4	1.3	1.4			1.0		1.5	1.1	1.6
	.7	.5	.9			.5		1.0	.8	1.1
Quick	2.0	2.2	2.2			4.8		3.3	2.1	2.1
	.9	1.0	1.2			.7		1.2	1.0	1.2
	.4	.4	.7			.4		.8	.5	.9
Sales/Receivables	19 19.6	16 23.5	21 17.0			5 72.4		13 28.4	23 15.7	45 8.1
	41 9.0	42 8.7	46 8.0			12 31.5		24 15.1	31 11.7	62 5.9
	56 6.6	61 6.0	67 5.5			59 6.2		72 5.0	61 6.0	67 5.5
Cost of Sales/Inventory										
Cost of Sales/Payables										
Sales/Working Capital	4.6	4.7	4.4			5.0		3.4	3.9	5.5
	15.2	16.1	14.1			NM		9.5	56.6	8.1
	-12.3	-8.1	-45.3			-7.0		NM	-19.3	69.2
EBIT/Interest	5.4	3.9	7.1					47.1	7.7	7.0
	(79) .6	(63) 1.3	(71) 3.1			(13) 6.5		(20) 3.0	(25) 3.8	
	-3.0	-4.1	-.7			-18.8		-.8	1.9	
Net Profit + Depr., Dep., Amort./Cur. Mat. L/T/D			3.0							
		(12)	2.7							
			1.0							
Fixed/Worth	.6	.7	.5			.2		.7	.6	.4
	1.1	1.3	1.0			1.1		1.0	1.0	4.5
	-1.6	-1.1	-2.6			2.2		22.0	-40.1	-1.1
Debt/Worth	.3	.3	.2			.2		.1	.5	.4
	1.3	1.3	.9			1.0		.2	.7	12.9
	-3.5	-2.6	-5.5			NM		76.6	-57.5	-2.7
% Profit Before Taxes/Tangible Net Worth	32.0	10.7	17.8					16.0	19.9	34.6
	(63) 2.5	(52) .8	(60) 3.6			(13) 7.6		(17) 4.7	(14) 12.0	
	-11.1	-16.1	-8.3			-6.8		-6.1	-1.6	
% Profit Before Taxes/Total Assets	7.2	3.8	9.0			.4		11.4	9.6	9.4
	-1.6	.1	3.0			-5.1		3.8	3.8	6.2
	-9.0	-8.3	-4.2			-8.9		-4.1	-3.2	.3
Sales/Net Fixed Assets	4.4	3.4	3.8			88.1		2.4	3.2	5.0
	2.1	1.7	2.1			.9		1.2	2.0	2.3
	1.2	1.2	1.1			.7		.7	1.1	2.0
Sales/Total Assets	1.1	1.0	.9			1.3		.9	.9	.9
	.7	.6	.7			.6		.5	.7	.7
	.5	.4	.5			.2		.4	.5	.5
% Depr., Dep., Amort./Sales	4.9	5.8	5.5					5.9	5.6	3.1
	(83) 9.3	(71) 10.0	(73) 8.7			(14) 11.8		9.1	(20) 6.7	
	15.1	16.2	15.7			14.0		16.4	9.0	
% Officers', Directors', Owners' Comp/Sales	9.3									
	(10) 14.4									
	32.8									
Net Sales ($)	2477685M	1834048M	2479403M		2627M	21669M	17020M	106092M	386587M	1945…
Total Assets ($)	3547446M	3218520M	3789133M		2770M	68426M	15472M	273830M	618295M	28…

© RMA 2011   M = $ thousand   MM = $ million
See Pages 9 through 22 for Explanation of Ratios and Data

Current Data Sorted by Assets   Comparative Historical Data

	0-500M	500M-2MM	2-10MM	10-50MM	50-100MM	100-250MM		ALL 4/1/06-3/31/07	ALL 4/1/07-3/31/08
							Type of Statement		
			7	4	3	9	Unqualified	25	25
		1	2	1	1		Reviewed	7	11
	1	2	2	1	1		Compiled	7	4
	1	1	1				Tax Returns	7	5
	3	3	8	3	7	1	Other	26	19
	0-500M	**500M-2MM**	**2-10MM**	**10-50MM**	**50-100MM**	**100-250MM**			
		9 (4/1-9/30/10)			54 (10/1/10-3/31/11)				
	5	7	20	9	12	10	**NUMBER OF STATEMENTS**	72	64
	%	%	%	%	%	%	**ASSETS**	%	%
			17.6		11.5	23.4	Cash & Equivalents	13.0	14.0
			19.9		8.6	7.3	Trade Receivables (net)	15.9	13.5
			6.2		.5	.2	Inventory	5.1	2.7
			2.2		1.3	2.5	All Other Current	5.1	4.0
			45.9		21.9	33.4	Total Current	39.1	34.1
			38.6		47.8	29.4	Fixed Assets (net)	35.5	41.5
			8.9		27.0	26.5	Intangibles (net)	17.8	19.3
			6.6		3.3	10.6	All Other Non-Current	7.6	5.1
			100.0		100.0	100.0	Total	100.0	100.0
							LIABILITIES		
			6.7		.1	.4	Notes Payable-Short Term	8.9	4.6
			5.4		9.8	1.6	Cur. Mat.-L.T.D.	2.5	5.2
			16.9		4.5	3.9	Trade Payables	18.1	11.6
			.0		.1	.3	Income Taxes Payable	.4	.3
			8.2		6.0	7.5	All Other Current	8.6	10.7
			37.1		20.5	13.7	Total Current	38.5	32.4
			36.3		42.1	33.5	Long-Term Debt	28.7	38.8
			.4		1.0	4.6	Deferred Taxes	1.2	.9
			14.8		5.5	3.7	All Other Non-Current	14.1	7.2
			11.3		30.9	44.4	Net Worth	17.5	20.6
			100.0		100.0	100.0	Total Liabilities & Net Worth	100.0	100.0
							INCOME DATA		
			100.0		100.0	100.0	Net Sales	100.0	100.0
							Gross Profit		
			92.1		102.3	87.1	Operating Expenses	93.1	92.9
			7.9		-2.3	12.9	Operating Profit	6.9	7.1
			2.4		9.3	2.6	All Other Expenses (net)	5.1	4.7
			5.5		-11.6	10.2	Profit Before Taxes	1.8	2.4
							RATIOS		
			2.3		1.7	3.8	Current	1.4	1.8
			1.1		.6	1.5		1.0	.9
			.5		.4	1.1		.6	.5
			2.1		1.6	3.5	Quick	1.3	1.4
			.7		.6	1.3		.7	.7
			.4		.3	.9		.5	.4
			8 44.6		20 18.3	21 17.4	Sales/Receivables	7 51.2	6 58.6
			19 19.3		29 12.8	32 11.4		25 14.4	20 18.3
			37 9.9		50 7.2	40 9.1		47 7.8	46 7.9
							Cost of Sales/Inventory		
							Cost of Sales/Payables		
			7.0		23.7	2.4	Sales/Working Capital	15.0	12.2
			NM		-18.1	14.7		-314.5	-51.2
			-9.0		-5.5	91.0		-11.3	-9.8
			12.0		1.5		EBIT/Interest	8.0	6.6
			(16) 8.1		(10) .0			(61) 2.6	(55) 2.5
			1.8		-1.1			.4	.9
							Net Profit + Depr., Dep., Amort./Cur. Mat. L/T/D	7.2	
								(11) 3.6	
								2.1	
			.3		1.9	.2	Fixed/Worth	.6	.6
			1.4		NM	2.0		5.7	2.7
			4.3		-1.4	-.9		-2.9	-2.4
			.7		1.7	.4	Debt/Worth	2.1	1.0
			1.4		NM	3.3		11.9	3.6
			17.1		-2.6	-2.2		-5.3	-5.1
			84.9				% Profit Before Taxes/Tangible Net Worth	98.0	35.8
			(17) 39.8					(40) 31.4	(40) 23.1
			23.9					7.0	7.8
			27.8		1.8	12.1	% Profit Before Taxes/Total Assets	20.6	13.5
			8.0		-5.6	5.1		4.3	4.1
			3.4		-10.3	1.0		-3.2	-2.0
			34.2		4.5	4.3	Sales/Net Fixed Assets	23.2	16.0
			6.2		1.2	1.8		5.3	2.5
			1.4		.7	1.5		1.1	1.2
			3.4		1.0	1.0	Sales/Total Assets	3.4	3.3
			2.0		.6	.6		1.4	1.1
			.7		.4	.4		.5	.6
			.8				% Depr., Dep., Amort./Sales	1.3	2.0
			(18) 2.4					(59) 6.2	(48) 7.0
			10.6					17.5	16.1
							% Officers', Directors' Owners' Comp/Sales	1.6	1.8
								(20) 3.1	(15) 2.8
								4.1	9.3
	174M	42000M	250947M	379815M	625853M	1294900M	Net Sales ($)	2528815M	2212336M
	..6M	10669M	110311M	254083M	878078M	1619991M	Total Assets ($)	2810700M	2471393M

M = $ thousand MM = $ million
See Pages 9 through 22 for Explanation of Ratios and Data

Comparative Historical Data | Current Data Sorted by Sales

21	25	23	Type of Statement						
				0-1MM	1-3MM	3-5MM	5-10MM	10-25MM	25MM & OVER
21	25	23	Unqualified		1	3	2	4	13
9	6	5	Reviewed		2	1	1	2	2
4	5	7	Compiled				1	3	1
7	10	3	Tax Returns	1			1		
19	21	25	Other	3	3	2		5	12
4/1/08-3/31/09 ALL	4/1/09-3/31/10 ALL	4/1/10-3/31/11 ALL			9 (4/1-9/30/10)			54 (10/1/10-3/31/11)	
60	67	63	NUMBER OF STATEMENTS	4	6	6	5	14	28
%	%	%	**ASSETS**	%	%	%	%	%	%
11.7	15.3	14.0	Cash & Equivalents					13.0	17.4
17.9	16.2	18.6	Trade Receivables (net)					27.3	14.6
2.7	2.6	2.6	Inventory					9.2	1.1
2.3	3.7	2.8	All Other Current					2.6	4.4
34.6	37.8	38.0	Total Current					52.1	37.5
36.1	35.6	39.3	Fixed Assets (net)					26.7	34.5
23.2	18.2	15.4	Intangibles (net)					12.9	21.4
6.0	8.4	7.3	All Other Non-Current					8.2	6.6
100.0	100.0	100.0	Total					100.0	100.0
			LIABILITIES						
4.4	5.8	5.4	Notes Payable-Short Term					7.6	3.9
4.4	6.5	4.7	Cur. Mat.-L.T.D.					4.8	5.3
10.0	9.1	12.5	Trade Payables					24.6	5.8
.1	.3	.1	Income Taxes Payable					.1	.1
11.6	15.3	15.4	All Other Current					4.4	10.9
30.5	36.9	38.1	Total Current					41.5	26.0
29.7	35.2	32.4	Long-Term Debt					27.1	32.8
.6	.9	1.1	Deferred Taxes					.3	2.0
3.8	8.5	9.3	All Other Non-Current					5.5	8.9
35.4	18.5	19.1	Net Worth					25.6	30.3
100.0	100.0	100.0	Total Liabilities & Net Worth					100.0	100.0
			INCOME DATA						
100.0	100.0	100.0	Net Sales					100.0	100.0
			Gross Profit						
90.9	91.7	91.5	Operating Expenses					96.7	91.9
9.1	8.3	8.5	Operating Profit					3.3	8.1
5.8	4.1	4.2	All Other Expenses (net)					2.4	5.5
3.3	4.2	4.3	Profit Before Taxes					.9	2.6
			RATIOS						
1.8	1.4	2.1	Current					2.4	2.5
1.0	.8	1.1						1.2	1.2
.6	.4	.5						.5	.6
1.7	1.3	2.0	Quick					2.1	2.0
.8	.6	.8						.8	1.1
.4	.3	.4						.4	.5
9 40.7	8 46.9	10 36.6	Sales/Receivables					20 18.2	18 20.2
27 13.7	21 17.4	26 13.8						35 10.4	27 13.4
47 7.7	38 9.5	48 7.6						57 6.4	50 7.3
			Cost of Sales/Inventory						
			Cost of Sales/Payables						
12.2	14.5	6.6	Sales/Working Capital					7.8	4.3
-203.1	-24.7	127.5						46.6	44.6
-11.9	-7.8	-7.5						-6.9	-14.6
7.5	11.5	11.5	EBIT/Interest					11.6	22.0
(47) 2.3	(60) 3.4	(50) 3.1						(11) 5.5	(25) 3.0
.2	.9	1.1						.5	.1
30.9			Net Profit + Depr., Dep., Amort./Cur. Mat. L/T/D						
(10) 8.3									
2.1									
.4	.3	.4	Fixed/Worth					.2	.4
2.8	2.3	1.9						1.3	2.1
-1.6	-1.3	-3.6						NM	-3.4
1.0	1.2	1.0	Debt/Worth					1.2	.5
6.1	4.9	3.1						3.4	2.7
-3.7	-5.6	-6.0						NM	-4.6
60.1	51.5	79.4	% Profit Before Taxes/Tangible Net Worth					82.8	73.4
(35) 20.6	(39) 21.5	(44) 30.8						(11) 54.2	(18) 26.7
6.6	7.6	9.4						27.6	8.3
15.1	16.0	16.0	% Profit Before Taxes/Total Assets					27.8	15.1
3.8	5.4	6.6						7.9	5.1
-2.2	.5	1.2						-3.0	-7.4
23.4	36.2	20.6	Sales/Net Fixed Assets					97.0	17.7
3.0	3.4	3.5						19.6	3.5
1.4	1.3	1.3						1.3	1.4
2.4	2.8	2.7	Sales/Total Assets					3.8	2.2
1.2	1.3	1.0						2.4	1.0
.4	.6	.6						.6	.5
1.7	1.4	1.5	% Depr., Dep., Amort./Sales					.4	1.5
(46) 6.7	(52) 8.3	(40) 6.9						(11) 2.1	(14) 4.9
15.0	17.7	17.6						22.7	16.0
1.5	.6		% Officers', Directors' Owners' Comp/Sales						
(16) 2.5	(12) 3.1								
7.4	9.3								
1811565M	2494963M	2596689M	Net Sales ($)	1357M	10197M	22791M	39505M	238471M	2284368M
2339127M	2648726M	2874178M	Total Assets ($)	956M	9236M	24447M	41474M	313789M	2484276M

M = $ thousand   MM = $ million
See Pages 9 through 22 for Explanation of Ratios and Data

Current Data Sorted by Assets

Comparative Historical Data

						Type of Statement		
	1	25	58	37	22	Unqualified	137	139
	2	9	2		1	Reviewed	22	18
3	4	5	4		2	Compiled	13	11
10	9	4				Tax Returns	16	31
11	15	38	45	13	17	Other	63	121
	38 (4/1-9/30/10)		299 (10/1/10-3/31/11)				4/1/06-3/31/07	4/1/07-3/31/08
0-500M	500M-2MM	2-10MM	10-50MM	50-100MM	100-250MM		ALL	ALL
24	31	81	109	50	42	NUMBER OF STATEMENTS	251	320
%	%	%	%	%	%	ASSETS	%	%
18.5	21.1	11.1	11.7	10.6	11.6	Cash & Equivalents	12.0	14.5
22.9	26.3	25.6	11.4	11.0	10.7	Trade Receivables (net)	17.4	17.5
6.5	6.3	3.9	1.3	3.2	2.8	Inventory	4.4	4.0
2.8	7.2	4.4	2.5	2.8	5.2	All Other Current	2.3	3.0
50.7	60.9	45.0	26.9	27.6	30.4	Total Current	36.0	39.1
36.1	23.3	38.5	52.0	50.4	42.7	Fixed Assets (net)	44.4	39.7
.9	8.4	5.5	10.1	13.0	19.3	Intangibles (net)	8.2	11.3
12.3	7.5	11.1	11.0	9.0	7.7	All Other Non-Current	11.4	9.9
100.0	100.0	100.0	100.0	100.0	100.0	Total	100.0	100.0
						LIABILITIES		
26.8	8.2	8.5	2.5	.8	.9	Notes Payable-Short Term	4.2	7.8
5.6	3.1	3.5	4.9	2.5	2.8	Cur. Mat.-L.T.D.	4.4	4.5
16.9	22.1	14.3	7.3	7.4	6.2	Trade Payables	11.7	11.6
.0	.0	.7	.3	.3	.4	Income Taxes Payable	.6	.3
28.8	9.3	13.8	7.9	7.5	12.1	All Other Current	8.9	13.1
78.0	42.7	40.8	22.9	18.3	22.4	Total Current	29.8	37.4
22.5	16.1	19.8	29.2	24.7	33.4	Long-Term Debt	25.6	25.2
.3	.3	.9	1.4	1.3	1.6	Deferred Taxes	1.3	.8
33.1	9.4	6.5	5.1	7.6	6.9	All Other Non-Current	6.0	9.3
-34.1	31.5	32.1	41.5	48.1	35.8	Net Worth	37.3	27.3
100.0	100.0	100.0	100.0	100.0	100.0	Total Liabilities & Net Worth	100.0	100.0
						INCOME DATA		
100.0	100.0	100.0	100.0	100.0	100.0	Net Sales	100.0	100.0
						Gross Profit		
95.2	92.8	93.9	90.1	90.4	87.1	Operating Expenses	89.1	91.7
4.8	7.2	6.1	9.9	9.6	12.9	Operating Profit	10.9	8.3
2.8	1.3	1.3	2.8	2.4	2.5	All Other Expenses (net)	2.2	2.2
2.0	5.9	4.8	7.0	7.2	10.4	Profit Before Taxes	8.7	6.1
						RATIOS		
1.3	2.6	1.8	2.2	2.2	1.9		2.1	2.1
.8	1.5	1.1	1.3	1.5	1.4	Current	1.3	1.2
.3	.8	.6	.7	.8	.8		.8	.8
1.1	1.7	1.6	1.8	1.9	1.5		1.7	1.6
.6	1.1	.8	1.0	1.1	1.0	Quick	1.1	1.0
.3	.6	.5	.6	.6	.5		.6	.6
0 UND	4 84.8	20 18.5	20 18.4	22 16.4	24 15.4		27 13.7	17 20.9
12 31.4	29 12.7	33 11.1	31 11.8	33 11.0	40 9.2	Sales/Receivables	40 9.2	34 10.9
35 10.3	55 6.6	53 6.9	46 7.9	44 8.3	51 7.2		56 6.6	57 6.4
						Cost of Sales/Inventory		
						Cost of Sales/Payables		
27.1	6.9	10.8	5.2	4.5	6.3		5.3	5.8
-154.0	25.3	57.3	15.0	10.9	11.1	Sales/Working Capital	17.8	21.3
-11.5	-46.7	-14.8	-15.7	-30.1	-21.8		-25.6	-20.1
6.1	46.5	19.9	11.7	14.3	13.5		9.9	10.0
(19) 3.2	(26) 10.8	(74) 5.8	(103) 4.1	(47) 3.4	(37) 4.1	EBIT/Interest	(210) 4.0	(266) 3.2
-2.1	-.3	1.9	1.0	.7	1.7		1.6	1.0
		5.3	7.1	7.8		Net Profit + Depr., Dep.,	5.2	10.8
		(25) 2.9	(51) 3.2	(27) 3.9		Amort./Cur. Mat. L/T/D	(92) 2.6	(111) 3.2
		1.2	2.3	2.2			1.6	1.8
1.3	.2	.3	.8	.9	1.0		.6	.6
UND	.5	1.2	1.4	1.6	2.3	Fixed/Worth	1.5	1.6
-1.8	18.8	2.8	4.1	3.6	-6.2		4.4	-6.9
2.1	.9	.8	.6	.6	1.1		.7	.8
UND	2.5	1.7	1.5	1.3	4.0	Debt/Worth	1.9	2.4
-3.8	26.5	5.9	5.1	3.9	-5.1		8.0	-13.9
549.9	82.1	68.1	27.5	22.8	60.3	% Profit Before Taxes/Tangible	45.2	55.2
(13) 17.7	(24) 60.4	(69) 20.0	(90) 10.9	(43) 11.9	(29) 10.8	Net Worth	(206) 17.7	(233) 14.7
-.3	1.0	4.4	-.3	-.8	6.5		5.4	4.1
16.7	29.6	18.7	13.7	9.9	13.7	% Profit Before Taxes/Total	12.9	13.9
6.3	8.7	7.8	5.1	4.9	4.9	Assets	6.3	5.2
-4.1	-2.8	1.3	-.1	.1	2.4		1.3	-.2
80.9	49.9	33.1	3.4	4.0	12.3		16.9	17.6
19.9	26.4	11.4	1.0	1.0	1.3	Sales/Net Fixed Assets	1.3	3.6
9.8	9.6	1.1	.7	.6	.7		.7	.8
12.1	4.9	3.8	1.4	1.3	1.2		2.2	2.8
4.9	3.7	2.1	.6	.6	.6	Sales/Total Assets	.7	1.1
2.4	1.8	.7	.4	.4	.4		.4	.5
.6	.4	1.0	8.8	5.9	3.7		3.0	2.3
(16) 1.9	(18) 1.6	(68) 5.3	(105) 17.4	(40) 19.2	(15) 10.8	% Depr., Dep., Amort./Sales	(200) 14.8	(250) 9.8
3.6	4.8	15.1	22.7	23.5	18.4		20.9	19.4
4.6	1.9	2.4				% Officers', Directors'	1.4	3.0
(10) 6.2	(14) 6.8	(18) 2.9				Owners' Comp/Sales	(38) 3.7	(43) 5.6
13.6	8.7	7.1					7.4	10.5
36008M	182825M	968165M	2793251M	2956786M	6204868M	Net Sales ($)	7049742M	11556539M
5124M	39696M	439694M	2710486M	3720373M	6477521M	Total Assets ($)	8371095M	12523005M

M = $ thousand　　MM = $ million
See Pages 9 through 22 for Explanation of Ratios and Data

Comparative Historical Data

Current Data Sorted by Sales

	109	169	143	Type of Statement						
	109	169	143	Unqualified	2	7	10	21	36	67
	35	39	14	Reviewed		1		4	6	3
	19	16	18	Compiled	1	3	2	5	2	5
	35	36	23	Tax Returns	6	4	3	6	3	1
	142	133	139	Other	9	13	12	23	27	55
	4/1/08-3/31/09 ALL	4/1/09-3/31/10 ALL	4/1/10-3/31/11 ALL		38 (4/1-9/30/10)		299 (10/1/10-3/31/11)			
					0-1MM	1-3MM	3-5MM	5-10MM	10-25MM	25MM & OVER
NUMBER OF STATEMENTS	340	393	337		18	27	28	59	74	131

Row	4/1/08-3/31/09	4/1/09-3/31/10	4/1/10-3/31/11	0-1MM	1-3MM	3-5MM	5-10MM	10-25MM	25MM & Over
ASSETS (%)	%	%	%	%	%	%	%	%	%
Cash & Equivalents	12.6	14.0	12.7	18.4	10.6	11.3	11.3	14.0	12.7
Trade Receivables (net)	20.9	17.0	16.8	23.5	12.1	13.4	17.6	15.3	18.2
Inventory	3.9	3.8	3.2	4.3	7.8	1.7	2.9	2.6	2.9
All Other Current	3.7	4.1	3.8	4.9	5.0	1.8	2.1	4.4	4.3
Total Current	41.1	39.0	36.6	51.1	35.5	28.3	33.9	36.2	38.1
Fixed Assets (net)	38.1	41.1	43.6	43.1	38.7	46.2	47.5	48.0	39.8
Intangibles (net)	10.4	10.4	9.8	.7	4.9	7.5	7.8	7.6	14.6
All Other Non-Current	10.3	9.5	10.1	5.2	20.9	18.0	10.9	8.2	7.5
Total	100.0	100.0	100.0	100.0	100.0	100.0	100.0	100.0	100.0
LIABILITIES									
Notes Payable-Short Term	7.6	5.2	5.7	14.3	9.1	6.4	10.4	2.6	3.4
Cur. Mat.-L.T.D.	4.5	4.6	3.8	1.1	7.1	4.4	3.2	3.9	3.6
Trade Payables	12.0	10.4	10.9	13.5	12.8	10.0	9.3	11.7	10.6
Income Taxes Payable	.3	.3	.4	.0	.1	.3	.3	.4	.5
All Other Current	13.3	11.5	11.4	20.9	17.3	6.7	9.6	8.0	12.7
Total Current	37.6	32.0	32.2	49.8	46.5	27.9	32.6	26.6	30.7
Long-Term Debt	26.1	22.9	25.1	13.7	27.1	22.4	29.6	18.9	28.3
Deferred Taxes	.8	1.2	1.1	.4	.1	1.3	1.6	.8	1.3
All Other Non-Current	8.3	7.6	8.4	26.9	4.2	7.2	13.6	6.0	6.0
Net Worth	27.1	36.3	33.2	8.9	22.1	41.2	22.6	47.7	33.7
Total Liabilties & Net Worth	100.0	100.0	100.0	100.0	100.0	100.0	100.0	100.0	100.0
INCOME DATA									
Net Sales	100.0	100.0	100.0	100.0	100.0	100.0	100.0	100.0	100.0
Gross Profit									
Operating Expenses	92.0	91.6	91.3	87.2	96.5	90.5	93.4	92.0	89.7
Operating Profit	8.0	8.4	8.7	12.8	3.5	9.5	6.6	8.0	10.3
All Other Expenses (net)	2.7	1.8	2.2	5.3	2.2	1.6	2.6	1.0	2.5
Profit Before Taxes	5.3	6.6	6.5	7.5	1.3	7.9	4.0	7.0	7.9
RATIOS									
Current	2.1	2.1	2.1	2.1	2.4	2.4	2.2	2.2	2.1
	1.2	1.3	1.2	1.0	.7	1.0	1.1	1.3	1.3
	.8	.8	.7	.5	.4	.7	.7	.8	.8
Quick	1.6	1.8	1.7	1.3	1.2	2.2	1.6	1.9	1.7
	1.0	.9	.9	.8	.5	.9	1.0	1.0	1.0
	.6	.6	.5	.5	.3	.5	.6	.6	.6
Sales/Receivables	19 19.4	17 21.9	19 19.7	0 UND	9 41.3	12 30.9	20 18.7	17 21.2	24 15.4
	35 10.5	32 11.3	31 11.7	35 10.4	18 19.8	22 16.3	29 12.6	30 12.1	37 10.0
	52 7.0	49 7.4	48 7.6	74 4.9	41 9.0	39 9.4	48 7.6	48 7.6	53 6.9
Cost of Sales/Inventory									
Cost of Sales/Payables									
Sales/Working Capital	6.1	6.2	6.3	5.1	10.4	11.6	7.8	5.6	6.1
	23.6	21.0	24.4	UND	-84.7	216.9	33.5	17.1	16.5
	-21.3	-23.4	-17.4	-5.2	-4.5	-11.2	-14.3	-38.9	-20.7
EBIT/Interest	9.9	12.1	14.3	6.0	12.7	14.1	10.8	12.2	19.4
	(287) 3.3	(349) 4.1	(306) 4.6	(10) 3.4	(26) 2.1	(26) 4.6	(56) 4.0	(68) 6.6	(120) 4.9
	.9	1.5	1.1	-1.3	-.5	1.2	.7	1.7	1.2
Net Profit + Depr., Dep., Amort./Cur. Mat. L/T/D	8.7	6.6	6.3			2.9	6.4	5.9	7.8
	(106) 3.4	(131) 3.4	(112) 3.4		(12) 1.5	(23) 2.4	(27) 3.9	(44) 4.1	
	1.9	1.9	2.0			.8	1.2	2.7	2.5
Fixed/Worth	.5	.6	.7	.9	.4	.6	.8	.7	.6
	1.5	1.3	1.4	2.5	1.1	1.4	1.6	1.1	1.6
	NM	5.8	5.7	UND	18.8	2.4	4.1	2.2	-67.0
Debt/Worth	.7	.7	.7	.8	.7	.8	.9	.5	.9
	2.6	1.8	1.9	7.1	1.7	1.2	1.7	1.2	2.8
	-48.4	10.9	14.1	UND	26.5	3.3	7.9	3.3	-124.1
% Profit Before Taxes/Tangible Net Worth	53.7	44.5	49.3	92.2	15.9	72.4	33.4	50.3	53.1
	(253) 16.8	(310) 15.4	(268) 13.2	(14) 12.2	(21) 5.3	(23) 11.8	(47) 10.0	(66) 12.2	(97) 19.8
	1.8	4.0	1.6	-2.5	-8.3	2.0	-1.7	4.3	6.5
% Profit Before Taxes/Total Assets	14.7	15.0	14.1	11.8	11.7	16.8	10._	14.0	19.7
	5.4	5.7	5.9	5.2	2.2	6.4		5.9	6.9
	-.8	1.2	.5	-.5	-3.4	.5		1.2	1.3
Sales/Net Fixed Assets	22.9	18.1	18.3	77.3	28.9	1_		13.8	17.5
	5.0	3.2	2.5	9.9	10.4			1.3	2.6
	.9	.8	.8	.7	.8			.7	1.0
Sales/Total Assets	3.0	2.6	2.6	5.0	4.1			2.1	2.1
	1.5	1.1	1.0	2.1	1.8			.7	1.1
	.5	.5	.5	.4	.6				.6
% Depr., Dep., Amort./Sales	2.1	2.3	2.7		1.1			5.5	2.2
	(261) 7.0	(311) 9.3	(262) 10.7		(22) 4.1	(23) 14._	(65) 14.0	(90) 16.7	6.7
	18.5	20.3	20.8			19.8	22.7	21.4 / 23.3	17.1
% Officers', Directors' Owners' Comp/Sales	1.9	2.3	2.3					1.8	2.1
	(49) 4.5	(64) 6.1	(48) 5.0				(10) 2.8	(11) 2.5	
	8.0	11.3	8.5					6.7	5.4
Net Sales ($)	11859267M	14737964M	13141903M	8648M	53266M	109080M	453068M	1180049M	11337792M
Total Assets ($)	11964160M	14971540M	13392894M	14223M	71295M	155054M	674072M	1846196M	10632054M

© RMA 2011

M = $ thousand   MM = $ million

See Pages 9 through 22 for Explanation of Ratios and Data

Current Data Sorted by Assets   Comparative Historical Data

0-500M	500M-2MM	2-10MM	10-50MM	50-100MM	100-250MM	Type of Statement	4/1/06-3/31/07 ALL	4/1/07-3/31/08 ALL
	1	5	14	7	11	Unqualified		26
1	3	9	1			Reviewed		15
1	3	4				Compiled		10
7	10	5		1		Tax Returns		15
4	6	15	10	6	4	Other		31
	15 (4/1-9/30/10)		113 (10/1/10-3/31/11)					
13	23	38	25	14	15	NUMBER OF STATEMENTS		97
%	%	%	%	%	%	**ASSETS**	%	%
17.9	18.4	13.3	17.7	9.5	6.8	Cash & Equivalents	D	11.7
20.8	27.6	28.5	21.1	14.2	10.2	Trade Receivables (net)	A	21.3
24.2	22.6	12.4	5.0	6.1	2.7	Inventory	T	10.6
3.4	3.2	3.9	3.0	5.5	6.7	All Other Current	A	5.0
66.4	71.8	58.1	46.8	35.3	26.4	Total Current		48.5
14.9	21.8	26.7	34.1	36.0	50.2	Fixed Assets (net)	N	38.6
6.6	1.8	9.6	7.3	18.6	16.7	Intangibles (net)	O	7.3
12.2	4.7	5.6	11.9	10.1	6.7	All Other Non-Current	T	5.6
100.0	100.0	100.0	100.0	100.0	100.0	Total		100.0
						LIABILITIES	A	
21.0	8.9	4.4	2.4	3.9	6.4	Notes Payable-Short Term	V	6.0
4.0	4.3	4.5	3.1	1.9	4.7	Cur. Mat.-L.T.D.	A	4.1
24.9	20.4	24.0	21.6	8.2	10.0	Trade Payables	I	15.1
.0	.0	.0	.1	.3	.4	Income Taxes Payable	L	.3
16.5	8.6	12.6	6.5	8.8	7.4	All Other Current	A	11.3
66.4	42.2	45.4	33.6	23.1	28.9	Total Current	B	36.8
27.0	14.6	28.7	18.3	12.4	28.7	Long-Term Debt	L	24.7
.1	.0	.1	.9	1.6	2.1	Deferred Taxes	E	.3
43.0	6.5	5.4	3.0	8.7	5.1	All Other Non-Current		5.9
-36.5	36.6	20.3	44.2	54.2	35.2	Net Worth		32.2
100.0	100.0	100.0	100.0	100.0	100.0	Total Liabilities & Net Worth		100.0
						INCOME DATA		
100.0	100.0	100.0	100.0	100.0	100.0	Net Sales		100.0
						Gross Profit		
97.4	94.6	91.1	91.0	91.2	84.7	Operating Expenses		93.1
2.6	5.4	8.9	9.0	8.8	15.3	Operating Profit		6.9
-.4	.3	3.5	.6	5.0	4.4	All Other Expenses (net)		1.7
3.0	5.1	5.5	8.4	3.7	10.8	Profit Before Taxes		5.2
						RATIOS		
7.4	8.5	1.8	2.8	2.2	1.9	Current		2.3
1.0	1.9	1.3	1.2	1.3	1.1	Current		1.5
.5	.8	1.0	.9	.8	.7	Current		1.0
3.6	5.4	1.4	2.7	1.7	1.0	Quick		1.6
.8	1.0	.8	1.1	.8	.8	Quick		1.0
.3	.7	.6	.7	.7	.4	Quick		.6
1 655.5	1 568.8	24 15.1	16 22.2	19 19.6	32 11.5	Sales/Receivables	22 16.7	
15 24.5	20 18.0	38 9.7	33 11.0	50 7.2	40 9.1	Sales/Receivables	35 10.5	
36 10.2	59 6.2	57 6.4	47 7.8	83 4.4	55 6.6	Sales/Receivables	57 6.4	
						Cost of Sales/Inventory		
						Cost of Sales/Payables		
10.9	9.3	9.1	5.9	3.7	4.1	Sales/Working Capital		6.7
-743.0	13.4	20.0	13.1	28.5	48.9	Sales/Working Capital		15.0
-9.2	-37.3	NM	-44.9	-21.7	-17.1	Sales/Working Capital		-131.4
	31.1	28.6	23.0	16.6	4.9	EBIT/Interest		13.1
(18) 8.6	(35) 6.2	(20) 6.5	(12) 5.8	(14) 3.1		EBIT/Interest	(83) 3.9	
1.6	2.1	1.3	-.5	1.8		EBIT/Interest		1.5
						Net Profit + Depr., Dep., Amort./Cur. Mat. L/T/D		9.8
						Net Profit + Depr., Dep., Amort./Cur. Mat. L/T/D	(12) 3.1	
						Net Profit + Depr., Dep., Amort./Cur. Mat. L/T/D		1.8
.3	.1	.4	.3	.4	1.2	Fixed/Worth		.5
-2.5	.4	1.3	.9	.8	2.7	Fixed/Worth		1.4
-.2	2.0	13.0	1.3	2.7	-3.3	Fixed/Worth		2.8
1.0	.3	1.6	.5	.3	1.2	Debt/Worth		.8
-21.3	1.4	4.0	1.3	1.0	3.3	Debt/Worth		2.0
-1.6	5.7	45.5	5.6	3.2	-5.9	Debt/Worth		8.6
	122.0	83.0	67.4	-28.6	49.5	% Profit Before Taxes/Tangible Net Worth		60.8
(20) 31.4	(30) 23.2	(24) 25.5	(12) 14.6	(11) 19.6		% Profit Before Taxes/Tangible Net Worth	(80) 24.6	
5.9	5.8	8.7	-.2	6.8		% Profit Before Taxes/Tangible Net Worth		6.8
53.9	41.2	15.6	14.6	15.6	7.9	% Profit Before Taxes/Total Assets		17.1
22.3	17.6	10.2	8.0	3.4	3.8	% Profit Before Taxes/Total Assets		7.0
-27.1	1.8	1.1	3.4	-4.3	1.4	% Profit Before Taxes/Total Assets		1.0
132.4	90.6	49.7	43.2	18.8	2.2	Sales/Net Fixed Assets		21.1
51.7	32.7	12.8	6.6	3.5	1.1	Sales/Net Fixed Assets		6.7
31.6	9.3	4.6	1.3	1.4	.6	Sales/Net Fixed Assets		1.5
8.5	8.1	3.7	3.5	1.2	.7	Sales/Total Assets		3.7
5.3	3.9	2.4	1.0	1.0	.6	Sales/Total Assets		1.8
3.9	3.3	1.1	.7	.7	.4	Sales/Total Assets		.7
	.5	.4	1.3	3.0		% Depr., Dep., Amort./Sales		1.1
(12) .8	(33) 1.9	(23) 5.9	(11) 9.0			% Depr., Dep., Amort./Sales	(83) 2.4	
3.1	7.4	14.5	12.9			% Depr., Dep., Amort./Sales		12.1
	.8	3.4				% Officers', Directors' Owners' Comp/Sales		2.4
(10) 1.4	(10) 4.7					% Officers', Directors' Owners' Comp/Sales	(24) 6.8	
3.1	9.3					% Officers', Directors' Owners' Comp/Sales		10.3
25621M	143772M	571920M	1212855M	1109182M	1952967M	Net Sales ($)		3158379M
3696M	25085M	183779M	518606M	1009225M	2457185M	Total Assets ($)		2671600M

© RMA 2011

M = $ thousand   MM = $ million
See Pages 9 through 22 for Explanation of Ratios and Data

Comparative Historical Data   Current Data Sorted by Sales

4/1/08-3/31/09 ALL	4/1/09-3/31/10 ALL	4/1/10-3/31/11 ALL	Type of Statement	0-1MM	1-3MM	3-5MM	5-10MM	10-25MM	25MM & OVER
32	36	38	Unqualified	2	1	4	2	8	24
11	13	14	Reviewed	2	1	1	2	4	4
13	9	8	Compiled	2	6	1	2	2	1
15	25	23	Tax Returns	2	6	3	5	5	2
40	39	45	Other	2	7	4	8	6	18
					15 (4/1-9/30/10)		113 (10/1/10-3/31/11)		
111	122	128	NUMBER OF STATEMENTS	8	14	13	19	25	49
%	%	%	**ASSETS**	%	%	%	%	%	%
12.0	14.5	14.4	Cash & Equivalents		13.2	5.4	19.6	16.6	15.7
19.4	17.3	22.4	Trade Receivables (net)		30.7	18.2	24.1	21.4	22.5
10.4	12.3	12.1	Inventory		19.2	15.7	18.5	11.1	7.7
4.8	4.6	4.1	All Other Current		1.4	4.0	3.7	3.6	5.4
46.5	48.7	53.0	Total Current		64.5	43.3	65.9	52.7	51.3
34.2	33.2	29.8	Fixed Assets (net)		17.5	40.1	24.6	26.7	31.2
9.4	11.0	9.2	Intangibles (net)		9.8	5.0	2.4	8.3	12.5
9.9	7.1	8.0	All Other Non-Current		8.3	11.5	7.1	12.3	5.0
100.0	100.0	100.0	Total		100.0	100.0	100.0	100.0	100.0
			LIABILITIES						
8.7	10.1	6.7	Notes Payable-Short Term		14.8	5.2	6.9	3.5	4.3
3.5	4.8	3.9	Cur. Mat.-L.T.D.		3.4	6.6	4.4	3.8	2.8
15.0	15.9	19.6	Trade Payables		20.9	20.4	18.2	19.7	22.2
.1	.1	.1	Income Taxes Payable		.0	.0	.2	.0	.2
12.3	11.8	10.1	All Other Current		10.1	6.3	16.1	10.1	9.8
39.7	42.7	40.3	Total Current		49.2	38.6	45.7	37.1	39.4
19.1	19.5	22.2	Long-Term Debt		21.1	41.4	18.3	19.3	15.6
.5	.4	.6	Deferred Taxes		.1	.9	.6	.0	1.2
5.3	8.2	9.3	All Other Non-Current		15.7	2.7	7.0	8.8	4.9
35.5	29.3	27.6	Net Worth		13.9	16.4	28.4	34.8	38.9
100.0	100.0	100.0	Total Liabilities & Net Worth		100.0	100.0	100.0	100.0	100.0
			INCOME DATA						
100.0	100.0	100.0	Net Sales		100.0	100.0	100.0	100.0	100.0
			Gross Profit						
91.0	91.0	91.6	Operating Expenses		93.5	92.0	94.8	92.9	90.7
9.0	9.0	8.4	Operating Profit		6.5	8.0	5.2	7.1	9.3
2.3	1.3	2.2	All Other Expenses (net)		.5	.8	.5	1.4	2.8
6.8	7.8	6.2	Profit Before Taxes		6.0	7.2	4.8	5.7	6.5
			RATIOS						
2.0	2.1	2.4	Current		6.9	2.4	3.6	2.6	2.1
1.4	1.2	1.3			1.2	1.2	1.4	1.5	1.2
.9	.8	.9			.8	.5	.8	1.0	.9
1.5	1.4	1.8	Quick		4.5	2.4	1.9	2.6	1.4
1.0	.8	.9			.9	.6	.9	1.0	.9
.5	.4	.6			.7	.2	.7	.7	.7
12 31.2	8 47.5	14 26.8	Sales/Receivables		10 36.6	2 171.7	4 98.4	14 26.1	22 16.9
28 13.0	25 14.7	33 10.9			36 10.2	25 14.7	24 15.3	35 10.4	37 9.8
50 7.2	46 8.0	55 6.6			60 6.0	73 5.0	46 8.0	49 7.4	55 6.6
			Cost of Sales/Inventory						
			Cost of Sales/Payables						
7.1	8.1	7.3	Sales/Working Capital		7.4	6.3	9.8	5.7	7.0
19.1	32.7	20.0			17.7	19.9	15.9	17.2	27.4
-71.9	-30.2	-41.2			-26.0	-10.8	-37.3	UND	-111.6
13.9	28.7	19.9	EBIT/Interest		129.1	12.8	9.5	23.8	35.6
(91) 5.4	(104) 6.4	(108) 5.0		(12) 8.4	(12) 3.0	(15) 3.0	(23) 9.3	(42) 6.9	
1.7	1.6	1.8			2.7	1.4	.3	1.5	2.7
17.1		28.0	Net Profit + Depr., Dep., Amort./Cur. Mat. L/T/D						
(13) 3.6		(15) 2.6							
1.6		1.0							
.3	.4	.3	Fixed/Worth		.3	.4	.3	.3	.3
1.1	.9	1.0			1.2	2.0	1.1	.8	.9
10.0	37.5	5.4			-2.3	90.2	3.7	1.6	2.3
.5	.7	.8	Debt/Worth		.8	1.4	.9	.7	.9
2.0	2.4	2.2			3.9	3.5	1.9	1.1	2.2
119.1	NM	16.1			-16.7	172.0	14.6	7.1	7.0
80.9	99.4	78.6	% Profit Before Taxes/Tangible Net Worth		355.5	113.4	107.8	54.8	78.0
(84) 25.6	(92) 35.8	(103) 24.5		(10) 43.6	(11) 24.5	(15) 20.2	(21) 21.6	(42) 30.4	
6.8	7.8	6.6			16.9	4.8	-1.6	6.2	9.4
23.1	26.8	18.5	% Profit Before Taxes/Total Assets		29.4	22.4	26.1	16.4	16.9
9.3	10.5	8.1			16.9	5.5	6.8	11.6	8.6
1.2	1.9	1.3			7.1	1.1	-.5	2.5	1.6
42.6	41.9	51.4	Sales/Net Fixed Assets		79.9	52.6	90.6	38.8	50.0
8.8	9.0	11.7			35.4	6.8	23.6	12.3	9.8
1.8	2.0	1.9			13.3	1.0	4.7	3.7	1.6
4.0	4.0	4.0	Sales/Total Assets		5.3	3.3	6.3	3.6	3.9
1.9	2.1	2.1			3.8	1.8	3.8	2.5	1.5
.9	.9	.8			1.7	.7	2.0	.9	.7
1.0	.7	.7	% Depr., Dep., Amort./Sales			2.9	.7	.8	.4
(81) 3.0	(90) 2.9	(91) 2.9			(11) 5.1	(11) 1.6	(24) 2.8	(32) 2.6	
11.0	11.0	11.4			25.2	11.9	9.8	8.9	
2.5	1.8	1.2	% Officers', Directors' Owners' Comp/Sales						
(32) 5.0	(36) 3.1	(33) 3.3							
7.8	7.6	6.2							
5120257M	5795849M	5016317M	Net Sales ($)	3372M	24103M	54413M	120795M	374494M	4439140M
3796638M	4028142M	4197576M	Total Assets ($)	14261M	10789M	63292M	63426M	276226M	3769582M

M = $ thousand   MM = $ million
See Pages 9 through 22 for Explanation of Ratios and Data

Current Data Sorted by Assets

Comparative Historical Data

						Type of Statement		
		4	3		5	Unqualified		7
1		8	1			Reviewed		2
	1	1				Compiled		3
1	3	1				Tax Returns		1
1	5	3	5	2	3	Other		12
	7 (4/1-9/30/10)		41 (10/1/10-3/31/11)				4/1/06-3/31/07 ALL	4/1/07-3/31/08 ALL
0-500M	500M-2MM	2-10MM	10-50MM	50-100MM	100-250MM			
3	9	17	9	2	8	NUMBER OF STATEMENTS		25
%	%	%	%	%	%		%	%
						ASSETS		
		16.4				Cash & Equivalents	D	16.5
		31.5				Trade Receivables (net)	A	28.5
		11.6				Inventory	T	14.6
		10.7				All Other Current	A	2.9
		70.2				Total Current		62.4
		18.2				Fixed Assets (net)	N	21.8
		6.3				Intangibles (net)	O	9.1
		5.4				All Other Non-Current	T	6.7
		100.0				Total		100.0
						LIABILITIES	A	
		4.0				Notes Payable-Short Term	V	15.7
		1.3				Cur. Mat.-L.T.D.	A	3.4
		35.5				Trade Payables	I	18.9
		.5				Income Taxes Payable	L	.3
		18.8				All Other Current	A	12.6
		60.1				Total Current	B	50.9
		6.2				Long-Term Debt	L	8.5
		.6				Deferred Taxes	E	.9
		3.0				All Other Non-Current		4.2
		30.1				Net Worth		35.5
		100.0				Total Liabilities & Net Worth		100.0
						INCOME DATA		
		100.0				Net Sales		100.0
						Gross Profit		
		99.1				Operating Expenses		92.2
		.9				Operating Profit		7.8
		.0				All Other Expenses (net)		.5
		.8				Profit Before Taxes		7.3
						RATIOS		
		1.4						1.8
		1.1				Current		1.3
		.9						.9
		1.2						1.4
		.8				Quick		1.0
		.5						.6
	17	21.5					23	15.9
	27	13.4				Sales/Receivables	38	9.7
	43	8.4					51	7.2
						Cost of Sales/Inventory		
						Cost of Sales/Payables		
		14.7						8.2
		78.1				Sales/Working Capital		18.1
		-97.3						-65.3
		73.3						12.6
	(15)	14.3				EBIT/Interest	(23)	4.4
		6.6						1.3
						Net Profit + Depr., Dep., Amort./Cur. Mat. L/T/D		
		.2						.4
		.7				Fixed/Worth		.6
		4.3						NM
		1.8						1.0
		4.3				Debt/Worth		1.8
		22.4						NM
		84.8				% Profit Before Taxes/Tangible Net Worth		64.2
	(14)	54.6					(19)	31.4
		15.3						16.2
		18.5				% Profit Before Taxes/Total Assets		19.1
		8.6						9.9
		2.8						2.8
		150.0				Sales/Net Fixed Assets		58.1
		58.9						23.7
		21.2						7.1
		7.3				Sales/Total Assets		3.7
		4.0						2.9
		2.3						1.6
		.2				% Depr., Dep., Amort./Sales		.4
	(15)	.5					(21)	1.3
		1.3						6.7
						% Officers', Directors' Owners' Comp/Sales		
1546M	71756M	570830M	566817M	182532M	1126537M	Net Sales ($)		1389514M
348M	10085M	87950M	216491M	136194M	1340726M	Total Assets ($)		917596M

M = $ thousand   MM = $ million
See Pages 9 through 22 for Explanation of Ratios and Data

Comparative Historical Data

Current Data Sorted by Sales

Type of Statement	4/1/08-3/31/09 ALL	4/1/09-3/31/10 ALL	4/1/10-3/31/11 ALL		0-1MM	1-3MM	3-5MM	5-10MM	10-25MM	25MM & OVER
					7 (4/1-9/30/10)			41 (10/1/10-3/31/11)		
Unqualified	9	6	12				1	1	1	9
Reviewed	3	7	10						6	3
Compiled	2	3	2		1	1				
Tax Returns	5	6	5		1	1	1		2	
Other	12	15	19		1	2	1		5	10
NUMBER OF STATEMENTS	31	37	48		4	4	3	1	14	22
	%	%	%		%	%	%	%	%	%
ASSETS										
Cash & Equivalents	10.6	10.8	12.7						17.5	15.6
Trade Receivables (net)	27.2	28.2	28.0						34.3	24.8
Inventory	11.9	14.5	12.6						13.3	7.3
All Other Current	4.2	5.4	9.4						9.8	7.0
Total Current	53.9	58.9	62.8						74.9	54.7
Fixed Assets (net)	17.8	16.9	19.2						15.1	18.2
Intangibles (net)	14.3	12.1	11.9						4.6	18.6
All Other Non-Current	14.0	12.0	6.1						5.3	8.5
Total	100.0	100.0	100.0						100.0	100.0
LIABILITIES										
Notes Payable-Short Term	11.5	17.2	8.0						4.7	4.6
Cur. Mat.-L.T.D.	2.6	3.8	3.0						1.3	1.5
Trade Payables	36.1	28.0	29.6						41.2	24.7
Income Taxes Payable	.5	.4	.6						.6	.8
All Other Current	12.2	16.3	12.4						15.2	15.6
Total Current	62.9	65.6	53.5						63.0	47.2
Long-Term Debt	18.5	18.9	12.6						6.4	16.0
Deferred Taxes	.7	.4	1.1						.4	2.1
All Other Non-Current	13.4	7.0	5.9						4.7	4.6
Net Worth	4.5	8.1	27.0						25.4	30.1
Total Liabilities & Net Worth	100.0	100.0	100.0						100.0	100.0
INCOME DATA										
Net Sales	100.0	100.0	100.0						100.0	100.0
Gross Profit										
Operating Expenses	92.8	93.6	97.2						100.7	94.9
Operating Profit	7.2	6.4	2.8						-.7	5.1
All Other Expenses (net)	3.0	2.8	1.4						.6	2.1
Profit Before Taxes	4.2	3.6	1.5						-1.3	3.0
RATIOS										
Current	1.6	1.7	1.7						1.5	1.5
	1.2	1.0	1.2						1.2	1.2
	.8	.6	.9						.9	.8
Quick	1.2	.9	1.2						1.3	1.3
	.8	.6	(47) .7						.8	.8
	.6	.4	.5						.5	.5
Sales/Receivables	18 20.0	13 27.7	19 18.7						13 28.2	19 19.2
	31 11.7	31 11.9	34 10.9						31 11.9	34 10.9
	55 6.7	51 7.1	46 7.9						45 8.0	57 6.4
Cost of Sales/Inventory										
Cost of Sales/Payables										
Sales/Working Capital	9.0	10.7	6.3						8.1	7.2
	50.5	-152.5	34.2						61.6	34.2
	-33.6	-9.8	-79.3						-103.0	-57.2
EBIT/Interest	5.0	16.7	36.3						17.9	59.9
	(26) 1.9	(33) 5.3	(42) 6.3						(12) 12.0	(21) 4.5
	-1.0	.6	2.5						3.6	2.4
Net Profit + Depr., Dep., Amort./Cur. Mat. L/T/D										
Fixed/Worth	.5	.3	.2						.2	.4
	2.7	2.1	1.2						1.0	1.6
	-.4	-.4	-26.2						NM	-.7
Debt/Worth	1.9	1.7	1.7						2.0	1.7
	11.5	-17.0	4.8						5.2	6.0
	-4.9	-2.9	-28.0						NM	-6.8
% Profit Before Taxes/Tangible Net Worth	98.2	84.5	84.8						100.0	84.7
	(19) 28.5	(18) 24.1	(34) 30.5						(11) 36.3	(13) 30.5
	11.7	11.2	-1.9						5.8	4.6
% Profit Before Taxes/Total Assets	10.8	18.2	17.9						18.3	14.2
	4.2	6.5	6.6						6.8	6.3
	-10.2	-.8	.0						1.0	3.2
Sales/Net Fixed Assets	213.4	120.5	120.3						113.1	79.1
	41.1	36.7	44.0						65.7	35.7
	11.2	12.3	10.0						20.6	4.3
Sales/Total Assets	4.3	5.9	5.2						8.5	5.2
	1.8	3.2	3.0						3.8	2.5
	1.1	1.7	1.1						2.4	.8
% Depr., Dep., Amort./Sales	.4	.5	.4						.3	.3
	(21) .9	(27) .9	(33) .8						(11) .9	(15) .6
	3.4	2.8	3.5						4.6	2.0
% Officers', Directors', Owners' Comp/Sales			.7							
		(11) 3.0								
			9.7							
Net Sales ($)	1605716M	2351557M	2520018M		1894M	8705M	12138M	6635M	245003M	2245643M
Total Assets ($)	1056762M	1316658M	1791794M		1386M	4848M	7772M	7694M	92015M	1678079M

Current Data Sorted by Assets

Comparative Historical Data

0-500M	500M-2MM	2-10MM	10-50MM	50-100MM	100-250MM	Type of Statement		4/1/06-3/31/07 ALL	4/1/07-3/31/08 ALL
	2	11	10	5	5	Unqualified			36
	4	6	3			Reviewed			9
2	7	11				Compiled			15
9	7	8				Tax Returns			12
2	8	23	20	10	8	Other			58
	26 (4/1-9/30/10)		135 (10/1/10-3/31/11)						
13	28	59	33	15	13	NUMBER OF STATEMENTS			130
%	%	%	%	%	%	**ASSETS**		%	%
18.6	12.7	10.6	12.7	8.3	12.0	Cash & Equivalents	D		14.5
43.0	27.4	32.8	27.0	12.3	20.6	Trade Receivables (net)	A		31.5
.0	4.5	8.8	8.6	4.7	3.0	Inventory	T		7.3
.3	7.2	3.8	5.2	2.7	4.4	All Other Current	A		4.8
62.0	51.8	56.0	53.6	28.0	40.0	Total Current			58.1
29.7	39.4	23.7	27.9	48.7	18.8	Fixed Assets (net)	N		24.4
7.5	1.5	6.9	12.2	11.2	32.3	Intangibles (net)	O		7.9
.8	7.2	13.5	6.4	12.2	9.0	All Other Non-Current	T		9.7
100.0	100.0	100.0	100.0	100.0	100.0	Total			100.0
						LIABILITIES	A		
67.2	10.4	7.5	4.9	.1	2.1	Notes Payable-Short Term	V		10.7
2.0	7.7	3.7	3.1	2.4	1.8	Cur. Mat.-L.T.D.	A		4.2
15.4	9.9	16.4	18.8	9.6	5.1	Trade Payables	I		17.5
.0	.6	.3	.1	1.9	.3	Income Taxes Payable	L		.4
12.2	13.7	10.5	15.8	13.3	18.2	All Other Current	A		16.6
96.8	42.2	38.5	42.6	27.3	27.4	Total Current	B		49.4
39.3	32.4	17.5	19.4	21.0	26.8	Long-Term Debt	L		19.5
.0	.0	.4	.7	.0	2.0	Deferred Taxes	E		.4
1.8	4.3	8.6	10.4	19.1	6.8	All Other Non-Current			6.6
-37.9	21.0	35.0	26.9	32.6	37.0	Net Worth			24.2
100.0	100.0	100.0	100.0	100.0	100.0	Total Liabilities & Net Worth			100.0
						INCOME DATA			
100.0	100.0	100.0	100.0	100.0	100.0	Net Sales			100.0
						Gross Profit			
82.9	85.8	92.8	93.4	89.8	91.4	Operating Expenses			91.4
17.1	14.2	7.2	6.6	10.2	8.6	Operating Profit			8.6
5.1	5.8	2.8	3.0	3.9	2.7	All Other Expenses (net)			2.4
12.1	8.3	4.4	3.6	6.3	5.9	Profit Before Taxes			6.2
						RATIOS			
22.8	2.5	2.7	1.7	1.7	2.4				1.9
.8	1.3	1.4	1.3	1.0	1.5	Current			1.3
.4	.4	.8	.8	.7	.7				.8
22.8	1.8	2.1	1.4	1.2	2.0				1.5
.8	.9	1.1	.9	.8	1.2	Quick			1.0
.3	.3	.6	.5	.5	.5				.5
0 UND	12 30.2	25 14.5	20 18.2	14 27.0	32 11.4			24	15.5
18 20.3	35 10.3	49 7.4	45 8.1	36 10.2	56 6.5	Sales/Receivables		44	8.3
60 6.1	58 6.3	88 4.2	62 5.9	55 6.6	83 4.4			71	5.1
						Cost of Sales/Inventory			
						Cost of Sales/Payables			
23.4	8.0	5.6	10.1	7.6	5.0				8.2
-48.0	24.9	11.9	18.9	480.8	10.5	Sales/Working Capital			19.8
-3.9	-10.0	-44.6	-13.7	-27.3	NM				-26.1
	14.4	38.1	20.7	14.3	8.7				9.7
(24) 5.5	(53) 5.7	(30) 3.4	4.5	(11) 2.0		EBIT/Interest		(100)	3.8
.6	1.2	1.6	.7	.9					1.2
		4.2	31.0						4.9
	(11) 2.2	(10) 6.5				Net Profit + Depr., Dep., Amort./Cur. Mat. L/T/D		(21)	2.4
	1.4	1.5							1.3
.2	.4	.2	.3	1.0	.4				.2
6.8	.9	.4	1.6	2.2	5.5	Fixed/Worth			1.0
-.1	6.2	3.0	-6.8	6.5	-.7				17.1
.3	1.0	.7	1.4	1.1	1.6				1.2
12.0	2.5	1.4	3.8	3.6	8.3	Debt/Worth			3.1
-1.9	16.3	6.7	-10.3	12.0	-2.3				69.6
	78.5	61.2	60.7	51.7		% Profit Before Taxes/Tangible Net Worth			86.8
(23) 20.9	(48) 24.4	(23) 28.3	(12) 25.9					(100)	33.1
	-2.5	2.7	13.3	.4					10.1
113.1	30.4	22.2	16.4	12.6	6.1				23.0
53.1	5.8	7.8	7.9	8.6	3.4	% Profit Before Taxes/Total Assets			7.0
4.7	-.7	.3	2.2	-.8	.8				.8
355.0	46.9	46.2	44.6	8.9	37.6				49.1
82.6	13.9	18.8	15.3	1.3	10.1	Sales/Net Fixed Assets			17.6
8.4	2.0	4.2	2.9	.8	3.7				6.2
17.7	4.9	3.4	2.8	1.4	1.4				3.8
4.3	2.7	2.2	1.8	.9	.8	Sales/Total Assets			2.6
2.2	1.1	1.3	1.3	.5	.6				1.3
	1.4	.9	1.3	3.2					.8
(25) 2.7	(48) 1.9	(29) 2.0	(12) 8.6			% Depr., Dep., Amort./Sales		(99)	1.9
	9.1	6.1	10.3	19.7					5.3
	2.1	1.6							2.2
(10) 4.9	(15) 2.9					% Officers', Directors' Owners' Comp/Sales		(33)	5.0
	9.3	5.3							11.7
39704M	97392M	787012M	1757433M	1298834M	2652229M	Net Sales ($)			5010857M
3957M	35250M	306485M	826929M	1105803M	2605668M	Total Assets ($)			3283391M

M = $ thousand   MM = $ million
See Pages 9 through 22 for Explanation of Ratios and Data

Comparative Historical Data | Current Data Sorted by Sales

			Type of Statement						
34	40	33	Unqualified	1	2		5	8	17
16	15	13	Reviewed	1	1	3	2	4	2
14	11	20	Compiled	3	2	5	4	6	
14	17	24	Tax Returns	10	3	4	3	2	2
71	89	71	Other	2	3	8	8	14	36
4/1/08-3/31/09 ALL	4/1/09-3/31/10 ALL	4/1/10-3/31/11 ALL		26 (4/1-9/30/10)			135 (10/1/10-3/31/11)		
				0-1MM	1-3MM	3-5MM	5-10MM	10-25MM	25MM & OVER
149	172	161	NUMBER OF STATEMENTS	17	11	20	22	34	57
%	%	%	**ASSETS**	%	%	%	%	%	%
15.1	14.0	11.9	Cash & Equivalents	11.7	9.1	8.9	10.6	17.5	10.9
31.9	24.9	28.6	Trade Receivables (net)	14.7	26.9	32.2	35.4	32.6	26.8
6.6	6.6	6.4	Inventory	.0	2.5	7.5	7.1	8.3	7.4
4.8	5.5	4.4	All Other Current	5.3	1.5	7.0	3.8	2.7	4.9
58.4	50.9	51.4	Total Current	31.7	39.9	55.6	56.9	61.1	50.0
26.7	29.0	29.7	Fixed Assets (net)	56.7	46.0	27.8	24.5	21.9	25.9
6.6	11.6	9.5	Intangibles (net)	5.2	5.1	5.7	5.2	7.5	15.9
8.4	8.5	9.4	All Other Non-Current	6.5	8.9	10.9	13.4	9.6	8.3
100.0	100.0	100.0	Total	100.0	100.0	100.0	100.0	100.0	100.0
			LIABILITIES						
9.3	9.4	11.2	Notes Payable-Short Term	24.5	31.9	11.6	10.1	10.1	4.0
4.6	3.9	3.9	Cur. Mat.-L.T.D.	4.9	11.1	5.8	4.5	2.3	2.1
18.4	15.2	14.1	Trade Payables	9.3	8.2	12.8	12.8	15.5	16.9
.3	.1	.4	Income Taxes Payable	.0	.0	.8	.3	.3	.6
15.1	18.3	13.2	All Other Current	12.7	7.0	11.7	8.3	13.3	16.8
47.6	46.8	42.7	Total Current	51.5	58.2	42.8	36.0	41.5	40.5
18.3	22.5	23.3	Long-Term Debt	52.2	56.6	17.3	15.4	16.2	17.7
.2	.7	.5	Deferred Taxes	.0	.1	.5	1.0	.2	.7
4.7	7.0	8.5	All Other Non-Current	2.4	8.4	6.0	7.1	12.1	9.6
29.2	23.0	24.9	Net Worth	-6.1	-23.3	33.4	40.5	30.1	31.5
100.0	100.0	100.0	Total Liabilities & Net Worth	100.0	100.0	100.0	100.0	100.0	100.0
			INCOME DATA						
100.0	100.0	100.0	Net Sales	100.0	100.0	100.0	100.0	100.0	100.0
			Gross Profit						
92.8	93.7	90.5	Operating Expenses	68.3	87.1	96.1	93.5	94.2	92.5
7.2	6.3	9.5	Operating Profit	31.7	12.9	3.9	6.5	5.8	7.5
2.7	1.9	3.7	All Other Expenses (net)	17.9	7.1	1.1	.5	1.8	2.0
4.6	4.4	5.8	Profit Before Taxes	13.8	5.8	2.8	6.1	4.0	5.5
			RATIOS						
2.0	1.7	2.2	Current	.9	18.3	2.7	2.2	3.2	1.7
1.2	1.1	1.3		.4	1.0	1.4	1.6	1.8	1.3
.8	.6	.7		.1	.3	.9	1.1	.8	.8
1.6	1.4	1.8	Quick	.7	17.3	2.5	1.8	2.4	1.4
1.0	.8	1.0		.3	.6	.9	1.3	1.3	1.0
.6	.5	.5		.1	.2	.5	.8	.6	.5
22 16.4	17 21.4	18 20.1	Sales/Receivables	0 UND	5 78.3	16 22.5	28 13.3	29 12.6	25 14.4
41 8.9	38 9.6	39 9.3		14 26.0	27 13.7	52 7.0	43 8.5	43 8.4	44 8.3
64 5.7	60 6.1	63 5.8		40 9.2	61 6.0	89 4.1	69 5.3	68 5.3	63 5.8
			Cost of Sales/Inventory						
			Cost of Sales/Payables						
7.2	10.7	6.2	Sales/Working Capital	NM	4.8	6.3	5.9	4.1	8.6
24.6	46.5	19.4		-4.4	-116.9	16.1	12.0	9.8	18.9
-43.4	-13.4	-27.9		-1.6	-3.3	-44.9	71.9	-35.1	-37.0
18.5	13.9	19.7	EBIT/Interest			5.6	17.8	49.5	25.2
(114) 4.2	(141) 3.7	(139) 4.5				(19) 1.2	(21) 7.3	(30) 4.1	(52) 5.1
.8	1.0	1.2				.0	2.5	.1	1.3
9.4	8.1	7.1	Net Profit + Depr., Dep., Amort./Cur. Mat. L/T/D						22.5
(23) 1.9	(30) 3.3	(26) 2.5							(11) 3.8
.7	1.1	1.4							1.3
.3	.3	.3	Fixed/Worth	.2	.3	.3	.2	.2	.3
.8	1.4	1.2		6.8	1.7	.7	.4	.7	1.6
7.4	-2.5	42.0		-15.7	-.4	1.8	2.0	-2.7	-12.0
.8	1.3	1.0	Debt/Worth	2.0	.4	.9	.9	.4	1.3
3.0	4.1	2.7		12.0	1.1	2.4	1.3	1.7	3.6
53.2	-5.4	134.1		-19.0	-6.7	9.7	4.2	-4.7	-62.7
69.3	66.0	66.5	% Profit Before Taxes/Tangible Net Worth	130.6		74.4	54.6	66.0	67.3
(116) 35.2	(119) 26.0	(122) 25.7		(12) 11.4		(18) 2.7	(19) 25.4	(24) 44.7	(42) 29.8
3.8	8.3	4.3		-5.2		-5.6	9.8	8.4	12.4
21.3	14.4	18.9	% Profit Before Taxes/Total Assets	19.0	43.1	10.1	20.6	26.7	13.2
6.7	6.4	7.6		3.0	7.8	.6	11.1	9.9	7.9
-.7	.9	.3		-1.7	-4.0	-3.0	2.2	.5	1.9
47.4	48.5	46.2	Sales/Net Fixed Assets	23.4	48.5	40.1	68.8	50.4	43.0
19.2	14.8	14.6		.8	2.3	14.6	19.2	17.7	14.7
5.6	3.7	3.1		.2	.5	3.9	4.1	5.2	3.4
3.7	3.3	3.5	Sales/Total Assets	2.2	3.1	4.5	3.4	3.5	3.3
2.7	2.0	1.9		.2	1.1	2.4	2.2	2.2	1.7
1.3	1.0	.9		.1	.4	1.6	1.4	1.6	.8
.7	1.1	1.1	% Depr., Dep., Amort./Sales	8.6		1.2	1.1	.9	.9
(113) 1.8	(123) 2.3	(124) 2.5		(12) 18.7		(16) 2.1	(19) 2.0	(28) 1.9	(41) 1.6
6.8	8.1	8.3		23.9		7.2	4.6	5.8	5.9
1.4	1.1	1.9	% Officers', Directors' Owners' Comp/Sales					1.5	
(36) 3.4	(32) 4.6	(35) 4.5						(12) 2.7	
9.7	13.1	9.8						13.2	
5524499M	6157303M	6632604M	Net Sales ($)	8115M	17520M	80794M	165045M	559462M	5801668M
3102250M	4221608M	4884092M	Total Assets ($)	19083M	44128M	40156M	96031M	407997M	4276697M

© RMA 2011

M = $ thousand   MM = $ million
See Pages 9 through 22 for Explanation of Ratios and Data

Current Data Sorted by Assets   **Comparative Historical Data**

Type of Statement

	0-500M	500M-2MM	2-10MM	10-50MM	50-100MM	100-250MM		4/1/06-3/31/07 ALL	4/1/07-3/31/08 ALL
Unqualified		1	19	29	16	12		63	61
Reviewed	1	9	20	12				23	17
Compiled	1	8	11		1	1		13	15
Tax Returns	15	9	6	1				30	29
Other	9	33	51	33	12	14		132	127
		47 (4/1-9/30/10)		277 (10/1/10-3/31/11)					
NUMBER OF STATEMENTS	26	60	107	75	29	27		261	249

Financial Data

0-500M	500M-2MM	2-10MM	10-50MM	50-100MM	100-250MM		4/1/06-3/31/07 ALL	4/1/07-3/31/08 ALL
%	%	%	%	%	%	**ASSETS**	%	%
41.0	24.2	20.7	18.1	15.8	23.7	Cash & Equivalents	16.7	20.3
17.2	37.2	31.8	24.3	12.9	17.9	Trade Receivables (net)	31.6	32.7
.8	2.1	1.1	1.9	1.6	.5	Inventory	3.2	2.7
.9	3.6	5.2	7.6	9.8	6.5	All Other Current	5.3	4.5
59.9	67.1	58.8	51.9	40.1	48.6	Total Current	56.7	60.2
20.2	17.1	26.2	24.0	23.5	12.8	Fixed Assets (net)	21.1	19.7
7.7	6.7	6.4	16.0	25.7	30.8	Intangibles (net)	12.5	11.1
12.3	9.1	8.6	8.1	10.6	7.8	All Other Non-Current	9.7	9.0
100.0	100.0	100.0	100.0	100.0	100.0	Total	100.0	100.0
						LIABILITIES		
17.3	12.2	6.5	4.6	.7	1.6	Notes Payable-Short Term	10.0	12.2
10.0	3.3	3.8	7.8	1.9	2.0	Cur. Mat.-L.T.D.	3.5	3.4
21.1	11.2	14.9	11.3	6.8	4.3	Trade Payables	13.9	11.8
1.2	.2	.3	.3	.5	.8	Income Taxes Payable	.8	.6
29.2	17.5	15.4	19.2	20.8	18.7	All Other Current	17.3	20.8
78.8	44.4	41.0	43.2	30.8	27.3	Total Current	45.5	48.8
28.0	14.5	12.4	16.4	27.1	25.6	Long-Term Debt	19.0	16.3
.0	.1	.7	1.1	.6	.8	Deferred Taxes	.6	.4
16.0	12.3	8.6	9.5	9.8	6.4	All Other Non-Current	9.9	10.7
-22.8	28.7	37.4	29.9	31.7	39.9	Net Worth	25.0	23.8
100.0	100.0	100.0	100.0	100.0	100.0	Total Liabilities & Net Worth	100.0	100.0
						INCOME DATA		
100.0	100.0	100.0	100.0	100.0	100.0	Net Sales	100.0	100.0
						Gross Profit		
90.0	94.6	93.2	93.3	87.3	91.0	Operating Expenses	92.8	91.8
10.0	5.4	6.8	6.7	12.7	9.0	Operating Profit	7.2	8.2
1.0	.7	1.3	3.0	3.8	1.7	All Other Expenses (net)	2.1	1.5
9.0	4.7	5.5	3.6	8.9	7.4	Profit Before Taxes	5.1	6.7
						RATIOS		
5.6	5.9	3.4	2.2	2.7	2.9		2.4	2.3
1.7	1.8	1.3	1.2	1.3	1.7	Current	1.3	1.4
.5	.8	.7	.9	.7	1.0		.9	.9
5.5	5.3	3.2	1.7	2.0	2.6		2.1	2.1
1.7	1.7	1.2	1.1	1.1	1.2	Quick	1.1	1.3
.3	.8	.7	.7	.4	.9		.7	.7
0 UND	12 30.9	23 15.8	26 13.8	21 17.3	24 15.5		26 13.8	28 12.8
0 UND	34 10.6	45 8.1	50 7.4	30 12.1	55 6.6	Sales/Receivables	48 7.6	49 7.5
35 10.4	56 6.5	62 5.9	67 5.5	56 6.6	68 5.3		68 5.3	70 5.2
						Cost of Sales/Inventory		
						Cost of Sales/Payables		
9.2	5.9	5.4	5.3	3.8	1.8		7.2	6.5
63.2	15.7	15.6	19.4	16.4	9.0	Sales/Working Capital	17.5	21.1
-10.7	-59.4	-21.7	-37.7	-13.2	-578.2		-39.2	-66.0
26.0	56.1	28.7	24.4	73.3	73.9		14.5	16.4
(20) 5.8	(48) 11.4	(78) 5.5	(59) 4.1	(27) 5.6	(19) 6.3	EBIT/Interest	(208) 3.6	(190) 5.1
.6	-.3	.8	-2.0	1.3	1.1		.4	1.0
		4.8	12.8				10.3	13.4
		(21) 1.8	(18) 2.7			Net Profit + Depr., Dep., Amort./Cur. Mat. L/T/D	(45) 3.3	(36) 1.8
		.6	-.2				1.2	.8
.0	.1	.2	.2	.3	.1		.2	.2
.3	.3	.7	1.3	2.2	.8	Fixed/Worth	.9	.7
-3.1	-3.6	9.4	-3.2	-.3	-.4		-1.7	-8.3
.8	.4	.4	1.2	.8	.7		.9	.9
8.2	2.1	2.1	2.3	8.6	2.5	Debt/Worth	2.8	2.6
-3.0	-12.9	15.1	-13.5	-2.8	-2.6		-7.7	-20.3
249.9	90.3	67.4	52.9	55.1	46.9		73.2	90.6
(16) 112.2	(42) 58.0	(86) 28.3	(51) 29.2	(17) 25.0	(18) 8.8	% Profit Before Taxes/Tangible Net Worth	(182) 32.7	(181) 42.0
11.6	25.7	4.2	8.1	11.7	-3.5		6.0	13.4
110.6	39.7	30.3	15.3	16.3	21.7		22.3	27.9
12.8	19.9	7.3	7.9	9.6	7.8	% Profit Before Taxes/Total Assets	8.3	11.0
-6.6	-.1	1.6	-4.1	3.4	-.4		-.9	.8
UND	166.1	41.9	38.1	21.2	22.3		63.5	66.4
77.7	34.9	12.6	10.0	10.5	15.1	Sales/Net Fixed Assets	18.4	19.2
15.0	14.5	3.8	4.2	3.5	7.9		6.4	8.2
9.8	5.3	3.3	2.4	1.9	1.7		3.5	3.9
6.8	3.6	2.2	1.5	1.0	1.0	Sales/Total Assets	2.0	2.3
2.8	2.2	1.5	.8	.6	.8		1.1	1.5
.6	.6	1.0	1.3	2.2	2.3		.9	.7
(12) .8	(35) 1.2	(80) 2.6	(64) 4.0	(17) 3.8	(13) 3.1	% Depr., Dep., Amort./Sales	(169) 2.6	(175) 2.2
6.6	3.6	5.7	7.4	8.1	4.6		5.9	4.8
4.3	4.2	2.4	.6				3.4	2.7
(16) 10.9	(27) 6.6	(28) 5.0	(10) 1.1			% Officers', Directors' Owners' Comp/Sales	(59) 5.8	(66) 6.8
31.0	10.1	8.8	5.6				11.3	10.5
54105M	269165M	1403432M	3157529M	3051221M	4951258M	Net Sales ($)	9257677M	7081062M
7276M	67608M	550712M	1743899M	2179246M	4314413M	Total Assets ($)	6289266M	5058850M

© RMA 2011

M = $ thousand   MM = $ million
See Pages 9 through 22 for Explanation of Ratios and Data

Comparative Historical Data

Current Data Sorted by Sales

4/1/08-3/31/09 ALL	4/1/09-3/31/10 ALL	4/1/10-3/31/11 ALL	Type of Statement	0-1MM	1-3MM	3-5MM	5-10MM	10-25MM	25MM & OVER
80	93	77	Unqualified		1	2	10	15	49
27	21	42	Reviewed	1	5	5	9	11	11
24	20	22	Compiled		4	4	5	5	4
22	34	31	Tax Returns	7	7	3	10	2	2
127	149	152	Other	5	27	13	29	30	48
				47 (4/1-9/30/10)			277 (10/1/10-3/31/11)		
280	317	324	**NUMBER OF STATEMENTS**	13	44	27	63	63	114
%	%	%	**ASSETS**	%	%	%	%	%	%
17.6	19.6	22.2	Cash & Equivalents	25.9	26.9	29.6	21.0	18.5	20.8
30.2	26.7	27.1	Trade Receivables (net)	25.8	27.2	22.9	30.8	28.5	25.3
2.3	1.8	1.4	Inventory	.9	1.1	.9	2.1	.8	1.7
5.5	5.1	5.6	All Other Current	.5	4.2	3.2	4.6	7.2	7.1
55.6	53.2	56.3	Total Current	53.2	59.4	56.6	58.4	55.1	55.0
20.7	21.7	22.2	Fixed Assets (net)	10.9	27.2	23.6	26.1	25.3	17.2
15.6	14.3	12.5	Intangibles (net)	17.4	7.3	5.6	4.7	12.0	20.2
8.1	10.7	9.0	All Other Non-Current	18.6	6.1	14.2	10.8	7.6	7.6
100.0	100.0	100.0	Total	100.0	100.0	100.0	100.0	100.0	100.0
			LIABILITIES						
10.3	13.1	7.1	Notes Payable-Short Term	9.6	13.4	8.2	7.5	5.8	4.5
6.3	3.9	4.8	Cur. Mat.-L.T.D.	2.1	7.6	1.5	4.5	5.3	4.7
12.6	10.8	12.3	Trade Payables	37.6	9.6	8.3	10.7	12.5	12.1
.3	.4	.4	Income Taxes Payable	2.5	.3	.2	.5	.2	.5
21.1	19.4	18.5	All Other Current	38.0	18.2	12.9	15.0	17.5	20.3
50.6	47.6	43.1	Total Current	89.8	49.1	31.0	38.2	41.3	42.0
19.3	18.3	17.4	Long-Term Debt	21.7	26.1	15.7	14.2	11.9	18.7
.6	.7	.6	Deferred Taxes	.0	.0	.7	1.0	.9	.6
8.1	10.7	10.0	All Other Non-Current	13.9	12.0	9.3	13.6	9.7	7.2
21.4	22.8	28.9	Net Worth	-25.4	12.7	43.3	33.0	36.3	31.5
100.0	100.0	100.0	Total Liabilities & Net Worth	100.0	100.0	100.0	100.0	100.0	100.0
			INCOME DATA						
100.0	100.0	100.0	Net Sales	100.0	100.0	100.0	100.0	100.0	100.0
			Gross Profit						
94.0	92.9	92.5	Operating Expenses	95.7	92.8	92.0	92.7	93.8	91.4
6.0	7.1	7.5	Operating Profit	4.3	7.2	8.0	7.3	6.2	8.6
2.2	2.4	1.8	All Other Expenses (net)	1.8	2.2	1.4	1.1	1.5	2.4
3.9	4.6	5.7	Profit Before Taxes	2.5	5.0	6.6	6.3	4.7	6.2
			RATIOS						
2.3	2.1	3.2	Current	6.0	4.1	6.3	3.9	2.4	2.6
1.3	1.2	1.4		.8	1.4	2.0	1.7	1.3	1.3
.8	.8	.8		.2	.6	.8	.8	.9	.9
2.1	1.9	2.9	Quick	5.9	3.8	5.6	3.5	2.2	2.1
1.1	(316) 1.0	1.2		.8	1.2	1.8	1.6	1.1	1.1
.6	.7	.7		.2	.4	.7	.7	.7	.7
23 15.8	20 18.1	16 22.4	Sales/Receivables	0 UND	0 UND	2 216.4	14 25.7	22 16.6	27 13.5
44 8.2	42 8.6	42 8.8		35 10.4	24 15.2	36 10.2	37 9.7	46 7.9	46 7.9
62 5.9	60 6.0	63 5.8		46 8.0	67 5.4	52 7.0	56 6.6	66 5.5	64 5.7
			Cost of Sales/Inventory						
			Cost of Sales/Payables						
6.9	7.4	5.1	Sales/Working Capital	4.3	4.0	4.3	5.0	6.7	4.9
20.5	27.1	16.3		-40.5	21.8	11.5	13.6	18.6	16.7
-34.9	-37.3	-31.1		-5.8	-5.5	-19.1	-66.0	-21.7	-79.6
14.8	17.6	32.5	EBIT/Interest	17.1	20.0	31.2	48.4	27.8	64.0
(223) 3.7	(251) 3.7	(251) 5.6		(10) 3.0	(33) 3.5	(20) 10.2	(52) 8.5	(48) 4.3	(88) 6.3
.4	.4	.6		-19.4	-1.0	.5	1.3	-2.3	.8
5.0	12.7	8.2	Net Profit + Depr., Dep., Amort./Cur. Mat. L/T/D				6.0	4.9	15.3
(46) 2.8	(50) 2.8	(54) 2.2					(11) 2.3	(18) 2.0	(21) 2.3
1.4	1.1	.9					.8	.7	1.3
.2	.2	.1	Fixed/Worth	.0	.2	.0	.2	.2	.1
1.2	1.0	.8		.1	.5	.3	.7	1.3	.9
-1.0	-3.3	-4.7		-1.3	-10.1	4.9	10.6	-36.6	-2.0
1.0	.9	.6	Debt/Worth	.8	.5	.2	.4	1.1	.8
4.4	3.1	2.7		10.9	3.1	1.4	1.9	2.5	2.8
-5.1	-10.2	-16.7		-1.4	-5.5	8.1	20.6	-36.9	-6.7
74.4	67.1	75.8	% Profit Before Taxes/Tangible Net Worth		92.0	78.8	81.2	90.1	59.4
(186) 30.9	(215) 26.0	(230) 32.3			(29) 41.2	(22) 32.5	(49) 39.3	(46) 42.8	(77) 28.8
9.7	8.4	5.6			2.0	12.6	5.6	16.3	4.4
19.3	18.1	27.0	% Profit Before Taxes/Total Assets	79.7	35.0	34.0	29.0	30.3	18.2
6.9	7.0	8.7		2.8	4.3	13.0	8.4	10.1	8.9
-.8	-1.8	.3		-7.9	-5.4	-.3	2.7	.9	.2
58.0	48.6	53.7	Sales/Net Fixed Assets	UND	52.4	131.7	37.9	56.8	42.1
17.0	14.4	15.7		61.8	14.1	16.6	17.0	10.1	17.5
6.4	6.6	5.5		9.3	2.8	3.6	5.2	4.8	7.4
3.7	3.8	3.6	Sales/Total Assets	4.7	4.0	5.0	4.5	3.3	3.0
2.3	1.9	2.0		2.0	2.3	2.2	2.9	1.9	1.7
1.2	1.1	1.1		.8	.9	1.3	1.8	1.2	.9
.7	.9	1.0	% Depr., Dep., Amort./Sales		.7	.7	1.0	1.7	.9
(177) 2.2	(204) 2.8	(221) 2.8			(25) 1.8	(18) 3.2	(50) 2.2	(47) 4.1	(76) 2.5
5.3	6.3	5.8			11.1	5.7	4.3	6.5	5.0
2.3	2.4	2.5	% Officers', Directors' Owners' Comp/Sales		7.9	2.8	1.8	2.8	
(65) 5.9	(67) 4.8	(82) 6.1			(16) 13.5	(10) 5.6	(25) 4.2	(14) 4.7	
11.7	12.6	13.0			20.0	14.0	7.5	9.0	
12580482M	11368362M	12886710M	Net Sales ($)	6883M	90626M	106826M	469119M	997511M	11215745M
8226720M	8915552M	8863154M	Total Assets ($)	7911M	104729M	65503M	282597M	632779M	7769635M

© RMA 2011

M = $ thousand   MM = $ million
See Pages 9 through 22 for Explanation of Ratios and Data

Current Data Sorted by Assets

Comparative Historical Data

						Type of Statement		
		1	1		2	Unqualified		2
						Reviewed		1
						Compiled		1
1	4					Tax Returns		1
2	4		6	3	3	Other		12
	5 (4/1-9/30/10)	3	25 (10/1/10-3/31/11)				4/1/06-3/31/07 ALL	4/1/07-3/31/08 ALL
0-500M	500M-2MM	2-10MM	10-50MM	50-100MM	100-250MM			
3	8	4	7	3	5	NUMBER OF STATEMENTS		17
%	%	%	%	%	%	ASSETS	%	%
						Cash & Equivalents	D	13.9
						Trade Receivables (net)	A	25.2
						Inventory	T	3.8
						All Other Current	A	3.7
						Total Current		46.5
						Fixed Assets (net)	N	14.0
						Intangibles (net)	O	28.1
						All Other Non-Current	T	11.4
						Total		100.0
						LIABILITIES	A	
						Notes Payable-Short Term	V	7.6
						Cur. Mat.-L.T.D.	A	2.7
						Trade Payables	I	8.1
						Income Taxes Payable	L	.0
						All Other Current	A	22.2
						Total Current	B	40.6
						Long-Term Debt	L	6.8
						Deferred Taxes	E	.1
						All Other Non-Current		7.9
						Net Worth		44.5
						Total Liabilties & Net Worth		100.0
						INCOME DATA		
						Net Sales		100.0
						Gross Profit		
						Operating Expenses		92.3
						Operating Profit		7.7
						All Other Expenses (net)		1.9
						Profit Before Taxes		5.8
						RATIOS		
								2.5
						Current		1.6
								.7
								2.4
						Quick		1.1
								.5
								15 24.0
						Sales/Receivables		43 8.4
								54 6.7
						Cost of Sales/Inventory		
						Cost of Sales/Payables		
								10.8
						Sales/Working Capital		28.1
								-9.3
								147.6
						EBIT/Interest		(11) 5.8
								.7
						Net Profit + Depr., Dep., Amort./Cur. Mat. L/T/D		
								.2
						Fixed/Worth		.7
								-.2
								.6
						Debt/Worth		1.5
								-3.3
						% Profit Before Taxes/Tangible Net Worth		62.5
								(11) 47.0
								13.8
						% Profit Before Taxes/Total Assets		29.3
								6.8
								1.9
						Sales/Net Fixed Assets		101.9
								33.8
								11.9
						Sales/Total Assets		6.1
								1.5
								.9
						% Depr., Dep., Amort./Sales		
						% Officers', Directors' Owners' Comp/Sales		
4779M	38468M	46997M	250834M	320128M	990737M	Net Sales ($)		819731M
1053M	8122M	18049M	136245M	198310M	809047M	Total Assets ($)		525773M

M = $ thousand   MM = $ million
See Pages 9 through 22 for Explanation of Ratios and Data

© RMA 2011

Comparative Historical Data | Current Data Sorted by Sales

	4/1/08-3/31/09 ALL	4/1/09-3/31/10 ALL	4/1/10-3/31/11 ALL	Type of Statement	0-1MM	1-3MM	3-5MM	5-10MM	10-25MM	25MM & OVER
	4	7	3	Unqualified		4				3
	2		1	Reviewed					1	
	2	3		Compiled						
	4	5	5	Tax Returns					1	
	18	15	21	Other		4	1	3	5	8
	30	30	30	**NUMBER OF STATEMENTS**		8	1	3	7	11
	%	%	%		%	%	%	%	%	%

Header date spans: left columns all = **ALL**, 30 statements each. Right side: **5 (4/1-9/30/10)** covers 0-1MM and 1-3MM; **25 (10/1/10-3/31/11)** covers 3-5MM through 25MM & OVER.

For the sort columns 0-1MM through 10-25MM the Assets/Liabilities percentages are marked **DATA NOT AVAILABLE** (only the 25MM & OVER column has values).

ASSETS

	08-09	09-10	10-11		25MM & OVER
Cash & Equivalents	17.6	28.5	26.1		30.7
Trade Receivables (net)	33.8	19.2	24.1		18.8
Inventory	1.5	3.3	1.2		.1
All Other Current	6.9	7.6	5.1		1.8
Total Current	59.7	58.5	56.5		51.3
Fixed Assets (net)	19.3	11.7	13.9		7.2
Intangibles (net)	12.9	22.2	21.1		36.8
All Other Non-Current	8.1	7.6	8.5		4.7
Total	100.0	100.0	100.0		100.0

LIABILITIES

	08-09	09-10	10-11		25MM & OVER
Notes Payable-Short Term	13.5	26.0	1.7		2.5
Cur. Mat.-L.T.D.	4.4	2.6	1.8		1.9
Trade Payables	18.7	11.8	11.2		9.8
Income Taxes Payable	2.8	.2	.3		.7
All Other Current	18.7	22.5	32.4		24.6
Total Current	58.0	63.1	47.3		39.4
Long-Term Debt	23.8	24.0	10.7		6.7
Deferred Taxes	.1	.2	.6		.9
All Other Non-Current	11.6	8.7	4.6		2.8
Net Worth	6.5	4.1	36.8		50.2
Total Liabilities & Net Worth	100.0	100.0	100.0		100.0

INCOME DATA

	08-09	09-10	10-11		25MM & OVER
Net Sales	100.0	100.0	100.0		100.0
Gross Profit					
Operating Expenses	92.7	95.1	92.0		86.9
Operating Profit	7.3	4.9	8.0		13.1
All Other Expenses (net)	2.9	1.0	1.3		1.3
Profit Before Taxes	4.5	3.9	6.7		11.9

RATIOS

	08-09	09-10	10-11		25MM & OVER
Current	2.1	2.4	2.6		2.0
	1.3	1.4	1.3		1.1
	.6	.9	.8		.8
Quick	1.8	2.4	2.3		2.0
	1.1	1.1	1.1		1.1
	.4	.7	.7		.8
Sales/Receivables	9 — 38.8	3 — 139.8	6 — 64.3		6 — 63.7
	35 — 10.5	23 — 16.2	40 — 9.1		30 — 12.1
	59 — 6.2	62 — 5.9	66 — 5.6		60 — 6.0
Cost of Sales/Inventory					
Cost of Sales/Payables					
Sales/Working Capital	9.1	8.1	5.8		5.2
	23.4	15.9	39.7		42.7
	-8.2	-25.6	-15.4		-19.9
EBIT/Interest	12.8	12.4	51.3		
	(22) .9	(22) 3.5	(19) 5.4		
	-2.5	-4.3	1.1		
Net Profit + Depr., Dep., Amort./Cur. Mat. L/T/D					
Fixed/Worth	.2	.1	.2		.2
	1.8	1.5	.5		.6
	-.4	-.4	-1.4		-1.7
Debt/Worth	1.4	1.8	.7		1.4
	4.9	13.3	2.9		4.0
	-2.9	-1.9	-10.0		-5.2
% Profit Before Taxes/Tangible Net Worth	102.9	90.4	124.4		
	(18) 42.4	(16) 45.1	(21) 61.9		
	-26.4	17.1	9.2		
% Profit Before Taxes/Total Assets	22.5	32.3	24.6		19.9
	2.8	9.0	8.7		12.2
	-11.3	-2.9	-1.0		8.1
Sales/Net Fixed Assets	89.8	116.7	60.7		85.4
	30.3	32.9	36.6		39.0
	13.3	19.3	16.6		26.0
Sales/Total Assets	5.1	6.0	3.3		2.3
	2.9	2.3	2.0		1.7
	1.3	1.3	1.3		1.0
% Depr., Dep., Amort./Sales	.6	.5	.4		
	(16) 1.7	(17) 1.4	(19) 1.7		
	4.4	2.7	5.2		
% Officers', Directors' Owners' Comp/Sales					

Dollar Data

	08-09	09-10	10-11		0-1MM	1-3MM	3-5MM	5-10MM	10-25MM	25MM & OVER
Net Sales ($)	977983M	1632322M	1651943M			16945M	4777M	21070M	120989M	1488162M
Total Assets ($)	500831M	1130920M	1170826M			6492M	1600M	10943M	61293M	1090498M

M = $ thousand   MM = $ million
See Pages 9 through 22 for Explanation of Ratios and Data

Current Data Sorted by Assets   Comparative Historical Data

Type of Statement	0-500M	500M-2MM	2-10MM	10-50MM	50-100MM	100-250MM		4/1/06-3/31/07 ALL	4/1/07-3/31/08 ALL
Unqualified		1	1	4	2	1		3	5
Reviewed		2	2					2	3
Compiled			1					1	
Tax Returns	7	4	1					1	3
Other	9	8	8	4	2	4		11	8
		8 (4/1-9/30/10)		53 (10/1/10-3/31/11)					
NUMBER OF STATEMENTS	16	15	13	8	4	5		18	19
	%	%	%	%	%	%		%	%
ASSETS									
Cash & Equivalents	46.9	26.9	22.4					13.6	13.3
Trade Receivables (net)	23.5	33.7	30.2					35.0	31.6
Inventory	.8	1.6	7.3					2.6	4.1
All Other Current	.3	10.4	3.5					7.6	4.5
Total Current	71.5	72.6	63.5					58.8	53.6
Fixed Assets (net)	14.2	14.3	18.2					15.6	15.1
Intangibles (net)	3.2	5.5	11.0					18.6	19.2
All Other Non-Current	11.1	7.5	7.3					7.0	12.1
Total	100.0	100.0	100.0					100.0	100.0
LIABILITIES									
Notes Payable-Short Term	27.9	4.9	8.3					15.4	38.7
Cur. Mat.-L.T.D.	1.2	2.2	.5					3.1	8.5
Trade Payables	27.2	20.4	14.5					8.0	6.6
Income Taxes Payable	.0	.2	.8					.8	.4
All Other Current	11.8	12.3	24.9					19.9	18.4
Total Current	68.2	40.1	49.1					47.2	72.6
Long-Term Debt	14.7	9.9	14.4					21.0	24.6
Deferred Taxes	.0	.7	.5					.5	.7
All Other Non-Current	4.4	.9	15.2					7.7	7.6
Net Worth	12.7	48.3	20.8					23.6	-5.5
Total Liabilities & Net Worth	100.0	100.0	100.0					100.0	100.0
INCOME DATA									
Net Sales	100.0	100.0	100.0					100.0	100.0
Gross Profit									
Operating Expenses	94.9	91.9	93.2					93.4	89.6
Operating Profit	5.1	8.1	6.8					6.6	10.4
All Other Expenses (net)	-.1	.5	2.8					2.5	5.6
Profit Before Taxes	5.2	7.6	4.0					4.2	4.7
RATIOS									
Current	4.9	12.1	4.8					2.5	2.4
	1.5	2.0	2.2					1.5	.9
	.5	.8	.7					.8	.6
Quick	4.9	7.8	4.3					1.7	2.3
	1.5	1.7	1.8					1.0	.8
	.5	.8	.4					.6	.3
Sales/Receivables	0 UND	4 96.3	11 33.3					38 9.5	15 24.4
	0 UND	31 11.7	53 6.9					60 6.1	45 8.0
	26 14.2	58 6.3	71 5.2					97 3.7	83 4.4
Cost of Sales/Inventory									
Cost of Sales/Payables									
Sales/Working Capital	23.9	4.3	4.8					5.5	6.5
	38.3	11.9	7.0					13.9	-60.7
	-23.4	-29.8	-7.2					-11.7	-9.1
EBIT/Interest								27.2	10.9
								(15) 9.2	(18) 2.0
								3.4	.1
Net Profit + Depr., Dep., Amort./Cur. Mat. L/T/D									
Fixed/Worth	.0	.0	.0					.4	.1
	.4	.2	1.0					4.0	1.6
	UND	.5	-.6					-.2	-.3
Debt/Worth	.5	.5	.8					1.1	1.2
	2.1	1.3	3.2					NM	10.2
	-73.8	18.9	-7.5					-3.1	-2.0
% Profit Before Taxes/Tangible Net Worth	209.8	105.6							51.9
	(11) 95.1	(13) 59.6						(10)	29.8
	20.2	14.8							8.4
% Profit Before Taxes/Total Assets	81.6	45.6	43.0					26.7	15.6
	47.5	17.6	9.6					14.6	6.5
	-2.0	5.2	.6					5.1	-1.2
Sales/Net Fixed Assets	UND	176.8	532.2					69.7	64.2
	164.6	111.2	46.2					15.9	22.1
	35.2	17.6	8.5					10.7	13.3
Sales/Total Assets	13.0	4.4	3.3					3.3	5.1
	9.1	3.3	2.4					2.1	2.6
	6.8	2.3	1.1					1.0	.9
% Depr., Dep., Amort./Sales									.3
								(10)	1.0
									3.7
% Officers', Directors' Owners' Comp/Sales									
Net Sales ($)	35005M	62791M	136391M	304730M	292217M	867853M		4246874M	902002M
Total Assets ($)	3181M	18109M	49769M	172510M	235493M	783769M		791662M	864962M

M = $ thousand   MM = $ million
See Pages 9 through 22 for Explanation of Ratios and Data

Comparative Historical Data / Current Data Sorted by Sales

	4/1/08-3/31/09 ALL	4/1/09-3/31/10 ALL	4/1/10-3/31/11 ALL		0-1MM	1-3MM	3-5MM	5-10MM	10-25MM	25MM & OVER
				Type of Statement		8 (4/1-9/30/10)			53 (10/1/10-3/31/11)	
Unqualified	41	12	9			1		1	1	6
Reviewed	11	9	4			2	1		1	
Compiled	16	1	1							1
Tax Returns	18	16	12		4	3	2	2	1	
Other	67	21	35		2	8	6	7	2	10
NUMBER OF STATEMENTS	153	59	61		6	14	9	10	5	17
	%	%	%	**ASSETS**	%	%	%	%	%	%
Cash & Equivalents	18.3	18.8	28.5			28.0		29.7		20.6
Trade Receivables (net)	24.3	34.4	27.4			28.6		37.1		21.6
Inventory	7.9	7.1	3.3			.9		6.2		4.1
All Other Current	4.3	3.0	6.0			1.0		10.2		9.3
Total Current	54.8	63.3	65.2			58.4		83.2		55.5
Fixed Assets (net)	25.6	17.3	14.8			29.0		5.2		11.2
Intangibles (net)	7.8	9.5	11.5			8.4		1.1		24.9
All Other Non-Current	11.8	9.9	8.5			4.2		10.4		8.3
Total	100.0	100.0	100.0			100.0		100.0		100.0
				LIABILITIES						
Notes Payable-Short Term	9.0	13.9	10.6			12.1		2.9		1.2
Cur. Mat.-L.T.D.	2.8	3.0	1.5			1.9		1.0		1.6
Trade Payables	10.7	14.6	17.3			11.3		26.2		7.6
Income Taxes Payable	.4	.2	.4			.3		.3		.5
All Other Current	16.1	20.1	19.3			11.5		16.9		28.5
Total Current	38.9	51.9	49.1			37.2		47.3		39.4
Long-Term Debt	18.9	13.8	14.2			29.7		8.2		16.6
Deferred Taxes	.5	.5	.7			.4		1.1		1.4
All Other Non-Current	7.9	8.6	6.8			5.0		3.2		9.9
Net Worth	33.8	25.2	29.2			27.7		40.1		32.8
Total Liabilities & Net Worth	100.0	100.0	100.0			100.0		100.0		100.0
				INCOME DATA						
Net Sales	100.0	100.0	100.0			100.0		100.0		100.0
Gross Profit										
Operating Expenses	92.9	93.1	93.2			94.3		91.2		93.2
Operating Profit	7.1	6.9	6.8			5.7		8.8		6.8
All Other Expenses (net)	2.2	1.4	1.2			1.6		.0		2.0
Profit Before Taxes	4.9	5.5	5.6			4.1		8.8		4.9
				RATIOS						
Current	3.2	2.4	3.7			4.7		5.7		2.4
	1.5	1.4	1.6			1.8		2.1		1.6
	1.0	1.0	.8			1.0		1.2		1.1
Quick	2.5	2.0	3.5			4.7		5.1		1.9
	1.2	1.2	1.5			1.6		1.9		1.2
	.6	.5	.6			.9		1.1		.8
Sales/Receivables	11 32.2	18 20.5	4 93.4			0 UND		7 55.9		26 14.3
	39 9.4	39 9.4	31 11.7			12 31.2		42 8.8		42 8.7
	61 6.0	63 5.8	58 6.3			33 11.1		61 6.0		67 5.5
Cost of Sales/Inventory										
Cost of Sales/Payables										
Sales/Working Capital	5.4	5.5	5.2			13.5		4.7		6.5
	13.9	19.7	16.4			30.0		8.4		13.9
	335.4	117.3	-40.0			NM		NM		62.8
EBIT/Interest	15.0	12.4	25.2							6.4
	(120) 3.1	(45) 3.6	(36) 7.1							(12) 2.3
	.5	.4	1.8							-1.2
Net Profit + Depr., Dep., Amort./Cur. Mat. L/T/D	31.2									
	(18) 5.5									
	1.5									
Fixed/Worth	.2	.1	.1			.2		.0		.2
	.7	.5	.4			.6		.1		.7
	5.0	1.7	-5.7			-7.9		.4		-.4
Debt/Worth	.8	.9	.8			.8		.8		1.6
	2.0	2.3	2.7			2.1		1.3		3.0
	16.8	19.5	-17.0			-213.3		11.8		-2.8
% Profit Before Taxes/Tangible Net Worth	51.9	54.4	106.4			110.9				74.4
	(120) 17.6	(46) 22.7	(44) 56.9			(10) 54.6				(11) 3.1
	3.7	.3	3.3			-13.6				-3.1
% Profit Before Taxes/Total Assets	16.8	12.3	50.6			67.6		57.6		15.9
	5.3	6.7	12.2			16.4		27.6		3.4
	-.5	-.8	1.3			-3.0		-1.9		-2.5
Sales/Net Fixed Assets	52.5	168.9	197.2			259.8		UND		36.3
	18.9	30.4	46.2			38.9		400.8		15.7
	4.7	10.6	14.4			17.1		29.9		10.1
Sales/Total Assets	4.0	5.0	6.1			11.4		5.1		2.3
	1.8	2.5	3.0			6.9		3.3		1.4
	.9	1.3	1.4			2.1		2.6		1.1
% Depr., Dep., Amort./Sales	.8	.4	.9							2.3
	(111) 1.8	(37) 1.6	(32) 2.1							(10) 3.8
	4.5	3.1	3.9							6.0
% Officers', Directors' Owners' Comp/Sales	2.2	2.8	2.3							
	(38) 6.1	(19) 6.3	(15) 6.8							
	9.1	22.6	9.6							
Net Sales ($)	4616574M	1737488M	1698987M		2839M	27568M	32800M	72671M	72754M	1490355M
Total Assets ($)	3786595M	1541380M	1262831M		906M	10728M	16959M	22662M	44455M	1167121M

M = $ thousand   MM = $ million
See Pages 9 through 22 for Explanation of Ratios and Data

FINANCE AND INSURANCE

FINANCE AND INSURANCE

Current Data Sorted by Assets   Comparative Historical Data

Type of Statement	0-500M	500M-2MM	2-10MM	10-50MM	50-100MM	100-250MM		4/1/06-3/31/07 ALL	4/1/07-3/31/08 ALL
Unqualified		1	9	43	10	18		79	58
Reviewed		2	19	10		2		35	33
Compiled	2	7	11	4				23	20
Tax Returns	5	10	7	2				22	14
Other	8	14	28	32	9	7		64	100
		32 (4/1-9/30/10)		228 (10/1/10-3/31/11)					
NUMBER OF STATEMENTS	15	34	74	91	19	27		223	225
ASSETS	%	%	%	%	%	%		%	%
Cash & Equivalents	26.2	16.8	6.5	6.7	5.3	2.9		7.2	5.8
Trade Receivables (net)	20.4	32.1	45.9	47.1	45.4	45.8		47.5	46.1
Inventory	6.9	2.1	3.9	4.5	4.8	3.6		3.8	5.1
All Other Current	19.5	7.0	7.9	8.5	6.0	10.0		7.6	11.9
Total Current	73.0	58.0	64.2	66.8	61.6	62.3		66.1	68.9
Fixed Assets (net)	25.2	19.7	17.5	8.1	5.4	11.3		17.3	10.2
Intangibles (net)	.9	3.7	.2	1.3	.3	1.8		.8	1.2
All Other Non-Current	1.0	18.5	18.0	23.7	32.7	24.7		15.8	19.7
Total	100.0	100.0	100.0	100.0	100.0	100.0		100.0	100.0
LIABILITIES									
Notes Payable-Short Term	16.3	16.6	20.7	29.8	31.3	13.8		29.0	27.8
Cur. Mat.-L.T.D.	19.3	8.9	7.9	5.3	.4	8.5		5.5	5.1
Trade Payables	1.9	4.0	2.5	2.7	4.4	5.5		3.9	4.1
Income Taxes Payable	1.5	.0	.0	.2	.0	.3		.1	.1
All Other Current	27.5	15.6	10.6	7.7	4.1	5.0		8.2	8.1
Total Current	66.5	45.1	41.7	45.7	40.3	33.0		46.6	45.2
Long-Term Debt	11.1	19.5	15.8	15.3	29.5	37.1		21.8	21.0
Deferred Taxes	.0	.6	.4	.6	.2	2.3		.4	.6
All Other Non-Current	4.0	6.0	10.0	8.5	5.8	3.2		7.9	9.3
Net Worth	18.0	28.8	32.1	30.0	24.2	24.3		23.3	23.9
Total Liabilities & Net Worth	100.0	100.0	100.0	100.0	100.0	100.0		100.0	100.0
INCOME DATA									
Net Sales	100.0	100.0	100.0	100.0	100.0	100.0		100.0	100.0
Gross Profit									
Operating Expenses	72.6	63.5	77.5	69.9	65.6	70.5		67.9	66.8
Operating Profit	27.4	36.5	22.5	30.1	34.4	29.5		32.1	33.2
All Other Expenses (net)	4.5	13.4	8.1	13.7	20.1	11.0		15.7	17.3
Profit Before Taxes	22.9	23.2	14.5	16.4	14.4	18.5		16.5	15.9
RATIOS									
Current	3.0	4.3	2.9	2.6	2.5	3.5		2.3	2.9
	1.5	1.3	1.5	1.4	1.4	1.4		1.3	1.4
	.8	.6	.7	1.1	1.1	1.2		1.1	1.1
Quick	3.0	4.3	2.3	1.9	2.2	3.1		2.1	2.2
	.6	1.1	1.4	1.2	1.4	1.2		1.2	1.2
	.1	.4	.2	.2	.5	.4		.4	.4
Sales/Receivables	0 UND	0 UND	9 40.8	16 22.2	34 10.8	9 39.3		8 44.9	6 63.2
	0 UND	24 14.9	199 1.8	296 1.2	236 1.5	378 1.0		281 1.3	281 1.3
	36 10.3	1428 .3	853 .4	1222 .3	979 .4	1609 .2		1217 .3	1117 .3
Cost of Sales/Inventory									
Cost of Sales/Payables									
Sales/Working Capital	.6	.5	.9	.6	1.0	.4		.7	.6
	20.4	7.7	2.7	1.7	2.0	1.0		2.3	2.0
	-4.0	-4.8	-8.8	9.2	6.1	3.3		24.2	20.5
EBIT/Interest		20.5	9.2	5.0	3.6	7.3		4.4	6.5
		(21) 7.2	(57) 3.1	(57) 3.2	(12) 2.4	(16) 2.6		(122) 2.7	(118) 2.5
		1.2	1.8	1.6	1.2	2.0		1.7	1.4
Net Profit + Depr., Dep., Amort./Cur. Mat. L/T/D								8.0	22.9
								(19) .9	(15) 1.5
								.1	.1
Fixed/Worth	.0	.0	.0	.0	.0	.0		.0	.0
	.0	.2	.1	.0	.0	.0		.1	.0
	6.1	1.8	1.3	.2	.1	.2		.8	.3
Debt/Worth	.5	.4	.8	1.5	2.3	2.1		2.0	1.9
	2.7	3.0	2.7	3.5	3.2	3.8		4.8	4.7
	-29.5	NM	9.6	5.6	6.9	5.7		9.7	10.9
% Profit Before Taxes/Tangible Net Worth	55.1	27.3	49.1	35.5	41.2	38.2		41.8	43.2
	(11) 21.7	(26) 12.8	(65) 17.5	(90) 17.6	(18) 12.4	12.0		(208) 22.7	(213) 20.5
	10.0	7.1	6.7	4.7	5.4	4.3		10.1	8.6
% Profit Before Taxes/Total Assets	16.7	10.5	8.5	8.7	8.7	6.9		8.6	7.7
	5.9	5.4	5.2	3.9	1.9	2.3		3.7	3.5
	1.1	1.6	1.6	1.2	1.1	1.3		1.4	1.1
Sales/Net Fixed Assets	UND	UND	402.7	133.5	156.6	134.1		185.8	348.0
	105.3	93.5	62.2	39.9	59.4	55.7		39.5	47.4
	4.4	1.9	3.7	8.6	23.8	5.0		5.7	12.4
Sales/Total Assets	8.3	.9	.8	.6	.5	.4		.6	.5
	.6	.3	.4	.3	.3	.2		.3	.3
	.2	.1	.3	.2	.1	.1		.2	.2
% Depr., Dep., Amort./Sales		1.0	.3	.4	.4	.3		.5	.4
		(13) 7.8	(46) .9	(66) .9	(11) .9	(13) .7		(147) 1.3	(142) 1.0
		50.6	42.3	2.5	1.8	1.5		7.3	2.6
% Officers', Directors' Owners' Comp/Sales			1.3					3.8	2.2
			(17) 3.3					(59) 8.6	(45) 5.7
			10.4					15.7	11.0
Net Sales ($)	22112M	144735M	315665M	1099869M	767363M	1817998M		3778614M	4310857M
Total Assets ($)	4163M	38807M	377208M	2345409M	1359266M	4344508M		7461224M	7877668M

M = $ thousand   MM = $ million
See Pages 9 through 22 for Explanation of Ratios and Data

Comparative Historical Data

Current Data Sorted by Sales

		Type of Statement						
84	88	81	Unqualified	3	7	10	14	26	21
36	37	33	Reviewed	7	15	5	1	3	2
17	25	24	Compiled	9	7		2	3	3
29	24	24	Tax Returns	11	6	4	1	1	1
99	88	98	Other	33	16	8	17	10	14
4/1/08-3/31/09 ALL	4/1/09-3/31/10 ALL	4/1/10-3/31/11 ALL		32 (4/1-9/30/10)			228 (10/1/10-3/31/11)		
				0-1MM	1-3MM	3-5MM	5-10MM	10-25MM	25MM & OVER
265	262	260	**NUMBER OF STATEMENTS**	63	51	27	35	43	41
%	%	%	**ASSETS**	%	%	%	%	%	%
5.2	6.1	8.6	Cash & Equivalents	11.8	11.2	3.9	3.0	9.3	7.6
46.8	46.0	43.0	Trade Receivables (net)	37.1	42.9	42.5	57.0	41.8	41.9
4.0	4.8	4.1	Inventory	2.1	1.3	2.5	2.9	7.1	9.5
8.0	7.5	8.7	All Other Current	9.7	7.2	15.0	7.6	10.8	3.9
64.0	64.4	64.4	Total Current	60.6	62.6	63.9	70.5	69.0	63.0
13.3	13.9	13.4	Fixed Assets (net)	18.9	16.2	6.1	8.1	9.8	14.8
.9	1.6	1.3	Intangibles (net)	1.3	.3	.4	.1	3.6	1.5
21.8	20.1	20.9	All Other Non-Current	19.2	20.9	29.6	21.3	17.6	20.8
100.0	100.0	100.0	Total	100.0	100.0	100.0	100.0	100.0	100.0
			LIABILITIES						
29.3	26.2	23.1	Notes Payable-Short Term	16.0	22.7	24.4	25.6	35.0	19.4
5.3	6.2	7.3	Cur. Mat.-L.T.D.	10.8	6.7	4.5	8.3	6.7	4.1
3.2	3.8	3.2	Trade Payables	1.0	1.7	2.9	3.7	5.0	6.2
.1	.2	.2	Income Taxes Payable	.4	.0	.0	.3	.4	.1
8.5	9.7	10.1	All Other Current	16.3	12.0	7.2	7.0	5.2	8.1
46.3	46.1	43.9	Total Current	44.5	43.1	39.1	44.8	52.3	37.9
19.8	22.7	19.0	Long-Term Debt	16.8	21.5	21.8	12.8	17.5	24.7
.4	.7	.7	Deferred Taxes	.6	.2	.2	.6	1.2	1.1
7.8	7.9	7.6	All Other Non-Current	6.6	10.8	9.4	10.2	4.6	4.9
25.7	22.5	28.7	Net Worth	31.4	24.4	29.6	31.6	24.5	31.4
100.0	100.0	100.0	Total Liabilities & Net Worth	100.0	100.0	100.0	100.0	100.0	100.0
			INCOME DATA						
100.0	100.0	100.0	Net Sales	100.0	100.0	100.0	100.0	100.0	100.0
			Gross Profit						
69.1	74.1	71.1	Operating Expenses	60.4	71.4	74.9	73.3	74.3	79.6
30.9	25.9	28.9	Operating Profit	39.6	28.6	25.1	26.7	25.7	20.4
15.7	12.7	11.7	All Other Expenses (net)	14.2	13.4	12.4	10.3	11.1	7.2
15.2	13.2	17.2	Profit Before Taxes	25.5	15.2	12.7	16.4	14.6	13.2
			RATIOS						
2.4	2.4	2.9		3.8	2.5	3.7	2.5	1.7	3.2
1.3	1.4	1.5	Current	1.5	1.5	1.6	1.6	1.4	1.6
.9	1.0	1.1		.6	.4	1.3	1.2	1.1	1.3
1.9	2.0	2.4		3.5	2.4	1.9	2.3	1.5	3.0
1.2	1.3	1.3	Quick	1.2	1.3	1.4	1.4	1.1	1.3
.3	.2	.3		.2	.2	.5	.5	.2	.6
14 25.2	5 76.4	6 65.4		0 UND	7 55.1	4 98.8	70 5.2	9 39.3	13 28.5
340 1.1	252 1.4	178 2.0	Sales/Receivables	168 2.2	472 .8	115 3.2	371 1.0	105 3.5	43 8.4
1295 .3	1193 .3	1025 .4		1536 .2	1313 .3	956 .4	1103 .3	818 .4	590 .6
			Cost of Sales/Inventory						
			Cost of Sales/Payables						
.7	.7	.7		.4	.7	.6	.7	1.2	1.3
2.2	2.0	2.0	Sales/Working Capital	1.5	1.4	1.4	1.5	2.1	5.2
-55.9	188.3	60.0		-3.7	-3.9	6.1	4.3	47.3	17.1
	4.8		5.8		7.2	16.2	4.3	3.4	7.7	5.4	7.4
(145) 2.4	(177) 2.4	(171) 3.1	EBIT/Interest	(32) 6.0	(30) 2.7	(18) 2.3	(25) 3.3	(29) 4.0	(37) 3.4
1.4	1.4	1.6		1.3	1.5	1.4	1.8	2.0	1.7
39.6	2.0	5.3							
(13) 2.8	(15) .5	(18) .3	Net Profit + Depr., Dep., Amort./Cur. Mat. L/T/D						
.2	.1	.1							
.0	.0	.0		.0	.0	.0	.0	.0	.0
.0	.1	.0	Fixed/Worth	.0	.0	.0	.0	.1	.1
.5	.7	.5		.9	1.4	.2	.1	.6	.5
1.6	1.6	1.2		.4	1.5	1.5	.9	2.1	1.7
3.9	3.5	3.4	Debt/Worth	2.7	3.6	4.0	2.8	4.6	3.1
10.7	7.7	7.0		9.6	7.3	7.3	5.8	8.4	4.1
25.2	30.8	38.9		35.4	30.5	18.7	45.5	41.6	46.1
(242) 14.0	(237) 13.2	(237) 17.0	% Profit Before Taxes/Tangible Net Worth	(52) 14.3	(46) 16.8	(25) 8.9	(34) 20.6	(40) 19.0	(40) 23.0
4.2	4.0	5.7		6.6	4.4	2.4	6.1	9.6	8.0
6.9	7.1	9.0		9.4	6.2	5.2	12.2	9.4	11.1
3.1	3.0	4.2	% Profit Before Taxes/Total Assets	4.9	3.2	1.5	4.6	4.6	5.6
.5	.6	1.3		.8	1.2	.6	1.9	1.3	2.2
201.4	235.9	264.0		UND	231.5	226.3	156.6	135.7	131.8
44.2	38.7	49.4	Sales/Net Fixed Assets	128.0	96.8	50.8	43.5	25.0	57.1
5.8	7.0	6.5		1.7	5.6	8.6	8.5	15.5	8.2
.4	.6	.7		.4	.5	.8	.7	1.0	1.3
.3	.3	.3	Sales/Total Assets	.2	.3	.4	.3	.4	.7
.2	.2	.2		.1	.1	.1	.2	.2	.4
.6	.4	.4		1.2	.3	.3	.4	.6	.3
(159) 1.1	(157) 1.1	(156) .9	% Depr., Dep., Amort./Sales	(25) 23.3	(38) 1.1	(14) .9	(24) .8	(31) 1.2	(24) .6
5.2	4.0	4.9		54.9	15.2	2.3	3.6	4.4	1.3
2.4	3.8	2.3							
(43) 7.6	(43) 7.4	(37) 7.1	% Officers', Directors' Owners' Comp/Sales						
16.3	19.3	15.7							
4093600M	5453004M	4167742M	Net Sales ($)	28675M	104701M	106719M	247174M	701388M	2979085M
9119247M	9259504M	8469361M	Total Assets ($)	153822M	504606M	676297M	864445M	2596122M	3674069M

© RMA 2011
M = $ thousand   MM = $ million
See Pages 9 through 22 for Explanation of Ratios and Data

Current Data Sorted by Assets   Comparative Historical Data

Type of Statement	0-500M	500M-2MM	2-10MM	10-50MM	50-100MM	100-250MM	4/1/06-3/31/07 ALL	4/1/07-3/31/08 ALL
Unqualified			14	32	13	20	81	75
Reviewed		1	13	11			27	28
Compiled	2	20	22	3	2		24	28
Tax Returns		7	4	4			25	25
Other	6	16	32	25	2	8	79	102
	50 (4/1-9/30/10)			207 (10/1/10-3/31/11)				
NUMBER OF STATEMENTS	8	44	85	75	17	28	236	258
ASSETS	%	%	%	%	%	%	%	%
Cash & Equivalents		7.9	6.0	6.1	8.4	9.6	8.3	6.5
Trade Receivables (net)		67.4	65.6	74.1	60.9	69.8	60.2	70.8
Inventory		.2	1.0	.7	1.5	.7	.9	1.5
All Other Current		7.0	5.6	6.7	5.7	4.3	10.4	5.4
Total Current		82.5	78.2	87.5	76.6	84.4	79.8	84.2
Fixed Assets (net)		3.0	6.3	3.9	3.8	5.4	7.1	5.8
Intangibles (net)		1.9	2.4	2.4	1.8	1.0	2.1	1.9
All Other Non-Current		12.5	13.0	6.2	17.9	9.2	10.9	8.1
Total		100.0	100.0	100.0	100.0	100.0	100.0	100.0
LIABILITIES								
Notes Payable-Short Term		30.3	31.9	38.6	24.4	29.0	35.4	41.1
Cur. Mat.-L.T.D.		2.3	1.7	2.6	1.8	6.4	2.3	2.8
Trade Payables		.9	1.4	2.0	1.3	5.2	2.3	2.1
Income Taxes Payable		.0	.3	.1	.0	.1	.2	.1
All Other Current		11.8	9.4	5.6	13.2	13.4	8.8	9.0
Total Current		45.3	44.6	49.0	40.8	54.1	48.9	55.1
Long-Term Debt		15.7	8.6	10.3	15.6	10.7	12.5	9.6
Deferred Taxes		.0	.0	.0	.0	.3	.1	.0
All Other Non-Current		12.5	19.5	12.0	14.6	6.6	10.4	11.5
Net Worth		26.5	27.3	28.8	29.0	28.4	28.2	23.7
Total Liabilities & Net Worth		100.0	100.0	100.0	100.0	100.0	100.0	100.0
INCOME DATA								
Net Sales		100.0	100.0	100.0	100.0	100.0	100.0	100.0
Gross Profit								
Operating Expenses		73.8	73.5	71.8	64.5	74.1	71.8	71.4
Operating Profit		26.2	26.5	28.2	35.5	25.9	28.2	28.6
All Other Expenses (net)		12.4	10.7	12.4	15.8	6.5	12.5	15.9
Profit Before Taxes		13.8	15.8	15.8	19.7	19.4	15.7	12.7
RATIOS								
Current		4.4	3.2	2.5	5.5	2.1	2.6	2.3
		2.4	1.8	1.6	1.6	1.5	1.5	1.4
		1.3	1.3	1.3	1.2	1.3	1.2	1.2
Quick		4.1	2.8	2.5	5.5	2.0	2.4	2.1
		1.6	1.5	1.5	1.6	1.4	1.4	1.3
		1.2	1.2	1.3	1.2	1.3	1.1	1.1
Sales/Receivables		140 2.6	128 2.9	272 1.3	108 3.4	128 2.9	102 3.6	176 2.1
		552 .7	663 .6	894 .4	676 .5	841 .4	556 .7	871 .4
		1004 .4	1156 .3	1334 .3	1517 .2	1304 .3	1337 .3	1370 .3
Cost of Sales/Inventory								
Cost of Sales/Payables								
Sales/Working Capital		.8	.6	.6	.4	.8	.7	.7
		1.6	1.4	1.2	.7	1.5	1.4	1.4
		3.6	4.4	1.9	2.4	3.0	5.0	5.7
EBIT/Interest		4.2	6.4	5.0		8.2	5.8	3.5
		(33) 2.5	(65) 2.8	(56) 2.6		(24) 3.6	(139) 2.9	(138) 2.0
		1.3	1.6	1.6		2.3	1.6	1.3
Net Profit + Depr., Dep., Amort./Cur. Mat. L/T/D							7.0	4.7
							(15) 2.3	(12) .9
							.3	.2
Fixed/Worth		.0	.0	.0	.0	.0	.0	.0
		.0	.1	.1	.1	.1	.1	.1
		.2	.3	.2	.3	.3	.4	.4
Debt/Worth		1.2	1.5	1.7	1.5	1.4	1.3	2.0
		3.8	3.8	3.4	4.6	2.9	3.6	4.2
		37.9	12.3	7.3	9.4	4.6	10.8	10.5
% Profit Before Taxes/Tangible Net Worth		56.2	52.6	38.0	51.1	53.5	44.0	38.4
		(37) 23.9	(74) 22.3	(70) 15.3	30.0	(24) 24.8	(216) 21.5	(231) 16.7
		8.3	4.9	6.8	9.7	12.1	7.6	5.3
% Profit Before Taxes/Total Assets		10.4	11.0	8.3	8.4	11.6	9.4	6.8
		3.5	4.8	3.9	3.9	7.7	4.3	3.2
		1.2	1.3	1.5	1.9	1.6	1.5	.9
Sales/Net Fixed Assets		UND	254.4	136.1	91.3	56.2	97.6	120.4
		204.7	30.7	34.0	36.1	25.6	27.9	30.6
		21.4	11.9	11.3	19.6	7.8	10.8	15.2
Sales/Total Assets		.7	.7	.5	.6	.9	.9	.6
		.5	.4	.3	.3	.3	.3	.3
		.2	.2	.2	.1	.2	.2	.2
% Depr., Dep., Amort./Sales		.7	.3	.4	.6	.9	.6	.6
		(19) 1.2	(57) .8	(52) 1.0	(12) 1.1	(25) 2.2	(161) 1.1	(169) 1.1
		2.0	2.1	1.8	1.9	3.4	2.3	2.3
% Officers', Directors' Owners' Comp/Sales		3.8	3.4	3.8			6.5	4.1
		(12) 4.6	(15) 14.5	(18) 7.2			(48) 12.3	(51) 11.7
		20.2	17.6	10.1			22.9	23.1
Net Sales ($)	13240M	64872M	347697M	975049M	483773M	2464041M	5171499M	4326682M
Total Assets ($)	2322M	50982M	457448M	1720997M	1294830M	4632708M	8136114M	7687990M

Comparative Historical Data

Current Data Sorted by Sales

			Type of Statement						
82	76	79	Unqualified	5	12	10	14	13	25
28	23	25	Reviewed	1	12	5	7		
33	55	49	Compiled	27	16	2	1	1	3
19	21	15	Tax Returns	8		2	1	3	1
134	122	89	Other	25	16	11	12	10	15
4/1/08-3/31/09	4/1/09-3/31/10	4/1/10-3/31/11			50 (4/1-9/30/10)			207 (10/1/10-3/31/11)	
ALL	ALL	ALL		0-1MM	1-3MM	3-5MM	5-10MM	10-25MM	25MM & OVER
296	297	257	NUMBER OF STATEMENTS	66	56	30	35	26	44
%	%	%	ASSETS	%	%	%	%	%	%
7.3	7.5	7.4	Cash & Equivalents	5.8	4.9	2.9	9.0	12.5	11.8
68.1	70.5	68.3	Trade Receivables (net)	65.8	72.8	77.0	70.6	64.6	61.1
1.4	1.4	.8	Inventory	.2	.7	.9	.1	1.5	1.6
6.3	4.9	6.0	All Other Current	4.3	8.5	1.5	9.7	9.5	3.3
83.1	84.3	82.5	Total Current	76.1	87.0	82.3	89.4	88.1	77.8
4.9	4.4	4.7	Fixed Assets (net)	4.1	3.7	4.6	2.8	4.9	8.4
1.4	2.4	2.1	Intangibles (net)	.9	2.1	4.3	1.7	.6	3.9
10.6	8.9	10.6	All Other Non-Current	18.9	7.2	8.8	6.1	6.3	9.9
100.0	100.0	100.0	Total	100.0	100.0	100.0	100.0	100.0	100.0
			LIABILITIES						
38.2	35.4	32.9	Notes Payable-Short Term	34.5	32.1	39.7	32.5	29.4	29.4
3.4	1.9	2.5	Cur. Mat.-L.T.D.	2.3	1.1	.7	3.4	3.1	4.9
2.7	2.0	2.0	Trade Payables	1.0	1.3	1.9	2.8	2.9	3.3
.1	.1	.1	Income Taxes Payable	.0	.4	.1	.0	.0	.2
7.4	10.2	9.8	All Other Current	8.0	11.8	6.3	11.8	15.1	7.4
51.7	49.6	47.3	Total Current	45.7	46.8	48.6	50.7	50.5	45.2
11.2	11.4	10.8	Long-Term Debt	15.1	6.0	7.6	11.3	13.9	10.6
.0	.0	.0	Deferred Taxes	.0	.0	.0	.0	.0	.2
9.9	13.7	14.3	All Other Non-Current	16.1	19.0	12.1	9.1	12.2	12.6
27.2	25.3	27.5	Net Worth	23.2	28.2	31.7	29.0	23.3	31.4
100.0	100.0	100.0	Total Liabilities & Net Worth	100.0	100.0	100.0	100.0	100.0	100.0
			INCOME DATA						
100.0	100.0	100.0	Net Sales	100.0	100.0	100.0	100.0	100.0	100.0
			Gross Profit						
77.1	74.7	72.9	Operating Expenses	72.2	68.4	73.6	73.9	72.9	78.4
22.9	25.3	27.1	Operating Profit	27.8	31.6	26.4	26.1	27.1	21.6
13.0	12.3	11.2	All Other Expenses (net)	14.5	13.5	10.9	7.9	10.4	6.8
9.9	13.0	15.9	Profit Before Taxes	13.3	18.1	15.5	18.3	16.7	14.7
			RATIOS						
2.8	2.7	3.2		3.3	3.5	2.7	2.1	4.9	2.3
1.5	1.6	1.7	Current	2.1	1.6	1.6	1.7	1.6	1.6
1.2	1.3	1.3		1.2	1.3	1.3	1.3	1.3	1.3
2.5	2.6	2.9		3.3	2.7	2.7	2.0	4.5	2.2
1.4	1.4	1.5	Quick	1.8	1.5	1.5	1.6	1.5	1.5
1.1	1.2	1.3		1.2	1.2	1.3	1.3	1.3	1.3
125 2.9	276 1.3	165 2.2		205 1.8	332 1.1	425 .9	375 1.0	71 5.1	71 5.1
697 .5	716 .5	680 .5	Sales/Receivables	695 .5	880 .4	972 .4	731 .5	536 .7	207 1.8
1147 .3	1207 .3	1176 .3		1229 .3	1187 .3	1358 .3	1259 .3	982 .4	953 .4
			Cost of Sales/Inventory						
			Cost of Sales/Payables						
.7	.7	.6		.5	.5	.5	.7	.8	1.3
1.7	1.3	1.3	Sales/Working Capital	1.0	1.2	1.0	1.1	1.6	2.8
3.9	3.0	3.1		3.4	3.0	1.9	1.6	3.3	7.1
4.2	4.9	5.3		3.4	5.3	4.6	7.6	9.0	7.5
(193) 2.2	(234) 2.7	(193) 2.8	EBIT/Interest	(47) 1.9	(38) 3.1	(24) 2.7	(27) 3.4	(19) 4.0	(38) 3.1
1.3	1.5	1.6		1.3	1.6	1.5	1.7	2.5	2.0
12.3	36.0	8.8							
(24) 4.5	(21) 5.2	(19) 1.6	Net Profit + Depr., Dep., Amort./Cur. Mat. L/T/D						
.1	1.5	.2							
.0	.0	.0		.0	.0	.0	.0	.0	.0
.1	.1	.1	Fixed/Worth	.0	.0	.1	.1	.1	.1
.4	.3	.3		.4	.2	.3	.2	.3	.5
1.5	1.5	1.5		1.2	1.5	1.0	1.7	2.5	1.2
4.0	3.9	3.5	Debt/Worth	5.1	3.3	2.9	3.5	5.7	2.8
11.4	10.0	9.6		66.3	7.0	8.4	6.0	10.6	6.6
44.3	47.2	49.7		42.0	49.7	38.1	41.2	67.0	58.4
(262) 17.2	(265) 20.6	(231) 21.5	% Profit Before Taxes/Tangible Net Worth	(54) 12.8	(51) 18.1	(27) 13.0	(25) 27.2	45.9	(39) 27.2
4.6	6.4	6.9		1.9	6.0	7.3	7.2	24.2	13.6
7.5	9.6	10.5		7.4	9.6	7.7	12.8	14.5	12.9
3.7	4.3	4.6	% Profit Before Taxes/Total Assets	2.6	4.5	4.1	4.1	7.0	8.6
.5	1.4	1.5		.3	1.8	1.3	1.5	4.2	4.0
121.4	138.5	186.0		UND	908.0	138.4	51.1	207.7	61.3
33.2	36.3	36.7	Sales/Net Fixed Assets	73.5	36.8	30.3	24.3	36.5	30.8
12.3	13.4	13.2		17.2	15.5	9.7	9.7	13.7	13.7
.8	.7	.7		.5	.6	.6	.5	.9	1.5
.3	.4	.4	Sales/Total Assets	.3	.3	.3	.3	.5	.9
.2	.2	.2		.1	.2	.2	.2	.3	.3
.5	.5	.5		.4	.3	.5	.3	.7	.9
(188) 1.2	(190) 1.1	(169) 1.0	% Depr., Dep., Amort./Sales	(35) .9	(35) .8	(23) 1.1	(26) .8	(17) 1.2	(33) 1.4
2.4	2.1	2.2		2.5	2.0	2.4	1.9	2.0	2.3
3.2	3.3	3.4		3.6	3.3				
(50) 7.7	(68) 7.6	(52) 6.3	% Officers', Directors' Owners' Comp/Sales	(12) 4.6	(15) 7.7				
18.8	15.8	15.1		15.5	14.6				
5785172M	5943353M	4348672M	Net Sales ($)	33268M	106406M	113012M	247183M	407945M	3440858M
10274047M	9528417M	8159287M	Total Assets ($)	165994M	410607M	408878M	1304695M	1154276M	4714837M

M = $ thousand   MM = $ million
See Pages 9 through 22 for Explanation of Ratios and Data

FINANCE—Real Estate Credit NAICS 522292

	Current Data Sorted by Assets							Comparative Historical Data	
Type of Statement									
Unqualified	3	5	39	67	31	21		421	247
Reviewed			3	4				23	13
Compiled	2	4	7	1	1			27	12
Tax Returns	6	6	5	3				46	28
Other	5	14	24	28	7	9		146	109
		36 (4/1-9/30/10)			259 (10/1/10-3/31/11)			4/1/06-3/31/07 ALL	4/1/07-3/31/08 ALL
	0-500M	500M-2MM	2-10MM	10-50MM	50-100MM	100-250MM			
NUMBER OF STATEMENTS	16	29	78	103	39	30		663	409
ASSETS	%	%	%	%	%	%		%	%
Cash & Equivalents	39.6	12.0	14.8	11.3	6.1	10.4		17.2	15.8
Trade Receivables (net)	14.5	19.3	27.4	30.9	25.1	22.1		30.4	25.2
Inventory	5.3	1.1	7.1	20.1	24.6	19.4		5.4	5.5
All Other Current	1.3	9.5	13.1	11.9	22.6	18.3		21.9	25.6
Total Current	60.7	41.9	62.4	74.2	78.4	70.1		74.9	72.2
Fixed Assets (net)	18.2	24.9	7.8	4.9	1.4	8.3		7.8	7.3
Intangibles (net)	1.1	4.5	1.4	1.7	1.1	4.5		1.7	2.0
All Other Non-Current	20.0	28.7	28.4	19.2	19.0	17.1		15.6	18.5
Total	100.0	100.0	100.0	100.0	100.0	100.0		100.0	100.0
LIABILITIES									
Notes Payable-Short Term	12.7	15.4	37.3	53.2	53.9	41.5		33.2	43.0
Cur. Mat.-L.T.D.	6.0	3.7	1.2	1.0	.3	3.6		1.4	1.8
Trade Payables	14.1	2.4	1.7	4.1	8.2	1.8		16.3	6.0
Income Taxes Payable	.0	.1	.1	.2	.0	.3		.2	.2
All Other Current	17.4	6.9	6.3	6.8	5.6	5.2		8.8	7.2
Total Current	50.2	28.6	46.6	65.3	68.0	52.4		59.8	58.1
Long-Term Debt	8.0	24.1	10.2	9.0	13.1	13.9		8.1	8.4
Deferred Taxes	.0	.0	.4	.3	.0	1.0		.2	.3
All Other Non-Current	6.2	2.1	8.3	1.9	2.0	3.0		2.7	3.8
Net Worth	35.6	45.3	34.4	23.5	16.9	29.7		29.1	29.4
Total Liabilities & Net Worth	100.0	100.0	100.0	100.0	100.0	100.0		100.0	100.0
INCOME DATA									
Net Sales	100.0	100.0	100.0	100.0	100.0	100.0		100.0	100.0
Gross Profit									
Operating Expenses	91.4	74.4	72.2	76.0	72.0	73.8		78.4	77.6
Operating Profit	8.6	25.6	27.8	24.0	28.0	26.2		21.6	22.4
All Other Expenses (net)	2.5	10.0	15.0	10.4	10.8	9.0		11.7	13.2
Profit Before Taxes	6.2	15.7	12.8	13.5	17.2	17.3		9.9	9.2
RATIOS									
Current	9.8	5.3	2.4	1.3	1.4	2.1		1.7	1.8
	1.2	1.2	1.3	1.1	1.1	1.1		1.2	1.2
	.4	.4	1.1	1.0	1.0	1.1		1.0	1.0
Quick	9.8	3.6	1.9	1.1	1.1	1.2		1.4	1.4
	1.1	.8	(77) 1.0	.9	.2	.6		1.0	(408) .9
	.1	.3	.3	.1	.1	.1		.1	.1
Sales/Receivables	0 UND	0 UND	0 UND	0 UND	3 129.6	6 61.3		0 UND	0 UND
	0 UND	0 796.0	40 9.1	28 13.0	18 20.7	29 12.6		15 24.1	9 41.6
	6 56.9	86 4.2	503 .7	531 .7	399 .9	950 .4		429 .9	430 .8
Cost of Sales/Inventory									
Cost of Sales/Payables									
Sales/Working Capital	5.0	2.6	1.2	2.1	2.3	1.1		2.0	1.3
	27.4	18.2	2.4	5.4	5.7	2.6		6.4	4.9
	-15.7	-3.4	22.8	14.9	10.0	8.7		33.6	44.0
EBIT/Interest		2.9	10.0	5.4	3.9	9.5		3.7	3.7
	(17) 1.8	(50) 3.7	(75) 2.8	(28) 2.8	(22) 3.3			(402) 1.4	(240) 1.3
		-.6	1.9	1.6	1.8	2.6		.7	.5
Net Profit + Depr., Dep., Amort./Cur. Mat. L/T/D				19.3				11.9	5.3
			(14) 6.7					(66) 2.1	(26) .1
			1.3					-1.4	-12.9
Fixed/Worth	.0	.0	.0	.0	.0	.0		.0	.0
	.3	.1	.0	.1	.1	.1		.1	.1
	1.6	1.6	.2	.3	.1	.2		.4	.3
Debt/Worth	.2	.2	1.1	2.6	5.5	1.3		1.4	1.4
	.9	1.8	2.6	4.9	7.9	4.5		4.1	3.7
	4.9	5.0	4.7	9.3	13.4	7.9		9.9	9.1
% Profit Before Taxes/Tangible Net Worth	74.9	30.3	22.2	48.7	62.5	50.0		33.0	25.9
	(13) 36.1	(28) 12.3	10.5	(101) 21.2	(37) 43.6	(28) 25.3		(636) 10.4	(386) 6.9
	5.6	.9	2.0	4.9	13.5	6.2		-4.0	-4.7
% Profit Before Taxes/Total Assets	47.3	10.9	6.8	7.4	6.6	7.1		7.0	5.9
	16.8	3.2	3.4	3.9	3.3	4.3		1.8	1.6
	-4.7	.7	.4	.7	1.7	1.5		-.7	-1.3
Sales/Net Fixed Assets	468.8	UND	198.4	220.4	106.1	80.3		105.1	132.3
	91.3	34.1	35.7	51.6	53.0	35.1		36.0	31.6
	14.3	1.1	5.9	11.8	21.6	5.8		15.3	11.5
Sales/Total Assets	5.5	1.0	.6	.6	.5	.5		1.3	.8
	3.1	.3	.3	.4	.3	.2		.5	.4
	1.2	.1	.1	.2	.2	.2		.2	.1
% Depr., Dep., Amort./Sales		.5	.3	.3	.4	.6		.5	.6
	(12) 6.7	(48) .9	(68) .7	(27) .7	(21) .7			(469) 1.1	(261) 1.2
		21.9	1.7	1.4	1.1	1.4		1.9	2.1
% Officers', Directors' Owners' Comp/Sales			2.7	1.4				2.0	3.0
		(18) 5.9	(19) 4.0					(215) 5.2	(86) 5.8
			15.4	8.7				12.5	12.3
Net Sales ($)	11069M	26953M	183696M	1157667M	982263M	1563473M		10406311M	6505606M
Total Assets ($)	3553M	32898M	434894M	2524171M	2670226M	4683768M		18828703M	12346643M

M = $ thousand   MM = $ million
See Pages 9 through 22 for Explanation of Ratios and Data

Comparative Historical Data | Current Data Sorted by Sales

Type of Statement					36 (4/1-9/30/10)			259 (10/1/10-3/31/11)		
Unqualified	182	177	166		9	25	27	25	46	34
Reviewed	15	6	7		4	2	1			
Compiled	12	12	15		10	3	1			1
Tax Returns	40	27	20		16	2	1		1	
Other	99	94	87		29	18	5	11	13	11
	4/1/08- 3/31/09 ALL	4/1/09- 3/31/10 ALL	4/1/10- 3/31/11 ALL		0-1MM	1-3MM	3-5MM	5-10MM	10-25MM	25MM & OVER
NUMBER OF STATEMENTS	348	316	295		68	50	35	36	60	46
ASSETS	%	%	%		%	%	%	%	%	%
Cash & Equivalents	13.2	14.1	13.0		10.3	20.0	14.2	12.4	12.1	10.3
Trade Receivables (net)	27.3	25.2	26.3		21.8	25.1	36.1	32.8	27.4	20.1
Inventory	6.2	13.5	14.5		1.7	7.7	13.7	14.4	24.1	29.0
All Other Current	21.1	17.4	13.5		9.3	11.7	10.7	15.5	18.4	15.6
Total Current	67.7	70.2	67.3		43.2	64.5	74.7	75.1	82.0	75.1
Fixed Assets (net)	8.4	7.5	8.2		14.2	11.8	5.8	4.1	3.6	6.7
Intangibles (net)	2.7	2.9	2.1		.4	3.6	1.9	1.6	1.4	4.3
All Other Non-Current	21.3	19.5	22.4		42.2	20.0	17.6	19.1	13.0	14.0
Total	100.0	100.0	100.0		100.0	100.0	100.0	100.0	100.0	100.0
LIABILITIES										
Notes Payable-Short Term	38.8	41.6	42.0		19.1	38.4	44.0	50.8	56.0	52.9
Cur. Mat.-L.T.D.	2.0	2.0	1.8		3.8	1.8	.7	.4	.6	2.2
Trade Payables	8.4	4.4	4.1		3.4	2.4	5.3	1.1	6.1	6.1
Income Taxes Payable	.1	.2	.1		.1	.1	.0	.5	.1	.3
All Other Current	8.1	7.6	7.0		8.3	8.7	6.2	4.7	7.3	4.9
Total Current	57.5	55.8	55.0		34.6	51.3	56.1	57.6	70.0	66.5
Long-Term Debt	9.2	10.5	11.8		20.3	14.3	8.8	13.2	6.8	4.2
Deferred Taxes	.3	.2	.3		.0	.0	.3	1.2	.3	.5
All Other Non-Current	3.6	4.3	4.0		9.5	2.8	3.8	1.4	1.5	2.5
Net Worth	29.3	29.3	28.9		35.6	31.5	31.0	26.6	21.4	26.3
Total Liabilities & Net Worth	100.0	100.0	100.0		100.0	100.0	100.0	100.0	100.0	100.0
INCOME DATA										
Net Sales	100.0	100.0	100.0		100.0	100.0	100.0	100.0	100.0	100.0
Gross Profit										
Operating Expenses	78.4	74.2	74.9		63.7	74.1	80.2	76.1	82.2	77.9
Operating Profit	21.6	25.8	25.1		36.3	25.9	19.8	23.9	17.8	22.1
All Other Expenses (net)	12.7	10.5	11.1		22.1	10.7	10.0	9.4	5.2	5.0
Profit Before Taxes	8.9	15.3	14.0		14.1	15.2	9.8	14.5	12.6	17.1
RATIOS										
Current	1.8	1.8	1.8		6.4	2.3	1.4	1.8	1.3	1.3
	1.1	1.2	1.1		1.3	1.3	1.2	1.2	1.1	1.1
	1.0	1.0	1.0		.3	1.1	1.0	1.1	1.1	1.1
Quick	1.3	1.4	1.3		3.2	1.6	1.2	1.3	1.1	1.1
	(347) .8	(294) .8	.9		(67) .9	1.1	1.0	1.0	.4	.4
	.1	.1	.1		.1	.3	.5	.2	.1	.1
Sales/Receivables	0 UND	0 UND	0 UND		0 UND	0 UND	1 390.3	0 UND	1 345.5	4 82.3
	19 18.8	15 23.7	18 20.7		0 UND	11 33.2	87 4.2	28 13.0	19 19.2	15 24.1
	662 .6	452 .8	473 .8		918 .4	404 .9	895 .4	566 .6	501 .7	103 3.6
Cost of Sales/Inventory										
Cost of Sales/Payables										
Sales/Working Capital	1.4	1.6	1.7		.4	1.6	2.2	1.6	2.6	2.3
	5.0	4.6	4.9		4.5	2.9	4.9	4.5	5.5	7.8
	82.5	15.3	19.0		-1.9	16.4	21.9	9.0	10.7	13.4
EBIT/Interest	3.4	6.5	7.1		5.7	10.3	4.5	8.6	4.2	9.1
	(219) 1.9	(207) 3.2	(200) 3.0		(25) 2.5	(33) 5.1	(23) 2.5	(27) 3.8	(49) 2.6	(43) 3.0
	1.1	1.7	1.7		1.1	2.0	1.6	1.7	1.5	2.1
Net Profit + Depr., Dep., Amort./Cur. Mat. L/T/D	5.2	13.1	13.7							
	(19) .5	(20) 1.9	(24) 3.3							
	.0	1.0	.6							
Fixed/Worth	.0	.0	.0		.0	.0	.0	.0	.0	.1
	.1	.1	.1		.0	.1	.0	.0	.1	.1
	.3	.2	.3		.4	.5	.4	.1	.2	.3
Debt/Worth	1.4	1.4	1.4		.8	1.3	1.3	1.9	3.0	1.7
	3.6	4.0	3.9		2.1	3.1	3.6	3.9	5.5	6.2
	8.6	7.8	7.9		6.0	7.3	6.3	8.1	9.7	8.9
% Profit Before Taxes/Tangible Net Worth	24.4	53.7	43.8		13.8	39.7	28.0	41.5	54.3	65.0
	(331) 8.9	(299) 21.1	(285) 16.0		(65) 4.0	(48) 20.2	(34) 15.1	(34) 17.5	28.7	(44) 44.3
	.6	4.3	5.5		-1.1	7.0	3.2	7.3	8.4	23.1
% Profit Before Taxes/Total Assets	5.1	9.2	7.3		4.9	11.4	6.6	7.6	7.4	11.9
	1.7	4.4	3.7		1.3	5.1	3.3	5.2	3.9	6.0
	.0	.8	.9		-.1	.8	.7	.9	1.6	2.8
Sales/Net Fixed Assets	172.4	152.5	162.3		UND	184.0	382.2	177.1	75.5	80.3
	36.2	49.8	49.0		119.3	32.3	49.8	61.4	40.1	38.6
	10.9	12.9	10.1		2.8	5.6	7.2	13.8	12.5	20.3
Sales/Total Assets	.7	.7	.6		.3	.7	.9	.6	.8	.8
	.3	.4	.4		.1	.4	.4	.4	.5	.5
	.1	.1	.1		.1	.1	.1	.3	.3	.4
% Depr., Dep., Amort./Sales	.7	.4	.4		1.0	.2	.4	.4	.4	.4
	(207) 1.3	(191) .8	(184) .8		(23) 2.9	(28) .7	(22) .9	(24) .6	(49) .7	(38) .7
	2.1	1.5	1.5		18.4	1.7	1.6	1.4	1.3	1.1
% Officers', Directors' Owners' Comp/Sales	3.3	3.2	2.5		3.0					
	(78) 7.3	(60) 6.5	(49) 6.1		(13) 13.5					
	14.2	14.0	18.4		28.0					
Net Sales ($)	3770623M	3996577M	3925121M		29801M	93385M	143563M	264998M	1003434M	2389940M
Total Assets ($)	9464493M	10197336M	10349510M		285776M	417995M	724696M	1063611M	2976483M	4880949M

© RMA 2011

M = $ thousand   MM = $ million
See Pages 9 through 22 for Explanation of Ratios and Data

FINANCE—Secondary Market Financing NAICS 522294

Current Data Sorted by Assets | **Comparative Historical Data**

Type of Statement

0-500M	500M-2MM	2-10MM	10-50MM	50-100MM	100-250MM	Type of Statement	4/1/06-3/31/07 ALL	4/1/07-3/31/08 ALL
	1	3	6	2	2	Unqualified	21	18
		3				Reviewed	2	3
	1	1				Compiled	4	1
1		4	2			Tax Returns	9	5
						Other	6	8
	12 (4/1-9/30/10)		14 (10/1/10-3/31/11)					
1	2	11	8	2	2	**NUMBER OF STATEMENTS**	42	35
%	%	%	%	%	%	**ASSETS**	%	%
		13.7				Cash & Equivalents	18.0	16.5
		41.5				Trade Receivables (net)	37.5	34.6
		3.0				Inventory	.7	.3
		9.2				All Other Current	8.3	10.6
		67.3				Total Current	64.4	62.0
		4.5				Fixed Assets (net)	21.7	20.0
		.7				Intangibles (net)	.5	.6
		27.4				All Other Non-Current	13.4	17.3
		100.0				Total	100.0	100.0
						LIABILITIES		
		10.2				Notes Payable-Short Term	21.3	19.7
		1.9				Cur. Mat.-L.T.D.	1.4	5.8
		3.6				Trade Payables	4.7	3.1
		.3				Income Taxes Payable	.1	.0
		13.2				All Other Current	7.0	4.8
		29.2				Total Current	34.6	33.3
		19.9				Long-Term Debt	23.6	22.0
		.0				Deferred Taxes	.0	.0
		13.0				All Other Non-Current	5.4	8.2
		37.9				Net Worth	36.4	36.5
		100.0				Total Liabilities & Net Worth	100.0	100.0
						INCOME DATA		
		100.0				Net Sales	100.0	100.0
						Gross Profit		
		71.8				Operating Expenses	64.5	65.1
		28.2				Operating Profit	35.5	34.9
		8.7				All Other Expenses (net)	16.9	17.2
		19.5				Profit Before Taxes	18.6	17.8
						RATIOS		
		34.2				Current	4.0	4.7
		2.2					1.8	2.0
		1.7					1.2	1.2
		26.5				Quick	3.9	3.3
		2.2					1.8	1.8
		1.2					1.1	1.2
		22 16.7				Sales/Receivables	0 UND	2 209.0
		34 10.6					32 11.6	63 5.8
		215 1.7					1139 .3	1325 .3
						Cost of Sales/Inventory		
						Cost of Sales/Payables		
		.7				Sales/Working Capital	.5	.7
		3.1					2.5	1.6
		18.9					32.2	4.7
						EBIT/Interest	8.2	8.2
							(18) 4.5	(14) 3.2
							1.4	1.3
						Net Profit + Depr., Dep., Amort./Cur. Mat. L/T/D		
		.0				Fixed/Worth	.0	.0
		.0					.1	.1
		.0					1.5	.8
		1.0				Debt/Worth	.8	.4
		1.2					2.1	3.1
		8.2					17.1	12.2
		23.2				% Profit Before Taxes/Tangible Net Worth	48.7	44.5
		8.0					(40) 15.5	(32) 14.8
		-2.2					7.8	8.8
		11.2				% Profit Before Taxes/Total Assets	9.9	11.7
		2.5					4.2	5.0
		-1.1					1.3	.8
		UND				Sales/Net Fixed Assets	UND	UND
		999.8					29.3	35.1
		45.3					3.0	2.8
		1.6				Sales/Total Assets	.8	.8
		.4					.3	.3
		.1					.1	.1
						% Depr., Dep., Amort./Sales	.7	.9
							(22) 1.6	(16) 3.2
							4.2	5.5
						% Officers', Directors' Owners' Comp/Sales	1.5	
							(11) 4.5	
							13.1	
2678M	2119M	71959M	31719M	39496M	29209M	Net Sales ($)	607890M	517597M
116M	2573M	47238M	268484M	116837M	306222M	Total Assets ($)	1022169M	1133106M

M = $ thousand   MM = $ million
See Pages 9 through 22 for Explanation of Ratios and Data

Comparative Historical Data | Current Data Sorted by Sales

			Type of Statement						
11	11	14	Unqualified	3	2	2	3	2	2
3	2	3	Reviewed	1		1		1	
	2		Compiled						
5	8	2	Tax Returns	1	1				
9	12	7	Other	1	2	3	1		
4/1/08-3/31/09 ALL	4/1/09-3/31/10 ALL	4/1/10-3/31/11 ALL		12 (4/1-9/30/10)			14 (10/1/10-3/31/11)		
				0-1MM	1-3MM	3-5MM	5-10MM	10-25MM	25MM & OVER
28	35	26	NUMBER OF STATEMENTS	6	5	6	4	3	2
%	%	%	ASSETS	%	%	%	%	%	%
12.3	15.3	14.4	Cash & Equivalents						
36.9	38.6	39.1	Trade Receivables (net)						
1.4	2.1	1.7	Inventory						
12.5	7.4	7.7	All Other Current						
63.2	63.4	63.0	Total Current						
11.7	9.9	7.2	Fixed Assets (net)						
1.0	2.7	1.0	Intangibles (net)						
24.1	23.9	28.8	All Other Non-Current						
100.0	100.0	100.0	Total						
			LIABILITIES						
23.0	24.0	23.8	Notes Payable-Short Term						
4.7	8.4	1.1	Cur. Mat.-L.T.D.						
1.7	4.3	2.3	Trade Payables						
.0	.0	.2	Income Taxes Payable						
7.0	11.5	8.8	All Other Current						
36.5	48.2	36.1	Total Current						
24.3	17.5	17.4	Long-Term Debt						
.1	.0	.0	Deferred Taxes						
6.6	11.1	6.6	All Other Non-Current						
32.6	23.1	39.9	Net Worth						
100.0	100.0	100.0	Total Liabilties & Net Worth						
			INCOME DATA						
100.0	100.0	100.0	Net Sales						
			Gross Profit						
61.6	72.8	71.4	Operating Expenses						
38.4	27.2	28.6	Operating Profit						
19.9	17.5	10.4	All Other Expenses (net)						
18.5	9.7	18.3	Profit Before Taxes						
			RATIOS						
5.5	4.5	14.3	Current						
2.0	1.4	2.1							
.9	1.1	1.3							
4.0	2.9	7.7	Quick						
1.5	1.4	1.9							
.7	.9	1.0							
3 107.5	9 40.8	0 UND	Sales/Receivables						
528 .7	173 2.1	63 5.8							
1497 .2	1579 .2	2000 .2							
			Cost of Sales/Inventory						
			Cost of Sales/Payables						
.4	.7	.2	Sales/Working Capital						
.8	2.1	1.6							
NM	14.8	49.4							
4.0	6.4	7.4	EBIT/Interest						
(13) 2.1	(19) 2.8	(11) 5.2							
1.1	1.5	.3							
			Net Profit + Depr., Dep., Amort./Cur. Mat. L/T/D						
.0	.0	.0	Fixed/Worth						
.0	.0	.0							
.9	.6	.2							
.8	.7	.6	Debt/Worth						
2.9	5.4	1.1							
10.1	43.6	8.3							
16.7	31.1	13.0	% Profit Before Taxes/Tangible Net Worth						
(26) 9.7	(27) 8.5	(25) 6.6							
4.6	-1.1	-4.7							
7.6	3.8	5.6	% Profit Before Taxes/Total Assets						
3.1	1.6	1.6							
.4	-.6	-2.4							
UND	UND	UND	Sales/Net Fixed Assets						
86.7	106.2	999.8							
7.9	10.3	5.2							
.3	.7	.8	Sales/Total Assets						
.2	.3	.2							
.1	.1	.1							
.6	1.0	.1	% Depr., Dep., Amort./Sales						
(14) 2.0	(17) 1.5	(12) .6							
4.9	7.5	4.8							
			% Officers', Directors' Owners' Comp/Sales						
211105M	344971M	177180M	Net Sales ($)	2688M	9905M	22422M	27481M	42900M	71784M
1029680M	1057572M	741470M	Total Assets ($)	57332M	29356M	130396M	158260M	308479M	57647M

© RMA 2011

M = $ thousand   MM = $ million

See Pages 9 through 22 for Explanation of Ratios and Data

Current Data Sorted by Assets   **Comparative Historical Data**

	0-500M	500M-2MM	2-10MM	10-50MM	50-100MM	100-250MM	Type of Statement	4/1/06-3/31/07 ALL	4/1/07-3/31/08 ALL
		5	16	51	21	25	Unqualified	122	144
	1	1	6	15	2	1	Reviewed	33	28
		2	13	4			Compiled	26	15
	3	8	14	1			Tax Returns	28	27
	3	14	30	36	14	12	Other	89	107
		48 (4/1-9/30/10)		250 (10/1/10-3/31/11)					
NUMBER OF STATEMENTS	7	30	79	107	37	38		298	321
	%	%	%	%	%	%	**ASSETS**	%	%
		15.2	14.8	9.2	8.7	5.6	Cash & Equivalents	9.6	8.8
		38.4	43.6	51.0	62.3	57.3	Trade Receivables (net)	46.9	53.7
		7.5	3.0	1.2	.0	3.4	Inventory	3.0	2.1
		7.9	4.8	13.7	10.4	8.6	All Other Current	12.2	10.1
		69.1	66.1	75.1	81.4	74.9	Total Current	71.7	74.7
		16.6	12.6	5.9	1.0	5.4	Fixed Assets (net)	9.5	6.8
		6.0	2.6	1.4	1.4	4.6	Intangibles (net)	2.8	1.7
		8.3	18.7	17.5	16.2	15.1	All Other Non-Current	16.1	16.8
		100.0	100.0	100.0	100.0	100.0	Total	100.0	100.0
							LIABILITIES		
		26.4	18.0	36.2	34.5	30.6	Notes Payable-Short Term	29.0	32.5
		2.8	3.3	2.7	2.3	4.2	Cur. Mat.-L.T.D.	4.2	3.6
		3.8	4.3	3.1	6.6	3.1	Trade Payables	4.3	5.1
		.0	.3	.1	.0	.1	Income Taxes Payable	.2	.1
		12.5	9.7	10.1	6.4	7.5	All Other Current	11.2	7.5
		45.6	35.6	52.2	49.8	45.4	Total Current	48.9	48.7
		8.9	20.1	15.0	19.4	19.4	Long-Term Debt	17.7	16.5
		.1	.2	.2	.1	.7	Deferred Taxes	.2	.2
		7.5	9.9	7.5	5.8	4.4	All Other Non-Current	8.8	9.0
		38.0	34.2	25.2	25.0	30.1	Net Worth	24.5	25.6
		100.0	100.0	100.0	100.0	100.0	Total Liabilities & Net Worth	100.0	100.0
							INCOME DATA		
		100.0	100.0	100.0	100.0	100.0	Net Sales	100.0	100.0
							Gross Profit		
		81.9	72.1	70.2	62.3	72.5	Operating Expenses	65.9	65.8
		18.1	27.9	29.8	37.7	27.5	Operating Profit	34.1	34.2
		5.0	14.1	11.6	16.6	9.4	All Other Expenses (net)	17.0	16.4
		13.0	13.8	18.1	21.1	18.1	Profit Before Taxes	17.2	17.8
							RATIOS		
		4.8	3.0	2.1	2.8	5.2	Current	2.6	2.5
		1.7	1.8	1.4	1.4	1.5		1.4	1.5
		.8	1.2	1.2	1.2	1.2		1.1	1.2
		3.5	2.8	1.8	2.0	3.6	Quick	2.2	2.2
		1.5	1.6	1.3	1.4	1.4		1.2	1.3
		.3	.9	.8	1.2	.9		.5	.8
		0 UND	22 16.5	19 19.5	29 12.5	244 1.5	Sales/Receivables	5 77.8	18 19.8
		40 9.1	290 1.3	753 .5	1582 .2	873 .4		227 1.6	771 .5
		888 .4	1109 .3	1481 .2	2000 .1	2000 .1		1436 .3	1725 .2
							Cost of Sales/Inventory		
							Cost of Sales/Payables		
		1.0	.6	.5	.2	.3	Sales/Working Capital	.6	.5
		2.5	1.6	1.1	.5	1.0		1.8	1.2
		-56.3	19.2	6.8	1.0	4.1		12.2	7.0
		18.9	4.1	4.2	5.5	6.0	EBIT/Interest	6.0	6.2
	(21)	4.6	(48) 2.9	(60) 2.7	(17) 3.8	(19) 3.7		(141) 2.5	(133) 2.7
		.3	1.2	1.6	1.6	1.2		1.1	1.5
							Net Profit + Depr., Dep., Amort./Cur. Mat. L/T/D	3.1	8.0
								(22) 1.1 (24) .9	
								.3	.4
		.0	.0	.0	.0	.0	Fixed/Worth	.0	.0
		.3	.0	.1	.0	.0		.0	.0
		3.8	.4	.3	.0	.2		.4	.2
		.3	1.0	1.7	2.3	1.8	Debt/Worth	1.7	1.8
		2.8	2.2	4.0	4.1	3.2		4.0	3.8
		17.2	10.1	9.9	7.4	6.4		12.6	10.1
		62.7	37.8	40.2	35.5	24.1	% Profit Before Taxes/Tangible Net Worth	36.7	34.4
	(26)	15.3	(71) 15.7	(101) 20.3	(35) 15.4	(36) 7.5		(261) 19.2	(294) 18.2
		4.0	3.6	5.8	5.6	4.2		7.2	6.5
		11.8	11.3	6.4	4.2	6.6	% Profit Before Taxes/Total Assets	7.9	6.9
		5.6	3.8	3.6	2.2	1.5		3.4	3.3
		.4	1.0	1.4	.8	.8		1.0	1.2
		UND	710.8	273.6	UND	114.7	Sales/Net Fixed Assets	510.1	555.9
		60.8	36.4	44.5	150.4	42.1		46.9	54.1
		3.4	9.5	7.0	45.4	11.8		11.7	13.9
		3.3	.8	.3	.2	.5	Sales/Total Assets	.6	.4
		.5	.3	.2	.1	.2		.3	.2
		.3	.2	.1	.1	.1		.1	.1
		.6	.6	.7	.4	.5	% Depr., Dep., Amort./Sales	.7	.4
	(14)	2.4	(43) 1.4	(60) 1.4	(12) 1.5	(17) 1.2		(181) 1.3	(180) 1.2
		5.4	4.8	3.3	4.2	3.0		2.7	2.6
			5.2	5.1			% Officers', Directors' Owners' Comp/Sales	6.1	5.2
			(25) 10.9	(16) 8.2				(54) 10.8	(63) 10.1
			19.5	18.3				25.2	19.9
	14699M	98814M	284422M	1274729M	449669M	2028662M	Net Sales ($)	3547200M	4687210M
	2384M	39229M	409851M	2744006M	2654557M	6082090M	Total Assets ($)	8328532M	12510136M

© RMA 2011

M = $ thousand   MM = $ million
See Pages 9 through 22 for Explanation of Ratios and Data

Comparative Historical Data / Current Data Sorted by Sales

						Type of Statement						
	100		134		118	Unqualified	10	16	14	33	23	22
	18		28		26	Reviewed	6	6	5	5	3	1
	19		14		19	Compiled	6	4	4	4	1	
	20		31		26	Tax Returns	9	9	1	4	3	
	84		122		109	Other	27	27	7	16	16	16
	4/1/08-3/31/09 ALL		4/1/09-3/31/10 ALL		4/1/10-3/31/11 ALL		48 (4/1-9/30/10)			250 (10/1/10-3/31/11)		
							0-1MM	1-3MM	3-5MM	5-10MM	10-25MM	25MM & OVER
	241		329		298	NUMBER OF STATEMENTS	58	62	31	62	46	39
	%		%		%	ASSETS	%	%	%	%	%	%
	8.6		10.7		11.4	Cash & Equivalents	14.7	11.4	6.7	9.3	13.2	11.4
	50.6		49.7		49.4	Trade Receivables (net)	40.4	45.6	56.6	57.1	54.1	44.9
	3.1		3.3		2.8	Inventory	1.7	3.9	1.8	1.6	3.5	4.3
	9.0		7.5		9.6	All Other Current	7.6	11.1	12.5	9.7	5.7	12.3
	71.3		71.1		73.1	Total Current	64.4	72.0	77.6	77.8	76.4	72.9
	7.7		8.4		8.3	Fixed Assets (net)	11.4	6.5	4.8	7.3	10.5	8.1
	2.9		2.9		2.6	Intangibles (net)	.6	2.6	.9	2.6	1.4	8.2
	18.0		17.5		16.0	All Other Non-Current	23.6	18.9	16.7	12.3	11.7	10.8
	100.0		100.0		100.0	Total	100.0	100.0	100.0	100.0	100.0	100.0
						LIABILITIES						
	30.7		27.3		28.6	Notes Payable-Short Term	26.9	25.3	33.9	36.5	22.7	26.7
	3.3		4.3		3.1	Cur. Mat.-L.T.D.	2.3	3.1	1.7	3.6	3.8	4.0
	4.2		4.6		4.0	Trade Payables	1.2	3.7	2.1	4.2	6.7	6.6
	.1		.2		.1	Income Taxes Payable	.0	.3	.1	.1	.1	.1
	8.5		9.0		9.3	All Other Current	5.9	11.0	11.4	8.4	8.8	12.3
	46.8		45.3		45.2	Total Current	36.4	43.4	49.3	52.8	41.9	49.7
	16.8		16.1		16.5	Long-Term Debt	13.1	21.2	15.7	15.1	17.6	15.5
	.1		.3		.2	Deferred Taxes	.3	.1	.0	.2	.1	1.0
	7.3		7.7		8.1	All Other Non-Current	8.7	8.7	10.4	7.1	9.2	4.5
	29.1		30.6		30.0	Net Worth	41.5	26.6	24.6	24.9	31.2	29.3
	100.0		100.0		100.0	Total Liabilities & Net Worth	100.0	100.0	100.0	100.0	100.0	100.0
						INCOME DATA						
	100.0		100.0		100.0	Net Sales	100.0	100.0	100.0	100.0	100.0	100.0
						Gross Profit						
	72.4		73.7		71.5	Operating Expenses	64.4	74.3	74.3	64.1	79.8	77.7
	27.6		26.3		28.5	Operating Profit	35.6	25.7	25.7	35.9	20.2	22.3
	14.8		9.8		11.7	All Other Expenses (net)	16.9	11.4	14.8	13.0	6.7	6.0
	12.9		16.5		16.7	Profit Before Taxes	18.7	14.3	10.9	22.9	13.5	16.2
						RATIOS						
	3.1		3.1		3.0		5.1	3.4	2.6	2.0	5.6	2.6
	1.5		1.5		1.5	Current	1.7	1.7	1.5	1.4	1.5	1.3
	1.1		1.1		1.2		1.1	1.2	1.2	1.2	1.3	1.1
	2.7		2.4		2.5		3.7	2.8	2.1	1.7	4.9	1.5
	1.3		1.4		1.4	Quick	1.6	1.4	1.5	1.3	1.4	1.1
	.7		.8		.9		1.0	.8	1.2	1.0	1.0	.7
25	14.9	17	21.6	21	17.1		13	29.2	21	17.5	22	16.5	63	5.8	15	23.8	17	22.0
502	.7	526	.7	609	.6	Sales/Receivables	719	.5	237	1.5	616	.6	1047	.3	910	.4	76	4.8
1526	.2	1439	.3	1552	.2		1396	.3	1375	.3	1687	.2	2000	.2	2000	.2	813	.4
						Cost of Sales/Inventory						
						Cost of Sales/Payables						
	.6		.6		.5		.3	.4	.4	.5	.3	1.4
	1.5		1.4		1.2	Sales/Working Capital	1.0	1.3	.9	1.0	.9	3.8
	16.6		10.8		7.0		7.3	7.5	2.1	3.7	10.4	31.5
	6.0		5.7		5.1		11.8	3.9	3.7	4.8	6.1	10.6
(110)	2.2	(196)	2.5	(168)	3.0	EBIT/Interest	(26)	3.0	(36)	2.8	(19)	3.3	(29)	3.4	(28)	2.5	(30)	3.7
	1.3		1.5		1.4		1.3	1.0	1.3	1.9	1.7	1.4
	2.4		5.5		7.9							
(18)	.3	(26)	2.1	(10)	2.1	Net Profit + Depr., Dep., Amort./Cur. Mat. L/T/D						
	.0		.1		.3							
	.0		.0		.0		.0	.0	.0	.0	.0	.0
	.0		.0		.0	Fixed/Worth	.0	.0	.1	.0	.1	.2
	.4		.4		.3		.2	.4	.2	.2	.3	.5
	1.4		1.4		1.3		.3	1.4	1.7	2.1	1.5	1.6
	3.8		3.2		3.1	Debt/Worth	1.8	3.4	3.4	3.9	3.1	3.3
	11.8		9.5		7.7		7.5	11.3	20.8	8.1	6.9	7.2
	27.7		33.0		38.9		24.0	27.7	32.3	40.2	36.7	55.7
(213)	12.3	(297)	15.1	(276)	15.8	% Profit Before Taxes/Tangible Net Worth	(54)	7.3	(55)	15.1	(28)	14.6	(60)	24.8	(45)	11.8	(34)	28.4
	2.8		4.8		4.6		2.4	1.9	1.2	7.0	4.9	11.1
	6.9		7.7		8.0		6.0	6.4	7.9	8.0	6.9	12.9
	2.3		3.2		3.5	% Profit Before Taxes/Total Assets	2.3	2.1	3.1	4.3	3.2	6.9
	.6		1.1		1.0		.9	.2	.9	1.6	1.1	1.5
	270.5		258.2		603.2		UND	UND	169.6	561.3	197.6	90.6
	43.1		45.0		47.7	Sales/Net Fixed Assets	219.2	29.5	45.2	59.0	43.1	47.4
	14.4		11.3		10.1		9.9	9.4	11.4	11.0	6.8	12.4
	.7		.6		.5		.3	.4	.3	.3	.9	1.8
	.3		.3		.2	Sales/Total Assets	.2	.2	.2	.2	.3	.6
	.1		.2		.1		.1	.1	.1	.1	.1	.3
	.5		.5		.6		.5	.7	.5	.9	.6	.4
(139)	1.2	(185)	1.3	(148)	1.5	% Depr., Dep., Amort./Sales	(20)	2.1	(32)	1.4	(18)	1.2	(35)	2.0	(26)	1.3	(17)	.9
	2.7		3.0		3.4		6.3	2.5	2.4	3.9	4.5	3.3
	4.2		4.3		3.5		11.0	4.1		5.3		
(41)	11.7	(64)	11.5	(60)	10.1	% Officers', Directors' Owners' Comp/Sales	(14)	13.4	(18)	9.5		(10)	14.3		
	17.9		20.0		15.9		23.3	14.0		33.3		
	4227075M		5251124M		4150995M	Net Sales ($)	33015M	126331M	120237M	445715M	704160M	2721537M
	9168676M		11549976M		11932117M	Total Assets ($)	254576M	850817M	742243M	2496788M	3538181M	4049512M

M = $ thousand   MM = $ million
See Pages 9 through 22 for Explanation of Ratios and Data

Current Data Sorted by Assets

Comparative Historical Data

						Type of Statement		
3	6	20	42	10	6	Unqualified	105	108
			1			Reviewed	4	8
1	1	1	1	1		Compiled	16	17
6	3	3	6	1		Tax Returns	31	22
4	4	10	14	3	6	Other	81	53
	16 (4/1-9/30/10)		131 (10/1/10-3/31/11)				4/1/06-3/31/07	4/1/07-3/31/08
0-500M	500M-2MM	2-10MM	10-50MM	50-100MM	100-250MM		ALL	ALL
14	14	34	58	15	12	NUMBER OF STATEMENTS	237	208
%	%	%	%	%	%	ASSETS	%	%
48.9	26.5	18.0	13.8	23.7	8.4	Cash & Equivalents	24.2	15.5
3.8	14.1	21.0	12.9	3.2	15.5	Trade Receivables (net)	22.8	22.7
.0	10.8	13.3	19.3	9.0	4.8	Inventory	5.5	6.5
13.5	1.5	25.0	29.0	28.3	24.7	All Other Current	15.6	22.7
66.2	53.0	77.4	75.0	64.2	53.5	Total Current	68.2	67.5
25.5	24.2	3.7	6.3	5.4	1.2	Fixed Assets (net)	14.0	13.2
.1	3.9	4.6	1.2	2.3	3.9	Intangibles (net)	2.4	2.0
8.1	18.9	14.3	17.5	28.0	41.4	All Other Non-Current	15.3	17.4
100.0	100.0	100.0	100.0	100.0	100.0	Total	100.0	100.0
						LIABILITIES		
5.4	14.2	42.8	48.9	33.3	45.2	Notes Payable-Short Term	35.7	37.6
7.9	1.0	.2	1.4	1.4	.2	Cur. Mat.-L.T.D.	1.9	2.7
3.9	1.8	6.7	3.3	1.8	1.3	Trade Payables	3.7	3.3
.8	.0	.1	.4	.8	.0	Income Taxes Payable	.7	.1
9.0	9.8	7.6	9.8	14.4	3.0	All Other Current	10.7	10.4
27.0	26.7	57.4	63.8	51.7	49.7	Total Current	52.7	54.1
12.3	23.5	6.1	8.8	12.7	25.0	Long-Term Debt	10.6	12.7
.0	.2	.2	.0	.9	.0	Deferred Taxes	.1	.1
.1	7.7	1.0	1.1	1.2	3.3	All Other Non-Current	3.2	3.8
60.6	41.9	35.4	26.3	33.5	22.0	Net Worth	33.3	29.2
100.0	100.0	100.0	100.0	100.0	100.0	Total Liabilties & Net Worth	100.0	100.0
						INCOME DATA		
100.0	100.0	100.0	100.0	100.0	100.0	Net Sales	100.0	100.0
						Gross Profit		
88.0	92.1	77.4	76.4	80.8	82.8	Operating Expenses	82.3	83.8
12.0	7.9	22.6	23.6	19.2	17.2	Operating Profit	17.7	16.2
4.4	5.3	7.5	6.9	4.7	6.7	All Other Expenses (net)	6.7	8.0
7.6	2.7	15.1	16.7	14.5	10.5	Profit Before Taxes	11.0	8.2
						RATIOS		
18.2	6.6	2.0	1.3	1.3	1.5		2.6	1.7
3.2	1.5	1.3	1.1	1.1	1.1	Current	1.2	1.2
.9	.2	1.1	1.1	1.0	1.0		1.0	1.0
12.8	2.5	1.8	1.1	1.1	1.3		2.4	1.3
2.0	1.3	.5	.2	.5	.3	Quick	1.0	.8
.7	.1	.1	.1	.1	.1		.3	.1
0 UND	0 UND	0 UND	0 UND	0 UND	3 123.2		0 UND	0 UND
0 UND	1 350.2	16 22.4	4 101.6	1 281.5	16 22.2	Sales/Receivables	8 44.8	9 41.0
0 UND	7 54.2	184 2.0	27 13.7	16 22.5	68 5.4		110 3.3	206 1.8
						Cost of Sales/Inventory		
						Cost of Sales/Payables		
8.2	2.1	1.2	2.4	5.5	2.6		3.1	1.8
9.6	8.2	4.1	5.2	7.7	4.5	Sales/Working Capital	11.0	6.5
-339.7	-13.4	14.1	12.4	112.1	NM		-155.0	69.0
		9.1	9.5	20.4			10.6	6.2
	(22) 3.4	(46) 3.2	(11) 3.7			EBIT/Interest	(161) 1.8	(133) 1.8
		2.0	2.2	2.5			.7	.5
						Net Profit + Depr., Dep.,	15.4	14.2
						Amort./Cur. Mat. L/T/D	(14) 2.0	(13) 1.0
							-1.6	-1.1
.0	.0	.0	.0	.0	.0		.0	.0
.2	.1	.0	.1	.1	.1	Fixed/Worth	.2	.1
1.1	6.9	.1	.3	.1	.1		.9	.5
.2	.4	1.0	1.8	1.0	2.1		.7	1.4
.4	1.5	2.5	4.0	2.8	5.6	Debt/Worth	3.0	3.8
1.1	12.1	5.3	8.3	6.6	10.8		8.1	8.5
231.7	29.5	58.0	59.7	34.3	42.8		56.4	38.0
(13) 18.5	(13) 7.7	(32) 22.2	(57) 28.0	28.3	17.9	% Profit Before Taxes/Tangible Net Worth	(222) 16.2	(199) 9.7
5.7	-8.1	6.8	13.0	11.2	2.8		-2.1	-4.6
141.9	18.7	16.3	10.9	10.5	6.3		16.7	7.4
25.0	3.0	5.2	5.0	4.9	2.3	% Profit Before Taxes/Total Assets	4.0	1.9
5.8	.0	2.3	2.4	2.2	.3		-.6	-.8
UND	155.2	843.5	109.1	406.6	928.8		105.7	98.1
63.8	32.1	101.2	44.1	26.4	48.8	Sales/Net Fixed Assets	33.2	28.0
13.8	1.2	15.3	12.3	16.2	24.3		12.3	8.3
6.8	2.3	1.1	.6	.9	.7		3.6	1.4
5.4	.8	.5	.4	.4	.3	Sales/Total Assets	.9	.5
3.5	.3	.3	.3	.1	.1		.4	.2
		.3	.4				.5	.6
		(23) .6	(43) .7			% Depr., Dep., Amort./Sales	(156) 1.1	(145) 1.3
		1.5	1.5				1.8	2.1
			3.1				2.7	4.1
			(10) 9.8			% Officers', Directors' Owners' Comp/Sales	(65) 9.5	(45) 10.4
			27.4				13.8	28.8
16705M	21091M	211511M	880678M	1101614M	4586570M	Net Sales ($)	7974664M	2167591M
3629M	15860M	193750M	1514699M	1041777M	1808321M	Total Assets ($)	4290025M	4444657M

M = $ thousand   MM = $ million
See Pages 9 through 22 for Explanation of Ratios and Data

Comparative Historical Data | | ## Current Data Sorted by Sales

			Type of Statement						
106	105	87	Unqualified	4	22	9	11	24	17
5	5	1	Reviewed		1				
11	6	5	Compiled	1	2	1	1		
21	21	13	Tax Returns	8	3		1		1
68	74	41	Other	6	10	8	5	4	8
4/1/08-3/31/09	4/1/09-3/31/10	4/1/10-3/31/11		16 (4/1-9/30/10)			131 (10/1/10-3/31/11)		
ALL	ALL	ALL		0-1MM	1-3MM	3-5MM	5-10MM	10-25MM	25MM & OVER
211	211	147	NUMBER OF STATEMENTS	19	38	18	18	28	26
%	%	%	ASSETS	%	%	%	%	%	%
15.7	18.1	19.9	Cash & Equivalents	22.9	26.0	26.3	12.0	9.9	20.5
20.1	26.3	13.3	Trade Receivables (net)	10.9	14.6	12.1	17.9	15.2	8.6
8.9	9.8	13.0	Inventory	5.2	9.0	4.7	19.6	24.5	13.3
18.1	15.6	23.6	All Other Current	9.6	22.1	19.9	21.8	23.5	39.9
62.8	69.8	69.8	Total Current	48.6	71.7	63.0	71.3	73.1	82.3
12.3	8.6	8.7	Fixed Assets (net)	27.7	6.2	11.7	4.3	5.8	2.6
2.5	1.8	2.5	Intangibles (net)	.2	2.8	3.7	5.0	1.0	2.9
22.3	19.8	19.0	All Other Non-Current	23.6	19.3	21.6	19.4	20.1	12.1
100.0	100.0	100.0	Total	100.0	100.0	100.0	100.0	100.0	100.0
			LIABILITIES						
41.4	42.5	38.1	Notes Payable-Short Term	13.9	33.4	18.2	45.6	59.7	48.2
2.9	2.2	1.6	Cur. Mat.-L.T.D.	5.5	.6	3.9	1.1	.6	.2
3.3	3.9	3.7	Trade Payables	2.0	5.1	2.4	.9	1.9	7.6
.1	.1	.3	Income Taxes Payable	.0	.4	.0	.3	.6	.5
8.8	9.7	9.1	All Other Current	1.6	12.2	13.0	8.1	6.1	11.4
56.5	58.4	52.9	Total Current	22.9	51.6	37.4	56.0	68.8	68.0
14.4	10.2	11.6	Long-Term Debt	27.5	10.9	17.6	8.8	9.6	1.0
.1	.1	.2	Deferred Taxes	.1	.0	.8	.3	.0	.0
3.0	3.6	1.8	All Other Non-Current	.0	3.2	3.3	1.4	1.1	1.1
26.0	27.8	33.5	Net Worth	49.3	34.3	40.9	33.5	20.6	29.8
100.0	100.0	100.0	Total Liabilities & Net Worth	100.0	100.0	100.0	100.0	100.0	100.0
			INCOME DATA						
100.0	100.0	100.0	Net Sales	100.0	100.0	100.0	100.0	100.0	100.0
			Gross Profit						
83.4	79.6	80.2	Operating Expenses	79.2	74.5	81.5	80.9	80.6	87.5
16.6	20.4	19.8	Operating Profit	20.8	25.5	18.5	19.1	19.4	12.5
7.9	8.3	6.4	All Other Expenses (net)	11.9	7.0	12.7	3.0	3.3	2.9
8.7	12.1	13.4	Profit Before Taxes	8.9	18.5	5.8	16.2	16.1	9.6
			RATIOS						
2.0	2.0	1.9		4.5	2.3	6.8	2.0	1.2	1.3
1.1	1.2	1.2	Current	1.5	1.2	1.8	1.1	1.1	1.1
.9	1.0	1.1		.2	1.1	1.1	1.0	1.1	1.1
1.5	1.5	1.5		3.9	1.7	6.8	1.3	1.0	.9
.5	.9	.3	Quick	1.2	1.0	.9	.3	.2	.2
.1	.1	.1		.2	.1	.3	.1	.1	.1
0 UND	0 UND	0 UND		0 UND	0 UND	0 UND	0 UND	0 807.7	1 708.4
6 59.0	13 28.2	4 84.3	Sales/Receivables	0 UND	0 UND	6 63.0	15 24.9	11 33.3	3 109.2
132 2.8	403 .9	33 11.2		7 55.3	49 7.5	39 9.5	52 7.0	28 13.1	34 10.7
			Cost of Sales/Inventory						
			Cost of Sales/Payables						
1.9	1.8	2.6		1.2	1.7	.9	2.0	3.4	5.5
9.4	6.1	6.4	Sales/Working Capital	8.4	4.7	2.6	5.5	6.8	7.9
-15.2	269.0	18.6		-21.2	17.5	NM	42.0	11.7	34.1
5.0	8.8	9.1		1.2	12.2		9.6	5.2	19.5
(135) 2.0	(132) 3.3	(99) 3.6	EBIT/Interest		(26) 3.8		(14) 4.1	(22) 3.2	(23) 3.4
.8	2.0	2.2			2.1		2.0	2.3	1.8
		24.7	Net Profit + Depr., Dep.,						
		(10) 2.4	Amort./Cur. Mat. L/T/D						
		1.1							
.0	.0	.0		.0	.0	.0	.0	.0	.0
.1	.1	.1	Fixed/Worth	.1	.0	.0	.0	.1	.1
.6	.4	.2		1.6	.2	.4	.2	.4	.2
1.2	1.3	1.0		.3	.8	.5	1.1	3.6	1.6
4.4	3.3	3.4	Debt/Worth	1.0	2.3	1.5	3.7	5.5	3.9
10.2	7.6	6.6		5.0	7.3	3.7	6.3	9.4	6.5
37.5	57.7	51.3	% Profit Before Taxes/Tangible	64.4	39.4	29.8	62.6	58.2	64.6
(192) 11.9	(193) 21.1	(142) 24.6	Net Worth	(18) 5.9	(36) 17.6	(16) 7.6	34.3	32.1	35.5
.1	6.8	8.4		-2.7	8.5	-.1	10.5	15.4	24.9
6.9	11.6	12.6	% Profit Before Taxes/Total	18.5	12.8	9.6	16.0	10.8	22.1
2.4	4.9	5.0	Assets	2.8	4.4	3.8	5.7	5.3	6.3
-.2	1.1	1.5		.4	1.6	-1.4	1.9	3.1	3.7
163.6	257.2	223.5		UND	330.5	737.7	184.3	70.0	843.5
43.3	48.3	51.6	Sales/Net Fixed Assets	16.5	80.4	177.8	46.8	22.2	54.9
10.6	14.9	15.0		1.4	14.5	28.9	18.8	8.0	31.5
1.5	1.5	1.0		4.2	1.1	1.9	.8	.6	1.6
.5	.5	.5	Sales/Total Assets	.5	.3	.4	.4	.4	.9
.2	.2	.2		.1	.2	.1	.3	.3	.7
.5	.5	.4			.3		.4	.4	.4
(136) 1.1	(138) .9	(98) .9	% Depr., Dep., Amort./Sales	(25) .7		(15) .5	(24) .8	(16) .8	
2.2	1.7	1.5			1.7		1.5	1.2	1.3
5.8	6.6	4.2	% Officers', Directors'		6.4				
(46) 9.0	(33) 14.9	(32) 10.5	Owners' Comp/Sales		(13) 12.1				
17.4	26.0	26.3			29.3				
1552604M	3465399M	6818169M	Net Sales ($)	10278M	77523M	72089M	132044M	434908M	6091327M
4196594M	7080365M	4578036M	Total Assets ($)	31487M	374941M	374002M	397591M	1471801M	1928214M

M = $ thousand   MM = $ million
See Pages 9 through 22 for Explanation of Ratios and Data

Current Data Sorted by Assets   Comparative Historical Data

0-500M	500M-2MM	2-10MM	10-50MM	50-100MM	100-250MM		4/1/06-3/31/07 ALL	4/1/07-3/31/08 ALL
						Type of Statement		
3	2	10	19	6	14	Unqualified	15	28
	1		1			Reviewed	5	2
4	3	1	1			Compiled	2	4
						Tax Returns		1
2	9	12	8	2	3	Other	21	36
		8 (4/1-9/30/10)	93 (10/1/10-3/31/11)				4/1/06-3/31/07	4/1/07-3/31/08
9	15	23	29	8	17	**NUMBER OF STATEMENTS**	43	71
%	%	%	%	%	%	**ASSETS**	%	%
	20.0	33.0	34.1		24.4	Cash & Equivalents	36.1	29.2
	19.2	16.7	22.8		19.4	Trade Receivables (net)	18.0	19.5
	.7	3.3	.7		.1	Inventory	1.8	2.4
	13.0	9.6	14.7		10.1	All Other Current	14.1	7.4
	52.8	62.7	72.3		53.9	Total Current	70.0	58.5
	25.1	16.4	11.3		7.0	Fixed Assets (net)	16.7	18.1
	10.6	7.8	11.4		29.8	Intangibles (net)	3.7	10.7
	11.4	13.1	5.1		9.3	All Other Non-Current	9.6	12.7
	100.0	100.0	100.0		100.0	Total	100.0	100.0
						LIABILITIES		
	18.2	13.9	9.8		9.3	Notes Payable-Short Term	11.1	10.0
	5.1	2.6	3.4		1.5	Cur. Mat.-L.T.D.	3.9	3.6
	12.8	10.3	12.9		13.1	Trade Payables	10.8	12.4
	.0	.6	.2		.1	Income Taxes Payable	.9	.3
	15.8	18.7	21.1		10.9	All Other Current	24.4	18.2
	52.0	46.1	47.4		35.1	Total Current	51.1	44.5
	48.5	7.7	24.2		20.1	Long-Term Debt	22.5	24.0
	.0	.4	.0		1.1	Deferred Taxes	.1	.3
	9.4	13.5	2.0		4.5	All Other Non-Current	3.3	7.3
	-9.9	32.3	26.4		39.2	Net Worth	23.0	23.8
	100.0	100.0	100.0		100.0	Total Liabilities & Net Worth	100.0	100.0
						INCOME DATA		
	100.0	100.0	100.0		100.0	Net Sales	100.0	100.0
						Gross Profit		
	93.4	90.3	81.4		87.9	Operating Expenses	89.4	91.7
	6.6	9.7	18.6		12.1	Operating Profit	10.6	8.3
	4.6	.6	2.1		2.0	All Other Expenses (net)	4.4	2.6
	2.0	9.1	16.4		10.1	Profit Before Taxes	6.1	5.7
						RATIOS		
	5.7	2.6	2.1		2.1		4.1	2.2
	1.2	1.5	1.5		1.5	Current	1.2	1.2
	.3	1.1	1.1		1.2		1.0	.9
	2.8	1.5	2.0		1.8		1.7	1.9
	1.1	1.0	1.2		1.3	Quick	1.1	1.1
	.2	.8	.7		1.0		.7	.7
	1 480.5	7 53.6	15 24.4		15 24.5		2 211.7	3 109.7
	18 20.6	32 11.4	41 8.9		34 10.7	Sales/Receivables	30 12.1	28 12.9
	35 10.5	70 5.2	77 4.7		94 3.9		73 5.0	57 6.4
						Cost of Sales/Inventory		
						Cost of Sales/Payables		
	3.9	4.1	1.5		3.6		3.1	4.7
	13.3	8.6	5.5		5.4	Sales/Working Capital	9.0	13.8
	-4.6	46.1	29.0		19.1		-354.3	-104.7
	9.0	58.4	30.9		10.9		13.0	14.0
	(12) 3.9	(19) 6.7	(18) 12.0		(16) 4.6	EBIT/Interest	(27) 2.8	(50) 2.7
	.5	1.6	4.3		1.8		1.0	.0
						Net Profit + Depr., Dep.,	26.5	15.3
						Amort./Cur. Mat. L/T/D	(11) 16.9	(16) 6.7
							2.8	1.6
	.1	.2	.1		.2		.1	.2
	1.2	.5	.3		.3	Fixed/Worth	.4	.6
	-.7	1.8	17.7		-.1		1.3	23.5
	.9	.6	1.1		.8		.7	.9
	4.5	2.3	3.1		9.9	Debt/Worth	2.9	3.5
	-2.1	5.1	192.3		-3.3		7.0	-7.4
		95.6	91.2		73.0	% Profit Before Taxes/Tangible	49.5	64.9
		(19) 23.0	(23) 48.5		(10) 42.0	Net Worth	(35) 15.1	(53) 22.0
		3.1	8.0		3.3		3.3	-6.4
	26.2	30.4	24.6		15.9	% Profit Before Taxes/Total	14.1	20.4
	7.1	12.9	13.2		4.7	Assets	3.5	8.1
	-5.0	1.2	3.9		1.5		.3	-2.4
	89.3	52.0	80.7		32.4		35.6	45.9
	19.8	11.2	27.7		14.6	Sales/Net Fixed Assets	13.1	15.4
	4.8	6.0	8.0		10.1		5.7	6.4
	4.1	2.5	2.1		1.3		2.1	2.7
	2.3	1.6	1.2		1.2	Sales/Total Assets	1.4	1.7
	.9	1.1	.6		.5		.6	.7
			.5	.7			1.2	1.4
		(18) 3.0	(21) 2.2			% Depr., Dep., Amort./Sales	(31) 2.2	(44) 2.1
		4.0	5.5				5.0	5.5
						% Officers', Directors'	1.6	1.8
						Owners' Comp/Sales	(16) 3.4	(17) 5.3
							12.9	13.6
12609M	58953M	341959M	864397M	1439983M	2591480M	Net Sales ($)	1337000M	2924124M
2387M	19360M	116392M	579740M	612708M	2617918M	Total Assets ($)	1401507M	2468796M

Comparative Historical Data   Current Data Sorted by Sales

Comparative Historical Data columns: **4/1/08-3/31/09 ALL**, **4/1/09-3/31/10 ALL**, **4/1/10-3/31/11 ALL**

Current Data column groups: **8 (4/1-9/30/10)** spans 0-1MM, 1-3MM, 3-5MM — **93 (10/1/10-3/31/11)** spans 5-10MM, 10-25MM, 25MM & OVER

4/1/08-3/31/09 ALL	4/1/09-3/31/10 ALL	4/1/10-3/31/11 ALL		0-1MM	1-3MM	3-5MM	5-10MM	10-25MM	25MM & OVER
			Type of Statement						
46	42	54	Unqualified	2	2	4	4	13	29
3	3	2	Reviewed	1				1	
8		2	Compiled						
11	5	9	Tax Returns	3	5				1
49	46	36	Other	2	5	5	11	4	9
117	98	101	**NUMBER OF STATEMENTS**	8	12	9	15	18	39
%	%	%	**ASSETS**	%	%	%	%	%	%
32.3	27.6	29.1	Cash & Equivalents		24.2		31.7	32.9	24.5
24.0	15.9	19.9	Trade Receivables (net)		14.6		23.8	23.3	18.2
1.7	2.2	1.1	Inventory		.7		.0	1.1	.3
8.8	12.4	12.1	All Other Current		23.4		15.8	10.6	12.0
66.8	58.0	62.2	Total Current		62.9		71.3	68.0	55.1
13.7	15.6	14.0	Fixed Assets (net)		16.0		16.1	16.3	9.5
9.8	17.6	14.9	Intangibles (net)		12.8		7.0	9.7	25.0
9.7	8.8	8.9	All Other Non-Current		8.4		5.6	6.1	10.4
100.0	100.0	100.0	Total		100.0		100.0	100.0	100.0
			LIABILITIES						
13.6	8.4	12.2	Notes Payable-Short Term		17.7		14.8	5.1	9.4
5.0	5.8	3.4	Cur. Mat.-L.T.D.		8.6		4.4	1.7	3.5
11.4	15.3	13.8	Trade Payables		26.1		15.2	13.7	13.6
.5	.5	.2	Income Taxes Payable		.0		.3	.7	.1
22.9	18.9	16.4	All Other Current		15.6		18.6	24.5	14.5
53.3	48.9	46.1	Total Current		68.1		53.3	45.6	41.2
16.7	19.6	23.3	Long-Term Debt		63.5		7.0	11.1	27.3
.1	.5	.3	Deferred Taxes		.0		.0	.3	.5
7.3	6.6	7.4	All Other Non-Current		17.2		14.2	.5	4.9
22.6	24.3	23.0	Net Worth		-48.8		25.4	42.5	26.2
100.0	100.0	100.0	Total Liabilities & Net Worth		100.0		100.0	100.0	100.0
			INCOME DATA						
100.0	100.0	100.0	Net Sales		100.0		100.0	100.0	100.0
			Gross Profit						
87.1	90.2	88.2	Operating Expenses		95.1		83.5	88.3	89.2
12.9	9.8	11.8	Operating Profit		4.9		16.5	11.7	10.8
2.1	2.8	2.1	All Other Expenses (net)		2.4		2.3	.1	2.3
10.9	7.0	9.7	Profit Before Taxes		2.5		14.1	11.6	8.5
			RATIOS						
2.1	1.8	2.7			3.4		3.3	3.0	1.9
1.3	1.2	1.5	Current		2.6		1.7	1.2	1.3
1.0	.8	1.1			.3		1.2	1.1	1.0
1.9	1.5	2.3			2.7		2.8	2.9	1.7
1.1	1.0	1.2	Quick		1.1		1.3	1.1	1.1
.7	.5	.6			.2		.9	.8	.6
4 91.0	4 81.1	7 53.1			0 UND		3 105.8	12 30.8	8 43.3
28 12.9	21 17.4	31 11.8	Sales/Receivables		6 64.5		29 12.4	39 9.5	28 12.9
92 3.9	50 7.2	66 5.5			29 12.7		131 2.8	66 5.5	54 6.8
			Cost of Sales/Inventory						
			Cost of Sales/Payables						
2.7	5.3	3.6			4.6		1.4	3.8	4.7
8.8	17.0	7.5	Sales/Working Capital		15.3		6.8	7.5	9.2
-75.9	-29.0	64.1			-4.8		20.3	42.9	80.3
27.7	19.5	24.8						136.2	13.4
(78) 4.9	(66) 3.3	(77) 5.5	EBIT/Interest					(11) 13.5	(36) 6.1
.9	-.7	1.6						1.9	.8
80.5	25.5	10.3							
(16) 13.9	(18) 4.7	(10) 4.0	Net Profit + Depr., Dep., Amort./Cur. Mat. L/T/D						
2.0	1.7	2.9							
.1	.1	.1			.1		.1	.1	.2
.3	.6	.5	Fixed/Worth		NM		.5	.3	.5
NM	-1.0	-1.1			-.1		1.3	1.3	-.1
.9	1.1	.8			1.8		.9	.6	1.1
4.3	4.6	3.1	Debt/Worth		-33.7		2.9	1.7	9.9
-12.1	-4.3	-5.4			-1.5		11.8	9.3	-2.4
82.1	87.2	83.6					48.6	132.3	87.7
(86) 25.4	(67) 34.0	(71) 43.4	% Profit Before Taxes/Tangible Net Worth				(12) 23.9	(16) 40.9	(23) 52.0
8.1	1.9	6.2					-25.0	5.1	6.2
20.9	20.3	23.5			89.9		23.2	36.5	20.3
5.8	5.4	10.7	% Profit Before Taxes/Total Assets		2.5		12.5	7.1	11.9
1.1	-3.3	1.1			-9.9		-.3	3.8	.5
82.0	57.7	54.4			126.5		46.2	51.8	56.9
25.9	15.9	23.0	Sales/Net Fixed Assets		30.4		15.2	17.3	27.7
6.5	6.2	8.7			12.8		5.7	5.6	13.2
2.5	2.5	2.9			6.1		2.1	2.5	2.9
1.4	1.3	1.4	Sales/Total Assets		4.4		1.2	1.5	1.3
.5	.6	.8			1.2		.5	.7	.9
.8	1.6	1.0						.7	1.3
(70) 2.4	(61) 3.1	(64) 2.9	% Depr., Dep., Amort./Sales					(17) 2.2	(21) 3.6
4.3	5.1	5.1						5.5	4.7
2.0	2.1								
(24) 5.0	(22) 4.9	(15) 5.5	% Officers', Directors' Owners' Comp/Sales						
10.0	10.1	10.2							
4244305M	4537676M	5309381M	Net Sales ($)	3996M	23686M	36120M	109962M	297946M	4837671M
3939846M	4138907M	3948505M	Total Assets ($)	11355M	10423M	38711M	135280M	260532M	3492204M

M = $ thousand   MM = $ million
See Pages 9 through 22 for Explanation of Ratios and Data

Current Data Sorted by Assets   Comparative Historical Data

	0-500M	500M-2MM	2-10MM	10-50MM	50-100MM	100-250MM	Type of Statement	4/1/06-3/31/07 ALL	4/1/07-3/31/08 ALL
	23	28	15	16	4	8	Unqualified	33	87
		1	4				Reviewed	7	4
	5		4	2			Compiled	14	18
	3	3	4				Tax Returns	9	13
	3	4	8	9	4	3	Other	32	30
		9 (4/1-9/30/10)		142 (10/1/10-3/31/11)					
	34	36	35	27	8	11	NUMBER OF STATEMENTS	95	152
	%	%	%	%	%	%	**ASSETS**	%	%
	64.8	64.8	32.8	27.8		20.9	Cash & Equivalents	31.0	45.1
	3.3	9.5	15.8	23.8		19.5	Trade Receivables (net)	26.9	17.7
	.0	2.0	.5	.3		1.9	Inventory	3.0	1.1
	6.8	2.6	6.4	15.4		9.4	All Other Current	8.7	5.7
	74.9	78.8	55.5	67.3		51.8	Total Current	69.6	69.6
	15.8	12.4	23.4	12.6		9.8	Fixed Assets (net)	12.1	15.5
	3.5	6.8	8.6	12.3		23.1	Intangibles (net)	4.0	4.9
	5.7	2.0	12.6	7.8		15.3	All Other Non-Current	14.2	10.0
	100.0	100.0	100.0	100.0		100.0	Total	100.0	100.0
							LIABILITIES		
	19.0	13.6	14.6	10.2		14.5	Notes Payable-Short Term	23.8	19.0
	1.8	1.4	4.7	1.9		8.8	Cur. Mat.-L.T.D.	1.2	3.8
	13.9	11.1	12.9	11.8		15.7	Trade Payables	8.2	11.6
	.0	.1	.3	.1		.3	Income Taxes Payable	.1	.2
	8.1	15.3	12.1	19.4		3.4	All Other Current	13.3	14.7
	42.8	41.4	44.6	43.4		42.7	Total Current	46.7	49.3
	2.6	6.3	11.4	9.6		9.8	Long-Term Debt	16.7	10.9
	.0	.0	.0	.0		1.2	Deferred Taxes	.2	.1
	15.8	10.0	8.5	11.8		5.3	All Other Non-Current	7.5	9.9
	38.9	42.3	35.5	35.1		41.0	Net Worth	29.0	29.8
	100.0	100.0	100.0	100.0		100.0	Total Liabilities & Net Worth	100.0	100.0
							INCOME DATA		
	100.0	100.0	100.0	100.0		100.0	Net Sales	100.0	100.0
							Gross Profit		
	92.7	88.9	82.6	89.1		91.3	Operating Expenses	77.8	82.6
	7.3	11.1	17.4	10.9		8.7	Operating Profit	22.2	17.4
	2.3	1.3	6.4	3.7		1.4	All Other Expenses (net)	8.7	6.7
	5.0	9.8	11.0	7.2		7.2	Profit Before Taxes	13.4	10.7
							RATIOS		
	5.5	4.4	2.4	2.6		1.9		3.1	3.1
	2.5	1.7	1.2	1.4		1.1	Current	1.6	1.6
	1.2	1.3	.7	1.1		1.0		1.0	1.1
	3.2	4.4	2.0	2.4		1.9		3.1	2.8
	2.4	1.7	1.1	1.2		.9	Quick	1.4	1.4
	1.2	1.3	.6	.5		.4		.9	1.0
	0 UND	0 UND	2 151.5	14 26.0		36 10.1		0 UND	0 UND
	2 201.6	5 77.6	6 63.2	53 6.9		47 7.7	Sales/Receivables	23 15.5	2 150.2
	8 47.0	20 18.3	34 10.6	115 3.2		116 3.1		155 2.4	56 6.6
							Cost of Sales/Inventory		
							Cost of Sales/Payables		
	2.0	1.7	3.6	1.4		4.0		2.0	2.1
	3.4	3.6	9.9	3.4		21.6	Sales/Working Capital	3.9	4.6
	14.4	7.1	-4.9	70.4		-31.9		50.2	20.0
	8.6	9.7	13.5	11.1				11.5	13.4
	(21) 4.0	(25) 2.9	(29) 4.5	(22) 2.7			EBIT/Interest	(62) 4.3	(113) 5.0
	1.5	1.1	1.1	.6				1.7	1.3
							Net Profit + Depr., Dep., Amort./Cur. Mat. L/T/D		16.1
								(18)	2.1
									.7
	.1	.1	.1	.1		.2		.0	.1
	.3	.3	.4	.2		.5	Fixed/Worth	.2	.3
	.6	1.0	6.3	.8		-1.0		1.0	1.2
	.3	.3	.8	1.4		.8		1.0	1.1
	1.0	2.2	2.3	3.2		3.6	Debt/Worth	3.1	2.7
	2.2	4.4	29.3	10.9		-4.4		9.1	7.9
	43.5	42.7	47.5	39.8			% Profit Before Taxes/Tangible Net Worth	70.0	47.9
	(29) 8.1	(32) 10.4	(28) 15.2	(23) 14.5				(84) 28.5	(132) 19.8
	1.7	2.9	2.0	2.2				6.8	6.5
	19.0	19.8	12.7	13.3		8.0	% Profit Before Taxes/Total Assets	22.8	16.5
	5.1	4.9	4.3	1.9		3.3		5.7	5.9
	.5	.5	.4	-.6		1.5		1.3	.8
	41.3	52.4	41.4	44.1		16.0	Sales/Net Fixed Assets	102.8	52.7
	14.5	11.8	7.6	19.8		10.1		24.8	17.9
	5.8	5.6	3.3	6.7		4.6		7.5	6.5
	1.5	1.3	1.7	1.4		1.3	Sales/Total Assets	1.8	1.7
	1.2	1.0	.9	.8		.6		1.0	1.1
	.9	.8	.3	.5		.4		.2	.5
	.8	.7	1.5	.7			% Depr., Dep., Amort./Sales	.9	.7
	(29) 1.3	(31) 1.1	(26) 2.0	(21) 3.0				(65) 1.9	(123) 1.7
	2.6	2.5	3.7	3.8				4.0	3.2
	11.2	8.9	5.7				% Officers', Directors' Owners' Comp/Sales	4.6	6.1
	(24) 16.5	(19) 13.0	(12) 10.5					(28) 12.4	(73) 11.1
	24.6	22.6	22.2					20.9	19.6
	17321M	64569M	230242M	575741M	147080M	1140875M	Net Sales ($)	3627367M	2467847M
	10760M	39253M	167825M	667356M	544236M	1520595M	Total Assets ($)	2735710M	3150060M

M = $ thousand   MM = $ million
See Pages 9 through 22 for Explanation of Ratios and Data

Comparative Historical Data | Current Data Sorted by Sales

						Type of Statement						
	98		124		94	Unqualified	40	20	4	6	10	14
	6		9		5	Reviewed	1	1	2		1	
	19		11		11	Compiled	5	4			2	
	11		19		10	Tax Returns	6	3	1		-	
	42		49		31	Other	4	4	3	4	7	9
	4/1/08-		4/1/09-		4/1/10-			9 (4/1-9/30/10)			142 (10/1/10-3/31/11)	
	3/31/09		3/31/10		3/31/11							
	ALL		ALL		ALL		0-1MM	1-3MM	3-5MM	5-10MM	10-25MM	25MM & OVER
	176		212		151	NUMBER OF STATEMENTS	56	32	10	10	20	23
	%		%		%	ASSETS	%	%	%	%	%	%
	43.9		47.5		45.2	Cash & Equivalents	60.1	48.1	38.4	34.2	31.2	24.6
	14.4		15.4		14.3	Trade Receivables (net)	6.7	16.4	14.8	27.8	19.2	19.3
	1.5		1.2		.8	Inventory	.0	.2	.5	.0	3.8	1.3
	5.8		4.8		7.3	All Other Current	4.5	5.1	18.9	7.9	7.6	11.4
	65.6		69.0		67.5	Total Current	71.4	69.8	72.5	69.9	61.9	56.5
	15.6		13.5		15.1	Fixed Assets (net)	17.3	15.0	12.9	11.1	18.1	9.9
	7.4		8.4		9.1	Intangibles (net)	4.6	10.4	7.6	3.2	7.2	23.3
	11.4		9.1		8.3	All Other Non-Current	6.7	4.9	7.0	15.8	12.9	10.4
	100.0		100.0		100.0	Total	100.0	100.0	100.0	100.0	100.0	100.0
						LIABILITIES						
	16.1		17.3		15.4	Notes Payable-Short Term	18.0	13.7	13.4	24.2	18.8	5.3
	4.6		3.6		2.8	Cur. Mat.-L.T.D.	1.8	3.6	2.9	.7	2.2	6.0
	8.6		10.3		12.3	Trade Payables	12.8	11.7	10.6	6.1	11.5	16.1
	.2		.2		.2	Income Taxes Payable	.1	.0	.4	.9	.3	.2
	14.6		11.0		12.7	All Other Current	8.2	10.3	22.8	23.9	18.7	12.8
	44.1		42.4		43.4	Total Current	40.8	39.3	50.1	55.8	51.6	40.3
	11.8		11.4		8.0	Long-Term Debt	4.9	11.1	2.4	4.2	11.4	12.5
	.1		.1		.2	Deferred Taxes	.0	.0	.0	.0	.0	1.3
	12.4		7.7		10.7	All Other Non-Current	13.0	10.4	9.4	6.1	11.5	7.4
	31.7		38.3		37.6	Net Worth	41.3	39.1	38.0	33.9	25.5	38.5
	100.0		100.0		100.0	Total Liabilities & Net Worth	100.0	100.0	100.0	100.0	100.0	100.0
						INCOME DATA						
	100.0		100.0		100.0	Net Sales	100.0	100.0	100.0	100.0	100.0	100.0
						Gross Profit						
	83.8		83.1		87.0	Operating Expenses	89.2	79.7	93.5	79.5	91.8	88.1
	16.2		16.9		13.0	Operating Profit	10.8	20.3	6.5	20.5	8.2	11.9
	5.5		5.2		3.6	All Other Expenses (net)	4.0	3.5	3.3	9.0	2.1	1.9
	10.7		11.7		9.4	Profit Before Taxes	6.8	16.8	3.1	11.4	6.1	10.1
						RATIOS						
	3.2		3.4		3.1		4.6	3.4	3.9	1.7	2.3	1.9
	1.5		1.6		1.5	Current	2.4	1.6	1.6	1.2	1.2	1.4
	1.0		1.1		1.1		1.2	1.1	1.1	1.0	.8	1.0
	3.0		3.3		2.9		4.2	3.1	3.9	1.6	2.3	1.9
	1.3		1.5		1.4	Quick	2.0	1.5	1.4	1.2	1.0	1.0
	.9		1.1		.9		1.1	1.1	.4	.7	.5	.5
0	UND	0	UND	1	719.0		0	UND	0	UND	0	UND	0	UND	6	61.6	19	19.0
2	172.5	3	114.1	7	51.2	Sales/Receivables	3	125.1	4	83.9	3	134.5	21	17.3	40	9.2	47	7.8
31	11.9	53	6.9	47	7.8		11	33.0	37	9.7	11	33.3	1809	.2	143	2.6	67	5.4
						Cost of Sales/Inventory						
						Cost of Sales/Payables						
	2.3		1.6		2.0		1.8	2.0	1.2	.7	3.2	3.7
	5.4		4.1		4.7	Sales/Working Capital	3.3	5.1	7.4	8.5	7.0	12.1
	36.3		18.5		24.9		12.9	10.8	NM	NM	-45.2	-31.9
	15.9		16.6		9.0		8.5	8.4			12.4	14.8
(124)	3.7	(154)	5.2	(110)	3.2	EBIT/Interest	(35)	3.1	(27)	2.9			(16)	3.8	(20)	4.3
	1.7		1.7		1.1		1.3	1.1			1.1	1.1
	9.3		9.9		5.7							
(29)	2.6	(33)	2.8	(21)	3.0	Net Profit + Depr., Dep., Amort./Cur. Mat. L/T/D						
	.5		1.0		1.3							
	.1		.1		.1		.1	.0	.1	.0	.2	.2
	.3		.3		.3	Fixed/Worth	.3	.4	.2	.1	.5	.5
	1.7		1.1		1.4		.8	1.6	.5	1.3	3.2	-.5
	1.0		.6		.7		.3	.9	.6	.6	1.4	.8
	3.0		1.8		2.2	Debt/Worth	1.3	3.2	1.9	4.9	2.9	3.5
	12.8		7.3		6.0		3.7	10.7	NM	9.8	10.4	-4.6
	49.1		44.8		40.1		33.3	62.7		38.0	44.7	69.6
(146)	25.6	(182)	20.6	(125)	11.1	% Profit Before Taxes/Tangible Net Worth	(49)	9.7	(26)	11.3			13.8	(16)	11.6	(16)	20.6
	9.0		6.3		2.7		1.7	2.9		-4.2	2.8	5.0
	15.9		16.9		13.3		11.9	16.4	24.9	6.0	12.7	18.0
	6.5		6.8		3.9	% Profit Before Taxes/Total Assets	4.0	4.2	2.3	1.5	4.0	5.9
	2.1		1.7		.5		.4	.6	-6.2	-2.3	.5	1.5
	54.1		54.3		42.0		30.7	52.4	92.3	93.4	40.2	26.4
	15.4		12.1		12.7	Sales/Net Fixed Assets	10.8	11.4	31.9	28.4	11.8	16.5
	6.2		5.8		5.4		5.1	4.2	5.7	2.9	4.2	8.9
	1.6		1.3		1.4		1.3	1.2	3.8	1.3	2.3	1.5
	1.0		.9		.9	Sales/Total Assets	.9	.9	1.5	.4	1.0	.9
	.5		.5		.6		.7	.5	.6	.1	.5	.6
	.9		.6		.8		.9	.6			.7	1.5
(136)	1.5	(160)	1.8	(120)	1.7	% Depr., Dep., Amort./Sales	(47)	1.6	(22)	1.6			(19)	2.1	(15)	3.1
	3.0		3.1		3.1		2.7	2.7			4.0	3.7
	6.8		7.0		8.8		11.1	8.9				
(66)	12.6	(88)	12.2	(59)	13.9	% Officers', Directors' Owners' Comp/Sales	(35)	15.8	(13)	12.8				
	26.4		22.5		23.5		23.5	23.3				
	4024922M		4424124M		2175828M	Net Sales ($)	28183M	61833M	39786M	71919M	325683M	1648424M
	3307047M		4543056M		2950025M	Total Assets ($)	48522M	160619M	68960M	328231M	499232M	1844461M

© RMA 2011

M = $ thousand   MM = $ million
See Pages 9 through 22 for Explanation of Ratios and Data

Current Data Sorted by Assets   Comparative Historical Data

0-500M	500M-2MM	2-10MM	10-50MM	50-100MM	100-250MM	Type of Statement	4/1/06-3/31/07 ALL	4/1/07-3/31/08 ALL
	4	7	6	3	5	Unqualified	42	45
		1			1	Reviewed	4	1
			1			Compiled	4	3
4	1	3				Tax Returns	3	2
3	3	6	2	1		Other	17	27
	8 (4/1-9/30/10)		43 (10/1/10-3/31/11)					
7	8	17	9	4	6	NUMBER OF STATEMENTS	70	78

0-500M %	500M-2MM %	2-10MM %	10-50MM %	50-100MM %	100-250MM %		%	%
						ASSETS		
		28.6				Cash & Equivalents	38.0	28.8
		15.7				Trade Receivables (net)	17.6	17.5
		5.9				Inventory	8.9	6.3
		6.0				All Other Current	9.6	9.1
		56.2				Total Current	74.1	61.6
		17.2				Fixed Assets (net)	10.6	9.8
		8.9				Intangibles (net)	3.8	6.9
		17.7				All Other Non-Current	11.5	21.7
		100.0				Total	100.0	100.0
						LIABILITIES		
		14.6				Notes Payable-Short Term	9.9	12.1
		2.7				Cur. Mat.-L.T.D.	1.1	1.2
		16.2				Trade Payables	17.2	13.7
		.0				Income Taxes Payable	.2	.3
		9.2				All Other Current	17.5	20.7
		42.8				Total Current	45.9	48.0
		21.1				Long-Term Debt	5.5	10.4
		1.0				Deferred Taxes	.3	.3
		6.1				All Other Non-Current	3.0	2.4
		28.9				Net Worth	45.4	38.8
		100.0				Total Liabilities & Net Worth	100.0	100.0
						INCOME DATA		
		100.0				Net Sales	100.0	100.0
						Gross Profit		
		88.4				Operating Expenses	77.2	74.6
		11.6				Operating Profit	22.8	25.4
		4.2				All Other Expenses (net)	3.0	4.0
		7.4				Profit Before Taxes	19.8	21.4
						RATIOS		
		2.2					2.9	4.3
		1.4				Current	1.3	1.4
		.8					1.1	1.0
		1.8					2.0	3.1
		1.2				Quick	1.1	1.1
		.6					.6	.5
	0	UND					0 UND	0 UND
	11	34.7				Sales/Receivables	12 30.5	14 25.8
	51	7.1					79 4.6	83 4.4
						Cost of Sales/Inventory		
						Cost of Sales/Payables		
		6.7					2.8	2.4
		11.8				Sales/Working Capital	4.8	5.2
		-63.1					28.9	-137.1
		59.3					177.5	21.7
	(10)	6.6				EBIT/Interest	(36) 6.4	(38) 3.2
		1.1					2.3	.8
						Net Profit + Depr., Dep., Amort./Cur. Mat. L/T/D		
		.1					.0	.0
		.1				Fixed/Worth	.1	.1
		2.8					.3	.5
		.9					.4	.5
		2.1				Debt/Worth	1.5	1.6
		4.3					4.7	6.1
		77.7				% Profit Before Taxes/Tangible	69.3	49.0
	(15)	27.1				Net Worth	(67) 26.5	(67) 19.9
		-.7					6.2	5.5
		45.2				% Profit Before Taxes/Total	35.5	25.5
		6.5				Assets	7.2	6.2
		-.6					1.9	1.2
		119.9					157.3	324.3
		28.2				Sales/Net Fixed Assets	54.7	74.2
		5.6					24.4	26.7
		4.4					2.6	2.4
		2.1				Sales/Total Assets	1.0	.9
		.4					.3	.3
		.3					.4	.3
	(14)	.8				% Depr., Dep., Amort./Sales	(51) .6	(48) .7
		5.4					1.5	1.3
							8.7	3.3
						% Officers', Directors' Owners' Comp/Sales	(15) 16.6	(12) 18.4
							33.6	35.0
11460M	23688M	271132M	218693M	336323M	480345M	Net Sales ($)	2677648M	2351609M
1608M	8779M	99018M	205989M	265900M	802555M	Total Assets ($)	2346093M	2710295M

Comparative Historical Data   Current Data Sorted by Sales

			Type of Statement						
32	31	25	Unqualified	1	4	2	2	4	12
3	1	2	Reviewed					2	
2	3	1	Compiled			1			
5	6	8	Tax Returns	3	1	1	1	1	1
21	22	15	Other	2	6		2	2	3
4/1/08-3/31/09 ALL	4/1/09-3/31/10 ALL	4/1/10-3/31/11 ALL		8 (4/1-9/30/10)			43 (10/1/10-3/31/11)		
				0-1MM	1-3MM	3-5MM	5-10MM	10-25MM	25MM & OVER
63	63	51	NUMBER OF STATEMENTS	6	11	4	5	9	16
%	%	%	ASSETS	%	%	%	%	%	%
32.6	30.7	33.5	Cash & Equivalents		34.5				49.8
17.2	16.5	14.2	Trade Receivables (net)		8.6				14.2
4.3	2.9	4.2	Inventory		.0				6.7
6.9	11.1	7.4	All Other Current		6.0				7.3
61.0	61.2	59.3	Total Current		49.1				78.0
17.4	13.6	12.1	Fixed Assets (net)		18.3				4.3
4.6	6.6	6.7	Intangibles (net)		3.1				4.0
17.0	18.6	21.9	All Other Non-Current		29.4				13.8
100.0	100.0	100.0	Total		100.0				100.0
			LIABILITIES						
6.5	8.8	16.4	Notes Payable-Short Term		9.3				4.7
4.4	1.3	2.7	Cur. Mat.-L.T.D.		8.6				.3
13.0	11.3	11.9	Trade Payables		10.2				18.5
.4	.1	.0	Income Taxes Payable		.0				.0
19.5	15.4	14.3	All Other Current		3.0				20.3
43.8	36.8	45.3	Total Current		31.1				43.8
13.4	8.1	12.2	Long-Term Debt		14.6				4.3
.0	.6	.4	Deferred Taxes		.0				.0
3.9	4.1	7.8	All Other Non-Current		4.1				6.7
38.9	50.4	34.3	Net Worth		50.1				45.2
100.0	100.0	100.0	Total Liabilities & Net Worth		100.0				100.0
			INCOME DATA						
100.0	100.0	100.0	Net Sales		100.0				100.0
			Gross Profit						
77.1	81.8	87.2	Operating Expenses		89.8				85.9
22.9	18.2	12.8	Operating Profit		10.2				14.1
8.7	3.3	1.9	All Other Expenses (net)		1.2				-.5
14.2	14.9	10.9	Profit Before Taxes		9.1				14.6
			RATIOS						
3.1	2.9	3.2	Current		3.8				3.0
1.6	1.9	1.5			1.4				1.8
1.0	1.1	1.1			.2				1.4
2.4	2.1	2.1	Quick		2.9				2.1
1.2	1.4	1.3			1.2				1.4
.5	.5	.6			.2				1.1
0 UND	0 UND	0 UND	Sales/Receivables		0 UND				0 UND
12 31.2	8 44.5	16 22.5			11 33.3				19 19.7
61 6.0	81 4.5	42 8.7			25 14.9				50 7.3
			Cost of Sales/Inventory						
			Cost of Sales/Payables						
2.3	2.4	3.2	Sales/Working Capital		1.7				3.9
5.0	4.5	7.1			21.7				5.1
93.3	241.0	75.2			-7.9				9.1
59.5	57.6	39.0	EBIT/Interest						
(35) 13.0	(33) 15.6	(32) 6.6							
1.2	2.7	1.0							
			Net Profit + Depr., Dep., Amort./Cur. Mat. L/T/D						
.0	.0	.0	Fixed/Worth		.0				.0
.1	.1	.1			.2				.1
.7	.5	1.0			1.0				.2
.7	.5	.6	Debt/Worth		.1				.7
1.8	1.2	1.7			1.0				1.4
6.0	3.1	3.9			3.0				2.9
48.1	80.9	74.0	% Profit Before Taxes/Tangible Net Worth		42.5				84.9
(57) 20.8	(59) 19.3	(44) 24.6		(10) 6.1				(15) 61.1
2.4	2.0	.7			-3.3				17.5
18.6	31.9	36.7	% Profit Before Taxes/Total Assets		41.0				54.0
5.7	6.5	6.5			5.1				21.3
.4	.5	.1			.0				3.2
83.7	356.2	136.9	Sales/Net Fixed Assets		73.9				241.6
32.8	39.3	38.0			31.4				43.4
6.2	17.5	14.0			15.6				20.7
2.0	2.0	3.2	Sales/Total Assets		3.2				3.7
.7	1.0	1.7			1.4				1.8
.3	.3	.7			.3				.9
.7	.6	.5	% Depr., Dep., Amort./Sales						.3
(42) 1.3	(35) .9	(36) .9						(11) .7
3.1	1.9	2.2							2.2
3.4	3.3	3.4	% Officers', Directors' Owners' Comp/Sales						
(17) 13.2	(14) 7.3	(12) 10.3							
20.5	29.7	27.1							
2637569M	3077773M	1341641M	Net Sales ($)	2769M	22188M	16435M	38424M	134801M	1127024M
3112435M	2654327M	1383849M	Total Assets ($)	7377M	62945M	24220M	41342M	342731M	905234M

M = $ thousand   MM = $ million
See Pages 9 through 22 for Explanation of Ratios and Data

FINANCE—Securities Brokerage NAICS 523120

| Current Data Sorted by Assets | | | | | | | Comparative Historical Data | |

Type of Statement

0-500M	500M-2MM	2-10MM	10-50MM	50-100MM	100-250MM	Type of Statement	4/1/06-3/31/07 ALL	4/1/07-3/31/08 ALL
2	7	15	15	9	7	Unqualified	64	59
	1	1	3			Reviewed	1	3
1	1					Compiled	11	7
15	6	3	1	1		Tax Returns	14	12
5	8	18	10	4	6	Other	43	36
	18 (4/1-9/30/10)		121 (10/1/10-3/31/11)					
23	23	37	29	14	13	**NUMBER OF STATEMENTS**	133	117
%	%	%	%	%	%	**ASSETS**	%	%
41.4	33.2	34.7	42.3	49.9	28.0	Cash & Equivalents	39.3	35.5
7.2	12.6	16.1	11.8	18.5	13.9	Trade Receivables (net)	17.5	13.2
.0	.0	1.4	4.4	.0	8.4	Inventory	2.3	3.9
11.0	11.8	10.0	14.5	6.5	31.0	All Other Current	10.5	9.9
59.7	57.6	62.1	72.9	74.9	81.3	Total Current	69.5	62.4
14.9	21.0	9.8	11.1	8.5	7.9	Fixed Assets (net)	9.9	11.0
7.8	8.0	5.1	1.5	1.7	5.5	Intangibles (net)	4.2	6.1
17.7	13.4	23.0	14.6	14.9	5.4	All Other Non-Current	16.4	20.4
100.0	100.0	100.0	100.0	100.0	100.0	Total	100.0	100.0
						LIABILITIES		
12.3	2.0	2.9	4.4	19.4	7.7	Notes Payable-Short Term	9.5	6.1
1.3	2.0	2.8	1.8	.4	2.0	Cur. Mat.-L.T.D.	1.4	2.8
9.8	8.7	13.7	18.1	11.3	20.6	Trade Payables	12.9	8.9
.0	.1	.9	.4	.1	.5	Income Taxes Payable	.9	.5
23.2	17.9	20.6	18.7	19.4	28.2	All Other Current	25.7	24.9
46.7	30.8	40.8	43.3	50.5	59.1	Total Current	50.3	43.2
12.6	18.2	15.4	6.1	4.7	4.0	Long-Term Debt	5.8	9.1
.0	.0	.0	.0	.0	.3	Deferred Taxes	.1	.0
18.0	.2	6.7	3.8	.8	9.0	All Other Non-Current	4.5	4.0
22.7	50.8	37.1	46.8	44.1	27.6	Net Worth	39.3	43.7
100.0	100.0	100.0	100.0	100.0	100.0	Total Liabilties & Net Worth	100.0	100.0
						INCOME DATA		
100.0	100.0	100.0	100.0	100.0	100.0	Net Sales	100.0	100.0
						Gross Profit		
88.3	88.9	89.5	82.8	78.3	94.9	Operating Expenses	83.9	82.0
11.7	11.1	10.5	17.2	21.7	5.1	Operating Profit	16.1	18.0
-.8	1.9	1.1	3.4	2.8	-.3	All Other Expenses (net)	2.6	4.2
12.5	9.2	9.4	13.8	18.9	5.4	Profit Before Taxes	13.4	13.9
						RATIOS		
3.2	2.8	3.0	3.4	2.2	1.8	Current	2.7	2.5
1.8	1.9	2.1	1.7	1.7	1.2		1.6	1.5
.6	1.2	1.3	1.2	1.1	1.1		1.1	1.0
2.5	2.2	2.7	3.2	2.2	1.3	Quick	2.3	2.2
1.0	1.6	1.9	1.5	1.5	1.0		1.4	1.3
.4	.6	.7	.7	1.0	.2		.7	.5
0 UND	0 UND	0 UND	2 176.6	0 UND	0 UND	Sales/Receivables	0 UND	0 UND
0 UND	2 153.0	14 25.8	22 16.5	18 20.6	44 8.2		11 33.7	7 51.7
0 UND	23 15.8	34 10.6	73 5.0	42 8.7	136 2.7		41 8.9	41 8.8
						Cost of Sales/Inventory		
						Cost of Sales/Payables		
8.5	4.6	3.6	1.4	1.4	1.1	Sales/Working Capital	2.9	3.4
37.2	27.6	12.0	2.8	3.8	2.9		7.3	12.1
-51.4	73.9	154.6	14.5	10.8	18.4		43.7	NM
40.8		108.0	48.4	280.2	9.2	EBIT/Interest	38.6	28.0
(10) 12.7	(19) 25.8	(16) 4.4	(11) 18.9	(11) 1.8			(76) 9.0	(62) 12.0
2.1		4.5	1.6	2.7	-.1		2.8	2.0
						Net Profit + Depr., Dep., Amort./Cur. Mat. L/T/D		
.0	.0	.0	.0	.0	.0	Fixed/Worth	.0	.0
.4	.1	.0	.1	.0	.2		.1	.1
-2.9	1.6	.3	.1	.2	1.0		.4	.3
.3	.3	.4	.4	1.0	1.9	Debt/Worth	.6	.4
1.7	.9	.9	1.5	1.1	4.6		1.4	1.2
-5.0	3.2	2.8	5.9	3.6	9.8		6.2	3.6
284.9	34.1	38.4	50.9	49.6	23.4	% Profit Before Taxes/Tangible Net Worth	71.2	65.5
(14) 68.4	(20) 12.3	(31) 21.3	15.6	(13) 34.1	(11) 4.7		(119) 32.4	(105) 21.7
.7	-15.9	1.7	1.3	14.6	-1.8		9.6	5.0
83.3	23.4	23.9	15.4	33.4	4.1	% Profit Before Taxes/Total Assets	38.1	28.5
24.7	3.7	8.7	4.0	14.3	.5		13.4	9.3
.7	-8.6	1.2	.8	4.0	-.4		2.5	1.7
UND	UND	722.6	113.0	UND	103.6	Sales/Net Fixed Assets	162.2	328.2
161.8	213.9	136.9	41.0	64.7	31.9		40.8	53.0
33.6	24.2	28.7	24.4	21.6	14.0		21.4	20.5
12.1	8.2	5.8	1.5	2.4	.8	Sales/Total Assets	4.5	4.2
5.9	3.0	2.2	.9	1.5	.6		1.9	1.8
4.2	.6	1.2	.3	.3	.1		.7	.8
.7	.3	.1	.5			% Depr., Dep., Amort./Sales	.4	.4
(11) .8	(12) 1.2	(24) .7	(20) .8				(90) .8	(75) .9
1.2	18.5	2.1	1.3				1.4	1.5
8.8						% Officers', Directors' Owners' Comp/Sales	7.6	4.7
(12) 19.7							(24) 17.8	(19) 12.8
33.2							25.8	27.9
30367M	113592M	646690M	780090M	2362460M	2324230M	Net Sales ($)	5416807M	6140279M
4019M	24681M	185688M	721010M	1020549M	2080715M	Total Assets ($)	4241264M	4423202M

M = $ thousand   MM = $ million
See Pages 9 through 22 for Explanation of Ratios and Data

Comparative Historical Data
Current Data Sorted by Sales

Hist 1	Hist 2	Hist 3	Type of Statement	0-1MM	1-3MM	3-5MM	5-10MM	10-25MM	25MM & OVER
66	62	55	Unqualified	2	5	3	5	16	24
1	3	5	Reviewed	1		1	1		2
2	4	2	Compiled	2					
15	15	26	Tax Returns	8	11	1	5		1
19	32	51	Other	8	4	3	11	11	14
4/1/08-3/31/09 ALL	4/1/09-3/31/10 ALL	4/1/10-3/31/11 ALL		18 (4/1-9/30/10)			121 (10/1/10-3/31/11)		
103	116	139	**NUMBER OF STATEMENTS**	21	20	8	22	27	41
%	%	%	**ASSETS**	%	%	%	%	%	%
37.4	33.2	38.0	Cash & Equivalents	31.0	35.0		28.9	43.5	46.0
15.6	17.2	13.2	Trade Receivables (net)	6.5	5.7		20.9	13.7	14.7
1.7	2.3	2.1	Inventory	.0	.0		5.5	2.1	2.7
11.3	9.0	13.0	All Other Current	7.8	11.2		12.2	16.6	13.4
66.1	61.7	66.3	Total Current	45.3	52.0		67.5	76.0	76.7
9.5	10.8	12.5	Fixed Assets (net)	33.3	13.7		7.7	6.6	7.3
5.7	6.7	5.0	Intangibles (net)	10.2	8.1		6.1	1.3	3.6
18.8	20.7	16.3	All Other Non-Current	11.2	26.3		18.7	16.1	12.4
100.0	100.0	100.0	Total	100.0	100.0		100.0	100.0	100.0
			LIABILITIES						
7.6	9.8	6.7	Notes Payable-Short Term	11.2	5.9		9.1	4.1	6.0
2.0	2.9	1.9	Cur. Mat.-L.T.D.	2.6	1.5		.2	2.7	1.7
9.9	12.8	13.5	Trade Payables	3.3	5.4		12.0	12.2	20.6
.4	.4	.4	Income Taxes Payable	.0	.1		.1	1.1	.5
19.9	17.4	20.8	All Other Current	8.9	25.1		17.6	20.7	27.3
39.7	43.3	43.3	Total Current	26.1	38.0		39.0	40.8	56.1
9.5	11.5	11.3	Long-Term Debt	31.1	11.7		8.9	11.0	2.0
.0	.3	.0	Deferred Taxes	.0	.0		.2	.0	.0
2.2	5.2	6.5	All Other Non-Current	5.1	24.0		5.8	.9	3.8
48.6	39.6	38.8	Net Worth	37.7	26.3		46.2	47.3	38.0
100.0	100.0	100.0	Total Liabilities & Net Worth	100.0	100.0		100.0	100.0	100.0
			INCOME DATA						
100.0	100.0	100.0	Net Sales	100.0	100.0		100.0	100.0	100.0
			Gross Profit						
87.5	83.4	87.2	Operating Expenses	75.8	90.5		90.9	88.1	91.3
12.5	16.6	12.8	Operating Profit	24.2	9.5		9.1	11.9	8.7
2.5	2.9	1.4	All Other Expenses (net)	6.2	2.5		1.3	-.4	-.8
10.0	13.7	11.4	Profit Before Taxes	17.9	7.0		7.7	12.3	9.4
			RATIOS						
3.1	3.3	2.8	Current	3.0	3.9		7.3	3.9	2.1
1.8	1.7	1.7		1.3	1.7		1.8	2.1	1.5
1.3	1.0	1.1		.4	.9		1.2	1.5	1.1
2.7	2.9	2.4	Quick	2.4	3.0		3.8	2.9	2.0
1.6	1.4	1.5		1.0	1.7		1.5	1.9	1.3
.7	.6	.6		.2	.4		.6	.8	.8
0 UND	0 UND	0 UND	Sales/Receivables	0 UND	0 UND		0 UND	0 UND	1 311.5
8 44.9	15 23.7	10 37.4		0 UND	9 41.7		2 182.2	17 20.9	16 22.3
34 10.7	40 9.1	34 10.8		4 83.7	56 6.5		43 8.5	32 11.4	36 10.2
			Cost of Sales/Inventory						
			Cost of Sales/Payables						
3.6	3.1	2.5	Sales/Working Capital	7.1	2.1		1.4	1.9	3.3
9.9	7.9	9.5		36.0	7.0		7.0	6.3	9.9
29.7	NM	60.8		-5.2	-320.1		43.8	16.3	22.2
32.5	32.9	53.7	EBIT/Interest		50.3		135.3	54.4	53.2
(52) 7.2	(68) 10.6	(76) 6.7		(11) 6.8			(11) 21.1	(15) 5.9	(26) 6.2
1.1	1.2	1.9			1.9		2.0	1.5	1.4
			Net Profit + Depr., Dep., Amort./Cur. Mat. L/T/D						
.0	.0	.0	Fixed/Worth	.0	.0		.0	.0	.0
.1	.1	.1		1.0	.1		.0	.0	.1
.2	.6	.4		UND	-3.2		.4	.1	.2
.4	.4	.4	Debt/Worth	.4	.3		.2	.4	1.0
1.0	1.2	1.3		2.4	11.5		1.5	.8	1.5
2.3	10.2	7.4		UND	-6.4		4.0	1.3	3.9
71.2	61.4	44.7	% Profit Before Taxes/Tangible Net Worth	205.0	43.8		22.8	46.7	44.7
(92) 29.0	(93) 23.2	(118) 18.1		(16) 45.5	(12) 10.5		(19) 12.9	(26) 11.5	(38) 21.6
2.6	4.0	1.0		-6.5	.6		1.7	.6	6.4
31.8	28.2	24.7	% Profit Before Taxes/Total Assets	43.8	32.6		13.2	33.9	21.5
13.6	8.6	5.9		17.7	5.9		4.6	5.2	9.8
.6	.2	.5		-1.6	.2		1.4	.5	.6
382.8	391.5	737.1	Sales/Net Fixed Assets	UND	293.2		UND	UND	445.6
70.3	67.9	83.8		63.6	85.6		105.9	221.4	53.5
26.4	22.9	25.3		.4	28.0		25.0	34.6	24.1
4.6	3.9	5.6	Sales/Total Assets	5.1	6.3		8.2	5.6	4.5
2.1	1.5	1.9		.7	3.6		2.0	1.6	1.6
.9	.6	.6		.2	.3		.5	1.0	.8
.3	.3	.4	% Depr., Dep., Amort./Sales	.9	.6		.3	.2	.5
(70) .7	(73) .8	(84) .8		(11) 3.8	(13) .7		(10) 1.1	(17) .4	(27) .7
1.7	2.3	1.9		21.9	1.4		2.0	3.5	1.4
6.7	4.1	3.7	% Officers', Directors' Owners' Comp/Sales						
(15) 18.5	(22) 8.2	(33) 16.0							
29.0	27.3	23.3							
6189125M	5139257M	6257429M	Net Sales ($)	9768M	34358M	30039M	161264M	430986M	5591014M
3241434M	3688502M	4036662M	Total Assets ($)	19425M	108136M	77458M	525811M	407380M	2898452M

M = $ thousand   MM = $ million
See Pages 9 through 22 for Explanation of Ratios and Data

FINANCE—Commodity Contracts Dealing   NAICS 523130

Current Data Sorted by Assets | Comparative Historical Data

Type of Statement

Type of Statement	0-500M	500M-2MM	2-10MM	10-50MM	50-100MM	100-250MM	4/1/06-3/31/07 ALL	4/1/07-3/31/08 ALL
Unqualified		1	4	6	2	3	13	7
Reviewed		2	2	1	1		3	3
Compiled		1	2	2			5	5
Tax Returns	2	2	3				6	6
Other	2	2	6	5			22	15

Sub-period headers: 3 (4/1-9/30/10) | 44 (10/1/10-3/31/11)

0-500M	500M-2MM	2-10MM	10-50MM	50-100MM	100-250MM		4/1/06-3/31/07 ALL	4/1/07-3/31/08 ALL
4	6	17	14	3	3	**NUMBER OF STATEMENTS**	49	36
%	%	%	%	%	%	**ASSETS**	%	%
		19.9	28.9			Cash & Equivalents	26.2	23.9
		29.9	19.5			Trade Receivables (net)	16.0	26.2
		10.0	6.6			Inventory	10.5	9.8
		6.2	9.9			All Other Current	9.4	5.3
		66.0	64.8			Total Current	62.0	65.2
		19.2	11.0			Fixed Assets (net)	15.9	19.8
		5.6	1.7			Intangibles (net)	1.2	1.2
		9.2	22.5			All Other Non-Current	21.0	13.8
		100.0	100.0			Total	100.0	100.0
						LIABILITIES		
		15.0	14.7			Notes Payable-Short Term	11.6	14.7
		.6	2.4			Cur. Mat.-L.T.D.	2.2	1.5
		12.1	3.6			Trade Payables	8.0	24.6
		.2	.3			Income Taxes Payable	.3	.2
		11.8	15.7			All Other Current	11.1	3.6
		39.8	36.8			Total Current	33.2	44.6
		8.5	18.8			Long-Term Debt	21.5	23.1
		.6	.0			Deferred Taxes	.0	.0
		4.0	4.2			All Other Non-Current	5.4	7.1
		47.1	40.3			Net Worth	39.9	25.2
		100.0	100.0			Total Liabilities & Net Worth	100.0	100.0
						INCOME DATA		
		100.0	100.0			Net Sales	100.0	100.0
						Gross Profit		
		82.3	65.5			Operating Expenses	61.7	67.8
		17.7	34.5			Operating Profit	38.3	32.2
		4.7	5.9			All Other Expenses (net)	8.9	7.4
		13.0	28.6			Profit Before Taxes	29.3	24.8
						RATIOS		
		4.1	4.6			Current	4.3	7.3
		1.7	1.3				2.0	2.6
		1.1	1.0				1.1	1.2
		3.7	3.6			Quick	4.2	5.0
		1.1	1.3				1.0	2.2
		.6	.8				.6	.9
		0 UND	15 24.4			Sales/Receivables	0 UND	1 581.2
		26 13.9	84 4.4				20 18.5	16 22.5
		77 4.7	282 1.3				47 7.7	57 6.4
						Cost of Sales/Inventory		
						Cost of Sales/Payables		
		2.2	.9			Sales/Working Capital	1.2	1.5
		24.8	3.5				5.4	6.0
		165.6	30.6				28.4	27.9
		85.1				EBIT/Interest	21.9	30.6
		(12) 12.5					(26) 7.2	(21) 15.6
		4.0					2.9	2.5
						Net Profit + Depr., Dep., Amort./Cur. Mat. L/T/D		
		.0	.0			Fixed/Worth	.0	.0
		.1	.1				.0	.2
		.7	.6				.6	1.3
		.4	.5			Debt/Worth	.5	.6
		1.1	2.0				1.9	1.4
		3.1	21.5				7.3	6.8
		71.0	51.8			% Profit Before Taxes/Tangible Net Worth	54.6	79.8
		(16) 29.6	(13) 24.2				(47) 26.6	(31) 37.0
		5.3	6.1				9.9	14.9
		23.0	33.4			% Profit Before Taxes/Total Assets	25.8	32.5
		11.3	3.3				6.5	10.2
		4.3	1.1				2.3	2.7
		632.5	190.9			Sales/Net Fixed Assets	UND	999.8
		40.6	14.9				69.9	26.4
		3.7	1.3				2.2	2.6
		6.1	.7			Sales/Total Assets	1.5	4.2
		1.6	.2				.3	.7
		.4	.1				.2	.2
		.1				% Depr., Dep., Amort./Sales	.5	.1
		(11) 1.3					(31) 1.6	(24) 1.4
		4.1					9.0	4.6
						% Officers', Directors' Owners' Comp/Sales	.9	
							(11) 7.2	
							23.5	
9198M	13554M	254808M	249045M	110227M	1282269M	Net Sales ($)	2730633M	2621812M
1129M	9185M	82212M	421389M	193535M	607420M	Total Assets ($)	1861392M	988991M

© RMA 2011

M = $ thousand   MM = $ million
See Pages 9 through 22 for Explanation of Ratios and Data

Comparative Historical Data | Current Data Sorted by Sales

Type of Statement

Type of Statement	4/1/08-3/31/09 ALL	4/1/09-3/31/10 ALL	4/1/10-3/31/11 ALL		0-1MM	1-3MM	3-5MM	5-10MM	10-25MM	25MM & OVER
							3 (4/1-9/30/10)		44 (10/1/10-3/31/11)	
Unqualified	10	14	16				2	3	5	6
Reviewed	5	2	4		3				1	
Compiled	4	2	5			1	1	1		2
Tax Returns	3	6	7		1		1	2	1	2
Other	14	19	15		6	3	2	1	1	2
NUMBER OF STATEMENTS	36	43	47		10	4	6	7	8	12

Financial Data

	4/1/08-3/31/09 ALL	4/1/09-3/31/10 ALL	4/1/10-3/31/11 ALL		0-1MM	1-3MM	3-5MM	5-10MM	10-25MM	25MM & OVER
	%	%	%		%	%	%	%	%	%
ASSETS										
Cash & Equivalents	19.0	28.6	23.6		15.4					17.1
Trade Receivables (net)	26.3	21.9	24.3		16.0					29.4
Inventory	13.4	8.9	9.5		.0					19.1
All Other Current	9.2	9.1	10.3		14.4					16.4
Total Current	68.0	68.5	67.8		45.7					82.0
Fixed Assets (net)	20.3	22.5	15.3		32.9					6.0
Intangibles (net)	1.2	1.7	2.9		.5					.7
All Other Non-Current	10.6	7.2	14.0		20.8					11.2
Total	100.0	100.0	100.0		100.0					100.0
LIABILITIES										
Notes Payable-Short Term	13.0	13.2	17.8		14.5					25.7
Cur. Mat.-L.T.D.	1.8	1.6	1.3		2.3					.1
Trade Payables	9.6	8.5	9.8		1.8					17.1
Income Taxes Payable	.2	.1	.2		.0					.0
All Other Current	14.1	16.7	12.5		6.4					7.4
Total Current	38.7	40.1	41.6		25.1					50.4
Long-Term Debt	25.5	17.2	12.8		26.5					5.8
Deferred Taxes	.0	.0	.2		.0					.0
All Other Non-Current	4.3	4.1	4.7		5.8					.9
Net Worth	31.5	38.6	40.7		42.6					42.9
Total Liabilties & Net Worth	100.0	100.0	100.0		100.0					100.0
INCOME DATA										
Net Sales	100.0	100.0	100.0		100.0					100.0
Gross Profit										
Operating Expenses	74.7	70.3	73.9		55.7					77.8
Operating Profit	25.3	29.7	26.1		44.3					22.2
All Other Expenses (net)	8.3	8.6	4.7		12.4					1.6
Profit Before Taxes	17.0	21.0	21.4		31.9					20.7
RATIOS										
Current	5.8	5.1	3.6		3.4					6.2
	2.5	1.4	1.3		1.4					1.6
	1.1	1.0	1.1		.6					1.1
Quick	4.2	3.4	3.4		3.4					2.9
	1.5	1.0	1.1		1.0					1.2
	.6	.5	.6		.1					.6
Sales/Receivables	0 UND	0 UND	7 56.0		0 UND					10 37.0
	12 30.6	22 16.9	35 10.5		0 UND					36 10.0
	69 5.3	66 5.5	94 3.9		83 4.4					87 4.2
Cost of Sales/Inventory										
Cost of Sales/Payables										
Sales/Working Capital	1.0	1.4	1.7		.4					1.6
	3.9	7.1	6.4		13.7					14.1
	42.2	999.8	65.9		-8.8					46.6
EBIT/Interest	9.9	16.5	32.0							35.5
	(25) 4.8	(24) 7.8	(33) 7.0						(11)	17.4
	1.7	3.7	2.2							4.8
Net Profit + Depr., Dep., Amort./Cur. Mat. L/T/D										
Fixed/Worth	.0	.0	.0		.0					.0
	.2	.2	.1		.2					.1
	1.1	1.0	.6		1.5					.4
Debt/Worth	.8	.5	.5		.5					.3
	2.6	2.4	1.7		1.0					2.1
	9.0	6.2	7.0		NM					5.6
% Profit Before Taxes/Tangible Net Worth	47.6	50.2	61.7							78.7
	(32) 28.2	(40) 24.1	(43) 29.4							55.1
	12.1	8.6	8.3							13.6
% Profit Before Taxes/Total Assets	17.0	17.4	23.9		13.4					26.2
	6.7	9.5	8.6		2.8					15.8
	2.4	2.2	1.7		1.2					5.8
Sales/Net Fixed Assets	855.0	590.4	626.3		UND					635.5
	31.3	38.8	42.5		23.3					62.9
	1.7	.9	6.0		.2					11.9
Sales/Total Assets	4.1	2.9	2.8		.7					6.0
	.7	.5	.8		.2					1.9
	.2	.1	.2		.1					.6
% Depr., Dep., Amort./Sales	.1	.6	.4							.0
	(23) 1.1	(29) 1.6	(30) 1.2						(10)	.7
	5.5	8.8	3.2							1.5
% Officers', Directors', Owners' Comp/Sales			.4							
		(10)	1.6							
			12.9							
Net Sales ($)	3820859M	2411412M	1919101M		4315M	6866M	21476M	52792M	134424M	1699228M
Total Assets ($)	1389676M	1137772M	1314870M		35899M	10966M	136991M	96163M	106434M	928417M

M = $ thousand   MM = $ million
See Pages 9 through 22 for Explanation of Ratios and Data

Current Data Sorted by Assets							Comparative Historical Data	

						Type of Statement		
	.1			1		Unqualified	10	7
	1		4			Reviewed	2	4
		1				Compiled	2	1
2	1	1	2	2	1	Tax Returns	3	2
3	1	1				Other	9	10
	2 (4/1-9/30/10)		21 (10/1/10-3/31/11)				4/1/06-3/31/07 ALL	4/1/07-3/31/08 ALL
0-500M	500M-2MM	2-10MM	10-50MM	50-100MM	100-250MM	NUMBER OF STATEMENTS	26	24
5	4	7	3	3	1			
%	%	%	%	%	%	ASSETS	%	%
						Cash & Equivalents	20.0	16.7
						Trade Receivables (net)	40.3	36.1
						Inventory	10.1	17.3
						All Other Current	10.5	12.3
						Total Current	80.9	82.4
						Fixed Assets (net)	10.6	8.3
						Intangibles (net)	.9	.0
						All Other Non-Current	7.5	9.3
						Total	100.0	100.0
						LIABILITIES		
						Notes Payable-Short Term	20.0	16.0
						Cur. Mat.-L.T.D.	1.0	.3
						Trade Payables	22.4	24.3
						Income Taxes Payable	.1	.0
						All Other Current	9.6	15.9
						Total Current	53.0	56.6
						Long-Term Debt	5.7	6.3
						Deferred Taxes	.0	.0
						All Other Non-Current	5.9	4.5
						Net Worth	35.4	32.6
						Total Liabilties & Net Worth	100.0	100.0
						INCOME DATA		
						Net Sales	100.0	100.0
						Gross Profit		
						Operating Expenses	90.8	89.8
						Operating Profit	9.2	10.2
						All Other Expenses (net)	-.4	-.5
						Profit Before Taxes	9.6	10.7
						RATIOS		
						Current	4.1	2.1
							1.3	1.3
							1.0	1.1
						Quick	3.9	1.7
							1.0	1.0
							.6	.4
						Sales/Receivables	25 14.6	17 21.4
							35 10.6	33 11.0
							62 5.9	60 6.0
						Cost of Sales/Inventory		
						Cost of Sales/Payables		
						Sales/Working Capital	3.4	4.2
							13.3	11.1
							214.6	28.3
						EBIT/Interest	30.8	6.6
							(23) 3.8	(19) 4.3
							2.3	2.3
						Net Profit + Depr., Dep., Amort./Cur. Mat. L/T/D		
						Fixed/Worth	.0	.0
							.0	.0
							.7	.7
						Debt/Worth	.8	.8
							3.7	3.5
							10.4	8.6
						% Profit Before Taxes/Tangible Net Worth	81.3	81.3
							(25) 46.5	35.2
							16.4	15.7
						% Profit Before Taxes/Total Assets	23.4	14.4
							6.8	6.5
							2.4	2.9
						Sales/Net Fixed Assets	UND	999.8
							360.1	598.6
							10.4	17.2
						Sales/Total Assets	5.2	4.9
							2.7	3.2
							1.0	.9
						% Depr., Dep., Amort./Sales	.0	.0
							(16) .1	(15) .7
							2.0	2.6
						% Officers', Directors' Owners' Comp/Sales		
1330M	22408M	226692M	700754M	1689359M	838888M	Net Sales ($)	1689901M	1530871M
999M	5995M	30949M	85405M	239255M	201509M	Total Assets ($)	459083M	879205M

M = $ thousand   MM = $ million
See Pages 9 through 22 for Explanation of Ratios and Data

Comparative Historical Data / Current Data Sorted by Sales

Note: For the six "Current Data Sorted by Sales" columns, the columns 0-1MM through 10-25MM are marked **DATA NOT AVAILABLE** for the Assets, Liabilities, Income Data and Ratios sections; only the 25MM & OVER column is populated.

4/1/08-3/31/09 ALL	4/1/09-3/31/10 ALL	4/1/10-3/31/11 ALL	Type of Statement	2 (4/1-9/30/10) 0-1MM	1-3MM	21 (10/1/10-3/31/11) 3-5MM	5-10MM	10-25MM	25MM & OVER
5	7	3	Unqualified				1	1	1
3	2	5	Reviewed			1	2		2
2	1	1	Compiled						1
2	5	4	Tax Returns	2		1			1
6	14	10	Other	3			1	1	5
18	29	23	**NUMBER OF STATEMENTS**	5		2	4	2	10
%	%	%	**ASSETS**	%	%	%	%	%	%
15.1	19.7	23.5	Cash & Equivalents						23.2
42.5	43.4	42.7	Trade Receivables (net)						59.0
15.3	7.5	6.7	Inventory						9.7
2.6	3.9	6.1	All Other Current						3.1
75.4	74.4	79.0	Total Current						95.1
11.2	9.6	8.9	Fixed Assets (net)						.4
.4	1.6	1.6	Intangibles (net)						2.7
12.9	14.4	10.6	All Other Non-Current						1.8
100.0	100.0	100.0	Total						100.0
			LIABILITIES						
16.3	16.2	7.3	Notes Payable-Short Term						.6
2.2	1.5	1.0	Cur. Mat.-L.T.D.						.3
26.4	24.3	32.2	Trade Payables						40.9
.1	.6	.3	Income Taxes Payable						.0
11.2	15.4	5.5	All Other Current						4.5
56.3	57.9	46.2	Total Current						46.3
6.5	7.0	34.7	Long-Term Debt						15.7
.0	.3	.8	Deferred Taxes						.0
2.9	.5	4.5	All Other Non-Current						9.6
34.3	34.2	13.9	Net Worth						28.4
100.0	100.0	100.0	Total Liabilities & Net Worth						100.0
			INCOME DATA						
100.0	100.0	100.0	Net Sales						100.0
			Gross Profit						
90.9	88.4	91.7	Operating Expenses						96.3
9.1	11.6	8.3	Operating Profit						3.7
-1.8	.2	1.6	All Other Expenses (net)						2.6
10.9	11.4	6.7	Profit Before Taxes						1.1
			RATIOS						
1.8 / 1.4 / 1.1	2.4 / 1.4 / 1.1	3.7 / 1.6 / 1.2	Current						15.9 / 1.6 / 1.3
1.4 / 1.0 / .4	2.4 / 1.2 / .6	2.9 / 1.5 / .6	Quick						15.5 / 1.4 / 1.2
11 34.4 / 22 16.4 / 49 7.5	8 46.9 / 28 13.0 / 50 7.2	8 48.4 / 28 13.1 / 49 7.4	Sales/Receivables						14 26.5 / 27 13.5 / 50 7.3
			Cost of Sales/Inventory						
			Cost of Sales/Payables						
14.5 / 31.2 / 160.6	9.5 / 26.0 / 105.7	8.2 / 22.4 / 57.7	Sales/Working Capital						6.1 / 20.2 / 60.1
10.5 / (13) 2.7 / 1.6	64.3 / (23) 12.4 / 2.2	97.6 / (16) 18.2 / 2.9	EBIT/Interest						
			Net Profit + Depr., Dep., Amort./Cur. Mat. L/T/D						
.0 / .2 / .7	.0 / .1 / .7	.0 / .0 / .5	Fixed/Worth						.0 / .0 / .0
1.4 / 2.6 / 8.9	.9 / 2.8 / 7.1	.8 / 3.7 / 5.8	Debt/Worth						3.4 / 3.7 / 5.6
96.2 / (17) 48.8 / 9.5	73.0 / (26) 36.7 / 8.8	69.3 / (21) 25.1 / 2.3	% Profit Before Taxes/Tangible Net Worth						61.6 / 46.5 / 23.6
28.1 / 7.1 / 1.1	26.0 / 7.8 / 2.2	15.5 / 8.6 / 2.5	% Profit Before Taxes/Total Assets						15.6 / 9.9 / 5.5
999.8 / 219.1 / 7.0	999.8 / 614.5 / 40.6	UND / 999.8 / 89.7	Sales/Net Fixed Assets						UND / 999.8 / 758.5
8.0 / 4.6 / 1.1	11.1 / 6.3 / 2.5	9.8 / 4.2 / 2.2	Sales/Total Assets						11.0 / 7.6 / 4.1
.0 / (11) 1.4 / 3.6	.0 / (17) .2 / 2.0	.0 / (12) .1 / 1.9	% Depr., Dep., Amort./Sales						
	(11) 1.6 / 2.6 / 7.7		% Officers', Directors' Owners' Comp/Sales						
1853983M	2806273M	3479431M	Net Sales ($)	1330M		7129M	25257M	47256M	3398459M
323047M	473719M	564112M	Total Assets ($)	999M		2748M	8599M	9809M	541957M

M = $ thousand   MM = $ million
See Pages 9 through 22 for Explanation of Ratios and Data

Current Data Sorted by Assets   **Comparative Historical Data**

Type of Statement	0-500M	500M-2MM	2-10MM	10-50MM	50-100MM	100-250MM		4/1/06-3/31/07 ALL	4/1/07-3/31/08 ALL
Unqualified	2	1	4	17	8	4		39	25
Reviewed		1	1	5				17	11
Compiled	1	1	4	3				12	14
Tax Returns	7	14	13	3	1	1		23	26
Other	10	14	28	13	10	6		82	68
	9 (4/1-9/30/10)			163 (10/1/10-3/31/11)					
NUMBER OF STATEMENTS	20	31	50	41	19	11		173	144
ASSETS	%	%	%	%	%	%		%	%
Cash & Equivalents	37.3	14.4	11.0	6.6	22.2	18.7		14.1	13.7
Trade Receivables (net)	10.3	5.1	13.7	21.6	6.5	3.8		17.8	12.4
Inventory	.0	4.0	1.9	4.6	4.3	13.5		5.5	4.6
All Other Current	7.3	11.5	11.6	12.7	9.7	.3		6.7	7.8
Total Current	54.9	35.0	38.3	45.6	42.6	36.2		44.1	38.5
Fixed Assets (net)	16.2	44.0	37.9	21.9	27.1	14.8		25.0	32.9
Intangibles (net)	4.8	12.3	4.9	3.2	8.2	1.1		4.2	4.0
All Other Non-Current	24.1	8.7	18.9	29.3	22.1	47.8		26.8	24.5
Total	100.0	100.0	100.0	100.0	100.0	100.0		100.0	100.0
LIABILITIES									
Notes Payable-Short Term	12.8	10.4	13.0	13.9	6.9	12.2		17.2	12.1
Cur. Mat.-L.T.D.	1.7	1.7	4.4	2.3	.2	5.8		3.9	4.9
Trade Payables	10.5	4.5	6.3	5.2	.7	.2		5.8	4.2
Income Taxes Payable	.0	.5	.0	.1	.1	.0		.1	.1
All Other Current	25.3	9.9	8.2	11.9	14.1	3.7		10.9	10.0
Total Current	50.3	27.0	31.9	33.4	22.1	21.8		37.9	31.3
Long-Term Debt	5.7	28.8	38.5	18.8	20.9	29.2		22.0	28.2
Deferred Taxes	.0	.0	.0	.0	.7	.3		.1	.1
All Other Non-Current	2.3	5.1	1.6	6.8	3.6	1.9		6.1	3.7
Net Worth	41.8	39.1	27.9	40.9	52.7	46.8		33.9	36.7
Total Liabilties & Net Worth	100.0	100.0	100.0	100.0	100.0	100.0		100.0	100.0
INCOME DATA									
Net Sales	100.0	100.0	100.0	100.0	100.0	100.0		100.0	100.0
Gross Profit									
Operating Expenses	69.7	74.3	68.6	62.4	50.3	58.2		67.9	59.3
Operating Profit	30.3	25.7	31.4	37.6	49.7	41.8		32.1	40.7
All Other Expenses (net)	3.0	9.2	16.5	12.6	9.2	26.5		13.8	15.0
Profit Before Taxes	27.2	16.5	14.9	24.9	40.5	15.3		18.3	25.8
RATIOS									
Current	6.8	2.6	3.8	2.0	31.2	48.6		2.1	3.2
	1.1	1.5	1.3	1.3	1.7	1.2		1.2	1.3
	.5	.3	.4	.6	.2	.2		.5	.4
Quick	6.6	1.7	2.1	1.4	16.9	48.6		1.6	2.0
	1.0	.9	.7	.6	1.6	.4		.7 (143)	.6
	.3	.2	.1	.1	.1	.1		.2	.1
Sales/Receivables	0 UND	0 UND	0 UND	0 UND	0 UND	0 UND		0 UND	0 UND
	0 UND	0 UND	0 UND	13 27.4	5 77.2	22 16.5		9 42.7	0 999.8
	2 167.3	4 84.0	38 9.5	66 5.5	32 11.4	65 5.6		66 5.5	34 10.6
Cost of Sales/Inventory									
Cost of Sales/Payables									
Sales/Working Capital	10.0	2.8	1.8	.7	.9	1.0		2.6	2.1
	432.2	17.0	13.7	8.8	5.8	17.0		13.4	25.0
	-53.6	-17.8	-6.5	-7.7	-5.0	-.8		-7.1	-4.6
EBIT/Interest		24.7	12.8	5.1	15.2			14.2	10.4
		(18) 5.4	(29) 4.8	(27) 2.8	(13) 5.4			(87) 4.4	(71) 5.5
		2.1	1.8	1.4	3.0			2.0	2.5
Net Profit + Depr., Dep., Amort./Cur. Mat. L/T/D								4.7	
								(18) 1.6	
								1.1	
Fixed/Worth	.0	.2	.0	.0	.1	.0		.0	.0
	.2	.9	1.0	.2	.5	.0		.2	.5
	1.2	-26.6	33.2	1.2	1.9	.4		2.6	6.6
Debt/Worth	.1	.7	.5	.4	.4	.1		.6	.5
	.9	1.9	2.5	1.8	1.1	1.8		1.9	2.0
	8.0	-29.7	275.5	9.2	8.6	4.7		8.3	18.1
% Profit Before Taxes/Tangible Net Worth	265.7	32.6	49.2	49.3	54.9	13.1		64.3	68.2
	(18) 65.6	(23) 13.9	(39) 16.1	(37) 20.5	(16) 16.9	3.7		(150) 14.1	(116) 18.2
	6.7	2.2	2.1	2.5	3.3	-1.3		3.2	4.9
% Profit Before Taxes/Total Assets	87.8	15.5	16.5	8.3	10.0	6.2		21.6	21.7
	44.2	4.3	5.3	3.6	4.4	1.3		5.1	6.1
	7.4	1.0	.5	1.4	3.1	-.5		.6	1.6
Sales/Net Fixed Assets	UND	161.3	304.4	UND	60.0	UND		UND	337.6
	422.8	4.0	10.3	35.2	14.8	262.7		21.3	13.4
	42.3	.2	.2	1.3	.1	3.4		2.5	.6
Sales/Total Assets	28.9	2.2	1.3	.7	1.3	.3		1.9	1.7
	6.4	.5	.3	.3	.2	.1		.4	.4
	1.4	.2	.1	.1	.1	.1		.1	.1
% Depr., Dep., Amort./Sales		.8	1.9	.9	.3			.9	1.2
		(21) 7.1	(31) 7.8	(25) 2.2	(10) 2.6			(102) 2.5	(86) 3.4
		20.6	20.5	15.0	15.2			10.2	13.6
% Officers', Directors' Owners' Comp/Sales								1.4	2.5
								(23) 8.1	(23) 6.7
								26.4	15.3
Net Sales ($)	37096M	88071M	265264M	642973M	2796644M	444609M		2879042M	2383313M
Total Assets ($)	3484M	39271M	246353M	923371M	1260333M	1744303M		4221898M	4009584M

Comparative Historical Data & Current Data Sorted by Sales

Type of Statement	4/1/08-3/31/09 ALL	4/1/09-3/31/10 ALL	4/1/10-3/31/11 ALL	0-1MM	1-3MM	3-5MM	5-10MM	10-25MM	25MM & OVER
Unqualified	53	43	36	3	8	3	5	4	13
Reviewed	11	13	7		4	1	2		
Compiled	11	9	9	3	2	1	2	1	
Tax Returns	25	26	39	27	7		2	1	2
Other	92	74	81	21	13	13	10	16	8
				9 (4/1-9/30/10)		163 (10/1/10-3/31/11)			
NUMBER OF STATEMENTS	192	165	172	54	34	18	21	22	23
	%	%	%	%	%	%	%	%	%
ASSETS									
Cash & Equivalents	13.1	14.6	15.4	13.8	16.1	18.5	5.8	13.5	26.0
Trade Receivables (net)	21.2	13.3	12.2	4.6	10.9	13.5	23.0	17.6	16.1
Inventory	1.8	3.3	3.7	2.7	.8	6.6	.1	2.6	12.5
All Other Current	13.7	9.4	10.4	4.4	14.2	15.7	7.9	16.9	10.8
Total Current	49.8	40.6	41.7	25.5	42.0	54.2	36.9	50.6	65.4
Fixed Assets (net)	23.1	26.7	30.0	47.9	31.5	16.8	25.2	15.0	14.7
Intangibles (net)	3.4	2.5	5.9	5.5	1.7	13.5	6.9	9.2	3.2
All Other Non-Current	23.7	30.1	22.4	21.0	24.8	15.5	30.9	25.2	16.8
Total	100.0	100.0	100.0	100.0	100.0	100.0	100.0	100.0	100.0
LIABILITIES									
Notes Payable-Short Term	19.5	14.8	12.0	7.7	15.7	7.8	20.9	12.9	10.8
Cur. Mat.-L.T.D.	2.3	1.9	2.7	2.4	1.0	6.7	3.9	1.9	2.8
Trade Payables	5.7	5.3	5.2	.4	2.0	14.9	4.8	7.4	11.7
Income Taxes Payable	.1	.1	.1	.0	.1	.0	.0	.0	.6
All Other Current	12.7	8.6	11.7	9.0	7.8	11.1	18.9	16.4	13.6
Total Current	40.3	30.7	31.8	19.6	26.6	40.5	48.6	38.6	39.5
Long-Term Debt	26.2	22.6	25.7	37.8	22.5	12.3	29.9	16.8	17.3
Deferred Taxes	.1	.0	.1	.0	.0	.0	.1	.3	.4
All Other Non-Current	6.2	4.9	3.8	3.5	.9	7.7	2.3	4.4	6.5
Net Worth	27.2	41.8	38.6	39.1	50.1	39.6	19.2	39.9	36.3
Total Liabilities & Net Worth	100.0	100.0	100.0	100.0	100.0	100.0	100.0	100.0	100.0
INCOME DATA									
Net Sales	100.0	100.0	100.0	100.0	100.0	100.0	100.0	100.0	100.0
Gross Profit									
Operating Expenses	67.1	65.9	65.6	55.5	63.4	66.0	63.8	76.8	83.2
Operating Profit	32.9	34.1	34.4	44.5	36.6	34.0	36.2	23.2	16.8
All Other Expenses (net)	14.6	13.6	12.5	20.2	12.4	8.8	7.1	9.9	5.2
Profit Before Taxes	18.3	20.5	21.9	24.3	24.1	25.3	29.1	13.4	11.7
RATIOS									
Current	2.6	3.8	2.8	3.6	4.1	4.0	1.7	2.3	2.6
	1.3	1.4	1.3	1.1	1.5	1.9	.6	1.3	1.5
	.5	.5	.5	.3	.4	1.1	.3	.6	1.1
Quick	1.9	2.9	2.1	2.9	2.4	2.0	1.3	1.9	1.6
	.9	1.0	.8	.9	.9	1.1	.4	.6	1.3
	.2	.2	.2	.1	.1	.4	.2	.2	.2
Sales/Receivables	0 UND	0 UND	0 UND	0 UND	0 UND	0 UND	6 59.4	0 UND	1 254.8
	5 77.2	2 203.3	1 276.2	0 UND	0 UND	0 UND	40 9.1	11 32.5	13 28.2
	69 5.3	41 9.0	34 10.6	5 68.7	5 70.3	37 9.8	113 3.2	49 7.4	46 8.0
Cost of Sales/Inventory									
Cost of Sales/Payables									
Sales/Working Capital	1.3	2.0	2.0	1.9	.7	1.3	5.4	4.6	2.7
	11.6	9.5	14.8	30.7	9.5	6.6	-45.7	15.1	7.4
	-12.1	-7.8	-10.5	-3.7	-30.6	NM	-1.6	-12.2	129.7
EBIT/Interest	7.3	25.3	17.2	9.4	6.1		18.4	32.3	25.1
	(101) 3.0	(84) 3.7	(100) 4.2	(22) 4.1	(20) 2.8		(17) 6.6	(12) 6.8	(20) 3.9
	1.4	1.2	2.1	1.9	1.8		2.6	2.3	1.5
Net Profit + Depr., Dep., Amort./Cur. Mat. L/T/D	17.8								
	(12) 10.3								
	2.0								
Fixed/Worth	.0	.0	.0	.0	.0	.0	.0	.0	.0
	.1	.1	.5	1.3	.3	.1	.5	.1	.1
	3.1	2.1	3.5	16.5	1.0	NM	NM	NM	.7
Debt/Worth	.8	.3	.5	.4	.2	.5	.9	.4	.8
	2.8	1.7	1.7	2.1	.9	1.8	1.8	2.1	1.8
	14.3	8.1	11.1	19.0	2.2	NM	NM	NM	8.6
% Profit Before Taxes/Tangible Net Worth	49.5	37.9	49.5	49.0	27.2	157.4	51.7	62.4	53.5
	(156) 16.1	(143) 9.5	(144) 15.6	(45) 7.1	(31) 6.8	(14) 46.6	(16) 24.9	(17) 24.4	(21) 37.0
	5.0	1.3	3.0	1.8	1.8	14.9	8.4	1.6	13.8
% Profit Before Taxes/Total Assets	15.4	11.1	19.8	8.4	7.9	33.7	30.4	29.8	34.6
	4.9	3.6	4.9	2.6	3.4	20.5	7.5	5.8	6.2
	1.1	.6	1.4	.3	1.7	5.1	4.1	1.4	1.7
Sales/Net Fixed Assets	549.2	UND	724.1	UND	UND	UND	613.8	295.7	395.3
	27.4	30.7	21.5	.5	11.7	164.9	55.0	38.0	27.1
	1.8	1.0	.6	.2	.2	10.1	1.4	8.6	10.8
Sales/Total Assets	1.7	1.5	1.7	.4	1.5	2.3	2.1	4.9	3.3
	.4	.2	.4	.2	.3	.9	.5	.8	1.5
	.1	.1	.1	.1	.1	.3	.1	.3	.6
% Depr., Dep., Amort./Sales	.6	.7	.9	3.7	.5		1.7	.4	.2
	(112) 1.6	(89) 2.4	(101) 3.5	(34) 14.7	(18) 3.5		(10) 4.7	(12) 1.1	(18) 1.2
	5.2	17.6	16.3	24.1	14.7		16.8	3.6	2.7
% Officers', Directors' Owners' Comp/Sales	4.9	3.9	4.8						
	(28) 12.8	(18) 9.6	(16) 10.4						
	20.6	22.9	25.3						
Net Sales ($)	3586580M	2739279M	4274657M	23331M	55145M	67977M	147880M	339321M	3641003M
Total Assets ($)	5064696M	4794079M	4217115M	219683M	492534M	257952M	567610M	937280M	1742056M

Current Data Sorted by Assets   Comparative Historical Data

0-500M	500M-2MM	2-10MM	10-50MM	50-100MM	100-250MM	Type of Statement	4/1/06-3/31/07 ALL	4/1/07-3/31/08 ALL
		8	7	10	8	Unqualified	38	36
	2	1	1	2		Reviewed	5	4
2		1	2			Compiled	11	10
7	9	3	2			Tax Returns	25	19
8	20	18	17	3	6	Other	44	58
17 (4/1-9/30/10)			120 (10/1/10-3/31/11)					
17	31	31	29	15	14	NUMBER OF STATEMENTS	123	127
%	%	%	%	%	%	ASSETS	%	%
35.1	27.6	26.0	11.8	19.1	29.1	Cash & Equivalents	29.2	26.2
10.3	20.2	23.1	21.2	11.8	10.2	Trade Receivables (net)	13.8	14.7
.0	.0	4.1	.9	.0	3.8	Inventory	.5	1.2
15.9	9.8	4.1	11.6	13.7	13.7	All Other Current	6.7	9.5
61.3	57.7	57.2	45.5	44.6	56.7	Total Current	50.2	51.6
17.8	19.5	18.0	24.6	10.0	10.2	Fixed Assets (net)	18.1	16.6
13.7	5.9	6.5	19.8	8.7	11.8	Intangibles (net)	7.6	5.7
7.2	16.9	18.3	10.2	36.7	21.2	All Other Non-Current	24.0	26.1
100.0	100.0	100.0	100.0	100.0	100.0	Total	100.0	100.0
						LIABILITIES		
61.9	22.3	4.6	11.8	3.1	8.1	Notes Payable-Short Term	16.8	15.1
8.5	3.0	4.8	1.3	2.4	1.3	Cur. Mat.-L.T.D.	2.5	2.4
5.6	1.7	9.1	9.3	5.7	5.0	Trade Payables	4.0	5.2
.0	.3	1.1	.0	.1	.2	Income Taxes Payable	.8	.3
41.9	17.2	13.2	6.3	13.2	13.1	All Other Current	18.6	18.4
117.9	44.4	32.8	28.8	24.5	27.7	Total Current	42.8	41.4
16.0	20.0	25.1	15.3	13.2	32.0	Long-Term Debt	20.2	16.9
.0	.1	.4	.3	.3	1.2	Deferred Taxes	.1	.3
.1	3.7	4.9	6.2	2.0	1.7	All Other Non-Current	7.1	8.2
-34.0	31.8	36.9	49.4	60.1	37.5	Net Worth	29.8	33.2
100.0	100.0	100.0	100.0	100.0	100.0	Total Liabilities & Net Worth	100.0	100.0
						INCOME DATA		
100.0	100.0	100.0	100.0	100.0	100.0	Net Sales	100.0	100.0
						Gross Profit		
90.0	73.7	69.7	64.7	57.4	64.5	Operating Expenses	68.3	69.4
10.0	26.3	30.3	35.3	42.6	35.5	Operating Profit	31.7	30.6
-.3	6.0	7.4	11.3	1.3	4.7	All Other Expenses (net)	6.1	5.8
10.2	20.3	22.8	24.0	41.3	30.8	Profit Before Taxes	25.6	24.8
						RATIOS		
5.1	6.9	8.9	3.6	3.5	4.0		4.7	5.0
.7	2.3	1.8	1.9	2.4	2.1	Current	1.8	1.9
.2	.8	1.0	1.0	1.0	1.2		.7	.9
1.9	5.9	5.8	3.5	3.5	2.6		4.7	3.8
.4	1.6	1.6	1.6	1.8	1.5	Quick	1.4	1.3
.1	.4	.9	.4	.7	.3		.5	.4
0 UND	0 UND	0 UND	0 UND	0 UND	0 UND		0 UND	0 UND
0 UND	0 UND	22 16.8	15 24.6	8 46.4	7 50.5	Sales/Receivables	4 89.7	2 214.3
8 43.3	56 6.5	39 9.4	86 4.2	41 9.0	40 9.1		39 9.4	41 9.0
						Cost of Sales/Inventory		
						Cost of Sales/Payables		
26.7	3.9	3.1	3.5	1.3	2.1		1.8	2.6
-30.7	13.6	11.9	6.6	5.9	3.5	Sales/Working Capital	8.3	9.7
-13.6	-34.8	-96.8	26.5	-51.1	13.4		-24.2	-28.4
177.1	40.3	45.5	129.9				23.6	41.5
(11) 12.9	(13) 8.3	(15) 4.7	(14) 33.6			EBIT/Interest	(67) 9.6	(64) 10.5
1.5	.6	1.9	2.6				2.8	2.2
						Net Profit + Depr., Dep., Amort./Cur. Mat. L/T/D		
.0	.0	.0	.0	.0	.0		.0	.0
.6	.2	.6	.2	.0	.1	Fixed/Worth	.2	.1
-.2	4.4	3.3	1.1	1.3	NM		3.6	2.9
.2	.2	.2	.8	.0	.6		.4	.4
-2.5	1.3	1.2	1.8	.5	2.0	Debt/Worth	1.5	1.6
-1.6	5.0	12.7	11.7	8.1	NM		39.0	20.8
	132.0	127.9	117.9	124.0	83.0		108.8	109.5
	(27) 72.7	(26) 21.9	(26) 59.0	(14) 41.2	(11) 25.3	% Profit Before Taxes/Tangible Net Worth	(97) 21.6	(105) 33.7
	17.2	4.2	8.7	8.9	13.7		4.0	6.6
288.2	72.3	31.1	34.5	43.0	39.8		33.0	36.7
87.8	13.7	10.5	6.3	22.1	9.3	% Profit Before Taxes/Total Assets	10.2	10.2
.0	4.9	1.9	2.2	5.5	2.3		1.9	2.1
UND	230.4	87.0	740.9	229.1	UND		999.8	999.8
128.8	38.2	24.6	42.9	45.3	46.4	Sales/Net Fixed Assets	48.8	51.0
41.0	20.8	2.5	2.5	22.6	12.2		14.9	12.1
24.4	4.0	3.6	1.7	1.8	1.8		3.3	3.2
10.8	2.1	1.3	.8	.9	.7	Sales/Total Assets	1.3	1.5
4.7	.3	.1	.1	.2	.2		.2	.3
	.4	.6	1.7	.6			.4	.5
	(17) 2.0	(16) 1.4	(13) 2.9	(11) .9		% Depr., Dep., Amort./Sales	(77) 1.2	(76) 1.2
	11.1	5.8	14.4	3.7			3.4	3.2
	5.4						10.5	7.6
	(12) 10.6					% Officers', Directors' Owners' Comp/Sales	(25) 23.3	(29) 22.5
	16.6						34.5	35.5
43775M	83462M	253864M	664163M	1103787M	2938839M	Net Sales ($)	1620725M	2301211M
3337M	31463M	159791M	627351M	1059545M	2431713M	Total Assets ($)	2644876M	2824370M

M = $ thousand   MM = $ million
See Pages 9 through 22 for Explanation of Ratios and Data

Comparative Historical Data | Current Data Sorted by Sales

		Comparative Historical Data		Type of Statement	0-1MM	1-3MM	3-5MM	5-10MM	10-25MM	25MM & OVER
	42	36	33	Unqualified	1		1	6	6	19
	10	7	6	Reviewed		3			2	1
	4	5	5	Compiled	2		1		1	1
	18	29	21	Tax Returns	9	9		3		1
	62	64	72	Other	16	17	5	8	12	14
	4/1/08-3/31/09 ALL	4/1/09-3/31/10 ALL	4/1/10-3/31/11 ALL		17 (4/1-9/30/10)			120 (10/1/10-3/31/11)		
NUMBER OF STATEMENTS	136	141	137		28	29	7	17	21	35
	%	%	%	**ASSETS**	%	%	%	%	%	%
	24.2	25.8	24.0	Cash & Equivalents	21.4	24.4		32.2	20.0	24.6
	15.8	15.1	17.9	Trade Receivables (net)	9.5	16.5		10.7	28.8	21.8
	.3	.6	1.5	Inventory	.0	.1		4.3	1.2	2.9
	8.5	9.8	10.5	All Other Current	13.4	10.3		3.6	14.6	10.4
	48.8	51.2	53.9	Total Current	44.4	51.4		50.9	64.7	59.6
	23.9	19.4	18.0	Fixed Assets (net)	22.7	27.9		10.6	13.7	9.3
	6.5	7.4	10.9	Intangibles (net)	10.1	8.2		12.5	12.5	12.4
	20.7	21.9	17.2	All Other Non-Current	22.8	12.5		26.0	9.1	18.7
	100.0	100.0	100.0	Total	100.0	100.0		100.0	100.0	100.0
				LIABILITIES						
	12.0	15.6	17.4	Notes Payable-Short Term	30.9	26.1		15.6	7.7	7.4
	3.8	4.4	3.5	Cur. Mat.-L.T.D.	1.5	6.5		7.1	2.5	1.7
	4.9	4.5	6.2	Trade Payables	2.6	4.6		2.1	11.6	10.1
	.3	.2	.3	Income Taxes Payable	.0	.3		1.7	.2	.1
	15.9	19.8	16.2	All Other Current	14.3	16.5		15.3	25.1	14.5
	36.9	44.4	43.7	Total Current	49.4	54.0		41.8	47.1	33.9
	25.3	25.7	20.1	Long-Term Debt	29.7	18.5		23.9	7.6	17.8
	.3	.3	.3	Deferred Taxes	.0	.1		.6	.6	.5
	6.3	8.3	3.6	All Other Non-Current	.9	5.3		1.2	9.0	2.1
	31.1	21.2	32.2	Net Worth	20.1	22.1		32.4	35.7	45.7
	100.0	100.0	100.0	Total Liabilities & Net Worth	100.0	100.0		100.0	100.0	100.0
				INCOME DATA						
	100.0	100.0	100.0	Net Sales	100.0	100.0		100.0	100.0	100.0
				Gross Profit						
	70.7	75.6	70.2	Operating Expenses	58.2	71.6		78.4	80.6	67.4
	29.3	24.4	29.8	Operating Profit	41.8	28.4		21.6	19.4	32.6
	8.1	6.2	6.0	All Other Expenses (net)	18.8	3.2		1.5	1.2	1.6
	21.2	18.2	23.8	Profit Before Taxes	23.0	25.2		20.1	18.2	31.1
				RATIOS						
	5.5	4.2	4.7	Current	16.5	2.9		6.4	3.0	3.4
	1.9	1.9	1.9		2.7	1.6		2.4	1.8	1.9
	.6	.9	.9		.4	.7		.8	1.1	1.2
	4.2	3.6	3.6	Quick	10.0	2.4		5.5	2.2	2.8
	1.4	1.3	1.5		1.3	1.2		1.7	1.2	1.6
	.4	.5	.4		.2	.3		.6	.6	.9
	0 UND	0 UND	0 UND	Sales/Receivables	0 UND	0 UND		0 UND	3 120.4	3 143.0
	1 414.9	2 177.8	7 48.7		0 UND	0 UND		4 94.6	25 14.4	35 10.4
	41 8.9	38 9.6	41 9.0		0 UND	48 7.6		21 17.0	51 7.1	68 5.4
				Cost of Sales/Inventory						
				Cost of Sales/Payables						
	3.3	3.3	3.2	Sales/Working Capital	.2	4.1		2.1	4.2	3.3
	16.5	11.6	9.5		29.4	24.3		8.5	9.5	5.9
	-11.7	-16.9	-59.1		-6.9	-22.4		-31.5	23.7	75.8
	36.2	47.4	52.4	EBIT/Interest		43.4			186.3	58.8
	(77) 7.2	(78) 7.4	(69) 9.4			(17) 4.7		(12) 35.5	(21) 22.2	
	1.9	1.2	1.9			1.5			5.1	4.2
	8.8	19.3	9.3	Net Profit + Depr., Dep., Amort./Cur. Mat. L/T/D						
	(11) 2.3	(10) 2.3	(11) 1.8							
	.7	.4	.2							
	.0	.0	.0	Fixed/Worth	.0	.0		.0	.1	.0
	.3	.4	.2		.1	.7		.1	.2	.1
	3.8	14.7	3.4		UND	4.7		.6	1.1	1.3
	.4	.3	.3	Debt/Worth	.1	.3		.1	.6	.5
	1.9	1.5	1.4		2.6	2.4		.7	1.9	1.3
	21.7	-154.2	15.8		-120.1	15.8		7.5	17.3	12.7
	118.6	84.7	124.4	% Profit Before Taxes/Tangible Net Worth	68.9	147.5		88.6	265.0	131.9
	(111) 41.7	(105) 22.2	(112) 41.2		(20) 15.0	(25) 69.5		(14) 32.8	(19) 48.2	(29) 55.6
	3.5	2.1	10.6		.7	12.8		4.5	20.8	25.1
	40.8	42.1	53.2	% Profit Before Taxes/Total Assets	10.5	89.9		49.6	45.9	60.1
	13.1	9.8	10.5		2.5	8.0		6.1	22.5	33.7
	1.0	.2	2.8		-.2	3.3		3.8	6.9	8.7
	410.0	208.1	250.2	Sales/Net Fixed Assets	UND	285.0		344.8	128.9	248.2
	32.8	35.0	44.6		69.2	34.9		68.2	62.7	51.6
	7.3	8.6	15.3		.3	9.3		23.6	20.8	17.0
	3.9	3.4	3.7	Sales/Total Assets	2.5	4.2		4.4	4.2	2.4
	1.6	1.6	1.5		.2	2.1		1.2	2.8	1.6
	.3	.3	.3		.0	.4		.2	1.0	.7
	.5	.6	.6	% Depr., Dep., Amort./Sales		.7			.4	.6
	(78) 1.8	(92) 1.5	(71) 1.8			(16) 1.9		(12) 1.1	(20) 1.1	
	4.3	5.0	6.1			11.8			1.9	3.7
	10.3	9.4	7.2	% Officers', Directors' Owners' Comp/Sales		8.3				
	(23) 20.2	(24) 18.7	(29) 11.8			(12) 13.5				
	38.2	27.2	20.3			21.5				
	4913207M	3482531M	5087890M	Net Sales ($)	12790M	57960M	26902M	127073M	306891M	4556274M
	3000777M	3519422M	4313200M	Total Assets ($)	82582M	117887M	89387M	495751M	368799M	3158794M

M = $ thousand   MM = $ million
See Pages 9 through 22 for Explanation of Ratios and Data

Current Data Sorted by Assets   Comparative Historical Data

	0-500M	500M-2MM	2-10MM	10-50MM	50-100MM	100-250MM		4/1/06-3/31/07 ALL	4/1/07-3/31/08 ALL
Type of Statement									
Unqualified	2	1	10	11	3	4		36	41
Reviewed		3	3	1		1		7	6
Compiled	3	3	4					10	10
Tax Returns	20	6	4		1			30	29
Other	18	13	11	12	1	3		54	65
	\<10 (4/1-9/30/10)\>			128 (10/1/10-3/31/11)					
NUMBER OF STATEMENTS	43	26	32	24	5	8		137	151
	%	%	%	%	%	%		%	%
ASSETS									
Cash & Equivalents	38.3	18.7	14.4	29.5				30.2	28.8
Trade Receivables (net)	9.3	18.8	25.5	21.9				18.9	18.6
Inventory	.0	1.0	1.8	3.0				.5	1.4
All Other Current	4.1	7.8	3.1	12.6				6.2	4.9
Total Current	51.7	46.4	44.8	66.9				55.7	53.7
Fixed Assets (net)	23.6	26.0	24.0	7.6				16.7	16.6
Intangibles (net)	6.1	10.3	12.5	4.6				7.0	12.3
All Other Non-Current	18.6	17.3	18.7	20.8				20.6	17.5
Total	100.0	100.0	100.0	100.0				100.0	100.0
LIABILITIES									
Notes Payable-Short Term	34.8	12.8	6.5	9.9				11.9	10.7
Cur. Mat.-L.T.D.	6.0	5.0	6.2	2.5				4.2	2.8
Trade Payables	2.2	5.0	6.1	5.6				4.3	3.6
Income Taxes Payable	.1	.2	.3	.1				.2	.1
All Other Current	22.0	15.9	13.8	21.7				17.2	18.5
Total Current	65.1	38.9	32.8	40.0				37.8	35.8
Long-Term Debt	25.4	22.8	38.9	9.2				17.5	18.6
Deferred Taxes	.0	.0	.7	.4				.5	.3
All Other Non-Current	9.6	5.3	4.4	4.4				8.2	4.7
Net Worth	-.1	32.9	23.2	46.0				36.1	40.6
Total Liabilities & Net Worth	100.0	100.0	100.0	100.0				100.0	100.0
INCOME DATA									
Net Sales	100.0	100.0	100.0	100.0				100.0	100.0
Gross Profit									
Operating Expenses	81.0	82.8	75.2	73.4				78.0	75.9
Operating Profit	19.0	17.2	24.8	26.6				22.0	24.1
All Other Expenses (net)	2.1	5.8	7.7	1.9				3.4	3.2
Profit Before Taxes	16.8	11.3	17.1	24.7				18.6	20.9
RATIOS									
Current	6.0	5.6	2.5	3.8				4.6	5.4
	1.0	1.4	1.1	1.8				1.6	1.8
	.3	.5	.7	1.1				.7	.8
Quick	4.7	3.7	2.5	3.5				4.2	4.3
	.9	.8	.8	1.1				1.4	1.5
	.2	.4	.6	.8				.5	.6
Sales/Receivables	0 UND	0 UND	0 UND	4 88.7				0 UND	0 UND
	0 UND	0 UND	13 28.6	36 10.2				10 35.2	8 47.6
	1 370.5	53 6.9	79 4.6	76 4.8				41 8.9	51 7.2
Cost of Sales/Inventory									
Cost of Sales/Payables									
Sales/Working Capital	28.6	5.5	6.8	2.7				4.2	4.5
	761.0	46.6	62.5	5.2				17.6	17.1
	-15.0	-7.6	-12.4	81.9				-33.2	-54.8
EBIT/Interest	349.0	49.7	74.2	125.0				64.8	91.7
	(23) 17.5	(14) 4.7	(20) 17.8	(17) 14.6				(89) 14.3	(93) 12.8
	3.2	1.4	3.0	7.1				3.7	1.5
Net Profit + Depr., Dep., Amort./Cur. Mat. L/T/D								7.9	
								(12) 2.4	
								1.0	
Fixed/Worth	.0	.0	.1	.0				.0	.1
	.3	.4	.9	.1				.2	.3
	-2.4	NM	21.1	.8				2.2	1.8
Debt/Worth	.5	.6	.6	.3				.3	.4
	2.7	2.1	3.1	1.0				1.7	1.2
	-3.3	NM	32.3	5.8				11.1	7.3
% Profit Before Taxes/Tangible Net Worth	908.3	77.3	260.0	101.7				138.5	225.5
	(25) 200.0	(20) 34.1	(26) 49.6	(21) 53.6				(114) 62.5	(126) 64.4
	41.2	9.2	10.9	11.0				13.3	13.9
% Profit Before Taxes/Total Assets	175.5	43.9	50.0	57.2				86.6	83.6
	79.6	7.0	16.8	9.7				20.5	26.2
	3.8	1.7	2.4	3.8				4.7	4.0
Sales/Net Fixed Assets	UND	173.0	69.5	99.3				171.9	119.3
	96.9	36.4	31.7	50.8				42.4	39.1
	23.0	7.7	9.9	16.7				14.7	14.6
Sales/Total Assets	21.0	3.5	3.4	2.7				5.5	5.1
	7.5	2.2	2.5	1.8				2.7	2.6
	4.6	.7	.7	.9				1.1	1.2
% Depr., Dep., Amort./Sales	.3	.8	.6	.5				.4	.5
	(15) 1.1	(17) 1.7	(25) 1.7	(16) .9				(78) 1.1	(97) 1.1
	1.5	16.3	13.8	1.8				2.3	2.3
% Officers', Directors' Owners' Comp/Sales	8.4							9.1	8.4
	(24) 20.6							(45) 21.7	(51) 20.7
	26.7							31.4	30.5
Net Sales ($)	85822M	81612M	450692M	870397M	1698523M	1156360M		2356077M	3958636M
Total Assets ($)	8237M	29924M	161966M	548877M	385191M	1404323M		2270579M	1961048M

© RMA 2011   M = $ thousand   MM = $ million
See Pages 9 through 22 for Explanation of Ratios and Data

Comparative Historical Data				Current Data Sorted by Sales					

				Type of Statement						
29	29	31	Unqualified	2	1	3	4	4	17
6	4	8	Reviewed	1	1	2	1	1	2
13	13	10	Compiled	2	1	2	3	2	
30	36	31	Tax Returns	14	10	4		1	2
72	68	58	Other	12	16	7	6	5	12
4/1/08-3/31/09 ALL	4/1/09-3/31/10 ALL	4/1/10-3/31/11 ALL		10 (4/1-9/30/10)			128 (10/1/10-3/31/11)		
				0-1MM	1-3MM	3-5MM	5-10MM	10-25MM	25MM & OVER
150	150	138	**NUMBER OF STATEMENTS**	31	29	18	14	13	33
%	%	%	**ASSETS**	%	%	%	%	%	%
28.2	25.1	25.7	Cash & Equivalents	22.9	38.7	26.0	13.5	17.8	25.0
17.8	15.4	17.3	Trade Receivables (net)	4.8	8.6	22.2	26.1	39.7	21.4
1.0	1.0	1.2	Inventory	.0	.0	.0	1.9	2.5	3.1
6.5	7.1	6.6	All Other Current	6.6	3.7	6.0	5.4	1.0	12.0
53.5	48.7	50.7	Total Current	34.3	51.1	54.1	47.0	61.0	61.4
20.7	22.5	20.8	Fixed Assets (net)	42.4	21.6	11.2	10.3	14.0	12.2
9.3	15.0	10.3	Intangibles (net)	4.8	7.7	11.0	23.8	9.1	12.4
16.5	13.8	18.1	All Other Non-Current	18.5	19.7	23.7	18.9	15.9	14.0
100.0	100.0	100.0	Total	100.0	100.0	100.0	100.0	100.0	100.0
			LIABILITIES						
15.2	22.6	16.8	Notes Payable-Short Term	27.1	15.3	10.4	17.7	28.6	7.1
3.0	4.8	5.4	Cur. Mat.-L.T.D.	3.1	6.1	7.6	10.8	2.6	4.6
5.1	4.7	4.1	Trade Payables	1.2	1.9	5.8	5.3	8.5	5.4
.4	.4	.3	Income Taxes Payable	.0	.2	.5	.0	.8	.6
15.8	18.5	18.9	All Other Current	13.2	18.7	16.0	16.7	22.1	25.6
39.4	51.1	45.5	Total Current	44.6	42.3	40.3	50.6	62.6	43.2
24.3	23.3	24.8	Long-Term Debt	45.3	20.0	11.1	39.0	5.2	18.8
.4	.4	.3	Deferred Taxes	.0	.1	.1	1.9	.0	.1
7.5	14.2	7.6	All Other Non-Current	9.2	6.7	4.8	2.7	4.1	11.9
28.4	11.1	21.8	Net Worth	.9	31.0	43.7	5.8	28.0	26.0
100.0	100.0	100.0	Total Liabilities & Net Worth	100.0	100.0	100.0	100.0	100.0	100.0
			INCOME DATA						
100.0	100.0	100.0	Net Sales	100.0	100.0	100.0	100.0	100.0	100.0
			Gross Profit						
80.1	79.1	77.8	Operating Expenses	68.2	80.1	84.2	90.0	79.4	75.5
19.9	20.9	22.2	Operating Profit	31.8	19.9	15.8	10.0	20.6	24.5
4.4	5.3	4.2	All Other Expenses (net)	14.3	1.9	.7	2.4	-.9	1.6
15.5	15.7	18.0	Profit Before Taxes	17.5	18.0	15.1	7.6	21.5	22.9
			RATIOS						
3.5	3.4	2.9		3.2	7.3	7.1	2.1	2.7	2.4
1.5	1.4	1.4	Current	.8	1.6	2.4	1.2	1.5	1.2
.9	.5	.6		.2	.5	.6	.6	.7	.9
2.9	2.9	2.7		1.9	6.6	7.1	1.8	2.5	2.0
1.3	1.1	.9	Quick	.6	1.5	2.4	.8	1.5	1.0
.6	.4	.4		.2	.5	.5	.5	.7	.6
0 UND	0 UND	0 UND		0 UND	0 UND	0 UND	2 166.2	4 89.0	4 87.1
5 67.5	4 88.6	3 114.6	Sales/Receivables	0 UND	0 UND	14 26.1	33 11.0	65 5.6	43 8.6
52 7.0	50 7.3	65 5.6		0 UND	3 135.0	83 4.4	86 4.2	92 4.0	82 4.5
			Cost of Sales/Inventory						
			Cost of Sales/Payables						
5.2	5.3	6.7		13.7	7.5	4.1	6.5	4.7	4.5
21.4	39.2	60.6	Sales/Working Capital	-31.2	54.1	42.8	NM	33.6	22.5
-66.1	-15.3	-19.1		-4.6	-18.6	-17.8	-7.1	-42.0	-53.6
64.7	37.8	74.2		20.4	406.0	58.9	164.8		85.3
(97) 7.6	(89) 5.2	(84) 15.1	EBIT/Interest	(10) 6.1	(19) 17.5	(11) 10.9	(11) 6.6		(25) 17.0
1.8	2.0	3.2		1.7	.8	3.0	1.4		5.6
6.6	13.2								
(13) 1.7	(12) 1.2		Net Profit + Depr., Dep., Amort./Cur. Mat. L/T/D						
.6	-.2								
.1	.1	.0		.0	.0	.0	.2	.0	.1
.5	.5	.4	Fixed/Worth	1.4	.4	.1	.9	.2	.3
8.3	-2.0	23.7		23.3	-12.6	NM	-.2	2.1	NM
.4	.4	.6		.8	.4	.2	.5	.8	.6
1.6	2.3	2.4	Debt/Worth	3.8	2.5	.8	3.3	2.0	2.3
NM	-3.0	-14.7		-4.3	-5.2	NM	-1.8	6.3	-9.1
138.6	112.8	148.2		147.9	628.7	108.8		269.9	115.5
(113) 50.8	(98) 44.2	(100) 62.3	% Profit Before Taxes/Tangible Net Worth	(22) 13.3	(19) 91.2	(14) 68.8		(12) 121.7	(24) 65.9
13.6	6.4	10.9		2.8	2.5	18.6		48.2	13.1
66.3	52.1	71.9		100.0	130.5	54.2	31.6	109.9	63.5
16.4	12.2	23.6	% Profit Before Taxes/Total Assets	6.1	63.9	19.0	16.8	42.4	25.2
2.8	1.5	3.6		1.7	.3	4.2	3.4	24.7	6.8
86.5	118.5	177.9		UND	UND	173.0	55.5	344.1	66.1
31.6	36.0	38.4	Sales/Net Fixed Assets	34.6	94.2	57.1	31.5	86.8	38.2
12.2	12.8	14.7		.2	15.8	18.4	19.8	24.9	20.2
5.2	5.7	5.8		5.7	8.9	5.9	3.9	8.2	3.4
2.5	2.1	2.6	Sales/Total Assets	2.2	6.0	2.4	3.0	3.3	2.2
1.4	.7	.9		.1	1.7	1.7	1.8	2.1	.8
.5	.7	.5		2.7	.4		.5		.5
(104) 1.1	(92) 1.3	(78) 1.3	% Depr., Dep., Amort./Sales	(15) 22.4	(12) 1.2		(11) 1.2		(22) .8
2.5	3.3	3.2		26.0	3.9		2.3		1.7
7.0	9.9	7.6		10.7	10.6				
(43) 15.0	(32) 16.0	(41) 17.0	% Officers', Directors' Owners' Comp/Sales	(10) 20.5	(16) 21.2				
24.2	28.4	25.9		25.4	28.3				
3995016M	4278754M	4343406M	Net Sales ($)	12931M	53981M	67117M	107571M	189716M	3912090M
2177934M	3625264M	2538518M	Total Assets ($)	39225M	168055M	72618M	60142M	67825M	2130653M

© RMA 2011

M = $ thousand   MM = $ million
See Pages 9 through 22 for Explanation of Ratios and Data

Current Data Sorted by Assets

Comparative Historical Data

Type of Statement	0-500M	500M-2MM	2-10MM	10-50MM	50-100MM	100-250MM	16 4/1/06- 3/31/07 ALL	12 4/1/07- 3/31/08 ALL
Unqualified		1	5	9	1	3	16	12
Reviewed			1				3	1
Compiled		2					1	6
Tax Returns		3	4				4	2
Other	1	1	5	7	1		21	12
	9 (4/1-9/30/10)			35 (10/1/10-3/31/11)				
NUMBER OF STATEMENTS	1	7	15	16	2	3	45	33
	%	%	%	%	%	%	%	%

ASSETS	0-500M	500M-2MM	2-10MM	10-50MM	50-100MM	100-250MM	ALL 06-07	ALL 07-08
Cash & Equivalents			33.6	35.5			28.8	33.7
Trade Receivables (net)			16.1	11.7			16.6	10.0
Inventory			.0	3.7			.6	3.4
All Other Current			5.5	3.4			4.8	4.0
Total Current			55.2	54.3			50.8	51.1
Fixed Assets (net)			20.7	8.5			24.5	17.5
Intangibles (net)			9.7	13.2			6.9	3.4
All Other Non-Current			14.3	24.0			17.8	27.9
Total			100.0	100.0			100.0	100.0
LIABILITIES								
Notes Payable-Short Term			3.8	1.7			3.5	1.2
Cur. Mat.-L.T.D.			6.6	2.9			3.1	1.4
Trade Payables			2.7	6.6			6.3	6.9
Income Taxes Payable			.1	2.8			.1	.1
All Other Current			17.6	25.7			10.9	11.8
Total Current			30.8	39.9			24.0	21.4
Long-Term Debt			42.1	15.4			14.6	12.7
Deferred Taxes			.6	1.5			.5	.7
All Other Non-Current			3.8	7.1			3.3	3.7
Net Worth			22.7	36.1			57.7	61.6
Total Liabilities & Net Worth			100.0	100.0			100.0	100.0
INCOME DATA								
Net Sales			100.0	100.0			100.0	100.0
Gross Profit								
Operating Expenses			74.7	79.3			65.6	68.1
Operating Profit			25.3	20.7			34.4	31.9
All Other Expenses (net)			6.5	4.8			7.9	6.0
Profit Before Taxes			18.8	16.0			26.5	26.0

RATIOS	0-500M	500M-2MM	2-10MM	10-50MM	50-100MM	100-250MM	ALL 06-07	ALL 07-08
Current			3.9	4.4			14.6	8.1
			1.8	1.6			2.3	2.7
			1.0	.7			1.1	1.6
Quick			2.7	4.4			14.4	6.8
			1.8	1.4			2.2	2.0
			.9	.3			.7	1.3
Sales/Receivables			0 UND	0 UND			0 UND	0 UND
			25 14.7	28 12.8			0 UND	10 36.0
			48 7.6	75 4.9			41 8.9	34 10.7
Cost of Sales/Inventory								
Cost of Sales/Payables								
Sales/Working Capital			2.2	1.8			1.9	.7
			7.8	5.8			4.9	3.0
			-328.5	UND			UND	36.6
EBIT/Interest							14.5	31.2
			(15) 6.9	(12) 5.7				
			3.6	.7				
Net Profit + Depr., Dep., Amort./Cur. Mat. L/T/D								
Fixed/Worth			.0	.0			.0	.0
			.5	.2			.2	.1
			13.2	UND			1.0	.6
Debt/Worth			.5	.6			.1	.2
			1.6	2.0			.7	.5
			-28.2	UND			3.4	1.5
% Profit Before Taxes/Tangible Net Worth			66.0	49.4			43.8	24.5
			(11) 16.1	(12) 31.3			(40) 19.4	(30) 11.1
			.2	5.8			6.8	2.7
% Profit Before Taxes/Total Assets			41.9	16.7			22.1	14.1
			10.9	9.4			8.7	6.6
			.5	.0			2.1	1.6
Sales/Net Fixed Assets			62.7	118.3			UND	UND
			27.6	44.9			37.0	37.2
			.4	8.7			1.0	4.9
Sales/Total Assets			3.0	1.9			2.4	2.6
			1.6	.5			.9	.6
			.2	.2			.1	.1
% Depr., Dep., Amort./Sales			1.1	.6			.6	.8
			(10) 1.5	(11) 1.0			(25) 2.0	(18) 1.8
			10.8	4.8			11.5	4.6
% Officers', Directors' Owners' Comp/Sales								
Net Sales ($)	2291M	7091M	105133M	362586M	135768M	549098M	2203428M	912367M
Total Assets ($)	466M	7685M	71053M	414231M	171858M	597637M	1609028M	1172343M

M = $ thousand   MM = $ million
See Pages 9 through 22 for Explanation of Ratios and Data

Comparative Historical Data | Current Data Sorted by Sales

					Type of Statement						
	13		12		19	Unqualified	1	3	3	2	6	4
	1		1		1	Reviewed		1				
	7		6		2	Compiled	1	1				
	1		3		7	Tax Returns	4	1		1	1	
	19		20		15	Other	3	1	1	2	2	6
	4/1/08-		4/1/09-		4/1/10-							
	3/31/09		3/31/10		3/31/11			9 (4/1-9/30/10)		35 (10/1/10-3/31/11)		
	ALL		ALL		ALL		0-1MM	1-3MM	3-5MM	5-10MM	10-25MM	25MM & OVER
	41		42		44	NUMBER OF STATEMENTS	9	7	4	5	9	10
	%		%		%	ASSETS	%	%	%	%	%	%
	23.2		31.9		33.2	Cash & Equivalents						42.8
	14.6		13.3		11.3	Trade Receivables (net)						14.6
	3.7		4.1		1.7	Inventory						7.4
	7.3		5.7		3.9	All Other Current						4.8
	48.8		55.0		50.1	Total Current						69.6
	21.7		23.4		17.4	Fixed Assets (net)						9.1
	5.6		4.7		13.0	Intangibles (net)						13.2
	23.9		17.0		19.4	All Other Non-Current						8.1
	100.0		100.0		100.0	Total						100.0
						LIABILITIES						
	3.1		2.8		4.0	Notes Payable-Short Term						.6
	3.3		2.0		3.6	Cur. Mat.-L.T.D.						2.1
	4.5		5.7		4.2	Trade Payables						10.7
	.2		1.0		1.0	Income Taxes Payable						4.2
	21.4		21.1		18.1	All Other Current						27.9
	32.5		32.7		30.9	Total Current						45.5
	16.4		26.4		25.3	Long-Term Debt						6.3
	.3		.2		1.0	Deferred Taxes						3.3
	7.2		5.6		6.1	All Other Non-Current						11.3
	43.7		35.1		36.7	Net Worth						33.5
	100.0		100.0		100.0	Total Liabilties & Net Worth						100.0
						INCOME DATA						
	100.0		100.0		100.0	Net Sales						100.0
						Gross Profit						
	73.8		76.0		79.2	Operating Expenses						89.6
	26.2		24.0		20.8	Operating Profit						10.4
	7.1		7.7		4.9	All Other Expenses (net)						1.0
	19.1		16.3		16.0	Profit Before Taxes						9.4
						RATIOS						
	2.4		4.2		4.5							2.9
	1.6		1.8		1.7	Current						1.6
	.9		1.0		1.0							1.3
	2.2		4.2		4.5							2.9
	1.1		1.3		1.7	Quick						1.4
	.5		.8		.7							.9
0	UND	0	UND	0	UND						12	29.7
23	15.8	30	12.1	23	15.9	Sales/Receivables					27	13.3
46	7.9	52	7.0	48	7.7						49	7.5
						Cost of Sales/Inventory						
						Cost of Sales/Payables						
	1.6		2.0		2.2							2.3
	9.7		7.6		6.2	Sales/Working Capital						5.8
	UND		-830.0		-138.5							11.7
	25.0		12.4		117.5							
(21)	5.5	(18)	7.0	(23)	7.9	EBIT/Interest						
	1.8		1.3		1.4							
						Net Profit + Depr., Dep., Amort./Cur. Mat. L/T/D						
	.0		.0		.0							.1
	.2		.5		.2	Fixed/Worth						.2
	2.7		1.7		10.2							NM
	.3		.5		.5							1.4
	1.3		1.6		1.5	Debt/Worth						1.9
	24.8		9.2		UND							NM
	41.8		31.2		64.1	% Profit Before Taxes/Tangible Net Worth						
(35)	14.4	(35)	8.9	(34)	17.3							
	3.8		1.0		.6							
	13.3		13.2		17.8	% Profit Before Taxes/Total Assets						18.3
	6.5		3.6		8.5							12.9
	.9		.2		.2							7.7
	999.8		857.8		104.3	Sales/Net Fixed Assets						71.8
	23.8		23.0		28.1							31.1
	.6		1.6		6.1							16.5
	1.7		2.4		2.1	Sales/Total Assets						2.5
	.5		.7		.7							1.9
	.1		.2		.2							.8
	.8		1.3		.8	% Depr., Dep., Amort./Sales						
(21)	2.4	(24)	2.3	(26)	1.3							
	11.5		9.3		5.3							
						% Officers', Directors' Owners' Comp/Sales						
	988463M		1011906M		1161967M	Net Sales ($)	4308M	14203M	14677M	34336M	160847M	933596M
	1124565M		973511M		1262930M	Total Assets ($)	37886M	32489M	71423M	70798M	397382M	652952M

M = $ thousand   MM = $ million
See Pages 9 through 22 for Explanation of Ratios and Data

Current Data Sorted by Assets

Comparative Historical Data

						Type of Statement		
1		3 3 3	7	7	3	Unqualified	11	14
						Reviewed	1	
2	1	1				Compiled	6	13
4	4	9	1	1		Tax Returns	6	6
5	5	8	11	5	2	Other	26	31
	6 (4/1-9/30/10)		77 (10/1/10-3/31/11)				4/1/06-3/31/07	4/1/07-3/31/08
0-500M	500M-2MM	2-10MM	10-50MM	50-100MM	100-250MM		ALL	ALL
12	10	24	19	13	5	NUMBER OF STATEMENTS	50	64
%	%	%	%	%	%	ASSETS	%	%
33.9	9.1	21.4	22.0	20.1		Cash & Equivalents	28.3	18.7
27.4	.5	6.9	12.8	8.5		Trade Receivables (net)	13.8	18.9
.0	1.6	1.6	.2	.0		Inventory	2.1	2.1
16.4	17.7	10.3	10.7	3.9		All Other Current	5.2	12.9
77.7	28.8	40.2	45.7	32.5		Total Current	49.5	52.6
15.1	34.6	33.3	8.3	10.9		Fixed Assets (net)	20.5	17.8
2.8	18.9	4.5	.2	4.0		Intangibles (net)	3.7	5.2
4.4	17.7	21.9	45.8	52.6		All Other Non-Current	26.3	24.4
100.0	100.0	100.0	100.0	100.0		Total	100.0	100.0
						LIABILITIES		
58.4	15.6	8.8	21.5	9.1		Notes Payable-Short Term	15.1	27.4
.0	.1	.6	1.9	4.2		Cur. Mat.-L.T.D.	2.4	2.3
10.7	.6	.3	5.2	1.2		Trade Payables	3.7	2.6
.0	.0	.2	.2	.0		Income Taxes Payable	.1	.0
17.7	7.6	16.2	5.8	4.5		All Other Current	8.0	7.9
86.8	23.9	26.1	34.5	19.1		Total Current	29.3	40.2
.0	9.3	26.6	16.8	48.4		Long-Term Debt	26.5	20.5
.0	.0	.0	.0	.0		Deferred Taxes	.4	.0
9.1	15.2	7.7	2.2	6.0		All Other Non-Current	.9	4.4
4.1	51.5	39.6	46.5	26.6		Net Worth	42.8	34.8
100.0	100.0	100.0	100.0	100.0		Total Liabilities & Net Worth	100.0	100.0
						INCOME DATA		
100.0	100.0	100.0	100.0	100.0		Net Sales	100.0	100.0
						Gross Profit		
81.1	74.1	48.3	52.2	46.6		Operating Expenses	67.4	51.7
18.9	25.9	51.7	47.8	53.4		Operating Profit	32.6	48.3
1.0	5.6	22.4	15.0	24.6		All Other Expenses (net)	16.0	23.4
17.9	20.2	29.3	32.8	28.8		Profit Before Taxes	16.7	24.9
						RATIOS		
9.0	3.5	5.1	4.7	3.5			5.1	4.4
1.7	2.1	2.0	1.2	1.7		Current	1.9	1.7
.7	.4	.4	.7	.5			.8	.9
8.5		3.3	4.1	3.5			3.9	3.3
1.5		.6	1.0	1.7		Quick	1.6	1.0
.4		.2	.2	.4			.4	.1
0 UND	0 UND	0 UND	0 UND	0 UND			0 UND	0 UND
4 81.3	0 UND	0 UND	11 34.0	1 566.8		Sales/Receivables	1 276.7	2 197.9
46 8.0	0 UND	13 27.1	44 8.3	59 6.2			52 7.0	86 4.3
						Cost of Sales/Inventory		
						Cost of Sales/Payables		
5.3	7.8	1.3	.7	.2			.4	.8
31.1	57.2	5.2	7.4	4.3		Sales/Working Capital	4.9	4.9
NM	-15.8	-3.6	-4.6	-4.7			-45.1	-36.5
		11.4					33.3	162.9
	(10)	6.1				EBIT/Interest	(20) 6.4	(13) 16.1
		3.1					-.9	2.0
						Net Profit + Depr., Dep., Amort./Cur. Mat. L/T/D		
.0	.1	.0	.0	.0			.0	.0
.2	.3	.4	.0	.0		Fixed/Worth	.1	.0
NM	4.7	4.8	.1	1.2			1.1	1.1
.3	.5	.3	.2	.4			.4	.4
1.5	2.1	2.3	.7	1.4		Debt/Worth	1.4	3.8
NM	3.8	77.9	9.7	49.8			4.8	79.6
		58.9	63.8	10.0			32.3	43.7
	(19)	9.1	(18) 23.7	(11) 4.6		% Profit Before Taxes/Tangible Net Worth	(46) 12.3	(51) 21.6
		4.7		8.4	2.9		1.8	4.7
41.6	28.7	9.1	19.8	4.9			21.4	7.5
32.8	10.9	4.6	5.8	1.9		% Profit Before Taxes/Total Assets	3.3	2.8
13.2	3.5	1.3	2.7	.1			.3	1.0
770.4	74.2	UND	UND	UND			UND	UND
34.0	30.1	8.4	328.3	UND		Sales/Net Fixed Assets	33.1	281.2
16.5	1.3	.2	9.5	9.2			1.1	10.0
15.4	2.7	.9	.9	.2			1.4	.4
4.3	1.0	.2	.2	.1		Sales/Total Assets	.2	.2
1.5	.5	.1	.1	.0			.1	.1
		1.1					1.1	1.0
	(15)	3.5				% Depr., Dep., Amort./Sales	(29) 2.1	(22) 2.9
		22.2					10.4	14.2
						% Officers', Directors' Owners' Comp/Sales		
17345M	13774M	120219M	447397M	196838M	121627M	Net Sales ($)	422857M	670215M
3363M	9244M	122698M	538788M	858438M	1027637M	Total Assets ($)	1534883M	2291084M

© RMA 2011

M = $ thousand   MM = $ million
See Pages 9 through 22 for Explanation of Ratios and Data

Comparative Historical Data

Current Data Sorted by Sales

			Type of Statement						
30	18	21	Unqualified	1	4		8	2	6
	2	3	Reviewed	2				1	
12	4	4	Compiled	4					
12	20	19	Tax Returns	9	6	3		1	
46	66	36	Other	11	11	2	6	4	2
4/1/08-3/31/09 ALL	4/1/09-3/31/10 ALL	4/1/10-3/31/11 ALL		0-1MM	1-3MM 6 (4/1-9/30/10)	3-5MM	5-10MM 77 (10/1/10-3/31/11)	10-25MM	25MM & OVER
100	110	83	**NUMBER OF STATEMENTS**	27	21	5	14	8	8
%	%	%	**ASSETS**	%	%	%	%	%	%
20.8	16.6	22.6	Cash & Equivalents	21.5	18.6		27.0		
19.0	18.1	11.4	Trade Receivables (net)	7.6	12.0		14.7		
2.7	.8	.7	Inventory	2.0	.0		.0		
8.8	8.8	10.7	All Other Current	16.6	2.5		15.0		
51.3	44.4	45.5	Total Current	47.6	33.1		56.8		
14.6	27.5	20.0	Fixed Assets (net)	28.8	17.3		5.1		
3.0	3.8	4.7	Intangibles (net)	5.6	5.1		1.5		
31.1	24.4	29.8	All Other Non-Current	17.9	44.4		36.6		
100.0	100.0	100.0	Total	100.0	100.0		100.0		
			LIABILITIES						
28.2	20.3	19.7	Notes Payable-Short Term	19.2	15.3		50.2		
2.0	4.6	1.4	Cur. Mat.-L.T.D.	.5	.8		1.7		
3.3	3.0	3.1	Trade Payables	4.2	1.3		4.3		
.1	.1	.1	Income Taxes Payable	.0	.0		.2		
8.7	10.7	10.2	All Other Current	9.5	12.3		1.8		
42.3	38.7	34.6	Total Current	33.3	29.7		58.2		
26.1	32.4	21.1	Long-Term Debt	21.2	25.7		6.9		
.1	.2	.0	Deferred Taxes	.0	.0		.0		
11.7	5.3	7.4	All Other Non-Current	7.0	11.3		5.6		
19.8	23.4	36.9	Net Worth	38.4	33.3		29.3		
100.0	100.0	100.0	Total Liabilities & Net Worth	100.0	100.0		100.0		
			INCOME DATA						
100.0	100.0	100.0	Net Sales	100.0	100.0		100.0		
			Gross Profit						
58.8	64.0	57.4	Operating Expenses	51.9	64.6		50.9		
41.2	36.0	42.6	Operating Profit	48.1	35.4		49.1		
18.9	13.8	15.1	All Other Expenses (net)	20.5	12.2		11.0		
22.3	22.2	27.5	Profit Before Taxes	27.6	23.1		38.1		
			RATIOS						
4.3	3.6	4.7		11.3	4.2		6.2		
1.5	1.5	1.7	Current	2.0	1.5		1.7		
.6	.5	.6		.4	.3		.7		
2.5	2.9	3.8		3.9	4.2		7.0		
(99) 1.1	1.2 (82)	1.3	Quick	.5	1.5	(13) 1.7			
.3	.4	.2		.2	.3		.3		
0 UND	0 UND	0 UND		0 UND	0 UND		0 UND		
0 904.7	0 UND	0 UND	Sales/Receivables	0 UND	0 UND		1 287.1		
71 5.1	52 7.0	25 14.7		14 25.3	27 13.4		55 6.6		
			Cost of Sales/Inventory						
			Cost of Sales/Payables						
1.3	.9	1.0		.7	1.2		.4		
6.2	10.3	6.4	Sales/Working Capital	5.0	29.4		4.8		
-13.3	-6.9	-7.2		-4.2	-7.9		-5.0		
18.9	18.2	22.7							
(44) 5.4	(47) 4.2	(32) 6.1	EBIT/Interest						
1.8	1.2	2.0							
	25.0		Net Profit + Depr., Dep.,						
	(10) 1.7		Amort./Cur. Mat. L/T/D						
	.8								
.0	.0	.0		.0	.0		.0		
.0	.1	.1	Fixed/Worth	.2	.0		.0		
1.0	2.4	1.4		4.8	2.4		.1		
.6	.5	.3		.1	.8		.2		
2.3	2.1	1.3	Debt/Worth	1.0	3.0		1.3		
27.6	8.2	9.7		94.8	39.6		6.6		
60.2	58.2	48.4	% Profit Before Taxes/Tangible	43.5	58.9		24.1		
(83) 18.0	(93) 12.5	(71) 16.4	Net Worth	(21) 6.5	(19) 38.2	(12) 11.5			
2.6	3.0	4.7		3.2	4.6		8.3		
12.4	19.3	16.6	% Profit Before Taxes/Total	15.2	20.2		20.7		
3.3	3.8	5.5	Assets	4.6	5.8		4.9		
.3	.5	1.8		1.0	1.6		3.0		
UND	UND	UND		UND	UND		UND		
173.6	40.3	39.1	Sales/Net Fixed Assets	25.7	208.3		UND		
9.1	.5	3.6		.2	10.8		28.2		
1.7	1.3	1.5		.9	2.9		.6		
.2	.3	.2	Sales/Total Assets	.2	.2		.2		
.1	.1	.1		.1	.0		.1		
.7	1.0	.7		1.8					
(38) 2.4	(55) 5.8	(37) 2.5	% Depr., Dep., Amort./Sales	(12) 16.9					
9.9	22.9	19.8		41.6					
	3.7	4.4	% Officers', Directors'						
	(13) 17.2	(12) 12.7	Owners' Comp/Sales						
	22.6	17.9							
1001419M	973144M	917200M	Net Sales ($)	12179M	41442M	17717M	101832M	123398M	620632M
3374631M	3043527M	2560168M	Total Assets ($)	86111M	645774M	100035M	591214M	715971M	421063M

© RMA 2011

M = $ thousand   MM = $ million
See Pages 9 through 22 for Explanation of Ratios and Data

Current Data Sorted by Assets   Comparative Historical Data

						Type of Statement	4/1/06-3/31/07 ALL	4/1/07-3/31/08 ALL
1			2	3	4	Unqualified	12	12
		2				Reviewed	1	
	3	1			1	Compiled		1
1	1					Tax Returns	1	2
1	1	2	6	3	3	Other	10	9
	1 (4/1-9/30/10)		34 (10/1/10-3/31/11)					
0-500M	500M-2MM	2-10MM	10-50MM	50-100MM	100-250MM			
3	5	5	8	6	8	NUMBER OF STATEMENTS	24	24
%	%	%	%	%	%		%	%

Label	ALL (4/1/06-3/31/07)	ALL (4/1/07-3/31/08)
ASSETS		
Cash & Equivalents	58.5	31.0
Trade Receivables (net)	9.8	19.2
Inventory	.0	1.9
All Other Current	4.3	15.2
Total Current	72.7	67.3
Fixed Assets (net)	3.9	11.8
Intangibles (net)	5.0	1.5
All Other Non-Current	18.4	19.4
Total	100.0	100.0
LIABILITIES		
Notes Payable-Short Term	7.5	10.9
Cur. Mat.-L.T.D.	1.7	.8
Trade Payables	13.2	21.7
Income Taxes Payable	.1	1.1
All Other Current	17.4	24.1
Total Current	39.9	58.6
Long-Term Debt	6.8	14.2
Deferred Taxes	.2	.4
All Other Non-Current	27.5	14.3
Net Worth	25.6	12.6
Total Liabilities & Net Worth	100.0	100.0
INCOME DATA		
Net Sales	100.0	100.0
Gross Profit		
Operating Expenses	87.3	85.4
Operating Profit	12.7	14.6
All Other Expenses (net)	.7	6.3
Profit Before Taxes	12.0	8.3
RATIOS		
Current	18.3 / 1.8 / 1.1	1.6 / 1.2 / .9
Quick	18.3 / 1.6 / 1.0	1.5 / 1.0 / .5
Sales/Receivables	0 UND / 10 37.2 / 105 3.5	0 UND / 30 12.3 / 132 2.8
Cost of Sales/Inventory		
Cost of Sales/Payables		
Sales/Working Capital	.4 / 3.5 / 29.5	1.0 / 11.0 / -22.9
EBIT/Interest	26.4 / (12) 15.9 / .3	17.8 / (15) 8.2 / 3.2
Net Profit + Depr., Dep., Amort./Cur. Mat. L/T/D		
Fixed/Worth	.0 / .0 / .4	.0 / .1 / 2.1
Debt/Worth	1.9 / 4.8 / 12.8	2.2 / 6.7 / 43.1
% Profit Before Taxes/Tangible Net Worth	32.5 / (22) 16.6 / 1.4	46.3 / (20) 20.5 / 8.6
% Profit Before Taxes/Total Assets	7.3 / 1.9 / .3	14.7 / 1.9 / .9
Sales/Net Fixed Assets	UND / UND / 29.6	UND / 63.6 / 14.6
Sales/Total Assets	1.2 / .3 / .1	2.5 / .7 / .1
% Depr., Dep., Amort./Sales		
% Officers', Directors' Owners' Comp/Sales		

0-500M	500M-2MM	2-10MM	10-50MM	50-100MM	100-250MM		ALL	ALL
4485M	17973M	56059M	91042M	617753M	1199240M	Net Sales ($)	610975M	887816M
1177M	4375M	25512M	163933M	503981M	1509321M	Total Assets ($)	1186018M	1543109M

© RMA 2011

M = $ thousand   MM = $ million
See Pages 9 through 22 for Explanation of Ratios and Data

Comparative Historical Data   Current Data Sorted by Sales

4/1/08-3/31/09 ALL	4/1/09-3/31/10 ALL	4/1/10-3/31/11 ALL	Type of Statement	0-1MM	1-3MM	3-5MM	5-10MM	10-25MM	25MM & OVER
12	15	10	Unqualified	1				4	5
2	3	2	Reviewed		1				1
2	2	5	Compiled	1	2		1		1
6	4	2	Tax Returns	1	1				
11	16	16	Other	1	1	2	3	4	5
				1 (4/1-9/30/10)			34 (10/1/10-3/31/11)		
33	40	35	NUMBER OF STATEMENTS	4	5	2	4	8	12
%	%	%	ASSETS	%	%	%	%	%	%
40.3	49.5	43.6	Cash & Equivalents						37.3
11.6	12.8	14.4	Trade Receivables (net)						14.0
.0	2.2	.2	Inventory						.3
5.8	5.3	7.5	All Other Current						8.3
57.7	69.9	65.7	Total Current						59.8
13.5	5.6	7.6	Fixed Assets (net)						8.8
6.0	5.7	6.7	Intangibles (net)						8.8
22.8	18.8	20.0	All Other Non-Current						22.6
100.0	100.0	100.0	Total						100.0
			LIABILITIES						
12.1	6.7	3.8	Notes Payable-Short Term						2.2
.8	3.9	1.7	Cur. Mat.-L.T.D.						2.0
15.6	10.6	6.0	Trade Payables						8.3
.1	.1	.2	Income Taxes Payable						.0
27.0	45.4	29.5	All Other Current						29.9
55.6	66.8	41.3	Total Current						42.5
14.8	11.6	12.4	Long-Term Debt						11.2
.1	.1	.0	Deferred Taxes						.1
3.7	6.9	8.3	All Other Non-Current						6.5
25.9	14.6	38.0	Net Worth						39.7
100.0	100.0	100.0	Total Liabilities & Net Worth						100.0
			INCOME DATA						
100.0	100.0	100.0	Net Sales						100.0
			Gross Profit						
84.6	90.0	86.1	Operating Expenses						90.4
15.4	10.0	13.9	Operating Profit						9.6
6.3	3.2	3.6	All Other Expenses (net)						-1.4
9.1	6.8	10.3	Profit Before Taxes						11.0
			RATIOS						
1.7	2.2	4.3	Current						2.2
1.1	1.2	1.5							1.4
.8	.9	1.0							1.1
1.7	2.1	4.3	Quick						2.2
.9	1.1	1.5							1.1
.7	.7	.9							.9
0 UND	0 857.8	0 999.8	Sales/Receivables						0 UND
13 27.6	18 20.0	22 16.4							24 15.2
91 4.0	66 5.5	133 2.7							107 3.4
			Cost of Sales/Inventory						
			Cost of Sales/Payables						
3.4	1.6	1.0	Sales/Working Capital						3.5
29.9	7.8	5.5							12.2
-5.1	-5.5	-119.1							NM
29.4	29.1	60.0	EBIT/Interest						
(20) 7.3	(24) 6.7	(16) 18.6							
1.8	2.6	3.6							
			Net Profit + Depr., Dep., Amort./Cur. Mat. L/T/D						
.0	.0	.0	Fixed/Worth						.0
.1	.0	.0							.1
1.7	.8	.3							1.1
1.5	1.3	.5	Debt/Worth						.7
5.2	4.8	2.2							2.1
16.2	16.2	11.5							9.8
33.9	42.6	55.8	% Profit Before Taxes/Tangible Net Worth						139.6
(28) 9.8	(33) 14.4	(31) 15.2						(11)	23.9
1.1	4.5	3.7							7.8
8.5	11.7	18.2	% Profit Before Taxes/Total Assets						36.8
2.2	3.4	5.1							12.4
.3	.6	.6							1.2
UND	UND	UND	Sales/Net Fixed Assets						828.6
51.2	114.6	81.5							28.1
16.9	31.9	19.7							11.3
1.6	2.2	2.0	Sales/Total Assets						2.8
.4	.8	.9							1.0
.2	.2	.3							.8
.8	.5	.5	% Depr., Dep., Amort./Sales						
(12) 2.0	(16) 1.6	(15) 1.6							
3.9	3.7	2.8							
			% Officers', Directors' Owners' Comp/Sales						
1824893M	1842034M	1986552M	Net Sales ($)	992M	9030M	8152M	25847M	134086M	1808445M
.1654699M	2182467M	2208299M	Total Assets ($)	6652M	8416M	32492M	65230M	698989M	1396520M

M = $ thousand   MM = $ million
See Pages 9 through 22 for Explanation of Ratios and Data

Current Data Sorted by Assets | Comparative Historical Data

0-500M	500M-2MM	2-10MM	10-50MM	50-100MM	100-250MM	Type of Statement	4/1/06-3/31/07 ALL	4/1/07-3/31/08 ALL
	1	3	21	10	8	Unqualified	48	40
					1	Reviewed		2
	1					Compiled	4	3
1	2	1				Tax Returns	8	3
1	1	5	12	8	10	Other	37	27
	12 (4/1-9/30/10)		74 (10/1/10-3/31/11)					
2	5	9	33	18	19	**NUMBER OF STATEMENTS**	97	75
%	%	%	%	%	%	**ASSETS**	%	%
			62.4	45.3	40.2	Cash & Equivalents	37.9	35.1
			8.4	16.7	13.1	Trade Receivables (net)	15.3	15.5
			.2	.2	.8	Inventory	1.0	.7
			8.9	6.7	3.9	All Other Current	3.9	4.6
			79.9	68.8	58.0	Total Current	58.1	55.8
			9.0	7.2	9.8	Fixed Assets (net)	16.4	18.1
			1.3	2.2	11.3	Intangibles (net)	9.4	8.8
			9.9	21.8	21.0	All Other Non-Current	16.0	17.3
			100.0	100.0	100.0	Total	100.0	100.0
						LIABILITIES		
			.4	.8	.3	Notes Payable-Short Term	5.6	3.5
			1.2	1.6	.9	Cur. Mat.-L.T.D.	1.9	2.1
			13.0	17.7	20.5	Trade Payables	10.8	12.4
			.6	.3	.1	Income Taxes Payable	.2	.2
			28.8	32.8	18.8	All Other Current	28.3	23.5
			44.1	53.1	40.5	Total Current	46.8	41.6
			5.4	8.2	15.5	Long-Term Debt	12.4	17.5
			.9	.1	1.6	Deferred Taxes	.3	.4
			7.9	2.1	1.0	All Other Non-Current	7.9	8.6
			41.7	36.6	41.4	Net Worth	32.7	31.9
			100.0	100.0	100.0	Total Liabilities & Net Worth	100.0	100.0
						INCOME DATA		
			100.0	100.0	100.0	Net Sales	100.0	100.0
						Gross Profit		
			94.2	97.8	96.3	Operating Expenses	96.2	95.9
			5.8	2.2	3.7	Operating Profit	3.8	4.1
			1.8	-.3	.8	All Other Expenses (net)	-.1	-.7
			4.0	2.5	2.9	Profit Before Taxes	3.9	4.9
						RATIOS		
			3.2	1.7	1.8		2.2	2.3
			1.6	1.4	1.4	Current	1.3	1.5
			1.2	.8	1.2		.9	1.0
			2.7	1.5	1.7		2.0	2.1
			1.4	1.2	1.3	Quick	1.2	1.4
			1.0	.8	1.0		.8	.8
		2 177.1	5 66.8	4 91.7		Sales/Receivables	3 108.7	4 99.6
		16 23.4	15 24.4	20 18.6			16 23.2	18 19.8
		23 15.6	23 16.0	27 13.3			39 9.4	39 9.4
						Cost of Sales/Inventory		
						Cost of Sales/Payables		
			3.8	11.4	7.4		6.6	6.1
			7.8	18.6	25.5	Sales/Working Capital	19.8	15.1
			28.5	-43.8	37.0		-55.5	163.1
			51.8				12.9	22.5
			(14) 12.1			EBIT/Interest	(52) 5.1	(46) 6.0
			-5.1				1.5	1.9
						Net Profit + Depr., Dep.,	20.8	
						Amort./Cur. Mat. L/T/D	(12) 6.3	
							1.8	
			.0	.0	.0		.1	.1
			.2	.1	.1	Fixed/Worth	.4	.3
			.5	.4	.7		3.1	1.1
			.6	.7	.8		.8	.7
			1.1	1.4	1.4	Debt/Worth	2.0	1.3
			4.4	4.1	3.2		14.6	9.7
			45.8	41.2	41.1		71.0	44.3
		(30) 11.7	(16) 7.9	(16) 13.0		% Profit Before Taxes/Tangible Net Worth	(81) 23.1	(65) 18.7
			.0	.5	7.5		6.2	5.7
			11.4	16.8	11.8		18.9	14.9
			4.4	4.3	5.1	% Profit Before Taxes/Total Assets	8.2	8.2
			-1.2	.4	2.9		.6	2.4
			999.8	283.6	999.8		165.1	154.6
			92.5	69.7	69.2	Sales/Net Fixed Assets	38.9	20.1
			16.5	32.6	10.9		10.3	8.4
			3.8	4.6	4.5		4.1	3.9
			1.9	3.6	3.0	Sales/Total Assets	3.0	2.2
			.9	2.7	1.4		1.5	1.2
			.2	.2	.2		.4	.3
		(22) .5	(16) .4	(12) .4		% Depr., Dep., Amort./Sales	(65) 1.0	(58) 1.5
			1.6	.8	2.6		2.7	2.9
						% Officers', Directors'	6.9	
						Owners' Comp/Sales	(12) 17.3	
							38.6	
5123M	17492M	250794M	2471563M	4973769M	8482201M	Net Sales ($)	13116850M	9971497M
769M	7117M	51540M	888601M	1341810M	3010558M	Total Assets ($)	5289526M	4103183M

M = $ thousand   MM = $ million
See Pages 9 through 22 for Explanation of Ratios and Data

Comparative Historical Data				Current Data Sorted by Sales					

			Type of Statement						
46	51	43	Unqualified	1	3	1	1		37
	1		Reviewed						
5	11	2	Compiled	1					1
2	1	4	Tax Returns		2	1	1		
26	33	37	Other	2	3		1	3	28
4/1/08-3/31/09 ALL	4/1/09-3/31/10 ALL	4/1/10-3/31/11 ALL		12 (4/1-9/30/10)			74 (10/1/10-3/31/11)		
				0-1MM	1-3MM	3-5MM	5-10MM	10-25MM	25MM & OVER
79	97	86	NUMBER OF STATEMENTS	4	8	2	3	3	66
%	%	%	ASSETS	%	%	%	%	%	%
43.5	43.0	47.1	Cash & Equivalents						48.6
15.0	16.3	12.8	Trade Receivables (net)						14.6
.5	.4	.3	Inventory						.4
4.7	5.4	7.5	All Other Current						6.2
63.6	65.1	67.6	Total Current						69.8
12.8	15.6	12.5	Fixed Assets (net)						10.1
8.1	7.3	5.6	Intangibles (net)						4.2
15.5	12.0	14.2	All Other Non-Current						16.0
100.0	100.0	100.0	Total						100.0
			LIABILITIES						
9.5	3.7	.5	Notes Payable-Short Term						.4
1.2	1.2	1.3	Cur. Mat.-L.T.D.						1.3
13.4	12.9	17.5	Trade Payables						18.2
.4	.2	.3	Income Taxes Payable						.4
28.4	26.2	24.7	All Other Current						25.0
52.8	44.2	44.3	Total Current						45.4
8.8	10.3	12.7	Long-Term Debt						10.4
.3	.5	.7	Deferred Taxes						.6
5.1	6.1	6.6	All Other Non-Current						4.5
33.0	39.0	35.7	Net Worth						39.1
100.0	100.0	100.0	Total Liabilities & Net Worth						100.0
			INCOME DATA						
100.0	100.0	100.0	Net Sales						100.0
			Gross Profit						
93.4	93.8	92.1	Operating Expenses						96.7
6.6	6.2	7.9	Operating Profit						3.3
.6	.4	2.1	All Other Expenses (net)						.1
6.0	5.7	5.9	Profit Before Taxes						3.2
			RATIOS						
2.3 1.5 1.0	3.3 1.6 1.0	2.4 1.4 1.1	Current						2.3 1.4 1.2
2.0 1.4 .9	3.0 1.5 .8	2.3 1.3 .9	Quick						2.1 1.3 1.0
(3) 134.6 (18) 20.3 (36) 10.0	(5) 77.4 (18) 20.4 (33) 10.9	(2) 149.1 (15) 24.6 (25) 14.9	Sales/Receivables						(4) 93.9 (16) 22.5 (23) 15.6
			Cost of Sales/Inventory						
			Cost of Sales/Payables						
7.3 15.9 -55.4	5.2 12.3 UND	5.8 17.1 77.5	Sales/Working Capital						7.3 17.1 46.6
(37) 25.6 9.7 1.6	(53) 58.4 6.6 1.9	(40) 51.5 6.6 1.4	EBIT/Interest						(30) 56.8 6.6 1.9
(11) 17.1 12.0 .4	(17) 18.6 4.0 1.1	(14) 9.6 5.8 1.5	Net Profit + Depr., Dep., Amort./Cur. Mat. L/T/D						(13) 9.7 5.5 1.4
.0 .2 .8	.0 .3 1.4	.0 .2 1.6	Fixed/Worth						.0 .1 .5
.6 1.3 11.4	.6 1.5 11.5	.7 1.3 14.6	Debt/Worth						.7 1.2 3.6
(65) 41.8 16.6 2.5	(81) 38.3 15.9 1.1	(73) 42.6 13.0 3.0	% Profit Before Taxes/Tangible Net Worth						(58) 44.2 11.7 3.2
11.6 5.0 1.1	13.8 6.1 .4	15.8 5.1 .6	% Profit Before Taxes/Total Assets						16.6 5.2 .7
295.7 60.9 13.0	362.1 43.6 10.9	625.0 71.3 19.2	Sales/Net Fixed Assets						509.8 70.3 21.1
4.0 2.8 1.2	4.2 2.4 1.0	4.6 2.8 1.4	Sales/Total Assets						4.7 3.4 1.9
(55) .2 .7 2.4	(65) .2 .8 2.8	(58) .2 .5 1.8	% Depr., Dep., Amort./Sales						(50) .2 .4 1.7
	(11) 4.7 7.5 14.2	(10) 4.1 7.5 10.2	% Officers', Directors' Owners' Comp/Sales						
12004306M 4268118M	12983816M 4754326M	16200942M 5300395M	Net Sales ($) Total Assets ($)	3158M 31799M	14161M 75290M	7011M 4097M	20667M 24177M	50084M 97430M	16105861M 5067602M

© RMA 2011

M = $ thousand   MM = $ million

See Pages 9 through 22 for Explanation of Ratios and Data

Current Data Sorted by Assets							Comparative Historical Data	
0-500M	500M-2MM	2-10MM	11 (4/1-9/30/10) 10-50MM	62 (10/1/10-3/31/11) 50-100MM	100-250MM	Type of Statement	4/1/06-3/31/07 ALL	4/1/07-3/31/08 ALL
	2	2	6	3	7	Unqualified	36	23
	1		1			Reviewed	2	
	2	3				Compiled	8	1
2	3		1	1		Tax Returns	7	3
4	2		10	11	12	Other	29	46
6	10	5	18	15	19	NUMBER OF STATEMENTS	82	73
%	%	%	%	%	%	ASSETS	%	%
	31.0		56.9	53.8	52.4	Cash & Equivalents	45.8	41.6
	27.8		15.0	11.4	15.8	Trade Receivables (net)	11.1	10.8
	.0		.0	.0	.0	Inventory	.1	.6
	2.7		2.3	1.6	10.0	All Other Current	8.7	9.8
	61.5		74.2	66.7	78.3	Total Current	65.8	62.8
	13.0		4.6	.6	1.6	Fixed Assets (net)	5.8	5.2
	7.5		1.1	.0	2.3	Intangibles (net)	3.5	4.1
	18.0		20.1	32.7	17.8	All Other Non-Current	24.9	27.9
	100.0		100.0	100.0	100.0	Total	100.0	100.0
						LIABILITIES		
	5.8		.3	2.1	.1	Notes Payable-Short Term	7.2	6.2
	2.0		.2	.0	.3	Cur. Mat.-L.T.D.	1.3	.5
	26.9		13.0	4.2	5.2	Trade Payables	14.5	8.2
	.2		.4	.3	.2	Income Taxes Payable	.7	.5
	13.7		41.4	38.7	43.8	All Other Current	25.9	32.5
	48.6		55.3	45.4	49.6	Total Current	49.7	48.0
	11.5		1.1	2.4	2.1	Long-Term Debt	14.7	11.8
	.0		.0	.0	.3	Deferred Taxes	.1	.1
	13.5		3.0	8.5	9.0	All Other Non-Current	18.3	9.1
	26.5		40.6	43.7	39.1	Net Worth	17.3	31.1
	100.0		100.0	100.0	100.0	Total Liabilities & Net Worth	100.0	100.0
						INCOME DATA		
	100.0		100.0	100.0	100.0	Net Sales	100.0	100.0
						Gross Profit		
	84.0		93.2	97.8	95.6	Operating Expenses	85.9	83.6
	16.0		6.8	2.2	4.4	Operating Profit	14.1	16.4
	-1.8		-3.6	-6.6	-1.8	All Other Expenses (net)	-1.8	-.7
	17.8		10.5	8.9	6.2	Profit Before Taxes	15.8	17.1
						RATIOS		
	2.3		2.0	3.1	2.4	Current	2.3	1.9
	1.2		1.5	1.9	1.8		1.5	1.4
	.9		1.0	1.0	1.0		.9	1.0
	1.9		1.9	3.1	2.2	Quick	2.2	1.7
	1.2		1.5	1.9	1.7		1.3	1.2
	.9		.9	1.0	.5		.8	.6
0 UND	0 UND	18 19.8	38 9.7	65 5.6		Sales/Receivables	0 UND	0 UND
17 21.1	76 4.8	53 6.8	91 4.0				23 15.8	33 11.2
224 1.6	99 3.7	91 4.0	173 2.1				64 5.7	81 4.5
						Cost of Sales/Inventory		
						Cost of Sales/Payables		
	1.9		1.0	.7	.6	Sales/Working Capital	1.1	1.3
	92.3		3.2	1.2	1.5		3.7	4.0
	-19.5		-35.6	-22.7	14.4		-43.1	112.3
						EBIT/Interest	73.3	25.1
							(32) 12.9	(32) 7.1
							2.9	3.4
						Net Profit + Depr., Dep., Amort./Cur. Mat. L/T/D		
	.0		.0	.0	.0	Fixed/Worth	.0	.0
	.3		.0	.0	.0		.0	.0
	.9		.1	.0	.1		.4	.1
	.6		.9	.7	.9	Debt/Worth	1.1	1.0
	2.8		1.4	1.1	1.6		2.3	1.9
	13.0		2.1	3.2	3.1		4.4	3.8
			29.1	9.5	12.5	% Profit Before Taxes/Tangible Net Worth	44.7	34.5
	(17) 12.7		5.4	(18) 8.4			(70) 22.0	(67) 19.9
	1.8		1.3	5.8			12.5	10.8
	6.3		11.6	4.3	6.2	% Profit Before Taxes/Total Assets	13.6	12.5
	2.9		4.5	2.6	3.3		6.0	7.9
	1.6		-.4	.1	1.7		2.8	2.8
	UND		UND	UND	648.7	Sales/Net Fixed Assets	UND	UND
	54.2		197.2	112.9	36.9		67.6	41.3
	13.2		17.3	33.9	19.7		22.1	18.7
	1.7		1.0	.6	.5	Sales/Total Assets	1.4	1.0
	.9		.5	.3	.4		.5	.5
	.2		.3	.2	.2		.4	.3
						% Depr., Dep., Amort./Sales	.6	.6
							(39) 1.2	(32) 1.1
							2.5	1.8
						% Officers', Directors' Owners' Comp/Sales	4.2	
							(13) 10.9	
							23.9	
6807M	14797M	23946M	267508M	401736M	1558890M	Net Sales ($)	1934552M	2119747M
1760M	11365M	17492M	420258M	1084841M	3258742M	Total Assets ($)	4027570M	4220942M

© RMA 2011

M = $ thousand   MM = $ million
See Pages 9 through 22 for Explanation of Ratios and Data

Comparative Historical Data — Current Data Sorted by Sales

4/1/08-3/31/09 ALL	4/1/09-3/31/10 ALL	4/1/10-3/31/11 ALL	Type of Statement	0-1MM	1-3MM	3-5MM	5-10MM	10-25MM	25MM & OVER
28	32	20	Unqualified	3		4		5	8
2	3	2	Reviewed		1		1		
	5	5	Compiled	1	1	2		1	
5	3	7	Tax Returns	2	1		1	1	2
44	39	39	Other	6	1		3	10	19
				11 (4/1-9/30/10)			62 (10/1/10-3/31/11)		
79	82	73	**NUMBER OF STATEMENTS**	12	4	6	5	17	29
%	%	%	**ASSETS**	%	%	%	%	%	%
47.7	44.8	49.5	Cash & Equivalents	42.1				60.0	51.6
12.9	13.8	15.7	Trade Receivables (net)	14.5				8.1	16.0
.0	.3	.0	Inventory	.0				.0	.0
9.4	8.3	4.2	All Other Current	3.2				1.7	7.3
70.0	67.2	69.4	Total Current	59.9				69.8	74.9
6.9	3.3	4.0	Fixed Assets (net)	11.9				3.1	2.1
5.8	2.5	5.3	Intangibles (net)	8.5				3.3	2.2
17.3	27.0	21.3	All Other Non-Current	19.7				23.9	20.8
100.0	100.0	100.0	Total	100.0				100.0	100.0
			LIABILITIES						
1.3	4.2	3.8	Notes Payable-Short Term	15.6				1.4	1.2
1.4	1.1	.7	Cur. Mat.-L.T.D.	1.9				.0	.3
12.5	13.6	10.6	Trade Payables	10.1				7.5	4.7
.6	.2	.3	Income Taxes Payable	.1				.2	.3
34.2	33.6	35.6	All Other Current	9.1				39.8	41.8
50.0	52.7	51.0	Total Current	36.9				48.9	48.3
8.9	4.0	5.0	Long-Term Debt	18.1				2.2	3.0
.2	.0	.1	Deferred Taxes	.0				.0	.2
13.1	9.0	6.7	All Other Non-Current	.4				6.9	7.5
27.9	34.2	37.2	Net Worth	44.5				42.1	40.9
100.0	100.0	100.0	Total Liabilities & Net Worth	100.0				100.0	100.0
			INCOME DATA						
100.0	100.0	100.0	Net Sales	100.0				100.0	100.0
			Gross Profit						
90.4	90.6	92.6	Operating Expenses	83.0				96.9	95.5
9.6	9.4	7.4	Operating Profit	17.0				3.1	4.5
-1.2	-1.1	-2.9	All Other Expenses (net)	-.1				-5.5	-2.5
10.8	10.6	10.2	Profit Before Taxes	17.0				8.5	7.0
			RATIOS						
2.6	1.9	2.1		7.0				3.1	2.1
1.7	1.5	1.6	Current	1.8				1.5	1.8
1.1	1.0	.9		.7				.8	1.1
2.5	1.7	2.1		6.9				3.1	2.1
1.3	1.3	1.5	Quick	1.5				1.5	1.8
.8	.7	.7		.7				1.5	.8
0 UND	2 188.6	7 51.7		0 UND			34 10.8		36 10.0
45 8.2	39 9.3	65 5.6	Sales/Receivables	0 UND			53 6.8		90 4.0
97 3.8	109 3.3	127 2.9		63 5.8			76 4.8		156 2.3
			Cost of Sales/Inventory						
			Cost of Sales/Payables						
1.0	1.0	.8		1.0				.7	.8
3.6	3.9	4.3	Sales/Working Capital	6.8				1.9	1.8
156.1	NM	-19.5		-13.6				-14.5	14.1
15.6	17.6	26.8							
(33) 4.9	(30) 3.6	(24) 11.9	EBIT/Interest						
-1.0	2.2	3.0							
			Net Profit + Depr., Dep., Amort./Cur. Mat. L/T/D						
.0	.0	.0		.0				.0	.0
.0	.0	.0	Fixed/Worth	.0				.0	.0
.3	.2	.1		.3				.0	.1
1.3	.8	.9		.2				.7	.9
2.4	2.0	1.6	Debt/Worth	1.1				1.1	1.4
13.8	4.6	3.6		4.8				3.6	2.8
45.3	20.7	16.4		41.5				9.5	14.9
(66) 12.6	(75) 9.8	(65) 7.9	% Profit Before Taxes/Tangible Net Worth	(10) 7.4				(15) 5.4	(28) 8.4
1.0	2.5	4.0		2.4				-7.5	4.5
12.2	7.0	7.9		8.8				6.4	8.3
4.8	3.3	3.3	% Profit Before Taxes/Total Assets	2.9				3.4	3.3
-.1	.4	1.2		1.3				-2.8	1.6
UND	UND	UND		UND				UND	UND
67.7	116.5	88.6	Sales/Net Fixed Assets	UND				108.9	51.3
20.4	21.7	27.6		11.9				26.7	26.2
1.0	1.2	1.0		1.7				.9	.6
.5	.5	.5	Sales/Total Assets	1.1				.5	.5
.3	.3	.3		.2				.2	.3
.2	.5	.4							
(31) 1.2	(28) 1.0	(21) .9	% Depr., Dep., Amort./Sales						
2.4	1.7	1.8							
	5.7	1.9							
	(10) 9.9	(15) 9.3	% Officers', Directors' Owners' Comp/Sales						
	22.1	22.8							
3013461M	2439278M	2273684M	Net Sales ($)	6707M	6236M	23216M	33223M	277555M	1926747M
5325827M	5236832M	4794458M	Total Assets ($)	9846M	7663M	65940M	75431M	730493M	3905085M

M = $ thousand   MM = $ million
See Pages 9 through 22 for Explanation of Ratios and Data

FINANCE—Direct Title Insurance Carriers NAICS 524127

Current Data Sorted by Assets | Comparative Historical Data

						Type of Statement		
1	1	6	6	1	1	Unqualified	25	20
		1			1	Reviewed	5	2
	1					Compiled	7	2
2	1	2				Tax Returns	13	11
2	6	5	3	2		Other	42	37
		4 (4/1-9/30/10)	38 (10/1/10-3/31/11)				4/1/06-3/31/07	4/1/07-3/31/08
0-500M	500M-2MM	2-10MM	10-50MM	50-100MM	100-250MM		ALL	ALL
5	9	14	9	3	2	NUMBER OF STATEMENTS	92	72
%	%	%	%	%	%	ASSETS	%	%
		42.9				Cash & Equivalents	40.0	32.8
		4.6				Trade Receivables (net)	6.2	6.7
		.1				Inventory	1.1	1.7
		5.7				All Other Current	8.9	10.7
		53.3				Total Current	56.2	51.8
		15.7				Fixed Assets (net)	19.0	19.1
		11.3				Intangibles (net)	7.2	9.8
		19.7				All Other Non-Current	17.6	19.3
		100.0				Total	100.0	100.0
						LIABILITIES		
		6.1				Notes Payable-Short Term	6.5	11.3
		2.2				Cur. Mat.-L.T.D.	1.8	1.6
		6.8				Trade Payables	8.9	9.8
		.0				Income Taxes Payable	.4	.8
		19.5				All Other Current	20.7	20.1
		34.6				Total Current	38.3	43.6
		6.6				Long-Term Debt	10.7	13.3
		1.3				Deferred Taxes	.5	.5
		13.7				All Other Non-Current	8.3	13.0
		43.8				Net Worth	42.2	29.6
		100.0				Total Liabilities & Net Worth	100.0	100.0
						INCOME DATA		
		100.0				Net Sales	100.0	100.0
						Gross Profit		
		96.2				Operating Expenses	94.4	101.7
		3.8				Operating Profit	5.6	-1.7
		.8				All Other Expenses (net)	-1.2	-2.6
		3.0				Profit Before Taxes	6.8	.9
						RATIOS		
		3.6				Current	2.6	3.0
		1.7					1.5	1.2
		1.2					1.0	.7
		3.5				Quick	2.4	2.3
		1.6					(91) 1.3	(71) 1.0
		1.0					.6	.5
		0 UND				Sales/Receivables	0 968.5	0 UND
		3 117.4					4 92.6	5 69.5
		16 22.4					12 30.0	15 24.5
						Cost of Sales/Inventory		
						Cost of Sales/Payables		
		5.8				Sales/Working Capital	6.2	7.4
		13.3					19.1	24.7
		31.2					999.8	-21.9
		20.6				EBIT/Interest	38.4	7.1
		(11) 11.3					(58) 9.2	(39) 1.6
		-.8					-.3	-6.1
		28.9				Net Profit + Depr., Dep., Amort./Cur. Mat. L/T/D		5.2
		4.6					(16)	(11) 1.2
		.5						-2.3
		.2				Fixed/Worth	.1	.1
		.5					.4	.4
		NM					1.3	NM
		.7				Debt/Worth	.5	.6
		1.4					1.0	1.3
		NM					7.4	-84.7
		58.0				% Profit Before Taxes/Tangible Net Worth	88.9	48.9
		(11) 31.6					(80) 31.8	(53) 3.2
		15.4					-5.0	-29.1
		26.5				% Profit Before Taxes/Total Assets	34.3	16.4
		8.4					9.3	1.0
		.1					-4.2	-19.0
		110.1				Sales/Net Fixed Assets	52.4	60.1
		20.4					18.8	17.2
		8.0					8.6	8.9
		2.9				Sales/Total Assets	4.0	4.2
		1.9					2.3	2.3
		1.2					1.3	1.3
		.3				% Depr., Dep., Amort./Sales	1.3	1.2
		(13) 1.8					(62) 2.0	(51) 2.1
		3.4					3.0	3.3
						% Officers', Directors' Owners' Comp/Sales	4.3	6.6
							(21) 9.0	(17) 14.2
							17.8	22.9
4771M	33504M	140372M	469651M	314885M	1505938M	Net Sales ($)	3700935M	3359721M
1237M	10327M	67393M	247437M	207292M	329116M	Total Assets ($)	1693159M	1672663M

M = $ thousand   MM = $ million
See Pages 9 through 22 for Explanation of Ratios and Data

Comparative Historical Data | | | | Current Data Sorted by Sales

			Type of Statement	0-1MM	1-3MM	3-5MM	5-10MM	10-25MM	25MM & OVER
17	9	16	Unqualified	1	2		2	3	8
2	2	1	Reviewed		1				
3	3	2	Compiled			1			1
8	8	5	Tax Returns	1		1			
21	17	18	Other	4	3	3	1	2	4
4/1/08- 3/31/09 ALL	4/1/09- 3/31/10 ALL	4/1/10- 3/31/11 ALL		4 (4/1-9/30/10)			38 (10/1/10-3/31/11)		
51	39	42	**NUMBER OF STATEMENTS**	6	8	4	6	5	13
%	%	%	**ASSETS**	%	%	%	%	%	%
33.3	31.6	36.0	Cash & Equivalents						37.0
7.0	5.3	7.4	Trade Receivables (net)						4.9
1.4	.3	.0	Inventory						.0
11.3	5.5	10.7	All Other Current						15.8
53.1	42.8	54.2	Total Current						57.7
18.7	24.1	15.2	Fixed Assets (net)						14.7
6.6	13.9	12.3	Intangibles (net)						13.6
21.7	19.3	18.4	All Other Non-Current						14.0
100.0	100.0	100.0	Total						100.0
			LIABILITIES						
17.1	9.9	6.8	Notes Payable-Short Term						6.7
1.7	2.1	2.9	Cur. Mat.-L.T.D.						4.6
7.2	5.6	9.7	Trade Payables						10.9
1.0	.6	.4	Income Taxes Payable						1.1
18.8	13.3	21.1	All Other Current						13.2
45.9	31.5	40.9	Total Current						36.5
13.6	24.1	12.5	Long-Term Debt						14.2
.3	.7	.8	Deferred Taxes						.8
10.7	13.3	12.1	All Other Non-Current						17.9
29.6	30.5	33.7	Net Worth						30.6
100.0	100.0	100.0	Total Liabilities & Net Worth						100.0
			INCOME DATA						
100.0	100.0	100.0	Net Sales						100.0
			Gross Profit						
102.2	92.6	92.2	Operating Expenses						94.1
-2.2	7.4	7.8	Operating Profit						5.9
1.4	2.9	.9	All Other Expenses (net)						-.4
-3.6	4.5	7.0	Profit Before Taxes						6.3
			RATIOS						
2.9	4.3	3.5	Current						2.5
1.6	1.5	1.6							1.9
.9	1.0	1.0							1.1
2.4	2.6	2.9	Quick						2.1
1.1	1.4	1.4							1.7
.5	.9	.6							.8
0 UND	0 UND	0 UND	Sales/Receivables						4 90.1
8 45.4	3 110.5	5 66.4							8 43.0
21 17.7	14 27.0	16 23.3							15 24.6
			Cost of Sales/Inventory						
			Cost of Sales/Payables						
5.5	6.7	5.1	Sales/Working Capital						3.3
13.4	18.4	12.7							8.8
-55.5	368.1	NM							162.7
6.0	37.1	33.3	EBIT/Interest						48.8
(28) -.5	(28) 5.3	(31) 6.6						(10)	27.0
-17.6	.4	1.4							5.5
			Net Profit + Depr., Dep., Amort./Cur. Mat. L/T/D						
.1	.2	.2	Fixed/Worth						.1
.3	.9	.5							.3
1.9	-.6	18.2							.9
.4	.6	.7	Debt/Worth						.9
1.8	1.8	2.4							1.3
16.0	-7.3	77.8							8.3
33.3	90.0	66.3	% Profit Before Taxes/Tangible Net Worth						72.8
(40) -4.4	(28) 22.7	(33) 27.9						(11)	27.9
-47.6	-1.5	-.9							6.9
11.5	32.9	24.4	% Profit Before Taxes/Total Assets						20.7
-4.6	6.3	6.7							6.8
-21.7	-1.5	.1							3.8
49.1	56.0	108.6	Sales/Net Fixed Assets						78.0
19.8	21.8	30.6							16.6
11.4	7.0	10.5							9.8
3.7	3.5	3.6	Sales/Total Assets						4.3
1.9	2.3	1.9							2.1
1.0	.8	1.0							.9
1.0	.7	.4	% Depr., Dep., Amort./Sales						.4
(36) 2.6	(27) 1.3	(34) 1.2						(11)	1.3
3.5	3.5	2.1							2.2
			% Officers', Directors' Owners' Comp/Sales						
1919185M	1172388M	2469121M	Net Sales ($)	3222M	16692M	15896M	44844M	70983M	2317484M
1162627M	880119M	862802M	Total Assets ($)	3821M	38646M	16967M	24466M	24737M	754165M

© RMA 2011

M = $ thousand   MM = $ million
See Pages 9 through 22 for Explanation of Ratios and Data

Current Data Sorted by Assets | **Comparative Historical Data**

0-500M	500M-2MM	2-10MM	10-50MM	50-100MM	100-250MM		4/1/06-3/31/07 ALL	4/1/07-3/31/08 ALL
						Type of Statement		
1	1	7	3	3	10	Unqualified	32	29
	2	1				Reviewed	3	3
		2				Compiled	1	2
4	3					Tax Returns	2	6
2	2	1	7	5	6	Other	24	25
10 (4/1-9/30/10)			50 (10/1/10-3/31/11)					
7	8	11	10	8	¹16	**NUMBER OF STATEMENTS**	62	65
%	%	%	%	%	%	**ASSETS**	%	%
		44.4	62.0		58.2	Cash & Equivalents	47.9	49.0
		7.2	12.1		6.1	Trade Receivables (net)	9.4	11.0
		.0	.2		.1	Inventory	.1	.0
		12.4	4.7		2.0	All Other Current	5.7	7.1
		64.0	79.0		66.4	Total Current	63.2	67.1
		9.3	3.9		3.0	Fixed Assets (net)	7.9	7.6
		2.2	3.8		9.2	Intangibles (net)	11.7	5.6
		24.5	13.3		21.4	All Other Non-Current	17.2	19.7
		100.0	100.0		100.0	Total	100.0	100.0
						LIABILITIES		
		.0	.0		.2	Notes Payable-Short Term	3.3	8.2
		.4	1.0		.3	Cur. Mat.-L.T.D.	4.0	2.5
		11.8	7.0		11.8	Trade Payables	13.4	11.7
		.0	.0		.3	Income Taxes Payable	.7	.8
		35.9	37.1		32.6	All Other Current	27.7	26.0
		48.2	45.0		45.3	Total Current	49.1	49.3
		7.6	5.1		5.3	Long-Term Debt	8.8	5.1
		.7	.0		1.0	Deferred Taxes	.2	.3
		3.6	2.8		7.6	All Other Non-Current	10.1	13.5
		39.8	47.1		40.8	Net Worth	31.7	31.9
		100.0	100.0		100.0	Total Liabilities & Net Worth	100.0	100.0
						INCOME DATA		
		100.0	100.0		100.0	Net Sales	100.0	100.0
						Gross Profit		
		87.2	82.6		94.3	Operating Expenses	86.1	88.8
		12.8	17.4		5.7	Operating Profit	13.9	11.2
		.4	-1.6		-2.6	All Other Expenses (net)	.0	-.2
		12.4	19.0		8.3	Profit Before Taxes	13.8	11.4
						RATIOS		
		2.2	4.4		2.4		2.4	2.7
		1.4	1.7		1.6	Current	1.2	1.6
		1.0	1.3		1.1		.8	1.0
		1.8	4.2		2.4		2.1	2.6
		1.1	1.6		1.5	Quick	1.1	1.4
		.5	1.3		1.1		.7	.8
		1 470.9	0 UND		9 41.2		0 UND	0 UND
		7 52.5	2 212.6		23 16.1	Sales/Receivables	11 32.7	8 46.2
		37 9.9	31 11.9		74 4.9		63 5.8	43 8.4
						Cost of Sales/Inventory		
						Cost of Sales/Payables		
		6.0	1.2		1.1		2.4	1.8
		8.1	3.9		2.5	Sales/Working Capital	10.3	4.9
		71.4	12.9		11.5		-7.5	UND
					36.6		34.5	21.7
					(12) 9.2	EBIT/Interest	(35) 8.9	(28) 9.1
					-.3		4.2	1.4
						Net Profit + Depr., Dep., Amort./Cur. Mat. L/T/D		
		.0	.0		.0		.0	.0
		.1	.0		.1	Fixed/Worth	.1	.0
		.4	.1		.3		2.2	1.4
		.7	.4		.9		1.0	1.3
		2.2	1.4		2.1	Debt/Worth	3.0	3.0
		3.3	6.2		6.2		26.7	8.0
		56.4	93.3		21.0		59.5	61.5
		12.3	18.5		(14) 11.1	% Profit Before Taxes/Tangible Net Worth	(48) 36.7	(57) 31.1
		-1.0	9.8		.1		11.9	9.9
		7.3	13.4		6.2		19.1	14.9
		4.4	9.5		4.0	% Profit Before Taxes/Total Assets	8.1	5.6
		-.3	5.7		.3		1.9	1.7
		UND	UND		256.6		UND	UND
		238.9	UND		42.2	Sales/Net Fixed Assets	64.6	127.9
		10.7	291.5		9.9		21.7	23.6
		2.6	3.1		.7		2.2	2.4
		.9	1.0		.4	Sales/Total Assets	.7	.7
		.5	.3		.3		.5	.4
							.5	.5
						% Depr., Dep., Amort./Sales	(26) 1.2	(27) 1.1
							1.6	2.2
								3.3
						% Officers', Directors' Owners' Comp/Sales		(10) 9.0
								15.2
5296M	28850M	76690M	440270M	566914M	1917897M	Net Sales ($)	2489434M	2824851M
1712M	9039M	57183M	258223M	627919M	2877136M	Total Assets ($)	3367493M	2968794M

M = $ thousand   MM = $ million
See Pages 9 through 22 for Explanation of Ratios and Data

Comparative Historical Data   Current Data Sorted by Sales

4/1/08-3/31/09 ALL	4/1/09-3/31/10 ALL	4/1/10-3/31/11 ALL	Type of Statement	0-1MM	1-3MM	3-5MM	5-10MM	10-25MM	25MM & OVER
33	25	25	Unqualified	2	4	1	3	2	13
3		1	Reviewed		1				
5	3	4	Compiled		2		1		1
4	10	7	Tax Returns	4	2			1	
29	19	23	Other	2	1	1	3	5	11
				10 (4/1-9/30/10)			**50 (10/1/10-3/31/11)**		
74	57	60	**NUMBER OF STATEMENTS**	8	10	2	7	8	25
%	%	%	**ASSETS**	%	%	%	%	%	%
52.1	48.5	51.1	Cash & Equivalents		66.1				54.2
9.7	8.7	11.6	Trade Receivables (net)		10.5				11.3
.2	.8	.6	Inventory		.0				.1
5.0	5.0	5.8	All Other Current		2.3				4.1
67.0	63.0	69.1	Total Current		78.9				69.8
5.4	3.8	5.7	Fixed Assets (net)		6.3				5.0
4.6	10.5	5.6	Intangibles (net)		4.9				8.9
23.0	22.7	19.7	All Other Non-Current		9.9				16.3
100.0	100.0	100.0	Total		100.0				100.0
			LIABILITIES						
4.7	10.6	4.9	Notes Payable-Short Term		9.5				.1
.6	2.0	.4	Cur. Mat.-L.T.D.		.2				.6
10.6	10.2	12.3	Trade Payables		6.8				14.0
.6	.6	.1	Income Taxes Payable		.2				.2
31.1	28.2	31.0	All Other Current		36.0				29.3
47.6	51.5	48.7	Total Current		52.8				44.3
6.5	5.4	7.0	Long-Term Debt		6.2				6.9
.4	.7	.6	Deferred Taxes		.1				1.0
15.0	13.0	6.4	All Other Non-Current		9.7				5.9
30.5	29.4	37.4	Net Worth		31.2				41.9
100.0	100.0	100.0	Total Liabilities & Net Worth		100.0				100.0
			INCOME DATA						
100.0	100.0	100.0	Net Sales		100.0				100.0
			Gross Profit						
88.9	89.3	86.8	Operating Expenses		85.8				95.8
11.1	10.7	13.2	Operating Profit		14.2				4.2
.4	.1	-.2	All Other Expenses (net)		1.5				-2.1
10.7	10.7	13.3	Profit Before Taxes		12.7				6.3
			RATIOS						
2.7 / 1.6 / 1.0	2.8 / 1.5 / .9	2.4 / 1.5 / 1.0	Current		3.5 / 1.5 / 1.0				2.5 / 1.7 / 1.1
2.7 / 1.4 / .8	2.7 / 1.4 / .7	2.1 / 1.4 / .9	Quick		3.4 / 1.4 / 1.0				2.3 / 1.4 / 1.1
0 UND / 7 48.9 / 44 8.3	0 UND / 7 50.6 / 43 8.5	0 867.6 / 15 24.7 / 48 7.6	Sales/Receivables		0 UND / 13 28.2 / 34 10.6				8 44.3 / 25 14.8 / 59 6.2
			Cost of Sales/Inventory						
			Cost of Sales/Payables						
1.4 / 4.4 / 133.4	1.7 / 6.6 / -20.7	1.7 / 7.7 / 97.1	Sales/Working Capital		2.8 / 7.8 / UND				1.7 / 7.6 / 17.4
(31) 23.3 / 9.5 / 1.7	(26) 31.2 / 7.8 / .4	(30) 40.5 / 9.7 / 2.0	EBIT/Interest					(15) 39.2 / 9.2 / 3.9	
			Net Profit + Depr., Dep., Amort./Cur. Mat. L/T/D						
.0 / .0 / .4	.0 / .0 / .2	.0 / .0 / .3	Fixed/Worth		.0 / .0 / .3				.0 / .1 / .3
.9 / 2.2 / 14.4	.8 / 2.7 / 9.8	.9 / 2.1 / 10.5	Debt/Worth		1.4 / 2.2 / 7.5				.8 / 1.5 / 8.6
(62) 57.9 / 16.9 / 2.6	(48) 53.1 / 13.8 / 1.4	(53) 41.9 / 13.8 / 3.8	% Profit Before Taxes/Tangible Net Worth					(21) 18.6 / 11.1 / 6.5	
15.2 / 4.8 / .5	18.5 / 4.3 / .1	11.5 / 5.6 / .6	% Profit Before Taxes/Total Assets		116.9 / 6.0 / -1.2				8.1 / 4.7 / 2.7
UND / 283.3 / 40.4	UND / 164.0 / 26.6	UND / 254.3 / 25.6	Sales/Net Fixed Assets		UND / 405.2 / 67.2				279.6 / 57.0 / 8.5
2.4 / .7 / .3	2.3 / .7 / .4	2.6 / .7 / .3	Sales/Total Assets		5.2 / 1.7 / .5				2.5 / .7 / .4
(25) .3 / .7 / 1.3	(21) .3 / .9 / 1.8	(24) .3 / .6 / 1.9	% Depr., Dep., Amort./Sales					(14) .4 / .6 / 1.8	
(10) 2.7 / 15.6 / 25.9		(10) 2.5 / 8.6 / 18.6	% Officers', Directors' Owners' Comp/Sales						
2695775M	2398420M	3035917M	Net Sales ($)	3932M	21374M	8313M	50856M	141666M	2609776M
4184720M	3127302M	3831212M	Total Assets ($)	11739M	23284M	5149M	135911M	701004M	2954125M

M = $ thousand   MM = $ million
See Pages 9 through 22 for Explanation of Ratios and Data

Current Data Sorted by Assets

Comparative Historical Data

						Type of Statement		
3	5	28	48	12	23	Unqualified	119	100
6	25	40	20	2		Reviewed	117	111
21	38	34	5			Compiled	114	100
123	88	40	1		3	Tax Returns	242	242
66	77	86	53	12	19	Other	247	297
	116 (4/1-9/30/10)		762 (10/1/10-3/31/11)				4/1/06-3/31/07	4/1/07-3/31/08
0-500M	500M-2MM	2-10MM	10-50MM	50-100MM	100-250MM		ALL	ALL
219	233	228	127	26	45	NUMBER OF STATEMENTS	839	850
%	%	%	%	%	%	ASSETS	%	%
29.5	24.0	27.2	33.0	29.1	37.3	Cash & Equivalents	30.1	30.6
9.0	14.5	20.0	20.7	16.8	12.5	Trade Receivables (net)	18.9	17.9
.1	.5	.5	.0	.3	.0	Inventory	.2	.2
4.0	4.5	7.6	6.9	11.0	9.4	All Other Current	5.5	5.7
42.5	43.5	55.4	60.7	57.3	59.2	Total Current	54.9	54.5
22.1	17.8	13.3	8.7	10.2	2.7	Fixed Assets (net)	14.3	13.6
21.4	23.0	17.1	15.2	15.2	26.7	Intangibles (net)	15.5	17.5
14.0	15.7	14.2	15.4	17.3	11.4	All Other Non-Current	15.3	14.4
100.0	100.0	100.0	100.0	100.0	100.0	Total	100.0	100.0
						LIABILITIES		
30.4	7.5	6.3	3.6	.9	2.7	Notes Payable-Short Term	11.1	9.6
5.6	4.9	3.2	2.2	2.9	.7	Cur. Mat.-L.T.D.	3.5	4.1
12.7	19.1	23.5	22.0	16.5	11.0	Trade Payables	21.8	20.6
.0	.0	.1	.4	.1	.3	Income Taxes Payable	.4	.7
16.9	16.7	17.3	20.6	29.6	32.2	All Other Current	19.8	18.5
65.6	48.4	50.5	48.7	50.0	46.9	Total Current	56.5	53.5
30.9	22.1	21.3	12.9	16.8	10.9	Long-Term Debt	18.2	21.1
.0	.0	.4	.5	.6	.7	Deferred Taxes	.3	.2
10.1	8.0	4.3	6.5	11.5	4.4	All Other Non-Current	6.7	6.0
-6.6	21.5	23.5	31.3	21.1	37.0	Net Worth	18.3	19.2
100.0	100.0	100.0	100.0	100.0	100.0	Total Liabilities & Net Worth	100.0	100.0
						INCOME DATA		
100.0	100.0	100.0	100.0	100.0	100.0	Net Sales	100.0	100.0
						Gross Profit		
87.9	90.3	89.5	87.7	90.3	89.6	Operating Expenses	87.2	87.3
12.1	9.7	10.5	12.3	9.7	10.4	Operating Profit	12.8	12.7
1.6	2.3	2.5	1.9	-.2	1.3	All Other Expenses (net)	1.4	1.6
10.5	7.4	7.9	10.4	9.9	9.1	Profit Before Taxes	11.4	11.0
						RATIOS		
2.3	1.6	1.5	1.6	1.5	1.6		1.5	1.7
.7	1.0	1.0	1.2	1.1	1.3	Current	1.0	1.1
.3	.5	.7	.9	1.0	.9		.6	.7
2.1	1.3	1.3	1.5	1.4	1.4		1.4	1.5
.6	.9	.9	1.1	1.0	1.0	Quick	1.0	1.0
.3	.4	.5	.8	.6	.7		.5	.5
0 UND	0 UND	2 168.7	18 20.6	8 43.5	14 25.2		0 UND	0 UND
0 UND	7 51.3	28 12.9	47 7.7	28 13.2	58 6.3	Sales/Receivables	19 19.5	17 21.1
8 48.5	38 9.5	84 4.3	91 4.0	66 5.5	118 3.1		75 4.9	64 5.7
						Cost of Sales/Inventory		
						Cost of Sales/Payables		
33.8	14.2	6.4	3.6	6.3	1.4		8.0	7.7
-47.7	-622.3	77.7	11.6	25.3	8.5	Sales/Working Capital	93.1	66.6
-9.1	-10.7	-10.9	-36.0	379.2	-56.6		-12.0	-14.0
19.0	15.2	21.2	27.5	45.6	51.7		21.6	23.1
(147) 4.4	(177) 5.0	(169) 5.5	(83) 9.8	(21) 21.0	(27) 11.0	EBIT/Interest	(611) 7.4	(600) 5.9
1.1	1.6	2.0	2.3	11.3	1.3		2.5	1.6
	4.5	13.6	9.0				6.6	9.3
(23) 1.1	(29) 4.7	(23) 2.6			Net Profit + Depr., Dep.,	(107) 2.7	(104) 3.2
.4	.7	1.5			Amort./Cur. Mat. L/T/D	1.4	1.3
.2	.3	.1	.1	.3	.0		.1	.1
4.8	1.4	.9	.3	.8	.1	Fixed/Worth	.6	.7
-.3	-.2	-.7	2.9	-1.5	-1.4		-1.2	-1.0
.9	1.5	1.6	1.5	2.9	1.9		1.6	1.7
-16.6	14.3	8.1	3.7	7.1	5.6	Debt/Worth	6.8	6.8
-1.8	-2.9	-6.0	33.8	-21.1	-9.9		-6.6	-5.5
401.7	101.0	77.4	72.3	96.5	41.6	% Profit Before Taxes/Tangible	119.2	146.5
(105) 114.1	(128) 30.3	(146) 24.6	(99) 28.8	(18) 34.6	(31) 16.2	Net Worth	(565) 39.7	(559) 44.7
14.7	5.1	6.4	8.9	9.9	3.0		12.0	10.3
65.9	26.1	14.3	14.0	17.8	9.5	% Profit Before Taxes/Total	25.4	26.6
21.3	9.7	5.7	5.9	7.4	2.9	Assets	10.0	9.6
2.1	1.4	1.4	2.2	2.3	.5		2.5	1.4
284.1	97.5	99.2	67.4	32.6	87.0		111.3	101.6
46.7	29.7	30.2	23.4	15.6	41.5	Sales/Net Fixed Assets	28.8	29.8
15.2	11.1	13.2	8.6	5.6	16.5		12.5	11.7
8.7	3.6	2.1	1.2	1.2	.8		3.1	3.2
4.5	2.0	1.3	.9	1.0	.4	Sales/Total Assets	1.6	1.6
2.3	1.3	.8	.6	.7	.3		.9	.9
.5	.6	.8	1.4	1.6	.2		.7	.8
(107) .9	(144) 1.5	(149) 1.5	(87) 2.1	(20) 2.4	(18) .7	% Depr., Dep., Amort./Sales	(533) 1.5	(519) 1.6
2.4	2.6	2.6	4.0	3.5	1.9		2.7	2.9
10.0	6.7	5.6	2.1			% Officers', Directors'	7.1	8.2
(135) 17.4	(148) 12.7	(84) 12.7	(14) 5.9			Owners' Comp/Sales	(382) 14.6	(365) 14.1
24.6	20.9	19.7	11.5				23.1	22.2
237525M	699278M	1776273M	3014092M	2683190M	6392217M	Net Sales ($)	13221096M	12287714M
48786M	248586M	1057083M	2950539M	1884600M	7515120M	Total Assets ($)	10296333M	12645205M

© RMA 2011

M = $ thousand   MM = $ million
See Pages 9 through 22 for Explanation of Ratios and Data

Comparative Historical Data | Current Data Sorted by Sales

	Comparative Historical Data				Current Data Sorted by Sales					
Type of Statement										
Unqualified	101	107	119		5	7	9	19	28	51
Reviewed	98	92	93		8	21	17	19	16	12
Compiled	98	106	98		17	32	20	16	10	3
Tax Returns	250	262	255		108	84	30	17	8	8
Other	309	312	313		70	75	36	40	42	50
	4/1/08-3/31/09 ALL	4/1/09-3/31/10 ALL	4/1/10-3/31/11 ALL		116 (4/1-9/30/10)			762 (10/1/10-3/31/11)		
					0-1MM	1-3MM	3-5MM	5-10MM	10-25MM	25MM & OVER
NUMBER OF STATEMENTS	856	879	878		208	219	112	111	104	124
	%	%	%		%	%	%	%	%	%
ASSETS										
Cash & Equivalents	29.6	29.7	28.3		23.3	26.5	28.2	32.3	33.4	32.3
Trade Receivables (net)	18.3	16.9	15.4		9.1	15.3	21.3	17.8	16.8	17.6
Inventory	.1	.2	.3		.5	.0	.3	.6	.5	.1
All Other Current	6.2	6.4	6.0		3.7	4.1	5.3	6.5	8.3	11.4
Total Current	54.2	53.1	50.1		36.5	46.0	55.0	57.3	59.1	61.4
Fixed Assets (net)	14.1	13.1	15.4		23.9	16.2	11.6	13.0	10.6	9.4
Intangibles (net)	17.8	17.6	19.9		23.8	23.6	19.0	13.9	13.5	18.3
All Other Non-Current	13.9	16.1	14.7		15.8	14.3	14.4	15.8	16.9	11.0
Total	100.0	100.0	100.0		100.0	100.0	100.0	100.0	100.0	100.0
LIABILITIES										
Notes Payable-Short Term	10.5	10.4	11.9		22.2	14.6	9.2	6.8	6.0	1.8
Cur. Mat.-L.T.D.	3.3	4.8	4.0		4.6	4.6	3.6	3.1	5.3	1.9
Trade Payables	20.0	19.1	18.6		11.7	17.0	27.5	21.5	23.1	18.4
Income Taxes Payable	.3	.3	.1		.0	.0	.2	.1	.2	.4
All Other Current	20.5	20.0	18.7		16.0	13.5	16.3	23.7	20.9	28.0
Total Current	54.6	54.5	53.2		54.5	49.7	56.8	55.3	55.4	50.5
Long-Term Debt	20.5	19.5	22.0		33.3	24.1	19.2	15.0	15.9	13.4
Deferred Taxes	.2	.1	.3		.3	.0	.2	.1	.5	.5
All Other Non-Current	6.9	7.6	7.3		9.3	6.1	5.7	7.0	8.1	6.9
Net Worth	17.8	18.2	17.2		2.6	20.1	18.1	22.6	20.1	28.6
Total Liabilities & Net Worth	100.0	100.0	100.0		100.0	100.0	100.0	100.0	100.0	100.0
INCOME DATA										
Net Sales	100.0	100.0	100.0		100.0	100.0	100.0	100.0	100.0	100.0
Gross Profit										
Operating Expenses	89.3	88.1	89.1		81.8	90.4	92.7	92.7	91.9	90.2
Operating Profit	10.7	11.9	10.9		18.2	9.6	7.3	7.3	8.1	9.8
All Other Expenses (net)	2.1	2.3	2.0		5.3	1.5	1.6	.8	.6	.0
Profit Before Taxes	8.6	9.5	8.9		12.9	8.1	5.6	6.5	7.5	9.8
RATIOS										
Current	1.7 / 1.1 / .6	1.7 / 1.0 / .6	1.7 / 1.0 / .6		2.0 / .7 / .2	1.9 / 1.0 / .4	1.4 / 1.0 / .6	1.6 / 1.1 / .8	1.9 / 1.1 / .9	1.6 / 1.2 / .9
Quick	1.5 / 1.0 / .5	1.6 / .9 / .4	1.5 / .9 / .4		1.7 / .6 / .2	1.6 / .9 / .3	1.3 / .9 / .5	1.5 / 1.0 / .7	1.5 / 1.0 / .6	1.4 / 1.0 / .7
Sales/Receivables	0 UND / 18 20.6 / 66 5.5	0 UND / 17 21.6 / 59 6.2	0 UND / 13 27.9 / 53 6.9		0 UND / 0 UND / 11 34.7	0 UND / 9 40.7 / 39 9.4	5 80.6 / 24 14.9 / 73 5.0	1 426.9 / 20 17.8 / 71 5.1	1 347.5 / 25 14.8 / 52 7.1	13 27.5 / 38 9.6 / 91 4.0
Cost of Sales/Inventory										
Cost of Sales/Payables										
Sales/Working Capital	8.0 / 97.7 / -10.8	7.3 / 83.8 / -10.2	9.4 / 118.3 / -11.1		14.6 / -39.1 / -6.3	11.1 / 627.5 / -11.0	10.6 / -112.3 / -10.3	6.8 / 66.1 / -14.3	6.3 / 27.8 / -23.1	5.4 / 19.6 / -102.5
EBIT/Interest	18.3 / (591) 5.0 / 1.3	25.5 / (624) 6.0 / 1.8	21.7 / (624) 5.7 / 1.7		12.0 / (135) 3.9 / 1.4	10.8 / (167) 3.7 / 1.2	9.6 / (83) 3.7 / 1.2	26.2 / (80) 9.9 / 3.5	36.6 / (71) 10.8 / 2.0	50.2 / (88) 16.1 / 2.7
Net Profit + Depr., Dep., Amort./Cur. Mat. L/T/D	6.9 / (80) 2.1 / .9	8.0 / (98) 1.9 / .8	9.6 / (96) 2.6 / .7			5.5 / (20) 2.0 / .2	4.3 / (16) 1.0 / -.1	5.4 / (10) 2.6 / 1.0	18.4 / (22) 4.2 / 1.4	19.5 / (24) 8.9 / 2.0
Fixed/Worth	.1 / .6 / -.8	.1 / .6 / -.8	.1 / .9 / -.5		.1 / 3.9 / -.2	.1 / 1.4 / -.4	.2 / .9 / -.3	.1 / .8 / -1.1	.1 / .6 / -.7	.1 / .6 / -35.8
Debt/Worth	1.4 / 6.7 / -4.4	1.3 / 6.2 / -4.4	1.5 / 8.4 / -3.3		1.2 / UND / -1.7	1.2 / 16.8 / -2.5	2.0 / 12.1 / -3.7	1.5 / 6.9 / -7.6	1.0 / 4.6 / -10.9	1.9 / 4.2 / -244.8
% Profit Before Taxes/Tangible Net Worth	112.6 / (552) 36.3 / 5.9	119.7 / (567) 31.3 / 6.3	114.1 / (527) 33.8 / 7.1		242.2 / (105) 48.7 / 5.1	104.8 / (122) 39.7 / 4.0	88.0 / (63) 24.8 / 5.3	81.0 / (74) 21.6 / 7.8	112.8 / (74) 37.3 / 8.2	98.8 / (89) 34.9 / 13.3
% Profit Before Taxes/Total Assets	23.3 / 6.7 / .4	21.7 / 7.1 / 1.1	24.6 / 7.7 / 1.6		45.1 / 8.5 / 1.7	26.5 / 8.6 / 1.2	13.1 / 5.0 / .3	20.6 / 6.9 / 1.6	24.2 / 7.7 / 2.5	16.2 / 8.2 / 2.5
Sales/Net Fixed Assets	115.7 / 32.7 / 13.5	131.6 / 33.5 / 13.7	99.6 / 32.1 / 12.0		207.8 / 32.1 / 7.3	142.1 / 33.8 / 13.5	93.7 / 33.0 / 14.9	110.5 / 35.8 / 13.4	73.3 / 28.1 / 12.4	68.7 / 24.4 / 10.2
Sales/Total Assets	3.5 / 1.7 / .8	3.2 / 1.6 / .8	3.5 / 1.6 / .8		4.6 / 1.8 / .6	4.4 / 2.2 / 1.2	3.0 / 1.7 / 1.0	3.6 / 1.7 / .8	2.6 / 1.5 / 1.0	1.9 / 1.0 / .6
% Depr., Dep., Amort./Sales	.8 / (487) 1.4 / 2.7	.7 / (495) 1.4 / 2.6	.7 / (525) 1.6 / 2.7		.8 / (88) 2.3 / 6.7	.6 / (131) 1.5 / 2.6	.7 / (70) 1.3 / 2.1	.6 / (77) 1.4 / 2.4	.8 / (81) 1.6 / 2.6	.8 / (78) 1.7 / 3.2
% Officers', Directors' Owners' Comp/Sales	6.6 / (371) 13.7 / 22.7	7.1 / (389) 13.4 / 22.5	(391) 13.7 / 21.6		9.9 / (111) 16.8 / 24.6	6.9 / (132) 16.2 / 23.4	6.8 / (56) 12.0 / 20.6	3.3 / (51) 7.8 / 15.4	2.7 / (20) 7.7 / 18.1	1.8 / (21) 8.4 / 20.0
Net Sales ($)	11552528M	10809436M	14802575M		107606M	395804M	450176M	795073M	1608920M	11444996M
Total Assets ($)	11639528M	12505704M	13704714M		158022M	333705M	403049M	966292M	1528378M	10315268M

© RMA 2011

M = $ thousand   MM = $ million
See Pages 9 through 22 for Explanation of Ratios and Data

Current Data Sorted by Assets | Comparative Historical Data

Type of Statement	0-500M	500M-2MM	2-10MM	10-50MM	50-100MM	100-250MM		4/1/06-3/31/07 ALL	4/1/07-3/31/08 ALL
Unqualified		2	12	12	8	7		18	20
Reviewed		1	3					1	3
Compiled		2	3					4	1
Tax Returns	7	2	1					2	4
Other	6	8	14	12	1	7		21	30
		20 (4/1-9/30/10)		88 (10/1/10-3/31/11)					
NUMBER OF STATEMENTS	13	15	33	24	9	14		46	58

	0-500M %	500M-2MM %	2-10MM %	10-50MM %	50-100MM %	100-250MM %		%	%
ASSETS									
Cash & Equivalents	32.9	24.0	28.0	28.9		32.9		28.6	26.6
Trade Receivables (net)	8.7	13.0	17.1	19.7		8.9		19.9	21.8
Inventory	.0	.0	.1	.4		.0		.0	.2
All Other Current	4.7	2.6	8.8	10.6		2.2		9.1	7.8
Total Current	46.2	39.6	54.0	59.6		43.9		57.6	56.5
Fixed Assets (net)	34.6	19.9	20.3	13.7		6.2		17.0	13.3
Intangibles (net)	6.7	26.6	8.4	15.0		37.9		12.9	11.7
All Other Non-Current	12.3	13.9	17.3	11.8		12.0		12.5	18.5
Total	100.0	100.0	100.0	100.0		100.0		100.0	100.0
LIABILITIES									
Notes Payable-Short Term	15.6	16.2	18.2	2.8		.9		11.0	8.4
Cur. Mat.-L.T.D.	.4	3.6	4.7	1.8		2.2		2.5	3.9
Trade Payables	6.8	17.2	14.6	16.5		11.9		12.4	18.1
Income Taxes Payable	.0	1.4	.5	.5		.1		.4	.3
All Other Current	10.0	11.0	34.4	26.1		15.6		33.7	25.9
Total Current	32.8	49.5	72.5	47.7		30.6		59.9	56.6
Long-Term Debt	23.9	12.4	8.2	18.5		17.5		17.3	15.0
Deferred Taxes	.0	.0	.3	1.1		2.1		.7	.8
All Other Non-Current	3.2	15.6	10.8	7.8		11.3		7.3	19.4
Net Worth	40.2	22.5	8.3	24.9		38.3		14.7	8.1
Total Liabilities & Net Worth	100.0	100.0	100.0	100.0		100.0		100.0	100.0
INCOME DATA									
Net Sales	100.0	100.0	100.0	100.0		100.0		100.0	100.0
Gross Profit									
Operating Expenses	80.3	83.1	93.5	90.2		95.1		93.9	91.9
Operating Profit	19.7	16.9	6.5	9.8		4.9		6.1	8.1
All Other Expenses (net)	6.7	1.3	-.1	.2		.8		-.6	1.2
Profit Before Taxes	13.1	15.7	6.6	9.6		4.1		6.8	6.9
RATIOS									
Current	3.9	2.0	1.8	2.3		2.0		2.0	2.1
	1.6	.7	1.0	1.4		1.3		1.1	.9
	.8	.4	.5	.9		1.0		.5	.6
Quick	3.3	1.8	1.3	1.7		1.8		1.6	1.9
	1.5	.7	.7	1.1		1.2		.8	.9
	.8	.2	.3	.6		1.0		.4	.4
Sales/Receivables	0 UND	0 UND	0 UND	12 30.7		13 28.4		8 46.5	6 66.2
	0 999.8	1 502.3	12 30.4	24 15.1		31 12.0		28 13.3	25 14.6
	26 14.3	16 22.2	36 10.2	56 6.5		73 5.0		49 7.5	45 8.2
Cost of Sales/Inventory									
Cost of Sales/Payables									
Sales/Working Capital	4.5	10.4	14.0	3.7		3.0		8.0	8.1
	35.5	-46.4	-280.3	13.2		11.1		93.2	-42.6
	-569.1	-16.7	-5.3	-34.9		NM		-7.2	-8.8
EBIT/Interest		72.7	130.5	52.7		9.1		18.3	26.0
	(14) 15.6	(25) 23.5	(15) 8.2			(10) 2.2		(31) 6.3	(42) 4.7
		4.7	-.3	3.0		1.0		1.3	1.7
Net Profit + Depr., Dep., Amort./Cur. Mat. L/T/D								9.0	22.0
								(13) 2.9	(12) 5.6
								.9	1.8
Fixed/Worth	.0	.1	.2	.0		.1		.2	.1
	.7	1.6	.6	.5		NM		.8	.5
	3.1	-.6	2.8	NM		-.4		-1.1	-1.1
Debt/Worth	.3	.4	1.2	.7		1.2		1.2	1.3
	1.3	14.4	2.8	2.2		NM		7.0	10.6
	3.8	-2.4	UND	-3.5		-2.4		-5.1	-3.9
% Profit Before Taxes/Tangible Net Worth	100.0		110.1	27.1				117.4	83.9
	(11) 21.3		(26) 42.8	(16) 15.8				(30) 34.2	(34) 43.7
	-1.7		8.5	3.5				11.5	14.9
% Profit Before Taxes/Total Assets	23.9	48.5	22.3	17.5		4.3		24.9	27.3
	4.3	25.3	9.8	5.5		3.4		8.0	13.1
	-20.2	1.2	-1.0	1.5		1.4		.3	1.6
Sales/Net Fixed Assets	UND	266.0	72.1	654.3		35.9		52.7	138.6
	24.7	42.7	24.9	27.6		16.7		23.0	25.2
	5.3	12.6	6.2	9.9		7.5		8.6	13.3
Sales/Total Assets	9.6	6.3	4.0	2.8		1.2		3.7	4.4
	3.2	3.0	2.2	1.8		.8		2.0	2.4
	1.1	1.1	1.1	1.1		.4		1.0	1.2
% Depr., Dep., Amort./Sales			.6	1.0		.2		1.2	.6
		(27) 1.1		(16) 1.9		(11) 2.2		(34) 2.0	(41) 1.8
			3.2	3.1		3.0		3.0	3.4
% Officers', Directors' Owners' Comp/Sales									
Net Sales ($)	15007M	98081M	499468M	1198406M	1089041M	2049376M		2111236M	3009437M
Total Assets ($)	2943M	20063M	181335M	547996M	659437M	2410832M		1299328M	1564872M

M = $ thousand   MM = $ million
See Pages 9 through 22 for Explanation of Ratios and Data

Comparative Historical Data

Current Data Sorted by Sales

			Type of Statement						
33	40	41	Unqualified		2	3	3	9	24
6	2	4	Reviewed			1	1	2	
4	4	5	Compiled		1		2	2	
8	13	10	Tax Returns	4	2	2	1		1
25	40	48	Other	7	4	5	3	10	19
4/1/08-	4/1/09-	4/1/10-							
3/31/09	3/31/10	3/31/11			20 (4/1-9/30/10)		88 (10/1/10-3/31/11)		
ALL	ALL	ALL		0-1MM	1-3MM	3-5MM	5-10MM	10-25MM	25MM & OVER
76	99	108	**NUMBER OF STATEMENTS**	11	9	11	10	23	44
%	%	%	**ASSETS**	%	%	%	%	%	%
32.1	27.5	28.9	Cash & Equivalents	26.0		30.4	32.9	28.1	27.3
22.0	17.3	14.9	Trade Receivables (net)	7.1		4.8	9.8	22.3	18.8
.2	1.3	.1	Inventory	.0		.0	.0	.5	.0
7.0	8.2	7.1	All Other Current	5.5		16.4	1.7	5.1	6.6
61.3	54.2	51.0	Total Current	38.7		51.6	44.4	56.0	52.6
11.6	19.1	17.7	Fixed Assets (net)	47.6		17.9	23.7	15.6	11.7
12.1	14.6	16.6	Intangibles (net)	8.6		14.5	11.6	11.6	22.4
15.0	12.0	14.7	All Other Non-Current	4.8		16.1	20.3	16.8	13.3
100.0	100.0	100.0	Total	100.0		100.0	100.0	100.0	100.0
			LIABILITIES						
7.1	6.2	10.7	Notes Payable-Short Term	19.7		9.0	4.2	9.8	12.8
2.3	3.9	2.8	Cur. Mat.-L.T.D.	1.0		1.9	1.8	5.2	2.3
19.1	11.9	14.1	Trade Payables	7.0		15.8	9.6	14.3	17.9
.3	.4	.5	Income Taxes Payable	.0		1.3	.6	.4	.3
22.9	26.5	23.3	All Other Current	5.5		24.3	28.3	32.3	23.2
51.7	48.9	51.4	Total Current	33.3		52.4	44.4	61.9	56.6
12.0	16.3	13.9	Long-Term Debt	34.4		10.5	9.4	13.0	13.3
.4	.4	.8	Deferred Taxes	.0		.3	.0	.5	1.6
9.0	10.7	10.0	All Other Non-Current	10.3		8.5	12.4	9.7	9.4
27.0	23.7	23.9	Net Worth	22.0		28.3	33.8	14.8	19.1
100.0	100.0	100.0	Total Liabilities & Net Worth	100.0		100.0	100.0	100.0	100.0
			INCOME DATA						
100.0	100.0	100.0	Net Sales	100.0		100.0	100.0	100.0	100.0
			Gross Profit						
93.6	88.2	89.6	Operating Expenses	67.5		87.7	96.2	93.0	93.6
6.4	11.8	10.4	Operating Profit	32.5		12.3	3.8	7.0	6.4
.6	1.6	1.0	All Other Expenses (net)	9.1		-.6	-2.5	.4	.3
5.8	10.2	9.4	Profit Before Taxes	23.3		12.9	6.3	6.6	6.1
			RATIOS						
2.1	2.2	2.0		1.7		1.4	2.6	2.4	1.7
1.3	1.2	1.1	Current	.7		.9	1.2	1.1	1.3
1.0	.7	.7		.4		.7	.6	.7	.8
1.9	1.8	1.7		1.7		1.0	2.5	1.7	1.7
1.2	1.0	1.0	Quick	.7		.6	1.2	.9	1.1
.7	.6	.6		.4		.2	.6	.6	.6
7 55.9	1 583.8	1 552.0		0 UND	0 UND	1 345.3	7 53.1	13 27.3	
30 12.0	17 21.3	17 21.4	Sales/Receivables	0 UND	0 UND	6 62.9	18 20.4	23 16.1	
47 7.7	39 9.4	35 10.5		25 14.8	18 19.9	22 16.4	55 6.7	44 8.4	
			Cost of Sales/Inventory						
			Cost of Sales/Payables						
6.0	5.9	7.4		4.4		10.2	7.1	9.5	5.7
25.1	29.0	39.1	Sales/Working Capital	-138.4		-117.1	426.6	39.4	23.9
-63.5	-15.9	-17.5		-3.4		-3.2	-33.3	-17.5	-25.6
37.8	38.6	52.7				149.2		87.1	39.5
(52) 4.7	(77) 10.6	(75) 8.3	EBIT/Interest	(10) 66.4			(18) 6.2	(29) 8.2	
.8	2.0	1.8		9.5				.5	1.8
5.0	12.7	24.1							30.6
(11) 3.2	(17) 2.5	(18) 3.7	Net Profit + Depr., Dep., Amort./Cur. Mat. L/T/D					(14) 4.6	
1.4	1.6	.9							1.3
.1	.2	.1		.2		.3	.1	.1	.1
.5	1.0	.7	Fixed/Worth	2.6		1.1	.9	.5	.7
-6.5	-2.0	-1.3		-2.1		-1.3	NM	10.4	-.8
1.1	1.2	1.0		1.3		1.2	.9	1.2	1.0
5.1	4.4	2.9	Debt/Worth	2.0		3.2	2.6	4.2	6.5
-17.4	-9.8	-4.8		-5.6		-12.0	NM	-4.5	-2.7
98.5	115.3	87.4	% Profit Before Taxes/Tangible Net Worth					128.2	36.3
(53) 38.2	(68) 35.5	(73) 26.5					(16) 42.8	(26) 14.3	
9.7	7.9	6.3						7.6	5.0
22.0	27.9	19.2	% Profit Before Taxes/Total Assets	11.4		32.2	29.3	22.4	17.5
6.7	8.4	5.4		3.8		13.0	15.3	10.6	4.1
-.6	2.2	1.3		-18.4		1.7	-.6	1.5	1.5
170.8	50.5	84.7		71.0		57.1	117.2	93.8	43.6
31.0	19.3	27.6	Sales/Net Fixed Assets	16.2		17.5	23.0	40.5	27.1
13.3	9.4	7.8		.2		7.2	4.7	18.7	8.3
4.0	3.8	3.6		2.9		3.0	6.3	4.1	3.5
2.2	1.8	1.7	Sales/Total Assets	1.0		1.2	2.8	2.2	1.6
.9	.8	.9		.1		1.0	.8	1.5	.8
.6	.8	.6						.6	1.0
(48) 1.3	(72) 1.9	(74) 1.5	% Depr., Dep., Amort./Sales					(20) .9	(30) 2.0
2.6	2.9	3.1						1.9	3.0
3.8	3.7	3.7							
(16) 6.5	(20) 7.0	(11) 5.7	% Officers', Directors' Owners' Comp/Sales						
11.6	10.2	7.1							
2976965M	3667818M	4949379M	Net Sales ($)	4015M	14345M	47231M	70256M	381659M	4431873M
1710346M	2285801M	3822606M	Total Assets ($)	10149M	41460M	38552M	43517M	214203M	3474725M

M = $ thousand   MM = $ million
See Pages 9 through 22 for Explanation of Ratios and Data

	Current Data Sorted by Assets						Type of Statement	Comparative Historical Data	
1	2	4	8	4	2		Unqualified	7	6
	1						Reviewed	1	
2		1					Compiled	1	2
7	1						Tax Returns	5	4
2	6	6	3	2	4		Other	11	15
	3 (4/1-9/30/10)		53 (10/1/10-3/31/11)					4/1/06- 3/31/07 ALL	4/1/07- 3/31/08 ALL
0-500M	500M-2MM	2-10MM	10-50MM	50-100MM	100-250MM				
12	10	11	11	6	6		NUMBER OF STATEMENTS	25	27
%	%	%	%	%	%		ASSETS	%	%
40.8	14.2	17.0	25.7				Cash & Equivalents	31.0	26.6
9.2	17.4	43.3	20.5				Trade Receivables (net)	24.9	28.6
.0	1.4	.2	.1				Inventory	.3	.0
11.1	16.5	3.4	12.1				All Other Current	9.2	11.1
61.1	49.5	63.9	58.5				Total Current	65.5	66.4
15.9	17.5	5.3	8.3				Fixed Assets (net)	18.9	9.8
6.0	29.8	2.6	18.5				Intangibles (net)	10.4	5.7
17.1	3.2	28.2	14.7				All Other Non-Current	5.2	18.1
100.0	100.0	100.0	100.0				Total	100.0	100.0
							LIABILITIES		
30.1	3.2	15.6	2.0				Notes Payable-Short Term	29.8	25.6
3.7	4.9	.0	3.1				Cur. Mat.-L.T.D.	3.2	1.0
6.6	6.3	16.0	11.3				Trade Payables	16.5	13.3
.0	.0	1.0	.5				Income Taxes Payable	.2	.3
14.4	34.2	12.7	25.9				All Other Current	18.1	23.7
54.8	48.7	45.4	42.7				Total Current	67.9	63.9
27.8	37.7	.1	10.6				Long-Term Debt	15.5	11.0
.0	.0	.3	2.2				Deferred Taxes	.2	.4
.4	29.2	15.7	20.2				All Other Non-Current	15.0	9.8
17.0	-15.6	38.5	24.3				Net Worth	1.5	14.9
100.0	100.0	100.0	100.0				Total Liabilities & Net Worth	100.0	100.0
							INCOME DATA		
100.0	100.0	100.0	100.0				Net Sales	100.0	100.0
							Gross Profit		
85.2	89.0	94.0	91.0				Operating Expenses	90.6	79.8
14.8	11.0	6.0	9.0				Operating Profit	9.4	20.2
.6	1.9	.2	.0				All Other Expenses (net)	.6	1.2
14.1	9.1	5.7	9.0				Profit Before Taxes	8.7	19.0
							RATIOS		
2.8	2.3	2.1	2.2					2.2	1.8
1.3	1.0	1.6	1.6				Current	1.3	1.4
.5	.5	.9	.8					1.1	.9
2.1	1.3	2.1	2.1					1.9	1.6
.9	.8	1.2	1.0				Quick	1.3	1.3
.2	.4	.9	.4					.8	.8
0 UND	0 UND	10 38.1	12 30.2					2 191.4	11 33.3
0 UND	17 22.1	41 8.9	41 8.8				Sales/Receivables	35 10.4	36 10.0
2 228.4	33 11.1	96 3.8	50 7.3					69 5.3	91 4.0
							Cost of Sales/Inventory		
							Cost of Sales/Payables		
11.4	6.4	1.0	2.2					5.5	3.5
NM	NM	46.0	11.3				Sales/Working Capital	9.5	11.6
-28.1	-11.2	-24.2	-20.8					74.5	-93.2
								9.4	31.9
							EBIT/Interest	(19) 4.7	(17) 10.7
								1.1	7.9
							Net Profit + Depr., Dep., Amort./Cur. Mat. L/T/D		
.0	.3	.0	.0					.4	.1
.4	-.3	.2	.4				Fixed/Worth	1.8	.4
-.3	-.1	.8	-.1					-.5	2.1
.4	1.3	.5	1.2					1.7	1.3
.8	-3.3	1.2	9.3				Debt/Worth	6.2	1.7
-12.3	-1.3	62.9	-2.7					-5.0	26.6
								124.9	221.0
							% Profit Before Taxes/Tangible Net Worth	(16) 66.6	(22) 75.7
								39.0	27.3
86.8	43.2	13.1	16.9					25.2	32.6
65.3	19.2	5.8	4.5				% Profit Before Taxes/Total Assets	14.2	15.5
14.0	1.2	1.8	-.2					1.9	10.2
UND	93.5	UND	UND					62.2	147.1
110.4	25.0	43.4	49.7				Sales/Net Fixed Assets	13.9	36.1
15.5	12.3	33.0	11.5					6.7	19.1
13.4	5.6	5.0	2.1					3.5	4.0
4.6	1.5	2.1	1.4				Sales/Total Assets	1.6	2.3
2.4	1.0	.2	.3					.8	.9
								.7	.5
							% Depr., Dep., Amort./Sales	(14) 1.5	(17) 1.4
								3.0	2.1
							% Officers', Directors' Owners' Comp/Sales		
26798M	30272M	123218M	400751M	576570M	1135389M		Net Sales ($)	1157558M	877594M
3341M	10750M	54817M	302072M	456781M	1013277M		Total Assets ($)	901497M	696595M

© RMA 2011

M = $ thousand   MM = $ million
See Pages 9 through 22 for Explanation of Ratios and Data

Comparative Historical Data | Current Data Sorted by Sales

Type of Statement

	4/1/08-3/31/09	4/1/09-3/31/10	4/1/10-3/31/11		0-1MM	1-3MM	3-5MM	5-10MM	10-25MM	25MM & OVER
Unqualified	15	10	21		3	3	1	1	3	10
Reviewed		1	1			1				
Compiled	2	7	3		2				1	
Tax Returns	4	5	8		4	2	2			
Other	12	23	23		4	3	2	2	3	9
	ALL	ALL	ALL		3 (4/1-9/30/10)			53 (10/1/10-3/31/11)		
NUMBER OF STATEMENTS	33	46	56		13	9	5	3	7	19
ASSETS	%	%	%		%	%	%	%	%	%
Cash & Equivalents	29.9	27.7	24.5		12.4					20.8
Trade Receivables (net)	26.2	23.1	22.3		30.0					24.1
Inventory	.3	.1	.3		1.1					.1
All Other Current	7.3	8.6	9.5		10.5					9.3
Total Current	63.8	59.5	56.7		54.0					54.3
Fixed Assets (net)	13.7	11.5	12.5		11.4					15.2
Intangibles (net)	10.3	16.5	14.1		17.7					16.6
All Other Non-Current	12.3	12.5	16.7		17.0					13.9
Total	100.0	100.0	100.0		100.0					100.0
LIABILITIES										
Notes Payable-Short Term	18.9	10.4	11.9		12.0					.5
Cur. Mat.-L.T.D.	2.4	1.9	2.9		4.8					3.0
Trade Payables	13.5	12.8	9.6		5.9					14.8
Income Taxes Payable	.5	.6	.3		.0					.4
All Other Current	24.4	20.9	20.8		9.9					24.0
Total Current	59.8	46.7	45.5		32.6					42.7
Long-Term Debt	11.6	12.2	18.1		24.4					11.8
Deferred Taxes	.5	.4	.8		.0					1.4
All Other Non-Current	11.8	10.4	15.2		4.5					14.5
Net Worth	16.5	30.3	20.4		38.6					29.6
Total Liabilities & Net Worth	100.0	100.0	100.0		100.0					100.0
INCOME DATA										
Net Sales	100.0	100.0	100.0		100.0					100.0
Gross Profit										
Operating Expenses	87.4	85.0	90.3		80.4					92.5
Operating Profit	12.6	15.0	9.7		19.6					7.5
All Other Expenses (net)	1.8	1.8	.5		3.0					-.2
Profit Before Taxes	10.9	13.1	9.2		16.6					7.7
RATIOS										
Current	2.4	1.8	2.1		2.2					2.1
	1.4	1.3	1.5		1.7					1.5
	1.1	.7	.8		.5					.9
Quick	2.3	1.7	1.7		2.0					1.8
	1.2	1.2	1.1		1.2					1.3
	.9	.5	.6		.3					.6
Sales/Receivables	4 81.7	8 43.7	4 94.6		0 UND				21	17.2
	29 12.7	35 10.3	24 15.3		13 27.2				43	8.5
	48 7.6	49 7.5	46 7.9		141 2.6				50	7.3
Cost of Sales/Inventory										
Cost of Sales/Payables										
Sales/Working Capital	5.2	5.7	4.8		.6					6.7
	16.1	16.9	14.1		10.5					13.0
	127.2	-24.1	-40.7		-32.3					-74.1
EBIT/Interest	71.9	54.4	41.0							47.6
	(22) 14.7	(29) 3.8	(34) 10.0						(14)	18.4
	3.0	-5.1	1.2							.7
Net Profit + Depr., Dep., Amort./Cur. Mat. L/T/D										
Fixed/Worth	.0	.0	.1		.0					.3
	.3	.3	.5		.8					.6
	NM	NM	-.2		-.3					-.5
Debt/Worth	.9	1.1	.8		.5					1.2
	1.9	2.7	2.3		1.4					3.6
	NM	-7.4	-4.9		-6.4					-7.4
% Profit Before Taxes/Tangible Net Worth	72.8	81.1	80.8							76.9
	(25) 54.3	(34) 35.6	(37) 37.5						(13)	37.5
	15.1	6.8	9.1							13.7
% Profit Before Taxes/Total Assets	31.3	20.4	29.9		48.8					16.9
	11.2	7.5	11.1		11.2					11.0
	3.3	-.7	1.4		1.4					1.5
Sales/Net Fixed Assets	162.2	359.1	171.7		UND					43.9
	41.8	33.9	36.8		36.3					16.8
	16.2	17.8	12.1		12.3					7.6
Sales/Total Assets	4.7	3.8	4.0		3.3					3.3
	2.8	1.7	1.5		.8					1.4
	.9	.4	.6		.2					1.0
% Depr., Dep., Amort./Sales	.4	.6	.8							1.1
	(24) 1.2	(24) 1.4	(32) 1.7						(14)	1.7
	2.1	2.4	3.1							3.3
% Officers', Directors' Owners' Comp/Sales		5.3	4.3							
	(13)	7.6	(14) 6.1							
		27.0	13.0							
Net Sales ($)	2184549M	1873209M	2292998M		7852M	18348M	19700M	22010M	98617M	2126471M
Total Assets ($)	1020893M	1403162M	1841038M		30154M	22205M	18266M	4779M	244028M	1521606M

© RMA 2011

M = $ thousand   MM = $ million
See Pages 9 through 22 for Explanation of Ratios and Data

Current Data Sorted by Assets   Comparative Historical Data

0-500M	500M-2MM	2-10MM	10-50MM	50-100MM	100-250MM	Type of Statement	4/1/06-3/31/07 ALL	4/1/07-3/31/08 ALL
1		4	5	3	3	Unqualified	27	15
1			1			Reviewed	3	2
1		1				Compiled	3	3
		3				Tax Returns	11	5
2	5	9	10	4	1	Other	27	31
	19 (4/1-9/30/10)		37 (10/1/10-3/31/11)					
5	7	17	16	7	4	**NUMBER OF STATEMENTS**	71	56
%	%	%	%	%	%	**ASSETS**	%	%
		18.5	43.2			Cash & Equivalents	23.9	23.8
		7.8	14.6			Trade Receivables (net)	13.2	15.2
		.0	.0			Inventory	2.6	2.0
		6.1	1.3			All Other Current	5.5	7.6
		32.4	59.0			Total Current	45.3	48.6
		29.5	9.2			Fixed Assets (net)	20.6	18.8
		3.0	4.6			Intangibles (net)	6.8	4.9
		35.1	27.2			All Other Non-Current	27.3	27.7
		100.0	100.0			Total	100.0	100.0
						LIABILITIES		
		4.9	23.6			Notes Payable-Short Term	7.7	11.6
		3.8	.7			Cur. Mat.-L.T.D.	2.8	4.5
		2.2	2.7			Trade Payables	5.2	6.3
		.0	.0			Income Taxes Payable	.2	.2
		7.8	10.8			All Other Current	16.0	12.3
		18.7	37.7			Total Current	31.9	34.9
		36.8	9.6			Long-Term Debt	15.9	21.5
		.0	.0			Deferred Taxes	.0	.7
		.6	12.7			All Other Non-Current	6.6	7.8
		43.9	40.0			Net Worth	45.6	35.2
		100.0	100.0			Total Liabilities & Net Worth	100.0	100.0
						INCOME DATA		
		100.0	100.0			Net Sales	100.0	100.0
						Gross Profit		
		63.9	59.6			Operating Expenses	65.4	63.1
		36.1	40.4			Operating Profit	34.6	36.9
		11.9	8.5			All Other Expenses (net)	4.0	7.6
		24.2	31.8			Profit Before Taxes	30.6	29.3
						RATIOS		
		15.6	20.7			Current	10.5	9.2
		2.8	2.0				1.8	1.6
		.4	1.0				.5	.7
		15.5	19.2			Quick	8.9	7.6
		2.6	2.0				1.4	1.0
		.3	1.0				.3	.4
		0 UND	0 UND			Sales/Receivables	0 UND	0 UND
		22 16.7	29 12.6				4 86.3	1 680.0
		51 7.2	61 5.9				36 10.1	54 6.8
						Cost of Sales/Inventory		
						Cost of Sales/Payables		
		1.5	2.3			Sales/Working Capital	2.5	2.8
		9.0	3.6				19.2	8.7
		-3.6	10.4				-10.3	-19.1
						EBIT/Interest	37.7	55.9
							(35) 6.7	(27) 4.6
							2.2	2.0
						Net Profit + Depr., Dep., Amort./Cur. Mat. L/T/D		
		.0	.0			Fixed/Worth	.0	.0
		.2	.1				.2	.1
		2.4	1.5				1.9	4.2
		.1	.1			Debt/Worth	.1	.2
		.7	.9				1.1	1.0
		5.3	27.8				8.3	29.9
		37.8	154.3			% Profit Before Taxes/Tangible Net Worth	114.2	115.6
		(16) 10.6	(13) 52.8				(60) 24.0	(46) 38.7
		2.0	.8				5.2	5.8
		9.8	72.7			% Profit Before Taxes/Total Assets	33.9	80.0
		4.5	13.2				10.1	9.5
		.6	.5				1.2	2.9
		188.2	UND			Sales/Net Fixed Assets	UND	222.6
		6.7	124.3				32.0	32.9
		.4	12.9				10.7	7.4
		1.2	1.9			Sales/Total Assets	2.6	3.0
		.3	.5				1.0	.9
		.1	.1				.2	.2
			.2			% Depr., Dep., Amort./Sales	.6	.6
			(10) 1.0				(37) 1.7	(29) 2.0
			2.4				6.6	7.3
						% Officers', Directors' Owners' Comp/Sales	3.7	
							(10) 10.2	
							38.3	
3070M	17792M	81324M	438032M	509445M	1132986M	Net Sales ($)	8777750M	1354813M
1239M	8947M	77851M	468158M	497417M	633193M	Total Assets ($)	2097658M	1494673M

M = $ thousand   MM = $ million
See Pages 9 through 22 for Explanation of Ratios and Data

Comparative Historical Data

Current Data Sorted by Sales

			Type of Statement						
26	21	16	Unqualified	1	2		3	3	7
3	3	2	Reviewed		2				
5	2	2	Compiled		1				1
8	6	5	Tax Returns	3	1	1			
24	26	31	Other	12	5		3	3	8
4/1/08-3/31/09 ALL	4/1/09-3/31/10 ALL	4/1/10-3/31/11 ALL		0-1MM	19 (4/1-9/30/10) 1-3MM	3-5MM	37 (10/1/10-3/31/11) 5-10MM	10-25MM	25MM & OVER
66	58	56	NUMBER OF STATEMENTS	16	11	1	6	6	16
%	%	%	ASSETS	%	%	%	%	%	%
22.8	20.1	32.2	Cash & Equivalents	21.0	34.3				38.8
11.1	13.3	11.1	Trade Receivables (net)	4.2	12.2				19.8
2.0	1.8	1.1	Inventory	.0	.3				3.6
6.8	6.1	6.8	All Other Current	9.8	8.8				2.2
42.7	41.3	51.1	Total Current	35.0	55.6				64.4
17.5	14.0	18.3	Fixed Assets (net)	30.5	11.5				10.7
7.2	3.0	4.3	Intangibles (net)	8.3	.5				6.1
32.6	41.7	26.4	All Other Non-Current	26.1	32.4				18.8
100.0	100.0	100.0	Total	100.0	100.0				100.0
			LIABILITIES						
9.0	7.6	12.8	Notes Payable-Short Term	1.5	28.9				11.2
4.2	2.7	1.8	Cur. Mat.-L.T.D.	1.2	1.2				.7
4.8	3.4	4.0	Trade Payables	3.0	4.3				3.6
.0	.1	.0	Income Taxes Payable	.0	.1				.1
13.2	11.7	8.7	All Other Current	1.3	9.7				10.1
31.1	25.5	27.3	Total Current	7.0	44.3				25.6
27.1	13.5	20.5	Long-Term Debt	40.1	9.5				5.9
.4	.9	.6	Deferred Taxes	.0	.4				.6
7.4	3.2	5.2	All Other Non-Current	3.4	1.1				12.3
34.0	57.0	46.5	Net Worth	49.4	44.7				55.6
100.0	100.0	100.0	Total Liabilities & Net Worth	100.0	100.0				100.0
			INCOME DATA						
100.0	100.0	100.0	Net Sales	100.0	100.0				100.0
			Gross Profit						
64.8	66.8	68.9	Operating Expenses	69.6	66.5				75.4
35.2	33.2	31.1	Operating Profit	30.4	33.5				24.6
10.6	8.4	8.1	All Other Expenses (net)	13.5	12.8				-.7
24.5	24.8	23.0	Profit Before Taxes	16.9	20.7				25.3
			RATIOS						
5.0	6.8	16.1		20.1	6.4				6.5
1.7	1.7	2.2	Current	2.6	1.0				4.0
.5	.6	1.0		.8	.9				1.4
4.3	4.9	13.7		20.0	2.6				6.2
1.1	1.5	1.7	Quick	1.7	1.0				3.1
.4	.4	.6		.3	.5				1.1
0 UND	0 UND	0 UND		0 UND	0 UND			0	754.0
0 730.3	5 73.3	25 14.4	Sales/Receivables	0 UND	3 113.3			30	12.1
47 7.8	44 8.3	48 7.7		84 4.3	35 10.4		18	44	8.3
			Cost of Sales/Inventory						
			Cost of Sales/Payables						
3.5	1.7	1.8		.8	1.6				2.8
14.0	8.6	4.0	Sales/Working Capital	4.0	9.0				4.5
-8.5	-6.1	NM		NM	-8.6				10.6
176.7	127.3	161.3							572.0
(35) 5.7	(29) 9.5	(29) 12.2	EBIT/Interest					(10)	86.7
3.0	2.4	1.6							-1.6
			Net Profit + Depr., Dep., Amort./Cur. Mat. L/T/D						
.0	.0	.0		.0	.0				.0
.1	.1	.1	Fixed/Worth	.4	.0				.1
8.6	.7	1.2		2.0	1.2				.3
.1	.1	.1		.1	.1				.1
1.4	.6	.7	Debt/Worth	1.9	.6				.2
-72.4	2.6	7.3		16.7	28.2				1.5
66.1	41.5	102.7	% Profit Before Taxes/Tangible Net Worth	26.0					125.3
(49) 20.2	(49) 13.5	(49) 11.7		(14) 8.3				(14)	65.7
3.8	1.7	1.3		-.1					4.6
54.3	30.2	40.7	% Profit Before Taxes/Total Assets	8.5	9.5				99.6
5.5	7.4	6.1		2.6	5.7				44.8
1.4	1.2	.5		-3.2	-1.3				5.5
UND	UND	UND		UND	UND				254.1
50.7	40.6	35.2	Sales/Net Fixed Assets	2.7	361.3				28.9
10.8	7.4	6.0		.3	6.7				12.7
2.4	2.1	1.8		.5	1.8				2.9
.8	.4	.7	Sales/Total Assets	.2	.6				2.0
.1	.1	.2		.1	.1				.8
.6	.7	.5							.6
(39) 1.2	(33) 1.2	(29) 1.3	% Depr., Dep., Amort./Sales					(14)	1.1
7.6	6.6	4.5							3.5
			% Officers', Directors' Owners' Comp/Sales						
1586311M	1282887M	2182649M	Net Sales ($)	6956M	20531M	3527M	35810M	89337M	2026488M
2028657M	2631580M	1686805M	Total Assets ($)	39526M	133353M	2685M	311940M	96860M	1102441M

© RMA 2011

M = $ thousand   MM = $ million
See Pages 9 through 22 for Explanation of Ratios and Data

Current Data Sorted by Assets

Comparative Historical Data

						Type of Statement		
1	2	4	5	8	6	Unqualified	26	36
	3	3	2			Reviewed	5	9
	2	9	2	1		Compiled	9	13
9	26	9	3			Tax Returns	28	50
5	7	24	17	4	9	Other	39	60
	21 (4/1-9/30/10)		140 (10/1/10-3/31/11)				4/1/06-3/31/07	4/1/07-3/31/08
0-500M	500M-2MM	2-10MM	10-50MM	50-100MM	100-250MM		ALL	ALL
15	40	49	29	13	15	**NUMBER OF STATEMENTS**	107	168
%	%	%	%	%	%	**ASSETS**	%	%
33.8	23.7	11.7	15.9	11.5	6.5	Cash & Equivalents	26.0	14.3
5.9	9.9	11.2	14.3	25.9	.7	Trade Receivables (net)	16.4	10.7
.5	1.1	2.0	2.9	.4	.1	Inventory	2.8	1.8
11.1	4.8	9.9	10.1	4.1	6.6	All Other Current	9.1	5.7
51.2	39.6	34.8	43.2	41.9	14.0	Total Current	54.4	32.4
13.5	42.3	42.1	35.7	8.3	47.1	Fixed Assets (net)	15.0	44.2
18.7	8.0	1.3	7.1	3.5	7.3	Intangibles (net)	5.6	4.3
16.6	10.2	21.8	14.0	46.4	31.7	All Other Non-Current	25.1	19.1
100.0	100.0	100.0	100.0	100.0	100.0	Total	100.0	100.0
						LIABILITIES		
17.2	9.5	10.3	9.4	7.2	10.0	Notes Payable-Short Term	11.3	11.3
1.5	2.9	6.0	3.7	1.8	7.1	Cur. Mat.-L.T.D.	3.2	3.1
6.9	5.5	4.8	2.6	5.4	2.7	Trade Payables	4.2	3.4
.0	.1	.2	.2	.0	.0	Income Taxes Payable	.3	.0
33.1	9.2	9.4	2.8	5.8	2.4	All Other Current	17.7	9.1
58.8	27.2	30.7	18.7	20.2	22.3	Total Current	36.6	27.0
16.2	34.4	26.6	36.0	34.5	31.8	Long-Term Debt	15.5	34.8
.0	.1	.1	.0	.1	.0	Deferred Taxes	.2	.3
4.3	3.8	4.6	1.3	7.5	2.5	All Other Non-Current	8.2	7.4
20.7	34.6	38.0	43.9	37.7	43.4	Net Worth	39.6	30.5
100.0	100.0	100.0	100.0	100.0	100.0	Total Liabilties & Net Worth	100.0	100.0
						INCOME DATA		
100.0	100.0	100.0	100.0	100.0	100.0	Net Sales	100.0	100.0
						Gross Profit		
83.3	66.1	60.8	62.5	70.5	64.6	Operating Expenses	62.2	60.5
16.7	33.9	39.2	37.5	29.5	35.4	Operating Profit	37.8	39.5
18.8	10.8	15.2	13.8	18.9	15.2	All Other Expenses (net)	11.8	20.2
-2.0	23.0	24.0	23.7	10.6	20.1	Profit Before Taxes	26.0	19.3
						RATIOS		
3.6	3.4	2.2	7.4	5.8	3.5		5.3	3.5
1.0	1.5	.8	3.1	1.7	.8	Current	1.5	1.1
.3	.8	.1	1.2	1.3	.2		.8	.3
2.4	3.1	2.1	7.2	5.3	2.0		3.1	2.9
.6	1.1	.7	2.3	1.7	.3	Quick	1.1	.8
.2	.5	.1	.3	1.0	.1		.3	.1
0 UND	0 UND	0 UND	0 UND	26 14.3	0 UND		0 UND	0 UND
0 UND	0 UND	0 UND	13 27.1	78 4.7	4 85.1	Sales/Receivables	0 UND	0 UND
0 999.8	21 17.3	34 10.8	65 5.6	471 .8	32 11.6		87 4.2	35 10.5
						Cost of Sales/Inventory		
						Cost of Sales/Payables		
14.1	3.1	3.2	.5	.4	2.2		1.3	2.4
UND	19.4	-11.8	2.1	2.1	-89.5	Sales/Working Capital	5.1	32.3
-3.0	-24.6	-2.9	8.0	15.7	-1.0		-8.4	-2.3
	24.8	15.7	76.0				28.4	12.5
	(22) 5.0	(30) 4.3	(14) 8.5			EBIT/Interest	(61) 7.9	(77) 4.1
	1.1	1.2	4.3				2.5	1.3
						Net Profit + Depr., Dep., Amort./Cur. Mat. L/T/D		
.0	.2	.1	.0	.0	.2		.0	.0
1.1	2.3	1.1	.8	.1	1.2	Fixed/Worth	.1	1.6
-.2	UND	6.2	3.3	2.7	4.8		.9	6.3
.6	.5	.4	.5	.3	.6		.2	.7
4.5	2.7	2.3	1.6	2.3	1.5	Debt/Worth	1.8	3.1
-2.0	UND	9.0	6.2	13.5	4.5		13.7	11.4
	98.8	43.9	44.3	15.9	53.3		58.9	33.0
	(30) 30.4	(44) 14.9	(25) 13.7	(11) 4.1	(13) 11.5	% Profit Before Taxes/Tangible Net Worth	(91) 15.6	(135) 10.5
	15.1	2.9	4.5	.1	-2.0		3.2	1.5
74.9	21.5	14.2	13.7	4.0	7.8		18.8	10.9
1.3	9.6	5.3	4.2	.4	3.0	% Profit Before Taxes/Total Assets	5.6	4.0
-10.1	.5	.4	1.0	-.6	-2.1		1.3	.0
UND	73.5	39.1	65.6	656.9	31.6		UND	100.9
83.5	2.8	2.3	10.9	45.1	.6	Sales/Net Fixed Assets	61.5	2.6
9.2	.2	.2	.2	3.8	.1		7.4	.2
12.2	2.1	1.0	.5	.9	.6		1.5	.7
3.8	.4	.2	.1	.1	.2	Sales/Total Assets	.4	.2
1.4	.2	.1	.1	.1	.1		.1	.1
	2.9	1.6	1.7		2.7		.6	2.0
	(26) 12.7	(34) 6.2	(15) 11.1		(11) 5.3	% Depr., Dep., Amort./Sales	(47) 2.7	(105) 8.0
	22.4	16.4	23.4		37.6		8.7	20.0
							3.2	4.5
						% Officers', Directors' Owners' Comp/Sales	(13) 8.5	(19) 9.0
							19.2	16.2
30261M	53919M	145595M	312597M	506333M	1804841M	Net Sales ($)	1576123M	6088659M
3443M	43414M	231742M	699691M	909882M	2333280M	Total Assets ($)	3171297M	4535727M

© RMA 2011

M = $ thousand   MM = $ million
See Pages 9 through 22 for Explanation of Ratios and Data

Comparative Historical Data | Current Data Sorted by Sales

Hist 1	Hist 2	Hist 3	Type of Statement	0-1MM	1-3MM	3-5MM	5-10MM	10-25MM	25MM & OVER
30	23	26	Unqualified	2	3	3	2	9	7
10	5	8	Reviewed	3	3	1	1		
13	14	14	Compiled	7	3	1	2	1	
50	49	47	Tax Returns	34	9	3	1		
77	86	66	Other	14	17	8	11	8	8
4/1/08-3/31/09 ALL	4/1/09-3/31/10 ALL	4/1/10-3/31/11 ALL		21 (4/1-9/30/10)			140 (10/1/10-3/31/11)		
180	177	161	NUMBER OF STATEMENTS	60	35	16	17	18	15
%	%	%	ASSETS	%	%	%	%	%	%
15.7	16.1	17.0	Cash & Equivalents	13.3	19.5	20.0	24.9	12.0	19.8
10.2	13.2	11.1	Trade Receivables (net)	4.8	6.8	19.6	22.6	19.0	15.2
1.4	1.6	1.5	Inventory	.1	1.4	.3	5.2	4.6	.5
5.1	7.6	8.0	All Other Current	10.0	9.8	.6	6.4	8.5	5.2
32.4	38.6	37.7	Total Current	28.3	37.6	40.5	59.0	44.2	40.7
42.8	39.9	36.0	Fixed Assets (net)	49.1	39.3	24.8	13.7	28.6	22.5
4.8	3.3	6.3	Intangibles (net)	6.2	5.9	3.3	4.6	8.3	10.7
20.0	18.2	19.9	All Other Non-Current	16.5	17.2	31.4	22.7	18.9	26.1
100.0	100.0	100.0	Total	100.0	100.0	100.0	100.0	100.0	100.0
			LIABILITIES						
10.9	13.6	10.3	Notes Payable-Short Term	10.8	6.8	4.4	17.2	15.4	9.1
3.6	3.1	4.2	Cur. Mat.-L.T.D.	4.4	5.0	1.1	4.5	6.5	1.5
2.6	2.7	4.6	Trade Payables	.8	4.2	7.7	14.2	4.1	7.4
.2	.2	.1	Income Taxes Payable	.0	.1	.0	.5	.2	.0
9.1	7.8	9.4	All Other Current	11.2	7.7	6.9	5.5	13.9	8.0
26.3	27.4	28.7	Total Current	27.3	23.8	20.1	41.9	40.1	26.1
36.4	37.4	30.4	Long-Term Debt	36.5	30.8	30.4	20.6	30.8	15.3
.2	.3	.1	Deferred Taxes	.0	.2	.0	.1	.0	.1
6.6	7.6	3.8	All Other Non-Current	4.0	2.4	1.9	5.4	3.6	7.2
30.5	27.4	37.1	Net Worth	32.3	42.8	47.6	32.0	25.5	51.4
100.0	100.0	100.0	Total Liabilties & Net Worth	100.0	100.0	100.0	100.0	100.0	100.0
			INCOME DATA						
100.0	100.0	100.0	Net Sales	100.0	100.0	100.0	100.0	100.0	100.0
			Gross Profit						
59.0	64.6	65.7	Operating Expenses	55.3	67.9	67.9	80.6	69.4	78.1
41.0	35.4	34.3	Operating Profit	44.7	32.1	32.1	19.4	30.6	21.9
19.8	18.0	14.5	All Other Expenses (net)	22.6	10.9	13.7	6.0	12.8	3.1
21.2	17.4	19.8	Profit Before Taxes	22.1	21.2	18.4	13.4	17.8	18.8
			RATIOS						
4.1	3.5	3.5	Current	3.4	3.3	9.3	3.6	4.4	3.2
1.2	1.4	1.4		1.0	1.7	1.8	1.4	1.3	1.4
.3	.4	.5		.3	.6	.4	.9	.6	.5
3.0	2.8	2.9	Quick	2.4	3.3	9.0	2.9	3.4	3.2
1.0	1.1	1.0		.8	1.0	1.7	1.3	.9	1.2
.2	.2	.2		.1	.1	.4	.5	.1	.3
0 UND	0 UND	0 UND	Sales/Receivables	0 UND	0 UND	0 999.8	2 167.3	0 UND	1 302.3
0 UND	0 UND	0 999.8		0 UND	0 UND	16 23.3	32 11.5	44 8.2	9 39.0
35 10.3	41 8.8	38 9.5		0 UND	33 11.2	109 3.4	64 5.7	84 4.3	68 5.4
			Cost of Sales/Inventory						
			Cost of Sales/Payables						
1.8	1.9	2.1	Sales/Working Capital	1.4	2.2	.9	3.5	.6	2.2
14.3	9.8	18.7		UND	17.2	13.7	22.0	7.3	11.2
-3.5	-5.7	-7.2		-4.4	-6.6	-7.2	-60.3	-7.7	-89.5
8.7	15.7	26.7	EBIT/Interest	12.2	17.0		91.5	34.0	307.7
(75) 4.0	(88) 5.1	(85) 5.0		(27) 4.3	(17) 3.9		(11) 34.1	(11) 8.5	(12) 11.1
1.5	1.3	1.6		.9	1.5		3.3	.2	2.8
			Net Profit + Depr., Dep., Amort./Cur. Mat. L/T/D						
.0	.0	.0	Fixed/Worth	.2	.0	.0	.0	.0	.1
1.2	1.0	1.1		2.5	1.1	.1	.1	.5	.5
6.2	8.0	6.4		UND	4.9	1.7	1.7	-2.1	1.2
.7	.7	.5	Debt/Worth	.5	.3	.2	.3	.5	.5
2.9	3.2	2.3		3.8	2.3	1.7	3.6	6.9	.9
13.1	19.4	13.9		UND	9.9	3.2	61.7	-8.0	2.5
32.8	35.4	45.5	% Profit Before Taxes/Tangible Net Worth	31.5	40.2	81.5	131.1	41.7	119.6
(150) 9.2	(144) 13.4	(132) 16.4		(46) 7.9	(31) 16.9	(15) 23.7	(14) 48.1	(12) 16.8	(14) 26.9
.7	.9	3.2		.7	5.2	4.1	7.5	5.0	5.1
8.1	9.0	14.9	% Profit Before Taxes/Total Assets	8.3	15.7	24.5	49.3	15.7	70.0
2.9	2.6	4.4		1.8	5.4	5.2	17.0	3.1	7.8
.0	.0	.1		-.4	.7	1.3	.9	-3.2	2.3
173.5	72.4	86.2	Sales/Net Fixed Assets	45.1	88.9	UND	422.5	43.7	71.8
2.5	4.3	7.1		.4	8.8	23.1	44.1	14.7	31.6
.2	.2	.2		.2	.2	1.5	15.5	.5	2.3
.6	.9	1.2	Sales/Total Assets	.3	1.3	3.4	5.2	.6	1.6
.1	.2	.2		.2	.3	.3	2.1	.3	.9
.1	.1	.1		.1	.1	.1	.7	.1	.6
2.9	2.7	1.8	% Depr., Dep., Amort./Sales	8.5	2.2		.5	3.4	.6
(106) 14.1	(105) 9.1	(97) 9.3		(40) 16.1	(20) 11.7		(10) 1.3	(11) 4.4	(10) 2.2
25.4	22.2	18.8		22.6	21.2		4.2	21.4	6.7
4.1	2.1	2.9	% Officers', Directors' Owners' Comp/Sales	3.4					
(18) 11.6	(23) 10.9	(25) 7.8		(10) 8.5					
15.4	15.6	16.4		28.1					
2826103M	1562705M	2853546M	Net Sales ($)	22674M	60992M	60832M	124868M	288121M	2296059M
4787222M	4347235M	4221452M	Total Assets ($)	170339M	337512M	365229M	307894M	1368783M	1671695M

© RMA 2011

M = $ thousand   MM = $ million
See Pages 9 through 22 for Explanation of Ratios and Data

REAL ESTATE AND RENTAL AND LEASING

Current Data Sorted by Assets   Comparative Historical Data

Type of Statement	0-500M	500M-2MM	2-10MM	10-50MM	50-100MM	100-250MM	4/1/06-3/31/07 ALL	4/1/07-3/31/08 ALL
Unqualified	8	83	145	60	19	19	249	251
Reviewed		11	22	17		3	45	57
Compiled	25	75	95	22	4		172	199
Tax Returns	217	667	489	59	2	2	859	961
Other	81	279	367	144	10	12	441	467
		152 (4/1-9/30/10)		2,785 (10/1/10-3/31/11)				
NUMBER OF STATEMENTS	331	1115	1118	302	35	36	1766	1935
ASSETS	%	%	%	%	%	%	%	%
Cash & Equivalents	14.3	5.8	4.7	6.7	9.4	9.1	6.9	6.8
Trade Receivables (net)	2.6	1.4	1.2	3.4	7.8	5.4	2.7	2.3
Inventory	1.4	1.1	1.0	2.4	1.9	2.4	3.5	3.2
All Other Current	3.6	1.6	2.0	3.1	4.5	1.1	2.6	2.4
Total Current	21.9	9.9	8.8	15.6	23.6	18.0	15.7	14.7
Fixed Assets (net)	67.9	82.6	82.3	72.5	54.2	64.0	75.2	76.2
Intangibles (net)	2.1	1.5	1.5	1.7	5.6	4.1	1.6	1.7
All Other Non-Current	8.1	6.0	7.3	10.2	16.6	13.9	7.6	7.4
Total	100.0	100.0	100.0	100.0	100.0	100.0	100.0	100.0
LIABILITIES								
Notes Payable-Short Term	8.0	3.8	2.8	5.0	5.3	7.4	6.2	6.1
Cur. Mat.-L.T.D.	4.7	4.7	3.2	2.9	5.0	2.4	3.9	4.0
Trade Payables	4.3	1.3	.9	1.8	4.4	1.7	1.9	2.1
Income Taxes Payable	.1	.0	.0	.1	.1	.1	.0	.0
All Other Current	13.5	6.3	5.0	6.0	4.9	3.9	6.4	6.9
Total Current	30.5	16.1	11.8	15.7	19.6	15.5	18.4	19.2
Long-Term Debt	66.6	77.1	69.9	59.4	50.1	68.2	66.7	68.9
Deferred Taxes	.0	.0	.0	.1	.0	.1	.0	.0
All Other Non-Current	6.7	3.3	3.5	3.6	4.1	3.9	3.5	3.1
Net Worth	-3.9	3.5	14.8	21.2	26.1	12.3	11.3	8.9
Total Liabilities & Net Worth	100.0	100.0	100.0	100.0	100.0	100.0	100.0	100.0
INCOME DATA								
Net Sales	100.0	100.0	100.0	100.0	100.0	100.0	100.0	100.0
Gross Profit								
Operating Expenses	71.9	65.4	66.8	72.8	79.0	78.7	70.4	70.2
Operating Profit	28.1	34.6	33.2	27.2	21.0	21.3	29.6	29.8
All Other Expenses (net)	16.4	24.4	25.5	22.0	15.0	20.9	21.5	23.0
Profit Before Taxes	11.7	10.2	7.7	5.3	6.0	.4	8.1	6.7

RATIOS

	0-500M	500M-2MM	2-10MM	10-50MM	50-100MM	100-250MM	4/1/06-3/31/07 ALL	4/1/07-3/31/08 ALL
Current	2.4	1.5	1.9	2.4	2.4	2.7	2.0	1.9
	.8	.5	.6	.8	1.1	1.5	.7	.7
	.2	.1	.1	.2	.4	.7	.2	.2
Quick	2.0	1.2	1.4	1.6	1.5	2.2	1.4	1.3
	(330) .5	.4	(1117) .4	.5	.9	1.2	(1763) .4	.4
	.1	.1	.1	.1	.3	.5	.1	.1
Sales/Receivables	0 UND	0 UND	0 UND	0 UND	0 UND	0 UND	0 UND	0 UND
	0 UND	0 UND	0 UND	1 324.8	14 26.7	5 77.9	0 UND	0 UND
	0 UND	0 UND	2 151.3	9 41.8	60 6.1	33 11.1	4 102.0	3 133.4
Cost of Sales/Inventory								
Cost of Sales/Payables								
Sales/Working Capital	10.1	19.5	7.2	3.6	6.4	2.4	7.6	9.1
	-25.0	-10.3	-11.5	-19.2	12.7	14.7	-19.7	-15.8
	-3.2	-2.6	-2.6	-2.6	-2.3	-15.4	-3.1	-3.0
EBIT/Interest	8.2	4.9	4.7	5.5	17.4	6.6	5.4	4.9
	(140) 3.7	(414) 2.5	(368) 2.4	(110) 2.1	(18) 3.0	(13) 2.1	(681) 2.5	(712) 2.4
	1.3	1.1	1.2	.7	-.2	1.0	1.3	1.1
Net Profit + Depr., Dep., Amort./Cur. Mat. L/T/D		4.6	4.8	1.4			3.2	2.3
		(12) 2.7	(28) 1.8	(11) .6			(41) 1.7	(41) 1.1
		1.0	.8	-.4			.8	.7
Fixed/Worth	1.0	2.4	2.1	1.3	.6	1.2	1.7	1.9
	7.6	8.0	5.5	4.4	2.3	4.4	5.4	5.7
	-3.4	-7.9	-49.3	35.5	7.5	NM	-26.7	-19.7
Debt/Worth	.8	1.9	1.7	1.4	1.7	1.4	1.6	1.8
	12.1	8.1	5.7	4.2	3.4	8.3	6.1	6.4
	-4.9	-9.4	-57.7	51.6	36.1	-278.3	-27.5	-21.4
% Profit Before Taxes/Tangible Net Worth	84.0	29.7	21.5	18.3	31.2	25.5	28.8	29.8
	(201) 23.5	(707) 10.1	(807) 5.0	(233) 5.3	(28) 8.1	(26) 1.8	(1250) 8.8	(1329) 7.6
	.7	-2.3	-3.2	-3.7	-4.3	-4.3	-2.8	-4.2
% Profit Before Taxes/Total Assets	22.6	6.7	4.2	3.9	6.5	3.8	6.6	6.4
	5.2	1.9	1.1	.9	.9	.2	1.8	1.4
	-1.1	-1.2	-1.4	-1.5	-1.1	-1.5	-1.0	-1.5
Sales/Net Fixed Assets	6.0	.4	.3	.4	5.9	1.1	.7	.6
	.5	.2	.2	.2	.2	.2	.3	.3
	.2	.1	.1	.1	.2	.2	.1	.2
Sales/Total Assets	1.6	.3	.2	.3	.5	.4	.5	.4
	.4	.2	.2	.2	.2	.2	.2	.2
	.2	.1	.1	.1	.1	.1	.1	.1
% Depr., Dep., Amort./Sales	5.6	11.6	14.0	9.3	3.1	7.5	8.7	9.1
	(250) 14.0	(965) 18.1	(942) 21.4	(247) 20.0	(28) 14.2	(25) 14.9	(1510) 16.7	(1696) 16.6
	23.1	26.4	30.9	29.4	25.3	22.4	25.2	25.0
% Officers', Directors' Owners' Comp/Sales	4.6	3.0	3.3	2.6			2.8	3.3
	(38) 8.4	(88) 4.9	(92) 6.2	(33) 4.8			(203) 6.7	(220) 6.0
	19.8	8.9	9.9	11.1			13.2	13.2
Net Sales ($)	111698M	549637M	1348784M	2286469M	1090130M	2110234M	5622159M	8004279M
Total Assets ($)	88785M	1332120M	4970639M	6244778M	2248820M	5778107M	12357034M	13712681M

M = $ thousand   MM = $ million
See Pages 9 through 22 for Explanation of Ratios and Data

Comparative Historical Data | Current Data Sorted by Sales

Type of Statement	4/1/08-3/31/09 ALL	4/1/09-3/31/10 ALL	4/1/10-3/31/11 ALL	0-1MM	1-3MM	3-5MM	5-10MM	10-25MM	25MM & OVER
Unqualified	264	308	334	198	40	23	25	25	23
Reviewed	68	70	53	19	15	6	2	7	4
Compiled	182	229	221	142	47	9	17	4	2
Tax Returns	1219	1527	1436	1207	181	22	16	6	4
Other	690	788	893	571	203	47	37	20	15
				152 (4/1-9/30/10)		2,785 (10/1/10-3/31/11)			
NUMBER OF STATEMENTS	2423	2922	2937	2137	486	107	97	62	48
ASSETS	%	%	%	%	%	%	%	%	%
Cash & Equivalents	6.8	6.5	6.5	5.0	8.6	14.2	13.4	13.6	13.0
Trade Receivables (net)	2.4	2.0	1.8	.7	2.8	3.1	5.8	8.6	20.1
Inventory	2.1	1.6	1.3	.6	1.9	2.0	5.3	8.4	6.2
All Other Current	2.1	1.5	2.1	1.7	3.2	3.9	3.6	3.1	4.9
Total Current	13.3	11.6	11.7	8.0	16.5	23.2	28.1	33.7	44.1
Fixed Assets (net)	76.3	78.6	79.2	84.6	72.5	62.5	52.9	50.3	37.9
Intangibles (net)	1.6	1.6	1.7	1.4	2.2	1.6	2.3	2.2	6.9
All Other Non-Current	8.8	8.2	7.4	6.1	8.8	12.7	16.7	13.8	11.1
Total	100.0	100.0	100.0	100.0	100.0	100.0	100.0	100.0	100.0
LIABILITIES									
Notes Payable-Short Term	5.1	3.6	4.1	3.8	3.8	4.8	7.6	5.8	9.2
Cur. Mat.-L.T.D.	4.7	4.2	3.9	4.0	3.8	3.7	3.2	1.9	2.7
Trade Payables	1.6	1.3	1.6	1.0	1.7	2.8	4.3	5.9	10.8
Income Taxes Payable	.1	.0	.0	.0	.1	.0	.1	.1	.0
All Other Current	7.8	7.5	6.6	5.7	7.9	11.8	9.4	7.4	11.9
Total Current	19.2	16.5	16.1	14.5	17.4	23.1	24.7	21.3	34.6
Long-Term Debt	69.8	73.1	70.9	73.2	72.4	62.9	53.0	49.4	39.3
Deferred Taxes	.0	.1	.0	.0	.0	.0	.0	.0	.3
All Other Non-Current	3.4	3.1	3.8	3.5	3.8	4.1	8.9	5.5	5.3
Net Worth	7.5	7.3	9.1	8.9	6.4	9.8	13.4	23.8	20.6
Total Liabilties & Net Worth	100.0	100.0	100.0	100.0	100.0	100.0	100.0	100.0	100.0
INCOME DATA									
Net Sales	100.0	100.0	100.0	100.0	100.0	100.0	100.0	100.0	100.0
Gross Profit									
Operating Expenses	69.0	67.5	67.8	64.8	72.0	75.7	81.8	84.3	87.8
Operating Profit	31.0	32.5	32.2	35.2	28.0	24.3	18.2	15.7	12.2
All Other Expenses (net)	23.9	24.2	23.5	26.5	18.2	13.9	10.7	10.3	7.5
Profit Before Taxes	7.1	8.3	8.7	8.6	9.9	10.3	7.5	5.4	4.8

RATIOS

Ratio	Hist 4/1/08-3/31/09	Hist 4/1/09-3/31/10	Hist 4/1/10-3/31/11	0-1MM	1-3MM	3-5MM	5-10MM	10-25MM	25MM & OVER
Current	1.8 / .6 / .2	1.8 / .6 / .1	1.8 / .6 / .2	1.5 / .5 / .1	2.4 / .7 / .2	4.3 / .9 / .3	3.4 / 1.4 / .5	3.1 / 1.3 / .7	2.4 / 1.5 / 1.0
Quick	(2421) 1.3 / .4 / .1	(2921) 1.4 / .4 / .1	(2935) 1.4 / .5 / .1	(2136) 1.2 / .4 / .1	1.7 / .5 / .1	2.2 / .7 / .2	3.0 / .9 / .3	(61) 2.1 / 1.0 / .5	1.6 / 1.1 / .5
Sales/Receivables	0 UND / 0 UND / 2 147.0	0 UND / 0 UND / 2 171.4	0 UND / 0 UND / 2 174.4	0 UND / 0 UND / 0 UND	0 UND / 0 UND / 4 92.1	0 UND / 1 542.3 / 7 51.3	0 UND / 3 105.8 / 21 17.3	1 356.0 / 13 28.0 / 35 10.5	5 80.8 / 32 11.5 / 64 5.7
Cost of Sales/Inventory									
Cost of Sales/Payables									
Sales/Working Capital	9.3 / -11.9 / -2.6	10.5 / -11.1 / -2.6	9.1 / -12.8 / -2.7	12.8 / -9.0 / -2.2	6.3 / -30.7 / -3.7	3.5 / -97.7 / -5.1	3.0 / 26.7 / -7.5	3.5 / 22.4 / -19.8	6.5 / 13.2 / NM
EBIT/Interest	(899) 4.6 / 2.2 / .9	(1054) 5.5 / 2.6 / 1.1	(1063) 5.5 / 2.5 / 1.1	(650) 4.8 / 2.5 / 1.1	(227) 5.2 / 2.5 / 1.3	(55) 12.4 / 2.7 / .1	(60) 6.8 / 1.9 / -.3	(39) 17.5 / 3.1 / 1.1	(32) 17.8 / 4.8 / 1.4
Net Profit + Depr., Dep., Amort./Cur. Mat. L/T/D	(52) 3.0 / 1.2 / .4	(41) 4.4 / 2.1 / .5	(59) 4.4 / 1.6 / .5	(21) 3.3 / 2.0 / .9	(14) 3.1 / 1.5 / .5				
Fixed/Worth	2.0 / 7.2 / -13.1	2.1 / 6.8 / -11.2	2.0 / 6.0 / -14.6	2.3 / 6.7 / -16.2	1.6 / 6.0 / -6.6	.8 / 4.6 / -9.8	.5 / 2.0 / 80.3	.5 / 1.5 / 7.0	.2 / 1.5 / NM
Debt/Worth	1.8 / 8.4 / -15.2	1.9 / 7.3 / -13.4	1.6 / 6.5 / -16.1	1.8 / 6.8 / -17.4	1.5 / 8.1 / -8.5	1.2 / 5.7 / -13.6	1.0 / 3.0 / NM	.7 / 3.0 / 11.2	1.1 / 3.2 / NM
% Profit Before Taxes/Tangible Net Worth	(1606) 28.0 / 7.4 / -4.2	(1939) 27.8 / 7.0 / -3.2	(2002) 26.7 / 7.6 / -2.7	(1457) 24.6 / 5.9 / -3.4	(306) 37.5 / 12.5 / .3	(76) 30.8 / 9.1 / -4.8	(73) 34.4 / 9.8 / -1.2	(54) 35.2 / 9.6 / .3	(36) 52.6 / 23.6 / 9.6
% Profit Before Taxes/Total Assets	6.1 / 1.3 / -1.6	6.0 / 1.3 / -1.5	5.8 / 1.5 / -1.3	5.1 / 1.2 / -1.4	8.9 / 2.5 / -.7	7.5 / 2.0 / -1.9	8.6 / 2.3 / -1.2	11.1 / 1.9 / -.1	11.6 / 4.5 / .3
Sales/Net Fixed Assets	.6 / .2 / .1	.5 / .2 / .1	.5 / .2 / .1	.3 / .2 / .1	1.0 / .3 / .2	2.9 / .6 / .2	12.7 / .7 / .2	9.9 / 1.1 / .3	32.6 / 6.5 / .5
Sales/Total Assets	.4 / .2 / .1	.3 / .2 / .1	.3 / .2 / .1	.3 / .2 / .1	.6 / .3 / .2	.9 / .3 / .2	1.3 / .3 / .2	1.8 / .5 / .2	2.3 / 1.1 / .4
% Depr., Dep., Amort./Sales	(2049) 9.8 / 17.7 / 26.7	(2512) 11.0 / 18.8 / 27.1	(2457) 11.6 / 19.2 / 28.4	(1819) 14.0 / 20.9 / 30.4	(387) 7.5 / 15.6 / 25.1	(84) 4.1 / 10.8 / 20.6	(80) 1.5 / 10.4 / 19.9	(54) 1.5 / 5.4 / 15.2	(33) .9 / 2.1 / 7.5
% Officers', Directors' Owners' Comp/Sales	(236) 3.5 / 6.5 / 11.3	(270) 2.7 / 5.3 / 11.0	(255) 3.0 / 5.6 / 10.7	(134) 3.7 / 6.9 / 13.4	(73) 2.3 / 4.6 / 7.7	(15) 2.8 / 5.9 / 7.3	(22) 2.1 / 5.4 / 14.3		
Net Sales ($)	8263148M	9240220M	7496952M	731946M	826392M	419316M	681451M	980340M	3857507M
Total Assets ($)	18088802M	22183155M	20663249M	4739989M	3757753M	1702784M	2766206M	3005017M	4691500M

M = $ thousand   MM = $ million
See Pages 9 through 22 for Explanation of Ratios and Data

Current Data Sorted by Assets

Comparative Historical Data

						Type of Statement		
5	23	69	72	16	18	Unqualified	241	206
13	54	138	84	17	8	Reviewed	282	248
43	298	410	109	6	2	Compiled	790	720
702	2812	2281	264	6	7	Tax Returns	3479	3887
197	1010	1375	425	59	34	Other	1494	1668
	327 (4/1-9/30/10)			10,230 (10/1/10-3/31/11)			4/1/06-3/31/07 ALL	4/1/07-3/31/08 ALL
0-500M	500M-2MM	2-10MM	10-50MM	50-100MM	100-250MM	NUMBER OF STATEMENTS		
960	4197	4273	954	104	69		6286	6729
%	%	%	%	%	%	ASSETS	%	%
10.0	4.2	4.1	4.5	4.4	7.0	Cash & Equivalents	5.1	5.0
2.5	1.1	1.3	2.6	2.4	2.0	Trade Receivables (net)	1.9	1.6
1.1	.5	.7	2.0	4.2	2.6	Inventory	1.4	1.1
1.8	1.2	1.5	2.7	2.1	2.3	All Other Current	1.7	1.8
15.5	7.0	7.7	11.8	13.2	13.9	Total Current	10.1	9.5
78.8	87.3	84.6	76.4	72.2	63.0	Fixed Assets (net)	82.3	83.2
1.6	1.4	1.8	2.1	1.9	5.3	Intangibles (net)	1.6	1.4
4.1	4.3	5.9	9.7	12.7	17.8	All Other Non-Current	5.9	5.9
100.0	100.0	100.0	100.0	100.0	100.0	Total	100.0	100.0
						LIABILITIES		
5.8	3.0	3.0	4.1	5.5	4.8	Notes Payable-Short Term	4.5	3.4
5.9	4.4	3.8	3.5	3.1	2.9	Cur. Mat.-L.T.D.	4.4	4.5
2.5	.6	.7	1.4	1.7	2.1	Trade Payables	1.4	1.2
.0	.0	.0	.0	.1	.2	Income Taxes Payable	.1	.0
10.4	3.5	3.1	4.0	4.0	4.3	All Other Current	4.6	4.3
24.6	11.6	10.7	13.0	14.4	14.3	Total Current	15.0	13.4
70.3	69.9	67.1	58.9	52.1	44.5	Long-Term Debt	65.8	67.3
.0	.0	.0	.1	.6	.6	Deferred Taxes	.1	.1
4.3	2.6	2.8	3.8	2.6	5.0	All Other Non-Current	2.6	3.1
.8	16.0	19.4	24.1	30.3	35.6	Net Worth	16.5	16.2
100.0	100.0	100.0	100.0	100.0	100.0	Total Liabilities & Net Worth	100.0	100.0
						INCOME DATA		
100.0	100.0	100.0	100.0	100.0	100.0	Net Sales	100.0	100.0
						Gross Profit		
50.0	46.1	48.8	57.6	69.0	68.2	Operating Expenses	49.5	48.8
50.0	53.9	51.2	42.4	31.0	31.8	Operating Profit	50.5	51.2
22.7	30.5	30.2	25.8	17.7	17.1	All Other Expenses (net)	28.7	30.2
27.3	23.4	21.0	16.7	13.3	14.7	Profit Before Taxes	21.7	21.1
						RATIOS		
1.6	1.7	1.9	2.2	1.8	2.4	Current	1.8	1.8
.5	.5	.6	.7	.8	1.3		.6	.5
.1	.1	.2	.2	.4	.5		.1	.2
1.3	1.4	1.5	1.5	1.2	1.8	Quick	1.4	1.3
(959) .4	(4196) .4	(4271) .4	.4	(103) .5	.8		(6282) .4	(6723) .4
.1	.1	.1	.1	.2	.2		.1	.1
0 UND	0 UND	0 UND	0 UND	0 UND	0 999.8	Sales/Receivables	0 UND	0 UND
0 UND	0 UND	0 UND	0 UND	5 75.2	5 76.4		0 UND	0 UND
0 UND	0 UND	0 UND	12 31.1	27 13.4	23 16.1		0 UND	0 UND
						Cost of Sales/Inventory		
						Cost of Sales/Payables		
14.4	11.5	7.2	4.5	3.9	3.6	Sales/Working Capital	9.3	9.7
-10.2	-8.4	-10.0	-13.3	-32.5	14.3		-10.7	-10.0
-2.8	-2.6	-2.7	-2.3	-2.9	-4.7		-2.3	-2.6
9.3	7.1	6.5	5.9	6.4	6.7	EBIT/Interest	7.5	6.8
(354) 4.7	(1144) 4.3	(1202) 3.9	(334) 3.3	(49) 3.0	(40) 3.2		(1763) 4.1	(1764) 4.0
2.6	2.8	2.3	1.6	1.2	1.1		2.2	2.2
	2.9	3.6	3.6	2.8	14.5	Net Profit + Depr., Dep., Amort./Cur. Mat. L/T/D	3.5	4.3
	(47) 1.6	(145) 1.9	(77) 1.9	(20) 1.5	(13) 3.3		(265) 1.7	(257) 1.9
	.7	.9	1.0	.8	1.5		1.0	.9
1.7	2.6	2.3	1.7	1.3	1.1	Fixed/Worth	2.3	2.3
4.8	5.5	5.2	4.0	2.8	2.3		5.2	5.2
-20.2	335.0	56.3	19.3	8.4	10.2		53.4	66.5
1.1	1.9	1.7	1.5	.9	.8	Debt/Worth	1.8	1.8
4.7	5.2	4.7	4.1	3.0	2.2		5.2	5.0
-16.2	521.2	64.6	22.2	8.5	15.5		67.3	81.4
50.4	37.0	29.5	25.1	13.2	15.8	% Profit Before Taxes/Tangible Net Worth	37.9	35.2
(670) 22.8	(3164) 16.1	(3302) 13.4	(785) 10.9	(87) 6.6	(57) 7.5		(4873) 16.7	(5208) 15.9
9.4	5.0	3.3	1.3	-1.0	-.2		5.2	4.5
16.0	7.8	6.2	5.0	4.4	5.5	% Profit Before Taxes/Total Assets	8.1	7.8
6.4	3.5	2.9	2.2	1.9	2.2		3.5	3.4
1.5	.6	.4	.0	-.8	-.6		.7	.6
.7	.3	.2	.3	.4	1.0	Sales/Net Fixed Assets	.3	.3
.3	.2	.2	.2	.2	.3		.2	.2
.2	.1	.1	.1	.1	.2		.1	.1
.6	.2	.2	.2	.2	.3	Sales/Total Assets	.3	.3
.2	.2	.1	.1	.1	.2		.2	.2
.2	.1	.1	.1	.1	.1		.1	.1
8.0	12.4	13.6	12.7	9.5	9.3	% Depr., Dep., Amort./Sales	10.8	11.1
(802) 14.5	(3792) 18.1	(3802) 19.5	(836) 19.4	(90) 18.7	(55) 16.4		(5772) 16.5	(6113) 16.6
21.3	24.5	26.8	27.7	28.8	23.4		23.0	23.3
5.6	2.7	2.2	1.2		2.5	% Officers', Directors' Owners' Comp/Sales	2.8	2.7
(54) 8.8	(199) 6.1	(276) 4.3	(92) 4.3		(14) 5.4		(458) 6.4	(429) 5.9
16.4	13.8	10.6	11.6		9.7		14.9	13.0
214228M	1399474M	4196701M	5879912M	2762836M	8318751M	Net Sales ($)	16165689M	20406044M
295921M	4994679M	18111661M	18715080M	7255110M	11083591M	Total Assets ($)	38104097M	39567965M

M = $ thousand   MM = $ million

See Pages 9 through 22 for Explanation of Ratios and Data

Comparative Historical Data | Current Data Sorted by Sales

			Type of Statement						
238	222	203	Unqualified	64	43	20	27	19	30
291	263	314	Reviewed	129	76	29	31	30	19
851	918	868	Compiled	642	153	37	21	10	5
5067	5789	6072	Tax Returns	5374	556	64	47	18	13
2144	2498	3100	Other	2250	514	120	98	75	43
4/1/08-3/31/09 ALL	4/1/09-3/31/10 ALL	4/1/10-3/31/11 ALL		327 (4/1-9/30/10)			10,230 (10/1/10-3/31/11)		
				0-1MM	1-3MM	3-5MM	5-10MM	10-25MM	25MM & OVER
8591	9690	10557	NUMBER OF STATEMENTS	8459	1342	270	224	152	110
%	%	%	ASSETS	%	%	%	%	%	%
5.0	4.7	4.8	Cash & Equivalents	4.3	5.7	6.9	9.3	9.0	9.1
1.5	1.3	1.5	Trade Receivables (net)	.7	2.2	4.5	7.7	12.8	13.9
1.0	.9	.8	Inventory	.2	1.3	3.5	4.3	10.1	13.2
1.5	1.3	1.6	All Other Current	1.3	2.1	3.4	3.1	4.0	3.9
9.0	8.2	8.6	Total Current	6.5	11.4	18.3	24.5	35.8	40.0
83.2	84.5	84.1	Fixed Assets (net)	87.3	78.5	69.4	59.6	48.2	43.9
1.5	1.7	1.7	Intangibles (net)	1.4	2.2	2.2	3.7	5.5	4.3
6.3	5.7	5.6	All Other Non-Current	4.7	7.9	10.1	12.2	10.5	11.9
100.0	100.0	100.0	Total	100.0	100.0	100.0	100.0	100.0	100.0
			LIABILITIES						
3.6	3.3	3.4	Notes Payable-Short Term	3.1	3.8	4.1	4.3	9.1	8.9
4.3	4.5	4.2	Cur. Mat.-L.T.D.	4.2	4.3	3.4	3.5	4.0	3.5
1.1	1.0	.9	Trade Payables	.4	1.2	2.9	4.8	5.8	10.8
.0	.0	.0	Income Taxes Payable	.0	.0	.0	.1	.1	.3
4.1	4.1	4.1	All Other Current	3.6	4.8	6.8	8.1	8.7	8.5
13.2	12.9	12.6	Total Current	11.4	14.2	17.3	20.7	27.7	32.1
68.1	68.1	67.5	Long-Term Debt	69.5	66.9	56.4	47.1	40.2	29.4
.0	.0	.0	Deferred Taxes	.0	.1	.1	.5	.4	.5
2.9	2.6	2.9	All Other Non-Current	2.7	3.5	3.4	6.8	5.2	5.7
15.7	16.3	17.0	Net Worth	16.5	15.4	22.8	24.9	26.5	32.4
100.0	100.0	100.0	Total Liabilties & Net Worth	100.0	100.0	100.0	100.0	100.0	100.0
			INCOME DATA						
100.0	100.0	100.0	Net Sales	100.0	100.0	100.0	100.0	100.0	100.0
			Gross Profit						
49.2	49.2	48.9	Operating Expenses	45.3	56.6	67.9	76.1	81.8	88.3
50.8	50.8	51.1	Operating Profit	54.7	43.4	32.1	23.9	18.2	11.7
30.3	29.7	29.0	All Other Expenses (net)	31.6	22.3	16.0	12.9	9.0	4.5
20.5	21.1	22.0	Profit Before Taxes	23.1	21.2	16.1	11.0	9.2	7.2
			RATIOS						
1.8	1.7	1.8		1.7	2.3	2.7	2.8	2.3	2.1
.6	.5	.6	Current	.5	.7	1.2	1.2	1.2	1.2
.2	.1	.2		.1	.2	.3	.4	.6	.8
1.3	1.4	1.4		1.3	1.8	1.8	1.7	1.7	1.3
(8587) .4	(9684) .4	(10552) .4	Quick	(8457) .4	(1340) .5	(269) .7	.8	.8	.7
.1	.1	.1		.1	.1	.2	.2	.3	.3
0 UND	0 UND	0 UND		0 UND	0 UND	0 UND	0 UND	2 235.7	3 114.8
0 UND	0 UND	0 UND	Sales/Receivables	0 UND	0 UND	2 196.2	3 118.5	15 24.1	20 18.4
0 UND	0 UND	0 UND		0 UND	7 56.0	13 27.7	28 13.1	46 8.0	44 8.3
			Cost of Sales/Inventory						
			Cost of Sales/Payables						
9.6	9.1	8.5		10.4	6.1	4.4	4.2	7.0	7.4
-9.9	-9.5	-9.8	Sales/Working Capital	-8.0	-21.0	54.2	49.2	33.8	26.6
-2.7	-2.6	-2.7		-2.5	-3.2	-4.3	-4.9	-8.6	-26.9
6.7	7.0	7.0		7.0	6.5	8.4	8.5	7.4	8.1
(2320) 3.9	(2779) 4.0	(3123) 4.1	EBIT/Interest	(2069) 4.3	(570) 3.5	(150) 3.2	(132) 2.7	(109) 3.2	(93) 3.8
2.1	2.2	2.4		2.8	1.6	1.2	1.3	1.4	1.3
3.7	3.3	3.5		2.7	4.0	3.7	7.2	4.0	7.4
(278) 1.9	(267) 1.6	(310) 1.8	Net Profit + Depr., Dep., Amort./Cur. Mat. L/T/D	(143) 1.5	(63) 2.2	(20) 1.9	(28) 2.9	(27) 1.9	(29) 2.1
.8	.8	1.0		.8	1.0	.7	1.0	.8	1.7
2.3	2.3	2.2		2.5	1.9	1.5	1.0	.5	.5
5.3	5.6	5.1	Fixed/Worth	5.3	5.2	3.8	2.8	2.3	1.3
128.5	118.2	94.9		92.8	-137.1	126.3	43.6	8.8	3.3
1.8	1.8	1.7		1.8	1.5	1.3	1.1	1.1	.9
5.2	5.3	4.8	Debt/Worth	4.8	5.4	3.8	3.6	3.5	2.1
180.5	164.1	125.6		114.4	-123.6	365.6	76.1	16.9	10.0
33.9	33.3	33.2		32.5	36.8	45.2	31.0	38.4	27.6
(6552) 14.9	(7378) 14.2	(8065) 14.6	% Profit Before Taxes/Tangible Net Worth	(6487) 14.3	(985) 16.4	(205) 17.4	(170) 11.5	(124) 14.5	(94) 13.2
3.5	3.1	3.9		4.0	4.1	3.0	.8	1.3	4.8
7.3	7.0	7.2		7.0	8.2	9.4	8.6	10.1	10.1
3.1	3.0	3.2	% Profit Before Taxes/Total Assets	3.1	3.9	3.8	3.3	3.9	3.4
.4	.3	.5		.5	.6	.2	-.1	.3	.5
.3	.3	.3		.2	.4	1.6	12.3	21.1	20.9
.2	.2	.2	Sales/Net Fixed Assets	.2	.2	.3	.6	1.6	6.6
.1	.1	.1		.1	.1	.2	.2	.3	.7
.2	.2	.2		.2	.3	.9	1.7	2.3	3.0
.2	.1	.1	Sales/Total Assets	.1	.2	.2	.3	.6	1.7
.1	.1	.1		.1	.1	.1	.1	.2	.4
11.7	12.6	12.5		13.5	10.6	5.5	1.9	1.7	1.1
(7807) 17.4	(8784) 18.5	(9377) 18.5	% Depr., Dep., Amort./Sales	(7558) 19.2	(1172) 16.7	(232) 14.1	(190) 12.2	(131) 6.6	(94) 2.9
24.3	25.4	25.5		26.2	24.2	22.3	22.6	16.1	8.3
2.1	2.4	2.4		3.0	3.1	2.7	1.2	.8	.3
(540) 5.2	(584) 5.3	(640) 5.6	% Officers', Directors' Owners' Comp/Sales	(312) 6.4	(172) 6.0	(42) 5.3	(59) 3.2	(23) 2.9	1.1
11.6	11.8	12.4		14.7	12.7	9.0	10.1	6.3	4.2
20685589M	19871403M	22771902M	Net Sales ($)	2685610M	2196775M	1046399M	1564042M	2366281M	12912795M
52875159M	56315124M	60456042M	Total Assets ($)	19312830M	13065590M	5197831M	6670892M	7061899M	9147000M

© RMA 2011

M = $ thousand   MM = $ million
See Pages 9 through 22 for Explanation of Ratios and Data

Current Data Sorted by Assets

Comparative Historical Data

Type of Statement	0-500M	500M-2MM	2-10MM	10-50MM	50-100MM	100-250MM		4/1/06-3/31/07 ALL	4/1/07-3/31/08 ALL
Unqualified	1		1	3	1	4		4	7
Reviewed			7	5	1	1		8	11
Compiled	3	23	28	2	1	1		26	23
Tax Returns	39	138	113	4	1	1		103	185
Other	21	64	84	15	2			62	93
	15 (4/1-9/30/10)			551 (10/1/10-3/31/11)					
NUMBER OF STATEMENTS	64	229	233	29	5	6		203	319
	%	%	%	%	%	%		%	%
ASSETS									
Cash & Equivalents	29.2	3.2	4.3	5.0				6.9	7.0
Trade Receivables (net)	1.6	1.2	.7	1.2				1.6	2.0
Inventory	1.6	.8	.9	.4				1.3	1.7
All Other Current	2.4	.8	1.3	1.9				2.3	2.2
Total Current	34.7	6.0	7.3	8.4				12.1	12.9
Fixed Assets (net)	53.6	87.5	85.9	79.4				80.4	80.3
Intangibles (net)	2.9	2.9	3.0	3.4				1.2	2.1
All Other Non-Current	8.8	3.5	3.8	8.8				6.2	4.7
Total	100.0	100.0	100.0	100.0				100.0	100.0
LIABILITIES									
Notes Payable-Short Term	6.5	3.5	2.8	9.5				7.8	3.6
Cur. Mat.-L.T.D.	4.5	4.1	3.5	4.9				4.5	4.3
Trade Payables	4.1	.6	.5	.4				1.1	1.3
Income Taxes Payable	.0	.0	.0	.2				.0	.1
All Other Current	35.4	5.8	5.6	3.9				8.4	10.0
Total Current	50.5	14.1	12.4	18.9				21.8	19.3
Long-Term Debt	45.0	82.7	73.9	62.6				67.2	68.1
Deferred Taxes	.0	.0	.1	.5				.0	.1
All Other Non-Current	15.8	3.7	3.0	1.3				3.9	4.0
Net Worth	-11.4	-.5	10.6	16.6				7.0	8.5
Total Liabilties & Net Worth	100.0	100.0	100.0	100.0				100.0	100.0
INCOME DATA									
Net Sales	100.0	100.0	100.0	100.0				100.0	100.0
Gross Profit									
Operating Expenses	81.2	61.3	61.9	67.2				63.7	62.2
Operating Profit	18.8	38.7	38.1	32.8				36.3	37.8
All Other Expenses (net)	6.3	25.0	27.2	24.1				20.6	23.9
Profit Before Taxes	12.5	13.7	11.0	8.7				15.7	13.9
RATIOS									
Current	2.2	1.0	1.3	2.2				3.0	2.2
	.7	.4	.4	.7				.7	.8
	.2	.1	.1	.2				.2	.3
Quick	2.1	.9	.9	1.3				1.9	1.8
	(63) .7	.3	.4	.6				.5	.6
	.2	.1	.1	.2				.1	.2
Sales/Receivables	0 UND	0 UND	0 UND	0 UND				0 UND	0 UND
	0 UND	0 UND	0 UND	6 63.5				0 UND	0 UND
	0 UND	0 UND	0 UND	22 16.9				1 373.0	3 128.0
Cost of Sales/Inventory									
Cost of Sales/Payables									
Sales/Working Capital	21.1	134.5	33.2	10.9				12.2	12.4
	-50.7	-8.0	-7.7	-22.0				-24.2	-34.3
	-5.1	-2.9	-3.1	-2.0				-3.7	-4.5
EBIT/Interest	6.1	4.8	3.8	3.6				4.8	8.8
	(30) 2.6	(92) 3.2	(67) 2.9	(11) 2.3				(71) 3.1	(117) 3.7
	.7	1.7	1.7	1.6				1.7	2.0
Net Profit + Depr., Dep., Amort./Cur. Mat. L/T/D								5.8	5.8
								(13) 2.6	2.6
								1.3	1.3
Fixed/Worth	.7	3.5	3.0	3.1				2.2	2.6
	2.7	24.2	10.2	7.8				6.7	9.2
	-1.8	-4.1	-9.1	NM				-10.0	-8.8
Debt/Worth	.4	3.1	2.5	2.9				1.8	2.0
	5.6	25.3	9.4	9.2				6.9	10.3
	-3.7	-5.3	-11.3	NM				-11.8	-10.8
% Profit Before Taxes/Tangible Net Worth	167.7	37.9	33.6	36.6				47.3	51.9
	(39) 44.4	(126) 20.6	(146) 11.1	(22) 7.3				(137) 16.1	(199) 21.9
	2.0	.5	.8	-11.9				4.8	3.8
% Profit Before Taxes/Total Assets	41.2	8.1	5.4	4.1				9.0	9.3
	6.8	2.7	2.0	2.0				3.9	3.2
	-.9	.1	-.4	-.8				.9	-.3
Sales/Net Fixed Assets	61.8	.4	.3	.4				.6	.6
	5.0	.2	.2	.2				.3	.3
	.5	.2	.1	.1				.2	.2
Sales/Total Assets	9.4	.3	.2	.3				.5	.5
	1.2	.2	.2	.1				.2	.2
	.4	.2	.1	.1				.2	.2
% Depr., Dep., Amort./Sales	2.1	10.8	13.3	14.2				7.8	7.6
	(40) 8.2	(199) 15.5	(182) 19.2	(24) 19.4				(180) 13.2	(271) 12.7
	16.3	21.5	27.0	24.7				19.2	18.5
% Officers', Directors' Owners' Comp/Sales	2.0	4.3	2.0					2.9	4.9
	(10) 5.3	(25) 7.6	(20) 5.6					(26) 7.9	(40) 10.5
	17.6	11.9	12.6					13.0	13.8
Net Sales ($)	26443M	87523M	202415M	501156M	146717M	393091M		344087M	1424935M
Total Assets ($)	14023M	289150M	896842M	628724M	354637M	980007M		1213547M	1880863M

M = $ thousand   MM = $ million

© RMA 2011

See Pages 9 through 22 for Explanation of Ratios and Data

Comparative Historical Data | Current Data Sorted by Sales

			Type of Statement						
13	6	9	Unqualified	7	3	1	3	2	3
8	19	19	Reviewed			6	1		
28	37	56	Compiled	49	5	1			
193	216	296	Tax Returns	272	18		2	2	2
164	159	186	Other	152	27	2		1	
4/1/08-3/31/09 ALL	4/1/09-3/31/10 ALL	4/1/10-3/31/11 ALL		15 (4/1-9/30/10) 0-1MM	1-3MM	3-5MM	551 (10/1/10-3/31/11) 5-10MM	10-25MM	25MM & OVER
406	437	566	NUMBER OF STATEMENTS	480	53	10	8	7	8
%	%	%	ASSETS	%	%	%	%	%	%
6.6	7.0	6.6	Cash & Equivalents	6.5	7.0	7.6			
2.1	1.8	1.1	Trade Receivables (net)	.8	1.8	3.7			
1.1	1.5	.9	Inventory	.5	1.7	1.9			
1.4	1.4	1.4	All Other Current	1.1	1.8	4.0			
11.3	11.7	10.1	Total Current	9.0	12.2	17.1			
81.1	81.2	82.4	Fixed Assets (net)	84.5	73.8	70.5			
1.9	2.0	2.9	Intangibles (net)	2.5	6.4	4.2			
5.8	5.2	4.6	All Other Non-Current	4.0	7.6	8.2			
100.0	100.0	100.0	Total	100.0	100.0	100.0			
			LIABILITIES						
4.7	3.5	3.8	Notes Payable-Short Term	3.4	4.4	10.5			
4.2	3.5	3.9	Cur. Mat.-L.T.D.	3.8	5.3	2.4			
1.5	1.3	1.0	Trade Payables	.8	.8	.6			
.1	.0	.0	Income Taxes Payable	.0	.0	.0			
6.0	6.3	8.9	All Other Current	9.3	9.1	4.6			
16.5	14.6	17.7	Total Current	17.3	19.6	18.1			
66.5	68.7	73.1	Long-Term Debt	75.6	66.8	51.1			
.0	.0	.1	Deferred Taxes	.0	.1	1.2			
5.5	2.8	4.7	All Other Non-Current	3.6	4.3	51.0			
11.5	13.9	4.5	Net Worth	3.6	9.1	-21.4			
100.0	100.0	100.0	Total Liabilties & Net Worth	100.0	100.0	100.0			
			INCOME DATA						
100.0	100.0	100.0	Net Sales	100.0	100.0	100.0			
			Gross Profit						
64.5	64.0	64.5	Operating Expenses	63.0	65.6	81.9			
35.5	36.0	35.5	Operating Profit	37.0	34.4	18.1			
23.4	23.5	23.7	All Other Expenses (net)	24.7	21.5	15.9			
12.0	12.6	11.8	Profit Before Taxes	12.3	12.9	2.2			
			RATIOS						
2.0	2.2	1.2		1.1	2.2	3.3			
.7	.6	.5	Current	.4	.7	.9			
.2	.2	.2		.1	.1	.3			
1.6	1.7	1.0		.9	1.8	1.7			
.6	.5 (565)	.4	Quick	(479) .4	.5	.8			
.1	.1	.1		.1	.1	.2			
0 UND	0 UND	0 UND		0 UND	0 UND	6 66.0			
0 UND	0 UND	0 UND	Sales/Receivables	0 UND	0 UND	15 24.9			
4 98.4	3 120.0	0 UND		0 UND	17 21.3	22 16.9			
			Cost of Sales/Inventory						
			Cost of Sales/Payables						
15.7	11.8	44.3		119.5	8.3	2.1			
-25.7	-19.7	-8.6	Sales/Working Capital	-7.9	-23.6	-523.7			
-3.2	-3.0	-3.1		-3.0	-3.2	-2.2			
4.7	5.0	4.5		5.3	3.7				
(142) 2.7	(166) 2.8	(204) 2.9	EBIT/Interest	(160) 3.1	(25) 2.3				
1.6	1.7	1.6		1.7	1.4				
7.8	2.3	3.8	Net Profit + Depr., Dep.,						
(14) 1.6	(13) 1.4	(16) 2.4	Amort./Cur. Mat. L/T/D						
.6	.7	1.2							
2.7	2.4	2.8		2.9	2.6	3.8			
7.4	6.6	10.7	Fixed/Worth	13.8	7.0	11.2			
-17.6	-24.0	-7.7		-7.0	-8.7	NM			
2.2	1.7	2.4		2.5	2.2	5.1			
8.1	6.6	12.0	Debt/Worth	14.9	9.1	13.1			
-19.3	-26.4	-9.1		-8.2	-9.4	NM			
40.9	40.4	39.2	% Profit Before Taxes/Tangible	38.4	56.2				
(282) 14.8	(294) 15.6	(342) 15.0	Net Worth	(283) 15.7	(33) 16.0				
1.0	1.2	.4		.5	5.7				
6.9	7.9	7.1	% Profit Before Taxes/Total	7.2	6.8	6.9			
2.7	2.7	2.4	Assets	2.4	3.0	.7			
.0	-.2	-.5		-.5	.5	-2.1			
.5	.4	.4		.4	1.1	3.1			
.3	.2	.2	Sales/Net Fixed Assets	.2	.2	.3			
.2	.2	.2		.2	.2	.2			
.4	.4	.3		.3	.5	1.0			
.2	.2	.2	Sales/Total Assets	.2	.2	.3			
.1	.1	.1		.1	.2	.1			
9.1	10.5	11.1		11.6	9.8				
(310) 14.2	(346) 15.4	(454) 16.8	% Depr., Dep., Amort./Sales	(384) 17.1	(41) 15.2				
20.5	22.9	22.9		23.0	23.1				
3.5	3.7	2.9	% Officers', Directors'	3.6	3.9				
(44) 7.0	(60) 7.1	(63) 6.5	Owners' Comp/Sales	(45) 7.5	(14) 13.5				
12.3	14.0	13.2		13.5	13.5				
938197M	1121534M	1357345M	Net Sales ($)	194932M	86853M	40745M	52278M	115687M	866850M
2388156M	2662511M	3163383M	Total Assets ($)	1000246M	421326M	172076M	302305M	412362M	855068M

M = $ thousand   MM = $ million
See Pages 9 through 22 for Explanation of Ratios and Data

Current Data Sorted by Assets   Comparative Historical Data

Type of Statement	0-500M	500M-2MM	2-10MM	10-50MM	50-100MM	100-250MM		4/1/06-3/31/07 ALL	4/1/07-3/31/08 ALL
Unqualified	3	10	27	23	5	5		98	82
Reviewed	3	21	36	19	3	1		125	89
Compiled	13	93	94	21				290	241
Tax Returns	133	461	363	40				831	902
Other	48	200	255	87	11	8		531	533
	80 (4/1-9/30/10)			1,903 (10/1/10-3/31/11)					
NUMBER OF STATEMENTS	200	785	775	190	19	14		1875	1847
ASSETS	%	%	%	%	%	%		%	%
Cash & Equivalents	16.1	5.5	4.9	6.3	5.3	3.2		6.2	6.2
Trade Receivables (net)	1.5	1.5	1.5	2.8	3.0	3.3		2.5	2.2
Inventory	2.7	.7	1.5	2.9	2.8	1.6		3.0	2.6
All Other Current	2.0	1.6	1.9	3.0	.9	3.8		2.3	2.5
Total Current	22.3	9.3	9.7	15.0	12.1	12.0		14.0	13.4
Fixed Assets (net)	68.3	83.0	81.4	71.5	72.9	71.2		77.5	78.2
Intangibles (net)	2.3	1.9	2.0	1.5	3.1	1.6		1.6	1.6
All Other Non-Current	7.1	5.8	6.9	12.0	12.0	15.2		6.9	6.7
Total	100.0	100.0	100.0	100.0	100.0	100.0		100.0	100.0
LIABILITIES									
Notes Payable-Short Term	8.2	4.1	3.6	5.8	1.7	1.3		4.8	3.9
Cur. Mat.-L.T.D.	4.3	4.4	4.7	2.8	2.3	6.6		4.3	4.5
Trade Payables	3.0	.8	.9	2.0	2.5	3.3		2.0	1.5
Income Taxes Payable	.0	.0	.1	.1	.1	.1		.0	.1
All Other Current	16.7	3.9	3.7	5.5	3.4	4.4		5.6	5.3
Total Current	32.3	13.2	12.9	16.2	9.9	15.7		16.7	15.2
Long-Term Debt	57.0	66.1	60.1	50.6	61.4	53.2		58.3	59.5
Deferred Taxes	.0	.0	.1	.2	.0	.0		.1	.1
All Other Non-Current	11.6	3.9	4.1	5.3	5.0	8.5		4.1	3.8
Net Worth	-.8	16.8	22.9	27.6	23.6	22.6		20.8	21.5
Total Liabilities & Net Worth	100.0	100.0	100.0	100.0	100.0	100.0		100.0	100.0
INCOME DATA									
Net Sales	100.0	100.0	100.0	100.0	100.0	100.0		100.0	100.0
Gross Profit									
Operating Expenses	57.1	49.3	53.8	59.8	73.0	73.7		54.3	52.8
Operating Profit	42.9	50.7	46.2	40.2	27.0	26.3		45.7	47.2
All Other Expenses (net)	15.0	26.6	28.2	22.4	20.4	15.4		24.7	25.9
Profit Before Taxes	27.9	24.1	18.0	17.8	6.6	10.9		21.0	21.3
RATIOS									
Current	2.7	1.7	2.2	2.6	3.5	1.2		2.0	2.1
	.8	.6	.6	.7	1.2	.8		.7	.7
	.2	.2	.2	.1	.3	.4		.2	.2
Quick	1.8	1.4	1.5	1.7	2.7	.7		1.3	1.4
	.7	.4	.4	.4	.6	.4		(1872) .4	(1845) .5
	.2	.1	.1	.1	.1	.1		.1	.1
Sales/Receivables	0 UND	0 UND	0 UND	0 UND	0 999.8	0 UND		0 UND	0 UND
	0 UND	0 UND	0 UND	0 UND	4 97.6	8 47.0		0 UND	0 UND
	0 UND	0 UND	1 710.0	16 22.5	20 18.2	48 7.7		2 163.0	1 331.0
Cost of Sales/Inventory									
Cost of Sales/Payables									
Sales/Working Capital	8.8	9.2	5.1	4.2	3.1	20.7		6.9	6.4
	-35.4	-9.3	-10.7	-10.0	10.4	-7.8		-14.1	-15.5
	-4.0	-2.8	-2.4	-1.3	-4.2	-1.5		-3.0	-2.9
EBIT/Interest	13.1	7.5	8.2	7.4				7.4	6.9
	(82) 5.9	(267) 4.6	(248) 3.5	(83) 3.3				(664) 4.0	(624) 3.7
	2.9	2.7	1.5	1.4				2.0	1.8
Net Profit + Depr., Dep., Amort./Cur. Mat. L/T/D			2.7	3.2				5.1	3.7
			(32) 1.9	(20) 1.5				(99) 2.0	(82) 2.0
			.8	.6				.8	1.0
Fixed/Worth	1.0	2.0	1.9	1.3	1.9	1.4		1.7	1.8
	3.3	4.6	4.4	3.2	4.2	3.7		3.9	4.1
	-7.6	42.8	23.8	10.7	9.0	NM		22.0	22.6
Debt/Worth	.5	1.4	1.5	1.3	2.3	1.8		1.3	1.4
	3.3	4.3	4.1	2.9	3.9	3.3		3.8	4.0
	-7.3	50.7	29.4	11.5	11.6	NM		31.5	27.1
% Profit Before Taxes/Tangible Net Worth	76.8	35.2	25.8	23.1	14.0	19.9		38.7	37.5
	(136) 24.8	(608) 15.9	(616) 10.9	(156) 10.5	(16) 3.4	(11) 6.3		(1500) 15.8	(1476) 16.6
	12.0	3.6	1.2	1.0	-2.7	.2		4.0	4.7
% Profit Before Taxes/Total Assets	29.4	9.4	5.7	6.1	2.8	6.0		9.5	8.7
	8.7	3.7	2.4	2.3	.9	.2		3.8	3.8
	1.4	.5	.0	.0	-1.0	-1.4		.5	.6
Sales/Net Fixed Assets	5.1	.3	.3	.5	.4	.8		.5	.4
	.5	.2	.2	.2	.3	.2		.2	.2
	.2	.1	.1	.1	.2	.1		.1	.1
Sales/Total Assets	1.5	.3	.2	.3	.3	.4		.3	.3
	.4	.2	.1	.1	.2	.2		.2	.2
	.2	.1	.1	.1	.1	.1		.1	.1
% Depr., Dep., Amort./Sales	5.6	11.1	12.7	7.8	9.7	8.5		8.3	9.0
	(151) 11.8	(684) 17.5	(684) 20.0	(168) 16.3	19.8	(13) 18.3		(1673) 15.8	(1621) 15.7
	18.3	25.3	28.5	28.5	26.9	21.6		23.5	22.7
% Officers', Directors' Owners' Comp/Sales	6.4	3.0	2.4	1.3				2.6	2.2
	(17) 9.8	(47) 5.5	(54) 7.1	(21) 3.8				(184) 6.3	(160) 5.4
	28.4	22.5	13.1	6.9				12.2	13.1
Net Sales ($)	72774M	314512M	1100465M	1474715M	372604M	588633M		11641641M	8903227M
Total Assets ($)	55515M	928149M	3395683M	3701119M	1350009M	2077896M		15774566M	12889684M

M = $ thousand   MM = $ million
See Pages 9 through 22 for Explanation of Ratios and Data

Comparative Historical Data | Current Data Sorted by Sales

			Type of Statement						
99	99	73	Unqualified	30	12	6	10	11	4
102	100	83	Reviewed	45	17	3	3	10	5
262	256	221	Compiled	159	45	7	6	2	2
1071	1008	997	Tax Returns	878	87	12	15	5	
584	607	609	Other	423	112	22	11	28	13
4/1/08-3/31/09	4/1/09-3/31/10	4/1/10-3/31/11		80 (4/1-9/30/10)			1,903 (10/1/10-3/31/11)		
ALL	ALL	ALL		0-1MM	1-3MM	3-5MM	5-10MM	10-25MM	25MM & OVER
2118	2070	1983	**NUMBER OF STATEMENTS**	1535	273	50	45	56	24
%	%	%	**ASSETS**	%	%	%	%	%	%
6.0	5.7	6.4	Cash & Equivalents	5.5	8.2	10.0	11.4	13.0	10.1
2.2	2.1	1.6	Trade Receivables (net)	.7	2.5	5.1	7.2	6.7	20.7
1.7	1.5	1.4	Inventory	.5	2.7	5.8	9.0	4.6	16.3
2.2	2.0	1.9	All Other Current	1.6	2.5	3.8	2.8	3.5	3.7
12.0	11.2	11.4	Total Current	8.4	15.9	24.6	30.3	27.8	50.7
79.5	79.7	79.6	Fixed Assets (net)	83.6	72.8	61.1	58.7	54.8	35.0
1.9	2.0	2.0	Intangibles (net)	1.8	2.2	4.6	2.7	1.9	1.3
6.5	7.1	7.1	All Other Non-Current	6.2	9.2	9.7	8.3	15.5	13.0
100.0	100.0	100.0	Total	100.0	100.0	100.0	100.0	100.0	100.0
			LIABILITIES						
4.4	3.9	4.4	Notes Payable-Short Term	4.0	5.6	5.1	9.9	4.5	9.8
4.8	5.3	4.4	Cur. Mat.-L.T.D.	4.3	5.2	3.2	2.7	3.5	4.8
1.4	1.3	1.2	Trade Payables	.5	2.3	4.6	2.0	5.9	16.7
.1	.0	.0	Income Taxes Payable	.0	.0	.1	.0	.3	.0
5.0	5.2	5.3	All Other Current	4.6	7.0	10.4	7.1	6.9	10.3
15.8	15.8	15.3	Total Current	13.4	20.1	23.4	21.7	21.1	41.6
64.2	64.7	61.2	Long-Term Debt	63.7	61.8	41.9	36.3	41.3	26.4
.0	.1	.0	Deferred Taxes	.0	.0	.3	.2	.4	.7
3.8	3.7	4.9	All Other Non-Current	4.4	6.4	11.1	5.0	7.4	4.7
16.2	15.8	18.5	Net Worth	18.5	11.7	23.3	36.9	29.7	26.7
100.0	100.0	100.0	Total Liabilties & Net Worth	100.0	100.0	100.0	100.0	100.0	100.0
			INCOME DATA						
100.0	100.0	100.0	Net Sales	100.0	100.0	100.0	100.0	100.0	100.0
			Gross Profit						
53.4	53.6	53.2	Operating Expenses	48.9	62.0	71.7	71.4	80.3	93.8
46.6	46.4	46.8	Operating Profit	51.1	38.0	28.3	28.6	19.7	6.2
27.1	25.2	25.5	All Other Expenses (net)	28.6	19.0	12.9	8.7	8.9	2.6
19.5	21.3	21.2	Profit Before Taxes	22.5	19.0	15.4	20.0	10.8	3.6
			RATIOS						
2.0	2.2	2.1		1.9	2.8	3.4	3.5	2.4	1.6
.7	.6	.6	Current	.6	.7	1.2	1.3	1.4	1.2
.2	.2	.2		.1	.1	.3	.4	.6	.7
1.5	1.6	1.5		1.4	1.7	2.1	1.5	2.1	1.1
.4 (2068)	.4	.4	Quick	.4	.4	.9	.7	1.1	.5
.1	.1	.1		.1	.1	.1	.2	.3	.3
0 UND	0 UND	0 UND		0 UND	0 UND	0 UND	0 UND	0 UND	9 42.3
0 UND	0 UND	0 UND	Sales/Receivables	0 UND	0 UND	2 171.7	0 999.8	9 40.2	27 13.6
1 446.6	2 214.3	0 UND		0 UND	6 64.9	15 25.1	15 23.9	22 16.3	55 6.7
			Cost of Sales/Inventory						
			Cost of Sales/Payables						
7.4	6.5	6.5		7.1	5.0	3.0	3.9	5.8	9.7
-13.4	-12.6	-11.0	Sales/Working Capital	-8.9	-19.6	22.3	54.2	17.7	24.0
-2.7	-2.4	-2.6		-2.4	-2.6	-4.3	-3.0	-10.3	-12.7
7.0	7.6	7.9		8.4	6.2	7.1	8.9	6.1	11.0
(668) 4.0	(756) 4.2	(695) 4.2	EBIT/Interest	(445) 4.8	(133) 3.2	(29) 3.8	(34) 2.9	(34) 2.4	(20) 1.7
1.9	2.0	2.0		2.7	1.3	1.1	1.2	1.0	1.1
3.0	2.8	2.9		2.6	3.5				
(91) 1.7	(77) 1.8	(66) 1.7	Net Profit + Depr., Dep., Amort./Cur. Mat. L/T/D	(24) 1.3	(17) 1.7				
.9	1.0	.9		.9	.7				
1.9	1.8	1.7		2.0	1.5	1.0	.6	.7	.3
4.5	4.6	4.2	Fixed/Worth	4.5	4.3	2.8	2.0	2.0	1.2
85.2	116.0	31.7		29.5	-16.9	6.8	7.2	7.1	3.8
1.5	1.5	1.4		1.4	1.2	1.2	.7	1.2	1.5
4.5	4.6	3.9	Debt/Worth	4.0	4.9	2.8	2.6	2.4	2.6
155.1	198.6	46.5		37.8	-18.6	8.8	9.0	9.8	5.9
33.5	33.3	30.8		30.4	35.2	44.8	43.1	32.9	22.2
(1610) 13.8	(1567) 14.6	(1543) 13.6	% Profit Before Taxes/Tangible Net Worth	(1206) 13.3	(189) 15.7	(42) 13.2	(38) 17.1	(47) 11.3	(21) 9.7
2.5	3.0	2.4		2.4	3.7	-.3	6.8	1.3	1.4
8.2	8.2	8.1		7.7	8.4	9.7	18.3	12.1	7.3
3.2	3.4	3.2	% Profit Before Taxes/Total Assets	3.0	4.0	4.6	4.3	2.7	3.1
.1	.2	.2		.2	.3	-.1	1.4	-.7	.1
.4	.4	.4		.3	.8	5.1	5.6	10.7	34.6
.2	.2	.2	Sales/Net Fixed Assets	.2	.3	.3	.7	1.7	15.8
.1	.1	.1		.1	.2	.2	.3	.3	.9
.3	.3	.3		.2	.5	1.5	1.7	2.2	4.2
.2	.2	.2	Sales/Total Assets	.1	.2	.3	.4	.8	2.0
.1	.1	.1		.1	.1	.1	.2	.2	.4
9.9	10.6	11.0		12.6	8.2	3.4	1.1	1.5	.5
(1874) 17.1	(1839) 17.3	(1719) 17.9	% Depr., Dep., Amort./Sales	(1323) 19.2	(240) 15.6	(46) 15.3	(39) 5.8	(50) 5.7	(21) 2.8
25.0	25.0	26.4		27.3	25.0	22.2	14.0	18.9	6.7
3.1	4.0	2.4		3.3	4.1	1.9	3.8	1.4	
(165) 6.3	(173) 7.1	(143) 6.0	% Officers', Directors' Owners' Comp/Sales	(74) 3.3	(33) 4.2	(10) 4.2	(11) 4.7	(11) 2.3	
12.5	13.2	13.5		18.4	11.6	12.8	12.4	8.2	
5639253M	5826073M	3923703M	Net Sales ($)	506351M	436408M	197643M	307701M	894116M	1581484M
14673104M	16954725M	11508371M	Total Assets ($)	3571155M	2205924M	867878M	935542M	2294782M	1633090M

M = $ thousand   MM = $ million
See Pages 9 through 22 for Explanation of Ratios and Data

Current Data Sorted by Assets   Comparative Historical Data

						Type of Statement		
3	3	4	18	5	5	Unqualified	69	63
1	4	16	9	2	1	Reviewed	53	53
15	29	37	5		1	Compiled	112	97
140	95	62	4	1	2	Tax Returns	372	404
84	79	96	36	3	8	Other	342	296
	69 (4/1-9/30/10)		698 (10/1/10-3/31/11)				4/1/06-3/31/07 ALL	4/1/07-3/31/08 ALL
0-500M	500M-2MM	2-10MM	10-50MM	50-100MM	100-250MM			
243	210	215	72	11	16	NUMBER OF STATEMENTS	948	913
%	%	%	%	%	%	ASSETS	%	%
35.1	17.1	11.4	14.5	26.5	19.8	Cash & Equivalents	19.3	16.8
5.2	5.3	6.0	11.0	2.3	9.5	Trade Receivables (net)	8.1	6.8
.4	1.3	2.8	5.8	2.2	4.9	Inventory	5.5	4.9
7.1	4.6	6.0	4.8	6.1	11.8	All Other Current	7.2	7.5
47.8	28.4	26.1	36.1	37.2	45.9	Total Current	40.0	36.0
31.6	50.7	55.2	45.7	53.5	25.1	Fixed Assets (net)	41.4	44.3
7.2	5.9	6.3	5.6	5.4	14.4	Intangibles (net)	5.4	6.4
13.4	15.1	12.3	12.6	3.9	14.5	All Other Non-Current	13.1	13.3
100.0	100.0	100.0	100.0	100.0	100.0	Total	100.0	100.0
						LIABILITIES		
21.9	10.0	9.5	12.7	4.6	4.3	Notes Payable-Short Term	13.1	13.3
3.8	4.3	3.8	4.3	4.6	4.0	Cur. Mat.-L.T.D.	3.8	4.5
5.3	2.5	4.0	3.4	3.3	5.4	Trade Payables	5.2	4.8
.1	.1	.0	.2	.1	.2	Income Taxes Payable	.1	.1
30.5	11.5	10.3	11.4	5.6	11.5	All Other Current	17.1	18.5
61.6	28.4	27.5	32.0	18.3	25.3	Total Current	39.3	41.2
27.9	43.4	47.5	30.0	44.6	30.6	Long-Term Debt	31.7	34.6
.0	.0	.0	.2	.1	.5	Deferred Taxes	.1	.1
23.4	8.1	6.7	3.6	.4	2.4	All Other Non-Current	7.6	5.7
-12.8	20.1	18.2	34.3	36.7	41.3	Net Worth	21.3	18.4
100.0	100.0	100.0	100.0	100.0	100.0	Total Liabilities & Net Worth	100.0	100.0
						INCOME DATA		
100.0	100.0	100.0	100.0	100.0	100.0	Net Sales	100.0	100.0
						Gross Profit		
89.0	76.1	73.1	79.5	80.7	89.4	Operating Expenses	79.0	80.7
11.0	23.9	26.9	20.5	19.3	10.6	Operating Profit	21.0	19.3
1.6	12.2	15.6	11.3	14.8	6.1	All Other Expenses (net)	8.9	9.8
9.4	11.7	11.3	9.2	4.5	4.5	Profit Before Taxes	12.1	9.5
						RATIOS		
3.7	2.8	2.3	2.7	3.3	3.2		2.5	2.2
1.2	1.1	1.0	1.6	2.0	1.6	Current	1.1	1.0
.4	.4	.2	.6	1.3	1.1		.4	.3
3.0	2.2	1.8	2.2	2.9	2.0		1.8	1.6
1.0	.8	.5	1.0	1.5	.8	Quick	(947) .7	.6
.3	.3	.1	.4	.6	.6		.2	.1
0 UND	0 UND	0 UND	0 UND	0 UND	7 50.2		0 UND	0 UND
0 UND	0 UND	0 UND	6 57.6	3 124.9	27 13.7	Sales/Receivables	0 UND	0 UND
1 676.0	5 80.0	13 28.7	40 9.2	25 14.7	49 7.4		10 36.0	8 46.7
						Cost of Sales/Inventory		
						Cost of Sales/Payables		
15.9	7.5	5.7	3.2	2.2	5.1		8.0	9.9
180.0	176.6	-492.0	10.9	8.9	10.3	Sales/Working Capital	144.5	779.8
-14.2	-8.3	-3.4	-15.5	22.7	32.1		-11.1	-7.8
18.5	10.8	6.4	6.1		9.2		16.7	10.2
(127) 3.4	(119) 3.8	(119) 2.9	(43) 2.9		(13) 4.9	EBIT/Interest	(563) 4.3	(512) 2.9
-1.9	.7	1.1	1.0		2.0		1.3	.1
		3.2				Net Profit + Depr., Dep.,	4.6	4.5
	(10)	1.9				Amort./Cur. Mat. L/T/D	(56) 1.8	(36) 1.6
		.5					.6	.4
.1	.5	.8	.2	.4	.2		.2	.3
1.0	2.5	4.3	1.3	1.5	.7	Fixed/Worth	1.6	1.9
-1.3	-24.3	-22.1	4.1	77.0	2.8		21.5	UND
.4	.9	1.7	.8	.6	.7		.9	1.0
3.4	3.7	6.7	1.9	2.4	2.2	Debt/Worth	3.1	3.5
-2.8	-18.5	-32.7	4.1	81.9	2.8		297.1	-40.0
172.8	64.8	40.2	30.8		38.5	% Profit Before Taxes/Tangible	89.9	77.9
(150) 52.4	(149) 18.8	(146) 14.7	(63) 12.1		(14) 12.8	Net Worth	(724) 31.7	(663) 22.0
1.9	2.0	3.4	2.0		-2.4		6.5	2.2
48.5	14.3	8.3	10.1	9.6	8.7	% Profit Before Taxes/Total	23.3	17.7
14.6	4.5	2.9	3.8	4.4	4.4	Assets	6.9	4.4
-8.2	-.1	.1	.4	-1.7	-.1		.3	-1.8
371.0	37.8	16.8	32.5	28.3	28.7		71.3	55.5
40.9	4.1	.7	2.2	1.5	22.8	Sales/Net Fixed Assets	14.7	11.4
8.8	.2	.2	.3	.2	2.1		.4	.4
12.6	4.2	1.8	2.0	2.1	1.7		5.2	5.4
5.9	1.0	.3	.5	.7	1.3	Sales/Total Assets	1.7	1.5
2.1	.2	.1	.2	.2	.4		.3	.3
.4	.8	1.5	.7	1.8	1.5		.7	.8
(127) 1.1	(149) 4.6	(168) 6.7	(61) 3.7	(10) 7.7	(11) 1.9	% Depr., Dep., Amort./Sales	(676) 2.2	(671) 2.8
3.7	19.2	17.4	16.2	18.9	13.6		11.4	12.6
3.0	1.9	1.9				% Officers', Directors'	2.2	2.7
(99) 6.4	(57) 3.3	(56) 3.3				Owners' Comp/Sales	(245) 5.7	(239) 5.4
16.3	10.5	9.0					14.0	15.7
334786M	667183M	1190937M	3069005M	1465316M	3362635M	Net Sales ($)	16840523M	11119705M
46536M	232975M	903465M	1510647M	857431M	2475725M	Total Assets ($)	7039898M	6749598M

M = $ thousand   MM = $ million
See Pages 9 through 22 for Explanation of Ratios and Data

Comparative Historical Data | Current Data Sorted by Sales

44 / 46 / 38 etc			Type of Statement	0-1MM	1-3MM	3-5MM	5-10MM	10-25MM	25MM & OVER
44	46	38	Unqualified	3	4	2	4	7	18
47	40	33	Reviewed	4	7	5	4	5	8
94	96	86	Compiled	36	23	6	9	11	1
366	363	304	Tax Returns	184	63	22	16	15	4
314	289	306	Other	118	76	25	28	30	29
4/1/08-3/31/09 ALL	4/1/09-3/31/10 ALL	4/1/10-3/31/11 ALL		69 (4/1-9/30/10)			698 (10/1/10-3/31/11)		
865	834	767	**NUMBER OF STATEMENTS**	345	173	60	61	68	60
%	%	%	**ASSETS**	%	%	%	%	%	%
18.0	20.0	21.1	Cash & Equivalents	16.6	25.5	24.0	28.6	20.4	25.0
6.8	6.0	6.0	Trade Receivables (net)	2.3	6.3	8.2	9.3	11.5	15.5
3.5	2.7	2.0	Inventory	1.8	2.2	4.1	.3	.6	3.4
6.3	5.3	6.0	All Other Current	4.6	6.8	5.4	4.5	9.9	8.8
34.6	34.0	35.1	Total Current	25.3	40.8	41.6	42.6	42.4	52.7
46.1	45.7	45.0	Fixed Assets (net)	57.8	39.9	35.3	35.4	27.5	24.7
6.3	6.2	6.6	Intangibles (net)	4.8	6.2	8.5	6.4	11.7	10.1
12.9	14.1	13.4	All Other Non-Current	12.1	13.1	14.6	15.5	18.4	12.5
100.0	100.0	100.0	Total	100.0	100.0	100.0	100.0	100.0	100.0
			LIABILITIES						
14.6	15.9	13.7	Notes Payable-Short Term	13.1	13.5	19.0	10.9	15.2	13.3
5.0	4.5	4.0	Cur. Mat.-L.T.D.	4.0	3.2	5.1	4.0	5.3	3.8
5.0	4.3	4.0	Trade Payables	2.7	3.0	5.4	5.0	5.9	8.9
.2	.1	.1	Income Taxes Payable	.0	.1	.2	.0	.1	.3
16.5	15.5	17.1	All Other Current	18.8	15.9	12.6	16.4	16.8	16.2
41.3	40.3	38.8	Total Current	38.6	35.7	42.3	36.3	43.2	42.6
35.0	36.7	38.1	Long-Term Debt	50.6	31.9	30.3	27.2	24.5	18.5
.1	.0	.0	Deferred Taxes	.0	.0	.0	.0	.1	.2
8.8	8.2	11.9	All Other Non-Current	13.5	11.8	16.8	8.8	9.1	4.8
14.9	14.7	11.2	Net Worth	-2.8	20.7	10.6	27.8	23.1	33.9
100.0	100.0	100.0	Total Liabilities & Net Worth	100.0	100.0	100.0	100.0	100.0	100.0
			INCOME DATA						
100.0	100.0	100.0	Net Sales	100.0	100.0	100.0	100.0	100.0	100.0
			Gross Profit						
82.4	79.9	80.0	Operating Expenses	68.1	85.0	93.8	90.1	94.7	93.1
17.6	20.1	20.0	Operating Profit	31.9	15.0	6.2	9.9	5.3	6.9
10.8	10.5	9.6	All Other Expenses (net)	16.6	5.5	2.5	4.3	2.8	1.4
6.8	9.7	10.4	Profit Before Taxes	15.2	9.5	3.7	5.6	2.5	5.6
			RATIOS						
2.1	2.8	2.9	Current	2.7	3.7	3.7	4.2	2.1	2.3
1.0	1.1	1.2		.8	1.5	1.4	1.7	1.1	1.4
.3	.3	.4		.2	.6	.6	.5	.5	1.0
1.6	2.1	2.3	Quick	1.8	3.2	2.9	3.5	2.0	2.1
(863) .6	(832) .7	.8		.5	1.0	.9	1.6	.8	1.1
.2	.2	.2		.1	.3	.4	.4	.3	.6
0 UND	0 UND	0 UND	Sales/Receivables	0 UND	0 UND	0 UND	0 UND	0 UND	2 174.3
0 UND	0 UND	0 UND		0 UND	0 UND	1 396.8	2 174.3	4 95.6	12 30.4
9 42.8	9 41.6	7 52.3		0 UND	8 44.7	10 37.2	15 23.8	13 28.9	43 8.4
			Cost of Sales/Inventory						
			Cost of Sales/Payables						
12.6	7.9	8.0	Sales/Working Capital	7.9	7.5	14.3	5.5	12.2	6.7
-999.8	177.3	105.6		-41.5	34.3	97.8	46.0	280.0	19.4
-6.8	-6.1	-8.5		-3.0	-27.6	-20.4	-35.9	-21.1	NM
7.6	9.0	9.7	EBIT/Interest	5.9	16.6	16.8	49.3	6.3	15.0
(482) 1.2	(471) 2.6	(428) 3.3		(135) 3.2	(110) 3.5	(40) 2.9	(45) 4.1	(52) 1.5	(46) 5.2
-2.9	-.6	.4		.1	1.0	-1.1	.5	-1.1	1.7
2.6	2.6	2.9	Net Profit + Depr., Dep., Amort./Cur. Mat. L/T/D						
(38) 1.7	(42) 1.3	(29) 1.7							
-1.6	.2	.5							
.4	.3	.3	Fixed/Worth	1.0	.2	.3	.2	.3	.2
2.4	2.0	2.2		3.8	1.5	1.1	1.3	1.5	.4
-30.9	-21.4	-12.0		-31.0	-7.3	-7.5	-6.9	-2.0	2.2
.9	.8	.8	Debt/Worth	1.5	.5	.4	.5	1.0	.6
4.3	3.4	3.5		5.6	2.6	2.5	1.9	3.7	2.0
-22.2	-12.4	-12.4		-8.7	-9.5	-13.3	-31.7	-6.8	7.3
40.1	50.5	70.5	% Profit Before Taxes/Tangible Net Worth	47.3	88.2	111.3	84.7	69.6	62.3
(615) 10.9	(589) 14.8	(531) 20.6		(232) 15.1	(119) 22.7	(42) 35.0	(44) 31.9	(44) 31.9	(50) 20.4
-6.4	.9	2.0		1.7	2.7	3.4	2.0	2.4	1.8
9.8	12.6	18.6	% Profit Before Taxes/Total Assets	11.3	22.8	37.1	31.9	17.6	17.3
1.5	3.4	4.6		3.0	6.1	4.5	9.2	5.7	9.2
-5.7	-2.0	-.8		-1.0	.1	-2.5	.0	-4.8	1.1
48.8	51.6	52.1	Sales/Net Fixed Assets	20.9	56.4	95.8	90.3	79.6	43.9
8.2	6.9	8.1		.4	15.7	30.3	20.0	31.7	27.7
.3	.3	.3		.1	1.5	5.8	5.5	7.5	6.6
5.2	4.8	5.3	Sales/Total Assets	1.7	6.7	12.9	7.7	9.1	5.4
1.4	1.1	1.4		.3	2.0	4.9	3.4	3.7	2.5
.2	.2	.2		.1	.6	1.4	1.2	1.8	1.2
1.0	1.0	.8	% Depr., Dep., Amort./Sales	5.1	.5	.4	.5	.5	.6
(641) 3.3	(621) 4.3	(526) 3.0		(227) 13.3	(108) 1.4	(40) .8	(47) 1.0	(53) 1.2	(51) 1.5
14.9	16.4	14.8		23.1	6.3	2.0	2.6	2.8	2.2
1.7	2.3	2.2	% Officers', Directors' Owners' Comp/Sales	4.8	3.0	1.4	1.3	.8	2.2
(221) 4.9	(221) 6.1	(226) 5.2		(76)	(63)	(21) 2.3	(28) 3.1	(26) 2.1	(12)
11.8	12.9	13.3		19.4	11.8	4.3	5.6	3.5	10.6
8892674M	10899980M	10089862M	Net Sales ($)	130020M	307614M	228785M	432682M	1035382M	7955379M
5829371M	8329032M	6026779M	Total Assets ($)	519733M	497812M	217001M	509070M	667615M	3615548M

M = $ thousand   MM = $ million
See Pages 9 through 22 for Explanation of Ratios and Data

Current Data Sorted by Assets   Comparative Historical Data

						Type of Statement		
4	13	15	7	2	2	Unqualified	23	38
1	3	8	1			Reviewed	8	10
9	9	13	1			Compiled	15	17
64	74	68	8	2	2	Tax Returns	64	77
50	55	69	22	7	4	Other	64	83
	38 (4/1-9/30/10)		475 (10/1/10-3/31/11)				4/1/06-3/31/07	4/1/07-3/31/08
0-500M	500M-2MM	2-10MM	10-50MM	50-100MM	100-250MM		ALL	ALL
128	154	173	39	11	8	NUMBER OF STATEMENTS	174	225
%	%	%	%	%	%	ASSETS	%	%
32.4	17.2	11.3	9.7	9.9		Cash & Equivalents	18.4	20.0
8.8	6.0	7.0	6.4	2.9		Trade Receivables (net)	6.4	7.0
1.8	3.1	3.4	9.7	4.6		Inventory	5.2	6.9
4.3	1.7	2.1	5.2	13.0		All Other Current	5.7	5.4
47.4	28.0	23.8	30.9	30.4		Total Current	35.8	39.3
35.6	52.7	61.8	49.9	43.5		Fixed Assets (net)	43.5	42.4
3.4	3.1	2.3	4.6	2.0		Intangibles (net)	3.2	2.8
13.7	16.2	12.0	14.6	24.1		All Other Non-Current	17.5	15.4
100.0	100.0	100.0	100.0	100.0		Total	100.0	100.0
						LIABILITIES		
16.9	8.3	5.6	4.0	3.1		Notes Payable-Short Term	10.1	9.2
5.4	2.9	2.3	2.1	1.4		Cur. Mat.-L.T.D.	4.2	7.9
4.8	4.0	2.2	2.8	2.1		Trade Payables	4.2	5.8
.2	.0	.3	.0	.0		Income Taxes Payable	.0	.0
37.5	13.8	8.5	12.9	13.0		All Other Current	12.3	14.8
64.9	28.9	18.8	21.8	19.7		Total Current	30.9	37.7
26.1	52.0	49.9	40.3	44.9		Long-Term Debt	33.9	41.0
.0	.0	.1	.1	.0		Deferred Taxes	.0	.0
3.5	3.9	5.5	1.2	4.2		All Other Non-Current	4.3	2.9
5.5	15.2	25.7	36.6	31.2		Net Worth	30.9	18.4
100.0	100.0	100.0	100.0	100.0		Total Liabilties & Net Worth	100.0	100.0
						INCOME DATA		
100.0	100.0	100.0	100.0	100.0		Net Sales	100.0	100.0
						Gross Profit		
84.4	68.9	74.1	72.1	67.9		Operating Expenses	81.8	82.9
15.6	31.1	25.9	27.9	32.1		Operating Profit	18.2	17.1
4.8	16.7	15.8	14.9	14.0		All Other Expenses (net)	8.8	9.6
10.7	14.4	10.2	12.9	18.1		Profit Before Taxes	9.4	7.5
						RATIOS		
3.9	2.3	2.5	3.0	4.1			3.4	3.4
1.0	.8	.8	1.1	2.2		Current	1.1	1.1
.3	.2	.2	.3	.5			.4	.4
3.4	2.0	1.9	1.7	2.8			2.7	2.1
(127) .9	.7	.6	.5	.6		Quick	.7 (224)	.7
.2	.1	.1	.1	.3			.1	.1
0 UND	0 UND	0 UND	0 UND	0 UND			0 UND	0 UND
0 UND	0 UND	0 839.2	3 110.6	12 30.6		Sales/Receivables	0 UND	1 326.2
4 91.4	11 32.3	22 16.9	29 12.7	37 9.8			17 21.6	18 20.5
						Cost of Sales/Inventory		
						Cost of Sales/Payables		
12.9	6.5	6.4	2.5	2.8			5.1	4.2
UND	-27.8	-25.5	34.8	5.7		Sales/Working Capital	66.4	61.3
-9.6	-3.3	-4.1	-1.9	-5.1			-6.1	-4.2
17.5	19.4	6.6	15.8				9.5	8.9
(59) 4.1	(65) 2.9	(81) 3.0	(18) 3.9			EBIT/Interest	(85) 3.4	(108) 3.3
1.5	.9	1.3	.4				.2	.7
						Net Profit + Depr., Dep., Amort./Cur. Mat. L/T/D		
.0	.3	.9	.2	.0			.2	.1
.9	3.4	2.8	1.9	.9		Fixed/Worth	1.6	1.6
28.7	-24.1	29.8	10.6	9.7			25.1	124.0
.3	.9	1.2	.5	1.0			.4	.7
2.9	5.0	3.5	2.9	6.5		Debt/Worth	2.6	3.2
-5.1	-18.4	43.6	11.8	59.7			176.1	-120.4
214.3	48.3	43.1	23.1	113.8			67.1	47.2
(89) 54.5	(108) 16.7	(138) 12.4	(33) 7.1	(10) 28.8		% Profit Before Taxes/Tangible Net Worth	(136) 14.0	(166) 14.6
16.5	3.9	-.3	.7	8.0			.0	-.4
56.1	12.0	8.5	4.5	10.3			15.1	12.5
14.0	4.4	3.2	2.1	2.6		% Profit Before Taxes/Total Assets	3.9	2.5
.5	.5	-.1	-1.0	1.3			-1.4	-1.4
UND	34.1	7.4	14.0	37.6			78.1	97.5
32.6	.8	.4	.3	.8		Sales/Net Fixed Assets	4.7	6.9
4.4	.2	.1	.1	.2			.3	.3
8.0	1.6	.9	.8	.9			2.4	2.1
2.7	.4	.2	.1	.2		Sales/Total Assets	.6	.8
1.0	.1	.1	.1	.1			.2	.2
.7	1.8	2.5	1.3				1.4	1.1
(54) 2.2	(104) 12.4	(129) 13.0	(30) 6.3			% Depr., Dep., Amort./Sales	(118) 6.8	(152) 5.9
8.9	21.4	21.9	21.8				18.7	14.5
6.6	2.6	2.0					2.8	4.3
(41) 11.0	(28) 4.8	(23) 4.1				% Officers', Directors' Owners' Comp/Sales	(31) 5.5	(46) 8.3
18.3	6.7	11.4					11.8	14.5
99892M	248611M	589779M	457344M	638436M	1993898M	Net Sales ($)	837634M	2209381M
26160M	170140M	797515M	745872M	800846M	1174346M	Total Assets ($)	1316811M	1707626M

© RMA 2011

M = $ thousand   MM = $ million
See Pages 9 through 22 for Explanation of Ratios and Data

Comparative Historical Data | Current Data Sorted by Sales

			Type of Statement						
48	63	43	Unqualified	14	13	7	3	4	2
12	20	13	Reviewed	3	3	2	3	2	
21	42	32	Compiled	16	10	1	3	1	1
145	234	218	Tax Returns	155	37	7	9	7	3
170	189	207	Other	91	52	21	18	15	10
4/1/08-3/31/09 ALL	4/1/09-3/31/10 ALL	4/1/10-3/31/11 ALL		38 (4/1-9/30/10) 0-1MM	1-3MM	3-5MM	475 (10/1/10-3/31/11) 5-10MM	10-25MM	25MM & OVER
396	548	513	NUMBER OF STATEMENTS	279	115	38	36	29	16
%	%	%	ASSETS	%	%	%	%	%	%
19.1	17.9	18.3	Cash & Equivalents	16.0	20.6	20.6	22.4	22.2	19.5
7.2	7.0	7.0	Trade Receivables (net)	3.8	8.1	11.9	13.1	12.4	20.0
4.3	2.8	3.4	Inventory	2.2	3.7	7.1	2.2	3.8	15.3
4.2	3.0	3.0	All Other Current	1.9	3.9	3.3	3.1	7.4	6.3
34.8	30.7	31.7	Total Current	24.0	36.2	42.8	40.9	45.8	61.2
46.5	50.6	51.1	Fixed Assets (net)	61.4	44.9	36.0	31.4	36.9	24.1
3.8	4.1	3.1	Intangibles (net)	2.1	2.9	4.0	8.6	4.2	6.5
14.9	14.5	14.0	All Other Non-Current	12.6	16.0	17.2	19.1	13.1	8.2
100.0	100.0	100.0	Total	100.0	100.0	100.0	100.0	100.0	100.0
			LIABILITIES						
8.0	8.9	9.0	Notes Payable-Short Term	10.7	7.2	3.5	11.8	6.2	5.6
4.3	3.2	3.2	Cur. Mat.-L.T.D.	3.2	3.7	4.1	2.6	1.3	1.0
4.2	4.5	3.5	Trade Payables	2.1	3.7	5.8	9.7	4.8	5.1
.0	.1	.1	Income Taxes Payable	.1	.0	1.0	.4	.0	.1
20.4	20.3	17.7	All Other Current	16.4	22.3	11.3	21.4	19.2	11.4
36.8	37.0	33.5	Total Current	32.4	36.8	25.7	45.9	31.5	23.1
44.6	41.5	43.8	Long-Term Debt	50.8	40.0	41.9	25.9	25.6	27.1
.0	.1	.0	Deferred Taxes	.1	.0	.0	.0	.2	.0
3.5	3.1	4.3	All Other Non-Current	4.1	3.9	2.1	6.6	2.6	14.2
15.1	18.3	18.3	Net Worth	12.5	19.3	30.3	21.6	40.1	35.6
100.0	100.0	100.0	Total Liabilties & Net Worth	100.0	100.0	100.0	100.0	100.0	100.0
			INCOME DATA						
100.0	100.0	100.0	Net Sales	100.0	100.0	100.0	100.0	100.0	100.0
			Gross Profit						
79.9	76.7	75.1	Operating Expenses	66.6	80.4	89.1	90.2	89.0	94.4
20.1	23.3	24.9	Operating Profit	33.4	19.6	10.9	9.8	11.0	5.6
12.5	14.0	13.1	All Other Expenses (net)	19.3	8.7	3.2	2.9	2.7	1.3
7.6	9.3	11.8	Profit Before Taxes	14.2	10.9	7.8	6.9	8.3	4.3
			RATIOS						
2.6	2.0	2.9		2.0	4.1	5.6	2.5	2.9	6.4
1.0	.8	.9	Current	.6	1.1	1.7	1.2	1.0	2.8
.3	.2	.2		.2	.2	.7	.4	.6	1.5
2.2	1.7	2.1		1.6	3.2	3.9	2.3	2.7	4.5
.5	.6 (512)	.7	Quick	.4 (114)	.8	1.2	1.0	.9	1.6
.1	.1	.2		.1	.2	.7	.4	.4	.5
0 UND	0 UND	0 UND		0 UND	0 UND	1 641.6	0 UND	0 UND	0 UND
0 999.8	0 UND	0 UND	Sales/Receivables	0 UND	0 756.3	6 57.9	8 48.4	13 28.6	24 15.5
14 26.1	14 25.6	14 26.2		1 463.0	12 29.4	32 11.2	35 10.4	32 11.3	49 7.5
			Cost of Sales/Inventory						
			Cost of Sales/Payables						
4.9	8.5	6.4		13.2	5.4	2.5	9.6	5.6	3.6
-94.4	-29.4	-50.3	Sales/Working Capital	-13.8	105.2	18.9	97.5	111.2	6.2
-3.7	-3.3	-4.2		-2.7	-6.2	-25.4	-6.6	-10.3	9.3
9.5	10.7	13.7		9.1	18.1	13.2	15.8	44.1	13.2
(185) 2.6	(256) 3.3	(232) 3.2	EBIT/Interest	(86) 3.1	(65) 2.6	(22) 3.8	(30) 3.7	(17) 5.4	(12) 3.6
.1	.9	1.2		1.2	.9	1.3	-.3	1.8	1.5
4.2	13.2	14.6							
(19) 1.3	(23) 3.1	(16) 4.2	Net Profit + Depr., Dep., Amort./Cur. Mat. L/T/D						
.0	1.3	2.7							
.1	.2	.2		.6	.1	.0	.5	.0	.1
1.9	2.3	2.3	Fixed/Worth	3.8	1.2	1.7	1.7	.9	.3
21.1	275.7	36.6		UND	11.4	9.3	NM	NM	8.6
.9	1.0	.9		1.3	.4	.4	1.4	.4	.5
3.9	4.3	4.0	Debt/Worth	5.9	1.9	2.2	3.6	1.6	2.0
-34.6	-39.7	-194.1		-35.2	33.0	21.1	NM	NM	25.5
55.9	47.0	59.9		55.5	46.0	77.7	109.9	105.9	67.6
(292) 10.8	(394) 15.1	(383) 17.4	% Profit Before Taxes/Tangible Net Worth	(200) 17.2	(90) 13.4	(30) 26.8	(27) 44.1	(22) 30.1	(14) 10.6
-3.8	.2	2.1		1.6	.4	2.0	8.6	9.1	1.9
12.7	12.2	13.9		10.3	13.3	24.3	34.7	35.4	31.2
2.0	3.2	3.9	% Profit Before Taxes/Total Assets	3.0	4.6	8.2	9.4	8.7	4.6
-2.0	-.8	.0		-.1	.1	1.2	-.6	1.8	.8
65.8	54.5	39.1		22.5	49.1	102.5	51.4	86.5	37.6
2.1	1.2	1.8	Sales/Net Fixed Assets	.3	6.9	16.7	18.1	12.4	24.8
.2	.2	.2		.1	.4	1.5	2.3	1.8	7.7
2.2	2.1	2.2		1.1	3.0	3.7	4.7	3.2	5.0
.5	.5	.6	Sales/Total Assets	.2	.7	1.4	2.2	1.8	2.4
.2	.1	.1		.1	.2	.8	1.0	.7	.9
2.0	1.8	1.7		9.0	.7	.6	.8	.9	.1
(261) 8.9	(391) 9.6	(330) 9.7	% Depr., Dep., Amort./Sales	(177) 17.8	(71) 3.7	(25) 2.2	(23) 2.1	(23) 2.1	(11) 1.2
18.8	19.4	19.9		25.1	12.9	5.1	4.3	11.9	1.8
4.3	3.1	3.2		6.0	3.0				
(68) 9.0	(102) 7.0	(99) 6.3	% Officers', Directors' Owners' Comp/Sales	(43) 9.7	(30) 5.7				
19.4	14.2	12.3		15.4	10.4				
3943306M	5422831M	4027960M	Net Sales ($)	105473M	195449M	150997M	255003M	477940M	2843098M
3121525M	4254321M	3714879M	Total Assets ($)	519181M	657469M	188979M	376176M	692370M	1280704M

© RMA 2011

M = $ thousand   MM = $ million
See Pages 9 through 22 for Explanation of Ratios and Data

REAL ESTATE—Nonresidential Property Managers   NAICS 531312

Current Data Sorted by Assets | **Comparative Historical Data**

Type of Statement (Number of Statements)

Type of Statement	0-500M	500M-2MM	2-10MM	10-50MM	50-100MM	100-250MM	4/1/06-3/31/07 ALL	4/1/07-3/31/08 ALL
Unqualified		2	5	8	4	3	14	12
Reviewed		3	11	5	1		18	11
Compiled	4	11	17	4			30	32
Tax Returns	25	47	38	9			65	71
Other	23	43	42	20	4	4	61	106

25 (4/1-9/30/10)   308 (10/1/10-3/31/11)

	0-500M	500M-2MM	2-10MM	10-50MM	50-100MM	100-250MM	4/1/06-3/31/07 ALL	4/1/07-3/31/08 ALL
NUMBER OF STATEMENTS	52	106	113	46	9	7	188	232
ASSETS	%	%	%	%	%	%	%	%
Cash & Equivalents	28.6	8.4	7.8	7.8			8.3	11.9
Trade Receivables (net)	5.0	5.8	5.5	5.8			5.8	4.8
Inventory	1.0	1.5	1.0	2.0			3.4	1.3
All Other Current	5.2	3.3	6.5	3.9			3.7	3.6
Total Current	39.8	19.1	20.9	19.5			21.2	21.5
Fixed Assets (net)	41.3	67.4	67.7	59.6			65.4	64.7
Intangibles (net)	2.4	2.6	2.7	6.5			3.3	1.8
All Other Non-Current	16.6	11.0	8.7	14.4			10.1	12.0
Total	100.0	100.0	100.0	100.0			100.0	100.0
LIABILITIES								
Notes Payable-Short Term	23.6	10.2	5.5	3.9			5.5	6.5
Cur. Mat.-L.T.D.	2.4	4.6	4.1	3.5			3.7	2.8
Trade Payables	17.6	3.8	2.1	4.3			3.5	2.9
Income Taxes Payable	.0	.0	.0	.0			.1	.1
All Other Current	24.5	3.9	7.1	8.3			7.2	9.4
Total Current	68.1	22.5	18.8	20.0			19.9	21.7
Long-Term Debt	39.2	55.1	54.3	44.6			52.4	51.0
Deferred Taxes	.0	.0	.0	.7			.0	.0
All Other Non-Current	23.3	4.1	6.1	5.3			3.3	4.0
Net Worth	-30.8	18.3	20.8	29.4			24.3	23.3
Total Liabilities & Net Worth	100.0	100.0	100.0	100.0			100.0	100.0
INCOME DATA								
Net Sales	100.0	100.0	100.0	100.0			100.0	100.0
Gross Profit								
Operating Expenses	76.9	57.9	60.0	71.2			59.6	61.4
Operating Profit	23.1	42.1	40.0	28.8			40.4	38.6
All Other Expenses (net)	9.9	23.0	22.4	17.7			20.8	19.7
Profit Before Taxes	13.2	19.1	17.6	11.1			19.6	18.9
RATIOS								
Current	2.8	2.7	2.8	1.7			2.9	2.3
	.9	1.0	.7	1.0			.9	.8
	.2	.3	.3	.2			.2	.2
Quick	2.4	1.8	1.8	1.5			1.9	1.9
	.5	.6	.5	.7			.6	.6
	.2	.1	.1	.1			.1	.2
Sales/Receivables	0 UND	0 UND	0 UND	0 UND			0 UND	0 UND
	0 UND	0 UND	0 UND	2 242.7			0 UND	0 UND
	0 UND	8 45.3	19 19.4	19 18.8			9 41.5	13 27.2
Cost of Sales/Inventory								
Cost of Sales/Payables								
Sales/Working Capital	14.5	7.4	6.3	7.4			5.1	6.3
	-172.1	UND	-15.0	NM			-40.4	-35.3
	-4.2	-4.6	-3.0	-1.8			-3.5	-3.2
EBIT/Interest	7.4	18.7	15.5	15.8			9.2	8.4
	(21) 2.3	(42) 4.1	(43) 4.6	(20) 2.7			(74) 4.0	(93) 4.3
	1.1	1.7	2.8	.8			1.9	1.6
Net Profit + Depr., Dep., Amort./Cur. Mat. L/T/D							5.6	4.9
							(10) 1.5	(10) 2.1
							.0	1.4
Fixed/Worth	.1	1.1	1.2	.5			1.0	.8
	2.4	3.3	4.3	3.5			3.9	3.3
	-1.0	84.3	65.9	16.5			30.3	64.5
Debt/Worth	.9	1.2	1.6	1.1			1.2	.9
	8.4	3.4	5.6	3.2			4.7	3.4
	-2.3	89.2	577.0	26.0			45.2	114.1
% Profit Before Taxes/Tangible Net Worth	91.3	43.6	34.3	22.3			45.2	47.1
	(32) 22.7	(81) 15.0	(87) 14.6	(36) 7.8			(151) 17.8	(178) 16.7
	.5	2.7	2.9	-.5			1.7	2.7
% Profit Before Taxes/Total Assets	31.7	9.7	7.6	5.7			10.5	12.1
	5.7	3.8	3.3	2.4			3.5	4.1
	.1	.3	.2	-.6			.3	.3
Sales/Net Fixed Assets	UND	2.5	2.2	4.2			6.2	10.9
	24.1	.3	.2	.2			.3	.3
	.9	.1	.1	.1			.1	.2
Sales/Total Assets	9.8	.8	.4	.4			.8	1.1
	2.2	.2	.2	.2			.2	.2
	.4	.1	.1	.1			.1	.1
% Depr., Dep., Amort./Sales	1.7	4.4	7.0	3.8			2.5	3.6
	(24) 5.3	(87) 13.2	(93) 17.0	(41) 14.9			(159) 11.9	(175) 12.2
	16.0	20.4	24.8	29.5			20.3	19.6
% Officers', Directors' Owners' Comp/Sales	4.1	3.0	2.8				3.0	3.0
	(11) 6.5	(17)	(14) 9.2				(18) 9.7	(23) 5.7
	21.0	19.3	17.4				17.0	14.4
Net Sales ($)	27530M	124709M	329543M	711996M	135168M	295109M	1022142M	1781986M
Total Assets ($)	11450M	120745M	529468M	945236M	617526M	1023584M	1596163M	2403171M

M = $ thousand   MM = $ million
See Pages 9 through 22 for Explanation of Ratios and Data

Comparative Historical Data				Current Data Sorted by Sales					
			Type of Statement						
18	20	22	Unqualified	1	2		3	9	7
14	17	20	Reviewed	7	5	1	3	3	1
35	37	36	Compiled	22	10	4			
123	108	119	Tax Returns	91	21	3	3		
144	123	136	Other	74	29	9	8	11	5
4/1/08-3/31/09 ALL	4/1/09-3/31/10 ALL	4/1/10-3/31/11 ALL		25 (4/1-9/30/10)			308 (10/1/10-3/31/11)		
				0-1MM	1-3MM	3-5MM	5-10MM	10-25MM	25MM & OVER
334	305	333	**NUMBER OF STATEMENTS**	195	67	17	17	24	13
%	%	%	**ASSETS**	%	%	%	%	%	%
9.6	12.2	11.3	Cash & Equivalents	8.8	10.4	16.1	23.4	21.0	14.1
5.1	4.3	5.7	Trade Receivables (net)	2.1	6.6	11.0	7.4	14.4	29.5
1.3	1.6	1.3	Inventory	.2	1.0	5.3	3.4	5.8	3.0
3.1	3.7	4.8	All Other Current	2.1	7.4	23.8	6.4	4.6	5.4
19.1	21.7	23.1	Total Current	13.2	25.3	56.3	40.7	45.8	52.1
66.5	65.0	62.3	Fixed Assets (net)	73.0	61.9	25.1	44.0	33.9	29.9
2.1	3.2	3.1	Intangibles (net)	2.6	3.3	5.2	4.9	1.5	6.8
12.3	10.0	11.5	All Other Non-Current	11.2	9.5	13.4	10.4	18.8	11.3
100.0	100.0	100.0	Total	100.0	100.0	100.0	100.0	100.0	100.0
			LIABILITIES						
5.6	7.3	9.7	Notes Payable-Short Term	9.2	10.6	22.7	7.6	3.9	8.8
3.4	4.7	3.9	Cur. Mat.-L.T.D.	4.1	5.0	.5	4.8	1.4	3.9
3.0	2.3	5.4	Trade Payables	4.9	2.2	10.8	6.4	9.5	12.7
.1	.0	.0	Income Taxes Payable	.0	.0	.3	.0	.0	.2
6.0	10.0	8.9	All Other Current	7.5	7.6	8.6	14.4	15.3	15.9
18.0	24.4	27.8	Total Current	25.7	25.4	42.8	33.2	30.0	41.5
53.9	48.3	50.2	Long-Term Debt	62.5	44.4	21.5	27.9	17.6	22.4
.0	.1	.1	Deferred Taxes	.0	.0	.0	.0	1.3	.0
4.7	5.1	7.8	All Other Non-Current	7.9	11.2	4.2	6.5	2.3	5.2
23.4	22.2	14.1	Net Worth	3.9	19.0	31.5	32.4	48.7	30.9
100.0	100.0	100.0	Total Liabilties & Net Worth	100.0	100.0	100.0	100.0	100.0	100.0
			INCOME DATA						
100.0	100.0	100.0	Net Sales	100.0	100.0	100.0	100.0	100.0	100.0
			Gross Profit						
61.4	65.7	63.8	Operating Expenses	53.7	70.2	89.7	83.4	80.5	92.8
38.6	34.3	36.2	Operating Profit	46.3	29.8	10.3	16.6	19.5	7.2
20.7	18.9	19.5	All Other Expenses (net)	26.1	15.6	8.5	6.0	3.4	2.8
18.0	15.4	16.6	Profit Before Taxes	20.2	14.2	1.8	10.6	16.1	4.4
			RATIOS						
2.8	2.7	2.4		2.1	2.8	3.4	1.7	6.1	2.6
.9	.9	.9	Current	.6	.9	1.0	1.3	1.8	1.3
.3	.2	.3		.2	.3	.7	1.0	.8	.7
2.3	2.2	1.8		1.6	1.8	2.2	1.5	5.1	2.4
.7	(304) .7	.6	Quick	.4	.5	.6	1.0	1.2	.9
.2	.2	.1		.1	.1	.1	.3	.5	.5
0 UND	0 UND	0 UND		0 UND	0 UND	0 UND	0 UND	5 70.4	17 22.0
0 UND	0 UND	0 UND	Sales/Receivables	0 UND	0 UND	4 96.0	6 63.6	13 28.3	34 10.9
12 30.7	8 44.6	11 32.2		0 UND	23 16.0	51 7.1	22 16.3	52 7.0	62 5.9
			Cost of Sales/Inventory						
			Cost of Sales/Payables						
7.9	5.5	7.0		9.3	6.8	3.1	8.3	2.5	4.7
-115.4	-79.7	-59.8	Sales/Working Capital	-10.5	-271.9	-105.3	25.2	5.5	24.2
-4.9	-3.4	-3.9		-3.2	-4.2	-5.0	769.5	-41.1	-40.1
8.6	9.3	14.0		7.7	10.4		51.1	50.2	14.1
(142) 4.2	(135) 4.2	(137) 4.2	EBIT/Interest	(53) 4.1	(32) 3.8		(12) 7.2	(19) 16.5	(12) 4.9
1.5	1.7	1.5		1.8	1.3		1.3	2.6	-.2
5.4	3.5	4.2							
(17) 3.1	(15) 2.4	(15) 2.4	Net Profit + Depr., Dep., Amort./Cur. Mat. L/T/D						
1.7	.6	.7							
1.1	1.0	.9		2.0	.8	.0	.5	.1	.0
3.6	3.6	3.4	Fixed/Worth	4.6	3.8	.6	1.2	.5	.5
15.3	15.6	70.3		UND	-197.0	NM	NM	2.5	37.1
1.1	1.0	1.2		1.7	1.3	.5	.9	.3	1.4
3.7	3.6	4.1	Debt/Worth	5.3	5.5	1.8	2.5	.9	2.2
19.3	19.2	UND		-56.7	-200.7	NM	-187.1	4.6	57.7
46.6	43.7	37.2		36.7	45.1	9.9	131.0	24.2	48.2
(272) 14.3	(247) 14.7	(250) 13.9	% Profit Before Taxes/Tangible Net Worth	(143) 13.9	(50) 17.5	(13) 1.1	(12) 23.3	(21) 16.0	(11) 8.6
3.3	1.9	1.8		2.9	.7	-23.2	2.4	1.8	-7.8
9.8	10.9	8.9		7.9	10.9	6.5	30.4	20.4	14.1
3.5	3.4	3.5	% Profit Before Taxes/Total Assets	3.2	3.6	.7	4.4	8.7	4.4
.4	.0	.2		.2	.0	-6.3	.6	2.0	-2.1
4.9	10.3	15.0		.8	19.3	121.7	82.2	45.1	146.9
.3	.2	.3	Sales/Net Fixed Assets	.2	.3	24.7	1.7	16.3	37.1
.2	.1	.1		.1	.2	1.1	.2	.3	.7
.8	1.0	.9		.3	1.3	3.4	4.1	3.4	5.1
.2	.2	.2	Sales/Total Assets	.2	.2	1.0	.4	1.1	2.6
.1	.1	.1		.1	.1	.2	.2	.2	.3
5.6	4.2	4.4		9.9	2.6	.3	4.2	.3	.3
(266) 14.5	(245) 15.6	(259) 14.2	% Depr., Dep., Amort./Sales	(151) 17.6	(53) 14.1	(14) .7	(11) 11.6	(20) 1.4	(10) 1.0
22.1	24.5	22.4		23.2	26.0	4.9	16.7	13.0	8.6
4.8	4.1	3.2		3.8	4.4				
(35) 8.8	(49) 9.8	(52) 8.6	% Officers', Directors' Owners' Comp/Sales	(16) 8.5	(18) 10.8				
12.4	19.6	18.1		19.9	17.9				
3039662M	1654231M	1624055M	Net Sales ($)	66743M	118400M	63878M	119779M	359332M	895923M
3243923M	2863515M	3248009M	Total Assets ($)	391844M	497352M	252818M	317569M	865996M	922430M

M = $ thousand   MM = $ million
See Pages 9 through 22 for Explanation of Ratios and Data

Current Data Sorted by Assets | Comparative Historical Data

Note: Columns for 0-500M, 500M-2MM, 10-50MM, 50-100MM and 100-250MM are marked **DATA NOT AVAILABLE**.

0-500M	500M-2MM	2-10MM	10-50MM	50-100MM	100-250MM	Type of Statement	4/1/06-3/31/07 ALL	4/1/07-3/31/08 ALL
		1	1	1		Unqualified	2	
		3				Reviewed	1	1
1		1				Compiled	4	1
6	2	2				Tax Returns	14	18
1	3	4	4			Other	7	4
	2 (4/1-9/30/10)		28 (10/1/10-3/31/11)					
8	6	10	5	1		NUMBER OF STATEMENTS	28	24
%	%	%	%	%	%		%	%
						ASSETS		
		20.3				Cash & Equivalents	19.6	23.4
		20.9				Trade Receivables (net)	14.5	12.5
		.0				Inventory	.4	11.9
		4.9				All Other Current	7.4	4.6
		46.2				Total Current	41.8	52.5
		35.2				Fixed Assets (net)	25.3	30.9
		4.4				Intangibles (net)	4.5	4.5
		14.2				All Other Non-Current	28.3	12.1
		100.0				Total	100.0	100.0
						LIABILITIES		
		11.4				Notes Payable-Short Term	33.3	31.1
		2.6				Cur. Mat.-L.T.D.	.8	3.8
		8.9				Trade Payables	16.0	1.3
		.0				Income Taxes Payable	.0	.0
		10.6				All Other Current	24.5	30.6
		33.4				Total Current	74.7	66.7
		25.8				Long-Term Debt	10.4	20.2
		.0				Deferred Taxes	.9	.0
		1.4				All Other Non-Current	2.8	1.8
		39.3				Net Worth	11.1	11.3
		100.0				Total Liabilities & Net Worth	100.0	100.0
						INCOME DATA		
		100.0				Net Sales	100.0	100.0
						Gross Profit		
		77.2				Operating Expenses	85.6	83.0
		22.8				Operating Profit	14.4	17.0
		6.3				All Other Expenses (net)	2.8	3.3
		16.5				Profit Before Taxes	11.6	13.7
						RATIOS		
		2.6				Current	1.9	17.3
		1.5					.9	1.1
		1.0					.4	.4
		2.5				Quick	1.7	6.2
		1.5					.5	.6
		.9					.2	.3
		0 UND				Sales/Receivables	0 UND	0 UND
		9 38.9					1 597.3	0 UND
		75 4.9					33 11.1	17 21.1
						Cost of Sales/Inventory		
						Cost of Sales/Payables		
		7.4				Sales/Working Capital	10.1	4.8
		11.6					UND	15.2
		NM					-12.0	-24.9
						EBIT/Interest	21.0	69.4
							(19) 3.9	(17) 5.3
							2.0	1.3
						Net Profit + Depr., Dep., Amort./Cur. Mat. L/T/D		
		.2				Fixed/Worth	.0	.0
		1.0					.2	.8
		2.6					4.8	2.6
		.6				Debt/Worth	.7	.5
		2.7					1.9	1.4
		3.6					UND	NM
		184.5				% Profit Before Taxes/Tangible Net Worth	244.6	109.7
		31.7					(22) 65.6	(18) 24.6
		6.1					10.6	2.6
		27.3				% Profit Before Taxes/Total Assets	89.9	75.9
		13.9					19.0	11.9
		1.0					1.4	.7
		39.0				Sales/Net Fixed Assets	UND	900.4
		12.3					32.8	34.4
		2.2					9.9	4.9
		4.2				Sales/Total Assets	8.2	6.9
		2.2					4.1	3.7
		.4					2.3	.7
						% Depr., Dep., Amort./Sales	.7	.3
							(14) 1.2	(16) .9
							3.0	2.6
						% Officers', Directors' Owners' Comp/Sales	8.4	6.0
							(16) 13.1	(16) 10.6
							19.1	17.5
8488M	16457M	181156M	134236M	147497M		Net Sales ($)	92221M	98930M
863M	5312M	55539M	104839M	84231M		Total Assets ($)	46667M	58909M

M = $ thousand   MM = $ million

See Pages 9 through 22 for Explanation of Ratios and Data

Comparative Historical Data

Current Data Sorted by Sales

2	4	6	Type of Statement		1			1	3	1
	2	1	Unqualified						1	
4	1	1	Reviewed							
8	7	10	Compiled		1					
2	3	12	Tax Returns	6	2	2				
4/1/08-3/31/09 ALL	4/1/09-3/31/10 ALL	4/1/10-3/31/11 ALL	Other	1	3	1		4	3
				0-1MM	2 (4/1-9/30/10) 1-3MM	3-5MM	5-10MM	28 (10/1/10-3/31/11) 10-25MM	25MM & OVER
16	17	30	NUMBER OF STATEMENTS	8	6	3	1	8	4
%	%	%	**ASSETS**	%	%	%	%	%	%
27.8	15.9	16.8	Cash & Equivalents						
10.9	21.9	21.3	Trade Receivables (net)						
6.2	.0	.2	Inventory						
1.6	4.4	6.2	All Other Current						
46.5	42.2	44.4	Total Current						
38.2	26.4	36.1	Fixed Assets (net)						
9.0	8.3	7.7	Intangibles (net)						
6.4	23.1	11.8	All Other Non-Current						
100.0	100.0	100.0	Total						
			LIABILITIES						
22.3	25.8	15.9	Notes Payable-Short Term						
3.2	2.7	2.1	Cur. Mat.-L.T.D.						
4.8	5.8	5.7	Trade Payables						
.4	.1	.3	Income Taxes Payable						
16.9	19.2	24.6	All Other Current						
47.6	53.7	48.7	Total Current						
20.0	24.8	14.9	Long-Term Debt						
.0	.1	.8	Deferred Taxes						
3.9	.4	6.2	All Other Non-Current						
28.6	20.9	29.5	Net Worth						
100.0	100.0	100.0	Total Liabilties & Net Worth						
			INCOME DATA						
100.0	100.0	100.0	Net Sales						
			Gross Profit						
87.5	86.5	88.7	Operating Expenses						
12.5	13.5	11.3	Operating Profit						
3.8	6.1	2.6	All Other Expenses (net)						
8.7	7.3	8.7	Profit Before Taxes						
			RATIOS						
2.4	5.4	2.2							
.8	.8	1.4	Current						
.5	.3	.7							
2.1	5.4	1.7							
.7	.7	1.2	Quick						
.2	.2	.7							
0 UND	0 UND	0 UND							
0 UND	12 30.9	6 56.6	Sales/Receivables						
22 16.2	34 10.9	57 6.4							
			Cost of Sales/Inventory						
			Cost of Sales/Payables						
15.2	10.2	8.7							
-542.6	-27.5	33.4	Sales/Working Capital						
-17.8	-4.5	-27.5							
5.7	9.9	27.0							
(10) 1.6	(14) 2.2	(23) 8.0	EBIT/Interest						
-9.7	.8	.2							
			Net Profit + Depr., Dep., Amort./Cur. Mat. L/T/D						
.2	.1	.2							
1.3	1.2	1.0	Fixed/Worth						
7.7	60.8	3.9							
.5	.6	.6							
1.5	2.0	2.2	Debt/Worth						
6.9	69.1	5.1							
116.3	125.9	69.4							
(13) 5.1	(14) 13.2	(25) 15.4	% Profit Before Taxes/Tangible Net Worth						
-47.0	-2.6	-15.5							
80.5	31.5	20.1							
4.9	4.2	8.1	% Profit Before Taxes/Total Assets						
-22.8	-1.6	-6.0							
200.4	173.8	54.3							
24.8	35.9	18.0	Sales/Net Fixed Assets						
2.5	8.6	6.2							
7.7	4.1	5.3							
3.8	2.4	3.3	Sales/Total Assets						
1.5	1.7	1.5							
.4		.8							
(12) 1.8	(24) 1.6		% Depr., Dep., Amort./Sales						
3.4		3.2							
			% Officers', Directors' Owners' Comp/Sales						
258977M	559217M	487834M	Net Sales ($)	3443M	11334M	11468M	5308M	139272M	317009M
126565M	234261M	250784M	Total Assets ($)	9476M	4957M	20888M	1604M	84170M	129689M

© RMA 2011

M = $ thousand   MM = $ million
See Pages 9 through 22 for Explanation of Ratios and Data

Current Data Sorted by Assets   Comparative Historical Data

							Type of Statement			
6	28	22	29	8	8		Unqualified		91	88
2	12	19	15	3	2		Reviewed		32	37
13	25	41	13	2	1		Compiled		83	106
140	313	269	55	4	3		Tax Returns		547	625
84	191	257	91	12	19		Other		369	471
	91 (4/1-9/30/10)			1,596 (10/1/10-3/31/11)					4/1/06-3/31/07	4/1/07-3/31/08
0-500M	500M-2MM	2-10MM	10-50MM	50-100MM	100-250MM				ALL	ALL
245	569	608	203	29	33		NUMBER OF STATEMENTS		1122	1327
%	%	%	%	%	%		ASSETS		%	%
27.0	12.3	6.0	7.6	6.3	8.8		Cash & Equivalents		10.9	8.9
5.7	5.1	3.1	5.8	10.8	7.2		Trade Receivables (net)		5.2	5.0
5.0	6.4	10.0	13.2	10.6	9.7		Inventory		20.0	18.6
4.3	3.2	3.1	5.1	3.2	3.5		All Other Current		5.1	4.8
42.0	27.0	22.2	31.7	30.9	29.1		Total Current		41.2	37.3
39.9	61.4	64.6	48.4	44.9	41.8		Fixed Assets (net)		41.1	45.7
3.5	2.0	2.2	1.4	4.4	4.3		Intangibles (net)		2.3	2.0
14.7	9.5	11.1	18.6	19.8	24.8		All Other Non-Current		15.4	15.0
100.0	100.0	100.0	100.0	100.0	100.0		Total		100.0	100.0
							LIABILITIES			
17.8	7.1	7.5	9.8	10.6	9.9		Notes Payable-Short Term		16.3	13.8
5.3	3.0	3.0	2.9	3.7	2.1		Cur. Mat.-L.T.D.		3.0	4.2
4.6	2.1	1.4	2.5	1.3	1.5		Trade Payables		3.4	3.3
.0	.0	.0	.0	.0	.4		Income Taxes Payable		.1	.1
21.1	8.4	6.7	10.3	3.9	9.7		All Other Current		11.0	10.2
48.8	20.7	18.7	25.5	19.5	23.7		Total Current		33.9	31.5
34.1	53.1	55.0	44.0	39.3	30.4		Long-Term Debt		36.6	42.5
.0	.0	.0	.5	.6	.9		Deferred Taxes		.1	.1
9.7	4.0	4.5	5.6	5.1	4.3		All Other Non-Current		4.7	5.0
7.4	22.3	21.9	24.5	35.5	40.8		Net Worth		24.8	20.9
100.0	100.0	100.0	100.0	100.0	100.0		Total Liabilities & Net Worth		100.0	100.0
							INCOME DATA			
100.0	100.0	100.0	100.0	100.0	100.0		Net Sales		100.0	100.0
							Gross Profit			
76.1	63.3	64.5	71.6	77.4	76.9		Operating Expenses		73.1	70.9
23.9	36.7	35.5	28.4	22.6	23.1		Operating Profit		26.9	29.1
9.2	21.2	24.0	17.1	11.4	11.3		All Other Expenses (net)		12.1	16.6
14.8	15.4	11.5	11.3	11.2	11.8		Profit Before Taxes		14.7	12.5
							RATIOS			
3.8	3.2	2.6	3.3	3.6	3.9				3.1	2.6
.9	.8	.9	1.2	1.6	1.4		Current		1.2	1.1
.3	.2	.2	.4	1.0	.3				.4	.3
2.5	1.8	1.4	1.5	2.9	1.4				1.5	1.3
.6	(568) .4	(607) .4	.5	1.2	.3		Quick	(1120)	.3 (1326)	.3
.2	.1	.1	.2	.2	.1				.1	.1
0 UND	0 UND	0 UND	0 UND	0 UND	0 UND			0	UND 0	UND
0 UND	0 UND	0 UND	0 999.8	2 157.7	7 52.2		Sales/Receivables	0	UND 0	UND
0 UND	1 274.4	4 102.1	16 22.8	193 1.9	17 22.1			8	47.7 8	45.1
							Cost of Sales/Inventory			
							Cost of Sales/Payables			
6.8	4.6	3.1	2.3	1.4	1.6				2.7	2.7
-208.3	-30.6	-62.5	18.9	3.4	15.7		Sales/Working Capital		24.1	45.7
-4.0	-3.3	-3.1	-4.0	NM	-2.8				-5.1	-4.5
14.0	9.5	7.4	10.1	11.7	7.6				10.9	8.8
(105) 3.3	(210) 3.9	(231) 3.5	(96) 3.2	(18) 3.7	(23) 3.0		EBIT/Interest	(569)	3.8 (598)	2.8
-.1	1.0	1.5	1.4	1.6	1.2				1.3	.8
		2.6	12.2						2.9	6.7
	(12)	2.1	(11) 5.2				Net Profit + Depr., Dep.,	(21)	1.4 (35)	2.2
		.8	1.2				Amort./Cur. Mat. L/T/D		.4	.9
.0	.5	1.0	.1	.1	.0				.0	.0
1.2	3.2	3.6	2.0	1.2	1.2		Fixed/Worth		1.1	1.8
48.3	32.2	26.5	11.6	5.4	3.2				6.5	17.2
.4	1.0	1.5	.9	.8	.7				1.0	1.3
2.8	4.1	4.3	3.5	4.2	2.5		Debt/Worth		3.8	4.4
-11.2	54.2	57.2	38.2	14.0	6.8				26.1	90.5
103.4	38.8	34.8	27.5	25.3	32.4		% Profit Before Taxes/Tangible		71.8	48.8
(172) 24.0	(444) 13.9	(481) 8.9	(163) 8.1	(26) 6.0	(30) 18.6		Net Worth	(920)	22.0 (1030)	15.4
5.7	.1	.3	.6	-1.2	1.2				4.2	.8
31.4	11.8	5.9	5.3	4.2	10.1		% Profit Before Taxes/Total		13.5	10.3
7.9	3.3	1.7	2.0	2.5	4.0		Assets		4.1	2.6
.0	-.1	-.4	-.6	.1	-.9				.2	-.4
UND	21.0	1.9	27.2	33.0	43.0				273.3	98.8
14.3	.3	.2	.6	.5	2.9		Sales/Net Fixed Assets		5.3	1.9
.5	.1	.1	.1	.2	.2				.3	.2
5.1	.8	.3	.4	.5	.7				1.4	1.1
1.3	.2	.1	.2	.2	.4		Sales/Total Assets		.5	.3
.3	.1	.1	.1	.1	.1				.2	.1
1.3	6.4	6.6	1.8	3.0	.6				.9	1.6
(124) 4.1	(368) 16.0	(450) 17.0	(143) 11.2	(22) 12.3	(23) 5.3		% Depr., Dep., Amort./Sales	(635)	5.6 (810)	8.9
16.3	23.8	26.5	22.1	22.3	23.6				16.9	18.4
5.6	2.2	1.5	1.9				% Officers', Directors'		2.1	2.2
(61) 11.0	(74) 4.6	(71) 3.7	(23) 4.9				Owners' Comp/Sales	(184)	5.4 (195)	5.1
23.5	14.9	9.3	11.1						14.4	14.3
201583M	558001M	1389905M	2401337M	775844M	5966434M		Net Sales ($)		9758464M	10404961M
60723M	655993M	2664099M	4338919M	2046633M	5102680M		Total Assets ($)		12207747M	15187587M

© RMA 2011   M = $ thousand   MM = $ million
See Pages 9 through 22 for Explanation of Ratios and Data

Comparative Historical Data | Current Data Sorted by Sales

			Type of Statement						
101	97	101	Unqualified	28	25	7	7	17	17
46	48	53	Reviewed	16	12	5	6	8	6
95	95	95	Compiled	49	23	6	4	9	4
743	817	784	Tax Returns	596	111	40	24	6	7
571	581	654	Other	377	130	45	37	35	30
4/1/08-3/31/09 ALL	4/1/09-3/31/10 ALL	4/1/10-3/31/11 ALL		91 (4/1-9/30/10) 0-1MM	1-3MM	3-5MM	1,596 (10/1/10-3/31/11) 5-10MM	10-25MM	25MM & OVER
1556	1638	1687	NUMBER OF STATEMENTS	1066	301	103	78	75	64
%	%	%	ASSETS	%	%	%	%	%	%
9.7	9.3	11.4	Cash & Equivalents	9.6	15.3	11.7	15.4	10.7	17.6
4.6	4.7	4.7	Trade Receivables (net)	2.1	6.2	9.4	13.3	10.7	16.2
13.8	12.5	8.5	Inventory	6.2	10.0	14.9	14.4	14.8	14.2
3.4	2.8	3.6	All Other Current	2.6	4.9	4.5	6.3	7.7	4.2
31.5	29.3	28.1	Total Current	20.5	36.4	40.4	49.5	43.8	52.3
53.3	55.0	57.2	Fixed Assets (net)	67.9	45.7	36.9	30.4	36.8	23.2
1.5	2.3	2.3	Intangibles (net)	1.9	2.7	2.8	4.4	2.2	4.3
13.7	13.4	12.4	All Other Non-Current	9.8	15.3	20.0	15.7	17.2	20.3
100.0	100.0	100.0	Total	100.0	100.0	100.0	100.0	100.0	100.0
			LIABILITIES						
11.1	11.4	9.3	Notes Payable-Short Term	8.3	9.7	13.0	12.7	6.6	17.0
4.2	4.0	3.3	Cur. Mat.-L.T.D.	3.5	3.2	3.1	2.7	3.7	2.3
2.7	2.8	2.2	Trade Payables	1.2	2.4	2.4	7.3	7.1	7.4
.0	.1	.0	Income Taxes Payable	.0	.0	.1	.0	.0	.2
10.4	11.2	9.8	All Other Current	8.5	12.4	8.4	14.7	10.2	14.4
28.4	29.4	24.7	Total Current	21.4	27.7	27.0	37.5	27.7	41.3
48.3	48.2	49.2	Long-Term Debt	56.2	45.9	32.0	27.2	33.0	22.3
.2	.1	.1	Deferred Taxes	.0	.1	.0	.0	1.5	.4
5.1	5.1	5.2	All Other Non-Current	3.9	7.2	9.0	6.7	9.1	5.1
17.9	17.1	20.8	Net Worth	18.5	19.1	32.0	28.6	28.7	30.8
100.0	100.0	100.0	Total Liabilities & Net Worth	100.0	100.0	100.0	100.0	100.0	100.0
			INCOME DATA						
100.0	100.0	100.0	Net Sales	100.0	100.0	100.0	100.0	100.0	100.0
			Gross Profit						
70.8	69.4	67.1	Operating Expenses	58.8	78.3	82.3	84.7	86.8	85.0
29.2	30.6	32.9	Operating Profit	41.2	21.7	17.7	15.3	13.2	15.0
19.0	20.1	19.6	All Other Expenses (net)	25.9	11.9	9.2	4.8	4.9	3.5
10.2	10.5	13.3	Profit Before Taxes	15.4	9.8	8.6	10.5	8.3	11.5
			RATIOS						
2.7	2.5	3.1		2.2	4.0	4.6	4.3	3.9	3.1
1.0	.9	1.0	Current	.6	1.4	1.3	1.3	1.5	1.4
.2	.2	.2		.1	.4	.5	.8	.8	.9
1.5	1.3	1.7		1.5	2.2	2.4	2.5	1.9	1.6
(1555) .4	(1635) .3	(1685) .4	Quick	.3	(300) .7	(102) .6	.8	.8	.9
.1	.1	.1		.1	.1	.2	.2	.2	.1
0 UND	0 UND	0 UND		0 UND	0 UND	0 UND	0 UND	0 UND	0 UND
0 UND	0 UND	0 UND	Sales/Receivables	0 UND	0 UND	0 999.8	1 324.1	5 68.6	6 62.0
7 50.9	5 69.6	4 84.0		0 UND	13 28.3	16 23.3	40 9.2	31 11.7	33 11.0
			Cost of Sales/Inventory						
			Cost of Sales/Payables						
3.0	3.8	3.5		4.3	2.5	3.7	3.0	3.4	4.1
UND	-50.6	-166.7	Sales/Working Capital	-10.6	18.9	17.0	19.3	10.4	25.0
-3.0	-2.8	-3.3		-2.3	-8.0	-9.3	-56.4	-31.6	-134.6
8.0	7.2	9.4		6.7	8.2	8.4	8.9	17.5	71.4
(632) 2.4	(671) 2.6	(683) 3.5	EBIT/Interest	(302) 3.4	(153) 2.9	(66) 3.6	(53) 4.0	(58) 6.0	(51) 7.9
.3	.6	1.2		1.1	.3	1.2	1.4	1.6	2.3
5.8	6.6	5.2							8.8
(42) 2.5	(45) 2.4	(39) 2.1	Net Profit + Depr., Dep., Amort./Cur. Mat. L/T/D					(10) 2.0	
.5	.8	.5							.3
.2	.3	.4		1.1	.1	.0	.1	.1	.0
2.8	2.8	2.7	Fixed/Worth	3.7	1.6	.8	.9	.7	.5
45.7	27.1	24.6		34.7	34.1	4.1	7.0	4.8	3.3
1.4	1.3	1.0		1.3	.8	.5	.6	.5	1.0
5.0	4.9	3.9	Debt/Worth	4.4	4.0	2.1	3.2	2.3	2.9
UND	942.6	63.4		230.8	UND	13.5	35.8	9.5	15.0
37.5	36.4	39.1		30.4	42.7	49.6	77.1	73.0	129.5
(1169) 10.9	(1244) 9.6	(1316) 12.0	% Profit Before Taxes/Tangible Net Worth	(816) 9.4	(227) 10.9	(89) 13.5	(63) 26.1	(63) 25.5	(58) 29.5
-.9	-.7	.7		.1	.4	.1	3.4	5.8	15.5
6.8	7.0	9.2		6.6	14.7	11.1	23.1	20.1	33.2
1.6	1.7	2.7	% Profit Before Taxes/Total Assets	1.9	2.9	2.9	7.0	6.4	9.4
-1.1	-.9	-.2		-.5	-.8	.0	1.5	1.0	4.1
25.0	25.2	22.5		1.0	87.5	103.4	178.4	47.6	153.6
.6	.4	.3	Sales/Net Fixed Assets	.2	2.1	7.8	19.8	9.7	33.5
.1	.1	.1		.1	.2	.6	1.6	.7	5.7
.7	.7	.8		.3	1.5	2.7	3.4	3.5	4.8
.2	.2	.2	Sales/Total Assets	.1	.4	.7	1.2	.8	1.9
.1	.1	.1		.1	.2	.2	.3	.4	.5
2.1	2.8	3.6		10.3	1.2	.7	.6	.6	.4
(1023) 12.3	(1094) 13.9	(1130) 14.6	% Depr., Dep., Amort./Sales	(734) 18.6	(183) 7.0	(60) 3.0	(46) 2.6	(61) 1.9	(46) 1.4
21.4	23.4	24.0		26.5	20.6	16.9	13.1	9.5	3.2
1.9	2.1	2.2		2.5	4.7	2.2	1.6	.6	.4
(212) 5.0	(218) 5.1	(236) 5.5	% Officers', Directors' Owners' Comp/Sales	(90) 9.2	(60) 8.4	(33) 4.0	(25) 3.0	(16) 1.8	(12) .9
12.1	12.6	13.8		20.0	18.9	9.7	4.1	4.1	4.2
8493209M	9677855M	11293104M	Net Sales ($)	361722M	535040M	386066M	552630M	1148350M	8309296M
14557198M	15751710M	14869047M	Total Assets ($)	2465672M	2225605M	1213097M	1446060M	2454232M	5064381M

M = $ thousand   MM = $ million
See Pages 9 through 22 for Explanation of Ratios and Data

Current Data Sorted by Assets

Comparative Historical Data

0-500M	500M-2MM	2-10MM	10-50MM	50-100MM	100-250MM		4/1/06-3/31/07 ALL	4/1/07-3/31/08 ALL
						Type of Statement		
		1	1	13	3	6 — Unqualified	20	23
	4	10	8			Reviewed	13	14
1	2	10	2			Compiled	24	19
7	5	7				Tax Returns	20	11
4	9	17	8	4	3	Other	35	30
	18 (4/1-9/30/10)		107 (10/1/10-3/31/11)					
12	21	45	31	7	9	**NUMBER OF STATEMENTS**	112	97
%	%	%	%	%	%	**ASSETS**	%	%
19.0	11.3	7.9	7.8			Cash & Equivalents	6.7	6.8
4.4	4.0	7.1	5.9			Trade Receivables (net)	5.8	4.6
8.9	17.4	8.4	12.4			Inventory	15.1	17.8
2.8	8.0	2.3	6.7			All Other Current	8.8	8.1
35.1	40.6	25.8	32.8			Total Current	36.5	37.3
53.1	53.3	62.5	54.1			Fixed Assets (net)	53.7	53.5
5.3	.0	2.5	1.4			Intangibles (net)	3.1	3.2
6.5	6.1	9.2	11.7			All Other Non-Current	6.7	5.9
100.0	100.0	100.0	100.0			Total	100.0	100.0
						LIABILITIES		
18.4	23.1	16.9	29.7			Notes Payable-Short Term	32.2	34.9
2.7	6.4	9.9	9.7			Cur. Mat.-L.T.D.	7.1	6.1
2.2	2.6	3.6	3.4			Trade Payables	5.6	3.9
.1	.0	.0	.2			Income Taxes Payable	.1	.2
23.2	10.7	5.6	5.1			All Other Current	9.5	5.9
46.6	42.8	35.9	48.1			Total Current	54.5	51.1
14.3	22.2	34.5	22.9			Long-Term Debt	31.8	26.2
.0	.0	.6	1.5			Deferred Taxes	.5	.7
7.5	.9	4.4	3.0			All Other Non-Current	2.7	4.5
31.6	34.2	24.6	24.6			Net Worth	10.4	17.5
100.0	100.0	100.0	100.0			Total Liabilities & Net Worth	100.0	100.0
						INCOME DATA		
100.0	100.0	100.0	100.0			Net Sales	100.0	100.0
						Gross Profit		
75.4	77.8	87.2	90.6			Operating Expenses	92.8	91.9
24.6	22.2	12.8	9.4			Operating Profit	7.2	8.1
2.6	5.1	3.3	3.9			All Other Expenses (net)	4.4	6.8
22.0	17.1	9.5	5.5			Profit Before Taxes	2.8	1.3
						RATIOS		
5.3	1.9	2.7	1.4			Current	1.3	1.2
.9	1.1	.8	.9				.6	.7
.2	.5	.2	.2				.2	.2
5.1	1.5	1.8	1.3			Quick	.5	.5
.3	.4	.4	.3				.2	.2
.1	.1	.1	.1				.1	.1
0 UND	0 UND	1 525.0	10 37.1			Sales/Receivables	3 121.3	4 90.4
0 UND	2 165.6	9 40.3	18 20.4				10 37.9	13 28.9
0 UND	18 19.8	26 14.1	38 9.5				23 15.6	25 14.7
						Cost of Sales/Inventory		
						Cost of Sales/Payables		
17.6	7.7	7.8	7.4			Sales/Working Capital	8.4	10.3
NM	29.8	-29.0	-13.6				-12.7	-24.3
-1.3	-4.0	-2.2	-1.4				-2.2	-2.4
	4.4	4.9	4.4			EBIT/Interest	2.3	1.8
	(15) 2.5	(39) 2.1	(30) 2.3				(101) 1.2	(84) 1.1
	1.7	1.2	1.1				.9	.7
						Net Profit + Depr., Dep.,	3.6	19.3
						Amort./Cur. Mat. L/T/D	(11) 1.6	(10) 3.6
							.6	1.6
.5	.8	1.1	.2			Fixed/Worth	.6	.3
1.5	1.8	2.7	3.4				3.8	3.2
-19.3	5.6	15.3	6.2				15.0	11.1
.7	.8	1.6	2.5			Debt/Worth	2.2	2.4
2.0	1.9	3.0	4.6				7.2	6.1
-22.9	5.9	18.4	14.4				38.9	17.3
	63.6	30.7	52.6			% Profit Before Taxes/Tangible	25.7	22.6
	(19) 17.1	(38) 15.0	(30) 19.8			Net Worth	(91) 7.3	(85) 11.0
	8.2	4.7	6.1				.0	-4.1
28.4	11.9	8.3	6.8			% Profit Before Taxes/Total	7.4	3.7
18.3	5.4	3.2	3.4			Assets	1.6	1.1
1.2	3.0	.4	.7				-.5	-1.2
481.7	31.3	3.3	21.1			Sales/Net Fixed Assets	17.3	12.5
1.8	1.4	1.0	1.0				2.0	1.4
.6	.6	.6	.6				.8	.8
3.1	1.3	1.2	.9			Sales/Total Assets	1.8	1.1
.7	.9	.7	.6				.8	.7
.5	.3	.4	.5				.5	.5
	18.7	9.5	11.9			% Depr., Dep., Amort./Sales	9.7	11.4
	(14) 22.0	(38) 25.7	(23) 25.6				(79) 20.1	(66) 21.5
	32.9	40.1	35.6				39.0	37.1
		2.1				% Officers', Directors'	1.7	2.1
	(19) 4.3					Owners' Comp/Sales	(41) 3.6	(31) 4.0
		6.6					6.8	7.3
5111M	23000M	330837M	552782M	492918M	954584M	Net Sales ($)	1968403M	1373745M
2913M	22097M	232912M	672430M	514061M	1183186M	Total Assets ($)	1885448M	1865883M

M = $ thousand   MM = $ million
See Pages 9 through 22 for Explanation of Ratios and Data

Comparative Historical Data | | | Type of Statement | Current Data Sorted by Sales

Comparative Historical Data			Type of Statement						
24	26	24	Unqualified	1	5	4	7	4	12
14	17	22	Reviewed	1	5	4	5	5	2
14	21	15	Compiled	2	6	3	2	2	
10	31	19	Tax Returns	13	6				
34	42	45	Other	9	13	3	5	5	10
4/1/08-3/31/09 ALL	4/1/09-3/31/10 ALL	4/1/10-3/31/11 ALL			18 (4/1-9/30/10)			107 (10/1/10-3/31/11)	
				0-1MM	1-3MM	3-5MM	5-10MM	10-25MM	25MM & OVER
96	137	125	NUMBER OF STATEMENTS	26	30	10	19	16	24
%	%	%	ASSETS	%	%	%	%	%	%
8.3	10.9	9.2	Cash & Equivalents	12.9	11.5	5.5	5.5	9.6	6.8
6.7	7.9	7.0	Trade Receivables (net)	2.9	3.9	4.4	4.0	3.9	20.7
16.0	12.5	12.5	Inventory	9.3	11.6	13.0	13.0	16.7	13.5
3.8	4.7	4.8	All Other Current	3.2	2.9	6.4	1.5	10.1	7.2
34.9	36.0	33.4	Total Current	28.2	29.9	29.3	24.0	40.3	48.3
52.4	53.2	55.3	Fixed Assets (net)	60.4	63.7	56.1	63.2	51.9	35.2
2.8	2.2	1.9	Intangibles (net)	.0	2.3	6.2	3.5	.6	1.5
9.9	8.6	9.3	All Other Non-Current	11.4	4.2	8.4	9.3	7.2	15.0
100.0	100.0	100.0	Total	100.0	100.0	100.0	100.0	100.0	100.0
			LIABILITIES						
27.6	27.4	22.8	Notes Payable-Short Term	13.9	20.3	17.0	30.1	27.6	28.9
7.6	7.2	8.5	Cur. Mat.-L.T.D.	5.4	9.8	13.2	6.5	8.4	9.7
4.5	5.2	3.1	Trade Payables	.8	1.9	4.3	2.4	2.5	7.3
.1	.2	.3	Income Taxes Payable	.1	.1	.0	.0	.3	1.1
6.6	9.8	7.8	All Other Current	14.2	6.4	4.0	5.7	7.7	6.1
46.4	49.7	42.4	Total Current	34.4	38.5	38.5	44.7	46.4	53.1
32.8	28.9	26.9	Long-Term Debt	22.6	36.8	20.0	27.8	25.6	22.1
.7	.5	.6	Deferred Taxes	.0	.2	.0	2.4	1.3	.2
4.5	2.7	4.0	All Other Non-Current	.7	4.7	10.1	6.3	1.1	4.4
15.6	18.1	26.1	Net Worth	42.2	19.9	31.4	18.7	25.6	20.3
100.0	100.0	100.0	Total Liabilities & Net Worth	100.0	100.0	100.0	100.0	100.0	100.0
			INCOME DATA						
100.0	100.0	100.0	Net Sales	100.0	100.0	100.0	100.0	100.0	100.0
			Gross Profit						
94.6	89.0	85.6	Operating Expenses	62.6	91.5	89.5	92.4	91.7	91.9
5.4	11.0	14.4	Operating Profit	37.4	8.5	10.5	7.6	8.3	8.1
3.0	3.3	3.7	All Other Expenses (net)	8.5	2.1	.8	4.0	2.2	2.2
2.4	7.7	10.8	Profit Before Taxes	28.8	6.4	9.7	3.6	6.1	5.9
			RATIOS						
1.5	1.5	1.9		6.6	1.8	2.0	2.1	1.4	1.5
.9	.8	1.1	Current	1.1	1.1	.4	1.2	1.1	1.0
.3	.2	.3		.3	.3	.2	.1	.2	.4
.9	.9	1.4		6.6	1.6	.5	1.7	.9	1.0
.3	.3	.4	Quick	.4	.4	.4	.3	.2	.3
.1	.1	.1		.1	.2	.1	.1	.1	.2
3 131.9	3 107.1	2 167.6		0 UND	1 279.1	6 57.7	4 86.7	4 102.1	15 24.2
12 31.1	13 28.3	11 33.3	Sales/Receivables	0 UND	9 38.8	11 33.5	10 37.6	15 24.6	31 11.9
30 12.3	29 12.4	32 11.3		6 58.8	25 14.5	22 16.8	34 10.6	30 12.3	43 8.4
			Cost of Sales/Inventory						
			Cost of Sales/Payables						
11.0	10.7	7.2		1.8	12.2	5.6	7.4	8.2	5.4
-79.8	-19.7	40.8	Sales/Working Capital	25.5	35.6	-6.6	18.3	39.8	NM
-3.1	-2.2	-2.0		-1.5	-3.3	-1.7	-1.5	-2.4	-1.6
2.6	5.8	4.8		10.0	4.1		2.8	4.7	4.9
(89) 1.4	(120) 1.7	(108) 2.3	EBIT/Interest	(16) 5.1	(28) 2.0		1.4	(14) 2.4	(23) 2.8
.5	1.1	1.4		2.4	1.3		.8	1.8	1.9
12.0	6.5	10.7	Net Profit + Depr., Dep., Amort./Cur. Mat. L/T/D						
(10) 2.7	(14) 2.8	(10) 1.6							
1.4	.8	.1							
.4	.7	.6		.7	1.3	.3	2.3	.3	.2
3.4	2.6	2.0	Fixed/Worth	1.2	4.9	2.8	3.8	2.6	1.2
16.2	8.6	7.7		2.9	284.7	9.8	17.4	5.8	6.6
2.3	1.9	1.6		.6	1.7	.8	2.8	1.6	2.7
7.3	4.3	3.8	Debt/Worth	1.6	6.6	2.2	4.9	3.8	6.1
33.8	15.6	12.5		4.1	445.3	9.7	16.8	13.8	9.3
32.1	39.6	47.4		42.3	59.5		32.5	62.5	67.2
(76) 14.3	(117) 15.4	(111) 19.7	% Profit Before Taxes/Tangible Net Worth	(23) 15.1	(24) 21.2	(16)	9.1	(15) 21.9	23.9
.2	2.1	7.8		7.9	6.0		-2.4	7.8	15.1
5.5	7.6	8.3		17.4	8.6	6.9	6.8	9.2	8.2
2.0	2.7	4.1	% Profit Before Taxes/Total Assets	6.7	3.0	5.1	1.8	3.8	4.6
-2.3	.2	.9		3.1	.6	.1	-.5	1.9	2.2
19.1	6.5	7.4		3.3	4.8	4.6	3.4	15.9	54.2
1.4	1.5	1.3	Sales/Net Fixed Assets	.6	1.2	1.4	1.0	1.7	3.6
.8	.8	.6		.2	.6	.7	.6	.8	.9
1.2	1.2	1.0		.7	1.2	1.0	.9	1.3	1.9
.7	.7	.7	Sales/Total Assets	.4	.7	.7	.6	.9	.7
.6	.5	.5		.2	.4	.6	.5	.5	.5
14.7	7.9	10.0		10.0	21.0		15.6	12.1	.2
(59) 31.6	(94) 22.7	(86) 25.3	% Depr., Dep., Amort./Sales	(19) 27.8	(24) 27.5	(15)	26.6	(10) 20.4	(10) .4
43.9	38.4	37.4		49.7	43.4		35.2	35.6	13.2
1.0	1.5	1.3			4.2				
(33) 2.8	(40) 2.9	(34) 3.2	% Officers', Directors' Owners' Comp/Sales	(14)	5.6				
4.4	7.2	5.8			8.8				
1820826M	2135919M	2359232M	Net Sales ($)	8708M	62249M	42020M	140867M	224943M	1880445M
2034269M	2693886M	2627599M	Total Assets ($)	35525M	99543M	60195M	216970M	328728M	1886638M

M = $ thousand   MM = $ million
See Pages 9 through 22 for Explanation of Ratios and Data

REAL ESTATE—Passenger Car Leasing NAICS 532112

Current Data Sorted by Assets							Comparative Historical Data	
1	1		12	4	4	Type of Statement		
		8	11	1	3	Unqualified	28	22
1	2	5	5			Reviewed	29	23
3	8	3				Compiled	24	30
1	3	11	9	3	4	Tax Returns	11	13
						Other	41	59
	21 (4/1-9/30/10)		82 (10/1/10-3/31/11)				4/1/06-3/31/07 ALL	4/1/07-3/31/08 ALL
0-500M	500M-2MM	2-10MM	10-50MM	50-100MM	100-250MM			
6	14	27	37	8	11	NUMBER OF STATEMENTS	133	147
%	%	%	%	%	%	ASSETS	%	%
	9.3	6.6	3.7		4.1	Cash & Equivalents	6.0	5.8
	4.8	10.0	10.7		9.2	Trade Receivables (net)	8.9	9.8
	4.0	3.7	4.0		.6	Inventory	7.9	6.9
	2.2	8.5	6.6		5.8	All Other Current	7.5	7.7
	20.3	28.8	24.9		19.7	Total Current	30.3	30.2
	72.4	52.8	43.3		63.0	Fixed Assets (net)	48.8	45.8
	2.4	1.4	1.8		.3	Intangibles (net)	1.7	1.4
	4.9	17.1	30.0		17.0	All Other Non-Current	19.1	22.6
	100.0	100.0	100.0		100.0	Total	100.0	100.0
						LIABILITIES		
	19.6	12.2	8.7		15.4	Notes Payable-Short Term	16.6	18.5
	18.2	6.4	10.9		2.6	Cur. Mat.-L.T.D.	8.4	7.0
	3.0	3.3	2.3		1.6	Trade Payables	5.2	3.4
	.0	.0	.3		.0	Income Taxes Payable	.3	.2
	6.8	7.0	3.4		3.5	All Other Current	6.7	3.9
	47.7	28.9	25.6		23.0	Total Current	37.2	33.1
	37.0	52.8	54.6		55.8	Long-Term Debt	40.7	44.9
	.1	.7	1.8		1.6	Deferred Taxes	.8	.8
	6.3	9.6	3.4		1.3	All Other Non-Current	4.4	4.9
	8.9	8.1	14.6		18.4	Net Worth	16.9	16.3
	100.0	100.0	100.0		100.0	Total Liabilities & Net Worth	100.0	100.0
						INCOME DATA		
	100.0	100.0	100.0		100.0	Net Sales	100.0	100.0
						Gross Profit		
	85.6	79.9	87.8		89.1	Operating Expenses	84.9	82.9
	14.4	20.1	12.2		10.9	Operating Profit	15.1	17.1
	4.0	15.2	9.2		4.5	All Other Expenses (net)	7.7	11.1
	10.4	4.9	3.0		6.4	Profit Before Taxes	7.4	6.0
						RATIOS		
	.7	4.0	4.8		2.7		1.8	2.9
	.4	1.8	.8		1.4	Current	1.0	1.1
	.2	.4	.2		.6		.2	.3
	.5	2.5	2.7		1.2		1.1	1.7
	.2	1.0	.3		.5	Quick	.3 (146)	.5
	.1	.1	.2		.2		.1	.1
0 UND	5 66.8	5 69.7		12 30.8			2 199.5	3 114.5
7 54.3	21 17.1	29 12.6		27 13.6		Sales/Receivables	12 31.1	17 21.0
29 12.6	166 2.2	79 4.6		31 11.9			36 10.3	51 7.1
						Cost of Sales/Inventory		
						Cost of Sales/Payables		
	NM	2.3	2.9		1.1		4.0	3.7
	-2.8	11.8	-7.3		15.8	Sales/Working Capital	-275.8	27.8
	-1.7	-4.0	-1.4		-2.5		-1.9	-3.5
	3.5	4.3	2.7				3.2	2.4
	(12) 2.0	(21) 1.3	(29) 1.6			EBIT/Interest	(101) 1.5	(106) 1.4
	1.1	1.0	1.0				1.2	1.1
						Net Profit + Depr., Dep., Amort./Cur. Mat. L/T/D	1.6	
							(13) .7	
							.3	
	2.2	1.1	.1		1.4		.2	.2
	31.6	5.9	2.9		3.6	Fixed/Worth	2.6	3.1
	-2.9	-11.6	8.0		38.4		8.1	11.0
	1.6	3.5	4.8		3.3		3.0	3.8
	31.7	8.8	8.1		3.9	Debt/Worth	6.7	8.1
	-5.0	-30.3	18.3		46.4		17.3	20.5
		82.7	25.4				38.8	32.6
	(19) 8.8	(34) 13.5				% Profit Before Taxes/Tangible Net Worth	(119) 15.7	(126) 13.6
	4.1	1.9					8.3	4.2
	9.6	6.0	2.7		3.2		5.1	4.3
	3.9	1.4	1.6		2.6	% Profit Before Taxes/Total Assets	2.0	1.7
	-1.7	-.3	.1		.6		.8	.3
	3.9	7.6	35.0		.9		29.9	36.7
	1.1	1.0	.9		.6	Sales/Net Fixed Assets	1.1	1.3
	.4	.5	.5		.5		.5	.5
	2.2	.7	.5		.6		.7	.7
	.9	.4	.4		.4	Sales/Total Assets	.5	.5
	.4	.2	.2		.2		.3	.3
	20.6	6.6	2.6				8.0	3.5
(11) 56.6	(20) 34.8	(27) 29.8				% Depr., Dep., Amort./Sales	(90) 39.9	(106) 25.1
	66.6	59.4	57.2				63.7	58.9
			2.6				1.1	2.6
		(11) 3.7				% Officers', Directors' Owners' Comp/Sales	(29) 3.8	(36) 5.2
		5.4					6.4	7.7
830M	35311M	100162M	571898M	181620M	869595M	Net Sales ($)	1453113M	1777787M
1171M	13925M	150511M	991276M	480288M	1944591M	Total Assets ($)	3132974M	4074451M

M = $ thousand   MM = $ million
See Pages 9 through 22 for Explanation of Ratios and Data

Comparative Historical Data — Current Data Sorted by Sales

4/1/08-3/31/09 ALL	4/1/09-3/31/10 ALL	4/1/10-3/31/11 ALL	Type of Statement	0-1MM	1-3MM	3-5MM	5-10MM	10-25MM	25MM & OVER
23	27	22	Unqualified	2	1		2	12	5
27	24	23	Reviewed	1	5	5	6	3	3
18	27	13	Compiled	2	3	5	2	1	
21	18	14	Tax Returns	9	1	1	1	1	1
60	38	31	Other	6	8	5	2	5	5
				21 (4/1-9/30/10)			82 (10/1/10-3/31/11)		
149	134	103	NUMBER OF STATEMENTS	20	18	16	13	22	14
%	%	%	**ASSETS**	%	%	%	%	%	%
5.5	6.0	5.4	Cash & Equivalents	6.2	5.0	5.4	4.6	5.3	6.0
13.2	9.0	9.6	Trade Receivables (net)	10.3	5.6	8.1	9.2	13.0	10.8
6.6	4.6	5.0	Inventory	10.0	.8	3.8	6.0	4.7	4.0
8.4	4.7	6.4	All Other Current	5.6	6.9	7.5	15.9	2.1	3.2
33.7	24.4	26.4	Total Current	32.1	18.3	24.8	35.7	25.1	24.0
46.4	53.3	52.8	Fixed Assets (net)	57.2	60.6	45.2	41.8	49.2	61.3
1.2	1.0	1.4	Intangibles (net)	.0	4.5	.0	.1	1.8	1.5
18.7	21.3	19.3	All Other Non-Current	10.6	16.6	29.9	22.4	23.9	13.2
100.0	100.0	100.0	Total	100.0	100.0	100.0	100.0	100.0	100.0
			LIABILITIES						
16.9	10.8	12.1	Notes Payable-Short Term	13.1	20.1	6.3	3.6	14.9	10.3
8.1	9.8	10.1	Cur. Mat.-L.T.D.	10.9	3.8	18.1	12.9	11.4	3.2
3.2	2.8	2.4	Trade Payables	1.8	.9	3.3	1.5	1.7	5.9
.2	.2	.1	Income Taxes Payable	.0	.1	.0	.2	.2	.0
6.2	7.1	6.4	All Other Current	15.3	5.3	2.5	2.8	3.7	7.3
34.6	30.8	31.1	Total Current	41.0	30.3	30.3	21.0	32.0	26.7
45.7	54.9	49.6	Long-Term Debt	41.4	39.4	55.2	69.9	48.2	51.2
.8	.9	1.2	Deferred Taxes	.8	1.2	1.1	.5	2.2	.8
3.9	5.3	5.5	All Other Non-Current	5.1	13.7	9.4	3.0	.7	1.1
15.1	8.2	12.7	Net Worth	11.7	15.5	4.1	5.7	16.9	20.2
100.0	100.0	100.0	Total Liabilities & Net Worth	100.0	100.0	100.0	100.0	100.0	100.0
			INCOME DATA						
100.0	100.0	100.0	Net Sales	100.0	100.0	100.0	100.0	100.0	100.0
			Gross Profit						
82.4	86.9	84.7	Operating Expenses	72.6	83.1	87.2	90.7	88.3	90.1
17.6	13.1	15.3	Operating Profit	27.4	16.9	12.8	9.3	11.7	9.9
12.3	10.6	9.4	All Other Expenses (net)	16.1	9.1	12.1	8.8	5.1	4.7
5.3	2.5	5.9	Profit Before Taxes	11.4	7.8	.7	.5	6.6	5.2
			RATIOS						
2.1	2.6	3.0	Current	2.5	3.3	14.3	5.5	2.8	4.5
1.1	1.0	1.0		.5	1.1	1.2	.9	.9	1.4
.3	.3	.2		.1	.3	.2	.4	.2	.5
1.6	1.5	2.0	Quick	1.4	2.0	9.2	2.6	2.7	3.3
.5	.5	.4		.3	.6	.6	.5	.3	.7
.1	.2	.1		.1	.1	.2	.2	.2	.1
2 161.7	4 88.2	3 109.0	Sales/Receivables	0 UND	9 38.8	1 434.2	4 85.8	7 56.1	5 70.0
14 25.7	15 24.8	20 17.8		9 42.2	30 12.0	21 17.1	10 37.4	24 15.4	17 21.4
54 6.7	38 9.7	51 7.2		129 2.8	62 5.9	130 2.8	38 9.5	50 7.4	29 12.4
			Cost of Sales/Inventory						
			Cost of Sales/Payables						
3.1	4.2	3.5	Sales/Working Capital	1.4	7.0	1.9	2.3	3.0	11.7
68.4	NM	-84.1		-3.6	135.7	NM	-38.8	NM	27.4
-2.2	-2.4	-1.8		-1.5	-2.6	-.9	-5.8	-1.4	-2.2
2.6	2.5	2.9	EBIT/Interest	2.3	4.3	1.3	1.7	2.9	7.4
(106) 1.3	(99) 1.4	(79) 1.7		(12) 2.0	(13) 1.3	(11) 1.2	(11) 1.2	(20) 1.9	(12) 2.7
1.0	1.0	1.0		1.3	.6	.9	.9	1.5	2.0
		1.0	Net Profit + Depr., Dep., Amort./Cur. Mat. L/T/D						
	(10) .8								
		-.1							
.2	1.4	.7	Fixed/Worth	1.3	.8	.1	.6	.1	1.4
3.1	5.8	3.8		4.3	7.2	4.4	2.9	3.1	3.7
8.1	86.3	20.0		NM	-10.2	NM	15.7	6.3	NM
3.7	3.9	3.6	Debt/Worth	2.6	3.9	4.6	6.6	4.2	2.8
7.5	10.2	7.6		13.2	12.7	5.7	16.3	5.5	3.7
21.8	600.3	46.4		-51.2	-12.3	NM	46.5	8.6	NM
26.4	22.5	35.0	% Profit Before Taxes/Tangible Net Worth	103.6	94.0	17.4	37.6	34.0	21.3
(129) 12.3	(102) 11.9	(83) 13.7		(14) 31.2	(13) 11.4	(12) 8.1	(12) 5.4	(21) 17.2	(11) 13.7
1.9	1.9	4.2		3.5	1.3	-1.1	-35.0	12.1	10.6
3.3	3.4	4.4	% Profit Before Taxes/Total Assets	6.2	6.3	1.7	1.9	4.4	6.4
1.0	1.2	1.9		2.5	1.1	.4	1.3	2.4	3.0
.0	.1	.1		-.2	-.8	-.4	-1.2	1.6	1.9
29.8	12.2	11.4	Sales/Net Fixed Assets	7.4	1.8	18.8	115.5	39.4	1.1
1.1	.8	.9		.7	.8	1.1	1.3	2.3	.8
.5	.5	.5		.3	.4	.4	.8	.6	.5
.6	.6	.6	Sales/Total Assets	.9	.7	.5	.7	.6	.7
.4	.4	.4		.3	.3	.4	.5	.4	.5
.2	.3	.2		.2	.2	.1	.2	.3	.4
3.8	6.3	6.0	% Depr., Dep., Amort./Sales	35.3	8.8	3.6	3.6	3.0	
(97) 27.5	(86) 36.9	(63) 30.3		(12) 55.2	(15) 50.4	(13) 20.7	(11) 28.9	(10) 6.5	
60.7	70.6	57.2		66.6	57.2	77.6	41.7	35.7	
1.8	2.3	2.6	% Officers', Directors' Owners' Comp/Sales						
(36) 3.7	(39) 3.4	(30) 4.5							
7.4	5.7	7.8							
2343406M	1732376M	1759416M	Net Sales ($)	8487M	35837M	59952M	91880M	392186M	1171074M
4930160M	3529629M	3581762M	Total Assets ($)	35148M	109073M	266286M	274731M	1050836M	1845688M

M = $ thousand   MM = $ million
See Pages 9 through 22 for Explanation of Ratios and Data

Current Data Sorted by Assets							Comparative Historical Data	
						Type of Statement		
1	1	7	18	13	16	Unqualified	61	50
1	5	23	43	2	1	Reviewed	55	53
5	12	21	3			Compiled	44	37
9	14	7				Tax Returns	39	34
12	19	36	37	14	15	Other	96	102
42 (4/1-9/30/10)		293 (10/1/10-3/31/11)					4/1/06-3/31/07	4/1/07-3/31/08
0-500M	500M-2MM	2-10MM	10-50MM	50-100MM	100-250MM		ALL	ALL
28	51	94	101	29	32	NUMBER OF STATEMENTS	295	276
%	%	%	%	%	%	**ASSETS**	%	%
14.4	15.7	8.8	6.7	4.4	3.1	Cash & Equivalents	8.4	7.5
9.4	5.6	10.7	10.9	15.3	13.0	Trade Receivables (net)	10.4	10.5
6.6	6.7	9.4	6.4	9.1	2.5	Inventory	9.0	7.8
3.0	3.6	4.2	4.6	7.1	5.5	All Other Current	4.2	4.1
33.3	31.6	33.1	28.5	35.9	24.0	Total Current	32.1	30.0
54.7	51.7	56.4	61.0	47.4	52.8	Fixed Assets (net)	58.2	61.8
.1	1.4	3.6	2.0	1.8	3.3	Intangibles (net)	1.3	1.7
12.0	15.3	6.9	8.5	14.9	20.0	All Other Non-Current	8.5	6.5
100.0	100.0	100.0	100.0	100.0	100.0	Total	100.0	100.0
						LIABILITIES		
35.5	13.0	8.3	9.4	9.7	3.4	Notes Payable-Short Term	11.0	11.4
8.7	12.0	11.2	11.7	8.5	11.2	Cur. Mat.-L.T.D.	10.1	11.7
3.1	3.7	5.7	4.9	3.4	2.4	Trade Payables	5.0	4.5
.0	.1	.1	.3	.1	.0	Income Taxes Payable	.3	.3
19.4	9.1	7.7	5.0	7.5	3.3	All Other Current	8.5	6.0
66.8	37.8	32.9	31.3	29.3	20.3	Total Current	34.8	33.9
36.9	30.8	33.9	32.2	36.3	47.8	Long-Term Debt	38.0	38.0
.0	.0	.5	2.8	2.9	5.4	Deferred Taxes	1.6	2.0
4.0	5.0	2.8	1.8	3.0	5.3	All Other Non-Current	4.3	3.9
-7.6	26.5	29.9	32.0	28.5	21.2	Net Worth	21.2	22.2
100.0	100.0	100.0	100.0	100.0	100.0	Total Liabilties & Net Worth	100.0	100.0
						INCOME DATA		
100.0	100.0	100.0	100.0	100.0	100.0	Net Sales	100.0	100.0
						Gross Profit		
79.0	80.7	86.1	90.4	86.1	89.2	Operating Expenses	85.7	86.6
21.0	19.3	13.9	9.6	13.9	10.8	Operating Profit	14.3	13.4
4.1	2.7	2.9	3.6	9.9	9.3	All Other Expenses (net)	3.6	5.8
16.9	16.7	11.0	6.0	4.1	1.5	Profit Before Taxes	10.7	7.6
						RATIOS		
3.7	3.2	2.1	1.4	1.6	1.5		1.5	1.6
.8	1.1	1.0	.9	1.0	1.0	Current	.9	.9
.1	.3	.4	.4	.5	.6		.4	.4
2.0	2.0	1.5	1.0	1.2	1.1		1.0	1.1
.3	.5	.5	.5	.5	.6	Quick	.5	.5
.1	.1	.2	.3	.2	.3		.2	.2
0 UND	**0** UND	**1** 279.8	**19** 19.1	**10** 37.8	**27** 13.5		**0** UND	**2** 183.2
0 UND	**1** 727.0	**24** 15.2	**34** 10.9	**37** 9.8	**40** 9.2	Sales/Receivables	**22** 16.5	**28** 12.9
17 21.4	**29** 12.4	**40** 9.1	**53** 6.9	**57** 6.4	**55** 6.6		**42** 8.8	**44** 8.2
						Cost of Sales/Inventory		
						Cost of Sales/Payables		
15.1	5.2	5.0	10.3	5.4	6.9		11.3	10.2
-107.3	207.0	164.4	-60.0	-182.8	NM	Sales/Working Capital	-55.3	-98.7
-2.4	-3.5	-4.5	-4.5	-4.9	-7.8		-4.3	-4.2
10.5	8.2	7.6	4.0	3.2	2.7		4.5	3.7
(17) 5.4	(45) 2.9	(84) 2.5	(96) 2.0	(24) 2.5	(24) 1.8	EBIT/Interest	(257) 2.3	(243) 1.8
1.9	.4	1.2	1.2	1.2	1.3		1.3	1.2
		2.8	2.0				1.8	2.5
		(10) 1.3	(38) 1.1			Net Profit + Depr., Dep., Amort./Cur. Mat. L/T/D	(52) 1.3	(56) 1.2
		.9	1.0				.9	.9
.3	.7	.9	1.3	.1	1.2		1.1	1.3
UND	1.6	1.8	2.1	1.6	2.4	Fixed/Worth	2.6	2.7
-2.2	-6.0	24.4	4.0	3.0	5.9		6.1	7.3
2.1	.6	.9	1.2	1.4	2.3		1.8	1.8
UND	2.9	2.6	2.6	3.1	5.8	Debt/Worth	3.9	3.6
-3.7	-23.6	27.1	5.5	6.8	17.2		10.3	10.2
221.6	46.7	41.1	23.7	24.6	17.8		38.7	30.2
(14) 65.1	(37) 15.8	(75) 21.2	(95) 11.9	(26) 11.1	(27) 12.0	% Profit Before Taxes/Tangible Net Worth	(251) 17.7	(237) 14.2
30.6	4.0	7.1	3.5	4.2	4.8		8.0	5.6
39.7	24.0	10.3	6.9	4.9	3.1		11.0	8.0
22.0	5.5	5.0	3.2	2.9	1.8	% Profit Before Taxes/Total Assets	4.0	3.3
4.5	-1.2	.6	.6	.4	.2		1.1	.9
33.3	6.3	4.9	4.2	17.1	15.5		4.7	3.8
2.5	2.0	1.3	1.5	2.7	1.1	Sales/Net Fixed Assets	1.3	1.2
1.5	1.2	.5	.6	.6	.5		.6	.6
2.1	1.7	1.4	1.7	1.1	.9		1.6	1.6
1.8	1.1	.7	.9	.6	.5	Sales/Total Assets	.8	.8
1.0	.8	.4	.5	.3	.2		.4	.4
15.2	6.1	7.7	6.5	2.5			6.5	6.0
(12) 31.5	(35) 17.6	(79) 20.9	(91) 15.2	(17) 6.9		% Depr., Dep., Amort./Sales	(228) 17.2	(210) 19.5
50.3	32.3	41.0	31.2	17.1			42.5	42.5
		1.3	1.6				1.3	1.0
		(17) 2.2	(18) 2.6			% Officers', Directors' Owners' Comp/Sales	(55) 3.5	(48) 3.2
		4.2	9.1				8.3	6.3
23373M	**98311M**	**675098M**	**3118082M**	**1508626M**	**2802238M**	Net Sales ($)	**6614891M**	**8551283M**
6539M	**61871M**	**561516M**	**2578958M**	**1916530M**	**4767053M**	Total Assets ($)	**7568739M**	**8665091M**

M = $ thousand MM = $ million

See Pages 9 through 22 for Explanation of Ratios and Data

Comparative Historical Data / Current Data Sorted by Sales

	4/1/08-3/31/09 ALL	4/1/09-3/31/10 ALL	4/1/10-3/31/11 ALL	0-1MM	1-3MM	3-5MM	5-10MM	10-25MM	25MM & OVER
Type of Statement		42 (4/1-9/30/10)				293 (10/1/10-3/31/11)			
Unqualified	58	45	56	1	6	2	4	14	29
Reviewed	67	62	75	3	8	10	18	19	17
Compiled	45	47	41	12	10	6	7	3	3
Tax Returns	39	33	30	16	8	2	2	2	
Other	117	117	133	23	19	12	12	24	43
NUMBER OF STATEMENTS	326	304	335	55	51	32	43	62	92
	%	%	%	%	%	%	%	%	%
ASSETS									
Cash & Equivalents	6.5	7.7	8.7	14.3	13.6	6.1	7.0	4.8	7.1
Trade Receivables (net)	11.7	10.5	10.5	5.7	5.6	9.8	11.8	13.1	14.0
Inventory	6.4	9.1	7.1	1.9	4.9	10.8	9.3	9.2	7.8
All Other Current	4.6	4.5	4.5	4.7	4.4	4.4	3.9	4.6	4.7
Total Current	29.3	31.7	30.9	26.7	28.4	31.1	32.0	31.8	33.6
Fixed Assets (net)	60.5	57.6	55.8	58.0	59.2	54.6	56.8	51.4	55.5
Intangibles (net)	1.5	1.7	2.3	2.8	1.7	1.0	2.1	3.5	2.1
All Other Non-Current	8.7	9.0	11.0	12.5	10.7	13.4	9.1	13.4	8.7
Total	100.0	100.0	100.0	100.0	100.0	100.0	100.0	100.0	100.0
LIABILITIES									
Notes Payable-Short Term	9.3	12.4	11.2	20.4	10.4	9.5	11.2	9.5	8.0
Cur. Mat.-L.T.D.	12.8	12.0	11.0	12.7	10.5	11.6	12.3	9.9	10.3
Trade Payables	4.4	5.0	4.4	1.8	1.7	4.8	4.6	7.2	5.3
Income Taxes Payable	.2	.2	.1	.1	.0	.0	.0	.4	.2
All Other Current	7.2	9.0	7.6	13.3	9.5	6.8	4.3	4.8	7.0
Total Current	33.9	38.5	34.5	48.3	32.2	32.7	32.4	31.8	30.8
Long-Term Debt	40.5	35.6	34.7	35.0	37.5	35.4	33.3	35.4	32.9
Deferred Taxes	1.8	1.9	1.8	.0	.1	.8	.9	2.4	4.0
All Other Non-Current	4.9	4.9	3.2	4.6	3.6	2.0	2.4	3.5	2.7
Net Worth	18.9	19.0	25.9	12.1	26.6	29.0	31.0	26.9	29.7
Total Liabilities & Net Worth	100.0	100.0	100.0	100.0	100.0	100.0	100.0	100.0	100.0
INCOME DATA									
Net Sales	100.0	100.0	100.0	100.0	100.0	100.0	100.0	100.0	100.0
Gross Profit									
Operating Expenses	88.5	90.7	86.3	71.5	79.9	87.4	85.5	92.9	94.1
Operating Profit	11.5	9.3	13.7	28.5	20.1	12.6	14.5	7.1	5.9
All Other Expenses (net)	5.9	5.1	4.4	5.0	3.9	4.5	6.8	3.7	3.7
Profit Before Taxes	5.5	4.2	9.4	23.5	16.2	8.2	7.7	3.5	2.2
RATIOS									
Current	1.8	1.6	1.7	3.6	3.2	1.3	1.6	1.3	1.6
	.9	.9	1.0	1.0	1.2	.8	.7	1.0	1.0
	.3	.4	.4	.1	.3	.3	.3	.6	.6
Quick	1.1	1.1	1.3	2.3	2.3	1.0	.9	1.1	1.2
	.5	.5	.5	.4	.6	.4	.3	.5	.6
	.2	.2	.2	.1	.2	.1	.1	.3	.3
Sales/Receivables	1 324.7	4 99.3	1 271.3	0 UND	0 UND	0 UND	7 54.1	23 16.2	20 17.8
	26 14.2	27 13.7	26 13.8	0 UND	6 56.3	28 13.0	26 14.1	32 11.4	34 10.8
	46 7.9	42 8.6	45 8.1	29 12.4	33 10.9	57 6.4	45 8.2	53 6.9	47 7.7
Cost of Sales/Inventory									
Cost of Sales/Payables									
Sales/Working Capital	9.4	8.3	7.2	2.3	2.8	13.5	13.2	11.7	11.1
	-36.4	-59.5	-117.0	94.3	18.7	-25.7	-14.8	-264.7	-116.1
	-4.0	-3.9	-4.6	-2.4	-2.8	-2.8	-3.1	-8.3	-10.0
EBIT/Interest	2.8	3.1	5.3	8.6	7.7	3.9	5.0	5.3	3.6
	(266) 1.5	(265) 1.5	(290) 2.2	(41) 5.0	(44) 3.0	(26) 2.0	(37) 2.0	(55) 1.8	(87) 2.0
	.9	.3	1.2	1.2	1.1	1.3	1.1	1.1	1.3
Net Profit + Depr., Dep., Amort./Cur. Mat. L/T/D	2.6	2.9	2.4					2.8	1.8
	(60) 1.2	(59) 1.3	(55) 1.2				(18)	1.3	(24) 1.0
	.9	.9	1.0					1.0	.8
Fixed/Worth	1.3	1.2	1.0	.7	.7	1.0	.9	1.1	1.2
	2.6	2.3	2.0	2.8	1.6	2.1	1.8	2.0	2.1
	10.7	11.7	6.3	-2.6	6.9	5.4	18.9	5.0	4.4
Debt/Worth	1.5	1.4	1.2	.6	.8	1.5	.9	1.3	1.5
	3.7	3.6	2.9	4.5	2.7	2.6	2.1	3.7	3.0
	20.6	26.5	13.4	-3.8	17.0	14.3	28.3	11.2	6.2
% Profit Before Taxes/Tangible Net Worth	25.4	25.4	30.7	64.8	43.3	28.3	37.7	26.6	25.8
	(270) 9.5	(244) 9.6	(274) 14.4	(33) 24.4	(42) 18.4	(28) 15.4	(34) 13.1	(53) 13.5	(84) 12.1
	1.5	.1	5.1	8.2	7.8	6.3	4.5	2.8	4.6
% Profit Before Taxes/Total Assets	5.7	5.9	8.9	24.6	14.5	9.2	8.2	6.6	5.5
	2.1	1.7	3.4	8.7	6.3	2.4	4.8	2.6	3.0
	-.8	-2.0	.6	1.5	.6	1.2	.3	.2	.7
Sales/Net Fixed Assets	4.5	4.9	5.5	4.1	2.1	9.4	15.6	6.3	7.3
	1.1	1.4	1.6	1.8	1.2	.8	1.5	1.9	2.4
	.6	.7	.7	.6	.5	.5	.7	.8	.9
Sales/Total Assets	1.7	1.5	1.5	1.6	1.1	1.0	1.3	1.7	1.9
	.7	.8	.9	.9	.6	.5	.9	.8	1.2
	.4	.4	.4	.3	.3	.4	.4	.4	.6
% Depr., Dep., Amort./Sales	6.8	5.6	6.1	13.3	20.8	12.7	10.4	5.2	3.4
	(247) 22.3	(232) 20.6	(241) 16.9	(32) 28.1	(39) 34.8	(28) 35.5	(36) 20.7	(51) 14.5	(55) 6.9
	42.5	38.8	35.5	50.3	60.3	43.9	25.7	30.9	11.8
% Officers', Directors' Owners' Comp/Sales	.8	1.4	1.6					2.1	1.2
	(52) 2.8	(56) 2.6	(49) 3.4				(12)	3.7	(13) 1.6
	7.1	8.0	7.3					5.3	6.2
Net Sales ($)	7209273M	6466322M	8225728M	27287M	94934M	125555M	306586M	1027020M	6644346M
Total Assets ($)	8964143M	8297885M	9892467M	60689M	209109M	344726M	606927M	2134256M	6536760M

© RMA 2011   M = $ thousand   MM = $ million
See Pages 9 through 22 for Explanation of Ratios and Data

Current Data Sorted by Assets

Comparative Historical Data

						Type of Statement		
		1	5	1	1	Unqualified	15	11
	5	4	3	1		Reviewed	14	10
6	3	4				Compiled	23	22
3	11	5	1			Tax Returns	15	12
3	4	6	8		1	Other	21	24
	11 (4/1-9/30/10)		65 (10/1/10-3/31/11)				4/1/06-3/31/07	4/1/07-3/31/08
0-500M	500M-2MM	2-10MM	10-50MM	50-100MM	100-250MM		ALL	ALL
12	23	20	17	2	2	NUMBER OF STATEMENTS	88	79
%	%	%	%	%	%	ASSETS	%	%
13.2	7.7	3.9	5.7			Cash & Equivalents	7.6	7.7
11.9	13.9	5.4	11.9			Trade Receivables (net)	13.6	12.5
13.4	13.8	26.2	8.0			Inventory	12.3	15.9
1.1	1.5	3.6	2.7			All Other Current	4.7	4.3
39.6	36.9	39.2	28.3			Total Current	38.2	40.4
49.3	47.3	49.4	38.8			Fixed Assets (net)	44.4	46.1
5.7	6.9	5.5	9.3			Intangibles (net)	5.3	4.9
5.4	8.9	6.0	23.6			All Other Non-Current	12.2	8.6
100.0	100.0	100.0	100.0			Total	100.0	100.0
						LIABILITIES		
31.3	9.6	28.9	13.6			Notes Payable-Short Term	18.5	17.1
10.1	7.5	9.3	6.5			Cur. Mat.-L.T.D.	7.7	8.2
14.9	11.2	7.1	5.3			Trade Payables	7.5	9.0
.0	.0	1.0	.0			Income Taxes Payable	.2	.1
29.5	6.5	9.6	9.6			All Other Current	7.1	7.0
85.8	34.8	55.9	35.0			Total Current	41.0	41.6
36.1	43.4	27.4	32.0			Long-Term Debt	22.3	30.5
.0	.3	.7	.0			Deferred Taxes	.7	.5
28.0	6.5	4.1	10.4			All Other Non-Current	7.8	9.5
-49.9	15.0	11.9	22.6			Net Worth	28.2	18.0
100.0	100.0	100.0	100.0			Total Liabilties & Net Worth	100.0	100.0
						INCOME DATA		
100.0	100.0	100.0	100.0			Net Sales	100.0	100.0
						Gross Profit		
96.8	89.8	88.5	88.1			Operating Expenses	90.4	89.3
3.2	10.2	11.5	11.9			Operating Profit	9.6	10.7
2.6	6.0	3.8	5.9			All Other Expenses (net)	3.6	6.4
.6	4.3	7.7	6.0			Profit Before Taxes	6.0	4.2
						RATIOS		
1.9	1.8	1.0	1.4				2.2	2.1
.8	.9	.6	.9			Current	1.0	1.0
.2	.3	.1	.4				.5	.3
1.6	1.3	.1	.9				1.3	1.4
.5	.4	.0	.6			Quick	.5	.4
.1	.2	.0	.2				.1	.1
0 UND	0 UND	0 UND	0 999.8				0 UND	0 UND
3 136.5	19 19.6	0 UND	9 40.9			Sales/Receivables	12 29.3	6 57.6
21 17.5	37 9.7	1 377.1	45 8.1				37 9.7	29 12.6
						Cost of Sales/Inventory		
						Cost of Sales/Payables		
10.7	7.0	-109.7	5.9				6.7	6.7
-114.4	-43.9	-9.7	-136.2			Sales/Working Capital	111.0	103.6
-2.7	-9.3	-3.0	-7.8				-7.1	-5.1
	9.0	5.6	8.1				7.4	3.5
(20)	3.8	(19) 2.8	(14) 3.4			EBIT/Interest	(77) 2.5	(65) 1.9
	1.0	1.7	1.3				.9	1.0
						Net Profit + Depr., Dep., Amort./Cur. Mat. L/T/D	3.5	4.5
							(16) 1.6	(15) 2.9
							.3	1.8
2.0	.7	1.4	.3				.4	.5
-4.4	3.8	NM	1.8			Fixed/Worth	1.6	4.1
-.5	-5.3	-1.2	-288.6				10.6	-16.0
2.4	1.2	2.1	2.4				.6	1.5
-8.3	3.7	NM	3.9			Debt/Worth	2.8	6.2
-2.1	-10.0	-6.9	-344.5				21.3	-23.3
	33.5	48.4	62.0			% Profit Before Taxes/Tangible Net Worth	45.2	58.2
(15)	27.8	(10) 27.3	(12) 21.9				(70) 30.9	(55) 22.1
	7.3	3.4	6.7				8.8	4.6
39.5	22.8	10.9	10.9			% Profit Before Taxes/Total Assets	13.9	9.0
-2.7	4.3	6.0	6.0				6.1	4.2
-19.5	.0	1.3	1.0				.5	.0
22.7	12.5	17.1	15.4				15.2	15.7
3.2	4.6	3.2	5.4			Sales/Net Fixed Assets	4.3	3.0
2.5	1.9	1.9	2.3				1.8	1.4
2.8	2.4	2.1	1.9				2.4	2.3
2.1	1.6	1.8	1.3			Sales/Total Assets	1.8	1.5
1.4	.7	1.3	.5				.8	.7
	2.6	16.4	3.2				3.4	3.5
(22)	6.7	(11) 29.2	(10) 7.7			% Depr., Dep., Amort./Sales	(67) 11.3	(61) 15.1
	17.8	31.4	17.2				28.9	31.2
	3.0					% Officers', Directors' Owners' Comp/Sales	2.1	2.6
(10)	5.5						(26) 4.9	(22) 4.5
	11.4						8.1	10.8
9405M	56876M	152730M	527337M	165834M	239459M	Net Sales ($)	968375M	860370M
3602M	26283M	87542M	470111M	151962M	297357M	Total Assets ($)	859505M	792676M

M = $ thousand   MM = $ million
See Pages 9 through 22 for Explanation of Ratios and Data

Comparative Historical Data / Current Data Sorted by Sales

Type of Statement

	4/1/08-3/31/09 ALL	4/1/09-3/31/10 ALL	4/1/10-3/31/11 ALL	0-1MM	1-3MM	3-5MM	5-10MM	10-25MM	25MM & OVER
Unqualified	10	14	8			1		1	6
Reviewed	14	14	13	1	3		3	2	3
Compiled	28	10	13	7	1	1	4		
Tax Returns	23	25	20	10	3	2	4	1	
Other	25	27	22	3	3	3	6	2	6
					11 (4/1-9/30/10)			65 (10/1/10-3/31/11)	
NUMBER OF STATEMENTS	100	90	76	21	10	7	17	6	15

ASSETS

				%	%	%	%	%	%
	%	%	%						
Cash & Equivalents	9.2	9.1	7.2	8.8	6.9		5.3		5.5
Trade Receivables (net)	12.6	10.6	10.7	6.4	10.2		4.6		12.7
Inventory	15.9	15.6	15.7	11.0	25.6		21.8		11.8
All Other Current	4.1	3.4	2.3	1.0	1.1		3.9		1.1
Total Current	41.9	38.7	35.9	27.2	43.7		35.7		31.2
Fixed Assets (net)	44.8	44.6	46.6	59.4	37.7		49.2		51.4
Intangibles (net)	3.2	4.8	6.8	7.7	3.3		4.1		8.1
All Other Non-Current	10.1	12.0	10.7	5.6	15.3		11.0		9.4
Total	100.0	100.0	100.0	100.0	100.0		100.0		100.0

LIABILITIES

Notes Payable-Short Term	21.9	14.9	19.6	11.4	34.1		27.8		20.2
Cur. Mat.-L.T.D.	8.6	7.5	8.2	10.1	1.8		10.8		5.8
Trade Payables	7.2	7.3	9.1	8.6	10.1		6.4		6.9
Income Taxes Payable	.2	.3	.3	.0	.0		.4		.2
All Other Current	8.7	10.2	11.5	18.1	1.8		7.0		11.1
Total Current	46.6	40.2	48.7	48.3	47.8		52.4		44.1
Long-Term Debt	28.9	37.9	33.8	53.5	21.7		24.3		20.4
Deferred Taxes	.3	.6	.4	.0	.7		.8		.7
All Other Non-Current	9.8	13.9	9.8	18.2	11.0		5.6		9.1
Net Worth	14.4	7.5	7.3	-20.0	18.8		16.9		25.7
Total Liabilties & Net Worth	100.0	100.0	100.0	100.0	100.0		100.0		100.0

INCOME DATA

Net Sales	100.0	100.0	100.0	100.0	100.0		100.0		100.0
Gross Profit									
Operating Expenses	89.8	88.8	90.2	84.3	96.5		90.9		92.1
Operating Profit	10.2	11.2	9.8	15.7	3.5		9.1		7.9
All Other Expenses (net)	4.8	6.5	4.6	8.8	5.0		3.4		1.4
Profit Before Taxes	5.5	4.6	5.1	6.9	-1.5		5.6		6.5

RATIOS

Current	2.0	2.1	1.4	1.4	5.9		1.3		1.1
	1.1	1.1	.8	.5	2.0		.8		.8
	.4	.4	.2	.1	.6		.1		.3
Quick	1.4	1.2	.9	.8	1.5		.8		.8
	.5	.5	.3	.3	.8		.1		.6
	.1	.2	.1	.1	.1		.0		.1
Sales/Receivables	0 UND	0 UND	0 UND	0 UND	0 UND		0 UND		0 999.8
	10 36.6	11 33.0	4 87.4	3 141.0	13 27.7		0 999.8		22 16.4
	37 9.9	33 11.2	35 10.3	25 14.7	39 9.3		2 222.5		49 7.4
Cost of Sales/Inventory									
Cost of Sales/Payables									
Sales/Working Capital	5.2	7.1	9.6	12.3	2.4		80.8		32.6
	47.7	118.9	-22.7	-9.3	13.4		-18.3		-17.2
	-5.6	-7.4	-4.4	-2.3	-14.6		-3.2		-6.9
EBIT/Interest	6.4	4.9	5.8	6.7			5.8		5.6
	(85) 1.9	(73) 2.6	(66) 3.3	(16) 1.0			(16) 2.9		4.3
	.8	1.1	1.0	-1.0			1.5		3.4
Net Profit + Depr., Dep., Amort./Cur. Mat. L/T/D	9.8	2.6							
	(11) 2.5	(10) 1.8							
	1.2	.6							
Fixed/Worth	.6	.6	.9	5.0	.2		.8		1.0
	1.8	3.0	4.0	-12.5	1.2		2.9		1.8
	-5.9	-4.7	-3.6	-2.8	NM		-2.5		-567.8
Debt/Worth	.9	1.1	1.5	4.1	.9		1.2		1.3
	3.1	4.7	5.4	-30.7	2.4		3.8		3.9
	-10.2	-11.8	-10.1	-5.9	NM		-8.2		-636.9
% Profit Before Taxes/Tangible Net Worth	52.7	49.9	57.8				44.5		145.4
	(72) 17.7	(64) 16.9	(46) 26.8				(10) 21.0	(11) 36.2	
	4.5	2.3	5.6				3.4		14.8
% Profit Before Taxes/Total Assets	13.9	10.6	12.8	19.6	5.0		13.5		13.1
	3.1	4.1	5.4	1.1	.8		6.1		6.7
	-.6	.3	.4	-10.4	-9.1		1.9		3.9
Sales/Net Fixed Assets	12.2	13.8	11.5	3.8	16.6		15.8		5.4
	5.1	4.9	3.9	2.0	5.2		3.4		2.4
	1.6	1.9	2.0	.4	4.0		2.0		1.5
Sales/Total Assets	2.5	2.8	2.3	1.9	2.5		2.2		1.9
	1.6	1.8	1.6	1.3	1.5		1.7		1.4
	.8	.8	.8	.3	1.0		1.4		1.0
% Depr., Dep., Amort./Sales	3.6	2.2	4.4	6.7			9.3		
	(70) 9.3	(72) 8.1	(52) 10.3	(18) 14.9			(10) 24.2		
	30.1	22.3	22.9	22.7			30.5		
% Officers', Directors' Owners' Comp/Sales	3.6	3.1	2.6						
	(31) 7.1	(38) 5.5	(23) 5.1						
	10.8	10.1	9.9						
Net Sales ($)	1338007M	1209335M	1151641M	9905M	19569M	25805M	123695M	101414M	871253M
Total Assets ($)	1330760M	1289414M	1036857M	15681M	25274M	40800M	124624M	71865M	758613M

© RMA 2011

M = $ thousand   MM = $ million

See Pages 9 through 22 for Explanation of Ratios and Data

REAL ESTATE—Home Health Equipment Rental NAICS 532291

	Current Data Sorted by Assets							Comparative Historical Data	
			Type of Statement			
1	1	2	3		2	Unqualified		8	6
2	1	5	4			Reviewed		12	12
3	1	3				Compiled		7	7
3	6	6				Tax Returns		8	12
2	13	11	5	1	3	Other		26	34
	9 (4/1-9/30/10)		65 (10/1/10-3/31/11)					4/1/06-3/31/07	4/1/07-3/31/08
0-500M	500M-2MM	2-10MM	10-50MM	50-100MM	100-250MM			ALL	ALL
8	21	27	12	1	5	NUMBER OF STATEMENTS		61	71
%	%	%	%	%	%	**ASSETS**		%	%
	14.3	4.1	8.8			Cash & Equivalents		8.1	13.0
	19.3	22.5	22.0			Trade Receivables (net)		21.5	22.2
	13.7	8.2	13.3			Inventory		9.1	5.5
	3.5	2.5	5.9			All Other Current		2.8	2.9
	50.9	37.2	50.0			Total Current		41.5	43.5
	37.6	49.3	35.3			Fixed Assets (net)		47.9	40.9
	1.2	6.5	3.5			Intangibles (net)		5.5	7.6
	10.3	7.0	11.3			All Other Non-Current		5.0	8.0
	100.0	100.0	100.0			Total		100.0	100.0
						LIABILITIES			
	16.7	6.7	7.8			Notes Payable-Short Term		11.0	9.8
	5.7	9.8	9.2			Cur. Mat.-L.T.D.		6.8	9.6
	6.5	9.3	11.2			Trade Payables		10.0	8.5
	.9	.4	.0			Income Taxes Payable		.2	.1
	8.0	6.7	10.2			All Other Current		6.4	10.4
	37.8	33.0	38.4			Total Current		34.3	38.4
	34.2	28.1	11.8			Long-Term Debt		32.1	29.4
	.0	.3	3.1			Deferred Taxes		.4	.6
	4.4	15.1	3.7			All Other Non-Current		3.5	3.7
	23.7	23.6	43.1			Net Worth		29.7	27.9
	100.0	100.0	100.0			Total Liabilties & Net Worth		100.0	100.0
						INCOME DATA			
	100.0	100.0	100.0			Net Sales		100.0	100.0
						Gross Profit			
	91.7	91.7	87.5			Operating Expenses		90.1	84.8
	8.3	8.3	12.5			Operating Profit		9.9	15.2
	1.4	5.6	1.8			All Other Expenses (net)		2.9	3.5
	6.9	2.7	10.7			Profit Before Taxes		7.0	11.6
						RATIOS			
	4.1	1.7	3.1					1.9	1.9
	1.6	1.0	1.4			Current		1.2	1.1
	.7	.7	.9					.7	.6
	2.7	1.3	2.3					1.5	1.4
	.9	.8	.8			Quick		.9	.9
	.7	.3	.3					.5	.5
2	235.2	16	22.9	11	32.6		2	182.2	2	238.9
32	11.3	44	8.3	49	7.4	Sales/Receivables	45	8.1	51	7.1
58	6.2	71	5.1	70	5.3		72	5.1	75	4.9
						Cost of Sales/Inventory			
						Cost of Sales/Payables			
	3.8	11.2	4.5					5.2	6.4
	14.4	228.8	9.7			Sales/Working Capital		53.8	49.7
	-61.1	-14.1	-33.8					-17.5	-8.9
	18.8	6.4	16.5					7.4	8.7
	5.9	(22) 2.8	4.6			EBIT/Interest	(51)	2.7	(60) 4.3
	1.2	-1.1	.1					.5	2.2
								3.0	4.4
						Net Profit + Depr., Dep., Amort./Cur. Mat. L/T/D	(14)	1.6	(12) 1.8
								.8	.9
	.3	.7	.3					.8	.7
	.9	2.0	.6			Fixed/Worth		1.5	2.2
	-13.4	49.1	1.9					4.9	-21.8
	.8	1.0	.5					1.0	.9
	1.4	3.1	1.9			Debt/Worth		2.3	2.8
	-28.1	115.5	3.2					7.0	-63.1
	45.2	63.1	27.7			% Profit Before Taxes/Tangible Net Worth		49.5	88.7
(15)	31.4	(21) 20.9	8.2				(51)	18.8	(52) 30.7
	.9	-8.3	-1.4					2.0	14.4
	29.6	18.3	14.5			% Profit Before Taxes/Total Assets		13.8	25.2
	15.9	4.0	3.0					5.0	11.4
	.4	-5.1	-.3					-1.6	1.7
	19.7	6.3	11.0					7.7	11.0
	6.8	3.7	7.1			Sales/Net Fixed Assets		4.2	4.7
	3.4	1.9	1.3					1.9	1.9
	3.1	2.4	2.2					2.2	2.4
	2.0	1.7	1.5			Sales/Total Assets		1.7	1.6
	1.1	1.1	.5					1.0	1.0
		6.0	1.2					3.9	2.8
		(23) 10.0	5.3			% Depr., Dep., Amort./Sales	(53)	6.9	(56) 6.4
		14.7	21.2					15.4	17.9
	4.0	2.1						3.9	1.5
(10)	11.4	(10) 4.0				% Officers', Directors' Owners' Comp/Sales	(18)	8.7	(14) 9.8
	18.8	8.0						17.9	21.4
14324M	47849M	224682M	434070M	61237M	485723M	Net Sales ($)		847271M	1162678M
2061M	23894M	119998M	296026M	76367M	709830M	Total Assets ($)		709573M	1119888M

M = $ thousand   MM = $ million
See Pages 9 through 22 for Explanation of Ratios and Data

Comparative Historical Data

Current Data Sorted by Sales

Type of Statement	4/1/08-3/31/09 ALL	4/1/09-3/31/10 ALL	4/1/10-3/31/11 ALL	0-1MM	1-3MM	3-5MM	5-10MM	10-25MM	25MM & OVER
				9 (4/1-9/30/10)			65 (10/1/10-3/31/11)		
Unqualified	5	8	7				1	2	4
Reviewed	8	12	11	1	1	3	1	3	2
Compiled	5	6	6	1		3		2	
Tax Returns	18	20	15	6	4	4	1		
Other	30	29	35	3	9	5	6	6	6
NUMBER OF STATEMENTS	66	75	74	11	14	15	9	13	12
ASSETS	%	%	%	%	%	%	%	%	%
Cash & Equivalents	10.1	8.2	10.6	23.9	10.8	11.9		6.2	4.6
Trade Receivables (net)	27.5	20.8	19.0	1.1	18.8	19.6		24.9	27.6
Inventory	9.4	9.8	9.7	5.3	14.5	6.8		13.8	12.7
All Other Current	3.6	2.2	3.6	4.3	4.3	2.3		3.7	1.4
Total Current	50.7	41.0	43.0	34.5	48.4	40.6		48.5	46.4
Fixed Assets (net)	36.7	44.9	39.8	54.9	37.1	41.1		41.5	22.8
Intangibles (net)	6.0	5.8	5.8	1.4	6.8	3.1		1.2	15.9
All Other Non-Current	6.6	8.3	11.4	9.2	7.7	15.1		8.8	15.0
Total	100.0	100.0	100.0	100.0	100.0	100.0		100.0	100.0
LIABILITIES									
Notes Payable-Short Term	11.3	7.9	9.3	20.1	7.9	8.3		9.3	4.3
Cur. Mat.-L.T.D.	8.7	8.7	8.4	7.8	3.9	9.5		12.1	5.5
Trade Payables	12.0	8.9	7.6	1.9	4.3	8.0		12.8	12.1
Income Taxes Payable	.2	.3	.4	.0	1.3	.0		.4	.1
All Other Current	8.6	7.7	8.1	9.5	3.9	7.8		8.1	12.5
Total Current	40.8	33.6	33.9	39.3	21.3	33.6		42.7	34.5
Long-Term Debt	21.4	32.8	26.7	51.3	32.0	23.9		14.8	14.8
Deferred Taxes	.5	.7	.8	.0	.0	.0		.5	2.8
All Other Non-Current	4.7	6.5	8.2	.5	20.5	.7		4.2	7.8
Net Worth	32.6	26.4	30.5	8.9	26.2	41.7		37.9	40.0
Total Liabilities & Net Worth	100.0	100.0	100.0	100.0	100.0	100.0		100.0	100.0
INCOME DATA									
Net Sales	100.0	100.0	100.0	100.0	100.0	100.0		100.0	100.0
Gross Profit									
Operating Expenses	89.7	88.4	90.6	86.2	93.8	91.1		89.2	94.0
Operating Profit	10.3	11.6	9.4	13.8	6.2	8.9		10.8	6.0
All Other Expenses (net)	2.6	4.0	3.5	11.4	.4	.5		5.0	2.0
Profit Before Taxes	7.7	7.6	5.9	2.4	5.8	8.4		5.8	3.9
RATIOS									
Current	2.1	1.9	2.2	2.1	9.1	3.2		1.6	2.3
	1.3	1.2	1.2	.8	3.5	1.2		1.0	1.3
	.8	.9	.7	.3	1.0	.6		.8	.9
Quick	1.5	1.6	1.6	2.1	5.8	2.6		1.1	2.0
	.9	.9	.9	.7	1.6	1.0		.8	1.0
	.6	.5	.4	.1	.7	.4		.3	.8
Sales/Receivables	17 21.4	7 52.7	0 UND	0 UND	0 UND	0 UND	18 20.7	36 10.1	
	51 7.2	46 8.0	37 9.9	0 UND	44 8.3	29 12.5	42 8.6	58 6.3	
	80 4.6	64 5.7	64 5.7	1 282.7	70 5.3	57 6.4	59 6.2	77 4.8	
Cost of Sales/Inventory									
Cost of Sales/Payables									
Sales/Working Capital	6.8	8.6	8.4	4.8	3.3	12.6		13.8	5.9
	43.2	37.7	57.1	-94.2	14.4	69.7		228.8	13.1
	-19.9	-27.4	-17.3	-2.5	NM	-28.0		-28.2	-54.1
EBIT/Interest	9.7	8.0	13.8		10.5	36.0		14.0	15.5
	(61) 3.7	(66) 4.1	(66) 3.9		(12) 5.9	(13) 11.1	(11) 5.1	4.1	
	1.5	1.1	.8		-.4	1.6	-1.6	-.1	
Net Profit + Depr., Dep., Amort./Cur. Mat. L/T/D	10.8	3.7	7.7						
	(10) 1.7	(11) 1.9	(15) 1.2						
	.6	1.2	.6						
Fixed/Worth	.4	.6	.5	.4	.2	.5		.7	.3
	1.5	1.7	1.3	12.9	.9	.8		1.2	.7
	-65.1	-99.1	14.0	-3.7	UND	6.7		2.2	17.6
Debt/Worth	.8	.9	.8	1.1	.5	.3		.8	.7
	1.8	2.6	2.3	12.2	1.2	1.6		2.4	3.2
	-73.4	-159.5	25.8	-4.9	UND	9.0		4.3	47.7
% Profit Before Taxes/Tangible Net Worth	76.1	69.3	57.4		45.6	88.3		59.5	63.3
	(49) 21.9	(56) 24.2	(60) 21.3		(11) 36.2	(12) 22.3	(12) 24.0	(10) 19.0	
	11.3	6.7	.4		3.2	3.0	-6.1	-.2	
% Profit Before Taxes/Total Assets	22.6	18.8	20.1	19.2	41.8	29.9		24.2	12.6
	7.0	6.8	6.4	.7	16.6	15.6		7.6	2.1
	1.9	.3	-.3	-5.6	-1.2	.2		-2.0	-2.2
Sales/Net Fixed Assets	22.5	12.3	14.2	20.1	26.1	29.8		7.1	11.0
	6.9	4.9	6.3	1.1	6.4	7.6		5.4	8.8
	3.0	2.2	2.3	.3	2.6	1.9		3.0	5.6
Sales/Total Assets	3.2	2.6	2.7	1.3	3.5	5.9		2.7	2.2
	1.9	1.8	1.6	.6	1.6	2.8		2.1	1.3
	1.2	.9	.9	.3	.9	1.3		1.8	.9
% Depr., Dep., Amort./Sales	1.8	2.3	3.1					2.6	1.0
	(48) 6.4	(55) 6.2	(50) 7.4				(11) 6.2	(10) 5.3	
	12.9	17.6	15.1					10.0	9.1
% Officers', Directors' Owners' Comp/Sales	3.0	3.0	2.5			3.2			
	(20) 4.5	(21) 5.7	(26) 5.6		(10) 6.6				
	8.9	17.0	13.9			14.9			
Net Sales ($)	1367061M	1234311M	1267885M	6807M	27768M	57656M	64389M	198995M	912270M
Total Assets ($)	1266479M	1231979M	1228176M	13020M	19284M	33066M	98060M	227338M	837408M

Current Data Sorted by Assets   Comparative Historical Data

0-500M	500M-2MM	2-10MM	10-50MM	50-100MM	100-250MM	Type of Statement	4/1/06-3/31/07 ALL	4/1/07-3/31/08 ALL
	1	1	1		1	Unqualified	2	3
	1	11	2			Reviewed	2	5
2	6	6				Compiled	12	9
12	8	4				Tax Returns	6	13
4	13	3	3	2		Other	12	13
	13 (4/1-9/30/10)		68 (10/1/10-3/31/11)					
18	29	25	6	2	1	NUMBER OF STATEMENTS	34	43
%	%	%	%	%	%	**ASSETS**	%	%
13.1	11.4	12.5				Cash & Equivalents	9.7	6.9
12.1	10.8	16.0				Trade Receivables (net)	12.2	10.6
12.2	5.5	7.8				Inventory	16.0	13.9
1.0	2.5	1.2				All Other Current	3.4	3.7
38.4	30.2	37.5				Total Current	41.3	35.2
41.4	60.4	53.8				Fixed Assets (net)	50.3	53.0
13.4	2.4	2.5				Intangibles (net)	3.3	2.8
6.7	7.0	6.2				All Other Non-Current	5.2	9.1
100.0	100.0	100.0				Total	100.0	100.0
						LIABILITIES		
19.6	20.4	8.7				Notes Payable-Short Term	19.8	16.0
15.0	8.1	9.1				Cur. Mat.-L.T.D.	9.0	13.8
8.1	7.2	6.2				Trade Payables	8.9	5.9
.1	.0	.1				Income Taxes Payable	.0	.2
6.3	3.0	10.3				All Other Current	13.7	11.8
49.1	38.8	34.3				Total Current	51.4	47.8
26.9	39.5	24.0				Long-Term Debt	23.9	32.8
.0	.1	1.2				Deferred Taxes	.2	.5
17.2	12.3	11.2				All Other Non-Current	11.2	10.2
6.8	9.3	29.3				Net Worth	13.3	8.7
100.0	100.0	100.0				Total Liabilities & Net Worth	100.0	100.0
						INCOME DATA		
100.0	100.0	100.0				Net Sales	100.0	100.0
						Gross Profit		
96.1	95.3	98.7				Operating Expenses	96.8	91.3
3.9	4.7	1.3				Operating Profit	3.2	8.7
2.8	2.4	2.5				All Other Expenses (net)	3.0	5.5
1.1	2.3	-1.2				Profit Before Taxes	.3	3.2
						RATIOS		
3.9	2.1	2.8					1.3	2.1
1.0	1.2	.9				Current	.7	.8
.2	.4	.5					.4	.4
3.4	2.0	2.3					.8	.9
.3	.6	.6				Quick	(33) .4	.4
.1	.2	.4					.2	.2
0 UND	0 UND	14 25.6					0 UND	0 UND
5 77.1	13 27.4	29 12.5				Sales/Receivables	10 37.3	17 22.1
18 20.2	40 9.1	50 7.3					35 10.4	30 12.0
						Cost of Sales/Inventory		
						Cost of Sales/Payables		
7.3	9.6	4.3					14.8	9.9
NM	78.4	-111.3				Sales/Working Capital	-25.6	-36.1
-6.5	-4.6	-6.7					-5.7	-3.9
14.6	4.9	4.5					4.8	3.8
(13) 5.5	(28) 2.2	(23) 2.2				EBIT/Interest	(31) 2.0	(36) .9
-.1	.1	-.8					.3	-.1
						Net Profit + Depr., Dep., Amort./Cur. Mat. L/T/D		
.4	1.2	.6					1.5	.9
1.6	3.9	2.0				Fixed/Worth	3.0	2.1
-.6	-3.1	11.3					-9.6	-5.1
.6	1.4	.7					1.6	1.3
6.2	5.6	2.1				Debt/Worth	4.9	4.0
-2.4	-5.6	10.9					-89.4	-8.4
101.2	38.2	38.1					37.6	68.0
(10) 41.7	(17) 32.6	(20) 8.2				% Profit Before Taxes/Tangible Net Worth	(24) 12.9	(27) 13.7
-9.7	5.8	-4.3					-5.5	-3.7
38.3	10.8	10.1					6.8	11.5
13.4	3.2	2.7				% Profit Before Taxes/Total Assets	2.3	1.1
-4.6	-1.3	-7.3					-2.9	-4.3
21.4	6.2	6.7					9.6	5.9
8.3	2.0	2.8				Sales/Net Fixed Assets	3.4	3.1
3.1	1.3	1.3					1.5	1.9
4.4	2.1	1.9					2.7	2.4
2.8	1.5	1.5				Sales/Total Assets	1.5	1.7
1.5	1.0	.9					.9	1.0
	6.9	5.2					4.9	5.5
	(25) 13.5	(22) 12.0				% Depr., Dep., Amort./Sales	(26) 10.1	(32) 10.7
	20.9	15.5					17.8	16.4
	4.9						2.7	2.5
	(17) 6.3					% Officers', Directors' Owners' Comp/Sales	(15) 7.6	(20) 4.8
	8.4						15.4	7.7
12321M	53821M	148203M	180463M	132863M	180789M	Net Sales ($)	323937M	776385M
4690M	33067M	93384M	149434M	127298M	146252M	Total Assets ($)	227965M	718472M

M = $ thousand   MM = $ million
See Pages 9 through 22 for Explanation of Ratios and Data

Comparative Historical Data				Type of Statement	Current Data Sorted by Sales					
5	4	4		Unqualified	1	2	2	5	2	2
7	13	14		Reviewed	2	2	2	1		2
12	16	14		Compiled	3	6	4	1		
12	19	24		Tax Returns	14	8	1	1		
22	30	25		Other	7	8	3	2	2	3
4/1/08-3/31/09	4/1/09-3/31/10	4/1/10-3/31/11				13 (4/1-9/30/10)		68 (10/1/10-3/31/11)		
ALL	ALL	ALL			0-1MM	1-3MM	3-5MM	5-10MM	10-25MM	25MM & OVER
58	82	81		NUMBER OF STATEMENTS	25	26	10	9	4	7
%	%	%		ASSETS	%	%	%	%	%	%
11.4	9.9	11.0		Cash & Equivalents	8.9	16.6	15.0			
17.1	12.4	12.7		Trade Receivables (net)	9.9	12.2	9.5			
10.1	14.2	7.4		Inventory	7.0	6.6	4.0			
3.1	2.4	2.7		All Other Current	.4	1.6	5.8			
41.6	38.8	33.8		Total Current	26.2	37.0	34.2			
42.4	47.9	53.6		Fixed Assets (net)	55.2	56.1	47.5			
6.0	6.5	5.2		Intangibles (net)	10.1	2.7	1.3			
10.0	6.8	7.4		All Other Non-Current	8.6	4.1	17.0			
100.0	100.0	100.0		Total	100.0	100.0	100.0			
				LIABILITIES						
16.1	15.2	15.8		Notes Payable-Short Term	16.6	25.0	4.0			
6.1	6.2	9.5		Cur. Mat.-L.T.D.	13.9	7.7	2.8			
6.5	6.5	7.0		Trade Payables	6.0	7.1	2.9			
.2	.1	.1		Income Taxes Payable	.0	.0	.1			
13.0	5.8	6.5		All Other Current	3.8	7.6	4.4			
41.9	34.0	38.9		Total Current	40.3	47.4	14.2			
32.6	34.3	31.4		Long-Term Debt	31.4	38.0	26.9			
.5	.5	.6		Deferred Taxes	.0	.1	1.8			
11.2	11.5	12.2		All Other Non-Current	14.3	12.9	21.4			
13.9	19.8	16.9		Net Worth	14.0	1.5	35.7			
100.0	100.0	100.0		Total Liabilities & Net Worth	100.0	100.0	100.0			
				INCOME DATA						
100.0	100.0	100.0		Net Sales	100.0	100.0	100.0			
				Gross Profit						
91.3	89.7	96.0		Operating Expenses	91.9	99.7	92.7			
8.7	10.3	4.0		Operating Profit	8.1	.3	7.3			
5.0	5.9	3.0		All Other Expenses (net)	4.8	2.1	4.8			
3.7	4.4	1.0		Profit Before Taxes	3.3	-1.9	2.5			
				RATIOS						
2.6	2.4	2.5			3.1	2.1	7.6			
.9	1.0	1.1		Current	.7	.8	2.4			
.4	.6	.4			.2	.4	.6			
1.4	1.5	1.9			2.6	1.6	4.0			
.5	.6	.6		Quick	.3	.6	2.0			
.2	.2	.2			.1	.1	.5			
0 UND	0 UND	0 UND			0 UND	0 UND	0 UND			
22 16.4	17 21.1	16 22.8		Sales/Receivables	10 38.2	9 42.6	22 16.6			
62 5.9	40 9.1	41 8.9			36 10.0	46 8.0	31 11.6			
				Cost of Sales/Inventory						
				Cost of Sales/Payables						
5.2	4.9	7.3			7.1	10.1	3.8			
-86.7	268.5	85.0		Sales/Working Capital	-12.1	-17.8	8.5			
-6.2	-8.9	-6.4			-2.6	-5.5	-15.1			
4.9	4.3	5.4			6.5	4.2				
(48) 1.5	(65) 1.7	(72) 2.2		EBIT/Interest	(19) 2.9	(25) 1.6				
-.5	-.7	-.1			1.4	-1.0				
	2.6	5.5		Net Profit + Depr., Dep.,						
	(11) 1.9	(11) 2.4		Amort./Cur. Mat. L/T/D						
	1.2	1.1								
.5	.7	.8			1.0	1.0	.4			
1.9	2.3	2.3		Fixed/Worth	3.8	8.9	.6			
-151.6	UND	-7.8			-10.5	-1.1	NM			
1.4	1.4	1.4			2.2	1.4	.3			
2.7	4.6	4.0		Debt/Worth	4.9	8.9	1.1			
-203.6	-42.1	-8.7			-8.0	-2.9	NM			
28.3	39.4	40.1		% Profit Before Taxes/Tangible	52.3	37.9				
(42) 8.3	(61) 12.3	(55) 14.5		Net Worth	(16) 33.0	(14) 14.0				
-2.7	-6.8	2.7			-4.1	4.5				
11.3	15.1	12.0		% Profit Before Taxes/Total	20.4	7.9	11.2			
1.8	3.0	3.2		Assets	9.0	2.4	2.5			
-3.4	-3.7	-3.1			-1.5	-10.1	-5.4			
17.7	13.7	8.8			9.0	9.0	13.8			
5.0	3.9	3.1		Sales/Net Fixed Assets	2.1	3.3	3.8			
2.0	1.7	1.4			.9	1.5	2.0			
2.5	2.3	2.6			2.8	2.9	2.1			
1.4	1.4	1.6		Sales/Total Assets	1.5	1.5	1.6			
.8	.7	1.0			.6	1.0	1.1			
2.9	5.0	6.0			9.1	5.3	4.3			
(49) 9.7	(61) 11.7	(63) 11.9		% Depr., Dep., Amort./Sales	(17) 14.8	(21) 8.5	11.0			
14.4	17.9	18.9			42.1	17.2	15.8			
3.4	3.1	4.1		% Officers', Directors'		4.5				
(21) 5.5	(29) 5.1	(33) 5.5		Owners' Comp/Sales		(14) 6.2				
7.4	9.9	6.7				9.1				
1590813M	872902M	708460M		Net Sales ($)	13599M	52853M	38524M	58336M	57819M	487329M
825935M	1126218M	554125M		Total Assets ($)	16840M	36946M	55296M	44313M	40771M	359959M

M = $ thousand   MM = $ million
See Pages 9 through 22 for Explanation of Ratios and Data

Current Data Sorted by Assets   Comparative Historical Data

Type of Statement	0-500M	500M-2MM	2-10MM	10-50MM	50-100MM	100-250MM	4/1/06-3/31/07 ALL	4/1/07-3/31/08 ALL
Unqualified		1	1	3	2	7	10	10
Reviewed			4	4	1	1	17	10
Compiled	6	8	4	1			20	23
Tax Returns	13	25	5			3	35	34
Other	9	19	18	4		1	61	61
	21 (4/1-9/30/10)			119 (10/1/10-3/31/11)				
NUMBER OF STATEMENTS	28	53	32	12	3	12	143	138
	%	%	%	%	%	%	%	%
ASSETS								
Cash & Equivalents	14.3	8.1	5.9	7.9		4.1	7.6	6.4
Trade Receivables (net)	6.5	8.9	10.4	12.4		17.0	8.4	9.7
Inventory	8.2	7.7	17.4	13.7		2.6	9.0	9.7
All Other Current	3.6	2.3	2.0	1.2		2.7	3.5	4.1
Total Current	32.7	27.0	35.6	35.2		26.4	28.5	29.9
Fixed Assets (net)	56.6	65.2	55.7	54.5		55.8	60.6	60.0
Intangibles (net)	5.0	3.2	4.2	5.2		5.7	3.3	3.7
All Other Non-Current	5.7	4.6	4.4	5.1		12.1	7.5	6.4
Total	100.0	100.0	100.0	100.0		100.0	100.0	100.0
LIABILITIES								
Notes Payable-Short Term	19.8	7.4	14.0	19.1		7.4	10.8	10.1
Cur. Mat.-L.T.D.	12.9	8.8	7.0	4.7		10.3	9.7	8.5
Trade Payables	8.3	5.1	4.8	7.1		7.8	4.6	5.4
Income Taxes Payable	.0	.2	.1	.1		1.1	.2	.1
All Other Current	11.2	6.9	6.9	5.2		9.0	7.2	5.5
Total Current	52.3	28.4	32.7	36.0		35.6	32.7	29.6
Long-Term Debt	49.2	44.5	41.2	41.6		52.3	34.7	38.3
Deferred Taxes	.0	.4	.5	.1		.4	.5	.6
All Other Non-Current	20.5	9.3	6.6	1.5		20.0	9.7	6.6
Net Worth	-22.0	17.4	18.9	20.7		-8.3	22.4	25.0
Total Liabilities & Net Worth	100.0	100.0	100.0	100.0		100.0	100.0	100.0
INCOME DATA								
Net Sales	100.0	100.0	100.0	100.0		100.0	100.0	100.0
Gross Profit								
Operating Expenses	92.5	86.5	79.7	85.4		92.8	84.4	85.4
Operating Profit	7.5	13.5	20.3	14.6		7.2	15.6	14.6
All Other Expenses (net)	1.8	6.1	11.4	3.8		8.3	5.5	5.9
Profit Before Taxes	5.7	7.4	8.9	10.8		-1.2	10.1	8.7
RATIOS								
Current	1.8	3.0	2.8	2.1		1.2	1.8	1.8
	.7	.9	1.2	1.4		.9	1.0	1.0
	.2	.3	.6	.6		.4	.3	.4
Quick	1.1	1.5	1.4	1.6		1.1	1.1	1.1
	.5	.5	.6	.7		.7	(142) .6	(136) .5
	.1	.2	.1	.5		.2	.1	.1
Sales/Receivables	0 UND	0 UND	0 UND	0 780.9		0 UND	0 UND	0 UND
	2 165.4	13 29.0	22 16.2	41 9.0		35 10.5	14 26.9	14 26.2
	11 33.0	33 11.0	61 6.0	90 4.1		72 5.1	33 11.0	39 9.5
Cost of Sales/Inventory								
Cost of Sales/Payables								
Sales/Working Capital	27.4	7.9	5.4	3.9		14.2	8.9	10.3
	-23.1	-41.6	62.9	18.2		-103.6	-302.6	UND
	-6.8	-6.3	-10.4	-13.0		-9.1	-4.3	-5.3
EBIT/Interest	4.2	4.4	7.0	15.2			5.3	5.2
	(27) 1.8	(43) 2.8	(25) 3.7	3.4			(122) 2.8	(120) 2.4
	-.6	.7	1.7	1.9			1.0	.8
Net Profit + Depr., Dep., Amort./Cur. Mat. L/T/D							5.5	4.9
							(14) 2.0	(12) 2.2
							1.5	1.6
Fixed/Worth	1.1	1.3	.6	.5		1.2	1.2	1.0
	NM	6.0	1.8	4.8		57.8	2.8	2.3
	-1.1	-4.0	8.4	NM		-2.1	-405.5	10.1
Debt/Worth	2.1	1.1	1.0	1.2		2.0	1.2	1.1
	-18.6	8.3	1.9	4.5		65.8	4.0	3.8
	-2.3	-6.0	9.3	NM		-5.8	-852.0	20.3
% Profit Before Taxes/Tangible Net Worth	76.0	32.1	42.8				66.4	51.5
	(13) 7.5	(34) 13.6	(25) 12.9				(107) 22.3	(114) 23.8
	-34.4	.2	4.1				9.8	7.8
% Profit Before Taxes/Total Assets	31.6	9.5	13.9	17.4		5.3	15.5	13.6
	3.3	5.1	5.1	7.4		-.1	6.9	5.5
	-9.9	-1.2	.7	2.7		-26.7	1.1	-.8
Sales/Net Fixed Assets	10.5	4.9	11.1	12.1		4.2	5.7	5.2
	4.9	1.7	3.1	3.1		2.2	2.4	2.5
	3.6	.7	.2	.6		.9	1.1	1.1
Sales/Total Assets	3.7	2.2	2.0	2.6		1.8	2.2	2.1
	2.8	1.4	1.4	1.2		1.2	1.3	1.4
	1.7	.5	.2	.4		.3	.6	.5
% Depr., Dep., Amort./Sales	5.8	6.3	4.0				7.5	7.5
	(19) 8.9	(42) 11.2	(25) 13.2				(121) 13.2	(110) 13.3
	16.2	25.0	27.7				25.6	21.2
% Officers', Directors' Owners' Comp/Sales	3.7	4.7					1.8	2.3
	(11) 11.5	(22) 8.9					(46) 4.5	(47) 5.2
	12.8	13.0					7.0	9.4
Net Sales ($)	21691M	87831M	179856M	377927M	98470M	2936681M	1704924M	2202984M
Total Assets ($)	8119M	62049M	148266M	265115M	196863M	2026815M	1808597M	1758507M

© RMA 2011

M = $ thousand   MM = $ million
See Pages 9 through 22 for Explanation of Ratios and Data

Comparative Historical Data · Current Data Sorted by Sales

	4/1/08-3/31/09 ALL	4/1/09-3/31/10 ALL	4/1/10-3/31/11 ALL		0-1MM	1-3MM	3-5MM	5-10MM	10-25MM	25MM & OVER
						21 (4/1-9/30/10)			119 (10/1/10-3/31/11)	
Type of Statement										
Unqualified	11	11	13			1		1	3	8
Reviewed	12	12	11				2		4	4
Compiled	13	22	19		1			1		
Tax Returns	39	44	46		5	8	2	1	3	
Other	46	41	51		16	18	6	4	4	3
NUMBER OF STATEMENTS	121	130	140		48	38	16	6	14	18
ASSETS	%	%	%		%	%	%	%	%	%
Cash & Equivalents	9.7	8.8	8.7		7.6	10.8	10.2		9.3	6.2
Trade Receivables (net)	8.5	6.6	9.7		4.0	10.8	11.1		19.0	13.6
Inventory	9.6	10.0	10.1		5.2	11.9	15.5		20.3	7.9
All Other Current	3.5	3.0	2.6		1.7	3.6	1.0		2.8	2.6
Total Current	31.3	28.5	31.1		18.6	37.1	37.7		51.5	30.3
Fixed Assets (net)	60.6	60.4	59.4		71.7	59.1	51.0		28.1	60.7
Intangibles (net)	2.8	3.3	4.1		3.3	2.0	5.7		10.4	5.6
All Other Non-Current	5.2	7.8	5.4		6.4	1.8	5.6		10.1	3.5
Total	100.0	100.0	100.0		100.0	100.0	100.0		100.0	100.0
LIABILITIES										
Notes Payable-Short Term	12.5	12.4	12.3		10.7	12.1	20.8		18.0	7.4
Cur. Mat.-L.T.D.	7.8	8.1	8.8		7.8	6.8	19.5		8.4	8.9
Trade Payables	5.3	4.5	6.0		4.8	6.1	6.9		4.7	9.3
Income Taxes Payable	.2	.1	.2		.1	.2	.1		.1	.7
All Other Current	6.2	6.0	7.8		7.6	6.3	10.8		6.2	8.8
Total Current	32.0	31.1	35.1		31.0	31.6	58.1		37.4	35.2
Long-Term Debt	39.1	44.3	44.6		62.1	29.6	45.3		23.8	43.7
Deferred Taxes	.6	.5	.6		.3	.2	.0		3.7	.1
All Other Non-Current	7.0	11.3	11.0		11.3	11.3	.0		1.9	14.0
Net Worth	21.3	12.8	8.7		-4.6	27.3	-14.3		33.2	7.0
Total Liabilties & Net Worth	100.0	100.0	100.0		100.0	100.0	100.0		100.0	100.0
INCOME DATA										
Net Sales	100.0	100.0	100.0		100.0	100.0	100.0		100.0	100.0
Gross Profit										
Operating Expenses	85.6	88.5	86.4		76.0	93.1	92.0		84.0	95.6
Operating Profit	14.4	11.5	13.6		24.0	6.9	8.0		16.0	4.4
All Other Expenses (net)	5.5	6.9	6.4		12.7	1.5	4.2		4.7	4.3
Profit Before Taxes	8.9	4.6	7.2		11.3	5.4	3.7		11.3	.1
RATIOS										
Current	2.3	2.1	2.1		2.7	4.0	2.1		3.6	1.3
	1.0	.8	.9		.6	1.3	.9		1.4	.9
	.4	.3	.4		.1	.7	.2		1.0	.6
Quick	1.8	1.1	1.3		1.0	2.1	1.4		1.9	.9
	.6	.5	.6		.4	.8	.7		.9	.7
	.1	.2	.2		.1	.3	.1		.3	.4
Sales/Receivables	0 UND	0 UND	0 UND		0 UND	5 73.3	0 800.7		0 UND	0 UND
	11 31.9	12 29.3	12 29.3		0 UND	22 16.8	16 23.0		14 25.6	35 10.3
	35 10.4	36 10.1	38 9.6		13 29.2	44 8.4	29 12.8		43 8.4	56 6.5
Cost of Sales/Inventory										
Cost of Sales/Payables										
Sales/Working Capital	7.5	9.5	6.6		16.2	4.4	6.9		3.1	22.3
	UND	-32.5	-78.7		-10.7	34.3	-72.2		8.7	-48.8
	-7.2	-4.7	-7.0		-2.6	-12.3	-3.2	NM		-10.5
EBIT/Interest	4.6	3.5	4.5		4.2	5.0	4.1		92.9	3.7
	(101) 2.6	(106) 1.0	(118) 2.8		(35) 1.8	(34) 3.2	3.2	(10)	5.4	(17) 2.1
	.3	-.9	.6		.2	.7	.9		1.5	-.5
Net Profit + Depr., Dep., Amort./Cur. Mat. L/T/D	4.5	4.6								
	(12) 2.5	(15) 1.6								
	1.1	1.0								
Fixed/Worth	.9	1.2	1.2		1.7	1.0	1.3		.2	1.2
	2.3	2.9	3.3		7.1	2.1	NM		.7	5.4
	103.4	-7.5	-4.0		-3.6	NM	-.7		NM	-4.0
Debt/Worth	1.0	1.2	1.3		1.7	.9	1.3		1.1	1.1
	3.0	2.9	4.2		8.2	2.1	NM		2.5	5.5
	133.4	-12.7	-6.1		-4.4	NM	-2.3		NM	-13.2
% Profit Before Taxes/Tangible Net Worth	44.1	30.2	41.7		40.0	31.2			86.8	53.7
	(93) 19.5	(91) 7.1	(91) 13.7		(27) 11.9	(29) 13.1		(11)	35.8	(13) 13.7
	2.2	-4.8	2.6		3.1	-3.0			19.7	-1.4
% Profit Before Taxes/Total Assets	11.6	7.9	10.6		8.0	11.0	13.9		19.0	6.9
	5.1	.4	4.5		2.8	5.4	6.0		10.6	1.9
	-.6	-5.0	-1.5		-1.6	-2.4	-.8		1.6	-9.0
Sales/Net Fixed Assets	7.8	5.4	5.9		4.4	7.5	8.8		34.1	4.3
	2.6	2.3	3.1		1.2	3.9	3.7		12.8	3.0
	.8	.6	1.0		.2	1.6	3.0		2.9	1.0
Sales/Total Assets	2.1	2.2	2.5		2.0	2.9	2.6		2.3	2.8
	1.4	1.3	1.5		.8	2.1	1.8		1.4	1.4
	.8	.4	.6		.2	1.0	1.5		.3	.8
% Depr., Dep., Amort./Sales	6.6	8.9	5.8		8.4	5.0	4.9		.7	
	(92) 13.3	(104) 16.2	(100) 11.2		(33) 16.2	(31) 11.0	(14) 8.8	(10)	4.4	
	28.2	28.7	21.9		25.8	20.2	15.4		35.2	
% Officers', Directors' Owners' Comp/Sales	3.2	2.9	2.6		8.7	3.2				
	(35) 4.6	(51) 5.8	(41) 7.5		(14) 12.5	(15) 7.5				
	6.7	11.5	12.5		15.9	11.7				
Net Sales ($)	1451582M	1148233M	3702456M		25533M	66578M	64155M	41889M	222760M	3281541M
Total Assets ($)	1526148M	1309845M	2707227M		60821M	70431M	34218M	46738M	551563M	1943456M

© RMA 2011

M = $ thousand   MM = $ million

See Pages 9 through 22 for Explanation of Ratios and Data

Current Data Sorted by Assets   Comparative Historical Data

						Type of Statement		
		5	4	7	6	Unqualified	11	8
	3	4	9	2		Reviewed	7	8
1	5	5	3			Compiled	8	15
17	19	12	1			Tax Returns	7	22
9	15	19	9		3	Other	20	21
	7 (4/1-9/30/10)		151 (10/1/10-3/31/11)				4/1/06-3/31/07	4/1/07-3/31/08
0-500M	500M-2MM	2-10MM	10-50MM	50-100MM	100-250MM		ALL	ALL
27	42	45	26	9	9	NUMBER OF STATEMENTS	53	74
%	%	%	%	%	%	ASSETS	%	%
21.5	10.1	7.4	10.2			Cash & Equivalents	8.0	10.0
6.9	12.6	16.7	10.6			Trade Receivables (net)	14.6	5.3
.4	2.9	4.1	10.8			Inventory	6.3	3.6
1.9	3.0	3.3	5.7			All Other Current	4.1	2.8
30.7	28.7	31.6	37.2			Total Current	33.1	21.7
58.9	54.3	56.6	55.5			Fixed Assets (net)	51.0	67.8
.0	1.5	1.6	.5			Intangibles (net)	1.7	1.1
10.4	15.5	10.2	6.9			All Other Non-Current	14.2	9.5
100.0	100.0	100.0	100.0			Total	100.0	100.0
						LIABILITIES		
18.4	3.3	3.9	2.5			Notes Payable-Short Term	6.1	8.4
11.2	11.6	7.3	5.8			Cur. Mat.-L.T.D.	6.6	12.6
4.3	5.9	6.5	5.1			Trade Payables	7.4	2.7
.0	.1	.1	.4			Income Taxes Payable	.1	.0
26.0	4.8	7.5	7.4			All Other Current	7.5	5.0
60.0	25.8	25.3	21.3			Total Current	27.7	28.7
56.6	62.3	43.3	23.6			Long-Term Debt	38.8	48.1
.0	.0	.7	.6			Deferred Taxes	.9	.4
2.7	7.1	5.6	3.5			All Other Non-Current	7.7	5.5
-19.2	4.8	25.0	50.9			Net Worth	25.0	17.4
100.0	100.0	100.0	100.0			Total Liabilties & Net Worth	100.0	100.0
						INCOME DATA		
100.0	100.0	100.0	100.0			Net Sales	100.0	100.0
						Gross Profit		
74.7	68.7	80.7	82.4			Operating Expenses	80.5	77.1
25.3	31.3	19.3	17.6			Operating Profit	19.5	22.9
11.0	12.4	8.7	1.5			All Other Expenses (net)	10.3	9.2
14.3	18.9	10.5	16.1			Profit Before Taxes	9.2	13.7
						RATIOS		
2.2	2.5	2.1	3.7				1.7	2.0
.3	1.2	1.1	1.6			Current	1.1	.8
.1	.4	.5	1.1				.4	.4
2.2	2.4	1.9	2.2				1.4	1.8
.3	.9	.9	1.0			Quick	.7	.6
.1	.3	.2	.4				.2	.2
0 UND	0 UND	4 89.9	10 36.8				0 UND	0 UND
0 UND	6 56.6	34 10.9	30 12.3			Sales/Receivables	22 16.4	12 29.7
22 16.5	55 6.6	68 5.3	45 8.2				68 5.4	35 10.5
						Cost of Sales/Inventory		
						Cost of Sales/Payables		
7.0	5.6	4.1	2.6				4.6	8.5
-8.6	39.8	34.8	13.2			Sales/Working Capital	38.3	-17.4
-1.7	-7.0	-6.5	51.5				-3.3	-3.4
6.9	14.1	10.2	13.7				9.9	7.6
(19) 2.2	(30) 4.7	(37) 2.7	(24) 5.6			EBIT/Interest	(34) 3.1	(54) 2.4
-.9	1.1	-.5	1.7				1.4	1.3
						Net Profit + Depr., Dep., Amort./Cur. Mat. L/T/D		
.5	.7	1.2	.6				.7	1.2
2.8	3.5	1.9	1.2			Fixed/Worth	1.8	2.6
-4.2	-14.9	9.0	1.6				7.7	-41.5
.5	1.1	1.0	.3				.9	.9
4.5	6.4	2.5	.9			Debt/Worth	2.8	2.8
-4.0	-20.2	13.2	2.0				11.4	-44.4
135.2	61.3	45.1	59.7				41.7	61.2
(16) 35.1	(27) 26.8	(36) 15.2	14.1			% Profit Before Taxes/Tangible Net Worth	(44) 14.3	(55) 17.1
17.0	6.5	-7.7	9.3				4.0	4.6
36.8	31.9	15.6	12.8				12.1	15.0
5.0	6.6	3.6	8.3			% Profit Before Taxes/Total Assets	3.5	4.6
-9.5	.0	-5.7	2.3				.2	.2
6.0	6.7	6.2	3.0				10.0	2.3
1.2	1.6	1.5	1.8			Sales/Net Fixed Assets	1.2	.7
.8	.4	.3	1.1				.4	.4
1.9	2.0	1.4	1.5				1.3	1.1
.8	.7	.7	.9			Sales/Total Assets	.5	.5
.6	.2	.3	.4				.2	.3
18.5	10.7	4.1	3.9				2.9	10.9
(19) 50.0	(31) 21.9	(39) 13.3	(22) 10.7			% Depr., Dep., Amort./Sales	(42) 16.9	(59) 24.9
68.1	52.2	40.0	23.3				47.8	51.9
						% Officers', Directors' Owners' Comp/Sales		1.3
							(13)	3.0
								7.0
7309M	72325M	243157M	638382M	196315M	601786M	Net Sales ($)	1271816M	974667M
6631M	49581M	222483M	623461M	587299M	1465559M	Total Assets ($)	1811629M	2059477M

M = $ thousand   MM = $ million
See Pages 9 through 22 for Explanation of Ratios and Data

Comparative Historical Data / Current Data Sorted by Sales

			Type of Statement	0-1MM	1-3MM	3-5MM	5-10MM	10-25MM	25MM & OVER
12	15	22	Unqualified		1	2	4	6	9
16	19	18	Reviewed	3	1	1	3	5	5
11	16	14	Compiled	4	2	1	5	2	
25	49	49	Tax Returns	31	12	2	3	1	
44	63	55	Other	23	10	2	5	12	3
4/1/08-3/31/09 ALL	4/1/09-3/31/10 ALL	4/1/10-3/31/11 ALL		7 (4/1-9/30/10)			151 (10/1/10-3/31/11)		
108	162	158	**NUMBER OF STATEMENTS**	61	26	8	20	26	17
%	%	%	**ASSETS**	%	%	%	%	%	%
8.0	9.9	10.8	Cash & Equivalents	12.9	8.1		13.1	8.3	10.0
14.1	10.1	11.4	Trade Receivables (net)	8.1	11.5		16.9	9.3	17.1
4.5	2.4	3.9	Inventory	.7	.7		11.4	6.1	3.2
3.0	3.5	3.3	All Other Current	2.8	4.4		5.4	1.5	4.9
29.6	25.9	29.4	Total Current	24.4	24.7		46.9	25.3	35.2
60.6	60.8	58.2	Fixed Assets (net)	61.4	64.1		38.8	66.4	53.3
2.0	2.1	1.0	Intangibles (net)	.6	.8		2.9	.5	.6
7.8	11.2	11.4	All Other Non-Current	13.5	10.5		11.4	7.8	10.9
100.0	100.0	100.0	Total	100.0	100.0		100.0	100.0	100.0
			LIABILITIES						
8.2	7.4	5.7	Notes Payable-Short Term	9.0	4.2		3.5	3.0	1.9
10.2	10.2	8.8	Cur. Mat.-L.T.D.	10.7	10.0		11.2	6.2	4.1
6.6	5.7	5.2	Trade Payables	2.1	4.2		5.6	9.3	11.2
.0	.0	.1	Income Taxes Payable	.1	.1		.5	.0	.1
8.1	8.6	9.4	All Other Current	12.0	9.7		10.2	4.0	10.3
33.2	32.0	29.3	Total Current	34.0	28.2		31.0	22.5	27.5
47.8	51.8	47.5	Long-Term Debt	67.7	47.7		30.6	31.4	29.0
.8	.8	.4	Deferred Taxes	.0	.0		1.7	.2	1.3
4.6	5.2	5.0	All Other Non-Current	3.6	12.1		4.4	1.6	5.2
13.6	10.2	17.9	Net Worth	-5.2	11.9		32.3	44.3	37.0
100.0	100.0	100.0	Total Liabilities & Net Worth	100.0	100.0		100.0	100.0	100.0
			INCOME DATA						
100.0	100.0	100.0	Net Sales	100.0	100.0		100.0	100.0	100.0
			Gross Profit						
77.7	74.2	75.1	Operating Expenses	65.4	82.6		83.3	78.3	85.1
22.3	25.8	24.9	Operating Profit	34.6	17.4		16.7	21.7	14.9
7.2	10.1	9.1	All Other Expenses (net)	17.5	4.5		3.8	3.2	3.5
15.2	15.7	15.8	Profit Before Taxes	17.2	12.9		12.9	18.4	11.4
			RATIOS						
2.0	1.7	2.5	Current	2.4	2.7		2.1	2.7	1.5
.8	.8	1.1		.9	1.0		1.2	1.1	1.2
.3	.3	.4		.2	.3		.8	.6	.9
1.4	1.5	2.0	Quick	2.1	2.2		1.8	1.9	1.1
.6	.5	.8		.4	.8		.8	.9	.9
.1	.2	.2		.1	.2		.3	.3	.7
0 UND	0 UND	0 UND	Sales/Receivables	0 UND	0 UND		7 53.7	9 41.1	23 16.2
24 15.1	10 35.7	22 16.7		0 UND	35 10.6		46 7.9	28 12.8	37 9.9
55 6.6	52 7.0	51 7.1		25 14.4	64 5.7		68 5.3	48 7.6	52 7.0
			Cost of Sales/Inventory						
			Cost of Sales/Payables						
7.1	8.0	5.1	Sales/Working Capital	4.3	5.2		4.0	6.4	11.7
-23.3	-16.5	36.2		-17.8	321.1		26.0	54.4	35.9
-3.2	-3.2	-5.3		-2.0	-3.1		-16.1	-8.3	-68.1
10.0	6.8	10.3	EBIT/Interest	8.0	10.1		10.6	14.9	7.4
(86) 3.5	(126) 2.9	(124) 3.9		(37) 2.4	(24) 2.5		(18) 3.6	(22) 7.6	2.3
1.6	1.1	1.0		-.4	.9		.5	3.4	1.1
3.3	10.6	5.8	Net Profit + Depr., Dep., Amort./Cur. Mat. L/T/D						
(17) 1.6	(16) 3.1	(15) 1.9							
.7	1.0	.7							
1.0	1.0	.8	Fixed/Worth	.7	1.3		.3	1.1	.4
1.9	2.4	1.8		3.0	2.0		1.4	1.7	1.4
12.1	UND	10.7		-13.0	-5.9		3.0	3.0	3.0
.9	1.0	.8	Debt/Worth	.7	1.0		.9	.4	1.1
3.3	3.4	2.2		4.5	3.0		2.6	1.4	2.0
27.1	-51.0	22.5		-8.9	-8.7		5.4	3.5	3.1
52.3	47.5	51.9	% Profit Before Taxes/Tangible Net Worth	51.0	61.2		54.0	43.8	37.3
(84) 19.7	(120) 12.4	(122) 16.4		(38) 17.2	(18) 26.5		(18) 14.6	(23) 13.2	13.2
6.7	1.9	5.5		4.7	3.1		1.8	8.2	13.2
14.8	15.6	17.9	% Profit Before Taxes/Total Assets	19.0	16.7		18.8	14.1	14.7
5.9	5.4	5.9		3.8	6.6		7.9	7.3	4.3
1.1	.4	-.1		-3.0	-1.1		-.5	4.0	.2
5.0	3.2	3.8	Sales/Net Fixed Assets	2.6	3.8		19.6	3.5	33.9
1.0	1.1	1.3		.8	1.1		2.9	1.3	1.9
.5	.5	.4		.3	.4		1.5	.3	.9
1.6	1.5	1.4	Sales/Total Assets	.8	1.5		2.0	1.7	2.4
.8	.6	.7		.5	.8		1.2	.9	.9
.2	.3	.3		.2	.3		.8	.3	.5
3.8	8.2	8.4	% Depr., Dep., Amort./Sales	18.4	15.1		1.3	8.7	1.1
(92) 21.6	(125) 21.7	(124) 20.2		(48) 45.5	(20) 24.5		(16) 8.2	(22) 18.5	(12) 5.7
48.4	39.5	43.9		67.4	54.9		13.2	28.0	9.6
.9	2.6	1.2	% Officers', Directors' Owners' Comp/Sales						
(18) 3.0	(33) 4.0	(24) 3.3							
7.3	9.5	4.7							
2324748M	1581112M	1759274M	Net Sales ($)	21121M	48511M	30263M	145767M	413324M	1100288M
2721026M	2747322M	2955014M	Total Assets ($)	68887M	86630M	113670M	224521M	1074001M	1387305M

M = $ thousand   MM = $ million
See Pages 9 through 22 for Explanation of Ratios and Data

Current Data Sorted by Assets   Comparative Historical Data

						Type of Statement		
1	2	13	29	13	15	Unqualified	66	68
3	6	42	28	8	3	Reviewed	95	113
6	14	18	7	2		Compiled	58	78
12	35	19	1			Tax Returns	57	47
7	14	52	53	11	12	Other	117	156
	75 (4/1-9/30/10)		351 (10/1/10-3/31/11)				4/1/06-3/31/07	4/1/07-3/31/08
0-500M	500M-2MM	2-10MM	10-50MM	50-100MM	100-250MM		ALL	ALL
29	71	144	118	34	30	NUMBER OF STATEMENTS	393	462
%	%	%	%	%	%	ASSETS	%	%
14.1	13.5	8.9	7.1	7.9	3.6	Cash & Equivalents	6.8	7.1
12.9	11.8	16.1	14.2	13.4	11.2	Trade Receivables (net)	14.5	13.4
1.1	10.2	11.0	12.1	17.8	7.5	Inventory	10.2	10.1
3.6	3.5	3.3	2.4	1.9	4.8	All Other Current	3.1	3.2
31.7	38.9	39.3	35.8	41.0	27.0	Total Current	34.7	33.9
56.9	48.5	52.9	53.7	47.6	61.9	Fixed Assets (net)	58.6	59.7
1.0	3.5	2.3	1.9	2.8	7.1	Intangibles (net)	1.5	1.7
10.5	9.1	5.5	8.7	8.6	3.9	All Other Non-Current	5.2	4.7
100.0	100.0	100.0	100.0	100.0	100.0	Total	100.0	100.0
						LIABILITIES		
9.3	6.7	10.1	10.5	8.0	5.3	Notes Payable-Short Term	10.4	9.7
8.8	11.6	8.1	8.6	7.0	4.6	Cur. Mat.-L.T.D.	10.9	10.3
8.9	4.6	5.7	5.2	6.5	5.2	Trade Payables	6.0	6.0
.0	.1	.4	.3	.7	.6	Income Taxes Payable	.3	.4
10.1	5.8	6.9	4.8	5.8	3.4	All Other Current	5.5	4.5
37.1	28.8	31.2	29.4	28.0	19.3	Total Current	33.0	30.8
34.2	34.6	25.4	26.7	28.7	34.0	Long-Term Debt	34.0	37.0
.1	.5	1.4	1.4	1.1	3.9	Deferred Taxes	.9	.8
11.6	6.1	4.3	3.1	3.3	5.0	All Other Non-Current	3.6	3.5
16.9	30.0	37.7	39.4	39.0	37.9	Net Worth	28.4	27.9
100.0	100.0	100.0	100.0	100.0	100.0	Total Liabilties & Net Worth	100.0	100.0
						INCOME DATA		
100.0	100.0	100.0	100.0	100.0	100.0	Net Sales	100.0	100.0
						Gross Profit		
77.4	83.8	90.8	92.9	94.1	88.6	Operating Expenses	84.4	84.6
22.6	16.2	9.2	7.1	5.9	11.4	Operating Profit	15.6	15.4
3.7	2.0	3.5	3.0	2.7	5.8	All Other Expenses (net)	3.4	4.0
18.9	14.3	5.7	4.1	3.2	5.6	Profit Before Taxes	12.2	11,3
						RATIOS		
2.1	3.6	2.6	2.0	2.6	2.8		1.8	2.0
1.0	1.4	1.3	1.1	1.7	1.6	Current	1.1	1.1
.4	.6	.6	.7	.9	.9		.6	.5
2.0	2.0	1.9	1.5	1.8	1.4		1.4	1.4
.9	(70) .6	.9	.7	.7	1.0	Quick	.7	.6
.3	.3	.3	.4	.4	.5		.3	.3
0 UND	0 UND	24 15.2	38 9.6	34 10.6	36 10.2		17 21.0	13 27.6
0 UND	11 32.5	46 7.9	58 6.3	45 8.1	50 7.2	Sales/Receivables	42 8.7	40 9.2
51 7.2	53 6.9	69 5.3	76 4.8	66 5.6	68 5.3		66 5.6	64 5.7
						Cost of Sales/Inventory		
						Cost of Sales/Payables		
6.5	5.1	3.7	5.6	3.2	3.2		7.0	7.1
UND	17.9	15.7	19.3	8.8	9.6	Sales/Working Capital	50.5	30.2
-7.0	-6.3	-7.8	-7.8	-13.4	-53.6		-6.2	-5.6
22.4	12.6	5.5	3.9	5.6	4.0		6.6	6.2
(21) 4.2	(65) 2.5	(129) 2.3	(111) 1.8	2.5	(29) 3.3	EBIT/Interest	(365) 3.3	(420) 3.0
1.0	.9	.3	.1	.8	1.2		1.7	1.5
		3.1	2.8				3.5	3.0
	(30) 1.7	(33) 1.4				Net Profit + Depr., Dep., Amort./Cur. Mat. L/T/D	(89) 1.5	(95) 1.6
	.8	.7					1.1	1.2
1.0	.6	.7	.7	.7	.9		1.1	1.0
2.0	1.5	1.3	1.4	1.1	2.2	Fixed/Worth	2.1	2.3
50.9	8.0	3.3	2.8	3.0	4.3		4.7	5.8
.8	.6	.7	.9	1.0	1.1		1.3	1.3
2.2	2.0	1.6	1.8	1.4	1.6	Debt/Worth	2.6	2.9
126.2	23.5	4.6	3.5	4.7	5.4		6.2	7.0
89.9	61.0	26.2	16.9	16.3	24.0		51.8	51.1
(23) 15.1	(56) 24.1	(133) 8.8	(111) 6.9	(32) 12.5	(26) 8.7	% Profit Before Taxes/Tangible Net Worth	(355) 27.2	(410) 27.5
5.3	1.3	-1.9	-1.9	-2.1	4.5		12.5	12.0
33.8	19.8	8.4	5.9	9.5	8.6		15.3	13.8
5.0	5.0	2.5	2.1	4.1	4.1	% Profit Before Taxes/Total Assets	7.3	6.7
-.1	-.5	-2.0	-3.1	-.6	-.7		2.5	1.9
8.8	7.6	6.1	3.9	8.0	1.5		4.1	4.1
2.0	2.2	1.6	1.4	1.6	1.0	Sales/Net Fixed Assets	1.6	1.5
.9	.9	.8	.7	.8	.5		.8	.7
2.4	1.9	1.4	1.3	1.3	1.0		1.5	1.5
.9	1.0	.9	.8	.7	.6	Sales/Total Assets	1.0	.9
.5	.6	.5	.5	.5	.4		.6	.5
10.6	7.9	6.1	7.2	5.4			6.7	6.2
(21) 16.7	(49) 21.1	(126) 15.0	(104) 13.3	(28) 11.9		% Depr., Dep., Amort./Sales	(327) 13.5	(401) 14.4
37.4	37.5	30.6	23.8	19.4			28.0	29.7
	2.3	2.7	1.1				2.4	1.6
(31)	5.2	(36) 4.6	(15) 1.7			% Officers', Directors' Owners' Comp/Sales	(99) 5.1	(101) 3.2
	7.3	7.9	6.0				8.7	7.1
16459M	109836M	830091M	2606629M	2196461M	3645057M	Net Sales ($)	8119047M	9920573M
7592M	76776M	724752M	2742873M	2241989M	4991804M	Total Assets ($)	7714163M	10279818M

© RMA 2011

M = $ thousand   MM = $ million
See Pages 9 through 22 for Explanation of Ratios and Data

Comparative Historical Data | Current Data Sorted by Sales

	Comparative Historical Data				Current Data Sorted by Sales					
				Type of Statement						
66	57	73		Unqualified	3	4	4	5	17	40
98	98	90		Reviewed	4	7	18	25	18	18
57	59	47		Compiled	13	12	9	6	3	4
46	42	67		Tax Returns	33	17	7	8	1	1
161	141	149		Other	22	26	16	19	32	34
4/1/08-3/31/09 ALL	4/1/09-3/31/10 ALL	4/1/10-3/31/11 ALL			75 (4/1-9/30/10)			351 (10/1/10-3/31/11)		
					0-1MM	1-3MM	3-5MM	5-10MM	10-25MM	25MM & OVER
428	397	426		**NUMBER OF STATEMENTS**	75	66	54	63	71	97
%	%	%		**ASSETS**	%	%	%	%	%	%
7.7	8.6	9.1		Cash & Equivalents	11.7	10.9	11.1	8.1	7.6	6.2
12.8	13.3	14.1		Trade Receivables (net)	8.4	13.2	14.4	15.2	17.4	15.7
12.8	11.2	10.8		Inventory	3.0	6.8	8.0	12.8	15.4	16.4
2.5	3.0	3.1		All Other Current	2.9	4.1	2.2	3.7	3.1	2.8
35.8	36.0	37.0		Total Current	25.9	35.0	35.7	39.7	43.6	41.1
56.8	54.7	52.8		Fixed Assets (net)	62.3	51.4	53.5	53.1	49.4	48.5
2.1	3.0	2.7		Intangibles (net)	3.3	3.3	1.6	1.3	1.5	4.1
5.3	6.3	7.5		All Other Non-Current	8.5	10.3	9.2	5.9	5.5	6.4
100.0	100.0	100.0		Total	100.0	100.0	100.0	100.0	100.0	100.0
				LIABILITIES						
10.1	9.7	9.1		Notes Payable-Short Term	5.2	7.2	8.1	9.3	13.5	10.5
9.6	9.8	8.5		Cur. Mat.-L.T.D.	10.9	8.9	8.5	8.8	9.8	5.5
5.1	4.8	5.7		Trade Payables	3.3	5.5	3.7	6.1	6.9	7.5
.2	.3	.3		Income Taxes Payable	.0	.3	.5	.4	.1	.7
5.5	5.5	6.0		All Other Current	4.1	9.8	5.0	5.3	4.7	6.9
30.5	30.0	29.6		Total Current	23.4	31.8	25.8	29.8	35.0	31.0
34.0	30.6	28.8		Long-Term Debt	36.9	29.7	29.0	27.3	20.8	28.5
.8	1.1	1.3		Deferred Taxes	.9	.8	1.0	1.6	1.3	1.9
3.3	4.6	4.7		All Other Non-Current	8.6	3.3	4.2	3.9	4.1	4.0
31.4	33.7	35.6		Net Worth	30.2	34.4	40.1	37.4	38.8	34.6
100.0	100.0	100.0		Total Liabilities & Net Worth	100.0	100.0	100.0	100.0	100.0	100.0
				INCOME DATA						
100.0	100.0	100.0		Net Sales	100.0	100.0	100.0	100.0	100.0	100.0
				Gross Profit						
85.9	91.4	89.4		Operating Expenses	71.5	88.1	92.4	96.4	94.6	94.1
14.1	8.6	10.6		Operating Profit	28.5	11.9	7.6	3.6	5.4	5.9
4.4	4.6	3.2		All Other Expenses (net)	6.7	3.4	1.4	2.2	2.3	2.8
9.7	4.0	7.4		Profit Before Taxes	21.8	8.5	6.2	1.3	3.1	3.1
				RATIOS						
2.2	2.2	2.4		Current	2.3	2.9	2.9	1.9	2.0	2.5
1.2	1.2	1.3			.9	1.2	1.9	1.3	1.3	1.4
.6	.6	.6			.3	.4	.8	.6	.8	.9
1.5	1.5	1.7		Quick	2.0	2.0	2.4	1.4	1.6	1.4
.7 (396)	.7 (425)	.7			(74) .7	.7	1.3	.7	.7	.7
.3	.3	.4			.1	.2	.4	.4	.4	.4
17 20.9	21 17.5	22 17.0		Sales/Receivables	0 UND	1 329.4	24 15.0	38 9.6	39 9.4	33 11.2
40 9.2	41 8.8	45 8.0			0 UND	40 9.1	47 7.8	54 6.8	57 6.4	47 7.7
63 5.8	64 5.7	69 5.3			61 6.0	70 5.2	68 5.4	77 4.7	72 5.1	65 5.6
				Cost of Sales/Inventory						
				Cost of Sales/Payables						
5.5	5.0	4.6		Sales/Working Capital	5.5	3.6	4.0	5.7	5.5	3.9
18.7	24.4	16.6			-40.0	21.0	9.4	18.9	14.3	12.2
-8.6	-6.6	-7.7			-2.7	-4.8	-12.6	-7.2	-15.3	-37.4
6.1	4.5	5.7		EBIT/Interest	17.0	6.3	8.9	3.7	5.0	4.4
(395) 2.8	(353) 1.6	(389) 2.2			(57) 3.6	(56) 2.5	(50) 1.9	2.0	(68) 1.8	(95) 2.3
1.1	-.4	.7			1.0	.2	.0	.1	.7	.7
3.7	2.8	3.0		Net Profit + Depr., Dep., Amort./Cur. Mat. L/T/D			3.8	2.3	2.6	5.9
(91) 1.8	(100) 1.2	(84) 1.6					(10) 2.1	(18) 1.3	(21) 1.4	(19) 2.1
1.1	.5	.9					.6	.8	.7	1.1
.9	.8	.7		Fixed/Worth	.9	.5	.7	.6	.6	.7
1.9	1.8	1.5			1.8	1.5	1.4	1.5	1.2	1.5
4.5	4.5	3.3			7.7	6.8	3.2	3.2	2.3	2.9
1.1	.9	.9		Debt/Worth	.7	.5	.5	1.0	1.0	1.1
2.5	2.1	1.7			2.1	1.8	1.2	1.7	1.7	1.7
6.5	5.7	4.8			9.0	9.7	4.6	4.8	3.4	4.5
41.1	24.6	26.4		% Profit Before Taxes/Tangible Net Worth	58.4	29.9	24.4	15.8	24.3	23.7
(380) 21.6	(348) 6.7	(381) 9.2			(62) 22.5	(54) 11.2	(49) 8.9	(60) 5.8	(69) 7.0	(87) 11.3
4.7	-11.2	-.3			4.1	-2.3	-2.8	-2.2	-3.9	.3
13.1	8.5	9.1		% Profit Before Taxes/Total Assets	21.6	10.9	11.6	5.2	6.9	7.8
6.2	1.4	2.7			6.1	2.2	2.3	1.8	2.4	3.2
.4	-4.7	-1.3			.0	-4.1	-3.4	-2.6	-2.8	-.9
4.6	4.9	5.9		Sales/Net Fixed Assets	2.6	4.0	7.5	6.2	6.8	7.2
1.6	1.4	1.6			.9	1.4	1.7	1.6	1.8	2.3
.8	.7	.8			.4	.7	.8	.9	.9	.9
1.5	1.4	1.4		Sales/Total Assets	.9	1.3	1.6	1.4	1.5	1.5
.9	.8	.8			.6	.7	.9	.9	1.0	1.0
.5	.5	.5			.3	.5	.5	.6	.6	.6
6.3	6.8	7.1		% Depr., Dep., Amort./Sales	16.5	11.3	7.2	5.6	6.3	4.5
(352) 13.8	(317) 14.4	(337) 14.8			(57) 32.6	(54) 21.7	(45) 14.8	(55) 13.2	(63) 12.0	(63) 9.1
27.3	30.3	28.1			51.5	41.6	25.1	21.0	24.2	15.6
1.2	2.2	1.8		% Officers', Directors' Owners' Comp/Sales	5.2	3.9	2.1			.7
(102) 3.7	(86) 4.2	(89) 4.1			(11) 7.3	(22) 5.5	(17) 3.7	(19) 4.2		(12) 1.1
7.5	7.4	7.2			19.1	7.7	7.1	7.1		1.4
10394268M	8742446M	9404533M		Net Sales ($)	34760M	124410M	209361M	461483M	1144041M	7430478M
11236597M	10872783M	10785786M		Total Assets ($)	78104M	235328M	298666M	637076M	1399030M	8137582M

Current Data Sorted by Assets   Comparative Historical Data

0-500M	500M-2MM	2-10MM	10-50MM	50-100MM	100-250MM	Type of Statement	4/1/06-3/31/07 ALL	4/1/07-3/31/08 ALL
	1	2	7	3	1	Unqualified	22	24
	5	10	4			Reviewed	8	17
4	5	8	4			Compiled	18	17
15	13	3	4			Tax Returns	29	21
7	9	11	10	2	1	Other	40	44
	22 (4/1-9/30/10)		103 (10/1/10-3/31/11)					
26	33	34	25	5	2	**NUMBER OF STATEMENTS**	117	123
%	%	%	%	%	%	**ASSETS**	%	%
23.6	13.8	8.1	4.9			Cash & Equivalents	7.3	7.6
10.9	12.4	13.1	16.7			Trade Receivables (net)	18.8	13.5
3.6	9.8	7.8	6.9			Inventory	8.5	7.3
4.5	7.1	8.6	6.7			All Other Current	6.4	6.7
42.5	43.1	37.6	35.3			Total Current	41.1	35.1
46.6	51.7	39.4	42.0			Fixed Assets (net)	40.2	42.4
2.8	1.2	3.8	4.5			Intangibles (net)	1.9	1.9
8.0	4.0	19.2	18.2			All Other Non-Current	16.8	20.5
100.0	100.0	100.0	100.0			Total	100.0	100.0
						LIABILITIES		
20.5	25.1	8.0	9.1			Notes Payable-Short Term	14.9	16.2
6.6	10.6	9.0	8.8			Cur. Mat.-L.T.D.	10.9	10.4
8.9	7.8	6.7	7.5			Trade Payables	9.5	5.7
.0	.1	.2	.0			Income Taxes Payable	.3	.3
9.8	7.3	8.8	12.1			All Other Current	6.6	7.2
45.9	50.8	32.8	37.5			Total Current	42.2	39.8
24.8	35.2	30.8	28.4			Long-Term Debt	34.4	31.6
.0	.1	.6	1.0			Deferred Taxes	.3	.6
8.4	5.5	3.6	4.8			All Other Non-Current	9.9	6.4
20.9	8.4	32.2	28.3			Net Worth	13.3	21.6
100.0	100.0	100.0	100.0			Total Liabilities & Net Worth	100.0	100.0
						INCOME DATA		
100.0	100.0	100.0	100.0			Net Sales	100.0	100.0
						Gross Profit		
77.4	84.5	78.0	80.5			Operating Expenses	76.3	74.0
22.6	15.5	22.0	19.5			Operating Profit	23.7	26.0
3.5	4.6	7.1	7.6			All Other Expenses (net)	11.6	12.3
19.1	10.9	14.8	11.8			Profit Before Taxes	12.1	13.8
						RATIOS		
5.9	3.5	1.5	1.7				1.5	1.4
1.3	1.0	.9	.9			Current	1.0	.9
.5	.2	.5	.3				.4	.4
2.7	1.9	1.2	1.2				1.1	1.1
.8	.5	.5	.4			Quick	.5	.4
.3	.2	.1	.1				.2	.1
0 UND	0 UND	0 UND	6 66.1				0 UND	0 UND
7 52.6	17 21.9	28 12.9	28 12.9			Sales/Receivables	28 13.0	23 16.1
23 16.1	36 10.2	59 6.2	67 5.4				55 6.6	45 8.1
						Cost of Sales/Inventory		
						Cost of Sales/Payables		
3.5	4.1	6.9	6.4				5.6	6.6
180.1	-281.0	-54.9	-40.1			Sales/Working Capital	-95.8	-22.3
-6.1	-2.2	-7.9	-3.1				-3.7	-2.2
17.6	10.3	5.0	5.0				7.2	5.7
(17) 7.8	(24) 3.5	(26) 2.0	(18) 2.2			EBIT/Interest	(89) 2.4	(88) 2.2
1.7	1.1	1.0	.8				1.2	1.3
						Net Profit + Depr., Dep.,	5.0	2.7
						Amort./Cur. Mat. L/T/D	(15) 2.2	(19) 1.3
							.8	.9
.3	.4	.1	.2				.1	.1
1.5	2.3	1.5	2.0			Fixed/Worth	1.2	1.5
NM	-5.4	6.7	4.5				10.7	9.7
.3	.6	1.0	2.0				1.5	1.8
2.9	4.4	2.7	3.3			Debt/Worth	5.6	5.7
-21.3	-8.1	23.7	8.0				31.1	30.1
208.6	51.9	26.0	52.0			% Profit Before Taxes/Tangible	52.7	43.7
(19) 31.1	(21) 27.3	(29) 15.2	(24) 17.4			Net Worth	(97) 23.7	(99) 23.2
3.5	10.3	1.6	2.8				10.7	9.1
36.0	16.8	8.0	8.9			% Profit Before Taxes/Total	11.7	11.8
10.6	5.3	3.8	3.5			Assets	4.4	4.4
-2.3	-2.3	.0	1.5				.9	1.3
16.7	17.3	35.7	74.6				43.3	36.5
2.1	1.7	2.2	5.2			Sales/Net Fixed Assets	6.8	3.9
.8	.6	.6	.7				.9	.7
2.7	2.2	1.6	2.0				1.9	1.4
.9	1.0	.6	.7			Sales/Total Assets	.7	.5
.5	.4	.2	.3				.3	.3
7.4	2.5	3.3	1.2				1.6	2.8
(17) 27.7	(22) 17.1	(25) 16.5	(16) 14.9			% Depr., Dep., Amort./Sales	(84) 8.5	(89) 15.4
67.9	53.9	60.6	25.5				50.1	49.9
	1.6						2.4	4.7
	(10) 7.5					% Officers', Directors' Owners' Comp/Sales	(28) 6.2	(25) 8.6
	13.0						14.5	13.8
21408M	57758M	203002M	526193M	222452M	200863M	Net Sales ($)	1099029M	1506604M
8327M	38422M	173491M	497967M	357951M	354441M	Total Assets ($)	2108902M	2685582M

Comparative Historical Data / Current Data Sorted by Sales

			Type of Statement						
21	18	14	Unqualified		2	1	5	2	4
18	9	19	Reviewed	4	3	5	3	2	2
12	17	21	Compiled	7	2	3	5	2	2
34	22	31	Tax Returns	22	7		2		
56	44	40	Other	16	5	4	6	2	7
4/1/08-	4/1/09-	4/1/10-			22 (4/1-9/30/10)		103 (10/1/10-3/31/11)		
3/31/09	3/31/10	3/31/11							
ALL	ALL	ALL		0-1MM	1-3MM	3-5MM	5-10MM	10-25MM	25MM & OVER
141	110	125	NUMBER OF STATEMENTS	49	19	13	21	8	15
%	%	%	ASSETS	%	%	%	%	%	%
7.5	11.1	11.9	Cash & Equivalents	15.0	14.1	12.2	7.2		3.3
15.5	14.5	14.2	Trade Receivables (net)	7.7	6.5	18.5	18.0		29.9
7.0	7.4	7.0	Inventory	2.4	8.2	12.7	6.2		13.8
7.3	8.4	6.9	All Other Current	8.1	10.2	.8	3.7		9.9
37.3	41.4	40.0	Total Current	33.2	38.9	44.3	35.1		56.8
41.3	41.5	43.4	Fixed Assets (net)	54.9	31.0	46.3	47.5		20.8
2.2	2.0	2.9	Intangibles (net)	1.1	4.7	2.1	4.8		3.9
19.2	15.1	13.7	All Other Non-Current	10.7	25.3	7.3	12.6		18.5
100.0	100.0	100.0	Total	100.0	100.0	100.0	100.0		100.0
			LIABILITIES						
15.8	10.4	15.8	Notes Payable-Short Term	25.3	10.2	4.6	9.4		16.0
10.0	9.3	8.4	Cur. Mat.-L.T.D.	5.6	18.2	8.3	12.2		1.8
6.8	6.9	7.4	Trade Payables	2.7	6.5	19.2	5.6		15.4
.1	.2	.1	Income Taxes Payable	.0	.0	.5	.0		.6
7.1	12.9	9.8	All Other Current	5.6	11.9	8.6	11.3		17.1
39.8	39.6	41.5	Total Current	39.2	46.8	41.1	38.5		50.9
34.4	30.3	30.0	Long-Term Debt	33.1	43.3	32.2	26.5		18.5
.4	.5	.4	Deferred Taxes	.0	.5	2.0	.4		.4
5.6	6.4	5.7	All Other Non-Current	7.6	.5	3.8	5.3		8.0
19.8	23.3	22.4	Net Worth	20.1	9.0	20.9	29.3		22.3
100.0	100.0	100.0	Total Liabilities & Net Worth	100.0	100.0	100.0	100.0		100.0
			INCOME DATA						
100.0	100.0	100.0	Net Sales	100.0	100.0	100.0	100.0		100.0
			Gross Profit						
78.5	84.8	80.4	Operating Expenses	70.4	80.6	89.0	90.1		89.0
21.5	15.2	19.6	Operating Profit	29.6	19.4	11.0	9.9		11.0
9.2	6.6	5.6	All Other Expenses (net)	7.8	3.4	8.0	4.9		1.0
12.3	8.6	14.0	Profit Before Taxes	21.8	16.0	3.1	5.0		9.9
			RATIOS						
1.9	2.4	2.4		4.6	3.1	2.5	1.4		1.6
.9	1.2	1.0	Current	.9	.9	.9	.9		1.1
.3	.5	.4		.4	.2	.5	.4		.7
1.4	1.8	1.5		2.0	2.1	1.3	1.2		1.1
.5	.7	.5	Quick	.5	.3	.9	.5		.6
.1	.2	.2		.1	.1	.4	.3		.3
0 UND	0 UND	0 UND		0 UND	0 UND	11 33.6	13 27.4	24 15.0	
17 21.6	19 19.2	21 17.5	Sales/Receivables	0 UND	6 60.9	21 17.5	48 7.7	45 8.1	
51 7.1	52 7.1	51 7.1		30 12.1	33 11.1	43 8.6	73 5.0	69 5.3	
			Cost of Sales/Inventory						
			Cost of Sales/Payables						
4.5	2.7	5.2		1.8	5.2	6.9	14.8		13.5
-66.2	17.4	-281.0	Sales/Working Capital	-41.6	-34.2	-47.0	-18.8		71.6
-3.2	-5.6	-4.5		-2.6	-3.0	-15.0	-3.4		-11.2
7.9	7.1	9,5		9.6	8.3	20.5	3.2		14.0
(98) 2.6	(91) 2.3	(92) 2.8	EBIT/Interest	(27) 2.9	(15) 2.7	(10) 3.1	(20) 1.2	(13)	5.4
1.3	1.0	1.2		1.3	1.8	-.8	.6		3.0
3.2									
(14) 1.3			Net Profit + Depr., Dep., Amort./Cur. Mat. L/T/D						
.4									
.1	.2	.3		.6	.0	.4	1.6		.1
1.2	1.8	1.7	Fixed/Worth	2.0	.7	1.5	3.9		1.1
5.5	7.4	7.4		14.8	-4.2	-3.9	6.4		3.0
1.5	1.5	1.0		.6	1.1	.8	1.5		2.6
4.3	3.8	3.3	Debt/Worth	3.2	2.7	2.0	6.5		4.7
18.3	26.3	26.2		NM	-8.3	-6.3	22.6		8.6
51.7	42.8	51.3		55.0	23.8		42.1		102.2
(115) 20.0	(87) 16.9	(100) 19.7	% Profit Before Taxes/Tangible Net Worth	(37) 23.1	(13) 15.0		(20) 7.7	(13)	29.4
7.5	2.6	9.5		8.3	12.3		-4.6		15.8
14.9	12.1	15.5		18.5	13.6	12.9	6.9		16.5
4.8	4.5	5.1	% Profit Before Taxes/Total Assets	5.1	6.7	3.9	1.4		8.5
.8	.0	.2		-1.1	3.6	-3.9	-1.4		5.3
30.7	37.6	20.6		3.5	129.4	55.1	18.9		96.5
4.3	2.6	2.3	Sales/Net Fixed Assets	1.0	7.8	2.1	1.7		12.0
.9	.8	.7		.4	2.1	.8	.7		4.0
1.8	1.7	2.0		.9	2.0	3.3	1.6		2.5
.7	.7	.8	Sales/Total Assets	.5	1.2	1.3	.8		1.9
.3	.4	.4		.2	.3	.5	.4		.7
2.2	2.4	2.9		13.9		2.4	4.6		
(93) 11.3	(70) 14.6	(83) 16.5	% Depr., Dep., Amort./Sales	(34) 28.3		(10) 19.7	(17) 18.5		
44.0	62.3	54.5		67.8		63.9	53.3		
2.9	4.2	1.8							
(35) 6.2	(19) 5.3	(24) 7.0	% Officers', Directors' Owners' Comp/Sales						
12.0	11.8	11.4							
1288523M	1612105M	1231676M	Net Sales ($)	21031M	35192M	50749M	156122M	126687M	841895M
2251517M	2952130M	1430599M	Total Assets ($)	58686M	94647M	72128M	231673M	161000M	812465M

M = $ thousand   MM = $ million
See Pages 9 through 22 for Explanation of Ratios and Data

Current Data Sorted by Assets   Comparative Historical Data

						Type of Statement		
1	3	9	36	9	11	Unqualified	87	87
5	11	48	28	3		Reviewed	87	93
10	31	30	10			Compiled	105	101
35	45	28				Tax Returns	115	109
22	53	59	48	16	9	Other	192	226
	68 (4/1-9/30/10)		492 (10/1/10-3/31/11)				4/1/06-3/31/07	4/1/07-3/31/08
0-500M	500M-2MM	2-10MM	10-50MM	50-100MM	100-250MM		ALL	ALL
73	143	174	122	28	20	NUMBER OF STATEMENTS	586	616
%	%	%	%	%	%	ASSETS	%	%
18.4	9.4	7.2	7.5	8.9	3.5	Cash & Equivalents	8.5	8.5
8.6	13.7	16.6	18.1	16.1	13.2	Trade Receivables (net)	15.9	15.1
1.1	6.9	5.5	8.1	7.8	5.6	Inventory	7.2	7.6
3.8	3.4	5.1	4.2	4.0	16.3	All Other Current	3.9	4.2
31.8	33.4	34.4	37.8	36.8	38.5	Total Current	35.4	35.4
55.4	55.1	53.4	49.8	52.1	37.7	Fixed Assets (net)	52.2	53.9
2.5	2.5	3.2	4.2	2.4	8.9	Intangibles (net)	2.6	2.2
10.2	9.1	8.9	8.1	8.7	14.8	All Other Non-Current	9.8	8.6
100.0	100.0	100.0	100.0	100.0	100.0	Total	100.0	100.0
						LIABILITIES		
16.7	8.0	9.0	8.8	11.9	8.8	Notes Payable-Short Term	10.3	11.0
14.7	9.1	10.1	9.7	7.9	6.4	Cur. Mat.-L.T.D.	8.9	9.9
4.4	6.7	6.1	6.4	5.0	3.6	Trade Payables	6.2	6.1
.4	.1	.6	.1	.2	.5	Income Taxes Payable	.3	.2
13.0	6.8	7.8	6.4	8.5	3.4	All Other Current	7.9	8.0
49.1	30.6	33.6	31.5	33.5	22.6	Total Current	33.7	35.2
48.8	32.3	29.7	25.7	33.7	41.5	Long-Term Debt	33.7	35.4
.0	.4	.3	1.9	1.9	1.4	Deferred Taxes	.8	.7
17.4	4.9	7.2	4.5	6.7	10.2	All Other Non-Current	4.8	4.4
-15.3	31.9	29.2	36.4	24.2	24.3	Net Worth	27.0	24.3
100.0	100.0	100.0	100.0	100.0	100.0	Total Liabilities & Net Worth	100.0	100.0
						INCOME DATA		
100.0	100.0	100.0	100.0	100.0	100.0	Net Sales	100.0	100.0
						Gross Profit		
75.6	83.7	83.8	86.8	82.8	79.4	Operating Expenses	78.9	81.0
24.4	16.3	16.2	13.2	17.2	20.6	Operating Profit	21.1	19.0
3.8	4.2	5.9	4.8	7.7	12.8	All Other Expenses (net)	6.6	6.4
20.5	12.1	10.3	8.3	9.4	7.7	Profit Before Taxes	14.5	12.6
						RATIOS		
3.5	2.9	2.0	2.0	2.0	2.0		2.3	1.9
1.1	1.0	1.1	1.3	1.0	1.3	Current	1.1	1.0
.3	.4	.6	.7	.7	.9		.5	.5
2.7	1.7	1.6	1.7	1.4	1.1		1.6	1.3
.9	.7	.7	.8	.7	.9	Quick	.7	.7
.2	.3	.3	.4	.3	.4		.3	.3
0 UND	0 UND	8 45.5	24 15.4	34 10.7	17 21.8		0 UND	0 UND
0 UND	21 17.2	34 10.8	47 7.8	46 7.9	42 8.7	Sales/Receivables	28 13.1	28 13.1
29 12.5	45 8.1	73 5.0	78 4.7	89 4.1	67 5.4		60 6.1	57 6.4
						Cost of Sales/Inventory		
						Cost of Sales/Payables		
5.1	5.8	5.6	4.2	3.1	1.4		6.0	6.2
69.0	142.4	90.4	14.8	NM	15.8	Sales/Working Capital	55.9	129.1
-4.8	-5.8	-7.8	-10.3	-5.5	-42.9		-6.1	-6.4
14.7	10.6	6.8	5.9	5.8	4.4		8.5	6.5
(66) 4.3	(117) 4.4	(149) 3.3	(112) 2.5	(25) 2.2	(14) 2.4	EBIT/Interest	(477) 3.6	(490) 2.9
1.2	.7	1.2	1.4	1.0	1.0		1.7	1.3
	12.2	4.8	4.2				4.5	4.3
	(16) 4.2	(33) 2.2	(32) 1.9			Net Profit + Depr., Dep., Amort./Cur. Mat. L/T/D	(91) 2.2	(98) 1.9
	1.6	1.1	1.1				1.1	1.3
.9	.8	.9	.5	.9	.3		.7	.7
27.0	1.6	1.7	1.7	2.3	1.7	Fixed/Worth	1.7	1.9
-.9	9.6	7.8	3.7	5.2	6.4		5.7	7.5
1.0	.6	.9	1.0	1.3	1.4		1.0	1.3
64.0	1.7	2.2	2.4	3.3	6.6	Debt/Worth	2.7	3.3
-2.3	10.1	10.7	6.4	18.2	14.6		10.8	12.8
171.2	51.3	37.4	32.4	45.2	31.3		62.2	54.8
(42) 47.6	(112) 18.2	(143) 16.9	(113) 14.1	(24) 16.5	(16) 16.9	% Profit Before Taxes/Tangible Net Worth	(501) 29.7	(521) 26.2
18.2	1.0	2.4	2.7	2.2	11.7		12.2	9.0
46.3	19.7	13.2	9.2	9.2	6.6		16.5	15.6
16.8	6.3	4.9	3.8	2.6	3.1	% Profit Before Taxes/Total Assets	7.2	6.2
-.5	-1.5	.2	.7	-.5	.8		2.1	1.1
5.9	6.5	5.7	6.5	6.3	15.1		7.1	7.3
2.3	2.5	2.1	2.1	1.3	1.9	Sales/Net Fixed Assets	2.4	2.1
.9	.7	.8	.7	.6	.7		.8	.7
2.3	2.3	1.8	1.5	1.2	1.0		1.8	1.9
1.2	1.1	1.0	.8	.7	.4	Sales/Total Assets	1.0	.9
.7	.5	.4	.4	.3	.2		.4	.4
10.7	6.5	6.9	5.4	4.0			4.6	4.6
(53) 30.0	(115) 15.6	(152) 12.9	(109) 13.1	(14) 12.8		% Depr., Dep., Amort./Sales	(491) 12.1	(500) 13.2
50.5	40.7	34.4	26.3	29.8			32.1	33.0
3.9	2.9	1.7	1.6				2.6	2.2
(17) 8.3	(35) 7.0	(40) 4.0	(24) 4.5			% Officers', Directors' Owners' Comp/Sales	(149) 5.3	(152) 4.5
14.9	10.1	6.3	9.6				8.9	8.5
32773M	259622M	1028949M	2963519M	1580937M	1878254M	Net Sales ($)	7263416M	8465540M
18993M	168381M	854096M	2796028M	1788457M	3185015M	Total Assets ($)	8708889M	10056888M

M = $ thousand   MM = $ million
See Pages 9 through 22 for Explanation of Ratios and Data

Comparative Historical Data / Current Data Sorted by Sales

Hist 1	Hist 2	Hist 3	Type of Statement	0-1MM	1-3MM	3-5MM	5-10MM	10-25MM	25MM & OVER
69	74	69	Unqualified	6	4	4	9	12	34
77	85	95	Reviewed	12	19	9	15	28	12
75	69	81	Compiled	24	28	9	12	8	
129	114	108	Tax Returns	59	31	7	9	2	
225	220	207	Other	51	37	21	31	33	34
4/1/08-3/31/09 ALL	4/1/09-3/31/10 ALL	4/1/10-3/31/11 ALL		68 (4/1-9/30/10)	492 (10/1/10-3/31/11)				
575	562	560	NUMBER OF STATEMENTS	152	119	50	76	83	80
%	%	%	**ASSETS**	%	%	%	%	%	%
9.5	9.2	9.2	Cash & Equivalents	12.1	10.7	8.9	7.7	6.9	5.7
13.7	14.1	15.0	Trade Receivables (net)	7.3	14.4	20.9	18.1	22.5	16.1
6.7	6.9	6.0	Inventory	.8	6.0	6.9	8.0	5.7	13.5
4.7	4.5	4.6	All Other Current	4.5	4.4	3.8	3.8	5.6	5.5
34.6	34.7	34.8	Total Current	24.7	35.5	40.5	37.5	40.7	40.9
53.3	53.2	52.7	Fixed Assets (net)	61.1	50.6	47.4	53.1	49.3	46.3
2.4	2.3	3.3	Intangibles (net)	3.2	2.6	1.6	2.7	4.6	4.8
9.7	9.8	9.2	All Other Non-Current	10.9	11.3	10.5	6.6	5.3	8.1
100.0	100.0	100.0	Total	100.0	100.0	100.0	100.0	100.0	100.0
			LIABILITIES						
9.7	10.8	9.8	Notes Payable-Short Term	10.5	11.3	7.1	8.0	9.1	10.6
10.1	10.3	10.1	Cur. Mat.-L.T.D.	11.2	11.6	7.9	10.6	10.1	6.6
5.2	5.3	5.9	Trade Payables	3.3	4.8	6.1	8.1	7.8	8.6
.2	.1	.3	Income Taxes Payable	.3	.2	.6	.7	.1	.3
6.9	7.7	7.8	All Other Current	8.0	6.5	5.0	7.4	8.6	10.7
32.1	34.2	34.0	Total Current	33.3	34.4	26.7	34.7	35.7	36.8
36.6	32.3	32.6	Long-Term Debt	44.8	34.0	24.1	27.1	23.3	27.4
.6	.6	.8	Deferred Taxes	.3	.1	.9	.5	1.3	2.2
5.1	5.8	7.4	All Other Non-Current	6.4	11.2	6.7	7.9	4.9	6.7
25.6	27.2	25.2	Net Worth	15.3	20.3	41.5	29.7	34.8	27.0
100.0	100.0	100.0	Total Liabilities & Net Worth	100.0	100.0	100.0	100.0	100.0	100.0
			INCOME DATA						
100.0	100.0	100.0	Net Sales	100.0	100.0	100.0	100.0	100.0	100.0
			Gross Profit						
80.1	82.6	83.2	Operating Expenses	71.6	81.7	87.1	90.3	89.5	91.4
19.9	17.4	16.8	Operating Profit	28.4	18.3	12.9	9.7	10.5	8.6
7.1	6.8	5.3	All Other Expenses (net)	8.8	4.3	4.1	3.5	3.8	4.3
12.8	10.6	11.5	Profit Before Taxes	19.6	14.0	8.8	6.2	6.7	4.3
			RATIOS						
1.9	2.2	2.3	Current	2.5	2.8	3.2	1.9	1.9	1.8
1.0	1.1	1.1		.9	1.1	1.7	1.1	1.2	1.1
.5	.5	.5		.2	.5	1.0	.7	.7	.8
1.4	1.5	1.7	Quick	1.8	1.9	2.1	1.6	1.4	1.1
.7	.7	.7		.6	.6	1.4	.7	.7	.7
.3	.3	.3		.2	.3	.6	.4	.5	.4
0 UND	0 UND	1 490.2	Sales/Receivables	0 UND	0 UND	10 35.3	14 25.8	30 12.1	27 13.7
23 15.8	27 13.3	31 11.8		0 UND	24 15.3	36 10.1	32 11.3	47 7.8	42 8.6
48 7.6	55 6.7	59 6.2		49 7.4	51 7.2	78 4.7	59 6.2	75 4.9	57 6.4
			Cost of Sales/Inventory						
			Cost of Sales/Payables						
6.6	5.5	5.2	Sales/Working Capital	3.6	3.9	4.0	8.0	5.5	8.4
154.6	40.9	49.4		-29.8	69.0	11.3	93.9	42.7	34.6
-6.6	-6.3	-6.6		-3.2	-5.8	-370.7	-10.5	-12.6	-15.0
6.7	6.0	8.4	EBIT/Interest	12.6	8.9	8.0	5.1	11.3	6.0
(457) 2.6	(454) 2.2	(483) 3.2		(114) 4.2	(104) 4.2	(43) 3.4	(70) 2.7	(77) 2.4	(75) 2.3
1.0	.5	1.1		1.2	.7	1.1	1.3	1.2	1.0
4.1	4.0	5.0	Net Profit + Depr., Dep., Amort./Cur. Mat. L/T/D		3.1		2.5	6.3	7.5
(79) 1.7	(76) 1.6	(87) 2.1			(12) 1.6		(14) 1.8	(29) 1.8	(18) 2.3
1.1	1.0	1.0			1.0		1.3	1.1	.9
.8	.7	.8	Fixed/Worth	.9	.7	.5	.9	.7	.7
2.1	1.8	1.8		2.4	1.7	1.0	1.8	1.8	1.9
8.2	9.5	9.6		-26.5	20.2	2.5	5.4	8.7	4.1
1.1	.9	.9	Debt/Worth	.9	.8	.5	1.1	.8	1.2
3.1	2.6	2.3		2.8	2.3	1.4	2.1	2.3	2.9
13.6	15.9	14.8		-34.3	37.5	3.4	8.6	12.1	6.7
54.6	40.0	40.8	% Profit Before Taxes/Tangible Net Worth	57.0	38.3	40.2	48.2	40.0	35.0
(479) 21.2	(456) 16.4	(450) 18.2		(109) 21.1	(93) 18.0	(44) 15.6	(66) 16.1	(68) 16.3	(70) 18.0
3.4	1.8	2.6		4.4	.2	1.6	4.7	2.4	4.2
15.5	13.6	14.1	% Profit Before Taxes/Total Assets	21.6	16.7	16.0	11.4	11.1	8.5
4.9	3.4	4.9		6.1	7.6	5.3	5.0	3.6	3.9
.0	-1.0	.1		-.2	-.6	.4	.9	.6	.1
7.0	6.3	6.0	Sales/Net Fixed Assets	2.7	7.4	9.2	7.0	7.9	7.2
2.0	1.8	2.2		.9	2.6	3.3	2.5	2.9	3.2
.7	.7	.8		.5	.9	1.0	1.2	1.5	1.2
1.8	1.5	1.8	Sales/Total Assets	.9	1.9	2.8	2.1	2.0	1.8
.9	.8	.9		.5	.9	1.2	1.3	1.4	1.3
.4	.4	.4		.3	.4	.4	.5	.6	.7
5.5	5.3	6.5	% Depr., Dep., Amort./Sales	16.7	7.9	4.1	7.3	5.3	3.4
(459) 15.2	(446) 16.6	(449) 15.1		(122) 37.2	(93) 17.6	(42) 9.7	(66) 12.8	(72) 8.3	(54) 5.8
33.0	35.5	35.2		59.8	39.4	24.1	28.2	19.8	11.0
2.2	2.2	1.9	% Officers', Directors' Owners' Comp/Sales	7.7	2.9	4.0	1.6	1.5	
(125) 5.5	(114) 4.5	(122) 4.9		(16) 12.6	(35) 6.8	(17) 7.6	(22) 2.2	(23) 3.4	
10.3	10.2	9.6		19.0	13.1	9.1	5.4	4.9	
7865076M	10671039M	7744054M	Net Sales ($)	62611M	218761M	198497M	536001M	1321805M	5406379M
9468348M	10084459M	8810970M	Total Assets ($)	198116M	417423M	374689M	818908M	1908531M	5093303M

M = $ thousand   MM = $ million
See Pages 9 through 22 for Explanation of Ratios and Data

Current Data Sorted by Assets   **Comparative Historical Data**

						Type of Statement		
3	4	3	7	3	2	Unqualified	18	12
	3	3	1			Reviewed	3	2
	2	2				Compiled	5	6
3	8	6				Tax Returns	13	15
1	4	11	6	1	1	Other	25	26
	5 (4/1-9/30/10)		69 (10/1/10-3/31/11)				4/1/06-3/31/07	4/1/07-3/31/08
0-500M	500M-2MM	2-10MM	10-50MM	50-100MM	100-250MM		ALL	ALL
7	21	25	14	4	3	NUMBER OF STATEMENTS	64	61
%	%	%	%	%	%	ASSETS	%	%
	34.2	11.1	21.4			Cash & Equivalents	13.4	10.9
	8.1	4.4	8.9			Trade Receivables (net)	12.2	11.7
	3.4	4.2	.3			Inventory	2.0	8.3
	1.6	11.4	10.7			All Other Current	5.9	5.0
	47.3	31.0	41.4			Total Current	33.5	35.8
	35.8	54.2	29.1			Fixed Assets (net)	45.6	46.6
	8.5	3.6	24.7			Intangibles (net)	9.0	6.0
	8.4	11.1	4.8			All Other Non-Current	11.9	11.6
	100.0	100.0	100.0			Total	100.0	100.0
						LIABILITIES		
	5.1	7.7	2.8			Notes Payable-Short Term	3.0	7.0
	6.0	5.3	3.4			Cur. Mat.-L.T.D.	5.4	3.7
	6.4	2.4	6.3			Trade Payables	8.4	8.8
	.0	.4	.3			Income Taxes Payable	.5	.0
	3.7	15.5	21.0			All Other Current	11.9	13.6
	21.2	31.4	33.9			Total Current	29.2	33.1
	23.1	36.7	15.2			Long-Term Debt	41.3	44.0
	.0	.0	.5			Deferred Taxes	.5	.4
	6.1	2.3	5.9			All Other Non-Current	6.3	4.7
	49.6	29.6	44.6			Net Worth	22.8	17.9
	100.0	100.0	100.0			Total Liabilities & Net Worth	100.0	100.0
						INCOME DATA		
	100.0	100.0	100.0			Net Sales	100.0	100.0
						Gross Profit		
	69.2	61.0	74.1			Operating Expenses	78.0	72.7
	30.8	39.0	25.9			Operating Profit	22.0	27.3
	8.0	18.0	2.5			All Other Expenses (net)	10.5	11.6
	22.8	21.0	23.4			Profit Before Taxes	11.4	15.7
						RATIOS		
	9.1	2.7	3.0				3.2	1.5
	2.0	.9	1.1			Current	1.2	.9
	.5	.2	.5				.4	.5
	5.9	1.7	2.8				2.1	1.3
	1.4	.2	.5			Quick	(63) 1.0	.6
	.3	.0	.2				.3	.1
0 UND	0 UND	0 UND					0 UND	0 UND
7 54.3	0 UND	32 11.5				Sales/Receivables	11 33.7	3 126.8
30 12.3	23 15.6	58 6.3					35 10.3	30 12.1
						Cost of Sales/Inventory		
						Cost of Sales/Payables		
	1.8	2.3	8.9				4.8	11.4
	12.6	-393.1	46.4			Sales/Working Capital	25.5	-31.0
	-11.5	-1.4	-8.2				-7.5	-5.9
		14.3	33.5				11.4	11.4
	(12)	5.1	(11) 16.3			EBIT/Interest	(43) 5.0	(37) 4.5
		2.1	3.8				1.5	1.5
						Net Profit + Depr., Dep.,	21.2	
						Amort./Cur. Mat. L/T/D	(11) 6.2	
							1.7	
	.0	.6	.4				.5	.5
	.6	2.3	1.9			Fixed/Worth	3.2	3.5
	8.5	NM	-.6				-8.2	-5.0
	.1	.8	.5				.9	1.3
	1.6	3.1	4.4			Debt/Worth	9.7	4.3
	11.5	NM	-4.2				-11.8	-14.0
	128.6	33.9				% Profit Before Taxes/Tangible	72.6	113.8
	(18) 53.7	(19) 15.3				Net Worth	(43) 36.9	(41) 34.2
	20.9	5.0					2.0	6.6
	44.7	13.3	36.5			% Profit Before Taxes/Total	17.7	19.9
	16.5	3.8	15.3			Assets	6.3	8.0
	4.2	.6	5.5				.1	.9
	UND	24.6	24.6				18.6	30.7
	18.0	.3	7.4			Sales/Net Fixed Assets	2.6	3.6
	.7	.2	2.6				.3	.3
	1.8	.7	1.7				2.0	2.2
	.6	.3	1.2			Sales/Total Assets	.7	.9
	.4	.1	.7				.2	.2
	.9	1.0	1.2				.8	1.7
	(12) 2.7	(21) 6.0	(10) 2.5			% Depr., Dep., Amort./Sales	(50) 4.2	(46) 5.3
	20.3	18.9	4.4				13.4	16.3
						% Officers', Directors'	1.5	2.7
						Owners' Comp/Sales	(10) 6.8	(11) 8.3
							25.4	31.4
3208M	27603M	145155M	332132M	179373M	1541922M	Net Sales ($)	1084176M	859047M
1885M	21943M	115930M	267072M	264588M	425669M	Total Assets ($)	1310707M	719907M

M = $ thousand   MM = $ million
See Pages 9 through 22 for Explanation of Ratios and Data

Comparative Historical Data / Current Data Sorted by Sales

			Type of Statement	0-1MM	1-3MM	3-5MM	5-10MM	10-25MM	25MM & OVER
21	22	22	Unqualified	6	3		2	2	9
4	1	7	Reviewed	2	2			2	1
3	4	4	Compiled	2	2				
10	17	17	Tax Returns	13	4				
26	24	24	Other	8	5	2	1	4	4
4/1/08-3/31/09	4/1/09-3/31/10	4/1/10-3/31/11			5 (4/1-9/30/10)		69 (10/1/10-3/31/11)		
ALL	ALL	ALL		0-1MM	1-3MM	3-5MM	5-10MM	10-25MM	25MM & OVER
64	68	74	NUMBER OF STATEMENTS	31	16	2	3	8	14
%	%	%	ASSETS	%	%	%	%	%	%
9.2	14.4	21.2	Cash & Equivalents	19.7	25.9				28.2
14.3	8.2	8.1	Trade Receivables (net)	3.2	6.4				13.3
3.3	2.1	3.6	Inventory	.8	8.4				4.5
4.0	8.4	7.8	All Other Current	6.2	6.3				7.1
30.8	33.1	40.7	Total Current	29.9	47.0				53.1
43.6	39.6	39.0	Fixed Assets (net)	50.0	44.5				22.9
12.4	11.9	9.7	Intangibles (net)	6.7	1.1				15.1
13.2	15.3	10.6	All Other Non-Current	13.4	7.4				8.9
100.0	100.0	100.0	Total	100.0	100.0				100.0
			LIABILITIES						
14.1	7.5	5.9	Notes Payable-Short Term	4.4	13.3				1.9
2.8	11.6	5.2	Cur. Mat.-L.T.D.	5.9	6.0				5.7
7.2	4.9	5.9	Trade Payables	2.4	5.4				10.3
.0	.1	.3	Income Taxes Payable	.2	.7				.4
11.8	11.9	13.2	All Other Current	9.2	3.6				25.3
35.9	36.0	30.5	Total Current	22.0	29.0				43.6
38.3	35.9	29.1	Long-Term Debt	43.2	22.8				14.6
.5	.3	.4	Deferred Taxes	.0	.1				1.6
7.4	6.5	4.2	All Other Non-Current	6.0	2.4				1.2
17.8	21.3	35.7	Net Worth	28.8	45.7				39.0
100.0	100.0	100.0	Total Liabilties & Net Worth	100.0	100.0				100.0
			INCOME DATA						
100.0	100.0	100.0	Net Sales	100.0	100.0				100.0
			Gross Profit						
70.2	74.6	70.2	Operating Expenses	62.6	65.7				78.1
29.8	25.4	29.8	Operating Profit	37.4	34.3				21.9
11.4	14.1	9.7	All Other Expenses (net)	17.9	5.1				2.8
18.4	11.3	20.1	Profit Before Taxes	19.4	29.2				19.1
			RATIOS						
2.3	2.9	4.0		4.3	6.9				2.8
1.0	1.0	1.2	Current	.7	1.8				1.2
.4	.5	.5		.1	.7				.9
1.4	1.4	2.4		2.4	6.4				2.7
.7	.6	.7	Quick	.3	1.5				.9
.3	.2	.1		.0	.2				.6
0 UND	0 UND	0 UND		0 UND	0 UND				0 999.8
14 25.6	5 68.1	5 76.0	Sales/Receivables	0 UND	3 116.5				18 20.1
44 8.3	29 12.7	33 11.2		7 51.6	30 12.0				47 7.8
			Cost of Sales/Inventory						
			Cost of Sales/Payables						
8.6	6.4	3.5		1.5	1.4				4.1
-816.0	208.0	30.1	Sales/Working Capital	-19.8	4.8				29.2
-5.7	-4.8	-4.9		-2.1	NM				-69.6
13.0	16.3	23.9		3.9	254.0				27.0
(40) 4.8	(44) 4.1	(40) 7.2	EBIT/Interest	(10) 3.0	(11) 8.7			(10)	12.5
1.9	1.0	3.0		2.3	3.4				4.4
8.8	8.9		Net Profit + Depr., Dep.,						
(10) 4.1	(10) 1.1		Amort./Cur. Mat. L/T/D						
2.0	.5								
.5	.5	.1		.0	.1				.2
3.1	2.7	1.4	Fixed/Worth	2.3	.7				1.3
111.2	-1.6	9.3		10.8	3.5				-.9
1.4	1.2	.5		.6	.3				1.2
5.2	5.9	2.5	Debt/Worth	3.1	1.3				5.1
213.2	-8.7	-87.2		-106.4	4.1				-22.0
163.2	57.2	71.8	% Profit Before Taxes/Tangible	39.8	172.8				
(49) 44.1	(43) 18.1	(55) 25.2	Net Worth	(23) 20.6	(14) 27.4				
20.3	.2	12.6		1.8	13.8				
24.2	14.9	25.0	% Profit Before Taxes/Total	19.5	43.3				36.5
7.7	3.7	8.5	Assets	4.9	12.6				16.6
1.3	-2.1	3.4		.6	3.2				4.9
23.5	33.8	114.5		UND	107.8				134.1
4.7	4.9	5.3	Sales/Net Fixed Assets	.7	2.2				17.1
.3	.3	.4		.2	.5				3.3
1.9	1.8	1.5		.8	1.3				2.6
.9	.7	.7	Sales/Total Assets	.4	.5				1.4
.2	.2	.3		.1	.3				.7
1.2	1.5	1.0		3.2	2.2				.3
(48) 3.8	(52) 3.9	(51) 3.8	% Depr., Dep., Amort./Sales	(17) 13.2	(13) 3.8			(11)	2.3
18.4	16.3	12.7		23.1	17.1				4.5
	2.1		% Officers', Directors'						
	(11) 8.8		Owners' Comp/Sales						
	16.8								
1026808M	2484571M	2229393M	Net Sales ($)	13947M	29325M	7604M	18207M	135985M	2024325M
997162M	1551292M	1097087M	Total Assets ($)	60778M	62113M	20594M	7427M	111736M	834439M

M = $ thousand   MM = $ million
See Pages 9 through 22 for Explanation of Ratios and Data

PROFESSIONAL, SCIENTIFIC, AND TECHNICAL SERVICES

Current Data Sorted by Assets   **Comparative Historical Data**

0-500M	500M-2MM	2-10MM	10-50MM	50-100MM	100-250MM	Type of Statement	4/1/06-3/31/07 ALL	4/1/07-3/31/08 ALL
4	10	20	46	17	12	Unqualified	110	100
8	24	102	75	9	4	Reviewed	187	176
79	89	75	15	3	2	Compiled	240	244
363	176	89	10	2	3	Tax Returns	517	469
265	286	243	133	21	14	Other	747	769
	119 (4/1-9/30/10)		2,080 (10/1/10-3/31/11)					
719	585	529	279	52	35	**NUMBER OF STATEMENTS**	1801	1758
%	%	%	%	%	%	**ASSETS**	%	%
39.7	33.8	28.9	29.2	35.7	43.2	Cash & Equivalents	31.9	31.9
7.8	13.9	22.7	24.6	15.4	10.5	Trade Receivables (net)	15.3	16.0
.4	.6	1.3	3.1	1.1	.0	Inventory	1.4	1.1
12.9	15.3	14.7	11.1	11.6	11.1	All Other Current	12.8	13.2
60.9	63.7	67.7	68.0	63.9	64.7	Total Current	61.4	62.3
21.2	18.5	16.6	18.0	23.8	23.8	Fixed Assets (net)	22.1	21.8
2.7	3.3	1.4	1.6	3.5	4.0	Intangibles (net)	2.8	2.4
15.2	14.4	14.4	12.4	8.8	7.5	All Other Non-Current	13.8	13.4
100.0	100.0	100.0	100.0	100.0	100.0	Total	100.0	100.0
						LIABILITIES		
47.9	21.2	15.8	5.4	5.6	5.1	Notes Payable-Short Term	25.6	26.6
6.3	3.7	2.8	2.6	2.8	3.3	Cur. Mat.-L.T.D.	4.6	4.6
3.1	2.4	3.6	3.8	2.3	.5	Trade Payables	3.0	2.8
.3	.3	1.0	1.0	.4	.0	Income Taxes Payable	.5	.4
43.8	31.3	26.0	22.1	25.2	14.2	All Other Current	32.3	31.9
101.3	59.0	49.3	34.9	36.3	23.2	Total Current	65.9	66.2
14.2	14.4	10.2	8.1	7.8	10.9	Long-Term Debt	14.8	13.3
.0	.1	.5	.6	.0	.0	Deferred Taxes	.2	.2
8.0	4.9	6.0	6.8	3.5	5.4	All Other Non-Current	7.1	5.8
-23.6	21.6	34.0	49.7	52.3	60.5	Net Worth	11.9	14.5
100.0	100.0	100.0	100.0	100.0	100.0	Total Liabilities & Net Worth	100.0	100.0
						INCOME DATA		
100.0	100.0	100.0	100.0	100.0	100.0	Net Sales	100.0	100.0
						Gross Profit		
85.4	82.7	78.9	75.7	66.5	61.0	Operating Expenses	79.7	79.5
14.6	17.3	21.1	24.3	33.5	39.0	Operating Profit	20.3	20.5
.8	2.0	2.1	1.5	1.9	.9	All Other Expenses (net)	1.3	1.5
13.8	15.3	19.0	22.8	31.7	38.1	Profit Before Taxes	18.9	19.1
						RATIOS		
1.6	2.5	3.3	5.5	4.8	11.2		2.8	2.9
.8	1.2	1.5	2.2	2.0	4.9	Current	1.2	1.2
.3	.7	.9	1.1	1.3	1.7		.6	.6
1.3	1.9	2.7	4.8	4.4	10.0		2.2	2.2
(715) .6	(583) .9	1.2	(278) 1.8	1.5	4.0	Quick	(1798) .9	(1753) 1.0
.2	.3	.5	.9	.8	1.1		.3	.3
0 UND	0 UND	0 UND	0 UND	0 UND	0 UND		0 UND	0 UND
0 UND	0 UND	5 69.6	15 24.2	8 47.7	3 120.5	Sales/Receivables	0 UND	0 UND
0 UND	10 35.1	62 5.9	74 4.9	40 9.0	16 23.1		17 21.9	21 17.3
						Cost of Sales/Inventory		
						Cost of Sales/Payables		
37.5	9.4	4.9	3.8	5.6	4.7		9.1	8.7
-91.2	64.1	16.9	8.0	10.7	6.8	Sales/Working Capital	92.1	65.2
-16.4	-20.7	-52.3	43.8	35.0	23.9		-25.2	-29.1
46.0	85.2	186.7	203.6	636.3	284.0		94.1	91.2
(499) 10.0	(462) 13.2	(454) 23.4	(243) 44.4	(44) 100.2	(28) 138.1	EBIT/Interest	(1426) 16.8	(1464) 17.8
1.0	1.1	3.3	5.6	25.9	22.2		1.9	2.4
2.1	7.3	12.6	8.5				10.4	7.1
(12) .2	(29) 1.5	(50) 2.0	(43) 2.5			Net Profit + Depr., Dep., Amort./Cur. Mat. L/T/D	(117) 2.1	(120) 2.5
-.6	.5	.9	1.4				1.0	.8
.0	.1	.1	.1	.2	.2		.2	.2
1.0	.3	.3	.3	.5	.3	Fixed/Worth	.7	.7
-.6	-14.7	1.9	.8	.7	.7		-12.8	UND
1.2	.8	.5	.3	.4	.1		.6	.6
17.7	2.6	2.0	1.0	.8	.5	Debt/Worth	2.9	2.9
-2.8	-41.0	12.2	3.2	2.2	2.0		-15.6	-26.5
783.6	327.5	296.6	192.5	305.8	355.9		402.5	388.0
(394) 173.1	(422) 82.3	(444) 103.7	(261) 83.8	(50) 187.0	(34) 180.7	% Profit Before Taxes/Tangible Net Worth	(1275) 139.5	(1273) 147.8
31.7	17.2	16.9	15.6	100.7	133.6		20.1	24.4
164.4	108.4	107.5	115.8	172.4	162.3		162.4	163.2
37.0	20.7	24.0	39.1	120.6	116.4	% Profit Before Taxes/Total Assets	40.5	43.6
1.8	1.8	3.6	5.1	25.0	71.6		2.0	3.2
816.0	171.3	129.2	43.4	28.8	25.0		103.3	107.4
92.7	58.7	41.4	24.3	18.1	15.6	Sales/Net Fixed Assets	37.9	39.3
29.1	22.3	19.9	14.4	11.6	11.0		17.8	17.8
19.5	7.6	4.9	4.2	5.0	3.9		9.7	9.7
9.3	4.4	3.0	2.6	3.5	3.2	Sales/Total Assets	4.6	4.6
4.6	2.4	1.9	1.7	2.3	2.5		2.5	2.5
.3	.3	.5	.7	1.1	.9		.5	.5
(305) .6	(329) .8	(371) .9	(244) 1.2	(44) 1.6	(20) 1.2	% Depr., Dep., Amort./Sales	(1211) .9	(1174) .9
1.3	1.5	1.5	1.8	2.0	2.3		1.5	1.5
12.6	9.2	5.2	9.0	7.6	4.9		11.9	11.7
(412) 23.0	(284) 23.2	(213) 19.2	(99) 25.9	(11) 15.6	(13) 18.2	% Officers', Directors' Owners' Comp/Sales	(791) 23.9	(777) 23.1
34.6	35.0	32.0	37.2	33.2	31.3		35.1	33.7
1800410M	3520415M	9435769M	20065225M	12692818M	23684865M	Net Sales ($)	73783173M	68261416M
149553M	627701M	2476190M	6362443M	3485549M	5755291M	Total Assets ($)	17028079M	16701460M

© RMA 2011

M = $ thousand   MM = $ million
See Pages 9 through 22 for Explanation of Ratios and Data

Comparative Historical Data / Current Data Sorted by Sales

			Type of Statement						
117	115	109	Unqualified	3	6	5	7	10	78
202	209	222	Reviewed	1	4	4	26	74	113
259	275	263	Compiled	24	64	33	59	54	29
566	654	643	Tax Returns	190	192	84	96	60	21
905	938	962	Other	113	191	120	185	164	189
4/1/08-3/31/09	4/1/09-3/31/10	4/1/10-3/31/11		119 (4/1-9/30/10)			2,080 (10/1/10-3/31/11)		
ALL	ALL	ALL		0-1MM	1-3MM	3-5MM	5-10MM	10-25MM	25MM & OVER
2049	2191	2199	NUMBER OF STATEMENTS	331	457	246	373	362	430
%	%	%	ASSETS	%	%	%	%	%	%
30.7	33.4	34.2	Cash & Equivalents	33.8	35.6	38.9	34.1	31.0	33.0
16.9	16.1	15.4	Trade Receivables (net)	9.3	12.7	14.3	16.1	20.8	18.4
1.5	1.3	1.0	Inventory	.5	.9	.8	.3	2.2	1.5
13.7	12.0	13.7	All Other Current	12.8	13.7	16.4	15.4	13.6	11.5
62.8	62.7	64.3	Total Current	56.4	62.8	70.4	65.8	67.6	64.4
21.1	21.0	19.1	Fixed Assets (net)	25.1	18.8	13.8	16.0	17.0	22.2
3.1	2.8	2.5	Intangibles (net)	2.3	2.4	2.8	3.7	1.6	2.2
13.0	13.5	14.2	All Other Non-Current	16.2	16.0	13.0	14.6	13.8	11.3
100.0	100.0	100.0	Total	100.0	100.0	100.0	100.0	100.0	100.0
			LIABILITIES						
27.6	26.0	26.0	Notes Payable-Short Term	35.3	38.8	30.8	27.5	18.6	7.5
4.4	4.4	4.1	Cur. Mat.-L.T.D.	6.4	3.8	3.0	4.4	3.4	3.8
3.2	2.9	3.1	Trade Payables	2.5	3.0	3.2	3.8	2.7	3.2
.5	.6	.5	Income Taxes Payable	.1	.2	.7	.7	.9	.7
29.6	30.6	32.5	All Other Current	33.7	39.4	36.8	30.5	31.6	24.5
65.2	64.4	66.3	Total Current	78.0	85.1	74.6	66.9	57.2	39.7
13.6	14.6	12.3	Long-Term Debt	20.5	15.0	7.5	10.2	9.9	9.9
.2	.2	.2	Deferred Taxes	.0	.2	.2	.3	.4	.4
5.1	6.9	6.4	All Other Non-Current	9.1	7.7	5.1	4.8	5.6	5.6
15.9	13.9	14.7	Net Worth	-7.6	-8.0	12.7	17.8	26.9	44.4
100.0	100.0	100.0	Total Liabilities & Net Worth	100.0	100.0	100.0	100.0	100.0	100.0
			INCOME DATA						
100.0	100.0	100.0	Net Sales	100.0	100.0	100.0	100.0	100.0	100.0
			Gross Profit						
79.4	80.7	81.1	Operating Expenses	79.0	86.3	81.5	83.8	81.0	74.4
20.6	19.3	18.9	Operating Profit	21.0	13.7	18.5	16.2	19.0	25.6
1.4	1.5	1.6	All Other Expenses (net)	4.7	1.0	.9	.5	.6	1.8
19.2	17.7	17.4	Profit Before Taxes	16.2	12.6	17.6	15.8	18.5	23.7
			RATIOS						
2.9	2.9	3.0		1.9	1.8	2.3	3.1	3.4	5.0
1.2	1.2	1.2	Current	.9	1.0	1.2	1.2	1.4	1.9
.6	.6	.6		.3	.4	.7	.6	.8	1.0
2.2	2.3	2.3		1.5	1.5	1.9	2.5	2.6	4.2
(2046) 1.0	(2187) 1.0	(2192) 1.0	Quick	(328) .7	(456) .7	1.0	(372) 1.0	(361) 1.1	(429) 1.5
.3	.4	.3		.2	.2	.4	.3	.4	.7
0 UND	0 UND	0 UND		0 UND	0 UND	0 UND	0 UND	0 UND	0 UND
0 UND	0 UND	0 UND	Sales/Receivables	0 UND	0 UND	0 UND	0 UND	2 155.0	5 67.7
31 11.9	24 15.1	18 20.2		0 UND	4 101.2	19 18.9	20 18.1	50 7.3	41 8.9
			Cost of Sales/Inventory						
			Cost of Sales/Payables						
8.6	8.0	8.0		11.4	15.0	10.9	7.9	5.9	5.7
57.1	51.2	54.0	Sales/Working Capital	-87.4	-618.8	60.8	52.2	26.6	16.6
-25.2	-29.2	-28.8		-7.9	-15.2	-37.6	-32.9	-49.8	198.0
108.6	118.6	124.0		23.3	52.0	103.7	122.2	183.8	265.0
(1647) 19.3	(1715) 17.9	(1730) 17.9	EBIT/Interest	(192) 8.2	(363) 10.8	(193) 18.0	(298) 12.5	(312) 24.5	(372) 69.8
2.1	1.8	2.2		1.5	1.0	2.6	1.6	2.1	7.7
6.3	7.5	7.2					4.4	8.1	8.3
(139) 1.9	(136) 1.8	(144) 2.0	Net Profit + Depr., Dep., Amort./Cur. Mat. L/T/D			(23) 1.6	(44) 2.3	(60) 2.4
.9	.6	.8					.3	.8	1.3
.1	.1	.1		.0	.0	.1	.1	.1	.2
.6	.6	.4	Fixed/Worth	1.4	.5	.3	.4	.4	.4
-38.0	-24.3	16.1		-1.5	-1.1	25.4	-99.9	3.1	1.1
.6	.6	.6		1.0	1.1	.8	.6	.6	.3
2.5	3.0	2.5	Debt/Worth	12.8	6.7	2.7	2.6	2.0	1.1
-20.8	-17.0	-36.2		-3.9	-4.1	-53.3	-28.2	16.0	3.6
355.1	340.1	335.1		277.6	332.4	656.5	323.7	314.9	302.3
(1465) 119.2	(1541) 118.2	(1605) 111.0	% Profit Before Taxes/Tangible Net Worth	(197) 78.6	(274) 79.6	(181) 166.8	(272) 108.7	(290) 113.3	(391) 148.6
20.7	17.7	19.1		16.7	15.9	24.1	14.4	18.6	31.2
154.2	129.0	131.9		79.8	95.2	172.9	120.6	122.5	160.0
41.2	31.0	31.1	% Profit Before Taxes/Total Assets	19.8	21.2	37.1	29.5	31.4	73.4
3.0	1.8	3.1		1.8	.7	5.0	2.2	2.6	6.8
130.7	158.6	170.9		736.0	308.6	283.3	232.5	146.6	49.0
40.8	43.3	49.0	Sales/Net Fixed Assets	41.8	70.0	88.0	73.7	45.8	26.4
17.8	17.8	19.4		11.3	22.9	35.2	28.9	22.4	15.5
9.1	8.9	8.8		6.7	11.5	12.5	11.5	8.2	6.4
4.5	4.2	4.3	Sales/Total Assets	3.3	5.0	5.8	5.1	3.9	4.0
2.3	2.2	2.4		1.3	2.4	2.7	2.7	2.3	2.6
.4	.4	.4		.7	.3	.3	.3	.4	.7
(1292) .9	(1354) .9	(1313) .9	% Depr., Dep., Amort./Sales	(151) 1.5	(208) .6	(121) .6	(209) .6	(261) .8	(363) 1.2
1.6	1.6	1.6		5.6	1.4	1.1	1.3	1.3	1.7
11.1	9.6	9.7		13.1	10.9	8.3	8.3	6.5	8.5
(877) 21.0	(1038) 22.0	(1032) 22.2	% Officers', Directors' Owners' Comp/Sales	(157) 22.0	(249) 19.6	(122) 19.6	(188) 25.5	(170) 21.8	(146) 20.9
34.2	34.1	34.5		32.6	33.9	34.7	34.0	37.4	36.5
87407896M	82554282M	71199502M	Net Sales ($)	172277M	876063M	952591M	2726606M	5814333M	60657632M
22186517M	19999008M	18856727M	Total Assets ($)	139208M	360262M	403209M	799376M	2029473M	15125199M

M = $ thousand   MM = $ million
See Pages 9 through 22 for Explanation of Ratios and Data

Current Data Sorted by Assets **Comparative Historical Data**

Type of Statement	0-500M	500M-2MM	2-10MM	10-50MM	50-100MM	100-250MM		4/1/06-3/31/07 ALL	4/1/07-3/31/08 ALL
Unqualified		1	2	5				11	3
Reviewed		1	4	4				3	2
Compiled	1	4	4					12	3
Tax Returns	16	6	2					29	20
Other	11	12	15	8	1			37	41
		5 (4/1-9/30/10)		88 (10/1/10-3/31/11)					
NUMBER OF STATEMENTS	28	24	27	13	1			92	69
ASSETS	%	%	%	%	%	%		%	%
Cash & Equivalents	42.4	34.6	29.6	25.1				33.5	27.6
Trade Receivables (net)	2.7	6.5	17.7	11.8				10.1	12.0
Inventory	.0	.0	2.3	1.8				.1	.4
All Other Current	8.2	6.0	13.9	10.9				6.5	8.4
Total Current	53.4	47.1	63.4	49.5				50.2	48.4
Fixed Assets (net)	15.7	25.6	14.8	20.9				21.4	23.5
Intangibles (net)	15.0	.8	13.8	12.4				9.7	11.5
All Other Non-Current	16.0	26.4	8.0	17.2				18.7	16.6
Total	100.0	100.0	100.0	100.0				100.0	100.0
LIABILITIES									
Notes Payable-Short Term	32.2	14.0	8.1	3.5				16.7	15.9
Cur. Mat.-L.T.D.	4.6	.7	2.0	4.3				1.7	1.9
Trade Payables	7.8	8.4	10.0	5.3				6.4	8.4
Income Taxes Payable	.0	.0	.0	.4				.5	.6
All Other Current	18.1	26.2	26.6	24.2				27.9	27.6
Total Current	62.7	49.3	46.7	37.7				53.2	54.3
Long-Term Debt	11.8	14.4	12.3	14.4				15.6	16.8
Deferred Taxes	.0	.0	.0	1.7				.5	.1
All Other Non-Current	25.8	3.3	2.8	4.2				3.3	4.7
Net Worth	-.3	32.9	38.1	42.0				27.4	24.1
Total Liabilties & Net Worth	100.0	100.0	100.0	100.0				100.0	100.0
INCOME DATA									
Net Sales	100.0	100.0	100.0	100.0				100.0	100.0
Gross Profit									
Operating Expenses	88.8	90.6	91.3	84.1				90.2	96.1
Operating Profit	11.2	9.4	8.7	15.9				9.8	3.9
All Other Expenses (net)	.4	4.4	.4	1.0				-.1	-.8
Profit Before Taxes	10.8	5.0	8.3	14.9				10.0	4.7
RATIOS									
Current	2.1	2.0	2.4	2.1				2.2	2.8
	1.1	.9	1.4	1.7				1.2	1.1
	.5	.4	1.0	1.0				.6	.6
Quick	2.1	2.0	1.9	2.0				2.2	2.3
	1.1	.8	1.0	1.3				1.1	1.0
	.4	.2	.6	.4				.4	.4
Sales/Receivables	0 UND	0 UND	4 84.7	5 77.0				0 UND	0 UND
	0 UND	1 600.1	8 44.6	23 16.1				2 189.6	3 130.9
	0 UND	6 59.5	33 11.0	41 9.0				17 21.4	20 18.6
Cost of Sales/Inventory									
Cost of Sales/Payables									
Sales/Working Capital	19.2	13.4	5.1	4.8				8.6	10.3
	UND	-48.0	13.2	11.1				33.2	75.9
	-15.5	-7.6	-99.0	NM				-19.6	-14.9
EBIT/Interest	17.2	21.6	51.1	42.0				17.0	28.0
	(19) .8	(12) 3.7	(23) 26.1	22.0				(63) 5.8	(51) 3.3
	-4.5	-3.3	1.6	3.4				.6	-3.0
Net Profit + Depr., Dep., Amort./Cur. Mat. L/T/D									
Fixed/Worth	.1	.1	.1	.3				.1	.3
	NM	.6	.6	.8				.5	.9
	-.2	2.7	-4.7	NM				3.7	-2.5
Debt/Worth	.8	.8	.7	.6				.6	.5
	-129.0	2.0	2.0	2.6				2.3	2.3
	-2.8	9.4	-12.1	NM				24.9	-8.4
% Profit Before Taxes/Tangible Net Worth	393.5	146.8	109.5	175.6				118.5	148.2
	(13) 214.6	(22) 15.8	(20) 61.9	(10) 22.0				(74) 51.9	(51) 31.1
	45.8	-6.9	19.4	12.3				3.1	-5.7
% Profit Before Taxes/Total Assets	85.9	29.7	30.9	38.8				45.3	32.7
	26.9	2.5	11.3	12.7				12.8	5.0
	-10.5	-5.2	1.9	4.1				.6	-12.1
Sales/Net Fixed Assets	283.6	44.0	59.2	39.8				75.4	38.9
	60.1	22.8	23.5	8.0				23.7	18.9
	14.0	12.5	9.2	4.6				8.4	8.9
Sales/Total Assets	10.7	4.5	2.7	2.3				4.2	5.3
	4.6	3.6	2.2	1.4				2.3	2.9
	3.0	1.3	1.1	1.0				1.0	1.3
% Depr., Dep., Amort./Sales	.3	.7	.6	1.6				.7	.8
	(14) .4	(18) 1.9	(20) 1.1	(10) 2.1				(60) 1.7	(51) 1.9
	2.2	2.8	2.8	2.5				3.7	4.0
% Officers', Directors' Owners' Comp/Sales	5.4							3.6	4.7
	(15) 12.6							(31) 7.7	(18) 9.5
	29.9							16.4	27.6
Net Sales ($)	34547M	90256M	302543M	487432M	62266M			1100597M	692954M
Total Assets ($)	5849M	28080M	121657M	296288M	81814M			712440M	420367M

(Columns 50-100MM and 100-250MM: DATA NOT AVAILABLE)

M = $ thousand   MM = $ million
See Pages 9 through 22 for Explanation of Ratios and Data

Comparative Historical Data | | Current Data Sorted by Sales

			Type of Statement						
5	10	8	Unqualified			2	1	2	4
4	4	5	Reviewed			2	1	2	
14	11	9	Compiled	1	2	2	1	3	
23	33	24	Tax Returns	11	8	3	1	1	
44	43	47	Other	8	10	4	12	7	6
4/1/08-3/31/09 ALL	4/1/09-3/31/10 ALL	4/1/10-3/31/11 ALL		5 (4/1-9/30/10)			88 (10/1/10-3/31/11)		
				0-1MM	1-3MM	3-5MM	5-10MM	10-25MM	25MM & OVER
90	101	93	**NUMBER OF STATEMENTS**	20	20	13	15	15	10
%	%	%	**ASSETS**	%	%	%	%	%	%
32.6	34.0	33.9	Cash & Equivalents	31.4	43.1	42.9	25.8	32.8	22.5
9.0	10.1	9.3	Trade Receivables (net)	2.2	2.3	11.9	16.8	15.7	13.7
1.4	.7	.9	Inventory	.0	.0	.0	1.3	2.7	2.3
6.0	7.6	9.7	All Other Current	7.6	9.9	2.1	7.2	18.7	13.3
49.1	52.4	53.8	Total Current	41.3	55.2	57.0	51.1	69.9	51.8
21.5	23.4	18.6	Fixed Assets (net)	26.6	14.5	13.8	21.1	13.0	22.1
14.5	10.5	11.2	Intangibles (net)	15.4	13.5	12.5	2.7	5.9	17.1
14.9	13.7	16.4	All Other Non-Current	16.7	16.8	16.8	25.1	11.2	9.0
100.0	100.0	100.0	Total	100.0	100.0	100.0	100.0	100.0	100.0
			LIABILITIES						
22.9	12.6	16.1	Notes Payable-Short Term	26.0	25.6	13.8	9.7	7.2	3.6
4.2	1.6	2.8	Cur. Mat.-L.T.D.	6.5	.1	1.0	2.2	1.9	5.8
7.9	14.6	8.2	Trade Payables	7.2	8.1	7.6	8.9	9.6	8.2
.2	.2	.1	Income Taxes Payable	.0	.0	.0	.1	.0	.5
20.1	23.7	23.4	All Other Current	19.4	18.9	23.5	26.3	35.6	17.4
55.2	52.7	50.7	Total Current	59.2	52.8	45.8	47.1	54.4	35.4
14.0	14.3	13.1	Long-Term Debt	22.3	4.3	18.4	11.5	6.6	18.0
.3	.2	.2	Deferred Taxes	.0	.0	.0	.0	.6	1.2
3.9	7.7	10.2	All Other Non-Current	7.3	31.5	3.5	3.1	.9	7.1
26.7	25.1	25.7	Net Worth	11.3	11.4	32.3	38.2	37.5	38.3
100.0	100.0	100.0	Total Liabilities & Net Worth	100.0	100.0	100.0	100.0	100.0	100.0
			INCOME DATA						
100.0	100.0	100.0	Net Sales	100.0	100.0	100.0	100.0	100.0	100.0
			Gross Profit						
93.7	92.1	89.1	Operating Expenses	84.0	89.6	98.2	92.6	89.0	81.1
6.3	7.9	10.9	Operating Profit	16.0	10.4	1.8	7.4	11.0	18.9
1.2	.9	1.6	All Other Expenses (net)	6.1	.2	-.1	.1	.4	2.0
5.1	7.0	9.3	Profit Before Taxes	9.9	10.2	1.9	7.3	10.6	16.8
			RATIOS						
2.6	2.3	2.1		2.3	2.1	2.2	2.1	2.3	2.1
1.1	1.1	1.2	Current	.8	1.0	1.3	1.1	1.7	1.6
.5	.6	.7		.4	.5	.8	.4	1.0	1.0
2.1	2.0	2.0		2.0	2.1	2.0	1.6	2.1	1.9
1.0	1.0	1.0	Quick	.7	1.0	1.2	.8	1.0	1.4
.3	.4	.4		.3	.3	.8	.2	.7	.5
0 UND	0 UND	0 UND		0 UND	0 UND	0 UND	1 353.5	4 84.7	5 68.4
3 130.4	1 279.8	2 211.6	Sales/Receivables	0 UND	0 UND	3 132.4	10 37.7	7 49.6	22 16.8
25 14.5	24 15.0	17 22.1		0 UND	4 96.7	17 21.1	33 11.0	29 12.5	41 8.8
			Cost of Sales/Inventory						
			Cost of Sales/Payables						
8.7	9.7	10.4		28.9	10.4	11.1	8.7	4.5	6.4
107.6	114.5	48.8	Sales/Working Capital	-28.9	UND	17.7	30.7	12.9	16.0
-8.8	-20.8	-18.0		-4.9	-17.4	-220.8	-12.4	81.6	NM
	19.0	26.5	32.4	24.7	17.2		33.4	84.2	60.6
(58) 1.8	(71) 10.5	(68) 6.9	EBIT/Interest	(12) -1.4	(11) 5.0	(12) 5.5	(14) 48.4	9.1
-6.1	.4	.3		-4.1	.2		3.5	24.2	3.1
		11.6	Net Profit + Depr., Dep., Amort./Cur. Mat. L/T/D						
	(10) 6.4								
		2.1							
.2	.2	.1		.1	.0	.1	.2	.2	.3
.9	.9	.6	Fixed/Worth	4.3	.9	.6	.6	.5	1.0
-.8	-4.9	-6.9		-.4	-.5	-1.2	2.0	.6	-10.5
.5	.6	.7		.9	.7	.6	.8	.7	.7
3.9	2.0	2.4	Debt/Worth	8.0	6.0	2.3	1.3	2.0	2.4
-4.4	-22.7	-12.1		-3.6	-6.1	-6.0	9.8	11.3	-45.5
84.2	168.3	147.9	% Profit Before Taxes/Tangible Net Worth	305.0	409.5		253.8	135.0	
(62) 27.4	(73) 71.0	(65) 51.3		(11) 15.2	(12) 107.3	(14) 46.5	(13) 82.2	
4.9	12.4	9.0		-5.6	44.1		2.0	22.4	
31.6	50.8	39.1	% Profit Before Taxes/Total Assets	45.3	60.4	17.6	23.3	38.2	53.4
4.7	16.2	11.5		1.0	26.9	1.9	11.3	28.8	18.5
-3.5	.4	-.3		-10.5	.1	-16.5	1.3	10.2	5.1
75.9	53.5	76.4	Sales/Net Fixed Assets	245.1	255.9	150.8	28.3	46.9	83.7
19.9	24.0	30.2		25.0	58.7	42.9	21.1	34.2	8.6
8.3	10.6	11.7		11.7	15.3	10.6	10.3	14.0	4.8
4.2	5.9	4.6	Sales/Total Assets	4.4	6.0	5.7	4.5	4.5	2.7
2.3	2.7	2.7		2.1	4.1	2.8	4.1	2.4	1.8
1.2	1.5	1.4		.4	2.0	1.5	2.3	1.4	1.0
1.2	.9	.6	% Depr., Dep., Amort./Sales	.4			1.0	.6	
(53) 2.3	(68) 1.6	(62) 1.7		(11) 2.0		(13) 2.0	1.1	
3.9	3.2	2.5		18.7			2.9	2.1	
5.7	4.7	3.7	% Officers', Directors' Owners' Comp/Sales						
(28) 11.4	(41) 9.3	(31) 6.8							
27.6	26.7	27.5							
1185962M	897930M	977044M	Net Sales ($)	10042M	35263M	51802M	103510M	254941M	521486M
877575M	464161M	533688M	Total Assets ($)	12096M	16666M	22486M	48247M	116998M	317195M

© RMA 2011

M = $ thousand   MM = $ million

See Pages 9 through 22 for Explanation of Ratios and Data

Current Data Sorted by Assets							Comparative Historical Data	
						Type of Statement		
		3			2	Unqualified	3	4
		1				Reviewed	2	1
	1	2				Compiled	1	1
4	1	1				Tax Returns		1
5	7	9	3		1	Other	5	7
	3 (4/1-9/30/10)		37 (10/1/10-3/31/11)				**4/1/06-3/31/07 ALL**	**4/1/07-3/31/08 ALL**
0-500M	**500M-2MM**	**2-10MM**	**10-50MM**	**50-100MM**	**100-250MM**			
9	9	16	3		3	**NUMBER OF STATEMENTS**	11	14
%	%	%	%	%	%	**ASSETS**	%	%
		22.6		**DATA NOT AVAILABLE**		Cash & Equivalents	30.4	34.5
		44.1				Trade Receivables (net)	36.9	25.8
		2.9				Inventory	.8	.2
		4.9				All Other Current	3.2	6.4
		74.5				Total Current	71.3	66.8
		16.6				Fixed Assets (net)	11.0	17.3
		4.4				Intangibles (net)	5.3	10.3
		4.5				All Other Non-Current	12.4	5.5
		100.0				Total	100.0	100.0
						LIABILITIES		
		7.0				Notes Payable-Short Term	11.5	11.4
		1.4				Cur. Mat.-L.T.D.	7.0	1.7
		3.3				Trade Payables	4.5	4.1
		.2				Income Taxes Payable	.4	.9
		7.8				All Other Current	31.1	36.5
		19.7				Total Current	54.5	54.6
		8.9				Long-Term Debt	9.8	4.6
		.0				Deferred Taxes	.0	.2
		12.2				All Other Non-Current	4.4	12.8
		59.2				Net Worth	31.3	27.8
		100.0				Total Liabilities & Net Worth	100.0	100.0
						INCOME DATA		
		100.0				Net Sales	100.0	100.0
						Gross Profit		
		80.5				Operating Expenses	85.2	86.3
		19.5				Operating Profit	14.8	13.7
		.4				All Other Expenses (net)	.9	.8
		19.2				Profit Before Taxes	13.9	12.9
						RATIOS		
		9.8					2.7	2.6
		5.3				Current	1.5	1.3
		2.6					.9	.9
		9.7					2.5	2.5
		4.2				Quick	1.3	1.3
		2.5					.9	.9
		37 10.0					**8** 44.4	**0** UND
		57 6.4				Sales/Receivables	**53** 6.9	**14** 26.8
		109 3.4					**79** 4.6	**72** 5.1
						Cost of Sales/Inventory		
						Cost of Sales/Payables		
		2.1					5.8	5.3
		5.7				Sales/Working Capital	12.6	17.8
		7.6					-125.5	NM
		148.6					33.1	9.7
		(12) 15.6				EBIT/Interest	(10) 3.7	(10) 3.9
		3.3					1.6	2.2
						Net Profit + Depr., Dep., Amort./Cur. Mat. L/T/D		
		.0					.2	.2
		.2				Fixed/Worth	.4	.6
		.4					1.0	NM
		.2					.8	.6
		.6				Debt/Worth	2.7	2.2
		1.1					21.0	NM
		86.8						360.7
		(15) 49.1				% Profit Before Taxes/Tangible Net Worth		(11) 38.8
		13.1						14.8
		62.5					54.7	42.0
		31.8				% Profit Before Taxes/Total Assets	13.5	17.8
		7.8					2.6	5.7
		181.0					56.6	48.6
		24.1				Sales/Net Fixed Assets	26.7	25.0
		10.9					18.1	16.0
		3.9					3.1	5.9
		2.1				Sales/Total Assets	2.7	3.5
		1.2					1.9	2.2
		.3						.8
		(13) 1.1				% Depr., Dep., Amort./Sales		(13) 1.7
		2.9						2.4
						% Officers', Directors' Owners' Comp/Sales		
23429M	**26364M**	**229530M**	**169818M**		**588399M**	Net Sales ($)	**263658M**	**374466M**
2004M	**10541M**	**97215M**	**75759M**		**518010M**	Total Assets ($)	**295644M**	**400346M**

M = $ thousand MM = $ million

See Pages 9 through 22 for Explanation of Ratios and Data

Comparative Historical Data | **Current Data Sorted by Sales**

			Type of Statement	0-1MM	1-3MM	3-5MM	5-10MM	10-25MM	25MM & OVER
6	5	5	Unqualified					1	4
2	1	1	Reviewed					1	
	2	3	Compiled		1			2	
4	7	6	Tax Returns		4	1		1	
12	13	25	Other	5	5	1	5	5	4
4/1/08-3/31/09	4/1/09-3/31/10	4/1/10-3/31/11			3 (4/1-9/30/10)			37 (10/1/10-3/31/11)	
ALL	ALL	ALL							
24	28	40	**NUMBER OF STATEMENTS**	5	10	2	6	9	8
%	%	%	**ASSETS**	%	%	%	%	%	%
30.1	33.1	26.8	Cash & Equivalents		27.9				
23.9	19.5	24.1	Trade Receivables (net)		10.2				
.3	.1	2.8	Inventory		2.1				
12.9	13.6	6.3	All Other Current		14.5				
67.3	66.3	60.0	Total Current		54.7				
20.0	14.3	20.7	Fixed Assets (net)		19.7				
3.4	10.2	11.1	Intangibles (net)		8.4				
9.3	9.2	8.2	All Other Non-Current		17.2				
100.0	100.0	100.0	Total		100.0				
			LIABILITIES						
13.0	17.5	14.0	Notes Payable-Short Term		23.6				
3.3	3.1	2.9	Cur. Mat.-L.T.D.		1.1				
4.8	4.8	2.7	Trade Payables		2.4				
.1	.0	.3	Income Taxes Payable		.0				
28.1	15.3	15.6	All Other Current		26.4				
49.3	40.7	35.5	Total Current		53.5				
12.7	12.3	12.9	Long-Term Debt		19.7				
.5	.3	.6	Deferred Taxes		.0				
11.8	7.6	8.3	All Other Non-Current		2.8				
25.7	39.1	42.7	Net Worth		23.9				
100.0	100.0	100.0	Total Liabilities & Net Worth		100.0				
			INCOME DATA						
100.0	100.0	100.0	Net Sales		100.0				
			Gross Profit						
84.5	80.4	85.5	Operating Expenses		87.7				
15.5	19.6	14.5	Operating Profit		12.3				
1.8	1.3	.8	All Other Expenses (net)		.9				
13.7	18.3	13.7	Profit Before Taxes		11.5				
			RATIOS						
3.5	2.8	5.4	Current		2.7				
1.6	1.6	2.3			2.1				
1.1	.8	1.2			.5				
2.0	2.5	4.6	Quick		2.4				
1.4	1.0	2.1			1.1				
.9	.5	.6			.4				
0 UND	0 UND	0 UND	Sales/Receivables		0 UND				
4 84.8	0 UND	34 10.8			0 UND				
61 6.0	49 7.5	59 6.2			1 395.1				
			Cost of Sales/Inventory						
			Cost of Sales/Payables						
7.1	6.5	5.5	Sales/Working Capital		7.3				
14.8	12.7	9.4			31.8				
135.6	-20.1	121.9			-52.0				
84.6	170.6	42.1	EBIT/Interest						
(18) 23.4	(21) 38.4	(31) 8.3							
3.8	3.4	1.5							
			Net Profit + Depr., Dep., Amort./Cur. Mat. L/T/D						
.1	.0	.1	Fixed/Worth		.1				
.6	.2	.4			.9				
1.4	3.9	NM			-2.0				
.6	.5	.5	Debt/Worth		.6				
1.3	1.2	1.0			2.0				
5.9	30.4	NM			-6.0				
188.1	245.1	125.0	% Profit Before Taxes/Tangible Net Worth						
(20) 65.5	(22) 80.9	(30) 69.5							
5.6	38.9	15.7							
108.5	68.9	47.7	% Profit Before Taxes/Total Assets		89.1				
18.4	37.1	16.7			36.1				
1.7	6.3	1.9			4.2				
74.7	284.7	97.8	Sales/Net Fixed Assets		UND				
19.5	59.2	27.9			46.7				
10.5	13.2	10.8			16.0				
5.4	4.7	4.9	Sales/Total Assets		20.3				
3.0	3.0	2.5			6.1				
2.3	1.6	1.1			2.3				
.6	.4	.4	% Depr., Dep., Amort./Sales						
(19) 1.7	(16) 1.7	(27) 1.2							
3.1	2.8	2.9							
		11.0	% Officers', Directors' Owners' Comp/Sales						
		(10) 19.8							
		23.7							
1012573M	937527M	1037540M	Net Sales ($)	2661M	20665M	8656M	42647M	137983M	824928M
448253M	376407M	703529M	Total Assets ($)	11487M	5855M	1609M	25264M	59039M	600275M

M = $ thousand   MM = $ million
See Pages 9 through 22 for Explanation of Ratios and Data

Current Data Sorted by Assets | Comparative Historical Data

Type of Statement

	0-500M	500M-2MM	2-10MM	10-50MM	50-100MM	100-250MM		4/1/06-3/31/07 ALL	4/1/07-3/31/08 ALL
Unqualified			6	10	2	5		22	19
Reviewed			3	3				5	7
Compiled	25	27	25	9	1	1		105	100
Tax Returns	146	56	15	4	1			149	165
Other	117	141	175	47	9	10		482	454
	195 (4/1-9/30/10)			644 (10/1/10-3/31/11)					
NUMBER OF STATEMENTS	288	225	224	73	13	16		763	745

	%	%	%	%	%	%		%	%
ASSETS									
Cash & Equivalents	25.7	12.6	13.2	15.6	21.1	14.8		17.4	17.1
Trade Receivables (net)	16.9	33.3	41.1	38.2	31.1	35.0		31.6	31.3
Inventory	1.8	3.9	5.3	4.4	.7	1.4		4.1	3.8
All Other Current	7.1	5.7	7.6	7.3	21.2	12.8		7.0	7.6
Total Current	51.4	55.5	67.1	65.5	74.0	64.0		60.2	59.8
Fixed Assets (net)	21.9	19.2	15.7	12.0	12.0	7.5		18.4	18.0
Intangibles (net)	13.5	15.3	8.3	9.2	7.0	15.8		9.7	11.9
All Other Non-Current	13.2	10.0	8.8	13.3	6.9	12.8		11.7	10.3
Total	100.0	100.0	100.0	100.0	100.0	100.0		100.0	100.0
LIABILITIES									
Notes Payable-Short Term	35.1	14.0	8.8	8.7	3.9	8.4		15.6	17.2
Cur. Mat.-L.T.D.	4.1	3.8	3.0	3.1	2.0	1.1		4.4	5.6
Trade Payables	3.5	1.9	3.3	6.1	4.2	11.8		4.2	3.8
Income Taxes Payable	.4	.4	.4	.0	.0	.0		.5	.3
All Other Current	25.2	13.2	15.7	19.9	17.4	20.7		17.9	19.8
Total Current	68.4	33.4	31.2	37.8	27.5	42.0		42.5	46.6
Long-Term Debt	22.3	21.5	14.2	12.3	9.3	7.1		16.9	17.8
Deferred Taxes	.1	.4	.3	.0	.0	.1		.2	.1
All Other Non-Current	7.9	6.0	6.5	8.5	4.2	15.2		7.7	8.1
Net Worth	1.3	38.7	47.8	41.4	59.1	35.7		32.6	27.3
Total Liabilties & Net Worth	100.0	100.0	100.0	100.0	100.0	100.0		100.0	100.0
INCOME DATA									
Net Sales	100.0	100.0	100.0	100.0	100.0	100.0		100.0	100.0
Gross Profit									
Operating Expenses	85.0	82.2	83.9	81.2	76.0	81.8		82.8	83.7
Operating Profit	15.0	17.8	16.1	18.8	24.0	18.2		17.2	16.3
All Other Expenses (net)	.9	4.4	3.0	3.0	1.6	1.4		1.8	2.0
Profit Before Taxes	14.0	13.4	13.1	15.8	22.3	16.8		15.4	14.3

RATIOS

	0-500M	500M-2MM	2-10MM	10-50MM	50-100MM	100-250MM		Hist1	Hist2
Current	2.6	4.0	4.7	4.7	8.1	2.8		3.9	3.6
	1.1	1.6	2.1	2.2	3.5	1.4		1.8	1.7
	.3	.8	1.4	1.4	1.4	1.1		1.0	.8
Quick	2.1	3.2	3.8	3.8	6.0	1.9		3.1	3.0
	(287) .9	1.4	1.8	2.0	2.4	1.1		(761) 1.4	(744) 1.3
	.2	.6	1.1	1.0	1.3	1.0		.7	.6
Sales/Receivables	0 UND	0 UND	38 9.6	40 9.2	27 13.4	15 24.6		0 UND	0 UND
	0 UND	47 7.8	57 6.4	63 5.8	55 6.7	58 6.3		45 8.1	42 8.7
	32 11.5	74 4.9	79 4.6	82 4.5	81 4.5	78 4.7		71 5.1	70 5.2
Cost of Sales/Inventory									
Cost of Sales/Payables									
Sales/Working Capital	12.9	4.6	4.3	3.7	3.6	4.8		5.2	5.4
	154.3	11.8	6.9	7.3	5.0	7.6		11.5	12.0
	-17.2	-34.6	14.2	16.2	17.8	49.7		-189.7	-65.2
EBIT/Interest	31.4	46.6	47.8	61.1	209.0	91.5		35.4	31.4
	(208) 8.8	(180) 6.4	(189) 11.2	(60) 20.6	(11) 47.7	(14) 24.8		(606) 8.9	(608) 8.9
	2.7	1.6	2.4	5.4	3.3	1.7		2.4	2.4
Net Profit + Depr., Dep., Amort./Cur. Mat. L/T/D			5.2	14.9				7.6	5.6
			(17) 1.5	(10) 4.5				(36) 2.4	(46) 2.1
			.8	2.9				1.1	1.0
Fixed/Worth	.0	.1	.1	.1	.2	.2		.1	.1
	.6	.3	.2	.2	.2	.5		.4	.4
	-2.6	129.3	.8	.5	.5	NM		3.1	22.1
Debt/Worth	.7	.5	.4	.4	.3	1.2		.5	.5
	6.2	2.0	1.1	1.2	.7	5.5		1.7	1.8
	-2.4	-44.4	4.5	9.7	1.9	NM		125.3	-27.9
% Profit Before Taxes/Tangible Net Worth	478.8	115.0	115.6	125.3	137.7	238.4		173.8	153.5
	(176) 118.4	(163) 36.7	(195) 39.0	(63) 72.5	100.1	(12) 114.9		(585) 77.6	(540) 72.3
	23.4	5.1	6.4	18.9	19.0	84.9		14.0	16.4
% Profit Before Taxes/Total Assets	111.3	42.1	55.8	56.8	79.9	63.6		75.7	70.8
	34.5	10.5	15.9	16.9	56.4	35.7		23.0	22.0
	6.8	1.2	1.7	4.4	2.3	2.4		4.2	4.1
Sales/Net Fixed Assets	999.8	91.3	52.5	46.6	23.9	43.5		78.5	83.6
	74.5	33.9	26.7	26.8	18.7	20.0		26.7	29.3
	18.9	15.5	13.9	17.1	14.1	10.8		13.4	15.5
Sales/Total Assets	11.2	3.7	3.3	3.2	2.7	2.8		4.6	4.7
	5.2	2.5	2.5	2.4	2.3	1.9		2.9	2.8
	2.8	1.4	1.8	1.7	1.7	.5		1.9	2.0
% Depr., Dep., Amort./Sales	.6	.9	.9	.9	1.1	1.1		1.0	.9
	(121) 1.4	(147) 1.5	(170) 1.5	(61) 1.6	1.7	(12) 1.8		(493) 1.6	(477) 1.5
	2.7	2.9	2.3	2.6	2.5	3.1		2.6	2.5
% Officers', Directors' Owners' Comp/Sales	14.2	11.8	16.2	5.8				13.9	14.2
	(199) 21.5	(106) 21.7	(98) 23.4	(29) 17.5				(366) 24.6	(366) 22.8
	29.8	31.3	31.7	29.8				32.7	30.9
Net Sales ($)	370932M	703858M	2570855M	4028726M	2819363M	8047169M		20016925M	16594587M
Total Assets ($)	59827M	243785M	994089M	1462249M	1047012M	2717805M		6427869M	5944918M

M = $ thousand   MM = $ million
See Pages 9 through 22 for Explanation of Ratios and Data

Comparative Historical Data				Current Data Sorted by Sales					
			Type of Statement						
36	37	23	Unqualified		1	1	2	5	14
15	9	7	Reviewed		1	1	3		2
82	81	88	Compiled	21	28	8	10	11	10
167	225	222	Tax Returns	100	70	23	15	9	5
490	480	499	Other	86	99	63	87	101	63
4/1/08-3/31/09	4/1/09-3/31/10	4/1/10-3/31/11			195 (4/1-9/30/10)		644 (10/1/10-3/31/11)		
ALL	ALL	ALL		0-1MM	1-3MM	3-5MM	5-10MM	10-25MM	25MM & OVER
790	832	839	**NUMBER OF STATEMENTS**	207	199	96	117	126	94
%	%	%	**ASSETS**	%	%	%	%	%	%
15.4	17.4	17.7	Cash & Equivalents	18.6	18.4	18.9	16.0	16.4	16.8
33.0	31.7	30.2	Trade Receivables (net)	14.6	30.2	30.9	38.5	40.1	39.9
4.1	3.3	3.5	Inventory	1.2	3.9	4.2	4.3	5.1	3.8
6.8	5.3	7.2	All Other Current	6.7	6.3	6.9	5.9	10.0	8.6
59.3	57.7	58.5	Total Current	41.1	58.7	60.9	64.7	71.6	69.1
19.0	18.4	18.2	Fixed Assets (net)	31.2	14.8	14.6	14.6	13.8	11.1
9.9	12.1	12.2	Intangibles (net)	15.7	15.1	12.7	8.3	6.7	10.1
11.8	11.8	11.1	All Other Non-Current	12.0	11.5	11.8	12.4	7.9	9.7
100.0	100.0	100.0	Total	100.0	100.0	100.0	100.0	100.0	100.0
			LIABILITIES						
17.6	18.2	19.1	Notes Payable-Short Term	24.2	29.0	23.0	9.0	9.9	8.4
4.5	5.1	3.6	Cur. Mat.-L.T.D.	4.1	3.6	3.1	4.5	2.8	2.7
4.8	3.8	3.4	Trade Payables	2.2	1.7	1.4	6.6	3.8	7.5
.4	.2	.3	Income Taxes Payable	.3	.3	.4	.8	.0	.1
18.8	19.2	18.8	All Other Current	13.3	20.8	27.6	19.2	17.1	19.7
46.0	46.5	45.3	Total Current	44.1	55.3	55.5	40.1	33.6	38.4
16.6	17.0	18.6	Long-Term Debt	30.7	22.4	10.3	10.9	11.8	10.5
.2	.3	.2	Deferred Taxes	.0	.4	.3	.0	.4	.2
7.0	6.2	7.2	All Other Non-Current	5.8	9.8	5.8	6.4	6.2	8.0
30.3	29.9	28.8	Net Worth	19.4	11.9	28.0	42.6	48.0	43.0
100.0	100.0	100.0	Total Liabilities & Net Worth	100.0	100.0	100.0	100.0	100.0	100.0
			INCOME DATA						
100.0	100.0	100.0	Net Sales	100.0	100.0	100.0	100.0	100.0	100.0
			Gross Profit						
84.0	84.1	83.4	Operating Expenses	75.9	87.1	89.4	86.7	83.9	81.5
16.0	15.9	16.6	Operating Profit	24.1	12.9	10.6	13.3	16.1	18.5
2.8	2.7	2.6	All Other Expenses (net)	5.8	1.4	.8	1.4	1.8	2.7
13.2	13.3	13.9	Profit Before Taxes	18.3	11.6	9.8	11.9	14.3	15.7
			RATIOS						
3.5	3.8	4.0		3.1	3.6	4.0	4.7	4.7	4.0
1.7	1.6	1.7	Current	1.1	1.6	1.5	2.2	2.0	2.2
.8	.8	.9		.3	.8	.8	1.0	1.4	1.3
2.9	3.2	3.1		2.1	2.9	3.2	3.8	3.4	3.6
1.4	1.3 (838)	1.4	Quick	(206) .8	1.2	1.3	1.7	1.7	1.8
.6	.6	.7		.2	.6	.6	.8	1.1	1.0
0 UND	0 UND	0 UND		0 UND	0 UND	0 UND	24 15.0	34 10.7	37 9.8
45 8.2	41 8.9	41 8.9	Sales/Receivables	0 UND	38 9.7	46 8.0	51 7.1	53 6.9	57 6.4
74 4.9	68 5.3	69 5.3		35 10.6	74 5.0	72 5.1	77 4.7	68 5.3	76 4.8
			Cost of Sales/Inventory						
			Cost of Sales/Payables						
5.4	5.6	5.2		9.1	5.6	5.2	4.3	5.2	4.3
12.3	15.5	12.5	Sales/Working Capital	208.5	18.1	14.2	8.9	7.3	7.4
-78.3	-45.7	-102.7		-8.8	-35.7	-36.9	164.2	14.4	19.1
33.8	33.7	46.0		33.8	28.3	67.7	39.6	52.7	94.8
(642) 8.5	(657) 9.6	(662) 10.5	EBIT/Interest	(131) 8.9	(167) 6.6	(83) 14.8	(91) 9.2	(110) 11.6	(80) 23.2
2.2	2.0	2.3		3.1	1.8	2.0	1.8	2.2	5.1
6.9	8.1	6.8						12.5	6.7
(50) 1.9	(34) 3.2	(40) 3.2	Net Profit + Depr., Dep., Amort./Cur. Mat. L/T/D				(13) 3.0	(11) 5.5
1.0	.7	1.3						1.1	3.2
.1	.1	.1		.0	.0	.1	.1	.1	.1
.4	.3	.3	Fixed/Worth	1.0	.3	.3	.2	.3	.3
5.3	4.3	4.3		-271.4	-4.7	NM	1.2	.7	.6
.6	.5	.5		.7	.6	.4	.4	.5	.5
1.9	1.9	1.9	Debt/Worth	3.8	3.1	1.9	1.1	1.1	1.2
63.1	UND	-90.0		-4.5	-3.2	-17.6	6.3	3.6	7.0
143.1	151.6	152.9		409.6	150.9	91.3	142.7	146.1	125.2
(605) 58.8	(629) 57.5	(622) 63.7	% Profit Before Taxes/Tangible Net Worth	(140) 85.1	(123) 64.9	(68) 33.0	(97) 43.6	(114) 65.7	(80) 83.7
13.9	8.8	10.0		17.4	9.4	3.1	5.4	7.6	18.6
66.6	68.0	64.2		97.1	60.6	48.7	63.6	67.3	60.0
18.2	18.7	20.3	% Profit Before Taxes/Total Assets	26.3	23.5	14.6	13.5	26.7	34.9
3.2	2.0	2.6		6.2	2.5	1.4	1.3	1.6	4.5
80.1	120.5	110.8		450.0	448.0	132.8	76.5	53.2	46.2
29.9	31.4	33.3	Sales/Net Fixed Assets	30.3	50.5	42.7	36.6	28.1	25.3
15.4	15.1	16.1		5.9	17.8	23.8	18.9	13.6	17.9
4.5	5.0	4.7		5.8	6.0	6.4	4.2	3.6	3.5
2.9	3.0	2.9	Sales/Total Assets	2.5	3.1	3.1	2.9	2.9	2.7
2.0	1.9	1.9		1.2	1.9	2.1	2.2	2.2	2.0
.9	.9	.9		1.1	.7	.7	.7	1.1	1.0
(538) 1.5	(511) 1.6	(524) 1.5	% Depr., Dep., Amort./Sales	(104) 2.9	(99) 1.4	(58) 1.3	(85) 1.2	(102) 1.5	(76) 1.5
2.5	2.8	2.5		10.9	2.4	1.9	2.0	2.3	2.2
11.8	10.9	13.1		11.4	13.5	17.6	17.0	16.5	6.2
(375) 21.4	(406) 21.9	(438) 21.8	% Officers', Directors' Owners' Comp/Sales	(121) 19.0	(116) 13.0	(60) 25.6	(51) 27.2	(55) 23.3	(35) 17.5
30.3	31.7	31.1		26.3	31.8	34.1	33.5	30.0	30.6
15157413M	18739443M	18540903M	Net Sales ($)	105148M	354402M	375582M	849251M	1899535M	14956985M
5826677M	6881308M	6524767M	Total Assets ($)	84240M	185993M	145611M	345325M	852769M	4910829M

© RMA 2011

M = $ thousand   MM = $ million
See Pages 9 through 22 for Explanation of Ratios and Data

Current Data Sorted by Assets   Comparative Historical Data

						Type of Statement		
		2	4	2	2	Unqualified	8	8
		2	1	1		Reviewed	2	2
2	1		1			Compiled	3	4
4	2	4				Tax Returns	5	2
4	6	5	9		4	Other	5	10
	12 (4/1-9/30/10)		44 (10/1/10-3/31/11)				4/1/06-3/31/07	4/1/07-3/31/08
0-500M	500M-2MM	2-10MM	10-50MM	50-100MM	100-250MM		ALL	ALL
10	9	13	15	3	6	NUMBER OF STATEMENTS	23	26
%	%	%	%	%	%	ASSETS	%	%
25.9		57.9	15.4			Cash & Equivalents	34.5	32.9
23.0		21.2	13.5			Trade Receivables (net)	16.4	16.5
.0		1.5	.1			Inventory	.4	.1
19.0		9.5	31.0			All Other Current	15.2	23.3
67.9		90.2	59.9			Total Current	66.5	72.8
15.5		7.8	9.7			Fixed Assets (net)	9.4	11.7
1.4		.2	12.2			Intangibles (net)	9.0	8.9
15.4		1.8	18.1			All Other Non-Current	15.1	6.6
100.0		100.0	100.0			Total	100.0	100.0
						LIABILITIES		
35.2		6.1	9.8			Notes Payable-Short Term	15.8	9.5
.0		.3	2.0			Cur. Mat.-L.T.D.	.6	.4
3.4		2.2	1.5			Trade Payables	3.6	3.4
.0		.0	.0			Income Taxes Payable	1.2	.0
51.3		67.2	48.7			All Other Current	31.0	45.5
89.9		75.8	62.1			Total Current	52.1	58.8
13.3		.5	10.6			Long-Term Debt	17.1	20.6
.0		.2	.2			Deferred Taxes	.5	.1
.0		1.3	19.6			All Other Non-Current	10.7	4.2
-3.2		22.3	7.6			Net Worth	19.6	16.3
100.0		100.0	100.0			Total Liabilities & Net Worth	100.0	100.0
						INCOME DATA		
100.0		100.0	100.0			Net Sales	100.0	100.0
						Gross Profit		
91.9		101.2	92.4			Operating Expenses	101.9	93.9
8.1		-1.2	7.6			Operating Profit	-1.9	6.1
-.3		-.3	.7			All Other Expenses (net)	.6	2.7
8.4		-.9	7.0			Profit Before Taxes	-2.6	3.4
						RATIOS		
2.4		1.5	1.1				2.8	1.7
1.2		1.3	1.0			Current	1.2	1.1
.7		1.0	.9				1.0	1.0
1.2		1.5	1.0				2.7	1.5
.9		1.0	.8			Quick	1.2	1.0
.1		.7	.1				.3	.1
0 UND		0 UND	7 52.6				0 UND	1 503.3
1 390.9		30 12.3	10 35.4			Sales/Receivables	14 26.0	9 38.5
16 22.3		41 8.8	46 7.9				28 13.2	29 12.6
						Cost of Sales/Inventory		
						Cost of Sales/Payables		
13.7		9.1	22.5				5.8	3.2
240.0		21.2	-18.7			Sales/Working Capital	28.5	20.5
-95.5		NM	-8.5				-307.3	-37.1
			36.1				18.2	20.6
		(13) 3.7				EBIT/Interest	(16) 2.9	(17) 3.2
		1.2					-13.0	-3.8
						Net Profit + Depr., Dep., Amort./Cur. Mat. L/T/D		
.0		.0	.4				.1	.1
.1		.2	4.4			Fixed/Worth	1.4	.7
NM		.6	-.2				-1.2	-.9
1.0		1.2	8.4				.8	1.3
2.0		2.5	-119.8			Debt/Worth	12.6	13.7
-2.5		NM	-6.3				-30.3	-7.9
		58.4				% Profit Before Taxes/Tangible Net Worth	168.1	107.5
		(10) 24.1					(16) 29.2	(17) 20.2
		7.0					11.6	5.3
61.1		10.3	6.8			% Profit Before Taxes/Total Assets	23.5	9.4
20.3		4.3	5.3				7.0	2.9
4.3		-1.2	.2				-5.6	-4.0
UND		UND	117.2			Sales/Net Fixed Assets	447.7	87.1
UND		76.3	26.1				24.7	12.8
18.5		23.5	7.6				11.6	7.6
48.6		5.7	1.3			Sales/Total Assets	10.5	3.0
10.7		1.9	.4				1.3	.6
1.7		.4	.3				.3	.3
			.7			% Depr., Dep., Amort./Sales	.5	.9
		(13) 1.8					(15) 1.6	(14) 1.9
		4.0					3.5	3.8
						% Officers', Directors' Owners' Comp/Sales		
77620M	74510M	341955M	831919M	105272M	4288351M	Net Sales ($)	2747047M	2899234M
2300M	9783M	71758M	309871M	273623M	1126458M	Total Assets ($)	1068767M	1240071M

© RMA 2011

M = $ thousand   MM = $ million
See Pages 9 through 22 for Explanation of Ratios and Data

Comparative Historical Data

Current Data Sorted by Sales

			Type of Statement		12 (4/1-9/30/10)		44 (10/1/10-3/31/11)		
7	8	10	Unqualified			2		4	4
2	7	4	Reviewed					1	3
3	2	4	Compiled	1	2	1			
5	13	10	Tax Returns	5	1	1	1	2	
19	17	28	Other	4	3	3	4	5	9
4/1/08-3/31/09 ALL	4/1/09-3/31/10 ALL	4/1/10-3/31/11 ALL		0-1MM	1-3MM	3-5MM	5-10MM	10-25MM	25MM & OVER
36	47	56	NUMBER OF STATEMENTS	10	6	5	7	12	16
%	%	%	ASSETS	%	%	%	%	%	%
27.8	33.9	34.3	Cash & Equivalents	63.0				21.9	19.9
17.5	7.8	15.3	Trade Receivables (net)	1.7				29.3	22.7
.3	.4	.4	Inventory	.0				.4	1.1
21.1	23.8	20.8	All Other Current	.7				30.7	25.0
66.6	65.9	70.8	Total Current	65.4				82.2	68.7
10.1	13.4	8.3	Fixed Assets (net)	5.5				4.9	9.7
10.1	5.7	8.1	Intangibles (net)	1.5				10.4	14.0
13.2	14.9	12.9	All Other Non-Current	27.9				2.5	7.6
100.0	100.0	100.0	Total	100.0				100.0	100.0
			LIABILITIES						
11.6	14.7	10.4	Notes Payable-Short Term	6.3				13.0	3.4
5.5	1.8	.7	Cur. Mat.-L.T.D.	.0				1.1	1.5
5.0	3.7	2.2	Trade Payables	1.9				3.5	2.3
.1	2.6	.6	Income Taxes Payable	.3				.0	.0
47.6	45.8	57.0	All Other Current	86.1				44.8	57.7
69.9	68.6	70.9	Total Current	94.6				62.4	65.0
13.8	8.6	7.6	Long-Term Debt	1.4				8.7	11.3
.1	.1	.1	Deferred Taxes	.0				.2	.0
12.3	15.8	6.1	All Other Non-Current	.7				3.5	2.4
3.9	6.9	15.3	Net Worth	3.3				25.1	21.3
100.0	100.0	100.0	Total Liabilities & Net Worth	100.0				100.0	100.0
			INCOME DATA						
100.0	100.0	100.0	Net Sales	100.0				100.0	100.0
			Gross Profit						
96.6	93.5	94.8	Operating Expenses	90.2				99.4	99.5
3.4	6.5	5.2	Operating Profit	9.8				.6	.5
.9	1.4	.5	All Other Expenses (net)	-.2				.6	1.2
2.5	5.1	4.7	Profit Before Taxes	10.0				.1	-.7
			RATIOS						
1.8	1.8	1.5	Current	1.1				2.7	1.4
1.3	1.0	1.0		1.0				1.0	1.1
1.0	1.0	.9		.4				.9	1.0
1.5	1.7	1.3	Quick	1.1				2.6	1.1
1.0	1.0	.9		1.0				.9	.8
.3	.1	.2		.4				.1	.1
3 130.5	0 UND	0 UND	Sales/Receivables	0 UND			7 54.3		2 166.5
9 42.4	1 325.4	7 50.7		0 UND			12 29.8		10 35.6
26 14.1	11 32.9	34 10.7		0 UND			34 10.7		45 8.0
			Cost of Sales/Inventory						
			Cost of Sales/Payables						
9.5	8.8	10.8	Sales/Working Capital	9.9				9.8	16.1
77.9	47.4	131.5		-31.9				87.4	170.3
-26.4	-16.5	-16.5		-.5				-127.1	NM
19.5	15.0	28.7	EBIT/Interest						32.1
(27) 1.3	(32) 5.8	(33) 3.1						(11)	3.1
-3.9	-1.7	-.1							-1.6
			Net Profit + Depr., Dep., Amort./Cur. Mat. L/T/D						
.1	.0	.0	Fixed/Worth	.0				.0	.2
2.0	.8	.5		.0				.3	.8
-.3	-.8	-2.1		UND				NM	NM
3.2	2.3	1.8	Debt/Worth	1.8				.7	2.0
57.0	23.1	12.1		UND				17.5	11.1
-5.6	-30.4	-21.0		-55.1				-7.6	NM
117.1	205.5	90.1	% Profit Before Taxes/Tangible Net Worth						108.7
(24) 51.9	(32) 42.7	(37) 27.3						(12)	21.6
-9.6	12.8	7.2							1.7
18.7	16.6	10.0	% Profit Before Taxes/Total Assets	9.7				7.7	11.6
2.9	5.3	4.7		5.2				3.1	4.0
-2.1	.2	.1		-1.5				-1.9	.0
598.5	303.0	885.2	Sales/Net Fixed Assets	UND				UND	845.4
26.0	30.9	45.5		UND				281.9	19.8
9.9	8.5	13.4		29.4				14.8	5.7
14.9	9.5	5.9	Sales/Total Assets	.9				14.2	21.9
1.6	1.4	.9		.3				1.7	2.2
.3	.3	.3		.3				1.1	.3
.2	.5	.3	% Depr., Dep., Amort./Sales						.1
(24) 1.1	(24) 1.4	(36) 1.4						(11)	1.5
3.9	2.8	2.9							11.5
	2.1	3.5	% Officers', Directors' Owners' Comp/Sales						
	(13) 8.2	(12) 7.7							
	12.7	14.5							
4249877M	4541762M	5719627M	Net Sales ($)	4270M	10148M	18443M	53034M	200935M	5432797M
1621390M	1920120M	1793793M	Total Assets ($)	12392M	9382M	67397M	108651M	297264M	1298707M

© RMA 2011

M = $ thousand   MM = $ million
See Pages 9 through 22 for Explanation of Ratios and Data

Current Data Sorted by Assets | **Comparative Historical Data**

0-500M	500M-2MM	2-10MM	10-50MM	50-100MM	100-250MM	Type of Statement	4/1/06-3/31/07 ALL	4/1/07-3/31/08 ALL
	3	7	7	1	5	Unqualified	9	9
	3	1	2			Reviewed	2	9
1	7	1				Compiled	8	18
32	13	2	1			Tax Returns	42	30
29	16	27	9	4	4	Other	75	66
	19 (4/1-9/30/10)		156 (10/1/10-3/31/11)					
62	42	38	19	5	9	NUMBER OF STATEMENTS	136	132
%	%	%	%	%	%	ASSETS	%	%
29.6	21.2	18.1	24.6			Cash & Equivalents	21.3	22.2
9.1	29.4	33.9	23.3			Trade Receivables (net)	25.5	22.6
.1	1.9	4.6	.6			Inventory	2.8	2.9
8.8	5.2	11.1	10.6			All Other Current	5.9	8.1
47.6	57.6	67.7	59.1			Total Current	55.4	55.8
20.0	20.2	13.6	11.2			Fixed Assets (net)	20.0	20.4
13.3	10.8	8.1	10.0			Intangibles (net)	9.9	9.6
19.2	11.4	10.6	19.6			All Other Non-Current	14.6	14.2
100.0	100.0	100.0	100.0			Total	100.0	100.0
						LIABILITIES		
33.6	19.0	5.5	10.7			Notes Payable-Short Term	14.9	15.3
2.3	2.9	2.8	2.3			Cur. Mat.-L.T.D.	3.1	5.2
4.7	4.2	6.8	10.9			Trade Payables	6.0	5.8
.0	1.0	.3	.7			Income Taxes Payable	.6	.8
30.9	18.5	29.5	39.8			All Other Current	22.3	22.3
71.5	45.6	45.0	64.3			Total Current	46.9	49.4
19.5	18.9	12.7	9.4			Long-Term Debt	15.0	17.8
.0	.6	.4	.7			Deferred Taxes	.2	.2
11.2	3.0	4.3	11.9			All Other Non-Current	6.8	11.7
-2.2	31.9	37.6	13.7			Net Worth	31.1	21.0
100.0	100.0	100.0	100.0			Total Liabilities & Net Worth	100.0	100.0
						INCOME DATA		
100.0	100.0	100.0	100.0			Net Sales	100.0	100.0
						Gross Profit		
85.3	86.2	89.3	88.8			Operating Expenses	86.2	88.8
14.7	13.8	10.7	11.2			Operating Profit	13.8	11.2
.8	1.7	.7	1.1			All Other Expenses (net)	1.9	.3
13.9	12.1	10.0	10.1			Profit Before Taxes	11.9	10.8
						RATIOS		
1.8	3.3	3.1	1.6				2.9	2.6
.7	1.7	1.7	1.0			Current	1.4	1.3
.3	.5	1.2	.5				.7	.6
1.5	3.3	2.8	1.4				2.3	2.3
.6	1.4	1.5	.9			Quick	1.1	1.1
.1	.4	.8	.4				.6	.4
0 UND	0 UND	0 UND	4 91.6				0 UND	0 UND
0 UND	13 27.1	43 8.4	38 9.5			Sales/Receivables	25 14.5	25 14.8
1 295.9	69 5.3	75 4.8	59 6.2				56 6.5	50 7.3
						Cost of Sales/Inventory		
						Cost of Sales/Payables		
31.8	5.3	6.0	5.0				7.3	7.6
-77.0	14.9	10.1	-104.4			Sales/Working Capital	32.0	20.1
-8.9	-12.6	18.6	-3.1				-23.1	-25.6
26.8	38.0	50.5	8.9				23.7	17.5
(36) 6.0	(33) 13.0	(28) 7.1	(14) 4.1			EBIT/Interest	(92) 5.9	(104) 4.5
-2.0	1.7	2.6	2.5				1.5	1.3
						Net Profit + Depr., Dep., Amort./Cur. Mat. L/T/D	(10) 3.8 / 1.5 / -1.2	
.0	.1	.1	.1				.1	.2
.5	.3	.3	1.2			Fixed/Worth	.4	.6
-2.1	-2.2	1.0	-.9				6.4	19.2
1.0	.5	.6	3.9				.5	1.0
UND	1.7	1.3	7.6			Debt/Worth	2.6	3.0
-1.9	-9.0	10.2	-12.1				-21.5	-21.0
715.0	103.6	97.8	69.0				109.7	143.8
(33) 96.7	(28) 54.8	(32) 39.6	(13) 46.2			% Profit Before Taxes/Tangible Net Worth	(100) 62.1	(97) 61.0
23.4	23.1	17.0	17.6				11.9	10.6
92.1	49.4	29.1	17.7				50.7	48.0
26.6	20.2	11.2	6.0			% Profit Before Taxes/Total Assets	14.3	14.9
-.8	5.1	4.1	3.2				2.2	1.1
UND	115.9	143.6	67.8				92.1	90.7
84.6	40.9	36.4	24.2			Sales/Net Fixed Assets	28.3	21.0
12.4	9.5	19.6	5.7				10.9	11.4
9.9	4.4	3.7	2.5				5.0	5.2
5.4	3.2	2.8	1.1			Sales/Total Assets	2.8	2.9
2.8	1.9	1.5	.5				1.6	1.5
1.1	.3	.6	.7				.9	1.0
(20) 1.7	(28) .9	(29) 1.2	(16) 1.4			% Depr., Dep., Amort./Sales	(79) 1.3	(85) 1.6
3.5	3.4	1.9	3.8				3.5	2.7
8.0	3.4	1.1					5.2	4.5
(34) 12.0	(19) 6.7	(13) 4.8				% Officers', Directors' Owners' Comp/Sales	(49) 9.0	(46) 13.0
26.1	16.3	23.2					18.9	20.3
56332M	167687M	667010M	765726M	430666M	5343736M	Net Sales ($)	4109536M	1844282M
9047M	46731M	182343M	424251M	286793M	1462039M	Total Assets ($)	1413177M	1215294M

M = $ thousand   MM = $ million
See Pages 9 through 22 for Explanation of Ratios and Data

Comparative Historical Data | **Current Data Sorted by Sales**

	4/1/08-3/31/09 ALL	4/1/09-3/31/10 ALL	4/1/10-3/31/11 ALL	Type of Statement	0-1MM	1-3MM	3-5MM	5-10MM	10-25MM	25MM & OVER
	20	18	23	Unqualified	1	2	2	1	6	13
	8	11	6	Reviewed		3		1		
	16	7	9	Compiled	2		2	2		1
	40	63	48	Tax Returns	24	13	5	5	1	
	81	82	89	Other	22	19	7	14	10	17
						19 (4/1-9/30/10)			156 (10/1/10-3/31/11)	
NUMBER OF STATEMENTS	165	181	175		49	36	19	23	18	30
	%	%	%	**ASSETS**	%	%	%	%	%	%
	22.1	23.9	23.1	Cash & Equivalents	27.9	26.2	24.7	17.6	24.2	14.0
	24.8	21.8	22.1	Trade Receivables (net)	6.2	15.8	30.0	36.8	29.7	34.9
	2.9	1.4	1.7	Inventory	.1	.8	2.2	2.3	3.5	3.5
	7.0	6.2	8.6	All Other Current	9.9	8.0	5.6	9.9	7.6	8.7
	56.8	53.2	55.5	Total Current	44.1	50.9	62.6	66.7	64.9	61.1
	18.5	19.1	17.0	Fixed Assets (net)	24.6	13.7	19.4	11.7	17.2	11.2
	12.3	12.3	13.2	Intangibles (net)	15.4	12.9	8.0	7.3	5.2	22.8
	12.4	15.4	14.2	All Other Non-Current	15.9	22.5	10.0	14.4	12.6	4.9
	100.0	100.0	100.0	Total	100.0	100.0	100.0	100.0	100.0	100.0
				LIABILITIES						
	15.5	12.9	19.1	Notes Payable-Short Term	24.3	33.1	15.8	16.7	3.2	7.2
	3.0	4.9	2.5	Cur. Mat.-L.T.D.	1.8	2.8	3.5	2.9	3.4	1.9
	7.2	6.2	5.8	Trade Payables	4.3	3.4	6.1	2.3	6.1	13.4
	.3	.3	.4	Income Taxes Payable	.0	.1	2.2	.0	.7	.5
	22.8	25.0	28.1	All Other Current	32.7	30.3	13.0	29.0	29.1	26.0
	49.0	49.3	55.9	Total Current	63.1	69.8	40.6	50.9	42.5	49.0
	14.8	21.2	16.9	Long-Term Debt	17.6	22.4	14.2	13.1	16.0	14.3
	.2	.2	.4	Deferred Taxes	.0	.1	.0	.9	.6	.9
	8.9	16.4	7.8	All Other Non-Current	5.6	9.8	6.7	3.3	12.7	10.5
	27.1	12.9	19.0	Net Worth	13.7	-2.1	38.6	31.8	28.1	25.2
	100.0	100.0	100.0	Total Liabilities & Net Worth	100.0	100.0	100.0	100.0	100.0	100.0
				INCOME DATA						
	100.0	100.0	100.0	Net Sales	100.0	100.0	100.0	100.0	100.0	100.0
				Gross Profit						
	90.0	87.9	87.2	Operating Expenses	80.4	92.0	86.3	84.3	93.8	91.1
	10.0	12.1	12.8	Operating Profit	19.6	8.0	13.7	15.7	6.2	8.9
	1.7	1.3	1.2	All Other Expenses (net)	1.0	.3	2.5	1.8	.8	1.5
	8.4	10.8	11.7	Profit Before Taxes	18.6	7.7	11.2	14.0	5.4	7.4
				RATIOS						
	2.4	3.2	2.5	Current	1.4	2.4	3.2	4.3	4.0	1.6
	1.3	1.2	1.2		.7	1.1	1.9	1.5	2.4	1.2
	.7	.6	.6		.3	.2	.8	.9	1.4	1.0
	2.1	2.8	2.1	Quick	1.2	1.8	3.2	2.8	3.5	1.3
	1.1	1.0	1.0		.6	.9	1.9	1.5	1.9	1.1
	.5	.4	.4		.1	.2	.4	.3	.9	.7
0	UND	0 UND	0 UND	Sales/Receivables	0 UND	0 UND	0 UND	0 999.8	5 70.7	37 9.9
21	17.0	13 27.1	8 47.1		0 UND	0 UND	9 40.9	40 9.2	38 9.6	50 7.3
49	7.5	54 6.7	51 7.1		2 212.8	34 10.7	90 4.1	78 4.7	54 6.8	72 5.1
				Cost of Sales/Inventory						
				Cost of Sales/Payables						
	8.3	6.2	7.6	Sales/Working Capital	31.0	9.5	5.2	6.3	5.0	8.9
	29.5	38.5	34.8		-29.5	112.9	17.5	10.2	7.9	22.8
	-24.6	-16.1	-20.2		-5.1	-14.2	-28.4	-54.8	15.4	441.6
	18.9	22.6	28.6	EBIT/Interest	23.0	16.9	34.0	31.9	48.7	24.9
(118)	4.9	(122) 5.6	(124) 7.3		(27) 7.0	(23) 2.8	(16) 13.0	(19) 14.0	(13) 4.9	(26) 5.6
	1.3	1.2	1.8		1.7	-2.2	2.1	7.4	1.9	2.0
	6.5	4.2	14.8	Net Profit + Depr., Dep., Amort./Cur. Mat. L/T/D						
(14)	1.8	(12) 3.1	(15) 6.6							
	.9	1.1	2.3							
	.1	.1	.1	Fixed/Worth	.0	.0	.1	.1	.1	.3
	.5	.7	.5		.5	.2	.2	.2	.6	2.4
	37.7	UND	-2.5		UND	-.6	3.4	-1.1	NM	-.3
	1.0	.7	.8	Debt/Worth	.9	1.0	.4	.6	.7	2.2
	5.0	4.6	4.8		10.2	9.4	1.3	2.0	2.2	8.7
	-21.6	-9.4	-4.3		-1.9	-2.3	-12.8	-12.1	NM	-3.9
	102.6	122.5	125.3	% Profit Before Taxes/Tangible Net Worth	710.0	99.8	113.7	194.3	66.2	98.5
(117)	48.7	(129) 49.2	(111) 55.1		(27) 84.5	(23) 47.3	(14) 75.2	(17) 55.1	(14) 28.2	(16) 66.6
	5.4	13.6	21.4		23.9	-2.3	54.4	26.4	15.3	26.7
	42.4	38.8	47.6	% Profit Before Taxes/Total Assets	93.4	27.7	63.8	64.7	19.7	19.5
	7.5	11.7	13.3		27.0	5.5	27.2	16.7	10.2	11.4
	.5	.6	3.2		4.4	-7.9	5.0	10.1	3.7	3.4
	84.2	86.6	177.0	Sales/Net Fixed Assets	UND	479.7	86.6	108.8	148.2	56.4
	24.6	23.5	37.7		27.5	99.3	33.5	63.3	32.7	29.4
	10.8	9.8	11.7		7.2	19.7	14.3	20.6	8.3	11.1
	5.7	5.0	5.3	Sales/Total Assets	6.1	9.3	3.9	4.5	4.7	3.7
	2.6	2.5	3.0		3.2	3.3	3.0	3.5	2.9	2.0
	1.3	1.1	1.5		1.3	1.4	2.0	2.0	1.7	1.3
	1.0	.9	.7	% Depr., Dep., Amort./Sales	1.2	.6	.6	.6	.8	.4
(103)	1.7	(102) 1.4	(101) 1.4		(20) 2.8	(13) 1.7	(12) 1.1	(19) 1.0	(16) 1.3	(21) 1.3
	2.6	2.8	3.1		3.9	3.5	3.2	1.5	2.1	3.1
	3.6	8.9	4.7	% Officers', Directors' Owners' Comp/Sales	8.4	6.0		3.7		
(49)	11.2	(66) 17.8	(71) 9.8		(24) 12.0	(15) 12.7		(13) 6.7		
	22.3	30.5	25.2		29.1	22.9		10.0		
	6529696M	6112608M	7431157M	Net Sales ($)	19679M	65359M	74631M	161506M	298970M	6811012M
	2418742M	2678154M	2411204M	Total Assets ($)	12592M	52729M	50311M	104333M	123600M	2067639M

M = $ thousand   MM = $ million
See Pages 9 through 22 for Explanation of Ratios and Data

Current Data Sorted by Assets | Comparative Historical Data

Type of Statement	0-500M	500M-2MM	2-10MM	10-50MM	50-100MM	100-250MM	4/1/06-3/31/07 ALL	4/1/07-3/31/08 ALL
Unqualified	3	1	11	21	3	5	36	28
Reviewed		11	73	37	4	1	102	104
Compiled	20	35	33	3			83	74
Tax Returns	72	43	14				91	90
Other	53	58	72	22	4	3	180	190
		53 (4/1-9/30/10)		549 (10/1/10-3/31/11)				
NUMBER OF STATEMENTS	148	148	203	83	11	9	492	486
ASSETS	%	%	%	%	%	%	%	%
Cash & Equivalents	28.6	17.4	10.7	12.1	19.8		14.4	14.3
Trade Receivables (net)	18.6	37.9	51.0	50.7	35.2		45.5	45.2
Inventory	.6	2.1	2.7	1.1	.0		2.1	2.1
All Other Current	6.7	5.8	8.1	10.2	20.7		7.0	5.9
Total Current	54.5	63.2	72.5	74.1	75.7		69.0	67.5
Fixed Assets (net)	29.3	21.8	17.3	14.2	11.2		18.8	19.4
Intangibles (net)	3.3	3.8	2.9	3.1	5.2		2.8	2.9
All Other Non-Current	12.9	11.2	7.3	8.6	7.9		9.4	10.1
Total	100.0	100.0	100.0	100.0	100.0		100.0	100.0
LIABILITIES								
Notes Payable-Short Term	38.1	12.5	7.8	6.4	1.7		15.3	16.0
Cur. Mat.-L.T.D.	4.9	2.4	2.2	1.9	1.6		3.6	3.8
Trade Payables	10.8	14.9	17.5	16.3	12.4		14.2	15.2
Income Taxes Payable	.0	1.6	2.8	2.5	2.6		2.1	1.7
All Other Current	32.3	13.3	14.6	23.0	34.9		20.4	19.3
Total Current	86.0	44.7	44.9	50.1	53.1		55.6	56.0
Long-Term Debt	15.9	12.4	8.0	7.1	4.0		10.3	10.6
Deferred Taxes	.0	.7	1.4	.9	.5		1.1	1.1
All Other Non-Current	18.8	6.5	3.4	5.4	3.4		4.6	7.2
Net Worth	-20.7	35.7	42.3	36.6	39.0		28.4	25.1
Total Liabilities & Net Worth	100.0	100.0	100.0	100.0	100.0		100.0	100.0
INCOME DATA								
Net Sales	100.0	100.0	100.0	100.0	100.0		100.0	100.0
Gross Profit								
Operating Expenses	94.8	94.3	94.2	96.4	94.7		92.1	91.7
Operating Profit	5.2	5.7	5.8	3.6	5.3		7.9	8.3
All Other Expenses (net)	1.1	1.8	2.0	.6	.5		.9	1.1
Profit Before Taxes	4.1	3.8	3.8	3.0	4.8		6.9	7.2
RATIOS								
Current	4.3	2.9	2.7	2.0	1.9		2.3	2.3
	1.0	1.5	1.6	1.5	1.3		1.5	1.5
	.2	.9	1.2	1.2	1.2		1.0	1.0
Quick	3.3	2.3	2.2	1.7	1.4		2.1	2.2
	.8	1.3	1.3	1.3	1.0		1.3	1.3
	.1	.7	1.0	.9	.7		.8	.8
Sales/Receivables	0 UND	0 UND	58 6.3	64 5.7	53 6.8		21 17.3	7 52.5
	0 UND	46 8.0	81 4.5	81 4.5	59 6.1		70 5.2	71 5.1
	37 9.9	86 4.3	105 3.5	131 2.8	88 4.2		98 3.7	103 3.6
Cost of Sales/Inventory								
Cost of Sales/Payables								
Sales/Working Capital	10.2	6.8	4.8	4.9	5.1		6.4	5.9
	237.1	13.6	8.6	8.6	7.8		13.1	13.2
	-13.8	-54.1	25.4	23.6	16.8		999.8	-207.7
EBIT/Interest	19.7	20.8	31.4	23.1			31.2	30.5
	(95) 5.9	(114) 3.0	(163) 5.1	(73) 7.4			(392) 11.2	(388) 9.0
	-2.0	-6.7	-.9	.8			2.6	2.5
Net Profit + Depr., Dep., Amort./Cur. Mat. L/T/D		4.1	4.2	7.6			6.5	7.5
		(13) 1.5	(51) 2.1	(27) 2.7			(96) 2.7	(92) 3.5
		-2.1	.3	1.1			1.3	1.2
Fixed/Worth	.2	.2	.2	.1	.2		.2	.1
	1.1	.5	.3	.3	.4		.4	.4
	-.7	3.1	.7	.6	.5		1.5	1.3
Debt/Worth	.5	.5	.7	1.3	1.2		.8	.7
	3.8	1.6	1.5	2.1	1.6		1.9	1.9
	-2.7	10.5	3.4	4.3	6.2		6.0	7.8
% Profit Before Taxes/Tangible Net Worth	137.1	62.8	39.2	35.8	60.3		73.7	77.7
	(86) 49.3	(117) 16.5	(190) 12.6	(81) 19.1	18.9		(413) 35.2	(411) 35.3
	-1.4	-9.8	-4.9	.9	9.7		10.8	12.6
% Profit Before Taxes/Total Assets	63.1	20.7	18.0	10.4	12.2		31.5	35.2
	14.0	3.5	3.9	3.7	4.2		12.4	12.5
	-12.7	-7.0	-2.2	-.1	1.7		2.3	3.1
Sales/Net Fixed Assets	109.2	59.7	38.5	37.6	30.3		48.8	65.7
	34.3	23.9	22.3	20.7	22.2		25.8	27.6
	13.8	10.2	11.3	10.8	9.5		14.3	13.5
Sales/Total Assets	10.6	4.0	3.0	2.5	2.4		4.2	4.3
	5.0	2.8	2.3	1.9	1.8		2.8	2.7
	3.4	1.9	1.7	1.5	1.0		2.0	2.1
% Depr., Dep., Amort./Sales	.4	.8	1.0	.8			.8	.7
	(83) 1.0	(101) 1.4	(168) 1.6	(73) 1.6			(362) 1.3	(372) 1.2
	1.9	2.6	2.4	2.6			1.9	1.9
% Officers', Directors' Owners' Comp/Sales	8.1	4.7	2.6	2.3			5.4	6.2
	(95) 13.6	(79) 9.7	(49) 6.4	(22) 3.7			(223) 10.5	(208) 11.6
	22.3	16.5	13.0	10.0			18.0	19.2
Net Sales ($)	238344M	518917M	2287033M	3467148M	1392800M	2876387M	12853282M	7474408M
Total Assets ($)	34262M	167467M	976134M	1779283M	738129M	1545593M	4734898M	3373499M

M = $ thousand   MM = $ million
See Pages 9 through 22 for Explanation of Ratios and Data

Comparative Historical Data   Current Data Sorted by Sales

Hist 1	Hist 2	Hist 3		0-1MM	1-3MM	3-5MM	5-10MM	10-25MM	25MM & OVER
			Type of Statement						
39	42	41	Unqualified	2	4	7	2	10	29
127	112	129	Reviewed	13	20	17	33	54	29
96	99	91	Compiled	39	52	20	22	16	3
112	127	129	Tax Returns	42	49	24	13	5	
221	222	212	Other				34	37	26
4/1/08-3/31/09 ALL	4/1/09-3/31/10 ALL	4/1/10-3/31/11 ALL		53 (4/1-9/30/10)			549 (10/1/10-3/31/11)		
595	602	602	**NUMBER OF STATEMENTS**	96	125	68	104	122	87
%	%	%	**ASSETS**	%	%	%	%	%	%
15.2	16.4	17.2	Cash & Equivalents	21.2	21.7	21.2	14.6	11.4	14.4
45.2	40.5	39.3	Trade Receivables (net)	22.6	28.6	33.1	49.4	51.9	48.1
2.5	1.5	1.7	Inventory	.8	1.2	3.4	1.9	2.7	.7
6.1	6.7	7.9	All Other Current	7.7	5.3	5.2	6.4	9.6	13.3
69.1	65.2	66.1	Total Current	52.3	56.8	62.9	72.2	75.7	76.5
19.0	21.5	20.8	Fixed Assets (net)	32.8	26.5	21.8	16.6	14.6	12.2
2.2	3.1	3.3	Intangibles (net)	4.2	4.0	3.3	2.7	2.5	3.3
9.7	10.2	9.8	All Other Non-Current	10.7	12.7	12.0	8.5	7.3	8.1
100.0	100.0	100.0	Total	100.0	100.0	100.0	100.0	100.0	100.0
			LIABILITIES						
15.0	18.8	16.0	Notes Payable-Short Term	25.9	25.6	20.7	9.7	8.9	5.1
3.2	3.4	2.9	Cur. Mat.-L.T.D.	3.8	4.9	2.1	1.7	2.0	2.0
15.8	14.5	14.9	Trade Payables	9.7	12.5	16.0	15.8	19.0	16.5
1.6	1.9	1.8	Income Taxes Payable	.0	.4	1.5	1.9	3.8	2.6
19.6	19.5	20.4	All Other Current	29.2	16.9	14.9	17.6	17.2	28.0
55.3	58.2	55.9	Total Current	68.7	60.4	55.1	46.7	50.9	54.2
10.1	11.1	10.8	Long-Term Debt	18.8	17.1	9.0	7.4	6.1	4.9
1.2	1.0	.8	Deferred Taxes	.0	.2	1.2	1.3	1.3	.7
4.8	5.9	8.3	All Other Non-Current	10.1	8.2	15.2	6.1	7.0	5.1
28.6	23.7	24.2	Net Worth	2.4	14.1	19.5	38.4	34.6	35.0
100.0	100.0	100.0	Total Liabilities & Net Worth	100.0	100.0	100.0	100.0	100.0	100.0
			INCOME DATA						
100.0	100.0	100.0	Net Sales	100.0	100.0	100.0	100.0	100.0	100.0
			Gross Profit						
93.8	97.2	94.7	Operating Expenses	89.4	92.9	97.3	98.0	96.1	95.4
6.2	2.8	5.3	Operating Profit	10.6	7.1	2.7	2.0	3.9	4.6
1.4	1.7	1.5	All Other Expenses (net)	5.4	1.2	-.2	.9	.7	.7
4.8	1.1	3.8	Profit Before Taxes	5.2	5.9	2.9	1.0	3.2	4.0
			RATIOS						
2.4	2.4	2.6	Current	4.2	2.8	4.0	3.2	2.3	1.8
1.5	1.4	1.4		1.1	1.1	1.5	2.0	1.5	1.3
.9	.9	1.0		.4	.6	.9	1.2	1.2	1.2
2.1	2.2	2.2	Quick	3.1	2.2	3.9	2.9	1.8	1.6
1.3	(601) 1.2	1.2		.8	1.0	1.3	1.6	1.3	1.2
.7	.7	.8		.2	.4	.6	1.0	1.0	.9
14 26.5	0 UND	0 UND	Sales/Receivables	0 UND	0 UND	0 UND	43 8.5	57 6.4	58 6.3
69 5.3	63 5.8	60 6.0		0 UND	32 11.5	38 9.6	75 4.9	79 4.6	74 4.9
104 3.5	102 3.6	91 4.0		49 7.4	75 4.9	90 4.1	113 3.2	101 3.6	93 3.9
			Cost of Sales/Inventory						
			Cost of Sales/Payables						
5.8	5.6	5.7	Sales/Working Capital	5.5	6.8	7.0	4.5	5.7	6.3
13.2	13.7	12.8		73.1	46.6	12.3	8.2	10.8	11.2
-130.3	-54.0	-234.2		-11.4	-16.5	-66.1	38.9	24.8	25.2
30.7	19.4	21.3	EBIT/Interest	9.8	20.0	22.5	21.1	28.5	40.4
(475) 7.2	(473) 2.3	(463) 5.3		(54) 2.7	(94) 7.2	(54) 1.0	(78) 2.3	(109) 7.5	(74) 7.9
1.1	-8.6	-1.9		-2.9	-1.1	-7.7	-7.4	-.5	2.2
9.8	5.9	5.5	Net Profit + Depr., Dep., Amort./Cur. Mat. L/T/D				4.0	8.7	7.0
(123) 3.3	(123) 1.6	(105) 2.5				(20) 2.1	(40) 2.5	(33) 3.3	
1.3	-1.1	.5					.4	.2	1.5
.2	.1	.2	Fixed/Worth	.1	.2	.2	.1	.2	.2
.4	.4	.4		1.2	.6	.4	.3	.3	.4
1.4	2.4	1.4		-1.6	UND	1.7	.6	.6	.6
.7	.7	.7	Debt/Worth	.4	.7	.5	.5	.8	1.3
2.0	1.9	1.9		2.9	2.4	1.9	1.1	1.9	2.3
6.6	7.3	7.0		-6.1	-17.3	7.1	3.3	3.4	4.4
71.0	47.6	52.0	% Profit Before Taxes/Tangible Net Worth	86.4	91.8	65.1	38.3	38.9	43.7
(504) 26.5	(496) 11.2	(494) 16.7		(63) 15.6	(90) 25.0	(53) 20.6	(89) 7.7	(115) 13.8	(84) 22.2
3.8	-20.6	-4.9		.0	-6.6	-10.9	-17.0	-2.0	3.8
24.8	17.6	21.7	% Profit Before Taxes/Total Assets	25.7	40.0	21.5	18.9	16.1	12.4
7.9	2.4	5.2		4.4	11.2	3.7	1.1	5.1	5.1
.5	-11.8	-3.4		-11.1	-4.4	-9.2	-6.6	-.9	1.3
61.1	54.6	54.7	Sales/Net Fixed Assets	66.6	93.3	57.3	57.1	39.9	36.7
25.9	23.4	23.4		19.6	24.1	22.8	26.8	22.9	22.8
14.1	10.9	11.3		6.4	11.1	10.0	13.2	13.8	11.3
4.3	4.3	3.9	Sales/Total Assets	4.7	5.4	6.2	3.5	3.3	3.0
2.7	2.6	2.6		3.0	3.1	3.3	2.5	2.4	2.2
2.0	1.7	1.8		.9	1.9	2.4	1.8	1.9	1.6
.8	.7	.8	% Depr., Dep., Amort./Sales	.8	.5	.6	1.0	.8	1.0
(427) 1.4	(453) 1.5	(442) 1.5		(54) 2.0	(83) 1.5	(47) 1.2	(81) 1.5	(102) 1.5	(75) 1.5
2.2	2.5	2.4		9.3	2.9	1.6	2.2	2.3	2.3
4.9	6.4	4.5	% Officers', Directors' Owners' Comp/Sales	8.1	5.8	7.0	3.5	1.3	3.0
(244) 10.7	(249) 12.4	(249) 9.6		(47) 15.0	(73) 12.3	(37) 9.6	(36) 8.5	(37) 4.0	(19) 6.3
18.2	19.5	17.9		24.7	19.1	16.4	14.5	11.1	15.4
14120626M	9757855M	10780629M	Net Sales ($)	53667M	243132M	270428M	754878M	1936508M	7522016M
5633092M	4513410M	5240868M	Total Assets ($)	50911M	106097M	98485M	347389M	893164M	3744822M

M = $ thousand   MM = $ million
See Pages 9 through 22 for Explanation of Ratios and Data

Current Data Sorted by Assets　　　　　　　Comparative Historical Data

	0-500M	500M-2MM	2-10MM	10-50MM	50-100MM	100-250MM	Type of Statement	7	7
			2	8	1		Unqualified		
	3	7	18	4	1		Reviewed	37	26
	4	8	3			1	Compiled	39	25
	27	19	5			1	Tax Returns	38	33
	21	27	11	5			Other	61	57
		18 (4/1-9/30/10)		158 (10/1/10-3/31/11)				4/1/06-3/31/07 ALL	4/1/07-3/31/08 ALL
NUMBER OF STATEMENTS	55	61	39	17	2	2		182	148
	%	%	%	%	%	%	ASSETS	%	%
	21.8	14.3	9.3	17.2			Cash & Equivalents	10.3	11.9
	19.7	34.3	37.1	32.7			Trade Receivables (net)	33.3	30.9
	6.1	9.1	4.9	8.2			Inventory	7.3	6.7
	3.5	3.8	6.1	4.6			All Other Current	3.0	4.0
	51.1	61.4	57.3	62.6			Total Current	54.0	53.6
	34.6	25.1	32.6	23.5			Fixed Assets (net)	36.5	33.9
	2.2	2.8	4.0	4.5			Intangibles (net)	3.0	4.2
	12.2	10.6	6.1	9.3			All Other Non-Current	6.5	8.4
	100.0	100.0	100.0	100.0			Total	100.0	100.0
							LIABILITIES		
	26.1	15.3	8.9	4.2			Notes Payable-Short Term	14.7	11.4
	5.3	4.9	4.8	3.3			Cur. Mat.-L.T.D.	6.2	7.2
	12.3	13.2	12.6	7.9			Trade Payables	13.3	13.4
	.0	.1	.9	3.3			Income Taxes Payable	.8	.5
	14.9	6.6	7.8	23.1			All Other Current	9.4	14.1
	58.7	40.3	34.9	41.7			Total Current	44.4	46.5
	29.4	17.6	16.9	13.9			Long-Term Debt	24.0	22.6
	.0	.2	.0	.1			Deferred Taxes	.7	.5
	8.9	5.6	5.6	5.0			All Other Non-Current	5.7	3.0
	2.9	36.3	42.5	39.3			Net Worth	25.2	27.5
	100.0	100.0	100.0	100.0			Total Liabilities & Net Worth	100.0	100.0
							INCOME DATA		
	100.0	100.0	100.0	100.0			Net Sales	100.0	100.0
							Gross Profit		
	92.3	92.3	93.8	94.8			Operating Expenses	94.4	94.3
	7.7	7.7	6.2	5.2			Operating Profit	5.6	5.7
	2.1	1.7	3.4	1.6			All Other Expenses (net)	1.3	1.0
	5.6	6.0	2.8	3.6			Profit Before Taxes	4.3	4.7
							RATIOS		
	3.7	3.7	3.0	1.9				2.2	2.5
	1.3	1.7	1.7	1.6			Current	1.3	1.4
	.4	1.0	1.0	.9				.9	.8
	3.0	2.8	2.2	1.6				1.8	2.1
	.8	1.1	1.4	1.0			Quick	1.1	1.1
	.3	.6	.9	.7				.6	.6
	0 UND	19 18.9	31 11.6	27 13.3				13 27.6	15 25.0
	8 43.2	48 7.7	48 7.6	57 6.4			Sales/Receivables	40 9.2	39 9.3
	25 14.8	67 5.4	79 4.6	75 4.9				63 5.8	61 6.0
							Cost of Sales/Inventory		
							Cost of Sales/Payables		
	10.1	4.9	5.4	4.7				7.9	7.0
	63.0	12.9	13.2	6.8			Sales/Working Capital	22.9	20.8
	-18.1	NM	239.0	-50.8				-80.2	-38.6
	13.0	10.4	9.8	35.4				11.7	12.4
	(43) 4.9	(51) 3.6	(33) 2.5	(13) 12.3			EBIT/Interest	(168) 4.1	(134) 3.5
	-1.5	-.4	-2.9	-.1				1.4	1.0
							Net Profit + Depr., Dep., Amort./Cur. Mat. L/T/D	3.2	3.4
								(32) 1.7	(23) 2.4
								1.3	1.5
	.5	.1	.4	.1				.5	.4
	1.8	.6	.7	.6			Fixed/Worth	1.2	.9
	-3.2	2.4	1.8	1.0				4.0	4.1
	.5	.6	.6	1.1				1.1	.8
	6.5	1.6	1.5	1.9			Debt/Worth	2.4	2.1
	-7.5	9.6	4.3	2.3				13.9	10.5
	220.6	78.6	27.1	35.6				65.7	61.2
	(33) 34.2	(51) 22.7	(34) 10.7	(14) 9.5			% Profit Before Taxes/Tangible Net Worth	(150) 26.0	(119) 27.4
	-6.8	1.7	-20.1	-3.4				7.2	8.5
	51.4	21.2	10.9	16.9				21.7	21.0
	13.1	4.8	3.0	4.3			% Profit Before Taxes/Total Assets	8.3	8.0
	-6.2	-1.1	-3.5	-1.3				1.8	.8
	64.4	33.6	17.9	41.8				23.6	24.9
	27.6	14.6	9.3	10.9			Sales/Net Fixed Assets	11.5	11.2
	8.2	7.3	4.2	5.5				5.3	5.9
	9.1	3.6	3.3	2.2				3.9	4.1
	5.5	2.7	2.3	1.6			Sales/Total Assets	3.0	2.9
	3.0	1.5	1.8	1.3				2.0	2.0
	.7	1.0	1.8	1.1				1.4	1.9
	(29) 2.6	(46) 2.4	(33) 3.1	(14) 2.0			% Depr., Dep., Amort./Sales	(147) 2.6	(120) 3.1
	5.2	4.3	5.3	6.0				4.6	4.7
	4.0	2.4	1.5					2.5	3.3
	(31) 7.4	(32) 7.2	(19) 3.0				% Officers', Directors' Owners' Comp/Sales	(91) 5.7	(70) 5.5
	10.1	10.8	4.7					9.6	8.7
	68757M	172328M	382651M	563787M	116072M	1312717M	Net Sales ($)	2101033M	2752603M
	12067M	66190M	162853M	336981M	121328M	494390M	Total Assets ($)	933493M	1006258M

© RMA 2011

M = $ thousand　　MM = $ million
See Pages 9 through 22 for Explanation of Ratios and Data

Comparative Historical Data | Current Data Sorted by Sales

Type of Statement									
Unqualified	6	6	11		1		1	3	6
Reviewed	35	33	33		6	4	11	7	5
Compiled	25	19	16	1	5	5	2	2	1
Tax Returns	57	61	52	22	16	7	4	2	1
Other	61	72	64	15	26	8	8	4	3
	4/1/08-3/31/09 ALL	4/1/09-3/31/10 ALL	4/1/10-3/31/11 ALL	\<-- 18 (4/1-9/30/10) --\>			\<-- 158 (10/1/10-3/31/11) --\>		
				0-1MM	1-3MM	3-5MM	5-10MM	10-25MM	25MM & OVER
NUMBER OF STATEMENTS	184	191	176	38	54	24	26	18	16
ASSETS	%	%	%	%	%	%	%	%	%
Cash & Equivalents	11.7	14.1	15.6	16.8	20.7	10.0	11.4	7.9	19.8
Trade Receivables (net)	31.0	30.0	29.5	19.3	27.9	36.5	30.8	45.7	28.3
Inventory	6.6	6.1	7.0	7.5	9.2	5.7	5.5	6.0	3.5
All Other Current	3.9	4.0	4.3	3.9	2.8	3.9	8.0	4.3	4.7
Total Current	53.2	54.3	56.4	47.5	60.7	56.0	55.8	63.9	56.3
Fixed Assets (net)	36.2	33.2	30.6	37.9	26.8	29.2	33.8	25.1	29.4
Intangibles (net)	2.2	3.2	3.0	1.3	2.8	2.2	4.3	5.5	3.9
All Other Non-Current	8.3	9.3	10.0	13.3	9.8	12.5	6.1	5.5	10.3
Total	100.0	100.0	100.0	100.0	100.0	100.0	100.0	100.0	100.0
LIABILITIES									
Notes Payable-Short Term	14.0	16.1	16.1	20.7	16.3	18.4	19.4	7.2	6.0
Cur. Mat.-L.T.D.	4.7	6.5	4.8	4.2	4.7	6.5	5.6	5.6	2.1
Trade Payables	9.3	13.1	12.1	9.5	12.3	16.9	11.6	14.5	8.5
Income Taxes Payable	.6	.8	.6	.0	.2	.0	.2	1.9	3.3
All Other Current	10.5	16.4	11.0	10.6	11.8	5.8	7.2	15.0	18.2
Total Current	39.1	52.8	44.6	45.1	45.2	47.6	43.9	44.1	38.2
Long-Term Debt	26.9	20.5	20.9	35.0	20.5	14.4	17.8	14.3	11.1
Deferred Taxes	.7	.3	.1	.0	.1	.0	.2	.1	.1
All Other Non-Current	4.9	7.0	6.8	12.8	4.0	5.8	1.8	10.9	6.7
Net Worth	28.5	19.4	27.7	7.1	30.2	32.2	36.2	30.6	44.1
Total Liabilities & Net Worth	100.0	100.0	100.0	100.0	100.0	100.0	100.0	100.0	100.0
INCOME DATA									
Net Sales	100.0	100.0	100.0	100.0	100.0	100.0	100.0	100.0	100.0
Gross Profit									
Operating Expenses	93.0	96.3	93.0	84.8	93.5	96.2	96.6	97.7	95.3
Operating Profit	7.0	3.7	7.0	15.2	6.5	3.8	3.4	2.3	4.7
All Other Expenses (net)	2.1	1.8	2.2	6.0	1.5	.8	.7	1.3	.5
Profit Before Taxes	4.9	1.9	4.8	9.2	5.0	3.0	2.7	1.0	4.2
RATIOS									
Current	2.7	2.4	3.3	4.9	3.6	2.6	3.0	2.0	2.6
	1.6	1.5	1.6	1.5	2.1	1.2	1.3	1.5	1.7
	.9	.7	.8	.4	.9	.7	.9	1.0	1.0
Quick	2.2	1.9	2.4	3.6	3.2	2.4	1.5	1.9	2.4
	1.1	1.1	1.1	.8	1.3	1.1	1.1	1.2	1.5
	.6	.5	.5	.2	.6	.4	.8	.8	.9
Sales/Receivables	12 29.4	8 45.7	9 42.3	0 UND	10 37.0	14 26.2	28 12.8	32 11.4	18 20.4
	37 9.8	39 9.4	32 11.4	7 53.8	26 14.2	49 7.4	42 8.7	53 6.9	36 10.3
	64 5.7	69 5.3	59 6.2	47 7.8	51 7.1	66 5.6	68 5.4	83 4.4	65 5.6
Cost of Sales/Inventory									
Cost of Sales/Payables									
Sales/Working Capital	5.7	6.5	6.4	5.7	5.3	9.2	6.3	7.4	5.5
	17.1	18.1	18.9	52.0	12.0	27.4	45.4	13.5	16.1
	-74.1	-25.7	-43.8	-7.5	-288.2	-69.6	-37.6	-331.6	NM
EBIT/Interest	10.9	8.4	12.9	11.0	14.4	12.0	6.6	19.9	18.3
	(155) 3.8	(154) 2.1	(144) 4.2	(25) 4.0	(44) 4.8	(21) 4.2	(23) 2.3	(17) 3.4	(14) 11.2
	1.4	-1.1	-.8	-1.0	-.5	-.5	-8.1	-.8	-.2
Net Profit + Depr., Dep., Amort./Cur. Mat. L/T/D	2.5	3.4	6.6						
	(27) 1.5	(28) 1.4	(16) 1.0						
	.7	-.3	.2						
Fixed/Worth	.3	.3	.3	.3	.1	.3	.4	.4	.2
	.9	.8	.9	2.4	.7	.7	.9	.6	.6
	3.5	86.7	33.5	-5.0	39.4	2.5	2.0	1.6	4.7
Debt/Worth	.8	.8	.6	.6	.6	.5	.5	.9	.7
	2.1	2.1	1.9	12.3	1.6	1.8	1.1	2.2	1.4
	5.8	UND	80.8	-7.8	77.2	10.4	7.1	7.3	6.8
% Profit Before Taxes/Tangible Net Worth	57.7	52.0	71.8	134.5	78.6	67.0	27.9	32.7	44.0
	(156) 20.0	(144) 15.0	(135) 18.4	(24) 42.3	(43) 21.4	(19) 14.4	(21) 8.3	(15) 11.1	(13) 23.4
	3.9	-4.0	-1.6	-5.0	1.8	-8.0	-25.2	3.8	-3.1
% Profit Before Taxes/Total Assets	20.6	16.6	22.2	36.7	25.2	15.8	16.2	13.0	20.5
	6.1	4.1	4.8	4.9	7.1	2.3	4.8	3.8	11.7
	.6	-4.7	-3.5	-6.8	-.3	-7.2	-10.8	-3.4	-1.3
Sales/Net Fixed Assets	23.6	28.9	36.0	41.0	58.6	25.5	18.4	27.0	44.4
	10.4	11.5	14.7	16.7	23.5	15.4	11.2	15.8	10.1
	4.7	5.2	6.4	4.1	6.5	7.6	5.4	7.8	5.0
Sales/Total Assets	4.0	4.1	4.1	6.4	5.4	4.0	3.3	4.0	3.1
	2.8	2.6	2.9	3.0	2.8	3.4	2.5	3.2	2.1
	1.7	1.6	1.8	.9	1.9	2.7	2.1	1.8	1.4
% Depr., Dep., Amort./Sales	1.6	1.5	1.2	1.5	.7	1.2	1.8	1.2	.9
	(140) 3.3	(140) 2.9	(124) 2.7	(19) 5.1	(35) 2.6	(18) 2.0	(25) 3.1	(16) 2.7	(11) 1.4
	5.3	4.8	5.1	11.7	4.6	4.5	5.3	3.4	4.0
% Officers', Directors' Owners' Comp/Sales	2.9	3.9	2.5	4.1	3.1	2.8	1.8		
	(93) 6.4	(88) 6.8	(85) 5.5	(18) 8.1	(32) 8.1	(10) 5.5	(16) 3.1		
	12.1	11.5	9.3	13.8	9.9	11.0	4.9		
Net Sales ($)	1841212M	1427877M	2616312M	19787M	100840M	93693M	181035M	280332M	1940625M
Total Assets ($)	807845M	716433M	1193809M	18543M	55174M	34816M	91965M	151825M	841486M

M = $ thousand   MM = $ million
See Pages 9 through 22 for Explanation of Ratios and Data

Current Data Sorted by Assets   **Comparative Historical Data**

						Type of Statement		
1	12	85	103	17	25	Unqualified	251	224
4	51	205	72	2	3	Reviewed	320	313
34	93	109	12	.	1	Compiled	237	199
151	106	53	3	1	1	Tax Returns	250	244
102	187	250	132	23	15	Other	533	589
	230 (4/1-9/30/10)		1,622 (10/1/10-3/31/11)				4/1/06-3/31/07	4/1/07-3/31/08
0-500M	500M-2MM	2-10MM	10-50MM	50-100MM	100-250MM		ALL	ALL
292	449	702	322	43	44	NUMBER OF STATEMENTS	1591	1569
%	%	%	%	%	%	ASSETS	%	%
30.0	15.6	14.0	13.1	9.8	13.0	Cash & Equivalents	13.3	14.2
19.8	43.5	49.0	45.7	40.9	32.4	Trade Receivables (net)	46.2	46.4
3.0	4.2	4.3	3.3	3.2	3.1	Inventory	4.0	3.9
4.4	4.3	7.2	10.7	10.7	9.8	All Other Current	7.2	7.0
57.2	67.6	74.4	72.8	64.7	58.3	Total Current	70.7	71.6
27.4	21.5	14.9	13.8	15.4	15.1	Fixed Assets (net)	18.4	18.1
3.6	3.0	2.8	5.6	15.6	18.1	Intangibles (net)	3.1	2.9
11.8	7.9	7.9	7.8	4.3	8.5	All Other Non-Current	7.8	7.4
100.0	100.0	100.0	100.0	100.0	100.0	Total	100.0	100.0
						LIABILITIES		
30.3	14.0	9.2	7.4	4.5	3.5	Notes Payable-Short Term	13.3	12.0
7.8	2.6	2.3	2.3	2.4	2.5	Cur. Mat.-L.T.D.	3.3	3.2
9.3	10.6	11.1	11.8	11.9	9.8	Trade Payables	10.9	11.0
.3	.6	2.0	3.7	3.5	2.8	Income Taxes Payable	2.0	1.7
20.3	11.8	15.8	18.0	16.7	20.1	All Other Current	16.9	17.0
67.9	39.5	40.4	43.3	39.0	38.6	Total Current	46.3	44.9
21.5	12.5	8.1	7.5	13.2	12.4	Long-Term Debt	11.5	11.9
.1	.7	1.2	1.7	.8	1.5	Deferred Taxes	1.0	1.0
7.0	5.4	3.9	5.5	7.2	6.9	All Other Non-Current	5.0	4.5
3.5	41.8	46.4	42.1	39.7	40.5	Net Worth	36.2	37.6
100.0	100.0	100.0	100.0	100.0	100.0	Total Liabilities & Net Worth	100.0	100.0
						INCOME DATA		
100.0	100.0	100.0	100.0	100.0	100.0	Net Sales	100.0	100.0
						Gross Profit		
94.9	92.3	93.7	94.7	93.4	94.3	Operating Expenses	92.4	92.3
5.1	7.7	6.3	5.3	6.6	5.7	Operating Profit	7.6	7.7
.6	2.3	1.4	1.0	2.1	1.4	All Other Expenses (net)	1.3	1.5
4.5	5.4	4.9	4.3	4.5	4.3	Profit Before Taxes	6.3	6.2
						RATIOS		
3.6	4.1	3.1	2.6	2.1	2.2		3.0	2.9
1.3	1.9	1.9	1.7	1.7	1.6	Current	1.7	1.7
.4	1.0	1.3	1.3	1.3	1.1		1.2	1.2
3.2	3.5	2.7	2.1	1.8	1.8		2.6	2.5
1.0	1.7	1.6	1.4	1.3	1.3	Quick	(1590) 1.5	(1567) 1.5
.3	.9	1.0	1.0	.9	.8		.9	.9
0 UND	25 14.7	50 7.3	57 6.4	61 6.0	57 6.4		41 8.8	42 8.7
0 UND	62 5.9	74 4.9	75 4.9	79 4.6	71 5.2	Sales/Receivables	66 5.5	69 5.3
42 8.7	93 3.9	101 3.6	100 3.6	103 3.5	81 4.5		93 3.9	96 3.8
						Cost of Sales/Inventory		
						Cost of Sales/Payables		
8.8	4.5	4.3	4.4	4.8	5.3		5.3	5.1
93.9	9.5	7.0	6.9	7.7	9.9	Sales/Working Capital	9.4	9.0
-23.2	121.4	16.7	15.7	11.7	38.9		30.5	28.0
23.7	30.8	38.1	27.3	23.4	26.5		27.9	25.5
(205) 4.3	(357) 5.8	(565) 8.5	(277) 8.1	(38) 10.2	(41) 10.6	EBIT/Interest	(1299) 8.1	(1283) 7.5
-3.1	.6	1.5	2.3	1.9	2.2		2.2	2.0
8.1	8.1	11.0	8.1	6.8	6.3		8.4	8.4
	(38) 2.2	(154) 3.3	(146) 2.4	(14) 1.9	(22) 2.0	Net Profit + Depr., Dep., Amort./Cur. Mat. L/T/D	(343) 3.4	(339) 2.8
	.2	1.1	.8	.9	.6		1.5	1.2
.1	.1	.1	.1	.2	.3		.1	.1
.7	.4	.2	.3	.4	.6	Fixed/Worth	.3	.3
-2.1	1.7	.6	.7	1.4	1.9		1.0	.9
.5	.4	.5	.8	.8	.9		.6	.6
2.6	1.3	1.2	1.5	1.6	2.0	Debt/Worth	1.5	1.4
-4.1	4.5	2.5	3.7	4.5	7.7		4.2	4.3
168.4	62.9	45.4	38.4	38.1	57.7		64.6	66.0
(194) 43.2	(398) 25.5	(667) 19.5	(305) 18.7	(35) 20.9	(36) 26.2	% Profit Before Taxes/Tangible Net Worth	(1408) 31.5	(1408) 30.6
.2	1.7	3.1	4.1	6.0	7.5		12.9	9.0
58.0	24.2	20.5	13.4	12.6	12.8		27.3	25.0
16.2	9.6	7.0	6.3	6.7	6.6	% Profit Before Taxes/Total Assets	11.5	10.8
-7.2	.1	1.1	1.4	2.4	1.9		3.0	2.5
163.1	61.0	65.4	50.6	43.0	45.3		56.8	60.7
38.4	24.1	27.3	23.5	18.8	12.7	Sales/Net Fixed Assets	24.0	24.8
15.4	10.1	11.7	10.6	10.1	7.4		12.5	11.5
11.4	3.9	3.1	2.6	2.3	2.3		3.7	3.7
5.6	2.6	2.4	2.1	1.8	1.6	Sales/Total Assets	2.6	2.6
2.9	1.9	1.7	1.6	1.3	1.2		2.0	1.9
.7	.7	.6	.7	1.1	1.3		.7	.7
(155) 1.4	(315) 1.6	(585) 1.4	(280) 1.4	(37) 1.6	(34) 2.2	% Depr., Dep., Amort./Sales	(1267) 1.4	(1250) 1.4
2.6	3.0	2.4	2.4	3.2	3.3		2.4	2.3
7.3	3.9	2.2	.7				3.6	3.7
(174) 13.0	(167) 5.3	(177) 5.3	(43) 2.4			% Officers', Directors' Owners' Comp/Sales	(516) 7.9	(511) 7.6
19.8	11.5	8.9	8.1				15.1	14.7
602516M	1707436M	8697913M	15325228M	7747317M	12885435M	Net Sales ($)	50111380M	48440781M
75080M	547347M	3432598M	6932503M	2987355M	7023727M	Total Assets ($)	19281735M	19812964M

© RMA 2011

M = $ thousand   MM = $ million
See Pages 9 through 22 for Explanation of Ratios and Data

Comparative Historical Data | | | Type of Statement | Current Data Sorted by Sales

			Type of Statement	0-1MM	1-3MM	3-5MM	5-10MM	10-25MM	25MM & OVER
249	222	243	Unqualified	1	6	4	24	56	152
324	353	337	Reviewed	3	23	26	88	136	61
218	219	248	Compiled	23	47	48	59	60	11
289	286	315	Tax Returns	84	108	36	53	27	7
657	634	709	Other	75	139	72	132	136	155
4/1/08-3/31/09 ALL	4/1/09-3/31/10 ALL	4/1/10-3/31/11 ALL		230 (4/1-9/30/10)			1,622 (10/1/10-3/31/11)		
1737	1714	1852	NUMBER OF STATEMENTS	186	323	186	356	415	386
%	%	%	ASSETS	%	%	%	%	%	%
14.2	15.8	16.6	Cash & Equivalents	20.3	22.2	14.6	16.0	15.6	12.7
44.4	41.8	41.9	Trade Receivables (net)	22.3	35.3	43.2	44.7	49.1	45.9
3.9	4.0	3.8	Inventory	2.8	3.9	5.4	4.4	3.5	3.2
6.7	7.2	6.8	All Other Current	4.3	5.0	5.2	6.0	7.1	10.9
69.2	68.7	69.2	Total Current	49.7	66.4	68.3	71.1	75.3	72.7
18.6	18.6	18.3	Fixed Assets (net)	37.1	21.1	19.4	16.3	13.8	13.1
3.6	4.6	4.1	Intangibles (net)	3.0	3.7	2.8	3.5	3.1	7.3
8.5	8.1	8.4	All Other Non-Current	10.1	8.8	9.4	9.0	7.8	6.9
100.0	100.0	100.0	Total	100.0	100.0	100.0	100.0	100.0	100.0
			LIABILITIES						
14.0	15.2	13.1	Notes Payable-Short Term	21.1	19.0	15.6	13.4	9.2	7.1
3.5	3.8	3.2	Cur. Mat.-L.T.D.	4.9	3.3	6.8	2.5	2.4	2.2
10.8	10.0	10.8	Trade Payables	10.5	8.2	10.7	10.4	11.0	13.3
1.7	1.7	1.7	Income Taxes Payable	.3	.3	1.2	1.6	2.5	3.3
16.5	16.2	16.0	All Other Current	14.4	13.7	12.7	15.4	17.7	19.2
46.5	47.0	45.0	Total Current	51.3	44.6	47.1	43.4	42.8	45.1
12.8	12.6	11.4	Long-Term Debt	28.5	15.8	11.9	7.8	6.6	7.6
.9	.9	1.0	Deferred Taxes	.1	.3	1.2	.8	1.7	1.4
6.3	6.2	5.2	All Other Non-Current	7.1	5.5	4.9	4.7	3.7	6.3
33.5	33.4	37.5	Net Worth	13.0	33.8	35.0	43.4	45.2	39.7
100.0	100.0	100.0	Total Liabilities & Net Worth	100.0	100.0	100.0	100.0	100.0	100.0
			INCOME DATA						
100.0	100.0	100.0	Net Sales	100.0	100.0	100.0	100.0	100.0	100.0
			Gross Profit						
93.4	95.0	93.7	Operating Expenses	84.3	95.2	95.3	94.6	94.1	95.2
6.6	5.0	6.3	Operating Profit	15.7	4.8	4.7	5.4	5.9	4.8
1.5	1.3	1.4	All Other Expenses (net)	7.1	.9	1.0	.4	.8	1.0
5.1	3.7	4.8	Profit Before Taxes	8.6	4.0	3.7	5.0	5.1	3.8
			RATIOS						
2.9	3.0	3.1		3.3	5.1	3.3	3.6	2.9	2.3
1.7	1.8	1.8	Current	1.2	2.0	1.9	2.0	1.8	1.6
1.1	1.1	1.2		.4	1.0	1.0	1.3	1.3	1.3
2.5	2.6	2.7		2.9	4.4	2.8	3.1	2.5	2.0
1.4	1.4	1.5	Quick	.9	1.8	1.5	1.7	1.6	1.3
.9	.9	.9		.3	.7	.9	1.0	1.0	.9
37 9.8	33 11.0	35 10.6		0 UND	0 UND	33 11.2	38 9.5	50 7.3	51 7.1
64 5.7	62 5.9	66 5.6	Sales/Receivables	3 108.3	51 7.1	69 5.3	70 5.2	69 5.3	70 5.2
94 3.9	93 3.9	94 3.9		71 5.1	100 3.6	95 3.9	98 3.7	97 3.8	90 4.0
			Cost of Sales/Inventory						
			Cost of Sales/Payables						
5.2	5.0	4.6		3.9	4.0	4.7	4.4	4.7	5.3
9.7	9.2	8.8	Sales/Working Capital	71.1	8.8	8.7	7.6	8.2	8.6
42.4	43.2	40.0		-5.6	999.8	269.6	21.7	17.7	19.7
26.2	24.8	30.7		16.6	21.8	25.3	31.5	53.3	29.1
(1444) 6.8	(1403) 5.5	(1483) 7.4	EBIT/Interest	(108) 3.0	(247) 3.9	(154) 6.0	(289) 7.4	(352) 11.8	(333) 10.1
1.2	.2	1.3		-2.9	-2.5	1.1	1.1	1.9	2.4
9.2	6.4	9.3			9.4	2.7	11.1	9.8	8.5
(393) 3.3	(342) 2.5	(380) 2.5	Net Profit + Depr., Dep., Amort./Cur. Mat. L/T/D	(16) 2.7	(25) .6	(61) 3.2	(115) 3.3	(161) 2.4
1.2	.8	.8			.6	-.4	1.1	.8	1.1
.1	.1	.1		.1	.1	.1	.1	.1	.1
.4	.3	.3	Fixed/Worth	1.3	.4	.4	.3	.2	.3
1.2	1.2	1.0		12.0	2.4	1.4	.7	.6	.7
.6	.6	.6		.6	.3	.6	.4	.6	.8
1.5	1.5	1.4	Debt/Worth	3.1	1.0	1.5	1.1	1.2	1.6
4.7	5.6	4.2		UND	15.0	4.6	2.8	3.0	3.9
59.7	50.4	53.1		65.3	69.3	63.7	48.3	51.6	47.6
(1505) 26.1	(1442) 20.0	(1635) 21.7	% Profit Before Taxes/Tangible Net Worth	(140) 21.2	(262) 18.7	(164) 26.8	(322) 18.9	(393) 22.9	(354) 21.2
5.0	.9	3.3		.0	-3.4	2.4	2.5	4.7	6.1
23.2	21.3	21.5		23.2	28.7	24.1	23.5	21.4	16.1
8.6	7.0	7.9	% Profit Before Taxes/Total Assets	4.1	7.9	9.9	7.1	9.2	7.7
.6	-1.0	.8		-4.7	-4.4	.9	.6	1.8	2.5
61.7	67.0	65.8		88.7	71.1	52.1	64.1	74.8	62.8
25.4	25.7	26.4	Sales/Net Fixed Assets	13.7	25.8	24.1	29.9	30.0	27.1
12.3	11.0	11.3		2.3	11.3	11.9	12.5	14.4	12.3
3.8	3.7	3.7		4.1	4.6	4.1	3.6	3.6	3.0
2.6	2.6	2.4	Sales/Total Assets	2.1	2.7	2.6	2.6	2.5	2.3
1.9	1.8	1.8		.6	1.8	1.9	1.9	1.9	1.7
.7	.7	.7		1.3	.9	.7	.7	.6	.6
(1349) 1.5	(1327) 1.5	(1406) 1.4	% Depr., Dep., Amort./Sales	(108) 3.2	(205) 1.7	(134) 1.5	(285) 1.4	(351) 1.2	(323) 1.4
2.5	2.6	2.6		12.0	2.9	2.5	2.4	2.2	2.3
3.4	4.2	3.4		7.6	5.6	3.9	3.0	1.9	1.0
(537) 7.5	(551) 8.9	(567) 7.2	% Officers', Directors' Owners' Comp/Sales	(72) 14.1	(148) 10.7	(75) 7.1	(132) 5.7	(92) 4.8	(48) 3.1
13.7	15.4	13.3		22.0	15.3	11.7	9.3	9.2	8.8
53653005M	45127541M	46965845M	Net Sales ($)	100298M	632285M	736914M	2553883M	6608662M	36333803M
21904315M	19972985M	20998610M	Total Assets ($)	121002M	307264M	317578M	1114487M	2843426M	16294853M

© RMA 2011

M = $ thousand   MM = $ million
See Pages 9 through 22 for Explanation of Ratios and Data

Current Data Sorted by Assets   Comparative Historical Data

0-500M	500M-2MM	2-10MM	10-50MM	50-100MM	100-250MM	Type of Statement	4/1/06-3/31/07 ALL	4/1/07-3/31/08 ALL
1	1	2		2	1	Unqualified	4	3
	1	3	1			Reviewed	9	10
2	4	1				Compiled	8	11
19	5	3				Tax Returns	22	24
8	12	7	2		1	Other	27	36
	8 (4/1-9/30/10)		68 (10/1/10-3/31/11)					
30	23	16	3	2	2	NUMBER OF STATEMENTS	70	84
%	%	%	%	%	%	**ASSETS**	%	%
14.8	9.1	19.1				Cash & Equivalents	16.5	14.9
33.8	35.7	32.2				Trade Receivables (net)	33.1	35.6
1.2	2.5	3.8				Inventory	1.7	2.9
4.8	6.1	6.1				All Other Current	5.7	4.9
54.6	53.4	61.2				Total Current	57.0	58.4
24.8	28.1	25.5				Fixed Assets (net)	30.2	27.6
.1	5.6	1.9				Intangibles (net)	4.6	6.6
20.9	12.8	11.4				All Other Non-Current	8.2	7.5
100.0	100.0	100.0				Total	100.0	100.0
						LIABILITIES		
28.4	7.2	3.9				Notes Payable-Short Term	17.0	12.2
10.2	3.5	4.5				Cur. Mat.-L.T.D.	4.5	6.2
5.8	6.1	5.3				Trade Payables	8.2	6.0
.0	2.6	.5				Income Taxes Payable	.9	2.0
20.7	18.9	14.7				All Other Current	11.3	10.3
65.1	38.3	28.9				Total Current	41.8	36.7
52.5	22.5	14.7				Long-Term Debt	19.6	19.8
1.0	1.8	.3				Deferred Taxes	.5	1.4
23.0	2.7	4.4				All Other Non-Current	5.4	6.1
-41.7	34.7	51.8				Net Worth	32.7	35.9
100.0	100.0	100.0				Total Liabilities & Net Worth	100.0	100.0
						INCOME DATA		
100.0	100.0	100.0				Net Sales	100.0	100.0
						Gross Profit		
97.7	98.5	93.6				Operating Expenses	92.0	94.1
2.3	1.5	6.4				Operating Profit	8.0	5.9
1.3	.1	1.3				All Other Expenses (net)	1.6	1.2
1.0	1.4	5.1				Profit Before Taxes	6.4	4.8
						RATIOS		
2.0	3.8	8.1				Current	2.6	4.4
.8	1.4	2.4					1.5	1.6
.2	.7	1.0					.9	1.1
1.6	3.8	6.0				Quick	2.5	3.4
.7	1.4	2.1					1.2	1.4
.2	.6	.9					.8	.9
0 UND	0 UND	34 10.7				Sales/Receivables	0 UND	9 39.7
30 12.3	47 7.7	49 7.4					50 7.2	64 5.7
87 4.2	84 4.4	111 3.3					93 3.9	87 4.2
						Cost of Sales/Inventory		
						Cost of Sales/Payables		
8.9	5.4	3.4				Sales/Working Capital	6.8	4.5
-76.6	41.0	6.1					13.5	9.3
-8.4	-67.6	NM					-51.7	193.2
6.0	21.2	10.8				EBIT/Interest	30.2	23.2
(29) .2	(18) 2.6	(13) 2.4					(64) 5.2	(73) 3.4
-5.9	-.8	.8					1.0	.6
						Net Profit + Depr., Dep., Amort./Cur. Mat. L/T/D	21.4	5.6
							(14) 4.3	(18) 1.6
							1.7	.8
.4	.2	.2				Fixed/Worth	.3	.3
2.2	.5	.5					.6	.5
-.3	-6.2	3.4					NM	1.8
1.1	.3	.2				Debt/Worth	.5	.5
14.5	1.7	.9					1.3	1.3
-1.9	-12.8	9.3					NM	4.3
328.3	78.0	53.4				% Profit Before Taxes/Tangible Net Worth	87.7	71.4
(16) 39.7	(15) 6.9	(15) 9.7					(53) 40.1	(70) 17.2
-19.2	-6.7	-3.6					9.6	1.9
28.4	17.2	16.9				% Profit Before Taxes/Total Assets	28.7	29.1
-2.8	4.6	4.1					11.0	7.1
-21.9	-3.1	-1.7					-.4	-1.1
66.2	60.4	19.9				Sales/Net Fixed Assets	33.2	25.0
19.1	12.9	9.7					12.2	12.9
10.3	4.4	3.5					6.5	6.8
5.4	4.0	2.8				Sales/Total Assets	4.4	4.0
3.5	2.5	1.7					2.5	2.5
2.5	1.6	1.1					1.6	1.8
1.5	.7	1.2				% Depr., Dep., Amort./Sales	1.5	1.5
(16) 2.1	(13) 1.3	(13) 2.4					(42) 2.5	(66) 2.7
4.6	3.3	6.4					5.5	5.2
11.8	5.1					% Officers', Directors' Owners' Comp/Sales	6.0	3.7
(19) 16.4	(11) 10.2						(32) 10.4	(44) 8.0
25.5	24.4						16.1	14.7
19731M	65285M	128529M	111167M	158268M	450414M	Net Sales ($)	1790185M	790824M
5324M	22482M	68889M	86351M	142497M	413093M	Total Assets ($)	729018M	514482M

M = $ thousand   MM = $ million
See Pages 9 through 22 for Explanation of Ratios and Data

Comparative Historical Data

Current Data Sorted by Sales

					Type of Statement						
	6		9	7	Unqualified		1		1	2	3
	9		7	5	Reviewed		1		4		
	8		7	7	Compiled	2	3		1	1	
	20		26	27	Tax Returns	16	6	2	3		
	32		23	30	Other	9	8	6	4		3
	4/1/08-		4/1/09-	4/1/10-			8 (4/1-9/30/10)		68 (10/1/10-3/31/11)		
	3/31/09		3/31/10	3/31/11							
	ALL		ALL	ALL		0-1MM	1-3MM	3-5MM	5-10MM	10-25MM	25MM & OVER
	75		72	76	NUMBER OF STATEMENTS	27	19	8	13	3	6
	%		%	%	ASSETS	%	%	%	%	%	%
	14.3		14.9	13.8	Cash & Equivalents	13.1	8.8		17.2		
	34.9		28.8	32.8	Trade Receivables (net)	32.7	42.3		38.6		
	1.8		1.7	2.2	Inventory	.8	3.3		2.1		
	4.6		5.4	6.2	All Other Current	8.0	3.5		10.1		
	55.6		50.8	55.1	Total Current	54.6	57.8		68.0		
	25.9		24.2	25.4	Fixed Assets (net)	27.2	24.7		13.7		
	7.8		8.6	4.8	Intangibles (net)	.0	.9		9.4		
	10.8		16.4	14.8	All Other Non-Current	18.4	16.6		8.8		
	100.0		100.0	100.0	Total	100.0	100.0		100.0		
					LIABILITIES						
	17.8		25.8	14.4	Notes Payable-Short Term	25.3	13.7		5.1		
	3.5		7.8	6.3	Cur. Mat.-L.T.D.	10.3	3.9		1.7		
	6.3		8.0	6.0	Trade Payables	5.5	4.6		8.6		
	1.7		.3	1.2	Income Taxes Payable	.0	1.5		3.0		
	10.7		11.4	19.2	All Other Current	21.3	19.9		28.4		
	40.0		53.2	47.0	Total Current	62.4	43.6		46.7		
	19.2		26.8	32.4	Long-Term Debt	53.5	26.0		8.3		
	.9		1.0	1.1	Deferred Taxes	.9	2.4		.1		
	6.7		15.5	11.8	All Other Non-Current	24.7	4.3		1.8		
	33.3		3.5	7.6	Net Worth	-41.7	23.7		43.1		
	100.0		100.0	100.0	Total Liabilties & Net Worth	100.0	100.0		100.0		
					INCOME DATA						
	100.0		100.0	100.0	Net Sales	100.0	100.0		100.0		
					Gross Profit						
	97.6		96.2	96.7	Operating Expenses	96.5	99.0		99.0		
	2.4		3.8	3.3	Operating Profit	3.5	1.0		1.0		
	1.3		2.4	1.2	All Other Expenses (net)	1.6	-.1		.6		
	1.0		1.4	2.1	Profit Before Taxes	1.8	1.0		.3		
					RATIOS						
	4.2		4.1	2.4		2.2	3.6		3.5		
	1.6		1.3	1.4	Current	1.1	1.4		1.5		
	1.0		.7	.6		.3	.6		.8		
	4.1		3.3	2.3		1.7	2.8		3.2		
	1.4		1.1	1.0	Quick	.9	1.4		1.4		
	.8		.5	.5		.3	.6		.4		
2	157.7	0	UND	0 UND		0 UND	12 31.2		0 UND		
53	6.8	49	7.4	48 7.6	Sales/Receivables	43 8.5	66 5.5		83 4.4		
84	4.4	93	3.9	89 4.1		87 4.2	94 3.9		109 3.3		
					Cost of Sales/Inventory						
					Cost of Sales/Payables						
	5.9		5.0	5.6		9.0	5.1		4.1		
	20.7		30.1	34.7	Sales/Working Capital	83.6	11.2		41.0		
	-293.0		-16.9	-15.9		-8.4	-32.6		-17.8		
	8.3		10.1	7.2		6.6	13.2				
(66)	3.1	(60)	3.3	(66) 1.9	EBIT/Interest	(25) 1.9	(17) -.6				
	-3.8		-4.8	-2.0		-3.6	-4.1				
				18.4	Net Profit + Depr., Dep.,						
			(10)	2.7	Amort./Cur. Mat. L/T/D						
				1.8							
	.3		.1	.2		.4	.3		.1		
	.9		.8	1.0	Fixed/Worth	2.0	.6		.4		
	10.6		-.6	-1.7		-.2	-22.5		NM		
	.5		.5	.6		.8	1.2		.2		
	2.1		3.0	3.1	Debt/Worth	9.0	3.7		.9		
	72.7		-2.8	-4.5		-1.8	-24.6		NM		
	62.1		48.5	80.8	% Profit Before Taxes/Tangible	340.9	54.7		138.5		
(57)	13.5	(44)	9.1	(50) 11.5	Net Worth	(15) 50.0	(13) 15.2		(10) -1.2		
	-21.4		-17.7	-7.6		-10.3	-24.5		-57.5		
	23.0		18.3	18.1	% Profit Before Taxes/Total	29.0	14.0		11.4		
	4.6		2.6	3.4	Assets	5.3	-.4		-.6		
	-12.9		-22.9	-8.5		-17.3	-9.1		-14.3		
	31.5		47.3	41.3		46.7	70.0		73.8		
	12.0		17.7	13.7	Sales/Net Fixed Assets	16.7	17.0		30.5		
	8.8		8.6	7.4		8.2	9.4		10.9		
	3.9		4.2	4.2		5.3	3.6		4.0		
	2.4		2.5	2.5	Sales/Total Assets	2.9	3.0		2.4		
	1.8		1.3	1.5		2.1	2.1		1.5		
	2.0		1.0	1.3		1.5			.7		
(56)	2.8	(54)	2.7	(47) 2.1	% Depr., Dep., Amort./Sales	(16) 2.1		(10) 1.0			
	5.2		4.0	4.8		4.6			2.6		
	5.2		5.9	6.7		9.6					
(30)	8.9	(35)	12.6	(35) 14.9	% Officers', Directors'	(16) 15.8					
	15.1		19.6	24.4	Owners' Comp/Sales	23.5					
	923992M		1052927M	933394M	Net Sales ($)	13198M	34591M	29507M	93216M	52621M	710261M
	564291M		938693M	738636M	Total Assets ($)	6569M	14588M	19891M	48616M	19476M	629496M

© RMA 2011

M = $ thousand   MM = $ million

See Pages 9 through 22 for Explanation of Ratios and Data

Current Data Sorted by Assets   Comparative Historical Data

						Type of Statement		
1	1	7	10	4	5	Unqualified	31	27
1	5	21	8	1		Reviewed	46	32
5	13	8	2			Compiled	31	35
13	28	12				Tax Returns	28	32
12	32	29	16	3	5	Other	65	72
	35 (4/1-9/30/10)		206 (10/1/10-3/31/11)				4/1/06-3/31/07	4/1/07-3/31/08
0-500M	500M-2MM	2-10MM	10-50MM	50-100MM	100-250MM		ALL	ALL
31	79	77	36	8	10	NUMBER OF STATEMENTS	201	198
%	%	%	%	%	%	ASSETS	%	%
19.2	13.4	11.6	8.6		5.8	Cash & Equivalents	11.6	10.7
20.6	32.7	31.9	31.7		21.6	Trade Receivables (net)	33.9	32.5
1.1	6.1	3.2	3.4		2.9	Inventory	3.5	4.1
3.4	2.7	3.4	4.8		2.5	All Other Current	3.7	3.7
44.3	54.9	50.1	48.5		32.8	Total Current	52.8	50.9
39.8	32.1	36.4	34.5		22.6	Fixed Assets (net)	35.2	37.9
.8	4.5	4.4	8.7		36.7	Intangibles (net)	5.3	4.4
15.1	8.5	9.2	8.3		7.9	All Other Non-Current	6.7	6.7
100.0	100.0	100.0	100.0		100.0	Total	100.0	100.0
						LIABILITIES		
27.8	10.8	5.8	6.4		.8	Notes Payable-Short Term	10.5	9.6
11.5	5.8	3.9	4.5		1.9	Cur. Mat.-L.T.D.	4.7	5.0
5.6	9.0	8.5	8.7		3.1	Trade Payables	9.4	10.0
.0	.3	.7	.5		.6	Income Taxes Payable	.5	.6
8.9	9.5	12.7	11.5		9.9	All Other Current	12.0	10.7
53.7	35.5	31.6	31.6		16.2	Total Current	37.1	35.9
33.0	19.7	14.3	14.5		20.9	Long-Term Debt	17.5	21.6
.0	.6	1.3	.5		3.9	Deferred Taxes	.6	.8
11.1	8.3	6.0	6.7		10.0	All Other Non-Current	6.6	5.4
2.2	35.9	46.9	46.7		49.0	Net Worth	38.2	36.3
100.0	100.0	100.0	100.0		100.0	Total Liabilities & Net Worth	100.0	100.0
						INCOME DATA		
100.0	100.0	100.0	100.0		100.0	Net Sales	100.0	100.0
						Gross Profit		
90.0	91.9	89.6	94.3		89.0	Operating Expenses	90.4	90.0
10.0	8.1	10.4	5.7		11.0	Operating Profit	9.6	10.0
2.8	2.6	1.6	.9		1.8	All Other Expenses (net)	1.5	2.5
7.2	5.5	8.9	4.8		9.2	Profit Before Taxes	8.2	7.4
						RATIOS		
3.0	3.8	3.0	2.5		2.9		2.7	2.9
1.3	1.9	1.8	1.7		2.2	Current	1.5	1.6
.5	.9	1.2	1.0		2.0		1.0	1.0
3.0	3.4	2.7	2.2		2.8		2.5	2.2
1.3	1.7	1.5	1.2		1.8	Quick	1.4 (197)	1.3
.3	.8	1.0	.8		1.7		.8	.8

0	UND	29	12.5	36	10.2	50	7.3	71	5.2		38	9.6	33	11.0
11	32.2	51	7.1	56	6.6	62	5.8	76	4.8	Sales/Receivables	63	5.8	55	6.6
48	7.6	66	5.6	84	4.4	84	4.4	100	3.6		83	4.4	75	4.9

						Cost of Sales/Inventory		
						Cost of Sales/Payables		
13.9	5.3	4.8	5.0		3.3	Sales/Working Capital	5.8	5.4
62.9	9.8	10.0	11.3		6.4		13.2	11.5
-6.6	-44.3	48.5	217.5		8.6		-175.5	-999.8
17.9	18.7	26.0	13.2			EBIT/Interest	18.6	14.5
(24) 4.2	(64) 3.2	(68) 8.7	(34) 5.8				(176) 5.4	(170) 5.2
1.2	-.4	3.4	2.1				2.2	1.7
	6.7	7.2	3.4			Net Profit + Depr., Dep., Amort./Cur. Mat. L/T/D	5.5	9.2
	(16) 1.9	(25) 2.8	(17) 1.9				(53) 2.9	(49) 4.1
	.2	1.1	1.2				1.9	2.1
.4	.3	.4	.6		.7	Fixed/Worth	.5	.4
5.0	.8	.8	1.1		1.2		.9	1.0
-3.1	9.4	1.4	2.4		-.9		2.0	2.8
.6	.5	.5	.5		.9	Debt/Worth	.6	.6
7.9	1.4	1.0	1.7		2.0		1.4	1.6
-6.4	13.1	2.1	5.0		-3.2		3.8	6.4
152.1	83.8	52.0	40.4			% Profit Before Taxes/Tangible Net Worth	61.1	59.2
(19) 42.8	(64) 30.5	(70) 25.2	(33) 23.0				(174) 30.9	(170) 32.8
7.7	3.0	7.3	11.1				11.4	11.8
55.5	31.8	22.5	11.2		9.3	% Profit Before Taxes/Total Assets	26.7	21.3
17.1	8.5	13.6	7.8		7.4		11.3	12.8
.7	-1.8	4.2	3.0		2.5		3.7	2.4
38.3	22.3	14.2	7.9		6.6	Sales/Net Fixed Assets	12.2	13.1
15.1	10.2	6.2	4.7		3.8		6.8	6.5
3.5	4.1	3.4	2.9		2.9		4.0	3.7
6.9	3.3	2.5	2.1		1.4	Sales/Total Assets	2.8	3.0
2.8	2.4	2.0	1.6		.8		2.2	2.2
1.6	1.4	1.3	1.2		.6		1.4	1.4
1.2	1.5	1.9	3.1			% Depr., Dep., Amort./Sales	1.9	1.9
(19) 3.7	(59) 2.8	(65) 3.1	(34) 4.4				(179) 3.5	(162) 3.5
12.1	6.2	5.8	6.2				5.2	5.3
7.4	4.1	1.9				% Officers', Directors' Owners' Comp/Sales	4.0	2.6
(13) 10.3	(43) 6.3	(31) 4.3					(63) 6.2	(60) 5.6
23.3	10.6	6.9					11.2	9.4
38587M	242726M	783033M	1357028M	698098M	1744139M	Net Sales ($)	2600531M	2998309M
8324M	91243M	384728M	741391M	510340M	1782239M	Total Assets ($)	1779781M	1891566M

M = $ thousand   MM = $ million
See Pages 9 through 22 for Explanation of Ratios and Data

Comparative Historical Data / Current Data Sorted by Sales

Current data periods: **35 (4/1-9/30/10)** and **206 (10/1/10-3/31/11)**

4/1/08-3/31/09 ALL	4/1/09-3/31/10 ALL	4/1/10-3/31/11 ALL	Type of Statement	0-1MM	1-3MM	3-5MM	5-10MM	10-25MM	25MM & OVER
38	35	27	Unqualified		1		4	6	16
29	33	36	Reviewed		3	4	9	13	7
31	22	28	Compiled	4	5	9	6	3	1
44	43	53	Tax Returns	16	14	9	11	2	1
93	97	97	Other	14	25	8	14	18	18
235	230	241	**NUMBER OF STATEMENTS**	34	48	30	44	42	43
%	%	%	**ASSETS**	%	%	%	%	%	%
11.8	13.6	12.4	Cash & Equivalents	11.1	12.8	15.8	13.7	12.9	8.5
32.4	29.6	30.1	Trade Receivables (net)	15.1	30.0	34.9	35.2	32.1	31.4
3.5	3.2	3.9	Inventory	1.0	5.0	7.0	3.8	3.6	3.2
4.4	4.6	3.5	All Other Current	3.7	2.3	.8	3.6	4.7	5.2
52.2	51.0	49.8	Total Current	31.0	50.1	58.5	56.2	53.3	48.2
35.5	34.2	34.2	Fixed Assets (net)	51.3	35.3	29.3	33.7	30.8	26.6
5.4	7.3	6.6	Intangibles (net)	4.6	2.5	3.7	4.7	4.2	18.9
7.0	7.5	9.4	All Other Non-Current	13.1	12.0	8.5	5.4	11.6	6.3
100.0	100.0	100.0	Total	100.0	100.0	100.0	100.0	100.0	100.0
			LIABILITIES						
9.5	9.5	10.0	Notes Payable-Short Term	22.1	13.6	8.2	4.7	7.4	6.0
4.4	5.2	5.5	Cur. Mat.-L.T.D.	11.8	4.1	8.3	3.4	4.2	3.4
8.3	6.9	8.0	Trade Payables	3.7	6.6	11.8	7.2	11.3	8.1
.6	.3	.4	Income Taxes Payable	.0	.0	.5	.4	1.1	.5
12.3	11.4	11.1	All Other Current	6.1	9.9	10.0	10.2	13.8	15.6
35.1	33.4	35.1	Total Current	43.7	34.2	38.8	25.9	37.8	33.6
19.8	18.4	18.6	Long-Term Debt	41.2	18.1	19.0	11.9	12.0	14.2
.8	.7	.9	Deferred Taxes	.0	.5	.2	2.4	.3	1.3
5.8	5.1	7.8	All Other Non-Current	11.9	10.6	11.8	4.1	3.8	6.3
38.5	42.4	37.7	Net Worth	3.2	36.5	30.2	55.7	46.1	44.7
100.0	100.0	100.0	Total Liabilties & Net Worth	100.0	100.0	100.0	100.0	100.0	100.0
			INCOME DATA						
100.0	100.0	100.0	Net Sales	100.0	100.0	100.0	100.0	100.0	100.0
			Gross Profit						
91.5	90.9	91.2	Operating Expenses	84.8	92.2	91.5	91.4	94.8	91.3
8.5	9.1	8.8	Operating Profit	15.2	7.8	8.5	8.6	5.2	8.7
1.8	2.1	2.0	All Other Expenses (net)	9.3	1.1	.4	.5	.5	1.3
6.7	7.0	6.8	Profit Before Taxes	5.9	6.6	8.1	8.1	4.7	7.5
			RATIOS						
3.0	3.2	3.0		2.4	3.6	3.5	5.1	2.5	2.2
1.6	1.8	1.8	Current	.7	2.0	1.9	2.3	1.6	1.7
1.0	1.0	1.0		.4	1.1	.9	1.4	1.0	1.0
2.4	2.8	2.7		2.4	3.1	3.5	4.7	2.1	1.9
1.3	1.5	1.6	Quick	.7	1.8	1.8	1.9	1.3	1.6
.8	.8	.8		.3	.8	.8	1.2	.7	.8
36 10.1	38 9.7	34 10.6		0 UND	30 12.1	29 12.8	41 9.0	45 8.2	53 6.9
56 6.5	55 6.6	55 6.6	Sales/Receivables	18 20.6	52 7.1	54 6.8	57 6.4	55 6.6	67 5.4
73 5.0	73 5.0	73 5.0		51 7.1	65 5.6	67 5.4	85 4.3	75 4.9	82 4.5
			Cost of Sales/Inventory						
			Cost of Sales/Payables						
5.0	5.2	5.5		7.3	6.7	5.9	4.1	7.0	6.4
12.2	11.4	11.4	Sales/Working Capital	-19.2	10.7	10.6	6.8	12.8	9.2
-107.4	-194.0	NM		-3.9	97.6	-123.4	18.2	NM	110.9
13.4	17.9	18.9		8.6	16.2	11.6	27.7	25.5	18.6
(202) 4.6	(191) 5.2	(205) 6.5	EBIT/Interest	(26) 2.1	(40) 4.6	(23) 3.8	(39) 10.3	(39) 8.9	(38) 7.2
1.7	1.0	1.8		.6	-1.7	1.6	3.2	.6	3.3
11.0	7.1	7.4					10.0	3.3	25.3
(61) 4.7	(52) 2.8	(66) 2.6	Net Profit + Depr., Dep., Amort./Cur. Mat. L/T/D			(15) 2.8	(15) 1.9	(20) 3.4	
2.2	1.3	1.1					2.0	.7	1.7
.4	.4	.4		.9	.4	.2	.2	.4	.7
.9	.9	1.0	Fixed/Worth	14.3	.9	.9	.7	.7	1.2
2.5	2.8	4.5		-2.2	2.1	-21.6	1.2	1.4	2.6
.6	.5	.5		.6	.5	.5	.3	.5	1.0
1.4	1.2	1.3	Debt/Worth	24.3	1.3	1.3	.9	1.1	1.8
4.8	6.7	9.1		-3.5	6.2	-33.5	1.5	3.2	7.0
60.0	66.1	58.7	% Profit Before Taxes/Tangible Net Worth	62.3	88.5	76.8	49.2	63.7	58.0
(200) 27.4	(193) 22.8	(200) 27.0		(19) 16.1	(42) 30.5	(22) 13.3	(42) 32.6	(39) 21.3	(36) 28.0
7.8	6.5	7.4		2.5	5.0	6.1	10.6	5.0	20.9
22.8	21.1	24.4	% Profit Before Taxes/Total Assets	18.1	30.7	35.3	26.1	25.2	11.2
8.5	7.5	9.5		5.1	12.8	6.9	15.4	10.3	8.2
1.9	.3	2.3		-.3	-.9	2.0	4.4	1.7	5.4
12.9	13.5	16.8		13.1	17.6	23.9	20.7	17.4	11.6
6.3	5.9	6.6	Sales/Net Fixed Assets	3.9	6.6	11.7	6.0	6.7	5.5
3.9	3.4	3.5		1.2	3.5	7.7	3.2	4.4	3.9
2.8	2.8	2.9		2.4	3.3	3.5	2.6	3.1	2.5
2.0	1.9	2.0	Sales/Total Assets	1.3	2.1	2.6	2.0	2.1	1.6
1.4	1.1	1.2		.6	1.4	1.7	1.6	1.5	1.1
2.0	2.1	2.0		3.1	1.3	1.3	2.3	1.7	3.1
(193) 3.9	(179) 3.8	(190) 3.8	% Depr., Dep., Amort./Sales	(24) 8.1	(37) 2.9	(23) 2.6	(35) 3.9	(37) 2.7	(34) 4.2
6.1	6.0	6.2		20.4	5.9	4.3	6.7	5.3	5.6
2.6	2.9	2.9		7.9	5.3	3.6	2.8	1.6	
(75) 4.9	(63) 6.2	(90) 6.1	% Officers', Directors' Owners' Comp/Sales	(13) 10.6	(21) 7.2	(16) 5.9	(23) 5.2	(12) 3.2	
8.1	11.0	9.9		23.3	12.7	7.1	8.6	6.7	
4890000M	4398189M	4863611M	Net Sales ($)	17947M	92928M	118121M	306401M	627436M	3700778M
3485207M	3275100M	3518265M	Total Assets ($)	34601M	51881M	68775M	172395M	339882M	2850731M

M = $ thousand   MM = $ million
See Pages 9 through 22 for Explanation of Ratios and Data

Current Data Sorted by Assets   Comparative Historical Data

Type of Statement	0-500M	500M-2MM	2-10MM	10-50MM	50-100MM	100-250MM		4/1/06-3/31/07 ALL	4/1/07-3/31/08 ALL
Unqualified	2	2	1					4	2
Reviewed		2	3	1				3	4
Compiled	2	4	1	1				10	8
Tax Returns	13	13	1					19	20
Other	10	19	10	5				23	27
	7 (4/1-9/30/10)			81 (10/1/10-3/31/11)					
NUMBER OF STATEMENTS	27	38	16	7				59	61
	%	%	%	%	%	%		%	%
ASSETS									
Cash & Equivalents	19.4	12.2	16.4					18.7	13.8
Trade Receivables (net)	19.7	32.3	31.9		D A T A	D A T A		25.4	29.4
Inventory	14.5	21.8	19.5					16.1	21.0
All Other Current	5.0	3.8	3.8		N O T	N O T		9.0	5.5
Total Current	58.5	70.1	71.6					69.2	69.8
Fixed Assets (net)	24.5	18.4	19.3		A V A I L A B L E	A V A I L A B L E		18.7	17.3
Intangibles (net)	1.0	2.9	3.7					3.2	2.7
All Other Non-Current	16.0	8.6	5.4					8.9	10.3
Total	100.0	100.0	100.0					100.0	100.0
LIABILITIES									
Notes Payable-Short Term	59.7	15.8	2.4					9.7	17.3
Cur. Mat.-L.T.D.	2.3	1.4	2.9					3.3	5.7
Trade Payables	11.1	15.3	12.1					13.2	18.0
Income Taxes Payable	.1	.0	.9					.5	.1
All Other Current	20.5	23.6	25.7					32.6	24.5
Total Current	93.6	56.0	44.0					59.2	65.6
Long-Term Debt	11.4	11.1	9.9					14.2	15.8
Deferred Taxes	.0	.0	.0					.7	.0
All Other Non-Current	13.9	4.3	3.3					10.6	5.9
Net Worth	-18.9	28.6	42.8					15.3	12.7
Total Liabilties & Net Worth	100.0	100.0	100.0					100.0	100.0
INCOME DATA									
Net Sales	100.0	100.0	100.0					100.0	100.0
Gross Profit									
Operating Expenses	87.9	95.3	90.6					95.1	93.7
Operating Profit	12.1	4.7	9.4					4.9	6.3
All Other Expenses (net)	2.3	.4	3.0					1.0	1.1
Profit Before Taxes	9.8	4.2	6.3					3.9	5.2
RATIOS									
Current	3.3	2.5	2.4					2.2	2.0
	1.0	1.4	1.7					1.3	1.3
	.4	1.0	1.2					.8	.9
Quick	2.6	1.4	2.0					1.3	1.6
	.6	1.0	1.2					.8	.7
	.1	.3	.5					.3	.3
Sales/Receivables	0 UND	10 37.9	13 28.3					3 126.3	8 43.7
	4 97.9	31 11.6	36 10.1					22 16.8	27 13.6
	36 10.2	67 5.5	71 5.1					45 8.1	49 7.4
Cost of Sales/Inventory									
Cost of Sales/Payables									
Sales/Working Capital	9.4	6.7	4.9					8.0	6.7
	-100.1	18.2	9.1					24.7	22.6
	-6.3	-205.0	26.0					-44.9	-43.2
EBIT/Interest	16.4	11.3	49.4					35.6	20.8
	(18) 4.8	(29) 4.4	(13) 8.4					(46) 3.9	(53) 6.0
	-3.3	1.0	4.3					-.7	1.9
Net Profit + Depr., Dep., Amort./Cur. Mat. L/T/D									
Fixed/Worth	.1	.2	.1					.2	.2
	1.0	.5	.2					.6	.6
	-.5	5.2	.7					-3.9	6.7
Debt/Worth	.4	.7	.6					1.0	1.1
	5.5	3.1	1.6					5.5	3.5
	-3.5	12.4	4.0					-8.6	44.5
% Profit Before Taxes/Tangible Net Worth	173.2	116.9	57.0					94.3	86.5
	(14) 52.3	(32) 15.6	38.0					(40) 59.2	(48) 45.9
	12.2	2.3	9.7					8.2	17.8
% Profit Before Taxes/Total Assets	40.0	21.8	17.1					22.3	24.6
	16.3	9.2	10.0					9.5	9.1
	.8	.6	3.3					-3.5	1.5
Sales/Net Fixed Assets	458.0	42.2	145.6					103.2	78.5
	57.7	17.6	34.9					27.6	37.9
	7.6	12.6	7.0					11.7	14.1
Sales/Total Assets	5.2	4.2	3.8					5.0	4.8
	3.5	2.8	1.9					3.5	3.4
	2.2	1.9	1.4					2.1	1.8
% Depr., Dep., Amort./Sales	.4	.4	.3					.4	.5
	(12) 1.8	(25) .7	(13) 1.8					(39) .9	(47) .9
	3.8	1.5	4.1					1.5	1.8
% Officers', Directors' Owners' Comp/Sales	5.7	4.3						2.9	2.4
	(11) 8.2	(20) 6.6						(30) 6.5	(30) 4.6
	13.6	7.5						9.6	7.2
Net Sales ($)	34023M	124950M	185483M	307720M				2902008M	1059035M
Total Assets ($)	6472M	39458M	73555M	114267M				507252M	272260M

© RMA 2011

M = $ thousand   MM = $ million
See Pages 9 through 22 for Explanation of Ratios and Data

Comparative Historical Data				Current Data Sorted by Sales					
			Type of Statement						
3	1	3	Unqualified	2					1
7	8	6	Reviewed			2	2	1	1
16	10	8	Compiled		3	2	1	1	1
33	28	27	Tax Returns	13	8	4	2		
29	38	44	Other	7	13	8	5	6	5
4/1/08-3/31/09 ALL	4/1/09-3/31/10 ALL	4/1/10-3/31/11 ALL			7 (4/1-9/30/10)		81 (10/1/10-3/31/11)		
				0-1MM	1-3MM	3-5MM	5-10MM	10-25MM	25MM & OVER
88	85	88	**NUMBER OF STATEMENTS**	22	24	16	10	8	8
%	%	%	**ASSETS**	%	%	%	%	%	%
17.0	22.1	14.6	Cash & Equivalents	17.7	15.4	7.4	18.0		
27.1	25.4	29.6	Trade Receivables (net)	13.0	29.0	37.0	33.7		
19.3	14.1	18.1	Inventory	12.2	21.7	27.4	21.0		
6.4	6.3	4.4	All Other Current	7.6	3.8	1.6	2.9		
69.9	67.9	66.7	Total Current	50.5	69.9	73.4	75.6		
19.8	22.1	19.9	Fixed Assets (net)	34.3	16.6	14.7	18.2		
1.6	3.1	2.7	Intangibles (net)	1.1	4.2	3.0	.0		
8.7	6.9	10.8	All Other Non-Current	14.1	9.4	8.9	6.1		
100.0	100.0	100.0	Total	100.0	100.0	100.0	100.0		
			LIABILITIES						
13.5	19.4	26.8	Notes Payable-Short Term	52.9	27.9	19.7	6.2		
4.0	2.0	1.9	Cur. Mat.-L.T.D.	2.1	1.6	1.6	4.1		
13.6	22.7	13.9	Trade Payables	6.9	11.8	22.6	15.5		
.2	1.5	.2	Income Taxes Payable	.2	.0	.0	.2		
24.6	24.6	23.6	All Other Current	18.9	25.0	18.6	26.8		
56.0	70.3	66.4	Total Current	80.8	66.3	62.4	52.9		
15.8	14.4	14.4	Long-Term Debt	20.9	11.0	5.2	5.2		
.1	.3	.1	Deferred Taxes	.0	.0	.1	.0		
7.9	4.0	7.7	All Other Non-Current	16.7	3.5	4.1	2.4		
20.2	11.2	11.5	Net Worth	-18.3	19.2	28.2	39.6		
100.0	100.0	100.0	Total Liabilties & Net Worth	100.0	100.0	100.0	100.0		
			INCOME DATA						
100.0	100.0	100.0	Net Sales	100.0	100.0	100.0	100.0		
			Gross Profit						
94.8	98.4	92.8	Operating Expenses	81.8	97.6	94.6	92.1		
5.2	1.6	7.2	Operating Profit	18.2	2.4	5.4	7.9		
.4	1.6	1.5	All Other Expenses (net)	4.8	.8	.1	.0		
4.9	.0	5.7	Profit Before Taxes	13.4	1.6	5.3	7.9		
			RATIOS						
2.1	2.4	2.4		2.7	3.3	1.5	2.5		
1.3	1.2	1.4	Current	1.4	1.3	1.4	1.4		
1.0	.7	.9		.4	.8	1.0	1.1		
1.4	1.6	1.5		1.5	2.8	1.4	2.3		
.8	.8	1.0	Quick	.6	.8	.9	1.0		
.3	.4	.3		.1	.3	.2	.4		
3 111.0	0 UND	4 92.6		0 UND	6 59.7	8 46.1	13 28.2		
25 14.9	24 15.1	31 11.7	Sales/Receivables	1 254.9	28 13.1	38 9.7	30 12.3		
54 6.7	47 7.8	66 5.5		37 9.9	61 6.0	62 5.9	52 7.0		
			Cost of Sales/Inventory						
			Cost of Sales/Payables						
8.1	8.2	8.1		6.0	4.9	12.3	9.0		
20.0	46.7	18.4	Sales/Working Capital	46.2	13.9	29.3	18.9		
UND	-15.6	-35.1		-6.1	-15.3	-71.2	44.3		
17.3	21.5	19.6		16.4	8.2	43.6			
(73) 5.3	(64) 1.7	(66) 5.2	EBIT/Interest	(14) 6.8	(17) 3.8	(15) 6.2			
1.1	-1.5	1.3		.9	-3.5	1.3			
	8.5								
	(10) 1.7		Net Profit + Depr., Dep., Amort./Cur. Mat. L/T/D						
	.1								
.1	.1	.1		.2	.0	.2	.3		
.5	.6	.5	Fixed/Worth	1.7	.2	.4	.5		
-47.0	NM	10.0		-.8	NM	3.3	.7		
.9	.7	.8		1.1	.3	1.7	.7		
2.9	2.8	3.2	Debt/Worth	4.9	2.2	4.9	1.7		
-38.4	-13.2	92.1		-4.6	-124.8	22.7	3.4		
75.3	93.0	114.4		177.9	27.5	168.7	120.6		
(63) 30.0	(61) 33.8	(67) 30.5	% Profit Before Taxes/Tangible Net Worth	(13) 67.2	(17) 11.1	(14) 31.9	48.5		
9.1	-6.2	5.7		13.2	-12.5	5.1	7.0		
25.9	26.3	22.3		35.2	20.4	26.0	32.9		
9.5	2.4	9.8	% Profit Before Taxes/Total Assets	16.3	9.4	9.4	19.9		
-.2	-11.2	1.3		1.9	-4.0	.4	2.8		
86.8	217.2	88.9		94.0	80.4	116.4	94.8		
29.7	26.7	27.7	Sales/Net Fixed Assets	9.9	27.9	25.1	16.6		
11.8	9.6	10.7		3.6	13.0	15.3	10.9		
4.9	5.4	4.2		3.7	3.9	4.8	5.0		
3.2	3.3	3.0	Sales/Total Assets	2.0	2.8	3.3	3.7		
2.1	2.0	1.8		1.3	1.8	2.6	1.7		
.4	.4	.4		.8	.7	.3			
(63) .9	(53) .9	(56) .9	% Depr., Dep., Amort./Sales	(12) 2.4	(10) 1.4	(12) .7			
1.8	3.0	2.3		5.8	1.9	1.8			
2.4	3.5	4.1			5.8	3.1			
(46) 5.2	(44) 7.1	(37) 6.3	% Officers', Directors' Owners' Comp/Sales		(10) 7.0	(11) 6.0			
8.8	13.7	8.5			13.6	7.4			
1284723M	2882128M	652176M	Net Sales ($)	11899M	39408M	66741M	74799M	92767M	366562M
473650M	566116M	233752M	Total Assets ($)	9045M	18780M	21746M	28092M	40471M	115618M

M = $ thousand MM = $ million

See Pages 9 through 22 for Explanation of Ratios and Data

Current Data Sorted by Assets   **Comparative Historical Data**

0-500M	500M-2MM	2-10MM	10-50MM	50-100MM	100-250MM	Type of Statement	4/1/06-3/31/07 ALL	4/1/07-3/31/08 ALL
	4	4	7	2	2	Unqualified	20	18
	4	15	2			Reviewed	22	21
3	6	4				Compiled	40	30
13	8	5				Tax Returns	36	25
14	12	19	7	1	1	Other	86	62
	19 (4/1-9/30/10)		110 (10/1/10-3/31/11)				204	156
30	30	47	16	3	3	NUMBER OF STATEMENTS	204	156
%	%	%	%	%	%	**ASSETS**	%	%
24.4	18.4	10.5	9.0			Cash & Equivalents	14.6	14.3
28.2	33.3	32.1	19.3			Trade Receivables (net)	29.0	30.4
2.2	10.2	13.4	3.8			Inventory	6.7	5.7
4.4	1.9	2.7	4.4			All Other Current	3.8	3.7
59.2	63.8	58.7	36.5			Total Current	54.2	54.0
29.3	27.4	32.2	29.1			Fixed Assets (net)	32.8	32.7
6.5	4.4	4.0	17.9			Intangibles (net)	4.8	4.3
5.0	4.3	5.1	16.4			All Other Non-Current	8.2	9.0
100.0	100.0	100.0	100.0			Total	100.0	100.0
						LIABILITIES		
46.7	13.2	7.8	3.4			Notes Payable-Short Term	12.7	18.1
3.3	4.0	5.8	1.9			Cur. Mat.-L.T.D.	8.0	4.0
12.2	13.0	12.3	7.0			Trade Payables	11.8	11.7
.0	.8	.4	.0			Income Taxes Payable	.4	.5
8.1	11.8	11.0	12.1			All Other Current	15.3	14.0
70.3	42.7	37.3	24.5			Total Current	48.1	48.3
12.5	18.9	15.1	23.2			Long-Term Debt	23.4	19.3
.0	.1	.5	.0			Deferred Taxes	.6	.4
33.1	5.6	6.2	10.5			All Other Non-Current	6.3	5.5
-15.9	32.7	41.0	41.8			Net Worth	21.6	26.5
100.0	100.0	100.0	100.0			Total Liabilities & Net Worth	100.0	100.0
						INCOME DATA		
100.0	100.0	100.0	100.0			Net Sales	100.0	100.0
						Gross Profit		
89.8	96.4	92.9	89.6			Operating Expenses	94.9	95.3
10.2	3.6	7.1	10.4			Operating Profit	5.1	4.7
4.2	.4	1.0	6.4			All Other Expenses (net)	1.4	1.3
6.0	3.2	6.1	4.0			Profit Before Taxes	3.7	3.4
						RATIOS		
9.6	3.3	2.5	2.7				2.5	2.4
1.0	1.7	1.4	1.5			Current	1.4	1.5
.3	1.1	1.1	1.3				.9	.9
9.0	3.2	1.9	2.3				2.2	2.1
.8	1.0	1.0	1.3			Quick	1.1	1.1
.3	.6	.7	.8				.6	.7
0 UND	15 24.3	29 12.7	33 10.9				19 18.8	17 21.0
25 14.8	39 9.3	51 7.2	49 7.4			Sales/Receivables	45 8.1	43 8.5
66 5.6	61 6.0	67 5.5	78 4.7				61 6.0	63 5.8
						Cost of Sales/Inventory		
						Cost of Sales/Payables		
13.0	5.5	7.5	4.5				7.0	6.7
NM	12.1	14.2	8.2			Sales/Working Capital	19.5	16.0
-9.7	NM	57.0	19.8				-53.9	-62.9
9.8	39.5	24.8	7.1				9.0	9.9
(21) 3.5	(26) 2.9	(44) 4.7	(14) 3.3			EBIT/Interest	(174) 3.4	(133) 3.3
-.2	-.2	1.6	1.6				.9	.8
						Net Profit + Depr., Dep.,	7.8	3.3
						Amort./Cur. Mat. L/T/D	(31) 2.3	(23) 1.7
							1.3	.8
.2	.3	.3	.4				.4	.4
1.1	.7	.8	.8			Fixed/Worth	1.2	.8
-.7	4.4	2.4	13.2				9.2	3.4
.1	.4	.7	.8				.8	.6
136.4	1.7	1.7	1.7			Debt/Worth	2.6	1.8
-1.9	10.1	4.9	16.0				26.3	10.2
183.2	71.9	59.1	24.6			% Profit Before Taxes/Tangible	52.6	68.8
(16) 68.2	(24) 24.3	(41) 19.9	(13) 8.5			Net Worth	(162) 20.0	(129) 24.0
14.6	-15.5	8.2	2.5				1.7	3.8
38.7	47.0	17.7	5.6			% Profit Before Taxes/Total	17.0	20.7
15.0	2.0	7.1	2.4			Assets	6.2	6.6
-.6	-8.7	2.3	.3				-.1	-.5
47.9	69.0	26.9	21.9				33.3	31.3
19.5	12.8	9.7	9.2			Sales/Net Fixed Assets	9.9	10.1
9.4	4.6	3.5	1.9				4.3	4.0
8.0	3.4	3.2	1.5				3.9	3.9
4.0	2.5	2.1	1.1			Sales/Total Assets	2.5	2.4
2.4	1.9	1.7	.6				1.6	1.6
.5	1.5	1.0	1.7				1.2	1.3
(15) 1.2	(22) 2.6	(41) 2.6	(12) 3.0			% Depr., Dep., Amort./Sales	(168) 2.5	(119) 2.5
1.7	3.9	5.3	5.4				4.7	4.6
3.0	3.3	2.8				% Officers', Directors'	3.7	3.4
(17) 8.3	(18) 7.2	(17) 6.0				Owners' Comp/Sales	(81) 7.3	(65) 6.9
14.6	13.2	9.4					13.8	13.6
44888M	90603M	532767M	499025M	115213M	784136M	Net Sales ($)	7341093M	3828919M
7998M	31445M	225614M	416345M	201133M	470712M	Total Assets ($)	3074964M	1993521M

M = $ thousand   MM = $ million
See Pages 9 through 22 for Explanation of Ratios and Data

	Comparative Historical Data			Current Data Sorted by Sales					
Type of Statement					19 (4/1-9/30/10)		110 (10/1/10-3/31/11)		
Unqualified	13	13	15		2			6	7
Reviewed	22	21	21		3	1	6	8	3
Compiled	26	19	13	2	6	2	3		
Tax Returns	35	36	26	6	8	6	6		
Other	72	54	54	11	13	3	10	9	8
	4/1/08-3/31/09 ALL	4/1/09-3/31/10 ALL	4/1/10-3/31/11 ALL	0-1MM	1-3MM	3-5MM	5-10MM	10-25MM	25MM & OVER
NUMBER OF STATEMENTS	168	143	129	19	32	12	25	23	18
	%	%	%	%	%	%	%	%	%
ASSETS									
Cash & Equivalents	14.2	18.8	15.8	15.4	20.3	20.1	13.7	12.9	12.2
Trade Receivables (net)	30.5	28.9	29.1	29.9	23.1	35.8	35.2	25.4	30.9
Inventory	7.7	6.6	8.5	1.7	7.4	9.6	7.0	16.9	8.4
All Other Current	4.8	3.5	3.2	5.1	2.9	.7	1.4	4.8	3.3
Total Current	57.3	57.8	56.6	52.1	53.8	66.3	57.3	60.0	54.8
Fixed Assets (net)	29.1	30.3	29.8	36.9	34.6	24.8	30.7	30.8	14.5
Intangibles (net)	5.4	4.2	6.8	8.6	4.5	4.3	4.9	1.1	20.7
All Other Non-Current	8.2	7.7	6.8	2.4	7.1	4.7	7.1	8.1	10.0
Total	100.0	100.0	100.0	100.0	100.0	100.0	100.0	100.0	100.0
LIABILITIES									
Notes Payable-Short Term	14.9	23.7	17.2	58.2	18.2	6.0	7.3	7.1	6.4
Cur. Mat.-L.T.D.	6.5	4.4	4.1	2.0	4.1	6.7	7.4	2.8	1.5
Trade Payables	11.6	12.2	11.4	12.5	7.2	16.2	10.0	15.5	11.3
Income Taxes Payable	.2	.3	.3	.0	.1	1.6	.6	.1	.1
All Other Current	13.5	13.0	11.2	7.2	10.3	9.5	9.1	11.4	20.7
Total Current	46.7	53.5	44.2	79.9	39.9	40.0	34.4	37.0	40.0
Long-Term Debt	19.1	15.0	16.7	19.8	16.3	30.5	13.8	13.6	12.5
Deferred Taxes	.2	.2	.2	.0	.4	.0	.2	.4	.1
All Other Non-Current	6.0	8.7	12.7	6.8	34.4	7.6	2.7	6.9	4.9
Net Worth	28.0	22.6	26.2	-6.6	9.0	21.9	49.0	42.2	42.5
Total Liabilties & Net Worth	100.0	100.0	100.0	100.0	100.0	100.0	100.0	100.0	100.0
INCOME DATA									
Net Sales	100.0	100.0	100.0	100.0	100.0	100.0	100.0	100.0	100.0
Gross Profit									
Operating Expenses	95.7	96.1	92.7	90.3	90.0	95.7	92.1	95.7	94.7
Operating Profit	4.3	3.9	7.3	9.7	10.0	4.3	7.9	4.3	5.3
All Other Expenses (net)	1.1	1.1	2.3	6.4	2.8	.9	1.4	.3	1.8
Profit Before Taxes	3.2	2.8	5.1	3.3	7.2	3.5	6.6	4.0	3.5
RATIOS									
Current	2.9	2.8	3.3	3.3	3.2	5.6	4.0	3.6	2.3
	1.4	1.4	1.4	.7	1.4	2.9	1.4	2.1	1.4
	1.0	.9	.9	.3	.9	1.2	1.1	1.1	1.2
Quick	2.3	2.2	2.9	3.3	3.1	5.0	4.0	2.2	2.1
	1.1	1.2	1.1	.6	.9	2.7	1.2	1.3	1.2
	.6	.6	.6	.2	.5	.8	1.0	.6	.9
Sales/Receivables	22 16.4	18 20.2	22 16.5	0 UND	0 UND	36 10.2	37 9.8	24 15.5	40 9.1
	40 9.2	38 9.5	43 8.4	29 12.5	27 13.5	53 6.9	55 6.6	40 9.1	49 7.4
	59 6.2	60 6.0	66 5.5	73 5.0	49 7.5	69 5.3	70 5.2	64 5.7	73 5.0
Cost of Sales/Inventory									
Cost of Sales/Payables									
Sales/Working Capital	7.7	6.0	6.0	6.6	5.8	5.0	9.8	4.6	5.0
	18.9	15.3	14.3	-16.1	24.2	7.4	15.8	8.4	12.9
	183.8	-58.2	-66.6	-2.2	-38.8	26.5	76.5	40.0	28.6
EBIT/Interest	13.5	11.0	17.8	6.9	18.3	145.5	17.1	23.7	82.3
	(150) 3.5	(120) 2.8	(110) 3.7	(13) 1.6	(28) 3.2	(11) 2.8	(21) 5.0	(20) 3.9	(17) 4.3
	-.1	-1.1	1.0	-.5	1.0	-1.7	1.1	.4	1.5
Net Profit + Depr., Dep., Amort./Cur. Mat. L/T/D	3.4	4.7	5.1						
	(24) 1.3	(24) 2.0	(15) 1.8						
	-.2	.3	.3						
Fixed/Worth	.4	.3	.3	.3	.4	.1	.3	.3	.3
	.9	.7	.8	2.6	1.0	.7	.9	.7	.5
	4.2	4.7	7.0	-.7	-25.0	NM	1.5	1.7	-.8
Debt/Worth	.7	.6	.5	.3	.7	.4	.3	.5	1.0
	2.2	2.0	1.7	271.0	2.1	2.1	1.6	1.3	1.5
	11.6	19.8	162.1	-1.9	-40.0	NM	3.1	3.3	-8.6
% Profit Before Taxes/Tangible Net Worth	61.2	45.2	70.6	180.6	74.7		82.9	28.8	97.9
	(134) 19.1	(114) 12.1	(98) 19.6	(10) 50.5	(23) 22.4		(24) 16.9	(19) 16.3	(13) 10.8
	1.6	-.3	2.6	-3.0	2.7		2.7	7.6	3.4
% Profit Before Taxes/Total Assets	19.4	15.3	21.1	30.3	21.2	48.0	32.7	12.0	12.6
	5.7	4.5	6.1	4.1	10.7	7.1	6.1	7.1	4.9
	-3.7	-4.5	-.4	-5.3	.1	-7.9	.2	-1.7	.3
Sales/Net Fixed Assets	41.4	38.4	38.7	20.2	35.6	136.0	32.1	25.8	59.0
	13.4	12.7	14.0	15.2	12.8	42.8	9.7	11.2	24.3
	4.8	5.5	4.0	2.4	4.5	4.8	3.5	2.5	10.8
Sales/Total Assets	4.5	4.2	3.7	3.8	4.6	4.4	3.2	3.3	3.0
	2.7	2.6	2.4	2.4	2.5	2.7	2.5	2.0	1.5
	1.7	1.9	1.4	1.1	1.6	1.9	1.7	1.4	1.0
% Depr., Dep., Amort./Sales	1.1	.9	1.0			1.2	1.0	1.5	1.0
	(125) 2.5	(113) 2.2	(95) 2.5		(26) 2.3		(22) 2.4	(18) 2.5	(13) 2.1
	5.3	4.5	4.5			4.5		4.6	4.7	4.3
% Officers', Directors' Owners' Comp/Sales	4.4	5.3	3.1	3.0	3.3		2.4		
	(77) 7.5	(65) 10.1	(54) 6.9	(10) 7.0	(18) 9.2		(12) 3.6		
	14.0	19.0	11.7	14.8	13.1		7.4		
Net Sales ($)	2879799M	1373045M	2066632M	11245M	64236M	46554M	182680M	342045M	1419872M
Total Assets ($)	1317493M	732035M	1353247M	7006M	69206M	18881M	91667M	236363M	930124M

M = $ thousand   MM = $ million
See Pages 9 through 22 for Explanation of Ratios and Data

Current Data Sorted by Assets   Comparative Historical Data

Type of Statement								
Unqualified							107	86
Reviewed							78	57
Compiled							51	38
Tax Returns							90	75
Other							248	260

	5 / 6 / 38 / 34	3 / 9 / 22 / 42 / 83	33 / 48 / 27 / 21 / 124	48 / 13 / 1 / 74	16 / 1 / 10	18 / 16		
		67 (4/1-9/30/10)		625 (10/1/10-3/31/11)			4/1/06-3/31/07	4/1/07-3/31/08
	0-500M	500M-2MM	2-10MM	10-50MM	50-100MM	100-250MM	ALL	ALL
NUMBER OF STATEMENTS	83	159	253	136	27	34	574	516
ASSETS	%	%	%	%	%	%	%	%
Cash & Equivalents	29.6	21.0	18.6	24.2	23.7	23.4	20.0	19.6
Trade Receivables (net)	27.0	45.8	47.2	34.3	29.3	20.3	42.4	41.0
Inventory	2.2	1.9	2.2	3.0	3.0	1.5	2.2	2.4
All Other Current	4.8	2.2	4.1	6.2	8.1	8.6	4.7	5.3
Total Current	63.5	71.0	72.2	67.8	64.2	53.8	69.3	68.2
Fixed Assets (net)	15.7	14.9	10.9	12.3	5.6	11.6	12.4	12.4
Intangibles (net)	5.2	5.4	6.4	13.5	24.5	28.9	9.6	10.1
All Other Non-Current	15.5	8.8	10.6	6.4	5.7	5.8	8.6	9.3
Total	100.0	100.0	100.0	100.0	100.0	100.0	100.0	100.0
LIABILITIES								
Notes Payable-Short Term	39.9	13.4	8.0	4.9	.1	.9	13.8	13.2
Cur. Mat.-L.T.D.	2.9	2.4	1.8	2.0	1.6	1.7	2.1	2.8
Trade Payables	11.9	11.2	11.7	9.6	9.5	9.0	11.0	10.8
Income Taxes Payable	.4	.4	.5	.4	.1	.5	.6	.8
All Other Current	18.7	22.5	22.5	25.9	33.3	19.2	24.3	21.0
Total Current	73.8	49.8	44.6	42.8	44.6	31.2	51.8	48.6
Long-Term Debt	13.3	11.9	7.2	6.5	9.2	7.4	10.4	10.0
Deferred Taxes	.0	.0	.6	.5	1.0	1.0	.5	.5
All Other Non-Current	20.8	11.3	7.9	11.8	5.0	8.9	11.8	7.9
Net Worth	-7.9	26.9	39.6	38.4	40.2	51.5	25.6	33.1
Total Liabilities & Net Worth	100.0	100.0	100.0	100.0	100.0	100.0	100.0	100.0
INCOME DATA								
Net Sales	100.0	100.0	100.0	100.0	100.0	100.0	100.0	100.0
Gross Profit								
Operating Expenses	90.1	89.9	91.7	94.3	90.1	88.1	94.4	94.5
Operating Profit	9.9	10.1	8.3	5.7	9.9	11.9	5.6	5.5
All Other Expenses (net)	1.0	2.2	.9	.7	1.3	2.0	.8	1.3
Profit Before Taxes	8.9	7.9	7.4	5.0	8.6	9.9	4.8	4.2
RATIOS								
Current	2.0	4.1	3.2	2.7	2.2	2.5	2.9	2.8
	1.1	1.7	1.8	1.6	1.3	1.5	1.5	1.6
	.5	1.0	1.1	1.1	1.1	1.1	1.0	1.0
Quick	1.7	3.9	-2.9	2.5	1.6	2.4	2.6	2.6
	.9	1.6	1.7	1.4	1.2	1.1	1.4	1.4
	.5	.9	1.0	.9	.8	.7	.9	.9
Sales/Receivables	0 UND	22 16.4	41 8.9	49 7.5	60 6.1	39 9.4	35 10.4	35 10.6
	8 43.1	47 7.8	60 6.1	62 5.9	74 4.9	56 6.6	58 6.3	58 6.3
	37 9.8	68 5.4	84 4.4	83 4.4	88 4.2	79 4.6	78 4.7	78 4.7
Cost of Sales/Inventory								
Cost of Sales/Payables								
Sales/Working Capital	17.9	5.8	5.2	3.6	3.2	3.0	5.9	5.8
	417.4	12.7	9.6	7.6	7.2	7.0	13.9	12.9
	-16.2	-161.2	34.1	36.2	38.8	58.6	-220.9	362.3
EBIT/Interest	23.2	42.8	80.5	48.7	300.8	26.3	29.5	19.9
	(60) 5.5	(107) 9.3	(188) 20.8	(95) 14.2	(23) 15.0	(23) 15.1	(451) 6.3	(373) 5.2
	1.1	1.7	5.3	3.2	.9	1.1	1.3	.9
Net Profit + Depr., Dep., Amort./Cur. Mat. L/T/D			14.4	16.7			26.1	30.0
			(26) 3.3	(26) 3.7			(70) 6.3	(61) 3.8
			1.3	2.2			1.2	.5
Fixed/Worth	.0	.0	.1	.1	.1	.1	.1	.1
	.7	.2	.2	.3	.2	.4	.3	.3
	-.3	3.3	.7	2.1	-.4	-2.2	2.9	1.9
Debt/Worth	.8	.5	.6	.7	.9	.8	.8	.6
	5.3	1.8	1.4	1.8	2.3	2.2	2.2	1.8
	-3.1	15.9	4.3	15.2	-4.8	-14.9	41.5	13.3
% Profit Before Taxes/Tangible Net Worth	283.9	92.7	81.9	57.4	105.2	66.1	78.6	70.5
	(48) 61.7	(127) 42.2	(224) 42.9	(108) 30.3	(18) 18.0	(25) 30.4	(440) 39.1	(407) 34.6
	3.1	14.1	17.9	12.2	4.0	4.5	11.5	9.3
% Profit Before Taxes/Total Assets	78.3	37.3	27.9	22.4	21.7	17.3	25.1	24.1
	20.1	14.3	14.4	10.5	10.8	8.8	11.4	9.3
	1.3	2.2	4.9	2.7	.8	1.4	1.3	.2
Sales/Net Fixed Assets	392.3	209.1	159.2	67.7	54.5	40.4	113.5	109.3
	112.8	65.6	40.2	29.5	26.7	16.8	42.1	36.2
	30.0	22.8	18.1	12.1	14.7	8.9	16.1	15.8
Sales/Total Assets	12.0	4.8	3.7	2.6	1.7	1.3	4.3	4.2
	6.4	3.5	2.6	1.7	1.2	.9	2.8	2.7
	4.0	2.3	1.8	1.1	.7	.6	1.6	1.5
% Depr., Dep., Amort./Sales	.2	.3	.3	.8	.8	.7	.4	.4
	(40) .4	(97) .7	(157) .8	(83) 1.9	(15) 1.9	(18) 2.2	(359) 1.1	(331) 1.1
	1.1	2.0	1.7	3.5	4.9	4.1	2.5	2.7
% Officers', Directors' Owners' Comp/Sales	7.0	2.6	1.7	1.4			3.7	3.1
	(37) 10.3	(62) 6.3	(50) 4.7	(16) 11.4			(160) 7.2	(149) 6.6
	18.2	11.2	8.7	23.5			12.8	13.5
Net Sales ($)	175127M	694666M	3304843M	5824986M	2920074M	5714734M	14248138M	12854996M
Total Assets ($)	20815M	187082M	1180697M	3047625M	2078163M	5104177M	7607978M	9278578M

© RMA 2011   M = $ thousand   MM = $ million
See Pages 9 through 22 for Explanation of Ratios and Data

Comparative Historical Data			Type of Statement	Current Data Sorted by Sales					
112	126	118	Unqualified			5	13	32	68
68	73	76	Reviewed	2	9	7	10	33	15
57	64	55	Compiled	5	11	9	19	9	2
105	101	102	Tax Returns	14	25	22	27	6	8
280	338	341	Other	22	43	42	70	82	82
4/1/08-3/31/09	4/1/09-3/31/10	4/1/10-3/31/11			67 (4/1-9/30/10)			625 (10/1/10-3/31/11)	
ALL	ALL	ALL		0-1MM	1-3MM	3-5MM	5-10MM	10-25MM	25MM & OVER
622	702	692	NUMBER OF STATEMENTS	43	88	85	139	162	175
%	%	%	ASSETS	%	%	%	%	%	%
21.7	23.4	22.0	Cash & Equivalents	21.6	24.2	24.2	18.1	23.6	21.6
40.8	38.4	39.9	Trade Receivables (net)	18.9	38.1	39.1	41.4	46.8	38.9
2.1	1.8	2.3	Inventory	1.4	2.8	2.2	1.6	1.9	3.3
5.1	6.0	4.5	All Other Current	1.1	2.9	3.5	4.6	4.8	6.4
69.7	69.6	68.8	Total Current	43.1	68.0	68.8	65.7	77.1	70.2
13.1	11.9	12.5	Fixed Assets (net)	32.4	13.3	13.2	13.2	9.5	9.0
8.8	9.8	9.2	Intangibles (net)	14.2	6.3	5.4	7.8	6.5	15.0
8.5	8.7	9.5	All Other Non-Current	10.3	12.4	12.5	13.2	7.0	5.8
100.0	100.0	100.0	Total	100.0	100.0	100.0	100.0	100.0	100.0
			LIABILITIES						
13.3	14.1	11.8	Notes Payable-Short Term	16.6	32.0	14.0	10.1	7.1	5.1
3.2	3.2	2.1	Cur. Mat.-L.T.D.	3.6	1.9	1.8	3.1	1.6	1.7
12.8	11.9	11.0	Trade Payables	8.1	9.5	9.8	10.5	12.0	12.3
.6	.6	.4	Income Taxes Payable	.8	.4	.2	.6	.5	.3
22.0	24.3	23.0	All Other Current	20.6	21.7	20.5	20.0	25.5	25.5
51.9	54.1	48.3	Total Current	49.7	65.5	46.2	44.3	46.7	45.0
12.3	9.5	9.0	Long-Term Debt	32.1	9.7	9.2	8.8	4.8	6.9
.4	.4	.4	Deferred Taxes	.0	.0	.1	.4	.7	.6
9.6	10.9	10.9	All Other Non-Current	27.4	16.0	11.6	8.0	7.7	9.1
25.8	25.1	31.4	Net Worth	-9.2	8.8	32.8	38.5	40.1	38.4
100.0	100.0	100.0	Total Liabilties & Net Worth	100.0	100.0	100.0	100.0	100.0	100.0
			INCOME DATA						
100.0	100.0	100.0	Net Sales	100.0	100.0	100.0	100.0	100.0	100.0
			Gross Profit						
94.0	93.5	91.4	Operating Expenses	72.1	93.8	93.6	93.1	92.0	91.8
6.0	6.5	8.6	Operating Profit	27.9	6.2	6.4	6.9	8.0	8.2
1.4	1.2	1.3	All Other Expenses (net)	8.8	1.2	.2	.7	.6	.9
4.5	5.3	7.4	Profit Before Taxes	19.1	5.0	6.2	6.1	7.4	7.3
			RATIOS						
2.8	2.8	3.0		2.1	3.2	3.9	3.9	2.6	2.5
1.5	1.6	1.6	Current	.9	1.3	1.7	2.0	1.7	1.6
1.0	1.0	1.0		.4	.7	1.0	1.1	1.1	1.1
2.6	2.5	2.7		1.7	3.1	3.7	3.6	2.5	2.4
(621) 1.3	(701) 1.4	1.4	Quick	.9	1.2	1.7	1.7	1.5	1.3
.8	.8	.9		.4	.6	.9	1.0	1.0	.9
31 11.6	29 12.7	33 10.9		0 UND	12 30.6	30 12.3	36 10.1	41 8.8	49 7.4
52 7.0	52 7.0	55 6.7	Sales/Receivables	1 459.5	43 8.5	49 7.5	53 6.9	59 6.1	62 5.9
74 4.9	75 4.9	76 4.8		33 11.0	73 5.0	71 5.2	76 4.8	82 4.4	81 4.5
			Cost of Sales/Inventory						
			Cost of Sales/Payables						
5.8	5.4	5.1		9.8	6.2	5.5	5.3	5.0	4.6
13.4	13.8	11.4	Sales/Working Capital	-124.5	31.6	9.0	11.6	10.3	9.6
-130.4	-174.0	395.3		-6.8	-18.3	475.5	139.9	30.4	36.9
29.7	27.2	53.2		8.7	22.3	44.3	61.0	81.5	58.2
(469) 7.1	(495) 7.4	(496) 14.1	EBIT/Interest	(24) 5.1	(65) 6.6	(56) 14.0	(106) 14.9	(116) 24.9	(129) 15.6
.9	.7	3.0		.0	1.6	1.7	2.2	6.2	3.8
10.8	14.1	19.1						23.2	24.2
(74) 4.0	(72) 3.4	(65) 3.6	Net Profit + Depr., Dep., Amort./Cur. Mat. L/T/D					(21) 3.2	(27) 6.5
.8	.5	1.9						1.3	3.4
.1	.1	.1		.0	.1	.0	.0	.0	.1
.3	.3	.2	Fixed/Worth	2.0	.4	.3	.2	.2	.3
5.1	6.0	1.9		-1.4	NM	1.2	1.1	.7	2.7
.7	.7	.7		1.2	.8	.5	.4	.7	.7
2.1	2.0	1.9	Debt/Worth	5.3	3.2	1.6	1.3	1.5	2.3
69.1	182.1	14.9		-2.0	-22.2	7.3	6.7	4.8	89.9
82.3	78.5	83.9		61.6	136.4	83.1	86.5	76.3	85.9
(473) 34.0	(530) 30.5	(550) 40.1	% Profit Before Taxes/Tangible Net Worth	(23) 20.7	(65) 52.2	(71) 44.1	(115) 40.3	(142) 41.6	(134) 35.1
6.9	9.8	14.1		4.3	12.0	15.1	8.0	18.7	15.6
26.2	24.4	29.9		54.1	41.8	35.4	29.5	27.9	24.1
10.1	10.0	13.6	% Profit Before Taxes/Total Assets	9.8	14.1	17.3	13.9	13.8	11.9
.2	.9	3.0		1.7	1.8	4.4	1.1	5.7	2.8
130.4	145.4	152.6		162.3	153.7	143.3	165.5	183.6	99.9
39.2	44.1	44.4	Sales/Net Fixed Assets	51.3	54.0	48.8	44.9	45.7	35.3
15.2	16.6	16.7		.3	19.6	17.3	18.7	18.5	15.1
4.6	4.3	4.2		5.4	5.4	4.8	4.6	3.8	3.2
2.9	2.8	2.6	Sales/Total Assets	2.1	3.1	2.9	2.9	2.7	1.9
1.6	1.6	1.5		.2	2.0	1.7	1.8	1.6	1.1
.4	.4	.3		1.0	.4	.3	.3	.3	.5
(376) 1.0	(409) 1.0	(410) .9	% Depr., Dep., Amort./Sales	(18) 5.7	(53) .8	(51) .9	(81) .9	(104) .8	(103) 1.2
2.6	2.2	2.2		22.9	2.0	1.7	2.0	1.8	3.1
3.0	2.7	2.6			5.8	5.9	4.8	1.7	1.0
(158) 5.9	(191) 6.0	(168) 6.9	% Officers', Directors' Owners' Comp/Sales		(37) 10.3	(27) 7.9	(45) 4.7	(25) 3.4	(25) 3.6
13.1	11.9	13.8			16.7	11.7	6.9	11.3	19.9
19137886M 10387008M	17538981M 11756229M	18634430M 11618559M	Net Sales ($) Total Assets ($)	18396M 20594M	181762M 72440M	326427M 185910M	977749M 502547M	2585136M 1304978M	14544960M 9532090M

© RMA 2011　　　M = $ thousand　　MM = $ million

See Pages 9 through 22 for Explanation of Ratios and Data

Current Data Sorted by Assets   Comparative Historical Data

0-500M	500M-2MM	2-10MM	10-50MM	50-100MM	100-250MM	Type of Statement	ALL 4/1/06-3/31/07	ALL 4/1/07-3/31/08
	4	55	66	18	23	Unqualified	125	102
1	24	74	24			Reviewed	77	75
5	21	33	2			Compiled	58	43
35	36	12	4		1	Tax Returns	66	63
30	74	147	94	22	14	Other	234	262
92 (4/1-9/30/10)			727 (10/1/10-3/31/11)					
71	159	321	190	40	38	**NUMBER OF STATEMENTS**	560	545
%	%	%	%	%	%	**ASSETS**	%	%
27.9	17.4	17.2	15.5	15.4	14.7	Cash & Equivalents	14.8	14.4
27.6	48.9	50.3	47.3	32.1	25.2	Trade Receivables (net)	47.0	45.4
6.9	3.4	5.2	3.7	4.0	5.6	Inventory	5.9	5.4
5.1	3.8	5.3	6.6	5.4	9.8	All Other Current	4.8	4.7
67.5	73.4	78.0	73.1	56.9	55.3	Total Current	72.4	70.0
15.0	14.3	9.0	8.5	7.5	8.7	Fixed Assets (net)	11.4	13.4
6.2	4.3	6.2	10.7	28.0	27.3	Intangibles (net)	7.7	9.4
11.3	7.9	6.8	7.8	7.6	8.7	All Other Non-Current	8.5	7.3
100.0	100.0	100.0	100.0	100.0	100.0	Total	100.0	100.0
						LIABILITIES		
38.4	16.8	8.9	8.2	7.2	2.2	Notes Payable-Short Term	13.8	13.1
4.2	2.8	2.0	1.8	1.7	2.6	Cur. Mat.-L.T.D.	3.7	2.8
13.6	16.9	16.3	20.3	14.7	12.6	Trade Payables	17.2	17.5
.0	.6	.8	.7	.8	.4	Income Taxes Payable	.6	.7
32.2	18.2	21.2	19.1	22.0	20.7	All Other Current	18.2	17.4
88.5	55.2	49.4	50.1	46.4	38.5	Total Current	53.4	51.6
16.4	14.8	6.1	6.3	8.8	14.8	Long-Term Debt	9.9	10.5
.0	.2	.3	.4	1.3	.7	Deferred Taxes	.3	.5
11.0	5.9	7.6	5.7	13.2	8.5	All Other Non-Current	7.5	7.7
-15.9	23.9	36.6	37.4	30.2	37.5	Net Worth	28.8	29.7
100.0	100.0	100.0	100.0	100.0	100.0	Total Liabilities & Net Worth	100.0	100.0
						INCOME DATA		
100.0	100.0	100.0	100.0	100.0	100.0	Net Sales	100.0	100.0
						Gross Profit		
94.4	93.8	94.9	94.3	91.5	92.2	Operating Expenses	94.3	94.4
5.6	6.2	5.1	5.7	8.5	7.8	Operating Profit	5.7	5.6
.3	.5	.4	.8	1.9	2.0	All Other Expenses (net)	1.0	.9
5.3	5.7	4.6	4.9	6.6	5.8	Profit Before Taxes	4.7	4.7
						RATIOS		
2.5	2.9	2.7	2.0	1.7	2.2		2.2	2.3
1.2	1.5	1.6	1.4	1.2	1.5	Current	1.5	1.4
.5	1.0	1.1	1.1	.9	1.0		1.0	1.0
2.2	2.9	2.4	1.8	1.6	1.7		2.0	2.0
.9	1.3	1.4	1.2	1.0	1.0	Quick	(559) 1.2	1.2
.3	.8	1.0	.9	.7	.6		.8	.8
0 UND	30 12.3	41 8.8	51 7.2	40 9.1	56 6.5		38 9.7	38 9.6
10 37.5	48 7.7	59 6.2	67 5.4	65 5.7	69 5.3	Sales/Receivables	59 6.2	56 6.5
34 10.8	67 5.4	74 5.0	81 4.5	85 4.3	87 4.2		79 4.6	77 4.7
						Cost of Sales/Inventory		
						Cost of Sales/Payables		
15.1	7.8	5.6	6.5	7.7	4.5		6.4	6.9
110.5	14.8	11.7	12.9	17.7	9.4	Sales/Working Capital	13.1	14.6
-17.0	-163.5	38.9	38.9	-53.4	71.2		98.3	-999.8
24.8	23.2	52.9	46.0	40.2	24.0		22.4	25.3
(47) 12.5	(124) 6.5	(252) 16.0	(156) 10.9	(36) 10.4	(28) 4.6	EBIT/Interest	(450) 5.7	(445) 5.7
-.3	1.2	3.7	3.1	2.4	.5		1.3	1.7
		24.6	20.6				15.8	11.5
	(51) 7.7	(39) 5.0				Net Profit + Depr., Dep., Amort./Cur. Mat. L/T/D	(75) 3.2	(74) 3.3
		1.2	1.8				.3	1.3
.0	.0	.1	.1	.1	.2		.1	.1
.5	.2	.2	.2	.5	.6	Fixed/Worth	.3	.3
-.9	1.6	.7	.8	-.3	-.2		1.9	2.6
1.0	.7	.7	1.0	2.3	1.0		.8	.9
4.0	2.4	1.7	2.4	5.1	5.6	Debt/Worth	2.1	2.4
-3.4	20.8	5.7	8.5	-4.3	-6.9		15.8	23.0
201.1	81.5	71.8	58.8	61.7	42.7		73.4	76.7
(44) 80.4	(124) 41.3	(276) 38.9	(163) 35.1	(24) 46.6	(23) 17.6	% Profit Before Taxes/Tangible Net Worth	(445) 36.0	(425) 38.8
21.9	9.9	12.7	16.6	23.5	.3		13.7	12.9
61.9	36.2	25.8	19.6	15.9	9.6		22.2	24.1
20.3	13.6	11.3	10.6	9.5	5.7	% Profit Before Taxes/Total Assets	9.5	10.4
.0	1.2	3.4	3.1	2.1	.0		1.6	1.9
999.8	472.6	172.8	173.9	92.9	93.7		121.4	122.9
75.7	64.7	70.1	76.2	43.8	23.4	Sales/Net Fixed Assets	50.4	43.3
23.3	22.3	25.9	23.8	17.7	7.6		20.6	17.4
11.5	5.2	4.2	3.5	2.4	1.7		4.3	4.3
6.0	4.0	3.2	2.5	1.5	1.2	Sales/Total Assets	3.0	2.9
4.0	2.6	2.1	1.5	.8	.8		1.8	1.8
.4	.3	.2	.3	.2	1.5		.4	.4
(38) 1.1	(96) .8	(227) .6	(139) .6	(22) .8	(22) 2.7	% Depr., Dep., Amort./Sales	(390) .9	(368) .9
2.0	2.1	1.4	1.1	2.9	4.1		2.0	2.2
4.4	3.3	1.6	1.2				2.9	2.5
(38) 7.6	(56) 6.0	(57) 3.8	(21) 3.4			% Officers', Directors' Owners' Comp/Sales	(135) 5.6	(136) 5.1
14.1	10.1	5.4	16.3				11.5	9.3
147932M	719448M	5255574M	12279949M	5096912M	8720991M	Net Sales ($)	18214895M	18391158M
17292M	173138M	1644639M	3944682M	2919724M	6562318M	Total Assets ($)	8208790M	10003424M

M = $ thousand   MM = $ million
See Pages 9 through 22 for Explanation of Ratios and Data

Comparative Historical Data | Current Data Sorted by Sales

Type of Statement	4/1/08-3/31/09 ALL	4/1/09-3/31/10 ALL	4/1/10-3/31/11 ALL	0-1MM	1-3MM	3-5MM	5-10MM	10-25MM	25MM & OVER
Unqualified	126	161	166		2	3	8	40	113
Reviewed	102	102	123	1	9	10	24	45	34
Compiled	53	53	61	2	9	11	16	17	6
Tax Returns	82	91	88	15	30	10	16	13	4
Other	283	368	381	15	41	38	63	93	131
				92 (4/1-9/30/10)			**727 (10/1/10-3/31/11)**		
NUMBER OF STATEMENTS	646	775	819	33	91	72	127	208	288
ASSETS	%	%	%	%	%	%	%	%	%
Cash & Equivalents	16.1	17.8	17.6	19.0	22.3	15.8	22.9	17.3	14.2
Trade Receivables (net)	45.5	44.8	45.3	30.7	34.1	46.6	41.0	50.0	48.7
Inventory	4.7	4.8	4.6	11.6	4.1	5.8	4.6	3.2	4.7
All Other Current	5.1	5.2	5.5	4.3	5.0	1.4	5.5	5.2	7.1
Total Current	71.4	72.7	73.0	65.7	65.6	69.6	74.0	75.7	74.6
Fixed Assets (net)	11.5	11.1	10.4	14.7	17.8	13.9	10.5	9.9	6.9
Intangibles (net)	8.8	8.9	8.9	8.7	8.8	4.6	7.4	7.1	12.0
All Other Non-Current	8.3	7.4	7.8	11.0	7.8	11.9	8.2	7.2	6.5
Total	100.0	100.0	100.0	100.0	100.0	100.0	100.0	100.0	100.0
LIABILITIES									
Notes Payable-Short Term	15.5	14.4	12.5	24.7	28.1	16.8	10.6	9.0	8.4
Cur. Mat.-L.T.D.	2.4	3.0	2.3	3.8	4.3	1.4	2.3	2.8	1.5
Trade Payables	18.0	17.5	16.9	18.0	10.1	17.4	13.8	15.6	21.0
Income Taxes Payable	.6	.5	.6	.0	.4	.4	.6	.8	.8
All Other Current	17.9	19.1	21.1	43.0	18.5	15.5	22.0	20.7	20.7
Total Current	54.4	54.5	53.4	89.4	61.4	51.5	49.3	48.9	52.3
Long-Term Debt	11.2	10.8	9.3	19.6	15.4	15.0	9.8	6.9	6.2
Deferred Taxes	.3	.4	.3	.0	.0	.3	.1	.4	.5
All Other Non-Current	7.5	6.2	7.5	7.5	9.9	7.8	7.4	6.2	6.2
Net Worth	26.5	28.1	29.5	-16.6	13.3	25.5	33.3	35.8	34.8
Total Liabilties & Net Worth	100.0	100.0	100.0	100.0	100.0	100.0	100.0	100.0	100.0
INCOME DATA									
Net Sales	100.0	100.0	100.0	100.0	100.0	100.0	100.0	100.0	100.0
Gross Profit									
Operating Expenses	94.5	94.3	94.2	87.3	94.1	96.3	95.3	93.8	94.3
Operating Profit	5.5	5.7	5.8	12.7	5.9	3.7	4.7	6.2	5.7
All Other Expenses (net)	1.4	1.3	.7	1.1	.8	.7	.3	.5	.8
Profit Before Taxes	4.2	4.4	5.1	11.6	5.1	2.9	4.4	5.7	4.9
RATIOS									
Current	2.3	2.2	2.4	2.9	2.4	3.7	3.7	2.6	2.0
	1.5	1.4	1.5	1.2	1.3	1.6	1.6	1.6	1.4
	1.0	1.0	1.1	.5	.8	.9	1.0	1.2	1.1
Quick	2.1	1.9	2.2	2.7	2.1	3.6	3.4	2.5	1.7
	1.3	1.3	1.3	.7	1.2	1.4	1.4	1.5	1.2
	.8	.8	.8	.3	.6	.8	.8	1.0	.9
Sales/Receivables	33 11.1	35 10.4	37 9.9	0 UND	17 21.0	34 10.7	33 11.1	43 8.4	49 7.5
	53 6.9	55 6.7	57 6.4	19 19.7	37 9.9	48 7.5	51 7.2	61 6.0	64 5.7
	72 5.1	73 5.0	74 4.9	61 6.0	60 6.1	77 4.7	69 5.3	74 4.9	80 4.5
Cost of Sales/Inventory									
Cost of Sales/Payables									
Sales/Working Capital	6.6	6.7	6.6	6.0	9.1	5.2	4.9	5.8	7.7
	14.0	14.4	14.1	24.7	18.1	13.4	11.8	10.7	15.7
	299.8	793.9	95.7	-10.7	-32.4	-97.0	-191.1	31.0	41.3
EBIT/Interest	26.5	32.6	37.4	14.1	16.7	16.6	26.9	53.9	49.0
	(510) 7.0	(604) 7.6	(643) 11.3	(20) 4.3	(71) 4.9	(52) 4.9	(89) 7.2	(166) 17.5	(245) 15.0
	1.1	1.1	2.4	-1.6	1.0	-.8	-.1	4.5	3.6
Net Profit + Depr., Dep., Amort./Cur. Mat. L/T/D	11.4	15.6	21.6				12.9	22.6	23.4
	(83) 3.5	(103) 3.4	(112) 5.0			(10) 3.6	(34) 5.7	(61) 7.3	
	.7	.6	1.8				.0	1.2	2.4
Fixed/Worth	.1	.1	.1	.0	.1	.0	.0	.1	.1
	.3	.3	.2	.3	.6	.2	.2	.2	.2
	2.2	2.8	1.4	-.7	-105.6	2.0	1.6	.6	.8
Debt/Worth	.9	.9	.8	.5	.9	.5	.6	.8	1.1
	2.4	2.4	2.3	3.1	3.6	1.9	1.7	1.6	2.8
	35.7	38.4	12.4	-2.4	-16.8	-82.9	10.8	5.8	9.7
% Profit Before Taxes/Tangible Net Worth	66.7	64.5	73.8	145.9	94.0	70.4	75.6	75.6	65.6
	(502) 35.7	(602) 30.1	(654) 38.9	(18) 87.2	(64) 39.5	(53) 25.5	(104) 36.6	(176) 41.8	(239) 37.3
	10.6	8.0	13.3	10.7	11.2	2.3	6.2	16.8	16.7
% Profit Before Taxes/Total Assets	22.4	21.8	24.3	64.6	27.0	24.9	31.0	29.6	19.3
	9.6	8.0	10.9	15.7	10.4	6.2	10.5	14.0	10.0
	.8	.3	2.6	-4.4	.8	-.1	.1	4.5	3.4
Sales/Net Fixed Assets	144.5	157.9	187.1	UND	245.4	358.9	186.3	172.8	182.5
	50.9	58.0	66.2	82.8	30.4	62.5	60.7	74.1	73.1
	22.1	20.9	22.9	19.7	12.4	27.1	19.6	29.2	26.5
Sales/Total Assets	4.4	4.3	4.4	6.0	5.0	5.1	4.8	4.3	3.9
	3.3	3.0	3.1	3.5	3.2	3.7	2.9	3.2	2.9
	2.0	1.9	1.8	1.4	1.8	2.2	1.8	2.1	1.7
% Depr., Dep., Amort./Sales	.3	.3	.3	.6	.4	.3	.3	.3	.2
	(431) .7	(490) .7	(544) .7	(14) 1.8	(60) 1.5	(43) .9	(79) .7	(145) .6	(203) .5
	1.7	1.6	1.7	3.5	3.3	1.7	1.7	1.4	1.4
% Officers', Directors' Owners' Comp/Sales	2.2	2.4	2.9	6.5	5.7	3.2	2.6	2.1	1.0
	(142) 4.7	(186) 5.2	(173) 5.4	(10) 13.5	(43) 9.4	(28) 5.1	(27) 4.5	(44) 3.6	(21) 2.5
	8.7	10.9	10.8	24.4	13.0	8.8	6.4	5.6	19.0
Net Sales ($)	23302122M	27717292M	32220806M	19726M	182066M	289655M	921928M	3270850M	27536581M
Total Assets ($)	11331466M	14067052M	15261793M	10794M	83292M	137902M	454450M	1348623M	13226732M

© RMA 2011   M = $ thousand   MM = $ million
See Pages 9 through 22 for Explanation of Ratios and Data

	Current Data Sorted by Assets							Comparative Historical Data	
Type of Statement	0-500M	500M-2MM	2-10MM	10-50MM	50-100MM	100-250MM		4/1/06-3/31/07 ALL	4/1/07-3/31/08 ALL
Unqualified			2	2	4	4		5	5
Reviewed			2	1				2	
Compiled		2	1					1	1
Tax Returns		5	4	3		1		7	2
Other								10	14
		3 (4/1-9/30/10)		28 (10/1/10-3/31/11)					
NUMBER OF STATEMENTS		7	9	6	4	5		25	22
ASSETS	%	%	%	%	%	%		%	%
Cash & Equivalents	D							13.5	11.0
Trade Receivables (net)	A							50.4	46.4
Inventory	T							1.9	3.3
All Other Current	A							5.4	8.5
Total Current								71.2	69.1
Fixed Assets (net)	N							11.3	12.5
Intangibles (net)	O							7.6	8.2
All Other Non-Current	T							9.9	10.2
Total								100.0	100.0
LIABILITIES	A								
Notes Payable-Short Term	V							13.6	17.1
Cur. Mat.-L.T.D.	A							1.1	3.7
Trade Payables	I							18.0	16.7
Income Taxes Payable	L							2.1	1.7
All Other Current	A							23.1	22.2
Total Current	B							57.9	61.4
Long-Term Debt	L							9.3	15.4
Deferred Taxes	E							.7	.5
All Other Non-Current								3.6	2.2
Net Worth								28.6	20.4
Total Liabilties & Net Worth								100.0	100.0
INCOME DATA									
Net Sales								100.0	100.0
Gross Profit								52.6	42.0
Operating Expenses								46.7	36.6
Operating Profit								5.9	5.4
All Other Expenses (net)								2.1	1.9
Profit Before Taxes								3.8	3.6
RATIOS									
Current								1.7	1.7
								1.2	1.2
								.9	.9
Quick								1.5	1.6
								1.1	1.0
								.6	.5
Sales/Receivables								24 15.1	22 16.7
								49 7.5	53 6.9
								92 4.0	86 4.3
Cost of Sales/Inventory								0 UND	0 UND
								0 UND	0 UND
								0 UND	3 113.6
Cost of Sales/Payables								4 88.8	9 41.5
								26 13.9	35 10.3
								67 5.4	56 6.5
Sales/Working Capital								12.1	8.6
								30.9	20.5
								NM	-33.4
EBIT/Interest								25.6	42.4
								(20) 7.6	(18) 5.9
								1.5	-.2
Net Profit + Depr., Dep., Amort./Cur. Mat. L/T/D									
Fixed/Worth								.1	.1
								.3	.3
								NM	-1.2
Debt/Worth								.8	1.2
								4.0	3.0
								-84.1	-5.0
% Profit Before Taxes/Tangible Net Worth								183.2	55.2
								(18) 46.5	(15) 43.5
								4.1	12.4
% Profit Before Taxes/Total Assets								27.3	28.4
								13.0	11.0
								-1.9	-3.4
Sales/Net Fixed Assets								123.0	116.3
								41.2	61.1
								26.6	24.8
Sales/Total Assets								5.8	4.2
								3.2	3.2
								2.3	2.3
% Depr., Dep., Amort./Sales								.5	.4
								(15) .7	(14) .7
								1.4	1.2
% Officers', Directors' Owners' Comp/Sales									
Net Sales ($)		65240M	142700M	171734M	320343M	882711M		660572M	1765383M
Total Assets ($)		8990M	47929M	142922M	246612M	778132M		333042M	700695M

Comparative Historical Data / Current Data Sorted by Sales

4/1/08-3/31/09 ALL	4/1/09-3/31/10 ALL	4/1/10-3/31/11 ALL	Type of Statement	0-1MM	1-3MM	3-5MM	5-10MM	10-25MM	25MM & OVER
3	4	12	Unqualified				1	3	8
1	1	3	Reviewed					1	2
2	3		Compiled						
1	3	3	Tax Returns			1		2	
8	10	13	Other		2	1	3	4	3
					3 (4/1-9/30/10)		28 (10/1/10-3/31/11)		
15	21	31	NUMBER OF STATEMENTS		2	2	4	10	13
%	%	%	**ASSETS**	%	%	%	%	%	%
10.0	17.1	15.5	Cash & Equivalents	DATA NOT AVAILABLE				12.2	15.9
50.4	36.0	36.3	Trade Receivables (net)					38.3	31.4
9.7	3.0	4.3	Inventory					5.8	4.4
7.3	3.5	10.5	All Other Current					8.6	9.0
77.4	59.6	66.7	Total Current					64.9	60.7
17.2	26.6	12.2	Fixed Assets (net)					13.3	16.0
4.3	6.0	10.8	Intangibles (net)					11.3	15.0
1.1	7.9	10.3	All Other Non-Current					10.4	8.3
100.0	100.0	100.0	Total					100.0	100.0
			LIABILITIES						
18.4	8.4	8.1	Notes Payable-Short Term					7.5	4.8
3.9	7.5	2.8	Cur. Mat.-L.T.D.					4.5	3.0
28.3	19.3	15.3	Trade Payables					14.5	17.8
2.4	.2	.3	Income Taxes Payable					.0	.7
24.6	15.5	21.4	All Other Current					22.5	18.5
77.6	50.9	47.9	Total Current					49.0	44.8
6.2	16.6	8.6	Long-Term Debt					8.9	11.6
.6	.7	.4	Deferred Taxes					.2	.6
.6	3.8	12.1	All Other Non-Current					17.9	2.9
14.9	28.0	31.1	Net Worth					23.9	40.2
100.0	100.0	100.0	Total Liabilties & Net Worth					100.0	100.0
			INCOME DATA						
100.0	100.0	100.0	Net Sales					100.0	100.0
47.1	45.4	47.4	Gross Profit					51.4	40.1
39.9	35.7	39.6	Operating Expenses					46.4	29.9
7.1	9.7	7.8	Operating Profit					5.0	10.2
2.4	2.5	3.4	All Other Expenses (net)					5.2	2.7
4.8	7.2	4.5	Profit Before Taxes					-.1	7.5
			RATIOS						
1.5	2.1	1.9						2.0	2.2
1.0	1.3	1.3	Current					1.3	1.3
.7	.7	.8						.4	.8
1.5	1.8	1.6						1.5	1.6
.7	1.0	1.1	Quick					1.1	.8
.3	.6	.5						.4	.5
29 12.6	**16** 22.5	**23** 15.8						**17** 21.5	**20** 18.6
52 7.0	**41** 9.0	**52** 7.0	Sales/Receivables					**46** 7.9	**57** 6.4
72 5.1	**74** 4.9	**81** 4.5						**87** 4.2	**77** 4.7
0 UND	**0** UND	**0** UND						**0** UND	**0** UND
3 112.3	**0** UND	**0** 999.8	Cost of Sales/Inventory					**0** UND	**0** 756.2
5 71.5	**8** 43.9	**9** 40.8						**10** 37.5	**13** 27.4
22 16.7	**14** 25.3	**19** 19.6						**15** 24.6	**20** 17.8
32 11.5	**42** 8.7	**41** 8.9	Cost of Sales/Payables					**35** 10.5	**60** 6.1
149 2.5	**115** 3.2	**128** 2.8						**103** 3.6	**107** 3.4
10.5	8.8	6.7						5.7	8.7
-393.1	21.7	20.3	Sales/Working Capital					29.3	24.6
-10.0	-18.2	-14.7						-6.7	-13.7
22.7	22.8	100.6							33.5
5.2	(18) 4.1	(24) 7.5	EBIT/Interest						(11) 7.1
-.2	1.0	1.7							2.4
			Net Profit + Depr., Dep., Amort./Cur. Mat. L/T/D						
.1	.2	.1						.1	.1
1.1	1.2	.3	Fixed/Worth					.2	.7
-.6	UND	45.8						NM	NM
1.8	1.0	1.0						1.9	1.1
6.6	6.0	2.5	Debt/Worth					4.4	2.5
-8.2	UND	52.6						NM	NM
	181.0	70.2							54.5
	(17) 76.9	(24) 31.8	% Profit Before Taxes/Tangible Net Worth						(10) 14.4
	33.2	7.2							-15.3
16.7	48.9	20.4						34.7	12.0
4.4	12.0	6.8	% Profit Before Taxes/Total Assets					13.0	5.6
-6.8	2.4	.8						-.1	.5
113.0	100.6	147.2						208.5	137.7
44.3	22.5	63.0	Sales/Net Fixed Assets					64.5	36.2
17.6	8.2	20.7						11.6	15.6
4.6	4.2	3.6						4.2	3.5
3.6	2.9	2.3	Sales/Total Assets					2.4	1.9
2.2	1.9	.9						.6	.9
.4	.7	.3							
(11) .9	(14) 2.7	(19) .6	% Depr., Dep., Amort./Sales						
1.2	5.4	1.9							
			% Officers', Directors' Owners' Comp/Sales						
782225M	**675775M**	**1582728M**	Net Sales ($)		**4396M**	**7822M**	**34479M**	**158567M**	**1377464M**
314950M	**490627M**	**1224585M**	Total Assets ($)		**5176M**	**2949M**	**19384M**	**163123M**	**1033953M**

M = $ thousand MM = $ million

See Pages 9 through 22 for Explanation of Ratios and Data

Current Data Sorted by Assets

Comparative Historical Data

						Type of Statement		
	4	23	25	14	5	Unqualified	81	59
2	16	49	11			Reviewed	57	61
11	17	14	2		1	Compiled	41	40
73	64	28	3	1	1	Tax Returns	102	93
51	93	94	37	17	9	Other	196	216
	60 (4/1-9/30/10)		605 (10/1/10-3/31/11)				4/1/06-3/31/07	4/1/07-3/31/08
0-500M	500M-2MM	2-10MM	10-50MM	50-100MM	100-250MM		ALL	ALL
137	194	208	78	32	16	**NUMBER OF STATEMENTS**	477	469
%	%	%	%	%	%	**ASSETS**	%	%
33.4	17.8	14.5	16.3	15.6	14.9	Cash & Equivalents	17.9	16.7
26.5	43.6	51.4	43.1	30.9	19.8	Trade Receivables (net)	42.5	42.3
3.2	3.1	3.1	4.4	1.3	4.4	Inventory	5.5	5.8
3.8	2.9	5.0	6.3	9.7	6.3	All Other Current	4.4	4.1
66.9	67.5	74.0	70.2	57.5	45.4	Total Current	70.3	69.0
18.2	17.2	12.4	10.2	14.8	13.0	Fixed Assets (net)	15.4	15.1
4.7	6.5	5.7	12.6	24.0	28.3	Intangibles (net)	6.3	7.6
10.2	8.9	7.9	7.0	3.8	13.3	All Other Non-Current	8.0	8.3
100.0	100.0	100.0	100.0	100.0	100.0	Total	100.0	100.0
						LIABILITIES		
26.9	13.4	9.5	9.1	4.9	.9	Notes Payable-Short Term	16.4	16.8
2.4	3.4	1.9	2.8	4.0	7.0	Cur. Mat.-L.T.D.	2.8	3.2
12.5	15.8	15.9	17.1	14.1	14.0	Trade Payables	15.8	16.1
.1	.4	.5	.2	.4	.1	Income Taxes Payable	.6	.4
23.6	16.1	18.6	21.4	17.0	15.2	All Other Current	18.4	18.7
65.5	49.0	46.5	50.6	40.3	37.3	Total Current	53.9	55.2
18.1	14.2	10.2	8.4	13.0	14.0	Long-Term Debt	11.8	13.0
.0	.2	.2	.2	1.2	2.4	Deferred Taxes	.4	.2
14.0	12.6	5.8	7.0	3.1	8.6	All Other Non-Current	11.1	10.6
2.4	24.0	37.3	33.8	42.3	37.8	Net Worth	22.8	21.1
100.0	100.0	100.0	100.0	100.0	100.0	Total Liabilities & Net Worth	100.0	100.0
						INCOME DATA		
100.0	100.0	100.0	100.0	100.0	100.0	Net Sales	100.0	100.0
						Gross Profit		
91.2	90.9	92.0	93.5	93.0	92.3	Operating Expenses	93.6	94.9
8.8	9.1	8.0	6.5	7.0	7.7	Operating Profit	6.4	5.1
.6	2.1	.9	1.5	2.2	2.3	All Other Expenses (net)	1.3	.8
8.2	7.1	7.1	4.9	4.8	5.4	Profit Before Taxes	5.1	4.3
						RATIOS		
3.8	3.3	2.5	2.3	1.8	2.2		2.6	2.5
1.5	1.4	1.6	1.4	1.5	1.2	Current	1.5	1.4
.7	.9	1.1	1.1	1.0	.8		1.0	.9
3.1	2.7	2.4	2.1	1.8	1.7		2.2	2.2
(136) 1.4	1.3	1.4	1.2	1.2	1.0	Quick	(476) 1.2	(468) 1.2
.6	.8	1.0	.9	.7	.5		.8	.7
0 UND	16 22.9	40 9.0	38 9.7	36 10.2	18 20.0		29 12.6	30 12.0
12 30.0	40 9.2	60 6.1	60 6.0	62 5.9	47 7.7	Sales/Receivables	52 7.0	48 7.5
35 10.4	63 5.8	79 4.6	79 4.6	73 5.0	68 5.4		76 4.8	69 5.3
						Cost of Sales/Inventory		
						Cost of Sales/Payables		
9.6	7.1	6.4	5.9	5.9	5.9		6.9	7.6
51.0	21.4	12.8	14.2	12.5	23.0	Sales/Working Capital	16.3	18.6
-60.0	-47.2	50.6	103.6	NM	-22.5		-241.5	-74.3
18.4	39.3	46.5	85.3	30.6	24.0		17.7	17.0
(90) 5.5	(151) 7.4	(161) 12.4	(64) 8.7	(27) 3.8	(14) 2.6	EBIT/Interest	(360) 5.1	(369) 5.5
.3	1.5	3.4	1.9	.0	.0		1.4	1.2
		17.4	14.6				19.4	10.1
	(22) 5.2	(21) 2.7			Net Profit + Depr., Dep.,	(46) 3.5	(47) 2.6
		2.2	1.0			Amort./Cur. Mat. L/T/D	.8	.9
.1	.0	.0	.1	.2	.1		.1	.1
.4	.4	.2	.1	.8	1.3	Fixed/Worth	.4	.4
-.8	7.2	.9	3.2	-6.2	-.4		22.2	10.3
.4	.6	.7	1.1	1.1	1.2		.9	.8
2.3	2.5	1.9	2.7	2.7	3.9	Debt/Worth	2.9	2.9
-3.4	54.0	6.1	42.2	-16.4	-3.2		-125.4	-54.1
165.4	100.0	80.8	82.5	74.6	57.3	% Profit Before Taxes/Tangible	75.4	96.4
(83) 70.3	(147) 56.0	(181) 46.5	(63) 50.6	(22) 36.3	(10) 27.4	Net Worth	(357) 37.4	(347) 42.0
25.1	17.9	23.3	16.6	6.7	2.6		11.7	12.0
71.3	40.1	27.9	24.4	14.4	10.1	% Profit Before Taxes/Total	26.6	27.8
22.8	14.3	13.6	8.1	7.6	5.4	Assets	10.3	11.2
2.7	2.1	6.3	2.7	-1.4	-.5		1.2	1.5
410.8	226.8	160.7	167.6	42.4	159.9		118.5	167.4
52.9	59.3	63.0	80.7	23.9	14.2	Sales/Net Fixed Assets	41.0	43.5
24.9	15.5	19.2	26.0	10.0	6.8		15.2	15.8
9.7	5.4	4.2	3.3	2.6	2.5		4.8	5.0
5.5	3.7	3.1	2.5	1.9	1.1	Sales/Total Assets	3.2	3.3
4.1	2.5	2.0	1.6	1.1	.9		2.0	2.1
.5	.2	.2	.3	.9			.4	.4
(68) 1.4	(107) .8	(145) .7	(53) .6	(24) 1.8		% Depr., Dep., Amort./Sales	(330) 1.0	(308) 1.0
2.2	2.6	1.7	1.9	3.4			2.3	2.8
4.9	3.8	1.6	1.3			% Officers', Directors'	3.3	2.9
(78) 8.4	(88) 7.1	(66) 2.9	(11) 3.6			Owners' Comp/Sales	(152) 6.0	(157) 6.4
17.2	10.6	5.4	15.3				12.6	11.7
262060M	882496M	3354274M	4465501M	4436394M	3926681M	Net Sales ($)	9139532M	12201138M
33406M	223124M	920124M	1681330M	2194873M	2478656M	Total Assets ($)	4666207M	5597101M

M = $ thousand   MM = $ million
See Pages 9 through 22 for Explanation of Ratios and Data

Comparative Historical Data				Current Data Sorted by Sales					
			Type of Statement			3	5	22	41
81	81	71	Unqualified						
72	68	78	Reviewed	1	6	5	16	33	17
53	47	45	Compiled	4	8	15	6	9	3
125	128	170	Tax Returns	33	54	31	27	19	6
205	294	301	Other	24	55	38	68	56	60
4/1/08-3/31/09	4/1/09-3/31/10	4/1/10-3/31/11		60 (4/1-9/30/10)			605 (10/1/10-3/31/11)		
ALL	ALL	ALL		0-1MM	1-3MM	3-5MM	5-10MM	10-25MM	25MM & OVER
536	618	665	**NUMBER OF STATEMENTS**	62	123	92	122	139	127
%	%	%	**ASSETS**	%	%	%	%	%	%
16.6	16.9	19.6	Cash & Equivalents	28.7	23.4	17.8	20.0	16.7	15.8
40.5	42.1	41.3	Trade Receivables (net)	18.1	33.1	42.5	45.9	52.2	43.3
5.3	4.2	3.2	Inventory	3.8	2.7	4.4	3.3	2.2	3.6
4.4	4.3	4.6	All Other Current	3.7	3.2	3.5	2.9	6.8	6.3
66.9	67.5	68.7	Total Current	54.2	62.5	68.2	72.1	77.9	68.9
15.9	15.0	14.9	Fixed Assets (net)	33.2	16.9	14.6	13.7	10.8	9.8
8.9	8.8	7.9	Intangibles (net)	5.6	9.7	5.1	5.8	5.4	14.3
8.4	8.7	8.5	All Other Non-Current	6.9	10.9	12.1	8.4	6.0	7.0
100.0	100.0	100.0	Total	100.0	100.0	100.0	100.0	100.0	100.0
			LIABILITIES						
14.6	14.8	13.8	Notes Payable-Short Term	19.8	22.0	15.4	12.2	9.0	8.3
3.9	4.1	2.8	Cur. Mat.-L.T.D.	2.3	2.8	2.0	1.9	1.6	3.5
14.7	15.7	15.2	Trade Payables	11.2	11.4	13.2	17.6	17.0	17.7
.4	.2	.4	Income Taxes Payable	.0	.2	.3	.4	.8	.2
17.1	18.4	19.1	All Other Current	30.7	13.4	15.8	19.8	18.2	21.5
50.7	53.3	51.1	Total Current	64.0	49.8	49.7	52.0	46.6	51.3
15.9	16.1	13.0	Long-Term Debt	22.8	19.1	10.8	13.6	9.2	7.6
.2	.2	.3	Deferred Taxes	.0	.0	.2	.3	.2	.8
10.3	11.1	9.5	All Other Non-Current	17.6	15.8	10.6	8.9	4.5	4.8
22.8	19.3	26.1	Net Worth	-4.4	15.3	28.7	25.3	39.5	35.5
100.0	100.0	100.0	Total Liabilities & Net Worth	100.0	100.0	100.0	100.0	100.0	100.0
			INCOME DATA						
100.0	100.0	100.0	Net Sales	100.0	100.0	100.0	100.0	100.0	100.0
			Gross Profit						
95.0	94.4	91.7	Operating Expenses	77.2	92.8	92.8	94.2	92.7	93.6
5.0	5.6	8.3	Operating Profit	22.8	7.2	7.2	5.8	7.3	6.4
1.1	1.4	1.4	All Other Expenses (net)	7.1	.8	.3	.5	.8	1.4
3.9	4.2	6.9	Profit Before Taxes	15.7	6.4	6.8	5.4	6.5	5.1
			RATIOS						
2.6	2.7	2.8		3.8	4.2	3.5	2.5	2.6	2.1
1.5	1.5	1.4	Current	1.3	1.4	1.4	1.5	1.6	1.4
1.0	.9	1.0		.3	.7	.9	1.0	1.2	1.0
2.3	2.3	2.4		3.3	3.8	3.1	2.4	2.4	1.9
1.3	1.2 (664)	1.3	Quick	1.0 (122)	1.4	1.3	1.3	1.5	1.2
.8	.7	.8		.3	.6	.8	.9	1.0	.8
26 14.1	26 14.1	17 21.7		0 UND	4 93.3	10 35.8	31 11.7	36 10.3	36 10.0
47 7.7	49 7.5	47 7.8	Sales/Receivables	2 223.2	30 12.0	37 9.7	51 7.1	54 6.7	57 6.4
69 5.3	70 5.2	68 5.3		43 8.4	62 5.9	67 5.4	77 4.7	70 5.3	71 5.2
			Cost of Sales/Inventory						
			Cost of Sales/Payables						
6.9	7.1	7.1		5.4	7.1	6.7	7.4	6.6	8.1
14.9	16.2	16.9	Sales/Working Capital	31.2	22.4	19.2	16.9	12.3	16.2
-381.2	-98.8	-256.5		-6.6	-36.8	-82.6	203.2	41.9	691.1
21.4	24.4	42.0		10.9	13.5	68.3	39.3	53.6	50.9
(428) 5.1	(487) 5.3	(507) 7.5	EBIT/Interest	(34) 5.5	(89) 4.3	(79) 8.9	(91) 8.9	(108) 13.5	(106) 11.5
1.2	1.0	1.8		1.4	-.2	1.5	2.0	4.8	1.9
9.8	14.4	10.7	Net Profit + Depr., Dep.,					14.8	11.1
(53) 3.4	(42) 3.8	(63) 2.8	Amort./Cur. Mat. L/T/D				(15) 5.1	(29) 2.6	
1.1	1.4	.9						2.5	.7
.1	.1	.1		.1	.1	.0	.1	.0	.1
.4	.3	.3	Fixed/Worth	1.3	.5	.3	.3	.1	.3
8.0	37.3	5.3		-3.3	-.8	2.8	1.6	.8	4.0
.8	.7	.6		1.0	.4	.4	.9	.6	1.1
2.7	2.7	2.3	Debt/Worth	5.5	2.3	1.9	2.3	1.7	2.7
-72.3	-70.9	45.6		-5.4	-3.8	14.8	11.0	5.4	52.5
75.2	77.7	91.4	% Profit Before Taxes/Tangible	237.8	116.3	87.4	110.5	83.5	89.2
(399) 36.8	(461) 33.4	(506) 51.0	Net Worth	(39) 45.9	(74) 61.5	(72) 45.1	(97) 54.9	(125) 52.5	(99) 48.9
11.6	7.4	19.8		16.5	19.1	13.4	20.2	29.0	14.5
29.3	24.3	34.3	% Profit Before Taxes/Total	65.6	42.7	43.4	32.3	34.7	19.5
10.7	8.4	13.2	Assets	11.3	14.8	16.2	13.1	15.0	8.9
.6	.5	3.2		.8	-1.1	2.5	4.1	6.7	2.8
165.9	172.4	183.0		66.8	179.6	238.0	185.2	326.4	170.3
43.9	52.2	58.3	Sales/Net Fixed Assets	19.2	52.5	57.9	51.3	88.2	62.0
14.8	15.9	18.6		6.0	23.4	18.5	17.2	33.5	19.9
4.7	4.9	5.3		5.3	5.8	6.0	5.1	5.2	3.7
3.4	3.2	3.3	Sales/Total Assets	2.8	4.0	3.9	3.3	3.4	2.7
2.0	1.9	2.2		.8	2.3	2.7	2.5	2.4	1.7
.4	.3	.3		1.3	.4	.3	.2	.2	.2
(346) 1.0	(387) .8	(402) .9	% Depr., Dep., Amort./Sales	(30) 2.7	(67) 1.4	(48) 1.0	(79) .8	(92) .5	(86) .7
2.4	2.5	2.3		8.5	3.3	2.0	1.4		1.9
2.9	2.2	2.8	% Officers', Directors'	10.4	5.6	4.1	1.8	1.5	1.3
(177) 6.2	(201) 5.6	(246) 6.0	Owners' Comp/Sales	(24) 22.9	(72) 8.6	(49) 7.0	(37) 3.2	(45) 2.6	(19) 2.5
10.8	10.2	10.7		29.3	12.5	9.4	5.0	5.3	9.2
13931296M	14904573M	17327406M	Net Sales ($)	27512M	231106M	365870M	872501M	2199158M	13631259M
6459643M	7623524M	7531513M	Total Assets ($)	32352M	102779M	116774M	317291M	815496M	6146821M

M = $ thousand   MM = $ million
See Pages 9 through 22 for Explanation of Ratios and Data

Current Data Sorted by Assets   Comparative Historical Data

0-500M	500M-2MM	2-10MM	10-50MM	50-100MM	100-250MM	Type of Statement	ALL	ALL
2	10	44	48	9	16	Unqualified	114	88
1	11	50	11			Reviewed	70	52
15	28	19	4			Compiled	52	49
63	52	20	4			Tax Returns	91	71
63	91	118	47	19	13	Other	224	210
	106 (4/1-9/30/10)		652 (10/1/10-3/31/11)				4/1/06-3/31/07	4/1/07-3/31/08
0-500M	500M-2MM	2-10MM	10-50MM	50-100MM	100-250MM		ALL	ALL
144	192	251	114	28	29	NUMBER OF STATEMENTS	551	470
%	%	%	%	%	%	**ASSETS**	%	%
32.8	17.3	16.6	16.9	16.4	20.6	Cash & Equivalents	19.1	19.6
21.0	38.4	42.1	37.2	29.8	23.3	Trade Receivables (net)	37.3	37.3
1.3	2.0	1.9	2.2	3.4	1.4	Inventory	3.0	2.0
5.2	6.0	7.7	7.4	8.8	9.3	All Other Current	6.8	5.8
60.3	63.7	68.4	63.6	58.5	54.6	Total Current	66.1	64.8
19.3	16.4	13.5	15.4	13.6	16.2	Fixed Assets (net)	15.6	15.2
5.1	4.9	5.9	10.0	17.6	20.1	Intangibles (net)	7.4	7.4
15.2	15.0	12.2	11.0	10.3	9.1	All Other Non-Current	10.8	12.6
100.0	100.0	100.0	100.0	100.0	100.0	Total	100.0	100.0
						LIABILITIES		
31.3	14.5	10.4	7.0	3.1	2.1	Notes Payable-Short Term	12.2	14.2
3.9	3.3	2.3	2.0	1.7	2.4	Cur. Mat.-L.T.D.	2.9	4.1
10.4	12.5	10.8	13.2	9.8	9.9	Trade Payables	10.9	10.1
.3	.7	.6	.7	.3	1.1	Income Taxes Payable	.8	.8
24.3	20.6	21.3	20.1	22.8	17.8	All Other Current	21.8	20.6
70.2	51.6	45.3	42.9	37.6	33.2	Total Current	48.6	49.8
15.9	9.1	10.1	12.6	20.5	12.4	Long-Term Debt	12.8	11.7
.0	.3	.5	.5	.6	.9	Deferred Taxes	.4	.5
8.9	8.4	9.6	4.6	6.5	4.1	All Other Non-Current	6.5	8.2
5.0	30.6	34.5	39.3	34.8	49.4	Net Worth	31.6	29.8
100.0	100.0	100.0	100.0	100.0	100.0	Total Liabilities & Net Worth	100.0	100.0
						INCOME DATA		
100.0	100.0	100.0	100.0	100.0	100.0	Net Sales	100.0	100.0
						Gross Profit		
89.3	89.4	90.6	89.4	91.2	92.6	Operating Expenses	90.0	90.1
10.7	10.6	9.4	10.6	8.8	7.4	Operating Profit	10.0	9.9
1.2	1.4	1.5	2.6	2.0	.3	All Other Expenses (net)	1.8	1.6
9.5	9.2	7.9	8.0	6.8	7.1	Profit Before Taxes	8.3	8.3
						RATIOS		
4.1	2.8	2.9	2.3	2.3	2.8		3.1	3.0
1.3	1.3	1.7	1.6	1.6	1.7	Current	1.5	1.5
.4	.9	1.1	1.1	1.2	1.1		.9	1.0
4.0	2.4	2.5	2.1	2.1	2.4		2.4	2.7
1.2	1.2	1.5	(113) 1.3	1.3	1.5	Quick	1.2	1.3
.3	.6	.8	.9	.7	.8		.7	.8
0 UND	8 46.7	27 13.3	40 9.2	40 9.0	31 11.9		11 34.4	7 50.5
0 UND	40 9.1	55 6.7	58 6.3	63 5.8	59 6.2	Sales/Receivables	45 8.0	48 7.5
36 10.2	63 5.8	76 4.8	84 4.3	75 4.8	77 4.8		73 5.0	76 4.8
						Cost of Sales/Inventory		
						Cost of Sales/Payables		
11.5	6.8	5.6	4.7	5.4	4.5		6.0	5.7
68.8	27.1	11.4	10.0	8.2	6.5	Sales/Working Capital	16.2	15.7
-16.5	-40.6	59.4	39.5	27.1	12.7		-147.9	-388.9
28.7	52.0	47.0	34.8	74.1	51.9		34.4	25.6
(81) 4.7	(142) 12.0	(187) 11.6	(76) 8.5	(23) 14.3	(24) 7.2	EBIT/Interest	(416) 7.9	(357) 6.7
-1.0	2.1	2.3	2.6	1.5	2.7		1.8	2.0
		7.5	11.3		11.2	Net Profit + Depr., Dep.,	9.0	18.2
	(27) 2.1	(21) 2.9			(10) 3.6	Amort./Cur. Mat. L/T/D	(70) 2.8	(52) 4.2
	.5	1.8			2.0		.5	1.5
.0	.1	.1	.1	.1	.2		.1	.1
.4	.4	.3	.2	.4	.4	Fixed/Worth	.3	.3
-13.5	5.2	2.0	1.3	-1.5	3.1		2.6	2.0
.3	.7	.6	.8	1.0	.7		.7	.7
3.5	2.0	2.0	2.1	1.6	1.4	Debt/Worth	2.1	2.3
-3.6	76.2	8.6	5.0	-14.3	24.4		17.9	12.7
181.1	115.1	86.0	54.4	64.9	69.0	% Profit Before Taxes/Tangible	83.4	81.8
(96) 76.8	(149) 47.4	(207) 38.2	(101) 22.0	(20) 44.8	(24) 29.2	Net Worth	(441) 39.5	(375) 37.9
15.5	12.7	8.7	9.1	14.2	10.2		10.8	11.0
77.2	42.4	27.8	19.8	23.0	11.8	% Profit Before Taxes/Total	34.4	30.5
20.9	17.3	12.5	7.6	13.8	8.5	Assets	11.9	12.1
-6.5	3.0	2.1	2.5	3.4	4.9		2.2	3.0
832.0	183.4	116.7	119.0	73.9	46.2		129.2	135.3
86.2	54.0	50.9	33.8	23.2	18.5	Sales/Net Fixed Assets	42.4	44.1
22.1	14.3	18.2	11.2	15.0	7.1		12.9	14.6
11.1	4.9	3.8	2.9	2.7	2.1		4.4	4.3
5.5	3.6	2.8	1.9	1.9	1.3	Sales/Total Assets	2.8	2.8
2.7	2.0	1.8	1.2	1.2	.9		1.7	1.6
.4	.4	.4	.5	.9	1.4		.5	.4
(63) .7	(122) .9	(167) .8	(89) 1.4	(15) 1.5	(20) 2.6	% Depr., Dep., Amort./Sales	(373) 1.0	(315) 1.0
2.2	2.1	2.0	3.6	3.4	4.0		2.1	2.1
4.8	3.2	2.7				% Officers', Directors'	3.6	3.4
(52) 12.2	(71) 7.8	(53) 4.7				Owners' Comp/Sales	(145) 8.4	(119) 8.6
22.1	14.0	14.4					16.2	16.7
247313M	943072M	3473890M	5183606M	4375859M	5949553M	Net Sales ($)	14297679M	16782558M
33930M	226414M	1151137M	2540915M	2064549M	4049014M	Total Assets ($)	7370251M	8546200M

M = $ thousand   MM = $ million
See Pages 9 through 22 for Explanation of Ratios and Data

Comparative Historical Data

Current Data Sorted by Sales

				Type of Statement						
108		130	129	Unqualified	3	4	4	21	33	64
73		78	73	Reviewed	1	4	7	17	30	14
46		61	66	Compiled	2	18	9	22	13	2
129		137	139	Tax Returns	44	49	16	16	11	3
248		310	351	Other	39	69	46	56	54	87
4/1/08-3/31/09 ALL		4/1/09-3/31/10 ALL	4/1/10-3/31/11 ALL		106 (4/1-9/30/10)			652 (10/1/10-3/31/11)		
					0-1MM	1-3MM	3-5MM	5-10MM	10-25MM	25MM & OVER
604		716	758	NUMBER OF STATEMENTS	89	144	82	132	141	170
%		%	%	ASSETS	%	%	%	%	%	%
19.6		20.4	20.0	Cash & Equivalents	22.1	21.7	23.6	18.2	18.0	19.0
36.2		34.8	35.3	Trade Receivables (net)	15.0	27.9	31.9	44.0	46.0	38.1
2.1		2.2	1.9	Inventory	1.7	1.2	1.1	3.0	2.0	2.1
6.6		7.0	6.8	All Other Current	6.1	7.6	6.2	5.5	5.8	8.7
64.4		64.4	64.0	Total Current	44.9	58.3	62.8	70.6	71.9	67.9
17.0		16.5	15.7	Fixed Assets (net)	24.7	19.7	17.0	14.1	12.6	11.1
6.6		6.5	7.1	Intangibles (net)	6.9	2.7	6.3	5.7	7.3	12.2
12.0		12.6	13.1	All Other Non-Current	23.5	19.3	14.0	9.6	8.3	8.8
100.0		100.0	100.0	Total	100.0	100.0	100.0	100.0	100.0	100.0
				LIABILITIES						
15.6		14.1	14.3	Notes Payable-Short Term	16.4	21.7	20.1	14.5	12.1	5.9
2.9		3.4	2.8	Cur. Mat.-L.T.D.	4.0	3.1	3.8	2.0	2.5	2.2
9.5		10.5	11.4	Trade Payables	11.7	7.2	10.0	15.4	9.9	13.8
.7		.4	.6	Income Taxes Payable	.6	.3	.5	.8	.7	.6
22.4		20.0	21.4	All Other Current	23.6	17.7	20.4	19.9	23.5	23.4
51.1		48.4	50.5	Total Current	56.3	49.9	54.8	52.6	48.7	45.9
11.7		12.0	11.8	Long-Term Debt	17.3	16.6	17.5	6.1	7.6	9.9
.4		.5	.4	Deferred Taxes	.0	.1	.7	.4	.6	.5
5.8		8.1	8.1	All Other Non-Current	14.0	5.2	8.7	9.2	7.6	6.6
31.0		31.0	29.2	Net Worth	12.4	28.2	18.3	31.6	35.5	37.1
100.0		100.0	100.0	Total Liabilities & Net Worth	100.0	100.0	100.0	100.0	100.0	100.0
				INCOME DATA						
100.0		100.0	100.0	Net Sales	100.0	100.0	100.0	100.0	100.0	100.0
				Gross Profit						
89.6		90.2	90.0	Operating Expenses	79.5	85.8	91.6	93.5	93.0	92.8
10.4		9.8	10.0	Operating Profit	20.5	14.2	8.4	6.5	7.0	7.2
2.0		1.8	1.6	All Other Expenses (net)	5.0	2.3	.8	.8	.7	.9
8.4		8.0	8.5	Profit Before Taxes	15.5	11.9	7.7	5.7	6.2	6.3
				RATIOS						
2.6		2.8	2.9		5.6	3.2	4.3	2.6	2.7	2.2
1.5		1.5	1.6	Current	1.4	1.3	1.7	1.6	1.7	1.5
1.0		.9	.9		.3	.7	.9	1.0	1.1	1.1
2.3		2.4	2.5		5.6	2.7	3.9	2.2	2.5	2.1
1.3		1.3 (757)	1.3	Quick	1.3 (143)	1.1	1.5	1.5	1.4	1.3
.8		.7	.7		.2	.6	.7	.8	.9	.9
6 57.9	8 47.1	8	44.6		0 UND	0 UND	0 850.7	30 12.3	32 11.6	35 10.4
45 8.1	42 8.6	45	8.2	Sales/Receivables	0 UND	28 13.0	30 12.1	49 7.5	54 6.7	57 6.4
70 5.2	67 5.5	72	5.1		37 10.0	69 5.3	62 5.9	72 5.1	75 4.9	76 4.8
				Cost of Sales/Inventory						
				Cost of Sales/Payables						
7.2		5.8	5.8		4.3	6.3	5.4	6.5	6.2	5.6
15.9		14.5	14.9	Sales/Working Capital	39.4	23.3	21.4	15.0	12.3	11.3
-304.4		-125.4	-94.5		-3.5	-27.3	-50.7	-650.2	60.4	43.2
29.9		31.0	43.5		32.0	31.7	42.6	58.2	45.4	53.7
(451) 8.0	(515) 8.4	(533)	10.0	EBIT/Interest	(43) 4.3	(98) 6.5	(57) 10.0	(94) 12.5	(117) 12.9	(124) 12.1
2.1		1.4	2.1		.3	1.3	.7	2.3	2.9	2.8
16.8		8.3	9.9						14.6	10.9
(74) 4.5	(73) 2.5	(74)	2.8	Net Profit + Depr., Dep., Amort./Cur. Mat. L/T/D				(19) 2.1	(39) 3.5
1.1		.4	1.3						.5	1.9
.1		.1	.1		.0	.0	.0	.1	.1	.1
.3		.3	.3	Fixed/Worth	.5	.4	.6	.3	.2	.2
2.3		2.8	2.9		22.9	4.0	-2.1	2.2	1.4	1.4
.7		.6	.6		.3	.5	.6	.5	.8	.8
2.0		1.9	2.0	Debt/Worth	2.7	2.1	2.7	2.0	2.0	2.0
12.4		16.0	21.1		-6.8	44.4	-8.0	9.8	6.6	8.9
90.4		80.8	94.1		101.5	110.6	120.2	105.5	90.4	69.1
(495) 38.7	(568) 33.7	(597)	38.3	% Profit Before Taxes/Tangible Net Worth	(61) 25.8	(113) 38.2	(58) 57.0	(107) 40.2	(119) 43.8	(139) 34.2
10.8		9.1	10.7		1.3	13.7	16.0	11.4	8.2	12.3
35.1		31.9	32.0		41.5	42.1	39.8	32.3	32.3	22.2
11.5		10.4	12.4	% Profit Before Taxes/Total Assets	7.0	13.5	15.4	13.8	13.8	10.3
1.4		1.2	1.9		-.8	1.4	.8	1.6	3.6	4.7
128.8		137.0	148.0		360.0	258.8	216.0	129.2	137.2	109.7
46.0		43.0	49.3	Sales/Net Fixed Assets	29.6	35.6	66.8	53.6	59.8	38.0
14.0		15.0	15.5		4.3	8.6	17.2	21.6	24.5	18.4
4.6		4.7	4.6		3.9	5.1	5.3	4.7	4.7	3.7
2.9		2.8	2.9	Sales/Total Assets	1.4	2.8	3.4	3.4	3.3	2.3
1.8		1.5	1.6		.5	1.4	2.0	2.2	2.2	1.4
.4		.5	.4		1.0	.5	.4	.3	.4	.5
(407) 1.0	(467) 1.0	(476)	1.0	% Depr., Dep., Amort./Sales	(36) 2.9	(85) 1.1	(49) .7	(89) .8	(99) .8	(118) 1.2
2.1		2.4	2.3		16.2	2.9	1.6	1.7	1.8	2.5
3.4		3.7	3.1		4.7	5.2	5.5	2.6	2.0	1.7
(166) 6.9	(191) 10.2	(189)	6.8	% Officers', Directors' Owners' Comp/Sales	(23) 19.2	(54) 12.0	(24) 9.8	(39) 5.5	(35) 3.2	(14) 3.5
12.8		17.3	16.3		26.1	19.7	13.8	11.7	7.4	6.2
22653996M		20531091M	20173293M	Net Sales ($)	40545M	272086M	322700M	983499M	2216431M	16338032M
9406455M		10385864M	10065959M	Total Assets ($)	91352M	260278M	134860M	380370M	861185M	8337914M

M = $ thousand   MM = $ million
See Pages 9 through 22 for Explanation of Ratios and Data

Current Data Sorted by Assets   **Comparative Historical Data**

0-500M	500M-2MM	2-10MM	10-50MM	50-100MM	100-250MM	Type of Statement	4/1/06-3/31/07 ALL	4/1/07-3/31/08 ALL
		12	9		3	Unqualified	29	20
	6	14	4			Reviewed	18	23
4	6	4	4			Compiled	17	15
10	7	2	2			Tax Returns	24	10
14	28	15	11		2	Other	65	51
	26 (4/1-9/30/10)		125 (10/1/10-3/31/11)					
28	47	47	24		5	**NUMBER OF STATEMENTS**	153	119
%	%	%	%	%	%	**ASSETS**	%	%
24.5	21.2	17.9	17.8			Cash & Equivalents	20.2	16.3
29.0	43.6	51.3	33.6			Trade Receivables (net)	41.3	44.7
.0	2.5	.6	1.0			Inventory	.2	.8
6.2	6.9	4.5	15.7			All Other Current	5.5	4.8
59.7	74.1	74.3	68.2			Total Current	67.2	66.6
13.6	10.3	12.8	8.4			Fixed Assets (net)	12.0	13.5
11.9	9.1	4.4	15.8			Intangibles (net)	8.4	6.2
14.7	6.5	8.5	7.7			All Other Non-Current	12.4	13.6
100.0	100.0	100.0	100.0			Total	100.0	100.0
						LIABILITIES		
59.4	11.6	9.9	10.9			Notes Payable-Short Term	16.1	21.3
.4	1.7	1.5	2.1			Cur. Mat.-L.T.D.	3.1	3.2
6.1	8.3	10.9	5.0			Trade Payables	8.4	10.4
.0	.3	.7	.6			Income Taxes Payable	.8	.7
33.2	21.4	22.1	30.2			All Other Current	24.7	27.5
99.0	43.4	45.1	48.7			Total Current	53.1	63.2
9.1	9.9	7.8	6.6			Long-Term Debt	17.8	7.4
.0	.5	.3	.4			Deferred Taxes	.3	.6
11.2	7.5	7.3	7.1			All Other Non-Current	6.1	6.3
-19.3	38.6	39.6	37.2			Net Worth	22.7	22.7
100.0	100.0	100.0	100.0			Total Liabilities & Net Worth	100.0	100.0
						INCOME DATA		
100.0	100.0	100.0	100.0			Net Sales	100.0	100.0
						Gross Profit		
97.3	90.6	95.9	98.8			Operating Expenses	95.0	95.7
2.7	9.4	4.1	1.2			Operating Profit	5.0	4.3
.2	1.0	.2	1.7			All Other Expenses (net)	1.6	.8
2.5	8.5	3.9	-.5			Profit Before Taxes	3.4	3.5
						RATIOS		
3.6	7.0	3.8	2.0			Current	2.1	2.4
1.2	1.9	1.5	1.2				1.3	1.3
.3	1.0	1.1	1.0				.9	.8
2.8	8.1	3.8	1.4			Quick	2.0	2.2
1.2	(46) 1.7	1.5	1.1				1.2	1.2
.2	.8	1.0	.8				.7	.7
0 UND	4 89.0	31 11.7	10 35.6			Sales/Receivables	5 68.6	12 30.5
19 19.0	40 9.1	46 8.0	46 7.9				38 9.7	44 8.3
42 8.6	55 6.6	66 5.6	70 5.2				60 6.0	62 5.9
						Cost of Sales/Inventory		
						Cost of Sales/Payables		
12.6	7.6	6.1	8.8			Sales/Working Capital	10.8	9.0
153.5	15.2	13.0	15.7				30.0	25.2
-9.6	UND	129.0	NM				-90.6	-85.1
37.4	32.4	36.4	46.5			EBIT/Interest	11.5	19.3
(14) 5.3	(33) 9.8	(37) 12.2	(21) 12.1				(127) 4.0	(97) 4.8
1.2	3.0	2.0	1.3				.9	1.0
						Net Profit + Depr., Dep., Amort./Cur. Mat. L/T/D	17.8	34.8
							(17) 3.5	(10) 16.9
							-1.6	3.6
.0	.0	.0	.1			Fixed/Worth	.1	.1
.0	.1	.2	.5				.3	.3
1.4	3.3	.8	NM				UND	25.0
.8	.2	.5	1.5			Debt/Worth	1.1	.7
8.8	2.6	1.4	2.6				4.4	2.7
-1.6	-15.6	5.9	NM				-44.9	-94.0
109.8	121.1	54.1	49.7			% Profit Before Taxes/Tangible Net Worth	108.5	68.0
(16) 59.1	(35) 50.0	(40) 21.5	(18) 16.2				(112) 31.3	(89) 32.8
-16.5	10.9	8.4	6.3				8.3	4.6
53.3	45.8	16.5	11.7			% Profit Before Taxes/Total Assets	23.3	22.8
14.3	14.4	8.4	3.7				7.8	8.9
-19.9	6.1	2.2	2.0				-.1	.6
UND	999.8	558.8	207.4			Sales/Net Fixed Assets	283.6	290.0
782.9	173.6	122.2	47.1				78.9	71.8
47.9	52.9	19.8	14.5				30.8	28.9
9.0	6.0	6.2	4.1			Sales/Total Assets	8.6	6.7
5.1	4.4	4.1	2.8				4.6	4.2
3.4	2.8	2.0	1.8				2.3	2.5
	.1	.1	.2			% Depr., Dep., Amort./Sales	.2	.2
	(28) .4	(30) .4	(16) 1.0				(102) .5	(82) .5
	1.2	2.0	1.5				1.2	1.0
3.3	2.5	.8				% Officers', Directors' Owners' Comp/Sales	2.3	1.4
(16) 8.0	(11) 3.8	(11) 2.2					(34) 7.1	(22) 3.5
24.7	8.1	6.1					12.6	7.9
40287M	453853M	1257026M	1892825M		1932273M	Net Sales ($)	6125637M	3957832M
6400M	56911M	216164M	486631M		913814M	Total Assets ($)	1351051M	1188674M

(Columns 50-100MM and 100-250MM marked "DATA NOT AVAILABLE")

M = $ thousand   MM = $ million
See Pages 9 through 22 for Explanation of Ratios and Data

Comparative Historical Data / Current Data Sorted by Sales

			Type of Statement		26 (4/1-9/30/10)		125 (10/1/10-3/31/11)		
				0-1MM	1-3MM	3-5MM	5-10MM	10-25MM	25MM & OVER
27	30	24	Unqualified				6	6	12
15	23	24	Reviewed		3		5	7	9
19	14	14	Compiled	4	1	3	2	4	
18	15	19	Tax Returns	3	5	5	3	1	2
75	65	70	Other	11	10	11	9	9	20
4/1/08-3/31/09 ALL	4/1/09-3/31/10 ALL	4/1/10-3/31/11 ALL							
154	147	151	**NUMBER OF STATEMENTS**	18	19	19	25	27	43
%	%	%	**ASSETS**	%	%	%	%	%	%
20.7	22.3	20.1	Cash & Equivalents	17.9	27.2	22.5	29.1	14.3	15.2
41.7	33.9	41.4	Trade Receivables (net)	19.9	35.6	33.2	42.4	59.8	44.4
.8	.5	1.3	Inventory	.0	.1	2.3	.2	.7	2.8
6.6	5.3	7.4	All Other Current	6.1	5.0	12.2	4.4	5.7	9.7
69.7	62.1	70.2	Total Current	43.9	68.0	70.2	76.1	80.6	72.1
13.6	15.3	11.2	Fixed Assets (net)	23.8	11.6	7.7	15.3	7.3	7.4
7.4	10.0	9.7	Intangibles (net)	17.7	9.7	15.0	1.3	3.5	12.7
9.3	12.6	8.9	All Other Non-Current	14.6	10.7	7.0	7.3	8.7	7.7
100.0	100.0	100.0	Total	100.0	100.0	100.0	100.0	100.0	100.0
			LIABILITIES						
15.8	16.9	19.7	Notes Payable-Short Term	50.5	37.9	16.0	9.3	11.5	11.8
2.0	3.5	1.4	Cur. Mat.-L.T.D.	.8	.2	1.6	2.7	1.2	1.5
8.7	10.2	8.0	Trade Payables	4.8	8.2	7.0	11.9	8.4	7.2
.5	.6	.4	Income Taxes Payable	.0	.0	.0	1.2	.1	.7
23.2	25.3	25.7	All Other Current	46.5	19.7	11.9	13.7	19.0	37.1
50.2	56.6	55.3	Total Current	102.5	66.0	36.4	38.8	40.2	58.2
14.7	13.5	8.4	Long-Term Debt	22.0	5.4	10.9	6.9	7.2	4.6
.4	.5	.4	Deferred Taxes	.0	.0	.0	.3	1.1	.6
6.2	5.4	8.1	All Other Non-Current	10.1	5.9	13.6	10.1	4.6	6.9
28.5	24.0	27.7	Net Worth	-34.6	22.7	39.0	43.8	47.0	29.6
100.0	100.0	100.0	Total Liabilities & Net Worth	100.0	100.0	100.0	100.0	100.0	100.0
			INCOME DATA						
100.0	100.0	100.0	Net Sales	100.0	100.0	100.0	100.0	100.0	100.0
			Gross Profit						
95.4	94.8	94.8	Operating Expenses	95.3	90.1	89.4	95.7	97.7	96.6
4.6	5.2	5.2	Operating Profit	4.7	9.9	10.6	4.3	2.3	3.4
1.0	1.5	.8	All Other Expenses (net)	3.3	-.3	.0	.2	.9	.8
3.6	3.7	4.5	Profit Before Taxes	1.4	10.3	10.6	4.1	1.4	2.6
			RATIOS						
2.6	2.5	4.0	Current	2.1	4.8	7.9	10.3	6.0	1.7
1.4	1.3	1.4		.5	1.4	2.5	2.6	2.1	1.2
1.0	.9	1.0		.1	1.0	1.1	1.2	1.2	1.0
2.5	2.4	3.4	Quick	1.8	4.8	6.5	10.3	5.2	1.4
1.2	1.2 (150)	1.3		.5	1.4	2.0	2.6	1.9 (42)	1.1
.8	.8	.9		.1	.9	.4	1.2	1.0	.9
9 42.1	9 39.0	8 45.5	Sales/Receivables	0 UND	9 39.8	1 497.6	8 45.5	34 10.6	8 47.0
36 10.1	35 10.6	40 9.1		12 29.8	40 9.1	31 11.7	47 7.8	47 7.8	42 8.7
59 6.2	53 6.9	60 6.1		35 10.4	59 6.2	55 6.6	70 5.2	60 6.1	64 5.7
			Cost of Sales/Inventory						
			Cost of Sales/Payables						
8.4	8.7	7.9	Sales/Working Capital	37.9	8.0	5.0	4.4	6.4	11.1
22.0	22.5	16.7		-16.5	16.2	9.4	10.0	11.0	38.3
-977.9	-141.8	-211.3		-4.0	-197.7	68.2	225.0	34.0	-428.7
21.7	14.9	33.0	EBIT/Interest		35.7	30.3	25.2	39.2	47.4
(123) 6.3	(106) 4.1	(110) 10.5		(11) 5.6	(14) 15.4	(17) 7.6	(21) 4.9	(38) 13.3	
1.3	-.1	2.2			1.0	3.1	.6	1.4	4.0
31.0	8.5	19.7	Net Profit + Depr., Dep., Amort./Cur. Mat. L/T/D						
(12) 12.2	(12) 2.1	(13) 2.8							
1.2	-.4	1.5							
.1	.0	.0	Fixed/Worth	.0	.0	.0	.0	.0	.1
.3	.3	.1		.2	.0	.1	.2	.1	.7
2.1	7.1	2.0		-6.6	.9	1.7	NM	.3	-1.2
.8	.6	.6	Debt/Worth	1.6	.5	.2	.2	.5	1.8
1.8	1.7	2.2		-6.3	2.0	2.7	.6	1.3	3.4
19.4	-808.2	-20.0		-1.5	419.0	-2.8	NM	3.8	-20.0
79.6	74.0	83.0	% Profit Before Taxes/Tangible Net Worth		121.1	148.5	52.6	49.6	68.5
(125) 33.8	(110) 28.9	(112) 26.5		(15) 67.3	(14) 60.6	(19) 11.1	(26) 19.2	(31) 33.5	
5.3	4.5	8.5			1.2	12.8	3.2	5.2	16.0
28.5	26.0	23.6	% Profit Before Taxes/Total Assets	28.4	54.3	57.3	33.2	21.1	15.9
10.1	7.0	9.4		.2	19.4	29.1	8.4	8.7	6.2
.7	-1.2	2.2		-24.1	.6	6.2	.8	1.3	3.5
383.8	364.0	999.8	Sales/Net Fixed Assets	UND	UND	937.8	330.6	999.8	389.7
76.0	62.5	133.4		317.6	206.6	92.9	71.4	324.2	122.2
21.6	15.3	33.1		17.7	33.7	47.1	13.1	38.0	45.3
6.9	6.5	6.2	Sales/Total Assets	6.7	5.1	5.7	4.5	7.4	8.7
4.2	3.7	4.2		3.4	3.7	4.0	3.6	5.2	4.2
2.1	1.8	2.2		1.8	1.9	2.2	1.9	3.5	2.4
.2	.3	.1	% Depr., Dep., Amort./Sales			.3	.2	.1	.1
(106) .6	(89) .7	(85) .7			(12) .7	(15) .9	(17) .3	(28) .3	
1.7	1.9	1.5				3.0	4.1	1.0	1.1
1.9	2.9	1.7	% Officers', Directors', Owners' Comp/Sales						
(45) 3.8	(40) 5.4	(40) 4.8							
10.0	14.9	10.3							
9053837M	6068615M	5576264M	Net Sales ($)	9801M	39239M	71771M	176944M	390226M	4888283M
2066991M	2234487M	1679920M	Total Assets ($)	4917M	18241M	26345M	94015M	108713M	1427689M

M = $ thousand   MM = $ million
See Pages 9 through 22 for Explanation of Ratios and Data

Current Data Sorted by Assets   Comparative Historical Data

0-500M	500M-2MM 24 (4/1-9/30/10)	2-10MM	10-50MM 175 (10/1/10-3/31/11)	50-100MM	100-250MM	Type of Statement	4/1/06-3/31/07 ALL	4/1/07-3/31/08 ALL
		7	7	2	7	Unqualified	15	19
	5	14	3			Reviewed	8	12
3	10	9	3			Compiled	11	15
12	7	2				Tax Returns	10	24
27	22	33	20	2	4	Other	61	67
42	44	65	33	4	11	**NUMBER OF STATEMENTS**	105	137
%	%	%	%	%	%	**ASSETS**	%	%
25.2	25.4	17.8	16.8		13.7	Cash & Equivalents	16.7	18.8
27.0	30.4	41.1	34.2		15.3	Trade Receivables (net)	35.9	30.7
3.4	2.7	3.0	6.8		9.2	Inventory	4.2	4.0
6.4	9.7	6.1	7.0		7.2	All Other Current	6.1	7.8
62.0	68.1	68.1	64.8		45.4	Total Current	62.9	61.3
14.4	15.9	15.4	13.7		13.4	Fixed Assets (net)	13.1	15.2
3.4	7.4	8.7	15.4		39.4	Intangibles (net)	11.3	10.1
20.2	8.6	7.8	6.2		1.8	All Other Non-Current	12.7	13.4
100.0	100.0	100.0	100.0		100.0	Total	100.0	100.0
						LIABILITIES		
33.7	14.4	8.8	6.4		4.1	Notes Payable-Short Term	15.5	16.8
7.7	2.9	3.4	3.3		3.1	Cur. Mat.-L.T.D.	1.6	2.4
15.2	9.6	15.4	12.5		9.8	Trade Payables	17.7	13.5
.0	.6	.3	.3		.3	Income Taxes Payable	.6	.6
24.9	18.5	18.6	28.9		14.4	All Other Current	18.6	22.9
81.4	46.0	46.6	51.4		31.6	Total Current	54.0	56.2
19.2	9.1	9.4	17.2		16.6	Long-Term Debt	12.2	10.8
.0	.0	.0	.4		.7	Deferred Taxes	.2	.2
8.7	8.2	6.3	10.9		13.6	All Other Non-Current	8.8	10.4
-9.2	36.7	37.7	20.1		37.4	Net Worth	24.9	22.5
100.0	100.0	100.0	100.0		100.0	Total Liabilities & Net Worth	100.0	100.0
						INCOME DATA		
100.0	100.0	100.0	100.0		100.0	Net Sales	100.0	100.0
						Gross Profit		
89.0	91.7	89.7	91.5		88.5	Operating Expenses	92.0	92.0
11.0	8.3	10.3	8.5		11.5	Operating Profit	8.0	8.0
1.0	.4	1.2	1.8		2.0	All Other Expenses (net)	1.1	1.3
9.9	7.9	9.1	6.7		9.5	Profit Before Taxes	6.8	6.7
						RATIOS		
2.8	4.8	3.2	2.1		3.9	Current	2.2	2.2
1.3	1.6	1.5	1.3		1.2		1.4	1.3
.4	1.1	1.0	1.0		1.0		.8	1.0
2.8	3.7	2.5	1.7		1.8	Quick	1.9	2.0
1.3	1.4	1.2	1.2		1.0		1.1	1.0
.2	.7	.8	.7		.6		.6	.6
0 UND	3 118.5	30 12.1	34 10.6		24 15.1	Sales/Receivables	29 12.8	13 28.8
7 52.2	26 14.2	49 7.4	58 6.3		49 7.4		49 7.4	47 7.8
47 7.8	57 6.4	73 5.0	87 4.2		61 6.0		69 5.3	68 5.4
						Cost of Sales/Inventory		
						Cost of Sales/Payables		
9.4	7.3	6.4	6.5		5.5	Sales/Working Capital	6.7	8.0
45.8	15.6	13.2	12.2		25.2		21.7	24.2
-23.8	63.9	999.8	NM		999.8		-33.4	-188.2
16.1	46.4	39.0	10.6		5.9	EBIT/Interest	16.2	29.1
(23) 2.9	(33) 21.8	(53) 12.0	(25) 4.9		(10) 2.8		(82) 3.4	(102) 4.5
-4.8	5.4	2.2	2.4		2.1		.0	1.3
						Net Profit + Depr., Dep., Amort./Cur. Mat. L/T/D	73.2	16.4
							(14) 18.6	(17) 4.6
							1.1	2.0
.0	.1	.1	.3		.1	Fixed/Worth	.1	.1
.3	.5	.4	1.1		2.4		.4	.4
-.6	4.4	2.6	-.6		-.2		-1.1	4.9
.8	.5	.6	1.5		2.0	Debt/Worth	.9	.9
1.8	1.7	2.2	7.7		11.5		3.3	3.7
-2.6	112.0	-12.5	-4.5		-2.5		-8.1	176.3
276.2	151.1	108.8	125.7			% Profit Before Taxes/Tangible Net Worth	95.2	104.6
(27) 58.1	(34) 56.8	(53) 47.8	(21) 39.9				(71) 48.5	(105) 44.1
5.4	18.0	8.2	19.3				20.6	3.1
78.3	47.4	35.8	18.5		9.5	% Profit Before Taxes/Total Assets	28.7	29.2
28.6	17.2	12.4	8.2		4.2		11.8	10.6
1.7	4.6	2.0	2.6		2.7		.7	.4
UND	146.0	82.0	58.1		97.6	Sales/Net Fixed Assets	104.2	135.9
65.8	54.2	29.9	25.5		22.3		38.4	36.5
22.2	15.0	16.7	12.6		10.1		14.6	11.1
14.0	6.5	3.7	2.9		2.1	Sales/Total Assets	4.2	4.2
5.0	3.5	2.7	2.0		1.2		2.8	2.7
2.6	1.9	2.0	1.3		.9		1.8	1.6
.6	.2	.4	.7			% Depr., Dep., Amort./Sales	.5	.5
(15) .7	(28) 1.1	(46) .9	(24) 1.6				(71) 1.1	(98) 1.3
2.0	1.8	2.1	2.8				2.6	2.5
3.8	5.3	1.6				% Officers', Directors' Owners' Comp/Sales	2.7	4.2
(19) 10.6	(13) 9.9	(19) 2.7					(31) 4.7	(38) 6.7
14.3	13.3	6.3					10.2	12.4
59880M	253006M	957830M	1672426M	326947M	2486399M	Net Sales ($)	3781817M	4202060M
9188M	50011M	320836M	690523M	290101M	1728141M	Total Assets ($)	2181947M	2907232M

M = $ thousand   MM = $ million
See Pages 9 through 22 for Explanation of Ratios and Data

Comparative Historical Data / Current Data Sorted by Sales

			Type of Statement	0-1MM	1-3MM	3-5MM	5-10MM	10-25MM	25MM & OVER
22	24	23	Unqualified					9	14
13	21	22	Reviewed		3		4	11	4
21	23	25	Compiled	1	7	3	6	6	2
28	29	21	Tax Returns	7	7	3	3	1	
74	76	108	Other	16	20	5	14	31	22
4/1/08-3/31/09 ALL	4/1/09-3/31/10 ALL	4/1/10-3/31/11 ALL			24 (4/1-9/30/10)			175 (10/1/10-3/31/11)	
158	173	199	NUMBER OF STATEMENTS	24	37	11	27	58	42
%	%	%	ASSETS	%	%	%	%	%	%
17.6	20.0	20.4	Cash & Equivalents	28.6	22.4	14.5	21.2	21.4	13.6
31.5	32.2	33.0	Trade Receivables (net)	22.9	28.1	40.3	32.9	39.4	32.6
4.1	5.5	4.2	Inventory	3.6	1.2	3.0	3.9	4.9	6.5
7.3	5.3	7.1	All Other Current	3.6	11.9	9.2	9.9	4.6	5.9
60.5	63.0	64.7	Total Current	58.8	63.6	67.1	67.9	70.3	58.6
14.8	14.7	14.8	Fixed Assets (net)	19.5	16.6	11.4	12.2	12.9	15.8
11.8	10.5	10.6	Intangibles (net)	3.8	4.4	9.6	14.2	9.7	19.2
13.0	11.8	9.9	All Other Non-Current	17.9	15.4	11.9	5.7	7.2	6.4
100.0	100.0	100.0	Total	100.0	100.0	100.0	100.0	100.0	100.0
			LIABILITIES						
22.4	11.6	14.6	Notes Payable-Short Term	43.5	16.4	18.7	7.0	8.8	8.6
3.3	2.9	4.1	Cur. Mat.-L.T.D.	9.6	4.1	1.4	2.8	3.0	4.3
13.9	14.8	13.1	Trade Payables	11.4	12.2	17.4	10.8	15.7	11.5
.1	.4	.3	Income Taxes Payable	.0	.8	.1	.0	.5	.2
18.3	19.7	21.3	All Other Current	18.2	24.1	19.4	17.0	20.2	25.3
58.0	49.4	53.5	Total Current	82.7	57.5	57.0	37.6	48.2	49.8
11.0	11.0	13.4	Long-Term Debt	20.2	15.4	20.8	7.1	8.5	16.8
.2	.3	.2	Deferred Taxes	.0	.0	.2	.0	.2	.5
13.8	8.6	8.5	All Other Non-Current	11.2	8.5	16.8	6.0	7.5	8.0
17.0	30.7	24.4	Net Worth	-14.0	18.6	5.2	49.4	35.6	25.0
100.0	100.0	100.0	Total Liabilities & Net Worth	100.0	100.0	100.0	100.0	100.0	100.0
			INCOME DATA						
100.0	100.0	100.0	Net Sales	100.0	100.0	100.0	100.0	100.0	100.0
			Gross Profit						
94.8	92.6	90.1	Operating Expenses	81.0	92.1	91.4	89.9	90.9	92.0
5.2	7.4	9.9	Operating Profit	19.0	7.9	8.6	10.1	9.1	8.0
1.5	1.3	1.4	All Other Expenses (net)	2.5	.6	2.0	.2	2.0	1.4
3.7	6.1	8.5	Profit Before Taxes	16.4	7.3	6.5	9.8	7.2	6.6
			RATIOS						
2.2	2.5	2.8		4.2	3.3	2.4	4.2	2.9	2.1
1.3	1.3	1.4	Current	1.5	1.5	1.6	1.7	1.4	1.2
.8	.9	1.0		.8	.8	1.1	1.2	1.0	1.0
1.9	1.9	2.2		2.7	3.1	2.0	3.0	2.2	1.7
1.0	1.2	1.2	Quick	1.3	1.3	1.3	1.3	1.2	1.0
.5	.7	.7		.2	.4	.7	.9	.8	.6
17 22.0	18 20.1	16 23.5		0 UND	0 UND	48 7.5	4 83.1	19 19.5	32 11.5
41 8.9	43 8.5	42 8.6	Sales/Receivables	21 17.0	26 14.1	53 6.9	40 9.0	48 7.6	49 7.5
60 6.0	68 5.3	65 5.6		65 5.6	57 6.4	63 5.8	64 5.7	78 4.7	74 5.0
			Cost of Sales/Inventory						
			Cost of Sales/Payables						
7.4	7.7	6.9		3.2	7.8	6.6	5.2	6.7	8.2
25.8	19.6	16.6	Sales/Working Capital	23.0	15.7	13.2	15.5	14.6	27.2
-29.2	-57.7	-367.9		-19.2	-52.2	60.1	35.8	-169.8	-349.0
22.5	24.7	30.5		26.5	34.3		43.2	45.2	7.1
(123) 3.3	(134) 3.7	(147) 7.5	EBIT/Interest	(15) 8.7	(24) 4.5		(21) 12.0	(44) 18.5	(35) 4.7
-1.2	.7	2.0		2.6	-1.9		2.7	2.9	2.1
6.9	4.3	21.8	Net Profit + Depr., Dep.,						
(21) 1.9	(15) 1.5	(18) 8.2	Amort./Cur. Mat. L/T/D						
-.4	.7	2.8							
.1	.1	.1		.0	.3	.0	.1	.1	.3
.6	.5	.4	Fixed/Worth	.3	.3	9.1	.2	.4	1.1
-1.2	-2.5	-9.1		-.2	-24.1	-.4	1.2	2.5	-.7
1.0	.8	.9		.6	.7	.3	.4	.8	1.5
3.8	3.4	2.4	Debt/Worth	1.9	2.1	142.7	1.7	2.2	7.8
-7.1	-12.2	-12.6		-2.2	-19.3	-3.3	9.4	17.2	-4.6
109.1	108.2	135.6	% Profit Before Taxes/Tangible	100.0	154.6		216.1	119.0	146.2
(107) 33.0	(122) 39.1	(144) 51.4	Net Worth	(15) 29.7	(26) 57.4		(24) 48.7	(46) 49.2	(27) 55.4
7.2	4.7	11.6		4.5	27.5		9.1	15.2	20.5
22.2	25.9	41.5	% Profit Before Taxes/Total	36.7	44.7	47.6	56.1	46.1	17.0
8.0	7.5	11.0	Assets	15.4	16.2	22.1	21.5	12.1	6.5
-1.4	.2	2.5		3.8	-1.6	3.3	2.5	2.4	2.6
134.3	111.6	104.1		414.2	291.3	87.5	306.3	103.8	54.4
31.4	35.2	37.3	Sales/Net Fixed Assets	50.6	51.9	50.4	47.3	38.6	25.0
13.8	12.8	15.3		6.9	14.7	29.1	17.1	17.0	12.3
4.3	4.6	4.5		4.8	5.9	4.2	5.7	4.5	3.2
3.0	2.7	2.8	Sales/Total Assets	2.1	4.1	3.1	3.1	2.8	2.7
1.8	1.7	1.7		.7	2.2	2.0	2.0	1.8	1.3
.6	.6	.5			.3		.3	.5	.5
(96) 1.3	(109) 1.4	(121) 1.0	% Depr., Dep., Amort./Sales		(18) 1.0		(20) .9	(39) 1.0	(29) 1.4
3.0	2.2	2.3			2.0		1.5	2.3	3.1
2.9	2.9	2.5		4.0	8.0		1.7	2.0	
(47) 4.4	(60) 6.5	(57) 6.3	% Officers', Directors'	(10) 12.6	(12) 9.9		(12) 3.4	(12) 4.7	
13.4	15.3	11.7	Owners' Comp/Sales	17.2	14.1		7.3	10.2	
8142211M	6096471M	5756488M	Net Sales ($)	10700M	71436M	45392M	199926M	910234M	4518800M
3642460M	3131834M	3088800M	Total Assets ($)	10549M	22335M	19463M	71763M	445378M	2519312M

M = $ thousand   MM = $ million
See Pages 9 through 22 for Explanation of Ratios and Data

Current Data Sorted by Assets   Comparative Historical Data

						Type of Statement		
		13	7	3	7	Unqualified	13	14
1	1	8	7	1	1	Reviewed	5	7
3	7	6	1			Compiled	12	14
6	5	3				Tax Returns	3	8
6	6	25	17	8	5	Other	35	42
	20 (4/1-9/30/10)		127 (10/1/10-3/31/11)				4/1/06-3/31/07	4/1/07-3/31/08
0-500M	500M-2MM	2-10MM	10-50MM	50-100MM	100-250MM		ALL	ALL
16	19	55	32	12	13	NUMBER OF STATEMENTS	68	85
%	%	%	%	%	%	ASSETS	%	%
17.3	18.7	10.2	9.7	11.4	15.1	Cash & Equivalents	10.2	13.3
30.0	51.8	48.4	41.3	36.7	36.8	Trade Receivables (net)	43.0	39.2
2.4	4.0	2.4	4.3	5.3	3.8	Inventory	5.4	4.4
15.6	1.1	9.8	7.4	2.7	7.7	All Other Current	6.3	7.2
65.2	75.7	70.9	62.6	56.1	63.5	Total Current	64.9	64.2
16.4	14.6	13.2	24.9	18.2	17.7	Fixed Assets (net)	17.7	15.6
.7	1.1	8.3	8.3	20.5	15.9	Intangibles (net)	8.1	10.9
17.7	8.5	7.6	4.2	5.2	2.9	All Other Non-Current	9.4	9.3
100.0	100.0	100.0	100.0	100.0	100.0	Total	100.0	100.0
						LIABILITIES		
34.1	12.8	18.2	9.4	10.9	3.8	Notes Payable-Short Term	12.6	14.9
3.9	3.0	2.5	3.4	1.5	1.2	Cur. Mat.-L.T.D.	5.4	2.8
6.1	21.4	19.2	20.5	11.5	23.1	Trade Payables	17.1	16.0
.6	.1	.3	.1	.2	.5	Income Taxes Payable	.6	.5
6.7	10.8	18.1	14.6	16.8	22.2	All Other Current	15.0	19.1
51.5	48.1	58.2	47.9	40.9	50.8	Total Current	50.8	53.3
8.2	8.7	8.6	11.6	9.8	14.8	Long-Term Debt	12.1	12.1
.0	.1	.2	.6	2.0	1.7	Deferred Taxes	.6	.2
12.9	6.2	6.2	5.9	15.0	.9	All Other Non-Current	3.6	7.1
27.3	36.9	26.8	34.0	32.2	31.9	Net Worth	33.0	27.2
100.0	100.0	100.0	100.0	100.0	100.0	Total Liabilties & Net Worth	100.0	100.0
						INCOME DATA		
100.0	100.0	100.0	100.0	100.0	100.0	Net Sales	100.0	100.0
						Gross Profit		
87.7	93.5	96.8	88.5	92.3	90.8	Operating Expenses	96.0	94.4
12.3	6.5	3.2	11.5	7.7	9.2	Operating Profit	4.0	5.6
2.2	-.1	.7	1.4	1.5	.8	All Other Expenses (net)	.3	1.9
10.1	6.6	2.5	10.2	6.2	8.4	Profit Before Taxes	3.7	3.8
						RATIOS		
5.8	4.0	2.3	2.1	1.6	1.7		2.3	2.3
1.8	1.8	1.4	1.4	1.3	1.5	Current	1.5	1.3
.6	1.0	.9	.9	1.0	1.0		.9	.9
5.6	4.0	2.0	1.9	1.5	1.4		1.9	1.8
.8	1.8	1.1	1.0	1.2	1.1	Quick	1.3	1.0
.5	.9	.7	.6	.8	.8		.7	.7
0 UND	24 15.0	33 11.1	32 11.5	38 9.6	38 9.7		27 13.4	25 14.6
10 35.3	35 10.4	48 7.6	47 7.7	59 6.2	53 6.9	Sales/Receivables	44 8.3	38 9.6
71 5.1	53 6.9	70 5.2	64 5.7	87 4.2	60 6.1		63 5.8	61 6.0
						Cost of Sales/Inventory		
						Cost of Sales/Payables		
4.8	8.3	7.2	5.6	7.9	8.3		8.5	9.4
16.3	15.3	17.1	17.4	18.8	15.1	Sales/Working Capital	19.9	24.9
-103.5	-189.2	-104.5	-102.0	445.5	187.5		-174.0	-159.9
	33.2	25.2	48.4		49.7		21.8	17.3
(16) 5.9	(45) 6.9	(29) 8.4		(12) 3.9	EBIT/Interest	(53) 4.9	(72) 5.3
	2.2	1.4	2.9		1.5		1.4	1.7
						Net Profit + Depr., Dep., Amort./Cur. Mat. L/T/D	38.0	32.5
							(13) 3.0	(11) 6.4
							1.7	1.4
.0	.0	.1	.2	.6	.4		.1	.1
.4	.5	.2	1.2	1.0	1.1	Fixed/Worth	.4	.5
NM	7.0	2.1	-8.6	-1.6	NM		3.9	4.0
.4	.3	.6	.9	.9	1.3		.9	.8
1.2	1.1	2.4	2.4	4.5	9.9	Debt/Worth	2.9	2.8
NM	15.3	10.7	-124.4	-12.4	NM		16.0	-50.1
87.1	110.6	71.0	44.8		42.9	% Profit Before Taxes/Tangible Net Worth	91.8	79.0
(12) 58.8	(16) 60.3	(45) 28.1	(23) 30.3		(10) 19.6		(56) 30.9	(63) 44.0
3.6	27.7	8.9	19.1		2.2		10.2	10.9
62.5	41.0	23.7	21.8	13.8	8.9	% Profit Before Taxes/Total Assets	20.9	27.3
15.3	29.5	11.6	8.4	6.0	5.4		8.8	9.0
-22.6	7.5	2.4	4.6	-1.2	.7		2.2	2.0
826.7	388.1	245.0	55.0	60.5	115.6		157.3	210.9
49.4	75.0	59.7	19.2	16.4	26.9	Sales/Net Fixed Assets	46.4	38.7
19.3	17.6	17.0	4.1	6.3	6.0		9.6	13.0
5.6	7.3	4.9	3.9	2.8	5.0		6.4	6.5
3.1	4.9	3.3	2.5	1.5	2.1	Sales/Total Assets	3.5	3.5
1.2	3.7	2.2	1.4	1.1	.9		2.2	2.0
	.3	.2	.5				.3	.4
(13) .6	(42) .7	(29) 1.4		% Depr., Dep., Amort./Sales	(45) .6	(48) .9
	1.0	2.6	3.4				2.7	2.2
	2.3	1.3					.8	1.4
(12) 3.5	(13) 1.7				% Officers', Directors' Owners' Comp/Sales	(16) 2.7	(17) 5.5
	10.0	4.0					4.8	7.7
48483M	112455M	1084366M	2700484M	1550663M	5541113M	Net Sales ($)	7833080M	5730996M
5235M	20540M	289633M	831488M	828172M	2014348M	Total Assets ($)	1476005M	2000834M

M = $ thousand   MM = $ million
See Pages 9 through 22 for Explanation of Ratios and Data

Comparative Historical Data — **Current Data Sorted by Sales**

			Type of Statement	0-1MM	1-3MM	3-5MM	5-10MM	10-25MM	25MM & OVER
27	32	30	Unqualified				3	7	20
13	18	19	Reviewed		2	1	4	3	9
8	14	17	Compiled	1	1	3	5	3	4
9	12	14	Tax Returns	4	3	1	4	1	1
51	59	67	Other	4	7		8	16	32
4/1/08-3/31/09 ALL	4/1/09-3/31/10 ALL	4/1/10-3/31/11 ALL			20 (4/1-9/30/10)		127 (10/1/10-3/31/11)		
108	135	147	**NUMBER OF STATEMENTS**	9	13	5	24	30	66
%	%	%	**ASSETS**	%	%	%	%	%	%
12.7	11.8	12.5	Cash & Equivalents		24.1		10.0	11.7	10.7
43.7	41.4	43.3	Trade Receivables (net)		24.6		48.2	48.5	43.6
5.0	4.7	3.4	Inventory		.2		5.5	2.4	3.7
5.0	5.8	8.0	All Other Current		17.6		9.8	2.8	8.0
66.3	63.6	67.2	Total Current		66.5		73.6	65.4	66.1
15.6	17.7	17.1	Fixed Assets (net)		18.3		14.1	17.2	17.9
8.0	7.2	8.2	Intangibles (net)		4.7		3.6	12.2	10.4
10.1	11.5	7.5	All Other Non-Current		10.6		8.7	5.2	5.6
100.0	100.0	100.0	Total		100.0		100.0	100.0	100.0
			LIABILITIES						
16.3	16.1	15.5	Notes Payable-Short Term		17.8		28.3	13.5	10.4
3.0	4.1	2.7	Cur. Mat.-L.T.D.		.3		2.9	3.7	2.2
22.5	18.4	18.0	Trade Payables		10.7		15.0	17.6	23.2
.2	.4	.3	Income Taxes Payable		.0		.0	.2	.3
17.1	12.3	15.4	All Other Current		13.7		15.9	10.6	19.8
59.1	51.3	51.9	Total Current		42.5		62.1	45.5	55.9
14.3	7.4	9.9	Long-Term Debt		7.2		11.7	8.8	10.1
.3	.4	.5	Deferred Taxes		.0		.0	.1	1.1
4.5	5.0	7.1	All Other Non-Current		2.5		13.4	5.6	5.2
21.7	36.0	30.6	Net Worth		47.7		12.9	39.9	27.7
100.0	100.0	100.0	Total Liabilities & Net Worth		100.0		100.0	100.0	100.0
			INCOME DATA						
100.0	100.0	100.0	Net Sales		100.0		100.0	100.0	100.0
			Gross Profit						
95.2	95.9	92.7	Operating Expenses		98.4		95.1	92.2	92.6
4.8	4.1	7.3	Operating Profit		1.6		4.9	7.8	7.4
.5	.8	1.0	All Other Expenses (net)		.0		1.1	.7	.9
4.3	3.3	6.4	Profit Before Taxes		1.6		3.8	7.1	6.5
			RATIOS						
1.8	2.1	2.2			4.7		3.3	2.3	1.6
1.2	1.2	1.4	Current		1.5		1.7	1.5	1.2
.9	.9	1.0			.7		1.0	1.0	.9
1.6	1.8	2.0			4.7		2.4	2.2	1.5
1.0	1.0	1.1	Quick		.9		1.3	1.3	1.0
.7	.7	.7			.5		.6	.9	.7
26 14.1	29 12.8	32 11.4		0 UND			29 12.8	41 8.9	33 11.1
39 9.3	45 8.1	47 7.8	Sales/Receivables	32 11.4			54 6.8	52 7.0	46 8.0
59 6.2	63 5.8	66 5.5		54 6.7			75 4.8	68 5.4	62 5.9
			Cost of Sales/Inventory						
			Cost of Sales/Payables						
11.8	9.1	6.9			6.0		5.8	7.0	10.7
38.6	33.9	16.5	Sales/Working Capital		16.5		12.0	15.3	31.7
-82.4	-42.3	-144.0			-10.7		UND	NM	-102.7
13.3	16.0	30.6					49.7	28.9	22.6
(91) 4.8	(112) 4.5	(117) 6.9	EBIT/Interest				(26) 6.0	13.1	(53) 5.0
1.3	.5	2.6					1.8	5.3	2.4
8.4	6.0	20.8							37.0
(18) 3.2	(26) 2.3	(26) 4.2	Net Profit + Depr., Dep., Amort./Cur. Mat. L/T/D					(17) 3.9	
1.2	.7	1.6						1.5	
.1	.1	.1			.0		.0	.1	.2
.4	.3	.5	Fixed/Worth		.3		.3	.5	.9
2.4	1.8	6.0			.9		UND	6.3	-7.7
1.0	.7	.8			.2		.7	.8	1.1
3.2	2.3	2.4	Debt/Worth		.8		1.6	1.7	5.2
86.5	7.3	30.8			7.2		UND	58.3	-103.9
85.4	55.9	69.7			88.2		70.2	85.1	54.3
(85) 35.0	(113) 20.2	(114) 29.6	% Profit Before Taxes/Tangible Net Worth		(12) 38.2		(19) 26.1	(24) 31.8	(48) 26.0
12.6	2.7	11.6			.3		17.1	19.1	9.9
19.4	16.8	28.6			38.6		40.9	26.8	13.6
7.0	5.9	10.2	% Profit Before Taxes/Total Assets		18.7		11.8	14.2	7.0
1.0	.0	2.2			-7.5		2.2	6.0	2.1
251.1	124.4	143.0			173.7		352.3	145.7	114.2
50.9	39.4	32.8	Sales/Net Fixed Assets		22.3		43.8	52.1	28.6
18.1	13.8	13.9			15.3		16.6	17.1	10.4
7.0	5.0	4.9			4.8		4.4	4.7	5.9
3.9	3.3	3.2	Sales/Total Assets		3.4		3.3	3.0	3.0
2.2	2.0	1.7			1.3		2.5	1.7	1.7
.4	.4	.4			.2		.4	.2	.4
(67) .9	(88) 1.0	(109) .8	% Depr., Dep., Amort./Sales		(10) 1.0		(16) 1.1	(24) .6	(51) .9
2.5	2.5	2.6			2.2		3.4	2.2	2.8
1.6	2.3	1.5						1.4	
(17) 3.5	(27) 3.4	(39) 2.5	% Officers', Directors' Owners' Comp/Sales					(12) 2.3	
11.0	6.9	7.3						5.8	
13110248M	8503553M	11037564M	Net Sales ($)	4598M	26527M	20201M	178396M	487312M	10320530M
2817040M	3036446M	3989416M	Total Assets ($)	2641M	29063M	4792M	71423M	207228M	3674269M

M = $ thousand   MM = $ million
See Pages 9 through 22 for Explanation of Ratios and Data

Current Data Sorted by Assets   Comparative Historical Data

	0-500M	500M-2MM	2-10MM	10-50MM	50-100MM	100-250MM	Type of Statement	4/1/06-3/31/07 ALL	4/1/07-3/31/08 ALL
		4	37	27	13	6	Unqualified	86	80
	2	12	41	9	1		Reviewed	62	42
	6	17	13	3		1	Compiled	45	41
	32	28	11	2			Tax Returns	48	48
	32	56	60	42	6	12	Other	160	154
		60 (4/1-9/30/10)		413 (10/1/10-3/31/11)					
NUMBER OF STATEMENTS	72	117	162	83	20	19		401	365
ASSETS	%	%	%	%	%	%		%	%
Cash & Equivalents	31.6	17.3	18.3	14.0	12.1	11.5		17.1	15.7
Trade Receivables (net)	27.0	42.4	50.6	47.0	30.1	30.9		43.2	42.8
Inventory	1.1	3.0	3.1	1.8	3.9	.9		2.3	2.5
All Other Current	7.2	4.8	5.2	8.8	9.7	12.3		7.7	6.7
Total Current	66.9	67.5	77.1	71.5	55.9	55.6		70.3	67.6
Fixed Assets (net)	16.4	19.6	10.0	10.5	18.2	5.3		15.3	16.1
Intangibles (net)	6.0	3.6	5.2	7.9	14.1	23.9		4.7	7.0
All Other Non-Current	10.8	9.3	7.7	10.0	11.8	15.1		9.7	9.2
Total	100.0	100.0	100.0	100.0	100.0	100.0		100.0	100.0
LIABILITIES									
Notes Payable-Short Term	40.2	13.8	9.2	9.0	4.2	6.4		14.7	12.7
Cur. Mat.-L.T.D.	5.7	2.4	1.4	2.0	2.7	2.2		3.4	3.1
Trade Payables	9.6	12.9	16.0	17.3	11.2	12.2		13.6	14.5
Income Taxes Payable	.3	.4	.9	.9	.2	.6		1.2	.8
All Other Current	27.1	15.6	18.6	16.9	22.1	20.5		18.7	19.6
Total Current	83.0	45.1	46.1	46.1	40.4	42.0		51.6	50.7
Long-Term Debt	10.6	14.2	5.4	5.8	19.3	20.3		11.5	14.1
Deferred Taxes	.0	.1	.6	.5	1.2	1.1		.7	.3
All Other Non-Current	4.1	7.4	5.1	4.9	9.4	9.2		6.9	8.4
Net Worth	2.2	33.2	42.8	42.7	29.7	27.5		29.3	26.5
Total Liabilties & Net Worth	100.0	100.0	100.0	100.0	100.0	100.0		100.0	100.0
INCOME DATA									
Net Sales	100.0	100.0	100.0	100.0	100.0	100.0		100.0	100.0
Gross Profit									
Operating Expenses	89.2	90.3	93.4	90.9	81.6	89.6		91.3	90.2
Operating Profit	10.8	9.7	6.6	9.1	18.4	10.4		8.7	9.8
All Other Expenses (net)	-.2	2.3	.7	1.3	7.2	1.7		1.4	2.0
Profit Before Taxes	11.0	7.4	5.9	7.8	11.3	8.7		7.3	7.9
RATIOS									
Current	4.1	3.7	3.6	2.4	2.1	1.9		2.5	2.6
	1.5	1.7	1.8	1.5	1.6	1.3		1.5	1.5
	.4	1.0	1.2	1.1	1.1	1.0		1.0	1.0
Quick	3.6	3.6	3.4	2.0	1.5	1.7		2.2	2.3
	1.1	1.4	1.5	1.3	1.1	1.2		1.3 (364)	1.3
	.3	.7	1.0	.9	.6	.5		.8	.8
Sales/Receivables	0 UND	14 25.8	40 9.2	47 7.8	26 14.0	41 9.0		27 13.5	21 17.0
	7 51.5	45 8.0	63 5.8	69 5.3	44 8.2	49 7.5		57 6.5	55 6.6
	40 9.2	74 4.9	87 4.2	86 4.2	64 5.7	95 3.8		88 4.1	86 4.2
Cost of Sales/Inventory									
Cost of Sales/Payables									
Sales/Working Capital	9.4	7.0	4.5	5.5	7.6	3.9		5.7	5.6
	48.3	12.1	8.6	10.7	10.4	14.6		12.6	13.6
	-17.4	325.1	25.4	42.3	38.6	89.5		97.7	UND
EBIT/Interest	77.8	42.5	56.5	48.4	183.8	16.9		27.4	20.1
	(38) 9.1	(81) 11.8	(119) 15.8	(63) 15.8	(16) 16.8	(16) 8.1		(312) 7.0	(271) 6.7
	-3.2	2.4	2.9	3.1	2.6	4.7		1.8	1.8
Net Profit + Depr., Dep., Amort./Cur. Mat. L/T/D			10.6	146.8				11.3	5.0
		(20) 3.6	(15) 6.8					(65) 3.7	(43) 2.4
			.3	1.0				1.4	1.3
Fixed/Worth	.0	.1	.0	.0	.2	.1		.1	.1
	.2	.3	.2	.1	.5	.3		.3	.3
	7.7	3.9	.5	.6	119.5	-.1		1.4	7.1
Debt/Worth	.4	.5	.4	.6	.8	1.2		.7	.7
	2.4	1.9	1.3	1.6	2.5	5.6		1.9	2.2
	-3.1	23.6	5.9	6.5	540.4	-2.3		10.8	50.4
% Profit Before Taxes/Tangible Net Worth	250.0	90.8	75.1	66.6	108.4	58.4		79.4	80.3
	(47) 91.3	(93) 38.6	(143) 38.3	(73) 24.6	(16) 41.6	(12) 45.3		(338) 38.3	(281) 34.0
	19.5	16.2	11.8	7.4	36.2	15.7		12.4	11.3
% Profit Before Taxes/Total Assets	84.5	29.8	27.9	18.7	29.4	14.3		29.6	27.2
	25.6	14.8	11.3	8.8	12.1	8.1		10.7	11.0
	.4	2.7	3.0	2.8	6.3	3.7		3.3	2.4
Sales/Net Fixed Assets	UND	132.7	175.2	157.2	41.6	87.8		107.5	115.2
	135.8	42.0	60.8	53.7	21.0	35.2		38.7	41.0
	23.0	13.3	21.3	23.8	7.2	18.5		14.8	15.3
Sales/Total Assets	12.7	4.7	3.9	3.5	2.4	2.5		4.1	4.0
	6.4	3.3	2.8	2.3	2.0	1.5		2.8	2.7
	3.3	1.9	2.1	1.2	1.3	.5		1.8	1.7
% Depr., Dep., Amort./Sales	.2	.4	.3	.4	.4	.5		.4	.4
	(27) .6	(73) .8	(123) .8	(61) .8	(14) 1.7	(12) 1.2		(295) 1.1	(259) 1.0
	2.1	2.0	1.6	2.0	3.0	3.1		2.2	2.2
% Officers', Directors' Owners' Comp/Sales	5.4	5.3	1.5					3.2	3.2
	(34) 10.5	(42) 8.0	(38) 3.4					(103) 6.8	(90) 6.3
	21.5	15.9	6.0					16.3	15.6
Net Sales ($)	127473M	463725M	2297851M	3963913M	3002875M	4801499M		15242730M	10382991M
Total Assets ($)	16881M	128554M	785802M	1731945M	1389245M	2981333M		5357656M	5551582M

M = $ thousand   MM = $ million
See Pages 9 through 22 for Explanation of Ratios and Data

Comparative Historical Data | Current Data Sorted by Sales

Type of Statement	4/1/08-3/31/09 ALL	4/1/09-3/31/10 ALL	4/1/10-3/31/11 ALL	60 (4/1-9/30/10) 0-1MM	1-3MM	3-5MM	413 (10/1/10-3/31/11) 5-10MM	10-25MM	25MM & OVER
Unqualified	78	90	87	1	4	3	8	20	51
Reviewed	53	50	65	2	3	6	17	31	6
Compiled	43	42	40	5	12	3	11	7	2
Tax Returns	76	74	73	17	19	16	13	8	
Other	165	187	208	25	35	22	28	42	56
NUMBER OF STATEMENTS	415	443	473	50	73	50	77	108	115
ASSETS	%	%	%	%	%	%	%	%	%
Cash & Equivalents	17.6	18.6	18.8	24.7	18.8	21.4	21.2	20.1	12.1
Trade Receivables (net)	41.6	39.5	42.7	18.8	36.9	40.9	45.3	50.9	48.1
Inventory	3.0	2.7	2.5	1.2	4.3	.9	3.0	2.5	2.2
All Other Current	6.1	7.3	6.5	7.1	5.0	3.0	4.4	6.7	10.0
Total Current	68.3	68.1	70.4	51.9	65.0	66.2	73.9	80.2	72.3
Fixed Assets (net)	14.9	15.3	13.6	31.1	15.9	18.4	13.7	6.9	8.7
Intangibles (net)	6.5	6.9	6.5	4.8	7.4	3.2	4.1	5.6	10.7
All Other Non-Current	10.3	9.7	9.4	12.2	11.8	12.3	8.2	7.2	8.3
Total	100.0	100.0	100.0	100.0	100.0	100.0	100.0	100.0	100.0
LIABILITIES									
Notes Payable-Short Term	17.7	16.2	14.7	41.7	18.1	12.9	12.1	8.5	9.2
Cur. Mat.-L.T.D.	4.3	3.3	2.5	3.6	5.4	1.5	1.9	1.2	2.3
Trade Payables	12.0	12.8	14.1	7.7	13.3	7.9	13.5	17.3	17.7
Income Taxes Payable	.8	.9	.6	.1	.4	.7	.2	1.2	.7
All Other Current	20.3	22.7	19.1	27.8	15.7	20.3	14.7	18.7	20.3
Total Current	54.9	55.9	51.0	81.0	52.9	43.3	42.3	46.8	50.1
Long-Term Debt	15.2	10.2	9.6	24.2	11.8	12.9	5.8	3.0	9.3
Deferred Taxes	.6	.3	.4	.0	.1	.0	.4	.6	.7
All Other Non-Current	6.0	7.4	5.8	7.0	4.8	8.5	6.8	3.1	6.7
Net Worth	23.3	26.3	33.1	-12.2	30.4	35.4	44.7	46.5	33.2
Total Liabilties & Net Worth	100.0	100.0	100.0	100.0	100.0	100.0	100.0	100.0	100.0
INCOME DATA									
Net Sales	100.0	100.0	100.0	100.0	100.0	100.0	100.0	100.0	100.0
Gross Profit									
Operating Expenses	90.8	92.1	90.9	79.8	92.9	93.5	91.3	92.5	91.6
Operating Profit	9.2	7.9	9.1	20.2	7.1	6.5	8.7	7.5	8.4
All Other Expenses (net)	2.6	2.0	1.4	4.4	.9	.7	.5	.6	2.0
Profit Before Taxes	6.6	5.9	7.7	15.8	6.2	5.8	8.3	6.9	6.4
RATIOS									
Current	2.4	2.5	3.1	2.7	4.5	4.1	4.6	3.0	2.1
	1.5	1.4	1.6	1.0	1.6	1.9	2.3	1.7	1.5
	1.0	1.0	1.0	.3	.9	1.1	1.3	1.2	1.1
Quick	2.1	2.1	2.8	2.6	3.8	3.7	4.6	2.8	1.8
	(414) 1.3	1.2	1.4	.6	1.4	1.8	2.1	1.5	1.3
	.8	.7	.8	.2	.6	1.0	.9	1.1	.8
Sales/Receivables	23 15.6	21 17.7	25 14.7	0 UND	14 26.7	10 36.8	19 19.6	38 9.7	43 8.6
	50 7.3	51 7.1	52 7.0	0 UND	39 9.4	50 7.3	51 7.1	63 5.8	61 5.9
	80 4.6	78 4.7	79 4.6	49 7.5	82 4.5	73 5.0	89 4.1	79 4.6	81 4.5
Cost of Sales/Inventory									
Cost of Sales/Payables									
Sales/Working Capital	6.0	6.2	5.6	7.5	5.5	4.9	4.4	5.8	6.6
	14.6	14.7	12.1	NM	11.0	14.2	10.7	9.0	12.9
	-131.3	-140.7	99.0	-3.7	-39.8	106.6	49.8	25.9	42.6
EBIT/Interest	27.0	42.4	46.4	70.0	25.5	40.4	45.1	77.5	52.0
	(322) 8.0	(335) 8.0	(333) 13.7	(27) 6.9	(45) 5.1	(36) 14.1	(52) 15.4	(81) 26.9	(92) 10.7
	2.0	1.6	2.8	-6.7	1.3	2.6	4.1	6.2	3.3
Net Profit + Depr., Dep., Amort./Cur. Mat. L/T/D	14.9	17.6	17.0					15.4	24.0
	(61) 3.0	(60) 2.6	(59) 3.8					(14) 3.9	(26) 4.1
	1.0	.9	.9					1.0	1.7
Fixed/Worth	.1	.1	.0	.0	.0	.1	.1	.0	.1
	.3	.3	.2	1.0	.3	.2	.2	.1	.3
	3.4	2.0	1.3	-1.5	1.6	5.2	.7	.4	2.4
Debt/Worth	.7	.7	.5	.8	.4	.4	.4	.4	.9
	2.1	2.1	1.6	5.6	1.6	1.6	.9	1.4	2.2
	47.4	22.5	12.1	-2.3	UND	14.1	6.1	3.4	19.5
% Profit Before Taxes/Tangible Net Worth	83.4	71.3	88.9	132.1	88.4	55.4	100.3	81.4	79.7
	(320) 36.0	(345) 32.7	(384) 39.4	(31) 66.0	(56) 41.3	(40) 29.5	(66) 36.9	(101) 40.3	(90) 46.3
	8.4	8.3	13.7	10.0	14.1	9.6	17.8	12.0	19.7
% Profit Before Taxes/Total Assets	28.6	25.7	29.9	79.8	26.9	25.1	43.5	25.3	27.7
	11.5	9.8	12.4	18.3	11.9	13.3	14.4	13.2	11.4
	1.7	.8	3.1	-6.1	1.5	3.6	4.7	3.4	4.3
Sales/Net Fixed Assets	151.9	143.9	179.4	UND	380.5	134.8	169.7	193.9	158.1
	43.8	43.8	54.2	17.5	50.0	45.0	51.5	78.5	50.6
	15.7	16.6	17.6	2.0	13.9	10.9	17.7	31.6	21.9
Sales/Total Assets	4.6	4.4	4.4	5.6	4.1	5.1	5.1	4.3	3.8
	2.8	3.0	2.9	1.7	2.9	3.5	3.0	3.0	2.7
	1.8	1.7	1.8	.6	1.8	1.9	2.0	2.2	1.8
% Depr., Dep., Amort./Sales	.5	.4	.3	1.2	.3	.4	.4	.3	.3
	(264) 1.2	(287) .9	(310) .8	(20) 2.9	(43) 1.6	(33) .8	(58) .8	(78) .7	(78) .9
	2.4	2.1	2.0	17.9	2.5	1.6	1.6	1.3	1.8
% Officers', Directors' Owners' Comp/Sales	3.1	2.3	3.5	5.6	4.2	5.5	1.5	2.2	
	(107) 8.2	(119) 5.0	(122) 6.9	(14) 12.8	(31) 8.6	(22) 8.4	(27) 4.6	(21) 4.6	
	17.0	9.8	14.4	26.2	18.3	15.7	8.1	11.7	
Net Sales ($)	15472197M	13614314M	14657336M	24091M	141547M	197051M	562323M	1691163M	12041161M
Total Assets ($)	7298284M	6757700M	7033760M	24125M	94724M	123262M	234759M	822926M	5733964M

© RMA 2011

M = $ thousand   MM = $ million
See Pages 9 through 22 for Explanation of Ratios and Data

Current Data Sorted by Assets   Comparative Historical Data

0-500M	500M-2MM	2-10MM	10-50MM	50-100MM	100-250MM	Type of Statement	ALL	ALL
	2	6	14	3	3	Unqualified	15	14
1	11	25	5			Reviewed	18	13
1	12	10				Compiled	14	6
15	11	7				Tax Returns	16	13
7	15	24	7	2		Other	31	36
	16 (4/1-9/30/10)		165 (10/1/10-3/31/11)				4/1/06-3/31/07	4/1/07-3/31/08
24	51	72	26	5	3	**NUMBER OF STATEMENTS**	94	82
%	%	%	%	%	%	**ASSETS**	%	%
30.3	11.8	12.0	14.7			Cash & Equivalents	11.1	10.8
19.0	41.9	51.6	49.4			Trade Receivables (net)	48.3	43.8
.4	2.3	2.6	.9			Inventory	2.1	2.2
.6	8.8	4.1	7.1			All Other Current	5.3	5.7
50.3	64.9	70.4	72.1			Total Current	66.9	62.5
28.9	24.6	17.5	13.8			Fixed Assets (net)	22.9	25.5
4.7	3.3	3.5	8.7			Intangibles (net)	4.4	3.1
16.0	7.2	8.6	5.4			All Other Non-Current	5.8	8.9
100.0	100.0	100.0	100.0			Total	100.0	100.0
						LIABILITIES		
16.6	20.1	12.7	8.9			Notes Payable-Short Term	14.9	14.7
26.2	5.6	3.2	2.9			Cur. Mat.-L.T.D.	3.3	4.5
7.4	15.6	15.1	17.4			Trade Payables	13.3	14.1
.0	.1	.9	.6			Income Taxes Payable	1.1	1.3
20.9	15.7	10.1	13.2			All Other Current	14.5	11.9
71.2	57.2	42.0	43.0			Total Current	47.2	46.5
18.0	18.4	7.8	8.7			Long-Term Debt	16.1	20.8
.0	.9	1.1	1.8			Deferred Taxes	.7	.5
2.0	7.1	3.0	2.8			All Other Non-Current	3.4	3.8
8.8	16.5	46.0	43.7			Net Worth	32.6	28.4
100.0	100.0	100.0	100.0			Total Liabilities & Net Worth	100.0	100.0
						INCOME DATA		
100.0	100.0	100.0	100.0			Net Sales	100.0	100.0
						Gross Profit		
88.5	92.6	93.7	91.0			Operating Expenses	92.7	93.1
11.5	7.4	6.3	9.0			Operating Profit	7.3	6.9
.3	2.8	.1	.6			All Other Expenses (net)	1.6	1.8
11.2	4.5	6.2	8.4			Profit Before Taxes	5.6	5.1
						RATIOS		
6.0	2.3	2.7	2.4				2.2	2.1
1.2	1.4	2.0	1.7			Current	1.5	1.4
.1	.8	1.5	1.3				1.1	1.1
6.0	2.0	2.5	2.0				1.8	1.9
1.2	1.2	1.8	1.6			Quick	1.3	1.2
.1	.7	1.2	1.0				.9	.8
0 UND	10 36.2	60 6.1	53 6.9				46 7.9	53 7.0
0 UND	51 7.2	76 4.8	72 5.1			Sales/Receivables	75 4.9	75 4.9
31 11.7	91 4.0	107 3.4	117 3.1				100 3.6	98 3.7
						Cost of Sales/Inventory		
						Cost of Sales/Payables		
7.4	8.9	4.7	4.0				6.0	5.9
559.9	20.5	7.7	8.1			Sales/Working Capital	13.9	12.6
-12.9	-28.6	15.3	19.5				72.5	92.0
13.4	27.9	33.0	35.8				23.6	21.3
(15) 3.3	(43) 4.7	(60) 10.8	(24) 17.1			EBIT/Interest	(82) 6.2	(67) 5.5
-1.4	-.9	2.3	7.2				2.2	1.7
		6.0	22.7			Net Profit + Depr., Dep.,	11.8	8.1
	(15) 1.7	(12) 5.5				Amort./Cur. Mat. L/T/D	(18) 3.2	(13) 1.6
		1.1	2.8				1.0	1.3
.2	.2	.1	.1				.2	.2
.7	.6	.3	.3			Fixed/Worth	.5	.6
-1.6	4.0	.6	.9				1.7	3.1
.4	.9	.5	1.0				1.0	.9
1.6	2.5	1.1	1.5			Debt/Worth	1.9	1.9
-4.7	34.7	2.1	3.8				5.0	6.1
313.1	84.7	52.5	56.5			% Profit Before Taxes/Tangible	61.9	52.2
(17) 129.4	(39) 25.3	(69) 29.8	(23) 31.9			Net Worth	(81) 28.5	(69) 28.6
27.0	4.0	7.8	14.8				13.2	14.4
149.2	25.5	21.8	15.5			% Profit Before Taxes/Total	24.8	23.5
47.5	8.9	11.7	12.4			Assets	10.5	9.4
5.3	.5	2.4	5.4				3.1	2.7
152.5	50.3	45.7	50.2				48.2	40.0
35.6	23.9	23.8	29.8			Sales/Net Fixed Assets	18.3	17.3
12.8	6.8	8.5	10.5				10.4	6.0
20.2	4.8	2.9	2.8				3.5	3.3
6.5	3.1	2.3	2.2			Sales/Total Assets	2.6	2.2
3.7	1.9	1.7	1.6				1.8	1.6
1.0	.8	.9	.8				.9	1.0
(10) 2.2	(38) 1.6	(61) 1.8	(22) 1.2			% Depr., Dep., Amort./Sales	(73) 1.7	(69) 2.1
3.8	6.2	2.8	2.0				3.2	3.9
4.5	3.8	2.1				% Officers', Directors'	3.6	2.4
(14) 10.9	(23) 6.7	(27) 5.1				Owners' Comp/Sales	(37) 9.2	(25) 5.6
19.2	12.2	8.0					14.4	13.2
46545M	220541M	966103M	1038125M	696114M	754371M	Net Sales ($)	1609693M	1509591M
5580M	58863M	323292M	480359M	395796M	581986M	Total Assets ($)	605201M	755692M

M = $ thousand   MM = $ million
See Pages 9 through 22 for Explanation of Ratios and Data

Comparative Historical Data — Current Data Sorted by Sales

			Type of Statement						
14	20	28	Unqualified		1	1	2	6	18
20	28	42	Reviewed	1	3	4	15	14	5
15	15	23	Compiled		5	6	7	5	
20	24	33	Tax Returns	7	10	5	6	3	2
57	57	55	Other	6	11	5	14	13	6
4/1/08-3/31/09 ALL	4/1/09-3/31/10 ALL	4/1/10-3/31/11 ALL		16 (4/1-9/30/10)	165 (10/1/10-3/31/11)				
				0-1MM	1-3MM	3-5MM	5-10MM	10-25MM	25MM & OVER
126	144	181	NUMBER OF STATEMENTS	14	30	21	44	41	31
%	%	%	ASSETS	%	%	%	%	%	%
15.4	15.0	14.4	Cash & Equivalents	28.8	15.2	10.2	12.7	14.5	12.6
38.7	44.2	43.0	Trade Receivables (net)	15.2	32.5	47.7	51.9	50.7	39.7
2.2	2.0	2.1	Inventory	.8	1.8	3.4	1.4	2.9	1.9
6.3	5.6	5.8	All Other Current	3.8	2.8	6.3	5.7	4.8	10.9
62.6	66.8	65.4	Total Current	48.5	52.4	67.5	71.7	73.0	65.0
22.3	19.2	20.8	Fixed Assets (net)	50.5	21.0	23.5	16.7	13.4	21.2
5.0	4.8	5.1	Intangibles (net)	.7	6.4	5.4	3.0	5.3	8.2
10.1	9.2	8.7	All Other Non-Current	.3	20.2	3.6	8.5	8.3	5.6
100.0	100.0	100.0	Total	100.0	100.0	100.0	100.0	100.0	100.0
			LIABILITIES						
13.1	11.0	14.4	Notes Payable-Short Term	7.1	24.5	14.4	9.4	6.1	25.8
4.8	3.8	6.9	Cur. Mat.-L.T.D.	11.0	18.1	5.5	5.5	3.1	2.3
13.0	11.5	14.4	Trade Payables	3.6	13.6	15.0	15.3	15.5	16.8
.9	.9	.5	Income Taxes Payable	.0	.1	.0	.6	1.0	.6
12.7	12.5	13.6	All Other Current	33.3	10.6	9.0	12.1	13.2	13.5
44.5	39.7	49.8	Total Current	55.0	66.9	44.0	42.9	39.0	58.9
15.9	13.4	12.9	Long-Term Debt	41.0	17.2	13.8	7.1	6.6	11.9
.4	.7	1.0	Deferred Taxes	.0	.5	.2	.8	1.9	1.7
4.6	3.5	4.3	All Other Non-Current	15.8	2.8	1.5	3.2	4.4	3.8
34.7	42.6	32.0	Net Worth	-11.8	12.6	40.5	45.9	48.1	23.8
100.0	100.0	100.0	Total Liabilities & Net Worth	100.0	100.0	100.0	100.0	100.0	100.0
			INCOME DATA						
100.0	100.0	100.0	Net Sales	100.0	100.0	100.0	100.0	100.0	100.0
			Gross Profit						
94.3	94.5	92.4	Operating Expenses	77.4	94.5	90.4	94.6	94.1	93.0
5.7	5.5	7.6	Operating Profit	22.6	5.5	9.6	5.4	5.9	7.0
1.4	.7	1.0	All Other Expenses (net)	9.5	.3	.8	.3	-.2	.7
4.3	4.8	6.6	Profit Before Taxes	13.1	5.2	8.9	5.2	6.1	6.3
			RATIOS						
2.4	2.8	2.5		3.7	1.8	2.7	2.8	2.4	2.3
1.6	1.8	1.6	Current	1.3	1.0	1.6	2.0	1.9	1.6
1.0	1.1	1.1		.1	.4	1.1	1.2	1.5	1.1
2.3	2.6	2.2		3.7	1.8	2.2	2.6	2.3	2.0
1.3	1.5	1.4	Quick	1.3	.8	1.4	1.8	1.7	1.3
.9	1.0	.9		.1	.4	.8	1.1	1.2	.9
33 11.0	35 10.5	36 10.2		0 UND	0 UND	36 10.2	42 8.6	52 7.0	41 9.0
59 6.2	63 5.8	66 5.5	Sales/Receivables	0 UND	40 9.1	85 4.3	81 4.5	68 5.4	60 6.1
83 4.4	91 4.0	93 3.9		22 16.3	91 4.0	99 3.7	110 3.3	82 4.5	86 4.3
			Cost of Sales/Inventory						
			Cost of Sales/Payables						
6.3	5.0	5.4		8.0	8.3	5.6	5.1	4.7	5.3
13.3	8.8	10.2	Sales/Working Capital	83.5	151.8	9.1	8.1	8.2	9.4
178.9	51.0	103.5		-4.7	-11.7	NM	22.1	15.2	122.2
23.8	34.5	30.0			7.6	51.0	16.7	34.6	36.0
(105) 7.4	(115) 8.3	(150) 7.9	EBIT/Interest	(25) 1.7	(20) 4.9	(35) 7.3	(34) 12.9	(29) 12.0	
1.5	1.2	1.7			-2.8	1.3	2.4	4.6	3.2
16.5	10.1	6.2						6.0	24.8
(15) 7.0	(20) 3.1	(35) 2.9	Net Profit + Depr., Dep., Amort./Cur. Mat. L/T/D				(14) 2.9	(11) 5.7	
1.4	.8	1.3						1.5	2.3
.2	.1	.1		.2	.1	.2	.2	.1	.2
.5	.4	.3	Fixed/Worth	1.8	.5	.8	.3	.2	.4
2.5	1.3	1.3		NM	-11.1	2.3	.6	.6	1.5
.7	.5	.7		1.2	.8	.5	.4	.6	1.0
1.6	1.1	1.5	Debt/Worth	3.2	2.3	2.0	1.1	1.2	1.6
6.6	4.0	4.1		-12.4	-5.2	7.1	3.1	2.0	4.6
56.0	47.3	62.3		227.8	49.4	87.3	39.5	59.2	61.3
(106) 24.3	(126) 20.1	(154) 29.7	% Profit Before Taxes/Tangible Net Worth	(10) 78.8	(21) 20.0	(18) 46.8	(40) 18.1	(39) 32.4	(26) 34.4
8.1	3.5	7.9		21.3	-17.2	6.5	6.5	17.8	19.8
21.0	23.8	27.5		86.4	28.7	39.7	21.4	24.6	16.6
8.9	9.2	11.4	% Profit Before Taxes/Total Assets	9.6	9.7	10.5	10.5	15.4	12.4
.5	.2	3.0		2.3	-7.9	3.0	2.8	5.1	4.1
49.1	56.5	52.2		122.1	137.8	30.9	43.5	60.5	49.7
21.2	20.8	26.1	Sales/Net Fixed Assets	7.9	31.5	17.2	24.6	35.7	24.2
9.1	8.8	9.5		.3	8.4	6.9	13.7	12.2	10.1
3.6	3.7	3.6		7.1	4.9	3.4	4.5	3.3	3.0
2.6	2.6	2.5	Sales/Total Assets	2.0	3.3	2.3	2.7	2.4	2.2
1.8	1.7	1.8		.2	1.9	1.7	1.9	1.9	1.8
1.0	.7	.9			1.1	.8	1.0	.7	.8
(93) 1.9	(119) 1.4	(135) 1.6	% Depr., Dep., Amort./Sales	(12) 3.6	(18) 1.8	(37) 1.5	(35) 1.4	(24) 1.0	
3.5	3.4	3.2			7.6	3.8	2.0	2.2	1.9
2.8	4.3	2.7			4.9	3.1	3.9	2.1	
(40) 8.9	(54) 7.9	(69) 5.2	% Officers', Directors' Owners' Comp/Sales	(14) 9.1	(10) 4.1	(20) 7.0	(15) 3.9		
14.9	13.7	12.2			11.8	6.9	13.3	7.0	
2326648M	2081202M	3721799M	Net Sales ($)	7026M	58680M	82967M	325813M	554161M	2693152M
1058086M	939104M	1845876M	Total Assets ($)	19574M	19771M	36550M	138296M	245529M	1386156M

M = $ thousand   MM = $ million
See Pages 9 through 22 for Explanation of Ratios and Data

Current Data Sorted by Assets   Comparative Historical Data

						Type of Statement		
1	3	20	17	8	11	Unqualified	21	24
1	4	20	8			Reviewed	10	12
2	5	7	1			Compiled	15	15
9	13	4			1	Tax Returns	18	14
18	32	68	20	6	4	Other	55	72
	32 (4/1-9/30/10)		251 (10/1/10-3/31/11)				4/1/06-3/31/07	4/1/07-3/31/08
0-500M	500M-2MM	2-10MM	10-50MM	50-100MM	100-250MM		ALL	ALL
31	57	119	46	14	16	**NUMBER OF STATEMENTS**	119	137
%	%	%	%	%	%	**ASSETS**	%	%
36.5	13.4	14.5	20.9	23.3	6.4	Cash & Equivalents	14.3	13.9
25.5	43.4	47.6	35.4	20.6	23.2	Trade Receivables (net)	43.6	46.0
1.3	1.9	2.6	2.3	.7	4.4	Inventory	3.0	3.3
8.0	4.0	7.5	5.6	4.0	16.3	All Other Current	5.6	7.1
71.3	62.7	72.3	64.2	48.5	50.3	Total Current	66.5	70.3
14.7	21.2	16.0	16.5	12.8	16.3	Fixed Assets (net)	17.2	16.0
5.1	3.4	6.4	10.1	32.4	26.5	Intangibles (net)	7.9	6.7
8.9	12.7	5.3	9.1	6.3	6.9	All Other Non-Current	8.4	6.9
100.0	100.0	100.0	100.0	100.0	100.0	Total	100.0	100.0
						LIABILITIES		
28.3	11.5	8.3	6.3	.9	10.6	Notes Payable-Short Term	13.4	13.3
5.0	3.3	1.6	2.7	1.6	2.9	Cur. Mat.-L.T.D.	3.2	2.5
7.1	13.5	11.6	11.7	6.8	5.0	Trade Payables	14.1	15.9
.0	.1	.9	1.2	.4	1.5	Income Taxes Payable	1.0	.7
18.1	21.5	17.8	16.9	18.3	17.3	All Other Current	21.8	19.2
58.5	49.9	40.2	38.8	27.9	37.3	Total Current	53.6	51.6
12.1	16.7	7.4	9.3	9.9	17.1	Long-Term Debt	13.3	10.0
.3	1.0	.7	.2	.9	1.8	Deferred Taxes	1.0	.6
6.3	1.9	3.4	6.5	10.9	9.7	All Other Non-Current	7.0	5.2
22.8	30.5	48.3	45.1	50.3	34.0	Net Worth	25.0	32.5
100.0	100.0	100.0	100.0	100.0	100.0	Total Liabilties & Net Worth	100.0	100.0
						INCOME DATA		
100.0	100.0	100.0	100.0	100.0	100.0	Net Sales	100.0	100.0
						Gross Profit		
93.3	87.9	91.0	95.4	88.1	88.5	Operating Expenses	90.4	92.0
6.7	12.1	9.0	4.6	11.9	11.5	Operating Profit	9.6	8.0
-.2	4.7	1.1	1.0	1.2	.9	All Other Expenses (net)	1.0	.7
6.9	7.4	7.9	3.5	10.8	10.5	Profit Before Taxes	8.6	7.3
						RATIOS		
6.5	2.2	3.4	2.8	3.7	1.9		2.3	2.2
1.3	1.4	2.1	1.6	1.7	1.4	Current	1.6	1.5
.8	.6	1.1	1.2	.9	1.0		1.0	1.0
6.5	2.1	3.0	2.7	3.3	1.6		2.2	2.0
1.2	1.3	1.7	1.5	1.7	.7	Quick	1.4	1.2
.5	.5	1.0	1.0	.8	.4		.8	.8

0	UND	2	175.6	39	9.2	41	8.9	25	14.5	18	20.6	Sales/Receivables	24	15.1	34	10.7

Continued data rows:

												Sales/Receivables		
14	26.9	46	7.9	60	6.1	58	6.3	41	8.9	61	6.0		61	6.0	58	6.3
55	6.6	68	5.3	91	4.0	84	4.3	65	5.6	87	4.2		89	4.1	82	4.5

						Cost of Sales/Inventory		
						Cost of Sales/Payables		
7.7	8.3	4.3	4.3	3.6	5.0	Sales/Working Capital	5.8	6.9
32.3	27.0	7.8	9.0	7.1	11.9		13.4	14.7
-42.8	-21.8	45.9	27.0	-255.5	NM		800.0	982.7

	21.5		48.6		62.6		46.4		105.2		18.6	EBIT/Interest		31.6		27.1
(20)	5.1	(41)	8.5	(88)	15.4	(33)	6.7	(11)	33.4	(15)	9.4		(93)	11.1	(106)	5.8
	-4.9		1.5		2.0		2.7		13.7		3.9			3.8		1.8

			19.2			Net Profit + Depr., Dep., Amort./Cur. Mat. L/T/D		4.7		9.5
	(15)	7.1						(11)	2.9	(17)	2.6
		1.2							1.0		.4

.0	.1	.1	.1	.1	.3	Fixed/Worth	.1	.1
.9	.3	.2	.3	.3	2.1		.3	.4
-1.6	10.2	.8	1.0	-11.8	-.3		2.8	2.6
.2	.8	.4	.5	.6	2.1	Debt/Worth	.9	.8
4.1	2.0	1.1	1.8	1.7	4.9		2.1	2.3
-11.5	9.3	4.3	5.0	-63.3	-8.0		UND	16.2

	184.4		76.2		76.7		67.2		118.5		63.3	% Profit Before Taxes/Tangible Net Worth		92.8		99.0
(22)	74.4	(45)	35.4	(112)	38.7	(39)	23.9	(10)	35.3	(11)	39.4		(90)	44.3	(112)	50.3
	8.3		10.8		9.0		2.5		7.4		25.4			19.9		15.5

56.3	37.5	31.5	19.4	23.2	12.1	% Profit Before Taxes/Total Assets	35.3	36.6
20.2	10.1	12.2	6.7	9.6	7.9		18.8	13.4
-4.9	.9	1.8	.4	3.6	6.3		3.9	2.0
UND	153.7	106.8	86.0	42.1	62.7	Sales/Net Fixed Assets	86.3	111.6
66.0	57.9	38.1	25.8	26.5	32.7		37.8	37.3
16.4	13.9	14.0	7.0	11.6	3.9		12.1	13.9
17.9	4.7	3.5	3.0	1.9	1.8	Sales/Total Assets	4.7	4.6
4.5	3.2	2.7	2.1	1.3	1.5		3.0	3.1
2.9	1.4	1.7	1.2	.6	.5		1.9	1.9

	.3		.4		.4		.5			% Depr., Dep., Amort./Sales		.5		.6
(12)	.8	(36)	1.1	(82)	1.1	(35)	1.6				(87)	1.1	(83)	1.0
	1.4		4.0		2.0		3.1					1.9		1.8

			2.6		2.2				% Officers', Directors' Owners' Comp/Sales		1.4		2.8
	(16)	3.8	(26)	3.6						(35)	5.0	(28)	5.0
		11.4		7.4							9.0		13.5

60333M	236557M	1635933M	2757024M	1442509M	4284332M	Net Sales ($)	4323073M	4850063M
7949M	69440M	559130M	1118248M	950166M	2528900M	Total Assets ($)	1974411M	2465929M

M = $ thousand   MM = $ million
See Pages 9 through 22 for Explanation of Ratios and Data

Comparative Historical Data				Current Data Sorted by Sales					
			Type of Statement						
35	52	60	Unqualified	1	2	1	4	19	33
20	32	33	Reviewed		1	2	7	17	6
25	14	15	Compiled		1	4	5	3	2
20	28	27	Tax Returns	8	5	4	6	3	1
84	112	148	Other	16	21	16	26	36	33
4/1/08- 3/31/09	4/1/09- 3/31/10	4/1/10- 3/31/11			32 (4/1-9/30/10)		251 (10/1/10-3/31/11)		
ALL	ALL	ALL		0-1MM	1-3MM	3-5MM	5-10MM	10-25MM	25MM & OVER
184	238	283	**NUMBER OF STATEMENTS**	25	30	27	48	78	75
%	%	%	**ASSETS**	%	%	%	%	%	%
19.9	17.7	17.7	Cash & Equivalents	14.5	29.3	17.2	14.1	18.0	16.3
38.0	42.1	39.6	Trade Receivables (net)	16.5	32.9	41.2	50.6	46.7	35.2
2.6	2.9	2.3	Inventory	.7	2.7	1.8	3.3	2.2	2.4
5.9	5.6	6.9	All Other Current	1.2	3.6	9.9	5.4	8.3	8.4
66.4	68.2	66.5	Total Current	32.9	68.5	70.2	73.3	75.2	62.2
19.3	16.4	16.9	Fixed Assets (net)	47.0	17.8	17.1	11.8	11.9	14.8
7.4	7.2	8.7	Intangibles (net)	3.3	5.0	4.0	7.4	7.3	16.0
6.9	8.1	8.0	All Other Non-Current	16.9	8.7	8.8	7.6	5.7	7.0
100.0	100.0	100.0	Total	100.0	100.0	100.0	100.0	100.0	100.0
			LIABILITIES						
12.6	10.7	10.6	Notes Payable-Short Term	20.1	13.7	16.6	8.6	8.0	7.9
3.0	3.1	2.6	Cur. Mat.-L.T.D.	1.6	1.3	6.9	2.6	1.9	2.5
12.8	12.6	10.9	Trade Payables	2.7	9.1	14.3	12.3	11.6	11.5
.5	.6	.7	Income Taxes Payable	.0	.0	.2	.4	.4	2.0
19.1	19.0	18.4	All Other Current	10.5	19.6	23.7	16.3	22.2	16.1
48.0	46.0	43.2	Total Current	34.8	43.8	61.6	40.2	44.1	40.0
13.2	14.4	10.8	Long-Term Debt	37.6	7.2	10.3	7.4	7.2	9.4
.7	.6	.7	Deferred Taxes	.4	1.4	.5	.9	.5	.7
11.7	7.0	4.6	All Other Non-Current	6.6	2.4	3.8	4.4	3.2	6.9
26.5	32.0	40.7	Net Worth	20.5	45.4	23.8	47.1	45.1	43.1
100.0	100.0	100.0	Total Liabilties & Net Worth	100.0	100.0	100.0	100.0	100.0	100.0
			INCOME DATA						
100.0	100.0	100.0	Net Sales	100.0	100.0	100.0	100.0	100.0	100.0
			Gross Profit						
90.1	92.8	91.1	Operating Expenses	72.2	93.0	97.6	88.2	94.5	92.5
9.9	7.2	8.9	Operating Profit	27.8	7.0	2.4	11.8	5.5	7.5
2.2	1.6	1.7	All Other Expenses (net)	13.5	-.2	.2	.4	.5	1.0
7.6	5.6	7.3	Profit Before Taxes	14.3	7.2	2.3	11.4	5.0	6.5
			RATIOS						
2.5	3.1	3.1		4.1	3.1	2.6	4.4	2.8	2.7
1.5	1.6	1.6	Current	.8	1.6	1.4	2.1	1.8	1.6
1.1	1.1	1.1		.2	1.0	.5	1.3	1.1	1.1
2.3	2.7	2.8		3.4	2.9	2.5	3.8	2.4	2.2
1.3	1.4	1.4	Quick	.7	1.5	1.1	2.1	1.5	1.4
.8	.9	.8		.2	.9	.5	1.1	1.0	.8
25 14.7	30 12.1	27 13.4		0 UND	0 UND	23 16.2	40 9.1	40 9.1	31 11.8
49 7.5	54 6.7	55 6.6	Sales/Receivables	0 UND	41 9.0	48 7.6	68 5.4	57 6.4	55 6.6
77 4.7	75 4.9	78 4.7		57 6.4	92 3.9	83 4.4	100 3.7	79 4.6	72 5.1
			Cost of Sales/Inventory						
			Cost of Sales/Payables						
5.7	5.3	5.0		7.4	3.8	6.9	4.0	5.1	5.6
15.4	13.0	9.5	Sales/Working Capital	-100.0	8.8	13.5	8.0	8.9	11.1
89.7	79.3	87.0		-3.5	NM	-31.0	32.8	64.1	43.7
28.4	38.3	42.7		7.2	54.0	49.6	102.0	43.8	45.0
(141) 8.4	(175) 8.0	(208) 12.8	EBIT/Interest	(12) 3.1	(22) 15.5	(21) 8.5	(35) 18.8	(58) 9.7	(60) 15.5
1.8	1.5	2.2		-3.1	-2.8	-4.9	6.6	1.6	3.9
13.2	19.6	17.5						21.8	27.6
(28) 3.4	(34) 2.3	(39) 3.3	Net Profit + Depr., Dep., Amort./Cur. Mat. L/T/D				(13) 3.3	(16) 3.3	9.7
1.3	1.2	1.4						.8	1.9
.1	.1	.1		.2	.0	.0	.0	.1	.1
.5	.4	.3	Fixed/Worth	4.2	.3	.7	.2	.2	.3
7.6	2.2	1.6		NM	1.1	-1.5	1.0	.8	2.7
.7	.7	.5		.3	.4	.6	.4	.6	.7
2.2	2.3	1.9	Debt/Worth	9.0	1.7	2.4	.8	1.6	2.0
57.4	12.5	7.3		NM	5.2	-11.5	3.1	4.7	9.3
83.2	77.9	77.3		100.0	113.4	60.8	77.5	78.8	74.4
(142) 38.6	(195) 36.6	(239) 38.0	% Profit Before Taxes/Tangible Net Worth	(19) 12.7	(27) 48.5	(18) 27.3	(41) 59.5	(73) 28.5	(61) 36.2
10.3	8.5	8.6		-4.9	1.7	10.5	22.7	6.8	13.8
28.9	26.6	29.3		19.0	32.2	33.2	50.3	23.8	22.1
14.8	10.0	10.1	% Profit Before Taxes/Total Assets	5.8	7.2	11.4	26.2	7.3	8.7
2.1	1.6	1.6		-.4	-4.4	-.4	5.8	1.2	3.4
117.5	125.9	114.0		64.8	213.3	127.6	174.9	118.1	95.1
30.8	38.7	40.5	Sales/Net Fixed Assets	7.2	59.4	60.5	45.5	45.2	33.5
9.3	11.6	12.8		.2	6.9	19.3	14.4	16.6	9.8
4.7	4.5	3.9		2.5	4.6	5.4	4.1	4.1	3.7
2.8	2.9	2.6	Sales/Total Assets	1.2	2.5	3.3	2.8	2.9	2.3
1.5	1.6	1.5		.2	1.2	2.1	1.7	2.2	1.3
.4	.4	.4		1.4	.4	.7	.4	.3	.4
(127) 1.2	(164) 1.0	(183) 1.3	% Depr., Dep., Amort./Sales	(14) 12.0	(14) 1.3	(16) 1.2	(29) 1.4	(60) .9	(50) 1.5
2.7	2.2	2.4		19.9	2.8	2.1	2.3	1.7	2.8
2.7	2.3	2.4					2.7	2.2	
(41) 7.5	(54) 4.8	(56) 4.2	% Officers', Directors' Owners' Comp/Sales				(13) 3.5	(17) 3.2	
14.8	11.2	12.1					7.2	5.3	
5880581M 2641159M	8004503M 3769377M	10416688M 5233833M	Net Sales ($) Total Assets ($)	10627M 22417M	54336M 40275M	103063M 58122M	347934M 156005M	1135077M 531379M	8765651M 4425635M

M = $ thousand   MM = $ million
See Pages 9 through 22 for Explanation of Ratios and Data

						Comparative Historical Data	
Current Data Sorted by Assets							
	4	16	33	11	10	**Type of Statement** Unqualified	77
1	3	13	7	1		Reviewed	17
1	3	8				Compiled	15
9	8	6				Tax Returns	19
3	24	34	32	7	15	Other	89
	66 (4/1-9/30/10)		183 (10/1/10-3/31/11)				4/1/06-3/31/07 ALL / 4/1/07-3/31/08
0-500M	500M-2MM	2-10MM	10-50MM	50-100MM	100-250MM		ALL
14	42	77	72	19	25	NUMBER OF STATEMENTS	217
%	%	%	%	%	%	**ASSETS**	% / %
37.7	23.5	15.7	21.5	26.9	11.8	Cash & Equivalents	19.2
25.1	33.3	35.4	28.8	22.6	14.5	Trade Receivables (net)	28.4
.5	5.3	6.1	5.7	1.4	2.9	Inventory	5.1
4.3	7.1	6.6	5.0	4.6	14.4	All Other Current	5.7
67.6	69.3	63.7	61.0	55.5	43.6	Total Current	58.3
19.8	16.5	21.4	25.5	23.3	21.0	Fixed Assets (net)	23.5
.4	4.8	4.2	5.6	3.3	21.9	Intangibles (net)	6.4
12.9	9.4	10.7	7.8	18.0	13.5	All Other Non-Current	11.8
100.0	100.0	100.0	100.0	100.0	100.0	Total	100.0
						LIABILITIES	
20.0	12.5	8.4	3.4	.5	1.8	Notes Payable-Short Term	7.8
2.9	1.7	1.6	1.7	.6	.9	Cur. Mat.-L.T.D.	2.3
7.0	10.3	11.2	8.8	7.9	6.2	Trade Payables	9.2
.0	.1	.7	.3	.7	.6	Income Taxes Payable	.4
22.8	15.3	14.0	15.9	25.5	20.7	All Other Current	20.3
52.7	39.9	35.9	30.1	35.3	30.3	Total Current	39.9
3.5	6.1	11.4	13.1	15.1	14.1	Long-Term Debt	12.9
1.5	.4	.7	.7	.1	1.2	Deferred Taxes	.3
4.3	1.5	5.1	6.8	4.7	16.0	All Other Non-Current	7.6
37.9	52.1	46.9	49.3	44.7	38.4	Net Worth	39.3
100.0	100.0	100.0	100.0	100.0	100.0	Total Liabilties & Net Worth	100.0
						INCOME DATA	
100.0	100.0	100.0	100.0	100.0	100.0	Net Sales	100.0
						Gross Profit	
88.7	91.3	92.3	91.0	88.8	94.4	Operating Expenses	93.2
11.3	8.7	7.7	9.0	11.2	5.6	Operating Profit	6.8
-.1	.1	1.4	.1	.0	2.0	All Other Expenses (net)	.7
11.4	8.6	6.3	9.0	11.1	3.5	Profit Before Taxes	6.2
						RATIOS	
4.1	4.5	3.6	3.2	2.4	1.8		3.7
2.4	1.7	2.0	2.4	1.8	1.3	Current	1.7
.7	1.2	1.1	1.4	1.1	1.1		1.1
3.3	4.1	3.1	2.9	1.8	1.7		2.9
2.1	1.6	1.4	1.8	1.5	.9	Quick	1.4
.6	.7	.8	1.1	.8	.5		.8
0 UND	12 31.5	26 13.9	39 9.4	17 21.3	33 10.9		27 13.5
4 90.9	40 9.2	54 6.7	58 6.3	41 8.8	47 7.8	Sales/Receivables	51 7.2
40 9.1	65 5.6	85 4.3	89 4.1	59 6.2	66 5.5		80 4.6
						Cost of Sales/Inventory	
						Cost of Sales/Payables	
8.8	3.2	3.6	2.7	2.4	6.1		3.4
17.7	7.3	7.8	5.1	7.3	8.3	Sales/Working Capital	9.2
-22.0	45.0	38.7	11.8	31.8	35.3		89.2
	67.3	33.7	71.4	229.6	9.0		15.6
(31) 11.4	(56) 11.9	(51) 8.0	(12) 55.5	(19) 5.2		EBIT/Interest	(151) 5.7
2.4	1.5	.8	-.2	.8			1.6
	41.4	14.0					8.9
(14) 8.7	(18) 5.7					Net Profit + Depr., Dep., Amort./Cur. Mat. L/T/D	(41) 4.4
4.2	2.2						1.5
.2	.1	.1	.1	.1	.3		.2
.4	.3	.3	.3	.4	.7	Fixed/Worth	.5
4.9	.8	1.0	1.3	1.6	-.9		1.8
.3	.3	.4	.5	.6	1.0		.4
1.7	.9	1.0	1.1	1.5	2.9	Debt/Worth	1.4
14.9	4.3	3.4	2.8	4.6	-14.8		5.8
109.9	77.4	53.7	46.0	41.3	45.7	% Profit Before Taxes/Tangible Net Worth	54.4
(12) 27.6	(38) 25.4	(70) 23.5	(65) 16.3	(18) 15.0	(18) 10.5		(189) 20.7
-118.4	4.6	6.0	-.5	2.8	4.5		1.9
74.2	32.4	26.1	26.9	18.7	10.6	% Profit Before Taxes/Total Assets	19.0
30.2	10.9	12.8	7.6	8.6	2.8		8.3
-7.7	2.8	1.1	-.5	.6	-1.2		.5
237.9	107.3	54.8	44.0	65.5	21.7	Sales/Net Fixed Assets	44.8
43.7	27.4	19.7	12.0	21.9	6.8		14.5
23.3	8.7	7.0	2.0	.6	2.0		4.3
13.4	4.2	3.4	2.1	2.6	1.7	Sales/Total Assets	3.1
6.5	2.8	2.2	1.3	.6	.7		1.8
3.6	1.4	1.5	.8	.3	.6		.9
	.5	.7	1.2	1.0	1.9	% Depr., Dep., Amort./Sales	1.0
(21) 1.2	(56) 1.7	(61) 3.0	(15) 2.3	(16) 3.2			(174) 2.3
4.1	3.4	6.0	11.0	7.4			4.3
	2.6					% Officers', Directors' Owners' Comp/Sales	3.2
(12) 9.7							(31) 7.5
16.2							16.6
23770M	137757M	836770M	2936864M	1891692M	4782657M	Net Sales ($)	9239155M
3104M	46717M	379509M	1798727M	1347663M	3999749M	Total Assets ($)	6850277M

M = $ thousand   MM = $ million
See Pages 9 through 22 for Explanation of Ratios and Data

Comparative Historical Data | | | Current Data Sorted by Sales

			Type of Statement						
81	92	74	Unqualified		4	1	13	17	39
24	21	25	Reviewed		1	5	5	7	7
9	8	12	Compiled	1	1	1	5	3	1
22	20	23	Tax Returns	6	10	3	1	3	
101	101	115	Other	8	15	11	17	20	44
4/1/08-3/31/09 ALL	4/1/09-3/31/10 ALL	4/1/10-3/31/11 ALL			66 (4/1-9/30/10)		183 (10/1/10-3/31/11)		
				0-1MM	1-3MM	3-5MM	5-10MM	10-25MM	25MM & OVER
237	242	249	**NUMBER OF STATEMENTS**	15	31	21	41	50	91
%	%	%	**ASSETS**	%	%	%	%	%	%
20.0	21.5	20.4	Cash & Equivalents	31.2	26.3	17.1	13.6	16.9	22.3
30.4	27.6	29.5	Trade Receivables (net)	21.8	21.7	36.9	29.4	35.4	28.4
4.5	5.3	4.9	Inventory	7.5	4.5	3.5	4.7	6.4	4.1
5.6	6.5	6.7	All Other Current	2.7	5.3	4.5	6.8	4.7	9.5
60.5	60.8	61.5	Total Current	63.2	57.9	62.1	54.5	63.5	64.2
23.9	22.8	21.8	Fixed Assets (net)	17.9	26.6	22.2	30.4	22.0	16.6
5.2	5.1	6.2	Intangibles (net)	8.7	.8	2.5	6.7	5.7	8.5
10.4	11.3	10.6	All Other Non-Current	10.8	14.8	13.2	8.4	8.7	10.7
100.0	100.0	100.0	Total	100.0	100.0	100.0	100.0	100.0	100.0
			LIABILITIES						
6.7	5.7	7.1	Notes Payable-Short Term	10.8	15.9	8.1	6.9	6.7	3.5
2.0	1.8	1.6	Cur. Mat.-L.T.D.	2.2	2.4	2.4	1.8	1.5	1.0
10.3	10.6	9.4	Trade Payables	6.8	3.5	12.0	10.5	11.3	9.6
.3	.5	.4	Income Taxes Payable	.0	.0	.2	.4	.7	.5
17.2	16.8	16.8	All Other Current	4.2	17.4	11.5	14.2	15.8	21.7
36.5	35.4	35.3	Total Current	24.0	39.1	34.2	33.8	36.0	36.3
14.6	10.3	11.1	Long-Term Debt	11.3	9.7	10.7	15.9	10.8	9.7
.4	.4	.7	Deferred Taxes	.4	.9	.1	.8	.7	.7
4.7	6.3	6.0	All Other Non-Current	9.5	3.9	2.3	2.8	5.8	8.6
43.8	47.6	46.9	Net Worth	54.7	46.4	52.7	46.7	46.8	44.7
100.0	100.0	100.0	Total Liabilties & Net Worth	100.0	100.0	100.0	100.0	100.0	100.0
			INCOME DATA						
100.0	100.0	100.0	Net Sales	100.0	100.0	100.0	100.0	100.0	100.0
			Gross Profit						
93.7	93.0	91.5	Operating Expenses	89.5	89.6	88.3	95.7	94.0	90.0
6.3	7.0	8.5	Operating Profit	10.5	10.4	11.7	4.3	6.0	10.0
2.1	1.2	.7	All Other Expenses (net)	2.2	.9	.3	.7	.3	.6
4.3	5.8	7.8	Profit Before Taxes	8.3	9.4	11.4	3.6	5.7	9.5
			RATIOS						
3.3	3.5	3.3		4.4	7.2	4.4	3.4	2.9	3.0
1.8	1.9	1.8	Current	2.7	2.0	1.7	2.0	2.0	1.8
1.2	1.2	1.2		1.4	.5	1.1	1.2	1.2	1.3
2.9	2.9	2.8		4.4	5.1	3.6	3.2	2.6	2.1
1.5	1.5	1.5	Quick	2.7	1.6	1.4	1.4	1.4	1.5
.9	.9	.8		.7	.2	1.0	.7	1.0	.8
32 11.4	28 13.2	26 14.1		0 UND	0 UND	11 32.6	26 14.3	31 11.9	32 11.3
52 7.0	48 7.7	51 7.2	Sales/Receivables	51 7.2	29 12.4	50 7.3	58 6.3	52 7.0	52 7.1
76 4.8	68 5.3	75 4.8		143 2.6	58 6.3	94 3.9	80 4.5	83 4.4	71 5.1
			Cost of Sales/Inventory						
			Cost of Sales/Payables						
3.9	3.2	3.3		1.4	3.2	3.8	2.8	3.7	3.7
7.8	7.6	7.3	Sales/Working Capital	2.4	7.1	11.3	7.6	7.1	7.3
37.7	24.7	26.6		9.3	-25.0	44.0	35.2	44.3	18.3
23.0	38.4	51.7			88.8	52.7	12.3	30.8	119.7
(163) 3.6	(168) 8.8	(176) 8.3	EBIT/Interest		(22) 9.8	(15) 12.4	(29) 6.4	(37) 8.5	(66) 11.9
-.5	1.4	1.3			-2.6	1.9	1.2	-2.9	2.1
15.3	9.4	34.5						28.1	82.7
(37) 4.3	(34) 3.5	(43) 7.8	Net Profit + Depr., Dep., Amort./Cur. Mat. L/T/D					(12) 8.1	(22) 10.6
1.6	1.4	2.9						4.6	2.8
.1	.1	.1		.1	.1	.1	.1	.1	.1
.4	.4	.3	Fixed/Worth	.2	.4	.4	.5	.3	.3
1.1	1.1	1.3		.4	2.3	.9	1.9	1.2	1.0
.4	.4	.5		.3	.2	.3	.3	.6	.5
1.1	1.0	1.1	Debt/Worth	1.2	1.1	.8	1.5	1.2	1.1
3.4	2.8	3.9		5.3	4.4	3.0	4.3	3.4	3.9
44.9	51.0	53.7		54.3	73.9	51.2	40.9	69.2	62.6
(214) 18.6	(216) 14.7	(221) 20.9	% Profit Before Taxes/Tangible Net Worth	(14) 15.2	(26) 16.8	(20) 28.7	(36) 16.7	(46) 22.5	(79) 24.3
-1.0	.7	3.8		-.5	-18.8	8.4	2.8	-4.2	9.2
18.3	19.7	26.1		20.0	39.3	33.8	15.4	28.2	27.9
5.4	7.0	8.6	% Profit Before Taxes/Total Assets	4.1	8.4	15.3	5.5	8.4	9.5
-1.1	.2	.6		.0	-.7	2.8	-.1	-1.7	1.9
67.4	44.6	57.4		234.0	71.4	39.0	42.2	41.4	67.0
16.5	14.6	19.0	Sales/Net Fixed Assets	29.2	21.3	15.4	12.7	19.5	21.9
3.5	3.5	4.0		2.7	3.3	5.0	1.2	5.6	6.1
3.1	2.8	3.2		3.8	3.2	3.7	3.3	3.6	2.9
1.9	1.7	1.8	Sales/Total Assets	1.0	2.1	1.8	1.7	2.2	1.7
1.0	1.0	.9		.6	1.3	1.4	.7	1.1	.9
.7	1.0	.9			1.4	.5	1.2	.9	.9
(176) 2.3	(187) 2.6	(178) 2.1	% Depr., Dep., Amort./Sales		(17) 2.4	(12) 2.7	(32) 2.6	(41) 1.7	(67) 2.0
5.5	5.9	4.6			8.0	7.0	5.4	3.4	3.8
3.0	3.9	1.8							
(34) 9.2	(33) 8.6	(34) 6.6	% Officers', Directors' Owners' Comp/Sales						
13.9	12.9	14.8							
11651357M	9982321M	10609510M	Net Sales ($)	8976M	61032M	85644M	294099M	760032M	9399727M
8568654M	7387910M	7575469M	Total Assets ($)	12928M	84292M	109472M	413489M	603895M	6351393M

M = $ thousand   MM = $ million
See Pages 9 through 22 for Explanation of Ratios and Data

Current Data Sorted by Assets   Comparative Historical Data

0-500M	500M-2MM	2-10MM	10-50MM	50-100MM	100-250MM		4/1/06-3/31/07 ALL	4/1/07-3/31/08 ALL
						Type of Statement		
	1	5	8	6	9	Unqualified	17	20
	1		2			Reviewed	5	5
1	4	1				Compiled	5	7
2	1					Tax Returns	4	2
2	2	7	8	2	6	Other	21	26
	18 (4/1-9/30/10)		50 (10/1/10-3/31/11)					
5	8	14	18	8	15	**NUMBER OF STATEMENTS**	52	60
%	%	%	%	%	%	**ASSETS**	%	%
		39.0	22.1		22.0	Cash & Equivalents	23.6	24.4
		20.0	24.1		19.6	Trade Receivables (net)	30.2	27.5
		2.6	.1		.5	Inventory	.5	1.3
		4.6	8.0		9.0	All Other Current	7.7	6.4
		66.1	54.3		51.2	Total Current	62.0	59.6
		22.4	16.4		24.2	Fixed Assets (net)	20.2	21.8
		2.5	4.0		3.5	Intangibles (net)	8.1	12.8
		9.0	25.3		21.2	All Other Non-Current	9.7	5.9
		100.0	100.0		100.0	Total	100.0	100.0
						LIABILITIES		
		1.7	3.9		.2	Notes Payable-Short Term	14.4	8.6
		1.0	.9		2.3	Cur. Mat.-L.T.D.	1.2	3.2
		4.6	8.8		5.8	Trade Payables	8.6	8.0
		.7	.1		.0	Income Taxes Payable	.1	1.5
		14.4	15.2		21.2	All Other Current	25.3	18.4
		22.4	29.0		29.6	Total Current	49.6	39.7
		6.1	7.6		17.9	Long-Term Debt	11.7	14.2
		.0	.3		.1	Deferred Taxes	.2	.2
		4.3	6.1		11.2	All Other Non-Current	5.4	8.3
		67.1	57.1		41.2	Net Worth	33.1	37.7
		100.0	100.0		100.0	Total Liabilties & Net Worth	100.0	100.0
						INCOME DATA		
		100.0	100.0		100.0	Net Sales	100.0	100.0
						Gross Profit		
		87.0	96.9		98.6	Operating Expenses	92.4	91.8
		13.0	3.1		1.4	Operating Profit	7.6	8.2
		2.8	-.4		3.2	All Other Expenses (net)	.4	1.5
		10.2	3.4		-1.8	Profit Before Taxes	7.2	6.7
						RATIOS		
		8.1	2.9		3.0		2.6	2.8
		3.5	2.1		1.8	Current	1.8	1.7
		1.4	1.3		1.4		1.0	1.1
		7.8	2.6		2.8		2.4	2.4
		2.9	1.7		1.7	Quick	1.3	1.4
		1.3	1.2		.6		.9	.9
		5 79.1	1 294.1		46 8.0		18 20.2	32 11.3
		39 9.4	40 9.1		58 6.3	Sales/Receivables	53 6.9	61 6.0
		59 6.2	73 5.0		86 4.2		75 4.9	76 4.8
						Cost of Sales/Inventory		
						Cost of Sales/Payables		
		2.1	4.3		2.2		3.6	3.8
		3.1	9.4		4.4	Sales/Working Capital	8.3	6.1
		15.1	78.9		16.7		-134.7	62.4
			39.4		103.3		26.7	32.6
			(10) 15.0		(10) 1.2	EBIT/Interest	(43) 6.8	(46) 9.4
			3.0		-2.1		1.1	1.3
								17.9
						Net Profit + Depr., Dep., Amort./Cur. Mat. L/T/D		(13) 4.5
								2.5
		.0	.0		.1		.1	.1
		.1	.2		.6	Fixed/Worth	.4	.7
		.8	.6		1.0		2.7	NM
		.1	.3		.4		.5	.5
		.3	.8		1.0	Debt/Worth	.9	2.1
		2.3	1.9		29.4		9.1	-19.6
		66.7	30.7		71.9		49.5	68.2
		11.1	22.2		(13) 5.9	% Profit Before Taxes/Tangible Net Worth	(42) 15.2	(44) 18.6
		2.7	4.6		-4.3		2.2	6.2
		24.7	18.6		10.2		19.3	25.4
		9.8	7.5		1.0	% Profit Before Taxes/Total Assets	6.9	8.1
		1.8	3.0		-4.5		.2	.3
		87.1	68.0		24.4		102.6	49.8
		37.2	27.7		5.6	Sales/Net Fixed Assets	24.1	13.8
		3.3	4.3		.7		4.2	5.1
		2.3	3.4		1.7		3.2	2.4
		1.5	1.7		.6	Sales/Total Assets	1.7	1.6
		1.0	.7		.4		1.1	.8
		.5	.9		1.3		.6	.8
	(13)	.7	(14) 1.5		(10) 4.9	% Depr., Dep., Amort./Sales	(40) 2.3	(44) 2.6
		1.7	3.1		9.7		4.3	4.8
							3.8	
						% Officers', Directors' Owners' Comp/Sales	(16) 8.7	
							28.3	
6150M	50406M	119765M	3976896M	857074M	2706997M	Net Sales ($)	1995312M	2352509M
1302M	9843M	77380M	474424M	624515M	2342088M	Total Assets ($)	1811727M	2079081M

M = $ thousand   MM = $ million
See Pages 9 through 22 for Explanation of Ratios and Data

Comparative Historical Data / Current Data Sorted by Sales

			Type of Statement				18 (4/1-9/30/10)	50 (10/1/10-3/31/11)	
31	35	29	Unqualified		1		6	3	19
8	5	3	Reviewed					2	1
3	6	6	Compiled	1	1	2	2		
7	4	3	Tax Returns	1			1	1	
21	18	27	Other	2	2	2	3	4	14
4/1/08-3/31/09 ALL	4/1/09-3/31/10 ALL	4/1/10-3/31/11 ALL		0-1MM	1-3MM	3-5MM	5-10MM	10-25MM	25MM & OVER
70	68	68	NUMBER OF STATEMENTS	4	4	5	12	9	34
%	%	%	ASSETS	%	%	%	%	%	%
26.6	23.0	26.9	Cash & Equivalents				38.4		19.5
31.0	30.0	25.6	Trade Receivables (net)				26.7		26.0
.8	1.0	.9	Inventory				.5		.8
4.3	6.6	6.6	All Other Current				3.0		8.4
62.7	60.6	60.1	Total Current				68.6		54.7
16.1	18.8	19.8	Fixed Assets (net)				11.3		21.0
7.2	6.8	3.8	Intangibles (net)				.0		5.6
14.1	13.7	16.3	All Other Non-Current				20.1		18.8
100.0	100.0	100.0	Total				100.0		100.0
			LIABILITIES						
9.4	10.6	6.4	Notes Payable-Short Term				1.9		2.1
4.0	1.9	1.6	Cur. Mat.-L.T.D.				.4		1.6
8.5	10.1	6.7	Trade Payables				5.5		8.9
.2	.1	.2	Income Taxes Payable				.2		.0
22.1	16.8	19.5	All Other Current				12.0		19.7
44.1	39.5	34.5	Total Current				20.1		32.3
11.7	10.2	13.7	Long-Term Debt				2.8		12.4
.4	.1	.2	Deferred Taxes				.0		.4
6.3	5.9	6.8	All Other Non-Current				5.9		8.9
37.5	44.4	44.8	Net Worth				71.2		46.0
100.0	100.0	100.0	Total Liabilities & Net Worth				100.0		100.0
			INCOME DATA						
100.0	100.0	100.0	Net Sales				100.0		100.0
			Gross Profit						
94.0	99.2	95.5	Operating Expenses				98.5		96.6
6.0	.8	4.5	Operating Profit				1.5		3.4
2.6	.9	1.6	All Other Expenses (net)				-.5		1.7
3.4	-.1	2.9	Profit Before Taxes				2.0		1.7
			RATIOS						
2.9	2.9	3.5	Current				13.5		2.9
2.0	1.7	2.1					3.1		1.7
1.1	1.1	1.3					1.4		1.3
2.7	2.6	3.0	Quick				12.7		2.4
1.5	1.5	1.7					3.0		1.5
.9	.7	1.0					1.3		.6
17 21.9	6 63.5	14 26.5	Sales/Receivables				3 142.0		31 11.9
57 6.4	53 6.8	52 7.0					43 8.6		58 6.3
86 4.3	84 4.3	74 5.0					68 5.4		75 4.9
			Cost of Sales/Inventory						
			Cost of Sales/Payables						
3.9	3.4	2.9	Sales/Working Capital				2.3		3.0
7.5	10.1	7.1					6.4		9.4
45.2	73.3	29.4					30.1		65.5
11.8	25.1	61.9	EBIT/Interest						47.0
(50) 1.8	(45) 6.0	(44) 8.6							(22) 8.6
-5.9	-3.8	-.1							.1
17.1			Net Profit + Depr., Dep., Amort./Cur. Mat. L/T/D						
(12) 4.3									
1.9									
.1	.1	.1	Fixed/Worth				.0		.1
.3	.3	.3					.1		.5
1.6	1.6	1.0					.2		.8
.5	.5	.3	Debt/Worth				.1		.4
1.1	1.3	1.1					.3		1.4
8.8	4.7	3.7					1.1		3.8
46.9	34.6	36.4	% Profit Before Taxes/Tangible Net Worth				37.0		33.6
(59) 8.0	(59) 7.6	(60) 15.1					7.2		(31) 16.4
-6.9	-5.0	2.1					-.5		3.1
12.8	12.9	16.6	% Profit Before Taxes/Total Assets				24.8		14.7
1.5	2.4	5.9					6.0		6.1
-5.1	-4.5	-.6					-.3		.8
89.0	75.7	69.6	Sales/Net Fixed Assets				91.1		44.2
23.4	24.7	19.0					57.6		15.9
5.2	4.5	4.4					13.2		2.4
2.9	3.4	2.9	Sales/Total Assets				4.2		2.9
1.6	2.1	1.7					2.1		1.6
.8	.9	.7					.5		.6
.7	.9	.7	% Depr., Dep., Amort./Sales				.6		1.1
(54) 1.7	(48) 1.8	(54) 1.5					(11) .7		(25) 2.1
3.2	3.6	3.4					1.2		7.8
5.4	6.6	3.7	% Officers', Directors' Owners' Comp/Sales						
(15) 9.3	(16) 15.3	(14) 17.5							
14.2	20.9	31.1							
2515838M	6259637M	7717288M	Net Sales ($)	2628M	8339M	19051M	92485M	141969M	7452816M
2087681M	2423251M	3529552M	Total Assets ($)	8787M	6985M	10992M	149955M	119845M	3232988M

M = $ thousand   MM = $ million
See Pages 9 through 22 for Explanation of Ratios and Data

Current Data Sorted by Assets   **Comparative Historical Data**

Type of Statement	0-500M	500M-2MM	2-10MM	10-50MM	50-100MM	100-250MM		4/1/06-3/31/07 ALL	4/1/07-3/31/08 ALL
Unqualified		1	7	13	4	1		31	26
Reviewed	1	11	37	20	1			76	52
Compiled	15	15	28	2				70	63
Tax Returns	47	35	24	1				72	68
Other	40	56	78	26	4	5		159	161
		44 (4/1-9/30/10)		428 (10/1/10-3/31/11)					
NUMBER OF STATEMENTS	103	118	174	62	9	6		408	370
ASSETS	%	%	%	%	%	%		%	%
Cash & Equivalents	28.0	19.2	20.3	21.9				14.9	16.2
Trade Receivables (net)	29.9	44.8	42.4	41.7				47.2	46.7
Inventory	2.3	2.9	3.4	1.6				3.6	3.1
All Other Current	3.0	3.8	6.4	6.6				4.5	5.9
Total Current	63.2	70.7	72.4	71.8				70.2	71.9
Fixed Assets (net)	20.7	14.0	14.6	11.1				15.8	13.4
Intangibles (net)	4.5	5.0	5.0	10.7				5.9	6.0
All Other Non-Current	11.7	10.3	8.0	6.4				8.1	8.7
Total	100.0	100.0	100.0	100.0				100.0	100.0
LIABILITIES									
Notes Payable-Short Term	40.1	11.0	4.8	4.8				12.1	12.6
Cur. Mat.-L.T.D.	5.9	2.8	1.5	1.9				3.7	4.0
Trade Payables	20.6	25.2	30.2	27.3				30.3	28.2
Income Taxes Payable	.1	.1	.3	.3				.4	.3
All Other Current	26.7	17.7	22.4	24.8				19.8	20.0
Total Current	93.3	56.9	59.1	59.1				66.3	65.1
Long-Term Debt	25.7	10.0	6.4	7.4				11.8	11.5
Deferred Taxes	.1	.3	.2	.1				.3	.2
All Other Non-Current	11.8	10.2	6.8	6.5				6.6	9.5
Net Worth	-30.9	22.6	27.6	26.9				15.0	13.7
Total Liabilties & Net Worth	100.0	100.0	100.0	100.0				100.0	100.0
INCOME DATA									
Net Sales	100.0	100.0	100.0	100.0				100.0	100.0
Gross Profit									
Operating Expenses	93.1	94.1	93.7	91.5				94.6	94.5
Operating Profit	6.9	5.9	6.3	8.5				5.4	5.5
All Other Expenses (net)	1.1	1.5	1.4	.8				1.3	1.3
Profit Before Taxes	5.8	4.4	4.9	7.7				4.0	4.2
RATIOS									
Current	2.0	2.3	2.2	1.9				1.7	1.8
	.8	1.3	1.2	1.2				1.1	1.1
	.4	.9	.9	.9				.8	.8
Quick	2.0	2.1	1.9	1.7				1.5	1.5
	.7	1.1	1.1	1.0			(407)	1.0 (368)	1.0
	.3	.7	.8	.8				.7	.7
Sales/Receivables	0 UND	23 16.0	30 12.2	48 7.6			30	12.2 26	14.0
	15 23.9	42 8.7	48 7.5	73 5.0			48	7.6 49	7.5
	40 9.0	62 5.8	68 5.3	120 3.0			73	5.0 71	5.1
Cost of Sales/Inventory									
Cost of Sales/Payables									
Sales/Working Capital	21.5	9.3	8.0	5.5				13.6	12.0
	-66.1	28.1	28.7	26.1				50.4	46.1
	-10.9	-48.9	-41.3	-28.1				-31.5	-37.3
EBIT/Interest	26.3	23.8	69.3	67.6				23.4	24.9
	(71) 6.5	(80) 4.9	(120) 13.6	(46) 13.4			(323)	5.5 (277)	6.0
	.6	.8	2.1	1.7				1.3	1.3
Net Profit + Depr., Dep., Amort./Cur. Mat. L/T/D			13.4	12.5				7.6	7.5
		(23)	4.1	(15) 4.6			(51)	2.6 (35)	2.4
			2.1	2.2				1.1	1.3
Fixed/Worth	.1	.1	.1	.2				.2	.2
	2.9	.4	.5	.6				.8	.5
	-.3	-1.8	15.8	-.7				-47.3	-3.7
Debt/Worth	1.2	.9	1.0	1.4				1.5	1.4
	-11.4	3.8	4.4	5.8				5.7	5.4
	-2.0	-11.9	87.1	-11.2				-59.3	-15.3
% Profit Before Taxes/Tangible Net Worth	426.0	86.0	85.6	111.3				98.9	95.0
	(50) 92.2	(84) 37.9	(138) 40.7	(44) 47.2			(296)	45.0 (259)	43.0
	18.2	5.3	6.4	17.0				11.5	14.9
% Profit Before Taxes/Total Assets	67.4	24.3	20.5	18.2				23.2	24.4
	22.0	6.8	8.1	9.8				7.3	7.2
	-3.5	.5	1.2	1.6				.8	.9
Sales/Net Fixed Assets	719.0	160.3	110.7	59.6				93.4	116.7
	61.9	56.3	36.1	28.9				36.7	46.0
	18.4	25.4	18.9	10.1				17.8	19.2
Sales/Total Assets	12.4	5.5	4.4	2.8				5.1	5.3
	6.0	3.7	2.9	1.8				3.5	3.7
	3.3	2.6	1.9	1.2				2.4	2.3
% Depr., Dep., Amort./Sales	.5	.3	.4	.5				.4	.4
	(47) 1.1	(81) .8	(133) 1.1	(52) 1.2			(313)	.9 (267)	.8
	2.2	1.6	2.0	2.9				1.8	1.8
% Officers', Directors' Owners' Comp/Sales	5.5	4.2	2.3	.4				3.0	2.7
	(63) 10.1	(60) 6.7	(56) 4.4	(14) 1.3			(167)	6.1 (160)	5.7
	16.4		8.2	4.9				11.4	12.0
Net Sales ($)	148623M	583732M	2515955M	2783661M	725299M	1335933M		7352154M	9144795M
Total Assets ($)	20599M	143135M	782611M	1396465M	624199M	1061982M		3291179M	3556690M

M = $ thousand   MM = $ million
See Pages 9 through 22 for Explanation of Ratios and Data

Comparative Historical Data

Current Data Sorted by Sales

			Type of Statement						
28	29	26	Unqualified		1	2	9	14	
55	67	70	Reviewed	2	2	4	17	25	20
59	61	60	Compiled	7	15	10	11	15	2
94	96	107	Tax Returns	26	29	16	24	11	1
170	195	209	Other	26	35	25	40	42	41
4/1/08-3/31/09 ALL	4/1/09-3/31/10 ALL	4/1/10-3/31/11 ALL		44 (4/1-9/30/10)		428 (10/1/10-3/31/11)			
				0-1MM	1-3MM	3-5MM	5-10MM	10-25MM	25MM & OVER
406	448	472	NUMBER OF STATEMENTS	61	81	56	94	102	78
%	%	%	ASSETS	%	%	%	%	%	%
16.9	18.9	21.9	Cash & Equivalents	29.0	20.6	21.6	20.6	20.6	21.0
44.6	40.7	39.8	Trade Receivables (net)	22.5	38.2	40.4	43.1	46.1	42.1
2.9	3.3	2.7	Inventory	.9	3.4	3.0	3.0	4.0	1.1
4.9	5.0	4.9	All Other Current	3.4	4.3	7.4	4.6	4.4	5.7
69.4	67.9	69.2	Total Current	55.8	66.6	72.5	71.3	75.1	69.9
15.1	15.7	15.0	Fixed Assets (net)	29.5	18.5	9.9	12.8	13.8	8.1
6.2	5.9	6.7	Intangibles (net)	3.9	4.8	5.8	6.6	4.2	14.9
9.4	10.6	9.0	All Other Non-Current	10.7	10.1	11.8	9.3	7.0	7.1
100.0	100.0	100.0	Total	100.0	100.0	100.0	100.0	100.0	100.0
			LIABILITIES						
15.9	17.2	13.9	Notes Payable-Short Term	32.1	27.7	12.3	10.3	5.5	1.8
3.5	3.1	2.9	Cur. Mat.-L.T.D.	6.9	3.7	3.8	1.3	1.7	1.7
29.9	27.5	26.6	Trade Payables	13.9	23.4	21.6	27.0	34.4	32.7
.2	.2	.2	Income Taxes Payable	.1	.1	.1	.0	.4	.3
19.1	22.9	22.3	All Other Current	29.1	16.9	18.8	23.2	23.7	21.9
68.7	70.9	65.8	Total Current	82.0	71.7	56.5	61.8	65.8	58.4
10.1	10.8	11.7	Long-Term Debt	43.8	11.5	8.5	4.9	4.7	6.5
.2	.2	.2	Deferred Taxes	.0	.4	.0	.1	.3	.5
8.5	7.9	8.6	All Other Non-Current	11.1	10.2	11.7	4.8	9.3	6.7
12.5	10.2	13.6	Net Worth	-37.0	6.2	23.3	28.4	20.0	27.8
100.0	100.0	100.0	Total Liabilities & Net Worth	100.0	100.0	100.0	100.0	100.0	100.0
			INCOME DATA						
100.0	100.0	100.0	Net Sales	100.0	100.0	100.0	100.0	100.0	100.0
			Gross Profit						
95.0	96.3	93.4	Operating Expenses	85.4	94.3	96.3	94.2	94.8	93.9
5.0	3.7	6.6	Operating Profit	14.6	5.7	3.7	5.8	5.2	6.1
1.3	1.1	1.3	All Other Expenses (net)	6.1	.8	.8	.4	.7	.5
3.7	2.6	5.3	Profit Before Taxes	8.5	4.9	2.9	5.4	4.5	5.6
			RATIOS						
1.8	1.7	2.1	Current	2.3	2.5	2.9	2.1	1.7	1.8
1.1	1.1	1.1		.9	1.1	1.5	1.1	1.2	1.1
.8	.7	.8		.3	.6	1.0	.9	.9	.9
1.6	1.5	1.8	Quick	2.3	2.0	2.6	1.8	1.5	1.6
1.0	(447) .9	1.0		.8	.9	1.3	1.0	1.0	1.1
.7	.6	.7		.2	.5	.9	.7	.8	.8
28 13.3	24 15.4	21 17.7	Sales/Receivables	0 UND	7 51.9	10 35.8	30 12.1	31 11.8	36 10.1
45 8.1	46 7.9	45 8.0		1 557.0	32 11.4	55 6.6	48 7.6	50 7.4	51 7.1
72 5.0	76 4.8	68 5.4		45 8.1	59 6.1	83 4.4	69 5.3	71 5.1	78 4.7
			Cost of Sales/Inventory						
			Cost of Sales/Payables						
12.0	10.1	8.9	Sales/Working Capital	7.4	9.4	5.4	8.0	11.3	9.8
51.9	65.2	39.1		-66.1	69.2	12.0	43.2	41.2	34.4
-27.0	-18.6	-27.1		-7.5	-15.1	-136.9	-26.6	-44.4	-33.1
24.5	20.9	38.7	EBIT/Interest	23.4	19.2	19.9	34.5	70.6	120.1
(312) 5.9	(336) 3.7	(328) 8.0		(30) 6.3	(61) 5.0	(33) 5.6	(69) 8.1	(78) 13.3	(57) 16.2
.7	-2.4	1.2		.9	.5	-3.6	1.2	1.7	2.0
7.0	9.1	14.1	Net Profit + Depr., Dep., Amort./Cur. Mat. L/T/D					13.0	67.2
(47) 2.1	(37) 2.1	(50) 4.3					(21) 3.6	(13) 10.9	
.6	.5	2.1						1.5	3.8
.2	.2	.1	Fixed/Worth	.0	.1	.1	.1	.2	.2
.6	.7	.6		16.9	1.2	.2	.5	.8	.7
-3.4	-1.1	-1.8		-.4	-1.3	2.2	29.2	-2.7	-.7
1.2	1.3	1.1	Debt/Worth	.8	1.1	.8	1.0	1.2	2.3
5.4	5.6	5.9		-30.1	5.4	2.4	4.5	5.7	8.0
-20.9	-6.5	-8.4		-1.9	-4.4	NM	NM	-25.2	-9.4
100.0	99.7	112.1	% Profit Before Taxes/Tangible Net Worth	504.2	127.7	51.0	88.7	116.2	110.0
(285) 36.3	(296) 31.1	(323) 43.3		(30) 86.3	(52) 36.6	(42) 22.4	(71) 51.2	(74) 48.5	(54) 45.5
7.0	.7	7.2		35.4	2.0	3.4	6.3	10.8	15.0
23.4	22.1	26.6	% Profit Before Taxes/Total Assets	58.8	38.2	15.9	23.5	23.4	17.0
7.4	5.1	8.8		13.0	11.2	5.7	8.0	10.3	7.3
-.1	-4.3	.6		.0	-.5	-2.8	1.5	.5	1.6
111.6	99.6	120.3	Sales/Net Fixed Assets	UND	258.9	144.9	108.6	104.2	91.3
40.3	37.5	40.6		25.7	54.0	44.6	47.7	35.9	43.7
18.8	16.1	18.4		8.4	17.3	20.2	23.7	19.5	18.3
5.5	5.1	5.3	Sales/Total Assets	7.9	8.6	4.1	4.6	5.1	4.6
3.7	3.4	3.3		3.0	3.9	2.9	3.0	3.6	2.8
2.3	1.8	1.9		1.1	2.4	1.7	2.0	2.1	1.4
.5	.5	.4	% Depr., Dep., Amort./Sales	.7	.7	.3	.4	.4	.4
(280) .9	(306) 1.1	(318) 1.0		(31) 1.9	(46) 1.1	(38) .8	(69) .9	(83) .9	(51) .8
2.0	2.1	2.1		11.4	2.9	1.8	2.0	1.6	2.3
2.5	3.2	3.8	% Officers', Directors' Owners' Comp/Sales	7.7	5.2	4.2	2.9	2.3	.7
(168) 5.8	(182) 5.8	(193) 6.7		(30) 12.4	(49) 9.7	(23) 6.7	(41) 5.0	(28) 4.6	(22) 1.8
11.3	11.1	12.3		17.9	15.7	11.4	9.4	7.9	4.3
9121021M	8527079M	8093203M	Net Sales ($)	29455M	153856M	223500M	681455M	1691028M	5313909M
4319658M	4271237M	4028991M	Total Assets ($)	27363M	62145M	100939M	288717M	640612M	2909215M

M = $ thousand   MM = $ million
See Pages 9 through 22 for Explanation of Ratios and Data

Current Data Sorted by Assets   **Comparative Historical Data**

0-500M	500M-2MM	2-10MM	10-50MM	50-100MM	100-250MM	Type of Statement	4/1/06-3/31/07 ALL	4/1/07-3/31/08 ALL
		8		2	1	Unqualified	21	15
	3	4	2	1		Reviewed	15	13
1	5	6				Compiled	12	11
4	4					Tax Returns	12	10
3	20	6	3	1	3	Other	33	16
	15 (4/1-9/30/10)			62 (10/1/10-3/31/11)				
8	32	24	5	4	4	**NUMBER OF STATEMENTS**	93	65
%	%	%	%	%	%	**ASSETS**	%	%
	13.0	26.8				Cash & Equivalents	18.8	23.6
	45.8	38.5				Trade Receivables (net)	40.8	41.3
	.2	.9				Inventory	2.5	3.5
	2.9	3.1				All Other Current	4.8	4.0
	62.0	69.3				Total Current	66.9	72.3
	16.1	14.3				Fixed Assets (net)	17.4	16.7
	9.0	6.4				Intangibles (net)	4.3	4.9
	13.0	10.0				All Other Non-Current	11.5	6.1
	100.0	100.0				Total	100.0	100.0
						LIABILITIES		
	14.0	6.6				Notes Payable-Short Term	13.2	13.9
	2.7	3.5				Cur. Mat.-L.T.D.	6.1	6.3
	7.5	16.7				Trade Payables	13.9	10.5
	.4	.5				Income Taxes Payable	.7	.7
	10.7	17.7				All Other Current	19.1	14.2
	35.4	45.0				Total Current	52.9	45.5
	11.8	12.9				Long-Term Debt	12.8	6.7
	.6	1.1				Deferred Taxes	.6	.5
	11.6	10.1				All Other Non-Current	11.4	10.6
	40.7	31.0				Net Worth	22.3	36.8
	100.0	100.0				Total Liabilties & Net Worth	100.0	100.0
						INCOME DATA		
	100.0	100.0				Net Sales	100.0	100.0
						Gross Profit		
	93.4	91.9				Operating Expenses	93.2	92.0
	6.6	8.1				Operating Profit	6.8	8.0
	.1	.0				All Other Expenses (net)	1.0	3.3
	6.4	8.1				Profit Before Taxes	5.7	4.6
						RATIOS		
	3.6	3.1					2.3	3.4
	1.6	1.4				Current	1.5	1.6
	1.0	1.0					.9	1.1
	3.6	3.0					1.9	3.2
	1.6	1.3				Quick	1.3	1.5
	1.0	.9					.8	.9
	11 32.6	24 15.5					31 11.6	23 15.9
	59 6.2	44 8.2				Sales/Receivables	53 6.9	51 7.1
	77 4.7	77 4.7					79 4.6	75 4.9
						Cost of Sales/Inventory		
						Cost of Sales/Payables		
	5.5	4.4					6.8	7.0
	15.3	11.4				Sales/Working Capital	12.8	11.3
	NM	NM					-158.6	131.0
	38.8	17.6					28.5	18.7
	(24) 13.9	(16) 4.1				EBIT/Interest	(75) 7.8	(50) 4.3
	.7	2.1					1.2	.9
						Net Profit + Depr., Dep.,	28.1	
						Amort./Cur. Mat. L/T/D	(17) 2.9	
							.5	
	.0	.0					.1	.1
	.2	.8				Fixed/Worth	.4	.3
	1.0	-2.2					2.6	1.7
	.3	.6					.8	.5
	1.0	2.0				Debt/Worth	2.0	1.5
	19.1	-15.4					13.6	9.3
	86.6	65.8				% Profit Before Taxes/Tangible	88.8	94.8
	(26) 21.8	(16) 20.2				Net Worth	(73) 43.8	(53) 20.8
	2.2	3.9					9.3	-3.7
	29.0	31.1				% Profit Before Taxes/Total	39.3	18.5
	11.9	7.0				Assets	10.0	7.4
	-.6	.4					.5	-1.5
	208.3	333.6					80.4	115.8
	45.2	43.4				Sales/Net Fixed Assets	36.4	29.4
	18.5	18.5					16.2	15.1
	5.1	4.3					4.6	5.1
	3.2	2.3				Sales/Total Assets	2.7	3.4
	2.0	1.2					1.8	2.0
	.9	.8					.5	.5
	(16) 1.2	(16) 1.4				% Depr., Dep., Amort./Sales	(75) 1.1	(47) 1.1
	1.6	2.4					2.1	2.1
	8.5						6.0	4.8
	(16) 13.6					% Officers', Directors'	(28) 14.7	(20) 8.0
	22.6					Owners' Comp/Sales	23.3	17.6
14379M	137828M	269842M	158373M	309582M	2028934M	Net Sales ($)	3028951M	3098599M
1947M	34867M	113191M	72311M	264922M	540920M	Total Assets ($)	1493880M	901622M

M = $ thousand   MM = $ million
See Pages 9 through 22 for Explanation of Ratios and Data

Comparative Historical Data | Current Data Sorted by Sales

			Type of Statement						
15	19	11	Unqualified	1	2	1	1	3	3
14	9	10	Reviewed	1	1	1	3	2	2
10	14	12	Compiled		3	2	3	4	
13	13	8	Tax Returns	2	3	3			
21	22	36	Other	1	11	7	6	3	8
4/1/08-3/31/09 ALL	4/1/09-3/31/10 ALL	4/1/10-3/31/11 ALL		15 (4/1-9/30/10)			62 (10/1/10-3/31/11)		
				0-1MM	1-3MM	3-5MM	5-10MM	10-25MM	25MM & OVER
73	77	77	NUMBER OF STATEMENTS	5	20	14	13	12	13
%	%	%	ASSETS	%	%	%	%	%	%
22.7	23.9	19.9	Cash & Equivalents		21.1	19.6	16.1	24.6	14.9
38.2	39.0	37.6	Trade Receivables (net)		34.7	41.9	44.4	40.0	40.7
3.8	2.9	1.6	Inventory		.5	.5	.0	1.1	7.2
4.5	3.5	3.4	All Other Current		2.3	1.7	3.0	4.8	6.1
69.3	69.2	62.5	Total Current		58.6	63.7	63.6	70.5	68.9
17.2	14.6	17.0	Fixed Assets (net)		20.0	15.6	11.5	13.8	11.3
4.3	5.4	9.0	Intangibles (net)		8.6	9.4	8.1	6.6	15.8
9.2	10.7	11.4	All Other Non-Current		12.8	11.4	16.9	9.1	4.0
100.0	100.0	100.0	Total		100.0	100.0	100.0	100.0	100.0
			LIABILITIES						
14.1	12.7	12.3	Notes Payable-Short Term		9.1	19.3	17.1	7.5	2.3
10.5	3.0	2.8	Cur. Mat.-L.T.D.		1.0	3.1	6.3	2.9	2.5
11.3	12.3	10.7	Trade Payables		7.8	8.7	15.0	15.7	9.4
.9	.7	.8	Income Taxes Payable		1.0	.8	.2	1.0	1.2
16.7	22.0	16.3	All Other Current		20.1	8.5	9.3	24.7	22.3
53.5	50.8	43.0	Total Current		38.9	40.4	47.9	51.7	37.6
8.2	11.5	13.4	Long-Term Debt		6.7	18.1	19.2	12.6	10.6
.7	.7	.6	Deferred Taxes		.9	.0	.0	2.2	.0
7.3	9.3	9.1	All Other Non-Current		5.6	18.7	13.1	2.7	8.8
30.3	27.7	33.9	Net Worth		47.8	22.8	19.7	30.9	42.9
100.0	100.0	100.0	Total Liabilities & Net Worth		100.0	100.0	100.0	100.0	100.0
			INCOME DATA						
100.0	100.0	100.0	Net Sales		100.0	100.0	100.0	100.0	100.0
			Gross Profit						
93.4	93.0	92.5	Operating Expenses		90.6	96.4	94.0	94.7	90.4
6.6	7.0	7.5	Operating Profit		9.4	3.6	6.0	5.3	9.6
2.4	1.7	.6	All Other Expenses (net)		1.5	-.5	.3	1.2	1.3
4.2	5.4	6.9	Profit Before Taxes		7.9	4.1	5.7	4.0	8.3
			RATIOS						
3.2	2.7	2.7			4.0	3.6	2.2	2.8	3.1
1.6	1.4	1.5	Current		1.5	1.6	1.0	1.3	2.1
1.0	.8	.9			.9	1.3	.8	.8	1.4
2.7	2.3	2.6			4.0	3.6	2.0	2.7	2.8
1.5	1.3	1.5	Quick		1.5	1.6	1.0	1.2	1.7
.9	.8	.7			.7	1.1	.7	.7	.8
13 27.2	25 14.5	13 27.7		12 30.0	0 UND	17 21.3	12 29.8	32 11.5	
44 8.2	45 8.1	52 7.0	Sales/Receivables	57 6.4	50 7.3	53 6.8	48 7.7	63 5.8	
68 5.4	68 5.4	70 5.2		103 3.5	72 5.1	68 5.3	63 5.8	71 5.2	
			Cost of Sales/Inventory						
			Cost of Sales/Payables						
6.9	6.1	5.5			4.3	5.6	13.5	5.9	4.5
14.1	21.6	14.3	Sales/Working Capital		7.5	15.3	90.3	22.1	6.6
-575.4	-47.1	-94.3			-39.0	NM	-27.4	NM	18.9
20.4	23.9	29.8			31.9	102.2			41.1
(51) 5.4	(58) 7.2	(58) 7.0	EBIT/Interest	(14) 8.7	(12) 2.7			(11) 28.3	
-1.8	1.1	1.9			-2.2	.6			6.9
	14.8		Net Profit + Depr., Dep.,						
	(13) 2.7		Amort./Cur. Mat. L/T/D						
	.9								
.1	.1	.1			.1	.0	.0	.1	.1
.3	.4	.5	Fixed/Worth		.3	.4	11.2	.6	.3
1.4	-8.0	13.7			3.9	NM	-5.2	NM	.7
.7	.9	.6			.3	.6	2.1	1.0	.8
1.4	2.3	1.7	Debt/Worth		.7	1.3	40.6	2.0	1.6
4.2	-30.9	NM			NM	-7.0	-16.7	NM	8.1
91.9	87.2	94.7	% Profit Before Taxes/Tangible		54.4	71.1			114.3
(61) 30.7	(56) 25.7	(58) 30.4	Net Worth	(15) 7.1	(10) 13.2			(12) 86.9	
1.5	3.5	4.0			4.0	-6.4			12.1
31.4	32.2	29.8	% Profit Before Taxes/Total		23.2	39.0	48.0	32.7	37.3
10.4	7.7	9.6	Assets		3.3	8.3	10.3	12.7	13.3
-2.3	-.1	.7			.9	-4.2	2.8	-19.7	4.5
82.6	112.6	204.5			67.5	269.5	999.8	208.9	154.3
43.0	36.0	41.7	Sales/Net Fixed Assets		34.3	75.6	41.7	52.1	47.3
18.7	19.3	17.2			11.3	12.7	21.9	18.7	13.8
5.4	4.9	4.7			3.3	6.4	4.7	5.5	3.9
3.2	3.3	2.7	Sales/Total Assets		1.9	3.9	3.7	3.1	2.4
2.4	2.2	1.6			1.1	2.6	2.4	1.9	1.1
.5	.4	.7			.9				
(53) 1.0	(60) 1.0	(46) 1.2	% Depr., Dep., Amort./Sales	(12) 1.6					
2.0	1.6	1.8			2.5				
4.8	6.0	6.5	% Officers', Directors'						
(22) 7.2	(28) 10.5	(31) 12.0	Owners' Comp/Sales						
11.6	16.1	16.5							
1424649M	1891481M	2918938M	Net Sales ($)	4392M	38589M	53365M	101066M	177676M	2543850M
705769M	1041493M	1028158M	Total Assets ($)	4004M	37007M	20564M	38511M	61176M	866896M

© RMA 2011

M = $ thousand   MM = $ million
See Pages 9 through 22 for Explanation of Ratios and Data

Current Data Sorted by Assets

Comparative Historical Data

							Type of Statement		
			1	4	1	1	Unqualified	4	4
	1		1				Reviewed	1	3
	1						Compiled	5	4
	1						Tax Returns		3
2	2						Other	5	8
2	3	6	2	2	1			4/1/06-	4/1/07-
	4 (4/1-9/30/10)		25 (10/1/10-3/31/11)					3/31/07	3/31/08
0-500M	500M-2MM	2-10MM	10-50MM	50-100MM	100-250MM			ALL	ALL
4	6	8	6	3	2		NUMBER OF STATEMENTS	15	22
%	%	%	%	%	%		ASSETS	%	%
							Cash & Equivalents	19.5	14.0
							Trade Receivables (net)	26.6	41.4
							Inventory	5.6	1.0
							All Other Current	7.4	2.8
							Total Current	59.0	59.2
							Fixed Assets (net)	19.0	21.9
							Intangibles (net)	5.9	11.8
							All Other Non-Current	16.1	7.1
							Total	100.0	100.0
							LIABILITIES		
							Notes Payable-Short Term	12.6	7.4
							Cur. Mat.-L.T.D.	1.8	3.0
							Trade Payables	13.3	27.5
							Income Taxes Payable	.2	.2
							All Other Current	23.6	13.3
							Total Current	51.6	51.4
							Long-Term Debt	6.4	32.5
							Deferred Taxes	.0	.4
							All Other Non-Current	18.0	3.8
							Net Worth	24.0	11.9
							Total Liabilties & Net Worth	100.0	100.0
							INCOME DATA		
							Net Sales	100.0	100.0
							Gross Profit		
							Operating Expenses	94.8	92.1
							Operating Profit	5.2	7.9
							All Other Expenses (net)	.6	4.3
							Profit Before Taxes	4.6	3.5
							RATIOS		
								1.7	2.6
							Current	1.3	1.2
								.6	.7
								1.5	2.5
							Quick	.8	1.0
								.5	.7
								3 108.2	25 14.3
							Sales/Receivables	42 8.7	47 7.7
								80 4.6	85 4.3
							Cost of Sales/Inventory		
							Cost of Sales/Payables		
								9.9	8.0
							Sales/Working Capital	32.0	39.8
								-7.4	-16.2
								62.1	7.6
							EBIT/Interest	(13) 9.7	(16) 1.8
								.4	-.3
							Net Profit + Depr., Dep., Amort./Cur. Mat. L/T/D		
								.1	.3
							Fixed/Worth	.8	2.8
								-3.8	-2.0
								.7	1.5
							Debt/Worth	3.0	12.7
								-10.9	-6.8
								175.4	104.9
							% Profit Before Taxes/Tangible Net Worth	(11) 16.0	(13) 41.0
								6.5	11.7
								24.3	18.8
							% Profit Before Taxes/Total Assets	7.1	4.1
								.1	-1.6
								98.2	80.9
							Sales/Net Fixed Assets	21.0	31.6
								6.4	8.4
								3.6	4.4
							Sales/Total Assets	2.0	2.8
								1.0	1.4
									.6
							% Depr., Dep., Amort./Sales	(20) 1.3	
								4.3	
							% Officers', Directors' Owners' Comp/Sales		
6823M	46216M	83743M	220905M	561668M	445645M		Net Sales ($)	7061967M	786942M
816M	8084M	39669M	175039M	227292M	246237M		Total Assets ($)	461202M	337030M

M = $ thousand   MM = $ million
See Pages 9 through 22 for Explanation of Ratios and Data

Comparative Historical Data   Current Data Sorted by Sales

			Type of Statement	0-1MM	1-3MM	3-5MM	5-10MM	10-25MM	25MM & OVER
6	6	7	Unqualified				1	1	5
4	2	2	Reviewed				2		
4	2	1	Compiled		1				
2	8	3	Tax Returns	1	1	1			
16	16	16	Other	1	1	3	2	4	5
4/1/08-3/31/09	4/1/09-3/31/10	4/1/10-3/31/11				4 (4/1-9/30/10)		25 (10/1/10-3/31/11)	
ALL	ALL	ALL							
32	34	29	NUMBER OF STATEMENTS	2	3	4	5	5	10
%	%	%	ASSETS	%	%	%	%	%	%
13.8	12.9	20.8	Cash & Equivalents						19.3
35.3	32.2	32.3	Trade Receivables (net)						24.0
3.1	2.4	2.5	Inventory						3.0
4.5	1.8	2.9	All Other Current						5.6
56.7	49.4	58.5	Total Current						51.9
20.6	21.4	15.4	Fixed Assets (net)						16.8
15.4	17.4	18.4	Intangibles (net)						28.3
7.2	11.8	7.7	All Other Non-Current						3.0
100.0	100.0	100.0	Total						100.0
			LIABILITIES						
12.4	17.2	15.4	Notes Payable-Short Term						4.5
3.5	2.2	1.6	Cur. Mat.-L.T.D.						.8
25.3	16.3	20.3	Trade Payables						19.0
.0	2.7	.1	Income Taxes Payable						.2
11.3	14.9	26.5	All Other Current						13.1
52.6	53.2	63.9	Total Current						37.6
20.3	18.5	10.8	Long-Term Debt						8.9
.8	.8	.2	Deferred Taxes						.6
5.3	7.0	3.4	All Other Non-Current						3.0
21.1	20.5	21.7	Net Worth						49.9
100.0	100.0	100.0	Total Liabilities & Net Worth						100.0
			INCOME DATA						
100.0	100.0	100.0	Net Sales						100.0
			Gross Profit						
96.1	99.3	94.0	Operating Expenses						95.9
3.9	.7	6.0	Operating Profit						4.1
4.2	1.9	1.2	All Other Expenses (net)						2.0
-.2	-1.1	4.8	Profit Before Taxes						2.1
			RATIOS						
1.6	1.5	1.9							2.1
1.1	1.1	1.1	Current						1.5
.8	.7	.6							1.1
1.4	1.4	1.5							1.8
.9	.9	1.0	Quick						1.2
.6	.6	.6							.9
29 12.6	12 31.0	12 30.2							10 36.0
51 7.2	52 7.0	46 8.0	Sales/Receivables						78 4.7
79 4.6	77 4.8	85 4.3							91 4.0
			Cost of Sales/Inventory						
			Cost of Sales/Payables						
9.1	9.2	7.2							4.8
57.3	323.3	50.6	Sales/Working Capital						11.1
-25.0	-14.2	-15.8							NM
8.3	4.6	21.8							
(25) 1.4	(26) -.5	(21) 2.6	EBIT/Interest						
-.1	-7.7	-4.8							
			Net Profit + Depr., Dep., Amort./Cur. Mat. L/T/D						
.3	.4	.2							.3
1.1	2.3	.5	Fixed/Worth						.4
-21.1	-1.0	-12.6							NM
2.2	1.2	1.7							.8
13.8	15.4	4.4	Debt/Worth						3.0
-13.9	-4.2	-11.5							NM
93.9	66.1	188.0							
(21) 32.8	(20) 1.2	(19) 36.9	% Profit Before Taxes/Tangible Net Worth						
-6.5	-102.5	-12.2							
11.5	9.5	33.7							13.9
1.9	-.9	7.7	% Profit Before Taxes/Total Assets						6.9
-3.7	-13.7	-.5							-15.6
71.3	87.5	121.9							70.7
17.4	21.6	29.3	Sales/Net Fixed Assets						25.2
5.8	7.6	9.2							7.0
4.4	4.7	4.1							2.2
2.0	2.3	2.3	Sales/Total Assets						1.5
.5	1.3	1.5							.9
.5	1.7	.6							
(24) 2.2	(18) 2.4	(18) 2.0	% Depr., Dep., Amort./Sales						
4.6	4.3	5.3							
	4.0								
	(13) 7.4		% Officers', Directors' Owners' Comp/Sales						
	9.3								
970467M	994235M	1365000M	Net Sales ($)	970M	6655M	16015M	43521M	79237M	1218602M
804828M	736528M	697137M	Total Assets ($)	285M	2046M	13170M	29862M	22058M	629716M

© RMA 2011

M = $ thousand   MM = $ million

See Pages 9 through 22 for Explanation of Ratios and Data

Current Data Sorted by Assets   Comparative Historical Data

0-500M	500M-2MM	2-10MM	10-50MM	50-100MM	100-250MM	Type of Statement	4/1/06-3/31/07 ALL	4/1/07-3/31/08 ALL
		3	6	1	3	Unqualified	10	12
		5	2		2	Reviewed	8	7
1	5	2				Compiled	7	12
2	3	2	1			Tax Returns	14	8
4	6	13	6		2	Other	33	45
	8 (4/1-9/30/10)		61 (10/1/10-3/31/11)					
7	14	25	15	1	7	NUMBER OF STATEMENTS	72	84
%	%	%	%	%	%	**ASSETS**	%	%
	16.6	16.9	7.7			Cash & Equivalents	7.0	11.0
	24.0	18.5	19.0			Trade Receivables (net)	23.9	22.5
	13.0	6.4	5.1			Inventory	8.9	6.2
	2.1	5.3	1.7			All Other Current	3.0	3.2
	55.7	47.1	33.5			Total Current	42.9	42.9
	22.4	40.7	36.4			Fixed Assets (net)	40.7	43.1
	11.1	4.2	13.8			Intangibles (net)	6.9	5.2
	10.8	7.9	16.2			All Other Non-Current	9.6	8.8
	100.0	100.0	100.0			Total	100.0	100.0
						LIABILITIES		
	10.5	4.8	5.3			Notes Payable-Short Term	11.2	12.9
	3.3	4.6	4.8			Cur. Mat.-L.T.D.	6.7	5.0
	12.6	11.8	7.4			Trade Payables	10.5	11.9
	.0	.1	.3			Income Taxes Payable	.0	.0
	11.7	12.3	8.4			All Other Current	10.3	11.1
	38.2	33.7	26.2			Total Current	38.7	40.9
	38.4	29.4	28.2			Long-Term Debt	31.6	30.2
	.0	.5	.3			Deferred Taxes	.1	.1
	8.9	2.4	19.2			All Other Non-Current	6.9	12.9
	14.6	34.0	26.2			Net Worth	22.6	15.9
	100.0	100.0	100.0			Total Liabilties & Net Worth	100.0	100.0
						INCOME DATA		
	100.0	100.0	100.0			Net Sales	100.0	100.0
						Gross Profit		
	90.8	90.4	90.5			Operating Expenses	84.3	86.2
	9.2	9.6	9.5			Operating Profit	15.7	13.8
	2.4	3.6	3.0			All Other Expenses (net)	4.8	4.0
	6.8	6.0	6.5			Profit Before Taxes	10.9	9.9
						RATIOS		
	3.9	2.5	1.8				1.7	2.5
	1.4	1.3	1.0			Current	1.2	1.2
	.8	.8	.8				.7	.7
	2.2	1.9	1.2				1.3	1.8
	1.0	1.1	.8			Quick	.9	.9
	.6	.5	.5				.4	.4
	23 16.1	17 21.6	42 8.7				17 22.0	12 29.4
	43 8.5	30 12.0	48 7.7			Sales/Receivables	38 9.7	38 9.7
	55 6.7	58 6.3	77 4.7				62 5.9	58 6.3
						Cost of Sales/Inventory		
						Cost of Sales/Payables		
	4.4	4.4	8.6				10.3	6.5
	17.7	22.0	934.0			Sales/Working Capital	37.0	25.1
	-24.2	-20.7	-15.2				-22.8	-16.2
	11.7	11.2	6.0				12.2	9.7
	(10) .4	(21) 2.7	3.2			EBIT/Interest	(61) 5.0	(72) 3.1
	-5.9	1.1	1.0				1.6	1.0
						Net Profit + Depr., Dep., Amort./Cur. Mat. L/T/D		
	.2	.2	.7				.5	.6
	NM	1.5	1.5			Fixed/Worth	1.4	1.4
	-.2	4.2	5.9				-38.7	20.8
	.3	1.1	.6				1.0	.9
	NM	2.1	1.3			Debt/Worth	2.8	2.3
	-3.1	9.2	16.3				-61.8	47.4
		39.7	26.7			% Profit Before Taxes/Tangible Net Worth	81.8	64.1
	(23) 19.8	(12) 6.6					(52) 41.3	(66) 32.4
		4.9	1.5				15.3	6.2
	22.8	16.8	10.3			% Profit Before Taxes/Total Assets	24.7	22.1
	6.4	6.5	3.5				10.2	9.3
	-7.4	.3	.1				2.5	-.9
	58.7	45.6	8.0			Sales/Net Fixed Assets	43.9	24.5
	21.8	3.5	2.4				5.6	5.6
	3.6	.9	1.1				1.0	1.2
	2.9	2.5	1.5			Sales/Total Assets	2.8	2.8
	1.9	1.5	.9				1.7	1.7
	1.3	.7	.4				.7	.8
	.2	.9	2.5			% Depr., Dep., Amort./Sales	.7	1.3
	(12) 1.6	(23) 6.1	(13) 12.7				(53) 4.6	(66) 4.6
	3.8	12.6	16.4				12.1	12.4
						% Officers', Directors' Owners' Comp/Sales	2.7	3.0
							(21) 4.0	(34) 4.7
							6.3	8.2
7787M	32595M	210831M	289839M	176470M	1016136M	Net Sales ($)	1491643M	1029640M
2116M	16795M	140660M	299875M	96885M	1325889M	Total Assets ($)	989234M	784367M

Comparative Historical Data   Current Data Sorted by Sales

4/1/08-3/31/09 ALL	4/1/09-3/31/10 ALL	4/1/10-3/31/11 ALL	Type of Statement	0-1MM	1-3MM 8 (4/1-9/30/10)	3-5MM	5-10MM	10-25MM 61 (10/1/10-3/31/11)	25MM & OVER
9	9	13	Unqualified			1	1	5	6
10	13	9	Reviewed		1		3	4	
7	12	8	Compiled	1	3	1	1	2	
13	14	8	Tax Returns	1	4	1	1	2	
39	24	31	Other	5	7	3	5	8	3
78	72	69	NUMBER OF STATEMENTS	7	15	7	10	21	9
%	%	%	ASSETS	%	%	%	%	%	%
10.4	12.3	12.3	Cash & Equivalents		13.1		14.6	13.1	
22.9	21.9	21.4	Trade Receivables (net)		25.2		14.1	22.0	
7.2	7.3	6.6	Inventory		10.2		5.8	7.8	
2.1	5.5	5.8	All Other Current		1.6		1.4	13.2	
42.7	47.0	46.0	Total Current		50.1		35.9	56.0	
40.3	39.0	34.1	Fixed Assets (net)		28.8		50.3	24.3	
8.3	6.4	10.4	Intangibles (net)		13.0		4.1	11.4	
8.7	7.6	9.6	All Other Non-Current		8.1		9.8	8.3	
100.0	100.0	100.0	Total		100.0		100.0	100.0	
			LIABILITIES						
11.7	10.2	7.5	Notes Payable-Short Term		17.2		4.8	3.6	
4.4	4.9	4.5	Cur. Mat.-L.T.D.		4.9		8.0	2.2	
9.8	12.6	11.9	Trade Payables		16.9		4.1	14.4	
.0	.0	.1	Income Taxes Payable		.0		.0	.1	
11.0	14.0	12.2	All Other Current		8.8		6.6	13.5	
37.0	41.7	36.2	Total Current		47.8		23.6	33.8	
28.1	41.3	34.4	Long-Term Debt		35.4		36.4	18.5	
.2	.3	.3	Deferred Taxes		.0		.1	.0	
4.4	4.3	9.1	All Other Non-Current		3.0		5.2	1.8	
30.4	12.5	20.0	Net Worth		13.8		34.7	45.9	
100.0	100.0	100.0	Total Liabilties & Net Worth		100.0		100.0	100.0	
			INCOME DATA						
100.0	100.0	100.0	Net Sales		100.0		100.0	100.0	
			Gross Profit						
86.6	91.5	90.7	Operating Expenses		94.7		90.8	93.9	
13.4	8.5	9.3	Operating Profit		5.3		9.2	6.1	
2.9	4.3	3.6	All Other Expenses (net)		2.0		3.2	1.0	
10.6	4.1	5.7	Profit Before Taxes		3.2		6.0	5.1	
			RATIOS						
2.4	2.0	2.2	Current		3.9		2.5	3.6	
1.3	1.1	1.3			1.1		1.1	1.3	
.8	.9	.8			.4		.8	.8	
1.9	1.6	1.5	Quick		3.9		2.3	1.7	
(77) 1.0	(71) .9	1.0			.7		.9	1.1	
.6	.4	.5			.4		.4	.5	
16 22.3	17 20.9	20 18.3	Sales/Receivables		19 19.4		27 13.4	13 27.9	
35 10.5	39 9.3	42 8.6			29 12.7		40 9.2	48 7.7	
48 7.6	57 6.4	61 6.0			51 7.1		52 7.1	65 5.7	
			Cost of Sales/Inventory						
			Cost of Sales/Payables						
8.4	6.9	4.8	Sales/Working Capital		3.7		5.0	4.4	
23.6	32.2	22.7			58.8		478.4	22.3	
-29.2	-45.7	-17.3			-9.4		-24.0	-18.8	
12.0	4.8	7.7	EBIT/Interest		4.3		9.6	10.4	
(70) 3.6	(62) 1.8	(58) 2.0		(12) .5			1.7	(16) 4.9	
1.2	.2	.4			-.6		1.2	.1	
10.3			Net Profit + Depr., Dep., Amort./Cur. Mat. L/T/D						
(10) 3.2									
.9									
.3	.6	.3	Fixed/Worth		.4		.4	.1	
1.1	1.7	2.6			12.5		1.3	.8	
3.4	-14.6	-1.3			-.2		6.8	2.7	
.9	1.5	1.0	Debt/Worth		.3		1.1	.4	
2.2	5.0	3.5			32.8		1.6	1.2	
5.8	-16.4	-4.2			-2.0		7.4	20.1	
81.6	46.6	39.7	% Profit Before Taxes/Tangible Net Worth					29.3	
(67) 31.4	(51) 10.8	(47) 18.4					(18) 16.8		
7.1	-11.8	.7						.4	
25.2	10.1	16.0	% Profit Before Taxes/Total Assets		18.3		18.1	12.7	
8.8	1.4	3.6			.4		3.3	4.3	
.5	-2.7	-1.0			-4.1		.5	.0	
28.4	28.3	26.2	Sales/Net Fixed Assets		39.5		12.9	61.6	
6.3	9.7	6.3			21.5		1.7	6.3	
1.2	1.0	1.1			2.4		.8	1.3	
3.4	2.7	2.4	Sales/Total Assets		3.2		1.9	2.7	
1.9	1.6	1.5			2.2		.8	1.5	
.7	.7	.6			.9		.6	.5	
1.0	1.1	1.1	% Depr., Dep., Amort./Sales		.6		2.1	.6	
(64) 3.9	(59) 3.9	(58) 3.6		(13) 1.5			10.6	(19) 3.9	
11.9	14.4	13.0			12.4		20.7	14.8	
3.4	3.2	4.3	% Officers', Directors' Owners' Comp/Sales						
(28) 5.1	(28) 5.2	(19) 7.4							
13.5	8.5	10.9							
2158521M	1846735M	1733658M	Net Sales ($)	3330M	28926M	27111M	67490M	308313M	1298488M
1344595M	1220077M	1882220M	Total Assets ($)	8586M	30225M	35417M	80059M	788497M	939436M

M = $ thousand   MM = $ million
See Pages 9 through 22 for Explanation of Ratios and Data

Current Data Sorted by Assets / Comparative Historical Data

0-500M	500M-2MM	2-10MM	10-50MM	50-100MM	100-250MM	Type of Statement	4/1/06-3/31/07 ALL	4/1/07-3/31/08 ALL
1		1	7	3	2	Unqualified	17	14
1	2	17	5			Reviewed	20	15
1	1	8	1			Compiled	20	18
3	8	3				Tax Returns	11	13
3	9	14	13	2	3	Other	45	43
	18 (4/1-9/30/10)		90 (10/1/10-3/31/11)					
9	20	43	26	5	5	NUMBER OF STATEMENTS	113	103
%	%	%	%	%	%	**ASSETS**	%	%
	19.0	12.6	11.0			Cash & Equivalents	11.7	14.1
	22.7	36.2	32.9			Trade Receivables (net)	39.0	36.0
	1.4	4.5	3.4			Inventory	3.7	4.6
	2.7	2.7	7.1			All Other Current	3.9	3.6
	45.8	56.0	54.4			Total Current	58.4	58.2
	27.4	32.4	19.5			Fixed Assets (net)	27.1	24.8
	15.1	5.1	18.0			Intangibles (net)	6.8	11.6
	11.7	6.5	8.1			All Other Non-Current	7.7	5.4
	100.0	100.0	100.0			Total	100.0	100.0
						LIABILITIES		
	4.1	11.8	4.3			Notes Payable-Short Term	8.5	7.9
	4.5	4.8	4.3			Cur. Mat.-L.T.D.	5.1	5.4
	14.4	19.0	18.2			Trade Payables	18.6	18.9
	.1	.1	.0			Income Taxes Payable	.1	.1
	20.4	14.8	19.8			All Other Current	19.2	17.5
	43.6	50.6	46.6			Total Current	51.5	49.7
	29.9	19.8	19.0			Long-Term Debt	18.6	22.9
	.0	.5	.2			Deferred Taxes	.3	.4
	5.7	9.7	9.8			All Other Non-Current	3.4	6.6
	20.7	19.5	24.4			Net Worth	26.3	20.4
	100.0	100.0	100.0			Total Liabilities & Net Worth	100.0	100.0
						INCOME DATA		
	100.0	100.0	100.0			Net Sales	100.0	100.0
						Gross Profit		
	89.2	94.4	94.3			Operating Expenses	94.0	94.9
	10.8	5.6	5.7			Operating Profit	6.0	5.1
	4.0	2.5	1.4			All Other Expenses (net)	1.3	1.4
	6.9	3.1	4.3			Profit Before Taxes	4.7	3.7
						RATIOS		
	3.7	1.4	1.8			Current	1.5	1.9
	1.2	1.1	1.0				1.1	1.1
	.3	.8	.7				.9	.8
	3.6	1.4	1.4			Quick	1.3	1.6
	1.0	1.0	.8				1.0	1.1
	.3	.6	.6				.7	.7
4	99.2	27 / 13.4	35 / 10.5			Sales/Receivables	26 / 13.9	31 / 11.9
18	20.6	49 / 7.5	52 / 7.0				50 / 7.2	50 / 7.3
44	8.3	63 / 5.8	81 / 4.5				68 / 5.4	60 / 6.1
						Cost of Sales/Inventory		
						Cost of Sales/Payables		
	13.8	10.5	6.6			Sales/Working Capital	13.7	10.6
	40.8	40.8	-566.3				82.8	74.7
	-10.4	-36.3	-12.7				-26.1	-32.4
	12.2	6.9	20.8			EBIT/Interest	16.3	24.8
	(14) 2.0	(36) 2.0	(22) 5.2				(101) 4.6	(97) 3.9
	-3.7	.4	1.9				1.1	1.2
						Net Profit + Depr., Dep., Amort./Cur. Mat. L/T/D	8.2	7.3
							(27) 3.3	(26) 3.3
							1.5	1.3
	.1	.7	.3			Fixed/Worth	.5	.5
	2.2	1.7	1.6				1.1	1.7
	-1.7	35.5	-1.8				8.1	-.9
	.5	1.8	1.0			Debt/Worth	1.2	1.4
	12.3	2.9	2.8				3.1	4.1
	-5.9	157.6	-6.9				36.6	-6.2
	218.0	58.0	44.7			% Profit Before Taxes/Tangible Net Worth	83.8	93.2
	(14) 38.0	(34) 11.9	(17) 22.7				(86) 42.7	(69) 38.3
	-3.5	-1.9	4.8				3.7	10.2
	18.8	13.1	11.7			% Profit Before Taxes/Total Assets	27.2	21.4
	5.2	3.5	7.0				8.4	7.6
	-6.1	-1.2	2.2				.8	.6
	80.8	21.2	20.8			Sales/Net Fixed Assets	31.5	27.5
	34.3	9.1	11.0				13.6	13.7
	7.7	4.1	6.4				6.2	8.1
	5.7	3.5	2.3			Sales/Total Assets	4.2	4.0
	3.0	2.6	1.9				3.0	2.6
	1.4	1.7	1.3				1.8	1.9
	.5	1.2	1.4			% Depr., Dep., Amort./Sales	1.2	1.0
	(13) 1.6	(35) 2.5	(23) 2.3				(97) 2.3	(88) 2.3
	4.8	4.8	4.4				4.2	4.0
		2.3				% Officers', Directors' Owners' Comp/Sales	1.8	2.0
		(17) 5.5					(43) 4.8	(35) 3.7
		8.7					8.1	6.4
12348M	81955M	538180M	1056042M	411545M	1075824M	Net Sales ($)	2927185M	2956738M
1853M	22104M	211453M	581920M	333156M	847190M	Total Assets ($)	1386235M	1654461M

M = $ thousand   MM = $ million
See Pages 9 through 22 for Explanation of Ratios and Data

Comparative Historical Data | | Current Data Sorted by Sales

4/1/08-3/31/09 ALL	4/1/09-3/31/10 ALL	4/1/10-3/31/11 ALL	Type of Statement	0-1MM	1-3MM	3-5MM	5-10MM	10-25MM	25MM & OVER
					18 (4/1-9/30/10)		90 (10/1/10-3/31/11)		
15	12	14	Unqualified		1	1	7	10	13
17	28	25	Reviewed	1			5	5	5
23	14	11	Compiled		1				
19	19	14	Tax Returns	3	5	3	1	2	
45	51	44	Other	2	4	6	4	13	15
119	124	108	NUMBER OF STATEMENTS	7	11	10	17	30	33
%	%	%		%	%	%	%	%	%
			ASSETS						
14.2	16.3	14.2	Cash & Equivalents		25.8	14.7	16.6	8.5	11.3
33.9	31.6	30.9	Trade Receivables (net)		17.9	30.3	33.5	38.9	30.1
3.4	3.6	3.3	Inventory		.4	2.2	6.2	3.2	3.8
4.7	4.7	3.8	All Other Current		.6	3.6	3.0	2.7	7.2
56.2	56.2	52.2	Total Current		44.8	50.8	59.3	53.4	52.4
25.7	24.8	26.0	Fixed Assets (net)		32.3	23.6	24.8	31.0	16.7
11.3	12.4	14.0	Intangibles (net)		15.1	9.5	8.3	7.5	24.7
6.8	6.5	7.7	All Other Non-Current		7.8	16.1	7.7	8.1	6.2
100.0	100.0	100.0	Total		100.0	100.0	100.0	100.0	100.0
			LIABILITIES						
12.0	7.0	6.9	Notes Payable-Short Term		3.9	8.5	6.7	13.2	3.3
5.7	7.8	4.2	Cur. Mat.-L.T.D.		4.6	5.6	3.8	5.1	3.7
16.7	15.3	17.8	Trade Payables		12.4	7.4	14.4	27.0	16.4
.2	.3	.1	Income Taxes Payable		.1	.0	.2	.1	.3
18.0	17.7	18.7	All Other Current		25.7	19.9	20.3	14.4	19.4
52.8	48.1	47.8	Total Current		46.7	41.3	45.4	59.9	43.0
29.0	22.0	24.0	Long-Term Debt		35.8	39.7	17.9	11.8	21.1
1.0	.3	.5	Deferred Taxes		.0	1.1	.0	.3	1.1
8.0	9.3	9.7	All Other Non-Current		17.0	6.2	13.7	5.8	11.7
9.2	20.4	18.0	Net Worth		.5	11.6	23.0	22.2	23.1
100.0	100.0	100.0	Total Liabilities & Net Worth		100.0	100.0	100.0	100.0	100.0
			INCOME DATA						
100.0	100.0	100.0	Net Sales		100.0	100.0	100.0	100.0	100.0
			Gross Profit						
95.6	95.0	93.5	Operating Expenses		94.9	96.7	97.0	96.1	93.2
4.4	5.0	6.5	Operating Profit		5.1	3.3	3.0	3.9	6.8
2.1	1.8	2.4	All Other Expenses (net)		4.4	2.1	.2	1.7	2.0
2.3	3.2	4.1	Profit Before Taxes		.7	1.2	2.8	2.1	4.8
			RATIOS						
1.8	1.9	1.7	Current		1.7	6.6	3.0	1.3	1.8
1.1	1.3	1.1			1.1	1.7	1.4	1.0	1.1
.7	.9	.7			.4	.6	.9	.7	.8
1.6	1.6	1.5	Quick		1.7	6.1	2.5	1.1	1.3
.9	1.0	.9			1.1	1.4	1.3	.9	.9
.6	.7	.6			.2	.6	.9	.5	.7
22 16.3	28 13.2	22 17.0	Sales/Receivables		3 113.5	1 264.9	39 9.4	23 15.8	36 10.2
41 8.9	45 8.1	46 8.0			19 19.6	44 8.4	55 6.6	42 8.6	49 7.4
63 5.8	69 5.3	65 5.6			33 10.9	71 5.2	66 5.5	64 5.7	74 4.9
			Cost of Sales/Inventory						
			Cost of Sales/Payables						
12.4	7.4	10.0	Sales/Working Capital		22.7	6.2	7.9	23.9	8.4
43.5	34.5	65.2			44.5	141.6	14.6	-554.7	31.3
-23.3	-43.6	-15.6			-10.5	-11.5	-66.9	-14.2	-35.5
9.2	12.2	10.0	EBIT/Interest				29.0	24.6	4.0	19.9
(104) 1.9	(108) 3.2	(89) 2.2				-1.3	(12) 3.4	(25) 1.9	(31) 6.1
.8	.9	.1				-18.9	1.1	-.1	1.7
2.5	3.5	5.2	Net Profit + Depr., Dep., Amort./Cur. Mat. L/T/D						6.1
(22) 1.4	(23) 1.4	(17) 2.3							(10) 2.7
.6	.3	1.3							1.3
.5	.3	.4	Fixed/Worth		.9	.1	.5	.9	.3
2.0	1.4	2.3			15.5	.3	2.1	1.6	2.4
-.7	-1.9	-1.1			-.1	-1.8	-2.3	4.9	-.4
1.7	1.2	1.5	Debt/Worth		.5	.6	.6	1.8	1.3
6.1	3.6	4.8			18.7	2.2	2.8	3.5	8.9
-5.8	-6.7	-4.8			-1.5	-6.1		10.9	-2.6
57.0	70.8	63.7	% Profit Before Taxes/Tangible Net Worth				119.3	62.5	93.2
(76) 18.7	(84) 24.9	(71) 21.0					(12) 6.3	(25) 16.2	(18) 32.7
.1	1.6	.6					-2.7	-2.5	6.5
14.8	15.9	11.8	% Profit Before Taxes/Total Assets		11.4	26.7	13.5	9.9	13.0
3.6	5.2	5.4			3.1	-5.8	5.4	4.3	9.7
-1.0	-2.0	-.2			-17.4	-16.4	-1.2	-.1	2.0
36.3	33.4	28.5	Sales/Net Fixed Assets		35.5	86.6	25.5	28.5	22.5
14.8	12.6	14.3			26.8	26.9	10.1	11.1	13.2
7.3	6.1	6.4			3.3	6.8	3.7	6.0	6.8
4.2	3.3	3.5	Sales/Total Assets		6.3	5.8	3.9	4.1	2.3
2.9	2.4	2.3			3.0	2.5	2.1	2.7	1.8
1.8	1.5	1.4			1.1	1.5	1.4	2.0	1.3
.8	1.2	1.2	% Depr., Dep., Amort./Sales				.5	1.2	1.4
(92) 2.6	(94) 2.8	(85) 2.3					(13) 1.9	(24) 2.4	(28) 2.5
4.8	5.2	4.6					4.0	3.8	4.9
2.4	1.9	2.2	% Officers', Directors' Owners' Comp/Sales						1.4
(43) 5.0	(44) 4.9	(32) 5.4						(10) 2.8	
11.2	9.3	9.1							7.2
3097872M	3411150M	3175894M	Net Sales ($)	2624M	19223M	35840M	129979M	468827M	2519401M
1690755M	2114650M	1997676M	Total Assets ($)	5085M	15870M	15919M	75461M	181887M	1703454M

M = $ thousand   MM = $ million
See Pages 9 through 22 for Explanation of Ratios and Data

Current Data Sorted by Assets

Comparative Historical Data

0-500M	500M-2MM	2-10MM	10-50MM	50-100MM	100-250MM	Type of Statement	4/1/06-3/31/07 ALL	4/1/07-3/31/08 ALL
		2	5		1	Unqualified	12	10
	1	6	5	1		Reviewed	11	7
	3					Compiled	7	5
4	1	3				Tax Returns	4	7
3	7	7	4		1	Other	19	26
	13 (4/1-9/30/10)		41 (10/1/10-3/31/11)					
7	12	18	14	1	2	**NUMBER OF STATEMENTS**	53	55
%	%	%	%	%	%	**ASSETS**	%	%
	9.7	17.0	11.2			Cash & Equivalents	15.9	8.9
	42.2	30.5	30.3			Trade Receivables (net)	31.1	41.7
	9.9	5.8	15.5			Inventory	10.2	6.8
	1.6	13.7	4.2			All Other Current	5.8	5.6
	63.4	67.0	61.2			Total Current	63.1	63.0
	9.6	26.2	19.6			Fixed Assets (net)	22.0	17.9
	8.9	2.8	15.3			Intangibles (net)	7.2	11.6
	18.1	4.1	3.8			All Other Non-Current	7.7	7.4
	100.0	100.0	100.0			Total	100.0	100.0
						LIABILITIES		
	8.8	15.6	6.5			Notes Payable-Short Term	8.0	10.1
	1.8	3.4	4.0			Cur. Mat.-L.T.D.	3.8	5.9
	24.3	14.0	15.9			Trade Payables	16.9	18.9
	.0	.3	.1			Income Taxes Payable	.4	.1
	13.5	20.1	16.8			All Other Current	19.0	13.5
	48.5	53.4	43.3			Total Current	48.1	48.5
	7.9	10.7	13.9			Long-Term Debt	14.4	12.2
	.0	.6	1.1			Deferred Taxes	.4	.1
	9.0	7.2	2.4			All Other Non-Current	5.3	13.5
	34.6	28.2	39.3			Net Worth	31.9	25.6
	100.0	100.0	100.0			Total Liabilities & Net Worth	100.0	100.0
						INCOME DATA		
	100.0	100.0	100.0			Net Sales	100.0	100.0
						Gross Profit		
	99.9	88.4	92.9			Operating Expenses	91.9	93.5
	.1	11.6	7.1			Operating Profit	8.1	6.5
	.6	4.0	1.1			All Other Expenses (net)	1.4	1.8
	-.5	7.6	6.0			Profit Before Taxes	6.8	4.7
						RATIOS		
	1.8	1.9	3.3				2.5	2.4
	1.3	1.3	1.6			Current	1.3	1.3
	1.1	.9	.9				.8	.9
	1.7	1.4	1.8				2.1	1.6
	1.2	1.0	1.2			Quick	.9	1.1
	.6	.5	.6				.5	.6
	29 12.6	29 12.7	20 18.2				16 22.4	33 11.1
	44 8.3	39 9.4	43 8.4			Sales/Receivables	36 10.3	47 7.7
	74 4.9	77 4.8	55 6.6				58 6.3	71 5.2
						Cost of Sales/Inventory		
						Cost of Sales/Payables		
	8.1	5.7	6.5				6.9	8.6
	17.4	20.2	12.6			Sales/Working Capital	34.5	24.0
	191.9	-25.3	-19.9				-24.7	-58.1
		54.7	38.9				20.7	12.1
	(17) 5.1	5.6				EBIT/Interest	(41) 5.0	(45) 5.6
		2.0	3.6				1.2	1.4
								5.7
						Net Profit + Depr., Dep., Amort./Cur. Mat. L/T/D		(13) 2.0
								1.1
	.0	.1	.2				.2	.2
	.3	.5	1.3			Fixed/Worth	.7	.6
	.8	1.9	-.5				NM	5.9
	.4	.9	.6				.7	1.0
	2.2	2.3	1.6			Debt/Worth	2.3	3.3
	5.2	4.8	-44.5				NM	31.2
	69.1	84.0					82.9	88.4
	(10) 20.2	(16) 34.8				% Profit Before Taxes/Tangible Net Worth	(40) 27.9	(42) 43.5
	1.3	12.9					12.4	4.0
	14.8	20.9	16.2				28.5	28.2
	8.5	9.2	7.4			% Profit Before Taxes/Total Assets	9.3	10.4
	-3.6	3.2	5.0				1.3	-1.4
	185.8	78.8	63.3				60.7	80.5
	40.0	12.8	28.9			Sales/Net Fixed Assets	22.2	25.3
	20.6	4.4	9.2				9.0	11.7
	5.3	2.9	3.6				4.3	3.8
	3.5	2.1	2.5			Sales/Total Assets	2.6	2.8
	2.6	1.5	1.5				1.8	1.8
		.5	.3					.5
		(16) 2.4	(13) 1.2			% Depr., Dep., Amort./Sales	(43) 1.3	(39) 1.7
		5.2	4.3					3.1	3.5
							2.3	2.6
						% Officers', Directors' Owners' Comp/Sales	(14) 3.4	(15) 6.0
							6.3	10.7
10293M	54756M	196002M	751567M	31709M	268683M	Net Sales ($)	1251951M	1550293M
1343M	14277M	89943M	314303M	50604M	340952M	Total Assets ($)	455788M	695112M

© RMA 2011

M = $ thousand   MM = $ million
See Pages 9 through 22 for Explanation of Ratios and Data

Comparative Historical Data | Current Data Sorted by Sales

4/1/08-3/31/09 ALL	4/1/09-3/31/10 ALL	4/1/10-3/31/11 ALL	Type of Statement	0-1MM	1-3MM	3-5MM	5-10MM	10-25MM	25MM & OVER
4	14	8	Unqualified	2			3	2	6
15	15	13	Reviewed				1	3	5
2	2	3	Compiled			2	2		
6	7	8	Tax Returns	1	4			1	
12	32	22	Other	2	2	5	5	3	5
					13 (4/1-9/30/10)		41 (10/1/10-3/31/11)		
39	70	54	**NUMBER OF STATEMENTS**	5	6	7	11	9	16
%	%	%	**ASSETS**	%	%	%	%	%	%
11.7	13.5	14.4	Cash & Equivalents				7.4		13.4
39.2	35.0	32.8	Trade Receivables (net)				38.4		27.9
10.0	8.4	8.2	Inventory				10.7		13.4
5.0	5.0	6.7	All Other Current				2.9		6.1
66.0	61.8	62.0	Total Current				59.4		60.7
22.2	21.6	17.8	Fixed Assets (net)				23.5		12.8
4.5	12.7	12.8	Intangibles (net)				3.5		23.4
7.3	3.8	7.4	All Other Non-Current				13.6		3.0
100.0	100.0	100.0	Total				100.0		100.0
			LIABILITIES						
13.2	12.4	14.3	Notes Payable-Short Term				8.4		5.7
3.6	6.9	9.5	Cur. Mat.-L.T.D.				3.3		3.3
18.4	20.2	18.4	Trade Payables				24.0		16.2
.0	.3	.1	Income Taxes Payable				.0		.1
12.2	19.9	19.8	All Other Current				16.8		17.3
47.4	59.7	62.1	Total Current				52.6		42.5
14.1	16.1	15.9	Long-Term Debt				14.5		11.9
.0	.7	.6	Deferred Taxes				.0		.2
6.5	5.5	6.8	All Other Non-Current				10.5		2.8
32.0	18.0	14.7	Net Worth				22.4		42.6
100.0	100.0	100.0	Total Liabilities & Net Worth				100.0		100.0
			INCOME DATA						
100.0	100.0	100.0	Net Sales				100.0		100.0
			Gross Profit						
91.4	94.8	93.7	Operating Expenses				95.7		94.0
8.6	5.2	6.3	Operating Profit				4.3		6.0
1.7	1.9	2.1	All Other Expenses (net)				1.9		1.2
6.9	3.4	4.2	Profit Before Taxes				2.4		4.9
			RATIOS						
2.7	2.3	1.9	Current				1.4		2.7
1.4	1.2	1.3					1.1		1.4
.9	.8	.9					.9		.8
1.8	1.7	1.6	Quick				1.3		1.7
1.2	.9	1.0					.9		1.0
.7	.5	.5					.5		.6
27 13.3	24 15.3	22 16.8	Sales/Receivables				27 13.4		22 16.8
50 7.3	42 8.6	40 9.2					44 8.4		43 8.6
74 4.9	63 5.8	56 6.5					67 5.5		54 6.7
			Cost of Sales/Inventory						
			Cost of Sales/Payables						
7.1	7.0	7.4	Sales/Working Capital				18.6		5.1
12.6	31.8	26.5					57.7		12.6
-49.6	-27.1	-22.5					-23.1		-24.3
11.9	13.5	12.9	EBIT/Interest				13.0		115.0
(30) 4.2	(62) 2.6	(48) 4.9					(10) 5.2		(15) 5.5
1.2	.6	2.0					.7		2.9
	2.2		Net Profit + Depr., Dep., Amort./Cur. Mat. L/T/D						
(11)	.3								
	-.4								
.1	.2	.1	Fixed/Worth				.2		.1
.6	1.2	.6					.7		.9
1.7	-1.0	-3.7					1.1		-.4
.8	1.1	.7	Debt/Worth				1.1		.6
2.2	3.4	2.6					2.7		2.3
6.7	-4.6	-44.5					5.4		-16.3
60.7	64.9	77.0	% Profit Before Taxes/Tangible Net Worth				115.2		38.2
(32) 27.5	(48) 17.4	(39) 26.2					(10) 20.1		(10) 22.5
11.7	2.9	11.8					8.2		10.6
21.0	12.9	17.0	% Profit Before Taxes/Total Assets				18.1		16.5
6.7	3.6	8.2					6.2		6.2
2.0	-.7	2.4					1.1		4.3
54.0	82.9	99.1	Sales/Net Fixed Assets				72.2		62.9
22.7	23.2	29.9					9.7		32.0
5.5	7.3	10.1					6.4		13.7
4.0	4.2	4.6	Sales/Total Assets				5.5		3.9
2.2	2.6	2.6					2.6		2.5
1.6	1.7	1.6					2.0		1.4
.6	.6	.3	% Depr., Dep., Amort./Sales						.5
(30) 1.5	(56) 1.4	(41) 1.2						(12)	1.2
3.3	3.9	3.2							2.7
2.5	1.0	2.7	% Officers', Directors' Owners' Comp/Sales						
(10) 5.6	(19) 4.8	(12) 5.9							
14.0	10.2	13.4							
1447504M	2470391M	1313010M	Net Sales ($)	3127M	10163M	28067M	78816M	139768M	1053069M
565455M	1216555M	811422M	Total Assets ($)	7773M	5304M	12154M	30896M	111807M	643488M

M = $ thousand   MM = $ million
See Pages 9 through 22 for Explanation of Ratios and Data

Current Data Sorted by Assets   Comparative Historical Data

Type of Statement	0-500M	500M-2MM	2-10MM	10-50MM	50-100MM	100-250MM		4/1/06-3/31/07 ALL	4/1/07-3/31/08 ALL
Unqualified	1		7	14	2	1		9	14
Reviewed	2		13	4				9	8
Compiled	2	6	8	1				15	14
Tax Returns	12	9	6	2	8	7		19	13
Other	14	20	28	12	8	7		51	45
		26 (4/1-9/30/10)		153 (10/1/10-3/31/11)					
NUMBER OF STATEMENTS	29	37	62	33	10	8		103	94
	%	%	%	%	%	%		%	%
ASSETS									
Cash & Equivalents	32.2	14.6	16.1	15.5	4.3			16.9	16.6
Trade Receivables (net)	22.7	32.7	37.4	25.3	22.4			37.0	41.2
Inventory	4.7	10.2	18.9	13.5	11.2			12.0	11.0
All Other Current	8.1	2.8	3.3	3.4	2.1			4.6	3.6
Total Current	67.6	60.4	75.7	57.7	40.0			70.6	72.4
Fixed Assets (net)	17.6	13.2	10.6	22.1	20.2			16.4	14.4
Intangibles (net)	4.2	13.9	5.8	11.6	25.7			6.7	5.4
All Other Non-Current	10.6	12.5	7.9	8.6	14.1			6.3	7.8
Total	100.0	100.0	100.0	100.0	100.0			100.0	100.0
LIABILITIES									
Notes Payable-Short Term	40.5	10.9	13.0	4.8	10.7			15.3	13.3
Cur. Mat.-L.T.D.	2.2	2.5	2.2	1.4	4.4			5.0	4.6
Trade Payables	15.3	22.3	21.1	10.9	12.5			20.3	18.9
Income Taxes Payable	.0	.4	1.3	1.0	1.3			.4	.3
All Other Current	22.0	17.8	11.6	18.9	15.7			18.2	18.5
Total Current	80.0	53.9	49.3	37.0	44.6			59.3	55.6
Long-Term Debt	7.9	13.3	9.8	14.5	17.3			18.3	19.8
Deferred Taxes	.0	.0	.2	.9	.2			.3	.1
All Other Non-Current	6.4	5.6	3.9	5.4	6.8			5.3	5.2
Net Worth	5.7	27.2	36.7	42.2	31.1			16.9	19.2
Total Liabilities & Net Worth	100.0	100.0	100.0	100.0	100.0			100.0	100.0
INCOME DATA									
Net Sales	100.0	100.0	100.0	100.0	100.0			100.0	100.0
Gross Profit									
Operating Expenses	85.5	92.5	93.9	91.8	95.1			91.6	93.9
Operating Profit	14.5	7.5	6.1	8.2	4.9			8.4	6.1
All Other Expenses (net)	1.6	1.1	1.2	2.3	2.2			1.6	1.2
Profit Before Taxes	12.9	6.4	4.8	5.9	2.8			6.8	4.9
RATIOS									
Current	3.9	2.4	3.1	3.3	1.4			2.2	2.2
	1.0	1.3	1.5	1.4	1.0			1.4	1.4
	.5	.9	1.2	1.0	.6			.9	1.0
Quick	1.6	1.9	2.2	2.9	1.0			1.5	1.7
	.7	1.1	1.0	1.1	.7			1.0	1.1
	.3	.6	.6	.5	.5			.6	.7
Sales/Receivables	0 UND	0 UND	25 14.8	35 10.3	38 9.5			23 16.2	29 12.6
	14 25.6	29 12.6	42 8.7	47 7.8	55 6.6			46 8.0	49 7.5
	41 8.8	47 7.8	67 5.5	66 5.6	60 6.1			68 5.4	64 5.7
Cost of Sales/Inventory									
Cost of Sales/Payables									
Sales/Working Capital	10.3	11.0	6.2	3.6	18.6			7.4	6.9
	999.8	34.8	12.4	10.6	534.7			23.8	16.1
	-16.8	-73.4	28.2	NM	-7.3			-63.6	390.6
EBIT/Interest	25.9	20.9	12.9	18.3				23.0	14.2
	(16) 9.6	(26) 4.6	(49) 5.2	(24) 7.1				(87) 4.1	(79) 4.1
	2.6	1.0	1.8	1.4				1.5	.9
Net Profit + Depr., Dep., Amort./Cur. Mat. L/T/D								6.1	13.1
								(18) 3.3	(21) 4.7
								1.2	.5
Fixed/Worth	.0	.1	.0	.1	.3			.1	.1
	.3	.4	.2	.4	NM			.5	.4
	30.1	-1.9	1.1	3.2	-.7			4.7	1.8
Debt/Worth	.8	.6	.7	.6	4.4			1.1	1.0
	5.3	5.8	2.1	2.0	NM			3.0	2.8
	NM	-5.6	8.7	4.8	-5.3			47.2	26.5
% Profit Before Taxes/Tangible Net Worth	315.6	71.0	90.9	29.0				87.6	68.0
	(22) 70.1	(27) 22.3	(51) 23.5	(27) 17.0				(79) 30.3	(72) 21.5
	32.2	-4.9	8.8	5.2				12.2	5.0
% Profit Before Taxes/Total Assets	59.3	24.6	18.0	13.5	14.8			25.4	19.0
	26.6	8.5	7.4	7.6	3.1			7.5	7.7
	4.1	-.7	1.3	2.3	-2.0			1.9	.1
Sales/Net Fixed Assets	397.9	158.1	507.0	51.1	174.4			97.8	133.7
	88.7	67.8	69.9	12.8	16.0			46.6	41.0
	14.7	23.3	23.6	4.2	1.7			14.7	13.0
Sales/Total Assets	10.7	5.6	4.2	2.3	1.6			4.1	5.0
	5.0	3.7	2.8	1.6	1.3			2.9	2.9
	1.6	2.9	1.9	1.1	.8			2.1	2.1
% Depr., Dep., Amort./Sales	.7	.3	.2	.9				.6	.4
	(13) 2.3	(24) .6	(45) .7	(26) 2.6				(74) 1.1	(71) 1.0
	5.4	2.1	1.4	7.4				2.2	2.2
% Officers', Directors' Owners' Comp/Sales	5.6	2.9	2.2					3.0	2.8
	(13) 9.3	(20) 6.4	(22) 3.0					(41) 4.7	(38) 4.8
	16.3	12.9	6.5					8.5	9.1
Net Sales ($)	50568M	161489M	841314M	1372187M	1031511M	1846841M		2698826M	4477065M
Total Assets ($)	7447M	40120M	274295M	752715M	761346M	1153851M		1116998M	1868305M

© RMA 2011

M = $ thousand   MM = $ million

See Pages 9 through 22 for Explanation of Ratios and Data

Comparative Historical Data / Current Data Sorted by Sales

		Comparative Historical Data				Current Data Sorted by Sales				
Type of Statement					0-1MM	1-3MM	3-5MM	5-10MM	10-25MM	25MM & OVER
Unqualified	18	21	25		2			3	6	14
Reviewed	17	17	19				2	3	12	2
Compiled	22	13	17			6	1	6	2	2
Tax Returns	27	33	29		8	9	4	5	2	1
Other	61	71	89		11	9	12	12	19	26
	4/1/08- 3/31/09 ALL	4/1/09- 3/31/10 ALL	4/1/10- 3/31/11 ALL			26 (4/1-9/30/10)			153 (10/1/10-3/31/11)	
NUMBER OF STATEMENTS	145	155	179		21	24	19	29	41	45
ASSETS	%	%	%		%	%	%	%	%	%
Cash & Equivalents	15.2	19.8	17.3		33.9	15.3	17.8	16.9	14.3	13.3
Trade Receivables (net)	36.2	33.6	30.6		12.7	36.6	22.4	34.0	38.2	30.3
Inventory	9.3	7.1	12.8		3.5	5.2	18.3	15.0	16.3	14.3
All Other Current	4.7	5.6	3.9		5.9	3.3	6.5	2.3	5.0	2.3
Total Current	65.4	66.1	64.6		55.8	60.4	65.0	68.2	73.8	60.2
Fixed Assets (net)	17.6	15.7	14.8		23.0	14.3	13.1	14.5	13.5	13.4
Intangibles (net)	9.0	10.2	10.9		7.8	20.7	5.0	6.5	5.2	17.7
All Other Non-Current	8.1	8.0	9.6		13.4	4.6	16.9	10.8	7.5	8.7
Total	100.0	100.0	100.0		100.0	100.0	100.0	100.0	100.0	100.0
LIABILITIES										
Notes Payable-Short Term	14.2	14.2	15.1		38.6	20.8	14.3	12.7	11.4	6.3
Cur. Mat.-L.T.D.	5.8	4.4	2.3		3.5	2.0	1.2	3.1	1.8	2.4
Trade Payables	17.5	20.6	17.6		3.5	20.1	17.9	21.7	21.2	17.0
Income Taxes Payable	.7	.4	.8		.0	.0	.8	.7	.7	1.8
All Other Current	18.1	19.1	16.2		14.7	12.8	24.8	13.8	13.7	19.0
Total Current	56.4	58.7	52.1		60.2	55.7	59.1	51.9	48.8	46.5
Long-Term Debt	17.8	14.9	12.1		12.9	24.9	8.0	10.7	7.4	12.0
Deferred Taxes	.3	.4	.3		.0	.0	.0	.4	.7	.2
All Other Non-Current	6.5	6.7	5.2		5.2	9.2	.4	2.7	6.3	5.8
Net Worth	19.1	19.3	30.3		21.7	10.2	32.6	34.3	36.9	35.5
Total Liabilities & Net Worth	100.0	100.0	100.0		100.0	100.0	100.0	100.0	100.0	100.0
INCOME DATA										
Net Sales	100.0	100.0	100.0		100.0	100.0	100.0	100.0	100.0	100.0
Gross Profit										
Operating Expenses	96.1	95.8	91.8		74.7	92.4	92.3	94.9	95.3	94.2
Operating Profit	3.9	4.2	8.2		25.3	7.6	7.7	5.1	4.7	5.8
All Other Expenses (net)	1.4	2.0	1.6		4.0	3.2	1.5	.6	.5	1.2
Profit Before Taxes	2.5	2.2	6.6		21.3	4.4	6.2	4.5	4.2	4.6
RATIOS										
Current	2.1	2.1	2.5		18.2	1.8	7.3	2.1	2.8	2.2
	1.3	1.2	1.3		1.8	1.1	1.0	1.3	1.5	1.2
	.9	.8	.9		.6	.7	.6	1.0	1.1	.9
Quick	1.5	1.8	1.8		15.0	1.4	2.4	2.0	2.0	1.4
	1.0	1.0	1.0		1.7	.9	.7	1.0	1.1	.9
	.6	.5	.5		.4	.7	.3	.6	.8	.5
Sales/Receivables	21 17.1	23 15.6	22 16.7		0 UND	18 19.9	0 UND	17 21.9	27 13.7	36 10.2
	38 9.5	41 8.8	40 9.1		0 UND	34 10.8	22 16.8	40 9.1	47 7.8	52 7.0
	58 6.3	62 5.9	61 6.0		44 8.3	53 6.9	41 8.8	59 6.1	67 5.4	63 5.8
Cost of Sales/Inventory										
Cost of Sales/Payables										
Sales/Working Capital	7.3	6.5	7.3		1.4	11.1	5.6	8.6	7.1	6.0
	25.9	24.8	19.2		13.2	89.5	177.0	19.9	10.6	21.2
	-43.0	-27.6	-61.7		UND	-20.9	-16.5	-371.5	27.0	-48.3
EBIT/Interest	(124) 12.3	(132) 12.1	(132) 13.5		25.6	7.8	37.8	50.9	12.6	18.1
	4.1	2.6	4.8		(10) 4.1	(17) 2.9	(16) 7.3	(21) 7.7	(31) 5.2	(37) 5.1
	.7	.6	1.4		2.2	.9	-.1	1.4	1.7	2.3
Net Profit + Depr., Dep., Amort./Cur. Mat. L/T/D	(31) 8.3	(21) 6.5	(21) 7.6							7.2
	2.1	1.7	1.9						(10)	2.6
	1.1	.8	1.3							1.3
Fixed/Worth	.2	.1	.1		.0	.3	.0	.1	.0	.1
	1.0	.8	.3		.3	20.1	.2	.5	.2	.6
	-2.4	-1.3	30.1		1.7	-.2	4.3	2.4	1.4	-2.2
Debt/Worth	1.2	1.1	.8		.1	2.6	.2	.9	.6	1.3
	3.6	4.2	2.8		1.0	61.7	2.8	2.5	1.8	4.4
	-10.1	-6.6	296.0		154.5	-2.6	21.6	6.5	6.7	-10.3
% Profit Before Taxes/Tangible Net Worth	(104) 73.7	(102) 52.7	(135) 73.9		174.9	72.0	225.8	70.1	48.0	96.3
	23.6	12.4	28.7		(17) 55.6	(13) 33.3	(15) 48.0	(24) 18.1	(35) 20.0	(31) 29.9
	.9	-4.3	9.5		8.6	-21.0	10.7	3.8	8.8	17.0
% Profit Before Taxes/Total Assets	20.0	16.8	20.3		59.3	24.0	50.0	19.3	15.9	18.0
	5.3	3.2	7.9		16.4	4.0	11.9	7.8	7.6	8.3
	-.7	-3.3	1.9		3.0	-1.1	3.4	-.1	1.8	2.5
Sales/Net Fixed Assets	73.7	120.4	169.6		UND	141.4	169.6	125.6	404.5	88.9
	27.9	30.7	48.4		16.6	45.3	98.4	33.1	62.1	26.4
	11.2	12.2	13.5		3.7	17.0	50.6	15.6	21.0	8.5
Sales/Total Assets	4.9	4.6	4.4		3.9	5.1	6.3	4.9	4.6	2.6
	3.0	2.5	2.6		1.3	3.1	3.3	3.1	3.2	1.9
	2.0	1.6	1.5		.3	1.9	1.7	2.3	2.1	1.4
% Depr., Dep., Amort./Sales	(117) .6	(112) .6	(122) .4		.6	.5	.4	.5	.2	.8
	1.5	1.4	1.1		(11) 2.8	(16) 1.2	(11) .6	(18) .9	(32) .6	(34) 1.9
	2.9	3.3	3.2		13.7	3.7	3.2	1.3	2.4	4.3
% Officers', Directors' Owners' Comp/Sales	(58) 2.4	(63) 2.6	(59) 2.6				4.4		2.2	1.9
	4.9	5.5	5.1			(14) 6.7		(13) 3.9	(15) 2.7	
	9.1	11.6	9.8			11.6		7.4	3.6	
Net Sales ($)	6228423M	4213893M	5303910M		10817M	47286M	76572M	211451M	643842M	4313942M
Total Assets ($)	2622109M	2271723M	2989774M		14854M	60400M	37468M	86790M	283074M	2507188M

M = $ thousand   MM = $ million
See Pages 9 through 22 for Explanation of Ratios and Data

Current Data Sorted by Assets   **Comparative Historical Data**

						Type of Statement		
						Unqualified	21	16
						Reviewed	9	9
	1	6	7	2	6	Compiled	25	11
2	2	12	3			Tax Returns	16	19
8	7	7	1	1		Other	32	34
2	7	1					4/1/06-	4/1/07-
2	25	19	12	3	1		3/31/07	3/31/08
	19 (4/1-9/30/10)		116 (10/1/10-3/31/11)				ALL	ALL
0-500M	500M-2MM	2-10MM	10-50MM	50-100MM	100-250MM	NUMBER OF STATEMENTS		
12	42	45	23	6	7		103	89
%	%	%	%	%	%	ASSETS	%	%
38.4	17.0	12.4	17.0			Cash & Equivalents	18.7	16.6
2.3	48.1	47.4	40.8			Trade Receivables (net)	36.3	38.3
.1	3.5	2.3	2.8			Inventory	1.8	1.2
8.1	2.2	4.7	9.7			All Other Current	4.1	6.5
48.8	70.8	66.7	70.2			Total Current	60.9	62.8
18.5	14.4	16.0	18.5			Fixed Assets (net)	21.6	20.2
8.4	5.1	7.8	4.1			Intangibles (net)	5.4	7.8
24.3	9.6	9.6	7.2			All Other Non-Current	12.1	9.3
100.0	100.0	100.0	100.0			Total	100.0	100.0
						LIABILITIES		
73.1	13.8	9.9	10.8			Notes Payable-Short Term	12.9	15.6
2.8	3.9	1.2	.9			Cur. Mat.-L.T.D.	4.2	5.9
5.3	16.9	18.4	15.0			Trade Payables	12.1	13.9
.0	.1	.4	.3			Income Taxes Payable	.5	.4
17.8	22.7	22.6	25.3			All Other Current	20.6	21.6
99.0	57.3	52.5	52.4			Total Current	50.2	57.5
15.2	10.6	10.8	7.9			Long-Term Debt	10.8	15.8
.0	.2	.6	1.3			Deferred Taxes	.4	.2
20.4	13.5	9.3	2.9			All Other Non-Current	5.9	6.4
-34.6	18.4	26.9	35.5			Net Worth	32.6	20.1
100.0	100.0	100.0	100.0			Total Liabilities & Net Worth	100.0	100.0
						INCOME DATA		
100.0	100.0	100.0	100.0			Net Sales	100.0	100.0
						Gross Profit		
95.7	91.3	92.0	91.9			Operating Expenses	89.9	94.6
4.3	8.7	8.0	8.1			Operating Profit	10.1	5.4
1.3	2.2	1.6	3.7			All Other Expenses (net)	1.5	1.7
3.0	6.5	6.5	4.4			Profit Before Taxes	8.6	3.7
						RATIOS		
2.0	4.3	2.1	2.9				2.8	2.4
.7	1.6	1.2	1.3			Current	1.5	1.3
.1	.7	.9	.9				.9	.9
.9	4.3	2.1	2.9				2.3	2.1
.4	1.5	1.1	1.1			Quick	1.3	1.1
.0	.6	.8	.7				.8	.7
0 UND	21 17.6	44 8.2	44 8.4				10 38.0	28 13.2
0 UND	43 8.5	64 5.7	63 5.8			Sales/Receivables	45 8.0	51 7.2
0 UND	69 5.3	79 4.6	81 4.5				68 5.3	68 5.3
						Cost of Sales/Inventory		
						Cost of Sales/Payables		
NM	5.8	10.0	4.9				7.2	8.6
-150.4	14.7	29.0	16.4			Sales/Working Capital	22.4	22.8
-9.6	-16.1	-59.0	-30.4				-61.1	-37.3
14.8	15.2	52.3	29.5				19.7	17.3
(10) .4	(31) 5.7	(35) 13.9	(18) 4.7			EBIT/Interest	(73) 7.2	(69) 2.9
-3.6	-1.4	4.0	.3				2.2	1.1
							9.1	7.6
						Net Profit + Depr., Dep., Amort./Cur. Mat. L/T/D	(15) 2.8	(13) 3.7
							1.8	2.0
.0	.1	.2	.2				.2	.2
.4	.2	.6	.4			Fixed/Worth	.5	.6
-1.1	UND	3.6	1.4				3.2	-1.8
.7	.5	1.2	1.1				.7	.8
NM	1.8	3.4	2.4			Debt/Worth	1.7	3.3
-1.6	-6.5	15.9	13.0				18.5	-10.2
	101.9	88.9	47.3				129.4	91.4
	(30) 42.7	(37) 43.8	(21) 20.3			% Profit Before Taxes/Tangible Net Worth	(84) 50.6	(61) 26.5
	8.4	12.5	1.1				14.9	8.4
19.5	31.8	20.1	14.3				35.7	23.0
5.0	8.9	11.4	4.5			% Profit Before Taxes/Total Assets	12.2	6.2
-20.9	-4.8	3.1	.6				4.4	.6
UND	102.0	95.1	50.9				62.5	54.7
95.1	61.2	32.7	22.0			Sales/Net Fixed Assets	24.2	28.4
40.6	28.0	13.1	7.4				11.0	11.3
31.8	6.1	4.2	3.5				5.1	4.5
9.1	3.2	2.7	2.2			Sales/Total Assets	3.1	3.0
4.4	2.2	2.2	1.5				2.2	2.1
	.6	.4	.7				.8	.7
(23) .9	(33) 1.0	(22) 1.2				% Depr., Dep., Amort./Sales	(78) 1.3	(68) 1.3
	1.3	2.1	2.0				2.5	2.1
5.8	1.9						3.6	2.8
(10) 9.0	(17) 3.6					% Officers', Directors' Owners' Comp/Sales	(35) 9.9	(27) 8.0
13.8	9.9						24.3	16.8
44477M	247248M	775444M	1233169M	572221M	1269731M	Net Sales ($)	2489991M	4874062M
2700M	50680M	232487M	523716M	401272M	1138705M	Total Assets ($)	1044180M	1558431M

© RMA 2011   M = $ thousand   MM = $ million
See Pages 9 through 22 for Explanation of Ratios and Data

Comparative Historical Data | Current Data Sorted by Sales

			Type of Statement						
22	25	22	Unqualified		1		2	3	16
14	14	17	Reviewed		1	1	3	8	4
13	16	18	Compiled		5	3	4	4	1
20	17	16	Tax Returns	1	4	3	4	2	1
43	66	62	Other	2	7	7	13	18	15
4/1/08-3/31/09 ALL	4/1/09-3/31/10 ALL	4/1/10-3/31/11 ALL			19 (4/1-9/30/10)		116 (10/1/10-3/31/11)		
				0-1MM	1-3MM	3-5MM	5-10MM	10-25MM	25MM & OVER
112	138	135	NUMBER OF STATEMENTS	5	18	14	26	35	37
%	%	%	ASSETS	%	%	%	%	%	%
19.2	16.7	17.4	Cash & Equivalents		13.6	24.3	19.5	13.6	18.5
35.4	37.6	40.5	Trade Receivables (net)		42.8	32.8	43.0	49.1	37.8
2.4	2.3	2.3	Inventory		1.5	4.0	1.2	3.1	2.5
5.4	5.9	5.2	All Other Current		6.6	2.4	2.3	6.1	7.6
62.4	62.5	65.5	Total Current		64.4	63.5	66.0	71.9	66.4
20.6	19.2	16.0	Fixed Assets (net)		18.3	14.1	15.8	14.4	12.8
8.0	8.7	8.6	Intangibles (net)		7.1	4.2	9.4	6.4	13.7
9.0	9.6	9.9	All Other Non-Current		10.2	18.2	8.7	7.3	7.2
100.0	100.0	100.0	Total		100.0	100.0	100.0	100.0	100.0
			LIABILITIES						
14.6	12.4	16.2	Notes Payable-Short Term		33.3	31.1	7.0	14.2	9.8
3.7	6.5	2.5	Cur. Mat.-L.T.D.		3.9	1.2	4.6	1.3	2.3
13.2	14.6	15.0	Trade Payables		8.4	12.0	15.5	22.1	14.4
.4	.2	.4	Income Taxes Payable		.1	.0	.0	.2	1.2
19.6	19.3	22.0	All Other Current		13.8	26.4	23.3	22.3	26.1
51.4	53.0	56.1	Total Current		59.5	70.8	50.3	60.0	53.8
12.5	16.3	11.5	Long-Term Debt		18.3	8.1	13.6	7.6	8.7
.3	.5	.6	Deferred Taxes		.0	.6	.0	1.6	.5
8.3	7.9	10.8	All Other Non-Current		26.6	8.6	8.3	9.8	6.2
27.4	22.3	21.0	Net Worth		-4.4	11.9	27.8	21.0	30.7
100.0	100.0	100.0	Total Liabilities & Net Worth		100.0	100.0	100.0	100.0	100.0
			INCOME DATA						
100.0	100.0	100.0	Net Sales		100.0	100.0	100.0	100.0	100.0
			Gross Profit						
95.7	93.7	92.0	Operating Expenses		89.6	94.8	96.5	92.4	94.2
4.3	6.3	8.0	Operating Profit		10.4	5.2	3.5	7.6	5.8
1.7	2.6	2.3	All Other Expenses (net)		3.4	.8	.7	1.1	1.2
2.7	3.7	5.7	Profit Before Taxes		7.0	4.4	2.9	6.5	4.6
			RATIOS						
2.5	2.3	2.7			12.2	3.3	3.2	2.1	2.0
1.3	1.4	1.3	Current		2.9	1.1	1.5	1.2	1.2
.9	1.0	.9			.9	.5	.9	.9	.9
2.2	2.1	2.4			8.2	3.1	3.0	2.1	1.9
(111) 1.2	1.2	1.1	Quick		2.2	.9	1.4	1.0	1.1
.8	.8	.7			.5	.5	.9	.7	.8
23 15.6	30 12.0	25 14.8		0 UND	0 UND	35 10.5	37 9.8	37 10.0	
47 7.7	50 7.3	54 6.7	Sales/Receivables	60 6.1	40 9.1	49 7.4	58 6.3	56 6.6	
64 5.7	77 4.7	76 4.8		140 2.6	64 5.7	70 5.2	80 4.6	79 4.6	
			Cost of Sales/Inventory						
			Cost of Sales/Payables						
7.2	6.0	6.3			2.6	7.1	7.8	9.5	6.0
28.5	18.3	24.9	Sales/Working Capital		5.7	NM	20.9	29.0	22.7
-49.9	-195.5	-35.1			-606.0	-9.4	-68.7	-37.2	-83.0
23.5	19.5	29.8			26.8	10.9	10.3	69.6	24.9
(93) 4.1	(103) 5.4	(105) 7.0	EBIT/Interest	(14) 8.9	(11) 5.1	(16) 3.8	(30) 15.9	(32) 5.8	
.9	.9	1.3		-.3	-2.5	-1.0	3.2	1.8	
20.7	8.6	13.3							11.7
(19) 2.7	(21) 4.4	(13) 7.4	Net Profit + Depr., Dep., Amort./Cur. Mat. L/T/D					(10) 7.3	
1.3	2.1	3.6							4.2
.2	.1	.1			.0	.0	.1	.1	.2
.6	.5	.5	Fixed/Worth		.2	.6	.6	.5	.8
UND	4.1	4.3			-26.7	-1.1	1.4	UND	3.3
.9	.8	.8			.3	.8	1.0	1.1	1.6
2.7	2.7	2.9	Debt/Worth		.8	5.7	1.9	3.1	4.5
UND	36.7	107.7			-2.0	-3.9	7.1	-462.6	27.5
82.6	64.3	86.7			60.3	101.8	99.5	86.7	
(85) 20.2	(106) 21.6	(103) 39.8	% Profit Before Taxes/Tangible Net Worth	(11) 26.9		(23) 13.3	(26) 53.8	(31) 30.8	
2.7	2.1	10.0		17.3		-3.3	20.0	10.5	
23.2	19.5	19.4			37.3	22.1	18.4	32.8	14.7
5.8	6.7	7.8	% Profit Before Taxes/Total Assets		13.6	9.8	4.8	11.1	6.1
-.1	-1.1	.7			-1.8	-22.1	-2.6	1.6	1.0
56.8	70.8	97.3			106.9	277.5	74.6	120.5	137.1
24.4	27.0	38.6	Sales/Net Fixed Assets		43.4	64.3	41.0	37.4	31.6
11.4	9.8	13.5			18.9	14.9	20.1	13.5	12.0
4.9	4.0	4.6			4.4	6.9	6.1	4.9	3.8
3.0	2.5	2.7	Sales/Total Assets		2.5	3.2	3.0	2.8	2.3
2.1	1.6	1.8			1.7	2.3	2.3	2.2	1.6
.9	.7	.6					.6	.6	.2
(79) 1.5	(100) 1.5	(90) 1.0	% Depr., Dep., Amort./Sales		(19) .9	(23) 1.4	(29) .8		
2.5	2.6	1.8					1.2	2.5	1.6
4.3	3.3	2.3					4.0	1.6	
(42) 9.8	(33) 8.2	(38) 4.4	% Officers', Directors' Owners' Comp/Sales			(10) 7.9	(10) 2.4		
21.4	16.3	8.9					9.3	6.1	
3465487M	3765111M	4142290M	Net Sales ($)	1249M	34445M	54517M	185070M	588002M	3279007M
1921247M	2314504M	2349560M	Total Assets ($)	5386M	27041M	15432M	71005M	275420M	1955276M

M = $ thousand   MM = $ million
See Pages 9 through 22 for Explanation of Ratios and Data

Current Data Sorted by Assets | Comparative Historical Data

	0-500M	500M-2MM	2-10MM	10-50MM	50-100MM	100-250MM		4/1/06-3/31/07 ALL	4/1/07-3/31/08 ALL
Type of Statement		7 (4/1-9/30/10)		42 (10/1/10-3/31/11)					
Unqualified				2	1	1		4	1
Reviewed		1						6	7
Compiled	2	1	3					10	4
Tax Returns	9	4	3		1			20	6
Other	7	7	4	1		2		19	15
NUMBER OF STATEMENTS	18	13	10	3	2	3		59	33
ASSETS	%	%	%	%	%	%		%	%
Cash & Equivalents	27.0	18.2	11.9					20.9	18.5
Trade Receivables (net)	10.9	15.7	12.6					9.4	10.9
Inventory	3.7	7.4	3.2					4.7	4.9
All Other Current	1.3	2.9	7.8					9.0	4.2
Total Current	42.8	44.1	35.4					44.0	38.4
Fixed Assets (net)	38.4	46.2	26.4					38.9	47.1
Intangibles (net)	10.7	4.5	20.5					4.4	10.5
All Other Non-Current	8.0	5.2	17.7					12.7	3.9
Total	100.0	100.0	100.0					100.0	100.0
LIABILITIES									
Notes Payable-Short Term	28.6	13.5	4.2					11.3	7.3
Cur. Mat.-L.T.D.	3.4	3.6	2.6					4.8	3.9
Trade Payables	12.2	10.9	11.5					7.0	10.8
Income Taxes Payable	.0	.3	.2					.3	.7
All Other Current	18.5	9.6	8.5					19.1	13.0
Total Current	62.7	37.9	27.0					42.4	35.7
Long-Term Debt	29.7	28.6	29.7					20.6	28.7
Deferred Taxes	.0	.0	.8					.4	.7
All Other Non-Current	.2	9.5	6.2					12.9	8.9
Net Worth	7.4	24.0	36.3					23.8	26.0
Total Liabilities & Net Worth	100.0	100.0	100.0					100.0	100.0
INCOME DATA									
Net Sales	100.0	100.0	100.0					100.0	100.0
Gross Profit									
Operating Expenses	93.8	92.6	90.9					91.2	95.4
Operating Profit	6.2	7.4	9.1					8.8	4.6
All Other Expenses (net)	1.0	2.3	3.6					1.5	1.8
Profit Before Taxes	5.2	5.1	5.5					7.3	2.9
RATIOS									
Current	2.2	3.8	2.8					3.2	1.7
	1.0	1.4	1.7					1.0	1.2
	.2	.3	.5					.4	.6
Quick	2.0	3.8	2.1					2.5	1.4
	.7	.7	1.4				(58)	.6	(32) .9
	.1	.2	.3					.2	.3
Sales/Receivables	0 UND	1 664.0	2 237.1				0	UND	1 384.9
	0 UND	4 83.0	21 17.7				2	217.0	5 72.2
	16 22.6	22 16.3	56 6.5				25	14.6	20 18.1
Cost of Sales/Inventory									
Cost of Sales/Payables									
Sales/Working Capital	18.6	9.2	7.2					5.6	7.5
	NM	35.2	10.5					569.7	75.1
	-9.3	-4.0	-22.1					-16.4	-22.7
EBIT/Interest	5.0	9.8						8.8	7.9
	(13) 3.0	5.5					(46)	3.2	(32) 2.7
	1.4	.8						-.3	.2
Net Profit + Depr., Dep., Amort./Cur. Mat. L/T/D									
Fixed/Worth	.8	.6	.5					.3	.8
	13.8	2.3	1.0					1.4	2.0
	-.9	NM	NM					18.0	-3.7
Debt/Worth	1.7	.7	.6					.8	1.0
	24.1	2.9	1.6					2.7	2.4
	-3.1	NM	NM					41.0	-6.9
% Profit Before Taxes/Tangible Net Worth	366.1	47.4						82.8	58.8
	(11) 35.4	(10) 24.4					(45)	31.4	(22) 30.0
	15.8	1.8						2.1	4.9
% Profit Before Taxes/Total Assets	18.9	15.8	10.7					29.5	16.3
	8.5	6.2	5.2					7.3	5.3
	1.8	-1.0	-3.7					-1.0	-5.4
Sales/Net Fixed Assets	52.7	16.9	22.6					20.1	8.7
	12.4	6.1	7.1					8.4	6.2
	6.1	1.7	4.9					3.9	3.0
Sales/Total Assets	6.3	4.4	2.5					4.3	3.0
	3.3	2.2	1.6					2.7	2.4
	1.6	.9	1.2					1.5	1.8
% Depr., Dep., Amort./Sales	2.1	3.2						1.7	2.4
	(10) 3.5	(11) 4.7					(44)	3.1	(29) 3.2
	4.9	7.0						5.0	6.2
% Officers', Directors' Owners' Comp/Sales	7.8							5.0	2.5
	(11) 14.6						(29)	9.8	(19) 8.8
	21.1							16.4	12.2
Net Sales ($)	19257M	46679M	79282M	233531M	294008M	948274M		1134450M	1060655M
Total Assets ($)	3606M	14371M	42687M	97947M	116007M	424973M		467766M	573752M

© RMA 2011

M = $ thousand   MM = $ million
See Pages 9 through 22 for Explanation of Ratios and Data

Comparative Historical Data | Current Data Sorted by Sales

	4/1/08-3/31/09 ALL	4/1/09-3/31/10 ALL	4/1/10-3/31/11 ALL	Type of Statement	0-1MM	1-3MM	3-5MM	5-10MM	10-25MM	25MM & OVER
	4	4	4	Unqualified			1	1		4
	7	3	1	Reviewed			2			
	6	8	6	Compiled	3	6	1			
	17	21	17	Tax Returns	5	4	1	3	1	1
	19	14	21	Other	7			3	3	3
					7 (4/1-9/30/10)			42 (10/1/10-3/31/11)		
	53	50	49	NUMBER OF STATEMENTS	15	10	5	7	4	8
	%	%	%		%	%	%	%	%	%
				ASSETS						
Cash & Equivalents	15.5	17.9	19.3		22.7	20.1				
Trade Receivables (net)	10.2	5.3	11.6		13.6	12.2				
Inventory	5.9	7.3	4.7		1.8	5.1				
All Other Current	2.5	3.1	3.4		1.2	.2				
Total Current	34.1	33.5	38.9		39.2	37.6				
Fixed Assets (net)	40.8	38.9	39.1		41.8	53.2				
Intangibles (net)	14.0	16.6	13.2		8.2	5.5				
All Other Non-Current	11.1	11.1	8.7		10.7	3.7				
Total	100.0	100.0	100.0		100.0	100.0				
				LIABILITIES						
Notes Payable-Short Term	13.5	24.0	14.9		13.5	13.2				
Cur. Mat.-L.T.D.	5.2	4.6	3.3		3.7	1.3				
Trade Payables	6.7	11.0	10.5		8.7	10.0				
Income Taxes Payable	.6	.1	.1		.0	.0				
All Other Current	18.4	15.9	13.5		17.8	13.1				
Total Current	44.4	55.7	42.3		43.8	37.6				
Long-Term Debt	27.8	33.2	29.2		24.4	43.8				
Deferred Taxes	.5	.2	.3		.0	.0				
All Other Non-Current	16.8	9.2	7.5		.0	.4				
Net Worth	10.4	1.8	20.8		31.8	18.1				
Total Liabilties & Net Worth	100.0	100.0	100.0		100.0	100.0				
				INCOME DATA						
Net Sales	100.0	100.0	100.0		100.0	100.0				
Gross Profit										
Operating Expenses	95.8	96.9	92.5		82.4	97.8				
Operating Profit	4.2	3.1	7.5		17.6	2.2				
All Other Expenses (net)	1.5	3.0	1.9		4.8	-.6				
Profit Before Taxes	2.7	.1	5.6		12.9	2.8				
				RATIOS						
Current	1.9	2.1	2.3		2.2	2.5				
	.7	.6	1.2		.8	1.3				
	.3	.3	.4		.2	.3				
Quick	1.4	1.3	2.1		2.2	2.5				
	.5	.4	.7		.7	1.1				
	.2	.2	.2		.1	.3				
Sales/Receivables	0 UND	0 UND	0 UND		0 UND	0 UND				
	4 96.5	1 364.3	4 90.5		2 212.0	2 161.8				
	15 24.2	8 44.9	21 17.5		47 7.8	16 23.3				
Cost of Sales/Inventory										
Cost of Sales/Payables										
Sales/Working Capital	12.1	13.1	10.2		4.5	18.6				
	-31.7	-32.9	56.6		-24.1	43.8				
	-9.2	-7.3	-10.7		-4.3	-27.7				
EBIT/Interest	6.1	4.4	8.6			7.2				
	(44) 1.6	(38) .0	(41) 3.5			4.1				
	-.9	-4.0	1.3			-1.6				
Net Profit + Depr., Dep., Amort./Cur. Mat. L/T/D										
Fixed/Worth	.8	.7	.8		.4	.7				
	4.3	NM	2.3		1.0	13.8				
	-.8	-.6	-1.0		4.1	-1.7				
Debt/Worth	1.3	.9	.8		.8	1.6				
	8.2	NM	3.3		2.4	14.6				
	-2.8	-2.1	-3.8		21.7	-4.7				
% Profit Before Taxes/Tangible Net Worth	42.0	121.0	75.4		69.9					
	(30) 15.6	(25) 8.9	(32) 26.1		(12) 26.1					
	-10.2	-9.4	6.3		7.5					
% Profit Before Taxes/Total Assets	14.3	12.8	14.9		17.1	30.0				
	2.2	-1.1	7.9		7.9	9.3				
	-8.6	-15.5	1.9		2.5	-3.0				
Sales/Net Fixed Assets	18.1	20.2	19.4		18.7	21.5				
	8.2	12.4	7.6		6.7	6.9				
	4.4	5.9	4.4		.7	4.5				
Sales/Total Assets	3.9	6.2	3.7		2.4	6.6				
	2.6	3.1	2.3		1.2	4.2				
	1.8	1.7	1.4		.6	2.2				
% Depr., Dep., Amort./Sales	1.8	1.6	3.1							
	(40) 3.5	(37) 3.0	(31) 4.1							
	5.7	5.8	6.6							
% Officers', Directors', Owners' Comp/Sales	4.0	3.5	2.2							
	(21) 9.8	(25) 8.7	(20) 6.6							
	15.9	18.4	15.7							
Net Sales ($)	2160688M	1105905M	1621031M		5510M	16306M	19920M	49025M	54457M	1475813M
Total Assets ($)	1059621M	550991M	699591M		6574M	4865M	9546M	22698M	16981M	638927M

© RMA 2011

M = $ thousand   MM = $ million
See Pages 9 through 22 for Explanation of Ratios and Data

Current Data Sorted by Assets   Comparative Historical Data

						Type of Statement		
	1		1			Unqualified	4	2
	3	4				Reviewed	2	2
	1	1				Compiled	6	4
1	2					Tax Returns	9	5
2	7	6	1	1		Other	7	14
	6 (4/1-9/30/10)		25 (10/1/10-3/31/11)				4/1/06-3/31/07	4/1/07-3/31/08
0-500M	500M-2MM	2-10MM	10-50MM	50-100MM	100-250MM		ALL	ALL
3	14	11	2	1		NUMBER OF STATEMENTS	28	27
%	%	%	%	%	%		%	%
	5.9	11.2				**ASSETS** Cash & Equivalents	12.1	13.0
	32.7	12.8				Trade Receivables (net)	26.9	20.2
	3.5	5.8				Inventory	4.8	7.8
	7.1	7.5				All Other Current	7.1	4.2
	49.2	37.3				Total Current	50.9	45.2
	38.5	50.6				Fixed Assets (net)	36.8	40.5
	4.9	.9				Intangibles (net)	5.0	4.7
	7.4	11.3				All Other Non-Current	7.3	9.6
	100.0	100.0				Total	100.0	100.0
	9.2	2.7				**LIABILITIES** Notes Payable-Short Term	8.8	16.7
	9.3	10.5				Cur. Mat.-L.T.D.	5.1	13.7
	8.5	7.0				Trade Payables	6.9	16.7
	.4	.1				Income Taxes Payable	.9	.3
	24.9	8.4				All Other Current	11.7	11.2
	52.4	28.7				Total Current	33.5	58.6
	17.4	29.5				Long-Term Debt	20.7	26.1
	.2	.8				Deferred Taxes	.3	.4
	1.6	6.0				All Other Non-Current	13.6	4.0
	28.3	34.9				Net Worth	31.9	10.8
	100.0	100.0				Total Liabilities & Net Worth	100.0	100.0
	100.0	100.0				**INCOME DATA** Net Sales	100.0	100.0
						Gross Profit		
	93.2	86.8				Operating Expenses	88.1	90.1
	6.8	13.2				Operating Profit	11.9	9.9
	3.9	-.1				All Other Expenses (net)	3.5	3.1
	2.9	13.3				Profit Before Taxes	8.4	6.8
	2.3	3.7				**RATIOS** Current	3.9	3.2
	.9	2.2					1.7	1.0
	.6	.7					.9	.6
	1.8	3.4				Quick	3.0	2.4
	.8	1.8					1.4	.7
	.4	.3					.4	.3
	0 UND	3 145.6				Sales/Receivables	4 95.6	4 100.8
	56 6.6	21 17.3					47 7.8	32 11.6
	62 5.9	78 4.7					76 4.8	63 5.8
						Cost of Sales/Inventory		
						Cost of Sales/Payables		
	8.2	4.6				Sales/Working Capital	5.6	7.1
	-54.7	7.6					9.7	-162.0
	-14.6	-27.2					-94.3	-10.0
	9.3	15.2				EBIT/Interest	18.7	8.6
	(12) 3.4	(10) 7.9					(23) 4.5	(20) 2.2
	-1.1	2.3					1.8	.1
						Net Profit + Depr., Dep., Amort./Cur. Mat. L/T/D		
	.4	.6				Fixed/Worth	.3	.5
	1.4	1.7					.9	1.3
	UND	13.7					2.3	-2.7
	.8	.7				Debt/Worth	.6	.7
	3.5	1.9					1.4	2.0
	UND	25.3					5.4	-7.2
	68.5					% Profit Before Taxes/Tangible Net Worth	76.1	82.3
	(12) 31.5						(25) 44.1	(20) 44.9
	-44.7						11.4	5.3
	20.9	25.8				% Profit Before Taxes/Total Assets	37.3	33.0
	5.3	14.7					10.5	8.8
	-13.3	7.8					2.4	.6
	23.4	9.8				Sales/Net Fixed Assets	20.5	22.2
	13.6	3.1					6.9	8.9
	3.5	1.6					3.8	3.3
	3.5	3.2				Sales/Total Assets	3.1	4.5
	2.5	1.2					2.4	2.5
	.9	.9					1.5	1.4
		2.5				% Depr., Dep., Amort./Sales	1.7	.9
		3.0					(24) 3.5	(18) 3.1
		7.9					6.7	3.8
						% Officers', Directors' Owners' Comp/Sales	6.0	5.9
							(10) 12.0	(11) 8.6
							17.7	15.8
5294M	46638M	108928M	59727M	40896M		Net Sales ($)	551738M	439095M
386M	17133M	53116M	45736M	64636M		Total Assets ($)	306073M	236851M

M = $ thousand   MM = $ million

See Pages 9 through 22 for Explanation of Ratios and Data

Comparative Historical Data

Current Data Sorted by Sales

Type of Statement									
	1	1	2		1			1	Unqualified
	4	6	7			3	2	1	1	Reviewed
	3	2	2			1				Compiled
	6	8	3	1	2					Tax Returns
	11	10	17	2	3	3	2	5	2	Other

	4/1/08-3/31/09 ALL	4/1/09-3/31/10 ALL	4/1/10-3/31/11 ALL	0-1MM	6 (4/1-9/30/10) 1-3MM	3-5MM	5-10MM	25 (10/1/10-3/31/11) 10-25MM	25MM & OVER
NUMBER OF STATEMENTS	25	27	31	4	7	7	4	6	3
	%	%	%	%	%	%	%	%	%
ASSETS									
Cash & Equivalents	12.1	12.1	7.2						
Trade Receivables (net)	24.7	18.4	24.1						
Inventory	8.1	5.6	3.9						
All Other Current	5.5	7.0	7.2						
Total Current	50.3	43.1	42.4						
Fixed Assets (net)	38.8	41.3	43.2						
Intangibles (net)	2.6	7.3	5.5						
All Other Non-Current	8.4	8.3	8.9						
Total	100.0	100.0	100.0						
LIABILITIES									
Notes Payable-Short Term	15.0	13.3	22.6						
Cur. Mat.-L.T.D.	11.4	7.0	8.5						
Trade Payables	20.1	12.1	16.5						
Income Taxes Payable	.9	.1	.3						
All Other Current	11.7	26.5	18.4						
Total Current	59.2	58.9	66.2						
Long-Term Debt	39.0	29.9	19.3						
Deferred Taxes	.9	.9	.7						
All Other Non-Current	4.8	7.3	4.6						
Net Worth	-3.9	3.0	9.3						
Total Liabilties & Net Worth	100.0	100.0	100.0						
INCOME DATA									
Net Sales	100.0	100.0	100.0						
Gross Profit									
Operating Expenses	88.2	95.3	90.0						
Operating Profit	11.8	4.7	10.0						
All Other Expenses (net)	4.2	3.2	2.0						
Profit Before Taxes	7.6	1.5	8.1						
RATIOS									
Current	2.7	1.5	2.5						
	1.1	.9	1.1						
	.4	.4	.6						
Quick	2.0	1.0	2.1						
	.7	.7	.8						
	.3	.2	.3						
Sales/Receivables	19 19.6	2 222.7	2 196.0						
	48 7.6	23 15.9	41 9.0						
	68 5.4	61 6.0	62 5.9						
Cost of Sales/Inventory									
Cost of Sales/Payables									
Sales/Working Capital	6.2	9.7	7.6						
	18.8	-75.0	23.3						
	-6.9	-11.7	-15.0						
EBIT/Interest	9.2	3.5	12.1						
	(21) 1.8	(22) 1.0	(25) 4.6						
	.1	-.5	.3						
Net Profit + Depr., Dep., Amort./Cur. Mat. L/T/D									
Fixed/Worth	.7	.9	.6						
	1.4	5.4	1.6						
	-31.5	-2.1	UND						
Debt/Worth	1.1	1.3	1.0						
	3.5	7.9	4.3						
	-44.3	-6.5	UND						
% Profit Before Taxes/Tangible Net Worth	51.9	36.0	57.2						
	(18) 19.7	(18) 7.7	(24) 39.7						
	1.2	-25.5	-36.0						
% Profit Before Taxes/Total Assets	21.3	8.0	26.6						
	9.7	.0	10.7						
	-.5	-7.4	-.8						
Sales/Net Fixed Assets	17.8	19.3	17.7						
	5.9	12.0	8.9						
	3.0	3.1	2.1						
Sales/Total Assets	3.9	5.8	3.8						
	2.4	1.9	2.5						
	.9	1.2	.9						
% Depr., Dep., Amort./Sales	2.1	3.3	2.2						
	(19) 3.8	(19) 4.6	(25) 2.9						
	7.7	6.1	7.0						
% Officers', Directors' Owners' Comp/Sales		4.5	2.4						
		(12) 6.4	(12) 4.7						
		18.7	9.9						
Net Sales ($)	304448M	196316M	261483M	1934M	14656M	27683M	25128M	77538M	114544M
Total Assets ($)	140088M	127408M	181007M	3356M	8063M	13974M	20347M	42670M	92597M

M = $ thousand   MM = $ million
See Pages 9 through 22 for Explanation of Ratios and Data

Current Data Sorted by Assets   **Comparative Historical Data**

Type of Statement	0-500M	500M-2MM	2-10MM	10-50MM	50-100MM	100-250MM	4/1/06-3/31/07 ALL	4/1/07-3/31/08 ALL
Unqualified	1	1	2		3		7	6
Reviewed	2	6	4				8	12
Compiled	38	36	9	1			70	72
Tax Returns	162	73	15			1	171	158
Other	78	59	23	3		1	105	103
		31 (4/1-9/30/10)		487 (10/1/10-3/31/11)				
NUMBER OF STATEMENTS	281	175	53	4	3	2	361	351
ASSETS	%	%	%	%	%	%	%	%
Cash & Equivalents	27.3	14.4	8.9				21.0	19.3
Trade Receivables (net)	5.1	2.5	5.6				6.0	6.7
Inventory	11.5	4.7	4.9				9.5	10.1
All Other Current	2.3	2.2	3.4				3.6	2.8
Total Current	46.2	23.7	22.8				40.1	38.9
Fixed Assets (net)	32.0	46.7	57.8				39.0	37.8
Intangibles (net)	11.7	20.1	8.7				11.1	12.7
All Other Non-Current	10.1	9.5	10.7				9.6	10.6
Total	100.0	100.0	100.0				100.0	100.0
LIABILITIES								
Notes Payable-Short Term	16.5	5.2	3.3				8.5	10.0
Cur. Mat.-L.T.D.	7.5	4.3	4.2				5.2	5.2
Trade Payables	15.5	4.4	5.7				9.7	8.3
Income Taxes Payable	.2	.0	.0				.4	.1
All Other Current	18.4	8.3	8.1				12.1	13.1
Total Current	58.3	22.2	21.3				36.0	36.6
Long-Term Debt	39.4	49.3	57.5				36.3	36.5
Deferred Taxes	.1	.1	.0				.1	.1
All Other Non-Current	16.9	7.1	3.3				7.6	7.8
Net Worth	-14.6	21.3	17.9				20.1	19.0
Total Liabilties & Net Worth	100.0	100.0	100.0				100.0	100.0
INCOME DATA								
Net Sales	100.0	100.0	100.0				100.0	100.0
Gross Profit								
Operating Expenses	93.0	86.3	82.3				89.8	89.8
Operating Profit	7.0	13.7	17.7				10.2	10.2
All Other Expenses (net)	.9	4.6	7.9				2.7	2.0
Profit Before Taxes	6.1	9.2	9.8				7.5	8.2
RATIOS								
Current	3.5	2.8	1.7				3.4	3.0
	1.2	.9	.8				1.3	1.2
	.4	.3	.3				.5	.5
Quick	2.5	2.0	1.0				2.3	2.1
	.7	(174) .6	.5				(359) .8	(350) .7
	.2	.1	.2				.3	.2
Sales/Receivables	0 UND	0 UND	0 UND				0 UND	0 UND
	0 UND	0 UND	1 727.5				0 UND	0 UND
	3 125.0	3 132.7	6 59.9				5 75.9	4 81.8
Cost of Sales/Inventory								
Cost of Sales/Payables								
Sales/Working Capital	19.9	16.1	16.4				14.1	17.3
	139.1	-209.1	-88.7				63.0	85.4
	-21.3	-14.1	-6.9				-26.6	-30.1
EBIT/Interest	17.3	15.3	16.0				17.7	16.4
	(207) 4.4	(147) 4.1	(42) 2.9				(272) 5.7	(279) 4.9
	.8	1.7	1.4				1.6	1.5
Net Profit + Depr., Dep., Amort./Cur. Mat. L/T/D							2.9	7.1
							(12) 1.7	(14) 3.5
							1.0	2.1
Fixed/Worth	.5	1.1	1.1				.5	.5
	2.5	6.3	9.2				2.1	2.2
	-.5	-1.9	-7.7				-1.9	-2.0
Debt/Worth	.8	1.2	1.9				.8	.8
	37.3	8.5	10.9				3.1	3.8
	-2.1	-3.9	-9.4				-4.3	-5.2
% Profit Before Taxes/Tangible Net Worth	293.3	154.3	95.1				172.3	227.0
	(145) 80.8	(107) 60.8	(33) 27.9				(236) 57.9	(232) 83.6
	22.7	13.0	5.5				18.9	31.2
% Profit Before Taxes/Total Assets	58.5	31.6	15.2				52.0	58.3
	20.3	13.6	4.0				19.3	21.1
	.0	3.1	1.9				2.4	3.9
Sales/Net Fixed Assets	101.6	21.0	12.8				43.9	63.9
	28.1	8.4	2.5				15.4	15.5
	12.4	1.9	.5				5.5	5.6
Sales/Total Assets	10.8	3.5	2.5				7.5	8.1
	6.6	2.0	1.4				4.3	3.8
	3.8	1.2	.5				2.3	2.1
% Depr., Dep., Amort./Sales	.7	1.8	2.5				.8	.9
	(162) 1.7	(113) 3.1	(41) 3.9				(246) 2.2	(242) 2.0
	3.2	5.9	10.1				3.8	3.8
% Officers', Directors' Owners' Comp/Sales	5.8	4.9	4.0				6.6	5.5
	(205) 8.9	(103) 8.0	(25) 7.4				(222) 10.8	(218) 9.4
	14.8	12.9	11.3				17.5	15.3
Net Sales ($)	420728M	449220M	402923M	167948M	367076M	1804881M	4192249M	6697572M
Total Assets ($)	60743M	178216M	209570M	75660M	202406M	389725M	1212145M	1671296M

Comparative Historical Data / Current Data Sorted by Sales

Type of Statement				0-1MM	1-3MM	3-5MM	5-10MM	10-25MM	25MM & OVER
6	8	7	Unqualified		2		2		3
11	13	12	Reviewed		4	4	3		1
78	74	84	Compiled	20	43	13	4	2	2
194	280	251	Tax Returns	83	126	24	14		4
107	132	164	Other	57	65	14	20	5	3
4/1/08-3/31/09 ALL	4/1/09-3/31/10 ALL	4/1/10-3/31/11 ALL		31 (4/1-9/30/10)			487 (10/1/10-3/31/11)		
396	507	518	**NUMBER OF STATEMENTS**	160	240	55	43	7	13
%	%	%	**ASSETS**	%	%	%	%	%	%
19.0	18.4	20.7	Cash & Equivalents	17.9	20.2	29.4	26.0		12.7
4.6	4.6	4.4	Trade Receivables (net)	3.2	4.5	2.9	5.2		14.8
11.0	8.4	8.6	Inventory	9.2	8.2	8.3	6.1		16.4
2.7	1.6	2.3	All Other Current	1.7	2.1	3.8	3.6		1.5
37.3	33.1	36.1	Total Current	32.0	35.0	44.3	40.9		45.3
36.7	40.5	39.7	Fixed Assets (net)	44.6	37.9	33.3	44.5		32.2
15.7	16.4	14.3	Intangibles (net)	13.8	17.4	10.4	4.5		10.1
10.4	10.0	9.9	All Other Non-Current	9.6	9.7	12.0	10.1		12.4
100.0	100.0	100.0	Total	100.0	100.0	100.0	100.0		100.0
			LIABILITIES						
10.2	12.2	11.2	Notes Payable-Short Term	14.6	11.0	8.7	5.0		6.8
5.4	5.8	6.0	Cur. Mat.-L.T.D.	5.2	6.3	9.0	4.4		4.9
9.2	8.2	10.6	Trade Payables	14.0	9.2	6.9	8.7		13.8
.1	.0	.1	Income Taxes Payable	.1	.1	.4	.0		.1
15.6	16.0	13.8	All Other Current	15.5	13.5	15.6	8.8		8.2
40.4	42.1	41.7	Total Current	49.4	40.0	40.7	26.9		33.8
38.9	45.4	44.3	Long-Term Debt	48.3	46.7	32.6	42.9		23.5
.1	.1	.1	Deferred Taxes	.1	.0	.0	.0		.0
5.7	4.5	11.9	All Other Non-Current	19.3	9.9	5.7	8.3		1.8
14.9	7.9	2.0	Net Worth	-17.1	3.3	21.0	21.9		41.0
100.0	100.0	100.0	Total Liabilities & Net Worth	100.0	100.0	100.0	100.0		100.0
			INCOME DATA						
100.0	100.0	100.0	Net Sales	100.0	100.0	100.0	100.0		100.0
			Gross Profit						
90.0	90.4	89.7	Operating Expenses	85.6	90.9	91.1	94.0		95.5
10.0	9.6	10.3	Operating Profit	14.4	9.1	8.9	6.0		4.5
3.1	3.4	2.9	All Other Expenses (net)	5.9	2.0	.8	.4		.0
6.9	6.2	7.4	Profit Before Taxes	8.5	7.1	8.1	5.6		4.5
			RATIOS						
2.9	2.5	3.1	Current	3.4	2.8	3.5	3.4		3.7
1.1	.9	1.0		.7	1.1	1.3	1.3		1.4
.4	.4	.4		.2	.4	.6	.8		.7
1.8	1.8	2.2	Quick	2.2	2.1	2.6	3.3		2.0
.6 (506)	.5 (517)	.6		.4 (239)	.7	.8	1.0		1.0
.2	.2	.2		.1	.2	.3	.4		.3
0 UND	0 UND	0 UND	Sales/Receivables	0 UND	0 UND	0 UND	0 UND	2	219.0
0 UND	0 UND	0 UND		0 UND	0 UND	0 UND	0 857.8	8	45.1
3 132.2	3 108.7	3 106.4		2 154.8	4 101.1	3 124.7	6 58.5	36	10.2
			Cost of Sales/Inventory						
			Cost of Sales/Payables						
19.2	20.4	17.6	Sales/Working Capital	16.9	20.8	19.5	13.7		7.9
400.0	-202.0	999.8		-50.0	275.5	94.6	56.3		19.4
-16.2	-15.1	-15.8		-7.7	-19.1	-31.2	-64.6		-197.4
12.7	12.2	16.8	EBIT/Interest	8.5	13.1	36.1	61.0		31.2
(301) 3.4	(391) 3.6	(404) 4.1		(111) 2.8	(190) 4.2	(46) 10.1	(39) 7.3	(12)	10.4
1.0	.9	1.3		.6	1.4	2.1	1.4		2.5
5.2	7.0	5.4	Net Profit + Depr., Dep., Amort./Cur. Mat. L/T/D						
(16) 4.1	(19) 4.8	(14) 1.5							
.7	1.1	.8							
.5	.7	.7	Fixed/Worth	.8	.8	.5	.4		.3
4.4	15.1	4.2		35.0	4.2	2.0	1.6		.7
-1.1	-.8	-.8		-.5	-.5	-2.3	-6.1		NM
1.1	1.2	1.0	Debt/Worth	1.0	1.1	.8	.7		.6
15.0	69.0	12.5		-90.7	12.7	4.9	2.1		1.4
-3.2	-2.7	-3.0		-2.0	-2.6	-3.9	-10.3		NM
180.8	201.1	180.8	% Profit Before Taxes/Tangible Net Worth	140.2	239.6	202.5	196.2		249.5
(220) 62.8	(265) 61.4	(292) 61.4		(78) 51.2	(135) 67.0	(33) 83.2	(30) 69.2	(10)	54.6
20.7	13.1	13.8		9.7	20.8	26.3	22.0		15.3
46.8	46.5	41.6	% Profit Before Taxes/Total Assets	36.8	40.2	68.8	45.7		36.2
14.9	13.6	14.2		8.0	16.0	31.6	17.9		13.1
.7	.0	1.9		-1.6	3.5	4.3	2.4		3.0
62.9	-45.3	52.6	Sales/Net Fixed Assets	38.0	56.7	100.5	44.9		75.3
20.5	15.6	15.7		11.1	18.6	21.0	17.7		11.0
6.7	4.6	4.4		1.9	5.6	8.4	4.3		6.2
9.3	7.6	7.8	Sales/Total Assets	5.6	8.2	10.7	8.9		6.4
4.4	3.8	3.8		2.9	4.0	6.2	5.2		3.0
2.0	1.8	1.8		1.1	2.0	2.3	2.5		2.7
1.0	1.1	1.1	% Depr., Dep., Amort./Sales	1.1	1.1	1.2	1.1		
(246) 2.0	(347) 2.5	(323) 2.4		(97) 3.6	(146) 2.2	(33) 2.0	(33) 2.3		
4.2	4.9	4.6		7.0	4.4	2.8	3.8		
5.3	5.8	5.4	% Officers', Directors' Owners' Comp/Sales	7.5	4.9	5.4	5.1		
(243) 9.0	(321) 9.6	(336) 8.4		(89) 11.0	(169) 7.7	(42) 8.0	(24) 8.9		
15.1	14.0	14.0		15.8	11.6	13.0	17.1		
3343372M	7263151M	3612776M	Net Sales ($)	95868M	415128M	210171M	307477M	84668M	2499464M
1013487M	1510029M	1116320M	Total Assets ($)	77682M	170334M	56878M	91232M	52015M	668179M

M = $ thousand   MM = $ million
See Pages 9 through 22 for Explanation of Ratios and Data

Current Data Sorted by Assets   Comparative Historical Data

0-500M	500M-2MM	2-10MM	10-50MM	50-100MM	100-250MM	Type of Statement	4/1/06-3/31/07 ALL	4/1/07-3/31/08 ALL
2	8	42	33	14	10	Unqualified	133	99
5	23	61	14	1		Reviewed	88	76
26	43	25	2			Compiled	133	105
159	129	49	6	1	2	Tax Returns	236	242
122	158	158	57	11	11	Other	336	331
	118 (4/1-9/30/10)		1,054 (10/1/10-3/31/11)					
314	361	335	112	27	23	**NUMBER OF STATEMENTS**	926	853
%	%	%	%	%	%	**ASSETS**	%	%
31.1	18.3	13.9	18.0	17.9	10.5	Cash & Equivalents	16.6	19.3
18.2	33.2	37.0	29.5	32.1	21.9	Trade Receivables (net)	28.9	28.3
3.4	5.9	6.8	3.0	1.1	2.2	Inventory	6.6	6.8
3.9	3.5	4.1	4.8	5.0	6.3	All Other Current	4.8	4.9
56.6	60.9	61.8	55.3	56.1	40.9	Total Current	56.9	59.3
24.0	24.7	21.8	25.2	22.8	19.0	Fixed Assets (net)	27.0	25.2
4.7	4.7	6.5	7.9	13.6	29.7	Intangibles (net)	5.5	4.9
14.7	9.7	9.9	11.6	7.5	10.5	All Other Non-Current	10.7	10.5
100.0	100.0	100.0	100.0	100.0	100.0	Total	100.0	100.0
						LIABILITIES		
23.2	11.8	9.5	8.7	7.8	7.9	Notes Payable-Short Term	13.0	14.5
4.2	3.2	2.8	2.3	2.4	1.6	Cur. Mat.-L.T.D.	4.3	3.5
7.9	11.2	13.6	11.6	11.3	8.1	Trade Payables	12.5	13.1
.2	.2	.3	.2	1.2	.3	Income Taxes Payable	.4	.4
22.6	12.8	12.3	12.2	18.7	16.8	All Other Current	18.1	17.6
58.1	39.2	38.6	35.0	41.5	34.7	Total Current	48.3	49.1
21.0	17.2	12.9	14.7	19.9	22.1	Long-Term Debt	20.5	18.2
.1	.1	.2	.2	.2	2.1	Deferred Taxes	.3	.2
15.3	6.6	7.8	6.1	7.5	33.5	All Other Non-Current	6.2	6.3
5.6	36.8	40.5	44.0	31.0	7.5	Net Worth	24.8	26.1
100.0	100.0	100.0	100.0	100.0	100.0	Total Liabilties & Net Worth	100.0	100.0
						INCOME DATA		
100.0	100.0	100.0	100.0	100.0	100.0	Net Sales	100.0	100.0
						Gross Profit		
89.7	91.5	92.0	91.6	86.9	91.4	Operating Expenses	90.8	89.8
10.3	8.5	8.0	8.4	13.1	8.6	Operating Profit	9.2	10.2
1.3	2.3	1.6	2.0	6.9	5.9	All Other Expenses (net)	2.1	2.1
9.0	6.2	6.4	6.4	6.2	2.7	Profit Before Taxes	7.1	8.2
						RATIOS		
4.0	4.0	3.4	3.2	2.1	1.7	Current	2.5	2.9
1.3	1.7	1.7	1.6	1.5	1.2		1.4	1.4
.5	.9	1.1	1.0	.9	1.0		.8	.8
3.5	3.5	2.9	2.7	1.9	1.4	Quick	2.1	2.4
1.1	1.5	1.4	1.3	1.1	1.1		1.1	1.1
.4	.6	.7	.8	.9	.7		.5	.6
0 UND	3 138.5	28 13.3	25 14.4	42 8.7	28 13.1	Sales/Receivables	1 673.4	0 UND
0 UND	32 11.4	49 7.4	49 7.4	55 6.7	67 5.5		33 11.0	29 12.8
27 13.6	57 6.4	73 5.0	69 5.3	75 4.9	126 2.9		62 5.9	62 5.9
						Cost of Sales/Inventory		
						Cost of Sales/Payables		
12.2	6.2	5.1	4.0	2.3	4.6	Sales/Working Capital	7.8	6.6
120.9	15.8	11.4	12.0	14.6	10.8		22.3	20.8
-21.4	-70.5	77.4	220.0	-39.8	189.5		-46.8	-54.3
17.3	24.8	43.4	31.7	48.3	11.1	EBIT/Interest	17.0	16.9
(177) 4.4	(278) 5.2	(269) 7.3	(85) 7.8	(20) 2.8	(21) 3.6		(715) 4.3	(644) 5.1
.7	1.0	1.5	1.8	1.1	.7		1.1	1.5
	4.8	7.9	32.1			Net Profit + Depr., Dep., Amort./Cur. Mat. L/T/D	6.5	7.2
	(17) 1.9	(35) 3.2	(18) 4.0				(99) 2.4	(71) 3.1
	-2.1	1.6	1.9				1.0	.9
.0	.1	.1	.1	.1	.6	Fixed/Worth	.1	.1
.6	.5	.4	.6	1.0	-2.0		.6	.6
-2.4	2.8	1.6	1.9	-.9	-.2		4.3	4.7
.4	.5	.5	.5	1.1	2.6	Debt/Worth	.7	.6
3.9	1.8	1.7	1.3	3.3	-9.4		2.5	2.3
-3.6	9.8	5.5	5.0	-4.1	-1.6		28.8	66.2
235.4	83.2	72.9	61.4	44.6		% Profit Before Taxes/Tangible Net Worth	86.5	93.6
(199) 80.0	(300) 33.4	(286) 33.9	(97) 30.5	(18) 10.4			(730) 37.1	(657) 40.6
19.4	3.9	4.9	10.1	2.7			7.9	11.3
83.4	31.2	25.8	20.2	16.2	11.3	% Profit Before Taxes/Total Assets	29.4	34.0
25.3	9.8	11.4	9.1	3.9	2.6		9.6	12.0
1.0	.1	1.4	1.8	.1	-2.4		.7	1.4
964.1	160.7	75.1	47.2	79.0	19.7	Sales/Net Fixed Assets	80.0	86.4
56.5	29.6	20.1	16.2	17.8	14.1		22.1	24.5
15.6	6.0	6.6	3.4	2.7	5.4		6.7	7.1
12.6	4.9	3.2	2.9	2.1	1.4	Sales/Total Assets	4.8	4.8
5.4	3.1	2.5	1.8	1.4	.6		3.0	2.8
2.9	1.7	1.6	.9	.4	.4		1.6	1.6
.4	.4	.6	.6	.5	1.2	% Depr., Dep., Amort./Sales	.6	.6
(148) 1.1	(236) 1.4	(254) 1.4	(94) 2.3	(21) 1.7	(10) 3.4		(672) 1.6	(584) 1.5
3.0	4.2	3.5	5.3	7.6	6.2		3.6	3.9
5.9	3.0	2.2	1.2			% Officers', Directors' Owners' Comp/Sales	2.8	3.3
(158) 10.7	(173) 7.0	(105) 4.0	(15) 2.4				(359) 6.1	(327) 6.2
20.0	11.4	7.1	4.6				11.9	13.0
548238M	1425217M	3625753M	4802189M	3533703M	5679352M	Net Sales ($)	12902099M	12909839M
73219M	386528M	1419640M	2305709M	1943373M	3793933M	Total Assets ($)	8076763M	7953824M

© RMA 2011   M = $ thousand   MM = $ million
See Pages 9 through 22 for Explanation of Ratios and Data

Comparative Historical Data | **Current Data Sorted by Sales**

Type of Statement	4/1/08-3/31/09 ALL	4/1/09-3/31/10 ALL	4/1/10-3/31/11 ALL	0-1MM	1-3MM	3-5MM	5-10MM	10-25MM	25MM & OVER
Unqualified	83	119	109	3	7	10	11	32	46
Reviewed	71	103	104	4	14	15	28	31	12
Compiled	90	128	96	12	26	21	23	8	6
Tax Returns	314	334	346	105	105	57	50	23	6
Other	283	373	517	92	111	84	82	84	64
				118 (4/1-9/30/10)		1,054 (10/1/10-3/31/11)			
NUMBER OF STATEMENTS	841	1057	1172	216	263	187	194	178	134
ASSETS	%	%	%	%	%	%	%	%	%
Cash & Equivalents	20.6	20.6	20.3	25.6	21.5	19.3	19.0	17.5	16.5
Trade Receivables (net)	28.1	27.3	29.6	12.8	23.5	35.1	34.2	41.1	39.6
Inventory	5.5	5.5	5.0	2.7	5.8	5.6	6.4	5.7	3.3
All Other Current	4.1	4.4	4.0	3.5	3.9	3.3	3.7	4.4	5.8
Total Current	58.3	57.8	59.0	44.6	54.7	63.3	63.4	68.6	65.2
Fixed Assets (net)	24.1	24.4	23.6	34.2	26.3	21.5	20.4	18.5	15.3
Intangibles (net)	5.6	6.1	6.2	3.9	6.1	4.9	6.9	5.8	11.5
All Other Non-Current	11.9	11.7	11.2	17.3	12.9	10.2	9.3	7.1	8.1
Total	100.0	100.0	100.0	100.0	100.0	100.0	100.0	100.0	100.0
LIABILITIES									
Notes Payable-Short Term	15.5	16.1	13.7	10.6	19.7	14.4	13.3	11.9	9.3
Cur. Mat.-L.T.D.	4.4	3.8	3.2	2.8	3.9	2.8	3.8	3.1	2.4
Trade Payables	11.4	10.6	11.0	5.7	10.3	10.9	12.1	14.9	14.2
Income Taxes Payable	.2	.2	.3	.0	.3	.2	.2	.1	.9
All Other Current	17.5	16.1	15.5	21.3	12.5	14.4	13.7	13.5	18.4
Total Current	49.1	46.7	43.6	40.4	46.7	42.6	43.2	43.6	45.2
Long-Term Debt	17.3	17.1	16.9	28.6	16.1	17.3	11.6	12.3	12.9
Deferred Taxes	.2	.2	.2	.1	.2	.1	.2	.2	.5
All Other Non-Current	7.4	7.2	9.8	12.3	11.2	10.4	7.5	5.2	11.3
Net Worth	26.0	28.8	29.5	18.6	25.9	29.6	37.5	38.7	30.1
Total Liabilities & Net Worth	100.0	100.0	100.0	100.0	100.0	100.0	100.0	100.0	100.0
INCOME DATA									
Net Sales	100.0	100.0	100.0	100.0	100.0	100.0	100.0	100.0	100.0
Gross Profit									
Operating Expenses	90.6	91.8	91.1	84.1	92.5	93.2	92.6	92.4	92.4
Operating Profit	9.4	8.2	8.9	15.9	7.5	6.8	7.4	7.6	7.6
All Other Expenses (net)	2.0	1.8	2.0	5.8	1.1	1.0	1.0	.6	2.3
Profit Before Taxes	7.4	6.4	6.9	10.0	6.5	5.8	6.3	7.0	5.3
RATIOS									
Current	3.0	3.3	3.5	4.6	4.4	3.5	4.0	2.7	2.4
	1.4	1.5	1.6	1.1	1.4	1.7	1.8	1.6	1.5
	.8	.8	.9	.4	.6	1.0	1.1	1.1	1.1
Quick	2.5	2.7	3.1	4.0	3.3	3.3	3.7	2.5	2.0
	1.2	1.2	1.3	1.0	1.1	1.5	1.4	1.4	1.3
	.5	.6	.6	.3	.4	.7	.7	.9	.9
Sales/Receivables	0 UND	0 UND	0 UND	0 UND	0 UND	10 35.9	14 26.3	23 15.8	31 11.9
	29 12.8	31 11.9	34 10.8	0 UND	22 16.5	39 9.5	40 9.2	48 7.5	51 7.2
	57 6.4	58 6.3	60 6.0	31 11.7	50 7.3	69 5.3	64 5.7	72 5.1	69 5.3
Cost of Sales/Inventory									
Cost of Sales/Payables									
Sales/Working Capital	7.1	6.8	6.1	6.7	6.7	6.0	5.6	6.5	5.5
	23.8	22.8	18.3	92.8	31.7	14.2	13.8	15.2	14.4
	-42.1	-40.2	-63.9	-9.7	-21.2	-226.2	112.9	82.1	109.0
EBIT/Interest	26.6	25.0	27.7	13.2	13.7	24.5	37.8	63.3	32.9
	(621) 6.5	(800) 5.3	(850) 6.1	(111) 3.0	(185) 2.8	(144) 4.9	(155) 8.6	(151) 16.6	(104) 8.9
	1.4	.7	1.2	.5	.1	1.2	2.0	2.7	2.1
Net Profit + Depr., Dep., Amort./Cur. Mat. L/T/D	7.1	6.8	8.6			8.6	7.1	23.3	12.8
	(58) 3.5	(77) 2.7	(86) 3.0			(11) 1.2	(19) 3.7	(20) 3.1	(27) 3.8
	1.5	.8	1.2			-1.3	1.3	.9	1.5
Fixed/Worth	.1	.1	.1	.0	.1	.1	.1	.1	.1
	.7	.6	.5	.9	.8	.4	.5	.3	.4
	6.8	6.3	4.8	98.5	-16.4	2.5	2.0	1.3	-14.1
Debt/Worth	.6	.6	.5	.5	.4	.5	.5	.6	.9
	2.7	1.9	2.0	2.8	1.9	2.0	1.6	1.5	2.7
	342.5	64.7	26.2	-23.8	-22.6	17.0	9.0	4.4	-20.2
% Profit Before Taxes/Tangible Net Worth	101.3	81.5	91.0	140.7	73.6	91.0	92.3	91.3	75.2
	(643) 43.8	(817) 32.6	(908) 36.6	(156) 37.2	(186) 25.8	(152) 34.2	(162) 38.0	(153) 45.1	(99) 42.2
	9.3	4.8	6.3	1.7	2.9	3.1	8.4	14.3	19.0
% Profit Before Taxes/Total Assets	36.8	31.0	33.6	41.3	37.7	36.2	30.2	33.8	22.6
	13.2	9.5	12.2	9.9	8.6	11.3	13.2	15.5	11.6
	.9	-.1	.8	-.3	-.4	.6	2.2	4.5	3.0
Sales/Net Fixed Assets	124.7	120.7	143.6	320.8	124.3	179.2	120.5	142.7	96.4
	31.9	28.1	28.5	16.9	23.9	38.3	28.6	34.5	30.8
	7.5	7.8	7.3	1.6	6.2	9.1	10.0	11.0	10.7
Sales/Total Assets	5.8	5.1	5.0	5.1	5.0	5.4	5.3	4.8	4.0
	3.0	2.9	2.9	2.0	3.0	3.2	3.0	3.0	2.7
	1.6	1.5	1.6	.6	1.7	2.1	1.9	2.2	1.4
% Depr., Dep., Amort./Sales	.5	.5	.5	1.2	.6	.4	.4	.4	.4
	(525) 1.5	(716) 1.5	(763) 1.5	(115) 3.7	(159) 1.7	(124) 1.0	(131) 1.5	(133) 1.1	(101) 1.1
	4.1	3.9	3.8	15.7	4.1	3.2	3.1	2.4	2.6
% Officers', Directors' Owners' Comp/Sales	2.8	3.4	3.1	8.2	4.6	3.3	2.3	1.7	.9
	(341) 6.1	(455) 7.2	(457) 7.0	(82) 14.4	(136) 8.3	(80) 7.0	(87) 4.9	(51) 2.5	(21) 2.3
	12.0	14.7	13.2	24.8	14.0	11.8	8.3	4.6	4.4
Net Sales ($)	16366600M	14078423M	19614452M	106988M	494476M	740634M	1395760M	2760744M	14115850M
Total Assets ($)	6377385M	8524632M	9922402M	138274M	290581M	595464M	708757M	1331946M	6857380M

M = $ thousand   MM = $ million
See Pages 9 through 22 for Explanation of Ratios and Data

MANAGEMENT OF
COMPANIES AND
ENTERPRISES

Current Data Sorted by Assets

Comparative Historical Data

Type of Statement		
Unqualified	7	9
Reviewed	1	
Compiled	4	6
Tax Returns	3	2
Other	7	9

							4/1/06-3/31/07	4/1/07-3/31/08
	5 4 (4/1-9/30/10)			23 (10/1/10-3/31/11)			ALL	ALL
0-500M	500M-2MM	2-10MM	10-50MM	50-100MM	100-250MM	NUMBER OF STATEMENTS	22	26
5	11	7	3	1				

%	%	%	%	%	%		%	%
						ASSETS		
		19.3				Cash & Equivalents	15.2	7.5
		5.2				Trade Receivables (net)	7.0	14.4
		9.6				Inventory	2.5	3.2
		1.1				All Other Current	5.9	11.4
		35.1				Total Current	30.6	36.5
		26.8				Fixed Assets (net)	29.9	17.0
		17.0				Intangibles (net)	5.2	3.3
		21.2				All Other Non-Current	34.3	43.2
		100.0				Total	100.0	100.0
						LIABILITIES		
		7.9				Notes Payable-Short Term	8.4	10.0
		2.5				Cur. Mat.-L.T.D.	2.7	1.4
		9.5				Trade Payables	1.8	9.0
		.0				Income Taxes Payable	.1	.1
		5.4				All Other Current	14.6	10.6
		25.2				Total Current	27.6	31.0
		36.4				Long-Term Debt	28.3	28.4
		.2				Deferred Taxes	.5	.5
		.2				All Other Non-Current	3.3	3.4
		38.0				Net Worth	40.3	36.7
		100.0				Total Liabilties & Net Worth	100.0	100.0
						INCOME DATA		
		100.0				Net Sales	100.0	100.0
						Gross Profit		
		65.1				Operating Expenses	57.8	55.9
		34.9				Operating Profit	42.2	44.1
		7.6				All Other Expenses (net)	9.5	9.6
		27.3				Profit Before Taxes	32.7	34.5
						RATIOS		
		2.7					2.4	1.8
		.8				Current	.8	1.1
		.1					.1	.2
		2.3					2.2	1.3
		.4				Quick	.4	.6
		.1					.1	.1
	0	UND					0 UND	0 UND
	0	UND				Sales/Receivables	0 UND	0 UND
	1	357.8					16 22.3	50 7.3
						Cost of Sales/Inventory		
						Cost of Sales/Payables		
		8.2					1.6	1.8
		-58.3				Sales/Working Capital	NM	10.8
		-10.9					-3.2	-2.8
							11.9	14.3
						EBIT/Interest	(15) 6.2	(18) 5.3
							1.8	2.5
						Net Profit + Depr., Dep., Amort./Cur. Mat. L/T/D		
		.1					.0	.0
		1.0				Fixed/Worth	.2	.3
		13.4					6.7	.7
		.5					.2	.2
		2.1				Debt/Worth	3.2	2.5
		23.2					15.6	11.9
							68.8	20.0
						% Profit Before Taxes/Tangible Net Worth	(20) 17.2	(23) 11.5
							7.6	4.8
		14.2					9.8	9.8
		8.0				% Profit Before Taxes/Total Assets	4.2	5.7
		3.7					1.8	1.0
		789.1					UND	UND
		42.3				Sales/Net Fixed Assets	6.7	35.0
		.4					.5	1.4
		4.0					.8	.6
		1.0				Sales/Total Assets	.2	.2
		.1					.1	.1
							4.1	3.1
						% Depr., Dep., Amort./Sales	(11) 14.6	(14) 4.9
							16.3	10.2
						% Officers', Directors' Owners' Comp/Sales		
3752M	147504M	47801M	166391M	7321M		Net Sales ($)	412167M	395807M
7179M	47486M	102013M	183194M	142741M		Total Assets ($)	972300M	1580016M

The left column between the header and the assets table contains the vertical text: **DATA NOT AVAILABLE**

M = $ thousand   MM = $ million
See Pages 9 through 22 for Explanation of Ratios and Data

Comparative Historical Data   ## Current Data Sorted by Sales

4/1/08-3/31/09 ALL	4/1/09-3/31/10 ALL	4/1/10-3/31/11 ALL	Type of Statement	0-1MM	1-3MM	3-5MM	5-10MM	10-25MM	25MM & OVER
3	5	5	Unqualified				3		2
1	3	2	Reviewed			1		1	
5	5	3	Compiled	2				1	
3	5	2	Tax Returns	1				1	
13	16	15	Other	6	4	2		2	1
				4 (4/1-9/30/10)			23 (10/1/10-3/31/11)		
25	34	27	**NUMBER OF STATEMENTS**	9	4	3	3	5	3
%	%	%	**ASSETS**	%	%	%	%	%	%
8.7	7.8	11.8	Cash & Equivalents						
19.6	18.1	11.4	Trade Receivables (net)						
6.1	6.6	5.2	Inventory						
4.3	6.0	1.3	All Other Current						
38.8	38.4	29.7	Total Current						
30.6	23.8	38.4	Fixed Assets (net)						
7.9	7.2	8.9	Intangibles (net)						
22.8	30.6	23.0	All Other Non-Current						
100.0	100.0	100.0	Total						
			LIABILITIES						
10.2	14.0	10.4	Notes Payable-Short Term						
1.3	1.5	3.5	Cur. Mat.-L.T.D.						
7.9	12.5	5.2	Trade Payables						
.3	.2	.0	Income Taxes Payable						
11.6	5.8	4.5	All Other Current						
31.3	34.0	23.7	Total Current						
25.5	17.5	30.7	Long-Term Debt						
.4	.4	.2	Deferred Taxes						
2.3	2.6	5.8	All Other Non-Current						
40.5	45.5	39.5	Net Worth						
100.0	100.0	100.0	Total Liabilties & Net Worth						
			INCOME DATA						
100.0	100.0	100.0	Net Sales						
			Gross Profit						
61.4	67.2	63.9	Operating Expenses						
38.6	32.8	36.1	Operating Profit						
16.6	12.2	7.3	All Other Expenses (net)						
22.0	20.6	28.8	Profit Before Taxes						
			RATIOS						
1.9	1.9	1.9							
1.1	1.2	1.1	Current						
.7	.3	.5							
1.5	1.3	1.7							
.8	.7	.9	Quick						
.4	.1	.2							
0 UND	0 UND	0 UND							
26 13.8	1 667.7	0 UND	Sales/Receivables						
69 5.3	42 8.6	32 11.3							
			Cost of Sales/Inventory						
			Cost of Sales/Payables						
1.9	4.6	8.0							
18.0	21.7	37.5	Sales/Working Capital						
-5.7	-4.2	-8.6							
24.4	6.3	12.6							
(17) 4.9	(17) 3.5	(19) 4.8	EBIT/Interest						
1.9	.9	2.0							
			Net Profit + Depr., Dep., Amort./Cur. Mat. L/T/D						
.0	.0	.1							
.8	.3	1.1	Fixed/Worth						
3.1	2.1	8.4							
.5	.3	.4							
2.1	1.3	2.7	Debt/Worth						
8.5	7.7	12.5							
27.3	28.1	43.8							
(21) 14.2	(30) 7.0	(23) 14.2	% Profit Before Taxes/Tangible Net Worth						
1.3	2.8	5.5							
12.6	7.5	11.4							
4.8	3.6	6.5	% Profit Before Taxes/Total Assets						
.9	.4	2.9							
114.3	UND	105.1							
8.2	44.6	4.6	Sales/Net Fixed Assets						
.4	2.6	.4							
1.0	1.9	1.5							
.3	.4	.3	Sales/Total Assets						
.1	.1	.1							
1.4	1.3	1.2							
(18) 4.5	(17) 5.2	(17) 4.1	% Depr., Dep., Amort./Sales						
13.4	11.7	16.4							
			% Officers', Directors' Owners' Comp/Sales						
273688M	488754M	372769M	Net Sales ($)	3642M	7629M	12038M	24004M	68806M	256650M
880307M	974903M	482613M	Total Assets ($)	33551M	42178M	68364M	168120M	34722M	135678M

M = $ thousand   MM = $ million
See Pages 9 through 22 for Explanation of Ratios and Data

Current Data Sorted by Assets

Comparative Historical Data

						Type of Statement		
2	3	10	40	14	19	Unqualified	100	86
1	8	24	12	2	3	Reviewed	67	59
8	24	49	11	1	1	Compiled	130	121
40	109	82	15	1	1	Tax Returns	221	244
26	66	87	59	16	16	Other	275	252
	74 (4/1-9/30/10)		675 (10/1/10-3/31/11)				4/1/06-3/31/07	4/1/07-3/31/08
0-500M	500M-2MM	2-10MM	10-50MM	50-100MM	100-250MM		ALL	ALL
77	210	252	137	34	39	NUMBER OF STATEMENTS	793	762
%	%	%	%	%	%	ASSETS	%	%
16.7	6.0	7.2	10.4	12.8	8.7	Cash & Equivalents	8.2	9.2
6.8	4.3	8.4	13.1	18.7	16.0	Trade Receivables (net)	7.0	8.0
4.4	2.2	4.9	6.6	10.9	7.5	Inventory	5.5	4.9
5.2	2.2	2.7	4.6	5.2	5.5	All Other Current	3.7	3.3
33.1	14.7	23.3	34.7	47.5	37.7	Total Current	24.4	25.5
48.0	74.1	57.4	45.3	33.3	30.6	Fixed Assets (net)	60.9	59.3
5.2	1.6	4.5	6.1	6.1	16.1	Intangibles (net)	3.5	3.3
13.7	9.6	14.8	13.9	13.0	15.6	All Other Non-Current	11.2	12.0
100.0	100.0	100.0	100.0	100.0	100.0	Total	100.0	100.0
						LIABILITIES		
10.2	5.2	5.4	6.3	5.9	3.4	Notes Payable-Short Term	6.1	5.3
8.0	3.7	3.8	4.0	2.6	3.2	Cur. Mat.-L.T.D.	4.4	4.1
4.8	1.3	3.6	6.6	11.3	5.5	Trade Payables	3.7	4.7
.1	.0	.1	.1	.1	.2	Income Taxes Payable	.1	.1
12.4	6.5	8.2	9.4	10.6	12.9	All Other Current	8.2	8.1
35.6	16.7	21.0	26.4	30.4	25.2	Total Current	22.6	22.3
45.9	54.9	41.3	27.7	23.3	27.5	Long-Term Debt	44.6	44.0
.0	.0	.1	.5	.6	2.3	Deferred Taxes	.3	.4
19.4	5.3	3.7	4.4	9.4	6.2	All Other Non-Current	5.1	4.3
-.9	23.1	33.8	41.0	36.3	38.9	Net Worth	27.5	29.0
100.0	100.0	100.0	100.0	100.0	100.0	Total Liabilities & Net Worth	100.0	100.0
						INCOME DATA		
100.0	100.0	100.0	100.0	100.0	100.0	Net Sales	100.0	100.0
						Gross Profit		
71.4	52.4	61.5	74.2	94.3	84.1	Operating Expenses	61.8	62.8
28.6	47.6	38.5	25.8	5.7	15.9	Operating Profit	38.2	37.2
8.2	21.5	16.2	8.4	2.3	5.3	All Other Expenses (net)	17.5	16.9
20.4	26.1	22.3	17.5	3.4	10.5	Profit Before Taxes	20.8	20.3
						RATIOS		
2.5	1.9	2.0	2.0	2.7	2.8		2.1	2.4
.8	.7	1.0	1.2	1.5	1.3	Current	1.0	1.1
.2	.2	.3	.6	1.1	.7		.3	.3
1.5	1.5	1.5	1.5	1.6	1.8		1.4	1.7
.5	.5	.6	.8	1.1	.8	Quick	(790) .6	.7
.2	.1	.2	.3	.6	.4		.2	.2
0 UND	0 UND	0 UND	0 UND	26 14.3	29 12.4		0 UND	0 UND
0 UND	0 UND	0 UND	21 17.8	42 8.6	42 8.6	Sales/Receivables	0 UND	0 UND
4 88.3	2 184.4	34 10.7	47 7.7	72 5.1	61 6.0		27 13.5	32 11.3
						Cost of Sales/Inventory		
						Cost of Sales/Payables		
13.6	7.5	7.0	5.4	4.1	3.1		6.3	5.6
-61.7	-13.7	213.1	25.3	9.4	11.5	Sales/Working Capital	UND	136.5
-3.9	-2.6	-4.4	-9.5	88.5	-13.1		-3.7	-3.7
12.4	8.9	14.0	16.0	6.8	10.3		10.3	8.9
(36) 3.5	(85) 4.2	(139) 5.8	(100) 5.2	(29) 2.8	(35) 3.7	EBIT/Interest	(397) 3.7	(388) 4.1
.8	1.8	2.1	2.1	1.2	1.1		1.6	1.6
	3.5	3.3	6.5	23.1	2.8		6.4	5.1
(10)	1.7 (19)	1.3 (32)	3.4 (13)	2.2 (16)	1.6	Net Profit + Depr., Dep., Amort./Cur. Mat. L/T/D	(94) 2.4	(84) 2.2
	.3	1.1	2.0	1.0	.8		1.0	1.0
.1	1.5	.7	.3	.4	.1		.9	.8
1.9	3.3	2.2	1.4	.9	1.4	Fixed/Worth	2.6	2.3
UND	15.3	5.8	3.8	2.6	-999.8		11.0	7.9
.5	1.3	.9	.7	.9	.7		1.1	.9
3.0	3.2	2.4	1.8	1.9	3.4	Debt/Worth	3.0	2.6
-7.7	20.0	8.5	5.2	5.0	-16.2		15.0	11.3
58.4	44.4	39.3	36.3	35.1	33.6	% Profit Before Taxes/Tangible Net Worth	41.7	36.5
(53) 26.2	(170) 17.4	(216) 15.5	(121) 15.8	(30) 19.5	(27) 20.4		(648) 18.9	(631) 17.0
2.6	6.1	3.9	3.7	1.6	5.2		6.4	5.2
17.9	9.3	11.1	11.2	10.3	11.1	% Profit Before Taxes/Total Assets	11.9	11.5
7.7	4.5	5.1	6.1	2.7	4.6		4.8	4.9
.0	.7	1.0	1.8	.7	.1		1.1	.9
112.8	.5	8.9	16.1	17.7	12.6	Sales/Net Fixed Assets	8.7	8.7
3.9	.2	.3	2.7	5.7	4.8		.4	.4
.3	.1	.1	.2	1.4	1.6		.2	.2
4.1	.3	1.4	1.7	2.1	1.3	Sales/Total Assets	1.4	1.5
1.1	.2	.2	.8	1.3	.8		.2	.2
.2	.1	.1	.2	.6	.3		.1	.1
1.9	10.9	3.5	1.5	1.0	1.1	% Depr., Dep., Amort./Sales	3.2	2.8
(44) 8.1	(170) 17.8	(209) 15.4	(126) 5.1	(31) 2.8	(30) 3.1		(658) 12.6	(654) 12.0
22.0	25.4	22.2	15.5	5.7	10.8		20.8	19.7
4.4	4.7	2.0	.4			% Officers', Directors' Owners' Comp/Sales	2.5	1.5
(20) 18.9	(15) 17.3	(42) 4.4	(16) 1.9				(102) 6.7	(97) 3.8
28.2	33.6	10.3	3.4				16.4	10.3
53466M	110450M	1178658M	4039319M	3715533M	6187237M	Net Sales ($)	13250110M	17092827M
21073M	238572M	1204574M	3177388M	2407758M	6367676M	Total Assets ($)	11006164M	12427990M

M = $ thousand   MM = $ million

© RMA 2011

See Pages 9 through 22 for Explanation of Ratios and Data

Comparative Historical Data

Current Data Sorted by Sales

4/1/08-3/31/09 ALL	4/1/09-3/31/10 ALL	4/1/10-3/31/11 ALL	Type of Statement	0-1MM	1-3MM	3-5MM	5-10MM	10-25MM	25MM & OVER
82	89	88	Unqualified	7	6	5	7	10	53
52	62	50	Reviewed	16	7	4	6	9	8
112	92	93	Compiled	57	11	5	8	7	5
227	259	248	Tax Returns	180	25	16	9	12	6
261	253	270	Other	125	36	15	24	19	51
				74 (4/1-9/30/10)			675 (10/1/10-3/31/11)		
734	755	749	**NUMBER OF STATEMENTS**	385	85	45	54	57	123
%	%	%	**ASSETS**	%	%	%	%	%	%
8.3	9.1	8.8	Cash & Equivalents	6.8	9.6	7.3	12.2	10.8	12.3
8.2	7.7	8.8	Trade Receivables (net)	2.2	8.0	8.4	16.6	16.1	23.4
5.5	4.5	4.8	Inventory	.6	3.4	14.0	9.1	11.5	10.8
3.6	3.3	3.4	All Other Current	2.6	2.5	2.8	3.1	5.7	6.0
25.6	24.7	25.8	Total Current	12.2	23.5	32.5	41.0	44.2	52.5
57.1	56.7	56.4	Fixed Assets (net)	73.7	53.6	48.4	34.5	36.0	26.2
5.0	4.7	4.7	Intangibles (net)	1.9	5.3	5.1	7.7	6.7	10.7
12.3	13.9	13.0	All Other Non-Current	12.1	17.6	14.1	16.8	13.1	10.6
100.0	100.0	100.0	Total	100.0	100.0	100.0	100.0	100.0	100.0
			LIABILITIES						
5.9	6.8	5.9	Notes Payable-Short Term	5.0	6.7	5.0	6.4	6.0	8.3
5.4	4.5	4.1	Cur. Mat.-L.T.D.	4.5	3.7	4.8	3.0	6.5	2.7
5.1	4.4	4.1	Trade Payables	.8	3.2	4.6	6.0	10.9	10.8
.1	.3	.1	Income Taxes Payable	.0	.1	.1	.1	.0	.2
8.0	10.0	8.7	All Other Current	6.1	9.1	9.7	10.0	10.3	14.9
24.6	26.0	22.9	Total Current	16.4	22.8	24.3	25.4	33.8	36.9
42.1	42.6	41.6	Long-Term Debt	56.0	37.0	34.2	26.9	27.3	15.3
.2	.3	.3	Deferred Taxes	.0	.2	.0	.2	.6	1.2
5.2	6.3	6.3	All Other Non-Current	4.3	7.4	17.4	11.3	5.1	5.9
27.9	24.8	28.9	Net Worth	23.3	32.7	24.1	36.2	33.2	40.7
100.0	100.0	100.0	Total Liabilities & Net Worth	100.0	100.0	100.0	100.0	100.0	100.0
			INCOME DATA						
100.0	100.0	100.0	Net Sales	100.0	100.0	100.0	100.0	100.0	100.0
			Gross Profit						
66.8	66.6	64.9	Operating Expenses	48.1	64.5	76.9	85.3	93.0	91.7
33.2	33.4	35.1	Operating Profit	51.9	35.5	23.1	14.7	7.0	8.3
16.1	15.6	14.2	All Other Expenses (net)	22.9	11.4	8.1	3.7	2.6	1.2
17.2	17.8	20.8	Profit Before Taxes	29.0	24.1	15.0	11.0	4.4	7.0
			RATIOS						
2.0	2.0	2.1	Current	1.7	2.2	3.1	3.5	1.9	2.5
1.0	.9	1.0		.6	.9	1.4	1.4	1.3	1.4
.3	.3	.3		.2	.3	.5	.9	.9	1.0
1.3	1.4	1.5	Quick	1.5	1.4	1.3	3.0	1.3	1.6
(733) .6	.6	.7		.4	.7	.6	1.0	.8	.9
.2	.2	.2		.1	.2	.2	.4	.3	.5
0 UND	0 UND	0 UND	Sales/Receivables	0 UND	0 UND	1 335.2	3 111.8	18 20.4	23 16.2
0 UND	0 999.8	0 UND		0 UND	0 UND	12 29.4	26 13.8	37 9.9	42 8.7
34 10.7	29 12.5	36 10.0		0 UND	21 17.3	33 11.2	58 6.3	48 7.6	59 6.2
			Cost of Sales/Inventory						
			Cost of Sales/Payables						
7.5	8.0	6.2	Sales/Working Capital	7.5	9.5	6.7	2.8	5.7	6.2
-173.9	-71.0	173.0		-10.2	-89.8	21.4	10.2	13.4	13.1
-3.5	-3.3	-4.2		-2.3	-3.6	-26.4	-59.0	-43.5	-146.9
8.9	8.4	12.2	EBIT/Interest	10.0	9.6	6.5	21.3	12.2	16.9
(398) 3.6	(415) 3.5	(424) 4.6		(139) 4.8	(45) 3.0	(29) 2.7	(47) 5.9	(48) 2.9	(116) 6.5
1.3	1.3	1.9		2.9	.5	1.3	1.9	1.1	2.1
8.7	4.3	4.5	Net Profit + Depr., Dep., Amort./Cur. Mat. L/T/D	4.2					7.7
(97) 2.8	(88) 1.8	(90) 2.1		(11) 2.0				(53)	3.2
1.0	.8	1.1		1.3					1.2
.7	.7	.6	Fixed/Worth	1.4	.1	.4	.2	.4	.2
2.5	2.6	2.2		3.2	1.6	1.5	1.3	1.3	.9
13.4	21.8	8.5		12.1	5.0	5.7	3.0	3.3	3.0
1.1	1.0	.9	Debt/Worth	1.0	.6	.6	.8	.9	.8
3.2	3.4	2.5		3.1	1.8	2.0	2.4	2.4	1.9
20.6	40.4	12.9		15.0	27.5	8.8	5.9	5.9	7.9
41.2	38.6	39.3	% Profit Before Taxes/Tangible Net Worth	35.7	35.6	54.3	41.2	41.2	41.7
(594) 16.3	(593) 14.8	(617) 16.7		(316) 15.5	(67) 12.0	(40) 13.5	(45) 15.7	(49) 19.3	(100) 26.7
3.1	3.1	3.9		5.0	-.4	3.7	3.7	.2	8.8
10.5	9.3	11.2	% Profit Before Taxes/Total Assets	8.7	13.1	9.5	12.7	13.7	15.7
4.3	4.2	5.1		4.3	4.9	3.9	6.2	6.1	8.4
.3	.3	1.0		.8	-.3	.9	1.5	.1	2.2
10.4	10.0	10.9	Sales/Net Fixed Assets	.4	32.5	15.8	56.1	15.0	35.5
.5	.5	.6		.2	.8	2.7	6.3	6.6	10.7
.2	.2	.2		.1	.2	.2	.8	2.0	3.7
1.6	1.3	1.4	Sales/Total Assets	.2	1.8	1.8	1.8	2.2	2.8
.3	.3	.3		.2	.3	.9	1.3	1.4	1.6
.1	.1	.1		.1	.2	.2	.3	.9	1.0
2.1	3.4	3.2	% Depr., Dep., Amort./Sales	13.4	4.5	1.2	1.2	1.1	.9
(603) 11.2	(620) 13.3	(610) 12.9		(307) 18.9	(65) 11.9	(38) 5.6	(41) 3.7	(52) 3.3	(107) 2.3
20.0	21.6	21.4		26.3	20.4	18.0	11.7	6.6	3.7
1.4	2.1	1.7	% Officers', Directors' Owners' Comp/Sales	14.3	4.4		1.8	.6	.2
(90) 3.0	(95) 5.2	(99) 4.6		(22) 19.4	(20) 11.5	(20)	3.8	(14) 2.4	(16) 1.3
11.9	13.4	15.3		28.1	17.3		5.5	5.1	1.9
18547998M	13073172M	15284663M	Net Sales ($)	126791M	152871M	169918M	395241M	900681M	13539161M
14695221M	12414948M	13417041M	Total Assets ($)	866316M	618013M	525654M	1198424M	1116286M	9092348M

© RMA 2011

M = $ thousand   MM = $ million
See Pages 9 through 22 for Explanation of Ratios and Data

ADMINISTRATIVE AND SUPPORT AND WASTE MANAGEMENT AND REMEDIATION SERVICES

Current Data Sorted by Assets							Comparative Historical Data	
						Type of Statement		
						Unqualified	64	48
3	2	14	20	5	11	Reviewed	28	21
10	6	15	5			Compiled	23	15
32	5	4				Tax Returns	54	48
33	39	12	1			Other	87	109
	45	38	25	10	6		4/1/06-3/31/07	4/1/07-3/31/08
	50 (4/1-9/30/10)		291 (10/1/10-3/31/11)				ALL	ALL
0-500M	500M-2MM	2-10MM	10-50MM	50-100MM	100-250MM			
78	97	83	51	15	17	**NUMBER OF STATEMENTS**	256	241
%	%	%	%	%	%	**ASSETS**	%	%
25.1	20.9	16.8	20.5	10.7	10.9	Cash & Equivalents	21.2	19.2
12.1	20.8	30.6	28.0	17.0	9.2	Trade Receivables (net)	23.4	25.9
1.0	.9	3.2	2.3	2.7	4.0	Inventory	2.8	3.3
7.3	8.6	10.0	7.3	10.2	13.5	All Other Current	6.8	8.9
45.6	51.3	60.5	58.0	40.6	37.5	Total Current	54.1	57.3
19.8	29.8	24.3	22.8	32.7	30.9	Fixed Assets (net)	24.8	23.9
3.8	3.2	6.5	8.2	14.6	14.8	Intangibles (net)	6.2	5.6
30.9	15.7	8.7	11.0	12.1	16.8	All Other Non-Current	14.8	13.2
100.0	100.0	100.0	100.0	100.0	100.0	Total	100.0	100.0
						LIABILITIES		
7.9	7.9	6.9	5.5	.6	1.9	Notes Payable-Short Term	10.2	11.6
2.0	4.9	3.8	1.9	3.2	2.1	Cur. Mat.-L.T.D.	3.3	4.4
10.9	9.4	12.0	8.4	6.0	3.6	Trade Payables	9.6	9.6
.3	.2	.2	.6	.2	.2	Income Taxes Payable	.8	.3
30.2	23.6	14.6	18.6	18.3	24.9	All Other Current	26.4	19.8
51.4	45.9	37.4	35.0	28.4	32.6	Total Current	50.3	45.7
15.0	21.8	17.8	17.3	26.1	21.4	Long-Term Debt	20.1	15.7
.0	.0	.1	.5	.4	.5	Deferred Taxes	.3	.1
16.7	8.8	6.8	5.9	15.1	4.2	All Other Non-Current	5.8	6.5
16.9	23.5	37.9	41.4	30.0	41.3	Net Worth	23.6	32.0
100.0	100.0	100.0	100.0	100.0	100.0	Total Liabilities & Net Worth	100.0	100.0
						INCOME DATA		
100.0	100.0	100.0	100.0	100.0	100.0	Net Sales	100.0	100.0
						Gross Profit		
84.8	86.8	87.7	88.4	95.4	92.0	Operating Expenses	88.4	89.4
15.2	13.2	12.3	11.6	4.6	8.0	Operating Profit	11.6	10.6
.3	3.6	3.9	3.8	3.3	2.5	All Other Expenses (net)	2.2	1.8
15.0	9.6	8.5	7.8	1.3	5.5	Profit Before Taxes	9.3	8.8
						RATIOS		
5.7	3.5	3.7	2.6	2.0	2.0		2.9	2.5
1.1	1.5	1.6	1.8	1.3	1.6	Current	1.3	1.3
.5	.7	1.0	1.2	.9	.6		.7	.8
3.1	2.5	1.9	1.9	1.5	1.8		2.1	1.9
.8	1.0	1.3	1.3	1.1	1.1	Quick	1.0 (240)	1.1
.2	.5	.6	.8	.5	.3		.5	.6
0 UND	0 UND	0 UND	10 37.6	23 16.1	14 25.5		0 UND	0 UND
0 UND	4 90.7	26 13.8	37 10.0	51 7.1	31 11.6	Sales/Receivables	24 15.4	26 14.1
13 28.5	32 11.5	69 5.3	62 5.8	72 5.1	61 6.0		56 6.5	56 6.5
						Cost of Sales/Inventory		
						Cost of Sales/Payables		
17.8	8.1	3.9	3.3	5.6	4.3		6.2	5.8
311.8	26.5	12.3	7.8	12.9	8.4	Sales/Working Capital	28.4	27.6
-21.1	-17.6	-505.3	23.7	-71.3	-5.9		-29.7	-62.9
36.0	29.6	32.2	30.1	8.8	11.3		16.2	21.9
(35) 11.0	(58) 6.4	(61) 9.9	(40) 8.3	(13) 2.2	(16) 5.9	EBIT/Interest	(188) 3.9	(178) 6.5
2.4	1.4	1.7	2.6	.3	.9		1.1	1.4
			22.0				12.8	12.3
			(14) 5.0			Net Profit + Depr., Dep., Amort./Cur. Mat. L/T/D	(27) 3.1	(31) 5.5
			2.3				.8	1.6
.0	.1	.0	.1	.3	.5		.1	.1
.2	.6	.3	.5	1.1	.8	Fixed/Worth	.9	.5
-6.6	-17.4	4.8	1.7	-3.9	-10.0		-12.9	4.8
.3	.6	.8	.7	.9	.6		.8	.8
1.6	2.0	2.0	1.6	4.4	1.4	Debt/Worth	3.2	2.3
-7.2	-16.3	13.8	4.1	-10.8	-194.6		-17.6	15.4
159.1	69.7	92.3	57.9		23.9		90.3	83.5
(50) 69.5	(67) 27.9	(69) 23.6	(46) 24.1		(12) 11.6	% Profit Before Taxes/Tangible Net Worth	(185) 38.2	(194) 36.4
2.9	6.4	6.9	6.8		2.3		8.2	9.0
90.4	26.8	22.0	21.2	8.0	9.1		27.9	26.6
28.6	8.7	6.2	9.0	4.6	2.9	% Profit Before Taxes/Total Assets	8.9	10.5
1.5	.9	.9	2.0	-3.4	.2		.7	1.4
UND	104.2	168.5	63.8	13.8	10.7		84.7	216.4
53.6	17.6	39.6	15.2	4.7	5.0	Sales/Net Fixed Assets	25.2	32.6
16.9	4.4	4.1	4.3	.9	.8		6.9	6.5
10.2	5.3	3.8	3.2	1.9	1.7		4.4	4.9
5.7	2.5	1.9	1.8	.8	.8	Sales/Total Assets	2.6	2.6
2.4	1.1	.9	1.0	.5	.4		1.2	1.3
.5	.7	.3	.9	1.9	1.8		.6	.4
(32) 1.1	(68) 2.3	(69) 1.2	(41) 2.7	(12) 4.9	(10) 5.6	% Depr., Dep., Amort./Sales	(185) 1.8	(154) 1.3
2.4	5.9	5.6	4.1	8.5	14.5		4.0	4.1
6.1	5.3	1.5					3.5	2.0
(26) 10.1	(23) 9.9	(21) 4.2				% Officers', Directors' Owners' Comp/Sales	(57) 8.4	(55) 7.8
26.8	16.0	15.5					22.3	14.2
104019M	413033M	980137M	2728590M	1217616M	2625348M	Net Sales ($)	7361079M	8221137M
17415M	110544M	394351M	1213114M	1095702M	2740936M	Total Assets ($)	4481105M	3937202M

M = $ thousand   MM = $ million
See Pages 9 through 22 for Explanation of Ratios and Data

Comparative Historical Data / Current Data Sorted by Sales

			Type of Statement						
54	47	52	Unqualified	2	1	4	7	9	31
21	40	29	Reviewed	5	3	7	8		4
19	16	19	Compiled	9	2	3	2	3	
84	67	84	Tax Returns	29	25	14	11	3	2
140	142	157	Other	34	32	14	24	18	35
4/1/08-3/31/09 ALL	4/1/09-3/31/10 ALL	4/1/10-3/31/11 ALL		0-1MM	1-3MM	3-5MM	5-10MM	10-25MM	25MM & OVER
					50 (4/1-9/30/10)		291 (10/1/10-3/31/11)		
318	312	341	NUMBER OF STATEMENTS	74	65	38	51	41	72
%	%	%	ASSETS	%	%	%	%	%	%
19.7	20.1	19.9	Cash & Equivalents	15.9	24.7	18.3	20.5	22.1	18.7
20.4	22.8	21.5	Trade Receivables (net)	6.0	18.5	23.4	29.9	35.7	25.2
2.5	2.5	1.9	Inventory	.0	1.9	.9	1.7	3.3	3.8
7.1	6.7	8.8	All Other Current	9.6	8.0	11.9	5.2	11.7	7.8
49.7	52.2	52.1	Total Current	31.5	53.1	54.5	57.3	72.7	55.5
27.3	24.5	25.3	Fixed Assets (net)	36.5	24.1	24.6	21.7	15.4	23.7
7.4	9.6	5.9	Intangibles (net)	3.5	5.2	4.0	4.6	5.2	11.6
15.6	13.7	16.7	All Other Non-Current	28.5	17.7	16.9	16.3	6.6	9.3
100.0	100.0	100.0	Total	100.0	100.0	100.0	100.0	100.0	100.0
			LIABILITIES						
9.7	12.2	6.7	Notes Payable-Short Term	4.3	7.4	17.5	5.1	6.9	3.8
3.8	3.0	3.3	Cur. Mat.-L.T.D.	1.5	4.2	3.4	3.8	3.2	3.8
9.9	10.8	9.8	Trade Payables	9.6	7.1	8.4	11.8	15.8	8.4
.3	.5	.3	Income Taxes Payable	.0	.2	.6	.0	.5	.4
22.0	19.1	22.0	All Other Current	27.3	21.0	15.6	22.4	22.1	20.5
45.8	45.5	42.0	Total Current	42.7	39.9	45.4	43.1	48.5	36.9
22.1	22.8	18.8	Long-Term Debt	29.6	23.2	9.4	13.6	10.1	17.3
.1	.2	.2	Deferred Taxes	.0	.0	.0	.1	.2	.5
7.1	9.4	9.7	All Other Non-Current	9.3	17.6	7.8	11.3	2.3	7.1
24.9	22.0	29.3	Net Worth	18.4	19.2	37.4	31.8	39.0	38.2
100.0	100.0	100.0	Total Liabilities & Net Worth	100.0	100.0	100.0	100.0	100.0	100.0
			INCOME DATA						
100.0	100.0	100.0	Net Sales	100.0	100.0	100.0	100.0	100.0	100.0
			Gross Profit						
87.5	90.2	87.4	Operating Expenses	75.6	84.6	93.2	92.2	91.5	93.5
12.5	9.8	12.6	Operating Profit	24.4	15.4	6.8	7.8	8.5	6.5
3.4	2.9	2.9	All Other Expenses (net)	8.3	3.5	.0	.3	.1	1.8
9.2	6.9	9.7	Profit Before Taxes	16.2	12.0	6.8	7.5	8.5	4.7
			RATIOS						
2.3	2.7	3.0		6.5	6.6	3.6	3.5	2.8	2.0
1.3	1.4	1.5	Current	.9	2.1	1.6	1.5	1.8	1.5
.6	.7	.8		.2	.8	.8	.8	1.1	1.0
2.0	2.3	2.2		2.0	2.8	1.8	2.8	1.8	1.8
(317) 1.0	1.1	1.1	Quick	.4	1.0	1.0	1.5	1.3	1.2
.4	.4	.5		.1	.5	.5	.8	.8	.7
0 UND	0 UND	0 UND		0 UND	0 UND	1 637.0	0 UND	1 539.4	16 22.6
18 20.8	19 19.1	13 27.1	Sales/Receivables	0 UND	1 710.0	17 21.8	31 11.9	27 13.8	37 9.9
50 7.3	54 6.8	50 7.3		1 243.9	27 13.6	38 9.6	62 5.9	68 5.3	61 6.0
			Cost of Sales/Inventory						
			Cost of Sales/Payables						
7.4	6.3	6.2		9.0	5.7	7.2	6.2	5.1	5.6
38.5	22.9	19.2	Sales/Working Capital	-161.6	17.5	21.7	21.3	11.6	13.9
-17.8	-49.3	-35.7		-7.9	-22.7	-37.5	-42.0	105.6	164.3
16.6	26.0	27.6		15.9	27.6	27.4	25.0	150.0	17.1
(228) 5.5	(228) 6.7	(223) 7.0	EBIT/Interest	(29) 6.7	(39) 6.6	(26) 5.1	(35) 6.3	(31) 26.4	(63) 6.2
1.4	1.1	1.6		2.6	1.9	.7	.3	4.6	1.6
7.3	7.5	15.1							10.0
(30) 2.7	(32) 2.5	(29) 4.6	Net Profit + Depr., Dep., Amort./Cur. Mat. L/T/D					(12)	5.3
1.3	1.0	2.1							2.6
.1	.1	.1		.0	.0	.0	.0	.0	.2
.9	.7	.5	Fixed/Worth	1.7	.3	.3	.5	.3	.6
19.5	26.7	7.5		-7.0	3.5	82.5	2.8	1.8	5.1
.8	.7	.6		.4	.3	.6	.7	.8	.7
2.8	2.8	2.0	Debt/Worth	6.9	1.2	1.2	1.3	1.5	2.1
UND	-41.7	-144.5		-8.4	-17.1	-533.3	12.9	13.3	22.0
111.6	74.7	88.7		101.2	101.4	72.3	87.3	104.4	57.3
(240) 38.7	(229) 40.0	(252) 24.6	% Profit Before Taxes/Tangible Net Worth	(46) 35.4	(47) 26.1	(28) 21.2	(40) 21.8	(35) 35.3	(56) 21.9
9.4	8.7	6.0		6.2	1.8	1.5	.0	9.2	4.5
32.6	26.1	28.5		56.4	40.2	24.5	24.5	41.6	15.8
8.8	9.3	8.4	% Profit Before Taxes/Total Assets	8.2	12.5	6.9	7.1	13.9	7.1
1.2	.1	.9		.9	.6	-.7	.0	3.6	.5
123.2	112.8	137.8		245.0	154.7	101.7	109.7	400.8	81.7
21.4	26.0	22.7	Sales/Net Fixed Assets	13.8	30.5	27.0	29.7	39.6	12.8
5.0	6.1	5.0		.5	6.4	10.5	8.2	7.2	3.8
4.7	4.5	5.0		5.0	5.2	5.7	5.5	5.1	3.5
2.4	2.5	2.3	Sales/Total Assets	1.3	2.2	3.1	3.2	3.2	1.9
1.0	1.2	1.0		.3	1.1	1.5	1.5	1.5	1.2
.6	.5	.6		3.2	.5	1.0	.6	.2	.7
(205) 2.0	(210) 1.8	(232) 2.1	% Depr., Dep., Amort./Sales	(39) 12.0	(48) 1.1	(25) 2.0	(36) 1.2	(31) .7	(53) 2.1
5.5	4.1	5.4		23.5	2.6	3.5	6.1	3.1	4.5
3.2	3.9	3.4		8.7	5.2	3.9	2.4		
(73) 9.1	(79) 7.9	(75) 8.9	% Officers', Directors' Owners' Comp/Sales	(13) 16.2	(22) 12.4	(14) 11.1	(16) 6.6		
17.9	20.1	18.0		32.6	21.5	22.0	10.2		
9473596M	10977076M	8068743M	Net Sales ($)	33953M	117780M	146819M	363677M	615261M	6791253M
5596866M	5183679M	5572062M	Total Assets ($)	71104M	128009M	131018M	208534M	438893M	4594504M

© RMA 2011

M = $ thousand   MM = $ million
See Pages 9 through 22 for Explanation of Ratios and Data

Current Data Sorted by Assets   **Comparative Historical Data**

	0-500M	500M-2MM	2-10MM	10-50MM	50-100MM	100-250MM	Type of Statement	4/1/06-3/31/07 ALL	4/1/07-3/31/08 ALL
		1	13	12	4	1	Unqualified	31	30
		4	9	2			Reviewed	14	9
	1	1	3				Compiled	4	6
	5	7	5				Tax Returns	7	9
		14	19	7	2	3	Other	28	30
		16 (4/1-9/30/10)		97 (10/1/10-3/31/11)					
NUMBER OF STATEMENTS	6	27	49	21	6	4		84	84
	%	%	%	%	%	%	**ASSETS**	%	%
		15.7	16.0	11.3			Cash & Equivalents	11.0	14.3
		46.9	47.3	36.4			Trade Receivables (net)	43.5	43.3
		3.9	2.2	2.6			Inventory	1.8	2.3
		9.0	5.6	12.0			All Other Current	8.5	6.5
		75.4	71.1	62.3			Total Current	64.7	66.5
		13.8	21.3	30.1			Fixed Assets (net)	22.2	23.3
		1.2	3.0	2.6			Intangibles (net)	3.8	2.3
		9.6	4.6	4.9			All Other Non-Current	9.3	7.9
		100.0	100.0	100.0			Total	100.0	100.0
							LIABILITIES		
		10.2	9.2	4.3			Notes Payable-Short Term	9.5	9.9
		3.4	3.2	1.4			Cur. Mat.-L.T.D.	5.1	4.5
		13.4	16.0	13.3			Trade Payables	14.2	13.2
		.2	.8	.0			Income Taxes Payable	1.0	.2
		15.4	16.5	17.6			All Other Current	16.1	17.5
		42.7	45.7	36.6			Total Current	45.8	45.4
		6.8	15.7	18.5			Long-Term Debt	14.6	13.1
		.3	1.6	.4			Deferred Taxes	.2	.3
		5.6	7.4	1.6			All Other Non-Current	4.2	2.7
		44.5	29.6	43.0			Net Worth	35.1	38.5
		100.0	100.0	100.0			Total Liabilities & Net Worth	100.0	100.0
							INCOME DATA		
		100.0	100.0	100.0			Net Sales	100.0	100.0
							Gross Profit		
		92.0	90.2	92.6			Operating Expenses	91.8	90.6
		8.0	9.8	7.4			Operating Profit	8.2	9.4
		1.2	1.8	1.3			All Other Expenses (net)	1.2	2.0
		6.8	7.9	6.1			Profit Before Taxes	7.0	7.4
							RATIOS		
		4.9	2.9	2.2				2.6	2.5
		2.3	1.6	1.8			Current	1.6	1.6
		1.3	1.2	1.5				1.2	1.1
		4.3	2.4	1.9				2.5	2.4
		1.9	1.4	1.3			Quick	(83) 1.3	1.5
		1.2	1.0	1.0				.9	.9
	11	32.9	35 10.5	35 10.4				23 15.6	27 13.3
	42	8.6	44 8.4	42 8.7			Sales/Receivables	50 7.3	52 7.1
	66	5.5	68 5.4	64 5.7				69 5.3	71 5.1
							Cost of Sales/Inventory		
							Cost of Sales/Payables		
		5.7	5.9	5.2				7.6	6.5
		9.1	13.2	8.0			Sales/Working Capital	14.9	14.0
		51.6	54.1	15.2				38.2	58.4
		64.4	19.7	61.7				23.0	31.3
	(21)	13.3	(37) 8.4	(16) 9.7			EBIT/Interest	(67) 8.7	(66) 9.1
		1.5	3.8	1.7				2.6	3.2
								10.3	24.4
			(20) 5.3				Net Profit + Depr., Dep., Amort./Cur. Mat. L/T/D	(23) 5.6	
								1.6	2.0
		.1	.1	.1				.1	.1
		.2	.5	.3			Fixed/Worth	.5	.4
		.5	1.7	1.6				2.1	1.5
		.5	.9	.9				.8	.6
		1.0	2.0	1.3			Debt/Worth	2.1	1.5
		5.3	7.0	2.4				7.1	7.7
		79.6	91.9	54.7				64.2	72.2
	(23)	51.8	(43) 35.1	(20) 32.1			% Profit Before Taxes/Tangible Net Worth	(73) 36.4	(76) 38.6
		30.3	10.3	2.7				17.9	20.0
		35.5	24.1	20.7				20.4	24.4
		26.1	11.7	14.2			% Profit Before Taxes/Total Assets	11.2	13.2
		11.6	4.1	1.3				4.4	3.4
		360.7	140.0	88.0				137.4	126.2
		46.3	38.7	18.7			Sales/Net Fixed Assets	32.1	20.3
		17.1	6.8	1.6				6.5	5.3
		5.6	5.1	3.7				4.7	4.3
		3.9	3.4	2.3			Sales/Total Assets	3.0	3.0
		2.1	1.9	1.0				1.7	1.4
		.5	.3	.5				.5	.3
	(18)	1.2	(37) .9	(18) 2.8			% Depr., Dep., Amort./Sales	(67) 1.3	(64) 1.0
		3.4	2.8	5.6				3.7	3.4
		1.5						1.0	.8
	(10)	4.9					% Officers', Directors' Owners' Comp/Sales	(17) 3.5	(19) 1.9
		5.9						8.8	10.0
	11094M	162860M	897722M	1452172M	1022857M	1060286M	Net Sales ($)	3114873M	3755832M
	1054M	36110M	237341M	518601M	411638M	743943M	Total Assets ($)	1177206M	1899437M

M = $ thousand   MM = $ million
See Pages 9 through 22 for Explanation of Ratios and Data

Comparative Historical Data | Current Data Sorted by Sales

4/1/08-3/31/09 ALL	4/1/09-3/31/10 ALL	4/1/10-3/31/11 ALL	Type of Statement	0-1MM	1-3MM	3-5MM	5-10MM	10-25MM	25MM & OVER
33	30	31	Unqualified		3	1	2	6	19
16	19	15	Reviewed		1		3	8	3
5	7	5	Compiled				2	1	1
12	16	17	Tax Returns	1			4	2	1
41	47	45	Other	3	7	5	12	8	15
					16 (4/1-9/30/10)		97 (10/1/10-3/31/11)		
107	119	113	NUMBER OF STATEMENTS	4	16	6	23	25	39
%	%	%	ASSETS	%	%	%	%	%	%
15.6	17.2	16.1	Cash & Equivalents		25.7		16.0	18.7	12.4
39.3	36.3	41.7	Trade Receivables (net)		24.8		44.4	42.2	51.0
2.0	2.6	2.4	Inventory		2.2		3.4	2.4	1.6
6.1	5.5	8.1	All Other Current		9.0		6.3	8.2	7.4
63.0	61.6	68.4	Total Current		61.7		70.1	71.5	72.4
22.8	25.8	22.1	Fixed Assets (net)		26.5		24.9	20.3	15.6
2.8	4.9	3.4	Intangibles (net)		5.6		1.3	.9	6.1
11.4	7.7	6.1	All Other Non-Current		6.2		3.7	7.2	6.0
100.0	100.0	100.0	Total		100.0		100.0	100.0	100.0
			LIABILITIES						
7.9	9.9	10.7	Notes Payable-Short Term		25.5		8.6	10.6	7.4
3.9	3.9	2.8	Cur. Mat.-L.T.D.		1.3		3.5	1.8	3.6
14.8	10.3	14.1	Trade Payables		6.8		12.6	11.8	19.4
.6	.3	.5	Income Taxes Payable		.0		1.6	.2	.2
15.9	16.1	17.3	All Other Current		17.3		16.2	17.9	18.9
43.0	40.5	45.4	Total Current		50.8		42.6	42.4	49.6
14.5	18.6	14.0	Long-Term Debt		16.5		20.6	10.1	9.5
.3	.2	.9	Deferred Taxes		.0		.8	.4	.5
2.2	4.7	6.0	All Other Non-Current		4.9		2.9	2.5	2.6
40.0	36.0	33.7	Net Worth		27.7		33.2	44.7	37.9
100.0	100.0	100.0	Total Liabilities & Net Worth		100.0		100.0	100.0	100.0
			INCOME DATA						
100.0	100.0	100.0	Net Sales		100.0		100.0	100.0	100.0
			Gross Profit						
91.6	90.5	91.8	Operating Expenses		83.4		90.4	93.4	95.0
8.4	9.5	8.2	Operating Profit		16.6		9.6	6.6	5.0
.8	2.6	1.5	All Other Expenses (net)		3.3		1.5	-.2	.7
7.6	6.9	6.7	Profit Before Taxes		13.3		8.1	6.8	4.3
			RATIOS						
2.4	2.6	2.7	Current		18.0		2.6	2.6	2.2
1.5	1.5	1.7			2.4		2.0	1.6	1.6
1.0	1.0	1.2			.7		1.3	1.2	1.2
1.9	2.4	2.4	Quick		9.2		2.4	2.3	2.2
1.3	1.3	1.3			1.7		1.7	1.4	1.3
.9	.9	1.0			.5		1.2	1.0	1.0
27 13.7	20 18.5	31 12.0	Sales/Receivables	0 UND		39 9.3	29 12.7	37 10.0	
48 7.6	43 8.5	44 8.4		56 6.5		48 7.7	36 10.0	48 7.6	
66 5.6	62 5.9	63 5.8		71 5.1		70 5.2	58 6.3	62 5.9	
			Cost of Sales/Inventory						
			Cost of Sales/Payables						
7.0	6.8	5.8	Sales/Working Capital		4.2		5.3	5.9	7.4
16.6	14.1	10.4			6.4		9.7	13.5	14.8
350.0	964.0	42.8			UND		17.4	56.1	38.1
		29.5	31.8	22.7	EBIT/Interest		34.2	19.5	28.9
(87) 11.4	(94) 6.9	(84) 8.3	EBIT/Interest		(19) 13.3		(19) 8.6	(30) 8.1	
2.6	1.2	1.6			2.2		4.8	2.3	
22.0	6.2	9.2	Net Profit + Depr., Dep., Amort./Cur. Mat. L/T/D					9.2	
(19) 8.6	(15) 2.0	(19) 2.8						(12) 2.2	
5.4	.3	1.6						1.6	
.1	.1	.1	Fixed/Worth		.2		.1	.1	.1
.4	.4	.3			.5		.5	.3	.2
1.1	2.6	1.7			UND		1.8	.7	1.3
.7	.7	.7	Debt/Worth		.1		.6	.6	.9
1.5	1.9	1.7			1.6		1.7	1.2	1.8
4.6	4.8	4.7			UND		4.6	3.0	4.0
74.3	60.1	79.3	% Profit Before Taxes/Tangible Net Worth		159.1		93.4	94.3	69.3
(99) 38.8	(102) 29.4	(100) 35.6		(12) 39.1		(19) 51.8	(24) 40.8	(37) 34.9	
12.3	5.8	13.3			15.4		17.9	8.4	20.9
25.5	23.2	26.0	% Profit Before Taxes/Total Assets		33.8		35.5	26.0	18.8
12.1	10.0	13.6			17.9		23.0	14.3	11.7
3.3	.5	3.8			-4.6		5.1	3.2	5.2
157.4	138.2	127.2	Sales/Net Fixed Assets		240.8		521.7	245.7	123.8
29.4	27.4	41.4			17.6		40.5	26.2	56.5
5.8	4.5	5.6			3.2		2.5	10.8	16.0
4.1	4.7	5.0	Sales/Total Assets		3.8		4.4	5.3	5.7
3.2	2.8	3.4			1.8		3.4	3.8	3.9
1.7	1.4	1.6			.9		1.3	2.0	2.3
.4	.4	.5	% Depr., Dep., Amort./Sales				.8	.3	.3
(70) 1.5	(82) 1.8	(82) 1.3					(14) 2.7	(21) 1.2	(30) .7
3.8	3.1	3.6					6.9	3.2	2.5
1.4	1.1	1.5	% Officers', Directors' Owners' Comp/Sales						
(22) 2.8	(24) 3.2	(24) 4.9							
5.5	5.4	7.3							
4988406M	4394957M	4606991M	Net Sales ($)	3024M	33289M	22501M	170638M	372899M	4004640M
2530255M	2053514M	1948687M	Total Assets ($)	10628M	28257M	9159M	101640M	158253M	1640750M

M = $ thousand   MM = $ million
See Pages 9 through 22 for Explanation of Ratios and Data

						Type of Statement		
	6	16	14	3	3	Unqualified		52
3	12	25	3			Reviewed		62
5	21	13	5			Compiled		41
43	28	4				Tax Returns		50
38	63	72	28	4	6	Other		130
	26 (4/1-9/30/10)		389 (10/1/10-3/31/11)				4/1/06-3/31/07	4/1/07-3/31/08
0-500M	500M-2MM	2-10MM	10-50MM	50-100MM	100-250MM		ALL	ALL
89	130	130	50	7	9	**NUMBER OF STATEMENTS**		335
%	%	%	%	%	%	**ASSETS**	%	%
25.4	17.0	10.9	9.7			Cash & Equivalents	D	13.8
34.7	58.5	63.3	46.8			Trade Receivables (net)	A	53.8
.6	.2	.2	.9			Inventory	T	.1
10.1	5.2	5.5	9.5			All Other Current	A	7.1
70.8	80.9	79.9	67.0			Total Current		74.9
12.6	7.4	8.9	11.6			Fixed Assets (net)	N	9.0
3.7	2.0	3.7	13.4			Intangibles (net)	O	5.4
12.8	9.7	7.5	8.0			All Other Non-Current	T	10.7
100.0	100.0	100.0	100.0			Total		100.0
						LIABILITIES	A	
32.6	21.1	21.9	11.8			Notes Payable-Short Term	V	21.8
5.9	1.9	1.5	2.3			Cur. Mat.-L.T.D.	A	3.0
7.9	7.0	8.8	10.0			Trade Payables	I	7.4
.1	.6	.7	.9			Income Taxes Payable	L	.7
27.4	21.6	21.2	22.1			All Other Current	A	21.7
73.9	52.1	54.0	47.1			Total Current	B	54.5
10.9	4.7	7.1	13.1			Long-Term Debt	L	8.6
.0	.0	.2	.2			Deferred Taxes	E	.2
20.5	9.4	3.4	10.4			All Other Non-Current		6.6
-5.2	33.9	35.3	29.2			Net Worth		30.1
100.0	100.0	100.0	100.0			Total Liabilties & Net Worth		100.0
						INCOME DATA		
100.0	100.0	100.0	100.0			Net Sales		100.0
						Gross Profit		
95.7	96.5	95.9	95.5			Operating Expenses		95.9
4.3	3.5	4.1	4.5			Operating Profit		4.1
1.0	.9	1.0	1.7			All Other Expenses (net)		1.3
3.3	2.6	3.1	2.8			Profit Before Taxes		2.8
						RATIOS		
3.1	3.0	2.4	2.4			Current		2.3
1.2	1.9	1.6	1.4					1.4
.7	1.1	1.1	.9					1.0
2.4	2.8	2.2	2.1			Quick		2.2
1.1	1.6	1.5	1.2					1.3
.4	1.0	1.1	.8					.9
0 UND	22 16.3	34 10.6	33 11.1			Sales/Receivables	23	15.9
13 28.6	40 9.0	49 7.4	45 8.1				39	9.4
37 9.9	57 6.4	65 5.6	61 6.0				56	6.5
						Cost of Sales/Inventory		
						Cost of Sales/Payables		
14.3	9.1	10.2	9.0			Sales/Working Capital		11.1
139.7	14.8	17.2	18.4					25.2
-39.5	74.6	61.0	-104.6					433.2
19.7	17.1	32.6	38.5			EBIT/Interest		12.5
(61) 4.9	(102) 6.2	(112) 8.5	(43) 6.1				(275)	4.2
.0	2.2	2.1	2.7					1.1
		70.4				Net Profit + Depr., Dep.,		14.1
	(10) 3.7					Amort./Cur. Mat. L/T/D	(34)	2.8
		-1.8						-.1
.0	.0	.0	.0			Fixed/Worth		.0
.2	.1	.1	.2					.2
4.5	.4	.5	-11.3					1.0
.6	.7	.7	1.1			Debt/Worth		.8
5.6	1.6	1.5	3.7					2.0
-4.2	8.3	7.3	-16.7					7.3
417.4	65.9	74.9	51.6			% Profit Before Taxes/Tangible		73.6
(63) 57.5	(110) 29.9	(112) 30.7	(36) 34.4			Net Worth	(277)	31.5
8.0	6.5	11.8	12.6					5.5
55.1	23.8	24.3	16.6			% Profit Before Taxes/Total		24.5
16.9	10.6	12.8	7.7			Assets		10.0
-7.4	3.8	3.3	2.5					.8
UND	924.3	477.7	219.1			Sales/Net Fixed Assets		435.5
198.0	202.4	155.9	107.6					131.8
49.2	77.8	55.6	35.6					54.8
14.3	7.9	6.0	5.5			Sales/Total Assets		7.8
7.6	5.8	4.7	3.9					5.6
4.8	3.7	3.6	2.5					4.1
.1	.1	.1	.2			% Depr., Dep., Amort./Sales		.1
(39) .5	(76) .2	(92) .2	(41) .4				(216)	.3
1.2	.5	.6	1.0					.6
3.3	1.4	1.2				% Officers', Directors'		1.4
(39) 5.3	(49) 2.6	(33) 2.4				Owners' Comp/Sales	(109)	3.2
9.8	6.7	8.2						8.7
204715M	1107046M	3127838M	4140987M	1648898M	4870299M	Net Sales ($)		14600806M
20066M	144871M	577177M	991575M	450295M	1376483M	Total Assets ($)		3069114M

Current Data Sorted by Assets   Comparative Historical Data

M = $ thousand   MM = $ million
See Pages 9 through 22 for Explanation of Ratios and Data

© RMA 2011

Comparative Historical Data				Current Data Sorted by Sales					
			Type of Statement						
52	45	42	Unqualified		2	2	2	5	31
57	61	43	Reviewed		2	4	6	21	10
59	43	44	Compiled		10	7	9	12	6
63	50	75	Tax Returns	14	25	17	12	4	3
141	155	211	Other	21	30	13	36	48	63
4/1/08-3/31/09 ALL	4/1/09-3/31/10 ALL	4/1/10-3/31/11 ALL		0-1MM	26 (4/1-9/30/10) 1-3MM	3-5MM	5-10MM	389 (10/1/10-3/31/11) 10-25MM	25MM & OVER
372	354	415	NUMBER OF STATEMENTS	35	69	43	65	90	113
%	%	%	ASSETS	%	%	%	%	%	%
16.4	14.4	15.8	Cash & Equivalents	18.1	22.1	22.3	14.9	14.7	10.3
46.6	51.5	53.1	Trade Receivables (net)	26.4	41.3	54.7	59.6	60.2	58.6
.5	.6	.3	Inventory	.0	.8	.3	.1	.0	.5
7.5	6.8	7.1	All Other Current	11.6	9.3	4.7	6.3	5.0	7.3
71.0	73.2	76.3	Total Current	56.1	73.5	82.0	80.9	79.9	76.7
10.1	10.0	9.4	Fixed Assets (net)	19.1	13.0	10.3	6.0	8.1	6.6
7.6	5.5	5.0	Intangibles (net)	7.1	3.5	1.5	3.1	3.1	9.1
11.3	11.3	9.3	All Other Non-Current	17.7	10.0	6.2	10.0	8.9	7.5
100.0	100.0	100.0	Total	100.0	100.0	100.0	100.0	100.0	100.0
			LIABILITIES						
21.6	20.3	22.0	Notes Payable-Short Term	26.6	27.8	24.5	28.1	17.6	16.2
3.0	3.1	2.6	Cur. Mat.-L.T.D.	.1	7.6	2.0	2.1	1.5	1.7
6.8	7.4	8.5	Trade Payables	15.4	2.8	3.5	7.4	10.5	10.9
.4	.5	.6	Income Taxes Payable	.0	.2	.3	.3	.4	1.5
19.9	22.7	23.0	All Other Current	23.7	25.8	20.6	18.6	22.5	24.8
51.8	54.0	56.8	Total Current	65.9	64.2	50.9	56.5	52.6	55.1
14.1	9.1	8.3	Long-Term Debt	17.1	8.3	6.2	4.3	7.1	9.6
.1	.2	.1	Deferred Taxes	.0	.0	.0	.0	.3	.3
7.6	5.8	9.8	All Other Non-Current	14.9	20.9	15.4	5.2	4.0	6.7
26.4	30.9	25.0	Net Worth	2.1	6.6	27.5	34.0	36.1	28.3
100.0	100.0	100.0	Total Liabilities & Net Worth	100.0	100.0	100.0	100.0	100.0	100.0
			INCOME DATA						
100.0	100.0	100.0	Net Sales	100.0	100.0	100.0	100.0	100.0	100.0
			Gross Profit						
95.9	98.5	96.1	Operating Expenses	90.5	96.5	96.3	96.4	96.6	96.9
4.1	1.5	3.9	Operating Profit	9.5	3.5	3.7	3.6	3.4	3.1
1.3	.9	1.0	All Other Expenses (net)	6.4	1.4	.6	.1	.2	.5
2.7	.7	2.9	Profit Before Taxes	3.1	2.1	3.1	3.5	3.3	2.6
			RATIOS						
2.8	2.8	2.7		3.4	3.1	3.3	2.7	2.8	2.0
1.6	1.5	1.6	Current	1.2	1.6	1.9	1.7	1.7	1.5
1.0	1.0	1.0		.2	.9	1.2	1.1	1.1	1.0
2.5	2.5	2.4		2.3	2.9	3.3	2.5	2.8	1.8
1.4	1.4	1.4	Quick	1.0	1.4	1.9	1.6	1.6	1.3
.8	.9	.9		.1	.6	1.1	1.0	1.0	.9
13 28.2	27 13.7	21 17.7		0 UND	0 UND	22 16.3	24 15.4	28 13.2	32 11.5
35 10.5	43 8.4	42 8.8	Sales/Receivables	19 18.9	27 13.7	41 8.9	42 8.6	42 8.6	46 7.9
51 7.1	63 5.8	61 6.0		77 4.7	53 6.9	60 6.1	62 5.9	58 6.3	64 5.7
			Cost of Sales/Inventory						
			Cost of Sales/Payables						
10.1	9.4	10.0		5.7	9.5	8.6	11.1	10.5	10.7
22.4	18.4	18.5	Sales/Working Capital	48.9	32.2	14.0	16.2	18.0	21.8
UND	NM	574.0		-11.1	-106.5	41.5	113.1	92.6	177.0
13.6	14.4	26.7		7.7	16.8	13.5	34.8	42.1	28.5
(292) 3.5	(283) 2.9	(331) 6.5	EBIT/Interest	(18) .7	(48) 4.5	(35) 5.5	(56) 7.1	(75) 8.5	(99) 7.1
.3	-2.2	1.9		-2.1	-.4	.9	2.9	2.0	3.0
9.3	10.4	15.8							105.4
(38) 2.1	(34) 2.4	(25) 2.3	Net Profit + Depr., Dep., Amort./Cur. Mat. L/T/D						(12) 3.6
-1.5	.0	.7							1.2
.0	.0	.0		.0	.0	.0	.0	.0	.0
.2	.2	.1	Fixed/Worth	.3	.2	.2	.1	.1	.1
1.3	1.1	1.1		-8.0	1.1	.8	.3	.5	3.1
.7	.6	.7		.5	.6	.7	.6	.6	1.1
1.9	1.8	1.9	Debt/Worth	5.3	2.7	1.4	1.5	1.3	2.5
26.9	11.1	14.7		-3.5	26.6	18.8	13.3	8.5	12.3
73.4	57.4	78.2		275.0	96.7	96.1	90.1	92.1	60.9
(287) 24.8	(288) 15.1	(332) 34.0	% Profit Before Taxes/Tangible Net Worth	(23) 47.0	(55) 26.7	(36) 27.0	(54) 44.6	(75) 39.7	(89) 31.0
2.0	-4.2	9.0		.0	-18.6	1.5	10.1	14.7	12.7
24.3	16.3	25.6		35.9	23.5	21.9	29.2	28.2	20.6
7.7	5.1	11.6	% Profit Before Taxes/Total Assets	3.4	6.6	8.0	14.2	15.3	9.9
-.7	-5.7	1.6		-8.1	-7.2	.1	5.1	4.3	3.7
507.8	438.7	490.5		UND	999.8	795.0	594.6	977.1	328.4
148.5	124.8	158.5	Sales/Net Fixed Assets	77.8	109.2	202.6	202.3	157.5	168.5
48.7	37.8	55.6		15.1	33.3	51.5	78.2	77.4	66.1
8.3	6.7	7.6		6.4	9.4	7.8	7.1	8.1	6.8
5.5	4.7	5.3	Sales/Total Assets	2.9	5.5	5.4	5.8	5.6	5.0
3.5	3.0	3.5		1.1	3.5	3.3	3.8	3.9	3.4
.1	.1	.1		.8	.2	.1	.1	.1	.1
(250) .3	(248) .4	(257) .3	% Depr., Dep., Amort./Sales	(13) 1.9	(38) .6	(24) .3	(42) .3	(54) .2	(86) .3
.6	.7	.7		22.9	1.6	1.1	.5	.4	.5
1.7	1.5	1.5		6.9	3.3	2.6	1.2	.6	1.2
(132) 3.5	(105) 2.8	(125) 3.7	% Officers', Directors' Owners' Comp/Sales	(12) 11.4	(31) 5.3	(19) 5.7	(22) 2.2	(22) 1.4	(19) 2.3
8.3	7.2	8.0		22.7	9.3	7.2	5.2	4.1	12.0
16493689M	13266747M	15099783M	Net Sales ($)	18184M	141215M	172587M	486951M	1459627M	12821219M
3874510M	3059295M	3560467M	Total Assets ($)	18371M	57596M	37480M	107629M	303175M	3036216M

M = $ thousand   MM = $ million
See Pages 9 through 22 for Explanation of Ratios and Data

Current Data Sorted by Assets   Comparative Historical Data

						Type of Statement		
1		21	26	6	3	Unqualified	67	53
	8	32	6			Reviewed	49	42
6	30	19	2		1	Compiled	46	45
19	20	5				Tax Returns	24	39
19	50	78	37	4	11	Other	140	136
	34 (4/1-9/30/10)		370 (10/1/10-3/31/11)				4/1/06-3/31/07	4/1/07-3/31/08
0-500M	500M-2MM	2-10MM	10-50MM	50-100MM	100-250MM		ALL	ALL
45	108	155	71	10	15	NUMBER OF STATEMENTS	326	315
%	%	%	%	%	%	ASSETS	%	%
25.3	14.0	8.5	10.7	14.4	11.4	Cash & Equivalents	13.5	13.3
36.7	58.9	60.0	53.3	37.4	52.0	Trade Receivables (net)	56.7	53.9
.3	.0	.4	.1	.8	.1	Inventory	.4	.4
8.0	4.5	9.4	8.7	6.2	7.7	All Other Current	6.1	5.9
70.2	77.5	78.3	72.8	58.7	71.2	Total Current	76.7	73.4
12.2	7.6	8.1	5.8	14.2	7.3	Fixed Assets (net)	8.2	9.4
1.9	5.3	5.3	11.2	11.8	15.4	Intangibles (net)	6.0	7.3
15.6	9.6	8.3	10.2	15.2	6.1	All Other Non-Current	9.1	10.0
100.0	100.0	100.0	100.0	100.0	100.0	Total	100.0	100.0
						LIABILITIES		
46.0	19.0	20.7	16.3	4.2	8.2	Notes Payable-Short Term	19.9	22.6
11.3	2.0	2.4	1.8	.4	3.9	Cur. Mat.-L.T.D.	1.2	1.8
9.5	5.6	6.6	7.7	12.8	10.0	Trade Payables	6.5	7.6
.1	.4	.5	.2	.1	3.2	Income Taxes Payable	.5	.5
36.8	20.0	19.6	26.4	25.4	26.7	All Other Current	24.9	23.6
103.7	47.0	49.7	52.4	42.8	51.9	Total Current	52.9	56.1
19.6	6.5	5.5	5.5	15.9	27.9	Long-Term Debt	6.4	9.4
.0	.2	.0	.4	.5	1.4	Deferred Taxes	.3	.1
16.5	7.8	6.9	7.8	4.4	11.1	All Other Non-Current	6.9	7.0
-39.8	38.6	37.8	33.8	36.3	7.7	Net Worth	33.5	27.5
100.0	100.0	100.0	100.0	100.0	100.0	Total Liabilties & Net Worth	100.0	100.0
						INCOME DATA		
100.0	100.0	100.0	100.0	100.0	100.0	Net Sales	100.0	100.0
						Gross Profit		
97.2	95.1	96.2	97.1	97.4	94.6	Operating Expenses	96.6	96.1
2.8	4.9	3.8	2.9	2.6	5.4	Operating Profit	3.4	3.9
1.6	.5	.8	.7	.7	2.2	All Other Expenses (net)	.5	.8
1.2	4.4	2.9	2.2	1.8	3.2	Profit Before Taxes	2.9	3.0
						RATIOS		
1.6	3.7	2.5	2.3	2.1	2.4		2.6	2.3
.9	1.7	1.6	1.4	1.8	1.7	Current	1.5	1.4
.4	1.1	1.1	1.0	1.0	1.1		1.1	1.0
1.5	3.4	2.3	2.0	1.9	2.4		2.4	2.2
.8	1.5	1.5	1.2	1.6	1.3	Quick	1.4	1.3
.3	1.1	1.0	.9	.9	.8		1.0	1.0
0 UND	26 14.3	31 11.6	29 12.7	38 9.7	50 7.4		26 13.9	24 15.0
17 21.2	36 10.0	45 8.0	40 9.2	46 8.0	62 5.8	Sales/Receivables	42 8.8	39 9.3
46 7.9	54 6.7	58 6.3	59 6.2	55 6.6	75 4.8		54 6.8	55 6.6
						Cost of Sales/Inventory		
						Cost of Sales/Payables		
20.8	9.4	9.2	11.6	8.2	7.7		10.8	10.9
-93.3	21.7	17.8	28.6	12.2	12.1	Sales/Working Capital	22.9	25.7
-9.0	91.7	65.3	286.4	NM	22.1		131.4	275.7
17.6	19.9	39.2	24.6		11.1		18.1	13.1
(33) 3.6	(83) 9.6	(136) 8.4	(60) 6.5		3.0	EBIT/Interest	(272) 5.9	(265) 5.3
-.7	2.7	2.1	3.0		.7		1.9	1.6
		89.0	50.0				40.4	30.8
	(16)	9.2	(18) 17.8			Net Profit + Depr., Dep., Amort./Cur. Mat. L/T/D	(39) 4.6	(36) 4.2
		1.1	1.9				1.1	-.2
.0	.0	.0	.1	.1	.3		.1	.1
.7	.1	.1	.2	.3	-.2	Fixed/Worth	.2	.2
-.2	.4	.6	.9	1.1	-.1		.6	.9
1.8	.7	.7	1.1	.9	6.8		.7	.9
UND	1.8	1.9	2.5	2.3	-6.7	Debt/Worth	2.0	2.5
-2.4	8.0	6.0	12.4	6.2	-3.1		5.9	8.7
181.7	94.0	60.9	78.4			% Profit Before Taxes/Tangible Net Worth	73.2	74.1
(23) 93.7	(92) 49.0	(135) 29.9	(58) 38.7				(282) 41.8	(260) 38.9
49.7	10.9	14.5	15.6				12.8	11.2
42.3	30.7	23.6	20.1	11.7	21.9	% Profit Before Taxes/Total Assets	24.1	20.7
8.6	14.5	11.1	11.3	5.2	7.4		11.8	11.5
-8.5	3.8	3.5	2.8	1.0	-1.2		3.0	2.0
UND	744.7	409.6	320.3	158.5	273.6		384.5	347.1
242.5	178.4	145.9	141.7	45.2	65.0	Sales/Net Fixed Assets	138.4	127.9
60.3	83.4	60.6	55.6	5.3	43.9		55.5	62.5
15.5	8.0	6.8	6.8	4.5	4.0		7.9	8.2
6.6	5.7	5.0	4.8	3.1	2.6	Sales/Total Assets	5.6	5.6
3.6	4.3	3.8	2.9	1.3	2.0		3.9	3.7
.1	.1	.1	.1		.2		.1	.1
(24) .2	(63) .2	(119) .2	(50) .3		(12) .7	% Depr., Dep., Amort./Sales	(240) .3	(226) .3
1.0	.4	.5	.5		1.1		.6	.5
1.4	1.5	1.3	.5				1.5	1.3
(22) 3.6	(42) 3.2	(48) 2.3	(12) .8			% Officers', Directors' Owners' Comp/Sales	(100) 2.9	(101) 2.7
9.3	4.4	4.2	3.9				6.8	6.7
194893M	898495M	4417825M	7921318M	2296768M	8639031M	Net Sales ($)	21763530M	22896790M
12106M	137828M	722907M	1555746M	754906M	2441391M	Total Assets ($)	4203209M	4762416M

M = $ thousand   MM = $ million
See Pages 9 through 22 for Explanation of Ratios and Data

Comparative Historical Data   Current Data Sorted by Sales

Hist 1	Hist 2	Hist 3		0-1MM	1-3MM	3-5MM	5-10MM	10-25MM	25MM & OVER
			Type of Statement						
60	55	57	Unqualified	1	1	1		6	48
57	67	46	Reviewed			2	11	16	17
49	43	58	Compiled	2	5	8	15	23	5
36	36	44	Tax Returns	6	10	8	9	7	4
167	178	199	Other	10	12	15	27	55	80
4/1/08-3/31/09 ALL	4/1/09-3/31/10 ALL	4/1/10-3/31/11 ALL		34 (4/1-9/30/10)			370 (10/1/10-3/31/11)		
369	379	404	**NUMBER OF STATEMENTS**	19	28	34	62	107	154
%	%	%	**ASSETS**	%	%	%	%	%	%
14.6	14.0	12.5	Cash & Equivalents	19.3	11.7	17.1	13.5	12.9	10.1
51.7	52.5	55.1	Trade Receivables (net)	28.1	49.5	49.3	60.7	58.1	56.3
.4	.1	.2	Inventory	.0	.4	.0	.2	.4	.1
6.6	7.6	7.7	All Other Current	8.1	7.3	5.1	2.9	8.0	9.9
73.2	74.2	75.5	Total Current	55.6	69.0	71.4	77.3	79.5	76.5
8.8	8.4	8.1	Fixed Assets (net)	32.7	12.8	3.9	6.1	7.4	6.5
7.8	6.6	6.5	Intangibles (net)	2.6	4.8	8.8	4.4	4.5	9.0
10.2	10.8	9.9	All Other Non-Current	9.2	13.5	15.9	12.2	8.6	7.9
100.0	100.0	100.0	Total	100.0	100.0	100.0	100.0	100.0	100.0
			LIABILITIES						
21.6	19.4	21.4	Notes Payable-Short Term	26.1	43.0	23.8	18.8	23.8	15.7
2.8	2.8	3.2	Cur. Mat.-L.T.D.	4.3	.3	13.2	3.9	3.0	1.2
7.7	7.6	7.1	Trade Payables	10.0	6.7	4.6	5.2	7.5	7.9
.6	.4	.5	Income Taxes Payable	.0	.2	.2	.6	.4	.6
19.8	22.0	23.2	All Other Current	27.3	29.3	15.1	16.2	21.0	27.8
52.5	52.1	55.4	Total Current	67.7	79.6	57.0	44.7	55.7	53.2
9.1	7.1	8.5	Long-Term Debt	15.9	10.5	5.4	7.2	9.5	7.6
.3	.2	.2	Deferred Taxes	.0	.0	.7	.0	.1	.3
6.9	8.6	8.5	All Other Non-Current	14.2	21.7	10.6	7.1	5.5	7.5
31.1	32.0	27.5	Net Worth	2.3	-11.8	26.3	41.0	29.2	31.4
100.0	100.0	100.0	Total Liabilties & Net Worth	100.0	100.0	100.0	100.0	100.0	100.0
			INCOME DATA						
100.0	100.0	100.0	Net Sales	100.0	100.0	100.0	100.0	100.0	100.0
			Gross Profit						
97.1	98.6	96.2	Operating Expenses	84.9	96.0	96.1	97.1	96.8	96.8
2.9	1.4	3.8	Operating Profit	15.1	4.0	3.9	2.9	3.2	3.2
.7	.6	.8	All Other Expenses (net)	8.3	.7	.2	.1	.5	.6
2.1	.8	3.0	Profit Before Taxes	6.7	3.3	3.7	2.8	2.7	2.6
			RATIOS						
2.5	2.5	2.5	Current	2.4	1.9	3.9	4.5	2.3	2.3
1.5	1.5	1.5		1.0	1.0	1.6	1.8	1.6	1.5
1.1	1.0	1.0		.3	.6	1.0	1.2	1.1	1.1
2.2	2.3	2.3	Quick	1.9	1.9	3.3	4.4	2.3	2.1
1.3	1.4	1.3		1.0	.9	1.3	1.8	1.4	1.3
.9	.9	.9		.2	.5	.8	1.1	1.0	.9
21 17.2	26 14.1	27 13.4	Sales/Receivables	0 UND	22 16.8	23 16.0	34 10.7	27 13.4	28 13.1
35 10.5	42 8.7	40 9.2		29 12.4	36 10.1	41 9.0	46 8.0	43 8.4	39 9.3
49 7.4	56 6.5	57 6.4		144 2.5	50 7.4	57 6.4	59 6.2	59 6.2	54 6.7
			Cost of Sales/Inventory						
			Cost of Sales/Payables						
11.3	10.2	9.9	Sales/Working Capital	5.1	18.9	7.8	7.6	10.3	11.2
23.4	20.8	22.0		-461.0	NM	19.0	13.4	19.6	22.6
233.0	209.4	291.8		-6.7	-9.3	NM	55.7	76.4	216.3
15.4	15.6	26.2	EBIT/Interest		14.6	19.1	23.5	26.5	39.6
(313) 3.8	(321) 3.3	(336) 7.0		(24) 2.6	(26) 7.9	(53) 8.6	(89) 6.6	(135) 9.0	
1.0	-2.1	2.0		.0	2.9	.9	1.9	2.7	
11.8	13.0	41.8	Net Profit + Depr., Dep., Amort./Cur. Mat. L/T/D					82.1	43.9
(49) 1.9	(45) 3.2	(45) 4.9					(12) 4.7	(29) 13.4	
.0	-.3	1.5					1.1	2.1	
.1	.0	.0	Fixed/Worth	.1	.0	.0	.0	.0	.1
.2	.2	.2		3.7	.5	.0	.1	.1	.2
.9	1.1	1.1		-2.7	-3.1	.7	.4	.6	.9
.7	.6	.8	Debt/Worth	2.7	1.4	.6	.6	.7	.8
2.1	1.8	2.3		7.0	11.3	2.8	1.6	1.8	2.5
9.6	9.3	14.3		-5.9	-6.2	33.4	5.6	7.2	10.6
62.3	51.9	85.7	% Profit Before Taxes/Tangible Net Worth	86.6	126.3	145.0	58.8	77.0	82.6
(303) 22.9	(308) 15.3	(324) 39.5		(13) 41.4	(15) 79.7	(28) 72.6	(52) 28.5	(90) 32.3	(126) 40.7
4.8	-2.9	14.5		9.1	14.5	9.0	3.2	13.9	19.0
18.1	15.2	25.7	% Profit Before Taxes/Total Assets	20.9	28.9	37.8	28.6	26.3	24.2
7.6	3.7	11.3		1.3	6.3	10.3	10.9	12.3	13.1
.2	-4.6	2.5		-2.9	-4.5	2.8	.3	4.1	3.9
341.9	353.1	470.2	Sales/Net Fixed Assets	163.0	999.8	UND	347.6	358.7	388.2
128.9	135.3	146.9		19.9	110.1	566.5	133.1	132.5	168.6
57.7	48.8	61.1		.6	45.1	105.5	60.3	65.1	69.4
8.0	6.9	7.3	Sales/Total Assets	3.1	8.4	6.8	6.7	7.8	7.8
5.6	4.9	5.1		1.1	5.3	4.6	4.8	5.2	5.6
3.7	3.6	3.6		.4	3.4	3.6	4.0	4.3	3.8
.1	.1	.1	% Depr., Dep., Amort./Sales	1.0	.1	.1	.1	.1	.1
(252) .3	(272) .3	(274) .2		(10) 3.6	(15) .6	(15) .1	(46) .2	(75) .2	(113) .3
.5	.6	.6		16.9	1.0	.3	.5	.5	.5
1.1	1.1	1.3	% Officers', Directors' Owners' Comp/Sales		2.4	3.2	1.7	1.1	.7
(115) 2.1	(131) 2.5	(124) 2.9		(14) 3.4	(17) 4.2	(21) 3.1	(35) 2.1	(33) 1.3	
5.2	4.9	4.9		8.1	5.4	5.3	3.8	3.0	
21760986M	29333582M	24368330M	Net Sales ($)	9567M	51683M	141411M	462858M	1772232M	21930579M
5077454M	6046474M	5624884M	Total Assets ($)	15355M	17055M	37028M	100295M	455503M	4999648M

M = $ thousand   MM = $ million
See Pages 9 through 22 for Explanation of Ratios and Data

Current Data Sorted by Assets | **Comparative Historical Data**

Type of Statement	0-500M	500M-2MM	2-10MM	10-50MM	50-100MM	100-250MM	4/1/06-3/31/07 ALL	4/1/07-3/31/08 ALL
Unqualified	1		3	9	1	2	5	9
Reviewed		3	8				4	3
Compiled	2	2						4
Tax Returns	2	6	3				3	5
Other	7	5	14	7	1	2	12	11
		3 (4/1-9/30/10)		75 (10/1/10-3/31/11)				
NUMBER OF STATEMENTS	12	16	28	16	2	4	24	32
	%	%	%	%	%	%	%	%
ASSETS								
Cash & Equivalents	32.1	25.0	24.4	12.4			26.6	14.6
Trade Receivables (net)	27.4	48.8	37.8	23.2			35.4	37.7
Inventory	.0	.0	.0	.0			.1	.0
All Other Current	11.3	5.4	12.4	16.3			14.7	14.8
Total Current	70.8	79.2	74.6	51.8			76.8	67.1
Fixed Assets (net)	16.7	6.1	11.8	6.9			8.8	6.3
Intangibles (net)	.2	5.2	5.5	28.0			7.5	8.9
All Other Non-Current	12.2	9.5	8.1	13.2			6.9	17.7
Total	100.0	100.0	100.0	100.0			100.0	100.0
LIABILITIES								
Notes Payable-Short Term	43.9	7.4	5.7	1.1			9.4	17.1
Cur. Mat.-L.T.D.	.4	2.4	1.3	1.9			.8	4.6
Trade Payables	5.2	12.1	5.5	3.3			7.2	6.4
Income Taxes Payable	.0	.0	.3	2.7			1.0	1.0
All Other Current	35.8	21.5	34.2	37.3			39.5	29.0
Total Current	85.2	43.4	47.0	46.3			57.9	58.1
Long-Term Debt	4.5	7.6	9.3	23.3			10.8	9.4
Deferred Taxes	.0	.0	.0	.6			.4	.1
All Other Non-Current	4.4	9.4	2.6	6.9			2.7	7.2
Net Worth	5.9	39.7	41.1	23.0			28.2	25.1
Total Liabilities & Net Worth	100.0	100.0	100.0	100.0			100.0	100.0
INCOME DATA								
Net Sales	100.0	100.0	100.0	100.0			100.0	100.0
Gross Profit								
Operating Expenses	96.5	96.1	94.7	93.7			96.3	92.9
Operating Profit	3.5	3.9	5.3	6.3			3.7	7.1
All Other Expenses (net)	.4	-.3	1.8	.8			.8	1.6
Profit Before Taxes	3.1	4.1	3.5	5.4			2.9	5.5
RATIOS								
Current	1.5	3.7	2.7	1.9			2.3	1.4
	1.0	1.8	1.7	1.1			1.3	1.1
	.7	1.4	1.0	.9			.9	.9
Quick	1.4	3.7	2.5	1.6			1.7	1.4
	1.0	1.7	1.3	.8			1.2	1.0
	.7	1.1	.9	.4			.9	.4
Sales/Receivables	0 UND	9 41.7	1 293.1	9 40.3			1 526.5	1 494.2
	0 UND	36 10.1	32 11.3	14 26.5			9 40.1	33 11.0
	14 26.5	52 7.0	55 6.6	49 7.4			53 6.9	63 5.8
Cost of Sales/Inventory								
Cost of Sales/Payables								
Sales/Working Capital	77.0	10.8	9.1	18.5			23.2	16.2
	999.8	19.0	20.9	177.8			78.5	147.7
	-138.4	66.7	NM	-207.0			-489.5	-84.1
EBIT/Interest		28.5	51.2	18.7			20.0	26.7
		(10) 11.1	(20) 15.5	(12) 4.8			(18) 6.4	(24) 4.5
		6.2	2.8	.5			3.8	1.6
Net Profit + Depr., Dep., Amort./Cur. Mat. L/T/D								
Fixed/Worth	.0	.0	.0	.2			.1	.0
	.5	.0	.1	1.5			.2	.2
	2.5	.4	1.0	.0			1.8	2.0
Debt/Worth	.8	.6	.6	2.7			1.8	1.8
	8.1	2.0	1.4	22.3			4.2	5.4
	NM	5.4	12.2	-2.3			16.1	24.8
% Profit Before Taxes/Tangible Net Worth		170.7	70.7				114.0	91.3
		(14) 72.4	(27) 26.9				(20) 80.4	(26) 37.5
		16.3	13.8				47.7	20.9
% Profit Before Taxes/Total Assets	58.1	38.1	18.7	10.6			24.8	17.9
	36.8	17.3	11.6	6.7			13.9	10.4
	10.7	7.4	1.4	-.5			4.2	3.4
Sales/Net Fixed Assets	UND	UND	877.0	336.0			943.3	999.8
	337.8	732.8	200.9	134.3			390.7	431.1
	50.4	113.0	44.8	40.4			62.2	47.4
Sales/Total Assets	53.1	14.6	16.6	9.7			20.4	15.1
	22.0	5.3	5.8	3.7			8.9	5.7
	7.7	3.6	3.6	1.8			4.3	2.5
% Depr., Dep., Amort./Sales			.1	.1			.1	.1
		(19) .1	(10) .4				(17) .1	(16) .4
			.6	.6			.5	2.0
% Officers', Directors' Owners' Comp/Sales							.2	1.2
							(10) 4.2	(10) 1.9
							8.5	4.6
Net Sales ($)	92286M	162500M	1699307M	2249499M	698428M	1487571M	3020762M	2943922M
Total Assets ($)	2965M	21379M	131429M	351197M	152165M	767254M	366107M	696302M

M = $ thousand   MM = $ million
See Pages 9 through 22 for Explanation of Ratios and Data

Comparative Historical Data   Current Data Sorted by Sales

4/1/08-3/31/09 ALL	4/1/09-3/31/10 ALL	4/1/10-3/31/11 ALL	Type of Statement	0-1MM	1-3MM	3 (4/1-9/30/10) 3-5MM	5-10MM	75 (10/1/10-3/31/11) 10-25MM	25MM & OVER
15	19	16	Unqualified		1		2	1	12
8	7	11	Reviewed			1	1	6	3
2	7	4	Compiled	1			2		1
5	6	11	Tax Returns	1		1	3	5	
25	32	36	Other	1	3	4	2	7	20
55	71	78	**NUMBER OF STATEMENTS**	2	5	6	10	19	36
%	%	%	**ASSETS**	%	%	%	%	%	%
27.7	31.8	23.2	Cash & Equivalents				26.0	17.0	23.7
29.9	26.4	35.2	Trade Receivables (net)				44.9	52.5	25.9
.0	.1	.1	Inventory				.0	.0	.2
12.0	14.7	11.3	All Other Current				1.9	8.5	16.4
69.6	73.0	69.8	Total Current				72.7	77.9	66.3
9.9	9.3	9.9	Fixed Assets (net)				7.7	8.7	6.8
7.3	8.9	10.4	Intangibles (net)				2.6	5.9	18.2
13.2	8.8	9.9	All Other Non-Current				17.0	7.4	8.7
100.0	100.0	100.0	Total				100.0	100.0	100.0
			LIABILITIES						
10.3	9.5	10.6	Notes Payable-Short Term				10.2	7.7	2.1
2.0	1.2	1.5	Cur. Mat.-L.T.D.				.6	2.3	1.7
7.0	4.2	6.1	Trade Payables				8.4	8.1	3.3
1.3	1.8	.7	Income Taxes Payable				.0	.2	1.3
43.5	42.8	32.9	All Other Current				24.5	25.1	43.3
64.1	59.5	51.8	Total Current				43.7	43.5	51.8
15.7	9.0	10.7	Long-Term Debt				18.3	8.9	10.6
.2	.3	.2	Deferred Taxes				.0	.0	.5
9.2	3.1	5.6	All Other Non-Current				3.2	7.9	5.5
10.8	28.0	31.7	Net Worth				34.8	39.8	31.6
100.0	100.0	100.0	Total Liabilities & Net Worth				100.0	100.0	100.0
			INCOME DATA						
100.0	100.0	100.0	Net Sales				100.0	100.0	100.0
			Gross Profit						
95.2	97.1	95.5	Operating Expenses				95.6	95.2	97.4
4.8	2.9	4.5	Operating Profit				4.4	4.8	2.6
.6	1.9	.8	All Other Expenses (net)				-.4	.0	.4
4.2	1.0	3.7	Profit Before Taxes				4.8	4.8	2.3
			RATIOS						
1.9	2.1	2.5					4.8	3.2	2.1
1.1	1.2	1.4	Current				1.7	1.8	1.2
.9	.9	1.0					1.3	1.4	1.0
1.7	1.8	2.2					4.8	3.1	1.7
1.0	1.0	1.3	Quick				1.7	1.5	1.0
.6	.6	.8					1.3	1.1	.5
0 897.1	0 UND	1 255.3					0 UND	8 45.0	2 225.2
9 42.5	5 67.8	22 16.7	Sales/Receivables				42 8.8	37 10.0	9 38.5
44 8.4	42 8.7	53 6.9					52 7.0	60 6.1	46 7.9
			Cost of Sales/Inventory						
			Cost of Sales/Payables						
16.6	11.4	11.2					9.9	7.5	17.3
119.3	115.1	31.4	Sales/Working Capital				13.9	12.8	140.1
-280.8	-497.4	NM					59.1	69.5	-746.2
45.6	27.7	30.1						52.5	26.2
(42) 8.6	(46) 3.7	(53) 9.8	EBIT/Interest					(14) 19.4	(26) 8.8
2.9	.5	2.8						4.4	.9
	12.7	5.6							5.7
	(11) 3.5	(12) 1.8	Net Profit + Depr., Dep., Amort./Cur. Mat. L/T/D						(11) 2.2
	.8	.8							1.1
.0	.0	.0					.0	.0	.1
.3	.2	.2	Fixed/Worth				.0	.1	.6
14.8	.9	1.4					.3	.5	-.8
1.5	1.2	.9					.7	.6	1.2
6.8	3.3	2.9	Debt/Worth				1.8	1.4	5.1
-107.5	14.3	22.3					9.8	3.9	-6.3
166.7	64.2	107.4						114.8	61.4
(40) 68.3	(59) 20.4	(64) 41.5	% Profit Before Taxes/Tangible Net Worth					(17) 60.9	(26) 29.9
12.5	.6	13.9						23.3	.7
27.8	16.7	26.8					26.6	50.0	17.8
9.7	2.7	10.5	% Profit Before Taxes/Total Assets				10.2	15.6	6.8
3.1	-.7	2.7					3.3	8.3	.4
999.8	999.8	977.7					UND	999.8	877.0
168.8	419.6	239.7	Sales/Net Fixed Assets				637.6	274.8	200.9
44.9	66.6	45.8					57.8	68.5	46.0
21.6	23.6	16.1					10.7	16.5	17.4
6.9	9.8	5.4	Sales/Total Assets				5.2	5.3	6.8
3.1	4.1	3.3					3.5	4.0	2.6
.1	.1	.1							.1
(35) .2	(37) .2	(45) .2	% Depr., Dep., Amort./Sales						(22) .1
.8	1.1	.5							.5
3.2	.8	1.3							
(11) 7.0	(16) 1.6	(16) 2.9	% Officers', Directors' Owners' Comp/Sales						
9.8	5.8	7.3							
4113094M	7891491M	6389591M	Net Sales ($)	1076M	9404M	25522M	70519M	298264M	5984806M
1025196M	1327616M	1426389M	Total Assets ($)	2676M	3953M	6062M	30290M	55314M	1328094M

M = $ thousand   MM = $ million
See Pages 9 through 22 for Explanation of Ratios and Data

Current Data Sorted by Assets — Comparative Historical Data

Type of Statement / Number of Statements

	0-500M	500M-2MM	2-10MM	10-50MM	50-100MM	100-250MM	Type of Statement	4/1/06-3/31/07 ALL	4/1/07-3/31/08 ALL
			2	4	2	1	Unqualified		4
			1				Reviewed	1	3
		3					Compiled	1	3
							Tax Returns	1	5
		1	11	4	3	3	Other	13	8
		3 (4/1-9/30/10)	32 (10/1/10-3/31/11)						
		4	14	8	5	4	NUMBER OF STATEMENTS	16	23

Financial Data

0-500M	500M-2MM	2-10MM	10-50MM	50-100MM	100-250MM		4/1/06-3/31/07 ALL	4/1/07-3/31/08 ALL
%	%	%	%	%	%	**ASSETS**	%	%
		10.3				Cash & Equivalents	14.7	13.3
		38.5				Trade Receivables (net)	40.3	35.2
		3.2				Inventory	.6	.6
		10.8				All Other Current	4.6	2.7
		62.8				Total Current	60.3	51.8
		21.1				Fixed Assets (net)	23.2	26.7
		13.8				Intangibles (net)	10.0	4.0
		2.3				All Other Non-Current	6.5	17.5
		100.0				Total	100.0	100.0
						LIABILITIES		
		17.2				Notes Payable-Short Term	9.5	12.7
		6.0				Cur. Mat.-L.T.D.	3.4	8.6
		9.2				Trade Payables	6.8	6.6
		.0				Income Taxes Payable	.2	.4
		30.7				All Other Current	16.7	14.1
		63.0				Total Current	36.6	42.5
		6.4				Long-Term Debt	14.1	18.4
		.4				Deferred Taxes	.5	.3
		18.0				All Other Non-Current	3.1	4.6
		12.2				Net Worth	45.7	34.3
		100.0				Total Liabilities & Net Worth	100.0	100.0
						INCOME DATA		
		100.0				Net Sales	100.0	100.0
						Gross Profit		
		96.2				Operating Expenses	91.3	92.7
		3.8				Operating Profit	8.7	7.3
		1.3				All Other Expenses (net)	1.6	1.6
		2.5				Profit Before Taxes	7.1	5.7
						RATIOS		
		2.8					2.8	2.5
		1.4				Current	2.0	1.8
		.4					1.3	.6
		2.5					2.6	2.1
		1.3				Quick	1.8	1.4
		.3					1.3	.4
	23	15.6					54 6.7	17 21.0
	38	9.6				Sales/Receivables	63 5.8	49 7.4
	54	6.8					77 4.7	66 5.5
						Cost of Sales/Inventory		
						Cost of Sales/Payables		
		9.1					5.3	6.0
		21.7				Sales/Working Capital	9.9	23.9
		-3.3					13.8	-196.4
		23.6					30.9	22.0
	(13)	8.1				EBIT/Interest	(14) 6.4	7.6
		-1.9					1.2	1.0
						Net Profit + Depr., Dep., Amort./Cur. Mat. L/T/D		
		.5					.4	.2
		1.2				Fixed/Worth	.6	.5
		-.1					1.2	2.3
		.8					.5	.7
		5.0				Debt/Worth	.9	2.2
		-1.8					5.4	6.3
						% Profit Before Taxes/Tangible Net Worth	53.3	163.8
							(13) 26.1	(20) 45.5
							13.0	10.1
		32.9					32.1	31.7
		12.6				% Profit Before Taxes/Total Assets	12.3	12.8
		-5.5					1.9	.2
		33.8					16.9	98.2
		21.7				Sales/Net Fixed Assets	11.3	20.3
		12.9					5.7	6.1
		4.8					3.2	4.0
		3.8				Sales/Total Assets	2.1	3.0
		1.8					1.7	1.6
		1.2					1.1	1.2
		1.8				% Depr., Dep., Amort./Sales	(13) 1.9	(14) 2.2
		2.4					3.9	3.3
						% Officers', Directors' Owners' Comp/Sales		
	24977M	208255M	385737M	608965M	1807249M	Net Sales ($)	1322692M	1192617M
	5546M	62749M	187327M	312397M	761754M	Total Assets ($)	658765M	592728M

© RMA 2011

M = $ thousand   MM = $ million
See Pages 9 through 22 for Explanation of Ratios and Data

Comparative Historical Data   Current Data Sorted by Sales

Type of Statement	8	7	9					2	7
Unqualified	8	7	9						7
Reviewed	2	2							
Compiled	1	2	1					1	
Tax Returns	2	2	3			1	2		
Other	7	15	22			2	3	8	9
	4/1/08-3/31/09 ALL	4/1/09-3/31/10 ALL	4/1/10-3/31/11 ALL	0-1MM	1-3MM	3-5MM	5-10MM	10-25MM	25MM & OVER
					3 (4/1-9/30/10)			32 (10/1/10-3/31/11)	
NUMBER OF STATEMENTS	20	28	35			3	5	11	16
ASSETS	%	%	%	%	%	%	%	%	%
Cash & Equivalents	9.4	9.7	12.7					11.4	13.1
Trade Receivables (net)	38.6	41.9	36.0	DATA	DATA			41.4	36.4
Inventory	.2	.4	3.1					9.4	.2
All Other Current	9.0	8.4	8.9	NOT	NOT			8.0	8.8
Total Current	57.2	60.4	60.6					70.2	58.5
Fixed Assets (net)	26.0	22.7	20.5	AVAILABLE	AVAILABLE			16.4	22.0
Intangibles (net)	7.2	8.9	14.5					10.5	12.6
All Other Non-Current	9.7	7.9	4.4					3.0	6.9
Total	100.0	100.0	100.0					100.0	100.0
LIABILITIES									
Notes Payable-Short Term	18.6	24.0	9.9					10.5	2.0
Cur. Mat.-L.T.D.	4.6	6.3	3.8					7.6	2.7
Trade Payables	5.6	11.1	9.6					7.1	8.3
Income Taxes Payable	.3	.6	.5					.1	.9
All Other Current	16.1	26.1	20.6					21.8	16.4
Total Current	45.1	68.1	44.3					47.2	30.4
Long-Term Debt	12.0	14.4	14.4					10.5	18.3
Deferred Taxes	.2	.4	.3					.4	.4
All Other Non-Current	5.4	5.5	8.1					12.8	3.8
Net Worth	37.3	11.6	32.8					29.1	47.1
Total Liabilities & Net Worth	100.0	100.0	100.0					100.0	100.0
INCOME DATA									
Net Sales	100.0	100.0	100.0					100.0	100.0
Gross Profit									
Operating Expenses	95.7	96.3	94.7					93.7	93.8
Operating Profit	4.3	3.7	5.3					6.3	6.2
All Other Expenses (net)	1.3	1.4	2.0					1.3	2.5
Profit Before Taxes	3.0	2.3	3.3					5.0	3.8
RATIOS									
Current	2.4	2.4	2.8					7.5	2.7
	1.2	1.4	1.7					1.6	1.9
	.9	.4	1.2					1.2	1.5
Quick	2.2	2.2	2.4					4.3	2.3
	1.2	1.2	1.5					1.4	1.7
	.9	.3	.8					.7	1.2
Sales/Receivables	37 9.9	35 10.4	26 14.0					21 17.6	37 10.0
	53 6.9	45 8.1	45 8.1					37 9.9	58 6.3
	69 5.3	60 6.1	64 5.7					79 4.6	66 5.5
Cost of Sales/Inventory									
Cost of Sales/Payables									
Sales/Working Capital	9.0	10.9	6.3					4.4	5.6
	29.9	19.1	12.4					10.5	10.7
	NM	-18.4	56.4					27.7	14.7
EBIT/Interest	7.2	20.2	12.8					14.6	13.1
	(18) 3.4	(25) 1.9	(31) 6.4					(10) 8.3	(14) 3.6
	.1	-.8	-1.9					-3.8	-7.2
Net Profit + Depr., Dep., Amort./Cur. Mat. L/T/D									
Fixed/Worth	.3	.3	.3					.1	.3
	.7	.9	.9					1.1	.6
	3.0	-1.3	-6.1					-6.1	1.9
Debt/Worth	.7	.5	.8					.3	.6
	2.6	3.7	2.8					6.9	1.6
	4.6	-2.6	-20.6					-20.6	3.3
% Profit Before Taxes/Tangible Net Worth	75.1	51.4	96.1						57.2
	(17) 43.7	(17) 40.7	(25) 43.9						(14) 17.0
	1.8	1.2	4.1						-13.9
% Profit Before Taxes/Total Assets	29.5	20.0	30.3					33.3	18.5
	7.9	4.4	12.0					14.3	10.0
	-2.5	-10.8	-4.4					-8.9	-4.6
Sales/Net Fixed Assets	40.6	47.6	32.7					60.3	29.4
	19.9	21.1	15.5					26.7	12.3
	8.0	10.9	11.1					13.6	7.2
Sales/Total Assets	4.4	5.1	4.3					4.8	3.9
	2.4	3.4	2.4					3.7	2.3
	2.0	2.1	1.7					1.9	1.6
% Depr., Dep., Amort./Sales	1.2	1.1	1.2					.9	1.4
	(14) 2.2	(19) 2.0	(28) 2.2					1.2	(10) 2.2
	3.7	3.0	3.1					2.3	3.3
% Officers', Directors' Owners' Comp/Sales									
Net Sales ($)	1375898M	2441258M	3035183M			12400M	38739M	159617M	2824427M
Total Assets ($)	562256M	909557M	1329773M			7151M	17229M	73958M	1231435M

M = $ thousand   MM = $ million
See Pages 9 through 22 for Explanation of Ratios and Data

	Current Data Sorted by Assets							Comparative Historical Data	
Type of Statement									
Unqualified			3	2	1	2		10	10
Reviewed		2	5	1				11	10
Compiled	1	5	2					16	15
Tax Returns	11	6	5		1			19	20
Other	10	13	13	3				30	36
			9 (4/1-9/30/10)		78 (10/1/10-3/31/11)			4/1/06-3/31/07	4/1/07-3/31/08
	0-500M	500M-2MM	2-10MM	10-50MM	50-100MM	100-250MM		ALL	ALL
NUMBER OF STATEMENTS	22	26	28	7	2	2		86	91
	%	%	%	%	%	%	**ASSETS**	%	%
Cash & Equivalents	17.8	19.3	14.9					11.7	14.4
Trade Receivables (net)	16.8	24.9	28.7					28.9	22.9
Inventory	4.3	7.3	6.5					9.0	8.1
All Other Current	4.6	9.6	1.6					2.8	2.2
Total Current	43.5	61.2	51.6					52.5	47.6
Fixed Assets (net)	30.7	21.4	33.9					29.3	32.2
Intangibles (net)	9.0	3.9	5.5					10.5	11.9
All Other Non-Current	16.6	13.5	9.0					7.7	8.3
Total	100.0	100.0	100.0					100.0	100.0
							LIABILITIES		
Notes Payable-Short Term	28.8	13.8	6.4					13.2	8.4
Cur. Mat.-L.T.D.	2.5	3.5	6.7					9.2	5.9
Trade Payables	15.5	16.5	14.2					12.0	10.9
Income Taxes Payable	.0	.1	.3					.1	.5
All Other Current	12.5	19.2	12.6					11.7	10.6
Total Current	59.2	53.1	40.1					46.2	36.2
Long-Term Debt	30.2	14.5	27.1					26.9	26.8
Deferred Taxes	.0	.4	.4					.2	.4
All Other Non-Current	18.2	7.9	12.9					5.7	5.7
Net Worth	-7.6	24.1	19.5					21.1	31.0
Total Liabilties & Net Worth	100.0	100.0	100.0					100.0	100.0
							INCOME DATA		
Net Sales	100.0	100.0	100.0					100.0	100.0
Gross Profit									
Operating Expenses	93.1	99.0	94.1					92.0	92.3
Operating Profit	6.9	1.0	5.9					8.0	7.7
All Other Expenses (net)	2.0	.3	1.5					2.2	1.6
Profit Before Taxes	4.9	.7	4.4					5.8	6.1
							RATIOS		
Current	1.5	3.4	2.3					2.1	2.4
	.7	1.3	1.1					1.3	1.5
	.4	.7	.7					.9	.8
Quick	.8	2.1	1.4					1.6	2.0
	.5	.8	1.0					.9	1.1
	.3	.5	.5					.6	.5
Sales/Receivables	0 UND	9 39.6	22 16.8					27 13.8	21 17.0
	6 57.0	33 11.0	37 9.9					40 9.0	36 10.3
	33 11.0	43 8.5	56 6.5					52 7.1	54 6.7
Cost of Sales/Inventory									
Cost of Sales/Payables									
Sales/Working Capital	29.9	6.3	7.2					9.3	8.2
	-25.9	46.7	49.5					25.5	18.9
	-10.4	-18.7	-12.5					-64.9	-21.8
EBIT/Interest	7.1	22.3	30.7					7.8	9.8
	(17) 3.5	(17) 4.7	4.0					(74) 3.6	(78) 3.7
	-1.7	-.9	1.2					1.5	1.6
Net Profit + Depr., Dep., Amort./Cur. Mat. L/T/D								4.5	3.6
								(19) 2.4	(15) 2.1
								1.5	1.4
Fixed/Worth	2.0	.3	.5					.5	.5
	-3.0	1.2	1.7					1.6	1.4
	-.4	-1.1	-2.8					12.2	-2.4
Debt/Worth	3.5	.8	.8					1.1	1.1
	-9.7	3.6	3.9					2.7	2.8
	-1.8	-10.5	-9.4					182.8	-8.7
% Profit Before Taxes/Tangible Net Worth		48.2	61.9					91.5	70.8
	(18) 24.1	(19) 38.7						(66) 31.0	(64) 38.0
	-23.1	3.6						12.4	8.4
% Profit Before Taxes/Total Assets	36.9	24.8	22.8					21.0	19.1
	10.6	8.9	10.2					7.2	9.0
	-12.0	-.1	.7					1.4	1.7
Sales/Net Fixed Assets	84.0	90.6	32.4					42.1	18.9
	16.4	28.5	12.2					9.8	8.7
	9.0	13.2	3.6					5.6	4.3
Sales/Total Assets	8.1	5.5	3.2					4.0	3.8
	4.7	3.2	2.6					2.6	2.3
	2.5	1.7	1.6					1.7	1.5
% Depr., Dep., Amort./Sales	.6	.4	1.7					1.4	2.5
	(13) 2.1	(14) 1.3	(25) 4.1					(68) 3.0	(75) 3.8
	3.8	4.1	6.7					5.2	6.3
% Officers', Directors' Owners' Comp/Sales	3.3		1.0					3.3	3.0
	(14) 10.5	(11) 6.7						(36) 5.8	(42) 6.1
	17.2	9.0						8.9	9.4
Net Sales ($)	28143M	104928M	297404M	322049M	834291M	254557M		1098249M	1070455M
Total Assets ($)	5109M	27241M	115933M	180605M	147053M	320790M		726468M	725758M

© RMA 2011

M = $ thousand   MM = $ million

See Pages 9 through 22 for Explanation of Ratios and Data

Comparative Historical Data — Current Data Sorted by Sales

Hist 4/1/08-3/31/09 ALL	Hist 4/1/09-3/31/10 ALL	Hist 4/1/10-3/31/11 ALL	Type of Statement	0-1MM	1-3MM	3-5MM	5-10MM	10-25MM	25MM & OVER
7	12	8	Unqualified				1	2	5
12	9	8	Reviewed				1	4	1
17	10	8	Compiled	2	1	2		4	1
27	15	24	Tax Returns	8	6	3	4		3
35	26	39	Other	7	9	6	8	6	3
				9 (4/1-9/30/10)			78 (10/1/10-3/31/11)		
98	72	87	**NUMBER OF STATEMENTS**	17	16	11	18	13	12
%	%	%	**ASSETS**	%	%	%	%	%	%
14.9	13.3	16.8	Cash & Equivalents	15.8	20.2	13.1	19.1	13.9	16.5
28.0	31.0	24.2	Trade Receivables (net)	13.8	19.0	20.3	30.7	39.0	24.0
9.5	8.6	5.8	Inventory	5.2	1.2	7.6	12.4	4.1	3.5
2.5	1.8	5.4	All Other Current	13.9	2.5	6.4	1.2	1.8	6.8
54.9	54.7	52.3	Total Current	48.6	42.9	47.4	63.3	58.7	50.8
31.9	27.1	27.9	Fixed Assets (net)	31.7	43.2	15.7	22.4	25.6	24.2
6.6	10.9	8.1	Intangibles (net)	8.5	5.6	9.8	2.3	5.4	20.7
6.6	7.3	11.7	All Other Non-Current	11.1	8.3	27.2	11.9	10.2	4.4
100.0	100.0	100.0	Total	100.0	100.0	100.0	100.0	100.0	100.0
			LIABILITIES						
12.9	13.3	14.2	Notes Payable-Short Term	18.6	21.0	16.7	6.3	17.1	5.5
5.9	5.3	4.6	Cur. Mat.-L.T.D.	4.0	4.5	2.5	5.9	4.6	5.6
11.8	15.8	14.9	Trade Payables	12.5	13.5	13.8	17.3	21.2	10.6
.1	1.2	.1	Income Taxes Payable	.0	.0	.0	.4	.1	.0
13.6	14.5	14.5	All Other Current	9.4	19.0	11.5	18.1	15.2	12.0
44.2	50.1	48.3	Total Current	44.5	57.9	44.5	47.9	58.3	33.8
25.6	19.5	22.9	Long-Term Debt	34.2	38.8	11.9	12.6	13.6	21.4
.3	.7	.3	Deferred Taxes	.0	.0	.8	.0	1.0	.7
6.4	7.3	12.3	All Other Non-Current	16.7	17.5	8.1	10.3	10.0	8.5
23.4	22.5	16.2	Net Worth	4.6	-14.2	34.6	29.2	17.1	35.6
100.0	100.0	100.0	Total Liabilities & Net Worth	100.0	100.0	100.0	100.0	100.0	100.0
			INCOME DATA						
100.0	100.0	100.0	Net Sales	100.0	100.0	100.0	100.0	100.0	100.0
			Gross Profit						
94.2	98.3	95.0	Operating Expenses	95.6	97.7	93.4	94.5	96.3	91.7
5.8	1.7	5.0	Operating Profit	4.4	2.3	6.6	5.5	3.7	8.3
1.3	1.1	1.5	All Other Expenses (net)	3.6	.5	1.0	.3	.8	2.6
4.5	.6	3.5	Profit Before Taxes	.8	1.8	5.6	5.2	3.0	5.8
			RATIOS						
2.5	2.0	2.5	Current	5.5	1.4	2.0	3.1	2.3	2.7
1.3	1.4	1.1		1.3	.6	.9	1.2	1.1	1.3
.9	.7	.7		.5	.5	.7	.7	.6	1.1
2.1	1.6	1.4	Quick	2.7	1.4	1.3	1.5	1.9	1.8
1.0	.9	.8		.5	.6	.8	1.1	.7	1.0
.6	.5	.5		.3	.4	.3	.6	.5	.8
22 16.5	21 17.6	8 48.3	Sales/Receivables	3 112.5	0 UND	0 UND	16 22.8	18 19.7	22 16.4
35 10.5	40 9.2	33 11.0		14 26.8	28 13.2	31 11.6	34 10.7	41 8.9	69 5.3
48 7.6	66 5.5	50 7.3		47 7.7	37 9.7	44 8.2	53 6.9	56 6.5	81 4.5
			Cost of Sales/Inventory						
			Cost of Sales/Payables						
7.8	9.4	8.7	Sales/Working Capital	2.5	UND	9.0	9.1	19.7	12.7
24.4	24.0	64.6		37.3	-20.5	-999.8	43.8	50.2	25.4
-30.9	-15.7	-16.4		-8.9	-9.9	-28.6	-18.6	-17.6	59.0
10.7	8.7	17.7	EBIT/Interest	5.1	12.8		36.1	15.2	22.7
(88) 2.7	(61) 2.3	(72) 4.1		(12) 1.5	(14) 2.9		(13) 6.0	4.7	(11) 7.7
.9	-.6	1.0		-3.0	-2.3		1.6	1.2	1.0
2.0	3.2	5.7	Net Profit + Depr., Dep., Amort./Cur. Mat. L/T/D						
(16) 1.7	(17) 1.9	(13) 2.5							
.6	.7	.9							
.4	.4	.5	Fixed/Worth	.3	4.0	.1	.3	.7	.4
1.5	1.6	1.9		2.5	-2.6	1.1	.9	1.9	1.2
-2.2	-2.1	-.8		-.8	-.6	-.8	-.8	-1.6	-2.4
.9	1.1	1.0	Debt/Worth	1.1	18.2	.8	.6	1.7	1.4
2.5	2.8	6.7		9.5	-9.9	2.3	3.5	4.3	2.6
-6.8	-6.5	-4.6		-2.2	-2.4	-17.9	-15.1	-8.3	-8.3
77.1	42.4	65.3	% Profit Before Taxes/Tangible Net Worth	136.9			51.0		
(67) 33.2	(45) 15.1	(53) 36.7		(10) 18.3			(13) 35.6		
7.1	-15.0	3.3		-23.1			5.8		
30.4	15.4	23.4	% Profit Before Taxes/Total Assets	28.9	17.9	27.0	30.7	22.7	22.1
7.7	2.2	9.8		5.0	9.4	5.4	10.6	10.6	11.2
-.9	-8.2	.3		-14.0	-15.8	.0	4.4	3.2	.3
28.9	30.0	37.5	Sales/Net Fixed Assets	30.7	24.8	109.3	42.8	43.3	25.3
11.7	14.7	15.7		15.2	15.4	50.1	24.2	20.9	9.3
5.4	5.4	6.4		3.3	4.2	5.3	9.0	9.9	5.6
4.6	4.3	5.0	Sales/Total Assets	4.0	5.4	5.1	5.5	4.8	3.1
2.9	2.8	2.8		1.9	2.8	3.2	2.9	3.3	1.7
1.9	2.1	1.7		.5	1.6	2.4	2.5	2.4	1.0
1.4	1.1	1.0	% Depr., Dep., Amort./Sales	1.5	.7		1.0	.7	1.3
(75) 3.0	(55) 2.7	(62) 2.8		(10) 3.1	(10) 3.8		(13) 2.8	1.7	(11) 3.6
6.6	5.4	5.5		6.3	11.0		5.1	3.5	5.7
3.6	3.6	2.8	% Officers', Directors', Owners' Comp/Sales						
(42) 6.1	(25) 8.8	(36) 7.6							
9.9	14.8	16.5							
1545097M	1262133M	1841372M	Net Sales ($)	8078M	25909M	44013M	126342M	196267M	1440763M
891013M	859549M	796731M	Total Assets ($)	6725M	12930M	18953M	45814M	61460M	650849M

Current Data Sorted by Assets   **Comparative Historical Data**

						Type of Statement		
1	13	24	27	5	5	Unqualified	41	40
2	5	12	2			Reviewed	22	16
2	10	7	1		1	Compiled	18	21
12	10	5	1			Tax Returns	23	26
8	18	28	28	4	5	Other	37	45
	25 (4/1-9/30/10)		211 (10/1/10-3/31/11)				4/1/06-3/31/07 ALL	4/1/07-3/31/08 ALL
0-500M	500M-2MM	2-10MM	10-50MM	50-100MM	100-250MM			
25	56	76	59	9	11	**NUMBER OF STATEMENTS**	141	148
%	%	%	%	%	%	**ASSETS**	%	%
36.7	33.5	27.0	18.6		14.8	Cash & Equivalents	21.4	26.8
14.2	24.0	29.5	22.3		23.0	Trade Receivables (net)	22.8	24.8
2.1	.9	.0	3.4		.0	Inventory	1.5	1.6
10.9	7.1	8.0	9.5		6.9	All Other Current	6.7	6.4
64.0	65.5	64.5	53.8		44.7	Total Current	52.5	59.6
20.7	12.8	22.5	17.5		10.0	Fixed Assets (net)	23.5	18.5
7.1	9.0	4.5	17.5		38.1	Intangibles (net)	11.5	9.7
8.2	12.7	8.5	11.2		7.2	All Other Non-Current	12.6	12.2
100.0	100.0	100.0	100.0		100.0	Total	100.0	100.0
						LIABILITIES		
45.9	14.0	5.6	8.6		2.6	Notes Payable-Short Term	11.8	10.9
6.0	3.0	4.6	4.0		3.5	Cur. Mat.-L.T.D.	7.9	4.6
6.4	11.4	10.2	7.7		6.3	Trade Payables	10.2	10.3
.4	.1	.1	.3		.3	Income Taxes Payable	.2	.2
16.7	17.3	18.5	17.6		11.2	All Other Current	16.5	17.7
75.3	45.8	38.9	38.1		23.8	Total Current	46.6	43.8
8.3	15.1	17.0	14.6		34.0	Long-Term Debt	17.0	16.5
.0	.1	.1	.5		2.1	Deferred Taxes	.2	.2
1.6	8.4	3.5	6.0		14.9	All Other Non-Current	4.8	8.5
14.7	30.6	40.4	40.8		25.2	Net Worth	31.3	31.1
100.0	100.0	100.0	100.0		100.0	Total Liabilities & Net Worth	100.0	100.0
						INCOME DATA		
100.0	100.0	100.0	100.0		100.0	Net Sales	100.0	100.0
						Gross Profit		
91.1	91.5	90.4	89.1		83.6	Operating Expenses	90.2	89.9
8.9	8.5	9.6	10.9		16.4	Operating Profit	9.8	10.1
-.1	1.9	2.0	2.9		6.6	All Other Expenses (net)	2.3	2.8
9.0	6.6	7.6	8.0		9.8	Profit Before Taxes	7.5	7.3
						RATIOS		
4.1	2.9	3.3	2.0		2.8		1.9	2.8
1.6	1.5	1.5	1.3		1.8	Current	1.2	1.5
.6	.9	1.0	.9		1.1		.7	.8
3.8	2.2	3.0	1.9		2.0		1.7	2.6
1.4	1.5	1.4	1.1		1.7	Quick	1.0	1.3
.6	.8	.9	.6		.9		.5	.7
0 UND	0 UND	14 26.1	18 20.0		15 23.9		9 40.1	9 39.3
0 UND	18 20.0	31 11.8	29 12.6		47 7.8	Sales/Receivables	26 13.8	24 15.0
15 24.0	38 9.7	45 8.0	43 8.6		70 5.2		46 8.0	46 7.9
						Cost of Sales/Inventory		
						Cost of Sales/Payables		
14.0	9.0	5.9	5.0		7.9		8.8	5.7
31.3	18.1	15.3	16.5		8.9	Sales/Working Capital	45.4	17.4
-39.2	-95.7	180.4	-88.2		32.6		-25.2	-45.1
18.3	31.2	55.3	35.9				20.3	14.9
(15) 5.6	(37) 5.1	(60) 5.5	(53) 7.3			EBIT/Interest	(122) 6.3	(114) 5.5
.1	1.1	1.0	2.2				1.0	1.8
					77.0		19.7	6.7
			(13) 4.8			Net Profit + Depr., Dep., Amort./Cur. Mat. L/T/D	(18) 2.6	(21) 2.3
			.9				1.1	-.9
.0	.1	.2	.2		.4		.3	.2
.5	.4	.4	.6		-.2	Fixed/Worth	1.1	.5
NM	NM	1.8	1.5		.0		10.8	2.6
.2	.7	.5	.8		1.2		.9	.7
2.1	2.7	1.9	2.8		-4.4	Debt/Worth	2.8	2.7
NM	-10.8	5.8	12.7		-1.5		30.7	23.7
329.9	129.4	87.6	106.1			% Profit Before Taxes/Tangible Net Worth	89.6	90.6
(19) 78.3	(40) 47.5	(69) 37.8	(48) 51.2				(109) 47.4	(118) 41.9
12.5	22.9	9.3	14.1				8.6	10.7
89.7	53.4	32.1	26.9		19.7	% Profit Before Taxes/Total Assets	30.7	29.7
24.6	18.4	11.4	12.7		12.3		11.4	9.7
4.0	1.7	1.8	2.3		2.3		.5	2.1
650.8	153.7	43.3	43.2		43.3	Sales/Net Fixed Assets	38.1	50.4
85.0	48.1	25.6	22.7		22.8		16.5	21.5
16.2	23.6	11.7	9.3		12.6		8.7	10.9
10.0	4.9	4.2	3.2		3.0	Sales/Total Assets	4.0	4.6
5.6	3.8	3.5	1.7		1.0		2.6	2.8
4.0	2.9	2.5	1.0		.8		1.4	1.5
.7	.4	1.1	1.3			% Depr., Dep., Amort./Sales	1.4	1.1
(14) 1.7	(39) .9	(59) 1.8	(46) 1.9				(107) 2.1	(119) 1.9
3.1	1.8	2.7	2.9				3.3	3.0
	2.3	2.6				% Officers', Directors' Owners' Comp/Sales	2.7	4.4
	(19) 4.9	(15) 4.7					(32) 6.2	(35) 5.6
	12.9	9.7					13.4	9.8
38660M	300956M	1206421M	2211587M	742985M	3778368M	Net Sales ($)	3259006M	3585516M
6083M	64948M	367643M	1181311M	624248M	1684226M	Total Assets ($)	1880043M	2309209M

M = $ thousand   MM = $ million
See Pages 9 through 22 for Explanation of Ratios and Data

Comparative Historical Data | Current Data Sorted by Sales

Type of Statement	4/1/08-3/31/09 ALL	4/1/09-3/31/10 ALL	4/1/10-3/31/11 ALL	0-1MM	1-3MM	3-5MM	5-10MM	10-25MM	25MM & OVER
Unqualified	56	72	75		4	5	12	19	35
Reviewed	22	25	21		2	1	4	12	2
Compiled	16	26	21	1	6	6	1	5	2
Tax Returns	25	28	28	9	8	5	5	1	
Other	75	77	91	5	12	5	14	27	28
				25 (4/1-9/30/10)			211 (10/1/10-3/31/11)		
NUMBER OF STATEMENTS	194	228	236	15	32	22	36	63	68
ASSETS	%	%	%	%	%	%	%	%	%
Cash & Equivalents	24.0	26.0	26.2	24.9	32.9	23.3	31.2	25.8	22.1
Trade Receivables (net)	25.8	24.6	23.8	6.8	20.3	22.6	25.3	27.6	25.4
Inventory	1.0	1.4	1.3	3.5	1.6	.0	.0	2.9	.4
All Other Current	9.4	10.4	8.2	.1	13.6	11.0	5.6	7.9	8.3
Total Current	60.2	62.4	59.7	35.3	68.5	56.9	62.1	64.2	56.3
Fixed Assets (net)	17.8	18.0	18.0	32.9	19.7	15.7	14.5	16.2	18.3
Intangibles (net)	11.7	11.0	12.4	18.2	6.0	7.1	10.1	11.5	17.8
All Other Non-Current	10.4	8.6	10.0	13.6	5.8	20.3	13.3	8.2	7.6
Total	100.0	100.0	100.0	100.0	100.0	100.0	100.0	100.0	100.0
LIABILITIES									
Notes Payable-Short Term	12.7	9.2	12.3	27.8	26.3	15.4	14.1	6.9	5.3
Cur. Mat.-L.T.D.	5.1	4.2	4.1	4.6	3.9	3.0	5.5	3.9	4.0
Trade Payables	9.4	10.5	9.0	.4	8.3	9.4	9.6	11.4	8.5
Income Taxes Payable	.4	.3	.2	.0	.6	.0	.0	.1	.3
All Other Current	21.4	19.4	17.2	2.8	19.0	24.1	13.2	17.1	19.6
Total Current	49.0	43.4	42.8	35.5	58.1	51.9	42.4	39.3	37.5
Long-Term Debt	16.8	16.4	16.3	53.0	5.7	22.7	14.8	9.7	17.9
Deferred Taxes	.3	.5	.3	.0	.1	.1	.0	.4	.6
All Other Non-Current	5.1	6.9	5.8	.0	6.8	4.2	8.4	6.0	5.5
Net Worth	28.9	32.7	34.8	11.5	29.3	21.1	34.3	44.5	38.3
Total Liabilities & Net Worth	100.0	100.0	100.0	100.0	100.0	100.0	100.0	100.0	100.0
INCOME DATA									
Net Sales	100.0	100.0	100.0	100.0	100.0	100.0	100.0	100.0	100.0
Gross Profit									
Operating Expenses	91.5	90.4	90.0	65.7	91.6	94.0	94.2	91.6	89.7
Operating Profit	8.5	9.6	10.0	34.3	8.4	6.0	5.8	8.4	10.3
All Other Expenses (net)	2.6	1.4	2.3	13.6	.6	1.2	2.2	1.3	2.0
Profit Before Taxes	5.9	8.2	7.7	20.8	7.8	4.9	3.6	7.1	8.3
RATIOS									
Current	2.3	2.8	2.8	6.0	4.3	1.9	3.6	2.5	2.3
	1.3	1.4	1.5	1.4	2.0	1.2	1.5	1.4	1.5
	.9	1.0	1.0	.2	1.2	.6	.9	1.1	1.0
Quick	1.8	2.2	2.3	6.0	4.3	1.8	3.6	2.4	2.0
	1.1	1.2	1.3	1.4	1.5	1.2	1.3	1.3	1.2
	.7	.7	.8	.2	.9	.5	.8	.8	.8
Sales/Receivables	8 44.6	8 46.7	8 44.1	0 UND	0 UND	0 UND	3 131.1	15 24.9	18 20.5
	27 13.7	27 13.6	26 13.8	0 UND	15 24.1	14 26.7	25 14.8	32 11.5	31 11.8
	50 7.3	45 8.2	43 8.5	0 UND	33 11.2	36 10.2	39 9.4	48 7.5	47 7.7
Cost of Sales/Inventory									
Cost of Sales/Payables									
Sales/Working Capital	6.2	7.0	7.2	2.8	3.8	12.4	6.8	7.2	7.7
	29.2	19.7	18.1	41.4	12.8	37.0	18.1	18.9	16.5
	-39.7	653.0	-192.5	-2.9	204.9	-12.8	-40.3	80.2	-178.1
EBIT/Interest	19.4	36.6	31.3		18.2	31.0	13.6	48.8	44.2
	(150) 5.4	(174) 7.9	(183) 5.6	(20) 4.5	(20) 10.5	(24) 3.3	(53) 8.0	(60) 8.3	
	1.2	1.9	1.5	.3	1.4	.0	1.6	1.5	
Net Profit + Depr., Dep., Amort./Cur. Mat. L/T/D	7.9	4.8	6.4					4.2	11.6
	(29) 2.5	(30) 2.7	(29) 2.4				(10) 2.1	(15) 2.4	
	.8	.6	.7				.4	.9	
Fixed/Worth	.2	.2	.2	.0	.1	.1	.1	.2	.3
	.7	.5	.5	3.0	.2	.9	.4	.4	.8
	7.2	2.8	5.6	-115.3	1.2	-3.6	-4.4	1.5	-3.0
Debt/Worth	1.0	.7	.7	2.2	.3	1.3	.7	.6	.8
	3.1	2.3	2.3	8.2	.9	7.1	2.1	1.9	2.7
	NM	13.3	31.5	-1.5	4.1	-13.7	-44.1	4.9	-15.9
% Profit Before Taxes/Tangible Net Worth	73.1	89.4	107.0		92.8	252.2	78.8	93.6	125.1
	(146) 38.4	(183) 49.5	(182) 45.2	(26) 42.4	(16) 72.0	(26) 42.5	(57) 44.8	(48) 45.5	
	8.8	22.7	13.5	6.5	20.5	14.8	12.1	17.6	
% Profit Before Taxes/Total Assets	24.6	34.1	35.1	16.7	52.7	66.6	35.8	32.2	31.7
	9.7	15.4	12.7	5.4	14.3	24.8	10.5	13.6	14.1
	1.0	3.8	2.3	1.1	-2.8	3.2	1.7	2.8	2.1
Sales/Net Fixed Assets	54.7	62.4	61.9	UND	91.5	331.1	94.1	44.0	43.2
	20.0	25.3	27.2	85.0	30.8	36.2	40.3	24.4	23.2
	11.3	11.6	13.7	.2	17.5	16.6	21.1	15.9	11.5
Sales/Total Assets	4.2	4.7	4.5	7.1	5.0	4.5	4.7	4.5	4.0
	2.7	3.1	3.3	.5	3.7	3.6	3.7	3.3	2.7
	1.4	1.5	1.6	.2	1.8	2.1	2.9	1.7	1.3
% Depr., Dep., Amort./Sales	1.0	.8	.8		.6	.8	.3	1.1	1.3
	(139) 2.0	(156) 1.7	(169) 1.8	(23) 1.8	(14) 1.2	(25) .9	(49) 1.8	(51) 1.8	
	3.1	2.8	2.7	3.0	2.9	1.7	2.5	3.3	
% Officers', Directors' Owners' Comp/Sales	2.9	2.5	2.9		8.3		1.7	2.1	2.5
	(41) 4.3	(51) 4.6	(53) 4.9	(11) 12.9		(10) 3.1	(10) 3.9	(12) 3.0	
	8.5	9.8	10.1	17.9		9.6	9.8	4.7	
Net Sales ($)	6585775M	6969291M	8278977M	5556M	58734M	90136M	254631M	1086552M	6783368M
Total Assets ($)	4058734M	4048188M	3928459M	16746M	42839M	45668M	147088M	591480M	3084638M

© RMA 2011

M = $ thousand   MM = $ million
See Pages 9 through 22 for Explanation of Ratios and Data

Current Data Sorted by Assets   Comparative Historical Data

Type of Statement	0-500M	500M-2MM	2-10MM	10-50MM	50-100MM	100-250MM		4/1/06-3/31/07 ALL	4/1/07-3/31/08 ALL
Unqualified		10	27	31	14	18		115	101
Reviewed	2	20	41	11	2			102	99
Compiled	11	22	37	4	2	1		83	78
Tax Returns	54	57	25	2	1			126	116
Other	40	74	119	52	19	14		248	247
	108 (4/1-9/30/10)			602 (10/1/10-3/31/11)					
NUMBER OF STATEMENTS	107	183	249	100	38	33		674	641
ASSETS	%	%	%	%	%	%		%	%
Cash & Equivalents	31.3	18.6	18.6	20.0	13.5	16.6		18.5	16.6
Trade Receivables (net)	18.8	27.6	29.9	29.8	22.4	17.7		29.3	29.7
Inventory	5.3	7.0	7.9	6.1	7.7	3.9		7.3	6.7
All Other Current	3.5	5.7	5.5	5.7	5.3	10.3		5.2	6.1
Total Current	58.9	58.9	61.9	61.5	48.9	48.5		60.3	59.2
Fixed Assets (net)	27.7	27.4	22.2	20.1	18.6	10.8		23.6	24.9
Intangibles (net)	3.0	5.0	7.0	11.6	22.2	31.3		7.0	7.1
All Other Non-Current	10.3	8.7	8.9	6.8	10.3	9.4		9.0	8.8
Total	100.0	100.0	100.0	100.0	100.0	100.0		100.0	100.0
LIABILITIES									
Notes Payable-Short Term	20.8	9.5	7.2	7.2	6.4	2.8		11.6	11.1
Cur. Mat.-L.T.D.	5.5	3.7	3.3	3.4	3.9	2.0		3.3	4.1
Trade Payables	11.8	14.3	14.4	12.2	10.6	6.9		13.7	11.2
Income Taxes Payable	1.4	.3	.2	.3	.3	.6		.5	.3
All Other Current	29.4	15.8	18.2	20.3	14.7	20.3		17.1	19.0
Total Current	69.0	43.5	43.3	43.5	35.9	32.7		46.3	45.8
Long-Term Debt	20.3	17.5	16.7	13.6	18.0	19.5		16.5	17.3
Deferred Taxes	.0	.2	.2	.8	.7	3.0		.3	.3
All Other Non-Current	12.4	4.8	8.3	10.3	14.2	4.8		7.8	6.4
Net Worth	-1.8	34.0	31.5	31.8	31.2	40.1		29.1	30.2
Total Liabilities & Net Worth	100.0	100.0	100.0	100.0	100.0	100.0		100.0	100.0
INCOME DATA									
Net Sales	100.0	100.0	100.0	100.0	100.0	100.0		100.0	100.0
Gross Profit									
Operating Expenses	89.6	87.1	91.5	88.9	92.9	90.4		89.9	89.9
Operating Profit	10.4	12.9	8.5	11.1	7.1	9.6		10.1	10.1
All Other Expenses (net)	1.9	4.5	2.0	1.9	3.1	4.0		1.9	2.5
Profit Before Taxes	8.6	8.4	6.5	9.1	4.0	5.6		8.2	7.7
RATIOS									
Current	3.5	3.7	2.9	2.2	2.0	2.4		2.4	2.6
	1.4	1.5	1.5	1.3	1.4	1.7		1.3	1.4
	.6	.8	.9	1.0	1.0	1.1		.9	.9
Quick	3.3	2.7	2.3	2.0	1.4	1.9		2.0	2.2
	1.1	1.1	1.1	1.1	1.0	1.3		1.1 (640)	1.1
	.3	.5	.7	.6	.4	.7		.6	.6
Sales/Receivables	0 UND	1 381.9	18 20.1	19 18.8	24 15.3	17 21.3		7 53.3	7 49.1
	2 162.0	24 15.5	41 9.0	49 7.4	42 8.8	46 7.9		36 10.1	38 9.5
	30 12.3	45 8.1	68 5.3	75 4.9	58 6.3	65 5.6		59 6.2	63 5.8
Cost of Sales/Inventory									
Cost of Sales/Payables									
Sales/Working Capital	10.6	7.4	6.1	4.7	5.8	4.6		7.1	6.6
	39.0	22.9	12.1	12.6	12.6	8.6		20.8	19.8
	-12.4	-28.0	-76.4	853.6	-127.1	52.3		-113.8	-59.6
EBIT/Interest	14.7	32.1	31.7	25.6	12.0	18.8		18.2	20.7
	(64) 2.9	(125) 5.4	(189) 4.8	(77) 7.6	(33) 3.5	(27) 7.3		(503) 4.7	(498) 5.4
	.1	1.4	1.7	2.1	1.3	1.5		1.4	1.3
Net Profit + Depr., Dep., Amort./Cur. Mat. L/T/D			6.5	10.4	12.0	28.6		10.4	10.6
		(10) 1.3	(33) 3.8	(12) 4.4	(10) 5.2			(99) 4.5	(92) 3.5
			.4	.6	1.9	2.6		1.9	1.1
Fixed/Worth	.1	.1	.1	.2	.3	.3		.1	.1
	1.2	.7	.5	.7	1.3	.7		.7	.7
	-3.2	5.2	6.0	13.4	-.6	-.4		3.4	3.3
Debt/Worth	.6	.5	.7	.9	1.2	1.1		.9	.8
	5.3	1.9	2.2	3.8	3.2	9.8		2.5	2.4
	-4.8	18.2	18.2	158.3	-5.0	-3.8		25.4	14.3
% Profit Before Taxes/Tangible Net Worth	210.6	96.5	63.1	67.5	41.2	52.5		81.1	87.0
	(69) 55.8	(145) 37.4	(195) 32.3	(77) 38.1	(26) 15.4	(20) 34.3		(536) 38.2	(515) 38.9
	9.2	5.5	7.7	11.8	5.8	15.7		10.3	8.7
% Profit Before Taxes/Total Assets	71.2	32.6	21.1	18.6	11.6	12.9		26.5	25.8
	18.2	10.4	8.6	8.0	4.1	6.8		9.2	9.5
	.2	.4	1.5	2.4	.9	.9		2.0	1.0
Sales/Net Fixed Assets	328.3	99.8	80.2	85.0	33.5	50.9		85.6	72.6
	35.4	28.4	22.7	19.3	12.0	16.9		21.1	20.0
	7.2	6.9	7.3	6.0	8.2	6.8		7.2	6.4
Sales/Total Assets	8.4	5.2	3.5	2.7	2.7	1.7		4.4	4.3
	4.5	3.4	2.3	1.8	1.5	1.1		2.6	2.5
	2.1	1.9	1.4	1.0	1.0	.5		1.5	1.4
% Depr., Dep., Amort./Sales	.5	.5	.7	.7	1.2	1.3		.6	.6
	(55) 1.4	(120) 1.6	(190) 1.5	(78) 1.9	(26) 2.1	(17) 2.3		(495) 1.6	(476) 1.6
	6.4	6.1	3.5	4.4	3.1	6.6		3.6	3.8
% Officers', Directors' Owners' Comp/Sales	5.4	2.9	2.1					2.3	2.4
	(50) 8.8	(68) 4.3	(63) 3.8					(223) 5.8	(212) 5.5
	13.2	10.1	8.1					10.9	10.9
Net Sales ($)	142376M	821894M	3840073M	4566251M	5119186M	8280708M		22026656M	18954331M
Total Assets ($)	25074M	209944M	1167410M	2200668M	2744290M	5494606M		10071860M	9302770M

© RMA 2011

M = $ thousand   MM = $ million
See Pages 9 through 22 for Explanation of Ratios and Data

Comparative Historical Data　　　　　　　　　　　　　　　Current Data Sorted by Sales

			Type of Statement						
116	115	100	Unqualified	6	3	4	8	21	58
88	102	76	Reviewed	5	9	9	15	27	11
100	93	77	Compiled	12	16	12	13	19	5
124	174	139	Tax Returns	42	38	23	18	14	4
273	359	318	Other	37	42	35	59	61	84
4/1/08-3/31/09 ALL	4/1/09-3/31/10 ALL	4/1/10-3/31/11 ALL		108 (4/1-9/30/10)			602 (10/1/10-3/31/11)		
				0-1MM	1-3MM	3-5MM	5-10MM	10-25MM	25MM & OVER
701	843	710	NUMBER OF STATEMENTS	102	108	83	113	142	162
%	%	%	ASSETS	%	%	%	%	%	%
15.7	18.2	20.3	Cash & Equivalents	20.8	22.1	22.4	18.7	20.5	18.7
29.0	28.2	26.7	Trade Receivables (net)	9.2	21.4	29.3	32.6	34.9	28.5
7.1	7.2	6.8	Inventory	4.4	5.4	10.6	7.3	7.5	6.3
6.4	6.1	5.5	All Other Current	3.7	3.7	5.9	4.8	6.9	7.0
58.2	59.7	59.3	Total Current	38.0	52.6	68.2	63.5	69.8	60.6
25.2	24.1	23.4	Fixed Assets (net)	49.1	29.8	18.2	18.5	16.3	15.0
7.5	7.7	8.5	Intangibles (net)	2.6	7.5	4.6	6.3	7.6	17.1
9.1	8.6	8.9	All Other Non-Current	10.3	10.1	9.0	11.7	6.4	7.3
100.0	100.0	100.0	Total	100.0	100.0	100.0	100.0	100.0	100.0
			LIABILITIES						
12.5	12.1	9.6	Notes Payable-Short Term	13.4	10.4	10.8	11.9	7.6	6.2
4.0	4.0	3.7	Cur. Mat.-L.T.D.	6.7	4.3	2.6	3.1	2.5	3.4
12.5	11.9	13.1	Trade Payables	6.5	13.6	13.2	15.8	14.5	13.8
.4	.5	.5	Income Taxes Payable	.6	1.0	.2	.3	.2	.4
16.3	19.5	19.5	All Other Current	15.8	17.5	23.8	16.7	22.3	20.4
45.6	47.9	46.4	Total Current	43.0	46.7	50.6	47.8	47.2	44.3
17.3	17.7	17.2	Long-Term Debt	37.5	22.4	12.3	12.6	9.6	13.3
.3	.3	.4	Deferred Taxes	.0	.1	.4	.2	.3	1.2
6.7	8.3	8.4	All Other Non-Current	5.9	6.8	10.1	8.5	6.6	11.7
30.1	25.7	27.5	Net Worth	13.5	23.9	26.5	30.8	36.3	29.4
100.0	100.0	100.0	Total Liabilities & Net Worth	100.0	100.0	100.0	100.0	100.0	100.0
			INCOME DATA						
100.0	100.0	100.0	Net Sales	100.0	100.0	100.0	100.0	100.0	100.0
			Gross Profit						
91.9	91.6	89.7	Operating Expenses	77.5	86.5	93.8	92.2	92.0	93.7
8.1	8.4	10.3	Operating Profit	22.5	13.5	6.2	7.8	8.0	6.3
2.9	2.9	2.8	All Other Expenses (net)	11.4	2.2	.6	1.4	.7	1.6
5.1	5.4	7.5	Profit Before Taxes	11.0	11.2	5.7	6.4	7.3	4.7
			RATIOS						
2.4	2.8	2.8		3.2	5.4	4.6	2.4	2.6	2.1
1.3	1.4	1.5	Current	1.0	1.4	1.8	1.5	1.6	1.4
.9	.9	.9		.3	.6	.9	.9	1.1	1.0
1.9	2.1	2.3		2.8	4.6	3.3	2.2	2.2	1.7
1.1	(842) 1.1	1.1	Quick	.7	1.1	1.3	1.1	1.2	1.1
.5	.5	.6		.2	.3	.5	.7	.8	.6
9　39.7	8　46.1	6　62.0		0　UND	0　UND	11　32.4	20　18.2	19　19.6	19　19.3
37　9.9	36　10.2	31　11.6	Sales/Receivables	0　UND	20　18.0	33　11.0	38　9.5	40　9.0	43　8.5
61　6.0	60　6.1	58　6.3		22　16.7	50　7.3	59　6.2	60　6.1	66　5.6	62　5.9
			Cost of Sales/Inventory						
			Cost of Sales/Payables						
6.7	5.7	6.6		5.7	6.3	5.2	7.4	6.9	6.6
23.7	15.8	16.3	Sales/Working Capital	UND	28.9	11.1	14.4	12.4	13.3
-48.1	-54.6	-55.7		-3.4	-12.0	-45.9	-73.4	93.7	NM
16.8	16.4	24.4		7.8	14.8	16.0	37.9	49.3	21.5
(562) 4.6	(637) 3.9	(515) 5.3	EBIT/Interest	(45) 2.3	(72) 3.7	(62) 4.6	(89) 4.3	(116) 10.2	(131) 6.2
1.0	.5	1.5		-.5	1.6	1.3	1.3	2.9	1.4
11.9	8.3	10.6						45.9	12.9
(89) 3.3	(79) 2.8	(71) 3.8	Net Profit + Depr., Dep., Amort./Cur. Mat. L/T/D				(18)	3.9	(31) 5.4
.8	.9	1.2						1.3	1.7
.2	.1	.1		.3	.1	.1	.1	.1	.2
.8	.7	.7	Fixed/Worth	2.4	1.0	.4	.5	.4	.7
6.0	11.4	16.6		UND	UND	-64.0	3.1	1.7	-1.5
.9	.8	.7		.9	.4	.5	.6	.7	1.0
2.5	2.5	2.5	Debt/Worth	4.3	2.8	1.9	2.0	1.9	3.5
32.7	378.0	-935.8		-22.5	-21.9	-17.9	11.1	7.6	-10.6
70.3	64.1	77.5		103.9	112.2	73.8	64.8	84.4	66.4
(539) 27.9	(640) 22.9	(532) 35.2	% Profit Before Taxes/Tangible Net Worth	(74) 12.6	(78) 50.4	(57) 28.7	(90) 34.2	(120) 40.1	(113) 37.1
3.6	2.7	8.4		2.1	16.5	.7	8.9	11.8	12.5
19.6	20.6	24.2		16.2	40.2	29.3	20.4	30.4	18.7
7.0	6.1	9.0	% Profit Before Taxes/Total Assets	3.5	17.0	10.9	8.7	12.8	7.4
-.1	-.5	1.2		-.6	3.7	.5	1.5	3.3	1.8
66.1	75.0	87.9		38.5	133.1	111.2	111.5	89.2	77.8
18.5	23.8	22.6	Sales/Net Fixed Assets	2.2	19.4	31.8	24.9	40.5	22.3
6.0	6.4	7.2		.2	6.2	9.7	9.6	13.5	9.2
4.2	4.1	4.2		2.5	5.1	4.7	4.5	4.5	3.7
2.5	2.5	2.4	Sales/Total Assets	.9	3.1	3.1	2.8	2.9	2.2
1.4	1.2	1.3		.2	1.3	1.6	1.8	2.0	1.2
.7	.6	.7		3.0	.7	.4	.7	.5	.6
(500) 1.7	(574) 1.7	(486) 1.6	% Depr., Dep., Amort./Sales	(66) 14.9	(69) 1.7	(59) 1.2	(70) 1.6	(112) 1.0	(110) 1.7
4.5	4.6	4.3		24.4	5.8	3.0	3.3	2.2	3.0
2.2	2.4	2.7		6.1	4.7	3.3	2.5	.8	.5
(228) 5.0	(236) 4.9	(194) 5.2	% Officers', Directors' Owners' Comp/Sales	(26) 10.9	(47) 6.9	(28) 8.4	(43) 3.6	(38) 2.9	(12) 2.9
10.4	11.1	10.5		15.0	11.3	13.7	5.7	6.3	7.6
22642162M	23152596M	22770488M	Net Sales ($)	42915M	212181M	329971M	785189M	2242681M	19157551M
11600157M	12929000M	11841992M	Total Assets ($)	112116M	205642M	161785M	650454M	1120957M	9591038M

M = $ thousand　　MM = $ million
See Pages 9 through 22 for Explanation of Ratios and Data

Current Data Sorted by Assets

Comparative Historical Data

0-500M	500M-2MM	2-10MM	10-50MM	50-100MM	100-250MM	Type of Statement		4/1/06-3/31/07 ALL	4/1/07-3/31/08 ALL
	3	4	9	1	1	Unqualified		16	12
2	5	8	5	1		Reviewed		11	16
2	6	6	1			Compiled		16	12
12	17	9	1			Tax Returns		22	21
7	13	19	11	2	2	Other		30	32
	35 (4/1-9/30/10)		112 (10/1/10-3/31/11)						
23	44	46	27	4	3	NUMBER OF STATEMENTS		95	93
%	%	%	%	%	%	ASSETS		%	%
49.4	36.5	31.6	42.0			Cash & Equivalents		29.3	33.0
15.3	13.5	17.3	19.5			Trade Receivables (net)		18.7	14.8
2.4	.5	.2	.1			Inventory		1.6	.8
6.1	6.3	14.5	10.0			All Other Current		8.7	7.7
73.2	56.8	63.6	71.7			Total Current		58.2	56.4
6.0	17.0	16.2	5.7			Fixed Assets (net)		18.5	20.2
4.4	10.7	6.3	13.0			Intangibles (net)		10.1	10.4
16.6	15.5	13.9	9.7			All Other Non-Current		13.2	13.0
100.0	100.0	100.0	100.0			Total		100.0	100.0
						LIABILITIES			
19.1	6.6	6.2	10.2			Notes Payable-Short Term		15.6	10.4
.9	6.5	1.1	.6			Cur. Mat.-L.T.D.		1.2	2.2
26.3	17.6	17.9	11.6			Trade Payables		20.4	19.7
.1	.2	.2	.3			Income Taxes Payable		.2	.8
23.7	27.3	38.8	40.8			All Other Current		29.9	37.2
70.2	58.3	64.3	63.5			Total Current		67.4	70.3
11.0	13.3	5.3	1.4			Long-Term Debt		9.9	11.5
.0	.1	.3	.3			Deferred Taxes		.1	.1
20.0	17.1	8.9	7.1			All Other Non-Current		7.8	9.1
-1.1	11.2	21.2	27.7			Net Worth		14.8	9.0
100.0	100.0	100.0	100.0			Total Liabilities & Net Worth		100.0	100.0
						INCOME DATA			
100.0	100.0	100.0	100.0			Net Sales		100.0	100.0
						Gross Profit			
98.2	98.4	93.2	94.2			Operating Expenses		96.2	95.0
1.8	1.6	6.8	5.8			Operating Profit		3.8	5.0
-.7	-.3	.3	-.1			All Other Expenses (net)		1.1	1.1
2.5	1.9	6.6	5.9			Profit Before Taxes		2.7	3.9
						RATIOS			
4.1	1.8	1.8	2.0					1.7	1.6
1.7	1.2	1.1	1.1			Current		1.0	.8
.8	.6	.6	.8					.6	.5
4.1	1.5	1.4	1.8					1.6	1.3
1.7	1.0	.8	1.0			Quick		.8	.7
.6	.5	.5	.6					.4	.3
0 UND	0 UND	1 270.6	2 223.0					1 402.9	0 UND
2 232.5	2 189.9	6 59.3	19 18.8			Sales/Receivables		7 53.1	5 79.8
8 48.0	12 29.3	39 9.3	58 6.3					42 8.8	29 12.4
						Cost of Sales/Inventory			
						Cost of Sales/Payables			
13.2	26.1	12.5	4.0					23.2	20.9
61.7	118.4	73.4	29.7			Sales/Working Capital		-721.0	-118.5
-245.0	-21.9	-8.9	-17.6					-15.6	-9.1
21.0	64.8	24.3	81.7					22.1	20.4
(10) 10.6	(24) 4.3	(27) 5.5	(12) 15.7			EBIT/Interest		(59) 4.8	(60) 6.1
1.9	1.6	2.6	2.1					1.0	.8
						Net Profit + Depr., Dep., Amort./Cur. Mat. L/T/D			22.0
								(12)	3.8
									1.1
.0	.1	.1	.1					.2	.2
.2	.5	.5	.3			Fixed/Worth		.8	1.1
-.8	-5.4	4.5	-33.3					-26.9	-.6
.5	1.1	1.1	1.3					1.4	1.1
2.3	2.8	2.8	5.8			Debt/Worth		5.6	7.5
-4.5	-4.1	148.1	-816.1					-49.8	-5.1
151.9	44.6	96.6	39.7					72.4	60.4
(15) 82.4	(30) 25.5	(36) 44.8	(20) 24.7			% Profit Before Taxes/Tangible Net Worth		(70) 35.1	(60) 25.4
21.8	7.8	17.2	7.6					15.3	12.4
66.3	21.0	21.8	11.7					14.8	14.8
25.1	9.1	7.3	5.7			% Profit Before Taxes/Total Assets		5.4	5.0
12.1	2.5	2.7	2.5					.4	-1.2
UND	495.2	187.3	101.2					147.6	153.6
242.2	89.4	66.6	55.3			Sales/Net Fixed Assets		59.5	41.9
107.0	20.3	18.2	20.2					13.0	10.4
31.0	10.7	5.2	3.0					8.2	10.3
9.9	4.5	2.5	1.8			Sales/Total Assets		3.3	3.0
6.8	2.4	1.2	1.0					1.6	1.5
	.1	.3	.3					.3	.2
(26)	.3	(35) 1.0	(22) .8			% Depr., Dep., Amort./Sales		(68) .8	(70) .6
	1.5	2.9	1.6					1.7	2.1
1.9	.7	2.3						1.3	.9
(11) 2.2	(18) 2.0	(17) 4.4				% Officers', Directors' Owners' Comp/Sales		(30) 4.4	(26) 3.0
3.7	7.6	7.2						10.1	7.0
84055M	375955M	1235310M	1401817M	523315M	338327M	Net Sales ($)		3181812M	3431306M
5434M	46559M	226466M	627933M	261748M	478333M	Total Assets ($)		1338204M	1403468M

© RMA 2011

M = $ thousand   MM = $ million
See Pages 9 through 22 for Explanation of Ratios and Data

Comparative Historical Data   **Current Data Sorted by Sales**

			Type of Statement						
8	14	18	Unqualified	1			2	4	11
15	10	21	Reviewed	1	1	2	5	4	8
14	23	15	Compiled		2	2	5	3	3
21	23	39	Tax Returns	5	14	5	9	3	3
38	59	54	Other	6	4	6	10	10	18
4/1/08-3/31/09 ALL	4/1/09-3/31/10 ALL	4/1/10-3/31/11 ALL		35 (4/1-9/30/10)			112 (10/1/10-3/31/11)		
				0-1MM	1-3MM	3-5MM	5-10MM	10-25MM	25MM & OVER
96	129	147	NUMBER OF STATEMENTS	13	21	15	31	24	43
%	%	%	**ASSETS**	%	%	%	%	%	%
35.1	37.1	37.8	Cash & Equivalents	29.6	45.7	43.4	38.0	34.4	36.2
16.2	15.5	16.8	Trade Receivables (net)	22.5	6.1	11.9	13.8	19.6	22.5
.1	.4	.6	Inventory	.0	.0	3.6	.4	.0	.6
9.7	8.8	9.5	All Other Current	7.3	3.4	10.8	13.7	5.2	12.1
61.0	61.8	64.7	Total Current	59.3	55.1	69.7	65.8	59.2	71.4
15.7	14.1	12.6	Fixed Assets (net)	31.3	12.5	12.9	8.6	12.2	10.0
6.8	10.3	9.2	Intangibles (net)	6.9	10.1	5.3	8.8	12.1	9.4
16.5	13.8	13.6	All Other Non-Current	2.7	22.3	12.2	16.7	16.5	9.2
100.0	100.0	100.0	Total	100.0	100.0	100.0	100.0	100.0	100.0
			LIABILITIES						
12.0	8.8	8.8	Notes Payable-Short Term	12.5	6.5	5.0	18.0	3.4	6.5
1.6	1.9	2.6	Cur. Mat.-L.T.D.	3.7	3.7	7.5	.6	4.4	.4
14.6	17.3	18.3	Trade Payables	15.4	13.6	21.0	18.6	19.9	19.4
.2	.2	.3	Income Taxes Payable	.0	.0	.2	.1	.5	.5
26.4	37.1	32.5	All Other Current	27.8	32.3	17.2	33.4	23.6	43.6
54.7	65.3	62.4	Total Current	59.4	56.2	50.9	70.8	51.8	70.3
8.0	14.8	8.3	Long-Term Debt	29.4	7.2	2.4	1.4	11.7	7.6
.1	.1	.3	Deferred Taxes	.1	.3	.0	.0	.4	.7
8.7	8.4	12.6	All Other Non-Current	2.3	32.9	9.8	17.5	6.1	6.8
28.5	11.4	16.3	Net Worth	8.8	3.5	36.8	10.2	29.9	14.6
100.0	100.0	100.0	Total Liabilities & Net Worth	100.0	100.0	100.0	100.0	100.0	100.0
			INCOME DATA						
100.0	100.0	100.0	Net Sales	100.0	100.0	100.0	100.0	100.0	100.0
			Gross Profit						
95.4	96.3	95.5	Operating Expenses	97.8	96.5	93.3	95.2	94.6	95.8
4.6	3.7	4.5	Operating Profit	2.2	3.5	6.7	4.8	5.4	4.2
.1	.9	-.1	All Other Expenses (net)	1.2	-1.8	.0	.0	.0	.3
4.5	2.8	4.6	Profit Before Taxes	1.0	5.3	6.7	4.8	5.4	3.9
			RATIOS						
3.2	1.6	2.0		1.7	1.8	3.1	1.9	3.3	1.9
1.3	1.0	1.2	Current	1.1	1.2	1.5	1.1	1.3	1.3
.8	.6	.7		.5	.6	.6	.6	.6	.9
2.3	1.5	1.7		1.5	1.6	3.0	1.4	3.1	1.5
1.1	.8	1.0	Quick	.9	1.1	1.2	1.0	.9	1.0
.5	.4	.6		.5	.4	.6	.4	.6	.6
0 742.1	0 999.8	0 999.8		0 UND	0 UND	0 999.8	0 UND	1 537.5	1 256.2
7 54.4	6 64.8	4 81.2	Sales/Receivables	3 111.0	4 85.5	7 50.6	1 403.6	22 16.4	7 52.5
26 14.0	25 14.7	31 11.7		79 4.6	12 31.6	20 17.8	9 40.7	41 8.9	49 7.5
			Cost of Sales/Inventory						
			Cost of Sales/Payables						
9.5	10.4	11.6		11.5	12.9	4.3	17.2	19.5	10.7
49.4	-947.2	65.5	Sales/Working Capital	55.5	33.3	10.8	84.4	104.4	112.6
-34.0	-12.0	-22.0		-4.7	-8.7	-84.8	-21.9	-22.5	-66.4
36.0	21.6	33.4			17.6		62.7	42.3	83.7
(53) 6.5	(75) 3.7	(76) 8.5	EBIT/Interest		(10) 2.8		(21) 15.0	(14) 14.4	(20) 6.7
1.8	-.4	1.9			1.0		2.6	8.3	2.0
		30.5	Net Profit + Depr., Dep., Amort./Cur. Mat. L/T/D						
	(13) 11.0							
		2.4							
.1	.1	.1		.1	.1	.0	.1	.1	.1
.4	.7	.4	Fixed/Worth	2.1	.3	.1	.2	.6	.4
2.4	-1.6	-33.3		-1.6	5.0	2.4	-.8	-6.7	-33.3
.6	1.1	1.1		1.2	1.1	.4	2.0	.5	1.1
1.9	6.5	4.3	Debt/Worth	UND	3.2	1.8	8.1	3.1	5.1
15.3	-7.0	-47.3		-3.4	150.3	8.2	-4.6	-55.3	-816.1
51.5	58.6	82.5			107.4	96.4	136.2	70.2	44.6
(77) 16.4	(87) 17.6	(106) 33.7	% Profit Before Taxes/Tangible Net Worth	(18) 34.7	(13) 32.1	(21) 71.0	(15) 41.1	(32) 26.4	
4.7	3.7	13.4			15.4	10.3	23.3	11.8	7.6
18.2	12.4	21.6		31.0	18.2	20.1	35.9	29.8	12.8
5.7	4.6	8.9	% Profit Before Taxes/Total Assets	6.6	8.9	12.6	10.4	14.2	5.7
.6	-.6	2.7		-9.9	3.1	4.0	2.9	7.4	1.7
301.5	240.2	277.0		UND	150.4	UND	999.8	192.7	157.6
58.3	48.6	73.7	Sales/Net Fixed Assets	32.9	97.8	40.3	106.3	53.8	68.4
18.2	14.9	22.3		.7	16.6	20.6	48.0	20.9	25.4
13.4	6.7	7.4		7.1	4.5	7.0	9.0	12.6	13.3
3.3	2.6	3.1	Sales/Total Assets	1.8	3.2	3.7	3.3	2.9	3.1
1.7	1.4	1.6		.6	1.5	.8	1.6	1.7	1.8
.3	.3	.2			.2		.1	.1	.2
(58) .8	(90) .7	(97) .7	% Depr., Dep., Amort./Sales	(11) .4		(19) .3	(16) .8	(35) .6	
2.5	2.4	1.7			1.5		2.4	2.7	1.2
1.3	1.6	1.0			2.0		2.3		
(35) 3.0	(43) 3.3	(52) 2.5	% Officers', Directors' Owners' Comp/Sales	(12) 5.2		(16) 3.0			
13.1	6.7	6.5			10.8		4.5		
1945610M	14477811M	3958779M	Net Sales ($)	5785M	45400M	58171M	230107M	390042M	3229274M
664155M	1936846M	1646473M	Total Assets ($)	11287M	20663M	46252M	90724M	153111M	1324436M

Current Data Sorted by Assets

Comparative Historical Data

0-500M	500M-2MM	2-10MM	10-50MM	50-100MM	100-250MM	Type of Statement	4/1/06-3/31/07 ALL	4/1/07-3/31/08 ALL
1		1	4	4	2	Unqualified	8	12
	1	3				Reviewed	2	3
		1	3			Compiled	6	9
3	5	3				Tax Returns	11	11
1	8	9	4	1	2	Other	15	29
	9 (4/1-9/30/10)		47 (10/1/10-3/31/11)					
5	14	17	11	5	4	**NUMBER OF STATEMENTS**	42	64
%	%	%	%	%	%	**ASSETS**	%	%
	20.2	29.4	35.3			Cash & Equivalents	24.2	30.3
	24.5	2.7	4.8			Trade Receivables (net)	10.1	7.3
	.1	.8	1.0			Inventory	1.5	2.0
	2.3	20.2	7.6			All Other Current	9.3	8.2
	47.1	53.1	48.8			Total Current	45.2	47.8
	36.9	34.5	37.9			Fixed Assets (net)	39.5	34.6
	5.8	2.3	3.6			Intangibles (net)	3.9	3.4
	10.2	10.1	9.8			All Other Non-Current	11.5	14.1
	100.0	100.0	100.0			Total	100.0	100.0
						LIABILITIES		
	6.9	6.9	.0			Notes Payable-Short Term	5.4	7.2
	5.4	4.0	3.0			Cur. Mat.-L.T.D.	4.7	4.6
	21.0	7.5	10.1			Trade Payables	11.1	14.5
	.0	.2	.0			Income Taxes Payable	.9	.1
	15.8	42.2	36.3			All Other Current	28.1	31.6
	49.2	60.9	49.5			Total Current	50.2	57.9
	29.9	16.6	25.4			Long-Term Debt	30.1	23.4
	.0	.3	.6			Deferred Taxes	.0	.4
	8.8	24.7	4.0			All Other Non-Current	9.8	11.5
	12.1	-2.5	20.5			Net Worth	9.9	6.7
	100.0	100.0	100.0			Total Liabilties & Net Worth	100.0	100.0
						INCOME DATA		
	100.0	100.0	100.0			Net Sales	100.0	100.0
						Gross Profit		
	96.4	98.2	94.1			Operating Expenses	94.0	95.7
	3.6	1.8	5.9			Operating Profit	6.0	4.3
	.9	-1.3	.7			All Other Expenses (net)	.8	.3
	2.7	3.2	5.2			Profit Before Taxes	5.2	4.0
						RATIOS		
	3.1	2.8	1.3			Current	1.6	1.3
	1.0	1.2	1.0				.8	.8
	.6	.3	.8				.4	.5
	3.1	1.5	1.1			Quick	1.4	1.1
	1.0	.4	.9				.6	.6
	.5	.2	.6				.3	.3
0 UND	0 999.8	1 429.7				Sales/Receivables	0 UND	0 UND
15 24.2	2 149.8	4 81.2					6 60.7	3 116.8
40 9.2	15 24.8	19 19.2					21 17.1	12 30.2
						Cost of Sales/Inventory		
						Cost of Sales/Payables		
	29.7	13.5	18.6			Sales/Working Capital	14.7	27.5
	NM	30.1	130.6				-32.3	-50.9
	-12.8	-5.1	-29.4				-8.0	-9.0
		20.2				EBIT/Interest	8.1	8.5
		(13) 3.2					(32) 2.5	(43) 2.1
		-.4					.2	.9
						Net Profit + Depr., Dep., Amort./Cur. Mat. L/T/D		
	.8	.2	.8			Fixed/Worth	.8	.3
	3.7	1.8	1.5				2.9	2.7
	-2.4	-4.5	3.8				-3.8	-6.0
	2.3	1.4	1.8			Debt/Worth	2.0	2.7
	12.2	4.7	7.0				3.7	8.2
	-9.9	-6.0	21.1				-30.1	-7.2
	94.1	81.8	233.5			% Profit Before Taxes/Tangible Net Worth	110.1	92.7
(10) 30.4	(12) 31.6	(10) 29.6				(28) 30.0	(43) 46.0
	9.2	14.4	18.3				-.9	6.1
	15.2	15.8	10.0			% Profit Before Taxes/Total Assets	21.3	16.8
	3.7	7.1	8.3				3.6	4.8
	1.8	-.3	3.5				-2.6	.1
	106.2	130.8	57.3			Sales/Net Fixed Assets	88.4	91.3
	15.6	42.7	15.7				10.0	13.7
	4.1	1.8	1.7				2.7	2.7
	6.7	5.1	2.3			Sales/Total Assets	4.0	4.9
	3.9	1.8	1.8				2.6	2.6
	2.4	1.0	1.1				1.6	1.2
	.4	.4	.4			% Depr., Dep., Amort./Sales	.4	.4
(11) 1.5	(14) 2.7	(10) 1.9				(32) 3.5	(47) 1.4
	4.8	6.3	4.4				6.2	7.3
						% Officers', Directors' Owners' Comp/Sales		1.1
							(13) 1.8
							7.8
9122M	62107M	225888M	405136M	668038M	857658M	Net Sales ($)	2439170M	3791407M
1360M	14664M	87657M	229165M	386542M	656456M	Total Assets ($)	982052M	1550061M

M = $ thousand   MM = $ million
See Pages 9 through 22 for Explanation of Ratios and Data

Comparative Historical Data

Current Data Sorted by Sales

			Type of Statement						
11	13	12	Unqualified		1			2	9
6	7	4	Reviewed			1	3		
7	10	4	Compiled			1		2	1
12	17	11	Tax Returns		5		2	2	2
21	19	25	Other	1	6	3	3	5	7
4/1/08-3/31/09 ALL	4/1/09-3/31/10 ALL	4/1/10-3/31/11 ALL			9 (4/1-9/30/10)		47 (10/1/10-3/31/11)		
				0-1MM	1-3MM	3-5MM	5-10MM	10-25MM	25MM & OVER
57	66	56	NUMBER OF STATEMENTS	1	12	5	8	11	19
%	%	%	ASSETS	%	%	%	%	%	%
30.2	28.0	29.9	Cash & Equivalents		19.1			33.3	41.8
9.2	7.6	10.0	Trade Receivables (net)		21.7			7.0	3.5
1.5	.5	.6	Inventory		.2			.6	.7
10.8	6.3	10.3	All Other Current		1.3			18.4	11.1
51.7	42.4	50.8	Total Current		42.3			59.3	57.1
30.1	36.1	31.4	Fixed Assets (net)		38.3			22.8	21.4
7.2	3.5	4.8	Intangibles (net)		7.3			7.2	3.3
11.0	18.0	13.0	All Other Non-Current		12.1			10.6	18.2
100.0	100.0	100.0	Total		100.0			100.0	100.0
			LIABILITIES						
5.3	5.2	5.5	Notes Payable-Short Term		2.9			.6	1.8
3.7	6.6	4.2	Cur. Mat.-L.T.D.		9.8			4.9	1.0
13.2	8.0	11.7	Trade Payables		24.1			12.0	9.4
.1	.2	.1	Income Taxes Payable		.0			.1	.2
29.8	30.8	29.9	All Other Current		8.0			55.0	34.7
52.1	50.8	51.5	Total Current		44.8			72.6	47.0
15.1	24.0	21.0	Long-Term Debt		39.1			16.5	12.5
.4	.2	.2	Deferred Taxes		.0			.6	.1
7.5	9.2	12.1	All Other Non-Current		13.9			22.4	7.3
24.9	15.9	15.1	Net Worth		2.1			-12.1	33.1
100.0	100.0	100.0	Total Liabilities & Net Worth		100.0			100.0	100.0
			INCOME DATA						
100.0	100.0	100.0	Net Sales		100.0			100.0	100.0
			Gross Profit						
97.1	96.2	95.8	Operating Expenses		94.3			96.0	95.7
2.9	3.8	4.2	Operating Profit		5.7			4.0	4.3
.7	1.3	.1	All Other Expenses (net)		1.3			.8	.1
2.3	2.6	4.1	Profit Before Taxes		4.5			3.3	4.2
			RATIOS						
1.6	1.4	2.1			1.9			2.7	2.3
1.0	.8	1.1	Current		1.0			1.2	1.3
.5	.4	.7			.7			.7	.9
1.4	1.1	1.4			1.9			2.5	1.7
.9	.6	.9	Quick		.9			.9	1.0
.4	.3	.4			.4			.3	.6
0 UND	0 UND	0 999.8		0 UND			0 999.8	0 UND	
6 65.5	2 156.2	5 69.2	Sales/Receivables	17 21.9			7 50.5	2 148.3	
17 21.8	10 37.0	17 21.6		39 9.5			14 25.6	9 38.5	
			Cost of Sales/Inventory						
			Cost of Sales/Payables						
12.6	29.5	12.6			49.4			15.2	5.3
170.9	-40.5	90.8	Sales/Working Capital		UND			45.6	30.1
-12.4	-6.6	-12.7			-28.4			-7.0	-32.9
11.5	9.7	24.0							
(36) 2.8	(34) 1.7	(35) 3.5	EBIT/Interest						
.5	.4	1.4							
			Net Profit + Depr., Dep., Amort./Cur. Mat. L/T/D						
.2	.3	.2			1.1			.0	.2
1.3	2.1	1.4	Fixed/Worth		4.9			1.8	.8
-4.5	-6.4	UND			-.6			.0	1.8
1.5	1.2	1.2			2.4			1.8	1.1
4.6	5.1	4.6	Debt/Worth		16.2			4.8	2.5
-10.5	-11.5	UND			-2.7			-3.4	10.4
51.1	86.4	82.3	% Profit Before Taxes/Tangible Net Worth						137.2
(42) 19.7	(44) 24.4	(43) 28.6							(17) 21.1
.9	9.2	9.4							5.0
12.4	13.4	15.0	% Profit Before Taxes/Total Assets		53.1			12.8	13.3
4.0	5.3	6.8			11.1			8.7	5.9
-.2	.1	1.8			1.8			2.2	1.7
83.2	57.0	90.2			77.8			219.8	57.3
15.5	17.0	24.9	Sales/Net Fixed Assets		19.1			123.0	39.9
3.4	2.6	2.9			3.3			3.2	11.2
5.1	4.2	4.5			6.1			7.0	2.7
2.8	2.0	2.3	Sales/Total Assets		3.6			3.1	1.8
1.5	1.4	1.1			2.2			1.1	.9
.4	.6	.4			.3				.4
(42) 2.1	(53) 2.4	(46) 1.4	% Depr., Dep., Amort./Sales	(11) 1.5				(16) 1.3	
5.6	8.2	6.0			4.8				2.0
1.1	.7	.9							
(15) 1.8	(19) 1.7	(18) 2.5	% Officers', Directors' Owners' Comp/Sales						
4.8	4.0	6.8							
4837804M	3984628M	2227949M	Net Sales ($)	489M	27529M	21566M	53084M	186043M	1939238M
1719057M	2030493M	1375844M	Total Assets ($)	111M	8652M	15357M	37128M	87503M	1227093M

M = $ thousand   MM = $ million
See Pages 9 through 22 for Explanation of Ratios and Data

Current Data Sorted by Assets

Comparative Historical Data

0-500M	500M-2MM	2-10MM	10-50MM	50-100MM	100-250MM	Type of Statement		4/1/06-3/31/07 ALL		4/1/07-3/31/08 ALL
		1	6	1	2	Unqualified		17		13
		2				Reviewed		1		2
		2				Compiled		5		3
1	1	1				Tax Returns		4		3
2	2	8	8	1	5	Other		13		19
2		5 (4/1-9/30/10)		40 (10/1/10-3/31/11)						
5	3	14	14	2	7	NUMBER OF STATEMENTS		40		40
%	%	%	%	%	%	ASSETS		%		%
		25.6	29.0			Cash & Equivalents		36.0		32.8
		20.0	14.1			Trade Receivables (net)		11.9		11.8
		3.0	1.0			Inventory		3.2		1.1
		3.9	17.0			All Other Current		9.4		13.5
		52.4	61.1			Total Current		60.5		59.2
		35.3	10.6			Fixed Assets (net)		21.4		22.8
		1.7	16.6			Intangibles (net)		3.4		6.9
		10.7	11.7			All Other Non-Current		14.7		11.1
		100.0	100.0			Total		100.0		100.0
						LIABILITIES				
		2.3	.6			Notes Payable-Short Term		5.6		3.8
		2.2	.4			Cur. Mat.-L.T.D.		2.6		5.4
		7.8	10.5			Trade Payables		11.3		13.5
		.0	1.5			Income Taxes Payable		.6		.8
		20.1	26.1			All Other Current		17.7		21.3
		32.4	39.1			Total Current		37.7		44.8
		26.0	3.8			Long-Term Debt		8.6		8.5
		.2	1.7			Deferred Taxes		.6		.1
		.4	15.5			All Other Non-Current		7.6		5.7
		41.1	39.8			Net Worth		45.4		40.8
		100.0	100.0			Total Liabilties & Net Worth		100.0		100.0
						INCOME DATA				
		100.0	100.0			Net Sales		100.0		100.0
						Gross Profit				
		93.4	94.5			Operating Expenses		89.9		88.6
		6.6	5.5			Operating Profit		10.1		11.4
		3.4	-.9			All Other Expenses (net)		1.1		1.9
		3.1	6.3			Profit Before Taxes		9.0		9.5
						RATIOS				
		3.4	3.1					4.1		2.5
		2.0	1.9			Current		1.7		1.6
		.6	.9					1.1		.9
		2.9	2.3					2.5		2.1
		1.6	1.2			Quick		1.5		1.0
		.6	.7					.8		.7
		2 173.5	5 71.5				0	UND	0	UND
		23 16.1	15 24.8			Sales/Receivables	5	80.6	7	54.4
		51 7.1	36 10.2				17	21.6	46	7.9
						Cost of Sales/Inventory				
						Cost of Sales/Payables				
		5.5	3.1					2.3		3.3
		25.4	8.4			Sales/Working Capital		10.8		9.2
		-7.5	-16.0					125.6		-145.4
		78.3						51.2		22.2
		(11) 12.9				EBIT/Interest	(27)	19.7	(23)	6.1
		1.0						4.0		1.1
						Net Profit + Depr., Dep., Amort./Cur. Mat. L/T/D				
		.1	.2					.0		.2
		1.4	.6			Fixed/Worth		.3		.6
		2.7	-.2					1.0		2.1
		.6	.7					.4		.5
		1.6	1.7			Debt/Worth		1.1		1.7
		4.4	-6.7					3.3		7.1
		117.7	56.8			% Profit Before Taxes/Tangible Net Worth		45.5		67.6
		20.3	(10) 31.6				(35)	15.0	(36)	19.2
		3.5	13.5					7.0		6.2
		18.7	14.6			% Profit Before Taxes/Total Assets		29.4		19.6
		6.7	6.2					8.1		8.0
		.5	3.1					2.7		.8
		54.1	58.0			Sales/Net Fixed Assets		244.1		116.1
		10.9	31.6					16.5		16.2
		2.4	15.6					4.2		4.6
		3.7	2.6			Sales/Total Assets		4.5		3.4
		1.9	1.2					1.5		1.4
		.9	.9					.8		.7
		1.5				% Depr., Dep., Amort./Sales		.7		.4
		(10) 2.9					(22)	2.5	(27)	2.6
		8.7						6.8		3.9
						% Officers', Directors' Owners' Comp/Sales				
41662M	7560M	234690M	561435M	119738M	570263M	Net Sales ($)		1147014M		1227038M
1738M	3321M	58453M	330831M	133448M	910307M	Total Assets ($)		979907M		1013801M

M = $ thousand   MM = $ million
See Pages 9 through 22 for Explanation of Ratios and Data

Comparative Historical Data

Current Data Sorted by Sales

			Type of Statement	0-1MM	1-3MM	3-5MM	5-10MM	10-25MM	25MM & OVER
17	13	10	Unqualified		1		1	3	6
6	4	2	Reviewed	1	1				
6	2	3	Compiled				3		
6	5	4	Tax Returns	2					1
17	21	26	Other		4		4	6	12
4/1/08-3/31/09	4/1/09-3/31/10	4/1/10-3/31/11				5 (4/1-9/30/10)	40 (10/1/10-3/31/11)		
ALL	ALL	ALL							
52	45	45	**NUMBER OF STATEMENTS**	3	6		8	9	19
%	%	%	**ASSETS**	%	%	%	%	%	%
28.3	27.7	26.8	Cash & Equivalents						28.8
14.2	16.9	17.4	Trade Receivables (net)						12.2
2.4	1.5	2.3	Inventory						2.1
7.9	11.6	8.7	All Other Current						11.4
52.8	57.7	55.1	Total Current						54.4
24.8	22.4	20.9	Fixed Assets (net)						15.7
8.0	8.5	11.1	Intangibles (net)						20.6
14.4	11.2	12.9	All Other Non-Current						9.4
100.0	100.0	100.0	Total						100.0
			LIABILITIES						
4.7	5.7	7.5	Notes Payable-Short Term						.3
1.9	.8	1.7	Cur. Mat.-L.T.D.						.3
10.4	14.7	12.6	Trade Payables						14.5
2.2	1.6	1.3	Income Taxes Payable						1.9
19.9	19.6	21.1	All Other Current						20.2
39.1	42.3	44.2	Total Current						37.2
13.2	9.4	14.3	Long-Term Debt						11.8
.3	.3	.7	Deferred Taxes						1.0
9.2	14.2	6.7	All Other Non-Current						8.0
38.1	34.0	34.1	Net Worth						42.0
100.0	100.0	100.0	Total Liabilties & Net Worth						100.0
			INCOME DATA						
100.0	100.0	100.0	Net Sales						100.0
			Gross Profit						
93.1	93.4	95.9	Operating Expenses						99.1
6.9	6.6	4.1	Operating Profit						.9
3.2	2.8	.1	All Other Expenses (net)						-.9
3.7	3.8	4.0	Profit Before Taxes						1.8
			RATIOS						
2.1	2.9	2.9	Current						2.2
1.2	1.4	1.3							1.6
1.0	.7	.8							1.0
2.0	2.8	2.1	Quick						1.9
1.0	1.0	1.0							1.0
.6	.5	.7							.8
4 97.2	5 72.8	5 77.8	Sales/Receivables						6 65.5
11 32.2	21 17.1	19 19.1							19 19.1
40 9.2	44 8.4	40 9.1							30 12.1
			Cost of Sales/Inventory						
			Cost of Sales/Payables						
4.4	2.1	4.1	Sales/Working Capital						3.4
18.3	12.5	35.0							31.0
-585.8	-23.5	-14.5							-53.6
11.6	25.0	42.5	EBIT/Interest						78.3
(32) 3.2	(26) 3.8	(26) 8.3						(11)	16.5
.8	-.3	.5							-20.0
			Net Profit + Depr., Dep., Amort./Cur. Mat. L/T/D						
.1	.2	.2	Fixed/Worth						.3
.6	.5	.9							.8
2.8	NM	13.8							-.7
.8	.8	.7	Debt/Worth						.7
1.8	1.2	1.8							1.6
4.4	NM	589.1							-7.3
45.8	32.0	95.1	% Profit Before Taxes/Tangible Net Worth						56.8
(43) 10.7	(34) 13.2	(36) 25.4						(14)	20.9
.0	-.7	12.6							16.1
16.1	11.1	15.2	% Profit Before Taxes/Total Assets						13.4
4.5	6.9	6.8							6.8
-1.1	-1.6	1.6							.2
97.4	64.8	62.2	Sales/Net Fixed Assets						69.0
12.2	13.1	19.4							19.4
3.4	4.1	3.3							3.6
2.8	3.3	3.5	Sales/Total Assets						4.6
1.4	1.2	1.3							.9
.9	.7	.8							.7
.5	.3	1.1	% Depr., Dep., Amort./Sales						.1
(36) 1.9	(28) 1.9	(28) 1.9						(11)	2.1
3.5	3.5	5.1							7.6
.8			% Officers', Directors' Owners' Comp/Sales						
(11) 6.7									
22.3									
3040687M	2016808M	1535348M	Net Sales ($)	1983M	14006M		56177M	157267M	1305915M
1994172M	1765936M	1438098M	Total Assets ($)	6797M	9626M		20691M	169802M	1231182M

(Current data columns 0-1MM, 1-3MM, 3-5MM, 5-10MM and 10-25MM for the Assets, Liabilities, Income and most Ratio rows are marked "DATA NOT AVAILABLE".)

M = $ thousand   MM = $ million
See Pages 9 through 22 for Explanation of Ratios and Data

Current Data Sorted by Assets

Comparative Historical Data

0-500M	500M-2MM	2-10MM	10-50MM	50-100MM	100-250MM	Type of Statement	4/1/06-3/31/07 ALL	4/1/07-3/31/08 ALL
	1	5	6	2	3	Unqualified	18	14
	4	11	6			Reviewed	19	16
3	6	8				Compiled	13	12
11	10	5				Tax Returns	9	12
5	18	17	12	4	4	Other	30	28
	17 (4/1-9/30/10)		124 (10/1/10-3/31/11)					
19	39	46	24	6	7	**NUMBER OF STATEMENTS**	89	82
%	%	%	%	%	%	**ASSETS**	%	%
26.2	19.8	9.6	9.1			Cash & Equivalents	10.6	13.9
39.0	44.3	48.4	49.2			Trade Receivables (net)	50.9	53.9
.1	2.0	1.2	1.1			Inventory	1.3	1.1
2.7	2.0	5.4	9.3			All Other Current	3.4	5.2
68.0	68.0	64.6	68.7			Total Current	66.1	74.1
16.8	21.6	17.0	15.9			Fixed Assets (net)	16.0	13.1
.3	4.7	8.6	10.0			Intangibles (net)	7.9	5.2
14.9	5.6	9.8	5.4			All Other Non-Current	9.9	7.6
100.0	100.0	100.0	100.0			Total	100.0	100.0
						LIABILITIES		
33.6	16.9	18.9	12.8			Notes Payable-Short Term	16.5	18.0
5.2	1.6	2.6	3.0			Cur. Mat.-L.T.D.	3.9	2.6
7.5	5.4	7.0	10.3			Trade Payables	7.3	7.4
.0	.2	.3	.4			Income Taxes Payable	4.5	.8
39.5	17.4	17.8	19.3			All Other Current	21.6	18.6
85.8	41.5	46.6	45.9			Total Current	53.8	47.4
15.4	10.1	11.6	11.3			Long-Term Debt	14.3	11.1
.0	.0	.0	.1			Deferred Taxes	.2	.4
27.8	1.5	7.2	7.1			All Other Non-Current	4.2	5.5
-29.1	46.9	34.5	35.7			Net Worth	27.5	35.7
100.0	100.0	100.0	100.0			Total Liabilites & Net Worth	100.0	100.0
						INCOME DATA		
100.0	100.0	100.0	100.0			Net Sales	100.0	100.0
						Gross Profit		
95.6	94.9	93.6	96.7			Operating Expenses	95.8	94.8
4.4	5.1	6.4	3.3			Operating Profit	4.2	5.2
.3	.6	.7	1.5			All Other Expenses (net)	.8	.8
4.2	4.5	5.6	1.8			Profit Before Taxes	3.4	4.4
						RATIOS		
3.5	3.4	2.4	2.3			Current	2.0	2.6
1.6	2.2	1.3	1.4				1.2	1.4
.8	1.0	.9	1.1				.9	1.1
3.4	3.4	2.2	2.0			Quick	1.9	2.6
1.6	2.1	1.1	1.4				1.2	1.3
.8	.9	.8	.9				.9	1.0
0 UND	26 13.9	31 11.6	43 8.6			Sales/Receivables	35 10.4	39 9.3
18 20.0	35 10.6	42 8.7	51 7.2				47 7.8	45 8.1
56 6.5	44 8.3	55 6.6	59 6.2				59 6.2	59 6.2
						Cost of Sales/Inventory		
						Cost of Sales/Payables		
8.2	8.2	12.7	11.2			Sales/Working Capital	11.8	11.1
22.6	15.0	34.5	18.8				32.1	23.6
-218.8	185.7	-172.2	53.3				-161.6	106.8
40.6	27.6	32.1	36.5			EBIT/Interest	16.0	13.9
(10) 10.3	(31) 8.9	(42) 8.8	(22) 6.5				(79) 4.1	(69) 4.4
-1.2	2.4	2.1	1.3				2.2	1.9
			8.2			Net Profit + Depr., Dep., Amort./Cur. Mat. L/T/D	10.0	9.8
			(10) 3.1				(24) 2.8	(16) 3.1
			-11.5				1.2	1.6
.0	.1	.1	.2			Fixed/Worth	.2	.1
.3	.5	.4	.3				.4	.4
-1.5	1.8	2.0	1.6				4.2	2.1
.3	.4	.9	.9			Debt/Worth	1.0	.6
13.6	1.1	1.6	2.3				2.8	2.5
-6.2	6.2	6.7	5.9				20.2	13.1
125.8	81.7	75.4	73.9			% Profit Before Taxes/Tangible Net Worth	68.5	75.3
(11) 100.0	(34) 36.3	(40) 34.2	(20) 28.9				(72) 38.1	(67) 36.6
39.0	10.7	20.1	16.1				15.7	15.9
46.2	38.6	21.3	19.2			% Profit Before Taxes/Total Assets	19.9	20.2
15.9	14.1	12.0	7.6				8.5	9.0
-.4	5.1	5.0	2.3				3.5	3.2
801.5	121.2	107.2	70.0			Sales/Net Fixed Assets	85.2	84.0
141.8	40.3	42.1	46.7				45.4	48.4
37.6	15.6	19.5	15.0				29.2	28.0
11.6	7.3	6.3	4.9			Sales/Total Assets	5.6	5.6
6.6	4.3	4.0	3.9				4.5	4.5
3.1	3.7	2.9	3.1				2.7	3.2
	.4	.3	.4			% Depr., Dep., Amort./Sales	.4	.4
(30)	.7	(36) .7	(22) .9				(78) .7	(58) .9
	1.8	1.5	4.0				1.3	1.2
2.5	2.4	1.3				% Officers', Directors' Owners' Comp/Sales	.9	1.1
(10) 6.5	(19) 4.3	(14) 2.7					(27) 2.4	(30) 2.0
12.3	8.4	6.2					4.9	4.6
38775M	242515M	937292M	1646152M	1302485M	2463368M	Net Sales ($)	6960345M	4143862M
5217M	42982M	221542M	440043M	448835M	1076115M	Total Assets ($)	1974700M	1189858M

M = $ thousand   MM = $ million
See Pages 9 through 22 for Explanation of Ratios and Data

Comparative Historical Data			Type of Statement	Current Data Sorted by Sales					
22	30	17	Unqualified		1			1	15
17	25	21	Reviewed			2	3	7	9
12	17	17	Compiled		3	4	3	4	2
12	16	26	Tax Returns	1	6	5	6	4	1
45	52	60	Other	2	9	2	10	13	24
4/1/08-3/31/09 ALL	4/1/09-3/31/10 ALL	4/1/10-3/31/11 ALL		0-1MM	17 (4/1-9/30/10) 1-3MM	3-5MM	124 (10/1/10-3/31/11) 5-10MM	10-25MM	25MM & OVER
108	140	141	**NUMBER OF STATEMENTS**	7	19	13	22	29	51
%	%	%	**ASSETS**	%	%	%	%	%	%
7.9	14.0	14.6	Cash & Equivalents		19.2	18.9	22.1	12.4	9.8
50.8	49.3	45.9	Trade Receivables (net)		49.0	29.5	40.4	45.9	53.9
1.3	1.3	1.4	Inventory		.1	7.7	.5	1.1	1.0
6.0	6.0	5.1	All Other Current		3.8	1.3	4.9	3.7	8.1
66.0	70.6	67.1	Total Current		72.1	57.4	67.9	63.2	72.7
16.3	14.0	17.3	Fixed Assets (net)		17.5	26.5	17.8	16.9	11.6
6.7	5.5	7.3	Intangibles (net)		4.7	5.4	4.6	10.5	9.0
11.0	9.9	8.3	All Other Non-Current		5.7	10.7	9.7	9.5	6.7
100.0	100.0	100.0	Total		100.0	100.0	100.0	100.0	100.0
			LIABILITIES						
21.0	18.8	18.7	Notes Payable-Short Term		21.2	16.2	16.0	16.5	15.4
2.7	2.9	2.7	Cur. Mat.-L.T.D.		.4	3.8	6.9	2.0	2.3
7.8	7.7	7.4	Trade Payables		5.4	5.3	8.9	5.8	8.7
.9	.6	.3	Income Taxes Payable		.0	.0	.3	.5	.3
18.5	21.2	21.3	All Other Current		7.5	51.8	13.9	23.3	22.0
51.0	51.2	50.3	Total Current		34.5	77.1	46.1	48.2	48.7
13.9	12.0	12.3	Long-Term Debt		10.5	21.7	7.6	14.3	9.2
.3	.1	.0	Deferred Taxes		.0	.0	.0	.0	.0
8.3	7.6	7.9	All Other Non-Current		7.6	3.6	4.4	12.7	2.4
26.6	29.1	29.5	Net Worth		47.4	-2.4	41.9	24.8	39.6
100.0	100.0	100.0	Total Liabilties & Net Worth		100.0	100.0	100.0	100.0	100.0
			INCOME DATA						
100.0	100.0	100.0	Net Sales		100.0	100.0	100.0	100.0	100.0
			Gross Profit						
95.7	95.8	94.8	Operating Expenses		95.3	98.2	95.7	96.2	95.4
4.3	4.2	5.2	Operating Profit		4.7	1.8	4.3	3.8	4.6
1.0	.7	.9	All Other Expenses (net)		.0	-.4	.4	1.3	1.1
3.3	3.5	4.2	Profit Before Taxes		4.7	2.2	3.9	2.5	3.4
			RATIOS						
1.8	2.1	2.7			6.3	2.4	2.7	2.7	2.0
1.3	1.5	1.4	Current		3.5	1.4	1.7	1.1	1.4
1.0	1.0	1.0			1.6	.6	.9	.9	1.2
1.7	2.1	2.5			6.3	2.4	2.7	2.7	1.7
1.2	1.3	1.3	Quick		3.4	.9	1.3	1.0	1.3
.8	.8	.8			1.6	.4	.6	.8	1.1
34 10.6	34 10.7	31 11.9		30 12.2	0 UND	21 17.1	33 11.1	36 10.1	
43 8.4	41 8.9	42 8.7	Sales/Receivables	45 8.1	33 10.9	36 10.3	42 8.7	45 8.1	
59 6.2	54 6.7	54 6.8		56 6.5	41 8.9	43 8.5	54 6.7	65 5.7	
			Cost of Sales/Inventory						
			Cost of Sales/Payables						
12.6	10.6	10.1			5.6	10.8	10.2	14.5	12.2
28.1	23.1	22.6	Sales/Working Capital		11.4	23.5	17.2	86.5	24.0
-259.2	UND	NM			44.4	-94.0	-97.6	-44.9	48.0
13.0	17.0	29.6			24.8	17.0	87.1	21.9	35.1
(98) 3.6	(126) 5.5	(117) 8.9	EBIT/Interest	(12) 16.4	(12) 2.5	(18) 13.0	(26) 5.1	(47) 9.4	
1.2	2.2	2.1			5.9	-.4	1.7	2.1	3.8
7.4	6.7	11.2							10.8
(27) 2.1	(37) 2.9	(24) 5.5	Net Profit + Depr., Dep., Amort./Cur. Mat. L/T/D					(17) 6.1	
.8	.9	2.6							2.7
.2	.1	.1			.0	.5	.1	.1	.1
.5	.3	.3	Fixed/Worth		.3	1.7	.3	.6	.3
2.0	2.0	2.2			.7	NM	1.3	-1.1	1.1
1.2	.9	.8			.2	1.0	.5	.7	1.0
2.2	1.9	1.8	Debt/Worth		.8	3.3	1.4	3.5	1.9
10.9	10.6	17.0			-134.0	NM	10.0	-6.6	3.7
101.6	79.2	81.7			101.4	50.4	87.0	134.7	77.4
(87) 29.5	(113) 32.6	(114) 34.7	% Profit Before Taxes/Tangible Net Worth	(14) 46.5	(10) 29.2	(20) 37.7	(20) 38.8	(45) 31.2	
6.0	11.1	18.2			19.4	6.1	12.1	21.3	19.3
18.3	22.0	25.9			46.2	15.6	39.3	30.8	21.7
6.9	10.1	12.5	% Profit Before Taxes/Total Assets		22.3	8.9	11.9	13.3	12.2
.7	3.2	4.1			11.3	-4.3	2.7	5.8	3.9
90.8	140.0	119.9			317.5	73.1	150.5	143.0	101.2
44.8	59.1	50.0	Sales/Net Fixed Assets		53.1	16.2	74.6	42.1	51.4
19.9	22.9	16.9			15.6	8.1	28.7	19.3	19.6
5.9	5.9	6.2			6.8	4.4	8.0	7.1	5.6
4.5	4.4	4.1	Sales/Total Assets		4.2	3.9	4.9	4.1	4.0
3.1	3.4	3.1			3.3	3.1	3.5	3.1	3.1
.4	.3	.4			.8		.4	.4	.2
(81) .8	(102) .7	(104) .7	% Depr., Dep., Amort./Sales		(11) 2.3	(16) .6	(24) 1.0	(41) .5	
1.3	1.4	1.7			3.9		1.1	1.7	1.2
1.3	1.6	1.9					2.4		
(33) 2.2	(40) 3.8	(45) 4.3	% Officers', Directors' Owners' Comp/Sales				(11) 3.0		
5.6	8.2	7.9					10.9		
8089752M	9659551M	6630587M	Net Sales ($)	3188M	35709M	51414M	161901M	466634M	5911741M
2226184M	2195757M	2234734M	Total Assets ($)	11552M	9447M	15319M	38977M	134195M	2025244M

Current Data Sorted by Assets   Comparative Historical Data

						Type of Statement		
1	2	6	16		13	Unqualified	19	20
1	12	36	5			Reviewed	49	50
5	12	10				Compiled	25	16
12	24	5				Tax Returns	21	34
14	26	29	25	9	1	Other	64	65
	41 (4/1-9/30/10)		223 (10/1/10-3/31/11)				4/1/06-3/31/07	4/1/07-3/31/08
0-500M	500M-2MM	2-10MM	10-50MM	50-100MM	100-250MM		ALL	ALL
33	76	86	46	9	14	NUMBER OF STATEMENTS	178	185
%	%	%	%	%	%	ASSETS	%	%
13.5	11.5	10.0	10.1		8.5	Cash & Equivalents	9.9	9.1
35.0	34.4	34.5	23.8		13.9	Trade Receivables (net)	36.2	35.4
11.4	14.1	10.7	8.2		5.1	Inventory	11.3	10.7
8.3	4.9	6.2	5.4		5.6	All Other Current	4.5	6.0
68.2	64.9	61.3	47.5		33.2	Total Current	62.1	61.2
16.7	19.9	15.8	12.3		6.0	Fixed Assets (net)	16.8	18.4
5.3	7.6	10.4	33.3		38.7	Intangibles (net)	12.1	12.9
9.8	7.5	12.4	7.0		22.1	All Other Non-Current	9.0	7.5
100.0	100.0	100.0	100.0		100.0	Total	100.0	100.0
						LIABILITIES		
29.9	11.6	13.0	8.7		7.7	Notes Payable-Short Term	11.4	10.9
7.3	3.2	5.9	4.5		1.2	Cur. Mat.-L.T.D.	4.7	6.0
28.9	16.7	12.9	12.8		7.3	Trade Payables	15.5	13.6
.4	.1	1.7	.3		.6	Income Taxes Payable	.4	.5
27.8	15.0	18.5	27.6		11.9	All Other Current	18.3	18.0
94.3	46.7	51.9	53.8		28.8	Total Current	50.3	49.0
39.3	20.3	14.6	30.7		48.7	Long-Term Debt	22.9	24.3
.1	.1	.3	.5		.7	Deferred Taxes	.3	.3
11.0	8.6	8.6	14.7		10.0	All Other Non-Current	12.7	6.1
-44.8	24.3	24.5	.2		11.8	Net Worth	13.8	20.3
100.0	100.0	100.0	100.0		100.0	Total Liabilities & Net Worth	100.0	100.0
						INCOME DATA		
100.0	100.0	100.0	100.0		100.0	Net Sales	100.0	100.0
						Gross Profit		
99.2	94.8	93.6	94.9		96.6	Operating Expenses	94.6	93.7
.8	5.2	6.4	5.1		3.4	Operating Profit	5.4	6.3
.7	.9	.9	4.1		8.2	All Other Expenses (net)	2.3	1.9
.1	4.2	5.5	1.0		-4.9	Profit Before Taxes	3.0	4.5
						RATIOS		
1.7	2.7	1.9	1.5		1.4		2.1	1.9
1.0	1.5	1.3	1.0		.8	Current	1.3	1.4
.4	.9	.8	.6		.8		.9	1.0
1.1	1.8	1.4	1.0		.9		1.5	1.5
.7	1.0	.9	.7		.6	Quick	1.0	1.0
.2	.6	.5	.4		.5		.6	.6
0 UND	25 14.3	30 12.4	20 18.0		10 37.9		27 13.7	25 14.5
22 16.7	39 9.3	50 7.3	41 8.8		39 9.5	Sales/Receivables	46 7.9	41 8.8
42 8.7	59 6.2	65 5.6	59 6.2		66 5.6		67 5.5	61 6.0
						Cost of Sales/Inventory		
						Cost of Sales/Payables		
16.5	6.4	6.9	10.3		10.8		7.6	8.9
192.0	13.0	15.9	-874.5		-36.8	Sales/Working Capital	18.7	17.9
-13.4	-44.0	-26.1	-11.0		-19.4		-57.8	-170.4
3.9	23.6	18.5	12.4				9.0	10.8
(21) 1.1	(65) 3.9	(79) 5.0	(42) 1.5			EBIT/Interest	(158) 3.6	(169) 3.7
-2.8	1.4	1.9	.3				.8	1.3
		6.4	6.9			Net Profit + Depr., Dep.,	7.4	6.4
		(25) 2.7	(12) 2.0			Amort./Cur. Mat. L/T/D	(47) 3.2	(41) 3.7
		1.1	.5				1.2	1.9
.0	.2	.2	.8		.0		.3	.2
1.5	.5	.6	-.9		NM	Fixed/Worth	1.0	.7
-1.1	-23.2	-5.9	-.1		-.1		-.8	-1.7
2.4	.7	1.2	2.5		.9		1.4	1.2
UND	2.1	3.7	-5.2		-6.7	Debt/Worth	3.8	3.3
-2.6	-33.4	-12.6	-1.5		-1.2		-5.1	-6.3
43.7	53.2	65.0	160.7			% Profit Before Taxes/Tangible	71.4	79.8
(18) 7.4	(55) 19.6	(61) 20.2	(21) 42.2			Net Worth	(118) 29.0	(126) 28.8
-25.5	2.6	6.6	11.8				6.8	9.3
31.6	21.1	15.0	10.6		5.6	% Profit Before Taxes/Total	19.2	20.0
1.3	6.8	8.4	3.3		.1	Assets	7.2	7.5
-12.7	.6	2.7	-4.6		-12.3		-.4	1.6
UND	45.0	50.8	54.5		66.5		48.7	52.1
109.6	23.7	22.5	23.6		29.0	Sales/Net Fixed Assets	21.6	22.0
30.1	11.7	12.4	12.1		17.7		11.7	11.1
9.2	4.0	3.0	3.1		1.4		3.9	4.1
5.1	2.9	2.3	1.7		.8	Sales/Total Assets	2.6	2.8
3.0	2.2	1.5	1.2		.5		1.6	1.7
.4	.8	.7	.7				.8	.9
(17) .8	(56) 1.4	(68) 1.5	(31) 2.6			% Depr., Dep., Amort./Sales	(129) 1.7	(136) 1.8
1.9	2.1	2.4	6.6				3.5	3.3
3.5	3.4	2.4				% Officers', Directors'	3.0	2.7
(12) 7.9	(41) 5.0	(25) 4.1				Owners' Comp/Sales	(60) 5.2	(73) 4.4
13.9	9.4	8.8					9.2	9.1
40572M	270098M	870115M	2441480M	1232568M	2269208M	Net Sales ($)	4128241M	3689240M
6562M	86090M	388838M	1123829M	597409M	2063802M	Total Assets ($)	2314457M	1995579M

M = $ thousand   MM = $ million
See Pages 9 through 22 for Explanation of Ratios and Data

Comparative Historical Data   Current Data Sorted by Sales

			Type of Statement						
36	44	38	Unqualified	1	2	1	4	7	24
58	43	54	Reviewed	1	5	9	13	23	3
27	28	27	Compiled	4	8	5	7	2	1
27	42	41	Tax Returns	6	18	9	6	2	1
83	93	104	Other	8	16	18	18	16	28
4/1/08-	4/1/09-	4/1/10-			41 (4/1-9/30/10)		223 (10/1/10-3/31/11)		
3/31/09	3/31/10	3/31/11							
ALL	ALL	ALL		0-1MM	1-3MM	3-5MM	5-10MM	10-25MM	25MM & OVER
231	250	264	**NUMBER OF STATEMENTS**	19	49	42	48	50	56
%	%	%	**ASSETS**	%	%	%	%	%	%
8.9	10.6	10.7	Cash & Equivalents	8.4	14.0	8.9	12.2	8.8	10.7
33.8	30.9	31.3	Trade Receivables (net)	23.6	36.0	29.6	31.7	36.9	25.8
10.3	10.1	10.8	Inventory	13.6	9.9	12.8	13.4	11.3	6.3
5.9	4.6	5.8	All Other Current	1.4	6.1	8.5	5.0	6.4	5.3
58.9	56.2	58.7	Total Current	46.9	66.0	59.8	62.3	63.3	48.0
16.7	18.3	15.7	Fixed Assets (net)	28.1	21.7	16.0	13.0	14.0	9.9
14.8	15.9	15.6	Intangibles (net)	10.9	5.5	12.0	13.1	16.3	30.4
9.6	9.6	10.0	All Other Non-Current	14.1	6.9	12.2	11.5	6.3	11.6
100.0	100.0	100.0	Total	100.0	100.0	100.0	100.0	100.0	100.0
			LIABILITIES						
11.9	12.7	13.9	Notes Payable-Short Term	19.2	21.1	12.6	14.8	7.6	11.6
5.4	4.3	4.6	Cur. Mat.-L.T.D.	6.6	4.8	3.9	2.6	8.7	2.5
14.2	15.7	15.6	Trade Payables	26.9	19.0	13.5	13.9	15.1	12.3
.7	.3	.7	Income Taxes Payable	.0	.7	.1	.9	1.6	.4
22.8	18.7	20.0	All Other Current	19.0	18.6	15.5	19.4	19.3	26.0
54.9	51.7	54.8	Total Current	71.6	64.2	45.7	51.6	52.4	52.7
26.1	26.3	24.9	Long-Term Debt	32.6	34.5	17.8	20.4	13.2	33.6
.4	.1	.3	Deferred Taxes	.0	.1	.1	.4	.5	.4
5.6	9.4	9.9	All Other Non-Current	5.2	11.2	10.8	6.8	9.6	12.7
13.0	12.5	10.1	Net Worth	-9.6	-10.0	25.7	20.8	24.4	.7
100.0	100.0	100.0	Total Liabilties & Net Worth	100.0	100.0	100.0	100.0	100.0	100.0
			INCOME DATA						
100.0	100.0	100.0	Net Sales	100.0	100.0	100.0	100.0	100.0	100.0
			Gross Profit						
94.4	95.6	95.2	Operating Expenses	99.8	93.6	94.3	94.2	96.0	95.8
5.6	4.4	4.8	Operating Profit	.2	6.4	5.7	5.8	4.0	4.2
2.8	2.2	1.9	All Other Expenses (net)	2.1	.4	1.2	1.7	1.6	4.3
2.8	2.2	2.9	Profit Before Taxes	-2.0	6.0	4.5	4.2	2.4	-.1
			RATIOS						
1.8	2.0	1.9		1.9	2.6	2.4	1.9	1.8	1.5
1.2	1.2	1.2	Current	1.0	1.3	1.4	1.3	1.1	1.0
.8	.7	.8		.5	.5	.8	.7	.8	.8
1.3	1.4	1.4		1.0	1.9	1.5	1.3	1.3	1.3
.9	.9	.8	Quick	.5	.9	.8	.9	.9	.7
.4	.5	.4		.1	.4	.5	.4	.5	.5
26 14.0	23 16.2	23 15.6		0 UND	22 16.7	24 15.4	26 14.2	39 9.3	21 17.5
42 8.6	38 9.7	41 8.9	Sales/Receivables	23 15.7	39 9.4	38 9.7	38 9.7	52 7.1	40 9.0
63 5.8	58 6.3	60 6.1		53 6.8	54 6.7	57 6.4	63 5.8	67 5.4	60 6.1
			Cost of Sales/Inventory						
			Cost of Sales/Payables						
8.7	8.4	7.8		11.7	6.5	6.2	7.4	7.9	10.2
29.2	29.3	26.2	Sales/Working Capital	99.8	17.5	24.9	15.9	33.3	-440.4
-22.1	-20.1	-20.5		-8.7	-19.7	-28.9	-21.9	-39.0	-12.7
13.0	12.5	16.6		3.6	21.5	8.0	14.6	27.0	33.8
(201) 3.4	(225) 3.0	(224) 3.2	EBIT/Interest	(13) .8	(38) 3.0	(33) 3.0	(46) 5.2	(47) 4.3	(47) 2.2
.6	.7	.8		-2.8	1.2	.8	1.8	.9	-.6
7.3	7.4	5.3	Net Profit + Depr., Dep.,				7.5	6.3	11.5
(52) 3.0	(34) 2.5	(43) 2.7	Amort./Cur. Mat. L/T/D			(12) 3.4	(14) 2.4	(10) 3.0	
1.2	1.5	1.1					1.1	.5	1.4
.2	.2	.2		.1	.1	.3	.1	.3	.2
1.3	1.0	.9	Fixed/Worth	9.2	.8	.6	.5	.7	NM
-.5	-.6	-.6		-1.3	-2.6	-.5	NM	-.7	-.1
1.4	1.2	1.3		3.0	.5	.9	1.3	1.3	2.1
5.4	4.2	7.9	Debt/Worth	UND	4.8	2.5	3.7	4.5	-19.9
-2.8	-3.8	-3.6		-2.9	-4.0	-10.8	NM	-5.9	-1.5
65.3	56.6	62.4	% Profit Before Taxes/Tangible	45.5	64.4	43.9	67.1	41.5	148.7
(136) 35.0	(156) 27.1	(162) 20.9	Net Worth	(11) 1.4	(29) 17.6	(29) 13.9	(36) 36.2	(31) 18.8	(26) 43.3
9.4	4.3	4.0		-32.1	2.3	.3	6.7	6.9	11.2
20.0	16.7	16.0		1.7	27.8	14.6	23.6	12.5	19.4
6.1	5.1	5.3	% Profit Before Taxes/Total	.0	8.6	5.5	9.3	5.4	3.6
-1.2	-2.4	-.5	Assets	-14.4	.9	-.2	1.0	.0	-7.3
53.2	53.5	72.0		UND	99.9	43.3	81.9	47.9	68.3
22.0	22.8	25.0	Sales/Net Fixed Assets	32.7	21.1	26.0	30.3	21.7	33.0
11.0	10.5	12.9		3.4	10.9	12.3	14.2	12.7	15.3
3.8	3.8	3.5		4.1	5.1	3.7	3.3	3.4	3.1
2.6	2.5	2.5	Sales/Total Assets	2.2	3.0	2.6	2.5	2.4	1.7
1.5	1.6	1.5		1.0	1.8	1.4	1.8	1.8	1.0
.7	.8	.7			.5	.6	.8	.7	.6
(160) 1.5	(173) 1.6	(183) 1.5	% Depr., Dep., Amort./Sales	(32) 1.4	(33) 1.5	(34) 1.4	(40) 1.6	(36) 1.5	
2.9	3.1	2.6		2.4	2.2	2.0	2.5	3.4	
3.1	3.0	2.9	% Officers', Directors'	3.5	3.8	2.4	2.1		
(67) 4.8	(98) 4.6	(83) 4.6	Owners' Comp/Sales	(21) 6.9	(20) 6.5	(20) 4.0	(11) 3.1		
9.2	10.4	8.9		14.6	9.2	8.0	5.3		
5849488M	5177143M	7124041M	Net Sales ($)	9196M	90600M	168534M	348789M	754645M	5752277M
3568706M	3036239M	4266530M	Total Assets ($)	7063M	47977M	90396M	182950M	460567M	3477577M

M = $ thousand   MM = $ million
See Pages 9 through 22 for Explanation of Ratios and Data

Current Data Sorted by Assets   Comparative Historical Data

0-500M	500M-2MM	2-10MM	10-50MM	50-100MM	100-250MM	Type of Statement	4/1/06-3/31/07 ALL	4/1/07-3/31/08 ALL
	1	1	2	1		Unqualified	2	3
	1	6	3			Reviewed	12	11
4	3	1	1			Compiled	19	20
12	11	4	1			Tax Returns	18	27
6	10	11	4	2		Other	27	18
	13 (4/1-9/30/10)		71 (10/1/10-3/31/11)				4/1/06-3/31/07 ALL	4/1/07-3/31/08 ALL
22	26	23	10	3		NUMBER OF STATEMENTS	78	79
%	%	%	%	%	%	ASSETS	%	%
28.9	20.9	14.5	16.3	D		Cash & Equivalents	18.7	14.6
14.3	15.5	21.8	15.7	A		Trade Receivables (net)	23.4	20.6
3.2	4.2	2.9	7.2	T		Inventory	3.2	3.6
1.6	4.7	9.0	2.4	A		All Other Current	5.4	6.4
48.0	45.4	48.2	41.7			Total Current	50.7	45.2
32.6	31.0	28.2	37.9	N		Fixed Assets (net)	31.8	35.3
13.7	11.7	14.1	17.3	O		Intangibles (net)	10.4	10.6
5.7	12.0	9.6	3.1	T		All Other Non-Current	7.1	9.0
100.0	100.0	100.0	100.0			Total	100.0	100.0
						LIABILITIES		
21.4	16.4	12.4	.3	A		Notes Payable-Short Term	4.9	8.6
7.4	6.2	5.3	1.7	V		Cur. Mat.-L.T.D.	7.1	7.7
10.0	8.6	9.5	12.4	A		Trade Payables	9.8	8.9
.1	.0	.4	.0	I		Income Taxes Payable	.3	.2
32.0	13.4	13.7	23.5	L		All Other Current	16.5	14.1
70.9	44.6	41.3	37.9	A		Total Current	38.6	39.5
39.9	13.6	19.0	20.2	B		Long-Term Debt	37.3	26.5
.0	.0	.2	.0	L		Deferred Taxes	.1	.2
12.1	.4	3.9	9.2	E		All Other Non-Current	5.9	5.0
-23.0	41.4	35.6	32.8			Net Worth	18.2	28.8
100.0	100.0	100.0	100.0			Total Liabilities & Net Worth	100.0	100.0
						INCOME DATA		
100.0	100.0	100.0	100.0			Net Sales	100.0	100.0
						Gross Profit		
89.6	91.9	95.6	96.5			Operating Expenses	93.3	94.2
10.4	8.1	4.4	3.5			Operating Profit	6.7	5.8
5.2	.3	.2	1.5			All Other Expenses (net)	1.6	1.7
5.2	7.8	4.1	2.0			Profit Before Taxes	5.2	4.1
						RATIOS		
1.4	3.2	1.8	2.4				2.6	2.7
.7	1.0	1.2	1.3			Current	1.5	1.3
.3	.4	1.0	.5				.8	.8
1.3	2.3	1.7	2.1				2.2	1.9
.6	.8	1.0	.8			Quick	1.2	.9
.3	.4	.5	.5				.7	.5
0 UND	0 UND	18 20.7	16 22.7				6 63.7	0 UND
4 91.7	13 28.0	22 16.8	21 17.7			Sales/Receivables	22 16.3	21 17.3
27 13.4	35 10.5	38 9.5	34 10.9				33 11.1	31 11.7
						Cost of Sales/Inventory		
						Cost of Sales/Payables		
314.3	13.3	13.9	7.4				11.5	11.5
-18.4	NM	58.2	NM			Sales/Working Capital	24.3	40.4
-8.3	-8.9	-87.0	-11.1				-49.0	-32.6
12.0	26.6	33.4					33.6	26.2
(18) 3.4	(22) 5.9	4.3				EBIT/Interest	(66) 5.1	(66) 4.1
1.4	-.8	.3					2.4	.9
							5.4	19.3
						Net Profit + Depr., Dep., Amort./Cur. Mat. L/T/D	(20) 2.6	(13) 6.7
							1.3	1.1
.3	.3	.8	.4				.5	.5
-22.0	1.0	1.6	1.6			Fixed/Worth	1.1	1.3
-.4	NM	5.8	-2.7				19.1	-4.6
2.4	.8	1.0	.7				1.1	.7
-5.8	1.6	3.6	2.4			Debt/Worth	2.2	2.6
-1.7	NM	32.4	-4.4				-11.5	-8.6
	31.8	141.1					109.5	129.2
	(20) 10.2	(18) 38.5				% Profit Before Taxes/Tangible Net Worth	(58) 42.1	(56) 50.3
	-12.7	.7					17.6	17.7
60.1	34.1	31.1	20.9				41.6	24.4
16.7	7.4	4.7	16.4			% Profit Before Taxes/Total Assets	13.8	8.6
1.4	-2.5	-.5	3.9				4.7	-.3
137.7	25.8	26.2	21.2				34.8	29.7
24.3	12.9	14.1	8.3			Sales/Net Fixed Assets	12.6	12.6
8.2	6.3	8.5	3.8				7.7	7.5
12.1	5.7	4.0	3.0				5.1	5.6
3.9	3.5	3.1	2.5			Sales/Total Assets	3.7	3.5
2.4	2.0	1.9	1.4				2.6	2.2
2.0	1.0	1.4					1.5	1.5
(12) 3.4	(16) 2.3	(20) 2.0				% Depr., Dep., Amort./Sales	(60) 2.4	(71) 2.5
7.2	3.3	4.0					3.9	4.0
5.8	3.5	2.2					3.2	3.2
(14) 8.6	(16) 5.7	(13) 3.1				% Officers', Directors' Owners' Comp/Sales	(49) 5.6	(52) 5.5
15.7	9.1	6.9					9.3	12.5
30762M	117637M	262651M	686316M	411717M		Net Sales ($)	1611998M	1011716M
6467M	30967M	88050M	275266M	215229M		Total Assets ($)	506482M	364440M

© RMA 2011

M = $ thousand   MM = $ million
See Pages 9 through 22 for Explanation of Ratios and Data

Comparative Historical Data | Current Data Sorted by Sales

			Type of Statement						
2	4	5	Unqualified		1	1			3
18	9	10	Reviewed		1	1	2	3	4
10	11	9	Compiled		4	3	5	5	1
24	25	27	Tax Returns	1	11	3	5	5	
24	43	33	Other	3	9	4	7	4	5
4/1/08-3/31/09	4/1/09-3/31/10	4/1/10-3/31/11		4		3			
ALL	ALL	ALL			13 (4/1-9/30/10)		71 (10/1/10-3/31/11)		
				0-1MM	1-3MM	3-5MM	5-10MM	10-25MM	25MM & OVER
78	92	84	NUMBER OF STATEMENTS	8	25	12	14	12	13
%	%	%	ASSETS	%	%	%	%	%	%
16.4	16.5	20.4	Cash & Equivalents		23.4	23.2	15.7	20.9	16.8
19.5	17.6	17.2	Trade Receivables (net)		17.6	12.8	15.0	23.0	22.1
4.6	3.6	3.9	Inventory		4.0	6.5	1.8	3.5	5.9
3.8	6.2	4.8	All Other Current		3.2	8.7	3.0	8.9	3.1
44.4	43.8	46.2	Total Current		48.2	51.2	35.5	56.3	47.8
32.1	29.8	30.6	Fixed Assets (net)		29.0	35.9	29.7	22.6	27.6
12.5	16.9	14.3	Intangibles (net)		11.0	5.3	25.1	17.6	16.8
11.0	9.5	8.9	All Other Non-Current		11.7	7.6	9.8	3.5	7.7
100.0	100.0	100.0	Total		100.0	100.0	100.0	100.0	100.0
			LIABILITIES						
14.4	9.5	14.3	Notes Payable-Short Term		24.1	26.2	2.9	12.6	1.1
10.6	5.6	5.7	Cur. Mat.-L.T.D.		6.8	5.0	6.2	5.6	4.0
8.9	8.0	9.5	Trade Payables		8.8	9.2	10.5	10.1	13.5
.1	.3	.1	Income Taxes Payable		.1	.5	.2	.0	.2
14.8	18.7	19.9	All Other Current		33.7	11.7	10.3	14.0	26.3
48.8	42.1	49.6	Total Current		73.4	52.5	30.0	42.3	45.1
32.3	36.8	23.3	Long-Term Debt		26.6	25.8	28.4	14.8	15.9
.1	.0	.1	Deferred Taxes		.0	.0	.0	.3	.0
16.6	4.9	6.4	All Other Non-Current		8.5	2.8	2.5	9.5	6.5
2.2	16.2	20.7	Net Worth		-8.4	18.9	39.1	33.1	32.4
100.0	100.0	100.0	Total Liabilities & Net Worth		100.0	100.0	100.0	100.0	100.0
			INCOME DATA						
100.0	100.0	100.0	Net Sales		100.0	100.0	100.0	100.0	100.0
			Gross Profit						
94.2	89.9	92.9	Operating Expenses		95.6	95.3	97.4	96.2	92.5
5.8	10.1	7.1	Operating Profit		4.4	4.7	2.6	3.8	7.5
1.3	2.1	1.8	All Other Expenses (net)		.3	-.3	.9	.7	1.0
4.5	8.1	5.2	Profit Before Taxes		4.1	4.9	1.7	3.1	6.5
			RATIOS						
2.4	2.5	2.0			1.6	3.2	1.8	2.2	1.9
1.2	1.2	1.0	Current		.7	.9	1.3	1.4	.8
.6	.6	.6			.4	.6	.7	1.0	.6
1.9	2.2	1.8			1.2	3.0	1.7	2.0	1.5
.9	1.0	.7	Quick		.6	.7	1.1	1.1	.8
.5	.5	.4			.3	.3	.5	.5	.5
3 138.2	0 UND	3 120.0		0 UND	0 UND	9 40.0	0 UND	16 23.2
20 18.3	19 19.7	19 19.3	Sales/Receivables	21 17.2	13 28.1	21 17.7	17 21.5	18 19.9
30 12.2	32 11.6	31 11.6		47 7.7	29 12.7	27 13.4	23 15.6	39 9.4
			Cost of Sales/Inventory						
			Cost of Sales/Payables						
11.1	10.0	12.7			21.8	9.5	12.8	16.5	8.7
82.7	64.9	-226.7	Sales/Working Capital		-22.7	-150.1	192.5	31.4	-22.8
-18.9	-18.0	-12.0			-8.0	-14.6	-42.8	-769.5	-13.6
8.1	19.0	17.8		12.7	28.4	34.6	27.5	51.7
(70) 3.5	(78) 5.5	(74) 4.4	EBIT/Interest	(21) 3.1	(10) 3.4	3.1	4.6	(11) 13.6
1.5	1.5	.6		-.2	1.4	-1.5	.0	1.8
17.1	17.6	6.6							
(17) 2.5	(15) 7.6	(15) 2.5	Net Profit + Depr., Dep., Amort./Cur. Mat. L/T/D						
.6	.4	1.7							
.7	.4	.5			.2	.7	.7	.6	.5
3.1	2.5	1.8	Fixed/Worth		1.9	2.4	2.0	1.3	1.3
-1.6	-1.5	-2.6			-1.6	-1.1	-2.9	NM	NM
1.2	1.0	1.0			1.3	1.4	.9	1.3	1.3
6.6	7.5	3.6	Debt/Worth		-74.0	2.8	7.8	2.8	3.6
-4.3	-5.2	-7.1			-2.3	-6.7	-6.9	NM	NM
81.8	72.3	95.0	% Profit Before Taxes/Tangible Net Worth	90.1		139.4		106.4
(47) 25.5	(52) 31.4	(54) 23.2		(12) 7.8	(10) 38.5	(10) 46.9
10.5	13.9	.3		-3.7	-89.7	23.3
18.7	24.1	29.8	% Profit Before Taxes/Total Assets		38.1	66.6	33.4	31.5	25.6
9.1	12.0	9.0			9.9	11.7	9.5	5.2	17.8
2.4	2.6	-.4			-1.7	1.6	-10.9	-3.3	6.3
34.4	37.9	29.8	Sales/Net Fixed Assets		54.9	60.6	25.3	29.6	35.9
14.1	14.6	14.8			17.4	14.2	13.4	23.6	13.1
8.8	7.7	7.0			7.1	6.2	8.0	12.0	4.6
5.0	4.4	4.5	Sales/Total Assets		4.6	7.0	3.7	6.7	3.3
3.2	2.9	3.0			3.2	3.1	3.2	5.4	2.7
2.2	1.7	1.9			2.2	1.8	2.1	3.2	1.7
1.6	1.5	1.5	% Depr., Dep., Amort./Sales	1.5		1.8		1.9
(57) 2.9	(58) 2.9	(57) 2.6		(16) 3.1	(10) 2.7	(10) 2.8
4.4	5.1	4.0		4.5	3.9	4.1
3.6	3.1	2.8	% Officers', Directors' Owners' Comp/Sales	5.0		2.8	
(47) 5.4	(53) 5.1	(47) 5.2		(14) 7.9	(11) 3.9
8.6	8.4	9.3		12.1	5.6
1727773M	1246452M	1509083M	Net Sales ($)	3294M	45429M	47315M	104011M	168543M	1140491M
612459M	523619M	615979M	Total Assets ($)	3488M	18111M	20214M	45802M	45090M	483274M

M = $ thousand   MM = $ million
See Pages 9 through 22 for Explanation of Ratios and Data

1374 ADMIN & WASTE MANAGEMENT SERVICES—Janitorial Services NAICS 561720

Current Data Sorted by Assets

Comparative Historical Data

						Type of Statement		
	5	10	13	4		Unqualified	29	34
1	13	38	3			Reviewed	49	57
6	20	14				Compiled	39	34
30	19	6		1		Tax Returns	63	60
19	44	41	12	5	5	Other	75	87

0-500M	500M-2MM	2-10MM	10-50MM	50-100MM	100-250MM		4/1/06-3/31/07 ALL	4/1/07-3/31/08 ALL
56	101	109	28	10	7	**NUMBER OF STATEMENTS**	255	272
%	%	%	%	%	%	**ASSETS**	%	%
21.8	15.2	10.7	12.1	6.3		Cash & Equivalents	12.5	13.3
27.0	39.4	46.9	44.9	37.1		Trade Receivables (net)	37.4	38.6
2.4	2.6	2.6	1.3	.3		Inventory	4.0	3.6
1.8	5.2	4.9	4.3	4.8		All Other Current	5.6	5.9
53.0	62.4	65.1	62.5	48.5		Total Current	59.5	61.5
25.2	19.7	17.2	14.7	19.6		Fixed Assets (net)	22.4	20.3
10.6	5.7	8.3	13.1	25.4		Intangibles (net)	8.0	8.2
11.2	12.1	9.3	9.7	6.5		All Other Non-Current	10.0	10.0
100.0	100.0	100.0	100.0	100.0		Total	100.0	100.0
						LIABILITIES		
19.6	13.3	10.9	11.9	3.1		Notes Payable-Short Term	15.4	14.7
8.2	5.3	2.9	6.4	2.8		Cur. Mat.-L.T.D.	4.0	4.6
10.1	14.4	14.1	11.3	7.3		Trade Payables	11.6	12.0
.1	.6	.2	.6	.1		Income Taxes Payable	.3	.4
18.4	15.4	16.5	18.4	21.7		All Other Current	17.9	16.8
56.4	48.9	44.6	48.5	35.0		Total Current	49.3	48.5
31.5	18.1	12.3	13.2	14.9		Long-Term Debt	19.5	18.4
.0	.1	.2	.7	1.9		Deferred Taxes	.4	.4
11.5	6.4	4.7	5.9	10.2		All Other Non-Current	6.0	6.2
.6	26.5	38.2	31.7	37.9		Net Worth	24.9	26.5
100.0	100.0	100.0	100.0	100.0		Total Liabilities & Net Worth	100.0	100.0
						INCOME DATA		
100.0	100.0	100.0	100.0	100.0		Net Sales	100.0	100.0
						Gross Profit		
94.9	93.5	94.3	95.2	94.6		Operating Expenses	95.2	93.9
5.1	6.5	5.7	4.8	5.4		Operating Profit	4.8	6.1
.4	.9	.7	.9	1.5		All Other Expenses (net)	.6	1.1
4.8	5.5	5.0	3.8	3.9		Profit Before Taxes	4.2	5.0
						RATIOS		
5.0	2.4	2.2	1.9	1.6			2.1	2.2
1.4	1.3	1.4	1.3	1.5		Current	1.4	1.4
.6	.9	1.1	1.0	.9			.9	1.0
4.0	2.0	2.0	1.9	1.6			1.9	1.8
1.3	1.2	1.2	1.1	1.4		Quick	(254) 1.2	1.2
.5	.7	.8	.9	.7			.6	.7
0 UND	16 22.9	29 12.5	29 12.7	18 20.8			17 20.9	17 21.1
18 20.7	26 14.2	38 9.7	43 8.6	53 6.9		Sales/Receivables	32 11.3	35 10.6
36 10.1	43 8.4	60 6.1	59 6.2	64 5.7			51 7.1	51 7.1
						Cost of Sales/Inventory		
						Cost of Sales/Payables		
13.6	10.0	10.2	11.9	12.4			11.9	11.8
95.6	35.3	23.1	22.3	31.4		Sales/Working Capital	31.8	29.0
-40.9	-110.7	109.3	NM	-89.0			-52.1	-208.5
27.0	28.8	28.1	14.4	67.7			15.8	16.6
(45) 9.2	(89) 5.9	(96) 8.3	(23) 5.6	10.4		EBIT/Interest	(232) 5.6	(230) 6.8
2.0	2.5	2.3	2.6	1.5			1.7	2.1
	9.0	11.0				Net Profit + Depr., Dep.,	13.1	13.4
	(15) 2.8	(23) 3.6				Amort./Cur. Mat. L/T/D	(48) 3.3	(55) 3.6
	1.3	1.7					1.2	1.8
.1	.2	.2	.2	.4			.3	.2
.9	.5	.5	.6	.8		Fixed/Worth	.9	.7
-1.1	4.3	1.3	125.7	NM			-22.9	3.8
.7	.8	.9	1.5	1.2			1.0	.9
5.0	1.9	2.2	4.1	5.2		Debt/Worth	2.5	2.4
-2.5	15.9	6.1	349.8	-2.6			-38.3	13.1
168.6	82.4	82.7	122.0			% Profit Before Taxes/Tangible	74.6	93.0
(33) 77.3	(81) 39.0	(101) 44.4	(22) 57.9			Net Worth	(184) 40.2	(215) 43.8
30.4	8.9	11.4	23.2				17.1	15.7
57.5	35.7	25.7	20.5	15.5		% Profit Before Taxes/Total	25.6	28.7
23.7	16.5	11.7	11.1	11.4		Assets	12.2	12.8
5.8	4.0	3.4	4.5	.5			3.2	3.2
149.7	97.4	78.2	94.8	141.9			63.7	75.8
31.7	35.5	43.8	41.9	51.9		Sales/Net Fixed Assets	29.6	32.8
13.9	13.2	19.1	15.5	19.8			12.3	14.9
9.2	6.6	5.8	4.5	4.2			6.1	5.8
5.7	4.4	3.9	3.4	3.1		Sales/Total Assets	4.1	4.2
3.3	3.0	2.7	2.7	2.4			2.7	2.9
.6	.4	.4	.2				.7	.5
(34) 1.0	(71) .9	(93) .9	(22) .7			% Depr., Dep., Amort./Sales	(198) 1.2	(207) 1.0
4.0	2.4	1.5	1.2				2.7	1.8
3.6	2.1	1.4					2.4	2.0
(30) 5.7	(48) 4.3	(44) 2.8				% Officers', Directors'	(121) 4.7	(112) 3.8
11.0	7.7	5.3				Owners' Comp/Sales	7.4	6.5
113759M	566997M	1990422M	2481847M	3806883M	2243281M	Net Sales ($)	10563876M	8843258M
12981M	106972M	471699M	675654M	708688M	1169697M	Total Assets ($)	2376111M	2364077M

M = $ thousand   MM = $ million
See Pages 9 through 22 for Explanation of Ratios and Data

Comparative Historical Data / Current Data Sorted by Sales

			Type of Statement						
39	36	34	Unqualified		2	1	2	7	22
50	55	55	Reviewed		3	4	9	23	16
32	29	40	Compiled	1	7	9	13	10	
63	77	56	Tax Returns	12	23	6	7	6	2
105	119	126	Other	13	22	14	21	27	29
4/1/08-3/31/09 ALL	4/1/09-3/31/10 ALL	4/1/10-3/31/11 ALL		42 (4/1-9/30/10)			269 (10/1/10-3/31/11)		
				0-1MM	1-3MM	3-5MM	5-10MM	10-25MM	25MM & OVER
289	316	311	**NUMBER OF STATEMENTS**	26	57	34	52	73	69
%	%	%	**ASSETS**	%	%	%	%	%	%
14.1	13.3	14.0	Cash & Equivalents	12.6	20.6	10.3	16.0	13.4	10.0
38.8	38.0	40.0	Trade Receivables (net)	18.5	28.3	39.2	39.8	49.5	48.2
2.8	3.0	2.3	Inventory	3.2	1.8	4.0	3.7	2.2	.8
4.3	5.0	4.3	All Other Current	1.8	3.7	6.0	4.7	5.1	3.8
60.0	59.4	60.6	Total Current	36.1	54.4	59.5	64.1	70.3	62.7
20.8	20.2	19.1	Fixed Assets (net)	35.0	23.8	20.4	18.9	13.9	14.1
9.1	10.9	9.9	Intangibles (net)	15.3	8.9	8.0	6.4	8.1	13.9
10.1	9.5	10.4	All Other Non-Current	13.5	12.9	12.0	10.5	7.7	9.2
100.0	100.0	100.0	Total	100.0	100.0	100.0	100.0	100.0	100.0
			LIABILITIES						
12.8	14.6	12.9	Notes Payable-Short Term	10.2	20.1	15.8	10.6	11.9	9.2
5.2	5.9	4.9	Cur. Mat.-L.T.D.	5.0	9.0	5.5	4.0	3.3	3.8
13.7	12.7	12.8	Trade Payables	10.5	9.1	15.8	11.7	17.4	11.1
.2	.5	.3	Income Taxes Payable	.0	.2	.0	.9	.2	.4
18.0	16.2	16.9	All Other Current	11.4	12.1	15.3	14.5	20.7	21.4
49.9	49.8	47.8	Total Current	37.1	50.5	52.5	41.6	53.5	45.9
22.1	17.8	18.1	Long-Term Debt	50.9	23.5	19.6	15.8	8.2	12.6
.2	.3	.2	Deferred Taxes	.0	.0	.0	.2	.5	.3
8.5	8.4	6.9	All Other Non-Current	22.8	7.2	5.1	2.8	5.2	6.4
19.2	23.7	27.0	Net Worth	-10.9	18.8	22.8	39.6	32.6	34.8
100.0	100.0	100.0	Total Liabilities & Net Worth	100.0	100.0	100.0	100.0	100.0	100.0
			INCOME DATA						
100.0	100.0	100.0	Net Sales	100.0	100.0	100.0	100.0	100.0	100.0
			Gross Profit						
94.9	95.2	94.3	Operating Expenses	92.5	90.0	94.1	95.2	96.2	95.8
5.1	4.8	5.7	Operating Profit	7.5	10.0	5.9	4.8	3.8	4.2
1.2	.7	.8	All Other Expenses (net)	2.5	1.6	.1	.3	.0	.9
3.9	4.0	4.9	Profit Before Taxes	5.0	8.3	5.7	4.5	3.8	3.3
			RATIOS						
1.8	2.0	2.3		5.1	3.7	2.2	3.5	1.6	1.9
1.3	1.2	1.4	Current	1.7	1.6	1.4	1.4	1.3	1.3
.9	.9	1.0		.6	.5	.9	1.0	1.1	1.0
1.7	1.8	2.1		4.1	3.1	1.8	3.5	1.6	1.9
1.2	1.1	1.2	Quick	1.7	1.3	1.1	1.2	1.2	1.2
.7	.7	.8		.5	.4	.6	.8	.8	.9
19 19.7	18 20.2	20 18.3		0 UND	8 43.7	21 17.7	17 20.9	23 16.0	30 12.2
32 11.5	31 11.7	33 11.2	Sales/Receivables	19 18.8	27 13.7	32 11.5	27 13.6	34 10.6	41 8.9
46 7.9	49 7.5	53 6.9		38 9.5	44 8.3	52 7.0	49 7.4	60 6.1	59 6.2
			Cost of Sales/Inventory						
			Cost of Sales/Payables						
14.1	13.5	11.2		9.2	6.9	10.3	9.1	15.3	12.1
35.3	42.3	32.3	Sales/Working Capital	35.8	21.7	33.4	37.5	33.0	23.8
-137.8	-67.6	-163.3		-12.9	-15.5	-60.9	972.0	165.8	257.3
15.8	22.5	27.6		23.4	24.1	20.8	38.1	26.8	32.2
(251) 3.9	(282) 7.2	(270) 6.9	EBIT/Interest	(20) 2.4	(47) 9.2	(31) 4.4	(48) 8.4	(62) 6.3	(62) 7.7
1.3	1.9	2.5		-3.2	2.5	1.8	3.0	2.2	2.8
14.0	11.8	8.1					11.1	6.9	11.0
(56) 4.6	(51) 3.7	(47) 3.1	Net Profit + Depr., Dep., Amort./Cur. Mat. L/T/D			(11) 5.1	(15) 2.4	(15) 4.6	
1.9	1.2	1.7				2.0	1.5	2.7	
.2	.2	.2		.3	.1	.1	.2	.2	.2
.7	.8	.6	Fixed/Worth	17.5	.8	.6	.4	.5	.6
-19.2	20.8	4.4		-.6	13.8	11.4	1.3	1.3	2.7
1.1	1.2	.9		.9	.6	.9	.5	1.3	1.1
2.8	3.2	2.7	Debt/Worth	-3.5	2.7	2.1	1.4	2.7	3.3
-32.4	-72.2	22.9		-2.2	-9.3	26.7	4.9	7.2	22.7
91.5	103.7	100.0		85.6	102.0	84.1	85.8	101.2	106.1
(213) 38.6	(234) 46.0	(247) 46.4	% Profit Before Taxes/Tangible Net Worth	(12) 58.8	(41) 53.9	(27) 37.5	(46) 37.4	(65) 57.1	(56) 48.9
13.1	10.4	15.0		19.7	20.3	6.9	11.6	12.6	22.0
26.1	28.6	29.6		30.0	43.6	33.4	28.7	29.5	19.5
10.8	11.7	13.4	% Profit Before Taxes/Total Assets	9.2	25.0	13.6	15.5	12.9	9.8
1.4	3.5	3.8		-7.4	4.8	1.6	4.2	3.4	4.0
104.5	90.7	91.3		35.0	128.9	90.3	96.5	103.2	97.2
35.2	38.4	36.7	Sales/Net Fixed Assets	11.8	21.6	32.3	36.6	57.5	43.8
15.8	15.5	15.9		5.9	9.2	11.6	17.6	26.6	22.6
6.3	6.8	6.4		6.2	5.4	5.7	7.4	7.0	6.3
4.5	4.6	4.2	Sales/Total Assets	2.8	3.5	4.3	4.9	4.8	4.1
2.9	2.8	2.8		1.7	2.2	2.9	3.0	3.4	2.9
.4	.5	.5		.9	.5	.7	.4	.4	.4
(215) .9	(218) .9	(229) .9	% Depr., Dep., Amort./Sales	(15) 3.1	(39) 1.9	(23) 1.1	(42) .8	(59) .7	(51) .7
1.9	2.0	1.8		6.0	4.0	2.7	1.4	1.2	1.2
2.1	2.6	1.9		7.8	2.8	2.3	2.7	1.3	1.1
(124) 4.2	(137) 5.0	(125) 4.2	% Officers', Directors' Owners' Comp/Sales	(10) 11.0	(33) 5.8	(19) 4.2	(18) 3.6	(33) 2.5	(12) 1.6
7.1	7.4	6.8		18.3	8.9	5.8	6.0	4.3	4.7
11348126M	12577136M	11203189M	Net Sales ($)	12576M	112216M	137661M	358393M	1157310M	9425033M
2906522M	3010756M	3145691M	Total Assets ($)	9135M	40352M	47518M	258753M	334255M	2455678M

M = $ thousand   MM = $ million
See Pages 9 through 22 for Explanation of Ratios and Data

Current Data Sorted by Assets   Comparative Historical Data

Type of Statement	0-500M	500M-2MM	2-10MM	10-50MM	50-100MM	100-250MM	4/1/06-3/31/07 ALL	4/1/07-3/31/08 ALL
Unqualified		3	7	10	6	1	26	26
Reviewed	3	27	48	7	1		87	79
Compiled	22	39	21				83	73
Tax Returns	138	74	11		1	2	149	182
Other	44	76	50	15	6	3	159	190
	48 (4/1-9/30/10)			567 (10/1/10-3/31/11)				
NUMBER OF STATEMENTS	207	219	137	32	14	6	504	550
ASSETS	%	%	%	%	%	%	%	%
Cash & Equivalents	14.7	10.2	9.9	8.4	6.7		10.7	10.1
Trade Receivables (net)	17.3	25.8	32.3	29.0	24.2		26.4	26.7
Inventory	4.1	5.5	8.1	3.9	10.4		5.8	6.4
All Other Current	3.5	3.4	5.5	7.0	5.2		3.5	4.1
Total Current	39.7	45.0	55.7	48.3	46.5		46.4	47.4
Fixed Assets (net)	45.8	37.1	33.5	42.2	41.2		43.4	42.3
Intangibles (net)	6.8	7.2	3.0	4.2	6.6		3.0	3.1
All Other Non-Current	7.8	10.8	7.8	5.2	5.8		7.1	7.2
Total	100.0	100.0	100.0	100.0	100.0		100.0	100.0
LIABILITIES								
Notes Payable-Short Term	24.1	12.5	9.6	8.9	6.6		11.1	12.5
Cur. Mat.-L.T.D.	8.0	5.8	5.0	5.7	7.5		6.8	8.2
Trade Payables	8.5	11.6	11.9	10.9	13.6		11.6	11.7
Income Taxes Payable	.1	.2	.4	.3	.0		.3	.3
All Other Current	11.1	9.5	10.1	13.1	11.7		12.6	10.8
Total Current	51.9	39.5	36.9	38.8	39.4		42.4	43.4
Long-Term Debt	43.2	27.1	15.7	23.9	24.2		32.1	31.6
Deferred Taxes	.0	.3	.6	.5	.6		.5	.4
All Other Non-Current	14.1	4.7	4.0	2.1	7.4		4.9	4.8
Net Worth	-9.3	28.4	42.8	34.7	28.5		20.0	19.8
Total Liabilties & Net Worth	100.0	100.0	100.0	100.0	100.0		100.0	100.0
INCOME DATA								
Net Sales	100.0	100.0	100.0	100.0	100.0		100.0	100.0
Gross Profit								
Operating Expenses	94.1	93.9	94.9	94.5	97.2		93.5	94.0
Operating Profit	5.9	6.1	5.1	5.5	2.8		6.5	6.0
All Other Expenses (net)	2.4	1.9	1.2	.8	.3		1.5	1.7
Profit Before Taxes	3.6	4.2	3.9	4.7	2.5		5.0	4.4
RATIOS								
Current	2.3	2.4	2.4	1.8	1.4		2.2	2.0
	.9	1.2	1.5	1.2	1.1		1.2	1.3
	.4	.7	1.0	1.0	.9		.7	.7
Quick	2.0	2.0	1.9	1.4	1.3		1.8	1.7
	(206) .7	(218) 1.0	1.1	1.0	.8		(503) 1.0	.9
	.3	.5	.7	.6	.6		.5	.4
Sales/Receivables	0 UND	15 24.1	27 13.3	33 11.0	38 9.5		7 53.2	7 54.8
	4 84.3	33 10.9	41 8.8	39 9.3	51 7.1		30 12.2	32 11.4
	24 15.1	54 6.8	68 5.4	62 5.9	59 6.2		52 7.0	55 6.6
Cost of Sales/Inventory								
Cost of Sales/Payables								
Sales/Working Capital	16.0	8.4	6.3	10.4	17.1		11.0	10.4
	-231.0	37.9	14.9	23.4	43.2		38.7	33.7
	-15.0	-19.5	-546.2	-81.9	-177.0		-30.1	-27.3
EBIT/Interest	9.9	9.3	16.9	21.7	7.8		11.4	9.5
	(176) 3.2	(199) 4.0	(129) 4.4	(30) 5.2	(13) 3.0		(465) 4.6	(510) 3.4
	.5	1.1	1.0	2.7	1.3		1.4	1.2
Net Profit + Depr., Dep., Amort./Cur. Mat. L/T/D		2.4	8.1	10.1			3.7	4.2
		(21) 1.1	(25) 2.2	(11) 2.3			(83) 2.2	(76) 2.2
		.3	.5	1.5			1.1	1.4
Fixed/Worth	.8	.5	.4	.6	1.2		.6	.6
	46.8	1.4	.7	1.4	2.6		1.6	1.7
	-1.0	16.3	1.9	2.3	3.3		7.2	11.2
Debt/Worth	1.4	.8	.5	1.0	1.7		1.2	1.1
	-58.8	2.7	1.3	2.1	3.5		2.8	2.9
	-3.0	126.9	4.1	3.1	5.5		17.6	32.7
% Profit Before Taxes/Tangible Net Worth	158.5	73.0	38.5	39.4	34.0		82.7	77.0
	(101) 38.6	(166) 26.5	(126) 20.0	(29) 28.0	(12) 14.8		(406) 35.0	(436) 34.1
	4.9	.6	1.1	12.2	3.5		11.0	10.0
% Profit Before Taxes/Total Assets	38.2	18.6	17.4	15.9	10.0		27.0	23.5
	11.2	7.2	5.9	8.9	4.6		10.3	9.3
	-2.7	-.1	.1	3.9	.5		1.7	.7
Sales/Net Fixed Assets	28.2	19.5	16.4	9.4	8.2		17.4	17.0
	12.0	9.1	8.9	6.1	5.0		8.3	8.9
	4.7	4.1	4.7	3.3	4.5		4.7	4.4
Sales/Total Assets	6.6	3.6	3.3	2.6	2.9		4.6	4.6
	4.3	2.5	2.3	2.3	2.4		3.1	3.0
	2.6	1.7	1.5	1.7	1.6		2.1	2.0
% Depr., Dep., Amort./Sales	2.0	1.9	1.9	3.0	3.9		2.1	2.0
	(142) 4.1	(171) 3.5	(118) 3.2	(29) 4.0	(10) 4.8		(416) 3.6	(467) 3.7
	7.1	6.2	5.6	5.6	6.0		5.7	6.1
% Officers', Directors' Owners' Comp/Sales	5.0	3.2	1.2				2.7	2.7
	(133) 7.5	(124) 5.0	(60) 2.2				(251) 4.7	(279) 4.3
	11.7	8.3	4.9				7.6	7.3
Net Sales ($)	226456M	699546M	1401900M	1306027M	2505839M	3910777M	10609644M	12720660M
Total Assets ($)	49243M	243771M	579594M	592817M	971682M	821883M	3131952M	3383236M

M = $ thousand   MM = $ million
See Pages 9 through 22 for Explanation of Ratios and Data

Comparative Historical Data | | | Current Data Sorted by Sales

					Type of Statement						
	30		26		27	Unqualified		2		4	3	18
	80		72		86	Reviewed	1	14	19	25	22	5
	71		76		82	Compiled	22	27	14	13	6	
	173		193		226	Tax Returns	83	85	32	17	6	3
	162		184		194	Other	33	63	25	27	22	24
	4/1/08-3/31/09		4/1/09-3/31/10		4/1/10-3/31/11			48 (4/1-9/30/10)		567 (10/1/10-3/31/11)		
	ALL		ALL		ALL		0-1MM	1-3MM	3-5MM	5-10MM	10-25MM	25MM & OVER
	516		551		615	NUMBER OF STATEMENTS	139	191	90	86	59	50
	%		%		%	ASSETS	%	%	%	%	%	%
	11.2		12.6		11.6	Cash & Equivalents	12.6	12.5	9.7	11.8	10.0	9.8
	26.1		22.8		24.5	Trade Receivables (net)	12.5	20.4	30.6	35.7	36.8	29.3
	6.5		6.5		5.6	Inventory	3.9	5.5	6.6	7.6	5.9	5.1
	4.2		3.5		4.2	All Other Current	3.6	3.3	4.2	4.4	6.4	5.9
	48.1		45.4		45.9	Total Current	32.6	41.7	51.1	59.5	59.2	50.1
	39.2		41.2		39.5	Fixed Assets (net)	49.2	42.1	34.1	30.9	29.8	39.0
	4.1		4.4		6.0	Intangibles (net)	8.9	6.8	5.0	2.9	2.7	5.8
	8.6		9.0		8.6	All Other Non-Current	9.4	9.4	9.8	6.7	8.3	5.1
	100.0		100.0		100.0	Total	100.0	100.0	100.0	100.0	100.0	100.0
						LIABILITIES						
	14.7		15.2		15.5	Notes Payable-Short Term	20.2	16.7	15.3	13.6	9.1	8.7
	7.2		6.6		6.4	Cur. Mat.-L.T.D.	7.0	6.5	6.1	6.0	6.3	5.1
	10.7		10.1		10.6	Trade Payables	6.0	8.4	15.1	14.3	15.5	11.1
	.3		.2		.2	Income Taxes Payable	.0	.2	.3	.2	.3	.2
	10.6		10.9		10.4	All Other Current	10.5	10.1	9.6	9.0	13.2	11.5
	43.5		43.0		43.0	Total Current	43.8	41.9	46.4	43.1	44.3	36.6
	30.9		31.7		29.9	Long-Term Debt	48.0	33.9	21.1	13.2	16.0	25.6
	.3		.3		.3	Deferred Taxes	.0	.1	.9	.3	.6	.5
	6.4		6.1		7.7	All Other Non-Current	16.6	6.9	3.9	3.5	3.3	5.1
	18.9		18.8		19.1	Net Worth	-8.4	17.2	27.7	39.8	35.8	32.2
	100.0		100.0		100.0	Total Liabilties & Net Worth	100.0	100.0	100.0	100.0	100.0	100.0
						INCOME DATA						
	100.0		100.0		100.0	Net Sales	100.0	100.0	100.0	100.0	100.0	100.0
						Gross Profit						
	94.2		95.0		94.3	Operating Expenses	91.6	94.3	95.1	96.5	95.3	95.0
	5.8		5.0		5.7	Operating Profit	8.4	5.7	4.9	3.5	4.7	5.0
	1.6		2.0		1.8	All Other Expenses (net)	5.1	1.3	.7	.3	.5	.6
	4.2		3.0		3.9	Profit Before Taxes	3.3	4.4	4.2	3.2	4.1	4.4
						RATIOS						
	2.2		2.2		2.2		2.3	2.4	2.2	2.3	2.2	2.2
	1.3		1.2		1.2	Current	.9	1.1	1.2	1.3	1.4	1.3
	.8		.7		.7		.3	.6	.7	1.0	1.0	1.0
	1.8		1.8		1.9		2.0	2.1	1.8	1.7	1.8	1.9
(514)	1.0		.9	(613)	.9	Quick	.6	(189) .8	1.0	1.1	1.2	1.0
	.4		.4		.5		.2	.4	.5	.8	.7	.7
6	57.4	6	61.2	5	69.2		0 UND	0 UND	15 24.2	26 14.2	28 12.9	32 11.4
30	12.4	27	13.7	28	12.9	Sales/Receivables	3 123.4	22 16.6	36 10.2	41 8.9	41 8.9	41 8.9
53	6.9	50	7.4	52	7.1		29 12.8	45 8.1	53 6.9	69 5.3	58 6.3	57 6.4
						Cost of Sales/Inventory						
						Cost of Sales/Payables						
	10.1		10.2		9.9		13.8	10.6	9.0	6.8	8.1	10.0
	29.0		36.8		38.4	Sales/Working Capital	-139.5	69.5	34.6	21.2	18.7	25.4
	-36.9		-24.6		-23.3		-7.9	-19.4	-19.4	-186.7	-754.7	-201.1
	9.8		11.3		11.2		7.5	10.1	10.2	20.8	22.9	16.6
(456)	3.2	(487)	2.9	(552)	4.1	EBIT/Interest	(113) 3.0	(173) 3.3	(84) 4.3	(81) 6.0	(55) 4.7	(46) 6.0
	1.0		.3		1.0		.2	1.0	.4	.9	1.2	1.6
	4.7		4.4		5.1			4.6	7.2	8.4	2.6	
(71)	2.2	(76)	1.8	(63)	2.0	Net Profit + Depr., Dep., Amort./Cur. Mat. L/T/D		(10) 1.3	(15) 2.0	(10) 1.7	(15) 1.9	
	.6		.7		.5			.2	.5	.2	.5	
	.6		.6		.5		.8	.6	.5	.4	.4	.6
	1.5		1.5		1.5	Fixed/Worth	122.5	2.4	1.2	.8	.7	1.4
	33.0		172.0		-14.3		-1.3	-3.0	6.9	1.7	3.2	2.8
	1.1		.8		.8		1.4	.8	.7	.6	.8	1.0
	2.8		2.8		3.1	Debt/Worth	-31.0	3.9	2.6	1.6	1.7	2.0
	64.7		-639.0		-18.0		-3.2	-8.2	23.0	4.1	6.3	4.1
	71.5		65.7		63.0	% Profit Before Taxes/Tangible Net Worth	94.1	77.9	57.2	44.1	54.9	41.9
(397)	27.2	(413)	20.9	(439)	25.3		(67) 22.6	(126) 28.7	(70) 20.0	(80) 23.8	(53) 27.7	(43) 23.6
	4.5		.0		3.0		-1.0	.6	4.2	1.6	3.8	9.7
	21.0		22.4		20.4	% Profit Before Taxes/Total Assets	21.4	24.4	20.4	17.4	21.2	17.9
	7.6		6.1		7.9		6.4	8.7	8.1	7.1	8.6	8.1
	.0		-2.4		.0		-3.5	-.1	-1.9	.1	.6	1.7
	19.6		18.5		20.1		19.0	21.3	22.3	21.9	21.1	15.1
	10.5		8.6		9.4	Sales/Net Fixed Assets	5.8	9.1	11.2	10.4	13.0	6.6
	4.6		4.3		4.3		2.0	4.3	6.4	6.2	7.5	4.5
	4.7		4.3		4.4		4.1	5.0	4.7	3.5	4.6	3.4
	3.0		2.8		2.7	Sales/Total Assets	2.2	2.9	2.8	2.7	3.3	2.5
	2.0		1.9		1.8		1.1	1.8	2.2	2.2	2.3	2.1
	1.8		2.1		2.0		2.6	2.4	1.7	2.0	1.4	1.9
(410)	3.6	(427)	3.9	(472)	3.7	% Depr., Dep., Amort./Sales	(106) 6.0	(129) 4.2	(77) 3.1	(68) 3.1	(52) 2.6	(40) 4.0
	5.3		6.1		6.1		11.9	6.4	4.3	5.0	4.6	4.9
	2.5		2.6		2.8	% Officers', Directors' Owners' Comp/Sales	5.8	4.6	2.4	1.3	1.2	.8
(258)	4.5	(285)	5.3	(329)	5.4		(78) 9.9	(114) 6.4	(50) 4.1	(51) 2.2	(24) 2.3	(12) 1.7
	8.4		8.8		9.3		14.1	9.1	6.7	4.6	3.9	5.8
	8583123M		8577746M		10050545M	Net Sales ($)	65742M	348297M	348300M	614058M	922864M	7751284M
	2879797M		3099988M		3258990M	Total Assets ($)	46550M	150201M	134490M	257463M	337186M	2333100M

M = $ thousand   MM = $ million
See Pages 9 through 22 for Explanation of Ratios and Data

Current Data Sorted by Assets

Comparative Historical Data

						Type of Statement		
	1	1				Unqualified	1	3
3	5					Reviewed	5	4
13	4	1				Compiled	5	3
15	6	8			1	Tax Returns	13	12
						Other	12	19
	7 (4/1-9/30/10)		53 (10/1/10-3/31/11)				4/1/06-3/31/07	4/1/07-3/31/08
0-500M	500M-2MM	2-10MM	10-50MM	50-100MM	100-250MM		ALL	ALL
31	16	10	1	2		NUMBER OF STATEMENTS	36	41
%	%	%	%	%	%	ASSETS	%	%
14.0	14.6	10.5				Cash & Equivalents	16.6	13.2
26.4	25.2	33.0			D	Trade Receivables (net)	25.0	22.9
1.4	1.7	6.6			A	Inventory	5.2	1.8
1.7	.8	5.5			T	All Other Current	3.3	1.5
43.5	42.3	55.6			A	Total Current	50.1	39.4
29.6	31.7	31.5			N	Fixed Assets (net)	30.2	37.4
14.9	6.3	5.3			O	Intangibles (net)	8.5	13.0
12.0	19.6	7.5			T	All Other Non-Current	11.2	10.2
100.0	100.0	100.0				Total	100.0	100.0
					A	LIABILITIES		
10.7	11.8	7.0			V	Notes Payable-Short Term	16.7	20.1
4.4	4.0	3.7			A	Cur. Mat.-L.T.D.	3.3	6.7
7.6	9.1	8.7			I	Trade Payables	9.4	9.2
.3	.0	.1			L	Income Taxes Payable	.0	.1
10.2	5.2	9.2			A	All Other Current	6.6	6.4
33.2	30.1	28.7			B	Total Current	36.1	42.5
31.5	20.1	16.3			L	Long-Term Debt	26.8	38.5
.0	.0	.0			E	Deferred Taxes	.3	.0
14.8	5.0	.1				All Other Non-Current	3.7	4.4
20.5	44.7	54.8				Net Worth	33.1	14.6
100.0	100.0	100.0				Total Liabilties & Net Worth	100.0	100.0
						INCOME DATA		
100.0	100.0	100.0				Net Sales	100.0	100.0
						Gross Profit		
91.2	95.2	91.6				Operating Expenses	91.3	93.7
8.8	4.8	8.4				Operating Profit	8.7	6.3
1.2	-.5	2.5				All Other Expenses (net)	.8	1.5
7.6	5.3	5.9				Profit Before Taxes	7.8	4.8
						RATIOS		
6.6	3.2	4.1					2.3	2.6
2.3	1.3	1.8				Current	1.3	1.0
.4	.5	1.2					.8	.5
5.9	3.0	3.4					2.1	1.9
2.3	1.3	1.5				Quick	1.0	1.0
.3	.5	1.1					.5	.3
0 UND	0 UND	39 9.5					0 UND	1 543.3
15 23.8	24 15.1	56 6.5				Sales/Receivables	19 19.0	15 24.5
44 8.4	66 5.6	123 3.0					47 7.8	51 7.2
						Cost of Sales/Inventory		
						Cost of Sales/Payables		
10.6	8.4	4.9					8.4	11.6
23.6	37.0	8.7				Sales/Working Capital	37.7	UND
-60.6	-30.7	NM					-63.2	-14.3
32.3	22.1	55.3					25.4	8.1
(25) 7.3	7.2	12.6				EBIT/Interest	(38) 6.2	4.0
1.4	1.1	3.7					1.3	1.2
						Net Profit + Depr., Dep., Amort./Cur. Mat. L/T/D		
.4	.3	.3					.3	.6
2.2	.7	.6				Fixed/Worth	1.4	2.2
-.8	2.1	1.6					121.8	-2.1
1.2	.5	.4					.7	1.4
21.0	1.4	1.0				Debt/Worth	2.9	14.2
-3.0	5.7	2.2					228.2	-4.8
154.6	78.1	72.9				% Profit Before Taxes/Tangible Net Worth	183.1	68.1
(17) 76.3	(14) 30.2	28.0					(28) 61.5	(22) 33.6
14.7	-.5	4.5					9.1	6.6
67.6	29.6	21.9				% Profit Before Taxes/Total Assets	31.4	24.9
16.2	14.2	5.8					12.6	9.8
.7	.2	3.2					1.9	.9
63.1	26.5	24.8				Sales/Net Fixed Assets	46.4	19.5
26.6	9.5	7.2					15.9	10.3
11.8	6.5	3.5					7.2	6.3
6.5	4.0	3.1				Sales/Total Assets	5.8	4.8
4.3	3.0	2.2					4.3	3.3
2.7	2.4	1.1					2.8	2.0
1.0							.8	1.6
(17) 2.3						% Depr., Dep., Amort./Sales	(27) 1.9	(30) 2.5
4.1							4.3	4.2
2.9	2.2					% Officers', Directors' Owners' Comp/Sales	3.5	2.3
(15) 5.6	(10) 10.6						(21) 5.0	(17) 7.3
7.7	14.0						7.5	10.4
30916M	49862M	83777M	24380M	365547M		Net Sales ($)	1147552M	182068M
7227M	16066M	45209M	22968M	140480M		Total Assets ($)	289299M	70672M

M = $ thousand   MM = $ million
See Pages 9 through 22 for Explanation of Ratios and Data

Comparative Historical Data | | Current Data Sorted by Sales

			Type of Statement						
4	2	2	Unqualified					1	1
4	7	2	Reviewed			1		1	
9	9	8	Compiled		6	1			
26	28	18	Tax Returns	1	5		3		
20	24	30	Other	10	14	2	7	1	1.
4/1/08-	4/1/09-	4/1/10-		5					
3/31/09	3/31/10	3/31/11			7 (4/1-9/30/10)		53 (10/1/10-3/31/11)		
ALL	ALL	ALL		0-1MM	1-3MM	3-5MM	5-10MM	10-25MM	25MM & OVER
63	70	60	**NUMBER OF STATEMENTS**	16	25	4	10	3	2
%	%	%	**ASSETS**	%	%	%	%	%	%
15.1	16.0	14.4	Cash & Equivalents	12.2	15.1		7.6		
23.6	25.1	26.5	Trade Receivables (net)	21.1	30.7		29.2		
3.5	4.6	2.6	Inventory	.7	1.3		9.2		
3.5	3.8	2.2	All Other Current	2.1	2.3		2.6		
45.7	49.5	45.7	Total Current	36.2	49.4		48.6		
34.0	28.0	30.6	Fixed Assets (net)	20.2	34.1		36.2		
11.2	11.9	10.7	Intangibles (net)	20.4	6.7		4.9		
9.2	10.6	13.0	All Other Non-Current	23.2	9.8		10.3		
100.0	100.0	100.0	Total	100.0	100.0		100.0		
			LIABILITIES						
18.7	22.6	9.8	Notes Payable-Short Term	10.2	10.9		10.4		
5.8	4.6	4.0	Cur. Mat.-L.T.D.	2.5	5.6		3.8		
8.5	9.0	8.0	Trade Payables	8.7	6.3		12.3		
.1	.0	.2	Income Taxes Payable	.0	.4		.0		
10.5	10.3	8.9	All Other Current	10.8	7.5		9.8		
43.7	46.5	31.0	Total Current	32.2	30.6		36.3		
31.5	31.7	24.8	Long-Term Debt	31.2	28.4		18.9		
.0	.1	.0	Deferred Taxes	.0	.0		.0		
4.4	6.2	9.1	All Other Non-Current	26.5	3.6		2.4		
20.4	15.5	35.0	Net Worth	10.0	37.4		42.4		
100.0	100.0	100.0	Total Liabilties & Net Worth	100.0	100.0		100.0		
			INCOME DATA						
100.0	100.0	100.0	Net Sales	100.0	100.0		100.0		
			Gross Profit						
90.9	94.3	92.5	Operating Expenses	90.1	93.5		93.2		
9.1	5.7	7.5	Operating Profit	9.9	6.5		6.8		
1.9	1.0	.9	All Other Expenses (net)	1.5	.3		2.2		
7.2	4.7	6.6	Profit Before Taxes	8.4	6.3		4.5		
			RATIOS						
3.0	3.2	4.9		7.8	4.4		2.3		
1.4	1.5	1.7	Current	2.9	1.7		1.2		
.6	.7	.8		.3	.7		.7		
2.7	2.9	4.1		6.1	4.2		1.7		
1.1	(69) 1.2	1.6	Quick	2.8	1.6		1.0		
.5	.6	.7		.2	.6		.6		
2 201.4	3 118.2	3 125.1		0 UND	0 UND		12 -29.5		
17 21.4	24 15.0	30 12.1	Sales/Receivables	10 38.1	31 11.9		42 8.7		
38 9.5	48 7.6	57 6.4		59 6.2	55 6.6		67 5.5		
			Cost of Sales/Inventory						
			Cost of Sales/Payables						
9.6	9.1	8.4		9.7	8.3		12.2		
36.9	25.0	19.3	Sales/Working Capital	31.1	13.0		29.9		
-19.0	-21.5	-104.3		-4.8	-121.2		-29.8		
17.9	19.6	31.0		21.2	39.7		28.1		
(58) 6.3	(66) 4.6	(54) 8.8	EBIT/Interest	(12) 2.0	(23) 12.8		7.8		
2.8	1.1	1.6		1.3	.9		3.1		
			Net Profit + Depr., Dep., Amort./Cur. Mat. L/T/D						
.3	.3	.3		.4	.3		.3		
1.0	.9	.8	Fixed/Worth	-6.3	.7		1.4		
-2.4	-1.6	-12.7		-.2	2.2		5.5		
.6	.8	.7		2.2	.9		.6		
2.9	1.6	1.6	Debt/Worth	-18.6	1.3		1.5		
-7.6	-4.6	-33.9		-2.1	7.4		7.1		
100.8	111.4	91.7			62.5				
(43) 54.2	(49) 30.8	(44) 36.2	% Profit Before Taxes/Tangible Net Worth		(20) 27.1				
21.8	8.4	3.3			-5.3				
46.5	27.1	42.3		75.8	53.1		30.8		
19.2	9.3	11.4	% Profit Before Taxes/Total Assets	8.5	15.9		10.7		
5.9	-1.2	2.3		1.1	-1.0		3.4		
36.7	56.6	43.3		96.8	36.7		36.5		
13.6	16.7	13.3	Sales/Net Fixed Assets	28.5	18.5		6.8		
7.7	8.2	7.1		13.3	8.6		5.7		
5.5	5.5	4.7		6.9	5.5		4.1		
3.7	3.5	3.3	Sales/Total Assets	3.5	3.9		3.1		
2.4	2.3	2.3		2.1	2.6		1.6		
1.6	.9	1.5		.2	1.5				
(44) 2.9	(38) 2.6	(36) 2.9	% Depr., Dep., Amort./Sales	(10) 3.0	(10) 3.1				
4.6	5.2	4.5		4.0	5.6				
3.2	3.1	2.0		3.7	2.6				
(32) 6.6	(46) 6.4	(30) 5.4	% Officers', Directors' Owners' Comp/Sales	(10) 6.2	(12) 7.9				
9.5	9.4	10.0		9.8	12.3				
452793M	260805M	554482M	Net Sales ($)	9396M	39100M	14978M	68668M	56793M	365547M
161748M	103130M	231950M	Total Assets ($)	3525M	16266M	5540M	32420M	33719M	140480M

M = $ thousand   MM = $ million
See Pages 9 through 22 for Explanation of Ratios and Data

Current Data Sorted by Assets   Comparative Historical Data

Type of Statement

Type of Statement	0-500M	500M-2MM	2-10MM	10-50MM	50-100MM	100-250MM	4/1/06-3/31/07 ALL	4/1/07-3/31/08 ALL
Unqualified	1		1	3	2		7	5
Reviewed		13	12	4			12	16
Compiled	2	4	4				19	18
Tax Returns	29	12	9				35	41
Other	12	15	10				37	28
		18 (4/1-9/30/10)		117 (10/1/10-3/31/11) 2				
NUMBER OF STATEMENTS	44	44	36	9	2		110	108

Data for columns 10-50MM, 50-100MM and 100-250MM: **DATA NOT AVAILABLE**

ASSETS (%)

	0-500M	500M-2MM	2-10MM	4/1/06-3/31/07 ALL	4/1/07-3/31/08 ALL
Cash & Equivalents	27.4	11.8	16.3	13.4	16.2
Trade Receivables (net)	22.5	30.6	36.2	36.7	32.2
Inventory	4.5	8.8	7.9	7.4	5.8
All Other Current	2.2	2.6	5.0	3.6	5.7
Total Current	56.6	53.8	65.4	61.1	60.0
Fixed Assets (net)	28.5	27.7	22.3	25.4	29.6
Intangibles (net)	3.5	5.5	4.2	6.1	3.3
All Other Non-Current	11.5	13.1	8.2	7.4	7.2
Total	100.0	100.0	100.0	100.0	100.0

LIABILITIES

	0-500M	500M-2MM	2-10MM	4/1/06-3/31/07 ALL	4/1/07-3/31/08 ALL
Notes Payable-Short Term	22.4	14.2	8.8	12.3	17.5
Cur. Mat.-L.T.D.	4.7	3.5	3.4	4.6	4.8
Trade Payables	8.1	14.5	17.7	13.9	11.6
Income Taxes Payable	.1	.8	.2	.2	.1
All Other Current	18.7	10.9	14.1	13.8	16.4
Total Current	54.0	43.9	44.1	44.7	50.4
Long-Term Debt	30.0	22.8	17.9	22.3	21.1
Deferred Taxes	.0	.1	.2	.3	.2
All Other Non-Current	11.2	9.5	3.5	7.0	6.7
Net Worth	4.8	23.7	34.4	25.6	21.6
Total Liabilities & Net Worth	100.0	100.0	100.0	100.0	100.0

INCOME DATA

	0-500M	500M-2MM	2-10MM	4/1/06-3/31/07 ALL	4/1/07-3/31/08 ALL
Net Sales	100.0	100.0	100.0	100.0	100.0
Gross Profit					
Operating Expenses	90.3	91.8	94.1	91.3	92.9
Operating Profit	9.7	8.2	5.9	8.7	7.1
All Other Expenses (net)	1.4	3.6	1.2	1.7	2.3
Profit Before Taxes	8.3	4.6	4.7	7.0	4.8

RATIOS

Ratio	0-500M	500M-2MM	2-10MM	4/1/06-3/31/07 ALL	4/1/07-3/31/08 ALL
Current	5.4	2.2	2.0	2.8	2.4
	1.5	1.1	1.5	1.4	1.4
	.5	.7	1.1	.9	.8
Quick	4.1	2.1	1.8	2.3	1.9
	1.4	.8	1.2	1.1	1.0
	.4	.4	.7	.7	.5
Sales/Receivables	0 UND	7 50.7	31 11.6	23 16.0	8 47.4
	7 54.7	29 12.5	45 8.1	42 8.8	37 9.9
	41 9.0	53 6.8	60 6.1	67 5.4	54 6.7
Cost of Sales/Inventory					
Cost of Sales/Payables					
Sales/Working Capital	8.8	10.7	6.5	8.1	7.7
	32.8	54.3	14.1	16.6	27.4
	-13.5	-19.4	53.2	-164.5	-41.6
EBIT/Interest	32.8	11.3	29.0	20.0	15.9
	(34) 5.1	(38) 4.4	(30) 4.4	(95) 5.3	(93) 5.5
	.9	.7	2.2	2.1	1.7
Net Profit + Depr., Dep., Amort./Cur. Mat. L/T/D				10.1	6.0
				(11) 6.6	(14) 3.1
				3.1	.5
Fixed/Worth	.1	.2	.1	.3	.3
	1.1	1.1	.4	1.0	.7
	-1.3	5.6	1.8	6.7	2.8
Debt/Worth	.6	.9	.8	.7	.7
	5.0	2.9	1.8	2.8	1.9
	-4.7	13.9	5.8	35.7	9.4
% Profit Before Taxes/Tangible Net Worth	133.1	73.8	73.4	138.7	71.2
	(27) 61.5	(37) 15.3	(29) 18.8	(87) 47.8	(85) 35.1
	7.5	-1.2	6.8	17.0	11.2
% Profit Before Taxes/Total Assets	58.5	16.9	19.1	35.4	30.3
	23.6	5.5	6.0	13.5	13.1
	.7	-1.2	2.0	4.1	2.0
Sales/Net Fixed Assets	183.3	72.7	66.4	38.3	49.6
	27.7	26.3	27.1	17.2	15.1
	10.5	9.1	7.0	7.3	6.7
Sales/Total Assets	8.4	5.1	3.5	4.5	5.4
	4.7	2.8	2.8	2.9	3.3
	2.5	2.1	1.7	2.0	2.1
% Depr., Dep., Amort./Sales	.8	.7	.6	.7	.9
	(24) 1.7	(32) 2.0	(29) 1.4	(81) 1.7	(79) 2.2
	3.1	4.8	5.1	4.0	5.3
% Officers', Directors' Owners' Comp/Sales	5.2	3.0	1.6	2.0	2.8
	(27) 10.1	(23) 5.7	(12) 3.8	(53) 4.3	(67) 6.1
	14.6	9.0	12.5	8.8	10.9

	0-500M	500M-2MM	2-10MM	10-50MM	50-100MM	4/1/06-3/31/07 ALL	4/1/07-3/31/08 ALL
Net Sales ($)	47800M	175266M	443596M	431013M	176930M	1137677M	1473264M
Total Assets ($)	10666M	51667M	161013M	141278M	159945M	433228M	467105M

M = $ thousand   MM = $ million
See Pages 9 through 22 for Explanation of Ratios and Data

Comparative Historical Data   Current Data Sorted by Sales

			Type of Statement						
7	9	7	Unqualified				1	1	5
19	28	29	Reviewed		6	4	10	5	4
20	16	10	Compiled		3	4	1	2	
43	38	50	Tax Returns	21	16	4	5	3	1
49	43	39	Other	12	7	3	7	9	1
4/1/08-3/31/09 ALL	4/1/09-3/31/10 ALL	4/1/10-3/31/11 ALL		0-1MM	18 (4/1-9/30/10) 1-3MM	3-5MM	117 (10/1/10-3/31/11) 5-10MM	10-25MM	25MM & OVER
138	134	135	**NUMBER OF STATEMENTS**	33	33	15	23	20	11
%	%	%	**ASSETS**	%	%	%	%	%	%
13.0	14.3	18.4	Cash & Equivalents	21.7	20.6	14.3	19.5	12.8	15.4
32.0	33.0	29.7	Trade Receivables (net)	16.2	22.1	37.3	38.9	42.8	40.1
5.7	7.2	6.8	Inventory	3.9	7.9	1.6	9.8	12.5	2.3
4.9	4.2	3.3	All Other Current	1.9	2.3	3.6	4.2	5.6	3.8
55.7	58.7	58.1	Total Current	43.6	52.7	56.7	72.4	73.8	61.6
31.0	25.6	26.3	Fixed Assets (net)	45.8	25.0	20.7	15.9	13.7	24.0
3.8	6.0	4.4	Intangibles (net)	3.0	5.6	9.9	2.6	2.3	5.1
9.5	9.6	11.1	All Other Non-Current	7.6	16.6	12.8	9.1	10.2	9.3
100.0	100.0	100.0	Total	100.0	100.0	100.0	100.0	100.0	100.0
			LIABILITIES						
13.7	13.4	14.4	Notes Payable-Short Term	17.8	20.4	12.4	12.4	8.3	3.9
5.5	4.2	3.7	Cur. Mat.-L.T.D.	3.9	5.1	5.3	1.7	3.2	2.1
11.9	12.1	13.1	Trade Payables	5.4	6.0	16.1	15.0	33.0	14.0
.1	.3	.3	Income Taxes Payable	.1	.1	.0	1.7	.1	.0
12.6	13.1	14.9	All Other Current	12.5	17.3	8.5	13.1	19.4	19.5
43.8	43.0	46.5	Total Current	39.7	48.9	42.3	43.9	63.9	39.6
22.0	22.1	23.3	Long-Term Debt	34.2	27.4	26.8	7.9	18.1	15.5
.1	.3	.1	Deferred Taxes	.0	.0	.2	.2	.0	.0
4.8	8.0	8.1	All Other Non-Current	12.3	8.0	3.8	2.2	13.5	4.4
29.3	26.6	21.9	Net Worth	13.8	15.7	26.8	45.8	4.4	40.5
100.0	100.0	100.0	Total Liabilties & Net Worth	100.0	100.0	100.0	100.0	100.0	100.0
			INCOME DATA						
100.0	100.0	100.0	Net Sales	100.0	100.0	100.0	100.0	100.0	100.0
			Gross Profit						
91.8	92.7	92.0	Operating Expenses	84.0	92.2	95.1	96.7	96.8	92.8
8.2	7.3	8.0	Operating Profit	16.0	7.8	4.9	3.3	3.2	7.2
2.4	1.1	2.0	All Other Expenses (net)	7.7	.4	1.1	-.7	-.3	.7
5.8	6.1	6.0	Profit Before Taxes	8.3	7.4	3.8	4.0	3.5	6.6
			RATIOS						
2.3	2.9	2.5	Current	5.1	2.6	2.4	3.0	1.7	2.2
1.4	1.6	1.4		1.3	1.5	1.4	1.7	1.2	1.6
.8	.9	.8		.4	.4	.9	1.2	.8	1.2
2.0	2.5	2.2	Quick	5.1	2.6	2.3	2.6	1.3	1.9
1.0	1.3	1.2		1.1	.7	1.2	1.5	.9	1.6
.5	.7	.6		.2	.2	.9	.8	.7	.9
9 41.0	9 41.7	5 71.3	Sales/Receivables	0 UND	0 UND	20 18.3	31 11.9	32 11.6	34 10.6
34 10.7	37 10.0	33 11.0		5 74.0	21 17.0	43 8.4	38 9.6	52 7.0	43 8.4
61 5.9	66 5.5	55 6.6		32 11.6	46 8.0	66 5.6	55 6.6	64 5.7	60 6.1
			Cost of Sales/Inventory						
			Cost of Sales/Payables						
7.7	6.9	7.9	Sales/Working Capital	8.4	7.1	11.1	4.5	7.2	9.2
23.0	14.8	23.4		37.0	74.9	37.9	11.5	24.5	15.4
-26.3	-244.0	-33.5		-10.7	-10.9	-62.0	37.9	-79.8	27.7
19.8	18.7	26.7	EBIT/Interest	10.3	28.9	10.1	17.1	26.7	90.8
(119) 5.6	(113) 5.6	(113) 4.7		(20) 2.8	(29) 10.3	4.5	(18) 4.0	4.9	39.8
1.6	1.4	1.4		.0	1.2	.7	1.3	2.4	4.2
13.2	7.7	6.3	Net Profit + Depr., Dep., Amort./Cur. Mat. L/T/D						
(20) 2.5	(21) 2.5	(11) 2.4							
.8	.5	1.1							
.3	.2	.1	Fixed/Worth	.4	.1	.3	.1	.1	.2
1.0	.7	.7		1.5	2.9	1.2	.3	.4	.5
6.6	5.8	5.7		NM	-2.8	-1.8	.8	1.9	.9
.8	.7	.9	Debt/Worth	.7	.7	2.1	.6	1.6	.9
2.5	2.0	2.4		3.1	4.2	3.7	.9	3.7	1.5
33.5	48.2	24.8		-14.5	-5.6	-5.5	3.6	6.6	6.1
83.3	87.7	88.2	% Profit Before Taxes/Tangible Net Worth	93.4	103.7	206.5	34.6	79.1	90.9
(106) 32.1	(104) 36.8	(104) 22.9		(24) 11.4	(21) 48.6	(10) 21.4	(22) 20.4	(16) 15.8	43.8
10.6	5.4	5.4		-11.7	4.9	-19.0	3.8	7.2	11.4
25.3	27.9	25.5	% Profit Before Taxes/Total Assets	39.8	55.2	23.6	17.3	18.5	31.2
12.8	11.7	8.6		6.5	14.7	13.7	8.6	5.8	21.7
1.6	.8	1.0		-5.0	.9	-.6	1.0	2.1	3.4
45.5	72.3	79.2	Sales/Net Fixed Assets	44.9	157.7	40.9	134.3	148.8	40.6
17.0	22.1	26.1		12.6	46.6	20.4	34.0	32.6	23.5
6.1	8.7	9.3		2.0	9.7	9.5	15.0	13.3	9.5
5.1	5.2	5.2	Sales/Total Assets	6.3	5.0	6.0	4.6	5.0	4.7
3.1	3.1	2.9		2.5	2.8	3.2	2.9	3.3	2.7
1.9	1.9	2.1		1.3	2.2	2.3	2.1	2.2	2.3
1.0	.8	.7	% Depr., Dep., Amort./Sales	1.2	.9	1.4	.4	.5	
(103) 2.3	(87) 1.6	(94) 1.5		(20) 3.1	(17) 2.3	(12) 2.9	(19) 1.1	(17) 1.1	
5.2	4.0	3.5		13.5	4.9	4.6	1.9	1.7	
2.3	3.4	3.2	% Officers', Directors' Owners' Comp/Sales	8.0	3.9				
(66) 4.7	(68) 6.8	(62) 6.7		(15) 10.8	(20) 7.2				
10.2	11.0	12.7		20.2	13.3				
1859301M	3193842M	1274605M	Net Sales ($)	16893M	61364M	56157M	181568M	304913M	653710M
708136M	906469M	524569M	Total Assets ($)	16687M	22550M	18632M	68609M	110677M	287414M

M = $ thousand   MM = $ million
See Pages 9 through 22 for Explanation of Ratios and Data

Current Data Sorted by Assets   **Comparative Historical Data**

0-500M	500M-2MM	2-10MM	10-50MM	50-100MM	100-250MM		4/1/06-3/31/07 ALL	4/1/07-3/31/08 ALL
						Type of Statement		
		1	5	1	1	Unqualified	3	5
	2	14	4			Reviewed	11	5
2	4	8				Compiled	5	5
9	12	5				Tax Returns	7	9
8	9	17	10		1	Other	24	21
16 (4/1-9/30/10)			97 (10/1/10-3/31/11)				4/1/06-3/31/07	4/1/07-3/31/08
19	27	45	19	1	2	**NUMBER OF STATEMENTS**	50	45
%	%	%	%	%	%	**ASSETS**	%	%
26.4	11.0	7.2	7.6			Cash & Equivalents	10.8	7.5
27.3	30.8	31.7	24.4			Trade Receivables (net)	28.7	25.6
4.0	11.1	16.8	13.8			Inventory	13.4	14.6
6.6	1.3	2.5	.9			All Other Current	3.2	3.0
64.3	54.2	58.2	46.7			Total Current	56.2	50.7
20.8	29.2	27.4	31.0			Fixed Assets (net)	33.0	34.1
3.9	4.6	9.1	19.0			Intangibles (net)	6.6	9.2
11.1	12.0	5.3	3.3			All Other Non-Current	4.1	6.0
100.0	100.0	100.0	100.0			Total	100.0	100.0
						LIABILITIES		
19.7	10.2	12.1	7.8			Notes Payable-Short Term	15.0	12.7
2.3	1.8	2.7	3.1			Cur. Mat.-L.T.D.	3.5	3.7
10.5	18.4	23.9	11.2			Trade Payables	20.7	15.3
.0	.1	.0	.4			Income Taxes Payable	.1	.0
14.0	9.0	14.4	3.8			All Other Current	12.8	13.4
46.5	39.5	53.1	26.4			Total Current	52.1	45.2
17.5	18.2	18.6	24.7			Long-Term Debt	21.7	31.8
.1	.0	.1	.5			Deferred Taxes	.1	.1
30.2	1.9	12.0	5.7			All Other Non-Current	7.1	10.3
5.6	40.4	16.2	42.7			Net Worth	18.9	12.7
100.0	100.0	100.0	100.0			Total Liabilties & Net Worth	100.0	100.0
						INCOME DATA		
100.0	100.0	100.0	100.0			Net Sales	100.0	100.0
						Gross Profit		
96.6	87.7	95.9	90.3			Operating Expenses	92.7	86.4
3.4	12.3	4.1	9.7			Operating Profit	7.3	13.6
.5	2.7	1.7	3.6			All Other Expenses (net)	4.2	6.1
2.9	9.5	2.4	6.1			Profit Before Taxes	3.0	7.5
						RATIOS		
8.4	2.8	1.6	3.1				1.5	1.5
2.0	1.5	1.1	1.6			Current	1.1	1.1
.5	.9	.8	1.1				.8	.8
8.4	2.3	1.1	2.2				1.3	1.1
1.1	1.2	.8	1.0			Quick	.8	.7
.5	.6	.5	.6				.4	.5
0 UND	21 17.8	33 11.2	30 12.1				22 16.5	26 14.0
3 113.9	33 11.0	39 9.3	35 10.5			Sales/Receivables	43 8.4	43 8.5
54 6.8	55 6.7	58 6.3	53 6.9				63 5.8	64 5.7
						Cost of Sales/Inventory		
						Cost of Sales/Payables		
6.3	7.0	10.9	4.7				10.7	10.8
41.7	21.1	41.6	13.1			Sales/Working Capital	50.2	28.0
-31.5	-91.9	-23.8	132.5				-55.7	-21.0
25.7	21.2	11.3	18.0				9.9	10.2
(14) 4.8	(22) 9.4	(40) 2.4	(18) 10.4			EBIT/Interest	(41) 2.9	(34) 1.9
1.9	5.3	-.1	3.5				.8	.4
						Net Profit + Depr., Dep., Amort./Cur. Mat. L/T/D		
.0	.2	.4	.4				.4	.4
.2	.6	1.6	1.1			Fixed/Worth	1.6	2.0
1.7	2.1	-.9	2.1				15.6	-20.6
.4	.6	1.2	1.7				2.5	2.0
1.2	1.6	5.0	2.1			Debt/Worth	5.1	4.1
-9.2	4.9	-5.1	5.6				NM	-7.1
132.5	114.9	30.9	114.1				98.8	87.8
(14) 51.2	(23) 36.6	(30) 21.8	(17) 32.5			% Profit Before Taxes/Tangible Net Worth	(38) 37.4	(32) 32.5
7.6	10.1	.6	15.9				2.8	1.4
68.7	29.2	11.2	24.2				14.2	17.1
9.9	15.1	3.8	12.2			% Profit Before Taxes/Total Assets	5.1	7.0
1.9	5.6	-2.4	2.4				.6	.2
UND	39.7	34.7	21.3				33.6	36.7
259.3	18.4	10.7	5.2			Sales/Net Fixed Assets	9.5	8.5
17.4	6.5	5.2	3.3				3.8	3.2
11.8	3.8	3.4	2.5				4.0	2.7
6.0	2.9	2.3	1.7			Sales/Total Assets	2.2	2.1
4.5	2.0	1.8	1.3				1.5	1.4
	1.1	1.0	.6				1.1	.8
	(22) 1.8	(38) 1.9	(18) 1.4			% Depr., Dep., Amort./Sales	(39) 1.7	(37) 2.0
	5.8	3.5	4.4				4.0	6.3
	3.5	1.5					1.7	1.7
	(12) 5.1	(11) 2.5				% Officers', Directors', Owners' Comp/Sales	(13) 3.6	(11) 3.7
	6.5	6.1					6.0	8.6
67101M	96026M	588118M	716105M	153298M	722733M	Net Sales ($)	1740996M	1161827M
4349M	31732M	239643M	366392M	61403M	354762M	Total Assets ($)	688436M	635369M

M = $ thousand   MM = $ million
See Pages 9 through 22 for Explanation of Ratios and Data

Comparative Historical Data   Current Data Sorted by Sales

	4/1/08-3/31/09 ALL	4/1/09-3/31/10 ALL	4/1/10-3/31/11 ALL	Type of Statement	0-1MM	1-3MM	3-5MM	5-10MM	10-25MM	25MM & OVER
	10	9	8	Unqualified					1	4
	12	9	20	Reviewed		1	1	2	14	2
	10	12	14	Compiled	2	2	3	4	3	
	12	16	26	Tax Returns	5	9	3	5	2	2
	19	42	45	Other	7	7	4	4	11	12
					16 (4/1-9/30/10)			97 (10/1/10-3/31/11)		
	63	88	113	NUMBER OF STATEMENTS	14	19	11	16	33	20
	%	%	%	ASSETS	%	%	%	%	%	%
	8.3	9.4	11.9	Cash & Equivalents	19.5	18.5	6.9	8.7	8.3	11.9
	29.3	25.0	29.4	Trade Receivables (net)	16.2	26.8	30.8	40.4	30.3	30.0
	16.3	13.4	12.6	Inventory	1.0	9.6	15.6	12.0	16.2	16.5
	4.7	2.5	2.6	All Other Current	6.7	3.5	.7	2.4	2.0	1.0
	58.7	50.4	56.5	Total Current	43.3	58.4	54.0	63.5	56.8	59.5
	30.9	34.2	27.1	Fixed Assets (net)	38.5	26.3	25.7	25.1	27.7	21.0
	4.4	8.0	8.8	Intangibles (net)	3.2	3.5	5.8	7.0	12.0	15.3
	6.0	7.4	7.6	All Other Non-Current	14.9	11.8	14.6	4.3	3.5	4.3
	100.0	100.0	100.0	Total	100.0	100.0	100.0	100.0	100.0	100.0
				LIABILITIES						
	14.9	15.4	11.9	Notes Payable-Short Term	12.9	14.1	12.8	9.6	10.9	12.2
	5.7	4.1	2.4	Cur. Mat.-L.T.D.	2.7	.9	2.2	3.4	2.8	2.6
	21.2	16.6	18.0	Trade Payables	3.6	21.2	14.2	24.4	18.7	20.6
	.1	.1	.1	Income Taxes Payable	.0	.0	.0	.2	.1	.3
	15.0	15.6	11.1	All Other Current	10.1	8.9	8.5	9.3	14.7	11.0
	56.9	51.8	43.6	Total Current	29.3	45.2	37.8	46.8	47.1	46.8
	19.7	27.0	19.4	Long-Term Debt	39.6	15.7	14.4	23.2	15.9	14.3
	.2	.1	.2	Deferred Taxes	.0	.1	.0	.0	.4	.0
	4.7	7.5	11.5	All Other Non-Current	20.7	15.5	2.1	23.0	6.7	5.3
	18.6	13.7	25.3	Net Worth	10.4	23.5	45.7	7.0	29.8	33.7
	100.0	100.0	100.0	Total Liabilities & Net Worth	100.0	100.0	100.0	100.0	100.0	100.0
				INCOME DATA						
	100.0	100.0	100.0	Net Sales	100.0	100.0	100.0	100.0	100.0	100.0
				Gross Profit						
	95.0	91.8	93.2	Operating Expenses	75.8	94.1	93.1	97.9	96.8	94.7
	5.0	8.2	6.8	Operating Profit	24.2	5.9	6.9	2.1	3.2	5.3
	2.9	3.5	2.1	All Other Expenses (net)	12.0	.4	.6	1.0	.6	.7
	2.1	4.8	4.8	Profit Before Taxes	12.2	5.5	6.3	1.1	2.6	4.6
				RATIOS						
	1.9	2.2	2.7	Current	6.6	4.7	2.8	1.9	2.1	1.9
	1.2	1.3	1.4		.9	2.1	1.7	1.3	1.3	1.4
	.8	.8	.9		.2	1.1	.9	1.0	.9	.9
	1.2	1.5	1.8	Quick	3.6	3.5	2.4	1.3	1.5	1.4
	.7	.8	.9		.4	1.3	1.5	1.0	.8	.9
	.4	.5	.5		.2	.5	.6	.8	.6	.5
	25 14.4	24 15.0	23 16.1	Sales/Receivables	0 UND	0 UND	29 12.4	35 10.4	33 11.2	28 12.8
	36 10.1	36 10.1	37 9.9		0 UND	30 12.1	33 11.0	49 7.5	39 9.4	36 10.1
	59 6.2	51 7.1	55 6.6		27 13.3	55 6.6	69 5.3	74 4.9	46 7.9	58 6.3
				Cost of Sales/Inventory						
				Cost of Sales/Payables						
	10.9	7.7	7.1	Sales/Working Capital	6.1	5.8	7.1	9.7	8.7	7.1
	36.0	20.3	19.3		NM	17.9	11.6	25.6	37.5	14.9
	-14.8	-19.5	-52.8		-2.6	92.2	-43.8	424.0	-70.6	-284.8
	10.7	7.9	16.1	EBIT/Interest		9.9	29.1	21.9	11.8	16.2
	(54) 3.0	(69) 2.8	(96) 5.7		(15) 5.6	13.3	(15) 4.2	(31) 2.5	(19) 10.2	
	-.1	.8	1.8			.9	4.3	2.3	.6	2.8
		9.1	13.1	Net Profit + Depr., Dep., Amort./Cur. Mat. L/T/D						
		(14) 4.8	(21) 3.5							
		1.2	1.1							
	.4	.5	.2	Fixed/Worth	.0	.2	.2	.2	.4	.3
	1.3	1.4	.9		.5	.8	.6	1.0	1.4	1.1
	-13.2	NM	3.1		NM	2.1	.8	-.8	2.7	5.9
	1.0	.9	.9	Debt/Worth	.3	.6	.5	.7	1.0	2.1
	3.3	3.6	2.2		1.4	1.6	1.1	3.2	2.4	3.7
	-36.5	-48.4	13.3		-27.4	10.5	4.1	-4.7	15.7	12.3
	54.6	62.7	78.7	% Profit Before Taxes/Tangible Net Worth	125.3	85.5	102.8		37.5	114.7
	(45) 27.3	(65) 23.2	(87) 26.9		(10) 37.1	(16) 29.3	(10) 30.0		(26) 22.4	(16) 44.7
	3.5	3.8	8.3		6.2	6.4	17.0		-.6	15.3
	16.1	16.3	19.0	% Profit Before Taxes/Total Assets	63.8	26.1	23.7	26.1	12.3	24.3
	4.9	8.0	8.1		4.2	8.0	16.5	7.8	6.5	9.4
	-3.1	.2	1.9		.1	1.8	5.0	2.2	-.3	2.6
	26.4	21.4	44.8	Sales/Net Fixed Assets	UND	151.8	27.6	57.7	34.4	68.8
	11.3	8.8	15.4		10.0	21.3	20.4	21.0	7.6	20.9
	4.7	4.1	5.4		-.1	9.8	6.5	9.6	5.1	5.6
	3.5	4.1	4.0	Sales/Total Assets	5.9	7.2	3.8	3.9	3.4	3.7
	2.6	2.4	2.7		1.5	3.4	3.0	2.8	2.2	2.5
	1.9	1.4	1.7		.1	2.1	2.0	2.4	1.7	1.8
	1.3	1.3	.9	% Depr., Dep., Amort./Sales		1.4	1.5	.7	.7	.4
	(51) 2.7	(70) 2.8	(88) 1.7			(12) 2.3	(10) 2.6	(13) 1.1	(27) 1.7	(19) 1.2
	3.7	6.2	4.0			7.7	3.9	2.3	3.5	2.6
	2.9	2.3	2.1	% Officers', Directors' Owners' Comp/Sales						
	(17) 4.1	(28) 5.4	(38) 3.8							
	8.9	11.7	6.6							
	1829259M	1998033M	2343381M	Net Sales ($)	6376M	35893M	39334M	104564M	500161M	1657053M
	568382M	825213M	1058281M	Total Assets ($)	24915M	16983M	19159M	35733M	238680M	722811M

© RMA 2011   M = $ thousand   MM = $ million
See Pages 9 through 22 for Explanation of Ratios and Data

Current Data Sorted by Assets   **Comparative Historical Data**

0-500M	500M-2MM	2-10MM	10-50MM	50-100MM	100-250MM		Type of Statement	4/1/06-3/31/07 ALL	4/1/07-3/31/08 ALL
		1	1	2			Unqualified	1	1
	1	2	2				Reviewed	1	2
	1	1					Compiled	1	3
5	1	2					Tax Returns	2	5
1	1	5	4	1			Other	3	4
	3 (4/1-9/30/10)		28 (10/1/10-3/31/11)						
6	4	11	7	3			NUMBER OF STATEMENTS	8	15
%	%	%	%	%	%			%	%
		17.9				D	Cash & Equivalents		27.5
		36.3				A	Trade Receivables (net)		23.6
		8.3				T	Inventory		5.1
		5.9				A	All Other Current		2.8
		68.4					Total Current		59.0
		20.2				N	Fixed Assets (net)		28.1
		.5				O	Intangibles (net)		2.8
		10.9				T	All Other Non-Current		10.1
		100.0					Total		100.0
						A	**LIABILITIES**		
		12.0				V	Notes Payable-Short Term		16.2
		.3				A	Cur. Mat.-L.T.D.		2.6
		11.9				I	Trade Payables		16.8
		.0				L	Income Taxes Payable		.0
		22.6				A	All Other Current		18.9
		46.8				B	Total Current		54.6
		13.2				L	Long-Term Debt		14.8
		.3				E	Deferred Taxes		.3
		7.5					All Other Non-Current		4.9
		32.3					Net Worth		25.3
		100.0					Total Liabilities & Net Worth		100.0
							INCOME DATA		
		100.0					Net Sales		100.0
							Gross Profit		
		93.8					Operating Expenses		95.9
		6.2					Operating Profit		4.1
		.4					All Other Expenses (net)		.6
		5.8					Profit Before Taxes		3.5
							RATIOS		
		2.9							2.7
		1.3					Current		1.5
		.9							1.0
		2.0							2.5
		1.1					Quick		1.1
		.8							.8
	8	47.0						2 171.5	
	41	9.0					Sales/Receivables	12 30.7	
	118	3.1						36 10.0	
							Cost of Sales/Inventory		
							Cost of Sales/Payables		
		7.9							6.7
		22.1					Sales/Working Capital		30.2
		-58.1							-176.7
									30.5
							EBIT/Interest	(11)	6.2
									1.8
							Net Profit + Depr., Dep., Amort./Cur. Mat. L/T/D		
		.2							.1
		.3					Fixed/Worth		.9
		4.9							2.5
		.7							.5
		2.6					Debt/Worth		3.2
		8.0							9.7
									167.9
							% Profit Before Taxes/Tangible Net Worth	(13)	60.3
									26.9
		27.6							35.4
		14.7					% Profit Before Taxes/Total Assets		21.1
		5.5							5.6
		85.4							51.6
		33.6					Sales/Net Fixed Assets		22.0
		12.6							7.0
		4.7							7.4
		2.9					Sales/Total Assets		4.4
		1.6							2.8
		.4							.6
	(10)	1.3					% Depr., Dep., Amort./Sales	(13)	1.2
		2.1							2.5
							% Officers', Directors' Owners' Comp/Sales		
12610M	9769M	154620M	187075M	200524M			Net Sales ($)	160876M	167918M
685M	5222M	51161M	116379M	226160M			Total Assets ($)	86960M	40473M

M = $ thousand   MM = $ million
See Pages 9 through 22 for Explanation of Ratios and Data

Comparative Historical Data

Current Data Sorted by Sales

			Type of Statement	0-1MM	1-3MM	3-5MM	5-10MM	10-25MM	25MM & OVER
6	5	4	Unqualified						4
3	4	5	Reviewed		1		2	1	1
3	1	2	Compiled				2		
4	2	8	Tax Returns	2	4		1	1	
8	15	12	Other		1	1	3	4	3
4/1/08- 3/31/09 ALL	4/1/09- 3/31/10 ALL	4/1/10- 3/31/11 ALL			3 (4/1-9/30/10)		28 (10/1/10-3/31/11)		
24	27	31	NUMBER OF STATEMENTS	2	6	1	8	6	8
%	%	%	ASSETS	%	%	%	%	%	%
21.9	15.3	23.5	Cash & Equivalents						
27.2	29.5	23.2	Trade Receivables (net)						
5.7	5.6	8.6	Inventory						
5.7	8.2	5.4	All Other Current						
60.5	58.5	60.7	Total Current						
21.3	20.8	23.8	Fixed Assets (net)						
10.9	14.1	6.4	Intangibles (net)						
7.4	6.6	9.1	All Other Non-Current						
100.0	100.0	100.0	Total						
			LIABILITIES						
9.4	10.9	22.1	Notes Payable-Short Term						
2.2	2.0	4.6	Cur. Mat.-L.T.D.						
12.5	15.0	10.5	Trade Payables						
.1	.0	.1	Income Taxes Payable						
17.5	25.8	39.0	All Other Current						
41.8	53.7	76.2	Total Current						
20.6	37.8	21.8	Long-Term Debt						
.3	.3	.1	Deferred Taxes						
26.4	10.8	6.1	All Other Non-Current						
10.9	-2.6	-4.3	Net Worth						
100.0	100.0	100.0	Total Liabilities & Net Worth						
			INCOME DATA						
100.0	100.0	100.0	Net Sales						
			Gross Profit						
93.1	96.2	91.1	Operating Expenses						
6.9	3.8	8.9	Operating Profit						
1.6	2.1	1.4	All Other Expenses (net)						
5.3	1.7	7.5	Profit Before Taxes						
			RATIOS						
3.0	2.8	2.1							
1.5	1.3	1.3	Current						
.9	.7	.7							
2.8	2.0	1.5							
1.3	1.1	.9	Quick						
.6	.4	.4							
13 28.2	**15** 24.9	**1** 260.3							
24 15.1	**24** 15.2	**26** 14.1	Sales/Receivables						
48 7.5	**54** 6.8	**67** 5.4							
			Cost of Sales/Inventory						
			Cost of Sales/Payables						
7.4	11.5	7.9							
15.6	25.2	33.7	Sales/Working Capital						
-133.1	-122.6	-23.3							
17.8	7.6	28.7							
(21) 3.7	(23) 2.4	(28) 4.6	EBIT/Interest						
2.1	1.7	1.5							
			Net Profit + Depr., Dep., Amort./Cur. Mat. L/T/D						
.3	.7	.2							
52.0	-504.0	1.0	Fixed/Worth						
-.3	-.5	73.6							
.9	1.8	1.1							
59.5	-999.8	8.0	Debt/Worth						
-3.4	-3.4	-22.0							
115.6	52.3	89.5	% Profit Before Taxes/Tangible						
(13) 37.9	(13) 19.5	(22) 44.9	Net Worth						
10.0	7.0	21.9							
32.7	15.1	24.3	% Profit Before Taxes/Total						
13.3	8.5	12.8	Assets						
3.7	2.8	3.0							
54.0	139.6	133.0							
19.1	35.0	45.6	Sales/Net Fixed Assets						
10.2	8.5	4.6							
5.2	4.6	5.2							
2.8	3.6	2.6	Sales/Total Assets						
1.7	1.4	1.4							
.4	.4	.5							
(18) 1.4	(18) 1.8	(24) 1.6	% Depr., Dep., Amort./Sales						
5.6	3.8	4.2							
		2.8	% Officers', Directors'						
	(14)	5.9	Owners' Comp/Sales						
		12.7							
677575M	701193M	564598M	Net Sales ($)	730M	9440M	3864M	59730M	104205M	386629M
491416M	545870M	399607M	Total Assets ($)	1702M	2147M	2396M	40077M	63576M	289709M

© RMA 2011

M = $ thousand   MM = $ million
See Pages 9 through 22 for Explanation of Ratios and Data

Current Data Sorted by Assets | Comparative Historical Data

0-500M	500M-2MM	2-10MM	10-50MM	50-100MM	100-250MM	Type of Statement	4/1/06-3/31/07 ALL	4/1/07-3/31/08 ALL
2	3	8	13	5	6	Unqualified	24	24
	6	30	5			Reviewed	11	12
4	13	15	2		1	Compiled	12	14
15	20	13				Tax Returns	24	24
14	36	42	13	4	2	Other	54	45
	37 (4/1-9/30/10)			235 (10/1/10-3/31/11)				
35	78	108	33	9	9	**NUMBER OF STATEMENTS**	125	119
%	%	%	%	%	%	**ASSETS**	%	%
27.6	18.2	15.2	12.4			Cash & Equivalents	15.3	13.8
15.1	33.2	31.2	34.1			Trade Receivables (net)	28.9	29.7
7.7	5.7	7.7	11.0			Inventory	8.3	7.8
3.6	4.9	6.7	4.8			All Other Current	4.3	5.4
53.9	62.0	60.8	62.3			Total Current	56.8	56.7
28.8	25.3	27.5	15.1			Fixed Assets (net)	28.2	27.3
5.2	4.8	2.4	18.4			Intangibles (net)	6.8	7.4
12.0	7.9	9.3	4.2			All Other Non-Current	8.3	8.6
100.0	100.0	100.0	100.0			Total	100.0	100.0
						LIABILITIES		
47.1	10.6	6.2	8.1			Notes Payable-Short Term	10.5	9.5
6.0	2.3	4.7	3.4			Cur. Mat.-L.T.D.	4.2	3.5
17.0	11.5	13.7	11.5			Trade Payables	13.3	14.9
.0	.6	.1	.6			Income Taxes Payable	.5	.4
19.5	28.2	21.3	15.1			All Other Current	14.6	16.4
89.6	53.2	46.0	38.7			Total Current	43.2	44.7
24.2	18.5	16.7	15.5			Long-Term Debt	17.6	22.1
.0	.5	.3	.3			Deferred Taxes	.7	.7
5.9	10.9	4.1	13.9			All Other Non-Current	7.0	4.2
-19.8	16.9	32.9	31.5			Net Worth	31.6	28.4
100.0	100.0	100.0	100.0			Total Liabilities & Net Worth	100.0	100.0
						INCOME DATA		
100.0	100.0	100.0	100.0			Net Sales	100.0	100.0
						Gross Profit		
89.2	91.6	92.4	93.0			Operating Expenses	92.3	88.3
10.8	8.4	7.6	7.0			Operating Profit	7.7	11.7
1.6	2.7	1.2	2.8			All Other Expenses (net)	1.0	2.9
9.2	5.6	6.5	4.2			Profit Before Taxes	6.7	8.9
						RATIOS		
4.4	3.3	2.1	2.3			Current	2.4	2.5
1.1	1.5	1.4	1.5				1.2	1.3
.4	.8	.9	1.2				.9	.8
3.1	2.6	1.8	1.8			Quick	1.8	2.3
.7	1.3	1.1	1.2				1.0	1.0
.4	.7	.6	.8				.6	.5
0 UND	4 90.1	13 27.1	36 10.2			Sales/Receivables	11 32.2	12 31.6
0 UND	25 14.5	38 9.7	53 6.9				37 10.0	45 8.2
23 16.1	52 7.1	56 6.5	76 4.8				62 5.8	70 5.2
						Cost of Sales/Inventory		
						Cost of Sales/Payables		
9.5	8.0	7.5	5.6			Sales/Working Capital	7.7	6.3
115.8	24.8	17.0	13.3				33.9	18.9
-10.9	-49.4	-62.3	39.9				-91.1	-26.4
14.6	14.1	18.8	27.4			EBIT/Interest	16.0	11.4
(22) 6.6	(51) 4.7	(87) 4.9	(28) 5.6				(106) 3.1	(87) 4.4
1.7	.1	1.4	1.1				1.1	1.1
		9.4				Net Profit + Depr., Dep., Amort./Cur. Mat. L/T/D	9.1	12.7
		(17) 5.2					(18) 2.1	(17) 5.5
		1.4					1.6	1.5
.3	.1	.1	.2			Fixed/Worth	.1	.2
3.1	.6	.7	.6				.8	.9
-.5	8.9	1.7	NM				3.5	8.3
.6	.6	.7	1.2			Debt/Worth	.8	1.0
8.2	1.4	1.6	2.9				2.8	3.6
-2.6	53.2	6.4	-9.6				22.3	15.7
139.2	89.2	57.7	77.0			% Profit Before Taxes/Tangible Net Worth	89.4	78.9
(21) 49.8	(60) 29.8	(95) 31.9	(24) 46.4				(102) 40.6	(95) 34.3
6.7	5.5	11.6	2.1				10.8	11.0
69.8	35.8	24.7	19.2			% Profit Before Taxes/Total Assets	25.8	24.1
27.5	7.9	11.0	9.1				9.0	9.1
4.3	-1.3	1.3	.8				.8	.9
166.0	99.8	93.9	76.6			Sales/Net Fixed Assets	91.8	41.5
20.4	23.8	21.6	23.0				14.6	15.1
6.8	7.8	4.5	5.9				4.9	4.5
7.9	5.2	4.6	3.5			Sales/Total Assets	4.4	3.8
4.7	3.6	2.9	2.1				2.6	2.2
2.5	2.4	1.7	.8				1.5	1.3
1.5	.3	.5	.7			% Depr., Dep., Amort./Sales	1.1	.8
(17) 2.2	(54) 1.4	(85) 1.3	(26) 2.2				(93) 2.5	(84) 2.0
7.1	4.2	4.4	5.1				6.6	4.9
6.2	2.8	1.8				% Officers', Directors' Owners' Comp/Sales	2.8	2.6
(19) 14.6	(27) 6.6	(28) 3.9					(47) 6.9	(37) 4.0
21.0	13.0	9.0					11.2	9.3
60130M	477732M	1612006M	2579188M	774954M	1826884M	Net Sales ($)	4040409M	4199439M
8683M	85702M	504308M	772536M	633195M	1442317M	Total Assets ($)	2392592M	3189911M

M = $ thousand   MM = $ million
See Pages 9 through 22 for Explanation of Ratios and Data

Comparative Historical Data | Current Data Sorted by Sales

			Type of Statement						
38	30	37	Unqualified	1	2	1		11	22
26	29	41	Reviewed	1	3	4	8	15	10
23	29	35	Compiled	2	7	2	13	7	4
48	65	48	Tax Returns	13	15	6	5	9	
61	102	111	Other	12	21	14	16	25	23
4/1/08-3/31/09 ALL	4/1/09-3/31/10 ALL	4/1/10-3/31/11 ALL			37 (4/1-9/30/10)		235 (10/1/10-3/31/11)		
				0-1MM	1-3MM	3-5MM	5-10MM	10-25MM	25MM & OVER
196	255	272	NUMBER OF STATEMENTS	29	48	27	42	67	59
%	%	%	ASSETS	%	%	%	%	%	%
17.3	16.1	16.9	Cash & Equivalents	15.8	22.0	17.0	13.7	17.1	15.6
26.3	23.8	29.2	Trade Receivables (net)	9.8	22.9	30.4	35.3	35.3	32.2
7.8	8.1	7.2	Inventory	6.5	3.8	2.8	8.8	11.3	6.4
5.5	4.5	6.0	All Other Current	4.8	1.7	8.3	3.3	7.5	9.2
56.9	52.5	59.3	Total Current	37.0	50.3	58.4	61.1	71.1	63.5
25.6	28.5	24.9	Fixed Assets (net)	51.7	31.0	24.5	26.1	17.3	14.8
8.5	9.6	7.3	Intangibles (net)	2.8	6.8	5.4	5.9	4.9	14.4
9.0	9.4	8.5	All Other Non-Current	8.4	11.9	11.7	7.0	6.7	7.3
100.0	100.0	100.0	Total	100.0	100.0	100.0	100.0	100.0	100.0
			LIABILITIES						
8.9	14.1	12.7	Notes Payable-Short Term	36.9	16.4	7.9	13.8	8.2	4.5
3.9	3.6	3.9	Cur. Mat.-L.T.D.	7.0	5.0	3.1	4.3	2.9	2.6
13.5	11.1	12.8	Trade Payables	7.7	13.8	11.4	12.1	14.5	13.8
.4	.4	.4	Income Taxes Payable	.0	.7	.1	.1	.3	.6
16.0	15.8	22.2	All Other Current	15.8	13.7	40.3	20.7	25.2	21.5
42.7	44.9	52.0	Total Current	67.4	49.7	62.8	51.0	51.1	43.1
19.8	20.3	18.1	Long-Term Debt	41.2	21.8	19.2	14.7	12.2	12.6
.6	.4	.4	Deferred Taxes	.0	.4	.9	.1	.4	.5
9.5	8.1	7.5	All Other Non-Current	2.4	9.4	18.5	5.2	4.8	8.0
27.5	26.3	22.0	Net Worth	-10.9	18.8	-1.5	29.0	31.4	35.9
100.0	100.0	100.0	Total Liabilities & Net Worth	100.0	100.0	100.0	100.0	100.0	100.0
			INCOME DATA						
100.0	100.0	100.0	Net Sales	100.0	100.0	100.0	100.0	100.0	100.0
			Gross Profit						
91.2	92.2	91.9	Operating Expenses	72.5	91.9	93.9	95.0	95.7	94.0
8.8	7.8	8.1	Operating Profit	27.5	8.1	6.1	5.0	4.3	6.0
1.9	2.1	1.9	All Other Expenses (net)	10.0	.5	1.6	1.5	.6	1.1
6.9	5.7	6.2	Profit Before Taxes	17.5	7.6	4.6	3.5	3.7	4.9
			RATIOS						
2.4	2.6	2.7		4.3	4.1	2.7	3.0	2.5	2.4
1.3	1.3	1.4	Current	1.1	1.3	1.6	1.4	1.5	1.5
.8	.8	.9		.5	.7	.6	.8	1.0	1.0
1.9	2.0	2.2		4.1	3.0	2.4	2.4	1.7	2.0
1.1	.9	1.1	Quick	.9	1.2	.9	1.2	1.1	1.1
.5	.4	.6		.1	.6	.4	.6	.6	.6
9 41.4	3 119.5	8 48.1		0 UND	0 UND	21 17.0	16 22.5	18 20.4	15 24.9
33 11.1	27 13.7	35 10.3	Sales/Receivables	0 UND	19 19.0	43 8.5	40 9.2	37 9.8	42 8.7
55 6.7	48 7.5	56 6.6		28 12.9	59 6.2	65 5.6	58 6.2	56 6.6	60 6.1
			Cost of Sales/Inventory						
			Cost of Sales/Payables						
7.8	8.8	7.4		4.8	8.2	4.6	7.5	8.0	7.3
25.2	27.9	20.7	Sales/Working Capital	119.0	34.6	11.6	19.5	17.2	20.4
-52.1	-22.1	-61.9		-7.9	-25.4	-10.3	-49.4	409.7	397.3
21.9	18.1	18.8		8.7	9.9	4.9	18.1	18.5	50.7
(161) 3.8	(198) 3.7	(203) 5.1	EBIT/Interest	(15) 7.0	(32) 4.9	(19) 2.1	(37) 5.0	(52) 6.0	(48) 11.0
1.2	.4	1.0		1.7	1.0	-6.3	-.4	1.1	2.5
5.6	11.1	8.1						8.1	13.2
(31) 1.6	(29) 3.2	(40) 4.2	Net Profit + Depr., Dep., Amort./Cur. Mat. L/T/D				(16) 5.2	(16) 5.1
.4	1.7	.9						1.1	.8
.2	.2	.2		.8	.3	.0	.2	.1	.1
.8	.9	.8	Fixed/Worth	3.2	1.1	.3	.9	.4	.5
7.1	-6.0	5.0		-7.8	NM	4.4	NM	1.5	1.6
.9	.8	.7		.5	.6	.5	.7	.7	.8
3.1	3.2	2.0	Debt/Worth	8.2	1.8	1.4	1.5	1.8	2.4
42.7	-8.8	24.6		-6.3	NM	-9.8	NM	6.7	14.4
89.1	60.0	69.7	% Profit Before Taxes/Tangible Net Worth	108.5	95.3	53.5	67.6	68.2	74.2
(151) 32.0	(181) 23.3	(211) 31.9		(19) 21.3	(36) 31.7	(19) 19.8	(32) 36.1	(58) 37.7	(47) 44.0
5.3	2.5	9.5		2.9	3.5	10.9	3.8	8.7	16.7
21.1	20.3	29.1		41.1	46.5	19.4	28.6	29.5	25.9
8.2	6.4	9.2	% Profit Before Taxes/Total Assets	10.9	8.9	6.7	9.7	12.7	9.1
.7	-1.7	.8		1.3	-.2	-5.5	-4.4	1.0	3.0
99.0	74.6	79.4		12.2	58.1	164.5	40.5	147.7	122.2
17.1	15.1	20.8	Sales/Net Fixed Assets	3.7	17.3	14.7	18.9	44.6	28.0
5.8	5.2	6.4		.3	3.5	6.1	5.5	10.1	8.3
4.3	4.7	4.9		3.7	4.7	3.9	4.6	5.5	6.1
2.6	2.4	3.0	Sales/Total Assets	1.3	2.7	2.9	3.2	3.5	3.1
1.2	1.1	1.5		.2	1.5	1.0	2.3	2.5	1.4
.6	.5	.5		2.3	1.4	.5	.7	.3	.3
(143) 2.1	(176) 2.3	(196) 1.5	% Depr., Dep., Amort./Sales	(21) 7.9	(29) 2.2	(19) 1.4	(31) 1.3	(51) .8	(45) 1.4
5.1	5.0	4.6		21.0	6.5	3.6	4.6	3.1	4.2
2.5	2.5	3.0			6.0		2.2	1.3	
(64) 5.1	(85) 5.1	(76) 6.5	% Officers', Directors' Owners' Comp/Sales	(25) 11.5		(17) 3.5	(15) 3.6	
8.2	9.8	13.2			14.7		6.9	6.5	
7100369M	7192441M	7330894M	Net Sales ($)	12724M	94757M	103875M	287591M	1085939M	5746008M
4090868M	3655078M	3446741M	Total Assets ($)	23931M	51085M	81784M	133305M	475682M	2680954M

M = $ thousand   MM = $ million
See Pages 9 through 22 for Explanation of Ratios and Data

Current Data Sorted by Assets   Comparative Historical Data

						Type of Statement		
		3	13	10	3	Unqualified	21	31
	12	15	9			Reviewed	31	24
7	20	17	2			Compiled	21	26
17	21	9	2			Tax Returns	39	52
6	20	33	30	5	4	Other	80	59
	37 (4/1-9/30/10)		221 (10/1/10-3/31/11)				4/1/06-3/31/07	4/1/07-3/31/08
0-500M	500M-2MM	2-10MM	10-50MM	50-100MM	100-250MM		ALL	ALL
30	73	77	56	15	7	**NUMBER OF STATEMENTS**	192	192
%	%	%	%	%	%	**ASSETS**	%	%
14.5	12.4	13.2	9.8	4.6		Cash & Equivalents	8.3	9.4
19.9	25.3	19.5	14.5	10.5		Trade Receivables (net)	17.8	16.4
.7	2.2	.8	.9	.8		Inventory	2.1	2.1
2.4	3.3	3.7	5.7	4.1		All Other Current	2.8	2.2
37.6	43.2	37.3	30.8	19.9		Total Current	31.1	30.1
38.2	40.2	49.3	53.1	53.5		Fixed Assets (net)	54.9	53.6
10.7	6.3	7.9	9.1	18.8		Intangibles (net)	6.1	8.4
13.5	10.3	5.5	7.0	7.8		All Other Non-Current	7.9	7.9
100.0	100.0	100.0	100.0	100.0		Total	100.0	100.0
						LIABILITIES		
30.6	8.4	4.9	2.4	1.9		Notes Payable-Short Term	5.8	5.8
6.6	5.8	7.8	7.1	5.6		Cur. Mat.-L.T.D.	8.5	8.1
6.5	13.7	11.4	8.3	5.8		Trade Payables	11.0	9.2
.3	.1	.5	.2	.0		Income Taxes Payable	.2	.1
19.9	5.5	10.2	7.4	6.7		All Other Current	9.5	8.7
63.8	33.5	34.9	25.4	20.0		Total Current	35.0	31.8
33.9	28.8	26.6	30.4	40.1		Long-Term Debt	38.0	41.3
.0	.5	1.1	1.7	.9		Deferred Taxes	.8	.7
12.4	17.7	2.1	5.9	6.9		All Other Non-Current	10.1	9.0
-10.2	19.4	35.3	36.7	32.2		Net Worth	16.1	17.1
100.0	100.0	100.0	100.0	100.0		Total Liabilities & Net Worth	100.0	100.0
						INCOME DATA		
100.0	100.0	100.0	100.0	100.0		Net Sales	100.0	100.0
						Gross Profit		
89.8	92.4	90.6	92.8	91.8		Operating Expenses	92.3	93.0
10.2	7.6	9.4	7.2	8.2		Operating Profit	7.7	7.0
1.1	2.0	1.9	1.6	2.6		All Other Expenses (net)	2.5	2.4
9.1	5.7	7.4	5.6	5.6		Profit Before Taxes	5.3	4.6
						RATIOS		
2.1	2.7	1.8	2.0	1.0			1.5	1.6
.4	1.2	1.0	1.1	.8		Current	.9	1.0
.2	.7	.7	.8	.6			.5	.6
2.0	2.0	1.7	1.5	1.0			1.3	1.4
.4	1.1	.9	.9	.8		Quick	.8	.8
.2	.5	.6	.6	.5			.5	.5
0 UND	14 25.8	20 17.9	26 13.9	28 13.2			15 24.0	13 27.1
4 102.3	31 11.8	32 11.5	35 10.3	37 9.8		Sales/Receivables	34 10.8	33 11.0
35 10.6	45 8.2	46 7.9	51 7.2	50 7.3			46 7.9	44 8.3
						Cost of Sales/Inventory		
						Cost of Sales/Payables		
15.5	10.2	11.3	7.3	62.7			19.3	15.4
-24.7	28.7	-420.4	42.4	-36.0		Sales/Working Capital	-78.3	-158.2
-4.6	-40.0	-22.1	-30.8	-10.2			-9.4	-12.9
18.2	7.4	10.4	8.7	13.2			5.5	5.4
(29) 6.9	(66) 3.5	(71) 5.7	(52) 5.7	(14) 4.4		EBIT/Interest	(180) 2.5	(175) 2.6
.7	.9	2.0	2.8	1.7			1.1	1.1
		2.9	2.3				3.0	2.8
	(22) 1.9	(23) 1.9			Net Profit + Depr., Dep.,	(43) 1.9	(44) 1.8
		1.2	1.4			Amort./Cur. Mat. L/T/D	1.2	1.3
.4	.7	1.0	1.0	1.8			1.5	1.3
-3.2	1.7	2.0	2.0	4.0		Fixed/Worth	3.8	3.8
-1.1	-8.6	5.3	7.3	-15.0			-19.9	-5.0
1.4	1.0	1.1	1.1	2.2			1.9	1.5
-7.2	1.9	2.3	2.5	4.3		Debt/Worth	4.8	4.8
-2.5	-15.8	10.1	8.2	-24.9			-37.1	-7.3
467.5	64.5	56.5	46.2	66.6		% Profit Before Taxes/Tangible	55.9	66.6
(13) 113.0	(51) 22.6	(65) 30.0	(48) 32.6	(10) 23.0		Net Worth	(137) 25.5	(133) 32.3
76.6	8.1	9.0	13.6	15.7			9.9	10.6
54.2	19.9	16.8	12.3	10.7		% Profit Before Taxes/Total	13.4	14.3
22.3	6.2	9.7	7.0	5.3		Assets	6.5	6.5
-1.8	.4	2.5	3.6	-2.8			1.2	.7
37.8	22.3	9.3	3.6	3.2			6.0	6.2
15.6	7.6	4.1	2.5	1.6		Sales/Net Fixed Assets	3.3	3.5
5.7	3.3	1.9	1.6	1.3			2.0	1.9
6.2	4.4	2.8	1.6	1.1			2.6	2.8
4.0	2.6	1.9	1.3	.9		Sales/Total Assets	1.7	1.7
2.0	1.5	1.2	1.0	.8			1.2	1.2
1.3	2.8	3.7	4.3	6.4			4.7	4.6
(20) 3.8	(58) 5.7	(70) 6.2	(55) 7.5	(11) 8.1		% Depr., Dep., Amort./Sales	(172) 7.7	(162) 7.6
12.0	8.6	9.9	11.2	9.9			11.1	11.2
3.5	2.0	1.5					2.4	1.6
(16) 5.2	(28) 4.4	(30) 4.2				% Officers', Directors'	(73) 5.7	(83) 4.1
12.5	8.5	5.7				Owners' Comp/Sales	7.8	6.6
32578M	272957M	791184M	1391574M	1086585M	939207M	Net Sales ($)	3438786M	4167555M
7818M	88210M	378190M	1161695M	1130473M	957991M	Total Assets ($)	2283259M	3680464M

'M = $ thousand   MM = $ million
See Pages 9 through 22 for Explanation of Ratios and Data

Comparative Historical Data | Current Data Sorted by Sales

						Type of Statement						
	28		37		29	Unqualified	1		1	1	8	18
	32		43		36	Reviewed	2	5	1	10	16	2
	30		50		46	Compiled	9	11	6	13	7	
	72		72		49	Tax Returns	12	10	8	12	5	2
	91		94		98	Other	8	20	10	11	26	23
	4/1/08- 3/31/09 ALL		4/1/09- 3/31/10 ALL		4/1/10- 3/31/11 ALL			37 (4/1-9/30/10)		221 (10/1/10-3/31/11)		
							0-1MM	1-3MM	3-5MM	5-10MM	10-25MM	25MM & OVER
	253		296		258	NUMBER OF STATEMENTS	32	46	26	47	62	45
	%		%		%	ASSETS	%	%	%	%	%	%
	10.9		11.8		11.7	Cash & Equivalents	14.4	12.4	14.0	12.0	10.0	10.0
	18.0		17.0		19.3	Trade Receivables (net)	10.5	20.5	24.2	23.2	21.9	13.8
	1.1		1.4		1.2	Inventory	.5	.1	1.6	2.6	1.2	.8
	3.3		3.2		3.9	All Other Current	6.9	2.5	2.2	2.7	5.4	3.2
	33.3		33.4		36.1	Total Current	32.4	35.5	41.9	40.5	38.6	27.9
	51.1		49.4		46.3	Fixed Assets (net)	44.4	48.9	41.2	42.9	46.8	50.8
	8.3		8.9		9.3	Intangibles (net)	13.2	5.3	2.5	10.4	8.1	15.2
	7.3		8.3		8.3	All Other Non-Current	10.1	10.2	14.3	6.1	6.5	6.1
	100.0		100.0		100.0	Total	100.0	100.0	100.0	100.0	100.0	100.0
						LIABILITIES						
	5.6		5.0		8.2	Notes Payable-Short Term	26.4	6.7	9.1	5.0	6.5	2.0
	9.1		7.5		6.8	Cur. Mat.-L.T.D.	4.1	7.4	4.9	7.9	7.5	7.4
	9.7		9.7		10.3	Trade Payables	3.5	8.1	11.5	12.9	13.2	9.9
	.2		.3		.3	Income Taxes Payable	.3	.2	.1	.0	.7	.2
	6.9		11.4		9.1	All Other Current	16.5	8.7	9.0	8.3	7.4	7.4
	31.4		33.9		34.7	Total Current	50.8	31.1	34.6	34.0	35.2	26.9
	43.0		37.5		29.8	Long-Term Debt	38.3	29.0	25.2	28.6	26.2	33.4
	.9		.8		1.2	Deferred Taxes	.1	.4	.8	1.0	1.6	2.8
	7.5		8.0		8.8	All Other Non-Current	2.3	25.0	15.4	4.2	4.0	4.5
	17.2		19.8		25.5	Net Worth	8.6	14.6	23.9	32.1	33.0	32.3
	100.0		100.0		100.0	Total Liabilities & Net Worth	100.0	100.0	100.0	100.0	100.0	100.0
						INCOME DATA						
	100.0		100.0		100.0	Net Sales	100.0	100.0	100.0	100.0	100.0	100.0
						Gross Profit						
	93.5		93.1		91.5	Operating Expenses	81.8	89.9	93.1	95.0	94.2	92.1
	6.5		6.9		8.5	Operating Profit	18.2	10.1	6.9	5.0	5.8	7.9
	2.9		2.3		1.8	All Other Expenses (net)	6.1	2.4	1.5	.5	.6	1.6
	3.7		4.6		6.6	Profit Before Taxes	12.1	7.7	5.4	4.5	5.3	6.3
						RATIOS						
	1.8		2.0		1.9		2.6	3.5	2.5	1.9	1.8	1.5
	1.1		1.0		1.0	Current	.6	1.0	1.2	1.2	1.0	1.0
	.6		.6		.6		.1	.5	.7	.7	.7	.6
	1.6		1.7		1.7		1.9	3.5	2.1	1.8	1.4	1.3
	.9	(295)	.8		.9	Quick	.4	.9	1.1	1.0	.9	.8
	.5		.5		.5		.1	.5	.7	.6	.5	.5
15	24.8	17	21.6	19	18.7		0 UND	25 14.9	17 21.6	18 20.8	26 14.1	26 14.0
31	11.7	31	11.6	32	11.5	Sales/Receivables	0 UND	33 11.1	34 10.7	32 11.5	36 10.2	33 11.1
41	8.8	45	8.2	45	8.0		27 13.4	48 7.6	47 7.8	45 8.1	51 7.2	43 8.4
						Cost of Sales/Inventory						
						Cost of Sales/Payables						
	16.2		11.2		10.0		6.5	8.3	8.2	11.8	9.0	12.3
	196.5		UND		174.5	Sales/Working Capital	-26.6	NM	52.7	52.9	397.6	-440.3
	-14.2		-14.3		-17.9		-3.2	-13.1	-37.6	-27.5	-23.2	-13.1
	5.8		7.5		10.6		15.5	14.9	18.9	8.8	8.8	10.6
(232)	2.9	(272)	3.2	(239)	4.6	EBIT/Interest	(24) 3.8	(44) 4.5	(25) 4.2	(44) 3.5	(59) 5.3	(43) 6.5
	1.0		1.1		1.9		.9	.6	1.8	1.6	2.2	2.8
	2.9		3.4		2.3						2.3	2.6
(54)	1.6	(57)	1.9	(63)	1.8	Net Profit + Depr., Dep., Amort./Cur. Mat. L/T/D				(27) 1.8	(17) 2.0
	1.0		1.4		1.2						1.2	1.2
	1.0		1.1		.9		.6	.7	.6	1.0	.9	1.3
	3.3		2.8		2.1	Fixed/Worth	NM	1.7	1.6	2.1	1.9	2.9
	-6.0		-7.2		-43.0		-.9	-3.6	4.2	10.7	7.5	-156.6
	1.6		1.4		1.1		1.1	.9	.8	1.2	1.2	1.8
	4.2		3.3		3.0	Debt/Worth	NM	1.8	2.0	3.7	2.8	5.6
	-11.6		-12.2		-83.9		-2.7	-6.8	11.7	18.9	8.5	-276.8
	59.2		50.2		61.4		133.6	92.0	91.9	55.5	52.2	59.1
(178)	29.3	(212)	25.7	(189)	30.0	% Profit Before Taxes/Tangible Net Worth	(16) 24.1	(30) 26.4	(23) 29.3	(37) 23.8	(51) 31.7	(32) 32.5
	7.1		6.4		12.3		4.1	10.8	10.0	4.9	12.7	20.7
	15.6		13.6		18.6		29.3	22.0	26.3	18.4	14.2	12.3
	5.5		6.3		7.6	% Profit Before Taxes/Total Assets	4.6	9.9	8.6	6.6	7.1	7.4
	.0		.4		1.5		-1.1	-1.4	.5	1.7	3.3	3.2
	8.7		8.1		10.3		19.3	15.3	15.2	14.7	8.2	3.4
	3.9		3.8		4.0	Sales/Net Fixed Assets	4.2	4.7	5.5	7.0	3.8	2.3
	2.0		1.9		2.0		1.1	1.9	3.4	3.3	2.3	1.6
	3.4		2.8		3.0		3.2	3.5	3.8	4.4	2.6	1.5
	1.9		1.7		1.7	Sales/Total Assets	1.5	1.9	2.4	2.7	1.7	1.2
	1.2		1.1		1.1		.4	1.2	1.6	1.5	1.3	.9
	5.0		4.5		3.5		3.1	3.4	3.2	2.9	2.9	5.0
(202)	7.5	(250)	7.6	(216)	6.4	% Depr., Dep., Amort./Sales	(23) 9.0	(39) 5.8	(22) 6.4	(40) 5.9	(57) 5.6	(35) 8.1
	10.6		10.8		10.1		22.8	10.6	10.3	8.9	8.5	11.0
	1.9		2.3		2.6		3.8	3.1	3.8	1.4	1.5	
(104)	4.0	(110)	4.5	(82)	4.5	% Officers', Directors' Owners' Comp/Sales	(10) 5.8	(19) 4.9	(13) 6.2	(17) 3.9	(19) 2.6	
	7.7		6.9		7.3		10.2	12.5	9.6	10.2	4.5	
	6402782M		5933994M		4514085M	Net Sales ($)	17554M	87951M	101506M	339333M	1027132M	2940609M
	4526778M		4131736M		3724377M	Total Assets ($)	39979M	64565M	55656M	174677M	700660M	2688840M

M = $ thousand   MM = $ million
See Pages 9 through 22 for Explanation of Ratios and Data

Current Data Sorted by Assets | **Comparative Historical Data**

						Type of Statement		
						Unqualified	3	4
		1	1			Reviewed		1
	3	3	1			Compiled	5	5
8	3	1				Tax Returns	5	6
2	1	1	4	2		Other	10	14
	2 (4/1-9/30/10)		29 (10/1/10-3/31/11)				4/1/06-3/31/07	4/1/07-3/31/08
0-500M	**500M-2MM**	**2-10MM**	**10-50MM**	**50-100MM**	**100-250MM**		**ALL**	**ALL**
10	7	6	6	2		**NUMBER OF STATEMENTS**	23	30
%	%	%	%	%	%	**ASSETS**	%	%
8.1					D	Cash & Equivalents	7.7	9.8
13.9					A	Trade Receivables (net)	17.5	17.6
.5					T	Inventory	1.1	1.5
1.0					A	All Other Current	1.5	3.0
23.4						Total Current	27.8	32.0
68.2					N	Fixed Assets (net)	51.4	52.2
.4					O	Intangibles (net)	15.0	10.6
7.9					T	All Other Non-Current	5.9	5.2
100.0						Total	100.0	100.0
					A	**LIABILITIES**		
4.3					V	Notes Payable-Short Term	3.7	15.1
13.6					A	Cur. Mat.-L.T.D.	10.8	7.6
26.2					I	Trade Payables	8.3	8.7
.0					L	Income Taxes Payable	.7	.0
8.4					A	All Other Current	4.9	5.3
52.4					B	Total Current	28.5	36.7
47.6					L	Long-Term Debt	48.8	39.8
.0					E	Deferred Taxes	.8	.4
13.5						All Other Non-Current	9.0	8.3
-13.5						Net Worth	12.8	14.7
100.0						Total Liabilties & Net Worth	100.0	100.0
						INCOME DATA		
100.0						Net Sales	100.0	100.0
						Gross Profit		
77.5						Operating Expenses	92.9	93.4
22.5						Operating Profit	7.1	6.6
7.9						All Other Expenses (net)	1.7	3.3
14.6						Profit Before Taxes	5.4	3.3
						RATIOS		
1.2							1.3	1.9
.4						Current	.8	.9
.1							.5	.3
1.2							1.1	1.6
.4						Quick	.7	.6
.1							.5	.3
0 UND							**11** 32.1	**17** 21.1
12 29.4						Sales/Receivables	**32** 11.3	**35** 10.4
46 8.0							**45** 8.1	**46** 7.9
						Cost of Sales/Inventory		
						Cost of Sales/Payables		
NM							44.4	13.2
-6.6						Sales/Working Capital	-57.5	-49.0
-4.1							-13.2	-5.9
							6.4	6.0
						EBIT/Interest	(21) 4.0	(26) 2.2
							1.6	.7
						Net Profit + Depr., Dep., Amort./Cur. Mat. L/T/D		
2.1							1.4	1.4
3.5						Fixed/Worth	4.7	33.2
-1.9							-1.6	-4.8
1.4							1.6	1.5
2.8						Debt/Worth	5.3	NM
-3.1							-3.8	-10.4
							133.3	59.0
						% Profit Before Taxes/Tangible Net Worth	(15) 45.7	(15) 34.9
							36.4	7.9
22.6							18.0	18.5
5.8						% Profit Before Taxes/Total Assets	11.8	7.9
1.2							2.8	-2.1
20.4							9.1	10.4
2.9						Sales/Net Fixed Assets	4.5	3.0
.2							1.5	1.3
3.6							3.2	3.4
1.7						Sales/Total Assets	1.9	1.7
.2							1.0	.9
							3.8	4.9
						% Depr., Dep., Amort./Sales	(22) 6.2	(23) 10.7
							13.4	13.6
							1.9	2.3
						% Officers', Directors' Owners' Comp/Sales	(10) 3.1	(16) 4.5
							8.8	9.6
6214M	28193M	45444M	229621M	138780M		Net Sales ($)	413653M	594042M
2954M	9047M	23376M	145497M	162032M		Total Assets ($)	245764M	592580M

M = $ thousand MM = $ million

See Pages 9 through 22 for Explanation of Ratios and Data

Comparative Historical Data   Current Data Sorted by Sales

			Type of Statement	0-1MM	1-3MM	3-5MM	5-10MM	10-25MM	25MM & OVER
4	3		Unqualified	1	2	1	1	2	1
4	4	2	Reviewed	6	3	2	1	1	
4	7	7	Compiled	1	1		1	3	4
6	10	12	Tax Returns						
6	26	10	Other						
4/1/08-3/31/09	4/1/09-3/31/10	4/1/10-3/31/11			2 (4/1-9/30/10)			29 (10/1/10-3/31/11)	
ALL	ALL	ALL							
24	50	31	NUMBER OF STATEMENTS	8	6	3	3	6	5
%	%	%	**ASSETS**	%	%	%	%	%	%
9.7	7.3	11.7	Cash & Equivalents						
19.1	16.2	20.3	Trade Receivables (net)						
1.8	3.3	1.1	Inventory						
1.7	3.4	2.3	All Other Current						
32.3	30.2	35.4	Total Current						
53.9	52.3	53.2	Fixed Assets (net)						
8.7	6.9	3.8	Intangibles (net)						
5.2	10.6	7.7	All Other Non-Current						
100.0	100.0	100.0	Total						
			LIABILITIES						
5.5	6.5	5.4	Notes Payable-Short Term						
10.2	9.6	10.2	Cur. Mat.-L.T.D.						
7.1	10.6	14.3	Trade Payables						
.0	.0	.0	Income Taxes Payable						
5.8	10.9	9.6	All Other Current						
28.7	37.7	39.5	Total Current						
36.9	41.5	36.1	Long-Term Debt						
.7	.8	.5	Deferred Taxes						
13.5	2.5	9.4	All Other Non-Current						
20.2	17.5	14.5	Net Worth						
100.0	100.0	100.0	Total Liabilities & Net Worth						
			INCOME DATA						
100.0	100.0	100.0	Net Sales						
			Gross Profit						
93.9	91.3	86.8	Operating Expenses						
6.1	8.7	13.2	Operating Profit						
2.3	2.3	2.9	All Other Expenses (net)						
3.8	6.4	10.3	Profit Before Taxes						
			RATIOS						
2.6	1.5	1.7							
.9	.8	.8	Current						
.6	.4	.5							
1.5	1.1	1.7							
.9	.6	.8	Quick						
.6	.3	.3							
28 12.9	7 52.2	13 27.2							
40 9.2	31 11.8	33 11.0	Sales/Receivables						
57 6.4	51 7.1	47 7.7							
			Cost of Sales/Inventory						
			Cost of Sales/Payables						
11.8	19.8	10.9							
-102.5	-37.4	-30.2	Sales/Working Capital						
-12.5	-8.3	-7.1							
6.4	8.0	20.0							
3.6 (46)	2.5 (28)	5.4	EBIT/Interest						
1.1	1.1	2.0							
			Net Profit + Depr., Dep., Amort./Cur. Mat. L/T/D						
1.1	1.1	.7							
2.6	2.5	2.7	Fixed/Worth						
NM	-16.0	19.7							
1.0	1.6	.8							
3.5	4.0	2.6	Debt/Worth						
NM	-29.7	30.5							
103.2	53.1	62.7	% Profit Before Taxes/Tangible Net Worth						
(18) 32.0	(35) 29.2	(24) 21.0							
10.0	9.7	12.8							
15.1	20.6	20.8	% Profit Before Taxes/Total Assets						
7.4	7.3	6.9							
.5	.4	2.8							
6.2	9.4	10.2							
2.0	3.8	4.4	Sales/Net Fixed Assets						
1.7	1.6	1.4							
1.9	2.9	3.3							
1.4	1.7	1.8	Sales/Total Assets						
1.1	1.0	.8							
5.8	2.6	2.7							
(21) 10.1	(40) 7.4	(26) 8.9	% Depr., Dep., Amort./Sales						
12.8	12.6	13.0							
1.5	2.1	3.0	% Officers', Directors' Owners' Comp/Sales						
(13) 3.9	(20) 3.4	(16) 4.2							
4.8	6.5	6.5							
490659M	616788M	448252M	Net Sales ($)	2126M	12159M	9776M	22045M	98018M	304128M
473366M	461201M	342906M	Total Assets ($)	3086M	4417M	7585M	5014M	78088M	244716M

M = $ thousand   MM = $ million
See Pages 9 through 22 for Explanation of Ratios and Data

Current Data Sorted by Assets **Comparative Historical Data**

Type of Statement

Type of Statement	0-500M	500M-2MM	2-10MM	10-50MM	50-100MM	100-250MM		4/1/06-3/31/07 ALL	4/1/07-3/31/08 ALL
Unqualified		1	1	9	2	4		7	9
Reviewed		1	12	3				16	16
Compiled		2	3					8	7
Tax Returns	2	1	2					3	9
Other	2	3	9	7	2	5		15	24
	4 (4/1-9/30/10)			67 (10/1/10-3/31/11)					
	0-500M	500M-2MM	2-10MM	10-50MM	50-100MM	100-250MM	**NUMBER OF STATEMENTS**	49	65
	4	8	27	19	4	9			

	0-500M %	500M-2MM %	2-10MM %	10-50MM %	50-100MM %	100-250MM %		%	%
							ASSETS		
			8.6	12.6			Cash & Equivalents	9.7	8.2
			31.1	25.2			Trade Receivables (net)	25.9	25.6
			1.9	2.4			Inventory	1.5	1.6
			3.6	4.3			All Other Current	3.0	2.7
			45.2	44.5			Total Current	40.1	38.1
			43.0	39.9			Fixed Assets (net)	45.7	47.3
			4.5	10.2			Intangibles (net)	5.6	7.3
			7.2	5.3			All Other Non-Current	8.6	7.2
			100.0	100.0			Total	100.0	100.0
							LIABILITIES		
			2.5	2.5			Notes Payable-Short Term	4.8	6.7
			7.8	5.9			Cur. Mat.-L.T.D.	5.8	9.0
			14.2	14.3			Trade Payables	11.3	13.4
			.0	.2			Income Taxes Payable	.1	.3
			8.2	8.5			All Other Current	9.2	9.2
			32.7	31.5			Total Current	31.1	38.7
			21.9	15.4			Long-Term Debt	22.0	30.8
			.5	1.0			Deferred Taxes	.3	.3
			2.5	5.7			All Other Non-Current	5.9	4.7
			42.4	46.5			Net Worth	40.6	25.6
			100.0	100.0			Total Liabilities & Net Worth	100.0	100.0
							INCOME DATA		
			100.0	100.0			Net Sales	100.0	100.0
							Gross Profit		
			95.0	92.0			Operating Expenses	89.6	89.7
			5.0	8.0			Operating Profit	10.4	10.3
			.7	.9			All Other Expenses (net)	1.3	2.2
			4.3	7.0			Profit Before Taxes	9.1	8.1
							RATIOS		
			1.9	1.7			Current	1.9	1.7
			1.5	1.3				1.3	1.2
			.8	1.0				1.0	.8
			1.8	1.4			Quick	1.7	1.5
			1.3	1.0				1.1	1.1
			.7	.8				.8	.6
			26 14.1	37 9.8			Sales/Receivables	26 14.0	25 14.3
			53 6.8	48 7.7				40 9.0	42 8.7
			68 5.3	67 5.4				64 5.7	67 5.4
							Cost of Sales/Inventory		
							Cost of Sales/Payables		
			8.4	8.8			Sales/Working Capital	9.8	11.0
			26.1	25.4				23.2	38.7
			-45.5	83.6				-136.2	-24.3
			13.1	64.8			EBIT/Interest	18.6	10.6
			(24) 4.5	(18) 8.9				(44) 6.4	(61) 5.2
			2.8	3.4				2.8	2.2
							Net Profit + Depr., Dep.,	3.9	6.2
							Amort./Cur. Mat. L/T/D	(14) 2.4	(13) 3.0
								1.4	1.8
			.6	.5			Fixed/Worth	.7	.8
			1.1	1.0				1.3	1.7
			2.1	3.2				3.2	NM
			1.0	.7			Debt/Worth	.6	.9
			1.4	1.3				2.0	2.4
			2.2	4.6				5.8	NM
			46.8	67.9			% Profit Before Taxes/Tangible	80.4	69.8
			(24) 18.7	(18) 30.1			Net Worth	(44) 39.4	(49) 35.3
			5.2	16.8				11.2	21.4
			19.4	14.9			% Profit Before Taxes/Total	25.3	22.2
			8.1	11.1			Assets	14.1	9.1
			2.0	6.7				5.6	2.5
			9.6	8.7			Sales/Net Fixed Assets	6.8	7.9
			5.6	5.6				4.4	4.1
			2.6	1.8				2.9	2.3
			3.0	2.5			Sales/Total Assets	2.8	2.5
			2.1	1.6				1.9	1.8
			1.5	1.1				1.2	1.2
			2.0	2.2			% Depr., Dep., Amort./Sales	2.7	2.5
			(26) 4.4	(17) 4.7				(46) 4.7	(56) 4.7
			6.2	7.5				6.9	7.7
							% Officers', Directors'	1.8	1.2
							Owners' Comp/Sales	(18) 3.6	(21) 3.0
								8.1	4.8
6072M	21508M	305235M	692974M	293111M	2341095M	Net Sales ($)	1078237M	1600044M
1130M	7863M	139620M	425782M	300015M	1527043M	Total Assets ($)	831073M	1452324M

M = $ thousand   MM = $ million
See Pages 9 through 22 for Explanation of Ratios and Data

Comparative Historical Data | **Current Data Sorted by Sales**

Current data date ranges: **4 (4/1-9/30/10)** covers 0-1MM, 1-3MM, 3-5MM; **67 (10/1/10-3/31/11)** covers 5-10MM, 10-25MM, 25MM & OVER.

	4/1/08-3/31/09 ALL	4/1/09-3/31/10 ALL	4/1/10-3/31/11 ALL	0-1MM	1-3MM	3-5MM	5-10MM	10-25MM	25MM & OVER
Type of Statement									
Unqualified	7	8	17				1	4	12
Reviewed	9	14	16			1	5	10	
Compiled	11	8	5		2	1	1	1	
Tax Returns	7	5	5		3	1	1		
Other	31	23	28	2	3	1	2	8	12
NUMBER OF STATEMENTS	65	58	71	2	8	4	10	23	24
ASSETS	%	%	%	%	%	%	%	%	%
Cash & Equivalents	8.1	8.2	9.3				4.4	12.3	10.0
Trade Receivables (net)	27.7	25.2	28.7				28.2	27.2	26.2
Inventory	2.0	1.7	2.6				1.3	2.2	1.9
All Other Current	3.5	5.1	3.3				4.0	3.2	5.0
Total Current	41.4	40.2	43.9				37.9	44.9	43.1
Fixed Assets (net)	42.3	39.6	40.7				48.9	46.0	32.5
Intangibles (net)	8.5	11.1	8.9				1.4	5.0	18.2
All Other Non-Current	7.8	9.1	6.6				11.9	4.1	6.2
Total	100.0	100.0	100.0				100.0	100.0	100.0
LIABILITIES									
Notes Payable-Short Term	12.8	7.5	2.8				3.1	1.5	1.6
Cur. Mat.-L.T.D.	8.1	8.3	6.5				11.6	5.5	4.2
Trade Payables	13.1	13.1	14.6				11.9	13.7	16.3
Income Taxes Payable	.5	.2	.1				.0	.0	.3
All Other Current	12.9	11.0	8.0				6.7	9.1	8.0
Total Current	47.4	40.1	32.0				33.4	29.8	30.3
Long-Term Debt	21.7	22.7	20.9				29.8	20.3	17.5
Deferred Taxes	.5	.9	1.0				1.3	.4	2.1
All Other Non-Current	3.6	4.7	3.5				.9	2.1	6.4
Net Worth	26.8	31.7	42.7				34.7	47.4	43.7
Total Liabilties & Net Worth	100.0	100.0	100.0				100.0	100.0	100.0
INCOME DATA									
Net Sales	100.0	100.0	100.0				100.0	100.0	100.0
Gross Profit									
Operating Expenses	91.1	96.5	92.6				95.5	93.1	92.7
Operating Profit	8.9	3.5	7.4				4.5	6.9	7.3
All Other Expenses (net)	2.1	1.4	1.0				1.1	.8	.7
Profit Before Taxes	6.8	2.1	6.5				3.4	6.1	6.6
RATIOS									
Current	1.7	1.8	1.8				1.7	1.9	1.7
	1.1	1.2	1.4				1.2	1.5	1.4
	.7	.7	1.0				.7	.8	1.2
Quick	1.5	1.4	1.7				1.4	1.8	1.4
	(64) 1.0	1.0	1.2				1.1	1.5	1.2
	.6	.6	.8				.7	.7	1.2
Sales/Receivables	26 14.1	36 10.1	32 11.3				36 10.1	25 14.5	40 9.2
	51 7.2	47 7.7	48 7.6				55 6.7	37 9.8	59 6.2
	75 4.8	62 5.9	68 5.3				64 5.7	67 5.4	74 4.9
Cost of Sales/Inventory									
Cost of Sales/Payables									
Sales/Working Capital	10.5	8.6	8.8				20.4	8.4	8.6
	45.3	31.5	20.8				38.3	17.4	12.7
	-12.7	-25.9	128.3				-13.0	-38.1	36.5
EBIT/Interest	12.2	11.1	18.4				10.4	29.4	22.3
	(64) 5.2	(55) 3.6	(65) 6.4				3.3	(21) 7.7	(22) 7.6
	.9	-.3	3.4				1.2	3.5	4.2
Net Profit + Depr., Dep., Amort./Cur. Mat. L/T/D	12.1	4.4	6.9						
	(16) 3.6	(17) 1.2	(18) 1.9						
	2.2	.9	1.5						
Fixed/Worth	.9	.7	.6				.9	.5	.8
	1.1	1.1	1.2				1.3	1.1	1.4
	8.9	3.5	2.9				2.8	2.1	3.4
Debt/Worth	1.0	1.0	1.0				1.3	.7	1.1
	2.2	1.8	1.7				1.8	1.2	2.4
	17.0	18.7	3.4				3.1	2.8	9.2
% Profit Before Taxes/Tangible Net Worth	59.8	36.2	62.2					48.1	87.7
	(50) 27.4	(45) 14.8	(66) 33.1					(22) 29.8	(23) 38.7
	10.4	-7.9	14.9					14.9	17.9
% Profit Before Taxes/Total Assets	18.0	14.3	19.8				14.2	20.2	12.6
	7.0	6.0	10.2				4.0	9.9	9.7
	-.2	-3.2	4.5				1.4	6.5	4.8
Sales/Net Fixed Assets	11.6	14.3	10.2				8.0	9.6	13.4
	3.8	5.0	5.6				3.8	4.6	4.4
	2.0	2.5	2.3				1.8	1.9	2.0
Sales/Total Assets	2.6	2.5	2.7				2.8	3.0	2.5
	1.7	1.6	1.9				1.9	1.9	1.3
	1.1	1.2	1.2				1.1	1.5	.9
% Depr., Dep., Amort./Sales	2.2	3.9	2.1				1.9	2.7	.9
	(58) 4.6	(45) 5.3	(61) 4.1				5.6	(22) 4.8	(18) 4.0
	7.5	9.1	6.0				8.7	7.4	5.0
% Officers', Directors' Owners' Comp/Sales	1.9		1.4						
	(16) 4.0	(19) 3.2							
	7.7		4.3						
Net Sales ($)	1978251M	1491693M	3659995M	1643M	17158M	15351M	78330M	376296M	3171217M
Total Assets ($)	1629671M	1129551M	2401453M	919M	7320M	7284M	48015M	253330M	2084585M

M = $ thousand   MM = $ million

See Pages 9 through 22 for Explanation of Ratios and Data

Current Data Sorted by Assets   Comparative Historical Data

0-500M	500M-2MM	2-10MM	10-50MM	50-100MM	100-250MM	Type of Statement	4/1/06-3/31/07 ALL	4/1/07-3/31/08 ALL
	3	3	13	2	1	Unqualified	37	30
	4	10	3			Reviewed	24	25
2	4	3	3	1		Compiled	16	15
	2	3				Tax Returns	13	10
	1	19	13	4		Other	41	41
	20 (4/1-9/30/10)		74 (10/1/10-3/31/11)					
2	14	38	32	7	1	NUMBER OF STATEMENTS	131	121
%	%	%	%	%	%	ASSETS	%	%
	18.2	10.2	7.7			Cash & Equivalents	11.7	13.6
	30.9	13.5	12.8			Trade Receivables (net)	20.5	18.7
	1.2	1.7	2.0			Inventory	2.4	2.2
	5.9	3.9	.7			All Other Current	2.2	3.0
	56.2	29.4	23.2			Total Current	36.8	37.5
	32.8	53.9	62.0			Fixed Assets (net)	48.2	46.9
	4.7	6.7	4.7			Intangibles (net)	5.1	6.5
	6.3	9.9	10.1			All Other Non-Current	9.9	9.1
	100.0	100.0	100.0			Total	100.0	100.0
						LIABILITIES		
	8.0	4.2	3.0			Notes Payable-Short Term	4.7	3.8
	4.4	9.4	7.0			Cur. Mat.-L.T.D.	5.4	5.8
	11.8	6.7	7.0			Trade Payables	10.3	10.3
	.1	.1	.1			Income Taxes Payable	.3	.4
	17.1	9.5	6.5			All Other Current	8.9	6.7
	41.4	29.9	23.6			Total Current	29.6	27.0
	9.0	25.1	32.5			Long-Term Debt	25.9	29.3
	.7	.4	.1			Deferred Taxes	.7	.6
	8.4	5.9	12.6			All Other Non-Current	4.8	7.3
	40.5	38.7	31.2			Net Worth	38.9	35.8
	100.0	100.0	100.0			Total Liabilities & Net Worth	100.0	100.0
						INCOME DATA		
	100.0	100.0	100.0			Net Sales	100.0	100.0
						Gross Profit		
	91.9	88.2	88.4			Operating Expenses	89.7	86.2
	8.1	11.8	11.6			Operating Profit	10.3	13.8
	.3	3.0	4.0			All Other Expenses (net)	1.4	1.8
	7.8	8.8	7.7			Profit Before Taxes	8.9	12.1
						RATIOS		
	3.1	2.0	2.1				2.1	2.1
	1.9	1.1	1.0			Current	1.1	1.2
	.8	.5	.4				.8	.9
	2.7	2.0	1.7				1.9	1.8
	1.4	.8	.8			Quick	1.0	1.1
	.8	.4	.4				.7	.7
11	32.6	24 14.9	37 9.8				25 14.7	21 17.3
23	15.9	32 11.4	49 7.5			Sales/Receivables	38 9.7	37 9.8
52	7.0	41 9.0	67 5.4				57 6.5	54 6.7
						Cost of Sales/Inventory		
						Cost of Sales/Payables		
	4.4	7.1	6.5				8.4	6.6
	26.6	67.4	NM			Sales/Working Capital	64.1	26.1
	-77.0	-4.7	-5.4				-32.2	-50.8
	38.1	10.7	5.6				13.0	10.8
(11)	6.8	(34) 5.8	(28) 3.1			EBIT/Interest	(118) 5.0	(108) 4.1
	4.4	.6	1.3				2.0	2.1
		2.6	3.7				4.7	3.9
		(10) 1.9	(12) 1.6			Net Profit + Depr., Dep., Amort./Cur. Mat. L/T/D	(39) 1.9	(41) 2.6
		1.2	1.0				1.4	1.6
	.2	1.0	.9				.7	.9
	.7	2.1	2.2			Fixed/Worth	1.4	1.7
	2.6	6.7	105.7				3.5	4.3
	.6	1.0	.8				.8	.9
	1.5	2.3	1.9			Debt/Worth	1.9	2.1
	6.7	8.8	185.8				4.8	10.8
	80.2	41.6	41.6				67.4	82.3
(13)	36.6	(34) 24.9	(25) 13.3			% Profit Before Taxes/Tangible Net Worth	(119) 32.5	(105) 39.3
	13.1	5.2	3.8				10.2	13.0
	28.3	16.9	9.9				18.0	26.4
	16.5	8.0	3.8			% Profit Before Taxes/Total Assets	8.3	9.0
	2.7	-.7	.7				3.1	4.3
	16.6	5.0	3.0				7.3	7.0
	9.1	2.1	1.0			Sales/Net Fixed Assets	3.5	3.4
	4.5	1.4	.6				1.7	1.6
	3.6	1.9	1.5				2.6	2.5
	2.9	1.0	.8			Sales/Total Assets	1.6	1.5
	1.7	.5	.3				1.0	.8
	2.5	5.6	6.2				3.3	3.5
(12)	4.5	(37) 8.6	12.1			% Depr., Dep., Amort./Sales	(117) 6.1	(103) 6.7
	7.8	14.7	19.3				9.7	10.6
			.3				1.2	2.0
		(11) 2.3				% Officers', Directors' Owners' Comp/Sales	(36) 2.3	(36) 3.4
		4.0					5.0	5.8
2756M	58185M	226824M	751997M	386146M	157647M	Net Sales ($)	2685406M	3029878M
746M	17830M	179383M	776301M	528091M	217259M	Total Assets ($)	2037750M	2692913M

Comparative Historical Data | Current Data Sorted by Sales

	39 / 31 / 22 ... (Comparative Historical)			Type of Statement	20 (4/1-9/30/10)			74 (10/1/10-3/31/11)		
					0-1MM	1-3MM	3-5MM	5-10MM	10-25MM	25MM & OVER

Type of Statement	4/1/08-3/31/09 ALL	4/1/09-3/31/10 ALL	4/1/10-3/31/11 ALL		0-1MM	1-3MM	3-5MM	5-10MM	10-25MM	25MM & OVER
Unqualified	39	31	22		1	2	3	4	4	8
Reviewed	24	19	17		1		3	8	4	1
Compiled	14	13	13		1	3	3	2	3	1
Tax Returns	16	11	5			3		1	1	
Other	41	35	37		3	6	7	6	5	10
NUMBER OF STATEMENTS	134	109	94		6	14	16	21	17	20
ASSETS	%	%	%		%	%	%	%	%	%
Cash & Equivalents	12.2	13.1	10.3			15.4	11.2	12.4	6.5	5.8
Trade Receivables (net)	14.7	14.5	16.1			8.3	20.4	14.3	20.0	17.2
Inventory	1.3	1.4	1.6			.1	2.4	.5	3.9	1.7
All Other Current	3.7	4.6	2.8			5.9	6.6	1.6	1.1	.7
Total Current	31.9	33.5	30.9			29.6	40.5	28.8	31.4	25.3
Fixed Assets (net)	51.3	50.3	53.6			58.9	40.1	57.0	54.8	59.9
Intangibles (net)	6.7	5.2	6.0			3.9	11.3	4.5	4.4	6.1
All Other Non-Current	10.1	10.9	9.5			7.6	8.0	9.8	9.4	8.7
Total	100.0	100.0	100.0			100.0	100.0	100.0	100.0	100.0
LIABILITIES										
Notes Payable-Short Term	3.3	5.5	4.2			4.6	1.6	2.2	8.8	4.0
Cur. Mat.-L.T.D.	6.0	4.7	7.2			6.9	9.8	7.6	8.4	5.5
Trade Payables	6.8	9.8	7.9			7.2	7.4	7.0	7.9	9.5
Income Taxes Payable	.1	.1	.1			.4	.0	.0	.0	.1
All Other Current	8.5	12.0	9.4			19.0	6.3	12.2	5.1	7.6
Total Current	24.8	32.1	28.9			38.1	25.1	28.9	30.1	26.7
Long-Term Debt	33.2	29.0	24.6			25.5	10.0	29.0	27.0	26.1
Deferred Taxes	.7	.8	.5			.0	1.0	.4	.6	.6
All Other Non-Current	7.9	8.8	9.1			5.0	11.2	10.7	8.8	9.1
Net Worth	33.5	29.3	37.0			31.4	52.7	31.0	33.4	37.5
Total Liabilities & Net Worth	100.0	100.0	100.0			100.0	100.0	100.0	100.0	100.0
INCOME DATA										
Net Sales	100.0	100.0	100.0			100.0	100.0	100.0	100.0	100.0
Gross Profit										
Operating Expenses	90.7	91.2	89.4			82.3	89.0	93.3	88.3	94.1
Operating Profit	9.3	8.8	10.6			17.7	11.0	6.7	11.7	5.9
All Other Expenses (net)	3.4	3.1	2.6			2.5	.9	2.4	2.3	1.4
Profit Before Taxes	5.9	5.6	7.9			15.2	10.1	4.3	9.4	4.6
RATIOS										
Current	2.2	2.8	2.2			2.7	5.9	2.0	2.0	1.6
	1.3	1.3	1.1			.6	1.8	1.0	1.2	.8
	.7	.6	.5			.3	.5	.5	.5	.7
Quick	1.8	2.3	2.0			2.4	3.3	1.8	1.7	1.3
	1.0	1.1	.9			.5	1.4	.8	1.0	.8
	.5	.5	.5			.2	.4	.4	.5	.5
Sales/Receivables	16 22.9	24 15.4	25 14.4		0 UND	25 14.7	33 11.1	18 19.9	34 10.7	
	34 10.9	37 10.0	39 9.3		26 14.3	45 8.1	41 9.0	30 12.0	50 7.4	
	49 7.5	50 7.3	54 6.8		48 7.6	60 6.1	56 6.6	48 7.6	62 5.9	
Cost of Sales/Inventory										
Cost of Sales/Payables										
Sales/Working Capital	6.8	5.5	6.0			4.1	4.5	11.7	12.3	12.2
	29.5	24.3	69.2			-11.0	10.4	92.0	46.4	-51.9
	-17.4	-13.6	-7.2			-2.1	-12.4	-4.4	-10.7	-10.7
EBIT/Interest	(117) 7.3	(91) 9.2	(81) 10.2		(12) 9.1	(14) 103.2	(18) 6.3	(15) 8.4	(19) 9.7	
	3.2	3.2	4.2		5.6	12.7	2.4	4.2	3.4	
	1.3	.8	1.2		-1.0	2.7	.6	3.0	1.1	
Net Profit + Depr., Dep., Amort./Cur. Mat. L/T/D	(51) 4.2	(30) 3.4	(28) 3.5						(10) 3.6	
	2.2	2.0	1.7						1.4	
	1.2	1.4	1.3						1.1	
Fixed/Worth	1.0	.8	.8			.8	.4	1.1	.8	.9
	1.9	1.8	1.9			3.8	.9	1.9	2.0	2.4
	7.4	8.8	7.2			7.7	2.5	NM	6.6	8.6
Debt/Worth	.9	.7	.8			.6	.4	.8	1.3	.9
	2.4	2.1	1.9			3.3	.9	2.1	1.9	2.5
	11.5	19.0	9.2			9.0	4.1	NM	27.5	16.2
% Profit Before Taxes/Tangible Net Worth	(116) 63.3	(90) 38.6	(81) 42.5		(12) 31.3	(14) 65.8	(16) 31.7	(15) 63.3	(18) 28.7	
	21.0	15.8	21.8		18.6	34.7	22.5	25.1	16.9	
	3.9	-.1	5.0		-5.2	8.1	-2.5	13.3	1.7	
% Profit Before Taxes/Total Assets	13.8	13.6	14.0			10.3	26.4	13.1	17.1	9.8
	5.4	4.6	6.3			7.8	12.6	3.6	9.7	3.8
	.6	-.6	.4			-.4	2.1	-1.0	3.3	.5
Sales/Net Fixed Assets	6.2	6.7	5.2			6.8	11.6	3.8	6.5	4.0
	2.5	2.2	2.0			1.2	4.7	2.0	3.0	1.7
	1.1	1.0	.9			.4	.9	.8	.9	1.3
Sales/Total Assets	2.2	2.4	2.1			1.9	3.0	1.8	2.8	1.7
	1.2	1.2	1.1			.6	1.3	.9	1.6	1.1
	.7	.6	.5			.3	.4	.5	.6	.8
% Depr., Dep., Amort./Sales	(121) 4.3	(92) 4.3	(88) 4.7		(11) 5.3	4.6	6.3	(16) 5.9	(18) 4.2	
	7.4	7.8	8.4		15.1	7.5	8.8	6.6	8.0	
	12.1	14.0	15.1		17.5	16.8	15.4	15.8	11.3	
% Officers', Directors', Owners' Comp/Sales	(33) 1.5	(30) 1.9	(22) 1.7							
	2.8	3.3	3.4							
	5.0	5.0	4.1							
Net Sales ($)	3143469M	2108479M	1583555M		3669M	27567M	66365M	141773M	266448M	1077733M
Total Assets ($)	3260098M	2675820M	1719610M		12300M	49752M	91601M	187116M	306187M	1072654M

M = $ thousand   MM = $ million
See Pages 9 through 22 for Explanation of Ratios and Data

Current Data Sorted by Assets   Comparative Historical Data

0-500M	500M-2MM	2-10MM	10-50MM	50-100MM	100-250MM	Type of Statement	4/1/06-3/31/07 ALL	4/1/07-3/31/08 ALL
	1					Unqualified	3	7
		2				Reviewed	3	5
2	3	1				Compiled	10	
2	6	4				Tax Returns		3
1	4	6	3	4		Other	6	8
	2 (4/1-9/30/10)		42 (10/1/10-3/31/11)					
5	14	13	6	5	1	NUMBER OF STATEMENTS	22	23
%	%	%	%	%	%	**ASSETS**	%	%
	14.4	6.5				Cash & Equivalents	6.7	4.2
	13.0	23.7				Trade Receivables (net)	21.5	19.4
	2.9	2.0				Inventory	.7	1.7
	7.2	7.9				All Other Current	2.5	3.4
	37.6	40.2				Total Current	31.3	28.7
	48.8	43.7				Fixed Assets (net)	54.1	56.9
	5.1	1.4				Intangibles (net)	6.8	8.1
	8.6	14.8				All Other Non-Current	7.8	6.3
	100.0	100.0				Total	100.0	100.0
						LIABILITIES		
	5.6	2.3				Notes Payable-Short Term	4.3	2.2
	7.5	3.5				Cur. Mat.-L.T.D.	8.3	6.5
	4.0	18.8				Trade Payables	13.1	10.9
	.2	.0				Income Taxes Payable	.3	.5
	18.6	5.4				All Other Current	9.7	5.4
	35.9	29.9				Total Current	35.7	25.6
	27.8	19.4				Long-Term Debt	35.3	38.0
	.0	.0				Deferred Taxes	2.0	.9
	6.4	17.0				All Other Non-Current	3.7	11.3
	29.8	33.7				Net Worth	23.3	24.2
	100.0	100.0				Total Liabilities & Net Worth	100.0	100.0
						INCOME DATA		
	100.0	100.0				Net Sales	100.0	100.0
						Gross Profit		
	82.8	90.2				Operating Expenses	92.0	88.0
	17.2	9.8				Operating Profit	8.0	12.0
	4.8	3.5				All Other Expenses (net)	1.5	1.8
	12.4	6.4				Profit Before Taxes	6.4	10.2
						RATIOS		
	2.7	2.0				Current	2.2	1.7
	1.7	1.4					1.0	1.0
	1.2	1.0					.6	.6
	2.2	1.7				Quick	1.8	1.2
	1.3	1.1					.9	.9
	.9	.4					.5	.5
	0 UND	22 16.9				Sales/Receivables	26 14.0	25 14.4
	28 13.1	28 12.9					32 11.3	37 9.8
	53 6.9	48 7.5					41 8.9	61 5.9
						Cost of Sales/Inventory		
						Cost of Sales/Payables		
	3.4	6.8				Sales/Working Capital	18.4	11.0
	22.5	80.7					NM	-320.3
	NM	-535.9					-14.3	-10.9
	36.1	25.7				EBIT/Interest	19.3	8.3
	(11) 5.7	(12) 12.0					(21) 4.3	(20) 5.9
	-2.9	2.3					1.9	1.4
						Net Profit + Depr., Dep., Amort./Cur. Mat. L/T/D		
	.5	.6				Fixed/Worth	1.0	1.2
	1.8	1.0					2.1	3.0
	NM	3.5					-9.4	11.6
	.3	.8				Debt/Worth	.8	1.2
	1.6	1.9					2.6	2.7
	NM	4.6					-17.5	12.6
	59.3	55.5				% Profit Before Taxes/Tangible Net Worth	81.7	71.2
	(11) 19.6	(11) 29.9					(16) 63.9	(19) 41.0
	3.4	22.0					24.0	23.8
	28.0	20.2				% Profit Before Taxes/Total Assets	30.9	23.2
	5.1	6.3					13.5	10.1
	-.6	2.5					4.0	2.7
	17.0	15.5				Sales/Net Fixed Assets	7.0	6.1
	3.9	3.1					3.5	3.3
	1.0	1.4					2.3	1.8
	3.2	3.5				Sales/Total Assets	3.2	3.0
	1.4	1.9					2.1	1.6
	.8	.7					1.4	1.1
		2.5				% Depr., Dep., Amort./Sales	2.5	3.1
	(11)	5.4					(19) 5.8	(19) 5.6
		7.3					10.3	9.3
						% Officers', Directors' Owners' Comp/Sales		
5641M	35748M	128864M	238159M	282590M	175795M	Net Sales ($)	1005001M	785963M
1077M	17356M	55172M	187189M	310557M	180035M	Total Assets ($)	467739M	670117M

M = $ thousand   MM = $ million
See Pages 9 through 22 for Explanation of Ratios and Data

Comparative Historical Data / Current Data Sorted by Sales

				Type of Statement						
8		10	6	Unqualified		1				5
13		5	2	Reviewed			1	1		
3		5	6	Compiled		1			1	1
5		7	12	Tax Returns	3	1	1	5	1	
10		16	18	Other	2	3	1	5	1	6
4/1/08-3/31/09		4/1/09-3/31/10	4/1/10-3/31/11		3	5				
ALL		ALL	ALL		**2 (4/1-9/30/10)**			**42 (10/1/10-3/31/11)**		
					0-1MM	1-3MM	3-5MM	5-10MM	10-25MM	25MM & OVER
39		43	44	**NUMBER OF STATEMENTS**	8	10	2	9	3	12
%		%	%	**ASSETS**	%	%	%	%	%	%
7.6		10.0	11.2	Cash & Equivalents		13.7				5.5
20.8		16.0	16.5	Trade Receivables (net)		11.0				20.6
2.8		2.2	2.2	Inventory		.5				2.3
4.6		2.8	5.5	All Other Current		12.2				3.0
35.8		31.1	35.3	Total Current		37.5				31.4
52.7		54.6	49.0	Fixed Assets (net)		43.5				57.7
6.3		6.2	4.0	Intangibles (net)		4.9				5.5
5.2		8.1	11.7	All Other Non-Current		14.1				5.5
100.0		100.0	100.0	Total		100.0				100.0
				LIABILITIES						
9.3		4.8	5.8	Notes Payable-Short Term		7.5				1.1
7.4		5.0	5.9	Cur. Mat.-L.T.D.		4.0				5.1
11.1		10.7	9.6	Trade Payables		4.6				13.5
.0		.1	.1	Income Taxes Payable		.0				.0
6.4		10.2	10.5	All Other Current		6.7				8.1
34.2		30.8	31.9	Total Current		22.8				27.8
29.3		27.7	27.1	Long-Term Debt		23.1				30.9
1.1		1.3	.0	Deferred Taxes		.0				.0
12.7		9.4	11.2	All Other Non-Current		19.6				12.4
22.7		30.8	29.8	Net Worth		34.5				28.9
100.0		100.0	100.0	Total Liabilties & Net Worth		100.0				100.0
				INCOME DATA						
100.0		100.0	100.0	Net Sales		100.0				100.0
				Gross Profit						
93.5		90.3	88.0	Operating Expenses		85.3				91.3
6.5		9.7	12.0	Operating Profit		14.7				8.7
1.3		3.7	3.5	All Other Expenses (net)		5.3				1.9
5.2		6.0	8.5	Profit Before Taxes		9.3				6.9
				RATIOS						
2.5		2.3	2.0			3.3				1.6
1.2		1.3	1.3	Current		1.8				1.3
.8		.8	1.0			.9				1.0
1.5		1.6	1.6			2.4				1.4
.9		1.1	1.1	Quick		1.0				1.0
.6		.5	.7			.6				.6
20 17.9	26 14.2	22 16.5		Sales/Receivables	0 UND				29 12.7	
37 9.8	37 10.0	32 11.3			36 10.1				33 11.1	
46 7.9	60 6.1	42 8.7			63 5.8				41 9.0	
				Cost of Sales/Inventory						
				Cost of Sales/Payables						
8.9		11.3	8.6			3.1				8.0
30.6		26.2	32.1	Sales/Working Capital		8.8				53.0
-33.6		-26.7	-303.9			-66.4				NM
12.7		12.0	17.8			36.0				7.9
(38) 3.3	(38) 1.4	(39) 4.8		EBIT/Interest		3.3			(10) 5.0	
.6		-.9	1.5			.1				1.5
				Net Profit + Depr., Dep., Amort./Cur. Mat. L/T/D						
.8		.8	.8			.9				1.3
3.0		1.5	1.6	Fixed/Worth		1.2				2.4
-17.2		10.3	11.7			22.8				NM
1.0		.7	1.0			.6				1.3
3.7		2.5	2.1	Debt/Worth		3.2				3.3
-27.5		13.1	14.9			40.4				NM
50.7		54.0	57.9	% Profit Before Taxes/Tangible Net Worth						
(28) 27.6	(33) 11.8	(35) 29.9								
6.2		-3.9	5.0							
16.3		17.4	20.3	% Profit Before Taxes/Total Assets		23.8				12.0
5.8		1.9	6.4			4.3				9.1
-2.0		-4.8	1.5			-3.2				1.7
6.6		3.9	11.2			37.9				2.8
3.7		2.3	2.9	Sales/Net Fixed Assets		3.3				1.7
2.1		1.2	1.3			.9				1.3
3.3		1.9	2.7			5.1				1.7
1.9		1.2	1.3	Sales/Total Assets		1.2				1.0
1.1		.8	.9			.5				.9
2.1		4.6	3.3			.8				
(34) 4.7	(33) 7.1	(33) 6.0		% Depr., Dep., Amort./Sales		6.1				
8.0		13.1	10.9			12.9				
1.3			2.1	% Officers', Directors' Owners' Comp/Sales						
(11) 2.4	(13) 3.9									
4.2			5.6							
1200090M		1176923M	866797M	Net Sales ($)	3502M	18953M	6472M	65455M	46446M	725969M
982419M		1165373M	751386M	Total Assets ($)	5891M	25196M	3114M	29300M	17329M	670556M

© RMA 2011

M = $ thousand   MM = $ million

See Pages 9 through 22 for Explanation of Ratios and Data

	Current Data Sorted by Assets							Comparative Historical Data	
Type of Statement									
1	1	8	8		7	Unqualified		7	9
2	4	24	5			Reviewed		24	23
2	9	4				Compiled		10	11
6	5	5				Tax Returns		6	8
3	8	15	10	1	2	Other		9	21
	23 (4/1-9/30/10)		107 (10/1/10-3/31/11)					4/1/06-3/31/07 ALL	4/1/07-3/31/08 ALL
0-500M	500M-2MM	2-10MM	10-50MM	50-100MM	100-250MM				
14	27	56	23	1	9	**NUMBER OF STATEMENTS**		56	72
%	%	%	%	%	%	**ASSETS**		%	%
30.1	11.6	7.8	10.8			Cash & Equivalents		9.5	9.2
21.2	44.4	38.3	41.9			Trade Receivables (net)		43.4	42.7
4.2	3.9	3.5	1.9			Inventory		3.1	2.7
8.1	6.1	7.8	10.2			All Other Current		10.9	8.8
63.6	65.9	57.4	64.9			Total Current		66.9	63.5
17.0	22.1	31.0	26.9			Fixed Assets (net)		21.9	26.5
10.3	2.2	4.0	3.9			Intangibles (net)		6.1	3.5
9.2	9.8	7.6	4.4			All Other Non-Current		5.1	6.5
100.0	100.0	100.0	100.0			Total		100.0	100.0
						LIABILITIES			
16.5	13.8	7.3	9.1			Notes Payable-Short Term		16.1	9.3
27.4	5.4	6.1	3.2			Cur. Mat.-L.T.D.		3.8	4.0
12.5	14.3	14.4	18.6			Trade Payables		16.5	12.5
.0	.4	.2	.1			Income Taxes Payable		1.3	.8
26.4	7.7	9.7	12.8			All Other Current		14.9	11.4
82.8	41.6	37.7	43.8			Total Current		52.5	38.0
20.0	21.2	18.6	13.1			Long-Term Debt		15.2	19.4
.0	.2	.4	.1			Deferred Taxes		.6	.2
12.4	1.7	5.9	7.7			All Other Non-Current		3.6	1.6
-15.3	35.4	37.4	35.3			Net Worth		28.0	40.8
100.0	100.0	100.0	100.0			Total Liabilities & Net Worth		100.0	100.0
						INCOME DATA			
100.0	100.0	100.0	100.0			Net Sales		100.0	100.0
						Gross Profit			
100.2	94.8	93.8	95.1			Operating Expenses		95.4	90.3
-.2	5.2	6.2	4.9			Operating Profit		4.6	9.7
.4	.9	1.3	.5			All Other Expenses (net)		1.0	2.3
-.7	4.2	4.9	4.4			Profit Before Taxes		3.6	7.4
						RATIOS			
1.9	2.8	2.2	1.9					1.9	2.7
1.1	1.5	1.5	1.5			Current		1.3	1.7
.5	1.0	1.1	1.2					1.0	1.2
1.6	2.8	2.0	1.6					1.5	2.4
1.1	1.1	1.2	1.2			Quick		1.1	1.3
.2	.7	.8	.8					.7	1.0
0 UND	44 8.2	44 8.4	49 7.5					40 9.2	33 10.9
0 UND	58 6.3	70 5.2	74 5.0			Sales/Receivables		74 5.0	68 5.4
55 6.7	83 4.4	92 4.0	83 4.4					96 3.8	93 3.9
						Cost of Sales/Inventory			
						Cost of Sales/Payables			
7.3	6.4	5.8	5.6					8.2	5.6
47.2	10.7	11.0	12.9			Sales/Working Capital		17.1	8.7
-18.1	218.7	64.3	21.9					233.0	29.0
	10.2	17.7	46.2					9.9	22.3
	(25) 5.3	(54) 4.7	(21) 9.4			EBIT/Interest		(50) 4.1	(63) 8.4
	1.5	1.5	2.5					1.8	2.5
						Net Profit + Depr., Dep.,		5.9	11.7
						Amort./Cur. Mat. L/T/D		(16) 3.0	(21) 5.1
								1.0	1.5
.0	.2	.3	.2					.2	.2
.2	.4	.8	.7			Fixed/Worth		.7	.6
-.5	3.1	2.9	1.4					4.7	1.2
.9	.5	.8	1.0					1.3	.6
5.8	1.9	1.8	1.9			Debt/Worth		2.4	1.6
-2.0	7.8	7.8	3.4					15.3	3.3
	42.6	39.8	68.9			% Profit Before Taxes/Tangible		63.9	60.9
	(23) 17.9	(49) 24.2	(20) 43.8			Net Worth		(45) 32.1	(65) 33.3
	7.2	10.8	25.9					11.6	16.5
14.2	14.0	18.5	22.0			% Profit Before Taxes/Total		17.9	23.9
2.1	6.2	8.2	12.1			Assets		9.0	11.3
-36.1	2.3	1.9	5.4					3.6	4.0
UND	30.5	19.3	40.9					37.5	32.9
55.0	18.9	9.2	15.1			Sales/Net Fixed Assets		12.6	15.0
31.9	6.0	4.5	3.5					6.6	6.4
5.1	3.1	2.6	3.0					3.7	3.3
2.8	2.6	2.1	2.4			Sales/Total Assets		2.6	2.4
1.9	1.5	1.4	1.6					1.9	1.8
	.9	1.6	.6					1.0	.9
	(23) 1.9	(50) 2.7	(22) 2.0			% Depr., Dep., Amort./Sales		(49) 1.7	(59) 2.1
	2.8	4.4	3.5					3.6	4.2
	2.7	1.4				% Officers', Directors'		2.2	2.1
	(14) 6.0	(32) 2.4				Owners' Comp/Sales		(25) 4.6	(30) 4.1
	9.0	5.3						7.5	8.8
11375M	92812M	546836M	1002791M	125184M	2178632M	Net Sales ($)		895279M	1475890M
3264M	34650M	264359M	394769M	87805M	1617712M	Total Assets ($)		724704M	702751M

© RMA 2011

M = $ thousand   MM = $ million

See Pages 9 through 22 for Explanation of Ratios and Data

Comparative Historical Data — Current Data Sorted by Sales

			Type of Statement						
12	21	25	Unqualified	1	1		1	9	13
36	34	35	Reviewed	1	4	4	12	11	3
4	11	15	Compiled	2	5	2	4	2	
8	18	16	Tax Returns	4	2	5	5		
28	38	39	Other	3	6	5	12	4	9
4/1/08-3/31/09 ALL	4/1/09-3/31/10 ALL	4/1/10-3/31/11 ALL		23 (4/1-9/30/10)			107 (10/1/10-3/31/11)		
				0-1MM	1-3MM	3-5MM	5-10MM	10-25MM	25MM & OVER
88	122	130	**NUMBER OF STATEMENTS**	11	18	16	34	26	25
%	%	%	**ASSETS**	%	%	%	%	%	%
11.5	11.5	11.6	Cash & Equivalents	35.2	8.0	15.6	7.5	8.6	10.2
39.7	37.0	37.8	Trade Receivables (net)	21.6	32.1	35.5	40.5	39.9	44.6
4.2	2.8	3.1	Inventory	4.7	3.5	.7	3.7	5.0	1.0
5.5	5.3	7.7	All Other Current	8.4	7.6	4.3	5.5	10.5	9.8
60.9	56.7	60.3	Total Current	69.9	51.2	56.0	57.2	64.0	65.6
25.5	30.0	25.6	Fixed Assets (net)	11.4	36.3	28.4	32.8	24.6	13.9
5.4	4.8	6.4	Intangibles (net)	4.9	5.6	9.1	1.9	4.0	14.5
8.2	8.6	7.7	All Other Non-Current	13.8	6.9	6.5	8.0	7.4	6.1
100.0	100.0	100.0	Total	100.0	100.0	100.0	100.0	100.0	100.0
			LIABILITIES						
12.1	11.7	9.5	Notes Payable-Short Term	24.4	7.0	8.2	9.9	8.1	6.7
5.5	6.2	7.4	Cur. Mat.-L.T.D.	26.4	8.5	5.3	7.7	4.2	2.6
13.1	14.1	15.0	Trade Payables	13.9	9.6	15.8	12.1	16.2	21.7
.4	.6	.2	Income Taxes Payable	.0	.1	.5	.2	.1	.2
10.7	9.7	11.6	All Other Current	33.1	6.2	6.3	7.6	12.8	13.5
41.8	42.2	43.7	Total Current	97.7	31.4	36.1	37.5	41.5	44.7
20.0	21.7	17.8	Long-Term Debt	13.5	27.2	20.7	21.4	16.3	7.8
.4	.9	.6	Deferred Taxes	.0	.2	.0	.6	.2	2.2
4.5	5.7	6.2	All Other Non-Current	15.8	3.8	8.7	7.2	1.7	5.6
33.3	29.4	31.6	Net Worth	-27.0	37.4	34.5	33.3	40.4	39.8
100.0	100.0	100.0	Total Liabilities & Net Worth	100.0	100.0	100.0	100.0	100.0	100.0
			INCOME DATA						
100.0	100.0	100.0	Net Sales	100.0	100.0	100.0	100.0	100.0	100.0
			Gross Profit						
93.6	95.9	94.8	Operating Expenses	97.0	94.5	98.0	94.3	94.8	93.0
6.4	4.1	5.2	Operating Profit	3.0	5.5	2.0	5.7	5.2	7.0
1.3	1.1	.9	All Other Expenses (net)	.3	1.5	.5	1.4	1.0	.4
5.1	3.0	4.2	Profit Before Taxes	2.8	4.0	1.5	4.3	4.2	6.6
			RATIOS						
2.3	2.5	2.2	Current	1.9	2.8	2.2	2.6	2.3	1.8
1.5	1.5	1.5		1.2	1.5	1.9	1.5	1.4	1.5
1.1	1.1	1.1		.5	.5	.9	1.1	1.1	1.2
1.9	2.2	2.0	Quick	1.6	2.7	2.1	2.2	1.9	1.5
1.3	1.3	1.2		1.1	1.1	1.6	1.2	1.1	1.4
1.0	.8	.8		.5	.3	.9	.7	.8	1.0
35 10.3	35 10.3	41 8.9	Sales/Receivables	0 UND	20 18.5	49 7.5	49 7.5	43 8.5	53 6.9
64 5.7	60 6.1	67 5.5		25 14.7	51 7.1	67 5.4	73 5.0	60 6.1	74 4.9
79 4.6	85 4.3	83 4.4		83 4.4	81 4.5	90 4.0	91 4.0	78 4.7	93 3.9
			Cost of Sales/Inventory						
			Cost of Sales/Payables						
6.2	6.3	6.0	Sales/Working Capital	6.7	4.7	5.2	5.0	6.3	6.0
12.8	13.4	11.3		13.0	9.1	8.4	12.2	11.9	11.8
45.5	84.8	76.2		-9.9	-43.4	NM	273.7	76.2	22.9
17.6	10.5	15.6	EBIT/Interest		16.1	11.9	22.7	13.8	25.8
(82) 4.8	(107) 3.2	(117) 5.3			(17) 5.3	(14) 4.9	(33) 4.4	(25) 4.7	(23) 10.1
1.0	-.6	1.6			1.2	1.3	1.1	1.5	2.6
3.9	5.1	6.3	Net Profit + Depr., Dep., Amort./Cur. Mat. L/T/D						
(16) 1.2	(32) 2.1	(23) 2.6							
.3	.5	1.2							
.2	.3	.2	Fixed/Worth	.0	.2	.3	.3	.2	.1
.6	.7	.8		.1	1.0	1.7	.8	.7	.8
1.5	3.2	3.4		-.2	9.1	NM	3.8	1.3	1.7
.8	.7	.8	Debt/Worth	1.0	.6	.8	.6	.8	1.3
1.7	1.6	2.1		2.4	2.5	3.2	2.1	1.5	2.4
6.2	6.5	9.2		-2.1	18.9	NM	9.0	4.4	5.6
56.8	47.6	47.6	% Profit Before Taxes/Tangible Net Worth		63.5	37.1	33.3	53.7	68.9
(74) 26.3	(98) 19.3	(107) 25.7			(15) 15.1	(12) 27.8	(29) 20.2	(24) 25.8	(20) 40.4
3.2	-4.9	10.4			2.8	9.1	9.7	5.4	19.2
25.8	18.0	17.7	% Profit Before Taxes/Total Assets	17.3	20.8	11.2	17.0	18.7	24.8
8.9	5.8	7.6		6.1	6.1	7.3	7.4	7.8	12.0
-.4	-2.6	1.8		-3.7	-8.0	1.8	.6	1.6	3.9
28.6	28.1	35.0	Sales/Net Fixed Assets	UND	26.4	23.8	20.0	29.8	69.6
13.2	9.6	12.1		57.0	7.2	13.3	6.8	11.8	28.0
4.9	3.9	5.0		50.5	3.1	3.3	3.9	6.0	8.1
3.1	3.2	2.9	Sales/Total Assets	4.9	2.9	3.1	2.6	3.1	3.0
2.3	2.1	2.1		2.0	1.7	2.2	1.9	2.2	2.4
1.8	1.5	1.5		1.6	1.5	1.2	1.4	1.9	1.6
1.0	1.4	1.1	% Depr., Dep., Amort./Sales		1.9	1.0	1.6	1.5	.6
(70) 2.2	(103) 2.9	(104) 2.1			(15) 2.9	(13) 1.8	(30) 3.3	(24) 2.6	(19) .9
4.9	5.8	4.1			7.3	2.9	5.0	3.3	2.1
2.5	2.8	1.5	% Officers', Directors' Owners' Comp/Sales			2.5	1.4		
(36) 4.2	(51) 5.8	(59) 3.0			(10) 6.3	(22) 2.6			
7.5	10.1	6.2			9.0	5.9			
1517527M	2213531M	3957630M	Net Sales ($)	4726M	37387M	63855M	250069M	412687M	3188906M
1196402M	1684133M	2402559M	Total Assets ($)	2138M	23745M	48059M	147673M	185338M	1995606M

© RMA 2011   M = $ thousand   MM = $ million
See Pages 9 through 22 for Explanation of Ratios and Data

| Current Data Sorted by Assets | | | | | | Comparative Historical Data | | |

	0-500M	500M-2MM	2-10MM	10-50MM	50-100MM	100-250MM	Type of Statement	4/1/06-3/31/07 ALL	4/1/07-3/31/08 ALL
		2	3	11	2	1	Unqualified	6	9
		4	12	3	1		Reviewed	17	13
	2	6	10	2	1		Compiled	7	11
	2	3	2				Tax Returns	7	9
	3	6	11	8		2	Other	19	21
		15 (4/1-9/30/10)		82 (10/1/10-3/31/11)					
NUMBER OF STATEMENTS	7	21	38	24	4	3		56	63
	%	%	%	%	%	%	ASSETS	%	%
		11.9	14.7	7.9			Cash & Equivalents	9.7	9.1
		22.5	17.5	18.9			Trade Receivables (net)	22.7	22.2
		9.7	5.9	7.2			Inventory	8.0	6.5
		3.3	5.3	2.0			All Other Current	4.2	5.1
		47.5	43.4	36.0			Total Current	44.5	43.0
		43.1	45.6	47.2			Fixed Assets (net)	40.0	44.4
		5.5	3.4	9.4			Intangibles (net)	4.8	5.7
		4.0	7.7	7.4			All Other Non-Current	10.6	6.9
		100.0	100.0	100.0			Total	100.0	100.0
							LIABILITIES		
		12.5	4.7	7.0			Notes Payable-Short Term	9.2	11.7
		3.5	3.2	8.2			Cur. Mat.-L.T.D.	4.8	8.2
		10.9	8.8	10.3			Trade Payables	13.6	10.2
		.0	.3	.0			Income Taxes Payable	.8	.5
		6.6	9.4	7.0			All Other Current	9.3	7.8
		33.6	26.4	32.5			Total Current	37.6	38.4
		22.5	22.4	18.7			Long-Term Debt	27.8	33.1
		.6	.3	.7			Deferred Taxes	.4	.7
		5.7	6.5	7.4			All Other Non-Current	4.6	5.1
		37.5	44.5	40.7			Net Worth	29.6	22.8
		100.0	100.0	100.0			Total Liabilities & Net Worth	100.0	100.0
							INCOME DATA		
		100.0	100.0	100.0			Net Sales	100.0	100.0
							Gross Profit		
		86.9	88.5	91.4			Operating Expenses	92.1	93.9
		13.1	11.5	8.6			Operating Profit	7.9	6.1
		5.8	3.6	3.6			All Other Expenses (net)	3.7	2.0
		7.3	7.9	5.0			Profit Before Taxes	4.2	4.2
							RATIOS		
		3.1	3.3	1.7				2.1	2.0
		1.5	1.7	1.0			Current	1.2	1.2
		.7	.7	.6				.7	.7
		2.4	2.3	1.3				1.6	1.5
		1.0	1.3	.6			Quick	1.0	.9
		.5	.6	.5				.4	.5
	4 91.2	**11** 32.2	**29** 12.4					**16** 22.4	**17** 21.2
	19 19.5	**33** 11.1	**42** 8.8				Sales/Receivables	**30** 12.3	**32** 11.5
	58 6.3	**46** 7.9	**55** 6.6					**48** 7.6	**46** 8.0
							Cost of Sales/Inventory		
							Cost of Sales/Payables		
		9.2	5.7	8.3				11.3	11.8
		33.3	21.6	NM			Sales/Working Capital	36.2	39.8
		-20.1	-16.0	-11.3				-24.6	-21.0
		20.2	14.2	11.4				8.9	21.2
		(15) 14.9	(30) 5.2	5.4			EBIT/Interest	(48) 2.5	(60) 3.9
		5.2	2.0	2.3				1.5	1.1
				3.8			Net Profit + Depr., Dep.,		17.2
			(14) 1.6				Amort./Cur. Mat. L/T/D	(17) 3.3
				1.1					1.9
		.3	.4	1.1				.4	.6
		1.5	1.4	1.8			Fixed/Worth	2.0	1.9
		59.8	2.7	3.2				8.4	-26.9
		.5	.3	1.1				.9	1.2
		2.4	1.6	1.8			Debt/Worth	3.1	2.3
		NM	4.3	6.7				14.6	-33.6
		90.6	66.5	64.9			% Profit Before Taxes/Tangible	49.5	79.3
		(16) 65.9	(34) 22.7	(21) 23.3			Net Worth	(46) 20.5	(47) 35.8
		14.7	7.9	8.7				7.6	6.2
		28.9	29.6	15.5			% Profit Before Taxes/Total	16.6	21.1
		21.2	9.1	6.5			Assets	4.7	8.5
		2.3	2.5	3.0				1.2	.4
		20.2	15.3	6.4				21.9	17.9
		14.2	4.6	4.2			Sales/Net Fixed Assets	5.7	6.2
		2.6	2.1	1.8				2.9	2.1
		4.7	3.4	2.2				4.0	3.9
		3.0	1.7	1.5			Sales/Total Assets	2.6	1.9
		1.8	1.0	1.1				1.1	1.1
		1.4	1.5	2.5				1.5	1.4
		(16) 3.4	(37) 3.0	(23) 4.6			% Depr., Dep., Amort./Sales	(51) 3.6	(58) 3.1
		12.5	6.4	10.1				9.2	7.1
			.7				% Officers', Directors'	1.0	.9
			(10) 2.4				Owners' Comp/Sales	(15) 2.1	(22) 2.8
			3.6					6.6	4.7
Net Sales ($)	9258M	100367M	458660M	765408M	606615M	601622M		1276855M	1934700M
Total Assets ($)	2028M	29517M	199743M	512652M	281115M	448494M		542462M	973837M

M = $ thousand   MM = $ million
See Pages 9 through 22 for Explanation of Ratios and Data

Comparative Historical Data | Current Data Sorted by Sales

				Type of Statement								
12	14	19		Unqualified	1	1	1	4	4	10		
18	21	20		Reviewed			2	8	5	3		
15	16	21		Compiled	4		4	7	4	2		
11	13	7		Tax Returns	1	3	1		1	1		
31	31	30		Other	3	3	4	3	7	10		
4/1/08-3/31/09 ALL	4/1/09-3/31/10 ALL	4/1/10-3/31/11 ALL			15 (4/1-9/30/10)			82 (10/1/10-3/31/11)				
					0-1MM	1-3MM	3-5MM	5-10MM	10-25MM	25MM & OVER		

H1	H2	H3	Item	0-1MM	1-3MM	3-5MM	5-10MM	10-25MM	25MM & OVER
87	95	97	**NUMBER OF STATEMENTS**	9	7	12	22	21	26
%	%	%	**ASSETS**	%	%	%	%	%	%
11.9	10.3	12.5	Cash & Equivalents			9.0	10.4	12.8	10.0
19.6	18.1	19.0	Trade Receivables (net)			23.4	19.4	20.5	22.3
5.2	8.4	8.2	Inventory			3.6	8.8	6.1	13.0
3.5	4.0	4.1	All Other Current			3.8	5.8	1.4	3.0
40.1	40.8	43.8	Total Current			39.8	44.4	40.9	48.2
44.1	47.6	41.3	Fixed Assets (net)			47.5	46.3	46.6	32.0
6.4	3.7	7.5	Intangibles (net)			4.3	3.1	8.4	12.4
9.4	8.0	7.4	All Other Non-Current			8.4	6.2	4.2	7.4
100.0	100.0	100.0	Total			100.0	100.0	100.0	100.0
			LIABILITIES						
8.1	7.6	8.2	Notes Payable-Short Term			16.2	3.0	3.2	7.6
5.6	6.0	4.7	Cur. Mat.-L.T.D.			2.9	6.0	5.7	4.7
11.7	11.8	9.8	Trade Payables			9.4	10.3	11.5	11.7
.1	.2	.1	Income Taxes Payable			.0	.3	.1	.2
9.3	9.8	7.6	All Other Current			10.2	7.0	7.9	7.7
34.8	35.4	30.5	Total Current			38.7	26.6	28.5	31.9
28.7	29.1	20.7	Long-Term Debt			24.6	17.3	22.2	14.6
.2	.2	.5	Deferred Taxes			.0	1.2	.0	.7
5.8	7.2	6.2	All Other Non-Current			10.8	.4	8.9	9.1
30.5	28.0	42.1	Net Worth			25.9	54.6	40.4	43.7
100.0	100.0	100.0	Total Liabilities & Net Worth			100.0	100.0	100.0	100.0
			INCOME DATA						
100.0	100.0	100.0	Net Sales			100.0	100.0	100.0	100.0
			Gross Profit						
91.3	95.3	88.6	Operating Expenses			93.7	90.4	90.1	94.0
8.7	4.7	11.4	Operating Profit			6.3	9.6	9.9	6.0
2.9	2.1	3.7	All Other Expenses (net)			.7	3.0	3.5	1.4
5.8	2.6	7.7	Profit Before Taxes			5.6	6.6	6.5	4.6
			RATIOS						
2.2	1.8	2.6	Current			3.3	5.1	2.3	2.1
1.3	1.1	1.5				.9	1.6	1.5	1.4
.7	.7	.7				.5	.8	1.0	.8
1.7	1.3	1.8	Quick			2.2	1.8	2.2	1.5
1.0	.8	.8				.6	.9	.9	.9
.4	.4	.5				.3	.6	.6	.5
9 41.2	19 19.0	14 26.3	Sales/Receivables	13 27.8	5 71.3	16 23.4			29 12.6
28 13.2	36 10.1	33 10.9		46 7.9	27 13.4	32 11.3			42 8.8
49 7.5	47 7.8	49 7.4		63 5.8	43 8.5	39 9.4			57 6.4
			Cost of Sales/Inventory						
			Cost of Sales/Payables						
12.3	11.2	8.4	Sales/Working Capital			7.8	8.2	8.8	7.9
35.1	84.9	33.3				NM	41.0	20.6	23.7
-19.7	-14.3	-17.3				-9.4	-15.5	-350.3	-20.7
14.2	7.3	17.6	EBIT/Interest			17.9	15.6	28.8	18.2
(74) 3.6	(90) 2.6	(80) 6.4			(11) 6.6	(18) 8.5	(20) 5.5	(24) 6.1	
1.5	-.2	2.4				1.9	3.7	1.9	2.5
11.9	7.1	10.5	Net Profit + Depr., Dep.,						7.4
(13) 2.3	(18) 2.0	(27) 1.9	Amort./Cur. Mat. L/T/D					(15) 1.9	
.6	1.2	1.2							1.3
.5	.7	.5	Fixed/Worth			1.1	.4	.7	.5
1.8	1.7	1.5				2.0	.9	1.9	1.1
9.5	4.1	4.4				5.9	2.0	3.9	3.6
.9	1.0	.6	Debt/Worth			1.8	.2	.6	.7
2.9	2.2	1.8				2.9	1.0	1.7	1.9
18.0	5.5	6.2				NM	2.4	5.7	12.0
72.7	33.3	80.7	% Profit Before Taxes/Tangible				80.8	72.2	62.6
(69) 38.0	(82) 15.2	(82) 28.7	Net Worth				(21) 21.1	(17) 40.3	(21) 25.4
13.6	1.3	10.1					9.0	10.7	10.0
27.7	9.7	26.7	% Profit Before Taxes/Total			22.7	30.2	40.0	18.3
7.7	4.1	12.0	Assets			9.5	15.7	12.7	8.2
2.1	-1.8	3.6				1.1	6.4	2.7	3.5
14.3	10.9	19.0	Sales/Net Fixed Assets			6.3	19.1	12.3	22.5
5.6	3.6	5.8				4.4	5.1	5.3	6.5
2.2	2.0	2.2				2.2	2.3	2.3	4.0
4.0	3.0	3.4	Sales/Total Assets			2.9	4.0	3.7	3.4
2.1	1.6	1.9				1.9	2.1	1.9	2.2
1.3	1.1	1.2				1.1	1.3	1.5	1.2
1.3	2.2	1.7	% Depr., Dep., Amort./Sales			2.1	1.3	2.4	1.0
(72) 2.8	(81) 4.8	(83) 3.3			(10) 3.8	(20) 2.4	3.5	(23) 2.3	
7.6	8.5	7.4				13.8	6.6	7.1	5.1
.9	.7	1.0	% Officers', Directors'						
(31) 2.5	(26) 2.6	(23) 2.6	Owners' Comp/Sales						
6.3	4.8	5.4							
3479947M	2297197M	2541930M	Net Sales ($)	4212M	13498M	43620M	168338M	369444M	1942818M
1430503M	1209899M	1473549M	Total Assets ($)	16635M	6336M	27229M	92096M	211938M	1119315M

M = $ thousand   MM = $ million
See Pages 9 through 22 for Explanation of Ratios and Data

Current Data Sorted by Assets

Comparative Historical Data

							Type of Statement		
1			8	9		2	Unqualified	20	18
1	3		15	8			Reviewed	20	33
4	3		5				Compiled	22	18
17	5		5	1			Tax Returns	33	28
6	9		13	11	2		Other	40	48
	20 (4/1-9/30/10)			108 (10/1/10-3/31/11)				4/1/06-3/31/07	4/1/07-3/31/08
0-500M	500M-2MM		2-10MM	10-50MM	50-100MM	100-250MM		ALL	ALL
29	20		46	29	2	2	NUMBER OF STATEMENTS	135	145
%	%		%	%	%	%	ASSETS	%	%
27.4	9.6		10.2	9.1			Cash & Equivalents	11.6	9.4
13.3	26.2		28.7	22.2			Trade Receivables (net)	26.6	25.4
4.1	2.8		3.4	5.4			Inventory	2.8	2.4
1.1	4.0		3.3	2.3			All Other Current	3.5	3.7
45.9	42.6		45.5	38.9			Total Current	44.6	40.9
40.6	38.7		35.7	44.4			Fixed Assets (net)	42.4	44.9
6.5	5.7		9.2	7.0			Intangibles (net)	5.5	5.6
7.0	12.9		9.6	9.7			All Other Non-Current	7.5	8.6
100.0	100.0		100.0	100.0			Total	100.0	100.0
							LIABILITIES		
17.9	5.2		5.1	7.2			Notes Payable-Short Term	7.8	5.0
5.4	6.7		6.8	7.0			Cur. Mat.-L.T.D.	6.7	7.2
13.1	10.0		10.8	9.0			Trade Payables	11.2	12.0
.1	.7		.5	.2			Income Taxes Payable	1.0	.7
26.0	6.9		7.6	5.6			All Other Current	8.4	6.7
62.6	29.6		30.9	28.9			Total Current	35.1	31.6
37.2	22.2		23.0	32.2			Long-Term Debt	27.9	29.8
.0	.5		.3	.2			Deferred Taxes	.3	.6
10.2	4.6		8.1	6.4			All Other Non-Current	2.7	9.3
-10.1	43.1		37.7	32.3			Net Worth	34.0	28.7
100.0	100.0		100.0	100.0			Total Liabilties & Net Worth	100.0	100.0
							INCOME DATA		
100.0	100.0		100.0	100.0			Net Sales	100.0	100.0
							Gross Profit		
93.0	96.5		93.6	89.3			Operating Expenses	93.0	93.8
7.0	3.5		6.4	10.7			Operating Profit	7.0	6.2
1.3	1.2		2.2	2.3			All Other Expenses (net)	1.8	1.8
5.8	2.3		4.2	8.4			Profit Before Taxes	5.1	4.5
							RATIOS		
5.5	2.0		2.5	1.7				2.1	2.2
1.1	1.2		1.5	1.2			Current	1.4	1.3
.3	1.0		.9	.8				.8	.8
5.5	1.9		2.3	1.4				1.9	2.0
1.0	1.1		1.3	.9			Quick	1.1 (144)	1.1
.3	.7		.6	.7				.6	.6
0 UND	6 63.1		34 10.7	29 12.4				16 22.6	20 18.4
4 90.3	34 10.8		47 7.8	49 7.4			Sales/Receivables	38 9.5	39 9.4
22 16.2	69 5.3		61 6.0	70 5.2				65 5.6	60 6.1
							Cost of Sales/Inventory		
							Cost of Sales/Payables		
12.6	7.8		6.3	7.9				7.7	8.6
118.5	23.9		13.3	21.8			Sales/Working Capital	22.9	36.5
-12.5	-554.3		-49.8	-30.4				-28.3	-24.7
11.3	9.0		27.7	6.1				15.0	7.5
(19) 2.7	(19) 3.0		(45) 5.2	(26) 4.1			EBIT/Interest	(123) 4.1	(127) 3.3
-.6	.3		1.3	2.4				1.0	1.3
							Net Profit + Depr., Dep., Amort./Cur. Mat. L/T/D	5.7	9.8
								(28) 2.2	(31) 2.3
								.8	1.0
.6	.5		.3	1.2				.6	.5
5.7	1.0		1.1	1.9			Fixed/Worth	1.3	1.9
-5.3	2.4		4.4	4.0				6.8	7.2
.9	.3		.7	1.3				.8	.8
UND	1.8		1.9	2.8			Debt/Worth	2.1	2.7
-5.2	8.0		7.0	9.0				8.3	11.5
328.6	48.3		54.6	56.9			% Profit Before Taxes/Tangible Net Worth	72.6	58.1
(16) 128.4	(17) 14.8		(39) 22.1	(25) 18.5				(109) 24.8	(119) 27.8
19.5	-8.4		1.5	12.5				.6	10.7
75.0	13.4		21.7	10.1			% Profit Before Taxes/Total Assets	22.7	16.1
13.3	3.2		7.2	7.0				7.5	7.4
.0	-2.2		.6	2.8				-.1	.7
71.1	13.4		18.8	7.7				13.5	11.3
11.7	6.2		7.2	3.4			Sales/Net Fixed Assets	6.2	5.5
5.1	3.4		3.1	1.7				3.0	2.4
8.2	3.6		2.8	2.3				3.5	3.0
4.0	2.2		2.1	1.3			Sales/Total Assets	2.1	2.0
2.8	1.1		1.4	.7				1.4	1.3
2.9	3.0		1.8	4.5				2.7	2.2
(18) 7.8	(17) 5.7		(40) 4.4	(28) 7.0			% Depr., Dep., Amort./Sales	(113) 4.8	(127) 4.9
14.2	10.4		8.1	10.4				8.2	9.3
4.4	5.8		2.3					2.5	2.4
(15) 6.6	(10) 7.9	(16)	3.8				% Officers', Directors' Owners' Comp/Sales	(53) 3.8	(62) 5.1
10.7	18.1		6.3					6.9	7.9
47711M	63957M		484101M	1066759M	69894M	168271M	Net Sales ($)	1919544M	2284023M
7074M	25235M		229097M	751696M	146337M	251905M	Total Assets ($)	1411431M	1539606M

© RMA 2011

M = $ thousand   MM = $ million
See Pages 9 through 22 for Explanation of Ratios and Data

Comparative Historical Data

Current Data Sorted by Sales

Type of Statement	4/1/08-3/31/09 ALL	4/1/09-3/31/10 ALL	4/1/10-3/31/11 ALL	0-1MM	1-3MM	3-5MM	5-10MM	10-25MM	25MM & OVER
Unqualified	18	16	20	2	3	4	4	5	8
Reviewed	36	25	27	1	4	7	9	5	
Compiled	17	22	12	1	4		3	2	2
Tax Returns	27	23	28	9	10	4	3	1	1
Other	46	39	41	8	6	2	7	8	10
				20 (4/1-9/30/10)			108 (10/1/10-3/31/11)		
NUMBER OF STATEMENTS	144	125	128	20	23	13	23	25	24
ASSETS	%	%	%	%	%	%	%	%	%
Cash & Equivalents	12.1	12.0	13.5	21.1	16.5	8.8	12.2	15.6	5.9
Trade Receivables (net)	25.4	24.2	22.6	9.1	19.4	23.4	21.2	29.5	30.9
Inventory	2.7	4.2	3.8	3.5	2.7	.7	3.2	6.1	5.0
All Other Current	3.4	4.1	2.6	3.2	1.1	2.6	4.6	2.0	2.4
Total Current	43.5	44.5	42.5	37.0	39.7	35.5	41.1	53.1	44.1
Fixed Assets (net)	39.6	41.0	39.9	42.0	43.4	44.2	42.3	32.5	37.7
Intangibles (net)	7.1	6.8	8.2	9.8	7.4	11.2	4.0	7.6	10.6
All Other Non-Current	9.8	7.8	9.4	11.2	9.6	9.1	12.6	6.7	7.6
Total	100.0	100.0	100.0	100.0	100.0	100.0	100.0	100.0	100.0
LIABILITIES									
Notes Payable-Short Term	7.6	9.3	8.4	3.7	18.4	3.5	4.1	8.4	9.3
Cur. Mat.-L.T.D.	6.8	6.9	6.4	7.5	5.9	7.1	6.7	4.7	6.9
Trade Payables	9.8	12.5	10.6	14.2	9.3	10.7	6.8	8.6	14.4
Income Taxes Payable	.7	.3	.4	.2	.0	1.0	.7	.3	.2
All Other Current	6.2	5.8	11.0	21.9	16.1	6.4	6.1	8.6	6.8
Total Current	31.0	34.7	36.7	47.6	49.7	28.7	24.3	30.6	37.6
Long-Term Debt	25.9	24.4	28.5	43.4	28.8	32.7	28.3	10.9	31.7
Deferred Taxes	.4	.8	.2	.5	.0	.0	.4	.3	.0
All Other Non-Current	5.3	8.2	7.6	7.4	11.9	5.8	7.2	7.4	5.1
Net Worth	37.3	31.9	27.0	.9	9.6	32.8	39.7	50.8	25.6
Total Liabilities & Net Worth	100.0	100.0	100.0	100.0	100.0	100.0	100.0	100.0	100.0
INCOME DATA									
Net Sales	100.0	100.0	100.0	100.0	100.0	100.0	100.0	100.0	100.0
Gross Profit									
Operating Expenses	92.0	94.2	92.9	92.0	93.1	96.7	93.1	91.9	92.6
Operating Profit	8.0	5.8	7.1	8.0	6.9	3.3	6.9	8.1	7.4
All Other Expenses (net)	1.6	1.8	2.0	2.4	3.2	.5	2.2	1.7	1.5
Profit Before Taxes	6.4	4.0	5.0	5.6	3.7	2.8	4.7	6.4	5.9
RATIOS									
Current	2.7	2.4	2.4	7.2	2.1	2.1	4.4	3.7	1.3
	1.4	1.3	1.3	1.5	.6	1.2	1.9	1.6	1.1
	.8	.8	.8	.3	.4	1.0	.9	1.0	.9
Quick	2.4	2.0	2.1	7.2	1.9	1.9	2.8	2.6	1.0
	1.2	1.0	1.1	1.4	.5	1.1	1.6	1.3	.9
	.6	.6	.6	.3	.2	.9	.7	1.0	.7
Sales/Receivables	24 15.5	25 14.6	13 29.1	0 UND	0 UND	13 27.7	19 19.1	34 10.6	34 10.8
	37 9.8	41 9.0	39 9.3	10 37.3	18 20.4	39 9.3	40 9.2	46 7.9	50 7.4
	65 5.7	67 5.4	52 7.0	37 9.8	43 8.4	50 7.3	52 7.0	77 4.8	66 5.5
Cost of Sales/Inventory									
Cost of Sales/Payables									
Sales/Working Capital	6.5	7.4	7.5	6.1	8.3	7.8	4.4	4.4	21.0
	25.0	24.6	31.3	49.2	-27.7	40.9	9.9	10.5	73.5
	-32.5	-24.6	-28.7	-12.1	-11.3	-466.4	-58.7	UND	-43.5
EBIT/Interest	11.3	8.5	9.0	12.1	5.4	7.8	10.4	76.1	7.0
	(134) 4.3	(112) 2.9	(113) 3.7	(14) 2.9	(19) 1.4	(12) 1.5	4.0	(23) 8.8	(22) 3.9
	1.8	1.0	1.1	-.1	-.6	.8	-.9	1.9	2.1
Net Profit + Depr., Dep., Amort./Cur. Mat. L/T/D	4.1	4.7	3.0						
	(30) 2.0	(24) 2.0	(20) 2.3						
	1.1	1.4	1.2						
Fixed/Worth	.5	.5	.6	.7	.4	1.1	.5	.2	1.1
	1.5	1.8	1.6	4.5	1.5	2.3	1.2	1.2	1.9
	5.0	11.1	9.8	-42.6	-13.5	NM	3.1	2.1	-50.0
Debt/Worth	.7	.8	.8	.9	.6	1.5	.7	.4	1.7
	1.9	2.7	2.5	6.4	12.4	5.7	1.7	1.4	5.2
	6.3	20.1	226.7	-7.0	-6.9	NM	4.6	2.1	-76.4
% Profit Before Taxes/Tangible Net Worth	52.9	49.6	66.3	208.9	62.8	75.0	41.8	53.6	108.9
	(120) 25.1	(99) 20.8	(99) 19.3	(13) 58.3	(15) 11.0	(10) 24.0	(21) 7.1	(23) 23.7	(17) 23.9
	12.3	3.9	3.2	4.5	-2.4	-.6	-22.2	6.8	17.3
% Profit Before Taxes/Total Assets	22.2	15.0	18.9	52.5	22.5	14.7	13.6	19.7	17.1
	9.8	5.3	7.0	12.5	1.7	3.4	3.3	8.9	7.0
	2.7	.0	.6	1.6	-4.3	-1.0	-3.8	1.3	3.8
Sales/Net Fixed Assets	14.1	15.2	15.2	13.5	47.1	7.9	9.7	23.9	18.6
	6.3	4.5	6.4	5.1	11.3	4.1	5.4	11.0	6.8
	2.8	2.4	3.0	1.6	3.3	3.0	2.2	2.9	2.9
Sales/Total Assets	3.0	2.7	3.4	4.6	6.7	3.3	3.1	2.8	3.3
	2.1	1.8	2.1	1.8	3.5	1.9	1.9	2.1	2.0
	1.4	1.2	1.2	.6	1.2	1.5	1.2	1.1	1.2
% Depr., Dep., Amort./Sales	2.5	2.0	2.4	4.2	3.2	3.4	2.7	1.7	1.5
	(124) 4.9	(108) 5.4	(106) 5.9	(13) 9.1	(17) 6.2	6.0	(19) 4.8	(22) 4.9	(22) 4.9
	8.9	10.1	10.6	24.9	11.5	8.9	12.4	9.9	9.0
% Officers', Directors' Owners' Comp/Sales	2.2	2.1	3.1		4.5	2.4			
	(60) 4.4	(40) 4.3	(46) 5.6		(12) 6.3	(10) 7.0			
	9.7	8.3	9.0		8.9	16.4			
Net Sales ($)	1988890M	1591795M	1900693M	10392M	43271M	50596M	161850M	379309M	1255275M
Total Assets ($)	1363086M	1239734M	1411344M	13017M	41875M	26387M	153837M	428936M	747292M

© RMA 2011

M = $ thousand   MM = $ million

See Pages 9 through 22 for Explanation of Ratios and Data

EDUCATIONAL SERVICES

Current Data Sorted by Assets　　　　　　　　　　Comparative Historical Data

0-500M	500M-2MM	2-10MM	10-50MM	50-100MM	100-250MM	Type of Statement	4/1/06-3/31/07 ALL	4/1/07-3/31/08 ALL
34	116	318	631	190	123	Unqualified	1037	1004
2	11	56	17	2		Reviewed	85	68
9	14	24	7	3		Compiled	52	47
24	30	27	3		1	Tax Returns	59	51
41	69	112	97	26	11	Other	247	277
	1,840 (4/1-9/30/10)			158 (10/1/10-3/31/11)				
110	240	537	755	221	135	**NUMBER OF STATEMENTS**	1480	1447
%	%	%	%	%	%	**ASSETS**	%	%
34.1	30.0	21.6	19.0	18.6	16.7	Cash & Equivalents	22.6	22.6
11.2	14.7	6.5	4.0	3.6	5.0	Trade Receivables (net)	6.5	6.6
1.5	.3	.2	.1	.1	.2	Inventory	.2	.3
6.9	3.8	3.1	2.5	2.6	3.0	All Other Current	4.2	4.0
53.8	48.7	31.4	25.6	25.0	24.9	Total Current	33.4	33.4
32.2	41.0	60.2	62.0	58.4	59.9	Fixed Assets (net)	54.3	54.9
3.8	1.8	.5	.6	.6	.9	Intangibles (net)	1.0	.7
10.2	8.5	7.9	11.8	16.0	14.3	All Other Non-Current	11.3	10.9
100.0	100.0	100.0	100.0	100.0	100.0	Total	100.0	100.0
						LIABILITIES		
12.7	4.2	2.7	1.3	1.0	1.0	Notes Payable-Short Term	2.8	2.6
2.1	2.7	2.4	1.7	1.6	2.1	Cur. Mat.-L.T.D.	2.2	2.1
8.2	6.9	3.4	2.1	1.6	2.5	Trade Payables	3.7	4.1
.0	.1	.1	.0	.0	.1	Income Taxes Payable	.1	.1
39.1	19.4	10.0	8.3	7.0	6.4	All Other Current	11.3	10.8
62.2	33.3	18.7	13.3	11.2	12.1	Total Current	20.2	19.7
21.6	22.0	32.2	31.5	34.1	37.7	Long-Term Debt	28.4	28.2
.0	.0	.0	.0	.0	.0	Deferred Taxes	.0	.0
11.0	5.7	5.0	4.8	3.9	3.9	All Other Non-Current	5.5	5.6
5.1	38.9	44.1	50.4	50.8	46.2	Net Worth	46.0	46.6
100.0	100.0	100.0	100.0	100.0	100.0	Total Liabilities & Net Worth	100.0	100.0
						INCOME DATA		
100.0	100.0	100.0	100.0	100.0	100.0	Net Sales	100.0	100.0
						Gross Profit		
96.4	94.2	94.1	94.8	94.8	94.4	Operating Expenses	92.9	91.5
3.6	5.8	5.9	5.2	5.2	5.6	Operating Profit	7.1	8.5
1.5	1.6	3.2	1.5	.4	1.4	All Other Expenses (net)	1.2	1.1
2.1	4.1	2.7	3.7	4.8	4.2	Profit Before Taxes	5.9	7.4
						RATIOS		
4.7	3.6	3.9	4.1	4.1	3.5		4.3	4.4
1.5	1.4	1.9	1.9	1.9	2.0	Current	1.9	1.9
.4	.8	.9	1.1	1.1	1.2		.9	1.0
3.9	3.2	3.5	3.7	3.8	3.2		3.9	3.9
1.1	1.4	1.7	1.6	1.7	1.7	Quick	1.6 (1445)	1.7
.4	.7	.8	.9	.9	1.0		.7	.8
0 UND	0 947.6	1 281.7	2 206.1	3 136.8	3 126.8		1 316.8	1 368.2
1 253.2	8 45.0	8 43.6	8 45.3	12 31.2	11 32.4	Sales/Receivables	7 53.6	7 52.2
15 24.8	32 11.3	28 12.9	26 13.9	35 10.3	57 6.4		28 13.0	26 14.1
						Cost of Sales/Inventory		
						Cost of Sales/Payables		
10.3	6.5	3.6	2.6	2.3	2.5		2.8	3.0
42.0	18.1	8.9	6.5	5.5	5.4	Sales/Working Capital	8.3	8.2
-20.1	-34.0	-75.3	46.9	28.4	27.4		-88.6	529.4
10.4	12.1	4.5	4.8	5.2	3.6		6.7	7.9
(50) 1.4	(147) 2.8	(412) 1.5	(650) 2.0	(194) 2.4	(120) 1.8	EBIT/Interest	(1109) 2.6	(1092) 2.9
-2.6	.6	.3	.7	1.0	.7		.9	1.1
						Net Profit + Depr., Dep.,	12.0	7.5
						Amort./Cur. Mat. L/T/D	(14) 3.4 (19) 3.8	
							1.7	.1
.1	.2	.7	.8	.7	.9		.6	.6
1.0	.8	1.4	1.2	1.0	1.5	Fixed/Worth	1.1	1.1
UND	2.6	3.2	2.0	2.0	2.8		2.3	2.3
.5	.4	.4	.5	.4	.4		.4	.4
1.7	1.0	1.2	1.0	.8	1.5	Debt/Worth	1.0	1.0
-4.9	5.7	3.6	2.0	1.9	2.9		2.7	2.6
85.5	35.3	15.6	8.7	9.2	8.9	% Profit Before Taxes/Tangible	16.8	19.3
(78) 19.4	(200) 12.9	(500) 4.5	(739) 3.2	(217) 3.5	(131) 4.0	Net Worth	(1383) 6.5	(1373) 8.6
-8.9	-.8	-4.1	-1.0	-.1	-.8		.4	1.0
31.0	15.3	6.3	4.1	4.1	3.7	% Profit Before Taxes/Total	7.6	8.8
6.4	5.2	1.7	1.4	1.9	1.6	Assets	3.1	3.9
-9.3	-1.7	-1.7	-.5	.0	-.5		-.1	.3
191.0	40.1	2.9	1.2	1.0	1.2		3.1	3.2
24.7	8.6	1.1	.8	.7	.8	Sales/Net Fixed Assets	1.1	1.1
7.6	2.1	.7	.5	.5	.5		.7	.7
8.7	3.7	1.4	.7	.6	.7		1.2	1.4
5.2	2.2	.7	.5	.4	.5	Sales/Total Assets	.7	.7
2.6	1.2	.5	.3	.3	.3		.4	.4
.6	1.0	2.8	4.1	3.7	3.3		2.7	2.6
(60) 1.7	(184) 2.1	(451) 4.7	(680) 6.0	(197) 6.0	(117) 5.1	% Depr., Dep., Amort./Sales	(1192) 4.6	(1160) 4.5
2.7	3.8	6.8	8.1	9.1	8.1		6.5	6.4
4.1	3.4	3.5	3.5			% Officers', Directors'	4.1	3.7
(25) 7.2	(42) 6.2	(57) 7.5	(48) 7.0			Owners' Comp/Sales	(177) 7.6	(153) 7.1
11.4	11.8	15.1	17.7				16.1	13.3
157227M	673611M	3291669M	11500812M	8091578M	14117465M	Net Sales ($)	24700690M	29106068M
25018M	265964M	3008060M	18244827M	15616439M	19881991M	Total Assets ($)	36506894M	35983798M

© RMA 2011

M = $ thousand　　MM = $ million
See Pages 9 through 22 for Explanation of Ratios and Data

Comparative Historical Data | Current Data Sorted by Sales

Hist 1	Hist 2	Hist 3	Type of Statement	0-1MM	1-3MM	3-5MM	5-10MM	10-25MM	25MM & OVER
1234	1303	1412	Unqualified	26	159	181	326	419	301
78	73	88	Reviewed	3	30	26	21	7	1
54	58	57	Compiled	13	23	7	7	7	
65	75	85	Tax Returns	32	38	6	4	5	
314	341	356	Other	33	97	57	66	72	31
4/1/08-3/31/09	4/1/09-3/31/10	4/1/10-3/31/11		1,840 (4/1-9/30/10)			158 (10/1/10-3/31/11)		
ALL	ALL	ALL							
1745	1850	1998	**NUMBER OF STATEMENTS**	107	347	277	424	510	333
%	%	%	**ASSETS**	%	%	%	%	%	%
23.2	21.5	21.6	Cash & Equivalents	20.2	22.8	23.2	21.3	19.6	23.2
7.1	6.3	6.4	Trade Receivables (net)	4.7	9.7	6.1	5.4	5.3	6.7
.3	.2	.2	Inventory	.5	.4	.2	.1	.2	.2
3.6	2.8	3.1	All Other Current	3.1	2.8	3.0	2.6	3.1	4.2
34.3	30.7	31.4	Total Current	28.5	35.7	32.4	29.4	28.2	34.4
52.9	59.0	56.8	Fixed Assets (net)	60.2	54.4	57.6	59.0	56.3	55.5
.9	.9	.9	Intangibles (net)	2.4	2.0	.8	.4	.4	.7
11.9	9.5	10.9	All Other Non-Current	9.0	7.9	9.2	11.2	15.0	9.4
100.0	100.0	100.0	Total	100.0	100.0	100.0	100.0	100.0	100.0
			LIABILITIES						
2.9	2.8	2.6	Notes Payable-Short Term	6.4	4.9	2.2	2.3	1.6	1.3
1.9	2.3	2.0	Cur. Mat.-L.T.D.	2.3	2.5	1.8	2.2	1.4	2.4
3.9	3.3	3.3	Trade Payables	1.9	4.8	3.8	2.7	2.7	3.7
.1	.1	.1	Income Taxes Payable	.0	.1	.0	.0	.1	.1
10.7	10.7	11.5	All Other Current	16.4	16.0	11.8	10.3	9.6	9.5
19.6	19.2	19.5	Total Current	27.0	28.3	19.7	17.5	15.4	16.8
28.3	31.4	30.7	Long-Term Debt	38.8	30.1	30.8	27.2	28.9	35.8
.0	.0	.0	Deferred Taxes	.0	.0	.0	.0	.0	.0
5.1	5.6	5.1	All Other Non-Current	5.4	6.6	5.1	5.0	4.5	4.7
47.0	43.8	44.6	Net Worth	28.7	35.0	44.3	50.3	51.1	42.7
100.0	100.0	100.0	Total Liabilities & Net Worth	100.0	100.0	100.0	100.0	100.0	100.0
			INCOME DATA						
100.0	100.0	100.0	Net Sales	100.0	100.0	100.0	100.0	100.0	100.0
			Gross Profit						
94.1	95.9	94.6	Operating Expenses	88.4	94.4	95.4	95.1	95.0	95.0
5.9	4.1	5.4	Operating Profit	11.6	5.6	4.6	4.9	5.0	5.0
2.9	4.4	1.8	All Other Expenses (net)	9.1	2.6	2.3	1.0	.6	1.3
3.0	-.3	3.5	Profit Before Taxes	2.5	3.0	2.3	3.9	4.4	3.7
			RATIOS						
4.4	3.9	4.0		4.0	4.2	4.2	4.5	3.8	3.7
2.0	1.8	1.9	Current	1.0	1.6	1.9	2.0	1.9	2.0
1.0	.9	1.0		.3	.7	.9	1.0	1.1	1.3
3.9	3.5	3.6		3.0	3.8	3.6	3.8	3.4	3.2
1.8	(1849) 1.6	1.6	Quick	.9	1.5	1.7	1.8	1.6	1.7
.8	.8	.8		.3	.6	.8	.8	.9	1.1
1 370.2	1 339.4	1 277.2		0 UND	0 837.5	2 217.2	2 175.6	2 174.6	1 396.4
7 51.8	7 54.6	8 43.6	Sales/Receivables	1 499.0	7 49.5	7 50.0	8 47.2	10 34.9	11 33.1
28 13.1	24 15.5	28 13.0		18 20.5	29 12.8	28 12.8	25 14.4	30 12.1	32 11.3
			Cost of Sales/Inventory						
			Cost of Sales/Payables						
3.0	3.2	3.2		6.7	4.3	3.2	2.6	2.9	3.2
7.9	9.0	8.3	Sales/Working Capital	221.7	12.5	8.6	6.9	7.1	7.2
178.8	-163.3	-318.0		-7.8	-29.2	-56.2	-151.3	60.6	24.2
4.9	3.7	5.0		2.6	4.9	3.4	7.5	5.4	4.2
(1321) 1.8	(1447) 1.2	(1573) 2.0	EBIT/Interest	(54) 1.1	(246) 1.6	(202) 1.4	(346) 2.3	(431) 2.3	(294) 2.2
.3	-.7	.6		-.6	.1	.3	.4	.8	1.1
7.9	10.2	4.1							
(16) 3.9	(17) 2.7	(13) 2.1	Net Profit + Depr., Dep., Amort./Cur. Mat. L/T/D						
1.5	1.8	.9							
.6	.7	.7		.6	.5	.7	.8	.7	.7
1.1	1.2	1.2	Fixed/Worth	2.1	1.4	1.3	1.1	1.1	1.3
2.3	2.5	2.4		23.6	4.0	2.8	1.9	1.9	2.3
.4	.4	.4		.6	.4	.5	.4	.4	.5
.9	1.1	1.0	Debt/Worth	2.3	1.5	1.1	.9	.9	1.2
2.7	2.6	2.7		40.3	4.7	3.4	1.9	1.9	2.8
14.9	11.8	12.3		39.8	18.5	13.1	11.0	10.5	11.2
(1631) 4.2	(1726) 1.5	(1865) 4.0	% Profit Before Taxes/Tangible Net Worth	(84) 3.9	(298) 3.5	(255) 3.1	(408) 3.7	(501) 3.7	(319) 5.9
-2.5	-6.5	-1.6		-7.8	-4.9	-4.5	-1.9	-.4	.1
6.2	5.0	5.6		8.8	8.4	4.4	5.3	4.7	5.1
1.8	.6	1.8	% Profit Before Taxes/Total Assets	.6	2.1	1.2	1.6	1.8	2.3
-1.3	-3.3	-.8		-3.5	-2.0	-1.9	-1.1	-.3	.1
3.6	2.6	2.7		11.9	16.5	4.0	1.8	1.4	2.3
1.1	1.0	1.0	Sales/Net Fixed Assets	1.3	1.5	1.0	.9	.8	1.1
.7	.6	.6		.4	.6	.5	.6	.5	.8
1.4	1.3	1.3		2.6	2.6	1.6	1.0	.8	1.4
.7	.6	.6	Sales/Total Assets	.8	.9	.6	.6	.5	.7
.4	.4	.4		.3	.5	.4	.4	.3	.5
2.6	2.6	2.9		2.0	1.9	2.7	3.7	3.8	2.3
(1402) 4.7	(1565) 4.7	(1689) 5.0	% Depr., Dep., Amort./Sales	(72) 5.2	(271) 3.8	(242) 5.1	(381) 5.4	(453) 6.0	(270) 3.7
6.7	7.1	7.4		12.6	6.8	7.2	7.9	8.1	5.5
3.6	3.7	3.7		5.7	3.7	2.8	4.2	3.0	3.3
(179) 7.6	(216) 7.1	(190) 6.5	% Officers', Directors' Owners' Comp/Sales	(20) 7.3	(49) 5.4	(25) 5.4	(29) 9.0	(43) 4.9	(24) 5.7
13.8	14.4	12.4		11.5	11.4	16.8	21.9	12.6	15.1
38437550M	36506660M	37832362M	Net Sales ($)	58332M	680768M	1091926M	3138678M	7948743M	24913915M
53819064M	51921585M	57042299M	Total Assets ($)	131904M	1096570M	1975803M	6168797M	18454047M	29215178M

M = $ thousand   MM = $ million

See Pages 9 through 22 for Explanation of Ratios and Data

Current Data Sorted by Assets   Comparative Historical Data

	0-500M	500M-2MM	2-10MM	10-50MM	50-100MM	100-250MM	Type of Statement	ALL 4/1/06-3/31/07	ALL 4/1/07-3/31/08
		4	11	23	11	11	Unqualified	37	41
	1		1				Reviewed		
		2					Compiled	2	1
							Tax Returns	1	
	1	2	3	6	3	1	Other	13	10
	1	63 (4/1-9/30/10)		17 (10/1/10-3/31/11)					
NUMBER OF STATEMENTS	2	8	15	29	14	12		53	52
	%	%	%	%	%	%	**ASSETS**	%	%
			32.3	23.2	18.6	18.7	Cash & Equivalents	19.2	20.7
			14.9	10.5	6.4	7.8	Trade Receivables (net)	12.6	10.0
			1.5	.9	.9	.2	Inventory	1.0	1.2
			1.8	1.8	3.4	.9	All Other Current	3.2	2.7
			50.5	36.4	29.4	27.6	Total Current	36.0	34.6
			44.1	43.6	51.5	57.1	Fixed Assets (net)	46.2	46.9
			.1	3.3	6.0	.1	Intangibles (net)	1.6	4.5
			5.3	16.6	13.2	15.2	All Other Non-Current	16.2	14.0
			100.0	100.0	100.0	100.0	Total	100.0	100.0
							LIABILITIES		
			1.7	2.5	.4	.0	Notes Payable-Short Term	.7	1.0
			.6	1.4	2.7	1.6	Cur. Mat.-L.T.D.	2.5	1.9
			1.9	3.8	3.8	3.1	Trade Payables	4.5	4.6
			.5	.3	.0	.0	Income Taxes Payable	.3	.3
			17.0	9.0	9.5	7.8	All Other Current	11.4	7.0
			21.7	17.0	16.5	12.5	Total Current	19.3	14.8
			21.2	17.2	23.3	31.1	Long-Term Debt	29.8	22.8
			.2	.3	.0	.0	Deferred Taxes	.3	.5
			1.8	8.0	6.5	4.2	All Other Non-Current	3.8	4.3
			55.2	57.4	53.7	52.2	Net Worth	46.7	57.7
			100.0	100.0	100.0	100.0	Total Liabilities & Net Worth	100.0	100.0
							INCOME DATA		
			100.0	100.0	100.0	100.0	Net Sales	100.0	100.0
							Gross Profit		
			81.8	90.8	95.1	92.9	Operating Expenses	93.0	91.1
			18.2	9.2	4.9	7.1	Operating Profit	7.0	8.9
			3.3	-1.3	-2.7	-.3	All Other Expenses (net)	.1	-1.0
			14.8	10.5	7.6	7.4	Profit Before Taxes	6.9	9.9
							RATIOS		
			11.5	5.4	2.8	3.9		4.1	5.2
			2.3	2.8	1.9	2.3	Current	1.8	2.6
			1.4	1.2	1.7	1.4		1.1	1.4
			11.5	5.2	2.6	3.9		3.7	4.9
			2.2	2.6	1.8	2.2	Quick	1.7	2.2
			1.3	1.0	1.3	1.3		.9	1.0
			(10) 37.2	(10) 37.9	(9) 41.4	(18) 20.7		(12) 31.0	(11) 34.6
			27 13.7	29 12.4	29 12.7	43 8.4	Sales/Receivables	23 16.2	25 14.7
			73 5.0	50 7.3	45 8.0	86 4.2		75 4.9	46 7.9
							Cost of Sales/Inventory		
							Cost of Sales/Payables		
			2.9	2.0	4.0	2.3		3.5	2.4
			7.1	5.8	5.9	6.3	Sales/Working Capital	7.8	4.5
			16.5	22.2	-10.4	9.4		34.1	13.8
				30.5	51.8	15.0		10.0	13.0
				(22) 7.0	(12) 7.6	(11) 4.5	EBIT/Interest	(43) 4.0	(43) 6.3
				3.1	3.0	2.1		2.0	2.8
							Net Profit + Depr., Dep., Amort./Cur. Mat. L/T/D		
			.2	.5	.7	.7		.7	.6
			1.0	.8	.8	1.2	Fixed/Worth	.9	.9
			1.1	1.2	1.0	1.7		1.3	1.2
			.4	.2	.4	.3		.4	.4
			.7	1.0	.6	1.0	Debt/Worth	1.1	.7
			3.3	2.3	.9	2.3		2.1	1.5
			47.5	48.4	14.0	18.3		38.1	30.9
			22.2	(28) 11.1	(13) 7.2	5.7	% Profit Before Taxes/Tangible Net Worth	(52) 9.0	(50) 10.4
			7.6	4.4	2.0	.3		3.5	5.2
			28.5	14.8	8.1	7.8		13.5	12.8
			9.3	6.1	5.6	3.6	% Profit Before Taxes/Total Assets	4.3	6.4
			4.2	1.5	2.0	.0		2.0	2.4
			16.2	6.7	3.2	1.1		5.4	5.9
			1.7	1.7	1.5	.9	Sales/Net Fixed Assets	2.2	1.4
			1.2	.8	1.0	.7		.9	.8
			1.8	1.4	1.1	.8		1.8	1.2
			1.0	.8	.8	.5	Sales/Total Assets	.9	.8
			.6	.4	.5	.4		.5	.5
			1.9	2.5	2.3	3.3		2.0	2.4
			(13) 2.7	(26) 4.8	4.5	4.2	% Depr., Dep., Amort./Sales	(49) 3.7	(46) 4.6
			5.6	6.6	6.2	6.9		5.6	6.4
							% Officers', Directors' Owners' Comp/Sales		
	3140M	25346M	105706M	568950M	945161M	1169807M	Net Sales ($)	2155121M	2399822M
	337M	10172M	89808M	650714M	957085M	2212223M	Total Assets ($)	2711356M	3425107M

© RMA 2011

M = $ thousand   MM = $ million
See Pages 9 through 22 for Explanation of Ratios and Data

Comparative Historical Data

Current Data Sorted by Sales

				Type of Statement						
57	48	60		Unqualified		4	3	16	14	23
1	4			Reviewed						
		2		Compiled		2				
1	1	2		Tax Returns		2				
13	13	16		Other	2	2	1	3		8
4/1/08-	4/1/09-	4/1/10-				63 (4/1-9/30/10)		17 (10/1/10-3/31/11)		
3/31/09	3/31/10	3/31/11			0-1MM	1-3MM	3-5MM	5-10MM	10-25MM	25MM & OVER
ALL	ALL	ALL								
72	66	80		NUMBER OF STATEMENTS	2	10	4	16	17	31
%	%	%		ASSETS	%	%	%	%	%	%
19.7	21.4	24.4		Cash & Equivalents		30.3		22.8	26.8	21.6
8.2	9.1	13.7		Trade Receivables (net)		28.1		9.4	15.0	9.3
.8	.8	.9		Inventory		.1		1.5	1.4	.8
3.1	4.4	1.8		All Other Current		1.7		2.5	1.4	2.0
31.8	35.7	40.8		Total Current		60.2		36.2	44.6	33.7
51.8	46.4	44.0		Fixed Assets (net)		36.2		51.0	39.1	48.8
1.7	3.3	2.3		Intangibles (net)		.0		.1	.2	5.7
14.7	14.6	12.9		All Other Non-Current		3.6		12.7	16.1	11.8
100.0	100.0	100.0		Total		100.0		100.0	100.0	100.0
				LIABILITIES						
1.2	1.2	2.5		Notes Payable-Short Term		.0		1.6	2.2	1.3
3.2	2.8	1.8		Cur. Mat.-L.T.D.		.2		2.9	.9	2.4
3.9	6.1	4.5		Trade Payables		8.6		3.7	3.1	4.5
.2	.1	.2		Income Taxes Payable		.3		.3	.2	.1
9.3	12.2	12.1		All Other Current		13.0		12.2	15.4	10.4
17.8	22.4	21.0		Total Current		22.0		20.7	21.8	18.7
26.1	20.9	19.6		Long-Term Debt		19.8		15.3	11.0	25.9
.2	.2	.4		Deferred Taxes		.0		1.4	.1	.2
5.0	4.8	5.8		All Other Non-Current		.7		7.4	8.2	6.3
50.9	51.7	53.2		Net Worth		57.5		55.2	58.8	48.9
100.0	100.0	100.0		Total Liabilties & Net Worth		100.0		100.0	100.0	100.0
				INCOME DATA						
100.0	100.0	100.0		Net Sales		100.0		100.0	100.0	100.0
				Gross Profit						
92.9	94.3	90.4		Operating Expenses		92.0		92.0	92.7	91.7
7.1	5.7	9.6		Operating Profit		8.0		8.0	7.3	8.3
1.3	2.6	-.5		All Other Expenses (net)		-.9		-.9	-1.7	-.9
5.8	3.1	10.1		Profit Before Taxes		8.9		8.8	9.0	9.3
				RATIOS						
3.2	2.7	4.3				16.0		6.3	4.3	2.8
1.8	1.7	2.2		Current		12.2		2.2	3.3	1.9
1.1	1.2	1.3				2.2		.7	1.5	1.3
3.1	2.4	4.1				14.4		5.3	4.1	2.5
1.7	1.5	2.1		Quick		10.7		2.1	3.0	1.9
.9	.9	1.2				2.2		.4	1.1	1.3

6	57.6	10	37.2	10	35.2			0	UND			7	52.8	11	34.3	13	28.0
17	22.0	23	15.8	28	12.8	Sales/Receivables		41	9.0			15	23.6	40	9.2	31	11.9
41	8.8	45	8.1	53	6.9			98	3.7			27	13.3	57	6.4	56	6.5

			Cost of Sales/Inventory						

			Cost of Sales/Payables						

3.2	3.3	2.9				1.8		3.1	2.4	4.3
6.9	7.8	6.2	Sales/Working Capital			3.4		8.6	4.2	7.2
69.4	36.9	14.3				9.4		NM	8.8	10.8

	9.8		27.4		34.3						34.8	152.5			31.4
(59)	4.4	(55)	3.2	(58)	8.2	EBIT/Interest	(11)	17.2	(11)		10.9		(29)		7.2
	1.8		.1		3.4						1.2	6.8			2.9

			Net Profit + Depr., Dep.,						
			Amort./Cur. Mat. L/T/D						

.6	.7	.5				.0		.6	.4	.7
.9	.9	.8	Fixed/Worth			.5		1.0	.7	.9
1.5	1.3	1.2				1.0		1.6	.9	1.5
.4	.5	.3				.1		.2	.2	.5
.8	.8	.8	Debt/Worth			.7		.7	.5	.9
1.6	1.5	2.4				3.7		2.3	2.0	2.5

	25.1		39.0		39.2	% Profit Before Taxes/Tangible			37.9		27.1	51.3			35.0
(68)	5.8	(64)	7.1	(77)	12.9	Net Worth			18.5		12.2	10.0	(29)		11.0
	1.8		-1.0		4.4				-1.4		1.4	.7			4.9
	8.3		16.0		15.5	% Profit Before Taxes/Total			27.9		15.5	23.1			11.4
	2.9		3.5		6.9	Assets			9.3		6.5	6.6			6.1
	1.1		-.9		2.4				-1.3		1.1	.6			2.7
	4.6		6.1		7.9				UND		6.5	11.0			5.9
	1.2		1.2		1.6	Sales/Net Fixed Assets			5.1		1.6	1.7			1.5
	.8		.8		.9				.5		1.0	.7			1.0
	1.5		2.0		1.7				2.6		1.1	1.9			1.3
	.7		.7		.8	Sales/Total Assets			1.2		.8	.8			.8
	.5		.5		.5				.4		.6	.4			.5

	2.5		2.3		2.2	% Depr., Dep., Amort./Sales					2.4	2.1			2.2
(69)	4.4	(60)	3.7	(71)	3.9					(15)	4.5	4.3	(29)		3.7
	7.0		6.3		6.1						6.1	6.8			5.6

			% Officers', Directors'						
			Owners' Comp/Sales						

2885334M	2874920M	2818110M		Net Sales ($)	1476M	17877M	17806M	112826M	299449M	2368676M
4194995M	3683554M	3920339M		Total Assets ($)	3193M	38128M	56089M	157137M	571181M	3094611M

© RMA 2011

M = $ thousand   MM = $ million
See Pages 9 through 22 for Explanation of Ratios and Data

Current Data Sorted by Assets   **Comparative Historical Data**

	0-500M	500M-2MM	2-10MM	10-50MM	50-100MM	100-250MM	4/1/06-3/31/07 ALL	4/1/07-3/31/08 ALL
Type of Statement								
Unqualified	2	7	50	186	161	240	597	505
Reviewed		1				1	6	10
Compiled	1		2				2	3
Tax Returns	3	1	3	3	3	1	1	5
Other	1	5	20	31	27	28	97	98
		703 (4/1-9/30/10)		74 (10/1/10-3/31/11)				
NUMBER OF STATEMENTS	7	14	75	220	191	270	703	621
ASSETS	%	%	%	%	%	%	%	%
Cash & Equivalents		31.8	20.9	18.1	14.4	15.1	15.9	16.4
Trade Receivables (net)		13.3	10.2	5.6	4.1	3.6	5.8	5.4
Inventory		2.6	1.1	.7	.2	.4	.5	.5
All Other Current		2.3	3.7	3.5	2.8	2.7	3.3	3.4
Total Current		50.0	35.8	27.9	21.5	21.8	25.6	25.8
Fixed Assets (net)		31.9	49.7	52.6	54.1	50.3	47.0	47.4
Intangibles (net)		5.5	1.1	1.0	1.1	1.3	1.5	1.1
All Other Non-Current		12.5	13.4	18.5	23.3	26.5	25.9	25.8
Total		100.0	100.0	100.0	100.0	100.0	100.0	100.0
LIABILITIES								
Notes Payable-Short Term		18.6	5.2	1.6	2.0	.6	1.7	1.6
Cur. Mat.-L.T.D.		6.1	3.2	2.1	1.4	1.1	1.5	1.4
Trade Payables		4.9	5.6	3.3	2.6	2.5	3.1	3.4
Income Taxes Payable		.0	.8	.1	.0	.0	.1	.2
All Other Current		5.2	13.7	7.6	5.7	4.8	7.4	5.9
Total Current		34.8	28.5	14.6	11.7	9.1	13.7	12.5
Long-Term Debt		25.6	24.0	27.4	28.5	26.7	24.4	26.7
Deferred Taxes		.9	.2	.0	.1	.0	.1	.1
All Other Non-Current		11.0	5.6	5.8	4.2	4.9	4.4	4.6
Net Worth		27.7	41.7	52.2	55.5	59.3	57.5	56.1
Total Liabilties & Net Worth		100.0	100.0	100.0	100.0	100.0	100.0	100.0
INCOME DATA								
Net Sales		100.0	100.0	100.0	100.0	100.0	100.0	100.0
Gross Profit								
Operating Expenses		85.8	93.0	90.7	92.7	90.9	90.7	88.7
Operating Profit		14.2	7.0	9.3	7.3	9.1	9.3	11.3
All Other Expenses (net)		2.3	2.3	1.9	.0	.1	-.4	-.1
Profit Before Taxes		11.9	4.7	7.4	7.4	9.0	9.7	11.4
RATIOS								
Current		7.4	2.8	4.1	3.4	3.8	3.9	4.1
		3.4	1.1	1.7	1.7	1.9	1.8	1.9
		1.1	.7	.9	.8	1.2	1.0	1.0
Quick		7.1	2.4	3.6	2.9	3.2	3.2	3.5
		3.3	1.0	1.3	1.1	1.6	1.4	1.5
		.2	.5	.7	.6	.9	.7	.8
Sales/Receivables		0 UND	5 80.3	6 62.3	8 43.7	8 44.4	7 51.1	7 55.0
		3 106.9	8 45.3	14 26.8	16 22.2	17 21.2	17 21.2	15 24.5
		37 9.9	23 15.7	30 12.0	35 10.5	32 11.5	36 10.2	34 10.7
Cost of Sales/Inventory								
Cost of Sales/Payables								
Sales/Working Capital		2.7	4.9	3.2	3.0	2.3	2.7	2.6
		3.7	37.8	8.6	9.1	5.9	8.0	7.3
		NM	-14.7	-39.4	-22.5	26.2	-171.2	206.6
EBIT/Interest			8.7	7.6	7.3	7.4	9.1	9.2
			(59) 2.7	(187) 3.3	(164) 4.2	(229) 3.8	(548) 4.3	(474) 5.0
			-.7	1.3	1.8	1.8	1.9	2.2
Net Profit + Depr., Dep., Amort./Cur. Mat. L/T/D							8.1	8.3
							(25) 2.4	(24) 2.4
							1.1	.8
Fixed/Worth		.0	.5	.6	.7	.6	.5	.6
		.9	1.1	1.0	.9	.9	.8	.8
		1.9	2.3	1.5	1.4	1.2	1.2	1.2
Debt/Worth		.5	.4	.4	.5	.4	.3	.4
		1.2	1.2	.8	.7	.6	.6	.7
		-3.3	3.2	1.7	1.3	1.1	1.2	1.2
% Profit Before Taxes/Tangible Net Worth		50.2	32.6	14.2	10.2	9.3	13.1	14.9
	(10) 17.9	(67) 8.6	(214) 5.8	(187) 5.8	(265) 5.5		(677) 6.9	(595) 8.7
		13.4	-2.2	1.5	2.4	2.0	2.4	3.8
% Profit Before Taxes/Total Assets		19.9	12.8	7.4	5.9	6.0	7.8	8.7
		7.0	3.6	3.0	3.1	3.2	4.1	4.7
		-.6	-2.3	.6	1.3	1.1	1.3	2.0
Sales/Net Fixed Assets		193.6	10.1	1.8	1.2	1.1	1.7	1.7
		12.5	2.0	1.1	.9	.8	1.0	1.0
		.6	.8	.7	.6	.6	.8	.7
Sales/Total Assets		2.8	1.7	.9	.6	.5	.7	.7
		1.6	.9	.6	.5	.4	.5	.5
		.4	.5	.4	.4	.3	.4	.4
% Depr., Dep., Amort./Sales		.8	2.0	3.8	4.8	4.9	4.1	3.9
	(11) 3.2	(67) 3.8	(204) 5.5	(182) 6.5	(247) 6.3		(639) 5.4	(554) 5.3
		21.0	7.1	7.4	8.6	8.3	6.9	7.1
% Officers', Directors', Owners' Comp/Sales				5.8	4.4	6.0	5.1	3.7
			(18) 16.6	(20) 10.2	(27) 10.4		(79) 8.8	(65) 7.7
				43.9	16.3	20.7	20.7	16.3
Net Sales ($)	5089M	38552M	670616M	4387202M	7749540M	19732744M	26167377M	24067575M
Total Assets ($)	2013M	19391M	442269M	6161489M	13957440M	43352405M	52483450M	47438602M

© RMA 2011

M = $ thousand   MM = $ million
See Pages 9 through 22 for Explanation of Ratios and Data

Comparative Historical Data | Current Data Sorted by Sales

Hist 1	Hist 2	Hist 3	Type of Statement	0-1MM	1-3MM	3-5MM	5-10MM	10-25MM	25MM & OVER
613	616	646	Unqualified	4	21	26	50	155	390
3	6	2	Reviewed		1				1
6	3	3	Compiled		2	1			
6	4	14	Tax Returns	3	4			3	4
113	112	112	Other	5	4	7	11	25	60
4/1/08-3/31/09 ALL	4/1/09-3/31/10 ALL	4/1/10-3/31/11 ALL			703 (4/1-9/30/10)			74 (10/1/10-3/31/11)	
741	741	777	**NUMBER OF STATEMENTS**	12	32	34	61	183	455
%	%	%	**ASSETS**	%	%	%	%	%	%
15.5	16.0	16.8	Cash & Equivalents	26.9	20.6	18.6	18.1	17.0	15.9
5.1	5.7	5.3	Trade Receivables (net)	9.5	5.8	7.2	5.0	5.9	4.8
.6	.5	.6	Inventory	1.8	.7	.8	.8	.5	.5
3.3	3.1	3.1	All Other Current	1.7	1.9	4.9	4.3	2.8	3.0
24.6	25.3	25.7	Total Current	39.8	29.0	31.5	28.2	26.2	24.1
48.0	51.9	51.2	Fixed Assets (net)	48.7	54.5	54.6	52.8	49.9	51.1
1.1	1.7	1.3	Intangibles (net)	2.6	.3	.8	1.9	.6	1.5
26.3	21.0	21.8	All Other Non-Current	9.0	16.3	13.1	17.2	23.3	23.2
100.0	100.0	100.0	Total	100.0	100.0	100.0	100.0	100.0	100.0
			LIABILITIES						
1.9	1.7	2.1	Notes Payable-Short Term	4.1	10.5	2.8	3.6	2.2	1.1
1.5	1.8	1.8	Cur. Mat.-L.T.D.	5.1	4.3	1.4	3.5	1.8	1.3
2.9	3.2	3.1	Trade Payables	1.3	3.0	2.1	2.7	3.4	3.1
.1	.0	.1	Income Taxes Payable	.0	.0	.0	.1	.4	.0
7.0	7.5	6.8	All Other Current	13.2	8.3	7.9	6.9	7.4	6.2
13.3	14.2	13.9	Total Current	23.7	26.1	14.3	16.8	15.2	11.8
26.3	27.2	27.5	Long-Term Debt	62.3	34.1	23.6	31.4	27.8	25.8
.0	.1	.1	Deferred Taxes	.1	.4	.3	.0	.0	.1
4.3	4.8	5.2	All Other Non-Current	7.1	6.3	5.8	4.9	4.2	5.5
56.1	53.7	53.3	Net Worth	6.9	33.2	56.0	46.9	52.9	56.8
100.0	100.0	100.0	Total Liabilties & Net Worth	100.0	100.0	100.0	100.0	100.0	100.0
			INCOME DATA						
100.0	100.0	100.0	Net Sales	100.0	100.0	100.0	100.0	100.0	100.0
			Gross Profit						
93.3	93.9	91.3	Operating Expenses	75.3	87.3	87.8	92.3	92.9	91.5
6.7	6.1	8.7	Operating Profit	24.7	12.7	12.2	7.7	7.1	8.5
5.6	9.5	.8	All Other Expenses (net)	5.5	6.5	2.8	3.8	1.4	-.5
1.1	-3.4	7.9	Profit Before Taxes	19.2	6.2	9.4	3.9	5.7	9.0
			RATIOS						
3.9	3.5	3.8		6.7	4.1	7.9	4.4	3.4	3.6
1.8	1.7	1.7	Current	2.0	1.6	2.5	1.7	1.5	1.8
1.0	.9	.9		1.0	.4	.9	.7	.8	1.1
3.4	2.9	3.1		6.3	3.9	6.6	3.8	2.8	3.1
1.4	1.4	1.4	Quick	1.7	1.2	2.2	1.4	1.2	1.5
.6	.7	.7		.8	.3	.7	.6	.5	.8
7 50.8	6 57.1	7 54.5		0 UND	1 587.6	4 92.3	3 114.6	6 64.4	9 41.8
16 23.2	16 22.8	15 23.8	Sales/Receivables	0 UND	8 46.2	11 33.2	12 31.6	13 28.4	17 21.6
36 10.3	35 10.4	31 11.6		16 22.7	28 13.2	34 10.6	26 14.0	34 10.7	31 11.6
			Cost of Sales/Inventory						
			Cost of Sales/Payables						
2.5	3.2	3.0		2.3	3.0	2.0	1.7	3.4	3.0
8.0	8.8	7.4	Sales/Working Capital	6.9	14.1	3.7	6.4	10.1	7.1
-140.4	-103.7	-104.6		-201.1	-3.3	-29.7	-25.3	-18.1	111.6
4.7	3.7	7.6			6.0	6.5	5.9	7.6	8.1
(590) 1.5	(612) .6	(652) 3.8	EBIT/Interest		(22) 2.9	(25) 2.8	(47) 2.3	(154) 3.1	(395) 4.2
-1.1	-3.6	1.6			.5	-.5	-.1	1.2	2.0
11.0	16.5	22.2	Net Profit + Depr., Dep.,						22.2
(30) 3.4	(37) 6.6	(29) 12.4	Amort./Cur. Mat. L/T/D					(17)	12.4
1.7	2.8	3.3							3.3
.5	.7	.6		.5	.6	.6	.6	.6	.6
.8	.9	.9	Fixed/Worth	.9	1.3	.9	1.1	.6	.9
1.2	1.5	1.4		2.2	3.5	1.7	2.5	1.4	1.3
.3	.4	.4		.2	.6	.3	.4	.4	.4
.6	.8	.7	Debt/Worth	1.2	1.5	.6	1.0	.8	.7
1.2	1.5	1.4		9.6	6.4	2.3	3.6	1.7	1.2
7.3	7.2	12.0		73.1	20.6	23.1	9.3	12.8	11.4
(708) 1.3	(715) -1.1	(749) 6.0	% Profit Before Taxes/Tangible Net Worth	(10) 15.2	(26) 7.4	(32) 5.6	(55) 3.1	(178) 5.1	(448) 6.3
-3.3	-10.1	1.8		2.8	1.6	-2.7	-2.5	.6	2.9
4.2	4.1	6.6		33.0	6.7	8.8	4.2	5.9	6.7
.7	-.7	3.3	% Profit Before Taxes/Total Assets	6.1	3.0	2.4	1.4	2.7	3.5
-2.1	-5.8	.7		-3.7	-2.0	-1.8	-1.8	-.1	1.5
1.5	1.5	1.5		71.4	5.4	2.8	1.6	1.7	1.3
.9	.9	.9	Sales/Net Fixed Assets	.7	.9	.8	.8	1.0	.9
.7	.6	.7		.2	.3	.3	.5	.7	.7
.7	.7	.7		1.4	1.1	.7	.9	.8	.7
.5	.5	.5	Sales/Total Assets	.4	.5	.5	.4	.5	.5
.3	.3	.3		.2	.2	.2	.2	.3	.4
4.2	4.3	4.3			3.1	2.5	4.4	4.1	4.4
(681) 5.6	(679) 6.0	(714) 5.9	% Depr., Dep., Amort./Sales		(24) 7.3	(31) 5.2	(56) 6.4	(172) 5.9	(422) 5.7
7.6	7.8	8.2			19.1	10.7	10.1	8.3	7.7
3.7	3.6	5.4						5.7	5.3
(83) 8.7	(93) 10.3	(74) 10.3	% Officers', Directors' Owners' Comp/Sales					(17) 7.9	(44) 11.0
18.5	19.7	21.0						17.8	21.3
29513898M	31617495M	32583743M	Net Sales ($)	5349M	67363M	130732M	451201M	3235477M	28693621M
63226488M	59939574M	63935007M	Total Assets ($)	15252M	248340M	394362M	1449026M	8071517M	53756510M

M = $ thousand   MM = $ million
See Pages 9 through 22 for Explanation of Ratios and Data

Current Data Sorted by Assets   Comparative Historical Data

0-500M	500M-2MM	2-10MM	10-50MM	50-100MM	100-250MM	Type of Statement		24	23
1	2	10	14	1	4	Unqualified		24	23
	2	2				Reviewed		1	1
						Compiled		2	1
5	2	3	1			Tax Returns		4	7
1	4	15	7			Other		11	10
	32 (4/1-9/30/10)		42 (10/1/10-3/31/11)					4/1/06-3/31/07 ALL	4/1/07-3/31/08 ALL
7	10	30	22	1	4	NUMBER OF STATEMENTS		42	42
%	%	%	%	%	%	**ASSETS**		%	%
	20.8	24.6	23.4			Cash & Equivalents		17.0	21.2
	17.0	22.9	15.3			Trade Receivables (net)		14.2	13.1
	2.6	.5	.6			Inventory		2.9	4.3
	4.2	3.2	3.8			All Other Current		7.7	4.3
	44.6	51.2	43.1			Total Current		41.8	43.0
	27.6	35.1	29.1			Fixed Assets (net)		41.1	36.4
	4.7	3.2	12.0			Intangibles (net)		6.3	8.2
	23.1	10.5	15.8			All Other Non-Current		10.8	12.4
	100.0	100.0	100.0			Total		100.0	100.0
						LIABILITIES			
	12.0	2.4	1.5			Notes Payable-Short Term		8.3	7.6
	.6	1.8	1.3			Cur. Mat.-L.T.D.		2.8	4.0
	14.5	7.8	6.8			Trade Payables		5.9	5.0
	.0	.2	.1			Income Taxes Payable		.1	.1
	10.5	14.2	17.4			All Other Current		14.8	19.1
	37.6	26.3	27.0			Total Current		31.8	35.8
	10.3	13.7	19.7			Long-Term Debt		19.1	16.3
	.0	.2	.3			Deferred Taxes		.1	.2
	42.1	24.4	5.8			All Other Non-Current		5.8	6.8
	10.0	35.5	47.1			Net Worth		43.2	40.8
	100.0	100.0	100.0			Total Liabilties & Net Worth		100.0	100.0
						INCOME DATA			
	100.0	100.0	100.0			Net Sales		100.0	100.0
						Gross Profit			
	94.8	95.9	90.4			Operating Expenses		97.9	95.2
	5.2	4.1	9.6			Operating Profit		2.1	4.8
	-.3	1.2	2.1			All Other Expenses (net)		1.3	1.4
	5.5	2.9	7.6			Profit Before Taxes		.8	3.4
						RATIOS			
	11.5	4.7	3.6					2.9	2.6
	2.0	1.8	1.8			Current		1.2	1.3
	.6	.7	.8					.7	.8
	9.5	4.5	3.2					2.3	1.8
	2.0	1.5	1.6			Quick		1.0	1.1
	.5	.7	.7					.4	.4
	0 UND	1 307.9	8 45.2					1 356.6	1 520.8
	12 31.2	22 16.3	26 14.2			Sales/Receivables		14 26.0	16 22.7
	58 6.3	51 7.2	65 5.6					53 6.9	46 8.0
						Cost of Sales/Inventory			
						Cost of Sales/Payables			
	4.9	4.7	2.7					6.0	4.7
	32.0	13.2	10.7			Sales/Working Capital		22.3	27.9
	-28.9	-26.5	-26.9					-37.2	-26.9
		72.8	38.7					11.7	12.7
		(17) 6.7	(14) 6.6			EBIT/Interest		(34) 1.8	(31) 2.1
		-2.7	3.7					-2.4	-.7
						Net Profit + Depr., Dep., Amort./Cur. Mat. L/T/D			
	.2	.1	.4					.2	.5
	3.1	.5	.8			Fixed/Worth		1.0	1.0
	-1.3	3.9	5.1					2.4	3.8
	.4	.4	.6					.5	.4
	3.5	1.0	1.1			Debt/Worth		1.2	1.5
	-6.0	4.5	20.1					6.1	19.4
		45.5	52.4			% Profit Before Taxes/Tangible Net Worth		35.3	29.8
		(26) 3.9	(18) 21.8					(36) 6.6	(34) 10.9
		-2.7	7.4					-.5	-3.6
	18.8	16.6	15.1			% Profit Before Taxes/Total Assets		12.5	11.3
	2.6	2.2	10.7					1.6	5.0
	-27.7	-3.1	4.0					-1.6	-3.1
	48.3	82.0	25.0			Sales/Net Fixed Assets		33.7	31.2
	23.2	7.4	5.1					5.4	5.9
	4.3	2.5	1.9					1.7	2.3
	3.6	2.6	2.2			Sales/Total Assets		2.4	2.9
	2.0	1.8	1.2					1.3	1.5
	1.1	.9	.7					.8	.9
		.8	1.9			% Depr., Dep., Amort./Sales		1.3	1.0
		(19) 2.8	(18) 3.1					(29) 2.6	(34) 2.3
		5.4	7.4					4.6	3.9
						% Officers', Directors' Owners' Comp/Sales			
9950M	60460M	340727M	680559M	178709M	934710M	Net Sales ($)		1694493M	1285924M
1294M	10689M	151016M	439719M	85089M	645194M	Total Assets ($)		826122M	1066058M

M = $ thousand   MM = $ million
See Pages 9 through 22 for Explanation of Ratios and Data

Comparative Historical Data | Current Data Sorted by Sales

			Type of Statement	0-1MM	1-3MM	3-5MM	5-10MM	10-25MM	25MM & OVER
18	22	32	Unqualified	1	4	2	5	10	10
2	1	4	Reviewed		2			1	1
1	3		Compiled						
3	10	11	Tax Returns	2	6	1	2		
20	23	27	Other	3	5	1	5	7	6
4/1/08-3/31/09 ALL	4/1/09-3/31/10 ALL	4/1/10-3/31/11 ALL		\<32 (4/1-9/30/10)\>			\<42 (10/1/10-3/31/11)\>		
44	59	74	**NUMBER OF STATEMENTS**	6	17	4	12	18	17
%	%	%	**ASSETS**	%	%	%	%	%	%
24.3	21.3	24.2	Cash & Equivalents		22.2		33.3	25.5	25.4
13.7	18.1	19.8	Trade Receivables (net)		13.8		22.0	14.7	27.5
2.4	1.2	1.3	Inventory		2.8		.5	.5	.5
5.4	7.5	3.7	All Other Current		1.9		2.6	5.1	4.6
45.7	48.1	49.1	Total Current		40.7		58.5	45.8	58.1
31.4	31.8	28.9	Fixed Assets (net)		39.5		20.5	30.5	16.2
10.3	10.0	7.7	Intangibles (net)		2.8		3.9	12.9	13.0
12.6	10.1	14.2	All Other Non-Current		17.0		17.2	10.7	12.8
100.0	100.0	100.0	Total		100.0		100.0	100.0	100.0
			LIABILITIES						
2.5	6.5	3.4	Notes Payable-Short Term		7.7		3.4	.6	2.7
2.2	2.9	1.5	Cur. Mat.-L.T.D.		1.5		.0	2.7	1.0
6.4	7.1	8.2	Trade Payables		3.3		9.7	4.9	15.5
.2	.3	.2	Income Taxes Payable		.5		.2	.2	.0
19.5	20.8	15.9	All Other Current		12.8		12.7	12.9	26.3
30.7	37.5	29.2	Total Current		25.8		26.0	21.4	45.4
20.1	18.2	13.5	Long-Term Debt		16.4		10.3	19.1	7.3
.1	.3	.2	Deferred Taxes		.0		.0	.7	.3
10.2	9.1	17.9	All Other Non-Current		35.8		10.8	10.8	13.5
38.9	34.9	39.1	Net Worth		22.1		53.0	48.1	33.4
100.0	100.0	100.0	Total Liabilties & Net Worth		100.0		100.0	100.0	100.0
			INCOME DATA						
100.0	100.0	100.0	Net Sales		100.0		100.0	100.0	100.0
			Gross Profit						
97.3	93.2	93.7	Operating Expenses		90.5		98.9	90.5	92.9
2.7	6.8	6.3	Operating Profit		9.5		1.1	9.5	7.1
1.2	2.0	1.3	All Other Expenses (net)		4.3		-.4	.2	1.6
1.5	4.8	5.1	Profit Before Taxes		5.2		1.6	9.3	5.5
			RATIOS						
3.9	3.6	4.7	Current		9.6		8.8	3.9	2.9
1.6	1.6	1.8			1.1		2.3	2.1	1.3
.7	.6	.8			.5		1.1	1.4	.8
3.5	3.1	4.5	Quick		9.6		8.7	3.9	2.7
1.5	1.3	1.6			1.0		2.3	1.8	1.1
.6	.4	.7			.5		.9	.9	.8
2 164.4	2 174.3	1 287.3	Sales/Receivables		0 UND		0 UND	3 126.2	2 191.7
24 15.5	27 13.4	23 15.6			8 46.9		28 13.1	30 12.3	27 13.4
46 7.9	49 7.5	51 7.2			21 17.1		76 4.8	51 7.2	61 6.0
			Cost of Sales/Inventory						
			Cost of Sales/Payables						
4.6	5.0	4.7	Sales/Working Capital		4.9		2.7	2.8	9.6
13.3	10.7	14.8			234.9		10.2	5.5	18.9
-20.7	-10.2	-95.9			-6.9		69.2	NM	-72.6
14.3	13.4	48.7	EBIT/Interest					84.7	42.2
(32) 3.6	(40) 3.8	(44) 7.0					(13) 7.3	7.3	(11) 12.8
-.8	-.3	.2						4.0	5.0
			Net Profit + Depr., Dep., Amort./Cur. Mat. L/T/D						
.3	.4	.1	Fixed/Worth		.1		.1	.4	.1
.8	1.0	.6			.4		.4	.6	.8
7.6	-4.6	4.8			4.8		10.5	4.8	NM
.7	.4	.4	Debt/Worth		.2		.4	.7	.8
1.9	1.4	1.2			1.2		.7	1.1	2.1
9.3	-14.2	8.7			4.2		13.6	9.1	NM
45.3	44.3	73.6	% Profit Before Taxes/Tangible Net Worth		74.1		24.2	39.1	123.2
(35) 11.9	(43) 10.8	(61) 21.2			(15) 9.5		(10) .3	(15) 24.9	(13) 74.9
3.1	1.7	.3			-1.1		-14.0	8.9	38.2
12.1	18.1	20.0	% Profit Before Taxes/Total Assets		26.0		18.1	14.1	32.8
2.7	4.7	6.9			1.8		.1	10.2	12.0
-3.2	-.9	-.9			-4.9		-6.7	4.3	6.5
37.5	35.3	53.7	Sales/Net Fixed Assets		100.1		60.1	17.1	154.7
7.6	12.3	10.9			30.8		38.7	5.3	36.5
2.5	2.3	2.8			.6		2.8	3.2	7.5
3.3	3.6	2.8	Sales/Total Assets		3.4		2.8	2.3	5.0
1.5	1.9	1.8			1.3		2.0	1.3	2.6
.8	.8	1.0			.6		1.5	1.0	1.7
1.4	1.1	.8	% Depr., Dep., Amort./Sales		.9			1.8	.2
(31) 3.1	(39) 2.0	(52) 2.1			(13) 2.0			(13) 2.1	(11) 2.3
5.7	4.6	4.6			9.2			3.7	3.9
1.8	4.8	3.0	% Officers', Directors' Owners' Comp/Sales						
(10) 7.9	(14) 8.6	(14) 7.3							
18.4	12.7	14.4							
1386758M	1458802M	2205115M	Net Sales ($)	3676M	33939M	16419M	92889M	290085M	1768107M
1046362M	1122320M	1333001M	Total Assets ($)	3813M	47348M	31968M	72625M	231599M	945648M

M = $ thousand   MM = $ million
See Pages 9 through 22 for Explanation of Ratios and Data

Current Data Sorted by Assets   Comparative Historical Data

						Type of Statement		
1	5	29	16	9	3	Unqualified	66	52
		1	1			Reviewed	5	6
5	1					Compiled	6	8
5	3	1				Tax Returns	12	12
5	10	21	16		7	Other	34	25

0-500M	500M-2MM	2-10MM	10-50MM	50-100MM	100-250MM		4/1/06-3/31/07 ALL	4/1/07-3/31/08 ALL
	59 (4/1-9/30/10)		80 (10/1/10-3/31/11)					
16	19	52	33	9	10	NUMBER OF STATEMENTS	123	103
%	%	%	%	%	%	**ASSETS**	%	%
27.1	23.1	23.1	19.7		21.6	Cash & Equivalents	22.1	20.9
12.3	16.0	23.6	20.7		18.1	Trade Receivables (net)	23.4	25.7
3.5	5.5	.7	.7		1.5	Inventory	1.4	1.6
3.3	4.1	4.8	2.9		4.7	All Other Current	3.5	3.6
46.2	48.7	52.1	44.0		46.0	Total Current	50.5	51.8
33.7	24.4	39.1	37.5		37.1	Fixed Assets (net)	35.0	33.5
6.5	12.5	4.1	8.4		10.6	Intangibles (net)	6.3	7.1
13.6	14.4	4.6	10.0		6.4	All Other Non-Current	8.3	7.6
100.0	100.0	100.0	100.0		100.0	Total	100.0	100.0
						LIABILITIES		
11.1	7.4	4.5	2.2		.1	Notes Payable-Short Term	6.1	4.6
5.5	1.8	2.1	1.8		4.2	Cur. Mat.-L.T.D.	2.5	3.2
12.8	8.5	4.2	14.5		3.1	Trade Payables	6.8	9.1
.0	.2	.3	.1		.7	Income Taxes Payable	.5	.3
21.9	26.9	23.6	30.1		32.6	All Other Current	23.2	22.9
51.2	44.7	34.7	48.7		40.5	Total Current	39.2	40.1
19.6	12.1	16.1	17.7		24.1	Long-Term Debt	15.1	13.4
.0	.1	.3	.3		.8	Deferred Taxes	.3	.1
5.6	8.5	6.5	7.9		4.7	All Other Non-Current	5.3	5.6
23.5	34.5	42.4	25.3		29.9	Net Worth	40.2	40.8
100.0	100.0	100.0	100.0		100.0	Total Liabilities & Net Worth	100.0	100.0
						INCOME DATA		
100.0	100.0	100.0	100.0		100.0	Net Sales	100.0	100.0
						Gross Profit		
90.8	85.4	92.3	88.7		81.9	Operating Expenses	92.0	92.2
9.2	14.6	7.7	11.3		18.1	Operating Profit	8.0	7.8
3.0	3.8	1.1	1.1		.7	All Other Expenses (net)	.9	.8
6.2	10.8	6.6	10.2		17.3	Profit Before Taxes	7.1	7.0
						RATIOS		
2.2	1.9	3.0	2.4		1.5		2.3	2.6
.9	1.2	1.4	1.2		1.1	Current	1.2	1.3
.3	.8	1.1	.8		1.0		.8	.9
1.0	1.9	2.7	1.9		1.3		2.2	2.3
.8	1.0	1.3	1.1		.9	Quick	1.1	1.2
.3	.3	1.0	.7		.8		.7	.9
0 UND	1 277.1	13 29.1	9 41.0		12 31.1		6 58.1	14 25.3
0 UND	21 17.2	46 7.9	32 11.6		43 8.5	Sales/Receivables	35 10.5	36 10.0
30 12.3	52 7.0	98 3.7	110 3.3		82 4.5		78 4.7	98 3.7
						Cost of Sales/Inventory		
						Cost of Sales/Payables		
22.4	4.2	3.2	5.5		7.9		4.9	5.4
UND	50.4	9.4	15.5		49.8	Sales/Working Capital	19.0	12.5
-6.8	-17.6	54.0	-23.4		-154.0		-15.4	-136.4
	21.9	37.8	25.6				14.9	23.8
	(14) 9.8	(43) 14.1	(30) 5.8			EBIT/Interest	(83) 4.5	(77) 8.8
	4.5	1.5	3.0				1.5	1.1
						Net Profit + Depr., Dep.,	3.4	12.3
						Amort./Cur. Mat. L/T/D	(22) 1.8 / (13) 3.1	
							.4	2.1
.0	.1	.4	.6		.8		.4	.4
.9	.9	.7	1.0		1.2	Fixed/Worth	.8	.8
NM	-7.8	1.4	2.9		2.5		2.4	1.8
1.1	.7	.8	.8		1.5		.6	.6
1.8	1.9	1.3	1.9		1.6	Debt/Worth	1.7	1.5
-17.9	-8.5	3.2	6.4		3.9		5.6	4.4
131.1	51.8	54.6	82.8			% Profit Before Taxes/Tangible	45.9	54.7
(11) 63.8	(12) 33.6	(48) 24.1	(29) 33.7			Net Worth	(103) 17.6	(91) 25.4
5.5	11.9	4.8	6.9				3.8	4.3
41.6	23.2	19.4	16.9		45.5	% Profit Before Taxes/Total	17.5	20.4
12.6	13.3	10.1	7.5		17.8	Assets	5.2	8.4
-15.8	4.6	1.9	2.9		10.8		1.2	.3
774.8	39.6	14.5	10.6		6.5		18.7	16.4
25.9	7.1	5.4	4.6		4.0	Sales/Net Fixed Assets	6.9	7.8
2.0	4.8	1.5	1.6		2.9		2.0	2.5
11.5	2.5	1.9	1.8		1.7		2.3	2.4
2.7	1.5	1.2	1.2		1.5	Sales/Total Assets	1.6	1.5
.7	1.1	.7	.7		1.2		.7	.8
	1.3	1.5	2.9				1.7	1.6
	(10) 4.0	(49) 2.9	(29) 3.5			% Depr., Dep., Amort./Sales	(99) 3.2	(82) 3.0
	5.4	6.3	5.2				5.1	4.8
10.0							2.2	3.2
(11) 19.8						% Officers', Directors' Owners' Comp/Sales	(24) 4.0	(21) 6.5
28.1							14.7	11.9
19876M	54440M	374159M	1691265M	930034M	2608108M	Net Sales ($)	3464217M	2092588M
3268M	24614M	274477M	737560M	685959M	1723524M	Total Assets ($)	2766346M	1726497M

Comparative Historical Data | Current Data Sorted by Sales

			Type of Statement						
74	65	63	Unqualified	1	9	6	12	17	18
2	1	2	Reviewed			1			
15	9	6	Compiled	4	1			1	
14	11	9	Tax Returns	2	5	1	1	1	
33	51	59	Other	9	12	7	10	7	14
4/1/08-3/31/09 ALL	4/1/09-3/31/10 ALL	4/1/10-3/31/11 ALL		0-1MM	1-3MM	3-5MM	5-10MM	10-25MM	25MM & OVER
					59 (4/1-9/30/10)		80 (10/1/10-3/31/11)		
138	137	139	NUMBER OF STATEMENTS	16	27	15	23	26	32
%	%	%	ASSETS	%	%	%	%	%	%
19.8	20.8	22.2	Cash & Equivalents	24.3	20.7	15.8	20.2	28.0	22.0
17.3	17.9	19.3	Trade Receivables (net)	13.6	15.8	17.8	23.5	23.6	19.3
1.4	1.7	1.7	Inventory	1.7	4.7	1.2	.6	.6	1.2
5.0	4.1	4.0	All Other Current	6.0	2.6	5.8	3.5	2.7	4.7
43.5	44.4	47.2	Total Current	45.5	43.7	40.7	47.9	54.8	47.2
38.2	34.8	35.4	Fixed Assets (net)	36.8	36.6	41.5	41.2	29.3	31.4
9.6	9.2	7.8	Intangibles (net)	9.6	5.3	6.6	7.6	7.5	9.9
8.7	11.5	9.7	All Other Non-Current	8.1	14.4	11.2	3.4	8.4	11.5
100.0	100.0	100.0	Total	100.0	100.0	100.0	100.0	100.0	100.0
			LIABILITIES						
4.8	3.1	4.5	Notes Payable-Short Term	9.1	7.5	2.2	3.0	6.1	.5
2.4	3.7	2.5	Cur. Mat.-L.T.D.	6.0	1.0	1.2	1.6	2.6	3.0
4.8	6.9	8.2	Trade Payables	13.8	3.0	3.5	3.4	7.1	16.3
.4	.5	.2	Income Taxes Payable	.0	.1	.1	.0	.6	.2
18.5	20.3	25.5	All Other Current	13.5	27.8	13.1	23.5	25.8	36.7
30.9	34.6	40.9	Total Current	42.4	39.4	20.1	31.4	42.2	56.7
18.2	16.1	16.7	Long-Term Debt	21.9	20.1	15.2	14.7	12.3	16.9
.3	.2	.3	Deferred Taxes	.0	.1	.0	.4	.3	.6
7.1	7.6	6.7	All Other Non-Current	11.0	6.1	7.9	6.5	5.2	5.6
43.5	41.4	35.5	Net Worth	24.4	34.3	56.8	47.0	40.0	20.1
100.0	100.0	100.0	Total Liabilities & Net Worth	100.0	100.0	100.0	100.0	100.0	100.0
			INCOME DATA						
100.0	100.0	100.0	Net Sales	100.0	100.0	100.0	100.0	100.0	100.0
			Gross Profit						
92.9	88.4	89.0	Operating Expenses	85.4	96.7	85.2	86.6	90.5	86.6
7.1	11.6	11.0	Operating Profit	14.6	3.3	14.8	13.4	9.5	13.4
1.5	2.2	1.6	All Other Expenses (net)	7.4	1.3	1.0	1.6	.1	.4
5.6	9.4	9.4	Profit Before Taxes	7.2	1.9	13.8	11.8	9.4	13.1
			RATIOS						
2.8	2.1	2.5	Current	2.7	3.0	2.5	3.2	2.7	1.7
1.3	1.3	1.3		1.0	1.5	1.7	1.4	1.2	1.2
.9	.9	.9		.4	.4	1.0	1.0	.9	.9
2.3	1.9	2.1	Quick	1.7	2.6	2.1	3.1	2.5	1.5
1.2 (136)	1.2	1.1		1.0	1.1	1.3	1.2	1.2	1.1
.7	.7	.7		.2	.3	.4	.9	.8	.8
5 79.5	8 43.2	7 51.4	Sales/Receivables	0 UND	5 80.4	3 125.5	11 34.7	11 34.0	14 25.3
28 13.2	28 13.2	30 12.1		0 UND	23 15.6	21 17.2	67 5.4	44 8.3	28 13.3
74 4.9	68 5.3	85 4.3		65 5.6	85 4.3	92 4.0	144 2.5	92 4.0	67 5.4
			Cost of Sales/Inventory						
			Cost of Sales/Payables						
5.0	4.7	4.9	Sales/Working Capital	8.6	2.8	3.1	4.1	5.2	6.6
16.0	11.5	18.1		UND	17.1	9.1	9.7	18.7	34.4
-56.3	-100.2	-32.1		-3.1	-19.7	344.6	154.8	-31.1	-45.8
25.3	23.9	42.0	EBIT/Interest	31.5	13.9	26.0	17.7	75.8	75.0
(98) 5.3	(100) 7.3	(111) 11.1		(10) 5.6	(20) 5.9	(10) 10.1	(21) 8.3	(22) 30.7	(28) 20.5
1.5	2.0	3.1		-.9	-.7	1.2	3.6	5.9	5.8
7.9	17.1	27.1	Net Profit + Depr., Dep., Amort./Cur. Mat. L/T/D						
(26) 1.9	(22) 5.4	(16) 8.6							
.5	2.8	3.1							
.4	.4	.4	Fixed/Worth	.2	.1	.3	.6	.4	.4
.9	.8	.9		1.0	1.3	.5	.9	.7	.9
2.3	2.1	1.9		NM	3.5	2.0	1.4	1.1	2.4
.8	.7	.8	Debt/Worth	1.1	.8	.2	.7	.8	1.1
1.5	1.6	1.5		1.8	1.6	1.0	1.3	1.5	1.6
3.9	4.1	3.8		-5.8	6.9	2.2	3.5	3.4	6.6
43.8	55.7	68.5	% Profit Before Taxes/Tangible Net Worth	101.8	53.5	68.8	47.3	68.3	125.1
(115) 17.4	(118) 19.4	(118) 32.7		(10) 42.7	(22) 30.1	(14) 14.8	(21) 25.2	(23) 31.2	(28) 59.5
2.5	5.1	8.2		-2.1	.0	3.4	5.7	17.8	18.1
17.7	17.7	22.1	% Profit Before Taxes/Total Assets	34.5	18.0	26.1	13.6	28.2	42.1
7.1	7.3	11.0		12.0	6.1	13.6	8.2	15.9	13.6
.2	1.8	3.9		-2.5	-1.1	1.5	3.9	6.6	5.7
12.6	15.1	14.1	Sales/Net Fixed Assets	54.3	21.9	9.6	15.1	20.8	10.8
4.8	5.4	5.2		4.8	5.9	2.8	3.5	8.2	6.2
2.0	1.8	1.9		1.1	.9	1.0	1.4	3.6	3.3
2.0	1.9	2.2	Sales/Total Assets	2.8	2.2	1.2	1.8	2.4	2.3
1.3	1.3	1.3		.8	1.3	.9	1.2	1.6	1.6
.7	.7	.8		.4	.5	.6	.6	1.3	1.0
1.8	1.5	2.0	% Depr., Dep., Amort./Sales		2.2	1.5	2.2	1.6	1.9
(113) 3.0	(119) 3.0	(108) 3.4		(20) 4.8	(13) 2.6	(20) 3.1	(22) 3.0	(24) 3.4	
5.4	5.3	5.3		11.5	4.8	5.6	4.7	4.7	
3.9	4.2	4.4	% Officers', Directors' Owners' Comp/Sales						
(24) 8.9	(16) 10.4	(22) 10.9							
19.0	25.0	21.0							
2394547M	4543889M	5677882M	Net Sales ($)	7227M	53752M	58714M	172425M	409420M	4976344M
2247452M	3058990M	3449402M	Total Assets ($)	8998M	73586M	87697M	238602M	317754M	2722765M

M = $ thousand   MM = $ million
See Pages 9 through 22 for Explanation of Ratios and Data

Current Data Sorted by Assets   Comparative Historical Data

						Type of Statement		
							20	27
	5	12	11	1	1	Unqualified		
		1				Reviewed	1	1
1	1					Compiled	3	1
6	3	2				Tax Returns	3	7
3	9	4	1	1		Other	5	13
	36 (4/1-9/30/10)		26 (10/1/10-3/31/11)				4/1/06-3/31/07	4/1/07-3/31/08
0-500M	500M-2MM	2-10MM	10-50MM	50-100MM	100-250MM		ALL	ALL
10	18	19	12	2	1	NUMBER OF STATEMENTS	32	49
%	%	%	%	%	%	ASSETS	%	%
38.6	21.5	12.6	14.3			Cash & Equivalents	19.3	20.8
.3	12.6	13.6	6.9			Trade Receivables (net)	6.2	6.0
.1	.8	.3	.7			Inventory	2.6	1.4
.0	.6	.5	.9			All Other Current	1.5	2.5
39.1	35.5	27.0	22.8			Total Current	29.6	30.6
35.5	42.3	63.4	48.8			Fixed Assets (net)	50.3	49.5
3.0	2.8	1.0	.9			Intangibles (net)	3.2	2.8
22.5	19.4	8.6	27.5			All Other Non-Current	16.9	17.1
100.0	100.0	100.0	100.0			Total	100.0	100.0
						LIABILITIES		
.4	.2	3.0	3.3			Notes Payable-Short Term	5.3	3.6
1.9	1.3	1.7	1.6			Cur. Mat.-L.T.D.	.9	.9
.0	3.3	2.3	3.0			Trade Payables	2.8	6.9
.0	2.5	4.0	.0			Income Taxes Payable	.0	.0
20.3	17.4	6.4	8.3			All Other Current	12.7	7.4
22.7	24.7	17.4	16.2			Total Current	21.7	18.9
69.3	28.8	24.5	31.7			Long-Term Debt	24.1	25.3
.0	.1	.0	.0			Deferred Taxes	.0	.0
2.9	1.3	2.8	.7			All Other Non-Current	1.7	6.5
5.2	45.0	55.3	51.4			Net Worth	52.5	49.3
100.0	100.0	100.0	100.0			Total Liabilities & Net Worth	100.0	100.0
						INCOME DATA		
100.0	100.0	100.0	100.0			Net Sales	100.0	100.0
						Gross Profit		
87.1	87.1	95.9	99.4			Operating Expenses	91.2	91.2
12.9	12.9	4.1	.6			Operating Profit	8.8	8.8
1.3	4.2	1.4	2.3			All Other Expenses (net)	.0	1.9
11.6	8.7	2.7	-1.7			Profit Before Taxes	8.8	6.9
						RATIOS		
8.2	5.6	3.5	3.0				4.6	5.0
1.9	1.4	1.5	1.6			Current	1.8	1.7
.6	.3	.5	.7				.7	.6
8.2	5.2	3.5	2.9				3.5	4.3
1.9	1.4	1.1	1.5			Quick	1.3	1.6
.6	.3	.4	.5				.5	.5
0 UND	0 UND	1 269.0	9 41.5				3 134.6	0 UND
0 UND	3 116.6	5 74.4	35 10.5			Sales/Receivables	11 32.0	5 76.1
1 263.9	19 19.1	47 7.7	86 4.3				20 18.7	28 13.3
						Cost of Sales/Inventory		
						Cost of Sales/Payables		
9.0	6.4	3.8	3.0				5.4	4.1
95.1	35.6	9.7	10.3			Sales/Working Capital	11.9	24.6
-51.8	-12.2	-17.6	-9.6				-23.1	-18.7
	40.7	17.0					16.9	14.6
	(11) 15.7	(15) 1.9				EBIT/Interest	(19) 3.5	(29) 4.4
	4.8	-.9					1.5	1.0
						Net Profit + Depr., Dep., Amort./Cur. Mat. L/T/D		
.1	.2	.6	.5				.6	.4
.9	1.1	1.2	1.0			Fixed/Worth	.9	.8
UND	7.4	2.3	1.6				2.1	2.0
.1	.3	.3	.3				.2	.2
1.6	1.2	.7	1.0			Debt/Worth	.6	.5
UND	8.6	1.6	2.5				3.0	2.9
	38.8	17.0	27.8			% Profit Before Taxes/Tangible Net Worth	40.1	39.8
(16) 21.9	(18) 2.0	(11) 3.4				(27) 7.5	(43) 8.3
	9.4	-5.3	-2.8				-1.5	.3
61.3	20.8	8.9	8.4			% Profit Before Taxes/Total Assets	24.3	17.8
22.1	8.4	2.1	.8				3.4	6.5
-5.3	2.9	-3.3	-1.4				-.3	.1
65.3	30.2	2.3	3.1				8.8	11.7
28.2	6.4	1.3	1.2			Sales/Net Fixed Assets	1.6	1.7
4.8	1.3	.6	.6				.9	.9
8.4	3.5	1.5	.9				2.4	2.2
5.2	1.3	.7	.6			Sales/Total Assets	.9	1.0
1.5	.6	.5	.3				.4	.5
		2.8	2.2				3.6	2.1
	(17) 4.9	(10) 4.0			% Depr., Dep., Amort./Sales	(24) 5.2	(38) 4.0
		6.2	7.6				7.0	6.2
						% Officers', Directors' Owners' Comp/Sales		
5188M	66648M	87208M	164901M	321262M	10394M	Net Sales ($)	146078M	253299M
1458M	22294M	92215M	276241M	146272M	132411M	Total Assets ($)	272050M	585768M

M = $ thousand   MM = $ million
See Pages 9 through 22 for Explanation of Ratios and Data

Comparative Historical Data | Current Data Sorted by Sales

			Type of Statement	0-1MM	1-3MM	3-5MM	5-10MM	10-25MM	25MM & OVER
32	28	30	Unqualified		4	7	9	7	3
1	1	1	Reviewed					1	
1	2	2	Compiled	2					
8	10	11	Tax Returns	7	3	1			
13	15	18	Other	6	7	2	1	2	
4/1/08- 3/31/09 ALL	4/1/09- 3/31/10 ALL	4/1/10- 3/31/11 ALL			36 (4/1-9/30/10)			26 (10/1/10-3/31/11)	
55	56	62	NUMBER OF STATEMENTS	15	14	10	10	10	3
%	%	%	ASSETS	%	%	%	%	%	%
20.4	22.2	19.7	Cash & Equivalents	28.0	15.8	18.6	22.5	13.2	
4.9	8.4	9.4	Trade Receivables (net)	.3	14.7	9.0	16.0	10.7	
.8	2.8	.5	Inventory	.2	.3	1.2	.7	.2	
3.2	2.5	.6	All Other Current	.7	.7	.2	.1	1.0	
29.4	36.0	30.1	Total Current	29.2	31.6	28.9	39.4	25.1	
53.1	42.6	49.8	Fixed Assets (net)	50.4	49.3	52.3	43.5	58.2	
2.7	2.1	1.8	Intangibles (net)	5.3	.1	.5	.1	2.3	
14.8	19.2	18.2	All Other Non-Current	15.1	18.9	18.3	17.0	14.5	
100.0	100.0	100.0	Total	100.0	100.0	100.0	100.0	100.0	
			LIABILITIES						
8.1	5.4	1.7	Notes Payable-Short Term	.3	1.5	2.0	.3	5.6	
1.8	1.1	1.6	Cur. Mat.-L.T.D.	1.2	1.8	1.6	1.6	1.7	
2.7	6.0	2.5	Trade Payables	.2	1.5	2.6	5.5	2.9	
.2	.9	1.9	Income Taxes Payable	.0	3.2	6.0	1.6	.0	
14.5	12.7	12.5	All Other Current	13.0	13.2	3.6	14.2	10.7	
27.3	26.0	20.2	Total Current	14.8	21.2	15.8	23.2	21.0	
19.2	16.9	34.8	Long-Term Debt	62.9	27.8	25.1	22.8	31.5	
.0	.0	.0	Deferred Taxes	.0	.1	.0	.0	.0	
5.4	4.9	1.9	All Other Non-Current	3.1	2.1	1.8	.8	1.6	
48.1	52.2	43.1	Net Worth	19.3	48.8	57.2	53.2	45.9	
100.0	100.0	100.0	Total Liabilities & Net Worth	100.0	100.0	100.0	100.0	100.0	
			INCOME DATA						
100.0	100.0	100.0	Net Sales	100.0	100.0	100.0	100.0	100.0	
			Gross Profit						
93.8	94.7	92.9	Operating Expenses	85.4	89.8	100.0	98.4	96.1	
6.2	5.3	7.1	Operating Profit	14.6	10.2	.0	1.6	3.9	
3.1	1.3	2.3	All Other Expenses (net)	7.1	1.8	.8	.5	.8	
3.1	4.0	4.8	Profit Before Taxes	7.5	8.5	-.7	1.1	3.1	
			RATIOS						
4.1	6.7	4.0	Current	5.9	5.0	21.4	4.0	1.8	
.9	1.3	1.5		1.2	1.5	3.3	2.6	1.0	
.6	.9	.5		.4	.6	.5	1.1	.7	
2.7	5.3	3.6	Quick	5.9	4.1	21.2	3.6	1.6	
.8	1.1	1.4		1.2	1.4	3.0	2.5	1.0	
.5	.5	.4		.4	.5	.4	1.1	.6	
0 UND	0 UND	0 UND	Sales/Receivables	0 UND	0 UND	0 UND	2 187.7	10 35.7	
4 84.9	4 93.3	4 90.1		0 UND	5 79.9	3 105.2	63 5.8	18 20.1	
29 12.7	31 11.9	37 9.9		1 269.0	50 7.4	7 50.3	104 3.5	42 8.7	
			Cost of Sales/Inventory						
			Cost of Sales/Payables						
4.8	5.0	5.4	Sales/Working Capital	9.9	3.0	4.3	2.5	7.9	
-58.2	28.7	37.2		98.0	10.9	100.7	5.9	NM	
-11.1	-96.9	-13.9		-14.3	-16.5	-9.3	NM	-9.1	
12.1	14.0	21.6	EBIT/Interest		20.4				
(41) 2.6	(35) 3.9	(42) 5.7		(11)	7.4				
-1.6	-.4	.6			2.6				
			Net Profit + Depr., Dep., Amort./Cur. Mat. L/T/D						
.4	.3	.3	Fixed/Worth	.1	.6	.1	.3	1.0	
1.1	.8	1.1		1.0	1.3	.9	1.1	1.5	
2.0	1.7	2.3		10.7	4.8	1.5	2.4	1.9	
.2	.2	.3	Debt/Worth	.1	.2	.1	.2	.7	
.8	.6	.9		1.1	.7	.6	1.0	1.0	
3.5	2.3	2.6		9.9	5.8	NM	2.0	2.4	
39.5	47.5	37.6	% Profit Before Taxes/Tangible Net Worth	68.4	36.4			28.6	
(51) 4.9	(52) 10.0	(57) 12.6		(14) 28.8	(13) 12.6			14.2	
-3.2	-5.4	-3.0		-8.0	3.0			1.5	
13.8	21.9	18.4	% Profit Before Taxes/Total Assets	28.2	18.4	13.9	22.8	9.7	
1.4	5.6	4.8		3.3	7.2	.1	-.6	4.8	
-2.8	-3.0	-2.0		-4.6	2.3	-2.6	-4.9	.9	
5.1	21.7	15.5	Sales/Net Fixed Assets	30.7	6.9	72.3	18.0	1.9	
1.3	5.8	2.2		5.7	1.5	2.4	4.3	1.2	
.7	1.2	.9		.3	.9	.9	.7	.5	
1.8	3.3	2.7	Sales/Total Assets	5.2	1.2	2.7	3.3	1.2	
.9	1.4	1.0		1.4	.7	1.2	1.4	.8	
.4	.7	.5		.3	.5	.7	.3	.3	
2.3	1.5	1.7	% Depr., Dep., Amort./Sales	.8					
(46) 4.6	(43) 3.0	(43) 4.0		(10) 2.0					
6.7	5.1	6.4		11.7					
4.7		3.7	% Officers', Directors' Owners' Comp/Sales						
(10) 6.6	(11)	4.3							
12.0		16.3							
535418M	517202M	655601M	Net Sales ($)	6936M	25636M	38099M	69567M	143484M	371879M
744299M	497496M	670891M	Total Assets ($)	10373M	39604M	57946M	113650M	340553M	108765M

M = $ thousand   MM = $ million
See Pages 9 through 22 for Explanation of Ratios and Data

Current Data Sorted by Assets   Comparative Historical Data

						Type of Statement		
			2	1		Unqualified	2	2
1			1			Reviewed	2	
1	3					Compiled	2	5
6	4		2			Tax Returns	6	4
4	6		7		1	Other	5	9
		10 (4/1-9/30/10)		29 (10/1/10-3/31/11)			4/1/06-3/31/07	4/1/07-3/31/08
0-500M	500M-2MM	2-10MM	10-50MM	50-100MM	100-250MM		ALL	ALL
12	13	12	1	1		NUMBER OF STATEMENTS	17	20
%	%	%	%	%	%	ASSETS	%	%
33.4	18.2	18.2			D	Cash & Equivalents	17.3	18.7
6.3	1.2	13.5			A	Trade Receivables (net)	2.3	4.6
9.5	3.2	1.6			T	Inventory	1.1	8.3
2.6	.4	3.8			A	All Other Current	4.0	4.2
51.9	23.0	37.2				Total Current	24.8	35.7
24.4	72.8	44.7			N	Fixed Assets (net)	55.5	52.8
5.4	1.6	10.3			O	Intangibles (net)	2.2	1.0
18.4	2.6	7.7			T	All Other Non-Current	17.5	10.4
100.0	100.0	100.0				Total	100.0	100.0
					A	LIABILITIES		
19.2	6.6	2.0			V	Notes Payable-Short Term	5.2	11.6
5.4	1.9	1.2			A	Cur. Mat.-L.T.D.	6.3	4.3
14.5	3.8	3.3			I	Trade Payables	3.6	6.8
.0	.0	5.7			L	Income Taxes Payable	.0	.0
15.2	8.0	28.1			A	All Other Current	11.8	13.8
54.3	20.3	40.2			B	Total Current	26.8	36.4
20.5	51.6	23.0			L	Long-Term Debt	47.7	32.1
.0	.0	.0			E	Deferred Taxes	.0	.2
25.4	14.8	6.3				All Other Non-Current	4.3	11.4
-.2	13.3	30.5				Net Worth	21.2	19.8
100.0	100.0	100.0				Total Liabilities & Net Worth	100.0	100.0
						INCOME DATA		
100.0	100.0	100.0				Net Sales	100.0	100.0
						Gross Profit		
94.5	78.8	89.2				Operating Expenses	86.3	90.4
5.5	21.2	10.8				Operating Profit	13.7	9.6
1.0	6.9	6.0				All Other Expenses (net)	3.2	6.3
4.5	14.3	4.8				Profit Before Taxes	10.4	3.3
						RATIOS		
7.4	4.1	2.5					3.1	1.6
1.9	.7	1.6				Current	.8	.6
.5	.1	.3					.4	.1
5.3	4.1	2.5					2.8	1.3
1.5	.5	1.3				Quick	.6	.4
.2	.1	.2					.2	.1
0 UND	0 UND	2 185.0					0 UND	0 UND
0 UND	0 UND	26 14.2				Sales/Receivables	0 UND	0 UND
2 152.4	0 UND	80 4.5					4 100.0	4 90.4
						Cost of Sales/Inventory		
						Cost of Sales/Payables		
6.2	9.5	2.1					10.7	17.4
69.8	-70.8	13.2				Sales/Working Capital	-80.0	-23.7
-58.6	-3.2	-4.5					-9.9	-6.0
							11.6	9.2
						EBIT/Interest	(11) 1.2	(13) 2.1
							.1	.1
						Net Profit + Depr., Dep., Amort./Cur. Mat. L/T/D		
.1	1.7	.3					.5	.3
1.0	4.8	.8				Fixed/Worth	2.8	2.7
-2.6	-33.6	15.3					28.3	18.3
1.1	1.6	.6					.4	1.4
6.7	4.0	1.8				Debt/Worth	2.9	4.2
-5.2	-35.7	16.1					28.5	NM
		78.8					79.0	84.6
	(10)	-2.0				% Profit Before Taxes/Tangible Net Worth	(15) 23.5	(15) 42.2
		-11.0					-5.7	-22.0
18.4	16.7	9.3					50.8	21.3
7.2	8.7	-1.2				% Profit Before Taxes/Total Assets	16.7	4.8
-1.6	-1.9	-2.9					-.1	-2.2
111.0	8.8	19.5					15.9	45.1
23.7	1.3	1.2				Sales/Net Fixed Assets	3.7	5.9
12.5	.5	.5					.9	.8
7.9	3.3	2.2					3.5	4.6
3.8	1.2	.9				Sales/Total Assets	1.4	2.1
2.1	.5	.2					.8	.8
	3.7						2.5	.9
	9.2					% Depr., Dep., Amort./Sales	(13) 4.6	(13) 3.7
	17.3						7.4	8.3
						% Officers', Directors' Owners' Comp/Sales		
22123M	23173M	74542M	4981M	25024M		Net Sales ($)	36058M	33938M
3532M	14496M	60396M	38853M	51308M		Total Assets ($)	63827M	28031M

M = $ thousand MM = $ million
See Pages 9 through 22 for Explanation of Ratios and Data

Comparative Historical Data
Current Data Sorted by Sales

4/1/08-3/31/09 ALL	4/1/09-3/31/10 ALL	4/1/10-3/31/11 ALL	Type of Statement	0-1MM	1-3MM	3-5MM	5-10MM	10-25MM	25MM & OVER
3	3	3	Unqualified				1	1	1
2	3	2	Reviewed		2				
2	1	4	Compiled	2	2				
2	6	12	Tax Returns	7	3		1	1	
8	9	18	Other	5	6	2	1	3	1
			10 (4/1-9/30/10)			**29 (10/1/10-3/31/11)**			
17	**19**	**39**	NUMBER OF STATEMENTS	**14**	**13**	**3**	**3**	**5**	**1**
%	%	%	**ASSETS**	%	%	%	%	%	%
13.9	18.6	22.2	Cash & Equivalents	12.8	24.0				
7.8	8.5	6.6	Trade Receivables (net)	4.8	6.3				
12.1	5.6	4.5	Inventory	1.2	6.9				
1.9	1.1	2.2	All Other Current	.6	5.1				
35.8	33.8	35.5	Total Current	19.4	42.3				
40.9	33.2	47.1	Fixed Assets (net)	67.6	47.2				
9.1	9.9	5.4	Intangibles (net)	3.6	2.1				
14.2	23.1	12.1	All Other Non-Current	9.5	8.4				
100.0	100.0	100.0	Total	100.0	100.0				
			LIABILITIES						
19.4	5.4	9.3	Notes Payable-Short Term	8.5	13.8				
6.8	2.6	2.7	Cur. Mat.-L.T.D.	1.5	5.4				
9.8	3.9	6.8	Trade Payables	4.8	8.4				
.0	.1	1.8	Income Taxes Payable	.0	.0				
24.6	15.1	16.3	All Other Current	7.4	13.4				
60.6	27.1	36.8	Total Current	22.2	41.0				
30.9	30.7	31.4	Long-Term Debt	40.9	36.0				
.0	.0	.0	Deferred Taxes	.0	.0				
24.5	5.5	14.9	All Other Non-Current	19.1	8.9				
-16.0	36.7	16.9	Net Worth	17.8	14.1				
100.0	100.0	100.0	Total Liabilities & Net Worth	100.0	100.0				
			INCOME DATA						
100.0	100.0	100.0	Net Sales	100.0	100.0				
			Gross Profit						
94.7	89.5	87.2	Operating Expenses	69.4	100.7				
5.3	10.5	12.8	Operating Profit	30.6	-.7				
3.2	6.1	4.8	All Other Expenses (net)	12.0	.3				
2.1	4.4	8.0	Profit Before Taxes	18.6	-1.0				
			RATIOS						
1.8	6.8	3.8	Current	5.5	4.1				
.5	.9	1.5		1.1	2.1				
.2	.2	.2		.1	.3				
1.3	4.6	3.2	Quick	3.3	4.1				
.2	.7	1.2		1.0	1.4				
.1	.1	.2		.1	.2				
0 UND	0 UND	0 UND	Sales/Receivables	0 UND	0 UND				
2 192.6	0 999.8	1 501.1		0 UND	1 258.8				
29 12.5	34 10.7	18 20.5		0 UND	30 12.1				
			Cost of Sales/Inventory						
			Cost of Sales/Payables						
26.8	4.9	5.2	Sales/Working Capital	5.9	2.3				
-16.7	-37.3	51.1		NM	13.9				
-3.4	-6.5	-4.2		-3.3	-8.5				
19.8	6.7	4.9	EBIT/Interest						
(14) 2.0	(11) 2.8	(24) 1.8							
.4	.0	-2.3							
			Net Profit + Depr., Dep., Amort./Cur. Mat. L/T/D						
.4	.2	.4	Fixed/Worth	1.4	.4				
2.3	.9	2.4		14.3	.9				
-.5	-4.4	-12.5		-48.5	-4.0				
1.2	.2	.8	Debt/Worth	2.3	.4				
3.9	2.8	3.9		14.6	1.1				
-1.8	-7.9	-16.5		-50.4	-6.1				
72.5	48.5	93.2	% Profit Before Taxes/Tangible Net Worth	412.9					
(10) 17.2	(14) 15.8	(28) 13.2		(10) 118.1					
-2.5	-5.3	-3.0		5.7					
13.4	20.3	11.9	% Profit Before Taxes/Total Assets	18.3	6.5				
4.0	3.8	6.3		8.5	-1.4				
-3.6	-4.8	-2.0		5.8	-4.6				
67.9	32.7	22.0	Sales/Net Fixed Assets	15.5	19.2				
7.9	16.1	6.2		1.3	4.6				
1.1	2.0	.6		.2	.8				
3.4	3.3	3.4	Sales/Total Assets	2.1	3.5				
1.5	1.9	2.0		1.0	2.1				
.9	.9	.5		.2	.6				
2.2	1.4	1.9	% Depr., Dep., Amort./Sales	9.2	.7				
(12) 4.4	(16) 2.8	(28) 4.9		(11) 11.7	(11) 2.5				
10.2	5.7	15.8		31.9	4.9				
			% Officers', Directors' Owners' Comp/Sales						
89823M	88558M	149843M	Net Sales ($)	8081M	20699M	13238M	20721M	62080M	25024M
98665M	78410M	168585M	Total Assets ($)	17497M	20575M	40582M	7937M	30686M	51308M

M = $ thousand   MM = $ million
See Pages 9 through 22 for Explanation of Ratios and Data

Current Data Sorted by Assets   ## Comparative Historical Data

Type of Statement	0-500M	500M-2MM	2-10MM	10-50MM	50-100MM	100-250MM	4/1/06-3/31/07 ALL	4/1/07-3/31/08 ALL
Unqualified	3	21	46	38	8	4	76	83
Reviewed	1	1	6	4	1		2	4
Compiled	5	4	3	2			10	9
Tax Returns	20	9	10		1	1	19	24
Other	19	18	22	13	1	2	33	42
		154 (4/1-9/30/10)			109 (10/1/10-3/31/11)			
NUMBER OF STATEMENTS	48	53	87	57	11	7	140	162
ASSETS	%	%	%	%	%	%	%	%
Cash & Equivalents	29.9	26.0	21.5	19.9	21.6		26.9	22.6
Trade Receivables (net)	12.5	21.2	9.4	7.7	4.3		12.0	12.5
Inventory	3.7	2.7	2.9	1.3	.0		2.3	1.6
All Other Current	3.6	3.0	4.2	3.7	4.3		3.8	5.6
Total Current	49.7	52.9	38.0	32.6	30.1		45.0	42.3
Fixed Assets (net)	29.8	39.0	50.7	53.8	38.2		38.1	46.5
Intangibles (net)	12.0	3.3	2.6	3.3	6.0		3.9	2.2
All Other Non-Current	8.5	4.9	8.6	10.3	25.7		13.0	9.0
Total	100.0	100.0	100.0	100.0	100.0		100.0	100.0
LIABILITIES								
Notes Payable-Short Term	13.4	4.9	3.9	1.2	.2		7.6	6.1
Cur. Mat.-L.T.D.	3.0	2.2	2.2	4.1	5.9		3.2	4.0
Trade Payables	9.9	6.8	5.1	4.2	2.9		5.9	6.2
Income Taxes Payable	.0	.0	.0	.4	.0		.3	.1
All Other Current	9.8	12.5	11.6	10.2	9.0		14.5	14.6
Total Current	36.2	26.5	22.8	20.2	18.0		31.5	31.0
Long-Term Debt	32.5	20.0	26.0	27.3	18.1		15.9	19.3
Deferred Taxes	.0	.0	.0	.2	.0		.0	.0
All Other Non-Current	33.9	5.7	10.9	5.9	11.4		9.8	6.4
Net Worth	-2.6	47.8	40.2	46.4	52.5		42.8	43.3
Total Liabilities & Net Worth	100.0	100.0	100.0	100.0	100.0		100.0	100.0
INCOME DATA								
Net Sales	100.0	100.0	100.0	100.0	100.0		100.0	100.0
Gross Profit								
Operating Expenses	93.7	88.8	93.4	88.6	81.4		94.1	89.8
Operating Profit	6.3	11.2	6.6	11.4	18.6		5.9	10.2
All Other Expenses (net)	1.3	2.4	4.2	2.8	4.2		1.2	1.5
Profit Before Taxes	5.0	8.8	2.3	8.5	14.4		4.7	8.7
RATIOS								
Current	9.7	5.4	5.1	3.8	7.7		4.8	3.3
	1.9	2.2	2.0	2.0	1.7		1.5	1.7
	.6	.9	1.0	1.2	1.5		.8	.9
Quick	9.4	4.3	4.0	3.3	2.8		3.9	2.8
	1.6	1.9	1.4	2.0	1.5		1.3	1.4
	.5	.8	.6	1.0	.6		.7	.6
Sales/Receivables	0 UND	1 404.0	3 143.6	3 114.7	0 UND		1 513.2	0 UND
	0 UND	23 15.9	8 43.9	14 26.1	11 34.6		14 26.0	10 36.7
	12 31.6	45 8.2	37 9.9	34 10.7	61 6.0		34 10.6	35 10.6
Cost of Sales/Inventory								
Cost of Sales/Payables								
Sales/Working Capital	10.7	4.5	3.4	2.6	1.6		4.3	4.5
	25.4	8.6	8.4	5.7	6.3		12.7	11.7
	-41.4	-194.6	-256.4	33.1	19.3		-32.2	-68.9
EBIT/Interest	13.8	16.1	7.2	12.0			11.4	13.2
	(23) 2.4	(33) 3.2	(59) 2.2	(46) 2.9			(91) 3.2	(122) 3.7
	.0	.6	.0	1.1			.6	1.6
Net Profit + Depr., Dep., Amort./Cur. Mat. L/T/D								
Fixed/Worth	.4	.1	.5	.7	.1		.4	.5
	1.6	.7	1.5	1.2	1.1		.7	1.0
	-.2	2.5	3.5	2.7	6.3		2.3	2.2
Debt/Worth	.4	.3	.4	.7	.2		.3	.5
	8.5	1.0	1.3	1.1	.8		1.0	1.0
	-1.7	3.0	4.4	3.1	12.5		5.8	3.4
% Profit Before Taxes/Tangible Net Worth	137.1	53.3	22.1	28.7			32.9	44.7
	(28) 43.5	(49) 23.0	(76) 5.9	(55) 8.3			(119) 10.8	(146) 18.3
	10.3	.7	-4.5	.1			.0	3.8
% Profit Before Taxes/Total Assets	49.7	19.1	7.9	11.4	12.9		14.3	20.5
	9.7	11.2	2.5	3.1	2.7		5.0	8.1
	1.0	.0	-2.2	.2	1.0		-.4	1.6
Sales/Net Fixed Assets	81.0	62.2	10.1	5.3	27.1		19.1	15.9
	26.5	6.4	2.1	1.0	10.3		5.3	4.0
	14.6	2.2	.8	.6	.6		1.5	1.1
Sales/Total Assets	8.7	3.6	1.8	1.3	1.2		3.3	2.9
	5.1	1.9	1.1	.6	.5		1.5	1.6
	3.2	1.1	.5	.4	.3		.6	.7
% Depr., Dep., Amort./Sales	.8	.9	1.9	2.2			1.1	1.2
	(23) 1.4	(37) 1.6	(75) 3.4	(50) 5.0			(109) 2.5	(123) 2.6
	3.1	3.5	7.0	7.4			4.9	5.1
% Officers', Directors' Owners' Comp/Sales	4.4	2.8	3.0				3.3	3.0
	(27) 6.6	(15) 9.3	(10) 4.6				(29) 6.8	(36) 6.4
	17.4	14.7	7.7				11.2	12.4
Net Sales ($)	61119M	154101M	571264M	1124370M	2237630M	1073365M	1782658M	2352552M
Total Assets ($)	10214M	64910M	406277M	1083834M	777695M	1016924M	1628906M	2053192M

M = $ thousand   MM = $ million
See Pages 9 through 22 for Explanation of Ratios and Data

Comparative Historical Data

Current Data Sorted by Sales

			Type of Statement	0-1MM	1-3MM	3-5MM	5-10MM	10-25MM	25MM & OVER
204	105	120	Unqualified	3	22	23	35	23	14
15	7	13	Reviewed	1	2	3	4	1	2
11	7	14	Compiled	5	3	1	4	1	
47	26	41	Tax Returns	17	13	6	2	1	3
68	75	75	Other	20	21	9	6	8	11
4/1/08-3/31/09 ALL	4/1/09-3/31/10 ALL	4/1/10-3/31/11 ALL		154 (4/1-9/30/10)			109 (10/1/10-3/31/11)		
345	220	263	NUMBER OF STATEMENTS	46	61	42	51	33	30
%	%	%	ASSETS	%	%	%	%	%	%
21.9	22.9	23.2	Cash & Equivalents	24.8	22.2	23.6	20.7	26.8	22.8
9.9	13.0	11.7	Trade Receivables (net)	7.0	11.1	18.7	8.5	11.8	15.1
1.8	1.4	2.5	Inventory	2.4	2.1	1.3	4.5	3.1	1.1
4.0	4.0	3.7	All Other Current	1.9	3.1	4.0	2.5	5.8	6.6
37.6	41.3	41.1	Total Current	36.2	38.5	47.6	36.3	47.6	45.7
44.9	44.2	44.1	Fixed Assets (net)	51.5	46.8	41.3	51.4	35.8	28.1
3.5	5.5	5.3	Intangibles (net)	6.4	6.4	3.4	1.4	3.8	12.8
13.9	9.0	9.5	All Other Non-Current	5.9	8.4	7.8	10.9	12.9	13.3
100.0	100.0	100.0	Total	100.0	100.0	100.0	100.0	100.0	100.0
			LIABILITIES						
4.9	6.9	5.0	Notes Payable-Short Term	8.6	5.0	5.7	5.9	2.0	.3
2.6	2.5	2.9	Cur. Mat.-L.T.D.	1.6	3.2	3.0	2.1	.7	8.0
5.0	5.1	6.0	Trade Payables	7.8	3.3	7.0	5.4	6.2	7.8
.2	.1	.1	Income Taxes Payable	.0	.0	.0	.0	.1	.7
14.8	15.8	10.9	All Other Current	7.4	7.3	11.5	5.9	15.5	26.0
27.5	30.3	24.9	Total Current	25.5	18.8	27.2	19.4	24.5	42.8
23.3	22.3	25.9	Long-Term Debt	37.7	30.6	20.6	28.8	13.9	13.9
.1	.1	.1	Deferred Taxes	.0	.0	.0	.0	.1	.5
8.6	10.3	12.9	All Other Non-Current	15.2	21.8	9.8	8.4	9.8	6.8
40.5	37.0	36.2	Net Worth	21.6	28.8	42.4	43.3	51.8	36.0
100.0	100.0	100.0	Total Liabilities & Net Worth	100.0	100.0	100.0	100.0	100.0	100.0
			INCOME DATA						
100.0	100.0	100.0	Net Sales	100.0	100.0	100.0	100.0	100.0	100.0
			Gross Profit						
92.4	93.0	91.0	Operating Expenses	84.8	92.5	95.4	91.0	91.1	91.1
7.6	7.0	9.0	Operating Profit	15.2	7.5	4.6	9.0	8.9	8.9
3.4	4.2	2.9	All Other Expenses (net)	7.1	3.1	1.5	2.8	.4	.7
4.2	2.8	6.1	Profit Before Taxes	8.0	4.4	3.1	6.3	8.5	8.2
			RATIOS						
4.1	3.9	4.8	Current	8.2	7.0	5.4	3.9	5.0	2.9
1.9	1.7	2.0		1.8	2.9	2.0	2.1	2.3	1.2
.9	.8	1.0		.5	1.1	.8	1.0	1.3	.6
3.6	3.6	3.9	Quick	8.0	5.8	4.8	3.5	4.3	2.0
1.5	1.4	1.7		1.5	2.2	1.8	1.9	2.1	1.0
.7	.6	.7		.4	.9	.7	.8	.8	.4
0　958.0	1　636.2	0　UND	Sales/Receivables	0　UND	0　UND	4　86.6	3　128.9	3　106.9	2　228.6
10　35.7	13　27.9	8　43.9		0　UND	7　50.9	31　11.9	12　31.2	17　22.0	10　36.1
35　10.5	38　9.6	36　10.1		15　23.6	25　14.4	69　5.3	32　11.2	42　8.7	34　10.8
			Cost of Sales/Inventory						
			Cost of Sales/Payables						
3.4	4.5	4.0	Sales/Working Capital	4.8	4.2	3.3	2.7	3.7	5.7
11.1	12.7	10.0		17.6	9.0	9.1	5.9	7.0	32.3
-115.4	-21.1	-239.9		-11.0	237.9	-22.9	357.4	30.0	-25.5
6.6	10.1	10.5	EBIT/Interest	10.8	4.9	20.3	8.0	18.2	30.6
(246) 2.1	(137) 2.5	(173) 2.9		(22) 2.2	(38) 2.0	(30) 3.7	(37) 2.4	(23) 5.1	(23) 6.5
.3	.4	.5		.1	-.4	-2.4	1.2	-.1	2.0
		7.7	Net Profit + Depr., Dep., Amort./Cur. Mat. L/T/D						
	(12)	2.5							
		.8							
.4	.4	.4	Fixed/Worth	.4	.6	.4	.7	.2	.3
1.0	1.1	1.3		1.5	1.6	.9	1.4	.7	1.0
2.5	2.9	3.5		10.8	4.8	2.4	2.5	1.3	-2.0
.4	.5	.4	Debt/Worth	.2	.5	.6	.5	.3	.5
1.2	1.3	1.3		1.6	2.1	1.3	1.1	.8	1.7
3.5	4.8	5.9		20.4	11.5	3.5	3.8	1.7	-10.4
24.1	32.5	37.5	% Profit Before Taxes/Tangible Net Worth	74.4	34.1	35.5	19.1	28.7	86.4
(306) 8.1	(189) 7.3	(221) 11.9		(36) 24.5	(49) 9.9	(37) 11.9	(46) 7.3	(31) 8.3	(22) 28.0
-1.2	-3.4	-.3		6.5	-4.4	-5.1	-.4	-1.6	8.1
10.5	15.0	14.7	% Profit Before Taxes/Total Assets	31.7	15.1	14.2	8.2	15.1	19.0
2.2	3.3	5.0		9.2	2.5	5.4	2.8	3.8	7.9
-1.4	-1.5	-.3		-1.0	-1.7	-2.0	-.2	-1.2	2.6
14.1	21.9	24.9	Sales/Net Fixed Assets	24.7	22.2	39.7	11.2	18.9	31.4
2.4	4.3	4.6		5.5	4.1	4.7	1.6	5.0	14.5
.8	.9	.9		.4	1.1	.9	.7	1.7	4.4
2.4	3.1	3.2	Sales/Total Assets	4.5	3.8	2.3	1.8	2.6	3.9
1.0	1.4	1.5		1.6	1.5	1.6	.7	1.7	1.8
.5	.6	.6		.3	.8	.7	.4	.7	.9
1.5	1.5	1.4	% Depr., Dep., Amort./Sales	1.5	1.3	1.7	1.2	1.3	1.3
(274) 3.3	(161) 3.0	(199) 2.9		(24) 3.9	(45) 3.2	(34) 2.9	(45) 4.7	(29) 2.0	(22) 2.7
6.1	6.1	5.7		10.1	5.8	5.0	7.7	3.5	4.3
3.4	3.2	3.9	% Officers', Directors' Owners' Comp/Sales	5.6	4.4				
(68) 6.5	(38) 6.3	(56) 6.5		(15) 9.3	(21) 6.5				
10.4	11.2	11.1		17.4	9.3				
5325230M	3624860M	5221849M	Net Sales ($)	23894M	114647M	159787M	366780M	520261M	4036480M
6605063M	3651425M	3359854M	Total Assets ($)	51387M	134107M	190083M	653518M	535551M	1795208M

© RMA 2011

M = $ thousand　　MM = $ million
See Pages 9 through 22 for Explanation of Ratios and Data

Current Data Sorted by Assets   Comparative Historical Data

Type of Statement	0-500M	500M-2MM	2-10MM	10-50MM	50-100MM	100-250MM	ALL 4/1/06-3/31/07	ALL 4/1/07-3/31/08
Unqualified	5	18	58	84	34	33	208	182
Reviewed	1	2	7	7			19	13
Compiled	3	1	4	2			19	12
Tax Returns	14	8	6				25	26
Other	10	12	32	26	3	4	68	79
		264 (4/1-9/30/10)			110 (10/1/10-3/31/11)			
NUMBER OF STATEMENTS	33	41	107	119	37	37	339	312
ASSETS	%	%	%	%	%	%	%	%
Cash & Equivalents	39.6	26.9	27.8	23.6	19.2	24.4	22.8	24.0
Trade Receivables (net)	18.8	17.6	16.2	11.7	7.6	7.7	14.3	16.0
Inventory	3.3	3.1	2.0	1.0	2.9	.4	1.8	2.0
All Other Current	3.0	3.3	3.6	4.4	2.4	4.1	3.7	4.2
Total Current	64.7	50.9	49.6	40.6	32.1	36.5	42.7	46.1
Fixed Assets (net)	21.1	35.8	34.6	40.1	43.7	37.2	41.1	38.1
Intangibles (net)	6.9	4.0	2.1	5.5	1.0	3.2	2.5	2.8
All Other Non-Current	7.2	9.2	13.8	13.8	23.2	23.1	13.7	12.9
Total	100.0	100.0	100.0	100.0	100.0	100.0	100.0	100.0
LIABILITIES								
Notes Payable-Short Term	20.4	11.9	3.4	2.2	2.4	.9	5.1	3.4
Cur. Mat.-L.T.D.	3.1	2.2	2.0	1.8	2.5	6.7	1.8	2.3
Trade Payables	18.1	10.8	6.7	5.5	3.0	2.4	6.2	5.9
Income Taxes Payable	.0	.1	.0	.1	.1	.0	.3	.1
All Other Current	26.2	12.6	13.8	16.2	10.3	12.9	15.1	16.9
Total Current	67.7	37.5	25.9	25.8	18.3	23.0	28.5	28.6
Long-Term Debt	9.2	20.8	19.3	23.5	28.6	17.1	21.9	22.6
Deferred Taxes	.0	.0	.0	.2	.0	.1	.0	.1
All Other Non-Current	28.2	7.0	6.5	4.5	2.0	3.4	6.2	9.5
Net Worth	-5.1	34.7	48.2	46.0	51.2	56.5	43.4	39.3
Total Liabilities & Net Worth	100.0	100.0	100.0	100.0	100.0	100.0	100.0	100.0
INCOME DATA								
Net Sales	100.0	100.0	100.0	100.0	100.0	100.0	100.0	100.0
Gross Profit								
Operating Expenses	95.9	91.1	93.3	94.0	90.9	90.3	92.0	91.3
Operating Profit	4.1	8.9	6.7	6.0	9.1	9.7	8.0	8.7
All Other Expenses (net)	.7	3.1	1.2	2.1	3.7	-.7	1.5	1.3
Profit Before Taxes	3.4	5.8	5.5	3.9	5.4	10.5	6.5	7.4
RATIOS								
Current	5.0	8.1	4.4	3.9	3.2	5.3	3.8	4.4
	1.4	2.5	2.2	2.0	1.7	1.5	1.6	1.9
	.5	.7	1.1	1.0	1.1	1.1	.9	1.0
Quick	5.0	6.6	4.1	3.6	2.7	4.4	3.3	3.5
	(32) 1.4	1.8	1.9	1.8	1.4	1.4	1.3	1.5
	.4	.5	.9	.9	1.0	.6	.7	.8
Sales/Receivables	0 UND	0 UND	6 61.5	5 76.3	7 55.8	1 368.4	2 177.0	2 223.2
	5 75.7	13 29.0	24 15.5	21 17.7	19 19.3	19 19.2	19 19.0	21 17.0
	31 11.8	40 9.2	54 6.8	56 6.5	49 7.4	70 5.2	49 7.4	55 6.6
Cost of Sales/Inventory								
Cost of Sales/Payables								
Sales/Working Capital	9.4	4.2	2.8	2.2	3.1	-1.7	3.7	3.3
	36.8	7.6	6.2	6.6	6.3	5.6	13.0	10.9
	-14.9	-35.1	35.1	231.8	17.5	67.1	-72.8	NM
EBIT/Interest	52.3	31.4	13.7	9.0	13.2	33.2	6.9	11.0
	(17) 5.0	(27) 2.1	(70) 2.5	(86) 2.9	(29) 4.0	(28) 5.4	(223) 2.6	(212) 3.1
	.8	.9	-.1	.7	1.6	1.7	1.1	1.2
Net Profit + Depr., Dep., Amort./Cur. Mat. L/T/D							12.5	15.0
							(10) 8.7	(11) 3.8
							1.2	1.5
Fixed/Worth	.0	.2	.1	.4	.3	.4	.3	.2
	.2	.8	.6	.9	.9	.7	.9	.8
	UND	2.7	1.5	2.2	1.5	1.1	2.3	2.0
Debt/Worth	.3	.5	.5	.5	.6	.2	.4	.4
	1.9	1.5	1.0	1.2	.9	.7	1.2	1.2
	-2.5	34.8	3.2	3.5	2.3	2.0	3.3	3.6
% Profit Before Taxes/Tangible Net Worth	67.0	31.7	29.7	22.1	9.9	14.2	24.8	27.9
	(22) 25.5	(32) 12.9	(99) 8.7	(110) 7.2	(36) 4.7	(35) 6.4	(304) 9.7	(273) 10.3
	2.9	-2.9	.4	-.6	-.2	3.0	1.1	2.0
% Profit Before Taxes/Total Assets	33.7	17.1	13.6	8.3	3.8	6.4	11.0	12.4
	11.9	4.5	3.7	2.2	2.0	3.2	3.5	4.2
	-10.2	-1.0	.0	-.8	-.4	1.0	.0	.3
Sales/Net Fixed Assets	UND	46.9	39.4	12.3	5.2	6.2	23.1	28.8
	62.2	10.9	7.7	2.6	1.6	1.3	3.1	5.3
	14.1	1.7	1.0	.7	.7	.7	.9	1.1
Sales/Total Assets	9.7	4.1	2.2	1.6	1.1	1.0	2.3	2.5
	5.1	1.8	1.2	.7	.6	.4	1.0	1.2
	2.6	1.0	.6	.4	.4	.3	.5	.6
% Depr., Dep., Amort./Sales	.3	.6	.9	1.4	2.0	1.9	1.4	1.1
	(15) 1.0	(31) 1.6	(83) 2.8	(98) 3.7	(34) 4.8	(30) 3.7	(245) 3.3	(235) 3.0
	2.6	5.0	5.5	6.6	6.1	7.5	5.9	5.2
% Officers', Directors' Owners' Comp/Sales	2.3		2.9	1.8			2.4	1.5
	(11) 9.0		(13) 4.5	(11) 4.1			(51) 5.1	(47) 6.8
	32.4		9.6	30.6			11.5	12.5
Net Sales ($)	55402M	129624M	968978M	2800326M	1875754M	3970024M	7213686M	9154602M
Total Assets ($)	8186M	48229M	592363M	2811273M	2548050M	5772698M	6522010M	7711899M

M = $ thousand   MM = $ million
See Pages 9 through 22 for Explanation of Ratios and Data

Comparative Historical Data | Current Data Sorted by Sales

128	224	232	Type of Statement						
128	224	232	Unqualified	5	24	21	45	53	84
10	22	17	Reviewed	1	5		2	5	4
3	14	10	Compiled		4	2	3		1
21	25	28	Tax Returns	14	6	5	2	1	
46	68	87	Other	8	16	13	14	19	17
4/1/08-3/31/09	4/1/09-3/31/10	4/1/10-3/31/11		264 (4/1-9/30/10)			110 (10/1/10-3/31/11)		
ALL	ALL	ALL		0-1MM	1-3MM	3-5MM	5-10MM	10-25MM	25MM & OVER
208	353	374	**NUMBER OF STATEMENTS**	28	55	41	66	78	106
%	%	%	**ASSETS**	%	%	%	%	%	%
28.5	24.5	26.2	Cash & Equivalents	19.9	28.2	26.1	26.7	31.7	22.6
15.5	13.0	13.4	Trade Receivables (net)	9.7	9.1	12.3	10.7	17.5	15.8
3.2	2.1	1.9	Inventory	2.2	1.3	4.5	.4	1.8	1.9
4.4	3.7	3.7	All Other Current	4.1	3.1	1.3	1.9	4.1	5.6
51.6	43.3	45.2	Total Current	36.0	41.8	44.2	39.8	55.1	45.9
30.6	40.3	36.4	Fixed Assets (net)	47.9	41.6	32.6	37.8	29.9	36.2
2.9	4.3	3.8	Intangibles (net)	8.2	1.7	4.0	2.4	2.8	5.4
14.8	12.1	14.5	All Other Non-Current	8.0	14.9	19.2	20.0	12.2	12.6
100.0	100.0	100.0	Total	100.0	100.0	100.0	100.0	100.0	100.0
			LIABILITIES						
5.6	8.0	5.1	Notes Payable-Short Term	7.1	6.4	7.0	9.2	2.5	2.5
1.5	3.9	2.6	Cur. Mat.-L.T.D.	2.5	2.3	2.1	3.3	2.7	2.4
7.6	6.0	7.0	Trade Payables	11.7	4.7	6.5	7.2	7.0	7.0
.2	.2	.0	Income Taxes Payable	.0	.0	.2	.0	.0	.1
18.1	14.9	15.1	All Other Current	4.4	13.9	10.2	16.7	13.8	20.3
33.0	33.0	29.8	Total Current	25.7	27.3	26.0	36.4	26.1	32.3
17.9	22.1	20.6	Long-Term Debt	36.2	23.3	20.5	21.7	15.3	18.3
.1	.0	.1	Deferred Taxes	.0	.0	.0	.1	.1	.2
8.1	6.7	7.1	All Other Non-Current	30.0	5.7	5.2	3.9	7.4	4.3
40.9	38.1	42.4	Net Worth	8.1	43.7	48.3	37.9	51.1	45.0
100.0	100.0	100.0	Total Liabilities & Net Worth	100.0	100.0	100.0	100.0	100.0	100.0
			INCOME DATA						
100.0	100.0	100.0	Net Sales	100.0	100.0	100.0	100.0	100.0	100.0
			Gross Profit						
93.4	94.8	93.0	Operating Expenses	87.7	92.1	93.2	92.4	94.5	93.8
6.6	5.2	7.0	Operating Profit	12.3	7.9	6.8	7.6	5.5	6.2
4.0	4.2	1.7	All Other Expenses (net)	8.9	1.9	2.0	4.1	-.8	.0
2.6	1.0	5.3	Profit Before Taxes	3.4	6.0	4.8	3.5	6.3	6.1
			RATIOS						
5.0	4.1	4.3	Current	7.3	5.2	5.8	4.5	4.6	2.7
2.1	1.8	1.9		2.6	2.4	2.5	1.8	2.2	1.6
1.0	1.0	1.1		.8	.7	1.3	.8	1.3	1.1
4.3	3.5	3.9	Quick	7.8	5.0	5.3	3.9	3.9	2.4
1.7	1.5 (373)	1.7		(27) 2.3	1.7	2.0	1.8	2.0	1.2
.8	.7	.8		.7	.4	.9	.7	1.1	.8
3 116.1	1 333.9	3 107.6	Sales/Receivables	0 UND	0 UND	2 183.1	3 107.1	7 55.0	7 50.6
23 16.1	16 22.4	19 19.3		5 69.3	8 46.5	17 21.6	14 25.2	26 13.9	24 15.2
49 7.4	44 8.3	50 7.2		52 7.0	20 18.1	41 8.9	56 6.5	56 6.5	60 6.0
			Cost of Sales/Inventory						
			Cost of Sales/Payables						
2.9	3.1	3.0	Sales/Working Capital	3.8	2.6	2.9	2.2	2.4	4.0
7.8	8.6	7.2		8.9	7.9	6.8	8.9	5.7	8.4
UND	-82.7	92.8		NM	-26.6	31.7	-13.9	17.7	74.7
9.0	10.5	15.0	EBIT/Interest	3.8	6.7	30.5	8.6	18.3	22.9
(129) 2.5	(263) 2.2	(257) 3.0		(19) 1.5	(33) 2.0	(28) 4.9	(46) 2.1	(47) 4.6	(84) 4.5
.3	-.4	1.1		.7	.0	-.2	-.2	1.5	1.7
13.7	7.6	7.8	Net Profit + Depr., Dep., Amort./Cur. Mat. L/T/D						41.8
(12) 5.7	(13) 3.6	(14) 3.7						(10)	4.9
1.6	1.6	1.2							2.9
.1	.2	.2	Fixed/Worth	.3	.1	.1	.3	.1	.4
.6	1.0	.8		1.6	.9	.5	.8	.6	.9
1.7	2.1	1.7		15.0	2.0	1.4	2.4	1.2	1.6
.3	.4	.4	Debt/Worth	.6	.3	.4	.4	.5	.5
1.1	1.3	1.0		2.4	.8	.8	1.2	1.0	1.2
3.5	3.5	3.5		UND	4.1	2.0	4.4	2.5	3.0
28.4	17.5	23.0	% Profit Before Taxes/Tangible Net Worth	27.5	25.4	26.2	13.4	28.2	23.0
(183) 6.0	(305) 4.0	(334) 7.9		(21) 6.2	(46) 9.6	(36) 6.4	(57) 1.6	(76) 10.6	(98) 7.9
-3.3	-5.3	.3		-6.5	.8	-1.5	-3.4	1.2	2.4
13.4	8.7	10.2	% Profit Before Taxes/Total Assets	8.4	12.4	15.2	8.9	13.4	8.6
1.8	1.3	3.1		1.5	4.2	3.7	1.2	4.4	3.4
-1.9	-2.9	-.3		-5.6	-.5	-2.5	-1.4	.6	.7
40.8	30.2	25.3	Sales/Net Fixed Assets	36.3	40.9	75.6	24.5	36.6	14.2
9.8	3.3	4.2		2.0	2.9	7.7	2.2	7.9	4.2
1.8	.9	.9		.8	.6	1.0	.7	1.5	1.1
2.9	2.3	2.2	Sales/Total Assets	2.4	3.8	2.8	1.8	2.1	2.0
1.4	1.1	1.0		1.0	.9	.9	.7	1.3	1.2
.7	.5	.5		.3	.3	.5	.3	.7	.5
.8	1.3	1.0	% Depr., Dep., Amort./Sales	3.6	.9	.8	.9	.7	1.2
(168) 2.0	(274) 3.4	(291) 3.0		(18) 5.0	(40) 3.2	(30) 3.3	(52) 3.6	(59) 2.4	(92) 2.6
4.6	5.6	6.1		11.3	7.8	5.4	8.9	6.3	5.5
4.3	4.1	2.9	% Officers', Directors' Owners' Comp/Sales						.9
(35) 8.0	(51) 8.2	(45) 6.6						(14)	3.0
18.6	12.7	12.9							12.0
5552332M	8060336M	9800108M	Net Sales ($)	16110M	100329M	159843M	471726M	1274827M	7777273M
6658056M	8871953M	11780799M	Total Assets ($)	30481M	247030M	301223M	1317732M	1869261M	8015072M

M = $ thousand   MM = $ million
See Pages 9 through 22 for Explanation of Ratios and Data

HEALTH CARE AND SOCIAL ASSISTANCE

Current Data Sorted by Assets   Comparative Historical Data

						Type of Statement		
3	19	83	86	34	22	Unqualified	199	201
6	28	73	32	1		Reviewed	141	132
311	227	113	13	1	2	Compiled	657	579
855	454	186	16	4	5	Tax Returns	1224	1107
503	473	369	139	20	17	Other	987	1015
	442 (4/1-9/30/10)			3,653 (10/1/10-3/31/11)			4/1/06-3/31/07 ALL	4/1/07-3/31/08 ALL
0-500M	500M-2MM	2-10MM	10-50MM	50-100MM	100-250MM			
1678	1201	824	286	60	46	NUMBER OF STATEMENTS	3208	3034
%	%	%	%	%	%	ASSETS	%	%
38.9	25.6	16.0	13.3	22.7	21.8	Cash & Equivalents	25.8	27.1
3.5	8.5	18.9	22.8	16.3	14.1	Trade Receivables (net)	11.1	10.2
1.1	1.2	.9	1.5	1.5	1.9	Inventory	1.1	1.0
3.8	3.7	3.0	5.3	5.8	2.8	All Other Current	4.0	4.6
47.3	39.1	38.8	42.9	46.3	40.5	Total Current	41.9	42.9
34.4	43.3	47.4	41.8	35.7	32.8	Fixed Assets (net)	42.0	42.1
4.8	5.0	3.4	4.4	6.6	15.9	Intangibles (net)	4.1	3.7
13.5	12.6	10.4	10.9	11.3	10.8	All Other Non-Current	12.1	11.3
100.0	100.0	100.0	100.0	100.0	100.0	Total	100.0	100.0
						LIABILITIES		
31.2	14.9	6.7	4.3	3.6	3.6	Notes Payable-Short Term	20.7	18.6
8.0	7.1	6.1	4.8	4.3	3.2	Cur. Mat.-L.T.D.	8.0	8.5
2.8	2.5	4.3	6.2	12.7	6.0	Trade Payables	3.5	3.1
.2	.2	.5	.6	1.0	.1	Income Taxes Payable	.5	.4
38.6	20.4	15.7	16.3	16.5	14.0	All Other Current	27.9	27.6
80.8	45.0	33.4	32.3	38.1	26.7	Total Current	60.7	58.3
27.6	31.3	35.2	27.1	23.0	21.0	Long-Term Debt	32.5	31.8
.0	.2	.2	.4	.5	.7	Deferred Taxes	.1	.2
7.1	5.8	3.5	3.5	7.0	5.5	All Other Non-Current	4.5	5.5
-15.6	17.7	28.1	36.8	31.5	46.6	Net Worth	2.2	4.3
100.0	100.0	100.0	100.0	100.0	100.0	Total Liabilities & Net Worth	100.0	100.0
						INCOME DATA		
100.0	100.0	100.0	100.0	100.0	100.0	Net Sales	100.0	100.0
						Gross Profit		
89.0	85.9	83.8	88.1	94.3	88.6	Operating Expenses	89.0	89.0
11.0	14.1	16.2	11.9	5.7	11.4	Operating Profit	11.0	11.0
.8	2.8	4.8	4.5	.9	2.8	All Other Expenses (net)	2.1	2.4
10.2	11.3	11.3	7.4	4.9	8.6	Profit Before Taxes	8.9	8.6
						RATIOS		
2.0	2.3	2.4	2.4	2.2	2.9		1.9	2.0
.7	.9	1.1	1.3	1.4	1.5	Current	.9	.9
.2	.3	.5	.9	.9	1.0		.3	.3
1.7	2.0	2.2	2.1	1.9	2.3		1.6	1.7
(1677) .6	(1198) .8	(822) 1.0	1.2	1.1	1.4	Quick	(3200) .7	(3027) .7
.2	.2	.4	.7	.7	.9		.2	.2
0 UND	0 UND	0 UND	5 67.4	2 155.0	12 31.4		0 UND	0 UND
0 UND	0 UND	1 454.8	31 11.8	29 12.5	38 9.6	Sales/Receivables	0 UND	0 UND
0 UND	0 UND	40 9.0	51 7.2	41 8.8	47 7.8		13 28.2	9 40.8
						Cost of Sales/Inventory		
						Cost of Sales/Payables		
48.8	21.8	10.0	8.4	6.4	8.9		24.2	22.4
-99.9	-206.3	117.0	23.8	16.4	17.6	Sales/Working Capital	-132.6	-205.2
-20.4	-19.9	-23.7	-60.8	NM	-780.7		-20.9	-22.5
30.5	28.3	24.8	21.9	15.2	122.5		17.7	16.7
(1128) 7.0	(923) 5.7	(633) 5.9	(236) 5.6	(51) 4.2	(43) 8.3	EBIT/Interest	(2496) 3.8	(2309) 3.8
1.0	1.0	1.3	1.5	1.5	3.4		.8	.8
5.3	4.2	5.3	4.7	4.3			3.3	3.6
(21) 2.1	(43) 2.4	(57) 1.8	(45) 1.5	(20) 1.9		Net Profit + Depr., Dep., Amort./Cur. Mat. L/T/D	(206) 1.7	(184) 1.6
.6	.9	1.1	.9	1.4			.9	.9
.2	.5	.6	.5	.3	.4		.6	.5
3.4	2.9	1.7	1.2	.9	1.0	Fixed/Worth	3.5	2.9
-1.0	-6.0	38.0	4.6	2.5	3.0		-3.3	-3.9
1.0	1.0	.9	.6	.7	.7		1.3	1.2
40.1	5.4	3.0	1.8	1.9	1.5	Debt/Worth	9.2	7.4
-3.0	-10.6	101.8	9.5	4.6	3.2		-6.7	-6.8
475.5	200.9	105.5	60.3	22.3	80.2		222.2	226.1
(900) 137.2	(802) 69.5	(630) 33.4	(250) 18.9	(51) 13.4	(38) 21.2	% Profit Before Taxes/Tangible Net Worth	(1999) 56.3	(1916) 59.5
27.8	11.6	7.0	3.4	3.6	8.7		6.0	7.1
113.9	55.2	30.3	17.4	8.9	19.4		54.4	54.8
30.3	13.7	7.7	6.1	4.4	8.8	% Profit Before Taxes/Total Assets	10.2	9.8
.0	.2	.7	.6	1.0	3.1		-.4	-.3
245.1	64.3	26.0	16.9	25.0	28.5		69.2	69.6
52.6	19.5	10.0	6.6	6.6	8.0	Sales/Net Fixed Assets	21.2	21.2
19.2	7.0	2.5	2.9	2.2	3.2		7.7	7.8
22.9	10.6	5.7	3.8	3.5	2.8		14.0	14.0
11.6	5.6	3.1	2.1	2.1	1.8	Sales/Total Assets	6.6	6.5
5.6	2.6	1.2	1.1	1.0	1.4		2.8	2.7
.4	.8	1.4	1.4	1.5	.9		.8	.8
(892) 1.0	(826) 1.8	(677) 2.6	(260) 2.7	(50) 3.1	(34) 1.7	% Depr., Dep., Amort./Sales	(2367) 1.8	(2215) 1.9
2.0	4.0	6.0	4.7	4.9	3.2		3.5	3.4
14.0	11.4	8.0	7.0				15.1	13.7
(1106) 23.2	(626) 22.7	(298) 21.5	(72) 20.8	(16) 25.6	(12) 24.4	% Officers', Directors' Owners' Comp/Sales	(1720) 25.8	(1634) 24.9
33.3	31.7	33.4	33.1	36.8	33.6		35.8	35.3
5267699M	9732856M	14581073M	16065747M	12854678M	32444357M	Net Sales ($)	110263769M	104989116M
364623M	1223886M	3745462M	6015625M	3991502M	7855488M	Total Assets ($)	18600243M	18078305M

M = $ thousand   MM = $ million
See Pages 9 through 22 for Explanation of Ratios and Data

Comparative Historical Data | Current Data Sorted by Sales

			Type of Statement						
198	222	247	Unqualified	5	12	13	34	51	132
140	162	140	Reviewed	2	6	7	18	41	66
646	698	667	Compiled	96	166	109	147	105	44
1324	1634	1520	Tax Returns	367	474	199	226	179	75
1263	1356	1521	Other	229	322	185	250	284	251
4/1/08-3/31/09 ALL	4/1/09-3/31/10 ALL	4/1/10-3/31/11 ALL		442 (4/1-9/30/10)			3,653 (10/1/10-3/31/11)		
				0-1MM	1-3MM	3-5MM	5-10MM	10-25MM	25MM & OVER
3571	4072	4095	NUMBER OF STATEMENTS	699	980	513	675	660	568
%	%	%	**ASSETS**	%	%	%	%	%	%
27.0	27.5	28.2	Cash & Equivalents	24.0	32.0	33.3	29.7	26.5	22.3
9.7	9.5	9.7	Trade Receivables (net)	4.1	5.1	7.4	12.2	14.4	18.2
1.0	1.0	1.1	Inventory	.7	1.0	1.4	1.4	1.0	1.4
4.4	4.2	3.7	All Other Current	2.6	4.3	3.1	3.5	3.6	5.4
42.0	42.2	42.8	Total Current	31.5	42.4	45.2	46.7	45.6	47.2
41.6	41.1	40.2	Fixed Assets (net)	51.3	36.5	37.1	39.3	39.6	37.2
4.1	4.5	4.7	Intangibles (net)	4.3	5.5	5.2	3.9	4.3	4.8
12.3	12.3	12.4	All Other Non-Current	12.9	15.6	12.5	10.1	10.6	10.8
100.0	100.0	100.0	Total	100.0	100.0	100.0	100.0	100.0	100.0
			LIABILITIES						
20.0	18.5	18.9	Notes Payable-Short Term	22.5	23.8	19.5	18.5	15.2	10.4
8.5	7.9	7.0	Cur. Mat.-L.T.D.	7.0	5.9	7.2	8.1	7.9	6.7
3.1	3.2	3.4	Trade Payables	1.9	2.7	2.9	3.5	3.8	6.7
.5	.4	.3	Income Taxes Payable	.1	.1	.3	.1	.3	.9
26.1	27.3	26.5	All Other Current	23.3	21.7	32.1	30.1	30.3	25.2
58.2	57.2	56.1	Total Current	54.9	54.1	61.9	60.2	57.3	49.9
31.9	32.6	30.1	Long-Term Debt	41.5	30.1	29.1	26.6	29.6	21.5
.2	.1	.2	Deferred Taxes	.0	.0	.2	.3	.2	.4
4.9	4.8	5.6	All Other Non-Current	8.7	6.0	7.8	3.3	4.2	3.7
4.9	5.2	8.0	Net Worth	-5.0	9.8	1.1	9.6	8.6	24.5
100.0	100.0	100.0	Total Liabilities & Net Worth	100.0	100.0	100.0	100.0	100.0	100.0
			INCOME DATA						
100.0	100.0	100.0	Net Sales	100.0	100.0	100.0	100.0	100.0	100.0
			Gross Profit						
87.9	87.8	87.1	Operating Expenses	71.4	86.3	88.9	91.7	93.3	93.2
12.1	12.2	12.9	Operating Profit	28.6	13.7	11.1	8.3	6.7	6.8
2.6	2.6	2.5	All Other Expenses (net)	10.1	2.3	.9	.1	.0	.6
9.5	9.6	10.4	Profit Before Taxes	18.5	11.4	10.2	8.2	6.7	6.2
			RATIOS						
2.0	2.1	2.3	Current	2.3	3.0	2.6	2.3	2.0	1.8
.9	.9	.9		.6	.9	.9	.9	1.0	1.1
.3	.3	.3		.2	.3	.3	.4	.4	.6
1.8	1.8	2.0	Quick	1.7	2.6	2.4	2.0	1.8	1.6
(3565) .7	(4065) .8	(4089) .8		(698) .5	(978) .8	(512) .8	.8	.9	(566) .9
.2	.2	.3		.2	.2	.3	.3	.3	.5
0 UND	0 UND	0 UND	Sales/Receivables	0 UND	0 UND	0 UND	0 UND	0 UND	0 UND
0 UND	0 UND	0 UND		0 UND	0 UND	0 UND	0 UND	0 UND	13 28.7
2 150.0	2 174.0	5 80.0		0 UND	0 UND	0 UND	15 24.2	31 11.9	37 9.8
			Cost of Sales/Inventory						
			Cost of Sales/Payables						
24.5	24.7	19.3	Sales/Working Capital	18.8	18.1	25.1	19.5	22.1	16.1
-182.9	-207.7	-337.5		-28.6	-303.3	-326.3	-439.5	-999.8	169.7
-20.1	-20.9	-21.6		-5.3	-17.3	-28.3	-27.8	-37.3	-40.8
22.5	22.7	27.9	EBIT/Interest	19.8	33.3	39.0	26.4	24.3	29.3
(2701) 4.2	(3073) 5.4	(3014) 6.3		(349) 6.2	(680) 7.5	(383) 8.3	(551) 5.5	(561) 5.2	(490) 5.5
.8	1.0	1.1		2.3	1.3	1.3	1.0	1.0	1.2
3.7	4.4	4.8	Net Profit + Depr., Dep., Amort./Cur. Mat. L/T/D			10.7	4.9	5.7	4.7
(204) 1.5	(245) 1.8	(194) 1.8		(11) 2.5	(27) 2.3	(47) 2.4	(97) 1.7		
.7	.8	1.0		.0	1.1	1.1	1.0		
.5	.5	.4	Fixed/Worth	.5	.3	.4	.4	.5	.5
2.8	2.7	2.3		3.8	2.0	3.2	2.4	2.1	1.4
-3.8	-3.4	-4.3		-4.9	-3.4	-1.5	-3.2	-7.4	11.4
1.1	1.1	.9	Debt/Worth	1.1	.7	.9	1.0	1.1	1.0
6.5	6.8	5.4		6.8	6.1	10.5	5.9	5.2	3.1
-6.9	-6.6	-7.4		-4.6	-6.1	-4.3	-6.8	-12.8	49.2
233.4	225.1	222.2	% Profit Before Taxes/Tangible Net Worth	165.9	340.8	241.9	242.1	171.5	125.0
(2264) 60.2	(2549) 59.3	(2671) 60.4		(444) 54.8	(630) 106.6	(296) 80.9	(426) 64.6	(437) 39.3	(438) 26.1
6.5	9.7	10.4		11.9	21.8	24.3	11.5	4.5	3.8
63.5	58.4	64.4	% Profit Before Taxes/Total Assets	67.7	88.1	79.6	57.6	37.9	31.0
11.3	12.0	13.9		12.9	26.1	22.1	13.0	9.2	7.0
-.3	.3	.4		1.5	1.1	.6	.0	-.3	.2
75.0	82.3	86.3	Sales/Net Fixed Assets	57.5	117.5	111.8	93.3	71.7	49.9
21.0	22.3	22.9		8.6	27.5	37.4	28.4	25.6	17.7
7.6	7.8	7.6		.3	8.1	12.2	12.1	10.6	7.5
13.4	13.5	13.1	Sales/Total Assets	6.5	12.1	17.6	16.7	16.8	10.8
6.5	6.4	5.8		2.5	5.8	8.3	8.5	7.4	4.9
2.7	2.6	2.6		.2	2.8	3.8	4.1	3.5	2.6
.8	.8	.8	% Depr., Dep., Amort./Sales	1.6	.6	.5	.7	.8	1.0
(2468) 1.9	(2860) 1.8	(2739) 1.7		(435) 9.2	(577) 1.6	(304) 1.4	(468) 1.4	(498) 1.6	(457) 1.8
4.0	3.7	3.7		19.0	4.0	2.8	2.7	2.7	3.0
12.3	12.3	12.5	% Officers', Directors' Owners' Comp/Sales	13.3	11.6	12.7	11.4	12.2	9.1
(1898) 23.8	(2193) 23.8	(2130) 23.0		(272) 22.9	(610) 19.3	(307) 24.1	(384) 26.6	(334) 25.1	(223) 25.3
33.8	34.0	33.0		30.1	29.4	33.4	35.4	35.0	35.8
66197860M	97386418M	90946410M	Net Sales ($)	371556M	1810245M	2011708M	4833984M	10351198M	71567719M
18538944M	22074414M	23196586M	Total Assets ($)	591562M	995876M	616703M	1144716M	2491654M	17356075M

M = $ thousand   MM = $ million
See Pages 9 through 22 for Explanation of Ratios and Data

Current Data Sorted by Assets   **Comparative Historical Data**

Type of Statement	0-500M	500M-2MM	2-10MM	10-50MM	50-100MM	100-250MM		4/1/06-3/31/07 ALL	4/1/07-3/31/08 ALL
Unqualified		4	4	4	3	3		13	9
Reviewed			4	1					
Compiled	5	3	7					15	11
Tax Returns	14	5	5					18	25
Other	11	11	8	4				19	13
	16 (4/1-9/30/10)			81 (10/1/10-3/31/11)					
NUMBER OF STATEMENTS	30	23	28	9	4	3		65	58
	%	%	%	%	%	%		%	%
ASSETS									
Cash & Equivalents	39.6	18.7	14.8					24.7	34.2
Trade Receivables (net)	9.8	8.1	28.2					17.6	7.2
Inventory	1.0	.7	2.3					2.3	.5
All Other Current	7.9	1.7	1.6					3.5	6.1
Total Current	58.3	29.2	47.0					48.1	48.0
Fixed Assets (net)	22.7	41.0	43.8					36.3	38.7
Intangibles (net)	3.8	11.4	2.6					4.8	5.1
All Other Non-Current	15.3	18.5	6.6					10.9	8.1
Total	100.0	100.0	100.0					100.0	100.0
LIABILITIES									
Notes Payable-Short Term	39.5	15.5	4.9					20.7	22.8
Cur. Mat.-L.T.D.	6.3	5.1	4.4					8.2	9.3
Trade Payables	5.2	5.2	3.7					3.3	4.3
Income Taxes Payable	.0	1.8	.0					.2	.0
All Other Current	32.2	26.8	14.0					29.4	30.3
Total Current	83.1	54.5	27.1					61.8	66.7
Long-Term Debt	11.0	35.9	36.6					22.5	35.8
Deferred Taxes	.0	.0	.8					.1	.4
All Other Non-Current	1.8	11.1	6.4					2.5	3.6
Net Worth	4.0	-1.4	29.2					13.2	-6.7
Total Liabilities & Net Worth	100.0	100.0	100.0					100.0	100.0
INCOME DATA									
Net Sales	100.0	100.0	100.0					100.0	100.0
Gross Profit									
Operating Expenses	89.6	84.1	85.9					86.2	88.4
Operating Profit	10.4	15.9	14.1					13.8	11.6
All Other Expenses (net)	.0	4.2	3.2					2.2	1.2
Profit Before Taxes	10.4	11.6	10.9					11.6	10.4
RATIOS									
Current	3.8	3.0	4.9					2.8	3.9
	1.3	.9	1.9					1.1	1.2
	.5	.2	.6					.4	.4
Quick	3.3	2.2	4.7					2.3	3.2
	.8	.8	1.8					.9	.9
	.4	.2	.6					.3	.3
Sales/Receivables	0 UND	0 UND	4 95.9					0 UND	0 UND
	0 UND	0 UND	28 12.9					1 470.2	0 UND
	0 UND	23 16.1	45 8.1					47 7.8	6 62.4
Cost of Sales/Inventory									
Cost of Sales/Payables									
Sales/Working Capital	24.5	7.3	4.9					6.6	11.5
	235.5	-132.0	16.9					658.3	95.0
	-65.0	-10.6	-32.6					-20.0	-36.7
EBIT/Interest	70.6	31.2	46.3					28.1	25.5
	(19) 26.2	(16) 4.3	(21) 3.4					(41) 3.7	(40) 5.1
	-2.2	.7	1.0					.2	1.5
Net Profit + Depr., Dep., Amort./Cur. Mat. L/T/D									
Fixed/Worth	.1	1.1	.4					.2	.3
	.6	-7.6	1.7					1.4	2.8
	-.5	-.6	16.2					16.5	-.9
Debt/Worth	.3	.6	.7					.5	.5
	2.2	-11.4	4.8					2.6	6.3
	-4.0	-2.2	44.0					UND	-3.7
% Profit Before Taxes/Tangible Net Worth	457.1	68.3	120.7					310.2	147.4
	(19) 247.6	(10) 29.8	(22) 18.5					(50) 24.6	(35) 27.8
	24.2	-1.7	3.1					.0	8.6
% Profit Before Taxes/Total Assets	196.9	45.1	46.0					78.0	82.7
	69.0	8.2	6.9					9.0	13.5
	-.5	-.6	.0					-.5	2.3
Sales/Net Fixed Assets	324.3	70.4	31.9					74.5	103.4
	100.8	14.2	9.0					18.7	25.0
	25.7	1.9	2.4					4.7	6.1
Sales/Total Assets	23.4	7.2	4.6					11.5	13.2
	11.9	2.4	2.5					4.4	4.5
	7.4	1.1	1.1					1.4	2.1
% Depr., Dep., Amort./Sales	.2	1.0	1.2					.6	.5
	(12) .3	(15) 2.0	(22) 2.5					(46) 1.3	(40) 1.9
	1.0	4.5	5.3					3.8	3.9
% Officers', Directors' Owners' Comp/Sales	6.8							9.1	13.3
	(21) 22.5							(24) 23.2	(24) 25.6
	33.9							38.5	33.6
Net Sales ($)	91601M	120882M	386688M	287605M	475276M	1239951M		1667389M	1928901M
Total Assets ($)	6047M	26696M	123467M	191164M	286625M	518022M		605090M	295433M

M = $ thousand   MM = $ million
See Pages 9 through 22 for Explanation of Ratios and Data

Comparative Historical Data | | Current Data Sorted by Sales

					Type of Statement						
	14		9	18	Unqualified		4	1	2	3	8
	1		4	5	Reviewed			2	1		2
	14		19	15	Compiled	5	1	2	1	4	2
	27		27	24	Tax Returns	5	6	2	6	5	
	26		29	35	Other	5	8	5	5	7	5
	4/1/08-		4/1/09-	4/1/10-			16 (4/1-9/30/10)		81 (10/1/10-3/31/11)		
	3/31/09		3/31/10	3/31/11							
	ALL		ALL	ALL		0-1MM	1-3MM	3-5MM	5-10MM	10-25MM	25MM & OVER
	82		88	97	NUMBER OF STATEMENTS	15	19	12	15	19	17
	%		%	%	ASSETS	%	%	%	%	%	%
	25.0		19.2	24.2	Cash & Equivalents	18.8	31.8	27.0	28.4	19.7	19.9
	14.3		14.8	15.7	Trade Receivables (net)	12.9	14.0	15.5	8.4	23.7	17.6
	.7		.4	1.3	Inventory	.0	1.7	2.8	1.1	.7	1.6
	5.9		3.8	4.9	All Other Current	3.8	3.5	3.6	4.3	4.4	9.4
	45.9		38.3	46.1	Total Current	35.5	51.1	48.8	42.2	48.6	48.5
	40.8		40.0	35.4	Fixed Assets (net)	37.3	36.2	35.2	36.9	31.2	36.2
	2.9		6.6	6.0	Intangibles (net)	5.6	.4	7.3	8.2	9.3	6.0
	10.3		15.0	12.5	All Other Non-Current	21.5	12.3	8.6	12.8	10.9	9.3
	100.0		100.0	100.0	Total	100.0	100.0	100.0	100.0	100.0	100.0
					LIABILITIES						
	14.3		17.0	17.9	Notes Payable-Short Term	14.6	19.4	38.5	25.2	13.6	2.7
	4.2		11.7	4.8	Cur. Mat.-L.T.D.	2.9	7.2	3.9	7.3	1.8	5.5
	6.0		6.4	4.9	Trade Payables	7.0	2.2	12.6	1.4	3.7	5.0
	.0		.1	.7	Income Taxes Payable	.0	.0	.0	2.8	.0	1.5
	24.9		24.9	22.4	All Other Current	11.8	27.2	36.9	15.5	25.6	18.5
	49.3		60.1	50.6	Total Current	36.4	56.0	91.9	52.3	44.7	33.2
	30.1		29.6	25.1	Long-Term Debt	26.6	23.4	40.1	25.4	21.6	19.0
	.4		.3	.3	Deferred Taxes	.0	.0	.0	.0	.0	1.4
	4.7		4.3	5.6	All Other Non-Current	13.2	.4	1.3	6.9	9.6	2.3
	15.6		5.7	18.3	Net Worth	23.8	20.2	-33.3	15.5	24.1	44.0
	100.0		100.0	100.0	Total Liabilities & Net Worth	100.0	100.0	100.0	100.0	100.0	100.0
					INCOME DATA						
	100.0		100.0	100.0	Net Sales	100.0	100.0	100.0	100.0	100.0	100.0
					Gross Profit						
	90.8		86.8	87.8	Operating Expenses	75.2	86.5	85.9	87.4	95.2	93.8
	9.2		13.2	12.2	Operating Profit	24.8	13.5	14.1	12.6	4.8	6.2
	3.3		3.7	2.3	All Other Expenses (net)	10.7	.2	1.5	.3	1.1	.9
	5.9		9.5	9.9	Profit Before Taxes	14.1	13.3	12.6	12.3	3.7	5.3
					RATIOS						
	3.2		2.2	3.4		2.2	5.3	3.1	3.3	7.2	2.6
	1.1		.9	1.4	Current	1.4	2.1	1.1	1.1	1.4	2.1
	.4		.4	.5		.6	.8	.4	.2	.2	.8
	2.8		1.8	2.9		2.2	4.7	2.1	2.9	4.7	2.3
	1.0		.8	1.0	Quick	.9	1.9	.8	.8	1.0	1.4
	.3		.3	.4		.1	.8	.4	.2	.0	.6
0	UND	0	UND	0 UND		0 UND	0 UND	0 UND	0 UND	0 UND	7 49.0
0	UND	1	428.1	1 276.4	Sales/Receivables	0 UND	0 UND	25 14.7	0 UND	28 13.0	26 14.1
36	10.0	42	8.6	38 9.5		16 22.4	20 18.7	34 10.7	38 9.6	60 6.1	39 9.4
					Cost of Sales/Inventory						
					Cost of Sales/Payables						
	11.4		11.3	6.2		17.7	6.1	6.1	32.6	6.0	5.8
	211.3		-302.2	57.3	Sales/Working Capital	178.7	26.4	NM	143.4	193.4	12.0
	-20.9		-13.1	-32.1		-7.7	-77.3	-15.6	-35.5	-11.4	-36.5
	27.0		16.7	44.0			37.7	87.3	48.2	42.8	-47.7
(57)	3.3	(68)	3.0	(70) 4.7	EBIT/Interest	(11) 3.0	4.5	(13) 12.0	(14) 4.3	(15) 4.4
	.5		-.1	1.0		-2.5	-.1	1.2	1.1	.7
					Net Profit + Depr., Dep., Amort./Cur. Mat. L/T/D						
	.4		.5	.3		.3	.1	.3	.2	.5	.5
	1.8		1.4	1.3	Fixed/Worth	1.5	1.1	9.4	2.5	3.4	.7
	-8.3		-2.7	-4.9		-5.7	-10.6	-1.5	-.7	-1.1	1.7
	.6		1.0	.4		.5	.3	.9	.3	.3	.7
	4.5		3.7	2.2	Debt/Worth	2.1	1.2	NM	10.2	9.3	1.1
	-13.2		-5.7	-7.5		-9.0	-12.0	-2.8	-3.1	-5.0	3.2
	137.5		120.4	177.7		235.5	250.0			339.2	66.2
(56)	30.5	(60)	26.6	(66) 25.8	% Profit Before Taxes/Tangible Net Worth	(11) 18.6	(14) 47.6		(11) 12.8	(15) 14.8
	5.3		-.2	3.2		-2.1	-1.7			4.7	.2
	25.7		50.8	60.5		61.5	102.0	90.9	105.7	32.7	18.6
	4.1		6.8	11.3	% Profit Before Taxes/Total Assets	8.2	23.3	12.2	45.1	3.5	5.9
	-.7		-1.7	.1		-1.9	-.2	-6.5	2.4	-.6	-.1
	89.2		47.7	93.2		61.3	133.5	198.1	114.5	68.4	34.5
	16.4		18.9	20.8	Sales/Net Fixed Assets	16.1	25.8	14.0	25.6	24.1	10.5
	4.0		3.7	4.0		.3	2.1	3.0	8.8	5.2	3.0
	8.5		10.2	9.5		9.9	9.9	13.1	14.5	9.4	4.2
	4.0		3.3	3.4	Sales/Total Assets	3.0	3.2	2.5	7.2	4.7	2.5
	1.6		1.4	1.5		.3	1.4	1.6	2.3	1.8	1.5
	.7		.9	.8			.3			1.5	.9
(61)	2.0	(66)	2.2	(64) 2.0	% Depr., Dep., Amort./Sales	(11) 1.1		(11) 2.3	(16) 2.1
	4.7		4.9	3.8			3.1			2.9	3.3
	14.6		10.4	8.0							
(31)	27.1	(32)	16.0	(37) 22.5	% Officers', Directors' Owners' Comp/Sales						
	35.2		31.2	32.7							
	1229216M		1436445M	2602003M	Net Sales ($)	7243M	35590M	46793M	104801M	293833M	2113743M
	547312M		737601M	1152021M	Total Assets ($)	11733M	16946M	21309M	30797M	121739M	949497M

© RMA 2011

M = $ thousand   MM = $ million
See Pages 9 through 22 for Explanation of Ratios and Data

Current Data Sorted by Assets

Comparative Historical Data

							Type of Statement		
3	4	1	9		6		Unqualified	17	19
2	1	10	1				Reviewed	12	19
137	80	16			2		Compiled	173	158
589	220	16	1		6		Tax Returns	465	520
280	145	33	13	2	8		Other	208	243
	91 (4/1-9/30/10)		1,495 (10/1/10-3/31/11)					4/1/06-3/31/07	4/1/07-3/31/08
0-500M	500M-2MM	2-10MM	10-50MM	50-100MM	100-250MM			ALL	ALL
1011	450	76	24	3	22		NUMBER OF STATEMENTS	875	959
%	%	%	%	%	%		ASSETS	%	%
27.5	16.5	8.1	14.7		13.2		Cash & Equivalents	20.7	21.1
3.2	5.0	13.3	10.3		6.2		Trade Receivables (net)	5.6	4.5
.5	.4	.9	1.8		1.6		Inventory	.5	.4
3.0	2.8	3.8	6.6		1.9		All Other Current	3.4	3.1
34.2	24.7	26.1	33.4		23.0		Total Current	30.1	29.0
40.5	44.0	49.1	38.2		35.0		Fixed Assets (net)	45.4	45.4
14.7	20.4	12.2	18.6		35.8		Intangibles (net)	15.1	14.8
10.6	10.9	12.6	9.9		6.3		All Other Non-Current	9.4	10.8
100.0	100.0	100.0	100.0		100.0		Total	100.0	100.0
							LIABILITIES		
17.1	8.0	5.1	3.5		5.4		Notes Payable-Short Term	13.4	15.1
8.4	6.0	5.6	3.4		3.1		Cur. Mat.-L.T.D.	8.1	8.4
2.2	1.2	3.0	7.3		2.1		Trade Payables	1.8	2.2
.1	.1	.7	.0		.1		Income Taxes Payable	.2	.2
19.7	6.5	5.3	19.5		16.2		All Other Current	22.4	19.4
47.5	21.8	19.7	33.7		26.8		Total Current	45.9	45.1
48.0	53.6	41.2	32.5		50.9		Long-Term Debt	46.5	46.9
.0	.1	.0	.2		3.7		Deferred Taxes	.1	.0
10.9	4.5	8.8	10.6		8.4		All Other Non-Current	6.7	6.9
-6.5	20.0	30.2	23.0		10.1		Net Worth	.8	1.0
100.0	100.0	100.0	100.0		100.0		Total Liabilities & Net Worth	100.0	100.0
							INCOME DATA		
100.0	100.0	100.0	100.0		100.0		Net Sales	100.0	100.0
							Gross Profit		
86.7	82.5	81.8	88.0		92.3		Operating Expenses	87.7	87.4
13.3	17.5	18.2	12.0		7.7		Operating Profit	12.3	12.6
1.8	4.9	7.4	1.8		3.3		All Other Expenses (net)	2.1	2.6
11.5	12.6	10.8	10.2		4.3		Profit Before Taxes	10.2	10.0
							RATIOS		
2.6	3.8	2.7	1.7		1.6			2.0	1.8
.9	1.3	1.2	.9		.9		Current	.8	.7
.3	.3	.2	.5		.6			.2	.2
2.2	3.7	2.1	1.3		1.4			1.8	1.6
(1009) .7	(449) 1.0	.9	.8		.6		Quick	(870) .7	(957) .5
.2	.2	.2	.4		.4			.2	.2
0 UND	0 UND	0 UND	0 UND		0 UND			0 UND	0 UND
0 UND	0 UND	0 UND	16 22.5		18 20.7		Sales/Receivables	0 UND	0 UND
0 UND	0 UND	30 12.2	20 17.8		29 12.6			0 UND	0 UND
							Cost of Sales/Inventory		
							Cost of Sales/Payables		
27.4	9.8	12.6	13.4		31.2			33.1	36.8
-175.9	75.7	76.0	-122.1		-96.7		Sales/Working Capital	-110.5	-64.0
-17.3	-16.1	-13.1	-19.1		-20.5			-17.1	-15.9
20.5	14.4	22.4	21.6		3.9			16.6	12.4
(760) 6.4	(373) 5.2	(62) 5.0	(22) 9.8		(20) 1.5		EBIT/Interest	(684) 4.6	(752) 4.0
1.6	1.5	1.7	2.6		.9			1.1	1.1
3.4	6.6						Net Profit + Depr., Dep.,	3.4	4.8
(12) 1.2	(12) 1.8						Amort./Cur. Mat. L/T/D	(27) 2.0	(26) 1.6
.6	.2							1.4	.6
.8	1.1	.7	.7		6.5			1.1	1.1
-51.9	38.7	2.6	2.9		-1.3		Fixed/Worth	36.8	188.0
-.6	-1.3	NM	NM		-.2			-.9	-1.0
1.4	1.7	1.4	1.5		9.2			1.7	2.0
-17.2	233.5	4.2	4.8		-2.9		Debt/Worth	243.0	-58.8
-2.2	-3.2	NM	-7.3		-1.6			-2.4	-2.5
432.1	178.8	133.4	193.1				% Profit Before Taxes/Tangible	370.0	356.4
(470) 144.4	(232) 85.5	(57) 47.5	(17) 83.9				Net Worth	(447) 119.0	(465) 123.3
45.5	24.2	4.4	45.4					28.1	33.7
93.3	40.9	40.7	29.4		10.2		% Profit Before Taxes/Total	71.6	66.5
34.7	17.0	7.5	15.1		2.6		Assets	21.0	19.2
4.0	2.2	.1	8.5		-.7			1.3	.8
59.1	19.6	16.0	11.1		11.6			37.3	38.2
18.3	7.4	5.3	6.2		7.6		Sales/Net Fixed Assets	14.2	12.4
7.8	2.7	1.1	3.5		4.7			5.7	5.2
10.3	3.3	3.3	3.1		3.7			9.2	8.7
5.5	2.0	1.5	2.6		2.2		Sales/Total Assets	4.5	4.2
3.0	1.3	.7	1.9		1.4			2.3	2.2
.9	1.9	1.8	2.2					1.2	1.2
(601) 2.3	(314) 4.2	(53) 3.1	(22) 3.4				% Depr., Dep., Amort./Sales	(594) 2.5	(649) 2.7
4.9	8.2	7.0	4.5					5.2	5.5
10.8	8.5	3.9					% Officers', Directors'	12.8	11.9
(727) 17.7	(295) 14.1	(31) 11.1					Owners' Comp/Sales	(614) 19.6	(664) 19.1
26.1	23.0	18.5						26.8	28.8
1340073M	1101855M	682329M	3813476M	204998M	16053358M		Net Sales ($)	18559817M	14421648M
229357M	415021M	292408M	662233M	196949M	3645407M		Total Assets ($)	3811253M	3250423M

M = $ thousand　　MM = $ million
See Pages 9 through 22 for Explanation of Ratios and Data

Comparative Historical Data | Current Data Sorted by Sales

			Type of Statement						
18	27	24	Unqualified	2	3	1		4	14
6	7	14	Reviewed		3	1	1	5	4
187	226	235	Compiled	88	99	23	14	7	4
657	792	832	Tax Returns	330	400	67	22	6	7
297	330	481	Other	189	201	42	12	12	25
4/1/08-3/31/09	4/1/09-3/31/10	4/1/10-3/31/11		91 (4/1-9/30/10)			1,495 (10/1/10-3/31/11)		
ALL	ALL	ALL		0-1MM	1-3MM	3-5MM	5-10MM	10-25MM	25MM & OVER
1165	1382	1586	**NUMBER OF STATEMENTS**	609	706	134	49	34	54
%	%	%	**ASSETS**	%	%	%	%	%	%
20.4	22.0	23.0	Cash & Equivalents	21.4	25.5	22.7	25.9	13.0	13.1
3.3	4.0	4.4	Trade Receivables (net)	2.8	3.9	6.0	5.1	21.0	12.9
.5	.4	.5	Inventory	.5	.3	.3	.2	1.6	3.4
3.6	2.9	3.1	All Other Current	3.1	2.7	3.6	1.4	6.9	5.5
27.7	29.3	30.9	Total Current	27.7	32.5	32.5	32.6	42.6	34.9
46.0	42.8	41.8	Fixed Assets (net)	44.4	38.9	44.4	48.5	42.7	35.8
16.7	17.0	16.6	Intangibles (net)	18.3	16.3	13.1	10.5	4.4	23.3
9.5	10.8	10.7	All Other Non-Current	9.7	12.3	10.0	8.4	10.3	5.9
100.0	100.0	100.0	Total	100.0	100.0	100.0	100.0	100.0	100.0
			LIABILITIES						
13.3	13.8	13.5	Notes Payable-Short Term	11.7	16.2	12.3	11.2	12.1	4.8
9.5	8.2	7.5	Cur. Mat.-L.T.D.	8.3	6.6	8.6	7.9	10.8	3.7
1.6	1.8	2.1	Trade Payables	2.1	1.5	2.4	1.1	5.8	6.4
.1	.1	.1	Income Taxes Payable	.0	.1	.1	.1	2.3	.0
16.6	19.0	15.2	All Other Current	13.2	14.7	19.8	23.7	24.7	19.8
41.1	43.0	38.4	Total Current	35.4	39.2	43.2	44.1	55.8	34.7
51.8	49.1	49.0	Long-Term Debt	56.9	45.7	41.3	48.0	25.3	37.6
.1	.1	.1	Deferred Taxes	.0	.0	.0	.2	.4	1.9
5.5	6.2	8.9	All Other Non-Current	8.9	9.0	10.6	3.5	9.3	8.4
1.6	1.5	3.6	Net Worth	-1.2	6.0	4.9	4.2	9.1	17.4
100.0	100.0	100.0	Total Liabilities & Net Worth	100.0	100.0	100.0	100.0	100.0	100.0
			INCOME DATA						
100.0	100.0	100.0	Net Sales	100.0	100.0	100.0	100.0	100.0	100.0
			Gross Profit						
87.0	87.1	85.4	Operating Expenses	82.5	86.6	87.1	88.2	91.1	92.5
13.0	12.9	14.6	Operating Profit	17.5	13.4	12.9	11.8	8.9	7.5
3.2	2.7	2.9	All Other Expenses (net)	5.3	1.6	.9	.8	.5	2.2
9.9	10.2	11.6	Profit Before Taxes	12.1	11.8	12.0	11.0	8.4	5.3
			RATIOS						
2.0	2.3	2.9		3.1	3.3	1.8	2.1	2.4	1.9
.7	.8	1.0	Current	.9	1.0	.9	1.1	1.1	1.0
.2	.2	.3		.2	.3	.3	.3	.6	.6
1.8	2.0	2.5		2.6	2.9	1.6	2.1	2.1	1.4
(1161) .6	(1381) .6	(1583) .8	Quick	(607) .7	(705) .9	.6	.9	.9	.7
.2	.2	.2		.2	.2	.2	.2	.3	.4
0 UND	0 UND	0 UND		0 UND	0 UND	0 UND	0 UND	0 UND	0 UND
0 UND	0 UND	0 UND	Sales/Receivables	0 UND	0 UND	0 UND	0 UND	9 38.5	18 19.8
0 UND	0 UND	0 UND		0 UND	0 UND	0 UND	0 UND	30 12.3	28 12.9
			Cost of Sales/Inventory						
			Cost of Sales/Payables						
34.1	25.8	19.3		15.0	20.8	34.1	32.8	17.1	15.8
-75.2	-111.7	-855.8	Sales/Working Capital	-129.0	678.0	-396.8	281.8	83.4	NM
-14.1	-14.9	-17.0		-11.2	-19.9	-20.1	-29.9	-39.3	-20.5
14.2	15.6	18.6		12.4	21.5	27.9	24.7	41.5	13.7
(939) 4.1	(1107) 4.4	(1240) 5.7	EBIT/Interest	(437) 4.2	(563) 6.5	(118) 7.1	(43) 8.7	(29) 16.0	(50) 3.8
1.2	1.3	1.5		1.5	1.7	1.4	1.1	2.9	1.1
4.8	7.9	7.4			6.3				10.6
(34) 1.2	(30) 2.5	(42) 1.6	Net Profit + Depr., Dep., Amort./Cur. Mat. L/T/D	(12) 1.4				(11) 2.8
.5	1.0	.6			.7				1.3
1.2	.9	.9		1.2	.7	.9	.7	.8	.9
-54.1	UND	42.5	Fixed/Worth	-25.7	10.5	23.1	37.6	1.5	9.0
-.9	-.9	-.8		-.6	-.8	-1.1	-2.1	-3.0	-1.2
1.9	1.6	1.5		1.8	1.3	1.7	1.3	.7	1.7
-30.2	-24.0	-137.8	Debt/Worth	-13.7	141.7	34.1	-137.6	1.8	19.4
-2.4	-2.4	-2.5		-2.1	-2.5	-2.9	-4.8	-7.7	-2.7
339.4	283.5	296.9		229.4	332.2	828.9	208.6	89.3	205.8
(547) 117.8	(660) 96.3	(783) 108.6	% Profit Before Taxes/Tangible Net Worth	(271) 87.5	(364) 122.3	(71) 151.4	(24) 119.8	(24) 49.7	(29) 75.9
29.4	24.2	30.9		12.7	44.3	80.2	30.5	2.9	20.2
63.0	61.0	71.5		57.7	82.2	100.4	83.5	49.1	22.6
19.0	19.7	24.6	% Profit Before Taxes/Total Assets	18.8	30.6	32.5	31.8	17.6	7.6
1.4	1.4	2.6		1.6	6.3	1.6	.3	1.5	.9
35.3	36.5	38.9		34.2	49.6	36.3	32.8	25.6	18.1
12.1	13.1	13.2	Sales/Net Fixed Assets	8.8	16.2	17.2	13.5	17.0	9.6
4.5	5.5	5.3		3.0	7.2	8.3	8.5	6.9	4.8
8.5	7.8	7.8		5.1	8.8	12.2	10.3	8.5	4.0
3.8	4.0	3.7	Sales/Total Assets	2.6	4.5	6.6	6.1	4.3	2.7
2.0	2.1	1.9		1.3	2.4	3.5	4.4	2.6	1.7
1.4	1.3	1.3		2.2	.9	1.0	1.3	.8	1.8
(781) 3.4	(910) 2.9	(1000) 2.8	% Depr., Dep., Amort./Sales	(364) 5.0	(433) 2.3	(102) 1.8	(40) 2.3	(28) 2.0	(33) 2.9
6.5	5.8	6.1		10.7	4.5	2.9	3.1	2.7	4.4
10.4	10.6	10.1		10.4	9.7	9.0	10.5	6.6	15.0
(802) 18.1	(965) 17.7	(1067) 16.6	% Officers', Directors' Owners' Comp/Sales	(372) 16.5	(533) 16.1	(91) 18.4	(40) 23.9	(17) 17.2	(14) 22.7
25.8	26.4	25.5		25.4	24.0	27.6	38.2	31.7	38.0
11970487M	19358930M	23196089M	Net Sales ($)	365372M	1189731M	518136M	335993M	489955M	20296902M
2956731M	5245972M	5441375M	Total Assets ($)	235884M	364418M	122386M	79333M	141377M	4497977M

M = $ thousand   MM = $ million
See Pages 9 through 22 for Explanation of Ratios and Data

Current Data Sorted by Assets — Comparative Historical Data

						Type of Statement		
1		1	1	2		Unqualified	1	
						Reviewed		
15	5	2				Compiled	14	19
76	14				2	Tax Returns	64	77
54	12		5		2	Other	42	34
	7 (4/1-9/30/10)		183 (10/1/10-3/31/11)				4/1/06-3/31/07	4/1/07-3/31/08
0-500M	500M-2MM	2-10MM	10-50MM	50-100MM	100-250MM		ALL	ALL
146	31	3	6	2	2	NUMBER OF STATEMENTS	121	130
%	%	%	%	%	%	ASSETS	%	%
28.2	12.9					Cash & Equivalents	23.8	23.4
5.7	6.2					Trade Receivables (net)	10.5	8.6
.9	.7					Inventory	.7	.5
1.8	1.5					All Other Current	4.5	4.8
36.7	21.3					Total Current	39.6	37.1
37.0	52.5					Fixed Assets (net)	36.3	35.7
10.6	12.6					Intangibles (net)	8.8	13.4
15.7	13.6					All Other Non-Current	15.3	13.8
100.0	100.0					Total	100.0	100.0
						LIABILITIES		
20.5	6.9					Notes Payable-Short Term	23.2	22.6
5.5	4.1					Cur. Mat.-L.T.D.	4.9	7.0
1.2	1.0					Trade Payables	2.8	5.5
.3	.4					Income Taxes Payable	.6	.5
16.0	5.5					All Other Current	16.6	12.4
43.5	17.9					Total Current	48.1	47.9
28.4	41.1					Long-Term Debt	22.9	34.7
.0	.0					Deferred Taxes	.0	.0
15.0	13.4					All Other Non-Current	7.0	10.0
13.1	27.6					Net Worth	22.0	7.4
100.0	100.0					Total Liabilities & Net Worth	100.0	100.0
						INCOME DATA		
100.0	100.0					Net Sales	100.0	100.0
						Gross Profit		
85.9	77.1					Operating Expenses	85.7	83.7
14.1	22.9					Operating Profit	14.3	16.3
1.0	6.7					All Other Expenses (net)	2.1	3.1
13.1	16.1					Profit Before Taxes	12.3	13.2
						RATIOS		
3.3	3.8						4.4	2.7
.8	.8					Current	1.6	1.0
.3	.3						.4	.3
3.3	3.8						3.6	2.4
.7	.7					Quick	1.3 (129)	.8
.2	.1						.2	.2
0 UND	0 UND						0 UND	0 UND
0 UND	0 UND					Sales/Receivables	0 UND	0 UND
0 UND	0 UND						5 76.4	0 UND
						Cost of Sales/Inventory		
						Cost of Sales/Payables		
23.8	12.1						10.4	20.8
-111.6	-109.4					Sales/Working Capital	88.8	-270.0
-15.5	-8.1						-16.9	-12.5
29.7	73.9						17.1	12.9
(91) 8.9	(22) 8.1					EBIT/Interest	(80) 4.5	(93) 5.8
3.2	3.9						1.8	2.0
						Net Profit + Depr., Dep., Amort./Cur. Mat. L/T/D		
.4	.3						.2	.3
1.5	2.8					Fixed/Worth	1.1	3.5
-2.2	-5.7						-7.8	-.9
.5	.3						.4	.5
3.9	3.5					Debt/Worth	2.4	34.2
-3.3	-7.2						-11.8	-2.9
523.3	103.3						247.6	412.5
(98) 116.2	(19) 50.9					% Profit Before Taxes/Tangible Net Worth	(86) 82.2	(71) 155.3
40.9	16.2						31.1	45.8
88.7	68.5						80.5	109.5
39.7	24.0					% Profit Before Taxes/Total Assets	27.9	31.1
10.4	4.1						3.3	4.6
61.4	18.8						52.8	52.5
17.6	5.8					Sales/Net Fixed Assets	16.1	20.3
7.3	1.0						5.9	7.4
8.1	3.6						7.8	11.0
4.6	1.5					Sales/Total Assets	3.6	4.5
2.4	.7						1.9	1.9
.7	1.5						.8	.9
(76) 1.7	(20) 3.2					% Depr., Dep., Amort./Sales	(59) 1.8	(77) 2.3
3.3	12.2						3.7	4.5
10.2	4.6						10.5	12.7
(103) 13.8	(15) 9.3					% Officers', Directors' Owners' Comp/Sales	(73) 15.4	(81) 19.9
22.9	16.1						24.0	27.4
131045M	79315M	18056M	519831M	80451M	1227676M	Net Sales ($)	2772957M	901972M
24143M	29145M	7141M	123005M	145300M	357553M	Total Assets ($)	947739M	328176M

M = $ thousand   MM = $ million
See Pages 9 through 22 for Explanation of Ratios and Data

Comparative Historical Data   Current Data Sorted by Sales

Comp 1	Comp 3	Comp 5	Type of Statement						
1			Unqualified	1			1	1	2
1			Reviewed						
12	20	22	Compiled	14	4	4			
64	79	92	Tax Returns	68	18	3			3
26	51	71	Other	47	14	4	1	1	4
4/1/08-3/31/09 ALL	4/1/09-3/31/10 ALL	4/1/10-3/31/11 ALL		7 (4/1-9/30/10) 0-1MM	1-3MM	3-5MM	183 (10/1/10-3/31/11) 5-10MM	10-25MM	25MM & OVER
104	153	190	NUMBER OF STATEMENTS	130	36	11	2	2	9
%	%	%	ASSETS	%	%	%	%	%	%
27.8	27.7	24.9	Cash & Equivalents	24.6	27.5	13.8			
9.3	11.0	7.1	Trade Receivables (net)	5.8	6.4	10.4			
.5	.2	1.1	Inventory	1.0	.3	2.1			
3.3	2.6	1.9	All Other Current	.9	3.3	5.3			
40.8	41.6	35.1	Total Current	32.2	37.5	31.7			
38.3	37.9	39.0	Fixed Assets (net)	39.9	40.7	37.2			
6.0	8.1	10.3	Intangibles (net)	12.8	7.2	1.6			
14.8	12.3	15.7	All Other Non-Current	15.1	14.6	29.5			
100.0	100.0	100.0	Total	100.0	100.0	100.0			
			LIABILITIES						
26.9	18.6	18.1	Notes Payable-Short Term	19.0	17.8	14.6			
4.3	3.8	5.0	Cur. Mat.-L.T.D.	6.2	1.4	5.8			
1.8	1.9	1.4	Trade Payables	1.3	.3	3.1			
.3	.1	.3	Income Taxes Payable	.1	1.1	.0			
10.1	12.9	13.8	All Other Current	15.3	11.8	6.2			
43.4	37.3	38.7	Total Current	41.9	32.5	29.8			
31.1	33.2	28.8	Long-Term Debt	33.4	22.0	25.5			
.0	.3	.0	Deferred Taxes	.0	.0	.0			
8.6	2.7	13.9	All Other Non-Current	13.8	10.3	41.0			
16.8	26.5	18.6	Net Worth	10.9	35.2	3.8			
100.0	100.0	100.0	Total Liabilties & Net Worth	100.0	100.0	100.0			
			INCOME DATA						
100.0	100.0	100.0	Net Sales	100.0	100.0	100.0			
			Gross Profit						
80.5	81.1	84.1	Operating Expenses	83.8	83.7	88.6			
19.5	18.9	15.9	Operating Profit	16.2	16.3	11.4			
2.7	2.2	1.9	All Other Expenses (net)	2.6	.6	-.6			
16.7	16.7	14.1	Profit Before Taxes	13.6	15.7	12.0			
			RATIOS						
3.3	4.0	3.2		3.2	4.3	2.3			
1.4	1.3	.8	Current	.6	1.0	.7			
.4	.4	.3		.2	.6	.4			
3.2	4.0	3.2		2.9	3.8	2.3			
1.2	1.2	.8	Quick	.5	1.0	.6			
.3	.3	.2		.1	.5	.2			
0 UND	0 UND	0 UND		0 UND	0 UND	0 UND			
0 UND	0 UND	0 UND	Sales/Receivables	0 UND	0 UND	0 UND			
0 UND	0 UND	0 UND		0 UND	0 UND	4 93.4			
			Cost of Sales/Inventory						
			Cost of Sales/Payables						
15.1	12.1	19.4		23.8	19.3	13.9			
75.9	68.2	-126.0	Sales/Working Capital	-59.9	NM	-127.9			
-25.1	-23.9	-15.5		-10.2	-29.1	-59.5			
38.9	38.6	34.0		29.3	43.6	188.6			
(70) 12.4	(101) 12.0	(123) 9.0	EBIT/Interest	(83) 8.6	(22) 17.4	(10) 7.2			
1.8	3.5	4.0		3.2	.9	4.7			
			Net Profit + Depr., Dep., Amort./Cur. Mat. L/T/D						
.3	.3	.4		.4	.5	.1			
1.1	1.1	1.5	Fixed/Worth	1.7	1.7	1.6			
UND	UND	-5.1		-1.4	-74.0	-3.3			
.4	.3	.4		.6	.3	.5			
2.0	2.5	2.8	Debt/Worth	4.9	2.1	2.4			
-85.7	-165.1	-4.3		-2.9	-20.9	-5.5			
496.7	415.3	289.8		493.3	284.8				
(77) 145.8	(114) 99.8	(129) 91.9	% Profit Before Taxes/Tangible Net Worth	(85) 101.5	(25) 90.7				
70.0	40.5	27.6		36.3	10.1				
135.1	99.3	80.9		79.7	89.6	68.5			
53.2	43.3	36.8	% Profit Before Taxes/Total Assets	34.3	41.7	36.9			
15.9	12.1	6.0		5.3	.2	25.9			
51.2	59.9	51.2		57.0	58.2	50.1			
15.2	15.2	15.9	Sales/Net Fixed Assets	16.0	13.9	17.9			
6.0	6.2	6.0		5.0	8.3	6.7			
8.6	7.4	7.2		7.3	7.0	11.0			
4.5	3.9	3.8	Sales/Total Assets	3.6	4.3	5.2			
2.2	2.0	1.8		1.7	3.1	2.2			
.6	.8	.8		.8	.6				
(68) 2.0	(89) 2.0	(106) 1.8	% Depr., Dep., Amort./Sales	(71) 1.9	(20) 1.8				
4.2	3.9	3.5		4.9	3.0				
10.9	8.6	9.3		10.3	5.7				
(68) 15.7	(93) 15.6	(123) 13.7	% Officers', Directors' Owners' Comp/Sales	(88) 13.7	(24) 11.7				
21.7	25.7	20.4		21.9	20.1				
1205613M	1760090M	2056374M	Net Sales ($)	57980M	57495M	44121M	12642M	24408M	1859728M
337105M	421249M	686287M	Total Assets ($)	28663M	17065M	10706M	76837M	13209M	539807M

M = $ thousand   MM = $ million

See Pages 9 through 22 for Explanation of Ratios and Data

Current Data Sorted by Assets | Comparative Historical Data

Type of Statement	0-500M	500M-2MM	2-10MM	10-50MM	50-100MM	100-250MM		4/1/06-3/31/07 ALL	4/1/07-3/31/08 ALL
Unqualified		2						6	7
Reviewed	3	5	4	2	1			5	5
Compiled	36	21	8					50	43
Tax Returns	89	26	10			2		93	87
Other	34	29	20	5	1			42	44
	19 (4/1-9/30/10)			279 (10/1/10-3/31/11)					
NUMBER OF STATEMENTS	162	83	42	7	2	2		196	186
	%	%	%	%	%	%		%	%
ASSETS									
Cash & Equivalents	24.5	19.2	12.7					17.7	18.7
Trade Receivables (net)	8.1	8.6	17.0					10.6	9.8
Inventory	14.3	7.6	5.9					13.3	11.6
All Other Current	1.0	2.7	4.1					2.8	2.8
Total Current	48.0	38.1	39.7					44.5	42.8
Fixed Assets (net)	33.5	39.7	45.5					36.5	39.1
Intangibles (net)	8.1	13.7	5.8					11.7	8.2
All Other Non-Current	10.4	8.5	9.0					7.4	9.9
Total	100.0	100.0	100.0					100.0	100.0
LIABILITIES									
Notes Payable-Short Term	10.9	8.9	7.0					8.3	12.2
Cur. Mat.-L.T.D.	7.9	6.8	7.9					8.9	7.1
Trade Payables	5.1	4.8	5.6					5.5	8.6
Income Taxes Payable	.2	.0	.0					.4	.3
All Other Current	15.3	12.4	15.5					16.5	16.0
Total Current	39.4	32.9	36.0					39.6	44.2
Long-Term Debt	43.9	33.4	28.3					36.5	39.3
Deferred Taxes	.1	.0	.1					.1	.1
All Other Non-Current	5.4	6.0	3.0					9.4	7.7
Net Worth	11.2	27.7	32.6					14.5	8.6
Total Liabilties & Net Worth	100.0	100.0	100.0					100.0	100.0
INCOME DATA									
Net Sales	100.0	100.0	100.0					100.0	100.0
Gross Profit									
Operating Expenses	89.3	88.1	86.0					89.1	91.4
Operating Profit	10.7	11.9	14.0					10.9	8.6
All Other Expenses (net)	1.1	2.2	4.1					1.9	1.4
Profit Before Taxes	9.5	9.7	10.0					8.9	7.3
RATIOS									
Current	4.3	3.9	1.9					2.6	2.8
	1.3	1.4	1.1					1.3	1.1
	.6	.7	.7					.6	.5
Quick	2.8	2.7	1.6					1.9	1.9
	(160) .9	.7	.8					(195) .7	.6
	.3	.3	.5					.3	.2
Sales/Receivables	0 UND	0 UND	0 UND					0 UND	0 UND
	0 UND	0 UND	20 18.4					0 UND	0 UND
	5 79.3	13 28.4	35 10.4					20 18.4	17 21.5
Cost of Sales/Inventory									
Cost of Sales/Payables									
Sales/Working Capital	15.0	11.7	15.1					15.7	15.5
	78.3	44.4	64.2					94.9	307.1
	-42.3	-31.4	-27.2					-30.1	-27.8
EBIT/Interest	19.8	20.1	38.2					16.4	11.9
	(122) 5.9	(72) 8.6	(38) 15.1					(166) 4.1	(148) 3.7
	1.1	1.4	1.7					.9	1.0
Net Profit + Depr., Dep., Amort./Cur. Mat. L/T/D									
Fixed/Worth	.4	.4	.7					.7	.6
	2.7	2.1	1.6					3.0	2.5
	-1.1	-2.4	4.1					-2.6	-3.5
Debt/Worth	.7	.8	1.0					1.4	1.0
	8.1	3.2	2.6					7.4	5.5
	-4.0	-5.8	8.3					-4.7	-6.7
% Profit Before Taxes/Tangible Net Worth	232.9	122.4	120.5					190.1	150.0
	(97) 96.5	(58) 48.2	(34) 28.5					(119) 58.6	(119) 43.1
	20.8	19.0	11.2					7.1	9.9
% Profit Before Taxes/Total Assets	69.7	39.3	28.5					57.0	47.8
	17.7	18.9	7.3					13.4	12.3
	1.1	1.1	1.7					.0	.6
Sales/Net Fixed Assets	91.7	29.9	16.3					55.8	43.8
	32.0	13.9	8.6					18.1	16.3
	9.6	5.5	3.3					7.4	7.6
Sales/Total Assets	11.6	7.1	5.3					9.1	9.3
	5.4	3.7	2.9					4.5	5.5
	3.1	1.6	1.5					2.7	2.6
% Depr., Dep., Amort./Sales	.8	1.4	1.6					1.4	1.1
	(85) 1.7	(56) 2.3	(35) 3.2					(137) 2.6	(134) 2.1
	3.5	5.6	4.8					4.2	3.8
% Officers', Directors' Owners' Comp/Sales	8.4	6.8	7.4					7.8	8.3
	(103) 13.3	(51) 15.6	(18) 16.7					(138) 13.5	(123) 14.2
	21.8	30.8	29.3					22.9	24.5
Net Sales ($)	293883M	416965M	843561M	251845M	150058M	1221770M		2869707M	4216963M
Total Assets ($)	38907M	80015M	200363M	105033M	142509M	393966M		821270M	1160827M

© RMA 2011

M = $ thousand   MM = $ million
See Pages 9 through 22 for Explanation of Ratios and Data

Comparative Historical Data   Current Data Sorted by Sales

Type of Statement	4/1/08-3/31/09 ALL	4/1/09-3/31/10 ALL	4/1/10-3/31/11 ALL	0-1MM	1-3MM	3-5MM	5-10MM	10-25MM	25MM & OVER
Unqualified	5	4	2					1	1
Reviewed	3	18	15	2	2	2	2	4	3
Compiled	47	45	65	11	22	13	12	6	1
Tax Returns	118	148	127	51	43	12	11	7	3
Other	80	85	89	25	24	6	13	11	10
				19 (4/1-9/30/10)			279 (10/1/10-3/31/11)		
NUMBER OF STATEMENTS	253	300	298	89	91	34	38	28	18
ASSETS	%	%	%	%	%	%	%	%	%
Cash & Equivalents	16.6	21.5	21.6	19.1	18.9	29.7	28.4	17.7	23.5
Trade Receivables (net)	8.5	9.2	9.6	8.6	7.5	12.0	7.1	17.2	13.9
Inventory	10.8	12.5	11.0	12.5	14.5	6.6	7.5	7.5	6.8
All Other Current	4.0	1.6	2.2	.7	.9	3.6	3.0	2.0	12.5
Total Current	40.0	44.8	44.4	41.0	41.8	51.8	46.0	44.4	56.7
Fixed Assets (net)	38.3	36.7	36.9	41.1	33.2	31.1	43.9	38.6	27.9
Intangibles (net)	10.2	10.5	9.3	10.3	11.4	8.9	3.6	8.9	7.0
All Other Non-Current	11.5	8.0	9.5	7.7	13.6	8.2	6.6	8.0	8.4
Total	100.0	100.0	100.0	100.0	100.0	100.0	100.0	100.0	100.0
LIABILITIES									
Notes Payable-Short Term	11.0	10.5	9.5	11.1	8.3	11.0	7.9	12.1	4.7
Cur. Mat.-L.T.D.	7.9	9.1	7.5	6.1	9.9	3.9	7.5	8.7	7.4
Trade Payables	5.3	5.8	5.1	3.4	5.1	7.0	6.8	4.8	7.3
Income Taxes Payable	.4	.1	.1	.0	.2	.0	.3	.0	.0
All Other Current	16.6	16.3	14.3	9.3	15.2	14.2	17.8	16.8	23.4
Total Current	41.2	41.8	36.6	30.0	38.7	36.1	40.3	42.4	42.8
Long-Term Debt	40.9	38.6	37.9	39.6	45.9	26.0	44.8	24.5	17.4
Deferred Taxes	.0	.1	.1	.0	.1	.0	.0	.1	.3
All Other Non-Current	7.1	6.2	5.1	6.2	3.9	6.6	6.8	3.7	1.9
Net Worth	10.8	13.4	20.3	24.2	11.4	31.3	8.1	29.3	37.7
Total Liabilities & Net Worth	100.0	100.0	100.0	100.0	100.0	100.0	100.0	100.0	100.0
INCOME DATA									
Net Sales	100.0	100.0	100.0	100.0	100.0	100.0	100.0	100.0	100.0
Gross Profit									
Operating Expenses	90.1	87.8	88.7	81.1	91.5	90.7	94.6	93.4	89.1
Operating Profit	9.9	12.2	11.3	18.9	8.5	9.3	5.4	6.6	10.9
All Other Expenses (net)	1.7	2.7	1.8	4.3	.8	.5	-.5	1.4	2.1
Profit Before Taxes	8.2	9.5	9.5	14.6	7.7	8.7	5.8	5.2	8.9
RATIOS									
Current	2.6 / 1.2 / .6	3.2 / 1.3 / .6	3.6 / 1.4 / .7	4.5 / 1.6 / .6	4.8 / 1.3 / .6	3.9 / 1.3 / .8	2.5 / 1.3 / .8	2.2 / .9 / .7	2.7 / 1.2 / .8
Quick	1.8 / (251) .7 / .2	2.1 / (299) .8 / .3	2.6 / (296) .9 / .4	2.8 / (88) 1.0 / .3	3.4 / (90) .7 / .1	3.6 / 1.1 / .6	2.3 / .8 / .5	1.7 / .9 / .5	1.9 / .8 / .5
Sales/Receivables	0 UND / 0 UND / 19 19.5	0 UND / 0 UND / 15 24.8	0 UND / 0 UND / 14 25.6	0 UND / 0 UND / 10 36.0	0 UND / 0 UND / 1 556.0	0 UND / 1 562.6 / 26 14.3	0 UND / 0 UND / 6 56.7	0 UND / 5 67.2 / 29 12.7	0 UND / 9 41.8 / 37 9.9
Cost of Sales/Inventory									
Cost of Sales/Payables									
Sales/Working Capital	15.8 / 110.9 / -31.0	15.3 / 75.6 / -30.6	12.9 / 58.6 / -35.7	8.1 / 28.5 / -19.0	13.6 / 58.2 / -48.9	13.2 / 54.4 / -42.7	22.5 / 102.3 / -241.4	20.9 / -211.6 / -34.7	9.0 / 190.3 / -31.0
EBIT/Interest	15.0 / (209) 4.2 / .7	21.1 / (233) 5.5 / 1.5	24.4 / (243) 7.2 / 1.4	15.8 / (57) 6.5 / 1.9	19.1 / (79) 6.0 / 1.0	149.1 / (29) 15.6 / 2.2	17.9 / (35) 5.7 / .9	24.7 / (26) 5.9 / 1.6	62.5 / (17) 29.2 / 7.3
Net Profit + Depr., Dep., Amort./Cur. Mat. L/T/D	6.1 / (12) 1.1 / .5	2.5 / (13) 1.6 / .8	5.9 / (11) 3.8 / 1.4						
Fixed/Worth	.6 / 3.9 / -1.6	.5 / 2.5 / -1.4	.4 / 2.0 / -3.4	.4 / 2.2 / -3.1	.6 / 4.4 / -1.1	.3 / .6 / -8.8	.5 / 2.7 / -.9	.7 / 1.8 / -33.1	.2 / .8 / 2.3
Debt/Worth	1.0 / 8.5 / -4.7	1.1 / 4.9 / -3.8	.8 / 3.6 / -6.3	.6 / 3.0 / -5.3	.8 / 7.6 / -3.8	.4 / 1.9 / -22.3	.9 / 4.2 / -4.4	1.0 / 3.4 / -69.2	.9 / 1.8 / 6.8
% Profit Before Taxes/Tangible Net Worth	211.2 / (158) 78.6 / 18.5	172.5 / (187) 70.1 / 14.0	190.7 / (199) 62.8 / 15.8	177.8 / (58) 70.0 / 22.1	261.8 / (54) 66.4 / 9.5	175.8 / (25) 59.7 / 20.2	179.2 / (26) 55.9 / 7.6	89.0 / (20) 29.7 / 12.6	198.3 / (16) 54.3 / 12.1
% Profit Before Taxes/Total Assets	50.1 / 15.5 / .0	55.3 / 18.5 / 1.9	50.2 / 16.7 / 1.1	56.2 / 17.4 / 3.0	50.7 / 16.7 / .0	63.5 / 24.9 / 2.8	40.1 / 12.0 / -.1	22.3 / 7.7 / 1.3	61.2 / 21.3 / 5.6
Sales/Net Fixed Assets	37.5 / 13.7 / 6.6	51.1 / 17.8 / 6.5	50.5 / 18.2 / 6.9	72.4 / 8.7 / 3.0	44.4 / 22.3 / 8.4	59.7 / 23.7 / 9.4	57.2 / 24.4 / 9.1	39.3 / 15.2 / 7.5	278.0 / 14.7 / 8.2
Sales/Total Assets	8.0 / 4.4 / 2.3	8.3 / 4.5 / 2.7	8.3 / 4.4 / 2.3	4.8 / 2.7 / 1.4	9.3 / 4.5 / 2.7	10.7 / 4.9 / 3.4	15.9 / 8.8 / 4.4	8.7 / 5.3 / 3.2	6.7 / 3.7 / 2.7
% Depr., Dep., Amort./Sales	1.7 / (168) 2.9 / 5.1	1.3 / (196) 2.5 / 4.3	1.2 / (184) 2.2 / 4.3	1.4 / (47) 4.3 / 9.6	.9 / (57) 1.9 / 3.7	1.8 / (19) 2.2 / 4.1	1.1 / (27) 1.6 / 3.4	1.6 / (23) 2.1 / 3.5	1.1 / (11) 2.8 / 5.3
% Officers', Directors' Owners' Comp/Sales	7.9 / (165) 14.2 / 22.1	8.1 / (183) 13.6 / 23.0	8.1 / (174) 14.6 / 24.9	7.7 / (45) 11.4 / 16.5	7.6 / (62) 13.1 / 20.1	7.3 / (19) 17.6 / 35.1	11.1 / (26) 27.2 / 34.0	11.1 / (17) 23.0 / 31.7	
Net Sales ($)	2528226M	3185274M	3178082M	51443M	166469M	133425M	266771M	439350M	2120624M
Total Assets ($)	1007665M	1150549M	960793M	41780M	60168M	39333M	55352M	103423M	660737M

© RMA 2011   M = $ thousand   MM = $ million
See Pages 9 through 22 for Explanation of Ratios and Data

Current Data Sorted by Assets   Comparative Historical Data

0-500M	500M-2MM	2-10MM	10-50MM	50-100MM	100-250MM	Type of Statement	4/1/06-3/31/07 ALL	4/1/07-3/31/08 ALL
						Type of Statement		
1	5	10	4	3		Unqualified	18	15
		1	1			Reviewed	1	2
5	6	1	1			Compiled	6	5
18	7					Tax Returns	21	14
3	6	7	4	1		Other	21	19
	34 (4/1-9/30/10)		50 (10/1/10-3/31/11)					
27	24	19	10	4		**NUMBER OF STATEMENTS**	67	55
%	%	%	%	%	%	**ASSETS**	%	%
49.8	22.1	20.4	18.8			Cash & Equivalents	31.0	26.7
7.0	27.2	36.4	19.7			Trade Receivables (net)	15.4	18.2
.0	.0	.0	.6			Inventory	.6	.4
4.1	3.1	2.5	7.5			All Other Current	4.3	5.2
60.9	52.4	59.3	46.6			Total Current	51.2	50.5
23.3	32.8	31.8	47.0			Fixed Assets (net)	36.0	32.7
1.7	5.5	.1	1.3			Intangibles (net)	3.3	7.3
14.1	9.3	8.8	5.0			All Other Non-Current	9.5	9.5
100.0	100.0	100.0	100.0			Total	100.0	100.0
						LIABILITIES		
35.5	7.8	3.8	2.7			Notes Payable-Short Term	23.9	20.8
2.8	1.2	.7	1.7			Cur. Mat.-L.T.D.	3.8	3.9
1.6	4.6	5.3	6.5			Trade Payables	2.9	4.2
.5	1.6	1.1	.0			Income Taxes Payable	.3	.2
21.4	19.1	15.5	19.9			All Other Current	21.8	22.0
61.9	34.3	26.3	30.7			Total Current	52.7	51.1
17.8	19.5	8.0	31.1			Long-Term Debt	32.0	15.9
.0	.0	.1	.0			Deferred Taxes	.1	.0
17.9	3.3	1.7	1.1			All Other Non-Current	3.2	8.0
2.4	42.9	63.9	37.0			Net Worth	12.0	24.9
100.0	100.0	100.0	100.0			Total Liabilities & Net Worth	100.0	100.0
						INCOME DATA		
100.0	100.0	100.0	100.0			Net Sales	100.0	100.0
						Gross Profit		
89.2	88.8	97.0	95.7			Operating Expenses	92.5	91.9
10.8	11.2	3.0	4.3			Operating Profit	7.5	8.1
-.1	2.8	-.7	1.7			All Other Expenses (net)	1.9	.1
10.9	8.4	3.7	2.6			Profit Before Taxes	5.6	8.0
						RATIOS		
5.7	4.6	3.3	3.7			Current	3.0	3.0
2.3	1.7	2.5	2.0				1.6	1.5
.7	.9	1.7	1.1				.9	.8
5.4	4.5	3.1	2.4			Quick	2.3	2.9
2.3	1.7	2.5	1.6				1.2	1.3
.7	.7	1.7	1.1				.8	.6
0 UND	0 UND	28 13.1	9 40.5			Sales/Receivables	0 UND	0 UND
0 UND	21 17.7	48 7.5	25 14.8				6 58.0	15 24.3
0 UND	39 9.3	77 4.7	43 8.5				44 8.4	39 9.3
						Cost of Sales/Inventory		
						Cost of Sales/Payables		
12.2	6.5	4.3	4.3			Sales/Working Capital	8.0	6.2
39.8	15.7	6.7	12.1				37.7	18.3
-43.2	NM	13.0	NM				-104.2	-28.0
67.0	33.0	18.6				EBIT/Interest	14.5	11.0
(15) 28.4	(17) 8.8	(14) 7.1					(50) 4.0	(42) 3.9
5.8	1.9	2.6					.9	1.2
						Net Profit + Depr., Dep., Amort./Cur. Mat. L/T/D		
.0	.1	.1	.4			Fixed/Worth	.3	.3
.4	.5	.4	1.2				.9	.7
-10.0	4.4	.7	NM				-999.8	2.8
.2	.5	.3	.5			Debt/Worth	.7	.5
.8	1.5	.4	1.5				2.0	1.5
-15.3	6.0	1.2	NM				-999.8	27.0
500.0	61.2	37.1				% Profit Before Taxes/Tangible Net Worth	174.4	98.7
(19) 114.0	(21) 36.2	8.2					(50) 33.4	(44) 16.2
70.4	2.9	3.2					4.6	1.9
114.5	31.6	19.9	7.1			% Profit Before Taxes/Total Assets	52.1	38.5
78.5	16.6	5.5	4.4				6.7	7.3
23.9	1.3	1.5	-.8				-3.8	.8
523.0	148.6	53.7	16.9			Sales/Net Fixed Assets	93.3	45.2
97.3	25.5	4.6	3.6				20.8	12.6
34.3	3.7	3.3	1.4				4.0	3.8
15.9	4.7	3.2	2.9			Sales/Total Assets	11.2	5.1
9.7	3.7	2.1	1.6				3.7	2.9
7.7	1.6	1.4	1.0				1.8	1.7
	.4	1.3	.7			% Depr., Dep., Amort./Sales	.6	.6
(16)	1.8	(17) 2.1	2.5				(53) 1.7	(40) 1.7
	3.3	3.0	4.8				2.7	3.2
4.9						% Officers', Directors' Owners' Comp/Sales	5.6	3.2
(20) 13.2							(27) 15.8	(15) 10.4
21.2							22.7	22.0
40632M	100207M	227386M	399407M	197041M		Net Sales ($)	2898144M	688500M
4006M	30397M	98965M	221150M	361613M		Total Assets ($)	386259M	330852M

(Middle columns under 50-100MM / 100-250MM: DATA NOT AVAILABLE)

Comparative Historical Data | | | Current Data Sorted by Sales

			Type of Statement						
18	17	23	Unqualified		2	3	8	6	4
1	10	2	Reviewed				1		1
9	6	13	Compiled						2
23	22	25	Tax Returns	3	3	2	3		
19	20	21	Other	12	7	5	1		2
4/1/08-3/31/09	4/1/09-3/31/10	4/1/10-3/31/11		2	4	1	2	6	6
ALL	ALL	ALL		34 (4/1-9/30/10)			50 (10/1/10-3/31/11)		
				0-1MM	1-3MM	3-5MM	5-10MM	10-25MM	25MM & OVER
70	75	84	**NUMBER OF STATEMENTS**	17	16	11	15	12	13
%	%	%	**ASSETS**	%	%	%	%	%	%
22.4	25.1	29.5	Cash & Equivalents	37.4	40.7	39.0	22.9	18.2	15.1
19.3	20.7	21.0	Trade Receivables (net)	2.9	9.1	23.4	35.8	33.1	28.8
.2	.2	.1	Inventory	.0	.1	.0	.0	.0	.5
5.7	5.0	3.7	All Other Current	5.1	1.7	.8	5.2	4.8	4.0
47.5	51.0	54.2	Total Current	45.4	51.6	63.2	63.9	56.0	48.5
35.5	34.6	30.3	Fixed Assets (net)	32.5	37.8	22.6	24.2	37.0	25.3
6.8	5.0	2.3	Intangibles (net)	1.7	4.3	4.6	2.1	.2	.9
10.2	9.4	13.2	All Other Non-Current	20.4	6.2	9.6	9.8	6.8	25.3
100.0	100.0	100.0	Total	100.0	100.0	100.0	100.0	100.0	100.0
			LIABILITIES						
19.8	7.4	14.8	Notes Payable-Short Term	41.1	17.2	5.9	5.0	5.3	5.3
2.6	2.0	1.6	Cur. Mat.-L.T.D.	1.6	3.6	.5	1.4	1.3	.6
5.5	6.8	3.8	Trade Payables	1.4	3.8	2.2	5.7	4.7	5.6
.0	.9	.9	Income Taxes Payable	.8	.0	.0	3.0	1.2	.0
20.1	17.3	18.5	All Other Current	18.7	22.9	14.1	19.7	14.8	18.7
47.9	34.4	39.7	Total Current	63.6	47.6	22.6	34.8	27.4	30.2
27.0	24.5	16.8	Long-Term Debt	24.4	25.0	7.7	7.8	24.2	8.3
.0	.0	.0	Deferred Taxes	.0	.0	.0	.1	.0	.0
7.2	6.5	7.2	All Other Non-Current	9.3	21.1	5.8	1.4	1.3	.9
18.0	34.6	36.2	Net Worth	2.7	6.3	63.8	55.9	47.2	60.6
100.0	100.0	100.0	Total Liabilities & Net Worth	100.0	100.0	100.0	100.0	100.0	100.0
			INCOME DATA						
100.0	100.0	100.0	Net Sales	100.0	100.0	100.0	100.0	100.0	100.0
			Gross Profit						
93.9	91.5	92.3	Operating Expenses	83.8	92.2	91.8	95.7	94.4	98.1
6.1	8.5	7.7	Operating Profit	16.2	7.8	8.2	4.3	5.6	1.9
1.8	2.4	.4	All Other Expenses (net)	2.8	1.0	-.6	-.5	1.4	-2.2
4.3	6.1	7.3	Profit Before Taxes	13.4	6.8	8.9	4.8	4.1	4.1
			RATIOS						
2.3	3.9	4.7		4.7	5.1	13.8	3.1	3.2	4.4
1.3	1.9	2.2	Current	2.1	2.1	4.9	2.0	2.2	2.1
.7	.9	1.2		.7	.3	1.2	1.6	1.7	1.3
2.0	3.8	3.9		4.4	4.3	13.8	2.7	2.9	4.2
1.1	1.8	2.1	Quick	2.1	2.0	4.9	2.0	1.8	1.5
.6	.8	1.1		.6	.2	1.2	1.6	1.6	1.3
0 UND	0 UND	0 UND		0 UND	0 UND	0 UND	5 79.4	18 20.4	14 25.8
17 21.1	20 18.7	18 20.0	Sales/Receivables	0 UND	0 UND	31 11.7	39 9.5	32 11.4	41 8.8
43 8.5	48 7.6	46 8.0		0 UND	14 25.9	46 7.9	60 6.1	49 7.5	63 5.8
			Cost of Sales/Inventory						
			Cost of Sales/Payables						
8.5	9.7	6.6		8.8	11.6	3.6	7.1	5.0	5.0
28.9	22.6	13.1	Sales/Working Capital	35.5	69.2	10.1	13.0	7.9	7.8
-86.4	-87.6	82.6		UND	-13.5	26.2	33.7	17.5	20.0
14.3	16.0	39.0			67.3		24.3	26.6	
(55) 2.5	(49) 2.9	(55) 8.8	EBIT/Interest	(11) 34.5		(11) 10.0	(10) 7.1		
.4	-.5	2.8			3.0		2.3	2.6	
			Net Profit + Depr., Dep., Amort./Cur. Mat. L/T/D						
.3	.3	.1		.3	.1	.2	.1	.1	.1
1.2	.7	.4	Fixed/Worth	.4	1.4	.4	.4	.6	.2
8.0	6.8	1.3		UND	-3.9	.7	.7	1.3	1.2
.7	.3	.3		.2	.3	.1	.4	.4	.2
2.4	1.2	.8	Debt/Worth	2.8	2.2	.4	.8	1.3	.5
82.6	7.9	3.2		-28.4	-6.0	1.5	1.3	1.9	2.4
92.9	97.5	80.3		403.5	210.6	121.6	75.0	59.6	24.9
(56) 14.2	(60) 23.2	(71) 26.7	% Profit Before Taxes/Tangible Net Worth	(12) 85.2	(11) 70.4	(10) 54.6	4.8	(11) 15.6	(12) 7.6
2.8	.5	4.8		16.9	13.6	5.7	.5	8.0	2.1
20.3	46.2	54.6		154.6	92.3	74.6	23.6	27.2	7.9
3.4	5.1	11.4	% Profit Before Taxes/Total Assets	68.8	24.0	27.8	3.0	7.2	4.3
-1.2	-.2	2.6		3.6	5.1	7.3	.4	5.1	.9
108.5	71.9	153.2		454.5	328.7	94.9	233.9	176.5	29.5-
19.5	20.4	24.4	Sales/Net Fixed Assets	49.7	32.4	26.4	28.4	4.9	10.7
2.8	4.4	4.0		6.5	10.3	3.4	4.4	2.1	2.4
7.7	6.6	8.1		19.1	10.9	8.6	6.7	3.7	3.6
3.4	3.5	3.7	Sales/Total Assets	8.1	6.6	3.4	3.9	2.0	2.0
1.7	1.8	1.5		1.7	2.2	1.5	2.6	1.2	.6
.5	.7	.7					.3	1.1	.7
(51) 1.5	(64) 1.3	(56) 2.0	% Depr., Dep., Amort./Sales			(10) 1.7	(10) 2.5	(12) 2.1	
3.2	3.0	3.4					2.5	3.5	4.4
6.2	4.6	4.7		4.7					
(26) 11.6	(27) 10.2	(35) 7.7	% Officers', Directors' Owners' Comp/Sales	(13) 15.7					
31.0	15.0	16.6		22.2					
698186M	970002M	964673M	Net Sales ($)	8490M	27631M	44745M	108627M	183259M	591921M
380080M	500884M	716131M	Total Assets ($)	6576M	7639M	19460M	39910M	100459M	542087M

© RMA 2011

M = $ thousand   MM = $ million
See Pages 9 through 22 for Explanation of Ratios and Data

Current Data Sorted by Assets | **Comparative Historical Data**

						Type of Statement		
	2	8	7		2	Unqualified	20	17
2	1	6	4	1		Reviewed	14	21
13	14	6				Compiled	38	18
72	11	4	1		2	Tax Returns	84	81
42	26	16	7	1	2	Other	56	59
	23 (4/1-9/30/10)		227 (10/1/10-3/31/11)				4/1/06-3/31/07	4/1/07-3/31/08
0-500M	500M-2MM	2-10MM	10-50MM	50-100MM	100-250MM		ALL	ALL
129	54	40	19	2	6	**NUMBER OF STATEMENTS**	212	196
%	%	%	%	%	%	**ASSETS**	%	%
35.9	19.8	13.8	13.5			Cash & Equivalents	23.1	26.1
8.2	29.3	33.3	22.4			Trade Receivables (net)	18.5	16.3
.4	.2	.2	.2			Inventory	1.0	.9
4.7	2.9	5.2	10.3			All Other Current	3.9	6.2
49.2	52.1	52.5	46.4			Total Current	46.5	49.5
32.2	30.5	23.8	34.1			Fixed Assets (net)	34.2	33.1
6.3	5.2	9.4	7.8			Intangibles (net)	5.8	5.4
12.3	12.2	14.4	11.8			All Other Non-Current	13.4	12.0
100.0	100.0	100.0	100.0			Total	100.0	100.0
						LIABILITIES		
24.0	14.6	6.7	3.0			Notes Payable-Short Term	19.7	22.7
4.4	7.9	3.0	2.8			Cur. Mat.-L.T.D.	5.4	6.0
4.1	4.5	3.1	3.8			Trade Payables	4.5	5.2
.0	.1	.1	.1			Income Taxes Payable	.1	.1
20.8	12.2	13.7	14.6			All Other Current	23.4	19.6
53.4	39.2	26.6	24.2			Total Current	53.1	53.5
22.0	17.1	19.5	18.8			Long-Term Debt	20.9	27.2
.0	1.3	.6	.3			Deferred Taxes	.3	.3
6.7	9.9	5.3	1.8			All Other Non-Current	3.3	4.4
18.0	32.6	48.0	54.8			Net Worth	22.3	14.6
100.0	100.0	100.0	100.0			Total Liabilties & Net Worth	100.0	100.0
						INCOME DATA		
100.0	100.0	100.0	100.0			Net Sales	100.0	100.0
						Gross Profit		
90.8	89.2	87.3	91.2			Operating Expenses	90.6	91.1
9.2	10.8	12.7	8.8			Operating Profit	9.4	8.9
.7	2.0	.6	.0			All Other Expenses (net)	1.1	1.6
8.5	8.8	12.0	8.8			Profit Before Taxes	8.4	7.2
						RATIOS		
4.1	3.8	4.4	3.0				2.3	3.0
1.4	1.4	2.1	2.0			Current	1.2	1.2
.4	.9	1.3	1.2				.4	.5
4.0	2.9	4.2	2.7				2.2	2.9
(128) 1.2	1.4	2.0	1.6			Quick	(211) 1.1	1.1
.3	.9	1.0	.7				.3	.4
0 UND	0 UND	26 14.0	20 18.5				0 UND	0 UND
0 UND	25 14.4	42 8.7	39 9.3			Sales/Receivables	0 UND	0 UND
0 UND	46 8.0	58 6.3	53 6.9				46 7.9	38 9.5
						Cost of Sales/Inventory		
						Cost of Sales/Payables		
14.9	9.4	6.2	2.8				10.9	10.5
80.7	30.3	11.5	9.1			Sales/Working Capital	77.0	55.2
-27.4	-97.7	89.7	26.4				-25.2	-24.4
22.7	21.1	44.5	30.2				21.4	18.6
(83) 7.0	(41) 7.6	(35) 12.3	6.7			EBIT/Interest	(153) 6.3	(144) 4.9
1.4	1.8	2.3	3.0				1.5	1.0
						Net Profit + Depr., Dep., Amort./Cur. Mat. L/T/D	8.5	2.5
							(12) 1.6	(15) 1.8
							.8	1.2
.2	.1	.1	.4				.3	.2
.7	.8	.4	.7			Fixed/Worth	.9	.9
43.6	3.6	2.5	1.0				25.6	UND
.4	.5	.4	.4				.5	.5
1.9	2.1	1.2	1.0			Debt/Worth	2.0	2.4
-10.6	17.9	3.6	2.4				UND	-27.5
378.9	87.5	95.5	44.0				194.1	135.3
(91) 147.7	(42) 44.0	(35) 38.2	(18) 10.7			% Profit Before Taxes/Tangible Net Worth	(159) 33.6	(143) 44.0
25.0	1.6	10.6	4.7				6.3	5.7
122.2	42.1	30.5	21.4				56.4	50.6
29.7	16.7	15.6	4.6			% Profit Before Taxes/Total Assets	13.5	12.8
1.7	2.3	7.0	3.6				.8	.0
154.3	65.5	104.2	26.7				106.6	84.1
42.5	21.8	21.3	5.4			Sales/Net Fixed Assets	25.1	22.8
12.6	7.1	7.7	1.5				7.9	6.8
13.4	5.4	3.9	3.4				9.6	9.1
7.2	3.5	3.0	1.1			Sales/Total Assets	4.1	3.9
3.3	2.0	1.7	.9				2.0	2.0
.5	.6	.5	.8				.5	.5
(74) 1.2	(38) 1.2	(36) 1.1	(18) 2.0			% Depr., Dep., Amort./Sales	(148) 1.6	(150) 1.2
2.7	2.9	2.3	3.9				2.6	2.7
5.8	8.4						6.7	6.1
(77) 13.9	(21) 13.8					% Officers', Directors' Owners' Comp/Sales	(93) 14.2	(99) 12.5
23.2	19.1						26.8	21.7
192228M	244939M	586795M	634844M	276350M	3379631M	Net Sales ($)	4339649M	4883279M
23868M	56086M	202279M	381747M	148865M	1080394M	Total Assets ($)	1345204M	1058195M

M = $ thousand   MM = $ million
See Pages 9 through 22 for Explanation of Ratios and Data

Comparative Historical Data			Type of Statement	Current Data Sorted by Sales					
11	18	19	Unqualified		3	3	2	5	6
10	22	14	Reviewed	1		1	2	3	7
10	36	33	Compiled	6	10	6	5	6	
69	96	90	Tax Returns	41	34	4	5	4	2
63	81	94	Other	32	17	12	9	18	6
4/1/08-3/31/09	4/1/09-3/31/10	4/1/10-3/31/11		23 (4/1-9/30/10)			227 (10/1/10-3/31/11)		
ALL	ALL	ALL		0-1MM	1-3MM	3-5MM	5-10MM	10-25MM	25MM & OVER
163	253	250	**NUMBER OF STATEMENTS**	80	64	26	23	36	21
%	%	%	**ASSETS**	%	%	%	%	%	%
25.8	24.8	26.8	Cash & Equivalents	28.1	36.4	25.9	20.8	17.7	15.3
18.5	18.6	18.3	Trade Receivables (net)	7.9	11.5	24.3	24.8	34.7	36.4
.6	.4	.3	Inventory	.4	.3	.2	.0	.1	.9
5.9	3.8	4.7	All Other Current	5.9	1.5	4.0	5.6	6.2	7.7
50.7	47.6	50.2	Total Current	42.3	49.7	54.4	51.3	58.7	60.3
29.8	32.4	30.2	Fixed Assets (net)	34.5	38.4	25.3	23.0	19.1	21.4
10.1	7.1	7.5	Intangibles (net)	8.5	2.3	8.2	8.4	8.5	15.4
9.4	12.8	12.2	All Other Non-Current	14.6	9.6	12.1	17.4	13.6	2.9
100.0	100.0	100.0	Total	100.0	100.0	100.0	100.0	100.0	100.0
			LIABILITIES						
18.6	18.3	17.2	Notes Payable-Short Term	22.2	17.8	26.8	13.2	6.3	7.3
3.9	6.8	4.7	Cur. Mat.-L.T.D.	4.7	3.5	4.5	3.6	9.3	2.3
3.1	4.0	4.1	Trade Payables	4.8	1.7	1.5	8.3	4.8	6.6
.2	.1	.1	Income Taxes Payable	.1	.0	.2	.2	.0	.0
16.0	16.8	16.9	All Other Current	15.8	15.5	25.3	12.7	17.6	18.0
41.8	46.0	42.9	Total Current	47.5	38.5	58.2	37.9	38.0	34.2
23.9	28.3	20.3	Long-Term Debt	23.9	20.5	20.9	10.2	19.8	17.4
.1	.1	.4	Deferred Taxes	.0	.0	.2	3.8	.1	.4
6.4	6.1	7.0	All Other Non-Current	9.5	6.2	3.6	7.1	5.5	6.1
27.8	19.5	29.4	Net Worth	19.0	34.9	17.1	41.0	36.7	41.9
100.0	100.0	100.0	Total Liabilities & Net Worth	100.0	100.0	100.0	100.0	100.0	100.0
			INCOME DATA						
100.0	100.0	100.0	Net Sales	100.0	100.0	100.0	100.0	100.0	100.0
			Gross Profit						
90.4	87.0	89.8	Operating Expenses	88.5	89.3	91.9	88.3	92.4	91.0
9.6	13.0	10.2	Operating Profit	11.5	10.7	8.1	11.7	7.6	9.0
1.5	2.1	1.0	All Other Expenses (net)	1.7	.6	2.2	-.3	.2	1.1
8.1	10.9	9.2	Profit Before Taxes	9.8	10.1	5.9	12.1	7.3	7.9
			RATIOS						
5.2	4.1	3.9	Current	4.1	5.2	3.0	4.2	3.0	2.9
1.6	1.3	1.5		1.4	1.8	1.1	1.8	2.0	1.8
.6	.5	.7		.4	.8	.5	1.0	1.3	1.2
4.1	3.8	3.6	Quick	3.9	5.3	2.3	3.5	2.7	2.9
1.3	1.2 (249)	1.4		1.3 (63)	1.9	1.0	1.5	1.9	1.6
.4	.4	.6		.2	.7	.4	.9	1.1	.7
0 UND	0 UND	0 UND	Sales/Receivables	0 UND	0 UND	0 UND	0 UND	11 34.3	19 19.2
0 UND	0 UND	0 UND		0 UND	0 UND	0 UND	30 12.4	37 9.9	47 7.7
49 7.5	44 8.3	40 9.1		0 UND	32 11.6	50 7.2	48 7.6	53 6.8	61 6.0
			Cost of Sales/Inventory						
			Cost of Sales/Payables						
7.5	9.3	9.8	Sales/Working Capital	12.0	9.7	12.3	9.4	6.3	6.8
30.1	38.9	27.4		73.4	36.5	182.4	21.3	12.4	10.3
-24.3	-26.1	-52.0		-10.3	-83.2	-29.0	-401.1	62.0	23.5
24.8	21.7	26.2	EBIT/Interest	19.8	27.9	21.0	33.9	34.7	144.1
(113) 6.7	(189) 7.1	(186) 7.7		(49) 5.5	(45) 7.6	(19) 1.7	(19) 10.4	(33) 12.9	27.8
1.4	1.8	1.9		2.0	1.3	-1.1	4.0	2.3	2.1
	10.6	19.1	Net Profit + Depr., Dep., Amort./Cur. Mat. L/T/D						22.7
	(16) 3.7	(24) 3.6							(11) 6.6
	1.7	1.6							1.9
.1	.1	.2	Fixed/Worth	.2	.2	.2	.1	.1	.2
.8	.8	.7		.8	.7	.9	.7	.3	.7
65.5	17.0	4.3		24.4	2.0	-1.8	1.6	1.0	13.4
.4	.6	.4	Debt/Worth	.4	.4	.4	.5	.5	.7
2.4	2.2	1.6		2.0	1.3	5.3	1.4	1.1	2.0
-26.3	-14.9	85.3		-8.0	3.7	-6.5	7.2	28.0	21.5
163.1	210.2	200.1	% Profit Before Taxes/Tangible Net Worth	325.0	311.0	189.1	137.2	121.6	114.4
(118) 68.3	(185) 66.7	(190) 62.3		(55) 103.2	(55) 69.7	(17) 53.3	(18) 63.7	(28) 33.2	(17) 57.9
10.4	16.0	10.4		8.8	7.6	-9.6	19.3	10.6	21.7
66.7	72.8	56.9	% Profit Before Taxes/Total Assets	99.4	90.7	58.1	57.1	32.8	41.9
18.5	22.5	21.1		22.2	26.5	13.2	23.0	13.2	20.0
2.7	3.2	3.1		2.1	1.2	-4.7	8.2	5.3	2.7
143.0	88.9	94.2	Sales/Net Fixed Assets	107.2	74.0	119.4	86.8	136.9	41.3
31.0	22.5	27.5		27.4	19.0	51.8	29.4	42.7	18.5
9.8	8.0	10.2		6.7	8.4	21.6	7.1	13.4	11.5
8.0	7.9	8.5	Sales/Total Assets	8.6	12.2	10.6	7.9	6.1	4.2
4.1	4.0	4.2		3.9	5.7	5.2	4.9	3.4	3.7
2.1	2.2	2.1		1.9	2.7	3.2	2.1	1.7	1.6
.5	.6	.6	% Depr., Dep., Amort./Sales	.7	.6	.4	.5	.5	.6
(108) 1.5	(173) 1.5	(173) 1.4		(44) 2.2	(44) 1.4	(18) .8	(18) 1.0	(29) 1.1	(20) 1.7
3.2	2.9	2.7		3.6	2.8	2.0	3.0	2.1	2.5
6.4	6.8	5.8	% Officers', Directors' Owners' Comp/Sales	9.8	5.1	5.3			
(79) 10.7	(108) 11.9	(109) 13.6		(43) 17.0	(38) 10.1	(10) 25.2			
18.4	20.1	20.1		23.3	15.9	32.2			
4488495M	6328356M	5314787M	Net Sales ($)	44123M	113276M	108285M	169128M	575647M	4304328M
929657M	1180297M	1893239M	Total Assets ($)	19181M	53639M	41647M	87385M	256981M	1434406M

© RMA 2011

M = $ thousand   MM = $ million
See Pages 9 through 22 for Explanation of Ratios and Data

Current Data Sorted by Assets   Comparative Historical Data

						Type of Statement		
						Unqualified		
						Reviewed		
3		2				Compiled	6	4
27	1					Tax Returns	18	21
10	4	1				Other	9	6
	2 (4/1-9/30/10)		46 (10/1/10-3/31/11)				4/1/06-3/31/07	4/1/07-3/31/08
0-500M	500M-2MM	2-10MM	10-50MM	50-100MM	100-250MM		ALL	ALL
40	5	3				NUMBER OF STATEMENTS	33	31
%	%	%	%	%	%	ASSETS	%	%
27.9						Cash & Equivalents	29.0	30.3
3.1			D	D	D	Trade Receivables (net)	6.6	.7
.8			A	A	A	Inventory	.1	.2
3.5			T	T	T	All Other Current	.9	5.2
35.3			A	A	A	Total Current	36.6	36.4
32.1						Fixed Assets (net)	34.8	40.4
17.0			N	N	N	Intangibles (net)	10.1	6.8
15.6			O	O	O	All Other Non-Current	18.5	16.4
100.0			T	T	T	Total	100.0	100.0
						LIABILITIES		
30.2			A	A	A	Notes Payable-Short Term	19.3	15.8
5.5			V	V	V	Cur. Mat.-L.T.D.	13.6	17.5
3.5			A	A	A	Trade Payables	3.4	.4
.8			I	I	I	Income Taxes Payable	.1	.0
23.7			L	L	L	All Other Current	23.7	20.6
63.7			A	A	A	Total Current	60.1	54.4
36.8			B	B	B	Long-Term Debt	41.2	41.0
.0			L	L	L	Deferred Taxes	.0	.0
6.5			E	E	E	All Other Non-Current	12.7	4.8
-6.9						Net Worth	-14.0	-.1
100.0						Total Liabilities & Net Worth	100.0	100.0
						INCOME DATA		
100.0						Net Sales	100.0	100.0
						Gross Profit		
89.7						Operating Expenses	87.2	89.0
10.3						Operating Profit	12.8	11.0
1.1						All Other Expenses (net)	2.8	2.3
9.2						Profit Before Taxes	10.1	8.6
						RATIOS		
1.5							1.7	1.7
.6						Current	.6	.8
.1							.2	.3
1.4							1.7	1.7
.3						Quick	.6	.8
.1							.2	.1
0 UND							0 UND	0 UND
0 UND						Sales/Receivables	0 UND	0 UND
0 UND							0 UND	0 UND
						Cost of Sales/Inventory		
						Cost of Sales/Payables		
128.5							61.8	46.1
-62.8						Sales/Working Capital	-39.4	-56.6
-14.5							-21.5	-13.4
10.6							18.4	19.7
(24) 2.5						EBIT/Interest	(25) 4.6	(25) 4.8
.6							.7	1.4
						Net Profit + Depr., Dep., Amort./Cur. Mat. L/T/D		
.4							.1	.6
3.5						Fixed/Worth	3.5	5.0
-.5							-.7	-1.0
.9							1.7	.6
66.0						Debt/Worth	5.6	-11.2
-1.9							-2.3	-2.7
364.7							356.1	128.0
(21) 134.6						% Profit Before Taxes/Tangible Net Worth	(18) 100.3	(14) 65.2
65.9							16.8	24.7
93.0							86.1	55.5
29.7						% Profit Before Taxes/Total Assets	21.3	17.5
-1.3							.5	1.1
117.6							173.5	145.0
21.1						Sales/Net Fixed Assets	30.3	23.5
12.7							7.9	9.8
10.6							12.9	13.2
6.5						Sales/Total Assets	5.0	6.0
3.9							2.3	2.9
.9							.5	.8
(23) 2.0						% Depr., Dep., Amort./Sales	(22) 1.5	(16) 2.0
3.5							3.4	6.3
13.2							19.0	15.3
(32) 18.6						% Officers', Directors' Owners' Comp/Sales	(22) 25.1	(23) 20.9
30.3							41.9	32.2
49371M	18364M	46023M				Net Sales ($)	47273M	57533M
7814M	4525M	14786M				Total Assets ($)	14563M	10071M

M = $ thousand   MM = $ million
See Pages 9 through 22 for Explanation of Ratios and Data

Comparative Historical Data   Current Data Sorted by Sales

		Comparative Historical Data		Type of Statement	2 (4/1-9/30/10)		46 (10/1/10-3/31/11)			
	5	13	5	Unqualified	2	1			2	
	22	39	28	Reviewed	18	9	1		1	
	5	9	15	Compiled / Tax Returns / Other	4	5	3	2		
	4/1/08-3/31/09	4/1/09-3/31/10	4/1/10-3/31/11		0-1MM	1-3MM	3-5MM	5-10MM	10-25MM	25MM & OVER
	ALL	ALL	ALL							
NUMBER OF STATEMENTS	32	61	48		24	15	4	2	3	
	%	%	%	ASSETS	%	%	%	%	%	%
Cash & Equivalents	31.7	25.9	26.6		31.9	19.1				D
Trade Receivables (net)	5.8	4.0	7.7		3.9	2.0				A
Inventory	.0	1.4	.8		1.3	.7				T
All Other Current	2.2	4.6	2.9		2.6	5.1				A
Total Current	39.8	36.0	38.1		39.7	26.8				
Fixed Assets (net)	31.9	32.3	30.4		25.1	35.5				N
Intangibles (net)	6.9	13.7	16.8		18.6	20.0				O
All Other Non-Current	21.4	18.0	14.7		16.6	17.7				T
Total	100.0	100.0	100.0		100.0	100.0				
				LIABILITIES						A
Notes Payable-Short Term	20.4	25.5	26.1		24.4	27.2				V
Cur. Mat.-L.T.D.	11.5	6.2	5.6		7.8	2.8				A
Trade Payables	2.4	4.0	3.3		5.4	.6				I
Income Taxes Payable	.0	.0	.7		1.3	.0				L
All Other Current	20.5	23.2	22.1		17.2	32.1				A
Total Current	54.8	58.9	57.7		56.1	62.8				B
Long-Term Debt	40.9	45.7	34.3		38.2	35.5				L
Deferred Taxes	.4	.0	.0		.0	.0				E
All Other Non-Current	2.3	4.0	5.4		10.2	.9				
Net Worth	1.6	-8.5	2.6		-4.5	.7				
Total Liabilities & Net Worth	100.0	100.0	100.0		100.0	100.0				
				INCOME DATA						
Net Sales	100.0	100.0	100.0		100.0	100.0				
Gross Profit										
Operating Expenses	86.6	88.9	88.8		88.2	88.6				
Operating Profit	13.4	11.1	11.2		11.8	11.4				
All Other Expenses (net)	2.5	2.9	1.0		.9	1.5				
Profit Before Taxes	10.9	8.1	10.2		10.9	9.8				
				RATIOS						
Current	4.1	5.7	1.8		2.2	1.0				
	1.2	.6	.7		.7	.3				
	.1	.1	.2		.2	.1				
Quick	3.2	5.1	1.6		1.6	.8				
	1.2	.6	.6		.5	.2				
	.1	.1	.1		.1	.1				
Sales/Receivables	0 UND	0 UND	0 UND		0 UND	0 UND				
	0 UND	0 UND	0 UND		0 UND	0 UND				
	0 UND	0 UND	0 UND		0 UND	0 UND				
Cost of Sales/Inventory										
Cost of Sales/Payables										
Sales/Working Capital	23.5	37.3	23.3		28.0	408.5				
	134.1	-46.3	-92.2		-88.9	-49.2				
	-8.8	-13.5	-16.7		-13.6	-13.8				
EBIT/Interest	43.8	14.4	16.9		17.3	11.2				
	(26) 12.7	(44) 3.4	(29) 4.3		(12) 2.2	(10) 4.4				
	.4	-.5	1.0		-2.3	1.7				
Net Profit + Depr., Dep., Amort./Cur. Mat. L/T/D										
Fixed/Worth	.3	.4	.4		.0	1.4				
	1.5	-40.5	2.6		2.1	5.3				
	-1.4	-.4	-.7		-.4	-.7				
Debt/Worth	.8	.8	.6		.5	1.4				
	4.2	-7.8	17.8		NM	29.0				
	-4.4	-2.1	-2.0		-1.7	-2.0				
% Profit Before Taxes/Tangible Net Worth	498.8	169.2	342.6		387.3					
	(21) 138.5	(27) 83.9	(27) 127.3		(12) 162.8					
	68.2	18.6	54.6		63.6					
% Profit Before Taxes/Total Assets	131.2	76.7	77.3		101.8	71.9				
	39.6	31.4	32.3		44.2	29.9				
	-2.7	-.9	3.9		-3.7	3.8				
Sales/Net Fixed Assets	194.7	70.9	89.4		294.5	47.5				
	38.5	25.8	20.5		23.6	20.3				
	12.0	13.5	11.8		12.1	14.3				
Sales/Total Assets	10.4	10.5	10.0		11.4	9.4				
	5.6	5.3	5.2		5.4	5.8				
	2.9	2.9	3.3		2.4	4.4				
% Depr., Dep., Amort./Sales	.3	.9	.8		1.0					
	(21) 1.0	(39) 1.9	(27) 1.5		(12) 2.5					
	3.4	3.8	3.3		5.0					
% Officers', Directors' Owners' Comp/Sales	14.2	11.6	10.8		14.6	6.9				
	(22) 20.9	(49) 19.3	(36) 17.7		(20) 20.8	(11) 13.1				
	35.0	30.8	27.3		31.5	18.4				
Net Sales ($)	49750M	110355M	113758M		14980M	24366M	13497M	14892M	46023M	
Total Assets ($)	10263M	24946M	27125M		4076M	4159M	2343M	1761M	14786M	

© RMA 2011

M = $ thousand   MM = $ million
See Pages 9 through 22 for Explanation of Ratios and Data

Current Data Sorted by Assets

	0-500M	500M-2MM	2-10MM	10-50MM	50-100MM	100-250MM		Comparative Historical Data 4/1/06-3/31/07 ALL	4/1/07-3/31/08 ALL
Type of Statement									
Unqualified		5	12	18	7	2		31	38
Reviewed		9	6					8	9
Compiled	15	7	6	1		1		41	29
Tax Returns	64	42	10	1		1		72	79
Other	40	40	25	9	1	2		76	68
		44 (4/1-9/30/10)		279 (10/1/10-3/31/11)					
NUMBER OF STATEMENTS	119	103	59	29	8	5		228	223
	%	%	%	%	%	%	ASSETS	%	%
	31.8	21.6	16.2	16.6			Cash & Equivalents	20.9	22.1
	8.0	19.1	20.7	18.2			Trade Receivables (net)	17.0	15.8
	4.5	3.5	2.0	.9			Inventory	2.6	3.0
	4.7	4.1	2.2	4.5			All Other Current	4.3	4.9
	49.1	48.4	41.0	40.3			Total Current	44.6	45.7
	30.6	31.5	39.7	40.6			Fixed Assets (net)	38.6	40.0
	3.8	8.2	10.1	6.1			Intangibles (net)	5.2	3.0
	16.5	11.9	9.3	13.0			All Other Non-Current	11.6	11.3
	100.0	100.0	100.0	100.0			Total	100.0	100.0
							LIABILITIES		
	30.3	11.3	3.5	4.7			Notes Payable-Short Term	14.0	17.6
	7.2	5.8	4.3	6.6			Cur. Mat.-L.T.D.	7.1	6.7
	4.5	5.4	5.9	4.8			Trade Payables	6.0	7.0
	.1	.6	.4	.2			Income Taxes Payable	.6	.4
	35.4	15.4	12.5	16.2			All Other Current	22.7	16.6
	77.4	38.5	26.6	32.4			Total Current	50.4	48.3
	29.6	28.7	25.8	22.1			Long-Term Debt	31.5	28.2
	.0	.0	.1	.6			Deferred Taxes	.3	.2
	11.4	5.8	3.3	11.6			All Other Non-Current	5.1	6.9
	-18.5	27.0	44.2	33.3			Net Worth	12.7	16.4
	100.0	100.0	100.0	100.0			Total Liabilities & Net Worth	100.0	100.0
							INCOME DATA		
	100.0	100.0	100.0	100.0			Net Sales	100.0	100.0
							Gross Profit		
	88.4	87.5	84.2	92.6			Operating Expenses	87.8	88.2
	11.6	12.5	15.8	7.4			Operating Profit	12.2	11.8
	.6	1.3	2.8	1.0			All Other Expenses (net)	2.4	1.9
	11.0	11.2	13.0	6.3			Profit Before Taxes	9.8	9.8
							RATIOS		
	3.6	3.8	3.5	2.8				2.7	2.5
	1.0	1.4	1.7	1.2			Current	1.2	1.3
	.3	.6	.8	1.0				.5	.6
	2.8	3.1	2.9	1.8				2.2	2.4
	(118) .8	1.3	1.6	1.1			Quick	(226) 1.0	(222) 1.1
	.2	.3	.6	.7				.4	.4
	0 UND	0 UND	0 UND	10 35.2				0 UND	0 UND
	0 UND	0 UND	34 10.8	30 12.1			Sales/Receivables	1 596.8	2 213.0
	0 UND	43 8.4	56 6.5	67 5.5				42 8.7	40 9.2
							Cost of Sales/Inventory		
							Cost of Sales/Payables		
	20.7	8.7	5.5	7.3				10.1	8.8
	-999.8	26.1	13.5	23.9			Sales/Working Capital	76.6	51.3
	-17.3	-25.3	-30.1	-246.7				-23.1	-22.8
	24.2	23.1	24.2	12.7				13.7	24.0
	(67) 3.5	(78) 9.8	(43) 6.1	(24) 3.6			EBIT/Interest	(164) 3.5	(171) 4.3
	.1	2.2	1.8	1.8				1.0	1.1
							Net Profit + Depr., Dep., Amort./Cur. Mat. L/T/D	5.3	
								(12) 2.9	
								1.3	
	.2	.2	.4	.6				.4	.4
	1.1	.7	1.2	1.1			Fixed/Worth	1.6	1.3
	-.6	-23.0	3.2	2.8				-3.0	-69.3
	.5	.4	.4	.7				.8	.7
	3.7	2.6	1.6	1.5			Debt/Worth	2.8	2.4
	-2.6	-21.8	7.6	10.1				-9.3	-24.8
	287.0	137.5	81.7	28.7				161.5	158.8
	(74) 93.9	(73) 50.9	(50) 28.7	(24) 9.8			% Profit Before Taxes/Tangible Net Worth	(162) 46.7	(163) 25.3
	15.4	21.3	6.6	1.2				6.7	3.0
	136.6	60.4	24.2	17.1				46.5	60.9
	28.3	19.8	8.3	4.7			% Profit Before Taxes/Total Assets	10.0	8.4
	.0	5.3	1.8	1.4				.3	-.1
	264.6	48.0	26.7	11.6				62.0	46.1
	53.7	17.2	6.4	2.6			Sales/Net Fixed Assets	13.9	11.8
	14.1	6.1	2.1	.9				3.9	3.8
	16.9	5.1	2.8	2.7				7.4	6.4
	7.1	3.4	1.6	1.4			Sales/Total Assets	3.5	3.3
	4.0	1.9	.7	.4				1.9	1.7
	.5	.9	1.3	2.3				.7	.9
	(60) .9	(69) 1.9	(51) 2.8	(24) 3.1			% Depr., Dep., Amort./Sales	(170) 2.3	(155) 2.2
	2.6	4.2	6.6	5.4				4.4	5.6
	7.3	3.9	2.0					5.4	6.1
	(63) 14.7	(49) 8.5	(14) 7.9				% Officers', Directors' Owners' Comp/Sales	(83) 11.9	(96) 14.6
	28.0	16.7	22.3					22.5	23.5
	290772M	501402M	552632M	2132710M	556969M	2231450M	Net Sales ($)	2985775M	2573984M
	22902M	109666M	272862M	734853M	540278M	877792M	Total Assets ($)	1319955M	1678940M

M = $ thousand   MM = $ million
See Pages 9 through 22 for Explanation of Ratios and Data

Comparative Historical Data

Current Data Sorted by Sales

					Type of Statement						
45		53		44	Unqualified	2	6	4	4	12	16
31		23		15	Reviewed		1	2	6	5	1
34		38		30	Compiled	7	8	6	3	3	3
87		124		117	Tax Returns	39	39	16	16	6	1
99		92		117	Other	20	38	16	17	18	8
4/1/08-3/31/09 ALL		4/1/09-3/31/10 ALL		4/1/10-3/31/11 ALL			44 (4/1-9/30/10)		279 (10/1/10-3/31/11)		
						0-1MM	1-3MM	3-5MM	5-10MM	10-25MM	25MM & OVER
296		330		323	NUMBER OF STATEMENTS	68	92	44	46	44	29
%		%		%	ASSETS	%	%	%	%	%	%
21.6		21.4		23.8	Cash & Equivalents	30.3	18.8	21.2	28.5	21.1	24.4
18.6		16.5		14.9	Trade Receivables (net)	5.4	16.1	13.0	24.7	15.6	19.0
2.9		3.2		3.2	Inventory	4.8	4.0	2.8	3.0	1.4	1.0
3.3		4.3		4.1	All Other Current	4.3	2.7	5.8	3.1	4.2	6.6
46.4		45.3		45.9	Total Current	45.0	41.7	42.8	59.3	42.2	51.1
36.7		36.7		33.3	Fixed Assets (net)	39.6	34.8	29.9	25.9	38.4	22.7
4.4		5.8		7.4	Intangibles (net)	4.9	5.2	11.6	6.1	7.1	16.2
12.5		12.2		13.4	All Other Non-Current	10.6	18.3	15.7	8.7	12.3	10.0
100.0		100.0		100.0	Total	100.0	100.0	100.0	100.0	100.0	100.0
					LIABILITIES						
16.1		14.9		16.0	Notes Payable-Short Term	19.5	16.4	16.6	14.7	15.6	8.0
5.8		6.1		6.0	Cur. Mat.-L.T.D.	8.3	4.8	7.4	4.0	5.0	7.1
7.8		5.7		5.0	Trade Payables	4.2	4.6	4.1	7.4	5.1	6.3
.1		.1		.3	Income Taxes Payable	.0	.4	.2	1.1	.0	.2
16.0		19.9		22.0	All Other Current	27.4	16.5	17.5	21.8	34.1	15.2
45.7		46.8		49.3	Total Current	59.4	42.7	45.8	48.9	59.9	36.8
26.9		30.8		27.4	Long-Term Debt	29.9	29.0	42.8	20.1	18.6	17.5
.2		.1		.1	Deferred Taxes	.0	.2	.0	.0	.1	.1
4.2		8.4		7.8	All Other Non-Current	14.1	5.8	5.3	6.9	4.3	10.1
22.9		13.8		15.4	Net Worth	-3.4	22.3	6.1	24.0	17.1	35.5
100.0		100.0		100.0	Total Liabilities & Net Worth	100.0	100.0	100.0	100.0	100.0	100.0
					INCOME DATA						
100.0		100.0		100.0	Net Sales	100.0	100.0	100.0	100.0	100.0	100.0
					Gross Profit						
87.5		89.9		87.7	Operating Expenses	81.7	87.1	85.9	91.5	94.7	89.9
12.5		10.1		12.3	Operating Profit	18.3	12.9	14.1	8.5	5.3	10.1
3.6		2.1		1.3	All Other Expenses (net)	3.6	1.2	1.0	.1	-.7	.8
8.9		8.1		11.0	Profit Before Taxes	14.7	11.6	13.1	8.4	5.9	9.3
					RATIOS						
2.8		2.5		3.4		6.5	3.7	3.8	2.7	2.2	3.1
1.4		1.3		1.3	Current	.9	1.3	1.4	1.8	1.0	1.4
.6		.5		.5		.2	.4	.6	1.0	.6	1.1
2.5		2.2		2.7		4.6	3.3	2.8	2.5	2.0	2.3
(295) 1.2		(322) 1.0		1.1	Quick	.5 (91)	1.2	1.0	1.6	.9	1.3
.4		.3		.3		.2	.4	.2	.8	.3	.9
0 UND	0 UND	0 UND				0 UND	0 UND	0 UND	0 UND	0 UND	11 34.1
12 30.7	2 228.3	0 UND			Sales/Receivables	0 UND	0 UND	0 UND	22 16.5	11 34.5	32 11.6
43 8.4	36 10.1	39 9.4				0 UND	43 8.5	37 9.9	51 7.1	37 9.8	52 7.1
					Cost of Sales/Inventory						
					Cost of Sales/Payables						
9.4		9.8		8.7		10.5	9.3	7.6	8.7	8.3	6.7
43.3		50.3		54.4	Sales/Working Capital	43.3 50.3 NM	60.5	25.0	20.9	NM	23.9
-25.4		-23.7		-24.6		-9.0	-15.7	-29.6	-807.8	-32.0	106.3
25.8		22.4		20.9		12.0	18.5	12.2	25.5	39.1	25.2
(230) 5.8	(249) 6.0	(222) 5.9			EBIT/Interest	(31) 3.5	(66) 5.7	(35) 5.6	(32) 7.3	(34) 5.4	(24) 11.2
1.0		1.2		1.4		1.1	.6	1.2	.3	1.5	2.1
8.8		23.6									
(24) 3.5	(12) 3.5				Net Profit + Depr., Dep., Amort./Cur. Mat. L/T/D						
.5		.7									
.4		.3		.3		.1	.4	.2	.1	.5	.3
1.2		1.3		1.0	Fixed/Worth	1.7	.9	1.2	.5	1.2	.8
-40.7		-45.0		-23.0		-4.5	UND	-.9	6.9	6.2	NM
.6		.7		.5		.2	.5	.5	.4	.6	.5
2.1		2.7		1.9	Debt/Worth	2.3	2.6	3.5	1.3	1.7	1.7
-30.5		-19.7		-11.6		-4.1	UND	-3.0	367.6	-36.4	-7.2
120.9		124.2		131.0		174.5	146.7	85.8	137.1	73.0	75.2
(210) 32.3	(237) 40.3	(231) 42.2			% Profit Before Taxes/Tangible Net Worth	(47) 60.6	(69) 50.9	(26) 27.1	(37) 78.3	(32) 24.9	(20) 22.6
6.5		6.8		8.0		12.4	15.2	.7	6.8	5.9	10.1
47.5		44.9		60.3		91.5	59.5	57.4	68.4	32.4	32.4
11.5		12.7		14.7	% Profit Before Taxes/Total Assets	18.9	20.5	14.3	15.0	5.3	15.2
-.1		.8		1.5		2.1	1.0	.4	.3	1.2	5.0
42.1		65.4		78.2		111.6	59.7	149.2	88.4	86.9	138.1
13.1		15.3		17.2	Sales/Net Fixed Assets	16.3	14.9	20.8	31.8	12.2	12.2
3.7		4.2		4.9		5.4	5.1	7.4	9.8	3.4	3.2
6.4		7.7		7.1		7.3	6.1	5.8	9.1	14.0	3.9
3.2		3.8		3.4	Sales/Total Assets	3.8	3.4	3.6	4.2	3.4	2.2
1.5		1.8		1.6		1.4	1.5	1.7	2.5	1.6	1.2
.8		.8		.8		.8	.9	.5	1.0	.8	2.4
(227) 2.2	(244) 2.1	(211) 2.1			% Depr., Dep., Amort./Sales	(35) 2.5	(62) 2.0	(32) 1.4	(31) 1.6	(34) 2.3	(17) 2.8
4.2		4.3		4.4		6.6	5.3	3.4	3.4	4.0	4.0
5.3		5.9		5.5		5.8	4.7	3.9	5.2	5.4	
(106) 11.6	(147) 11.9	(128) 11.3			% Officers', Directors' Owners' Comp/Sales	(30) 13.0	(44) 11.0	(18) 8.3	(17) 10.2	(16) 19.3	
23.6		22.9		25.0		32.7	18.1	21.8	27.5	37.4	
4993551M		8996080M		6265935M	Net Sales ($)	34592M	168002M	168770M	330755M	722932M	4840884M
2375716M		2716232M		2558353M	Total Assets ($)	33953M	118568M	105691M	139626M	467059M	1693456M

M = $ thousand   MM = $ million
See Pages 9 through 22 for Explanation of Ratios and Data

Current Data Sorted by Assets   Comparative Historical Data

0-500M	500M-2MM	2-10MM	10-50MM	50-100MM	100-250MM	Type of Statement	4/1/06-3/31/07 ALL	4/1/07-3/31/08 ALL
1	6	8	13	3	2	Unqualified	23	18
		1				Reviewed		1
1						Compiled	1	
1		1				Tax Returns	2	2
3	3	4	3	1		Other	13	13
	30 (4/1-9/30/10)		21 (10/1/10-3/31/11)				13 ALL	13 ALL
6	9	14	16	4	2	**NUMBER OF STATEMENTS**	39	34
%	%	%	%	%	%	**ASSETS**	%	%
		15.5	23.8			Cash & Equivalents	18.0	15.3
		9.2	11.5			Trade Receivables (net)	14.9	18.9
		1.7	2.7			Inventory	2.3	1.1
		1.7	2.4			All Other Current	6.3	5.8
		28.2	40.3			Total Current	41.5	41.2
		54.9	41.1			Fixed Assets (net)	40.9	44.8
		2.6	.2			Intangibles (net)	1.8	2.6
		14.3	18.4			All Other Non-Current	15.9	11.4
		100.0	100.0			Total	100.0	100.0
						LIABILITIES		
		.7	.9			Notes Payable-Short Term	2.7	3.4
		3.2	.6			Cur. Mat.-L.T.D.	1.5	3.2
		3.5	2.7			Trade Payables	6.7	7.6
		.0	.0			Income Taxes Payable	.3	.3
		3.9	5.3			All Other Current	9.4	9.6
		11.3	9.6			Total Current	20.6	24.2
		22.6	11.7			Long-Term Debt	18.1	23.3
		.0	.0			Deferred Taxes	.0	.0
		1.5	.6			All Other Non-Current	1.7	1.8
		64.6	78.1			Net Worth	59.7	50.7
		100.0	100.0			Total Liabilities & Net Worth	100.0	100.0
						INCOME DATA		
		100.0	100.0			Net Sales	100.0	100.0
						Gross Profit		
		86.8	93.6			Operating Expenses	93.1	91.9
		13.2	6.4			Operating Profit	6.9	8.1
		3.7	-1.3			All Other Expenses (net)	.2	-.6
		9.5	7.7			Profit Before Taxes	6.6	8.7
						RATIOS		
		6.6	6.2			Current	4.1	3.5
		2.2	4.0				2.7	2.0
		1.2	3.2				1.3	1.1
		6.0	5.0			Quick	3.6	3.2
		1.9	3.6				2.0	1.7
		.8	2.5				1.0	1.0
		4 97.3	14 26.0			Sales/Receivables	7 49.5	5 73.0
		21 17.7	42 8.8				24 15.5	31 11.6
		35 10.5	51 7.1				62 5.9	58 6.3
						Cost of Sales/Inventory		
						Cost of Sales/Payables		
		2.8	3.0			Sales/Working Capital	3.7	4.8
		9.7	4.0				7.8	10.5
		33.5	5.7				17.5	64.2
		11.4				EBIT/Interest	15.5	24.9
		(11) 7.9					(32) 4.8	(28) 6.0
		4.3					.7	2.3
						Net Profit + Depr., Dep., Amort./Cur. Mat. L/T/D		
		.5	.3			Fixed/Worth	.2	.4
		.7	.5				.6	.8
		1.6	.9				1.5	1.9
		.1	.1			Debt/Worth	.2	.3
		.4	.2				.6	.8
		1.6	.7				1.2	2.5
		19.4	12.0			% Profit Before Taxes/Tangible Net Worth	26.6	46.8
		(13) 10.0	8.1				(38) 6.6	(32) 15.5
		3.1	5.1				.2	2.4
		11.8	11.1			% Profit Before Taxes/Total Assets	8.1	18.0
		6.3	7.3				2.5	6.5
		3.3	2.8				-.4	.8
		3.0	3.8			Sales/Net Fixed Assets	9.4	10.7
		2.2	2.6				3.5	3.4
		1.5	1.9				2.0	2.0
		1.5	1.3			Sales/Total Assets	2.7	2.6
		1.1	1.0				1.4	1.7
		.7	.8				.9	1.0
		2.1	2.3			% Depr., Dep., Amort./Sales	1.7	1.4
		(13) 3.2	3.2				(36) 3.0	(31) 2.7
		5.3	4.3				3.6	3.5
						% Officers', Directors', Owners' Comp/Sales		
10690M	24577M	103811M	378134M	165256M	241029M	Net Sales ($)	685567M	517104M
1844M	9978M	83955M	351032M	270590M	343439M	Total Assets ($)	542766M	456982M

© RMA 2011

M = $ thousand   MM = $ million
See Pages 9 through 22 for Explanation of Ratios and Data

Comparative Historical Data | Current Data Sorted by Sales

			Type of Statement	0-1MM	1-3MM	3-5MM	5-10MM	10-25MM	25MM & OVER
34	33	33	Unqualified	1	7	3	3	9	10
	1	1	Reviewed				1		
1		1	Compiled	1					
2	4	2	Tax Returns		1		1		
14	17	14	Other	3	3	1	1	5	1
4/1/08-3/31/09	4/1/09-3/31/10	4/1/10-3/31/11			30 (4/1-9/30/10)			21 (10/1/10-3/31/11)	
ALL	ALL	ALL							
51	55	51	NUMBER OF STATEMENTS	5	11	4	6	14	11
%	%	%	ASSETS	%	%	%	%	%	%
23.8	18.2	22.8	Cash & Equivalents		29.3			15.6	23.1
13.6	11.0	12.1	Trade Receivables (net)		7.4			15.1	11.7
2.0	1.5	1.5	Inventory		.6			2.0	3.2
6.2	2.3	2.4	All Other Current		3.3			2.3	2.5
45.6	33.0	38.9	Total Current		40.7			35.1	40.5
37.1	49.8	43.2	Fixed Assets (net)		58.1			42.4	34.2
2.7	4.5	2.0	Intangibles (net)		.1			.0	5.7
14.6	12.7	16.0	All Other Non-Current		1.1			22.6	19.6
100.0	100.0	100.0	Total		100.0			100.0	100.0
			LIABILITIES						
4.3	1.9	4.9	Notes Payable-Short Term		1.4			6.5	.5
2.3	1.8	2.0	Cur. Mat.-L.T.D.		4.1			2.9	.5
7.7	4.6	4.7	Trade Payables		2.7			7.4	3.8
.0	.1	.0	Income Taxes Payable		.0			.0	.0
8.7	5.6	8.3	All Other Current		4.6			6.9	5.8
23.0	14.0	19.8	Total Current		12.7			23.7	10.7
13.0	26.2	15.9	Long-Term Debt		22.5			13.1	13.3
.0	.0	.1	Deferred Taxes		.0			.0	.4
1.4	3.7	2.1	All Other Non-Current		.0			1.9	1.0
62.6	56.0	62.1	Net Worth		64.8			61.3	74.5
100.0	100.0	100.0	Total Liabilities & Net Worth		100.0			100.0	100.0
			INCOME DATA						
100.0	100.0	100.0	Net Sales		100.0			100.0	100.0
			Gross Profit						
91.4	92.3	90.4	Operating Expenses		85.6			97.4	92.4
8.6	7.7	9.6	Operating Profit		14.4			2.6	7.6
1.1	2.1	.7	All Other Expenses (net)		4.6			-1.3	-.9
7.5	5.7	8.9	Profit Before Taxes		9.7			3.9	8.6
			RATIOS						
4.2	4.5	5.1	Current		15.9			4.0	5.1
2.3	2.5	2.4			2.1			1.7	3.4
1.2	1.2	1.2			1.2			.8	2.7
3.8	3.7	4.7	Quick		15.9			3.6	4.7
1.9	2.2	2.1			1.8			1.6	2.8
.9	.9	.8			.8			.5	2.1
10 35.7	5 71.5	8 44.1	Sales/Receivables		1 316.6			14 26.0	27 13.6
27 13.7	22 16.6	27 13.6			4 101.7			31 11.7	41 8.9
44 8.3	38 9.6	41 8.8			21 17.0			57 6.4	51 7.2
			Cost of Sales/Inventory						
			Cost of Sales/Payables						
2.8	3.4	3.3	Sales/Working Capital		2.5			4.1	2.7
5.9	6.5	6.6			12.0			9.7	5.4
60.5	33.7	34.4			34.6			-26.4	6.7
35.7	14.5	21.2	EBIT/Interest					21.7	
(34) 3.1	(41) 2.7	(34) 6.5						(13) 5.6	
-1.3	.2	1.6						-.6	
			Net Profit + Depr., Dep., Amort./Cur. Mat. L/T/D						
.3	.4	.3	Fixed/Worth		.2			.3	.3
.5	1.0	.7			1.0			.7	.5
.9	2.4	1.3			1.8			1.3	.9
.2	.2	.1	Debt/Worth		.2			.2	.1
.4	.7	.4			.4			.4	.3
1.7	2.2	1.4			1.2			1.0	.8
35.5	13.8	19.4	% Profit Before Taxes/Tangible Net Worth		37.0			9.9	14.4
(48) 4.1	(48) 6.6	(46) 9.0			17.0			(13) 4.2	(10) 11.3
-6.5	-5.9	2.7			6.7			.5	5.1
16.9	10.0	12.3	% Profit Before Taxes/Total Assets		20.2			6.4	11.3
2.9	3.5	6.7			6.7			3.2	10.0
-3.7	-3.1	1.9			4.7			-.5	2.8
13.9	5.8	6.2	Sales/Net Fixed Assets		14.3			5.1	4.9
4.5	2.5	2.8			2.4			2.9	3.6
2.2	1.4	1.9			1.7			.9	2.1
2.3	1.7	1.7	Sales/Total Assets		2.3			1.5	1.4
1.4	1.2	1.1			1.4			1.1	1.0
.8	.7	.7			1.2			.6	.9
1.5	1.9	1.9	% Depr., Dep., Amort./Sales		.9			2.0	2.1
(43) 2.5	(45) 2.9	(46) 2.9			3.0			3.0 (10)	3.1
3.4	4.6	4.3			3.5			4.8	4.3
			% Officers', Directors' Owners' Comp/Sales						
1201654M	1099743M	923497M	Net Sales ($)	3597M	19347M	14766M	49143M	242355M	594289M
1008015M	1024244M	1060838M	Total Assets ($)	3827M	17477M	11524M	54069M	327147M	646794M

© RMA 2011

M = $ thousand   MM = $ million
See Pages 9 through 22 for Explanation of Ratios and Data

Current Data Sorted by Assets　　　　　　　　　　　　**Comparative Historical Data**

Type of Statement	0-500M	500M-2MM	2-10MM	10-50MM	50-100MM	100-250MM		4/1/06-3/31/07 ALL	4/1/07-3/31/08 ALL
Unqualified		13	59	48	3	1		61	84
Reviewed			2					1	
Compiled			4	1				3	5
Tax Returns	9	5	1					5	6
Other	3	10	24	11	1			27	23
	140 (4/1-9/30/10)			55 (10/1/10-3/31/11)					
NUMBER OF STATEMENTS	12	28	90	60	4	1		97	118
	%	%	%	%	%	%		%	%
ASSETS									
Cash & Equivalents	33.2	16.6	23.6	21.3				19.7	20.7
Trade Receivables (net)	18.4	28.3	19.1	14.8				19.6	20.2
Inventory	.0	.3	.1	.2				.3	.5
All Other Current	2.7	9.7	3.5	2.7				5.2	4.6
Total Current	54.3	54.8	46.4	39.0				44.8	46.0
Fixed Assets (net)	33.3	38.7	44.7	49.4				45.1	40.5
Intangibles (net)	6.3	2.5	.8	3.6				1.5	2.4
All Other Non-Current	6.1	4.0	8.1	8.0				8.6	11.2
Total	100.0	100.0	100.0	100.0				100.0	100.0
LIABILITIES									
Notes Payable-Short Term	19.6	6.1	2.6	3.8				2.5	3.2
Cur. Mat.-L.T.D.	10.0	2.7	2.3	2.4				2.7	2.2
Trade Payables	5.9	9.5	8.4	4.5				5.9	8.9
Income Taxes Payable	.0	.0	.2	.0				.3	.1
All Other Current	17.1	23.1	15.1	11.6				12.7	12.0
Total Current	52.6	41.3	28.6	22.4				24.1	26.4
Long-Term Debt	16.9	11.5	20.1	25.8				23.8	22.9
Deferred Taxes	.0	.0	.1	.0				.0	.1
All Other Non-Current	.6	10.8	2.3	2.5				2.1	3.0
Net Worth	30.5	36.4	48.9	49.4				49.9	47.6
Total Liabilties & Net Worth	100.0	100.0	100.0	100.0				100.0	100.0
INCOME DATA									
Net Sales	100.0	100.0	100.0	100.0				100.0	100.0
Gross Profit									
Operating Expenses	81.9	99.0	93.8	94.3				94.7	94.5
Operating Profit	18.1	1.0	6.2	5.7				5.3	5.5
All Other Expenses (net)	1.9	1.4	2.6	1.8				1.5	.3
Profit Before Taxes	16.2	-.4	3.6	4.0				3.8	5.2
RATIOS									
Current	7.9	2.4	3.0	2.9				3.8	3.1
	2.1	1.5	1.9	2.1				1.9	2.0
	.2	.8	1.1	1.3				1.3	1.2
Quick	7.5	2.4	3.0	2.6				3.3	2.8
	2.0	1.1	1.8	1.8				1.8	1.7
	.2	.4	1.0	1.2				1.1	1.1
Sales/Receivables	0 UND	8 43.1	17 21.6	12 29.3				17 21.5	17 22.1
	0 UND	31 11.6	32 11.4	30 12.1				31 12.0	32 11.3
	35 10.4	48 7.6	44 8.3	51 7.1				51 7.1	46 8.0
Cost of Sales/Inventory									
Cost of Sales/Payables									
Sales/Working Capital	5.8	8.9	5.3	4.9				4.0	5.4
	12.5	18.4	9.8	7.4				10.5	9.8
	-11.5	-26.2	51.4	21.0				39.4	33.2
EBIT/Interest		9.4	10.6	9.3				9.2	9.5
		(19) 2.8	(71) 3.7	(56) 2.5				(79) 2.7	(95) 2.9
		-6.2	.8	1.3				.7	1.0
Net Profit + Depr., Dep., Amort./Cur. Mat. L/T/D									
Fixed/Worth	.0	.3	.5	.6				.5	.5
	.3	.8	.9	1.1				.8	.9
	NM	2.8	1.7	2.0				1.6	1.8
Debt/Worth	.1	.4	.4	.5				.4	.5
	1.9	1.6	.9	1.0				.8	1.0
	-60.9	3.7	2.2	2.2				1.8	2.3
% Profit Before Taxes/Tangible Net Worth		34.9	20.7	11.0				13.6	25.7
	(24)	3.5	(85) 5.9	(56) 5.8				(89) 6.1	(108) 7.1
		-4.0	.0	.9				-1.1	.1
% Profit Before Taxes/Total Assets	51.3	13.1	11.6	6.4				8.4	12.3
	23.7	.4	2.9	2.5				3.0	3.3
	2.7	-6.8	-.1	.5				-.7	.1
Sales/Net Fixed Assets	60.9	62.0	12.8	4.9				9.2	15.5
	27.4	7.5	3.9	2.9				3.3	4.2
	5.2	3.8	2.1	1.7				2.0	2.2
Sales/Total Assets	7.0	4.9	3.2	1.9				2.7	3.2
	3.1	2.9	1.9	1.3				1.5	1.8
	1.0	2.0	1.3	1.0				1.0	1.1
% Depr., Dep., Amort./Sales		.8	1.1	1.9				1.5	1.3
	(20)	1.5	(81) 2.0	2.5				(91) 2.7	(108) 2.3
		3.3	2.9	3.5				3.8	3.3
% Officers', Directors' Owners' Comp/Sales								1.6	
								(12) 6.0	
								14.2	
Net Sales ($)	12991M	108408M	1010439M	2072301M	468594M	57973M		1777072M	2658130M
Total Assets ($)	2874M	35091M	462128M	1251872M	290753M	169343M		1082051M	1545424M

M = $ thousand   MM = $ million
See Pages 9 through 22 for Explanation of Ratios and Data

Comparative Historical Data | Current Data Sorted by Sales

4/1/08-3/31/09 ALL	4/1/09-3/31/10 ALL	4/1/10-3/31/11 ALL	Type of Statement	0-1MM	1-3MM	3-5MM	5-10MM	10-25MM	25MM & OVER
77	91	124	Unqualified	1	8	10	31	40	34
1		2	Reviewed	1					1
6	3	4	Compiled			1	2		1
11	12	16	Tax Returns	8	1	3	3		1
37	33	49	Other	4	5	13	5	15	7
				140 (4/1-9/30/10)			55 (10/1/10-3/31/11)		
132	139	195	**NUMBER OF STATEMENTS**	14	14	27	41	55	44
%	%	%	**ASSETS**	%	%	%	%	%	%
21.2	22.1	22.4	Cash & Equivalents	23.1	30.7	20.7	20.2	23.0	21.8
19.9	20.4	18.7	Trade Receivables (net)	14.6	21.5	15.7	19.0	19.6	19.6
.2	.1	.2	Inventory	.0	.2	.0	.1	.2	.3
5.3	5.3	4.1	All Other Current	2.9	2.5	2.2	8.2	3.2	3.4
46.6	47.9	45.4	Total Current	40.6	54.9	38.7	47.6	46.0	45.2
41.8	40.4	44.2	Fixed Assets (net)	54.2	41.6	49.2	45.2	43.9	38.0
2.6	4.4	3.0	Intangibles (net)	.1	.0	2.8	2.3	1.7	7.2
9.0	7.3	7.5	All Other Non-Current	5.2	3.4	9.3	5.0	8.4	9.6
100.0	100.0	100.0	Total	100.0	100.0	100.0	100.0	100.0	100.0
			LIABILITIES						
3.1	5.6	4.5	Notes Payable-Short Term	15.5	1.2	4.0	3.4	3.7	4.3
2.6	3.1	2.8	Cur. Mat.-L.T.D.	9.9	1.8	1.5	1.8	3.0	2.4
6.2	7.1	7.2	Trade Payables	6.5	7.9	3.7	6.7	9.7	6.5
.1	.1	.1	Income Taxes Payable	.0	.0	.0	.0	.3	.0
11.7	16.0	15.1	All Other Current	12.3	22.4	9.5	16.0	16.4	14.6
23.6	32.0	29.6	Total Current	44.2	33.3	18.7	28.0	33.1	27.8
21.6	21.0	21.0	Long-Term Debt	20.1	19.9	21.7	17.9	21.1	24.1
.0	.0	.0	Deferred Taxes	.0	.0	.0	.0	.0	.0
2.3	3.0	3.4	All Other Non-Current	.5	9.1	7.8	3.2	.2	2.5
52.4	44.1	45.9	Net Worth	35.6	37.7	51.8	51.0	44.2	45.5
100.0	100.0	100.0	Total Liabilities & Net Worth	100.0	100.0	100.0	100.0	100.0	100.0
			INCOME DATA						
100.0	100.0	100.0	Net Sales	100.0	100.0	100.0	100.0	100.0	100.0
			Gross Profit						
94.8	95.9	93.9	Operating Expenses	81.1	90.2	97.3	95.7	94.8	94.0
5.2	4.1	6.1	Operating Profit	18.9	9.8	2.7	4.3	5.2	6.0
.7	.4	2.0	All Other Expenses (net)	7.2	3.6	1.6	.4	2.6	1.0
4.5	3.7	4.1	Profit Before Taxes	11.8	6.2	1.1	3.9	2.5	5.0
			RATIOS						
3.2	2.8	2.9	Current	4.2	5.7	6.0	3.8	2.3	2.5
2.1	1.9	1.9		1.1	1.6	2.4	2.3	1.8	1.7
1.3	1.2	1.2		.1	.9	1.6	1.2	1.1	1.2
3.1	2.6	2.8	Quick	3.4	5.7	5.8	3.4	2.2	2.2
1.9	1.7	1.7		1.1	1.5	2.4	2.2	1.7	1.5
1.0	1.0	1.0		.1	.8	1.3	1.0	1.0	1.1
14 25.7	14 25.9	12 31.2	Sales/Receivables	0 UND	0 UND	18 19.9	13 27.5	21 17.2	7 53.1
32 11.4	30 12.0	30 12.0		0 UND	28 13.1	35 10.3	32 11.3	32 11.3	24 15.2
47 7.8	46 7.9	48 7.6		39 9.3	49 7.4	58 6.3	47 7.7	44 8.3	47 7.7
			Cost of Sales/Inventory						
			Cost of Sales/Payables						
5.1	5.8	5.6	Sales/Working Capital	5.3	5.8	3.0	4.4	6.3	6.9
9.4	10.9	10.2		68.9	7.8	5.8	8.1	10.4	12.5
28.5	39.1	46.6		-3.6	-25.4	23.8	42.5	44.4	40.1
10.2	8.3	9.9	EBIT/Interest			7.4	11.2	9.4	12.2
(100) 3.0	(107) 3.4	(157) 3.1		(23) 2.1	(31) 4.5		(47) 4.5	(41) 3.0	3.1
.9	1.0	1.3				-.8	1.3	1.1	1.6
		22.7	Net Profit + Depr., Dep.,						
	(10)	5.7	Amort./Cur. Mat. L/T/D						
		2.4							
.4	.4	.5	Fixed/Worth	.2	.2	.6	.4	.7	.5
.9	1.0	.9		1.2	.8	.9	.9	.9	1.0
1.6	1.9	2.0		7.0	UND	1.7	2.1	1.3	2.4
.4	.5	.5	Debt/Worth	.2	.3	.3	.4	.6	.6
.9	1.1	1.0		.8	2.2	.7	.7	1.0	1.1
1.8	2.9	2.4		7.7	UND	1.5	2.2	2.4	3.8
24.2	21.4	19.4	% Profit Before Taxes/Tangible	51.8	31.3	19.1	11.4	16.8	26.1
(125) 8.2	(123) 6.6	(177) 5.9	Net Worth	(13) 2.1	(11) 6.7	(25) 2.7	(38) 3.9	(51) 7.6	(39) 7.9
.9	-.3	.5		-4.7	.0	-4.8	.4	1.0	2.0
14.0	9.7	10.4	% Profit Before Taxes/Total	24.5	30.8	7.6	7.5	7.4	12.2
4.3	3.1	2.8	Assets	1.8	4.1	1.7	1.7	4.5	3.2
.1	-.2	.1		-1.3	-5.0	-3.2	-.1	.4	1.0
18.9	25.5	12.6	Sales/Net Fixed Assets	21.6	UND	5.6	25.9	9.4	14.0
4.6	4.3	3.9		2.6	4.2	2.9	3.8	3.9	4.9
2.1	2.2	2.1		.3	1.3	2.0	1.9	2.4	2.7
3.6	3.9	3.1	Sales/Total Assets	3.0	3.1	2.2	3.7	3.2	3.5
1.7	1.8	1.8		.6	2.1	1.4	2.0	1.8	1.9
1.2	1.2	1.1		.2	.8	1.0	1.2	1.3	1.2
1.1	.9	1.3	% Depr., Dep., Amort./Sales	1.0		1.9	.9	1.3	1.2
(111) 2.1	(122) 1.8	(174) 2.1		(12) 3.2		(23) 2.7	(38) 1.9	(50) 1.9	(42) 1.9
3.2	2.5	3.3		15.9		4.7	3.4	2.5	2.8
2.9	5.9	2.1	% Officers', Directors'						
(17) 8.9	(24) 11.6	(26) 6.1	Owners' Comp/Sales						
14.6	25.0	11.6							
2397367M	2296461M	3730706M	Net Sales ($)	6786M	24567M	107194M	318096M	882487M	2391576M
1413395M	1333839M	2212061M	Total Assets ($)	16115M	43449M	93084M	210274M	502601M	1346538M

M = $ thousand   MM = $ million
See Pages 9 through 22 for Explanation of Ratios and Data

Current Data Sorted by Assets

	1		1	2	4	4
2	1		1			
2		1	3			
2	2	3		1		3
	3 (4/1-9/30/10)			26 (10/1/10-3/31/11)		
0-500M	500M-2MM	2-10MM	10-50MM	50-100MM	100-250MM
6	4	5	3	4	7
%	%	%	%	%	%

Comparative Historical Data

Type of Statement	12	11
Unqualified		
Reviewed		
Compiled	1	
Tax Returns	1	
Other	5	7
	4/1/06-	4/1/07-
	3/31/07	3/31/08
	ALL	ALL
NUMBER OF STATEMENTS	19	18
	%	%
ASSETS		
Cash & Equivalents	45.8	39.1
Trade Receivables (net)	9.3	12.0
Inventory	.5	1.1
All Other Current	5.8	4.1
Total Current	61.3	56.2
Fixed Assets (net)	16.3	21.2
Intangibles (net)	12.2	11.4
All Other Non-Current	10.2	11.1
Total	100.0	100.0
LIABILITIES		
Notes Payable-Short Term	1.8	.3
Cur. Mat.-L.T.D.	3.1	1.7
Trade Payables	11.8	11.2
Income Taxes Payable	.5	.6
All Other Current	27.9	18.8
Total Current	45.1	32.5
Long-Term Debt	16.6	19.5
Deferred Taxes	.1	.1
All Other Non-Current	13.0	3.7
Net Worth	25.2	44.2
Total Liabilities & Net Worth	100.0	100.0
INCOME DATA		
Net Sales	100.0	100.0
Gross Profit		
Operating Expenses	89.0	90.4
Operating Profit	11.0	9.6
All Other Expenses (net)	6.2	3.0
Profit Before Taxes	4.8	6.6
RATIOS		
Current	1.8	2.7
	1.5	1.5
	1.1	1.3
Quick	1.6	2.7
	1.3	1.4
	.8	1.2
Sales/Receivables	0 UND	0 UND
	3 127.7	4 82.2
	14 26.9	33 11.1
Cost of Sales/Inventory		
Cost of Sales/Payables		
Sales/Working Capital	6.5	3.8
	19.8	8.5
	89.4	22.2
EBIT/Interest	19.4	95.0
	(13) 9.0	(13) 6.5
	1.5	1.5
Net Profit + Depr., Dep., Amort./Cur. Mat. L/T/D		
Fixed/Worth	.1	.1
	.4	.4
	-14.4	1.8
Debt/Worth	1.4	.8
	2.1	1.4
	-187.5	6.8
% Profit Before Taxes/Tangible Net Worth	49.6	44.1
	(13) 24.6	(16) 25.0
	12.9	2.8
% Profit Before Taxes/Total Assets	14.1	22.0
	8.8	14.3
	.9	.7
Sales/Net Fixed Assets	105.6	144.7
	48.4	28.8
	12.4	10.2
Sales/Total Assets	3.9	2.9
	2.0	1.8
	1.1	1.1
% Depr., Dep., Amort./Sales	.5	.9
	(13) .9	(14) 2.0
	5.0	5.8
% Officers', Directors' Owners' Comp/Sales		

14535M	25223M	61138M	191728M	678197M	2452206M	Net Sales ($)	2525078M	3463481M
938M	6157M	17137M	104342M	356136M	1297697M	Total Assets ($)	1146275M	1547201M

© RMA 2011

M = $ thousand   MM = $ million
See Pages 9 through 22 for Explanation of Ratios and Data

Comparative Historical Data | Current Data Sorted by Sales

			Type of Statement						
12	15	12	Unqualified		1		1		10
	1		Reviewed						
1	1	3	Compiled	1	1		1	1	
2	3	3	Tax Returns		2	1			
8	11	11	Other	1	1	3			4
4/1/08-3/31/09 ALL	4/1/09-3/31/10 ALL	4/1/10-3/31/11 ALL		0-1MM	3 (4/1-9/30/10) 1-3MM	3-5MM	5-10MM	26 (10/1/10-3/31/11) 10-25MM	25MM & OVER
23	31	29	NUMBER OF STATEMENTS	2	4	6	1	2	14
%	%	%	ASSETS	%	%	%	%	%	%
46.7	34.3	31.1	Cash & Equivalents						36.3
11.3	9.2	9.8	Trade Receivables (net)						7.2
.0	.1	.1	Inventory						.1
3.5	5.2	5.5	All Other Current						8.2
61.5	48.7	46.5	Total Current						51.8
16.8	22.8	27.2	Fixed Assets (net)						8.6
7.2	6.3	11.2	Intangibles (net)						19.3
14.4	22.2	15.1	All Other Non-Current						20.3
100.0	100.0	100.0	Total						100.0
			LIABILITIES						
2.5	17.7	8.3	Notes Payable-Short Term						.3
1.7	1.3	2.4	Cur. Mat.-L.T.D.						2.8
10.6	12.2	9.1	Trade Payables						11.5
.1	1.0	.1	Income Taxes Payable						.2
21.4	21.2	16.0	All Other Current						13.8
36.2	53.4	35.9	Total Current						28.5
14.2	14.3	19.6	Long-Term Debt						12.4
.2	.5	.8	Deferred Taxes						1.6
1.3	1.9	8.5	All Other Non-Current						2.7
48.1	29.9	35.2	Net Worth						54.8
100.0	100.0	100.0	Total Liabilities & Net Worth						100.0
			INCOME DATA						
100.0	100.0	100.0	Net Sales						100.0
			Gross Profit						
94.7	91.8	93.8	Operating Expenses						94.3
5.3	8.2	6.2	Operating Profit						5.7
2.7	1.5	.1	All Other Expenses (net)						-.4
2.6	6.7	6.1	Profit Before Taxes						6.2
			RATIOS						
2.9	2.0	2.5							2.5
1.6	1.4	1.6	Current						1.6
1.2	.8	1.2							1.2
2.5	1.9	2.4							2.2
1.6	.9	1.5	Quick						1.3
1.1	.4	.8							.9
1 721.7	0 UND	0 UND						3	130.9
9 39.5	7 53.0	7 54.1	Sales/Receivables					8	45.1
22 16.5	22 16.5	15 23.6						15	24.7
			Cost of Sales/Inventory						
			Cost of Sales/Payables						
4.6	10.8	6.1							4.5
13.6	61.2	16.8	Sales/Working Capital						12.7
36.5	-31.8	207.4							30.3
24.6	28.9	22.8							44.9
(15) 8.2	(21) 9.0	(21) 6.4	EBIT/Interest					(10)	20.3
1.9	.9	1.9							5.4
			Net Profit + Depr., Dep., Amort./Cur. Mat. L/T/D						
.0	.0	.1							.1
.2	.5	.8	Fixed/Worth						.2
1.0	2.6	-3.6							-4.0
.4	.6	.6							.4
1.2	1.3	1.5	Debt/Worth						1.0
1.9	15.4	-8.8							-16.6
63.1	98.7	49.3							36.8
(21) 14.9	(24) 5.0	(19) 12.2	% Profit Before Taxes/Tangible Net Worth					(10)	11.7
1.0	-19.2	6.7							7.7
15.3	42.9	22.1							14.4
8.6	3.3	6.8	% Profit Before Taxes/Total Assets						6.5
-.1	-2.4	1.8							3.5
144.8	185.6	43.8							54.6
34.4	57.1	27.0	Sales/Net Fixed Assets						30.7
16.0	10.3	9.8							16.7
4.7	7.6	5.1							2.7
2.4	2.6	2.4	Sales/Total Assets						1.8
1.8	1.6	1.3							1.1
.5	.5	.5							.4
(17) 1.4	(22) 1.4	(21) 1.3	% Depr., Dep., Amort./Sales					(10)	.8
2.1	3.1	1.8							1.7
			% Officers', Directors' Owners' Comp/Sales						
3573362M	3440936M	3423027M	Net Sales ($)	1772M	8402M	20750M	7942M	29048M	3355113M
1450823M	1206600M	1782407M	Total Assets ($)	14811M	4173M	6721M	1935M	5508M	1749259M

M = $ thousand   MM = $ million
See Pages 9 through 22 for Explanation of Ratios and Data

HEALTH CARE—Kidney Dialysis Centers NAICS 621492

Current Data Sorted by Assets

Comparative Historical Data

Type of Statement	0-500M	500M-2MM	2-10MM	10-50MM	50-100MM	100-250MM		4/1/06-3/31/07 ALL	4/1/07-3/31/08 ALL
Unqualified		2	2	2	3			4	8
Reviewed			3					2	3
Compiled		2	4	1	1			1	3
Tax Returns	6	1	2					10	11
Other	2	11	13	4	3	2		27	24
		12 (4/1-9/30/10)		52 (10/1/10-3/31/11)					
NUMBER OF STATEMENTS	8	16	24	7	7	2		44	49
ASSETS	%	%	%	%	%	%		%	%
Cash & Equivalents		11.9	9.4					19.5	17.5
Trade Receivables (net)		31.9	25.6					25.4	26.0
Inventory		1.9	1.2					2.7	2.5
All Other Current		1.0	6.7					3.2	5.5
Total Current		46.6	43.0					50.8	51.6
Fixed Assets (net)		38.9	43.1					39.0	32.2
Intangibles (net)		1.6	6.9					5.9	7.0
All Other Non-Current		12.9	7.0					4.3	9.1
Total		100.0	100.0					100.0	100.0
LIABILITIES									
Notes Payable-Short Term		13.4	6.3					6.8	8.7
Cur. Mat.-L.T.D.		14.5	7.5					8.9	5.1
Trade Payables		11.8	5.7					5.8	7.4
Income Taxes Payable		.0	.7					.6	.1
All Other Current		28.3	13.1					23.9	21.0
Total Current		67.9	33.2					46.0	42.2
Long-Term Debt		22.5	21.7					29.4	23.8
Deferred Taxes		.0	.1					.1	.0
All Other Non-Current		8.8	4.6					6.4	3.9
Net Worth		.8	40.4					18.1	30.0
Total Liabilities & Net Worth		100.0	100.0					100.0	100.0
INCOME DATA									
Net Sales		100.0	100.0					100.0	100.0
Gross Profit									
Operating Expenses		85.1	81.9					88.0	86.1
Operating Profit		14.9	18.1					12.0	13.9
All Other Expenses (net)		1.8	3.0					3.5	3.0
Profit Before Taxes		13.2	15.1					8.5	10.9
RATIOS									
Current		2.2	2.6					3.6	3.2
		.8	1.8					1.7	1.5
		.4	.7					.8	.9
Quick		2.0	2.2					3.3	2.9
		.8	1.3					1.4	1.1
		.4	.5					.6	.7
Sales/Receivables		10 36.3	18 20.6					0 UND	18 20.2
		43 8.5	48 7.7					53 6.8	48 7.5
		65 5.6	64 5.7					73 5.0	68 5.3
Cost of Sales/Inventory									
Cost of Sales/Payables									
Sales/Working Capital		10.5	5.8					5.6	5.2
		-123.2	7.3					10.5	14.4
		-8.3	-20.1					-66.8	-265.5
EBIT/Interest		18.1	21.4					24.0	19.1
		5.4	(20) 9.9					(33) 7.2	(38) 7.8
		-1.0	2.8					1.8	2.4
Net Profit + Depr., Dep., Amort./Cur. Mat. L/T/D									
Fixed/Worth		.5	.4					.6	.3
		6.2	1.4					2.4	.9
		-1.5	10.5					-2.7	UND
Debt/Worth		1.0	.4					.4	.4
		10.1	1.5					5.8	2.0
		-3.2	11.7					-7.3	-11.5
% Profit Before Taxes/Tangible Net Worth		581.2	158.6					102.0	127.5
		(10) 152.5	(20) 42.2					(27) 50.1	(35) 47.3
		25.1	15.5					13.5	7.4
% Profit Before Taxes/Total Assets		68.4	43.5					28.4	38.2
		14.6	16.4					11.5	14.4
		-8.3	5.6					1.0	3.4
Sales/Net Fixed Assets		31.7	11.5					22.6	32.9
		11.4	5.5					7.1	6.6
		4.1	3.1					3.4	3.9
Sales/Total Assets		5.5	3.0					4.3	3.7
		2.5	1.7					2.0	2.1
		2.1	1.3					1.3	1.3
% Depr., Dep., Amort./Sales		1.6	1.6					1.0	1.7
		(12) 3.4	(21) 2.9					(41) 2.2	(42) 2.9
		6.4	4.7					4.4	4.6
% Officers', Directors' Owners' Comp/Sales								4.9	4.7
								(19) 8.1	(10) 31.9
								18.7	41.3
Net Sales ($)	16702M	83135M	244987M	264682M	516294M	325381M		557086M	1195225M
Total Assets ($)	2371M	20448M	102052M	173497M	532226M	236751M		363816M	843566M

M = $ thousand   MM = $ million
See Pages 9 through 22 for Explanation of Ratios and Data

Comparative Historical Data | Current Data Sorted by Sales

Current Data date ranges: **12 (4/1-9/30/10)** covers 0-1MM, 1-3MM, 3-5MM columns; **52 (10/1/10-3/31/11)** covers 5-10MM, 10-25MM, 25MM columns.

	4/1/08-3/31/09 ALL	4/1/09-3/31/10 ALL	4/1/10-3/31/11 ALL	Type of Statement	0-1MM	1-3MM	3-5MM	5-10MM	10-25MM	25MM & OVER
	10	11	9	Unqualified		2			4	3
	4	7	3	Reviewed				2	1	
	3	2	8	Compiled	1	1	1	1	2	2
	9	8	9	Tax Returns		5	1	1		
	31	41	35	Other	2	7	8	4	7	9
	57	69	64	NUMBER OF STATEMENTS	3	15	10	8	14	14
	%	%	%	**ASSETS**	%	%	%	%	%	%
	17.7	13.0	13.6	Cash & Equivalents		17.6	7.5		15.2	11.0
	25.0	25.9	22.4	Trade Receivables (net)		16.1	28.9		26.5	19.2
	2.2	2.6	1.5	Inventory		1.1	1.4		2.1	2.1
	3.9	6.0	5.7	All Other Current		3.6	6.3		5.5	4.0
	48.9	47.5	43.2	Total Current		38.5	44.1		49.4	36.4
	35.1	34.2	38.5	Fixed Assets (net)		43.3	39.4		31.3	32.0
	10.6	8.8	9.2	Intangibles (net)		2.5	9.0		10.0	22.7
	5.4	9.5	9.1	All Other Non-Current		15.7	7.5		9.3	8.9
	100.0	100.0	100.0	Total		100.0	100.0		100.0	100.0
				LIABILITIES						
	5.5	1.5	11.2	Notes Payable-Short Term		20.0	12.0		3.4	.6
	4.4	7.2	8.9	Cur. Mat.-L.T.D.		13.1	12.9		9.6	5.5
	8.0	11.4	6.8	Trade Payables		5.8	7.4		10.4	6.7
	.0	.3	.3	Income Taxes Payable		.0	.0		1.2	.0
	17.6	22.8	17.7	All Other Current		22.4	3.4		29.9	8.3
	35.5	43.1	45.0	Total Current		61.2	35.6		54.7	21.2
	30.0	21.1	21.7	Long-Term Debt		34.8	17.5		17.6	14.4
	.1	.1	.0	Deferred Taxes		.0	.0		.2	.0
	5.1	8.9	8.6	All Other Non-Current		15.9	6.9		2.8	13.3
	29.3	26.8	24.6	Net Worth		-11.9	40.0		24.7	51.1
	100.0	100.0	100.0	Total Liabilities & Net Worth		100.0	100.0		100.0	100.0
				INCOME DATA						
	100.0	100.0	100.0	Net Sales		100.0	100.0		100.0	100.0
				Gross Profit						
	90.6	88.4	86.1	Operating Expenses		88.1	76.8		89.8	89.6
	9.4	11.6	13.9	Operating Profit		11.9	23.2		10.2	10.4
	1.9	2.7	1.5	All Other Expenses (net)		.9	2.2		.6	.8
	7.5	9.0	12.4	Profit Before Taxes		11.0	21.0		9.6	9.6
				RATIOS						
	2.9	3.5	2.7	Current		2.1	7.0		2.2	4.0
	1.8	1.8	1.6			.6	2.3		1.4	3.0
	.9	.7	.6			.2	.9		.7	1.8
	2.7	3.1	2.4	Quick		2.1	6.9		1.6	3.3
	1.4	1.5	1.2			.4	1.1		1.3	2.4
	.7	.5	.4			.1	.6		.7	1.2
	8 47.8	10 35.1	1 307.0	Sales/Receivables		0 UND	22 16.4		19 18.7	26 14.2
	53 6.9	51 7.2	46 7.9			10 37.1	43 8.5		43 8.4	58 6.3
	65 5.6	69 5.3	65 5.7			68 5.3	69 5.3		53 6.8	67 5.4
				Cost of Sales/Inventory						
				Cost of Sales/Payables						
	5.7	4.9	5.4	Sales/Working Capital		5.4	4.7		6.2	4.1
	11.6	8.7	20.3			-56.1	6.3		21.9	4.5
	-83.4	-35.3	-11.9			-8.2	-113.7		-73.1	41.0
	14.2	35.4	16.2	EBIT/Interest		16.8			19.8	10.4
	(51) 4.5	(50) 8.8	(55) 6.7			(14) 3.6			10.3	(11) 3.8
	1.6	1.2	1.5			-.1			.3	1.5
		47.0		Net Profit + Depr., Dep., Amort./Cur. Mat. L/T/D						
		(13) 9.3								
		1.0								
	.5	.4	.4	Fixed/Worth		.1	.4		.8	.4
	1.1	1.0	1.6			9.4	1.6		1.4	.9
	-6.8	-6.0	-4.3			-1.5	NM		-1.6	NM
	.7	.5	.5	Debt/Worth		.8	.3		1.2	.4
	1.9	1.8	2.9			22.3	2.0		1.9	1.0
	-16.2	-6.6	-6.3			-3.8	NM		-7.1	NM
	115.5	96.9	167.6	% Profit Before Taxes/Tangible Net Worth						109.4
	(39) 32.7	(49) 30.3	(46) 57.1							(11) 34.9
	4.7	6.0	6.7							9.4
	32.3	31.0	38.2	% Profit Before Taxes/Total Assets		54.5	56.3		36.1	18.9
	10.6	10.0	10.7			10.1	36.1		8.8	7.2
	1.3	.9	1.2			-1.8	13.5		-1.8	2.2
	16.4	19.4	13.3	Sales/Net Fixed Assets		17.1	5.7		27.3	6.7
	6.7	8.8	5.6			6.2	5.3		8.6	5.0
	3.7	3.7	3.6			4.0	3.4		3.7	4.2
	3.8	3.5	3.7	Sales/Total Assets		4.8	2.1		5.0	2.0
	1.7	2.0	2.0			2.2	1.8		2.5	1.4
	1.2	1.3	1.3			1.7	1.5		1.7	1.1
	1.7	1.3	1.8	% Depr., Dep., Amort./Sales		2.7			1.3	2.4
	(53) 3.1	(61) 2.4	(55) 3.0			(10) 6.1			2.3	2.9
	4.7	3.8	4.7			7.1			3.4	4.0
	2.6	4.4	2.9	% Officers', Directors' Owners' Comp/Sales						
	(12) 7.7	(17) 8.0	(12) 7.3							
	34.1	33.2	32.0							
	1725392M	1384215M	1451181M	Net Sales ($)	1739M	32288M	40546M	61626M	205028M	1109954M
	1229370M	923818M	1067345M	Total Assets ($)	3219M	15251M	23014M	27715M	164346M	833800M

M = $ thousand   MM = $ million
See Pages 9 through 22 for Explanation of Ratios and Data

Current Data Sorted by Assets   **Comparative Historical Data**

						Type of Statement		
1	2	21	8	2	2	Unqualified	25	25
2	10	12	5	1		Reviewed	6	12
13	11	13				Compiled	23	41
19	27	20	1			Tax Returns	46	54
23	28	79	13	1	2	Other	73	97
	18 (4/1-9/30/10)		298 (10/1/10-3/31/11)				4/1/06-3/31/07	4/1/07-3/31/08
0-500M	500M-2MM	2-10MM	10-50MM	50-100MM	100-250MM		ALL	ALL
58	78	145	27	4	4	NUMBER OF STATEMENTS	173	229
%	%	%	%	%	%	ASSETS	%	%
36.1	19.9	14.5	17.4			Cash & Equivalents	19.4	19.0
4.8	12.5	20.9	20.6			Trade Receivables (net)	15.8	14.1
1.4	3.6	3.0	4.6			Inventory	2.5	2.8
4.8	3.1	1.2	7.4			All Other Current	3.6	1.9
47.1	39.2	39.6	50.0			Total Current	41.3	37.7
37.5	48.5	49.5	42.0			Fixed Assets (net)	45.4	49.9
7.0	6.0	7.3	2.7			Intangibles (net)	5.3	4.9
8.4	6.4	3.6	5.3			All Other Non-Current	8.0	7.5
100.0	100.0	100.0	100.0			Total	100.0	100.0
						LIABILITIES		
31.1	9.9	3.1	3.9			Notes Payable-Short Term	10.4	13.5
15.2	10.4	7.0	6.4			Cur. Mat.-L.T.D.	7.3	9.0
2.0	7.7	5.6	4.6			Trade Payables	4.6	4.6
.9	.0	.3	.7			Income Taxes Payable	.0	.0
30.3	11.7	9.9	12.4			All Other Current	17.6	13.3
79.5	39.7	26.0	28.1			Total Current	40.0	40.4
39.3	39.0	37.4	23.9			Long-Term Debt	31.3	36.8
.0	.0	.0	.3			Deferred Taxes	.1	.0
12.3	5.0	3.1	1.8			All Other Non-Current	2.1	3.7
-31.1	16.3	33.6	46.0			Net Worth	26.5	19.0
100.0	100.0	100.0	100.0			Total Liabilities & Net Worth	100.0	100.0
						INCOME DATA		
100.0	100.0	100.0	100.0			Net Sales	100.0	100.0
						Gross Profit		
89.3	80.0	76.2	80.2			Operating Expenses	81.5	78.8
10.7	20.0	23.8	19.8			Operating Profit	18.5	21.2
1.1	2.7	3.6	1.7			All Other Expenses (net)	2.2	2.5
9.6	17.2	20.2	18.1			Profit Before Taxes	16.3	18.7
						RATIOS		
2.4	2.5	3.1	3.7			Current	3.6	2.8
.7	1.1	1.8	2.5				1.3	1.4
.2	.4	1.0	1.2				.6	.5
2.1	2.3	2.6	3.2			Quick	3.0	2.5
.6	.8	1.5	2.0				1.2	1.2
.2	.3	.8	1.0				.4	.4
0 UND	0 UND	14 26.0	27 13.7			Sales/Receivables	0 UND	0 UND
0 UND	0 UND	37 9.9	42 8.6				18 20.0	23 16.0
0 UND	30 12.2	53 6.9	63 5.7				51 7.2	46 8.0
						Cost of Sales/Inventory		
						Cost of Sales/Payables		
40.3	13.9	6.9	4.9			Sales/Working Capital	6.2	8.4
-71.3	408.4	11.8	6.8				28.6	34.5
-21.5	-18.0	-147.7	17.6				-29.0	-22.0
18.6	63.0	47.2	47.9			EBIT/Interest	34.9	37.9
(43) 6.9	(67) 11.5	(126) 14.7	(26) 23.1				(141) 7.7	(200) 10.2
1.2	1.8	4.4	11.1				1.8	1.9
		24.3				Net Profit + Depr., Dep., Amort./Cur. Mat. L/T/D	6.2	18.3
	(12) 9.3						(12) 2.4	(13) 4.0
		4.0					.7	.8
.2	.8	.6	.5			Fixed/Worth	.5	.7
5.8	2.4	1.5	.9				1.7	1.8
-.8	-3.6	6.0	2.0				10.1	-16.3
1.4	.6	.7	.5			Debt/Worth	.6	.7
-9.6	4.0	1.8	.9				2.4	2.7
-2.3	-9.4	7.0	2.9				17.8	-15.3
211.8	295.4	164.1	104.3			% Profit Before Taxes/Tangible Net Worth	192.5	279.1
(26) 86.7	(54) 126.2	(120) 95.0	(24) 59.6				(134) 75.2	(167) 95.1
15.8	48.7	43.9	23.5				21.2	28.3
103.6	100.7	66.2	47.7			% Profit Before Taxes/Total Assets	66.8	70.6
27.1	29.9	30.2	28.6				23.7	27.0
1.0	6.1	6.9	7.8				3.8	2.9
181.0	18.6	8.6	9.8			Sales/Net Fixed Assets	21.5	19.3
37.5	7.3	4.3	3.4				7.8	5.2
12.7	3.8	2.2	2.0				2.7	2.5
25.3	5.1	2.6	2.7			Sales/Total Assets	5.4	4.7
8.9	3.0	1.8	1.6				2.4	2.2
4.5	2.0	1.2	.9				1.4	1.4
.9	2.2	3.0	3.1			% Depr., Dep., Amort./Sales	1.8	2.1
(27) 1.7	(64) 4.3	(139) 4.9	(24) 4.5				(144) 3.7	(196) 4.1
3.0	7.5	8.7	5.7				6.1	7.6
14.8		1.8				% Officers', Directors' Owners' Comp/Sales	6.5	5.9
(26) 23.3		(24) 4.7					(50) 16.9	(63) 14.3
33.9		10.3					29.2	26.2
193883M	396128M	1359182M	1050436M	218820M	627080M	Net Sales ($)	1889902M	2565124M
15798M	93340M	678365M	507457M	301249M	827231M	Total Assets ($)	1201986M	1457460M

© RMA 2011

M = $ thousand   MM = $ million
See Pages 9 through 22 for Explanation of Ratios and Data

Comparative Historical Data   Current Data Sorted by Sales

			Type of Statement						
27	30	36	Unqualified			6	6	13	11
22	23	30	Reviewed		3	6	8	11	2
59	44	37	Compiled	5	8	11	8	4	1
62	81	67	Tax Returns	10	17	14	12	13	1
104	127	146	Other	14	19	36	38	26	13
4/1/08-3/31/09 ALL	4/1/09-3/31/10 ALL	4/1/10-3/31/11 ALL			18 (4/1-9/30/10)		298 (10/1/10-3/31/11)		
				0-1MM	1-3MM	3-5MM	5-10MM	10-25MM	25MM & OVER
274	305	316	NUMBER OF STATEMENTS	29	47	73	72	67	28
%	%	%	ASSETS	%	%	%	%	%	%
19.0	17.3	19.8	Cash & Equivalents	21.9	15.6	16.5	24.1	21.2	19.6
14.7	16.0	15.6	Trade Receivables (net)	6.1	9.2	15.4	16.7	19.9	23.1
2.7	2.3	2.9	Inventory	.1	2.8	3.6	3.2	2.6	4.4
2.8	2.7	2.9	All Other Current	4.1	1.9	2.8	2.2	1.8	8.2
39.2	38.4	41.2	Total Current	32.1	29.4	38.3	46.1	45.6	55.3
46.6	45.6	45.7	Fixed Assets (net)	46.3	55.3	52.2	42.3	43.7	25.6
6.1	8.3	7.7	Intangibles (net)	6.9	9.3	6.3	6.1	7.3	14.2
8.0	7.7	5.4	All Other Non-Current	14.6	6.0	3.2	5.5	3.5	4.9
100.0	100.0	100.0	Total	100.0	100.0	100.0	100.0	100.0	100.0
			LIABILITIES						
12.1	13.3	10.0	Notes Payable-Short Term	12.9	16.6	8.6	11.8	6.1	3.9
10.7	7.4	9.2	Cur. Mat.-L.T.D.	8.0	11.1	9.3	12.5	7.3	3.4
4.4	5.2	5.3	Trade Payables	1.5	6.1	7.5	5.0	3.6	7.0
.2	.4	.4	Income Taxes Payable	.0	.0	.7	.3	.3	.7
16.4	14.0	14.2	All Other Current	15.4	10.8	11.2	15.7	16.7	15.9
43.8	40.4	39.0	Total Current	37.7	44.7	37.3	45.4	34.1	30.8
34.1	35.7	36.7	Long-Term Debt	44.0	51.9	39.8	37.8	25.2	19.4
.1	.1	.1	Deferred Taxes	.0	.0	.0	.1	.0	.5
6.6	4.4	5.2	All Other Non-Current	10.8	11.6	4.4	2.2	3.3	2.9
15.4	19.4	19.1	Net Worth	7.4	-8.3	18.4	14.5	37.4	46.3
100.0	100.0	100.0	Total Liabilities & Net Worth	100.0	100.0	100.0	100.0	100.0	100.0
			INCOME DATA						
100.0	100.0	100.0	Net Sales	100.0	100.0	100.0	100.0	100.0	100.0
			Gross Profit						
80.6	80.1	80.1	Operating Expenses	64.5	87.9	86.9	79.3	73.0	84.8
19.4	19.9	19.9	Operating Profit	35.5	12.1	13.1	20.7	27.0	15.2
3.4	3.4	2.8	All Other Expenses (net)	12.2	3.3	2.5	1.5	.8	1.1
16.0	16.5	17.1	Profit Before Taxes	23.3	8.8	10.7	19.2	26.1	14.2
			RATIOS						
2.8	2.8	2.9		2.3	1.8	2.3	3.3	3.2	3.4
1.3	1.5	1.5	Current	.7	.9	1.1	1.8	2.1	2.0
.5	.5	.6		.3	.4	.6	1.0	1.1	1.2
2.5	2.4	2.6		1.9	1.8	1.9	3.0	2.7	3.0
1.1	1.1	1.2	Quick	.6	.7	.8	1.6	2.0	1.7
.3	.4	.5		.2	.2	.4	.9	1.0	.8
0 UND	0 UND	0 UND		0 UND	0 UND	0 UND	0 UND	0 UND	11 34.7
17 21.7	24 15.2	26 13.8	Sales/Receivables	0 UND	0 UND	29 12.7	29 12.8	38 9.7	37 9.8
45 8.2	47 7.7	46 7.9		0 UND	32 11.5	52 7.1	46 8.0	50 7.3	50 7.4
			Cost of Sales/Inventory						
			Cost of Sales/Payables						
8.7	7.8	7.7		7.6	13.2	14.2	7.8	6.2	6.3
33.5	29.2	24.7	Sales/Working Capital	-41.5	-130.0	501.0	16.0	10.5	12.0
-22.5	-25.6	-28.5		-8.4	-13.5	-15.0	NM	162.1	37.7
	34.1	39.8	42.8			14.8	42.0	41.8	67.9	28.7
(232) 8.8	(261) 11.0	(270) 13.0	EBIT/Interest	(40) 4.4	(69) 6.4	(68) 16.6	(59) 37.1	(25) 15.8	
1.8	2.7	3.1			.6	.8	6.0	12.9	5.7
7.7	6.6	10.9							
(15) 3.3	(19) 2.3	(22) 4.3	Net Profit + Depr., Dep., Amort./Cur. Mat. L/T/D						
1.8	1.4	1.5							
.7	.5	.6		.0	1.4	1.0	.6	.6	.4
1.9	1.6	1.7	Fixed/Worth	2.5	7.1	2.5	1.1	1.0	.6
-10.3	13.5	-9.4		NM	-2.0	-5.4	NM	2.8	-1.1
.7	.7	.7		1.3	2.1	.7	.6	.6	.5
2.6	2.6	2.5	Debt/Worth	3.8	13.3	4.0	1.8	1.3	1.1
-16.9	64.1	-10.9		-3.1	-3.4	-9.9	-9.8	3.4	-6.1
192.9	183.3	188.4		70.5	257.7	193.1	173.7	233.2	160.5
(195) 75.4	(234) 79.2	(226) 91.3	% Profit Before Taxes/Tangible Net Worth	(21) 44.5	(27) 100.0	(50) 77.2	(51) 88.5	(57) 121.7	(20) 81.7
22.7	20.0	33.1		15.9	-4.1	15.8	56.6	75.4	16.0
65.0	69.1	67.3		35.5	57.5	60.2	81.3	91.4	54.0
20.7	24.6	29.0	% Profit Before Taxes/Total Assets	9.9	12.7	20.0	36.0	55.8	15.4
3.1	4.7	6.1		3.3	-3.9	-.1	18.2	22.1	7.6
22.2	24.5	18.6		UND	11.3	18.5	15.6	15.6	39.2
6.9	6.6	6.2	Sales/Net Fixed Assets	11.6	5.4	4.9	6.0	6.1	11.0
2.5	2.6	2.9		.2	2.5	2.2	3.4	3.2	6.1
5.8	5.1	4.3		4.5	4.8	4.6	4.7	3.7	6.4
2.3	2.2	2.4	Sales/Total Assets	1.2	2.7	2.5	2.4	2.4	2.7
1.3	1.2	1.4		.2	1.5	1.2	1.7	1.7	1.3
2.1	2.2	2.5		1.9	1.8	2.6	2.9	2.6	1.3
(222) 4.0	(248) 3.8	(261) 4.4	% Depr., Dep., Amort./Sales	(17) 14.1	(36) 5.2	(66) 5.4	(58) 4.0	(60) 3.5	(24) 3.7
8.2	7.5	7.7		16.4	9.7	10.1	6.1	5.6	5.1
3.6	5.8	4.3				1.1	4.0	4.8	
(77) 8.2	(80) 14.6	(60) 16.3	% Officers', Directors' Owners' Comp/Sales		(16) 8.7	(11) 16.3	(16) 7.5		
26.7	33.0	31.3			29.8	33.3	31.8		
3585593M	4286828M	3845529M	Net Sales ($)	16920M	96474M	293428M	526440M	987440M	1924827M
1904892M	2908497M	2423440M	Total Assets ($)	37518M	55260M	184483M	233269M	530457M	1382453M

© RMA 2011

M = $ thousand   MM = $ million
See Pages 9 through 22 for Explanation of Ratios and Data

Current Data Sorted by Assets   Comparative Historical Data

	0-500M	500M-2MM	2-10MM	10-50MM	50-100MM	100-250MM	4/1/06-3/31/07 ALL	4/1/07-3/31/08 ALL
Type of Statement								
Unqualified	3	1	37	48	8	5	111	95
Reviewed		4	9	3			19	14
Compiled	6	4	7	1			33	29
Tax Returns	16	27	12	2			35	38
Other	22	18	47	31	4	4	100	101
	100 (4/1-9/30/10)			219 (10/1/10-3/31/11)				
NUMBER OF STATEMENTS	47	54	112	85	12	9	298	277
	%	%	%	%	%	%	%	%
ASSETS								
Cash & Equivalents	26.5	16.8	14.3	19.3	16.8		21.1	17.7
Trade Receivables (net)	12.3	15.8	19.1	15.9	13.9		19.1	20.0
Inventory	1.7	4.8	1.7	.9	2.2		1.2	1.5
All Other Current	5.9	4.3	3.2	5.8	5.4		4.0	5.0
Total Current	46.3	41.8	38.4	41.9	38.3		45.5	44.2
Fixed Assets (net)	30.7	39.3	51.2	48.0	40.7		42.8	43.2
Intangibles (net)	9.4	6.3	2.4	2.3	8.4		4.0	3.9
All Other Non-Current	13.6	12.6	8.0	7.8	12.7		7.7	8.7
Total	100.0	100.0	100.0	100.0	100.0		100.0	100.0
LIABILITIES								
Notes Payable-Short Term	19.9	5.7	3.5	2.3	1.4		7.7	7.4
Cur. Mat.-L.T.D.	5.4	5.8	5.3	3.8	2.1		5.3	5.4
Trade Payables	7.8	7.8	7.3	6.7	8.4		6.6	6.8
Income Taxes Payable	.7	.1	.1	.2	.5		.2	.3
All Other Current	17.8	10.3	8.5	12.9	7.5		13.3	13.2
Total Current	51.7	29.7	24.6	25.9	20.0		33.1	33.1
Long-Term Debt	33.6	32.4	27.6	24.3	33.9		27.1	28.7
Deferred Taxes	.5	.0	.3	.0	.2		.4	.2
All Other Non-Current	9.4	14.0	9.0	4.7	3.9		4.2	3.9
Net Worth	4.8	23.9	38.5	45.0	42.0		35.3	34.1
Total Liabilities & Net Worth	100.0	100.0	100.0	100.0	100.0		100.0	100.0
INCOME DATA								
Net Sales	100.0	100.0	100.0	100.0	100.0		100.0	100.0
Gross Profit								
Operating Expenses	94.6	84.7	85.9	93.5	92.5		89.1	87.8
Operating Profit	5.4	15.3	14.1	6.5	7.5		10.9	12.2
All Other Expenses (net)	.8	1.8	3.5	.5	1.3		2.7	2.6
Profit Before Taxes	4.6	13.5	10.6	6.0	6.2		8.2	9.6
RATIOS								
Current	5.0	3.6	3.1	3.1	2.7		3.2	3.5
	1.6	1.6	1.6	2.0	1.7		1.7	1.6
	.5	.6	.9	1.2	1.3		.9	.8
Quick	4.1	2.3	2.8	2.7	2.2		2.8	2.8
	1.2	1.3	1.5	(84) 1.7	1.2		(297) 1.5	1.3
	.2	.6	.8	1.0	1.0		.7	.6
Sales/Receivables	0 UND	0 UND	16 23.0	20 18.5	19 19.2		0 UND	0 813.5
	0 UND	2 174.1	33 11.1	35 10.5	35 10.4		33 11.2	33 11.2
	1 422.8	38 9.7	52 7.1	52 7.0	57 6.5		54 6.8	56 6.5
Cost of Sales/Inventory								
Cost of Sales/Payables								
Sales/Working Capital	18.4	8.3	6.5	4.7	6.1		5.7	5.1
	55.7	24.8	14.6	8.5	9.5		15.3	14.5
	-52.7	-27.0	-114.2	25.1	30.3		-139.2	-54.4
EBIT/Interest	11.4	57.1	27.7	12.6	60.3		22.6	19.4
	(24) 4.7	(38) 16.8	(93) 5.2	(71) 5.6	4.9		(226) 5.8	(217) 5.2
	-1.0	3.3	1.1	1.4	2.7		1.4	1.2
Net Profit + Depr., Dep., Amort./Cur. Mat. L/T/D							6.5	9.0
							(19) 1.5	(14) 6.5
							.6	2.3
Fixed/Worth	.1	.4	.6	.6	.4		.4	.5
	.8	1.4	1.0	1.0	1.3		1.0	1.1
	-8.3	NM	3.1	1.6	NM		6.2	4.8
Debt/Worth	.5	.7	.5	.5	.6		.5	.6
	2.5	2.3	1.1	1.1	1.2		1.4	1.3
	-2.8	NM	3.9	2.3	NM		10.3	7.2
% Profit Before Taxes/Tangible Net Worth	240.6	229.0	82.8	26.4			68.4	80.7
	(34) 51.9	(41) 88.2	(103) 20.6	(78) 11.9			(240) 19.6	(229) 19.7
	-.9	19.3	2.0	4.9			2.7	3.2
% Profit Before Taxes/Total Assets	52.5	72.4	27.2	12.3	10.3		22.8	30.2
	14.6	28.5	7.9	5.9	5.5		7.0	7.5
	-8.2	2.9	.5	1.3	2.6		.2	.5
Sales/Net Fixed Assets	187.7	26.7	7.1	4.7	11.9		18.6	16.9
	49.8	10.0	3.5	2.8	4.0		5.3	4.6
	12.0	5.7	1.6	1.7	2.1		2.3	2.1
Sales/Total Assets	14.3	4.6	2.7	1.9	2.1		3.4	3.4
	6.4	2.6	1.6	1.4	1.3		2.0	1.9
	3.5	1.8	1.0	1.0	.7		1.0	1.1
% Depr., Dep., Amort./Sales	.4	1.1	1.6	2.0	1.8		1.3	1.3
	(23) 1.1	(44) 2.3	(107) 2.9	(78) 3.0	(11) 2.8		(259) 3.0	(236) 2.7
	3.1	4.8	5.9	4.5	4.9		6.2	5.1
% Officers', Directors' Owners' Comp/Sales	4.0	3.8	2.6	2.3			4.3	4.2
	(14) 10.0	(18) 7.4	(11) 5.3	(12) 9.4			(52) 9.0	(52) 7.1
	16.4	21.8	8.6	33.1			27.1	18.2
Net Sales ($)	95576M	200797M	1046119M	2713935M	1260087M	1487483M	6782191M	5320406M
Total Assets ($)	11317M	59939M	588782M	1723956M	833004M	1446868M	3666670M	3371779M

© RMA 2011

M = $ thousand   MM = $ million
See Pages 9 through 22 for Explanation of Ratios and Data

Comparative Historical Data | Current Data Sorted by Sales

115	110	102	Type of Statement		7	3	16	35	41
12	19	16	Unqualified						
22	29	18	Reviewed		2	4	2	6	2
48	59	57	Compiled	1	6	3	3	4	1
106	119	126	Tax Returns	14	12	12	12	5	2
			Other	15	25	9	22	37	18
4/1/08-	4/1/09-	4/1/10-			100 (4/1-9/30/10)		219 (10/1/10-3/31/11)		
3/31/09	3/31/10	3/31/11							
ALL	ALL	ALL		0-1MM	1-3MM	3-5MM	5-10MM	10-25MM	25MM & OVER
303	336	319	NUMBER OF STATEMENTS	30	52	31	55	87	64
%	%	%	ASSETS	%	%	%	%	%	%
19.7	20.1	17.9	Cash & Equivalents	14.6	20.4	17.3	17.3	16.9	19.4
18.8	18.4	16.2	Trade Receivables (net)	11.4	10.0	17.0	15.0	20.7	18.2
1.6	1.9	2.0	Inventory	.5	3.4	4.1	1.5	1.8	1.3
5.3	4.7	4.6	All Other Current	4.7	4.0	3.6	3.9	4.6	6.0
45.4	45.1	40.7	Total Current	31.2	37.8	42.0	37.8	44.0	44.9
41.1	40.6	44.1	Fixed Assets (net)	50.1	42.5	43.3	47.6	44.8	39.0
5.2	4.8	5.6	Intangibles (net)	9.9	6.2	2.7	6.5	1.3	9.6
8.2	9.5	9.6	All Other Non-Current	8.8	13.5	12.0	8.1	9.9	6.4
100.0	100.0	100.0	Total	100.0	100.0	100.0	100.0	100.0	100.0
			LIABILITIES						
8.8	6.2	5.8	Notes Payable-Short Term	19.7	9.8	5.6	2.5	3.7	1.8
6.1	4.9	4.8	Cur. Mat.-L.T.D.	5.8	5.8	9.1	5.0	3.5	3.2
6.3	6.8	7.2	Trade Payables	3.5	7.5	10.2	5.9	7.8	7.6
.2	.1	.2	Income Taxes Payable	.0	.0	.1	.0	.5	.3
14.0	13.5	11.3	All Other Current	13.5	12.0	7.7	9.0	11.4	13.3
35.5	31.5	29.3	Total Current	42.6	35.1	32.7	22.3	26.9	26.3
27.4	27.6	28.6	Long-Term Debt	48.5	30.6	38.7	31.0	19.2	23.5
.4	.3	.3	Deferred Taxes	.7	.0	.5	.0	.2	.5
6.3	5.5	8.4	All Other Non-Current	13.2	2.7	8.4	13.1	10.6	3.7
30.5	35.1	33.4	Net Worth	-5.0	31.6	19.7	33.6	43.2	46.1
100.0	100.0	100.0	Total Liabilities & Net Worth	100.0	100.0	100.0	100.0	100.0	100.0
			INCOME DATA						
100.0	100.0	100.0	Net Sales	100.0	100.0	100.0	100.0	100.0	100.0
			Gross Profit						
90.5	87.8	89.4	Operating Expenses	85.2	84.5	90.2	88.6	90.5	94.0
9.5	12.2	10.6	Operating Profit	14.8	15.5	9.8	11.4	9.5	6.0
2.2	2.6	1.9	All Other Expenses (net)	9.2	5.1	.7	.0	.5	.1
7.3	9.6	8.7	Profit Before Taxes	5.6	10.4	9.2	11.5	9.0	5.9
			RATIOS						
3.7	3.5	3.2		4.0	3.5	2.6	4.3	3.2	2.5
1.8	1.7	1.7	Current	1.3	1.5	1.4	2.2	1.9	1.8
.9	.9	1.0		.4	.5	.6	1.0	1.2	1.3
2.8	3.1	2.6		3.9	2.3	1.9	4.1	2.5	2.3
1.5 (335)	1.4 (318)	1.5	Quick	1.1	.9	1.3	2.0 (86)	1.5	1.5
.7	.7	.8		.2	.3	.3	.8	.9	1.0
0 UND	0 UND	0 UND		0 UND	0 UND	0 UND	0 UND	18 20.3	20 18.4
31 11.9	28 12.9	29 12.7	Sales/Receivables	0 UND	0 UND	24 15.2	24 15.3	35 10.5	35 10.5
52 7.1	50 7.3	49 7.4		48 7.6	34 10.6	50 7.2	50 7.3	49 7.4	52 7.0
			Cost of Sales/Inventory						
			Cost of Sales/Payables						
5.0	5.8	6.5		8.2	8.9	9.9	6.1	5.9	5.7
13.1	16.5	15.4	Sales/Working Capital	52.4	45.5	23.9	16.9	8.9	10.5
-84.0	-87.3	-818.9		-2.7	-15.5	-24.1	259.1	54.7	26.3
16.6	28.5	23.3		7.7	22.0	19.4	48.1	32.7	19.4
(230) 3.3	(257) 6.0	(247) 5.5	EBIT/Interest	(13) .2	(32) 8.6	(26) 6.0	(46) 6.4	(72) 5.2	(58) 5.6
.8	1.3	1.6		-1.6	1.3	1.0	2.2	1.1	2.4
18.0	12.9	4.1							4.4
(14) 6.6	(27) 5.2	(22) 1.8	Net Profit + Depr., Dep., Amort./Cur. Mat. L/T/D					(14)	1.9
.5	1.1	1.1							1.1
.4	.4	.6		1.0	.3	.6	.7	.5	.6
1.0	1.0	1.1	Fixed/Worth	4.9	.8	1.3	1.3	.9	.9
4.3	3.7	4.0		NM	9.9	7.3	12.9	1.4	1.7
.6	.6	.6		1.1	.6	.8	.5	.4	.6
1.3	1.4	1.3	Debt/Worth	8.7	1.6	2.4	1.5	.9	1.1
9.9	7.1	6.2		NM	18.1	20.9	15.2	1.8	3.0
60.2	100.8	78.6		100.0	95.9	238.5	156.6	70.7	36.2
(243) 12.6	(277) 24.3	(270) 19.7	% Profit Before Taxes/Tangible Net Worth	(23) 31.5	(42) 39.2	(25) 55.4	(45) 23.4	(80) 16.0	(55) 12.0
.8	3.4	5.5		-18.1	8.9	15.8	7.5	2.0	6.4
26.1	37.0	28.4		13.4	40.9	43.4	35.0	23.1	13.5
5.5	9.3	7.7	% Profit Before Taxes/Total Assets	2.8	11.7	18.8	10.7	6.1	6.6
-.1	.3	1.2		-9.7	.7	.3	2.6	.5	2.9
16.2	17.4	15.5		44.0	31.4	22.1	16.7	8.6	11.9
5.6	6.3	4.8	Sales/Net Fixed Assets	5.3	10.0	7.1	4.1	3.6	4.5
2.6	2.4	2.2		.3	1.4	3.1	2.0	2.2	2.7
3.8	3.9	3.5		2.9	5.8	5.8	3.7	2.8	2.7
2.0	1.9	1.8	Sales/Total Assets	1.3	2.4	2.6	1.8	1.6	1.7
1.1	1.1	1.0		.2	.7	1.7	1.1	1.1	1.1
1.6	1.6	1.6		3.0	1.0	1.9	1.0	1.6	1.7
(248) 3.0	(271) 3.0	(270) 2.8	% Depr., Dep., Amort./Sales	(18) 5.8	(40) 2.8	(24) 2.9	(47) 2.4	(82) 2.7	(59) 2.7
5.5	5.5	4.9		30.1	10.9	5.8	5.9	4.2	4.1
3.4	3.2	3.2			5.0		4.4		
(48) 6.8	(60) 9.8	(55) 7.2	% Officers', Directors' Owners' Comp/Sales	(13) 7.2		(11) 7.8			
17.3	20.8	17.4			17.8		27.2		
7537356M	7138527M	6803997M	Net Sales ($)	13541M	99250M	118825M	395339M	1307743M	4869299M
5170930M	3979168M	4663866M	Total Assets ($)	33398M	152484M	55155M	257636M	926998M	3238195M

M = $ thousand   MM = $ million
See Pages 9 through 22 for Explanation of Ratios and Data

Current Data Sorted by Assets   Comparative Historical Data

Type of Statement	0-500M	500M-2MM	2-10MM	10-50MM	50-100MM	100-250MM	4/1/06-3/31/07 ALL	4/1/07-3/31/08 ALL
Unqualified		1	7	14	5	5	51	35
Reviewed		1	13	5			20	19
Compiled	9	14	17	3			29	21
Tax Returns	22	11	15	1			23	24
Other	14	16	35	23	10	8	85	107
		27 (4/1-9/30/10)		222 (10/1/10-3/31/11)				
NUMBER OF STATEMENTS	45	43	87	46	15	13	208	206
ASSETS	%	%	%	%	%	%	%	%
Cash & Equivalents	34.4	19.6	13.9	17.1	10.5	9.0	15.3	15.8
Trade Receivables (net)	7.1	24.6	28.2	23.3	22.9	17.0	22.8	21.8
Inventory	1.8	2.3	2.2	2.6	2.5	5.9	2.5	3.0
All Other Current	4.2	4.1	2.7	2.8	9.1	11.0	3.4	3.6
Total Current	47.5	50.6	47.0	45.7	45.0	42.9	44.1	44.2
Fixed Assets (net)	36.2	33.5	40.0	37.7	30.2	21.5	41.0	40.2
Intangibles (net)	4.7	6.3	5.6	9.2	22.3	29.4	7.7	8.4
All Other Non-Current	11.6	9.7	7.4	7.3	2.6	6.2	7.2	7.1
Total	100.0	100.0	100.0	100.0	100.0	100.0	100.0	100.0
LIABILITIES								
Notes Payable-Short Term	28.8	9.4	8.4	2.8	1.7	.9	9.1	9.0
Cur. Mat.-L.T.D.	13.2	15.5	7.4	6.5	4.1	2.6	6.9	7.4
Trade Payables	5.4	8.2	9.5	6.7	9.8	5.6	8.5	7.9
Income Taxes Payable	.0	.6	.6	.4	1.3	.0	.2	.5
All Other Current	38.8	16.7	16.3	11.8	13.5	11.2	16.8	12.6
Total Current	86.2	50.5	42.3	28.3	30.4	20.4	41.5	37.4
Long-Term Debt	27.1	33.2	26.5	24.3	-15.4	27.0	25.5	31.8
Deferred Taxes	.0	.3	.5	.3	1.1	1.0	.4	1.0
All Other Non-Current	6.6	7.4	4.8	3.4	15.6	9.6	5.1	8.8
Net Worth	-20.0	8.6	26.0	43.8	37.6	41.9	27.6	21.0
Total Liabilities & Net Worth	100.0	100.0	100.0	100.0	100.0	100.0	100.0	100.0
INCOME DATA								
Net Sales	100.0	100.0	100.0	100.0	100.0	100.0	100.0	100.0
Gross Profit								
Operating Expenses	91.6	86.9	89.8	91.3	88.6	86.3	88.7	89.7
Operating Profit	8.4	13.1	10.2	8.7	11.4	13.7	11.3	10.3
All Other Expenses (net)	1.0	2.6	2.9	.9	1.7	2.1	1.5	2.1
Profit Before Taxes	7.4	10.4	7.3	7.8	9.7	11.6	9.7	8.2
RATIOS								
Current	3.0	2.2	2.3	2.5	2.4	2.6	2.3	2.5
	.7	1.2	1.3	1.7	1.6	2.1	1.4	1.6
	.2	.4	.7	1.1	1.0	1.5	.8	.8
Quick	2.6	1.8	1.9	2.3	1.9	1.9	2.1	2.2
	.5	1.1	1.1	1.4	1.4	1.3	1.1	1.3
	.1	.4	.6	1.0	.9	.8	.6	.6
Sales/Receivables	0 UND	0 UND	20 18.6	29 12.4	35 10.4	42 8.8	0 UND	5 72.5
	0 UND	19 19.4	39 9.3	47 7.7	48 7.6	53 6.9	41 9.0	41 8.8
	1 641.3	43 8.4	61 6.0	66 5.6	68 5.4	69 5.3	62 5.9	58 6.3
Cost of Sales/Inventory								
Cost of Sales/Payables								
Sales/Working Capital	106.0	10.6	8.5	6.2	5.9	2.8	7.1	6.7
	-85.7	40.9	28.3	8.5	11.9	5.1	25.7	17.3
	-9.0	-19.3	-21.1	60.1	845.7	8.9	-39.9	-35.7
EBIT/Interest	12.6	44.2	13.4	30.1	44.9	52.0	19.4	13.6
	(24) 1.0	(39) 9.0	(77) 3.5	(36) 6.7	(12) 7.2	10.1	(177) 6.0	(171) 4.3
	-4.0	2.1	.7	3.2	1.3	2.9	2.1	1.2
Net Profit + Depr., Dep., Amort./Cur. Mat. L/T/D			5.0	4.6			8.8	9.0
			(13) 1.8	(12) 2.1			(32) 3.7	(30) 3.7
			.9	1.1			1.5	1.3
Fixed/Worth	.1	.4	.7	.5	.6	.4	.5	.5
	3.3	1.1	1.4	1.2	1.7	.7	1.2	1.2
	-1.5	9.4	5.5	2.6	-4.5	-1.2	13.5	UND
Debt/Worth	.6	1.2	.9	.6	.5	.6	.7	.8
	13.1	3.0	2.5	1.4	1.6	1.5	1.8	1.9
	-3.0	-15.3	12.7	4.5	-13.6	-4.4	16.9	-147.7
% Profit Before Taxes/Tangible Net Worth	822.7	230.1	77.5	49.2	156.9		92.1	71.8
	(25) 218.2	(32) 64.8	(74) 32.0	(40) 26.1	(10) 31.4		(162) 36.0	(153) 28.2
	.9	15.8	.4	11.4	15.3		11.2	7.5
% Profit Before Taxes/Total Assets	231.1	57.9	30.5	21.8	29.3	25.7	34.5	26.4
	16.2	26.0	7.1	12.8	6.9	6.7	10.3	8.0
	-2.3	3.5	-.6	6.1	5.1	3.0	2.1	.7
Sales/Net Fixed Assets	172.5	38.9	16.2	12.4	15.3	9.7	20.1	21.7
	44.7	14.4	8.6	7.4	5.0	3.4	7.2	7.5
	10.9	5.6	2.5	2.5	3.8	3.1	2.7	2.6
Sales/Total Assets	24.3	8.1	3.5	2.5	2.3	1.5	3.7	3.8
	10.3	3.3	2.2	1.7	1.5	.9	2.2	2.1
	5.0	2.5	1.3	1.4	1.3	.7	1.2	1.1
% Depr., Dep., Amort./Sales	.5	1.0	1.6	2.1	1.9		1.5	1.6
	(22) 1.5	(27) 3.8	(80) 3.8	(42) 3.8	(12) 4.0		(174) 3.0	(164) 3.7
	3.8	6.6	7.9	5.9	5.5		6.0	7.8
% Officers', Directors' Owners' Comp/Sales	7.3	3.2	3.5				4.8	2.7
	(15) 11.7	(19) 7.0	(26) 8.8				(60) 11.2	(53) 11.3
	16.7	14.2	17.5				25.8	20.3
Net Sales ($)	120267M	247288M	1145358M	2009811M	1819588M	2322578M	6203932M	6480955M
Total Assets ($)	8566M	47389M	421678M	1007012M	1055573M	2112490M	4565051M	4658427M

M = $ thousand   MM = $ million
See Pages 9 through 22 for Explanation of Ratios and Data

Comparative Historical Data | **Current Data Sorted by Sales**

Current Data date ranges: **27 (4/1-9/30/10)** covers 0-1MM / 1-3MM / 3-5MM; **222 (10/1/10-3/31/11)** covers 5-10MM / 10-25MM / 25MM & OVER.

4/1/08-3/31/09 ALL	4/1/09-3/31/10 ALL	4/1/10-3/31/11 ALL	Type of Statement	0-1MM	1-3MM	3-5MM	5-10MM	10-25MM	25MM & OVER
50	50	32	Unqualified	1			2	8	21
16	25	19	Reviewed		1	1	2	10	5
23	24	43	Compiled	4	8	7	12	9	3
40	51	49	Tax Returns	10	11	8	12	4	4
108	124	106	Other	5	19	7	12	23	40
237	274	249	**NUMBER OF STATEMENTS**	20	39	23	40	54	73
%	%	%	**ASSETS**	%	%	%	%	%	%
13.4	16.7	18.7	Cash & Equivalents	27.2	19.5	12.3	20.2	20.6	15.8
24.0	23.9	22.0	Trade Receivables (net)	7.1	16.7	29.0	22.3	28.7	21.4
2.8	2.2	2.4	Inventory	1.9	2.9	.7	2.4	2.3	2.9
5.2	3.0	4.0	All Other Current	3.3	3.0	3.1	4.0	3.2	5.8
45.3	45.8	47.1	Total Current	39.4	42.1	45.1	48.9	54.8	45.9
38.1	36.6	36.2	Fixed Assets (net)	47.7	37.7	46.5	32.3	34.0	32.8
9.3	8.7	8.5	Intangibles (net)	3.4	8.1	1.9	7.8	4.5	15.5
7.2	9.0	8.2	All Other Non-Current	9.6	12.1	6.6	11.0	6.7	5.8
100.0	100.0	100.0	Total	100.0	100.0	100.0	100.0	100.0	100.0
			LIABILITIES						
6.9	7.3	10.5	Notes Payable-Short Term	37.0	12.1	22.1	5.2	7.9	3.4
8.0	7.7	9.2	Cur. Mat.-L.T.D.	15.7	8.2	10.8	17.1	5.4	6.0
9.5	8.5	7.8	Trade Payables	10.9	5.1	11.4	5.3	8.8	8.0
.8	.6	.5	Income Taxes Payable	.0	.7	.0	.0	1.0	.5
12.9	17.5	19.2	All Other Current	31.1	24.2	19.3	25.6	14.9	12.9
38.1	41.5	47.2	Total Current	94.7	50.3	63.6	53.1	38.0	30.9
25.1	26.1	26.7	Long-Term Debt	37.0	26.8	33.0	36.2	16.6	24.1
.3	.3	.4	Deferred Taxes	.0	.2	.1	.3	.6	.5
3.3	8.0	6.2	All Other Non-Current	7.5	6.0	5.0	5.2	6.6	6.6
33.2	24.0	19.5	Net Worth	-39.2	16.7	-1.8	5.1	38.2	37.8
100.0	100.0	100.0	Total Liabilities & Net Worth	100.0	100.0	100.0	100.0	100.0	100.0
			INCOME DATA						
100.0	100.0	100.0	Net Sales	100.0	100.0	100.0	100.0	100.0	100.0
			Gross Profit						
89.7	88.4	89.6	Operating Expenses	87.9	88.0	91.5	93.2	87.3	90.3
10.3	11.6	10.4	Operating Profit	12.1	12.0	8.5	6.8	12.7	9.7
1.7	1.7	2.0	All Other Expenses (net)	9.1	2.0	1.5	1.9	1.4	.8
8.6	9.9	8.3	Profit Before Taxes	3.0	10.0	7.0	4.9	11.4	8.9
			RATIOS						
2.6	2.6	2.4	Current	5.5	2.9	1.4	2.9	2.8	2.4
1.4	1.5	1.4		.6	1.1	.8	1.4	1.4	1.7
.9	.9	.7		.2	.4	.4	.4	.9	1.2
2.2	2.2	2.0	Quick	5.4	2.3	1.4	2.1	2.4	2.2
(236) 1.2	1.2	1.1		.3	.9	.8	1.2	1.3	1.4
.7	.7	.5		.1	.3	.4	.4	.7	.8
21 17.8	13 29.1	0 UND	Sales/Receivables	0 UND	0 UND	0 UND	0 UND	19 19.6	26 14.0
44 8.3	39 9.4	33 10.9		0 UND	0 UND	37 9.9	33 11.2	39 9.3	45 8.1
59 6.2	61 6.0	56 6.5		0 UND	57 6.5	131 2.8	46 8.0	65 5.6	57 6.4
			Cost of Sales/Inventory						
			Cost of Sales/Payables						
6.2	7.0	7.7	Sales/Working Capital	64.8	13.5	21.2	8.0	8.2	6.0
17.5	17.6	27.6		-13.6	506.3	-390.9	28.1	24.5	9.3
-46.3	-60.9	-28.4		-6.4	-9.3	-7.4	-30.2	-42.6	56.0
21.4	28.3	26.5	EBIT/Interest		8.7	10.3	37.1	35.4	40.1
(208) 5.0	(227) 6.8	(201) 4.5			(29) 2.4	(21) 3.1	(33) 6.2	(47) 4.5	(62) 10.4
1.4	2.3	1.2			-.1	1.1	.7	1.7	3.1
7.6	9.9	5.0	Net Profit + Depr., Dep., Amort./Cur. Mat. L/T/D				5.9	5.6	
(44) 4.2	(46) 2.4	(41) 2.5					(11) 1.8	(22) 2.8	
1.5	1.3	1.0					1.2	1.0	
.5	.4	.5	Fixed/Worth	.1	.4	1.1	.3	.3	.5
1.1	1.1	1.3		2.8	2.2	2.2	1.2	.9	1.1
6.6	8.2	11.3		NM	-6.7	-1.6	-5.9	2.9	19.2
.7	.6	.7	Debt/Worth	.5	1.2	1.4	.7	.4	.7
2.1	1.8	2.6		4.9	7.9	5.6	3.4	1.5	1.8
18.2	31.2	52.8		-3.7	-7.6	-4.1	-7.2	5.4	78.0
97.2	101.3	110.0	% Profit Before Taxes/Tangible Net Worth	451.4	269.1	250.4	90.9	86.5	91.0
(187) 36.9	(213) 39.2	(190) 37.0		(14) 13.2	(27) 70.2	(16) 50.2	(28) 37.5	(48) 26.8	(57) 38.6
7.3	10.4	4.4		-18.0	-.7	2.5	1.9	4.6	12.5
29.9	35.5	34.9	% Profit Before Taxes/Total Assets	69.9	57.9	46.5	40.0	57.7	24.9
11.1	12.7	11.2		-2.0	15.0	15.9	13.9	11.9	12.3
1.2	2.9	1.0		-19.6	-.3	.7	-.4	1.8	4.2
20.0	24.7	26.3	Sales/Net Fixed Assets	96.6	42.0	35.0	50.2	38.8	13.4
7.1	7.5	9.6		10.9	11.7	6.1	12.2	10.3	8.1
2.9	3.2	3.5		3.0	3.4	2.3	3.7	3.5	4.1
3.5	3.9	5.0	Sales/Total Assets	7.4	9.6	6.6	6.7	4.6	3.2
2.0	2.2	2.5		4.5	2.8	2.7	2.4	3.0	1.7
1.2	1.3	1.5		1.9	1.4	1.3	1.7	1.6	1.3
1.8	1.9	1.7	% Depr., Dep., Amort./Sales	2.7	1.5	3.2	1.1	1.5	1.8
(189) 3.8	(212) 3.8	(191) 3.6		(12) 4.8	(25) 4.0	(19) 6.6	(29) 2.8	(44) 3.0	(62) 2.9
7.8	6.3	6.3		26.5	9.1	8.8	5.1	6.2	5.3
2.9	2.8	3.4	% Officers', Directors' Owners' Comp/Sales		5.7		3.2	3.6	1.8
(53) 8.5	(65) 8.5	(69) 8.2			(13) 8.6		(15) 7.5	(15) 7.2	(15) 10.8
15.2	16.7	17.6			18.9		14.2	12.6	42.4
7977926M	8613558M	7664890M	Net Sales ($)	10816M	74671M	90997M	277927M	891540M	6318939M
5707933M	6193601M	4652708M	Total Assets ($)	6681M	48854M	48350M	119020M	406104M	4023699M

M = $ thousand   MM = $ million
See Pages 9 through 22 for Explanation of Ratios and Data

Current Data Sorted by Assets   Comparative Historical Data

0-500M	500M-2MM	2-10MM	10-50MM	50-100MM	100-250MM		Hist 4/1/06-3/31/07 ALL	Hist 4/1/07-3/31/08 ALL
						Type of Statement		
1	1	16	7	1	2	Unqualified	25	16
	4	11	6			Reviewed	16	26
6	13	20	3			Compiled	40	25
11	28	9	2			Tax Returns	30	31
11	34	57	22			Other	85	107
	13 (4/1-9/30/10)		255 (10/1/10-3/31/11)					
29	80	113	40	3	3	**NUMBER OF STATEMENTS**	196	205
%	%	%	%	%	%	**ASSETS**	%	%
31.1	14.3	13.5	9.2			Cash & Equivalents	14.6	12.4
6.0	12.6	16.8	18.7			Trade Receivables (net)	17.2	17.7
.2	.1	.6	.4			Inventory	.6	.4
4.4	3.6	4.8	6.4			All Other Current	3.6	4.3
41.8	30.6	35.8	34.7			Total Current	36.1	34.8
49.5	49.8	47.6	44.1			Fixed Assets (net)	49.6	49.6
4.6	6.3	6.0	12.9			Intangibles (net)	5.6	6.8
4.1	13.3	10.6	8.2			All Other Non-Current	8.7	8.8
100.0	100.0	100.0	100.0			Total	100.0	100.0
						LIABILITIES		
33.3	10.9	4.3	3.8			Notes Payable-Short Term	6.1	7.8
23.3	15.5	10.0	10.1			Cur. Mat.-L.T.D.	10.0	10.7
7.8	4.6	3.9	4.0			Trade Payables	5.1	5.3
.0	.2	.2	.2			Income Taxes Payable	.2	.4
14.5	9.2	12.3	10.3			All Other Current	14.9	13.2
78.9	40.4	30.7	28.4			Total Current	36.4	37.4
53.7	47.3	28.2	33.9			Long-Term Debt	36.1	36.5
.1	.0	.0	.0			Deferred Taxes	.1	.1
6.2	13.2	3.7	4.0			All Other Non-Current	5.7	6.2
-39.0	-.8	37.4	33.7			Net Worth	21.7	19.8
100.0	100.0	100.0	100.0			Total Liabilities & Net Worth	100.0	100.0
						INCOME DATA		
100.0	100.0	100.0	100.0			Net Sales	100.0	100.0
						Gross Profit		
85.8	86.8	83.9	84.4			Operating Expenses	84.5	86.6
14.2	13.2	16.1	15.6			Operating Profit	15.5	13.4
1.0	2.9	1.7	2.5			All Other Expenses (net)	3.0	2.6
13.1	10.3	14.5	13.1			Profit Before Taxes	12.5	10.7
						RATIOS		
3.2	2.3	2.4	2.5				2.5	2.1
.9	.8	1.2	1.3			Current	1.1	1.0
.2	.2	.6	.9				.6	.6
2.4	2.2	1.9	1.8				2.0	1.9
.9	.6	1.0	1.2	(195)		Quick	1.0	.9
.2	.2	.4	.4				.4	.4
0 UND	0 UND	0 UND	26 14.3				0 UND	0 UND
0 UND	0 UND	30 12.1	39 9.2			Sales/Receivables	38 9.7	37 9.7
0 UND	38 9.5	43 8.5	56 6.5				57 6.4	55 6.6
						Cost of Sales/Inventory		
						Cost of Sales/Payables		
50.7	19.0	9.1	9.7				9.1	9.7
-491.5	-269.2	35.2	19.3			Sales/Working Capital	96.5	999.8
-12.9	-7.8	-17.7	NM				-14.2	-12.0
29.9	11.2	41.4	22.9				17.3	14.0
(17) 7.8	(69) 4.0	(102) 10.4	(39) 6.4			EBIT/Interest	(170) 5.3	(174) 4.1
.1	.8	3.7	2.3				1.2	1.0
		6.6					4.1	2.5
	(12) 3.4					Net Profit + Depr., Dep., Amort./Cur. Mat. L/T/D	(12) 3.0	(14) 1.4
		1.7					.8	.5
.4	1.2	.5	.8				.7	.9
2.2	4.0	1.6	1.5			Fixed/Worth	1.9	2.5
-.6	-1.2	6.2	7.3				NM	-15.0
.9	1.7	.6	.7				.9	1.1
-8.9	6.4	2.0	1.4			Debt/Worth	2.4	3.1
-2.1	-4.9	7.3	8.4				-24.2	-32.3
371.1	146.6	108.0	67.7				150.2	118.7
(14) 81.9	(49) 86.4	(89) 57.0	(32) 42.6			% Profit Before Taxes/Tangible Net Worth	(144) 61.0	(149) 46.5
15.3	13.5	20.3	22.1				21.3	9.4
192.6	39.3	46.0	29.7				41.4	40.4
25.2	16.4	19.2	13.8			% Profit Before Taxes/Total Assets	16.2	10.8
.8	-1.2	3.3	3.0				1.0	-.2
222.0	12.0	10.9	7.3				9.5	9.8
17.0	5.7	4.8	4.1			Sales/Net Fixed Assets	4.1	4.2
5.7	2.9	2.1	2.2				2.0	2.2
26.3	4.2	3.1	2.8				3.7	3.5
6.1	2.4	1.9	1.8			Sales/Total Assets	2.0	1.9
3.1	1.4	1.1	1.0				1.1	1.1
1.2	2.6	3.6	5.0				3.6	4.4
(15) 5.1	(63) 5.3	(99) 7.6	(38) 6.8			% Depr., Dep., Amort./Sales	(167) 7.7	(174) 8.1
15.0	14.3	13.8	12.3				12.8	13.6
	5.1	2.4	3.7				4.8	4.3
	(25) 9.6	(22) 11.4	(14) 8.6			% Officers', Directors' Owners' Comp/Sales	(47) 9.8	(45) 10.9
	16.3	26.9	22.6				20.5	25.8
94742M	363146M	1375696M	1612465M	491451M	513323M	Net Sales ($)	3352071M	3381016M
7139M	91874M	527805M	797926M	219315M	572042M	Total Assets ($)	2215494M	1886849M

© RMA 2011

M = $ thousand   MM = $ million
See Pages 9 through 22 for Explanation of Ratios and Data

Comparative Historical Data | Current Data Sorted by Sales

4/1/08-3/31/09 ALL	4/1/09-3/31/10 ALL	4/1/10-3/31/11 ALL	Type of Statement	0-1MM	1-3MM	3-5MM	5-10MM	10-25MM	25MM & OVER
19	18	28	Unqualified	3	2	3	3	7	10
29	23	21	Reviewed		1	3	4	6	7
33	35	42	Compiled	5	11	10	6	9	1
36	39	50	Tax Returns	8	18	10	7	7	
113	122	127	Other	12	24	15	21	31	24
				13 (4/1-9/30/10)			255 (10/1/10-3/31/11)		
230	237	268	NUMBER OF STATEMENTS	28	56	41	41	60	42
%	%	%	ASSETS	%	%	%	%	%	%
13.2	14.9	14.9	Cash & Equivalents	15.0	18.1	14.4	14.0	14.1	12.9
14.2	16.8	14.8	Trade Receivables (net)	4.0	12.2	9.8	19.7	19.2	19.2
.3	.6	.3	Inventory	.2	.1	.0	1.4	.2	.3
4.0	3.6	4.6	All Other Current	2.9	5.7	3.4	4.5	3.9	6.8
31.7	35.8	34.7	Total Current	22.2	36.1	27.7	39.6	37.4	39.2
54.6	49.8	47.8	Fixed Assets (net)	59.0	49.7	55.7	41.7	46.6	37.9
6.5	7.1	7.4	Intangibles (net)	6.8	5.9	4.6	10.8	6.1	10.8
7.1	7.3	10.2	All Other Non-Current	11.9	8.3	12.1	7.9	9.9	12.1
100.0	100.0	100.0	Total	100.0	100.0	100.0	100.0	100.0	100.0
			LIABILITIES						
7.5	9.9	9.2	Notes Payable-Short Term	17.6	11.5	11.8	4.9	4.4	9.3
12.6	12.5	13.0	Cur. Mat.-L.T.D.	15.8	14.5	15.1	8.3	14.2	10.0
5.8	7.0	4.7	Trade Payables	3.7	4.5	5.0	5.3	4.7	4.5
.2	.3	.2	Income Taxes Payable	.0	.0	.3	.0	.1	.7
10.8	11.7	12.0	All Other Current	5.0	8.1	9.5	7.3	14.3	25.5
36.9	41.5	39.1	Total Current	42.1	38.6	41.7	25.7	37.7	50.0
44.7	36.5	37.4	Long-Term Debt	60.4	41.6	50.8	29.5	25.6	28.1
.0	.1	.1	Deferred Taxes	.1	.0	.0	.0	.0	.5
5.9	4.7	6.8	All Other Non-Current	14.6	8.3	13.4	2.9	.9	5.2
12.5	17.2	16.6	Net Worth	-17.3	11.5	-5.9	41.8	35.7	16.2
100.0	100.0	100.0	Total Liabilities & Net Worth	100.0	100.0	100.0	100.0	100.0	100.0
			INCOME DATA						
100.0	100.0	100.0	Net Sales	100.0	100.0	100.0	100.0	100.0	100.0
			Gross Profit						
85.7	87.6	85.3	Operating Expenses	82.2	83.7	86.0	81.3	86.7	90.6
14.3	12.4	14.7	Operating Profit	17.8	16.3	14.0	18.7	13.3	9.4
3.5	2.5	2.1	All Other Expenses (net)	8.7	2.7	1.9	.7	.5	.8
10.8	9.9	12.6	Profit Before Taxes	9.1	13.6	12.1	18.0	12.8	8.6
			RATIOS						
1.8	1.9	2.4	Current	2.5	3.1	1.6	3.7	1.8	1.8
.9	1.0	1.1		.7	1.0	.9	1.5	1.3	1.1
.4	.4	.4		.2	.4	.3	.9	.6	.4
1.6	1.8	2.0	Quick	2.2	2.8	1.5	3.7	1.7	1.5
(229) .8	.8	1.0		.6	.7	.6	1.4	1.2	1.0
.3	.3	.3		.2	.4	.2	.7	.6	.2
0 UND	0 UND	0 UND	Sales/Receivables	0 UND	0 UND	0 UND	0 UND	0 UND	0 UND
26 14.0	26 14.0	24 15.3		0 UND	0 UND	0 UND	36 10.0	31 11.9	30 12.0
47 7.8	46 7.9	42 8.8		49 7.4	36 10.0	37 9.9	63 5.8	38 9.5	52 7.0
			Cost of Sales/Inventory						
			Cost of Sales/Payables						
12.8	12.2	11.1	Sales/Working Capital	9.8	7.2	38.5	5.9	14.9	11.8
-70.7	-327.6	63.1		-252.7	NM	-235.1	27.4	38.5	81.2
-10.8	-10.6	-14.5		-3.0	-7.5	-6.9	-356.7	-29.0	-21.8
12.4	14.7	23.4	EBIT/Interest	7.0	16.3	11.7	44.0	36.0	17.2
(196) 4.1	(208) 4.6	(233) 6.4		(17) 3.5	(49) 4.0	(37) 5.6	(39) 14.7	(52) 15.4	(39) 7.0
.9	1.2	2.0		-.6	1.0	.4	4.3	3.1	2.3
3.1	3.2	6.6	Net Profit + Depr., Dep., Amort./Cur. Mat. L/T/D						
(17) 1.2	(15) 2.0	(16) 2.2							
.8	1.0	1.4							
1.1	1.0	.8	Fixed/Worth	2.7	1.0	1.2	.5	.5	.7
3.7	2.6	2.1		27.3	3.9	3.3	1.5	1.2	1.9
-5.0	-6.8	-3.9		-.8	-2.0	-1.1	4.0	2.2	-1.8
1.3	1.1	.8	Debt/Worth	2.6	1.0	1.1	.6	.6	.9
5.8	3.7	2.9		NM	5.1	3.9	1.4	1.2	3.5
-9.6	-8.6	-8.8		-3.1	-4.9	-2.4	6.6	3.4	-5.0
132.9	115.2	129.1	% Profit Before Taxes/Tangible Net Worth	66.9	160.6	155.4	143.0	94.6	122.7
(156) 60.0	(166) 53.9	(188) 56.2		(14) 20.5	(35) 76.2	(25) 83.0	(33) 57.0	(53) 55.3	(28) 50.1
8.1	15.6	18.8		-8.1	8.8	31.8	26.3	11.9	12.5
33.2	42.2	43.8	% Profit Before Taxes/Total Assets	17.1	38.5	59.1	46.8	51.1	27.5
11.0	14.0	18.5		4.1	18.0	19.6	24.1	26.6	15.9
-1.5	1.6	1.7		-4.2	.2	.0	7.6	3.0	4.0
8.3	10.8	12.0	Sales/Net Fixed Assets	8.7	12.0	9.7	10.2	18.7	23.1
3.6	4.6	5.2		2.1	4.4	5.5	5.5	5.2	7.2
1.8	2.3	2.7		.5	1.8	2.3	3.1	3.3	4.5
3.7	3.7	3.8	Sales/Total Assets	2.3	2.6	4.6	2.9	4.4	6.2
1.9	2.0	2.2		1.0	1.9	2.8	1.9	2.8	3.0
1.1	1.2	1.3		.3	1.0	1.6	1.2	1.8	1.9
4.7	3.8	3.8	% Depr., Dep., Amort./Sales	14.1	3.5	2.6	4.4	3.3	2.5
(191) 8.4	(202) 6.9	(215) 6.7		(21) 26.0	(43) 9.8	(33) 5.4	(36) 7.7	(54) 5.9	(28) 5.4
14.5	12.5	13.8		36.3	25.2	12.5	12.4	9.5	7.3
7.1	5.0	4.1	% Officers', Directors' Owners' Comp/Sales		4.6	5.6		3.4	3.5
(58) 13.6	(56) 13.7	(67) 9.8		(16) 8.9	(13) 9.8		(15) 22.9	(13) 18.7	
23.5	23.5	22.5		14.3	19.8		31.7	23.6	
3659940M	4073446M	4450823M	Net Sales ($)	17445M	108963M	161257M	295894M	942339M	2924925M
2198651M	2150317M	2216101M	Total Assets ($)	46539M	84033M	80652M	187382M	447474M	1370021M

M = $ thousand   MM = $ million
See Pages 9 through 22 for Explanation of Ratios and Data

Current Data Sorted by Assets   Comparative Historical Data

Type of Statement	0-500M	500M-2MM	2-10MM	10-50MM	50-100MM	100-250MM		4/1/06-3/31/07 ALL	4/1/07-3/31/08 ALL
Unqualified	2	15	45	56	19	10		108	99
Reviewed	1	5	16	6				25	21
Compiled	13	26	13	3	1	2		32	24
Tax Returns	55	38	13	1				58	85
Other	45	65	81	47	10	8		137	161
		109 (4/1-9/30/10)		487 (10/1/10-3/31/11)					
NUMBER OF STATEMENTS	116	149	168	113	30	20		360	390
ASSETS	%	%	%	%	%	%		%	%
Cash & Equivalents	30.0	18.3	17.6	21.0	20.0	10.9		20.1	19.9
Trade Receivables (net)	20.4	35.2	34.5	26.8	22.2	16.4		34.8	35.7
Inventory	.9	1.8	2.4	1.6	.9	1.0		1.4	1.5
All Other Current	4.6	3.6	4.2	4.0	2.6	2.4		3.9	4.9
Total Current	55.9	58.9	58.7	53.4	45.6	30.8		60.3	61.9
Fixed Assets (net)	18.7	21.3	25.3	23.0	12.4	11.6		23.5	19.9
Intangibles (net)	9.5	10.4	3.7	9.7	30.4	51.4		4.9	6.5
All Other Non-Current	15.9	9.5	12.3	13.9	11.6	6.2		11.4	11.7
Total	100.0	100.0	100.0	100.0	100.0	100.0		100.0	100.0
LIABILITIES									
Notes Payable-Short Term	20.3	14.0	7.7	3.1	2.8	.5		9.6	10.2
Cur. Mat.-L.T.D.	11.7	2.8	2.8	2.4	2.8	2.2		2.7	2.8
Trade Payables	7.9	8.1	9.4	7.9	8.2	8.2		8.2	7.3
Income Taxes Payable	.0	.2	.2	.5	.3	.1		.2	.4
All Other Current	28.0	18.3	15.0	13.7	14.9	9.9		20.1	18.0
Total Current	67.9	43.4	35.2	27.7	28.9	20.8		40.7	38.7
Long-Term Debt	14.1	17.4	14.8	13.9	16.5	39.9		15.1	15.4
Deferred Taxes	.0	.0	.3	.4	1.0	2.5		.1	.1
All Other Non-Current	16.3	8.8	3.6	6.6	8.1	6.1		6.7	7.6
Net Worth	1.6	30.4	46.1	51.4	45.5	30.8		37.5	38.1
Total Liabilities & Net Worth	100.0	100.0	100.0	100.0	100.0	100.0		100.0	100.0
INCOME DATA									
Net Sales	100.0	100.0	100.0	100.0	100.0	100.0		100.0	100.0
Gross Profit									
Operating Expenses	92.4	90.3	91.9	94.1	89.8	87.0		93.8	93.0
Operating Profit	7.6	9.7	8.1	5.9	10.2	13.0		6.2	7.0
All Other Expenses (net)	.7	1.8	1.2	.5	.7	2.6		.4	.6
Profit Before Taxes	6.9	7.9	6.8	5.3	9.5	10.4		5.7	6.4
RATIOS									
Current	3.1	3.8	2.9	3.4	2.7	2.1		3.6	3.5
	1.3	1.8	1.7	2.1	1.8	1.5		1.8	1.8
	.4	.8	1.1	1.3	1.1	1.3		1.1	1.1
Quick	2.7	3.5	2.6	3.0	2.4	1.9		3.3	3.3
	1.1	1.6	1.5	2.0	1.6	1.4		1.7	1.6
	.3	.7	1.0	1.0	1.0	1.1		.9	.9
Sales/Receivables	0 UND	1 578.7	26 14.1	32 11.5	38 9.7	30 12.0		23 15.7	21 17.5
	0 UND	34 10.8	44 8.3	45 8.1	49 7.4	38 9.5		44 8.3	43 8.4
	24 15.3	52 7.0	61 6.0	59 6.1	61 6.0	56 6.6		62 5.9	61 6.0
Cost of Sales/Inventory									
Cost of Sales/Payables									
Sales/Working Capital	18.7	6.5	5.6	4.1	4.6	8.3		6.0	6.2
	132.4	14.8	12.0	8.7	8.1	16.6		12.3	12.7
	-28.7	-47.2	80.9	32.2	36.6	29.8		103.6	104.2
EBIT/Interest	(67) 55.3	(117) 44.4	(128) 39.0	(87) 23.5	(27) 86.5	(17) 8.1		(261) 21.0	(289) 23.7
	15.2	9.6	7.1	9.5	11.5	2.7		5.7	7.2
	4.0	1.8	3.2	3.1	5.0	1.4		1.3	1.8
Net Profit + Depr., Dep., Amort./Cur. Mat. L/T/D			(13) 29.1	(10) 14.7				(19) 14.1	(28) 16.8
			4.3	6.4				4.8	3.8
			1.5	1.1				1.2	1.7
Fixed/Worth	.0	.1	.1	.2	.3	2.0		.1	.1
	.4	.4	.4	.5	1.6	-.2		.4	.4
	-13.2	12.8	1.4	1.2	-.2	-.1		1.9	1.4
Debt/Worth	.5	.5	.5	.3	.9	6.5		.4	.5
	3.3	1.8	1.1	.8	5.7	-1.7		1.1	1.3
	-4.1	-17.8	3.5	3.4	-2.9	-1.6		6.4	6.1
% Profit Before Taxes/Tangible Net Worth	(76) 278.2	(111) 104.2	(153) 71.0	(98) 36.6	(17) 60.5			(301) 76.2	(327) 84.3
	125.2	50.7	29.0	13.5	19.4			27.2	28.5
	53.4	12.2	8.3	3.5	7.4			5.7	6.6
% Profit Before Taxes/Total Assets	120.1	37.9	25.4	16.7	18.7	11.1		28.6	33.3
	49.8	18.8	9.8	8.4	11.6	8.3		9.9	11.5
	12.2	2.5	3.7	1.8	6.5	2.0		1.4	2.4
Sales/Net Fixed Assets	999.8	143.1	51.5	75.2	54.1	67.5		132.8	155.6
	119.9	41.5	18.7	12.1	26.1	23.9		28.5	37.5
	39.8	12.9	4.9	3.8	6.4	7.3		5.8	9.4
Sales/Total Assets	15.2	4.9	3.8	2.8	2.2	1.5		5.0	5.0
	9.0	3.7	2.6	1.7	1.5	1.1		2.9	3.2
	5.1	2.3	1.5	1.3	1.0	.9		1.5	1.7
% Depr., Dep., Amort./Sales	(47) .3	(99) .4	(131) .5	(93) .8	(23) .6			(262) .5	(282) .4
	.6	.9	1.2	1.7	1.2			1.2	1.0
	1.6	2.2	2.4	2.7	1.7			2.7	2.2
% Officers', Directors' Owners' Comp/Sales	(53) 2.6	(55) 3.1	(38) 2.3					(83) 2.8	(100) 3.1
	5.1	5.1	4.5					6.8	5.2
	9.5	8.8	8.4					13.0	8.9
Net Sales ($)	278613M	609511M	2308388M	5637084M	3369718M	4189125M		13854009M	8583959M
Total Assets ($)	27156M	170551M	806830M	2560060M	2049638M	3220711M		4055659M	4186073M

M = $ thousand   MM = $ million
See Pages 9 through 22 for Explanation of Ratios and Data

Comparative Historical Data | Current Data Sorted by Sales

Right-side groups: **109 (4/1-9/30/10)** covers 0-1MM, 1-3MM, 3-5MM · **487 (10/1/10-3/31/11)** covers 5-10MM, 10-25MM, 25MM & OVER

Type of Statement

Type of Statement	4/1/08-3/31/09 ALL	4/1/09-3/31/10 ALL	4/1/10-3/31/11 ALL	0-1MM	1-3MM	3-5MM	5-10MM	10-25MM	25MM & OVER
Unqualified	123	128	147	1	9	10	19	37	72
Reviewed	31	36	28	4	2	2	9	9	5
Compiled	35	40	58	21	20	12	8	8	6
Tax Returns	85	83	107	23	31	26	22	4	3
Other	182	216	256		45	35	42	43	68
Number of Statements	456	503	596	49	107	85	100	101	154

ASSETS (%)

	4/1/08-3/31/09	4/1/09-3/31/10	4/1/10-3/31/11	0-1MM	1-3MM	3-5MM	5-10MM	10-25MM	25MM & OVER
Cash & Equivalents	18.8	21.5	20.8	26.3	24.2	17.9	20.0	18.1	20.4
Trade Receivables (net)	35.9	34.0	29.2	14.1	25.3	29.5	32.5	36.0	30.1
Inventory	1.3	1.1	1.7	.6	2.3	1.3	2.2	2.4	1.0
All Other Current	4.5	3.4	3.9	2.4	4.4	2.1	4.7	3.8	4.8
Total Current	60.5	60.0	55.6	43.4	56.1	50.7	59.4	60.3	56.3
Fixed Assets (net)	21.1	18.9	21.5	34.3	20.5	23.8	21.8	22.6	15.8
Intangibles (net)	7.4	9.1	10.6	6.7	11.6	10.4	6.6	3.5	18.4
All Other Non-Current	11.0	12.0	12.4	15.6	11.8	15.1	12.2	13.5	9.5
Total	100.0	100.0	100.0	100.0	100.0	100.0	100.0	100.0	100.0

LIABILITIES

	4/1/08-3/31/09	4/1/09-3/31/10	4/1/10-3/31/11	0-1MM	1-3MM	3-5MM	5-10MM	10-25MM	25MM & OVER
Notes Payable-Short Term	11.0	10.0	10.4	12.1	14.9	18.0	13.7	5.8	3.2
Cur. Mat.-L.T.D.	3.7	2.9	4.5	7.1	7.7	5.6	3.8	3.0	2.1
Trade Payables	8.4	8.6	8.4	1.8	8.3	9.6	7.2	10.0	9.6
Income Taxes Payable	.4	.3	.2	.1	.0	.1	.5	.1	.4
All Other Current	18.1	21.2	18.0	20.8	23.5	16.8	14.5	15.7	17.5
Total Current	41.6	43.0	41.4	41.8	54.5	50.1	39.8	34.6	32.9
Long-Term Debt	15.9	13.7	16.1	30.4	16.0	15.8	13.1	13.2	15.5
Deferred Taxes	.2	.7	.3	.0	.0	.1	.2	.2	.8
All Other Non-Current	9.8	6.6	8.2	13.2	13.9	7.3	6.4	2.9	7.9
Net Worth	32.5	36.0	34.0	14.5	15.5	26.6	40.6	49.1	42.9
Total Liabilities & Net Worth	100.0	100.0	100.0	100.0	100.0	100.0	100.0	100.0	100.0

INCOME DATA

	4/1/08-3/31/09	4/1/09-3/31/10	4/1/10-3/31/11	0-1MM	1-3MM	3-5MM	5-10MM	10-25MM	25MM & OVER
Net Sales	100.0	100.0	100.0	100.0	100.0	100.0	100.0	100.0	100.0
Gross Profit									
Operating Expenses	93.3	93.2	91.8	81.9	90.6	92.4	93.8	94.1	92.4
Operating Profit	6.7	6.8	8.2	18.1	9.4	7.6	6.2	5.9	7.6
All Other Expenses (net)	1.6	1.0	1.2	6.4	1.1	.7	.7	.1	.8
Profit Before Taxes	5.1	5.8	7.1	11.7	8.3	6.9	5.5	5.7	6.8

RATIOS

	4/1/08-3/31/09	4/1/09-3/31/10	4/1/10-3/31/11	0-1MM	1-3MM	3-5MM	5-10MM	10-25MM	25MM & OVER
Current	3.5	3.3	3.1	3.9	4.6	2.7	3.1	3.0	3.0
	1.9	1.8	1.7	1.1	1.9	1.6	1.7	2.0	1.8
	1.1	1.0	1.0	.3	.5	.8	.8	1.3	1.2
Quick	3.2	3.1	2.8	3.9	4.4	2.6	2.8	2.8	2.5
	1.7	1.6	1.5	1.1	1.6	1.4	1.5	1.7	1.5
	.9	.9	.8	.3	.4	.7	.7	1.2	1.0
Sales/Receivables	24 15.5	19 18.9	10 35.0	0 UND	0 UND	0 UND	14 26.9	32 11.4	31 12.0
	44 8.2	38 9.5	37 9.8	0 UND	15 24.2	37 10.0	35 10.4	47 7.8	43 8.6
	64 5.7	56 6.5	55 6.6	30 12.2	42 8.6	55 6.6	53 6.8	63 5.8	56 6.6
Cost of Sales/Inventory									
Cost of Sales/Payables									
Sales/Working Capital	5.7	6.3	6.2	11.2	5.4	7.2	7.6	5.4	5.2
	12.6	15.4	15.4	174.0	19.9	27.9	15.8	10.1	12.2
	89.8	-999.8	-936.2	-14.3	-20.6	-98.8	-73.2	25.4	34.0
EBIT/Interest	26.6	26.7	37.4	25.3	44.0	103.7	47.7	29.1	26.8
	(331) 7.8	(362) 7.1	(443) 9.6	(21) 4.8	(72) 10.3	(68) 11.2	(79) 8.5	(83) 8.7	(120) 9.5
	1.3	1.7	2.9	1.5	1.3	3.4	2.3	3.1	4.1
Net Profit + Depr., Dep., Amort./Cur. Mat. L/T/D	6.7	23.0	12.5						11.3
	(35) 2.4	(39) 3.7	(41) 3.0					(24)	2.8
	1.1	1.8	1.6						2.0
Fixed/Worth	.1	.1	.1	.0	.0	.1	.1	.1	.2
	.4	.4	.5	.6	.5	.8	.4	.4	.7
	2.0	2.7	4.5	50.6	-7.0	UND	2.1	1.1	-3.4
Debt/Worth	.5	.4	.5	.4	.4	.5	.4	.4	.6
	1.2	1.4	1.5	3.9	1.9	2.0	1.2	.8	1.9
	11.7	12.8	21.3	NM	-4.9	-11.8	7.0	2.4	-25.8
% Profit Before Taxes/Tangible Net Worth	75.5	91.7	94.9	148.2	153.0	124.8	74.2	59.3	80.3
	(363) 25.4	(398) 29.7	(461) 34.3	(37) 41.8	(70) 80.3	(61) 53.8	(85) 31.5	(95) 24.0	(113) 22.8
	3.2	5.9	8.8	10.9	15.9	12.3	7.4	5.6	7.6
% Profit Before Taxes/Total Assets	30.5	33.6	35.3	46.7	68.9	48.0	33.8	23.4	20.7
	9.5	11.4	12.4	14.3	29.2	19.4	14.2	10.1	10.6
	.5	2.2	3.5	2.3	3.0	5.5	2.4	2.7	4.5
Sales/Net Fixed Assets	139.6	159.4	135.9	644.8	263.2	111.1	187.1	59.4	79.9
	35.6	44.3	31.7	33.7	51.4	41.5	42.2	22.3	28.5
	7.4	11.2	7.2	1.0	15.6	9.3	6.7	5.7	7.2
Sales/Total Assets	4.7	5.5	5.0	7.5	7.4	6.2	5.5	4.2	3.5
	3.0	3.2	2.9	2.2	3.9	3.8	3.6	2.6	2.2
	1.6	1.7	1.5	.4	2.1	2.1	2.0	1.4	1.4
% Depr., Dep., Amort./Sales	.4	.4	.5	1.2	.5	.6	.3	.5	.6
	(337) 1.0	(350) 1.0	(402) 1.2	(21) 5.5	(58) 1.5	(58) 1.1	(71) .8	(82) 1.3	(112) 1.2
	2.2	2.2	2.4	13.6	3.5	2.3	1.4	2.4	2.0
% Officers', Directors' Owners' Comp/Sales	2.3	2.3	2.6	5.4	3.4	2.9	2.3	1.4	.4
	(108) 5.7	(125) 5.0	(155) 4.8	(11) 8.8	(38)	(41) 5.1	(41) 4.5	(14) 3.2	(10)
	10.2	10.2	8.8	18.4	11.1	8.7	8.0	5.8	7.6
Net Sales ($)	12201616M	12583706M	16392439M	26603M	209539M	330747M	706185M	1622397M	13496968M
Total Assets ($)	6648118M	6372925M	8834946M	34859M	91717M	125641M	282652M	840291M	7459786M

M = $ thousand   MM = $ million
See Pages 9 through 22 for Explanation of Ratios and Data

HEALTH CARE—Ambulance Services NAICS 621910

Current Data Sorted by Assets							Comparative Historical Data	
0-500M	500M-2MM	2-10MM	10-50MM	50-100MM	100-250MM	Type of Statement	16	14
	2	15	8	2		Unqualified	16	14
	4	7	3			Reviewed	9	9
	5	6	2	1		Compiled	12	10
10	7	8				Tax Returns	10	9
4	11	18	10	2	2	Other	18	30
	34 (4/1-9/30/10)			95 (10/1/10-3/31/11)			4/1/06-3/31/07 ALL	4/1/07-3/31/08 ALL
0-500M	500M-2MM	2-10MM	10-50MM	50-100MM	100-250MM	**NUMBER OF STATEMENTS**		
16	29	54	23	5	2		65	72
%	%	%	%	%	%	**ASSETS**	%	%
34.8	19.2	16.4	11.7			Cash & Equivalents	16.4	18.7
11.0	14.2	30.0	30.8			Trade Receivables (net)	26.9	29.3
2.9	.3	.6	1.4			Inventory	1.8	1.0
2.5	.6	3.5	6.7			All Other Current	4.0	3.3
51.3	34.4	50.6	50.6			Total Current	49.2	52.3
33.1	38.3	41.3	38.1			Fixed Assets (net)	42.1	35.9
4.6	4.9	1.8	3.1			Intangibles (net)	3.0	4.5
11.1	22.5	6.3	8.1			All Other Non-Current	5.7	7.4
100.0	100.0	100.0	100.0			Total	100.0	100.0
						LIABILITIES		
13.0	4.7	5.9	5.7			Notes Payable-Short Term	9.4	8.7
7.6	5.2	5.9	4.3			Cur. Mat.-L.T.D.	6.0	5.7
7.5	8.9	6.2	6.3			Trade Payables	4.9	4.3
.0	.4	.4	.9			Income Taxes Payable	.6	.4
14.6	5.7	12.1	9.2			All Other Current	9.0	7.1
42.7	24.9	30.4	26.3			Total Current	29.9	26.2
19.4	24.8	20.5	16.4			Long-Term Debt	34.9	29.0
.0	.2	.7	1.2			Deferred Taxes	.7	.0
3.7	2.2	3.7	2.3			All Other Non-Current	3.1	5.1
34.3	47.8	44.6	53.7			Net Worth	31.3	39.7
100.0	100.0	100.0	100.0			Total Liabilties & Net Worth	100.0	100.0
						INCOME DATA		
100.0	100.0	100.0	100.0			Net Sales	100.0	100.0
						Gross Profit		
89.8	89.6	93.1	92.1			Operating Expenses	90.2	91.7
10.2	10.4	6.9	7.9			Operating Profit	9.8	8.3
1.2	2.2	1.9	.5			All Other Expenses (net)	1.1	2.2
9.0	8.1	5.1	7.4			Profit Before Taxes	8.7	6.1
						RATIOS		
3.8	5.5	4.1	3.1			Current	3.7	3.8
1.5	2.1	1.9	2.1				1.9	2.2
.6	.5	1.1	1.4				1.0	1.4
3.5	5.5	4.1	2.9			Quick	3.5	3.4
1.1	2.0	1.7	1.5				1.6	2.1
.4	.5	1.0	1.4				.8	1.3
0 UND	0 UND	30 12.1	34 10.7			Sales/Receivables	0 UND	21 17.1
0 UND	12 31.4	48 7.6	68 5.4				45 8.1	51 7.2
0 UND	42 8.7	62 5.9	87 4.2				78 4.7	78 4.7
						Cost of Sales/Inventory		
						Cost of Sales/Payables		
9.7	4.8	4.2	4.1			Sales/Working Capital	5.2	3.9
113.6	20.5	13.0	6.8				10.2	8.4
-35.5	-27.2	71.0	17.6				-999.8	32.1
	18.3	13.6	23.0			EBIT/Interest	16.4	14.1
	(23) 6.2	(45) 5.5	(21) 6.7				(56) 5.1	(63) 5.5
	2.8	2.8	2.2				1.6	1.2
		2.2				Net Profit + Depr., Dep., Amort./Cur. Mat. L/T/D	6.3	5.0
		(10) 1.5					(14) 3.3	(11) 2.5
		.4					1.2	1.8
.1	.5	.5	.3			Fixed/Worth	.4	.4
.7	.9	1.1	.8				1.0	.8
NM	2.8	2.8	1.8				3.0	2.7
.3	.3	.3	.2			Debt/Worth	.4	.5
1.4	.8	1.2	.8				1.1	1.2
NM	3.6	7.9	3.1				4.9	4.2
229.2	61.1	46.9	25.5			% Profit Before Taxes/Tangible Net Worth	49.9	50.3
(12) 28.8	(26) 27.1	(48) 20.7	(22) 14.2				(57) 19.9	(61) 26.8
-7.4	-.3	3.3	6.0				10.8	7.7
98.0	29.6	14.3	18.5			% Profit Before Taxes/Total Assets	22.0	22.2
9.8	12.3	6.8	6.1				8.9	9.9
-8.2	2.2	.6	1.3				1.9	1.1
177.4	27.5	10.5	8.7			Sales/Net Fixed Assets	11.7	14.8
19.8	11.6	5.8	5.1				6.0	6.8
6.7	2.5	2.7	2.4				3.7	3.7
14.5	6.9	3.2	2.2			Sales/Total Assets	3.5	2.9
9.0	2.7	2.0	1.9				2.2	2.0
3.0	1.2	1.2	1.0				1.5	1.4
.4	3.4	2.8	1.9			% Depr., Dep., Amort./Sales	2.6	2.4
(10) 2.1	(16) 6.3	(53) 4.5	4.1				(60) 3.9	(62) 4.2
4.2	8.7	6.2	6.3				6.6	6.6
		1.7				% Officers', Directors' Owners' Comp/Sales	1.6	1.8
		(11) 2.6					(23) 3.8	(21) 2.8
		3.4					4.9	6.9
48202M	133008M	703108M	737116M	321623M	535155M	Net Sales ($)	1079583M	998848M
4751M	32802M	312164M	436046M	310695M	356328M	Total Assets ($)	574222M	660008M

M = $ thousand   MM = $ million
See Pages 9 through 22 for Explanation of Ratios and Data

Comparative Historical Data

Current Data Sorted by Sales

				Type of Statement						
21	20	27		Unqualified	1	3		8	8	7
17	11	14		Reviewed	3	1		7	7	3
11	13	16		Compiled	3	3	4	2	4	1
12	24	25		Tax Returns	2	3	4	3	4	
35	41	47		Other	4	5	4	6	9	
4/1/08-	4/1/09-	4/1/10-			4	6	8	6	6	17
3/31/09	3/31/10	3/31/11				34 (4/1-9/30/10)		95 (10/1/10-3/31/11)		
ALL	ALL	ALL			0-1MM	1-3MM	3-5MM	5-10MM	10-25MM	25MM & OVER
96	109	129		NUMBER OF STATEMENTS	14	18	16	19	34	28
%	%	%		ASSETS	%	%	%	%	%	%
15.6	16.1	18.0		Cash & Equivalents	20.5	25.4	19.2	17.1	20.1	9.5
31.7	26.3	23.9		Trade Receivables (net)	9.0	19.1	10.3	21.3	31.9	34.4
1.3	.8	1.0		Inventory	.6	.6	3.0	.7	.4	1.4
2.3	5.3	3.6		All Other Current	.7	.6	3.4	2.5	3.3	8.0
50.9	48.5	46.5		Total Current	30.7	45.7	35.9	41.6	55.7	53.3
36.6	37.9	39.2		Fixed Assets (net)	55.7	38.5	37.8	39.2	34.4	37.9
3.4	6.8	3.4		Intangibles (net)	2.5	2.1	3.4	3.7	3.9	4.0
9.1	6.8	10.9		All Other Non-Current	11.1	13.7	22.9	15.6	6.0	4.9
100.0	100.0	100.0		Total	100.0	100.0	100.0	100.0	100.0	100.0
				LIABILITIES						
10.7	9.6	6.2		Notes Payable-Short Term	1.2	1.4	19.6	2.8	3.3	9.8
8.2	5.8	5.8		Cur. Mat.-L.T.D.	1.4	4.6	4.4	11.5	5.7	6.0
5.8	4.5	7.1		Trade Payables	10.0	6.3	7.1	3.5	7.4	8.2
.2	.5	.4		Income Taxes Payable	.0	.6	.0	.1	.4	.8
13.8	11.3	10.6		All Other Current	.7	4.4	10.5	6.8	17.6	13.6
38.7	31.5	30.1		Total Current	13.3	17.3	41.6	24.6	34.4	38.5
22.7	28.3	21.5		Long-Term Debt	39.8	19.1	19.1	24.8	15.1	20.7
.4	.6	.6		Deferred Taxes	.0	.4	.0	.2	1.0	1.2
3.9	4.3	3.3		All Other Non-Current	4.7	1.3	2.3	4.2	1.7	5.8
34.3	35.3	44.5		Net Worth	42.2	61.9	37.0	46.2	47.7	33.8
100.0	100.0	100.0		Total Liabilities & Net Worth	100.0	100.0	100.0	100.0	100.0	100.0
				INCOME DATA						
100.0	100.0	100.0		Net Sales	100.0	100.0	100.0	100.0	100.0	100.0
				Gross Profit						
94.0	91.2	91.6		Operating Expenses	77.6	95.4	91.8	92.5	91.6	95.5
6.0	8.8	8.4		Operating Profit	22.4	4.6	8.2	7.5	8.4	4.5
1.4	1.6	1.7		All Other Expenses (net)	13.0	-.2	.5	.0	.4	.8
4.6	7.3	6.7		Profit Before Taxes	9.4	4.8	7.8	7.5	8.1	3.7
				RATIOS						
3.4	3.8	3.7			9.9	8.6	2.5	6.3	3.9	2.2
1.6	1.7	1.8		Current	3.6	2.7	1.0	2.3	1.7	1.4
.9	.9	1.0			.5	1.6	.4	1.1	1.2	1.0
3.3	3.3	3.4			9.8	8.6	2.1	6.2	3.7	1.9
1.5	1.4	1.5		Quick	3.4	2.4	.7	2.1	1.4	1.1
.7	.8	.8			.5	1.6	.4	1.0	1.0	.8
26 14.0	0 UND	0 UND			0 UND	0 UND	0 UND	24 15.3	21 17.4	35 10.5
50 7.3	41 8.9	43 8.5		Sales/Receivables	18 20.0	5 73.2	0 UND	45 8.2	53 6.9	56 6.5
81 4.5	66 5.5	69 5.3			70 5.2	64 5.7	36 10.1	87 4.2	72 5.1	71 5.1
				Cost of Sales/Inventory						
				Cost of Sales/Payables						
5.4	5.8	4.7			1.7	4.2	11.8	3.1	6.6	6.3
11.8	16.0	14.5		Sales/Working Capital	5.1	8.2	NM	6.8	15.2	20.1
-46.5	-65.7	629.4			-3.8	26.0	-28.9	51.6	113.2	420.0
13.9	17.0	15.5			14.8	23.4	13.9	36.7	14.3	
(84) 3.6	(93) 5.6	(103) 5.6		EBIT/Interest	(11) 5.8	(13) 7.8	(17) 5.5	(30) 6.5	(26) 5.4	
1.2	2.9	1.7			2.8	2.0	2.1	3.1	1.3	
4.4	4.7	2.6								2.3
(16) 2.8	(24) 2.8	(25) 1.6		Net Profit + Depr., Dep., Amort./Cur. Mat. L/T/D					(11) 1.7	
2.0	1.9	1.1								1.0
.4	.5	.5			.3	.1	.5	.5	.4	.7
1.0	1.1	1.0		Fixed/Worth	1.4	.7	.9	1.2	1.0	1.6
2.5	5.1	2.9			4.8	1.0	NM	2.8	1.6	3.2
.6	.4	.3			.3	.1	.3	.1	.3	.7
1.4	1.9	1.2		Debt/Worth	1.6	.5	2.0	2.9	1.2	2.9
5.7	7.7	4.6			5.0	1.3	NM	4.8	2.4	8.4
58.3	68.6	48.2		% Profit Before Taxes/Tangible Net Worth	33.2	42.6	126.6	29.4	49.0	64.1
(79) 21.9	(87) 33.8	(114) 19.4			(12) 11.0	(17) 13.2	(12) 39.4	(17) 18.6	(31) 21.9	(25) 22.7
4.3	9.4	3.6			-7.4	-.5	1.8	2.5	4.9	7.4
16.4	27.0	19.5		% Profit Before Taxes/Total Assets	11.1	42.6	53.0	12.0	26.4	19.0
8.8	11.5	7.8			2.9	8.6	7.3	7.7	7.9	8.9
.8	3.2	.5			-4.7	-.1	-.7	.5	4.2	.6
16.7	13.8	15.0		Sales/Net Fixed Assets	6.4	39.6	25.1	10.9	19.9	9.7
7.2	7.3	6.3			.9	5.8	16.1	5.8	7.1	6.5
4.0	4.3	3.1			.2	2.0	4.6	1.7	4.7	3.9
4.0	3.5	3.6		Sales/Total Assets	1.1	4.2	11.7	2.5	3.7	3.3
2.4	2.2	2.1			.6	2.0	5.4	1.6	2.6	2.1
1.3	1.6	1.1			.2	1.0	1.9	.9	1.6	1.7
2.9	2.1	2.6		% Depr., Dep., Amort./Sales		3.9	2.4	3.6	2.6	1.9
(78) 4.1	(90) 3.5	(108) 4.3			(12) 7.2	(11) 3.0	(18) 4.6	(31) 4.5	(27) 3.4	
6.2	5.6	6.5			10.2	6.1	7.3	5.7	4.1	
2.6	1.9	2.1		% Officers', Directors' Owners' Comp/Sales					1.6	
(23) 4.7	(33) 4.0	(29) 3.4						(14) 2.7		
7.2	7.8	5.1							4.0	
1809580M	7892524M	2478212M		Net Sales ($)	7137M	36792M	62780M	135268M	513274M	1722961M
992716M	2343736M	1452786M		Total Assets ($)	20546M	31978M	41538M	116194M	218656M	1023874M

M = $ thousand   MM = $ million
See Pages 9 through 22 for Explanation of Ratios and Data

Current Data Sorted by Assets   **Comparative Historical Data**

	0-500M	500M-2MM	2-10MM	10-50MM	50-100MM	100-250MM	Type of Statement	28	22
			4	20	7	2	Unqualified	28	22
			1				Reviewed		
				1			Compiled	1	1
			1				Tax Returns	1	
	2	1	4	3	2	1	Other	18	16
	2							4/1/06-	4/1/07-
		24 (4/1-9/30/10)		27 (10/1/10-3/31/11)				3/31/07	3/31/08
	0-500M	500M-2MM	2-10MM	10-50MM	50-100MM	100-250MM		ALL	ALL
NUMBER OF STATEMENTS	4	1	10	24	9	3		48	39
	%	%	%	%	%	%	ASSETS	%	%
			23.5	18.7			Cash & Equivalents	20.4	19.4
			21.6	16.3			Trade Receivables (net)	21.5	23.6
			7.2	4.6			Inventory	5.3	6.3
			2.8	1.4			All Other Current	4.6	3.0
			55.1	40.9			Total Current	51.8	52.3
			27.1	44.9			Fixed Assets (net)	32.5	35.2
			5.0	.3			Intangibles (net)	1.6	.5
			12.8	13.8			All Other Non-Current	14.1	12.2
			100.0	100.0			Total	100.0	100.0
							LIABILITIES		
			6.2	2.0			Notes Payable-Short Term	4.2	5.5
			.5	2.6			Cur. Mat.-L.T.D.	1.2	1.6
			25.3	7.5			Trade Payables	9.8	12.3
			.0	.0			Income Taxes Payable	.1	.1
			8.1	6.8			All Other Current	7.9	8.5
			40.1	18.9			Total Current	23.2	28.0
			2.7	16.5			Long-Term Debt	14.1	15.7
			.0	.0			Deferred Taxes	.0	.0
			1.2	3.1			All Other Non-Current	3.2	1.2
			56.0	61.5			Net Worth	59.5	55.0
			100.0	100.0			Total Liabilities & Net Worth	100.0	100.0
							INCOME DATA		
			100.0	100.0			Net Sales	100.0	100.0
							Gross Profit		
			90.0	95.9			Operating Expenses	92.4	96.1
			10.0	4.1			Operating Profit	7.6	3.9
			.7	-1.4			All Other Expenses (net)	-.4	-1.5
			9.3	5.5			Profit Before Taxes	8.0	5.5
							RATIOS		
			4.9	4.5			Current	4.3	4.3
			2.1	2.8				2.8	2.6
			1.1	1.6				1.6	1.8
			4.2	3.9			Quick	3.5	3.8
			2.0	2.5				2.3	2.2
			.9	1.3				1.4	1.1
			32 11.4	35 10.5			Sales/Receivables	27 13.5	37 9.9
			37 9.8	42 8.6				42 8.6	49 7.4
			49 7.5	49 7.5				52 7.0	60 6.0
							Cost of Sales/Inventory		
							Cost of Sales/Payables		
			3.8	2.8			Sales/Working Capital	3.6	3.1
			9.8	5.8				5.3	5.2
			NM	12.5				12.0	11.4
				35.0			EBIT/Interest	23.4	20.5
				(19) 6.2				(31) 6.5	(28) 8.6
				5.2				3.3	3.4
							Net Profit + Depr., Dep., Amort./Cur. Mat. L/T/D		
			.2	.5			Fixed/Worth	.2	.3
			.4	.8				.6	.5
			NM	1.3				1.3	1.1
			.2	.3			Debt/Worth	.2	.3
			.3	.6				.7	.6
			NM	1.1				1.4	1.1
				18.7			% Profit Before Taxes/Tangible Net Worth	36.4	17.3
				9.8				(47) 12.4	(37) 10.5
				6.5				6.2	6.2
			36.4	8.6			% Profit Before Taxes/Total Assets	16.5	9.8
			2.2	6.6				7.2	6.4
			-5.0	4.6				3.2	2.8
			25.7	4.7			Sales/Net Fixed Assets	23.2	13.0
			10.6	2.6				4.7	4.4
			5.4	2.2				2.7	2.2
			3.4	1.6			Sales/Total Assets	2.4	2.1
			2.0	1.3				1.6	1.4
			1.2	1.0				1.0	1.1
				2.1			% Depr., Dep., Amort./Sales	.7	1.8
				3.2				(40) 2.5	(35) 2.6
				4.1				3.1	3.7
							% Officers', Directors' Owners' Comp/Sales		
	6819M	94M	155721M	822515M	782962M	679741M	Net Sales ($)	1895536M	1931827M
	1109M	1232M	67688M	628851M	682183M	446386M	Total Assets ($)	1117544M	1336918M

M = $ thousand   MM = $ million

See Pages 9 through 22 for Explanation of Ratios and Data

Comparative Historical Data | | | Current Data Sorted by Sales

			Type of Statement	0-1MM	1-3MM	3-5MM	5-10MM	10-25MM	25MM & OVER
31	38	33	Unqualified		1			10	22
1	1	1	Reviewed					1	
1		1	Compiled					1	1
3		3	Tax Returns		2				
13	13	13	Other	1	2			4	6
4/1/08-3/31/09 ALL	4/1/09-3/31/10 ALL	4/1/10-3/31/11 ALL				24 (4/1/1-9/30/10)		27 (10/1/10-3/31/11)	
49	52	51	NUMBER OF STATEMENTS	1	5			16	29
%	%	%	ASSETS	%	%			%	%
18.1	15.8	18.6	Cash & Equivalents			D	D	24.3	17.9
17.3	20.8	17.7	Trade Receivables (net)			A	A	17.3	17.4
7.8	6.7	9.8	Inventory			T	T	5.3	9.2
2.6	2.1	1.6	All Other Current			A	A	1.8	1.9
45.9	45.3	47.7	Total Current					48.6	46.4
36.4	39.2	38.4	Fixed Assets (net)			N	N	39.8	39.7
2.5	1.8	1.4	Intangibles (net)			O	O	.5	.6
15.2	13.7	12.6	All Other Non-Current			T	T	11.1	13.3
100.0	100.0	100.0	Total					100.0	100.0
			LIABILITIES			A	A		
1.5	2.1	3.3	Notes Payable-Short Term			V	V	3.9	1.7
1.8	1.5	2.4	Cur. Mat.-L.T.D.			A	A	1.2	2.0
8.5	10.0	12.2	Trade Payables			I	I	16.2	8.6
.1	.1	.0	Income Taxes Payable			L	L	.0	.0
8.1	9.3	8.4	All Other Current			A	A	5.7	8.9
20.0	23.1	26.3	Total Current			B	B	26.9	21.2
16.8	17.0	17.0	Long-Term Debt			L	L	10.2	15.3
.0	.0	.0	Deferred Taxes			E	E	.0	.0
.9	2.5	1.9	All Other Non-Current					1.7	2.4
62.4	57.3	54.8	Net Worth					61.2	61.1
100.0	100.0	100.0	Total Liabilities & Net Worth					100.0	100.0
			INCOME DATA						
100.0	100.0	100.0	Net Sales					100.0	100.0
			Gross Profit						
95.1	94.5	92.0	Operating Expenses					95.4	95.8
4.9	5.5	8.0	Operating Profit					4.6	4.2
.8	-.1	.2	All Other Expenses (net)					-.5	-1.7
4.1	5.6	7.8	Profit Before Taxes					5.2	6.0
			RATIOS						
3.4	3.7	4.4	Current					4.9	4.2
2.5	2.1	2.5						3.2	2.5
1.8	1.4	1.6						1.7	1.8
2.8	3.3	3.6	Quick					4.4	3.6
2.1	1.5	1.9						2.8	1.8
1.1	.9	1.0						1.6	1.0
34 10.7	34 10.7	34 10.8	Sales/Receivables					34 10.7	36 10.1
46 7.9	42 8.7	42 8.7						39 9.4	43 8.4
57 6.4	51 7.1	48 7.5						47 7.7	49 7.5
			Cost of Sales/Inventory						
			Cost of Sales/Payables						
3.3	4.0	2.9	Sales/Working Capital					2.6	3.0
5.8	7.0	6.2						4.7	4.4
12.5	16.7	13.5						11.0	11.7
13.8	31.6	65.4	EBIT/Interest					82.1	51.8
(36) 5.9	(42) 14.7	(37) 12.3						(10) 7.2	(24) 13.6
1.5	4.1	5.3						5.0	5.9
			Net Profit + Depr., Dep., Amort./Cur. Mat. L/T/D						
.4	.5	.4	Fixed/Worth					.4	.4
.6	.6	.6						.6	.6
.9	.9	1.2						1.2	1.1
.4	.3	.3	Debt/Worth					.2	.3
.6	.6	.6						.4	.6
1.0	1.3	1.1						1.0	.9
17.7	18.4	24.5	% Profit Before Taxes/Tangible Net Worth					11.0	20.1
(48) 7.4	(50) 12.2	(48) 10.2						(14) 8.5	11.3
.4	4.3	6.5						-.6	6.5
10.8	10.0	12.6	% Profit Before Taxes/Total Assets					9.1	12.3
4.7	7.7	7.0						5.7	7.1
.0	1.3	4.0						-.6	4.2
9.3	8.2	9.8	Sales/Net Fixed Assets					10.6	6.1
3.4	3.5	3.2						2.8	3.1
2.6	2.3	2.4						1.9	2.4
1.9	2.2	1.9	Sales/Total Assets					2.0	1.6
1.3	1.5	1.4						1.1	1.4
1.0	1.0	1.0						1.0	1.2
1.8	1.9	2.1	% Depr., Dep., Amort./Sales					2.2	2.2
(48) 2.6	(49) 2.8	(46) 3.0						(15) 2.9	(27) 3.3
3.5	3.3	4.1						4.3	4.1
			% Officers', Directors' Owners' Comp/Sales						
2586112M	3010679M	2447852M	Net Sales ($)	94M	9274M			292240M	2146244M
1945086M	1996571M	1827449M	Total Assets ($)	1232M	6230M			240355M	1579632M

M = $ thousand   MM = $ million
See Pages 9 through 22 for Explanation of Ratios and Data

Current Data Sorted by Assets   **Comparative Historical Data**

0-500M	500M-2MM	2-10MM	10-50MM	50-100MM	100-250MM	Type of Statement	4/1/06-3/31/07 ALL	4/1/07-3/31/08 ALL
	4	31	37	8	8	Unqualified	120	113
1	1	7	3	1		Reviewed	19	20
5	8	8	1			Compiled	26	17
17	11	1			1	Tax Returns	29	39
21	19	36	28	8	8	Other	94	109
	72 (4/1-9/30/10)		200 (10/1/10-3/31/11)					
44	43	83	68	17	17	NUMBER OF STATEMENTS	288	298
%	%	%	%	%	%	ASSETS	%	%
33.1	12.3	21.8	20.3	16.5	8.9	Cash & Equivalents	16.6	15.0
9.3	24.1	26.3	24.8	24.0	23.9	Trade Receivables (net)	26.3	26.8
3.6	3.9	3.8	1.4	3.9	6.2	Inventory	3.0	3.1
5.1	4.7	5.0	4.7	3.8	4.0	All Other Current	3.7	3.9
51.2	45.0	56.9	51.3	48.1	43.0	Total Current	49.6	48.8
31.7	37.4	28.6	33.9	28.9	18.8	Fixed Assets (net)	31.0	34.5
4.3	4.2	3.0	7.1	9.4	24.3	Intangibles (net)	7.3	7.6
12.9	13.4	11.5	7.8	13.5	13.9	All Other Non-Current	12.1	9.1
100.0	100.0	100.0	100.0	100.0	100.0	Total	100.0	100.0
						LIABILITIES		
20.9	11.1	5.8	4.3	1.8	2.5	Notes Payable-Short Term	8.8	8.8
13.9	1.9	4.4	2.1	2.5	4.3	Cur. Mat.-L.T.D.	3.8	5.5
7.1	10.6	7.9	6.4	8.4	8.4	Trade Payables	9.1	9.4
.0	.0	.0	.1	.0	.2	Income Taxes Payable	.6	.4
21.2	11.7	15.4	18.2	18.8	11.6	All Other Current	15.9	15.9
63.2	35.2	33.5	31.1	31.5	26.9	Total Current	38.1	40.0
25.4	28.7	16.9	18.1	26.2	19.0	Long-Term Debt	23.9	23.6
.0	.0	.0	.4	.0	1.4	Deferred Taxes	.2	.2
29.9	6.5	7.0	4.8	6.0	9.5	All Other Non-Current	5.2	4.6
-18.5	29.6	42.5	45.5	36.2	43.2	Net Worth	32.6	31.6
100.0	100.0	100.0	100.0	100.0	100.0	Total Liabilities & Net Worth	100.0	100.0
						INCOME DATA		
100.0	100.0	100.0	100.0	100.0	100.0	Net Sales	100.0	100.0
						Gross Profit		
87.7	86.5	91.7	92.5	94.4	93.9	Operating Expenses	89.7	89.6
12.3	13.5	8.3	7.5	5.6	6.1	Operating Profit	10.3	10.4
1.8	4.1	2.3	1.7	.6	1.2	All Other Expenses (net)	2.1	2.4
10.5	9.4	6.0	5.8	5.0	4.9	Profit Before Taxes	8.2	7.9
						RATIOS		
2.8	2.3	3.9	3.0	2.0	2.2	Current	2.6	2.7
1.0	1.0	1.8	1.8	1.5	1.7		1.5	1.4
.5	.6	1.1	1.1	1.0	1.2		1.0	.8
2.4	1.7	3.8	2.9	1.6	2.0	Quick	2.3	2.3
.8	.9	1.5	1.6	1.1	1.4		1.4	1.2
.4	.5	1.0	1.0	.9	1.0		.8	.7
0 UND	0 UND	11 33.7	21 17.5	24 15.0	33 10.9	Sales/Receivables	8 46.4	11 32.0
0 UND	29 12.7	37 9.8	43 8.6	38 9.6	42 8.7		39 9.3	39 9.3
2 169.0	48 7.7	56 6.6	65 5.6	51 7.1	54 6.8		61 5.9	62 5.9
						Cost of Sales/Inventory		
						Cost of Sales/Payables		
33.5	7.9	4.3	3.5	9.0	6.7	Sales/Working Capital	6.0	6.3
NM	627.3	10.8	8.6	13.1	11.9		14.3	20.2
-25.1	-19.0	58.3	53.2	NM	26.8		-619.1	-63.4
7.9	19.5	22.1	14.6	28.8	27.9	EBIT/Interest	13.0	17.1
(22) 1.9	(34) 7.3	(64) 4.7	(52) 4.6	(15) 4.2	(15) 4.7		(217) 3.9	(233) 4.0
-3.2	3.1	.9	2.1	1.6	3.3		1.1	1.2
			5.2			Net Profit + Depr., Dep., Amort./Cur. Mat. L/T/D	(24) 6.7	5.7
			(13) 2.4				3.1	(34) 1.2
			1.4				1.9	.3
.1	.1	.1	.2	.5	.2	Fixed/Worth	.3	.4
2.1	.8	.6	.6	.9	.8		.8	1.1
-11.7	6.7	2.0	1.7	-4.3	13.8		4.3	10.7
1.5	.9	.4	.5	.9	.6	Debt/Worth	.5	.6
8.5	2.0	1.0	1.1	1.9	2.9		1.7	2.0
-5.8	25.9	4.7	4.3	-12.3	32.3		10.8	31.8
963.9	76.4	59.8	48.6	70.0	141.9	% Profit Before Taxes/Tangible Net Worth	62.0	55.1
(29) 148.8	(34) 20.7	(70) 15.3	(61) 14.7	(12) 19.1	(14) 30.8		(230) 17.9	(229) 21.7
11.7	10.5	1.2	4.4	1.8	.5		3.2	5.3
220.6	27.7	18.5	13.6	16.0	13.6	% Profit Before Taxes/Total Assets	22.3	22.9
12.7	10.3	6.1	4.7	6.9	8.7		7.0	7.6
-10.9	2.6	-.2	.9	1.5	3.5		.8	1.5
278.0	106.2	57.5	24.7	27.3	81.0	Sales/Net Fixed Assets	43.6	36.7
36.4	11.2	15.6	5.7	6.9	17.6		9.8	9.7
13.1	2.9	4.2	2.0	2.9	3.0		3.3	3.3
18.1	4.5	3.5	2.4	2.9	2.5	Sales/Total Assets	3.6	4.0
8.0	2.6	2.2	1.5	1.9	1.5		2.2	2.1
3.4	1.3	1.3	.9	1.4	1.0		1.1	1.2
.3	1.0	1.1	1.1	1.7	.9	% Depr., Dep., Amort./Sales	1.3	.9
(20) 1.0	(32) 2.4	(62) 2.4	(65) 2.6	(13) 2.4	(15) 1.3		(233) 2.5	(243) 2.4
4.0	6.8	4.9	4.3	3.6	3.8		4.6	4.4
2.8	5.3					% Officers', Directors' Owners' Comp/Sales	5.4	4.3
(21) 13.2	(10) 8.1						(48) 11.5	(45) 7.3
26.2	14.9						25.9	24.5
114266M	160601M	1165381M	2976044M	2849779M	6091192M	Net Sales ($)	12975800M	12419348M
9535M	50487M	427279M	1650493M	1193482M	2942013M	Total Assets ($)	6772995M	6109414M

© RMA 2011

M = $ thousand   MM = $ million

See Pages 9 through 22 for Explanation of Ratios and Data

Comparative Historical Data | **Current Data Sorted by Sales**

			Type of Statement						
108	98	88	Unqualified	2	6	6	8	23	43
18	15	13	Reviewed		2		1	4	6
21	30	21	Compiled	3	3	4	5	6	
45	46	30	Tax Returns	14	6	7	1	1	1
124	109	120	Other	10	18	12	19	19	42
4/1/08-3/31/09	4/1/09-3/31/10	4/1/10-3/31/11		72 (4/1-9/30/10)			200 (10/1/10-3/31/11)		
ALL	ALL	ALL		0-1MM	1-3MM	3-5MM	5-10MM	10-25MM	25MM & OVER
316	298	272	**NUMBER OF STATEMENTS**	29	35	29	34	53	92
%	%	%	**ASSETS**	%	%	%	%	%	%
17.6	19.4	20.6	Cash & Equivalents	20.0	19.5	24.4	21.3	19.2	20.6
24.7	22.3	22.5	Trade Receivables (net)	5.9	18.9	20.6	23.3	25.0	28.1
2.8	3.5	3.4	Inventory	4.4	2.9	2.6	4.7	3.8	2.7
4.1	4.1	4.8	All Other Current	3.4	6.8	5.6	5.0	3.7	4.6
49.2	49.3	51.3	Total Current	33.6	48.1	53.2	54.3	51.6	56.1
34.2	33.7	31.2	Fixed Assets (net)	54.4	29.9	31.6	32.0	27.4	26.1
6.8	7.3	6.1	Intangibles (net)	3.6	3.7	4.5	1.1	8.3	9.0
9.9	9.8	11.4	All Other Non-Current	8.3	18.3	10.6	12.5	12.7	8.8
100.0	100.0	100.0	Total	100.0	100.0	100.0	100.0	100.0	100.0
			LIABILITIES						
8.7	7.8	8.3	Notes Payable-Short Term	13.7	11.1	16.7	8.1	6.5	3.9
5.9	4.0	4.8	Cur. Mat.-L.T.D.	14.3	2.6	2.4	2.5	4.6	4.5
8.8	8.5	7.9	Trade Payables	5.7	9.9	7.0	7.9	8.1	8.0
.1	.1	.1	Income Taxes Payable	.0	.0	.0	.0	.0	.2
14.9	13.5	16.4	All Other Current	17.2	14.0	16.3	14.5	12.4	20.1
38.4	34.0	37.5	Total Current	50.9	37.4	42.5	33.0	31.6	36.6
25.8	21.7	21.2	Long-Term Debt	38.5	30.1	22.9	16.6	17.5	15.5
.2	.3	.2	Deferred Taxes	.0	.0	.0	.0	.2	.5
7.5	7.5	10.2	All Other Non-Current	37.2	15.3	8.5	2.6	4.3	6.4
28.1	36.5	31.0	Net Worth	-26.7	17.1	26.1	47.7	46.3	41.0
100.0	100.0	100.0	Total Liabilities & Net Worth	100.0	100.0	100.0	100.0	100.0	100.0
			INCOME DATA						
100.0	100.0	100.0	Net Sales	100.0	100.0	100.0	100.0	100.0	100.0
			Gross Profit						
90.0	90.8	90.7	Operating Expenses	81.4	87.1	91.6	94.3	90.3	93.8
10.0	9.2	9.3	Operating Profit	18.6	12.9	8.4	5.7	9.7	6.2
3.0	2.8	2.2	All Other Expenses (net)	9.9	3.5	.6	1.5	-1.2	.5
7.0	6.5	7.1	Profit Before Taxes	8.7	9.4	7.8	4.3	8.5	5.7
			RATIOS						
2.8	2.9	3.0		3.0	2.3	4.1	5.3	3.8	2.5
1.5	1.6	1.6	Current	1.0	1.1	1.5	1.6	1.9	1.7
.9	1.0	.9		.3	.7	.6	1.1	1.1	1.1
2.6	2.3	2.4		2.1	1.6	2.1	4.2	3.4	2.2
1.4	1.4	1.3	Quick	.6	.9	1.3	1.5	1.5	1.4
.7	.8	.6		.1	.5	.6	1.0	.7	1.0
5 69.3	3 105.3	2 219.0		0 UND	0 UND	0 UND	11 33.6	21 17.4	21 17.7
35 10.6	33 11.0	33 10.9	Sales/Receivables	0 UND	3 121.2	11 31.9	36 10.1	39 9.4	41 9.0
61 5.9	54 6.8	53 6.9		2 236.2	36 10.0	47 7.8	54 6.7	57 6.4	57 6.4
			Cost of Sales/Inventory						
			Cost of Sales/Payables						
6.0	6.1	5.9		11.5	8.5	6.4	3.9	4.6	6.4
16.0	14.4	14.7	Sales/Working Capital	-100.3	43.7	60.1	12.6	13.7	10.1
-107.4	680.1	-143.4		-6.8	-26.9	-54.9	65.2	138.3	40.0
17.6	21.2	18.9		3.6	19.0	24.3	34.3	18.8	24.7
(244) 5.2	(219) 5.2	(202) 4.8	EBIT/Interest	(12) 1.2	(23) 5.1	(22) 6.3	(26) 5.5	(47) 2.1	(72) 6.3
1.0	1.4	1.5		-2.6	2.8	-.1	2.0	-.1	3.2
8.7	10.1	5.9							5.7
(38) 2.1	(29) 2.6	(30) 3.2	Net Profit + Depr., Dep., Amort./Cur. Mat. L/T/D					(23)	3.8
1.2	1.6	1.7							1.6
.3	.2	.2		1.0	.0	.2	.2	.1	.2
1.1	.9	.8	Fixed/Worth	4.9	1.1	.7	.6	.6	.7
5.0	3.3	4.8		-270.9	-56.4	15.3	1.3	2.1	2.5
.6	.6	.7		1.3	1.5	.7	.4	.4	.6
1.8	1.6	1.6	Debt/Worth	5.2	6.4	2.0	.8	1.0	1.4
16.4	6.2	10.6		-4.4	-8.3	NM	3.5	4.9	8.1
69.9	64.6	69.4		279.6	295.1	35.9		86.7	63.7
(248) 20.2	(251) 14.4	(220) 18.3	% Profit Before Taxes/Tangible Net Worth	(20) 51.6	(25) 33.5	(22) 17.7	(31) 14.8	(46) 11.3	(76) 24.1
3.2	2.1	4.3		5.3	11.4	6.3	1.2	-1.2	6.3
25.8	21.5	20.0		36.5	21.8	28.4	18.8	37.0	16.2
7.2	6.4	6.9	% Profit Before Taxes/Total Assets	6.3	8.0	11.4	5.9	4.4	8.8
.0	.3	.6		-5.9	1.2	.0	.1	-1.2	2.7
42.5	42.9	57.0		29.1	348.6	149.4	44.7	63.4	44.7
11.7	10.4	12.9	Sales/Net Fixed Assets	4.7	15.1	29.7	12.1	13.0	13.1
2.8	3.0	3.2		.3	2.9	5.9	3.1	3.0	3.6
4.2	4.1	4.3		5.6	4.2	18.8	3.6	3.8	3.4
2.2	2.1	2.2	Sales/Total Assets	1.8	1.8	4.1	2.2	2.1	2.2
1.1	1.1	1.2		.2	.8	1.6	1.1	1.1	1.5
1.1	1.1	1.0		1.5	2.2	.3	1.0	1.2	1.0
(245) 2.6	(230) 2.3	(207) 2.3	% Depr., Dep., Amort./Sales	(18) 6.9	(22) 4.9	(21) 1.1	(26) 1.6	(42) 2.8	(78) 1.9
4.8	4.1	4.4		27.7	7.4	4.2	4.4	4.3	3.6
5.3	4.2	3.7				3.1			9.5
(50) 9.8	(60) 7.9	(48) 10.3	% Officers', Directors' Owners' Comp/Sales			(11) 15.4		(10)	14.9
25.6	16.7	24.3				27.9			33.9
11332833M	12693628M	13357263M	Net Sales ($)	12342M	68618M	113724M	240955M	793638M	12127986M
5820088M	6726600M	6273289M	Total Assets ($)	16979M	91485M	47185M	156437M	505603M	5455600M

M = $ thousand   MM = $ million
See Pages 9 through 22 for Explanation of Ratios and Data

Current Data Sorted by Assets

Comparative Historical Data

						Type of Statement		
3	7	30	106	82	92	Unqualified	385	317
1	3	8	6	3	2	Reviewed	11	8
5	5	8	8	1	2	Compiled	21	20
6	4	7	1			Tax Returns	14	20
3	11	54	88	44	51	Other	248	237
	305 (4/1-9/30/10)		328 (10/1/10-3/31/11)				4/1/06-3/31/07	4/1/07-3/31/08
0-500M	500M-2MM	2-10MM	10-50MM	50-100MM	100-250MM		ALL	ALL
18	30	107	201	130	147	NUMBER OF STATEMENTS	679	602
%	%	%	%	%	%	ASSETS	%	%
39.3	23.8	14.7	13.0	13.4	13.6	Cash & Equivalents	14.5	11.8
4.5	14.5	27.9	19.1	15.6	12.1	Trade Receivables (net)	17.7	18.3
1.2	1.4	3.2	2.1	2.0	2.0	Inventory	2.2	2.3
6.4	3.6	2.5	3.1	4.3	2.9	All Other Current	3.7	3.4
51.4	43.2	48.3	37.4	35.3	30.6	Total Current	38.0	35.8
31.2	42.7	42.4	49.5	46.3	42.4	Fixed Assets (net)	43.1	44.0
8.1	5.2	3.6	2.0	1.3	4.8	Intangibles (net)	2.0	2.4
9.3	8.9	5.6	11.1	17.1	22.2	All Other Non-Current	16.8	17.8
100.0	100.0	100.0	100.0	100.0	100.0	Total	100.0	100.0
						LIABILITIES		
45.5	9.1	3.8	2.3	1.8	1.2	Notes Payable-Short Term	2.1	2.5
2.5	5.4	5.4	3.9	3.0	2.3	Cur. Mat.-L.T.D.	3.3	3.4
7.8	2.9	10.7	6.8	6.6	4.8	Trade Payables	6.3	7.4
.2	.6	.1	.1	.1	.0	Income Taxes Payable	.1	.1
29.7	12.2	10.9	12.2	9.9	8.9	All Other Current	11.2	10.4
85.8	30.2	30.9	25.2	21.5	17.1	Total Current	23.1	23.8
28.2	33.1	29.1	31.3	29.1	25.9	Long-Term Debt	28.5	27.9
.0	.1	.1	.1	.0	.1	Deferred Taxes	.1	.1
.9	4.2	6.1	4.2	5.3	7.6	All Other Non-Current	4.8	4.7
-14.7	32.4	33.8	39.2	44.0	49.2	Net Worth	43.5	43.6
100.0	100.0	100.0	100.0	100.0	100.0	Total Liabilties & Net Worth	100.0	100.0
						INCOME DATA		
100.0	100.0	100.0	100.0	100.0	100.0	Net Sales	100.0	100.0
						Gross Profit		
86.9	82.4	85.4	92.2	95.9	95.1	Operating Expenses	94.0	94.1
13.1	17.6	14.6	7.8	4.1	4.9	Operating Profit	6.0	5.9
.1	4.0	3.1	1.5	.7	.3	All Other Expenses (net)	.5	.5
13.0	13.6	11.4	6.3	3.3	4.6	Profit Before Taxes	5.5	5.4
						RATIOS		
5.4	7.5	2.9	2.7	2.9	2.7		2.9	2.7
1.2	2.3	1.7	1.7	1.9	2.0	Current	1.9	1.8
.5	.4	1.1	1.2	1.2	1.3		1.2	1.2
5.3	6.8	2.6	2.3	2.4	2.2		2.4	2.3
.8	2.1	1.6	1.5	1.6	1.7	Quick	1.6 (601)	1.5
.3	.3	.9	1.0	1.0	1.0		1.0	1.0
0 UND	0 UND	30 12.1	36 10.1	38 9.7	36 10.0		37 10.0	37 10.0
0 UND	0 UND	43 8.6	48 7.7	45 8.1	43 8.4	Sales/Receivables	49 7.4	48 7.5
0 UND	42 8.7	58 6.3	59 6.1	54 6.8	50 7.2		60 6.0	61 6.0
						Cost of Sales/Inventory		
						Cost of Sales/Payables		
18.1	6.7	5.8	4.8	4.6	4.7		4.9	5.2
NM	25.9	11.4	9.5	8.3	7.5	Sales/Working Capital	8.3	9.3
-19.9	-9.3	54.5	26.0	29.8	19.0		27.1	40.1
64.6	35.3	29.4	10.4	6.8	8.6		8.3	8.9
(14) 15.6	(22) 4.1	(92) 7.4	(180) 3.3	(121) 2.8	(140) 3.5	EBIT/Interest	(600) 3.7	(542) 3.5
4.8	1.0	2.3	1.3	1.3	.9		1.3	1.1
			19.0		2.8		8.0	6.7
		(10) 2.6		(11) 1.6		Net Profit + Depr., Dep., Amort./Cur. Mat. L/T/D	(30) 4.0	(38) 3.6
			1.3		.3		1.8	1.6
.2	.4	.6	.7	.7	.6		.6	.6
2.3	1.0	.9	1.1	1.0	.8	Fixed/Worth	.9	.9
-.5	NM	2.9	2.8	1.9	1.4		1.6	1.9
.6	.4	.6	.6	.6	.5		.5	.5
7.4	1.5	1.1	1.2	1.1	1.0	Debt/Worth	1.0	1.0
-2.3	-287.2	7.5	3.8	2.6	1.8		2.5	3.1
679.2	106.8	90.7	38.1	12.3	10.9		18.0	21.5
(10) 156.2	(22) 26.2	(87) 28.3	(181) 8.5	(119) 5.3	(132) 6.0	% Profit Before Taxes/Tangible Net Worth	(617) 8.1	(542) 9.0
11.8	-5.4	7.8	2.1	1.2	.4		2.1	2.5
246.7	57.2	32.1	11.3	6.6	6.1		8.6	8.3
50.4	6.5	9.5	4.0	3.0	3.1	% Profit Before Taxes/Total Assets	4.1	4.1
3.5	-.5	2.9	.4	.3	.1		.4	.2
UND	38.3	12.4	4.7	3.7	3.2		5.2	5.3
41.9	11.6	5.2	2.6	2.5	2.2	Sales/Net Fixed Assets	2.7	2.6
9.5	1.6	2.9	1.5	1.7	1.5		1.8	1.8
19.2	5.0	3.0	1.7	1.6	1.2		1.8	1.9
10.9	1.9	2.0	1.3	1.1	.9	Sales/Total Assets	1.2	1.2
3.8	.7	1.3	.9	.8	.7		.9	.8
.6	1.4	2.1	2.8	3.8	4.0		3.2	3.1
(12) 2.7	(23) 5.5	(100) 3.3	(197) 4.3	(128) 4.8	(98) 5.2	% Depr., Dep., Amort./Sales	(582) 4.4	(530) 4.6
4.8	10.0	5.5	6.4	6.2	6.7		5.8	6.1
9.6		5.1	1.7	6.8	10.2		7.0	6.7
(10) 20.5	(12)	21.6	(13) 9.7	(13) 9.0	(10) 19.7	% Officers', Directors' Owners' Comp/Sales	(71) 14.4	(69) 17.6
40.6		40.5	39.5	18.4	40.1		37.8	37.4
52340M	127950M	1256041M	7602408M	11196065M	23680868M	Net Sales ($)	48064321M	44328410M
4428M	32817M	574595M	5216228M	9149255M	23833228M	Total Assets ($)	43606580M	39495844M

M = $ thousand   MM = $ million
See Pages 9 through 22 for Explanation of Ratios and Data

Comparative Historical Data | Current Data Sorted by Sales

4/1/08-3/31/09 ALL	4/1/09-3/31/10 ALL	4/1/10-3/31/11 ALL	Type of Statement	0-1MM	1-3MM	3-5MM	5-10MM	10-25MM	25MM & OVER
321	284	320	Unqualified	9	6	3	13	55	234
10	13	23	Reviewed		3	1	3	8	8
22	21	21	Compiled	3	1	4	5	4	4
22	13	18	Tax Returns	5	4	3	3	2	1
233	237	251	Other	4	18	12	11	51	155
					305 (4/1-9/30/10)			328 (10/1/10-3/31/11)	
608	**568**	**633**	**NUMBER OF STATEMENTS**	21	32	23	35	120	402
%	%	%	**ASSETS**	%	%	%	%	%	%
11.9	14.4	14.8	Cash & Equivalents	6.1	19.4	22.7	26.3	14.1	13.6
17.0	17.6	17.6	Trade Receivables (net)	3.0	11.3	16.8	19.2	24.2	16.8
2.1	2.2	2.2	Inventory	.5	.9	1.2	3.7	2.6	2.2
3.7	3.5	3.3	All Other Current	3.4	3.4	.7	2.2	2.7	3.7
34.7	37.6	37.9	Total Current	13.1	35.0	41.5	51.4	43.7	36.3
46.2	44.7	45.1	Fixed Assets (net)	71.7	49.3	40.3	38.7	45.9	44.0
2.6	2.6	3.1	Intangibles (net)	1.5	8.1	5.7	3.7	1.7	3.0
16.5	15.1	13.8	All Other Non-Current	13.7	7.6	12.4	6.2	8.7	16.6
100.0	100.0	100.0	Total	100.0	100.0	100.0	100.0	100.0	100.0
			LIABILITIES						
2.6	3.1	3.7	Notes Payable-Short Term	34.9	9.2	3.5	1.0	3.3	2.0
3.4	3.9	3.6	Cur. Mat.-L.T.D.	4.2	8.2	3.7	2.7	4.8	3.0
5.5	6.0	6.8	Trade Payables	2.5	2.5	9.8	7.2	9.1	6.5
.1	.0	.1	Income Taxes Payable	.0	.0	.7	.0	.1	.1
10.6	11.7	11.3	All Other Current	12.2	12.3	3.7	12.0	11.3	11.5
22.2	24.7	25.5	Total Current	53.8	32.3	21.4	22.9	28.5	23.1
30.2	29.3	29.2	Long-Term Debt	54.1	45.0	34.6	26.4	27.2	27.2
.0	.1	.1	Deferred Taxes	.0	.1	.0	.1	.0	.1
5.4	5.1	5.5	All Other Non-Current	1.2	1.0	3.1	1.4	5.9	6.4
42.1	40.8	39.7	Net Worth	-8.9	21.6	40.9	49.2	38.4	43.3
100.0	100.0	100.0	Total Liabilties & Net Worth	100.0	100.0	100.0	100.0	100.0	100.0
			INCOME DATA						
100.0	100.0	100.0	Net Sales	100.0	100.0	100.0	100.0	100.0	100.0
			Gross Profit						
94.2	93.3	91.9	Operating Expenses	68.2	72.2	80.2	91.1	94.4	94.7
5.8	6.7	8.1	Operating Profit	31.8	27.8	19.8	8.9	5.6	5.3
2.0	1.5	1.4	All Other Expenses (net)	16.9	10.4	4.2	-1.4	-.1	.4
3.8	5.2	6.7	Profit Before Taxes	14.9	17.4	15.7	10.3	5.6	4.9
			RATIOS						
2.6	3.0	2.8	Current	1.5	4.5	6.4	4.7	2.8	2.7
1.8	1.9	1.8		.2	1.2	2.7	2.4	1.8	1.9
1.3	1.3	1.2		.2	.5	1.1	1.7	1.2	1.2
2.3	2.4	2.5	Quick	1.1	4.3	6.4	3.6	2.6	2.3
1.5	1.6	1.5		.2	1.2	2.7	2.1	1.5	1.5
1.0	1.1	.9		.1	.4	.9	1.4	1.0	1.0
37 9.8	36 10.2	34 10.8	Sales/Receivables	0 UND	0 UND	0 UND	18 20.5	39 9.4	37 9.9
48 7.5	45 8.1	44 8.4		0 UND	0 UND	40 9.1	42 8.8	48 7.7	45 8.2
60 6.1	55 6.7	55 6.7		27 13.4	40 9.1	58 6.3	67 5.5	64 5.7	53 6.9
			Cost of Sales/Inventory						
			Cost of Sales/Payables						
5.3	4.7	5.0	Sales/Working Capital	28.7	6.0	3.4	4.9	4.9	5.0
9.4	8.6	9.5		-4.7	42.0	10.3	7.5	9.4	9.1
24.9	24.0	37.4		-1.0	-11.4	79.7	19.8	33.3	27.6
6.5	8.3	11.5	EBIT/Interest	10.1	32.0	34.6	162.7	14.9	8.6
(549) 2.1	(517) 2.9	(569) 3.6		(13) 4.9	(21) 6.6	(16) 12.1	(30) 9.9	(109) 4.3	(380) 3.2
-.4	.9	1.4		1.7	1.7	1.4	2.3	1.2	1.3
9.2	5.6	5.2	Net Profit + Depr., Dep., Amort./Cur. Mat. L/T/D						4.3
(31) 4.8	(23) 2.9	(36) 2.8						(30)	2.6
1.8	1.6	.9							.6
.7	.7	.6	Fixed/Worth	1.6	.4	.5	.4	.6	.6
1.0	1.0	1.0		2.9	1.7	1.3	.7	1.0	1.0
1.9	2.0	2.1		NM	NM	6.1	1.6	2.8	1.6
.6	.6	.5	Debt/Worth	1.4	.8	.3	.3	.5	.6
1.1	1.1	1.1		3.6	3.1	1.1	.8	1.1	1.1
2.7	2.9	3.4		-208.5	-6.7	21.4	1.9	4.1	2.5
15.3	17.2	29.2	% Profit Before Taxes/Tangible Net Worth	40.9	48.0	266.8	62.5	42.8	16.4
(543) 4.8	(500) 6.6	(551) 8.1		(15) 15.8	(22) 28.9	(18) 39.2	(32) 24.1	(102) 9.0	(362) 7.0
-4.2	.0	1.6		5.9	11.5	5.9	7.2	.6	1.3
7.2	9.0	10.8	% Profit Before Taxes/Total Assets	6.7	38.3	72.1	37.2	17.3	7.7
2.2	3.1	4.3		3.5	6.5	19.0	6.2	5.1	3.5
-2.2	-.5	.5		1.4	1.7	.4	2.7	.3	.4
4.5	4.7	5.3	Sales/Net Fixed Assets	2.8	19.8	31.4	7.9	8.8	4.4
2.4	2.6	2.8		.5	2.8	3.5	5.0	3.1	2.7
1.7	1.8	1.8		.1	.2	1.7	2.8	1.7	1.9
1.7	1.7	1.8	Sales/Total Assets	.9	2.9	2.9	3.0	2.6	1.6
1.1	1.2	1.2		.3	1.2	1.3	1.7	1.4	1.2
.8	.8	.8		.1	.2	.9	1.3	.9	.9
3.2	3.3	2.9	% Depr., Dep., Amort./Sales	6.6	4.2	1.9	1.9	2.4	3.1
(540) 4.6	(481) 4.7	(558) 4.5		(19) 13.0	(24) 13.6	(21) 5.2	(30) 3.9	(115) 3.8	(349) 4.5
6.1	6.1	6.3		24.7	25.4	10.9	4.9	5.8	5.9
5.1	6.2	7.9	% Officers', Directors' Owners' Comp/Sales					2.0	7.8
(64) 13.5	(66) 13.8	(65) 15.3						(12) 7.1	(34) 10.7
37.0	36.5	39.8						42.4	39.1
45792607M	39889287M	43915672M	Net Sales ($)	10614M	58160M	90083M	256382M	2071858M	41428575M
42589129M	36954669M	38810551M	Total Assets ($)	52940M	160584M	229985M	190091M	1841992M	36334959M

M = $ thousand   MM = $ million
See Pages 9 through 22 for Explanation of Ratios and Data

Current Data Sorted by Assets   Comparative Historical Data

						Type of Statement		
						Unqualified	229	229
						Reviewed	3	1
						Compiled	3	2
						Tax Returns	1	1
4	4	10	57	61	95	Other	94	113
	208 (4/1-9/30/10)		157 (10/1/10-3/31/11)				4/1/06-3/31/07	4/1/07-3/31/08
1	1	12	35	42	43		ALL	ALL
0-500M	500M-2MM	2-10MM	10-50MM	50-100MM	100-250MM	NUMBER OF STATEMENTS	330	346
5	5	22	92	103	138			
%	%	%	%	%	%	ASSETS	%	%
		12.9	13.6	13.7	12.1	Cash & Equivalents	11.1	11.2
		23.9	16.9	14.6	12.8	Trade Receivables (net)	15.9	15.6
		4.3	2.2	2.0	1.7	Inventory	1.9	1.8
		4.8	4.4	3.5	3.1	All Other Current	3.4	2.8
		46.0	37.0	33.7	29.7	Total Current	32.3	31.5
		43.8	48.4	45.8	46.3	Fixed Assets (net)	44.5	43.6
		.7	.5	.8	1.0	Intangibles (net)	.9	.9
		9.5	14.1	19.7	23.0	All Other Non-Current	22.4	23.9
		100.0	100.0	100.0	100.0	Total	100.0	100.0
						LIABILITIES		
		2.6	.9	.6	.6	Notes Payable-Short Term	1.0	.8
		3.7	2.7	2.6	1.7	Cur. Mat.-L.T.D.	2.6	2.4
		17.6	6.4	6.2	5.6	Trade Payables	6.2	6.6
		.0	.0	.0	.0	Income Taxes Payable	.0	.0
		25.7	9.9	10.2	9.9	All Other Current	9.8	9.4
		49.6	19.9	19.6	17.8	Total Current	19.6	19.1
		27.6	27.6	27.8	27.7	Long-Term Debt	28.1	27.1
		.0	.0	.0	.1	Deferred Taxes	.0	.0
		3.5	3.6	9.0	8.6	All Other Non-Current	4.0	4.5
		19.2	48.9	43.7	45.8	Net Worth	48.2	49.3
		100.0	100.0	100.0	100.0	Total Liabilities & Net Worth	100.0	100.0
						INCOME DATA		
		100.0	100.0	100.0	100.0	Net Sales	100.0	100.0
						Gross Profit		
		97.1	99.0	98.0	96.3	Operating Expenses	96.3	96.7
		2.9	1.0	2.0	3.7	Operating Profit	3.7	3.3
		.5	.9	.5	.8	All Other Expenses (net)	.4	-.1
		2.5	.1	1.5	2.8	Profit Before Taxes	3.3	3.5
						RATIOS		
		2.1	3.1	2.8	2.7	Current	2.6	2.5
		1.4	2.0	1.8	1.8		1.9	1.8
		.8	1.2	1.2	1.3		1.3	1.3
		1.9	2.5	2.4	2.4	Quick	2.2	2.2
		1.1	1.6	1.5	1.5		1.5	1.6
		.8	1.0	1.0	.9		1.0	1.0
		28 13.2	40 9.1	37 9.8	38 9.6	Sales/Receivables	42 8.7	42 8.8
		45 8.1	47 7.8	46 8.0	45 8.1		50 7.4	50 7.3
		56 6.5	56 6.6	55 6.7	51 7.2		58 6.3	58 6.2
						Cost of Sales/Inventory		
						Cost of Sales/Payables		
		6.8	3.8	4.6	4.5	Sales/Working Capital	5.1	5.0
		18.0	7.8	8.9	9.2		8.7	8.3
		-42.8	24.6	27.4	21.2		21.5	25.6
		6.4	4.3	4.4	5.8	EBIT/Interest	7.1	6.3
		(17) 3.1	(85) 2.0	(98) 1.7	(135) 2.6		(312) 3.3	(329) 3.0
		-.6	-.1	.6	1.4		1.1	1.2
						Net Profit + Depr., Dep., Amort./Cur. Mat. L/T/D		
		.6	.7	.8	.7	Fixed/Worth	.6	.6
		.9	.9	1.1	1.0		.9	.9
		1.7	1.6	1.5	1.4		1.3	1.2
		.4	.5	.7	.6	Debt/Worth	.5	.6
		1.1	.9	1.3	1.0		.9	.9
		4.1	1.7	2.5	1.9		1.6	1.5
		15.1	8.9	8.3	10.2	% Profit Before Taxes/Tangible Net Worth	11.0	10.4
		(18) 7.3	(88) 3.1	(99) 4.0	(131) 5.0		(309) 6.2	(331) 6.4
		-21.6	-3.5	-2.0	1.3		.9	.6
		9.7	4.2	3.9	5.2	% Profit Before Taxes/Total Assets	5.9	5.5
		4.3	1.4	1.7	2.4		3.2	2.7
		-6.2	-1.9	-.9	.6		.1	.1
		6.4	3.9	3.5	2.8	Sales/Net Fixed Assets	3.4	3.4
		4.1	2.7	2.4	2.2		2.4	2.4
		3.0	1.8	2.0	1.6		1.9	1.9
		2.8	1.5	1.5	1.3	Sales/Total Assets	1.4	1.4
		1.9	1.3	1.1	.9		1.1	1.1
		1.6	.9	.9	.8		.8	.8
		1.8	3.8	3.9	4.3	% Depr., Dep., Amort./Sales	3.8	3.8
		(21) 3.1	4.6	(102) 4.9	(100) 5.2		(297) 4.9	(298) 4.6
		4.7	6.5	6.0	6.1		5.8	5.7
						% Officers', Directors' Owners' Comp/Sales	1.6	2.0
							(11) 20.3	(16) 10.6
							40.8	17.2
999M	20694M	271397M	3290649M	8950393M	23674893M	Net Sales ($)	30914081M	34155607M
924M	7416M	141272M	2566895M	7544108M	22755494M	Total Assets ($)	29191942M	33396848M

M = $ thousand   MM = $ million

See Pages 9 through 22 for Explanation of Ratios and Data

Comparative Historical Data | | | | ## Current Data Sorted by Sales

Hist 1	Hist 2	Hist 3	Type of Statement	0-1MM	1-3MM	3-5MM	5-10MM	10-25MM	25MM & OVER
245	207	231	Unqualified	5		2	8	19	197
			Reviewed						
1			Compiled						
			Tax Returns						
134	116	134	Other	2	1	1	6	18	106
4/1/08-3/31/09 ALL	4/1/09-3/31/10 ALL	4/1/10-3/31/11 ALL		208 (4/1-9/30/10)			157 (10/1/10-3/31/11)		
380	323	365	**NUMBER OF STATEMENTS**	7	1	3	14	37	303
%	%	%	**ASSETS**	%	%	%	%	%	%
11.5	11.0	12.9	Cash & Equivalents				19.5	14.2	12.7
15.2	14.7	15.1	Trade Receivables (net)				19.4	18.6	14.6
1.8	2.1	2.0	Inventory				3.9	2.5	1.9
3.0	2.9	3.7	All Other Current				6.9	4.1	3.5
31.5	30.7	33.7	Total Current				49.7	39.4	32.8
46.2	47.1	46.5	Fixed Assets (net)				40.5	50.4	46.2
.7	.8	.8	Intangibles (net)				.1	.9	.8
21.5	21.4	19.0	All Other Non-Current				9.6	9.3	20.2
100.0	100.0	100.0	Total				100.0	100.0	100.0
			LIABILITIES						
.7	.5	.8	Notes Payable-Short Term				2.4	1.4	.7
2.1	2.2	2.4	Cur. Mat.-L.T.D.				1.7	2.6	2.3
6.0	5.9	6.7	Trade Payables				8.9	10.7	6.3
.0	.0	.0	Income Taxes Payable				.0	.0	.0
10.6	9.6	11.1	All Other Current				22.7	14.3	10.2
19.4	18.2	21.0	Total Current				35.6	28.9	19.4
27.6	26.2	28.7	Long-Term Debt				16.8	29.7	27.3
.0	.0	.0	Deferred Taxes				.0	.0	.0
6.9	6.1	7.1	All Other Non-Current				.7	4.1	7.8
46.2	49.5	43.2	Net Worth				46.9	37.3	45.5
100.0	100.0	100.0	Total Liabilities & Net Worth				100.0	100.0	100.0
			INCOME DATA						
100.0	100.0	100.0	Net Sales				100.0	100.0	100.0
			Gross Profit						
97.5	97.5	97.3	Operating Expenses				97.6	100.7	97.4
2.5	2.5	2.7	Operating Profit				2.4	-.7	2.6
2.1	.8	.8	All Other Expenses (net)				.0	.8	.6
.4	1.6	1.8	Profit Before Taxes				2.4	-1.5	2.0
			RATIOS						
2.5	2.5	2.8					3.8	3.2	2.8
1.7	1.8	1.8	Current				1.6	2.0	1.8
1.3	1.3	1.2					1.1	1.1	1.3
2.3	2.1	2.3					2.8	2.5	2.3
1.5	1.5	1.5	Quick				1.1	1.6	1.5
1.0	1.0	.9					.8	.9	1.0
39 9.3	38 9.6	38 9.6					26 14.0	43 8.5	38 9.6
49 7.5	46 7.9	46 8.0	Sales/Receivables				44 8.3	49 7.4	46 8.0
57 6.4	54 6.7	54 6.8					46 7.9	64 5.7	53 6.9
			Cost of Sales/Inventory						
			Cost of Sales/Payables						
5.1	5.5	4.6					4.7	3.7	4.6
9.6	9.1	9.0	Sales/Working Capital				10.0	7.5	8.9
24.4	21.2	29.1					213.1	36.4	25.8
4.4	4.9	5.1						4.6	5.1
(354) 1.8	(308) 2.6	(340) 2.5	EBIT/Interest			(32)		1.6 (292)	2.5
-.5	.4	.7						-1.9	.9
			Net Profit + Depr., Dep., Amort./Cur. Mat. L/T/D						
.7	.7	.7					.5	.7	.7
1.0	1.0	1.0	Fixed/Worth				.7	1.1	1.0
1.5	1.4	1.5					1.1	1.7	1.5
.6	.6	.6					.4	.6	.6
1.1	.9	1.1	Debt/Worth				.6	1.2	1.1
1.9	1.7	2.0					2.3	2.5	1.9
9.0	9.2	9.6					11.2	11.1	9.6
(365) 2.4	(317) 3.6	(344) 4.4	% Profit Before Taxes/Tangible Net Worth		(13)		5.3 (33)	1.5 (290)	4.5
-6.6	-.9	-1.2					-7.3	-16.6	-1.0
4.3	4.8	4.6					6.1	5.7	4.3
1.0	1.8	2.1	% Profit Before Taxes/Total Assets				3.3	.9	2.1
-3.0	-.6	-.6					-3.9	-7.9	-.4
3.0	3.1	3.4					17.0	4.4	3.3
2.3	2.3	2.4	Sales/Net Fixed Assets				3.2	2.3	2.4
1.8	1.7	1.8					1.8	1.5	1.8
1.3	1.4	1.5					2.9	1.7	1.4
1.0	1.0	1.1	Sales/Total Assets				2.0	1.1	1.1
.8	.8	.9					.8	.9	.9
3.7	4.0	3.8					1.0	3.5	3.9
(322) 4.9	(274) 5.0	(324) 4.8	% Depr., Dep., Amort./Sales				2.0 (36)	4.9 (264)	4.8
5.9	6.0	6.0					5.2	7.5	5.8
4.0	10.1								
(17) 11.2	(10) 21.1		% Officers', Directors', Owners' Comp/Sales						
17.7	41.6								
40264786M	33447591M	36209025M	Net Sales ($)	2613M	1074M	11832M	116796M	653562M	35423148M
38525970M	31586656M	33016109M	Total Assets ($)	2909M	25688M	15936M	93194M	594530M	32283852M

© RMA 2011

M = $ thousand   MM = $ million
See Pages 9 through 22 for Explanation of Ratios and Data

Current Data Sorted by Assets | Comparative Historical Data

						Type of Statement		
3	1	14	28	3		Unqualified	54	57
8		1	2			Reviewed		1
3						Compiled	4	2
5	2	2				Tax Returns	3	
1	2	9	8		2	Other	23	25
	49 (4/1-9/30/10)		45 (10/1/10-3/31/11)				4/1/06-3/31/07	4/1/07-3/31/08
0-500M	500M-2MM	2-10MM	10-50MM	50-100MM	100-250MM		ALL	ALL
20	5	26	38	3	2	NUMBER OF STATEMENTS	84	85
%	%	%	%	%	%	ASSETS	%	%
22.5		21.8	19.6			Cash & Equivalents	20.0	18.6
6.0		21.9	14.0			Trade Receivables (net)	17.1	19.0
.0		.2	.4			Inventory	.4	.5
4.6		3.5	3.1			All Other Current	3.7	4.9
33.2		47.5	37.0			Total Current	41.2	43.0
27.2		42.7	46.8			Fixed Assets (net)	46.1	43.2
5.6		1.4	4.3			Intangibles (net)	2.2	3.1
33.9		8.5	11.9			All Other Non-Current	10.4	10.8
100.0		100.0	100.0			Total	100.0	100.0
						LIABILITIES		
33.6		3.1	1.2			Notes Payable-Short Term	3.9	3.3
2.5		1.9	2.8			Cur. Mat.-L.T.D.	2.7	2.3
4.0		5.4	6.0			Trade Payables	6.3	5.7
.0		.4	.0			Income Taxes Payable	.1	.3
62.6		21.3	10.1			All Other Current	11.0	14.2
102.7		32.1	20.0			Total Current	24.0	25.8
14.9		24.0	22.8			Long-Term Debt	23.7	21.5
.0		.0	.0			Deferred Taxes	.0	.0
13.9		7.4	1.2			All Other Non-Current	2.5	3.6
-31.6		36.5	55.9			Net Worth	49.7	49.1
100.0		100.0	100.0			Total Liabilities & Net Worth	100.0	100.0
						INCOME DATA		
100.0		100.0	100.0			Net Sales	100.0	100.0
						Gross Profit		
97.8		85.3	92.7			Operating Expenses	93.1	95.9
2.2		14.7	7.3			Operating Profit	6.9	4.1
-1.4		2.7	2.3			All Other Expenses (net)	1.8	.5
3.6		12.1	4.9			Profit Before Taxes	5.1	3.7
						RATIOS		
4.2		3.7	3.0			Current	3.5	2.8
.3		1.8	2.1				1.8	1.9
.1		.8	1.4				1.1	1.1
3.9		3.6	2.7			Quick	3.0	2.7
.2		1.5	1.8				1.6	1.6
.1		.7	1.0				.9	1.0
0 UND		8 45.9	16 22.6			Sales/Receivables	17 21.9	17 20.9
0 UND		32 11.3	31 11.9				40 9.2	37 9.9
12 29.8		39 9.3	45 8.1				52 7.0	59 6.2
						Cost of Sales/Inventory		
						Cost of Sales/Payables		
11.1		4.6	4.2			Sales/Working Capital	4.9	4.7
-18.0		13.1	7.9				10.7	10.5
-4.2		-67.1	23.5				68.3	49.0
53.2		19.8	10.7			EBIT/Interest	6.3	12.2
(14) 7.2		(20) 6.5	(35) 6.7				(68) 3.4	(68) 3.0
-1.0		2.7	1.6				.2	1.4
						Net Profit + Depr., Dep., Amort./Cur. Mat. L/T/D		
.2		.5	.7			Fixed/Worth	.5	.5
1.5		1.2	1.0				.9	.9
-.9		12.4	1.3				1.6	1.4
1.0		.6	.5			Debt/Worth	.4	.5
3.2		1.1	.9				1.0	.9
-2.9		21.1	1.6				2.8	2.2
75.9		40.9	20.0			% Profit Before Taxes/Tangible Net Worth	16.6	22.4
(12) 27.1		(22) 18.9	8.2				(78) 6.1	(79) 6.6
-3.2		3.7	.7				-.6	1.6
47.3		33.3	11.1			% Profit Before Taxes/Total Assets	10.6	11.8
21.8		11.2	4.2				3.4	3.2
-1.4		3.6	.3				-.6	.6
114.7		21.9	4.4			Sales/Net Fixed Assets	5.9	7.6
23.4		4.7	3.2				3.1	3.3
8.8		2.7	2.1				2.0	1.9
9.4		3.5	1.9			Sales/Total Assets	2.2	2.5
4.5		2.3	1.4				1.4	1.5
2.1		1.4	1.0				1.0	1.1
.5		.9	1.8			% Depr., Dep., Amort./Sales	1.7	1.5
(15) .9		(22) 1.7	2.7				(75) 2.5	(81) 2.7
1.8		2.6	4.2				3.6	3.7
						% Officers', Directors' Owners' Comp/Sales	8.4	
							(10) 15.3	
							33.8	
30740M	14343M	369382M	1315164M	384968M	586759M	Net Sales ($)	4562677M	2036852M
3771M	5282M	131988M	888604M	183203M	365693M	Total Assets ($)	1392979M	1526606M

M = $ thousand   MM = $ million
See Pages 9 through 22 for Explanation of Ratios and Data

Comparative Historical Data / Current Data Sorted by Sales

			Type of Statement						
56	46	49	Unqualified	3	2	2	3	17	22
3	5	11	Reviewed	8					3
4	2	3	Compiled		2		1		
1	5	9	Tax Returns	2		1	4		
28	27	22	Other	3	2	3	2	3	9
4/1/08- 3/31/09 ALL	4/1/09- 3/31/10 ALL	4/1/10- 3/31/11 ALL		0-1MM	49 (4/1-9/30/10) 1-3MM	3-5MM	5-10MM	45 (10/1/10-3/31/11) 10-25MM	25MM & OVER
92	85	94	**NUMBER OF STATEMENTS**	16	8	6	10	20	34
%	%	%	**ASSETS**	%	%	%	%	%	%
19.1	17.9	21.1	Cash & Equivalents	20.4			30.2	20.5	19.7
18.0	18.9	14.9	Trade Receivables (net)	7.6			2.8	23.0	20.0
.6	.5	.3	Inventory	.0			.1	.2	.7
3.5	4.0	3.5	All Other Current	2.1			4.7	3.0	3.2
41.2	41.3	39.8	Total Current	30.1			37.8	46.6	43.7
42.9	42.6	40.3	Fixed Assets (net)	34.5			46.6	38.4	39.5
4.7	5.3	4.2	Intangibles (net)	.4			5.3	3.4	2.7
11.3	10.8	15.8	All Other Non-Current	34.7			10.3	11.6	14.1
100.0	100.0	100.0	Total	100.0			100.0	100.0	100.0
			LIABILITIES						
3.8	12.6	8.6	Notes Payable-Short Term	2.3			3.2	3.7	1.0
2.4	3.7	2.5	Cur. Mat.-L.T.D.	1.2			1.2	1.7	3.4
5.9	8.6	5.9	Trade Payables	5.0			1.2	7.4	8.2
.1	.1	.1	Income Taxes Payable	.0			.0	.0	.3
13.3	13.5	25.5	All Other Current	69.7			12.2	13.0	16.9
25.6	38.4	42.7	Total Current	78.1			17.8	25.8	29.8
27.8	27.7	22.9	Long-Term Debt	21.5			27.1	18.8	21.0
.1	.0	.0	Deferred Taxes	.0			.0	.0	.1
9.4	4.5	7.0	All Other Non-Current	11.7			10.3	9.4	5.2
37.1	29.4	27.3	Net Worth	-11.2			44.7	45.9	44.0
100.0	100.0	100.0	Total Liabilites & Net Worth	100.0			100.0	100.0	100.0
			INCOME DATA						
100.0	100.0	100.0	Net Sales	100.0			100.0	100.0	100.0
			Gross Profit						
95.2	93.6	91.6	Operating Expenses	93.0			85.5	95.4	93.0
4.8	6.4	8.4	Operating Profit	7.0			14.5	4.6	7.0
3.2	2.4	1.6	All Other Expenses (net)	2.0			1.1	-.3	.8
1.6	4.0	6.8	Profit Before Taxes	5.0			13.3	4.9	6.2
			RATIOS						
3.1	2.8	3.0		5.2			7.9	3.6	2.8
2.0	1.8	1.8	Current	1.2			1.8	2.3	1.9
1.2	1.0	.7		.1			.5	1.2	1.0
2.8	2.5	2.8		4.2			7.1	3.3	2.6
1.7	1.6	1.6	Quick	1.2			1.3	2.2	1.7
.9	.8	.6		.1			.5	.9	.9
16 23.2	18 20.0	7 48.8		0 UND			0 UND	24 15.2	22 16.8
39 9.3	37 9.8	28 13.0	Sales/Receivables	9 40.3			0 UND	40 9.1	32 11.3
54 6.7	55 6.7	41 9.0		16 22.9			17 21.6	44 8.2	48 7.6
			Cost of Sales/Inventory						
			Cost of Sales/Payables						
5.1	4.6	5.7		4.8			7.0	4.9	5.8
8.9	11.4	13.0	Sales/Working Capital	NM			19.2	6.9	10.5
39.5	-365.2	-42.0		-3.9			-83.6	48.0	NM
10.5	8.8	14.6						20.0	11.5
(76) 2.0	(71) 3.1	(77) 6.4	EBIT/Interest				(16) 5.8	(32) 7.9	
-.9	.4	1.6						1.2	3.3
	16.2	39.9							
	(10) 3.1	(11) 16.3	Net Profit + Depr., Dep., Amort./Cur. Mat. L/T/D						
	.2	2.8							
.6	.7	.5		.2			.6	.4	.6
1.0	1.1	1.0	Fixed/Worth	1.7			1.1	.8	1.0
2.4	3.1	2.0		NM			14.1	1.4	1.3
.5	.6	.6		.9			.7	.4	.6
1.0	1.3	1.1	Debt/Worth	2.0			1.1	.9	.9
3.7	6.5	4.7		-3.9			22.2	2.0	2.0
18.4	28.3	43.5		41.7				23.0	40.6
(79) 6.0	(68) 6.6	(78) 11.0	% Profit Before Taxes/Tangible Net Worth	(11) 7.1				(18) 6.2	(30) 10.8
-5.9	-1.7	1.4		-5.8				1.5	3.1
9.6	12.4	25.9		31.7			130.4	13.3	20.6
2.5	4.1	7.5	% Profit Before Taxes/Total Assets	5.3			44.6	5.5	6.6
-2.6	-1.3	.6		-4.2			3.2	.8	1.5
8.6	10.0	17.7		30.4			97.6	11.3	9.4
3.4	3.5	4.3	Sales/Net Fixed Assets	14.2			3.6	4.7	4.2
2.0	2.2	2.6		2.8			2.7	2.2	2.7
2.3	2.7	3.3		4.6			15.6	2.9	2.6
1.5	1.8	2.0	Sales/Total Assets	2.5			2.3	1.7	1.7
1.0	1.1	1.3		1.4			1.4	1.0	1.3
1.5	1.5	1.1		.7				1.2	1.3
(81) 2.5	(79) 2.4	(81) 2.0	% Depr., Dep., Amort./Sales	(12) .9				(19) 2.2	(32) 2.2
3.7	3.6	3.5		3.0				3.6	3.6
		.7							
	(10)	2.5	% Officers', Directors' Owners' Comp/Sales						
		26.0							
2987261M	2603123M	2701356M	Net Sales ($)	8346M	12559M	25208M	71667M	320377M	2263199M
2272749M	1937680M	1578541M	Total Assets ($)	11811M	21310M	15024M	38892M	215808M	1275696M

M = $ thousand   MM = $ million
See Pages 9 through 22 for Explanation of Ratios and Data

Current Data Sorted by Assets | **Comparative Historical Data**

0-500M	500M-2MM	2-10MM	10-50MM	50-100MM	100-250MM	Type of Statement	4/1/06-3/31/07 ALL	4/1/07-3/31/08 ALL
1	1	6	26	13	11	Unqualified	64	58
	1	2	2			Reviewed	1	4
1	1	2	1			Compiled	7	7
5	2	3	3			Tax Returns	6	8
7	5	17	18	5	6	Other	46	50
	42 (4/1-9/30/10)		97 (10/1/10-3/31/11)					
14	10	30	50	18	17	NUMBER OF STATEMENTS	124	127
%	%	%	%	%	%	ASSETS	%	%
34.4	25.0	15.6	13.4	13.5	13.4	Cash & Equivalents	16.7	18.7
4.3	9.8	26.4	25.9	13.0	17.0	Trade Receivables (net)	22.5	18.9
4.0	.1	3.6	2.0	.9	1.3	Inventory	1.0	2.0
1.5	1.6	2.1	2.9	4.8	1.8	All Other Current	4.3	5.6
44.2	36.5	47.7	44.2	32.1	33.5	Total Current	44.4	45.1
34.6	47.0	40.9	43.5	41.4	34.5	Fixed Assets (net)	35.4	38.2
3.8	14.3	5.1	3.1	4.0	11.4	Intangibles (net)	2.9	3.6
16.9	2.2	6.3	9.1	22.5	20.7	All Other Non-Current	17.3	13.0
100.0	100.0	100.0	100.0	100.0	100.0	Total	100.0	100.0
						LIABILITIES		
26.9	79.9	7.1	5.4	.6	.7	Notes Payable-Short Term	8.2	8.1
4.0	.2	4.9	4.8	4.1	2.8	Cur. Mat.-L.T.D.	3.8	4.8
9.8	.1	10.7	8.5	4.0	4.9	Trade Payables	9.4	7.8
.0	.2	.1	.1	.1	.0	Income Taxes Payable	.2	.0
31.3	13.8	14.0	13.7	8.5	14.1	All Other Current	20.3	12.8
72.0	94.2	36.8	32.5	17.2	22.5	Total Current	41.8	33.5
39.1	15.2	24.4	25.8	26.7	32.9	Long-Term Debt	22.4	26.9
.0	.0	.5	.2	.0	.5	Deferred Taxes	.1	.1
.5	8.5	6.0	3.2	6.5	9.1	All Other Non-Current	2.9	4.2
-12.0	-17.9	32.2	38.3	49.6	35.0	Net Worth	32.8	35.3
100.0	100.0	100.0	100.0	100.0	100.0	Total Liabilities & Net Worth	100.0	100.0
						INCOME DATA		
100.0	100.0	100.0	100.0	100.0	100.0	Net Sales	100.0	100.0
						Gross Profit		
95.5	81.7	87.1	90.1	90.1	92.0	Operating Expenses	91.3	90.9
4.5	18.3	12.9	9.9	9.9	8.0	Operating Profit	8.7	9.1
.4	1.5	2.8	.9	.3	1.8	All Other Expenses (net)	2.5	1.6
4.1	16.8	10.0	9.0	9.5	6.2	Profit Before Taxes	6.2	7.5
						RATIOS		
1.8	7.9	4.0	2.5	3.0	3.0		2.6	3.0
.6	1.3	1.6	1.7	1.8	1.9	Current	1.5	1.7
.3	.1	.9	1.1	1.5	.8		.8	.9
1.8	7.4	3.1	2.3	2.7	2.8		2.2	2.5
.5	1.2	1.2	1.6	1.7	1.5	Quick	1.2	1.4
.3	.0	.7	.8	1.2	.7		.7	.7
0 UND	0 UND	0 UND	32 11.3	38 9.7	32 11.2		14 25.2	11 33.3
0 UND	0 UND	35 10.4	44 8.4	49 7.4	48 7.6	Sales/Receivables	47 7.7	46 8.0
3 119.2	16 22.2	50 7.2	68 5.4	55 6.7	64 5.7		65 5.6	67 5.5
						Cost of Sales/Inventory		
						Cost of Sales/Payables		
142.8	5.7	6.7	5.8	3.6	2.7		4.8	4.8
-43.3	NM	20.4	10.6	8.1	9.8	Sales/Working Capital	13.7	11.0
-21.0	-10.9	-43.9	NM	12.4	-40.0		-33.8	-148.5
42.6		21.6	51.7	18.4	5.1		10.9	15.3
(11) 9.1		(21) 6.9	(45) 8.2	(17) 4.2	(16) 3.7	EBIT/Interest	(94) 3.8	(100) 3.5
1.0		.4	2.6	1.5	1.1		.9	1.3
						Net Profit + Depr., Dep., Amort./Cur. Mat. L/T/D		
.8	.2	.6	.6	.5	.4		.4	.4
6.5	1.5	1.3	1.1	.9	2.8	Fixed/Worth	.8	1.0
-.3	-1.6	-4.7	3.8	3.2	-6.6		2.9	8.0
1.9	.4	.4	.6	.5	.5		.5	.5
20.9	2.8	1.6	1.6	.9	4.1	Debt/Worth	1.2	1.6
-2.7	-2.7	-10.1	7.3	7.0	-13.0		8.4	17.5
		139.9	118.6	30.8	16.2	% Profit Before Taxes/Tangible Net Worth	35.5	69.9
		(21) 53.4	(44) 38.9	(17) 9.7	(12) 8.0		(102) 11.2	(101) 10.8
		16.0	4.8	5.0	-7.6		3.7	3.5
79.1	169.3	39.0	32.3	9.6	7.5	% Profit Before Taxes/Total Assets	13.6	26.4
42.0	26.1	12.6	11.0	4.5	5.7		5.1	5.4
-5.3	11.0	.1	2.4	.8	.0		.1	.8
176.7	126.5	15.9	10.3	2.9	9.4	Sales/Net Fixed Assets	21.1	16.8
56.0	35.5	9.5	3.6	2.0	4.0		4.8	4.5
20.0	14.6	2.6	1.9	1.3	1.6		2.3	2.1
31.6	17.0	4.0	2.6	1.3	1.8	Sales/Total Assets	2.7	2.9
10.4	11.0	2.9	1.6	.9	.9		1.5	1.6
3.3	1.5	1.3	1.1	.5	.5		.8	.7
		.7	1.6	3.6	2.1	% Depr., Dep., Amort./Sales	1.4	1.6
		(24) 2.7	(49) 2.8	4.4	(14) 3.8		(108) 2.8	(109) 3.2
		5.4	5.0	6.1	5.7		4.9	5.0
						% Officers', Directors' Owners' Comp/Sales	11.2	4.6
							(18) 22.4	(18) 8.0
							29.6	19.8
66807M	142123M	539138M	2164318M	1216886M	2860249M	Net Sales ($)	5763915M	5234318M
3842M	13580M	155812M	1158546M	1427549M	2640654M	Total Assets ($)	5389820M	5137682M

© RMA 2011

M = $ thousand   MM = $ million
See Pages 9 through 22 for Explanation of Ratios and Data

Comparative Historical Data | | | Current Data Sorted by Sales

					Type of Statement						
54		68		58	Unqualified	1	3	1	6	5	42
2		12		5	Reviewed		1	1		1	2
9		8		5	Compiled					3	2
8		8		13	Tax Returns		1	1	1	3	3
51		75		58	Other	4	1		7	14	30
4/1/08-		4/1/09-		4/1/10-		3	2	2			
3/31/09		3/31/10		3/31/11			42 (4/1-9/30/10)		97 (10/1/10-3/31/11)		
ALL		ALL		ALL		0-1MM	1-3MM	3-5MM	5-10MM	10-25MM	25MM & OVER
124		171		139	NUMBER OF STATEMENTS	8	7	5	14	26	79
%		%		%	ASSETS	%	%	%	%	%	%
15.6		15.3		16.8	Cash & Equivalents				16.8	17.7	13.8
20.2		19.0		19.9	Trade Receivables (net)				16.5	23.5	22.8
1.3		1.9		2.2	Inventory				3.6	2.1	2.2
6.0		5.4		2.6	All Other Current				1.5	2.5	3.1
43.2		41.5		41.5	Total Current				38.4	45.7	41.8
37.5		40.6		40.9	Fixed Assets (net)				49.1	35.4	40.6
2.1		5.2		5.5	Intangibles (net)				1.4	12.8	4.4
17.1		12.7		11.9	All Other Non-Current				11.1	6.1	13.3
100.0		100.0		100.0	Total				100.0	100.0	100.0
					LIABILITIES						
10.8		3.2		12.1	Notes Payable-Short Term				19.1	10.7	11.7
3.6		3.3		4.1	Cur. Mat.-L.T.D.				1.9	4.2	4.3
8.1		7.3		7.5	Trade Payables				14.6	8.6	7.0
.2		.2		.1	Income Taxes Payable				.0	.1	.2
12.1		18.0		14.9	All Other Current				25.8	15.1	14.6
34.8		32.0		38.6	Total Current				61.5	38.7	37.8
23.4		30.3		27.0	Long-Term Debt				33.8	13.6	26.1
.1		.1		.2	Deferred Taxes				.0	.6	.1
4.6		3.8		5.1	All Other Non-Current				.2	8.6	4.7
37.0		33.8		28.9	Net Worth				4.5	38.6	31.3
100.0		100.0		100.0	Total Liabilties & Net Worth				100.0	100.0	100.0
					INCOME DATA						
100.0		100.0		100.0	Net Sales				100.0	100.0	100.0
					Gross Profit						
91.9		88.9		89.6	Operating Expenses				89.0	90.5	90.5
8.1		11.1		10.4	Operating Profit				11.0	9.5	9.5
3.6		3.3		1.3	All Other Expenses (net)				.8	-.6	.6
4.5		7.8		9.0	Profit Before Taxes				10.2	10.1	8.8
					RATIOS						
3.0		2.7		2.5					3.4	2.4	2.5
1.8		1.7		1.6	Current				1.3	1.4	1.7
1.1		1.0		.8					.6	.6	1.1
2.5		2.3		2.4					3.1	2.2	2.3
1.5		1.4		1.5	Quick				1.1	1.0	1.5
.8		.8		.7					.5	.5	.9

14	26.0	8	48.5	7	51.4	Sales/Receivables	0	UND	0	UND			32	11.3
47	7.7	38	9.5	39	9.4		18	20.1	39	9.3			47	7.7
64	5.7	55	6.7	53	6.8		43	8.5	47	7.8			58	6.3
						Cost of Sales/Inventory								
						Cost of Sales/Payables								
	5.2		6.4		6.1	Sales/Working Capital						15.7	8.8	5.4
	11.4		13.4		14.3							69.7	27.4	10.3
	175.6		155.5		-50.4							-29.1	-31.8	95.8
	16.4		19.6		20.8	EBIT/Interest						37.2	25.6	18.2
(100)	4.0	(128)	3.4	(116)	6.8		(11)	9.1	(17)	7.4	(73)	5.2		
	.5		1.0		1.4			-.1		3.3		1.8		
				4.3		Net Profit + Depr., Dep., Amort./Cur. Mat. L/T/D								
		(14)	2.5											
			-.9											
	.4		.4		.5	Fixed/Worth						.9	.4	.5
	.8		.9		1.3							2.3	1.2	1.1
	3.1		10.1		10.5							-.5	11.3	5.7
	.4		.5		.5	Debt/Worth						.6	.5	.6
	1.0		1.5		1.7							2.0	1.9	1.4
	7.2		14.8		26.9							-3.4	NM	9.8
	48.7		82.4		112.8	% Profit Before Taxes/Tangible Net Worth							320.6	84.6
(101)	9.3	(138)	21.8	(109)	28.9					(20)	76.6	(65)	17.8	
	.3		.9		6.4								22.6	6.4
	15.4		24.0		33.5	% Profit Before Taxes/Total Assets						49.4	47.8	29.0
	3.8		6.7		8.7							18.5	13.6	7.0
	-1.0		.0		2.1							-1.1	2.3	2.7
	15.9		21.4		17.5	Sales/Net Fixed Assets						54.3	26.3	10.4
	3.9		4.7		5.7							4.6	11.6	4.0
	1.8		1.6		2.0							1.4	3.7	2.0
	2.8		3.1		3.2	Sales/Total Assets						5.7	6.9	2.6
	1.5		1.5		1.8							2.4	3.2	1.5
	.7		.8		1.0							1.0	1.6	1.0
	1.8		1.2		1.5	% Depr., Dep., Amort./Sales						1.1	.7	2.0
(106)	3.7	(155)	2.7	(120)	3.2		(11)	3.6	(20)	2.4	(74)	3.3		
	5.1		5.5		5.5							10.5	4.0	5.0
	3.5		5.0		3.8	% Officers', Directors' Owners' Comp/Sales								5.5
(19)	9.7	(29)	11.4	(28)	10.0								(13)	8.8
	24.8		28.4		30.8									34.8
5144051M		8339835M		6989521M	Net Sales ($)	4423M	13873M	17983M	109859M	434830M	6408553M
5074935M		6187651M		5399983M	Total Assets ($)	9857M	29258M	12657M	121446M	283176M	4943589M

M = $ thousand   MM = $ million
See Pages 9 through 22 for Explanation of Ratios and Data

Current Data Sorted by Assets							Comparative Historical Data	
						Type of Statement		
2	31	147	228	45	34	Unqualified	549	508
2	29	99	23	2	3	Reviewed	123	125
10	32	61	15	2	1	Compiled	158	137
38	45	52	10			Tax Returns	128	120
58	192	324	164	50	34	Other	526	574
	410 (4/1-9/30/10)		1,323 (10/1/10-3/31/11)				4/1/06-3/31/07	4/1/07-3/31/08
0-500M	500M-2MM	2-10MM	10-50MM	50-100MM	100-250MM		ALL	ALL
110	329	683	440	99	72	NUMBER OF STATEMENTS	1484	1464
%	%	%	%	%	%	**ASSETS**	%	%
30.1	14.4	12.0	10.9	10.4	11.5	Cash & Equivalents	11.9	11.7
18.7	33.1	21.4	11.8	11.3	9.6	Trade Receivables (net)	21.2	21.4
.9	.4	.2	.2	.3	.3	Inventory	.5	.4
4.5	4.2	3.3	3.5	4.6	3.5	All Other Current	3.7	5.4
54.2	52.1	37.0	26.4	26.5	25.0	Total Current	37.2	38.8
31.1	32.5	48.6	54.1	49.6	55.6	Fixed Assets (net)	45.4	44.4
2.9	4.6	4.5	5.5	5.4	4.7	Intangibles (net)	4.1	3.8
11.8	10.8	9.9	14.0	18.4	14.8	All Other Non-Current	13.3	13.0
100.0	100.0	100.0	100.0	100.0	100.0	Total	100.0	100.0
						LIABILITIES		
17.9	5.7	4.0	2.2	1.3	1.1	Notes Payable-Short Term	4.5	5.8
3.6	2.4	4.7	3.2	2.8	3.9	Cur. Mat.-L.T.D.	2.9	3.2
20.4	15.5	9.6	5.8	5.4	3.8	Trade Payables	10.5	10.8
.0	.1	.1	.0	.0	.0	Income Taxes Payable	.1	.1
41.9	27.3	14.3	10.3	8.2	9.3	All Other Current	18.3	17.3
83.8	51.0	32.6	21.4	17.7	18.2	Total Current	36.3	37.1
24.6	27.1	44.6	47.3	41.5	49.0	Long-Term Debt	41.0	40.5
.0	.1	.1	.0	.2	.1	Deferred Taxes	.1	.1
14.2	10.9	5.1	7.4	12.0	13.4	All Other Non-Current	8.8	8.5
-22.5	10.9	17.6	23.8	28.5	19.4	Net Worth	13.8	13.8
100.0	100.0	100.0	100.0	100.0	100.0	Total Liabilties & Net Worth	100.0	100.0
						INCOME DATA		
100.0	100.0	100.0	100.0	100.0	100.0	Net Sales	100.0	100.0
						Gross Profit		
91.7	86.6	85.8	88.5	91.0	92.9	Operating Expenses	90.8	89.4
8.3	13.4	14.2	11.5	9.0	7.1	Operating Profit	9.2	10.6
2.2	3.1	6.4	5.4	4.0	3.0	All Other Expenses (net)	4.5	5.1
6.1	10.2	7.8	6.2	5.0	4.2	Profit Before Taxes	4.6	5.5
						RATIOS		
2.0	2.0	2.2	2.6	2.6	2.2		2.1	2.2
1.0	1.2	1.3	1.4	1.6	1.4	Current	1.2	1.3
.3	.6	.8	.8	.9	.9		.8	.8
2.0	1.9	2.0	2.2	1.9	1.8		2.0	1.9
1.0	1.1	1.2	1.2	1.2	1.1	Quick	1.1	1.1
.3	.5	.7	.7	.7	.8		.6	.6
0 UND	**6** 64.1	**12** 30.0	**20** 18.5	**23** 15.9	**24** 15.1		**15** 23.6	**13** 27.5
1 258.7	**29** 12.7	**34** 10.7	**33** 10.9	**33** 11.1	**32** 11.4	Sales/Receivables	**34** 10.9	**34** 10.7
24 15.5	**39** 9.3	**48** 7.6	**45** 8.1	**45** 8.2	**40** 9.1		**47** 7.7	**47** 7.8
						Cost of Sales/Inventory		
						Cost of Sales/Payables		
18.8	12.9	8.7	5.3	4.6	4.9		8.4	8.2
386.6	48.2	27.7	18.3	13.2	18.9	Sales/Working Capital	35.6	27.3
-15.8	-16.1	-19.3	-27.4	-79.9	-51.5		-22.2	-22.8
22.4	38.0	10.0	6.0	5.1	4.6		5.4	4.9
(59) 4.8	(209) 10.3	(543) 3.4	(380) 2.4	(81) 2.0	(67) 2.5	EBIT/Interest	(1196) 2.3	(1126) 2.2
.9	2.0	1.3	1.3	1.0	1.3		.9	.9
		7.3	5.9		11.0		7.4	6.5
		(63) 2.7	(34) 3.6		(11) 3.6	Net Profit + Depr., Dep., Amort./Cur. Mat. L/T/D	(97) 2.8	(103) 3.0
		1.7	1.5		.4		1.0	1.5
.2	.3	.7	1.1	.8	1.7		.8	.7
1.2	1.3	3.2	2.9	2.1	4.7	Fixed/Worth	2.8	2.5
-.7	-7.9	-7.5	-442.3	24.9	-17.6		-8.4	-9.0
1.0	.8	1.2	1.1	1.0	2.3		1.3	1.2
7.0	3.8	4.4	3.8	2.9	5.8	Debt/Worth	5.0	4.3
-2.6	-12.5	-16.8	-103.7	37.2	-23.8		-14.0	-14.3
169.5	124.2	74.4	26.9	26.9	44.3		59.8	54.3
(64) 67.3	(223) 64.0	(466) 32.3	(326) 11.5	(75) 8.2	(52) 13.1	% Profit Before Taxes/Tangible Net Worth	(1019) 17.7	(1024) 18.2
26.5	26.3	11.6	2.8	1.3	5.5		3.9	3.9
62.5	36.2	17.2	7.9	5.6	7.1		11.9	12.8
22.9	16.3	6.6	3.3	2.4	3.6	% Profit Before Taxes/Total Assets	3.8	4.2
-.7	4.6	1.4	.5	-.1	.8		-.4	-.1
192.3	69.6	13.9	3.2	3.6	3.1		19.7	19.8
43.6	20.0	3.3	1.5	1.5	1.2	Sales/Net Fixed Assets	3.0	3.1
13.1	3.4	1.1	.7	.6	.7		1.1	1.2
12.0	5.5	2.8	1.3	1.6	1.2		3.0	3.1
6.8	3.8	1.5	.8	.7	.8	Sales/Total Assets	1.3	1.4
4.0	1.6	.7	.5	.3	.4		.6	.7
.3	.4	1.4	2.4	2.0	2.7		1.1	1.1
(62) .8	(270) 1.1	(633) 2.8	(422) 4.2	(97) 4.9	(70) 4.2	% Depr., Dep., Amort./Sales	(1371) 2.9	(1307) 2.7
2.4	3.8	5.9	7.5	10.1	8.8		6.3	5.9
4.1	1.7	1.4	1.9	2.0			2.2	2.1
(23) 6.2	(49) 4.0	(97) 4.0	(59) 4.0	(12) 6.0		% Officers', Directors' Owners' Comp/Sales	(206) 4.5	(230) 4.3
9.7	7.4	6.4	13.6	13.6			8.5	9.5
179871M	**1493133M**	**6004725M**	**11010520M**	**7789543M**	**11268880M**	Net Sales ($)	**31501453M**	**32100782M**
26662M	**408393M**	**3471083M**	**9877280M**	**7091506M**	**10485384M**	Total Assets ($)	**31092073M**	**28882403M**

M = $ thousand MM = $ million

See Pages 9 through 22 for Explanation of Ratios and Data

Comparative Historical Data | Current Data Sorted by Sales

			Type of Statement						
449	513	487	Unqualified	16	26	31	95	178	141
129	174	158	Reviewed	10	14	15	45	64	10
130	117	121	Compiled	14	23	19	33	26	6
155	149	145	Tax Returns	40	44	20	29	10	2
644	685	822	Other	95	122	101	205	163	136
4/1/08-3/31/09 ALL	4/1/09-3/31/10 ALL	4/1/10-3/31/11 ALL		410 (4/1-9/30/10)			1,323 (10/1/10-3/31/11)		
				0-1MM	1-3MM	3-5MM	5-10MM	10-25MM	25MM & OVER
1507	1638	1733	**NUMBER OF STATEMENTS**	175	229	186	407	441	295
%	%	%	**ASSETS**	%	%	%	%	%	%
11.5	12.2	13.2	Cash & Equivalents	10.7	15.8	15.5	13.1	12.6	12.4
21.7	20.2	19.9	Trade Receivables (net)	3.4	9.9	23.7	27.0	23.3	20.3
.2	.3	.3	Inventory	.2	.3	.4	.3	.3	.3
4.0	3.5	3.7	All Other Current	3.4	2.6	3.9	3.4	3.7	4.9
37.4	36.1	37.2	Total Current	17.7	28.6	43.5	43.8	39.9	38.0
44.9	46.2	46.2	Fixed Assets (net)	65.8	54.2	40.9	40.2	43.7	43.5
3.7	5.3	4.8	Intangibles (net)	5.1	7.3	4.0	4.1	4.5	4.3
14.0	12.4	11.9	All Other Non-Current	11.4	9.8	11.6	12.0	11.8	14.2
100.0	100.0	100.0	Total	100.0	100.0	100.0	100.0	100.0	100.0
			LIABILITIES						
4.7	3.8	4.4	Notes Payable-Short Term	4.4	10.4	5.0	3.6	3.0	2.8
3.1	3.7	3.6	Cur. Mat.-L.T.D.	5.8	3.9	4.2	2.7	3.7	3.1
10.4	9.5	9.9	Trade Payables	2.5	9.7	11.0	11.0	11.9	9.5
.1	.0	.1	Income Taxes Payable	.0	.1	.1	.2	.0	.1
19.6	17.9	16.9	All Other Current	10.3	21.9	21.9	18.9	14.0	15.4
37.9	34.9	35.1	Total Current	23.1	46.0	42.1	36.5	32.7	30.9
41.7	41.4	40.7	Long-Term Debt	63.0	54.4	35.6	32.9	36.5	37.0
.1	.1	.1	Deferred Taxes	.0	.0	.1	.2	.1	.1
7.4	7.8	8.1	All Other Non-Current	4.3	12.3	7.4	7.6	7.9	8.6
12.9	15.8	16.1	Net Worth	9.6	-12.7	14.9	22.8	22.8	23.5
100.0	100.0	100.0	Total Liabilites & Net Worth	100.0	100.0	100.0	100.0	100.0	100.0
			INCOME DATA						
100.0	100.0	100.0	Net Sales	100.0	100.0	100.0	100.0	100.0	100.0
			Gross Profit						
88.6	87.7	87.6	Operating Expenses	57.0	81.6	90.5	92.6	93.2	93.3
11.4	12.3	12.4	Operating Profit	43.0	18.4	9.5	7.4	6.8	6.7
6.3	5.1	5.0	All Other Expenses (net)	19.1	9.8	3.0	2.3	2.2	1.8
5.1	7.2	7.4	Profit Before Taxes	23.9	8.6	6.5	5.1	4.5	4.9
			RATIOS						
2.1	2.1	2.2		2.2	2.1	2.5	2.3	2.4	2.1
1.2	1.2	1.3	Current	.6	1.0	1.4	1.4	1.4	1.4
.7	.7	.7		.1	.3	.8	.9	.9	.9
1.9	2.0	2.0		1.9	1.9	2.3	2.1	2.0	1.9
(1506) 1.1	1.1	1.1	Quick	.4	.9	1.2	1.4	1.2	1.1
.6	.6	.6		.1	.2	.7	.8	.7	.8
14 26.8	11 32.2	11 34.5		0 UND	0 UND	10 37.8	24 15.1	27 13.4	28 13.1
34 10.7	32 11.3	32 11.5	Sales/Receivables	0 UND	4 100.7	31 11.7	35 10.5	37 9.9	36 10.3
48 7.6	44 8.3	44 8.3		5 74.0	26 14.0	45 8.1	46 7.9	46 7.9	46 8.0
			Cost of Sales/Inventory						
			Cost of Sales/Payables						
9.4	8.9	8.4		6.7	11.0	9.0	9.1	7.5	7.8
34.0	34.2	28.7	Sales/Working Capital	-22.1	-238.5	24.1	20.8	22.4	19.3
-15.5	-19.5	-21.3		-3.3	-8.2	-26.7	-37.7	-37.2	-92.1
6.3	9.5	11.0		11.9	5.9	16.2	12.5	10.1	11.5
(1173) 2.3	(1268) 3.1	(1339) 3.1	EBIT/Interest	(88) 4.4	(140) 2.1	(145) 3.3	(318) 3.3	(379) 3.0	(269) 3.5
.7	1.3	1.3		1.5	.8	1.3	1.4	1.2	1.6
7.1	7.3	6.7					6.8	6.6	9.0
(94) 3.6	(118) 3.6	(124) 3.3	Net Profit + Depr., Dep., Amort./Cur. Mat. L/T/D			(28) 3.0	(43) 3.4	(36) 4.8
1.0	1.6	1.5					1.5	1.8	2.6
.7	.7	.7		1.6	1.1	.4	.5	.7	.8
3.0	3.0	2.7	Fixed/Worth	8.7	-166.4	1.9	1.8	2.0	2.0
-6.4	-8.9	-13.4		-6.3	-1.6	-24.9	35.5	-32.0	24.9
1.3	1.3	1.2		1.8	2.6	1.0	.9	1.0	1.1
5.2	4.9	4.1	Debt/Worth	10.7	-32.4	3.3	3.1	3.1	3.4
-11.8	-13.0	-17.5		-7.2	-3.2	-24.7	395.3	-47.9	40.9
71.7	74.8	71.0		86.6	115.9	76.1	78.4	62.7	55.9
(1011) 22.2	(1128) 28.7	(1206) 26.0	% Profit Before Taxes/Tangible Net Worth	(109) 30.6	(107) 50.7	(130) 26.3	(309) 29.7	(324) 22.9	(227) 18.2
2.2	6.1	6.7		10.2	10.5	11.0	7.7	5.1	5.8
13.7	16.7	18.0		12.2	21.3	20.0	22.1	16.7	14.2
4.3	5.9	6.0	% Profit Before Taxes/Total Assets	4.8	5.4	8.9	7.8	5.4	5.2
-.9	.6	.9		.3	-.2	1.1	1.7	1.1	1.7
22.7	19.6	17.6		1.7	20.9	39.2	31.0	15.5	13.2
3.3	3.1	3.0	Sales/Net Fixed Assets	.4	1.9	6.1	5.1	3.2	3.2
1.1	1.1	1.0		.2	.5	1.3	1.6	1.5	1.3
3.4	3.3	3.4		.7	4.0	4.3	4.2	3.2	2.8
1.4	1.4	1.4	Sales/Total Assets	.2	1.1	1.9	2.0	1.5	1.4
.6	.7	.6		.1	.4	.8	.9	.8	.8
1.0	1.2	1.2		5.4	1.5	.8	.7	1.3	1.2
(1371) 2.8	(1482) 2.9	(1554) 3.1	% Depr., Dep., Amort./Sales	(151) 18.1	(176) 6.4	(156) 2.9	(365) 2.5	(421) 2.7	(285) 2.4
5.9	5.9	6.2		28.0	13.3	5.3	4.5	5.0	4.4
1.6	1.7	1.7		4.0	3.6	1.6	1.4	1.6	1.8
(181) 3.5	(217) 3.9	(247) 4.2	% Officers', Directors' Owners' Comp/Sales	(19) 5.2	(39) 5.0	(29) 4.4	(68) 3.2	(56) 4.1	(36) 4.4
7.2	7.8	7.8		9.7	6.4	7.8	7.8	8.4	13.4
31076987M	36304439M	37746672M	Net Sales ($)	93824M	435215M	742763M	3056763M	6628301M	26789806M
27822741M	30224820M	31360308M	Total Assets ($)	478409M	885951M	824334M	2996693M	7001997M	19172924M

© RMA 2011

M = $ thousand   MM = $ million
See Pages 9 through 22 for Explanation of Ratios and Data

Current Data Sorted by Assets   Comparative Historical Data

Type of Statement	0-500M	500M-2MM	2-10MM	10-50MM	50-100MM	100-250MM	ALL 4/1/06-3/31/07	ALL 4/1/07-3/31/08
Unqualified	2	9	44	53	9	9	78	86
Reviewed	1		2					1
Compiled	1		1	2			2	4
Tax Returns	4	4	2				9	5
Other	1	7	19	11	1	1	18	24
		131 (4/1-9/30/10)		52 (10/1/10-3/31/11)				

	0-500M	500M-2MM	2-10MM	10-50MM	50-100MM	100-250MM	Label	ALL 4/1/06-3/31/07	ALL 4/1/07-3/31/08
NUMBER OF STATEMENTS	9	20	68	66	10	10		107	120
	%	%	%	%	%	%	**ASSETS**	%	%
		17.0	17.3	19.0	11.9	6.8	Cash & Equivalents	18.8	17.1
		31.1	17.8	15.4	16.6	10.6	Trade Receivables (net)	16.9	19.6
		.0	.3	.2	.0	.1	Inventory	.1	.1
		2.8	2.5	2.7	4.4	1.4	All Other Current	2.7	4.3
		50.9	37.9	37.3	32.9	19.0	Total Current	38.5	41.2
		41.3	53.1	49.6	54.6	32.0	Fixed Assets (net)	50.0	47.7
		2.3	3.0	2.0	.7	9.3	Intangibles (net)	1.4	1.1
		5.5	6.0	11.1	11.8	39.7	All Other Non-Current	10.1	10.0
		100.0	100.0	100.0	100.0	100.0	Total	100.0	100.0
							LIABILITIES		
		5.3	3.1	2.1	5.2	6.5	Notes Payable-Short Term	3.9	4.4
		2.3	2.9	3.8	3.8	3.9	Cur. Mat.-L.T.D.	2.2	2.7
		5.3	6.8	6.5	6.9	7.4	Trade Payables	7.0	7.9
		.1	.4	.0	.3	.0	Income Taxes Payable	.2	.2
		15.3	13.0	11.8	11.5	4.6	All Other Current	11.6	13.4
		28.3	26.2	24.3	27.7	22.5	Total Current	24.9	28.7
		30.8	31.7	26.0	40.5	37.5	Long-Term Debt	33.5	31.3
		.3	.2	.0	.0	.0	Deferred Taxes	.0	.0
		1.1	2.4	3.4	8.6	8.2	All Other Non-Current	1.9	2.6
		39.5	39.4	46.3	23.2	31.8	Net Worth	39.7	37.5
		100.0	100.0	100.0	100.0	100.0	Total Liabilities & Net Worth	100.0	100.0
							INCOME DATA		
		100.0	100.0	100.0	100.0	100.0	Net Sales	100.0	100.0
							Gross Profit		
		97.0	90.9	95.8	91.2	89.1	Operating Expenses	93.6	94.1
		3.0	9.1	4.2	8.8	10.9	Operating Profit	6.4	5.9
		1.1	4.2	.1	6.7	3.2	All Other Expenses (net)	2.0	1.4
		1.9	4.9	4.2	2.1	7.6	Profit Before Taxes	4.4	4.5
							RATIOS		
		4.9	2.6	2.5	1.7	1.8	Current	2.6	3.0
		1.8	1.5	1.7	1.1	1.1		1.6	1.4
		.9	.9	1.1	.7	.5		.9	.9
		4.1	2.6	2.5	1.5	1.6	Quick	2.5	2.8
		1.7	1.3	1.4	1.0	1.0		1.4	1.1
		.9	.8	1.0	.6	.5		.8	.7
	0 UND	20 18.6	25 14.6	0 UND	26 13.9		Sales/Receivables	14 25.6	23 15.6
	28 12.9	32 11.5	34 10.7	43 8.5	36 10.1			32 11.4	34 10.7
	39 9.5	38 9.7	46 8.0	68 5.3	39 9.3			51 7.1	48 7.5
							Cost of Sales/Inventory		
							Cost of Sales/Payables		
		3.6	5.8	5.4	6.9	10.8	Sales/Working Capital	5.2	5.2
		19.1	18.1	12.9	33.5	NM		13.4	15.9
		NM	-88.7	52.9	-24.0	-10.0		-131.9	-89.2
		8.3	5.8	7.7		3.9	EBIT/Interest	5.3	4.7
		(19) 2.7	(54) 3.2	(60) 3.2		2.9		(81) 2.1	(89) 2.5
		-.6	1.5	1.7		2.2		1.0	1.1
							Net Profit + Depr., Dep., Amort./Cur. Mat. L/T/D		
		.2	.8	.7	1.5	.8	Fixed/Worth	.5	.7
		.8	1.5	1.1	1.3	1.3		1.3	1.4
		3.0	2.9	2.1	4.7	3.8		3.3	3.3
		.5	.6	.6	1.8	1.4	Debt/Worth	.6	.6
		1.1	1.7	1.2	4.8	3.0		1.5	1.7
		6.1	5.4	2.6	6.8	19.9		4.2	4.5
		20.5	19.5	18.4	14.3		% Profit Before Taxes/Tangible Net Worth	18.9	20.9
		(19) 5.0	(62) 11.5	9.9	7.8			(94) 6.8	(106) 9.9
		-8.2	5.1	3.7	1.9			.6	3.8
		10.4	7.5	7.1	2.8	3.8	% Profit Before Taxes/Total Assets	7.7	7.9
		3.0	3.8	3.6	1.7	1.7		2.7	3.6
		-3.1	1.4	1.5	.5	1.4		.1	.5
		35.7	5.9	4.6	4.1	3.5	Sales/Net Fixed Assets	6.0	5.8
		11.4	3.1	3.1	2.4	2.8		2.6	3.1
		1.7	1.8	2.0	1.2	1.4		1.6	2.0
		6.0	2.5	1.9	1.7	1.4	Sales/Total Assets	2.3	2.4
		2.9	1.7	1.4	1.3	1.0		1.5	1.6
		1.2	1.0	1.1	.7	.1		.9	1.2
		.6	1.6	1.7	2.4	2.1	% Depr., Dep., Amort./Sales	1.5	1.5
		(19) 1.6	(66) 2.2	(62) 2.6	3.1	3.5		(103) 2.6	(108) 2.5
		3.7	3.4	3.7	12.9	5.6		4.0	3.5
			1.0				% Officers', Directors' Owners' Comp/Sales	3.5	2.6
		(10) 1.5						(16) 4.7	(13) 4.4
		4.1						16.0	24.7
	7656M	97498M	704554M	2304257M	890509M	1303578M	Net Sales ($)	2511451M	3662286M
	2093M	25826M	372743M	1467765M	685308M	1519910M	Total Assets ($)	2190039M	2800442M

© RMA 2011

M = $ thousand   MM = $ million
See Pages 9 through 22 for Explanation of Ratios and Data

Comparative Historical Data | Current Data Sorted by Sales

				Type of Statement						
85		108	126	Unqualified	3	7	5	24	34	53
2		2	3	Reviewed	2	1				
5		3	4	Compiled	1				2	1
9		4	10	Tax Returns	4	4	1		1	
37		53	40	Other	2	4	6	9	7	12
4/1/08-3/31/09 ALL		4/1/09-3/31/10 ALL	4/1/10-3/31/11 ALL		131 (4/1-9/30/10)			52 (10/1/10-3/31/11)		
138		170	183	NUMBER OF STATEMENTS	12	15	12	34	44	66
					0-1MM	1-3MM	3-5MM	5-10MM	10-25MM	25MM & OVER
%		%	%	ASSETS	%	%	%	%	%	%
17.1		16.1	17.3	Cash & Equivalents	23.4	18.5	16.2	18.8	17.2	15.5
19.3		20.4	18.0	Trade Receivables (net)	8.1	8.5	26.1	20.5	16.2	20.3
.2		.2	.2	Inventory	.1	.1	.0	.3	.3	.2
3.5		4.0	2.8	All Other Current	3.8	3.6	1.2	1.8	2.9	3.2
40.1		40.7	38.3	Total Current	35.4	30.7	43.4	41.4	36.6	39.2
47.6		48.1	48.3	Fixed Assets (net)	47.5	62.3	43.9	50.5	48.8	44.7
3.1		1.9	3.4	Intangibles (net)	12.3	1.2	3.9	3.0	1.8	3.5
9.2		9.2	9.9	All Other Non-Current	4.8	5.7	8.8	5.1	12.7	12.6
100.0		100.0	100.0	Total	100.0	100.0	100.0	100.0	100.0	100.0
				LIABILITIES						
5.4		4.3	3.3	Notes Payable-Short Term	.0	2.6	4.6	2.6	3.3	4.2
3.4		3.2	3.3	Cur. Mat.-L.T.D.	4.1	5.0	.6	2.2	3.7	3.7
7.1		6.4	7.1	Trade Payables	13.5	1.6	4.7	6.1	6.3	8.7
.2		.1	.2	Income Taxes Payable	.0	.0	.1	.1	.0	.4
13.6		13.3	13.1	All Other Current	20.9	9.0	10.4	12.1	12.9	13.7
29.6		27.3	27.1	Total Current	38.5	18.1	20.4	23.1	26.2	30.9
29.0		30.0	32.5	Long-Term Debt	71.6	57.0	20.7	28.3	30.3	25.7
.0		.1	.1	Deferred Taxes	.0	.1	.0	.3	.0	.2
3.7		4.0	4.2	All Other Non-Current	15.7	5.0	2.4	1.0	2.6	5.0
37.6		38.7	36.0	Net Worth	-25.9	19.8	56.5	47.4	40.9	38.2
100.0		100.0	100.0	Total Liabilities & Net Worth	100.0	100.0	100.0	100.0	100.0	100.0
				INCOME DATA						
100.0		100.0	100.0	Net Sales	100.0	100.0	100.0	100.0	100.0	100.0
				Gross Profit						
94.3		94.5	93.3	Operating Expenses	76.4	85.0	95.9	92.8	94.8	97.2
5.7		5.5	6.7	Operating Profit	23.6	15.0	4.1	7.2	5.2	2.8
2.4		2.8	2.5	All Other Expenses (net)	16.7	8.8	.5	2.7	.4	.3
3.2		2.7	4.1	Profit Before Taxes	6.9	6.2	3.7	4.5	4.8	2.6
				RATIOS						
2.2		2.7	2.5		5.9	4.6	4.0	2.8	2.7	1.9
1.3		1.4	1.5	Current	1.1	1.2	2.0	2.2	1.5	1.4
.9		1.0	.9		.3	.5	1.1	1.1	1.1	.9
2.0		2.6	2.4		5.4	4.4	3.8	2.7	2.6	1.6
1.1		1.3	1.4	Quick	1.0	.8	2.0	1.8	1.3	1.3
.7		.8	.9		.2	.2	1.1	1.0	.9	.9
17	22.0	20	18.4	23	16.1	Sales/Receivables	0	UND	0	UND	13	27.9	25	14.6	24	15.1	28	12.9

| 33 | 11.1 | 34 | 10.6 | 32 | 11.4 | | 0 | UND | 4 | 81.1 | 32 | 11.3 | 33 | 11.1 | 31 | 11.9 | 38 | 9.6 |
| 46 | 8.0 | 51 | 7.2 | 41 | 8.8 | | 30 | 12.2 | 29 | 12.6 | 77 | 4.7 | 41 | 8.9 | 38 | 9.7 | 48 | 7.6 |

				Cost of Sales/Inventory						

| | | | | Cost of Sales/Payables | | | | | | |

6.6		6.5	5.9	Sales/Working Capital	2.9	3.0	5.4	4.1	5.8	9.0
25.1		17.2	17.1		NM	42.4	9.6	10.0	19.2	18.5
-50.2		-401.7	-97.3		-3.1	-9.6	94.9	90.2	164.9	-70.6

4.4		5.2	5.5	EBIT/Interest		19.5	11.3	6.2	5.5	4.8
(113)	2.0	(140)	2.3	(156)	2.9		(12)	3.3	(10)	3.8	(28)	4.1	(39)	2.9	(62)	2.5
	.9		.8		1.6			1.7		-6.9		1.6		1.7		1.4

				2.0	Net Profit + Depr., Dep., Amort./Cur. Mat. L/T/D						
		(12)	1.2								
			.3								

.6		.7	.7	Fixed/Worth	.3	.7	.4	.7	.8	.8
1.4		1.2	1.3		2.4	4.5	.7	1.2	1.4	1.4
2.9		2.7	2.5		-3.2	39.5	1.7	1.9	2.4	2.4
.7		.7	.6	Debt/Worth	1.2	.6	.3	.5	.6	.9
1.8		1.5	1.6		2.2	3.8	1.0	1.0	1.3	1.9
4.1		4.3	4.5		-6.0	39.4	1.7	2.6	3.6	4.5
19.1		21.2	19.4	% Profit Before Taxes/Tangible Net Worth		24.8	18.0	22.1	25.0	15.8
(129)	5.3	(161)	8.3	(171)	10.1		(12)	11.7	5.7	(32)	11.3	(43)	10.3	(64)	7.9
	-.8		.7		3.4			4.1	-5.3		3.1		5.1		3.2
5.4		7.8	7.0	% Profit Before Taxes/Total Assets	6.2	12.2	8.4	9.8	7.1	5.4
1.5		2.6	3.2		2.1	5.2	3.2	4.5	3.7	2.5
-.3		-.2	.8		.0	1.3	-2.9	1.0	1.5	.6
8.4		7.9	6.1	Sales/Net Fixed Assets	67.6	3.4	6.3	8.3	5.9	6.1
3.6		3.4	3.1		1.8	1.8	3.9	2.8	3.2	3.5
2.1		2.0	1.8		.2	1.2	1.7	1.5	1.7	2.6
2.7		2.5	2.2	Sales/Total Assets	3.1	1.4	2.7	2.8	2.5	2.1
1.6		1.7	1.5		.9	1.1	1.4	1.6	1.6	1.6
1.2		1.2	1.1		.2	.6	.8	1.0	1.0	1.4
1.5		1.6	1.7	% Depr., Dep., Amort./Sales		1.7	1.7	1.4	1.7	1.6
(122)	2.3	(156)	2.4	(173)	2.4		(14)	3.7	2.5	(31)	2.4	2.4	(63)	2.2
	3.6		3.4		3.6			6.6	3.2		3.5		3.8		3.2
2.8		1.2	1.5	% Officers', Directors' Owners' Comp/Sales						
(15)	6.0	(23)	2.7	(26)	3.9						
	12.5		4.6		8.1						
4121118M		5064276M	5308052M	Net Sales ($)	5853M	28615M	47727M	259698M	649784M	4316375M
2857567M		3487884M	4073645M	Total Assets ($)	12403M	41683M	38396M	323812M	845547M	2811804M

M = $ thousand   MM = $ million
See Pages 9 through 22 for Explanation of Ratios and Data

Current Data Sorted by Assets

								Comparative Historical Data	
		19	66	68	4	4	Type of Statement		
			3				Unqualified	189	171
	1	4	3				Reviewed	7	4
	6	5	1	1			Compiled	6	6
	4	12	29	28	5	5	Tax Returns	8	10
							Other	61	70
		169 (4/1-9/30/10)		99 (10/1/10-3/31/11)				4/1/06-3/31/07	4/1/07-3/31/08
	0-500M	500M-2MM	2-10MM	10-50MM	50-100MM	100-250MM		ALL	ALL
	11	40	102	97	9	9	NUMBER OF STATEMENTS	271	261
	%	%	%	%	%	%	ASSETS	%	%
	23.6	23.1	18.2	18.1			Cash & Equivalents	15.3	14.7
	16.2	16.6	18.1	14.0			Trade Receivables (net)	17.5	16.3
	.0	.0	.1	.2			Inventory	.2	.2
	.9	5.2	3.2	2.4			All Other Current	2.9	3.8
	40.7	45.0	39.6	34.8			Total Current	36.0	35.0
	28.0	50.2	51.9	53.6			Fixed Assets (net)	51.4	52.5
	3.1	.4	1.3	1.5			Intangibles (net)	1.9	1.5
	28.1	4.4	7.2	10.1			All Other Non-Current	10.7	11.0
	100.0	100.0	100.0	100.0			Total	100.0	100.0
							LIABILITIES		
	9.5	4.5	2.1	1.7			Notes Payable-Short Term	4.3	4.2
	4.6	1.6	2.7	3.4			Cur. Mat.-L.T.D.	3.2	2.9
	.3	5.1	5.6	4.8			Trade Payables	5.8	5.3
	1.0	.0	.2	.0			Income Taxes Payable	.1	.0
	38.8	15.3	10.6	11.4			All Other Current	12.8	12.8
	54.3	26.6	21.1	21.4			Total Current	26.2	25.3
	23.4	23.3	30.0	30.4			Long-Term Debt	32.0	32.9
	.0	.0	.0	.1			Deferred Taxes	.0	.0
	13.9	2.0	2.9	4.7			All Other Non-Current	4.4	4.7
	8.4	48.2	45.9	43.5			Net Worth	37.4	37.1
	100.0	100.0	100.0	100.0			Total Liabilities & Net Worth	100.0	100.0
							INCOME DATA		
	100.0	100.0	100.0	100.0			Net Sales	100.0	100.0
							Gross Profit		
	88.8	94.1	95.9	95.7			Operating Expenses	94.8	94.8
	11.2	5.9	4.1	4.3			Operating Profit	5.2	5.2
	1.3	2.2	1.2	1.2			All Other Expenses (net)	2.4	2.1
	9.9	3.7	2.9	3.1			Profit Before Taxes	2.8	3.1
							RATIOS		
	3.8	3.0	3.3	2.5				2.3	2.5
	1.2	1.8	1.8	1.6			Current	1.4	1.6
	.5	.8	1.3	1.2				.9	1.0
	3.5	2.8	3.0	2.2				2.1	2.3
	1.2	1.7	1.7	1.5			Quick	1.3	1.4
	.5	.5	1.1	1.1				.8	.9
	0 UND	0 UND	19 19.7	19 19.2				18 20.5	15 24.9
	0 UND	8 43.1	36 10.0	36 10.1			Sales/Receivables	35 10.4	34 10.8
	36 10.0	37 9.9	51 7.2	48 7.6				50 7.3	48 7.6
							Cost of Sales/Inventory		
							Cost of Sales/Payables		
	37.8	5.8	5.5	5.7				6.6	5.7
	77.6	15.4	10.5	10.7			Sales/Working Capital	20.3	14.0
	-35.7	-26.3	24.3	52.1				-58.3	196.5
		23.5	7.4	7.3				5.1	5.1
	(26) 1.7	(89) 2.4	(91) 2.9				EBIT/Interest	(222) 2.2	(213) 2.3
	-.7	1.0	1.3					1.0	.9
							Net Profit + Depr., Dep., Amort./Cur. Mat. L/T/D	4.7	
								(15) 1.4	
								.7	
	.4	.2	.6	.8				.7	.7
	.8	1.0	1.1	1.3			Fixed/Worth	1.4	1.5
	-.8	2.0	2.0	2.4				3.2	2.8
	.4	.6	.6	.7				.8	.6
	2.6	.9	1.1	1.4			Debt/Worth	1.6	1.6
	-14.5	1.9	2.7	2.6				4.2	3.7
		77.5	19.7	12.6			% Profit Before Taxes/Tangible Net Worth	20.0	19.3
	(37) 12.0	(97) 7.6	(92) 6.9					(238) 6.9	(233) 7.8
	-7.2	.0	1.5					.2	.6
	57.9	43.5	8.3	6.1			% Profit Before Taxes/Total Assets	7.6	6.9
	11.7	6.1	2.6	2.5				2.9	2.5
	-8.3	-3.0	-.4	.6				-.1	-.7
	119.9	46.5	6.7	4.3			Sales/Net Fixed Assets	6.3	6.1
	26.8	3.8	2.8	2.4				2.8	2.4
	8.5	1.1	1.7	1.4				1.5	1.3
	8.0	4.2	2.3	1.8			Sales/Total Assets	2.2	2.2
	4.3	1.9	1.7	1.2				1.4	1.3
	1.4	.7	1.0	.8				.8	.7
		.8	1.6	1.9			% Depr., Dep., Amort./Sales	1.5	1.8
	(33) 1.8	(98) 2.4	(91) 2.9					(254) 2.6	(242) 2.8
	5.0	3.9	4.1					4.6	5.1
		4.1		1.4			% Officers', Directors' Owners' Comp/Sales	2.8	4.1
	(10) 6.5		(12) 4.3					(20) 6.3	(22) 7.5
	8.8		9.7					10.0	21.5
	8877M	110977M	983620M	2843672M	560134M	1052871M	Net Sales ($)	5963871M	4742171M
	1929M	43477M	556469M	2139021M	623406M	1568458M	Total Assets ($)	4455449M	4549380M

M = $ thousand   MM = $ million
See Pages 9 through 22 for Explanation of Ratios and Data

Comparative Historical Data   **Current Data Sorted by Sales**

Type of Statement	4/1/08-3/31/09 ALL	4/1/09-3/31/10 ALL	4/1/10-3/31/11 ALL	0-1MM	1-3MM	3-5MM	5-10MM	10-25MM	25MM & OVER
					169 (4/1-9/30/10)			99 (10/1/10-3/31/11)	
Unqualified	86	150	161	10	16	9	32	50	44
Reviewed	5	2	3			1	1	1	
Compiled	7	4	8	3	2	2	1		
Tax Returns	10	12	13	2	6	2	1	1	1
Other	53	87	83	7	8	6	18	22	22
NUMBER OF STATEMENTS	161	255	268	22	32	20	53	74	67
	%	%	%	%	%	%	%	%	%
ASSETS									
Cash & Equivalents	16.1	15.7	18.8	17.0	22.7	21.7	19.3	18.9	16.3
Trade Receivables (net)	19.9	15.7	15.8	3.4	11.4	17.5	17.6	16.8	18.9
Inventory	.2	.1	.1	.0	.0	.0	.0	.2	.3
All Other Current	3.4	2.7	3.0	4.8	1.8	5.1	2.9	3.0	2.3
Total Current	39.5	34.3	37.7	25.3	35.9	44.4	39.8	38.9	37.8
Fixed Assets (net)	49.3	53.2	51.5	58.5	56.5	49.0	49.3	51.7	49.3
Intangibles (net)	1.5	1.9	1.6	.5	1.3	.5	2.4	.7	2.5
All Other Non-Current	9.7	10.6	9.2	15.7	6.2	6.1	8.5	8.6	10.4
Total	100.0	100.0	100.0	100.0	100.0	100.0	100.0	100.0	100.0
LIABILITIES									
Notes Payable-Short Term	4.2	2.8	2.6	6.3	6.2	1.6	1.6	1.2	2.4
Cur. Mat.-L.T.D.	2.7	5.1	2.8	2.2	2.6	2.1	2.7	3.8	2.4
Trade Payables	6.3	5.1	5.1	.8	2.9	5.0	5.3	5.4	7.0
Income Taxes Payable	.0	.1	.1	.0	.3	.0	.0	.2	.0
All Other Current	13.4	13.3	12.4	23.5	7.4	10.5	12.8	12.2	11.6
Total Current	26.6	26.4	23.0	32.8	19.5	19.1	22.4	22.7	23.4
Long-Term Debt	28.9	31.3	29.4	34.1	34.7	28.4	24.7	28.5	30.3
Deferred Taxes	.1	.0	.1	.0	.0	.0	.1	.0	.2
All Other Non-Current	1.9	5.9	4.5	1.3	7.9	1.5	3.8	2.7	7.4
Net Worth	42.5	36.4	43.0	31.7	37.9	51.0	49.1	46.1	38.7
Total Liabilities & Net Worth	100.0	100.0	100.0	100.0	100.0	100.0	100.0	100.0	100.0
INCOME DATA									
Net Sales	100.0	100.0	100.0	100.0	100.0	100.0	100.0	100.0	100.0
Gross Profit									
Operating Expenses	97.2	95.3	95.4	91.6	92.5	93.5	95.1	97.2	96.8
Operating Profit	2.8	4.7	4.6	8.4	7.5	6.5	4.9	2.8	3.2
All Other Expenses (net)	1.4	2.5	1.3	4.0	2.8	1.2	1.0	.8	.4
Profit Before Taxes	1.3	2.2	3.3	4.4	4.6	5.3	3.9	1.9	2.7
RATIOS									
Current	2.7	2.8	2.9	4.2	4.1	3.8	3.4	2.6	2.0
	1.7	1.6	1.7	.9	2.3	2.1	1.9	1.6	1.6
	1.0	1.0	1.1	.4	1.1	1.8	1.1	1.3	1.1
Quick	2.7	2.5	2.7	4.1	4.1	3.5	3.2	2.2	1.9
	1.4	1.4	1.6	.6	2.2	2.1	1.7	1.5	1.4
	.9	.8	1.0	.1	1.1	1.6	.9	1.2	1.0
Sales/Receivables	19 19.4	13 27.8	13 28.7	0 UND	0 UND	13 27.9	15 23.6	23 16.1	21 17.0
	37 9.9	33 10.9	34 10.9	0 UND	7 50.1	31 11.7	40 9.2	34 10.6	40 9.1
	52 7.0	50 7.3	47 7.7	28 13.1	36 10.1	41 9.0	51 7.2	47 7.8	52 7.0
Cost of Sales/Inventory									
Cost of Sales/Payables									
Sales/Working Capital	6.0	6.6	5.7	2.7	5.5	5.0	5.0	6.7	7.5
	13.7	15.0	11.3	UND	9.3	9.0	8.4	12.2	13.3
	351.5	999.8	56.2	-5.1	76.6	18.3	30.6	32.9	56.5
EBIT/Interest	5.7	5.1	7.6	12.7	3.0	9.0	10.6	5.5	7.0
	(130) 2.6	(205) 1.8	(231) 2.4	(13) 1.1	(24) 1.2	(17) 3.5	(47) 3.4	(65) 2.4	(65) 3.4
	.4	.2	1.0	-3.4	-1.0	.9	1.2	.8	1.5
Net Profit + Depr., Dep., Amort./Cur. Mat. L/T/D									
Fixed/Worth	.6	.8	.7	.6	.8	.5	.6	.7	.8
	1.2	1.4	1.2	1.5	1.6	.9	1.0	1.2	1.4
	2.4	2.9	2.4	10.6	5.0	1.9	1.7	2.0	2.5
Debt/Worth	.6	.7	.6	.4	.6	.4	.6	.6	.9
	1.1	1.4	1.2	.9	1.5	.8	1.0	1.1	1.8
	3.1	3.9	2.7	10.1	5.3	2.8	2.4	2.5	2.7
% Profit Before Taxes/Tangible Net Worth	19.7	18.8	20.2	14.9	70.4	81.1	21.4	13.3	20.3
	(148) 7.6	(228) 6.7	(249) 7.1	(18) 1.9	(30) 4.6	(19) 10.9	(49) 7.3	(70) 5.0	(63) 9.7
	-4.1	-1.3	.5	-11.1	-6.2	.4	1.7	-.9	2.3
% Profit Before Taxes/Total Assets	8.9	6.6	8.3	10.2	9.1	33.3	10.1	6.1	8.1
	3.2	2.0	2.7	-.4	1.1	7.9	3.3	2.4	3.4
	-2.4	-.9	.0	-5.6	-3.0	.2	.3	-.2	1.2
Sales/Net Fixed Assets	7.1	6.0	6.2	4.2	26.2	18.9	6.6	5.5	5.6
	3.5	2.6	2.7	1.2	1.9	3.2	2.6	2.6	2.9
	2.0	1.5	1.4	.4	.8	1.4	1.3	1.7	1.8
Sales/Total Assets	2.7	2.2	2.2	1.0	3.5	4.1	2.5	2.1	2.2
	1.8	1.4	1.4	.5	1.2	1.8	1.3	1.6	1.5
	1.1	.9	.8	.3	.5	.9	.8	.9	1.1
% Depr., Dep., Amort./Sales	1.5	1.7	1.7	3.0	1.2	1.0	1.2	1.7	1.7
	(151) 2.1	(232) 2.8	(243) 2.7	(16) 9.8	(25) 3.7	(16) 2.3	(50) 3.1	(71) 2.6	(65) 2.4
	3.4	4.3	4.2	25.5	5.7	4.4	4.2	3.6	3.9
% Officers', Directors' Owners' Comp/Sales	4.2	3.9	2.3						
	(23) 8.3	(27) 8.1	(33) 6.9						
	11.1	11.3	10.4						
Net Sales ($)	2506062M	4977347M	5560151M	10535M	59987M	82585M	388761M	1181405M	3836878M
Total Assets ($)	1780799M	4375838M	4932760M	26381M	99627M	63228M	406214M	926515M	3410795M

M = $ thousand   MM = $ million
See Pages 9 through 22 for Explanation of Ratios and Data

Current Data Sorted by Assets   Comparative Historical Data

Type of Statement	0-500M	500M-2MM	2-10MM	10-50MM	50-100MM	100-250MM	4/1/06-3/31/07 ALL	4/1/07-3/31/08 ALL
Unqualified		5	47	80	60	53	189	174
Reviewed		9	19	7	1		29	26
Compiled	2	5	11	4		1	30	34
Tax Returns	9	9	15	2	1		13	19
Other	16	17	58	64	25	17	114	125
		151 (4/1-9/30/10)		386 (10/1/10-3/31/11)				
NUMBER OF STATEMENTS	27	45	150	157	87	71	375	378
	%	%	%	%	%	%	%	%
ASSETS								
Cash & Equivalents	22.5	13.1	10.5	9.5	10.6	8.8	10.7	10.1
Trade Receivables (net)	25.6	18.4	9.5	4.8	4.6	2.3	9.1	9.9
Inventory	.3	.4	.3	1.1	.2	.1	.2	.2
All Other Current	2.9	5.7	1.4	1.9	1.4	2.2	3.1	2.9
Total Current	51.2	37.6	21.6	17.3	16.7	13.4	23.1	23.1
Fixed Assets (net)	27.8	45.6	65.3	68.0	63.3	62.7	60.1	59.5
Intangibles (net)	8.3	3.3	2.7	2.3	3.6	1.4	3.0	2.6
All Other Non-Current	12.7	13.5	10.4	12.4	16.4	22.5	13.8	14.8
Total	100.0	100.0	100.0	100.0	100.0	100.0	100.0	100.0
LIABILITIES								
Notes Payable-Short Term	5.0	6.3	2.6	2.0	1.1	.6	2.9	2.7
Cur. Mat.-L.T.D.	1.2	3.6	4.3	3.2	3.4	2.3	2.0	2.9
Trade Payables	26.2	9.5	3.6	2.2	2.5	1.9	5.0	4.4
Income Taxes Payable	1.3	.0	.1	.0	.0	.0	.1	.0
All Other Current	71.0	27.3	10.7	7.1	5.9	6.8	12.1	13.2
Total Current	104.7	46.7	21.3	14.5	12.9	11.6	22.1	23.2
Long-Term Debt	24.0	37.9	66.2	52.2	54.1	45.6	50.5	49.2
Deferred Taxes	1.5	.0	.1	.1	.3	.0	.1	.4
All Other Non-Current	9.2	8.1	4.1	16.3	32.4	33.3	15.4	13.5
Net Worth	-39.4	7.3	8.3	16.9	.2	9.4	11.9	13.7
Total Liabilties & Net Worth	100.0	100.0	100.0	100.0	100.0	100.0	100.0	100.0
INCOME DATA								
Net Sales	100.0	100.0	100.0	100.0	100.0	100.0	100.0	100.0
Gross Profit								
Operating Expenses	96.7	91.3	83.3	90.5	93.8	96.2	91.1	91.1
Operating Profit	3.3	8.7	16.7	9.5	6.2	3.8	8.9	8.9
All Other Expenses (net)	2.7	2.7	11.0	6.5	5.7	5.9	6.2	5.6
Profit Before Taxes	.6	6.1	5.7	3.0	.5	-2.2	2.8	3.2
RATIOS								
Current	2.3	1.6	2.6	2.7	3.3	2.4	2.4	2.4
	.5	.9	1.0	1.4	1.5	1.3	1.3	1.3
	.4	.4	.4	.6	.9	.7	.7	.7
Quick	1.9	1.5	2.3	2.1	2.9	1.6	2.0	2.1
	.5	.8	.8	1.1	1.3	1.0	1.1	1.0
	.4	.3	.3	.6	.7	.6	.5	.5
Sales/Receivables	0 UND	0 UND	1 316.3	3 115.8	11 32.5	9 39.1	4 83.1	3 108.3
	5 68.9	10 35.0	11 33.0	20 18.1	18 20.0	18 20.7	22 16.4	20 18.2
	30 12.2	30 12.1	31 11.6	33 11.0	38 9.6	29 12.4	41 9.0	38 9.7
Cost of Sales/Inventory								
Cost of Sales/Payables								
Sales/Working Capital	36.5	15.8	7.6	4.8	2.3	3.1	5.6	5.9
	-133.1	-86.4	-999.8	20.1	10.8	16.4	24.5	24.0
	-12.0	-12.5	-6.6	-12.8	-81.8	-6.4	-19.6	-15.6
EBIT/Interest	5.0	96.7	5.9	3.3	3.0	2.0	3.5	3.7
	(13) .3	(32) 6.2	(115) 1.6	(137) 1.6	(77) 1.8	(64) 1.1	(295) 1.8	(306) 1.9
	-19.5	1.0	.7	.8	1.1	.1	.9	.9
Net Profit + Depr., Dep., Amort./Cur. Mat. L/T/D							6.7	6.3
							(12) 2.7	(11) 2.0
							1.2	1.2
Fixed/Worth	.5	.5	1.3	1.7	2.6	2.7	1.3	1.3
	1.9	2.0	15.8	5.1	-166.3	9.6	4.1	3.8
	-.2	-12.8	-5.3	-6.8	-4.2	-6.8	-8.0	-12.4
Debt/Worth	1.3	.8	1.5	1.7	3.2	3.8	1.6	1.5
	-6.0	2.7	18.2	5.9	-210.8	15.0	6.5	5.6
	-2.0	-24.3	-7.1	-9.8	-6.2	-10.5	-12.8	-19.9
% Profit Before Taxes/Tangible Net Worth	211.5	105.7	51.3	20.3	17.6	14.0	36.3	42.5
	(12) 76.0	(32) 44.6	(88) 18.4	(108) 7.8	(43) 8.8	(41) 3.8	(257) 9.5	(260) 10.4
	31.0	12.6	.1	.8	4.8	-2.3	1.8	1.2
% Profit Before Taxes/Total Assets	49.4	28.8	11.9	3.9	2.9	1.8	6.0	7.1
	4.1	9.2	3.3	1.6	1.3	.1	1.9	1.9
	-38.5	-.4	-1.0	-.5	-.5	-1.8	-.5	-.6
Sales/Net Fixed Assets	359.6	29.7	3.4	1.0	.7	.6	2.3	3.0
	49.4	6.3	1.0	.6	.5	.3	.8	.9
	19.2	1.6	.5	.4	.3	.2	.4	.4
Sales/Total Assets	10.2	4.5	1.5	.6	.4	.3	1.2	1.4
	8.0	2.9	.6	.5	.3	.2	.5	.6
	5.5	.9	.3	.3	.2	.2	.3	.3
% Depr., Dep., Amort./Sales	.2	.7	2.7	6.0	9.5	11.3	2.9	2.8
	(17) .6	(40) 1.9	(139) 6.8	(151) 9.2	(84) 12.1	(68) 15.8	(358) 7.0	(359) 6.4
	1.5	5.5	14.2	13.7	15.4	18.6	12.3	11.8
% Officers', Directors' Owners' Comp/Sales			1.5	3.0			1.5	2.7
			(19) 3.9	(22) 5.2			(45) 3.6	(49) 4.8
			13.5	11.0			15.6	10.9
Net Sales ($)	45349M	154588M	817890M	2540201M	3090112M	3077316M	7580701M	7682723M
Total Assets ($)	6014M	49907M	796004M	4149928M	6280704M	9937256M	12477395M	13127485M

© RMA 2011   M = $ thousand   MM = $ million
See Pages 9 through 22 for Explanation of Ratios and Data

Comparative Historical Data | Current Data Sorted by Sales

4/1/08-3/31/09 ALL	4/1/09-3/31/10 ALL	4/1/10-3/31/11 ALL	Type of Statement	0-1MM	1-3MM	3-5MM	5-10MM	10-25MM	25MM & OVER
232	234	245	Unqualified	4	15	19	39	109	59
33	32	36	Reviewed	4	8	5	5	13	1
26	24	23	Compiled	3	7	4	3	5	1
48	31	36	Tax Returns	7	15	7	3	3	1
166	174	197	Other	19	47	17	32	56	26
				151 (4/1-9/30/10)			386 (10/1/10-3/31/11)		
505	495	537	**NUMBER OF STATEMENTS**	37	92	52	82	186	88
%	%	%	**ASSETS**	%	%	%	%	%	%
11.1	10.9	10.8	Cash & Equivalents	8.3	9.4	10.5	11.7	11.4	11.4
11.3	9.5	7.9	Trade Receivables (net)	7.4	6.8	8.9	9.4	7.4	8.4
.4	.2	.5	Inventory	.1	.1	.4	.4	1.0	.3
3.2	3.0	2.1	All Other Current	1.3	3.4	1.8	1.9	1.4	2.9
26.0	23.7	21.3	Total Current	17.0	19.8	21.6	23.3	21.1	23.0
56.2	57.9	61.9	Fixed Assets (net)	70.7	65.3	65.4	59.1	61.2	56.5
2.8	3.0	2.9	Intangibles (net)	4.4	3.3	3.7	2.3	2.1	3.7
15.0	15.5	13.9	All Other Non-Current	8.0	11.7	9.2	15.2	15.6	16.8
100.0	100.0	100.0	Total	100.0	100.0	100.0	100.0	100.0	100.0
			LIABILITIES						
2.7	4.2	2.3	Notes Payable-Short Term	2.3	4.4	5.6	1.2	.8	2.6
4.3	4.0	3.3	Cur. Mat.-L.T.D.	5.6	3.4	4.1	3.8	2.6	2.9
5.2	4.9	4.4	Trade Payables	8.5	5.7	4.4	4.1	3.3	4.1
.0	.1	.1	Income Taxes Payable	.0	.4	.2	.0	.0	.1
13.4	12.8	12.8	All Other Current	25.7	18.6	13.4	13.2	8.6	9.3
25.7	26.0	23.0	Total Current	42.1	32.6	27.7	22.2	15.4	19.1
46.5	49.5	52.9	Long-Term Debt	80.4	58.3	58.8	50.3	49.0	43.1
.3	.5	.2	Deferred Taxes	.0	.4	.0	.1	.1	.3
14.8	18.1	16.7	All Other Non-Current	8.8	7.0	5.8	12.7	24.1	24.8
12.7	6.0	7.2	Net Worth	-31.3	1.7	7.7	14.8	11.5	12.7
100.0	100.0	100.0	Total Liabilities & Net Worth	100.0	100.0	100.0	100.0	100.0	100.0
			INCOME DATA						
100.0	100.0	100.0	Net Sales	100.0	100.0	100.0	100.0	100.0	100.0
			Gross Profit						
92.6	91.9	90.2	Operating Expenses	70.8	85.5	88.4	91.9	94.4	93.5
7.4	8.1	9.8	Operating Profit	29.2	14.5	11.6	8.1	5.6	6.5
7.0	5.9	7.0	All Other Expenses (net)	24.4	9.0	9.1	5.2	4.5	3.5
.4	2.2	2.8	Profit Before Taxes	4.8	5.4	2.5	2.9	1.0	2.9
			RATIOS						
2.4	2.5	2.4	Current	1.7	1.6	2.5	2.3	3.1	2.4
1.3	1.3	1.2		.3	.7	.9	1.4	1.3	1.3
.7	.6	.6		.0	.3	.5	.6	.8	.9
2.1	2.0	2.1	Quick	1.5	1.5	2.3	2.0	2.6	1.8
1.0	1.1	1.0		.2	.5	.9	1.1	1.2	1.0
.5	.5	.5		.0	.3	.5	.5	.7	.7
4 82.4	5 74.0	4 99.1	Sales/Receivables	0 UND	0 999.8	0 780.1	3 138.3	13 28.1	14 25.5
22 17.0	19 18.9	16 22.8		0 UND	3 104.3	8 47.7	19 19.6	22 16.9	24 15.0
38 9.5	34 10.7	32 11.6		20 17.9	14 25.4	23 15.5	33 11.1	36 10.1	38 9.6
			Cost of Sales/Inventory						
			Cost of Sales/Payables						
6.1	6.1	5.9	Sales/Working Capital	6.0	15.4	10.9	6.7	4.2	4.7
23.3	31.7	41.5		-7.8	-32.2	-115.4	17.1	16.8	20.7
-14.8	-11.7	-11.7		-2.3	-4.0	-12.1	-11.6	-25.8	-40.8
3.8	3.9	3.8	EBIT/Interest	3.2	6.3	2.9	4.6	3.2	3.9
(408) 1.3	(383) 1.5	(438) 1.6		(16) 1.0	(64) 1.5	(41) 1.5	(71) 1.4	(164) 1.7	(82) 2.1
.1	.5	.7		.2	-.3	.9	.7	.9	1.0
8.1	6.3	5.2	Net Profit + Depr., Dep., Amort./Cur. Mat. L/T/D						
(23) 2.9	(12) 2.7	(18) 2.3							
2.1	.8	.6							
1.2	1.4	1.7	Fixed/Worth	2.0	1.8	1.6	1.1	1.8	1.5
3.9	5.7	7.2		-12.7	33.0	43.0	4.2	5.4	3.9
-6.4	-5.0	-5.2		-2.7	-3.8	-3.1	-5.4	-7.1	-19.8
1.3	1.7	1.9	Debt/Worth	4.3	1.8	1.5	1.4	1.8	2.1
5.5	8.0	9.7		-11.8	33.1	47.5	5.3	7.3	5.7
-11.0	-7.5	-7.5		-2.8	-6.0	-5.2	-9.0	-10.3	-34.7
36.6	36.8	35.3	% Profit Before Taxes/Tangible Net Worth	67.7	44.5	66.4	37.3	20.6	27.5
(341) 8.0	(302) 11.0	(324) 11.2		(15) 17.6	(48) 28.4	(29) 12.5	(56) 11.0	(115) 9.3	(61) 10.4
-3.7	-1.8	1.7		-2.6	3.8	-.1	.0	1.9	2.7
7.5	7.8	5.8	% Profit Before Taxes/Total Assets	4.7	11.4	7.2	9.1	3.7	6.1
1.1	1.7	1.7		-.4	3.1	1.9	1.2	1.5	1.8
-2.2	-1.5	-1.0		-1.9	-3.7	-.8	-.9	-.9	.0
4.6	3.7	2.4	Sales/Net Fixed Assets	2.9	8.3	5.1	3.0	1.5	2.7
1.0	.8	.6		.3	.8	.8	.8	.6	.8
.4	.4	.3		.1	.3	.5	.4	.3	.5
1.7	1.5	1.2	Sales/Total Assets	.9	2.0	1.7	1.3	.7	1.4
.6	.5	.5		.2	.6	.6	.6	.4	.5
.3	.3	.2		.1	.3	.4	.2	.2	.3
2.3	2.8	4.0	% Depr., Dep., Amort./Sales	8.9	2.2	2.6	3.8	5.3	2.9
(463) 6.2	(466) 7.2	(499) 9.2		(30) 23.4	(80) 8.8	(47) 6.9	(77) 7.1	(182) 10.2	(83) 7.2
11.7	13.0	14.9		38.3	19.3	11.0	13.2	14.8	13.4
2.5	2.6	2.4	% Officers', Directors' Owners' Comp/Sales		2.7			1.9	2.3
(64) 5.2	(54) 5.3	(69) 4.9			(18) 5.0			(19) 8.0	(15) 4.9
9.2	11.9	9.6			6.4			24.1	9.4
10028324M	8994926M	9725456M	Net Sales ($)	18971M	172097M	197687M	617712M	3105707M	5613282M
17241637M	17805355M	21219813M	Total Assets ($)	116520M	422028M	365797M	1868919M	9579813M	8866736M

M = $ thousand   MM = $ million
See Pages 9 through 22 for Explanation of Ratios and Data

Current Data Sorted by Assets   **Comparative Historical Data**

0-500M	500M-2MM	2-10MM	10-50MM	50-100MM	100-250MM	Type of Statement	4/1/06-3/31/07 ALL	4/1/07-3/31/08 ALL
	5	22	18	6	2	Unqualified	47	38
	1	12	4		2	Reviewed	5	12
7	3	5	3			Compiled	7	8
21	9	7	1			Tax Returns	12	15
15	16	18	17	4	2	Other	36	56
\- 42 (4/1-9/30/10) \-		\- 158 (10/1/10-3/31/11) \-						
43	34	64	43	10	6	**NUMBER OF STATEMENTS**	107	129
%	%	%	%	%	%	**ASSETS**	%	%
35.1	17.9	8.9	11.3	9.2		Cash & Equivalents	10.7	12.4
9.9	12.8	5.4	3.4	7.0		Trade Receivables (net)	8.6	7.6
.7	.1	.2	.1	.9		Inventory	.1	.7
6.9	1.6	1.9	.6	1.2		All Other Current	2.8	5.0
52.6	32.4	16.4	15.4	18.3		Total Current	22.1	25.8
29.7	59.4	74.8	69.4	56.1		Fixed Assets (net)	62.4	61.4
5.5	2.7	2.4	6.4	6.1		Intangibles (net)	2.8	2.1
12.2	5.5	6.4	8.7	19.4		All Other Non-Current	12.7	10.6
100.0	100.0	100.0	100.0	100.0		Total	100.0	100.0
						LIABILITIES		
12.2	4.0	.1	3.0	2.5		Notes Payable-Short Term	2.3	3.4
11.2	3.1	3.3	3.3	2.2		Cur. Mat.-L.T.D.	4.5	4.4
13.4	7.9	2.9	2.4	3.6		Trade Payables	5.0	5.3
1.6	.0	.0	.0	.0		Income Taxes Payable	.0	.1
38.2	16.8	8.7	5.5	11.0		All Other Current	20.8	19.5
76.6	31.7	14.9	14.2	19.2		Total Current	32.6	32.7
20.8	50.1	74.7	58.8	64.6		Long-Term Debt	47.5	51.9
.0	.0	.0	.0	.0		Deferred Taxes	.0	.0
11.5	3.7	6.7	14.3	14.9		All Other Non-Current	6.4	10.1
-8.9	14.4	3.6	12.7	1.3		Net Worth	13.5	5.2
100.0	100.0	100.0	100.0	100.0		Total Liabilities & Net Worth	100.0	100.0
						INCOME DATA		
100.0	100.0	100.0	100.0	100.0		Net Sales	100.0	100.0
						Gross Profit		
93.6	85.9	85.1	89.0	93.2		Operating Expenses	88.0	88.6
6.4	14.1	14.9	11.0	6.8		Operating Profit	12.0	11.4
1.7	5.4	10.5	11.8	4.6		All Other Expenses (net)	5.9	9.1
4.7	8.6	4.4	-.8	2.2		Profit Before Taxes	6.2	2.4
						RATIOS		
2.3	3.0	2.4	3.0	3.4		Current	2.1	2.5
1.4	1.0	1.3	.9	.8			1.1	1.0
.4	.4	.7	.4	.5			.4	.4
2.1	2.3	2.4	2.5	3.4		Quick	1.9	2.3
1.3	.8 (63)	1.2	.9	.8			1.0 (128)	.9
.3	.3	.5	.3	.4			.4	.3
0 UND	0 UND	0 UND	2 239.7	15 23.9		Sales/Receivables	1 349.0	0 UND
3 114.0	5 76.1	3 135.1	6 62.0	30 12.3			13 27.1	6 57.8
7 53.7	26 14.0	10 38.4	27 13.7	42 8.6			32 11.3	30 12.0
						Cost of Sales/Inventory		
						Cost of Sales/Payables		
17.7	7.7	5.4	3.9	3.1		Sales/Working Capital	10.4	7.4
53.4	NM	40.8	-61.3	-17.8			133.0	171.7
-12.1	-7.0	-17.8	-8.4	-6.3			-9.1	-8.5
33.0	7.8	2.7	3.5			EBIT/Interest	5.8	3.6
(23) 6.0	(24) 2.5	(53) 1.9	(30) 1.9				(71) 1.9	(90) 1.3
1.0	1.1	.9	.6				.9	.6
						Net Profit + Depr., Dep., Amort./Cur. Mat. L/T/D		
.1	.4	2.2	2.1	6.1		Fixed/Worth	1.0	1.2
.9	5.0	23.7	26.3	-11.9			5.2	5.5
-.9	-4.7	-3.2	-6.9	-2.3			-17.3	-8.6
.8	.8	2.7	2.6	7.8		Debt/Worth	.8	1.5
3.7	18.4	24.3	27.5	-18.8			5.2	10.7
-2.2	-7.1	-5.3	-9.2	-4.3			-21.3	-10.7
145.2	91.2	35.3	33.8			% Profit Before Taxes/Tangible Net Worth	33.7	45.4
(28) 55.2	(19) 46.4	(35) 7.4	(25) 5.1				(74) 13.4	(74) 10.2
30.3	5.6	-.7	-5.5				-3.3	.5
62.0	18.3	7.8	4.6	9.1		% Profit Before Taxes/Total Assets	8.9	9.3
16.7	3.7	2.3	1.3	3.5			3.4	.8
.0	-.1	-.4	-2.2	-.8			-1.0	-1.2
183.2	11.5	1.1	.8	3.2		Sales/Net Fixed Assets	5.0	5.9
41.2	1.3	.7	.5	.9			1.4	1.0
13.6	.6	.4	.3	.4			.5	.4
10.7	2.8	1.0	.6	.9		Sales/Total Assets	1.8	2.0
6.4	.9	.5	.3	.4			.9	.7
3.4	.5	.4	.2	.3			.4	.3
.4	2.2	4.3	5.8	3.2		% Depr., Dep., Amort./Sales	2.0	2.8
(28) 1.1	(28) 5.4	(61) 7.8	(42) 11.0	7.7			(101) 4.8	(117) 6.0
3.0	9.3	12.6	15.1	10.6			9.8	12.6
		5.1				% Officers', Directors' Owners' Comp/Sales	4.1	6.0
	(12) 5.9						(17) 8.7	(24) 9.1
		21.9					12.0	16.8
47559M	70040M	237698M	519095M	560785M	442397M	Net Sales ($)	848676M	1200256M
8326M	39297M	322874M	898500M	681979M	932487M	Total Assets ($)	1390269M	1979682M

M = $ thousand   MM = $ million
See Pages 9 through 22 for Explanation of Ratios and Data

Comparative Historical Data | | | | Current Data Sorted by Sales

			Type of Statement						
112	61	53	Unqualified	7	9	12	7	12	6
10	10	19	Reviewed		4	4	7	2	2
10	16	18	Compiled	5	7	4	1	1	
26	44	38	Tax Returns	17	19	1	1		
89	53	72	Other	20	22	8	9	8	5
4/1/08-3/31/09 ALL	4/1/09-3/31/10 ALL	4/1/10-3/31/11 ALL		42 (4/1-9/30/10)			158 (10/1/10-3/31/11)		
				0-1MM	1-3MM	3-5MM	5-10MM	10-25MM	25MM & OVER
247	184	200	NUMBER OF STATEMENTS	49	61	29	25	23	13
%	%	%	ASSETS	%	%	%	%	%	%
15.1	15.1	16.4	Cash & Equivalents	20.0	19.9	13.1	12.4	14.6	5.3
11.1	6.4	7.4	Trade Receivables (net)	3.9	5.3	4.8	16.2	11.7	11.2
.2	.2	.3	Inventory	.5	.1	.1	.1	.4	.7
2.6	3.1	2.6	All Other Current	6.5	1.1	1.8	.5	2.2	.9
29.0	24.7	26.7	Total Current	30.9	26.4	19.9	29.3	28.9	18.2
55.8	59.3	60.5	Fixed Assets (net)	57.2	62.1	71.1	58.0	52.2	60.9
2.4	2.7	4.2	Intangibles (net)	4.6	3.7	2.7	4.7	4.6	6.9
12.9	13.3	8.6	All Other Non-Current	7.3	7.8	6.3	8.0	14.3	14.0
100.0	100.0	100.0	Total	100.0	100.0	100.0	100.0	100.0	100.0
			LIABILITIES						
4.8	4.0	4.1	Notes Payable-Short Term	10.6	2.9	2.5	.1	1.5	2.0
4.8	4.1	4.9	Cur. Mat.-L.T.D.	2.3	9.6	2.2	2.4	3.1	7.2
5.5	7.3	5.9	Trade Payables	4.5	7.4	2.4	9.4	5.6	6.0
.0	.0	.4	Income Taxes Payable	1.4	.0	.0	.1	.0	.0
19.8	18.6	15.7	All Other Current	24.7	15.6	4.9	15.0	15.0	8.9
34.9	34.0	31.0	Total Current	43.4	35.3	12.1	27.0	25.2	24.2
43.1	51.6	55.1	Long-Term Debt	49.8	54.4	79.8	46.6	40.5	65.1
.0	.0	.0	Deferred Taxes	.0	.0	.0	.0	.0	.0
7.1	9.0	9.4	All Other Non-Current	8.9	9.8	3.4	7.7	22.9	2.8
14.8	5.4	4.5	Net Worth	-2.1	.5	4.7	18.7	11.3	8.0
100.0	100.0	100.0	Total Liabilties & Net Worth	100.0	100.0	100.0	100.0	100.0	100.0
			INCOME DATA						
100.0	100.0	100.0	Net Sales	100.0	100.0	100.0	100.0	100.0	100.0
			Gross Profit						
91.9	87.3	88.5	Operating Expenses	86.5	90.0	82.6	88.9	94.5	90.5
8.1	12.7	11.5	Operating Profit	13.5	10.0	17.4	11.1	5.5	9.5
6.5	9.9	7.7	All Other Expenses (net)	8.3	8.0	10.1	7.9	3.5	5.7
1.6	2.8	3.8	Profit Before Taxes	5.2	2.0	7.2	3.2	2.0	3.8
			RATIOS						
2.2	2.2	2.5		2.3	2.7	2.5	2.6	2.7	2.1
1.2	1.0	1.2	Current	1.0	1.3	1.3	1.2	1.2	.7
.6	.4	.5		.4	.4	.7	.6	.5	.4
2.0	1.7	2.3		1.9	2.6	2.2	2.5	2.3	2.1
1.0	.8 (199)	1.1	Quick	.7	1.3 (28)	1.1	1.1	1.2	.7
.5	.2	.4		.2	.4	.5	.5	.5	.4
2 173.6	0 UND	0 UND		0 UND	0 UND	0 999.8	2 151.4	16 22.7	10 37.4
18 20.0	4 89.7	4 91.0	Sales/Receivables	0 UND	2 213.2	3 139.4	8 48.5	29 12.4	28 13.2
42 8.8	20 18.2	23 15.7		6 64.1	8 43.0	7 53.8	40 9.2	39 9.4	39 9.3
			Cost of Sales/Inventory						
			Cost of Sales/Payables						
6.8	9.0	7.2		10.9	7.4	6.9	6.2	5.1	8.9
39.2	NM	63.3	Sales/Working Capital	317.0	81.2	45.1	36.4	45.8	-20.5
-14.4	-6.8	-10.0		-4.8	-11.1	-20.0	-20.9	-9.1	-6.2
4.7	6.7	4.7		4.7	25.5	2.9	10.4	3.0	4.3
(185) 1.6	(126) 1.8	(144) 2.0	EBIT/Interest	(26) 1.7	(44) 2.2	(27) 2.0	(17) 2.3	(19) 1.6	(11) 2.5
.4	1.0	.9		.9	.7	1.2	1.0	.3	.9
			Net Profit + Depr., Dep., Amort./Cur. Mat. L/T/D						
1.0	1.1	1.1		1.3	.6	1.8	.7	2.1	2.6
2.6	7.7	11.4	Fixed/Worth	13.9	7.1	-11.5	3.6	7.2	-8.2
-12.4	-4.3	-3.9		-3.4	-5.4	-3.4	-10.1	-2.4	-3.1
1.1	1.7	1.7		2.2	1.2	1.6	1.1	1.8	2.3
3.6	12.4	17.6	Debt/Worth	88.2	8.1	-14.4	13.5	8.8	-10.2
-15.0	-5.9	-5.9		-4.8	-6.7	-5.1	-10.3	-6.0	-5.6
22.7	68.9	68.9		86.1	116.7	32.3	66.2	46.5	
(174) 7.4	(106) 11.7	(113) 16.4	% Profit Before Taxes/Tangible Net Worth	(25) 32.7	(39) 31.4	(12) 12.5	(17) 13.6	(15) 6.4	
-3.9	1.9	.9		4.4	3.1	3.0	-.2	-5.1	
6.8	8.1	9.6		12.5	24.4	7.9	8.3	6.9	13.8
1.2	2.2	2.9	% Profit Before Taxes/Total Assets	2.8	4.3	3.2	2.5	2.2	5.8
-2.3	-.6	-1.0		-1.5	-2.0	.9	.0	-1.5	-.7
5.8	8.7	11.9		28.4	36.7	1.2	9.3	10.1	5.7
1.7	.9	.9	Sales/Net Fixed Assets	.9	.9	.8	1.1	.7	1.4
.6	.4	.4		.2	.4	.5	.4	.6	.4
2.1	2.5	2.9		4.4	4.3	1.1	3.0	1.9	1.5
.9	.7	.7	Sales/Total Assets	.7	.8	.6	.7	.6	.8
.4	.3	.4		.2	.4	.4	.3	.4	.3
1.8	2.6	2.6		2.1	2.2	5.0	2.3	1.4	2.3
(220) 4.0	(159) 6.9	(175) 6.6	% Depr., Dep., Amort./Sales	(39) 6.1	(50) 7.2	(28) 7.8	(22) 4.3	8.3	4.9
10.3	14.3	12.2		20.3	13.0	10.1	12.8	10.9	10.2
5.1	5.0	2.7		2.6	2.7				
(21) 6.4	(31) 6.5	(38) 5.9	% Officers', Directors' Owners' Comp/Sales	(10) 6.4	(13) 8.3				
15.9	11.4	11.0		13.6	12.3				
4537967M	2004492M	1877574M	Net Sales ($)	23678M	118091M	108676M	180079M	359743M	1087307M
5756804M	2843097M	2883463M	Total Assets ($)	69435M	230371M	213056M	356320M	735774M	1278507M

© RMA 2011

M = $ thousand   MM = $ million
See Pages 9 through 22 for Explanation of Ratios and Data

Current Data Sorted by Assets   Comparative Historical Data

Type of Statement	0-500M	500M-2MM	2-10MM	10-50MM	50-100MM	100-250MM	4/1/06-3/31/07 ALL	4/1/07-3/31/08 ALL
Unqualified	2	11	49	46	8	4	102	85
Reviewed	1	1	2	1			7	6
Compiled		2	5		1		5	7
Tax Returns	10	8	5	1		2	9	14
Other	11	8	28	12	1	2	57	46
		104 (4/1-9/30/10)		117 (10/1/10-3/31/11)				
NUMBER OF STATEMENTS	24	30	89	60	10	8	180	158
ASSETS	%	%	%	%	%	%	%	%
Cash & Equivalents	29.3	19.5	16.1	15.5	11.8		15.9	16.6
Trade Receivables (net)	9.5	15.9	15.4	12.8	9.9		14.3	15.5
Inventory	.1	.5	.2	.1	.1		.2	.3
All Other Current	11.4	1.5	2.7	2.2	3.6		3.7	2.4
Total Current	50.4	37.4	34.5	30.6	25.3		34.1	34.7
Fixed Assets (net)	33.2	52.9	56.0	49.4	45.6		53.1	51.9
Intangibles (net)	1.8	1.3	1.9	3.0	10.0		3.0	3.4
All Other Non-Current	14.5	8.4	7.6	17.1	19.0		9.8	10.1
Total	100.0	100.0	100.0	100.0	100.0		100.0	100.0
LIABILITIES								
Notes Payable-Short Term	12.7	8.0	3.2	3.1	.4		4.3	6.0
Cur. Mat.-L.T.D.	5.6	3.4	2.6	3.4	2.2		2.9	2.4
Trade Payables	16.1	5.6	4.7	4.9	5.0		5.3	5.3
Income Taxes Payable	.0	.0	.0	.0	.0		.0	.0
All Other Current	51.2	9.5	12.3	9.2	10.0		12.6	11.0
Total Current	85.6	26.5	22.8	20.7	17.6		25.1	24.6
Long-Term Debt	6.3	41.2	34.4	28.6	44.6		35.0	29.7
Deferred Taxes	.0	.0	.0	.0	.0		.0	.0
All Other Non-Current	16.5	7.3	7.0	5.1	7.9		6.5	5.8
Net Worth	-8.4	24.9	35.7	45.5	29.9		33.4	39.9
Total Liabilities & Net Worth	100.0	100.0	100.0	100.0	100.0		100.0	100.0
INCOME DATA								
Net Sales	100.0	100.0	100.0	100.0	100.0		100.0	100.0
Gross Profit								
Operating Expenses	97.2	93.6	89.3	96.2	87.6		93.8	93.1
Operating Profit	2.8	6.4	10.7	3.8	12.4		6.2	6.9
All Other Expenses (net)	.5	4.0	4.2	2.6	5.0		2.5	2.5
Profit Before Taxes	2.4	2.3	6.6	1.1	7.4		3.7	4.4
RATIOS								
Current	2.8	4.4	2.8	3.5	4.0		2.8	3.0
	.8	1.8	1.6	1.9	1.9		1.6	1.6
	.2	.6	.8	1.1	.6		.8	.9
Quick	2.1	3.3	2.6	3.3	3.9		2.5	2.6
	.6	1.7	1.3	1.7	1.6		1.3	1.5
	.2	.4	.7	1.0	.5		.7	.9
Sales/Receivables	0 UND	0 UND	7 50.3	20 18.2	12 29.3		4 85.9	5 79.7
	0 UND	22 16.4	28 12.9	36 10.2	34 10.8		29 12.8	30 12.1
	3 144.9	31 11.9	42 8.6	50 7.3	71 5.1		42 8.8	48 7.6
Cost of Sales/Inventory								
Cost of Sales/Payables								
Sales/Working Capital	14.2	4.6	5.6	3.7	1.7		6.3	4.6
	-68.5	16.5	16.8	7.7	5.8		16.1	14.5
	-6.9	-14.0	-38.8	107.9	-13.4		-46.6	-111.6
EBIT/Interest	10.1	5.1	6.3	4.3	5.2		8.4	9.7
	(10) 7.1	(22) 1.6	(71) 2.2	(45) 1.8	2.8		(145) 2.2	(122) 2.8
	1.0	1.0	.8	.0	1.1		1.0	1.5
Net Profit + Depr., Dep., Amort./Cur. Mat. L/T/D								
Fixed/Worth	.3	.6	.7	.6	1.0		.6	.6
	1.8	1.7	1.5	1.1	1.5		1.5	1.5
	-2.5	26.4	7.0	2.4	-2.2		6.1	4.9
Debt/Worth	.5	.7	.6	.4	1.0		.5	.5
	1.6	2.4	1.5	1.1	2.5		1.7	1.3
	-5.5	37.4	8.0	3.3	-5.8		8.3	6.3
% Profit Before Taxes/Tangible Net Worth	68.1	40.8	24.8	12.1			22.4	24.4
	(16) 43.7	(24) 18.3	(72) 8.4	(54) 5.1			(153) 9.2	(138) 11.3
	14.2	6.3	-.2	-.6			-.9	2.6
% Profit Before Taxes/Total Assets	39.7	11.6	9.0	4.2	4.9		9.2	10.0
	21.1	5.5	3.6	2.0	3.4		3.7	4.4
	2.3	-.2	-.3	-.4	.1		-.1	.8
Sales/Net Fixed Assets	64.2	20.3	5.8	4.5	2.9		5.7	7.0
	19.7	2.8	2.4	1.9	1.6		2.6	2.6
	9.2	1.1	.7	.9	1.0		1.2	1.1
Sales/Total Assets	8.7	5.2	2.3	1.6	1.1		2.4	2.3
	5.1	1.6	1.3	1.0	.6		1.3	1.3
	3.0	.7	.5	.4	.4		.7	.7
% Depr., Dep., Amort./Sales	.5	1.2	1.5	2.0	2.4		1.9	1.8
	(17) 1.4	(23) 2.7	(82) 3.0	(57) 3.2	3.8		(163) 3.2	(145) 2.8
	1.9	5.3	7.5	5.4	8.5		5.2	5.3
% Officers', Directors' Owners' Comp/Sales			1.7				2.9	1.7
		(14) 4.5					(27) 6.4	(28) 5.4
			11.8				8.9	9.6
Net Sales ($)	26223M	80018M	640949M	1468336M	475059M	2450690M	2702658M	2361502M
Total Assets ($)	5780M	32418M	430293M	1297159M	626873M	1343869M	2477101M	2167072M

M = $ thousand   MM = $ million
See Pages 9 through 22 for Explanation of Ratios and Data

Comparative Historical Data   Current Data Sorted by Sales

Hist 1	Hist 2	Hist 3	Type of Statement	0-1MM	1-3MM	3-5MM	5-10MM	10-25MM	25MM & OVER
118	106	120	Unqualified	5	14	18	25	30	28
6	8	5	Reviewed	2			1	2	
11	8	8	Compiled	2	3	1	1		1
14	22	26	Tax Returns	10	9		3	2	2
58	60	62	Other	15	12	6	12	11	6
4/1/08-3/31/09 ALL	4/1/09-3/31/10 ALL	4/1/10-3/31/11 ALL		104 (4/1-9/30/10)			117 (10/1/10-3/31/11)		
207	204	221	NUMBER OF STATEMENTS	34	38	25	42	45	37
%	%	%	ASSETS	%	%	%	%	%	%
16.5	15.4	17.8	Cash & Equivalents	14.8	16.8	15.6	25.7	16.6	15.6
15.3	16.3	13.9	Trade Receivables (net)	4.0	7.3	13.9	16.6	18.2	21.6
.1	.4	.2	Inventory	.0	.2	.5	.2	.2	.2
2.6	3.1	3.5	All Other Current	1.5	6.4	2.5	3.3	3.0	3.7
34.6	35.2	35.4	Total Current	20.3	30.7	32.5	45.7	37.9	41.2
49.1	50.8	50.3	Fixed Assets (net)	63.2	61.5	53.8	40.5	43.6	43.8
2.8	2.6	2.6	Intangibles (net)	1.5	1.6	.5	3.2	4.2	3.6
13.5	11.4	11.7	All Other Non-Current	15.1	6.2	13.2	10.6	14.3	11.5
100.0	100.0	100.0	Total	100.0	100.0	100.0	100.0	100.0	100.0
			LIABILITIES						
5.1	6.1	4.6	Notes Payable-Short Term	5.9	8.3	5.3	2.8	3.3	3.0
3.5	2.7	3.3	Cur. Mat.-L.T.D.	6.3	2.8	2.5	1.6	3.3	3.5
5.0	5.4	6.8	Trade Payables	5.0	6.3	5.2	7.3	5.2	11.4
.0	.0	.0	Income Taxes Payable	.0	.0	.0	.1	.0	.0
11.6	13.1	15.4	All Other Current	7.7	28.8	13.7	14.6	9.4	18.0
25.2	27.3	30.2	Total Current	25.0	46.2	26.7	26.5	21.1	36.0
29.7	34.7	31.2	Long-Term Debt	41.3	42.7	33.4	22.7	20.7	31.2
.1	.1	.0	Deferred Taxes	.0	.0	.0	.0	.1	.0
7.3	6.5	8.4	All Other Non-Current	10.1	11.0	6.4	5.7	5.2	12.4
37.6	31.3	30.2	Net Worth	23.7	.1	33.4	45.1	52.9	20.4
100.0	100.0	100.0	Total Liabilities & Net Worth	100.0	100.0	100.0	100.0	100.0	100.0
			INCOME DATA						
100.0	100.0	100.0	Net Sales	100.0	100.0	100.0	100.0	100.0	100.0
			Gross Profit						
93.2	93.8	92.8	Operating Expenses	85.3	88.2	97.7	93.9	95.7	96.1
6.8	6.2	7.2	Operating Profit	14.7	11.8	2.3	6.1	4.3	3.9
4.0	3.5	3.3	All Other Expenses (net)	8.7	6.4	1.2	1.5	.5	1.7
2.8	2.8	4.0	Profit Before Taxes	6.0	5.4	1.2	4.6	3.7	2.1
			RATIOS						
3.0	3.0	3.1	Current	3.0	3.5	2.9	4.1	3.6	2.2
1.5	1.5	1.6		.8	1.4	1.7	2.0	1.7	1.4
.8	.8	.8		.2	.3	.9	1.3	1.1	.8
2.8	2.7	2.9	Quick	2.7	2.8	2.8	3.5	3.4	2.1
1.4	1.4	1.4		.6	1.1	1.6	1.9	1.6	1.1
.7	.7	.6		.1	.3	.8	1.1	1.0	.7
4 89.6	3 108.8	5 71.1	Sales/Receivables	0 UND	0 UND	12 31.5	10 37.3	24 15.4	18 20.7
29 12.4	29 12.7	27 13.6		0 UND	16 22.5	28 12.9	30 12.1	35 10.4	38 9.6
46 7.9	48 7.6	42 8.7		15 24.7	28 13.1	41 8.8	48 7.6	46 8.0	63 5.8
			Cost of Sales/Inventory						
			Cost of Sales/Payables						
5.9	5.5	5.1	Sales/Working Capital	4.2	5.3	5.3	4.2	5.0	5.8
16.2	21.1	15.6		-68.5	25.2	16.9	7.9	9.4	21.3
-45.0	-43.1	-31.8		-5.6	-7.6	-46.2	24.5	90.7	-16.3
6.1	6.1	5.8	EBIT/Interest	5.2	5.2	4.1	11.3	5.8	4.2
(169) 1.8	(160) 2.1	(166) 2.1		(21) 1.4	(26) 1.9	(19) 1.5	(31) 3.4	(38) 3.5	(31) 1.7
.3	.6	.8		.2	.6	.8	.8	1.2	1.0
			Net Profit + Depr., Dep., Amort./Cur. Mat. L/T/D						
.5	.6	.6	Fixed/Worth	.7	1.0	.7	.5	.4	.8
1.2	1.3	1.4		2.7	2.7	1.9	.8	.9	1.7
4.6	6.4	4.5		-16.9	-20.6	3.7	1.6	1.7	5.8
.5	.5	.6	Debt/Worth	.7	.6	.7	.4	.4	1.0
1.3	1.5	1.5		2.4	2.9	1.4	.8	.7	2.7
6.6	10.7	10.4		-19.6	-25.3	5.3	3.6	2.1	14.0
26.0	28.4	27.1	% Profit Before Taxes/Tangible Net Worth	49.7	44.4	24.6	15.8	19.9	18.9
(183) 6.0	(170) 8.0	(179) 8.5		(24) 18.3	(26) 21.2	(21) 6.0	(36) 8.7	(42) 5.6	(30) 10.5
-2.3	-1.1	.8		1.7	1.4	-3.5	.2	1.1	2.3
7.7	9.3	8.6	% Profit Before Taxes/Total Assets	14.6	16.9	8.8	9.9	5.8	5.5
2.5	3.4	3.3		3.3	5.5	1.4	6.8	3.2	3.4
-1.0	-.7	-.2		-1.3	-.4	-2.1	.1	.2	.2
7.2	9.0	9.5	Sales/Net Fixed Assets	10.7	12.5	6.7	18.5	5.7	7.3
2.7	2.8	2.7		.8	1.4	2.3	3.3	3.2	4.6
1.1	1.1	1.0		.2	.4	1.1	1.8	1.5	1.7
2.3	2.6	2.5	Sales/Total Assets	4.3	3.9	3.2	2.4	2.3	2.5
1.3	1.4	1.3		.6	1.1	1.4	1.6	1.4	1.7
.6	.6	.6		.2	.3	.7	.9	.8	.9
2.0	1.8	1.6	% Depr., Dep., Amort./Sales	1.8	1.5	2.5	1.1	1.9	1.5
(189) 2.9	(180) 3.0	(195) 3.0		(26) 6.8	(34) 4.9	(20) 2.9	(39) 2.6	(42) 3.0	(34) 2.4
5.0	5.5	6.0		18.1	12.1	5.4	5.2	3.7	4.0
3.1	4.1	2.1	% Officers', Directors' Owners' Comp/Sales						
(33) 5.9	(25) 6.4	(35) 6.3							
10.9	12.1	11.3							
4425843M	3726694M	5141275M	Net Sales ($)	19447M	73955M	95418M	314541M	727611M	3910303M
4101974M	3261640M	3736392M	Total Assets ($)	50442M	150657M	120754M	391055M	671858M	2351626M

    M = $ thousand   MM = $ million
See Pages 9 through 22 for Explanation of Ratios and Data

Current Data Sorted by Assets   Comparative Historical Data

Type of Statement	0-500M	500M-2MM	2-10MM	10-50MM	50-100MM	100-250MM	4/1/06-3/31/07 ALL	4/1/07-3/31/08 ALL
Unqualified	8	34	113	112	16	9	223	243
Reviewed	2	1	2	2			5	7
Compiled	1	1	2				7	7
Tax Returns	13	10	6				12	15
Other	21	25	31	24	2	2	82	76
		321 (4/1-9/30/10)		116 (10/1/10-3/31/11)				
NUMBER OF STATEMENTS	45	71	154	138	18	11	329	348
ASSETS	%	%	%	%	%	%	%	%
Cash & Equivalents	31.6	26.3	18.9	16.7	13.7	16.8	20.1	22.2
Trade Receivables (net)	19.7	23.5	18.5	12.8	10.4	4.2	17.6	15.7
Inventory	.9	.9	.3	.5	.1	.2	.7	.5
All Other Current	4.3	2.7	4.0	3.2	4.4	5.1	3.6	4.2
Total Current	56.5	53.5	41.8	33.2	28.6	26.3	42.0	42.7
Fixed Assets (net)	26.4	37.4	48.1	48.4	46.3	53.5	42.2	44.0
Intangibles (net)	4.2	1.9	.8	1.0	.8	7.6	1.5	.8
All Other Non-Current	12.9	7.2	9.4	17.4	24.3	12.6	14.2	12.6
Total	100.0	100.0	100.0	100.0	100.0	100.0	100.0	100.0
LIABILITIES								
Notes Payable-Short Term	11.5	4.5	3.6	1.8	.4	.8	4.5	3.4
Cur. Mat.-L.T.D.	2.0	1.9	2.0	1.1	1.2	.8	1.5	2.0
Trade Payables	8.6	11.5	9.5	5.5	6.0	2.4	7.4	6.7
Income Taxes Payable	.0	.0	.0	.0	.0	.0	.2	.0
All Other Current	25.6	11.2	9.9	8.5	4.8	7.1	9.7	8.7
Total Current	47.7	29.2	25.0	17.0	12.5	11.0	23.4	20.8
Long-Term Debt	29.5	18.0	17.6	20.9	19.8	23.4	20.2	18.6
Deferred Taxes	.0	.0	.0	.0	.0	.6	.0	.0
All Other Non-Current	5.8	3.9	3.4	2.8	9.2	6.1	4.2	3.4
Net Worth	17.0	48.9	53.9	59.3	58.5	58.9	52.2	57.2
Total Liabilities & Net Worth	100.0	100.0	100.0	100.0	100.0	100.0	100.0	100.0
INCOME DATA								
Net Sales	100.0	100.0	100.0	100.0	100.0	100.0	100.0	100.0
Gross Profit								
Operating Expenses	94.6	94.0	97.6	96.2	102.4	91.0	94.8	93.9
Operating Profit	5.4	6.0	2.4	3.8	-2.4	9.0	5.2	6.1
All Other Expenses (net)	.3	1.2	.7	-.5	.3	1.2	.2	.9
Profit Before Taxes	5.1	4.8	1.7	4.3	-2.7	7.9	5.1	5.2
RATIOS								
Current	5.0	6.4	3.3	3.7	2.9	3.8	4.3	4.4
	1.8	2.1	1.8	1.9	2.0	2.6	2.1	2.3
	.8	1.2	1.0	1.1	1.3	1.5	1.3	1.3
Quick	4.0	5.7	2.9	3.2	2.4	2.3	3.8	4.0
	1.4	1.9	1.6	1.6	1.6	1.8	1.9	2.0
	.7	1.2	.9	1.1	.8	.9	1.1	1.0
Sales/Receivables	0 UND	5 70.1	8 43.3	13 27.9	24 15.2	2 155.8	9 39.4	4 95.8
	5 80.6	29 12.7	31 11.6	35 10.5	34 10.6	26 14.2	30 12.2	29 12.8
	27 13.6	56 6.6	49 7.4	55 6.6	59 6.2	32 11.5	51 7.1	49 7.5
Cost of Sales/Inventory								
Cost of Sales/Payables								
Sales/Working Capital	9.6	3.7	5.2	4.1	3.6	2.3	4.0	3.6
	55.2	9.9	11.9	8.7	8.8	5.1	9.1	7.8
	-93.1	65.0	316.9	65.3	NM	25.1	35.1	36.8
EBIT/Interest	21.1	13.4	9.3	12.4	5.2	11.4	9.7	10.2
	(20) 3.5	(46) 4.5	(116) 1.7	(108) 2.7	(14) 1.3	(10) 4.5	(220) 3.5	(236) 3.0
	1.1	1.1	-1.6	.5	-1.2	3.5	.8	.4
Net Profit + Depr., Dep., Amort./Cur. Mat. L/T/D								
Fixed/Worth	.1	.3	.4	.5	.4	.7	.3	.3
	.5	.7	.9	.8	.7	1.0	.8	.7
	3.5	1.6	1.5	1.3	1.2	1.6	1.4	1.3
Debt/Worth	.2	.3	.3	.3	.3	.3	.2	.2
	1.3	.9	.7	.6	.5	.7	.7	.6
	NM	2.8	2.1	1.6	1.3	1.1	1.9	1.6
% Profit Before Taxes/Tangible Net Worth	88.7	29.8	13.7	8.9	5.0		17.6	14.2
	(34) 18.5	(65) 4.0	(147) 3.5	(137) 4.2	(17) .6		(306) 7.1	(335) 5.8
	3.2	-2.4	-4.1	-.8	-8.1		.1	-1.5
% Profit Before Taxes/Total Assets	45.0	12.6	7.3	5.2	2.7	7.4	9.6	9.3
	8.5	1.9	1.6	2.0	.2	4.0	3.7	2.9
	.6	-2.0	-2.7	-.6	-3.9	1.7	-.2	-1.0
Sales/Net Fixed Assets	148.9	32.0	10.2	4.5	3.9	2.7	14.2	14.0
	69.3	9.7	3.3	2.1	2.4	1.1	3.4	3.3
	11.9	2.4	1.3	1.0	.7	.5	1.5	1.3
Sales/Total Assets	10.0	3.5	2.9	1.5	1.2	.9	2.6	2.3
	6.8	2.1	1.6	.9	.6	.5	1.4	1.3
	3.3	1.0	.8	.5	.5	.4	.7	.7
% Depr., Dep., Amort./Sales	.5	.6	1.1	1.9	1.8	2.3	1.3	1.2
	(28) 1.2	(57) 1.9	(144) 2.3	(126) 3.1	2.3	6.5	(289) 2.4	(306) 2.3
	3.2	2.7	3.7	5.1	9.8	8.9	4.0	3.9
% Officers', Directors' Owners' Comp/Sales	2.5	2.8	1.2				2.8	2.9
	(22) 5.4	(11) 10.3	(12) 2.8				(38) 5.7	(35) 6.4
	15.6	33.6	4.3				10.5	11.9
Net Sales ($)	66770M	242688M	1628946M	3328686M	1241091M	1473113M	6708133M	6049248M
Total Assets ($)	9350M	86929M	786884M	2845762M	1341518M	1762238M	5060833M	5209319M

M = $ thousand   MM = $ million
See Pages 9 through 22 for Explanation of Ratios and Data

Comparative Historical Data			Type of Statement	Current Data Sorted by Sales					
246	262	292	Unqualified	10	37	30	49	97	69
6	5	7	Reviewed	4			1	2	
7	3	4	Compiled	2		1	1		
16	23	29	Tax Returns	6	9	5	7	2	
76	94	105	Other	22	22	18	17	17	9
4/1/08-3/31/09	4/1/09-3/31/10	4/1/10-3/31/11		321 (4/1-9/30/10)			116 (10/1/10-3/31/11)		
ALL	ALL	ALL		0-1MM	1-3MM	3-5MM	5-10MM	10-25MM	25MM & OVER
351	387	437	**NUMBER OF STATEMENTS**	44	68	54	75	118	78
%	%	%	**ASSETS**	%	%	%	%	%	%
20.6	20.5	20.5	Cash & Equivalents	26.4	21.5	18.8	17.1	20.3	20.9
18.1	15.1	16.9	Trade Receivables (net)	11.2	13.8	18.4	16.3	18.8	19.6
.5	.4	.5	Inventory	.3	.9	.3	1.3	.1	.4
3.4	3.5	3.6	All Other Current	3.4	3.0	2.7	2.7	4.0	5.2
42.6	39.5	41.5	Total Current	41.4	39.2	40.2	37.4	43.3	46.1
42.8	47.7	44.3	Fixed Assets (net)	48.7	43.9	47.5	51.1	40.7	38.7
.8	.8	1.6	Intangibles (net)	2.1	2.3	1.2	2.0	.8	1.6
13.8	12.0	12.6	All Other Non-Current	7.9	14.6	11.2	9.4	15.2	13.6
100.0	100.0	100.0	Total	100.0	100.0	100.0	100.0	100.0	100.0
			LIABILITIES						
3.4	4.3	3.8	Notes Payable-Short Term	5.5	2.8	7.1	4.8	3.2	1.5
1.1	1.5	1.7	Cur. Mat.-L.T.D.	1.2	1.8	2.0	2.3	1.6	1.1
7.3	7.8	8.2	Trade Payables	2.8	5.8	8.5	6.9	10.0	11.7
.0	.0	.0	Income Taxes Payable	.0	.0	.0	.0	.0	.0
9.9	10.4	11.0	All Other Current	9.2	13.4	11.0	8.5	10.1	13.6
21.6	24.0	24.6	Total Current	18.7	23.7	28.6	22.5	24.8	27.8
17.2	20.5	20.2	Long-Term Debt	31.9	21.8	22.0	22.9	14.8	16.4
.0	.0	.0	Deferred Taxes	.0	.0	.0	.0	.0	.1
3.0	4.6	3.8	All Other Non-Current	2.5	5.4	4.0	1.7	3.3	6.0
58.1	50.9	51.3	Net Worth	46.9	49.1	45.4	52.9	57.0	49.8
100.0	100.0	100.0	Total Liabilties & Net Worth	100.0	100.0	100.0	100.0	100.0	100.0
			INCOME DATA						
100.0	100.0	100.0	Net Sales	100.0	100.0	100.0	100.0	100.0	100.0
			Gross Profit						
97.6	99.0	96.3	Operating Expenses	86.6	95.1	95.2	98.4	98.3	98.4
2.4	1.0	3.7	Operating Profit	13.4	4.9	4.8	1.6	1.7	1.6
1.8	1.6	.3	All Other Expenses (net)	3.0	1.2	.2	.8	-1.1	.0
.6	-.6	3.4	Profit Before Taxes	10.3	3.7	4.6	.8	2.8	1.6
			RATIOS						
3.9	3.7	3.7		7.5	5.6	4.1	3.5	2.9	2.9
2.1	2.0	2.0	Current	2.4	2.6	1.9	2.0	1.8	1.7
1.3	1.0	1.1		1.0	1.0	.9	.9	1.2	1.0
3.6	3.5	3.2		7.1	4.7	3.9	3.5	2.7	2.3
1.8	1.8	1.7	Quick	2.3	2.0	1.8	1.4	1.7	1.5
1.0	.9	1.0		.8	.9	.9	.9	1.1	1.0
11 32.7	6 66.1	7 53.4		0 UND	0 UND	4 99.2	12 30.1	15 24.1	18 19.8
33 11.0	26 14.0	30 12.2	Sales/Receivables	5 72.1	18 20.5	32 11.4	30 12.0	35 10.3	31 12.0
54 6.7	44 8.2	50 7.3		34 10.6	43 8.5	47 7.7	51 7.1	55 6.6	45 8.1
			Cost of Sales/Inventory						
			Cost of Sales/Payables						
3.8	4.5	4.5		2.7	3.7	5.0	4.2	5.6	5.6
9.0	10.5	10.5	Sales/Working Capital	9.6	8.4	13.6	9.9	10.3	12.8
37.4	754.0	166.7		-241.8	NM	-109.9	-149.1	50.1	171.2
6.7	4.7	10.6		18.5	5.6	8.9	7.2	14.2	12.1
(247) 1.4	(269) 1.2	(314) 2.7	EBIT/Interest	(24) 2.8	(43) 2.2	(37) 1.5	(58) 1.1	(95) 4.4	(57) 3.5
-1.9	-3.0	.1		.9	.1	-.1	-2.8	1.0	.8
			Net Profit + Depr., Dep., Amort./Cur. Mat. L/T/D						
.3	.5	.4		.2	.3	.4	.6	.4	.4
.7	.9	.8	Fixed/Worth	.8	.7	1.0	1.0	.7	.7
1.2	1.6	1.6		1.8	1.7	1.9	1.9	1.1	1.3
.2	.3	.3		.2	.2	.3	.3	.3	.4
.6	.7	.7	Debt/Worth	.6	.7	.7	.7	.6	.8
1.3	1.9	2.0		2.0	2.2	3.6	2.2	1.5	2.2
11.5	8.6	13.3		34.5	11.1	25.5	10.0	12.0	12.1
(338) 1.7	(365) .6	(409) 4.1	% Profit Before Taxes/Tangible Net Worth	(41) 9.2	(59) 4.0	(51) 2.1	(71) .6	(113) 5.4	(74) 4.6
-6.0	-5.9	-1.9		-1.5	-3.6	-4.9	-5.7	.3	-.2
5.8	4.2	7.4		16.0	5.9	11.4	7.1	7.2	5.5
.6	.3	2.1	% Profit Before Taxes/Total Assets	6.9	2.0	1.2	.4	2.6	1.8
-3.2	-4.0	-1.2		-.8	-2.6	-2.4	-3.9	.0	-.1
13.0	10.2	14.1		37.9	23.9	22.5	6.2	13.9	13.3
3.1	2.9	3.2	Sales/Net Fixed Assets	3.4	3.8	2.9	2.6	3.1	4.8
1.2	1.1	1.3		.5	.8	1.1	1.0	1.9	2.1
2.5	2.9	2.9		4.4	3.2	2.5	2.2	2.6	3.2
1.3	1.3	1.4	Sales/Total Assets	1.0	1.2	1.4	1.2	1.5	1.7
.7	.7	.7		.4	.6	.8	.6	.8	1.0
1.2	1.3	1.3		1.3	.9	1.0	1.8	1.1	1.0
(319) 2.2	(339) 2.3	(384) 2.4	% Depr., Dep., Amort./Sales	(31) 3.6	(57) 2.7	(47) 2.6	(68) 3.1	(109) 2.0	(72) 2.1
4.0	4.5	4.4		8.9	6.6	4.2	5.0	3.5	3.1
2.5	2.4	2.4		3.9	3.4				
(41) 5.5	(37) 6.2	(54) 4.6	% Officers', Directors' Owners' Comp/Sales	(10) 10.4	(18) 6.3				
15.7	12.3	14.0		17.9	17.1				
8469766M	6406904M	7981294M	Net Sales ($)	22595M	123721M	207125M	546181M	1894730M	5186942M
6040500M	4908119M	6832681M	Total Assets ($)	43714M	245226M	216888M	670964M	1672099M	3983790M

© RMA 2011

M = $ thousand   MM = $ million

See Pages 9 through 22 for Explanation of Ratios and Data

Current Data Sorted by Assets   Comparative Historical Data

						Type of Statement		
5	20	84	44	11	3	Unqualified	101	109
	3	2	1			Reviewed	1	5
1	4	1				Compiled	4	5
5	8	3	1			Tax Returns	8	9
6	10	22	18	2		Other	34	43
	187 (4/1-9/30/10)		67 (10/1/10-3/31/11)				4/1/06- 3/31/07	4/1/07- 3/31/08
0-500M	500M-2MM	2-10MM	10-50MM	50-100MM	100-250MM		ALL	ALL
17	45	112	64	13	3	NUMBER OF STATEMENTS	148	171
%	%	%	%	%	%	ASSETS	%	%
17.9	30.9	17.3	22.2	16.7		Cash & Equivalents	20.5	20.5
20.3	19.6	19.5	14.6	18.2		Trade Receivables (net)	19.0	18.3
2.7	.0	.5	.6	.1		Inventory	.9	.8
.7	5.5	3.7	3.4	4.4		All Other Current	4.7	3.0
41.6	56.0	41.0	40.8	39.5		Total Current	45.0	42.7
41.4	31.7	48.8	44.5	38.7		Fixed Assets (net)	44.9	45.0
5.2	6.6	1.4	3.9	.8		Intangibles (net)	1.8	2.5
11.8	5.7	8.7	10.8	21.0		All Other Non-Current	8.3	9.8
100.0	100.0	100.0	100.0	100.0		Total	100.0	100.0
						LIABILITIES		
18.2	3.3	3.3	3.5	1.0		Notes Payable-Short Term	3.2	3.2
7.0	3.8	2.1	2.1	1.9		Cur. Mat.-L.T.D.	2.0	2.3
13.5	4.4	5.4	7.8	9.4		Trade Payables	7.2	8.0
.0	.0	.0	.4	.4		Income Taxes Payable	.0	.0
11.8	16.3	13.8	9.4	11.5		All Other Current	12.7	14.8
50.4	27.8	24.7	23.2	24.2		Total Current	25.1	28.4
70.8	23.6	24.4	23.8	27.8		Long-Term Debt	22.1	25.6
.0	.0	.1	.1	.0		Deferred Taxes	.1	.1
13.2	2.3	2.3	3.9	5.2		All Other Non-Current	3.7	3.6
-34.5	46.3	48.4	49.1	42.8		Net Worth	48.9	42.3
100.0	100.0	100.0	100.0	100.0		Total Liabilties & Net Worth	100.0	100.0
						INCOME DATA		
100.0	100.0	100.0	100.0	100.0		Net Sales	100.0	100.0
						Gross Profit		
82.5	90.8	96.5	95.7	97.7		Operating Expenses	94.4	95.8
17.5	9.2	3.5	4.3	2.3		Operating Profit	5.6	4.2
8.3	1.0	1.0	1.1	.7		All Other Expenses (net)	.5	1.0
9.3	8.3	2.5	3.2	1.6		Profit Before Taxes	5.1	3.2
						RATIOS		
2.3	5.9	3.0	3.7	5.7			3.3	3.3
1.0	2.8	2.1	1.7	1.6	Current	1.9	1.7
.3	1.1	1.1	1.0	1.2		1.1	1.0
2.2	5.5	2.8	3.2	5.5			2.8	3.0
1.0	2.5	1.9	1.5	1.2	Quick	(147) 1.7	1.5
.2	.9	1.0	.9	.9		.9	.8
0 UND	0 UND	19 19.1	11 34.8	18 19.7			13 27.5	8 46.2
0 UND	21 17.2	31 11.7	28 12.8	46 7.9		Sales/Receivables	31 11.7	27 13.6
21 17.4	43 8.5	43 8.4	47 7.8	58 6.3			48 7.6	45 8.2
						Cost of Sales/Inventory		
						Cost of Sales/Payables		
11.6	4.6	5.9	3.6	2.5			4.5	5.3
UND	7.4	10.1	12.0	10.4	Sales/Working Capital	10.2	13.4
-8.9	189.3	61.6	-272.9	29.0		117.9	302.5
	61.9	13.1	11.1	3.7			11.6	7.1
	(30) 8.2	(95) 2.9	(53) 3.1	(12) 1.7	EBIT/Interest	(110) 3.7	(122) 2.7
	2.0	.6	.7	.9		1.3	.8
						Net Profit + Depr., Dep., Amort./Cur. Mat. L/T/D		
.3	.1	.6	.5	.3			.5	.4
2.5	.6	.9	.9	1.2	Fixed/Worth	1.0	1.0
-.6	2.1	1.7	2.4	2.2		1.7	2.2
2.7	.3	.5	.4	.5			.4	.4
-6.5	.7	.8	1.4	1.7	Debt/Worth	1.0	.9
-1.8	3.7	2.3	3.2	4.4		2.9	3.2
	63.9	15.1	15.0	7.6	% Profit Before Taxes/Tangible		22.7	19.6
	(38) 18.1	(106) 4.7	(56) 5.8	(12) 2.5	Net Worth	(138) 10.7	(152) 9.1
	2.2	-2.5	.5	.9		3.0	2.3
45.1	30.1	7.6	8.1	2.2	% Profit Before Taxes/Total	12.9	9.9
4.2	12.1	2.3	3.4	.6	Assets	4.2	3.9
.8	3.1	-.6	-.2	-.1		.9	.0
66.5	44.7	8.1	6.7	4.9		10.9	13.0
21.4	12.0	3.2	2.7	3.0	Sales/Net Fixed Assets	3.5	3.6
2.5	4.9	1.7	1.3	1.5		2.0	1.9
9.6	3.8	2.6	1.9	1.6		2.5	2.9
4.6	2.4	1.7	1.4	1.4	Sales/Total Assets	1.8	1.7
1.5	1.9	1.0	.6	.6		1.1	1.1
.6	.8	1.2	1.7	2.3		1.3	1.4
(11) 1.7	(38) 1.2	(107) 2.4	(59) 3.0	(12) 3.0	% Depr., Dep., Amort./Sales	(134) 2.5	(152) 2.6
6.7	2.5	3.9	4.5	5.8		4.0	4.0
	2.3	1.7					2.7	1.3
	(11) 5.5	(10) 3.3			% Officers', Directors' Owners' Comp/Sales	(21) 5.8	(20) 4.7
	7.9	9.3				19.6	6.3
21852M	171775M	1052526M	2287645M	1092491M	269992M	Net Sales ($)	2797770M	3007958M
4295M	51765M	556921M	1405497M	831317M	381100M	Total Assets ($)	1941468M	1873149M

M = $ thousand   MM = $ million
See Pages 9 through 22 for Explanation of Ratios and Data

Comparative Historical Data | Current Data Sorted by Sales

Hist 1	Hist 2	Hist 3	Type of Statement	0-1MM	1-3MM	3-5MM	5-10MM	10-25MM	25MM & OVER
122	144	167	Unqualified	3	20	18	43	47	36
6	6	6	Reviewed	2	3				1
5	4	6	Compiled	1	3	1	1		
9	10	17	Tax Returns	4	8	3	1		1
58	44	58	Other	7	7	9	10	16	9
4/1/08-3/31/09 ALL	4/1/09-3/31/10 ALL	4/1/10-3/31/11 ALL		187 (4/1-9/30/10)			67 (10/1/10-3/31/11)		
200	208	254	NUMBER OF STATEMENTS	17	41	31	55	63	47
%	%	%	**ASSETS**	%	%	%	%	%	%
22.9	20.1	20.8	Cash & Equivalents	17.8	17.9	26.8	19.5	20.4	22.8
19.9	18.3	18.2	Trade Receivables (net)	10.2	13.3	13.5	17.7	22.2	23.5
.6	.6	.5	Inventory	2.6	.1	.5	.2	.5	.6
4.4	4.4	3.8	All Other Current	.6	2.7	3.8	3.6	5.5	3.7
47.8	43.4	43.3	Total Current	31.3	34.0	44.6	41.0	48.5	50.6
41.5	44.9	43.5	Fixed Assets (net)	50.7	45.9	45.7	51.5	38.7	34.6
1.6	1.8	3.2	Intangibles (net)	6.4	5.5	1.3	1.6	3.2	3.0
9.2	9.9	10.0	All Other Non-Current	11.7	14.6	8.4	5.9	9.6	11.8
100.0	100.0	100.0	Total	100.0	100.0	100.0	100.0	100.0	100.0
			LIABILITIES						
6.5	4.6	4.2	Notes Payable-Short Term	1.1	8.9	2.9	2.0	5.6	2.8
2.7	2.4	2.7	Cur. Mat.-L.T.D.	6.6	3.0	4.8	1.4	2.2	1.9
7.7	5.9	6.5	Trade Payables	6.5	2.4	7.5	4.8	6.3	12.0
.0	.0	.1	Income Taxes Payable	.0	.0	.0	.0	.4	.2
15.6	14.9	12.8	All Other Current	2.7	6.8	10.5	14.8	18.3	13.4
32.5	27.7	26.4	Total Current	16.8	21.1	25.6	22.9	32.8	30.2
20.2	24.2	27.5	Long-Term Debt	78.7	33.7	28.5	22.9	18.2	20.7
.1	.0	.1	Deferred Taxes	.0	.0	.0	.0	.2	.1
5.2	5.6	3.6	All Other Non-Current	2.8	5.9	2.3	1.6	3.8	4.9
42.0	42.5	42.5	Net Worth	1.7	39.2	43.5	52.6	45.0	44.2
100.0	100.0	100.0	Total Liabilties & Net Worth	100.0	100.0	100.0	100.0	100.0	100.0
			INCOME DATA						
100.0	100.0	100.0	Net Sales	100.0	100.0	100.0	100.0	100.0	100.0
			Gross Profit						
96.2	96.3	94.4	Operating Expenses	77.6	88.8	96.5	97.4	97.0	97.0
3.8	3.7	5.6	Operating Profit	22.4	11.2	3.5	2.6	3.0	3.0
1.1	1.9	1.5	All Other Expenses (net)	12.1	1.4	1.4	.5	.4	.6
2.7	1.9	4.1	Profit Before Taxes	10.2	9.9	2.1	2.1	2.6	2.4
			RATIOS						
3.5	3.6	3.5	Current	5.7	5.0	5.1	3.9	2.7	3.1
2.1	2.0	2.0		2.0	2.4	1.7	2.3	1.8	1.6
1.1	1.1	1.1		.4	.7	1.3	1.4	.9	1.2
3.2	3.4	3.1	Quick	3.9	4.7	4.5	3.1	2.4	2.6
1.7	1.8	1.6		1.9	2.0	1.6	2.2	1.6	1.4
.9	.9	.9		.3	.7	1.1	1.1	.7	1.0
14 25.4	18 20.8	10 37.9	Sales/Receivables	0 UND	0 UND	10 36.8	14 25.9	12 30.5	25 14.6
31 11.8	31 11.7	29 12.8		0 UND	19 19.1	27 13.6	30 12.1	31 11.8	35 10.4
47 7.8	47 7.8	46 7.9		23 15.9	38 9.6	36 10.3	41 9.0	51 7.2	50 7.3
			Cost of Sales/Inventory						
			Cost of Sales/Payables						
4.4	4.6	5.0	Sales/Working Capital	4.2	4.1	4.0	5.0	6.0	5.6
10.9	8.9	11.0		18.5	8.5	10.0	9.0	13.5	12.2
116.1	74.6	218.4		-7.6	-48.3	32.7	25.2	-36.3	36.4
7.2	7.1	13.3	EBIT/Interest		26.7	9.9	14.8	13.3	11.9
(153) 2.7	(170) 2.3	(201) 3.2		(33) 5.3	(20) 5.2	(48) 2.3	(52) 3.3	(43) 2.7	
.3	.3	.8			1.2	.7	.3	.7	1.1
		3.3	Net Profit + Depr., Dep.,						
	(10) 2.1		Amort./Cur. Mat. L/T/D						
		.4							
.3	.5	.4	Fixed/Worth	.2	.3	.4	.7	.3	.4
.9	1.0	.9		2.5	.9	.9	.9	.9	.8
1.9	2.1	2.2		-1.4	NM	2.0	1.7	2.4	2.0
.5	.5	.4	Debt/Worth	.7	.1	.4	.3	.6	.6
1.0	1.2	1.1		11.7	.8	.9	.7	1.3	1.6
2.8	2.8	4.0		-3.9	NM	2.5	1.6	4.4	3.8
23.3	14.3	18.6	% Profit Before Taxes/Tangible	49.5	45.1	31.6	13.2	21.6	16.8
(182) 6.7	(189) 5.6	(223) 6.6	Net Worth	(10) 8.7	(31) 10.8	(28) 7.9	(52) 4.0	(58) 6.9	(44) 6.7
-.9	-2.3	-.5		-1.6	1.8	-.7	-3.2	.0	1.7
10.8	8.0	10.8	% Profit Before Taxes/Total	29.6	34.5	12.1	7.0	9.3	8.2
2.9	2.6	3.6	Assets	7.8	7.1	2.8	2.3	3.1	1.8
-.7	-1.1	-.4		-.3	.2	-.9	-1.4	.0	.4
26.9	9.9	15.7	Sales/Net Fixed Assets	49.6	21.8	15.5	6.3	20.7	18.2
4.4	3.4	4.0		3.2	4.6	4.1	2.9	4.4	4.6
1.8	1.8	1.7		.4	1.0	1.4	1.6	2.2	2.6
3.3	2.6	2.9	Sales/Total Assets	1.6	2.8	3.4	2.6	3.2	3.2
1.8	1.6	1.7		1.2	1.7	1.6	1.5	1.9	1.8
1.0	1.0	.9		.4	.6	.8	1.0	1.1	1.4
1.1	1.3	1.2	% Depr., Dep., Amort./Sales	2.8	1.0	1.3	1.7	.9	1.1
(179) 2.3	(191) 2.4	(230) 2.4		(10) 13.6	(36) 2.7	(29) 2.1	(51) 2.5	(60) 2.1	(44) 2.3
4.1	3.9	4.0		15.8	6.0	3.7	4.0	3.7	3.2
5.1	1.2	2.3	% Officers', Directors'	5.5					
(24) 6.7	(29) 4.3	(30) 4.6	Owners' Comp/Sales	(11) 7.7					
11.0	7.3	9.0		10.4					
3922747M	3688218M	4896281M	Net Sales ($)	8577M	84858M	119399M	388199M	1029302M	3265946M
2353122M	2402714M	3230895M	Total Assets ($)	16583M	120604M	99926M	318155M	741827M	1933800M

M = $ thousand   MM = $ million
See Pages 9 through 22 for Explanation of Ratios and Data

Current Data Sorted by Assets   **Comparative Historical Data**

Type of Statement	0-500M	500M-2MM	2-10MM	10-50MM	50-100MM	100-250MM		4/1/06-3/31/07 ALL	4/1/07-3/31/08 ALL
Unqualified	10	59	246	214	35	15		509	526
Reviewed	1	5	6					8	3
Compiled	1	2	4	1	1			17	10
Tax Returns	8	9	5			1		13	23
Other	12	33	96	57	10	2		144	168
		608 (4/1-9/30/10)		225 (10/1/10-3/31/11)					
NUMBER OF STATEMENTS	32	108	357	272	46	18		691	730
ASSETS	%	%	%	%	%	%		%	%
Cash & Equivalents	30.9	26.0	21.9	17.5	17.8	16.6		20.6	20.5
Trade Receivables (net)	20.5	19.4	18.9	15.2	11.9	6.4		16.9	17.9
Inventory	1.9	1.3	1.0	1.4	.6	4.2		1.4	1.3
All Other Current	11.4	5.5	4.2	3.4	4.5	1.4		5.3	5.3
Total Current	64.6	52.2	46.1	37.5	34.9	28.5		44.2	45.0
Fixed Assets (net)	25.5	38.3	43.0	46.0	41.0	41.6		42.3	41.9
Intangibles (net)	3.1	1.7	.9	.9	1.2	.4		.9	.8
All Other Non-Current	6.5	7.8	10.0	15.6	22.9	29.5		12.5	12.2
Total	100.0	100.0	100.0	100.0	100.0	100.0		100.0	100.0
LIABILITIES									
Notes Payable-Short Term	4.1	3.0	2.8	2.4	1.5	5.0		4.1	4.2
Cur. Mat.-L.T.D.	1.3	1.8	1.6	2.3	1.5	2.8		2.0	1.7
Trade Payables	9.9	5.2	7.0	6.2	7.0	2.9		7.0	7.3
Income Taxes Payable	.1	.2	.1	.0	.0	.0		.1	.1
All Other Current	53.0	10.8	11.2	9.3	10.0	12.8		11.6	11.1
Total Current	68.4	21.0	22.7	20.3	20.0	23.5		24.7	24.4
Long-Term Debt	26.2	14.5	17.2	21.5	25.8	19.5		18.2	19.0
Deferred Taxes	.0	.0	.0	.0	.2	.0		.0	.0
All Other Non-Current	6.9	4.3	2.9	4.1	5.7	5.5		2.5	3.5
Net Worth	-1.9	60.1	57.2	54.1	48.2	51.5		54.5	53.0
Total Liabilities & Net Worth	100.0	100.0	100.0	100.0	100.0	100.0		100.0	100.0
INCOME DATA									
Net Sales	100.0	100.0	100.0	100.0	100.0	100.0		100.0	100.0
Gross Profit									
Operating Expenses	98.1	98.0	96.3	96.9	96.2	93.6		96.6	96.3
Operating Profit	1.9	2.0	3.7	3.1	3.8	6.4		3.4	3.7
All Other Expenses (net)	1.9	.1	.8	.0	.1	1.4		.2	.3
Profit Before Taxes	-.1	1.9	2.8	3.0	3.7	5.0		3.2	3.4
RATIOS									
Current	4.5	5.5	3.8	3.6	2.9	2.6		3.6	3.6
	2.2	2.6	2.2	2.1	1.8	1.1		2.0	1.9
	.6	1.3	1.2	1.3	1.1	.5		1.2	1.1
Quick	3.9	4.9	3.5	2.9	2.2	2.6		3.1	3.1
	1.3	2.1	1.9	1.8	1.6	1.1		1.7	1.6
	.3	1.1	1.1	1.1	.9	.4		1.0	1.0
Sales/Receivables	0 UND	4 102.8	15 24.9	20 17.9	8 47.9	15 24.2		13 29.0	13 28.7
	8 47.9	25 14.6	34 10.7	36 10.1	24 15.1	36 10.2		32 11.6	33 10.9
	31 11.7	45 8.1	50 7.3	53 6.9	52 7.1	73 5.0		50 7.4	55 6.7
Cost of Sales/Inventory									
Cost of Sales/Payables									
Sales/Working Capital	6.3	3.9	4.2	3.6	3.3	4.7		4.2	4.3
	16.5	7.1	8.6	8.0	7.3	NM		9.1	9.5
	-30.7	38.2	28.1	26.8	NM	-5.7		36.7	51.0
EBIT/Interest	19.8	21.5	10.3	9.7	4.2	9.2		7.7	8.9
	(13) 4.7	(63) 3.4	(259) 2.4	(224) 3.3	(38) 2.1	(15) 3.0		(476) 2.9	(514) 2.6
	-.6	.4	.0	1.0	.8	.4		.4	.8
Net Profit + Depr., Dep., Amort./Cur. Mat. L/T/D									
Fixed/Worth	.1	.1	.3	.5	.4	.2		.3	.3
	.2	.5	.8	.8	.9	.9		.8	.7
	4.8	1.1	1.3	1.4	1.7	2.4		1.3	1.4
Debt/Worth	.5	.2	.3	.3	.6	.4		.3	.3
	1.9	.5	.7	.8	1.0	.8		.7	.7
	NM	1.3	1.6	1.6	2.6	2.9		1.6	1.8
% Profit Before Taxes/Tangible Net Worth	72.5	21.5	13.0	11.4	11.1	5.1		13.6	12.6
	(24) 18.7	(103) 4.4	(348) 3.6	(267) 4.4	(45) 3.3	2.2		(659) 4.9	(703) 4.9
	-15.6	-5.1	-2.8	.0	-.7	-2.4		-.8	-.7
% Profit Before Taxes/Total Assets	20.2	12.3	7.4	6.1	5.1	3.4		7.6	7.3
	1.2	3.0	1.7	2.4	1.3	1.0		2.5	2.7
	-16.2	-2.7	-1.4	.0	-.4	-.5		-.6	-.6
Sales/Net Fixed Assets	147.7	32.8	12.2	5.4	5.6	5.5		11.9	13.5
	50.3	9.3	4.6	2.6	2.5	1.7		3.7	3.6
	16.8	2.3	1.8	1.5	1.0	.6		1.7	1.7
Sales/Total Assets	7.9	3.5	2.6	1.7	1.6	1.0		2.4	2.5
	5.0	2.2	1.7	1.2	.9	.4		1.5	1.5
	2.9	1.2	1.0	.7	.5	.2		.8	.8
% Depr., Dep., Amort./Sales	.6	.6	1.0	1.5	2.1	.6		1.2	1.2
	(20) 1.4	(86) 1.7	(317) 1.8	(261) 2.7	(43) 3.0	(17) 3.2		(614) 2.2	(644) 2.2
	1.9	3.0	3.3	4.0	7.9	6.2		3.8	3.7
% Officers', Directors' Owners' Comp/Sales		3.1	1.4	1.7				3.0	2.7
		(11) 3.9	(24) 7.4	(21) 4.1				(66) 7.8	(71) 6.6
		8.6	17.5	12.7				15.4	13.7
Net Sales ($)	38530M	368022M	3598355M	7250644M	4050763M	4737016M		14851298M	13826589M
Total Assets ($)	6647M	135652M	1908591M	5753347M	3133770M	2859058M		9093666M	10743927M

M = $ thousand   MM = $ million
See Pages 9 through 22 for Explanation of Ratios and Data

Comparative Historical Data — Current Data Sorted by Sales

			Type of Statement						
577	480	579	Unqualified	16	70	52	114	182	145
6	8	12	Reviewed	2	4	1		5	
10	14	9	Compiled	2		2	2	2	1
26	28	23	Tax Returns	7	8	2	4	1	1
192	194	210	Other	16	41	25	28	65	35
4/1/08-3/31/09 ALL	4/1/09-3/31/10 ALL	4/1/10-3/31/11 ALL		608 (4/1-9/30/10)			225 (10/1/10-3/31/11)		
				0-1MM	1-3MM	3-5MM	5-10MM	10-25MM	25MM & OVER
811	724	833	NUMBER OF STATEMENTS	43	123	82	148	255	182
%	%	%	ASSETS	%	%	%	%	%	%
19.5	20.7	21.0	Cash & Equivalents	22.0	25.2	17.7	23.1	19.6	19.8
16.5	17.6	17.2	Trade Receivables (net)	8.9	12.3	13.5	18.8	19.4	19.6
1.2	1.4	1.3	Inventory	.5	1.2	1.5	.8	1.1	1.9
5.3	4.8	4.3	All Other Current	6.5	4.8	3.3	4.2	4.6	3.9
42.4	44.4	43.8	Total Current	38.9	43.4	35.9	46.8	44.6	45.1
43.7	42.2	42.6	Fixed Assets (net)	51.9	44.7	52.0	38.6	42.5	37.8
1.0	1.0	1.1	Intangibles (net)	2.2	1.8	.3	1.0	1.0	.9
12.8	12.3	12.6	All Other Non-Current	6.8	10.1	11.8	13.6	11.9	16.1
100.0	100.0	100.0	Total	100.0	100.0	100.0	100.0	100.0	100.0
			LIABILITIES						
3.8	3.9	2.7	Notes Payable-Short Term	3.1	2.0	2.7	2.3	3.1	2.9
1.8	1.8	1.9	Cur. Mat.-L.T.D.	1.5	1.7	1.8	1.5	2.2	2.1
6.6	6.5	6.5	Trade Payables	5.0	3.7	4.1	6.3	7.3	9.0
.1	.1	.1	Income Taxes Payable	.0	.0	.2	.1	.1	.0
10.3	12.6	12.1	All Other Current	32.0	8.4	7.4	10.0	11.7	14.3
22.6	24.9	23.3	Total Current	41.6	15.8	16.1	20.2	24.4	28.4
19.1	17.7	19.1	Long-Term Debt	32.0	15.6	23.8	17.5	17.9	19.4
.0	.0	.0	Deferred Taxes	.0	.0	.0	.0	.0	.1
3.0	4.4	3.8	All Other Non-Current	6.9	2.6	1.5	2.5	4.2	5.6
55.3	53.0	53.7	Net Worth	19.2	66.0	58.5	59.8	53.5	46.6
100.0	100.0	100.0	Total Liabilities & Net Worth	100.0	100.0	100.0	100.0	100.0	100.0
			INCOME DATA						
100.0	100.0	100.0	Net Sales	100.0	100.0	100.0	100.0	100.0	100.0
			Gross Profit						
96.9	97.9	96.7	Operating Expenses	94.0	93.8	96.4	98.2	97.3	97.5
3.1	2.1	3.3	Operating Profit	6.0	6.2	3.6	1.8	2.7	2.5
1.7	1.4	.5	All Other Expenses (net)	5.4	2.0	.3	-.3	-.2	.1
1.4	.6	2.8	Profit Before Taxes	.7	4.2	3.2	2.1	2.9	2.4
			RATIOS						
3.9	3.6	3.9		8.8	7.2	5.5	4.4	3.3	2.6
2.0	1.9	2.1	Current	1.9	3.0	2.7	2.6	2.0	1.7
1.2	1.2	1.2		.6	1.5	1.3	1.5	1.2	1.1
3.2	3.2	3.4		8.0	6.4	5.4	3.6	2.9	2.2
1.7	1.7	1.8	Quick	1.4	2.6	2.2	2.1	1.8	1.4
1.0	1.0	1.0		.4	1.1	.9	1.3	1.0	1.0
12 31.5	13 29.2	13 28.7		0 UND	1 497.2	6 62.0	20 18.0	21 17.4	17 21.2
31 11.9	31 11.6	33 11.1	Sales/Receivables	6 62.0	21 17.1	31 11.8	37 10.0	35 10.3	36 10.2
51 7.2	49 7.4	51 7.2		34 10.6	43 8.6	50 7.3	52 7.1	53 6.9	52 7.0
			Cost of Sales/Inventory						
			Cost of Sales/Payables						
4.3	4.7	4.0		2.4	3.1	3.1	3.4	4.4	6.2
9.3	9.9	8.5	Sales/Working Capital	12.6	5.2	8.4	6.6	9.2	10.9
45.7	44.3	33.7		-17.0	22.4	22.0	20.7	34.0	88.3
6.4	6.7	10.3		3.1	9.4	15.3	15.6	11.0	8.7
(588) 1.6	(516) 1.6	(612) 2.9	EBIT/Interest	(20) .5	(76) 1.8	(61) 1.5	(94) 2.9	(208) 3.6	(153) 3.1
-1.3	-1.6	.5		-.9	-.6	-.7	.4	.7	1.1
			Net Profit + Depr., Dep., Amort./Cur. Mat. L/T/D						
.4	.4	.3		.2	.2	.4	.2	.4	.4
.8	.8	.8	Fixed/Worth	1.1	.6	.9	.6	.8	.8
1.4	1.4	1.4		3.2	1.3	1.2	1.3	1.4	1.4
.3	.3	.3		.3	.1	.2	.2	.4	.5
.7	.8	.7	Debt/Worth	1.0	.4	.4	.6	.8	1.0
1.7	1.8	1.7		3.2	1.1	1.2	1.5	1.7	2.0
12.1	14.9	13.2		9.3	15.1	9.0	15.0	13.1	13.9
(784) 1.6	(694) 2.8	(805) 3.8	% Profit Before Taxes/Tangible Net Worth	(36) -.2	(119) 3.4	(77) 2.0	(147) 3.3	(249) 4.9	(177) 5.4
-5.7	-4.7	-1.9		-13.0	-3.4	-3.5	-3.3	-1.0	.0
6.6	7.0	7.1		3.2	10.5	7.2	7.9	6.9	6.8
.8	1.4	1.9	% Profit Before Taxes/Total Assets	-.5	1.8	1.2	1.5	2.7	2.4
-3.2	-3.0	-1.1		-5.5	-2.8	-2.7	-1.6	-.5	.0
11.4	13.2	11.8		37.2	13.6	6.9	13.2	10.1	10.8
3.4	4.0	3.8	Sales/Net Fixed Assets	1.2	2.3	2.2	4.3	3.7	5.0
1.4	1.7	1.6		.6	.7	1.0	2.1	1.9	2.6
2.5	2.8	2.5		3.6	2.1	2.0	2.4	2.6	2.9
1.4	1.5	1.5	Sales/Total Assets	.8	1.0	1.1	1.5	1.6	1.7
.7	.8	.8		.3	.5	.6	.9	1.0	1.1
1.2	1.1	1.1		1.4	1.5	1.5	1.0	1.2	.9
(731) 2.4	(625) 2.2	(744) 2.1	% Depr., Dep., Amort./Sales	(30) 3.4	(96) 3.0	(71) 2.7	(137) 1.9	(240) 2.1	(170) 1.8
3.8	3.9	3.7		10.4	5.9	4.8	3.2	3.6	3.0
2.9	2.5	2.4			3.8			1.8	1.3
(84) 6.6	(74) 6.1	(68) 4.6	% Officers', Directors' Owners' Comp/Sales		(11) 4.7			(20) 4.1	(16) 3.4
14.3	13.8	14.5			17.1			14.8	9.4
15732387M	15874106M	20043330M	Net Sales ($)	23665M	248851M	324054M	1099051M	4145001M	14202708M
12381963M	11473874M	13797065M	Total Assets ($)	48854M	401197M	518635M	1222519M	3515236M	8090624M

M = $ thousand   MM = $ million
See Pages 9 through 22 for Explanation of Ratios and Data

Current Data Sorted by Assets | **Comparative Historical Data**

0-500M	500M-2MM	2-10MM	10-50MM	50-100MM	100-250MM		4/1/06-3/31/07 ALL	4/1/07-3/31/08 ALL
						Type of Statement		
1	4	5	9	1		Unqualified	13	9
						Reviewed		
1						Compiled	1	1
	1					Tax Returns		7
2	1	4	4			Other	1	1
	24 (4/1-9/30/10)		9 (10/1/10-3/31/11)					
4	6	9	13	1		**NUMBER OF STATEMENTS**	15	18
%	%	%	%	%	%	**ASSETS**	%	%
			19.4		D	Cash & Equivalents	23.9	16.3
			7.1		A	Trade Receivables (net)	9.0	10.1
			9.4		T	Inventory	19.1	7.9
			2.8		A	All Other Current	2.4	11.5
			38.7			Total Current	54.3	45.8
			49.4		N	Fixed Assets (net)	35.8	41.6
			.2		O	Intangibles (net)	.0	2.3
			11.8		T	All Other Non-Current	9.8	10.3
			100.0			Total	100.0	100.0
					A	**LIABILITIES**		
			.0		V	Notes Payable-Short Term	2.1	.7
			3.2		A	Cur. Mat.-L.T.D.	.8	2.0
			4.2		I	Trade Payables	3.0	4.0
			.0		L	Income Taxes Payable	.0	.0
			2.1		A	All Other Current	7.4	24.8
			9.5		B	Total Current	13.3	31.4
			10.3		L	Long-Term Debt	5.7	16.8
			.0		E	Deferred Taxes	.0	.0
			1.0			All Other Non-Current	1.8	1.0
			79.2			Net Worth	79.2	50.8
			100.0			Total Liabilties & Net Worth	100.0	100.0
						INCOME DATA		
			100.0			Net Sales	100.0	100.0
						Gross Profit		
			89.3			Operating Expenses	91.6	98.9
			10.7			Operating Profit	8.4	1.1
			-.6			All Other Expenses (net)	-1.2	-.6
			11.4			Profit Before Taxes	9.7	1.6
						RATIOS		
			7.7				14.7	8.6
			6.1			Current	8.8	3.1
			2.6				3.0	.9
			6.6				12.6	4.8
			3.0			Quick	3.6	2.7
			1.6				1.6	.2
			0 UND				**2** 183.6	**0** UND
			5 78.0			Sales/Receivables	**6** 60.8	**2** 160.4
			9 41.7				**21** 17.1	**19** 19.4
						Cost of Sales/Inventory		
						Cost of Sales/Payables		
			4.7				2.9	6.6
			6.8			Sales/Working Capital	4.9	8.9
			13.0				9.6	-125.7
								28.1
						EBIT/Interest		(14) 5.1
								-1.5
						Net Profit + Depr., Dep., Amort./Cur. Mat. L/T/D		
			.4				.2	.4
			.7			Fixed/Worth	.5	.6
			.9				.6	1.5
			.1				.1	.1
			.2			Debt/Worth	.1	.8
			.4				.4	2.3
			16.0				19.6	14.8
			8.4			% Profit Before Taxes/Tangible Net Worth	(14) 7.1	(15) 5.3
			2.7				4.4	-8.8
			13.3				14.0	11.9
			7.0			% Profit Before Taxes/Total Assets	6.1	3.4
			2.4				2.5	-6.2
			11.6				24.0	15.5
			2.8			Sales/Net Fixed Assets	5.1	8.0
			1.5				1.6	2.0
			2.9				4.1	4.7
			1.6			Sales/Total Assets	1.5	2.5
			1.0				.8	1.1
			1.1				.6	.9
			1.7			% Depr., Dep., Amort./Sales	1.2	(16) 1.2
			3.1				3.2	2.7
						% Officers', Directors' Owners' Comp/Sales		
4109M	55701M	75266M	447977M	209558M		Net Sales ($)	245263M	176941M
1234M	8200M	50286M	238869M	65960M		Total Assets ($)	143313M	70381M

M = $ thousand MM = $ million

See Pages 9 through 22 for Explanation of Ratios and Data

Comparative Historical Data   Current Data Sorted by Sales

Type of Statement

10	21	20		2	1	2	4	3	8
			Unqualified						
	1		Reviewed						
2	3	1	Compiled	1					
8	8	1	Tax Returns		1				
3	8	11	Other	2	3	1		2	3
4/1/08-3/31/09 ALL	4/1/09-3/31/10 ALL	4/1/10-3/31/11 ALL		0-1MM	1-3MM	3-5MM	5-10MM	10-25MM	25MM & OVER
					24 (4/1-9/30/10)			9 (10/1/10-3/31/11)	

23	33	33	**NUMBER OF STATEMENTS**	5	5	3	4	5	11
%	%	%	**ASSETS**	%	%	%	%	%	%
17.6	21.6	22.3	Cash & Equivalents						21.6
8.0	5.9	10.4	Trade Receivables (net)						4.8
10.8	14.4	10.6	Inventory						21.0
14.5	2.2	3.3	All Other Current						2.8
50.9	44.1	46.5	Total Current						50.3
37.2	45.0	43.6	Fixed Assets (net)						39.1
2.0	.4	.1	Intangibles (net)						.2
9.9	10.4	9.9	All Other Non-Current						10.4
100.0	100.0	100.0	Total						100.0
			LIABILITIES						
4.6	2.8	2.3	Notes Payable-Short Term						1.2
5.3	.9	2.9	Cur. Mat.-L.T.D.						5.1
3.8	6.1	6.4	Trade Payables						3.0
.0	.0	.0	Income Taxes Payable						.0
22.7	3.7	4.1	All Other Current						2.8
36.5	13.5	15.7	Total Current						12.0
8.3	9.8	9.1	Long-Term Debt						8.4
.0	.0	.0	Deferred Taxes						.0
2.3	5.2	4.8	All Other Non-Current						1.2
52.8	71.5	70.4	Net Worth						78.5
100.0	100.0	100.0	Total Liabilties & Net Worth						100.0
			INCOME DATA						
100.0	100.0	100.0	Net Sales						100.0
			Gross Profit						
96.8	91.7	92.0	Operating Expenses						99.5
3.2	8.3	8.0	Operating Profit						.5
.4	.4	.2	All Other Expenses (net)						.6
2.8	7.9	7.7	Profit Before Taxes						-.1
			RATIOS						
9.7	14.1	13.7	Current						11.0
4.5	6.9	6.1							7.0
1.0	1.8	1.8							3.4
6.0	6.1	7.2	Quick						7.2
2.4	3.5	3.0							3.6
.2	1.3	1.3							1.3
0 UND	0 999.8	0 839.7	Sales/Receivables						0 912.0
2 148.4	3 118.9	7 53.8							4 90.8
15 24.8	10 37.2	36 10.0							6 64.9
			Cost of Sales/Inventory						
			Cost of Sales/Payables						
4.0	5.0	3.5	Sales/Working Capital						4.2
9.1	7.0	6.1							8.6
-676.7	13.2	13.0							11.3
56.3	21.6	49.1	EBIT/Interest						
(16) 8.7	(17) 6.1	(17) 6.0							
-1.1	-4.0	2.4							
			Net Profit + Depr., Dep., Amort./Cur. Mat. L/T/D						
.1	.3	.3	Fixed/Worth						.1
.6	.6	.6							.5
1.6	.9	.9							.9
.1	.1	.1	Debt/Worth						.1
.4	.3	.3							.2
3.4	.5	.8							.4
31.9	35.7	14.9	% Profit Before Taxes/Tangible Net Worth						10.9
(20) 14.1	(32) 16.9	(32) 6.8							5.6
1.7	-1.9	-1.4							-4.2
17.4	22.8	10.6	% Profit Before Taxes/Total Assets						9.1
6.0	11.4	6.2							3.9
-1.0	-2.7	-.6							-4.1
23.1	14.9	20.7	Sales/Net Fixed Assets						29.9
7.3	5.7	4.1							14.2
2.5	2.4	1.8							4.1
3.4	3.8	3.4	Sales/Total Assets						5.0
2.5	2.2	1.4							3.2
1.3	1.3	1.0							2.0
.6	.7	.9	% Depr., Dep., Amort./Sales						.5
(22) 1.7	(28) 1.3	(29) 1.4							.9
3.1	2.1	3.4							1.7
			% Officers', Directors' Owners' Comp/Sales						
945922M	1705237M	792611M	Net Sales ($)	2448M	10663M	13037M	32841M	73941M	659681M
201839M	449949M	364549M	Total Assets ($)	3848M	15360M	11435M	25463M	74171M	234272M

M = $ thousand   MM = $ million
See Pages 9 through 22 for Explanation of Ratios and Data

Current Data Sorted by Assets   Comparative Historical Data

0-500M	500M-2MM	2-10MM	10-50MM	50-100MM	100-250MM	Type of Statement	4/1/06-3/31/07 ALL	4/1/07-3/31/08 ALL
1	6	10	7	1	2	Unqualified	14	16
1						Reviewed	1	1
	1					Compiled		1
		1				Tax Returns	1	
2	2	3		1		Other	2	7
	32 (4/1-9/30/10)		6 (10/1/10-3/31/11)					
4	9	14	7	2	2	NUMBER OF STATEMENTS	18	25
%	%	%	%	%	%	**ASSETS**	%	%
		17.3				Cash & Equivalents	19.5	17.7
		5.6				Trade Receivables (net)	5.1	4.5
		.1				Inventory	.1	.3
		3.9				All Other Current	5.7	6.5
		26.9				Total Current	30.4	29.0
		61.2				Fixed Assets (net)	63.5	55.3
		.0				Intangibles (net)	.0	.0
		11.9				All Other Non-Current	6.1	15.7
		100.0				Total	100.0	100.0
						LIABILITIES		
		.7				Notes Payable-Short Term	1.3	1.0
		.5				Cur. Mat.-L.T.D.	1.0	1.0
		1.0				Trade Payables	2.9	2.4
		.0				Income Taxes Payable	.0	.0
		3.5				All Other Current	2.1	8.2
		5.8				Total Current	7.4	12.5
		11.3				Long-Term Debt	15.1	14.6
		.0				Deferred Taxes	.0	.0
		.4				All Other Non-Current	.4	.5
		82.4				Net Worth	77.1	72.4
		100.0				Total Liabilties & Net Worth	100.0	100.0
						INCOME DATA		
		100.0				Net Sales	100.0	100.0
						Gross Profit		
		93.1				Operating Expenses	89.9	92.4
		6.9				Operating Profit	10.1	7.6
		-.2				All Other Expenses (net)	-.2	-.4
		7.1				Profit Before Taxes	10.3	8.0
						RATIOS		
		10.7				Current	12.6	5.3
		4.6					4.9	3.1
		1.7					1.8	1.5
		10.7				Quick	12.0	4.6
		2.4					3.6	1.6
		1.6					.9	1.0
		1 409.0				Sales/Receivables	1 463.8	0 UND
		14 25.6					12 30.3	7 54.1
		28 12.9					41 9.0	30 12.0
						Cost of Sales/Inventory		
						Cost of Sales/Payables		
		2.1				Sales/Working Capital	2.5	3.1
		4.7					4.2	7.6
		12.2					8.4	15.3
						EBIT/Interest		13.7
							(15) 7.8	7.8
								2.2
						Net Profit + Depr., Dep., Amort./Cur. Mat. L/T/D		
		.5				Fixed/Worth	.6	.4
		.7					.8	.8
		1.0					1.2	1.1
		.1				Debt/Worth	.1	.1
		.2					.2	.3
		.3					.5	.7
		14.0				% Profit Before Taxes/Tangible Net Worth	11.8	14.6
		2.5					6.1	6.2
		-2.6					.1	1.6
		11.9				% Profit Before Taxes/Total Assets	9.1	11.6
		1.9					5.1	3.8
		-2.0					.1	1.3
		1.6				Sales/Net Fixed Assets	1.8	2.8
		1.0					1.1	1.2
		.8					.8	.7
		.9				Sales/Total Assets	1.2	1.2
		.7					.7	.7
		.5					.5	.5
		2.8				% Depr., Dep., Amort./Sales	2.8	2.2
		3.9					(16) 3.9	(21) 3.1
		5.6					4.9	5.6
						% Officers', Directors' Owners' Comp/Sales		
2424M	11251M	73051M	66683M	37581M	169315M	Net Sales ($)	50819M	274588M
867M	11394M	85236M	108237M	122208M	239398M	Total Assets ($)	71056M	329150M

© RMA 2011

M = $ thousand   MM = $ million
See Pages 9 through 22 for Explanation of Ratios and Data

Comparative Historical Data				Current Data Sorted by Sales					
18	23	27	Type of Statement						
1	1	1	Unqualified	4	7	4	5	5	2
1	1	1	Reviewed	1					
		1	Compiled	1					
			Tax Returns		1				
8	9	8	Other	3	1	1	2	1	
4/1/08-	4/1/09-	4/1/10-			32 (4/1-9/30/10)		6 (10/1/10-3/31/11)		
3/31/09	3/31/10	3/31/11		0-1MM	1-3MM	3-5MM	5-10MM	10-25MM	25MM & OVER
ALL	ALL	ALL							
28	34	38	NUMBER OF STATEMENTS	9	9	5	7	6	2
%	%	%	ASSETS	%	%	%	%	%	%
17.9	16.9	17.8	Cash & Equivalents						
11.3	8.9	7.7	Trade Receivables (net)						
.3	.2	.3	Inventory						
5.8	3.1	2.6	All Other Current						
35.2	29.1	28.4	Total Current						
51.6	56.6	62.0	Fixed Assets (net)						
1.0	.0	.7	Intangibles (net)						
12.2	14.2	8.9	All Other Non-Current						
100.0	100.0	100.0	Total						
			LIABILITIES						
3.5	4.0	2.4	Notes Payable-Short Term						
.4	1.1	.8	Cur. Mat.-L.T.D.						
3.7	2.5	1.8	Trade Payables						
.0	.0	.0	Income Taxes Payable						
3.6	4.3	3.8	All Other Current						
11.3	11.8	8.8	Total Current						
11.3	21.1	15.9	Long-Term Debt						
.0	.0	.0	Deferred Taxes						
1.0	1.2	3.1	All Other Non-Current						
76.5	65.8	72.1	Net Worth						
100.0	100.0	100.0	Total Liabilties & Net Worth						
			INCOME DATA						
100.0	100.0	100.0	Net Sales						
			Gross Profit						
96.3	98.8	95.0	Operating Expenses						
3.7	1.2	5.0	Operating Profit						
-.6	2.2	-.1	All Other Expenses (net)						
4.3	-1.0	5.1	Profit Before Taxes						
			RATIOS						
8.8	5.4	7.4	Current						
3.7	3.1	3.4							
1.1	1.4	1.7							
6.4	4.0	7.2	Quick						
2.7	2.3	2.9							
.8	1.3	1.6							
1 469.3	2 204.1	8 44.5	Sales/Receivables						
22 16.3	22 16.8	20 18.6							
56 6.5	48 7.6	32 11.4							
			Cost of Sales/Inventory						
			Cost of Sales/Payables						
2.8	3.2	2.7	Sales/Working Capital						
4.7	4.8	5.6							
55.2	14.2	10.5							
29.8	14.8	11.0	EBIT/Interest						
(19) 1.3	(23) 1.9	(24) 1.7							
-3.2	-2.2	.6							
			Net Profit + Depr., Dep., Amort./Cur. Mat. L/T/D						
.4	.5	.6	Fixed/Worth						
.7	.9	.9							
1.0	1.3	1.3							
.1	.2	.1	Debt/Worth						
.2	.4	.2							
.6	1.2	.9							
4.8	6.9	13.3	% Profit Before Taxes/Tangible Net Worth						
.5	-.6	2.1							
-3.6	-7.7	-1.7							
3.9	4.0	10.4	% Profit Before Taxes/Total Assets						
.4	-.4	1.5							
-2.6	-5.0	-.9							
3.6	3.0	2.3	Sales/Net Fixed Assets						
1.7	1.3	.9							
.7	.7	.7							
1.4	1.2	1.1	Sales/Total Assets						
.8	.8	.7							
.4	.5	.5							
2.0	1.9	2.8	% Depr., Dep., Amort./Sales						
(24) 2.9	(29) 3.1	(35) 4.3							
5.3	5.7	6.3							
			% Officers', Directors' Owners' Comp/Sales						
204468M	797560M	360305M	Net Sales ($)	5872M	16500M	17886M	53042M	97690M	169315M
298961M	684050M	567340M	Total Assets ($)	8234M	33657M	27779M	74942M	183330M	239398M

M = $ thousand   MM = $ million
See Pages 9 through 22 for Explanation of Ratios and Data

Current Data Sorted by Assets							Comparative Historical Data	

0-500M	500M-2MM	2-10MM	10-50MM	50-100MM	100-250MM	Type of Statement		
1	9	35	21	8	1	Unqualified	32	30
	1		1			Reviewed	2	2
						Compiled		
						Tax Returns	1	2
2	1			3	2	Other	13	14
2	9	10	10				4/1/06-3/31/07	4/1/07-3/31/08
	79 (4/1-9/30/10)		37 (10/1/10-3/31/11)				ALL	ALL
5	20	45	32	11	3	**NUMBER OF STATEMENTS**	48	48
%	%	%	%	%	%	**ASSETS**	%	%
	18.6	13.7	10.1	20.4		Cash & Equivalents	12.4	18.5
	11.7	8.5	11.1	9.4		Trade Receivables (net)	6.8	7.7
	.4	3.8	4.5	4.2		Inventory	4.6	3.6
	1.9	3.3	3.7	6.1		All Other Current	5.2	6.6
	32.7	29.3	29.4	40.1		Total Current	29.0	36.4
	39.7	50.0	41.6	31.3		Fixed Assets (net)	47.3	43.5
	.3	1.6	.7	.5		Intangibles (net)	.8	1.5
	27.3	19.1	28.3	28.1		All Other Non-Current	22.9	18.7
	100.0	100.0	100.0	100.0		Total	100.0	100.0
						LIABILITIES		
	.7	3.2	2.3	.8		Notes Payable-Short Term	7.1	2.8
	4.6	2.2	3.8	2.0		Cur. Mat.-L.T.D.	4.9	2.0
	2.6	2.8	4.8	1.4		Trade Payables	4.4	2.6
	.2	.0	.0	.0		Income Taxes Payable	.0	.0
	11.6	9.5	7.1	10.1		All Other Current	4.8	4.0
	19.6	17.7	18.0	14.3		Total Current	21.2	11.5
	20.9	25.7	26.5	40.0		Long-Term Debt	28.2	29.7
	.0	.0	.0	.0		Deferred Taxes	.0	.0
	2.3	2.2	6.0	4.1		All Other Non-Current	2.7	3.4
	57.2	54.4	49.5	41.6		Net Worth	48.0	55.4
	100.0	100.0	100.0	100.0		Total Liabilities & Net Worth	100.0	100.0
						INCOME DATA		
	100.0	100.0	100.0	100.0		Net Sales	100.0	100.0
						Gross Profit		
	90.3	93.6	87.0	74.3		Operating Expenses	90.7	92.2
	9.7	6.4	13.0	25.7		Operating Profit	9.3	7.8
	.2	2.1	3.5	11.6		All Other Expenses (net)	2.8	2.3
	9.5	4.3	9.5	14.1		Profit Before Taxes	6.6	5.6
						RATIOS		
	9.5	5.7	4.2	11.3			3.5	6.8
	2.2	2.1	1.9	2.6		Current	1.6	4.7
	.6	.9	1.1	1.1			.9	1.5
	6.0	4.8	3.2	4.9			2.4	5.3
	2.2	1.7	1.2	1.5		Quick	1.0	2.6
	.4	.5	.7	1.0			.5	1.0
0 UND	6 63.4	16 22.4	0 UND				0 UND	2 185.5
5 79.7	20 18.0	30 12.3	5 77.3			Sales/Receivables	21 17.0	22 16.9
49 7.5	46 7.9	63 5.8	112 3.3				58 6.3	60 6.0
						Cost of Sales/Inventory		
						Cost of Sales/Payables		
	2.7	1.8	2.0	.8			2.0	1.5
	9.7	5.8	5.3	1.4		Sales/Working Capital	7.9	3.0
	-14.7	-44.0	58.6	4.1			-21.8	12.1
	8.4	8.7	17.7				7.5	13.4
	(10) 2.0	(39) 2.2	(25) 4.1			EBIT/Interest	(31) 2.8	(33) 1.8
	-10.2	-1.2	1.2				1.0	-.6
						Net Profit + Depr., Dep., Amort./Cur. Mat. L/T/D		
	.2	.4	.3	.1			.3	.2
	.6	1.0	.8	.7		Fixed/Worth	.9	.7
	1.7	1.7	1.5	2.2			1.8	1.3
	.2	.3	.3	.5			.5	.2
	.4	.9	1.0	1.6		Debt/Worth	1.0	.6
	1.2	2.0	2.3	3.9			2.9	1.7
	35.2	19.0	14.8	13.3			15.9	18.3
	(18) 4.5	(43) 7.4	(30) 6.8	11.5		% Profit Before Taxes/Tangible Net Worth	(43) 4.6	(44) 4.1
	-3.5	-4.6	1.4	2.0			-.9	-.3
	19.5	7.7	10.8	6.5			7.3	8.2
	1.9	2.7	3.0	2.1		% Profit Before Taxes/Total Assets	1.6	2.5
	-3.4	-2.2	.6	.4			-.5	-1.0
	15.6	3.8	4.6	4.6			4.9	3.5
	2.9	1.0	1.8	1.7		Sales/Net Fixed Assets	1.5	1.4
	1.0	.4	.7	.5			.4	.4
	1.3	1.1	1.1	.4			.9	1.2
	1.0	.5	.5	.2		Sales/Total Assets	.4	.6
	.4	.3	.3	.1			.2	.2
	.7	1.2	1.2	.9			1.4	1.7
	(17) 1.4	(42) 3.2	(30) 3.5	(10) 4.2		% Depr., Dep., Amort./Sales	(42) 3.9	(40) 3.1
	7.8	6.7	10.0	8.8			7.7	12.0
						% Officers', Directors' Owners' Comp/Sales		
4377M	28229M	204314M	517535M	180074M	69313M	Net Sales ($)	322818M	299894M
762M	20854M	246840M	665944M	733939M	324844M	Total Assets ($)	745910M	553679M

© RMA 2011

M = $ thousand   MM = $ million
See Pages 9 through 22 for Explanation of Ratios and Data

Comparative Historical Data

Current Data Sorted by Sales

Comparative Historical Data			Type of Statement	Current Data Sorted by Sales					
44	64	75	Unqualified	12	17	10	13	16	7
1	1	2	Reviewed	1					1
2			Compiled						
2	2	3	Tax Returns	3					
19	32	36	Other	7	8	6	6	6	3
4/1/08-3/31/09	4/1/09-3/31/10	4/1/10-3/31/11			79 (4/1-9/30/10)		37 (10/1/10-3/31/11)		
ALL	ALL	ALL		0-1MM	1-3MM	3-5MM	5-10MM	10-25MM	25MM & OVER
68	99	116	**NUMBER OF STATEMENTS**	23	25	16	19	22	11
%	%	%	**ASSETS**	%	%	%	%	%	%
9.7	11.1	15.6	Cash & Equivalents	12.8	16.3	17.4	17.4	10.7	24.2
8.2	9.0	10.1	Trade Receivables (net)	7.8	6.2	10.8	5.8	18.3	13.9
4.5	4.2	3.2	Inventory	1.4	1.1	1.8	10.0	4.0	.0
3.5	4.8	3.5	All Other Current	4.0	1.6	5.4	2.0	4.8	4.4
25.9	29.1	32.4	Total Current	26.1	25.1	35.4	35.1	37.8	42.5
45.1	45.6	43.3	Fixed Assets (net)	45.1	54.8	42.7	33.4	41.1	35.4
2.6	.6	.9	Intangibles (net)	.7	1.0	.0	2.8	.7	.2
26.4	24.6	23.3	All Other Non-Current	28.1	19.1	21.8	28.8	20.4	21.8
100.0	100.0	100.0	Total	100.0	100.0	100.0	100.0	100.0	100.0
			LIABILITIES						
2.7	3.2	2.2	Notes Payable-Short Term	1.4	2.5	.9	4.0	2.8	.7
2.7	2.3	3.1	Cur. Mat.-L.T.D.	2.0	3.5	3.8	6.3	1.1	2.2
4.4	4.0	3.5	Trade Payables	4.3	2.2	1.6	2.6	4.5	7.3
.0	.0	.0	Income Taxes Payable	.0	.0	.2	.0	.0	.0
4.2	5.5	9.7	All Other Current	10.6	8.3	8.9	5.2	13.8	11.3
14.0	15.0	18.5	Total Current	18.3	16.6	15.4	18.1	22.1	21.5
25.9	33.7	26.5	Long-Term Debt	26.5	27.4	17.0	34.7	26.6	23.4
.0	.0	.0	Deferred Taxes	.0	.0	.0	.0	.0	.0
3.8	3.1	5.0	All Other Non-Current	3.2	8.8	1.9	2.4	5.9	6.8
56.3	48.2	50.0	Net Worth	52.1	47.1	65.6	44.8	45.3	48.3
100.0	100.0	100.0	Total Liabilties & Net Worth	100.0	100.0	100.0	100.0	100.0	100.0
			INCOME DATA						
100.0	100.0	100.0	Net Sales	100.0	100.0	100.0	100.0	100.0	100.0
			Gross Profit						
89.3	90.2	89.6	Operating Expenses	95.8	88.2	88.5	79.4	91.0	96.2
10.7	9.8	10.4	Operating Profit	4.2	11.8	11.5	20.6	9.0	3.8
3.1	5.9	2.8	All Other Expenses (net)	2.3	2.1	-.4	7.6	4.0	-.4
7.6	4.0	7.6	Profit Before Taxes	1.8	9.7	11.9	13.0	5.1	4.2
			RATIOS						
5.4	4.2	5.2		6.2	8.3	8.8	2.8	3.7	6.2
2.4	2.2	2.1	Current	2.2	2.5	3.2	2.2	1.5	2.6
1.0	1.1	1.0		.6	.6	1.3	1.4	1.0	1.1
3.0	2.8	3.9		3.9	5.0	6.1	2.5	2.5	4.9
1.7	1.3	1.6	Quick	2.2	2.5	1.8	1.1	1.2	2.2
.7	.6	.6		.3	.4	1.0	.5	.8	.9
1 677.5	3 123.8	3 117.7		0 UND	1 466.7	16 23.2	12 29.5	7 51.5	1 391.1
21 17.8	21 17.0	23 15.7	Sales/Receivables	2 150.0	17 21.7	32 11.6	23 15.8	28 13.1	30 12.1
65 5.6	49 7.4	50 7.3		41 9.0	47 7.8	85 4.3	33 11.0	83 4.4	43 8.5
			Cost of Sales/Inventory						
			Cost of Sales/Payables						
1.7	1.9	1.8		1.9	2.0	1.2	2.0	3.4	2.3
6.0	6.3	5.7	Sales/Working Capital	7.2	4.4	2.5	4.1	6.5	7.0
116.9	56.9	UND		-9.8	-10.1	25.0	18.2	132.2	69.5
8.1	14.9	11.4		3.0	7.2	19.5	14.7	13.4	31.9
(41) 1.2	(62) 1.9	(88) 2.9	EBIT/Interest	(15) -1.2	(20) 1.7	(11) 4.6	(14) 4.3	(17) 1.9	13.5
-1.1	.0	-.4		-13.5	-.9	4.0	-.1	-.6	1.4
			Net Profit + Depr., Dep., Amort./Cur. Mat. L/T/D						
.2	.3	.3		.3	.5	.2	.1	.1	.3
.7	.9	.8	Fixed/Worth	1.0	.9	.6	.4	1.2	.7
1.4	2.1	1.6		1.6	3.4	.8	2.6	2.5	1.1
.3	.3	.3		.3	.3	.1	.3	.3	.5
.7	1.0	.9	Debt/Worth	.6	.6	.5	1.7	1.5	1.1
1.8	2.4	2.5		3.1	3.6	1.1	3.5	2.2	2.4
8.9	9.7	15.1	% Profit Before Taxes/Tangible Net Worth	12.1	18.4	14.8	17.8	22.1	17.7
(65) 3.0	(91) 3.4	(109) 6.1		(20) 1.2	(24) 2.5	6.9	(17) 12.6	(21) 8.1	9.4
-3.4	-1.6	-1.8		-8.7	-9.6	3.2	.2	-.8	1.5
5.6	5.8	8.4	% Profit Before Taxes/Total Assets	4.3	7.3	7.3	13.9	9.2	9.7
1.1	1.6	2.6		.0	1.7	3.4	2.1	2.8	3.7
-2.0	-.8	-1.5		-6.6	-1.9	2.7	-1.3	.1	.6
5.4	4.4	5.2	Sales/Net Fixed Assets	4.1	2.5	5.9	20.0	5.5	8.4
1.5	1.4	1.8		.8	.7	1.8	2.9	3.2	2.5
.5	.6	.5		.4	.4	.8	.5	.8	1.6
.7	.9	1.1	Sales/Total Assets	1.0	.7	1.1	.9	1.7	1.7
.4	.5	.5		.4	.5	.6	.5	.7	1.2
.3	.2	.3		.3	.3	.3	.2	.3	.4
1.4	1.4	1.0	% Depr., Dep., Amort./Sales	.9	1.3	1.3	1.0	1.0	.9
(52) 2.8	(84) 3.6	(106) 3.1		(21) 5.2	(22) 4.0	(14) 3.7	(16) 2.7	2.2	1.5
7.4	8.6	7.8		13.0	8.6	4.9	18.8	5.5	8.0
		3.9	% Officers', Directors' Owners' Comp/Sales						
	(12)	6.6							
		13.6							
621131M	1015670M	1003842M	Net Sales ($)	13651M	42938M	63148M	130296M	354372M	399437M
1288066M	1967712M	1993183M	Total Assets ($)	39538M	130442M	122524M	475809M	701483M	523387M

© RMA 2011

M = $ thousand   MM = $ million
See Pages 9 through 22 for Explanation of Ratios and Data

Current Data Sorted by Assets   **Comparative Historical Data**

	0-500M	500M-2MM	2-10MM	10-50MM	50-100MM	100-250MM		4/1/06-3/31/07 ALL	4/1/07-3/31/08 ALL
Type of Statement									
Unqualified	6	14	90	71	6	3		205	188
Reviewed		1	3					5	9
Compiled		3	1		5			8	5
Tax Returns	1	5	1					9	11
Other	4	11	26	26	8	2		56	50
		183 (4/1-9/30/10)		99 (10/1/10-3/31/11)					
NUMBER OF STATEMENTS	11	34	121	97	14	5		283	263
	%	%	%	%	%	%		%	%
ASSETS									
Cash & Equivalents	22.8	27.1	19.1	18.9	17.4			17.8	18.1
Trade Receivables (net)	46.7	19.5	20.2	15.6	14.7			18.7	19.3
Inventory	1.5	3.2	3.4	2.6	5.0			2.8	3.3
All Other Current	2.7	3.3	2.9	2.5	1.5			4.9	2.8
Total Current	73.7	53.0	45.5	39.5	38.6			44.3	43.6
Fixed Assets (net)	13.7	38.0	44.8	47.9	50.3			45.0	45.1
Intangibles (net)	.0	2.8	1.2	1.1	.3			1.1	1.5
All Other Non-Current	12.5	6.2	8.5	11.5	10.8			9.7	9.8
Total	100.0	100.0	100.0	100.0	100.0			100.0	100.0
LIABILITIES									
Notes Payable-Short Term	15.0	7.2	3.5	1.2	2.6			3.6	4.2
Cur. Mat.-L.T.D.	.6	2.6	2.0	2.3	1.3			2.1	2.3
Trade Payables	4.9	5.6	6.6	7.2	7.1			6.4	6.6
Income Taxes Payable	1.3	.2	.1	.0	.0			.1	.1
All Other Current	20.9	13.9	12.7	9.5	8.6			11.1	12.5
Total Current	42.7	29.5	24.9	20.1	19.6			23.2	25.7
Long-Term Debt	6.9	18.3	18.7	20.4	24.9			19.2	19.3
Deferred Taxes	.0	.0	.0	.0	.0			.1	.0
All Other Non-Current	6.4	.2	4.7	3.1	3.0			3.5	3.4
Net Worth	44.0	52.1	51.8	56.4	52.5			53.9	51.5
Total Liabilities & Net Worth	100.0	100.0	100.0	100.0	100.0			100.0	100.0
INCOME DATA									
Net Sales	100.0	100.0	100.0	100.0	100.0			100.0	100.0
Gross Profit									
Operating Expenses	95.9	94.0	96.9	95.1	95.6			95.8	96.2
Operating Profit	4.1	6.0	3.1	4.9	4.4			4.2	3.8
All Other Expenses (net)	1.5	1.5	1.0	.5	-.6			.7	.6
Profit Before Taxes	2.5	4.5	2.1	4.4	5.0			3.5	3.2
RATIOS									
Current	3.6	6.2	3.6	3.5	3.4			3.6	3.2
	1.6	2.5	2.0	2.3	1.8			2.0	1.9
	1.4	1.0	1.3	1.5	1.3			1.2	1.1
Quick	3.6	5.3	3.2	2.9	2.7			3.2	2.7
	1.6	2.1	1.7	2.1	1.5			1.6	1.6
	1.2	1.0	1.1	1.3	1.0			1.0	1.0
Sales/Receivables	18 20.8	3 106.2	12 31.5	17 20.9	12 30.0			13 28.6	15 24.1
	33 11.0	29 12.7	35 10.5	36 10.2	22 16.7			32 11.4	33 11.1
	72 5.1	53 6.9	51 7.2	48 7.6	37 9.8			49 7.5	47 7.7
Cost of Sales/Inventory									
Cost of Sales/Payables									
Sales/Working Capital	5.4	3.7	5.1	4.2	4.0			4.7	4.8
	18.6	9.4	9.4	7.0	9.2			9.8	10.7
	86.1	297.7	24.5	16.1	17.0			32.1	53.7
EBIT/Interest		12.8	9.3	10.3	24.4			7.5	10.1
		(26) 2.8	(101) 4.0	(79) 4.9	(11) 4.2			(230) 3.4	(208) 3.7
		-4.0	.6	1.5	3.0			.3	1.2
Net Profit + Depr., Dep., Amort./Cur. Mat. L/T/D									
Fixed/Worth	.0	.2	.4	.5	.6			.4	.5
	.1	.8	.9	.9	1.0			.9	.9
	4.0	4.0	1.4	1.3	1.4			1.4	1.5
Debt/Worth	.3	.3	.4	.4	.5			.4	.4
	1.2	.7	.8	.7	1.0			.8	.9
	3.8	8.0	1.9	1.4	1.9			1.6	1.7
% Profit Before Taxes/Tangible Net Worth	150.3	44.6	15.5	13.8	20.2			14.4	14.7
	(10) 61.8	(30) 12.0	(116) 6.3	(95) 7.6	9.6			(277) 6.2	(251) 6.5
	-15.5	-7.4	-1.1	1.3	4.2			-1.8	.5
% Profit Before Taxes/Total Assets	37.3	16.9	7.9	8.3	11.2			8.4	7.6
	15.2	6.3	3.4	3.5	5.5			3.4	3.2
	-13.5	-3.5	-.4	.6	1.6			-.8	.2
Sales/Net Fixed Assets	UND	70.8	9.8	5.3	4.4			9.9	10.6
	201.3	7.1	3.7	2.9	3.1			3.3	3.3
	20.3	2.9	1.9	1.5	.9			1.9	1.9
Sales/Total Assets	7.1	4.6	2.5	1.9	1.9			2.6	2.5
	3.5	2.3	1.6	1.3	1.6			1.6	1.6
	2.3	1.5	1.0	.8	.7			1.0	1.1
% Depr., Dep., Amort./Sales		.8	1.4	1.9	1.6			1.5	1.6
		(29) 2.2	(110) 2.8	(94) 3.1	(13) 2.8			(259) 2.7	(242) 2.9
		3.5	4.0	4.0	6.0			4.1	4.2
% Officers', Directors' Owners' Comp/Sales								3.1	3.9
								(30) 9.8	(28) 9.1
								37.9	34.4
Net Sales ($)	16114M	114654M	1270311M	3654907M	1176165M	2300439M		5967530M	6328351M
Total Assets ($)	3599M	40453M	674037M	2210100M	917941M	881131M		3697314M	3845222M

© RMA 2011   M = $ thousand   MM = $ million
See Pages 9 through 22 for Explanation of Ratios and Data

Comparative Historical Data | | | Current Data Sorted by Sales

						Type of Statement						
	199		159		190	Unqualified	6	18	17	36	62	51
	6		3		4	Reviewed		1			3	
	2		8		4	Compiled		1	1	2		
	10		11		7	Tax Returns	3		2	2		
	81		80		77	Other	1	13	11	9	20	23
	4/1/08-3/31/09 ALL		4/1/09-3/31/10 ALL		4/1/10-3/31/11 ALL		183 (4/1-9/30/10)			99 (10/1/10-3/31/11)		
							0-1MM	1-3MM	3-5MM	5-10MM	10-25MM	25MM & OVER
	298		261		282	NUMBER OF STATEMENTS	10	33	31	49	85	74
	%		%		%	ASSETS	%	%	%	%	%	%
	19.1		19.0		19.9	Cash & Equivalents	25.0	19.4	17.7	20.9	20.1	19.4
	18.6		20.3		19.4	Trade Receivables (net)	12.5	24.3	15.1	17.7	18.4	22.0
	3.1		4.1		3.1	Inventory	1.5	2.2	3.9	3.0	2.7	4.1
	3.5		3.4		2.7	All Other Current	2.9	1.8	1.4	2.7	2.8	3.6
	44.1		46.8		45.1	Total Current	41.9	47.8	38.1	44.3	44.0	49.1
	44.8		42.1		43.8	Fixed Assets (net)	47.1	41.7	52.3	44.2	44.1	40.1
	1.4		1.2		1.5	Intangibles (net)	.3	.2	1.0	3.6	1.1	1.6
	9.7		9.9		9.6	All Other Non-Current	10.7	10.3	8.6	7.9	10.8	9.2
	100.0		100.0		100.0	Total	100.0	100.0	100.0	100.0	100.0	100.0
						LIABILITIES						
	4.8		5.6		3.5	Notes Payable-Short Term	7.1	6.5	6.1	4.1	1.7	2.2
	1.8		2.2		2.1	Cur. Mat.-L.T.D.	.9	2.4	2.9	1.7	2.2	1.7
	6.5		7.8		6.7	Trade Payables	.6	4.3	4.6	4.6	6.0	11.6
	.2		.1		.1	Income Taxes Payable	.0	.6	.1	.1	.0	.0
	12.8		13.0		11.9	All Other Current	2.6	12.4	6.6	15.1	11.8	13.2
	26.1		28.7		24.3	Total Current	11.2	26.2	20.3	25.7	21.8	28.7
	17.3		17.4		19.0	Long-Term Debt	20.5	18.1	23.3	17.5	17.8	19.7
	.1		.0		.0	Deferred Taxes	.0	.0	.0	.0	.0	.0
	3.2		3.7		3.7	All Other Non-Current	.6	5.3	2.7	3.0	3.9	4.0
	53.4		50.2		53.0	Net Worth	67.8	50.3	53.6	53.8	56.5	47.6
	100.0		100.0		100.0	Total Liabilties & Net Worth	100.0	100.0	100.0	100.0	100.0	100.0
						INCOME DATA						
	100.0		100.0		100.0	Net Sales	100.0	100.0	100.0	100.0	100.0	100.0
						Gross Profit						
	96.8		96.6		95.8	Operating Expenses	85.0	96.0	96.6	94.6	96.9	96.4
	3.2		3.4		4.2	Operating Profit	15.0	4.0	3.4	5.4	3.1	3.6
	1.1		1.0		.9	All Other Expenses (net)	4.7	3.3	.7	.4	.1	.5
	2.1		2.4		3.3	Profit Before Taxes	10.3	.7	2.6	5.1	3.0	3.1
						RATIOS						
	3.6		3.3		3.6		27.3	5.6	6.0	3.5	3.6	2.8
	2.0		1.9		2.2	Current	6.5	2.6	2.3	1.9	2.6	2.0
	1.3		1.2		1.4		1.5	1.1	1.1	1.1	1.4	1.4
	3.1		2.7		3.2		27.1	4.9	5.4	2.6	3.0	2.4
	1.6		1.5		1.8	Quick	5.6	2.3	2.3	1.8	2.0	1.5
	1.0		1.0		1.2		1.5	1.0	1.0	1.1	1.3	1.2
15	24.2	14	26.2	15	24.0		0 UND	18 20.5	4 83.9	15 24.1	16 23.1	15 23.9
32	11.3	31	11.6	33	11.0	Sales/Receivables	0 UND	33 11.0	28 12.9	30 12.3	36 10.2	33 10.9
45	8.1	53	6.9	50	7.3		63 5.8	58 6.3	51 7.2	53 6.9	48 7.7	48 7.6
						Cost of Sales/Inventory						
						Cost of Sales/Payables						
	4.6		5.0		4.7		1.0	3.2	5.2	5.3	4.3	5.5
	9.7		11.6		8.7	Sales/Working Capital	3.2	7.7	9.8	9.2	7.3	10.3
	32.1		30.1		19.8		5.5	211.8	60.3	22.8	16.2	17.5
	7.4		13.2		10.3			4.5	5.8	13.9	11.2	11.3
(244)	2.2	(216)	3.5	(227)	4.1	EBIT/Interest	(27) .7	(27) 3.3	(43) 4.1	(69) 4.4	(57) 4.7	
	-.7		-.5		1.0			-3.1	.1	.8	1.6	1.9
						Net Profit + Depr., Dep., Amort./Cur. Mat. L/T/D						
	.5		.4		.4		.0	.1	.5	.5	.4	.5
	.9		.8		.9	Fixed/Worth	.6	.8	1.1	.9	.8	.8
	1.3		1.4		1.4		3.2	2.2	1.9	1.8	1.1	1.3
	.4		.4		.4		.0	.3	.4	.5	.4	.6
	.7		.9		.8	Debt/Worth	.2	.7	.8	.8	.7	1.0
	1.5		2.4		1.7		2.4	1.8	1.8	1.8	1.3	2.0
	12.6		17.9		16.9	% Profit Before Taxes/Tangible Net Worth	28.8	28.5	20.3	21.9	14.3	18.2
(289)	3.7	(249)	6.6	(269)	7.2		6.2	(29) 1.0	(30) 3.8	(46) 7.1	(82) 7.3	(72) 9.2
	-3.2		-3.5		.2		.8	-4.6	-4.7	.2	.5	2.2
	7.4		9.4		9.0	% Profit Before Taxes/Total Assets	16.0	11.9	8.6	13.9	8.3	9.8
	1.8		3.1		3.9		4.5	.0	3.4	4.2	4.1	3.9
	-2.0		-2.2		.1		.4	-5.0	-1.9	.5	.2	1.0
	10.0		16.5		10.8	Sales/Net Fixed Assets	UND	62.3	8.8	10.2	7.3	13.8
	3.2		3.6		3.5		3.3	3.3	2.2	3.1	3.6	4.5
	1.9		2.0		1.8		.2	1.0	1.1	1.6	2.1	2.6
	2.5		2.6		2.5	Sales/Total Assets	1.7	2.8	2.8	2.3	2.2	3.1
	1.6		1.6		1.6		.8	1.5	1.5	1.4	1.6	1.9
	1.0		1.1		1.0		.2	.7	.7	1.0	1.0	1.3
	1.4		1.4		1.6	% Depr., Dep., Amort./Sales		1.4	1.8	1.9	1.5	1.4
(270)	2.7	(228)	2.6	(254)	2.8		(27) 3.0	(28) 3.8	(44) 2.8	(79) 2.9	(69) 2.2	
	4.1		4.0		4.0			5.2	5.1	4.0	3.6	3.4
	5.3		2.2		5.0	% Officers', Directors' Owners' Comp/Sales						
(33)	7.7	(34)	3.8	(26)	9.3							
	31.9		8.8		19.3							
	6757440M		8433012M		8532590M	Net Sales ($)	5486M	65651M	121864M	366447M	1401420M	6571722M
	4322266M		4405106M		4727261M	Total Assets ($)	15345M	69815M	111994M	282976M	1109635M	3137496M

M = $ thousand   MM = $ million
See Pages 9 through 22 for Explanation of Ratios and Data

Current Data Sorted by Assets

Comparative Historical Data

0-500M	500M-2MM	2-10MM	10-50MM	50-100MM	100-250MM		4/1/06-3/31/07 ALL	4/1/07-3/31/08 ALL
						Type of Statement		
5	19	51	17	3	1	Unqualified	75	78
	3	6	1			Reviewed	11	8
27	20	11	1			Compiled	45	44
141	59	32	2	2		Tax Returns	176	177
96	65	45	14	2	1	Other	105	111
135 (4/1-9/30/10)			489 (10/1/10-3/31/11)					
269	166	145	35	7	2	NUMBER OF STATEMENTS	412	418
%	%	%	%	%	%	**ASSETS**	%	%
32.2	16.4	11.9	20.4			Cash & Equivalents	21.5	19.5
6.1	7.8	9.5	9.0			Trade Receivables (net)	8.3	8.8
.4	.1	.3	.0			Inventory	.3	.5
3.5	2.1	1.2	4.4			All Other Current	4.2	3.8
42.3	26.4	23.0	33.9			Total Current	34.3	32.6
36.4	59.0	65.2	48.5			Fixed Assets (net)	49.7	50.0
10.0	5.9	2.3	3.0			Intangibles (net)	7.0	7.4
11.3	8.7	9.5	14.6			All Other Non-Current	9.0	10.0
100.0	100.0	100.0	100.0			Total	100.0	100.0
						LIABILITIES		
11.9	6.0	3.3	1.9			Notes Payable-Short Term	5.9	5.9
3.3	2.3	2.3	2.5			Cur. Mat.-L.T.D.	4.5	5.1
5.9	3.9	5.2	5.5			Trade Payables	5.0	6.0
.2	.1	.0	.1			Income Taxes Payable	.0	.1
24.8	9.6	8.3	12.2			All Other Current	20.4	16.6
46.1	21.8	19.1	22.2			Total Current	35.7	33.7
30.6	49.2	45.6	26.6			Long-Term Debt	37.3	40.1
.0	.0	.1	.4			Deferred Taxes	.1	.1
23.3	6.1	3.7	7.0			All Other Non-Current	9.5	8.4
-.1	22.8	31.5	43.8			Net Worth	17.4	17.8
100.0	100.0	100.0	100.0			Total Liabilities & Net Worth	100.0	100.0
						INCOME DATA		
100.0	100.0	100.0	100.0			Net Sales	100.0	100.0
						Gross Profit		
94.6	86.1	83.8	93.0			Operating Expenses	90.1	89.4
5.4	13.9	16.2	7.0			Operating Profit	9.9	10.6
.4	6.8	9.5	1.2			All Other Expenses (net)	4.2	3.7
5.0	7.1	6.7	5.9			Profit Before Taxes	5.6	7.0
						RATIOS		
4.9	3.9	2.4	2.4				2.9	2.9
1.4	1.3	1.4	1.6			Current	1.1	1.2
.4	.5	.5	.9				.4	.5
4.5	3.8	2.3	2.1				2.4	2.5
1.3	1.3	1.2	1.6			Quick	(410) .9	1.1
.3	.4	.3	.8				.3	.3
0 UND	0 UND	0 UND	6 56.2				0 UND	0 UND
0 UND	0 UND	5 70.7	16 22.9			Sales/Receivables	0 UND	0 UND
0 921.0	11 32.7	25 14.7	31 11.9				15 25.1	16 22.5
						Cost of Sales/Inventory		
						Cost of Sales/Payables		
18.9	7.7	10.3	4.8				15.3	12.6
123.9	65.5	45.9	13.7			Sales/Working Capital	228.6	87.5
-28.5	-20.1	-17.4	-94.9				-20.3	-18.7
15.1	5.9	6.6	20.3				9.5	11.5
(146) 4.0	(118) 2.7	(95) 2.4	(31) 5.4			EBIT/Interest	(281) 2.6	(286) 3.7
.2	1.2	1.0	2.2				.9	1.2
							8.3	11.8
						Net Profit + Depr., Dep., Amort./Cur. Mat. L/T/D	(19) 3.6	(16) 4.5
							1.8	2.1
.3	.6	.9	.5				.6	.6
1.3	3.9	2.6	1.2			Fixed/Worth	2.0	1.6
-1.2	-11.2	27.7	3.8				-8.1	-10.3
.4	.6	.8	.5				.7	.6
3.2	4.1	2.8	1.3			Debt/Worth	2.7	2.6
-2.5	-12.4	27.0	4.4				-10.0	-11.9
194.6	42.6	34.0	30.7				88.3	108.0
(168) 73.7	(111) 16.1	(116) 11.3	(31) 13.6			% Profit Before Taxes/Tangible Net Worth	(283) 29.6	(296) 29.0
23.2	3.4	.9	4.1				4.3	6.0
63.5	12.1	6.5	14.1				28.6	37.0
21.5	4.3	3.0	6.8			% Profit Before Taxes/Total Assets	8.3	8.8
.0	.6	.2	1.1				.0	.9
87.2	10.8	5.5	14.8				33.7	28.1
24.4	2.2	1.2	2.6			Sales/Net Fixed Assets	8.0	8.7
11.2	.8	.5	1.3				1.6	1.7
11.4	2.3	2.0	3.1				6.2	6.0
7.0	1.4	.8	1.4			Sales/Total Assets	2.9	3.2
4.4	.7	.4	.8				1.0	1.2
.8	1.6	1.9	2.1				1.2	1.0
(169) 1.6	(132) 3.1	(121) 3.6	(32) 3.2			% Depr., Dep., Amort./Sales	(311) 2.4	(316) 2.2
3.0	6.5	9.0	4.0				4.6	4.1
3.0	2.9	2.3					2.5	2.6
(131) 5.0	(58) 5.9	(39) 5.0				% Officers', Directors' Owners' Comp/Sales	(146) 5.8	(163) 5.9
9.1	11.5	8.5					9.4	10.6
318740M	342390M	1062123M	1260558M	2687377M	37032M	Net Sales ($)	7739800M	2896137M
50986M	179650M	615395M	594736M	514275M	229611M	Total Assets ($)	1939757M	1401519M

M = $ thousand   MM = $ million
See Pages 9 through 22 for Explanation of Ratios and Data

Comparative Historical Data | Current Data Sorted by Sales

			Type of Statement						
76	92	96	Unqualified	5	15	18	20	21	17
9	27	10	Reviewed	1		2	4	2	1
42	55	59	Compiled	27	24	5	2		1
173	201	236	Tax Returns	106	110	13	4		3
139	171	223	Other	93	79	19	7	17	8
4/1/08-	4/1/09-	4/1/10-			135 (4/1-9/30/10)		489 (10/1/10-3/31/11)		
3/31/09	3/31/10	3/31/11							
ALL	ALL	ALL		0-1MM	1-3MM	3-5MM	5-10MM	10-25MM	25MM & OVER
439	546	624	NUMBER OF STATEMENTS	232	228	57	37	40	30
%	%	%	ASSETS	%	%	%	%	%	%
22.8	20.9	22.3	Cash & Equivalents	21.1	25.4	17.5	19.2	23.8	19.3
7.9	8.0	7.5	Trade Receivables (net)	4.7	4.9	15.7	11.2	11.7	22.3
.3	.3	.3	Inventory	.2	.3	.9	.1	.2	.1
3.4	2.5	2.7	All Other Current	2.1	3.2	1.7	2.6	4.4	2.5
34.3	31.7	32.7	Total Current	28.0	33.8	35.9	33.1	40.1	44.1
49.0	50.8	49.8	Fixed Assets (net)	56.7	45.8	51.7	52.5	41.2	30.9
6.7	7.0	7.1	Intangibles (net)	8.6	7.8	1.0	.6	5.8	10.2
10.0	10.5	10.5	All Other Non-Current	6.8	12.6	11.4	13.7	12.9	14.8
100.0	100.0	100.0	Total	100.0	100.0	100.0	100.0	100.0	100.0
			LIABILITIES						
8.4	6.2	7.7	Notes Payable-Short Term	9.4	6.2	7.8	15.3	1.6	3.7
5.0	5.3	2.7	Cur. Mat.-L.T.D.	2.3	3.5	1.8	3.1	2.4	1.6
5.9	4.9	5.1	Trade Payables	3.0	4.5	5.2	9.3	8.8	15.1
.2	.0	.1	Income Taxes Payable	.1	.1	.2	.0	.0	.1
15.9	22.4	15.9	All Other Current	16.9	17.5	14.7	10.4	9.5	14.1
35.4	38.8	31.5	Total Current	31.7	32.0	29.7	38.1	22.4	34.6
37.9	37.4	38.8	Long-Term Debt	50.1	37.4	32.4	28.2	17.5	16.3
.0	.1	.1	Deferred Taxes	.0	.0	.0	.2	.0	1.0
9.1	9.8	13.1	All Other Non-Current	11.9	20.0	3.0	4.4	5.6	9.3
17.6	14.0	16.5	Net Worth	6.4	10.5	34.9	29.0	54.5	38.8
100.0	100.0	100.0	Total Liabilties & Net Worth	100.0	100.0	100.0	100.0	100.0	100.0
			INCOME DATA						
100.0	100.0	100.0	Net Sales	100.0	100.0	100.0	100.0	100.0	100.0
			Gross Profit						
90.7	90.5	89.6	Operating Expenses	83.1	92.7	94.2	95.4	93.0	96.5
9.3	9.5	10.4	Operating Profit	16.9	7.3	5.8	4.6	7.0	3.5
4.4	4.4	4.4	All Other Expenses (net)	9.1	1.9	1.8	.1	.4	1.4
4.9	5.1	6.0	Profit Before Taxes	7.8	5.4	4.0	4.5	6.6	2.1
			RATIOS						
3.4	2.8	3.8		4.2	4.9	3.5	2.2	2.8	2.2
1.3	1.0	1.4	Current	1.1	1.8	1.1	1.5	1.9	1.2
.4	.3	.5		.3	.5	.5	.8	1.1	.9
3.1	2.5	3.2		3.8	4.8	3.0	2.1	2.6	1.8
1.1	1.0	1.3	Quick	.9	1.4	1.1	1.3	1.7	1.2
.3	.3	.4		.2	.5	.4	.8	1.0	.7
0 UND	0 UND	0 UND		0 UND	0 UND	0 UND	1 642.1	5 77.7	8 48.4
0 UND	0 UND	0 UND	Sales/Receivables	0 UND	0 UND	11 34.5	13 28.9	15 24.6	18 20.7
10 35.5	11 32.2	11 32.9		2 201.8	4 100.2	37 9.9	35 10.5	31 11.6	31 11.8
			Cost of Sales/Inventory						
			Cost of Sales/Payables						
12.1	14.4	11.4		11.5	14.7	8.2	11.0	9.1	13.0
78.0	999.8	84.6	Sales/Working Capital	220.2	84.4	43.3	34.1	17.5	81.7
-25.6	-15.3	-25.0		-14.5	-32.0	-26.5	-35.9	102.7	-129.4
10.0	9.4	9.9		4.9	10.1	10.1	8.4	23.5	24.8
(300) 3.1	(361) 2.7	(397) 3.1	EBIT/Interest	(127) 1.8	(146) 3.3	(46) 3.0	(27) 4.5	(28) 7.7	(23) 11.0
1.0	.7	1.0		.2	1.2	1.0	2.2	2.3	2.7
7.9	8.6	11.7	Net Profit + Depr., Dep.,						
(20) 1.9	(18) 2.4	(18) 5.0	Amort./Cur. Mat. L/T/D						
.5	1.3	1.8							
.5	.7	.5		.8	.5	.4	.5	.3	.4
1.7	2.0	2.1	Fixed/Worth	6.1	2.2	1.3	1.1	.8	1.2
-22.7	-6.2	-16.0		-4.2	-4.9	5.0	4.0	1.2	3.9
.7	.7	.6		.8	.5	.6	.3	.3	.9
2.6	3.5	3.1	Debt/Worth	9.5	5.1	1.6	1.2	.8	1.6
-11.4	-8.7	-13.0		-6.3	-5.2	4.5	4.9	2.5	9.6
93.4	73.8	84.3		96.6	142.1	39.0	24.5	33.4	50.3
(314) 23.9	(366) 20.9	(433) 24.1	% Profit Before Taxes/Tangible Net Worth	(142) 27.0	(144) 43.2	(50) 9.7	(33) 13.3	(38) 12.4	(26) 21.7
3.9	1.4	4.5		5.1	7.2	.2	5.5	4.3	4.3
26.7	26.5	22.8		22.5	43.7	10.8	10.5	12.7	16.9
5.9	5.9	6.4	% Profit Before Taxes/Total Assets	4.3	12.4	3.9	4.8	6.4	5.6
-.3	-.4	.4		-.3	1.4	-.1	2.9	1.2	.6
34.3	28.1	30.2		23.8	46.1	16.9	9.9	19.3	55.0
9.0	8.2	8.7	Sales/Net Fixed Assets	4.0	15.3	6.5	4.3	7.3	19.8
1.7	1.6	1.2		.6	2.4	1.4	1.2	2.4	5.7
6.8	6.4	6.8		6.0	8.8	4.6	3.3	4.1	6.9
3.2	3.1	2.7	Sales/Total Assets	1.5	4.5	2.1	1.5	2.2	4.3
1.0	1.0	.9		.4	1.5	.9	.9	1.2	1.9
1.1	1.0	1.1		1.6	.8	1.5	1.4	1.0	.4
(333) 2.2	(412) 2.3	(459) 2.6	% Depr., Dep., Amort./Sales	(166) 3.8	(163) 2.1	(43) 2.6	(32) 2.3	(32) 1.9	(23) 2.1
4.5	4.7	5.1		10.7	3.9	4.6	3.5	3.5	3.5
2.7	2.7	2.9		2.4	3.4	3.0			
(179) 4.8	(175) 5.5	(238) 5.2	% Officers', Directors' Owners' Comp/Sales	(85) 5.3	(103) 5.6	(24) 4.5			
8.3	11.0	9.9		11.6	8.8	6.2			
2981409M	5317596M	5708220M	Net Sales ($)	130055M	379665M	221443M	269102M	656391M	4051564M
1721672M	2295982M	2184653M	Total Assets ($)	196898M	215613M	167514M	184077M	576495M	844056M

M = $ thousand　　MM = $ million
See Pages 9 through 22 for Explanation of Ratios and Data

ARTS, ENTERTAINMENT, AND RECREATION

Current Data Sorted by Assets   Comparative Historical Data

						Type of Statement				
5	3	26	21	8	8	Unqualified			74	58
1	1	5				Reviewed			12	9
2	5	4	1			Compiled			26	6
7	12	4			1	Tax Returns			35	32
8	13	9	16	2	1	Other			56	47
		81 (4/1-9/30/10)		82 (10/1/10-3/31/11)					4/1/06-3/31/07	4/1/07-3/31/08
0-500M	500M-2MM	2-10MM	10-50MM	50-100MM	100-250MM				ALL	ALL
23	34	48	38	10	10	NUMBER OF STATEMENTS			203	152
%	%	%	%	%	%	**ASSETS**			%	%
22.2	25.6	11.3	15.2	8.2	13.8	Cash & Equivalents			16.9	18.5
8.9	10.9	5.3	3.7	1.2	2.1	Trade Receivables (net)			5.2	6.2
4.0	2.8	2.6	.7	.3	.2	Inventory			2.8	3.4
4.9	8.3	4.1	3.8	.8	8.4	All Other Current			4.1	4.9
40.0	47.6	23.2	23.3	10.4	24.5	Total Current			28.9	33.0
38.2	36.4	54.6	51.6	60.6	43.8	Fixed Assets (net)			48.7	46.2
5.6	3.7	4.0	1.4	5.8	5.5	Intangibles (net)			5.0	5.7
16.2	12.3	18.1	23.6	23.3	26.2	All Other Non-Current			17.5	15.1
100.0	100.0	100.0	100.0	100.0	100.0	Total			100.0	100.0
						LIABILITIES				
24.0	7.9	5.8	2.5	.2	1.5	Notes Payable-Short Term			10.7	5.4
2.5	1.4	2.0	2.9	2.2	.7	Cur. Mat.-L.T.D.			3.0	2.4
20.7	12.0	5.8	6.4	3.1	4.1	Trade Payables			7.2	7.0
.0	.2	.2	.0	.0	.0	Income Taxes Payable			.2	.1
19.9	11.2	9.8	12.1	4.5	36.8	All Other Current			13.5	11.6
67.1	32.7	23.5	24.0	10.1	43.2	Total Current			34.7	26.4
13.6	18.4	19.2	17.8	28.5	16.7	Long-Term Debt			21.2	22.1
.0	.0	.0	.1	.0	.0	Deferred Taxes			.0	.4
7.3	7.1	13.5	2.7	19.1	2.6	All Other Non-Current			4.0	12.4
11.9	41.8	43.8	55.4	42.3	37.4	Net Worth			40.0	38.7
100.0	100.0	100.0	100.0	100.0	100.0	Total Liabilities & Net Worth			100.0	100.0
						INCOME DATA				
100.0	100.0	100.0	100.0	100.0	100.0	Net Sales			100.0	100.0
						Gross Profit				
97.5	94.4	97.5	99.8	106.3	98.2	Operating Expenses			94.9	92.7
2.5	5.6	2.5	.2	-6.3	1.8	Operating Profit			5.1	7.3
2.5	1.2	3.0	-.1	.3	-.7	All Other Expenses (net)			1.3	.9
.0	4.3	-.5	.4	-6.6	2.5	Profit Before Taxes			3.8	6.5
						RATIOS				
2.8	2.4	2.5	2.2	2.1	5.0				2.1	3.4
1.2	1.4	1.0	1.0	1.1	1.7	Current			.9	1.3
.2	.9	.4	.7	.5	.6				.4	.6
2.4	2.4	2.0	1.5	1.7	1.7				1.4	2.6
.8	(33) 1.1	.7	.8	.9	.7	Quick			.6	1.0
.1	.4	.3	.4	.5	.2				.2	.3
0 UND	0 UND	1 263.6	3 144.8	0 UND	3 131.2				0 UND	0 UND
0 UND	1 553.4	8 48.7	12 29.5	3 111.9	14 26.1	Sales/Receivables			3 130.6	3 128.1
10 35.8	14 25.2	29 12.4	37 10.0	24 14.9	31 11.7				13 29.0	14 25.7
						Cost of Sales/Inventory				
						Cost of Sales/Payables				
16.2	7.9	9.1	5.0	4.9	3.0				10.0	5.3
208.6	24.4	951.3	NM	NM	8.9	Sales/Working Capital			-71.8	36.2
-13.0	-30.3	-9.6	-7.1	-11.7	-5.7				-9.2	-18.1
11.5	32.6	4.0	20.6						11.8	17.5
(15) 2.0	(20) 3.1	(39) 1.4	(32) 2.6			EBIT/Interest			(153) 2.4	(112) 3.5
-18.7	.8	-5.1	-1.2						-.1	.5
									31.2	
						Net Profit + Depr., Dep., Amort./Cur. Mat. L/T/D			(13) 4.1	
									1.3	
.2	.2	.6	.4	.9	.5				.4	.4
1.3	1.0	1.1	.7	1.0	.8	Fixed/Worth			1.2	1.2
-11.1	4.8	7.0	2.0	-14.0	NM				3.2	5.6
.4	.5	.3	.3	.3	.1				.3	.3
1.3	1.1	.9	.7	.7	.4	Debt/Worth			1.1	1.1
-13.9	4.2	7.2	1.9	-18.0	NM				4.2	7.0
62.9	56.5	20.6	11.0						48.3	47.6
(17) 5.6	(27) 4.4	(42) 1.8	(36) .8			% Profit Before Taxes/Tangible Net Worth			(170) 13.0	(124) 10.9
-26.8	-1.2	-9.5	-6.6						-2.8	-3.8
29.4	15.8	4.3	7.2	3.9	17.3				22.4	18.8
.8	3.1	-.1	.6	-1.8	3.2	% Profit Before Taxes/Total Assets			3.3	5.3
-30.3	-1.4	-7.7	-3.1	-3.3	-1.6				-2.2	-1.8
119.2	25.7	10.2	2.9	2.7	4.4				13.5	11.7
9.7	9.3	1.8	1.4	.7	1.3	Sales/Net Fixed Assets			3.6	4.0
5.6	2.1	.7	.8	.2	.2				1.3	1.3
6.0	4.5	2.1	1.2	1.0	.9				3.7	3.3
4.1	2.1	1.0	.6	.5	.4	Sales/Total Assets			1.5	1.5
2.9	1.1	.4	.4	.2	.2				.7	.4
.9	.6	2.8	3.5		1.2				1.5	1.5
(14) 2.4	(26) 1.8	(46) 3.9	(34) 6.1		5.8	% Depr., Dep., Amort./Sales			(179) 3.1	(128) 3.0
4.4	5.0	9.7	10.7		17.1				5.3	5.6
									2.8	3.7
						% Officers', Directors' Owners' Comp/Sales			(55) 4.6	(39) 5.3
									12.2	12.8
27984M	118242M	353722M	625266M	433214M	2306684M	Net Sales ($)			2867301M	1377246M
6461M	40668M	238569M	733600M	706611M	1524510M	Total Assets ($)			2707607M	1784877M

M = $ thousand   MM = $ million
See Pages 9 through 22 for Explanation of Ratios and Data

Comparative Historical Data   Current Data Sorted by Sales

4/1/08-3/31/09 ALL	4/1/09-3/31/10 ALL	4/1/10-3/31/11 ALL	Type of Statement	0-1MM	1-3MM	3-5MM	5-10MM	10-25MM	25MM & OVER
85	71	71	Unqualified	5	11	8	20	14	13
8	5	7	Reviewed	1			1	4	1
11	18	12	Compiled	4	4	2	2		
24	30	24	Tax Returns	11	5	3	4		1
60	42	49	Other	8	12	2	11	9	7
				81 (4/1-9/30/10)			82 (10/1/10-3/31/11)		
188	**166**	**163**	**NUMBER OF STATEMENTS**	**29**	**32**	**15**	**38**	**27**	**22**
%	%	%	**ASSETS**	%	%	%	%	%	%
17.1	16.0	16.7	Cash & Equivalents	13.2	21.0	17.2	16.9	14.1	17.5
7.0	3.9	6.1	Trade Receivables (net)	4.5	4.3	5.3	9.7	7.3	3.9
2.6	1.7	2.1	Inventory	.9	3.1	2.5	1.0	4.1	1.4
5.2	4.2	5.1	All Other Current	5.0	4.8	12.2	5.1	3.3	2.9
31.8	25.8	30.0	Total Current	23.5	33.2	37.1	32.7	28.8	25.7
45.5	51.0	47.5	Fixed Assets (net)	59.6	45.9	39.4	40.2	53.2	45.0
3.8	6.3	3.8	Intangibles (net)	5.1	4.3	1.6	1.9	1.4	8.8
18.8	16.9	18.7	All Other Non-Current	11.7	16.6	21.9	25.2	16.6	20.5
100.0	100.0	100.0	Total	100.0	100.0	100.0	100.0	100.0	100.0
			LIABILITIES						
9.3	5.9	7.4	Notes Payable-Short Term	14.8	7.3	9.1	6.5	1.8	5.3
2.8	2.4	2.1	Cur. Mat.-L.T.D.	1.4	2.4	1.2	1.5	1.9	4.3
7.3	6.4	9.1	Trade Payables	10.1	8.5	12.9	9.2	6.1	9.4
.2	.1	.1	Income Taxes Payable	.0	.0	.4	.0	.4	.0
12.1	9.9	13.4	All Other Current	5.4	17.3	9.7	11.6	10.7	27.0
31.8	24.7	32.1	Total Current	31.7	35.5	33.2	28.9	20.9	46.1
22.6	25.6	18.3	Long-Term Debt	21.9	19.5	15.9	10.1	21.9	23.5
.4	.0	.0	Deferred Taxes	.0	.0	.0	.0	.0	.1
9.9	7.9	8.4	All Other Non-Current	5.3	2.7	12.8	13.1	7.8	10.7
35.3	41.8	41.1	Net Worth	41.1	42.3	38.1	47.9	49.5	19.5
100.0	100.0	100.0	Total Liabilities & Net Worth	100.0	100.0	100.0	100.0	100.0	100.0
			INCOME DATA						
100.0	100.0	100.0	Net Sales	100.0	100.0	100.0	100.0	100.0	100.0
			Gross Profit						
96.6	99.3	98.0	Operating Expenses	90.4	98.3	104.5	99.7	103.8	93.0
3.4	.7	2.0	Operating Profit	9.6	1.7	-4.5	.3	-3.8	7.0
2.0	2.8	1.4	All Other Expenses (net)	7.1	1.3	1.9	-1.1	-.5	.5
1.4	-2.0	.6	Profit Before Taxes	2.5	.4	-6.4	1.4	-3.3	6.5
			RATIOS						
2.9	2.5	2.4	Current	3.1	2.5	2.4	2.6	2.5	1.6
1.2	1.0	1.1		.9	1.3	1.9	1.0	1.0	.8
.5	.6	.5		.2	.4	.6	.7	.6	.3
2.2	2.0	2.1	Quick	2.6	2.3	2.1	1.9	1.8	1.4
(187) .9	(165) .8	(162) .8		.8	1.1	1.0	(37) .8	.7	.7
.3	.3	.3		.2	.3	.2	.5	.2	.3
0 999.8	0 UND	0 UND	Sales/Receivables	0 UND	0 UND	0 UND	5 69.6	2 198.5	2 219.6
5 74.5	3 106.4	6 65.8		0 UND	1 288.3	6 58.2	15 24.6	7 55.7	5 74.8
24 15.3	20 18.2	23 15.7		14 26.5	14 25.3	26 14.0	46 8.0	19 19.3	20 18.6
			Cost of Sales/Inventory						
			Cost of Sales/Payables						
5.4	6.2	7.9	Sales/Working Capital	11.4	5.1	8.2	5.2	9.4	9.4
44.8	228.2	88.1		-100.2	23.8	10.2	403.9	71.0	-53.6
-13.6	-12.9	-10.9		-2.9	-18.9	-13.0	-14.8	-6.4	-12.5
9.8	4.7	9.4	EBIT/Interest	7.8	6.0	15.2	19.3	5.3	27.7
(138) 1.9	(116) 1.0	(122) 1.6		(20) 1.0	(23) 1.3	(10) 1.2	(26) 5.3	(22) .9	(21) 2.9
-1.1	-4.5	-1.9		-7.1	-1.4	-6.0	-.4	-7.3	.1
11.6	18.1		Net Profit + Depr., Dep., Amort./Cur. Mat. L/T/D						
(12) 2.4	(13) 4.5								
1.1	1.5								
.4	.5	.4	Fixed/Worth	.7	.1	.4	.4	.6	.7
1.0	1.1	1.0		1.2	.9	.8	.7	1.0	5.2
3.6	5.9	5.8		5.1	5.0	10.3	1.1	2.2	-2.6
.3	.2	.3	Debt/Worth	.2	.3	.3	.2	.4	.5
.8	.8	.9		1.0	.7	1.0	.4	.9	5.4
4.2	5.5	6.2		4.6	5.1	9.8	2.1	3.7	-11.8
31.6	10.0	20.7	% Profit Before Taxes/Tangible Net Worth	9.0	21.0	19.9	27.7	19.0	35.2
(158) 6.2	(132) -.2	(137) 1.4		(24) 1.4	(28) -.3	(12) 1.0	(33) 4.4	(26) -.6	(14) 7.9
-4.9	-10.2	-5.4		-5.1	-5.4	-10.3	-3.8	-14.4	-5.0
12.8	5.3	8.8	% Profit Before Taxes/Total Assets	7.7	5.9	3.2	11.0	6.3	16.7
1.7	.0	.7		.2	-.2	-2.5	1.5	-1.8	6.1
-4.1	-6.5	-4.4		-5.6	-4.4	-7.9	-4.3	-5.1	-1.9
10.4	7.7	11.9	Sales/Net Fixed Assets	8.2	22.7	24.6	13.0	4.3	7.0
3.4	2.8	2.7		1.8	6.7	8.4	2.0	1.6	4.0
1.2	.7	.9		.2	.8	1.2	1.0	.5	1.9
2.9	2.3	2.7	Sales/Total Assets	2.8	3.7	4.5	2.1	2.3	2.1
1.3	1.0	1.3		.8	1.3	2.2	.8	1.1	1.5
.5	.4	.5		.1	.5	.7	.5	.4	.9
1.9	2.2	1.8	% Depr., Dep., Amort./Sales	2.0	.8	1.8	2.1	3.1	1.4
(159) 3.5	(142) 4.1	(138) 4.1		(22) 5.9	(25) 3.2	(13) 4.5	(32) 3.9	(25) 4.3	(21) 2.9
6.2	8.1	8.7		16.0	7.8	7.4	8.0	9.8	7.1
2.6	2.9	3.7	% Officers', Directors' Owners' Comp/Sales						
(33) 6.6	(27) 4.4	(21) 7.9							
11.3	12.5	13.2							
2500801M	2717815M	3865112M	Net Sales ($)	16658M	57092M	58140M	272475M	416099M	3044648M
3800914M	4212677M	3250419M	Total Assets ($)	59720M	76629M	123051M	567792M	856311M	1566916M

M = $ thousand   MM = $ million
See Pages 9 through 22 for Explanation of Ratios and Data

Current Data Sorted by Assets | Comparative Historical Data

	0-500M	500M-2MM	2-10MM	10-50MM	50-100MM	100-250MM		4/1/06-3/31/07 ALL	4/1/07-3/31/08 ALL
Type of Statement									
Unqualified		2	6	10	2	1		34	32
Reviewed	1	3	1			1		2	1
Compiled	1	3	1					5	2
Tax Returns	4	4	4	4		1		3	5
Other								21	17
	0-500M	33 (4/1-9/30/10) 500M-2MM	2-10MM	16 (10/1/10-3/31/11) 10-50MM	50-100MM	100-250MM			
NUMBER OF STATEMENTS	6	12	12	14	2	3		65	57
	%	%	%	%	%	%		%	%
ASSETS									
Cash & Equivalents		23.8	19.4	26.5				22.5	18.5
Trade Receivables (net)		7.0	7.4	3.0				7.2	11.0
Inventory		8.9	.8	.0				1.4	2.3
All Other Current		1.9	8.1	4.5				5.9	3.5
Total Current		41.6	35.7	34.0				37.0	35.3
Fixed Assets (net)		41.3	33.0	22.9				24.7	25.8
Intangibles (net)		.9	1.0	.0				1.2	1.6
All Other Non-Current		16.1	30.3	43.2				37.0	37.3
Total		100.0	100.0	100.0				100.0	100.0
LIABILITIES									
Notes Payable-Short Term		14.2	5.1	3.6				7.6	10.0
Cur. Mat.-L.T.D.		1.2	.4	3.0				1.6	2.3
Trade Payables		6.1	11.2	2.4				14.9	8.7
Income Taxes Payable		.0	.0	.0				.8	.0
All Other Current		4.4	7.7	6.8				13.4	8.5
Total Current		25.9	24.4	15.8				38.2	29.4
Long-Term Debt		20.9	20.2	18.5				12.6	11.1
Deferred Taxes		.0	.0	.0				.0	.0
All Other Non-Current		7.4	1.4	10.3				10.7	11.7
Net Worth		45.8	54.0	55.4				38.5	47.7
Total Liabilities & Net Worth		100.0	100.0	100.0				100.0	100.0
INCOME DATA									
Net Sales		100.0	100.0	100.0				100.0	100.0
Gross Profit									
Operating Expenses		103.6	102.8	84.0				93.3	92.3
Operating Profit		-3.6	-2.8	16.0				6.7	7.7
All Other Expenses (net)		-1.1	-.4	2.3				.8	1.5
Profit Before Taxes		-2.5	-2.4	13.7				5.9	6.2
RATIOS									
Current		7.8	10.3	4.6				2.8	3.8
		1.6	1.5	2.3				1.2	1.1
		.7	.3	.8				.6	.5
Quick		5.4	10.0	3.3				2.0	3.5
		1.0	.4	1.9				.9	.8
		.5	.2	.3				.3	.2
Sales/Receivables	0 UND	0 UND	0 UND				1	454.9	2 238.0
	0 UND	8 43.9	10 37.8				9	40.6	11 33.3
	39 9.3	32 11.3	26 14.2				38	9.7	57 6.4
Cost of Sales/Inventory									
Cost of Sales/Payables									
Sales/Working Capital		5.7	1.8	3.2				4.5	4.4
		90.0	NM	6.1				27.1	45.5
		-19.4	-6.0	-14.0				-8.7	-8.0
EBIT/Interest								12.6	30.7
							(43)	4.1	(42) 2.8
								-.7	-1.7
Net Profit + Depr., Dep., Amort./Cur. Mat. L/T/D									
Fixed/Worth		.1	.1	.0				.1	.0
		.8	.4	.0				.3	.2
		2.6	1.3	.7				1.4	1.3
Debt/Worth		.5	.4	.1				.2	.2
		1.0	.7	.2				.6	.5
		3.9	2.0	1.1				2.7	1.4
% Profit Before Taxes/Tangible Net Worth		11.7	27.2	25.0				14.0	19.2
	(11)	3.4	3.3	(13) 4.7			(54)	2.5	(51) 5.9
		-25.1	-9.1	-1.1				-6.5	-6.3
% Profit Before Taxes/Total Assets		7.1	9.0	20.6				8.2	9.2
		1.2	2.0	3.1				1.9	3.0
		-11.4	-4.2	-.5				-4.0	-4.9
Sales/Net Fixed Assets		132.9	25.5	106.8				39.5	35.9
		8.4	5.1	35.3				16.0	11.7
		1.7	.9	1.9				2.1	2.3
Sales/Total Assets		2.2	1.7	1.1				2.0	1.6
		1.6	1.0	.6				1.0	.8
		.7	.4	.3				.4	.4
% Depr., Dep., Amort./Sales				.7				.8	.6
			(12) 2.0				(48)	1.3	(47) 1.3
				5.0				4.0	3.4
% Officers', Directors' Owners' Comp/Sales									
Net Sales ($)	3601M	19453M	61566M	235157M	80104M	165650M		1074932M	746836M
Total Assets ($)	1204M	12971M	61026M	283455M	155157M	598266M		1763094M	1505080M

M = $ thousand   MM = $ million
See Pages 9 through 22 for Explanation of Ratios and Data

Comparative Historical Data / Current Data Sorted by Sales

4/1/08-3/31/09 ALL	4/1/09-3/31/10 ALL	4/1/10-3/31/11 ALL	Type of Statement	0-1MM	1-3MM	3-5MM	5-10MM	10-25MM	25MM & OVER
36	22	21	Unqualified	1	4	2	4	8	2
1	3	1	Reviewed		1				
1	2	6	Compiled	3	1		1		1
3	3	4	Tax Returns	2	2				1
19	12	17	Other	3	6	2	1	3	2
				33 (4/1-9/30/10)			16 (10/1/10-3/31/11)		
60	42	49	**NUMBER OF STATEMENTS**	9	14	4	6	11	5
%	%	%	**ASSETS**	%	%	%	%	%	%
24.4	17.4	20.8	Cash & Equivalents		14.9			24.0	
8.3	8.3	4.8	Trade Receivables (net)		6.9			4.4	
.9	1.0	2.8	Inventory		8.5			.9	
5.1	4.4	4.6	All Other Current		2.0			4.6	
38.6	31.1	33.0	Total Current		32.4			33.8	
23.1	30.0	33.1	Fixed Assets (net)		53.0			15.2	
1.0	5.5	1.6	Intangibles (net)		3.9			.9	
37.2	33.5	32.3	All Other Non-Current		10.7			50.0	
100.0	100.0	100.0	Total		100.0			100.0	
			LIABILITIES						
8.3	8.9	10.0	Notes Payable-Short Term		14.9			4.5	
1.6	1.0	2.6	Cur. Mat.-L.T.D.		5.7			3.7	
5.5	6.2	6.1	Trade Payables		8.3			3.4	
.2	.0	.0	Income Taxes Payable		.0			.0	
9.4	6.8	5.8	All Other Current		4.6			10.5	
25.0	23.0	24.5	Total Current		33.6			22.1	
13.3	22.5	19.9	Long-Term Debt		19.5			13.9	
.3	.3	.1	Deferred Taxes		.0			.0	
15.8	11.3	5.9	All Other Non-Current		2.9			12.7	
45.6	42.9	49.6	Net Worth		44.1			51.2	
100.0	100.0	100.0	Total Liabilities & Net Worth		100.0			100.0	
			INCOME DATA						
100.0	100.0	100.0	Net Sales		100.0			100.0	
			Gross Profit						
96.5	97.8	96.7	Operating Expenses		98.4			94.0	
3.5	2.2	3.3	Operating Profit		1.6			6.0	
4.2	5.9	.8	All Other Expenses (net)		1.3			.3	
-.7	-3.7	2.5	Profit Before Taxes		.3			5.6	
			RATIOS						
5.2	4.3	3.8	Current		2.9			3.4	
1.5	1.8	2.0			.8			1.3	
.5	.3	.7			.4			.7	
4.6	4.0	2.9	Quick		1.2			3.3	
1.1	1.3	1.0			.4			1.3	
.2	.1	.3			.2			.3	
2 235.1	1 499.3	0 UND	Sales/Receivables	0 UND				9 40.7	
11 34.5	10 36.5	6 64.4		0 UND				20 18.4	
39 9.3	40 9.2	33 11.0		38 9.6				33 10.9	
			Cost of Sales/Inventory						
			Cost of Sales/Payables						
2.8	4.6	4.4	Sales/Working Capital		5.8			2.4	
11.7	24.1	13.3			-20.7			8.5	
-7.8	-4.9	-7.8			-6.9			-7.4	
8.3	3.3	8.3	EBIT/Interest		7.0				
(43) .2	(32) -2.9	(32) 1.4		(10) 1.5					
-6.4	-25.7	-4.8			-6.9				
			Net Profit + Depr., Dep., Amort./Cur. Mat. L/T/D						
.0	.1	.0	Fixed/Worth		.6			.0	
.2	.5	.4			1.1			.0	
1.2	1.3	1.3			2.9			.4	
.2	.3	.2	Debt/Worth		.5			.2	
.5	.8	.7			1.8			.3	
1.7	3.0	2.1			3.2			.9	
9.1	9.2	15.4	% Profit Before Taxes/Tangible Net Worth		22.5			9.9	
(53) -2.4	(36) -7.2	(45) 3.4		(13) 3.4			(10) 1.4		
-10.3	-42.4	-7.2			-22.2			-10.9	
5.7	3.8	8.8	% Profit Before Taxes/Total Assets		10.7			9.8	
-1.0	-4.3	2.2			-.3			2.2	
-5.8	-16.8	-4.7			-9.4			-4.8	
54.6	45.2	57.2	Sales/Net Fixed Assets		35.8			91.7	
19.4	9.1	7.2			3.3			23.0	
2.1	1.8	1.6			.6			3.3	
1.7	2.2	1.8	Sales/Total Assets		2.2			1.4	
.8	1.0	.9			1.6			.7	
.4	.4	.4			.5			.5	
.7	1.0	.8	% Depr., Dep., Amort./Sales						
(49) 1.0	(28) 1.9	(36) 2.2							
4.2	4.1	5.0							
			% Officers', Directors' Owners' Comp/Sales						
1463696M	572572M	565531M	Net Sales ($)	4488M	26104M	15926M	42883M	171704M	304426M
1793422M	958838M	1112079M	Total Assets ($)	7718M	39478M	31903M	55899M	301982M	675099M

M = $ thousand   MM = $ million
See Pages 9 through 22 for Explanation of Ratios and Data

Current Data Sorted by Assets   **Comparative Historical Data**

	0-500M	500M-2MM	2-10MM	10-50MM	50-100MM	100-250MM	Type of Statement	4/1/06-3/31/07 ALL	4/1/07-3/31/08 ALL
	1		3	8	10	24	Unqualified	63	51
			4	4			Reviewed	6	10
		2	2	1			Compiled	5	5
	11	7	4				Tax Returns	10	13
	6	11	13	8	6	16	Other	40	54
		50 (4/1-9/30/10)		91 (10/1/10-3/31/11)					
	18	20	26	21	16	40	**NUMBER OF STATEMENTS**	124	133
	%	%	%	%	%	%	**ASSETS**	%	%
	26.4	14.3	15.1	8.8	16.0	8.5	Cash & Equivalents	12.5	15.4
	2.6	6.1	6.8	3.4	18.8	7.2	Trade Receivables (net)	10.7	9.8
	1.3	3.0	1.6	.6	.2	.5	Inventory	1.1	1.3
	3.3	5.2	3.6	5.2	5.8	7.0	All Other Current	4.9	6.8
	33.6	28.5	27.0	18.0	40.9	23.3	Total Current	29.2	33.3
	36.0	34.6	35.1	38.3	10.3	26.4	Fixed Assets (net)	30.8	29.2
	15.2	16.3	23.6	31.2	27.1	23.9	Intangibles (net)	23.3	22.4
	15.1	20.6	14.3	12.6	21.8	26.4	All Other Non-Current	16.7	15.2
	100.0	100.0	100.0	100.0	100.0	100.0	Total	100.0	100.0
							LIABILITIES		
	6.0	22.9	5.6	31.3	18.0	5.4	Notes Payable-Short Term	11.9	14.3
	1.4	2.9	3.2	4.3	2.3	7.4	Cur. Mat.-L.T.D.	3.5	4.6
	13.5	10.9	3.4	3.6	8.7	5.7	Trade Payables	7.4	6.9
	.0	.0	.3	.0	.0	.1	Income Taxes Payable	.2	.1
	34.0	20.8	13.8	23.9	56.2	17.7	All Other Current	19.8	28.1
	55.0	57.5	26.3	63.0	85.1	36.3	Total Current	42.7	54.0
	21.4	35.9	18.8	35.9	77.0	50.8	Long-Term Debt	33.5	33.5
	.0	.3	.1	.0	.0	1.2	Deferred Taxes	.1	.2
	2.3	19.2	6.5	26.6	20.8	32.8	All Other Non-Current	21.4	19.5
	21.3	-12.9	48.2	-25.5	-82.9	-21.1	Net Worth	2.3	-7.2
	100.0	100.0	100.0	100.0	100.0	100.0	Total Liabilities & Net Worth	100.0	100.0
							INCOME DATA		
	100.0	100.0	100.0	100.0	100.0	100.0	Net Sales	100.0	100.0
							Gross Profit		
	91.5	97.2	94.6	100.1	106.5	98.2	Operating Expenses	94.9	93.1
	8.5	2.8	5.4	-.1	-6.5	1.8	Operating Profit	5.1	6.9
	1.1	2.9	4.6	7.2	4.6	5.4	All Other Expenses (net)	4.2	3.8
	7.3	-.1	.7	-7.3	-11.2	-3.5	Profit Before Taxes	.8	3.0
							RATIOS		
	14.5	2.4	2.1	.9	.9	1.3		1.7	1.6
	1.4	.6	1.0	.6	.5	.7	Current	.9	.8
	.5	.2	.5	.3	.2	.5		.4	.3
	12.3	1.9	1.9	.9	.7	.8		1.4	1.3
	1.3	.4	.8	.4	.4	.5	Quick	.8	.5
	.1	.1	.3	.1	.2	.2		.3	.2
	0 UND	0 UND	7 54.9	4 82.8	20 17.9	11 33.0		9 40.5	6 66.0
	0 UND	3 137.6	24 15.1	13 28.9	48 7.6	22 16.6	Sales/Receivables	27 13.6	20 18.2
	10 36.1	13 28.3	52 7.0	25 14.6	94 3.9	46 8.0		51 7.2	41 8.8
							Cost of Sales/Inventory		
							Cost of Sales/Payables		
	6.8	7.0	3.5	NM	-41.5	13.7		9.5	9.3
	53.2	-20.0	475.2	-9.2	-3.4	-15.9	Sales/Working Capital	-40.6	-17.8
	-6.2	-3.8	-3.9	-3.1	-1.9	-4.2		-3.8	-3.5
	16.8	3.0	9.3	1.7	1.3	1.6		4.9	3.9
	(11) 5.4	(16) .1	(16) .7	(18) -.2	(14) -.7	(38) .6	EBIT/Interest	(96) 1.0	(110) .7
	-2.0	-11.5	-6.4	-1.8	-4.2	-2.4		-1.4	-2.1
							Net Profit + Depr., Dep., Amort./Cur. Mat. L/T/D		
	.4	1.1	.2	.9	NM	3.1		.9	.9
	1.0	NM	1.0	6.2	-.2	-.5	Fixed/Worth	NM	-10.6
	5.2	-.3	-3.3	-.9	-.1	-.2		-.2	-.1
	.2	1.9	.5	1.5	-2.9	NM		1.9	1.9
	1.0	NM	1.1	-10.8	-1.8	-2.9	Debt/Worth	-11.4	-12.8
	NM	-3.1	-5.2	-2.1	-1.3	-1.6		-1.8	-1.7
	273.5	19.0	19.6	11.3		10.4	% Profit Before Taxes/Tangible	39.4	57.8
	(14) 30.2	(10) 3.4	(18) 3.6	(10) 2.2		(10) -3.8	Net Worth	(59) 7.6	(62) 14.3
	4.3	-95.7	-8.7	-12.9		-31.8		-2.9	-5.4
	29.8	5.6	8.4	2.3	.0	2.4	% Profit Before Taxes/Total	10.7	10.1
	10.1	-1.0	.7	-2.8	-12.5	-1.2	Assets	.1	-.4
	1.3	-33.4	-3.9	-4.9	-29.6	-10.0		-7.3	-13.7
	55.8	29.3	17.4	12.0	72.3	20.7		45.3	45.3
	9.8	9.0	5.8	4.9	17.2	5.9	Sales/Net Fixed Assets	8.5	11.2
	1.5	2.3	.5	.8	5.9	2.3		1.7	1.9
	3.4	3.1	1.1	1.7	1.8	1.2		1.5	1.8
	1.6	1.9	.7	.6	1.3	.9	Sales/Total Assets	.9	1.0
	.7	.7	.3	.2	1.0	.5		.5	.6
	1.1	1.3	1.3	3.6	.9	1.6		1.2	1.2
	(12) 1.8	(13) 6.2	(22) 3.1	(17) 6.8	(11) 1.9	(19) 2.3	% Depr., Dep., Amort./Sales	(88) 3.7	(100) 3.6
	8.0	9.5	8.0	14.1	2.6	8.5		7.8	8.3
								3.3	3.6
							% Officers', Directors' Owners' Comp/Sales	(19) 8.8	(23) 8.3
								16.3	17.7
	11307M	46389M	79559M	622781M	1661239M	5987226M	Net Sales ($)	8237650M	7215850M
	4670M	23042M	113161M	558826M	1159369M	7013863M	Total Assets ($)	8462856M	7445233M

© RMA 2011

M = $ thousand   MM = $ million
See Pages 9 through 22 for Explanation of Ratios and Data

Comparative Historical Data | Current Data Sorted by Sales

			Type of Statement	0-1MM	1-3MM	3-5MM	5-10MM	10-25MM	25MM & OVER
56	47	46	Unqualified	1	1		3	2	39
9	7	8	Reviewed	1	2		2	2	
2	4	5	Compiled			1			
9	19	22	Tax Returns	14	6	2			
54	61	60	Other	5	20	4	4	3	24
4/1/08-3/31/09 ALL	4/1/09-3/31/10 ALL	4/1/10-3/31/11 ALL		50 (4/1-9/30/10)			91 (10/1/10-3/31/11)		
130	138	141	NUMBER OF STATEMENTS	23	32	7	9	7	63
%	%	%	ASSETS	%	%	%	%	%	%
15.4	14.3	13.7	Cash & Equivalents	17.9	16.7				11.2
8.8	8.4	7.1	Trade Receivables (net)	2.6	3.6				10.0
1.0	1.2	1.2	Inventory	.4	2.3				.5
5.7	5.0	5.2	All Other Current	1.8	6.2				7.2
31.0	29.0	27.2	Total Current	22.6	28.7				28.9
31.0	32.1	30.3	Fixed Assets (net)	51.5	32.8				21.5
19.4	20.8	23.1	Intangibles (net)	9.7	23.2				24.8
18.6	18.1	19.3	All Other Non-Current	16.1	15.4				24.8
100.0	100.0	100.0	Total	100.0	100.0				100.0
			LIABILITIES						
11.2	6.4	13.3	Notes Payable-Short Term	13.9	6.7				18.2
3.1	4.1	4.2	Cur. Mat.-L.T.D.	1.2	3.4				5.5
7.2	5.8	7.0	Trade Payables	10.7	5.7				6.4
.0	.1	.1	Income Taxes Payable	.0	.0				.1
19.0	20.5	24.8	All Other Current	27.5	13.8				32.4
40.5	36.8	49.4	Total Current	53.3	29.6				62.6
36.5	40.4	39.8	Long-Term Debt	27.9	27.1				56.5
.2	.3	.4	Deferred Taxes	.0	.0				.8
18.2	23.4	19.8	All Other Non-Current	2.3	8.0				31.5
4.5	-.9	-9.4	Net Worth	16.5	35.2				-51.4
100.0	100.0	100.0	Total Liabilities & Net Worth	100.0	100.0				100.0
			INCOME DATA						
100.0	100.0	100.0	Net Sales	100.0	100.0				100.0
			Gross Profit						
95.8	97.0	97.8	Operating Expenses	91.9	97.3				101.9
4.2	3.0	2.2	Operating Profit	8.1	2.7				-1.9
5.4	4.8	4.5	All Other Expenses (net)	5.8	3.2				4.6
-1.2	-1.8	-2.3	Profit Before Taxes	2.3	-.5				-6.5
			RATIOS						
1.6	1.7	1.7	Current	13.0	1.8				1.0
.8	.8	.7		1.3	.6				.7
.5	.4	.4		.1	.3				.4
1.2	1.2	1.4	Quick	5.1	1.5				.7
.6	.6	.5		1.3	.4				.5
.3	.3	.2		.1	.1				.2
7 54.9	6 58.6	4 90.3	Sales/Receivables	0 UND	0 UND				12 31.3
23 16.0	18 20.5	16 22.7		0 UND	6 57.2				21 17.4
44 8.3	42 8.6	40 9.1		27 13.7	29 12.8				55 6.7
			Cost of Sales/Inventory						
			Cost of Sales/Payables						
13.0	10.6	11.2	Sales/Working Capital	6.5	6.9				88.3
-28.4	-16.4	-14.2		19.6	-20.0				-9.4
-5.3	-4.4	-3.6		-1.6	-5.2				-3.2
2.7	2.9	2.7	EBIT/Interest	4.9	6.5				1.6
(100) .7	(108) .4	(113) .3		(16) 2.5	(21) -.4				(58) -.2
-2.2	-1.9	-2.6		-1.5	-7.5				-2.9
			Net Profit + Depr., Dep., Amort./Cur. Mat. L/T/D						
.7	.8	.7	Fixed/Worth	.5	.4				2.5
9.4	19.0	18.6		1.2	2.0				-.4
-.3	-.3	-.2		-4.3	-1.1				-.1
1.2	1.6	1.4	Debt/Worth	.2	.8				-6.1
-188.7	-7.5	-6.1		1.4	2.8				-2.4
-2.3	-2.2	-2.0		-5.0	-5.1				-1.5
21.0	26.8	24.9	% Profit Before Taxes/Tangible Net Worth	45.4	23.0				17.9
(64) 3.9	(64) 2.5	(64) 6.4		(16) 8.6	(22) 3.1				(13) 5.9
-16.0	-27.6	-9.5		-3.1	-17.9				-34.2
5.1	6.4	5.9	% Profit Before Taxes/Total Assets	9.2	9.5				2.3
.2	-.5	-.6		2.6	-.3				-5.2
-8.8	-9.0	-9.9		-2.4	-6.3				-23.8
52.0	28.4	24.5	Sales/Net Fixed Assets	39.7	29.9				38.7
8.7	5.7	6.6		1.5	8.4				10.6
1.6	1.6	2.2		.4	3.8				4.0
1.5	1.7	1.6	Sales/Total Assets	1.3	2.1				1.5
.9	.9	1.0		.6	1.1				1.1
.5	.5	.5		.3	.4				.6
1.0	1.7	1.6	% Depr., Dep., Amort./Sales	1.8	1.2				1.4
(88) 3.2	(93) 3.7	(94) 3.3		(14) 14.8	(27) 2.8				(34) 2.2
8.7	9.3	8.0		24.5	7.6				3.7
5.1	5.0	4.8	% Officers', Directors' Owners' Comp/Sales						
(16) 9.6	(14) 6.6	(16) 7.1							
14.9	13.9	21.8							
8185833M	8089347M	8408501M	Net Sales ($)	8917M	65312M	27109M	64682M	113671M	8128810M
10223798M	9698000M	8872931M	Total Assets ($)	24053M	107206M	40563M	112689M	276939M	8311481M

M = $ thousand   MM = $ million
See Pages 9 through 22 for Explanation of Ratios and Data

Current Data Sorted by Assets   Comparative Historical Data

Type of Statement	0-500M	500M-2MM	2-10MM	10-50MM	50-100MM	100-250MM	4/1/06-3/31/07 ALL	4/1/07-3/31/08 ALL
Unqualified			2	6	4	1	23	13
Reviewed		1		1			2	7
Compiled	1		1				5	5
Tax Returns	3		1				7	9
Other	2	4	8	2	1	2	16	14
		7 (4/1-9/30/10)		32 (10/1/10-3/31/11)				
NUMBER OF STATEMENTS	6	5	11	9	5	3	53	48
ASSETS	%	%	%	%	%	%	%	%
Cash & Equivalents			17.0				12.8	16.0
Trade Receivables (net)			6.0				7.4	5.2
Inventory			.2				2.8	1.8
All Other Current			6.6				3.4	2.1
Total Current			29.9				26.4	25.1
Fixed Assets (net)			57.0				61.1	65.6
Intangibles (net)			.1				4.1	4.1
All Other Non-Current			13.0				8.4	5.2
Total			100.0				100.0	100.0
LIABILITIES								
Notes Payable-Short Term			2.7				5.3	12.9
Cur. Mat.-L.T.D.			2.2				6.0	8.4
Trade Payables			4.6				13.9	8.6
Income Taxes Payable			.0				.0	.1
All Other Current			4.3				19.4	16.9
Total Current			13.8				44.6	46.9
Long-Term Debt			28.5				27.5	39.8
Deferred Taxes			1.0				.2	.7
All Other Non-Current			10.9				11.3	10.1
Net Worth			45.8				16.3	2.5
Total Liabilities & Net Worth			100.0				100.0	100.0
INCOME DATA								
Net Sales			100.0				100.0	100.0
Gross Profit								
Operating Expenses			90.0				94.0	90.3
Operating Profit			10.0				6.0	9.7
All Other Expenses (net)			4.7				2.1	3.4
Profit Before Taxes			5.3				3.9	6.3
RATIOS								
Current			5.9				1.5	1.5
			1.2				.7	.7
			.2				.4	.2
Quick			5.0				1.3	1.3
			.6				(52) .5	.5
			.2				.2	.2
Sales/Receivables			(1) 688.7				(3) 125.6	(2) 182.3
			(20) 18.7				(10) 35.1	(7) 49.3
			(44) 8.2				(23) 15.6	(23) 15.8
Cost of Sales/Inventory								
Cost of Sales/Payables								
Sales/Working Capital			2.7				17.3	13.6
			9.1				-22.9	-13.8
			-5.3				-6.6	-5.4
EBIT/Interest							16.0	10.8
							(47) 3.5	(43) 3.6
							-.3	.9
Net Profit + Depr., Dep., Amort./Cur. Mat. L/T/D								
Fixed/Worth			.2				1.0	1.1
			1.7				2.1	3.1
			10.6				21.1	NM
Debt/Worth			.2				.9	.9
			.9				2.0	3.4
			9.8				27.0	-9.0
% Profit Before Taxes/Tangible Net Worth			49.6				39.9	47.4
		(10) 13.2					(41) 18.6	(35) 16.0
			-16.5				-4.0	6.7
% Profit Before Taxes/Total Assets			8.7				16.8	19.1
			1.5				2.7	5.5
			-13.1				-5.8	-.4
Sales/Net Fixed Assets			5.6				4.5	3.4
			1.1				2.5	1.7
			.5				1.3	1.0
Sales/Total Assets			1.2				2.5	2.1
			.9				1.6	1.2
			.3				.9	.6
% Depr., Dep., Amort./Sales			2.5				2.5	3.0
		(10) 6.7					(50) 4.3	(45) 5.4
			14.7				6.8	7.9
% Officers', Directors' Owners' Comp/Sales								
Net Sales ($)	4382M	8396M	51668M	359474M	594982M	356836M	2554045M	1393790M
Total Assets ($)	1872M	6373M	61134M	292054M	328563M	439117M	1963209M	1413981M

M = $ thousand   MM = $ million
See Pages 9 through 22 for Explanation of Ratios and Data

Comparative Historical Data / Current Data Sorted by Sales

			Type of Statement	0-1MM	1-3MM	3-5MM	5-10MM	10-25MM	25MM & OVER
8	11	13	Unqualified			1	1	2	9
7	2	2	Reviewed		1				1
3	2	1	Compiled	1					
3	15	4	Tax Returns	3			1		
23	31	19	Other	4	7		3		5
4/1/08-3/31/09 ALL	4/1/09-3/31/10 ALL	4/1/10-3/31/11 ALL			7 (4/1-9/30/10)		32 (10/1/10-3/31/11)		
44	61	39	NUMBER OF STATEMENTS	8	8	1	5	2	15
%	%	%	ASSETS	%	%	%	%	%	%
18.4	13.5	16.8	Cash & Equivalents						15.0
7.2	6.5	7.0	Trade Receivables (net)						6.1
3.2	2.8	3.8	Inventory						4.5
1.9	2.0	3.3	All Other Current						3.4
30.8	24.9	31.0	Total Current						29.0
55.1	61.6	54.9	Fixed Assets (net)						62.0
4.9	4.3	3.2	Intangibles (net)						4.6
9.3	9.3	10.9	All Other Non-Current						4.4
100.0	100.0	100.0	Total						100.0
			LIABILITIES						
5.9	6.9	5.3	Notes Payable-Short Term						6.6
10.2	9.4	2.5	Cur. Mat.-L.T.D.						2.1
6.3	5.1	5.7	Trade Payables						7.2
.0	.0	.1	Income Taxes Payable						.1
17.9	22.7	21.1	All Other Current						17.1
40.2	44.2	34.7	Total Current						33.1
27.9	39.5	24.6	Long-Term Debt						30.2
.0	1.0	.9	Deferred Taxes						1.2
5.2	6.5	9.4	All Other Non-Current						15.4
26.7	8.8	30.5	Net Worth						20.0
100.0	100.0	100.0	Total Liabilities & Net Worth						100.0
			INCOME DATA						
100.0	100.0	100.0	Net Sales						100.0
			Gross Profit						
95.5	94.1	91.5	Operating Expenses						95.6
4.5	5.9	8.5	Operating Profit						4.4
3.2	5.5	2.9	All Other Expenses (net)						3.1
1.4	.4	5.6	Profit Before Taxes						1.3
			RATIOS						
2.3	2.0	2.9	Current						1.7
.8	.6	1.0							1.0
.3	.2	.4							.4
1.6	1.9	2.0	Quick						1.2
.6	.4	.8							.8
.3	.1	.2							.2
5　70.3	1　423.6	4　101.3	Sales/Receivables						5　75.0
12　31.1	10　36.4	11　32.3							8　43.4
31　11.7	24　15.1	26　14.0							25　14.6
			Cost of Sales/Inventory						
			Cost of Sales/Payables						
12.2	8.5	5.2	Sales/Working Capital						11.3
-21.9	-19.5	405.4							-79.1
-5.5	-3.8	-6.5							-13.1
11.0	7.0	12.5	EBIT/Interest						8.4
(36) 2.4	(47) 1.0	(28) 2.3							(13) 2.6
-.2	-1.3	-2.9							-2.8
			Net Profit + Depr., Dep., Amort./Cur. Mat. L/T/D						
.8	.8	.4	Fixed/Worth						1.0
1.8	2.1	1.2							1.3
UND	-3.9	10.6							-16.7
.4	.6	.3	Debt/Worth						.5
2.3	1.4	.9							1.2
UND	-5.4	9.8							-22.8
29.1	36.6	33.1	% Profit Before Taxes/Tangible Net Worth						26.0
(33) 10.9	(43) 12.4	(31) 12.4							(11) 8.7
-2.7	-4.0	-9.7							-9.7
15.1	11.5	16.5	% Profit Before Taxes/Total Assets						14.6
4.4	1.1	3.6							1.4
-2.4	-5.9	-7.6							-7.6
4.5	5.0	5.6	Sales/Net Fixed Assets						3.3
2.2	2.1	1.9							1.9
1.1	.7	1.0							1.5
2.0	2.0	1.7	Sales/Total Assets						1.9
1.2	1.0	1.2							1.2
.8	.5	.7							.9
2.9	3.4	3.0	% Depr., Dep., Amort./Sales						3.0
(40) 4.9	(53) 7.0	(33) 5.0							(14) 3.8
7.2	13.8	11.4							5.8
	1.8		% Officers', Directors' Owners' Comp/Sales						
	(10) 7.0								
	9.4								
1377109M	1715339M	1375738M	Net Sales ($)	4388M	16318M	4595M	39145M	40957M	1270335M
1295253M	1862385M	1129113M	Total Assets ($)	4991M	30517M	1192M	32679M	60352M	999382M

© RMA 2011

M = $ thousand　　MM = $ million
See Pages 9 through 22 for Explanation of Ratios and Data

Current Data Sorted by Assets

Comparative Historical Data

						Type of Statement		
						Unqualified	41	38
3	2	6	18	4	6	Reviewed	11	8
	1	6	2			Compiled	7	10
1	3	2	2			Tax Returns	16	33
13	9	3	1	1		Other	19	34
8	13	8	10	4	3		4/1/06-3/31/07	4/1/07-3/31/08
	46 (4/1-9/30/10)		83 (10/1/10-3/31/11)				ALL	ALL
0-500M	500M-2MM	2-10MM	10-50MM	50-100MM	100-250MM	NUMBER OF STATEMENTS		
25	28	25	33	9	9		94	123
%	%	%	%	%	%		%	%
						ASSETS		
20.1	20.1	10.9	14.4			Cash & Equivalents	18.0	14.3
6.8	8.1	10.6	9.9			Trade Receivables (net)	7.7	8.5
.8	4.8	2.4	.2			Inventory	3.4	2.4
11.6	7.7	5.6	5.0			All Other Current	5.8	3.7
39.4	40.7	29.4	29.5			Total Current	35.0	29.0
37.9	37.9	51.1	54.1			Fixed Assets (net)	48.9	51.8
3.2	2.9	9.0	7.1			Intangibles (net)	4.0	3.6
19.6	18.5	10.5	9.3			All Other Non-Current	12.2	15.6
100.0	100.0	100.0	100.0			Total	100.0	100.0
						LIABILITIES		
16.3	9.6	7.4	4.7			Notes Payable-Short Term	9.9	6.9
6.2	1.7	3.6	3.9			Cur. Mat.-L.T.D.	5.9	3.5
10.2	5.9	7.1	3.6			Trade Payables	6.3	5.2
.0	.3	.0	2.0			Income Taxes Payable	.0	.8
16.6	18.9	9.7	12.7			All Other Current	11.1	10.7
49.3	36.4	27.7	26.9			Total Current	33.2	27.2
25.0	12.3	17.9	13.2			Long-Term Debt	27.1	23.5
.0	.0	.8	.1			Deferred Taxes	.0	.1
27.9	9.1	14.7	7.1			All Other Non-Current	16.9	13.0
-2.3	42.2	38.9	52.8			Net Worth	22.8	36.3
100.0	100.0	100.0	100.0			Total Liabilities & Net Worth	100.0	100.0
						INCOME DATA		
100.0	100.0	100.0	100.0			Net Sales	100.0	100.0
						Gross Profit		
85.4	94.0	93.4	91.3			Operating Expenses	85.3	84.3
14.6	6.0	6.6	8.7			Operating Profit	14.7	15.7
2.6	2.4	4.8	2.0			All Other Expenses (net)	5.6	5.3
12.0	3.6	1.8	6.7			Profit Before Taxes	9.2	10.4
						RATIOS		
1.9	3.1	2.0	2.8				3.5	3.6
.7	1.3	1.0	1.2			Current	1.1	1.1
.4	.6	.5	.7				.5	.4
1.5	3.1	1.3	2.6				2.7	2.6
.4	.9	.6	1.1			Quick	.8	.8
.2	.2	.2	.6				.4	.3
0 UND	0 UND	0 UND	6 62.3				0 UND	0 UND
0 UND	1 601.3	2 163.2	18 20.5			Sales/Receivables	8 47.7	6 59.1
1 283.3	14 26.1	30 12.4	51 7.1				27 13.7	34 10.6
						Cost of Sales/Inventory		
						Cost of Sales/Payables		
13.8	9.7	9.2	2.4				6.1	3.7
-213.0	39.4	999.8	16.4			Sales/Working Capital	269.1	79.3
-19.9	-35.1	-12.9	-14.5				-8.3	-10.0
38.7	27.3	15.6	15.7				11.1	18.6
(16) 6.8	(17) 4.0	(16) 1.9	(24) 4.1			EBIT/Interest	(58) 3.8	(85) 4.1
1.2	1.0	-2.6	-2.0				.8	1.2
						Net Profit + Depr., Dep., Amort./Cur. Mat. L/T/D		
.2	.1	.8	.7				.4	.5
1.4	.9	1.6	1.4			Fixed/Worth	1.4	1.1
-6.9	NM	UND	2.3				NM	4.4
1.4	.3	.6	.3				.3	.3
7.5	1.0	1.7	.9			Debt/Worth	2.0	1.1
-5.2	NM	UND	1.8				-221.4	5.3
186.4	30.6	37.5	66.4				51.4	32.5
(17) 72.6	(21) 1.7	(19) 11.4	(30) 3.2			% Profit Before Taxes/Tangible Net Worth	(69) 13.6	(100) 12.8
8.2	-4.2	-4.5	-2.8				1.1	2.1
55.8	21.8	12.1	8.6				19.3	15.3
11.5	5.5	2.9	2.4			% Profit Before Taxes/Total Assets	4.7	4.9
-3.4	-.6	-3.9	-2.0				-1.3	-.7
152.7	197.3	30.9	3.2				32.9	22.0
23.2	12.6	2.8	1.2			Sales/Net Fixed Assets	2.1	1.8
1.9	.8	.7	.4				.6	.3
11.4	5.5	2.9	1.1				3.0	2.0
3.9	2.1	1.2	.5			Sales/Total Assets	1.1	.7
1.0	.6	.7	.3				.3	.3
.6	.5	1.3	3.6				1.4	1.9
(15) 2.1	(19) 2.6	(20) 5.4	(28) 6.7			% Depr., Dep., Amort./Sales	(73) 6.4	(101) 6.1
8.8	6.3	9.5	13.7				12.3	12.3
	2.1						3.4	3.7
	(10) 3.3					% Officers', Directors' Owners' Comp/Sales	(18) 5.5	(19) 6.4
	5.1						17.9	13.3
40255M	150205M	189105M	664720M	621304M	964051M	Net Sales ($)	1150321M	2025691M
7249M	32745M	103398M	800733M	653094M	1460391M	Total Assets ($)	1721877M	2386156M

M = $ thousand   MM = $ million
See Pages 9 through 22 for Explanation of Ratios and Data

Comparative Historical Data / Current Data Sorted by Sales

			Type of Statement	0-1MM	1-3MM	3-5MM	5-10MM	10-25MM	25MM & OVER
58	61	39	Unqualified	1	5	5	10	9	9
10	9	9	Reviewed		2	4		2	1
21	15	8	Compiled	4			2	2	
21	34	27	Tax Returns	10	7	4	3	1	2
32	43	46	Other	8	8	5	7	4	14
4/1/08-3/31/09 ALL	4/1/09-3/31/10 ALL	4/1/10-3/31/11 ALL		46 (4/1-9/30/10)			83 (10/1/10-3/31/11)		
142	162	129	NUMBER OF STATEMENTS	23	22	18	22	18	26
%	%	%	**ASSETS**	%	%	%	%	%	%
16.9	16.1	15.4	Cash & Equivalents	9.0	16.4	15.0	17.7	17.1	17.5
8.3	7.8	8.3	Trade Receivables (net)	2.8	6.2	9.1	7.6	17.4	8.4
1.7	1.1	1.8	Inventory	2.3	1.4	.7	4.8	.7	.8
5.0	4.2	7.3	All Other Current	4.0	13.6	3.4	7.0	6.5	8.4
31.8	29.2	32.8	Total Current	18.2	37.5	28.2	37.1	41.7	35.0
49.3	47.8	45.1	Fixed Assets (net)	62.2	48.8	43.1	45.4	36.4	33.9
6.2	8.9	7.6	Intangibles (net)	1.1	2.9	8.6	4.1	9.1	18.4
12.6	14.2	14.6	All Other Non-Current	18.6	10.8	20.1	13.5	12.8	12.7
100.0	100.0	100.0	Total	100.0	100.0	100.0	100.0	100.0	100.0
			LIABILITIES						
3.4	4.7	7.9	Notes Payable-Short Term	9.2	11.5	10.7	6.6	5.5	4.6
4.4	5.5	3.5	Cur. Mat.-L.T.D.	4.6	5.1	1.1	1.6	7.6	1.6
6.1	6.6	5.9	Trade Payables	1.4	10.0	6.3	6.0	7.6	4.9
.0	.3	.6	Income Taxes Payable	.0	.0	.0	.4	.0	2.6
12.9	14.1	14.0	All Other Current	8.4	8.9	19.1	16.0	16.9	16.0
26.9	31.2	31.9	Total Current	23.6	35.6	37.1	30.6	37.7	29.7
29.2	29.7	19.8	Long-Term Debt	28.4	23.3	12.1	14.6	5.0	28.9
.3	.3	.3	Deferred Taxes	.0	.0	1.2	.0	.0	.6
7.6	10.2	13.3	All Other Non-Current	5.6	30.6	16.6	7.8	7.0	12.0
36.1	28.6	34.7	Net Worth	42.4	10.4	33.0	47.0	50.3	28.8
100.0	100.0	100.0	Total Liabilities & Net Worth	100.0	100.0	100.0	100.0	100.0	100.0
			INCOME DATA						
100.0	100.0	100.0	Net Sales	100.0	100.0	100.0	100.0	100.0	100.0
			Gross Profit						
84.3	90.2	90.6	Operating Expenses	80.1	96.4	88.3	95.4	98.9	87.0
15.7	9.8	9.4	Operating Profit	19.9	3.6	11.7	4.6	1.1	13.0
6.1	5.7	3.6	All Other Expenses (net)	7.8	2.7	2.6	1.6	-1.4	6.6
9.7	4.2	5.7	Profit Before Taxes	12.1	.9	9.0	3.0	2.5	6.4
			RATIOS						
4.0	3.1	2.5		2.9	3.6	1.8	3.0	2.4	2.1
1.3	1.1	1.0	Current	1.2	1.0	.5	1.0	1.2	1.1
.5	.4	.5		.3	.5	.2	.6	.8	.6
2.9	2.7	1.8		1.9	2.2	1.6	2.2	1.9	1.8
1.1	.9	.8	Quick	.7	.9	.5	.7	1.0	.8
.4	.3	.3		.0	.3	.2	.3	.7	.5
0 UND	0 UND	0 UND		0 UND	0 UND	0 UND	0 999.8	11 32.5	4 95.7
7 49.2	9 40.8	5 73.3	Sales/Receivables	0 UND	1 284.4	2 157.2	2 158.4	21 17.0	6 57.9
26 14.2	23 15.6	21 17.0		6 60.0	7 54.3	22 16.9	42 8.7	42 8.6	42 8.7
			Cost of Sales/Inventory						
			Cost of Sales/Payables						
3.6	5.6	6.9		3.5	6.7	13.1	6.2	5.1	8.1
25.3	51.8	200.5	Sales/Working Capital	30.0	354.5	-35.4	NM	27.5	495.0
-12.5	-9.7	-17.0		-10.7	-70.2	-4.4	-11.6	-34.2	-7.9
6.7	12.7	15.9		5.1	14.7	37.2	19.3	21.1	12.4
(95) 3.1	(110) 2.2	(89) 3.6	EBIT/Interest	(12) 3.9	(15) 1.4	(11) .9	(18) 4.7	(12) 3.8	(21) 2.8
.6	-1.4	-.6		1.2	-1.3	-7.3	-.6	-5.1	1.7
			Net Profit + Depr., Dep., Amort./Cur. Mat. L/T/D						
.5	.7	.5		.6	.5	.2	.2	.6	.6
1.2	1.6	1.4	Fixed/Worth	1.6	1.2	1.2	1.0	.8	2.8
10.2	-17.0	10.6		3.3	-1.0	NM	2.1	9.2	-.2
.3	.4	.3		.2	.2	.8	.5	.3	.5
1.2	2.1	1.6	Debt/Worth	1.6	2.3	1.8	1.0	1.5	2.6
28.4	-16.9	17.3		3.9	-2.6	-6.1	2.2	17.3	-3.1
42.8	29.5	60.0		45.2	12.4	96.6	58.9	86.4	29.8
(114) 9.6	(117) 6.3	(100) 8.4	% Profit Before Taxes/Tangible Net Worth	(20) 7.5	(15) -4.1	(13) 11.9	(19) 8.9	(16) 41.8	(17) 15.0
-.1	-5.6	-2.3		-.5	-6.1	-7.1	-4.5	-.9	5.3
13.8	9.8	19.4		7.6	33.6	30.6	24.1	17.1	13.7
2.7	2.1	3.6	% Profit Before Taxes/Total Assets	3.1	.0	1.6	5.4	3.9	3.9
-1.3	-4.2	-1.7		-.3	-6.1	-2.7	-1.7	-1.4	.9
17.9	22.1	38.9		3.2	79.8	74.6	90.2	48.9	38.4
1.7	2.6	2.9	Sales/Net Fixed Assets	.7	11.0	6.2	4.9	5.8	3.4
.5	.6	.6		.2	.7	1.0	.4	.8	.9
1.8	2.6	3.4		1.0	7.7	10.1	4.6	4.1	2.3
.7	.8	1.0	Sales/Total Assets	.4	3.2	1.1	2.6	1.3	.8
.3	.3	.4		.2	.6	.6	.3	.5	.4
2.2	1.9	1.3		6.0	.7	1.0	.5	1.3	1.9
(115) 5.0	(119) 5.3	(99) 5.8	% Depr., Dep., Amort./Sales	(15) 13.1	(17) 3.7	(13) 3.7	(17) 2.7	(15) 5.8	(22) 5.8
10.9	11.6	10.6		20.7	7.5	9.0	14.6	7.5	9.8
3.6	3.9	2.6							
(22) 5.6	(24) 6.9	(25) 5.5	% Officers', Directors' Owners' Comp/Sales						
10.4	11.2	11.3							
3201839M	4469713M	2629640M	Net Sales ($)	9843M	38703M	69980M	164317M	318137M	2028660M
4208974M	5393117M	3057610M	Total Assets ($)	49371M	41137M	95205M	365454M	501688M	2004755M

M = $ thousand   MM = $ million
See Pages 9 through 22 for Explanation of Ratios and Data

Current Data Sorted by Assets | | | | | | **Comparative Historical Data**

						Type of Statement			
1	7	26	53	15	21	Unqualified		139	115
		2	1			Reviewed		3	5
	2					Compiled		3	7
1	1	2			1	Tax Returns		7	3
4		15	18	8	10	Other		41	45
	119 (4/1-9/30/10)		69 (10/1/10-3/31/11)					4/1/06- 3/31/07	4/1/07- 3/31/08
0-500M	500M-2MM	2-10MM	10-50MM	50-100MM	100-250MM			ALL	ALL
6	10	45	72	24	31	NUMBER OF STATEMENTS		193	175
%	%	%	%	%	%	ASSETS		%	%
	10.9	16.6	11.6	7.6	7.3	Cash & Equivalents		12.5	13.8
	3.7	6.9	2.5	2.1	2.0	Trade Receivables (net)		4.3	5.4
	3.3	5.9	1.0	2.1	1.7	Inventory		2.5	2.9
	3.6	1.0	4.0	5.4	2.6	All Other Current		3.4	3.8
	21.5	30.3	19.1	17.1	13.6	Total Current		22.8	25.8
	56.3	52.6	58.4	52.1	45.6	Fixed Assets (net)		50.4	48.2
	.6	.6	1.5	.1	.2	Intangibles (net)		.5	.5
	21.6	16.5	21.1	30.6	40.6	All Other Non-Current		26.4	25.5
	100.0	100.0	100.0	100.0	100.0	Total		100.0	100.0
						LIABILITIES			
	2.6	3.2	2.0	1.3	.5	Notes Payable-Short Term		3.6	3.6
	2.8	.6	1.2	.4	.7	Cur. Mat.-L.T.D.		.8	1.0
	8.6	3.3	1.8	1.5	1.9	Trade Payables		3.9	3.6
	.0	.2	.0	.0	.0	Income Taxes Payable		.1	.0
	9.1	3.3	2.3	3.2	1.6	All Other Current		2.9	4.8
	23.1	10.6	7.3	6.4	4.7	Total Current		11.3	13.0
	26.5	4.3	13.1	11.5	16.1	Long-Term Debt		11.7	16.3
	.0	.0	.0	.0	.0	Deferred Taxes		.0	.0
	18.3	2.4	2.7	3.3	2.2	All Other Non-Current		2.0	3.5
	32.0	82.7	76.9	78.8	77.0	Net Worth		75.0	67.3
	100.0	100.0	100.0	100.0	100.0	Total Liabilities & Net Worth		100.0	100.0
						INCOME DATA			
	100.0	100.0	100.0	100.0	100.0	Net Sales		100.0	100.0
						Gross Profit			
	88.8	93.9	92.4	93.3	87.6	Operating Expenses		88.6	83.9
	11.2	6.1	7.6	6.7	12.4	Operating Profit		11.4	16.1
	1.7	-.6	3.5	.1	4.5	All Other Expenses (net)		.9	2.6
	9.6	6.7	4.1	6.6	7.9	Profit Before Taxes		10.5	13.4
						RATIOS			
	3.0	9.5	10.7	6.2	5.1			6.5	7.7
	.8	3.0	3.0	2.9	2.9	Current		2.5	2.9
	.2	1.4	1.1	1.4	1.7			1.3	1.1
	2.3	9.1	6.4	2.9	3.7			5.3	5.4
	.5	2.1	1.7	2.1	2.0	Quick		1.7	1.6
	.2	1.0	.6	.4	.7			.7	.7
0 UND	0 UND	2 170.0	4 90.7	5 76.7		2 216.2	2 146.0
0 UND	5 70.2	9 38.8	14 26.9	7 49.2	Sales/Receivables		12 31.7	18 20.0
6 63.6	62 5.9	34 10.7	60 6.1	50 7.3			48 7.6	54 6.8
						Cost of Sales/Inventory			
						Cost of Sales/Payables			
	13.8	1.4	1.6	1.8	1.9			1.6	1.6
	-41.8	5.3	4.0	3.6	2.8	Sales/Working Capital		4.4	4.7
	-5.4	15.9	121.1	23.3	7.5			18.6	35.7
		35.8	10.5	14.1	24.4			9.9	14.5
	(28) 4.7	(44) 1.3	(18) 4.8	(23) 7.1	EBIT/Interest		(129) 1.8	(115) 3.6
	-6.7	-3.5	-4.3	-1.4			-.6	-.2
						Net Profit + Depr., Dep., Amort./Cur. Mat. L/T/D			
	.3	.3	.5	.5	.3			.3	.3
	1.2	.6	.8	.7	.6	Fixed/Worth		.7	.7
	3.3	1.0	1.1	1.0	1.0			.9	1.0
	.3	.0	.1	.1	.1			.1	.1
	1.2	.1	.2	.2	.3	Debt/Worth		.2	.2
	7.8	.3	.6	.5	.4			.5	.8
		11.6	7.7	6.6	5.3	% Profit Before Taxes/Tangible Net Worth		10.2	16.2
	2.8	(71) .6	1.9	1.3		(187) 2.5	(165) 3.3
	-.8	-3.5	-2.1	-2.8			-1.1	-1.9
	19.6	5.1	4.9	3.9	4.6	% Profit Before Taxes/Total Assets		6.8	11.1
	-6.6	2.2	.4	1.5	1.1			1.5	2.4
	-6.6	-.6	-2.3	-2.0	-2.1			-1.1	-1.2
	46.8	5.9	1.1	.7	1.0			1.3	2.3
	1.7	.9	.5	.4	.4	Sales/Net Fixed Assets		.7	.7
	.3	.3	.3	.2	.2			.4	.4
	2.9	.9	.5	.3	.3			.6	.6
	1.0	.4	.3	.2	.2	Sales/Total Assets		.3	.3
	.3	.2	.2	.1	.1			.2	.2
		2.1	7.2	7.6	4.4	% Depr., Dep., Amort./Sales		4.3	2.7
	(38) 4.0	(66) 13.5	(22) 13.0	(29) 10.1		(170) 8.7	(147) 7.1
	15.4	20.3	21.6	14.9			14.9	13.2
						% Officers', Directors' Owners' Comp/Sales		3.3	4.4
								(21) 7.4	(22) 6.6
								22.2	12.7
3553M	25282M	144669M	604026M	471397M	1165866M	Net Sales ($)		2192689M	2323268M
1679M	12723M	237913M	1749859M	1753537M	4591598M	Total Assets ($)		7469434M	7220773M

M = $ thousand   MM = $ million
See Pages 9 through 22 for Explanation of Ratios and Data

Comparative Historical Data			Type of Statement	Current Data Sorted by Sales					
126	120	123	Unqualified	10	18	22	27	34	12
5	6	3	Reviewed		1	1		1	
3	6	2	Compiled	1		1			
9	9	5	Tax Returns	2		1			
52	43	55	Other	10	11	7	4	14	9
4/1/08-3/31/09 ALL	4/1/09-3/31/10 ALL	4/1/10-3/31/11 ALL		119 (4/1-9/30/10)			69 (10/1/10-3/31/11)		
				0-1MM	1-3MM	3-5MM	5-10MM	10-25MM	25MM & OVER
195	184	188	NUMBER OF STATEMENTS	23	30	32	32	50	21
%	%	%	**ASSETS**	%	%	%	%	%	%
13.3	12.0	11.5	Cash & Equivalents	9.8	13.4	12.4	7.9	14.1	8.9
3.7	4.3	4.0	Trade Receivables (net)	4.2	4.8	5.5	3.0	3.2	3.4
2.8	3.9	3.1	Inventory	5.8	1.2	4.8	.8	3.5	3.3
3.4	3.1	3.3	All Other Current	.1	4.7	3.9	2.8	3.8	3.1
23.2	23.3	21.9	Total Current	19.8	24.1	26.6	14.5	24.6	18.8
52.9	52.5	53.4	Fixed Assets (net)	68.7	52.4	55.5	52.9	48.5	47.2
.6	.3	.8	Intangibles (net)	.0	2.2	.8	.9	.4	.1
23.3	23.9	23.9	All Other Non-Current	11.6	21.3	17.1	31.7	26.4	33.9
100.0	100.0	100.0	Total	100.0	100.0	100.0	100.0	100.0	100.0
			LIABILITIES						
4.2	5.5	4.2	Notes Payable-Short Term	20.6	2.4	3.1	1.2	1.4	1.5
.8	1.0	1.1	Cur. Mat.-L.T.D.	1.7	2.0	1.3	.5	.5	.8
3.2	3.6	3.2	Trade Payables	5.9	1.9	3.9	1.8	3.2	3.5
.0	.0	.1	Income Taxes Payable	.4	.0	.2	.0	.0	.0
4.2	4.1	4.2	All Other Current	10.7	2.2	4.8	3.1	1.6	6.4
12.5	14.2	12.7	Total Current	39.3	8.5	13.3	6.6	6.8	12.2
12.9	14.3	12.0	Long-Term Debt	13.2	9.8	13.6	11.5	11.4	13.5
.1	.0	.0	Deferred Taxes	.0	.0	.0	.0	.0	.0
3.2	3.9	3.4	All Other Non-Current	.5	.4	7.1	1.1	4.7	5.2
71.3	67.6	71.9	Net Worth	47.0	81.3	66.0	80.8	77.1	69.1
100.0	100.0	100.0	Total Liabilities & Net Worth	100.0	100.0	100.0	100.0	100.0	100.0
			INCOME DATA						
100.0	100.0	100.0	Net Sales	100.0	100.0	100.0	100.0	100.0	100.0
			Gross Profit						
93.6	97.2	92.6	Operating Expenses	99.9	98.0	97.6	88.7	88.9	84.1
6.4	2.8	7.4	Operating Profit	.1	2.0	2.4	11.3	11.1	15.9
5.0	5.4	2.0	All Other Expenses (net)	-.5	.5	4.6	5.1	-.9	5.1
1.4	-2.6	5.4	Profit Before Taxes	.5	1.5	-2.2	6.2	12.0	10.8
			RATIOS						
6.0	7.2	6.8		8.4	11.5	12.0	5.9	4.9	5.5
2.3	2.2	2.7	Current	2.5	3.0	2.7	2.6	3.0	1.9
1.0	1.0	1.1		.2	1.0	1.1	1.1	1.8	.7
4.4	5.1	5.1		8.3	9.1	5.6	5.5	3.6	4.1
1.4	1.5	1.7	Quick	2.5	2.0	1.2	1.7	2.1	1.2
.5	.5	.6		.2	.6	1.2	.8	.9	.2
1 274.5	1 725.5	1 421.8		0 UND	2 160.5	2 217.4	3 126.7	4 100.9	1 254.8
11 34.8	11 33.4	8 48.5	Sales/Receivables	0 UND	8 46.8	6 64.2	19 19.5	9 40.6	7 49.4
41 9.0	50 7.3	41 8.8		11 32.3	80 4.5	26 14.2	60 6.1	41 8.9	39 9.4
			Cost of Sales/Inventory						
			Cost of Sales/Payables						
1.8	1.8	1.8		2.2	1.0	1.2	2.0	1.9	2.8
6.5	4.3	4.6	Sales/Working Capital	7.0	2.6	3.8	5.7	3.6	7.5
-126.0	NM	83.2		-5.2	NM	92.4	31.8	10.7	-16.9
8.9	6.7	17.7		6.4	23.6	11.9	4.3	88.9	14.2
(132) .8	(119) -.6	(123) 3.3	EBIT/Interest	(16) .3	(15) 2.1	(19) 1.5	(20) .3	(35) 7.4	(18) 6.5
-7.2	-7.5	-2.5		-11.8	-1.7	-4.0	-5.5	.1	-1.3
			Net Profit + Depr., Dep., Amort./Cur. Mat. L/T/D						
.4	.4	.4		.9	.3	.5	.4	.3	.3
.7	.8	.7	Fixed/Worth	1.1	.8	.7	.7	.7	.8
1.1	1.1	1.1		1.4	1.0	1.1	.9	1.0	1.2
.1	.1	.1		.1	.0	.1	.0	.1	.1
.2	.3	.2	Debt/Worth	.3	.2	.2	.1	.2	.4
.7	.8	.6		1.3	.5	1.1	.5	.5	.8
9.6	7.8	7.8		3.3	4.5	13.8	4.8	12.6	7.3
(189) -.5	(178) -1.5	(184) 1.3	% Profit Before Taxes/Tangible Net Worth	(21) .0	-.5	(31) .9	(31) .6	4.3	3.5
-6.5	-5.3	-2.4		-5.7	-4.1	-3.6	-2.4	-1.8	-.7
6.5	5.2	5.1		2.7	3.8	8.2	4.2	8.8	4.5
-.5	-.9	.9	% Profit Before Taxes/Total Assets	-.2	-.4	.4	.1	2.9	2.1
-4.8	-4.5	-2.1		-6.4	-2.5	-2.8	-2.3	-1.5	-.3
1.6	1.4	1.4		.9	1.6	3.9	1.0	1.2	2.4
.6	.6	.5	Sales/Net Fixed Assets	.3	.4	.5	.5	.7	1.1
.3	.3	.3		.2	.2	.2	.3	.3	.5
.6	.5	.5		.3	.4	1.0	.5	.5	1.0
.3	.3	.3	Sales/Total Assets	.2	.2	.3	.2	.2	.4
.2	.2	.1		.2	.2	.2	.1	.1	.3
4.0	4.4	4.0		3.3	3.4	3.7	5.1	5.0	3.0
(163) 8.5	(160) 9.5	(167) 9.6	% Depr., Dep., Amort./Sales	(17) 20.0	(26) 13.7	(28) 11.9	(30) 11.2	(46) 8.9	(20) 8.7
14.3	17.2	19.6		29.3	23.0	23.8	19.1	14.6	10.8
1.6	2.9	1.7							
(20) 6.7	(23) 6.0	(17) 4.3	% Officers', Directors' Owners' Comp/Sales						
14.6	14.9	10.0							
2391781M	2145985M	2414793M	Net Sales ($)	13153M	54254M	127170M	236107M	780783M	1203326M
7730159M	7482266M	8347309M	Total Assets ($)	78828M	338636M	634158M	1045266M	3672662M	2577759M

M = $ thousand   MM = $ million
See Pages 9 through 22 for Explanation of Ratios and Data

Current Data Sorted by Assets   Comparative Historical Data

0-500M	500M-2MM	2-10MM	10-50MM	50-100MM	100-250MM	Type of Statement	4/1/06-3/31/07 ALL	4/1/07-3/31/08 ALL
1		1	3	1	1	Unqualified	11	11
		8	7	1		Reviewed	10	19
1	2	6	1			Compiled	10	13
8	6	3	6			Tax Returns	17	21
10	6	23	13	4	2	Other	25	20
	7 (4/1-9/30/10)		107 (10/1/10-3/31/11)					
20	14	41	30	6	3	NUMBER OF STATEMENTS	73	84
%	%	%	%	%	%	ASSETS	%	%
11.5	12.4	11.7	8.8			Cash & Equivalents	11.8	12.6
2.0	2.1	1.4	1.7			Trade Receivables (net)	.8	1.3
1.5	1.4	1.8	1.5			Inventory	1.6	4.2
3.4	2.4	5.8	3.8			All Other Current	2.0	1.5
18.3	18.3	20.6	15.8			Total Current	16.2	19.6
73.0	64.4	64.7	74.8			Fixed Assets (net)	72.8	70.3
5.5	9.5	1.6	2.0			Intangibles (net)	2.8	1.8
3.1	7.9	13.0	7.4			All Other Non-Current	8.2	8.2
100.0	100.0	100.0	100.0			Total	100.0	100.0
						LIABILITIES		
13.9	9.6	2.5	4.1			Notes Payable-Short Term	2.8	6.5
9.6	5.3	3.5	3.4			Cur. Mat.-L.T.D.	3.8	4.6
1.1	12.1	3.4	2.0			Trade Payables	2.9	4.6
.0	.0	.0	.0			Income Taxes Payable	.1	.1
15.9	7.9	11.0	9.5			All Other Current	11.9	12.1
40.5	34.9	20.4	19.1			Total Current	21.6	27.9
41.7	44.9	43.3	40.8			Long-Term Debt	34.5	49.8
.0	.0	.9	.4			Deferred Taxes	.7	.7
6.8	55.7	3.2	20.3			All Other Non-Current	8.8	5.8
11.0	-35.4	32.2	19.4			Net Worth	34.4	15.8
100.0	100.0	100.0	100.0			Total Liabilities & Net Worth	100.0	100.0
						INCOME DATA		
100.0	100.0	100.0	100.0			Net Sales	100.0	100.0
						Gross Profit		
85.2	93.1	78.3	89.8			Operating Expenses	90.2	88.7
14.8	6.9	21.7	10.2			Operating Profit	9.8	11.3
3.4	2.0	8.6	7.0			All Other Expenses (net)	4.4	4.5
11.4	4.9	13.1	3.3			Profit Before Taxes	5.4	6.7
						RATIOS		
3.5	7.4	2.9	1.7			Current	1.6	2.1
.4	.8	.8	.6				.7	.9
.1	.2	.4	.3				.2	.3
3.5	5.8	2.6	1.2			Quick	1.5	1.8
.2	.8	.7	.4				.4	.4
.1	.1	.2	.2				.1	.1
0 UND	0 UND	0 UND	0 999.8			Sales/Receivables	0 UND	0 UND
0 UND	0 UND	0 986.5	2 180.1				0 999.8	0 999.8
0 UND	3 133.0	8 48.4	9 38.5				4 103.0	4 100.6
						Cost of Sales/Inventory		
						Cost of Sales/Payables		
NM	13.0	7.2	9.7			Sales/Working Capital	10.8	11.9
-12.4	NM	-98.4	-21.3				-32.6	-46.0
-3.0	-4.8	-11.8	-4.4				-5.7	-6.1
13.1	10.7	7.0	3.6			EBIT/Interest	3.7	4.6
(14) 3.4	(12) 2.7	(33) 3.7	(27) 1.8				(67) 1.6	(71) 2.2
1.0	.4	1.2	.9				.4	1.2
						Net Profit + Depr., Dep., Amort./Cur. Mat. L/T/D	3.1	16.6
							(13) 2.3	(15) 2.6
							1.1	1.3
1.1	1.4	.8	1.3			Fixed/Worth	1.0	1.2
9.3	8.2	2.0	3.1				3.2	2.8
-4.1	-1.4	6.0	20.3				13.4	23.7
1.5	.9	.7	.7			Debt/Worth	.4	.8
13.2	9.3	1.7	2.7				2.5	2.6
-4.7	-2.9	10.2	23.2				17.8	24.2
179.9		41.7	43.5			% Profit Before Taxes/Tangible Net Worth	34.9	34.4
(11) 132.0		(34) 21.6	(25) 18.1				(61) 7.7	(64) 17.0
.0		3.4	-.5				-1.2	4.3
63.6	20.9	14.8	9.1			% Profit Before Taxes/Total Assets	10.1	14.0
8.4	2.2	6.8	2.9				3.0	4.5
1.3	-4.0	.8	-.5				-1.8	.5
8.8	6.7	3.6	1.3			Sales/Net Fixed Assets	2.4	2.8
2.8	2.9	1.7	.9				1.1	1.6
.9	1.6	.7	.5				.6	.7
5.3	3.3	1.5	1.1			Sales/Total Assets	1.4	2.1
2.0	1.4	1.0	.6				.8	.9
.5	.9	.5	.4				.5	.6
2.4	7.6	6.4	7.0			% Depr., Dep., Amort./Sales	6.2	4.1
(16) 5.5	(12) 9.9	(34) 8.3	(29) 11.5				(68) 10.1	(83) 8.5
12.0	16.6	13.8	15.2				17.0	12.4
						% Officers', Directors' Owners' Comp/Sales	1.4	2.7
							(22) 5.0	(23) 6.9
							16.8	13.6
16142M	28730M	210998M	438497M	276363M	238870M	Net Sales ($)	1039375M	999623M
5311M	14712M	219952M	574925M	375864M	524143M	Total Assets ($)	1095069M	1158862M

© RMA 2011

M = $ thousand   MM = $ million
See Pages 9 through 22 for Explanation of Ratios and Data

Comparative Historical Data | Current Data Sorted by Sales

4/1/08-3/31/09 ALL	4/1/09-3/31/10 ALL	4/1/10-3/31/11 ALL	Type of Statement	0-1MM	1-3MM	3-5MM	5-10MM	10-25MM	25MM & OVER
13	6	7	Unqualified		1		1	2	3
16	14	16	Reviewed		1		7	4	2
19	24	10	Compiled	2		3	5		
19	25	23	Tax Returns	9	5	5	2	2	
44	40	58	Other	14	11	8	6	12	7
				7 (4/1-9/30/10)			107 (10/1/10-3/31/11)		
111	109	114	**NUMBER OF STATEMENTS**	25	18	18	21	20	12
%	%	%	**ASSETS**	%	%	%	%	%	%
11.0	8.9	10.4	Cash & Equivalents	9.7	8.2	13.5	11.1	11.4	7.4
1.6	1.4	1.6	Trade Receivables (net)	.3	3.1	2.0	2.0	1.3	1.5
3.3	4.6	1.6	Inventory	.6	3.1	.8	1.4	2.4	1.4
3.6	1.2	4.3	All Other Current	3.7	7.2	1.4	3.8	5.5	4.5
19.6	16.1	17.9	Total Current	14.3	21.5	17.6	18.3	20.6	14.8
66.4	72.2	69.9	Fixed Assets (net)	72.4	64.9	76.0	69.5	63.0	75.0
2.8	2.0	3.3	Intangibles (net)	5.7	5.5	.8	3.0	2.4	1.4
11.2	9.7	8.9	All Other Non-Current	7.6	8.2	5.6	9.1	14.0	8.8
100.0	100.0	100.0	Total	100.0	100.0	100.0	100.0	100.0	100.0
			LIABILITIES						
4.0	5.9	6.4	Notes Payable-Short Term	9.2	8.7	1.7	6.9	2.9	8.7
6.3	6.7	5.1	Cur. Mat.-L.T.D.	6.0	5.9	2.4	5.6	3.4	7.6
4.4	3.6	3.6	Trade Payables	.8	10.0	2.0	3.5	3.4	2.5
.3	.1	.0	Income Taxes Payable	.0	.0	.1	.0	.0	.0
12.5	12.8	10.8	All Other Current	15.2	18.4	3.8	10.5	7.1	7.2
27.5	29.1	25.8	Total Current	31.2	43.1	10.0	26.5	16.9	26.1
39.8	45.9	40.4	Long-Term Debt	46.9	50.9	55.6	29.9	32.8	19.5
.7	.8	1.0	Deferred Taxes	.0	.1	.7	1.1	.6	5.2
10.3	11.6	15.0	All Other Non-Current	19.2	20.8	7.4	3.3	29.9	4.4
21.7	12.6	17.8	Net Worth	2.8	-14.8	26.3	39.2	19.8	44.8
100.0	100.0	100.0	Total Liabilities & Net Worth	100.0	100.0	100.0	100.0	100.0	100.0
			INCOME DATA						
100.0	100.0	100.0	Net Sales	100.0	100.0	100.0	100.0	100.0	100.0
			Gross Profit						
90.2	90.7	85.0	Operating Expenses	72.1	83.2	90.5	93.1	88.0	87.7
9.8	9.3	15.0	Operating Profit	27.9	16.8	9.5	6.9	12.0	12.3
4.4	4.1	6.0	All Other Expenses (net)	14.8	1.6	5.8	3.9	3.1	3.2
5.4	5.2	9.0	Profit Before Taxes	13.1	15.2	3.8	3.0	9.0	9.1
			RATIOS						
2.0	1.5	2.6	Current	3.5	1.9	3.6	3.6	2.0	1.5
.7	.6	.7		.3	.5	.9	.5	1.2	.4
.2	.2	.2		.1	.3	.3	.2	.4	.1
1.6	1.2	1.8	Quick	3.5	1.7	3.4	3.4	1.4	.6
(110) .5	.3	.4		.2	.3	.7	.5	.9	.2
.1	.1	.1		.1	.1	.3	.2	.1	.1
0 UND	0 UND	0 UND	Sales/Receivables	0 UND	0 UND	0 UND	0 999.8	0 999.8	2 206.5
1 714.0	0 999.8	0 959.3		0 UND	0 UND	1 588.0	3 112.8	1 382.0	3 107.0
4 90.9	3 114.2	7 49.3		0 UND	7 53.9	10 36.3	8 46.5	8 46.1	10 35.2
			Cost of Sales/Inventory						
			Cost of Sales/Payables						
12.6	24.0	12.6	Sales/Working Capital	32.5	16.8	11.1	6.2	8.1	18.7
-33.2	-23.0	-28.4		-10.5	-17.5	-549.1	-30.4	86.1	-7.1
-5.4	-4.5	-4.9		-2.6	-4.4	-10.3	-4.3	-8.4	-2.2
3.9	4.6	7.4	EBIT/Interest	7.2	8.6	14.6	7.1	10.1	9.2
(88) 1.8	(88) 1.6	(94) 2.8		(15) 1.3	(15) 2.6	(15) 2.9	(20) 2.0	(18) 2.9	(11) 4.4
.0	.2	1.0		1.0	.6	.4	.9	1.6	2.5
4.6	3.4	3.9	Net Profit + Depr., Dep., Amort./Cur. Mat. L/T/D						
(14) 2.9	(16) 2.3	(20) 2.4							
1.5	1.5	1.3							
1.0	1.3	.9	Fixed/Worth	1.3	1.3	.9	.9	.7	1.0
2.6	3.8	2.9		7.8	3.5	3.7	2.2	1.6	1.8
18.2	-10.0	23.8		-5.4	-1.4	NM	8.3	14.6	6.6
.6	.8	.7	Debt/Worth	2.0	1.0	.6	.7	.6	.3
2.6	3.7	2.7		10.3	2.6	3.2	1.7	2.1	2.1
575.3	-13.3	42.8		-5.9	-2.9	NM	7.7	17.9	7.2
37.4	40.7	54.9	% Profit Before Taxes/Tangible Net Worth	143.7	43.4	52.8	36.0	88.8	52.3
(86) 13.7	(72) 13.3	(87) 21.2		(14) 33.1	(11) 36.0	(14) 19.0	(19) 9.5	(17) 21.2	19.0
-.4	.8	2.5		-.4	17.8	-1.7	-1.7	9.5	2.1
11.2	8.3	15.2	% Profit Before Taxes/Total Assets	17.0	31.0	14.0	13.3	14.4	10.0
4.0	1.9	5.6		3.4	12.1	3.1	2.6	8.1	6.5
-2.9	-2.9	.3		.2	-1.1	-4.0	-.3	2.3	1.6
3.7	3.5	3.8	Sales/Net Fixed Assets	5.8	9.3	3.6	3.5	2.5	1.3
1.3	1.3	1.3		1.8	1.9	1.1	.9	1.7	.9
.6	.5	.6		.4	1.1	.4	.6	1.1	.7
1.9	2.1	1.6	Sales/Total Assets	2.0	2.6	1.4	1.7	1.5	.9
.8	.8	.9		.6	1.1	.7	.8	1.1	.8
.5	.4	.5		.3	.5	.4	.5	.7	.6
4.6	5.4	5.9	% Depr., Dep., Amort./Sales	3.9	7.4	7.2	7.3	5.4	6.2
(98) 9.6	(99) 10.0	(99) 9.0		(19) 5.6	(13) 9.1	(17) 10.8	11.8	(18) 7.5	(11) 8.3
13.8	14.3	13.6		12.2	18.4	16.2	14.1	9.6	11.2
1.5	3.8	1.7	% Officers', Directors' Owners' Comp/Sales						
(22) 5.2	(30) 5.5	(25) 4.8							
8.6	10.9	6.7							
1362861M	1061394M	1209600M	Net Sales ($)	10846M	31460M	73233M	152544M	308071M	633446M
2022629M	1720020M	1714907M	Total Assets ($)	26996M	47697M	117993M	216236M	329629M	976356M

© RMA 2011

M = $ thousand   MM = $ million
See Pages 9 through 22 for Explanation of Ratios and Data

Current Data Sorted by Assets   Comparative Historical Data

						Type of Statement		
		1	4	4	4	Unqualified	27	13
		6				Reviewed	5	6
	1	3				Compiled	5	6
1	2	3				Tax Returns	9	12
3	4	9	8	2	12	Other	32	45
	20 (4/1-9/30/10)		47 (10/1/10-3/31/11)				4/1/06-	4/1/07-
							3/31/07	3/31/08
0-500M	500M-2MM	2-10MM	10-50MM	50-100MM	100-250MM		ALL	ALL
4	7	22	12	6	16	NUMBER OF STATEMENTS	78	82
%	%	%	%	%	%	ASSETS	%	%
		18.0	16.1		18.9	Cash & Equivalents	18.8	20.2
		6.7	1.6		1.4	Trade Receivables (net)	4.3	5.0
		6.8	2.6		.6	Inventory	4.3	3.5
		2.3	1.5		1.0	All Other Current	2.4	2.0
		33.7	21.8		21.8	Total Current	29.8	30.7
		47.6	61.4		76.5	Fixed Assets (net)	60.2	59.3
		11.1	5.5		.6	Intangibles (net)	6.2	5.9
		7.6	11.2		1.1	All Other Non-Current	3.8	4.1
		100.0	100.0		100.0	Total	100.0	100.0
						LIABILITIES		
		4.9	1.8		.0	Notes Payable-Short Term	3.7	5.1
		7.8	11.9		3.4	Cur. Mat.-L.T.D.	8.0	5.3
		4.5	4.3		2.7	Trade Payables	8.5	5.2
		.1	.0		.0	Income Taxes Payable	.2	.0
		9.4	12.9		7.9	All Other Current	10.2	12.2
		26.8	30.8		13.9	Total Current	30.5	27.7
		30.1	43.7		31.1	Long-Term Debt	32.7	31.6
		.7	.0		.2	Deferred Taxes	.1	.1
		13.1	3.6		1.5	All Other Non-Current	6.3	5.1
		29.3	21.8		53.2	Net Worth	30.4	35.6
		100.0	100.0		100.0	Total Liabilities & Net Worth	100.0	100.0
						INCOME DATA		
		100.0	100.0		100.0	Net Sales	100.0	100.0
						Gross Profit		
		96.2	84.8		71.4	Operating Expenses	80.6	79.8
		3.8	15.2		28.6	Operating Profit	19.4	20.2
		3.8	4.4		3.5	All Other Expenses (net)	2.9	3.9
		.0	10.7		25.1	Profit Before Taxes	16.6	16.3
						RATIOS		
		1.9	1.2		2.1		2.2	3.4
		1.3	.7		1.4	Current	1.2	1.6
		.8	.5		1.0		.5	.8
		1.7	.8		2.0		1.9	3.0
		.9	.5		1.2	Quick	.9	1.2
		.2	.4		.9		.4	.5
0 UND	0 UND	1 566.1		1 304.3			1 560.6	0 UND
0 UND	0 UND	1 287.8		2 196.5		Sales/Receivables	2 198.5	2 199.8
15 24.5		4 95.4		6 62.8			6 65.1	6 56.6
						Cost of Sales/Inventory		
						Cost of Sales/Payables		
		8.7	NM		14.3		11.7	6.8
		24.1	-16.3		28.4	Sales/Working Capital	68.9	26.3
		-25.4	-7.5		NM		-11.4	-24.9
		11.5	13.9		23.2		25.5	29.5
		(17) 1.1	6.3		(15) 14.9	EBIT/Interest	(68) 3.8	(67) 6.4
		-1.0	.6		8.2		.8	.9
						Net Profit + Depr., Dep., Amort./Cur. Mat. L/T/D		
		.4	1.2		1.2		.9	.8
		.9	1.5		1.5	Fixed/Worth	1.7	1.4
		-8.1	NM		1.9		NM	8.1
		.4	.5		.5		.5	.4
		1.5	1.0		.8	Debt/Worth	1.6	1.4
		-9.8	NM		2.3		-40.3	7.9
		64.2			108.2		113.6	90.0
		(16) 17.6			(15) 43.2	% Profit Before Taxes/Tangible Net Worth	(58) 39.6	(64) 47.8
		.6			10.3		10.6	14.6
		16.3	17.2		40.5		62.5	42.7
		3.6	11.4		27.1	% Profit Before Taxes/Total Assets	14.8	15.3
		-4.9	-.8		5.7		1.8	.2
		6.5	2.3		1.8		5.8	4.4
		2.6	1.5		1.2	Sales/Net Fixed Assets	2.5	2.3
		1.0	1.4		.9		1.6	1.1
		1.8	1.2		1.2		2.5	2.2
		1.0	1.1		1.0	Sales/Total Assets	1.7	1.3
		.7	.9		.8		.9	.8
		8.8	6.6				3.6	3.7
		(18) 10.9	(11) 8.2			% Depr., Dep., Amort./Sales	(64) 7.3	(66) 7.3
		16.3	11.4				11.6	11.7
							1.4	1.9
						% Officers', Directors' Owners' Comp/Sales	(18) 2.7	(15) 4.6
							6.9	7.7
2884M	7029M	207532M	409574M	322317M	2800895M	Net Sales ($)	5510845M	6218450M
1356M	4943M	103860M	347602M	420608M	2662118M	Total Assets ($)	3404939M	4056349M

M = $ thousand   MM = $ million
See Pages 9 through 22 for Explanation of Ratios and Data

Comparative Historical Data | **Current Data Sorted by Sales**

12	13	13	Type of Statement						
2	2	6	Unqualified		2	2	2	2	11
4	6	4	Reviewed		3	1			
3	8	6	Compiled		3				
46	35	38	Tax Returns	3	3	1	2	6	
4/1/08-3/31/09	4/1/09-3/31/10	4/1/10-3/31/11	Other	5					21
ALL	ALL	ALL		0-1MM	1-3MM	3-5MM	5-10MM	10-25MM	25MM & OVER
				20 (4/1-9/30/10)			47 (10/1/10-3/31/11)		
67	64	67	**NUMBER OF STATEMENTS**	8	11	4	4	8	32
%	%	%	**ASSETS**	%	%	%	%	%	%
14.6	14.5	16.9	Cash & Equivalents		8.4				17.2
2.9	2.7	3.5	Trade Receivables (net)		2.4				4.9
4.9	5.7	3.6	Inventory		4.1				1.9
2.3	4.8	1.6	All Other Current		1.0				1.1
24.7	27.6	25.6	Total Current		15.9				25.1
63.3	61.7	60.5	Fixed Assets (net)		63.4				67.8
5.1	4.5	7.3	Intangibles (net)		12.0				3.8
6.9	6.3	6.6	All Other Non-Current		8.7				3.3
100.0	100.0	100.0	Total		100.0				100.0
			LIABILITIES						
6.5	5.4	6.2	Notes Payable-Short Term		5.1				.2
8.0	6.3	6.7	Cur. Mat.-L.T.D.		13.5				6.6
7.5	7.2	4.1	Trade Payables		2.9				2.9
.1	.0	.0	Income Taxes Payable		.0				.0
9.2	10.5	8.5	All Other Current		4.4				11.9
31.3	29.4	25.6	Total Current		25.8				21.7
26.6	36.1	37.0	Long-Term Debt		55.2				35.2
.1	.1	.4	Deferred Taxes		.2				.3
6.1	4.3	12.2	All Other Non-Current		13.0				2.7
35.9	30.1	24.7	Net Worth		5.7				40.2
100.0	100.0	100.0	Total Liabilities & Net Worth		100.0				100.0
			INCOME DATA						
100.0	100.0	100.0	Net Sales		100.0				100.0
			Gross Profit						
83.6	88.5	84.2	Operating Expenses		97.5				72.9
16.4	11.5	15.8	Operating Profit		2.5				27.1
3.5	2.4	4.4	All Other Expenses (net)		4.2				5.1
12.9	9.0	11.4	Profit Before Taxes		-1.7				22.0
			RATIOS						
1.6	2.3	1.9	Current		1.7				1.8
.9	1.0	1.1			.9				1.2
.5	.4	.7			.4				.8
1.0	1.6	1.7	Quick		1.6				1.5
.7	.6	.9			.4				1.0
.3	.1	.4			.1				.7
0 999.8	0 UND	0 UND	Sales/Receivables	0 UND				1 340.7	
2 206.0	1 372.9	1 259.7		0 UND				2 155.4	
6 64.2	5 74.8	5 73.7		4 94.2				6 56.7	
			Cost of Sales/Inventory						
			Cost of Sales/Payables						
15.5	8.4	9.7	Sales/Working Capital		18.5				14.3
-40.4	646.5	39.8			-26.9				41.0
-7.6	-7.8	-16.6			-4.6				-37.9
18.8	17.8	15.2	EBIT/Interest		10.8				21.5
(57) 5.5	(58) 3.5	(60) 5.1			1.0				(29) 13.8
.4	-.3	1.2			-1.6				3.4
			Net Profit + Depr., Dep., Amort./Cur. Mat. L/T/D						
.9	.8	.9	Fixed/Worth		1.2				1.2
1.6	1.4	1.5			4.8				1.5
7.7	NM	-197.8			-1.4				2.5
.5	.5	.6	Debt/Worth		1.1				.5
1.3	1.0	1.3			3.9				.9
7.9	NM	-246.9			-2.7				2.7
84.7	56.8	69.6	% Profit Before Taxes/Tangible Net Worth						85.2
(54) 36.3	(48) 17.9	(50) 31.1						(28)	45.2
5.3	.2	4.8							10.3
36.9	23.1	24.3	% Profit Before Taxes/Total Assets		6.8				37.7
14.7	4.9	11.5			.0				21.5
-1.1	-1.6	.8			-19.9				5.7
4.1	4.2	3.4	Sales/Net Fixed Assets		3.6				2.0
2.0	2.1	1.7			1.9				1.3
1.2	1.3	1.1			1.0				1.1
1.9	2.0	1.5	Sales/Total Assets		2.0				1.2
1.3	1.3	1.0			.9				1.0
.8	.8	.8			.7				.8
4.5	5.6	6.7	% Depr., Dep., Amort./Sales		9.0				5.9
(50) 7.2	(52) 7.6	(43) 9.5		(10)	11.1			(15)	8.2
9.9	10.6	12.7			16.5				9.5
1.9	2.3	2.3	% Officers', Directors' Owners' Comp/Sales						
(15) 4.2	(18) 4.4	(15) 5.2							
10.9	6.9	7.4							
4243140M	2556439M	3750231M	Net Sales ($)	4936M	18148M	14502M	29706M	127148M	3555791M
3748134M	2501070M	3540487M	Total Assets ($)	6185M	20615M	17435M	23910M	102855M	3369487M

M = $ thousand   MM = $ million
See Pages 9 through 22 for Explanation of Ratios and Data

Current Data Sorted by Assets   **Comparative Historical Data**

0-500M	500M-2MM	2-10MM	10-50MM	50-100MM	100-250MM		4/1/06-3/31/07 ALL	4/1/07-3/31/08 ALL
						Type of Statement		
	1	4	10	9	11	Unqualified	51	40
	2	1				Reviewed		
		4				Compiled	3	2
7	5	2	1			Tax Returns	8	11
2	2	5	20	11	13	Other	56	51
	27 (4/1-9/30/10)		84 (10/1/10-3/31/11)					
9	10	17	31	20	24	**NUMBER OF STATEMENTS**	118	104
%	%	%	%	%	%		%	%
						ASSETS		
	23.5	14.1	16.1	17.1	13.1	Cash & Equivalents	22.1	20.4
	.0	2.5	1.2	1.9	1.2	Trade Receivables (net)	1.0	1.3
	1.8	6.8	.6	1.2	.5	Inventory	.7	.5
	4.0	4.3	2.2	3.1	1.1	All Other Current	4.5	3.0
	29.3	27.8	20.1	23.4	15.8	Total Current	28.3	25.2
	45.1	59.1	60.7	71.4	71.8	Fixed Assets (net)	63.5	66.4
	21.8	5.1	9.0	3.5	7.6	Intangibles (net)	3.9	4.0
	3.7	8.0	10.3	1.8	4.8	All Other Non-Current	4.3	4.4
	100.0	100.0	100.0	100.0	100.0	Total	100.0	100.0
						LIABILITIES		
	.9	.9	12.1	.1	.9	Notes Payable-Short Term	5.0	3.2
	2.4	26.8	20.4	4.0	3.6	Cur. Mat.-L.T.D.	4.4	4.8
	3.7	5.0	2.7	3.1	3.3	Trade Payables	4.1	3.9
	2.2	.0	.0	.0	.3	Income Taxes Payable	.0	.0
	6.4	13.3	10.6	8.2	6.2	All Other Current	11.8	10.4
	15.6	46.0	45.9	15.5	14.3	Total Current	25.4	22.3
	24.2	36.3	25.4	31.2	44.0	Long-Term Debt	28.1	34.9
	.0	.0	.0	.0	.0	Deferred Taxes	.3	.1
	39.9	6.7	9.3	4.8	4.0	All Other Non-Current	1.8	4.0
	20.3	11.0	19.4	48.4	37.7	Net Worth	44.4	38.7
	100.0	100.0	100.0	100.0	100.0	Total Liabilities & Net Worth	100.0	100.0
						INCOME DATA		
	100.0	100.0	100.0	100.0	100.0	Net Sales	100.0	100.0
						Gross Profit		
	99.7	95.2	79.0	79.1	75.9	Operating Expenses	72.6	74.2
	.3	4.8	21.0	20.9	24.1	Operating Profit	27.4	25.8
	1.6	2.5	6.3	3.5	11.8	All Other Expenses (net)	3.6	4.0
	-1.3	2.4	14.6	17.3	12.3	Profit Before Taxes	23.7	21.8
						RATIOS		
	11.0	1.7	2.4	2.2	1.5	Current	2.4	2.2
	1.5	.9	.8	1.2	1.2		1.2	1.2
	1.0	.3	.4	.8	.7		.8	.7
	9.9	1.4	1.9	1.8	1.4	Quick	2.1	2.0
	1.3	(16) .7	.6	1.1	1.1		1.0	1.1
	.4	.2	.8	.8	.6		.6	.6
0 UND	0 UND	1 670.9	0 964.1	1 337.2		Sales/Receivables	0 999.8	0 999.8
0 UND	1 388.5	1 285.1	1 268.0	2 199.0			1 438.8	1 372.5
0 UND	5 67.0	4 98.1	5 72.5	5 71.0			3 126.0	3 112.1
						Cost of Sales/Inventory		
						Cost of Sales/Payables		
	7.4	10.8	9.3	7.6	13.6	Sales/Working Capital	11.9	11.4
	40.2	-94.7	-37.9	53.0	38.5		57.7	69.8
	NM	-10.3	-7.1	-25.7	-15.2		-29.4	-19.0
		3.3	25.7	31.8	13.0	EBIT/Interest	(89) 33.1	(78) 27.2
		(16) 1.2	(25) 5.9	(17) 15.4	(20) 4.4		11.3	9.7
		-1.2	1.3	4.5	1.4		2.9	3.0
						Net Profit + Depr., Dep., Amort./Cur. Mat. L/T/D		
	4.1	1.6	.9	1.0	1.4	Fixed/Worth	.9	.9
	-4.0	4.0	1.8	1.5	1.9		1.4	1.6
	-1.1	-2.4	-21.5	2.5	4.8		3.6	5.3
	4.1	1.9	.5	.5	.8	Debt/Worth	.3	.4
	-7.0	5.2	1.4	1.0	1.4		.9	1.4
	-4.6	-4.6	-37.6	1.9	4.7		4.1	6.9
		125.3	83.0	82.2	61.4	% Profit Before Taxes/Tangible Net Worth	(104) 124.1	(84) 148.3
		(12) 30.0	(23) 16.9	(17) 57.7	(21) 38.1		78.1	72.8
		-12.3	7.9	19.8	13.0		31.9	29.2
	9.6	20.1	48.2	41.5	26.0	% Profit Before Taxes/Total Assets	68.5	59.8
	.6	2.4	15.1	19.4	8.7		32.5	31.2
	-16.3	-8.2	3.4	7.1	1.5		6.6	5.7
	14.5	6.4	4.8	3.0	1.6	Sales/Net Fixed Assets	4.6	4.0
	4.8	2.9	2.1	1.6	1.1		2.1	1.9
	1.8	1.4	1.0	1.1	.8		1.4	1.1
	3.1	2.4	1.8	1.7	.9	Sales/Total Assets	2.4	2.2
	2.8	1.7	.9	1.2	.7		1.5	1.4
	1.3	.9	.6	.9	.6		1.0	.8
		3.6	5.5	4.0	6.3	% Depr., Dep., Amort./Sales	(103) 3.6	(83) 3.8
		(15) 4.5	(30) 6.8	(18) 6.2	(13) 8.3		5.8	6.2
		6.6	9.1	9.7	10.2		8.1	8.9
						% Officers', Directors' Owners' Comp/Sales	(13) 1.7	(14) 2.1
							4.3	3.1
							16.4	7.4
14748M	28240M	172925M	1248803M	1933143M	3051476M	Net Sales ($)	8194227M	9620075M
1702M	11596M	82273M	826999M	1363536M	3872278M	Total Assets ($)	5669045M	6691547M

M = $ thousand   MM = $ million
See Pages 9 through 22 for Explanation of Ratios and Data

Comparative Historical Data — Current Data Sorted by Sales

Hist 1	Hist 2	Hist 3	Type of Statement	0-1MM	1-3MM	3-5MM	5-10MM	10-25MM	25MM & OVER
36	38	35	Unqualified		1		2	5	27
1	2	3	Reviewed		1	1	1		
3	8	4	Compiled		1	1			1
7	14	16	Tax Returns	5	5	2	3	1	
62	72	53	Other	2	3	2	4	9	33
4/1/08-3/31/09 ALL	4/1/09-3/31/10 ALL	4/1/10-3/31/11 ALL			27 (4/1-9/30/10)			84 (10/1/10-3/31/11)	
109	134	111	NUMBER OF STATEMENTS	7	11	6	11	15	61
%	%	%	**ASSETS**	%	%	%	%	%	%
19.7	19.0	17.5	Cash & Equivalents		20.9		20.1	10.7	17.1
1.9	2.3	1.6	Trade Receivables (net)		1.4		3.1	.6	1.6
.6	.9	1.9	Inventory		9.9		1.3	.8	.8
2.2	2.9	2.9	All Other Current		6.8		2.1	2.7	2.4
24.4	25.1	24.0	Total Current		39.1		26.6	14.8	22.0
65.6	62.7	60.4	Fixed Assets (net)		47.2		48.2	68.0	67.9
3.2	5.9	8.5	Intangibles (net)		6.9		17.5	9.3	5.6
6.8	6.3	7.1	All Other Non-Current		6.9		7.7	7.8	4.5
100.0	100.0	100.0	Total		100.0		100.0	100.0	100.0
			LIABILITIES						
2.3	2.5	4.6	Notes Payable-Short Term		4.2		.7	1.3	6.3
3.7	9.0	12.1	Cur. Mat.-L.T.D.		4.7		20.6	26.3	9.7
4.5	3.7	4.3	Trade Payables		6.3		1.4	3.1	4.0
.1	.1	.3	Income Taxes Payable		.0		1.5	.0	.1
10.6	10.9	9.4	All Other Current		7.6		7.0	6.5	11.2
21.3	26.2	30.6	Total Current		22.8		31.4	37.2	31.4
32.7	34.2	32.8	Long-Term Debt		26.2		23.7	33.9	32.9
.1	.0	.0	Deferred Taxes		.0		.0	.0	.0
5.5	7.1	10.6	All Other Non-Current		46.4		2.6	9.7	5.7
40.4	32.5	25.9	Net Worth		4.7		42.3	19.2	30.0
100.0	100.0	100.0	Total Liabilities & Net Worth		100.0		100.0	100.0	100.0
			INCOME DATA						
100.0	100.0	100.0	Net Sales		100.0		100.0	100.0	100.0
			Gross Profit						
78.6	79.6	84.2	Operating Expenses		96.0		92.4	88.3	77.6
21.4	20.4	15.8	Operating Profit		4.0		7.6	11.7	22.4
4.3	4.5	5.5	All Other Expenses (net)		4.2		2.1	11.2	5.5
17.2	15.9	10.3	Profit Before Taxes		-.2		5.5	.5	16.9
			RATIOS						
2.1	2.1	1.9	Current		1.9		1.9	2.7	1.7
1.3	1.1	1.2			1.0		1.7	.8	1.1
.8	.5	.6			.6		.8	.3	.6
1.9	1.8	1.6	Quick		3.7		1.9	2.0	1.5
1.1 (132)	.9 (110)	1.0			(10) .8		1.5	.6	1.0
.6	.4	.5			.3		.3	.3	.6
0 768.4	0 999.8	0 999.8	Sales/Receivables		0 UND		0 UND	0 999.8	1 444.5
1 260.8	1 315.3	1 295.2			0 UND		1 388.5	1 251.0	1 257.2
4 82.2	3 120.5	4 95.3			3 108.0		22 16.7	4 95.3	4 82.2
			Cost of Sales/Inventory						
			Cost of Sales/Payables						
10.6	12.0	11.1	Sales/Working Capital		15.0		8.7	6.4	13.7
39.0	116.2	63.0			390.5		11.1	-37.9	74.1
-23.3	-15.0	-15.3			-18.7		-45.5	-6.3	-14.2
28.4	31.0	14.3	EBIT/Interest		136.2			9.6	19.0
(82) 10.9	(109) 5.8	(93) 4.2					1.6	(13) 3.5	(51) 6.5
2.5	1.7	.7					.3	-.2	1.8
			Net Profit + Depr., Dep., Amort./Cur. Mat. L/T/D						
.9	1.0	1.0	Fixed/Worth		.7		.7	1.3	1.0
1.4	1.9	2.0			32.0		2.3	2.2	1.8
7.4	37.7	-5.8			-1.4		-2.4	-1.7	4.5
.4	.5	.6	Debt/Worth		.5		.5	.9	.6
1.1	1.5	1.9			31.8		4.4	2.0	1.3
7.8	-139.1	-8.4			-5.0		-4.7	-2.9	4.7
107.8	96.1	71.0	% Profit Before Taxes/Tangible Net Worth					45.7	78.4
(91) 58.6	(100) 45.7	(81) 35.6						(10) 12.6	(50) 51.2
19.9	16.9	10.6						-15.0	17.2
49.2	38.9	27.6	% Profit Before Taxes/Total Assets		3.7		22.3	15.1	42.8
20.3	13.9	10.0			-2.4		3.4	5.2	19.7
5.0	.5	-.7			-10.9		-1.2	-6.0	4.4
3.4	4.0	4.8	Sales/Net Fixed Assets		23.1		7.0	2.9	3.2
1.6	1.7	1.8			4.1		3.5	1.4	1.6
1.0	1.1	1.1			1.3		1.6	.8	1.1
1.9	2.1	2.3	Sales/Total Assets		3.0		2.8	1.0	1.8
1.2	1.1	1.1			1.6		1.7	.9	1.0
.8	.8	.7			.6		.7	.6	.7
4.2	4.8	3.8	% Depr., Dep., Amort./Sales		1.9		3.7	6.4	4.2
(86) 6.3	(103) 6.8	(92) 6.4			(10) 5.2		(10) 4.6	7.0	(46) 6.3
8.7	9.8	9.1			12.7		8.2	9.5	9.3
2.4	1.7	1.0	% Officers', Directors' Owners' Comp/Sales						
(11) 3.8	(19) 3.8	(14) 2.9							
5.0	5.2	5.8							
7904068M	7792600M	6449335M	Net Sales ($)	4338M	22185M	24063M	82139M	261310M	6055300M
7057498M	7413417M	6158384M	Total Assets ($)	2791M	25675M	19097M	68623M	537125M	5505073M

M = $ thousand   MM = $ million
See Pages 9 through 22 for Explanation of Ratios and Data

Current Data Sorted by Assets   Comparative Historical Data

0-500M	500M-2MM	2-10MM	10-50MM	50-100MM	100-250MM	Type of Statement		
			3	4	3	Unqualified	5	6
	1	3				Reviewed		1
1	1	1				Compiled	3	3
1	1					Tax Returns		4
2	1	4	7	3	5	Other	13	15
	8 (4/1-9/30/10)		28 (10/1/10-3/31/11)				4/1/06-3/31/07 ALL	4/1/07-3/31/08 ALL
3	3	8	11	3	8	NUMBER OF STATEMENTS	21	29
%	%	%	%	%	%	ASSETS	%	%
			18.2			Cash & Equivalents	16.2	14.1
			3.8			Trade Receivables (net)	4.2	5.3
			1.8			Inventory	2.3	1.5
			9.3			All Other Current	6.1	7.8
			33.1			Total Current	28.8	28.7
			47.7			Fixed Assets (net)	47.0	56.1
			8.9			Intangibles (net)	19.5	11.5
			10.2			All Other Non-Current	4.8	3.8
			100.0			Total	100.0	100.0
						LIABILITIES		
			4.3			Notes Payable-Short Term	2.5	.5
			7.8			Cur. Mat.-L.T.D.	3.8	5.2
			4.3			Trade Payables	2.6	5.8
			.0			Income Taxes Payable	.2	.0
			15.9			All Other Current	6.5	13.7
			32.2			Total Current	15.7	25.3
			26.2			Long-Term Debt	38.1	40.5
			.9			Deferred Taxes	.8	.2
			2.5			All Other Non-Current	6.4	7.1
			38.2			Net Worth	39.0	27.0
			100.0			Total Liabilities & Net Worth	100.0	100.0
						INCOME DATA		
			100.0			Net Sales	100.0	100.0
						Gross Profit		
			78.7			Operating Expenses	78.5	85.2
			21.3			Operating Profit	21.5	14.8
			2.8			All Other Expenses (net)	7.0	4.1
			18.5			Profit Before Taxes	14.5	10.8
						RATIOS		
			1.4			Current	2.6	2.0
			.9				1.8	1.3
			.5				1.0	.7
			1.4			Quick	2.3	1.6
			.8				1.3	.9
			.4				.7	.5
		2	241.6			Sales/Receivables	0 981.9	0 UND
		7	50.7				5 67.5	6 58.5
		28	13.2				21 17.1	19 18.9
						Cost of Sales/Inventory		
						Cost of Sales/Payables		
			11.3			Sales/Working Capital	6.7	8.0
			-35.6				13.6	56.3
			-10.7				-567.9	-33.1
						EBIT/Interest	13.1	12.1
							(19) 5.2	(27) 3.1
							1.6	.8
						Net Profit + Depr., Dep., Amort./Cur. Mat. L/T/D		
			.8			Fixed/Worth	.8	1.3
			1.1				2.6	2.7
			2.9				-2.2	-12.5
			.4			Debt/Worth	.8	.9
			3.0				2.0	3.5
			6.0				-4.7	-17.0
			193.3			% Profit Before Taxes/Tangible Net Worth	79.7	71.9
			(10) 65.9				(13) 33.5	(20) 23.0
			-.6				15.9	-2.9
			83.6			% Profit Before Taxes/Total Assets	28.9	22.9
			10.5				17.0	6.7
			.4				3.2	-.9
			10.4			Sales/Net Fixed Assets	7.8	5.3
			2.3				3.7	3.3
			1.0				1.5	1.1
			2.2			Sales/Total Assets	2.3	2.5
			1.0				1.1	1.1
			.6				.8	.7
			2.0			% Depr., Dep., Amort./Sales	2.0	2.7
			3.5				(13) 3.5	(21) 3.5
			6.7				6.7	10.2
						% Officers', Directors' Owners' Comp/Sales		
1261M	15267M	86404M	249820M	157375M	959266M	Net Sales ($)	1536782M	1430518M
982M	3870M	47249M	238413M	212050M	1430179M	Total Assets ($)	1414975M	1296171M

M = $ thousand   MM = $ million
See Pages 9 through 22 for Explanation of Ratios and Data

Comparative Historical Data | Current Data Sorted by Sales

			Type of Statement	0-1MM	1-3MM	3-5MM	5-10MM	10-25MM	25MM & OVER
6	5	10	Unqualified				4	1	5
2	2	2	Reviewed		1		1		
			Compiled						
3			Tax Returns				1		
5	2	2	Other	1			1		
10	17	22		2	1	1	3	5	10
4/1/08-3/31/09	4/1/09-3/31/10	4/1/10-3/31/11			8 (4/1-9/30/10)			28 (10/1/10-3/31/11)	
ALL	ALL	ALL		0-1MM	1-3MM	3-5MM	5-10MM	10-25MM	25MM & OVER
26	26	36	**NUMBER OF STATEMENTS**	3	2	1	9	6	15
%	%	%	**ASSETS**	%	%	%	%	%	%
17.2	24.4	20.9	Cash & Equivalents						22.0
2.4	4.4	4.3	Trade Receivables (net)						3.1
7.0	3.9	1.2	Inventory						.9
4.9	6.8	4.2	All Other Current						2.0
31.5	39.5	30.5	Total Current						28.0
52.9	48.5	48.0	Fixed Assets (net)						53.6
11.5	6.7	15.5	Intangibles (net)						13.7
4.2	5.2	5.9	All Other Non-Current						4.8
100.0	100.0	100.0	Total						100.0
			LIABILITIES						
6.0	4.4	2.3	Notes Payable-Short Term						1.2
3.6	12.1	7.3	Cur. Mat.-L.T.D.						6.3
6.5	8.9	5.1	Trade Payables						3.0
.8	1.0	.0	Income Taxes Payable						.0
12.8	13.6	11.2	All Other Current						12.0
29.7	40.1	26.0	Total Current						22.6
35.8	32.6	29.9	Long-Term Debt						33.2
.1	.1	.6	Deferred Taxes						.1
6.9	11.3	11.7	All Other Non-Current						6.6
27.5	15.9	31.8	Net Worth						37.5
100.0	100.0	100.0	Total Liabilities & Net Worth						100.0
			INCOME DATA						
100.0	100.0	100.0	Net Sales						100.0
			Gross Profit						
89.7	95.2	84.5	Operating Expenses						85.0
10.3	4.8	15.5	Operating Profit						15.0
4.3	4.6	4.6	All Other Expenses (net)						4.7
6.0	.2	10.9	Profit Before Taxes						10.2
			RATIOS						
2.4	2.3	1.6	Current						1.4
1.3	1.1	.8							.6
.6	.7	.5							.4
1.5	2.1	1.6	Quick						1.4
.9	1.0	.7							.5
.4	.4	.4							.4
0 UND	0 UND	0 816.5	Sales/Receivables						2 232.5
1 253.7	1 331.8	5 70.4							5 67.7
13 27.3	22 16.9	35 10.5							38 9.6
			Cost of Sales/Inventory						
			Cost of Sales/Payables						
5.9	11.1	13.9	Sales/Working Capital						19.9
79.4	42.0	-21.4							-17.6
-11.1	-14.6	-9.5							-5.6
(25) 22.2	(23) 12.0	(32) 7.6	EBIT/Interest					(14)	7.7
5.9	3.6	4.5							4.0
.7	-.3	.2							-.5
			Net Profit + Depr., Dep., Amort./Cur. Mat. L/T/D						
1.1	1.0	1.2	Fixed/Worth						1.3
3.1	3.0	2.6							2.0
-4.8	-4.7	NM							8.5
.8	.5	1.2	Debt/Worth						.5
4.0	3.9	4.6							2.0
-7.4	-12.6	NM							9.9
(17) 60.0	(18) 61.0	(27) 124.5	% Profit Before Taxes/Tangible Net Worth					(12)	116.9
19.2	23.0	64.3							61.7
1.3	1.7	-4.0							-2.8
15.6	14.9	25.6	% Profit Before Taxes/Total Assets						25.2
10.0	4.7	9.4							5.3
-.9	-2.7	-.6							-2.5
5.1	8.8	6.3	Sales/Net Fixed Assets						5.7
2.9	3.2	1.9							1.4
1.3	1.3	1.0							.7
2.3	2.6	2.0	Sales/Total Assets						2.2
1.2	1.3	1.0							1.0
.6	.7	.6							.4
3.0	3.0	3.7	% Depr., Dep., Amort./Sales						
(20) 6.1	(21) 5.5	(26) 9.0							
10.5	12.9	19.9							
			% Officers', Directors' Owners' Comp/Sales						
1316200M	860405M	1469393M	Net Sales ($)	1261M	2470M	4959M	64936M	117855M	1277912M
1271681M	908813M	1932743M	Total Assets ($)	982M	3972M	44887M	70094M	111506M	1701302M

M = $ thousand   MM = $ million
See Pages 9 through 22 for Explanation of Ratios and Data

Current Data Sorted by Assets | Comparative Historical Data

0-500M	500M-2MM	2-10MM	10-50MM	50-100MM	100-250MM		Type of Statement	4/1/06-3/31/07 ALL	4/1/07-3/31/08 ALL
2	5	110	134	10	2		Unqualified	261	268
2	12	68	17				Reviewed	99	106
14	43	48	2				Compiled	141	141
31	59	43	5				Tax Returns	100	87
16	57	157	88	5	7		Other	303	306
	188 (4/1-9/30/10)		749 (10/1/10-3/31/11)						
65	176	426	246	15	9		**NUMBER OF STATEMENTS**	904	908
%	%	%	%	%	%		**ASSETS**	%	%
23.3	8.9	6.6	6.9	7.6			Cash & Equivalents	7.4	6.8
3.4	4.2	4.6	4.2	5.3			Trade Receivables (net)	4.8	4.8
11.1	2.9	1.7	1.2	.7			Inventory	2.1	2.0
1.9	1.8	1.8	2.1	.5			All Other Current	1.5	1.4
39.8	17.8	14.7	14.4	14.0			Total Current	15.9	14.9
44.3	69.3	79.4	79.3	81.5			Fixed Assets (net)	77.6	78.8
6.7	4.8	1.1	.6	.4			Intangibles (net)	1.8	1.4
9.2	8.0	4.8	5.7	4.1			All Other Non-Current	4.7	4.9
100.0	100.0	100.0	100.0	100.0			Total	100.0	100.0
							LIABILITIES		
13.4	8.7	3.0	.9	.2			Notes Payable-Short Term	4.9	4.1
7.5	5.9	2.9	2.0	3.2			Cur. Mat.-L.T.D.	4.0	4.4
7.9	4.7	2.4	2.0	1.7			Trade Payables	3.1	3.0
.1	.1	.1	.0	.0			Income Taxes Payable	.2	.1
42.1	24.1	8.4	6.2	10.1			All Other Current	9.3	10.4
70.9	43.6	16.9	11.2	15.1			Total Current	21.5	22.0
50.7	51.0	44.6	28.4	23.7			Long-Term Debt	40.1	40.5
.0	.6	.1	.1	.1			Deferred Taxes	.1	.1
33.1	21.5	6.4	7.9	11.1			All Other Non-Current	8.0	9.7
-54.7	-16.6	32.1	52.5	50.0			Net Worth	30.3	27.7
100.0	100.0	100.0	100.0	100.0			Total Liabilties & Net Worth	100.0	100.0
							INCOME DATA		
100.0	100.0	100.0	100.0	100.0			Net Sales	100.0	100.0
							Gross Profit		
98.3	97.6	98.0	101.9	101.5			Operating Expenses	96.6	97.2
1.7	2.4	2.0	-1.9	-1.5			Operating Profit	3.4	2.8
1.1	4.6	4.3	.8	.4			All Other Expenses (net)	4.1	4.3
.6	-2.2	-2.2	-2.7	-1.8			Profit Before Taxes	-.7	-1.4
							RATIOS		
1.2	1.2	1.6	2.0	1.2				1.7	1.7
.6	.5	.9	1.3	1.1			Current	.9	.9
.3	.2	.5	.8	.7				.5	.4
.8	.8	1.4	1.8	1.2				1.4	1.3
.3	.4	(425) .7	1.1	1.0			Quick	(901) .7	(907) .7
.1	.1	.5	.5					.3	.3
0 UND	0 UND	3 128.5	15 24.5	16 23.2				1 336.8	1 257.5
0 UND	2 219.6	23 15.6	27 13.5	32 11.2			Sales/Receivables	18 20.2	19 18.9
1 340.8	10 34.8	37 9.8	42 8.8	57 6.4				37 9.8	37 9.9
							Cost of Sales/Inventory		
							Cost of Sales/Payables		
60.7	59.8	10.5	6.0	12.7				10.7	11.8
-23.6	-12.2	-86.3	16.1	156.0			Sales/Working Capital	-80.5	-52.4
-7.3	-4.1	-7.8	-21.5	-11.1				-8.0	-6.9
3.0	1.9	1.7	2.2	1.4				2.3	2.1
(40) .2	(150) .9	(383) .6	(216) .2	(11) -.1			EBIT/Interest	(748) 1.0	(763) .9
-6.8	-.6	-.7	-1.8	-1.4				-.2	-.4
	2.1	4.4	4.8				Net Profit + Depr., Dep.,	4.8	3.9
	(10) 1.1	(25) 1.9	(22) 2.3				Amort./Cur. Mat. L/T/D	(64) 3.0	(67) 2.4
	.8	-.1	.6					1.1	.7
.7	2.0	1.4	1.0	1.1				1.2	1.3
-71.5	6.1	2.4	1.3	1.4			Fixed/Worth	2.1	2.1
-.4	-1.4	8.2	2.3	1.7				7.9	9.4
1.5	1.6	.7	.2	.4				.5	.6
-34.4	6.9	1.9	.6	.7			Debt/Worth	1.5	1.6
-1.7	-2.8	10.8	1.8	1.1				9.3	11.3
106.0	17.0	3.8	2.8	6.1			% Profit Before Taxes/Tangible	8.3	6.6
(30) 13.0	(106) .0	(349) -2.5	(230) -1.6	(13) -.1			Net Worth	(723) .9	(729) .0
-62.2	-12.2	-11.0	-6.6	-3.2				-6.5	-7.7
26.6	3.9	1.9	1.7	3.2			% Profit Before Taxes/Total	3.6	2.7
-.6	-.5	-1.2	-1.1	-.1			Assets	.1	-.5
-26.3	-8.0	-4.1	-3.5	-2.2				-3.8	-4.1
41.4	3.0	1.1	.7	.6				1.3	1.2
9.2	1.4	.7	.5	.5			Sales/Net Fixed Assets	.7	.7
4.2	.7	.5	.4	.3				.5	.5
6.3	1.7	.8	.6	.4				.9	.9
3.5	1.0	.6	.4	.4			Sales/Total Assets	.6	.6
1.9	.6	.4	.3	.3				.4	.4
1.7	3.8	7.6	10.0	9.7				7.0	6.9
(48) 3.6	(157) 7.4	(391) 10.3	(227) 12.6	12.0			% Depr., Dep., Amort./Sales	(815) 9.7	(823) 9.6
8.1	11.3	13.3	16.2	14.8				12.7	12.8
3.1	3.7	3.0	2.6				% Officers', Directors'	3.1	3.1
(22) 5.3	(46) 6.7	(72) 7.0	(19) 4.5				Owners' Comp/Sales	(155) 7.7	(138) 6.7
12.7	13.7	19.0	18.7					17.0	14.5
59468M	251620M	1375236M	2323408M	494368M	1607680M		Net Sales ($)	5102614M	5113414M
14185M	208572M	2262491M	4707807M	1025789M	1600098M		Total Assets ($)	7436957M	7928848M

© RMA 2011

M = $ thousand   MM = $ million
See Pages 9 through 22 for Explanation of Ratios and Data

Comparative Historical Data | Current Data Sorted by Sales

Type of Statement										
	249	257	263	Unqualified	2	29	71	115	34	12
	103	112	99	Reviewed	9	42	33	14		1
	98	113	107	Compiled	36	60	8	2	1	
	107	130	138	Tax Returns	61	62	9	5	1	
	283	280	330	Other	42	111	78	63	24	12
	4/1/08-3/31/09 ALL	4/1/09-3/31/10 ALL	4/1/10-3/31/11 ALL		188 (4/1-9/30/10)		749 (10/1/10-3/31/11)			
					0-1MM	1-3MM	3-5MM	5-10MM	10-25MM	25MM & OVER
NUMBER OF STATEMENTS	840	892	937		150	304	199	199	60	25

ASSETS	%	%	%		%	%	%	%	%	%
Cash & Equivalents	7.5	7.9	8.2		9.5	7.7	7.8	7.8	10.1	9.3
Trade Receivables (net)	4.7	4.3	4.4		1.5	4.1	6.2	4.5	5.0	7.6
Inventory	2.6	2.3	2.4		4.3	2.6	2.1	1.3	1.1	3.5
All Other Current	1.2	1.3	1.8		1.4	1.5	2.0	1.7	4.9	1.1
Total Current	16.0	15.9	16.9		16.7	16.0	18.1	15.3	21.1	21.6
Fixed Assets (net)	77.3	76.1	75.1		69.7	75.2	76.1	79.2	72.5	71.1
Intangibles (net)	1.3	2.0	2.1		5.4	2.9	.6	.3	.4	3.0
All Other Non-Current	5.5	6.0	5.9		8.2	5.9	5.1	5.2	6.0	4.4
Total	100.0	100.0	100.0		100.0	100.0	100.0	100.0	100.0	100.0

LIABILITIES										
Notes Payable-Short Term	4.2	3.7	4.2		9.7	5.9	1.6	1.2	1.1	1.8
Cur. Mat.-L.T.D.	3.8	4.3	3.5		5.5	3.7	3.6	2.3	2.0	3.4
Trade Payables	3.4	3.6	3.1		3.8	3.3	3.3	2.2	2.1	5.8
Income Taxes Payable	.1	.1	.1		.0	.2	.1	.0	.0	.1
All Other Current	11.0	13.7	13.2		18.5	15.3	12.4	8.6	7.2	14.9
Total Current	22.4	25.5	24.2		37.5	28.4	21.0	14.3	12.3	25.9
Long-Term Debt	40.2	40.0	41.5		56.9	51.4	34.4	26.2	26.9	41.3
Deferred Taxes	.1	.1	.2		.0	.4	.0	.0	.2	.1
All Other Non-Current	10.0	10.3	11.6		21.4	14.0	6.6	5.8	8.3	17.8
Net Worth	27.3	24.2	22.5		-15.9	5.8	38.0	53.7	52.3	14.9
Total Liabilities & Net Worth	100.0	100.0	100.0		100.0	100.0	100.0	100.0	100.0	100.0

INCOME DATA										
Net Sales	100.0	100.0	100.0		100.0	100.0	100.0	100.0	100.0	100.0
Gross Profit										
Operating Expenses	99.8	99.8	99.0		94.8	97.2	100.5	103.1	100.6	96.7
Operating Profit	.2	.2	1.0		5.2	2.8	-.5	-3.1	-.6	3.3
All Other Expenses (net)	3.6	3.3	3.1		7.7	5.1	1.1	-.5	.6	1.8
Profit Before Taxes	-3.3	-3.0	-2.1		-2.6	-2.3	-1.6	-2.7	-1.2	1.5

RATIOS										
Current	1.7	1.7	1.7		1.2	1.4	2.0	2.0	3.6	1.9
	1.0	.9	1.0		.5	.7	1.1	1.2	1.3	1.0
	.5	.4	.5		.2	.3	.7	.7	.9	.6
Quick	1.4	1.4	1.4		.8	1.1	1.6	1.7	1.8	1.5
	(839) .7	(890) .7	(936) .7		.3	(303) .5	.9	.9	1.1	.6
	.3	.2	.3		.1	.2	.5	.5	.6	.4
Sales/Receivables	2 186.5	1 391.6	1 351.7		0 UND	0 UND	16 22.6	15 24.0	15 24.6	14 25.4
	19 19.0	17 21.1	17 21.0		0 UND	7 49.6	32 11.5	25 14.4	26 13.8	22 16.6
	35 10.4	35 10.4	35 10.3		4 83.8	32 11.4	42 8.8	38 9.5	48 7.5	35 10.3
Cost of Sales/Inventory										
Cost of Sales/Payables										
Sales/Working Capital	11.2	11.6	10.5		56.0	22.9	7.9	7.2	3.6	8.6
	-160.8	-59.3	-127.3		-11.4	-22.1	85.8	23.4	15.3	-994.2
	-7.4	-6.9	-7.8		-3.1	-5.3	-14.5	-20.0	-92.1	-7.6
EBIT/Interest	1.7	1.9	1.8		1.6	1.8	1.6	1.9	2.9	3.6
	(700) .5	(752) .5	(807) .5		(110) .5	(269) .6	(184) .5	(173) .3	(50) .7	(21) .6
	-.9	-1.2	-.9		-1.2	-.7	-.9	-1.7	-1.5	-1.6
Net Profit + Depr., Dep., Amort./Cur. Mat. L/T/D	3.9	3.5	3.9			2.1	7.5	4.3		
	(66) 2.2	(69) 1.5	(60) 1.8			(20) 1.1	(10) 3.2	(11) 1.7		
	.4	.6	.6			-.2	1.4	1.0		
Fixed/Worth	1.2	1.2	1.2		2.0	1.7	1.1	1.0	.9	1.1
	2.1	2.2	2.2		5.5	5.0	1.7	1.5	1.2	1.9
	9.7	28.6	13.4		-1.7	-5.6	3.8	2.3	1.7	-8.1
Debt/Worth	.6	.5	.6		1.6	1.1	.4	.3	.3	.4
	1.6	1.8	1.7		6.6	5.1	1.2	.8	.6	2.6
	12.6	54.5	16.6		-3.0	-8.5	4.0	1.8	1.2	-10.5
% Profit Before Taxes/Tangible Net Worth	4.8	4.5	4.8		10.6	8.5	1.5	3.4	4.5	16.3
	(670) -1.4	(688) -1.5	(734) -1.5		(90) .0	(206) -1.9	(176) -2.2	(188) -1.8	(56) .0	(18) 5.5
	-10.5	-10.9	-8.8		-12.2	-16.6	-9.2	-7.2	-4.2	-2.9
% Profit Before Taxes/Total Assets	2.1	2.0	2.2		2.2	2.7	1.1	2.0	2.9	6.7
	-1.2	-1.2	-1.1		-1.0	-1.1	-1.1	-1.3	-.1	1.4
	-5.2	-4.9	-4.5		-8.0	-5.6	-3.6	-3.7	-3.0	-2.5
Sales/Net Fixed Assets	1.2	1.3	1.3		3.4	1.7	1.1	1.0	1.0	2.9
	.7	.7	.7		.8	.8	.7	.7	.7	.9
	.5	.5	.5		.4	.5	.5	.5	.5	.5
Sales/Total Assets	.9	.9	.9		1.4	1.1	.8	.7	.7	1.6
	.6	.6	.6		.7	.6	.6	.5	.6	.7
	.4	.4	.4		.4	.5	.4	.4	.4	.4
% Depr., Dep., Amort./Sales	6.6	6.9	7.0		4.6	6.0	7.7	8.5	3.6	3.6
	(772) 9.6	(822) 10.3	(843) 10.2		(126) 9.3	(272) 9.5	(184) 10.1	(187) 11.8	(53) 10.7	(21) 6.9
	12.6	13.9	13.6		16.3	13.0	13.0	15.0	12.9	12.0
% Officers', Directors' Owners' Comp/Sales	3.3	2.8	3.3		3.7	3.3	3.4	2.4		
	(134) 7.4	(139) 6.7	(161) 6.3		(44) 7.0	(60) 7.0	(28) 6.9	(21) 5.1		
	17.0	16.0	17.2		13.4	16.9	25.2	18.6		
Net Sales ($)	4689497M	4809586M	6111780M		90797M	570827M	792801M	1364514M	896649M	2396192M
Total Assets ($)	8729475M	8880453M	9818942M		215005M	1012456M	1548027M	2822686M	1787150M	2433618M

© RMA 2011

M = $ thousand   MM = $ million
See Pages 9 through 22 for Explanation of Ratios and Data

Current Data Sorted by Assets   Comparative Historical Data

Type of Statement	0-500M	500M-2MM	2-10MM	10-50MM	50-100MM	100-250MM		4/1/06-3/31/07 ALL	4/1/07-3/31/08 ALL
Unqualified			3	15	3	1		13	20
Reviewed		3	3	3		1		8	5
Compiled	1	2	1					5	5
Tax Returns	2	1	2						1
Other		4	4	11	2	2		13	18
	44 (4/1-9/30/10)			20 (10/1/10-3/31/11)					
NUMBER OF STATEMENTS	3	10	13	29	6	3		39	49

ASSETS	%	%	%	%	%	%		%	%
Cash & Equivalents		12.6	19.1	8.2				7.5	7.8
Trade Receivables (net)		1.2	.7	1.6				1.3	1.6
Inventory		4.0	2.9	2.7				4.0	2.9
All Other Current		.9	1.2	2.0				3.4	3.8
Total Current		18.7	24.0	14.5				16.3	16.2
Fixed Assets (net)		76.7	59.1	71.5				74.2	69.7
Intangibles (net)		1.7	.2	3.4				1.5	1.8
All Other Non-Current		2.9	16.7	10.6				8.0	12.3
Total		100.0	100.0	100.0				100.0	100.0

LIABILITIES									
Notes Payable-Short Term		41.8	1.1	2.5				8.1	4.3
Cur. Mat.-L.T.D.		5.7	6.6	2.2				3.5	3.7
Trade Payables		7.3	4.5	4.5				7.1	5.8
Income Taxes Payable		.0	.1	.2				.3	.2
All Other Current		14.1	14.2	9.9				9.2	12.5
Total Current		68.9	26.6	19.2				28.3	26.5
Long-Term Debt		46.3	24.7	29.3				25.7	25.0
Deferred Taxes		.1	.8	2.3				2.2	1.3
All Other Non-Current		3.5	5.5	3.8				8.6	9.1
Net Worth		-18.8	42.5	45.4				35.1	38.2
Total Liabilities & Net Worth		100.0	100.0	100.0				100.0	100.0

INCOME DATA									
Net Sales		100.0	100.0	100.0				100.0	100.0
Gross Profit									
Operating Expenses		91.5	88.5	95.1				94.2	91.9
Operating Profit		8.5	11.5	4.9				5.8	8.1
All Other Expenses (net)		3.3	2.1	4.6				.5	1.7
Profit Before Taxes		5.1	9.4	.3				5.3	6.3

RATIOS									
Current		1.7	1.6	1.1				.9	1.0
		.6	.9	.6				.4	.4
		.3	.3	.4				.2	.2
Quick		1.6	1.4	.8				.6	.5
		.4	.6	.3				.2	.2
		.2		.1				.1	.1
Sales/Receivables		0 UND	0 UND	2 221.3				1 671.9	1 583.1
		0 UND	0 999.8	4 82.1				3 112.0	4 103.4
		3 120.9	7 53.6	7 50.9				7 48.7	11 33.3
Cost of Sales/Inventory									
Cost of Sales/Payables									
Sales/Working Capital		NM	25.7	NM				-113.4	120.7
		-13.1	-67.0	-12.9				-9.9	-7.9
		-9.1	-4.2	-5.4				-4.1	-4.3
EBIT/Interest			12.8	6.6				12.7	5.8
		(11)	2.7	(27) 2.8				(36) 4.3	(47) 1.8
			1.0	.4				.2	.1
Net Profit + Depr., Dep., Amort./Cur. Mat. L/T/D								14.7	6.3
								(10) 2.0	(21) 2.8
								.7	1.4
Fixed/Worth		1.2	.6	1.0				1.1	1.2
		3.8	1.3	1.8				1.9	1.8
		-80.0	2.3	2.3				3.5	3.4
Debt/Worth		.3	.5	.5				.3	.6
		4.3	1.2	1.3				1.5	1.4
		-117.3	2.3	2.2				6.6	5.2
% Profit Before Taxes/Tangible Net Worth			24.6	18.8				33.5	22.1
		(11)	6.0	(27) 9.9				(34) 9.9	(43) 9.4
			2.7	-5.8				-1.1	-1.5
% Profit Before Taxes/Total Assets		26.8	15.5	7.9				13.2	10.6
		9.2	3.8	2.4				4.7	3.6
		-1.5	.8	-2.1				-3.4	-1.4
Sales/Net Fixed Assets		2.9	2.9	1.7				2.4	1.9
		2.4	1.2	1.1				1.2	1.3
		1.1	1.0	.4				.9	.9
Sales/Total Assets		2.2	1.5	1.1				1.4	1.3
		1.4	1.1	.8				.9	.9
		1.0	.8	.4				.7	.7
% Depr., Dep., Amort./Sales			6.6	7.1				5.7	5.5
		(10)	9.2	(27) 11.5				(32) 9.0	(46) 10.1
			15.7	15.5				12.2	12.3
% Officers', Directors' Owners' Comp/Sales									1.6
								(11)	4.6
									9.5

	0-500M	500M-2MM	2-10MM	10-50MM	50-100MM	100-250MM			
Net Sales ($)	3615M	18583M	111214M	598605M	411927M	202812M		1044269M	1381878M
Total Assets ($)	598M	11544M	70105M	784187M	407664M	514208M		1429106M	1508627M

M = $ thousand   MM = $ million
See Pages 9 through 22 for Explanation of Ratios and Data

Comparative Historical Data   **Current Data Sorted by Sales**

Hist 1	Hist 2	Hist 3	Type of Statement	0-1MM	1-3MM	3-5MM	5-10MM	10-25MM	25MM & OVER
16	22	22	Unqualified		2	3	5	10	7
9	12	10	Reviewed				1	3	1
4	7	4	Compiled		4				
1		5	Tax Returns	2	2		1		
23	16	23	Other	3	3	2		9	6
4/1/08-3/31/09 ALL	4/1/09-3/31/10 ALL	4/1/10-3/31/11 ALL			44 (4/1-9/30/10)			20 (10/1/10-3/31/11)	
53	57	64	NUMBER OF STATEMENTS	5	11	5	7	22	14
%	%	%	ASSETS	%	%	%	%	%	%
7.2	8.8	10.7	Cash & Equivalents		12.1			15.2	5.7
1.9	1.4	1.4	Trade Receivables (net)		1.2			1.6	2.1
4.1	1.7	3.2	Inventory		6.9			4.3	1.6
2.4	3.2	1.6	All Other Current		.6			2.0	2.4
15.6	15.1	17.0	Total Current		20.8			23.1	11.8
73.4	72.1	67.5	Fixed Assets (net)		66.6			67.8	62.1
2.8	3.2	3.5	Intangibles (net)		1.5			1.6	8.9
8.2	9.6	12.0	All Other Non-Current		11.0			7.4	17.1
100.0	100.0	100.0	Total		100.0			100.0	100.0
			LIABILITIES						
3.1	4.8	8.7	Notes Payable-Short Term		7.9			2.8	1.2
3.1	4.5	4.5	Cur. Mat.-L.T.D.		4.4			2.7	5.6
4.9	4.3	5.8	Trade Payables		10.8			5.5	5.3
.4	.2	.2	Income Taxes Payable		.0			.2	.4
11.7	13.6	13.9	All Other Current		9.5			10.7	13.5
23.2	27.4	33.1	Total Current		32.6			21.7	26.0
26.0	20.6	29.4	Long-Term Debt		37.6			27.1	21.1
1.9	1.9	1.4	Deferred Taxes		.1			2.1	1.9
8.0	7.1	9.1	All Other Non-Current		28.0			2.2	11.9
40.8	42.9	27.1	Net Worth		1.7			46.9	39.1
100.0	100.0	100.0	Total Liabilities & Net Worth		100.0			100.0	100.0
			INCOME DATA						
100.0	100.0	100.0	Net Sales		100.0			100.0	100.0
			Gross Profit						
89.2	92.1	93.2	Operating Expenses		94.9			95.1	91.4
10.8	7.9	6.8	Operating Profit		5.1			4.9	8.6
3.5	3.0	4.1	All Other Expenses (net)		1.5			4.5	5.2
7.3	4.9	2.7	Profit Before Taxes		3.6			.4	3.3
			RATIOS						
1.0	1.2	1.1			.7			1.3	1.0
.6	.6	.6	Current		.6			.6	.6
.2	.2	.3			.3			.5	.2
.7	.8	.8			.7			.9	.7
.3	.3	.4	Quick		.3			.4	.3
.1	.1	.1			.2			.2	.1
0 761.2	0 915.5	0 994.6		0 UND			1 331.8	5 76.5
5 71.4	4 87.6	4 92.0	Sales/Receivables	0 979.0			4 85.9	7 53.8
10 36.3	8 44.0	7 50.4		6 66.1			8 44.9	13 28.4
			Cost of Sales/Inventory						
			Cost of Sales/Payables						
NM	50.1	313.9			-25.4			24.6	NM
-9.7	-11.0	-12.8	Sales/Working Capital		-12.2			-13.1	-11.8
-4.9	-3.8	-5.4			-7.6			-6.5	-4.6
(50) 22.8	(54) 11.2	(54) 7.1						(21) 6.5	(13) 18.0
4.2	2.2	2.8	EBIT/Interest					3.4	4.0
1.0	.6	1.2						.2	1.3
(18) 6.4	(19) 9.1	(13) 4.3							
2.9	4.4	2.3	Net Profit + Depr., Dep., Amort./Cur. Mat. L/T/D						
1.5	2.0	.4							
1.2	1.1	1.0			1.9			1.0	.9
1.8	1.7	1.8	Fixed/Worth		5.3			1.6	1.6
3.1	3.8	8.7			-.8			2.3	10.1
.8	.6	.6			1.1			.5	.6
1.3	1.3	1.3	Debt/Worth		7.0			1.2	1.3
3.3	4.3	11.0			-2.6			2.0	NM
(46) 31.8	(47) 22.1	(51) 24.6						17.2	(11) 40.7
18.6	6.6	11.6	% Profit Before Taxes/Tangible Net Worth					9.6	18.8
4.9	-1.2	.3						-5.8	9.0
14.8	9.3	11.9			17.4			7.5	13.5
6.0	3.3	3.6	% Profit Before Taxes/Total Assets		5.7			3.8	6.0
-.2	-1.1	-2.3			-5.2			-2.6	-.5
1.8	2.0	2.2			7.2			2.0	2.4
1.3	1.2	1.2	Sales/Net Fixed Assets		2.8			1.2	1.2
.8	.8	.9			1.2			.4	.8
1.3	1.3	1.4			4.3			1.2	1.3
.9	.9	.9	Sales/Total Assets		1.4			.9	.9
.6	.7	.5			1.1			.4	.7
(48) 6.3	(53) 6.7	(56) 6.4		(10) 5.0				(20) 7.4	(12) 6.3
9.6	10.0	9.6	% Depr., Dep., Amort./Sales	7.4				11.5	7.1
13.1	13.4	12.8		9.7				16.9	10.7
			% Officers', Directors' Owners' Comp/Sales						
1762040M	1415453M	1346756M	Net Sales ($)	2792M	20906M	21892M	53443M	370406M	877317M
2187596M	1895868M	1788306M	Total Assets ($)	19862M	14230M	34174M	71476M	536961M	1111603M

M = $ thousand   MM = $ million
See Pages 9 through 22 for Explanation of Ratios and Data

Current Data Sorted by Assets | **Comparative Historical Data**

0-500M	500M-2MM	2-10MM	10-50MM	50-100MM	100-250MM	Type of Statement	4/1/06-3/31/07 ALL	4/1/07-3/31/08 ALL
			5	2		Unqualified	9	13
	5	12	3			Reviewed	26	19
3	11	7	3			Compiled	34	24
7	25	7	1	1		Tax Returns	35	46
6	20	36	11	2		Other	55	58
19 (4/1-9/30/10)		148 (10/1/10-3/31/11)						
16	61	62	23	5		NUMBER OF STATEMENTS	159	160
%	%	%	%	%	%	**ASSETS**	%	%
24.9	10.3	11.4	5.9		DATA NOT AVAILABLE	Cash & Equivalents	9.0	9.4
10.0	8.0	4.1	4.4			Trade Receivables (net)	6.9	6.1
10.5	14.4	6.1	5.8			Inventory	12.8	12.4
2.6	1.0	2.7	.6			All Other Current	1.7	2.1
48.1	33.8	24.4	16.7			Total Current	30.3	29.9
32.8	52.1	62.8	65.2			Fixed Assets (net)	56.8	55.7
6.6	4.5	6.5	6.4			Intangibles (net)	5.5	5.5
12.5	9.6	6.3	11.7			All Other Non-Current	7.4	8.8
100.0	100.0	100.0	100.0			Total	100.0	100.0
						LIABILITIES		
11.6	6.2	4.0	5.2			Notes Payable-Short Term	7.4	8.1
5.9	2.6	3.0	4.4			Cur. Mat.-L.T.D.	5.3	5.8
6.3	3.1	2.1	2.8			Trade Payables	3.7	3.3
.0	.0	.0	.0			Income Taxes Payable	.1	.1
25.2	9.5	13.6	4.3			All Other Current	9.3	10.6
49.1	21.4	22.8	16.7			Total Current	25.8	27.9
55.8	43.4	55.3	53.7			Long-Term Debt	47.3	50.4
.0	.0	.1	.4			Deferred Taxes	.1	.1
31.7	11.6	15.4	2.2			All Other Non-Current	7.4	7.0
-36.6	23.6	6.5	27.0			Net Worth	19.5	14.6
100.0	100.0	100.0	100.0			Total Liabilties & Net Worth	100.0	100.0
						INCOME DATA		
100.0	100.0	100.0	100.0			Net Sales	100.0	100.0
						Gross Profit		
92.5	88.7	85.4	84.3			Operating Expenses	86.6	86.4
7.5	11.3	14.6	15.7			Operating Profit	13.4	13.6
.9	6.3	6.9	10.3			All Other Expenses (net)	7.7	8.4
6.6	4.9	7.8	5.3			Profit Before Taxes	5.8	5.3
						RATIOS		
3.2	4.8	3.0	2.4				2.8	2.4
1.6	1.7	1.5	1.1			Current	1.3	1.1
.8	.9	.4	.4				.7	.6
3.1	3.2	2.0	2.2				2.1	1.7
1.1	.9	.9	.5			Quick	.7	.6
.2	.3	.3	.3				.2	.2
0 UND	**0** UND	**2** 146.9	**8** 45.6				**4** 99.0	**3** 113.5
5 75.9	**10** 36.9	**14** 26.5	**16** 22.9			Sales/Receivables	**16** 22.2	**13** 28.7
17 21.3	**45** 8.0	**37** 9.9	**36** 10.3				**40** 9.1	**28** 12.9
						Cost of Sales/Inventory		
						Cost of Sales/Payables		
10.3	3.7	3.6	4.9				6.1	6.2
18.2	12.0	14.9	61.6			Sales/Working Capital	26.7	38.6
NM	-38.1	-5.2	-4.3				-13.9	-9.3
11.0	6.5	4.6	3.5				4.3	5.3
(12) 1.6	(51) 3.4	(50) 2.0	(18) 1.5			EBIT/Interest	(126) 1.5	(125) 1.7
.7	1.3	.7	.7				.8	1.0
							3.5	
						Net Profit + Depr., Dep., Amort./Cur. Mat. L/T/D	(11) .9	
							.2	
.5	.6	1.0	1.0				1.0	1.2
-14.6	2.8	3.5	2.3			Fixed/Worth	3.4	5.9
-.2	-159.2	-3.5	29.0				-6.4	-6.4
.5	.9	.8	.4				1.2	1.4
-26.8	5.1	6.6	2.4			Debt/Worth	4.6	8.3
-2.0	-16.1	-4.8	51.9				-11.7	-9.9
	77.6	29.9	19.2				36.4	36.2
	(43) 17.1	(37) 5.8	(18) 3.1			% Profit Before Taxes/Tangible Net Worth	(111) 18.0	(105) 13.3
	3.9	-4.6	-2.0				.9	-2.3
19.7	11.1	9.5	5.8				9.2	8.8
2.8	4.3	2.8	1.2			% Profit Before Taxes/Total Assets	3.2	2.2
-2.9	-.2	-1.1	-.4				-.6	-.8
21.3	8.7	2.0	1.3				4.3	6.1
11.9	2.0	.9	.6			Sales/Net Fixed Assets	1.5	1.6
4.1	.7	.5	.3				.6	.5
4.6	1.8	1.0	.8				1.5	1.5
3.0	1.0	.6	.5			Sales/Total Assets	.9	.8
1.5	.5	.3	.2				.4	.3
	1.3	4.5	7.4				3.3	2.7
	(52) 3.1	(51) 8.7	(22) 11.5			% Depr., Dep., Amort./Sales	(145) 7.4	(137) 6.3
	8.9	13.0	18.0				12.1	12.2
	1.7	2.0					2.3	2.0
	(18) 3.1	(16) 6.1				% Officers', Directors' Owners' Comp/Sales	(47) 3.9	(52) 3.6
	7.7	9.7					10.2	8.2
8817M	94109M	193835M	203463M	494624M		Net Sales ($)	830125M	1721111M
3640M	72713M	270370M	417843M	351185M		Total Assets ($)	1026866M	1251357M

M = $ thousand MM = $ million

See Pages 9 through 22 for Explanation of Ratios and Data

Comparative Historical Data | Current Data Sorted by Sales

			Type of Statement						
10	9	7	Unqualified	2	11	2	3	1	3
14	33	20	Reviewed				2	3	
25	25	24	Compiled	8	8	3	3	2	
47	39	41	Tax Returns	22	15	2	1		1
74	69	75	Other	25	21	12	14		1
4/1/08-3/31/09 ALL	4/1/09-3/31/10 ALL	4/1/10-3/31/11 ALL		19 (4/1-9/30/10)			148 (10/1/10-3/31/11)		
				0-1MM	1-3MM	3-5MM	5-10MM	10-25MM	25MM & OVER
170	175	167	NUMBER OF STATEMENTS	57	55	19	23	8	5
%	%	%	ASSETS	%	%	%	%	%	%
8.8	8.9	11.7	Cash & Equivalents	12.0	10.2	14.6	12.7		
6.2	5.2	6.7	Trade Receivables (net)	4.9	7.4	7.6	5.7		
13.8	12.9	9.9	Inventory	5.8	10.8	13.5	13.4		
2.4	2.5	1.8	All Other Current	2.0	1.3	3.4	1.3		
31.2	29.4	30.1	Total Current	24.6	29.8	39.1	33.1		
55.9	57.2	55.3	Fixed Assets (net)	59.4	54.8	52.4	57.0		
4.7	5.5	5.7	Intangibles (net)	7.0	5.7	3.4	4.8		
8.2	7.9	8.9	All Other Non-Current	8.9	9.7	5.0	5.1		
100.0	100.0	100.0	Total	100.0	100.0	100.0	100.0		
			LIABILITIES						
7.1	6.6	5.8	Notes Payable-Short Term	6.5	3.5	3.9	8.6		
5.3	4.9	3.5	Cur. Mat.-L.T.D.	2.8	4.2	1.4	3.7		
3.3	3.4	3.1	Trade Payables	2.3	3.6	1.8	2.7		
.1	.1	.0	Income Taxes Payable	.0	.0	.1	.0		
8.6	11.2	12.2	All Other Current	11.9	16.0	8.6	6.2		
24.4	26.2	24.7	Total Current	23.5	27.4	15.8	21.2		
50.3	51.4	49.9	Long-Term Debt	59.8	40.7	46.1	44.1		
.1	.2	.1	Deferred Taxes	.0	.0	.0	.4		
8.6	15.4	13.4	All Other Non-Current	21.4	13.9	7.2	1.8		
16.6	6.8	11.9	Net Worth	-4.7	18.1	31.0	32.5		
100.0	100.0	100.0	Total Liabilties & Net Worth	100.0	100.0	100.0	100.0		
			INCOME DATA						
100.0	100.0	100.0	Net Sales	100.0	100.0	100.0	100.0		
			Gross Profit						
86.3	88.9	87.6	Operating Expenses	83.7	87.7	90.8	91.1		
13.7	11.1	12.4	Operating Profit	16.3	12.3	9.2	8.9		
7.7	8.2	6.5	All Other Expenses (net)	10.2	4.9	3.6	5.8		
6.0	3.0	6.0	Profit Before Taxes	6.2	7.4	5.6	3.1		
			RATIOS						
3.7	2.8	3.2		3.4	2.8	6.2	2.5		
1.4	1.2	1.4	Current	1.3	1.3	2.8	1.4		
.7	.5	.7		.6	.4	2.1	.9		
2.6	1.7	2.2		2.9	2.0	4.5	1.6		
.7 (174)	.5	.9	Quick	1.0	.6	2.4	.9		
.2	.2	.3		.2	.2	.2			
3 132.4	4 83.2	2 225.8		0 UND	4 84.9	3 119.7	4 102.7		
19 19.2	16 22.8	13 28.7	Sales/Receivables	4 101.1	17 21.7	18 20.9	13 28.7		
33 11.1	32 11.3	37 9.7		45 8.1	36 10.0	48 7.6	46 8.0		
			Cost of Sales/Inventory						
			Cost of Sales/Payables						
4.8	5.4	4.3		5.1	4.3	2.9	2.8		
16.8	28.5	17.5	Sales/Working Capital	19.3	16.4	4.8	17.2		
-16.2	-6.9	-12.5		-9.2	-4.8	5.6	-104.2		
3.7	3.6	5.2		5.2	5.0	9.9	8.0		
(143) 1.8	(132) 1.5	(135) 2.3	EBIT/Interest	(36) 2.1	(52) 2.3	(15) 2.8	(20) 1.0		
.8	.5	.8		.7	1.0	-.8	-.3		
		4.0	Net Profit + Depr., Dep.,						
	(12)	2.4	Amort./Cur. Mat. L/T/D						
		.6							
.9	1.2	.8		1.1	1.0	.5	.8		
3.2	4.8	2.9	Fixed/Worth	16.7	3.3	2.0	1.4		
-5.4	-3.9	-4.9		-2.9	-3.3	-5.0	4.4		
1.0	.9	.8		.8	1.0	.3	.7		
4.9	8.0	4.3	Debt/Worth	19.3	5.7	3.3	1.3		
-10.2	-6.5	-6.4		-4.0	-8.2	-6.9	9.4		
33.0	25.6	30.7	% Profit Before Taxes/Tangible	33.2	32.8	77.9	16.8		
(119) 12.9	(106) 6.5	(110) 10.9	Net Worth	(32) 13.6	(34) 11.3	(14) 19.5	(19) -.8		
1.9	-3.9	-.9		1.7	2.7	-6.3	-8.0		
7.6	6.2	9.6	% Profit Before Taxes/Total	8.2	8.8	13.1	6.4		
2.7	1.8	2.8	Assets	2.5	3.5	9.8	.2		
-.7	-2.0	-.8		-1.2	-.1	-.9	-2.5		
4.3	3.1	5.7		4.5	5.2	8.1	6.7		
1.4	1.1	1.4	Sales/Net Fixed Assets	.8	1.6	1.8	1.1		
.6	.5	.6		.3	.6	.7	.5		
1.3	1.2	1.4		1.4	1.6	1.4	1.0		
.7	.7	.8	Sales/Total Assets	.6	.9	1.1	.7		
.4	.4	.4		.3	.5	.5	.4		
3.1	3.8	3.1		5.5	2.0	4.1	3.5		
(143) 6.3	(148) 7.7	(136) 7.2	% Depr., Dep., Amort./Sales	(37) 9.8	(51) 5.6	(16) 6.8	(22) 7.6		
11.3	14.9	12.5		19.3	11.3	9.5	15.0		
2.4	2.2	2.1		2.8	1.8				
(51) 4.9	(50) 5.2	(45) 6.5	% Officers', Directors' Owners' Comp/Sales	(14) 7.0	(15) 6.9				
8.9	9.2	10.0		11.5	9.0				
735460M	764936M	994848M	Net Sales ($)	31473M	104382M	73305M	159619M	111172M	514897M
897491M	1255846M	1115751M	Total Assets ($)	74035M	188343M	96598M	347862M	96230M	312683M

M = $ thousand   MM = $ million
See Pages 9 through 22 for Explanation of Ratios and Data

Current Data Sorted by Assets | Comparative Historical Data

Type of Statement

	0-500M	500M-2MM	2-10MM	10-50MM	50-100MM	100-250MM		4/1/06-3/31/07 ALL	4/1/07-3/31/08 ALL
Unqualified	2		26	48	13	3		70	70
Reviewed	2	7	26	19	1			46	43
Compiled	10	17	19	7	1	1		62	60
Tax Returns	67	51	21	2		1		103	114
Other	50	64	63	34	10	8		167	159
	83 (4/1-9/30/10)			490 (10/1/10-3/31/11)					
NUMBER OF STATEMENTS	131	139	155	110	25	13		448	446

0-500M	500M-2MM	2-10MM	10-50MM	50-100MM	100-250MM		4/1/06-3/31/07 ALL	4/1/07-3/31/08 ALL
%	%	%	%	%	%	**ASSETS**	%	%
20.6	11.5	9.7	9.4	8.3	2.4	Cash & Equivalents	10.8	11.4
3.6	3.2	2.3	2.8	1.8	8.0	Trade Receivables (net)	4.2	3.6
5.0	1.7	1.1	.9	1.5	1.6	Inventory	1.7	1.7
3.6	2.3	2.1	2.0	3.3	2.9	All Other Current	2.0	2.8
32.9	18.7	15.1	15.1	15.0	14.8	Total Current	18.8	19.6
53.7	69.8	75.9	72.8	67.7	60.2	Fixed Assets (net)	66.3	66.4
5.9	3.4	2.5	4.2	11.4	15.6	Intangibles (net)	5.2	5.4
7.5	8.1	6.5	7.9	5.9	9.4	All Other Non-Current	9.8	8.7
100.0	100.0	100.0	100.0	100.0	100.0	Total	100.0	100.0
						LIABILITIES		
17.9	4.0	2.1	2.4	3.7	3.3	Notes Payable-Short Term	5.0	5.3
9.6	5.8	3.9	4.8	4.2	3.5	Cur. Mat.-L.T.D.	4.2	5.3
9.3	5.1	3.4	2.4	2.5	4.2	Trade Payables	3.7	3.9
.0	.1	.1	.1	2.4	.2	Income Taxes Payable	.0	.0
14.1	16.1	6.7	8.3	18.0	10.6	All Other Current	12.3	12.6
50.9	31.1	16.2	18.0	30.8	21.8	Total Current	25.3	27.1
48.8	48.4	48.0	42.7	27.1	41.8	Long-Term Debt	40.8	38.3
.0	.0	.0	.0	.5	1.1	Deferred Taxes	.1	.1
19.5	12.5	6.8	7.1	10.7	18.5	All Other Non-Current	9.9	13.0
-19.3	7.9	29.0	32.1	30.9	16.8	Net Worth	23.8	21.5
100.0	100.0	100.0	100.0	100.0	100.0	Total Liabilities & Net Worth	100.0	100.0
						INCOME DATA		
100.0	100.0	100.0	100.0	100.0	100.0	Net Sales	100.0	100.0
						Gross Profit		
94.3	90.4	88.9	91.9	94.6	90.2	Operating Expenses	90.2	90.4
5.7	9.6	11.1	8.1	5.4	9.8	Operating Profit	9.8	9.6
1.5	3.6	6.8	5.0	2.6	7.0	All Other Expenses (net)	4.9	5.2
4.2	5.9	4.3	3.1	2.8	2.7	Profit Before Taxes	4.8	4.5
						RATIOS		
2.5	2.4	2.2	2.3	1.5	1.9		2.0	2.4
.7	.7	.9	1.0	.5	.6	Current	.9	.9
.2	.2	.3	.4	.2	.3		.3	.3
1.9	1.9	1.8	1.8	1.0	1.4		1.7	1.8
(130) .5	(138) .4	.7	.9	.3	.5	Quick	(447) .7	(444) .7
.1	.2	.2	.3	.1	.1		.2	.2
0 UND	0 UND	0 UND	1 347.7	1 351.8	2 224.2		0 UND	0 UND
0 UND	0 UND	5 70.4	7 50.5	5 78.9	9 41.0	Sales/Receivables	3 131.4	2 196.9
0 UND	8 46.1	18 20.6	14 26.6	13 28.2	28 13.1		17 21.6	16 23.1
						Cost of Sales/Inventory		
						Cost of Sales/Payables		
21.9	13.9	8.1	6.1	12.7	8.1		12.6	11.3
-69.4	-30.9	-97.2	332.9	-9.2	-13.6	Sales/Working Capital	-80.3	-94.3
-7.7	-6.0	-7.3	-11.3	-4.7	-5.5		-8.5	-8.7
8.0	8.4	4.0	4.7	2.8	4.0		6.2	5.9
(83) 2.4	(118) 2.4	(128) 1.8	(99) 2.1	(20) 1.6	(12) 1.9	EBIT/Interest	(361) 2.1	(366) 1.6
.2	.5	.2	.0	.4	-1.8		.7	.4
		6.0	4.8				10.3	5.5
	(15) 2.8	(23) 2.3				Net Profit + Depr., Dep., Amort./Cur. Mat. L/T/D	(35) 3.0	(37) 2.7
		1.3	1.0				1.1	1.1
.7	1.6	1.3	1.1	1.1	1.7		1.2	1.2
4.6	8.7	2.5	2.5	3.5	28.1	Fixed/Worth	2.6	2.8
-1.0	-2.9	37.5	8.2	NM	-3.3		UND	-19.1
1.0	1.1	.7	.7	.5	2.9		.8	.7
15.9	10.0	2.2	1.9	3.2	31.4	Debt/Worth	2.5	2.7
-2.3	-5.0	65.9	9.8	NM	-5.1		-112.2	-21.9
88.2	98.0	36.8	18.1	21.6			42.5	48.9
(70) 38.0	(86) 33.1	(122) 7.7	(88) 6.1	(19) 4.8		% Profit Before Taxes/Tangible Net Worth	(331) 11.4	(323) 12.2
6.2	2.0	-1.8	-1.6	-1.8			.0	-1.2
37.1	24.3	8.1	7.3	5.1	4.4		11.9	13.8
9.8	4.7	2.1	3.0	2.1	2.8	% Profit Before Taxes/Total Assets	3.0	2.7
-2.3	-2.2	-1.9	-1.8	-2.2	-3.6		-1.1	-1.9
25.0	4.2	1.7	1.5	2.8	2.0		5.2	4.6
7.5	2.1	.8	.8	.8	1.1	Sales/Net Fixed Assets	1.3	1.5
3.3	.9	.5	.5	.7	.6		.6	.7
6.8	2.4	1.0	.8	1.2	1.1		2.1	2.2
3.9	1.4	.6	.6	.6	.7	Sales/Total Assets	.9	.9
2.1	.8	.4	.4	.5	.5		.5	.6
1.8	4.4	5.4	6.0	5.9			4.3	4.0
(85) 3.4	(118) 6.8	(141) 7.8	(105) 8.3	(23) 7.5		% Depr., Dep., Amort./Sales	(381) 7.1	(372) 6.7
8.0	11.9	12.6	11.8	10.2			10.9	10.0
4.1	3.5	3.2	1.7				3.4	3.2
(55) 8.3	(48) 6.3	(29) 4.8	(14) 4.3			% Officers', Directors' Owners' Comp/Sales	(105) 6.7	(115) 5.5
13.9	12.9	7.3	7.6				11.1	10.8
104520M	233277M	702216M	1727175M	1847797M	2240867M	Net Sales ($)	4736480M	4371789M
29018M	147907M	804886M	2116581M	1715113M	2014321M	Total Assets ($)	5047789M	5993886M

M = $ thousand   MM = $ million
See Pages 9 through 22 for Explanation of Ratios and Data

Comparative Historical Data | | Current Data Sorted by Sales

			Type of Statement						
75	75	92	Unqualified	5	12	10	17	25	23
39	49	55	Reviewed	2	14	10	12	15	2
63	65	55	Compiled	15	23	5	9	1	2
136	136	142	Tax Returns	74	55	8	3	1	1
193	193	229	Other	60	77	31	17	19	25
4/1/08-3/31/09	4/1/09-3/31/10	4/1/10-3/31/11			83 (4/1-9/30/10)			490 (10/1/10-3/31/11)	
ALL	ALL	ALL		0-1MM	1-3MM	3-5MM	5-10MM	10-25MM	25MM & OVER
506	518	573	**NUMBER OF STATEMENTS**	156	181	64	58	61	53
%	%	%	**ASSETS**	%	%	%	%	%	%
9.5	11.0	12.4	Cash & Equivalents	15.0	13.0	9.0	8.7	14.4	8.0
4.2	3.2	3.0	Trade Receivables (net)	2.6	3.0	3.3	2.4	2.1	5.9
1.3	1.8	2.1	Inventory	3.3	2.3	1.0	.8	1.0	2.0
3.2	3.1	2.5	All Other Current	1.7	2.5	3.4	2.9	2.2	4.0
18.3	19.0	20.0	Total Current	22.6	20.8	16.6	14.9	19.7	19.9
67.6	66.8	68.1	Fixed Assets (net)	65.4	69.1	72.8	73.6	68.3	60.5
6.0	5.8	4.5	Intangibles (net)	4.8	3.4	3.1	2.6	4.6	11.3
8.2	8.4	7.4	All Other Non-Current	7.3	6.8	7.5	9.0	7.4	8.4
100.0	100.0	100.0	Total	100.0	100.0	100.0	100.0	100.0	100.0
			LIABILITIES						
6.3	6.6	6.3	Notes Payable-Short Term	15.4	3.0	3.8	1.2	2.5	4.0
5.4	5.3	5.8	Cur. Mat.-L.T.D.	7.2	6.2	3.7	3.9	4.9	6.3
4.8	4.1	5.0	Trade Payables	7.1	5.3	2.5	1.9	4.5	4.2
.1	.1	.2	Income Taxes Payable	.0	.1	.1	.0	.2	1.3
13.4	10.0	11.6	All Other Current	10.5	11.6	13.8	8.9	9.2	17.5
30.0	26.2	28.9	Total Current	40.3	26.2	23.9	15.8	21.2	33.3
42.2	42.4	46.2	Long-Term Debt	56.0	46.1	42.7	48.9	34.0	33.2
.1	.1	.1	Deferred Taxes	.0	.1	.0	.0	.0	.6
11.2	11.4	11.6	All Other Non-Current	14.3	11.7	10.1	7.2	7.9	14.5
16.5	20.0	13.2	Net Worth	-10.6	16.0	23.3	28.1	36.9	18.4
100.0	100.0	100.0	Total Liabilities & Net Worth	100.0	100.0	100.0	100.0	100.0	100.0
			INCOME DATA						
100.0	100.0	100.0	Net Sales	100.0	100.0	100.0	100.0	100.0	100.0
			Gross Profit						
92.9	91.5	91.4	Operating Expenses	91.2	91.5	90.7	91.1	90.3	93.7
7.1	8.5	8.6	Operating Profit	8.8	8.5	9.3	8.9	9.7	6.3
5.1	4.3	4.3	All Other Expenses (net)	5.1	4.1	4.8	5.2	2.9	2.7
1.9	4.2	4.3	Profit Before Taxes	3.8	4.4	4.5	3.7	6.8	3.6
			RATIOS						
2.0	2.0	2.2		2.5	2.4	2.2	2.5	2.3	1.3
.8	.8	.8	Current	.6	.9	.9	1.0	1.0	.6
.3	.3	.3		.2	.3	.3	.4	.4	.2
1.3	1.6	1.8		1.9	2.0	1.7	1.6	2.0	1.0
.6 (515)	.6 (571)	.6	Quick	(154) .4	.6	.7	.9	.8	.4
.2	.2	.2		.1	.2	.2	.3	.3	.2
0 UND	0 UND	0 UND		0 UND	0 UND	1 367.9	1 287.2	0 UND	2 221.4
3 140.8	1 271.3	1 277.0	Sales/Receivables	0 UND	1 557.0	6 57.1	9 41.6	4 102.4	8 44.7
17 21.3	16 23.2	12 30.1		0 UND	13 28.8	18 20.2	16 22.2	12 30.2	19 19.3
			Cost of Sales/Inventory						
			Cost of Sales/Payables						
16.6	13.1	11.7		17.1	10.0	10.6	8.1	6.9	21.6
-36.5	-55.4	-59.8	Sales/Working Capital	-27.3	-103.7	-171.8	NM	262.8	-13.6
-6.8	-6.8	-7.0		-5.9	-8.4	-7.6	-10.6	-11.2	-5.5
4.3	4.9	5.1		3.7	6.7	7.7	4.1	5.5	4.9
(418) 1.4	(431) 1.8	(460) 2.0	EBIT/Interest	(105) 1.4	(148) 2.2	(55) 1.6	(53) 1.9	3.0	(48) 2.2
-.4	.3	.3		.4	-.1	.2	.5	1.0	.3
3.8	4.9	5.3			10.3			2.7	4.9
(46) 1.7	(39) 2.6	(53) 2.5	Net Profit + Depr., Dep., Amort./Cur. Mat. L/T/D	(11) 4.3		(10) 2.1	(16) 2.5		
.4	.8	1.5			2.4			1.1	1.3
1.3	1.2	1.2		1.2	1.1	1.2	1.4	1.0	1.1
3.1	3.1	3.3	Fixed/Worth	11.7	2.8	2.5	2.2	2.4	5.7
-14.9	-24.6	-7.2		-1.7	-8.6	14.9	NM	5.9	-4.0
.9	.8	.8		1.2	.7	.7	1.0	.6	.7
3.3	3.0	3.2	Debt/Worth	23.0	2.8	2.7	2.2	1.8	5.8
-17.3	-24.7	-10.4		-2.9	-10.5	21.6	NM	6.0	-7.9
52.4	56.6	61.5		57.5	81.5	40.2	24.6	47.3	56.1
(360) 7.9	(372) 14.0	(392) 12.0	% Profit Before Taxes/Tangible Net Worth	(87) 17.0	(127) 18.1	(50) 10.2	(44) 5.5	(51) 13.9	(33) 5.2
-5.3	-1.3	.0		.2	-1.0	-4.4	.3	4.8	-1.4
10.2	12.2	13.7		18.8	14.9	10.3	7.7	10.2	9.1
1.4	2.8	3.3	% Profit Before Taxes/Total Assets	3.0	3.3	2.7	2.2	5.5	3.3
-4.0	-2.7	-1.9		-2.2	-3.3	-2.3	-.3	1.2	-2.5
4.9	4.7	4.4		9.0	4.7	3.1	1.3	3.6	5.2
1.4	1.4	1.5	Sales/Net Fixed Assets	2.5	1.7	1.0	.8	1.0	1.9
.6	.7	.7		.7	.7	.6	.6	.7	.8
2.1	2.1	2.5		4.0	2.7	1.7	.9	1.9	1.9
.9	1.0	1.0	Sales/Total Assets	1.5	1.2	.8	.6	.8	1.0
.5	.5	.5		.6	.6	.5	.5	.5	.6
4.5	4.8	4.5		3.3	4.0	4.6	6.0	5.2	5.2
(416) 7.1	(436) 7.6	(480) 7.2	% Depr., Dep., Amort./Sales	(108) 7.9	(152) 7.4	(60) 7.0	(55) 7.2	(59) 6.8	(46) 6.8
11.0	11.4	11.1		14.4	12.9	11.0	9.5	8.6	9.6
3.2	3.3	3.6		5.8	3.1	1.2	3.4		
(131) 6.3	(138) 6.3	(149) 6.2	% Officers', Directors' Owners' Comp/Sales	(59) 8.5	(52) 5.0	(13) 3.8	(13) 3.9		
13.2	12.2	12.9		15.6	12.3	13.8	5.0		
5113917M	4890502M	6855852M	Net Sales ($)	83961M	324143M	254836M	406544M	930415M	4855953M
5563009M	5961467M	6827826M	Total Assets ($)	135634M	446577M	374644M	749336M	1200769M	3920866M

M = $ thousand   MM = $ million
See Pages 9 through 22 for Explanation of Ratios and Data

Current Data Sorted by Assets | Comparative Historical Data

0-500M	500M-2MM	2-10MM	10-50MM	50-100MM	100-250MM	Type of Statement	4/1/06-3/31/07 ALL	4/1/07-3/31/08 ALL
	2	7	1			Unqualified	4	5
1	5	10	2			Reviewed	12	13
18	24	5				Compiled	33	39
20	30	11		2		Tax Returns	61	56
18	20		2			Other	22	38
	37 (4/1-9/30/10)		141 (10/1/10-3/31/11)					
57	81	33	5	2		**NUMBER OF STATEMENTS**	132	151
%	%	%	%	%	%	**ASSETS**	%	%
22.3	9.3	5.0				Cash & Equivalents	13.1	15.1
3.2	.9	1.2				Trade Receivables (net)	.6	1.3
5.5	2.6	2.5				Inventory	4.1	3.9
4.8	2.7	2.7				All Other Current	2.2	3.1
35.7	15.5	11.4				Total Current	20.0	23.5
51.8	70.6	73.2				Fixed Assets (net)	62.9	62.8
2.6	7.8	4.5				Intangibles (net)	5.0	4.9
9.9	6.1	10.9				All Other Non-Current	12.1	8.8
100.0	100.0	100.0				Total	100.0	100.0
						LIABILITIES		
15.0	5.3	8.8				Notes Payable-Short Term	7.7	4.9
5.1	8.6	3.8				Cur. Mat.-L.T.D.	5.7	7.3
8.7	4.5	2.8				Trade Payables	5.0	4.8
.0	.1	.1				Income Taxes Payable	.1	.0
17.6	14.6	7.2				All Other Current	13.9	18.9
46.4	33.1	22.8				Total Current	32.4	35.9
52.1	59.9	67.3				Long-Term Debt	57.9	60.0
.0	.1	.2				Deferred Taxes	.2	.2
45.2	16.3	1.9				All Other Non-Current	14.7	19.2
-43.7	-9.5	7.9				Net Worth	-5.2	-15.2
100.0	100.0	100.0				Total Liabilities & Net Worth	100.0	100.0
						INCOME DATA		
100.0	100.0	100.0				Net Sales	100.0	100.0
						Gross Profit		
99.3	93.7	86.0				Operating Expenses	92.6	91.3
.7	6.3	14.0				Operating Profit	7.4	8.7
1.4	5.1	10.3				All Other Expenses (net)	4.0	5.7
-.8	1.2	3.7				Profit Before Taxes	3.4	2.9
						RATIOS		
2.8	1.4	1.2				Current	1.7	1.7
.9	.7	.5					.8	.8
.3	.2	.2					.3	.3
1.8	.8	.7				Quick	1.2	1.1
(56) .6	.3	.4					(131) .5	(150) .5
.1	.1	.2					.1	.1
0 UND	0 UND	0 UND				Sales/Receivables	0 UND	0 UND
0 UND	0 UND	0 999.8					0 UND	0 UND
1 710.5	1 637.7	2 189.0					1 422.8	2 229.3
						Cost of Sales/Inventory		
						Cost of Sales/Payables		
16.0	26.7	41.0				Sales/Working Capital	20.0	22.8
-271.5	-29.2	-15.2					-49.0	-36.7
-12.8	-5.1	-6.4					-9.4	-8.8
3.0	3.5	1.9				EBIT/Interest	3.7	3.1
(34) .4	(71) 1.3	(29) .8					(118) 1.6	(120) 1.2
-2.3	.1	.3					.8	.3
						Net Profit + Depr., Dep., Amort./Cur. Mat. L/T/D	2.3	2.0
							(15) 1.8	(12) 1.3
							.9	.5
.5	2.7	3.3				Fixed/Worth	2.2	2.5
24.2	-15.0	24.0					55.6	-148.3
-.5	-1.6	-9.7					-1.9	-1.7
.7	3.2	4.5				Debt/Worth	2.7	2.5
59.4	-19.9	25.7					87.1	-64.0
-1.7	-2.9	-11.8					-3.7	-3.5
48.5	41.2	73.9				% Profit Before Taxes/Tangible Net Worth	78.1	58.2
(29) 11.9	(39) 15.4	(23) 6.2					(68) 22.6	(73) 20.7
-4.8	-12.9	-11.8					4.6	.9
18.1	9.4	6.0				% Profit Before Taxes/Total Assets	10.8	12.7
-1.6	1.4	-.5					3.3	1.8
-14.1	-4.6	-3.3					-1.2	-4.3
25.9	2.8	1.3				Sales/Net Fixed Assets	5.9	6.9
6.6	1.5	.7					1.9	1.9
3.3	1.0	.5					1.3	1.0
6.3	1.7	.8				Sales/Total Assets	2.8	3.2
3.4	1.1	.5					1.3	1.1
2.2	.8	.4					.9	.8
1.5	3.9	5.0				% Depr., Dep., Amort./Sales	3.2	2.9
(45) 3.1	(78) 6.5	(32) 9.0					(125) 6.6	(136) 5.8
5.1	9.9	15.3					9.6	9.4
4.1	3.2					% Officers', Directors' Owners' Comp/Sales	3.5	2.9
(27) 6.6	(30) 9.7						(74) 6.0	(66) 5.6
11.4	13.4						12.4	11.2
48183M	119108M	92578M	72429M	131714M		Net Sales ($)	262276M	1324514M
13399M	90588M	145101M	91978M	111423M		Total Assets ($)	219660M	604673M

Columns 10-50MM, 50-100MM, 100-250MM: DATA NOT AVAILABLE.

M = $ thousand   MM = $ million
See Pages 9 through 22 for Explanation of Ratios and Data

Comparative Historical Data | Current Data Sorted by Sales

Hist 4/1/08-3/31/09 ALL	Hist 4/1/09-3/31/10 ALL	Hist 4/1/10-3/31/11 ALL	Type of Statement	0-1MM	1-3MM	3-5MM	5-10MM	10-25MM	25MM & OVER
6	3	3	Unqualified	1	1			1	
11	15	15	Reviewed	2	5	5	2	1	
44	49	52	Compiled	26	22	3	1		
60	75	55	Tax Returns	32	19	3	1		
24	37	53	Other	20	22	4	3	1	3
				37 (4/1-9/30/10)			141 (10/1/10-3/31/11)		
145	179	178	NUMBER OF STATEMENTS	81	69	15	7	3	3
%	%	%	ASSETS	%	%	%	%	%	%
13.6	12.2	12.5	Cash & Equivalents	14.7	11.4	10.1			
.6	.6	1.7	Trade Receivables (net)	1.9	1.5	.1			
3.8	4.6	3.5	Inventory	3.5	3.0	3.3			
2.4	2.6	3.6	All Other Current	4.5	2.8	1.7			
20.3	20.0	21.2	Total Current	24.6	18.7	15.2			
65.9	66.4	65.2	Fixed Assets (net)	62.8	66.9	72.7			
3.8	4.1	5.4	Intangibles (net)	4.3	6.6	3.5			
10.0	9.5	8.2	All Other Non-Current	8.3	7.7	8.6			
100.0	100.0	100.0	Total	100.0	100.0	100.0			
			LIABILITIES						
8.5	4.9	9.2	Notes Payable-Short Term	8.5	7.2	9.5			
5.1	5.7	6.4	Cur. Mat.-L.T.D.	5.7	7.3	7.6			
3.8	5.0	5.5	Trade Payables	4.5	6.4	5.9			
.0	.0	.1	Income Taxes Payable	.0	.2	.1			
11.5	17.4	14.0	All Other Current	15.3	13.1	15.7			
28.9	33.0	35.2	Total Current	34.0	34.2	38.8			
59.2	59.7	58.4	Long-Term Debt	66.4	50.5	62.5			
.2	.1	.1	Deferred Taxes	.0	.2	.4			
15.9	17.1	23.2	All Other Non-Current	27.3	21.8	15.2			
-4.2	-9.9	-16.8	Net Worth	-27.7	-6.6	-16.9			
100.0	100.0	100.0	Total Liabilities & Net Worth	100.0	100.0	100.0			
			INCOME DATA						
100.0	100.0	100.0	Net Sales	100.0	100.0	100.0			
			Gross Profit						
92.8	96.3	94.4	Operating Expenses	93.1	94.2	96.6			
7.2	3.7	5.6	Operating Profit	6.9	5.8	3.4			
5.7	3.9	4.9	All Other Expenses (net)	6.5	2.9	5.9			
1.5	-.3	.8	Profit Before Taxes	.4	2.9	-2.6			
			RATIOS						
1.9	1.3	1.5		2.0	1.6	1.0			
.7	.7	.7	Current	.9	.7	.5			
.3	.3	.3		.3	.3	.1			
1.1	.9	1.0		1.5	1.0	.5			
.4 (178)	.4 (177)	.4	Quick	(80) .4	.4	.3			
.2	.1	.1		.1	.1	.1			
0 UND	0 UND	0 UND		0 UND	0 UND	0 UND			
0 UND	0 UND	0 UND	Sales/Receivables	0 UND	0 UND	0 UND			
0 999.8	1 435.2	1 443.2		0 UND	1 273.4	0 UND			
			Cost of Sales/Inventory						
			Cost of Sales/Payables						
19.4	34.5	24.8		15.8	25.6	-232.2			
-34.5	-28.8	-33.5	Sales/Working Capital	-153.0	-29.2	-15.4			
-7.4	-7.5	-6.8		-7.7	-6.9	-6.1			
2.1	2.1	2.7		1.7	4.4	1.7			
(119) 1.1	(150) 1.0	(141) .9	EBIT/Interest	(54) .7	(59) 1.9	.7			
.1	-.1	-.1		-1.0	.6	-.3			
3.0	3.1	2.5	Net Profit + Depr., Dep.,						
(12) 1.2	(13) 1.1	(16) 1.4	Amort./Cur. Mat. L/T/D						
.7	.1	.3							
1.7	1.9	2.0		1.3	2.0	3.8			
14.2	22.1	32.7	Fixed/Worth	UND	25.3	45.1			
-1.9	-2.0	-1.5		-.8	-1.9	-1.5			
1.9	2.1	2.1		1.9	2.1	3.5			
51.8	32.0	39.0	Debt/Worth	-149.5	27.2	48.6			
-4.1	-3.5	-2.9		-1.9	-3.3	-3.1			
37.2	31.5	47.6	% Profit Before Taxes/Tangible	39.2	71.4				
(75) 14.2	(93) 6.0	(94) 13.6	Net Worth	(40) 6.4	(38) 22.0				
-6.2	-13.1	-11.9		-11.4	5.1				
7.8	6.0	8.9	% Profit Before Taxes/Total	9.1	12.2	5.6			
1.3	.0	.5	Assets	-1.0	4.3	-1.4			
-4.0	-6.4	-7.2		-9.8	-2.6	-7.5			
5.0	5.8	5.6		7.0	4.5	4.8			
1.8	1.9	1.9	Sales/Net Fixed Assets	2.1	1.8	1.4			
1.0	1.0	1.0		.9	1.1	.7			
2.4	2.6	2.5		2.7	2.1	3.5			
1.2	1.2	1.2	Sales/Total Assets	1.3	1.2	1.2			
.7	.8	.8		.7	.8	.6			
4.4	3.5	3.1		2.6	3.1	4.4			
(134) 7.0	(170) 6.4	(161) 5.8	% Depr., Dep., Amort./Sales	(70) 6.0	(65) 5.5	(14) 5.9			
10.5	10.2	9.6		11.0	8.7	9.1			
4.0	2.7	3.2	% Officers', Directors'	6.6	3.0				
(65) 7.7	(78) 6.3	(65) 7.0	Owners' Comp/Sales	(33) 11.2	(22) 4.8				
11.5	9.8	12.7		13.5	8.0				
398267M	576261M	464012M	Net Sales ($)	46625M	116667M	57814M	46670M	38828M	157408M
446536M	610333M	452489M	Total Assets ($)	51233M	119093M	55776M	37632M	45112M	143643M

© RMA 2011

M = $ thousand   MM = $ million

See Pages 9 through 22 for Explanation of Ratios and Data

Current Data Sorted by Assets   Comparative Historical Data

Type of Statement	0-500M	500M-2MM	2-10MM	10-50MM	50-100MM	100-250MM	4/1/06-3/31/07 ALL	4/1/07-3/31/08 ALL
Unqualified	2	3	15	25	4	9	60	58
Reviewed	1		18	3			29	24
Compiled	13	19	15	1			42	44
Tax Returns	48	27	13	1	7	1	81	70
Other	28	34	36	19	7	4	125	127
		69 (4/1-9/30/10)		277 (10/1/10-3/31/11)				
NUMBER OF STATEMENTS	92	83	97	49	11	14	337	323
ASSETS	%	%	%	%	%	%	%	%
Cash & Equivalents	25.1	14.5	11.7	10.7	6.8	19.1	16.6	16.3
Trade Receivables (net)	3.6	5.7	6.4	5.5	2.0	5.4	6.1	4.2
Inventory	10.4	6.0	4.6	4.6	2.1	1.3	6.0	4.6
All Other Current	6.8	2.9	3.0	2.5	2.7	2.6	4.5	4.3
Total Current	45.8	29.2	25.8	23.2	13.5	28.5	33.2	29.5
Fixed Assets (net)	41.2	59.7	62.3	54.4	72.6	52.7	54.5	54.7
Intangibles (net)	4.1	4.4	4.5	8.1	6.5	8.9	4.5	5.7
All Other Non-Current	8.9	6.7	7.4	14.3	7.4	9.8	7.8	10.1
Total	100.0	100.0	100.0	100.0	100.0	100.0	100.0	100.0
LIABILITIES								
Notes Payable-Short Term	23.8	5.1	4.4	3.6	3.8	.2	8.0	6.6
Cur. Mat.-L.T.D.	3.8	2.9	3.5	4.5	1.8	2.6	5.9	4.4
Trade Payables	11.5	5.3	4.3	4.8	2.2	4.6	9.0	6.7
Income Taxes Payable	.1	.1	.1	.0	.0	.0	.1	.1
All Other Current	31.0	10.2	7.9	11.1	3.3	13.0	15.5	16.9
Total Current	70.2	23.5	20.2	24.0	11.1	20.4	38.5	34.8
Long-Term Debt	17.9	45.0	29.6	22.8	12.9	21.1	37.1	32.1
Deferred Taxes	.3	.2	.2	.6	.9	1.5	.2	.2
All Other Non-Current	24.7	18.3	8.5	8.1	5.4	10.5	9.2	9.4
Net Worth	-13.0	13.1	41.4	44.5	69.7	46.5	15.1	23.4
Total Liabilities & Net Worth	100.0	100.0	100.0	100.0	100.0	100.0	100.0	100.0
INCOME DATA								
Net Sales	100.0	100.0	100.0	100.0	100.0	100.0	100.0	100.0
Gross Profit								
Operating Expenses	96.1	88.3	90.6	91.0	95.7	87.0	90.2	89.9
Operating Profit	3.9	11.7	9.4	9.0	4.3	13.0	9.8	10.1
All Other Expenses (net)	.4	6.0	4.2	4.3	5.2	4.7	4.0	4.2
Profit Before Taxes	3.5	5.8	5.1	4.7	-.9	8.3	5.8	5.9
RATIOS								
Current	3.2	2.7	2.9	2.0	3.5	3.0	2.4	2.3
	1.3	1.1	1.4	1.1	1.0	1.3	1.1	1.0
	.3	.3	.6	.5	.4	.8	.4	.5
Quick	2.7	2.2	2.7	1.3	3.2	2.3	1.7	1.8
	(91) .4	(82) .6	1.0	(48) .7	.5	1.2	(336) .6	.7
	.1	.1	.3	.3	.2	.6	.2	.2
Sales/Receivables	0 UND	0 UND	0 999.8	2 165.5	2 147.3	1 311.3	0 UND	0 UND
	0 UND	0 999.8	9 42.3	9 41.6	6 62.1	6 61.3	1 303.8	0 832.8
	0 UND	5 75.7	21 17.4	43 8.4	20 18.5	41 8.9	13 27.4	8 48.5
Cost of Sales/Inventory								
Cost of Sales/Payables								
Sales/Working Capital	15.6	9.3	5.5	7.3	5.0	4.7	7.8	10.3
	138.5	227.8	20.3	106.6	182.8	30.0	84.4	-999.8
	-10.6	-6.5	-11.0	-9.8	-5.9	-97.9	-9.9	-11.1
EBIT/Interest	11.6	13.2	5.4	6.4	11.8	16.7	6.2	8.9
	(46) 1.9	(60) 1.7	(80) 1.8	(40) 1.5	(10) 2.6	(10) 10.2	(256) 2.4	(233) 2.5
	-.2	.2	.2	-1.8	-2.8	.3	.3	.6
Net Profit + Depr., Dep., Amort./Cur. Mat. L/T/D			15.9				4.8	15.1
			(13) 4.5				(19) 2.6	(22) 2.8
			1.3				1.3	1.2
Fixed/Worth	.3	.7	.8	.7	.9	.6	.8	.8
	1.6	2.3	1.4	1.5	1.3	1.4	2.0	1.9
	-2.2	-4.0	4.4	4.8	1.8	NM	-122.0	-25.2
Debt/Worth	.4	.3	.3	.4	.1	.5	.7	.5
	4.0	4.4	1.2	1.1	.5	1.2	2.7	2.3
	-3.7	-6.4	9.5	5.1	1.0	NM	-24.7	-26.4
% Profit Before Taxes/Tangible Net Worth	119.2	57.8	34.4	29.8	8.4	56.6	52.4	62.0
	(63) 22.0	(52) 19.3	(78) 6.0	(41) 7.2	(10) 1.2	(11) 25.8	(245) 18.6	(238) 15.8
	-7.0	2.0	-1.3	-4.8	-3.4	.3	2.0	.7
% Profit Before Taxes/Total Assets	36.1	20.1	10.3	10.5	7.4	17.7	18.2	19.5
	7.2	3.2	2.4	3.4	.7	5.4	5.1	5.4
	-5.8	-4.2	-2.0	-3.1	-2.4	-2.4	-2.1	-1.2
Sales/Net Fixed Assets	56.3	10.8	4.6	5.3	.8	2.1	13.7	9.9
	13.8	1.9	1.2	1.3	.5	1.6	2.6	2.6
	5.1	.6	.6	.5	.3	.9	1.0	1.0
Sales/Total Assets	6.8	2.7	1.5	1.4	.6	1.1	3.0	2.9
	4.7	1.1	.8	.7	.4	.9	1.5	1.3
	2.7	.6	.5	.4	.3	.4	.7	.7
% Depr., Dep., Amort./Sales	1.2	1.7	4.0	3.6	7.3		2.4	2.5
	(59) 2.6	(64) 6.4	(82) 7.0	(42) 7.9	10.8		(261) 5.5	(258) 5.8
	5.5	13.6	11.5	11.3	15.0		9.9	9.4
% Officers', Directors' Owners' Comp/Sales	4.0	3.4	2.1				2.8	1.9
	(49) 7.4	(32) 7.3	(21) 4.7				(79) 6.4	(85) 4.9
	11.4	14.4	6.3				12.0	9.9
Net Sales ($)	110900M	176189M	528349M	1199673M	337953M	2656607M	6801969M	7839425M
Total Assets ($)	21255M	92737M	409901M	1247975M	712928M	2298485M	5043077M	5157534M

M = $ thousand   MM = $ million
See Pages 9 through 22 for Explanation of Ratios and Data

Comparative Historical Data

Current Data Sorted by Sales

			Type of Statement						
59	48	55	Unqualified	1	6	7	9	13	19
21	22	25	Reviewed	3	6	3	5	5	3
44	37	48	Compiled	19	17	5	4	3	
71	96	90	Tax Returns	47	34	5	1	2	1
105	125	128	Other	31	43	12	8	13	21
4/1/08-3/31/09 ALL	4/1/09-3/31/10 ALL	4/1/10-3/31/11 ALL		69 (4/1-9/30/10)			277 (10/1/10-3/31/11)		
				0-1MM	1-3MM	3-5MM	5-10MM	10-25MM	25MM & OVER
300	328	346	NUMBER OF STATEMENTS	101	106	32	27	36	44
%	%	%	ASSETS	%	%	%	%	%	%
16.4	15.0	15.9	Cash & Equivalents	15.2	17.7	19.0	16.2	14.1	12.7
4.8	4.2	5.2	Trade Receivables (net)	3.1	3.5	4.6	14.7	7.6	6.7
3.8	5.4	6.3	Inventory	6.4	5.1	8.1	5.3	7.6	7.0
3.0	4.6	3.9	All Other Current	3.6	5.6	3.4	2.0	2.7	3.0
28.0	29.1	31.3	Total Current	28.3	31.8	35.1	38.1	31.9	29.4
56.4	55.3	54.9	Fixed Assets (net)	62.8	54.9	52.8	47.2	50.1	46.6
6.2	7.3	5.2	Intangibles (net)	3.9	4.7	2.5	4.4	4.1	12.4
9.4	8.3	8.7	All Other Non-Current	5.0	8.6	9.6	10.2	13.9	11.5
100.0	100.0	100.0	Total	100.0	100.0	100.0	100.0	100.0	100.0
			LIABILITIES						
13.4	10.6	9.4	Notes Payable-Short Term	17.4	7.9	5.7	4.4	7.1	2.3
4.4	3.6	3.5	Cur. Mat.-L.T.D.	3.9	3.2	4.5	4.9	1.9	2.8
5.1	6.5	6.5	Trade Payables	7.1	5.9	3.3	8.1	6.4	7.8
.3	.5	.1	Income Taxes Payable	.1	.0	.0	.1	.0	.1
12.3	17.3	15.1	All Other Current	16.6	19.2	8.3	10.0	9.0	14.8
35.5	38.4	34.5	Total Current	45.2	36.2	21.8	27.6	24.5	27.8
34.5	34.0	28.3	Long-Term Debt	43.1	27.0	21.8	14.0	18.5	19.2
.2	.2	.4	Deferred Taxes	.3	.2	.0	.4	.3	1.2
7.2	13.2	15.1	All Other Non-Current	21.6	14.8	18.4	8.6	5.1	10.7
22.6	14.2	21.7	Net Worth	-10.2	21.8	38.0	49.5	51.6	41.1
100.0	100.0	100.0	Total Liabilities & Net Worth	100.0	100.0	100.0	100.0	100.0	100.0
			INCOME DATA						
100.0	100.0	100.0	Net Sales	100.0	100.0	100.0	100.0	100.0	100.0
			Gross Profit						
91.1	92.4	91.6	Operating Expenses	90.3	91.7	93.6	94.0	93.3	89.8
8.9	7.6	8.4	Operating Profit	9.7	8.3	6.4	6.0	6.7	10.2
4.1	4.3	3.7	All Other Expenses (net)	6.0	2.6	3.0	1.7	2.6	3.6
4.8	3.3	4.7	Profit Before Taxes	3.6	5.7	3.5	4.3	4.1	6.7
			RATIOS						
3.0	2.6	2.8	Current	4.0	2.4	4.9	3.6	2.6	1.9
1.2	1.0	1.2		1.0	1.0	1.5	2.0	1.2	1.1
.5	.4	.4		.2	.4	.5	1.1	.7	.5
2.4	1.9	2.2	Quick	3.7	2.1	3.3	3.0	2.1	1.3
.8	.6 (343) .7			(100) .3	(105) .7	.9	1.4	(43) .8	.7
.3	.2	.2		.1	.2	.2	.9	.4	.3
0 UND	0 UND	0 UND	Sales/Receivables	0 UND	0 UND	0 999.8	2 178.8	1 358.1	2 205.5
1 591.3	1 607.4	2 234.4		0 UND	0 999.8	8 48.2	11 34.5	7 50.6	9 40.9
12 29.7	9 41.8	13 27.3		2 189.2	9 39.8	21 17.6	87 4.2	20 18.4	29 12.5
			Cost of Sales/Inventory						
			Cost of Sales/Payables						
6.5	8.3	7.8	Sales/Working Capital	11.8	9.8	4.2	3.7	7.9	9.9
59.5	722.7	67.2		333.0	309.3	13.7	11.6	80.3	201.3
-11.8	-7.6	-9.2		-5.2	-10.1	-17.6	51.3	-18.7	-10.2
8.5	7.0	8.4	EBIT/Interest	4.2	6.7	9.8	10.7	7.0	16.7
(228) 2.7	(253) 2.3	(246) 1.8		(61) 1.2	(73) 1.7	(25) 1.8	(18) 3.1	(31) 2.4	(38) 4.3
.5	.3	-.1		-.5	.2	.7	-11.4	-2.4	.8
4.5	4.1	5.7	Net Profit + Depr., Dep., Amort./Cur. Mat. L/T/D						6.9
(24) 3.0	(24) 2.9	(32) 2.6						(13) 2.6	
.8	1.0	1.5							1.8
.9	.8	.6	Fixed/Worth	.7	.8	.3	.5	.3	.8
1.7	1.9	1.5		3.1	1.8	1.0	.8	1.0	1.7
55.3	-6.5	UND		-4.9	-5.7	3.4	2.6	1.7	NM
.5	.5	.4	Debt/Worth	.3	.5	.3	.2	.4	.6
1.6	2.3	1.6		4.6	2.4	.9	.7	.7	1.5
UND	-7.8	-43.5		-6.2	-10.6	6.7	3.8	2.4	NM
43.1	36.6	47.6	% Profit Before Taxes/Tangible Net Worth	44.4	67.5	48.3	27.0	34.1	59.8
(227) 12.5	(226) 7.8	(255) 11.5		(67) 9.4	(73) 15.9	(26) 5.0	(23) 11.5	(33) 11.1	(33) 30.8
-.2	-2.9	-2.5		-7.5	-2.3	.6	-3.4	-.6	1.0
15.8	13.1	16.5	% Profit Before Taxes/Total Assets	15.2	20.7	22.7	18.1	15.9	17.2
4.2	2.9	3.4		1.3	5.6	2.4	5.0	2.9	5.6
-2.2	-3.8	-2.8		-5.8	-2.0	-1.8	-3.0	-1.4	-1.0
9.0	12.9	13.4	Sales/Net Fixed Assets	10.1	18.7	12.0	10.0	10.3	12.9
2.2	2.5	2.5		1.6	3.6	2.2	2.2	2.7	2.0
.8	.9	.8		.5	.9	.8	.8	.7	1.2
2.7	2.9	3.3	Sales/Total Assets	3.7	4.2	2.1	3.0	2.8	1.9
1.1	1.3	1.2		1.1	1.6	1.2	1.0	1.2	1.0
.5	.6	.6		.4	.7	.6	.6	.5	.7
3.1	2.1	2.4	% Depr., Dep., Amort./Sales	2.6	1.7	3.2	3.6	2.9	2.0
(234) 6.1	(262) 5.3	(266) 6.2		(74) 8.1	(79) 5.5	(24) 6.2	(24) 6.0	(29) 7.1	(36) 7.1
11.1	10.6	11.2		19.3	9.1	8.8	9.8	9.5	11.7
4.0	2.4	3.5	% Officers', Directors' Owners' Comp/Sales	5.0	3.8	2.2			
(74) 6.1	(94) 5.1	(104) 6.6		(38) 10.0	(38) 6.5	(11) 3.8			
13.2	9.5	11.3		15.2	8.7	8.4			
4029350M	4646323M	5009671M	Net Sales ($)	54256M	187975M	125959M	195540M	552809M	3893132M
4325135M	3951271M	4783281M	Total Assets ($)	79408M	196152M	184550M	279452M	682174M	3361545M

ACCOMMODATION AND
FOOD SERVICES

ACCOMMODATION AND
FOOD SERVICES

Current Data Sorted by Assets   Comparative Historical Data

						Type of Statement		
	7	30	43	19	8	Unqualified	140	139
3	9	46	39	3	2	Reviewed	95	94
28	67	151	27	2		Compiled	289	275
146	294	407	39	2	1	Tax Returns	798	930
45	126	372	135	19	21	Other	485	545
	115 (4/1-9/30/10)		1,976 (10/1/10-3/31/11)				4/1/06- 3/31/07	4/1/07- 3/31/08
0-500M	500M-2MM	2-10MM	10-50MM	50-100MM	100-250MM		ALL	ALL
222	503	1006	283	45	32	NUMBER OF STATEMENTS	1807	1983
%	%	%	%	%	%	ASSETS	%	%
27.7	7.8	5.6	5.8	5.7	8.4	Cash & Equivalents	8.8	9.5
6.3	1.8	1.4	2.0	1.8	3.5	Trade Receivables (net)	2.4	2.3
1.7	.5	.4	1.1	.7	1.7	Inventory	1.0	1.0
2.2	1.5	1.3	1.9	3.7	2.6	All Other Current	2.1	2.2
37.8	11.5	8.6	10.9	11.9	16.1	Total Current	14.2	15.0
43.0	78.0	81.7	77.6	71.8	76.5	Fixed Assets (net)	75.8	74.4
6.6	3.6	3.3	3.7	3.8	3.0	Intangibles (net)	3.4	3.4
12.6	6.8	6.4	7.8	12.4	4.4	All Other Non-Current	6.5	7.2
100.0	100.0	100.0	100.0	100.0	100.0	Total	100.0	100.0
						LIABILITIES		
9.5	2.0	1.4	2.9	3.5	2.7	Notes Payable-Short Term	2.9	2.5
2.2	4.5	3.2	3.7	3.6	8.8	Cur. Mat.-L.T.D.	3.0	3.8
9.1	1.9	1.3	1.8	2.1	3.5	Trade Payables	2.6	2.9
.3	.0	.0	.1	.1	.1	Income Taxes Payable	.1	.1
36.5	8.8	6.2	7.5	9.6	7.0	All Other Current	10.0	9.2
57.6	17.3	12.2	16.1	18.8	22.2	Total Current	18.5	18.4
28.5	71.1	74.1	60.4	52.7	51.2	Long-Term Debt	64.3	64.4
.0	.0	.0	.3	.4	.3	Deferred Taxes	.1	.1
19.2	5.7	4.8	6.7	4.2	3.5	All Other Non-Current	6.0	5.8
-5.3	5.9	8.8	16.5	23.9	22.8	Net Worth	11.1	11.3
100.0	100.0	100.0	100.0	100.0	100.0	Total Liabilties & Net Worth	100.0	100.0
						INCOME DATA		
100.0	100.0	100.0	100.0	100.0	100.0	Net Sales	100.0	100.0
						Gross Profit		
94.3	85.6	83.5	87.7	92.7	93.5	Operating Expenses	82.3	81.4
5.7	14.4	16.5	12.3	7.3	6.5	Operating Profit	17.7	18.6
2.7	10.4	13.6	11.6	10.0	7.2	All Other Expenses (net)	10.9	11.4
3.0	4.0	2.9	.8	-2.7	-.7	Profit Before Taxes	6.8	7.2
						RATIOS		
2.6	1.9	1.9	1.8	1.6	1.6		2.3	2.4
.9	.6	.8	.7	.7	.9	Current	.9	1.0
.2	.2	.2	.3	.2	.4		.3	.3
2.4	1.6	1.6	1.3	1.1	1.2		1.9	2.0
.7	(502) .5	(1002) .6	.5	.5	.7	Quick	(1805) .7	(1976) .7
.2	.2	.2	.2	.2	.3		.2	.2
0 UND	0 UND	0 UND	3 134.1	4 84.3	5 74.8		0 UND	0 UND
0 UND	0 UND	3 126.0	6 58.2	8 45.1	9 38.9	Sales/Receivables	3 116.8	3 125.7
4 90.4	5 74.9	8 48.5	12 29.3	16 22.9	29 12.5		9 41.5	9 40.1
						Cost of Sales/Inventory		
						Cost of Sales/Payables		
21.3	17.8	13.9	11.0	8.4	15.8		12.4	11.4
-103.0	-24.8	-33.3	-19.7	-17.1	-86.5	Sales/Working Capital	-135.2	-283.5
-9.7	-5.6	-6.2	-4.1	-3.1	-4.7		-7.6	-8.3
6.8	3.0	2.5	2.7	2.7	2.5		3.1	3.1
(95) 1.9	(365) 1.6	(730) 1.4	(206) 1.3	(34) 1.2	(30) .9	EBIT/Interest	(1375) 1.8	(1486) 1.8
.0	.7	.7	.5	.1	-.1		1.1	1.1
		5.9	3.0			Net Profit + Depr., Dep.,	5.2	6.7
		(25) 2.8	(34) 1.6			Amort./Cur. Mat. L/T/D	(78) 2.4	(81) 3.2
		1.0	.4				1.5	1.2
.4	2.4	3.6	2.2	1.8	1.7		2.5	2.4
2.3	14.3	11.7	6.6	3.4	3.5	Fixed/Worth	7.2	7.2
-1.6	-6.5	-8.8	-18.3	NM	15.2		-14.4	-12.9
.6	1.9	3.3	2.0	1.2	1.2		2.2	2.1
4.3	17.0	12.9	7.6	2.9	3.9	Debt/Worth	7.7	7.7
-2.9	-8.3	-10.9	-21.4	NM	17.5		-15.8	-15.2
120.0	47.0	31.7	24.1	11.7	11.7	% Profit Before Taxes/Tangible	60.6	62.0
(139) 29.2	(297) 13.0	(622) 10.4	(196) 3.3	(34) 3.5	(26) -.8	Net Worth	(1195) 21.2	(1315) 22.0
-3.1	-2.7	-5.5	-6.6	-12.2	-14.2		3.5	3.2
30.4	8.1	5.4	4.0	3.9	3.3	% Profit Before Taxes/Total	9.6	9.7
5.0	2.0	1.3	.3	-.5	-.7	Assets	3.6	3.5
-7.0	-2.1	-2.2	-3.0	-3.8	-3.8		-.4	-.5
57.6	1.3	.7	.8	.9	1.0		1.3	1.2
13.5	.6	.5	.4	.5	.6	Sales/Net Fixed Assets	.6	.6
4.0	.4	.3	.3	.3	.4		.4	.4
8.0	.9	.5	.6	.6	.7		.9	.8
4.1	.5	.4	.3	.5	.4	Sales/Total Assets	.5	.5
1.7	.3	.3	.2	.2	.3		.4	.4
1.1	5.6	8.2	8.1	8.1	7.1		5.8	5.7
(158) 2.9	(443) 9.0	(913) 11.8	(252) 12.3	(40) 11.9	(21) 11.0	% Depr., Dep., Amort./Sales	(1637) 8.8	(1764) 8.7
5.6	13.4	17.6	19.4	16.1	13.8		12.4	12.6
3.7	2.8	1.7	.9			% Officers', Directors'	2.4	2.2
(95) 5.8	(162) 4.3	(217) 3.9	(42) 2.9			Owners' Comp/Sales	(532) 4.3	(545) 4.2
9.4	7.5	7.4	6.2				7.5	7.8
217889M	521877M	2255780M	2917406M	1417381M	3679930M	Net Sales ($)	12252255M	12990211M
51414M	641876M	4807031M	5535033M	3095548M	4826904M	Total Assets ($)	16158284M	18862413M

© RMA 2011   M = $ thousand   MM = $ million

See Pages 9 through 22 for Explanation of Ratios and Data

Comparative Historical Data | Current Data Sorted by Sales

			Type of Statement						
135	115	107	Unqualified	3	11	20	23	17	33
110	124	102	Reviewed	9	36	16	18	15	8
268	316	275	Compiled	88	132	29	15	10	1
893	1009	889	Tax Returns	447	364	40	29	7	2
641	683	718	Other	185	302	85	69	39	38
4/1/08-3/31/09 ALL	4/1/09-3/31/10 ALL	4/1/10-3/31/11 ALL		0-1MM	1-3MM	3-5MM	5-10MM	10-25MM	25MM & OVER
					115 (4/1-9/30/10)			1,976 (10/1/10-3/31/11)	
2047	2247	2091	NUMBER OF STATEMENTS	732	845	190	154	88	82
%	%	%	ASSETS	%	%	%	%	%	%
8.7	8.4	8.5	Cash & Equivalents	8.5	8.2	9.7	9.1	8.9	7.9
2.4	2.5	2.1	Trade Receivables (net)	1.2	1.9	3.1	4.2	3.7	4.4
.9	.8	.7	Inventory	.4	.4	.9	2.0	1.8	2.0
2.0	1.8	1.6	All Other Current	1.3	1.3	1.5	2.3	4.6	2.9
14.1	13.5	12.9	Total Current	11.4	11.8	15.2	17.7	19.0	17.2
74.3	74.9	75.9	Fixed Assets (net)	77.8	77.5	72.2	71.4	65.5	70.4
3.8	3.5	3.8	Intangibles (net)	4.0	3.7	2.7	3.3	5.4	3.6
7.8	8.0	7.5	All Other Non-Current	6.8	7.0	9.9	7.6	10.1	8.8
100.0	100.0	100.0	Total	100.0	100.0	100.0	100.0	100.0	100.0
			LIABILITIES						
3.4	2.7	2.7	Notes Payable-Short Term	3.1	2.1	2.6	2.8	4.8	3.2
4.0	3.9	3.6	Cur. Mat.-L.T.D.	3.3	3.4	4.0	4.4	3.0	6.4
2.7	3.1	2.4	Trade Payables	2.0	2.1	2.8	3.1	3.8	4.7
.1	.1	.1	Income Taxes Payable	.0	.1	.0	.1	.1	.1
10.7	11.2	10.3	All Other Current	11.8	9.3	7.9	11.2	10.8	10.5
20.9	21.1	19.1	Total Current	20.2	17.0	17.4	21.7	22.5	25.0
65.4	66.5	65.9	Long-Term Debt	66.4	68.7	67.0	61.4	55.1	49.5
.0	.0	.1	Deferred Taxes	.0	.0	.1	.4	.2	.5
5.6	6.8	6.8	All Other Non-Current	7.3	6.2	6.4	8.1	7.8	5.1
8.0	5.7	8.2	Net Worth	6.0	8.1	9.2	8.6	14.3	19.9
100.0	100.0	100.0	Total Liabilities & Net Worth	100.0	100.0	100.0	100.0	100.0	100.0
			INCOME DATA						
100.0	100.0	100.0	Net Sales	100.0	100.0	100.0	100.0	100.0	100.0
			Gross Profit						
84.8	88.4	86.1	Operating Expenses	84.3	85.5	86.8	90.4	89.9	94.2
15.2	11.6	13.9	Operating Profit	15.7	14.5	13.2	9.6	10.1	5.8
11.0	12.4	11.2	All Other Expenses (net)	14.0	10.9	9.4	6.8	7.1	6.4
4.2	-.8	2.7	Profit Before Taxes	1.7	3.6	3.8	2.8	3.0	-.6
			RATIOS						
2.0	1.7	1.9		2.0	2.1	1.8	1.7	1.6	1.6
.8	.6	.7	Current	.6	.8	.8	.8	.8	.9
.3	.2	.2		.2	.3	.3	.4	.4	.3
1.6	1.5	1.6		1.6	1.8	1.5	1.4	1.1	1.1
(2044) .6	(2245) .5	(2086) .6	Quick	(730) .5	(842) .7	.6	.5	.6	.6
.2	.2	.2		.1	.2	.3	.2	.2	.2
0 UND	0 UND	0 UND		0 UND	0 UND	2 216.6	3 126.3	4 87.7	5 69.0
2 149.4	2 146.9	3 143.0	Sales/Receivables	0 UND	3 115.0	5 78.0	6 60.2	8 44.8	8 45.8
8 45.4	8 45.7	8 46.1		3 133.0	8 47.7	10 36.6	14 26.2	14 25.6	21 17.4
			Cost of Sales/Inventory						
			Cost of Sales/Payables						
14.9	18.0	15.2		17.0	15.3	12.7	13.2	13.6	17.2
-44.9	-22.4	-30.3	Sales/Working Capital	-19.7	-46.5	-52.1	-24.5	-37.6	-34.4
-6.2	-4.9	-5.8		-4.6	-6.6	-8.1	-8.5	-5.5	-5.4
2.9	2.4	2.8		2.5	2.8	3.3	2.6	4.2	3.4
(1515) 1.6	(1555) 1.2	(1460) 1.5	EBIT/Interest	(434) 1.3	(600) 1.6	(146) 1.6	(135) 1.5	(72) 1.3	(73) 1.0
.7	.2	.6		.5	.8	.6	.5	.6	-.1
6.0	2.4	4.0			4.3	6.1	4.7	4.0	4.5
(93) 2.8	(73) 1.5	(74) 2.0	Net Profit + Depr., Dep., Amort./Cur. Mat. L/T/D	(18) 1.3	(11) 1.0	(15) 2.0	(14) 2.4	(12) 1.8
1.1	.6	.7			.6	.0	1.3	.7	.2
2.6	2.7	2.5		2.6	3.2	1.9	1.9	1.7	1.7
8.7	10.8	8.8	Fixed/Worth	9.6	10.8	9.0	5.5	4.3	3.4
-9.1	-7.0	-8.2		-8.4	-8.6	-6.6	-5.5	-11.3	NM
2.5	2.5	2.3		2.2	2.9	2.2	1.8	1.7	1.2
10.3	13.0	10.5	Debt/Worth	11.3	13.4	13.2	7.6	5.8	3.3
-10.7	-8.5	-10.0		-10.0	-10.4	-9.5	-6.8	-16.4	NM
50.3	26.6	37.7		32.0	47.4	41.3	30.2	38.5	16.7
(1293) 15.3	(1363) 4.9	(1314) 9.6	% Profit Before Taxes/Tangible Net Worth	(456) 6.8	(523) 14.0	(115) 10.0	(96) 10.7	(62) 6.5	(62) 2.6
-1.4	-12.2	-5.2		-6.9	-3.7	-5.1	-.7	-2.6	-13.5
7.6	4.5	6.3		5.5	7.4	7.5	6.1	7.4	4.7
2.2	.0	1.3	% Profit Before Taxes/Total Assets	.6	1.8	1.9	1.7	.9	.0
-2.2	-4.2	-2.5		-2.5	-2.3	-3.1	-2.6	-1.7	-4.5
1.3	1.2	1.1		.9	1.0	1.5	1.8	2.0	1.7
.6	.5	.5	Sales/Net Fixed Assets	.4	.5	.7	.9	.8	.9
.4	.3	.3		.3	.3	.4	.5	.4	.5
.8	.8	.8		.6	.7	.9	1.1	1.0	1.0
.5	.4	.4	Sales/Total Assets	.4	.4	.5	.7	.6	.7
.3	.3	.3		.2	.3	.3	.4	.4	.5
6.2	6.9	6.6		7.0	7.3	5.8	4.8	5.8	6.6
(1791) 9.6	(1991) 11.2	(1827) 10.6	% Depr., Dep., Amort./Sales	(639) 11.3	(736) 11.1	(170) 9.4	(139) 8.8	(77) 9.2	(66) 8.2
14.7	16.8	15.9		16.7	16.8	14.8	12.5	13.5	11.5
2.2	2.3	2.1		3.3	1.7	1.7	1.3	.8	
(530) 4.4	(576) 4.4	(523) 4.2	% Officers', Directors' Owners' Comp/Sales	(222) 5.8	(208) 3.6	(35) 4.4	(36) 2.9	(16) 1.7	
7.3	7.9	7.7		9.4	6.6	13.9	4.8	4.6	
11054434M	11528331M	11010263M	Net Sales ($)	413163M	1492521M	716240M	1089712M	1357479M	5941148M
18413725M	19491656M	18957806M	Total Assets ($)	1348446M	4030080M	1614842M	1997714M	2642932M	7323792M

M = $ thousand   MM = $ million
See Pages 9 through 22 for Explanation of Ratios and Data

Current Data Sorted by Assets   Comparative Historical Data

0-500M	500M-2MM	2-10MM	10-50MM	50-100MM	100-250MM		4/1/06-3/31/07 ALL	4/1/07-3/31/08 ALL
		1	8	9	10	Unqualified	16	26
		2	1		1	Reviewed	2	2
		2				Compiled	1	2
		1	1			Tax Returns	2	
2	3	6	11	16	19	Other	29	30
2	3	12	21	25	30	**NUMBER OF STATEMENTS**	50	60
%	%	%	%	%	%	**ASSETS**	%	%
		15.2	13.0	19.0	14.3	Cash & Equivalents	16.2	17.4
		1.6	.8	2.3	1.5	Trade Receivables (net)	1.2	1.0
		1.3	.6	.5	2.2	Inventory	.7	.8
		1.8	3.3	1.1	1.4	All Other Current	2.1	1.8
		19.9	17.7	22.9	19.4	Total Current	20.2	21.0
		67.5	76.1	68.8	72.4	Fixed Assets (net)	70.3	73.5
		7.9	2.8	3.9	1.7	Intangibles (net)	6.8	2.7
		4.7	3.3	4.4	6.5	All Other Non-Current	2.7	2.8
		100.0	100.0	100.0	100.0	Total	100.0	100.0
						LIABILITIES		
		.5	1.8	.6	5.9	Notes Payable-Short Term	1.0	1.2
		1.8	3.6	8.3	9.4	Cur. Mat.-L.T.D.	4.3	3.6
		3.5	2.7	2.1	2.2	Trade Payables	3.4	3.7
		.0	.0	.3	.0	Income Taxes Payable	.1	.0
		19.1	9.3	10.2	8.1	All Other Current	10.2	11.2
		24.9	17.4	21.5	25.6	Total Current	19.0	19.7
		55.7	37.8	26.6	28.9	Long-Term Debt	35.3	36.3
		.2	.1	.0	1.1	Deferred Taxes	.5	.1
		2.0	3.6	1.0	11.1	All Other Non-Current	6.9	3.3
		17.2	41.1	51.0	33.3	Net Worth	38.2	40.6
		100.0	100.0	100.0	100.0	Total Liabilities & Net Worth	100.0	100.0
						INCOME DATA		
		100.0	100.0	100.0	100.0	Net Sales	100.0	100.0
						Gross Profit		
		86.2	86.4	79.8	82.4	Operating Expenses	77.1	74.2
		13.8	13.6	20.2	17.6	Operating Profit	22.9	25.8
		4.2	5.8	4.0	4.2	All Other Expenses (net)	5.2	4.4
		9.6	7.8	16.3	13.4	Profit Before Taxes	17.7	21.4
						RATIOS		
		1.8	1.7	1.9	2.0		1.8	1.8
		1.0	.8	1.1	1.1	Current	1.2	1.2
		.4	.6	.5	.9		.7	.7
		1.6	1.3	1.8	1.8		1.5	1.7
		.9	.5	1.0	1.0	Quick	1.0	1.1
		.3	.3	.5	.6		.6	.5
		1 653.8	1 452.2	1 353.1	1 273.5		1 457.0	1 726.6
		2 215.6	2 232.2	2 154.9	2 192.3	Sales/Receivables	3 145.2	2 217.5
		6 59.9	3 104.5	4 87.4	4 86.6		5 78.8	4 82.7
						Cost of Sales/Inventory		
						Cost of Sales/Payables		
		12.9	13.7	9.4	9.9		10.4	12.1
		NM	-52.6	115.3	41.6	Sales/Working Capital	52.8	38.9
		-11.4	-10.7	-12.2	-33.8		-37.6	-18.6
			3.6	26.0	21.9		60.7	37.9
			(17) 1.3	(23) 11.5	(28) 9.2	EBIT/Interest	(39) 6.3	(51) 7.9
			.0	1.5	.8		2.5	1.7
						Net Profit + Depr., Dep., Amort./Cur. Mat. L/T/D		
		1.2	1.2	1.0	1.1		1.0	1.1
		-10.1	2.2	1.5	1.7	Fixed/Worth	1.9	1.6
		-2.9	3.7	2.8	4.8		7.2	4.3
		.6	.8	.5	.4		.5	.5
		-19.5	1.6	.9	1.5	Debt/Worth	1.4	1.1
		-5.3	3.2	2.1	4.7		7.9	4.6
			59.6	72.5	66.3	% Profit Before Taxes/Tangible Net Worth	97.3	134.1
			(19) 6.6	(23) 32.8	(24) 41.4		(41) 48.1	(49) 60.0
			-10.1	5.4	9.3		22.5	26.9
		30.2	17.6	32.4	33.1	% Profit Before Taxes/Total Assets	46.2	72.1
		6.0	1.8	15.7	11.9		18.1	22.5
		-3.2	-1.9	-.2	-.3		3.9	3.5
		4.8	1.9	3.4	1.8		2.5	2.5
		1.2	1.4	1.8	1.1	Sales/Net Fixed Assets	1.6	1.8
		.5	.8	1.1	.9		.9	1.1
		2.7	1.3	1.7	1.0		1.8	1.8
		.7	1.1	1.2	.8	Sales/Total Assets	1.1	1.3
		.4	.7	.7	.7		.7	
			4.1	6.0	5.5	% Depr., Dep., Amort./Sales	4.4	4.2
			(10) 7.4	7.2	(19) 7.4		(40) 6.6	(41) 6.5
			12.6	9.6	8.9		9.5	9.8
						% Officers', Directors' Owners' Comp/Sales		
1092M	1497M	111806M	780563M	2459591M	4771561M	Net Sales ($)	5351793M	8495224M
903M	3115M	68634M	659659M	1802520M	5216213M	Total Assets ($)	4330275M	6337226M

M = $ thousand   MM = $ million
See Pages 9 through 22 for Explanation of Ratios and Data

Comparative Historical Data | Current Data Sorted by Sales

	13	24	28	Type of Statement	0-1MM	1-3MM	3-5MM	5-10MM	10-25MM	25MM & OVER
Unqualified	13	24	28				1	1	6	22
Reviewed	1	3	4				1	1	1	
Compiled		2	2						1	
Tax Returns	3	4	2						1	
Other	43	46	57		6	2		2	5	42
	4/1/08-3/31/09 ALL	4/1/09-3/31/10 ALL	4/1/10-3/31/11 ALL			25 (4/1-9/30/10)		68 (10/1/10-3/31/11)		
NUMBER OF STATEMENTS	60	79	93		6	2	3	4	13	65
	%	%	%	**ASSETS**	%	%	%	%	%	%
	12.5	16.0	16.0	Cash & Equivalents					11.2	16.8
	3.6	2.4	1.5	Trade Receivables (net)					.5	1.9
	.7	.7	1.2	Inventory					.7	1.3
	4.0	2.9	1.9	All Other Current					2.6	1.7
	20.8	22.1	20.6	Total Current					15.0	21.7
	71.8	68.0	70.8	Fixed Assets (net)					70.6	72.1
	2.1	3.9	4.0	Intangibles (net)					4.2	2.4
	5.3	6.1	4.6	All Other Non-Current					10.1	3.9
	100.0	100.0	100.0	Total					100.0	100.0
				LIABILITIES						
	1.3	1.8	2.6	Notes Payable-Short Term					.6	3.4
	14.9	17.3	6.4	Cur. Mat.-L.T.D.					3.3	8.0
	4.7	3.3	2.5	Trade Payables					2.9	2.2
	.1	.2	.1	Income Taxes Payable					.0	.1
	11.9	10.0	10.0	All Other Current					5.6	10.0
	33.0	32.6	21.4	Total Current					12.3	23.8
	30.2	34.6	34.1	Long-Term Debt					44.0	27.1
	.1	.3	.4	Deferred Taxes					.9	.4
	5.9	9.1	7.3	All Other Non-Current					5.2	5.6
	30.8	23.4	36.7	Net Worth					37.6	43.1
	100.0	100.0	100.0	Total Liabilties & Net Worth					100.0	100.0
				INCOME DATA						
	100.0	100.0	100.0	Net Sales					100.0	100.0
				Gross Profit						
	82.2	83.6	83.0	Operating Expenses					91.9	80.2
	17.8	16.4	17.0	Operating Profit					8.1	19.8
	5.2	5.6	4.8	All Other Expenses (net)					7.5	3.9
	12.6	10.8	12.2	Profit Before Taxes					.6	15.9
				RATIOS						
	1.6 / .8 / .5	2.1 / 1.1 / .5	1.9 / 1.1 / .6	Current					2.0 / 1.2 / .7	1.9 / 1.1 / .6
	1.5 / .7 / .3	1.8 / (77) 1.0 / .4	1.7 / 1.0 / .4	Quick					1.8 / .8 / .4	1.7 / 1.0 / .5
	1 483.6 / 2 182.2 / 5 74.0	1 451.2 / 2 217.2 / 4 91.7	1 379.2 / 2 202.0 / 4 94.2	Sales/Receivables					1 403.1 / 2 234.0 / 3 113.4	1 337.2 / 2 188.9 / 4 87.0
				Cost of Sales/Inventory						
				Cost of Sales/Payables						
	15.2 / -50.3 / -10.0	11.4 / 83.4 / -16.9	10.3 / 59.5 / -14.5	Sales/Working Capital					11.1 / 52.5 / -10.7	10.3 / 76.3 / -15.9
	14.4 / (52) 6.0 / 1.1	14.6 / (67) 6.4 / 1.0	16.1 / (82) 3.7 / .3	EBIT/Interest					(12) 2.1 / 1.0 / .2	(57) 22.0 / 9.6 / 1.2
				Net Profit + Depr., Dep., Amort./Cur. Mat. L/T/D						
	1.2 / 1.9 / 8.7	1.0 / 1.8 / -30.2	1.1 / 1.9 / 5.3	Fixed/Worth					.9 / 2.5 / 6.7	1.1 / 1.6 / 3.2
	.7 / 1.4 / 9.8	.5 / 1.7 / -50.6	.6 / 1.4 / 5.1	Debt/Worth					.9 / 2.3 / 7.1	.4 / 1.1 / 3.0
	89.2 / (48) 38.2 / 17.9	70.3 / (57) 39.5 / 8.4	72.5 / (75) 32.8 / 1.7	% Profit Before Taxes/Tangible Net Worth					(12) 54.7 / .5 / -9.2	(56) 71.4 / 35.0 / 9.3
	35.1 / 13.0 / -.4	28.6 / 9.4 / -1.6	29.0 / 8.3 / -1.5	% Profit Before Taxes/Total Assets					4.1 / .8 / -2.1	34.1 / 15.0 / 1.9
	1.9 / 1.3 / .9	2.8 / 1.6 / .9	2.4 / 1.3 / .9	Sales/Net Fixed Assets					2.1 / 1.0 / .7	2.4 / 1.4 / 1.0
	1.4 / 1.0 / .7	1.7 / 1.0 / .7	1.4 / .9 / .6	Sales/Total Assets					1.0 / .7 / .5	1.5 / 1.0 / .8
	5.8 / (28) 7.5 / 11.2	4.9 / (53) 6.6 / 9.1	5.5 / (61) 7.2 / 9.9	% Depr., Dep., Amort./Sales					6.4 / (37) 8.8 / 11.9	5.0 / 6.5 / 8.8
		(11) 2.5 / 6.7 / 13.8		% Officers', Directors' Owners' Comp/Sales						
	6417783M	6496012M	8126110M	Net Sales ($)	3465M	4321M	11071M	29084M	251512M	7826657M
	6611135M	6625493M	7751044M	Total Assets ($)	6368M	12597M	21348M	18025M	515109M	7177597M

M = $ thousand   MM = $ million
See Pages 9 through 22 for Explanation of Ratios and Data

	Current Data Sorted by Assets						Comparative Historical Data	
							8	4
						Type of Statement		
						Unqualified	8	4
		1		1	1	1	Reviewed	9	3
	1			3			Compiled	18	18
2	7	6	1			Tax Returns	34	36
16	19	12	2			Other	15	26
6	10	12	1	1	1		4/1/06-3/31/07	4/1/07-3/31/08
	3 (4/1-9/30/10)		101 (10/1/10-3/31/11)				ALL	ALL
0-500M	500M-2MM	2-10MM	10-50MM	50-100MM	100-250MM			
24	37	31	8	2	2	NUMBER OF STATEMENTS	84	87
%	%	%	%	%	%	**ASSETS**	%	%
23.2	9.7	6.7				Cash & Equivalents	10.4	8.8
3.2	1.8	.4				Trade Receivables (net)	2.2	2.0
5.3	3.9	1.3				Inventory	5.8	3.4
5.6	.6	.7				All Other Current	1.4	2.2
37.3	15.9	9.1				Total Current	19.7	16.4
52.6	68.9	68.2				Fixed Assets (net)	64.4	70.0
5.0	7.6	4.5				Intangibles (net)	6.4	5.7
5.1	7.6	18.2				All Other Non-Current	9.5	7.9
100.0	100.0	100.0				Total	100.0	100.0
						LIABILITIES		
5.1	1.8	.6				Notes Payable-Short Term	5.4	5.1
1.7	4.5	2.2				Cur. Mat.-L.T.D.	3.5	3.4
.2	3.1	.6				Trade Payables	1.8	1.9
.0	.1	.0				Income Taxes Payable	.0	.0
20.1	11.4	5.5				All Other Current	13.1	8.3
27.1	20.9	8.9				Total Current	23.7	18.8
37.3	70.8	51.9				Long-Term Debt	50.7	59.3
.0	.0	.1				Deferred Taxes	.0	.1
7.4	12.4	3.5				All Other Non-Current	12.0	12.2
28.2	-4.2	35.6				Net Worth	13.5	9.6
100.0	100.0	100.0				Total Liabilities & Net Worth	100.0	100.0
						INCOME DATA		
100.0	100.0	100.0				Net Sales	100.0	100.0
						Gross Profit		
83.9	81.7	83.0				Operating Expenses	84.3	82.2
16.1	18.3	17.0				Operating Profit	15.7	17.8
2.7	12.2	9.8				All Other Expenses (net)	7.6	10.1
13.4	6.1	7.2				Profit Before Taxes	8.0	7.8
						RATIOS		
4.7	1.9	3.9					2.6	2.1
1.9	1.1	1.0				Current	.8	.7
1.1	.3	.4					.3	.3
3.9	1.8	3.3					1.7	1.4
1.5	.9	.7				Quick	.4	.5
.3	.2	.2					.2	.1
0 UND	0 UND	0 UND					0 UND	0 UND
0 UND	0 UND	0 UND				Sales/Receivables	0 UND	0 UND
0 UND	3 105.6	0 UND					4 83.3	3 111.8
						Cost of Sales/Inventory		
						Cost of Sales/Payables		
5.9	11.7	18.1					6.6	14.5
24.8	97.0	535.3				Sales/Working Capital	-41.8	-19.9
151.6	-7.6	-10.6					-6.3	-7.0
22.3	3.4	7.1					7.8	3.6
(13) 3.0	(23) 2.4	(22) 2.2				EBIT/Interest	(65) 1.9	(59) 2.1
1.7	1.0	.1					.9	.8
						Net Profit + Depr., Dep., Amort./Cur. Mat. L/T/D		
.4	2.9	.9					1.2	1.8
1.6	-60.0	2.7				Fixed/Worth	4.8	7.0
NM	-1.8	16.2					-4.0	-3.3
.3	3.0	.4					1.9	1.7
3.5	-74.3	1.9				Debt/Worth	6.0	6.8
NM	-3.6	15.3					-7.1	-5.8
448.8	29.0	35.1					31.5	59.0
(18) 37.6	(18) 11.5	(25) 8.1				% Profit Before Taxes/Tangible Net Worth	(55) 11.0	(55) 27.9
10.4	-.5	-3.5					-1.3	3.5
27.8	14.9	10.7					17.5	12.2
9.9	4.1	3.0				% Profit Before Taxes/Total Assets	3.2	4.6
.8	-2.2	-1.8					-.8	-.7
17.8	2.6	1.5					4.3	3.1
4.0	.9	.7				Sales/Net Fixed Assets	1.0	.9
1.6	.4	.4					.5	.5
5.3	1.1	.9					1.7	1.5
1.9	.6	.4				Sales/Total Assets	.8	.7
1.1	.4	.2					.4	.4
3.5	4.3	5.5					3.9	4.7
(18) 9.7	(32) 11.8	(26) 12.3				% Depr., Dep., Amort./Sales	(73) 7.5	(71) 8.7
16.8	16.2	18.5					15.0	13.1
	6.0						3.8	3.8
	(13) 6.8					% Officers', Directors' Owners' Comp/Sales	(28) 5.9	(36) 7.5
	13.9						12.5	11.0
16461M	40675M	81174M	150501M	49964M	115231M	Net Sales ($)	405826M	507058M
6076M	46622M	138545M	159493M	125768M	225819M	Total Assets ($)	639304M	661868M

M = $ thousand MM = $ million
See Pages 9 through 22 for Explanation of Ratios and Data

Comparative Historical Data

Current Data Sorted by Sales

	Hist 1	Hist 2	Hist 3	Type of Statement	0-1MM	1-3MM	3-5MM	5-10MM	10-25MM	25MM & OVER
	2		4	Unqualified						
	6	5	4	Reviewed	1			1	1	2
	13	21	16	Compiled	6	6	3	1	2	1
	34	47	49	Tax Returns	29	15	3	1	1	
	22	31	31	Other	20	3	2			2
	4/1/08-3/31/09 ALL	4/1/09-3/31/10 ALL	4/1/10-3/31/11 ALL		3 (4/1-9/30/10)			101 (10/1/10-3/31/11)		
NUMBER OF STATEMENTS	77	104	104		56	24	8	5	6	5
	%	%	%	**ASSETS**	%	%	%	%	%	%
	11.5	8.6	12.0	Cash & Equivalents	11.0	15.2				
	2.3	1.2	1.6	Trade Receivables (net)	1.6	1.9				
	5.4	3.8	3.1	Inventory	2.7	3.8				
	1.4	1.1	2.0	All Other Current	2.5	1.0				
	20.5	14.7	18.7	Total Current	17.8	21.8				
	69.1	72.1	64.2	Fixed Assets (net)	68.7	60.4				
	3.4	5.7	6.5	Intangibles (net)	6.9	5.7				
	7.0	7.5	10.6	All Other Non-Current	6.6	12.0				
	100.0	100.0	100.0	Total	100.0	100.0				
				LIABILITIES						
	4.0	2.9	2.2	Notes Payable-Short Term	2.3	2.5				
	3.2	4.4	3.0	Cur. Mat.-L.T.D.	3.7	1.8				
	1.5	1.5	1.5	Trade Payables	.5	4.0				
	.0	1.0	.1	Income Taxes Payable	.0	.1				
	9.3	8.4	11.5	All Other Current	7.8	12.9				
	18.0	18.2	18.4	Total Current	14.4	21.2				
	52.1	63.0	55.4	Long-Term Debt	65.8	46.1				
	.0	.0	.0	Deferred Taxes	.0	.1				
	10.9	7.3	7.9	All Other Non-Current	10.1	5.6				
	19.0	11.4	18.4	Net Worth	9.7	27.0				
	100.0	100.0	100.0	Total Liabilities & Net Worth	100.0	100.0				
				INCOME DATA						
	100.0	100.0	100.0	Net Sales	100.0	100.0				
				Gross Profit						
	85.8	79.7	83.5	Operating Expenses	80.8	87.1				
	14.2	20.3	16.5	Operating Profit	19.2	12.9				
	7.9	10.1	8.5	All Other Expenses (net)	12.0	3.5				
	6.3	10.1	8.1	Profit Before Taxes	7.2	9.3				
				RATIOS						
	4.1	2.6	3.0		3.5	3.8				
	1.3	.8	1.2	Current	1.3	.9				
	.4	.3	.4		.3	.4				
	3.2	2.2	2.1		2.7	3.0				
	(76) .7	.6	.9	Quick	1.0	.6				
	.2	.1	.2		.3	.2				
	0 UND	0 UND	0 UND		0 UND	0 UND				
	0 UND	0 UND	0 UND	Sales/Receivables	0 UND	0 UND				
	2 231.2	2 183.3	2 231.9		0 UND	1 358.9				
				Cost of Sales/Inventory						
				Cost of Sales/Payables						
	6.6	9.3	11.1		12.7	6.5				
	90.5	-114.3	64.3	Sales/Working Capital	40.0	NM				
	-9.0	-7.0	-10.8		-11.5	-11.4				
	6.2	5.7	5.5		3.4	5.5				
	(55) 2.3	(66) 2.4	(69) 2.5	EBIT/Interest	(31) 2.3	(19) 2.2				
	1.2	1.2	1.0		1.0	.5				
				Net Profit + Depr., Dep., Amort./Cur. Mat. L/T/D						
	1.1	1.4	1.0		1.5	.8				
	3.6	6.4	4.8	Fixed/Worth	8.6	3.5				
	-5.0	-3.7	-7.1		-7.0	-5.8				
	.7	.9	.8		1.2	.5				
	3.9	7.7	5.1	Debt/Worth	9.0	3.2				
	-7.0	-6.2	-11.0		-8.4	-15.4				
	46.3	67.4	48.5	% Profit Before Taxes/Tangible Net Worth	45.2	52.4				
	(51) 19.6	(66) 17.9	(67) 13.0		(34) 11.5	(16) 12.4				
	.7	3.6	2.6		-3.3	1.8				
	12.7	13.5	13.6	% Profit Before Taxes/Total Assets	13.7	12.6				
	4.3	4.3	4.7		1.9	5.5				
	-1.0	-.1	-1.0		-3.2	-.9				
	2.8	2.3	3.2	Sales/Net Fixed Assets	2.3	4.8				
	1.0	.8	1.0		.7	1.4				
	.5	.4	.5		.3	.7				
	1.6	1.3	1.2	Sales/Total Assets	1.1	2.1				
	.8	.6	.7		.5	.9				
	.4	.3	.4		.3	.6				
	3.7	5.2	5.2	% Depr., Dep., Amort./Sales	7.9	3.5				
	(69) 8.8	(87) 10.4	(88) 11.2		(44) 14.9	(21) 9.6				
	15.3	18.1	16.5		19.3	13.6				
	2.6	2.7	3.4	% Officers', Directors' Owners' Comp/Sales	4.2	5.5				
	(28) 5.5	(35) 5.8	(35) 6.3		(14) 6.1	(11) 7.7				
	9.2	10.8	8.6		8.0	12.9				
	356328M	1183808M	454006M	Net Sales ($)	28244M	45888M	31789M	34798M	83876M	229411M
	570055M	1033571M	702323M	Total Assets ($)	69952M	62455M	39903M	45162M	140685M	344166M

M = $ thousand   MM = $ million
See Pages 9 through 22 for Explanation of Ratios and Data

Current Data Sorted by Assets

Comparative Historical Data

	0-500M	500M-2MM	2-10MM	10-50MM	50-100MM	100-250MM		Type of Statement	4/1/06-3/31/07 ALL	4/1/07-3/31/08 ALL
	2	2	5	2				Unqualified	15	7
	3	9	7					Reviewed	7	4
	1	1	2					Compiled	7	5
		6	2					Tax Returns	14	22
			4	3				Other	14	17
		8 (4/1-9/30/10)	2	40 (10/1/10-3/31/11)						
NUMBER OF STATEMENTS	6	17	20	5				NUMBER OF STATEMENTS	57	55
	%	%	%	%	%	%		**ASSETS**	%	%
Cash & Equivalents		10.9	2.5					Cash & Equivalents	15.2	8.4
Trade Receivables (net)		1.4	3.1					Trade Receivables (net)	1.4	3.3
Inventory		4.2	.6					Inventory	1.1	1.7
All Other Current		3.8	.5	DATA	DATA			All Other Current	1.2	4.6
Total Current		20.3	6.8	NOT	NOT			Total Current	18.9	17.8
Fixed Assets (net)		73.0	66.3	AVAILABLE	AVAILABLE			Fixed Assets (net)	65.3	65.5
Intangibles (net)		2.4	5.7					Intangibles (net)	5.2	4.4
All Other Non-Current		4.3	21.2					All Other Non-Current	10.7	12.2
Total		100.0	100.0					Total	100.0	100.0
								LIABILITIES		
Notes Payable-Short Term		8.0	3.5					Notes Payable-Short Term	2.1	5.1
Cur. Mat.-L.T.D.		1.8	3.2					Cur. Mat.-L.T.D.	4.6	4.0
Trade Payables		1.2	1.9					Trade Payables	3.1	3.4
Income Taxes Payable		.0	.0					Income Taxes Payable	.0	.0
All Other Current		12.7	7.1					All Other Current	13.5	14.5
Total Current		23.7	15.6					Total Current	23.3	27.1
Long-Term Debt		38.6	38.6					Long-Term Debt	40.5	41.8
Deferred Taxes		.0	.0					Deferred Taxes	.0	.1
All Other Non-Current		9.9	26.9					All Other Non-Current	11.6	13.2
Net Worth		27.7	18.9					Net Worth	24.6	17.8
Total Liabilities & Net Worth		100.0	100.0					Total Liabilities & Net Worth	100.0	100.0
								INCOME DATA		
Net Sales		100.0	100.0					Net Sales	100.0	100.0
Gross Profit								Gross Profit		
Operating Expenses		90.0	88.2					Operating Expenses	88.2	87.4
Operating Profit		10.0	11.8					Operating Profit	11.8	12.6
All Other Expenses (net)		6.3	3.0					All Other Expenses (net)	4.3	7.5
Profit Before Taxes		3.7	8.8					Profit Before Taxes	7.5	5.1
								RATIOS		
Current		2.8	1.1					Current	3.7	1.8
		.8	.1						.7	.5
		.3	.1						.3	.2
Quick		.6	.9					Quick	3.2	1.2
		.4	.1						.6	.3
		.1	.0						.2	.0
Sales/Receivables	0 UND	0 UND						Sales/Receivables	0 UND	0 UND
	0 UND	1 406.6							0 UND	0 UND
	4 81.3	7 54.6							8 47.7	3 112.4
Cost of Sales/Inventory								Cost of Sales/Inventory		
Cost of Sales/Payables								Cost of Sales/Payables		
Sales/Working Capital		87.5	76.9					Sales/Working Capital	8.6	9.0
		-20.6	-10.2						-42.8	-11.5
		-8.0	-3.3						-10.0	-4.6
EBIT/Interest		6.7	5.0					EBIT/Interest	9.1	6.9
	(13)	1.6 (16)	2.0						(46) 1.5	(41) 1.5
		.8	.7						.1	.1
Net Profit + Depr., Dep., Amort./Cur. Mat. L/T/D								Net Profit + Depr., Dep., Amort./Cur. Mat. L/T/D		
Fixed/Worth		1.5	1.0					Fixed/Worth	1.2	1.2
		3.4	8.2						2.5	3.7
		NM	-8.6						-6.5	-5.9
Debt/Worth		.8	1.4					Debt/Worth	.8	.7
		3.9	20.8						2.8	3.6
		NM	-11.2						-10.7	-6.9
% Profit Before Taxes/Tangible Net Worth		27.4	68.5					% Profit Before Taxes/Tangible Net Worth	43.1	51.8
	(13)	6.3 (13)	4.5						(40) 7.4	(37) 12.8
		-2.1	-7.9						-1.2	-2.6
% Profit Before Taxes/Total Assets		9.8	4.7					% Profit Before Taxes/Total Assets	19.7	14.0
		1.4	2.7						2.7	1.3
		-.6	-1.1						-1.7	-2.3
Sales/Net Fixed Assets		6.5	2.0					Sales/Net Fixed Assets	3.3	4.1
		1.6	.9						1.3	1.1
		.5	.7						.6	.6
Sales/Total Assets		2.3	.9					Sales/Total Assets	1.6	1.5
		1.4	.7						.7	.7
		.4	.5						.4	.4
% Depr., Dep., Amort./Sales		3.9	4.6					% Depr., Dep., Amort./Sales	4.5	4.5
	(14)	4.9 (19)	7.5						(46) 6.2	(50) 6.7
		12.4	9.7						10.3	12.2
% Officers', Directors' Owners' Comp/Sales								% Officers', Directors' Owners' Comp/Sales	3.3	5.1
									(17) 6.3	(16) 8.0
									12.7	13.4
Net Sales ($)	7101M	26699M	85808M	44528M				Net Sales ($)	322552M	357066M
Total Assets ($)	1590M	21036M	97120M	79180M				Total Assets ($)	586602M	386880M

© RMA 2011

M = $ thousand   MM = $ million
See Pages 9 through 22 for Explanation of Ratios and Data

Comparative Historical Data   ## Current Data Sorted by Sales

			Type of Statement						
8	7	7	Unqualified		2	2	1	2	
2	9	7	Reviewed		2	5			
8	7	6	Compiled		4		1	1	
13	15	16	Tax Returns	6	9	1			
9	14	12	Other	6	2	1	2	1	
4/1/08-3/31/09 ALL	4/1/09-3/31/10 ALL	4/1/10-3/31/11 ALL			8 (4/1-9/30/10)		40 (10/1/10-3/31/11)		
40	52	48	**NUMBER OF STATEMENTS**	12	19	9	4	4	25MM & OVER
%	%	%	**ASSETS**	%	%	%	%	%	%
12.8	9.7	6.3	Cash & Equivalents	1.5	10.7				D
3.5	1.7	1.8	Trade Receivables (net)	.2	4.1				A
2.0	2.0	2.2	Inventory	4.3	1.8				T
2.1	2.3	1.6	All Other Current	4.6	.7				A
20.3	15.7	11.9	Total Current	10.7	17.3				
67.3	64.7	66.7	Fixed Assets (net)	80.4	62.0				N
2.3	4.8	5.3	Intangibles (net)	7.5	2.1				O
10.1	14.8	16.2	All Other Non-Current	1.4	18.6				T
100.0	100.0	100.0	Total	100.0	100.0				
			LIABILITIES						A
5.6	7.7	6.9	Notes Payable-Short Term	10.1	6.0				V
4.8	4.3	5.3	Cur. Mat.-L.T.D.	14.3	2.5				A
1.6	2.5	1.8	Trade Payables	.5	2.1				I
.0	.0	.0	Income Taxes Payable	.0	.0				L
12.7	7.1	19.1	All Other Current	1.6	38.9				A
24.7	21.5	33.0	Total Current	26.5	49.5				B
37.6	34.2	41.7	Long-Term Debt	53.1	40.0				L
.0	.0	.0	Deferred Taxes	.0	.0				E
6.0	19.1	20.8	All Other Non-Current	10.4	24.4				
31.7	25.1	4.5	Net Worth	10.0	-13.9				
100.0	100.0	100.0	Total Liabilities & Net Worth	100.0	100.0				
			INCOME DATA						
100.0	100.0	100.0	Net Sales	100.0	100.0				
			Gross Profit						
93.0	91.9	90.8	Operating Expenses	78.8	96.3				
7.0	8.1	9.2	Operating Profit	21.2	3.7				
2.9	3.6	3.7	All Other Expenses (net)	12.5	1.5				
4.1	4.5	5.5	Profit Before Taxes	8.7	2.2				
			RATIOS						
2.6	1.6	1.0		3.2	1.2				
1.1	.5	.3	Current	.3	.6				
.2	.1	.1		.1	.1				
1.4	1.2	.6		.4	1.0				
.8	.3	.1	Quick	.1	.4				
.1	.1	.0		.0	.1				
0 UND	0 UND	0 UND		0 UND	0 UND				
1 293.0	0 UND	0 UND	Sales/Receivables	0 UND	1 469.2				
9 41.8	3 104.5	5 76.2		1 341.3	7 53.2				
			Cost of Sales/Inventory						
			Cost of Sales/Payables						
9.3	12.9	NM		68.2	64.8				
91.1	-21.0	-13.6	Sales/Working Capital	-12.3	-19.2				
-7.5	-8.0	-4.0		-1.8	-8.2				
6.5	9.1	4.1			3.6				
(34) 2.3	(39) 2.9	(39) 1.8	EBIT/Interest	(16) 1.8					
.3	1.2	.7			.0				
			Net Profit + Depr., Dep., Amort./Cur. Mat. L/T/D						
.9	1.1	1.5		1.5	1.6				
1.8	2.6	5.4	Fixed/Worth	-12.9	4.8				
NM	-12.8	-6.7		-2.3	-2.6				
.4	.8	1.0		.6	1.0				
1.4	2.9	8.7	Debt/Worth	-14.2	5.0				
NM	-15.1	-8.1		-3.5	-6.5				
23.3	25.2	29.7	% Profit Before Taxes/Tangible Net Worth		39.9				
(30) 7.7	(36) 10.8	(30) 5.9		(13) 19.0					
-3.4	.0	-1.9			-3.9				
10.7	12.4	5.0	% Profit Before Taxes/Total Assets	4.9	4.7				
2.1	3.0	2.3		1.2	2.8				
-3.7	-.6	-1.5		-1.3	-5.9				
2.6	4.3	3.5	Sales/Net Fixed Assets	2.9	6.7				
1.6	1.4	1.4		.5	2.0				
.7	.7	.6		.2	.9				
1.7	1.4	1.8	Sales/Total Assets	.8	3.1				
.8	.9	.8		.4	1.4				
.4	.5	.5		.2	.7				
4.3	3.4	4.3	% Depr., Dep., Amort./Sales	5.0	2.5				
(35) 5.3	(47) 5.1	(42) 5.9		(10) 13.9	(17) 4.5				
8.5	7.9	9.1		26.3	7.9				
1.7	2.7	2.0	% Officers', Directors' Owners' Comp/Sales		1.8				
(16) 4.5	(20) 7.7	(16) 4.0		(11) 2.8					
9.9	12.5	8.9			9.1				
155074M	175470M	164136M	Net Sales ($)	5681M	41806M	34559M	27394M	54696M	
303604M	206861M	198926M	Total Assets ($)	15234M	37253M	50199M	48163M	48077M	

M = $ thousand   MM = $ million
See Pages 9 through 22 for Explanation of Ratios and Data

Current Data Sorted by Assets

Comparative Historical Data

Type of Statement	0-500M	500M-2MM	2-10MM	10-50MM	50-100MM	100-250MM	4/1/06-3/31/07 ALL	4/1/07-3/31/08 ALL
Unqualified	3	9	14	53	29	22	157	129
Reviewed	12	32	65	43	4		162	130
Compiled	198	165	123	21	1	3	465	499
Tax Returns	702	429	122	13	2	3	1053	1083
Other	390	353	274	132	31	35	902	951
	236 (4/1-9/30/10)			3,047 (10/1/10-3/31/11)				
NUMBER OF STATEMENTS	1305	988	598	262	67	63	2739	2792
ASSETS	%	%	%	%	%	%	%	%
Cash & Equivalents	18.9	13.4	11.8	10.3	7.1	7.5	14.5	13.7
Trade Receivables (net)	1.8	1.8	2.2	2.2	1.9	2.3	2.4	2.6
Inventory	9.2	4.7	3.6	2.9	2.8	3.3	6.0	6.2
All Other Current	3.5	2.5	2.5	2.2	2.0	4.9	3.2	3.2
Total Current	33.4	22.4	20.1	17.6	13.8	18.1	26.1	25.6
Fixed Assets (net)	44.3	53.7	59.3	59.4	64.2	47.5	53.5	53.1
Intangibles (net)	10.7	10.5	9.9	15.1	15.3	28.0	9.9	11.4
All Other Non-Current	11.5	13.4	10.8	7.9	6.7	6.5	10.5	9.9
Total	100.0	100.0	100.0	100.0	100.0	100.0	100.0	100.0
LIABILITIES								
Notes Payable-Short Term	9.0	3.8	3.5	1.8	.9	.9	5.2	5.2
Cur. Mat.-L.T.D.	3.8	3.5	5.5	5.5	4.3	5.2	4.3	4.8
Trade Payables	13.6	8.5	7.5	6.3	6.7	9.0	10.0	10.1
Income Taxes Payable	.2	.1	.1	.1	.1	.1	.1	.2
All Other Current	28.4	15.1	13.8	10.7	9.1	12.8	19.2	19.8
Total Current	54.9	31.1	30.4	24.4	21.1	28.0	38.8	40.1
Long-Term Debt	27.9	36.8	40.6	42.0	48.0	38.2	34.9	36.5
Deferred Taxes	.0	.0	.0	.4	.4	2.8	.1	.1
All Other Non-Current	20.2	10.1	6.9	6.5	13.3	14.9	11.3	11.3
Net Worth	-3.1	22.0	22.1	26.8	17.3	16.1	14.9	12.0
Total Liabilities & Net Worth	100.0	100.0	100.0	100.0	100.0	100.0	100.0	100.0
INCOME DATA								
Net Sales	100.0	100.0	100.0	100.0	100.0	100.0	100.0	100.0
Gross Profit	60.9	61.2	60.9	60.1	61.2	60.9	60.0	60.1
Operating Expenses	58.2	56.6	55.5	54.9	55.9	56.9	55.2	56.0
Operating Profit	2.7	4.6	5.4	5.1	5.2	4.0	4.8	4.1
All Other Expenses (net)	.4	1.2	1.8	1.7	3.2	3.1	1.4	1.5
Profit Before Taxes	2.3	3.4	3.5	3.4	2.1	1.0	3.4	2.6

RATIOS

Ratio	0-500M	500M-2MM	2-10MM	10-50MM	50-100MM	100-250MM	4/1/06-3/31/07 ALL	4/1/07-3/31/08 ALL
Current	1.9	1.6	1.3	1.1	.8	1.1	1.5	1.5
	.8	.8	.7	.7	.6	.6	.7	.7
	.3	.3	.3	.4	.4	.4	.3	.3
Quick	1.2	1.1	.9	.8	.6	.6	1.0	1.0
	(1289) .4	(983) .5	(594) .5	.5	.5	.4	(2712) .4	(2769) .4
	.1	.1	.2	.2	.2	.2	.1	.1
Sales/Receivables	0 UND	0 UND	0 UND	0 999.8	1 500.6	0 749.4	0 UND	0 UND
	0 UND	0 UND	0 999.8	1 351.7	2 214.2	3 110.7	0 UND	0 UND
	0 999.8	1 372.3	2 170.8	4 85.3	6 60.5	6 63.0	2 210.0	2 182.5
Cost of Sales/Inventory	5 68.1	6 60.0	7 54.4	7 52.8	7 55.9	8 46.8	5 66.5	6 64.4
	10 37.1	11 33.5	10 35.2	10 36.5	10 37.9	12 29.9	10 37.0	10 36.8
	17 21.6	19 19.6	17 21.1	16 22.1	15 24.3	17 21.9	17 21.4	17 21.0
Cost of Sales/Payables	0 UND	3 108.2	10 36.3	14 25.2	19 18.9	15 24.0	3 118.6	2 156.5
	9 39.7	18 20.5	22 16.5	26 14.3	37 9.9	29 12.6	18 19.8	17 21.1
	28 13.0	38 9.5	40 9.0	41 8.8	52 7.0	50 7.3	36 10.1	37 9.8
Sales/Working Capital	40.4	33.9	44.2	112.7	-49.5	150.5	40.1	49.1
	-97.0	-78.2	-39.0	-28.7	-18.1	-25.6	-56.2	-49.6
	-16.3	-12.8	-11.0	-12.8	-12.5	-14.4	-14.5	-13.4
EBIT/Interest	12.9	11.3	10.2	6.5	3.8	3.5	9.1	7.5
	(743) 2.6	(787) 3.2	(547) 3.3	(255) 2.7	(65) 1.9	(62) 1.9	(2138) 3.0	(2180) 2.5
	-.9	.4	1.2	1.3	1.4	.3	1.0	.5
Net Profit + Depr., Dep., Amort./Cur. Mat. L/T/D	22.6	6.3	7.9	3.8	4.0		5.3	5.4
	(11) 6.9	(29) 2.2	(44) 2.8	(59) 2.2	(29) 2.3		(200) 2.6	(183) 2.2
	1.5	.2	1.6	1.3	1.5		1.4	1.0
Fixed/Worth	.6	.9	1.4	1.6	2.0	2.8	1.0	1.1
	2.8	3.3	4.1	5.1	68.4	-3.9	3.4	4.0
	-1.0	-3.8	-6.9	-5.5	-2.7	-.7	-3.8	-3.0
Debt/Worth	.6	.9	1.2	1.4	1.7	4.5	1.0	1.1
	6.5	4.3	4.6	6.4	80.1	-7.2	5.1	5.7
	-2.6	-6.4	-9.9	-9.1	-5.3	-2.1	-6.1	-4.6
% Profit Before Taxes/Tangible Net Worth	147.9	75.0	69.2	58.0	33.5	57.6	98.3	99.2
	(743) 55.6	(624) 30.8	(398) 31.3	(166) 28.6	(35) 15.4	(23) 15.0	(1731) 37.5	(1724) 37.2
	8.9	7.5	6.3	7.3	7.9	-.8	9.8	7.5
% Profit Before Taxes/Total Assets	42.1	21.5	18.0	11.7	6.9	8.3	25.8	24.8
	11.5	8.2	6.8	5.9	4.0	3.4	9.2	7.6
	-7.0	-1.0	.8	1.3	2.0	-4.2	.5	-2.3
Sales/Net Fixed Assets	46.9	12.5	7.7	5.7	3.6	6.5	16.3	16.6
	15.5	5.5	4.0	3.6	2.9	4.3	6.8	6.8
	7.0	2.6	2.0	2.1	2.0	3.0	3.1	3.0
Sales/Total Assets	9.6	4.0	3.4	2.7	2.3	2.6	5.7	5.7
	5.8	2.6	2.2	1.9	1.7	1.9	3.3	3.2
	3.7	1.7	1.3	1.4	1.4	1.4	1.9	1.9
% Depr., Dep., Amort./Sales	.8	1.4	2.1	2.7	3.3	2.6	1.3	1.3
	(950) 1.7	(833) 2.5	(540) 3.2	(253) 3.8	(59) 4.0	(17) 3.2	(2351) 2.4	(2357) 2.5
	3.4	4.3	5.0	5.1	4.8	3.7	3.9	4.2
% Officers', Directors' Owners' Comp/Sales	2.3	1.9	1.1	1.1	.6		2.3	2.2
	(613) 4.6	(429) 3.5	(228) 2.5	(54) 2.4	(10) 2.1		(1132) 4.3	(1158) 4.2
	8.1	5.9	4.9	6.0	11.9		7.9	7.4
Net Sales ($)	1806324M	2942479M	6983323M	11926408M	9388905M	26992323M	46931992M	46442489M
Total Assets ($)	306862M	991524M	2695972M	5559629M	4892766M	10144075M	19548771M	22147813M

M = $ thousand   MM = $ million
See Pages 9 through 22 for Explanation of Ratios and Data

Comparative Historical Data / Current Data Sorted by Sales

			Type of Statement						
141	135	130	Unqualified	2	8	17	7	12	101
126	172	156	Reviewed	2	20	17	25	54	38
502	498	511	Compiled	70	228	71	51	62	29
1102	1309	1271	Tax Returns	377	612	134	93	37	18
1086	1073	1215	Other	185	455	139	125	121	190
4/1/08-3/31/09 ALL	4/1/09-3/31/10 ALL	4/1/10-3/31/11 ALL		236 (4/1-9/30/10) 0-1MM	1-3MM	3-5MM	3,047 (10/1/10-3/31/11) 5-10MM	10-25MM	25MM & OVER
2957	3187	3283	NUMBER OF STATEMENTS	636	1323	361	301	286	376
%	%	%	ASSETS	%	%	%	%	%	%
13.9	14.7	14.8	Cash & Equivalents	14.3	15.9	17.2	13.6	14.9	10.4
2.1	2.0	1.9	Trade Receivables (net)	1.2	1.9	1.7	2.5	2.8	2.4
6.4	6.2	6.1	Inventory	8.2	6.5	6.0	5.0	4.6	3.5
3.2	2.8	2.9	All Other Current	2.9	3.0	3.8	2.3	2.1	2.8
25.6	25.7	25.7	Total Current	26.6	27.2	28.7	23.4	24.3	19.1
52.6	52.8	51.5	Fixed Assets (net)	52.9	48.6	50.3	53.8	54.9	56.3
10.9	11.4	11.3	Intangibles (net)	10.0	10.9	8.9	11.3	10.7	17.3
11.0	10.2	11.5	All Other Non-Current	10.5	13.2	12.1	11.5	10.1	7.3
100.0	100.0	100.0	Total	100.0	100.0	100.0	100.0	100.0	100.0
			LIABILITIES						
6.2	5.4	5.5	Notes Payable-Short Term	9.2	6.5	3.7	2.5	3.6	1.6
4.7	5.0	4.2	Cur. Mat.-L.T.D.	4.1	3.1	4.1	5.2	6.7	5.8
10.1	9.7	10.1	Trade Payables	8.4	11.2	10.8	11.1	9.9	8.4
.2	.1	.1	Income Taxes Payable	.1	.1	.2	.0	.2	.1
20.6	21.5	19.6	All Other Current	26.4	19.5	19.7	18.1	15.2	12.9
41.8	41.7	39.6	Total Current	48.2	40.5	38.5	36.8	35.5	28.7
35.9	36.3	34.6	Long-Term Debt	33.8	33.5	31.4	36.3	36.3	40.2
.1	.1	.1	Deferred Taxes	.0	.0	.0	.0	.1	.8
11.7	13.2	13.4	All Other Non-Current	21.4	14.9	9.0	8.4	4.6	9.4
10.6	8.7	12.2	Net Worth	-3.4	11.0	21.0	18.6	23.5	20.9
100.0	100.0	100.0	Total Liabilities & Net Worth	100.0	100.0	100.0	100.0	100.0	100.0
			INCOME DATA						
100.0	100.0	100.0	Net Sales	100.0	100.0	100.0	100.0	100.0	100.0
60.3	61.3	60.9	Gross Profit	60.9	61.0	61.6	61.0	60.2	60.4
56.9	57.5	56.9	Operating Expenses	59.1	57.0	56.6	56.0	54.7	55.7
3.3	3.8	4.0	Operating Profit	1.8	4.1	5.1	5.0	5.6	4.7
1.4	1.3	1.1	All Other Expenses (net)	1.2	.9	.8	1.2	1.5	1.7
1.9	2.5	2.9	Profit Before Taxes	.6	3.2	4.3	3.8	4.1	3.0
			RATIOS						
1.5	1.6	1.6		2.3	1.8	1.6	1.3	1.2	1.0
.7	.7	.7	Current	.8	.8	.8	.7	.7	.6
.3	.3	.3		.3	.3	.4	.3	.4	.4
1.0	1.0	1.1		1.4	1.2	1.1	.9	.9	.7
(2937) .4	(3160) .4	(3258) .4	Quick	(627) .4	(1309) .4	(359) .5	.4	.5	.4
.1	.1	.1		.1	.1	.1	.1	.2	.2
0 UND	0 UND	0 UND		0 UND	0 UND	0 UND	0 UND	0 UND	0 999.8
0 UND	0 UND	0 UND	Sales/Receivables	0 UND	0 UND	0 999.8	0 999.8	1 490.1	1 286.8
1 255.3	1 276.1	1 289.7		0 UND	1 580.3	1 266.8	2 182.9	3 141.1	4 83.2
6 62.8	6 64.4	6 60.5		5 68.7	6 65.4	7 55.0	7 55.8	7 53.6	7 53.5
10 36.4	10 35.1	10 35.6	Cost of Sales/Inventory	11 31.9	10 35.6	10 35.3	10 36.1	10 36.6	10 36.6
17 21.3	18 20.2	17 21.1		21 17.3	17 21.4	18 19.8	17 22.0	15 23.6	15 24.4
2 233.7	1 424.0	2 170.0		0 UND	0 UND	10 35.7	8 43.6	11 32.8	15 24.0
16 22.4	16 22.5	17 21.7	Cost of Sales/Payables	3 123.3	14 25.6	21 17.0	22 16.6	23 15.8	26 14.0
35 10.4	36 10.2	36 10.1		24 15.5	35 10.3	40 9.2	38 9.7	39 9.3	43 8.5
49.7	42.6	43.7		32.4	39.4	30.3	55.8	71.2	595.5
-45.2	-51.2	-60.6	Sales/Working Capital	-99.8	-77.9	-113.9	-44.3	-41.2	-26.6
-12.3	-12.4	-13.4		-10.9	-14.2	-16.4	-12.6	-12.8	-14.1
7.5	9.1	10.3		5.6	12.2	14.1	12.0	12.3	7.0
(2277) 2.3	(2407) 2.8	(2459) 2.9	EBIT/Interest	(372) 1.4	(913) 2.7	(275) 3.7	(269) 3.7	(263) 4.1	(367) 2.9
.0	.4	.5		-2.0	.1	.3	1.1	1.6	1.4
4.4	4.9	5.8			6.5	12.1	21.7	4.2	4.7
(188) 1.8	(218) 2.4	(181) 2.3	Net Profit + Depr., Dep., Amort./Cur. Mat. L/T/D	(21) 1.9	(10) 4.5	(19) 5.8	(35) 2.5	(94) 2.3
.8	1.2	1.4			.3	1.3	1.6	1.5	1.4
1.0	1.0	.9		.9	.7	.8	1.3	1.2	1.8
4.3	4.3	3.7	Fixed/Worth	5.4	3.1	2.2	4.0	3.2	8.0
-2.5	-2.3	-2.4		-1.3	-2.0	-4.4	-3.7	-5.9	-2.4
1.1	1.0	.9		.8	.7	.7	1.2	1.1	1.5
6.3	6.1	5.4	Debt/Worth	9.2	5.0	2.8	5.1	4.0	9.5
-4.4	-4.3	-4.4		-3.0	-3.8	-8.4	-7.0	-9.6	-4.4
99.1	94.1	95.3		87.9	113.5	102.5	80.5	81.9	68.7
(1782) 34.1	(1924) 36.5	(1989) 35.1	% Profit Before Taxes/Tangible Net Worth	(357) 27.4	(802) 40.1	(240) 32.8	(189) 40.2	(187) 37.0	(214) 30.8
4.3	7.2	7.6		.2	9.9	6.0	9.8	8.9	8.4
22.9	23.9	24.8		22.6	31.2	28.2	22.7	22.2	14.4
5.9	7.3	7.7	% Profit Before Taxes/Total Assets	3.2	9.5	10.3	7.8	8.5	6.1
-3.7	-2.0	-1.1		-9.1	-2.1	-.3	.6	2.2	1.6
18.4	17.6	18.7		23.9	27.3	21.0	13.1	10.6	7.1
6.8	6.7	6.9	Sales/Net Fixed Assets	7.5	9.2	7.4	5.7	5.7	4.2
3.1	3.0	3.1		2.7	3.9	3.8	3.0	3.0	2.8
5.9	5.7	5.7		6.3	6.8	5.8	4.5	4.2	3.2
3.3	3.2	3.2	Sales/Total Assets	3.4	3.9	3.4	2.9	2.8	2.3
1.9	1.8	1.9		1.7	2.1	1.9	1.7	1.9	1.6
1.3	1.3	1.3		1.2	1.0	1.2	1.5	1.9	2.4
(2461) 2.6	(2652) 2.7	(2652) 2.6	% Depr., Dep., Amort./Sales	(472) 2.5	(1030) 2.2	(311) 2.1	(269) 2.8	(257) 3.0	(313) 3.4
4.3	4.5	4.3		5.0	3.9	3.7	4.6	4.4	4.5
2.0	2.0	1.8		2.3	2.2	1.8	1.3	1.0	.9
(1176) 3.8	(1297) 4.0	(1340) 3.7	% Officers', Directors' Owners' Comp/Sales	(295) 5.3	(593) 4.0	(145) 3.3	(131) 2.5	(106) 2.3	(70) 2.4
7.1	7.0	6.7		9.2	6.8	6.1	4.4	3.8	5.6
56407256M	56991284M	60039762M	Net Sales ($)	410887M	2392627M	1382501M	2139742M	4493034M	49220971M
21935029M	25318175M	24590828M	Total Assets ($)	194780M	903093M	558648M	1034478M	1886864M	20012965M

M = $ thousand   MM = $ million
See Pages 9 through 22 for Explanation of Ratios and Data

Current Data Sorted by Assets | **Comparative Historical Data**

Type of Statement	0-500M	500M-2MM	2-10MM	10-50MM	50-100MM	100-250MM		ALL	ALL
Unqualified	2	4	11	32	12	13		96	82
Reviewed	7	22	46	32	3			77	64
Compiled	135	207	184	27	1			203	260
Tax Returns	308	155	72	8	3	2		259	316
Other	172	190	198	103	15	24		327	374
		126 (4/1-9/30/10)		1,862 (10/1/10-3/31/11)				4/1/06-3/31/07	4/1/07-3/31/08
NUMBER OF STATEMENTS	624	578	511	202	34	39		962	1096
ASSETS	%	%	%	%	%	%		%	%
Cash & Equivalents	19.4	15.9	15.0	11.0	11.8	5.8		14.8	13.9
Trade Receivables (net)	2.3	1.1	1.3	1.2	3.1	1.8		1.3	1.2
Inventory	7.4	3.0	2.8	2.2	2.0	1.9		3.7	3.9
All Other Current	1.8	1.8	1.5	2.0	3.4	2.7		3.2	2.3
Total Current	30.9	21.8	20.6	16.4	20.3	12.1		23.0	21.4
Fixed Assets (net)	47.2	49.8	50.3	54.8	48.6	46.8		53.8	52.7
Intangibles (net)	12.7	19.1	20.7	20.0	23.5	33.6		15.3	16.3
All Other Non-Current	9.3	9.3	8.3	8.8	7.6	7.5		7.9	9.6
Total	100.0	100.0	100.0	100.0	100.0	100.0		100.0	100.0
LIABILITIES									
Notes Payable-Short Term	9.7	2.4	2.8	3.3	2.4	.6		4.6	4.3
Cur. Mat.-L.T.D.	7.0	7.3	9.0	6.6	5.4	3.0		5.5	6.9
Trade Payables	11.9	7.2	5.9	5.6	5.6	4.9		7.9	7.8
Income Taxes Payable	.1	.1	.0	.1	.2	.7		.1	.1
All Other Current	24.8	13.7	10.0	9.8	7.4	9.3		14.4	19.4
Total Current	53.4	30.8	27.7	25.3	21.0	18.4		32.6	38.5
Long-Term Debt	35.5	42.4	46.5	44.1	48.9	46.1		43.2	45.4
Deferred Taxes	.1	.0	.0	.2	.4	2.5		.2	.2
All Other Non-Current	16.3	7.9	6.1	4.9	6.4	11.3		8.8	10.5
Net Worth	-5.3	18.9	19.7	25.5	23.3	21.8		15.2	5.5
Total Liabilities & Net Worth	100.0	100.0	100.0	100.0	100.0	100.0		100.0	100.0
INCOME DATA									
Net Sales	100.0	100.0	100.0	100.0	100.0	100.0		100.0	100.0
Gross Profit	61.4	63.8	63.1	60.5	60.3	53.1		59.8	61.4
Operating Expenses	57.9	58.0	57.5	54.3	54.2	47.7		54.8	56.8
Operating Profit	3.6	5.8	5.6	6.2	6.1	5.4		5.1	4.6
All Other Expenses (net)	.5	1.2	1.3	1.2	2.7	4.5		1.5	1.7
Profit Before Taxes	3.1	4.5	4.3	5.1	3.4	.9		3.6	2.9
RATIOS									
Current	2.0	1.6	1.2	1.2	1.1	1.0		1.5	1.2
	.7	.7	.7	.7	.7	.7		.7	.6
	.3	.3	.4	.3	.4	.4		.3	.3
Quick	1.4	1.3	1.0	.9	1.0	.7		1.1	.9
	(621) .5	(577) .5	.5	.4	.6	.3		(956) .5	(1088) .4
	.1	.2	.2	.2	.3	.2		.1	.1
Sales/Receivables	0 UND	0 UND	0 UND	0 UND	0 UND	0 749.4		0 UND	0 UND
	0 UND	0 UND	0 999.8	0 999.8	1 289.9	1 248.4		0 UND	0 UND
	0 999.8	0 817.0	1 361.8	2 189.2	4 93.5	5 70.2		1 400.3	1 414.3
Cost of Sales/Inventory	5 79.1	5 66.7	6 59.2	5 72.3	5 68.9	4 86.6		5 78.3	5 72.0
	8 45.0	9 42.9	9 42.4	8 43.4	7 51.8	7 50.7		8 45.8	8 43.2
	12 30.9	12 31.2	11 32.4	11 33.3	10 35.2	11 32.1		12 30.9	12 30.4
Cost of Sales/Payables	0 UND	4 81.9	6 62.8	12 30.6	15 24.1	8 43.5		6 65.4	4 99.7
	8 43.3	16 22.7	16 22.3	22 16.3	23 15.6	19 19.3		17 22.0	14 25.5
	23 15.9	32 11.5	31 11.8	33 11.2	50 7.3	40 9.2		32 11.4	31 11.9
Sales/Working Capital	40.0	35.8	58.0	86.9	197.1	238.5		54.7	95.2
	-79.0	-44.8	-44.5	-31.2	-30.3	-33.2		-52.7	-39.5
	-14.9	-14.8	-14.9	-13.1	-16.1	-14.7		-14.3	-13.1
EBIT/Interest	15.3	10.9	8.6	8.7	6.5	4.6		7.6	7.4
	(411) 3.6	(509) 4.2	(481) 3.9	(193) 3.8	(32) 2.7	(38) 2.4		(812) 2.9	(965) 2.7
	-.3	1.5	1.5	2.1	1.7	.4		1.0	.8
Net Profit + Depr., Dep., Amort./Cur. Mat. L/T/D		3.2	5.6	5.8		9.6		4.3	7.0
		(14) 3.0	(31) 2.4	(46) 2.6		(14) 3.0		(97) 2.1	(95) 2.7
		.9	1.2	1.4		.9		1.4	1.3
Fixed/Worth	.8	1.2	1.8	1.5	2.6	3.0		1.3	1.7
	4.6	13.3	-999.8	5.6	NM	12.8		6.5	86.3
	-1.3	-1.5	-1.7	-2.3	-2.3	-.6		-2.0	-1.7
Debt/Worth	.7	1.4	2.1	1.3	2.4	2.8		1.2	1.9
	13.9	17.0	-709.5	8.6	NM	27.7		9.0	-110.3
	-2.6	-3.3	-3.5	-4.1	-4.1	-2.2		-4.0	-3.3
% Profit Before Taxes/Tangible Net Worth	164.0	120.6	101.7	61.0	75.8	65.2		98.0	114.8
	(339) 56.5	(306) 55.4	(254) 41.8	(116) 31.0	(17) 19.7	(20) 24.8		(548) 38.8	(542) 45.6
	14.3	18.6	13.0	15.1	5.9	7.0		13.4	12.8
% Profit Before Taxes/Total Assets	47.8	25.2	20.0	14.2	10.4	8.5		22.9	22.5
	13.7	12.8	9.8	8.2	5.7	3.9		8.9	7.7
	-3.4	1.9	2.2	3.8	1.8	-4.2		.4	-.9
Sales/Net Fixed Assets	33.8	14.6	10.5	6.7	7.3	6.9		12.4	13.2
	12.3	7.1	5.8	4.1	4.3	4.4		6.1	6.7
	6.2	3.4	3.4	2.4	2.2	2.6		2.9	3.2
Sales/Total Assets	9.0	4.5	3.8	2.8	2.4	2.0		5.0	5.1
	5.6	3.0	2.6	2.0	1.7	1.6		3.0	3.2
	3.3	1.8	1.6	1.5	1.3	1.2		1.8	1.9
% Depr., Dep., Amort./Sales	1.2	1.7	2.5	2.6	2.6	2.9		1.8	1.8
	(477) 2.4	(463) 3.0	(442) 3.8	(191) 3.5	(29) 3.2	(19) 3.4		(845) 2.9	(956) 2.8
	4.2	4.9	5.4	4.9	4.9	3.9		4.3	4.4
% Officers', Directors' Owners' Comp/Sales	2.5	1.4	.9	.9				1.9	1.6
	(251) 3.8	(214) 2.9	(168) 1.8	(50) 1.6				(358) 3.6	(424) 3.2
	6.5	4.8	3.9	3.2				6.3	5.4
Net Sales ($)	784801M	2115413M	6261678M	9587914M	5488312M	10128499M		29808506M	21518858M
Total Assets ($)	142265M	615925M	2286323M	4262585M	2379735M	6151302M		12012619M	10292280M

© RMA 2011

M = $ thousand   MM = $ million

See Pages 9 through 22 for Explanation of Ratios and Data

Comparative Historical Data   Current Data Sorted by Sales

Type of Statement	4/1/08-3/31/09 ALL	4/1/09-3/31/10 ALL	4/1/10-3/31/11 ALL	0-1MM	1-3MM	3-5MM	5-10MM	10-25MM	25MM & OVER
Unqualified	95	118	74	1	2	1	5	11	54
Reviewed	78	112	110	2	8	14	21	31	34
Compiled	373	452	554	73	133	72	129	113	34
Tax Returns	481	591	548	199	212	55	35	37	10
Other	474	617	702	114	187	62	93	109	137
				126 (4/1-9/30/10)			1,862 (10/1/10-3/31/11)		
NUMBER OF STATEMENTS	1501	1890	1988	389	542	204	283	301	269
ASSETS	%	%	%	%	%	%	%	%	%
Cash & Equivalents	12.7	13.6	16.0	14.9	17.7	16.7	17.2	16.3	11.9
Trade Receivables (net)	1.2	1.6	1.6	2.1	1.6	1.2	1.6	1.1	1.8
Inventory	4.0	4.2	4.2	6.4	4.6	3.6	3.5	3.5	2.4
All Other Current	2.7	3.0	1.8	1.7	1.8	2.0	1.4	1.8	2.2
Total Current	20.5	22.4	23.6	25.2	25.6	23.5	23.7	22.6	18.3
Fixed Assets (net)	51.5	50.8	49.5	52.1	47.7	50.6	47.1	49.7	51.2
Intangibles (net)	18.7	18.0	18.0	13.3	16.4	18.6	21.3	19.9	21.7
All Other Non-Current	9.3	8.8	8.9	9.5	10.2	7.3	7.9	7.8	8.9
Total	100.0	100.0	100.0	100.0	100.0	100.0	100.0	100.0	100.0
LIABILITIES									
Notes Payable-Short Term	5.3	3.9	4.8	9.9	5.7	2.1	2.6	2.2	3.1
Cur. Mat.-L.T.D.	6.3	7.2	7.5	5.4	6.7	8.1	9.1	9.9	6.9
Trade Payables	7.7	7.5	8.1	8.4	9.5	8.5	7.2	7.4	6.4
Income Taxes Payable	.1	.1	.1	.1	.1	.1	.0	.2	.2
All Other Current	15.9	17.6	15.6	17.4	19.8	16.1	13.8	11.4	11.1
Total Current	35.3	36.3	36.1	41.2	41.8	34.8	32.8	31.0	27.7
Long-Term Debt	46.7	47.2	41.6	37.7	39.5	39.6	46.9	46.4	42.3
Deferred Taxes	.1	.1	.1	.0	.1	.0	.0	.1	.5
All Other Non-Current	9.5	8.7	9.8	20.2	8.4	10.0	4.8	6.9	6.2
Net Worth	8.4	7.8	12.3	1.0	10.2	15.7	15.6	15.6	23.2
Total Liabilities & Net Worth	100.0	100.0	100.0	100.0	100.0	100.0	100.0	100.0	100.0
INCOME DATA									
Net Sales	100.0	100.0	100.0	100.0	100.0	100.0	100.0	100.0	100.0
Gross Profit	60.9	62.0	62.3	60.4	63.1	63.9	64.0	62.4	60.1
Operating Expenses	57.3	57.3	57.2	57.7	57.2	57.8	58.5	57.3	54.5
Operating Profit	3.6	4.7	5.1	2.7	6.0	6.1	5.5	5.1	5.6
All Other Expenses (net)	1.4	1.1	1.1	1.5	.9	1.1	1.0	.7	1.6
Profit Before Taxes	2.2	3.6	4.0	1.2	5.0	5.0	4.5	4.4	4.0
RATIOS									
Current	1.2	1.4	1.5	3.0	1.6	1.7	1.2	1.2	1.1
	.6	.7	.7	.8	.7	.7	.7	.7	.7
	.3	.3	.3	.2	.3	.4	.3	.4	.4
Quick	.9	1.0	1.2	1.8	1.3	1.3	1.0	1.0	.9
	(1495) .4	(1877) .4	(1984) .5	(387) .5	(540) .5	.5	.5	.6	.5
	.1	.1	.2	.1	.1	.2	.2	.2	.2
Sales/Receivables	0 UND	0 UND	0 UND	0 UND	0 UND	0 UND	0 UND	0 UND	0 UND
	0 UND	0 UND	0 UND	0 UND	0 UND	0 UND	0 999.8	0 999.8	1 630.9
	1 450.8	1 453.8	1 495.2	0 UND	0 999.8	0 999.8	1 391.3	1 364.7	3 143.9
Cost of Sales/Inventory	5 68.5	5 69.1	5 68.8	4 81.5	5 77.6	6 63.1	6 57.2	6 58.1	5 70.0
	9 42.2	9 42.3	9 43.6	8 43.5	8 46.4	8 44.0	9 40.6	9 42.6	8 45.0
	12 30.1	12 31.5	11 32.0	16 23.2	11 32.5	12 31.0	11 32.3	11 33.5	11 33.8
Cost of Sales/Payables	3 122.9	3 138.3	4 97.6	0 UND	3 121.8	6 58.0	6 64.4	7 50.6	11 33.5
	15 24.2	15 24.0	15 24.1	4 86.0	15 24.7	17 21.2	17 21.9	17 21.5	21 17.6
	30 12.1	28 13.2	29 12.4	21 17.5	29 12.7	32 11.4	29 12.6	30 12.2	34 10.7
Sales/Working Capital	104.1	59.9	44.0	24.6	40.5	35.2	76.4	90.8	159.6
	-36.0	-44.5	-48.9	-80.9	-51.5	-53.2	-37.5	-55.9	-31.2
	-12.7	-14.7	-14.6	-10.0	-13.2	-17.2	-15.9	-18.1	-14.3
EBIT/Interest	6.6	9.1	10.4	5.0	14.3	12.3	11.6	9.9	8.9
	(1304) 2.3	(1622) 3.4	(1664) 3.8	(254) 1.9	(422) 4.2	(177) 5.1	(269) 4.5	(287) 4.3	(255) 3.9
	.6	1.2	1.3	-1.2	1.2	1.4	1.4	2.0	1.9
Net Profit + Depr., Dep., Amort./Cur. Mat. L/T/D	4.7	3.9	5.2				4.3	4.5	5.9
	(107) 2.1	(151) 2.1	(116) 2.5				(21) 2.0	(15) 2.8	(66) 2.5
	1.1	1.1	1.3				.7	1.0	1.4
Fixed/Worth	1.8	1.5	1.2	.8	1.0	1.3	1.6	1.8	1.8
	-102.3	22.5	11.9	6.8	6.3	7.4	-8.3	-159.0	7.9
	-1.3	-1.3	-1.5	-1.6	-1.4	-2.0	-1.0	-1.5	-2.0
Debt/Worth	2.2	1.8	1.3	.6	1.0	1.5	1.7	2.1	1.8
	-47.8	42.1	22.7	17.4	10.8	10.8	-14.6	-103.8	11.1
	-2.9	-2.8	-3.2	-2.9	-3.1	-3.8	-2.5	-3.5	-3.7
% Profit Before Taxes/Tangible Net Worth	103.1	130.6	118.1	99.1	154.9	143.8	94.6	108.2	78.0
	(731) 38.0	(978) 50.9	(1052) 46.7	(207) 32.8	(301) 55.3	(118) 69.0	(124) 42.2	(149) 48.3	(153) 37.3
	7.9	16.9	14.6	3.9	16.5	19.2	17.3	19.6	14.6
% Profit Before Taxes/Total Assets	18.3	23.6	25.6	20.8	37.0	27.9	23.2	22.2	15.7
	6.1	9.4	10.3	5.2	14.5	14.9	10.6	11.0	7.7
	-1.4	1.0	1.3	-5.8	1.1	2.3	2.2	3.9	3.2
Sales/Net Fixed Assets	13.6	14.4	15.6	18.1	24.4	15.0	16.4	12.2	8.0
	6.3	6.4	7.1	6.5	8.9	7.9	7.8	7.0	5.1
	3.1	3.4	3.6	2.5	4.3	3.9	4.4	4.3	3.0
Sales/Total Assets	4.7	5.0	5.3	6.0	6.6	5.5	4.8	4.6	3.3
	2.9	3.0	3.1	2.7	3.7	3.5	3.2	3.3	2.3
	1.7	1.8	1.8	1.5	2.2	2.1	1.9	2.1	1.6
% Depr., Dep., Amort./Sales	1.9	1.8	1.8	1.6	1.5	1.6	2.0	2.1	2.5
	(1274) 3.2	(1591) 3.2	(1621) 3.2	(302) 3.3	(424) 2.6	(158) 2.8	(234) 3.5	(269) 3.5	(234) 3.3
	4.9	4.9	4.8	5.7	4.7	4.4	5.0	4.8	4.5
% Officers', Directors' Owners' Comp/Sales	1.4	1.5	1.4	2.8	1.8	1.0	1.0	.9	.8
	(562) 3.0	(660) 3.1	(695) 3.0	(141) 5.1	(215) 3.4	(80) 2.6	(96) 2.0	(106) 1.8	(57) 1.6
	5.7	5.6	5.1	8.1	4.7	4.8	3.6	3.6	3.6
Net Sales ($)	30224552M	34025855M	34366617M	239080M	994552M	801854M	2051289M	4637916M	25641926M
Total Assets ($)	13390780M	16878193M	15838135M	130546M	403742M	314307M	805628M	1698687M	12485225M

M = $ thousand   MM = $ million
See Pages 9 through 22 for Explanation of Ratios and Data

Current Data Sorted by Assets | **Comparative Historical Data**

	0-500M	500M-2MM	2-10MM	10-50MM	50-100MM	100-250MM	Type of Statement	4/1/06-3/31/07 ALL	4/1/07-3/31/08 ALL
		1	2	1		1	Unqualified	7	5
		3	4	4			Reviewed	7	9
	5	4	1	3			Compiled	10	5
	36	7	7				Tax Returns	42	67
	10	7	8	3	1	2	Other	38	39
		10 (4/1-9/30/10)		94 (10/1/10-3/31/11)					
NUMBER OF STATEMENTS	51	22	16	11	1	3		104	125
	%	%	%	%	%	%	**ASSETS**	%	%
Cash & Equivalents	13.8	12.2	14.8	6.2				11.8	10.3
Trade Receivables (net)	2.6	1.7	4.9	2.7				2.5	1.2
Inventory	4.7	2.6	4.7	4.2				4.8	3.6
All Other Current	3.1	2.1	.7	2.3				1.2	1.3
Total Current	24.3	18.6	25.0	15.5				20.3	16.4
Fixed Assets (net)	52.4	48.0	52.7	48.3				48.4	55.4
Intangibles (net)	12.4	19.5	16.3	22.0				15.7	15.8
All Other Non-Current	10.9	13.9	6.0	14.2				15.6	12.5
Total	100.0	100.0	100.0	100.0				100.0	100.0
							LIABILITIES		
Notes Payable-Short Term	10.9	4.2	7.1	4.0				10.4	6.1
Cur. Mat.-L.T.D.	8.9	6.9	6.7	7.3				6.5	4.9
Trade Payables	9.8	8.2	8.6	7.2				5.9	5.6
Income Taxes Payable	.0	.7	.0	.0				.2	.0
All Other Current	20.0	13.1	5.4	8.9				15.3	12.3
Total Current	49.5	32.9	27.8	27.3				38.3	28.9
Long-Term Debt	50.1	60.6	38.8	37.1				36.1	47.5
Deferred Taxes	.0	.0	.0	.6				.1	.0
All Other Non-Current	25.1	9.7	23.8	21.2				11.8	13.9
Net Worth	-24.7	-3.3	9.6	13.8				13.7	9.7
Total Liabilities & Net Worth	100.0	100.0	100.0	100.0				100.0	100.0
							INCOME DATA		
Net Sales	100.0	100.0	100.0	100.0				100.0	100.0
Gross Profit									
Operating Expenses	95.1	95.4	96.4	88.3				92.5	94.9
Operating Profit	4.9	4.6	3.6	11.7				7.5	5.1
All Other Expenses (net)	2.1	1.6	1.8	3.1				1.9	3.0
Profit Before Taxes	2.8	3.0	1.8	8.6				5.6	2.1
							RATIOS		
	1.6	1.0	1.5	.9				1.6	1.4
Current	.6	.5	.9	.6				.7	.7
	.3	.3	.4	.5				.1	.2
	1.1	1.0	1.2	.5				1.3	1.0
Quick	.3	.3	(15) .9	.4				(103) .5	.4
	.1	.0	.3	.3				.1	.1
	0 UND	0 UND	0 UND	1 519.6				0 UND	0 UND
Sales/Receivables	0 UND	0 UND	1 284.4	4 103.0				0 UND	0 UND
	0 UND	3 144.1	7 55.4	15 23.9				1 284.2	0 UND
							Cost of Sales/Inventory		
							Cost of Sales/Payables		
	43.8	NM	19.7	-39.7				45.8	86.4
Sales/Working Capital	-49.8	-18.3	-363.6	-24.8				-51.7	-37.5
	-10.5	-6.2	-11.2	-7.8				-9.3	-11.4
	4.7	5.2	10.8	16.0				8.4	6.8
EBIT/Interest	(43) 1.4	(20) 1.9	3.4	5.6				(83) 2.7	(103) 2.6
	-1.7	.5	.2	1.5				1.5	.3
							Net Profit + Depr., Dep., Amort./Cur. Mat. L/T/D		
	1.5	14.6	1.2	2.1				1.0	1.3
Fixed/Worth	-22.0	-2.5	11.0	5.2				6.0	-129.3
	-.9	-.6	-2.1	-.8				-1.2	-1.4
	1.6	16.3	1.3	1.5				.9	1.3
Debt/Worth	-8.9	-4.0	12.3	13.3				10.1	-92.8
	-2.0	-2.5	-5.2	-2.4				-3.2	-2.8
	142.3						% Profit Before Taxes/Tangible Net Worth	139.8	129.3
	(24) 45.1							(61) 56.8	(60) 67.2
	-2.8							17.7	17.2
	22.1	16.6	15.4	17.4			% Profit Before Taxes/Total Assets	24.9	23.3
	3.4	8.5	7.0	9.9				8.4	6.2
	-12.1	-1.5	-2.2	1.0				1.7	-1.3
	16.5	11.4	6.3	6.9			Sales/Net Fixed Assets	12.0	9.4
	8.7	4.8	4.3	3.3				6.3	5.0
	4.9	3.2	2.0	1.6				2.9	2.5
	6.5	3.4	3.0	1.9			Sales/Total Assets	4.0	3.8
	3.7	2.1	2.0	1.4				2.6	2.4
	2.0	1.7	.8	1.2				1.6	1.4
	2.2	2.7	3.4	2.0			% Depr., Dep., Amort./Sales	2.2	2.4
	(39) 3.1	(19) 3.9	(13) 4.8	3.7				(85) 3.7	(111) 4.1
	5.9	6.5	7.7	7.2				5.3	6.6
	3.3						% Officers', Directors' Owners' Comp/Sales	2.1	2.9
	(23) 8.4							(32) 4.4	(42) 4.6
	13.8							8.7	8.0
Net Sales ($)	42294M	61364M	143079M	255378M	90609M	839443M		3951314M	2007215M
Total Assets ($)	10405M	22398M	62815M	203883M	91618M	435987M		1220721M	694303M

© RMA 2011

M = $ thousand   MM = $ million
See Pages 9 through 22 for Explanation of Ratios and Data

Comparative Historical Data / Current Data Sorted by Sales

4/1/08-3/31/09 ALL	4/1/09-3/31/10 ALL	4/1/10-3/31/11 ALL	Type of Statement	0-1MM	1-3MM	3-5MM	5-10MM	10-25MM	25MM & OVER
4	7	5	Unqualified		1	1			3
2	16	11	Reviewed		2	1	3	4	1
9	24	13	Compiled		1	2		1	3
31	52	44	Tax Returns	6	18	2		1	
58	31	31	Other	23	1	2	2	1	3
				9	8	4		5	
				10 (4/1-9/30/10)			94 (10/1/10-3/31/11)		
104	130	104	**NUMBER OF STATEMENTS**	38	30	10	5	11	10
%	%	%	**ASSETS**	%	%	%	%	%	%
8.3	12.7	13.3	Cash & Equivalents	10.9	15.7	13.6		12.1	14.9
3.3	3.2	2.9	Trade Receivables (net)	2.9	1.2	3.1		3.5	3.5
6.7	4.9	4.4	Inventory	4.5	3.3	3.4		3.4	6.0
2.9	2.9	2.6	All Other Current	2.0	2.9	1.5		2.4	3.4
21.2	23.6	23.1	Total Current	20.3	23.1	21.6		21.4	27.8
50.0	45.7	51.1	Fixed Assets (net)	55.4	50.1	40.4		55.1	48.3
19.3	20.1	15.1	Intangibles (net)	12.9	17.8	16.9		18.6	8.9
9.5	10.6	10.8	All Other Non-Current	11.4	8.9	21.0		4.8	15.0
100.0	100.0	100.0	Total	100.0	100.0	100.0		100.0	100.0
			LIABILITIES						
4.7	3.7	7.9	Notes Payable-Short Term	10.5	11.5	.7		2.1	4.8
5.1	6.2	7.7	Cur. Mat.-L.T.D.	7.6	9.0	4.7		8.6	4.4
7.7	4.8	8.8	Trade Payables	10.6	6.8	8.6		9.2	6.1
.1	.0	.1	Income Taxes Payable	.0	.5	.1		.0	.0
16.3	10.2	15.0	All Other Current	23.7	10.6	7.4		9.9	12.8
33.9	24.8	39.6	Total Current	52.5	38.3	21.5		29.8	28.0
44.9	41.4	47.8	Long-Term Debt	59.6	49.3	41.5		36.4	23.7
.0	.0	.1	Deferred Taxes	.0	.0	.0		.0	.6
18.0	13.4	20.5	All Other Non-Current	31.5	7.4	14.3		22.7	28.8
3.1	20.4	-7.9	Net Worth	-43.5	5.0	22.7		11.1	18.9
100.0	100.0	100.0	Total Liabilities & Net Worth	100.0	100.0	100.0		100.0	100.0
			INCOME DATA						
100.0	100.0	100.0	Net Sales	100.0	100.0	100.0		100.0	100.0
			Gross Profit						
99.4	94.4	94.7	Operating Expenses	94.2	98.0	96.1		89.9	92.8
.6	5.6	5.3	Operating Profit	5.8	2.0	3.9		10.1	7.2
2.2	1.9	2.0	All Other Expenses (net)	2.2	2.0	.4		3.3	1.2
-1.6	3.7	3.3	Profit Before Taxes	3.7	.0	3.5		6.8	6.1
			RATIOS						
1.1	2.0	1.3	Current	1.5	1.2	2.5		1.0	1.5
.6	.9	.6		.5	.5	.6		.7	.7
.2	.4	.3		.1	.3	.4		.5	.5
.7	1.2	1.0	Quick	1.1	1.0	2.4		.9	.7
(102) .4	(128) .6	(103) .4		.3	(29) .3	.4		.3	.5
.1	.2	.2		.0	.2	.1		.3	.3
0 UND	0 UND	0 UND	Sales/Receivables	0 UND	0 UND	0 UND		0 999.8	0 UND
0 UND	0 UND	0 UND		0 UND	0 UND	4 99.2		1 519.6	5 74.8
4 89.6	1 366.1	3 108.6		0 900.0	0 UND	8 46.8		15 23.9	9 39.7
			Cost of Sales/Inventory						
			Cost of Sales/Payables						
118.1	26.1	56.4	Sales/Working Capital	39.7	73.2	22.9		113.9	14.9
-36.4	-153.3	-40.6		-20.5	-51.7	-38.5		-52.5	-25.4
-10.3	-18.9	-9.6		-5.4	-9.8	-15.9		-9.5	-15.1
4.0	8.2	6.2	EBIT/Interest	4.4	4.3	7.7		6.9	21.5
(82) 1.6	(110) 3.1	(94) 2.1		(32) 1.3	(26) 1.3	3.8		3.9	10.7
-2.3	.9	-.3		-1.1	-3.0	.7		.1	-7.0
			Net Profit + Depr., Dep., Amort./Cur. Mat. L/T/D						
1.7	1.1	1.6	Fixed/Worth	1.4	3.9	.6		2.1	1.0
-8.6	10.1	UND		-2.5	33.5	12.4		16.4	1.6
-.8	-1.3	-.9		-.4	-.9	-1.1		-1.0	NM
2.5	1.2	1.6	Debt/Worth	2.1	3.7	1.4		1.7	.6
-15.0	27.3	UND		-3.9	39.0	21.0		29.6	1.4
-2.6	-3.3	-2.5		-1.6	-2.6	-2.9		-4.5	NM
127.3	105.9	97.6	% Profit Before Taxes/Tangible Net Worth	166.0	94.8				
(46) 51.3	(70) 34.8	(52) 37.4		(12) 58.2	(17) 19.8				
4.9	4.7	-1.0		21.1	-21.4				
18.1	21.9	17.3	% Profit Before Taxes/Total Assets	20.0	16.0	16.2		15.7	23.1
4.0	8.5	6.4		3.4	2.1	7.4		6.1	11.1
-7.3	-.4	-3.4		-8.4	-11.0	-.5		-2.1	-6.9
11.5	14.5	12.5	Sales/Net Fixed Assets	14.0	13.8	29.9		9.4	6.9
5.0	5.4	6.3		5.8	7.2	4.4		4.9	5.0
2.4	2.8	3.3		3.0	4.7	3.1		1.6	2.4
3.8	3.7	4.4	Sales/Total Assets	4.0	6.0	4.4		4.2	2.7
2.3	2.1	2.4		2.4	3.6	2.3		1.9	2.0
1.4	1.2	1.5		1.4	1.9	1.2		1.4	1.3
2.1	2.5	2.4	% Depr., Dep., Amort./Sales	2.3	2.6				
(85) 3.8	(104) 4.5	(83) 3.7		(28) 3.7	(26) 3.5				
7.0	7.3	6.7		8.6	5.4				
2.6	1.9	3.0	% Officers', Directors' Owners' Comp/Sales	4.1	3.2				
(28) 5.2	(31) 5.1	(40) 6.8		(13) 9.1	(17) 6.8				
8.9	9.4	10.7		18.3	10.9				
1543136M	1243686M	1432167M	Net Sales ($)	18366M	50644M	37548M	32827M	175207M	1117575M
721248M	565537M	827106M	Total Assets ($)	10160M	21870M	21250M	20510M	126661M	626655M

© RMA 2011   M = $ thousand   MM = $ million
See Pages 9 through 22 for Explanation of Ratios and Data

Current Data Sorted by Assets | Comparative Historical Data

Type of Statement	0-500M	500M-2MM	2-10MM	10-50MM	50-100MM	100-250MM		4/1/06-3/31/07 ALL	4/1/07-3/31/08 ALL
Unqualified	2	2	3	7		1		9	13
Reviewed	1	5	12	3				8	5
Compiled		9	7					4	10
Tax Returns	16	11	6					2	17
Other	8	8	15	3	5	1		15	23
		18 (4/1-9/30/10)		107 (10/1/10-3/31/11)					
NUMBER OF STATEMENTS	27	35	43	13	6	1		38	68

	0-500M %	500M-2MM %	2-10MM %	10-50MM %	50-100MM %	100-250MM %		ALL %	ALL %
ASSETS									
Cash & Equivalents	15.9	13.4	14.8	10.3				13.3	11.9
Trade Receivables (net)	14.0	16.2	32.7	24.4				25.3	21.5
Inventory	7.2	6.3	9.8	12.1				8.0	7.9
All Other Current	.9	7.2	4.5	3.2				5.2	4.8
Total Current	38.0	43.0	61.8	50.1				51.7	46.1
Fixed Assets (net)	46.7	31.9	24.5	29.2				27.8	33.4
Intangibles (net)	6.9	9.0	6.9	8.2				4.7	10.2
All Other Non-Current	8.4	16.1	6.8	12.5				15.8	10.3
Total	100.0	100.0	100.0	100.0				100.0	100.0
LIABILITIES									
Notes Payable-Short Term	28.0	12.0	7.0	7.4				8.1	6.3
Cur. Mat.-L.T.D.	4.4	4.1	3.4	2.3				3.6	4.0
Trade Payables	15.3	11.8	21.1	14.9				17.7	15.2
Income Taxes Payable	.0	3.6	.6	.0				1.2	.1
All Other Current	18.1	20.1	16.0	11.5				17.5	17.2
Total Current	65.7	51.6	48.2	36.2				48.1	42.9
Long-Term Debt	22.7	20.7	15.0	22.9				18.3	27.2
Deferred Taxes	.0	.0	.1	.3				.1	.2
All Other Non-Current	22.1	17.3	13.1	4.2				11.2	7.0
Net Worth	-10.6	10.3	23.6	36.3				22.3	22.7
Total Liabilities & Net Worth	100.0	100.0	100.0	100.0				100.0	100.0
INCOME DATA									
Net Sales	100.0	100.0	100.0	100.0				100.0	100.0
Gross Profit									
Operating Expenses	95.0	96.2	95.8	95.3				95.0	91.8
Operating Profit	5.0	3.8	4.2	4.7				5.0	8.2
All Other Expenses (net)	1.2	1.7	1.7	1.4				1.5	3.7
Profit Before Taxes	3.8	2.1	2.5	3.4				3.5	4.5
RATIOS									
Current	2.2	1.9	2.3	2.0				1.8	2.1
	.8	1.0	1.3	1.3				1.1	1.1
	.2	.5	.8	.9				.5	.4
Quick	1.5	1.3	1.9	1.4				1.4	1.4
	(26) .4	.6	1.1	.9				.8	.8
	.1	.4	.6	.8				.4	.3
Sales/Receivables	0 UND	0 UND	5 68.3	18 20.0				9 42.4	1 305.1
	0 UND	8 45.2	26 14.2	27 13.4				14 26.7	16 22.5
	7 52.1	26 14.0	42 8.8	37 9.9				40 9.1	37 10.0
Cost of Sales/Inventory									
Cost of Sales/Payables									
Sales/Working Capital	32.9	18.2	11.9	8.4				15.6	14.8
	-59.6	999.8	24.9	27.2				93.8	77.4
	-10.1	-13.0	-51.1	-128.9				-20.7	-16.8
EBIT/Interest	12.0	6.7	22.4	21.7				13.8	20.0
	(25) 5.1	(27) 2.8	(39) 9.6	(12) 5.4				(29) 4.1	(60) 5.6
	.3	.3	1.5	.2				.6	1.6
Net Profit + Depr., Dep., Amort./Cur. Mat. L/T/D								5.5	7.6
								(10) 3.7	(11) 3.3
								1.9	1.5
Fixed/Worth	.9	.7	.4	.2				.3	.4
	81.5	8.0	.9	.8				1.0	1.7
	-1.2	-1.2	-13.3	2.7				NM	-7.4
Debt/Worth	.5	1.0	1.4	1.4				.7	1.2
	-26.2	23.6	3.8	1.7				3.4	3.9
	-2.9	-3.9	-98.5	6.1				NM	-29.6
% Profit Before Taxes/Tangible Net Worth	135.4	157.5	84.8	50.0				57.8	111.6
	(13) 34.8	(20) 19.3	(31) 16.7	(12) 25.6				(29) 33.5	(49) 46.3
	-11.5	3.2	1.2	-20.3				11.1	18.0
% Profit Before Taxes/Total Assets	22.4	16.9	19.8	19.4				14.2	20.4
	12.2	4.8	7.6	7.2				9.4	10.1
	-6.5	1.8	.4	-1.9				-1.4	1.6
Sales/Net Fixed Assets	29.7	66.9	90.3	90.2				36.4	45.4
	11.8	17.6	25.0	11.6				16.9	11.4
	6.7	5.8	9.2	3.8				7.4	5.6
Sales/Total Assets	8.2	6.2	6.5	3.9				5.1	5.4
	5.6	3.7	3.9	2.9				3.2	3.3
	3.8	2.2	2.2	2.0				2.1	2.1
% Depr., Dep., Amort./Sales	1.9	.5	.4	.7				.6	1.0
	(16) 2.9	(30) 1.1	(37) 1.0	1.9				(30) 1.8	(54) 2.1
	3.7	4.1	3.0	3.3				3.1	4.0
% Officers', Directors' Owners' Comp/Sales	1.2	.9	1.2						1.7
	(15) 7.2	(17) 4.2	(15) 2.1					(26)	2.8
	9.3	11.6	6.0						12.6
Net Sales ($)	32144M	156838M	904456M	948366M	1336156M	1073699M		1474936M	3494590M
Total Assets ($)	5312M	35432M	201966M	336656M	434247M	104336M		461050M	1086235M

M = $ thousand   MM = $ million
See Pages 9 through 22 for Explanation of Ratios and Data

Comparative Historical Data			Type of Statement	Current Data Sorted by Sales					
18	12	13	Unqualified		1	1		3	8
10	10	22	Reviewed	1	1	3	3	5	9
18	16	17	Compiled	1	1	6	6	2	1
22	30	33	Tax Returns	12	6	8	2	3	2
27	36	40	Other	4	10		5	6	15
4/1/08-	4/1/09-	4/1/10-				18 (4/1-9/30/10)	107 (10/1/10-3/31/11)		
3/31/09	3/31/10	3/31/11							
ALL	ALL	ALL		0-1MM	1-3MM	3-5MM	5-10MM	10-25MM	25MM & OVER
95	104	125	NUMBER OF STATEMENTS	18	19	18	16	19	35
%	%	%	ASSETS	%	%	%	%	%	%
10.2	12.6	13.6	Cash & Equivalents	12.1	16.1	16.4	9.8	13.5	13.5
19.8	20.3	22.9	Trade Receivables (net)	16.1	4.5	15.4	32.7	33.2	30.2
10.5	8.1	8.7	Inventory	5.3	5.9	5.3	8.8	13.6	11.1
2.4	4.5	4.8	All Other Current	.6	.4	11.6	5.6	4.7	5.7
43.0	45.5	50.1	Total Current	34.1	26.9	48.7	56.8	64.9	60.5
34.8	35.7	31.4	Fixed Assets (net)	58.5	44.0	24.7	27.2	19.5	22.4
12.9	7.9	8.2	Intangibles (net)	5.0	17.7	1.1	6.5	9.6	8.3
9.4	10.9	10.3	All Other Non-Current	2.5	11.4	25.5	9.5	5.9	8.7
100.0	100.0	100.0	Total	100.0	100.0	100.0	100.0	100.0	100.0
			LIABILITIES						
10.4	12.3	13.2	Notes Payable-Short Term	25.2	10.3	13.7	17.4	10.1	8.1
3.3	3.9	3.6	Cur. Mat.-L.T.D.	2.6	3.9	2.3	9.0	1.6	3.3
17.7	14.5	16.5	Trade Payables	5.6	15.8	12.3	20.8	21.5	19.9
.2	.1	1.3	Income Taxes Payable	.0	.0	.5	8.7	.3	.2
19.0	18.8	17.2	All Other Current	10.4	16.3	24.9	19.5	11.9	19.2
50.6	49.6	51.8	Total Current	43.8	46.3	53.7	75.3	45.3	50.7
29.0	28.9	20.7	Long-Term Debt	21.4	31.3	13.2	23.3	10.0	22.9
.2	.3	.1	Deferred Taxes	.0	.0	.1	.0	.2	.3
6.1	11.0	14.7	All Other Non-Current	24.1	18.7	23.3	7.2	16.1	6.0
14.0	10.1	12.7	Net Worth	10.7	3.7	9.8	-5.8	28.4	20.1
100.0	100.0	100.0	Total Liabilities & Net Worth	100.0	100.0	100.0	100.0	100.0	100.0
			INCOME DATA						
100.0	100.0	100.0	Net Sales	100.0	100.0	100.0	100.0	100.0	100.0
			Gross Profit						
94.9	92.8	95.7	Operating Expenses	89.3	96.5	99.0	97.1	95.7	96.1
5.1	7.2	4.3	Operating Profit	10.7	3.5	1.0	2.9	4.3	3.9
2.6	2.4	1.7	All Other Expenses (net)	6.4	.7	-.5	.5	1.9	1.3
2.5	4.7	2.7	Profit Before Taxes	4.3	2.7	1.5	2.4	2.4	2.6
			RATIOS						
1.7	1.8	2.0		3.4	2.3	1.5	1.6	2.5	1.6
1.1	1.1	1.2	Current	.8	.7	1.0	1.0	1.3	1.3
.4	.6	.7		.2	.3	.4	.7	.8	.9
1.1	1.2	1.5		2.0	2.2	1.2	1.3	2.4	1.3
.8	.8	(124) .8	Quick	.5	(18) .6	.6	.7	1.0	.9
.3	.4	.4		.1	.3	.1	.4	.6	.7
0 UND	0 999.8	0 UND		0 UND	0 UND	0 UND	0 816.1	10 38.4	16 23.3
14 25.2	16 22.4	15 24.2	Sales/Receivables	0 UND	0 UND	6 62.2	29 12.4	20 18.6	26 14.2
32 11.4	32 11.5	30 12.0		9 41.5	11 33.8	14 25.2	45 8.1	42 8.8	31 11.9
			Cost of Sales/Inventory						
			Cost of Sales/Payables						
19.3	17.0	15.2		19.1	10.3	15.9	17.9	14.6	12.6
121.9	125.5	90.8	Sales/Working Capital	-94.2	-59.6	NM	-455.1	24.4	40.9
-21.6	-14.3	-20.5		-6.3	-15.1	-9.8	-28.2	-51.1	-77.1
10.9	15.8	13.1		22.5	7.0	10.4	10.9	18.0	24.3
(80) 3.1	(88) 3.7	(110) 4.6	EBIT/Interest	(14) 9.3	(18) 1.8	(12) 3.5	(15) 4.1	(17) 6.0	(34) 5.9
.7	.5	.7		.1	-4.5	1.7	.8	1.4	1.1
7.0	7.0	4.4							4.4
(17) 3.1	(14) 2.8	(20) 3.2	Net Profit + Depr., Dep., Amort./Cur. Mat. L/T/D						(12) 3.4
1.4	.3	.8							1.3
.5	.3	.5		.8	1.2	.1	.4	.5	.2
2.1	2.6	1.6	Fixed/Worth	18.8	-27.6	1.7	1.7	.9	.9
-2.5	-2.0	-2.0		-3.2	-.7	-3.4	-1.7	-.7	-21.2
1.7	1.6	1.3		.4	1.3	.8	2.9	1.4	1.4
6.7	7.0	5.9	Debt/Worth	19.8	-91.3	5.5	9.9	2.9	2.9
-4.1	-4.7	-5.5		-4.6	-2.9	-27.2	-2.4	-9.9	-134.1
77.8	98.7	65.7		67.4		200.8	76.2	77.0	53.3
(63) 38.0	(67) 40.9	(80) 20.1	% Profit Before Taxes/Tangible Net Worth	(10) 27.4	(13) 18.3	(10) 29.1	(12) 18.0	(26) 26.6
14.3	6.1	-3.9		-11.0		8.4	-11.4	2.3	-2.6
17.9	22.3	18.2		27.1	15.4	17.2	16.7	15.6	20.8
5.5	6.9	6.9	% Profit Before Taxes/Total Assets	8.4	4.6	7.9	6.1	4.9	8.8
-1.2	.3	-.7		-5.3	-7.3	1.8	-.2	.4	.6
41.3	36.4	71.1		11.5	22.0	67.0	89.4	155.6	95.7
12.6	12.4	19.4	Sales/Net Fixed Assets	6.8	7.7	32.7	20.3	30.5	34.3
4.6	4.5	6.2		3.3	4.3	6.1	8.5	9.3	11.6
5.4	5.9	6.3		5.9	5.7	6.4	7.5	7.6	6.5
3.2	3.2	4.1	Sales/Total Assets	3.7	3.1	4.2	4.2	4.9	4.1
2.0	2.0	2.2		1.7	1.9	2.2	3.1	2.5	2.5
.6	.8	.5		2.5	1.4	.5	.4	.3	.4
(79) 1.9	(88) 1.8	(101) 1.6	% Depr., Dep., Amort./Sales	(13) 3.4	(14) 3.8	(15) .8	(13) 1.2	(15) .9	(31) 1.4
3.9	3.2	3.5		6.6	6.9	2.1	2.3	3.0	2.4
1.9	1.8	1.2			1.7				1.2
(31) 5.3	(33) 3.4	(51) 2.9	% Officers', Directors' Owners' Comp/Sales	(12) 3.8				(13) 2.1
8.8	7.6	9.2			9.9				13.7
3341136M	3030712M	4451659M	Net Sales ($)	8866M	30685M	65692M	122764M	299115M	3924537M
1160919M	1438213M	1117949M	Total Assets ($)	5753M	11407M	24569M	34151M	76155M	965914M

M = $ thousand   MM = $ million
See Pages 9 through 22 for Explanation of Ratios and Data

Current Data Sorted by Assets   Comparative Historical Data

	0-500M	500M-2MM	2-10MM	10-50MM	50-100MM	100-250MM	Type of Statement	4/1/06-3/31/07 ALL	4/1/07-3/31/08 ALL
	1				1	1	Unqualified	5	5
	1	1	7	3			Reviewed	5	3
	9	8	7	2			Compiled	13	14
	32	27	3				Tax Returns	29	33
	12	15	10	2		1	Other	18	31
		18 (4/1-9/30/10)		125 (10/1/10-3/31/11)					
	55	51	27	7	1	2	NUMBER OF STATEMENTS	70	86
	%	%	%	%	%	%	**ASSETS**	%	%
	20.6	13.7	15.4				Cash & Equivalents	18.0	18.4
	10.9	16.5	14.9				Trade Receivables (net)	18.6	17.3
	6.3	5.8	3.2				Inventory	4.0	5.9
	2.5	2.8	1.4				All Other Current	2.9	2.7
	40.3	38.8	34.9				Total Current	43.4	44.3
	39.9	41.8	41.1				Fixed Assets (net)	43.1	37.6
	7.4	7.9	7.5				Intangibles (net)	5.6	8.1
	12.4	11.6	16.5				All Other Non-Current	7.9	10.0
	100.0	100.0	100.0				Total	100.0	100.0
							LIABILITIES		
	9.7	4.8	6.0				Notes Payable-Short Term	9.7	6.8
	7.7	3.8	2.5				Cur. Mat.-L.T.D.	3.4	2.9
	15.8	13.5	11.5				Trade Payables	14.5	11.9
	.2	.2	.3				Income Taxes Payable	1.4	.2
	30.6	17.6	16.3				All Other Current	25.4	19.9
	63.9	39.9	36.6				Total Current	54.3	41.7
	27.0	31.3	37.7				Long-Term Debt	30.3	35.2
	.0	.0	.1				Deferred Taxes	.1	.1
	14.4	7.1	13.5				All Other Non-Current	11.8	15.7
	-5.3	21.6	12.0				Net Worth	3.5	7.4
	100.0	100.0	100.0				Total Liabilities & Net Worth	100.0	100.0
							INCOME DATA		
	100.0	100.0	100.0				Net Sales	100.0	100.0
							Gross Profit		
	94.6	90.3	94.3				Operating Expenses	92.2	93.5
	5.4	9.7	5.7				Operating Profit	7.8	6.5
	2.0	3.6	2.1				All Other Expenses (net)	2.5	1.9
	3.4	6.1	3.6				Profit Before Taxes	5.3	4.6
							RATIOS		
	1.7	1.4	2.4				Current	1.6	1.9
	.6	1.0	1.1					.8	1.2
	.3	.5	.3					.3	.5
	1.3	1.2	2.0				Quick	1.4	1.7
	.5	.6	(26) .9					.7	1.0
	.1	.4	.2					.3	.3
	0 UND	0 UND	0 UND					0 UND	0 UND
	0 UND	10 38.0	5 79.5				Sales/Receivables	6 61.1	11 34.6
	10 38.1	21 17.5	29 12.6					25 14.9	27 13.5
							Cost of Sales/Inventory		
							Cost of Sales/Payables		
	36.8	22.2	12.8				Sales/Working Capital	23.8	17.3
	-64.2	252.1	94.4					-77.1	69.5
	-8.4	-13.6	-5.9					-11.3	-11.8
	13.1	14.7	20.6				EBIT/Interest	10.3	11.6
	(34) 2.0	(34) 3.7	(23) 5.3					(54) 3.7	(61) 3.0
	-.3	.9	1.7					1.4	-.1
							Net Profit + Depr., Dep., Amort./Cur. Mat. L/T/D		7.0
								(10)	1.5
									-.1
	.5	.6	.4				Fixed/Worth	.5	.3
	3.9	2.4	1.5					3.1	2.0
	-.8	-6.8	70.3					-2.5	-8.3
	.9	1.4	1.0				Debt/Worth	1.3	1.2
	6.4	4.7	2.7					6.2	5.3
	-2.6	-20.5	73.1					-5.7	-13.7
	141.4	71.7	45.7				% Profit Before Taxes/Tangible Net Worth	111.9	98.6
	(30) 63.7	(35) 33.8	(21) 30.1					(44) 42.0	(59) 46.3
	1.1	11.7	8.4					15.0	17.5
	44.8	27.1	12.7				% Profit Before Taxes/Total Assets	28.4	23.8
	7.1	7.2	7.9					9.1	10.2
	-2.1	.2	3.0					1.6	-1.3
	51.9	31.8	18.7				Sales/Net Fixed Assets	33.4	38.7
	22.1	7.4	8.9					15.3	14.3
	10.3	3.0	2.7					3.6	3.5
	9.2	5.5	4.1				Sales/Total Assets	7.1	5.3
	6.6	2.9	2.2					3.8	3.6
	3.4	.9	1.2					1.6	1.6
	.7	1.3	1.6				% Depr., Dep., Amort./Sales	.8	.7
	(42) 1.9	(47) 2.1	(24) 2.5					(48) 2.1	(62) 2.0
	5.9	5.7	7.0					3.5	3.9
	3.0	2.7	2.2				% Officers', Directors' Owners' Comp/Sales	2.6	2.6
	(20) 4.9	(25) 4.5	(12) 4.2					(34) 4.7	(43) 4.0
	9.8	7.0	6.8					7.9	6.1
	70640M	199380M	301441M	398324M	198887M	594344M	Net Sales ($)	940310M	1550099M
	12513M	55446M	119878M	133855M	59432M	233992M	Total Assets ($)	306977M	467131M

© RMA 2011

M = $ thousand   MM = $ million
See Pages 9 through 22 for Explanation of Ratios and Data

Comparative Historical Data — Current Data Sorted by Sales

				Type of Statement	0-1MM	1-3MM	3-5MM	5-10MM	10-25MM	25MM & OVER
	3	7	3	Unqualified		1				2
	7	13	12	Reviewed		3		4	2	3
	25	31	26	Compiled		5	5	5	1	3
	49	70	62	Tax Returns	7	27	5	4	2	
	36	37	40	Other	5	16	4	3	8	4
	4/1/08-3/31/09 ALL	4/1/09-3/31/10 ALL	4/1/10-3/31/11 ALL		| 18 (4/1-9/30/10) |			| 125 (10/1/10-3/31/11) |		
NUMBER OF STATEMENTS	120	158	143		36	52	14	16	13	12
	%	%	%	**ASSETS**	%	%	%	%	%	%
Cash & Equivalents	15.1	15.1	16.6		12.5	19.1	20.0	19.2	13.0	14.7
Trade Receivables (net)	13.4	8.5	14.0		7.5	9.6	15.4	21.5	31.5	22.2
Inventory	5.4	6.3	5.8		3.9	6.3	6.7	5.8	5.1	9.5
All Other Current	4.2	2.6	2.5		.0	3.9	4.6	3.4	.7	1.7
Total Current	38.2	32.5	38.9		23.9	38.9	46.7	50.0	50.4	48.1
Fixed Assets (net)	44.0	46.2	41.2		53.4	41.9	37.7	31.6	22.3	38.1
Intangibles (net)	6.3	8.8	7.5		10.6	6.8	4.9	2.5	9.9	8.2
All Other Non-Current	11.5	12.5	12.4		12.1	12.3	10.7	15.9	17.4	5.6
Total	100.0	100.0	100.0		100.0	100.0	100.0	100.0	100.0	100.0
				LIABILITIES						
Notes Payable-Short Term	7.9	9.3	6.9		9.1	5.8	9.5	4.6	6.1	5.9
Cur. Mat.-L.T.D.	5.3	5.0	5.2		5.9	5.5	2.5	6.1	3.6	4.8
Trade Payables	12.8	10.6	13.8		11.9	11.6	17.2	14.3	24.4	12.7
Income Taxes Payable	.1	.1	.2		.0	.4	.0	.0	.5	.0
All Other Current	26.4	29.9	22.3		15.2	26.6	31.0	18.1	21.5	21.6
Total Current	52.5	55.0	48.4		42.1	49.9	60.2	43.2	56.1	44.9
Long-Term Debt	30.7	33.0	30.8		43.4	30.4	21.3	16.9	30.6	24.2
Deferred Taxes	.0	.0	.0		.0	.0	.0	.0	.0	.3
All Other Non-Current	7.2	14.2	10.8		5.4	19.0	8.4	2.5	12.5	3.3
Net Worth	9.6	-2.2	10.1		9.0	.7	10.1	37.5	.7	27.2
Total Liabilities & Net Worth	100.0	100.0	100.0		100.0	100.0	100.0	100.0	100.0	100.0
				INCOME DATA						
Net Sales	100.0	100.0	100.0		100.0	100.0	100.0	100.0	100.0	100.0
Gross Profit										
Operating Expenses	93.3	92.9	93.0		87.1	93.7	96.0	95.4	96.8	97.0
Operating Profit	6.7	7.1	7.0		12.9	6.3	4.0	4.6	3.2	3.0
All Other Expenses (net)	2.6	3.3	2.6		7.4	1.4	.8	1.0	-.3	.4
Profit Before Taxes	4.1	3.8	4.4		5.6	4.8	3.2	3.6	3.5	2.7
				RATIOS						
Current	1.6	1.3	1.6		1.2	1.6	2.2	1.9	2.1	1.6
	1.0	.6	.9		.5	1.0	1.5	1.2	1.1	1.2
	.4	.2	.3		.2	.4	.3	.3	.7	.4
Quick	1.3	.9	1.4		1.0	1.2	2.0	1.6	1.8	1.5
	.6	.5	(142) .6		.4	(51) .7	.8	.9	1.1	.7
	.2	.1	.2		.1	.3	.3	.1	.5	.2
Sales/Receivables	0 UND	0 UND	0 UND		0 UND	0 UND	0 UND	2 156.7	6 58.0	4 94.4
	6 66.2	2 225.5	2 155.0		0 UND	0 UND	11 34.0	15 24.0	20 17.9	15 24.6
	22 16.8	15 24.3	18 19.7		2 179.3	15 24.4	22 16.4	36 10.0	27 13.4	34 10.9
Cost of Sales/Inventory										
Cost of Sales/Payables										
Sales/Working Capital	22.9	60.1	21.0		84.2	30.5	14.7	7.4	18.7	14.1
	-458.3	-35.6	-107.2		-19.5	-385.2	62.9	48.0	252.1	NM
	-10.4	-7.0	-10.3		-3.6	-13.8	-12.0	-11.6	-25.5	-9.5
EBIT/Interest	(96) 13.3	(115) 8.5	(100) 13.4		(19) 6.4	(37) 16.6	(10) 24.4	(13) 38.3	(10) 16.9	(11) 9.8
	3.0	2.4	3.6		1.1	3.5	4.8	5.3	8.9	6.0
	.6	.1	.9		-1.8	.4	.8	.2	2.4	1.5
Net Profit + Depr., Dep., Amort./Cur. Mat. L/T/D	(11) 12.9	(16) 4.5	(12) 5.6							
	2.1	2.3	1.8							
	1.1	1.3	1.1							
Fixed/Worth	.7	.9	.5		1.1	.8	.3	.3	.3	.4
	2.5	3.5	2.4		8.8	4.3	.9	.7	1.0	1.3
	-5.2	-3.4	-3.8		-2.5	-1.4	NM	3.1	-.5	2.3
Debt/Worth	1.6	1.8	1.1		.8	1.4	.8	.7	1.2	1.0
	4.5	8.3	4.3		8.8	14.2	4.1	2.5	2.7	1.6
	-9.7	-5.4	-5.2		-3.2	-17.9	6.1	-3.3		6.2
% Profit Before Taxes/Tangible Net Worth	105.8	92.2	79.0		110.9	121.7	64.5	46.3		53.0
	(80) 42.2	(95) 34.4	(94) 33.7		(20) 43.0	(30) 32.6	(10) 33.0	(15) 25.0		(10) 28.1
	8.3	5.1	10.0		3.3	8.7	8.1	2.9		14.9
% Profit Before Taxes/Total Assets	25.0	19.5	23.1		16.3	31.8	28.0	23.5	21.6	19.8
	7.7	3.9	7.1		4.3	9.6	7.4	5.3	15.1	9.5
	-1.0	-2.3	.2		-1.8	-.3	-5.3	2.9	10.6	2.0
Sales/Net Fixed Assets	38.4	30.2	38.4		30.0	36.6	75.8	42.5	71.4	24.9
	11.1	7.9	12.2		3.2	11.4	13.9	16.7	32.7	10.1
	3.1	2.5	3.7		1.0	4.4	6.7	3.8	17.2	5.0
Sales/Total Assets	6.4	6.3	6.7		6.3	7.8	7.4	5.3	7.4	4.9
	3.5	2.8	3.7		1.7	3.7	5.4	2.8	4.8	3.6
	1.7	1.4	1.7		.5	2.3	2.9	1.6	3.3	2.5
% Depr., Dep., Amort./Sales	.8	1.5	1.1		1.1	1.2	.7	1.0		1.4
	(97) 1.9	(130) 2.1	(122) 2.2		(33) 5.9	(43) 2.1	(12) 2.0	(15) 1.8		(10) 2.3
	4.2	4.4	5.4		7.4	4.5	4.8	2.7		5.2
% Officers', Directors' Owners' Comp/Sales	2.4	2.4	2.7			2.7				
	(52) 4.4	(73) 4.8	(60) 4.4			(25) 4.7				
	7.0	8.7	7.4			7.4				
Net Sales ($)	1990905M	3364442M	1763016M		20546M	97688M	50896M	113294M	186738M	1293854M
Total Assets ($)	688297M	1120677M	615116M		18813M	50982M	15137M	53322M	39907M	436955M

M = $ thousand   MM = $ million
See Pages 9 through 22 for Explanation of Ratios and Data

Current Data Sorted by Assets   Comparative Historical Data

Type of Statement								
			1			Unqualified	4	2
15	8	3	1			Reviewed	5	5
80	33	9	4	1	2	Compiled	26	25
37	18	9	1	1		Tax Returns	111	102
	14 (4/1-9/30/10)		209 (10/1/10-3/31/11)			Other	46	55
0-500M	500M-2MM	2-10MM	10-50MM	50-100MM	100-250MM		4/1/06-3/31/07 ALL	4/1/07-3/31/08 ALL
132	59	21	6	2	3	NUMBER OF STATEMENTS	192	189
%	%	%	%	%	%	**ASSETS**	%	%
17.8	13.7	8.9				Cash & Equivalents	14.0	16.9
1.2	.4	2.0				Trade Receivables (net)	1.5	1.2
11.4	4.5	5.1				Inventory	9.3	8.7
1.9	1.6	4.3				All Other Current	4.0	3.0
32.2	20.2	20.3				Total Current	28.8	29.8
46.4	59.3	57.2				Fixed Assets (net)	47.5	47.4
12.6	11.9	12.7				Intangibles (net)	14.5	14.4
8.9	8.5	9.8				All Other Non-Current	9.1	8.4
100.0	100.0	100.0				Total	100.0	100.0
						LIABILITIES		
7.4	2.6	5.1				Notes Payable-Short Term	5.5	7.2
3.0	1.7	1.7				Cur. Mat.-L.T.D.	3.1	3.8
6.7	6.1	3.5				Trade Payables	5.6	8.5
.0	.0	.0				Income Taxes Payable	.2	.1
18.8	15.6	9.3				All Other Current	19.9	17.4
36.0	25.9	19.6				Total Current	34.3	37.0
26.4	31.2	28.7				Long-Term Debt	32.5	32.6
.0	.0	.2				Deferred Taxes	.0	.1
29.4	8.6	6.1				All Other Non-Current	15.8	18.6
8.1	34.3	45.4				Net Worth	17.4	11.7
100.0	100.0	100.0				Total Liabilities & Net Worth	100.0	100.0
						INCOME DATA		
100.0	100.0	100.0				Net Sales	100.0	100.0
58.8	66.8	61.7				Gross Profit	58.7	60.3
53.9	61.0	56.8				Operating Expenses	53.9	56.5
4.9	5.8	4.9				Operating Profit	4.8	3.7
.7	.9	.9				All Other Expenses (net)	1.2	.9
4.2	4.9	4.0				Profit Before Taxes	3.6	2.8
						RATIOS		
3.8	2.0	2.1					3.1	2.8
1.4	1.1	1.1				Current	1.1	1.3
.5	.4	.3					.3	.4
2.0	1.5	1.0					2.0	1.7
(131) .6	(58) .8	.2				Quick	(188) .4	(186) .7
.1	.2	.1					.1	.1
0 UND	0 UND	0 UND					0 UND	0 UND
0 UND	0 UND	0 UND				Sales/Receivables	0 UND	0 UND
0 UND	0 UND	1 393.7					1 490.7	0 999.8
8 43.0	10 35.2	11 34.5					8 46.9	8 45.5
16 22.3	20 18.7	22 17.0				Cost of Sales/Inventory	16 22.5	15 25.0
35 10.6	34 10.8	39 9.5					29 12.6	25 14.9
0 UND	0 UND	1 353.8					0 UND	0 UND
2 150.3	18 20.3	16 23.0				Cost of Sales/Payables	3 136.8	8 46.4
17 21.3	39 9.3	36 10.0					26 14.2	27 13.5
19.8	23.7	17.8					17.4	17.5
73.9	352.0	189.1				Sales/Working Capital	485.7	68.5
-28.2	-14.3	-14.5					-16.7	-17.1
16.6	12.5	10.2					12.5	9.9
(70) 3.2	(39) 2.6	(20) 2.8				EBIT/Interest	(133) 2.3	(134) 2.1
.7	1.1	1.4					.7	.2
						Net Profit + Depr., Dep., Amort./Cur. Mat. L/T/D		5.9
							(10)	2.1
								-.4
.6	1.0	.7					.8	.7
1.9	2.2	2.0				Fixed/Worth	3.7	4.1
-1.6	14.8	5.1					-1.5	-1.2
.4	.8	.5					.8	.8
2.8	2.2	1.7				Debt/Worth	5.9	8.3
-3.0	17.0	9.0					-2.9	-2.8
126.5	73.5	49.4				% Profit Before Taxes/Tangible	94.6	78.9
(82) 50.6	(46) 38.6	(17) 17.1				Net Worth	(109) 38.6	(107) 40.5
.5	-1.9	4.0					12.6	1.8
38.3	27.2	19.7				% Profit Before Taxes/Total	31.3	25.1
12.4	7.3	3.6				Assets	8.0	5.7
-2.8	.1	1.0					-1.3	-5.3
38.5	7.2	5.0					26.1	25.3
13.9	3.8	2.7				Sales/Net Fixed Assets	7.9	7.6
4.7	2.0	1.4					3.7	3.7
8.1	3.4	2.5					5.0	5.6
4.5	2.0	1.3				Sales/Total Assets	3.1	3.1
2.5	1.3	1.1					1.7	1.8
1.0	1.8	1.6					1.3	1.2
(94) 2.1	(52) 3.1	(17) 1.8				% Depr., Dep., Amort./Sales	(152) 2.3	(160) 2.2
3.6	6.3	5.7					4.0	4.3
2.2	2.0					% Officers', Directors'	2.3	2.6
(56) 4.7	(30) 4.4					Owners' Comp/Sales	(87) 4.4	(88) 4.8
9.5	6.5						7.2	8.9
116096M	123090M	245024M	1094249M	577595M	1605836M	Net Sales ($)	3356360M	5080841M
26983M	54293M	84611M	148787M	160005M	645048M	Total Assets ($)	941646M	838565M

© RMA 2011

M = $ thousand   MM = $ million
See Pages 9 through 22 for Explanation of Ratios and Data

Comparative Historical Data | Current Data Sorted by Sales

			Type of Statement						
3	2	1	Unqualified						1
2	1		Reviewed						
33	28	27	Compiled	11	11	2	3		
128	118	129	Tax Returns	62	48	7	5		7
42	55	66	Other	27	23	7	6	2	1
4/1/08-3/31/09 ALL	4/1/09-3/31/10 ALL	4/1/10-3/31/11 ALL		14 (4/1-9/30/10)			209 (10/1/10-3/31/11)		
				0-1MM	1-3MM	3-5MM	5-10MM	10-25MM	25MM & OVER
208	204	223	NUMBER OF STATEMENTS	100	82	16	14	2	9
%	%	%	ASSETS	%	%	%	%	%	%
13.5	16.4	15.4	Cash & Equivalents	15.7	15.5	17.8	7.8		
1.2	1.4	1.0	Trade Receivables (net)	.4	1.7	1.6	1.7		
8.4	7.6	8.8	Inventory	10.1	8.3	5.7	5.8		
4.8	2.5	1.9	All Other Current	1.3	2.1	7.1	.8		
27.8	27.9	27.2	Total Current	27.5	27.7	32.2	16.2		
48.9	46.9	51.6	Fixed Assets (net)	50.5	53.9	41.7	54.3		
14.6	17.1	12.2	Intangibles (net)	13.4	10.3	13.1	17.0		
8.6	8.1	9.1	All Other Non-Current	8.6	8.2	12.9	12.5		
100.0	100.0	100.0	Total	100.0	100.0	100.0	100.0		
			LIABILITIES						
6.4	5.9	5.7	Notes Payable-Short Term	5.3	6.9	2.5	1.0		
3.1	2.0	2.4	Cur. Mat.-L.T.D.	2.7	2.7	.7	1.7		
8.1	5.9	6.1	Trade Payables	5.4	6.0	12.8	6.2		
.1	.1	.0	Income Taxes Payable	.0	.1	.0	.0		
19.9	17.8	16.5	All Other Current	17.5	14.2	35.1	9.0		
37.4	31.7	30.8	Total Current	30.9	29.8	51.2	17.8		
33.1	29.6	28.3	Long-Term Debt	29.7	29.1	18.6	23.9		
.2	.1	.1	Deferred Taxes	.0	.0	.0	.3		
15.9	20.9	21.9	All Other Non-Current	28.7	18.2	6.1	7.5		
13.4	17.7	19.0	Net Worth	10.6	23.0	24.1	50.4		
100.0	100.0	100.0	Total Liabilities & Net Worth	100.0	100.0	100.0	100.0		
			INCOME DATA						
100.0	100.0	100.0	Net Sales	100.0	100.0	100.0	100.0		
59.7	60.0	61.2	Gross Profit	58.5	62.6	70.0	67.1		
55.1	56.1	56.1	Operating Expenses	53.5	58.4	61.8	57.9		
4.6	4.0	5.1	Operating Profit	5.0	4.2	8.1	9.2		
1.1	.9	.9	All Other Expenses (net)	1.0	.6	.9	.8		
3.6	3.0	4.3	Profit Before Taxes	4.1	3.6	7.2	8.5		
			RATIOS						
2.0	3.2	2.8	Current	4.3	2.1	2.2	1.9		
.9	1.0	1.2		1.6	1.0	1.2	1.1		
.4	.4	.4		.5	.4	.4	.3		
1.2	2.2	1.8	Quick	2.2	1.4	1.7	1.3		
(205) .4	(202) .5	(221) .6		(99) .7	.6	(15) .5	.4		
.1	.1	.1		.1	.1	.2	.1		
0 UND	0 UND	0 UND	Sales/Receivables	0 UND	0 UND	0 UND	0 UND		
0 UND	0 UND	0 UND		0 UND	0 UND	0 UND	0 UND		
0 UND	0 UND	0 UND		0 UND	0 UND	0 UND	3 109.8		
9 42.5	7 52.7	9 39.8	Cost of Sales/Inventory	10 35.2	9 39.7	9 41.8	11 34.7		
15 24.0	15 24.5	19 19.5		20 18.6	18 20.1	15 25.0	17 21.4		
29 12.6	26 14.2	34 10.8		37 9.8	34 10.8	25 14.5	30 12.1		
0 UND	0 UND	0 UND	Cost of Sales/Payables	0 UND	0 UND	0 790.4	8 47.8		
9 42.4	4 90.2	5 74.0		0 UND	9 42.2	13 28.7	21 17.6		
30 12.3	24 15.0	26 14.3		18 20.6	31 11.8	72 5.1	35 10.5		
27.0	19.0	21.8	Sales/Working Capital	19.6	25.2	11.7	27.6		
-157.2	UND	121.4		59.7	676.3	89.1	NM		
-15.0	-24.9	-19.4		-20.5	-20.0	-14.6	-15.4		
8.8	8.7	13.6	EBIT/Interest	5.3	13.3	15.8	36.7		
(153) 2.7	(140) 2.3	(138) 2.7		(49) 1.5	(56) 2.7	(11) 3.3	(13) 12.2		
.2	.4	1.0		.5	1.3	-2.5	2.2		
			Net Profit + Depr., Dep., Amort./Cur. Mat. L/T/D						
1.1	.8	.8	Fixed/Worth	.7	1.0	.5	1.1		
4.0	3.2	2.2		3.2	2.3	1.1	1.9		
-1.3	-1.8	-3.2		-1.6	-4.5	2.2	2.4		
1.0	.8	.5	Debt/Worth	.4	.6	.5	.6		
6.1	6.2	2.4		4.1	2.6	1.0	1.6		
-3.7	-3.4	-4.6		-2.8	-7.7	2.4	2.1		
77.4	97.8	87.7	% Profit Before Taxes/Tangible Net Worth	87.2	102.7	149.7	68.3		
(122) 38.2	(127) 40.6	(151) 34.9		(59) 30.8	(60) 33.8	(14) 51.5	(12) 49.4		
4.3	3.1	.8		.0	-2.1	7.3	9.0		
25.2	28.1	31.9	% Profit Before Taxes/Total Assets	24.3	31.4	68.5	42.2		
6.7	7.7	8.3		9.6	7.3	8.3	19.7		
-4.1	-1.6	-1.6		-3.4	-.6	2.1	4.5		
18.3	27.1	25.1	Sales/Net Fixed Assets	28.2	23.7	28.0	13.2		
7.7	8.6	6.4		8.9	5.8	8.6	4.2		
3.5	3.4	2.5		2.1	2.7	2.8	2.2		
5.5	5.8	6.1	Sales/Total Assets	6.8	6.2	4.6	4.5		
3.2	3.1	3.2		3.3	3.3	2.1	2.5		
1.8	1.6	1.6		1.4	2.0	1.2	1.5		
1.6	1.6	1.2	% Depr., Dep., Amort./Sales	1.1	1.6	.8	1.5		
(170) 2.8	(162) 2.8	(170) 2.5		(74) 2.5	(65) 2.8	(14) 1.7	(11) 1.8		
4.6	5.0	4.7		4.7	5.5	4.4	3.3		
2.2	2.4	2.3	% Officers', Directors' Owners' Comp/Sales	2.3	2.3				
(88) 3.9	(104) 4.6	(98) 4.9		(40) 5.7	(39) 3.8				
7.3	9.1	8.9		11.5	7.3				
3295620M	2407176M	3761890M	Net Sales ($)	52651M	139025M	60858M	98418M	36410M	3374528M
989206M	780191M	1119727M	Total Assets ($)	23289M	57000M	35310M	58328M	22372M	923428M

© RMA 2011

M = $ thousand   MM = $ million
See Pages 9 through 22 for Explanation of Ratios and Data

OTHER SERVICES (EXCEPT PUBLIC ADMINISTRATION)

	Current Data Sorted by Assets							Comparative Historical Data	
	1			4	2	2	**Type of Statement** Unqualified	6	5
	6	4	7	3			Reviewed	23	28
	41	26	21				Compiled	72	77
	201	68	11	4	3	2	Tax Returns	203	217
	93	58	25	10		4	Other	123	116
		62 (4/1-9/30/10)		534 (10/1/10-3/31/11)				4/1/06- 3/31/07	4/1/07- 3/31/08
	0-500M	500M-2MM	2-10MM	10-50MM	50-100MM	100-250MM		ALL	ALL
	342	156	64	21	5	8	**NUMBER OF STATEMENTS**	427	443
	%	%	%	%	%	%	**ASSETS**	%	%
	20.6	15.0	11.4	9.9			Cash & Equivalents	14.3	14.3
	10.6	12.6	12.0	10.3			Trade Receivables (net)	11.8	11.7
	15.6	18.2	18.3	13.6			Inventory	19.8	18.4
	3.3	2.4	3.9	1.9			All Other Current	2.3	3.1
	50.0	48.3	45.6	35.7			Total Current	48.1	47.4
	33.5	34.3	37.4	37.0			Fixed Assets (net)	36.5	36.2
	5.6	7.5	7.9	12.3			Intangibles (net)	7.5	6.5
	10.8	9.9	9.0	15.0			All Other Non-Current	7.9	9.9
	100.0	100.0	100.0	100.0			Total	100.0	100.0
							LIABILITIES		
	16.1	6.4	6.4	7.6			Notes Payable-Short Term	10.8	9.9
	5.5	3.6	4.1	7.2			Cur. Mat.-L.T.D.	4.6	5.1
	16.8	12.0	14.2	11.4			Trade Payables	14.5	15.9
	.2	.0	.2	.1			Income Taxes Payable	.1	.1
	19.3	9.5	8.1	10.7			All Other Current	14.0	14.9
	57.9	31.4	33.0	37.0			Total Current	44.0	45.9
	29.7	31.0	28.8	27.0			Long-Term Debt	32.2	31.3
	.0	.2	.5	.2			Deferred Taxes	.1	.0
	15.6	10.3	4.9	8.5			All Other Non-Current	13.1	10.2
	-3.2	27.1	32.8	27.3			Net Worth	10.6	12.6
	100.0	100.0	100.0	100.0			Total Liabilties & Net Worth	100.0	100.0
							INCOME DATA		
	100.0	100.0	100.0	100.0			Net Sales	100.0	100.0
							Gross Profit		
	95.3	91.1	92.9	83.3			Operating Expenses	95.0	94.2
	4.7	8.9	7.1	16.7			Operating Profit	5.0	5.8
	.9	3.3	3.8	7.7			All Other Expenses (net)	1.4	1.7
	3.8	5.5	3.4	9.0			Profit Before Taxes	3.6	4.1
							RATIOS		
	2.5	3.7	2.7	1.5				2.5	2.4
	1.0	1.7	1.4	1.1			Current	1.3	1.2
	.5	.8	.8	.7				.7	.7
	1.6	2.3	1.3	1.0				1.3	1.6
	(339) .6	.8	.6	.6			Quick	(426) .6	(440) .6
	.2	.3	.3	.4				.3	.2
	0 UND	0 999.8	2 165.4	1 378.2				0 UND	0 UND
	2 205.7	11 33.8	12 29.2	10 34.9			Sales/Receivables	6 61.8	5 72.6
	10 37.0	23 15.9	32 11.3	46 8.0				17 21.6	18 19.9
							Cost of Sales/Inventory		
							Cost of Sales/Payables		
	18.9	6.8	6.6	10.1				13.6	13.2
	322.6	19.3	29.1	99.9			Sales/Working Capital	51.4	51.5
	-24.0	-59.6	-25.8	-19.6				-31.5	-34.2
	10.7	8.9	9.9	18.5				7.9	8.2
	(224) 3.4	(119) 3.7	(54) 3.6	(17) 6.7			EBIT/Interest	(339) 2.7	(326) 3.0
	1.0	1.3	1.4	1.3				.8	1.2
			4.8					2.7	6.3
		(10) 2.9					Net Profit + Depr., Dep., Amort./Cur. Mat. L/T/D	(24) 1.6	(36) 2.1
			.9					.8	1.2
	.4	.2	.5	.6				.4	.4
	2.2	1.4	1.4	3.5			Fixed/Worth	2.2	1.7
	-1.7	-27.5	14.9	-25.3				-2.9	-5.4
	.9	.6	1.1	1.4				1.2	.8
	7.7	3.0	2.0	5.2			Debt/Worth	5.0	3.5
	-3.3	-20.2	25.0	-63.6				-6.0	-11.3
	158.6	54.7	33.6	76.7				84.0	97.8
	(209) 50.0	(112) 26.4	(49) 13.1	(15) 29.5			% Profit Before Taxes/Tangible Net Worth	(282) 30.7	(305) 38.0
	7.2	2.6	3.0	12.6				5.5	10.1
	39.7	21.0	15.5	16.4				25.2	28.9
	14.0	8.1	4.7	3.7			% Profit Before Taxes/Total Assets	6.9	9.1
	-.4	.7	1.0	2.8				-.8	1.3
	83.0	59.0	24.0	24.8				42.5	43.0
	26.1	16.7	11.3	9.2			Sales/Net Fixed Assets	15.7	16.2
	10.5	3.4	2.1	.9				5.2	6.1
	10.7	4.2	3.9	3.5				5.8	6.7
	5.8	2.7	2.3	1.7			Sales/Total Assets	3.8	3.9
	3.8	1.6	1.4	.4				2.2	2.4
	.6	.6	1.2	.8				.7	.8
	(212) 1.4	(119) 1.4	(57) 2.0	(20) 2.0			% Depr., Dep., Amort./Sales	(331) 1.8	(335) 1.7
	2.7	3.0	3.5	4.9				3.8	3.9
	4.5	2.2	1.5					3.5	3.9
	(236) 6.4	(90) 4.3	(27) 2.5				% Officers', Directors' Owners' Comp/Sales	(256) 5.8	(260) 5.9
	9.6	7.7	4.2					9.7	9.7
	364181M	472819M	660697M	1049817M	931244M	4655899M	Net Sales ($)	6858857M	7841371M
	63143M	153802M	268174M	404772M	308879M	1310124M	Total Assets ($)	1849518M	2249921M

M = $ thousand   MM = $ million
See Pages 9 through 22 for Explanation of Ratios and Data

Comparative Historical Data

Current Data Sorted by Sales

			Type of Statement						
8	7	9	Unqualified		1			1	7
20	16	20	Reviewed		6	4	2	4	4
64	54	88	Compiled	30	27	13	13	5	
238	282	289	Tax Returns	138	105	23	11	4	8
139	158	190	Other	66	64	19	18	13	10
4/1/08-3/31/09	4/1/09-3/31/10	4/1/10-3/31/11			62 (4/1-9/30/10)		534 (10/1/10-3/31/11)		
ALL	ALL	ALL		0-1MM	1-3MM	3-5MM	5-10MM	10-25MM	25MM & OVER
469	517	596	NUMBER OF STATEMENTS	234	203	59	44	27	29
%	%	%	ASSETS	%	%	%	%	%	%
15.4	15.8	17.8	Cash & Equivalents	17.7	18.0	19.3	17.9	13.5	18.0
12.0	11.3	11.2	Trade Receivables (net)	8.7	11.7	17.1	15.3	9.9	10.3
19.7	18.0	16.4	Inventory	12.8	18.3	18.7	24.2	15.6	15.9
2.7	3.2	3.2	All Other Current	2.9	2.9	3.7	3.4	4.9	4.2
49.9	48.2	48.5	Total Current	42.0	50.9	58.9	60.8	43.9	48.4
33.5	35.0	34.3	Fixed Assets (net)	40.9	32.4	27.3	24.7	28.0	29.4
6.9	7.0	6.6	Intangibles (net)	6.1	6.7	4.8	3.8	14.1	10.6
9.6	9.9	10.6	All Other Non-Current	11.0	9.9	9.1	10.7	14.1	11.5
100.0	100.0	100.0	Total	100.0	100.0	100.0	100.0	100.0	100.0
			LIABILITIES						
13.9	14.0	12.1	Notes Payable-Short Term	11.9	15.5	7.8	9.7	5.6	9.3
6.4	6.0	4.8	Cur. Mat.-L.T.D.	6.2	3.3	4.2	3.9	5.9	5.7
15.5	15.4	14.9	Trade Payables	13.7	14.5	18.6	15.7	17.6	16.6
.1	.1	.2	Income Taxes Payable	.1	.2	.1	.3	.1	.2
17.7	17.9	15.3	All Other Current	18.9	12.0	17.3	9.5	11.7	16.3
53.6	53.3	47.3	Total Current	50.8	45.5	48.1	39.1	41.0	48.1
32.0	35.2	29.8	Long-Term Debt	34.6	30.8	19.7	24.5	24.2	17.1
.1	.1	.1	Deferred Taxes	.0	.0	.1	.5	.7	.1
13.7	9.2	12.6	All Other Non-Current	17.4	11.9	5.3	9.1	4.3	6.5
.8	2.1	10.2	Net Worth	-2.9	11.8	26.8	26.8	29.9	28.3
100.0	100.0	100.0	Total Liabilities & Net Worth	100.0	100.0	100.0	100.0	100.0	100.0
			INCOME DATA						
100.0	100.0	100.0	Net Sales	100.0	100.0	100.0	100.0	100.0	100.0
			Gross Profit						
95.7	94.5	93.5	Operating Expenses	91.0	94.2	96.8	96.1	96.4	95.0
4.3	5.5	6.5	Operating Profit	9.0	5.8	3.2	3.9	3.6	5.0
1.5	2.3	2.1	All Other Expenses (net)	3.7	1.3	.7	1.1	.3	1.6
2.9	3.2	4.4	Profit Before Taxes	5.3	4.5	2.5	2.7	3.3	3.3
			RATIOS						
2.3	2.3	2.7		2.8	2.9	3.0	3.1	1.7	1.7
1.2	1.1	1.2	Current	.9	1.4	1.4	1.7	1.1	1.1
.6	.5	.6		.3	.8	.8	1.0	.8	.8
1.5	1.3	1.7		1.9	1.9	1.9	2.5	1.0	1.0
(467) .6	(516) .5	(593) .7	Quick	(233) .5	(201) .8	.9	.9	.6	.6
.2	.2	.2		.1	.3	.5	.4	.3	.4
0 UND	0 UND	0 UND		0 UND	0 UND	3 121.5	2 168.4	2 209.7	1 378.2
5 70.3	4 91.0	4 86.5	Sales/Receivables	1 383.3	5 69.3	14 26.6	13 27.9	7 50.5	10 38.3
17 21.0	15 24.9	16 23.4		10 36.0	15 24.5	28 13.0	31 11.9	17 21.3	25 14.6
			Cost of Sales/Inventory						
			Cost of Sales/Payables						
12.3	13.3	11.5		16.0	11.1	8.4	6.9	21.8	9.9
88.3	126.7	75.7	Sales/Working Capital	-159.7	54.1	25.2	17.2	61.6	131.8
-24.6	-19.8	-25.3		-12.3	-60.0	-96.1	412.3	-21.2	-25.3
8.4	9.7	10.3		7.0	11.6	11.9	7.1	11.7	20.3
(374) 2.9	(392) 2.5	(424) 3.6	EBIT/Interest	(143) 2.3	(152) 3.9	(48) 3.5	(33) 3.4	(24) 6.2	(24) 10.7
.9	.6	1.1		.8	1.4	1.1	1.3	1.9	1.2
4.6	5.8	5.5							
(29) 2.2	(23) 1.4	(28) 2.7	Net Profit + Depr., Dep., Amort./Cur. Mat. L/T/D						
.8	.7	1.0							
.4	.4	.3		.5	.3	.3	.2	.5	.4
2.6	2.6	1.7	Fixed/Worth	4.1	1.4	.8	1.2	1.9	1.4
-1.6	-1.4	-2.5		-1.6	-6.2	-69.1	14.5	-2.6	-2.6
1.2	1.1	.9		.9	.8	.7	.9	1.2	1.2
5.6	7.7	4.3	Debt/Worth	9.1	4.3	1.6	3.1	3.3	1.8
-4.2	-4.4	-5.8		-3.1	-7.3	-22.4	25.0	-11.6	-8.1
92.4	100.0	90.9		100.0	132.9	49.4	53.0	54.3	76.7
(296) 30.1	(308) 30.8	(393) 31.1	% Profit Before Taxes/Tangible Net Worth	(139) 34.9	(140) 36.5	(43) 24.4	(34) 18.8	(18) 31.2	(19) 34.3
6.7	4.5	5.5		.8	7.2	3.4	2.3	18.9	21.6
24.0	27.2	28.0		33.1	29.8	21.8	21.2	17.0	28.6
7.3	7.5	9.6	% Profit Before Taxes/Total Assets	9.8	8.7	10.1	9.6	8.7	13.5
-.9	-.4	.5		-.4	.5	.7	.3	3.4	2.0
60.9	48.5	58.7		63.3	59.4	69.1	83.0	40.1	34.9
19.7	18.3	19.2	Sales/Net Fixed Assets	16.7	24.6	27.0	22.3	13.9	16.0
6.3	5.9	6.9		4.8	8.8	8.0	11.2	9.2	5.6
6.9	6.8	7.3		9.6	7.3	6.6	5.8	4.8	6.1
3.9	3.9	4.2	Sales/Total Assets	4.4	4.6	4.0	3.6	4.0	3.2
2.3	2.1	2.3		2.0	2.4	2.4	2.2	2.4	2.0
.7	.8	.7		.9	.6	.8	.6	.5	.6
(347) 1.5	(390) 1.7	(416) 1.5	% Depr., Dep., Amort./Sales	(141) 2.4	(140) 1.2	(49) 1.4	(38) 1.1	(25) 1.4	(23) 1.4
3.3	3.0	2.9		4.8	2.5	2.5	2.2	2.1	2.4
3.1	2.9	3.3		5.5	3.5	2.2	1.0	1.0	.8
(290) 5.5	(326) 5.2	(364) 5.7	% Officers', Directors' Owners' Comp/Sales	(142) 7.8	(138) 5.2	(32) 3.4	(29) 1.7	(10) 2.0	(13) 4.3
9.1	9.1	8.7		11.1	8.0	5.5	6.0	5.0	15.4
6939033M	6205688M	8134657M	Net Sales ($)	130671M	345283M	238025M	308282M	414581M	6697815M
2328782M	1686598M	2508894M	Total Assets ($)	64354M	145863M	91635M	134104M	185732M	1887206M

M = $ thousand   MM = $ million
See Pages 9 through 22 for Explanation of Ratios and Data

Current Data Sorted by Assets   Comparative Historical Data

						Type of Statement		
						Unqualified	2	1
						Reviewed	5	2
						Compiled	5	1
						Tax Returns	10	8
1 9 5	1 5	1 1 1	1		2	Other	13	4
	2 (4/1-9/30/10)			25 (10/1/10-3/31/11)			4/1/06-3/31/07	4/1/07-3/31/08
0-500M	500M-2MM	2-10MM	10-50MM	50-100MM	100-250MM		ALL	ALL
15	6	3	1		2	NUMBER OF STATEMENTS	35	16
%	%	%	%	%	%	ASSETS	%	%
9.0						Cash & Equivalents	11.5	13.5
11.3						Trade Receivables (net)	6.6	6.3
24.2						Inventory	18.1	21.2
1.4				D		All Other Current	2.0	3.4
45.9				A		Total Current	38.2	44.4
21.3				T		Fixed Assets (net)	33.7	34.8
16.0				A		Intangibles (net)	15.1	15.9
16.8						All Other Non-Current	13.1	4.9
100.0				N		Total	100.0	100.0
				O		LIABILITIES		
17.3				T		Notes Payable-Short Term	2.2	4.7
3.4						Cur. Mat.-L.T.D.	4.2	4.4
21.7				A		Trade Payables	10.1	13.2
.0				V		Income Taxes Payable	.0	.0
19.2				A		All Other Current	16.4	5.7
61.6				I		Total Current	32.9	28.0
49.2				L		Long-Term Debt	31.3	27.1
.0				A		Deferred Taxes	.3	.9
20.7				B		All Other Non-Current	17.3	21.4
-31.5				L		Net Worth	18.3	22.6
100.0				E		Total Liabilities & Net Worth	100.0	100.0
						INCOME DATA		
100.0						Net Sales	100.0	100.0
						Gross Profit		
96.4						Operating Expenses	93.0	96.0
3.6						Operating Profit	7.0	4.0
.9						All Other Expenses (net)	3.4	.8
2.7						Profit Before Taxes	3.6	3.1
						RATIOS		
2.2							2.7	4.3
.9						Current	1.4	1.8
.2							.8	1.0
.9							1.2	1.5
.3						Quick	.6	1.0
.0							.2	.4
1 456.0							1 335.7 0 UND	
3 126.0						Sales/Receivables	3 133.5 3 104.7	
11 34.4							10 37.6 10 35.3	
						Cost of Sales/Inventory		
						Cost of Sales/Payables		
24.3							12.0	8.6
-387.7						Sales/Working Capital	22.6	23.5
-7.7							-20.8	NM
4.6							6.2	17.1
(12) 1.7						EBIT/Interest	(25) 1.5 (13) 2.0	
-1.3							-.1	1.4
						Net Profit + Depr., Dep., Amort./Cur. Mat. L/T/D		
1.0							.5	.7
-.6						Fixed/Worth	5.1	8.4
-.1							-.9	-.6
14.0							.9	.9
-2.5						Debt/Worth	11.8	13.3
-1.7							-3.1	-3.3
						% Profit Before Taxes/Tangible Net Worth	49.7	
							(21) 13.6	
							-5.2	
23.7							13.8	33.4
10.9						% Profit Before Taxes/Total Assets	2.9	5.2
-5.2							-3.8	2.8
147.0							25.9	55.0
32.1						Sales/Net Fixed Assets	11.1	17.6
12.9							5.7	6.3
8.8							4.8	4.9
4.4						Sales/Total Assets	3.1	3.6
2.5							1.4	3.1
.5							1.1	1.1
(11) .8						% Depr., Dep., Amort./Sales	(29) 1.9 (12) 2.6	
2.3							3.4	3.2
2.6							1.8	2.9
(10) 7.1						% Officers', Directors' Owners' Comp/Sales	(18) 2.8 (12) 5.4	
10.4							5.0	8.3
12090M	25176M	31712M	69752M		69452M	Net Sales ($)	295336M	111430M
2652M	7904M	11306M	44053M		236548M	Total Assets ($)	395643M	122770M

M = $ thousand   MM = $ million
See Pages 9 through 22 for Explanation of Ratios and Data

Comparative Historical Data   **Current Data Sorted by Sales**

			Type of Statement						
1			Unqualified					1	
2	2	1	Reviewed		1		1	1	
4	3	3	Compiled		3		1	1	
10	12	16	Tax Returns	9	2	1	1	1	1
8	9	7	Other	3					2
4/1/08-	4/1/09-	4/1/10-			2 (4/1-9/30/10)		25 (10/1/10-3/31/11)		
3/31/09	3/31/10	3/31/11							
ALL	ALL	ALL		0-1MM	1-3MM	3-5MM	5-10MM	10-25MM	25MM & OVER
25	26	27	**NUMBER OF STATEMENTS**	12	6	1	2	3	3
%	%	%	**ASSETS**	%	%	%	%	%	%
7.9	12.3	9.8	Cash & Equivalents	6.9					
7.4	6.2	8.9	Trade Receivables (net)	4.7					
16.8	13.9	18.0	Inventory	18.4					
4.8	2.6	2.6	All Other Current	2.6					
36.9	35.0	39.3	Total Current	32.5					
39.4	36.6	25.2	Fixed Assets (net)	28.5					
13.2	11.7	18.5	Intangibles (net)	23.4					
10.6	16.6	17.1	All Other Non-Current	15.6					
100.0	100.0	100.0	Total	100.0					
			LIABILITIES						
11.6	3.4	11.2	Notes Payable-Short Term	12.9					
2.5	1.4	3.4	Cur. Mat.-L.T.D.	1.8					
20.0	12.8	17.1	Trade Payables	10.7					
.0	.1	.1	Income Taxes Payable	.0					
19.2	22.5	13.5	All Other Current	20.2					
53.3	40.2	45.2	Total Current	45.6					
27.2	32.2	39.6	Long-Term Debt	55.6					
.3	.1	.6	Deferred Taxes	.0					
4.4	15.3	14.8	All Other Non-Current	19.9					
14.8	12.1	-.2	Net Worth	-21.1					
100.0	100.0	100.0	Total Liabilties & Net Worth	100.0					
			INCOME DATA						
100.0	100.0	100.0	Net Sales	100.0					
			Gross Profit						
93.5	95.9	91.0	Operating Expenses	86.9					
6.5	4.1	9.0	Operating Profit	13.1					
3.5	4.1	5.2	All Other Expenses (net)	7.1					
2.9	.0	3.8	Profit Before Taxes	6.0					
			RATIOS						
1.6	3.0	2.2		1.8					
.8	1.0	1.1	Current	.7					
.3	.3	.4		.2					
.7	1.5	.9		1.0					
.2	.3	.5	Quick	.1					
.1	.2	.1		.0					
1 621.9	1 675.1	1 295.6		0 UND					
4 97.7	2 190.2	3 126.0	Sales/Receivables	2 223.5					
8 46.8	8 46.8	13 27.3		7 51.0					
			Cost of Sales/Inventory						
			Cost of Sales/Payables						
38.8	14.6	16.1		25.6					
-38.3	NM	51.9	Sales/Working Capital	-491.1					
-8.4	-13.7	-9.8		-5.2					
8.0	5.7	8.4							
(17) 1.4	(18) 1.6	(22) 3.1	EBIT/Interest						
-5.4	-4.2	.9							
			Net Profit + Depr., Dep., Amort./Cur. Mat. L/T/D						
.6	.5	.6		1.0					
2.2	3.0	10.0	Fixed/Worth	-5.5					
-3.7	18.9	-.5		-.2					
1.1	1.1	1.9		10.2					
4.0	6.2	28.5	Debt/Worth	-8.0					
-8.1	NM	-2.2		-1.7					
82.2	45.2	234.5	% Profit Before Taxes/Tangible Net Worth	16.5					
(16) 17.9	(20) 17.5	(15) 40.0							
-8.5	.9	10.2							
14.8	10.8	17.5	% Profit Before Taxes/Total Assets	16.5					
1.6	2.9	6.0		7.4					
-9.5	-13.8	-1.4		-1.4					
32.6	22.6	69.8		150.0					
18.7	13.5	21.8	Sales/Net Fixed Assets	25.5					
5.7	5.4	8.4		5.9					
9.2	5.2	6.5		8.3					
5.0	3.2	3.3	Sales/Total Assets	2.8					
1.6	1.6	1.6		1.4					
.9	1.0	.6							
(22) 1.6	(22) 1.8	(22) 1.9	% Depr., Dep., Amort./Sales						
2.9	2.5	2.7							
	2.2	2.7							
	(10) 4.8	(13) 5.3	% Officers', Directors' Owners' Comp/Sales						
	14.3	9.6							
98377M	174607M	208182M	Net Sales ($)	6397M	7624M	4839M	15013M	35105M	139204M
50824M	189902M	302463M	Total Assets ($)	3174M	2248M	1428M	5522M	9490M	280601M

M = $ thousand   MM = $ million
See Pages 9 through 22 for Explanation of Ratios and Data

Current Data Sorted by Assets   **Comparative Historical Data**

						Type of Statement		
	1	1 2	2	1		Unqualified	2	2
						Reviewed	2	1
9	8	1				Compiled	19	23
16	7	3				Tax Returns	23	25
22	9	4	3			Other	18	17
	8 (4/1-9/30/10)		81 (10/1/10-3/31/11)				4/1/06-3/31/07	4/1/07-3/31/08
0-500M	500M-2MM	2-10MM	10-50MM	50-100MM	100-250MM		ALL	ALL
47	25	11	5	1		NUMBER OF STATEMENTS	64	68
%	%	%	%	%	%	**ASSETS**	%	%
16.7	12.9	9.7				Cash & Equivalents	11.3	12.8
17.6	12.3	12.7				Trade Receivables (net)	17.0	18.0
15.5	13.6	15.8				Inventory	18.8	21.1
3.5	1.9	3.1				All Other Current	3.4	1.9
53.2	40.7	41.3				Total Current	50.5	53.8
32.6	47.3	41.0		D		Fixed Assets (net)	35.2	35.0
5.4	7.4	9.0		A		Intangibles (net)	5.5	4.2
8.7	4.6	8.7		T		All Other Non-Current	8.8	7.0
100.0	100.0	100.0		A		Total	100.0	100.0
						LIABILITIES		
13.0	7.6	9.4		N		Notes Payable-Short Term	8.0	10.9
4.3	3.6	3.9		O		Cur. Mat.-L.T.D.	4.1	2.8
16.1	16.1	17.8		T		Trade Payables	14.1	12.9
.0	.1	.1				Income Taxes Payable	.2	.0
16.1	6.1	6.5		A		All Other Current	16.8	14.2
49.4	33.5	37.7		V		Total Current	43.2	40.9
25.3	35.5	37.9		A		Long-Term Debt	34.3	30.6
.0	.0	.0		I		Deferred Taxes	.0	.1
16.6	8.9	5.3		L		All Other Non-Current	11.2	11.0
8.8	22.1	19.1		A		Net Worth	11.3	17.5
100.0	100.0	100.0		B		Total Liabilities & Net Worth	100.0	100.0
				L		**INCOME DATA**		
100.0	100.0	100.0		E		Net Sales	100.0	100.0
						Gross Profit		
94.4	87.0	89.5				Operating Expenses	95.2	94.0
5.6	13.0	10.5				Operating Profit	4.8	6.0
1.3	8.1	7.6				All Other Expenses (net)	1.9	2.6
4.3	4.9	2.9				Profit Before Taxes	2.9	3.4
						RATIOS		
2.4	1.7	1.5					2.5	2.9
1.4	1.0	1.1				Current	1.3	1.7
.7	.6	.7					.7	1.1
1.8	1.3	1.2					1.9	2.0
.8	.6	.5				Quick	.6	.8
.3	.2	.3					.2	.3
1 689.0	0 UND	2 188.8					2 222.8	2 161.7
6 63.2	10 37.2	15 24.7				Sales/Receivables	13 28.8	17 21.3
17 21.0	21 17.1	36 10.2					28 12.9	31 11.7
						Cost of Sales/Inventory		
						Cost of Sales/Payables		
9.7	13.8	10.8					9.6	7.7
51.8	332.3	53.8				Sales/Working Capital	32.6	17.2
-30.8	-14.3	-33.0					-69.6	148.0
17.8	11.3	13.9					7.5	7.5
(30) 4.2	(18) 2.0	(10) 4.3				EBIT/Interest	(53) 2.9	(55) 2.6
-1.2	-.3	1.2					1.2	.4
						Net Profit + Depr., Dep., Amort./Cur. Mat. L/T/D		
.2	.9	.7					.4	.3
1.4	2.7	3.4				Fixed/Worth	1.4	1.1
-1.3	-2.5	-3.6					-10.4	5.4
.6	1.1	1.9					.9	.6
1.8	2.8	9.7				Debt/Worth	2.7	2.1
-2.9	-6.9	-5.0					-11.4	19.6
72.5	43.4						40.1	48.6
(32) 28.6	(18) 2.5					% Profit Before Taxes/Tangible Net Worth	(44) 22.0	(52) 23.4
1.0	-8.0						3.4	-1.4
28.7	13.1	20.3					18.9	17.8
9.0	.9	6.9				% Profit Before Taxes/Total Assets	7.4	6.2
-2.4	-4.3	-1.6					.6	-2.0
78.0	21.3	27.1					39.2	41.0
28.3	8.7	7.9				Sales/Net Fixed Assets	15.1	16.9
7.1	1.8	2.9					4.3	6.0
7.2	3.7	4.0					5.2	4.9
4.8	2.3	2.3				Sales/Total Assets	3.3	3.0
3.3	.7	1.3					1.8	2.1
.3	.7						.8	.9
(32) .9	(19) 1.4					% Depr., Dep., Amort./Sales	(55) 1.6	(51) 1.6
1.9	3.3						3.8	2.6
5.0	2.4						2.3	2.0
(28) 7.9	(13) 4.4					% Officers', Directors' Owners' Comp/Sales	(41) 5.9	(40) 4.9
10.7	7.9						9.1	9.0
53602M	66510M	130855M	222364M	151338M		Net Sales ($)	1744285M	577315M
10538M	25534M	36841M	152196M	82518M		Total Assets ($)	389604M	207040M

M = $ thousand   MM = $ million
See Pages 9 through 22 for Explanation of Ratios and Data

Comparative Historical Data | Current Data Sorted by Sales

			Type of Statement						
1	2	5	Unqualified		1		1	1	3
3	3	2	Reviewed						1
15	20	18	Compiled	6	7	2	3		
40	23	26	Tax Returns	14	8	1	2	1	
24	23	38	Other	15	12	5	2	1	3
4/1/08-3/31/09 ALL	4/1/09-3/31/10 ALL	4/1/10-3/31/11 ALL		0-1MM	8 (4/1-9/30/10) 1-3MM	3-5MM	81 (10/1/10-3/31/11) 5-10MM	10-25MM	25MM & OVER
83	71	89	NUMBER OF STATEMENTS	35	28	8	8	3	7
%	%	%	ASSETS	%	%	%	%	%	%
15.7	13.9	14.1	Cash & Equivalents	13.4	16.5				
15.5	14.8	15.1	Trade Receivables (net)	14.6	14.5				
18.8	19.4	15.1	Inventory	11.3	19.0				
3.1	4.5	2.9	All Other Current	1.9	2.7				
53.1	52.6	47.2	Total Current	41.2	52.7				
33.7	35.5	38.3	Fixed Assets (net)	43.8	33.5				
4.6	6.8	6.9	Intangibles (net)	6.9	6.9				
8.6	5.1	7.6	All Other Non-Current	8.1	6.9				
100.0	100.0	100.0	Total	100.0	100.0				
			LIABILITIES						
9.2	12.5	10.4	Notes Payable-Short Term	13.5	11.0				
6.4	2.6	4.0	Cur. Mat.-L.T.D.	2.8	5.3				
13.1	12.0	15.9	Trade Payables	8.7	22.7				
.1	.2	.0	Income Taxes Payable	.0	.0				
12.5	13.1	11.6	All Other Current	10.7	12.9				
41.3	40.4	41.9	Total Current	35.7	51.9				
22.7	25.1	30.9	Long-Term Debt	32.3	33.4				
.1	.3	.0	Deferred Taxes	.0	.0				
11.7	9.0	12.2	All Other Non-Current	12.5	19.0				
24.2	25.2	15.1	Net Worth	19.6	-4.3				
100.0	100.0	100.0	Total Liabilties & Net Worth	100.0	100.0				
			INCOME DATA						
100.0	100.0	100.0	Net Sales	100.0	100.0				
			Gross Profit						
93.0	93.5	91.7	Operating Expenses	84.9	97.5				
7.0	6.5	8.3	Operating Profit	15.1	2.5				
2.1	2.2	4.0	All Other Expenses (net)	8.7	.7				
5.0	4.3	4.2	Profit Before Taxes	6.5	1.9				
			RATIOS						
2.6	3.1	2.3		2.9	1.8				
1.5	1.5	1.2	Current	1.4	1.1				
.7	.9	.6		.5	.7				
1.5	2.5	1.5		2.3	1.4				
(82) .7	.8	.7	Quick	.8	.6				
.3	.3	.3		.3	.2				
1 427.7	1 381.5	1 403.0		0 UND	3 128.6				
13 27.9	14 26.2	9 39.3	Sales/Receivables	2 207.0	10 38.3				
33 11.2	37 9.8	22 16.7		23 15.8	18 20.5				
			Cost of Sales/Inventory						
			Cost of Sales/Payables						
8.3	7.5	10.5		8.5	15.0				
33.7	21.0	95.1	Sales/Working Capital	60.4	76.9				
-24.8	-156.9	-24.4		-16.9	-24.7				
6.4	6.1	12.2		11.2	27.4				
(67) 2.6	(58) 2.1	(64) 3.4	EBIT/Interest	(20) 2.0	(20) 2.6				
1.0	.6	.2		.7	-.6				
14.7			Net Profit + Depr., Dep.,						
(10) 7.3			Amort./Cur. Mat. L/T/D						
.6									
.2	.3	.4		.2	.4				
1.0	1.3	1.7	Fixed/Worth	1.8	4.6				
40.7	12.5	-2.7		13.9	-.7				
.5	.6	.9		.5	1.3				
2.1	2.3	2.6	Debt/Worth	1.7	8.3				
77.1	-55.3	-4.6		-4.3	-2.5				
89.3	60.7	54.0		37.8	74.2				
(63) 26.8	(53) 12.5	(62) 21.0	% Profit Before Taxes/Tangible Net Worth	(26) 16.7	(15) 32.2				
.0	-1.4	-5.8		-2.5	-17.5				
22.6	15.0	24.9		24.7	27.8				
4.5	3.4	5.2	% Profit Before Taxes/Total Assets	5.1	.0				
.0	-1.1	-2.1		-.4	-7.6				
34.1	35.5	37.7		42.8	48.1				
16.6	19.1	16.0	Sales/Net Fixed Assets	10.5	18.0				
7.7	4.6	5.5		3.5	5.5				
5.4	4.5	6.1		6.1	5.5				
3.5	2.9	3.6	Sales/Total Assets	3.3	4.0				
2.2	1.9	1.8		1.0	2.4				
.8	.7	.6		.5	.3				
(69) 1.4	(55) 1.9	(66) 1.5	% Depr., Dep., Amort./Sales	(21) 1.9	(21) 1.0				
2.4	3.0	2.8		9.1	2.4				
1.9	2.1	2.6		5.7	3.7				
(41) 5.2	(35) 4.8	(46) 6.1	% Officers', Directors' Owners' Comp/Sales	(17) 8.9	(16) 7.5				
8.8	8.2	9.1		11.0	10.1				
701879M	1769501M	624669M	Net Sales ($)	16712M	47167M	31009M	53183M	47836M	428762M
282945M	602897M	307627M	Total Assets ($)	13548M	14908M	12552M	17277M	36171M	213171M

M = $ thousand   MM = $ million
See Pages 9 through 22 for Explanation of Ratios and Data

Current Data Sorted by Assets   **Comparative Historical Data**

0-500M	500M-2MM	2-10MM	10-50MM	50-100MM	100-250MM	Type of Statement	ALL	ALL
1	1	3			1	Unqualified	2	10
9	11	1				Reviewed	13	16
26	17	7			1	Compiled	61	41
99	72	14	1		1	Tax Returns	133	137
48	46	21	4	2		Other	96	95
	56 (4/1-9/30/10)		330 (10/1/10-3/31/11)				4/1/06-3/31/07	4/1/07-3/31/08
173	145	54	9	2	3	NUMBER OF STATEMENTS	305	299
%	%	%	%	%	%	ASSETS	%	%
24.7	17.4	14.4				Cash & Equivalents	13.8	15.0
12.9	11.7	11.5				Trade Receivables (net)	14.5	13.4
11.1	8.2	9.5				Inventory	12.8	11.9
3.9	4.0	2.1				All Other Current	2.9	3.2
52.6	41.3	37.5				Total Current	44.0	43.5
34.6	40.6	41.9				Fixed Assets (net)	40.7	39.5
3.5	5.5	9.3				Intangibles (net)	5.4	8.5
9.3	12.6	11.3				All Other Non-Current	9.9	8.6
100.0	100.0	100.0				Total	100.0	100.0
						LIABILITIES		
18.9	8.5	6.7				Notes Payable-Short Term	11.8	14.7
3.8	3.6	3.6				Cur. Mat.-L.T.D.	4.2	4.4
16.1	13.5	14.4				Trade Payables	18.7	16.2
.2	.2	.0				Income Taxes Payable	.3	.1
21.8	11.0	9.4				All Other Current	14.5	12.1
60.9	36.7	34.1				Total Current	49.4	47.4
24.0	30.0	33.1				Long-Term Debt	34.9	30.2
.2	.1	.1				Deferred Taxes	.1	.2
27.7	6.4	7.6				All Other Non-Current	8.4	12.8
-12.8	26.8	25.1				Net Worth	7.3	9.4
100.0	100.0	100.0				Total Liabilities & Net Worth	100.0	100.0
						INCOME DATA		
100.0	100.0	100.0				Net Sales	100.0	100.0
						Gross Profit		
96.7	90.7	89.1				Operating Expenses	94.7	93.8
3.3	9.3	10.9				Operating Profit	5.3	6.2
.7	2.0	4.4				All Other Expenses (net)	2.2	1.4
2.7	7.2	6.6				Profit Before Taxes	3.1	4.7
						RATIOS		
2.3	2.6	1.8					1.8	2.1
1.0	1.1	1.0				Current	1.0	1.0
.5	.6	.6					.5	.6
1.7	1.9	1.3					1.4	1.5
(172) .7	.8	.8				Quick	(303) .6	(298) .7
.3	.4	.4					.3	.3
0 UND	1 340.5	5 66.7					0 999.8	0 UND
3 113.2	10 37.8	11 32.3				Sales/Receivables	9 39.6	8 44.5
12 29.9	17 21.2	18 20.6					20 18.7	19 18.8
						Cost of Sales/Inventory		
						Cost of Sales/Payables		
23.1	12.5	19.2					18.3	17.9
UND	65.6	NM				Sales/Working Capital	UND	267.0
-18.6	-23.3	-20.9					-21.0	-28.1
8.9	13.4	14.9					9.2	8.5
(118) 3.6	(110) 3.3	(44) 7.2				EBIT/Interest	(265) 3.0	(250) 2.6
-.3	1.3	1.5					1.0	.9
						Net Profit + Depr., Dep., Amort./Cur. Mat. L/T/D	4.2	3.3
							(26) 1.6	(24) 2.4
							.6	.8
.5	.4	.8					.6	.7
3.8	1.8	2.3				Fixed/Worth	2.5	2.9
-1.0	33.1	NM					-4.4	-2.1
1.0	.8	1.4					1.4	1.3
53.2	2.8	4.6				Debt/Worth	5.1	4.8
-3.5	56.1	NM					-7.6	-6.7
91.3	78.0	68.9				% Profit Before Taxes/Tangible Net Worth	110.7	124.8
(90) 33.1	(112) 31.2	(41) 43.1					(209) 39.3	(197) 42.0
3.6	9.4	13.9					9.1	6.4
32.4	19.6	19.7				% Profit Before Taxes/Total Assets	26.0	24.1
8.8	8.3	7.8					8.8	8.1
-4.4	.9	1.6					.2	.0
71.0	27.8	30.2				Sales/Net Fixed Assets	34.9	35.5
23.5	12.1	9.2					13.8	14.5
10.3	3.4	3.2					5.8	5.5
10.2	4.6	4.5				Sales/Total Assets	7.0	7.2
6.5	3.1	2.7					4.5	4.3
3.9	1.7	1.8					2.6	2.5
.5	.7	1.1				% Depr., Dep., Amort./Sales	.9	.7
(110) 1.0	(112) 1.4	(46) 1.7					(246) 1.6	(232) 1.5
2.3	2.7	3.1					3.0	2.6
3.9	2.8	1.1				% Officers', Directors' Owners' Comp/Sales	2.8	2.4
(105) 6.2	(86) 4.1	(25) 2.0					(193) 4.5	(188) 4.3
9.1	6.5	3.6					7.9	8.1
237921M	467110M	656817M	491569M	1058691M	2305468M	Net Sales ($)	4668632M	7658377M
37646M	144657M	221121M	171248M	149370M	500123M	Total Assets ($)	1001930M	1298484M

© RMA 2011

M = $ thousand   MM = $ million
See Pages 9 through 22 for Explanation of Ratios and Data

Comparative Historical Data			Type of Statement	Current Data Sorted by Sales					
7	8	6	Unqualified					2	4
20	18	21	Reviewed		4	3	3	11	
45	43	51	Compiled	9	27	4	8		3
143	165	187	Tax Returns	47	90	24	20	4	2
85	105	121	Other	32	48	13	10	12	6
4/1/08-3/31/09	4/1/09-3/31/10	4/1/10-3/31/11		56 (4/1-9/30/10)			330 (10/1/10-3/31/11)		
ALL	ALL	ALL		0-1MM	1-3MM	3-5MM	5-10MM	10-25MM	25MM & OVER
300	339	386	**NUMBER OF STATEMENTS**	88	169	44	41	29	15
%	%	%	**ASSETS**	%	%	%	%	%	%
17.8	19.2	20.1	Cash & Equivalents	22.3	19.1	22.9	19.8	17.3	15.3
13.2	13.4	12.2	Trade Receivables (net)	6.8	11.9	16.8	16.9	16.4	12.3
11.3	9.5	9.7	Inventory	9.9	9.1	8.7	11.9	10.7	11.4
2.7	3.1	3.6	All Other Current	2.8	4.1	4.2	4.3	1.9	1.3
44.9	45.1	45.5	Total Current	41.8	44.2	52.7	53.0	46.3	40.2
37.3	36.0	37.9	Fixed Assets (net)	49.5	37.2	30.1	31.2	31.7	31.0
6.0	8.4	5.5	Intangibles (net)	2.4	5.3	4.8	3.9	13.3	16.5
11.8	10.5	11.1	All Other Non-Current	6.3	13.3	12.4	12.0	8.7	12.3
100.0	100.0	100.0	Total	100.0	100.0	100.0	100.0	100.0	100.0
			LIABILITIES						
11.1	9.8	13.1	Notes Payable-Short Term	16.7	14.4	9.2	10.1	5.1	12.0
5.0	3.8	3.8	Cur. Mat.-L.T.D.	4.0	3.6	2.5	3.7	5.0	7.7
17.6	15.9	14.6	Trade Payables	7.4	15.1	21.0	17.1	20.3	15.9
.2	.1	.2	Income Taxes Payable	.0	.3	.2	.3	.0	.0
19.7	16.9	15.5	All Other Current	19.2	15.5	12.5	15.4	12.3	9.1
53.6	46.6	47.2	Total Current	47.3	48.8	45.3	46.6	42.6	44.7
29.1	31.8	27.7	Long-Term Debt	36.8	28.0	21.4	17.5	23.8	23.9
.2	.2	.2	Deferred Taxes	.0	.2	.1	.2	.5	.1
12.8	9.0	16.7	All Other Non-Current	25.2	13.9	19.6	11.1	9.3	18.0
4.3	12.6	8.2	Net Worth	-9.4	9.0	13.6	24.6	23.8	13.3
100.0	100.0	100.0	Total Liabilties & Net Worth	100.0	100.0	100.0	100.0	100.0	100.0
			INCOME DATA						
100.0	100.0	100.0	Net Sales	100.0	100.0	100.0	100.0	100.0	100.0
			Gross Profit						
95.2	95.3	93.2	Operating Expenses	85.4	94.9	95.8	96.5	95.6	96.9
4.8	4.7	6.8	Operating Profit	14.6	5.1	4.2	3.5	4.4	3.1
2.0	2.0	1.8	All Other Expenses (net)	5.5	1.1	.5	-.1	.0	.3
2.8	2.7	5.0	Profit Before Taxes	9.1	4.0	3.7	3.6	4.4	2.8
			RATIOS						
2.1	2.0	2.2		2.7	2.4	3.2	1.8	1.9	1.4
1.0	1.1	1.1	Current	1.0	1.0	1.3	1.2	.9	1.0
.6	.6	.6		.4	.5	.8	.7	.6	.8
1.5	1.6	1.6		1.9	1.6	2.5	1.4	1.3	1.0
.7	.7 (385)	.7	Quick	.6 (168)	.7	1.0	.8	.8	.8
.3	.3	.4		.2	.3	.5	.5	.4	.4
0 UND	1 541.0	0 UND		0 UND	0 UND	5 77.0	6 61.2	9 42.4	6 63.4
8 43.7	7 49.1	8 47.6	Sales/Receivables	0 UND	6 63.7	11 34.4	10 36.8	14 26.9	11 33.0
15 24.0	14 25.7	15 24.8		12 30.5	14 26.3	21 17.2	17 21.4	18 20.0	16 22.3
			Cost of Sales/Inventory						
			Cost of Sales/Payables						
19.4	16.3	18.2		11.6	19.6	10.9	20.4	15.8	35.7
-999.8	149.3	188.6	Sales/Working Capital	291.5	-999.8	26.9	52.8	-209.2	215.9
-18.5	-26.8	-20.2		-12.5	-19.9	-30.4	-39.8	-22.5	-36.8
7.2	9.6	11.7		13.6	8.0	13.8	15.6	18.8	15.8
(236) 2.3	(258) 3.0	(284) 3.7	EBIT/Interest	(55) 2.5	(122) 3.6	(30) 3.1	(37) 5.0	(26) 9.4	(14) 2.8
.4	.8	1.1		-.7	1.1	1.1	1.9	1.5	1.9
4.4	6.6	5.2							
(19) 1.4	(27) 2.3	(23) 1.5	Net Profit + Depr., Dep., Amort./Cur. Mat. L/T/D						
.6	1.2	.5							
.6	.5	.5		.6	.5	.2	.6	.7	1.3
2.7	2.3	2.3	Fixed/Worth	4.1	2.6	1.3	1.3	1.9	2.9
-1.9	-2.4	-2.7		-3.8	-1.6	-6.3	NM	-1.7	-2.7
1.4	1.0	1.1		1.3	1.0	.5	1.4	1.4	3.1
7.0	5.4	5.7	Debt/Worth	8.8	5.4	5.9	3.1	4.3	12.6
-5.9	-6.3	-6.5		-5.1	-5.1	-12.3	NM	-9.0	-5.6
104.8	106.1	89.2		87.4	70.5	80.7	105.8	107.8	136.0
(199) 30.8	(229) 39.7	(252) 35.4	% Profit Before Taxes/Tangible Net Worth	(53) 30.8	(109) 25.4	(29) 41.3	(31) 41.7	(20) 49.6	(10) 81.6
6.3	5.0	8.1		2.2	5.1	12.1	21.1	19.5	39.7
19.1	22.0	23.7		23.9	24.7	25.0	20.7	24.3	15.6
5.2	7.7	8.4	% Profit Before Taxes/Total Assets	5.7	8.4	8.9	10.1	12.5	10.2
-1.4	-.5	.5		-5.5	.4	.8	2.1	4.0	3.4
41.2	43.9	44.5		27.9	49.8	44.3	42.7	41.1	31.2
18.0	19.5	16.4	Sales/Net Fixed Assets	7.1	19.1	18.7	19.6	16.3	15.2
7.1	8.0	5.8		1.5	6.9	9.8	11.1	7.1	9.7
7.6	7.4	6.6		5.4	8.3	5.4	7.1	5.0	5.8
4.5	4.5	4.2	Sales/Total Assets	2.5	5.0	3.9	5.4	3.5	4.5
2.5	2.6	2.3		1.0	2.5	2.6	3.4	2.5	2.9
.8	.7	.6		.7	.6	.4	.9	1.0	.9
(238) 1.7	(264) 1.4	(277) 1.4	% Depr., Dep., Amort./Sales	(52) 2.5	(123) 1.4	(33) 1.0	(35) 1.2	(24) 1.5	(10) 1.8
3.0	2.6	2.7		8.1	2.5	1.9	1.7	2.9	2.1
3.0	2.6	2.7		6.2	3.2	2.8	1.2	1.0	
(179) 5.1	(219) 4.8	(221) 5.0	% Officers', Directors' Owners' Comp/Sales	(33) 7.9	(112) 5.3	(30) 5.2	(27) 2.8	(14) 1.6	
7.8	7.7	7.5		13.3	8.1	6.8	4.5	2.2	
2449796M	6030364M	5217576M	Net Sales ($)	45890M	309061M	170348M	264844M	466996M	3960437M
947951M	1464296M	1224165M	Total Assets ($)	42002M	111326M	52518M	75305M	143558M	799456M

M = $ thousand   MM = $ million
See Pages 9 through 22 for Explanation of Ratios and Data

Current Data Sorted by Assets

Comparative Historical Data

0-500M	500M-2MM	2-10MM	10-50MM	50-100MM	100-250MM	Type of Statement	4/1/06-3/31/07 ALL	4/1/07-3/31/08 ALL
	2		1	1		Unqualified	1	1
		2	2			Reviewed	1	4
3	1	4	1			Compiled	4	6
17	13	7	1			Tax Returns	11	10
12	11	10	3	1	1	Other	6	8
	3 (4/1-9/30/10)		90 (10/1/10-3/31/11)					
32	27	23	8	2	1	NUMBER OF STATEMENTS	23	29
%	%	%	%	%	%	**ASSETS**	%	%
20.6	12.2	7.8				Cash & Equivalents	15.7	18.1
6.8	4.1	2.8				Trade Receivables (net)	6.7	2.7
21.4	6.4	5.8				Inventory	17.9	9.0
5.3	4.0	3.8				All Other Current	1.4	3.0
54.2	26.7	20.2				Total Current	41.7	32.8
32.0	49.3	59.2				Fixed Assets (net)	42.5	50.9
6.5	19.1	11.7				Intangibles (net)	8.8	8.6
7.3	4.9	8.9				All Other Non-Current	7.1	7.7
100.0	100.0	100.0				Total	100.0	100.0
						LIABILITIES		
4.3	3.2	1.2				Notes Payable-Short Term	10.4	1.2
5.6	2.0	3.9				Cur. Mat.-L.T.D.	3.1	3.7
22.4	12.1	10.6				Trade Payables	18.5	8.0
.0	.0	.0				Income Taxes Payable	.0	.0
19.1	7.4	2.6				All Other Current	13.4	7.1
51.5	24.8	18.4				Total Current	45.5	20.0
47.6	57.6	64.4				Long-Term Debt	32.4	39.0
.0	.0	.4				Deferred Taxes	.4	.0
19.6	13.0	3.6				All Other Non-Current	7.1	30.3
-18.7	4.5	13.1				Net Worth	14.7	10.7
100.0	100.0	100.0				Total Liabilties & Net Worth	100.0	100.0
						INCOME DATA		
100.0	100.0	100.0				Net Sales	100.0	100.0
						Gross Profit		
93.7	90.7	86.1				Operating Expenses	92.2	90.0
6.3	9.3	13.9				Operating Profit	7.8	10.0
1.1	2.8	8.7				All Other Expenses (net)	2.2	4.4
5.2	6.5	5.2				Profit Before Taxes	5.6	5.7
						RATIOS		
3.0	2.0	1.5				Current	3.2	4.4
1.9	1.1	.9					.9	1.6
.7	.7	.5					.4	.8
1.9	1.7	1.2				Quick	2.7	3.3
.7	(26) .7	.4					.4	1.1
.1	.4	.3					.2	.3
0 UND	0 999.8	0 UND				Sales/Receivables	1 426.5	0 UND
0 UND	1 244.0	2 235.6					4 100.9	1 323.6
7 49.3	4 86.0	9 42.0					8 45.2	3 116.0
						Cost of Sales/Inventory		
						Cost of Sales/Payables		
9.2	16.4	10.8				Sales/Working Capital	12.9	8.1
22.0	139.0	-147.2					-65.0	28.0
-77.3	-17.9	-14.1					-10.9	-56.9
11.3	6.9	4.8				EBIT/Interest	10.8	11.6
(16) 2.9	(20) 2.2	(19) 1.6					(14) 2.0	(25) 2.4
.0	-.1	1.4					-1.1	1.4
						Net Profit + Depr., Dep., Amort./Cur. Mat. L/T/D		
.0	2.6	2.5				Fixed/Worth	.2	.7
1.5	-22.9	13.3					1.8	2.0
-.8	-1.1	-3.4					-4.9	-3.1
1.1	5.5	5.4				Debt/Worth	.6	1.2
NM	-25.6	13.1					10.5	5.4
-2.4	-2.5	-4.9					-4.4	-4.9
223.8	99.1	57.7				% Profit Before Taxes/Tangible Net Worth	69.4	67.4
(16) 66.7	(11) 62.7	(13) 19.1					(13) 27.4	(18) 34.0
19.6	14.1	5.3					13.8	12.7
32.9	19.9	8.4				% Profit Before Taxes/Total Assets	34.7	24.4
15.0	10.3	3.2					7.8	6.9
-8.4	1.1	.5					-.6	-2.8
UND	39.2	3.6				Sales/Net Fixed Assets	33.2	15.4
20.3	4.9	1.3					14.9	5.5
4.9	1.5	.5					1.6	1.4
7.6	2.7	1.5				Sales/Total Assets	10.0	4.4
3.9	1.7	.9					2.5	2.3
2.2	.9	.3					1.0	1.0
.8	1.3	2.3				% Depr., Dep., Amort./Sales	1.0	1.5
(17) 2.1	(19) 3.8	5.4					(20) 1.8	(27) 2.6
5.1	6.5	8.0					6.0	6.4
3.7	3.6					% Officers', Directors' Owners' Comp/Sales	1.8	1.9
(13) 5.6	(11) 4.8						(11) 2.3	(10) 4.1
10.9	6.0						5.1	7.9
24646M	59581M	110877M	324151M	160261M	109133M	Net Sales ($)	182316M	711304M
5391M	27532M	104608M	195387M	138832M	102157M	Total Assets ($)	144182M	578172M

M = $ thousand   MM = $ million
See Pages 9 through 22 for Explanation of Ratios and Data

Comparative Historical Data | Current Data Sorted by Sales

			Type of Statement						
1	2	4	Unqualified		1			1	2
3	1	4	Reviewed				1	2	1
2	6	9	Compiled	4	2	1		2	1
19	23	38	Tax Returns	16	17	3		1	
12	22	38	Other	16	11	4	1	3	3
4/1/08-3/31/09	4/1/09-3/31/10	4/1/10-3/31/11		3 (4/1-9/30/10)			90 (10/1/10-3/31/11)		
ALL	ALL	ALL		0-1MM	1-3MM	3-5MM	5-10MM	10-25MM	25MM & OVER
37	54	93	**NUMBER OF STATEMENTS**	36	31	8	2	9	7
%	%	%	**ASSETS**	%	%	%	%	%	%
11.6	8.9	13.6	Cash & Equivalents	13.5	14.4				
1.5	3.1	4.7	Trade Receivables (net)	4.7	5.0				
9.3	10.7	11.6	Inventory	10.3	15.8				
3.6	2.5	4.2	All Other Current	3.9	4.9				
25.9	25.3	34.0	Total Current	32.3	40.1				
55.2	58.8	44.4	Fixed Assets (net)	48.0	42.9				
12.8	12.0	13.9	Intangibles (net)	10.1	12.7				
6.1	3.9	7.7	All Other Non-Current	9.6	4.3				
100.0	100.0	100.0	Total	100.0	100.0				
			LIABILITIES						
2.2	4.6	3.0	Notes Payable-Short Term	2.9	3.3				
6.4	4.0	3.9	Cur. Mat.-L.T.D.	4.9	2.7				
8.6	11.0	14.9	Trade Payables	9.8	20.2				
.0	.0	.0	Income Taxes Payable	.0	.0				
21.9	11.7	10.0	All Other Current	8.7	15.5				
39.1	31.3	31.9	Total Current	26.3	41.7				
50.7	56.3	53.7	Long-Term Debt	60.7	50.8				
.2	.1	.2	Deferred Taxes	.0	.3				
17.4	23.6	12.4	All Other Non-Current	18.2	10.6				
-7.3	-11.4	1.8	Net Worth	-5.3	-3.4				
100.0	100.0	100.0	Total Liabilities & Net Worth	100.0	100.0				
			INCOME DATA						
100.0	100.0	100.0	Net Sales	100.0	100.0				
			Gross Profit						
84.5	91.4	91.0	Operating Expenses	88.0	93.0				
15.5	8.6	9.0	Operating Profit	12.0	7.0				
7.2	4.5	3.6	All Other Expenses (net)	6.1	2.4				
8.2	4.1	5.4	Profit Before Taxes	5.9	4.6				
			RATIOS						
1.5	1.6	2.1		2.5	2.7				
.9	.8	1.2	Current	1.3	1.3				
.3	.3	.6		.7	.6				
1.0	.9	1.6		1.8	1.9				
(36) .3	.4	(92) .6	Quick	(35) .7	.7				
.2	.2	.2		.2	.2				
0 UND	0 UND	0 UND		0 UND	0 UND				
2 180.9	0 759.3	1 244.0	Sales/Receivables	0 UND	1 266.8				
4 98.8	4 85.9	7 53.4		10 37.3	5 74.3				
			Cost of Sales/Inventory						
			Cost of Sales/Payables						
26.8	43.2	11.2		10.6	11.4				
-116.5	-44.4	75.7	Sales/Working Capital	30.0	65.8				
-7.4	-8.1	-17.7		-46.1	-29.9				
4.9	5.3	6.9		5.9	5.9				
(25) 2.0	(42) 2.3	(66) 2.4	EBIT/Interest	(21) 1.5	(20) 1.6				
.0	1.3	1.2		-.5	.0				
			Net Profit + Depr., Dep., Amort./Cur. Mat. L/T/D						
1.1	1.2	.7		.8	.2				
8.8	102.8	7.4	Fixed/Worth	-18.2	4.3				
-1.0	-1.9	-1.8		-1.1	-4.1				
2.6	2.6	2.6		2.7	2.7				
11.9	-45.1	-66.2	Debt/Worth	-16.6	12.7				
-2.6	-3.6	-2.8		-2.9	-3.1				
68.7	56.8	90.1		125.8	91.7				
(21) 26.2	(26) 25.5	(45) 34.2	% Profit Before Taxes/Tangible Net Worth	(16) 55.2	(16) 21.6				
3.6	3.8	9.6		19.6	4.9				
8.8	12.9	18.7		18.4	20.0				
4.4	6.4	6.9	% Profit Before Taxes/Total Assets	7.8	5.4				
-3.2	-1.0	-.2		-5.5	-5.9				
12.7	9.1	45.3		38.0	366.9				
5.7	2.5	5.3	Sales/Net Fixed Assets	4.5	7.5				
.7	.8	1.4		.9	1.3				
3.6	3.7	3.3		3.6	5.6				
1.7	1.5	1.8	Sales/Total Assets	1.3	2.3				
.6	.6	.9		.5	1.0				
2.3	2.5	1.3		1.8	1.1				
(30) 3.8	(42) 3.8	(68) 3.1	% Depr., Dep., Amort./Sales	(25) 3.3	(21) 4.4				
12.9	13.4	6.8		8.6	7.1				
2.6	1.9	3.3			3.5				
(12) 3.6	(18) 4.1	(31) 4.2	% Officers', Directors' Owners' Comp/Sales		(14) 4.5				
8.5	8.4	7.2			6.3				
242826M	213435M	788649M	Net Sales ($)	19451M	50625M	29432M	15449M	171350M	502342M
186853M	165325M	573907M	Total Assets ($)	34399M	35450M	25028M	10835M	135985M	332210M

M = $ thousand   MM = $ million
See Pages 9 through 22 for Explanation of Ratios and Data

Current Data Sorted by Assets   Comparative Historical Data

0-500M	500M-2MM	2-10MM	10-50MM	50-100MM	100-250MM	Type of Statement	ALL 4/1/06-3/31/07	ALL 4/1/07-3/31/08
	1	1	2		3	Unqualified	13	6
	4	5	7			Reviewed	12	8
28	31	15	1			Compiled	102	53
79	66	21	2	1	2	Tax Returns	135	117
33	41	47	11	3	1	Other	81	100
	29 (4/1-9/30/10)		376 (10/1/10-3/31/11)					
140	143	89	23	4	6	NUMBER OF STATEMENTS	343	284
%	%	%	%	%	%	**ASSETS**	%	%
22.0	6.8	4.7	8.5			Cash & Equivalents	9.5	8.5
2.9	2.1	2.4	.7			Trade Receivables (net)	3.1	2.2
6.6	2.9	2.3	1.7			Inventory	3.5	3.3
4.0	2.4	1.2	.6			All Other Current	1.3	2.8
35.6	14.1	10.7	11.5			Total Current	17.3	16.8
44.3	68.2	72.1	74.4			Fixed Assets (net)	67.4	67.5
8.7	10.3	8.0	6.4			Intangibles (net)	8.3	9.1
11.4	7.4	9.2	7.7			All Other Non-Current	6.9	6.6
100.0	100.0	100.0	100.0			Total	100.0	100.0
						LIABILITIES		
10.7	5.8	2.0	2.0			Notes Payable-Short Term	4.7	6.0
4.3	3.6	3.7	4.8			Cur. Mat.-L.T.D.	6.4	4.0
15.9	2.3	3.0	2.5			Trade Payables	5.0	5.5
.4	.0	.1	.0			Income Taxes Payable	.2	.2
23.8	12.6	5.8	7.1			All Other Current	9.5	10.9
55.1	24.3	14.6	16.3			Total Current	25.7	26.7
44.4	62.4	66.7	46.9			Long-Term Debt	60.8	63.5
.1	.0	.0	.1			Deferred Taxes	.0	.0
22.7	10.8	4.4	7.8			All Other Non-Current	11.1	11.1
-22.3	2.5	14.4	28.9			Net Worth	2.3	-1.3
100.0	100.0	100.0	100.0			Total Liabilities & Net Worth	100.0	100.0
						INCOME DATA		
100.0	100.0	100.0	100.0			Net Sales	100.0	100.0
						Gross Profit		
91.7	86.4	80.3	86.6			Operating Expenses	88.3	87.3
8.3	13.6	19.7	13.4			Operating Profit	11.7	12.7
3.1	10.6	12.8	5.7			All Other Expenses (net)	9.9	9.7
5.2	3.0	6.9	7.7			Profit Before Taxes	1.7	3.0
						RATIOS		
2.2	2.4	1.4	1.3				1.9	2.2
1.0	.5	.7	.6			Current	.6	.8
.3	.1	.2	.4				.2	.2
1.5	1.7	1.2	1.2				1.3	1.4
.5	.3	.3	.3			Quick	.4 (282)	.5
.1	.1	.1	.2				.1	.1
0 UND	0 UND	0 UND	0 771.4				0 UND	0 UND
0 UND	0 UND	1 724.0	1 373.8			Sales/Receivables	0 UND	0 UND
1 487.0	1 327.5	2 147.5	2 237.4				2 164.0	2 212.1
						Cost of Sales/Inventory		
						Cost of Sales/Payables		
26.1	19.0	36.2	27.9				24.6	20.7
UND	-18.0	-23.7	-13.5			Sales/Working Capital	-26.8	-31.9
-10.8	-4.1	-4.9	-8.1				-5.2	-4.8
14.5	4.3	4.7	4.5				3.0	4.2
(79) 5.8	(100) 2.1	(67) 2.0	(19) 2.4			EBIT/Interest	(247) 1.4	(202) 1.6
1.9	1.2	1.0	1.2				.5	.9
							7.9	4.2
						Net Profit + Depr., Dep., Amort./Cur. Mat. L/T/D	(15) 2.4	(14) 1.3
							.9	.5
.8	2.6	2.9	1.6				2.1	2.2
22.7	92.6	10.4	2.8			Fixed/Worth	35.1	23.9
-.6	-1.6	-7.5	-13.8				-2.9	-2.3
1.1	3.1	3.1	1.4				2.2	2.2
95.9	213.0	9.9	2.0			Debt/Worth	79.0	40.7
-2.0	-2.9	-9.0	-15.7				-4.2	-3.7
225.8	79.9	50.3	32.6				60.0	62.7
(74) 69.2	(72) 28.5	(58) 19.3	(17) 22.0			% Profit Before Taxes/Tangible Net Worth	(180) 21.8	(154) 24.7
3.9	1.1	1.1	13.3				.0	1.0
50.7	9.9	8.0	11.8				8.6	11.1
14.6	2.8	3.3	3.7			% Profit Before Taxes/Total Assets	1.4	2.1
.2	-1.8	.0	.6				-4.3	-3.4
68.5	3.7	1.4	2.4				6.9	5.1
10.5	.9	.6	1.1			Sales/Net Fixed Assets	1.3	1.2
2.6	.4	.3	.5				.4	.4
7.7	1.3	1.0	1.6				2.3	2.2
3.8	.6	.5	.9			Sales/Total Assets	.9	.7
1.6	.3	.3	.3				.4	.4
1.2	4.3	4.2	3.8				3.2	3.8
(96) 4.0	(121) 11.3	(74) 10.0	(22) 5.9			% Depr., Dep., Amort./Sales	(282) 8.6	(225) 9.7
10.8	24.7	20.6	10.5				19.5	20.9
4.0	2.1	3.1					3.1	2.8
(58) 5.8	(43) 4.9	(22) 4.5				% Officers', Directors' Owners' Comp/Sales	(112) 6.3	(89) 6.2
9.0	10.2	8.1					10.9	11.7
118128M	179332M	272022M	494326M	508061M	3793333M	Net Sales ($)	3844160M	1793632M
29032M	155284M	343620M	427997M	222270M	1042881M	Total Assets ($)	1910973M	1327240M

© RMA 2011

M = $ thousand   MM = $ million

See Pages 9 through 22 for Explanation of Ratios and Data

Comparative Historical Data   Current Data Sorted by Sales

			Type of Statement						
			Unqualified	1			2		4
5	5	7	Reviewed	2	2		3	6	3
14	16	16	Compiled	45	20	3	6	1	3
54	59	75	Tax Returns	107	50	6	4	1	3
141	170	171	Other	64	39	8	12	5	8
116	110	136							
4/1/08-3/31/09	4/1/09-3/31/10	4/1/10-3/31/11		29 (4/1-9/30/10)			376 (10/1/10-3/31/11)		
ALL	ALL	ALL		0-1MM	1-3MM	3-5MM	5-10MM	10-25MM	25MM & OVER
330	360	405	**NUMBER OF STATEMENTS**	219	111	17	27	13	18
%	%	%	**ASSETS**	%	%	%	%	%	%
10.1	10.7	11.7	Cash & Equivalents	12.7	11.7	8.3	8.8	8.2	10.1
2.4	1.7	2.3	Trade Receivables (net)	1.0	4.0	4.7	2.9	7.9	1.1
3.7	3.8	4.1	Inventory	2.1	6.2	8.5	8.2	4.3	4.5
2.9	2.9	2.6	All Other Current	2.1	2.7	7.4	1.4	7.0	.8
19.0	19.1	20.7	Total Current	17.9	24.6	29.0	21.3	27.5	16.5
63.2	63.3	61.0	Fixed Assets (net)	66.6	52.5	51.4	56.7	54.3	65.7
8.5	9.6	9.0	Intangibles (net)	7.0	12.6	9.7	11.9	7.2	7.5
9.2	8.0	9.3	All Other Non-Current	8.4	10.3	9.9	10.1	11.1	10.3
100.0	100.0	100.0	Total	100.0	100.0	100.0	100.0	100.0	100.0
			LIABILITIES						
6.1	4.9	6.4	Notes Payable-Short Term	8.2	5.0	2.7	2.6	5.1	2.8
4.6	5.4	4.4	Cur. Mat.-L.T.D.	4.6	2.9	1.9	4.0	4.1	13.9
4.3	4.0	7.3	Trade Payables	7.7	6.7	8.7	8.0	4.7	5.4
.2	.1	.2	Income Taxes Payable	.2	.0	.0	.2	.1	.0
15.8	15.9	14.7	All Other Current	15.2	14.9	10.8	15.0	12.3	12.7
30.9	30.3	32.9	Total Current	36.0	29.5	24.1	29.8	26.3	34.8
57.2	59.2	55.9	Long-Term Debt	61.1	53.5	44.8	51.8	31.9	41.9
.0	.1	.1	Deferred Taxes	.0	.0	.0	.1	.0	.9
10.7	12.7	13.4	All Other Non-Current	16.0	8.7	26.4	7.1	8.2	10.5
1.2	-2.3	-2.3	Net Worth	-13.2	8.3	4.8	11.2	33.7	11.9
100.0	100.0	100.0	Total Liabilities & Net Worth	100.0	100.0	100.0	100.0	100.0	100.0
			INCOME DATA						
100.0	100.0	100.0	Net Sales	100.0	100.0	100.0	100.0	100.0	100.0
			Gross Profit						
90.7	89.3	86.9	Operating Expenses	85.1	87.5	90.1	91.5	93.5	89.3
9.3	10.7	13.1	Operating Profit	14.9	12.5	9.9	8.5	6.5	10.7
8.7	9.4	8.1	All Other Expenses (net)	11.5	4.8	4.0	2.3	2.3	4.0
.7	1.3	5.0	Profit Before Taxes	3.4	7.7	5.9	6.1	4.2	6.7
			RATIOS						
2.2	2.0	2.0		2.0	2.7	2.3	1.1	1.8	1.2
.7	.7	.7	Current	.5	1.0	.8	.7	.9	.7
.2	.2	.2		.1	.4	.5	.4	.2	.5
1.6	1.2	1.4		1.6	2.0	.8	.6	1.2	1.0
.4	(359) .4	.4	Quick	.4	.4	.5	.3	.3	.4
.1	.1	.1		.1	.1	.2	.2	.1	.2
0 UND	0 UND	0 UND		0 UND	0 UND	0 UND	0 999.8	1 457.3	0 804.7
0 UND	0 UND	0 UND	Sales/Receivables	0 UND	0 999.8	0 999.8	1 273.2	1 341.5	1 259.6
2 182.1	1 271.2	1 269.7		0 UND	3 133.6	2 163.9	5 66.7	10 37.2	4 101.1
			Cost of Sales/Inventory						
			Cost of Sales/Payables						
19.6	25.5	26.8		26.0	16.2	51.4	103.7	21.4	97.5
-48.8	-41.9	-43.3	Sales/Working Capital	-13.9	190.4	-51.9	-39.1	-63.2	-46.8
-5.4	-5.1	-6.2		-3.6	-12.0	-14.8	-9.7	-10.4	-13.1
3.5	4.7	6.4		4.8	7.0	21.5	7.4	9.6	4.1
(219) 1.7	(238) 1.6	(273) 2.3	EBIT/Interest	(124) 2.0	(89) 2.6	(13) 5.1	(21) 2.4	(11) 4.5	(15) 2.2
.5	.6	1.2		1.1	1.3	1.9	1.5	1.5	1.1
3.9	2.9	2.3							
(22) 1.7	(21) 2.5	(18) 1.8	Net Profit + Depr., Dep., Amort./Cur. Mat. L/T/D						
1.0	1.7	1.2							
1.8	2.0	1.5		2.3	1.3	1.0	1.6	.4	1.1
11.8	28.5	13.4	Fixed/Worth	66.8	9.7	2.8	5.5	2.4	2.2
-2.3	-1.9	-1.7		-1.5	-1.2	-5.0	-1.8	4.6	-8.4
1.7	2.3	1.8		2.6	1.7	1.7	1.7	1.5	.6
23.3	120.3	21.5	Debt/Worth	109.5	12.0	9.9	5.8	2.0	4.0
-3.7	-3.1	-3.2		-2.9	-3.0	-11.5	-5.2	5.8	-2.1
44.0	38.4	86.0		82.3	125.8	136.6	56.7	40.4	25.2
(179) 15.6	(182) 16.1	(226) 29.2	% Profit Before Taxes/Tangible Net Worth	(113) 28.1	(63) 32.9	(11) 81.6	(17) 37.8	(11) 32.0	(11) 21.9
-1.5	-2.1	3.9		.7	5.0	2.8	18.6	9.2	9.9
8.4	9.6	15.4		10.1	30.4	35.3	12.8	12.5	15.0
1.6	1.8	4.5	% Profit Before Taxes/Total Assets	2.7	9.7	17.0	5.0	8.4	5.4
-5.1	-4.0	-.2		-2.4	1.3	-2.0	.6	.5	1.1
9.4	8.2	9.3		5.9	28.2	33.6	8.7	33.5	4.8
1.5	1.3	1.7	Sales/Net Fixed Assets	.8	2.3	4.3	3.1	3.8	2.4
.5	.5	.5		.3	.9	1.2	.9	1.1	1.4
2.8	2.6	3.1		1.9	5.9	9.3	2.7	3.9	2.8
.9	.8	1.0	Sales/Total Assets	.5	1.3	1.9	1.6	2.3	1.3
.4	.4	.4		.3	.6	.6	.7	1.0	1.0
3.0	2.9	3.0		6.0	1.2	.9	1.4	1.6	3.3
(262) 8.4	(298) 8.0	(319) 7.8	% Depr., Dep., Amort./Sales	(172) 13.7	(85) 4.2	(13) 5.6	(24) 3.8	(12) 2.9	(13) 4.4
18.9	22.3	18.9		25.6	10.1	6.7	6.9	5.1	5.6
2.4	2.7	2.8		4.1	2.0				
(116) 5.1	(124) 5.3	(132) 4.9	% Officers', Directors' Owners' Comp/Sales	(64) 7.3	(49) 4.6				
9.2	9.2	9.3		11.1	6.9				
4436632M	1001842M	5365202M	Net Sales ($)	95416M	184176M	60987M	183802M	177713M	4663108M
1585779M	1032971M	2221084M	Total Assets ($)	207717M	197686M	53588M	212773M	103623M	1445697M

M = $ thousand   MM = $ million
See Pages 9 through 22 for Explanation of Ratios and Data

Current Data Sorted by Assets

Comparative Historical Data

						Type of Statement		
				1		Unqualified	9	5
	1	2	3			Reviewed	7	6
6	8	5				Compiled	28	18
30	15	10	1		1	Tax Returns	51	34
21	13	6	1			Other	40	34
	14 (4/1-9/30/10)		110 (10/1/10-3/31/11)				4/1/06-3/31/07	4/1/07-3/31/08
0-500M	500M-2MM	2-10MM	10-50MM	50-100MM	100-250MM		ALL	ALL
57	37	23	5	1	1	NUMBER OF STATEMENTS	135	97
%	%	%	%	%	%	ASSETS	%	%
18.5	13.4	9.2				Cash & Equivalents	13.0	13.9
13.2	11.0	17.9				Trade Receivables (net)	14.1	16.2
21.9	16.4	17.1				Inventory	21.3	18.6
2.2	3.1	.6				All Other Current	1.9	2.4
55.8	43.9	44.8				Total Current	50.3	51.1
28.7	38.3	37.4				Fixed Assets (net)	34.5	35.5
6.1	6.5	5.8				Intangibles (net)	7.1	5.9
9.4	11.3	12.0				All Other Non-Current	8.2	7.5
100.0	100.0	100.0				Total	100.0	100.0
						LIABILITIES		
15.7	9.4	4.0				Notes Payable-Short Term	9.2	8.0
3.3	5.9	2.8				Cur. Mat.-L.T.D.	3.6	5.1
24.8	14.8	15.7				Trade Payables	13.4	14.2
.1	.0	.2				Income Taxes Payable	.9	.7
15.7	9.2	8.1				All Other Current	11.3	10.7
59.6	39.3	30.8				Total Current	38.3	38.8
23.5	31.4	29.1				Long-Term Debt	28.6	24.0
.0	.0	.0				Deferred Taxes	.1	.1
26.8	4.7	4.6				All Other Non-Current	16.0	11.3
-9.8	24.6	35.5				Net Worth	16.9	25.7
100.0	100.0	100.0				Total Liabilties & Net Worth	100.0	100.0
						INCOME DATA		
100.0	100.0	100.0				Net Sales	100.0	100.0
						Gross Profit		
97.9	92.8	90.5				Operating Expenses	93.6	95.5
2.1	7.2	9.5				Operating Profit	6.4	4.5
-.1	2.9	1.9				All Other Expenses (net)	2.1	1.1
2.2	4.3	7.6				Profit Before Taxes	4.3	3.4
						RATIOS		
2.3	3.1	2.3					2.5	2.6
1.1	1.3	1.5				Current	1.4	1.4
.6	.4	1.0					.9	.9
1.4	1.8	1.5					1.7	1.6
.7	.6	.9				Quick	.7	.7
.2	.2	.4					.3	.4
0 UND	1 686.0'	2 181.2					0 UND	2 147.2
5 73.6	5 69.1	16 22.3				Sales/Receivables	10 35.0	14 26.5
21 17.2	20 18.6	36 10.2					30 12.2	23 15.6
						Cost of Sales/Inventory		
						Cost of Sales/Payables		
11.0	7.3	8.1					9.4	9.9
55.8	58.4	28.3				Sales/Working Capital	26.0	31.5
-28.6	-10.4	999.8					-73.5	-116.0
23.0	11.1	15.5					7.0	10.5
(29) 3.6	(31) 4.6	(19) 5.8				EBIT/Interest	(110) 2.5	(81) 3.6
.9	2.1	2.3					1.1	.8
						Net Profit + Depr., Dep., Amort./Cur. Mat. L/T/D	4.8	
							(11) 2.9	
							1.0	
.3	.3	.2					.3	.4
1.1	1.6	1.2				Fixed/Worth	1.3	1.2
-.8	-3.2	6.3					-4.0	43.6
.6	1.0	.7					.7	.8
11.3	3.0	2.4				Debt/Worth	4.3	2.2
-2.7	-7.1	19.9					-5.1	74.2
89.2	74.1	61.2				% Profit Before Taxes/Tangible Net Worth	62.8	74.6
(33) 34.0	(25) 25.8	(20) 24.0					(89) 27.5	(76) 32.1
14.6	5.4	10.4					5.1	9.1
23.5	14.9	15.3				% Profit Before Taxes/Total Assets	20.1	21.8
11.9	8.5	9.6					6.7	8.0
.0	1.6	3.1					.4	1.1
57.7	31.6	31.1				Sales/Net Fixed Assets	55.8	43.6
22.3	16.1	7.3					13.1	12.0
8.6	2.0	1.3					5.3	5.3
8.3	3.6	3.2				Sales/Total Assets	5.1	5.8
4.6	2.1	2.3					3.0	3.2
2.5	1.4	.7					1.9	2.0
.9	.6	1.4				% Depr., Dep., Amort./Sales	1.0	.8
(39) 1.7	(27) 1.4	(21) 1.7					(97) 2.3	(76) 2.0
2.6	4.9	5.1					4.2	3.8
3.5	2.6					% Officers', Directors' Owners' Comp/Sales	2.9	2.9
(26) 7.0	(20) 4.3						(68) 6.1	(46) 6.7
11.7	7.3						10.1	13.8
58879M	116033M	208116M	121216M	93760M	746370M	Net Sales ($)	3202564M	1433640M
11206M	39263M	99281M	78488M	69513M	138123M	Total Assets ($)	991436M	630974M

M = $ thousand   MM = $ million
See Pages 9 through 22 for Explanation of Ratios and Data

Comparative Historical Data			Type of Statement	Current Data Sorted by Sales					
3	3	1	Unqualified					1	1
9	7	6	Reviewed					4	2
25	16	19	Compiled	5	3	5	4	2	
63	68	57	Tax Returns	24	20	5	2	5	1
47	52	41	Other	17	11	6	1	6	
4/1/08-3/31/09 ALL	4/1/09-3/31/10 ALL	4/1/10-3/31/11 ALL		14 (4/1-9/30/10)			110 (10/1/10-3/31/11)		
				0-1MM	1-3MM	3-5MM	5-10MM	10-25MM	25MM & OVER
147	146	124	NUMBER OF STATEMENTS	46	34	16	7	17	4
%	%	%	ASSETS	%	%	%	%	%	%
12.0	15.2	14.5	Cash & Equivalents	12.8	12.2	30.8		12.3	
11.0	16.3	12.8	Trade Receivables (net)	8.8	15.1	13.5		20.6	
15.8	16.3	18.5	Inventory	20.2	17.1	18.9		19.7	
1.9	2.0	2.1	All Other Current	1.7	1.9	1.7		4.7	
40.7	49.9	47.9	Total Current	43.5	46.3	65.0		57.3	
43.7	33.8	35.2	Fixed Assets (net)	38.3	37.5	17.8		27.9	
8.8	9.0	6.9	Intangibles (net)	6.5	7.0	5.5		6.2	
6.9	7.4	10.1	All Other Non-Current	11.7	9.2	11.8		8.6	
100.0	100.0	100.0	Total	100.0	100.0	100.0		100.0	
			LIABILITIES						
9.5	7.0	11.4	Notes Payable-Short Term	15.1	13.9	3.6		4.9	
6.4	3.6	4.1	Cur. Mat.-L.T.D.	5.3	2.5	5.3		2.9	
9.6	20.1	19.1	Trade Payables	18.7	19.6	15.5		17.9	
.2	.0	.1	Income Taxes Payable	.1	.0	.0		.4	
7.0	22.3	11.6	All Other Current	14.7	9.7	10.4		13.2	
32.8	53.1	46.2	Total Current	54.0	45.7	34.7		39.2	
37.1	32.1	28.7	Long-Term Debt	32.4	35.3	10.2		18.0	
.1	.0	.0	Deferred Taxes	.0	.0	.0		.0	
10.4	8.4	14.8	All Other Non-Current	30.3	8.8	4.2		2.2	
19.5	6.5	10.3	Net Worth	-16.8	10.1	50.8		40.6	
100.0	100.0	100.0	Total Liabilties & Net Worth	100.0	100.0	100.0		100.0	
			INCOME DATA						
100.0	100.0	100.0	Net Sales	100.0	100.0	100.0		100.0	
			Gross Profit						
91.1	94.7	94.6	Operating Expenses	95.6	93.0	95.6		93.5	
8.9	5.3	5.4	Operating Profit	4.4	7.0	4.4		6.5	
4.2	2.0	1.3	All Other Expenses (net)	1.3	2.6	-.3		.7	
4.7	3.3	4.1	Profit Before Taxes	3.2	4.3	4.7		5.8	
			RATIOS						
2.0	2.3	2.3		1.9	3.0	4.5		2.1	
1.1	1.1	1.2	Current	1.1	1.1	2.5		1.5	
.6	.6	.6		.4	.5	1.3		.9	
1.4	1.6	1.4		.9	1.9	2.9		1.3	
.6	.6	.6	Quick	.6	.5	1.2		.8	
.2	.2	.2		.1	.3	.6		.4	
0 UND	1 628.0	0 989.8		0 UND	0 999.8	1 528.8		3 139.2	
6 57.8	7 52.2	7 52.4	Sales/Receivables	5 68.7	3 105.8	6 61.7		19 18.8	
22 16.5	25 14.6	24 15.2		24 15.1	15 23.8	19 19.6		38 9.6	
			Cost of Sales/Inventory						
			Cost of Sales/Payables						
12.0	10.6	10.5		11.1	10.1	5.0		6.6	
88.6	64.5	52.0	Sales/Working Capital	53.2	65.5	17.6		32.1	
-18.6	-15.3	-21.2		-7.6	-12.2	76.3		-103.0	
6.4	10.5	12.0		11.1	8.4	55.1		40.2	
(118) 2.5	(107) 2.8	(86) 4.6	EBIT/Interest	(24) 2.8	(25) 3.1	(12) 8.8		(16) 7.3	
.9	.9	2.1		.0	1.7	5.5		5.2	
5.5			Net Profit + Depr., Dep.,						
(16) 1.8			Amort./Cur. Mat. L/T/D						
1.0									
.6	.3	.4		.5	.5	.1		.2	
2.8	2.1	1.7	Fixed/Worth	58.0	3.1	.3		.7	
-2.6	-1.3	-2.5		-.9	-1.3	1.1		7.4	
1.1	.9	.9		1.3	.6	.3		.8	
4.1	4.5	4.2	Debt/Worth	69.4	4.6	.8		2.2	
-5.0	-4.9	-6.7		-2.5	-5.5	7.9		8.2	
93.3	85.5	71.9	% Profit Before Taxes/Tangible	80.7	65.1	95.4		61.2	
(99) 35.2	(91) 23.7	(81) 29.0	Net Worth	(24) 34.5	(20) 29.9	(15) 31.6		(15) 39.4	
10.1	8.1	13.5		6.9	15.5	5.4		9.6	
19.3	19.6	17.4	% Profit Before Taxes/Total	17.5	18.4	26.1		22.5	
5.6	5.3	9.3	Assets	6.9	10.5	12.8		12.7	
-.1	-.5	1.5		-2.2	1.1	4.3		5.5	
29.1	91.6	38.5		26.0	39.0	117.4		40.4	
8.0	21.0	16.0	Sales/Net Fixed Assets	15.7	18.0	38.6		16.1	
2.2	4.8	4.8		3.4	1.9	16.6		8.8	
4.4	5.5	5.8		5.7	6.8	8.1		4.3	
2.5	3.1	2.5	Sales/Total Assets	2.5	2.6	4.3		2.4	
1.3	1.3	1.8		1.6	1.3	2.4		1.8	
1.0	.6	1.0		1.3	.6	.5		1.0	
(116) 2.1	(105) 1.9	(94) 1.7	% Depr., Dep., Amort./Sales	(34) 2.1	(25) 1.5	(11) 1.1		(15) 1.4	
6.4	3.9	3.4		3.4	7.8	2.3		1.7	
2.4	2.2	2.8		4.2	3.0	4.8			
(67) 4.5	(67) 4.5	(57) 5.5	% Officers', Directors' Owners' Comp/Sales	(18) 8.2	(18) 5.0	(11) 4.8			
10.8	8.8	8.6		13.6	7.0	7.6			
2918220M	1020588M	1344374M	Net Sales ($)	26575M	54549M	59233M	50140M	241810M	912067M
929883M	524975M	435874M	Total Assets ($)	16561M	36820M	17545M	20432M	100342M	244174M

© RMA 2011

M = $ thousand   MM = $ million
See Pages 9 through 22 for Explanation of Ratios and Data

Current Data Sorted by Assets

0-500M	500M-2MM	2-10MM	10-50MM	50-100MM	100-250MM		Comparative Historical Data 4/1/06-3/31/07 ALL	4/1/07-3/31/08 ALL
		1 4 1	2		1	**Type of Statement**	3	5
						Unqualified	3	5
1	3	4 1 6				Reviewed	5	8
4	4					Compiled	3	7
1	5	8	2	1		Tax Returns	8	11
			40 (10/1/10-3/31/11)			Other	12	12
0-500M	4 (4/1-9/30/10) 500M-2MM	2-10MM	10-50MM	50-100MM	100-250MM			
6	12	20	4	1	1	**NUMBER OF STATEMENTS**	31	43
%	%	%	%	%	%		%	%
						ASSETS		
	13.7	14.9				Cash & Equivalents	20.7	12.3
	29.2	36.5				Trade Receivables (net)	33.8	39.2
	22.0	16.2				Inventory	9.1	13.2
	2.3	3.1				All Other Current	3.9	4.9
	67.3	70.7				Total Current	67.5	69.6
	22.9	15.4				Fixed Assets (net)	15.7	22.8
	2.7	4.3				Intangibles (net)	12.1	2.8
	7.0	9.6				All Other Non-Current	4.7	4.8
	100.0	100.0				Total	100.0	100.0
						LIABILITIES		
	12.8	14.9				Notes Payable-Short Term	10.1	17.9
	2.5	1.8				Cur. Mat.-L.T.D.	6.6	6.8
	11.6	15.5				Trade Payables	15.0	16.8
	.0	.0				Income Taxes Payable	.1	.3
	8.6	11.9				All Other Current	22.6	15.8
	35.6	44.0				Total Current	54.4	57.6
	19.6	13.7				Long-Term Debt	12.3	24.4
	.0	.0				Deferred Taxes	.0	.0
	2.9	10.9				All Other Non-Current	7.4	9.2
	41.9	31.4				Net Worth	25.9	8.8
	100.0	100.0				Total Liabilities & Net Worth	100.0	100.0
						INCOME DATA		
	100.0	100.0				Net Sales	100.0	100.0
						Gross Profit		
	96.4	94.0				Operating Expenses	93.1	95.5
	3.6	6.0				Operating Profit	6.9	4.5
	.4	1.2				All Other Expenses (net)	1.0	1.0
	3.1	4.8				Profit Before Taxes	5.9	3.6
						RATIOS		
	8.8	2.4					2.3	2.0
	1.8	1.9				Current	1.3	1.3
	1.5	1.1					1.1	1.0
	2.4	2.1					2.1	1.8
	1.2	1.2				Quick	1.1 (42)	1.0
	.8	.9					.7	.6
0	UND	29 12.6					16 22.2	24 15.0
30	12.2	41 9.0				Sales/Receivables	44 8.3	43 8.5
50	7.3	58 6.3					52 7.1	60 6.1
						Cost of Sales/Inventory		
						Cost of Sales/Payables		
	6.2	7.8					7.9	9.7
	11.7	11.0				Sales/Working Capital	22.8	17.7
	17.4	33.8					80.8	UND
		15.0					40.0	9.2
	(18)	8.7				EBIT/Interest	(27) 6.1	(35) 2.3
		3.1					1.7	.0
								12.3
						Net Profit + Depr., Dep., Amort./Cur. Mat. L/T/D	(10)	4.7
								1.1
	.1	.2					.2	.2
	.6	.6				Fixed/Worth	.5	.8
	1.1	2.2					-10.9	UND
	.3	1.0					.9	1.0
	1.6	1.3				Debt/Worth	3.7	3.1
	6.0	11.4					-8.9	-15.2
	87.0	75.8					117.7	62.8
(11)	15.3	(16) 34.7				% Profit Before Taxes/Tangible Net Worth	(22) 54.3	(32) 33.8
	10.8	28.9					7.6	12.7
	32.6	18.3					38.1	22.5
	10.1	14.6				% Profit Before Taxes/Total Assets	13.3	6.9
	-6.5	3.3					1.2	-2.2
	58.7	70.5					131.2	69.5
	26.9	24.3				Sales/Net Fixed Assets	45.6	32.3
	10.5	13.8					20.5	9.8
	4.6	4.2					5.9	5.3
	3.8	2.9				Sales/Total Assets	3.5	3.5
	2.7	2.0					1.9	2.6
	.6	.6					.4	.4
(10)	.9	(14) .9				% Depr., Dep., Amort./Sales	(22) .6	(36) .7
	2.1	1.7					1.6	1.7
							3.3	3.0
						% Officers', Directors' Owners' Comp/Sales	(12) 5.0	(17) 7.0
							10.1	10.4
6872M	51199M	303165M	274581M	205981M	20447M	Net Sales ($)	417258M	751406M
1911M	12737M	106848M	121069M	66626M	247306M	Total Assets ($)	210641M	219863M

© RMA 2011

M = $ thousand   MM = $ million
See Pages 9 through 22 for Explanation of Ratios and Data

Comparative Historical Data | Current Data Sorted by Sales

			Type of Statement	0-1MM	1-3MM	3-5MM	5-10MM	10-25MM	25MM & OVER
3	7	4	Unqualified				2	1	3
5	4	4	Reviewed					1	1
8	5	5	Compiled	1	1	2		1	1
9	15	14	Tax Returns	2	3		5	4	
19	20	17	Other		3	1	5	6	2
4/1/08-3/31/09 ALL	4/1/09-3/31/10 ALL	4/1/10-3/31/11 ALL				4 (4/1-9/30/10)	40 (10/1/10-3/31/11)		
44	51	44	**NUMBER OF STATEMENTS**	3	7	3	12	13	6
%	%	%	**ASSETS**	%	%	%	%	%	%
11.7	10.7	12.4	Cash & Equivalents				16.1	12.9	
33.8	32.1	32.4	Trade Receivables (net)				29.4	32.7	
22.1	16.8	17.6	Inventory				18.9	19.0	
3.2	4.2	3.0	All Other Current				2.2	3.9	
70.7	63.8	65.4	Total Current				66.6	68.5	
21.3	21.2	19.4	Fixed Assets (net)				15.8	15.3	
3.8	10.8	6.4	Intangibles (net)				5.3	7.9	
4.1	4.2	8.7	All Other Non-Current				12.2	8.3	
100.0	100.0	100.0	Total				100.0	100.0	
			LIABILITIES						
16.0	13.6	13.8	Notes Payable-Short Term				21.7	11.1	
4.0	6.2	3.0	Cur. Mat.-L.T.D.				2.0	1.0	
18.7	19.9	13.7	Trade Payables				11.2	14.8	
.3	.4	.2	Income Taxes Payable				.0	.0	
17.4	18.4	12.3	All Other Current				7.2	12.8	
56.4	58.4	43.0	Total Current				42.0	39.8	
21.5	31.5	15.9	Long-Term Debt				13.4	14.2	
.1	.5	.4	Deferred Taxes				.0	.9	
9.4	7.8	6.3	All Other Non-Current				5.2	12.7	
12.6	1.8	34.4	Net Worth				39.4	32.4	
100.0	100.0	100.0	Total Liabilities & Net Worth				100.0	100.0	
			INCOME DATA						
100.0	100.0	100.0	Net Sales				100.0	100.0	
			Gross Profit						
95.8	95.5	93.5	Operating Expenses				91.9	94.0	
4.2	4.5	6.5	Operating Profit				8.1	6.0	
1.2	.8	1.2	All Other Expenses (net)				.7	1.7	
3.0	3.6	5.3	Profit Before Taxes				7.3	4.3	
			RATIOS						
3.1	1.6	2.6					6.7	2.3	
1.3	1.2	1.7	Current				1.7	1.9	
.9	.9	1.1					1.0	1.2	
1.7	1.4	2.2					2.3	2.0	
.9	.8	1.1	Quick				1.2	1.1	
.5	.5	.8					.8	.8	
24 15.0	23 15.6	27 13.4					13 28.9	28 13.1	
36 10.2	37 10.0	41 9.0	Sales/Receivables				36 10.0	35 10.4	
56 6.6	58 6.3	58 6.3					61 5.9	57 6.4	
			Cost of Sales/Inventory						
			Cost of Sales/Payables						
8.0	10.9	7.6					8.3	5.8	
23.3	38.3	12.0	Sales/Working Capital				17.0	9.8	
-55.9	-53.4	36.1					184.6	25.4	
13.2	12.7	14.1					104.0	13.6	
(35) 2.1	(46) 3.2	(37) 5.9	EBIT/Interest				(11) 8.4	(11) 8.2	
-.7	.9	2.4					5.1	2.8	
	3.2		Net Profit + Depr., Dep.,						
	(10) 1.3		Amort./Cur. Mat. L/T/D						
	.3								
.3	.4	.2					.3	.1	
1.1	1.7	.7	Fixed/Worth				.8	.4	
-15.3	-.6	2.4					1.0	-.5	
1.4	1.4	.8					.6	.9	
3.5	4.5	1.7	Debt/Worth				3.0	1.3	
-91.2	-2.9	10.3					11.4	-7.1	
91.3	79.3	75.8	% Profit Before Taxes/Tangible				183.1		
(32) 19.9	(30) 38.6	(36) 34.7	Net Worth				(11) 84.3		
.6	7.5	14.8					29.2		
17.9	18.3	18.3	% Profit Before Taxes/Total				42.8	18.7	
4.2	5.6	11.9	Assets				15.1	12.3	
-1.8	-.5	2.5					4.5	1.8	
45.9	60.8	59.4					81.3	74.7	
25.9	25.6	24.1	Sales/Net Fixed Assets				24.4	24.4	
10.9	13.1	12.5					13.0	12.7	
4.2	4.5	4.1					4.5	4.5	
3.1	3.2	3.1	Sales/Total Assets				2.9	2.6	
2.4	2.1	2.2					1.5	2.1	
.4	.9	.6							
(31) .8	(39) 1.5	(32) 1.0	% Depr., Dep., Amort./Sales						
2.2	2.5	1.8							
3.0	2.3	2.9	% Officers', Directors'						
(17) 4.9	(20) 4.9	(15) 4.3	Owners' Comp/Sales						
9.6	9.3	11.0							
790059M	1132518M	862245M	Net Sales ($)	1569M	12031M	12578M	85788M	210077M	540202M
266755M	432341M	556497M	Total Assets ($)	914M	3484M	3350M	39950M	314658M	194141M

M = $ thousand   MM = $ million
See Pages 9 through 22 for Explanation of Ratios and Data

Current Data Sorted by Assets   Comparative Historical Data

Type of Statement	0-500M	500M-2MM	2-10MM	10-50MM	50-100MM	100-250MM		4/1/06-3/31/07 ALL	4/1/07-3/31/08 ALL
Unqualified			3	7		2		16	13
Reviewed		2	14	4				29	24
Compiled	3	7	4	1				26	20
Tax Returns	8	8	3	7				39	26
Other	2	10	29	7		2		49	47
		17 (4/1-9/30/10)		99 (10/1/10-3/31/11)					
NUMBER OF STATEMENTS	13	27	53	19		4		159	130
ASSETS	%	%	%	%	%	%		%	%
Cash & Equivalents	18.2	13.9	13.0	4.0				9.9	12.8
Trade Receivables (net)	35.0	33.7	34.2	32.4				30.8	32.5
Inventory	18.5	18.2	17.3	15.1	D			21.0	19.6
All Other Current	1.4	7.3	3.9	2.6	A			3.6	3.2
Total Current	73.1	73.2	68.5	54.0	T			65.3	68.1
Fixed Assets (net)	14.7	18.9	21.2	25.9	A			25.3	21.0
Intangibles (net)	6.2	1.0	3.8	15.2	N			3.8	5.3
All Other Non-Current	6.0	7.0	6.6	4.9	O			5.7	5.6
Total	100.0	100.0	100.0	100.0	T			100.0	100.0
LIABILITIES									
Notes Payable-Short Term	12.2	5.4	10.2	8.9	A			13.3	11.3
Cur. Mat.-L.T.D.	2.7	6.4	2.6	4.0	V			4.3	5.3
Trade Payables	17.3	11.0	12.2	10.4	A			14.0	14.5
Income Taxes Payable	.0	.1	.1	.5	I			.5	.3
All Other Current	4.3	8.6	14.1	18.7	L			13.4	11.0
Total Current	36.5	31.4	39.2	42.4	A			45.5	42.4
Long-Term Debt	8.1	23.5	11.6	14.4	B			24.4	16.6
Deferred Taxes	.1	.0	.9	.4	L			.3	.2
All Other Non-Current	18.9	7.1	8.0	3.4	E			5.8	3.8
Net Worth	36.5	38.0	40.3	39.4				24.0	37.0
Total Liabilities & Net Worth	100.0	100.0	100.0	100.0				100.0	100.0
INCOME DATA									
Net Sales	100.0	100.0	100.0	100.0				100.0	100.0
Gross Profit									
Operating Expenses	96.0	89.3	92.3	89.7				93.3	91.5
Operating Profit	4.0	10.7	7.7	10.3				6.7	8.5
All Other Expenses (net)	.1	.2	1.0	1.1				1.4	1.3
Profit Before Taxes	3.9	10.5	6.7	9.2				5.2	7.2
RATIOS									
Current	4.2	5.0	3.1	1.9				3.0	3.0
	3.6	2.8	1.8	1.3				1.7	1.8
	1.8	1.3	1.3	1.1				1.2	1.1
Quick	3.2	3.4	2.2	1.4				2.0	2.1
	1.9	1.5	1.2	.9				1.0 (129)	1.1
	1.5	.6	.8	.6				.6	.7
Sales/Receivables	0 UND	18 20.5	34 10.9	44 8.3				32 11.4	27 13.3
	29 12.6	36 10.1	48 7.5	59 6.2				46 7.9	43 8.5
	50 7.3	60 6.1	68 5.3	85 4.3				60 6.1	58 6.3
Cost of Sales/Inventory									
Cost of Sales/Payables									
Sales/Working Capital	6.7	3.1	5.4	6.1				5.4	5.1
	9.9	8.2	7.6	18.5				11.4	10.5
	20.8	14.8	29.3	75.1				33.8	86.1
EBIT/Interest		13.1	18.8	102.8				9.3	14.5
	(25) 6.8	(42) 4.9	(18) 8.7					(146) 3.3	(110) 5.6
		1.9	1.3	3.1				1.6	1.6
Net Profit + Depr., Dep., Amort./Cur. Mat. L/T/D			15.5					7.0	4.9
		(11) 6.5						(37) 2.6	(24) 2.8
		1.5						1.5	1.0
Fixed/Worth	.0	.1	.1	.3				.3	.2
	.3	.3	.4	1.0				.8	.5
	5.6	1.4	2.2	2.8				4.4	1.7
Debt/Worth	.2	.5	.6	1.2				.9	.7
	.7	1.4	1.8	2.2				2.3	1.7
	155.1	6.5	3.8	5.5				15.9	8.6
% Profit Before Taxes/Tangible Net Worth	96.0	95.3	53.9	47.9				59.6	75.5
	(11) 25.7	(23) 27.3	(47) 25.3	(16) 33.8				(128) 34.1	(112) 41.0
	2.3	12.4	4.6	11.1				9.7	7.4
% Profit Before Taxes/Total Assets	38.9	25.3	22.8	14.9				19.3	27.4
	10.1	12.2	8.4	10.1				9.3	13.1
	.3	3.6	.8	4.7				2.2	1.6
Sales/Net Fixed Assets	UND	48.6	49.4	24.6				35.1	48.2
	41.1	24.4	23.1	9.3				13.9	16.0
	11.2	7.4	8.6	6.2				7.1	8.7
Sales/Total Assets	5.8	4.4	3.4	2.2				3.7	3.7
	4.5	2.7	2.2	1.8				2.5	2.5
	2.5	1.8	1.7	1.0				1.8	1.8
% Depr., Dep., Amort./Sales		1.0	.6	1.4				1.0	.8
	(15) 1.8	(42) 1.3	(18) 2.9					(131) 1.9	(100) 1.6
		2.5	2.3	4.5				3.4	2.9
% Officers', Directors' Owners' Comp/Sales		2.4	2.3					3.2	3.5
	(19) 4.8	(15) 4.2						(73) 6.8	(57) 5.5
		7.5	5.7					10.4	9.0
Net Sales ($)	17498M	94584M	550157M	739319M		596643M		2698177M	1952568M
Total Assets ($)	3852M	29608M	221826M	397787M		577473M		1563843M	997001M

Comparative Historical Data | **Current Data Sorted by Sales**

Type of Statement — right side date headers: **17 (4/1-9/30/10)** spans 0-1MM, 1-3MM, 3-5MM; **99 (10/1/10-3/31/11)** spans 5-10MM, 10-25MM, 25MM & OVER.

Item	4/1/08-3/31/09 ALL	4/1/09-3/31/10 ALL	4/1/10-3/31/11 ALL	0-1MM	1-3MM	3-5MM	5-10MM	10-25MM	25MM & OVER
Type of Statement									
Unqualified	9	12	12				2	2	8
Reviewed	18	24	20			2	5	11	2
Compiled	10	26	14			3	1	3	
Tax Returns	20	22	20	2	5	4	4		1
Other	27	45	50	4	7	5	13	13	5
NUMBER OF STATEMENTS	84	129	116	10	17	19	25	29	16
ASSETS	%	%	%	%	%	%	%	%	%
Cash & Equivalents	11.0	13.0	12.0	19.2	17.2	9.6	15.3	8.3	6.3
Trade Receivables (net)	39.4	31.2	33.3	21.2	34.3	32.2	35.9	34.3	35.4
Inventory	17.1	17.4	17.1	9.9	20.3	19.8	13.6	19.9	15.6
All Other Current	2.7	4.7	4.2	.0	7.9	3.9	5.2	2.6	4.3
Total Current	70.2	66.2	66.6	50.3	79.7	65.4	70.1	65.1	61.7
Fixed Assets (net)	21.1	23.7	20.4	34.9	10.9	27.0	22.3	17.6	15.6
Intangibles (net)	3.4	4.0	6.7	7.6	1.0	2.1	3.6	8.9	18.8
All Other Non-Current	5.4	6.1	6.3	7.1	8.4	5.5	4.1	8.4	4.0
Total	100.0	100.0	100.0	100.0	100.0	100.0	100.0	100.0	100.0
LIABILITIES									
Notes Payable-Short Term	10.7	12.3	8.8	5.6	8.1	13.1	5.3	10.7	8.4
Cur. Mat.-L.T.D.	4.9	3.7	3.7	.9	8.0	3.5	3.2	3.4	2.4
Trade Payables	15.2	11.9	12.0	5.6	12.4	13.6	10.5	13.3	13.4
Income Taxes Payable	.2	.5	.1	.1	.0	.0	.3	.1	.2
All Other Current	11.7	13.9	12.2	2.5	4.3	14.7	15.5	12.9	16.9
Total Current	42.7	42.3	36.7	14.7	32.8	44.9	34.7	40.5	41.4
Long-Term Debt	16.1	17.3	14.7	23.1	19.2	18.8	14.3	8.2	12.2
Deferred Taxes	.2	.5	.7	.1	.0	1.3	.1	.7	-1.8
All Other Non-Current	3.0	3.4	9.3	25.4	8.0	2.2	4.7	11.4	11.9
Net Worth	38.0	36.5	38.6	36.6	40.0	32.7	46.0	39.2	32.7
Total Liabilities & Net Worth	100.0	100.0	100.0	100.0	100.0	100.0	100.0	100.0	100.0
INCOME DATA									
Net Sales	100.0	100.0	100.0	100.0	100.0	100.0	100.0	100.0	100.0
Gross Profit									
Operating Expenses	91.0	94.0	91.7	82.3	90.4	97.9	87.4	93.0	95.9
Operating Profit	9.0	6.0	8.3	17.7	9.6	2.1	12.6	7.0	4.1
All Other Expenses (net)	1.2	1.5	1.0	2.0	.5	1.1	-.2	.4	3.3
Profit Before Taxes	7.8	4.5	7.3	15.7	9.1	1.0	12.8	6.5	.7
RATIOS									
Current	2.9	3.1	3.5	7.5	4.9	2.9	3.7	2.5	2.4
	1.7	1.5	1.9	3.9	2.8	1.4	2.4	1.6	1.6
	1.1	1.1	1.2	1.7	1.8	1.0	1.5	1.2	1.2
Quick	2.2	2.1	2.2	7.5	3.1	1.6	3.2	1.5	1.6
	1.2	1.0	1.4	2.9	1.7	.9	1.8	1.2	1.1
	.8	.6	.7	1.0	.9	.6	.8	.7	.7
Sales/Receivables	33 11.0	29 12.8	29 12.6	0 UND	3 115.4	28 12.9	38 9.6	32 11.3	48 7.6
	46 8.0	42 8.8	48 7.6	17 21.5	35 10.5	51 7.1	47 7.8	48 7.5	58 6.2
	59 6.2	58 6.3	68 5.4	83 4.4	57 6.4	73 5.0	62 5.9	64 5.7	82 4.5
Cost of Sales/Inventory									
Cost of Sales/Payables									
Sales/Working Capital	6.7	5.9	5.3	2.6	3.0	4.7	5.4	6.2	5.4
	10.0	11.7	8.7	8.1	7.0	12.5	6.2	12.0	9.1
	34.8	67.0	26.1	32.9	14.3	869.8	21.4	32.8	27.8
EBIT/Interest	(75) 25.0	(112) 12.2	(94) 20.4		29.4	5.6	44.3	43.6	70.6
	6.9	4.1	5.3		(13) 6.2	(18) 1.8	(20) 12.7	(24) 6.5	(15) 3.3
	3.0	.9	1.7		3.1	1.1	3.9	4.2	.9
Net Profit + Depr., Dep., Amort./Cur. Mat. L/T/D	(15) 13.1	(27) 3.6	(24) 11.8						
	4.1	2.6	3.9						
	1.6	1.2	1.2						
Fixed/Worth	.2	.2	.2	.3	.0	.2	.1	.2	.3
	.5	.6	.4	.7	.2	.5	.3	.6	.8
	1.3	1.6	2.3	17.5	.7	1.6	2.9	2.1	-2.3
Debt/Worth	.6	.7	.5	.1	.4	1.4	.5	.6	1.8
	1.3	2.1	1.8	.8	1.1	2.2	.8	1.7	2.8
	3.4	4.7	7.6	39.1	8.6	4.2	5.7	7.6	-15.4
% Profit Before Taxes/Tangible Net Worth	(76) 67.5	(114) 45.9	(98) 62.2		(15) 97.4	(18) 25.0	(22) 103.4	(23) 56.7	(11) 48.3
	34.9	22.0	26.7		53.9	9.8	32.9	30.3	27.6
	14.3	2.9	6.9		14.4	1.6	13.5	9.2	1.3
% Profit Before Taxes/Total Assets	25.8	17.3	22.2	28.1	41.9	9.8	29.5	20.3	14.4
	11.6	6.9	9.9	9.0	22.0	3.0	18.5	10.6	5.5
	5.4	.2	1.3	-3.2	4.9	.6	7.9	2.4	-.4
Sales/Net Fixed Assets	48.3	44.0	48.4	13.2	139.7	38.3	82.4	52.8	31.7
	18.6	14.9	17.3	8.4	40.8	10.4	25.4	20.8	14.3
	8.5	6.1	7.9	3.1	14.6	5.3	9.3	9.6	6.8
Sales/Total Assets	4.0	3.7	3.5	2.4	5.0	3.6	3.5	4.0	2.6
	2.8	2.4	2.2	1.2	3.0	2.0	2.8	2.4	2.0
	2.0	1.7	1.6	1.0	2.0	1.5	1.8	1.7	1.2
% Depr., Dep., Amort./Sales	(61) .8	(106) .8	(85) .9		(10) .4	(12) .9	(16) 1.0	(26) .7	(15) 1.0
	1.6	1.8	1.8		1.3	1.8	2.1	1.3	2.3
	3.3	3.8	3.0		1.8	4.7	3.4	2.2	3.6
% Officers', Directors', Owners' Comp/Sales	(33) 2.7	(49) 3.1	(45) 2.4		(13) 2.6		(12) 2.6		
	6.3	6.3	5.0		5.4		5.2		
	10.3	9.7	7.4		9.5		7.2		
Net Sales ($)	1349720M	2267479M	1998201M	5966M	31597M	75601M	178979M	455591M	1250467M
Total Assets ($)	722090M	1175752M	1230546M	6217M	13395M	38333M	120215M	218311M	834075M

M = $ thousand   MM = $ million
See Pages 9 through 22 for Explanation of Ratios and Data

Current Data Sorted by Assets   **Comparative Historical Data**

0-500M	500M-2MM	2-10MM	10-50MM	50-100MM	100-250MM	Type of Statement	4/1/06-3/31/07 ALL	4/1/07-3/31/08 ALL
		9	8	6	6	Unqualified	25	28
	12	30	12			Reviewed	38	49
12	20	20				Compiled	51	56
45	60	17	3	1	2	Tax Returns	89	97
25	41	48	10	2	1	Other	88	99
	64 (4/1-9/30/10)		326 (10/1/10-3/31/11)					
82	133	124	33	9	9	**NUMBER OF STATEMENTS**	291	329
%	%	%	%	%	%	**ASSETS**	%	%
14.2	9.3	8.9	9.6			Cash & Equivalents	10.5	10.1
26.0	32.1	30.3	28.0			Trade Receivables (net)	32.5	31.4
16.8	18.0	18.1	14.0			Inventory	18.5	18.6
3.5	2.4	4.3	7.5			All Other Current	3.7	3.2
60.6	61.9	61.6	59.1			Total Current	65.2	63.2
25.7	28.1	28.1	25.4			Fixed Assets (net)	25.6	27.1
6.9	2.9	4.7	10.1			Intangibles (net)	3.2	3.8
6.9	7.1	5.6	5.5			All Other Non-Current	6.0	5.9
100.0	100.0	100.0	100.0			Total	100.0	100.0
						LIABILITIES		
20.4	9.8	11.7	6.5			Notes Payable-Short Term	13.3	11.4
6.2	5.0	3.2	3.8			Cur. Mat.-L.T.D.	4.7	5.4
18.4	15.1	12.6	12.1			Trade Payables	15.9	17.0
.0	.1	.7	.1			Income Taxes Payable	.2	.3
11.5	11.3	8.6	17.4			All Other Current	11.4	10.9
56.6	41.3	36.8	39.8			Total Current	45.6	44.9
35.3	19.1	15.9	15.2			Long-Term Debt	24.6	22.6
.0	.6	.6	1.2			Deferred Taxes	.3	.3
13.3	6.7	3.8	6.2			All Other Non-Current	5.4	5.7
-5.2	32.4	43.0	37.6			Net Worth	24.1	26.6
100.0	100.0	100.0	100.0			Total Liabilities & Net Worth	100.0	100.0
						INCOME DATA		
100.0	100.0	100.0	100.0			Net Sales	100.0	100.0
						Gross Profit		
95.3	93.0	92.5	93.0			Operating Expenses	93.8	93.0
4.7	7.0	7.5	7.0			Operating Profit	6.2	7.0
.9	2.2	1.5	2.1			All Other Expenses (net)	1.0	1.2
3.8	4.8	6.0	4.9			Profit Before Taxes	5.2	5.8
						RATIOS		
2.5	3.0	2.6	2.1			Current	2.5	2.6
1.3	1.6	1.7	1.5				1.5	1.5
.8	1.1	1.1	1.1				1.1	1.0
1.6	2.2	1.8	1.4			Quick	1.6	1.7
(81) .8	1.1	1.1	1.1				1.0	1.0
.3	.4	.6	.6				.6	.6
0 UND	23 15.6	36 10.1	45 8.1			Sales/Receivables	25 14.8	26 14.1
23 15.9	41 8.9	47 7.7	59 6.2				41 8.9	41 8.9
45 8.2	58 6.3	64 5.7	73 5.0				58 6.3	59 6.2
						Cost of Sales/Inventory		
						Cost of Sales/Payables		
9.2	6.5	4.6	4.1			Sales/Working Capital	6.7	6.6
31.4	14.8	10.2	10.3				12.7	13.7
-36.2	56.3	42.2	20.7				90.2	422.4
11.1	11.9	15.2	13.3			EBIT/Interest	14.5	13.3
(70) 3.2	(116) 4.9	(113) 6.0	(29) 2.5				(252) 4.5	(302) 4.0
-.4	1.0	1.6	1.2				1.5	1.5
	3.2	7.9	6.6			Net Profit + Depr., Dep., Amort./Cur. Mat. L/T/D	4.9	4.4
	(11) 1.5	(33) 2.1	(12) 1.6				(44) 2.2	(48) 2.1
	.3	1.3	1.0				1.4	1.0
.3	.2	.3	.3			Fixed/Worth	.3	.3
1.3	.6	.6	.8				.9	.9
-3.3	5.3	1.3	2.3				3.1	3.5
1.2	.7	.7	1.1			Debt/Worth	1.0	.9
6.7	2.1	1.6	2.7				2.3	2.5
-5.5	33.1	3.6	6.8				10.3	11.9
82.2	64.1	42.8	57.5			% Profit Before Taxes/Tangible Net Worth	73.0	73.8
(52) 31.8	(108) 22.0	(116) 19.1	(28) 18.1				(239) 33.6	(271) 34.2
1.7	4.1	5.1	4.6				10.8	9.6
30.4	17.4	16.3	11.8			% Profit Before Taxes/Total Assets	22.1	24.5
9.5	7.1	7.7	3.8				9.3	9.1
-6.0	.1	1.2	.8				2.2	1.8
80.3	45.7	27.0	20.3			Sales/Net Fixed Assets	37.1	31.1
21.3	16.0	11.1	7.4				14.7	14.4
8.5	5.3	3.9	4.0				7.3	6.7
5.7	3.7	3.0	2.1			Sales/Total Assets	4.1	3.9
3.5	2.7	1.9	1.4				2.8	2.8
2.4	1.4	1.4	1.0				2.0	1.9
.9	.8	.9	1.0			% Depr., Dep., Amort./Sales	.8	.9
(49) 2.5	(102) 1.8	(95) 1.8	(32) 3.3				(243) 1.5	(264) 1.8
4.8	4.7	3.3	5.1				2.9	3.7
4.6	2.8	2.0				% Officers', Directors' Owners' Comp/Sales	3.2	2.6
(50) 7.3	(67) 5.3	(48) 3.6					(142) 5.5	(172) 4.8
12.8	8.6	5.7					10.3	7.6
94354M	397627M	1275076M	1092563M	2382528M	2691523M	Net Sales ($)	4114285M	11022140M
22512M	150091M	585407M	663275M	632778M	1349799M	Total Assets ($)	1894537M	3375811M

M = $ thousand   MM = $ million
See Pages 9 through 22 for Explanation of Ratios and Data

Comparative Historical Data | Current Data Sorted by Sales

Type of Statement									
Unqualified	21	17	29	1	3	4	20	10	19
Reviewed	42	59	54	10	19	3	16	21	5
Compiled	57	62	55	36	46	14	24	5	2
Tax Returns	121	130	125	23	35	21	17	2	3
Other	115	110	127					20	11
	4/1/08-3/31/09 ALL	4/1/09-3/31/10 ALL	4/1/10-3/31/11 ALL	0-1MM	1-3MM	3-5MM	5-10MM	10-25MM	25MM & OVER
				64 (4/1-9/30/10)			326 (10/1/10-3/31/11)		
NUMBER OF STATEMENTS	356	378	390	70	103	42	77	58	40
ASSETS	%	%	%	%	%	%	%	%	%
Cash & Equivalents	12.4	9.9	10.3	11.3	10.6	11.5	9.7	8.0	11.2
Trade Receivables (net)	27.9	26.8	29.6	18.9	26.4	36.5	35.3	33.7	32.8
Inventory	17.3	18.9	17.2	13.7	18.4	15.7	22.4	18.0	10.9
All Other Current	2.9	3.1	3.9	4.1	2.3	4.9	2.4	5.6	7.3
Total Current	60.5	58.7	61.1	48.1	57.7	68.6	69.7	65.2	62.1
Fixed Assets (net)	29.2	30.5	27.1	38.9	29.5	22.5	21.4	24.0	20.8
Intangibles (net)	3.7	4.1	5.6	6.2	5.5	3.1	2.3	5.8	13.3
All Other Non-Current	6.6	6.7	6.2	6.8	7.3	5.8	6.5	5.0	3.7
Total	100.0	100.0	100.0	100.0	100.0	100.0	100.0	100.0	100.0
LIABILITIES									
Notes Payable-Short Term	11.1	10.9	12.1	17.7	11.0	12.1	11.7	12.2	5.9
Cur. Mat.-L.T.D.	5.0	4.6	4.5	5.9	4.4	6.8	3.9	3.0	3.3
Trade Payables	14.3	14.0	14.6	13.3	15.8	14.6	15.5	12.8	15.0
Income Taxes Payable	.2	.2	.3	.0	.1	.1	.9	.5	.2
All Other Current	9.8	10.8	11.0	11.1	9.3	13.6	9.8	12.2	13.6
Total Current	40.3	40.5	42.6	48.0	40.5	47.2	41.7	40.6	37.8
Long-Term Debt	23.9	23.8	21.3	41.8	24.7	13.8	10.5	13.4	16.6
Deferred Taxes	1.0	.4	.5	.4	.2	.0	.9	1.0	1.0
All Other Non-Current	6.4	5.3	7.3	9.3	9.4	8.3	5.0	3.0	8.2
Net Worth	28.4	30.1	28.3	.5	25.2	30.7	41.9	41.9	36.4
Total Liabilities & Net Worth	100.0	100.0	100.0	100.0	100.0	100.0	100.0	100.0	100.0
INCOME DATA									
Net Sales	100.0	100.0	100.0	100.0	100.0	100.0	100.0	100.0	100.0
Gross Profit									
Operating Expenses	93.4	95.2	93.5	88.3	95.0	95.0	93.9	94.7	94.7
Operating Profit	6.6	4.8	6.5	11.7	5.0	5.0	6.1	5.3	5.3
All Other Expenses (net)	1.6	1.5	1.7	4.6	1.1	.8	.7	1.2	1.4
Profit Before Taxes	5.1	3.4	4.8	7.1	3.9	4.1	5.4	4.1	3.9
RATIOS									
Current	3.0	2.8	2.6	2.7	2.6	2.5	3.3	2.4	2.2
	1.7	1.6	1.5	1.2	1.5	1.5	1.7	1.7	1.5
	1.1	1.0	1.1	.5	.9	.9	1.2	1.2	1.1
Quick	1.9	1.9	1.8	1.8	1.9	2.2	2.4	1.6	1.7
	(355) 1.1	(377) 1.0	(389) 1.1	(69) .6	1.0	1.1	1.1	1.1	1.1
	.6	.5	.5	.2	.4	.6	.6	.7	.9
Sales/Receivables	17 21.9	22 16.8	25 14.6	0 UND	16 22.3	34 10.9	35 10.5	39 9.3	39 9.4
	37 9.8	39 9.3	44 8.4	22 16.5	38 9.6	42 8.7	48 7.7	56 6.6	56 6.6
	56 6.6	56 6.5	60 6.1	44 8.4	56 6.5	61 6.0	61 6.0	70 5.2	66 5.5
Cost of Sales/Inventory									
Cost of Sales/Payables									
Sales/Working Capital	6.2	5.8	5.7	7.4	7.3	5.4	4.2	5.1	8.4
	12.8	13.6	13.4	44.8	16.4	10.7	9.9	10.1	13.4
	152.4	-874.3	104.9	-10.7	-37.7	-129.8	31.4	26.3	22.1
EBIT/Interest	10.8	9.9	13.4	8.8	12.0	10.4	18.4	13.6	19.3
	(318) 4.2	(330) 2.5	(346) 4.7	(52) 3.1	(95) 3.1	(36) 6.5	(72) 5.8	(52) 5.8	(39) 5.5
	1.2	.0	1.1	-1.0	.9	.5	1.8	1.9	1.5
Net Profit + Depr., Dep., Amort./Cur. Mat. L/T/D	6.7	8.1	5.2				3.0	12.6	11.6
	(56) 2.3	(59) 2.2	(65) 2.1				(18) 1.7	(18) 2.6	(16) 3.0
	.6	1.1	1.2				1.1	1.6	1.3
Fixed/Worth	.3	.3	.3	.3	.3	.2	.2	.3	.3
	.8	.8	.7	1.5	1.0	.8	.4	.6	.6
	3.3	4.2	3.5	-3.2	UND	3.3	.9	1.5	NM
Debt/Worth	.9	.7	.8	.8	.9	.8	.7	1.0	1.1
	2.2	2.1	2.2	4.9	2.6	2.7	1.5	1.9	3.3
	10.1	16.1	11.6	-6.0	-49.4	15.9	4.1	3.2	NM
% Profit Before Taxes/Tangible Net Worth	68.4	40.4	58.8	58.5	66.7	65.8	64.1	43.0	76.8
	(291) 25.2	(309) 14.0	(315) 22.6	(47) 18.4	(75) 23.5	(35) 24.0	(74) 22.6	(54) 21.3	(30) 26.1
	9.2	-1.1	4.5	-.5	4.4	4.0	6.4	4.1	14.2
% Profit Before Taxes/Total Assets	21.2	16.4	18.9	21.0	18.3	20.2	20.9	15.6	20.6
	7.5	3.3	7.3	4.9	5.6	7.8	8.7	6.9	8.0
	.5	-2.7	.4	-3.8	-.2	-.2	2.0	1.1	1.6
Sales/Net Fixed Assets	31.5	32.8	38.2	42.7	45.1	30.1	47.6	28.2	28.7
	14.9	12.6	13.8	11.9	13.9	15.8	17.1	10.3	13.3
	5.3	4.7	5.3	2.1	5.0	8.3	6.9	5.0	5.6
Sales/Total Assets	3.9	3.6	3.6	3.6	3.8	3.6	3.5	3.0	3.4
	2.6	2.4	2.4	2.0	2.6	2.9	2.2	2.0	2.2
	1.7	1.6	1.5	1.0	1.5	1.6	1.6	1.5	1.3
% Depr., Dep., Amort./Sales	1.0	.9	.9	1.1	1.2	.6	.9	.9	.8
	(273) 2.0	(302) 2.0	(292) 1.9	(46) 3.6	(70) 2.5	(32) 1.5	(61) 1.7	(47) 1.8	(36) 1.5
	3.7	4.2	4.3	9.7	5.2	2.9	3.1	4.1	4.1
% Officers', Directors' Owners' Comp/Sales	2.8	2.9	2.5	5.4	3.5	2.4	1.9	2.0	
	(182) 4.6	(182) 5.5	(173) 5.3	(37) 8.7	(57) 5.6	(18) 4.3	(34) 3.4	(20) 3.7	
	7.7	9.0	8.9	14.1	9.1	7.6	5.5	8.1	
Net Sales ($)	5425792M	5600415M	7933671M	41263M	202207M	167223M	536277M	887992M	6098709M
Total Assets ($)	2913165M	2763258M	3403862M	40189M	99289M	78832M	257335M	507205M	2421012M

© RMA 2011

M = $ thousand   MM = $ million
See Pages 9 through 22 for Explanation of Ratios and Data

Current Data Sorted by Assets   Comparative Historical Data

						Type of Statement		
			1			Unqualified	1	1
	3	7	1			Reviewed	4	5
		4				Compiled	6	4
10	4	3	2			Tax Returns	9	10
5	4	11	3			Other	12	8
	13 (4/1-9/30/10)		45 (10/1/10-3/31/11)				4/1/06-3/31/07	4/1/07-3/31/08
0-500M	500M-2MM	2-10MM	10-50MM	50-100MM	100-250MM		ALL	ALL
15	11	25	7			NUMBER OF STATEMENTS	32	28
%	%	%	%	%	%	ASSETS	%	%
22.4	17.3	12.0				Cash & Equivalents	12.2	15.2
17.0	43.3	26.0				Trade Receivables (net)	28.2	31.1
17.8	15.0	15.8				Inventory	13.1	20.9
.6	.2	4.4				All Other Current	6.1	1.8
57.8	75.9	58.1				Total Current	59.6	69.0
31.5	15.5	27.2	D	D		Fixed Assets (net)	27.1	22.8
.1	1.1	7.5	A	A		Intangibles (net)	3.9	5.0
10.6	7.5	7.2	T	T		All Other Non-Current	9.4	3.2
100.0	100.0	100.0	A	A		Total	100.0	100.0
						LIABILITIES		
49.8	3.9	3.6	N	N		Notes Payable-Short Term	18.3	8.5
10.7	1.9	2.1	O	O		Cur. Mat.-L.T.D.	3.4	5.6
25.9	11.9	13.5	T	T		Trade Payables	10.8	11.6
.0	.0	.4				Income Taxes Payable	.9	1.2
18.7	27.4	19.6	A	A		All Other Current	14.2	10.5
105.2	45.0	39.3	V	V		Total Current	47.5	37.4
27.6	13.9	18.2	A	A		Long-Term Debt	21.4	24.1
.0	.0	1.2	I	I		Deferred Taxes	.6	.5
3.3	13.3	1.4	L	L		All Other Non-Current	4.3	5.4
-36.1	27.8	39.9	A	A		Net Worth	26.3	32.6
100.0	100.0	100.0	B	B		Total Liabilities & Net Worth	100.0	100.0
			L	L		INCOME DATA		
100.0	100.0	100.0	E	E		Net Sales	100.0	100.0
						Gross Profit		
91.5	98.5	91.6				Operating Expenses	93.9	94.7
8.5	1.5	8.4				Operating Profit	6.1	5.3
.1	.7	2.6				All Other Expenses (net)	1.4	2.0
8.4	.8	5.8				Profit Before Taxes	4.7	3.4
						RATIOS		
2.3	4.8	2.5					3.0	3.7
1.2	2.6	1.6				Current	1.3	1.7
.3	1.5	1.0					.9	1.1
1.4	3.9	1.5					2.1	2.4
.7	1.6	1.0				Quick	1.0	1.0
.1	.6	.7					.5	.5
0 UND	15 24.5	12 31.2					11 34.3	23 15.9
2 189.9	44 8.4	33 11.1				Sales/Receivables	26 14.1	36 10.1
29 12.5	73 5.0	52 7.0					60 6.1	61 5.9
						Cost of Sales/Inventory		
						Cost of Sales/Payables		
15.1	5.5	7.5					9.6	6.4
114.6	6.0	20.8				Sales/Working Capital	23.2	10.2
-6.9	14.6	248.8					-33.4	73.1
	7.5	70.7	25.2				9.4	18.1
(11) 6.3	(10) 21.1	(21) 6.6				EBIT/Interest	(28) 5.2	(24) 4.2
3.2	.1	2.4					1.7	1.8
						Net Profit + Depr., Dep., Amort./Cur. Mat. L/T/D		
.2	.2	.1					.3	.2
.8	.6	1.0				Fixed/Worth	1.1	.5
-.4	3.5	1.9					6.8	3.7
.7	.7	.7					1.1	.9
-5.8	2.1	2.6				Debt/Worth	2.9	2.3
-2.1	48.0	7.4					124.2	38.9
		71.2					66.7	81.2
	(21)	38.0				% Profit Before Taxes/Tangible Net Worth	(25) 46.0	(23) 44.9
		5.4					21.9	23.0
36.0	21.9	23.3					28.8	25.3
10.9	13.4	13.1				% Profit Before Taxes/Total Assets	15.0	12.1
5.8	4.1	2.3					2.5	1.7
224.0	120.7	28.9					34.9	63.3
20.6	30.6	16.8				Sales/Net Fixed Assets	15.8	20.7
7.4	13.0	7.3					8.4	11.3
9.0	4.4	4.3					4.5	3.5
5.4	3.4	2.9				Sales/Total Assets	3.4	2.9
2.9	2.4	1.9					2.0	2.0
		1.2					.8	1.2
	(19)	1.7				% Depr., Dep., Amort./Sales	(28) 2.0	(21) 1.8
		2.7					3.4	3.2
		3.0					3.4	2.0
	(10)	5.9				% Officers', Directors' Owners' Comp/Sales	(17) 5.0	(12) 4.5
		6.9					9.3	11.0
22504M	53577M	335685M	156827M			Net Sales ($)	242447M	1393837M
3504M	16197M	118770M	96361M			Total Assets ($)	94553M	482737M

M = $ thousand   MM = $ million
See Pages 9 through 22 for Explanation of Ratios and Data

Comparative Historical Data | Current Data Sorted by Sales

				Type of Statement						
2	1	1		Unqualified				1		
11	12	11		Reviewed			2	2	5	2
5	7	4		Compiled				1	3	
12	13	19		Tax Returns			6	4		1
26	22	23		Other	3	5	3	2	9	2
4/1/08-3/31/09	4/1/09-3/31/10	4/1/10-3/31/11			4	3		2		
ALL	ALL	ALL			**13 (4/1-9/30/10)**			**45 (10/1/10-3/31/11)**		
					0-1MM	1-3MM	3-5MM	5-10MM	10-25MM	25MM & OVER
56	55	58		**NUMBER OF STATEMENTS**	7	8	11	10	17	5
%	%	%		**ASSETS**	%	%	%	%	%	%
10.0	15.1	15.6		Cash & Equivalents			26.5	19.8	8.2	
24.9	26.2	25.8		Trade Receivables (net)			18.6	38.1	26.5	
16.6	19.2	16.8		Inventory			17.9	10.9	17.4	
3.7	5.8	2.7		All Other Current			.1	6.0	2.9	
55.2	66.3	60.9		Total Current			63.2	74.9	55.0	
26.0	22.4	24.7		Fixed Assets (net)			20.6	19.6	25.4	
4.2	3.5	4.5		Intangibles (net)			1.1	1.0	9.1	
14.6	7.8	9.9		All Other Non-Current			15.1	4.6	10.5	
100.0	100.0	100.0		Total			100.0	100.0	100.0	
				LIABILITIES						
7.4	23.5	15.7		Notes Payable-Short Term			16.0	2.8	3.6	
3.5	10.1	4.3		Cur. Mat.-L.T.D.			7.5	.8	2.9	
16.6	18.0	16.0		Trade Payables			31.4	11.3	14.9	
.3	.2	.2		Income Taxes Payable			.0	.0	.6	
21.7	18.0	21.9		All Other Current			10.9	25.2	17.6	
49.7	69.8	58.1		Total Current			66.0	40.1	39.5	
19.7	18.6	18.3		Long-Term Debt			17.9	8.9	20.6	
.4	.6	.5		Deferred Taxes			.0	.3	1.7	
6.9	4.5	4.0		All Other Non-Current			13.8	4.1	2.0	
23.4	6.5	19.1		Net Worth			2.3	46.6	36.2	
100.0	100.0	100.0		Total Liabilities & Net Worth			100.0	100.0	100.0	
				INCOME DATA						
100.0	100.0	100.0		Net Sales			100.0	100.0	100.0	
				Gross Profit						
92.7	95.8	93.4		Operating Expenses			94.8	95.4	95.0	
7.3	4.2	6.6		Operating Profit			5.2	4.6	5.0	
1.5	.8	1.1		All Other Expenses (net)			.1	.3	.3	
5.8	3.4	5.5		Profit Before Taxes			5.1	4.3	4.7	
				RATIOS						
2.6	2.5	2.6					3.3	4.2	2.0	
1.4	1.6	1.5		Current			1.6	2.0	1.4	
.6	.9	1.0					.3	1.3	1.0	
1.7	1.4	1.6					2.1	4.0	1.4	
.7	.9	.9		Quick			.7	1.5	.7	
.2	.4	.5					.2	.8	.6	
4 95.3	2 186.1	5 79.7			1 273.6	13 27.4	11 32.7			
35 10.6	34 10.9	30 12.2		Sales/Receivables	15 23.6	53 6.9	36 10.1			
58 6.3	51 7.1	53 6.9			44 8.4	68 5.4	54 6.7			
				Cost of Sales/Inventory						
				Cost of Sales/Payables						
7.8	5.9	5.9					4.5	3.3	10.2	
26.2	13.6	18.2		Sales/Working Capital			6.1	10.3	24.5	
-10.2	-48.1	NM					-9.3	30.8	374.5	
17.1	24.2	34.2					39.6		16.9	
(44) 3.4	(47) 6.4	(49) 7.2		EBIT/Interest			7.7	(16) 6.8		
1.6	.4	2.9					2.6		2.3	
				Net Profit + Depr., Dep., Amort./Cur. Mat. L/T/D						
.3	.1	.2					.3	.0	.2	
.8	.5	.8		Fixed/Worth			1.2	.3	1.4	
4.3	2.4	NM					-.4	.8	NM	
1.1	.7	.7					1.5	.5	1.0	
3.4	2.3	2.2		Debt/Worth			2.4	1.2	2.9	
9.9	24.6	-248.1					-3.1	2.9	NM	
103.8	70.3	63.8		% Profit Before Taxes/Tangible Net Worth			151.9	71.2		
(46) 34.6	(44) 25.7	(43) 21.1					33.4	(13) 25.9		
12.5	10.0	6.6					4.8	2.9		
24.4	20.7	22.0		% Profit Before Taxes/Total Assets			21.9	27.3	26.8	
8.4	6.9	11.3					9.0	14.8	15.0	
3.4	.2	4.0					4.7	3.5	2.3	
42.4	66.0	47.1		Sales/Net Fixed Assets			47.8	UND	30.1	
17.9	20.9	19.4					18.7	30.8	17.8	
6.5	9.4	7.5					13.0	7.2	7.0	
4.1	4.6	4.7		Sales/Total Assets			9.0	4.5	4.6	
2.6	3.3	3.0					3.4	3.4	2.8	
1.9	2.1	2.0					2.4	1.6	2.2	
.7	.4	.9		% Depr., Dep., Amort./Sales					1.1	
(45) 1.9	(40) 1.3	(39) 1.7						(14) 1.7		
4.2	2.1	2.7							2.6	
3.4	2.6	2.9		% Officers', Directors' Owners' Comp/Sales						
(18) 4.3	(26) 4.7	(26) 5.5								
6.5	8.4	6.8								
898772M	711707M	568593M		Net Sales ($)	3219M	11624M	41399M	79071M	260271M	173009M
446292M	280035M	234832M		Total Assets ($)	5665M	8893M	24074M	35664M	96959M	63577M

M = $ thousand   MM = $ million
See Pages 9 through 22 for Explanation of Ratios and Data

Current Data Sorted by Assets

Comparative Historical Data

						Type of Statement		
		1	1			Unqualified		
	2	3	1			Reviewed	1	2
	2	3	2			Compiled	6	4
2	2	3	1			Tax Returns	10	8
25	12	5	1			Other	12	20
10	12	7	4				9	14
	7 (4/1-9/30/10)		86 (10/1/10-3/31/11)				4/1/06-	4/1/07-
							3/31/07	3/31/08
0-500M	500M-2MM	2-10MM	10-50MM	50-100MM	100-250MM		ALL	ALL
37	28	19	9			NUMBER OF STATEMENTS	38	48
%	%	%	%	%	%	ASSETS	%	%
18.6	13.3	11.4				Cash & Equivalents	13.1	15.3
15.3	23.8	24.2				Trade Receivables (net)	32.8	28.8
11.9	15.4	24.0				Inventory	16.6	15.6
4.2	2.2	4.8				All Other Current	2.4	1.9
50.0	54.8	64.4				Total Current	65.0	61.6
28.6	29.9	22.0	D	D		Fixed Assets (net)	28.5	27.4
8.5	8.5	5.6	A	A		Intangibles (net)	2.8	4.8
12.9	6.8	7.9	T	T		All Other Non-Current	3.7	6.2
100.0	100.0	100.0	A	A		Total	100.0	100.0
						LIABILITIES		
12.1	11.3	7.6	N	N		Notes Payable-Short Term	6.5	12.9
6.1	1.3	4.4	O	O		Cur. Mat.-L.T.D.	4.8	3.0
15.7	6.5	16.3	T	T		Trade Payables	13.6	10.3
.0	.1	.2				Income Taxes Payable	.6	.1
11.7	7.2	13.8	A	A		All Other Current	10.8	10.1
45.6	26.3	42.4	V	V		Total Current	36.3	36.4
11.9	22.4	18.6	A	A		Long-Term Debt	28.6	27.0
.0	.0	.5	I	I		Deferred Taxes	.1	.0
21.0	7.7	5.0	L	L		All Other Non-Current	5.1	5.7
21.4	43.6	33.5	A	A		Net Worth	29.9	30.9
100.0	100.0	100.0	B	B		Total Liabilties & Net Worth	100.0	100.0
			L	L		INCOME DATA		
100.0	100.0	100.0	E	E		Net Sales	100.0	100.0
						Gross Profit		
91.8	96.1	94.1				Operating Expenses	89.1	90.2
8.2	3.9	5.9				Operating Profit	10.9	9.8
.6	1.7	1.1				All Other Expenses (net)	1.6	.7
7.6	2.2	4.8				Profit Before Taxes	9.3	9.1
						RATIOS		
3.9	5.1	5.7					2.8	3.8
1.2	1.8	1.6				Current	1.8	1.9
.4	1.1	.9					1.2	1.1
2.5	4.2	3.2					2.1	2.9
.8	1.1	.8				Quick	1.2	1.1
.1	.5	.4					.9	.6

							Sales/Receivables				
0	UND	2	192.9	15	24.3			12	30.6	3	106.8
2	182.0	23	15.9	28	12.9			39	9.4	33	11.2
18	19.8	59	6.2	51	7.1			71	5.1	50	7.4

0-500M	500M-2MM	2-10MM	10-50MM	50-100MM	100-250MM		ALL	ALL
						Cost of Sales/Inventory		
						Cost of Sales/Payables		
10.9	4.5	4.7					6.1	5.7
165.0	12.6	8.4				Sales/Working Capital	10.1	13.1
-25.7	92.3	-41.5					31.0	178.5
22.8	11.3	23.0					21.5	20.5
(23) 4.1	(23) 2.7	(18) 4.5				EBIT/Interest	(33) 6.1	(40) 7.7
1.2	-.5	2.2					2.1	2.7
						Net Profit + Depr., Dep., Amort./Cur. Mat. L/T/D		
.3	.2	.1					.1	.2
.9	.6	.7				Fixed/Worth	.6	.7
-13.0	1.7	-100.7					3.8	2.3
.3	.6	.5					.9	.5
2.0	1.7	3.2				Debt/Worth	1.8	1.4
-17.2	4.6	-222.2					16.2	5.6
116.3	57.1	38.0				% Profit Before Taxes/Tangible	90.6	94.1
(27) 53.0	(24) 17.3	(14) 19.4				Net Worth	(30) 41.7	(40) 46.6
16.0	3.1	6.5					16.9	20.4
45.3	28.1	17.1				% Profit Before Taxes/Total	32.0	42.6
14.5	4.9	8.1				Assets	12.8	19.9
1.6	-.8	3.4					5.0	4.8
91.7	38.4	77.6					62.5	36.0
25.5	13.0	27.5				Sales/Net Fixed Assets	17.1	19.6
9.7	4.8	5.1					6.3	5.9
6.9	3.3	4.0					4.1	4.8
4.4	2.3	2.2				Sales/Total Assets	2.8	3.4
2.7	1.4	1.8					2.1	2.5
.5	.6	.4					.6	1.0
(23) 1.1	(18) 1.3	(16) 1.5				% Depr., Dep., Amort./Sales	(27) 1.6	(36) 1.7
3.3	4.4	2.4					3.4	3.8
3.5	3.4					% Officers', Directors'	1.9	3.4
(22) 6.7	(16) 7.9					Owners' Comp/Sales	(25) 3.2	(26) 5.7
11.2	9.2						6.2	11.5

0-500M	500M-2MM	2-10MM	10-50MM				ALL	ALL
37187M	73447M	178708M	1294111M			Net Sales ($)	1266662M	2847364M
8323M	29398M	67846M	188714M			Total Assets ($)	233042M	407570M

M = $ thousand   MM = $ million
See Pages 9 through 22 for Explanation of Ratios and Data

Comparative Historical Data | Current Data Sorted by Sales

			Type of Statement						
12	3	2	Unqualified				1		1
14	6	6	Reviewed		1	1	3	1	
19	13	9	Compiled	2	1		3	3	
37	42	43	Tax Returns	14	17	5	5	1	1
42	22	33	Other	8	11	3	4	2	5
4/1/08-3/31/09 ALL	4/1/09-3/31/10 ALL	4/1/10-3/31/11 ALL		0-1MM	7 (4/1-9/30/10) 1-3MM	3-5MM	86 (10/1/10-3/31/11) 5-10MM	10-25MM	25MM & OVER
124	86	93	NUMBER OF STATEMENTS	24	30	9	16	7	7
%	%	%	ASSETS	%	%	%	%	%	%
12.7	13.9	16.3	Cash & Equivalents	17.6	17.7		12.0		
25.0	20.6	20.2	Trade Receivables (net)	13.7	22.6		30.7		
16.0	18.9	15.1	Inventory	15.2	10.6		20.5		
4.0	4.7	4.0	All Other Current	2.2	5.2		3.4		
57.7	58.1	55.5	Total Current	48.7	56.1		66.5		
29.6	29.5	27.4	Fixed Assets (net)	30.2	26.9		16.1		
7.2	4.8	7.6	Intangibles (net)	6.4	9.4		11.2		
5.4	7.5	9.5	All Other Non-Current	14.7	7.6		6.2		
100.0	100.0	100.0	Total	100.0	100.0		100.0		
			LIABILITIES						
10.0	13.4	9.8	Notes Payable-Short Term	11.0	11.2		14.5		
6.0	6.1	3.8	Cur. Mat.-L.T.D.	5.0	4.3		4.3		
11.8	11.4	12.4	Trade Payables	11.1	7.0		15.1		
.4	.2	.1	Income Taxes Payable	.0	.0		.2		
11.9	13.7	10.6	All Other Current	10.7	10.7		12.7		
40.0	44.8	36.8	Total Current	37.9	33.2		46.9		
26.2	27.8	16.8	Long-Term Debt	15.0	15.0		19.6		
.5	.1	.1	Deferred Taxes	.0	.0		.0		
6.0	5.8	11.9	All Other Non-Current	11.5	17.5		4.0		
27.3	21.5	34.5	Net Worth	35.6	34.2		29.5		
100.0	100.0	100.0	Total Liabilities & Net Worth	100.0	100.0		100.0		
			INCOME DATA						
100.0	100.0	100.0	Net Sales	100.0	100.0		100.0		
			Gross Profit						
92.7	92.4	93.9	Operating Expenses	87.6	97.2		93.8		
7.3	7.6	6.1	Operating Profit	12.4	2.8		6.2		
1.8	1.7	1.1	All Other Expenses (net)	3.2	-.5		1.0		
5.5	5.9	5.1	Profit Before Taxes	9.2	3.3		5.2		
			RATIOS						
2.7	3.4	4.5		3.3	4.7		12.1		
1.6	1.5	1.7	Current	1.3	1.9		1.4		
1.1	.7	.9		.7	.8		1.0		
2.0	2.1	3.3		2.6	4.5		6.9		
(123) 1.1	.8	1.0	Quick	.9	1.1		.9		
.6	.3	.3		.2	.5		.4		
11 32.4	0 UND	0 UND		0 UND	0 UND		12 31.2		
31 11.9	22 16.5	15 23.6	Sales/Receivables	0 UND	17 21.3		34 10.8		
47 7.8	46 7.9	47 7.7		22 16.6	57 6.4		62 5.8		
			Cost of Sales/Inventory						
			Cost of Sales/Payables						
7.0	6.1	5.6		9.7	5.3		5.0		
16.5	17.7	13.2	Sales/Working Capital	100.1	12.6		10.9		
56.3	-28.5	-74.8		-53.1	-77.6		NM		
13.0	19.3	18.5		15.1	15.2		22.2		
(103) 4.2	(67) 3.0	(73) 4.4	EBIT/Interest	(13) 4.1	(24) 4.1		(14) 4.5		
1.2	.4	1.4		.8	.5		2.0		
10.1			Net Profit + Depr., Dep.,						
(18) 2.8			Amort./Cur. Mat. L/T/D						
1.3									
.3	.2	.2		.3	.1		.2		
1.0	1.3	.7	Fixed/Worth	.8	.8		.7		
5.7	-2.1	3.8		NM	4.5		-25.6		
.7	.7	.5		.3	.5		.5		
2.6	2.5	1.6	Debt/Worth	1.8	1.7		3.5		
43.0	-10.9	10.3		NM	12.4		-58.5		
76.3	61.2	70.8	% Profit Before Taxes/Tangible	79.3	122.8		61.7		
(98) 30.0	(61) 22.3	(74) 25.7	Net Worth	(18) 47.8	(25) 18.6		(11) 37.2		
5.7	-2.2	7.7		8.2	7.8		9.6		
26.2	29.3	29.4	% Profit Before Taxes/Total	44.9	39.0		22.0		
9.5	8.3	9.3	Assets	11.2	10.8		10.4		
1.2	-2.0	1.9		1.4	.0		4.0		
46.9	59.2	59.0		85.0	43.6		110.0		
15.7	17.1	19.3	Sales/Net Fixed Assets	12.5	27.8		31.2		
5.4	5.8	6.1		4.9	8.7		9.0		
4.5	5.3	4.5		4.7	5.0		4.1		
2.8	2.8	2.7	Sales/Total Assets	2.9	3.1		2.6		
1.8	1.8	1.8		1.1	2.0		1.9		
.9	.8	.5		.5	.7		.3		
(97) 1.9	(59) 1.7	(65) 1.2	% Depr., Dep., Amort./Sales	(13) 1.7	(20) 1.3		(14) 1.0		
4.0	4.5	3.5		3.3	4.3		2.2		
3.2	2.8	2.7		2.9	4.8		1.9		
(52) 5.3	(47) 5.1	(48) 6.1	% Officers', Directors' Owners' Comp/Sales	(12) 6.4	(18) 7.5		(10) 2.6		
8.1	9.2	9.3		9.4	12.8		6.5		
3154841M	834639M	1583453M	Net Sales ($)	11510M	49134M	34384M	107985M	104669M	1275771M
1380170M	349237M	294281M	Total Assets ($)	6482M	18840M	14013M	42200M	58015M	154731M

© RMA 2011

M = $ thousand   MM = $ million
See Pages 9 through 22 for Explanation of Ratios and Data

Current Data Sorted by Assets | | | | | | | Comparative Historical Data

0-500M	500M-2MM	2-10MM	10-50MM	50-100MM	100-250MM	Type of Statement	4/1/06-3/31/07 ALL	4/1/07-3/31/08 ALL
2	1	2	4	2		Unqualified	7	7
	2	2	2			Reviewed	10	2
12	11	8	1			Compiled	19	15
60	22	6		1		Tax Returns	88	61
21	16	8	3		2	Other	50	60
	13 (4/1-9/30/10)		176 (10/1/10-3/31/11)					
95	**52**	**26**	**10**	**4**	**2**	**NUMBER OF STATEMENTS**	**174**	**145**
%	%	%	%	%	%	ASSETS	%	%
26.3	15.6	18.9	16.9			Cash & Equivalents	19.5	17.8
2.3	3.3	7.8	13.5			Trade Receivables (net)	2.1	1.9
10.9	6.7	7.9	16.2			Inventory	12.9	13.9
2.2	2.3	4.2	4.1			All Other Current	1.7	2.3
41.6	28.0	38.8	50.8			Total Current	36.2	35.9
41.6	51.0	42.5	28.0			Fixed Assets (net)	43.6	46.7
5.5	11.9	5.8	9.1			Intangibles (net)	9.7	8.3
11.4	9.1	12.9	12.0			All Other Non-Current	10.5	9.0
100.0	100.0	100.0	100.0			Total	100.0	100.0
						LIABILITIES		
13.5	2.6	2.6	5.7			Notes Payable-Short Term	12.9	10.7
2.8	7.2	3.9	5.5			Cur. Mat.-L.T.D.	3.2	3.2
6.5	4.5	7.9	11.0			Trade Payables	8.2	6.6
.1	.0	.1	.6			Income Taxes Payable	.1	.2
35.4	10.7	18.7	21.2			All Other Current	25.4	21.5
58.3	25.0	33.2	44.0			Total Current	49.8	42.3
30.6	37.9	23.2	45.5			Long-Term Debt	31.0	30.3
.0	.0	.0	.7			Deferred Taxes	.1	.1
21.6	10.2	16.0	8.1			All Other Non-Current	13.7	14.0
-10.5	26.9	27.6	1.7			Net Worth	5.4	13.4
100.0	100.0	100.0	100.0			Total Liabilities & Net Worth	100.0	100.0
						INCOME DATA		
100.0	100.0	100.0	100.0			Net Sales	100.0	100.0
						Gross Profit		
96.1	82.5	95.0	86.9			Operating Expenses	94.1	94.8
3.9	17.5	5.0	13.1			Operating Profit	5.9	5.2
2.3	5.4	1.0	2.1			All Other Expenses (net)	1.8	1.3
1.7	12.2	4.0	10.9			Profit Before Taxes	4.0	3.9
						RATIOS		
3.1	3.3	2.0	2.0				1.7	2.1
.9	1.4	1.0	1.4			Current	.8	1.0
.3	.6	.5	.8				.3	.5
2.0	2.2	1.1	1.0				1.0	1.2
.6	.9	.6	.8			Quick	(172) .4	(144) .5
.2	.2	.2	.4				.1	.2
0 UND	0 UND	0 UND	3 131.9				0 UND	0 UND
0 UND	0 UND	1 662.4	20 18.2			Sales/Receivables	0 UND	0 UND
0 UND	1 537.8	12 29.3	39 9.3				0 UND	0 999.8
						Cost of Sales/Inventory		
						Cost of Sales/Payables		
23.7	18.0	13.7	7.4				26.4	22.8
-300.8	99.8	NM	16.3			Sales/Working Capital	-52.0	UND
-10.5	-21.6	-18.1	-16.8				-13.0	-16.1
8.0	22.6	24.7					11.0	11.3
(63) 1.9	(42) 4.5	8.6				EBIT/Interest	(130) 3.5	(107) 3.7
-1.8	1.9	1.3					1.0	.8
							6.3	
						Net Profit + Depr., Dep., Amort./Cur. Mat. L/T/D	(11) 3.6	
							.5	
.3	.7	.8	.3				.8	.6
3.2	4.0	2.0	1.7			Fixed/Worth	2.5	2.2
-1.3	-3.4	56.9	NM				-2.4	-4.1
.5	.5	1.0	1.2				1.3	.8
10.5	4.6	3.0	2.4			Debt/Worth	6.0	3.2
-2.6	-6.0	77.2	NM				-4.7	-6.4
82.6	114.6	108.6					144.2	116.1
(49) 25.8	(30) 63.4	(21) 51.8				% Profit Before Taxes/Tangible Net Worth	(105) 52.6	(98) 47.8
4.3	22.9	16.1					13.5	16.3
41.5	28.4	18.7	29.8				28.3	28.2
7.3	11.9	9.9	13.8			% Profit Before Taxes/Total Assets	9.9	10.5
-6.6	3.5	1.1	5.8				-.4	.0
57.3	15.1	14.0	23.3				26.6	23.7
15.5	7.1	7.9	13.2			Sales/Net Fixed Assets	11.7	9.9
7.0	1.3	3.5	3.0				5.5	4.6
8.6	4.7	4.1	2.2				7.0	6.8
5.0	2.1	2.6	2.1			Sales/Total Assets	4.1	4.0
2.7	1.0	1.8	1.5				2.2	1.9
1.0	1.0	1.5					.9	1.1
(68) 2.4	(37) 2.0	(24) 3.1				% Depr., Dep., Amort./Sales	(123) 2.2	(111) 2.2
4.1	4.5	4.1					3.5	3.6
4.2	2.4	1.9					2.9	2.7
(53) 8.0	(17) 3.1	(15) 3.6				% Officers', Directors' Owners' Comp/Sales	(82) 5.1	(69) 4.6
13.7	8.1	6.9					10.1	10.0
88174M	175408M	304317M	364436M	853433M	1654732M	Net Sales ($)	1839278M	2112820M
18383M	56509M	97120M	205335M	294455M	381755M	Total Assets ($)	761430M	816099M

© RMA 2011

M = $ thousand   MM = $ million
See Pages 9 through 22 for Explanation of Ratios and Data

Comparative Historical Data — Current Data Sorted by Sales

			Type of Statement						
8	5	11	Unqualified	2	1	1		2	5
4	5	6	Reviewed				1	3	2
18	24	32	Compiled	8	11	4	4	4	1
106	102	89	Tax Returns	53	21	6	6	2	1
67	61	51	Other	14	16	3	6	3	6
4/1/08-3/31/09 ALL	4/1/09-3/31/10 ALL	4/1/10-3/31/11 ALL		13 (4/1-9/30/10) 0-1MM	1-3MM	3-5MM	176 (10/1/10-3/31/11) 5-10MM	10-25MM	25MM & OVER
203	197	189	NUMBER OF STATEMENTS	77	49	14	17	17	15
%	%	%	ASSETS	%	%	%	%	%	%
17.4	18.3	21.3	Cash & Equivalents	21.7	21.8	25.9	16.9	25.2	13.7
3.4	3.7	4.0	Trade Receivables (net)	2.1	3.3	9.2	1.4	9.5	7.8
12.2	10.4	9.6	Inventory	8.8	10.0	5.5	7.5	11.7	16.0
2.4	2.5	2.8	All Other Current	2.5	1.4	.2	3.9	6.4	5.8
35.5	34.9	37.6	Total Current	35.1	36.6	40.9	29.8	52.8	43.3
48.3	46.5	43.8	Fixed Assets (net)	48.2	42.4	40.8	46.7	32.3	38.6
5.9	10.3	7.8	Intangibles (net)	5.6	10.8	9.3	5.5	6.3	11.5
10.3	8.3	10.8	All Other Non-Current	11.2	10.2	9.0	18.0	8.6	6.7
100.0	100.0	100.0	Total	100.0	100.0	100.0	100.0	100.0	100.0
			LIABILITIES						
13.7	8.8	8.2	Notes Payable-Short Term	10.3	10.8	3.5	2.4	4.5	4.5
4.5	3.9	4.3	Cur. Mat.-L.T.D.	4.7	4.1	5.5	3.1	3.5	4.0
7.0	7.5	6.4	Trade Payables	5.1	5.3	3.3	12.0	8.8	10.5
.1	.1	.1	Income Taxes Payable	.0	.2	.0	.1	.0	.5
24.2	25.6	24.9	All Other Current	24.8	30.4	22.2	20.8	24.3	15.0
49.4	45.9	43.9	Total Current	44.8	50.9	34.4	38.3	41.2	34.6
37.2	30.8	32.8	Long-Term Debt	39.8	28.5	38.4	21.3	8.9	46.0
.0	.0	.0	Deferred Taxes	.0	.0	.0	.0	.4	.1
14.8	15.2	16.4	All Other Non-Current	20.1	16.8	15.4	21.0	3.4	6.8
-1.4	8.1	6.9	Net Worth	-4.7	3.8	11.8	19.4	46.2	12.6
100.0	100.0	100.0	Total Liabilities & Net Worth	100.0	100.0	100.0	100.0	100.0	100.0
			INCOME DATA						
100.0	100.0	100.0	Net Sales	100.0	100.0	100.0	100.0	100.0	100.0
			Gross Profit						
96.0	92.7	91.6	Operating Expenses	90.1	91.2	95.1	96.6	93.5	89.5
4.0	7.3	8.4	Operating Profit	9.9	8.8	4.9	3.4	6.5	10.5
2.1	2.0	2.9	All Other Expenses (net)	5.1	2.0	.8	1.0	.0	1.9
1.9	5.3	5.5	Profit Before Taxes	4.7	6.8	4.1	2.4	6.4	8.6
			RATIOS						
1.7	2.0	2.6		3.2	3.5	10.2	2.0	2.3	1.8
.8	.9	1.1	Current	1.2	.9	1.0	.7	1.4	1.5
.3	.3	.4		.3	.4	.3	.3	.8	.6
1.0	1.1	1.8		2.0	2.4	10.1	1.1	1.6	1.0
.4 (196)	.4	.7	Quick	.7	.7	.7	.2	.8	.9
.1	.1	.2		.2	.3	.2	.1	.4	.1
0 UND	0 UND	0 UND		0 UND	0 UND	0 UND	0 UND	0 UND	0 UND
0 UND	0 UND	0 UND	Sales/Receivables	0 UND	0 UND	0 UND	0 UND	1 324.9	4 103.5
0 UND	0 UND	1 300.5		0 UND	0 UND	6 57.1	1 567.2	13 27.6	28 12.8
			Cost of Sales/Inventory						
			Cost of Sales/Payables						
32.3	21.6	18.2		20.8	18.4	9.8	21.6	16.5	7.7
-70.9	-195.5	225.0	Sales/Working Capital	123.9	-300.8	NM	-26.8	29.0	16.3
-10.6	-14.5	-14.4		-9.2	-19.7	-12.0	-15.4	-25.5	-66.0
6.1	12.1	13.6		5.7	17.1	10.9	23.4	99.1	28.8
(153) 1.6	(147) 4.3	(145) 3.9	EBIT/Interest	(50) 2.4	(37) 3.4	(12) 2.3	8.8	(16) 15.0	(13) 4.4
-.3	1.3	.9		-.7	.9	.1	-1.5	7.1	1.3
		14.9							
	(13)	4.9	Net Profit + Depr., Dep., Amort./Cur. Mat. L/T/D						
		2.8							
.8	.6	.5		.4	.5	1.0	.9	.3	.5
5.3	3.1	3.2	Fixed/Worth	5.6	4.4	37.6	6.4	.9	2.0
-2.1	-1.7	-2.0		-1.5	-1.6	-3.5	-2.0	2.1	-1.2
1.6	.8	.7		.6	.5	2.3	.8	.5	1.0
8.9	5.0	5.2	Debt/Worth	6.5	6.2	57.9	7.3	1.0	1.7
-3.8	-3.6	-3.8		-2.8	-3.9	-7.5	-4.7	9.2	-2.8
95.7	92.7	98.8		58.5	143.4		114.8	144.1	146.9
(121) 46.6	(123) 50.4	(112) 41.0	% Profit Before Taxes/Tangible Net Worth	(40) 24.3	(27) 58.3	(10) 39.2	(16) 70.2	(11) 42.7
6.7	14.0	13.7		12.6	14.7		12.8	20.4	6.6
23.2	30.1	32.2		27.2	47.5	15.5	27.6	42.4	42.4
5.1	11.3	9.4	% Profit Before Taxes/Total Assets	7.3	13.7	5.8	10.1	17.9	18.2
-5.3	.5	.0		-7.7	1.5	-3.7	-4.9	7.0	1.2
22.4	25.3	24.9		32.2	23.9	22.3	25.7	44.6	17.6
9.3	10.1	10.9	Sales/Net Fixed Assets	9.6	11.0	9.7	8.8	13.1	7.9
3.8	4.7	4.1		1.7	5.0	3.8	4.6	8.9	4.9
6.8	6.0	6.2		6.9	7.2	5.7	6.0	6.4	2.9
3.9	3.6	3.5	Sales/Total Assets	3.0	3.9	2.8	4.3	4.7	2.2
2.2	1.7	1.7		1.0	2.1	1.7	2.1	3.1	1.6
.9	1.0	1.1		1.7	.8	1.1	.6	1.1	1.0
(152) 2.1	(158) 1.8	(142) 2.4	% Depr., Dep., Amort./Sales	(55) 3.2	(36) 1.6	(11) 2.0	(15) 1.1	(13) 2.1	(12) 2.5
3.8	3.5	4.1		6.5	4.0	3.7	4.2	3.1	3.0
3.8	2.3	2.9		3.8	2.7		3.0		
(98) 6.0	(86) 4.6	(89) 6.2	% Officers', Directors' Owners' Comp/Sales	(37) 8.3	(23) 6.2	(11) 5.8		
10.5	11.2	10.1		18.2	9.7		8.2		
1604397M	2788639M	3440500M	Net Sales ($)	36577M	84328M	53262M	115366M	263608M	2887359M
651221M	711407M	1053557M	Total Assets ($)	23922M	28719M	24685M	35409M	79528M	861294M

© RMA 2011

M = $ thousand   MM = $ million
See Pages 9 through 22 for Explanation of Ratios and Data

Current Data Sorted by Assets   Comparative Historical Data

	0-500M	500M-2MM	2-10MM	10-50MM	50-100MM	100-250MM	Type of Statement	4/1/06-3/31/07 ALL	4/1/07-3/31/08 ALL
						1	Unqualified	1	4
		1	1	1			Reviewed		1
			1				Compiled	1	2
	13	6					Tax Returns	8	6
	7	6					Other	3	4
		3 (4/1-9/30/10)		40 (10/1/10-3/31/11)					
NUMBER OF STATEMENTS	20	13	3	4	1	2		13	17
	%	%	%	%	%	%	ASSETS	%	%
	29.8	9.8					Cash & Equivalents	18.9	19.7
	4.8	12.2					Trade Receivables (net)	5.2	11.2
	10.5	1.2					Inventory	12.4	10.5
	1.3	3.4					All Other Current	7.6	2.6
	46.3	26.7					Total Current	44.1	44.0
	38.2	55.2					Fixed Assets (net)	44.0	46.6
	6.4	10.0					Intangibles (net)	4.0	4.9
	9.0	8.1					All Other Non-Current	7.8	4.5
	100.0	100.0					Total	100.0	100.0
							LIABILITIES		
	16.2	7.2					Notes Payable-Short Term	4.1	49.3
	3.5	3.4					Cur. Mat.-L.T.D.	7.0	4.5
	2.7	3.9					Trade Payables	1.8	6.7
	.0	.0					Income Taxes Payable	.0	.0
	25.9	4.6					All Other Current	27.5	25.2
	48.3	19.0					Total Current	40.4	85.7
	35.5	40.6					Long-Term Debt	53.1	37.6
	.0	.0					Deferred Taxes	.0	.1
	11.5	23.9					All Other Non-Current	17.8	25.7
	4.7	16.5					Net Worth	-11.3	-49.1
	100.0	100.0					Total Liabilties & Net Worth	100.0	100.0
							INCOME DATA		
	100.0	100.0					Net Sales	100.0	100.0
							Gross Profit		
	91.4	89.1					Operating Expenses	90.6	96.6
	8.6	10.9					Operating Profit	9.4	3.4
	1.1	6.5					All Other Expenses (net)	2.7	1.6
	7.6	4.3					Profit Before Taxes	6.7	1.8
							RATIOS		
	6.2	5.6						4.7	1.6
	1.6	1.2					Current	1.3	.9
	.6	.4						.3	.5
	5.3	4.8						2.1	1.2
	1.3	1.2					Quick	.2	.5
	.3	.1						.1	.1
	0 UND	0 UND						0 UND	0 UND
	0 UND	0 UND					Sales/Receivables	0 UND	0 UND
	0 UND	3 116.4						0 UND	7 49.3
							Cost of Sales/Inventory		
							Cost of Sales/Payables		
	11.0	5.5						7.8	9.0
	44.7	41.4					Sales/Working Capital	24.9	-57.3
	-14.2	-8.5						-5.1	-6.1
	16.2	14.0						7.2	10.7
	(15) 11.0	(10) 6.0					EBIT/Interest	(10) 1.5	(16) 3.3
	1.8	.9						-.3	-3.2
							Net Profit + Depr., Dep., Amort./Cur. Mat. L/T/D		
	.3	1.1						.7	.4
	1.1	18.0					Fixed/Worth	-319.5	1.9
	-1.1	-3.3						-1.5	-3.6
	.4	.8						1.6	.8
	15.4	18.3					Debt/Worth	-337.0	2.5
	-2.8	-5.0						-4.3	-2.4
	175.5								131.8
	(12) 79.6						% Profit Before Taxes/Tangible Net Worth		(10) 44.1
	39.1								7.2
	68.1	27.6						36.0	29.9
	41.2	10.5					% Profit Before Taxes/Total Assets	5.6	11.5
	6.9	-.9						-8.9	-21.8
	44.7	20.6						29.9	20.9
	18.4	3.8					Sales/Net Fixed Assets	4.7	9.0
	5.8	1.9						1.7	2.8
	6.9	2.6						2.7	7.0
	3.7	1.9					Sales/Total Assets	1.4	2.2
	2.4	.5						1.2	1.5
	1.2	1.9						2.4	2.0
	(12) 2.7	(10) 5.6					% Depr., Dep., Amort./Sales	(11) 7.6	(14) 4.6
	11.3	-15.1						14.5	8.7
							% Officers', Directors' Owners' Comp/Sales		
	13323M	33836M	12595M	141548M	75607M	148352M	Net Sales ($)	17060M	79416M
	3972M	13693M	10790M	109834M	62647M	304655M	Total Assets ($)	9004M	55632M

M = $ thousand   MM = $ million
See Pages 9 through 22 for Explanation of Ratios and Data

Comparative Historical Data   Current Data Sorted by Sales

Type of Statement									
	3	1	1	1		1			1
		3	2						1
	2	4	1			1			
	14	8	19	12	6				
	5	10	20	9	4		1	2	4
	4/1/08-3/31/09 ALL	4/1/09-3/31/10 ALL	4/1/10-3/31/11 ALL			3 (4/1-9/30/10)		40 (10/1/10-3/31/11)	
				0-1MM	1-3MM	3-5MM	5-10MM	10-25MM	25MM & OVER
NUMBER OF STATEMENTS	24	26	43	22	10	2	1	2	6
	%	%	%	%	%	%	%	%	%
ASSETS									
Cash & Equivalents	14.0	15.5	18.9	24.7	12.9				
Trade Receivables (net)	4.6	4.0	7.3	7.1	10.7				
Inventory	10.7	14.3	6.5	8.9	3.4				
All Other Current	6.0	1.5	2.0	.5	2.2				
Total Current	35.4	35.2	34.7	41.2	29.2				
Fixed Assets (net)	54.2	49.4	41.2	44.2	45.8				
Intangibles (net)	7.4	10.5	13.4	7.7	5.8				
All Other Non-Current	3.0	4.9	10.7	6.9	19.2				
Total	100.0	100.0	100.0	100.0	100.0				
LIABILITIES									
Notes Payable-Short Term	15.6	17.4	11.2	12.5	6.0				
Cur. Mat.-L.T.D.	6.9	2.9	4.5	3.5	4.5				
Trade Payables	6.8	6.4	3.9	3.0	5.0				
Income Taxes Payable	.0	.0	.0	.0	.0				
All Other Current	28.4	18.2	17.8	22.7	6.6				
Total Current	57.7	45.0	37.4	41.6	22.1				
Long-Term Debt	32.4	31.2	31.3	37.5	36.0				
Deferred Taxes	.0	.0	.1	.0	.0				
All Other Non-Current	13.6	20.1	14.6	15.8	24.1				
Net Worth	-3.7	3.7	16.6	5.2	17.8				
Total Liabilities & Net Worth	100.0	100.0	100.0	100.0	100.0				
INCOME DATA									
Net Sales	100.0	100.0	100.0	100.0	100.0				
Gross Profit									
Operating Expenses	87.7	92.9	91.5	89.6	93.4				
Operating Profit	12.3	7.1	8.5	10.4	6.6				
All Other Expenses (net)	3.9	3.8	4.0	5.0	-.4				
Profit Before Taxes	8.4	3.3	4.5	5.5	7.0				
RATIOS									
Current	2.8	3.9	3.7	4.6	5.6				
	.5	1.5	1.2	1.6	1.3				
	.2	.3	.4	.4	.6				
Quick	1.4	2.6	3.2	4.4	4.6				
	.3	.6	.9	1.3	1.1				
	.1	.1	.1	.1	.3				
Sales/Receivables	0 UND	0 UND	0 UND	0 UND	0 UND				
	0 UND	0 UND	0 UND	0 UND	0 UND				
	15 24.3	6 57.7	10 35.5	0 UND	26 14.0				
Cost of Sales/Inventory									
Cost of Sales/Payables									
Sales/Working Capital	26.2	7.7	11.4	6.0	26.1				
	-13.9	47.1	64.8	44.7	53.1				
	-3.9	-6.4	-8.0	-8.8	-27.6				
EBIT/Interest	15.3	6.2	12.8	16.1					
	(20) 4.1	(22) 2.4	(35) 3.7	(16) 7.6					
	.2	.1	.9	.4					
Net Profit + Depr., Dep., Amort./Cur. Mat, L/T/D									
Fixed/Worth	.9	.5	.6	.2	.6				
	UND	10.9	1.4	4.1	9.6				
	-1.2	-1.4	-1.8	-1.2	-7.4				
Debt/Worth	1.2	.8	.7	.5	.9				
	UND	24.6	6.9	17.7	10.3				
	-3.5	-2.6	-6.0	-3.1	-13.7				
% Profit Before Taxes/Tangible Net Worth	93.6	103.7	139.6	167.4					
	(13) 21.5	(14) 42.0	(28) 40.7	(13) 68.8					
	-5.4	2.4	-.2	-.7					
% Profit Before Taxes/Total Assets	30.3	18.4	42.2	55.8	39.9				
	10.2	7.3	13.2	21.9	19.7				
	-3.7	-1.6	-.1	-.9	.9				
Sales/Net Fixed Assets	14.7	16.4	27.2	50.3	27.0				
	5.1	9.8	7.6	10.7	4.6				
	1.5	2.8	2.7	1.5	2.9				
Sales/Total Assets	3.9	4.8	3.9	5.4	4.4				
	2.4	2.7	2.2	2.5	2.6				
	.9	1.2	1.2	1.1	1.9				
% Depr., Dep., Amort./Sales	1.6	2.4	2.1	1.4					
	(18) 4.6	(21) 3.8	(32) 4.6	(14) 8.8					
	10.4	9.3	10.4	13.3					
% Officers', Directors' Owners' Comp/Sales		2.5	1.4						
	(13)	4.7	(11) 7.2						
		19.8	11.2						
Net Sales ($)	84282M	1049139M	425261M	10789M	19400M	8809M	5032M	27528M	353703M
Total Assets ($)	35752M	568420M	505591M	8302M	9615M	5347M	3688M	21982M	456657M

M = $ thousand   MM = $ million
See Pages 9 through 22 for Explanation of Ratios and Data

Current Data Sorted by Assets   Comparative Historical Data

Type of Statement	0-500M	500M-2MM	2-10MM	10-50MM	50-100MM	100-250MM		4/1/06-3/31/07 ALL	4/1/07-3/31/08 ALL
Unqualified			2					9	5
Reviewed	4	3	7	3				25	26
Compiled	19	29	19	2				106	77
Tax Returns	75	73	22			1		108	123
Other	13	35	23	7	8	3		77	74
		59 (4/1-9/30/10)		289 (10/1/10-3/31/11)					
NUMBER OF STATEMENTS	111	140	73	12	8	4		325	305

	%	%	%	%	%	%		%	%
ASSETS									
Cash & Equivalents	19.9	13.1	9.8	6.2				10.7	10.7
Trade Receivables (net)	18.8	13.6	8.4	6.7				15.3	15.2
Inventory	8.2	4.1	3.0	5.3				5.1	4.9
All Other Current	1.9	2.5	2.5	6.1				2.5	2.4
Total Current	48.8	33.3	23.6	24.3				33.6	33.2
Fixed Assets (net)	34.0	44.4	49.8	49.0				41.7	41.3
Intangibles (net)	6.3	10.2	6.7	11.6				9.7	9.6
All Other Non-Current	10.9	12.2	19.9	15.2				15.1	15.9
Total	100.0	100.0	100.0	100.0				100.0	100.0
LIABILITIES									
Notes Payable-Short Term	12.1	4.8	3.3	2.5				4.7	5.8
Cur. Mat.-L.T.D.	8.4	4.3	3.0	4.4				4.1	4.0
Trade Payables	8.4	4.9	3.2	1.2				6.3	7.3
Income Taxes Payable	.1	.2	.2	.0				.2	.2
All Other Current	29.9	9.6	4.3	5.0				9.5	11.4
Total Current	58.9	23.8	14.0	13.2				24.8	28.7
Long-Term Debt	33.7	44.6	42.9	26.8				42.6	39.4
Deferred Taxes	.1	.1	.4	.0				.1	.1
All Other Non-Current	14.7	8.3	12.5	15.9				10.9	12.6
Net Worth	-7.4	23.3	30.2	44.1				21.6	19.1
Total Liabilities & Net Worth	100.0	100.0	100.0	100.0				100.0	100.0
INCOME DATA									
Net Sales	100.0	100.0	100.0	100.0				100.0	100.0
Gross Profit									
Operating Expenses	93.6	89.5	89.4	86.2				92.7	92.4
Operating Profit	6.4	10.5	10.6	13.8				7.3	7.6
All Other Expenses (net)	1.4	3.2	4.7	3.3				2.3	2.8
Profit Before Taxes	5.0	7.2	5.8	10.5				5.0	4.8
RATIOS									
Current	3.9	4.8	3.3	10.0				3.5	3.3
	1.4	2.0	1.5	1.6				1.6	1.7
	.6	.9	.8	1.1				.8	.8
Quick	2.7	3.6	2.9	3.5				2.8	2.6
	1.1	1.7	1.3	1.1				1.3 (304)	1.2
	.3	.5	.7	.6				.5	.5
Sales/Receivables	0 UND	12 31.5	17 22.1	18 20.5				14 26.2	12 29.6
	18 20.6	27 13.6	30 12.0	37 9.9				31 11.9	30 12.2
	32 11.4	44 8.3	42 8.6	52 7.0				46 7.9	44 8.3
Cost of Sales/Inventory									
Cost of Sales/Payables									
Sales/Working Capital	9.8	5.2	4.9	2.7				5.9	5.9
	25.8	12.3	17.2	7.3				16.3	16.8
	-16.2	-41.5	-52.9	31.2				-27.2	-35.9
EBIT/Interest	10.5	7.8	6.0					6.2	6.1
	(72) 4.8	(121) 2.9	(66) 2.0					(269) 2.4	(245) 2.2
	1.0	1.4	1.2					1.0	1.0
Net Profit + Depr., Dep., Amort./Cur. Mat. L/T/D		9.7	5.8					3.9	3.5
		(13) 3.3	(15) 2.8					(40) 1.7	(43) 1.4
		1.2	1.4					1.2	.7
Fixed/Worth	.3	.7	.9	1.1				.6	.6
	1.3	2.4	2.3	1.7				1.7	1.8
	-.8	-3.9	39.8	3.1				-5.5	-8.7
Debt/Worth	.6	.7	1.2	.8				.8	.8
	3.8	4.1	3.2	2.4				2.9	2.8
	-3.3	-7.9	68.4	5.2				-13.0	-13.9
% Profit Before Taxes/Tangible Net Worth	135.9	52.0	25.7	27.5				38.5	43.7
	(72) 36.3	(95) 28.2	(57) 12.2	(11) 9.8				(231) 14.6	(214) 13.8
	7.7	4.4	1.8	4.0				1.1	1.1
% Profit Before Taxes/Total Assets	31.0	16.3	7.6	7.7				12.4	13.1
	14.6	6.7	3.2	3.9				4.8	4.7
	.0	1.3	.5	2.0				-.4	-.4
Sales/Net Fixed Assets	27.7	10.1	4.3	2.7				10.1	10.8
	16.4	4.3	1.8	1.2				5.0	5.2
	6.3	1.8	1.1	.7				1.9	1.8
Sales/Total Assets	5.4	2.3	1.3	1.0				2.6	2.7
	3.4	1.4	.9	.5				1.5	1.6
	2.3	.9	.7	.3				.8	.7
% Depr., Dep., Amort./Sales	1.4	1.7	2.4	3.1				2.0	1.8
	(88) 2.2	(123) 3.3	(70) 3.8	(11) 4.7				(278) 3.3	(274) 3.2
	3.4	5.5	6.1	6.5				6.0	5.6
% Officers', Directors' Owners' Comp/Sales	6.0	5.6	4.3					6.9	7.1
	(71) 8.7	(88) 9.8	(46) 7.3					(197) 10.4	(200) 10.5
	15.8	14.4	10.9					15.3	14.5
Net Sales ($)	101420M	230917M	270556M	123916M	159538M	1297037M		919950M	1738157M
Total Assets ($)	27004M	144853M	302204M	219145M	507539M	779202M		1089380M	1169469M

M = $ thousand   MM = $ million
See Pages 9 through 22 for Explanation of Ratios and Data

Comparative Historical Data | Current Data Sorted by Sales

	4/1/08-3/31/09 ALL	4/1/09-3/31/10 ALL	4/1/10-3/31/11 ALL	0-1MM	1-3MM	3-5MM	5-10MM	10-25MM	25MM & OVER
					59 (4/1-9/30/10)		289 (10/1/10-3/31/11)		
Type of Statement									
Unqualified	11	14	2		1			1	
Reviewed	32	29	17	1	8	3	2	3	
Compiled	85	77	69	22	31	11	4	1	
Tax Returns	133	162	171	82	70	14	4	1	1
Other	81	80	89	23	30	10	13	7	6
NUMBER OF STATEMENTS	342	362	348	128	140	38	23	12	7
ASSETS	%	%	%	%	%	%	%	%	%
Cash & Equivalents	11.0	11.8	14.0	15.4	14.2	13.5	13.6	5.4	
Trade Receivables (net)	13.6	13.8	13.9	12.8	15.5	12.6	13.7	13.1	
Inventory	5.4	4.7	5.3	7.1	4.4	2.8	4.7	3.8	
All Other Current	3.4	2.2	2.4	2.1	2.7	2.6	1.6	2.4	
Total Current	33.5	32.5	35.6	37.4	36.7	31.5	33.5	24.7	
Fixed Assets (net)	43.6	42.2	41.8	43.9	39.6	47.4	36.5	41.8	
Intangibles (net)	7.4	10.0	8.5	7.5	8.9	6.9	8.5	10.9	
All Other Non-Current	15.5	15.3	14.2	11.2	14.7	14.3	21.5	22.6	
Total	100.0	100.0	100.0	100.0	100.0	100.0	100.0	100.0	
LIABILITIES									
Notes Payable-Short Term	6.1	5.2	6.6	8.5	5.5	7.9	3.7	4.0	
Cur. Mat.-L.T.D.	4.8	4.9	5.2	7.1	4.4	4.7	2.9	2.6	
Trade Payables	6.5	5.7	5.4	4.3	6.3	5.8	7.0	4.4	
Income Taxes Payable	.2	.2	.1	.0	.2	.3	.2	.1	
All Other Current	10.7	7.7	14.5	27.7	7.7	6.5	5.3	3.9	
Total Current	28.3	23.7	31.9	47.6	24.1	25.2	19.1	15.0	
Long-Term Debt	40.4	39.9	39.6	45.5	35.1	43.8	34.6	38.7	
Deferred Taxes	.1	.1	.1	.0	.2	.3	.3	.3	
All Other Non-Current	12.3	10.9	12.7	15.5	10.5	6.3	11.8	14.4	
Net Worth	19.0	25.4	15.6	-8.5	30.1	24.5	34.2	31.6	
Total Liabilities & Net Worth	100.0	100.0	100.0	100.0	100.0	100.0	100.0	100.0	
INCOME DATA									
Net Sales	100.0	100.0	100.0	100.0	100.0	100.0	100.0	100.0	
Gross Profit									
Operating Expenses	91.5	91.5	90.6	87.8	91.9	92.5	96.6	89.8	
Operating Profit	8.5	8.5	9.4	12.2	8.1	7.5	3.4	10.2	
All Other Expenses (net)	2.7	2.6	3.0	5.9	1.2	1.0	2.0	2.2	
Profit Before Taxes	5.8	6.0	6.4	6.3	6.9	6.5	1.3	8.0	
RATIOS									
Current	3.1	3.9	4.2	3.6	5.2	4.0	3.4	4.0	
	1.5	1.7	1.7	1.3	2.1	1.4	1.5	2.9	
	.7	.8	.7	.5	.9	.8	1.0	1.2	
Quick	2.3	3.2	3.2	2.5	3.8	3.4	3.3	3.6	
	1.1	1.4	1.3	.9	1.7	1.3	1.3	2.2	
	.5	.6	.5	.3	.7	.7	.8	.8	
Sales/Receivables	10 37.5	15 24.3	8 43.4	0 UND	11 33.1	13 28.2	23 16.2	17 21.6	
	26 13.9	29 12.8	25 14.7	20 18.2	27 13.7	25 14.9	28 13.2	53 6.9	
	43 8.4	44 8.2	43 8.4	42 8.7	42 8.7	39 9.3	47 7.8	73 5.0	
Cost of Sales/Inventory									
Cost of Sales/Payables									
Sales/Working Capital	6.2	5.8	5.9	7.1	5.3	5.3	4.9	2.9	
	20.3	15.7	18.2	25.6	12.3	17.6	25.1	6.6	
	-20.5	-40.7	-34.5	-10.7	-72.4	-39.1	550.7	22.1	
EBIT/Interest	8.5	7.1	8.6	5.8	10.7	7.1	4.9	10.2	
	(281) 2.6	(299) 2.7	(277) 2.8	(89) 2.4	(115) 4.0	(36) 3.2	(20) 2.7	(11) 3.6	
	1.3	1.3	1.3	1.0	1.4	1.3	1.3	1.4	
Net Profit + Depr., Dep., Amort./Cur. Mat. L/T/D	2.5	2.9	5.5		5.8				
	(45) 1.3	(33) 1.2	(39) 2.8		(19) 2.6				
	.9	.7	1.1		1.4				
Fixed/Worth	.5	.6	.6	.8	.5	.8	.9	.7	
	1.8	1.9	2.1	6.6	1.3	1.3	1.6	2.5	
	-5.6	-6.4	-6.6	-.8	98.2	-54.8	3.1	NM	
Debt/Worth	.7	.8	.9	1.5	.5	.8	1.1	.8	
	2.6	3.4	3.6	12.4	2.3	2.3	2.4	4.9	
	-16.0	-14.8	-11.0	-3.3	178.7	-92.4	11.7	NM	
% Profit Before Taxes/Tangible Net Worth	43.3	43.8	47.5	115.1	53.2	26.3	33.0		
	(239) 15.9	(253) 17.6	(241) 21.5	(76) 34.4	(106) 25.7	(27) 15.0	(20) 13.7		
	3.8	5.3	4.6	3.4	5.3	5.6	1.7		
% Profit Before Taxes/Total Assets	14.4	12.9	17.3	17.5	21.1	12.3	9.0	6.5	
	5.3	5.4	6.3	6.9	7.1	6.3	3.4	3.1	
	1.0	.7	.9	.0	1.2	1.3	.8	1.5	
Sales/Net Fixed Assets	10.3	11.0	14.1	17.7	17.6	11.0	10.4	2.8	
	4.5	4.6	4.9	4.8	5.6	3.5	4.7	1.4	
	1.6	1.5	1.8	1.3	2.0	1.7	3.0	1.0	
Sales/Total Assets	2.7	2.4	3.0	3.0	3.4	2.3	2.7	1.0	
	1.6	1.4	1.6	1.6	1.7	1.5	1.9	.6	
	.7	.7	.9	.8	1.1	1.1	.8	.3	
% Depr., Dep., Amort./Sales	2.0	1.7	1.8	2.0	1.6	2.2	2.0		
	(301) 3.3	(320) 3.4	(298) 3.0	(100) 4.1	(128) 2.7	(36) 3.2	(20) 2.7		
	6.0	6.2	5.2	8.1	4.9	4.6	3.2		
% Officers', Directors' Owners' Comp/Sales	6.9	6.2	5.6	5.7	5.6	4.4	6.1		
	(192) 9.5	(214) 9.6	(208) 8.7	(65) 9.6	(98) 8.7	(29) 7.1	(14) 8.7		
	14.0	14.7	14.0	15.7	13.9	12.6	14.0		
Net Sales ($)	1288233M	1767784M	2183384M	73423M	247777M	144153M	149937M	177908M	1390186M
Total Assets ($)	1332939M	1591710M	1979947M	81000M	224400M	127876M	195316M	434841M	916514M

Current Data Sorted by Assets | Comparative Historical Data

0-500M	500M-2MM	2-10MM	10-50MM	50-100MM	100-250MM	Type of Statement	4/1/06-3/31/07 ALL	4/1/07-3/31/08 ALL
		1	2	1	2	Unqualified	6	7
	4	2				Reviewed	4	7
	4	1				Compiled	10	9
3	4	4				Tax Returns	13	11
13		12	9			Other	18	20
		12 (4/1-9/30/10)	50 (10/1/10-3/31/11)					
16	12	20	11	1	2	**NUMBER OF STATEMENTS**	51	54
%	%	%	%	%	%	**ASSETS**	%	%
14.4	11.1	5.4	3.1			Cash & Equivalents	10.3	10.6
13.0	9.2	10.4	12.1			Trade Receivables (net)	14.4	13.4
10.3	13.3	16.1	7.8			Inventory	12.8	7.4
.0	.3	1.5	9.3			All Other Current	2.6	2.0
37.7	33.9	33.4	32.4			Total Current	40.1	33.4
40.8	42.3	32.8	16.7			Fixed Assets (net)	32.3	30.4
4.4	8.3	1.6	7.0			Intangibles (net)	4.1	3.3
17.1	15.4	32.2	44.0			All Other Non-Current	23.5	32.9
100.0	100.0	100.0	100.0			Total	100.0	100.0
						LIABILITIES		
7.6	2.8	3.4	2.3			Notes Payable-Short Term	8.4	3.4
6.6	4.6	1.0	1.3			Cur. Mat.-L.T.D.	4.7	1.6
2.4	5.3	1.7	1.6			Trade Payables	5.4	5.2
.0	.1	.0	.0			Income Taxes Payable	.2	.1
34.8	7.9	15.6	18.6			All Other Current	6.2	10.0
51.3	20.7	21.8	23.7			Total Current	24.9	20.2
42.8	13.4	28.1	12.4			Long-Term Debt	24.5	26.3
.0	3.1	.0	.0			Deferred Taxes	.1	.6
14.8	18.2	27.6	30.1			All Other Non-Current	18.6	25.3
-8.9	44.6	22.6	33.8			Net Worth	31.9	27.6
100.0	100.0	100.0	100.0			Total Liabilities & Net Worth	100.0	100.0
						INCOME DATA		
100.0	100.0	100.0	100.0			Net Sales	100.0	100.0
						Gross Profit		
92.8	89.6	96.0	89.5			Operating Expenses	87.9	90.7
7.2	10.4	4.0	10.5			Operating Profit	12.1	9.3
2.2	.9	-1.1	1.0			All Other Expenses (net)	2.3	2.1
5.0	9.4	5.0	9.5			Profit Before Taxes	9.8	7.2
						RATIOS		
3.1	5.7	4.6	3.9				8.3	6.0
1.0	3.9	2.7	2.4			Current	2.5	2.7
.3	1.2	1.3	1.6				1.2	1.5
1.8	4.4	2.5	2.3				5.7	4.9
.7	2.0	1.0	.5			Quick	1.6	1.6
.3	.3	.4	.3				.7	.8
0 UND	8 43.1	25 14.5	58 6.3				21 17.2	24 15.5
7 51.5	27 13.5	53 6.8	75 4.9			Sales/Receivables	58 6.3	58 6.3
42 8.7	38 9.6	163 2.2	164 2.2				118 3.1	127 2.9
						Cost of Sales/Inventory		
						Cost of Sales/Payables		
5.6	3.4	1.0	1.4				1.2	1.6
NM	4.4	2.8	2.3			Sales/Working Capital	4.3	4.5
-6.2	751.3	21.8	5.2				23.6	11.1
2.2	21.8	4.0					8.0	6.0
(11) 1.2	(11) 13.0	(17) 2.4				EBIT/Interest	(39) 3.4	(46) 2.7
-1.4	2.1	.5					1.7	1.2
						Net Profit + Depr., Dep., Amort./Cur. Mat. L/T/D		6.0
							(11)	4.9
								1.7
.7	.4	.5	.4				.4	.4
NM	.9	.9	.7			Fixed/Worth	.9	1.1
-.8	2.4	3.5	1.5				4.7	6.5
1.5	.5	.9	.3				.7	.5
NM	1.8	3.1	5.1			Debt/Worth	3.6	3.7
-2.4	4.9	6.6	13.0				14.2	26.7
	57.1	13.2	18.6			% Profit Before Taxes/Tangible Net Worth	51.2	27.9
	(11) 23.2	(17) 5.9	(10) 14.1				(44) 13.4	(46) 12.7
	11.7	.0	3.6				4.1	2.9
28.3	24.9	5.7	3.6			% Profit Before Taxes/Total Assets	8.5	7.0
1.8	9.4	1.6	3.0				4.4	3.4
-8.1	3.9	-.9	1.2				1.4	1.1
17.9	7.2	2.5	6.4			Sales/Net Fixed Assets	6.1	4.9
5.5	3.7	1.0	2.3				2.4	2.5
2.0	2.6	.8	1.5				1.1	1.0
3.3	1.8	.4	.6			Sales/Total Assets	1.3	1.3
1.9	1.6	.3	.3				.5	.4
.6	.4	.2	.2				.3	.3
3.5	2.3	3.8	2.3			% Depr., Dep., Amort./Sales	1.2	2.2
(12) 4.2	(11) 3.8	(19) 4.8	3.2				(39) 2.8	(47) 3.3
7.2	6.1	7.8	4.3				4.1	7.8
						% Officers', Directors' Owners' Comp/Sales	3.6	5.9
							(11) 7.6	(13) 13.4
							16.1	20.0
5208M	19953M	38076M	63540M	13996M	148186M	Net Sales ($)	680762M	616609M
3742M	16259M	111905M	173731M	52948M	357395M	Total Assets ($)	846561M	1179193M

M = $ thousand   MM = $ million
See Pages 9 through 22 for Explanation of Ratios and Data

Comparative Historical Data   Current Data Sorted by Sales

			Type of Statement						
7	7	6	Unqualified		1	1		2	2
10	6	2	Reviewed			2			
8	10	8	Compiled	5	3				
10	9	21	Tax Returns	16	3	2			
18	21	25	Other	3	15	3	2	2	
4/1/08-3/31/09 ALL	4/1/09-3/31/10 ALL	4/1/10-3/31/11 ALL		12 (4/1-9/30/10) 0-1MM	1-3MM	3-5MM	50 (10/1/10-3/31/11) 5-10MM	10-25MM	25MM & OVER
53	53	62	NUMBER OF STATEMENTS	24	22	8	2	4	2
%	%	%	ASSETS	%	%	%	%	%	%
9.5	9.4	8.2	Cash & Equivalents	12.4	5.1				
15.3	12.3	11.6	Trade Receivables (net)	10.8	11.0				
11.3	7.5	12.5	Inventory	12.0	13.2				
1.2	1.9	2.2	All Other Current	.0	1.1				
37.3	31.1	34.6	Total Current	35.2	30.5				
36.6	39.1	34.1	Fixed Assets (net)	37.7	32.1				
5.3	4.7	4.6	Intangibles (net)	3.4	6.9				
20.9	25.1	26.7	All Other Non-Current	23.7	30.6				
100.0	100.0	100.0	Total	100.0	100.0				
			LIABILITIES						
10.3	4.5	4.0	Notes Payable-Short Term	6.0	3.4				
2.2	2.6	4.0	Cur. Mat.-L.T.D.	4.5	3.2				
6.5	3.4	2.6	Trade Payables	2.1	2.9				
.0	.0	.0	Income Taxes Payable	.0	.1				
9.5	16.9	19.1	All Other Current	27.5	15.7				
28.5	27.3	29.7	Total Current	40.1	25.3				
23.7	21.3	25.0	Long-Term Debt	37.2	19.7				
.7	.7	.6	Deferred Taxes	1.5	.0				
18.1	20.0	22.2	All Other Non-Current	18.2	21.2				
29.1	30.7	22.6	Net Worth	3.1	33.8				
100.0	100.0	100.0	Total Liabilities & Net Worth	100.0	100.0				
			INCOME DATA						
100.0	100.0	100.0	Net Sales	100.0	100.0				
			Gross Profit						
95.0	90.3	92.2	Operating Expenses	96.7	87.5				
5.0	9.7	7.8	Operating Profit	3.3	12.5				
1.8	2.1	.7	All Other Expenses (net)	1.4	.5				
3.2	7.6	7.1	Profit Before Taxes	1.9	12.1				
			RATIOS						
6.0	4.9	4.7	Current	4.5	5.4				
2.4	2.4	2.7		1.8	2.7				
.9	.7	.7		.5	.9				
3.1	3.3	2.5	Quick	2.9	2.8				
1.4	1.4	1.0		.8	.7				
.6	.6	.3		.3	.2				
13 27.5	24 15.1	10 36.1	Sales/Receivables	0 UND	24 15.5				
55 6.7	59 6.2	40 9.2		19 19.0	46 8.0				
164 2.2	133 2.8	85 4.3		46 7.9	126 2.9				
			Cost of Sales/Inventory						
			Cost of Sales/Payables						
1.7	1.9	1.8	Sales/Working Capital	3.0	1.6				
6.3	6.6	4.5		9.8	3.9				
-76.0	-5.6	-14.3		-6.2	NM				
4.9	5.7	8.0	EBIT/Interest	2.2	12.7				
(43) 1.9	(44) 3.3	(50) 2.4		(19) 1.2	(18) 3.8				
.3	.9	.5		-1.4	2.1				
			Net Profit + Depr., Dep., Amort./Cur. Mat. L/T/D						
.6	.6	.5	Fixed/Worth	.5	.5				
1.0	1.2	1.0		1.5	1.1				
13.2	6.1	-4.1		-1.3	2.9				
.7	.4	.8	Debt/Worth	1.6	.8				
4.4	2.9	3.0		4.2	3.0				
23.4	11.1	13.8		-4.6	6.6				
24.3	29.7	24.4	% Profit Before Taxes/Tangible Net Worth	20.9	32.2				
(42) 4.4	(43) 13.1	(49) 11.0		(16) 3.4	(19) 15.0				
-2.2	1.1	3.8		-8.7	5.9				
5.8	11.4	7.7	% Profit Before Taxes/Total Assets	7.2	9.8				
1.9	3.7	3.2		1.1	5.6				
-.9	.4	.1		-7.0	1.7				
6.1	3.9	4.5	Sales/Net Fixed Assets	11.0	3.7				
2.4	1.8	2.5		3.6	2.3				
1.2	.8	1.0		.9	.9				
1.7	1.1	1.5	Sales/Total Assets	2.8	1.5				
.6	.5	.4		.6	.4				
.3	.3	.3		.2	.2				
2.5	3.3	3.2	% Depr., Dep., Amort./Sales	3.5	2.9				
(42) 4.6	(45) 4.7	(56) 4.1		(20) 4.5	(20) 4.1				
7.5	8.3	7.4		8.7	5.9				
2.4	4.0	3.3	% Officers', Directors' Owners' Comp/Sales						
(16) 5.6	(12) 11.1	(11) 7.5							
11.3	16.5	22.8							
381292M	305415M	288959M	Net Sales ($)	10431M	38500M	28336M	11093M	52413M	148186M
914359M	809576M	715980M	Total Assets ($)	30254M	117702M	68815M	38886M	102928M	357395M

M = $ thousand   MM = $ million
See Pages 9 through 22 for Explanation of Ratios and Data

Current Data Sorted by Assets   Comparative Historical Data

Type of Statement	0-500M	500M-2MM	2-10MM	10-50MM	50-100MM	100-250MM		2	3
Unqualified	4	1	5	2				2	3
Reviewed		1	3	1				2	4
Compiled	20	13	3					15	13
Tax Returns	4	6	3					34	18
Other			8					17	29
	9 (4/1-9/30/10)			62 (10/1/10-3/31/11)				4/1/06-3/31/07 ALL	4/1/07-3/31/08 ALL
NUMBER OF STATEMENTS	28	21	19	3				70	67

Columns 50-100MM and 100-250MM: DATA NOT AVAILABLE

	%	%	%	%	%	%		%	%
ASSETS									
Cash & Equivalents	10.8	7.8	8.1					12.8	14.4
Trade Receivables (net)	.1	3.9	6.2					1.6	4.0
Inventory	2.2	1.3	4.1					1.8	2.9
All Other Current	2.3	3.7	1.3					1.8	1.0
Total Current	15.4	16.7	19.8					18.0	22.3
Fixed Assets (net)	57.9	64.1	63.2					66.8	59.8
Intangibles (net)	13.3	12.6	8.7					8.5	10.2
All Other Non-Current	13.4	6.6	8.3					6.6	7.6
Total	100.0	100.0	100.0					100.0	100.0
LIABILITIES									
Notes Payable-Short Term	5.4	9.4	5.7					5.8	5.9
Cur. Mat.-L.T.D.	5.9	6.2	8.2					10.7	8.3
Trade Payables	4.7	3.9	4.0					4.3	3.4
Income Taxes Payable	.2	.0	.5					.0	.1
All Other Current	20.5	5.4	4.9					7.4	18.9
Total Current	36.8	24.9	23.3					28.2	36.6
Long-Term Debt	64.8	69.8	39.1					47.8	51.1
Deferred Taxes	.0	.4	.0					.0	.1
All Other Non-Current	7.0	5.3	7.5					8.7	8.3
Net Worth	-8.7	-.3	30.2					15.3	3.9
Total Liabilities & Net Worth	100.0	100.0	100.0					100.0	100.0
INCOME DATA									
Net Sales	100.0	100.0	100.0					100.0	100.0
Gross Profit									
Operating Expenses	98.1	92.4	92.9					91.1	92.0
Operating Profit	1.9	7.6	7.1					8.9	8.0
All Other Expenses (net)	3.2	4.2	4.9					4.6	4.3
Profit Before Taxes	-1.4	3.4	2.2					4.3	3.6
RATIOS									
Current	1.8	3.1	1.6					1.7	2.2
	.3	.5	.7					.5	.9
	.1	.3	.3					.1	.3
Quick	.9	.9	1.2					1.3	1.9
	.2	.4	.4					.5	.6
	.1	.2	.3					.1	.1
Sales/Receivables	0 UND	0 UND	0 UND					0 UND	0 UND
	0 UND	0 UND	6 56.2					0 UND	0 UND
	0 UND	2 239.5	29 12.7					1 321.5	4 94.1
Cost of Sales/Inventory									
Cost of Sales/Payables									
Sales/Working Capital	63.9	14.7	16.7					27.4	23.3
	-13.4	-13.6	-83.7					-28.5	-148.8
	-1.9	-5.7	-6.2					-5.9	-7.0
EBIT/Interest	8.6	2.4	7.9					7.3	5.2
	(21) .5	(15) .9	(16) 2.2					(58) 2.6	(60) 2.1
	-2.3	.2	1.1					.7	.7
Net Profit + Depr., Dep., Amort./Cur. Mat. L/T/D									
Fixed/Worth	1.1	2.0	1.0					1.2	1.4
	6.6	-41.8	2.4					3.0	6.1
	-1.1	-.7	-13.3					-15.8	-4.8
Debt/Worth	.5	1.2	.8					1.0	.9
	5.8	-54.8	1.9					3.9	6.5
	-2.7	-2.5	-17.5					-15.5	-6.7
% Profit Before Taxes/Tangible Net Worth	182.8		43.4					51.7	86.4
	(17) 50.0		(13) 10.7					(48) 19.0	(40) 19.2
	-5.3		.8					1.5	6.4
% Profit Before Taxes/Total Assets	18.4	7.6	9.9					17.9	22.5
	-2.0	.1	2.7					4.6	6.7
	-16.3	-2.9	-.8					-1.5	-1.9
Sales/Net Fixed Assets	11.4	3.5	4.4					5.5	7.3
	2.7	2.2	1.9					2.5	3.0
	1.2	.9	1.6					1.0	1.2
Sales/Total Assets	3.9	2.3	2.1					2.5	3.9
	1.7	1.2	1.5					1.5	1.7
	.8	.6	.5					.8	.8
% Depr., Dep., Amort./Sales	4.1	5.0	4.0					4.3	6.5
	(24) 14.6	(17) 12.7	(17) 13.4					(59) 10.4	(53) 10.5
	21.0	20.8	19.2					15.6	18.0
% Officers', Directors', Owners' Comp/Sales		2.5	1.0					2.6	2.7
		(13) 5.2	(13) 3.9					(31) 6.7	(34) 4.8
		10.4	6.5					10.3	8.3
Net Sales ($)	11846M	51372M	108191M	131798M				736431M	310700M
Total Assets ($)	5696M	25387M	68187M	81071M				446299M	201196M

© RMA 2011

M = $ thousand   MM = $ million

See Pages 9 through 22 for Explanation of Ratios and Data

Comparative Historical Data | Current Data Sorted by Sales

Type of Statement				0-1MM	1-3MM	3-5MM	5-10MM	10-25MM	25MM & OVER
Unqualified									
Reviewed					2	1	2	2	2
Compiled				3	2	1	2		
Tax Returns				24	8	3		1	
Other				8	3	2	3	2	
	4/1/08-3/31/09	4/1/09-3/31/10	4/1/10-3/31/11		9 (4/1-9/30/10)		62 (10/1/10-3/31/11)		
	ALL	ALL	ALL	0-1MM	1-3MM	3-5MM	5-10MM	10-25MM	25MM & OVER
NUMBER OF STATEMENTS	69	71	71	35	15	7	7	5	2

	%	%	%	%	%	%	%	%	%
ASSETS									
Cash & Equivalents	11.6	11.7	9.1	6.6	13.5				
Trade Receivables (net)	2.7	3.9	3.1	.3	2.8				
Inventory	3.3	1.7	2.5	.7	3.1				
All Other Current	2.4	3.9	2.4	1.9	2.4				
Total Current	19.9	21.2	17.0	9.5	21.8				
Fixed Assets (net)	62.6	61.0	61.4	65.8	58.6				
Intangibles (net)	7.5	8.0	11.4	13.1	15.4				
All Other Non-Current	10.0	9.7	10.2	11.6	4.2				
Total	100.0	100.0	100.0	100.0	100.0				
LIABILITIES									
Notes Payable-Short Term	7.5	6.7	6.4	5.7	9.2				
Cur. Mat.-L.T.D.	9.2	7.5	6.6	4.1	11.2				
Trade Payables	3.7	4.0	4.3	2.7	4.0				
Income Taxes Payable	.1	.2	.2	.2	.7				
All Other Current	11.4	6.1	11.4	16.1	7.7				
Total Current	32.0	24.5	29.0	28.8	32.8				
Long-Term Debt	45.5	60.2	57.5	74.6	44.5				
Deferred Taxes	.1	.2	.1	.0	.0				
All Other Non-Current	6.7	8.2	6.5	6.0	11.3				
Net Worth	15.8	6.9	6.8	-9.4	11.4				
Total Liabilties & Net Worth	100.0	100.0	100.0	100.0	100.0				
INCOME DATA									
Net Sales	100.0	100.0	100.0	100.0	100.0				
Gross Profit									
Operating Expenses	90.4	93.4	94.9	94.6	94.1				
Operating Profit	9.6	6.6	5.1	5.4	5.9				
All Other Expenses (net)	4.2	4.1	3.9	6.2	2.2				
Profit Before Taxes	5.3	2.5	1.3	-.8	3.7				
RATIOS									
Current	2.3	2.8	1.7	2.0	2.6				
	.6	.8	.4	.3	.4				
	.2	.2	.2	.1	.3				
Quick	1.8	1.5	1.0	1.0	1.2				
	.4	.4	.4	.3	.3				
	.1	.2	.2	.1	.2				
Sales/Receivables	0 UND	0 UND	0 UND	0 UND	0 UND				
	0 UND	0 UND	0 UND	0 UND	0 UND				
	2 157.5	7 51.8	2 217.3	0 UND	6 56.2				
Cost of Sales/Inventory									
Cost of Sales/Payables									
Sales/Working Capital	23.2	8.9	36.4	60.4	15.0				
	-22.6	-71.0	-15.0	-11.8	-11.2				
	-4.6	-6.7	-5.7	-1.9	-4.7				
EBIT/Interest	(55) 5.9	(53) 4.6	(54) 6.2	(23) 4.0	9.5				
	1.9	1.6	1.5	.5	1.8				
	1.0	.6	.0	-1.5	.2				
Net Profit + Depr., Dep., Amort./Cur. Mat. L/T/D									
Fixed/Worth	.9	.8	1.1	2.0	.8				
	10.4	6.3	5.5	UND	36.3				
	-4.1	-2.5	-2.0	-1.5	-.9				
Debt/Worth	.7	.7	.9	1.3	.4				
	11.0	8.5	5.5	UND	37.7				
	-6.0	-4.2	-3.2	-3.1	-2.4				
% Profit Before Taxes/Tangible Net Worth	(37) 49.8	(41) 53.9	(42) 58.3	(18) 76.4					
	17.4	19.6	12.0	5.1					
	2.5	-7.2	-1.3	-4.7					
% Profit Before Taxes/Total Assets	16.0	12.8	11.7	7.1	56.3				
	3.6	3.6	1.0	-1.1	4.1				
	-.8	-3.3	-6.7	-16.2	-4.2				
Sales/Net Fixed Assets	5.7	6.5	6.2	3.7	6.7				
	2.4	2.4	2.2	1.4	2.2				
	1.4	1.1	1.2	.7	1.2				
Sales/Total Assets	2.4	2.2	2.1	1.8	3.3				
	1.4	1.4	1.5	1.0	1.4				
	.8	.7	.8	.4	.9				
% Depr., Dep., Amort./Sales	(65) 4.6	(62) 4.5	(61) 4.7	(30) 6.0	(13) 5.0				
	9.1	8.0	13.4	17.8	7.4				
	16.6	15.8	19.3	22.1	14.7				
% Officers', Directors', Owners' Comp/Sales	(22) 3.1	(29) 2.6	(34) 2.0	(10) 3.2					
	6.5	4.4	4.6	5.5					
	9.3	7.7	6.9	11.3					
Net Sales ($)	482924M	572930M	303207M	11774M	24476M	28157M	50321M	80579M	107900M
Total Assets ($)	329551M	501316M	180341M	25015M	17583M	15963M	26265M	32680M	62835M

M = $ thousand   MM = $ million
See Pages 9 through 22 for Explanation of Ratios and Data

Current Data Sorted by Assets   Comparative Historical Data

						Type of Statement		
1	2	4	4			Unqualified	10	7
3	5	9	2			Reviewed	16	17
26	23	6	1			Compiled	30	22
10	22	10	3			Tax Returns	56	55
		18	6			Other	37	35
		13 (4/1-9/30/10)	**142 (10/1/10-3/31/11)**				**4/1/06- 3/31/07**	**4/1/07- 3/31/08**
0-500M	**500M-2MM**	**2-10MM**	**10-50MM**	**50-100MM**	**100-250MM**		**ALL**	**ALL**
40	52	47	16			**NUMBER OF STATEMENTS**	149	136
%	%	%	%	%	%	**ASSETS**	%	%
13.1	10.2	8.5	9.0	D	D	Cash & Equivalents	12.8	11.8
5.5	10.1	15.3	14.0	A	A	Trade Receivables (net)	11.0	10.2
1.8	1.3	4.9	5.1	T	T	Inventory	2.9	2.4
1.9	4.3	4.7	1.2	A	A	All Other Current	2.7	2.3
22.2	25.9	33.4	29.4			Total Current	29.4	26.7
50.1	57.0	45.9	55.6	N	N	Fixed Assets (net)	49.0	53.4
16.5	9.7	8.7	5.4	O	O	Intangibles (net)	9.9	10.2
11.2	7.4	12.0	9.7	T	T	All Other Non-Current	11.8	9.6
100.0	100.0	100.0	100.0			Total	100.0	100.0
				A	A	**LIABILITIES**		
8.7	11.1	4.8	3.0	V	V	Notes Payable-Short Term	5.4	5.8
11.3	6.9	7.2	4.2	A	A	Cur. Mat.-L.T.D.	7.8	9.4
4.4	5.6	8.7	7.8	I	I	Trade Payables	6.9	5.0
.1	.1	.1	.2	L	L	Income Taxes Payable	.2	.2
20.6	12.2	8.9	6.6	A	A	All Other Current	8.4	9.8
45.1	36.0	29.7	21.8	B	B	Total Current	28.8	30.1
49.1	43.3	39.2	36.5	L	L	Long-Term Debt	43.8	42.7
.0	.2	.0	.8	E	E	Deferred Taxes	.3	.2
17.5	11.3	3.7	6.5			All Other Non-Current	6.2	5.8
-11.8	9.3	27.4	34.4			Net Worth	20.9	21.2
100.0	100.0	100.0	100.0			Total Liabilities & Net Worth	100.0	100.0
						INCOME DATA		
100.0	100.0	100.0	100.0			Net Sales	100.0	100.0
						Gross Profit		
94.5	88.1	90.6	91.5			Operating Expenses	91.6	91.1
5.5	11.9	9.4	8.5			Operating Profit	8.4	8.9
1.2	5.4	3.0	2.4			All Other Expenses (net)	3.5	3.9
4.2	6.4	6.4	6.1			Profit Before Taxes	4.9	5.1
						RATIOS		
3.0	2.4	1.6	1.8				2.8	2.1
.6	.7	1.0	1.2			Current	1.2	1.0
.2	.3	.6	.9				.6	.4
2.9	1.9	1.4	1.6				2.1	1.7
.4	.6	.8	1.0			Quick	1.0	.7
.2	.2	.4	.7				.4	.2
0 UND	0 UND	10 35.8	13 27.5				0 UND	0 UND
0 UND	2 217.7	23 15.9	34 10.6			Sales/Receivables	8 45.9	6 60.8
8 46.7	30 12.3	33 10.9	46 7.9				26 14.3	29 12.4
						Cost of Sales/Inventory		
						Cost of Sales/Payables		
33.1	20.1	15.9	10.0				12.0	14.3
-29.8	-31.3	496.9	55.9			Sales/Working Capital	80.1	-301.3
-11.1	-6.3	-10.6	-58.2				-24.4	-12.6
8.2	4.8	10.8	6.8				9.0	6.4
(32) 1.8	(41) 2.5	(43) 4.1	2.8			EBIT/Interest	(122) 3.3	(111) 2.8
.5	1.3	2.1	2.0				1.2	.8
		21.4					4.0	3.5
		(10) 1.3				Net Profit + Depr., Dep., Amort./Cur. Mat. L/T/D	(13) 1.9	(20) 2.3
		1.1					1.3	1.2
1.0	2.0	.8	1.0				.7	.9
-7.0	NM	3.1	2.1			Fixed/Worth	2.1	3.2
-.6	-1.6	-5.0	11.6				-8.5	-9.1
1.1	3.5	.7	1.0				.9	1.0
-13.7	NM	3.3	2.0			Debt/Worth	2.8	4.7
-1.7	-4.1	-6.5	13.2				-13.0	-11.5
158.6	80.0	59.0	43.2				86.0	67.9
(18) 58.0	(26) 29.2	(31) 21.9	(14) 13.4			% Profit Before Taxes/Tangible Net Worth	(106) 31.0	(93) 22.4
13.5	8.4	7.5	2.8				12.7	6.6
46.0	16.7	14.7	13.0				23.1	16.8
8.4	5.8	7.6	5.2			% Profit Before Taxes/Total Assets	7.5	5.9
-1.5	2.1	2.4	2.3				1.1	-.4
17.8	10.7	9.8	5.4				13.7	9.8
8.7	4.4	5.1	3.1			Sales/Net Fixed Assets	5.7	5.1
4.6	1.1	1.9	1.2				2.2	2.0
6.7	3.3	2.9	1.9				3.7	3.6
3.6	1.8	1.9	1.5			Sales/Total Assets	2.4	2.2
2.0	.7	.9	.9				1.2	1.1
2.3	3.2	3.1	2.5				2.5	2.8
(29) 3.8	(39) 5.5	(44) 5.1	4.0			% Depr., Dep., Amort./Sales	(131) 4.6	(117) 4.3
6.6	12.5	9.2	8.0				7.3	8.2
5.3	3.1	1.5					3.8	2.9
(22) 9.2	(24) 5.2	(25) 3.3				% Officers', Directors' Owners' Comp/Sales	(79) 5.7	(63) 6.4
12.7	8.4	7.7					9.4	9.0
32154M	119181M	380825M	454749M			Net Sales ($)	1008293M	1659676M
7976M	53521M	205528M	301193M			Total Assets ($)	446613M	557969M

© RMA 2011

M = $ thousand   MM = $ million
See Pages 9 through 22 for Explanation of Ratios and Data

Comparative Historical Data | Current Data Sorted by Sales

Hist	Hist	Hist	Type of Statement	0-1MM	1-3MM	3-5MM	5-10MM	10-25MM	25MM & OVER
13	12	8	Unqualified				4	2	2
17	11	14	Reviewed	1		1	6	5	1
28	31	15	Compiled	2	3	4	2	3	1
63	58	62	Tax Returns	34	15	7	2	2	
37	39	56	Other	14	14	6	13	5	4
4/1/08-3/31/09 ALL	4/1/09-3/31/10 ALL	4/1/10-3/31/11 ALL		13 (4/1-9/30/10)			142 (10/1/10-3/31/11)		
158	151	155	**NUMBER OF STATEMENTS**	51	32	18	27	19	8
%	%	%	**ASSETS**	%	%	%	%	%	%
9.4	10.3	10.3	Cash & Equivalents	9.1	11.2	19.5	6.3	9.2	
10.1	10.6	10.9	Trade Receivables (net)	2.8	10.2	13.7	17.1	18.1	
3.1	3.1	2.9	Inventory	.9	2.8	.7	3.6	8.6	
2.0	2.4	3.5	All Other Current	1.8	4.4	8.1	1.7	5.1	
24.6	26.4	27.6	Total Current	14.6	28.5	42.0	28.8	40.9	
51.3	52.8	51.7	Fixed Assets (net)	59.9	54.4	42.2	47.0	46.3	
11.5	11.0	10.7	Intangibles (net)	15.8	9.2	5.9	11.1	3.9	
12.6	9.8	10.0	All Other Non-Current	9.7	7.8	9.9	13.1	9.0	
100.0	100.0	100.0	Total	100.0	100.0	100.0	100.0	100.0	
			LIABILITIES						
5.6	8.4	7.7	Notes Payable-Short Term	5.9	9.5	8.0	13.1	2.7	
8.1	8.8	7.8	Cur. Mat.-L.T.D.	7.7	10.4	9.3	6.1	6.2	
5.5	4.7	6.5	Trade Payables	3.0	6.3	8.3	6.5	12.6	
.2	.1	.1	Income Taxes Payable	.0	.1	.4	.1	.3	
9.8	15.2	12.8	All Other Current	16.0	9.4	20.6	10.9	6.4	
29.2	37.2	35.0	Total Current	32.6	35.7	46.6	36.7	28.1	
41.5	43.6	42.8	Long-Term Debt	58.0	40.8	34.9	30.3	36.2	
.2	.2	.2	Deferred Taxes	.0	.0	.6	.0	.7	
5.6	10.8	10.1	All Other Non-Current	16.1	12.7	1.5	7.7	2.4	
23.5	8.2	11.9	Net Worth	-6.7	10.8	16.4	25.4	32.5	
100.0	100.0	100.0	Total Liabilities & Net Worth	100.0	100.0	100.0	100.0	100.0	
			INCOME DATA						
100.0	100.0	100.0	Net Sales	100.0	100.0	100.0	100.0	100.0	
			Gross Profit						
92.5	92.6	90.9	Operating Expenses	86.1	92.5	93.7	92.2	95.2	
7.5	7.4	9.1	Operating Profit	13.9	7.5	6.3	7.8	4.8	
3.8	3.1	3.3	All Other Expenses (net)	7.3	2.1	.8	1.0	1.6	
3.7	4.3	5.8	Profit Before Taxes	6.6	5.4	5.6	6.8	3.2	
			RATIOS						
2.1	2.1	2.0	Current	2.7	3.1	2.6	1.6	2.2	
1.0	.9	.9		.6	.6	1.0	.8	1.3	
.4	.4	.3		.2	.2	.6	.5	.9	
1.6	1.8	1.8	Quick	1.9	2.1	2.6	1.2	1.8	
.8	.7	.7		.4	.6	.8	.7	1.0	
.3	.3	.3		.2	.2	.3	.3	.7	
0 UND	0 UND	0 UND	Sales/Receivables	0 UND	0 UND	11 34.4	10 35.8	10 35.9	
9 38.6	10 36.8	10 35.8		0 UND	5 75.3	20 17.9	23 15.9	27 13.7	
32 11.5	29 12.5	30 12.2		6 63.8	25 14.6	33 11.0	37 9.8	39 9.3	
			Cost of Sales/Inventory						
			Cost of Sales/Payables						
17.5	15.9	18.7	Sales/Working Capital	48.3	19.1	9.6	29.3	9.6	
-299.2	-151.7	-75.7		-26.5	-29.8	NM	-45.8	41.1	
-11.6	-11.9	-10.4		-7.4	-7.8	-9.5	-13.8	-76.0	
(132) 5.0 / 2.3 / .7	(129) 5.2 / 2.3 / .7	(132) 7.9 / 2.7 / 1.3	EBIT/Interest	(37) 4.5 / 1.8 / .6	(28) 7.6 / 2.6 / 1.1	(14) 7.0 / 3.3 / 1.7	(26) 32.6 / 3.4 / 2.1	8.4 / 3.1 / 2.2	
(20) 3.2 / 1.6 / 1.0	(12) 4.8 / 1.2 / .9	(16) 2.9 / 1.2 / .3	Net Profit + Depr., Dep., Amort./Cur. Mat. L/T/D						
.9	1.1	1.0	Fixed/Worth	5.1	.9	.7	.8	.8	
3.0	3.8	6.1		-19.1	-16.2	3.2	3.6	1.4	
-6.9	-1.6	-1.9		-.7	-1.6	-13.4	-1.4	5.5	
.9	1.0	1.0	Debt/Worth	6.6	1.0	.9	.7	.7	
4.4	5.2	10.5		-22.3	-24.7	8.2	3.3	1.5	
-9.0	-3.5	-4.6		-3.4	-4.1	-16.2	-3.9	16.3	
(101) 42.2 / 19.3 / 3.8	(88) 53.2 / 20.5 / -.1	(89) 64.7 / 25.9 / 8.4	% Profit Before Taxes/Tangible Net Worth	(24) 135.8 / 26.1 / 5.2	(15) 53.9 / 22.2 / 2.2	(12) 87.1 / 53.7 / 20.4	(16) 48.7 / 24.4 / 15.6	(16) 51.4 / 11.8 / 4.8	
12.3	17.0	18.4	% Profit Before Taxes/Total Assets	11.7	30.1	18.6	20.2	12.7	
4.1	4.3	6.8		3.8	6.1	12.1	12.6	6.8	
-1.1	-1.2	2.0		.0	.9	3.0	3.9	2.0	
7.8	9.5	11.0	Sales/Net Fixed Assets	10.5	14.4	16.6	11.0	12.1	
4.3	5.2	5.3		4.3	6.5	4.9	6.5	5.9	
2.0	2.2	2.3		.7	3.2	3.3	2.5	2.3	
3.1	3.8	3.6	Sales/Total Assets	3.3	5.3	3.1	3.8	3.8	
1.8	1.9	2.1		1.7	3.1	2.1	2.6	2.4	
1.0	1.1	1.1		.7	1.5	1.2	1.3	1.6	
(139) 3.1 / 5.0 / 8.0	(135) 2.8 / 4.8 / 8.6	(128) 2.9 / 4.8 / 9.5	% Depr., Dep., Amort./Sales	(38) 3.0 / 6.6 / 15.0	(25) 2.5 / 5.0 / 9.3	(15) 3.0 / 5.4 / 12.4	(23) 3.1 / 5.0 / 7.9	3.0 / 4.2 / 5.8	
(73) 3.6 / 5.6 / 9.9	(77) 2.5 / 4.7 / 9.4	(76) 3.0 / 5.4 / 8.9	% Officers', Directors' Owners' Comp/Sales	(21) 3.0 / 8.6 / 13.5	(18) 2.5 / 7.0 / 9.1	(11) 3.1 / 4.4 / 6.5	(16) 1.5 / 3.9 / 7.1		
845715M	979536M	986909M	Net Sales ($)	25970M	59876M	70347M	195031M	291008M	344677M
571698M	561249M	568218M	Total Assets ($)	30964M	42002M	42911M	107060M	149761M	195520M

M = $ thousand   MM = $ million
See Pages 9 through 22 for Explanation of Ratios and Data

Current Data Sorted by Assets | Comparative Historical Data

Type of Statement

0-500M	500M-2MM	2-10MM	10-50MM	50-100MM	100-250MM	Type of Statement	14 4/1/06-3/31/07 ALL	16 4/1/07-3/31/08 ALL
	1	2	7		1	Unqualified	14	16
		13	5	1		Reviewed	13	15
1	4	3	1			Compiled	11	14
1	4	4	3			Tax Returns	7	9
2	2	11	12	1	1	Other	25	26
		19 (4/1-9/30/10)		56 (10/1/10-3/31/11)			70 ALL	80 ALL
3	11	32	25	2	2	**NUMBER OF STATEMENTS**	70	80

0-500M	500M-2MM	2-10MM	10-50MM	50-100MM	100-250MM		4/1/06-3/31/07 ALL	4/1/07-3/31/08 ALL
%	%	%	%	%	%	**ASSETS**	%	%
	12.7	9.4	11.4			Cash & Equivalents	9.4	11.4
	21.7	23.2	17.7			Trade Receivables (net)	19.7	19.3
	6.4	10.9	11.6			Inventory	8.5	6.9
	1.4	2.4	3.3			All Other Current	2.0	1.9
	42.3	45.9	44.0			Total Current	39.6	39.4
	38.1	41.4	41.7			Fixed Assets (net)	46.9	48.2
	7.6	4.4	6.7			Intangibles (net)	5.6	5.0
	12.0	8.2	7.6			All Other Non-Current	8.0	7.4
	100.0	100.0	100.0			Total	100.0	100.0
						LIABILITIES		
	2.0	5.4	9.4			Notes Payable-Short Term	6.9	5.8
	4.5	5.4	2.9			Cur. Mat.-L.T.D.	5.4	6.1
	5.6	11.6	12.0			Trade Payables	10.0	8.6
	.0	.1	.3			Income Taxes Payable	.3	.2
	3.1	7.3	5.3			All Other Current	8.5	7.4
	15.2	29.8	29.9			Total Current	31.0	28.1
	38.6	25.8	24.6			Long-Term Debt	27.6	28.3
	1.2	.3	.2			Deferred Taxes	.4	.5
	3.6	5.0	7.4			All Other Non-Current	5.0	6.0
	41.4	39.0	37.9			Net Worth	36.1	37.1
	100.0	100.0	100.0			Total Liabilities & Net Worth	100.0	100.0
						INCOME DATA		
	100.0	100.0	100.0			Net Sales	100.0	100.0
						Gross Profit		
	86.7	95.2	94.1			Operating Expenses	94.9	93.2
	13.3	4.8	5.9			Operating Profit	5.1	6.8
	2.6	.9	1.9			All Other Expenses (net)	1.9	1.7
	10.7	3.9	4.0			Profit Before Taxes	3.2	5.0
						RATIOS		
	4.5	2.2	3.0			Current	2.0	2.6
	2.8	1.5	1.7				1.3	1.6
	1.5	1.0	1.1				.9	.9
	4.0	1.8	1.9			Quick	1.4	2.1
	1.8	1.0	1.1				1.0	1.1
	1.0	.5	.8				.6	.7
15 23.6	32 11.5	31 11.6				Sales/Receivables	28 13.0	29 12.5
34 10.7	37 9.8	35 10.6					36 10.2	34 10.8
39 9.4	43 8.5	41 9.0					42 8.8	39 9.4
						Cost of Sales/Inventory		
						Cost of Sales/Payables		
	5.9	6.8	4.7			Sales/Working Capital	9.1	7.6
	9.8	14.3	11.4				34.1	15.5
	16.7	204.7	65.3				-63.5	-68.1
		11.9	16.3			EBIT/Interest	10.8	12.1
	(31)	3.6	6.9				(64) 2.9	(73) 4.1
		.8	2.2				1.1	1.4
						Net Profit + Depr., Dep., Amort./Cur. Mat. L/T/D	7.2	8.4
							(17) 2.5	(22) 3.9
							1.3	1.4
	.3	.5	.4			Fixed/Worth	.7	.7
	.9	.8	1.0				1.3	1.4
	3.2	2.6	6.3				3.6	4.3
	.3	.6	.5			Debt/Worth	.6	.7
	1.6	1.5	2.1				1.7	1.5
	2.9	3.9	12.3				6.9	5.3
	80.4	38.2	37.1			% Profit Before Taxes/Tangible Net Worth	31.6	47.0
	(10) 12.9	(28) 14.5	(21) 14.8				(61) 13.1	(71) 16.4
	.5	1.9	5.2				.7	6.0
	28.7	17.3	11.1			% Profit Before Taxes/Total Assets	13.1	15.8
	8.0	4.7	7.0				5.3	7.5
	1.3	-.8	2.9				-.1	1.9
	23.2	9.3	6.6			Sales/Net Fixed Assets	8.3	7.7
	8.9	5.8	3.9				4.9	4.3
	2.7	3.0	2.5				2.5	2.4
	2.7	2.6	1.9			Sales/Total Assets	2.7	2.7
	2.0	2.0	1.7				2.1	2.0
	1.5	1.4	1.4				1.4	1.5
	1.7	3.0	2.4			% Depr., Dep., Amort./Sales	2.9	3.0
	2.7	(28) 4.3	(22) 5.2				(64) 4.6	(73) 4.2
	5.5	7.7	8.1				7.1	7.0
		2.6				% Officers', Directors' Owners' Comp/Sales	2.3	2.8
	(16)	4.7					(25) 4.9	(33) 4.9
		6.3					14.6	7.0
5271M	25272M	345437M	985247M	214225M	446162M	Net Sales ($)	1514358M	1994170M
1001M	11922M	164706M	602866M	119150M	292825M	Total Assets ($)	717948M	1027568M

M = $ thousand   MM = $ million
See Pages 9 through 22 for Explanation of Ratios and Data

Comparative Historical Data

Current Data Sorted by Sales

	4/1/08-3/31/09 ALL	4/1/09-3/31/10 ALL	4/1/10-3/31/11 ALL	Type of Statement	0-1MM	1-3MM	3-5MM	5-10MM	10-25MM	25MM & OVER
	13	11	11	Unqualified		1	1	1	4	4
	15	14	19	Reviewed			1	4	9	6
	11	8	9	Compiled		4		1	1	1
	10	9	9	Tax Returns	1	2	3	3		
	32	33	27	Other		2	3	5	6	12
		19 (4/1-9/30/10)						56 (10/1/10-3/31/11)		
	81	75	75	NUMBER OF STATEMENTS	1	9	8	14	20	23
	%	%	%	ASSETS	%	%	%	%	%	%
	8.9	11.5	11.8	Cash & Equivalents				10.1	12.3	9.8
	20.0	22.7	20.2	Trade Receivables (net)				21.2	21.3	21.1
	10.5	6.7	10.0	Inventory				6.6	14.3	12.1
	1.8	2.8	2.5	All Other Current				3.4	1.4	4.0
	41.2	43.7	44.5	Total Current				41.3	49.3	47.0
	47.5	45.3	41.5	Fixed Assets (net)				44.0	37.6	41.5
	5.2	6.0	6.1	Intangibles (net)				3.9	9.1	4.0
	6.1	5.0	7.9	All Other Non-Current				10.8	4.1	7.5
	100.0	100.0	100.0	Total				100.0	100.0	100.0
				LIABILITIES						
	10.5	8.0	5.9	Notes Payable-Short Term				6.3	3.8	9.9
	3.9	4.9	4.0	Cur. Mat.-L.T.D.				7.9	3.9	2.2
	8.8	8.6	10.1	Trade Payables				6.8	12.6	13.7
	.1	.2	.2	Income Taxes Payable				.0	.5	.1
	10.3	9.6	5.9	All Other Current				6.6	6.5	7.1
	33.5	31.2	26.1	Total Current				27.5	27.3	32.9
	27.0	22.4	26.1	Long-Term Debt				32.3	18.3	21.5
	.4	.4	.5	Deferred Taxes				.0	.7	.3
	3.8	4.9	5.4	All Other Non-Current				5.6	7.1	6.4
	35.3	41.1	41.9	Net Worth				34.5	46.6	38.9
	100.0	100.0	100.0	Total Liabilities & Net Worth				100.0	100.0	100.0
				INCOME DATA						
	100.0	100.0	100.0	Net Sales				100.0	100.0	100.0
				Gross Profit						
	92.7	94.7	93.5	Operating Expenses				94.3	95.2	94.3
	7.3	5.3	6.5	Operating Profit				5.7	4.8	5.7
	2.8	1.6	1.4	All Other Expenses (net)				.3	1.4	1.0
	4.5	3.8	5.1	Profit Before Taxes				5.4	3.4	4.6
				RATIOS						
	2.6	2.6	3.1					2.7	3.1	2.9
	1.4	1.9	1.7	Current				1.4	2.1	1.7
	.8	.9	1.1					.9	1.1	1.2
	1.8	2.2	2.2					2.3	2.1	1.8
	.9	1.2	1.2	Quick				.9	1.3	1.1
	.5	.5	.8					.4	.6	.8
27	13.4	30 / 12.0	31 / 12.0					32 / 11.3	32 / 11.5	31 / 11.9
35	10.6	36 / 10.2	35 / 10.4	Sales/Receivables				39 / 9.3	37 / 9.9	34 / 10.9
41	9.0	42 / 8.8	41 / 9.0					44 / 8.3	42 / 8.6	42 / 8.6
				Cost of Sales/Inventory						
				Cost of Sales/Payables						
	7.5	7.1	6.4					6.6	5.2	6.2
	22.2	12.2	10.9	Sales/Working Capital				13.2	8.5	9.5
	-25.6	-63.7	62.9					-45.3	73.2	56.0
	9.0	12.8	16.0					14.1	16.0	20.8
(66)	3.9	(63) 3.8	(71) 6.7	EBIT/Interest				3.2	(19) 6.9	7.5
	.7	1.1	1.8					.8	.8	3.0
	5.8	9.3	6.3							
(17)	3.4	(15) 5.0	(12) 2.6	Net Profit + Depr., Dep., Amort./Cur. Mat. L/T/D						
	1.8	1.0	.8							
	.7	.7	.5					.5	.5	.5
	1.4	1.2	.9	Fixed/Worth				.9	.8	.9
	4.6	2.6	2.9					2.9	4.8	2.9
	.6	.5	.5					.8	.4	.5
	2.1	1.9	1.5	Debt/Worth				1.8	1.2	1.2
	8.5	3.6	4.9					3.2	10.3	6.7
	55.5	38.5	41.0					57.5	29.0	38.8
(75)	18.3	(66) 21.4	(66) 14.7	% Profit Before Taxes/Tangible Net Worth		(12) 20.4	(17) 12.4			(21) 14.8
	3.5	5.2	4.7					9.0	.7	6.3
	13.7	15.5	16.7					24.9	12.1	11.7
	3.8	6.6	6.7	% Profit Before Taxes/Total Assets				4.2	6.1	7.0
	.3	.5	.7					-1.1	.0	3.5
	8.5	7.7	9.6					11.2	8.3	6.8
	4.3	4.3	5.5	Sales/Net Fixed Assets				3.4	6.3	3.6
	2.5	2.6	2.9					2.8	3.0	3.0
	2.6	2.6	2.5					2.5	2.5	2.1
	2.0	1.8	1.8	Sales/Total Assets				1.9	2.1	1.8
	1.3	1.4	1.5					1.4	1.2	1.6
	2.2	2.5	2.3					3.5	2.6	2.0
(71)	4.4	(67) 4.4	(66) 4.4	% Depr., Dep., Amort./Sales		(13) 6.1	(18) 4.1			(19) 4.4
	7.1	6.9	7.4					8.6	7.8	6.7
	1.8	1.7	2.9							
(29)	4.0	(24) 3.7	(30) 3.9	% Officers', Directors' Owners' Comp/Sales						
	6.8	9.1	5.9							
	1814865M	1507996M	2021614M	Net Sales ($)	113M	16104M	31666M	106494M	281442M	1585795M
	950594M	848317M	1192470M	Total Assets ($)	520M	7195M	25543M	65458M	189225M	904529M

M = $ thousand   MM = $ million
See Pages 9 through 22 for Explanation of Ratios and Data

Current Data Sorted by Assets							Comparative Historical Data	
						Type of Statement		
1	3	1	2			Unqualified	3	1
		1				Reviewed		1
1	1	3				Compiled	3	2
20	3	3	1			Tax Returns	10	15
14	11	7	3	1		Other	5	4
	14 (4/1-9/30/10)		62 (10/1/10-3/31/11)				**4/1/06-3/31/07**	**4/1/07-3/31/08**
0-500M	**500M-2MM**	**2-10MM**	**10-50MM**	**50-100MM**	**100-250MM**		**ALL**	**ALL**
36	18	15	6	1		**NUMBER OF STATEMENTS**	21	23
%	%	%	%	%	%	**ASSETS**	%	%
24.4	19.5	8.3			**DATA NOT AVAILABLE**	Cash & Equivalents	12.7	21.3
5.3	2.0	9.5				Trade Receivables (net)	6.5	3.3
4.4	1.1	3.9				Inventory	3.6	4.0
3.5	1.5	2.2				All Other Current	4.3	2.9
37.5	24.1	24.0				Total Current	27.1	31.5
43.5	57.4	63.0				Fixed Assets (net)	63.7	62.2
11.9	12.6	2.4				Intangibles (net)	2.9	3.4
7.0	5.9	10.6				All Other Non-Current	6.3	2.8
100.0	100.0	100.0				Total	100.0	100.0
						LIABILITIES		
3.3	23.3	5.1				Notes Payable-Short Term	5.6	12.6
2.9	2.3	3.1				Cur. Mat.-L.T.D.	1.7	1.6
1.9	1.6	1.5				Trade Payables	3.5	2.1
.0	.0	.0				Income Taxes Payable	.0	.0
18.8	7.7	3.2				All Other Current	65.0	28.7
26.9	34.9	12.8				Total Current	75.9	45.0
52.3	43.5	49.6				Long-Term Debt	34.3	35.3
.0	.0	.0				Deferred Taxes	.0	.0
13.1	5.0	3.4				All Other Non-Current	6.0	29.8
7.7	16.7	34.3				Net Worth	-16.1	-10.1
100.0	100.0	100.0				Total Liabilties & Net Worth	100.0	100.0
						INCOME DATA		
100.0	100.0	100.0				Net Sales	100.0	100.0
						Gross Profit		
90.4	81.2	85.8				Operating Expenses	85.8	85.9
9.6	18.8	14.2				Operating Profit	14.2	14.1
2.3	10.8	9.8				All Other Expenses (net)	3.9	5.5
7.3	7.9	4.4				Profit Before Taxes	10.3	8.5
						RATIOS		
5.7	4.6	6.5					6.5	4.5
1.8	1.3	1.6				Current	.9	1.0
.9	.3	.4					.2	.4
4.6	4.5	2.1					3.9	3.0
1.6	.7	.7				Quick	.6	.8
.3	.1	.3					.2	.3
0 UND	0 UND	0 UND					0 UND	0 UND
0 UND	0 UND	0 UND				Sales/Receivables	0 999.8	0 UND
4 83.9	3 134.8	23 16.1					15 25.2	1 411.3
						Cost of Sales/Inventory		
						Cost of Sales/Payables		
9.8	14.6	5.4					9.1	9.9
31.0	57.9	32.9				Sales/Working Capital	-105.6	UND
NM	-6.1	-12.5					-16.9	-16.5
14.8	7.2	5.1					6.2	13.8
(24) 2.3	(11) 1.6	(11) 1.6				EBIT/Interest	(16) 1.9	(15) 4.4
.8	.5	.9					1.0	1.5
						Net Profit + Depr., Dep., Amort./Cur. Mat. L/T/D		
.3	.8	.5					.6	1.8
2.7	2.9	2.8				Fixed/Worth	3.2	12.3
-1.3	-3.5	-70.0					-2.9	-1.8
.5	.8	.6					.5	1.4
5.3	6.2	1.9				Debt/Worth	2.7	13.0
-3.6	-3.4	-86.1					-4.9	-3.8
196.1	84.3	44.4					79.8	179.4
(21) 34.8	(11) 13.3	(11) 1.0				% Profit Before Taxes/Tangible Net Worth	(15) 10.1	(14) 57.7
5.6	2.6	-.9					-4.0	17.2
32.5	14.4	10.7					17.4	50.1
11.6	2.5	.7				% Profit Before Taxes/Total Assets	4.4	19.1
-.8	-2.6	-.3					-3.9	1.7
48.7	6.3	3.0					7.2	24.0
17.0	1.9	.9				Sales/Net Fixed Assets	1.3	4.7
4.2	.7	.6					.8	1.5
6.7	2.1	1.0					2.9	7.3
3.7	.9	.5				Sales/Total Assets	.9	2.6
1.8	.5	.4					.5	1.0
1.5	1.8	4.9					2.4	1.4
(22) 3.0	(14) 4.9	(13) 6.9				% Depr., Dep., Amort./Sales	(16) 5.2	(14) 3.5
5.1	11.8	12.0					8.9	7.6
5.3								2.7
(19) 10.3						% Officers', Directors' Owners' Comp/Sales		(12) 6.9
15.3								13.9
20842M	20066M	48467M	85395M	36004M		Net Sales ($)	473337M	30611M
6807M	17240M	62649M	119078M	64029M		Total Assets ($)	223522M	22673M

M = $ thousand MM = $ million

See Pages 9 through 22 for Explanation of Ratios and Data

	Comparative Historical Data			Type of Statement	Current Data Sorted by Sales					
				Unqualified	2	2	1	1	1	
	2	11	7	Reviewed				1		
	1	2	1	Compiled	3	2				
	3	5	5	Tax Returns	20	7				
	15	20	27	Other	20	12	1		1	2
	9	20	36			14 (4/1-9/30/10)		62 (10/1/10-3/31/11)		
	4/1/08-3/31/09 ALL	4/1/09-3/31/10 ALL	4/1/10-3/31/11 ALL		0-1MM	1-3MM	3-5MM	5-10MM	10-25MM	25MM & OVER
	30	58	76	NUMBER OF STATEMENTS	45	23	2	2	2	2
	%	%	%	**ASSETS**	%	%	%	%	%	%
	12.5	18.1	18.5	Cash & Equivalents	21.4	14.1				
	4.2	5.4	5.2	Trade Receivables (net)	4.0	2.4				
	5.6	3.3	3.1	Inventory	1.9	6.4				
	.8	1.2	2.5	All Other Current	1.9	4.3				
	23.1	28.0	29.3	Total Current	29.3	27.2				
	60.5	59.5	52.2	Fixed Assets (net)	51.6	54.1				
	4.6	2.0	9.3	Intangibles (net)	12.7	5.4				
	11.8	10.6	9.2	All Other Non-Current	6.4	13.4				
	100.0	100.0	100.0	Total	100.0	100.0				
				LIABILITIES						
	16.9	12.4	8.2	Notes Payable-Short Term	2.3	21.8				
	1.1	4.2	2.7	Cur. Mat.-L.T.D.	3.2	1.8				
	4.7	6.2	1.6	Trade Payables	1.3	1.9				
	.0	.9	.0	Income Taxes Payable	.0	.0				
	6.0	9.8	11.9	All Other Current	16.1	6.4				
	28.7	33.5	24.4	Total Current	22.9	32.0				
	36.2	32.3	47.8	Long-Term Debt	57.2	37.6				
	.0	.1	.0	Deferred Taxes	.0	.0				
	9.4	5.0	8.2	All Other Non-Current	7.0	12.9				
	25.7	29.1	19.6	Net Worth	12.9	17.5				
	100.0	100.0	100.0	Total Liabilities & Net Worth	100.0	100.0				
				INCOME DATA						
	100.0	100.0	100.0	Net Sales	100.0	100.0				
				Gross Profit						
	89.7	88.3	86.5	Operating Expenses	84.2	90.0				
	10.3	11.7	13.5	Operating Profit	15.8	10.0				
	5.5	7.6	6.5	All Other Expenses (net)	8.7	3.0				
	4.8	4.0	7.0	Profit Before Taxes	7.1	7.0				
				RATIOS						
	4.3	2.6	4.7		5.4	4.6				
	.9	1.3	1.6	Current	1.5	1.6				
	.4	.3	.7		.5	.7				
	3.1	2.2	4.0		4.6	2.1				
	.7	1.1	1.1	Quick	1.4	.7				
	.2	.3	.2		.1	.2				
	0 UND	0 UND	0 UND		0 UND	0 UND				
	0 UND	2 209.0	0 UND	Sales/Receivables	0 UND	0 UND				
	5 67.8	20 18.1	6 63.9		2 217.3	9 42.7				
				Cost of Sales/Inventory						
				Cost of Sales/Payables						
	11.8	7.2	7.8		13.4	7.3				
	-135.0	71.1	34.7	Sales/Working Capital	36.4	36.8				
	-14.2	-4.8	-19.7		-28.6	-12.5				
	25.4	9.6	7.2		7.1	7.0				
(24)	3.7	(39) 2.3	(51) 2.2	EBIT/Interest	(26) 2.2	(18) 2.1				
	.2	.8	.8		.9	.6				
				Net Profit + Depr., Dep., Amort./Cur. Mat. L/T/D						
	.6	.6	.5		.4	.9				
	2.5	1.5	2.3	Fixed/Worth	8.5	2.5				
	-32.4	7.9	-4.0		-2.2	51.9				
	.8	.5	.5		.5	.9				
	2.8	1.6	2.6	Debt/Worth	7.6	2.6				
	-43.4	21.7	-5.7		-3.9	-86.1				
	66.3	32.6	87.4	% Profit Before Taxes/Tangible	193.1	90.5				
(22)	23.2	(46) 10.3	(50) 15.1	Net Worth	(25) 22.4	(17) 27.7				
	-5.3	-1.0	.1		1.8	-.2				
	20.3	14.1	19.4	% Profit Before Taxes/Total	20.4	16.4				
	3.3	2.1	3.9	Assets	6.0	2.7				
	-4.8	-1.8	-.5		.1	-1.9				
	12.3	10.1	23.9		29.7	9.8				
	1.8	1.4	4.1	Sales/Net Fixed Assets	5.9	3.0				
	.8	.4	.8		.7	.9				
	4.6	3.2	3.6		5.3	3.1				
	1.3	.7	1.3	Sales/Total Assets	1.8	1.1				
	.5	.3	.5		.5	.7				
	2.3	1.7	2.0		2.0	1.8				
(27)	3.3	(50) 4.0	(54) 4.7	% Depr., Dep., Amort./Sales	(33) 4.5	(14) 4.8				
	7.5	8.6	7.9		10.1	5.7				
	4.8	3.1	4.5	% Officers', Directors'	5.0	3.0				
(13)	8.9	(19) 6.0	(32) 7.1	Owners' Comp/Sales	(20) 8.4	(10) 7.8				
	13.1	11.2	12.1		14.8	8.9				
	97112M	533298M	210774M	Net Sales ($)	22650M	41766M	7862M	14426M	23668M	100402M
	143290M	582657M	269803M	Total Assets ($)	49105M	51961M	13630M	22611M	26472M	106024M

© RMA 2011

M = $ thousand   MM = $ million
See Pages 9 through 22 for Explanation of Ratios and Data

Current Data Sorted by Assets

Comparative Historical Data

						Type of Statement		
	1	2	2	1		Unqualified	1	3
	2	2				Reviewed	5	5
	1	1				Compiled	3	1
5	1	3	1			Tax Returns	8	7
6	8	8	2		1	Other	14	13
	13 (4/1-9/30/10)		34 (10/1/10-3/31/11)				4/1/06-3/31/07	4/1/07-3/31/08
0-500M	500M-2MM	2-10MM	10-50MM	50-100MM	100-250MM		ALL	ALL
11	13	16	5	1	1	NUMBER OF STATEMENTS	31	29
%	%	%	%	%	%	ASSETS	%	%
29.3	10.4	9.7				Cash & Equivalents	14.9	14.1
12.2	11.3	16.2				Trade Receivables (net)	18.7	21.5
9.7	4.3	5.6				Inventory	6.5	13.6
.2	9.8	5.3				All Other Current	3.6	2.0
51.4	35.8	36.8				Total Current	43.7	51.1
36.2	56.7	45.1				Fixed Assets (net)	44.1	39.7
1.3	1.1	10.4				Intangibles (net)	5.1	4.4
12.0	6.3	7.7				All Other Non-Current	7.0	4.7
100.0	100.0	100.0				Total	100.0	100.0
						LIABILITIES		
6.6	4.8	4.7				Notes Payable-Short Term	15.3	5.9
12.6	7.0	5.1				Cur. Mat.-L.T.D.	6.1	7.8
13.7	6.0	7.9				Trade Payables	13.2	10.9
.0	.0	.0				Income Taxes Payable	.2	.2
44.3	12.1	12.0				All Other Current	14.3	12.7
77.1	29.9	29.7				Total Current	49.2	37.4
20.5	29.5	24.9				Long-Term Debt	28.8	27.6
.0	.7	.0				Deferred Taxes	.9	.4
15.8	5.2	5.8				All Other Non-Current	18.0	4.4
-13.4	34.6	39.6				Net Worth	3.0	30.2
100.0	100.0	100.0				Total Liabilities & Net Worth	100.0	100.0
						INCOME DATA		
100.0	100.0	100.0				Net Sales	100.0	100.0
						Gross Profit		
97.8	79.7	93.5				Operating Expenses	96.6	92.2
2.2	20.3	6.5				Operating Profit	3.4	7.8
.7	11.8	2.1				All Other Expenses (net)	2.8	2.9
1.5	8.6	4.4				Profit Before Taxes	.7	4.8
						RATIOS		
9.0	1.5	4.7					1.9	2.6
1.2	.9	1.2				Current	1.1	1.5
.2	.4	.5					.7	.8
9.0	1.0	3.4					1.8	1.7
1.0	.6	1.1				Quick	.9	.9
.2	.4	.3					.5	.4
0 UND	0 UND	5 80.2					10 35.6	13 29.1
0 UND	15 23.8	23 15.8				Sales/Receivables	23 15.8	32 11.5
6 61.4	27 13.5	50 7.2					46 8.0	44 8.4
						Cost of Sales/Inventory		
						Cost of Sales/Payables		
19.1	11.6	4.6					9.1	7.1
192.7	-91.2	49.7				Sales/Working Capital	74.8	27.4
-8.3	-4.7	-8.9					-13.7	-65.9
		9.7					5.0	21.1
	(14) 2.3					EBIT/Interest	(26) 2.0	(26) 2.9
		.0					-.4	.3
						Net Profit + Depr., Dep., Amort./Cur. Mat. L/T/D		
.2	.7	.6					.6	.4
1.0	2.4	1.6				Fixed/Worth	1.8	1.2
-.6	5.1	3.7					12.3	3.7
.2	1.1	.8					1.1	.9
2.5	2.8	2.2				Debt/Worth	2.7	1.9
-1.9	6.2	9.7					28.9	6.0
	19.3	36.5					53.7	75.2
	(12) 9.0	(13) 27.3				% Profit Before Taxes/Tangible Net Worth	(24) 19.6	(25) 23.4
	4.5	-2.0					2.4	6.2
13.0	6.8	15.1					11.8	26.9
4.7	2.2	7.1				% Profit Before Taxes/Total Assets	5.3	5.8
-.9	1.3	-2.7					-5.3	-1.0
UND	16.2	14.5					10.8	18.7
17.1	3.3	4.5				Sales/Net Fixed Assets	4.3	7.8
8.6	.2	1.6					3.7	3.6
8.6	3.0	2.9					3.3	4.2
6.3	2.2	1.5				Sales/Total Assets	2.3	2.7
5.3	.2	1.0					1.6	1.8
	2.8	2.3					3.4	2.2
	(11) 4.7	(13) 3.3				% Depr., Dep., Amort./Sales	(29) 4.6	(25) 3.9
	15.8	7.8					7.1	6.9
							5.1	5.3
						% Officers', Directors' Owners' Comp/Sales	(16) 7.3	(13) 7.0
							10.6	10.4
14741M	29006M	176175M	201792M	71979M	418327M	Net Sales ($)	164370M	563776M
2210M	16769M	85080M	142709M	56658M	164328M	Total Assets ($)	71480M	146564M

© RMA 2011

M = $ thousand   MM = $ million
See Pages 9 through 22 for Explanation of Ratios and Data

Comparative Historical Data / Current Data Sorted by Sales

	4/1/08-3/31/09 ALL	4/1/09-3/31/10 ALL	4/1/10-3/31/11 ALL	Type of Statement	0-1MM	1-3MM	3-5MM	5-10MM	10-25MM	25MM & OVER
	4	5	6	Unqualified			1		2	3
	3	2	4	Reviewed		2			2	
	5	3	2	Compiled				1		
	8	9	10	Tax Returns	3	3	3		1	1
	16	15	25	Other	9	6	2	1	4	3
						13 (4/1-9/30/10)		34 (10/1/10-3/31/11)		
	36	34	47	NUMBER OF STATEMENTS	12	9	9	2	8	7
	%	%	%	**ASSETS**	%	%	%	%	%	%
	10.2	13.6	14.9	Cash & Equivalents	17.6					
	21.6	14.8	13.6	Trade Receivables (net)	7.7					
	9.6	8.2	5.9	Inventory	4.4					
	1.8	2.7	5.9	All Other Current	1.1					
	43.3	39.2	40.2	Total Current	30.8					
	35.0	45.4	46.3	Fixed Assets (net)	63.1					
	10.9	7.7	5.4	Intangibles (net)	.8					
	10.9	7.7	8.2	All Other Non-Current	6.0					
	100.0	100.0	100.0	Total	100.0					
				LIABILITIES						
	15.4	6.5	4.9	Notes Payable-Short Term	3.8					
	11.3	7.7	7.9	Cur. Mat.-L.T.D.	12.2					
	10.9	8.3	8.9	Trade Payables	4.2					
	.0	.1	.0	Income Taxes Payable	.0					
	20.0	14.2	19.3	All Other Current	14.0					
	57.6	36.8	41.1	Total Current	34.3					
	21.6	31.4	24.7	Long-Term Debt	51.5					
	.2	.3	.2	Deferred Taxes	.0					
	4.4	2.1	7.8	All Other Non-Current	14.5					
	16.2	29.3	26.3	Net Worth	-.3					
	100.0	100.0	100.0	Total Liabilties & Net Worth	100.0					
				INCOME DATA						
	100.0	100.0	100.0	Net Sales	100.0					
				Gross Profit						
	94.8	91.5	90.5	Operating Expenses	78.5					
	5.2	8.5	9.5	Operating Profit	21.5					
	2.9	3.7	4.1	All Other Expenses (net)	14.7					
	2.3	4.8	5.4	Profit Before Taxes	6.8					
				RATIOS						
	1.8	1.9	3.6	Current	7.5					
	1.1	1.1	1.0		.6					
	.5	.5	.4		.1					
	1.2	1.3	2.1	Quick	7.2					
	.8	.9	.9		.4					
	.3	.4	.3		.1					
11	32.1	0 UND	0 UND	Sales/Receivables	0 UND					
28	13.0	21 17.4	15 24.4		0 UND					
51	7.1	34 10.8	32 11.3		0 UND					
				Cost of Sales/Inventory						
				Cost of Sales/Payables						
	9.1	10.3	8.0	Sales/Working Capital	7.7					
	58.6	54.5	192.7		-49.8					
	-10.2	-12.2	-8.3		-4.3					
	6.0	2.3	7.1	EBIT/Interest						
	(35) 1.8	(25) .7	(37) 3.6							
	-.3	-2.2	1.0							
				Net Profit + Depr., Dep., Amort./Cur. Mat. L/T/D						
	.3	.5	.5	Fixed/Worth	1.6					
	1.4	1.4	1.9		4.7					
	-39.6	3.7	11.2		UND					
	1.0	1.0	.7	Debt/Worth	1.0					
	2.6	1.9	2.4		3.8					
	-9.8	5.3	11.9		UND					
	44.1	15.3	28.8	% Profit Before Taxes/Tangible Net Worth						
	(25) 12.0	(28) 6.0	(37) 13.7							
	-8.4	-13.1	3.5							
	10.2	9.7	14.7	% Profit Before Taxes/Total Assets	6.9					
	2.5	1.5	6.6		1.8					
	-3.8	-7.6	.4		-3.2					
	55.0	16.6	16.2	Sales/Net Fixed Assets	21.3					
	9.1	7.9	7.6		1.4					
	3.9	2.5	2.2		.2					
	4.1	3.6	4.4	Sales/Total Assets	5.6					
	2.4	2.2	2.3		.8					
	1.0	1.4	1.1		.1					
	1.3	1.2	2.6	% Depr., Dep., Amort./Sales						
	(24) 2.9	(28) 3.7	(34) 3.7							
	7.4	7.2	7.2							
	2.1	4.2	5.1	% Officers', Directors' Owners' Comp/Sales						
	(15) 4.7	(12) 5.5	(14) 8.0							
	9.5	7.7	11.9							
	285416M	328013M	912020M	Net Sales ($)	6038M	16201M	32659M	14645M	119873M	722604M
	173421M	166665M	467754M	Total Assets ($)	15288M	7679M	17562M	9909M	96130M	321186M

© RMA 2011

M = $ thousand   MM = $ million
See Pages 9 through 22 for Explanation of Ratios and Data

Current Data Sorted by Assets   Comparative Historical Data

	0-500M	500M-2MM	2-10MM	10-50MM	50-100MM	100-250MM		4/1/06-3/31/07 ALL	4/1/07-3/31/08 ALL
Type of Statement									
Unqualified	1		1	9	4	2		8	9
Reviewed		4	3	2				3	3
Compiled		2	2	1				4	7
Tax Returns	6	5	5	2				8	9
Other	2	5	8	10		2		22	27
		10 (4/1-9/30/10)		66 (10/1/10-3/31/11)					
NUMBER OF STATEMENTS	9	16	19	24	4	4		45	55
	%	%	%	%	%	%		%	%
ASSETS									
Cash & Equivalents		27.6	5.8	11.4				19.1	11.9
Trade Receivables (net)		11.1	15.3	4.0				14.6	12.8
Inventory		3.4	.0	.0				.1	.0
All Other Current		.9	2.9	3.7				2.1	4.2
Total Current		43.0	24.0	19.1				35.9	29.0
Fixed Assets (net)		36.9	65.8	68.4				48.2	47.9
Intangibles (net)		8.4	5.7	2.2				7.1	6.1
All Other Non-Current		11.7	4.5	10.3				8.7	17.0
Total		100.0	100.0	100.0				100.0	100.0
LIABILITIES									
Notes Payable-Short Term		5.0	3.3	1.6				4.3	4.7
Cur. Mat.-L.T.D.		9.1	6.6	8.6				2.3	3.5
Trade Payables		5.8	5.2	3.0				7.3	9.9
Income Taxes Payable		.1	.0	.1				.0	.0
All Other-Current		8.4	8.5	8.2				14.1	12.4
Total Current		28.4	23.7	21.4				28.0	30.5
Long-Term Debt		34.9	40.3	55.3				38.1	43.8
Deferred Taxes		.0	.0	.1				.4	.2
All Other Non-Current		9.5	9.9	1.4				4.8	10.2
Net Worth		27.1	26.0	21.8				28.7	15.3
Total Liabilities & Net Worth		100.0	100.0	100.0				100.0	100.0
INCOME DATA									
Net Sales		100.0	100.0	100.0				100.0	100.0
Gross Profit									
Operating Expenses		82.8	84.2	78.2				77.9	81.5
Operating Profit		17.2	15.8	21.8				22.1	18.5
All Other Expenses (net)		5.3	9.5	16.4				7.8	7.5
Profit Before Taxes		11.9	6.3	5.4				14.3	11.0
RATIOS									
		4.1	3.1	2.6				3.1	1.9
Current		1.5	1.3	1.1				1.2	1.0
		.6	.8	.6				.6	.6
		4.1	2.6	1.6				2.5	1.7
Quick		1.3	1.0	1.0				1.1 (54)	.9
		.6	.7	.3				.5	.6
	0 UND	0 UND	0 UND				0 731.4	0 999.8
Sales/Receivables	0 UND	12 30.9	3 143.9				8 46.5	4 100.9
	26 13.8	44 8.4	11 34.2				27 13.5	20 18.2
Cost of Sales/Inventory									
Cost of Sales/Payables									
		6.3	9.5	5.5				7.8	14.0
Sales/Working Capital		19.7	25.8	38.7				50.9	-371.7
		-27.9	-27.4	-9.7				-10.5	-8.6
		18.1	7.4	9.8				14.5	15.8
EBIT/Interest		(12) 8.5	(15) 3.0	(17) 3.0				(34) 5.1	(39) 5.6
		5.1	1.0	1.6				1.3	2.0
Net Profit + Depr., Dep., Amort./Cur. Mat. L/T/D									
		.2	1.1	1.4				.4	1.0
Fixed/Worth		.9	3.4	2.8				1.7	2.8
		NM	9.1	19.8				-18.0	-2.6
		.9	1.4	1.5				.9	1.0
Debt/Worth		2.4	5.0	4.0				3.1	6.9
		NM	14.8	23.9				-22.4	-6.4
		55.8	80.2	47.6				69.7	146.1
% Profit Before Taxes/Tangible Net Worth		(12) 47.9	(16) 28.0	(19) 20.6				(28) 26.8	(36) 42.0
		16.7	.1	-.1				4.5	10.9
		26.1	11.3	10.0				20.4	26.8
% Profit Before Taxes/Total Assets		9.4	3.2	3.1				6.0	10.0
		5.7	.0	-.9				1.5	1.3
		49.4	6.3	1.5				31.3	28.3
Sales/Net Fixed Assets		16.3	1.2	.4				5.5	6.6
		2.0	.3	.2				.4	.5
		4.4	3.0	1.0				4.0	3.6
Sales/Total Assets		2.9	.8	.3				.9	1.2
		.4	.2	.2				.3	.3
		.6	1.7	4.3				.5	1.5
% Depr., Dep., Amort./Sales		(12) 3.4	(18) 5.8	(22) 11.8				(36) 2.5	(42) 3.5
		7.6	10.2	22.0				6.8	9.2
								2.2	2.0
% Officers', Directors' Owners' Comp/Sales								(14) 6.4	(12) 8.7
								14.4	26.3
Net Sales ($)	7314M	42062M	145701M	513432M	176773M	560872M		1294744M	1762276M
Total Assets ($)	1855M	16421M	96480M	597761M	292128M	662373M		835016M	1197352M

© RMA 2011

M = $ thousand   MM = $ million
See Pages 9 through 22 for Explanation of Ratios and Data

Comparative Historical Data | Current Data Sorted by Sales

			Type of Statement						
15	20	17	Unqualified	1	2	2	3	4	5
5	11	9	Reviewed		2	2	1	3	1
2	9	5	Compiled	1		3		1	
15	14	18	Tax Returns	6	7		3	1	1
27	33	27	Other	9		2	4	4	4
4/1/08-3/31/09 ALL	4/1/09-3/31/10 ALL	4/1/10-3/31/11 ALL		0-1MM	10 (4/1-9/30/10) 1-3MM	3-5MM	66 (10/1/10-3/31/11) 5-10MM	10-25MM	25MM & OVER
64	87	76	**NUMBER OF STATEMENTS**	17	15	9	11	13	11
%	%	%	**ASSETS**	%	%	%	%	%	%
15.6	13.3	14.7	Cash & Equivalents	16.1	14.1		11.3	11.1	17.8
15.5	12.7	9.9	Trade Receivables (net)	.9	8.9		10.6	18.0	12.0
.1	1.7	.7	Inventory	.0	.0		.0	.0	.0
3.3	4.1	2.9	All Other Current	1.5	1.2		3.2	8.3	1.5
34.4	31.9	28.2	Total Current	18.4	24.2		25.1	37.3	31.3
40.0	51.7	53.5	Fixed Assets (net)	64.9	58.7		57.1	49.6	35.3
7.8	7.8	7.5	Intangibles (net)	1.8	10.1		3.9	6.4	22.7
17.7	8.6	10.8	All Other Non-Current	15.0	7.0		13.9	6.7	10.8
100.0	100.0	100.0	Total	100.0	100.0		100.0	100.0	100.0
			LIABILITIES						
6.5	8.4	4.5	Notes Payable-Short Term	2.7	4.4		8.3	6.6	2.3
5.7	6.9	7.4	Cur. Mat.-L.T.D.	17.8	3.6		5.9	3.4	4.1
9.4	6.8	4.1	Trade Payables	.6	1.8		3.1	6.9	6.8
.1	.1	.0	Income Taxes Payable	.0	.0		.1	.0	.2
17.1	15.2	10.6	All Other Current	9.2	13.2		8.6	10.1	17.8
38.8	37.4	26.7	Total Current	30.4	23.0		26.0	27.0	31.2
43.8	43.5	46.0	Long-Term Debt	52.1	58.9		43.9	40.7	36.7
.6	.3	.3	Deferred Taxes	.0	.0		.0	.1	2.0
5.6	5.5	6.1	All Other Non-Current	4.7	11.8		2.7	2.8	7.6
11.2	13.3	20.9	Net Worth	12.8	6.4		27.4	29.4	22.5
100.0	100.0	100.0	Total Liabilities & Net Worth	100.0	100.0		100.0	100.0	100.0
			INCOME DATA						
100.0	100.0	100.0	Net Sales	100.0	100.0		100.0	100.0	100.0
			Gross Profit						
84.8	82.4	83.0	Operating Expenses	68.0	90.9		83.2	80.1	93.8
15.2	17.6	17.0	Operating Profit	32.0	9.1		16.8	19.9	6.2
5.0	10.1	10.3	All Other Expenses (net)	12.1	12.8		5.5	12.3	3.5
10.2	7.5	6.7	Profit Before Taxes	19.9	-3.7		11.3	7.6	2.7
			RATIOS						
2.0	2.0	2.8		2.1	4.2		4.0	3.8	1.2
1.0	.9	1.1	Current	.8	1.0		1.3	1.3	1.0
.6	.5	.6		.1	.5		.6	.9	.5
2.0	1.6	2.0		2.1	3.9		1.6	2.0	1.1
.9	.7	1.0	Quick	.8	1.0		.7	.7	1.0
.5	.4	.4		.1	.5		.3	.5	.5
0 999.8	0 UND	0 UND		0 UND	0 UND		0 759.4	2 200.9	4 89.4
12 29.2	8 45.7	5 68.9	Sales/Receivables	0 UND	0 UND		9 41.5	25 14.6	28 13.0
30 12.4	37 10.0	29 12.5		7 49.4	22 16.7		42 8.7	39 9.3	35 10.3
			Cost of Sales/Inventory						
			Cost of Sales/Payables						
11.7	12.5	7.5		7.8	9.9		6.1	3.5	38.7
NM	-166.7	41.9	Sales/Working Capital	-38.1	144.1		22.6	18.4	644.6
-15.5	-7.8	-10.1		-4.9	-20.9		-4.2	NM	-8.0
7.3	10.2	8.8						19.0	
(48) 3.6	(58) 3.2	(54) 3.4	EBIT/Interest				(12)	5.3	
1.3	1.4	1.5						1.8	
	17.1		Net Profit + Depr., Dep.,						
	(10) 3.5		Amort./Cur. Mat. L/T/D						
	.1								
.8	1.3	.8		.4	.3		1.1	.8	1.1
3.0	4.0	3.2	Fixed/Worth	4.1	3.7		2.7	2.2	6.1
-18.5	-5.6	-44.8		NM	-1.8		26.3	NM	-.1
2.0	1.7	1.4		1.1	1.8		1.6	.5	4.0
7.9	5.6	5.0	Debt/Worth	5.3	6.2		2.4	2.7	15.2
-16.2	-9.2	-34.4		NM	-3.0		73.0	NM	-1.8
118.2	104.7	51.7	% Profit Before Taxes/Tangible	73.6				45.7	
(44) 37.2	(61) 31.1	(55) 25.9	Net Worth	(13) 25.9			(10)	18.6	
7.5	1.3	1.4		-1.2				9.4	
18.8	13.4	12.7	% Profit Before Taxes/Total	18.7	6.6		19.3	14.5	10.2
6.0	4.1	4.1	Assets	6.0	.8		7.4	4.1	4.4
.0	-.2	.1		-1.1	-.5		1.2	2.4	.3
26.8	25.9	19.7		23.3	30.8		8.3	11.1	25.3
10.2	1.6	1.4	Sales/Net Fixed Assets	.4	1.2		.4	1.6	15.5
.8	.3	.3		.2	.3		.3	.6	1.2
5.5	3.7	3.4		1.6	4.3		2.1	3.5	3.2
1.6	1.2	.8	Sales/Total Assets	.3	1.1		.4	.9	1.5
.4	.2	.2		.2	.3		.2	.4	1.0
.8	.9	1.9		1.4	4.7		4.2	1.3	
(47) 3.3	(74) 5.8	(65) 6.2	% Depr., Dep., Amort./Sales	(14) 6.4	(12) 8.0		6.6	(12) 5.3	
8.6	13.0	14.4		18.1	18.8		17.8	11.9	
1.4	1.7	1.4	% Officers', Directors'						
(15) 2.7	(21) 4.2	(15) 3.4	Owners' Comp/Sales						
12.6	13.0	12.3							
2637924M	2325808M	1446154M	Net Sales ($)	9745M	28846M	30797M	76129M	206702M	1093935M
1736064M	1955832M	1667018M	Total Assets ($)	46449M	78230M	108479M	209218M	333635M	891007M

© RMA 2011   M = $ thousand   MM = $ million
See Pages 9 through 22 for Explanation of Ratios and Data

Current Data Sorted by Assets | Comparative Historical Data

0-500M	500M-2MM	2-10MM	10-50MM	50-100MM	100-250MM	Type of Statement	4/1/06-3/31/07 ALL	4/1/07-3/31/08 ALL
	3	6	9	3	7	Unqualified	25	30
1	5	11	4			Reviewed	20	18
21	19	16	1	1		Compiled	48	30
122	69	17	1		1	Tax Returns	146	173
48	51	40	11	4	2	Other	110	123
48 (4/1-9/30/10)		425 (10/1/10-3/31/11)						
192	147	90	26	8	10	**NUMBER OF STATEMENTS**	349	374
%	%	%	%	%	%	**ASSETS**	%	%
24.5	14.9	14.8	15.2		34.1	Cash & Equivalents	20.0	18.6
12.0	15.5	17.0	12.1		6.2	Trade Receivables (net)	17.1	16.8
4.4	4.3	11.1	8.4		3.7	Inventory	5.1	6.5
2.6	3.2	3.9	3.1		15.1	All Other Current	5.2	4.4
43.4	37.9	46.8	38.8		59.1	Total Current	47.4	46.3
37.0	42.6	36.3	44.6		23.3	Fixed Assets (net)	38.7	38.5
8.8	8.2	4.8	7.2		13.1	Intangibles (net)	5.7	6.7
10.8	11.3	12.1	9.4		4.5	All Other Non-Current	8.3	8.4
100.0	100.0	100.0	100.0		100.0	Total	100.0	100.0
						LIABILITIES		
11.3	8.6	6.5	1.6		.7	Notes Payable-Short Term	14.3	10.8
5.4	5.0	3.5	5.3		.4	Cur. Mat.-L.T.D.	5.1	4.0
7.0	6.6	9.5	13.5		5.8	Trade Payables	7.4	8.7
.0	.2	.1	.2		.3	Income Taxes Payable	.2	.1
22.1	14.7	12.5	11.6		9.5	All Other Current	19.3	17.6
45.9	35.0	32.2	32.2		16.7	Total Current	46.3	41.2
33.8	33.7	26.4	24.2		18.3	Long-Term Debt	28.1	29.6
.0	.0	.3	.1		.4	Deferred Taxes	.1	.2
22.3	8.2	7.5	1.6		5.8	All Other Non-Current	7.4	7.9
-1.9	23.2	33.6	41.9		58.7	Net Worth	18.1	21.2
100.0	100.0	100.0	100.0		100.0	Total Liabilties & Net Worth	100.0	100.0
						INCOME DATA		
100.0	100.0	100.0	100.0		100.0	Net Sales	100.0	100.0
						Gross Profit		
91.5	89.3	86.6	89.8		91.0	Operating Expenses	90.5	91.3
8.5	10.7	13.4	10.2		9.0	Operating Profit	9.5	8.7
1.6	4.2	3.4	3.0		.5	All Other Expenses (net)	2.4	2.5
6.9	6.4	10.1	7.3		8.5	Profit Before Taxes	7.1	6.3
						RATIOS		
3.1	3.6	3.0	1.7		6.5		2.9	3.1
1.1	1.3	1.3	1.3		3.7	Current	1.2	1.2
.4	.5	.6	.9		2.4		.5	.6
2.9	3.0	2.2	1.5		6.0		2.2	2.0
(191) .9	.9 (89)	.8	.9		2.0	Quick	.9	.8
.3	.3	.3	.6		1.2		.3	.4
0 UND	0 UND	0 UND	2 157.3		0 UND		0 UND	0 UND
0 UND	1 390.8	11 34.7	26 13.8		17 21.7	Sales/Receivables	3 130.8	5 78.9
7 52.0	34 10.8	51 7.1	55 6.6		48 7.6		35 10.5	34 10.9
						Cost of Sales/Inventory		
						Cost of Sales/Payables		
14.3	11.0	5.2	7.1		1.6		9.0	9.5
226.1	52.8	21.3	18.6		2.6	Sales/Working Capital	45.8	65.1
-19.1	-12.6	-17.7	-51.4		5.0		-15.0	-19.6
18.8	13.5	34.3	16.8				12.5	11.6
(127) 4.9	(114) 3.3	(71) 6.2	(20) 2.8			EBIT/Interest	(273) 3.7	(285) 3.5
1.4	1.0	2.0	1.6				1.1	1.0
							12.6	20.3
						Net Profit + Depr., Dep., Amort./Cur. Mat. L/T/D	(24) 2.6	(22) 2.4
							1.1	1.0
.2	.5	.1	.3		.2		.3	.2
2.1	1.8	1.0	1.2		.4	Fixed/Worth	1.7	1.4
-1.2	-15.3	6.7	3.6		.9		-18.8	-27.2
.9	1.0	.7	.8		.2		.8	.8
4.7	2.9	2.4	2.0		.6	Debt/Worth	3.3	3.2
-2.8	-28.2	9.6	4.0		1.0		-15.5	-26.2
152.1	80.5	75.8	38.7				101.1	108.2
(112) 62.4	(105) 24.0	(72) 37.9	(25) 9.9			% Profit Before Taxes/Tangible Net Worth	(245) 36.9	(268) 50.2
13.7	3.3	13.3	-.9				7.2	14.8
56.2	25.2	25.9	10.1		11.2		33.2	33.5
18.7	5.0	11.0	3.8		7.8	% Profit Before Taxes/Total Assets	9.3	12.0
1.9	.0	3.4	-.6		3.7		.0	.8
74.2	37.4	55.9	20.7		14.3		47.7	51.3
20.7	8.2	20.5	5.5		7.4	Sales/Net Fixed Assets	11.6	11.2
6.8	2.6	1.4	1.2		2.7		3.0	2.7
7.9	3.6	3.3	1.6		1.5		5.0	4.7
4.4	2.3	1.7	1.2		1.0	Sales/Total Assets	2.8	2.7
2.4	1.2	.7	.6		.7		1.4	1.4
.8	1.4	.7	1.8				1.0	1.0
(120) 2.2	(97) 3.7	(67) 2.2	(22) 3.9			% Depr., Dep., Amort./Sales	(254) 2.5	(277) 2.4
5.1	8.6	8.2	9.0				6.6	7.1
3.1	2.5	2.0					3.4	3.1
(111) 6.9	(67) 5.6	(31) 2.9				% Officers', Directors' Owners' Comp/Sales	(134) 6.5	(166) 6.4
14.7	8.3	7.0					12.2	12.4
221716M	513273M	1002603M	776429M	1789765M	2168999M	Net Sales ($)	6710279M	5474001M
42433M	157570M	386997M	522758M	532038M	1859050M	Total Assets ($)	2086452M	2283191M

Comparative Historical Data / Current Data Sorted by Sales

H: 4/1/08-3/31/09 ALL	H: 4/1/09-3/31/10 ALL	H: 4/1/10-3/31/11 ALL	Type of Statement	0-1MM	1-3MM	3-5MM	5-10MM	10-25MM	25MM & OVER
37	37	28	Unqualified		1	4	3	7	13
39	34	21	Reviewed	1	1	4	7	3	5
53	103	58	Compiled	17	16	5	14	5	1
214	280	210	Tax Returns	92	76	23	7	10	2
151	218	156	Other	50	44	15	21	12	14
				48 (4/1-9/30/10)			425 (10/1/10-3/31/11)		
494	672	473	**NUMBER OF STATEMENTS**	160	138	51	52	37	35
%	%	%	**ASSETS**	%	%	%	%	%	%
18.1	19.0	19.3	Cash & Equivalents	20.4	18.5	17.5	17.8	17.5	23.8
18.0	15.8	14.0	Trade Receivables (net)	7.9	13.4	18.1	27.6	18.7	12.6
7.6	8.2	5.8	Inventory	3.5	4.6	3.2	11.8	11.0	10.8
4.1	2.8	3.3	All Other Current	1.6	3.0	4.4	1.7	7.3	9.2
47.8	45.9	42.4	Total Current	33.4	39.5	43.2	58.9	54.4	56.4
36.8	37.0	38.7	Fixed Assets (net)	48.2	38.5	43.5	22.0	26.6	27.3
6.0	5.8	7.8	Intangibles (net)	8.2	10.5	3.8	3.1	8.3	7.8
9.4	11.3	11.0	All Other Non-Current	10.2	11.5	9.6	16.0	10.7	8.5
100.0	100.0	100.0	Total	100.0	100.0	100.0	100.0	100.0	100.0
			LIABILITIES						
9.9	12.1	8.9	Notes Payable-Short Term	9.7	8.6	10.0	9.8	6.8	5.4
4.6	4.6	4.7	Cur. Mat.-L.T.D.	3.7	6.2	5.8	5.0	3.5	3.1
10.1	9.1	7.6	Trade Payables	6.0	6.5	5.2	11.8	11.9	12.1
.6	.2	.1	Income Taxes Payable	.1	.1	.1	.1	.3	.1
17.0	17.7	16.9	All Other Current	19.2	15.9	16.3	15.3	17.7	13.5
42.1	43.6	38.3	Total Current	38.7	37.4	37.4	42.0	40.2	34.1
30.0	29.0	31.1	Long-Term Debt	37.0	34.9	38.9	15.8	19.5	12.5
.1	.1	.1	Deferred Taxes	.0	.0	.0	.2	.4	.3
6.7	9.6	13.4	All Other Non-Current	11.9	20.6	15.1	8.1	5.9	5.4
21.1	17.6	17.1	Net Worth	12.4	7.2	8.6	33.8	33.9	47.7
100.0	100.0	100.0	Total Liabilities & Net Worth	100.0	100.0	100.0	100.0	100.0	100.0
			INCOME DATA						
100.0	100.0	100.0	Net Sales	100.0	100.0	100.0	100.0	100.0	100.0
			Gross Profit						
91.7	91.7	89.7	Operating Expenses	85.3	92.6	89.8	89.7	95.2	93.2
8.3	8.3	10.3	Operating Profit	14.7	7.4	10.2	10.3	4.8	6.8
3.6	3.0	2.9	All Other Expenses (net)	6.1	1.4	2.1	.3	1.0	1.4
4.7	5.3	7.4	Profit Before Taxes	8.6	6.0	8.2	10.0	3.8	5.4
			RATIOS						
2.7	3.7	3.1	Current	3.3	3.1	2.3	3.6	2.0	3.4
1.2	1.3	1.3		1.2	1.1	1.2	1.6	1.4	1.8
.6	.5	.6		.3	.5	.5	.7	1.0	1.2
2.1	2.7	2.4	Quick	2.9	2.9	1.8	2.7	1.5	2.4
.9 (671)	1.0 (471)	1.0		.8	.9	.8 (51)	1.3 (36)	1.1	1.2
.3	.3	.3		.2	.3	.3	.6	.4	.7
0 UND	0 UND	0 UND	Sales/Receivables	0 UND	0 UND	0 UND	6 61.7	0 UND	2 147.9
6 58.0	5 77.0	0 999.8		0 UND	0 UND	8 46.8	27 13.6	14 26.7	15 24.2
34 10.7	37 9.9	31 11.8		3 110.3	26 13.8	43 8.4	55 6.7	43 8.4	40 9.1
			Cost of Sales/Inventory						
			Cost of Sales/Payables						
8.7	7.2	9.7	Sales/Working Capital	11.6	12.7	7.1	5.1	10.6	4.1
47.2	38.2	65.6		138.5	526.3	72.7	17.4	21.3	9.7
-20.7	-17.0	-17.8		-9.2	-14.8	-12.6	-39.3	541.7	169.1
12.9	14.1	18.5	EBIT/Interest	15.0	15.7	10.0	175.5	32.7	84.9
(378) 3.3	(499) 3.0	(343) 4.5		(93) 3.1	(112) 4.4	(42) 3.8	(40) 6.0	(30) 7.2	(26) 15.4
.6	.4	1.4		1.0	1.4	1.4	1.3	1.0	3.6
14.0	25.3	12.7	Net Profit + Depr., Dep., Amort./Cur. Mat. L/T/D						
(33) 5.5	(40) 2.3	(20) 3.3							
.8	.7	1.5							
.2	.2	.2	Fixed/Worth	.2	.7	.4	.1	.1	.2
1.2	1.4	1.5		2.1	2.6	2.9	.2	.6	.6
-38.6	-21.4	-6.6		-4.2	-1.2	-43.2	1.8	3.9	1.2
.8	.7	.8	Debt/Worth	.8	1.4	1.3	.4	.9	.4
3.5	3.1	2.7		2.9	5.7	3.8	1.2	3.0	1.0
-30.7	-17.6	-12.6		-5.2	-4.0	-48.4	3.7	11.8	2.5
84.0	71.2	96.9	% Profit Before Taxes/Tangible Net Worth	113.7	99.6	100.4	98.0	60.7	54.8
(358) 28.9	(485) 24.4	(330) 37.2		(100) 43.0	(86) 51.4	(37) 19.9	(45) 40.0	(31) 25.6	(31) 21.0
1.8	2.6	6.1		5.5	8.6	.8	9.6	.0	5.5
24.0	22.6	35.1	% Profit Before Taxes/Total Assets	42.4	37.1	19.8	43.1	23.3	21.5
6.7	6.7	10.0		10.4	10.8	7.5	18.6	7.6	7.9
-1.2	-1.1	.8		.0	1.2	.8	2.2	.2	1.6
60.1	59.9	55.8	Sales/Net Fixed Assets	48.3	39.8	55.1	136.4	112.4	49.6
14.2	12.8	12.9		7.3	12.1	7.1	42.2	26.2	14.1
3.2	3.2	3.1		1.2	4.4	2.5	11.7	6.7	4.3
4.9	4.4	5.1	Sales/Total Assets	4.3	5.2	3.4	5.8	5.0	7.0
2.6	2.5	2.7		2.1	3.3	2.3	3.2	3.3	2.1
1.2	1.3	1.3		.6	1.8	1.1	1.8	1.6	1.1
.9	.8	.9	% Depr., Dep., Amort./Sales	1.0	1.2	1.3	.7	.3	.7
(356) 2.1	(474) 2.6	(319) 2.9		(103) 4.9	(93) 2.9	(36) 3.5	(30) 1.8	(30) 1.2	(27) 1.9
5.8	7.1	7.2		12.5	6.2	8.5	4.4	3.7	3.3
2.8	3.0	2.7	% Officers', Directors' Owners' Comp/Sales	4.3	2.8	2.4	1.8	1.2	
(231) 5.1	(285) 5.7	(212) 5.8		(67) 8.3	(77) 4.8	(25) 5.6	(22) 3.6	(17) 3.2	
9.7	10.8	11.1		16.4	8.0	10.9	7.7	7.0	
5045837M	7583258M	6472785M	Net Sales ($)	72855M	244611M	202451M	365995M	596128M	4990745M
2486263M	3520629M	3500846M	Total Assets ($)	79920M	118879M	220121M	212325M	305824M	2563777M

Current Data Sorted by Assets   Comparative Historical Data

Type of Statement	0-500M	500M-2MM	2-10MM	10-50MM	50-100MM	100-250MM	4/1/06-3/31/07 ALL	4/1/07-3/31/08 ALL
Unqualified	5	22	128	252	74	45	398	351
Reviewed	3	26	154	77		1	122	133
Compiled	9	77	198	45			223	208
Tax Returns	1	5	5	2			8	17
Other	123	298	786	290	24	16	1188	1198
		942 (4/1-9/30/10)		1,724 (10/1/10-3/31/11)				
NUMBER OF STATEMENTS	141	428	1271	666	98	62	1939	1907
ASSETS	%	%	%	%	%	%	%	%
Cash & Equivalents	50.6	19.9	8.7	10.5	23.0	26.5	16.3	16.6
Trade Receivables (net)	1.6	.8	.7	1.5	4.0	5.7	1.8	1.8
Inventory	.5	.3	.2	.4	.2	.6	.3	.4
All Other Current	2.0	1.4	.7	1.2	4.0	3.8	1.6	1.5
Total Current	54.7	22.3	10.3	13.7	31.3	36.6	20.1	20.3
Fixed Assets (net)	36.1	72.6	86.6	78.1	41.2	28.3	72.4	72.6
Intangibles (net)	.5	.3	.2	.3	.1	.6	.3	.2
All Other Non-Current	8.7	4.8	2.9	7.9	27.4	34.6	7.3	6.9
Total	100.0	100.0	100.0	100.0	100.0	100.0	100.0	100.0
LIABILITIES								
Notes Payable-Short Term	5.0	1.9	1.5	1.6	3.0	2.1	2.7	2.5
Cur. Mat.-L.T.D.	7.0	1.7	1.7	1.7	2.0	1.1	1.4	1.7
Trade Payables	2.8	1.1	.7	1.2	1.6	3.1	1.3	1.4
Income Taxes Payable	.0	.0	.0	.0	.0	.0	.0	.0
All Other Current	17.4	3.3	1.8	3.1	8.3	13.0	4.1	3.8
Total Current	32.3	8.0	5.8	7.6	14.9	19.3	9.5	9.5
Long-Term Debt	37.5	41.8	33.4	29.1	16.2	14.1	28.7	29.0
Deferred Taxes	.0	.0	.0	.0	.0	.0	.0	.0
All Other Non-Current	2.0	1.7	.7	2.2	11.4	19.6	1.9	2.1
Net Worth	28.2	48.5	60.1	61.1	57.4	46.9	59.8	59.4
Total Liabilities & Net Worth	100.0	100.0	100.0	100.0	100.0	100.0	100.0	100.0
INCOME DATA								
Net Sales	100.0	100.0	100.0	100.0	100.0	100.0	100.0	100.0
Gross Profit								
Operating Expenses	89.5	86.9	86.9	89.0	89.3	94.9	86.1	85.9
Operating Profit	10.5	13.1	13.1	11.0	10.7	5.1	13.9	14.1
All Other Expenses (net)	4.7	6.9	7.6	6.2	3.5	1.1	5.1	5.8
Profit Before Taxes	5.8	6.2	5.4	4.7	7.2	4.0	8.8	8.3
RATIOS								
Current	13.0	13.0	8.1	6.7	7.2	5.1	10.2	9.9
	3.4	3.0	2.4	2.5	2.6	2.4	3.0	2.9
	1.0	.7	.9	1.0	1.2	.9	1.0	1.0
Quick	13.0	12.1	7.4	6.3	6.3	4.2	9.5	9.0
	3.3	2.8	2.3	2.2	2.2	1.9	2.7	2.6
	1.0	.6	.8	.8	1.0	.8	.9	.8
Sales/Receivables	0 UND	0 UND	0 UND	0 UND	0 UND	13 28.0	0 UND	0 UND
	0 UND	0 UND	0 UND	0 UND	11 32.5	32 11.4	0 UND	0 UND
	0 UND	0 UND	0 UND	5 70.5	36 10.1	68 5.3	2 188.3	2 215.3
Cost of Sales/Inventory								
Cost of Sales/Payables								
Sales/Working Capital	4.0	2.5	3.5	2.9	1.1	.9	2.8	2.9
	10.5	8.6	9.9	7.6	3.8	2.9	7.7	7.8
	UND	-40.9	-81.0	-402.5	29.3	-33.8	233.6	UND
EBIT/Interest	4.0	2.8	3.0	3.5	8.4	5.0	4.9	4.5
	(52) 1.3	(231) 1.5	(861) 1.5	(472) 1.5	(73) 2.9	(43) 1.4	(1160) 2.2	(1117) 2.1
	.4	.8	.6	.6	.2	-.3	1.1	.9
Net Profit + Depr., Dep., Amort./Cur. Mat. L/T/D								
Fixed/Worth	.0	.8	1.1	1.0	.2	.3	.8	.9
	.4	1.4	1.4	1.3	.7	.5	1.2	1.3
	1.8	2.3	2.1	1.9	1.1	1.2	1.8	1.8
Debt/Worth	.1	.2	.3	.2	.4	.5	.2	.2
	.6	.8	.6	.6	.6	1.1	.6	.6
	4.9	2.1	1.3	1.1	1.6	2.4	1.3	1.3
% Profit Before Taxes/Tangible Net Worth	38.3	9.9	5.5	5.7	8.6	5.3	10.6	10.6
	(119) 8.2	(397) 2.3	(1256) 1.3	(658) 1.2	3.0	(59) 1.5	(1896) 3.4	(1857) 3.1
	-1.3	-1.5	-.9	-1.3	-.8	-1.7	.1	-.3
% Profit Before Taxes/Total Assets	19.9	5.7	3.2	3.5	3.6	1.7	5.8	5.9
	3.9	1.4	.8	.8	1.4	.5	2.0	1.8
	-2.6	-.8	-.6	-.8	-.7	-.9	.0	-.2
Sales/Net Fixed Assets	UND	1.3	.5	.6	4.0	3.0	.9	.9
	34.4	.4	.3	.3	1.2	1.4	.4	.4
	1.0	.3	.2	.2	.4	.8	.3	.2
Sales/Total Assets	6.1	.7	.4	.4	.5	.4	.5	.5
	2.0	.4	.3	.3	.3	.3	.3	.3
	.6	.2	.2	.2	.2	.1	.2	.2
% Depr., Dep., Amort./Sales	2.3	3.2	5.6	5.0	1.6	1.8	3.1	3.4
	(22) 4.7	(150) 7.3	(592) 9.1	(441) 9.0	(84) 3.8	(57) 2.8	(882) 6.3	(817) 6.7
	10.7	13.2	13.0	12.4	10.2	4.8	9.9	10.6
% Officers', Directors' Owners' Comp/Sales	6.3	6.7	5.4	3.4			6.3	5.6
	(16) 12.3	(58) 16.3	(148) 12.2	(66) 7.2			(303) 11.6	(309) 13.0
	21.8	24.2	24.1	22.0			23.4	22.7
Net Sales ($)	69153M	347110M	2581392M	5129182M	2674855M	3191810M	14027492M	10126196M
Total Assets ($)	31736M	525517M	6538481M	12894160M	6660543M	9147787M	25399799M	25694391M

Comparative Historical Data			Type of Statement	Current Data Sorted by Sales					
483	507	526	Unqualified	31	88	95	113	116	83
213	264	261	Reviewed	43	140	39	26	13	
259	291	329	Compiled	142	138	30	15	4	
16	10	13	Tax Returns	9	1	2	1		
1422	1324	1537	Other	747	509	125	81	43	32
4/1/08-3/31/09	4/1/09-3/31/10	4/1/10-3/31/11		942 (4/1-9/30/10)			1,724 (10/1/10-3/31/11)		
ALL	ALL	ALL		0-1MM	1-3MM	3-5MM	5-10MM	10-25MM	25MM & OVER
2393	2396	2666	**NUMBER OF STATEMENTS**	972	876	291	236	176	115
%	%	%	**ASSETS**	%	%	%	%	%	%
15.2	13.9	14.1	Cash & Equivalents	14.4	11.3	13.4	13.9	19.2	26.9
1.5	1.4	1.2	Trade Receivables (net)	.5	.6	1.2	2.4	3.9	5.0
.4	.3	.3	Inventory	.1	.2	.2	.5	.5	1.2
1.3	1.0	1.2	All Other Current	.9	.7	.8	1.4	3.1	5.5
18.4	16.7	16.8	Total Current	15.9	12.9	15.6	18.3	26.8	38.5
74.6	76.5	76.5	Fixed Assets (net)	80.3	82.2	80.2	72.9	54.9	32.4
.2	.2	.3	Intangibles (net)	.2	.2	.2	.6	.5	.4
6.7	6.6	6.4	All Other Non-Current	3.6	4.7	4.0	8.2	17.8	28.7
100.0	100.0	100.0	Total	100.0	100.0	100.0	100.0	.100.0	100.0
			LIABILITIES						
2.7	2.7	1.9	Notes Payable-Short Term	2.3	1.7	.8	1.2	2.6	2.6
2.2	2.0	2.0	Cur. Mat.-L.T.D.	2.1	2.0	2.4	1.3	2.2	1.3
1.2	1.1	1.1	Trade Payables	.7	.7	1.0	1.2	3.0	4.4
.0	.0	.0	Income Taxes Payable	.0	.0	.0	.0	.0	.0
4.2	3.5	3.7	All Other Current	3.7	2.2	2.8	4.7	8.2	8.5
10.3	9.4	8.6	Total Current	8.7	6.6	7.1	8.4	16.1	16.8
30.8	33.8	32.8	Long-Term Debt	35.0	36.6	33.2	29.8	17.9	13.8
.0	.0	.0	Deferred Taxes	.0	.0	.0	.0	.0	.0
2.2	2.0	2.1	All Other Non-Current	.7	1.0	1.5	3.6	6.7	14.3
56.7	54.9	56.4	Net Worth	55.5	55.9	58.2	58.1	59.3	55.1
100.0	100.0	100.0	Total Liabilities & Net Worth	100.0	100.0	100.0	100.0	100.0	100.0
			INCOME DATA						
100.0	100.0	100.0	Net Sales	100.0	100.0	100.0	100.0	100.0	100.0
			Gross Profit						
89.1	88.7	87.9	Operating Expenses	84.7	87.8	90.0	90.0	94.6	95.3
10.9	11.3	12.1	Operating Profit	15.3	12.2	10.0	10.0	5.4	4.7
6.8	7.2	6.7	All Other Expenses (net)	9.1	6.6	5.9	4.8	2.0	.5
4.0	4.1	5.4	Profit Before Taxes	6.2	5.7	4.1	5.2	3.4	4.1
			RATIOS						
8.4	8.0	8.2		10.8	8.3	7.3	6.1	5.2	6.6
2.5	2.6	2.6	Current	2.5	2.6	3.0	2.3	2.1	2.5
.9	.9	.9		.7	1.0	1.2	.9	.9	1.1
7.8	7.4	7.5		10.3	7.6	6.9	5.6	4.6	4.8
(2392) 2.2	2.3	2.3	Quick	2.4	2.5	2.8	2.1	1.9	1.6
.7	.8	.8		.7	.9	1.0	.8	.8	.8
0 UND	0 UND	0 UND		0 UND	0 UND	0 UND	0 UND	0 UND	1 507.3
0 UND	0 UND	0 UND	Sales/Receivables	0 UND	0 UND	0 UND	0 986.8	4 95.1	13 27.7
1 267.1	1 294.2	1 577.5		0 UND	0 UND	2 183.8	11 34.0	31 11.7	35 10.5
			Cost of Sales/Inventory						
			Cost of Sales/Payables						
3.3	3.2	3.0		3.0	3.5	3.0	3.4	2.3	2.0
9.6	9.2	8.6	Sales/Working Capital	9.2	9.5	7.5	8.7	6.8	6.2
-77.9	-81.0	-95.7		-30.8	UND	53.6	-68.1	-49.1	75.0
3.2	3.1	3.2		2.7	3.0	3.2	4.7	6.6	11.4
(1502) 1.5	(1558) 1.4	(1732) 1.5	EBIT/Interest	(518) 1.5	(595) 1.4	(228) 1.4	(185) 1.7	(125) 1.7	(81) 2.9
.4	.5	.6		.8	.6	.4	.5	.1	.0
			Net Profit + Depr., Dep., Amort./Cur. Mat. L/T/D						
.9	1.0	1.0		1.0	1.0	1.0	.9	.4	.2
1.3	1.4	1.3	Fixed/Worth	1.4	1.4	1.3	1.3	1.0	.5
2.0	2.1	2.0		2.1	2.1	2.0	1.9	1.5	1.1
.2	.3	.3		.3	.3	.2	.3	.2	.4
.6	.7	.6	Debt/Worth	.6	.7	.6	.7	.6	.7
1.4	1.5	1.4		1.4	1.4	1.4	1.4	1.3	1.4
6.9	6.2	6.5		6.3	6.2	6.3	8.6	6.4	13.2
(2322) 1.1	(2333) 1.2	(2587) 1.6	% Profit Before Taxes/Tangible Net Worth	(940) 1.5	(848) 1.5	(283) 1.1	(233) 3.1	(172) 1.2	(111) 3.9
-2.2	-2.1	-1.0		-.6	-1.0	-2.0	-1.7	-2.2	-2.3
3.8	3.5	3.7	% Profit Before Taxes/Total Assets	3.3	3.8	3.5	4.8	3.2	5.8
.6	.7	.9		.8	.8	.9	1.6	.7	2.0
-1.3	-1.2	-.7		-.4	-.7	-1.0	-.9	-1.5	-1.4
.8	.7	.7		.5	.5	.6	.9	2.3	7.0
.4	.4	.4	Sales/Net Fixed Assets	.3	.3	.4	.5	.8	3.1
.2	.2	.2		.2	.2	.3	.4	.5	1.2
.5	.5	.5		.4	.5	.5	.5	.6	1.3
.3	.3	.3	Sales/Total Assets	.2	.3	.3	.4	.4	.6
.2	.2	.2		.1	.2	.2	.3	.2	.4
3.9	4.5	4.1		4.8	5.8	5.7	4.1	2.1	1.2
(1116) 7.2	(1187) 8.1	(1346) 8.4	% Depr., Dep., Amort./Sales	(275) 10.5	(431) 9.4	(192) 9.4	(186) 8.0	(157) 6.0	(105) 2.2
10.7	12.3	12.3		16.5	13.0	13.0	10.7	9.8	4.7
5.9	5.1	4.4		8.2	3.5	3.0	2.7	1.1	1.0
(318) 13.3	(312) 12.8	(301) 12.2	% Officers', Directors' Owners' Comp/Sales	(134) 16.1	(90) 7.3	(31) 12.4	(24) 6.9	(12) 2.8	(10) 3.7
23.5	24.7	22.7		25.1	20.6	30.2	20.8	17.0	9.8
14375459M	14053686M	13993502M	Net Sales ($)	500355M	1570457M	1117460M	1641941M	2723059M	6440230M
34857681M	33925080M	35798224M	Total Assets ($)	2563541M	6180038M	3797156M	4897220M	8554107M	9806162M

M = $ thousand   MM = $ million
See Pages 9 through 22 for Explanation of Ratios and Data

Current Data Sorted by Assets | Comparative Historical Data

Type of Statement	1	3	14	29	6	13		23	33
Unqualified									
Reviewed									
Compiled									1
Tax Returns								2	
Other	3	3	3	1 5	6	13		9	14
		60 (4/1-9/30/10)		21 (10/1/10-3/31/11)				4/1/06-3/31/07	4/1/07-3/31/08
	0-500M	500M-2MM	2-10MM	10-50MM	50-100MM	100-250MM		ALL	ALL
NUMBER OF STATEMENTS	4	6	17	35	6	13		34	48
	%	%	%	%	%	%		%	%
ASSETS									
Cash & Equivalents			28.0	17.7		40.3		33.1	34.0
Trade Receivables (net)			9.9	11.3		8.7		8.4	5.2
Inventory			.3	.0		.0		.4	1.0
All Other Current			2.2	3.8		2.5		4.5	3.2
Total Current			40.4	32.8		51.5		46.4	43.3
Fixed Assets (net)			32.3	40.8		9.9		25.7	25.6
Intangibles (net)			.1	1.1		.2		.6	1.4
All Other Non-Current			27.2	25.4		38.4		27.3	29.6
Total			100.0	100.0		100.0		100.0	100.0
LIABILITIES									
Notes Payable-Short Term			5.6	4.5		.3		4.2	3.3
Cur. Mat.-L.T.D.			3.2	.9		.3		.4	.3
Trade Payables			4.0	7.6		2.9		2.4	2.5
Income Taxes Payable			.0	.0		.0		.0	.0
All Other Current			5.8	7.7		6.5		5.3	5.2
Total Current			18.6	20.7		10.1		12.3	11.3
Long-Term Debt			17.8	24.7		12.6		14.7	18.7
Deferred Taxes			.0	.0		.0		.0	.0
All Other Non-Current			1.9	2.7		6.6		1.1	2.2
Net Worth			61.7	51.9		70.6		71.9	67.8
Total Liabilities & Net Worth			100.0	100.0		100.0		100.0	100.0
INCOME DATA									
Net Sales			100.0	100.0		100.0		100.0	100.0
Gross Profit									
Operating Expenses			78.1	81.8		74.3		68.4	71.4
Operating Profit			21.9	18.2		25.7		31.6	28.6
All Other Expenses (net)			-.6	7.6		4.2		3.4	4.0
Profit Before Taxes			22.5	10.6		21.4		28.2	24.7
RATIOS									
Current			10.7	7.9		58.5		14.2	26.4
			1.7	2.0		8.5		6.9	6.5
			1.1	1.2		1.6		2.7	1.5
Quick			10.6	7.8		52.2		13.8	24.5
			1.5	1.6		8.5		4.1	4.6
			1.1	1.1		1.3		1.6	1.4
Sales/Receivables			0 UND	8 48.0		0 UND		0 UND	0 UND
			48 7.7	26 14.2		19 19.3		2 236.5	1 271.8
			119 3.1	117 3.1		113 3.2		20 17.9	19 18.9
Cost of Sales/Inventory									
Cost of Sales/Payables									
Sales/Working Capital			.8	1.2		.2		.4	.4
			3.6	4.8		.8		1.9	1.5
			23.4	16.2		4.1		5.8	11.3
EBIT/Interest			10.1	9.7				75.3	17.9
			(10) 3.8	(20) 3.5				(14) 4.7	(19) 3.8
			-1.0	1.1				2.2	1.2
Net Profit + Depr., Dep., Amort./Cur. Mat. L/T/D									
Fixed/Worth			.0	.1		.0		.0	.0
			.4	.9		.1		.2	.2
			1.2	3.6		.5		.9	.9
Debt/Worth			.2	.1		.1		.0	.0
			.5	1.0		.2		.3	.3
			1.4	4.0		1.0		.8	1.4
% Profit Before Taxes/Tangible Net Worth			9.9	13.6		13.5		24.4	17.3
			(16) 7.8	(33) 4.3		(12) 5.9		6.1	(46) 5.9
			-.1	.0		.8		2.3	1.4
% Profit Before Taxes/Total Assets			7.9	4.0		9.2		11.9	9.8
			3.6	.6		2.3		4.8	3.6
			-1.3	-1.0		.2		1.7	.3
Sales/Net Fixed Assets			316.2	20.8		162.0		455.8	88.4
			3.1	1.4		3.1		1.7	2.7
			.3	.3		1.2		.4	.5
Sales/Total Assets			.7	.5		.4		.9	.6
			.2	.3		.2		.3	.2
			.1	.1		.1		.1	.1
% Depr., Dep., Amort./Sales			1.7	1.1		.3		.6	.6
			(11) 2.9	(26) 4.9		(11) 2.4		(25) 2.7	(39) 2.8
			14.2	12.0		6.2		8.8	9.1
% Officers', Directors' Owners' Comp/Sales									
Net Sales ($)	1592M	12285M	41396M	401050M	80183M	549587M		268127M	602274M
Total Assets ($)	568M	7022M	92820M	877646M	484452M	1896645M		1244405M	2655653M

© RMA 2011

M = $ thousand   MM = $ million
See Pages 9 through 22 for Explanation of Ratios and Data

Comparative Historical Data			Type of Statement	Current Data Sorted by Sales					
47	52	66	Unqualified	9	11	8	15	10	13
	2		Reviewed						
			Compiled						
		1	Tax Returns	1					
10	19	14	Other	4	4	2	2	2	
4/1/08- 3/31/09 ALL	4/1/09- 3/31/10 ALL	4/1/10- 3/31/11 ALL		0-1MM	1-3MM	3-5MM	5-10MM	10-25MM	25MM & OVER
					60 (4/1-9/30/10)		21 (10/1/10-3/31/11)		
57	73	81	**NUMBER OF STATEMENTS**	14	15	10	17	12	13
%	%	%	**ASSETS**	%	%	%	%	%	%
32.1	32.6	27.0	Cash & Equivalents	37.0	24.3	26.7	22.9	25.2	26.9
7.2	8.4	9.8	Trade Receivables (net)	4.8	6.6	11.8	12.2	5.0	18.4
.7	.7	.3	Inventory	.3	1.1	.0	.3	.0	.1
4.4	2.7	4.8	All Other Current	7.4	9.5	3.9	.3	3.5	4.5
44.4	44.3	42.0	Total Current	49.5	41.5	42.4	35.7	33.7	49.8
26.1	30.4	28.3	Fixed Assets (net)	35.4	26.5	32.8	36.1	18.9	17.5
1.6	.4	.5	Intangibles (net)	.1	.3	.4	1.3	.8	.0
27.9	24.9	29.3	All Other Non-Current	15.0	31.8	24.4	26.8	46.6	32.7
100.0	100.0	100.0	Total	100.0	100.0	100.0	100.0	100.0	100.0
			LIABILITIES						
1.2	2.8	4.8	Notes Payable-Short Term	9.8	.4	10.4	4.9	1.9	2.5
.4	.6	1.4	Cur. Mat.-L.T.D.	2.6	2.5	1.6	.8	.3	.6
2.6	3.9	6.2	Trade Payables	7.8	3.9	1.8	7.9	3.9	10.7
.0	.1	.0	Income Taxes Payable	.0	.0	.0	.0	.0	.0
8.3	10.7	7.6	All Other Current	3.3	9.5	5.9	6.4	12.8	8.0
12.6	18.2	20.0	Total Current	23.4	16.3	19.7	20.0	19.0	21.8
15.1	15.5	17.1	Long-Term Debt	10.8	17.8	23.9	33.9	7.2	4.9
.0	.0	.0	Deferred Taxes	.0	.0	.0	.0	.0	.0
3.8	2.8	3.1	All Other Non-Current	.0	2.7	.8	4.8	3.2	6.6
68.6	63.5	59.8	Net Worth	65.8	63.1	55.6	41.4	70.5	66.7
100.0	100.0	100.0	Total Liabilties & Net Worth	100.0	100.0	100.0	100.0	100.0	100.0
			INCOME DATA						
100.0	100.0	100.0	Net Sales	100.0	100.0	100.0	100.0	100.0	100.0
			Gross Profit						
89.5	83.0	82.0	Operating Expenses	76.6	89.3	89.2	77.4	75.1	86.0
10.5	17.0	18.0	Operating Profit	23.4	10.7	10.8	22.6	24.9	14.0
10.1	10.7	3.8	All Other Expenses (net)	1.3	7.1	1.6	10.4	2.1	-2.6
.3	6.3	14.2	Profit Before Taxes	22.1	3.6	9.2	12.2	22.8	16.6
			RATIOS						
23.5	12.9	9.0		26.1	8.4	5.3	10.2	8.4	35.8
4.6	2.5	2.5	Current	5.3	2.7	2.7	2.8	1.8	2.0
2.3	1.3	1.2		.8	1.1	1.3	1.1	.9	1.4
23.5	11.9	9.0		24.8	8.4	4.7	10.0	8.3	29.3
4.6	2.3	2.3	Quick	4.1	2.4	2.1	2.8	1.4	1.6
1.6	1.1	1.1		.6	1.1	1.2	1.1	.6	1.2
0 UND	0 UND	0 UND		0 UND	1 508.5	0 UND	1 352.9	0 UND	12 31.3
9 42.5	8 44.0	22 16.5	Sales/Receivables	0 UND	55 6.7	39 9.3	32 11.3	7 50.3	42 8.8
39 9.4	61 6.0	103 3.5		12 30.8	117 3.1	177 2.1	93 3.9	41 8.9	130 2.8
			Cost of Sales/Inventory						
			Cost of Sales/Payables						
.4	.7	.8		.3	.9	.4	.9	.6	1.0
1.5	2.8	3.4	Sales/Working Capital	1.9	2.1	4.1	4.3	5.4	3.5
5.5	13.6	12.7		-142.3	7.0	NM	18.8	NM	10.9
5.2	10.1	11.6					41.1		
(26) .2	(31) 2.8	(42) 4.2	EBIT/Interest				(11) 6.0		
-4.9	-1.2	1.0					-.8		
			Net Profit + Depr., Dep., Amort./Cur. Mat. L/T/D						
.0	.0	.0		.0	.0	.0	.1	.0	.0
.2	.3	.4	Fixed/Worth	.6	.2	.3	1.0	.2	.1
.8	.8	1.3		1.6	.8	3.1	UND	.7	.9
.0	.1	.1		.0	.1	.1	.4	.1	.1
.3	.5	.5	Debt/Worth	.3	.6	.7	1.0	.3	.2
1.0	1.5	1.7		.8	1.2	3.2	UND	.7	2.5
4.4	11.1	13.1	% Profit Before Taxes/Tangible Net Worth	10.0	6.0	56.0	18.8	15.3	13.4
(55) -1.1	(69) 2.5	(76) 4.6		(13) 7.9	(14) 1.2	4.4	(14) 2.5	4.3	9.7
-5.4	-2.6	-.1		.3	-2.3	.4	-5.9	.3	1.2
3.4	6.3	7.9	% Profit Before Taxes/Total Assets	8.0	2.8	8.8	6.1	11.3	9.2
-1.4	1.2	1.9		4.8	.3	2.3	.0	1.4	4.1
-3.6	-2.0	-.9		-2.9	-4.1	.0	-3.1	.2	.5
55.5	55.2	66.0		242.1	999.8	31.0	13.8	21.1	184.3
3.7	2.5	4.1	Sales/Net Fixed Assets	4.4	33.5	1.2	2.3	10.9	13.6
.6	.4	.5		.2	.3	.6	.2	.9	2.6
.6	.7	.8		1.4	.4	.6	.4	1.0	1.5
.3	.3	.3	Sales/Total Assets	.2	.2	.3	.2	.4	.4
.1	.1	.1		.1	.1	.2	.1	.2	.3
.7	.5	.6					1.4	.3	.3
(44) 2.8	(58) 2.0	(60) 2.4	% Depr., Dep., Amort./Sales				(15) 3.4	1.6	(11) 1.5
7.7	7.7	10.4					17.9	9.0	2.5
			% Officers', Directors' Owners' Comp/Sales						
1188089M	1064506M	1086093M	Net Sales ($)	7032M	30595M	40180M	123094M	192484M	692708M
3385999M	3154483M	3359153M	Total Assets ($)	45304M	167070M	210203M	770328M	714414M	1451834M

M = $ thousand   MM = $ million
See Pages 9 through 22 for Explanation of Ratios and Data

Current Data Sorted by Assets   Comparative Historical Data

0-500M	500M-2MM	2-10MM	10-50MM	50-100MM	100-250MM	Type of Statement	ALL 4/1/06-3/31/07	ALL 4/1/07-3/31/08
2	5	19	19	6	2	Unqualified	75	65
		1				Reviewed	1	
		1				Compiled		2
						Tax Returns	1	1
4	2	14	7		1	Other	18	23
4 (4/1-9/30/10)	61		22 (10/1/10-3/31/11)					
6	7	35	26	6	3	**NUMBER OF STATEMENTS**	95	91
%	%	%	%	%	%	**ASSETS**	%	%
		25.7	24.3			Cash & Equivalents	24.1	24.5
		13.8	17.1			Trade Receivables (net)	20.0	16.8
		.4	1.2			Inventory	.5	.8
		5.1	8.2			All Other Current	6.7	5.2
		45.0	50.8			Total Current	51.3	47.3
		44.6	38.2			Fixed Assets (net)	34.1	34.9
		1.8	.8			Intangibles (net)	.4	1.3
		8.6	10.3			All Other Non-Current	14.3	16.5
		100.0	100.0			Total	100.0	100.0
						LIABILITIES		
		2.2	2.7			Notes Payable-Short Term	4.8	5.4
		1.6	2.1			Cur. Mat.-L.T.D.	1.5	1.3
		9.4	5.6			Trade Payables	7.5	6.2
		.3	.0			Income Taxes Payable	.2	.1
		7.0	17.3			All Other Current	10.2	11.5
		20.5	27.6			Total Current	24.2	24.6
		22.0	18.8			Long-Term Debt	15.3	18.3
		.0	.0			Deferred Taxes	.1	.1
		1.1	2.2			All Other Non-Current	3.2	4.0
		56.4	51.3			Net Worth	57.2	53.0
		100.0	100.0			Total Liabilties & Net Worth	100.0	100.0
						INCOME DATA		
		100.0	100.0			Net Sales	100.0	100.0
						Gross Profit		
		87.9	96.8			Operating Expenses	94.2	94.3
		12.1	3.2			Operating Profit	5.8	5.7
		2.3	.1			All Other Expenses (net)	.7	1.0
		9.8	3.1			Profit Before Taxes	5.0	4.7
						RATIOS		
		6.1	3.1			Current	4.6	5.4
		2.0	1.7				2.2	2.0
		1.1	1.2				1.2	1.2
		4.9	2.7			Quick	4.1	4.1
		1.8	1.4				1.9	1.8
		.9	1.0				1.0	1.0
	1	331.4	20 18.4			Sales/Receivables	8 43.7	7 55.8
	25	14.5	36 10.3				34 10.8	28 13.0
	42	8.6	50 7.3				53 6.9	53 6.9
						Cost of Sales/Inventory		
						Cost of Sales/Payables		
		3.8	4.0			Sales/Working Capital	2.7	2.2
		7.8	8.7				8.2	10.1
		75.6	24.8				24.9	29.6
		25.8	10.0			EBIT/Interest	9.1	10.4
	(24)	5.8	(20) 3.3				(62) 3.4	(56) 3.4
		2.3	2.1				1.2	1.0
						Net Profit + Depr., Dep., Amort./Cur. Mat. L/T/D		
		.3	.3			Fixed/Worth	.1	.2
		.9	.6				.5	.6
		1.3	1.4				1.0	1.4
		.3	.4			Debt/Worth	.3	.3
		.7	1.1				.6	.8
		1.5	2.1				1.6	2.1
		22.3	11.1			% Profit Before Taxes/Tangible Net Worth	19.3	19.0
	(34)	9.4	6.0				(86) 8.4	7.9
		1.4	2.3				.7	.3
		14.8	4.2			% Profit Before Taxes/Total Assets	11.7	6.9
		4.6	2.8				3.7	3.4
		1.4	1.0				.1	.0
		12.3	13.8			Sales/Net Fixed Assets	29.8	33.4
		3.7	3.8				5.1	4.2
		2.0	2.0				2.2	2.0
		2.1	2.2			Sales/Total Assets	2.2	2.0
		1.6	1.4				1.4	1.2
		.7	1.0				.9	.7
		1.3	1.3			% Depr., Dep., Amort./Sales	1.2	1.2
	(30)	2.1	(24) 2.3				(82) 2.1	(77) 2.3
		3.8	3.5				3.5	3.5
						% Officers', Directors' Owners' Comp/Sales	4.7	3.2
							(13) 11.8	(16) 9.0
							18.4	22.1
4369M	22936M	318635M	880703M	276095M	446452M	Net Sales ($)	2094685M	2843963M
1567M	8185M	191124M	528224M	438719M	521302M	Total Assets ($)	1934357M	2428628M

M = $ thousand   MM = $ million
See Pages 9 through 22 for Explanation of Ratios and Data

Comparative Historical Data   Current Data Sorted by Sales

77	73	53	Type of Statement	3	3	8	5	19	15
1	1	1	Unqualified						
		1	Reviewed		1				
			Compiled		1				
2	1		Tax Returns						
21	12	28	Other	7	3	2	3	6	7
4/1/08-	4/1/09-	4/1/10-			61 (4/1-9/30/10)			22 (10/1/10-3/31/11)	
3/31/09	3/31/10	3/31/11		0-1MM	1-3MM	3-5MM	5-10MM	10-25MM	25MM & OVER
ALL	ALL	ALL							
101	87	83	**NUMBER OF STATEMENTS**	10	8	10	8	25	22
%	%	%	**ASSETS**	%	%	%	%	%	%
26.8	25.8	25.4	Cash & Equivalents	32.5		27.3		23.4	23.9
16.6	17.9	15.3	Trade Receivables (net)	6.9		23.5		12.6	20.3
.5	1.5	.8	Inventory	1.9		.3		.6	1.3
3.3	4.2	6.6	All Other Current	.6		2.2		8.9	5.5
47.2	49.5	48.0	Total Current	41.9		53.3		45.5	51.1
35.1	32.4	38.6	Fixed Assets (net)	44.4		29.1		46.7	30.9
2.3	.8	1.0	Intangibles (net)	.1		.0		1.3	1.6
15.4	17.3	12.4	All Other Non-Current	13.6		17.6		6.5	16.4
100.0	100.0	100.0	Total	100.0		100.0		100.0	100.0
			LIABILITIES						
2.5	2.8	3.4	Notes Payable-Short Term	1.7		1.3		3.2	1.5
1.0	1.9	1.3	Cur. Mat.-L.T.D.	2.2		.3		1.5	1.7
9.1	10.2	9.7	Trade Payables	11.9		9.7		9.9	11.8
.1	.1	.2	Income Taxes Payable	.0		.0		.1	.0
11.1	14.6	10.8	All Other Current	5.2		2.6		13.5	17.1
23.8	29.6	25.5	Total Current	20.9		13.9		28.2	32.1
18.2	15.6	17.2	Long-Term Debt	20.7		10.3		23.2	16.8
.0	.0	.1	Deferred Taxes	.0		.0		.0	.0
3.8	2.7	2.3	All Other Non-Current	.3		1.1		2.7	3.9
54.2	52.1	54.9	Net Worth	58.0		74.8		46.0	47.1
100.0	100.0	100.0	Total Liabilties & Net Worth	100.0		100.0		100.0	100.0
			INCOME DATA						
100.0	100.0	100.0	Net Sales	100.0		100.0		100.0	100.0
			Gross Profit						
95.0	94.9	92.9	Operating Expenses	87.2		89.8		95.1	97.2
5.0	5.1	7.1	Operating Profit	12.8		10.2		4.9	2.8
3.4	2.2	1.6	All Other Expenses (net)	8.5		.5		1.3	.7
1.6	2.8	5.6	Profit Before Taxes	4.3		9.8		3.6	2.1
			RATIOS						
4.5	4.3	3.9		8.1		9.0		2.7	2.4
2.0	2.0	2.0	Current	2.5		5.2		1.8	1.7
1.2	1.3	1.1		1.0		3.3		1.1	1.1
3.9	3.5	3.4		8.1		8.8		2.3	2.0
1.8	1.8	1.7	Quick	2.2		4.5		1.2	1.3
1.1	1.0	.9		.8		3.3		.8	1.0
4 85.3	4 85.3	4 84.2		0 UND	19 19.3		7 54.7	17 21.1	
30 12.1	35 10.5	28 13.1	Sales/Receivables	4 88.0	45 8.1		33 11.2	40 9.2	
53 6.9	54 6.8	49 7.4		42 8.7	63 5.8		42 8.7	55 6.6	
			Cost of Sales/Inventory						
			Cost of Sales/Payables						
2.5	3.1	3.9		4.6		2.0		4.6	4.4
6.5	6.5	7.8	Sales/Working Capital	5.4		3.8		11.0	13.9
30.8	29.7	55.0		NM		4.8		178.8	42.2
4.5	8.9	19.5						12.2	9.9
(59) 1.2	(60) 2.3	(58) 4.8	EBIT/Interest				(19) 2.9	(18) 4.3	
-2.0	.5	2.0						1.4	1.1
			Net Profit + Depr., Dep., Amort./Cur. Mat. L/T/D						
.2	.1	.2		.0		.1		.3	.2
.4	.5	.7	Fixed/Worth	.9		.3		1.0	.7
1.4	1.4	1.3		1.9		.7		2.2	1.3
.3	.3	.3		.2		.1		.6	.7
.9	.7	.8	Debt/Worth	.4		.3		1.1	1.4
1.8	2.6	2.0		3.5		.8		3.4	2.5
13.3	13.7	18.2	% Profit Before Taxes/Tangible Net Worth			37.6		18.8	19.2
(98) 1.7	(84) 2.5	(81) 7.6				11.4	(24) 4.9	9.3	
-9.1	-5.8	1.3				4.3		2.0	2.9
5.3	7.6	8.2	% Profit Before Taxes/Total Assets	25.1		20.7		5.0	8.4
.4	.9	3.8		2.1		7.0		2.9	3.6
-3.5	-2.8	.8		-5.3		3.3		.9	1.3
18.8	58.1	22.6	Sales/Net Fixed Assets	UND		14.9		11.7	39.9
4.5	5.3	4.1		17.2		4.1		3.1	5.8
1.9	2.3	2.0		.6		2.2		2.1	2.6
2.1	2.6	2.3	Sales/Total Assets	4.4		2.2		2.1	2.5
1.2	1.4	1.5		.8		1.3		1.5	1.7
.7	.7	.8		.2		.9		.9	1.2
1.0	.8	1.2						1.7	.5
(88) 2.0	(76) 1.9	(70) 2.1	% Depr., Dep., Amort./Sales				(22) 2.5	(20) 1.7	
3.9	3.3	3.6						3.7	2.9
2.6	2.3		% Officers', Directors' Owners' Comp/Sales						
(11) 8.1	(11) 4.8								
13.5	7.6								
2660877M	2756757M	1949190M	Net Sales ($)	5424M	15344M	40692M	56846M	374934M	1455950M
2569269M	1827531M	1689121M	Total Assets ($)	16301M	35866M	123897M	46933M	369967M	1096157M

M = $ thousand   MM = $ million
See Pages 9 through 22 for Explanation of Ratios and Data

Current Data Sorted by Assets							Comparative Historical Data	

						Type of Statement		
1	5	12	15	5	3	Unqualified	13	17
1						Reviewed		
		2				Compiled		1
		3	5			Tax Returns		1
	1		12			Other	4	4
		41 (4/1-9/30/10)		12 (10/1/10-3/31/11)			4/1/06-3/31/07 ALL	4/1/07-3/31/08 ALL
0-500M	500M-2MM	2-10MM	10-50MM	50-100MM	100-250MM			
2	6	17	20	5	3	NUMBER OF STATEMENTS	17	23
%	%	%	%	%	%	ASSETS	%	%
		23.6	24.6			Cash & Equivalents	23.8	18.8
		17.8	13.9			Trade Receivables (net)	13.1	14.8
		7.4	5.6			Inventory	.8	6.9
		4.7	7.1			All Other Current	2.1	6.5
		53.5	51.1			Total Current	39.8	47.1
		29.6	26.5			Fixed Assets (net)	40.3	29.8
		1.3	2.5			Intangibles (net)	.4	.5
		15.6	19.8			All Other Non-Current	19.4	22.6
		100.0	100.0			Total	100.0	100.0
						LIABILITIES		
		6.9	1.1			Notes Payable-Short Term	.9	6.5
		.2	1.4			Cur. Mat.-L.T.D.	1.1	1.0
		2.6	10.4			Trade Payables	6.3	4.2
		.0	.0			Income Taxes Payable	.0	.0
		7.8	19.2			All Other Current	10.4	14.0
		17.5	32.2			Total Current	18.7	25.8
		10.4	9.8			Long-Term Debt	13.9	10.4
		.0	.0			Deferred Taxes	.0	.0
		1.5	6.7			All Other Non-Current	2.9	3.1
		70.5	51.3			Net Worth	64.5	60.7
		100.0	100.0			Total Liabilties & Net Worth	100.0	100.0
						INCOME DATA		
		100.0	100.0			Net Sales	100.0	100.0
						Gross Profit		
		94.9	97.3			Operating Expenses	89.1	95.4
		5.1	2.7			Operating Profit	10.9	4.6
		.4	-1.6			All Other Expenses (net)	2.1	-1.6
		4.7	4.3			Profit Before Taxes	8.9	6.1
						RATIOS		
		11.4	5.8			Current	5.9	3.3
		3.7	1.9				2.6	2.0
		1.7	1.2				1.3	1.2
		9.1	4.9			Quick	3.5	2.3
		2.8	1.5				2.2	1.4
		1.2	.6				1.1	.7
	0 UND		6 59.5			Sales/Receivables	2 183.2	0 UND
	14 25.5		27 13.7				27 13.7	21 17.4
	49 7.5		73 5.0				111 3.3	62 5.9
						Cost of Sales/Inventory		
						Cost of Sales/Payables		
		1.6	1.9			Sales/Working Capital	2.0	4.5
		3.8	5.3				4.3	8.6
		19.8	8.9				79.3	39.8
						EBIT/Interest		14.2
							(12)	3.9
								-.3
						Net Profit + Depr., Dep., Amort./Cur. Mat. L/T/D		
		.0	.0			Fixed/Worth	.1	.1
		.2	.3				.5	.5
		.9	1.1				1.1	.7
		.1	.3			Debt/Worth	.2	.2
		.3	1.1				.5	.7
		1.1	3.9				1.4	1.6
		2.7	12.6			% Profit Before Taxes/Tangible Net Worth	14.2	12.4
		-1.1 (19)	5.9				8.3	4.3
		-5.2	-1.8				-5.8	-2.2
		1.7	10.3			% Profit Before Taxes/Total Assets	11.0	10.5
		-.7	1.6				2.5	3.2
		-3.3	.0				-4.7	-.6
		55.6	88.7			Sales/Net Fixed Assets	19.6	65.3
		5.9	9.4				2.4	8.1
		2.5	.8				1.3	2.1
		2.5	1.2			Sales/Total Assets	1.6	2.5
		1.4	.7				.9	1.5
		.4	.2				.5	.6
		.3	.3			% Depr., Dep., Amort./Sales	1.5	.4
		(15) 1.0	(16) 1.5				(12) 2.9	(20) 1.7
		2.2	3.4				6.7	3.8
						% Officers', Directors' Owners' Comp/Sales		
4868M	18493M	170444M	427486M	1058424M	110979M	Net Sales ($)	409495M	463137M
824M	8002M	95297M	412756M	383724M	492237M	Total Assets ($)	420607M	395208M

M = $ thousand   MM = $ million
See Pages 9 through 22 for Explanation of Ratios and Data

Comparative Historical Data / Current Data Sorted by Sales

Type of Statement	30	32	41	3	7	3	6	12	10
Unqualified	30	32	41	3	7	3	6	12	10
Reviewed	-1	1							
Compiled	1			1					
Tax Returns	1	2	2						
Other	8	11	9	1	1	1	3	1	2
	4/1/08-3/31/09 ALL	4/1/09-3/31/10 ALL	4/1/10-3/31/11 ALL	41 (4/1-9/30/10) 0-1MM	1-3MM	3-5MM	12 (10/1/10-3/31/11) 5-10MM	10-25MM	25MM & OVER
NUMBER OF STATEMENTS	41	46	53	5	9	4	10	13	12
ASSETS	%	%	%	%	%	%	%	%	%
Cash & Equivalents	23.2	27.5	27.3				24.9	24.4	36.1
Trade Receivables (net)	9.4	17.1	14.9				17.2	12.5	20.2
Inventory	8.9	2.3	4.9				10.9	2.5	5.2
All Other Current	3.3	1.6	4.8				4.8	9.3	.8
Total Current	44.8	48.5	51.9				57.7	48.6	62.3
Fixed Assets (net)	36.0	36.3	26.1				28.4	21.3	16.8
Intangibles (net)	1.2	2.4	1.4				.0	3.6	.5
All Other Non-Current	18.1	12.8	20.6				13.8	26.5	20.4
Total	100.0	100.0	100.0				100.0	100.0	100.0
LIABILITIES									
Notes Payable-Short Term	2.7	2.7	2.7				4.8	2.1	.0
Cur. Mat.-L.T.D.	.8	1.3	.8				.4	.3	.5
Trade Payables	3.0	5.8	6.4				4.0	3.1	16.7
Income Taxes Payable	.0	.0	.0				.0	.0	.0
All Other Current	9.3	15.2	13.9				8.4	13.2	12.2
Total Current	15.7	25.0	23.7				17.7	18.7	29.4
Long-Term Debt	17.6	16.3	10.2				6.9	5.1	11.0
Deferred Taxes	.0	.0	.0				.0	.0	.0
All Other Non-Current	1.5	4.1	3.5				.4	8.3	3.9
Net Worth	65.2	54.7	62.6				75.1	68.0	55.6
Total Liabilities & Net Worth	100.0	100.0	100.0				100.0	100.0	100.0
INCOME DATA									
Net Sales	100.0	100.0	100.0				100.0	100.0	100.0
Gross Profit									
Operating Expenses	96.6	96.9	94.6				98.9	92.0	92.9
Operating Profit	3.4	3.1	5.4				1.1	8.0	7.1
All Other Expenses (net)	.2	1.8	-.6				-.4	-2.5	1.1
Profit Before Taxes	3.1	1.3	6.0				1.4	10.5	6.1
RATIOS									
Current	9.0	8.5	7.3				8.0	9.7	6.5
	3.7	2.5	2.8				5.3	3.6	2.6
	1.5	1.1	1.3				2.1	1.5	1.3
Quick	6.0	5.7	5.6				6.9	6.1	5.1
	2.8	2.4	1.9				3.7	3.1	2.5
	1.1	1.0	1.0				1.2	.9	1.2
Sales/Receivables	0 UND	1 287.6	1 305.1				9 39.5	0 UND	6 58.6
	10 34.9	20 17.9	17 21.2				29 12.7	35 10.6	15 25.1
	61 6.0	59 6.2	53 6.9				86 4.2	57 6.4	37 9.8
Cost of Sales/Inventory									
Cost of Sales/Payables									
Sales/Working Capital	1.8	3.0	2.0				1.5	1.9	5.6
	4.1	6.1	5.8				4.1	5.0	8.4
	13.5	41.1	23.2				9.6	7.4	32.1
EBIT/Interest	9.8	5.0	12.4						
	(20) 1.0	(21) .7	(23) 1.5						
	-1.0	-4.6	-.2						
Net Profit + Depr., Dep., Amort./Cur. Mat. L/T/D									
Fixed/Worth	.0	.1	.0				.0	.0	.0
	.4	.6	.2				.2	.2	.2
	.9	1.9	.8				.8	.7	.3
Debt/Worth	.1	.3	.1				.2	.1	.1
	.6	.7	.4				.3	.3	.8
	1.0	2.6	1.3				.5	1.2	2.7
% Profit Before Taxes/Tangible Net Worth	14.8	11.4	9.4				15.5	12.6	24.6
	(40) 2.6	(45) 3.5	(51) 3.1				-.1	(12) 7.0	(11) 4.8
	-4.8	-13.9	-2.3				-5.1	-2.9	-1.6
% Profit Before Taxes/Total Assets	6.6	5.9	4.5				13.3	12.2	10.3
	1.6	.3	1.3				.2	3.5	2.0
	-2.7	-5.3	-1.0				-3.2	-1.2	-.6
Sales/Net Fixed Assets	27.3	94.2	67.6				63.1	53.4	362.6
	3.9	4.7	9.1				18.2	9.1	31.5
	1.4	1.2	1.5				1.2	3.6	3.7
Sales/Total Assets	1.8	2.6	2.4				3.4	1.7	4.2
	.9	1.1	.9				1.3	.8	2.4
	.4	.5	.3				.2	.6	.6
% Depr., Dep., Amort./Sales	.7	.4	.3					.8	.1
	(33) 2.4	(36) 1.3	(41) 1.1					(10) 1.5	(10) .4
	4.6	3.7	3.3					2.1	1.6
% Officers', Directors' Owners' Comp/Sales									
Net Sales ($)	850400M	661033M	1790694M	2954M	17514M	16137M	66725M	225750M	1461614M
Total Assets ($)	693456M	752584M	1392840M	17441M	70117M	17762M	121001M	420955M	745564M

M = $ thousand   MM = $ million
See Pages 9 through 22 for Explanation of Ratios and Data

Current Data Sorted by Assets   **Comparative Historical Data**

						Type of Statement	4/1/06-3/31/07 ALL	4/1/07-3/31/08 ALL
	2	10	5	5	4	Unqualified	13	17
						Reviewed		2
	1	1				Compiled	5	1
						Tax Returns	1	2
1	3	2	6	2		Other	4	8
0-500M	500M-2MM	2-10MM	10-50MM	50-100MM	100-250MM			
	27 (4/1-9/30/10)		15 (10/1/10-3/31/11)					
1	6	13	11	7	4	**NUMBER OF STATEMENTS**	23	30
%	%	%	%	%	%		%	%
						ASSETS		
		21.1	20.9			Cash & Equivalents	17.4	26.4
		11.6	11.3			Trade Receivables (net)	7.6	16.3
		.7	.9			Inventory	3.1	1.3
		3.5	1.5			All Other Current	3.1	2.5
		36.9	34.6			Total Current	31.2	46.6
		47.5	49.1			Fixed Assets (net)	39.6	29.9
		.0	.1			Intangibles (net)	.2	.1
		15.6	16.1			All Other Non-Current	29.0	23.4
		100.0	100.0			Total	100.0	100.0
						LIABILITIES		
		.3	3.3			Notes Payable-Short Term	2.1	2.3
		.7	.3			Cur. Mat.-L.T.D.	.7	1.3
		8.0	2.7			Trade Payables	3.0	5.1
		.0	.0			Income Taxes Payable	.0	.1
		3.5	5.2			All Other Current	7.8	12.0
		12.5	11.5			Total Current	13.6	20.8
		8.7	10.4			Long-Term Debt	12.2	9.9
		.0	.0			Deferred Taxes	.0	.0
		3.9	.8			All Other Non-Current	1.7	7.2
		74.9	77.3			Net Worth	72.5	62.1
		100.0	100.0			Total Liabilities & Net Worth	100.0	100.0
						INCOME DATA		
		100.0	100.0			Net Sales	100.0	100.0
						Gross Profit		
		97.5	95.0			Operating Expenses	86.1	89.9
		2.5	5.0			Operating Profit	13.9	10.1
		.5	.0			All Other Expenses (net)	-1.2	-1.7
		2.0	5.0			Profit Before Taxes	15.1	11.8
						RATIOS		
		11.0	8.3				7.7	8.1
		5.0	5.0			Current	2.3	2.9
		2.2	1.4				1.5	1.4
		10.2	8.2				6.0	8.1
		3.9	4.0			Quick	1.7	2.9
		2.1	1.3				1.0	.8
		2 150.4	18 20.5				1 564.0	0 UND
		28 13.0	38 9.6			Sales/Receivables	8 48.3	8 46.5
		43 8.4	84 4.3				27 13.4	46 8.0
						Cost of Sales/Inventory		
						Cost of Sales/Payables		
		2.3	1.6				2.9	2.3
		3.5	2.9			Sales/Working Capital	8.2	6.1
		17.4	11.2				16.4	21.3
							13.0	35.9
						EBIT/Interest	(13) 4.3	(20) 7.0
							-.5	4.6
						Net Profit + Depr., Dep., Amort./Cur. Mat. L/T/D		
		.2	.4				.1	.1
		.7	.5			Fixed/Worth	.5	.4
		1.0	.9				1.0	.9
		.1	.1				.2	.2
		.2	.2			Debt/Worth	.3	.6
		.5	.6				.9	1.0
		6.9	10.9				17.3	21.8
		.2	4.7			% Profit Before Taxes/Tangible Net Worth	7.6	12.7
		-4.2	-.6				.1	2.8
		5.9	8.5				10.0	13.7
		.0	2.3			% Profit Before Taxes/Total Assets	6.2	6.5
		-2.5	-.5				.1	.7
		28.4	4.7				6.8	47.8
		1.3	1.4			Sales/Net Fixed Assets	1.8	3.7
		.6	.4				.8	1.1
		1.8	1.2				1.0	1.9
		.6	.5			Sales/Total Assets	.6	.8
		.4	.3				.4	.5
		.8	1.8				.9	.6
		3.6	(10) 3.1			% Depr., Dep., Amort./Sales	(19) 1.7	(25) 1.4
		8.4	10.3				4.4	3.7
						% Officers', Directors' Owners' Comp/Sales		
739M	8778M	72180M	182571M	286896M	394006M	Net Sales ($)	426183M	637414M
310M	6655M	70277M	236895M	426406M	623195M	Total Assets ($)	533561M	1015215M

© RMA 2011

M = $ thousand   MM = $ million
See Pages 9 through 22 for Explanation of Ratios and Data

Comparative Historical Data | Current Data Sorted by Sales

18	14	26	Type of Statement		5	2	3	6	10
1	1		Unqualified						
			Reviewed						
	1	2	Compiled	1	1				
		1	Tax Returns						
10	8	14	Other	3	2	3	3	1	2
4/1/08-3/31/09 ALL	4/1/09-3/31/10 ALL	4/1/10-3/31/11 ALL		27 (4/1-9/30/10)			15 (10/1/10-3/31/11)		
				0-1MM	1-3MM	3-5MM	5-10MM	10-25MM	25MM & OVER
29	24	42	**NUMBER OF STATEMENTS**	4	8	5	6	7	12
%	%	%	**ASSETS**	%	%	%	%	%	%
28.4	20.7	23.0	Cash & Equivalents						21.7
8.5	9.4	10.7	Trade Receivables (net)						15.2
1.4	1.8	1.3	Inventory						1.5
6.5	3.6	3.7	All Other Current						3.1
44.8	35.4	38.7	Total Current						41.5
31.8	40.1	38.8	Fixed Assets (net)						21.0
.5	.1	.0	Intangibles (net)						.0
22.9	24.5	22.5	All Other Non-Current						37.4
100.0	100.0	100.0	Total						100.0
			LIABILITIES						
4.0	.8	1.0	Notes Payable-Short Term						2.6
2.7	1.5	.5	Cur. Mat.-L.T.D.						.3
3.6	5.8	5.0	Trade Payables						5.3
.0	.0	.0	Income Taxes Payable						.0
9.2	7.1	4.4	All Other Current						5.7
19.4	15.1	11.0	Total Current						13.9
9.5	8.0	8.5	Long-Term Debt						5.2
.0	.0	.0	Deferred Taxes						.0
5.0	8.1	3.6	All Other Non-Current						7.9
66.1	68.8	76.9	Net Worth						72.9
100.0	100.0	100.0	Total Liabilties & Net Worth						100.0
			INCOME DATA						
100.0	100.0	100.0	Net Sales						100.0
			Gross Profit						
91.7	96.8	94.9	Operating Expenses						95.6
8.3	3.2	5.1	Operating Profit						4.4
2.2	2.9	.2	All Other Expenses (net)						-.6
6.1	.3	4.9	Profit Before Taxes						5.0
			RATIOS						
9.1	9.6	9.6							5.4
4.2	3.0	4.8	Current						3.6
1.5	1.7	1.6							1.7
8.1	6.2	9.3							5.1
2.2	2.7	4.0	Quick						2.6
.9	1.3	1.4							1.2
0 UND	0 UND	5 77.3							7 51.2
8 48.2	7 51.9	25 14.4	Sales/Receivables						25 14.5
42 8.7	37 9.7	62 5.9							105 3.5
			Cost of Sales/Inventory						
			Cost of Sales/Payables						
1.6	2.5	2.0							2.2
2.9	4.8	3.3	Sales/Working Capital						3.8
11.9	23.2	9.1							7.1
10.2	17.1	17.3							
(18) 2.9	(17) 1.0	(23) 3.3	EBIT/Interest						
-4.1	-9.9	-.6							
			Net Profit + Depr., Dep., Amort./Cur. Mat. L/T/D						
.1	.2	.1							.0
.4	.6	.5	Fixed/Worth						.3
.8	1.0	.8							.5
.1	.1	.1							.1
.6	.3	.2	Debt/Worth						.3
1.2	.8	.5							.6
22.7	4.6	8.8							15.5
1.5	(23) -.2	2.9	% Profit Before Taxes/Tangible Net Worth						5.6
-5.7	-4.3	-1.1							-.3
6.4	4.5	7.7							12.2
1.3	-.7	2.1	% Profit Before Taxes/Total Assets						3.1
-3.6	-3.5	-.9							-.2
15.8	19.0	20.8							34.0
2.7	3.2	3.2	Sales/Net Fixed Assets						5.9
1.0	.9	.6							1.9
.9	2.1	1.4							1.4
.6	.8	.7	Sales/Total Assets						.8
.4	.5	.4							.6
1.2	1.2	1.1							.9
(25) 1.8	(20) 2.2	(38) 2.3	% Depr., Dep., Amort./Sales						(11) 1.3
4.1	4.3	5.0							2.3
			% Officers', Directors' Owners' Comp/Sales						
732885M	762525M	945170M	Net Sales ($)	2321M	15904M	17136M	44071M	101146M	764592M
1323056M	861462M	1363738M	Total Assets ($)	2453M	55725M	34532M	71970M	289149M	909909M

M = $ thousand   MM = $ million
See Pages 9 through 22 for Explanation of Ratios and Data

	Current Data Sorted by Assets							Comparative Historical Data	
Type of Statement									
Unqualified	11	48	125	114	17	18		311	329
Reviewed	2		1					6	5
Compiled	1	1	2					16	12
Tax Returns	4	3	4					14	7
Other	8	27	63	36	8	5		99	123
		363 (4/1-9/30/10)			135 (10/1/10-3/31/11)			4/1/06-3/31/07	4/1/07-3/31/08
	0-500M	500M-2MM	2-10MM	10-50MM	50-100MM	100-250MM		ALL	ALL
NUMBER OF STATEMENTS	26	79	195	150	25	23		446	476
	%	%	%	%	%	%		%	%
ASSETS									
Cash & Equivalents	44.5	32.0	22.0	20.5	25.2	22.6		20.7	22.3
Trade Receivables (net)	22.4	17.9	15.2	13.2	13.5	6.3		14.5	14.4
Inventory	.5	2.5	1.2	2.7	.1	.8		2.4	1.5
All Other Current	4.8	4.3	5.2	5.2	7.9	3.6		4.8	5.1
Total Current	72.2	56.7	43.8	41.6	46.7	33.2		42.5	43.3
Fixed Assets (net)	22.7	32.1	42.3	39.2	23.7	23.8		41.4	38.4
Intangibles (net)	.8	.5	.3	.9	.2	.2		1.1	.8
All Other Non-Current	4.3	10.6	13.6	18.4	29.5	42.7		15.1	17.5
Total	100.0	100.0	100.0	100.0	100.0	100.0		100.0	100.0
LIABILITIES									
Notes Payable-Short Term	6.6	5.4	2.7	1.4	.3	2.8		3.2	2.9
Cur. Mat.-L.T.D.	1.0	1.2	1.7	2.1	2.3	4.0		2.1	2.3
Trade Payables	16.8	8.7	6.5	5.8	5.2	3.9		6.2	6.0
Income Taxes Payable	.0	.0	.0	.0	.0	.0		.1	.1
All Other Current	9.6	11.4	9.8	10.6	15.6	11.8		9.8	9.4
Total Current	34.0	26.7	20.7	20.0	23.4	22.5		21.4	20.6
Long-Term Debt	10.5	15.2	17.0	16.5	19.3	12.4		20.6	18.4
Deferred Taxes	.0	.0	.0	.0	.0	.0		.0	.0
All Other Non-Current	5.3	4.8	3.5	3.8	3.6	12.1		2.7	3.2
Net Worth	50.2	53.4	58.7	59.7	53.7	53.0		55.3	57.8
Total Liabilities & Net Worth	100.0	100.0	100.0	100.0	100.0	100.0		100.0	100.0
INCOME DATA									
Net Sales	100.0	100.0	100.0	100.0	100.0	100.0		100.0	100.0
Gross Profit									
Operating Expenses	93.8	93.5	95.1	96.2	93.7	87.1		93.4	93.4
Operating Profit	6.2	6.5	4.9	3.8	6.3	12.9		6.6	6.6
All Other Expenses (net)	.5	.6	1.7	.2	.6	3.0		1.3	1.1
Profit Before Taxes	5.7	5.9	3.2	3.6	5.7	9.9		5.3	5.6
RATIOS									
Current	9.2	8.6	5.1	5.1	5.1	5.2		4.8	4.7
	2.6	2.8	2.2	2.3	2.4	2.1		2.0	2.1
	1.4	1.2	1.3	1.4	1.3	.9		1.2	1.2
Quick	9.2	7.5	4.5	3.8	5.0	2.9		3.6	4.0
	2.5	2.2	1.9	1.8	2.3	1.2		1.6	1.8
	1.2	1.1	1.0	1.1	1.3	.5		1.0	1.0
Sales/Receivables	0 UND	0 UND	5 68.5	11 34.5	18 20.6	3 136.8		4 95.2	5 77.3
	12 29.6	24 15.3	23 16.1	30 12.3	34 10.9	25 14.5		24 15.2	26 13.9
	31 11.7	49 7.5	44 8.4	56 6.6	59 6.1	79 4.6		48 7.6	48 7.5
Cost of Sales/Inventory									
Cost of Sales/Payables									
Sales/Working Capital	3.6	2.5	3.4	2.0	1.4	1.8		3.1	3.4
	6.2	6.3	8.1	6.0	4.4	6.3		8.0	7.4
	17.2	36.2	22.7	16.8	23.7	-64.4		35.0	28.4
EBIT/Interest	14.7	9.1	14.5	10.0	12.7	50.5		7.8	9.3
	(12) 2.9	(39) 2.6	(121) 3.1	(107) 3.1	(17) 6.1	(18) 3.3		(281) 2.4	(297) 2.6
	-6.0	-1.7	.5	.4	1.7	1.6		.8	.5
Net Profit + Depr., Dep., Amort./Cur. Mat. L/T/D									
Fixed/Worth	.0	.1	.2	.3	.1	.0		.2	.2
	.2	.3	.7	.6	.2	.5		.7	.6
	.8	1.4	1.3	1.2	.9	.9		1.4	1.2
Debt/Worth	.1	.1	.2	.2	.4	.2		.2	.2
	.7	.6	.6	.7	.7	.9		.8	.7
	4.5	2.5	1.2	1.5	2.3	2.2		1.9	1.6
% Profit Before Taxes/Tangible Net Worth	20.4	23.6	16.8	10.5	14.5	10.5		15.1	17.0
	(22) 8.0	(73) 9.8	(189) 4.1	(147) 3.5	(24) 5.2	(22) 5.0		(430) 4.8	(464) 6.4
	-17.2	-2.9	-.6	-1.4	1.1	1.3		-.9	-1.0
% Profit Before Taxes/Total Assets	19.1	11.6	9.0	5.6	5.4	4.1		7.5	9.0
	6.7	5.2	2.3	1.7	2.5	2.5		2.4	3.2
	-5.1	-2.4	-.8	-.9	-.1	.8		-.5	-.8
Sales/Net Fixed Assets	106.8	61.5	28.4	7.9	16.6	20.7		14.7	20.3
	51.1	18.1	4.1	2.8	3.4	6.9		3.6	4.0
	9.8	1.8	1.1	1.2	1.2	.8		1.1	1.3
Sales/Total Assets	3.5	3.3	2.4	1.8	1.2	.9		2.4	2.3
	2.4	1.6	1.3	.8	.7	.3		1.1	1.1
	1.3	.8	.6	.5	.3	.2		.5	.5
% Depr., Dep., Amort./Sales	.5	.5	.8	1.2	.8	.9		1.0	.9
	(16) 1.2	(59) 1.4	(166) 2.0	(138) 2.3	(22) 1.6	(19) 1.7		(375) 2.1	(401) 2.0
	2.7	3.7	4.3	4.4	3.5	6.1		4.5	3.9
% Officers', Directors' Owners' Comp/Sales			5.9					6.4	3.0
		(14)	10.2					(39) 11.8	(29) 9.9
			30.2					16.5	24.1
Net Sales ($)	20347M	236201M	1800888M	4987706M	2155911M	2322636M		10150563M	9052605M
Total Assets ($)	7157M	100552M	1003416M	3422688M	1777000M	3572748M		8190704M	8527616M

M = $ thousand   MM = $ million
See Pages 9 through 22 for Explanation of Ratios and Data

Comparative Historical Data | Current Data Sorted by Sales

			Type of Statement						
357	347	333	Unqualified	25	55	36	58	88	71
7	8	3	Reviewed	3					
10	5	4	Compiled	4					
9	8	11	Tax Returns	6	2		2	1	
124	133	147	Other	20	30	14	24	33	26
4/1/08-3/31/09 ALL	4/1/09-3/31/10 ALL	4/1/10-3/31/11 ALL		363 (4/1-9/30/10)			135 (10/1/10-3/31/11)		
				0-1MM	1-3MM	3-5MM	5-10MM	10-25MM	25MM & OVER
507	501	498	**NUMBER OF STATEMENTS**	58	87	50	84	122	97
%	%	%	**ASSETS**	%	%	%	%	%	%
20.0	22.3	24.5	Cash & Equivalents	32.4	21.9	23.3	22.7	22.4	27.0
13.1	14.8	14.9	Trade Receivables (net)	10.0	11.5	20.0	15.9	16.0	16.2
1.8	1.3	1.8	Inventory	.7	2.7	.8	2.0	.7	3.1
4.8	4.8	5.1	All Other Current	2.7	6.4	4.1	5.5	6.0	4.5
39.7	43.3	46.3	Total Current	45.8	42.5	48.2	46.1	45.1	50.8
42.3	39.3	36.9	Fixed Assets (net)	47.1	41.1	34.7	36.1	33.2	33.7
.8	.6	.5	Intangibles (net)	.1	.5	.4	.7	.3	.9
17.2	16.8	16.2	All Other Non-Current	7.0	15.9	16.7	17.1	21.4	14.5
100.0	100.0	100.0	Total	100.0	100.0	100.0	100.0	100.0	100.0
			LIABILITIES						
2.6	2.7	2.9	Notes Payable-Short Term	7.2	1.6	4.3	3.2	2.3	1.0
1.9	1.7	1.8	Cur. Mat.-L.T.D.	1.0	2.5	1.0	1.5	2.1	2.1
6.7	6.2	7.0	Trade Payables	6.8	3.3	6.2	8.5	7.5	8.8
.0	.2	.0	Income Taxes Payable	.0	.0	.0	.0	.0	.1
9.8	10.5	10.7	All Other Current	6.6	5.6	9.9	10.4	11.1	17.7
21.1	21.2	22.4	Total Current	21.7	13.0	21.5	23.6	23.0	29.7
20.6	18.5	16.1	Long-Term Debt	19.6	20.9	14.9	12.9	15.9	13.5
.0	.0	.0	Deferred Taxes	.0	.0	.0	.1	.0	.0
3.9	4.0	4.3	All Other Non-Current	2.4	4.3	4.0	3.2	5.3	5.1
54.4	56.3	57.2	Net Worth	56.3	61.8	59.5	60.2	55.8	51.7
100.0	100.0	100.0	Total Liabilities & Net Worth	100.0	100.0	100.0	100.0	100.0	100.0
			INCOME DATA						
100.0	100.0	100.0	Net Sales	100.0	100.0	100.0	100.0	100.0	100.0
			Gross Profit						
96.1	97.0	94.7	Operating Expenses	89.2	92.8	93.6	97.1	96.1	96.2
3.9	3.0	5.3	Operating Profit	10.8	7.2	6.4	2.9	3.9	3.8
2.2	2.2	1.0	All Other Expenses (net)	4.7	1.5	1.8	.1	.1	-.2
1.6	.8	4.3	Profit Before Taxes	6.1	5.8	4.6	2.8	3.8	4.0
			RATIOS						
4.7	4.8	5.7		9.3	10.0	8.1	4.3	4.5	3.6
2.1	2.3	2.3	Current	3.2	3.8	2.7	2.1	2.1	1.8
1.1	1.2	1.3		1.1	1.6	1.6	1.4	1.3	1.1
4.0	3.7	4.8		9.2	9.2	7.6	3.5	3.8	2.7
(506) 1.8	1.9	1.9	Quick	2.2	2.8	2.6	1.7	1.9	1.6
.9	1.0	1.0		.8	1.3	1.2	1.1	1.0	1.0
4 93.0	7 55.1	6 64.2		0 UND	0 834.3	11 33.3	10 36.5	13 28.3	10 36.9
23 16.0	27 13.4	25 14.5	Sales/Receivables	6 57.6	20 18.5	36 10.3	26 13.8	30 12.0	26 14.3
47 7.8	54 6.8	49 7.5		39 9.4	47 7.8	68 5.3	54 6.7	51 7.2	45 8.1
			Cost of Sales/Inventory						
			Cost of Sales/Payables						
2.9	2.8	2.6		1.6	1.6	1.8	2.8	3.5	4.7
8.3	7.2	6.7	Sales/Working Capital	5.0	3.9	4.7	7.8	8.0	11.3
69.6	30.8	22.7		36.4	16.2	13.0	22.6	24.4	42.1
6.8	8.8	13.0		4.9	8.1	13.1	12.9	16.6	19.0
(326) 1.7	(322) 2.3	(314) 3.1	EBIT/Interest	(29) 1.8	(53) 1.6	(27) 3.1	(51) 3.4	(83) 3.3	(71) 3.8
-.8	-1.1	.3		-2.7	-1.0	1.0	1.1	-.2	1.2
			Net Profit + Depr., Dep., Amort./Cur. Mat. L/T/D						
.3	.2	.1		.1	.1	.1	.1	.2	.3
.7	.6	.6	Fixed/Worth	.7	.5	.5	.6	.5	.6
1.4	1.2	1.2		1.6	1.4	1.1	1.2	1.1	1.1
.3	.3	.2		.1	.1	.2	.2	.3	.3
.7	.7	.6	Debt/Worth	.4	.5	.5	.5	.7	1.0
1.8	1.8	1.6		2.8	1.4	1.6	1.3	1.3	2.0
11.0	11.7	14.1		12.9	19.2	16.2	12.6	17.6	12.8
(481) 1.8	(483) 3.4	(477) 5.0	% Profit Before Taxes/Tangible Net Worth	(53) 3.2	(84) 5.7	(48) 5.1	(81) 5.4	(118) 4.1	(93) 7.3
-5.5	-4.5	-1.2		-3.8	-3.0	-.2	.3	-2.3	1.1
5.4	6.0	7.7		8.0	9.2	7.1	8.5	8.3	6.3
.8	1.2	2.5	% Profit Before Taxes/Total Assets	2.2	2.5	3.2	3.0	1.6	2.9
-3.4	-3.0	-.9		-2.5	-2.3	-.3	-.1	-1.3	.3
16.1	20.5	30.2		52.5	39.2	38.5	39.9	17.8	22.3
3.1	3.8	4.5	Sales/Net Fixed Assets	1.4	2.3	3.6	3.8	4.7	7.1
1.1	1.3	1.3		.5	.8	.9	1.2	2.0	3.0
2.0	2.2	2.2		1.7	1.3	1.9	2.6	2.4	3.1
1.1	1.1	1.1	Sales/Total Assets	.7	.7	1.1	1.0	1.3	1.9
.5	.5	.5		.3	.4	.4	.6	.6	.9
1.0	.9	.8		1.5	1.2	.7	.8	.8	.7
(431) 2.2	(431) 2.2	(420) 1.9	% Depr., Dep., Amort./Sales	(42) 4.3	(68) 3.3	(36) 2.2	(74) 2.3	(109) 1.8	(91) 1.4
4.6	4.4	4.2		14.8	7.4	4.6	4.5	3.0	3.1
2.1	2.9	2.3							
(34) 8.5	(44) 5.5	(28) 10.2	% Officers', Directors' Owners' Comp/Sales						
18.8	16.1	29.2							
10038971M	10562276M	11523689M	Net Sales ($)	33224M	164437M	199396M	624182M	2018540M	8483910M
8473172M	9515603M	9883561M	Total Assets ($)	93257M	340457M	397510M	730862M	2838162M	5483313M

M = $ thousand   MM = $ million
See Pages 9 through 22 for Explanation of Ratios and Data

Current Data Sorted by Assets

Comparative Historical Data

						Type of Statement		
13	36	135	158	36	15	Unqualified	266	280
2	3	14	5			Reviewed	14	8
10	15	15	4			Compiled	22	18
17	24	14	3			Tax Returns	28	41
29	39	100	58	11	3	Other	116	118
	469 (4/1-9/30/10)			290 (10/1/10-3/31/11)			4/1/06-3/31/07	4/1/07-3/31/08
0-500M	500M-2MM	2-10MM	10-50MM	50-100MM	100-250MM		ALL	ALL
71	117	278	228	47	18	NUMBER OF STATEMENTS	446	465
%	%	%	%	%	%	ASSETS	%	%
35.3	21.5	19.1	17.2	20.4	12.7	Cash & Equivalents	21.3	23.3
17.0	9.3	7.7	5.7	5.0	2.7	Trade Receivables (net)	7.2	8.2
2.8	1.3	.9	.9	1.7	.4	Inventory	1.5	1.1
2.5	1.8	1.8	2.5	2.6	3.6	All Other Current	3.5	3.0
57.6	34.0	29.6	26.2	29.7	19.3	Total Current	33.4	35.6
38.5	53.5	53.7	54.9	47.3	34.0	Fixed Assets (net)	51.3	49.1
.1	1.2	.7	.7	.6	.5	Intangibles (net)	.5	.5
3.7	11.4	16.0	18.2	22.3	46.2	All Other Non-Current	14.8	14.7
100.0	100.0	100.0	100.0	100.0	100.0	Total	100.0	100.0
						LIABILITIES		
9.8	2.4	2.7	1.2	1.2	1.6	Notes Payable-Short Term	3.7	3.2
1.6	1.8	1.9	1.4	1.2	2.0	Cur. Mat.-L.T.D.	2.0	1.9
16.5	3.9	4.7	3.0	3.6	3.3	Trade Payables	4.0	4.2
.1	.1	.0	.0	.0	.0	Income Taxes Payable	.0	.0
16.9	6.6	7.5	6.0	7.2	6.3	All Other Current	7.7	8.0
44.9	14.7	16.8	11.6	13.2	13.2	Total Current	17.4	17.4
31.7	27.6	19.9	20.6	19.7	15.9	Long-Term Debt	21.4	20.2
.0	.0	.0	.0	.0	.0	Deferred Taxes	.0	.0
6.1	3.4	3.9	2.9	2.5	4.3	All Other Non-Current	4.0	3.8
17.3	54.3	59.4	64.8	64.7	66.6	Net Worth	57.2	58.6
100.0	100.0	100.0	100.0	100.0	100.0	Total Liabilities & Net Worth	100.0	100.0
						INCOME DATA		
100.0	100.0	100.0	100.0	100.0	100.0	Net Sales	100.0	100.0
						Gross Profit		
95.9	92.5	95.6	95.5	92.5	91.0	Operating Expenses	93.3	92.6
4.1	7.5	4.4	4.5	7.5	9.0	Operating Profit	6.7	7.4
2.3	2.8	1.7	1.3	-.1	6.2	All Other Expenses (net)	1.2	1.4
1.8	4.7	2.7	3.2	7.6	2.8	Profit Before Taxes	5.4	6.1
						RATIOS		
8.0	8.1	5.3	5.3	4.5	3.0		5.9	6.5
2.6	3.2	2.2	2.6	2.0	1.9	Current	2.3	2.5
1.1	1.1	1.0	1.2	1.0	.4		1.0	1.1
7.8	7.1	5.1	4.1	3.7	2.1		5.2	5.5
2.2	3.1	2.0	2.2	1.6	1.2	Quick	1.8	2.1
1.1	1.1	.9	1.0	.8	.3		.8	.8
0 UND	0 UND	1 541.9	2 192.4	2 178.0	0 UND		0 936.6	1 557.4
1 341.3	2 148.5	12 30.2	14 26.3	15 23.9	9 40.8	Sales/Receivables	11 33.3	12 29.6
20 18.3	26 14.0	40 9.0	35 10.6	36 10.2	42 8.7		33 11.1	36 10.1
						Cost of Sales/Inventory		
						Cost of Sales/Payables		
3.1	3.1	2.9	2.3	2.6	2.2		2.5	2.2
8.7	6.7	7.1	5.2	7.7	3.8	Sales/Working Capital	7.9	6.8
59.5	69.0	-190.3	21.4	999.8	-4.4		250.0	66.7
4.6	4.8	4.4	6.3	9.8	4.9		6.6	7.9
(34) 1.7	(64) 2.2	(183) 1.5	(177) 1.9	(34) 2.6	(11) 2.5	EBIT/Interest	(281) 2.3	(301) 2.3
-1.1	.2	-.9	-.3	1.0	.9		.4	.6
						Net Profit + Depr., Dep., Amort./Cur. Mat. L/T/D	24.7	
							(10) 3.7	
							1.1	
.0	.3	.4	.5	.3	.0		.4	.3
.7	1.0	.9	.9	.7	.3	Fixed/Worth	.9	.8
2.3	1.8	1.6	1.3	1.5	1.4		1.5	1.4
.2	.1	.2	.2	.2	.1		.2	.2
.8	.7	.5	.5	.5	.4	Debt/Worth	.5	.5
9.0	1.8	1.3	1.0	1.1	1.1		1.4	1.2
24.4	15.2	10.6	7.3	10.5	5.8	% Profit Before Taxes/Tangible Net Worth	11.1	13.5
(57) 6.4	(109) 4.6	(264) 2.2	(225) 1.7	2.6	1.0		(421) 3.2	(445) 4.7
-5.1	-4.6	-2.0	-2.0	-.5	-1.6		-1.5	-1.1
15.6	7.4	5.0	4.2	7.3	3.6	% Profit Before Taxes/Total Assets	7.2	8.3
2.4	2.6	1.3	1.0	1.4	.7		1.9	2.3
-4.8	-2.2	-1.8	-1.4	-.4	-1.4		-1.3	-.9
132.0	8.6	4.9	2.2	5.2	11.6		5.2	6.8
8.1	1.9	1.3	.8	.8	.9	Sales/Net Fixed Assets	1.2	1.5
1.9	.6	.5	.5	.5	.5		.6	.7
4.5	1.8	1.2	.7	.8	.4		1.3	1.3
2.2	.8	.7	.5	.5	.3	Sales/Total Assets	.7	.7
1.0	.4	.4	.3	.3	.1		.3	.4
1.1	1.2	1.8	3.3	1.9	3.4	% Depr., Dep., Amort./Sales	1.9	2.0
(42) 2.9	(76) 3.4	(222) 3.8	(206) 6.7	(41) 6.4	(15) 6.9		(349) 4.7	(359) 4.5
7.5	8.2	8.6	10.4	10.3	12.0		7.7	7.8
3.7	.6	1.7	3.6			% Officers', Directors' Owners' Comp/Sales	5.0	4.5
(11) 27.5	(15) 4.4	(14) 7.2	(14) 7.0				(42) 10.6	(50) 10.6
31.6	6.0	18.3	14.2				32.4	21.2
49031M	223510M	1446492M	3282959M	2268586M	765479M	Net Sales ($)	4061897M	4692191M
19149M	140640M	1450179M	4956516M	3141477M	2751333M	Total Assets ($)	6921121M	8233753M

M = $ thousand   MM = $ million
See Pages 9 through 22 for Explanation of Ratios and Data

Comparative Historical Data / Current Data Sorted by Sales

			Type of Statement						
304	331	393	Unqualified	24	62	63	107	77	60
10	21	24	Reviewed	8	12	1	3		
30	38	44	Compiled	27	12	2	2		1
40	40	58	Tax Returns	42	9	3	3	1	
151	216	240	Other	61	60	27	40	30	22
4/1/08-3/31/09 ALL	4/1/09-3/31/10 ALL	4/1/10-3/31/11 ALL		469 (4/1-9/30/10)			290 (10/1/10-3/31/11)		
				0-1MM	1-3MM	3-5MM	5-10MM	10-25MM	25MM & OVER
535	646	759	NUMBER OF STATEMENTS	162	155	96	155	108	83
%	%	%	**ASSETS**	%	%	%	%	%	%
22.7	21.5	20.4	Cash & Equivalents	21.1	18.4	21.2	21.0	19.8	21.2
7.4	8.1	7.9	Trade Receivables (net)	6.3	6.8	8.1	8.2	8.5	11.7
1.0	1.2	1.2	Inventory	1.0	1.4	.9	.8	1.0	2.4
3.4	3.0	2.2	All Other Current	1.3	2.2	1.3	2.3	2.8	3.8
34.5	33.8	31.6	Total Current	29.7	28.8	31.5	32.3	32.1	39.1
49.6	52.5	51.7	Fixed Assets (net)	61.9	56.2	49.1	47.9	47.9	38.7
.7	.6	.7	Intangibles (net)	.3	1.1	.8	.5	.7	.7
15.1	13.1	15.9	All Other Non-Current	8.0	13.9	18.6	19.3	19.2	21.5
100.0	100.0	100.0	Total	100.0	100.0	100.0	100.0	100.0	100.0
			LIABILITIES						
2.6	2.9	2.7	Notes Payable-Short Term	3.2	4.0	1.5	1.9	1.5	4.2
1.7	2.2	1.7	Cur. Mat.-L.T.D.	1.6	2.8	.9	1.2	1.4	2.0
4.0	4.1	5.1	Trade Payables	5.5	3.7	4.1	4.3	5.8	8.3
.0	.1	.0	Income Taxes Payable	.0	.1	.0	.0	.0	.0
7.0	8.5	7.7	All Other Current	7.0	6.2	8.5	7.4	9.3	9.8
15.3	17.8	17.2	Total Current	17.4	16.8	15.0	14.8	18.0	24.2
20.6	23.5	22.3	Long-Term Debt	31.8	24.0	15.2	21.2	19.2	14.9
.0	.0	.0	Deferred Taxes	.0	.0	.0	.0	.0	.0
4.1	4.8	3.7	All Other Non-Current	2.0	4.8	2.6	3.1	6.4	3.6
60.0	53.9	56.8	Net Worth	48.9	54.4	67.2	61.0	56.4	57.3
100.0	100.0	100.0	Total Liabilities & Net Worth	100.0	100.0	100.0	100.0	100.0	100.0
			INCOME DATA						
100.0	100.0	100.0	Net Sales	100.0	100.0	100.0	100.0	100.0	100.0
			Gross Profit						
95.1	96.5	94.8	Operating Expenses	92.2	95.0	96.0	95.2	95.9	96.1
4.9	3.5	5.2	Operating Profit	7.8	5.0	4.0	4.8	4.1	3.9
3.9	2.7	1.8	All Other Expenses (net)	5.8	1.6	-.1	.5	1.3	-.2
1.0	.7	3.4	Profit Before Taxes	2.1	3.4	4.1	4.3	2.8	4.0
			RATIOS						
6.1	5.6	5.6		10.2	7.2	8.5	4.2	3.9	3.7
2.4	2.3	2.5	Current	3.4	2.5	3.1	2.3	2.4	2.0
1.1	1.0	1.1		1.1	.9	1.2	1.2	1.0	1.0
5.7	5.1	5.0		10.0	5.3	7.3	3.8	3.4	3.3
(534) 1.9	2.0	2.1	Quick	3.1	1.9	2.7	2.0	1.9	1.7
.8	.8	.9		1.1	.6	1.0	1.1	.8	.9
1 658.9	0 UND	0 999.8		0 UND	0 999.8	1 326.8	2 209.2	4 82.9	7 52.8
11 34.6	9 42.4	10 35.3	Sales/Receivables	0 UND	7 50.7	13 27.3	13 28.0	15 25.0	22 17.0
36 10.0	36 10.2	35 10.4		17 21.8	42 8.6	37 9.8	38 9.7	37 9.8	41 8.9
			Cost of Sales/Inventory						
			Cost of Sales/Payables						
2.3	2.4	2.7		2.1	2.9	2.4	2.8	2.8	3.6
6.5	6.4	6.3	Sales/Working Capital	5.6	7.1	4.8	6.0	6.9	7.3
103.7	436.0	114.9		45.0	-33.0	55.8	46.2	-461.5	142.5
4.2	4.3	5.6		3.5	3.7	4.2	6.8	8.2	10.3
(362) 1.1	(422) 1.1	(503) 1.8	EBIT/Interest	(88) 1.7	(109) 1.2	(54) .9	(116) 2.3	(74) 2.3	(62) 2.7
-2.7	-2.4	-.3		-.2	-.4	-2.8	.6	.0	.5
			Net Profit + Depr., Dep., Amort./Cur. Mat. L/T/D						
.3	.4	.4		.5	.4	.4	.4	.4	.2
.8	.9	.9	Fixed/Worth	1.1	1.0	.7	.7	.9	.5
1.4	1.6	1.5		1.8	1.7	1.3	1.3	1.6	1.2
.2	.2	.2		.1	.2	.1	.2	.2	.3
.5	.6	.5	Debt/Worth	.5	.5	.4	.5	.7	.6
1.2	1.5	1.3		1.7	1.4	1.0	1.2	2.2	1.2
7.7	7.0	10.4	% Profit Before Taxes/Tangible Net Worth	9.4	11.6	7.4	10.0	10.0	11.7
(515) .8	(608) .8	(720) 2.3		(148) 1.6	(142) 1.3	(93) 2.3	(151) 4.0	(104) 1.8	(82) 3.7
-5.7	-5.3	-2.2		-2.3	-3.0	-3.4	-.5	-2.1	-1.9
4.8	4.1	5.3	% Profit Before Taxes/Total Assets	4.8	6.2	4.9	5.3	5.3	5.3
.5	.3	1.4		1.2	.6	1.3	2.4	.9	2.0
-3.6	-3.6	-1.6		-1.9	-2.4	-1.9	-.3	-1.3	-1.2
5.4	5.9	5.5		3.6	3.6	6.1	5.1	5.4	17.1
1.2	1.2	1.3	Sales/Net Fixed Assets	.7	1.0	1.4	1.5	1.5	4.4
.6	.6	.5		.3	.5	.5	.7	.7	1.1
1.2	1.2	1.2		1.0	1.1	1.1	1.3	1.4	1.7
.6	.6	.6	Sales/Total Assets	.5	.6	.6	.6	.7	.9
.4	.3	.4		.2	.3	.3	.4	.4	.5
1.9	2.0	2.0		2.5	2.3	2.3	2.0	2.0	1.5
(418) 4.5	(510) 4.7	(602) 4.6	% Depr., Dep., Amort./Sales	(98) 6.6	(115) 5.9	(77) 6.2	(142) 4.4	(98) 4.0	(72) 2.7
8.4	8.9	9.1		16.2	11.1	9.7	8.5	8.1	6.8
3.5	2.6	1.9		1.3	3.1				
(49) 7.1	(54) 7.0	(57) 5.9	% Officers', Directors' Owners' Comp/Sales	(21) 6.3	(16) 5.8				
25.8	14.6	17.3		31.0	10.0				
5749889M	7533462M	8036057M	Net Sales ($)	78488M	299751M	366609M	1122924M	1724799M	4443486M
9980617M	11373463M	12459294M	Total Assets ($)	303160M	732409M	841595M	2147891M	3470040M	4964199M

M = $ thousand   MM = $ million
See Pages 9 through 22 for Explanation of Ratios and Data

Current Data Sorted by Assets   Comparative Historical Data

0-500M	500M-2MM	2-10MM	10-50MM	50-100MM	100-250MM	Type of Statement	4/1/06-3/31/07 ALL	4/1/07-3/31/08 ALL
9	12	64	70	11	16	Unqualified	144	134
1	7	4	2			Reviewed	13	10
3	3	2	1			Compiled	9	11
5	6	3				Tax Returns	17	14
23	26	38	18	7	3	Other	83	65
	145 (4/1-9/30/10)		189 (10/1/10-3/31/11)					
41	54	111	91	18	19	NUMBER OF STATEMENTS	266	234
%	%	%	%	%	%	**ASSETS**	%	%
47.9	36.3	39.0	40.6	32.3	30.4	Cash & Equivalents	38.7	39.4
11.8	14.4	8.2	10.9	8.3	13.7	Trade Receivables (net)	13.9	10.6
.1	2.5	.6	1.0	.5	4.2	Inventory	2.2	1.9
4.4	2.3	3.8	3.5	4.1	2.9	All Other Current	4.3	4.0
64.1	55.6	51.6	56.0	45.2	51.1	Total Current	59.2	55.9
26.8	34.0	32.8	23.3	13.4	16.6	Fixed Assets (net)	23.5	27.2
1.8	1.7	1.2	2.1	4.5	2.7	Intangibles (net)	1.5	1.2
7.3	8.7	14.3	18.6	36.9	29.6	All Other Non-Current	15.8	15.7
100.0	100.0	100.0	100.0	100.0	100.0	Total	100.0	100.0
						LIABILITIES		
6.9	7.2	3.1	.9	.1	8.5	Notes Payable-Short Term	3.9	3.3
4.2	1.3	2.0	1.3	1.3	.3	Cur. Mat.-L.T.D.	1.5	2.3
6.2	9.1	8.1	9.5	5.2	5.6	Trade Payables	11.7	9.3
.1	.0	.0	.2	.1	.1	Income Taxes Payable	.3	.1
26.2	12.8	12.8	14.2	23.5	9.7	All Other Current	15.3	13.8
43.6	30.5	26.1	26.2	30.2	24.2	Total Current	32.7	28.9
19.4	18.5	12.7	9.4	9.1	11.1	Long-Term Debt	14.0	12.5
.0	.1	.0	.1	.1	.1	Deferred Taxes	.1	.1
4.4	8.0	9.2	12.9	12.6	13.0	All Other Non-Current	7.7	9.4
32.6	42.9	52.1	51.4	48.0	51.5	Net Worth	45.5	49.1
100.0	100.0	100.0	100.0	100.0	100.0	Total Liabilities & Net Worth	100.0	100.0
						INCOME DATA		
100.0	100.0	100.0	100.0	100.0	100.0	Net Sales	100.0	100.0
						Gross Profit		
94.8	94.9	95.5	95.1	98.9	94.5	Operating Expenses	92.3	95.6
5.2	5.1	4.5	4.9	1.1	5.5	Operating Profit	7.7	4.4
.3	1.9	1.7	-.4	-.8	-.7	All Other Expenses (net)	.4	.3
4.9	3.1	2.7	5.3	1.9	6.2	Profit Before Taxes	7.3	4.1
						RATIOS		
11.6	9.4	7.6	4.4	3.3	7.0	Current	5.6	5.1
3.1	2.6	2.2	2.2	1.5	2.0		2.0	2.1
.9	.9	1.2	1.2	1.0	1.0		1.1	1.3
11.5	6.5	6.5	3.8	3.1	7.0	Quick	4.9	5.0
3.1	2.4	2.1	2.2	1.1	1.7		1.8	1.9
.8	.7	1.0	1.0	.9	.6		1.0	1.1
0 UND	3 111.8	1 333.8	5 66.8	7 49.9	12 30.7	Sales/Receivables	5 69.8	5 78.1
5 72.3	15 23.6	10 36.1	15 24.5	24 15.4	25 14.6		19 19.1	16 23.4
30 12.1	44 8.3	25 14.6	41 8.9	45 8.1	60 6.1		38 9.5	36 10.2
						Cost of Sales/Inventory		
						Cost of Sales/Payables		
2.7	2.0	1.9	1.7	1.9	.9	Sales/Working Capital	2.2	2.2
5.7	5.1	4.9	3.4	7.7	4.2		5.2	4.7
UND	-20.5	34.1	18.6	NM	-96.9		42.7	22.7
7.8	5.8	6.2	20.9			EBIT/Interest	17.7	12.6
(17) 2.0	(26) 2.4	(47) 1.8	(39) 5.1				(148) 6.5	(113) 4.0
.1	.9	-1.1	1.1				1.1	1.2
						Net Profit + Depr., Dep., Amort./Cur. Mat. L/T/D	16.9	14.6
							(14) 8.5	(13) 8.6
							3.3	2.3
.0	.1	.1	.1	.0	.0	Fixed/Worth	.1	.1
.2	.7	.4	.3	.2	.2		.3	.4
1.1	1.9	1.4	.9	1.0	.8		.9	1.0
.1	.3	.2	.4	.6	.3	Debt/Worth	.4	.4
.7	1.0	1.0	.7	.9	1.0		1.0	.9
NM	8.2	2.3	2.0	4.2	2.8		3.0	2.1
22.1	13.9	17.8	13.4	12.5	18.3	% Profit Before Taxes/Tangible Net Worth	24.7	20.8
(31) 15.6	(47) 2.5	(104) 4.6	(85) 7.5	(17) 4.3	8.3		(244) 12.1	(219) 8.4
.0	-6.8	-2.0	1.1	-6.6	-1.9		3.1	-.2
19.1	6.1	6.4	7.7	8.7	6.4	% Profit Before Taxes/Total Assets	12.7	9.9
7.2	1.9	2.3	4.4	1.8	3.4		5.5	3.7
-.8	-2.9	-1.5	.2	-1.6	-1.2		.8	-.6
UND	47.0	31.9	19.9	93.1	147.1	Sales/Net Fixed Assets	46.2	38.7
51.0	8.0	5.0	8.6	16.7	8.7		8.9	7.0
2.0	1.4	1.2	2.3	3.1	2.2		2.7	2.3
3.5	2.3	1.5	1.3	1.0	1.2	Sales/Total Assets	2.1	1.9
2.1	1.2	1.0	.8	.7	.8		1.2	1.1
1.1	.8	.6	.5	.5	.4		.6	.6
.5	.5	1.3	1.5	.6	1.4	% Depr., Dep., Amort./Sales	.9	1.1
(17) 1.9	(42) 2.0	(83) 2.5	(76) 2.3	(15) 3.0	(11) 2.1		(205) 1.9	(181) 1.9
3.3	4.1	5.0	3.9	5.2	4.5		3.0	3.5
						% Officers', Directors' Owners' Comp/Sales	2.3	4.9
							(36) 9.5	(24) 10.0
							17.3	27.9
22696M	137642M	859663M	2535426M	950245M	2812942M	Net Sales ($)	6315000M	6155217M
8740M	70944M	544504M	2078384M	1291645M	2969520M	Total Assets ($)	4862534M	4518702M

© RMA 2011

M = $ thousand   MM = $ million
See Pages 9 through 22 for Explanation of Ratios and Data

Comparative Historical Data | Current Data Sorted by Sales

			Type of Statement $						
154	160	182	Unqualified	8	31	16	25	55	47
16	14	14	Reviewed	2	9	1		1	1
9	14	9	Compiled	5		1	2		1
14	12	14	Tax Returns	9	2	1	1	1	
77	103	115	Other	34	26	15	14	13	13
4/1/08-3/31/09	4/1/09-3/31/10	4/1/10-3/31/11		145 (4/1-9/30/10)			189 (10/1/10-3/31/11)		
ALL	ALL	ALL		0-1MM	1-3MM	3-5MM	5-10MM	10-25MM	25MM & OVER
270	303	334	**NUMBER OF STATEMENTS**	58	68	34	42	70	62
%	%	%	**ASSETS**	%	%	%	%	%	%
36.6	37.7	39.3	Cash & Equivalents	37.3	41.9	33.3	40.4	42.1	37.5
11.2	12.8	10.7	Trade Receivables (net)	9.4	5.9	12.8	10.6	10.4	16.3
2.8	2.0	1.2	Inventory	.2	1.0	2.2	1.2	.5	2.3
3.8	3.1	3.5	All Other Current	3.3	2.9	3.8	4.3	3.8	3.3
54.3	55.6	54.6	Total Current	50.3	51.7	52.1	56.5	56.9	59.4
28.8	28.2	27.7	Fixed Assets (net)	38.1	37.8	35.3	23.3	21.5	12.8
1.9	1.4	1.9	Intangibles (net)	1.2	.8	1.3	2.1	2.5	3.1
14.9	14.8	15.8	All Other Non-Current	10.5	9.7	11.2	18.0	19.1	24.7
100.0	100.0	100.0	Total	100.0	100.0	100.0	100.0	100.0	100.0
			LIABILITIES						
3.8	4.1	3.8	Notes Payable-Short Term	7.8	3.9	3.2	2.5	2.7	2.2
2.4	2.8	1.9	Cur. Mat.-L.T.D.	3.3	2.5	2.4	2.2	.5	.7
9.0	10.9	8.1	Trade Payables	4.5	3.9	11.0	8.8	9.4	12.6
.1	.2	.1	Income Taxes Payable	.1	.0	.0	.1	.2	.1
14.1	16.0	15.2	All Other Current	17.1	13.5	5.9	18.4	15.2	18.4
29.4	34.1	29.1	Total Current	32.8	23.9	22.6	32.0	28.1	34.0
10.9	12.7	13.3	Long-Term Debt	21.7	19.2	12.3	10.6	6.9	8.3
.2	.1	.1	Deferred Taxes	.0	.0	.1	.0	.2	.1
10.3	9.7	9.8	All Other Non-Current	6.3	4.2	7.5	7.8	15.8	15.3
49.3	43.5	47.8	Net Worth	39.2	52.8	57.5	49.6	49.0	42.3
100.0	100.0	100.0	Total Liabilities & Net Worth	100.0	100.0	100.0	100.0	100.0	100.0
			INCOME DATA						
100.0	100.0	100.0	Net Sales	100.0	100.0	100.0	100.0	100.0	100.0
			Gross Profit						
97.8	96.6	95.3	Operating Expenses	91.0	97.0	95.8	94.6	95.6	97.5
2.2	3.4	4.7	Operating Profit	9.0	3.0	4.2	5.4	4.4	2.5
3.6	2.0	.7	All Other Expenses (net)	4.4	.9	1.2	.5	-1.2	-.7
-1.3	1.4	3.9	Profit Before Taxes	4.7	2.1	3.0	4.9	5.6	3.2
			RATIOS						
5.4	5.6	6.7		11.5	13.2	8.9	5.6	4.5	3.9
2.0	2.2	2.2	Current	1.9	3.0	2.7	1.9	2.3	1.7
1.2	1.1	1.1		.8	.9	1.3	1.0	1.4	1.1
4.7	5.1	5.9		10.8	12.0	8.5	4.1	4.4	3.3
1.8	2.1	2.1	Quick	1.9	3.0	2.4	1.7	2.2	1.6
.9	.9	.9		.7	.8	1.3	.9	1.3	1.0
5 75.2	3 114.5	3 115.8		0 UND.	1 326.1	1 640.9	2 227.7	6 63.3	12 30.8
16 22.3	15 24.6	14 26.6	Sales/Receivables	4 100.3	12 30.5	18 19.7	10 36.8	12 31.0	25 14.8
35 10.4	39 9.3	37 9.9		30 12.1	33 10.9	42 8.7	35 10.4	30 12.2	46 7.9
			Cost of Sales/Inventory						
			Cost of Sales/Payables						
2.3	2.0	1.9		2.1	1.6	1.9	1.8	2.0	2.0
5.6	4.9	4.7	Sales/Working Capital	5.3	3.7	4.9	6.0	3.8	7.6
27.5	61.9	37.5		-32.8	-23.2	12.2	155.1	17.3	71.3
4.6	9.2	12.2		6.2	5.7	4.8	5.1	30.9	18.8
(131) .7	(145) 2.3	(146) 2.7	EBIT/Interest	(23) 2.0	(35) 2.3	(16) 1.8	(16) 2.8	(30) 6.4	(26) 5.9
-4.1	-1.1	.4		.5	-1.5	.7	.8	.2	1.0
4.7	19.0	16.0							
(18) 2.3	(17) 3.2	(17) 7.9	Net Profit + Depr., Dep., Amort./Cur. Mat. L/T/D						
-.3	.2	1.0							
.1	.1	.1		.0	.1	.2	.1	.1	.0
.5	.4	.4	Fixed/Worth	.6	.6	.6	.3	.3	.2
1.2	1.3	1.1		1.7	1.5	1.4	.9	.7	.9
.4	.4	.3		.1	.2	.2	.3	.4	.6
1.0	.9	.8	Debt/Worth	.7	.6	.5	1.1	.7	1.1
2.6	2.5	2.5		3.7	2.3	1.8	2.7	2.2	3.3
13.4	15.1	16.6		19.8	14.8	11.3	20.9	16.0	17.0
(257) -.4	(274) 2.9	(303) 6.5	% Profit Before Taxes/Tangible Net Worth	(48) 4.3	(61) 4.3	(33) 2.0	(39) 8.5	(64) 8.2	(58) 7.0
-14.6	-10.1	-1.9		-1.6	-3.9	-3.1	.8	1.1	-2.0
4.9	8.3	8.1		13.7	7.1	6.2	8.1	8.6	6.7
-.3	1.3	3.0	% Profit Before Taxes/Total Assets	2.4	1.9	.8	4.5	5.2	3.1
-7.5	-5.4	-1.0		-1.0	-2.1	-1.5	.3	.5	-1.0
41.4	32.1	45.5		518.5	21.7	12.1	43.9	29.6	129.3
6.7	6.8	8.5	Sales/Net Fixed Assets	3.4	3.0	4.7	11.5	9.3	17.2
1.8	1.9	1.6		.8	1.2	1.3	2.1	3.6	7.5
1.8	2.0	1.6		2.1	1.4	1.6	1.5	2.1	1.8
1.1	1.0	1.0	Sales/Total Assets	1.0	.8	1.0	1.0	1.1	1.0
.6	.6	.6		.4	.6	.5	.6	.6	.7
.9	1.1	1.2		.6	1.7	.9	1.3	1.3	.6
(207) 2.2	(241) 2.0	(244) 2.3	% Depr., Dep., Amort./Sales	(30) 2.8	(53) 2.7	(24) 2.9	(35) 2.1	(56) 2.3	(46) 1.9
4.1	3.9	4.2		10.3	5.3	5.3	3.4	3.6	3.1
4.4	2.7	1.7							
(25) 8.7	(26) 6.0	(27) 8.2	% Officers', Directors' Owners' Comp/Sales						
19.9	10.8	18.6							
6481515M	6595203M	7318614M	Net Sales ($)	24660M	119813M	137149M	303474M	1193493M	5540025M
4929000M	5254040M	6963737M	Total Assets ($)	58570M	171786M	223328M	382275M	1473603M	4654175M

M = $ thousand   MM = $ million
See Pages 9 through 22 for Explanation of Ratios and Data

Current Data Sorted by Assets | **Comparative Historical Data**

0-500M	500M-2MM	2-10MM	10-50MM	50-100MM	100-250MM	Type of Statement	4/1/06-3/31/07 ALL	4/1/07-3/31/08 ALL
1	10	49	69	15	23	Unqualified	135	140
1	2	4	1			Reviewed	8	3
1	1	2	1			Compiled	5	2
5	5	2	1			Tax Returns	5	5
3	12	20	18	4	5	Other	49	42
	131 (4/1-9/30/10)			124 (10/1/10-3/31/11)				
11	30	77	90	19	28	**NUMBER OF STATEMENTS**	202	192
%	%	%	%	%	%	**ASSETS**	%	%
39.6	40.2	44.6	41.9	39.1	23.3	Cash & Equivalents	37.5	39.4
28.5	11.9	10.2	5.9	3.5	4.7	Trade Receivables (net)	12.0	10.3
3.6	1.9	.8	.8	1.9	.2	Inventory	1.3	1.1
5.4	3.9	5.8	4.2	6.4	1.8	All Other Current	4.4	3.9
77.0	57.9	61.4	52.8	50.9	30.1	Total Current	55.1	54.7
19.5	31.9	27.2	23.3	24.2	21.4	Fixed Assets (net)	25.1	27.1
.0	.3	1.5	.8	6.4	.8	Intangibles (net)	1.8	.7
3.4	9.8	9.9	23.1	18.5	47.7	All Other Non-Current	18.1	17.4
100.0	100.0	100.0	100.0	100.0	100.0	Total	100.0	100.0
						LIABILITIES		
7.2	6.7	1.5	.7	.3	.2	Notes Payable-Short Term	2.2	2.9
.6	2.4	.8	.9	.8	.4	Cur. Mat.-L.T.D.	.9	1.0
3.0	11.3	7.9	6.3	8.1	4.7	Trade Payables	9.0	8.9
.0	.0	.0	1.1	.2	.0	Income Taxes Payable	.4	.4
10.2	21.8	16.5	13.1	17.6	15.1	All Other Current	12.8	12.9
21.0	42.3	26.8	22.1	27.1	20.4	Total Current	25.3	26.1
22.7	14.4	12.5	10.6	16.4	11.1	Long-Term Debt	12.5	12.3
.0	.0	.4	.1	1.2	.0	Deferred Taxes	.1	.2
23.9	8.4	9.5	12.1	14.1	11.8	All Other Non-Current	9.7	11.7
32.4	34.9	50.9	55.1	41.2	56.7	Net Worth	52.4	49.8
100.0	100.0	100.0	100.0	100.0	100.0	Total Liabilities & Net Worth	100.0	100.0
						INCOME DATA		
100.0	100.0	100.0	100.0	100.0	100.0	Net Sales	100.0	100.0
						Gross Profit		
92.6	93.2	95.0	96.3	95.7	96.0	Operating Expenses	93.8	93.2
7.4	6.8	5.0	3.7	4.3	4.0	Operating Profit	6.2	6.8
2.6	3.9	.0	-2.1	-.9	-1.2	All Other Expenses (net)	-.8	-1.0
4.8	3.0	4.9	5.8	5.2	5.2	Profit Before Taxes	7.0	7.8
						RATIOS		
40.0	9.5	6.6	7.3	3.5	3.4	Current	5.0	5.3
8.2	2.1	2.4	2.3	1.8	1.2		2.5	2.6
1.3	1.0	1.3	1.2	.8	.6		1.3	1.3
39.0	7.1	6.5	6.8	3.5	3.4	Quick	4.6	5.0
7.9	2.0	2.0	2.1	1.3	1.1		2.2	2.3
.8	.9	1.1	1.0	.6	.6		1.1	1.2
0 UND	0 UND	2 186.8	4 81.4	5 68.4	12 29.2	Sales/Receivables	5 74.1	5 75.3
21 17.1	13 28.3	10 36.8	12 29.8	18 20.5	20 18.3		16 23.0	15 24.4
43 8.5	36 10.3	32 11.4	23 16.1	24 14.9	39 9.5		39 9.4	37 9.7
						Cost of Sales/Inventory		
						Cost of Sales/Payables		
3.3	1.9	1.3	1.4	1.2	3.7	Sales/Working Capital	2.2	2.0
7.2	7.2	3.4	3.0	4.7	12.3		4.5	4.0
7.9	-835.6	14.4	20.7	-16.6	-12.7		17.8	14.3
	12.9	16.3	8.9	35.9	43.6	EBIT/Interest	23.0	21.7
	(13) 3.1	(35) 2.5	(45) 3.7	(11) 4.6	(19) 5.4		(100) 5.8	(86) 6.1
	.5	1.2	.7	1.7	.9		2.3	1.2
						Net Profit + Depr., Dep., Amort./Cur. Mat. L/T/D	10.8	15.3
							(11) 6.0	(12) 11.7
							4.5	3.8
.0	.1	.2	.1	.1	.1	Fixed/Worth	.1	.1
.3	.9	.5	.3	.6	.4		.3	.4
.9	3.0	1.1	.8	1.7	.6		1.0	1.1
.1	.3	.4	.4	.4	.3	Debt/Worth	.4	.4
4.5	1.5	.8	.8	2.0	.7		.8	.8
131.0	3.9	2.0	1.4	3.9	1.2		1.9	2.0
	14.3	12.9	13.3	14.4	10.1	% Profit Before Taxes/Tangible Net Worth	24.1	17.9
	(26) 5.5	(74) 4.7	(89) 6.3	(16) 7.1	(27) 5.6		(191) 9.6	(182) 10.7
	-5.4	-1.3	.2	3.5	-1.4		1.1	2.3
23.0	7.2	7.0	7.2	5.5	7.0	% Profit Before Taxes/Total Assets	11.8	11.4
.4	2.4	2.2	3.3	2.1	3.2		5.5	5.1
-6.0	-4.3	-.6	.1	1.1	-.3		.4	.9
UND	60.4	30.3	23.0	10.3	8.8	Sales/Net Fixed Assets	30.4	21.5
120.3	22.5	6.8	5.7	4.4	3.6		8.8	5.9
7.1	1.6	2.0	1.8	2.3	1.4		2.1	2.1
5.3	3.0	1.7	1.1	.8	.8	Sales/Total Assets	1.8	1.5
2.2	1.6	1.0	.7	.7	.5		1.0	.9
1.5	.8	.6	.5	.4	.4		.6	.6
	.8	1.3	1.3	2.4	2.0	% Depr., Dep., Amort./Sales	1.2	1.3
	(19) 2.3	(65) 2.4	(82) 2.1	(16) 3.5	(24) 3.4		(161) 2.2	(166) 2.2
	3.7	4.4	4.0	7.0	5.5		3.3	3.5
						% Officers', Directors' Owners' Comp/Sales	3.1	2.8
							(24) 6.9	(11) 6.8
							22.4	27.9
8752M	102529M	657049M	1882127M	1182038M	3418492M	Net Sales ($)	4853996M	4651308M
3090M	36603M	411049M	2064434M	1276680M	4255903M	Total Assets ($)	5434337M	5170141M

M = $ thousand   MM = $ million
See Pages 9 through 22 for Explanation of Ratios and Data

Comparative Historical Data | Current Data Sorted by Sales

				Type of Statement						
160	146	167		Unqualified	4	20	11	32	48	52
5	4	8		Reviewed	1	3			2	2
11	7	5		Compiled	1	2	2			
4	10	13		Tax Returns	8	1		2	2	
44	59	62		Other	8	13	4	8	12	17
4/1/08-3/31/09 ALL	4/1/09-3/31/10 ALL	4/1/10-3/31/11 ALL			131 (4/1-9/30/10)			124 (10/1/10-3/31/11)		
					0-1MM	1-3MM	3-5MM	5-10MM	10-25MM	25MM & OVER
224	226	255		**NUMBER OF STATEMENTS**	22	39	17	42	64	71
%	%	%		**ASSETS**	%	%	%	%	%	%
37.9	38.3	40.2		Cash & Equivalents	37.8	44.0	44.5	44.0	37.4	38.0
10.3	9.8	8.5		Trade Receivables (net)	6.4	10.0	16.3	8.5	7.1	7.8
1.3	1.6	1.1		Inventory	2.4	.7	1.1	1.2	.6	1.1
4.2	3.2	4.6		All Other Current	3.5	5.2	1.8	4.7	5.5	4.4
53.7	52.9	54.4		Total Current	50.2	60.0	63.7	58.3	50.6	51.4
25.4	28.9	25.2		Fixed Assets (net)	38.7	32.1	21.9	24.6	26.1	17.6
1.8	1.4	1.3		Intangibles (net)	.4	1.0	1.0	.2	1.1	2.8
19.1	16.9	19.1		All Other Non-Current	10.6	6.8	13.4	16.8	22.3	28.2
100.0	100.0	100.0		Total	100.0	100.0	100.0	100.0	100.0	100.0
				LIABILITIES						
2.2	2.8	1.8		Notes Payable-Short Term	6.3	.7	7.9	1.0	1.0	.9
.9	1.5	1.0		Cur. Mat.-L.T.D.	.8	1.5	2.9	.7	.9	.5
8.1	7.4	7.2		Trade Payables	2.0	3.7	11.5	7.9	8.2	8.4
.7	.6	.4		Income Taxes Payable	.0	.0	.0	.2	1.5	.1
14.2	14.6	15.6		All Other Current	9.3	9.2	13.8	19.6	16.4	18.3
26.0	26.8	26.1		Total Current	18.5	15.0	36.0	29.4	28.0	28.4
13.7	15.6	12.6		Long-Term Debt	24.8	12.6	10.2	11.2	13.1	9.8
.1	.3	.2		Deferred Taxes	.0	.0	1.5	.0	.4	.1
11.6	11.3	11.5		All Other Non-Current	5.6	15.5	4.1	8.3	12.4	14.0
48.6	46.1	49.6		Net Worth	51.1	56.9	48.2	51.1	46.2	47.7
100.0	100.0	100.0		Total Liabilties & Net Worth	100.0	100.0	100.0	100.0	100.0	100.0
				INCOME DATA						
100.0	100.0	100.0		Net Sales	100.0	100.0	100.0	100.0	100.0	100.0
				Gross Profit						
96.6	97.5	95.3		Operating Expenses	85.2	97.6	97.0	98.0	94.2	96.2
3.4	2.5	4.7		Operating Profit	14.8	2.4	3.0	2.0	5.8	3.8
3.8	1.9	-.4		All Other Expenses (net)	6.2	.2	-.6	-1.6	-1.0	-1.3
-.4	.6	5.0		Profit Before Taxes	8.5	2.2	3.7	3.6	6.8	5.1
				RATIOS						
5.2	5.3	6.7			26.7	11.4	5.7	7.8	5.4	4.2
2.3	2.2	2.1		Current	4.7	5.2	3.0	1.8	1.8	1.8
1.3	1.3	1.1			1.3	1.7	1.0	1.0	1.1	1.0
4.9	4.5	6.5			18.0	10.1	5.5	7.5	5.4	3.5
2.1	1.9	1.8		Quick	4.5	4.2	2.9	1.7	1.5	1.4
1.1	1.1	1.0			1.2	1.7	1.0	.8	1.0	.9
6 57.9	3 106.6	4 93.2			0 UND	0 UND	11 34.4	4 89.6	4 102.9	6 57.3
16 23.3	14 26.2	14 26.7		Sales/Receivables	0 UND	10 37.7	24 15.5	14 25.8	11 32.0	18 20.5
37 9.9	32 11.5	28 13.1			22 16.3	22 16.5	48 7.5	28 13.1	26 13.9	31 11.8
				Cost of Sales/Inventory						
				Cost of Sales/Payables						
1.8	1.8	1.6			1.5	.9	1.6	1.3	2.4	2.3
4.3	4.6	4.4		Sales/Working Capital	1.9	3.3	2.7	3.6	4.7	7.4
14.4	20.1	30.9			7.6	7.3	NM	-279.6	56.8	165.0
9.0	6.7	13.5			12.7	3.1		5.3	16.8	36.9
(108) 1.8	(115) 2.1	(126) 3.4		EBIT/Interest	(10) 3.3	(15) 2.1	(21) 2.3	(32) 4.4	(41) 5.3	
-2.8	-1.7	1.2			1.4	.7	.0	1.4	1.5	
3.1	9.7			Net Profit + Depr., Dep.,						
(14) 1.3	(15) 2.7			Amort./Cur. Mat. L/T/D						
-17.0	1.1									
.1	.2	.1			.0	.0	.2	.1	.2	.1
.4	.5	.4		Fixed/Worth	.9	.6	.3	.5	.4	.4
1.2	1.2	1.0			1.0	1.1	1.3	1.1	1.1	.8
.4	.4	.4			.1	.3	.3	.3	.4	.5
1.0	1.0	.8		Debt/Worth	.5	.7	.5	1.0	.8	1.1
1.7	2.5	2.2			2.9	1.7	2.9	2.1	1.8	2.3
11.6	11.4	13.4		% Profit Before Taxes/Tangible	11.3	8.2	13.1	10.3	15.9	15.3
(208) .5	(210) .8	(241) 5.8		Net Worth	(19) 6.3	3.2	(16) 4.8	(41) 4.7	(59) 8.2	(67) 6.5
-14.8	-9.8	-.4			-3.4	-4.9	-.5	-1.5	1.6	1.6
5.6	5.0	7.0		% Profit Before Taxes/Total	8.3	4.5	5.9	6.9	8.9	7.0
.1	.3	2.8		Assets	1.2	2.0	2.9	2.5	4.0	3.2
-7.2	-6.3	-.2			-2.5	-3.2	-.3	-1.1	.6	1.0
23.1	18.4	30.0			UND	37.1	21.1	26.8	19.8	31.6
6.5	5.0	5.6		Sales/Net Fixed Assets	3.3	2.6	5.2	4.0	6.6	8.3
2.1	1.9	1.8			.3	1.1	2.1	1.6	2.4	3.5
1.4	1.5	1.4			1.5	1.6	1.5	1.4	1.4	1.2
.9	.9	.8		Sales/Total Assets	.4	.8	.9	.8	.9	.8
.6	.5	.5			.2	.5	.5	.5	.6	.6
1.3	1.5	1.3			3.0	2.3	1.0	1.3	1.2	1.3
(193) 2.3	(191) 2.5	(211) 2.5		% Depr., Dep., Amort./Sales	(11) 6.0	(31) 3.7	(13) 1.9	(38) 2.2	(57) 2.1	(61) 2.3
3.5	4.7	4.4			13.3	5.2	4.4	3.9	3.6	4.5
2.7	3.3	2.1		% Officers', Directors'						
(14) 8.0	(17) 8.3	(15) 7.5		Owners' Comp/Sales						
25.8	29.9	23.1								
6792129M	7507235M	7250987M		Net Sales ($)	11020M	75210M	66612M	317057M	983539M	5797549M
7229900M	7176157M	8047759M		Total Assets ($)	24457M	122809M	108465M	621239M	1244603M	5926186M

Current Data Sorted by Assets

Comparative Historical Data

0-500M	500M-2MM	2-10MM	10-50MM	50-100MM	100-250MM	Type of Statement	4/1/06-3/31/07 ALL	4/1/07-3/31/08 ALL
	6	27	23	3	8	Unqualified	38	49
		1	1			Reviewed	2	3
	2	2			2	Compiled	1	5
1	3	1				Tax Returns	3	7
2	3	8	6	2	1	Other	16	14
	60 (4/1-9/30/10)		42 (10/1/10-3/31/11)					
3	14	39	30	5	11	**NUMBER OF STATEMENTS**	60	78
%	%	%	%	%	%	**ASSETS**	%	%
	56.0	37.7	48.5		55.2	Cash & Equivalents	39.8	41.8
	4.8	2.6	4.7		5.7	Trade Receivables (net)	5.1	4.0
	3.0	.0	.1		.1	Inventory	.0	.4
	3.3	1.9	2.7		3.3	All Other Current	4.0	5.9
	67.1	42.1	56.0		64.3	Total Current	48.9	52.0
	24.0	51.6	28.3		18.6	Fixed Assets (net)	33.5	35.8
	1.5	.0	.0		1.2	Intangibles (net)	.1	.1
	7.5	6.3	15.7		16.0	All Other Non-Current	17.5	12.1
	100.0	100.0	100.0		100.0	Total	100.0	100.0
						LIABILITIES		
	.0	1.5	.3		1.0	Notes Payable-Short Term	.6	1.3
	.8	1.7	.4		.4	Cur. Mat.-L.T.D.	2.2	.9
	11.3	1.5	2.0		3.9	Trade Payables	2.9	4.1
	.1	.0	.0		.0	Income Taxes Payable	.0	.0
	17.5	6.4	14.0		4.0	All Other Current	9.0	7.1
	29.7	11.1	16.7		9.3	Total Current	14.9	13.5
	5.8	20.2	9.7		3.9	Long-Term Debt	16.1	17.3
	.0	.0	.1		.0	Deferred Taxes	.1	.0
	3.8	2.4	8.0		6.0	All Other Non-Current	4.0	7.8
	60.7	66.3	65.4		80.9	Net Worth	65.0	61.4
	100.0	100.0	100.0		100.0	Total Liabilities & Net Worth	100.0	100.0
						INCOME DATA		
	100.0	100.0	100.0		100.0	Net Sales	100.0	100.0
						Gross Profit		
	90.2	98.8	95.0		81.1	Operating Expenses	92.5	93.4
	9.8	1.2	5.0		18.9	Operating Profit	7.5	6.6
	1.4	.6	.2		-1.2	All Other Expenses (net)	-.1	.6
	8.3	.6	4.9		20.1	Profit Before Taxes	7.6	6.0
						RATIOS		
	17.0	41.9	62.0		620.3		25.1	40.5
	5.0	3.9	5.5		5.2	Current	5.9	5.6
	2.1	1.9	2.2		2.7		2.2	2.4
	17.0	41.8	61.8		613.6		25.1	40.3
	4.2	3.9	5.4		5.1	Quick	5.3	5.2
	1.5	1.5	2.0		2.6		1.9	1.8
0 UND	0 UND	0 UND			0 UND		0 UND	0 UND
8 47.1	0 UND	13 27.2			25 14.8	Sales/Receivables	8 44.7	0 999.8
21 17.6	16 22.4	30 12.1			39 9.3		25 14.6	20 18.3
						Cost of Sales/Inventory		
						Cost of Sales/Payables		
	1.0	1.0	.9		.2		1.5	1.6
	3.1	3.8	2.1		2.9	Sales/Working Capital	3.5	3.0
	4.5	13.7	4.5		5.7		6.6	7.7
		8.2	3.1				8.0	15.2
	(21) .8	(14) .8				EBIT/Interest	(33) 2.5	(43) 2.5
	-1.3	-8.9					-.2	-2.0
						Net Profit + Depr., Dep., Amort./Cur. Mat. L/T/D		
	.0	.1	.0		.0		.0	.0
	.2	1.0	.2		.4	Fixed/Worth	.5	.5
	.8	1.3	.9		.5		1.3	1.3
	.1	.0	.0		.0		.2	.0
	.4	.4	.3		.0	Debt/Worth	.5	.4
	.7	1.1	.9		1.0		1.2	1.3
	14.0	9.0	9.6		10.3		12.5	17.7
	(13) 6.2	(38) -.7	(28) 3.0		6.9	% Profit Before Taxes/Tangible Net Worth	(58) 6.2	(72) 6.1
	-2.7	-7.4	-2.7		4.0		-2.4	-4.3
	10.0	4.7	5.7		10.2		9.3	12.9
	2.9	-.2	1.5		4.5	% Profit Before Taxes/Total Assets	3.7	2.8
	-2.6	-4.6	-3.3		3.4		-1.9	-3.0
	316.3	7.6	38.4		520.2		47.9	33.5
	17.3	1.5	5.9		6.6	Sales/Net Fixed Assets	4.2	4.1
	2.4	.6	1.7		2.9		1.3	1.1
	2.0	1.3	1.2		1.2		1.4	1.6
	1.1	.7	.7		.4	Sales/Total Assets	.9	.9
	.5	.4	.2		.2		.4	.5
	.6	1.1	.9				1.6	.9
	(11) .9	(31) 2.5	(23) 2.1			% Depr., Dep., Amort./Sales	(46) 2.8	(63) 1.9
	4.4	6.0	3.9				4.6	4.6
							7.7	7.1
						% Officers', Directors' Owners' Comp/Sales	(10) 15.7	(21) 13.6
							27.0	27.1
831M	23556M	169960M	605504M	190087M	1311888M	Net Sales ($)	1128631M	1495172M
421M	16218M	195410M	831149M	376022M	2088998M	Total Assets ($)	1320742M	1527054M

M = $ thousand   MM = $ million
See Pages 9 through 22 for Explanation of Ratios and Data

Comparative Historical Data

Current Data Sorted by Sales

				Type of Statement						
54		60	67	Unqualified	5	12	5	15	12	18
3		3	2	Reviewed		1		1		
1		5	6	Compiled	1	2	1		1	1
6		7	5	Tax Returns	3		2			
22		31	22	Other	4	5	2	4	5	2
4/1/08-3/31/09 ALL		4/1/09-3/31/10 ALL	4/1/10-3/31/11 ALL		60 (4/1-9/30/10)			42 (10/1/10-3/31/11)		
					0-1MM	1-3MM	3-5MM	5-10MM	10-25MM	25MM & OVER
86		106	102	NUMBER OF STATEMENTS	13	20	10	20	18	21
%		%	%	ASSETS	%	%	%	%	%	%
48.4		48.2	45.7	Cash & Equivalents	47.9	43.5	55.6	37.6	47.6	48.0
4.7		4.0	3.8	Trade Receivables (net)	1.4	1.8	3.5	4.5	2.2	8.0
.4		.2	.5	Inventory	.1	.0	4.1	.1	.0	.3
3.5		3.5	2.5	All Other Current	1.0	3.2	.0	2.2	1.2	5.5
57.0		55.9	52.5	Total Current	50.4	48.5	63.2	44.4	51.0	61.7
30.9		33.7	35.2	Fixed Assets (net)	44.5	47.2	17.9	44.2	24.9	26.3
.1		.1	.4	Intangibles (net)	.0	.0	2.2	.0	.7	.0
12.1		10.3	11.9	All Other Non-Current	5.1	4.2	16.7	11.4	23.3	12.0
100.0		100.0	100.0	Total	100.0	100.0	100.0	100.0	100.0	100.0
				LIABILITIES						
.8		1.9	.8	Notes Payable-Short Term	2.8	.8	.0	.6	.2	.7
1.0		1.5	1.0	Cur. Mat.-L.T.D.	.7	1.8	.5	1.2	.6	.6
4.4		2.5	3.2	Trade Payables	.8	1.2	13.8	2.4	1.3	3.8
.0		.0	.0	Income Taxes Payable	.1	.0	.0	.0	.0	.0
6.8		10.4	9.5	All Other Current	6.2	5.2	10.2	9.3	7.1	17.6
13.0		16.3	14.5	Total Current	10.7	9.1	24.4	13.5	9.2	22.7
14.2		11.6	14.8	Long-Term Debt	28.8	17.0	7.8	15.4	10.9	10.0
.0		.0	.0	Deferred Taxes	.0	.0	.0	.0	.0	.1
8.7		3.9	4.5	All Other Non-Current	.4	.4	4.6	4.0	5.3	10.9
64.0		68.2	66.2	Net Worth	60.1	73.5	63.2	67.0	74.7	56.3
100.0		100.0	100.0	Total Liabilties & Net Worth	100.0	100.0	100.0	100.0	100.0	100.0
				INCOME DATA						
100.0		100.0	100.0	Net Sales	100.0	100.0	100.0	100.0	100.0	100.0
				Gross Profit						
93.7		95.0	94.3	Operating Expenses	93.0	98.4	88.4	98.1	90.6	93.6
6.3		5.0	5.7	Operating Profit	7.0	1.6	11.6	1.9	9.4	6.4
1.9		2.9	.4	All Other Expenses (net)	3.5	-.1	-1.0	.0	.9	-.3
4.3		2.0	5.3	Profit Before Taxes	3.5	1.7	12.6	1.9	8.5	6.8
				RATIOS						
42.5		64.5	49.2		45.1	47.3	794.0	10.8	62.0	57.4
6.1		6.8	5.5	Current	12.3	4.1	29.6	4.3	7.3	2.9
2.4		2.1	2.2		1.1	2.8	8.0	1.6	2.0	2.2
42.4		63.5	46.6		45.1	44.7	794.0	10.7	61.8	57.2
5.9		6.1	5.0	Quick	12.3	4.0	29.6	4.3	6.7	2.7
2.2		1.8	2.0		1.1	2.8	4.8	1.5	1.9	1.9
0	UND	0 UND	0 UND		0 UND	0 UND	0 UND	0 UND	0 UND	1 257.3
1	688.7	1 299.4	3 118.7	Sales/Receivables	0 UND	0 UND	0 UND	13 27.2	0 UND	26 13.9
26	14.2	22 16.4	26 13.8		22 16.7	16 23.2	10 37.5	38 9.7	23 16.0	38 9.5
				Cost of Sales/Inventory						
				Cost of Sales/Payables						
1.1		1.3	1.0		1.0	.7	.9	1.1	1.3	.9
2.5		2.9	2.5	Sales/Working Capital	2.0	2.8	1.9	4.5	2.2	2.9
6.5		7.8	6.4		NM	3.9	4.9	15.6	8.8	8.4
	14.6	6.6	9.9					16.9		16.8
(44)	2.2	(46) .5	(46) 1.4	EBIT/Interest				(10) 1.5	(11) 13.4	
	-.1	-4.0	-1.0					-4.7		-.8
				Net Profit + Depr., Dep., Amort./Cur. Mat. L/T/D						
.0		.1	.0		.1	.1	.0	.0	.0	.0
.3		.4	.5	Fixed/Worth	.8	.7	.0	.7	.2	.4
.9		1.0	1.2		1.6	1.2	1.1	1.3	.8	1.1
.0		.0	.0		.1	.0	.0	.1	.0	.0
.3		.3	.3	Debt/Worth	.3	.4	.2	.4	.2	.7
.9		1.0	1.0		1.0	.6	.7	1.4	.5	1.0
15.1		12.9	9.6	% Profit Before Taxes/Tangible Net Worth	5.6	8.7		8.1	10.7	10.5
(83)	4.9	(102) .7	(97) 2.6		(12) .0	-.7		-.5	(17) 5.1	(19) 5.7
	-4.0	-8.5	-5.1		-10.0	-5.6		-8.6	-1.9	1.3
10.1		9.3	7.0	% Profit Before Taxes/Total Assets	6.1	7.2	13.0	4.6	9.5	7.6
3.0		.1	1.9		1.5	-.1	5.4	-.4	3.0	3.4
-2.8		-6.0	-3.3		-5.7	-3.6	-.1	-5.2	-2.5	-2.7
60.6		28.2	45.0	Sales/Net Fixed Assets	94.3	11.8	UND	26.2	137.7	254.2
4.4		4.4	4.2		3.5	1.1	52.8	1.9	7.5	6.6
1.5		1.3	1.1		.2	.6	6.0	1.2	1.9	2.4
1.5		1.4	1.3	Sales/Total Assets	1.5	1.1	2.2	1.5	1.2	1.4
.8		.9	.7		.5	.6	.8	.9	.8	1.1
.5		.5	.4		.1	.4	.4	.2	.5	.5
.9		1.0	.7	% Depr., Dep., Amort./Sales		1.1		.6	.6	.5
(69)	2.2	(80) 2.1	(79) 2.0		(17) 2.5		(14) 2.0	(15) 1.6	(18) 1.7	
	4.3	4.4	4.4			5.6		7.3	3.2	2.5
5.2		6.3	6.5	% Officers', Directors' Owners' Comp/Sales						
(16)	11.1	(18) 16.1	(11) 12.8							
	26.6	32.2	19.3							
2042583M		2569269M	2301826M	Net Sales ($)	6069M	38667M	37136M	141071M	281875M	1797008M
1998866M		2802757M	3508218M	Total Assets ($)	23057M	75652M	59934M	347781M	636114M	2365680M

© RMA 2011   M = $ thousand   MM = $ million
See Pages 9 through 22 for Explanation of Ratios and Data

Current Data Sorted by Assets | Comparative Historical Data

Type of Statement	0-500M	500M-2MM	2-10MM	10-50MM	50-100MM	100-250MM	4/1/06-3/31/07 ALL	4/1/07-3/31/08 ALL
Unqualified	25	43	47	48	22	13	171	140
Reviewed	7	10	1	1			11	18
Compiled	7	3	5				18	16
Tax Returns	6	8	4				14	12
Other	30	31	38	30	1	5	109	113
		163 (4/1-9/30/10)		222 (10/1/10-3/31/11)				
NUMBER OF STATEMENTS	75	95	95	79	23	18	323	299
ASSETS	%	%	%	%	%	%	%	%
Cash & Equivalents	68.9	48.8	28.7	21.1	24.3	20.2	33.7	37.5
Trade Receivables (net)	7.0	9.7	6.4	9.7	6.0	6.4	8.3	8.4
Inventory	.4	1.0	2.6	1.4	.8	5.8	1.4	1.2
All Other Current	5.0	6.2	4.6	4.1	5.3	3.6	5.2	4.5
Total Current	81.3	65.8	42.3	36.3	36.4	36.0	48.6	51.5
Fixed Assets (net)	6.9	21.3	41.1	47.6	39.0	33.8	35.8	34.6
Intangibles (net)	.9	.4	.8	.8	1.3	4.2	.9	1.1
All Other Non-Current	10.9	12.5	15.8	15.3	23.3	26.0	14.6	12.8
Total	100.0	100.0	100.0	100.0	100.0	100.0	100.0	100.0
LIABILITIES								
Notes Payable-Short Term	8.0	3.3	2.7	.7	.3	5.7	4.8	2.3
Cur. Mat.-L.T.D.	4.5	1.8	1.6	1.3	1.8	1.7	2.0	3.0
Trade Payables	9.5	7.5	5.6	3.3	3.4	3.4	6.6	6.6
Income Taxes Payable	.0	.4	.2	.0	.2	.1	.1	.2
All Other Current	19.9	9.0	7.5	11.7	10.1	10.4	12.5	11.9
Total Current	41.9	21.9	17.5	17.0	15.8	21.2	26.2	24.0
Long-Term Debt	43.9	24.1	24.5	15.2	14.4	26.8	22.5	21.9
Deferred Taxes	.0	.0	.0	.1	.1	.3	.1	.1
All Other Non-Current	5.4	8.1	6.7	4.1	4.2	5.0	5.7	4.5
Net Worth	8.9	45.8	51.3	63.7	65.5	46.6	45.6	49.5
Total Liabilities & Net Worth	100.0	100.0	100.0	100.0	100.0	100.0	100.0	100.0
INCOME DATA								
Net Sales	100.0	100.0	100.0	100.0	100.0	100.0	100.0	100.0
Gross Profit								
Operating Expenses	87.2	85.7	92.1	97.7	90.9	95.9	91.1	89.7
Operating Profit	12.8	14.3	7.9	2.3	9.1	4.1	8.9	10.3
All Other Expenses (net)	1.8	2.4	2.4	1.0	1.5	1.7	2.2	2.3
Profit Before Taxes	11.1	11.9	5.5	1.3	7.6	2.5	6.7	8.0
RATIOS								
Current	14.4	9.7	6.0	4.2	2.9	4.2	5.6	7.0
	4.3	4.0	2.7	2.1	2.3	1.2	2.2	2.7
	1.4	1.5	1.3	1.2	1.2	1.0	1.1	1.1
Quick	14.4	9.6	5.2	3.4	2.3	3.0	4.6	6.7
	4.3	3.7	2.4	1.9	1.5	.9	1.8	2.2
	1.3	1.2	.9	1.0	1.0	.6	.8	.9
Sales/Receivables	0 UND	2 229.7	1 281.7	3 125.4	6 58.1	12 31.6	0 841.1	1 711.0
	5 72.9	7 54.4	11 34.5	16 23.4	16 23.4	30 12.3	10 37.3	8 43.4
	17 21.6	32 11.6	29 12.6	47 7.7	38 9.6	62 5.9	35 10.5	26 14.3
Cost of Sales/Inventory								
Cost of Sales/Payables								
Sales/Working Capital	1.8	1.9	2.2	2.5	1.6	2.6	2.1	1.9
	4.2	4.1	4.2	6.3	5.4	18.7	6.0	4.1
	21.6	25.1	30.3	24.9	14.4	NM	45.9	32.8
EBIT/Interest	11.9	10.2	7.4	8.6	15.3	2.9	11.7	10.2
	(29) 4.6	(40) 3.6	(60) 1.9	(55) 1.8	(15) 3.4	(15) 1.6	(189) 3.1	(155) 3.3
	-.4	.4	.3	-.8	.9	-4.1	.3	.8
Net Profit + Depr., Dep., Amort./Cur. Mat. L/T/D								6.8
							(13) 3.0	
								1.3
Fixed/Worth	.0	.0	.1	.3	.1	.0	.0	.0
	.0	.1	.7	.8	.4	1.2	.5	.5
	.0	1.1	1.6	1.2	1.1	1.7	1.1	1.1
Debt/Worth	.1	.1	.2	.2	.2	.7	.2	.2
	.7	.7	.6	.5	.5	1.5	.7	.6
	-20.7	3.1	3.9	1.2	1.2	3.8	2.6	2.0
% Profit Before Taxes/Tangible Net Worth	57.5	34.8	13.7	9.4	7.1	8.2	18.0	20.7
	(55) 25.8	(84) 16.7	(88) 5.8	(78) 2.3	3.2	(17) 3.5	(289) 6.1	(272) 6.6
	-.3	1.8	-2.2	-2.4	1.2	-1.5	-1.8	-1.1
% Profit Before Taxes/Total Assets	38.8	23.7	6.8	5.7	4.6	3.0	10.8	12.2
	20.7	8.5	3.3	1.1	2.5	1.5	3.3	3.3
	-1.6	1.2	-1.0	-1.5	.6	-.5	-1.2	-.6
Sales/Net Fixed Assets	UND	UND	38.4	6.4	6.1	27.4	113.7	547.3
	UND	137.9	2.1	1.8	1.2	2.1	4.2	4.1
	271.0	8.1	.6	.5	.5	.4	.9	.9
Sales/Total Assets	3.3	2.3	1.2	1.1	.7	1.0	1.8	1.5
	2.1	1.3	.7	.7	.5	.4	.8	.9
	1.4	.7	.4	.4	.2	.2	.4	.5
% Depr., Dep., Amort./Sales	.4	.3	1.4	2.0	1.9	.5	1.5	1.6
	(14) .8	(41) .8	(61) 4.7	(67) 4.1	3.4	(14) 1.5	(205) 3.8	(184) 3.9
	1.3	2.9	9.0	9.6	10.4	7.8	8.1	7.9
% Officers', Directors' Owners' Comp/Sales	2.7	5.6	8.0				4.5	1.9
	(15) 8.8	(13) 8.2	(16) 13.0				(29) 12.9	(19) 6.2
	17.7	29.9	21.6				25.6	14.0
Net Sales ($)	50243M	221762M	408173M	1692565M	864730M	2097649M	3623612M	3576179M
Total Assets ($)	18309M	107650M	445314M	1747354M	1651375M	2905672M	5359557M	4899800M

© RMA 2011

M = $ thousand   MM = $ million
See Pages 9 through 22 for Explanation of Ratios and Data

Comparative Historical Data | Current Data Sorted by Sales

4/1/08-3/31/09 ALL	4/1/09-3/31/10 ALL	4/1/10-3/31/11 ALL	Type of Statement	0-1MM	1-3MM	3-5MM	5-10MM	10-25MM	25MM & OVER
195	174	198	Unqualified	36	43	25	23	36	35
15	11	19	Reviewed	11	6	1			1
23	15	15	Compiled	9	4	1		1	
13	16	18	Tax Returns	9	7	2			
143	132	135	Other	44	22	19	22	16	12
				163 (4/1-9/30/10)		222 (10/1/10-3/31/11)			
389	348	385	**NUMBER OF STATEMENTS**	109	82	48	45	53	48
%	%	%	**ASSETS**	%	%	%	%	%	%
35.8	35.2	39.3	Cash & Equivalents	56.1	41.8	38.5	24.0	24.1	28.8
8.8	9.0	8.0	Trade Receivables (net)	4.8	8.4	7.0	8.2	11.0	12.1
1.1	1.2	1.6	Inventory	.6	.6	2.4	2.4	1.6	3.9
4.7	4.7	5.0	All Other Current	3.8	4.1	7.3	6.8	6.1	4.0
50.4	50.0	53.8	Total Current	65.2	54.8	55.2	41.3	42.8	48.8
33.1	36.7	30.4	Fixed Assets (net)	22.6	30.3	28.3	41.5	41.0	28.5
.7	.9	.9	Intangibles (net)	.6	.2	.2	1.8	.5	3.2
15.8	12.4	14.8	All Other Non-Current	11.6	14.7	16.3	15.4	15.8	19.5
100.0	100.0	100.0	Total	100.0	100.0	100.0	100.0	100.0	100.0
			LIABILITIES						
6.0	4.7	3.5	Notes Payable-Short Term	3.9	5.3	1.3	4.6	1.7	2.5
2.6	2.8	2.2	Cur. Mat.-L.T.D.	3.3	2.7	1.2	1.2	1.4	1.3
7.2	6.1	6.1	Trade Payables	5.9	5.0	8.2	8.8	5.3	4.8
.1	.1	.1	Income Taxes Payable	.0	.2	.7	.0	.1	.0
12.3	12.2	11.4	All Other Current	12.1	8.5	11.1	10.8	11.7	15.5
28.1	25.8	23.3	Total Current	25.3	21.6	22.4	25.4	20.2	24.1
21.8	25.7	25.8	Long-Term Debt	35.8	36.8	18.1	13.5	13.9	16.5
.0	.0	.0	Deferred Taxes	.0	.0	.0	.1	.0	.2
6.3	4.3	6.0	All Other Non-Current	4.7	4.3	4.6	11.2	8.7	5.6
43.8	44.2	44.8	Net Worth	34.3	37.2	54.8	49.8	57.1	53.7
100.0	100.0	100.0	Total Liabilities & Net Worth	100.0	100.0	100.0	100.0	100.0	100.0
			INCOME DATA						
100.0	100.0	100.0	Net Sales	100.0	100.0	100.0	100.0	100.0	100.0
			Gross Profit						
92.7	91.8	90.8	Operating Expenses	83.2	89.0	94.8	97.1	95.5	96.3
7.3	8.2	9.2	Operating Profit	16.8	11.0	5.2	2.9	4.5	3.7
3.7	4.5	1.9	All Other Expenses (net)	2.6	3.9	.3	1.2	1.3	-.1
3.6	3.7	7.3	Profit Before Taxes	14.3	7.1	4.9	1.7	3.2	3.7
			RATIOS						
5.8	6.0	6.7	Current	18.2	8.4	5.6	4.5	3.9	4.3
2.5	2.4	3.0		5.5	3.5	2.7	1.7	2.0	2.2
1.0	1.2	1.3		1.4	1.6	1.2	1.1	1.3	1.1
5.4	5.7	6.5	Quick	17.6	7.8	4.5	3.7	3.1	3.2
2.1	(347) 2.1	2.3		5.3	3.4	2.4	1.5	1.8	1.8
.8	1.0	1.0		1.2	1.4	.9	.8	.9	.9
2 163.6	1 473.4	2 233.3	Sales/Receivables	0 UND	2 220.0	2 235.6	2 212.1	5 76.3	9 39.9
11 32.5	10 35.0	9 41.2		5 68.2	10 36.2	4 84.2	8 44.5	16 22.4	28 12.9
32 11.3	36 10.2	32 11.5		19 19.4	35 10.4	17 21.9	24 15.2	38 9.6	62 5.9
			Cost of Sales/Inventory						
			Cost of Sales/Payables						
2.0	2.1	1.9	Sales/Working Capital	1.4	2.3	2.1	2.7	2.5	2.1
4.9	4.9	4.9		2.7	4.2	5.7	7.7	7.0	6.0
256.8	30.5	25.4		23.4	15.1	45.0	59.6	28.2	29.6
7.6	9.6	8.4	EBIT/Interest	7.4	8.0	14.9	14.0	9.8	5.5
(225) 1.6	(204) 2.7	(214) 2.5		(46) 2.5	(46) 2.3	(25) 5.1	(28) 1.6	(37) 4.1	(32) 2.2
-1.3	.2	.2		-.4	.3	.6	-.4	-1.1	1.1
6.5	45.8		Net Profit + Depr., Dep., Amort./Cur. Mat. L/T/D						
(16) 2.6	(14) 8.1	2.1							
.0	2.1								
.0	.0	.0	Fixed/Worth	.0	.0	.0	.3	.2	.1
.5	.5	.3		.3	.3	.3	.9	.8	.4
1.3	1.3	1.2		.9	1.5	.7	1.4	1.2	1.3
.3	.2	.2	Debt/Worth	.1	.2	.2	.2	.2	.4
.8	.8	.6		.5	.7	.5	.6	.6	.9
3.6	2.7	2.3		2.7	5.4	2.1	3.7	1.8	1.9
16.1	17.3	21.4	% Profit Before Taxes/Tangible Net Worth	32.5	33.0	19.8	14.1	13.0	11.6
(348) 3.9	(311) 4.2	(345) 6.6		(92) 12.9	(72) 7.2	(45) 8.1	(40) 3.7	(50) 2.6	(46) 4.3
-5.8	-4.4	-.6		.8	-3.0	-1.0	-2.0	-1.9	.5
9.6	9.2	14.3	% Profit Before Taxes/Total Assets	28.8	20.9	9.5	7.5	6.4	5.6
1.6	2.0	3.8		9.8	5.9	4.9	2.8	2.1	2.6
-3.4	-2.8	-.6		.0	-1.7	-.2	-1.5	-.6	.3
335.6	351.2	UND	Sales/Net Fixed Assets	UND	UND	387.4	42.0	7.6	46.2
5.5	5.6	10.8		UND	28.9	17.4	2.2	2.1	6.3
1.1	.8	1.0		1.2	.8	1.2	.6	.8	1.2
1.8	1.7	1.9	Sales/Total Assets	1.9	2.1	2.1	1.8	1.5	1.6
1.0	.8	1.0		1.0	1.1	1.1	.8	.9	.8
.5	.4	.5		.5	.5	.5	.4	.4	.5
1.3	1.2	1.0	% Depr., Dep., Amort./Sales	1.0	.5	.8	1.4	1.3	.8
(240) 3.3	(220) 4.0	(220) 2.9		(23) 6.7	(45) 1.7	(34) 3.1	(30) 4.3	(47) 3.5	(41) 2.0
7.8	9.4	8.5		14.4	8.3	11.0	10.3	6.8	4.0
4.6	5.3	5.1	% Officers', Directors' Owners' Comp/Sales	7.3	5.4				
(36) 9.0	(43) 8.1	(53) 11.3		(21) 17.6	(15) 9.0				
15.5	23.1	24.1		29.9	13.7				
5037478M	4896269M	5335122M	Net Sales ($)	52472M	143187M	189596M	325250M	865580M	3759037M
6152411M	5458144M	6875674M	Total Assets ($)	86105M	189074M	284205M	579309M	1687223M	4049758M

© RMA 2011

M = $ thousand   MM = $ million
See Pages 9 through 22 for Explanation of Ratios and Data

Current Data Sorted by Assets   Comparative Historical Data

	0-500M	500M-2MM	2-10MM	10-50MM	50-100MM	100-250MM	Type of Statement	ALL 4/1/06-3/31/07	ALL 4/1/07-3/31/08
		1	4	4	3	2	Unqualified	14	12
		6	6	3			Reviewed	20	11
	4	1	6	1	1		Compiled	7	16
	9	5	2			1	Tax Returns	37	25
	12	11	12	5	2		Other	46	41
		17 (4/1-9/30/10)		83 (10/1/10-3/31/11)					
NUMBER OF STATEMENTS	25	24	30	13	6	2		124	105
	%	%	%	%	%	%	**ASSETS**	%	%
Cash & Equivalents	26.1	17.5	8.5	25.1			Cash & Equivalents	13.9	15.4
	8.9	26.0	17.1	9.9			Trade Receivables (net)	17.8	14.7
	11.9	12.3	7.4	8.8			Inventory	12.8	10.4
	4.7	3.3	1.7	1.9			All Other Current	6.9	3.0
	51.6	59.1	34.7	45.8			Total Current	51.4	43.5
	29.1	22.6	49.3	35.2			Fixed Assets (net)	33.0	42.0
	8.9	5.0	3.2	.1			Intangibles (net)	4.8	4.3
	10.2	13.3	12.8	18.9			All Other Non-Current	10.8	10.2
	100.0	100.0	100.0	100.0			Total	100.0	100.0
							LIABILITIES		
	46.1	12.0	7.0	6.1			Notes Payable-Short Term	11.8	13.2
	6.0	3.0	1.4	.6			Cur. Mat.-L.T.D.	3.2	5.5
	15.3	16.0	5.4	10.4			Trade Payables	12.2	9.3
	.0	.0	.4	.1			Income Taxes Payable	.7	.3
	9.4	12.1	5.9	7.2			All Other Current	12.1	11.1
	76.9	43.0	20.1	24.3			Total Current	40.0	39.4
	27.7	34.5	25.4	16.9			Long-Term Debt	23.0	31.6
	.0	.1	.4	.0			Deferred Taxes	.3	.1
	6.6	7.2	3.5	2.0			All Other Non-Current	3.4	3.5
	-11.2	15.2	50.6	56.8			Net Worth	33.2	25.4
	100.0	100.0	100.0	100.0			Total Liabilities & Net Worth	100.0	100.0
							INCOME DATA		
	100.0	100.0	100.0	100.0			Net Sales	100.0	100.0
							Gross Profit		
	84.4	89.9	78.3	78.7			Operating Expenses	83.4	82.0
	15.6	10.1	21.7	21.3			Operating Profit	16.6	18.0
	.3	3.6	6.3	1.8			All Other Expenses (net)	6.9	7.2
	15.3	6.5	15.4	19.5			Profit Before Taxes	9.7	10.8
							RATIOS		
	1.9	3.4	3.1	17.2				2.7	2.2
	.9	1.8	1.6	1.5			Current	1.4	1.2
	.3	1.0	.8	1.0				.9	.6
	1.1	3.0	2.2	17.2				2.0	1.7
	.6	1.3	1.3	1.0			Quick	.8	.8
	.2	.7	.6	.5				.3	.2
	0 UND	0 UND	0 UND	0 UND				0 UND	0 UND
	0 UND	16 22.7	19 19.2	3 108.7			Sales/Receivables	11 33.9	5 80.3
	5 74.6	55 6.7	38 9.5	35 10.5				44 8.4	39 9.3
							Cost of Sales/Inventory		
							Cost of Sales/Payables		
	22.4	4.0	6.7	1.6				6.8	8.4
	-154.3	14.3	20.4	18.6			Sales/Working Capital	20.5	40.2
	-5.3	NM	-20.7	NM				-55.7	-22.0
	25.3	25.9	19.1					10.5	9.1
	(16) 11.1	(13) 3.1	(21) 6.8				EBIT/Interest	(84) 3.2	(72) 5.1
	1.3	.1	4.1					.5	1.1
							Net Profit + Depr., Dep.,	10.8	5.1
							Amort./Cur. Mat. L/T/D	(18) 4.6	(11) 2.5
								1.6	1.1
	.0	.1	.5	.0				.2	.3
	.7	.5	.9	.4			Fixed/Worth	.8	1.2
	-3.9	41.8	2.5	2.1				15.3	5.6
	.5	.4	.4	.3				.6	.6
	2.4	1.0	1.0	.8			Debt/Worth	2.2	2.1
	-3.4	NM	2.7	2.1				61.8	12.9
	274.4	78.5	51.6	22.9			% Profit Before Taxes/Tangible	64.5	47.9
	(15) 53.4	(18) 16.4	(28) 18.0	6.0			Net Worth	(99) 22.3	(83) 21.0
	18.2	.4	7.1	3.0				5.8	4.5
	80.9	26.8	22.0	13.1			% Profit Before Taxes/Total	20.2	17.2
	30.9	6.9	8.6	3.7			Assets	5.6	6.5
	6.6	-3.3	3.1	1.2				.0	.4
	237.7	128.1	16.9	84.6				42.2	36.4
	39.0	27.6	1.8	7.6			Sales/Net Fixed Assets	12.3	7.2
	7.2	8.0	.5	.7				2.1	1.1
	6.9	5.1	3.1	2.6				4.3	4.7
	4.5	3.3	1.1	.8			Sales/Total Assets	2.0	1.6
	2.6	1.8	.2	.3				.6	.5
	.4	.2	1.4	.4				.8	1.0
	(13) .7	(16) 1.1	(26) 4.5	(10) 1.6			% Depr., Dep., Amort./Sales	(96) 2.1	(84) 2.3
	3.9	3.8	12.4	5.5				5.5	7.2
	3.6	2.4						2.4	1.5
	(11) 7.2	(12) 6.5					% Officers', Directors'	(35) 3.3	(30) 2.3
	17.8	20.6					Owners' Comp/Sales	11.3	6.6
	37306M	107116M	207954M	435794M	304644M	887776M	Net Sales ($)	4160941M	2427861M
	6973M	29628M	136738M	262126M	408161M	362973M	Total Assets ($)	1712164M	1328845M

M = $ thousand   MM = $ million
See Pages 9 through 22 for Explanation of Ratios and Data

Comparative Historical Data				Current Data Sorted by Sales					
			Type of Statement						
11	12	14	Unqualified		3	1	2	3	5
16	15	15	Reviewed	1	4	1	2	6	1
13	14	13	Compiled	2	5		3	1	2
23	15	16	Tax Returns	8	5	3			
44	40	42	Other	9	13	6	7	4	3
4/1/08-3/31/09 ALL	4/1/09-3/31/10 ALL	4/1/10-3/31/11 ALL		17 (4/1-9/30/10)			83 (10/1/10-3/31/11)		
				0-1MM	1-3MM	3-5MM	5-10MM	10-25MM	25MM & OVER
107	96	100	**NUMBER OF STATEMENTS**	20	30	11	14	14	11
%	%	%	**ASSETS**	%	%	%	%	%	%
16.8	13.4	17.5	Cash & Equivalents	15.8	19.1	20.6	9.7	24.2	14.9
14.2	16.0	15.4	Trade Receivables (net)	2.5	18.4	12.9	17.6	27.3	15.1
15.3	10.7	11.2	Inventory	4.1	13.6	8.7	8.8	12.7	20.8
5.4	2.9	3.1	All Other Current	1.6	3.2	.7	6.4	1.7	5.7
51.7	43.1	47.2	Total Current	24.0	54.4	43.0	42.5	65.9	56.5
34.7	39.4	35.5	Fixed Assets (net)	49.5	29.6	37.6	34.5	24.7	38.9
2.6	6.8	4.6	Intangibles (net)	11.0	1.5	5.4	4.8	3.5	1.9
11.0	10.7	12.6	All Other Non-Current	15.3	14.5	14.1	18.2	5.9	2.6
100.0	100.0	100.0	Total	100.0	100.0	100.0	100.0	100.0	100.0
			LIABILITIES						
13.1	10.2	17.9	Notes Payable-Short Term	12.7	24.1	.0	39.3	14.7	5.4
3.6	3.2	3.0	Cur. Mat.-L.T.D.	.8	5.9	.6	2.3	2.9	2.4
10.1	.7.0	11.2	Trade Payables	3.0	15.1	8.8	4.9	18.6	16.6
.2	.2	.1	Income Taxes Payable	.5	.0	.1	.3	.0	.0
16.8	6.6	8.4	All Other Current	8.7	4.1	11.2	9.2	14.4	8.5
43.8	27.2	40.7	Total Current	25.7	49.1	20.7	55.9	50.5	32.9
29.7	32.3	26.9	Long-Term Debt	22.8	28.8	22.9	31.0	36.0	15.9
.1	.7	.2	Deferred Taxes	.0	.2	.0	.2	.4	.6
8.7	5.2	5.0	All Other Non-Current	.2	7.8	12.2	5.1	1.7	2.6
17.8	34.6	27.3	Net Worth	51.3	14.1	44.1	7.8	11.4	47.9
100.0	100.0	100.0	Total Liabilities & Net Worth	100.0	100.0	100.0	100.0	100.0	100.0
			INCOME DATA						
100.0	100.0	100.0	Net Sales	100.0	100.0	100.0	100.0	100.0	100.0
			Gross Profit						
85.8	81.4	83.3	Operating Expenses	60.3	85.8	89.0	84.7	95.4	95.1
14.2	18.6	16.7	Operating Profit	39.7	14.2	11.0	15.3	4.6	4.9
5.2	5.8	3.2	All Other Expenses (net)	13.1	-.2	.5	2.6	.6	1.2
9.0	12.9	13.5	Profit Before Taxes	26.6	14.4	10.5	12.7	3.9	3.7
			RATIOS						
2.6	3.4	3.1		1.9	3.3	3.8	2.7	7.8	2.7
1.5	1.8	1.4	Current	.8	1.5	2.7	1.0	1.8	1.4
.8	.8	.8		.4	.7	1.2	.7	1.0	1.0
1.8	2.6	2.4		1.6	3.0	3.8	1.6	4.5	1.9
.7	1.0	1.0	Quick	.7	.9	1.4	.9	1.5	.9
.2	.4	.4		.3	.4	.7	.3	.7	.3
0 UND	0 UND	0 UND		0 UND	0 UND	0 UND	0 UND	5 80.4	7 52.7
7 49.4	9 42.8	3 115.2	Sales/Receivables	0 UND	3 133.9	0 UND	4 87.4	25 14.7	37 10.0
33 10.9	47 7.8	40 9.2		0 UND	48 7.6	29 12.4	47 7.8	37 9.7	42 8.6
			Cost of Sales/Inventory						
			Cost of Sales/Payables						
6.0	4.6	6.6		16.7	3.8	4.4	7.0	6.4	3.7
29.4	22.9	26.4	Sales/Working Capital	-36.0	24.9	14.3	NM	14.1	34.3
-26.8	-45.4	-34.0		-4.4	-24.1	35.5	-40.8	NM	619.3
14.7	14.2	22.8			21.9		11.3	49.4	
(76) 4.1	(69) 3.7	(65) 6.6	EBIT/Interest		(18) 9.2		(12) 5.2	(12) 5.6	
.8	.5	1.6			3.4		1.0	.6	
5.7	5.3		Net Profit + Depr., Dep.,						
(12) 3.9	(13) 1.4		Amort./Cur. Mat. L/T/D						
.7	.9								
.2	.3	.2		.1	.1	.0	.2	.1	.4
.9	.9	.7	Fixed/Worth	.9	.6	.6	2.1	.4	.6
9.6	5.5	2.9		2.1	-54.8	3.7	-239.7	2.6	2.8
.8	.6	.4		.4	.4	.2	.6	.1	.8
1.9	1.6	1.1	Debt/Worth	1.1	.9	1.2	2.9	1.1	1.0
84.5	8.9	6.4		6.8	-83.3	4.0	-381.1	3.2	2.8
42.7	34.4	53.5		69.6	68.5	82.6	56.0	42.2	21.2
(81) 15.9	(77) 14.0	(82) 17.9	% Profit Before Taxes/Tangible Net Worth	(17) 17.6	(21) 18.5	(10) 35.8	(10) 38.9	(13) 14.0	9.6
2.8	.7	4.9		3.5	4.4	2.5	7.9	7.1	3.8
18.9	19.0	28.3		37.8	36.4	35.7	21.9	28.4	9.7
5.4	4.5	7.5	% Profit Before Taxes/Total Assets	6.1	8.8	8.3	14.9	6.4	4.3
.0	-1.0	2.0		1.5	2.8	-3.1	.6	1.3	1.5
80.3	32.1	62.5		137.1	48.3	185.1	119.1	147.7	30.0
14.1	5.8	10.9	Sales/Net Fixed Assets	.4	13.4	8.7	12.6	23.3	6.3
1.7	.6	1.4		.1	5.5	1.6	1.5	6.0	.9
6.2	3.2	4.5		2.2	4.3	5.5	3.5	6.6	3.5
2.3	1.7	2.2	Sales/Total Assets	.3	3.2	1.9	2.4	4.4	1.7
.6	.4	.6		.1	1.2	.8	.7	1.4	.6
.6	.9	.6		.7	.4		1.1	.6	.5
(82) 1.5	(72) 3.0	(71) 1.9	% Depr., Dep., Amort./Sales	(11) 18.6	(21) 1.9		(10) 2.2	(12) 1.3	(10) 1.8
6.4	8.2	7.0		22.8	5.2		5.5	1.7	5.5
1.8	2.1	2.3			3.6				
(31) 4.1	(18) 5.8	(31) 5.7	% Officers', Directors' Owners' Comp/Sales		(12) 5.4				
9.5	9.0	19.4			10.5				
5667577M	2703065M	1980590M	Net Sales ($)	10197M	56543M	42368M	106982M	218945M	1545555M
1874564M	1588287M	1206599M	Total Assets ($)	55284M	56994M	85347M	137742M	99142M	772090M

M = $ thousand   MM = $ million
See Pages 9 through 22 for Explanation of Ratios and Data

PUBLIC ADMINISTRATION

Current Data Sorted by Assets   Comparative Historical Data

Type of Statement

0-500M	500M-2MM	2-10MM	10-50MM	50-100MM	100-250MM	Type of Statement	4/1/06-3/31/07	4/1/07-3/31/08
1	3	18	34	23	30	Unqualified	53	63
				1	1	Reviewed		1
	1					Compiled	1	3
3	6	6	14	3	3	Tax Returns	3	5
	121 (4/1-9/30/10)		26 (10/1/10-3/31/11)			Other	8	8
4	10	24	48	27	34	**NUMBER OF STATEMENTS**	ALL 65	ALL 80

0-500M %	500M-2MM %	2-10MM %	10-50MM %	50-100MM %	100-250MM %		4/1/06-3/31/07 ALL %	4/1/07-3/31/08 ALL %
						ASSETS		
	35.3	19.3	22.6	18.5	21.0	Cash & Equivalents	21.2	23.7
	3.0	14.4	9.8	4.1	5.2	Trade Receivables (net)	11.3	5.1
	9.1	2.1	1.1	.1	.1	Inventory	2.3	.7
	.0	2.8	5.4	3.1	1.8	All Other Current	3.4	4.7
	47.4	38.5	38.9	25.8	28.1	Total Current	38.2	34.2
	45.8	49.1	47.4	64.7	61.5	Fixed Assets (net)	53.9	56.6
	.0	.1	.5	.9	.6	Intangibles (net)	.3	.7
	6.8	12.3	13.3	8.7	9.8	All Other Non-Current	7.6	8.5
	100.0	100.0	100.0	100.0	100.0	Total	100.0	100.0
						LIABILITIES		
	4.4	4.6	2.1	.2	1.5	Notes Payable-Short Term	1.8	2.0
	2.3	2.4	3.8	1.9	3.1	Cur. Mat.-L.T.D.	1.4	1.6
	1.4	6.7	3.7	2.5	2.0	Trade Payables	4.5	3.0
	.0	.9	1.2	.0	.0	Income Taxes Payable	.0	.1
	8.4	10.0	18.2	5.1	5.3	All Other Current	4.1	5.8
	16.5	24.6	29.0	9.7	11.8	Total Current	11.8	12.5
	23.4	22.2	26.8	27.0	28.9	Long-Term Debt	22.4	23.3
	.0	.0	.0	.0	.0	Deferred Taxes	.1	.0
	3.2	2.4	3.9	11.2	1.3	All Other Non-Current	11.5	4.3
	56.9	50.9	40.3	52.2	58.0	Net Worth	54.3	59.9
	100.0	100.0	100.0	100.0	100.0	Total Liabilities & Net Worth	100.0	100.0
						INCOME DATA		
	100.0	100.0	100.0	100.0	100.0	Net Sales	100.0	100.0
						Gross Profit		
	80.1	81.4	89.2	87.3	93.9	Operating Expenses	84.2	80.4
	19.9	18.6	10.8	12.7	6.1	Operating Profit	15.8	19.6
	16.7	6.2	7.7	2.0	2.3	All Other Expenses (net)	2.3	5.3
	3.2	12.4	3.1	10.7	3.8	Profit Before Taxes	13.5	14.3
						RATIOS		
	8.4	4.0	3.1	5.8	5.3	Current	8.1	7.2
	2.3	1.8	2.1	3.9	3.2		3.2	3.3
	.1	.3	1.1	1.9	1.6		1.6	1.8
	8.4	3.8	2.9	5.5	5.3	Quick	8.1	6.8
	1.3	1.7	1.7	3.8	2.9		2.8	2.7
	.1	.3	1.0	1.8	1.4		1.4	1.3
	0 UND	0 963.6	2 179.7	12 31.6	3 104.4	Sales/Receivables	0 999.8	0 972.5
	0 UND	19 19.6	24 15.3	28 12.8	21 17.7		32 11.6	18 20.1
	0 UND	59 6.2	47 7.8	67 5.4	44 8.4		69 5.3	41 8.8
						Cost of Sales/Inventory		
						Cost of Sales/Payables		
	2.3	3.2	2.7	1.1	1.6	Sales/Working Capital	1.4	1.5
	21.2	8.1	6.0	2.2	2.8		3.5	2.7
	-4.0	-5.1	35.5	5.1	7.5		6.9	9.0
		35.8	10.2	24.2	5.0	EBIT/Interest	14.2	17.0
		(18) 2.8	(31) 2.0	(25) 5.9	(27) 2.0		(42) 6.2	(52) 5.9
		.3	.7	1.4	.1		3.0	2.0
						Net Profit + Depr., Dep., Amort./Cur. Mat. L/T/D		
	.2	.3	.0	.9	.9	Fixed/Worth	.2	.6
	.7	.9	1.0	1.0	1.0		1.0	1.0
	2.9	2.0	1.4	1.6	1.4		1.3	1.5
	.1	.3	.3	.3	.3	Debt/Worth	.3	.2
	.6	1.1	.9	.5	.5		.6	.6
	7.6	2.1	4.0	.8	1.7		1.2	1.3
		33.6	8.0	7.2	6.3	% Profit Before Taxes/Tangible Net Worth	17.4	14.2
		8.5	(44) 1.6	(24) 4.1	(33) 2.0		(63) 8.8	(77) 5.5
		-3.9	-1.7	-2.0	-2.6		4.0	1.4
	6.9	8.4	3.5	4.6	3.0	% Profit Before Taxes/Total Assets	8.2	7.6
	1.7	1.4	.4	3.2	1.0		5.4	3.3
	-1.9	-2.9	-2.3	-.4	-1.8		1.9	1.1
	UND	404.8	UND	.6	.8	Sales/Net Fixed Assets	42.7	1.5
	3.9	1.4	1.2	.5	.5		.6	.6
	.5	.3	.3	.4	.3		.3	.3
	2.8	2.1	1.5	.4	.5	Sales/Total Assets	.9	.6
	1.2	.7	.6	.3	.3		.4	.4
	.3	.2	.3	.2	.2		.3	.2
		3.1	5.0	5.4	4.3	% Depr., Dep., Amort./Sales	3.8	4.7
		(14) 5.4	(30) 8.8	(21) 8.8	(23) 11.0		(37) 9.6	(49) 8.9
		11.1	12.9	13.3	18.6		15.6	14.9
						% Officers', Directors' Owners' Comp/Sales		4.5
								(10) 6.8
								16.7
3264M	24132M	365267M	1497119M	687587M	3150625M	Net Sales ($)	1458201M	2174528M
649M	13159M	133588M	1269630M	1878344M	5612115M	Total Assets ($)	2224883M	4021140M

M = $ thousand   MM = $ million
See Pages 9 through 22 for Explanation of Ratios and Data

Comparative Historical Data | Current Data Sorted by Sales

Hist 1	Hist 2	Hist 3	Type of Statement	0-1MM	1-3MM	3-5MM	5-10MM	10-25MM	25MM & OVER
72	103	109	Unqualified	3	11	6	14	28	47
1			Reviewed						
1	5	2	Compiled		1				1
3	5	1	Tax Returns		1				
17	21	35	Other	7	4	2	4	9	9
4/1/08-3/31/09 ALL	4/1/09-3/31/10 ALL	4/1/10-3/31/11 ALL		121 (4/1-9/30/10)			26 (10/1/10-3/31/11)		
94	134	147	NUMBER OF STATEMENTS	10	17	8	18	37	57
%	%	%	ASSETS	%	%	%	%	%	%
25.6	21.4	23.3	Cash & Equivalents	24.4	25.3		15.8	19.6	26.8
5.5	7.6	7.7	Trade Receivables (net)	.9	2.8		10.2	11.9	7.6
.9	1.0	1.4	Inventory	3.8	.5		5.1	.1	.9
5.6	3.8	3.3	All Other Current	.0	1.7		2.8	2.2	5.6
37.6	33.8	35.7	Total Current	29.0	30.3		33.9	33.8	41.0
53.7	55.6	53.1	Fixed Assets (net)	61.6	55.2		48.4	57.4	48.5
.3	.2	.5	Intangibles (net)	.1	.3		.1	.7	.6
8.4	10.4	10.7	All Other Non-Current	9.3	14.2		17.6	8.1	10.0
100.0	100.0	100.0	Total	100.0	100.0		100.0	100.0	100.0
			LIABILITIES						
3.5	1.7	2.1	Notes Payable-Short Term	6.2	2.3		2.6	.1	2.7
1.6	2.2	2.9	Cur. Mat.-L.T.D.	1.9	3.5		1.2	2.0	4.1
4.1	4.0	3.5	Trade Payables	.4	2.3		1.8	2.7	5.7
.5	.3	.5	Income Taxes Payable	.0	.0		.0	.6	.9
6.3	9.1	10.9	All Other Current	7.2	8.2		19.7	11.8	9.9
16.0	17.3	19.9	Total Current	15.7	16.2		25.4	17.2	23.3
20.7	24.7	25.6	Long-Term Debt	35.5	30.9		22.3	21.7	26.8
.0	.1	.0	Deferred Taxes	.0	.0		.0	.0	.0
6.9	4.0	4.3	All Other Non-Current	.3	2.0		3.5	10.4	2.6
56.2	53.8	50.2	Net Worth	48.5	50.9		48.8	50.7	47.3
100.0	100.0	100.0	Total Liabilties & Net Worth	100.0	100.0		100.0	100.0	100.0
			INCOME DATA						
100.0	100.0	100.0	Net Sales	100.0	100.0		100.0	100.0	100.0
			Gross Profit						
86.9	90.0	88.0	Operating Expenses	51.9	88.9		83.2	89.9	95.4
13.1	10.0	12.0	Operating Profit	48.1	11.1		16.8	10.1	4.6
4.3	4.9	5.5	All Other Expenses (net)	22.8	8.5		5.2	4.0	2.6
8.8	5.2	6.5	Profit Before Taxes	25.3	2.6		11.6	6.1	2.0
			RATIOS						
6.2	5.1	4.6	Current	11.5	5.7		4.4	5.6	4.1
3.0	2.5	2.7		.4	2.3		2.9	3.4	2.8
1.5	1.1	1.2		.2	.3		1.5	1.4	1.3
5.6	4.8	4.1	Quick	4.6	5.5		4.2	5.5	3.7
2.8	2.1	2.2		.4	1.9		2.4	3.2	2.2
1.2	.9	1.2		.2	.3		1.4	1.2	1.2
2 171.9	5 76.0	1 376.2	Sales/Receivables	0 UND	0 UND		10 36.3	8 43.6	2 149.8
13 27.2	23 15.7	20 18.5		0 UND	22 16.3		27 13.8	42 8.6	15 23.8
37 10.0	46 7.9	48 7.5		18 19.7	39 9.5		47 7.8	89 4.1	41 8.8
			Cost of Sales/Inventory						
			Cost of Sales/Payables						
1.4	1.8	1.9	Sales/Working Capital	1.8	1.4		2.6	1.4	2.1
3.3	3.9	4.5		-4.8	5.9		3.5	2.6	4.6
13.2	99.6	18.9		-.8	-4.2		10.7	12.2	15.6
8.6	5.9	11.1	EBIT/Interest				28.4	16.7	5.4
(67) 3.7	(101) 2.0	(106) 2.6				(16)	5.0	(30) 4.4	(42) 2.0
.1	-1.1	.4					2.0	-.3	.1
			Net Profit + Depr., Dep., Amort./Cur. Mat. L/T/D						
.5	.7	.5	Fixed/Worth	.1	.4		.1	.7	.1
1.0	1.0	1.0		1.8	1.0		.9	1.0	1.0
1.5	1.5	1.6		3.1	3.1		1.2	1.4	1.4
.2	.3	.3	Debt/Worth	.5	.2		.3	.3	.4
.5	.7	.6		1.2	.9		.5	.6	.6
1.2	1.7	2.0		2.3	3.7		2.2	2.3	2.0
15.3	8.6	9.4	% Profit Before Taxes/Tangible Net Worth		7.0		22.6	7.7	7.4
(91) 5.2	(128) 2.1	(138) 2.5		(16)	1.2	(17)	5.2	(35) 1.8	(53) 1.9
.8	-3.1	-2.3			-20.6		1.6	-3.0	-3.5
8.1	4.2	4.8	% Profit Before Taxes/Total Assets	13.5	4.9		8.2	4.0	3.4
2.8	1.1	1.3		3.5	.4		2.4	.8	.8
.0	-1.4	-1.8		.8	-2.8		.4	-1.8	-2.3
8.9	3.9	4.2	Sales/Net Fixed Assets	UND	5.6		185.2	1.6	719.8
.6	.6	.7		.2	.5		1.1	.5	.9
.4	.3	.4		.1	.2		.4	.3	.5
.8	1.0	1.3	Sales/Total Assets	.8	2.0		1.1	.6	1.7
.4	.4	.4		.1	.5		.4	.3	.6
.2	.2	.2		.1	.1		.3	.2	.4
4.5	5.0	4.5	% Depr., Dep., Amort./Sales		4.7		2.5	5.5	3.6
(55) 10.2	(88) 8.9	(95) 8.4		(14)	8.3	(13)	4.6	(27) 10.3	(33) 6.6
16.7	15.7	13.8			20.9		11.2	18.5	10.8
1.3	3.0	1.2	% Officers', Directors' Owners' Comp/Sales						
(14) 8.6	(15) 8.9	(10) 7.7							
20.9	26.1	21.5							
2897555M	4631603M	5727994M	Net Sales ($)	4177M	28916M	34868M	125760M	647701M	4886572M
4917901M	7884151M	8907485M	Total Assets ($)	28855M	207369M	110219M	349474M	2273863M	5937705M

M = $ thousand   MM = $ million
See Pages 9 through 22 for Explanation of Ratios and Data

Current Data Sorted by Assets   Comparative Historical Data

						Type of Statement		
2	2	6	19	18	7	Unqualified	29	28
1			1			Reviewed		
						Compiled	1	
						Tax Returns		
1	54 (4/1-9/30/10)	1	5		1	Other	2	6
			10 (10/1/10-3/31/11)				4/1/06-3/31/07	4/1/07-3/31/08
0-500M	500M-2MM	2-10MM	10-50MM	50-100MM	100-250MM		ALL	ALL
3	3	7	25	18	8	**NUMBER OF STATEMENTS**	32	34
%	%	%	%	%	%	**ASSETS**	%	%
			15.1	12.9		Cash & Equivalents	36.0	24.4
			3.6	6.8		Trade Receivables (net)	3.8	4.8
			.3	.3		Inventory	.4	.1
			2.5	1.7		All Other Current	3.4	2.1
			21.4	21.7		Total Current	43.6	31.4
			70.0	72.3		Fixed Assets (net)	48.4	59.5
			.8	.5		Intangibles (net)	1.2	.3
			7.7	5.5		All Other Non-Current	6.8	8.8
			100.0	100.0		Total	100.0	100.0
						LIABILITIES		
			1.6	.2		Notes Payable-Short Term	2.7	.8
			2.0	2.7		Cur. Mat.-L.T.D.	3.0	2.7
			1.4	1.5		Trade Payables	2.7	3.9
			.0	.0		Income Taxes Payable	1.0	.0
			2.8	5.3		All Other Current	6.7	2.9
			7.8	9.7		Total Current	16.1	10.3
			27.0	34.1		Long-Term Debt	27.1	26.9
			.2	.0		Deferred Taxes	.0	.0
			3.4	1.9		All Other Non-Current	2.6	2.8
			61.6	54.3		Net Worth	54.2	59.9
			100.0	100.0		Total Liabilities & Net Worth	100.0	100.0
						INCOME DATA		
			100.0	100.0		Net Sales	100.0	100.0
						Gross Profit		
			84.5	89.4		Operating Expenses	88.7	88.3
			15.5	10.6		Operating Profit	11.3	11.7
			4.8	4.4		All Other Expenses (net)	-.5	-1.5
			10.7	6.2		Profit Before Taxes	11.8	13.2
						RATIOS		
			4.4	4.1			6.1	8.9
			2.6	2.3		Current	3.5	4.7
			1.4	1.3			1.6	2.3
			3.8	3.8			5.5	7.4
			2.2	2.3		Quick	3.2	4.6
			1.1	1.2			1.4	1.5
			1 538.4	25 14.3			0 UND	5 68.0
			25 14.5	46 8.0		Sales/Receivables	14 25.5	19 19.7
			54 6.8	160 2.3			44 8.3	40 9.1
						Cost of Sales/Inventory		
						Cost of Sales/Payables		
			1.8	1.1			1.4	1.2
			3.7	3.2		Sales/Working Capital	2.5	2.5
			8.9	9.3			7.3	5.5
			5.6	4.9			7.4	11.1
			(21) 3.1	(16) 2.3		EBIT/Interest	(23) 3.4	(26) 4.1
			1.4	1.2			1.8	2.3
						Net Profit + Depr., Dep., Amort./Cur. Mat. L/T/D		
			.9	.9			.1	.8
			1.3	1.3		Fixed/Worth	.9	.9
			1.7	1.9			1.3	1.2
			.4	.3			.3	.3
			.7	.7		Debt/Worth	.6	.4
			.9	1.2			1.2	1.4
			9.3	7.8			11.9	10.5
			3.7	(17) 2.0		% Profit Before Taxes/Tangible Net Worth	(30) 6.3	(32) 4.8
			-.1	.7			2.0	1.1
			4.3	3.7			6.2	6.3
			3.0	1.3		% Profit Before Taxes/Total Assets	3.8	3.0
			-.1	.4			1.0	.4
			.6	.8			UND	1.4
			.3	.3		Sales/Net Fixed Assets	.8	.5
			.2	.2			.4	.4
			.3	.4			.8	.9
			.2	.2		Sales/Total Assets	.4	.4
			.2	.1			.2	.2
			8.7	6.6			4.5	5.5
			(20) 14.2	(16) 13.9		% Depr., Dep., Amort./Sales	(20) 7.7	(25) 11.1
			20.8	20.3			14.0	17.3
						% Officers', Directors' Owners' Comp/Sales		
1468M	6255M	27576M	344477M	387499M	243332M	Net Sales ($)	412517M	768813M
629M	3208M	43956M	618224M	1267369M	1369653M	Total Assets ($)	1169080M	1662860M

M = $ thousand   MM = $ million
See Pages 9 through 22 for Explanation of Ratios and Data

Comparative Historical Data

Current Data Sorted by Sales

28	56	54	Type of Statement	0-1MM	1-3MM	3-5MM	5-10MM	10-25MM	25MM & OVER
			Unqualified	6	10	2	10	16	10
	1	1	Reviewed		1				
		1	Compiled				1		
			Tax Returns						
			Other	1	2	2		2	1
7	6	8			54 (4/1-9/30/10)			10 (10/1/10-3/31/11)	
4/1/08-3/31/09	4/1/09-3/31/10	4/1/10-3/31/11							
ALL	ALL	ALL							
35	63	64	**NUMBER OF STATEMENTS**	7	13	4	13	16	11
%	%	%	**ASSETS**	%	%	%	%	%	%
26.6	22.3	14.9	Cash & Equivalents		21.9		7.4	16.4	19.9
10.0	4.9	5.2	Trade Receivables (net)		4.3		3.0	5.9	7.4
.1	.2	.3	Inventory		.2		.2	.1	1.1
2.4	5.0	1.6	All Other Current		.5		.7	1.3	5.7
39.2	32.5	22.1	Total Current		26.9		11.3	23.8	34.1
53.8	60.5	68.7	Fixed Assets (net)		62.1		83.5	65.2	55.5
.4	.5	.9	Intangibles (net)		3.5		.3	.2	.6
6.6	6.4	8.3	All Other Non-Current		7.5		5.0	10.8	9.8
100.0	100.0	100.0	Total		100.0		100.0	100.0	100.0
			LIABILITIES						
.8	.7	.7	Notes Payable-Short Term		2.2		1.0	.1	.1
2.0	2.1	2.4	Cur. Mat.-L.T.D.		2.3		1.8	2.3	3.5
3.9	2.6	1.5	Trade Payables		.9		.8	1.8	3.0
.9	.5	.0	Income Taxes Payable		.0		.0	.0	.0
4.8	5.2	4.0	All Other Current		2.3		2.4	5.2	6.6
12.4	11.2	8.5	Total Current		7.6		5.9	9.4	13.2
20.5	29.1	30.8	Long-Term Debt		34.1		31.1	29.2	31.8
.0	.0	.1	Deferred Taxes		.0		.0	.0	.5
2.4	2.7	2.9	All Other Non-Current		1.4		1.3	3.0	4.0
64.8	57.1	57.7	Net Worth		56.8		61.7	58.5	50.5
100.0	100.0	100.0	Total Liabilities & Net Worth		100.0		100.0	100.0	100.0
			INCOME DATA						
100.0	100.0	100.0	Net Sales		100.0		100.0	100.0	100.0
			Gross Profit						
89.8	89.0	87.9	Operating Expenses		87.8		86.1	92.4	89.4
10.2	11.0	12.1	Operating Profit		12.2		13.9	7.6	10.6
3.3	3.4	5.0	All Other Expenses (net)		5.1		3.2	3.2	6.8
6.9	7.5	7.1	Profit Before Taxes		7.1		10.7	4.4	3.8
			RATIOS						
5.0	4.7	4.2	Current		8.8		3.6	4.3	4.2
3.4	2.5	2.7			2.9		2.1	2.7	2.8
1.5	1.7	1.3			1.9		1.2	1.5	.9
4.9	4.6	3.9	Quick		8.5		3.4	3.9	3.4
3.4	2.3	2.5			2.8		1.9	2.7	2.2
1.3	1.5	1.2			1.4		1.0	1.4	.9
9 40.2	10 36.6	11 33.8	Sales/Receivables	0 UND	24 15.3		23 15.9		10 37.6
38 9.6	28 13.1	32 11.4		20 18.6	47 7.7		36 10.1		24 15.2
65 5.6	50 7.3	69 5.3		68 5.4	110 3.3		98 3.7		61 5.9
			Cost of Sales/Inventory						
			Cost of Sales/Payables						
1.4	1.6	1.7	Sales/Working Capital		1.4		2.0	1.7	2.2
3.0	3.4	3.8			2.0		6.2	3.1	2.8
7.9	6.5	10.0			10.7		23.0	5.2	-32.0
6.8	5.1	5.3	EBIT/Interest				5.6	6.9	4.5
(30) 2.9	(52) 2.4	(54) 2.4					2.5	(13) 2.1	2.1
-.4	.8	.9					.3	-11.2	.8
			Net Profit + Depr., Dep., Amort./Cur. Mat. L/T/D						
.2	.9	.9	Fixed/Worth		.7		1.1	.8	.8
1.0	1.1	1.3			1.1		1.3	1.1	1.2
1.3	1.6	1.7			1.7		1.7	1.7	1.4
.3	.3	.3	Debt/Worth		.3		.4	.3	.6
.5	.7	.8			.8		.7	.7	.9
.8	1.1	1.1			1.1		1.0	1.3	1.3
9.0	7.6	8.8	% Profit Before Taxes/Tangible Net Worth		11.7		8.7	6.9	9.5
3.3 (62)	1.9 (62)	2.6		(12) 5.8			2.5	1.7 (10)	2.0
-4.5	-3.8	-.4			.2		-.5	.0	-3.6
5.0	4.8	4.3	% Profit Before Taxes/Total Assets		6.5		4.2	2.9	6.8
2.3	1.0	1.5			3.1		1.4	1.0	1.3
-3.5	-.8	-.4			-.3		-.4	.0	-.6
4.9	1.4	.8	Sales/Net Fixed Assets		.9		.3	.8	.9
.5	.5	.3			.4		.2	.3	.8
.3	.3	.2			.2		.2	.2	.4
.8	.8	.4	Sales/Total Assets		.5		.3	.4	.8
.3	.4	.2			.2		.2	.2	.5
.2	.2	.1			.1		.1	.1	.3
6.8	4.5	7.0	% Depr., Dep., Amort./Sales				9.7	5.2	
(21) 11.0	(48) 8.8	(52) 14.2					(11) 15.9	(14) 12.6	
14.2	18.2	20.7					20.4	20.2	
			% Officers', Directors' Owners' Comp/Sales						
772788M	2310105M	1010607M	Net Sales ($)	3198M	24465M	16547M	111736M	267675M	586986M
1743110M	3308378M	3303039M	Total Assets ($)	35784M	143982M	73100M	735486M	1232641M	1082046M

© RMA 2011   M = $ thousand   MM = $ million
See Pages 9 through 22 for Explanation of Ratios and Data

Current Data Sorted by Assets | Comparative Historical Data

Type of Statement	0-500M	500M-2MM	8 — 2-10MM	17 — 10-50MM	10 — 50-100MM	13 — 100-250MM	22	30
Unqualified			8	17	10	13	22	30
Reviewed				1				
Compiled			1					
Tax Returns								
Other			1 2	3 8	1	1	10	13
		49 (4/1-9/30/10)		8 (10/1/10-3/31/11)			4/1/06-3/31/07 ALL	4/1/07-3/31/08 ALL
NUMBER OF STATEMENTS			11	21	11	14	32	43
ASSETS	%	%	%	%	%	%	%	%
Cash & Equivalents	DATA	DATA	23.1	19.0	11.4	13.0	24.0	31.8
Trade Receivables (net)	NOT	NOT	9.1	6.5	13.3	6.0	10.7	11.6
Inventory	AVAILABLE	AVAILABLE	3.2	.5	1.1	.2	1.1	.3
All Other Current			.2	3.6	1.1	.8	5.2	2.8
Total Current			35.5	29.6	26.8	20.1	41.0	46.5
Fixed Assets (net)			57.1	55.5	65.6	74.8	53.9	41.2
Intangibles (net)			1.3	.3	.0	.7	.0	.3
All Other Non-Current			6.0	14.6	7.6	4.5	5.0	12.1
Total			100.0	100.0	100.0	100.0	100.0	100.0
LIABILITIES								
Notes Payable-Short Term			.4	.2	.2	.2	1.8	1.0
Cur. Mat.-L.T.D.			1.8	1.4	1.3	2.7	2.6	1.2
Trade Payables			3.2	1.7	2.2	1.9	4.4	4.0
Income Taxes Payable			.0	.2	.0	.0	.9	.6
All Other Current			4.2	7.4	3.3	4.3	4.6	8.8
Total Current			9.5	11.0	7.1	9.0	14.2	15.6
Long-Term Debt			34.0	15.4	17.9	27.5	24.8	19.5
Deferred Taxes			1.1	.0	.0	.0	1.4	.0
All Other Non-Current			.7	1.4	9.6	3.9	6.1	4.0
Net Worth			54.7	72.3	65.5	59.6	53.5	60.8
Total Liabilities & Net Worth			100.0	100.0	100.0	100.0	100.0	100.0
INCOME DATA								
Net Sales			100.0	100.0	100.0	100.0	100.0	100.0
Gross Profit								
Operating Expenses			92.8	90.7	91.9	94.2	80.2	90.5
Operating Profit			7.2	9.3	8.1	5.8	19.8	9.5
All Other Expenses (net)			1.7	3.2	1.2	1.3	.2	2.6
Profit Before Taxes			5.5	6.0	6.9	4.5	19.6	6.8
RATIOS								
Current			25.8	7.9	8.5	5.5	6.6	5.6
			5.8	2.9	3.0	2.7	3.8	3.3
			1.4	1.3	1.4	1.4	1.8	2.0
Quick			25.8	7.1	7.7	5.4	5.8	4.9
			5.7	2.6	3.0	2.5	2.4	3.1
			1.4	1.0	1.3	1.2	1.7	1.9
Sales/Receivables			3 138.3	9 39.5	25 14.5	19 19.5	10 38.2	8 43.8
			26 14.0	29 12.7	50 7.3	38 9.6	39 9.5	27 13.3
			55 6.6	84 4.4	86 4.2	76 4.8	77 4.7	62 5.9
Cost of Sales/Inventory								
Cost of Sales/Payables								
Sales/Working Capital			1.0	1.3	1.3	1.3	1.5	1.8
			2.3	2.5	2.2	2.9	2.2	2.8
			10.7	14.8	14.1	15.0	5.5	5.4
EBIT/Interest				6.6	6.5	8.0	12.5	17.9
			(17) 2.0	(10) 1.4		2.2	(23) 5.5	(29) 4.6
			-1.7	-.9		-1.0	2.6	1.8
Net Profit + Depr., Dep., Amort./Cur. Mat. L/T/D								
Fixed/Worth			.6	.6	.9	1.1	.6	.0
			1.2	.9	1.0	1.2	1.1	.8
			5.4	1.2	1.1	1.6	1.4	1.2
Debt/Worth			.2	.2	.2	.4	.5	.2
			.4	.2	.5	.6	.8	.5
			5.1	.6	.8	1.1	1.3	1.0
% Profit Before Taxes/Tangible Net Worth			18.5	8.8	5.9	4.9	23.5	18.4
			(10) 2.9	1.8	1.3	2.0	(31) 9.0	(41) 4.7
			-5.3	-2.2	-1.6	-2.2	3.9	1.7
% Profit Before Taxes/Total Assets			4.7	6.0	4.8	2.7	10.4	9.4
			1.0	.8	1.1	1.3	4.5	2.8
			-8.8	-1.6	-1.1	-1.6	2.1	.7
Sales/Net Fixed Assets			2.7	1.9	.6	.6	4.5	UND
			.9	.4	.4	.4	1.0	1.0
			.3	.3	.2	.3	.3	.4
Sales/Total Assets			1.0	.8	.4	.5	1.3	1.9
			.4	.3	.3	.3	.5	.6
			.2	.2	.2	.2	.2	.3
% Depr., Dep., Amort./Sales				5.3		3.4	4.6	2.9
				(13) 11.0		(11) 7.4	(21) 5.7	(19) 7.5
				19.1		13.2	16.7	16.1
% Officers', Directors' Owners' Comp/Sales								
Net Sales ($)			28220M	330987M	400975M	738168M	1150894M	1552865M
Total Assets ($)			50754M	554186M	815061M	2124995M	1843430M	2159845M

© RMA 2011

M = $ thousand   MM = $ million
See Pages 9 through 22 for Explanation of Ratios and Data

Comparative Historical Data   Current Data Sorted by Sales

			Type of Statement						
52	70	48	Unqualified	1	9	2	8	10	18
1	1	1	Reviewed						
		1	Compiled	1					
		1	Tax Returns			1			
13	14	7	Other	1		2		2	2
4/1/08-3/31/09 ALL	4/1/09-3/31/10 ALL	4/1/10-3/31/11 ALL			49 (4/1-9/30/10)		8 (10/1/10-3/31/11)		
				0-1MM	1-3MM	3-5MM	5-10MM	10-25MM	25MM & OVER
66	85	57	NUMBER OF STATEMENTS	3	9	5	8	12	20
%	%	%	**ASSETS**	%	%	%	%	%	%
30.9	22.9	16.8	Cash & Equivalents					17.9	14.6
7.9	8.3	8.2	Trade Receivables (net)					4.0	13.7
.8	1.0	1.1	Inventory					.7	.8
3.6	3.9	1.8	All Other Current					1.9	2.6
43.2	36.1	27.8	Total Current					24.6	31.7
49.5	56.2	62.5	Fixed Assets (net)					62.6	61.4
.2	.7	.5	Intangibles (net)					.2	.4
7.1	7.0	9.1	All Other Non-Current					12.7	6.5
100.0	100.0	100.0	Total					100.0	100.0
			LIABILITIES						
1.9	1.6	.2	Notes Payable-Short Term					.1	.2
1.3	1.9	1.8	Cur. Mat.-L.T.D.					1.4	2.3
3.9	3.2	2.1	Trade Payables					1.2	2.6
.5	.4	.1	Income Taxes Payable					.0	.0
9.4	6.7	5.2	All Other Current					2.6	8.4
16.8	13.8	9.5	Total Current					5.3	13.5
19.3	21.8	22.4	Long-Term Debt					17.2	20.7
.0	.0	.2	Deferred Taxes					.0	.0
2.7	5.4	3.5	All Other Non-Current					2.3	7.1
61.2	59.1	64.5	Net Worth					75.1	58.7
100.0	100.0	100.0	Total Liabilities & Net Worth					100.0	100.0
			INCOME DATA						
100.0	100.0	100.0	Net Sales					100.0	100.0
			Gross Profit						
92.0	92.4	92.2	Operating Expenses					89.8	97.4
8.0	7.6	7.8	Operating Profit					10.2	2.6
-.4	1.8	2.1	All Other Expenses (net)					-.8	.8
8.4	5.9	5.7	Profit Before Taxes					11.1	1.8
			RATIOS						
5.9	6.8	7.9	Current					8.2	7.7
3.8	2.6	3.4						4.8	2.4
1.9	1.6	1.4						1.8	1.3
5.6	6.5	7.1	Quick					7.6	7.3
3.4	2.3	2.9						4.7	2.4
1.7	1.3	1.2						1.7	1.1
9 39.1	8 46.6	14 25.6	Sales/Receivables					12 31.2	23 15.9
27 13.3	25 14.7	34 10.7						27 13.6	60 6.1
55 6.6	55 6.7	79 4.6						53 6.9	86 4.3
			Cost of Sales/Inventory						
			Cost of Sales/Payables						
1.5	1.3	1.3	Sales/Working Capital					1.1	1.9
3.0	2.3	2.4						1.7	3.1
6.2	10.3	12.4						12.0	16.3
10.6	6.5	6.8	EBIT/Interest						9.9
(54) 3.4	(72) 2.0	(50) 2.0							2.3
.6	-.2	-1.2							-1.0
			Net Profit + Depr., Dep., Amort./Cur. Mat. L/T/D						
.0	.6	.7	Fixed/Worth					.6	.8
.9	1.0	1.0						.9	1.1
1.2	1.5	1.4						1.1	1.4
.2	.3	.2	Debt/Worth					.1	.3
.5	.7	.4						.3	.6
1.0	1.3	.9						.6	1.2
11.5	7.4	5.8	% Profit Before Taxes/Tangible Net Worth					5.9	5.8
(65) 5.2	(83) 1.9	(56) 1.9						.6	2.1
-.4	-2.3	-1.9						-4.5	-2.6
7.6	4.7	4.2	% Profit Before Taxes/Total Assets					5.1	4.2
3.3	.9	1.1						.5	1.6
-.3	-1.4	-1.6						-4.0	-2.0
UND	1.8	1.1	Sales/Net Fixed Assets					.8	1.6
.6	.7	.4						.4	.5
.3	.3	.3						.2	.4
1.4	.9	.6	Sales/Total Assets					.4	1.0
.4	.4	.3						.3	.4
.2	.2	.2						.2	.3
4.0	4.4	4.9	% Depr., Dep., Amort./Sales						4.9
(41) 9.6	(51) 9.7	(41) 9.8						(15)	7.0
15.7	13.1	14.6							13.2
3.7			% Officers', Directors' Owners' Comp/Sales						
(12) 13.2									
27.1									
2414053M	3146493M	1498350M	Net Sales ($)	2233M	17022M	21777M	57245M	182301M	1217772M
3935444M	5146232M	3544996M	Total Assets ($)	23998M	105713M	80988M	188898M	750923M	2394476M

M = $ thousand   MM = $ million
See Pages 9 through 22 for Explanation of Ratios and Data

Current Data Sorted by Assets   **Comparative Historical Data**

	0-500M	500M-2MM	2-10MM	10-50MM	50-100MM	100-250MM	Type of Statement	17	15
							Unqualified		
							Reviewed		
			1	5	2	4	Compiled		
				1			Tax Returns		
							Other	20	15
	2	14 (4/1-9/30/10)	3	23 (10/1/10-3/31/11)	6	9		20 4/1/06-3/31/07 ALL	15 4/1/07-3/31/08 ALL
NUMBER OF STATEMENTS	2		4	10	8	13		37	30
	%	%	%	%	%	%		%	%
ASSETS									
Cash & Equivalents		D		33.5		14.7		19.7	20.2
Trade Receivables (net)		A		3.3		2.0		4.0	3.3
Inventory		T		.9		.5		1.2	1.3
All Other Current		A		5.0		3.1		3.0	2.2
Total Current				42.7		20.3		28.0	27.0
Fixed Assets (net)		N		54.1		74.8		69.4	70.9
Intangibles (net)		O		.1		.5		.9	.2
All Other Non-Current		T		3.0		4.4		1.7	1.8
Total				100.0		100.0		100.0	100.0
LIABILITIES		A							
Notes Payable-Short Term		V		.8		.3		1.0	1.5
Cur. Mat.-L.T.D.		A		3.0		3.2		1.6	8.5
Trade Payables		I		2.4		.8		2.7	2.1
Income Taxes Payable		L		.0		.0		.0	.0
All Other Current		A		20.4		8.6		12.6	17.9
Total Current		B		26.5		12.8		18.0	30.1
Long-Term Debt		L		40.7		28.7		22.1	18.6
Deferred Taxes		E		.0		.2		.0	.0
All Other Non-Current				10.0		1.6		2.6	.7
Net Worth				22.8		56.6		57.2	50.6
Total Liabilties & Net Worth				100.0		100.0		100.0	100.0
INCOME DATA									
Net Sales				100.0		100.0		100.0	100.0
Gross Profit									
Operating Expenses				84.8		77.5		70.0	70.3
Operating Profit				15.2		22.5		30.0	29.7
All Other Expenses (net)				7.0		.8		3.8	.5
Profit Before Taxes				8.2		21.7		26.2	29.2
RATIOS									
Current				3.2		2.3		2.8	2.4
				1.5		1.5		1.7	1.2
				1.1		1.1		.9	.6
Quick				3.0		2.0		2.4	2.0
				1.3		1.1		1.4	1.0
				.8		.9		.9	.5
Sales/Receivables				1 432.2		2 229.3		1 526.3	1 288.0
				2 204.6		3 121.9		4 88.2	3 134.8
				10 37.8		10 37.6		9 41.0	6 57.0
Cost of Sales/Inventory									
Cost of Sales/Payables									
Sales/Working Capital				3.9		8.0		7.1	9.7
				8.5		21.4		20.9	38.3
				NM		131.8		-120.6	-15.6
EBIT/Interest						29.4		388.3	53.1
				(12)		11.2		(29) 39.6	(22) 22.8
						6.3		7.7	8.2
Net Profit + Depr., Dep., Amort./Cur. Mat. L/T/D									
Fixed/Worth				.7		.9		.9	.9
				.9		1.5		1.1	1.3
				2.9		2.2		1.7	3.0
Debt/Worth				.4		.2		.2	.2
				1.0		.8		.4	.7
				2.7		1.6		1.5	3.0
% Profit Before Taxes/Tangible Net Worth						62.7		159.8	168.9
						(12) 28.2		(35) 86.8	(29) 87.5
						13.1		16.7	15.7
% Profit Before Taxes/Total Assets				16.3		30.2		97.6	96.9
				3.8		16.2		39.9	44.1
				2.0		8.5		5.5	13.6
Sales/Net Fixed Assets				5.1		1.5		4.2	3.1
				2.4		.9		2.3	2.3
				1.2		.8		1.3	1.2
Sales/Total Assets				2.1		1.0		2.5	2.4
				1.2		.7		1.8	1.6
				.7		.7		.9	.9
% Depr., Dep., Amort./Sales								2.6	3.0
								(27) 5.4	(20) 4.9
								6.5	8.2
% Officers', Directors' Owners' Comp/Sales									
Net Sales ($)	1505M		31804M	350946M	425689M	2129258M		5154011M	4515377M
Total Assets ($)	676M		23733M	252902M	586679M	2430894M		2941349M	2905409M

M = $ thousand   MM = $ million
See Pages 9 through 22 for Explanation of Ratios and Data

Comparative Historical Data

Current Data Sorted by Sales

16	7	12	Type of Statement						
			Unqualified				1	2	9
			Reviewed						
	1	1	Compiled				1		
			Tax Returns						
16	17	24	Other	1					16
4/1/08-3/31/09 ALL	4/1/09-3/31/10 ALL	4/1/10-3/31/11 ALL		0-1MM	14 (4/1-9/30/10) 1-3MM	3-5MM	23 (10/1/10-3/31/11) 5-10MM	10-25MM	25MM & OVER
32	25	37	**NUMBER OF STATEMENTS**	1	2	1	3	5	25
%	%	%	**ASSETS**	%	%	%	%	%	%
22.0	19.6	28.0	Cash & Equivalents						22.8
1.9	7.5	3.6	Trade Receivables (net)						3.0
.4	.3	.7	Inventory						.4
2.8	3.0	6.4	All Other Current						5.5
27.2	30.4	38.7	Total Current						31.8
70.4	66.4	56.1	Fixed Assets (net)						63.1
.1	.1	.2	Intangibles (net)						.3
2.3	3.1	5.0	All Other Non-Current						4.8
100.0	100.0	100.0	Total						100.0
			LIABILITIES						
1.1	2.9	.7	Notes Payable-Short Term						1.0
4.0	2.6	2.3	Cur. Mat.-L.T.D.						2.5
3.6	2.0	2.5	Trade Payables						2.4
.0	.0	.4	Income Taxes Payable						.5
20.9	9.7	13.0	All Other Current						11.1
29.7	17.2	18.8	Total Current						17.5
21.7	26.3	25.5	Long-Term Debt						31.1
.0	.0	.1	Deferred Taxes						.1
2.9	3.3	4.5	All Other Non-Current						6.3
45.7	53.3	51.1	Net Worth						45.0
100.0	100.0	100.0	Total Liabilties & Net Worth						100.0
			INCOME DATA						
100.0	100.0	100.0	Net Sales						100.0
			Gross Profit						
72.6	77.1	83.1	Operating Expenses						80.0
27.4	22.9	16.9	Operating Profit						20.0
4.1	3.5	2.0	All Other Expenses (net)						3.4
23.3	19.4	14.9	Profit Before Taxes						16.6
			RATIOS						
2.1	2.3	3.1	Current						2.8
1.5	1.6	1.8							1.5
.7	1.2	1.2							1.1
1.9	2.1	2.6	Quick						2.4
1.0	1.4	1.3							1.2
.5	1.0	1.0							.9
1 307.8	1 381.7	1 294.9	Sales/Receivables					1 294.9
2 179.1	3 122.6	3 113.7							3 121.9
7 54.7	13 27.3	24 15.5							20 18.2
			Cost of Sales/Inventory						
			Cost of Sales/Payables						
10.6	9.4	3.3	Sales/Working Capital						3.8
26.0	11.9	8.8							10.4
-22.0	37.0	27.9							43.8
38.4	69.9	29.8	EBIT/Interest						27.8
(19) 9.9	(20) 11.1	(30) 10.0						(23) 10.4	
1.2	3.5	2.5							3.1
			Net Profit + Depr., Dep., Amort./Cur. Mat. L/T/D						
.9	.8	.5	Fixed/Worth						.7
1.3	1.1	1.0							1.0
3.0	1.9	1.7							1.8
.2	.3	.2	Debt/Worth						.3
.8	.6	.7							.8
2.8	1.3	1.9							1.6
114.4	90.7	47.3	% Profit Before Taxes/Tangible Net Worth						54.6
(29) 58.6	(24) 34.2	(35) 13.3						(23) 21.3	
6.2	7.6	7.8							6.6
62.1	53.5	21.0	% Profit Before Taxes/Total Assets						25.3
38.6	19.7	9.4							14.4
4.3	4.8	3.8							4.4
3.2	3.1	4.3	Sales/Net Fixed Assets						3.4
2.1	1.3	1.2							1.2
1.2	.9	.8							.9
2.2	2.0	1.4	Sales/Total Assets						1.4
1.5	1.0	.8							.9
.7	.6	.6							.7
2.4	2.9	1.6	% Depr., Dep., Amort./Sales						2.7
(20) 4.4	(11) 6.8	(22) 5.0						(15) 5.7	
5.7	8.3	7.0							7.2
			% Officers', Directors' Owners' Comp/Sales						
3400775M	2544736M	2939202M	Net Sales ($)	272M	3649M	4409M	25394M	77386M	2828092M
2684449M	2377743M	3294884M	Total Assets ($)	402M	8111M	5480M	43358M	186890M	3050643M

M = $ thousand   MM = $ million
See Pages 9 through 22 for Explanation of Ratios and Data

Current Data Sorted by Assets | **Comparative Historical Data**

Type of Statement	0-500M	500M-2MM	2-10MM	10-50MM	50-100MM	100-250MM	4/1/06-3/31/07 ALL	4/1/07-3/31/08 ALL
Unqualified	5	13	45	67	29	41	194	183
Reviewed	1		1				5	5
Compiled	1		3				4	2
Tax Returns							2	2
Other	4	8	11	9	1	5	41	40
		194 (4/1-9/30/10)		50 (10/1/10-3/31/11)				
NUMBER OF STATEMENTS	9	23	60	76	30	46	246	232
	%	%	%	%	%	%	%	%
ASSETS								
Cash & Equivalents		47.6	33.9	32.6	19.9	18.0	28.3	29.2
Trade Receivables (net)		13.5	11.1	5.1	5.8	3.8	9.0	7.3
Inventory		.3	1.4	.1	.4	.3	1.2	1.1
All Other Current		9.9	5.3	4.8	1.7	2.4	5.3	4.7
Total Current		71.2	51.7	42.6	27.8	24.4	43.8	42.3
Fixed Assets (net)		18.1	42.5	49.8	64.5	63.4	47.8	51.0
Intangibles (net)		.0	1.0	.4	.2	.2	.4	.2
All Other Non-Current		10.7	4.9	7.2	7.5	12.0	8.0	6.6
Total		100.0	100.0	100.0	100.0	100.0	100.0	100.0
LIABILITIES								
Notes Payable-Short Term		3.1	.5	1.4	.1	.1	2.3	1.8
Cur. Mat.-L.T.D.		1.7	1.8	1.6	1.4	2.7	1.8	1.7
Trade Payables		11.1	5.9	3.4	2.6	2.5	5.2	4.3
Income Taxes Payable		2.0	.5	.6	.0	.0	.5	.3
All Other Current		15.8	10.9	7.5	2.9	2.8	7.1	6.7
Total Current		33.6	19.5	14.6	7.1	8.1	16.9	14.8
Long-Term Debt		5.6	17.5	22.2	22.3	32.1	21.8	23.3
Deferred Taxes		.0	.0	.0	.0	.2	.0	.0
All Other Non-Current		4.7	4.4	5.8	3.2	3.2	4.5	3.8
Net Worth		56.1	58.6	57.3	67.5	56.5	56.8	58.1
Total Liabilities & Net Worth		100.0	100.0	100.0	100.0	100.0	100.0	100.0
INCOME DATA								
Net Sales		100.0	100.0	100.0	100.0	100.0	100.0	100.0
Gross Profit								
Operating Expenses		94.3	89.9	89.4	91.3	90.7	88.7	87.8
Operating Profit		5.7	10.1	10.6	8.7	9.3	11.3	12.2
All Other Expenses (net)		2.7	3.0	4.2	2.5	1.0	1.8	1.9
Profit Before Taxes		3.1	7.1	6.4	6.2	8.3	9.5	10.3
RATIOS								
Current		6.4	7.1	6.2	6.4	4.9	7.1	6.4
		2.5	3.4	3.9	3.4	2.6	3.3	3.2
		1.4	1.7	1.7	2.4	1.6	1.7	1.8
Quick		6.0	6.6	6.1	4.9	4.8	6.1	6.0
		2.1	3.0	3.4	3.3	2.3	2.7	2.8
		1.4	1.4	1.4	2.4	1.4	1.4	1.4
Sales/Receivables		0 UND	1 277.1	3 139.2	29 12.6	15 24.7	4 82.6	6 65.4
		4 85.5	26 14.1	22 16.7	42 8.7	37 10.0	25 14.8	20 17.9
		35 10.4	50 7.3	42 8.6	68 5.4	55 6.7	47 7.7	41 9.0
Cost of Sales/Inventory								
Cost of Sales/Payables								
Sales/Working Capital		2.5	1.6	1.1	.9	1.6	1.4	1.4
		4.5	4.3	2.6	2.0	2.9	3.2	2.8
		23.5	10.9	8.8	3.3	5.7	7.8	7.4
EBIT/Interest			11.1	11.7	13.2	8.7	8.4	10.2
		(38) 1.6	(55) 3.2	(25) 1.7	(41) 2.4		(168) 4.0	(152) 4.2
			.8	.1	-2.0	.9	1.5	1.5
Net Profit + Depr., Dep., Amort./Cur. Mat. L/T/D								
Fixed/Worth		.0	.0	.2	.8	.9	.2	.4
		.0	.7	.9	1.0	1.2	.9	1.0
		.9	1.1	1.4	1.2	1.5	1.3	1.3
Debt/Worth		.3	.2	.2	.2	.3	.2	.3
		.6	.7	.4	.3	.7	.6	.6
		1.5	1.5	1.2	.5	2.4	1.4	1.4
% Profit Before Taxes/Tangible Net Worth		13.9	13.1	6.5	4.8	8.4	15.1	15.1
		(21) 4.3	(59) 2.6	(72) 3.0	(29) 1.3	2.1	(240) 6.8	(225) 5.9
		-5.3	-1.5	-1.7	-2.6	-1.5	.7	1.3
% Profit Before Taxes/Total Assets		6.5	7.8	4.8	3.6	5.8	7.8	7.5
		3.3	1.4	2.0	.8	1.3	3.3	3.2
		.0	-.5	-1.3	-1.8	-.6	.3	.4
Sales/Net Fixed Assets		UND	UND	21.2	.6	.8	19.0	13.5
		UND	2.3	.8	.4	.4	1.0	.8
		18.3	.4	.3	.3	.3	.4	.4
Sales/Total Assets		5.2	2.5	.9	.3	.5	1.4	1.2
		2.6	.9	.4	.3	.3	.5	.5
		1.0	.2	.2	.2	.2	.3	.2
% Depr., Dep., Amort./Sales			1.8	4.8	5.9	5.7	1.8	2.4
		(36) 7.8	(53) 12.0	(23) 10.6	(39) 9.9		(151) 5.9	(135) 7.1
			13.5	22.0	17.6	16.3	12.6	11.0
% Officers', Directors' Owners' Comp/Sales							3.5	2.3
							(28) 14.9	(19) 8.5
							31.5	15.6
Net Sales ($)	11504M	95660M	476603M	1769314M	729218M	3178012M	9080859M	6970509M
Total Assets ($)	2234M	26001M	313882M	2044441M	2119045M	7054532M	11612842M	10604440M

M = $ thousand   MM = $ million
See Pages 9 through 22 for Explanation of Ratios and Data

Comparative Historical Data				Current Data Sorted by Sales					

Type of Statement

220	196	200	Unqualified	9	29	18	35	49	60
1	7	2	Reviewed	1		1			
6	9	4	Compiled	1		1	1	1	
3	2		Tax Returns						
47	65	38	Other	11		2	6	9	7
4/1/08-3/31/09 ALL	4/1/09-3/31/10 ALL	4/1/10-3/31/11 ALL		0-1MM	194 (4/1-9/30/10) 1-3MM	3-5MM	50 (10/1/10-3/31/11) 5-10MM	10-25MM	25MM & OVER
277	279	244	**NUMBER OF STATEMENTS**	22	32	22	42	59	67
%	%	%	**ASSETS**	%	%	%	%	%	%
31.7	28.3	30.0	Cash & Equivalents	33.5	28.2	32.7	29.3	25.8	33.1
7.4	8.2	8.0	Trade Receivables (net)	5.0	5.0	13.8	7.1	8.4	8.7
.6	.7	.5	Inventory	.0	.3	.1	.2	1.4	.3
5.0	4.7	5.5	All Other Current	2.0	6.4	12.4	3.9	5.2	5.1
44.8	41.9	44.0	Total Current	40.5	39.9	59.0	40.4	40.8	47.2
46.7	49.5	47.6	Fixed Assets (net)	51.3	55.0	34.2	47.9	49.0	45.9
.3	.9	.4	Intangibles (net)	.2	.6	.7	.1	.9	.1
8.2	7.8	8.0	All Other Non-Current	8.1	4.5	6.2	11.5	9.3	6.8
100.0	100.0	100.0	Total	100.0	100.0	100.0	100.0	100.0	100.0
			LIABILITIES						
.9	2.4	.9	Notes Payable-Short Term	2.6	.8	.4	.2	1.7	.4
1.7	2.0	1.8	Cur. Mat.-L.T.D.	3.2	1.3	.7	1.4	2.3	1.6
5.1	4.0	4.8	Trade Payables	2.8	2.7	3.4	3.9	6.5	5.9
.1	.3	.8	Income Taxes Payable	.0	3.1	.5	.0	.5	.7
8.6	7.3	8.2	All Other Current	7.2	5.2	11.1	8.9	7.8	8.8
16.3	16.0	16.4	Total Current	15.9	13.1	16.0	14.5	18.8	17.4
20.1	23.7	22.9	Long-Term Debt	51.3	21.6	10.0	15.5	23.5	22.7
.0	.0	.0	Deferred Taxes	.0	.0	.0	.0	.0	.1
3.6	4.2	4.4	All Other Non-Current	1.7	3.8	5.2	7.0	2.4	5.4
59.9	56.0	56.2	Net Worth	31.1	61.5	68.8	63.0	55.3	54.4
100.0	100.0	100.0	Total Liabilties & Net Worth	100.0	100.0	100.0	100.0	100.0	100.0
			INCOME DATA						
100.0	100.0	100.0	Net Sales	100.0	100.0	100.0	100.0	100.0	100.0
			Gross Profit						
88.2	92.4	90.6	Operating Expenses	84.5	86.5	91.8	89.9	91.4	93.9
11.8	7.6	9.4	Operating Profit	15.5	13.5	8.2	10.1	8.6	6.1
2.6	3.8	2.8	All Other Expenses (net)	6.8	2.4	2.0	4.4	1.0	2.6
9.2	3.8	6.6	Profit Before Taxes	8.7	11.1	6.2	5.8	7.6	3.6
			RATIOS						
7.1	7.4	6.4		6.5	6.6	12.7	7.4	4.8	6.2
3.5	3.1	3.3	Current	3.2	3.8	4.6	3.6	2.8	3.3
1.9	1.6	1.7		1.3	2.1	2.3	1.4	1.6	1.7
6.7	6.4	5.6		6.1	6.2	11.1	6.7	4.5	5.5
3.1	2.9 (243)	3.1	Quick	3.1	3.6 (21)	3.1	3.3	2.3	3.2
1.6	1.3	1.5		1.3	1.9	2.0	1.1	1.4	1.6
2 148.8	0 999.8	3 115.8		0 UND	0 UND	5 78.0	4 85.1	9 39.0	11 34.6
17 21.4	19 19.2	25 14.3	Sales/Receivables	0 UND	29 12.4	25 14.6	36 10.1	25 14.5	23 15.9
42 8.7	52 7.1	49 7.5		72 5.0	61 6.0	38 9.7	58 6.3	49 7.4	46 7.9
			Cost of Sales/Inventory						
			Cost of Sales/Payables						
1.3	1.5	1.5		1.1	1.0	1.5	.9	1.7	1.7
3.0	2.8	3.2	Sales/Working Capital	2.6	2.7	3.0	2.5	3.9	3.4
7.3	8.9	9.0		32.4	6.3	7.5	10.9	10.1	8.9
10.6	8.0	9.7		3.9	7.4	13.5	11.1	13.4	8.1
(187) 4.0	(180) 2.2	(173) 2.4	EBIT/Interest	(12) 2.6	(24) 3.0	(13) 1.7	(26) 2.6	(47) 2.6	(51) 1.9
1.1	-.3	.6		1.2	.7	.9	-.4	.4	.6
			Net Profit + Depr., Dep., Amort./Cur. Mat. L/T/D						
.1	.2	.0		.0	.2	.0	.2	.3	.0
.9	.9	.9	Fixed/Worth	1.0	1.0	.3	.8	.9	.8
1.2	1.4	1.2		1.8	1.6	1.3	1.1	1.2	1.2
.2	.2	.2		.3	.2	.1	.2	.3	.3
.5	.6	.5	Debt/Worth	.6	.5	.3	.5	.6	.6
1.2	1.6	1.3		3.2	1.0	.8	1.3	1.6	1.5
12.8	7.5	9.0		10.6	14.1	7.8	7.3	7.8	9.3
(267) 5.0	(267) 1.1	(234) 2.4	% Profit Before Taxes/Tangible Net Worth	(21) 3.3	(30) 3.6	(21) 2.0	(41) .9	(55) 2.0	(66) 2.4
.0	-3.2	-1.7		.2	-.6	-1.6	-3.0	-2.2	-4.0
7.3	4.1	6.2		7.5	9.4	6.9	4.1	5.6	6.0
2.9	.8	1.5	% Profit Before Taxes/Total Assets	1.6	2.2	2.6	.6	1.1	1.5
-.1	-1.8	-.9		.2	-.1	-.4	-1.0	-.8	-1.8
118.3	34.1	173.0		UND	14.4	UND	3.7	20.4	UND
.8	.8	.8	Sales/Net Fixed Assets	1.0	.4	30.0	1.1	.5	1.0
.4	.3	.3		.2	.2	.7	.3	.3	.5
1.4	1.5	1.8		1.0	1.4	2.6	1.2	1.8	1.9
.4	.5	.5	Sales/Total Assets	.4	.3	1.1	.4	.3	.6
.3	.2	.2		.1	.1	.4	.2	.2	.3
4.0	3.8	4.7		10.5	7.7	1.0	4.8	4.1	2.9
(166) 8.0	(160) 8.2	(157) 9.7	% Depr., Dep., Amort./Sales	(10) 18.8	(22) 17.8	(12) 9.7	(31) 12.0	(41) 9.4	(41) 6.2
13.4	15.9	16.4		31.9	27.1	19.2	16.4	16.2	10.8
3.9	5.3	2.6							
(19) 11.0	(30) 8.9	(22) 5.8	% Officers', Directors' Owners' Comp/Sales						
18.2	18.1	13.1							
8477845M	6180462M	6260311M	Net Sales ($)	14419M	60139M	85663M	278601M	960008M	4861481M
13993055M	11715031M	11560135M	Total Assets ($)	72445M	307578M	186754M	1055113M	3250093M	6688152M

© RMA 2011

M = $ thousand   MM = $ million
See Pages 9 through 22 for Explanation of Ratios and Data

Current Data Sorted by Assets   Comparative Historical Data

0-500M	500M-2MM	2-10MM	10-50MM	50-100MM	100-250MM	Type of Statement	4/1/06-3/31/07 ALL	4/1/07-3/31/08 ALL
3	11	22	10	1	1	Unqualified	25	36
	2	3				Reviewed	9	13
	5	2				Compiled	8	11
5	1	1		1		Tax Returns	11	7
1	11	10	3			Other	16	10
	55 (4/1-9/30/10)		38 (10/1/10-3/31/11)					
9	30	38	13	2	1	NUMBER OF STATEMENTS	69	77
%	%	%	%	%	%	ASSETS	%	%
	30.5	25.6	23.0			Cash & Equivalents	22.2	20.7
	11.3	8.3	17.4			Trade Receivables (net)	10.9	12.6
	.2	1.3	4.0			Inventory	2.2	2.2
	1.8	6.8	1.9			All Other Current	2.4	2.8
	43.7	42.1	46.3			Total Current	37.7	38.2
	53.7	53.7	39.9			Fixed Assets (net)	58.1	56.6
	.2	.4	7.8			Intangibles (net)	.3	.8
	2.4	3.8	6.0			All Other Non-Current	3.9	4.3
	100.0	100.0	100.0			Total	100.0	100.0
						LIABILITIES		
	5.1	3.3	2.2			Notes Payable-Short Term	2.9	4.0
	1.8	2.3	3.5			Cur. Mat.-L.T.D.	2.5	2.9
	2.3	3.9	6.2			Trade Payables	4.0	5.2
	.1	.0	.3			Income Taxes Payable	.0	.0
	4.0	4.9	11.0			All Other Current	4.8	5.2
	13.3	14.4	23.1			Total Current	14.2	17.4
	16.5	31.2	24.2			Long-Term Debt	21.2	20.9
	.7	.2	.6			Deferred Taxes	.0	.2
	1.1	1.0	4.6			All Other Non-Current	1.4	1.0
	68.4	53.2	47.5			Net Worth	63.3	60.6
	100.0	100.0	100.0			Total Liabilities & Net Worth	100.0	100.0
						INCOME DATA		
	100.0	100.0	100.0			Net Sales	100.0	100.0
						Gross Profit		
	98.4	91.9	95.4			Operating Expenses	86.2	87.3
	1.6	8.1	4.6			Operating Profit	13.8	12.7
	2.7	2.8	2.4			All Other Expenses (net)	4.1	4.1
	-1.1	5.3	2.2			Profit Before Taxes	9.7	8.6
						RATIOS		
	12.0	9.5	9.1				11.7	8.2
	4.6	3.8	2.1			Current	5.4	3.3
	1.6	1.8	1.2				1.5	1.5
	11.0	6.8	8.9				11.6	7.6
	4.0	3.7	1.6			Quick	5.4	3.0
	1.5	1.3	1.0				1.2	1.2
	0 UND	0 UND	1 309.5				0 UND	0 UND
	3 123.8	4 89.3	17 21.4			Sales/Receivables	4 101.0	1 520.3
	34 10.7	24 15.2	71 5.2				34 10.7	37 9.8
						Cost of Sales/Inventory		
						Cost of Sales/Payables		
	2.5	1.3	1.5				1.4	1.5
	4.2	3.5	2.9			Sales/Working Capital	2.6	3.3
	11.4	9.0	27.2				11.4	14.6
	11.3	7.9	7.0				7.8	11.3
	(23) 1.0	(27) 2.8	(11) 4.2			EBIT/Interest	(49) 4.4	(54) 4.0
	-10.2	1.6	1.0				1.5	.5
						Net Profit + Depr., Dep., Amort./Cur. Mat. L/T/D		
	.4	.3	.5				.5	.5
	.9	1.0	.9			Fixed/Worth	1.0	.8
	1.3	1.6	1.6				1.4	1.4
	.1	.3	.4				.2	.2
	.3	.6	1.5			Debt/Worth	.5	.5
	1.1	2.2	4.5				1.2	1.8
	15.7	15.7	32.0			% Profit Before Taxes/Tangible Net Worth	21.0	23.3
	(29) .0	(37) 5.2	(12) 6.8				(68) 7.2	(75) 7.7
	-12.3	-1.6	-10.8				1.4	.3
	9.2	8.2	7.0			% Profit Before Taxes/Total Assets	10.4	9.8
	-.7	2.4	4.2				3.9	3.4
	-8.8	-1.9	-2.8				1.0	-.3
	21.4	10.6	17.9				3.8	7.8
	1.4	1.0	2.5			Sales/Net Fixed Assets	.8	.9
	.5	.5	.9				.4	.3
	2.1	1.3	1.8				1.1	1.8
	.9	.7	.7			Sales/Total Assets	.5	.5
	.5	.3	.4				.3	.2
	2.7	4.1	2.1				2.8	1.6
	(17) 7.2	(26) 11.0	(12) 5.0			% Depr., Dep., Amort./Sales	(45) 12.1	(59) 10.4
	12.5	22.1	9.1				26.8	18.8
							2.5	2.1
						% Officers', Directors' Owners' Comp/Sales	(12) 4.1	(12) 5.1
							9.3	11.6
4508M	53563M	138562M	382135M	600260M	117437M	Net Sales ($)	242166M	375306M
2563M	39873M	166007M	277752M	119389M	247926M	Total Assets ($)	276913M	329150M

© RMA 2011

M = $ thousand   MM = $ million
See Pages 9 through 22 for Explanation of Ratios and Data

Comparative Historical Data | | | | Current Data Sorted by Sales | | | | | |

Comp 1	Comp 2	Comp 3	Type of Statement	0-1MM	1-3MM	3-5MM	5-10MM	10-25MM	25MM & OVER
44	38	48	Unqualified	7	16	8	7	6	4
15	6	5	Reviewed	2		1	1	1	
5	7	7	Compiled	2	2	3			
8	8	8	Tax Returns	5	2				1
22	27	25	Other	11	6	2	3		3
4/1/08-3/31/09 ALL	4/1/09-3/31/10 ALL	4/1/10-3/31/11 ALL		55 (4/1-9/30/10)			38 (10/1/10-3/31/11)		
94	86	93	**NUMBER OF STATEMENTS**	27	26	14	11	7	8
%	%	%	**ASSETS**	%	%	%	%	%	%
23.3	23.5	27.6	Cash & Equivalents	23.9	24.7	40.8	38.8		
11.6	10.8	10.8	Trade Receivables (net)	3.4	5.5	18.7	21.1		
1.7	2.0	1.5	Inventory	1.0	.4	2.7	.6		
3.7	3.1	3.7	All Other Current	4.4	2.1	5.1	5.0		
40.3	39.3	43.7	Total Current	32.8	32.7	67.3	65.4		
52.7	52.7	49.2	Fixed Assets (net)	62.2	64.4	26.8	32.5		
.8	2.2	1.8	Intangibles (net)	.7	1.1	.1	.0		
6.2	5.8	5.3	All Other Non-Current	4.3	1.9	5.8	2.1		
100.0	100.0	100.0	Total	100.0	100.0	100.0	100.0		
			LIABILITIES						
3.8	3.5	4.1	Notes Payable-Short Term	4.0	2.2	3.7	10.6		
3.2	3.3	3.3	Cur. Mat.-L.T.D.	2.6	4.2	2.0	1.5		
3.2	4.0	4.1	Trade Payables	1.7	2.2	4.4	10.1		
.0	.2	.1	Income Taxes Payable	.0	.0	.2	.0		
5.5	5.2	5.3	All Other Current	.9	4.0	8.5	7.5		
15.6	16.2	16.8	Total Current	9.2	12.6	18.8	29.7		
22.7	21.8	27.1	Long-Term Debt	25.2	33.8	29.0	16.3		
.1	.4	.4	Deferred Taxes	.3	.1	1.2	.0		
3.6	2.0	1.5	All Other Non-Current	.5	1.4	.8	1.8		
58.0	59.6	54.2	Net Worth	64.9	52.1	50.2	52.1		
100.0	100.0	100.0	Total Liabilities & Net Worth	100.0	100.0	100.0	100.0		
			INCOME DATA						
100.0	100.0	100.0	Net Sales	100.0	100.0	100.0	100.0		
			Gross Profit						
92.0	92.0	94.3	Operating Expenses	94.3	94.4	93.9	94.2		
8.0	8.0	5.7	Operating Profit	5.7	5.6	6.1	5.8		
2.2	2.2	2.5	All Other Expenses (net)	2.1	2.7	4.7	1.0		
5.8	5.9	3.2	Profit Before Taxes	3.5	2.9	1.4	4.8		
			RATIOS						
8.5	6.6	9.4		14.0	9.5	6.9	4.6		
3.1	3.5	3.7	Current	5.9	4.1	3.5	3.7		
1.5	1.5	1.4		1.4	1.8	2.7	1.4		
8.4	6.4	9.1		11.0	9.2	6.9	4.3		
2.8	3.1	3.5	Quick	4.6	3.8	3.5	3.7		
1.3	1.3	1.2		1.3	1.3	2.6	1.2		
0 UND	0 UND	0 UND		0 UND	0 UND	0 UND	2 188.0		
7 48.8	5 67.6	8 45.7	Sales/Receivables	0 UND	2 190.3	25 14.9	9 39.3		
29 12.7	29 12.7	35 10.4		23 16.0	20 18.4	56 6.5	67 5.4		
			Cost of Sales/Inventory						
			Cost of Sales/Payables						
1.8	1.9	1.6		1.0	1.6	2.6	2.7		
4.4	4.4	4.1	Sales/Working Capital	2.5	4.1	3.7	2.8		
13.6	10.4	10.8		14.6	11.6	5.3	7.8		
6.4	8.1	8.2		9.0	6.9	13.3			
(73) 3.5	(60) 2.9	(69) 2.8	EBIT/Interest	(17) 1.9	(20) 1.6	(10) 4.5			
1.4	.7	.4		-2.1	-1.4	-1.7			
			Net Profit + Depr., Dep., Amort./Cur. Mat. L/T/D						
.4	.5	.3		.7	.7	.0	.2		
.9	.9	.9	Fixed/Worth	1.0	1.0	.3	.5		
1.4	1.7	1.5		1.5	3.1	1.2	1.3		
.3	.2	.2		.1	.2	.1	.2		
.6	.5	.6	Debt/Worth	.4	.4	.5	1.2		
1.5	1.9	2.0		1.2	2.8	1.4	2.2		
18.0	17.4	17.5		20.9	9.4	17.9	17.9		
(91) 6.9	(83) 5.6	(89) 5.8	% Profit Before Taxes/Tangible Net Worth	(24) 1.6	2.8	(13) 11.2	9.2		
.1	-.5	-5.1		-3.3	-13.8	-21.2	.0		
9.6	9.1	8.2		8.2	7.2	10.6	14.7		
3.5	3.3	3.6	% Profit Before Taxes/Total Assets	1.4	1.8	5.1	3.8		
-.2	-.4	-4.1		-3.1	-6.3	-16.4	.0		
8.8	10.6	17.9		2.4	2.1	UND	37.5		
1.1	1.1	1.4	Sales/Net Fixed Assets	.5	1.0	17.9	10.4		
.4	.4	.6		.3	.6	1.6	.9		
2.0	1.9	1.8		.6	1.0	2.1	2.6		
.7	.7	.8	Sales/Total Assets	.4	.8	1.6	1.7		
.3	.3	.4		.2	.4	1.0	.7		
2.3	3.9	3.3		7.6	6.8				
(67) 7.8	(61) 8.5	(62) 7.2	% Depr., Dep., Amort./Sales	(16) 14.8	(17) 14.0				
18.8	19.1	14.9		32.7	21.0				
2.4	2.5	1.2							
(15) 3.9	(13) 4.4	(13) 3.4	% Officers', Directors' Owners' Comp/Sales						
8.1	11.3	6.4							
746514M	1024833M	1296465M	Net Sales ($)	13316M	45236M	51872M	74966M	91591M	1019484M
893732M	666735M	853510M	Total Assets ($)	37144M	78333M	42899M	73663M	121514M	499957M

M = $ thousand   MM = $ million
See Pages 9 through 22 for Explanation of Ratios and Data

Current Data Sorted by Assets   Comparative Historical Data

						Type of Statement		
1	8	32	43	24	28	Unqualified	83	102
		1				Reviewed		
						Compiled	3	2
1	3	10	6	1	1	Tax Returns	1	3
	148 (4/1-9/30/10)		11 (10/1/10-3/31/11)			Other	18	18
0-500M	500M-2MM	2-10MM	10-50MM	50-100MM	100-250MM		4/1/06-3/31/07 ALL	4/1/07-3/31/08 ALL
2	11	43	49	25	29	**NUMBER OF STATEMENTS**	105	125
%	%	%	%	%	%	**ASSETS**	%	%
	32.6	25.9	25.1	14.4	16.2	Cash & Equivalents	25.8	30.8
	22.8	19.6	7.3	11.6	6.9	Trade Receivables (net)	11.3	8.0
	1.0	.2	1.8	.2	.2	Inventory	.6	.9
	1.7	3.5	5.7	1.8	4.6	All Other Current	3.7	4.6
	58.1	49.3	39.9	28.1	27.9	Total Current	41.5	44.3
	29.3	36.5	53.5	64.6	61.5	Fixed Assets (net)	46.5	45.9
	2.3	2.5	.8	.3	.1	Intangibles (net)	.7	1.1
	10.2	11.7	5.9	7.0	10.5	All Other Non-Current	11.2	8.7
	100.0	100.0	100.0	100.0	100.0	Total	100.0	100.0
						LIABILITIES		
	4.6	6.6	1.6	2.6	.9	Notes Payable-Short Term	2.8	1.4
	.4	3.0	2.7	2.3	3.9	Cur. Mat.-L.T.D.	3.1	3.3
	6.6	8.0	5.8	1.4	2.9	Trade Payables	6.2	6.9
	.0	.0	.0	.0	.0	Income Taxes Payable	.0	.2
	17.4	15.5	8.9	6.1	10.3	All Other Current	12.8	9.3
	29.0	33.1	18.9	12.4	17.9	Total Current	25.0	21.0
	2.6	13.7	27.3	34.4	30.5	Long-Term Debt	29.7	28.8
	.0	.1	.0	.0	.0	Deferred Taxes	.0	.1
	.3	13.6	1.9	1.6	9.8	All Other Non-Current	5.2	7.4
	68.0	39.4	51.9	51.7	41.8	Net Worth	40.1	42.6
	100.0	100.0	100.0	100.0	100.0	Total Liabilties & Net Worth	100.0	100.0
						INCOME DATA		
	100.0	100.0	100.0	100.0	100.0	Net Sales	100.0	100.0
						Gross Profit		
	90.8	94.3	98.2	93.1	94.9	Operating Expenses	94.4	93.3
	9.2	5.7	1.8	6.9	5.1	Operating Profit	5.6	6.7
	.3	.6	.4	3.1	.4	All Other Expenses (net)	1.3	1.3
	8.9	5.1	1.4	3.7	4.7	Profit Before Taxes	4.3	5.3
						RATIOS		
	7.6	3.1	3.2	2.9	2.1		5.1	4.7
	2.1	1.6	1.7	2.1	1.8	Current	2.2	2.5
	1.1	1.0	1.1	1.3	1.1		1.1	1.5
	7.6	2.9	3.1	2.8	2.1		4.5	4.1
	2.1	1.4	1.4	1.8	1.4	Quick	2.0	2.2
	.9	.8	.9	1.3	.9		.9	1.2
	11 32.5	2 180.5	0 999.8	9 39.2	7 54.5		1 508.5	0 UND
	30 12.1	23 15.8	13 28.0	33 11.2	20 18.0	Sales/Receivables	10 36.3	7 50.7
	66 5.5	53 6.9	27 13.5	48 7.6	45 8.2		45 8.1	33 11.1
						Cost of Sales/Inventory		
						Cost of Sales/Payables		
	5.1	4.0	5.2	2.8	5.1		3.7	3.3
	5.9	18.7	10.5	7.5	7.1	Sales/Working Capital	9.8	6.6
	206.4	-383.6	100.3	41.9	NM		116.1	24.1
		7.6	4.0	3.4	4.0		5.8	8.4
	(25)	3.0	(37) 1.4	(22) 1.2	(23) 1.3	EBIT/Interest	(67) 2.1	(75) 4.0
		1.6	-1.1	.4	.8		.2	1.5
						Net Profit + Depr., Dep., Amort./Cur. Mat. L/T/D		
	.1	.2	.3	.8	1.1		.5	.4
	.4	.9	1.1	1.4	1.4	Fixed/Worth	1.0	1.0
	.8	2.3	2.0	2.6	2.7		2.2	2.0
	.1	.3	.4	.3	.6		.5	.4
	.7	1.2	1.2	1.1	1.5	Debt/Worth	1.4	1.2
	1.1	3.4	2.0	2.5	2.7		3.4	3.0
	61.9	23.3	10.6	5.4	9.7	% Profit Before Taxes/Tangible	16.2	21.0
	12.1	(36) 6.1	2.7	(24) 1.5	(27) 2.8	Net Worth	(100) 6.7	(114) 9.0
	-10.2	-.8	-2.0	-1.8	-2.4		-.1	3.3
	30.5	11.3	4.7	2.6	4.2		6.8	8.5
	5.9	3.7	.4	.5	1.5	% Profit Before Taxes/Total Assets	2.8	4.0
	-6.0	1.5	-.9	-.9	-.9		-.5	1.0
	55.0	66.1	7.9	1.5	2.7		10.4	12.2
	7.9	10.5	2.0	.9	.8	Sales/Net Fixed Assets	2.2	2.2
	2.0	1.7	1.1	.6	.6		1.2	1.1
	3.6	2.7	1.9	.9	1.1		2.1	2.3
	1.5	1.6	1.1	.6	.6	Sales/Total Assets	1.0	1.1
	1.1	.7	.7	.3	.4		.7	.7
		.9	1.4	2.9	2.3		1.0	.9
	(34)	1.8	(40) 3.0	(22) 5.0	(27) 3.7	% Depr., Dep., Amort./Sales	(78) 2.6	(86) 2.3
		3.3	4.7	7.1	5.9		3.8	4.0
						% Officers', Directors'	1.6	1.6
						Owners' Comp/Sales	(18) 6.0	(16) 5.9
							14.3	15.1
4217M	33301M	459535M	1967031M	1151600M	3709769M	Net Sales ($)	3952834M	6674942M
547M	13297M	234676M	1377962M	1719272M	4741377M	Total Assets ($)	4174005M	4918226M

M = $ thousand   MM = $ million

See Pages 9 through 22 for Explanation of Ratios and Data

Comparative Historical Data   **Current Data Sorted by Sales**

	Hist 1	Hist 2	Hist 3		0-1MM	1-3MM	3-5MM	5-10MM	10-25MM	25MM & OVER
Type of Statement										
Unqualified	125	124	136		3	12	7	11	29	74
Reviewed	3	2	1				1			
Compiled	1	2								
Tax Returns	1									
Other	26	28	22		2	3	2	1	8	6
	4/1/08-3/31/09 ALL	4/1/09-3/31/10 ALL	4/1/10-3/31/11 ALL			148 (4/1-9/30/10)			11 (10/1/10-3/31/11)	
NUMBER OF STATEMENTS	156	156	159		5	15	10	12	37	80
	%	%	%		%	%	%	%	%	%
ASSETS										
Cash & Equivalents	25.5	24.1	22.4			17.5	23.2	23.4	24.1	22.3
Trade Receivables (net)	9.9	8.2	12.7			17.5	4.1	19.3	17.9	9.7
Inventory	.5	.8	.8			.9	.0	.2	.5	1.1
All Other Current	4.4	3.1	4.0			2.2	5.8	1.4	4.1	4.6
Total Current	40.4	36.2	39.9			38.1	33.1	44.2	46.6	37.7
Fixed Assets (net)	47.3	51.0	50.3			50.3	49.9	43.7	43.3	55.0
Intangibles (net)	1.1	.7	1.1			.1	6.3	1.2	1.0	.5
All Other Non-Current	11.2	12.2	8.7			11.5	10.7	10.9	9.0	6.7
Total	100.0	100.0	100.0			100.0	100.0	100.0	100.0	100.0
LIABILITIES										
Notes Payable-Short Term	2.1	1.7	3.3			2.1	2.8	6.7	5.6	1.6
Cur. Mat.-L.T.D.	2.8	2.7	2.7			1.4	5.8	2.4	2.1	2.9
Trade Payables	5.2	5.2	5.1			2.8	2.9	3.7	7.2	5.2
Income Taxes Payable	.0	.0	.0			.0	.0	.0	.0	.0
All Other Current	10.6	9.7	11.2			11.1	6.3	18.2	11.6	10.9
Total Current	20.8	19.2	22.4			17.4	17.7	30.9	26.5	20.7
Long-Term Debt	26.0	25.4	23.8			17.3	17.3	24.7	23.8	26.8
Deferred Taxes	.1	.1	.0			.0	.0	.0	.2	.0
All Other Non-Current	3.5	5.1	6.4			1.8	2.4	4.4	10.2	5.9
Net Worth	49.5	50.2	47.4			63.5	62.6	39.9	39.3	46.6
Total Liabilities & Net Worth	100.0	100.0	100.0			100.0	100.0	100.0	100.0	100.0
INCOME DATA										
Net Sales	100.0	100.0	100.0			100.0	100.0	100.0	100.0	100.0
Gross Profit										
Operating Expenses	93.9	96.7	95.2			95.9	91.3	91.0	97.0	96.4
Operating Profit	6.1	3.3	4.8			4.1	8.7	9.0	3.0	3.6
All Other Expenses (net)	2.7	2.5	.9			-.3	1.0	6.4	.5	.4
Profit Before Taxes	3.4	.8	3.9			4.4	7.7	2.6	2.5	3.2
RATIOS										
Current	4.6	4.0	3.0			5.1	4.6	3.1	3.0	2.7
	2.2	2.0	1.8			2.1	1.7	2.0	1.7	1.8
	1.2	1.3	1.1			1.1	.4	1.1	1.0	1.2
Quick	4.4	3.9	2.8			5.1	3.3	3.0	2.8	2.3
	1.7	1.8	1.5			2.1	1.6	2.0	1.3	1.5
	1.0	1.1	.9			.8		1.0	.8	1.1
Sales/Receivables	2 216.3	2 195.3	4 96.4			10 37.9	0 UND	4 89.0	6 60.0	4 91.5
	14 26.4	14 25.9	22 16.9			30 12.1	12 29.7	27 13.6	25 14.3	18 20.7
	42 8.7	33 11.2	44 8.4			60 6.1	20 18.3	45 8.0	58 6.3	37 9.7
Cost of Sales/Inventory										
Cost of Sales/Payables										
Sales/Working Capital	2.9	3.4	4.7			5.1	3.1	2.5	3.6	5.4
	7.6	7.3	8.6			9.2	15.9	5.5	8.4	9.3
	40.5	26.6	76.8			146.9	-8.1	170.4	-250.3	46.6
EBIT/Interest	6.4	4.3	4.8						5.7	4.4
	(109) 2.1	(112) 1.2	(113) 2.0					(28)	2.3	(63) 1.4
	.8	-.7	.6						.7	.6
Net Profit + Depr., Dep., Amort./Cur. Mat. L/T/D										
Fixed/Worth	.4	.5	.3			.3	.1	.2	.3	.5
	1.0	1.0	1.1			.8	1.0	1.0	1.0	1.3
	1.9	1.9	2.2			2.0	2.4	NM	2.4	2.1
Debt/Worth	.4	.3	.4			.1	.2	.4	.4	.5
	1.0	.8	1.1			.4	.5	1.0	1.3	1.2
	2.1	2.2	2.2			1.8	1.5	NM	3.6	1.9
% Profit Before Taxes/Tangible Net Worth	14.7	7.6	11.5			13.6			12.1	10.3
	(148) 4.3	(149) 1.7	(148) 3.8			(14) 4.4		(34)	3.3	(77) 2.8
	-.3	-5.8	-1.8			-7.9			-.9	-2.2
% Profit Before Taxes/Total Assets	6.5	4.6	6.4			8.5	14.9	5.2	7.6	4.3
	2.0	.8	2.0			3.2	4.2	2.6	1.8	1.4
	-.5	-2.8	-.8			-4.8	-1.4	-3.4	-.2	-.9
Sales/Net Fixed Assets	8.3	5.6	13.0			7.9	43.2	12.7	20.2	6.0
	2.0	1.5	2.0			1.2	2.0	3.6	3.3	1.4
	1.0	.8	.8			.8	.5	1.4	1.0	.8
Sales/Total Assets	1.7	1.5	2.0			3.6	1.4	2.1	2.1	2.0
	1.0	.8	1.0			.9	.7	1.3	1.2	.9
	.6	.5	.6			.4	.4	.7	.6	.6
% Depr., Dep., Amort./Sales	1.6	2.0	1.6			2.4		1.4	1.4	1.6
	(120) 3.0	(123) 3.3	(132) 3.0			(11) 3.7	(10) 2.6	(33) 2.6	(68) 3.3	
	4.8	5.1	4.9			6.0		3.6	5.6	4.8
% Officers', Directors' Owners' Comp/Sales	2.3	2.3	3.2							2.7
	(18) 7.7	(23) 7.3	(16) 6.5						(15)	5.2
	19.2	14.3	15.0							12.4
Net Sales ($)	5605142M	6098055M	7325453M		3298M	30931M	36868M	83252M	627869M	6543235M
Total Assets ($)	5939363M	7529500M	8087131M		22269M	46086M	68230M	188177M	831630M	6930739M

© RMA 2011

M = $ thousand   MM = $ million
See Pages 9 through 22 for Explanation of Ratios and Data

Current Data Sorted by Assets | Comparative Historical Data

	0-500M	500M-2MM	2-10MM	10-50MM	50-100MM	100-250MM		4/1/06-3/31/07 ALL	4/1/07-3/31/08 ALL
Type of Statement									
Unqualified	1	3	5	11	1	3		22	20
Reviewed		1						3	
Compiled									1
Tax Returns									
Other				5		1		6	8
		23 (4/1-9/30/10)		11 (10/1/10-3/31/11)					
NUMBER OF STATEMENTS	1	4	8	16	1	4		31	29
	%	%	%	%	%	%		%	%
ASSETS									
Cash & Equivalents				31.2				33.2	35.5
Trade Receivables (net)				15.2				19.3	16.7
Inventory				.6				.8	1.5
All Other Current				7.2				2.3	2.6
Total Current				54.2				55.6	56.3
Fixed Assets (net)				23.0				23.5	29.4
Intangibles (net)				.3				5.0	2.1
All Other Non-Current				22.5				15.9	12.3
Total				100.0				100.0	100.0
LIABILITIES									
Notes Payable-Short Term				2.2				2.8	4.0
Cur. Mat.-L.T.D.				.3				2.6	1.0
Trade Payables				9.3				5.8	6.1
Income Taxes Payable				3.7				.1	.2
All Other Current				20.0				15.3	15.4
Total Current				35.4				26.7	26.7
Long-Term Debt				10.8				16.8	15.3
Deferred Taxes				.0				.1	.0
All Other Non-Current				7.3				2.6	4.1
Net Worth				46.4				53.9	53.9
Total Liabilties & Net Worth				100.0				100.0	100.0
INCOME DATA									
Net Sales				100.0				100.0	100.0
Gross Profit									
Operating Expenses				97.5				91.5	89.0
Operating Profit				2.5				8.5	11.0
All Other Expenses (net)				-.9				-.2	1.9
Profit Before Taxes				3.3				8.7	9.1
RATIOS									
Current				3.1				4.8	4.9
				1.6				2.1	2.5
				1.1				1.3	1.2
Quick				2.8				4.5	4.4
				1.4				1.8	2.4
				.8				1.2	1.2
Sales/Receivables				2 152.0				8 45.7	6 65.9
				26 14.1				31 11.8	38 9.5
				55 6.6				53 6.9	54 6.8
Cost of Sales/Inventory									
Cost of Sales/Payables									
Sales/Working Capital				4.0				3.0	2.4
				12.3				6.3	5.7
				40.2				12.9	16.3
EBIT/Interest								9.2	14.7
							(22)	5.7 (17)	4.8
								2.0	2.5
Net Profit + Depr., Dep., Amort./Cur. Mat. L/T/D									
Fixed/Worth				.1				.2	.0
				.3				.5	.5
				.8				.8	1.4
Debt/Worth				.3				.4	.3
				1.2				.9	.9
				6.0				2.7	2.2
% Profit Before Taxes/Tangible Net Worth				30.9				29.9	22.6
			(15)	6.5			(30)	13.3	9.6
				.5				-.4	3.5
% Profit Before Taxes/Total Assets				14.5				14.6	9.2
				1.8				5.7	3.4
				-1.3				-.1	1.5
Sales/Net Fixed Assets				68.6				25.5	63.3
				23.1				8.3	6.3
				2.0				4.7	3.9
Sales/Total Assets				3.7				2.9	3.1
				1.0				2.0	1.8
				.4				.9	.5
% Depr., Dep., Amort./Sales				.3				.6	.5
			(14)	1.6			(28)	1.3 (21)	1.7
				5.0				2.7	3.6
% Officers', Directors' Owners' Comp/Sales									
Net Sales ($)	1607M	9580M	110484M	998762M	3552M	2379886M		1904190M	1904918M
Total Assets ($)	270M	6496M	27669M	486417M	76315M	754161M		1149461M	1130792M

M = $ thousand   MM = $ million
See Pages 9 through 22 for Explanation of Ratios and Data

Comparative Historical Data | **Current Data Sorted by Sales**

4/1/08-3/31/09 ALL	4/1/09-3/31/10 ALL	4/1/10-3/31/11 ALL	Type of Statement	0-1MM	1-3MM	3-5MM	5-10MM	10-25MM	25MM & OVER
18	28	24	Unqualified		4	3	2	6	9
1	1		Reviewed						
	1	1	Compiled		1				
1	2	1	Tax Returns					1	
3	6	8	Other		1			2	5
					23 (4/1-9/30/10)		11 (10/1/10-3/31/11)		
23	38	34	NUMBER OF STATEMENTS		6	3	2	9	14
%	%	%	ASSETS	%	%	%	%	%	%
33.7	29.3	27.3	Cash & Equivalents	DATA NOT AVAILABLE					39.8
20.3	20.4	22.2	Trade Receivables (net)						23.6
1.1	1.9	.3	Inventory						.5
5.4	4.4	6.3	All Other Current						7.7
60.5	56.0	56.2	Total Current						71.6
25.8	30.8	24.1	Fixed Assets (net)						14.4
2.2	2.1	.2	Intangibles (net)						.1
11.5	11.1	19.5	All Other Non-Current						13.9
100.0	100.0	100.0	Total						100.0
			LIABILITIES						
3.2	4.6	2.7	Notes Payable-Short Term						1.8
1.1	2.2	.5	Cur. Mat.-L.T.D.						.2
11.2	6.8	6.9	Trade Payables						5.4
.0	.0	1.8	Income Taxes Payable						4.4
18.1	13.2	22.9	All Other Current						33.0
33.6	26.8	34.8	Total Current						44.8
8.7	8.5	10.2	Long-Term Debt						8.0
.0	.0	.0	Deferred Taxes						.0
6.2	7.6	7.7	All Other Non-Current						2.3
51.5	57.1	47.3	Net Worth						44.8
100.0	100.0	100.0	Total Liabilities & Net Worth						100.0
			INCOME DATA						
100.0	100.0	100.0	Net Sales						100.0
			Gross Profit						
96.0	94.8	96.8	Operating Expenses						95.7
4.0	5.2	3.2	Operating Profit						4.3
.4	.9	-.6	All Other Expenses (net)						-.4
3.6	4.3	3.8	Profit Before Taxes						4.7
			RATIOS						
3.1	5.1	3.8							3.0
1.9	2.1	1.6	Current						1.7
1.3	1.2	1.1							1.2
2.9	4.2	3.3							2.9
1.6	1.9	1.4	Quick						1.7
.8	1.1	.9							1.2
3 132.6	**2** 161.6	**7** 52.1							**3** 116.8
34 10.7	**23** 15.9	**34** 10.7	Sales/Receivables						**24** 15.4
57 6.5	**51** 7.2	**53** 6.9							**53** 6.9
			Cost of Sales/Inventory						
			Cost of Sales/Payables						
4.1	3.2	3.7							6.2
11.8	6.7	12.3	Sales/Working Capital						14.2
25.0	23.5	40.1							35.8
36.1	18.6	30.1							
(12) 9.6	(16) 6.1	(14) 1.6	EBIT/Interest						
-4.2	-1.6	.2							
			Net Profit + Depr., Dep., Amort./Cur. Mat. L/T/D						
.1	.1	.1							.1
.3	.5	.4	Fixed/Worth						.2
.8	1.1	.8							.7
.6	.2	.4							.7
.9	.6	1.0	Debt/Worth						.9
2.1	2.2	4.7							3.3
47.8	19.8	30.1							47.0
(22) 6.8	(37) 7.0	(33) 4.7	% Profit Before Taxes/Tangible Net Worth						(13) 30.9
-2.5	-3.6	-4.7							-6.5
16.2	11.2	14.0							24.2
3.6	3.4	.8	% Profit Before Taxes/Total Assets						13.8
-1.9	-1.5	-1.3							-1.9
70.3	35.2	79.2							285.5
10.4	9.6	23.1	Sales/Net Fixed Assets						59.6
5.5	2.6	2.5							24.0
4.4	3.2	4.0							5.2
3.0	1.6	2.0	Sales/Total Assets						3.6
1.1	.9	.6							1.5
.4	.9	.4							.1
(16) 1.0	(30) 1.9	(29) 1.1	% Depr., Dep., Amort./Sales						(11) .2
1.4	3.3	3.5							2.4
			% Officers', Directors' Owners' Comp/Sales						
870688M	990210M	3503871M	Net Sales ($)		11817M	11223M	15309M	144734M	3320788M
678620M	788975M	1351328M	Total Assets ($)		34721M	92072M	6764M	165436M	1052335M

M = $ thousand MM = $ million

See Pages 9 through 22 for Explanation of Ratios and Data

Current Data Sorted by Assets   Comparative Historical Data

0-500M	500M-2MM	2-10MM	10-50MM	50-100MM	100-250MM	Type of Statement	4/1/06-3/31/07 ALL	4/1/07-3/31/08 ALL
	3	10	23	13	14	Unqualified	39	45
	2	1		1		Reviewed	8	7
			3			Compiled	5	5
		1				Tax Returns	3	5
	1	5	9	4	4	Other	21	18
	56 (4/1-9/30/10)		38 (10/1/10-3/31/11)					
	6	17	35	18	18	NUMBER OF STATEMENTS	76	80

0-500M	500M-2MM	2-10MM	10-50MM	50-100MM	100-250MM		4/1/06-3/31/07	4/1/07-3/31/08
%	%	%	%	%	%	**ASSETS**	%	%
		14.1	15.2	12.8	12.4	Cash & Equivalents	14.2	13.7
		6.6	7.5	2.1	3.9	Trade Receivables (net)	15.3	9.3
		5.6	.4	.2	1.0	Inventory	2.9	2.9
		.5	1.5	3.0	1.9	All Other Current	2.5	2.5
		26.7	24.6	18.1	19.2	Total Current	34.8	28.4
		68.1	68.1	68.9	66.6	Fixed Assets (net)	55.1	59.2
		.6	1.0	.5	.3	Intangibles (net)	2.0	2.0
		4.6	6.3	12.6	13.8	All Other Non-Current	8.1	10.5
		100.0	100.0	100.0	100.0	Total	100.0	100.0
						LIABILITIES		
		3.3	.7	.4	.0	Notes Payable-Short Term	3.4	2.3
		4.9	2.8	2.0	1.5	Cur. Mat.-L.T.D.	3.0	3.6
		4.6	4.0	1.9	2.3	Trade Payables	7.5	5.3
		.0	.0	.0	.0	Income Taxes Payable	.1	.0
		1.7	2.8	3.7	2.7	All Other Current	6.4	4.5
		14.4	10.2	8.1	6.5	Total Current	20.3	15.8
		40.3	32.3	26.9	29.2	Long-Term Debt	31.1	29.4
		.0	.5	.0	.0	Deferred Taxes	.1	.3
		1.8	4.9	1.3	2.4	All Other Non-Current	1.7	2.5
		43.5	52.1	63.7	62.0	Net Worth	46.8	52.1
		100.0	100.0	100.0	100.0	Total Liabilities & Net Worth	100.0	100.0
						INCOME DATA		
		100.0	100.0	100.0	100.0	Net Sales	100.0	100.0
						Gross Profit		
		84.2	84.2	93.3	92.0	Operating Expenses	87.1	83.7
		15.8	15.8	6.7	8.0	Operating Profit	12.9	16.3
		10.9	6.7	2.7	.7	All Other Expenses (net)	3.3	3.4
		4.9	9.1	3.9	7.3	Profit Before Taxes	9.5	12.8
						RATIOS		
		5.4	4.6	6.6	5.0	Current	4.2	4.0
		2.3	2.2	1.5	3.1		1.9	2.0
		.9	1.3	.7	1.7		1.1	1.1
		5.4	4.5	4.4	5.0	Quick	4.2	3.3
		1.9	2.1	1.4	2.4		1.4	1.6
		.7	1.1	.5	1.5		.9	.8
		15 23.6	23 15.8	14 26.0	25 14.4	Sales/Receivables	21 17.5 23 16.0	
		35 10.3	36 10.1	28 12.9	48 7.6		33 11.1 36 10.2	
		60 6.1	60 6.1	37 9.9	62 5.8		58 6.3 55 6.6	
						Cost of Sales/Inventory		
						Cost of Sales/Payables		
		1.2	1.4	1.1	1.0	Sales/Working Capital	2.3	1.6
		3.1	3.9	5.3	2.3		8.8	6.5
		NM	9.4	-5.9	4.0		101.7	60.6
		8.6	10.5	2.9	3.6	EBIT/Interest	8.3	6.2
		(10) 3.3	(27) 2.6	(13) 2.2	(16) 2.2		(63) 2.9 (64) 3.6	
		1.8	1.2	.3	1.6		1.1	2.2
						Net Profit + Depr.,.Dep., Amort./Cur. Mat. L/T/D		
		.8	.9	.9	1.0	Fixed/Worth	.7	.8
		1.5	1.4	1.1	1.2		1.2	1.3
		4.6	1.9	1.8	1.3		2.1	2.0
		.3	.4	.2	.4	Debt/Worth	.4	.4
		1.0	.9	.5	.7		1.0	.8
		6.1	2.0	1.4	.9		3.5	1.8
		5.9	13.5	3.9	6.8	% Profit Before Taxes/Tangible Net Worth	25.5	11.8
		(14) 2.2	(33) 3.2	1.9	2.8		(69) 5.7 (74) 5.2	
		-3.5	.5	-1.5	.9		.9	1.9
		4.0	7.1	2.5	3.0	% Profit Before Taxes/Total Assets	10.5	6.5
		.9	1.7	1.3	1.6		2.7	3.3
		-.8	.3	-.5	.7		.1	.9
		3.9	.9	.5	.7	Sales/Net Fixed Assets	11.0	4.0
		.2	.2	.2	.3		.7	.5
		.1	.1	.1	.2		.2	.2
		1.0	.6	.2	.4	Sales/Total Assets	2.4	1.6
		.2	.2	.2	.2		.4	.2
		.1	.1	.1	.1		.1	.1
		14.5	6.7	9.3	7.0	% Depr., Dep., Amort./Sales	2.8	4.5
		(13) 21.7	(34) 15.2	(17) 17.0	(16) 15.5		(66) 11.4 (77) 11.5	
		34.4	25.4	37.0	24.2		21.6	19.9
						% Officers', Directors' Owners' Comp/Sales	3.3	3.1
							(18) 5.9 (17) 4.3	
							10.1	8.5
	24643M	45304M	420134M	368445M	797707M	Net Sales ($)	884482M	1233432M
	7482M	82860M	865459M	1366438M	2833446M	Total Assets ($)	1749781M	3446738M

M = $ thousand   MM = $ million
See Pages 9 through 22 for Explanation of Ratios and Data

Comparative Historical Data | Current Data Sorted by Sales

Hist 1	Hist 2	Hist 3	Type of Statement	0-1MM	1-3MM	3-5MM	5-10MM	10-25MM	25MM & OVER
45	61	63	Unqualified	10	9	5	12	15	12
5	7	3	Reviewed		1			1	
6	6	4	Compiled			1	1	1	1
9		1	Tax Returns			1	1	1	1
31	19	23	Other	3	3		8	5	3
4/1/08-3/31/09 ALL	4/1/09-3/31/10 ALL	4/1/10-3/31/11 ALL		56 (4/1-9/30/10)			38 (10/1/10-3/31/11)		
96	93	94	**NUMBER OF STATEMENTS**	13	13	8	21	23	16
%	%	%	**ASSETS**	%	%	%	%	%	%
11.4	12.9	13.8	Cash & Equivalents	10.2	8.9		13.6	15.7	18.8
10.1	6.6	6.6	Trade Receivables (net)	1.0	5.6		4.4	5.6	13.3
1.7	1.5	1.9	Inventory	.0	6.2		.2	2.5	1.3
1.8	2.1	1.6	All Other Current	.4	1.2		.9	1.1	5.0
25.0	23.1	23.9	Total Current	11.6	22.0		19.2	24.9	38.4
63.8	66.1	66.9	Fixed Assets (net)	83.0	72.4		70.8	62.7	50.0
1.3	2.7	.7	Intangibles (net)	.3	.1		.5	1.2	.4
9.9	8.1	8.5	All Other Non-Current	5.0	5.5		9.6	11.1	11.2
100.0	100.0	100.0	Total	100.0	100.0		100.0	100.0	100.0
			LIABILITIES						
3.1	2.6	1.4	Notes Payable-Short Term	.4	2.1		1.4	2.7	.0
4.1	4.6	3.1	Cur. Mat.-L.T.D.	1.9	3.5		3.0	4.6	1.8
5.0	3.0	3.4	Trade Payables	.5	1.9		3.2	2.7	7.3
.0	.0	.1	Income Taxes Payable	.0	.0		.0	.2	.0
3.4	3.7	3.3	All Other Current	.5	.8		.9	3.0	8.5
15.7	13.9	11.2	Total Current	3.3	8.3		8.5	13.2	17.7
31.2	30.1	32.3	Long-Term Debt	49.5	43.5		32.6	30.1	18.1
.1	.1	.2	Deferred Taxes	.0	.0		.0	.9	.0
2.9	1.6	2.9	All Other Non-Current	.3	1.4		2.9	3.5	2.6
50.1	54.2	53.3	Net Worth	47.0	46.9		56.0	52.3	61.7
100.0	100.0	100.0	Total Liabilities & Net Worth	100.0	100.0		100.0	100.0	100.0
			INCOME DATA						
100.0	100.0	100.0	Net Sales	100.0	100.0		100.0	100.0	100.0
			Gross Profit						
86.1	85.2	87.9	Operating Expenses	75.4	85.0		86.4	90.3	95.7
13.9	14.8	12.1	Operating Profit	24.6	15.0		13.6	9.7	4.3
5.1	7.3	5.7	All Other Expenses (net)	19.2	10.0		5.9	1.5	-1.7
8.8	7.4	6.4	Profit Before Taxes	5.4	5.0		7.7	8.2	6.1
			RATIOS						
4.9	4.9	4.9		7.2	4.7		6.1	5.4	3.2
1.8	1.9	2.2	Current	2.3	2.2		2.7	1.9	2.5
.9	.9	1.3		1.2	1.4		.9	1.1	1.5
4.8	4.6	4.6		7.2	4.7		5.2	5.2	2.8
1.6	1.7	1.9	Quick	2.2	1.5		2.1	1.7	1.9
.8	.6	1.0		1.1	.7		.8	.8	1.3
20 18.0	13 27.7	19 18.7		0 UND	18 19.8		10 36.0	23 15.8	19 19.7
38 9.5	33 11.1	35 10.4	Sales/Receivables	35 10.4	28 12.9		36 10.1	36 10.3	35 10.3
61 6.0	48 7.6	51 7.2		56 6.5	50 7.3		65 5.6	50 7.2	55 6.6
			Cost of Sales/Inventory						
			Cost of Sales/Payables						
1.9	1.4	1.4		1.0	1.2		1.1	1.2	2.3
6.7	6.0	3.9	Sales/Working Capital	2.1	4.2		2.7	3.9	4.2
-36.6	-14.3	15.7		15.8	6.8		-31.9	55.6	9.3
9.3	6.6	6.2					8.1	5.2	42.2
(73) 3.1	(69) 2.6	(70) 2.3	EBIT/Interest		(15) 2.2	(19) 2.4	(15) 4.9		
1.3	.8	1.2					.6	1.8	2.3
			Net Profit + Depr., Dep., Amort./Cur. Mat. L/T/D						
.9	.9	1.0		1.0	1.1		1.0	1.0	.5
1.2	1.2	1.3	Fixed/Worth	1.8	1.5		1.3	1.3	1.0
2.2	2.2	1.9		4.0	2.1		2.1	2.4	1.3
.4	.3	.4		.2	.4		.3	.3	.4
1.0	.8	.8	Debt/Worth	1.5	1.0		.7	.7	.7
2.1	1.9	2.0		3.3	2.2		1.7	2.1	.9
8.1	7.8	6.9		2.5	3.2		11.8	8.9	12.9
(87) 3.4	(83) 2.3	(88) 2.6	% Profit Before Taxes/Tangible Net Worth	(11) .5	(11) 1.8	(20) 2.5	(22) 3.6	6.9	
.4	-.5	-.1		-2.5	.1		-2.0	1.5	1.6
5.3	5.6	3.6		1.0	2.2		6.6	4.0	4.8
2.0	1.3	1.5	% Profit Before Taxes/Total Assets	.1	.9		2.1	2.2	3.7
.1	-.3	-.2		-.8	-.7		-.8	1.1	1.2
2.6	1.1	.9		.2	.6		.7	1.8	7.5
.3	.3	.2	Sales/Net Fixed Assets	.1	.2		.3	.3	.8
.1	.1	.1		.1	.1		.1	.2	.5
1.0	.6	.5		.2	.4		.4	.9	1.3
.2	.2	.2	Sales/Total Assets	.1	.1		.2	.2	.6
.1	.1	.1		.1	.1		.1	.1	.3
3.6	7.1	8.5		17.4	14.5		9.1	6.3	1.8
(87) 14.9	(83) 18.2	(83) 16.7	% Depr., Dep., Amort./Sales	(12) 29.1	(11) 26.0	(18) 16.2	(21) 15.4	(14) 5.9	
23.1	27.4	28.2		41.1	34.1		35.9	19.8	9.1
3.2		1.1							
(20) 6.1		(12) 3.2	% Officers', Directors' Owners' Comp/Sales						
7.8		6.3							
1525014M	1549335M	1656233M	Net Sales ($)	7789M	25112M	31587M	142643M	376103M	1072999M
4556536M	3912737M	5155685M	Total Assets ($)	91258M	155036M	174408M	977668M	1890496M	1866819M

M = $ thousand   MM = $ million
See Pages 9 through 22 for Explanation of Ratios and Data

Current Data Sorted by Assets | **Comparative Historical Data**

Type of Statement

Type of Statement	0-500M	500M-2MM	2-10MM	10-50MM	50-100MM	100-250MM	ALL 4/1/06-3/31/07	ALL 4/1/07-3/31/08
Unqualified	2	8	20	34	7	6	83	90
Reviewed			2				3	3
Compiled	1						1	
Tax Returns							3	2
Other	4	4	13	12	6		29	35

Date ranges: 75 (4/1-9/30/10); 44 (10/1/10-3/31/11)

	0-500M	500M-2MM	2-10MM	10-50MM	50-100MM	100-250MM	ALL 4/1/06-3/31/07	ALL 4/1/07-3/31/08
NUMBER OF STATEMENTS	7	12	35	46	13	6	119	130
	%	%	%	%	%	%	%	%
ASSETS								
Cash & Equivalents		22.2	7.7	16.9	16.8		17.5	16.1
Trade Receivables (net)		2.3	3.0	7.5	1.6		5.7	7.7
Inventory		4.3	1.4	3.4	.3		2.9	5.5
All Other Current		2.2	4.9	1.5	2.2		4.8	4.2
Total Current		30.9	16.9	29.3	20.9		30.9	33.6
Fixed Assets (net)		54.6	57.8	51.3	63.7		51.5	44.3
Intangibles (net)		1.3	4.3	.8	.1		.8	.3
All Other Non-Current		13.2	21.0	18.6	15.2		16.8	21.8
Total		100.0	100.0	100.0	100.0		100.0	100.0
LIABILITIES								
Notes Payable-Short Term		1.3	4.3	5.5	.1		3.8	4.1
Cur. Mat.-L.T.D.		1.6	1.7	2.3	1.6		2.2	2.6
Trade Payables		6.8	2.0	2.4	1.4		3.4	3.0
Income Taxes Payable		.0	.0	.1	.0		.1	.4
All Other Current		15.9	7.1	6.2	2.0		4.9	5.0
Total Current		25.7	15.0	16.4	5.1		14.3	15.1
Long-Term Debt		25.5	28.1	28.9	17.0		33.5	33.7
Deferred Taxes		.0	.9	.0	.0		.0	.0
All Other Non-Current		.7	2.0	3.5	1.2		3.7	3.4
Net Worth		48.1	53.9	51.1	76.8		48.5	47.8
Total Liabilities & Net Worth		100.0	100.0	100.0	100.0		100.0	100.0
INCOME DATA								
Net Sales		100.0	100.0	100.0	100.0		100.0	100.0
Gross Profit								
Operating Expenses		94.0	90.2	89.7	93.1		90.7	90.6
Operating Profit		6.0	9.8	10.3	6.9		9.3	9.4
All Other Expenses (net)		6.1	5.0	5.1	1.7		3.4	4.4
Profit Before Taxes		.0	4.8	5.3	5.2		5.9	5.0
RATIOS								
Current		4.2	3.5	4.5	8.4		5.7	6.2
		1.2	1.5	1.8	4.4		2.2	2.4
		.6	.3	1.1	1.9		1.2	1.3
Quick		1.8	2.2	3.3	6.7		4.3	4.9
		1.1	.9	1.5	4.4		1.6	1.6
		.6	.3	.7	1.5		.8	.6
Sales/Receivables	0	UND	1 594.0	3 112.1	5 77.7		1 527.1	1 336.0
	3	113.7	10 35.9	16 23.1	6 56.6		7 53.7	8 44.4
	18	20.6	22 16.6	42 8.7	24 15.0		35 10.4	36 10.1
Cost of Sales/Inventory								
Cost of Sales/Payables								
Sales/Working Capital		3.5	2.6	2.1	1.4		2.3	1.5
		24.9	10.3	6.9	3.0		4.8	3.6
		-4.3	-3.2	NM	12.4		22.3	24.7
EBIT/Interest			6.8	8.4	13.2		8.9	10.5
			(27) 3.2	(29) 3.7	(12) 6.5		(84) 2.6	(95) 2.3
			-.1	.9	-.1		.7	.3
Net Profit + Depr., Dep., Amort./Cur. Mat. L/T/D								
Fixed/Worth		.4	.3	.3	.6		.4	.2
		1.2	1.3	1.1	.8		1.0	.8
		2.7	2.4	1.6	1.2		2.2	1.8
Debt/Worth		.1	.3	.3	.1		.3	.3
		1.5	.7	.9	.2		.9	1.0
		2.8	1.6	2.7	.5		3.4	3.7
% Profit Before Taxes/Tangible Net Worth		5.7	9.8	15.9	10.6		13.2	10.6
		(11) 2.1	(34) 3.8	(44) 6.2	2.1		(110) 5.0	(123) 3.7
		-6.7	-4.3	-3.4	-3.5		-1.0	-1.7
% Profit Before Taxes/Total Assets		2.5	5.1	8.4	5.8		6.7	5.5
		1.0	1.7	2.6	1.9		2.1	1.0
		-3.6	-1.4	-1.6	-2.7		-.8	-1.1
Sales/Net Fixed Assets		4.7	2.6	4.2	1.0		4.1	6.8
		1.9	.6	1.3	.6		.7	1.4
		.2	.2	.5	.4		.5	.6
Sales/Total Assets		1.4	.8	1.0	.5		.9	.7
		.7	.4	.5	.4		.5	.4
		.2	.2	.3	.3		.2	.2
% Depr., Dep., Amort./Sales		.7	1.8	1.5	5.8		2.3	1.3
		3.2	(31) 8.1	(40) 4.8	(12) 10.7		(102) 6.0	(108) 4.4
		17.5	14.0	10.0	14.3		12.1	10.5
% Officers', Directors' Owners' Comp/Sales							4.4	
							(11) 17.4	
							24.9	
Net Sales ($)	1972M	13426M	110417M	835048M	383145M	232643M	1101804M	1651244M
Total Assets ($)	2187M	13412M	200049M	1173970M	906230M	907758M	2234103M	3837946M

Comparative Historical Data | Current Data Sorted by Sales

		Comparative Historical		Type of Statement		Current Data Sorted by Sales				
72	84	77		Unqualified	13	13	6	16	14	15
1	1	2		Reviewed	1	1				
7	2	1		Compiled	1		1			
1		1		Tax Returns	1					
26	21	39		Other	9	10	1	3	11	5
4/1/08-3/31/09 ALL	4/1/09-3/31/10 ALL	4/1/10-3/31/11 ALL			0-1MM	75 (4/1-9/30/10) 1-3MM	3-5MM	5-10MM	44 (10/1/10-3/31/11) 10-25MM	25MM & OVER
107	109	119		NUMBER OF STATEMENTS	23	24	8	19	25	20
%	%	%		ASSETS	%	%	%	%	%	%
15.1	15.7	15.3		Cash & Equivalents	14.7	9.5		12.6	21.5	17.2
5.9	6.1	4.2		Trade Receivables (net)	.5	6.9		2.5	3.9	8.2
4.7	2.7	2.7		Inventory	4.0	1.8		5.7	.3	.8
3.7	3.4	2.8		All Other Current	1.6	4.4		3.7	1.3	1.7
29.4	27.9	25.0		Total Current	20.7	22.5		24.4	26.9	27.9
46.9	52.7	54.0		Fixed Assets (net)	59.2	60.6		43.0	56.3	56.2
1.0	1.2	1.7		Intangibles (net)	.3	2.6		4.6	.4	1.3
22.7	18.2	19.3		All Other Non-Current	19.8	14.3		27.9	16.4	14.6
100.0	100.0	100.0		Total	100.0	100.0		100.0	100.0	100.0
				LIABILITIES						
3.4	2.4	3.8		Notes Payable-Short Term	6.5	5.7		5.4	1.5	.5
2.4	2.8	1.9		Cur. Mat.-L.T.D.	2.3	2.0		2.8	1.4	1.9
3.5	3.3	2.4		Trade Payables	.9	1.7		1.8	2.1	3.2
.0	.0	.0		Income Taxes Payable	.0	.1		.0	.0	.0
4.7	5.4	6.6		All Other Current	10.6	6.7		5.3	4.1	7.5
13.9	13.9	14.8		Total Current	20.2	16.2		15.3	9.1	13.0
33.0	34.6	30.2		Long-Term Debt	48.2	32.1		26.4	22.8	23.6
.0	.3	.3		Deferred Taxes	.0	.0		.0	.0	.0
3.7	3.2	2.2		All Other Non-Current	.5	.9		4.4	1.4	4.4
49.4	48.0	52.5		Net Worth	31.1	50.8		53.8	66.6	59.0
100.0	100.0	100.0		Total Liabilities & Net Worth	100.0	100.0		100.0	100.0	100.0
				INCOME DATA						
100.0	100.0	100.0		Net Sales	100.0	100.0		100.0	100.0	100.0
				Gross Profit						
92.4	94.1	90.2		Operating Expenses	89.5	89.6		87.6	89.1	96.3
7.6	5.9	9.8		Operating Profit	10.5	10.4		12.4	10.9	3.7
4.2	4.8	5.2		All Other Expenses (net)	13.7	5.3		7.0	2.2	-1.4
3.4	1.1	4.5		Profit Before Taxes	-3.2	5.1		5.3	8.7	5.1
				RATIOS						
5.6	5.2	4.9		Current	3.6	4.7		9.0	6.7	4.3
2.3	2.3	2.1			.8	1.5		2.7	3.8	2.0
1.0	1.1	.9			.2	.5		.5	1.2	1.4
4.0	4.2	3.9		Quick	2.8	3.5		2.9	6.1	4.1
1.3	1.5	1.5			.8	1.3		1.5	3.8	1.6
.7	.7	.7			.2	.5		.5	1.2	1.1
1 510.0	2 157.9	1 422.3		Sales/Receivables	0 UND	2 191.2		1 591.2	5 79.5	3 113.0
9 42.0	8 44.6	7 54.6			0 UND	18 20.6		5 77.8	15 23.6	8 45.8
31 11.6	32 11.5	26 14.0			9 40.4	59 6.2		12 31.0	29 12.8	28 12.9
				Cost of Sales/Inventory						
				Cost of Sales/Payables						
2.2	1.6	2.1		Sales/Working Capital	3.5	2.2		1.4	1.6	4.8
5.9	4.8	6.2			-5.9	7.8		5.9	4.2	8.8
-944.5	43.2	-80.2			-.9	-15.8		-11.5	25.8	23.4
12.4	6.7	7.8		EBIT/Interest	4.2	5.3		24.1	10.8	9.5
(74) 2.4	(74) 1.3	(83) 3.3			(13) 1.2	(17) 2.9	(13)	2.9	(19) 5.2	(18) 4.1
-.2	-.5	.6			-.3	-.1		.9	.7	.3
				Net Profit + Depr., Dep., Amort./Cur. Mat. L/T/D						
.2	.5	.4		Fixed/Worth	.4	.4		.2	.5	.7
.8	1.0	1.0			1.9	1.3		.7	.9	.9
1.8	2.0	1.9			7.7	2.5		1.3	1.4	1.3
.2	.4	.2		Debt/Worth	.2	.3		.2	.1	.3
.8	.8	.7			1.4	.9		.9	.5	.6
3.3	2.4	2.2			25.1	2.6		2.6	.9	1.8
12.2	9.2	11.1		% Profit Before Taxes/Tangible Net Worth	5.7	9.8		11.2	15.1	15.8
(99) 4.5	(101) 1.5	(112) 4.1			(19) -4.8	(23) 3.7		4.5	(24) 6.2	(19) 6.0
-1.6	-3.9	-3.6			-11.1	-4.1		-1.4	-.9	-3.0
4.6	3.0	5.5		% Profit Before Taxes/Total Assets	2.5	4.4		6.5	7.3	8.6
1.9	.3	1.9			-.6	1.2		.8	2.9	4.9
-1.0	-2.0	-1.8			-4.0	-1.4		-.6	-1.3	-1.7
5.2	3.0	2.8		Sales/Net Fixed Assets	2.3	2.2		11.3	2.3	3.6
1.1	.9	1.0			.3	.6		2.1	1.0	1.3
.4	.4	.4			.1	.3		.5	.6	.7
.7	.8	.9		Sales/Total Assets	.6	.6		.9	.9	2.0
.5	.4	.5			.2	.3		.5	.6	.8
.2	.2	.2			.1	.2		.2	.3	.4
1.9	2.4	1.9		% Depr., Dep., Amort./Sales	1.6	1.9		1.4	2.0	2.2
(94) 5.4	(92) 6.6	(104) 5.7			(20) 12.5	(20) 8.6	(16)	3.5	(23) 6.1	(18) 5.3
12.7	13.0	12.6			28.9	14.5		9.1	10.9	10.6
4.8	2.7	3.8		% Officers', Directors' Owners' Comp/Sales						
(11) 16.7	(12) 7.3	(12) 7.2								
23.0	18.8	16.9								
2500828M	1440944M	1576651M		Net Sales ($)	8635M	45118M	31869M	141005M	437628M	912396M
3455466M	3818664M	3203606M		Total Assets ($)	59859M	183755M	106560M	438623M	1138630M	1276179M

M = $ thousand   MM = $ million
See Pages 9 through 22 for Explanation of Ratios and Data

Current Data Sorted by Assets | Comparative Historical Data

Type of Statement	0-500M	500M-2MM	2-10MM	10-50MM	50-100MM	100-250MM	ALL 4/1/06-3/31/07	ALL 4/1/07-3/31/08
Unqualified	1	4	14	25	6	4	74	65
Reviewed	1							1
Compiled		1	4	3		1	8	6
Tax Returns							3	2
Other	1	5	8	5	4	2	17	22
		60 (4/1-9/30/10)		29 (10/1/10-3/31/11)				
NUMBER OF STATEMENTS	3	10	26	33	10	7	102	96
	%	%	%	%	%	%	%	%
ASSETS								
Cash & Equivalents		23.1	17.5	24.5	24.6		17.7	16.3
Trade Receivables (net)		11.7	7.9	12.5	7.5		12.7	16.1
Inventory		3.3	3.8	.2	.0		2.0	3.0
All Other Current		4.1	5.6	4.8	6.1		4.8	5.1
Total Current		42.2	34.7	42.0	38.3		37.2	40.6
Fixed Assets (net)		47.0	42.2	38.5	34.4		37.1	35.9
Intangibles (net)		.6	.2	.7	.1		.4	.5
All Other Non-Current		10.1	22.9	18.9	27.2		25.2	23.0
Total		100.0	100.0	100.0	100.0		100.0	100.0
LIABILITIES								
Notes Payable-Short Term		8.7	9.5	4.9	3.4		3.9	7.0
Cur. Mat.-L.T.D.		3.6	1.9	2.6	8.2		3.4	3.2
Trade Payables		5.0	4.6	2.5	1.5		5.0	3.5
Income Taxes Payable		.0	.0	.0	.0		.0	.0
All Other Current		16.2	2.4	7.4	2.7		7.0	8.8
Total Current		33.6	18.4	17.4	15.8		19.4	22.5
Long-Term Debt		12.3	29.9	32.7	34.6		36.7	35.5
Deferred Taxes		.0	.0	.0	.0		.0	.0
All Other Non-Current		27.0	4.9	3.4	4.1		5.4	3.4
Net Worth		27.2	46.8	46.5	45.4		38.5	38.6
Total Liabilities & Net Worth		100.0	100.0	100.0	100.0		100.0	100.0
INCOME DATA								
Net Sales		100.0	100.0	100.0	100.0		100.0	100.0
Gross Profit								
Operating Expenses		89.7	75.7	77.0	78.5		78.0	78.3
Operating Profit		10.3	24.3	23.0	21.5		22.0	21.7
All Other Expenses (net)		7.5	9.4	13.7	16.5		9.4	11.3
Profit Before Taxes		2.7	14.9	9.2	5.1		12.6	10.4
RATIOS								
Current		4.1	6.5	5.2	5.8		5.5	5.3
		1.2	2.0	2.4	3.4		1.9	2.0
		.7	1.0	1.2	1.5		.9	1.2
Quick		3.5	5.2	4.2	4.5		4.3	4.2
		1.2	1.6	2.1	2.7		1.3	1.6
		.4	.3	1.0	1.5		.5	.6
Sales/Receivables		0 UND	0 UND	0 UND	27 13.4		0 UND	0 UND
		21 17.5	7 55.5	18 20.3	57 6.4		22 16.8	20 18.5
		44 8.3	64 5.7	80 4.5	248 1.5		81 4.5	128 2.9
Cost of Sales/Inventory								
Cost of Sales/Payables								
Sales/Working Capital		1.8	1.1	.5	.4		.8	.6
		45.6	3.9	1.5	.9		5.4	4.5
		-3.7	NM	19.2	2.2		-32.3	19.8
EBIT/Interest			5.2	9.6			8.0	6.6
			(17) 1.3	(23) 2.0			(62) 3.0	(57) 1.7
			-.3	1.0			1.2	-.2
Net Profit + Depr., Dep., Amort./Cur. Mat. L/T/D								
Fixed/Worth		.8	.3	.0	.0		.0	.0
		1.4	.8	.9	.4		.7	.5
		UND	1.3	1.2	1.1		1.6	1.5
Debt/Worth		1.0	.4	.5	.6		.5	.5
		2.7	.9	1.1	1.2		1.3	1.4
		UND	5.4	5.3	3.3		4.4	3.4
% Profit Before Taxes/Tangible Net Worth			23.1	15.0	3.5		18.2	16.1
		(25)	3.1	(32) 3.6	1.3		(92) 6.8	(90) 4.8
			-5.0	-1.2	-1.9		.1	-2.0
% Profit Before Taxes/Total Assets		26.1	13.1	8.4	2.0		6.6	5.3
		-.8	1.5	1.1	.3		2.6	2.0
		-4.1	-.7	-.8	-.8		.0	-1.0
Sales/Net Fixed Assets		15.2	53.8	142.1	34.8		80.1	87.4
		2.6	1.6	1.2	3.4		2.2	2.5
		.4	.3	.2	.1		.4	.5
Sales/Total Assets		1.8	.8	.4	.2		.6	.8
		.8	.3	.2	.2		.3	.3
		.2	.2	.1	.1		.1	.1
% Depr., Dep., Amort./Sales			.9	.4			.8	.6
		(16)	4.2	(28) 3.2			(66) 2.8	(65) 1.6
			11.4	10.1			8.1	6.2
% Officers', Directors' Owners' Comp/Sales								
Net Sales ($)	1695M	8974M	85417M	310451M	136533M	208255M	831537M	808275M
Total Assets ($)	643M	9419M	149899M	779143M	720517M	932148M	2675693M	2932143M

M = $ thousand   MM = $ million
See Pages 9 through 22 for Explanation of Ratios and Data

Comparative Historical Data | | | | ## Current Data Sorted by Sales

			Type of Statement						
60	57	54	Unqualified	12	12	5	9	9	7
	3	1	Reviewed		1				
5	5	9	Compiled	2	4	2	1		
		1	Tax Returns						
26	25	25	Other	8	5	1	7	1	3
4/1/08-3/31/09 ALL	4/1/09-3/31/10 ALL	4/1/10-3/31/11 ALL		0-1MM	60 (4/1-9/30/10) 1-3MM	3-5MM	29 (10/1/10-3/31/11) 5-10MM	10-25MM	25MM & OVER
91	91	89	**NUMBER OF STATEMENTS**	22	22	8	17	10	10
%	%	%	**ASSETS**	%	%	%	%	%	%
21.2	19.7	23.1	Cash & Equivalents	23.1	16.5		24.6	34.7	20.7
15.1	14.9	10.2	Trade Receivables (net)	13.4	8.6		8.2	7.6	18.5
1.9	2.7	1.6	Inventory	1.7	2.2		.0	1.8	.8
4.6	3.5	5.0	All Other Current	.9	6.2		7.6	11.0	2.2
42.8	40.9	39.9	Total Current	39.1	33.4		40.5	55.1	42.3
30.6	33.1	38.6	Fixed Assets (net)	51.0	44.2		35.1	9.7	45.4
.7	.3	.4	Intangibles (net)	.2	.8		.4	.4	.1
25.9	25.7	21.1	All Other Non-Current	9.7	21.5		24.1	34.8	12.2
100.0	100.0	100.0	Total	100.0	100.0		100.0	100.0	100.0
			LIABILITIES						
6.0	4.9	6.1	Notes Payable-Short Term	6.6	7.9		3.4	2.8	7.5
3.9	4.8	3.0	Cur. Mat.-L.T.D.	2.6	2.7		3.8	4.3	2.0
3.1	4.0	3.2	Trade Payables	.8	4.1		3.0	6.8	5.3
.0	.0	.0	Income Taxes Payable	.0	.0		.0	.0	.0
6.5	9.6	6.7	All Other Current	5.3	9.5		2.7	11.9	6.8
19.6	23.3	19.0	Total Current	15.2	24.1		12.9	25.8	21.7
36.9	33.9	28.9	Long-Term Debt	29.9	29.1		31.9	35.1	18.8
.0	.0	.0	Deferred Taxes	.0	.0		.0	.0	.0
4.1	4.1	6.7	All Other Non-Current	7.4	7.9		7.2	4.3	2.5
39.4	38.8	45.4	Net Worth	47.5	38.9		47.9	34.8	57.0
100.0	100.0	100.0	Total Liabilities & Net Worth	100.0	100.0		100.0	100.0	100.0
			INCOME DATA						
100.0	100.0	100.0	Net Sales	100.0	100.0		100.0	100.0	100.0
			Gross Profit						
75.1	81.2	77.4	Operating Expenses	71.9	85.9		70.5	84.2	89.3
24.9	18.8	22.6	Operating Profit	28.1	14.1		29.5	15.8	10.7
13.7	10.9	11.6	All Other Expenses (net)	14.2	16.4		13.6	-.3	5.5
11.1	7.9	11.0	Profit Before Taxes	13.9	-2.3		15.9	16.1	5.2
			RATIOS						
7.4	5.4	5.6		7.1	4.3		6.2	3.7	3.8
3.4	2.5	2.4	Current	2.5	1.1		3.5	2.7	2.4
1.3	1.4	1.2		1.2	.4		1.9	1.3	1.4
5.0	4.6	4.6		5.9	3.6		6.1	2.6	3.2
2.4	2.0	2.0	Quick	2.5	.8		3.4	1.7	2.3
1.1	1.2	.8		1.2	.4		1.5	1.0	1.4
0 UND	5 66.8	0 UND		0 UND	0 UND	2 207.8	10 38.2		4 85.7
25 14.4	45 8.2	26 13.8	Sales/Receivables	37 9.8	7 55.5	26 13.8	31 11.7		37 9.9
194 1.9	123 3.0	69 5.3		158 2.3	56 6.6	65 5.6	69 5.3		110 3.3
			Cost of Sales/Inventory						
			Cost of Sales/Payables						
.5	.6	.7		.6	1.7		.5	.5	1.4
1.8	1.7	2.0	Sales/Working Capital	1.2	10.2		1.2	2.0	2.9
14.4	9.0	34.4		NM	-5.3		4.1	15.9	17.7
6.5	7.5	9.6		15.2	1.6		8.7		
(62) 2.7	(65) 2.4	(59) 1.9	EBIT/Interest	(10) 1.2	(14) -.1	(12) 2.0			
.5	.6	.3		-1.5	-5.9		1.6		
			Net Profit + Depr., Dep., Amort./Cur. Mat. L/T/D						
.0	.0	.0		.0	.4		.0	.0	.1
.4	.7	.9	Fixed/Worth	1.1	1.0		.9	.1	.8
1.7	1.6	1.2		20.3	1.8		1.1	.6	1.0
.6	.6	.4		.2	.4		.6	.9	.3
1.6	1.5	1.1	Debt/Worth	1.0	2.3		1.1	1.7	.5
3.6	3.8	4.4		33.2	8.1		1.9	4.3	2.0
10.7	8.4	16.7		9.1	20.3		9.7	18.8	4.6
(84) 3.6	(83) 2.1	(85) 3.1	% Profit Before Taxes/Tangible Net Worth	(19) 1.8	(21) -1.3		4.8	16.1	2.7
-1.9	-2.6	-1.5		-1.6	-16.6		1.4	-3.7	-4.2
5.5	4.1	8.2		4.6	11.6		6.2	10.0	3.7
2.0	.9	1.3	% Profit Before Taxes/Total Assets	.5	-.8		1.6	6.9	1.4
-.9	-.9	-.8		-.5	-4.5		.3	-.9	-2.0
92.8	43.2	44.4		54.4	15.2		115.4	100.1	20.1
3.3	2.5	1.8	Sales/Net Fixed Assets	.5	1.1		.9	19.6	1.2
.5	.4	.3		.1	.2		.2	4.8	.7
.5	.8	.6		.2	.8		.4	.8	1.6
.2	.2	.3	Sales/Total Assets	.1	.3		.2	.4	.5
.1	.1	.1		.1	.1		.1	.2	.3
.8	.6	.6		2.2	2.3		.6	.1	
(63) 3.1	(68) 2.9	(65) 2.7	% Depr., Dep., Amort./Sales	(11) 8.8	(17) 3.9	(14) 9.0	.6		
6.6	9.8	10.4		19.8	13.5		13.4	1.7	
			% Officers', Directors' Owners' Comp/Sales						
839530M	715852M	751325M	Net Sales ($)	12758M	42658M	31866M	120595M	160072M	383376M
3404604M	3089947M	2591769M	Total Assets ($)	131243M	249708M	115961M	758118M	504424M	832315M

© RMA 2011

M = $ thousand   MM = $ million
See Pages 9 through 22 for Explanation of Ratios and Data

Current Data Sorted by Assets

							Comparative Historical Data	
1	8	30 2	26	10 1	7	Type of Statement Unqualified	100	66
						Reviewed	3	4
1	1	3 1				Compiled	5	6
		1				Tax Returns	1	2
2	5	9	11	1	1	Other	30	32
	81 (4/1-9/30/10)		39 (10/1/10-3/31/11)				4/1/06-3/31/07 ALL	4/1/07-3/31/08 ALL
0-500M	500M-2MM	2-10MM	10-50MM	50-100MM	100-250MM	NUMBER OF STATEMENTS	139	110
4	14	45	37	12	8			
%	%	%	%	%	%	**ASSETS**	%	%
	27.8	21.9	21.5	25.4		Cash & Equivalents	22.2	24.1
	18.1	10.6	8.3	5.1		Trade Receivables (net)	12.7	11.8
	3.3	7.2	.1	.3		Inventory	2.0	1.4
	6.8	6.8	6.9	15.0		All Other Current	6.0	5.4
	55.9	46.6	36.8	45.8		Total Current	42.9	42.6
	35.4	33.5	39.8	37.4		Fixed Assets (net)	35.2	34.5
	.0	1.4	.8	.5		Intangibles (net)	1.6	1.2
	8.7	18.6	22.6	16.4		All Other Non-Current	20.3	21.7
	100.0	100.0	100.0	100.0		Total	100.0	100.0
						LIABILITIES		
	3.8	1.8	.8	2.1		Notes Payable-Short Term	4.0	5.8
	1.7	2.1	3.8	4.6		Cur. Mat.-L.T.D.	1.9	1.7
	9.8	4.4	2.2	2.7		Trade Payables	6.8	6.4
	.0	.0	.0	.0		Income Taxes Payable	.0	.4
	7.2	7.6	8.4	12.3		All Other Current	8.0	8.5
	22.5	15.9	15.3	21.7		Total Current	20.7	22.8
	19.6	23.1	35.7	30.5		Long-Term Debt	24.2	27.5
	.0	.0	.0	.0		Deferred Taxes	.1	.1
	6.8	2.9	3.5	1.3		All Other Non-Current	5.2	4.2
	51.1	58.2	45.5	46.5		Net Worth	49.9	45.3
	100.0	100.0	100.0	100.0		Total Liabilities & Net Worth	100.0	100.0
						INCOME DATA		
	100.0	100.0	100.0	100.0		Net Sales	100.0	100.0
						Gross Profit		
	92.2	86.9	80.3	81.0		Operating Expenses	81.8	81.0
	7.8	13.1	19.7	19.0		Operating Profit	18.2	19.0
	2.2	6.7	10.0	9.4		All Other Expenses (net)	5.8	8.0
	5.5	6.3	9.8	9.6		Profit Before Taxes	12.4	11.0
						RATIOS		
	11.3	10.2	5.5	7.4			4.4	5.5
	1.8	3.5	2.2	1.6		Current	2.2	2.3
	1.1	1.5	.9	1.1			1.3	1.1
	9.6	7.6	5.2	3.6			3.2	5.4
	1.8	2.0	1.7	1.2		Quick	1.8	1.9
	.8	.9	.5	.6			1.0	.8
	0 UND	0 UND	1 674.9	0 UND			1 330.7	2 183.3
	22 16.4	7 50.6	9 42.7	30 12.3		Sales/Receivables	23 15.8	18 20.3
	50 7.3	40 9.1	42 8.7	92 4.0			62 5.9	55 6.7
						Cost of Sales/Inventory		
						Cost of Sales/Payables		
	2.3	.6	.8	.7			1.7	1.2
	12.0	3.1	2.6	2.5		Sales/Working Capital	5.2	4.7
	56.1	16.0	NM	58.5			19.6	62.7
		4.1	5.3				10.4	5.5
		(25) 1.8	(23) 2.0			EBIT/Interest	(66) 4.1	(59) 2.2
		-1.0	.8				1.1	.5
						Net Profit + Depr., Dep., Amort./Cur. Mat. L/T/D		
	.0	.1	.0	.1			.1	.1
	.4	.4	.9	.8		Fixed/Worth	.7	.7
	1.6	1.2	1.5	2.6			1.3	1.3
	.4	.3	.5	.5			.4	.5
	1.2	.8	1.4	.9		Debt/Worth	1.1	1.2
	2.2	1.4	3.4	4.0			2.6	3.6
	29.2	11.5	11.0	17.3		% Profit Before Taxes/Tangible Net Worth	21.7	14.8
	7.2	3.6	(36) 1.4	(11) 10.6			(134) 6.8	(104) 4.8
	-9.2	-2.8	-2.4	-.7			-.8	-1.1
	11.5	5.7	5.9	11.0		% Profit Before Taxes/Total Assets	8.0	5.1
	3.2	1.7	.6	2.2			3.0	2.2
	-3.0	-1.7	-.6	-.2			-.3	-.7
	175.7	36.8	159.2	34.4			22.6	26.3
	14.7	5.1	1.2	1.0		Sales/Net Fixed Assets	3.2	4.4
	1.4	.5	.2	.4			.4	.4
	2.7	2.0	.6	.4			1.9	1.6
	1.2	.3	.2	.3		Sales/Total Assets	.4	.4
	.6	.1	.1	.2			.1	.1
	.3	1.0	3.0	1.7			.9	1.3
	(10) 1.3	(34) 2.7	(29) 7.9	(10) 4.9		% Depr., Dep., Amort./Sales	(96) 2.3	(79) 2.8
	2.4	14.9	18.2	13.7			10.7	7.7
						% Officers', Directors' Owners' Comp/Sales		4.4
								(11) 11.9
								27.5
4631M	28784M	220599M	526652M	334511M	476586M	Net Sales ($)	1513275M	1202402M
1012M	15334M	241723M	742092M	908472M	1151560M	Total Assets ($)	3104435M	2570260M

M = $ thousand   MM = $ million
See Pages 9 through 22 for Explanation of Ratios and Data

Comparative Historical Data | Current Data Sorted by Sales

			Type of Statement					
80	62	82	Unqualified	11	22	8	15	11	15
3	3	3	Reviewed	2			1		
5	3	5	Compiled	5					
1	3	1	Tax Returns		1				
28	33	29	Other	7	8	4	8	8	2
4/1/08- 3/31/09	4/1/09- 3/31/10	4/1/10- 3/31/11			81 (4/1-9/30/10)			39 (10/1/10-3/31/11)	
ALL	ALL	ALL		0-1MM	1-3MM	3-5MM	5-10MM	10-25MM	25MM & OVER
117	104	120	**NUMBER OF STATEMENTS**	25	31	12	16	19	17
%	%	%	**ASSETS**	%	%	%	%	%	%
25.2	24.6	23.8	Cash & Equivalents	26.9	20.8	25.9	17.4	25.4	27.0
13.6	8.4	10.3	Trade Receivables (net)	5.9	7.1	4.8	18.2	11.9	17.4
2.1	.9	3.2	Inventory	8.0	3.4	.6	.7	2.5	.5
5.0	4.4	7.0	All Other Current	2.8	7.5	12.2	6.8	9.2	6.6
46.0	38.3	44.3	Total Current	43.6	38.8	43.6	43.1	49.1	51.6
36.9	42.0	36.3	Fixed Assets (net)	38.0	34.6	34.0	41.5	38.9	30.4
.4	.4	.8	Intangibles (net)	.1	1.3	.3	2.1	1.0	.2
16.7	19.2	18.6	All Other Non-Current	18.3	25.3	22.2	13.3	11.0	17.9
100.0	100.0	100.0	Total	100.0	100.0	100.0	100.0	100.0	100.0
			LIABILITIES						
4.6	3.4	1.6	Notes Payable-Short Term	1.4	2.3	.5	1.2	2.6	.5
1.6	1.9	2.7	Cur. Mat.-L.T.D.	2.9	3.4	2.0	2.7	3.4	1.0
6.3	5.3	4.5	Trade Payables	1.1	3.6	2.4	6.6	6.0	8.8
.0	.0	.0	Income Taxes Payable	.0	.0	.1	.0	.0	.0
10.7	9.4	8.7	All Other Current	3.8	3.3	2.4	10.3	11.5	25.6
23.1	20.0	17.5	Total Current	9.2	12.6	7.5	20.9	23.5	35.9
23.0	28.6	27.8	Long-Term Debt	32.7	27.5	40.0	25.5	24.1	18.6
.0	.0	.0	Deferred Taxes	.0	.0	.0	.0	.0	.0
4.5	4.1	3.5	All Other Non-Current	3.0	3.2	4.7	4.0	4.5	2.6
49.4	47.3	51.2	Net Worth	55.0	56.7	47.8	49.6	48.0	42.9
100.0	100.0	100.0	Total Liabilities & Net Worth	100.0	100.0	100.0	100.0	100.0	100.0
			INCOME DATA						
100.0	100.0	100.0	Net Sales	100.0	100.0	100.0	100.0	100.0	100.0
			Gross Profit						
88.5	86.1	85.3	Operating Expenses	76.7	84.2	74.4	92.0	92.8	93.0
11.5	13.9	14.7	Operating Profit	23.3	15.8	25.6	8.0	7.2	7.0
6.6	11.2	7.2	All Other Expenses (net)	11.5	9.3	16.6	2.5	2.5	.3
4.9	2.8	7.5	Profit Before Taxes	11.8	6.5	9.0	5.5	4.8	6.7
			RATIOS						
5.4	4.9	7.7		26.5	9.6	9.1	3.7	4.1	2.1
2.5	2.0	2.5	Current	5.0	3.4	5.0	2.6	1.8	1.4
1.0	1.2	1.2		1.2	.4	2.4	1.3	1.2	1.1
5.0	4.7	5.4		10.0	7.2	7.8	3.4	2.0	1.6
2.2	1.6	1.8	Quick	2.5	2.1	2.6	2.0	1.7	1.1
.8	.8	.7		.8	.4	.7	1.0	.9	1.0
4 99.8	0 UND	0 906.4		0 UND	0 UND	0 808.3	7 51.2	1 349.9	9 42.8
19 19.1	9 41.2	13 27.4	Sales/Receivables	1 271.0	7 51.7	3 110.1	42 8.6	28 12.9	41 9.0
49 7.4	43 8.5	45 8.0		16 22.5	47 7.7	39 9.4	53 6.9	42 8.6	77 4.7
			Cost of Sales/Inventory						
			Cost of Sales/Payables						
1.8	1.3	.9		.4	.5	.6	1.9	2.0	4.1
4.4	5.1	3.8	Sales/Working Capital	1.8	2.4	2.2	4.2	8.1	7.4
225.0	23.7	22.8		44.8	-5.1	15.4	22.8	46.0	117.5
	11.8	11.8	5.1		4.1	5.2		2.5	8.8	19.4
(65) 2.0	(54) 2.6	(69) 2.0	EBIT/Interest	(11) 2.1	(20) 1.8	(11) 2.5	(12) 2.8	(12) 2.3
-.8	-.1	.5		.8	-.5	-.5	1.1	.5
			Net Profit + Depr., Dep., Amort./Cur. Mat. L/T/D						
.1	.1	.1		.0	.0	.1	.4	.3	.0
.7	.8	.6	Fixed/Worth	.3	.6	.6	1.0	1.0	.6
1.7	1.5	1.4		1.7	1.0	2.5	1.5	1.4	1.3
.3	.4	.4		.3	.4	.1	.5	.6	.7
1.0	.9	1.0	Debt/Worth	.9	.8	.9	1.1	1.4	1.2
2.5	2.7	1.9		2.2	1.5	5.1	2.5	1.8	5.0
12.7	12.9	12.8		12.4	7.3	10.6	19.5	15.2	18.4
(109) 2.8	(98) 2.7	(118) 3.2	% Profit Before Taxes/Tangible Net Worth	3.0	1.5	(11) 3.6	3.5	7.3	(16) 4.7
-5.2	-4.2	-2.2		-.1	-4.4	-.4	-3.9	-1.4	-13.6
5.9	4.7	6.6		6.2	6.9	5.1	6.2	6.3	10.9
.9	.8	1.6	% Profit Before Taxes/Total Assets	1.7	1.1	2.1	1.4	3.6	1.8
-2.2	-1.6	-.8		.0	-2.6	.1	-.7	-.3	-1.1
42.6	34.9	43.3		69.4	35.6	UND	13.6	38.0	135.1
4.3	2.2	2.6	Sales/Net Fixed Assets	1.6	1.9	1.7	3.1	3.1	7.6
.5	.2	.4		.2	.2	.3	.5	.4	.8
1.8	1.4	1.4		.7	.7	.7	2.7	2.3	2.6
.6	.3	.4	Sales/Total Assets	.1	.2	.2	1.1	1.1	.8
.2	.1	.1		.1	.1	.1	.2	.2	.4
1.0	.9	1.2		1.4	1.2		1.2	.8	.7
(87) 2.0	(82) 3.7	(92) 3.9	% Depr., Dep., Amort./Sales	(19) 13.4	(23) 3.6	(13) 6.1	(17) 2.4	(12) 2.2
5.8	16.0	14.3		22.3	22.4	13.4	6.8	5.7
	3.0	3.1							
	(17) 7.5	(10) 6.7	% Officers', Directors' Owners' Comp/Sales						
	17.8	28.1							
2364355M	1057916M	1591763M	Net Sales ($)	14248M	49084M	47505M	121202M	293428M	1066296M
2440742M	2158283M	3060193M	Total Assets ($)	111791M	263198M	260631M	355469M	761597M	1307507M

M = $ thousand   MM = $ million
See Pages 9 through 22 for Explanation of Ratios and Data

CONSTRUCTION— PERCENTAGE OF COMPLETION BASIS OF ACCOUNTING*

Current Data Sorted by Revenue   Comparative Historical Data

Type of Statement

0-1MM	1-10MM	10-50MM	50 & OVER	ALL		4/1/06-3/31/07 ALL	4/1/07-3/31/08 ALL	4/1/08-3/31/09 ALL	4/1/09-3/31/10 ALL	4/1/10-3/31/11 ALL
			9	10	Unqualified	26	26	25	18	10
			1	1	Reviewed	3	3	6	3	1
1	1		1	2	Compiled	20	17	22	19	2
3	1			4	Tax Returns	5	2	7	9	4
1	5	1	3	10	Other	40	28	24	31	10
0 (4/1-9/30/10)		27 (10/1/10-3/31/11)								
5	8	1	13	27	**NUMBER OF STATEMENTS**	94	76	84	80	27
%	%	%	%	%	**ASSETS**	%	%	%	%	%
			10.9	9.6	Cash & Equivalents	11.8	9.9	11.7	13.1	9.6
			11.1	16.6	A/R - Progress Billings	34.9	32.5	29.5	22.6	16.6
			1.3	.7	A/R - Current Retention	.0	.0	.8	.1	.7
			3.4	9.4	Inventory	7.5	6.8	5.0	5.7	9.4
			.4	.2	Cost & Est. Earnings In Excess Billings	.2	.1	.1	.2	.2
			4.2	2.7	All Other Current	4.4	3.0	1.6	3.2	2.7
			31.4	39.2	Total Current	58.8	52.3	48.8	44.9	39.2
			57.1	44.3	Fixed Assets (net)	30.1	33.6	37.5	40.6	44.3
			.5	1.4	Joint Ventures & Investments	1.4	.8	.9	1.2	1.4
			5.8	6.7	Intangibles (net)	3.5	5.9	4.8	4.0	6.7
			5.2	8.4	All Other Non-Current	6.2	7.4	8.0	9.3	8.4
			100.0	100.0	Total	100.0	100.0	100.0	100.0	100.0
					LIABILITIES					
			1.1	7.2	Notes Payable-Short Term	8.6	6.8	6.5	6.9	7.2
			5.5	8.1	A/P - Trade	11.5	9.2	8.8	7.2	8.1
			.0	.0	A/P - Retention	.3	.0	.1	.0	.0
			3.0	1.4	Billings in Excess of Costs & Est. Earnings	.4	.3	.1	.2	1.4
			.6	.3	Income Taxes Payable	.5	.5	.1	.3	.3
			.4	2.7	Cur. Mat.-L/T/D	2.0	3.8	2.5	3.7	2.7
			5.7	4.0	All Other Current	8.7	6.5	6.3	5.2	4.0
			16.3	23.6	Total Current	31.9	27.0	24.4	23.6	23.6
			25.9	26.5	Long-Term Debt	15.4	16.8	20.6	22.4	26.5
			5.7	2.8	Deferred Taxes	1.1	1.8	1.7	1.7	2.8
			2.6	5.1	All Other Non-Current	3.6	5.5	5.0	5.0	5.1
			49.5	42.0	Net Worth	48.0	48.9	48.3	47.3	42.0
			100.0	100.0	Total Liabilities & Net Worth	100.0	100.0	100.0	100.0	100.0
					INCOME DATA					
			100.0	100.0	Contract Revenues	100.0	100.0	100.0	100.0	100.0
					Gross Profit					
			93.1	89.8	Operating Expenses	83.2	85.0	83.0	91.7	89.8
			6.9	10.2	Operating Profit	16.8	15.0	17.0	8.3	10.2
			3.4	3.3	All Other Expenses (net)	2.4	1.7	2.2	1.8	3.3
			3.6	6.8	Profit Before Taxes	14.4	13.4	14.8	6.6	6.8
					RATIOS					
			3.1	2.7	Current	3.1	3.0	4.2	3.5	2.7
			2.0	1.7		2.0	1.8	2.0	2.2	1.7
			1.4	1.3		1.2	1.1	1.2	1.1	1.3
			4.6	31.5	Receivables/Payables	6.7	10.3	10.1	10.0	31.5
		(12)	3.0	(24) 3.0		(90) 3.3	3.3	(81) 4.3	(72) 3.3	(24) 3.0
			1.2	1.3		1.7	1.9	2.4	1.7	1.3
		51	7.1	26 14.1	Revenues/Receivables	46 8.0	50 7.3	44 8.3	35 10.4	26 14.1
		75	4.8	55 6.6		66 5.6	70 5.2	70 5.2	53 6.8	55 6.6
		86	4.2	87 4.2		88 4.1	90 4.1	86 4.3	69 5.3	87 4.2
					Cost of Revenues/Payables					
			3.2	4.1	Revenues/Working Capital	3.7	4.2	4.5	3.4	4.1
			4.1	7.7		6.9	7.3	7.3	7.3	7.7
			11.1	20.0		16.5	40.5	19.8	45.4	20.0
			12.6	8.7	EBIT/Interest	(88) 23.7	(66) 18.2	(81) 24.9	(70) 8.4	(24) 8.7
		(12)	2.4	(24) 3.3		11.4	8.2	10.2	2.8	3.3
			-.4	.5		4.6	3.8	2.9	-1.0	.5
					Net Profit + Depr., Dep., Amort./Cur. Mat. L/T/D	(11) 20.7	(11) 73.4			
						11.3	6.0			
						7.5	1.1			
			.8	.5	Fixed/Worth	.2	.2	.3	.4	.5
			1.8	1.8		.6	.7	1.0	.9	1.8
			2.0	2.6		1.3	1.9	2.1	2.6	2.6
			.7	.7	Debt/Worth	.4	.4	.4	.3	.7
			1.2	1.8		1.0	1.2	1.2	.9	1.8
			1.9	5.9		2.7	2.6	3.6	3.6	5.9
			22.5	25.5	% Profit Before Taxes/Tangible Net Worth	64.4	54.6	75.9	23.1	25.5
			6.9	(23) 10.5		(90) 42.4	(70) 29.6	(77) 35.3	(70) 7.9	(23) 10.5
			-19.9	-13.9		23.4	15.9	19.5	-8.2	-13.9
			8.4	19.7	% Profit Before Taxes/Total Assets	27.6	22.1	27.4	12.7	19.7
			3.1	5.3		17.6	13.4	14.5	4.2	5.3
			-5.3	.5		8.0	6.0	7.2	-3.7	.5
				2.2	% Depr., Dep., Amort./Revenues	(53) .9	(41) 1.4	(49) 2.0	(49) 2.3	(12) 2.2
			(12)	7.5		2.9	3.7	4.2	4.7	7.5
				19.9		5.8	7.4	9.7	11.4	19.9
				3.5	% Officers', Directors' Owners' Comp/Revenues		3.9	4.3	4.2	3.5
				(24) 5.8			(18) 7.3	(26) 7.1	(22) 7.1	(24) 5.8
				10.8			10.0	13.0	9.6	10.8
3335M	22304M	45746M	9638123M	9709508M	Contract Revenues ($)	28400657M	23858274M	31950373M	20941799M	9709508M
2636M	21998M	27801M	17970352M	18022787M	Total Assets ($)	40507716M	33013528M	39179109M	33995654M	18022787M

M = $ thousand   MM = $ million
See Pages 9 through 22 for Explanation of Ratios and Data

Current Data Sorted by Revenue   **Comparative Historical Data**

Type of Statement

0-1MM	1-10MM	10-50MM	50 & OVER	ALL	Type of Statement	4/1/06-3/31/07	4/1/07-3/31/08	4/1/08-3/31/09	4/1/09-3/31/10	4/1/10-3/31/11
	1	1	2	4	Unqualified	27	28	8	9	4
17	15	4		36	Reviewed	69	71	33	37	36
13	32	7		52	Compiled	95	84	61	65	52
38	65	8	6	117	Tax Returns	202	171	151	128	117
10	33	16	3	62	Other	165	145	102	93	62
32 (4/1-9/30/10)		239 (10/1/10-3/31/11)								
0-1MM	1-10MM	10-50MM	50 & OVER	ALL		ALL	ALL	ALL	ALL	ALL
61	148	47	15	271	NUMBER OF STATEMENTS	558	499	355	332	271

Assets

0-1MM	1-10MM	10-50MM	50 & OVER	ALL	ASSETS	4/1/06-3/31/07	4/1/07-3/31/08	4/1/08-3/31/09	4/1/09-3/31/10	4/1/10-3/31/11
%	%	%	%	%		%	%	%	%	%
6.7	9.4	9.1	9.3	8.7	Cash & Equivalents	8.0	7.4	7.0	9.2	8.7
2.9	7.8	6.7	3.0	6.2	A/R - Progress Billings	6.4	6.5	6.6	6.9	6.2
.0	1.8	4.0	1.2	1.8	A/R - Current Retention	.4	.2	.5	.5	1.8
46.7	50.5	47.2	64.8	49.9	Inventory	54.6	55.3	53.9	50.9	49.9
.6	.8	4.5	2.8	1.5	Cost & Est. Earnings In Excess of Billings	2.2	2.5	1.9	2.2	1.5
4.6	6.7	3.4	6.0	5.6	All Other Current	5.5	6.7	6.3	6.1	5.6
61.4	77.0	75.0	87.1	73.7	Total Current	77.0	78.6	76.1	75.7	73.7
22.0	10.5	5.7	5.9	12.0	Fixed Assets (net)	11.8	11.0	13.3	12.4	12.0
1.4	3.3	4.4	.5	2.9	Joint Ventures & Investments	2.3	2.6	2.2	2.7	2.9
1.5	.9	1.1	.0	1.0	Intangibles (net)	.6	.7	.9	.7	1.0
13.8	8.3	13.8	6.4	10.4	All Other Non-Current	8.3	7.1	7.4	8.4	10.4
100.0	100.0	100.0	100.0	100.0	Total	100.0	100.0	100.0	100.0	100.0

Liabilities

0-1MM	1-10MM	10-50MM	50 & OVER	ALL	LIABILITIES	4/1/06-3/31/07	4/1/07-3/31/08	4/1/08-3/31/09	4/1/09-3/31/10	4/1/10-3/31/11
31.0	33.8	30.5	23.7	32.0	Notes Payable-Short Term	34.5	37.6	38.4	35.4	32.0
5.4	8.9	9.9	3.6	8.0	A/P - Trade	8.6	7.8	8.2	8.0	8.0
.0	.2	.1	.0	.2	A/P - Retention	.3	.3	.2	.2	.2
1.0	1.7	1.8	1.0	1.5	Billings in Excess of Costs & Est. Earnings	2.1	1.0	1.6	2.0	1.5
.1	.1	.0	.0	.1	Income Taxes Payable	.0	.1	.2	.1	.1
7.6	2.5	4.8	6.2	4.3	Cur. Mat.-L/T/D	4.1	4.9	3.8	2.9	4.3
9.8	9.1	8.5	12.8	9.4	All Other Current	9.9	8.2	6.9	8.9	9.4
54.9	56.3	55.6	47.3	55.4	Total Current	59.4	59.8	59.3	57.4	55.4
22.6	15.8	10.5	22.4	16.8	Long-Term Debt	15.2	15.7	16.5	17.4	16.8
.0	.1	.0	.0	.0	Deferred Taxes	.2	.1	.1	.1	.0
11.9	7.5	2.7	11.2	7.9	All Other Non-Current	7.6	7.7	7.4	7.6	7.9
10.7	20.3	31.2	19.1	19.9	Net Worth	17.5	16.6	16.7	17.5	19.9
100.0	100.0	100.0	100.0	100.0	Total Liabilities & Net Worth	100.0	100.0	100.0	100.0	100.0

Income Data

0-1MM	1-10MM	10-50MM	50 & OVER	ALL	INCOME DATA	4/1/06-3/31/07	4/1/07-3/31/08	4/1/08-3/31/09	4/1/09-3/31/10	4/1/10-3/31/11
100.0	100.0	100.0	100.0	100.0	Contract Revenues	100.0	100.0	100.0	100.0	100.0
23.4	16.4	15.0	17.0	17.8	Gross Profit	20.5	17.7	18.0	18.3	17.8
20.3	14.9	13.1	13.6	15.7	Operating Expenses	14.9	14.9	15.3	16.4	15.7
3.0	1.5	1.9	3.4	2.0	Operating Profit	5.6	2.8	2.7	1.9	2.0
4.2	1.5	1.5	1.9	2.1	All Other Expenses (net)	1.5	1.9	2.2	1.7	2.1
-1.1	.1	.4	1.5	-.1	Profit Before Taxes	4.0	1.0	.5	.2	-.1

Ratios

0-1MM	1-10MM	10-50MM	50 & OVER	ALL	RATIOS	4/1/06-3/31/07	4/1/07-3/31/08	4/1/08-3/31/09	4/1/09-3/31/10	4/1/10-3/31/11
5.0	2.4	1.8	4.2	2.4	Current	2.0	2.2	2.2	2.6	2.4
1.3	1.4	1.3	2.3	1.4		1.3	1.2	1.3	1.3	1.4
.5	1.0	1.1	1.6	.9		1.0	1.0	1.0	.9	.9
.7	1.9	1.3	1.8	1.5	Receivables/Payables	1.2	1.0	1.4	1.2	1.5
(25) .1	(110) .2	(44) .5	(12) .4	(191) .3		(424) .1	(394) .1	(260) .1	(245) .1	(191) .3
.0	.0	.0	.0	.0		.0	.0	.0	.0	.0
0 UND	0 UND	0 UND	0 UND	0 UND	Revenues/Receivables	0 UND	0 UND	0 UND	0 UND	0 UND
0 UND	0 UND	4 86.1	2 179.8	0 UND		0 UND	0 UND	0 UND	0 UND	0 UND
0 UND	17 21.0	30 12.2	13 29.1	14 26.1		6 57.0	7 54.0	8 47.0	8 43.3	14 26.1
0 UND	0 UND	8 48.5	6 999.8	0 UND	Cost of Revenues/Payables	0 UND	0 UND	0 UND	0 UND	0 UND
0 UND	10 36.4	16 22.3	6 64.9	10 36.9		10 38.2	10 36.3	7 48.7	8 43.3	10 36.9
25 14.7	26 14.0	42 8.7	20 18.3	27 13.6		28 13.1	26 13.8	26 14.0	28 13.0	27 13.6
1.1	2.7	3.2	1.6	2.5	Revenues/Working Capital	4.0	3.3	2.9	2.4	2.5
11.5	8.6	10.0	3.5	8.7		13.0	10.4	9.0	9.8	8.7
-7.9	-74.6	45.0	15.3	-71.0		UND	159.7	-428.5	-43.5	-71.0
4.5	7.4	8.1		6.9	EBIT/Interest	13.4	8.1	6.0	8.8	6.9
(48) 1.2	(115) 2.7	(38) 1.6		(210) 2.0		(448) 3.5	(407) 2.0	(284) 1.4	(270) 1.3	(210) 2.0
-1.1	.1	.6		-.1		1.2	.4	-.4	-.8	-.1
				25.3	Net Profit + Depr., Dep., Amort./Cur. Mat. L/T/D	13.1	18.2	23.1	3.5	25.3
			(10)	13.1		(22) 3.7	(28) 3.9	(17) 1.9	(17) .5	(10) 13.1
				1.1		1.2	1.1	.2	-1.8	1.1
.0	.0	.0	.0	.0	Fixed/Worth	.0	.0	.0	.0	.0
.2	.2	.1	.1	.1		.2	.2	.2	.2	.1
12.5	2.2	.4	.3	1.9		2.3	2.1	2.6	3.4	1.9
1.8	1.4	1.2	1.0	1.5	Debt/Worth	2.0	2.0	1.7	1.4	1.5
6.1	5.8	2.4	3.3	3.9		5.6	5.6	5.4	4.6	3.9
-26.8	35.0	5.1	22.1	34.1		31.0	39.8	86.8	44.9	34.1
52.0	54.0	24.6	97.6	41.5	% Profit Before Taxes/Tangible Net Worth	74.4	52.4	38.2	38.2	41.5
(43) 9.3	(121) 14.1	(44) 5.7	(14) 16.7	(222) 10.5		(463) 34.0	(404) 17.8	(279) 6.9	(263) 7.8	(222) 10.5
-8.2	-11.0	-3.1	4.9	-8.0		8.7	.3	-10.2	-7.9	-8.0
7.6	10.0	7.5	8.3	9.1	% Profit Before Taxes/Total Assets	13.5	9.0	6.2	8.1	9.1
.6	2.0	1.2	3.6	1.8		4.5	2.3	.7	.7	1.8
-3.1	-3.2	-1.0	1.3	-2.6		.3	-1.4	-3.2	-3.4	-2.6
1.0	.2	.1		.2	% Depr., Dep., Amort./Revenues	.2	.2	.2	.3	.2
(29) 1.8	(98) .5	(37) .2		(170) .6		(325) .5	(309) .5	(217) .6	(197) .7	(170) .6
5.7	1.2	.7		1.3		1.2	1.2	1.2	1.6	1.3
2.7	1.7	.6		1.7	% Officers', Directors' Owners' Comp/Revenues	1.6	1.5	1.6	1.7	1.7
(26) 6.0	(78) 3.0	(18) 1.7		(131) 3.0		(288) 3.2	(253) 2.8	(173) 3.2	(164) 3.1	(131) 3.0
10.0	4.3	2.5		5.5		6.2	5.5	6.6	5.7	5.5
33163M	571015M	1076632M	71307771M	72988581M	Contract Revenues ($)	138951848M	57759246M	28436314M	79940276M	72988581M
60707M	597226M	1236832M	48328942M	50223707M	Total Assets ($)	77391611M	50831635M	33542288M	53992673M	50223707M

© RMA 2011

M = $ thousand   MM = $ million
See Pages 9 through 22 for Explanation of Ratios and Data

Current Data Sorted by Revenue | Comparative Historical Data

Current columns: 0-1MM and 1-10MM under **2 (4/1-9/30/10)**; 10-50MM and 50 & OVER under **26 (10/1/10-3/31/11)**.

Item	0-1MM	1-10MM	10-50MM	50 & OVER	ALL		4/1/06-3/31/07 ALL	4/1/07-3/31/08 ALL	4/1/08-3/31/09 ALL	4/1/09-3/31/10 ALL	4/1/10-3/31/11 ALL
Type of Statement											
Unqualified			1		1		3	1	3	3	1
Reviewed		4	3		7		10	12	6	8	7
Compiled		1			1		3	3	6	6	1
Tax Returns		5	1	1	7		9	16	6	10	7
Other	1	3	4	4	12		14	8	8	10	12
NUMBER OF STATEMENTS	1	13	9	5	28		39	40	29	40	28
	%	%	%	%	%		%	%	%	%	%
ASSETS											
Cash & Equivalents		18.2			18.7		12.0	11.9	10.5	14.9	18.7
A/R - Progress Billings		20.5			11.4		28.9	18.9	11.9	13.7	11.4
A/R - Current Retention		5.8			16.9		1.0	.1	1.5	1.3	16.9
Inventory		20.5			24.2		22.0	15.7	39.4	25.8	24.2
Cost & Est. Earnings In Excess Billings		1.5			2.0		5.3	2.1	1.1	2.2	2.0
All Other Current		12.2			9.9		9.4	8.1	12.6	11.3	9.9
Total Current		78.8			83.0		78.6	56.8	76.9	69.1	83.0
Fixed Assets (net)		15.3			10.1		13.1	25.5	16.0	20.6	10.1
Joint Ventures & Investments		.0			.4		3.3	2.8	1.1	1.7	.4
Intangibles (net)		.0			1.8		.9	2.7	.0	.4	1.8
All Other Non-Current		5.9			4.7		4.1	12.2	6.0	8.2	4.7
Total		100.0			100.0		100.0	100.0	100.0	100.0	100.0
LIABILITIES											
Notes Payable-Short Term		25.5			19.3		20.2	14.1	17.1	21.5	19.3
A/P - Trade		13.4			18.2		19.6	10.8	15.3	11.6	18.2
A/P - Retention		.8			4.1		.1	1.4	.9	.4	4.1
Billings in Excess of Costs & Est. Earnings		2.3			4.6		3.0	4.0	2.2	1.9	4.6
Income Taxes Payable		.0			.0		.0	.0	.1	.1	.0
Cur. Mat.-L/T/D		9.8			7.1		2.8	5.2	3.3	10.8	7.1
All Other Current		3.9			4.9		6.4	12.4	7.5	6.9	4.9
Total Current		55.7			58.2		52.2	47.9	46.3	53.2	58.2
Long-Term Debt		12.9			11.0		15.2	26.0	26.0	30.6	11.0
Deferred Taxes		.0			.0		.3	.1	.1	.3	.0
All Other Non-Current		9.3			5.7		14.3	7.6	2.4	4.7	5.7
Net Worth		22.0			25.1		18.0	18.4	25.2	11.2	25.1
Total Liabilities & Net Worth		100.0			100.0		100.0	100.0	100.0	100.0	100.0
INCOME DATA											
Contract Revenues		100.0			100.0		100.0	100.0	100.0	100.0	100.0
Gross Profit		16.9			16.0		19.7	24.8	13.6	23.4	16.0
Operating Expenses		13.2			12.1		14.7	21.0	14.9	23.3	12.1
Operating Profit		3.7			3.9		5.0	3.7	-1.2	.1	3.9
All Other Expenses (net)		.1			2.0		1.0	1.8	2.7	2.8	2.0
Profit Before Taxes		3.6			2.0		3.9	1.9	-3.9	-2.7	2.0
RATIOS											
Current		3.1			2.2		2.8	3.0	3.1	3.9	2.2
		1.9			1.4		1.5	1.3	1.5	1.6	1.4
		.8			1.2		1.1	.5	1.0	1.1	1.2
Receivables/Payables		6.3			3.0		3.0	3.6	1.1	2.3	3.0
		(11) 2.3			(25) 1.3		(33) 1.8	(31) 1.3	(27) .3	(33) .6	(25) 1.3
		.8			.5		.7	.0	.0	.0	.5
Revenues/Receivables		0 999.8			0 818.5		0 UND	0 UND	0 UND	0 UND	0 818.5
		27 13.5			45 8.1		34 10.7	2 159.0	4 96.5	4 82.0	45 8.1
		71 5.2			75 4.9		68 5.4	54 6.8	44 8.3	49 7.4	75 4.9
Cost of Revenues/Payables		1 568.3			9 38.5		5 67.3	0 UND	15 24.4	1 333.9	9 38.5
		13 27.3			35 10.4		24 15.2	11 31.9	31 11.6	28 12.9	35 10.4
		40 9.1			78 4.7		47 7.8	41 8.8	63 5.8	58 6.2	78 4.7
Revenues/Working Capital		5.2			4.7		5.1	6.6	1.7	1.4	4.7
		8.1			8.9		9.5	18.4	11.2	6.4	8.9
		-20.0			21.3		29.4	-7.9	37.8	157.5	21.3
EBIT/Interest					63.5		12.0	21.2	21.0	7.3	63.5
					(15) 7.6		(31) 4.8	(33) 2.3	(20) 3.5	(29) 1.5	(15) 7.6
					2.2		1.0	.4	1.1	-2.9	2.2
Net Profit + Depr., Dep., Amort./Cur. Mat. L/T/D											
Fixed/Worth		.1			.0		.0	.1	.0	.0	.0
		.4			.1		.3	.4	.2	.3	.1
		4.5			1.0		.8	9.1	1.0	7.7	1.0
Debt/Worth		1.2			1.4		1.4	1.5	1.3	1.1	1.4
		2.7			3.1		3.1	5.1	4.3	2.4	3.1
		17.4			8.8		14.7	117.8	15.7	10.4	8.8
% Profit Before Taxes/Tangible Net Worth		80.3			68.3		81.2	74.1	32.8	28.6	68.3
		(11) 17.8			(24) 17.2		(35) 34.8	(31) 21.4	(25) 9.5	(33) 1.5	(24) 17.2
		2.7			3.9		4.9	-.3	-5.2	-21.8	3.9
% Profit Before Taxes/Total Assets		21.1			12.2		18.8	13.7	6.8	9.7	12.2
		4.8			4.4		7.9	3.4	3.2	.7	4.4
		.4			.8		.1	-.9	-2.5	-6.0	.8
% Depr., Dep., Amort./Revenues		.2			.1		.2	.3	.2	.4	.1
		(10) .3			(17) .2		(25) .6	(24) 1.5	(16) .8	(24) .7	(17) .2
		1.4			.7		1.2	2.7	2.2	1.8	.7
% Officers', Directors' Owners' Comp/Revenues					.8		.9	1.5	1.0	1.4	.8
					(12) 1.8		(15) 2.9	(20) 2.1	(10) 2.7	(17)	(12) 1.8
					2.2		5.0	7.9	11.6	11.5	2.2
Contract Revenues ($)	171M	56266M	232209M	1327992M	1616638M		3312017M	10557982M	6008892M	5589802M	1616638M
Total Assets ($)	2175M	27691M	102194M	6313319M	6445379M		5192073M	14682719M	7603974M	8343364M	6445379M

M = $ thousand   MM = $ million

See Pages 9 through 22 for Explanation of Ratios and Data

Current Data Sorted by Revenue   Comparative Historical Data

	0-1MM	1-10MM	10-50MM	50 & OVER	ALL		4/1/06-3/31/07 ALL	4/1/07-3/31/08 ALL	4/1/08-3/31/09 ALL	4/1/09-3/31/10 ALL	4/1/10-3/31/11 ALL
Type of Statement											
Unqualified	1	1	1	1	4		8	13	3	2	4
Reviewed	1	1	1		3		7	19	2	6	3
Compiled		1	2		3		20	21	9	10	3
Tax Returns	3	5	1		9		29	31	19	6	9
Other		6	1	1	8		23	32	16	15	8
	4 (4/1-9/30/10)		23 (10/1/10-3/31/11)								
NUMBER OF STATEMENTS	5	14	6	2	27		87	116	49	39	27
	%	%	%	%	%	**ASSETS**	%	%	%	%	%
Cash & Equivalents		9.3			11.0		9.3	6.9	6.9	6.8	11.0
A/R - Progress Billings		12.2			9.7		5.0	3.8	3.4	4.7	9.7
A/R - Current Retention		1.8			3.3		.0	.1	.4	1.0	3.3
Inventory		26.9			30.2		55.8	57.5	58.1	53.6	30.2
Cost & Est. Earnings In Excess Billings		4.8			2.5		2.2	4.0	.6	.7	2.5
All Other Current		2.6			8.1		5.8	5.5	4.6	8.5	8.1
Total Current		57.5			65.0		78.1	77.8	73.9	75.3	65.0
Fixed Assets (net)		21.0			18.7		13.0	13.6	15.1	15.5	18.7
Joint Ventures & Investments		.0			.5		1.2	1.3	1.1	2.9	.5
Intangibles (net)		.0			.0		.8	.3	.0	.0	.0
All Other Non-Current		21.5			15.8		6.9	6.9	9.8	6.3	15.8
Total		100.0			100.0		100.0	100.0	100.0	100.0	100.0
						LIABILITIES					
Notes Payable-Short Term		20.9			18.1		38.5	39.5	31.2	20.0	18.1
A/P - Trade		8.4			10.1		8.9	6.5	7.5	4.4	10.1
A/P - Retention		.6			.3		.5	.3	.0	.0	.3
Billings in Excess of Costs & Est. Earnings		.6			1.5		.5	.7	.3	.6	1.5
Income Taxes Payable		.0			.0		.0	.0	.1	.0	.0
Cur. Mat.-L/T/D		3.1			2.0		4.0	2.6	3.6	5.0	2.0
All Other Current		7.3			8.3		10.0	8.6	5.1	9.0	8.3
Total Current		40.7			40.3		62.5	58.3	47.9	39.0	40.3
Long-Term Debt		19.2			20.6		11.7	14.2	20.5	17.6	20.6
Deferred Taxes		.0			.0		.1	.4	.2	.2	.0
All Other Non-Current		16.8			12.5		7.1	6.8	14.6	12.5	12.5
Net Worth		23.2			26.7		18.5	20.2	16.7	30.7	26.7
Total Liabilities & Net Worth		100.0			100.0		100.0	100.0	100.0	100.0	100.0
						INCOME DATA					
Contract Revenues		100.0			100.0		100.0	100.0	100.0	100.0	100.0
Gross Profit		31.6			27.2		18.4	18.1	17.4	17.1	27.2
Operating Expenses		25.6			22.8		12.1	14.2	16.3	19.3	22.8
Operating Profit		6.0			4.4		6.3	3.9	1.0	-2.2	4.4
All Other Expenses (net)		3.5			4.0		1.3	3.1	3.7	4.4	4.0
Profit Before Taxes		2.5			.4		5.0	.9	-2.7	-6.6	.4
						RATIOS					
Current		2.8			3.9		1.7	1.9	2.9	4.3	3.9
		1.3			1.4		1.3	1.2	1.5	1.7	1.4
		.7			1.1		1.0	1.1	1.1	1.0	1.1
Receivables/Payables		1.5			1.6		.8	.9	.4	2.0	1.6
		(12) .0		(25)	.1		(63) .1	(97) .1	(41) .0	(35) .1	(25) .1
		.0			.0		.0		.0	.0	.0
Revenues/Receivables	0 UND				0 UND		0 UND	0 UND	0 UND	0 UND	0 UND
	0 999.8				0 999.8		0 UND	0 999.8	0 UND	1 479.0	0 999.8
	15 23.8				27 13.6		6 62.8	7 55.7	2 158.3	9 41.3	27 13.6
Cost of Revenues/Payables	0 UND				1 411.9		0 UND	1 422.7	1 258.2	0 797.0	1 411.9
	31 11.8				17 21.4		13 28.9	12 30.0	16 22.2	12 30.9	17 21.4
	42 8.7				41 8.8		28 13.0	34 10.7	51 7.1	29 12.8	41 8.8
Revenues/Working Capital		4.5			2.6		3.3	3.4	1.6	.8	2.6
		25.5			16.5		15.8	9.2	4.3	6.1	16.5
		-23.1			493.5		-47.8	-140.5	42.9	50.0	493.5
EBIT/Interest					5.2		13.9	5.5	4.2	2.2	5.2
				(17)	2.1		(70) 4.0	(83) 1.8	(41) .8	(23) 1.1	(17) 2.1
					1.3		1.0	.9	-.8	-3.1	1.3
Net Profit + Depr., Dep., Amort./Cur. Mat. L/T/D											
Fixed/Worth		.0			.0		.0	.0	.0	.0	.0
		.2			.1		.2	.1	.2	.2	.1
		2.6			1.1		1.6	1.0	1.4	.8	1.1
Debt/Worth		1.7			1.8		2.0	2.0	1.5	1.1	1.8
		3.2			4.1		4.9	5.7	2.9	2.4	4.1
		22.2			9.9		35.7	24.3	23.0	6.3	9.9
% Profit Before Taxes/Tangible Net Worth		104.2			34.7		59.5	60.2	30.2	9.0	34.7
		(12) 29.5		(24)	13.2		(75) 32.5	(101) 16.4	(41) 5.3	(33) -2.5	(24) 13.2
		.3			.4		5.5	1.4	-6.6	-22.8	.4
% Profit Before Taxes/Total Assets		6.7			6.0		16.7	7.6	3.0	3.2	6.0
		2.9			2.4		6.7	1.7	.1	-2.0	2.4
		-.8			.1		.3	-1.3	-2.9	-8.1	.1
% Depr., Dep., Amort./Revenues					.1		.2	.1	.3	.2	.1
				(20)	.4		(52) .4	(63) .4	(26) .5	(24) .5	(20) .4
					1.6		.9	1.3	1.4	1.5	1.6
% Officers', Directors' Owners' Comp/Revenues							1.1	1.0	.8	1.3	
							(39) 3.0	(44) 2.7	(20) 1.8	(10) 1.8	
							4.8	5.3	4.0	5.2	
Contract Revenues ($)	3792M	58725M	163905M	395393M	621815M		46391476M	16442642M	1697106M	514409M	621815M
Total Assets ($)	2950M	81784M	235298M	361729M	681761M		42797135M	15806132M	2773168M	1224331M	681761M

M = $ thousand   MM = $ million
See Pages 9 through 22 for Explanation of Ratios and Data

CONSTRUCTION—% OF COMPLETION—Residential Remodelers NAICS 236118

Current Data Sorted by Revenue | Comparative Historical Data

0-1MM	1-10MM	10-50MM	50 & OVER	ALL	Type of Statement	4/1/06-3/31/07 ALL	4/1/07-3/31/08 ALL	4/1/08-3/31/09 ALL	4/1/09-3/31/10 ALL	4/1/10-3/31/11 ALL
	2	1		3	Unqualified		1			
2	3	2		7	Reviewed	4	4	3	3	3
2	7	1	2	12	Compiled	6	3	4	6	7
4	6	1	1	13	Tax Returns	14	20	14	14	12
					Other	12	9	8	4	13
8	18	5	4	35	**NUMBER OF STATEMENTS**	36	37	29	27	35
%	%	%	%	%	**ASSETS**	%	%	%	%	%
	17.2			18.0	Cash & Equivalents	16.6	15.3	21.3	24.1	18.0
	20.7			21.2	A/R - Progress Billings	17.3	14.3	18.2	12.5	21.2
	5.4			5.2	A/R - Current Retention	1.1	1.0	.0	.0	5.2
	14.0			10.8	Inventory	14.9	13.5	14.7	11.6	10.8
	6.9			5.7	Cost & Est. Earnings In Excess Billings	1.3	3.3	1.0	1.7	5.7
	6.1			3.2	All Other Current	12.9	10.3	7.4	2.4	3.2
	70.2			64.2	Total Current	64.2	57.7	62.6	52.3	64.2
	25.5			24.9	Fixed Assets (net)	22.9	27.2	22.1	33.8	24.9
	.0			.0	Joint Ventures & Investments	1.2	.0	.4	2.0	.0
	.5			3.1	Intangibles (net)	3.1	2.5	2.7	.0	3.1
	3.8			7.8	All Other Non-Current	8.6	12.5	12.1	11.8	7.8
	100.0			100.0	Total	100.0	100.0	100.0	100.0	100.0
					LIABILITIES					
	30.4			24.0	Notes Payable-Short Term	10.4	25.6	21.2	15.0	24.0
	14.9			14.0	A/P - Trade	12.0	20.1	10.2	17.9	14.0
	.0			.0	A/P - Retention	3.0	.0	.0	.0	.0
	5.2			4.5	Billings in Excess of Costs & Est. Earnings	3.2	4.7	3.3	1.1	4.5
	.2			.1	Income Taxes Payable	.0	.0	.0	.0	.1
	2.1			2.3	Cur. Mat.-L/T/D	6.2	4.0	4.5	8.2	2.3
	11.2			16.4	All Other Current	8.8	12.6	14.0	18.2	16.4
	64.0			61.3	Total Current	43.7	67.1	53.1	60.4	61.3
	8.4			9.5	Long-Term Debt	20.0	20.6	15.9	27.1	9.5
	.6			.3	Deferred Taxes	.0	.0	1.1	.0	.3
	6.0			5.0	All Other Non-Current	10.3	13.5	6.4	10.6	5.0
	21.0			23.9	Net Worth	26.0	-1.2	23.6	1.8	23.9
	100.0			100.0	Total Liabilties & Net Worth	100.0	100.0	100.0	100.0	100.0
					INCOME DATA					
	100.0			100.0	Contract Revenues	100.0	100.0	100.0	100.0	100.0
	32.8			35.4	Gross Profit	30.3	30.2	36.3	33.1	35.4
	30.5			30.5	Operating Expenses	26.5	30.2	31.6	28.2	30.5
	2.3			5.0	Operating Profit	3.8	.0	4.7	4.8	5.0
	.9			.4	All Other Expenses (net)	.4	.9	.7	.5	.4
	1.4			4.5	Profit Before Taxes	3.4	-.9	4.0	4.3	4.5
					RATIOS					
	2.6			2.5	Current	3.9	1.7	3.8	4.0	2.5
	1.3			1.2		1.6	.9	1.3	.9	1.2
	.8			.7		.9	.4	.6	.5	.7
	6.1			6.1	Receivables/Payables	5.1	3.6	8.8	1.6	6.1
	(15) 1.7		(27)	1.7		(28) 1.4	(22) .6	(19) 2.7	(20) .8	(27) 1.7
	1.2			1.2		.3	.2	1.0	.2	1.2
1	500.4		0	862.8	Revenues/Receivables	0 UND	0 UND	0 UND	0 UND	0 862.8
32	11.3		31	11.8		8 43.3	0 UND	6 58.3	4 82.1	31 11.8
50	7.3		50	7.3		32 11.5	18 20.0	40 9.2	14 25.3	50 7.3
0	UND		0	UND	Cost of Revenues/Payables	0 UND	0 UND	0 UND	0 UND	0 UND
26	14.1		20	18.5		14 25.6	15 24.5	5 68.8	9 40.1	20 18.5
39	9.4		38	9.7		31 11.6	33 10.9	20 18.5	19 19.2	38 9.7
	6.0			6.6	Revenues/Working Capital	8.8	9.0	7.8	5.5	6.6
	18.9			61.4		17.5	-259.2	28.6	-260.1	61.4
	-30.1			-25.8		-61.6	-11.2	-21.2	-25.6	-25.8
	49.1			27.6	EBIT/Interest	36.0	6.5	28.8	37.0	27.6
	(15) 7.1		(29)	7.1		(30) 6.6	(26) 1.8	(22) 5.7	(23) 14.0	(29) 7.1
	-8.7			-3.1		.2	-1.6	1.3	-.6	-3.1
					Net Profit + Depr., Dep., Amort./Cur. Mat. L/T/D					
	.1			.1	Fixed/Worth	.0	.2	.1	.3	.1
	.5			.6		.3	1.8	.4	1.5	.6
	2.4			3.8		6.3	-2.7	4.4	UND	3.8
	.6			.5	Debt/Worth	.8	1.3	1.2	.7	.5
	2.2			2.6		2.4	6.3	2.4	5.6	2.6
	8.9			13.3		19.6	-7.9	15.0	UND	13.3
	37.8			93.4	% Profit Before Taxes/Tangible Net Worth	85.2	99.1	115.3	102.3	93.4
	(15) 30.6		(28)	32.4		(29) 41.7	(24) 28.5	(24) 64.2	(21) 53.3	(28) 32.4
	-14.2			-7.7		17.5	3.3	15.5	2.1	-7.7
	25.0			25.3	% Profit Before Taxes/Total Assets	37.4	19.3	37.5	44.3	25.3
	10.0			8.6		12.7	1.6	17.2	20.0	8.6
	-17.6			-4.8		-.4	-9.2	.9	-4.8	-4.8
	.7			.6	% Depr., Dep., Amort./Revenues	.3	.4	.5	.4	.6
	(13) .9		(23)	.9		(16) 1.2	(23) 1.1	(18) 1.0	(23) .9	(23) .9
	1.9			2.0		2.3	1.9	2.1	2.2	2.0
	2.2			2.8	% Officers', Directors' Owners' Comp/Revenues	2.3	2.3	3.4	3.5	2.8
	(11) 3.7		(22)	4.9		(15) 4.6	(20) 5.3	(18) 5.6	(18) 5.1	(22) 4.9
	5.1			8.7		8.7	9.5	11.3	7.8	8.7
3668M	76980M	114576M	4086003M	4281227M	Contract Revenues ($)	5774697M	4824907M	289684M	86698M	4281227M
1495M	31037M	36526M	817635M	886693M	Total Assets ($)	1537369M	1154223M	72207M	23180M	886693M

M = $ thousand   MM = $ million
See Pages 9 through 22 for Explanation of Ratios and Data

Current Data Sorted by Revenue   **Comparative Historical Data**

0-1MM	1-10MM	10-50MM	50 & OVER	ALL	Type of Statement	4/1/06-3/31/07	4/1/07-3/31/08	4/1/08-3/31/09	4/1/09-3/31/10	4/1/10-3/31/11
	2	5	1	8	Unqualified	31	23	20	19	8
	22	22	1	45	Reviewed	48	42	34	35	45
1	6			7	Compiled	11	15	11	8	7
2	7	2		11	Tax Returns	16	18	10	6	11
2	6	13	13	34	Other	14	35	17	20	34
	17 (4/1-9/30/10)		88 (10/1/10-3/31/11)			ALL	ALL	ALL	ALL	ALL
5	43	42	15	105	**NUMBER OF STATEMENTS**	120	133	92	88	105
%	%	%	%	%	**ASSETS**	%	%	%	%	%
	16.9	19.4	21.8	18.2	Cash & Equivalents	17.4	18.6	21.2	23.0	18.2
	32.7	23.1	12.2	25.9	A/R - Progress Billings	37.2	38.1	35.6	33.9	25.9
	7.7	27.7	33.1	19.0	A/R - Current Retention	4.0	2.9	2.6	2.6	19.0
	4.3	1.2	2.6	3.0	Inventory	6.4	2.7	2.2	2.4	3.0
	6.6	6.3	5.6	6.1	Cost & Est. Earnings In Excess Billings	4.7	4.0	4.5	4.1	6.1
	6.3	4.4	4.5	5.0	All Other Current	5.6	6.3	6.5	6.4	5.0
	74.5	82.1	79.9	77.2	Total Current	75.4	72.6	72.6	72.4	77.2
	16.8	12.6	14.1	14.8	Fixed Assets (net)	17.6	18.2	19.0	18.6	14.8
	.4	.0	.1	.4	Joint Ventures & Investments	.8	.5	.4	.7	.4
	2.3	1.2	1.7	1.6	Intangibles (net)	.7	1.1	1.5	1.8	1.6
	6.0	4.2	4.1	5.9	All Other Non-Current	5.5	7.7	6.4	6.5	5.9
	100.0	100.0	100.0	100.0	Total	100.0	100.0	100.0	100.0	100.0
					LIABILITIES					
	5.4	4.0	.4	4.1	Notes Payable-Short Term	7.0	7.6	3.6	5.3	4.1
	30.0	37.6	29.4	32.9	A/P - Trade	26.5	25.6	25.2	25.8	32.9
	1.2	2.1	4.7	2.0	A/P - Retention	.9	1.7	1.7	1.2	2.0
	5.9	11.0	13.8	8.8	Billings in Excess of Costs & Est. Earnings	8.1	7.8	9.2	7.9	8.8
	.6	.1	.7	.4	Income Taxes Payable	.6	.4	.3	.5	.4
	1.5	1.7	2.2	2.3	Cur. Mat.-L/T/D	3.4	3.2	2.9	2.3	2.3
	7.7	5.8	6.6	6.7	All Other Current	9.2	6.8	6.4	7.7	6.7
	52.3	62.3	57.8	57.1	Total Current	55.8	52.9	49.3	50.7	57.1
	6.4	4.7	9.5	6.7	Long-Term Debt	10.7	10.7	9.1	7.5	6.7
	.9	.3	.4	.5	Deferred Taxes	.6	.7	.9	.7	.5
	8.9	2.6	1.3	5.4	All Other Non-Current	3.4	3.8	5.0	4.5	5.4
	31.5	30.1	31.0	30.2	Net Worth	29.5	31.9	35.8	36.5	30.2
	100.0	100.0	100.0	100.0	Total Liabilities & Net Worth	100.0	100.0	100.0	100.0	100.0
					INCOME DATA					
	100.0	100.0	100.0	100.0	Contract Revenues	100.0	100.0	100.0	100.0	100.0
	19.6	11.4	10.5	16.4	Gross Profit	17.2	19.4	17.1	19.2	16.4
	19.5	9.1	8.2	14.3	Operating Expenses	13.9	14.7	12.8	16.6	14.3
	.1	2.4	2.3	2.1	Operating Profit	3.3	4.7	4.3	2.6	2.1
	.0	.2	-.5	.0	All Other Expenses (net)	-.1	.0	.1	.5	.0
	.1	2.2	2.9	2.1	Profit Before Taxes	3.4	4.7	4.2	2.2	2.1
					RATIOS					
	2.3	1.6	1.7	1.8	Current	1.7	1.9	2.0	1.8	1.8
	1.5	1.3	1.3	1.4		1.4	1.3	1.4	1.4	1.4
	1.2	1.2	1.2	1.2		1.1	1.1	1.2	1.2	1.2
	2.1	2.1	2.0	2.0	Receivables/Payables	3.2	2.8	2.6	2.3	2.0
	1.3	1.2	1.3 (104)	1.3		(113) 1.5	(122) 1.5	(88) 1.4	(86) 1.4	(104) 1.3
	.8	1.0	1.0	.9		1.0	1.0	.9	1.0	.9
27 13.4	34 10.6	44 8.2	34 10.9		Revenues/Receivables	23 15.7	33 11.2	23 15.9	30 12.1	34 10.9
47 7.8	59 6.2	59 6.1	55 6.7			48 7.6	48 7.6	39 9.4	50 7.3	55 6.7
80 4.5	78 4.7	66 5.5	75 4.9			74 4.9	73 5.0	60 6.0	67 5.4	75 4.9
19 19.5	26 14.2	35 10.3	26 14.3		Cost of Revenues/Payables	13 28.2	15 23.7	18 20.5	18 19.8	26 14.3
41 8.9	47 7.7	46 7.9	44 8.2			34 10.7	38 9.7	30 12.1	39 9.4	44 8.2
62 5.8	63 5.8	60 6.0	62 5.9			57 6.4	60 6.0	52 7.0	59 6.2	62 5.9
	4.8	9.2	9.5	7.4	Revenues/Working Capital	8.0	8.7	7.8	7.1	7.4
	10.6	17.9	14.3	13.7		16.2	16.7	14.8	12.8	13.7
	25.6	33.1	30.6	32.8		37.6	49.6	38.3	32.5	32.8
	19.0	48.5	412.9	31.8	EBIT/Interest	39.0	32.2	69.6	67.8	31.8
(32)	1.5	(35) 6.2	(11) 26.9	(82) 4.5		(109) 10.1	(112) 9.0	(74) 15.4	(66) 6.3	(82) 4.5
	-7.6	1.2	1.6	-1.1		2.9	3.6	2.2	-.4	-1.1
	5.7	13.3		7.9	Net Profit + Depr., Dep., Amort./Cur. Mat. L/T/D	5.4	10.9	12.9	6.1	7.9
(12)	1.4	(13) 6.2		(27) 5.4		(39) 3.5	(37) 3.4	(24) 5.4	(17) 3.2	(27) 5.4
	-4.0	3.0		.3		1.0	1.5	2.3	.2	.3
	.1	.1	.1	.1	Fixed/Worth	.2	.2	.2	.1	.1
	.3	.3	.2	.3		.4	.4	.4	.4	.3
	1.0	.8	.9	.8		1.1	.9	.8	1.0	.8
	.8	1.4	1.3	1.1	Debt/Worth	1.2	1.0	.9	.8	1.1
	1.4	2.5	2.3	2.2		2.4	1.9	2.0	1.8	2.2
	3.0	4.5	3.8	3.8		6.2	4.4	3.6	3.2	3.8
	26.3	41.8	46.4	35.4	% Profit Before Taxes/Tangible Net Worth	62.6	52.2	51.9	49.9	35.4
(38)	6.0	(40) 14.4	(14) 25.2	(96) 12.3		(109) 30.7	(123) 33.7	(90) 30.8	(82) 20.7	(96) 12.3
	-23.7	1.5	8.5	.1		11.5	12.3	14.4	.6	.1
	6.3	13.0	14.9	11.2	% Profit Before Taxes/Total Assets	17.7	23.1	20.4	16.4	11.2
	1.6	3.7	5.3	3.3		7.7	9.8	9.9	5.3	3.3
	-9.8	.3	2.5	-1.8		2.6	3.9	2.7	-1.2	-1.8
	.5	.2	.3	.3	% Depr., Dep., Amort./Revenues	.3	.3	.3	.4	.3
(36)	1.0	(40) .5	(10) .4	(88) .7		(108) .8	(115) .8	(82) .8	(69) .8	(88) .7
	2.2	1.2	1.8	1.9		1.5	1.8	1.6	1.9	1.9
	1.7	1.1		1.2	% Officers', Directors' Owners' Comp/Revenues	1.4	1.0	.9	1.1	1.2
(20)	2.4	(20) 2.0		(45) 2.2		(56) 2.8	(57) 2.1	(37) 2.3	(36) 3.3	(45) 2.2
	4.4	2.8		3.8		4.3	5.0	4.1	6.9	3.8
4391M	212460M	1096036M	5064371M	6377258M	Contract Revenues ($)	47794599M	8516638M	31034859M	10494772M	6377258M
14880M	97343M	362012M	2758586M	3232821M	Total Assets ($)	16179798M	2949634M	9777481M	6040337M	3232821M

Current Data Sorted by Revenue · **Comparative Historical Data**

	0-1MM	1-10MM	10-50MM	50 & OVER	ALL	4/1/06-3/31/07 ALL	4/1/07-3/31/08 ALL	4/1/08-3/31/09 ALL	4/1/09-3/31/10 ALL	4/1/10-3/31/11 ALL
Type of Statement										
Unqualified	1	10	17	22	50	98	98	86	66	50
Reviewed	3	87	70	7	167	171	159	159	127	167
Compiled	3	14	1	2	20	26	26	23	18	20
Tax Returns	4	17	6	3	30	31	34	16	18	30
Other	3	33	31	24	91	76	57	46	49	91
	63 (4/1-9/30/10)		295 (10/1/10-3/31/11)							
NUMBER OF STATEMENTS	14	161	125	58	358	402	374	330	278	358
ASSETS	%	%	%	%	%	%	%	%	%	%
Cash & Equivalents	25.5	22.4	26.5	29.4	25.1	21.3	21.8	24.6	28.5	25.1
A/R - Progress Billings	18.2	30.2	26.6	22.8	27.2	39.6	39.2	38.1	32.5	27.2
A/R - Current Retention	3.2	11.7	19.0	18.1	14.9	2.8	3.0	3.1	3.0	14.9
Inventory	1.7	2.0	.5	5.6	2.0	4.0	3.1	3.1	2.3	2.0
Cost & Est. Earnings In Excess Billings	1.0	5.3	5.7	3.5	5.0	4.7	4.8	3.9	3.7	5.0
All Other Current	10.2	3.0	6.0	6.8	5.0	5.4	6.6	5.8	6.6	5.0
Total Current	59.8	74.5	84.4	86.1	79.2	77.8	78.5	78.6	76.6	79.2
Fixed Assets (net)	34.3	16.3	8.9	5.8	12.7	14.1	13.8	13.6	15.1	12.7
Joint Ventures & Investments	1.2	.8	.8	2.7	1.1	1.9	2.3	1.7	1.2	1.1
Intangibles (net)	.0	1.0	.4	1.7	.9	.8	.8	1.0	1.1	.9
All Other Non-Current	4.7	7.4	5.5	3.7	6.0	5.4	4.6	5.0	6.1	6.0
Total	100.0	100.0	100.0	100.0	100.0	100.0	100.0	100.0	100.0	100.0
LIABILITIES										
Notes Payable-Short Term	6.5	9.8	2.7	1.3	5.8	6.8	6.8	4.7	7.4	5.8
A/P - Trade	8.5	25.1	37.3	30.5	29.6	30.2	31.1	29.2	26.3	29.6
A/P - Retention	.5	1.4	3.4	4.9	2.6	1.8	1.8	2.4	2.1	2.6
Billings in Excess of Costs & Est. Earnings	9.8	7.6	8.9	9.5	8.5	7.6	7.5	8.8	6.9	8.5
Income Taxes Payable	1.0	.6	.2	.2	.4	.5	.3	.4	.3	.4
Cur. Mat.-L/T/D	9.9	2.3	1.6	.8	2.1	2.0	2.1	2.0	2.0	2.1
All Other Current	9.8	6.7	6.1	10.5	7.2	8.9	8.5	7.4	9.4	7.2
Total Current	45.9	53.5	60.1	57.7	56.2	57.7	58.2	54.9	54.4	56.2
Long-Term Debt	13.9	9.1	4.0	4.3	6.7	7.5	7.3	6.6	7.0	6.7
Deferred Taxes	.6	.3	.3	.4	.3	.5	.5	.5	.6	.3
All Other Non-Current	47.6	3.2	2.5	2.2	4.5	2.2	2.2	2.2	2.9	4.5
Net Worth	-8.1	34.0	33.1	35.5	32.2	32.0	31.8	35.9	35.1	32.2
Total Liabilities & Net Worth	100.0	100.0	100.0	100.0	100.0	100.0	100.0	100.0	100.0	100.0
INCOME DATA										
Contract Revenues	100.0	100.0	100.0	100.0	100.0	100.0	100.0	100.0	100.0	100.0
Gross Profit	32.7	19.1	11.6	11.8	15.8	17.2	16.4	15.4	17.4	15.8
Operating Expenses	32.5	18.5	10.1	9.5	14.7	12.9	12.8	12.2	15.8	14.7
Operating Profit	.1	.6	1.5	2.3	1.1	4.3	3.6	3.2	1.6	1.1
All Other Expenses (net)	1.2	.2	.0	.4	.2	-.1	.3	.2	.4	.2
Profit Before Taxes	-1.0	.4	1.4	1.8	.9	4.4	3.3	3.0	1.3	.9
RATIOS										
Current	3.6	2.1	1.7	1.9	2.0	1.9	1.8	1.9	2.1	2.0
	2.4	1.5	1.4	1.4	1.4	1.4	1.4	1.4	1.5	1.4
	1.3	1.1	1.2	1.2	1.1	1.2	1.2	1.2	1.2	1.1
Receivables/Payables		2.9	1.6	1.9	2.2	2.1	1.9	2.1	1.9	2.2
		(156) 1.6	(124) 1.2	(57) 1.2	(346) 1.3	(381) 1.3	(356) 1.3	(319) 1.3	(266) 1.3	(346) 1.3
		1.0	1.0	.9	.9	.9	.9	.9	.9	.9
Revenues/Receivables	0 UND	32 11.4	38 9.5	36 10.2	33 11.0	30 12.2	27 13.7	29 12.8	23 15.5	33 11.0
	19 19.6	54 6.7	54 6.8	56 6.5	54 6.8	49 7.4	48 7.6	48 7.7	44 8.3	54 6.8
	89 4.1	84 4.3	71 5.1	70 5.2	76 4.8	70 5.2	69 5.3	66 5.6	64 5.7	76 4.8
Cost of Revenues/Payables	0 UND	22 16.6	36 10.1	25 14.8	25 14.6	22 16.8	21 17.1	20 18.5	20 18.4	25 14.6
	22 16.9	40 9.2	52 7.0	54 6.7	46 7.9	40 9.2	43 8.5	39 9.4	40 9.0	46 7.9
	34 10.9	70 5.2	70 5.2	78 4.7	70 5.2	58 6.3	61 6.0	60 6.1	58 6.3	70 5.2
Revenues/Working Capital	2.4	5.3	7.8	6.2	6.2	8.3	8.2	8.0	6.5	6.2
	12.0	11.0	12.8	12.7	11.8	14.8	14.7	13.6	12.0	11.8
	NM	92.5	26.8	20.3	30.4	33.7	37.2	25.7	27.8	30.4
EBIT/Interest	13.7	16.0	79.5	137.3	37.9	47.2	54.1	48.5	35.6	37.9
	(10) -.8	(122) 3.4	(91) 11.2	(43) 16.9	(266) 6.2	(312) 11.7	(297) 12.1	(248) 10.0	(202) 5.3	(266) 6.2
	-29.0	-6.1	1.9	4.2	-.5	3.2	2.5	2.5	-4.9	-.5
Net Profit + Depr., Dep., Amort./Cur. Mat. L/T/D		7.3	7.4	21.8	8.3	16.5	10.8	11.9	13.0	8.3
		(26) 2.9	(17) 2.6	(10) 7.0	(53) 2.7	(88) 5.5	(84) 4.5	(83) 3.8	(57) 4.6	(53) 2.7
		.1	.8	1.8	.8	2.5	1.3	1.4	.2	.8
Fixed/Worth	.1	.1	.1	.1	.1	.1	.1	.1	.1	.1
	.7	.3	.1	.1	.2	.2	.2	.2	.2	.2
	-.3	.9	.4	.2	.5	.6	.6	.5	.6	.5
Debt/Worth	.5	.8	1.3	1.3	.9	1.1	1.1	1.0	.8	.9
	.7	1.5	2.2	2.3	2.0	1.9	2.2	1.8	1.7	2.0
	-2.6	3.8	4.1	3.3	3.9	4.0	4.4	3.6	3.5	3.9
% Profit Before Taxes/Tangible Net Worth	28.9	31.9	30.0	33.2	31.0	54.2	50.1	48.1	36.6	31.0
	(10) 3.2	(143) 9.5	(121) 13.8	(57) 16.5	(331) 12.0	(380) 30.5	(354) 26.1	(314) 22.4	(260) 11.9	(331) 12.0
	-39.3	-5.1	2.7	6.0	.3	12.0	9.0	5.6	-6.4	.3
% Profit Before Taxes/Total Assets	31.2	9.2	9.1	9.2	9.2	18.6	16.3	15.2	13.7	9.2
	2.2	2.0	3.2	4.2	3.4	9.5	7.6	7.0	4.0	3.4
	-67.6	-6.5	.5	1.7	-.8	3.2	2.0	1.4	-3.7	-.8
% Depr., Dep., Amort./Revenues	.7	.5	.2	.1	.3	.2	.3	.2	.2	.3
	(10) 2.8	(138) .9	(108) .4	(47) .3	(303) .5	(336) .5	(311) .5	(286) .5	(231) .6	(303) .5
	5.7	1.8	.8	.6	1.2	1.1	1.2	1.2	1.7	1.2
% Officers', Directors' Owners' Comp/Revenues	5.3	2.0	1.2	.8	1.5	1.3	1.1	1.3	1.4	1.5
	(11) 8.3	(83) 3.5	(50) 1.6	(10) 1.5	(154) 2.6	(211) 2.6	(187) 2.4	(148) 3.1	(133) 3.4	(154) 2.6
	12.6					4.6	4.5	6.0	6.7	5.3
Contract Revenues ($)	8190M	777590M	2530719M	53855836M	57172335M	68776588M	66762127M	74343772M	106919533M	57172335M
Total Assets ($)	4806M	369097M	983179M	37509251M	38866333M	37193126M	38690253M	36047329M	50228561M	38866333M

M = $ thousand   MM = $ million
See Pages 9 through 22 for Explanation of Ratios and Data

Current Data Sorted by Revenue | **Comparative Historical Data**

Current column groupings: **14 (4/1-9/30/10)** and **77 (10/1/10-3/31/11)**

0-1MM	1-10MM	10-50MM	50 & OVER	ALL		4/1/06-3/31/07 ALL	4/1/07-3/31/08 ALL	4/1/08-3/31/09 ALL	4/1/09-3/31/10 ALL	4/1/10-3/31/11 ALL
	4	4	3	11	**Type of Statement** — Unqualified	27	19	20	14	11
	21	10		31	Reviewed	45	34	32	26	31
2	7			9	Compiled	12	11	15	12	9
1	2		1	4	Tax Returns	9	6	5	5	4
	8	15	13	36	Other	15	18	12	5	36
3	42	29	17	91	**NUMBER OF STATEMENTS**	108	88	84	62	91
%	%	%	%	%	**ASSETS**	%	%	%	%	%
	17.8	19.9	16.3	17.8	Cash & Equivalents	17.1	15.4	16.3	17.8	17.8
	26.4	19.2	8.3	20.3	A/R - Progress Billings	30.5	30.6	31.6	29.2	20.3
	7.7	17.0	20.6	12.8	A/R - Current Retention	2.7	1.9	2.1	.9	12.8
	3.5	2.3	2.1	2.9	Inventory	2.7	2.2	2.5	4.3	2.9
	4.2	8.3	6.2	5.7	Cost & Est. Earnings In Excess Billings	3.9	3.4	3.1	4.0	5.7
	2.5	4.3	4.0	3.3	All Other Current	6.0	6.4	5.4	4.2	3.3
	62.1	71.0	57.6	62.8	Total Current	63.0	59.9	60.9	60.3	62.8
	29.8	23.0	28.9	28.2	Fixed Assets (net)	31.5	33.3	32.2	30.8	28.2
	.5	1.1	.2	.6	Joint Ventures & Investments	.8	.7	.6	.4	.6
	3.5	.0	9.6	3.4	Intangibles (net)	.2	.9	1.2	2.4	3.4
	4.1	4.9	3.7	5.0	All Other Non-Current	4.6	5.3	5.0	6.1	5.0
	100.0	100.0	100.0	100.0	Total	100.0	100.0	100.0	100.0	100.0
					LIABILITIES					
	8.0	2.6	3.0	5.1	Notes Payable-Short Term	9.6	8.1	6.3	7.3	5.1
	19.2	26.8	16.4	20.9	A/P - Trade	16.6	15.0	14.1	16.4	20.9
	.2	1.2	.2	.5	A/P - Retention	.8	.7	.9	.2	.5
	3.0	7.8	5.9	5.0	Billings in Excess of Costs & Est. Earnings	5.1	4.4	4.3	3.1	5.0
	.0	.6	.2	.3	Income Taxes Payable	.3	.1	.2	.1	.3
	5.0	2.9	3.3	4.8	Cur. Mat.-L/T/D	5.5	5.8	5.9	4.6	4.8
	3.1	4.2	6.1	4.0	All Other Current	6.9	6.7		6.5	4.0
	38.5	46.2	35.0	40.5	Total Current	44.8	40.9	37.7	38.2	40.5
	13.3	10.4	11.0	12.9	Long-Term Debt	13.3	16.5	15.0	15.0	12.9
	.4	1.2	1.4	.9	Deferred Taxes	.9	1.8	1.4	2.3	.9
	4.0	2.8	2.4	3.7	All Other Non-Current	4.7	3.2	3.9	3.3	3.7
	43.8	39.4	50.1	42.0	Net Worth	36.3	37.7	42.0	41.1	42.0
	100.0	100.0	100.0	100.0	Total Liabilities & Net Worth	100.0	100.0	100.0	100.0	100.0
					INCOME DATA					
	100.0	100.0	100.0	100.0	Contract Revenues	100.0	100.0	100.0	100.0	100.0
	20.5	16.0	17.0	19.0	Gross Profit	25.0	27.4	24.6	23.7	19.0
	20.5	13.7	12.8	18.0	Operating Expenses	19.8	22.2	22.3	22.5	18.0
	.1	2.3	4.3	1.1	Operating Profit	5.2	5.2	2.3	1.2	1.1
	-.4	-.1	.0	-.3	All Other Expenses (net)	.2	.0	.4	.0	-.3
	.5	2.4	4.2	1.4	Profit Before Taxes	5.0	5.1	1.9	1.2	1.4
					RATIOS					
	2.7	1.9	2.4	2.4	Current	2.1	2.1	2.3	2.5	2.4
	1.8	1.4	1.7	1.6		1.5	1.5	1.5	1.5	1.6
	1.2	1.3	1.3	1.2		1.1	1.1	1.3	1.1	1.2
	3.8	2.5	2.9	3.2	Receivables/Payables	4.4	5.5	3.7	3.0	3.2
	2.1	1.2	2.3	1.7		(101) 1.9	(85) 2.3	(83) 2.4	(60) 1.9	1.7
	1.3	.8	.8	1.0		1.2	1.6	1.6	1.6	1.0
	41 9.0	38 9.7	36 10.2	38 9.5	Revenues/Receivables	29 12.6	27 13.5	36 10.2	29 12.5	38 9.5
	50 7.3	53 6.8	58 6.3	51 7.1		54 6.8	57 6.5	52 7.0	48 7.6	51 7.1
	67 5.5	67 5.4	74 5.0	67 5.5		82 4.5	80 4.5	74 4.9	72 5.0	67 5.5
	14 26.0	24 15.3	19 19.5	22 16.8	Cost of Revenues/Payables	12 29.9	10 36.6	14 26.3	15 23.8	22 16.8
	34 10.7	44 8.3	34 10.8	38 9.6		33 11.0	26 13.9	30 12.2	31 11.8	38 9.6
	51 7.1	54 6.8	48 7.6	52 7.0		50 7.3	54 6.8	43 8.5	60 6.1	52 7.0
	5.6	6.4	4.8	6.1	Revenues/Working Capital	6.5	6.2	5.7	5.3	6.1
	10.5	10.2	9.7	10.9		12.3	11.4	9.6	10.9	10.9
	36.0	17.8	14.0	25.7		40.2	30.8	20.1	56.2	25.7
	12.5	12.0	25.7	12.4	EBIT/Interest	19.2	12.8	19.1	10.2	12.4
	(35) 1.3	(25) 3.5	(15) 10.0	(78) 3.2		(101) 6.5	(77) 4.4	(72) 4.0	(51) 2.6	(78) 3.2
	-2.2	1.2	7.1	-1.4		2.1	1.3	-.1	-3.0	-1.4
	6.7			5.7	Net Profit + Depr., Dep., Amort./Cur. Mat. L/T/D	3.9	4.6	4.9	6.3	5.7
	(11) 2.7		(22) 2.6			(38) 2.4	(27) 1.7	(18) 2.5	(18) 2.8	(22) 2.6
	-.1			.5		1.5	1.2	1.0	1.5	.5
	.3	.3	.4	.3	Fixed/Worth	.3	.3	.3	.3	.3
	.6	.6	.7	.6		.8	.8	.7	.6	.6
	1.3	.9	1.2	1.2		1.5	1.3	1.4	1.4	1.2
	.4	.9	.7	.6	Debt/Worth	.8	.8	.7	.6	.6
	1.3	1.6	.9	1.5		1.7	1.5	1.5	1.1	1.5
	3.9	2.5	2.5	3.1		3.3	3.1	2.9	2.9	3.1
	38.8	23.1	28.0	27.7	% Profit Before Taxes/Tangible Net Worth	53.5	41.8	34.2	34.1	27.7
	(40) 6.4	(28) 7.5	21.6	(86) 9.8		(102) 23.8	(80) 15.7	(79) 11.5	(56) 8.8	(86) 9.8
	-9.6	1.5	12.2	-.4		7.9	5.6	-3.5	.6	-.4
	15.1	9.9	8.1	9.9	% Profit Before Taxes/Total Assets	21.9	17.7	12.1	14.2	9.9
	1.7	3.2	6.6	4.7		9.7	5.7	4.4	3.3	4.7
	-7.5	.5	5.6	-1.5		2.0	1.1	-3.9	-1.7	-1.5
	2.3	.9	1.2	1.2	% Depr., Dep., Amort./Revenues	1.6	1.7	2.2	2.1	1.2
	(39) 3.4	(27) 1.9	(10) 1.9	(79) 3.0		(103) 3.0	(81) 3.5	(69) 4.1	(50) 3.6	(79) 3.0
	5.5	3.8	2.9	4.8		4.8	6.0	6.8	6.6	4.8
	2.4	.8		1.4	% Officers', Directors' Owners' Comp/Revenues	1.0	1.5	1.9	1.3	1.4
	(23) 3.5	(14) 1.2		(40) 2.7		(56) 2.3	(47) 3.2	(47) 3.4	(25) 2.5	(40) 2.7
	6.6	2.1		4.9		4.0	5.4	6.0	5.9	4.9
1176M	213307M	591956M	8739107M	9545546M	Contract Revenues ($)	1539617M	2097834M	3604883M	4498342M	9545546M
1222M	100873M	238944M	8033562M	8374601M	Total Assets ($)	702439M	1174683M	1983786M	3264021M	8374601M

M = $ thousand   MM = $ million
See Pages 9 through 22 for Explanation of Ratios and Data

Current Data Sorted by Revenue   Comparative Historical Data

					Type of Statement					
1		2	1	4	Unqualified	19	8	3	4	4
2	7	2		11	Reviewed	25	22	14	17	11
3	8			11	Compiled	22	26	18	16	11
26	8		2	36	Tax Returns	58	79	44	42	36
13	8	6		27	Other	45	52	39	33	27
						4/1/06-	4/1/07-	4/1/08-	4/1/09-	4/1/10-
						3/31/07	3/31/08	3/31/09	3/31/10	3/31/11
11 (4/1-9/30/10)		78 (10/1/10-3/31/11)				ALL	ALL	ALL	ALL	ALL
0-1MM	1-10MM	10-50MM	50 & OVER	ALL	NUMBER OF STATEMENTS	169	187	118	112	89
45	31	10	3	89						
%	%	%	%	%	ASSETS	%	%	%	%	%
2.8	4.4	5.4		3.7	Cash & Equivalents	6.3	5.4	3.8	4.4	3.7
.2	5.4	9.1		3.2	A/R - Progress Billings	3.5	4.6	4.5	4.2	3.2
.0	.3	3.1		.4	A/R - Current Retention	.8	.5	.2	.2	.4
27.0	35.3	9.1		28.1	Inventory	38.2	38.8	34.4	29.4	28.1
.0	.4	3.2		.5	Cost & Est. Earnings In Excess Billings	.7	1.1	.7	.9	.5
5.0	4.7	1.2		5.3	All Other Current	5.3	6.4	5.6	7.6	5.3
35.1	50.5	31.0		41.2	Total Current	54.7	56.7	49.1	46.6	41.2
54.7	32.6	46.3		45.2	Fixed Assets (net)	30.5	27.6	33.3	39.4	45.2
2.9	8.2	9.9		5.4	Joint Ventures & Investments	3.3	3.4	4.4	3.6	5.4
.3	.1	.7		.3	Intangibles (net)	.3	1.3	1.5	1.8	.3
7.1	8.6	12.1		7.9	All Other Non-Current	11.2	11.0	11.7	8.7	7.9
100.0	100.0	100.0		100.0	Total	100.0	100.0	100.0	100.0	100.0
					LIABILITIES					
30.9	14.0	5.9		22.6	Notes Payable-Short Term	23.1	20.4	17.1	13.7	22.6
1.2	1.5	8.1		2.1	A/P - Trade	4.2	3.3	3.7	2.9	2.1
.0	.0	.0		.0	A/P - Retention	.8	.8	.1	.0	.0
.7	.2	1.9		.6	Billings in Excess of Costs & Est. Earnings	.3	.6	1.1	.5	.6
.0	.0	.1		.0	Income Taxes Payable	.0	.0	.0	.0	.0
.5	2.9	7.5		2.1	Cur. Mat.-L/T/D	2.3	4.4	4.2	7.5	2.1
4.3	3.2	4.5		3.9	All Other Current	7.1	6.0	5.1	4.9	3.9
37.5	21.9	27.9		31.3	Total Current	38.0	35.6	31.2	29.5	31.3
49.5	33.5	41.2		42.0	Long-Term Debt	30.6	31.5	37.4	37.0	42.0
.0	.8	.7		.4	Deferred Taxes	.4	.2	.0	.3	.4
9.6	18.7	4.4		12.3	All Other Non-Current	11.7	11.0	8.5	7.2	12.3
3.3	25.1	25.7		14.0	Net Worth	19.3	21.7	22.8	25.9	14.0
100.0	100.0	100.0		100.0	Total Liabilties & Net Worth	100.0	100.0	100.0	100.0	100.0
					INCOME DATA					
100.0	100.0	100.0		100.0	Contract Revenues	100.0	100.0	100.0	100.0	100.0
					Gross Profit					
74.0	88.1	78.2		79.6	Operating Expenses	82.4	83.8	88.6	85.0	79.6
26.0	11.9	21.8		20.4	Operating Profit	17.6	16.2	11.4	15.0	20.4
27.7	12.5	14.9		20.5	All Other Expenses (net)	7.9	9.9	10.0	17.1	20.5
-1.7	-.5	6.9		-.1	Profit Before Taxes	9.7	6.3	1.4	-2.2	-.1
					RATIOS					
4.9	6.9	3.7		4.9		4.5	4.7	4.7	5.5	4.9
1.1	2.7	1.7		1.5	Current	1.5	1.6	1.3	1.4	1.5
.2	.7	.7		.5		.8	.8	.6	.6	.5
8.8	4.9			5.1		1.7	2.2	2.3	4.6	5.1
(21) .0	(24) .2		(57) .2		Receivables/Payables	(124) .1	(129) .1	(84) .1	(68) .5	(57) .2
.0	.0			.0		.0	.0	.0	.0	.0
0 UND	0 UND	0 UND		0 UND		0 UND	0 UND	0 UND	0 UND	0 UND
0 UND	0 UND	23 16.0		0 UND	Revenues/Receivables	0 UND	0 UND	0 UND	0 UND	0 UND
0 UND	6 63.4	31 12.0		5 77.3		5 80.1	6 57.0	10 36.7	8 48.5	5 77.3
					Cost of Revenues/Payables					
.6	1.0	3.6		.7		1.4	.8	1.3	.7	.7
12.9	2.7	9.7		4.2	Revenues/Working Capital	6.5	4.1	7.7	5.3	4.2
-2.0	-12.4	-22.9		-5.6		-20.9	-13.9	-8.3	-5.8	-5.6
	2.8			5.4		9.3	5.5	3.3	4.1	5.4
(22) 1.1			(39) 1.4		EBIT/Interest	(115) 3.2	(111) 1.5	(77) 1.2	(51) 1.5	(39) 1.4
-.6				.8		1.2	.5	-.4	-.5	.8
					Net Profit + Depr., Dep., Amort./Cur. Mat. L/T/D					
.0	.1	1.2		.0		.0	.0	.0	.0	.0
3.4	.2	2.4		1.9	Fixed/Worth	.7	.5	.8	1.1	1.9
-75.2	3.4	4.6		8.9		5.0	5.8	7.6	11.1	8.9
2.6	.7	1.9		1.7		1.8	1.4	1.5	1.2	1.7
9.8	2.7	2.9		4.9	Debt/Worth	4.7	6.5	4.8	3.4	4.9
-31.4	22.8	9.7		-210.9		33.4	70.9	34.8	26.4	-210.9
30.9	14.7			17.2		63.0	37.3	22.1	10.3	17.2
(28) 1.4	(25) 4.4		(65) 4.2		% Profit Before Taxes/ Tangible Net Worth	(139) 24.6	(147) 8.7	(96) 4.8	(91) .0	(65) 4.2
-10.2	-4.6			-7.1		5.9	-3.6	-10.4	-7.5	-7.1
2.2	5.3	5.3		3.5		13.4	7.7	4.9	3.1	3.5
.3	.2	1.8		.3	% Profit Before Taxes/ Total Assets	4.8	1.4	.5	.0	.3
-2.1	-1.5	.1		-1.6		-.1	-1.1	-3.2	-2.7	-1.6
6.7	.5			1.7		1.7	.8	.9	1.3	1.7
(25) 17.8	(23) 2.3		(58) 12.0		% Depr., Dep., Amort./ Revenues	(99) 1.5	(102) 2.4	(71) 3.0	(68) 7.5	(58) 12.0
28.4	16.8			18.8		9.7	11.8	16.9	19.9	18.8
				.4		2.4	2.3	1.8	.8	.4
			(15) 2.9		% Officers', Directors' Owners' Comp/Revenues	(36) 4.5	(38) 4.8	(26) 3.2	(24) 3.3	(15) 2.9
				5.3		6.5	7.1	6.8	6.4	5.3
18763M	100059M	187787M	403388M	709997M	Contract Revenues ($)	6864316M	1888207M	2259339M	849933M	709997M
167560M	461106M	802176M	3782668M	5213510M	Total Assets ($)	17878891M	6105175M	4099390M	5824551M	5213510M

Current Data Sorted by Revenue | **Comparative Historical Data**

0-1MM	1-10MM	10-50MM	50 & OVER	ALL		4/1/06-3/31/07 ALL	4/1/07-3/31/08 ALL	4/1/08-3/31/09 ALL	4/1/09-3/31/10 ALL	4/1/10-3/31/11 ALL
1	8	24	11	44	Unqualified	68	85	49	47	44
2	23	17	1	43	Reviewed	53	54	40	37	43
1	2	2		5	Compiled	9	10	5	8	5
3	5			8	Tax Returns	8	5	5	9	8
1	17	46	31	95	Other	33	28	21	19	95
	31 (4/1-9/30/10)		164 (10/1/10-3/31/11)		**Type of Statement**					
8	55	89	43	195	NUMBER OF STATEMENTS	171	182	120	120	195
%	%	%	%	%	**ASSETS**	%	%	%	%	%
	16.8	22.6	19.7	20.3	Cash & Equivalents	16.1	15.1	15.7	17.9	20.3
	22.4	14.4	5.8	15.6	A/R - Progress Billings	27.8	28.7	26.2	27.4	15.6
	7.9	16.9	17.9	13.9	A/R - Current Retention	2.9	3.4	2.8	2.1	13.9
	2.7	4.1	4.8	3.9	Inventory	4.3	3.0	3.9	3.2	3.9
	4.1	4.6	4.1	4.2	Cost & Est. Earnings In Excess Billings	3.9	3.5	2.5	2.3	4.2
	5.8	3.0	5.3	4.2	All Other Current	3.6	3.8	4.9	4.2	4.2
	59.6	65.6	57.6	62.1	Total Current	58.5	57.4	55.9	57.1	62.1
	32.5	29.5	31.3	30.8	Fixed Assets (net)	33.0	34.9	36.0	34.0	30.8
	.3	.3	.6	.4	Joint Ventures & Investments	1.9	1.1	1.5	.9	.4
	.6	.6	2.3	.9	Intangibles (net)	.9	.8	.8	1.4	.9
	6.9	4.0	8.2	5.7	All Other Non-Current	5.7	5.8	5.7	6.7	5.7
	100.0	100.0	100.0	100.0	Total	100.0	100.0	100.0	100.0	100.0
					LIABILITIES					
	7.1	2.7	1.5	3.6	Notes Payable-Short Term	6.0	5.1	4.6	5.6	3.6
	14.0	16.5	13.4	15.1	A/P - Trade	15.8	15.6	15.5	16.1	15.1
	.0	.4	1.4	.5	A/P - Retention	.6	.8	.5	.6	.5
	2.7	4.8	5.3	4.2	Billings in Excess of Costs & Est. Earnings	4.1	4.4	3.3	3.9	4.2
	.3	.2	.3	.3	Income Taxes Payable	.6	.4	.4	.2	.3
	5.5	3.9	3.1	4.1	Cur. Mat.-L/T/D	4.8	5.5	6.5	5.1	4.1
	3.0	6.3	6.7	5.5	All Other Current	7.7	8.7	5.7	6.5	5.5
	32.7	34.6	31.7	33.2	Total Current	39.6	40.5	36.6	37.9	33.2
	13.6	10.4	14.5	12.4	Long-Term Debt	14.6	15.1	14.9	14.1	12.4
	1.4	.9	1.1	1.0	Deferred Taxes	1.9	1.4	1.6	1.1	1.0
	2.5	2.3	4.0	2.7	All Other Non-Current	3.3	3.2	5.3	1.6	2.7
	49.9	51.8	48.7	50.7	Net Worth	40.6	39.8	41.7	45.4	50.7
	100.0	100.0	100.0	100.0	Total Liabilities & Net Worth	100.0	100.0	100.0	100.0	100.0
					INCOME DATA					
	100.0	100.0	100.0	100.0	Contract Revenues	100.0	100.0	100.0	100.0	100.0
	24.6	16.1	12.6	18.6	Gross Profit	20.6	21.2	19.9	21.3	18.6
	22.4	12.1	9.9	15.5	Operating Expenses	15.6	16.0	16.4	18.8	15.5
	2.2	4.0	2.7	3.2	Operating Profit	5.0	5.2	3.5	2.5	3.2
	.1	-.2	.0	-.1	All Other Expenses (net)	.1	.3	.4	.5	-.1
	2.2	4.3	2.7	3.2	Profit Before Taxes	5.0	4.9	3.1	2.0	3.2
					RATIOS					
	3.9	3.0	2.3	2.8		2.0	2.2	2.2	2.2	2.8
	1.8	2.1	1.8	1.8	Current	1.6	1.5	1.6	1.6	1.8
	1.3	1.4	1.4	1.4		1.1	1.2	1.2	1.1	1.4
	4.2	3.8	2.1	3.5		3.5	3.7	3.8	4.0	3.5
(54)	2.7	2.0	1.7	(193) 2.0	Receivables/Payables	(169) 2.0	(181) 2.0	(118) 2.0	(117) 1.8	(193) 2.0
	1.3	1.1	1.5	1.2		1.3	1.3	1.3	1.3	1.2
25 14.7	23 16.1	25 14.7	25 14.8		Revenues/Receivables	29 12.5	29 12.6	30 12.0	27 13.7	25 14.8
48 7.6	47 7.8	43 8.5	47 7.8			48 7.5	47 7.7	49 7.5	45 8.1	47 7.8
69 5.3	73 6.0	60 6.1	71 5.2			70 5.2	67 5.5	66 5.5	67 5.4	71 5.2
11 33.8	12 30.0	16 23.4	13 28.2		Cost of Revenues/Payables	15 23.7	15 24.5	11 33.1	13 29.1	13 28.2
22 16.3	23 15.6	26 14.1	25 14.7			30 12.2	28 13.0	26 14.1	27 13.4	25 14.7
40 9.2	48 7.6	40 9.2	43 8.5			45 8.1	42 8.7	46 8.0	52 7.1	43 8.5
	4.8	4.9	5.3	4.8	Revenues/Working Capital	6.9	7.5	6.5	6.0	4.8
	10.0	8.0	9.4	8.3		12.1	11.8	12.3	12.1	8.3
	17.8	15.0	14.5	15.0		35.4	28.2	26.2	32.4	15.0
	10.3	31.7	22.8	19.7	EBIT/Interest	20.1	14.8	13.1	15.1	19.7
(45)	3.5	(85) 7.3	(39) 6.4	(173) 5.8		(155) 6.6	(165) 5.9	(106) 4.6	(108) 4.5	(173) 5.8
	1.3	1.4	2.1	1.5		3.1	2.4	1.5	-.8	1.5
	4.5	4.7	3.7	4.0	Net Profit + Depr., Dep., Amort./Cur. Mat. L/T/D	4.9	4.2	3.4	4.6	4.0
(11)	2.1	(22) 2.6	(10) 2.5	(43) 2.5		(70) 2.4	(59) 2.1	(40) 2.0	(26) 2.1	(43) 2.5
	.6	1.4	1.6	1.3		1.5	1.4	.9	.7	1.3
	.3	.3	.4	.3	Fixed/Worth	.4	.5	.5	.4	.3
	.7	.6	.7	.7		.7	.8	.8	.7	.7
	1.3	.9	1.1	1.0		1.4	1.4	1.4	1.4	1.0
	.4	.4	.7	.5	Debt/Worth	.8	.8	.6	.6	.5
	1.2	.8	1.1	1.0		1.4	1.3	1.3	1.3	1.0
	2.2	1.8	2.2	2.0		2.6	2.7	2.5	2.5	2.0
	31.9	33.9	25.9	27.9	% Profit Before Taxes/Tangible Net Worth	41.6	47.6	31.4	32.4	27.9
(53)	8.2	(88) 13.7	9.6	(192) 11.1		(164) 26.2	(174) 24.4	(114) 12.3	(114) 12.0	(192) 11.1
	2.3	3.1	2.0	2.4		11.2	9.0	3.3	-1.8	2.4
	9.8	13.5	11.6	12.8	% Profit Before Taxes/Total Assets	17.5	17.0	13.0	13.0	12.8
	4.0	6.7	5.5	5.5		9.4	9.2	5.4	5.7	5.5
	.8	1.2	.9	.9		4.2	2.7	1.1	-1.7	.9
	2.2	1.8	2.3	1.9	% Depr., Dep., Amort./Revenues	1.8	2.1	2.4	1.7	1.9
(52)	4.0	(86) 2.9	(33) 3.0	(177) 3.1		(158) 3.0	(166) 3.1	(110) 3.3	(108) 3.5	(177) 3.1
	5.6	4.4	4.2	4.7		4.3	4.6	4.9	5.5	4.7
	2.7	1.2		1.3	% Officers', Directors' Owners' Comp/Revenues	1.3	1.3	1.4	1.2	1.3
(28)	4.0	(35) 2.0		(74) 2.9		(76) 2.3	(78) 2.7	(61) 2.2	(62) 2.2	(74) 2.9
	5.2	4.7		4.8		4.7	5.3	4.0	5.9	4.8
4308M	269040M	2096849M	27318725M	29688922M	Contract Revenues ($)	14560141M	15109325M	13593931M	24664202M	29688922M
3237M	144305M	996008M	13706201M	14849751M	Total Assets ($)	7648964M	8348429M	7028336M	22560228M	14849751M

M = $ thousand   MM = $ million
See Pages 9 through 22 for Explanation of Ratios and Data

Current Data Sorted by Revenue   **Comparative Historical Data**

Type of Statement

	0-1MM	1-10MM	10-50MM	50 & OVER	ALL	4/1/06-3/31/07 ALL	4/1/07-3/31/08 ALL	4/1/08-3/31/09 ALL	4/1/09-3/31/10 ALL	4/1/10-3/31/11 ALL
Unqualified		1	2	1	4	18	16	11	12	4
Reviewed		10	8	2	21	14	24	16	20	21
Compiled		3			3	5	7	3	2	3
Tax Returns		2		1	6	7	3	2	7	6
Other		7	12	15	34	6	9	12	14	34

Current period statement counts: 8 (4/1-9/30/10)   60 (10/1/10-3/31/11)

	0-1MM	1-10MM	10-50MM	50 & OVER	ALL	4/1/06-3/31/07 ALL	4/1/07-3/31/08 ALL	4/1/08-3/31/09 ALL	4/1/09-3/31/10 ALL	4/1/10-3/31/11 ALL
NUMBER OF STATEMENTS	4	23	22	19	68	50	59	44	55	68

ASSETS (%)

	0-1MM	1-10MM	10-50MM	50 & OVER	ALL	4/1/06-3/31/07	4/1/07-3/31/08	4/1/08-3/31/09	4/1/09-3/31/10	4/1/10-3/31/11
Cash & Equivalents		18.6	25.0	21.1	20.9	13.0	16.3	20.7	19.2	20.9
A/R - Progress Billings		30.5	10.7	8.3	17.0	32.2	33.2	35.2	30.8	17.0
A/R - Current Retention		6.1	24.5	26.3	17.3	.9	1.4	1.0	1.6	17.3
Inventory		2.2	2.0	2.0	2.0	4.0	3.7	1.0	1.8	2.0
Cost & Est. Earnings In Excess Billings		4.3	5.6	4.2	4.4	3.3	3.1	3.6	3.3	4.4
All Other Current		6.8	7.0	3.1	5.4	5.6	6.2	4.8	3.7	5.4
Total Current		68.4	74.7	64.9	67.0	59.0	63.9	66.4	60.4	67.0
Fixed Assets (net)		27.2	17.6	23.1	24.5	32.1	27.4	26.7	32.6	24.5
Joint Ventures & Investments		.0	.0	.0	.0	.2	.3	1.1	1.1	.0
Intangibles (net)		.4	.3	3.3	1.2	1.4	1.7	.5	.8	1.2
All Other Non-Current		4.0	7.4	8.7	7.3	7.3	6.8	5.3	5.1	7.3
Total		100.0	100.0	100.0	100.0	100.0	100.0	100.0	100.0	100.0

LIABILITIES

	0-1MM	1-10MM	10-50MM	50 & OVER	ALL	4/1/06-3/31/07	4/1/07-3/31/08	4/1/08-3/31/09	4/1/09-3/31/10	4/1/10-3/31/11
Notes Payable-Short Term		8.5	4.3	1.6	10.4	7.3	5.3	9.9	7.0	10.4
A/P - Trade		15.7	23.4	19.9	19.5	14.8	17.5	20.8	15.8	19.5
A/P - Retention		.0	1.4	2.2	1.1	.9	.3	.3	.3	1.1
Billings in Excess of Costs & Est. Earnings		3.5	5.9	13.3	6.8	4.5	5.5	4.8	4.7	6.8
Income Taxes Payable		.1	.1	.3	.2	.4	.3	.1	.2	.2
Cur. Mat.-L/T/D		6.8	2.8	2.8	5.7	6.8	5.9	4.8	5.1	5.7
All Other Current		6.6	7.4	8.1	8.5	10.0	9.0	5.9	6.0	8.5
Total Current		41.2	45.4	48.2	52.2	44.7	43.7	46.6	39.1	52.2
Long-Term Debt		12.6	9.1	15.6	14.1	21.5	14.3	12.2	14.2	14.1
Deferred Taxes		.9	.4	1.2	.8	.8	1.1	1.3	.9	.8
All Other Non-Current		3.1	.8	6.6	5.7	4.7	4.4	4.4	4.6	5.7
Net Worth		42.2	44.3	28.4	27.1	28.3	36.4	35.5	41.0	27.1
Total Liabilities & Net Worth		100.0	100.0	100.0	100.0	100.0	100.0	100.0	100.0	100.0

INCOME DATA

	0-1MM	1-10MM	10-50MM	50 & OVER	ALL	4/1/06-3/31/07	4/1/07-3/31/08	4/1/08-3/31/09	4/1/09-3/31/10	4/1/10-3/31/11
Contract Revenues		100.0	100.0	100.0	100.0	100.0	100.0	100.0	100.0	100.0
Gross Profit		25.2	13.8	16.2	19.9	30.6	25.7	21.2	26.9	19.9
Operating Expenses		23.3	11.4	8.8	16.8	22.8	19.4	18.5	22.7	16.8
Operating Profit		1.9	2.4	7.3	3.1	7.9	6.3	2.7	4.2	3.1
All Other Expenses (net)		.0	.2	.6	.3	.9	.3	.5	.8	.3
Profit Before Taxes		1.9	2.2	6.8	2.8	7.0	6.0	2.2	3.4	2.8

RATIOS

	0-1MM	1-10MM	10-50MM	50 & OVER	ALL	4/1/06-3/31/07	4/1/07-3/31/08	4/1/08-3/31/09	4/1/09-3/31/10	4/1/10-3/31/11
Current		3.0	2.9	1.6	2.6	1.7	2.2	2.2	2.2	2.6
		1.9	1.6	1.4	1.5	1.4	1.5	1.5	1.6	1.5
		1.3	1.2	1.1	1.2	1.1	1.1	1.2	1.1	1.2
Receivables/Payables		6.5	2.3	2.4	4.0	5.9	4.1	3.9	5.3	4.0
		(22) 2.6	1.2	1.4	(65) 1.6	(47) 2.1	2.0	(52) 2.2	(65) 2.2	1.6
		1.5	.9	1.1	1.0	1.3	1.3	1.1	1.2	1.0
Revenues/Receivables		40 9.1	31 11.9	57 6.4	39 9.4	31 12.0	31 11.9	37 9.8	29 12.5	39 9.4
		69 5.3	53 6.9	72 5.1	63 5.8	55 6.7	55 6.7	54 6.8	55 6.6	63 5.8
		93 3.9	72 5.1	89 4.1	87 4.2	75 4.9	91 4.0	91 4.1	86 4.3	87 4.2
Cost of Revenues/Payables		14 25.7	20 18.6	38 9.5	20 18.5	8 44.3	18 20.1	19 19.4	7 54.4	20 18.5
		30 12.0	38 9.5	51 7.1	38 9.5	29 12.5	31 11.7	31 11.6	29 12.6	38 9.5
		49 7.5	61 6.0	70 5.2	63 5.8	49 7.4	60 6.0	53 6.8	52 7.0	63 5.8
Revenues/Working Capital		3.7	3.7	7.9	4.5	7.9	5.9	5.7	4.7	4.5
		7.2	7.6	9.4	9.3	13.9	12.6	11.1	9.8	9.3
		16.4	28.6	28.2	28.4	41.1	38.6	35.6	90.4	28.4
EBIT/Interest		9.2	64.6	53.3	30.4	20.6	17.2	29.5	24.1	30.4
		(21) 1.0	(19) 7.5	18.2	(63) 5.6	(48) 7.0	(56) 5.4	(39) 7.0	(52) 6.1	(63) 5.6
		-4.3	1.9	4.6	.4	2.5	2.6	1.1	-.3	.4
Net Profit + Depr., Dep., Amort./Cur. Mat. L/T/D					18.9	16.9	14.9	18.6	8.9	18.9
				(14)	4.2	(17) 3.5	(25) 4.1	(16) 3.4	(13) 3.1	(14) 4.2
					.4	1.0	1.6	1.0	.3	.4
Fixed/Worth		.2	.1	.4	.3	.3	.3	.2	.3	.3
		.7	.4	.9	.5	.9	.8	.6	.5	.5
		.9	.5	1.8	1.2	1.9	1.5	1.6	1.6	1.2
Debt/Worth		.6	.6	1.8	.9	.9	.7	.7	.6	.9
		1.0	1.4	2.5	1.7	1.4	1.9	1.7	1.3	1.7
		2.4	2.6	7.5	4.1	5.5	4.0	5.1	2.8	4.1
% Profit Before Taxes/Tangible Net Worth		30.1	25.5	59.8	37.5	53.0	51.5	42.0	35.0	37.5
		(21) 2.4	13.6	(18) 41.3	(61) 18.2	(43) 30.9	(53) 22.3	(41) 17.1	(51) 16.3	(61) 18.2
		-10.5	.9	21.8	.6	9.5	6.8	2.5	.1	.6
% Profit Before Taxes/Total Assets		14.0	10.8	16.3	12.7	20.1	17.1	16.1	16.8	12.7
		.1	4.8	9.4	4.6	8.4	8.0	6.8	5.3	4.6
		-8.7	.4	2.5	-1.3	3.9	2.2	-.4	-.6	-1.3
% Depr., Dep., Amort./Revenues		1.7	.7		1.0	1.4	.9	.7	1.0	1.0
		(21) 3.5	1.6		(56) 2.4	(47) 3.5	(55) 2.5	(37) 2.0	(48) 2.7	(56) 2.4
		6.1	3.3		3.8	5.2	4.8	4.7	4.9	3.8
% Officers', Directors' Owners' Comp/Revenues		2.0	1.4		1.8	1.5	1.3	1.7		1.8
		(13) 4.1	(10) 2.2		(29) 2.8	(25) 3.0	(30) 3.0	(18) 2.6	(21) 4.7	(29) 2.8
		5.3	2.9		4.8	7.0	4.6	6.6	6.2	4.8
Contract Revenues ($)	3011M	120835M	464725M	12060067M	12648638M	2126436M	1045430M	6369802M	1846474M	12648638M
Total Assets ($)	443M	72235M	207408M	8602178M	8882264M	2291730M	538704M	5377672M	1677847M	8882264M

Current Data Sorted by Revenue — **Comparative Historical Data**

Type of Statement	0-1MM	1-10MM	10-50MM	50 & OVER	ALL		4/1/06-3/31/07	4/1/07-3/31/08	4/1/08-3/31/09	4/1/09-3/31/10	4/1/10-3/31/11
Unqualified	1	13	1	1	2		4	8	7	3	2
Reviewed	1	7	9	1	24		24	27	26	25	24
Compiled	1	7	1		9		17	13	9	14	9
Tax Returns	4	7		4	11		20	15	12	8	11
Other	2	15	10		31		22	21	9	15	31
	12 (4/1-9/30/10)		65 (10/1/10-3/31/11)				ALL	ALL	ALL	ALL	ALL
NUMBER OF STATEMENTS	8	42	21	6	77		87	84	63	65	77

	0-1MM %	1-10MM %	10-50MM %	50 & OVER %	ALL %		4/1/06-3/31/07 %	4/1/07-3/31/08 %	4/1/08-3/31/09 %	4/1/09-3/31/10 %	4/1/10-3/31/11 %
ASSETS											
Cash & Equivalents		10.3	7.9		9.7		13.7	13.9	13.3	12.7	9.7
A/R - Progress Billings		29.7	30.9		27.5		33.6	34.3	33.8	38.5	27.5
A/R - Current Retention		9.9	13.1		10.8		1.7	2.1	2.4	1.5	10.8
Inventory		2.8	1.3		3.1		2.6	3.1	3.0	2.6	3.1
Cost & Est. Earnings In Excess Billings		2.7	6.8		3.7		.8	1.4	1.8	1.8	3.7
All Other Current		3.3	3.3		4.3		4.4	4.3	4.1	4.9	4.3
Total Current		58.7	63.3		59.0		56.6	59.0	58.3	62.0	59.0
Fixed Assets (net)		30.1	32.2		32.0		35.2	32.2	33.3	27.5	32.0
Joint Ventures & Investments		.1	.0		.1		.1	.3	.9	.1	.1
Intangibles (net)		1.8	.3		1.5		1.4	2.3	2.6	2.5	1.5
All Other Non-Current		9.3	4.1		7.4		6.7	6.1	5.0	8.0	7.4
Total		100.0	100.0		100.0		100.0	100.0	100.0	100.0	100.0
LIABILITIES											
Notes Payable-Short Term		13.2	10.9		14.9		8.9	11.8	11.6	12.0	14.9
A/P - Trade		15.4	20.8		16.2		16.5	17.5	14.5	16.3	16.2
A/P - Retention		.0	.2		.2		.4	.3	.0	.1	.2
Billings in Excess of Costs & Est. Earnings		3.0	3.3		3.3		2.3	2.4	2.7	3.1	3.3
Income Taxes Payable		.0	.0		.0		.7	.5	.3	.5	.0
Cur. Mat.-L/T/D		7.6	3.9		5.5		4.6	4.7	5.0	4.4	5.5
All Other Current		6.1	5.6		7.1		6.3	6.9	6.6	6.6	7.1
Total Current		45.3	44.6		47.3		39.7	44.2	40.7	42.8	47.3
Long-Term Debt		11.3	11.8		13.5		23.3	18.8	18.0	14.1	13.5
Deferred Taxes		.6	2.8		1.3		.6	.8	.7	.7	1.3
All Other Non-Current		7.7	8.9		8.1		3.8	2.0	8.3	5.7	8.1
Net Worth		35.1	31.9		29.8		32.6	34.2	32.4	36.7	29.8
Total Liabilities & Net Worth		100.0	100.0		100.0		100.0	100.0	100.0	100.0	100.0
INCOME DATA											
Contract Revenues		100.0	100.0		100.0		100.0	100.0	100.0	100.0	100.0
Gross Profit		25.5	14.4		23.2		31.8	29.5	24.2	25.0	23.2
Operating Expenses		28.0	12.0		23.7		26.6	25.1	21.6	24.6	23.7
Operating Profit		-2.5	2.4		-.5		5.3	4.4	2.7	.4	-.5
All Other Expenses (net)		.3	.4		1.0		.9	1.0	.6	.3	1.0
Profit Before Taxes		-2.8	2.0		-1.5		4.4	3.4	2.0	.1	-1.5
RATIOS											
Current		2.7	2.2		2.4		2.8	2.4	2.4	2.9	2.4
		1.5	1.4		1.5		1.5	1.3	1.5	1.7	1.5
		.8	1.1		1.0		.9	1.0	1.0	1.0	1.0
Receivables/Payables		6.4	3.5		5.5		7.9	3.9	6.1	7.8	5.5
		(38) 2.8	2.4	(72)	2.6		(81) 2.9	(79) 2.4	(59) 3.3	(64) 3.2	(72) 2.6
		1.8	1.6		1.6		1.2	1.7	1.7	1.8	1.6
Revenues/Receivables		26 14.2	44 8.4	31	11.9		19 19.2	21 17.4	29 12.7	31 11.7	31 11.9
		60 6.0	59 6.2	54	6.8		52 7.1	49 7.5	52 7.0	60 6.1	54 6.8
		89 4.1	80 4.6	85	4.3		81 4.5	80 4.6	72 5.1	83 4.4	85 4.3
Cost of Revenues/Payables		6 58.5	16 22.3	10	37.0		4 96.1	12 31.2	6 62.9	10 35.0	10 37.0
		20 18.6	38 9.6	26	14.2		22 16.9	23 16.2	20 18.3	24 14.9	26 14.2
		44 8.3	55 6.6	49	7.5		44 8.3	51 7.2	42 8.6	48 7.6	49 7.5
Revenues/Working Capital		6.1	9.8		6.6		6.9	8.3	6.8	5.9	6.6
		12.9	13.4		12.5		21.1	18.9	14.3	10.6	12.5
		-29.2	47.1		-188.4		-99.3	NM	125.2	237.7	-188.4
EBIT/Interest		5.2	7.2		6.6		13.4	10.9	15.9	13.2	6.6
		(38) 1.2	1.8	(72)	1.8		(81) 4.3	(82) 4.7	(60) 2.5	(57) 2.3	(72) 1.8
		-12.5	.4		-4.7		1.2	.7	.6	-5.6	-4.7
Net Profit + Depr., Dep., Amort./Cur. Mat. L/T/D					7.4		9.8	10.7	7.1	4.6	7.4
				(14)	3.4		(20) 4.9	(23) 2.8	(11) 4.3	(16) 2.7	(14) 3.4
					1.2		1.4	1.0	2.0	.6	1.2
Fixed/Worth		.3	.6		.4		.3	.3	.4	.3	.4
		.7	1.2		1.0		1.0	.8	.8	.6	1.0
		1.8	1.6		2.2		3.8	2.1	3.9	1.3	2.2
Debt/Worth		.6	.8		.6		.7	.8	.9	.6	.6
		1.3	3.5		1.8		2.2	2.2	2.4	1.3	1.8
		4.4	4.4		4.4		5.9	5.2	7.6	3.3	4.4
% Profit Before Taxes/Tangible Net Worth		29.6	32.3		28.3		62.6	69.3	54.3	37.1	28.3
		(35) 3.5	(19) 1.6	(64)	3.6		(74) 30.7	(75) 23.1	(53) 13.4	(57) 12.4	(64) 3.6
		-23.0	-4.0		-9.4		6.4	5.0	2.3	-17.6	-9.4
% Profit Before Taxes/Total Assets		8.2	6.7		7.8		20.9	19.5	15.7	16.8	7.8
		.4	1.4		2.0		8.6	6.8	3.9	4.0	2.0
		-16.1	-.6		-6.9		1.0	-.1	-1.5	-8.5	-6.9
% Depr., Dep., Amort./Revenues		1.8	1.9		1.8		1.3	.9	1.5	1.4	1.8
		(37) 2.4	(19) 2.7	(66)	2.5		(73) 2.5	(71) 2.4	(53) 2.6	(60) 2.8	(66) 2.5
		3.2	3.8		4.3		5.3	4.9	4.7	4.9	4.3
% Officers', Directors' Owners' Comp/Revenues		2.5			1.9		2.1	1.8	1.9	1.9	1.9
		(25) 5.0		(39)	3.2		(48) 4.5	(48) 3.7	(35) 4.1	(38) 4.2	(39) 3.2
		8.0			7.7		8.4	8.7	9.2	8.4	7.7
Contract Revenues ($)	4748M	135719M	429385M	31621573M	32191425M		1300679M	12336218M	5251846M	24751762M	32191425M
Total Assets ($)	4683M	58024M	214467M	12587039M	12864213M		645701M	7968552M	2859822M	22364101M	12864213M

M = $ thousand   MM = $ million
See Pages 9 through 22 for Explanation of Ratios and Data

CONSTRUCTION-% OF COMPLETION—Structural Steel and Precast Concrete Contractors NAICS 238120

Current Data Sorted by Revenue   **Comparative Historical Data**

0-1MM	1-10MM	10-50MM	50 & OVER	ALL	Type of Statement	4/1/06-3/31/07 ALL	4/1/07-3/31/08 ALL	4/1/08-3/31/09 ALL	4/1/09-3/31/10 ALL	4/1/10-3/31/11 ALL
	1		2	3	Unqualified	5	6	6	6	3
1	14	7	1	23	Reviewed	20	16	15	15	23
1	3	1		5	Compiled	8	6	6	4	5
1				1	Tax Returns	2	6	2	3	1
1	6	8	3	18	Other	6	5	9	8	18
8 (4/1-9/30/10)		42 (10/1/10-3/31/11)								
4	24	16	6	50	NUMBER OF STATEMENTS	41	39	38	36	50
%	%	%	%	%	ASSETS	%	%	%	%	%
	18.8	14.1		16.7	Cash & Equivalents	10.8	14.2	16.5	25.3	16.7
	32.0	18.6		25.2	A/R - Progress Billings	46.6	49.1	43.5	35.8	25.2
	17.6	29.6		19.6	A/R - Current Retention	1.2	1.8	3.6	2.7	19.6
	2.5	2.8		2.9	Inventory	4.3	3.6	2.8	1.7	2.9
	2.2	5.1		3.5	Cost & Est. Earnings In Excess Billings	3.8	2.6	3.9	2.4	3.5
	4.5	2.3		3.4	All Other Current	5.4	3.1	5.1	4.6	3.4
	77.6	72.6		71.4	Total Current	72.0	74.4	75.5	72.5	71.4
	15.4	17.5		18.2	Fixed Assets (net)	22.1	21.0	19.9	19.4	18.2
	.4	.0		.2	Joint Ventures & Investments	1.2	.0	.1	.3	.2
	.6	3.0		1.3	Intangibles (net)	.3	.4	.2	.1	1.3
	6.1	6.9		9.0	All Other Non-Current	4.4	4.2	4.4	7.7	9.0
	100.0	100.0		100.0	Total	100.0	100.0	100.0	100.0	100.0
					LIABILITIES					
	9.9	14.4		11.2	Notes Payable-Short Term	10.0	16.6	5.7	10.3	11.2
	15.3	16.0		14.9	A/P - Trade	16.9	22.0	15.0	11.4	14.9
	.0	.9		.3	A/P - Retention	.0	.0	1.3	1.0	.3
	5.2	9.4		6.9	Billings in Excess of Costs & Est. Earnings	4.4	5.9	6.4	4.1	6.9
	.2	.4		.2	Income Taxes Payable	.7	.3	.6	.0	.2
	1.9	2.1		2.1	Cur. Mat.-L/T/D	3.1	2.0	2.4	3.0	2.1
	5.5	7.3		6.3	All Other Current	7.3	7.2	8.8	5.9	6.3
	37.9	50.6		41.9	Total Current	42.4	53.9	40.1	35.8	41.9
	5.4	6.1		11.9	Long-Term Debt	9.1	9.9	10.3	11.5	11.9
	.1	.7		.4	Deferred Taxes	.5	.6	.7	1.1	.4
	20.6	3.4		11.1	All Other Non-Current	2.3	3.9	1.5	3.8	11.1
	36.0	39.3		34.7	Net Worth	45.7	31.7	47.4	47.7	34.7
	100.0	100.0		100.0	Total Liabilities & Net Worth	100.0	100.0	100.0	100.0	100.0
					INCOME DATA					
	100.0	100.0		100.0	Contract Revenues	100.0	100.0	100.0	100.0	100.0
	15.0	16.8		17.8	Gross Profit	24.2	23.5	24.0	26.2	17.8
	18.1	17.4		18.9	Operating Expenses	17.6	21.1	17.5	22.9	18.9
	-3.1	-.6		-1.1	Operating Profit	6.7	2.4	6.4	3.2	-1.1
	.0	.1		.1	All Other Expenses (net)	.7	-.1	.1	.1	.1
	-3.1	-.6		-1.3	Profit Before Taxes	6.0	2.4	6.3	3.1	-1.3
					RATIOS					
	5.0	1.7		2.5	Current	3.1	2.3	2.9	4.1	2.5
	1.7	1.3		1.6		2.1	1.8	1.9	2.3	1.6
	1.3	1.2		1.3		1.2	1.0	1.3	1.4	1.3
	18.9	4.5		5.7	Receivables/Payables	5.7	5.7	5.3	6.6	5.7
	5.3	2.9	(48)	3.4		(39) 3.0	(36) 2.3	(35) 3.0	(34) 4.1	(48) 3.4
	2.9	2.5		2.5		1.5	1.5	2.2	1.7	2.5
	53 6.9	75 4.9		58 6.2	Revenues/Receivables	32 11.4	41 8.9	47 7.7	32 11.6	58 6.2
	87 4.2	86 4.3		85 4.3		57 6.4	66 5.5	56 6.5	57 6.4	85 4.3
	122 3.0	105 3.5		108 3.4		72 5.4	85 4.9	75 4.9	73 5.0	108 3.4
	4 83.5	21 17.2		17 21.5	Cost of Revenues/Payables	12 30.6	8 47.5	9 39.2	13 38.1	17 21.5
	25 14.7	37 10.0		28 12.8		23 16.0	26 14.1	21 17.2	21 17.5	28 12.8
	40 9.0	47 7.8		46 8.0		39 9.4	58 6.3	36 10.0	26 14.1	46 8.0
	3.3	5.9		4.3	Revenues/Working Capital	5.3	6.4	4.9	3.8	4.3
	5.8	9.6		7.2		7.9	10.8	7.6	5.8	7.2
	15.4	25.5		15.7		35.8	152.1	22.2	13.6	15.7
	6.3	15.9		8.7	EBIT/Interest	57.6	21.1	63.2	35.4	8.7
(19)	.6	(14) 5.0	(42)	2.5		(38) 8.4	(34) 5.6	(35) 10.8	(28) 4.4	(42) 2.5
	-19.7	.6		-5.0		1.4	1.3	6.0	1.1	-5.0
				3.3	Net Profit + Depr., Dep., Amort./Cur. Mat. L/T/D	8.9		53.2		3.3
			(12)	3.1		(13) 3.7		(10) 14.5		(12) 3.1
				-.1		1.8		2.5		-.1
	.1	.1		.1	Fixed/Worth	.2	.1	.1	.1	.1
	.4	.4		.4		.4	.5	.4	.5	.4
	.7	.9		1.0		.8	2.2	.6	.7	1.0
	.4	1.0		.7	Debt/Worth	.5	.8	.4	.4	.7
	1.0	1.5		1.3		1.1	1.5	1.2	.7	1.3
	2.2	2.3		2.2		2.7	6.0	2.3	1.8	2.2
	10.6	20.8		21.8	% Profit Before Taxes/Tangible Net Worth	62.6	50.8	62.6	42.2	21.8
(21)	.0	(15) 15.2	(45)	5.5		(39) 26.4	(33) 26.7	(36) 33.0	(34) 12.4	(45) 5.5
	-15.9	2.1		-11.1		3.3	11.2	11.4	.8	-11.1
	4.1	8.8		8.5	% Profit Before Taxes/Total Assets	29.0	21.2	28.9	28.2	8.5
	-2.8	4.7		1.9		10.1	8.0	14.5	5.0	1.9
	-14.6	.8		-8.7		1.9	1.1	6.4	.1	-8.7
	1.0	1.1		1.1	% Depr., Dep., Amort./Revenues	.6	.5	.3	.5	1.1
(22)	1.6	(14) 1.4	(42)	1.6		(37) 1.1	(33) 1.0	(32) .9	(28) 1.6	(42) 1.6
	3.2	3.9		3.2		2.3	2.3	2.1	2.7	3.2
				2.6	% Officers', Directors' Owners' Comp/Revenues	1.8	1.5	.8	1.0	2.6
			(18)	5.7		(22) 3.8	(23) 5.7	(17) 3.9	(19) 4.2	(18) 5.7
				8.8		5.9	9.5	7.2	13.5	8.8
2326M	115887M	348336M	8164247M	8630796M	Contract Revenues ($)	933909M	7791812M	761765M	35222235M	8630796M
2226M	68647M	191134M	5902329M	6164336M	Total Assets ($)	485758M	4430386M	295147M	21872885M	6164336M

© RMA 2011

M = $ thousand   MM = $ million
See Pages 9 through 22 for Explanation of Ratios and Data

Current Data Sorted by Revenue | **Comparative Historical Data**

0-1MM	1-10MM	10-50MM	50 & OVER	ALL	Type of Statement	4/1/06-3/31/07 ALL	4/1/07-3/31/08 ALL	4/1/08-3/31/09 ALL	4/1/09-3/31/10 ALL	4/1/10-3/31/11 ALL
		2		2	Unqualified	3	2	3		2
1	22	7		30	Reviewed	30	20	15	14	30
1	1			2	Compiled	8	7	6	7	2
1	3			4	Tax Returns	8	12	10	7	4
1	6	3		10	Other	4	7	3	4	10
11 (4/1-9/30/10)		37 (10/1/10-3/31/11)								
4	32	12		48	NUMBER OF STATEMENTS	53	48	37	32	48
%	%	%	%	%	**ASSETS**	%	%	%	%	%
	14.0	18.3	DATA NOT AVAILABLE	16.0	Cash & Equivalents	11.1	12.9	12.9	15.0	16.0
	24.0	4.5		19.8	A/R - Progress Billings	41.4	42.1	36.0	40.3	19.8
	24.8	36.0		26.6	A/R - Current Retention	5.6	1.7	5.6	1.9	26.6
	2.2	.6		1.6	Inventory	1.0	4.9	2.5	1.2	1.6
	2.9	6.4		3.5	Cost & Est. Earnings In Excess Billings	3.5	2.7	2.4	1.4	3.5
	4.8	7.3		5.6	All Other Current	5.0	4.4	8.5	3.7	5.6
	72.6	73.1		73.1	Total Current	67.6	68.7	67.8	63.5	73.1
	16.7	18.1		16.1	Fixed Assets (net)	23.4	22.1	24.7	25.6	16.1
	3.5	.1		2.6	Joint Ventures & Investments	1.5	1.3	.5	2.3	2.6
	.3	.0		.4	Intangibles (net)	.0	.7	1.2	1.7	.4
	6.9	8.7		7.8	All Other Non-Current	7.5	7.2	5.8	6.9	7.8
	100.0	100.0		100.0	Total	100.0	100.0	100.0	100.0	100.0
					LIABILITIES					
	18.4	17.9		17.6	Notes Payable-Short Term	11.6	10.5	12.8	23.9	17.6
	12.3	15.4		13.0	A/P - Trade	15.5	20.7	15.1	12.3	13.0
	.0	1.3		.3	A/P - Retention	.0	.1	.0	.0	.3
	6.5	5.0		5.6	Billings in Excess of Costs & Est. Earnings	8.6	5.7	6.3	2.5	5.6
	.4	.1		.3	Income Taxes Payable	.4	.3	.2	.1	.3
	2.2	2.7		2.3	Cur. Mat.-L/T/D	3.1	3.1	2.7	2.8	2.3
	5.6	6.0		6.0	All Other Current	8.7	8.1	9.0	6.9	6.0
	45.4	48.4		45.2	Total Current	47.9	48.4	46.2	48.5	45.2
	5.3	5.5		5.5	Long-Term Debt	9.9	15.3	16.0	14.3	5.5
	.4	.4		.4	Deferred Taxes	.5	.7	.5	.3	.4
	3.7	4.3		3.6	All Other Non-Current	3.4	5.0	7.2	9.8	3.6
	45.2	41.4		45.4	Net Worth	38.2	30.6	30.2	27.1	45.4
	100.0	100.0		100.0	Total Liabilties & Net Worth	100.0	100.0	100.0	100.0	100.0
					INCOME DATA					
	100.0	100.0		100.0	Contract Revenues	100.0	100.0	100.0	100.0	100.0
	17.6	16.4		19.0	Gross Profit	25.3	26.8	24.2	25.2	19.0
	24.3	15.7		22.9	Operating Expenses	20.8	24.8	20.7	24.4	22.9
	-6.6	.6		-3.9	Operating Profit	4.5	2.0	3.6	.8	-3.9
	.0	2.2		.6	All Other Expenses (net)	.2	.1	.4	-.1	.6
	-6.7	-1.6		-4.5	Profit Before Taxes	4.4	1.9	3.1	.8	-4.5
					RATIOS					
	3.8	3.3		3.5		2.0	1.9	2.2	3.7	3.5
	1.7	1.9		1.9	Current	1.6	1.6	1.5	1.8	1.9
	1.0	1.0		1.0		1.2	1.2	1.1	1.0	1.0
	22.3	4.3		12.4		8.1	4.5	6.0	7.7	12.4
	5.1	2.2		3.9	Receivables/Payables	(50) 3.4	(46) 2.8	(32) 3.6	(28) 5.5	3.9
	2.3	1.8		2.2		2.2	1.7	2.2	3.2	2.2
	62 5.9	**52** 7.0		**55** 6.6		**35** 10.6	**36** 10.2	**13** 29.0	**33** 11.2	**55** 6.6
	83 4.4	**66** 5.5		**80** 4.6	Revenues/Receivables	**63** 5.8	**57** 6.4	**48** 7.6	**57** 6.5	**80** 4.6
	113 3.2	**81** 4.5		**104** 3.5		**84** 4.3	**83** 4.4	**84** 4.3	**85** 4.3	**104** 3.5
	3 110.3	**22** 16.7		**6** 56.5		**6** 62.5	**10** 38.1	**4** 87.6	**4** 88.0	**6** 56.5
	20 18.7	**32** 11.3		**26** 13.9	Cost of Revenues/Payables	**17** 21.7	**26** 14.2	**21** 17.3	**15** 25.2	**26** 13.9
	50 7.3	**47** 7.7		**40** 9.0		**35** 10.5	**53** 6.9	**33** 11.0	**33** 11.1	**40** 9.0
	3.6	4.1		4.0		7.9	6.7	7.3	4.9	4.0
	8.4	7.7		7.5	Revenues/Working Capital	10.5	12.2	14.6	9.1	7.5
	81.7	NM		81.7		42.5	53.4	100.8	-185.6	81.7
	4.8			6.0		18.8	17.7	12.0	17.2	6.0
	(27) -1.1			(37) 2.2	EBIT/Interest	(46) 6.7	(44) 3.4	(32) 2.9	(28) 6.6	(37) 2.2
	-11.4			-10.6		2.0	.6	-.6	-8.5	-10.6
						9.2				
					Net Profit + Depr., Dep., Amort./Cur. Mat. L/T/D	(14) 3.1				
						1.4				
	.2	.2		.1		.3	.2	.2	.2	.1
	.4	.5		.4	Fixed/Worth	.5	.4	.5	.4	.4
	.7	.9		.7		1.1	1.3	1.6	2.3	.7
	.3	.4		.4		.9	.9	.7	.3	.4
	1.3	1.3		1.1	Debt/Worth	1.7	1.8	1.5	.9	1.1
	3.7	8.2		4.1		2.9	10.3	5.4	3.7	4.1
	10.7	33.6		22.6		59.0	45.9	80.1	54.8	22.6
	(30) -2.6	(11) 3.6		(45) .4	% Profit Before Taxes/ Tangible Net Worth	(50) 25.5	(42) 18.4	(33) 30.6	(25) 9.3	(45) .4
	-56.3	-9.1		-37.8		4.0	5.1	-6.0	-19.8	-37.8
	4.7	10.0		6.6		22.0	15.1	35.5	25.1	6.6
	-4.2	1.2		-.1	% Profit Before Taxes/ Total Assets	7.9	4.2	5.9	3.0	-.1
	-27.5	-5.9		-22.2		1.4	.3	-2.7	-15.2	-22.2
	1.4	.9		1.3		.8	.8	1.0	1.0	1.3
	(29) 2.5	1.5		(43) 2.1	% Depr., Dep., Amort./ Revenues	(44) 1.4	(38) 1.7	(31) 1.3	(27) 1.6	(43) 2.1
	3.6	2.6		3.3		2.4	2.7	2.2	3.4	3.3
	1.7			2.7		2.5	2.8	1.9	2.7	2.7
	(16) 4.8			(22) 4.7	% Officers', Directors' Owners' Comp/Revenues	(30) 4.0	(30) 4.6	(23) 3.3	(20) 3.1	(22) 4.7
	5.9			5.9		8.0	8.2	6.2	5.8	5.9
2115M	**106801M**	**219759M**		**328675M**	Contract Revenues ($)	**298397M**	**11599329M**	**252020M**	**4596064M**	**328675M**
683M	**52860M**	**110998M**		**164541M**	Total Assets ($)	**110686M**	**3908385M**	**85772M**	**1651203M**	**164541M**

M = $ thousand MM = $ million

See Pages 9 through 22 for Explanation of Ratios and Data

Current Data Sorted by Revenue — Comparative Historical Data

0-1MM	1-10MM	10-50MM	50 & OVER	ALL	Type of Statement	4/1/06-3/31/07	4/1/07-3/31/08	4/1/08-3/31/09	4/1/09-3/31/10	4/1/10-3/31/11
		1		1	Unqualified	2	2	1	1	1
	8	6	1	15	Reviewed	14	12	13	12	15
					Compiled	9	7	7	3	
2				2	Tax Returns	5	2	4	2	2
	3	1	1	5	Other	10	3	3	2	5
	7 (4/1-9/30/10)		16 (10/1/10-3/31/11)		**NUMBER OF STATEMENTS**	ALL	ALL	ALL	ALL	ALL
2	11	8	2	23		40	26	28	20	23
%	%	%	%	%	**ASSETS**	%	%	%	%	%
	13.0			19.7	Cash & Equivalents	12.4	9.8	20.5	25.7	19.7
	32.4			26.6	A/R - Progress Billings	54.5	56.8	49.6	42.8	26.6
	16.7			19.4	A/R - Current Retention	.9	1.8	1.1	3.1	19.4
	3.9			6.6	Inventory	8.9	7.9	7.7	3.2	6.6
	4.8			4.0	Cost & Est. Earnings In Excess Billings	2.8	2.8	2.4	4.3	4.0
	7.7			3.8	All Other Current	2.9	3.4	2.9	7.9	3.8
	78.5			80.0	Total Current	82.3	82.5	84.2	87.0	80.0
	14.7			12.9	Fixed Assets (net)	10.8	13.4	11.9	6.9	12.9
	.0			1.4	Joint Ventures & Investments	1.4	.1	.9	1.2	1.4
	.4			.8	Intangibles (net)	.3	1.0	.1	.2	.8
	6.5			4.8	All Other Non-Current	5.2	3.0	2.9	4.7	4.8
	100.0			100.0	Total	100.0	100.0	100.0	100.0	100.0
					LIABILITIES					
	6.5			5.2	Notes Payable-Short Term	9.9	15.5	18.0	7.6	5.2
	15.6			14.8	A/P - Trade	30.1	25.0	23.1	13.3	14.8
	.0			.2	A/P - Retention	.3	.0	.7	.1	.2
	5.1			5.6	Billings in Excess of Costs & Est. Earnings	5.9	8.9	4.9	7.5	5.6
	3.2			1.6	Income Taxes Payable	.2	.4	.4	.7	1.6
	2.7			3.5	Cur. Mat.-L/T/D	2.6	3.5	2.5	1.1	3.5
	7.5			7.7	All Other Current	8.3	7.3	6.2	7.5	7.7
	40.5			38.5	Total Current	57.3	60.6	55.8	37.9	38.5
	6.0			6.2	Long-Term Debt	8.1	8.6	6.5	3.1	6.2
	.6			.3	Deferred Taxes	.1	.3	.3	.2	.3
	.2			2.4	All Other Non-Current	5.9	5.0	5.2	5.2	2.4
	52.6			52.5	Net Worth	28.5	25.5	32.2	53.6	52.5
	100.0			100.0	Total Liabilities & Net Worth	100.0	100.0	100.0	100.0	100.0
					INCOME DATA					
	100.0			100.0	Contract Revenues	100.0	100.0	100.0	100.0	100.0
	25.3			28.9	Gross Profit	28.0	27.0	33.7	30.0	28.9
	27.7			25.6	Operating Expenses	25.1	24.0	29.7	22.7	25.6
	-2.4			3.3	Operating Profit	2.9	3.0	3.9	7.3	3.3
	.1			.6	All Other Expenses (net)	-.1	.8	.1	.1	.6
	-2.4			2.7	Profit Before Taxes	3.0	2.2	3.8	7.3	2.7
					RATIOS					
	3.0			4.2	Current	1.6	1.9	2.8	3.9	4.2
	2.1			2.3		1.5	1.5	1.8	2.2	2.3
	1.2			1.2		1.2	1.1	1.2	1.7	1.2
	4.5			4.6	Receivables/Payables	3.2	4.3	4.4	4.3	4.6
	3.4			3.4		(39) 1.9	2.5	2.1	3.5	3.4
	2.3			2.1		1.2	1.8	1.4	2.0	2.1
	66 5.6		62 5.9		Revenues/Receivables	45 8.2	53 6.9	38 9.6	31 11.7	62 5.9
	81 4.5		78 4.7			59 6.2	74 4.9	59 6.1	56 6.5	78 4.7
	89 4.1		89 4.1			84 4.3	101 3.6	90 4.1	74 4.9	89 4.1
	16 22.2		16 22.2		Cost of Revenues/Payables	29 12.7	26 13.8	20 18.1	17 21.4	16 22.2
	25 14.3		28 13.1			46 8.0	41 8.9	39 9.4	24 15.3	28 13.1
	38 9.7		40 9.1			61 6.0	64 5.7	58 6.3	28 13.2	40 9.1
	4.8			4.0	Revenues/Working Capital	7.6	7.4	6.2	4.2	4.0
	6.7			6.0		12.9	10.8	10.4	8.0	6.0
	19.4			14.1		28.4	30.6	29.4	9.9	14.1
	2.5			21.3	EBIT/Interest	(32) 12.1	(23) 17.0	(23) 22.0	(17) 95.1	(17) 21.3
	(10) -1.7		(17) 1.7			3.9	4.8	9.8	25.2	1.7
	-39.4			-11.6		.8	1.6	2.8	6.4	-11.6
					Net Profit + Depr., Dep., Amort./Cur. Mat. L/T/D					
	.1			.1	Fixed/Worth	.1	.2	.0	.0	.1
	.2			.2		.3	.4	.3	.1	.2
	.5			.5		1.4	1.1	.6	.2	.5
	.4			.3	Debt/Worth	1.5	1.3	.5	.4	.3
	.8			.7		2.1	1.9	1.5	1.0	.7
	1.7			1.7		7.5	4.4	2.7	1.1	1.7
	8.9			41.7	% Profit Before Taxes/ Tangible Net Worth	67.0	43.9	78.5	69.7	41.7
	-13.0		(22) 10.4			(36) 19.0	(22) 26.3	(26) 29.7	30.4	(22) 10.4
	-25.9			-14.5		5.2	7.5	8.2	11.4	-14.5
	2.4			15.1	% Profit Before Taxes/ Total Assets	23.2	18.0	38.5	28.9	15.1
	-8.3			6.1		4.0	5.9	7.7	13.8	6.1
	-18.7			-8.3		-.9	1.3	4.1	5.8	-8.3
	1.0			.5	% Depr., Dep., Amort./ Revenues	.2	.5	.3	.4	.5
	(10) 1.5		(20) 1.2			(34) .5	(24) .9	(24) .6	(16) .6	(20) 1.2
	2.0			1.9		1.1	1.5	1.8	1.2	1.9
				2.1	% Officers', Directors' Owners' Comp/Revenues	2.4	3.0	2.0	1.7	2.1
			(10) 3.5			(29) 3.7	(14) 7.5	(15) 5.4	(12) 5.0	(10) 3.5
				7.3		7.3	9.9	9.6	12.1	7.3
472M	56354M	143241M	150526M	350593M	Contract Revenues ($)	1438839M	814614M	938669M	361448M	350593M
431M	30175M	65169M	90533M	186308M	Total Assets ($)	371899M	274050M	347489M	194199M	186308M

M = $ thousand   MM = $ million
See Pages 9 through 22 for Explanation of Ratios and Data

Current Data Sorted by Revenue						Comparative Historical Data				

Type of Statement — Left period groups: 10 (4/1–9/30/10) covers 0-1MM & 1-10MM; 57 (10/1/10–3/31/11) covers 10-50MM, 50 & OVER, ALL.

0-1MM	1-10MM	10-50MM	50 & OVER	ALL	Type of Statement	4/1/06-3/31/07 ALL	4/1/07-3/31/08 ALL	4/1/08-3/31/09 ALL	4/1/09-3/31/10 ALL	4/1/10-3/31/11 ALL
		1		1	Unqualified	12	7	3	2	1
	23	8		31	Reviewed	42	40	29	27	31
2	9			11	Compiled	12	16	8	9	11
3	5	1		9	Tax Returns	8	5	8	7	9
	7	5	3	15	Other	17	10	8	11	15
5	44	15	3	67	**NUMBER OF STATEMENTS**	91	78	56	56	67
%	%	%	%	%	**ASSETS**	%	%	%	%	%
	15.4	25.4		16.6	Cash & Equivalents	11.4	16.3	16.1	13.9	16.6
	29.6	14.7		27.7	A/R - Progress Billings	46.5	40.0	42.6	41.4	27.7
	18.3	29.1		19.6	A/R - Current Retention	2.7	1.8	1.8	1.7	19.6
	7.3	2.4		6.7	Inventory	6.1	4.6	4.5	8.5	6.7
	3.6	5.3		3.9	Cost & Est. Earnings In Excess Billings	4.4	4.6	4.3	3.2	3.9
	3.8	6.6		4.0	All Other Current	3.6	5.9	4.0	3.5	4.0
	78.0	83.5		78.5	Total Current	74.7	73.2	73.2	72.2	78.5
	16.4	10.2		15.8	Fixed Assets (net)	17.7	18.2	18.9	20.7	15.8
	.0	.0		.0	Joint Ventures & Investments	.1	.4	.6	.1	.0
	.5	1.7		.7	Intangibles (net)	1.7	1.5	1.2	1.7	.7
	5.1	4.6		5.0	All Other Non-Current	5.8	6.8	6.1	5.3	5.0
	100.0	100.0		100.0	Total	100.0	100.0	100.0	100.0	100.0
					LIABILITIES					
	19.5	1.4		14.0	Notes Payable-Short Term	8.7	6.5	10.2	10.1	14.0
	26.1	16.1		24.6	A/P - Trade	20.6	20.4	20.2	19.1	24.6
	.0	.2		.0	A/P - Retention	.5	.3	.6	.2	.0
	4.0	12.7		5.6	Billings in Excess of Costs & Est. Earnings	6.7	4.7	4.1	4.0	5.6
	.3	.0		.2	Income Taxes Payable	.4	.5	.3	.1	.2
	6.7	1.7		7.2	Cur. Mat.-L/T/D	3.4	3.1	3.0	3.0	7.2
	9.2	6.9		10.3	All Other Current	8.5	8.4	8.5	6.6	10.3
	65.7	39.1		62.0	Total Current	48.8	43.7	46.7	43.0	62.0
	9.5	4.0		10.8	Long-Term Debt	10.1	8.9	10.3	10.2	10.8
	.5	.2		.4	Deferred Taxes	.4	.7	.7	1.4	.4
	5.3	2.5		4.4	All Other Non-Current	4.3	2.2	3.4	4.0	4.4
	19.0	54.3		22.5	Net Worth	36.5	44.5	38.8	41.5	22.5
	100.0	100.0		100.0	Total Liabilities & Net Worth	100.0	100.0	100.0	100.0	100.0
					INCOME DATA					
	100.0	100.0		100.0	Contract Revenues	100.0	100.0	100.0	100.0	100.0
	22.7	24.5		25.7	Gross Profit	29.6	29.3	29.6	26.9	25.7
	21.7	17.6		23.2	Operating Expenses	23.7	23.3	24.4	25.3	23.2
	1.0	6.9		2.5	Operating Profit	5.9	6.0	5.3	1.5	2.5
	.2	-.6		.0	All Other Expenses (net)	.1	.4	.2	.0	.0
	.8	7.5		2.5	Profit Before Taxes	5.8	5.6	5.1	1.5	2.5
					RATIOS					
	2.5	3.2		2.9	Current	2.4	2.7	2.8	2.4	2.9
	1.4	2.0		1.7		1.6	1.7	1.6	1.7	1.7
	1.0	1.6		1.1		1.2	1.3	1.1	1.3	1.1
	3.1	4.2		3.7	Receivables/Payables	4.5	4.5	6.0	4.6	3.7
	(42) 2.2	3.1		(64) 2.3		(90) 2.5	(76) 2.3	(53) 2.6	(55) 2.2	(64) 2.3
	1.6	1.7		1.7		1.6	1.4	1.4	1.4	1.7
	33 11.1	36 10.2		30 12.2	Revenues/Receivables	43 8.6	32 11.5	27 13.3	33 11.1	30 12.2
	66 5.5	48 7.6		53 6.9		59 6.2	48 7.6	53 6.9	54 6.7	53 6.9
	86 4.3	82 4.5		83 4.4		76 4.8	71 5.1	73 5.0	77 4.8	83 4.4
	20 18.5	17 21.3		17 21.3	Cost of Revenues/Payables	15 24.3	15 24.7	11 33.5	15 25.0	17 21.3
	32 11.4	36 10.0		33 11.1		28 13.3	32 11.6	26 14.3	29 12.6	33 11.1
	52 7.0	43 8.5		50 7.3		51 7.2	49 7.4	50 7.3	52 7.0	50 7.3
	6.7	4.6		6.1	Revenues/Working Capital	6.7	5.5	6.9	7.1	6.1
	16.0	6.7		12.6		12.3	11.2	15.4	11.5	12.6
	NM	8.5		32.7		26.3	22.3	64.4	20.5	32.7
	13.1	158.8		47.4	EBIT/Interest	22.7	30.8	34.8	18.3	47.4
	(41) 2.2	(14) 53.0		(62) 3.7		(82) 7.4	(67) 9.4	(47) 8.0	(48) 4.6	(62) 3.7
	-5.0	17.6		-3.4		2.6	2.7	1.2	-.7	-3.4
				2.4	Net Profit + Depr., Dep., Amort./Cur. Mat. L/T/D	13.2	13.8		10.3	2.4
				(10) 1.1		(20) 4.5	(16) 5.3		(14) 2.4	(10) 1.1
				-5.5		1.8	2.2		.7	-5.5
	.2	.1		.1	Fixed/Worth	.2	.1	.1	.2	.1
	.5	.2		.5		.4	.3	.4	.4	.5
	1.3	.2		.9		.9	.8	.9	1.2	.9
	.7	.4		.6	Debt/Worth	.9	.6	.5	.5	.6
	2.0	1.0		1.5		1.8	1.2	1.5	1.6	1.5
	7.0	1.5		3.9		3.0	2.2	3.5	3.4	3.9
	26.0	56.7		34.0	% Profit Before Taxes/Tangible Net Worth	53.7	70.7	67.6	37.6	34.0
	(36) 3.3	29.9		(56) 12.3		(83) 29.4	(73) 35.3	(49) 35.5	(53) 6.3	(56) 12.3
	-8.8	9.1		-3.7		11.3	10.8	5.8	-11.0	-3.7
	17.8	27.0		22.3	% Profit Before Taxes/Total Assets	30.5	28.5	28.5	22.8	22.3
	1.5	20.1		5.3		9.8	12.0	12.1	3.5	5.3
	-10.4	6.3		-3.6		4.6	3.4	.8	-5.6	-3.6
	.8	.5		.7	% Depr., Dep., Amort./Revenues	.6	.8	1.0	.6	.7
	(38) 1.5	(14) .9		(58) 1.3		(75) 1.0	(67) 1.3	(46) 1.5	(50) 1.6	(58) 1.3
	2.2	1.7		2.3		2.2	2.1	2.0	2.4	2.3
	2.6			2.5	% Officers', Directors' Owners' Comp/Revenues	1.9	2.1	1.9	1.9	2.5
	(25) 3.4			(39) 3.5		(53) 3.1	(52) 4.7	(35) 3.1	(37) 3.6	(39) 3.5
	4.8			6.2		7.0	7.8	6.3	5.2	6.2
3653M	208694M	225893M	823187M	1261427M	Contract Revenues ($)	5381093M	596818M	446313M	631640M	1261427M
866M	75053M	91311M	366035M	533265M	Total Assets ($)	3807916M	225859M	144742M	208200M	533265M

M = $ thousand   MM = $ million
See Pages 9 through 22 for Explanation of Ratios and Data

Current Data Sorted by Revenue   Comparative Historical Data

						Type of Statement					
		4	6	4	14	Unqualified	31	24	15	17	14
1	80	44	5	130		Reviewed	115	100	80	80	130
1	25	1	1	28		Compiled	36	27	21	29	28
6	15	1	2	23		Tax Returns	43	41	34	30	23
8	18	27	10	63		Other	55	55	31	35	63

	54 (4/1-9/30/10)		204 (10/1/10-3/31/11)				4/1/06-3/31/07	4/1/07-3/31/08	4/1/08-3/31/09	4/1/09-3/31/10	4/1/10-3/31/11
0-1MM	1-10MM	10-50MM	50 & OVER	ALL			ALL	ALL	ALL	ALL	ALL
16	142	78	22	258		NUMBER OF STATEMENTS	280	247	181	191	258
%	%	%	%	%		ASSETS	%	%	%	%	%
23.2	16.8	14.2	13.6	16.2		Cash & Equivalents	12.4	14.0	14.6	17.3	16.2
22.3	33.0	23.7	18.5	28.3		A/R - Progress Billings	47.4	46.4	41.2	40.2	28.3
.8	10.5	29.4	20.6	16.5		A/R - Current Retention	1.8	1.9	2.5	1.3	16.5
12.9	7.5	3.1	1.8	6.0		Inventory	7.1	6.9	6.3	5.8	6.0
.0	5.4	9.7	5.1	6.3		Cost & Est. Earnings In Excess Billings	4.2	4.7	4.4	4.8	6.3
.3	2.9	4.2	9.8	3.7		All Other Current	5.2	5.1	5.9	5.7	3.7
59.5	76.2	84.2	69.4	77.0		Total Current	78.0	79.0	74.9	75.0	77.0
33.5	15.3	11.2	20.1	15.6		Fixed Assets (net)	15.1	13.9	17.4	17.2	15.6
.0	.8	.2	.1	.5		Joint Ventures & Investments	.7	.4	.4	.7	.5
1.0	1.0	.6	3.1	1.0		Intangibles (net)	1.2	1.5	1.4	.7	1.0
6.0	6.7	3.8	7.3	5.8		All Other Non-Current	5.0	5.2	5.9	6.4	5.8
100.0	100.0	100.0	100.0	100.0		Total	100.0	100.0	100.0	100.0	100.0
						LIABILITIES					
20.6	11.0	10.5	11.1	11.5		Notes Payable-Short Term	12.0	9.9	10.4	12.0	11.5
11.2	17.8	22.0	18.5	18.7		A/P - Trade	20.5	20.0	16.5	17.5	18.7
.0	.5	.1	.1	.3		A/P - Retention	.2	.2	.1	.1	.3
.1	6.2	8.2	10.2	6.7		Billings in Excess of Costs & Est. Earnings	5.8	7.1	7.7	6.5	6.7
7.4	.4	.0	.7	.7		Income Taxes Payable	.2	.2	.5	.3	.7
9.9	4.0	2.0	2.8	3.6		Cur. Mat.-L/T/D	2.4	2.7	3.3	3.7	3.6
9.5	7.9	8.8	9.4	8.4		All Other Current	9.4	8.2	8.8	8.9	8.4
58.7	47.7	51.7	52.6	50.0		Total Current	50.5	48.2	47.3	48.9	50.0
24.7	8.5	4.0	7.9	8.1		Long-Term Debt	11.4	11.7	10.2	11.0	8.1
.0	.7	.3	.3	.5		Deferred Taxes	.6	.5	.7	.6	.5
14.0	3.6	3.0	4.0	4.1		All Other Non-Current	3.9	3.9	4.0	4.6	4.1
2.7	39.6	41.0	35.1	37.4		Net Worth	33.7	35.6	37.7	34.8	37.4
100.0	100.0	100.0	100.0	100.0		Total Liabilities & Net Worth	100.0	100.0	100.0	100.0	100.0
						INCOME DATA					
100.0	100.0	100.0	100.0	100.0		Contract Revenues	100.0	100.0	100.0	100.0	100.0
49.2	26.7	16.9	23.1	24.8		Gross Profit	26.8	27.4	28.9	30.1	24.8
50.9	26.8	13.8	21.2	23.9		Operating Expenses	22.5	21.8	24.4	28.3	23.9
-1.7	-.1	3.1	1.9	.9		Operating Profit	4.3	5.5	4.4	1.8	.9
.4	.1	.1	.6	.2		All Other Expenses (net)	.5	.4	.5	.4	.2
-2.0	-.2	3.0	1.2	.7		Profit Before Taxes	3.8	5.1	3.9	1.4	.7
						RATIOS					
2.5	2.8	2.3	1.8	2.5			2.6	2.6	2.7	2.6	2.5
1.3	1.7	1.6	1.5	1.6	Current		1.6	1.7	1.7	1.7	1.6
.3	1.2	1.2	1.2	1.2			1.2	1.2	1.3	1.1	1.2
	3.0	4.8	4.6	3.9	4.4		4.5	4.8	5.3	4.7	4.4
(11)	2.4	(138) 2.6	2.8	(21) 2.0	(248) 2.6	Receivables/Payables	(265) 2.5	(240) 2.6	(171) 3.0	(183) 2.7	(248) 2.6
	.6	1.8	1.6	1.7	1.6		1.7	1.5	1.7	1.7	1.6
0 UND	42 8.8	50 7.3	41 9.0	43 8.6			40 9.0	40 9.1	35 10.4	34 10.7	43 8.6
8 43.3	57 6.4	71 5.1	61 6.0	60 6.0		Revenues/Receivables	61 6.0	59 6.2	52 7.0	49 7.4	60 6.0
58 6.3	81 4.5	84 4.3	80 4.5	82 4.5			81 4.5	78 4.7	72 5.1	72 5.0	82 4.5
0 UND	16 22.3	17 21.1	21 17.1	16 22.3			15 23.8	15 25.0	11 33.2	11 32.5	16 22.3
4 91.0	28 12.9	27 13.6	29 12.5	27 13.5		Cost of Revenues/Payables	30 12.3	28 12.9	23 16.1	25 14.7	27 13.5
59 6.1	45 8.1	46 7.9	41 8.9	45 8.2			49 7.4	48 7.7	41 9.0	42 8.8	45 8.2
5.9	4.5	5.4	7.3	5.1			6.5	5.8	6.4	5.2	5.1
27.3	9.3	8.8	9.9	9.5		Revenues/Working Capital	9.8	9.5	10.0	10.2	9.5
-30.0	29.6	19.0	22.4	27.9			22.7	22.0	21.2	48.5	27.9
7.8	9.8	27.5	11.5	11.4			19.0	25.0	32.3	13.6	11.4
(13) 2.8	(113) 2.0	(66) 6.3	(19) 7.5	(211) 4.3		EBIT/Interest	(249) 6.3	(217) 6.9	(160) 9.2	(165) 4.3	(211) 4.3
-4.2	-7.0	1.7	2.2	-2.4			1.7	2.2	1.6	-1.2	-2.4
	3.5	11.6		7.8			13.2	10.9	9.8	9.6	7.8
(34) 1.6	(14) 2.9		(54) 2.0		Net Profit + Depr., Dep., Amort./Cur. Mat. L/T/D	(55) 5.0	(38) 4.2	(32) 3.9	(35) 2.9	(54) 2.0
.8	.0		.8			1.5	.9	1.2	1.4	.8
.4	.1	.1	.2	.1			.1	.1	.2	.1	.1
.7	.3	.2	.4	.3		Fixed/Worth	.3	.3	.3	.4	.3
-1.4	1.1	.5	.9	.8			.8	.8	1.0	1.1	.8
.9	.5	1.0	1.2	.7			.8	.8	.7	.7	.7
5.2	1.3	1.5	1.7	1.5		Debt/Worth	1.8	1.7	1.6	1.6	1.5
-4.2	4.2	3.1	2.9	3.8			4.6	4.8	3.6	4.4	3.8
52.3	19.0	30.6	25.5	26.8			57.4	63.8	54.8	44.2	26.8
(10) 7.8	(127) 4.0	(76) 14.6	(20) 18.0	(233) 8.9		% Profit Before Taxes/ Tangible Net Worth	(248) 29.9	(219) 31.2	(159) 27.8	(168) 18.2	(233) 8.9
-23.4	-18.8	2.0	1.7	-6.4			12.0	10.1	1.4	-1.9	-6.4
19.8	10.7	12.2	8.1	11.4			21.0	24.8	23.6	17.2	11.4
-4.2	1.5	5.8	5.7	3.7		% Profit Before Taxes/ Total Assets	9.7	11.0	7.9	5.0	3.7
-20.8	-9.9	.9	.2	-4.6			2.1	2.8	1.5	-2.4	-4.6
	.6	.5	.5	.6			.5	.4	.5	.5	.6
(11) 1.7	(126) 1.3	(74) .8	(14) 1.0	(225) 1.1		% Depr., Dep., Amort./ Revenues	(236) 1.0	(194) .9	(148) 1.0	(164) 1.1	(225) 1.1
3.4	2.1	1.3	3.1	1.8			1.6	1.5	2.1	2.0	1.8
	3.1	1.2		2.4			2.1	2.3	2.4	3.4	2.4
(79) 5.2	(33) 2.1		(128) 4.5		% Officers', Directors' Owners' Comp/Revenues	(167) 4.2	(141) 4.1	(109) 4.8	(118) 5.4	(128) 4.5
8.0	3.3		7.7			7.3	7.8	8.4	9.1	7.7
9119M	649430M	1709994M	17318370M	19686913M		Contract Revenues ($)	6016563M	8309209M	48104221M	26630772M	19686913M
2862M	356228M	677856M	6419639M	7456585M		Total Assets ($)	1993266M	2438338M	24767710M	10442463M	7456585M

M = $ thousand   MM = $ million
See Pages 9 through 22 for Explanation of Ratios and Data

Current Data Sorted by Revenue | Comparative Historical Data

0-1MM	1-10MM	10-50MM	50 & OVER	ALL	Type of Statement	4/1/06-3/31/07	4/1/07-3/31/08	4/1/08-3/31/09	4/1/09-3/31/10	4/1/10-3/31/11
1		2	1	4	Unqualified	22	18	6	14	4
2	61	55	4	122	Reviewed	108	101	76	81	122
4	26	4	3	37	Compiled	41	51	37	29	37
9	37	2	3	51	Tax Returns	42	62	54	44	51
2	29	19	8	58	Other	48	35	36	38	58
\(49 (4/1-9/30/10)\)		\(223 (10/1/10-3/31/11)\)								
ALL	ALL	ALL	ALL	ALL		ALL	ALL	ALL	ALL	ALL
18	153	82	19	272	NUMBER OF STATEMENTS	261	267	209	206	272
%	%	%	%	%	**ASSETS**	%	%	%	%	%
35.0	17.1	12.5	11.4	16.5	Cash & Equivalents	11.4	14.7	14.5	17.6	16.5
15.2	27.9	20.7	33.8	25.3	A/R - Progress Billings	42.7	40.4	38.7	37.5	25.3
.8	10.8	33.0	18.6	17.4	A/R - Current Retention	2.6	1.5	1.9	1.4	17.4
14.4	9.3	4.1	3.0	7.6	Inventory	8.8	7.8	9.8	8.7	7.6
.1	4.0	7.3	3.7	4.7	Cost & Est. Earnings In Excess Billings	3.9	2.9	2.5	2.6	4.7
1.7	5.0	5.1	10.2	5.2	All Other Current	4.4	5.5	5.1	5.0	5.2
67.1	74.0	82.7	80.8	76.6	Total Current	73.8	72.8	72.4	72.8	76.6
19.0	16.5	11.0	14.0	14.8	Fixed Assets (net)	17.5	17.3	18.8	17.9	14.8
.0	.0	.2	.2	.1	Joint Ventures & Investments	.5	.7	.9	.8	.1
4.4	2.5	.9	.1	2.0	Intangibles (net)	1.5	2.2	2.0	2.1	2.0
9.5	7.0	5.2	4.9	6.4	All Other Non-Current	6.6	7.0	5.9	6.5	6.4
100.0	100.0	100.0	100.0	100.0	Total	100.0	100.0	100.0	100.0	100.0
					LIABILITIES					
9.4	13.0	5.2	10.1	10.2	Notes Payable-Short Term	9.8	8.9	12.9	12.7	10.2
11.1	22.7	26.6	29.1	23.5	A/P - Trade	23.1	21.5	21.9	22.8	23.5
.1	.2	1.6	1.1	.7	A/P - Retention	.1	.2	.2	.4	.7
.6	5.1	10.4	9.9	6.7	Billings in Excess of Costs & Est. Earnings	6.0	6.6	5.9	5.1	6.7
.1	.3	.2	.0	.2	Income Taxes Payable	.3	.2	.3	.2	.2
3.1	3.8	1.8	2.4	3.1	Cur. Mat.-L/T/D	3.6	4.2	3.7	5.0	3.1
17.7	8.6	9.2	13.1	9.7	All Other Current	9.6	11.1	10.0	10.5	9.7
42.1	53.7	55.0	65.7	54.2	Total Current	52.5	52.9	54.9	56.7	54.2
13.4	12.7	4.1	10.8	10.0	Long-Term Debt	12.9	12.5	17.0	17.0	10.0
.0	.7	.2	.1	.5	Deferred Taxes	.5	.4	.3	.4	.5
4.7	3.9	2.3	1.2	3.3	All Other Non-Current	5.3	5.7	6.5	4.6	3.3
39.7	29.1	38.5	22.2	32.1	Net Worth	28.9	28.4	21.3	21.3	32.1
100.0	100.0	100.0	100.0	100.0	Total Liabilities & Net Worth	100.0	100.0	100.0	100.0	100.0
					INCOME DATA					
100.0	100.0	100.0	100.0	100.0	Contract Revenues	100.0	100.0	100.0	100.0	100.0
40.8	27.9	17.8	21.5	25.2	Gross Profit	27.5	30.7	30.0	29.4	25.2
35.8	26.7	15.9	20.1	23.6	Operating Expenses	23.2	26.1	26.7	26.5	23.6
4.9	1.2	1.9	1.4	1.7	Operating Profit	4.3	4.6	3.4	2.9	1.7
1.0	.3	.0	.2	.2	All Other Expenses (net)	.4	.3	.8	.5	.2
3.9	.9	2.0	1.3	1.5	Profit Before Taxes	4.0	4.3	2.6	2.4	1.5
					RATIOS					
9.0	2.2	2.1	1.7	2.2	Current	2.0	2.0	2.4	2.3	2.2
1.8	1.4	1.4	1.4	1.4		1.4	1.4	1.5	1.5	1.4
.7	1.0	1.2	1.1	1.1		1.1	1.1	1.1	1.0	1.1
5.4	3.6	3.2	2.6	3.3	Receivables/Payables	3.6	4.0	3.8	3.3	3.3
(13) 1.3	(148) 1.8	(18) 2.0	2.0	(261) 1.9		(246) 2.2	(245) 2.1	(194) 1.9	(197) 1.9	(261) 1.9
.7	1.2	1.5	1.2	1.2		1.3	1.2	1.4	1.0	1.2
0 UND	29 12.6	50 7.3	48 7.7	32 11.4	Revenues/Receivables	30 12.3	24 15.5	18 20.0	20 18.6	32 11.4
23 15.9	46 7.9	63 5.8	58 6.3	53 6.9		56 6.6	47 7.8	47 7.7	40 9.0	53 6.9
43 8.5	77 4.8	81 4.5	84 4.4	78 4.7		76 4.8	70 5.2	71 5.1	67 5.4	78 4.7
0 UND	18 19.9	22 16.4	29 12.6	19 19.5	Cost of Revenues/Payables	18 20.8	15 24.7	15 25.2	18 20.7	19 19.5
16 22.8	31 11.8	36 10.2	35 10.5	33 11.1		33 11.1	28 13.3	26 13.8	27 13.3	33 11.1
53 6.8	52 7.0	54 6.8	54 6.8	53 6.9		49 7.4	47 7.8	49 7.5	45 8.1	53 6.9
5.6	5.8	7.2	7.6	6.7	Revenues/Working Capital	7.7	8.2	7.3	6.8	6.7
11.2	12.0	12.7	13.2	12.4		15.2	16.0	13.6	15.3	12.4
-48.9	NM	23.2	206.7	43.9		57.0	85.8	94.0	521.3	43.9
7.5	12.0	53.5	34.6	20.5	EBIT/Interest	17.5	23.8	17.6	15.2	20.5
(12) 3.9	(133) 3.6	(76) 9.5	(15) 5.4	(236) 4.6		(229) 6.1	(234) 5.5	(178) 4.5	(177) 5.4	(236) 4.6
-1.4	-1.7	1.7	-1.8	-.5		1.7	1.6	1.0	.8	-.5
	5.9	7.6		6.0	Net Profit + Depr., Dep., Amort./Cur. Mat. L/T/D	9.3	15.8	5.3	7.7	6.0
	(27) 2.3	(18) 2.3		(46) 2.1		(61) 2.7	(53) 3.2	(32) 2.6	(38) 2.6	(46) 2.1
	-.3	-1.7		-.4		1.0	1.2	1.4	-.1	-.4
.0	.1	.1	.2	.1	Fixed/Worth	.2	.2	.2	.1	.1
.6	.5	.2	.3	.3		.5	.4	.4	.4	.3
-4.5	1.8	.5	78.7	1.2		1.2	1.9	2.9	2.6	1.2
.2	.7	.9	1.1	.8	Debt/Worth	.9	1.0	1.0	.9	.8
3.4	2.1	1.8	2.6	1.9		2.2	2.3	2.4	2.0	1.9
-32.6	9.5	3.4	452.1	5.8		5.2	9.2	18.2	10.5	5.8
318.4	32.3	35.0	40.2	35.5	% Profit Before Taxes/ Tangible Net Worth	58.2	69.3	66.7	46.6	35.5
(12) 37.4	(124) 8.8	(81) 12.7	(15) 18.8	(232) 11.7		(224) 31.3	(222) 32.5	(164) 26.8	(162) 20.0	(232) 11.7
1.8	-5.1	1.8	11.6	.5		6.9	10.0	7.6	2.4	.5
54.8	13.3	12.7	9.8	13.2	% Profit Before Taxes/ Total Assets	21.0	23.7	19.4	17.6	13.2
7.2	3.0	4.6	5.5	4.4		9.7	9.2	7.4	6.5	4.4
.1	-3.2	.9	-2.9	-1.6		1.2	2.0	.6	-.8	-1.6
.7	.8	.4	.2	.6	% Depr., Dep., Amort./ Revenues	.6	.6	.5	.7	.6
(10) 1.2	(120) 1.3	(79) .7	(10) .5	(219) 1.0		(221) 1.0	(217) 1.0	(170) 1.1	(171) 1.1	(219) 1.0
2.9	2.1	1.2	.9	1.7		1.7	1.7	1.9	1.9	1.7
	2.9	1.1		2.0	% Officers', Directors' Owners' Comp/Revenues	1.9	2.0	2.5	2.8	2.0
	(95) 4.5	(38) 1.7		(149) 3.6		(162) 3.8	(169) 4.4	(125) 4.4	(125) 5.0	(149) 3.6
	7.2	2.9		6.4		7.3	7.7	8.2	8.2	6.4
11753M	715961M	1748668M	26931149M	29407531M	Contract Revenues ($)	14535238M	30337111M	24041075M	58656308M	29407531M
5235M	271306M	591976M	8377290M	9245807M	Total Assets ($)	5080035M	8293981M	6055177M	13672430M	9245807M

M = $ thousand   MM = $ million
See Pages 9 through 22 for Explanation of Ratios and Data

Current Data Sorted by Revenue   Comparative Historical Data

Type of Statement

0-1MM	1-10MM	10-50MM	50 & OVER	ALL		4/1/06-3/31/07 ALL	4/1/07-3/31/08 ALL	4/1/08-3/31/09 ALL	4/1/09-3/31/10 ALL	4/1/10-3/31/11 ALL
	1	3		4	Unqualified	11	9	8	8	4
	20	17	2	39	Reviewed	33	40	29	25	39
2	9		1	12	Compiled	10	11	10	7	12
1	5		2	8	Tax Returns	14	13	9	8	8
1	10	7	2	20	Other	14	14	9	13	20
	12 (4/1-9/30/10)		71 (10/1/10-3/31/11)							
4	45	27	7	83	**NUMBER OF STATEMENTS**	82	87	65	61	83

Assets

0-1MM	1-10MM	10-50MM	50 & OVER	ALL		4/1/06-3/31/07	4/1/07-3/31/08	4/1/08-3/31/09	4/1/09-3/31/10	4/1/10-3/31/11
%	%	%	%	%		%	%	%	%	%
	12.3	14.4		13.1	Cash & Equivalents	11.6	16.4	11.7	17.6	13.1
	40.7	36.0		35.6	A/R - Progress Billings	52.7	50.0	54.6	47.5	35.6
	17.2	19.2		18.8	A/R - Current Retention	2.0	2.5	2.3	1.4	18.8
	2.8	2.2		2.8	Inventory	5.1	4.9	6.1	4.9	2.8
	3.8	7.6		5.1	Cost & Est. Earnings In Excess Billings	4.6	3.6	2.9	2.2	5.1
	4.5	3.8		4.8	All Other Current	3.9	3.6	6.3	4.9	4.8
	81.4	83.2		80.2	Total Current	80.0	81.0	83.9	78.5	80.2
	11.0	7.1		10.5	Fixed Assets (net)	12.5	11.2	10.7	12.0	10.5
	.0	.3		.1	Joint Ventures & Investments	.1	1.1	.1	.3	.1
	.3	2.3		1.6	Intangibles (net)	.6	.3	.5	.7	1.6
	7.3	7.1		7.6	All Other Non-Current	6.9	6.5	5.0	8.5	7.6
	100.0	100.0		100.0	Total	100.0	100.0	100.0	100.0	100.0

Liabilities

0-1MM	1-10MM	10-50MM	50 & OVER	ALL		4/1/06-3/31/07	4/1/07-3/31/08	4/1/08-3/31/09	4/1/09-3/31/10	4/1/10-3/31/11
	14.6	13.8		17.7	Notes Payable-Short Term	10.1	11.9	12.6	9.9	17.7
	15.1	10.4		13.1	A/P - Trade	15.2	12.5	14.2	16.6	13.1
	.2	.0		.2	A/P - Retention	.1	.3	.1	.0	.2
	4.0	6.5		5.0	Billings in Excess of Costs & Est. Earnings	5.4	10.1	7.9	6.8	5.0
	.0	.7		.3	Income Taxes Payable	.2	.1	.1	.0	.3
	2.7	1.3		2.6	Cur. Mat.-L/T/D	1.9	2.3	1.4	1.4	2.6
	8.5	9.6		9.5	All Other Current	11.7	10.3	9.8	10.8	9.5
	45.1	42.3		48.3	Total Current	44.6	47.5	46.1	45.6	48.3
	4.5	5.6		8.0	Long-Term Debt	6.4	9.3	7.3	5.5	8.0
	.6	.2		.4	Deferred Taxes	.6	.4	.5	.5	.4
	7.5	.7		6.3	All Other Non-Current	7.3	7.7	3.8	8.8	6.3
	42.3	51.2		37.1	Net Worth	41.1	35.1	42.4	39.5	37.1
	100.0	100.0		100.0	Total Liabilities & Net Worth	100.0	100.0	100.0	100.0	100.0

Income Data

0-1MM	1-10MM	10-50MM	50 & OVER	ALL		4/1/06-3/31/07	4/1/07-3/31/08	4/1/08-3/31/09	4/1/09-3/31/10	4/1/10-3/31/11
	100.0	100.0		100.0	Contract Revenues	100.0	100.0	100.0	100.0	100.0
	20.3	17.0		19.0	Gross Profit	23.7	24.3	25.4	24.8	19.0
	19.7	16.0		18.8	Operating Expenses	19.4	19.5	20.6	23.4	18.8
	.6	1.0		.3	Operating Profit	4.3	4.9	4.8	1.4	.3
	.2	.1		.1	All Other Expenses (net)	.2	.5	.1	.3	.1
	.4	.9		.1	Profit Before Taxes	4.1	4.4	4.7	1.1	.1

Ratios

0-1MM	1-10MM	10-50MM	50 & OVER	ALL		4/1/06-3/31/07	4/1/07-3/31/08	4/1/08-3/31/09	4/1/09-3/31/10	4/1/10-3/31/11
	3.4	3.8		3.2	Current	2.9	2.9	3.6	3.6	3.2
	1.9	2.0		1.8		1.9	1.8	1.9	2.0	1.8
	1.3	1.5		1.3		1.3	1.4	1.3	1.3	1.3
	6.4	8.9		8.4	Receivables/Payables	7.8	7.3	7.7	9.6	8.4
	(43) 4.2	5.8	(77)	4.5		(79) 4.7	(79) 4.8	(64) 4.9	(60) 4.8	(77) 4.5
	3.1	4.2		3.2		2.9	3.3	2.9	2.7	3.2
	62 · 5.9	63 · 5.8	60	6.1	Revenues/Receivables	40 · 9.1	37 · 9.7	50 · 7.3	44 · 8.3	60 · 6.1
	79 · 4.6	82 · 4.4	78	4.7		59 · 6.2	67 · 5.5	63 · 5.8	54 · 6.8	78 · 4.7
	107 · 3.4	93 · 3.9	101	3.6		77 · 4.7	81 · 4.5	87 · 4.2	69 · 5.3	101 · 3.6
	11 · 33.0	9 · 38.6	9	41.8	Cost of Revenues/Payables	9 · 40.3	7 · 50.3	9 · 40.9	8 · 46.1	9 · 41.8
	20 · 18.4	16 · 22.9	18	19.8		16 · 22.5	17 · 21.0	17 · 21.6	15 · 24.9	18 · 19.8
	38 · 9.6	23 · 16.1	30	12.1		27 · 13.4	24 · 15.1	30 · 12.0	28 · 13.1	30 · 12.1
	4.8	3.6		5.1	Revenues/Working Capital	6.4	6.4	5.5	4.7	5.1
	8.2	6.3		8.2		10.0	9.6	8.4	8.5	8.2
	15.6	11.5		15.9		20.0	16.3	16.4	18.6	15.9
	11.0	16.8		13.8	EBIT/Interest	31.5	44.4	35.4	24.2	13.8
	(43) 3.4	(23) 3.5	(76)	2.6		(72) 12.0	(72) 9.2	(55) 8.6	(49) 3.8	(76) 2.6
	-.7	-.8		-.5		1.9	2.3	1.5	-6.7	-.5
					Net Profit + Depr., Dep., Amort./Cur. Mat. L/T/D	31.1	12.8	42.3		
						(14) 8.2	(17) 4.3	(11) 4.6		
						3.7	2.7	2.1		
	.1	.1		.1	Fixed/Worth	.1	.1	.1	.1	.1
	.2	.1		.2		.2	.2	.2	.1	.2
	.4	.2		.4		.6	.4	.4	.5	.4
	.3	.6		.4	Debt/Worth	.5	.6	.6	.4	.4
	1.5	1.0		1.4		1.2	1.5	1.5	1.0	1.4
	3.0	1.6		2.8		2.7	2.6	3.0	2.5	2.8
	27.7	19.0		19.7	% Profit Before Taxes/Tangible Net Worth	54.3	58.0	53.9	32.9	19.7
	(41) 7.7	3.4	(75)	5.2		(75) 32.6	(80) 33.3	(61) 33.3	(55) 16.1	(75) 5.2
	-.5	-2.9		-2.9		6.7	9.3	8.9	-10.1	-2.9
	8.6	9.1		7.0	% Profit Before Taxes/Total Assets	26.9	30.7	26.2	16.9	7.0
	2.2	2.2		1.7		13.1	11.0	10.3	4.7	1.7
	-1.4	-1.5		-1.5		1.2	3.1	1.3	-6.8	-1.5
	.6	.4		.5	% Depr., Dep., Amort./Revenues	.3	.3	.3	.5	.5
	(34) .8	(24) .7	(66)	.8		(66) .6	(70) .6	(51) .6	(51) .7	(66) .8
	1.1	1.0		1.1		1.0	1.0	1.1	1.6	1.1
	2.4	1.7		1.9	% Officers', Directors' Owners' Comp/Revenues	2.2	1.7	1.8	2.0	1.9
	(25) 5.0	(12) 3.9	(44)	4.4		(51) 4.1	(57) 2.6	(37) 3.3	(30) 4.0	(44) 4.4
	7.6	7.4		7.4		7.1	7.6	6.8	11.1	7.4
2731M	193906M	524899M	4592856M	5314392M	Contract Revenues ($)	14564606M	11179995M	8423309M	779420M	5314392M
832M	76005M	230678M	1496825M	1804340M	Total Assets ($)	2338829M	2968525M	2531323M	297755M	1804340M

M = $ thousand   MM = $ million
See Pages 9 through 22 for Explanation of Ratios and Data

Current Data Sorted by Revenue   **Comparative Historical Data**

Type of Statement	0-1MM	1-10MM	10-50MM	50 & OVER	ALL		4/1/06-3/31/07	4/1/07-3/31/08	4/1/08-3/31/09	4/1/09-3/31/10	4/1/10-3/31/11
Unqualified		2	2		4		2	2	1	2	4
Reviewed	1	14	2		17		25	20	14	18	17
Compiled	2	5			7		9	15	9	6	7
Tax Returns	1	2			3		8	12	5	5	3
Other	1	3	2		6		10	7	5	14	6
	9 (4/1-9/30/10)		28 (10/1/10-3/31/11)				4/1/06-3/31/07	4/1/07-3/31/08	4/1/08-3/31/09	4/1/09-3/31/10	4/1/10-3/31/11
	0-1MM	1-10MM	10-50MM	50 & OVER	ALL		ALL	ALL	ALL	ALL	ALL
NUMBER OF STATEMENTS	5	26	6		37		54	56	34	45	37

(The 50 & OVER column is marked **DATA NOT AVAILABLE**.)

	0-1MM %	1-10MM %	10-50MM %	50 & OVER	ALL %		06/07 %	07/08 %	08/09 %	09/10 %	10/11 %
ASSETS											
Cash & Equivalents		12.3			17.3		12.4	19.4	19.2	17.2	17.3
A/R - Progress Billings		37.0			34.5		46.2	43.7	39.2	44.4	34.5
A/R - Current Retention		10.7			9.8		1.9	2.0	.3	.3	9.8
Inventory		3.3			2.8		3.4	2.5	2.4	2.3	2.8
Cost & Est. Earnings In Excess Billings		7.6			6.9		5.0	2.8	3.2	5.4	6.9
All Other Current		4.5			3.5		4.0	4.7	3.4	5.2	3.5
Total Current		75.4			74.8		72.8	75.1	67.5	74.8	74.8
Fixed Assets (net)		17.8			15.9		17.8	16.4	17.3	16.1	15.9
Joint Ventures & Investments		.0			.0		.7	1.1	.8	.6	.0
Intangibles (net)		.1			1.7		.3	1.3	2.2	1.1	1.7
All Other Non-Current		6.8			7.6		8.4	6.2	12.1	7.4	7.6
Total		100.0			100.0		100.0	100.0	100.0	100.0	100.0
LIABILITIES											
Notes Payable-Short Term		13.0			13.7		15.5	13.2	12.4	13.4	13.7
A/P - Trade		14.1			12.2		19.6	15.5	15.7	13.4	12.2
A/P - Retention		.0			.0		.0	.1	.0	.0	.0
Billings in Excess of Costs & Est. Earnings		2.9			2.1		3.3	2.1	2.6	3.0	2.1
Income Taxes Payable		1.5			1.2		.5	.2	.1	.2	1.2
Cur. Mat.-L/T/D		2.5			1.9		4.6	2.8	3.0	2.2	1.9
All Other Current		6.3			10.1		9.4	12.0	7.6	10.0	10.1
Total Current		40.4			41.1		52.9	45.9	41.4	42.2	41.1
Long-Term Debt		6.7			6.2		13.0	12.7	8.9	10.1	6.2
Deferred Taxes		1.5			1.5		.4	.6	.9	.6	1.5
All Other Non-Current		8.2			7.3		2.7	6.9	7.5	6.8	7.3
Net Worth		43.3			44.0		31.0	33.8	41.3	40.4	44.0
Total Liabilities & Net Worth		100.0			100.0		100.0	100.0	100.0	100.0	100.0
INCOME DATA											
Contract Revenues		100.0			100.0		100.0	100.0	100.0	100.0	100.0
Gross Profit		29.3			30.1		30.6	32.6	36.5	28.6	30.1
Operating Expenses		28.2			29.1		25.9	26.8	31.2	27.6	29.1
Operating Profit		1.1			.9		4.7	5.8	5.3	1.0	.9
All Other Expenses (net)		.3			-.1		.1	.4	-.5	.1	-.1
Profit Before Taxes		.8			1.0		4.6	5.5	5.8	.9	1.0

RATIOS

	1-10MM	50 & OVER	ALL		06/07	07/08	08/09	09/10	10/11
Current	3.3		3.6		2.5	3.3	4.7	3.2	3.6
	1.7		2.0		1.7	1.9	1.8	2.0	2.0
	1.2		1.3		1.1	1.1	1.1	1.3	1.3
Receivables/Payables	5.9		7.8		(50) 7.6	(50) 8.7	(30) 11.5	(43) 9.4	(36) 7.8
	4.0		(36) 4.1		3.6	3.8	4.1	4.2	4.1
	2.3		2.5		1.5	2.3	2.1	1.9	2.5
Revenues/Receivables	48 7.6	41 8.9	8.9		33 11.2	29 12.7	27 13.7	29 12.4	41 8.9
	64 5.7	62 5.9	5.9		62 5.9	54 6.8	47 7.7	56 6.6	62 5.9
	92 4.0	86 4.2	4.2		79 4.6	77 4.8	79 4.6	72 5.1	86 4.2
Cost of Revenues/Payables	17 21.3	11 31.9	31.9		7 53.3	6 57.7	0 UND	8 43.8	11 31.9
	28 13.2	24 15.0	15.0		21 17.5	16 22.6	14 26.7	14 26.0	24 15.0
	36 10.1	34 10.6	10.6		38 9.5	34 10.8	34 10.9	37 9.7	34 10.6
Revenues/Working Capital	4.4		4.0		5.2	6.1	7.0	5.0	4.0
	10.2		8.1		11.9	12.3	9.9	8.7	8.1
	22.0		17.8		225.6	42.7	152.8	22.6	17.8
EBIT/Interest	(24) 9.8	(31) 19.4	19.4		(46) 19.2	(46) 18.5	(28) 21.2	(38) 21.7	(31) 19.4
	6.1		7.9		4.9	5.4	6.8	3.8	7.9
	-3.7		-2.5		2.0	1.8	1.3	-3.2	-2.5
Net Profit + Depr., Dep., Amort./Cur. Mat. L/T/D					(12) 8.2	(14) 9.1			
					2.6	2.7			
					1.6	1.4			
Fixed/Worth	.2		.1		.1	.1	.1	.1	.1
	.4		.3		.3	.3	.3	.3	.3
	.9		.9		1.1	1.5	.9	.8	.9
Debt/Worth	.6		.4		.7	.5	.3	.5	.4
	1.6		1.3		1.3	1.3	1.0	1.0	1.3
	2.5		2.5		3.5	5.8	3.2	3.0	2.5
% Profit Before Taxes/Tangible Net Worth	(25) 43.3	(34) 31.9	31.9		(45) 55.2	(47) 55.0	(31) 74.5	(39) 26.0	(34) 31.9
	7.2		8.6		20.7	26.3	28.2	12.0	8.6
	-16.2		-14.2		4.7	6.0	1.6	-6.0	-14.2
% Profit Before Taxes/Total Assets	12.6		13.1		30.8	29.6	41.5	14.5	13.1
	4.3		6.8		6.3	12.8	13.1	3.6	6.8
	-6.6		-6.1		1.9	3.1	.4	-9.4	-6.1
% Depr., Dep., Amort./Revenues	(22) .7	(31) .7	.7		(45) .6	(43) .6	(28) .7	(37) .7	(31) .7
	1.3		1.2		.9	1.0	1.4	1.1	1.2
	2.5		2.3		1.8	2.0	2.1	2.3	2.3
% Officers', Directors' Owners' Comp/Revenues	(16) 2.5	(23) 2.6	2.6		(29) 1.9	(33) 2.2	(23) 2.6	(21) 2.1	(23) 2.6
	4.0		4.0		4.7	5.4	5.5	3.5	4.0
	5.3		7.0		9.1	8.8	6.3		7.0

	0-1MM	1-10MM	10-50MM	50 & OVER	ALL		06/07	07/08	08/09	09/10	10/11
Contract Revenues ($)	1769M	106760M	126627M		235156M		5392101M	2049461M	522849M	282326M	235156M
Total Assets ($)	1176M	41662M	47291M		90129M		723616M	521621M	228821M	104809M	90129M

© RMA 2011

M = $ thousand   MM = $ million
See Pages 9 through 22 for Explanation of Ratios and Data

Current Data Sorted by Revenue   Comparative Historical Data

Current data columns 0-1MM and 1-10MM are marked **DATA NOT AVAILABLE**.

	0-1MM	1-10MM	10-50MM	50 & OVER	ALL		4/1/06-3/31/07 ALL	4/1/07-3/31/08 ALL	4/1/08-3/31/09 ALL	4/1/09-3/31/10 ALL	4/1/10-3/31/11 ALL
						Type of Statement					
			1		1	Unqualified	3	2		1	1
		3	9		12	Reviewed	10	10	6	7	12
	1	2			3	Compiled	7	9	4	2	3
	1				1	Tax Returns	6	6	7	2	1
		2	2		4	Other	8	5	4	4	4
						1 (4/1-9/30/10) 20 (10/1/10-3/31/11)					
	2	7	12		21	**NUMBER OF STATEMENTS**	34	32	21	16	21
	%	%	%	%	%	**ASSETS**	%	%	%	%	%
			6.9		8.1	Cash & Equivalents	6.6	6.4	12.9	11.9	8.1
			34.2		26.6	A/R - Progress Billings	51.7	47.3	41.6	41.6	26.6
			25.9		20.6	A/R - Current Retention	1.4	.1	.0	.0	20.6
			4.0		13.0	Inventory	11.5	17.1	9.8	11.8	13.0
			11.5		8.3	Cost & Est. Earnings In Excess Billings	4.1	2.3	2.3	5.2	8.3
			2.3		2.2	All Other Current	3.6	3.4	7.3	4.3	2.2
			84.7		78.8	Total Current	78.8	76.6	73.8	74.8	78.8
			7.8		12.2	Fixed Assets (net)	12.4	14.9	19.4	16.5	12.2
			.0		.0	Joint Ventures & Investments	.1	.1	1.4	1.0	.0
			4.7		2.7	Intangibles (net)	1.9	2.0	2.1	.7	2.7
			2.9		6.4	All Other Non-Current	6.8	6.4	3.2	7.0	6.4
			100.0		100.0	Total	100.0	100.0	100.0	100.0	100.0
						LIABILITIES					
			11.4		12.5	Notes Payable-Short Term	28.6	22.9	18.6	48.5	12.5
			18.1		15.2	A/P - Trade	28.6	20.1	13.4	17.3	15.2
			.2		.2	A/P - Retention	.2	.0	.0	.0	.2
			7.6		8.1	Billings in Excess of Costs & Est. Earnings	2.9	4.0	2.4	3.3	8.1
			.0		.4	Income Taxes Payable	.3	.2	.1	.0	.4
			1.3		1.0	Cur. Mat.-L/T/D	1.2	2.2	2.3	2.5	1.0
			10.4		9.9	All Other Current	9.5	20.8	20.2	5.9	9.9
			49.1		47.2	Total Current	71.3	70.2	57.0	77.5	47.2
			7.6		11.1	Long-Term Debt	13.0	11.9	18.4	4.7	*11.1
			.1		.1	Deferred Taxes	.2	.0	.0	.0	.1
			7.0		9.4	All Other Non-Current	1.4	2.5	13.0	8.5	9.4
			36.2		32.2	Net Worth	14.0	15.4	11.6	9.2	32.2
			100.0		100.0	Total Liabilities & Net Worth	100.0	100.0	100.0	100.0	100.0
						INCOME DATA					
			100.0		100.0	Contract Revenues	100.0	100.0	100.0	100.0	100.0
			20.5		24.5	Gross Profit	27.8	26.0	27.1	27.3	24.5
			17.7		21.8	Operating Expenses	25.9	23.6	24.8	25.3	21.8
			2.8		2.7	Operating Profit	1.9	2.4	2.3	2.0	2.7
			.7		.9	All Other Expenses (net)	.5	.7	.4	.3	.9
			2.1		1.8	Profit Before Taxes	1.4	1.7	2.0	1.7	1.8
						RATIOS					
			2.2		2.5	Current	2.3	2.3	3.9	3.5	2.5
			1.9		1.8		1.4	1.1	2.1	1.6	1.8
			1.4		1.3		.9	.9	1.2	1.0	1.3
			8.2		6.0	Receivables/Payables	10.3	4.6	7.0	5.7	6.0
			3.0	(20)	3.0		(32) 2.8	(31) 2.1	(20) 4.8	2.2	(20) 3.0
			2.2		2.2		1.6	1.4	1.4	1.8	2.2
		54	6.7	38	9.7	Revenues/Receivables	35 10.6	21 17.4	12 29.3	30 12.2	38 9.7
		76	4.8	70	5.2		47 7.8	58 6.3	43 8.5	59 6.2	70 5.2
		95	3.9	77	4.7		83 4.4	71 5.1	63 5.8	75 4.9	77 4.7
		13	28.2	9	39.5	Cost of Revenues/Payables	5 68.2	19 19.7	2 167.4	12 31.2	9 39.5
		27	13.6	25	14.5		29 12.6	26 14.1	14 25.6	25 14.8	25 14.5
		51	7.2	45	8.1		42 8.7	44 8.2	36 10.3	45 8.2	45 8.1
			7.0		6.8	Revenues/Working Capital	7.1	8.4	6.6	5.3	6.8
			8.2		8.6		15.5	41.4	11.6	17.0	8.6
			14.7		15.0		-77.0	-28.4	41.9	NM	15.0
			7.7		6.6	EBIT/Interest	8.3	8.1	17.8	8.8	6.6
		(11)	5.5	(19)	4.9		(31) 2.4	(31) 4.1	5.9	(14) 2.1	(19) 4.9
			1.4		1.5		.1	1.2	1.1	.3	1.5
						Net Profit + Depr., Dep., Amort./Cur. Mat. L/T/D	24.3				
							(10) 3.3				
							.7				
			.1		.1	Fixed/Worth	.1	.1	.1	.1	.1
			.2		.3		.3	.4	.4	.2	.3
			.4		.5		-1.5	NM	6.0	2.2	.5
			1.6		1.2	Debt/Worth	.9	1.1	.9	1.2	1.2
			2.9		2.8		2.6	3.4	2.3	1.6	2.8
			3.6		4.1		-17.9	NM	NM	3.4	4.1
			40.6		33.9	% Profit Before Taxes/Tangible Net Worth	35.7	66.6	40.6	48.1	33.9
			20.7	(20)	11.0		(25) 27.7	(24) 22.3	(16) 20.0	(14) 10.5	(20) 11.0
			2.0		3.9		-2.6	3.4	3.1	-2.0	3.9
			14.6		9.0	% Profit Before Taxes/Total Assets	18.4	19.4	18.3	16.0	9.0
			6.2		5.0		5.1	5.6	5.9	2.6	5.0
			.6		1.0		-4.0	.1	.3	-5.7	1.0
			.2		.4	% Depr., Dep., Amort./Revenues	.3	.3	.2	.5	.4
		(10)	.7	(19)	.8		(23) .7	(25) .8	(14) .8	(10) .9	(19) .8
			1.1		1.5		1.2	1.7	1.1	1.6	1.5
					1.3	% Officers', Directors' Owners' Comp/Revenues	2.4	2.2	1.7	1.6	1.3
				(13)	2.2		(22) 5.6	(18) 3.1	(13) 4.3	(11) 8.1	(13) 2.2
					6.6		9.6	6.8	9.2	10.1	6.6
1534M	30604M	261268M		293406M	Contract Revenues ($)	247845M	301998M	162817M	155709M	293406M
612M	13239M	98460M		112311M	Total Assets ($)	75304M	90728M	50787M	63051M	112311M

M = $ thousand   MM = $ million
See Pages 9 through 22 for Explanation of Ratios and Data

Current Data Sorted by Revenue　　　　　Comparative Historical Data

					Type of Statement					
2	5	11	1	19	Unqualified	38	35	28	19	19
2	48	12	1	63	Reviewed	92	82	46	61	63
6	13			19	Compiled	35	26	25	12	19
8	11	1	2	22	Tax Returns	26	22	27	18	22
4	13	20	4	41	Other	30	33	34	28	41
23 (4/1-9/30/10)		141 (10/1/10-3/31/11)				4/1/06-3/31/07	4/1/07-3/31/08	4/1/08-3/31/09	4/1/09-3/31/10	4/1/10-3/31/11
0-1MM	1-10MM	10-50MM	50 & OVER	ALL		ALL	ALL	ALL	ALL	ALL
22	90	44	8	164	NUMBER OF STATEMENTS	221	198	160	138	164
%	%	%	%	%	ASSETS	%	%	%	%	%
12.4	11.9	11.9		12.1	Cash & Equivalents	8.5	9.4	9.7	11.3	12.1
15.0	28.1	21.4		23.6	A/R - Progress Billings	29.3	29.9	26.7	24.8	23.6
.0	5.8	18.3		8.4	A/R - Current Retention	1.5	1.4	2.1	1.5	8.4
6.4	2.5	.9		3.0	Inventory	3.8	3.0	2.8	2.8	3.0
1.3	2.5	4.7		3.0	Cost & Est. Earnings In Excess Billings	2.4	2.2	3.0	3.0	3.0
1.2	5.0	6.9		5.2	All Other Current	4.5	4.3	5.4	4.1	5.2
36.3	55.8	64.1		55.3	Total Current	49.9	50.2	49.7	47.5	55.3
47.1	35.6	27.9		35.2	Fixed Assets (net)	44.3	41.8	43.0	45.0	35.2
1.3	1.3	.7		1.1	Joint Ventures & Investments	.7	.7	.6	.8	1.1
3.4	.6	3.0		1.6	Intangibles (net)	.8	1.4	1.2	.9	1.6
11.9	6.8	4.3		6.7	All Other Non-Current	4.3	5.8	5.6	5.8	6.7
100.0	100.0	100.0		100.0	Total	100.0	100.0	100.0	100.0	100.0
					LIABILITIES					
19.1	13.4	7.2		12.2	Notes Payable-Short Term	7.3	7.5	9.8	8.6	12.2
17.4	14.9	20.9		16.7	A/P - Trade	14.1	12.6	13.1	12.6	16.7
.0	.1	.5		.2	A/P - Retention	.2	.2	.2	.1	.2
2.0	3.1	5.9		4.0	Billings in Excess of Costs & Est. Earnings	3.4	4.1	3.3	2.5	4.0
.0	.1	.2		.1	Income Taxes Payable	.2	.2	.3	.0	.1
6.4	7.8	4.8		6.8	Cur. Mat.-L/T/D	8.1	8.8	7.9	8.9	6.8
13.1	4.1	6.8		6.1	All Other Current	5.3	4.6	5.5	5.9	6.1
58.0	43.5	46.2		46.1	Total Current	38.6	38.1	40.0	38.6	46.1
24.1	17.6	10.0		16.4	Long-Term Debt	21.7	22.9	20.8	24.6	16.4
.2	.8	1.0		.7	Deferred Taxes	1.2	1.4	1.1	1.3	.7
13.5	7.3	1.6		6.8	All Other Non-Current	2.9	5.8	3.0	3.8	6.8
4.2	30.7	41.2		30.0	Net Worth	35.5	31.8	35.1	31.6	30.0
100.0	100.0	100.0		100.0	Total Liabilities & Net Worth	100.0	100.0	100.0	100.0	100.0
					INCOME DATA					
100.0	100.0	100.0		100.0	Contract Revenues	100.0	100.0	100.0	100.0	100.0
50.6	26.0	14.2		26.2	Gross Profit	30.3	29.7	30.6	31.9	26.2
47.1	26.3	14.4		25.9	Operating Expenses	24.7	24.7	28.7	31.4	25.9
3.5	-.2	-.2		.4	Operating Profit	5.6	5.0	2.0	.6	.4
1.3	.1	-.2		.2	All Other Expenses (net)	.8	1.1	.6	1.5	.2
2.2	-.3	.0		.1	Profit Before Taxes	4.8	3.9	1.3	-.9	.1
					RATIOS					
1.8	2.7	2.0		2.0		1.8	2.0	2.1	2.1	2.0
.8	1.3	1.4		1.4	Current	1.3	1.3	1.3	1.3	1.4
.5	.8	1.2		.9		1.0	1.0	.9	.8	.9

	7.2		6.1		2.9		4.7		3.6		5.1		5.7		7.2	4.7
(18)	2.3	(83)	2.9		2.1	(151)	2.4	Receivables/Payables	(207)	2.2	(182)	2.6	(149)	2.8	(125)	2.7	(151)	2.4
	1.1		1.5		1.3		1.3		1.4		1.5		1.5		1.5	1.3

Receivables/Payables:
0-1MM		1-10MM		10-50MM		50&OVER		ALL	Label	06/07		07/08		08/09		09/10		10/11
0	UND	25	14.4	39	9.5			25	14.6	Revenues/Receivables	31	11.6	31	11.8	31	11.9	28	13.2	25	14.6
33	11.0	55	6.7	70	5.2			55	6.7		53	7.0	56	6.5	48	7.6	49	7.5	55	6.7
53	6.9	81	4.5	90	4.1			80	4.6		77	4.7	81	4.5	72	5.1	72	5.1	80	4.6
0	UND	10	35.1	18	20.2			11	34.5	Cost of Revenues/Payables	16	22.3	10	35.0	9	38.8	5	73.0	11	34.5
23	15.9	24	15.3	41	8.9			28	13.2		31	11.8	28	13.0	26	14.0	24	15.4	28	13.2
67	5.5	47	7.7	62	5.9			57	6.4		50	7.4	47	7.8	47	7.8	52	7.0	57	6.4

	7.1		7.1		7.4		7.3		8.6		8.0		6.6		6.7	7.3
	-47.3		21.8		11.6		16.8	Revenues/Working Capital		18.7		18.2		18.0		19.2	16.8
	-8.1		-32.0		25.2		-32.5			-119.1		-158.5		-59.8		-36.0	-32.5

	5.1		7.2		9.0		7.1			10.5		8.5		8.3		4.3		7.1
(17)	1.3	(82)	2.0	(41)	3.0	(147)	2.1	EBIT/Interest	(209)	4.3	(188)	2.8	(143)	1.9	(123)	1.2	(147)	2.1
	-2.2		-1.3		-1.0		-1.2			1.4		1.1		-1.2		-3.4		-1.2
			2.4		2.4		2.6			4.0		2.4		2.9		2.9		2.6
		(17)	1.1	(10)	1.5	(30)	1.5	Net Profit + Depr., Dep., Amort./Cur. Mat. L/T/D	(63)	2.0	(61)	1.5	(36)	2.0	(34)	1.4	(30)	1.5
			.2		-.9		-.2			.9		1.1		1.0		.7		-.2

	.5		.5		.4		.5			.7		.6		.6		.6	.5
	3.3		1.0		.7		1.0	Fixed/Worth		1.2		1.2		1.1		1.2	1.0
	-4.5		2.5		1.2		2.5			2.3		2.0		2.6		2.8	2.5
	.6		.9		.8		.8			1.1		1.0		.8		.8	.8
	5.0		1.6		1.8		1.8	Debt/Worth		1.8		1.8		1.7		1.6	1.8
	-5.3		7.6		3.0		6.3			3.3		4.3		4.3		4.6	6.3

	46.7		29.5		25.9		27.2			51.6		41.9		31.5		20.9		27.2
(14)	18.7	(78)	9.7	(43)	7.8	(142)	8.1	% Profit Before Taxes/ Tangible Net Worth	(209)	22.6	(180)	17.5	(142)	7.6	(114)	3.2	(142)	8.1
	-2.1		-10.9		-4.4		-7.9			3.9		2.1		-7.3		-19.8		-7.9

	17.6		9.8		8.3		9.3			17.4		14.3		14.6		8.0	9.3
	4.4		2.4		3.4		2.9	% Profit Before Taxes/ Total Assets		8.2		5.5		3.1		.8	2.9
	-4.8		-5.8		-2.6		-4.1			1.3		.5		-4.9		-11.4	-4.1

	2.6		3.3		2.5		3.1			3.0		3.1		4.0		4.2		3.1
(19)	5.1	(77)	5.8		4.2	(145)	5.1	% Depr., Dep., Amort./ Revenues	(197)	5.4	(177)	5.6	(141)	6.5	(118)	7.4	(145)	5.1
	10.8		8.4		5.6		7.7			8.3		8.4		9.1		11.7		7.7
	6.0		2.1		1.4		2.0			2.2		2.0		2.4		2.2		2.0
(13)	10.3	(39)	3.7	(18)	2.2	(73)	4.0	% Officers', Directors' Owners' Comp/Revenues	(111)	3.2	(100)	4.1	(70)	4.6	(53)	4.8	(73)	4.0
	14.7		5.9		3.3		7.5			6.2		6.2		7.8		9.5		7.5

12013M	356318M	951712M	6830875M	8150918M	Contract Revenues ($)	38123492M	66001098M	42605534M	4950012M	8150918M
7110M	183265M	498817M	4119710M	4808902M	Total Assets ($)	16198292M	26833564M	17114825M	4055686M	4808902M

M = $ thousand　　MM = $ million
See Pages 9 through 22 for Explanation of Ratios and Data

Current Data Sorted by Revenue   Comparative Historical Data

0-1MM	1-10MM	10-50MM	50 & OVER	ALL	Type of Statement	ALL	ALL	ALL	ALL	ALL
1	3	3		6	Unqualified	7	8	10	5	6
	36	18	2	57	Reviewed	47	37	31	36	57
	17	2		19	Compiled	31	26	23	20	19
8	20			28	Tax Returns	28	36	36	33	28
4	24	10	5	43	Other	33	26	23	29	43
21 (4/1-9/30/10)		132 (10/1/10-3/31/11)				4/1/06-3/31/07	4/1/07-3/31/08	4/1/08-3/31/09	4/1/09-3/31/10	4/1/10-3/31/11
13	100	33	7	153	NUMBER OF STATEMENTS	146	133	123	123	153
%	%	%	%	%	**ASSETS**	%	%	%	%	%
11.8	13.2	17.6		13.9	Cash & Equivalents	13.5	14.0	11.3	14.8	13.9
24.5	23.4	30.9		24.7	A/R - Progress Billings	34.5	35.9	33.5	34.1	24.7
4.1	13.3	17.8		13.5	A/R - Current Retention	1.0	1.6	1.1	.8	13.5
2.3	8.1	3.3		6.4	Inventory	9.4	8.0	8.8	9.2	6.4
.0	4.0	6.5		4.5	Cost & Est. Earnings In Excess Billings	1.9	2.2	3.1	2.9	4.5
3.7	3.5	2.3		3.1	All Other Current	4.7	4.4	6.3	2.9	3.1
46.3	65.5	78.4		66.0	Total Current	65.0	65.9	64.1	64.7	66.0
36.1	23.2	15.5		23.2	Fixed Assets (net)	26.3	24.5	25.7	21.2	23.2
.0	.2	.9		.3	Joint Ventures & Investments	.4	.6	.1	.5	.3
7.7	3.2	1.0		3.3	Intangibles (net)	1.9	2.8	3.4	2.9	3.3
9.9	7.8	4.2		7.1	All Other Non-Current	6.5	6.2	6.7	10.7	7.1
100.0	100.0	100.0		100.0	Total	100.0	100.0	100.0	100.0	100.0
					LIABILITIES					
15.6	10.6	9.5		10.5	Notes Payable-Short Term	17.2	14.2	13.9	14.6	10.5
8.3	17.1	18.2		16.7	A/P - Trade	16.1	19.6	18.4	17.8	16.7
1.1	.2	.5		.3	A/P - Retention	.2	.2	.2	.1	.3
.0	4.4	7.2		4.6	Billings in Excess of Costs & Est. Earnings	2.6	2.8	2.7	2.4	4.6
.0	.2	.6		.2	Income Taxes Payable	.2	.2	.1	.1	.2
10.7	5.7	3.4		5.6	Cur. Mat.-L/T/D	5.7	5.0	10.0	5.3	5.6
12.0	6.6	8.4		7.4	All Other Current	9.2	7.9	9.8	8.8	7.4
47.7	44.8	47.8		45.4	Total Current	51.1	50.0	55.1	49.1	45.4
46.5	14.7	6.9		16.3	Long-Term Debt	17.4	20.6	21.0	23.8	16.3
.0	.3	.4		.4	Deferred Taxes	.6	.1	1.4	.5	.4
1.1	6.5	2.6		5.1	All Other Non-Current	2.9	3.4	4.6	3.3	5.1
4.6	33.6	42.2		32.8	Net Worth	27.9	25.8	17.9	23.4	32.8
100.0	100.0	100.0		100.0	Total Liabilities & Net Worth	100.0	100.0	100.0	100.0	100.0
					INCOME DATA					
100.0	100.0	100.0		100.0	Contract Revenues	100.0	100.0	100.0	100.0	100.0
55.6	28.6	19.1		28.4	Gross Profit	33.1	32.6	31.9	33.9	28.4
46.6	26.3	17.1		25.5	Operating Expenses	28.2	27.3	29.6	29.5	25.5
9.1	2.3	2.0		3.0	Operating Profit	4.9	5.3	2.3	4.4	3.0
1.0	.4	.4		.5	All Other Expenses (net)	.6	.7	.6	.7	.5
8.1	1.9	1.5		2.5	Profit Before Taxes	4.3	4.7	1.6	3.7	2.5
					RATIOS					
3.1	2.7	2.3		2.6	Current	2.2	2.4	2.6	2.5	2.6
.9	1.5	1.6		1.5		1.4	1.5	1.5	1.4	1.5
.4	.9	1.3		1.0		1.0	1.0	.9	.9	1.0
	5.2	5.6		5.4	Receivables/Payables	5.0	4.7	5.6	5.8	5.4
	(95) 2.4	3.0		(144) 2.6		(135) 2.2	(126) 2.4	(114) 2.2	(108) 2.4	(144) 2.6
	1.3	1.5		1.3		1.2	1.1	1.0	1.2	1.3
0 UND	21 17.4	38 9.7		24 14.9	Revenues/Receivables	13 28.0	22 16.3	19 19.4	14 25.4	24 14.9
17 22.0	50 7.3	71 5.1		52 7.0		40 9.2	43 8.5	42 8.8	39 9.4	52 7.0
68 5.4	67 5.4	90 4.1		74 4.9		74 5.4	69 5.3	64 5.7	66 5.5	74 4.9
0 UND	7 51.3	17 21.3		9 40.3	Cost of Revenues/Payables	8 43.3	9 40.5	7 53.4	8 48.6	9 40.3
10 36.5	21 17.5	24 14.9		23 15.8		24 15.3	25 14.8	22 16.4	22 16.5	23 15.8
32 11.4	54 6.8	53 6.9		53 6.9		46 8.0	49 7.4	47 7.8	46 8.0	53 6.9
8.1	5.9	7.1		6.5	Revenues/Working Capital	8.2	8.3	6.8	6.3	6.5
-135.0	11.9	10.2		11.3		16.5	15.3	15.5	18.5	11.3
-13.7	-174.4	18.6		936.5		-666.6	UND	-74.3	-65.7	936.5
40.7	15.8	13.0		15.3	EBIT/Interest	14.6	14.8	12.3	20.2	15.3
(12) 3.1	(92) 4.4	(24) 3.8		(134) 4.1		(128) 5.3	(123) 5.2	(109) 2.8	(108) 5.6	(134) 4.1
1.0	.7	-.9		.8		1.3	1.7	-.2	1.2	.8
	8.9			8.0	Net Profit + Depr., Dep., Amort./Cur. Mat. L/T/D	7.2	14.8	5.2	8.8	8.0
	(16) 1.5			(24) 2.1		(33) 2.4	(21) 7.0	(19) 2.6	(18) 3.4	(24) 2.1
	.3			.8		.8	1.8	1.3	.3	.8
.6	.2	.1		.2	Fixed/Worth	.2	.3	.2	.1	.2
UND	.5	.3		.5		.7	.6	.6	.7	.5
-1.1	1.5	1.0		1.8		2.0	2.7	8.1	2.8	1.8
1.0	.6	.5		.6	Debt/Worth	.9	.9	.7	.8	.6
UND	1.6	1.5		1.8		1.9	2.7	2.1	2.3	1.8
-4.6	4.0	3.0		6.0		5.5	10.6	38.5	18.4	6.0
	49.7	41.5		51.5	% Profit Before Taxes/ Tangible Net Worth	79.1	79.1	49.1	73.8	51.5
	(85) 17.6	(32) 17.9		(129) 20.0		(129) 31.3	(110) 38.9	(96) 19.7	(99) 26.7	(129) 20.0
	-.5	-3.5		.4		7.9	9.1	3.8	3.5	.4
35.9	16.1	14.7		16.7	% Profit Before Taxes/ Total Assets	25.9	25.5	18.3	25.6	16.7
13.1	5.2	5.6		5.6		10.3	10.1	5.3	10.0	5.6
-.1	-1.3	-.9		-.9		1.5	1.4	-2.2	.0	-.9
	1.0	.5		.8	% Depr., Dep., Amort./ Revenues	1.2	.8	1.0	.7	.8
	(80) 1.9	(28) .9		(119) 1.8		(112) 2.3	(108) 1.8	(92) 2.0	(94) 1.6	(119) 1.8
	3.3	2.8		3.2		3.3	3.3	3.7	3.2	3.2
	2.7			2.5	% Officers', Directors' Owners' Comp/Revenues	2.7	1.7	2.4	2.6	2.5
	(53) 4.1			(70) 4.1		(95) 4.5	(84) 3.9	(78) 4.2	(76) 4.7	(70) 4.1
	5.4			7.4		7.2	6.6	6.9	8.5	7.4
7878M	440740M	784165M	4437205M	5669988M	Contract Revenues ($)	10670425M	25225136M	22991743M	926661M	5669988M
3575M	184087M	325561M	4268751M	4781974M	Total Assets ($)	3522291M	8639005M	8446341M	346370M	4781974M

CONSTRUCTION
FINANCIAL MANAGEMENT
ASSOCIATION DATA

About the Construction Financial Management Association (CFMA) Data
Web site: www.cfma.org

Once again, we are delighted to include excerpts from *CFMA's 2011 Construction Industry Annual Financial Survey.* CFMA is **The Source and Resource for Construction Financial Professionals** and has nearly 6,700 members in 87 chapters throughout the U.S. and Canada.

The data presented are based on a survey to which approximately 4,000 general members employed within U.S. and Canadian construction firms were invited to respond. Additionally, this data was augmented by several hundred firms outside of CFMA member ranks. Of the **612** companies submitting data for the survey, **608** provided detailed financial statements and other required information and were included in the final respondent population. The data submitted were compiled and analyzed by Moss Adams LLP in cooperation with CFMA. Moss Adams was not engaged to and did not audit or review this information and, accordingly, does not express an opinion or any other form of assurance on it.

Almost all companies **(97.3%)** included in the survey recognize contract revenue and profit in accordance with the percentage of completion method of accounting. Likewise, our Statement Studies contractor data primarily reflects only this method of accounting. It is entirely possible that some of the same contractor companies are included in both the CFMA and Statement Studies data presentations. The inclusion of the CFMA data has not affected our Statement Studies contractor composite data.

Fiscal year-end closing dates reflected in the CFMA survey range from 3/31/10 through 3/31/11. The CFMA data are most comparable to the RMA contractor data from 4/1/10 through 3/31/11 appearing in this edition.

The survey respondents were classified into three categories of construction based on the type of work performed. Classification was based on the level of contract volume reported for various NAICS codes. A contractor was included in a classification if at least one half of its annual contract revenue was attributable to that classification. CFMA categorized certain NAICS codes together. The classifications and NAICS codes included in each are as follows:

NAICS Codes
INDUSTRIAL AND NONRESIDENTIAL CONTRACTORS:
236210 Industrial Building Construction
236220 Commercial and Institutional Building Construction

HEAVY AND HIGHWAY CONTRACTORS:
237110 Water and Sewer Line and Related Structures Construction
237120 Oil and Gas Pipeline and Related Structures Construction
237130 Power and Communication Line and Related Structures Construction
237210 Land Subdivision
237310 Highway, Street, and Bridge Construction
237990 Other Heavy and Civil Engineering Construction

SPECIALTY TRADES CONTRACTORS:
238110 Poured Concrete Foundation and Structure Contractors
238120 Structural Steel and Precast Concrete Contractors
238130 Framing Contractors
238140 Masonry Contractors
238150 Glass and Glazing Contractors
238160 Roofing Contractors
238170 Siding Contractors
238190 Other Foundation, Structure, and Building Exterior Contractors
238210 Electrical Contractors
238220 Plumbing, Heating, and Air-Conditioning Contractors
238290 Other Building Equipment Contractors
238310 Drywall and Insulation Contractors
238320 Painting and Wall Covering Contractors
238330 Flooring Contractors
238340 Tile and Terrazzo Contractors
238350 Finish Carpentry Contractors
238390 Other Building Finishing Contractors
238910 Site Preparation Contractors
238990 All Other Specialty Trade Contractors
561621 Security Systems Services (except Locksmiths)
562910 Environmental Remediation Services

The CFMA financial data includes balance sheets, statements of earnings, and financial ratios. The balance sheets and statements of earning represent a weighted average of all companies included in each classification. Percentages are presented for each dollar amount in the financial statements. Due to rounding, the totals may not agree to the sum of various accounts. Such variations are few and insignificant.

The financial ratios are calculated from the composite balance sheets and statements of earning data. They are not averages of ratios for all companies included in the classification.

If you wish to purchase *CFMA's 2011 Construction Industry Annual Financial Survey* or have questions regarding the data, contact Fern Oram, Associate Director of Project Management; Construction Financial Management Association, 100 Village Blvd, Suite 200, Princeton, NJ 08540; Phone 609-452-8000; Fax 609-452-0474; E-mail foram@cfma.org.

Interpretation of the
Construction Financial Management Association (CFMA) Data

CFMA's data should only be regarded as general information. It cannot be used to establish industry norms for a number of reasons, including the following:

(1) The financial statements used in the composite are not selected by any random or statistically reliable method. CFMA members voluntarily submitted their financial data. Note that contractors' statements have no upper asset/sales limit.
(2) Many companies provide varied services; CFMA includes a contractor in a classification if at least one-half (1/2) of its annual contract revenue was completed within that classification.
(3) Some of the NAICS group samples may be rather small in relation to the total number of firms in a given industry category. A relatively small sample can increase the chances that some of our composites do not fully represent an industry group.
(4) There is the chance that an extreme statement can be present in a sample, causing a disproportionate influence on the industry composite. This is particularly true in a relatively small sample.
(5) Companies within the same industry may differ in their method of operations, which in turn can directly influence their financial statements. Since such differences affect financial data included in our sample, our composite calculations could be significantly affected.
(6) Other considerations that can result in variation among different companies engaged in the same general line of business are: different labor markets; geographical location; different accounting methods; quality of service rendered; sources and methods of financing; and terms of sale.

The use of CFMA data may be helpful when considered with other methods of financial analysis. Nevertheless, RMA and CFMA do not recommend the use of CFMA's data to establish norms or parameters for a given industry or grouping, or the industry as a whole. Although CFMA believes that its data is accurate and representative within the confines of the aforementioned reasons, RMA and CFMA specifically make no representations regarding the accuracy of representativeness of the figures printed in this supplement of the RMA Annual Statement Studies.

Reprinted with permission © 2011 by the Construction Financial Management Association.

All Companies
Composite

Balance Sheet

	2011 Participants		2010 Participants	
	Amount	Percent	Amount	Percent
Current assets:		%		%
Cash and cash equivalents	$ 9,823,474	21.3	$ 8,766,996	21.4
Marketable securities and short-term investments	3,453,753	7.5	1,986,410	4.8
Receivables:				
Contract receivables currently due	13,687,224	29.7	13,045,413	31.8
Retainages on contracts	3,841,412	8.3	3,615,830	8.8
Unbilled work	176,724	0.4	174,294	0.4
Other receivables	598,519	1.3	1,355,980	3.3
Less allowance for doubtful accounts	(113,906)	(0.2)	(128,389)	(0.3)
Total receivables, net	18,189,973	39.5	18,063,127	44.1
Inventories	964,616	2.1	860,268	2.1
Costs and recognized earnings in excess of billings on uncompleted contracts	1,955,477	0.0	1,564,898	3.8
Investments in and advances to construction joint ventures	617,014	1.3	385,004	0.9
Income taxes:				
Current / refundable	43,447	0.1	108,670	0.3
Deferred	144,307	0.3	72,017	0.2
Other current assets	1,090,882	2.4	1,114,023	2.7
Total current assets	36,282,943	78.7	32,921,414	80.3
Property, plant and equipment	15,093,410	32.7	13,034,502	31.8
Less accumulated depreciation	(8,693,225)	(18.9)	(7,403,240)	(18.1)
Property, plant and equipment, net	6,400,186	13.9	5,631,262	13.7
Noncurrent assets:				
Long-term investments	628,809	1.4	598,193	1.5
Deferred income taxes	38,107	0.1	86,257	0.2
Other assets	2,737,375	5.9	1,739,115	4.2
Total noncurrent assets	3,404,291	7.4	2,423,565	5.9
Total assets	$ 46,087,420	100.0 %	$ 40,976,241	100.0 %

	2011 Participants		2010 Participants	
	Amount	Percent	Amount	Percent
Current liabilities:		%		%
Current maturity on long-term debt	$ 537,754	1.2	$ 577,865	1.4
Notes payable and lines of credit	928,503	2.0	478,425	1.2
Accounts payable:				
Trade, including currently due to subcontractors	11,009,286	23.9	10,178,510	24.8
Subcontracts retainages	2,452,522	5.3	2,475,727	6.0
Other	312,566	0.7	376,304	0.9
Total accounts payable	13,774,374	29.9	13,030,541	31.8
Accrued expenses	2,786,830	6.0	2,636,468	6.4
Billings in excess of costs and recognized earnings on uncompleted contracts	5,842,272	12.7	5,346,141	13.0
Income taxes:				
Current	64,599	0.1	91,693	0.2
Deferred	20,434	0.0	20,862	0.1
Other current liabilities	796,813	1.7	540,454	1.3
Total current liabilities	24,751,579	53.7	22,722,448	55.5
Noncurrent liabilities:				
Long-term debt, excluding current maturities	3,017,904	6.5	2,641,282	6.4
Deferred income taxes	139,495	0.3	147,056	0.4
Other	1,187,566	2.6	908,700	2.2
Total liabilities	29,096,544	63.1	26,419,486	64.5
Minority interests	254,000	0.6	136,520	0.3
Net worth:				
Common stock, par value	3,124,577	6.8	3,404,987	8.3
Preferred stock, stated value	104,385	0.2	21,227	0.1
Additional paid-in capital	1,924,472	4.2	840,332	2.1
Retained earnings	12,030,503	26.1	10,444,684	25.5
Treasury stock	(1,216,798)	(2.6)	(724,705)	(1.8)
Excess value of marketable securities	10,690	0.0	10,478	0.0
Other equity	759,047	1.6	423,232	1.0
Total net worth	16,736,877	36.3	14,420,235	35.2
Total liabilities and net worth	$ 46,087,420	100.0 %	$ 40,976,241	100.0 %

All Companies
Composite

Statement of Earnings

	2011 Participants		2010 Participants	
	Amount	Percent	Amount	Percent
Contract revenue	$ 103,308,454	98.7 %	$ 103,086,320	98.6 %
Other revenue	1,396,527	1.3	1,459,634	1.4
Total revenue	104,704,981	100.0	104,545,963	100.0
Contract cost	(92,801,744)	(88.6)	(91,909,826)	(87.9)
Other cost	(977,242)	(0.9)	(1,054,837)	(1.0)
Total cost	(93,778,986)	(89.6)	(92,964,663)	(88.9)
Gross profit	10,925,995	10.4	11,581,300	11.1
Selling, general and administrative expenses:				
Payroll	(3,058,204)	(2.9)	(2,781,097)	(2.7)
Professional fees	(189,595)	(0.2)	(193,097)	(0.2)
Sales and marketing costs	(233,914)	(0.2)	(225,596)	(0.2)
Technology costs	(157,829)	(0.2)	(147,422)	(0.1)
Administrative bonuses	(513,644)	(0.5)	(546,369)	(0.5)
Other	(3,500,717)	(3.3)	(4,047,246)	(3.9)
Total SG&A expenses	(7,653,904)	(7.3)	(7,940,827)	(7.6)
Income from operations	3,272,092	3.1	3,640,473	3.5
Interest income	140,124	0.1	111,746	0.1
Interest expense	(114,411)	(0.1)	(107,236)	(0.1)
Other income / (expense), net	90,580	0.1	58,257	0.1
Net earnings / (loss) before income taxes	3,388,384	3.2	3,703,240	3.5
Income tax (expense) / benefit	(229,331)	(0.2)	(317,405)	(0.3)
Net earnings	$ 3,159,054	3.0 %	$ 3,385,835	3.2 %
Average backlog	$ 111,779,895		$ 52,824,730	

Number of Participants

	Number
2011	608
2010	623

Financial Ratios

	2011 Participants		2010 Participants	
	Average	Median	Average	Median
Liquidity Ratios				
Current Ratio	1.5	1.6	1.4	1.7
Quick Ratio	1.3	1.4	1.3	1.4
Days of Cash	33.8	25.3	30.2	26.4
Working Capital Turnover	9.1	8.3	10.3	8.5
Profitability Ratios				
Return on Assets	7.4 %	4.8 %	9.0 %	7.1 %
Return on Equity	20.3 %	11.3 %	25.7 %	17.1 %
Times Interest Earned	30.6	9.2	35.5	14.8
Leverage Ratios				
Debt to Equity	1.7	1.4	1.8	1.3
Revenue to Equity	6.3	6.0	7.2	6.0
Asset Turnover	2.3	2.5	2.6	2.7
Fixed Asset Ratio	38.2 %	24.0 %	39.1 %	23.0 %
Equity to SG&A Expense	2.2	1.7	1.8	1.6
Underbillings to Equity	12.7 %	7.0 %	12.1 %	6.0 %
Backlog to Equity	6.7	3.4	3.7	1.3
Efficiency Ratios				
Backlog to Working Capital	9.7	3.3	5.2	1.7
Months in Backlog	12.8	5.5	6.1	3.2
Days in Accounts Receivable	48.7	50.9	49.1	46.1
Days in Inventory	3.7	0.0	3.3	0.0
Days in Accounts Payable	43.5	35.6	40.9	30.6
Operating Cycle	42.7	45.5	41.8	44.6

Industrial & Nonresidential Contractors

Composite

Balance Sheet

	2011 Participants		2010 Participants	
	Amount	Percent	Amount	Percent
Current assets:				
Cash and cash equivalents	$ 12,298,587	23.1 %	$ 12,010,978	23.5 %
Marketable securities and short-term investments	7,001,194	13.1	2,975,512	5.8
Receivables:				
Contract receivables currently due	17,819,633	33.4	19,311,172	37.7
Retainages on contracts	6,209,339	11.7	6,088,446	11.9
Unbilled work	83,699	0.2	127,308	0.2
Other receivables	618,134	1.2	2,915,571	5.7
Less allowance for doubtful accounts	(59,789)	(0.1)	(104,705)	(0.2)
Total receivables, net	24,671,015	46.3	28,337,792	55.4
Inventories	41,198	0.1	73,951	0.1
Costs and recognized earnings in excess of billings on uncompleted contracts	2,243,560	4.2	1,835,954	3.6
Investments in and advances to construction joint ventures	199,324	0.4	468,167	0.9
Income taxes:				
Current / refundable	36,218	0.1	262,653	0.5
Deferred	124,390	0.2	30,014	0.1
Other current assets	1,185,733	2.2	936,129	1.8
Total current assets	47,801,229	89.7	46,931,151	91.7
Property, plant and equipment	6,409,849	12.0	5,502,378	10.8
Less accumulated depreciation	(3,914,187)	(7.3)	(3,391,839)	(6.6)
Property, plant and equipment, net	2,495,662	4.7	2,110,539	4.1
Noncurrent assets:				
Long-term investments	764,637	1.4	1,146,272	2.2
Deferred income taxes	68,983	0.1	78,537	0.2
Other assets	2,166,384	4.1	907,531	1.8
Total noncurrent assets	3,000,005	5.6	2,132,340	4.2
Total assets	$ 53,296,895	100.0 %	$ 51,174,029	100.0 %

	2011 Participants		2010 Participants	
	Amount	Percent	Amount	Percent
Current liabilities:				
Current maturity on long-term debt	$ 158,570	0.3 %	$ 231,658	0.5 %
Notes payable and lines of credit	345,625	0.6	189,884	0.4
Accounts payable:				
Trade, including currently due to subcontractors	18,512,779	34.7	20,329,820	39.7
Subcontracts retainages	6,042,771	11.3	6,638,359	13.0
Other	421,281	0.8	616,994	1.2
Total accounts payable	24,976,831	46.9	27,585,173	53.9
Accrued expenses	3,586,852	6.7	2,992,177	5.8
Billings in excess of costs and recognized earnings on uncompleted contracts	7,207,438	13.5	5,548,926	10.8
Income taxes:				
Current	36,578	0.1	89,152	0.2
Deferred	17,029	0.0	11,804	0.0
Other current liabilities	482,585	0.9	213,093	0.4
Total current liabilities	36,811,307	69.1	36,861,868	72.0
Noncurrent liabilities:				
Long-term debt, excluding current maturities	949,287	1.8	1,082,389	2.1
Deferred income taxes	57,937	0.1	74,332	0.1
Other	1,208,463	2.3	683,860	1.3
Total liabilities	39,026,995	73.2	38,702,449	75.6
Minority interests	27,224	0.1	59,123	0.1
Net worth:				
Common stock, par value	2,115,566	4.0	2,421,976	4.7
Preferred stock, stated value	45,373	0.1	6,728	0.0
Additional paid-in capital	1,947,458	3.7	980,041	1.9
Retained earnings	9,649,298	18.1	8,608,485	16.8
Treasury stock	(1,375,146)	(2.6)	(322,214)	(0.6)
Excess value of marketable securities	18,254	0.0	11,654	0.0
Other equity	1,841,873	3.5	705,787	1.4
Total net worth	14,242,676	26.7	12,412,457	24.3
Total liabilities and net worth	$ 53,296,895	100.0 %	$ 51,174,029	100.0 %

Industrial & Nonresidential Contractors

Composite

Statement of Earnings

	2011 Participants		2010 Participants	
	Amount	Percent	Amount	Percent
Contract revenue	$ 148,810,925	99.9 %	$ 161,430,978	99.7 %
Other revenue	153,756	0.1	525,963	0.3
Total revenue	148,964,681	100.0	161,956,941	100.0
Contract cost	(137,643,392)	(92.4)	(151,091,829)	(93.3)
Other cost	(78,504)	(0.1)	(417,298)	(0.3)
Total cost	(137,721,896)	(92.5)	(151,509,127)	(93.5)
Gross profit	11,242,785	7.5	10,447,814	6.5
Selling, general and administrative expenses:				
Payroll	(3,444,417)	(2.3)	(2,896,816)	(1.8)
Professional fees	(219,202)	(0.1)	(197,776)	(0.1)
Sales and marketing costs	(276,444)	(0.2)	(256,952)	(0.2)
Technology costs	(193,994)	(0.1)	(156,345)	(0.1)
Administrative bonuses	(602,136)	(0.4)	(521,364)	(0.3)
Other	(3,162,348)	(2.1)	(3,198,835)	(2.0)
Total SG&A expenses	(7,898,539)	(5.3)	(7,228,088)	(4.5)
Income from operations	3,344,246	2.2	3,219,726	2.0
Interest income	259,808	0.2	193,990	0.1
Interest expense	(66,546)	(0.0)	(52,188)	(0.0)
Other income / (expense), net	167,420	0.1	(59,409)	(0.0)
Net earnings / (loss) before income taxes	3,704,928	2.5	3,302,119	2.0
Income tax (expense) / benefit	(300,137)	(0.2)	(200,375)	(0.1)
Net earnings	$ 3,404,791	2.3 %	$ 3,101,743	1.9 %
Average backlog	$ 165,477,234		$ 101,323,289	

Number of Participants

	Number
2011	211
2010	191

Financial Ratios

	2011 Participants		2010 Participants	
	Average	Median	Average	Median
Liquidity Ratios				
Current Ratio	1.3	1.4	1.3	1.4
Quick Ratio	1.2	1.3	1.2	1.3
Days of Cash	29.7	28.6	26.7	31.5
Working Capital Turnover	13.6	10.5	16.1	12.4
Profitability Ratios				
Return on Assets	7.0 %	4.5 %	6.5 %	5.8 %
Return on Equity	26.0 %	16.0 %	26.6 %	19.8 %
Times Interest Earned	56.7	8.2	64.3	22.2
Leverage Ratios				
Debt to Equity	2.7	2.2	3.1	2.0
Revenue to Equity	10.5	9.3	13.0	10.6
Asset Turnover	2.8	3.0	3.2	3.4
Fixed Asset Ratio	17.5 %	12.0 %	17.0 %	13.0 %
Equity to SG&A Expense	1.8	1.6	1.7	1.6
Underbillings to Equity	16.3 %	7.0 %	15.8 %	5.0 %
Backlog to Equity	11.6	6.6	8.2	3.7
Efficiency Ratios				
Backlog to Working Capital	15.1	6.1	10.1	4.7
Months in Backlog	13.3	7.2	7.5	4.5
Days in Accounts Receivable	44.4	44.4	49.2	38.5
Days in Inventory	0.1	0.0	0.2	0.0
Days in Accounts Payable	49.5	43.6	49.8	36.2
Operating Cycle	24.8	-32.9	26.3	34.0

Heavy & Highway Contractors
Composite

Balance Sheet

	2011 Participants		2010 Participants	
	Amount	Percent	Amount	Percent
Current assets:				
Cash and cash equivalents	$ 20,707,311	24.9 %	$ 13,836,711	23.8 %
Marketable securities and short-term investments	4,414,341	5.3	2,736,059	4.7
Receivables:				
Contract receivables currently due	16,414,059	19.8	10,162,270	17.5
Retainages on contracts	5,218,201	6.3	3,499,791	6.0
Unbilled work	570,729	0.7	360,593	0.6
Other receivables	1,358,683	1.6	1,562,932	2.7
Less allowance for doubtful accounts	(242,200)	(0.3)	(131,025)	(0.2)
Total receivables, net	23,319,472	28.1	15,454,562	26.6
Inventories	2,345,619	2.8	2,098,409	3.6
Costs and recognized earnings in excess of billings on uncompleted contracts	2,906,372	3.5	2,097,462	3.6
Investments in and advances to construction joint ventures	2,785,829	3.4	1,128,434	1.9
Income taxes:				
Current / refundable	77,147	0.1	27,770	0.0
Deferred	494,244	0.6	213,694	0.4
Other current assets	1,884,190	2.3	1,894,247	3.3
Total current assets	58,934,524	71.0	39,487,348	67.9
Property, plant and equipment	42,756,425	51.5	36,940,016	63.5
Less accumulated depreciation	(26,279,009)	(31.6)	(22,063,524)	(37.9)
Property, plant and equipment, net	16,477,416	19.8	14,876,491	25.6
Noncurrent assets:				
Long-term investments	1,339,490	1.6	691,814	1.2
Deferred income taxes	28,155	0.0	269,497	0.5
Other assets	6,250,621	7.5	2,823,836	4.9
Total noncurrent assets	7,618,266	9.2	3,785,146	6.5
Total assets	$ 83,030,207	100.0 %	$ 58,148,986	100.0 %

	2011 Participants		2010 Participants	
	Amount	Percent	Amount	Percent
Current liabilities:				
Current maturity on long-term debt	$ 1,574,605	1.9 %	$ 1,575,032	2.7 %
Notes payable and lines of credit	1,410,524	1.7	436,864	0.8
Accounts payable:				
Trade, including currently due to subcontractors	13,372,336	16.1	8,940,265	15.4
Subcontracts retainages	1,384,009	1.7	1,432,155	2.5
Other	280,567	0.3	394,892	0.7
Total accounts payable	15,036,912	18.1	10,767,311	18.5
Accrued expenses	4,223,056	5.1	3,365,917	5.8
Billings in excess of costs and recognized earnings on uncompleted contracts	10,735,923	12.9	7,333,829	12.6
Income taxes:				
Current	223,450	0.3	272,755	0.5
Deferred	7,639	0.0	48,496	0.1
Other current liabilities	623,431	0.8	407,806	0.7
Total current liabilities	33,835,541	40.8	24,208,011	41.6
Noncurrent liabilities:				
Long-term debt, excluding current maturities	5,703,085	6.9	6,229,081	10.7
Deferred income taxes	566,108	0.7	588,460	1.0
Other	2,901,328	3.5	1,805,508	3.1
Total liabilities	43,006,061	51.8	32,831,060	56.5
Minority interests	1,186,138	1.4	397,907	0.7
Net worth:				
Common stock, par value	5,436,411	6.5	4,410,466	7.6
Preferred stock, stated value	26,214	0.0	22,273	0.0
Additional paid-in capital	5,283,044	6.4	3,158,685	5.4
Retained earnings	29,342,228	35.3	18,395,337	31.6
Treasury stock	(1,604,054)	(1.9)	(1,338,491)	(2.3)
Excess value of marketable securities	2,918	0.0	10,696	0.0
Other equity	351,248	0.4	261,053	0.4
Total net worth	38,838,009	46.8	24,920,020	42.9
Total liabilities and net worth	$ 83,030,207	100.0 %	$ 58,148,986	100.0 %

Heavy & Highway Contractors

Composite

Statement of Earnings

	2011 Participants		2010 Participants	
	Amount	Percent	Amount	Percent
Contract revenue	$ 150,432,717	98.7 %	$ 117,898,262	98.7 %
Other revenue	2,032,556	1.3	1,609,197	1.3
Total revenue	152,465,273	100.0	119,507,459	100.0
Contract cost	(134,321,538)	(88.1)	(103,912,736)	(87.0)
Other cost	(1,390,686)	(0.9)	(1,004,964)	(0.8)
Total cost	(135,712,275)	(89.0)	(104,917,701)	(87.8)
Gross profit	16,752,998	11.0	14,589,758	12.2
Selling, general and administrative expenses:				
Payroll	(3,804,551)	(2.5)	(2,832,923)	(2.4)
Professional fees	(259,845)	(0.2)	(241,470)	(0.2)
Sales and marketing costs	(193,698)	(0.1)	(128,197)	(0.1)
Technology costs	(193,895)	(0.1)	(132,413)	(0.1)
Administrative bonuses	(532,477)	(0.3)	(576,984)	(0.5)
Other	(4,547,225)	(3.0)	(4,453,665)	(3.7)
Total SG&A expenses	(9,531,691)	(6.3)	(8,365,653)	(7.0)
Income from operations	7,221,307	4.7	6,224,105	5.2
Interest income	200,525	0.1	132,920	0.1
Interest expense	(317,685)	(0.2)	(289,358)	(0.2)
Other income / (expense), net	505,519	0.3	291,650	0.2
Net earnings / (loss) before income taxes	7,609,667	5.0	6,359,317	5.3
Income tax (expense) / benefit	(474,785)	(0.3)	(498,610)	(0.4)
Net earnings	$ 7,134,902	4.7 %	$ 5,860,707	4.9 %
Average backlog	$ 176,904,418		$ 71,600,040	

Number of Participants

	Number
2011	103
2010	110

Financial Ratios

	2011 Participants		2010 Participants	
	Average	Median	Average	Median
Liquidity Ratios				
Current Ratio	1.7	1.7	1.6	1.7
Quick Ratio	1.4	1.5	1.3	1.4
Days of Cash	48.9	33.3	41.7	25.0
Working Capital Turnover	6.1	6.8	7.8	8.1
Profitability Ratios				
Return on Assets	9.2 %	6.4 %	10.9 %	8.7 %
Return on Equity	19.6 %	12.2 %	25.5 %	17.3 %
Times Interest Earned	25.0	17.8	23.0	9.5
Leverage Ratios				
Debt to Equity	1.1	0.9	1.3	1.3
Revenue to Equity	3.9	4.0	4.8	5.1
Asset Turnover	1.8	1.9	2.1	2.3
Fixed Asset Ratio	42.4 %	50.0 %	59.7 %	58.0 %
Equity to SG&A Expense	4.1	3.1	3.0	2.3
Underbillings to Equity	9.0 %	5.0 %	9.9 %	7.0 %
Backlog to Equity	4.6	2.5	2.9	1.7
Efficiency Ratios				
Backlog to Working Capital	7.0	3.5	4.7	3.1
Months in Backlog	13.9	7.6	7.2	4.9
Days in Accounts Receivable	41.4	39.6	34.9	44.4
Days in Inventory	6.2	0.5	7.2	0.0
Days in Accounts Payable	36.2	32.1	32.0	28.3
Operating Cycle	60.3	50.1	51.8	43.4

Specialty Trade Contractors
Composite

Balance Sheet

Assets	2011 Participants		2010 Participants	
	Amount	Percent	Amount	Percent
Current assets:				
Cash and cash equivalents	$ 3,989,790	15.0 %	$ 4,632,598	17.0 %
Marketable securities and short-term investments	559,166	2.1	804,169	3.0
Receivables:				
Contract receivables currently due	9,325,981	35.1	9,669,365	35.5
Retainages on contracts	1,742,077	6.6	2,282,868	8.4
Unbilled work	113,889	0.4	128,279	0.5
Other receivables	350,048	1.3	379,730	1.4
Less allowance for doubtful accounts	(113,304)	(0.4)	(150,927)	(0.6)
Total receivables, net	11,418,692	43.0	12,309,345	45.2
Inventories	1,152,693	4.3	833,398	3.1
Costs and recognized earnings in excess of billings on uncompleted contracts	1,411,295	5.3	1,205,418	4.4
Investments in and advances to construction joint ventures	32,099	0.1	14,237	0.1
Income taxes:				
Current / refundable	32,301	0.1	43,108	0.2
Deferred	40,141	0.2	51,594	0.2
Other current assets	704,438	2.6	813,350	3.0
Total current assets	19,340,615	72.8	20,707,217	76.0
Property, plant and equipment	10,297,830	38.7	8,683,990	31.9
Less accumulated depreciation	(5,321,276)	(20.0)	(4,468,067)	(16.4)
Property, plant and equipment, net	4,976,554	18.7	4,215,922	15.5
Noncurrent assets:				
Long-term investments	309,955	1.2	263,346	1.0
Deferred income taxes	21,691	0.1	30,778	0.1
Other assets	1,935,069	7.3	2,031,611	7.5
Total noncurrent assets	2,266,715	8.5	2,325,735	8.5
Total assets	$ 26,583,883	100.0 %	$ 27,248,874	100.0 %

Liabilities and Net Worth	2011 Participants		2010 Participants	
	Amount	Percent	Amount	Percent
Current liabilities:				
Current maturity on long-term debt	$ 369,410	1.4 %	$ 447,317	1.6 %
Notes payable and lines of credit	1,283,431	4.8	696,077	2.6
Accounts payable:				
Trade, including currently due to subcontractors	4,241,092	16.0	3,998,842	14.7
Subcontracts retainages	246,413	0.9	257,391	0.9
Other	252,953	1.0	216,311	0.8
Total accounts payable	4,740,458	17.8	4,472,544	16.4
Accrued expenses	1,691,542	6.4	2,212,580	8.1
Billings in excess of costs and recognized earnings on uncompleted contracts	2,890,144	10.9	4,221,240	15.5
Income taxes:				
Current	28,105	0.1	23,558	0.1
Deferred	23,547	0.1	13,397	0.0
Other current liabilities	1,160,606	4.4	869,100	3.2
Total current liabilities	12,187,242	45.8	12,955,812	47.5
Noncurrent liabilities				
Long-term debt, excluding current maturities	2,727,051	10.3	2,323,351	8.5
Deferred income taxes	34,549	0.1	37,227	0.1
Other	575,038	2.2	765,114	2.8
Total liabilities	15,523,880	58.4	16,081,504	59.0
Minority interests	101,214	0.4	77,098	0.3
Net worth:				
Common stock, par value	3,622,508	13.6	3,173,461	11.6
Preferred stock, stated value	196,266	0.7	33,179	0.1
Additional paid-in capital	733,595	2.8	(260,839)	(1.0)
Retained earnings	7,424,905	27.9	8,670,385	31.8
Treasury stock	(1,028,713)	(3.9)	(784,749)	(2.9)
Excess value of marketable securities	8,195	0.0	9,570	0.0
Other equity	2,034	0.0	249,265	0.9
Total net worth	10,958,790	41.2	11,090,272	40.7
Total liabilities and net worth	$ 26,583,883	100.0 %	$ 27,248,874	100.0 %

Specialty Trade Contractors

Composite

Statement of Earnings

	2011 Participants		2010 Participants	
	Amount	Percent	Amount	Percent
Contract revenue	$ 51,249,247	96.2 %	$ 60,390,290	97.5 %
Other revenue	2,045,631	3.8	1,536,708	2.5
Total revenue	53,294,878	100.0	61,926,998	100.0
Contract cost	(43,435,627)	(81.5)	(50,090,133)	(80.9)
Other cost	(1,427,155)	(2.7)	(1,116,264)	(1.8)
Total cost	(44,862,782)	(84.2)	(51,206,397)	(82.7)
Gross profit	8,432,096	15.8	10,720,601	17.3
Selling, general and administrative expenses:				
Payroll	(2,602,201)	(4.9)	(2,835,048)	(4.6)
Professional fees	(141,574)	(0.3)	(182,179)	(0.3)
Sales and marketing costs	(229,254)	(0.4)	(250,315)	(0.4)
Technology costs	(119,748)	(0.2)	(159,327)	(0.3)
Administrative bonuses	(476,235)	(0.9)	(562,463)	(0.9)
Other	(3,279,070)	(6.2)	(3,960,202)	(6.4)
Total SG&A expenses	(6,848,082)	(12.8)	(7,949,534)	(12.8)
Income from operations	1,584,014	3.0	2,771,067	4.5
Interest income	28,452	0.1	44,213	0.1
Interest expense	(66,314)	(0.1)	(73,095)	(0.1)
Other income / (expense), net	(122,275)	(0.2)	22,560	0.0
Net earnings / (loss) before income taxes	1,423,878	2.7	2,764,745	4.5
Income tax (expense) / benefit	(85,259)	(0.2)	(274,846)	(0.4)
Net earnings	$ 1,338,619	2.5 %	$ 2,489,900	4.0 %
Average backlog	$ 51,889,394		$ 15,697,953	

Number of Participants

	Number
2011	260
2010	286

Financial Ratios

	2011 Participants		2010 Participants	
	Average	Median	Average	Median
Liquidity Ratios				
Current Ratio	1.6	1.8	1.6	1.8
Quick Ratio	1.3	1.5	1.4	1.6
Days of Cash	27.0	17.3	26.9	19.7
Working Capital Turnover	7.5	6.7	8.0	6.7
Profitability Ratios				
Return on Assets	5.4 %	4.2 %	10.2 %	7.4 %
Return on Equity	13.0 %	8.3 %	24.9 %	16.7 %
Times Interest Earned	22.5	6.8	38.8	17.6
Leverage Ratios				
Debt to Equity	1.4	1.2	1.5	1.0
Revenue to Equity	4.9	4.9	5.6	4.9
Asset Turnover	2.0	2.3	2.3	2.6
Fixed Asset Ratio	45.4 %	27.0 %	38.0 %	24.0 %
Equity to SG&A Expense	1.6	1.4	1.4	1.4
Underbillings to Equity	13.9 %	8.0 %	12.0 %	8.0 %
Backlog to Equity	4.7	2.3	1.4	0.5
Efficiency Ratios				
Backlog to Working Capital	7.3	1.8	2.0	0.8
Months in Backlog	11.7	3.5	3.0	1.9
Days in Accounts Receivable	64.6	59.2	57.5	54.3
Days in Inventory	9.2	0.7	5.9	0.7
Days in Accounts Payable	36.1	31.0	29.6	26.7
Operating Cycle	64.7	52.8	60.7	55.2

CFMA Comparative Financial Data

Balance Sheet
Most Recent Year-End

	All Companies		Industrial & Nonresidential		Heavy & Highway		Specialty Trade	
	Amount	Percent	Amount	Percent	Amount	Percent	Amount	Percent
Current assets:								
Cash and cash equivalents	$ 9,823,474	21.3 %	$ 12,298,587	23.1 %	$ 20,707,311	24.9 %	$ 3,989,790	15.0 %
Marketable securities and short-term investments	3,453,753	7.5	7,001,194	13.1	4,414,341	5.3	559,166	2.1
Receivables:								
Contract receivables currently due	13,687,224	29.7	17,819,633	33.4	16,414,059	19.8	9,325,981	35.1
Retainages on contracts	3,841,412	8.3	6,209,339	11.7	5,218,201	6.3	1,742,077	6.6
Unbilled work	176,724	0.4	83,699	0.2	570,729	0.7	113,869	0.4
Other receivables	598,519	1.3	618,134	1.2	1,358,683	1.6	350,048	1.3
Less allowance for doubtful accounts	(113,906)	(0.2)	(59,789)	(0.1)	(242,200)	(0.3)	(113,304)	(0.4)
Total receivables, net	18,189,973	39.5	24,671,015	46.3	23,319,472	28.1	11,418,692	43.0
Inventories	964,616	2.1	41,198	0.1	2,345,619	2.8	1,152,693	4.3
Costs and recognized earnings in excess of billings on uncompleted contracts	1,955,477	4.2	2,243,560	4.2	2,906,372	3.5	1,411,295	5.3
Investments in and advances to construction joint ventures	617,014	1.3	199,324	0.4	2,785,829	3.4	32,099	0.1
Income taxes:								
Current / refundable	43,447	0.1	36,218	0.1	77,147	0.1	32,301	0.1
Deferred	144,307	0.3	124,389	0.2	494,244	0.6	40,141	0.2
Other current assets	1,090,882	2.4	1,185,733	2.2	1,884,190	2.3	704,438	2.6
Total current assets	36,282,943	78.7	47,801,229	89.7	58,904,524	71.0	19,340,615	72.8
Property, plant and equipment	9,093,410	32.7	6,409,849	12.0	42,756,425	51.5	10,297,830	38.7
Less accumulated depreciation	(8,693,225)	(18.9)	(3,914,187)	(7.3)	(26,279,009)	(31.6)	(5,321,276)	(20.0)
Property, plant and equipment, net	6,400,186	13.9	2,495,662	4.7	16,477,416	19.8	4,976,554	18.7
Noncurrent assets:								
Long-term investments	628,809	1.4	764,637	1.4	1,339,490	1.6	309,955	1.2
Deferred income taxes	38,107	0.1	68,983	0.1	28,155	0.0	21,691	0.1
Other assets	2,737,375	5.9	2,166,384	4.1	6,250,621	7.5	1,935,069	7.3
Total noncurrent assets	3,404,291	7.4	3,000,005	5.6	7,618,266	9.2	2,266,715	8.5
Total assets	$ 46,087,420	100.0 %	$ 53,296,895	100.0 %	$ 83,030,207	100.0 %	$ 26,583,883	100.0 %

CFMA Comparative Financial Data

	All Companies		Industrial & Nonresidential		Heavy & Highway		Specialty Trade	
	Amount	Percent	Amount	Percent	Amount	Percent	Amount	Percent
Current liabilities:								
Current maturity on long-term debt	$ 537,754	1.2 %	$ 158,570	0.3 %	$ 1,574,605	1.9 %	$ 369,410	1.4 %
Notes payable and lines of credit	928,503	2.0	345,625	0.6	1,410,524	1.7	1,283,431	4.8
Accounts payable:								
Trade, including currently due to subcontractors	11,009,286	23.9	18,512,779	34.7	13,372,336	16.1	4,241,092	16.0
Subcontracts retainages	2,452,522	5.3	6,042,771	11.3	1,384,009	1.7	246,413	0.9
Other	312,566	0.7	421,281	0.8	280,567	0.3	252,953	1.0
Total accounts payable	13,774,374	29.9	24,976,831	46.9	15,036,912	18.1	4,740,458	17.8
Accrued expenses	2,786,830	6.0	3,588,652	6.7	4,223,056	5.1	1,691,542	6.4
Billings in excess of costs and recognized earnings on uncompleted contracts	5,842,272	12.7	7,207,438	13.5	10,735,923	12.9	2,890,144	10.9
Income taxes:								
Current	64,599	0.1	36,578	0.1	223,450	0.3	28,105	0.1
Deferred	20,434	0.0	17,029	0.0	7,639	0.0	23,547	0.1
Other current liabilities	796,813	1.7	482,585	0.9	623,431	0.8	1,160,606	4.4
Total current liabilities	24,751,579	53.7	36,811,307	69.1	33,835,541	40.8	12,187,242	45.8
Noncurrent liabilities								
Long-term debt, excluding current maturities	3,017,904	6.5	949,287	1.8	5,703,085	6.9	2,727,051	10.3
Deferred income taxes	139,495	0.3	57,937	0.1	566,108	0.7	34,549	0.1
Other	1,187,566	2.6	1,208,463	2.3	2,901,328	3.5	575,038	2.2
Total liabilities	29,096,544	63.1	39,026,995	73.2	43,006,061	51.8	15,523,880	58.4
Minority interests	254,000	0.6	27,224	0.1	1,186,138	1.4	101,214	0.4
Net worth:								
Common stock, par value	3,124,577	6.8	2,115,566	4.0	5,436,411	6.5	3,622,508	13.6
Preferred stock, stated value	104,385	0.2	45,373	0.1	26,214	0.0	196,266	0.7
Additional paid-in capital	1,924,472	4.2	1,947,458	3.7	5,283,044	6.4	733,595	2.8
Retained earnings	12,030,503	26.1	9,649,298	18.1	29,342,228	35.3	7,424,905	27.9
Treasury stock	(1,216,798)	(2.6)	(1,375,146)	(2.6)	(1,604,054)	(1.9)	(1,028,713)	(3.9)
Excess value of marketable securities	10,690	0.0	18,254	0.0	2,918	0.0	8,195	0.0
Other equity	759,047	1.6	1,841,873	3.5	351,248	0.4	2,034	0.0
Total net worth	16,736,877	36.3	14,242,676	26.7	38,838,009	46.8	10,958,790	41.2
Total liabilities and net worth	$ 46,087,420	100.0 %	$ 53,296,895	100.0 %	$ 83,030,207	100.0 %	$ 26,583,883	100.0 %

CFMA Comparative Financial Data

Statement of Earnings
Most Recent Year-End

	All Companies		Industrial & Nonresidential		Heavy & Highway		Specialty Trade	
	Amount	Percent	Amount	Percent	Amount	Percent	Amount	Percent
Contract revenue	$ 103,308,454	98.7 %	$ 148,810,925	99.9 %	$ 150,432,717	98.7 %	$ 51,249,247	96.2 %
Other revenue	1,396,527	1.3	153,756	0.1	2,032,556	1.3	2,045,631	3.8
Total revenue	104,704,981	100.0	148,964,681	100.0	152,465,273	100.0	53,294,878	100.0
Contract cost	(92,801,744)	(88.6)	(137,643,392)	(92.4)	(134,321,588)	(88.1)	(43,435,627)	(81.5)
Other cost	(977,242)	(0.9)	(78,504)	(0.1)	(1,390,686)	(0.9)	(1,427,155)	(2.7)
Total cost	(93,778,986)	(89.6)	(137,721,896)	(92.5)	(135,712,275)	(89.0)	(44,862,782)	(84.2)
Gross profit	10,925,995	10.4	11,242,785	7.5	16,752,998	11.0	8,432,096	15.8
Selling, general and administrative expenses:								
Payroll	(3,058,204)	(2.9)	(3,444,417)	(2.3)	(3,804,551)	(2.5)	(2,602,201)	(4.9)
Professional fees	(189,595)	(0.2)	(219,202)	(0.1)	(259,845)	(0.2)	(141,574)	(0.3)
Sales and marketing costs	(233,914)	(0.2)	(276,444)	(0.2)	(193,698)	(0.1)	(229,254)	(0.4)
Technology costs	(157,829)	(0.2)	(193,094)	(0.1)	(193,895)	(0.1)	(119,748)	(0.2)
Administrative bonuses	(513,644)	(0.5)	(602,136)	(0.4)	(532,477)	(0.3)	(476,235)	(0.9)
Other	(3,500,717)	(3.3)	(3,162,348)	(2.1)	(4,547,225)	(3.0)	(3,279,070)	(6.2)
Total SG&A expenses	(7,653,904)	(7.3)	(7,898,539)	(5.3)	(9,531,691)	(6.3)	(6,848,082)	(12.8)
Income from operations	3,272,092	3.1	3,344,246	2.2	7,221,307	4.7	1,584,014	3.0
Interest income	140,124	0.1	259,808	0.2	200,525	0.1	28,452	0.1
Interest expense	(114,411)	(0.1)	(66,546)	(0.0)	(317,685)	(0.2)	(66,314)	(0.1)
Other income / (expense), net	90,580	0.1	167,420	0.1	505,519	0.3	(122,275)	(0.2)
Net earnings / (loss) before income taxes	3,388,384	3.2	3,704,928	2.5	7,609,667	5.0	1,423,878	2.7
Income tax (expense) / benefit	(229,331)	(0.2)	(300,137)	(0.2)	(474,765)	(0.3)	(85,259)	(0.2)
Net earnings	$ 3,159,054	3.0 %	$ 3,404,791	2.3 %	$ 7,134,902	4.7 %	$ 1,338,619	2.5 %
Average backlog	$ 111,779,895		$ 165,477,234		$ 176,904,418		$ 51,889,394	

Number of Participants

	All Companies		Industrial & Nonresidential		Heavy & Highway		Specialty Trade	
	Number		Number		Number		Number	
2011	608		191		110		286	
2010	623		275		126		336	

1696

CFMA Comparative Financial Data

Financial Ratios
Most Recent Year-End

	All Companies		Industrial & Nonresidential		Heavy & Highway		Specialty Trade	
	Average	Median	Average	Median	Average	Median	Average	Median
Liquidity Ratios								
Current Ratio	1.5	1.6	1.3	1.4	1.7	1.7	1.6	1.8
Quick Ratio	1.3	1.4	1.2	1.3	1.4	1.5	1.3	1.5
Days of Cash	33.8	25.3	29.7	28.6	48.9	33.3	27.0	17.3
Working Capital Turnover	9.1	8.3	13.6	10.5	6.1	6.8	7.5	6.7
Profitability Ratios								
Return on Assets	7.4 %	4.8 %	7.0 %	4.5 %	9.2 %	6.4 %	5.4 %	4.2 %
Return on Equity	20.3 %	11.3 %	26.0 %	16.0 %	19.6 %	12.2 %	13.0 %	8.3 %
Times Interest Earned	30.6	9.2	56.7	8.2	25.0	17.8	22.5	6.8
Leverage Ratios								
Debt to Equity	1.7	1.4	2.7	2.2	1.1	0.9	1.4	1.2
Revenue to Equity	6.3	6.0	10.5	9.3	3.9	4.0	4.9	4.9
Asset Turnover	2.3	2.5	2.8	3.0	1.8	1.9	2.0	2.3
Fixed Asset Ratio	38.2 %	24.0 %	17.5 %	12.0 %	42.4 %	50.0 %	45.4 %	27.0 %
Equity to SG&A Expense	2.2	1.7	1.8	1.6	4.1	3.1	1.6	1.4
Underbillings to Equity	12.7 %	7.0 %	16.3 %	7.0 %	9.0 %	5.0 %	13.9 %	8.0 %
Backlog to Equity	6.7	3.4	11.6	6.6	4.6	2.5	4.7	2.3
Efficiency Ratios								
Backlog to Working Capital	9.7	3.3	15.1	6.1	7.0	3.5	7.3	1.8
Months in Backlog	12.8	5.5	13.3	7.2	13.9	7.6	11.7	3.5
Days in Accounts Receivable	48.7	50.9	44.4	44.4	41.4	39.6	64.6	59.2
Days in Inventory	3.7	0.0	0.1	0.0	6.2	0.5	9.2	0.7
Days in Accounts Payable	43.5	35.6	49.5	43.6	36.2	32.1	36.1	31.0
Operating Cycle	42.7	45.5	24.8	32.9	60.3	50.1	64.7	52.8

TEXT—KEY WORD INDEX OF INDUSTRIES APPEARING IN THE STATEMENT STUDIES

STATEMENT STUDIES KEY WORD INDEX

A complete description of each industry category listed below begins on page 35.

STATEMENT STUDIES KEY WORD INDEX

A complete description of each industry category listed below begins on page 35.

STATEMENT STUDIES KEY WORD INDEX

A complete description of each industry category listed below begins on page 35.

STATEMENT STUDIES KEY WORD INDEX

A complete description of each industry category listed below begins on page 35.

STATEMENT STUDIES KEY WORD INDEX

A complete description of each industry category listed below begins on page 35.

STATEMENT STUDIES KEY WORD INDEX

A complete description of each industry category listed below begins on page 35.

RMA'S CREDIT &
LENDING DICTIONARY

A

Absentee Owner: landlord who does not reside in his or her rental property.

Abstract of Title: condensed history of title to land and real property, consisting of ownership transfers and any conveyances or liens that may affect future ownership.

Acceleration Clause: provision in note or contract that allows holder to declare remaining balance due and payable immediately upon default in an obligation. Usual causes of default are failure to pay interest or principal installments in a timely manner, an adverse change in financing conditions, or failure to meet loan covenants.

Acceptance: drawee's signed agreement to honor draft as presented, which consists of signature alone, but will frequently be evidenced by drawee writing word "accepted," date it is payable, and signature. Sometimes called Trade Acceptance or Banker's Acceptance, depending upon function of acceptor.

Accommodation: 1. lending or extending credit to borrower. 2. loan or commitment to lend money.

Accord and Satisfaction: agreement between two or more persons or entities that satisfies or discharges obligation or settles claim or lawsuit. Generally involves disputed matter in which one party agrees to give and other party agrees to accept something in satisfaction different from, and usually less than, that originally asked for.

Account: 1. statement showing balance along with detailed explanation covering debits and credits. 2. right of payment for goods sold or leased or for services rendered on open account basis. 3. summarized record of financial transaction. 4. customer.

Accountant: person in charge of and skilled in the recording of financial transactions and maintenance of financial records.

Accounting: 1. theory and system of classifying, recording, summarizing, and auditing books of firm. 2. art of analyzing, interpreting, and reporting financial position and operating results of business.

Account Manager: 1. sometimes called Relationship Manager or Account Officer. 2. person responsible for overseeing all matters relating to a specific client or group of customers.

Account Number: unique identification number used to designate specific customer.

Accounts Payable: short-term liability representing amounts due trade creditors.

Accounts Payable Department: section of business office responsible for processing open account balances and paying amounts owed for goods and services purchased.

Accounts Receivable: money due to a business by its customers for goods sold or services performed on open account (or credit). Usually refers to short-term receivables.

Accounts Receivable Aging Report: report by customer that lists age of accounts receivable generally by 30-day intervals from invoice or due date. See also Aging of Accounts Receivable.

Accounts Receivable Financing: form of secured lending in which borrowings are typically limited to percentage of receivables pledged as collateral.

Accrual Accounting: basis of accounting in which expenses are recorded when incurred and revenues are recognized when earned, regardless of when cash is actually paid or received.

Accrue: 1. something gained, added, or accumulated, such as profit from a business transaction. 2. right to sue has become exercisable.

Accrued Expenses: short-term liabilities that represent expenses for goods used but not yet paid.

Accrued Income: income earned but not yet collected.

Accrued Interest: interest accumulated since last interest payment due date.

Accrued Liabilities: expenses or obligations for goods or services incurred but not yet paid.

ACH: see *Automated Clearinghouse*.

Acid Test: ratio between company's most liquid assets (generally, cash and accounts receivable) and current liabilities that represents the degree to which current liabilities can be paid with those assets.

Acknowledgment: 1. declaration making known receipt of something done or to be done; confirmation of receipt of order or of terms of contract. 2. statement of notary or other competent officer certifying that signature on document was personally signed by individual whose signature is affixed to instrument.

Acquisition: merger or taking over of controlling interest of one business by another.

Acquisition and Development Loan: loan made for the purpose of purchasing a property and completing all on-site improvements such as street layout, utility installation, and community area grading necessary to bring the site to a buildable state.

Acquittal: 1. release from obligation or contract. 2. to have accusation of crime dismissed by some formal legal procedure.

Active Account: 1. customer who makes frequent purchases. 2. bank account in which regular deposits or withdrawals are made.

Activity Charge: service charge imposed for check or deposit activity or any other maintenance charge.

Act of God: event that could not be prevented by reasonable foresight, is caused exclusively by forces and violence of nature, and is uninfluenced by human power (storm, flood, earthquake, or lightning).

Additional Dating: means of extending credit beyond normal sales terms, granted to induce buyers to place orders in advance of season or for other special reasons. See also *Advance Dating and Dating*.

Adjudication: judgment rendered by court, primarily used in bankruptcy proceedings.

Adjustable Interest Rate: interest rate on loan that may be adjusted up or down at specific intervals. Index used in determining adjusted interest rate and potential frequency of adjustments must be stated in loan documents.

Adjustable Rate Mortgage: loan is pursuant to an agreement executed at the inception of the loan that permits creditor to adjust interest rate from time to time based on a specific interest rate index.

Adjuster: person who deals with insured party to settle amount of loss, claim, or debt.

Adjustment: 1. settlement of disputed account. 2. change or concession in price or terms. 3. determining amount one is to receive in settlement of claim. 4. in accounting, entry made to correct or compensate for error or difference in account.

Adjustment Bureau: organization that supervises debt extensions and compromise arrangements or oversees orderly liquidation of troubled businesses for benefit of creditors.

Advance: 1. payment made before it is due. 2. disbursement of loan proceeds.

Advance Dating: additional time granted customers to pay for goods received and to earn available discounts. See also Additional Dating and Dating.

Advancement of Costs: prepayment of necessary legal expenses. Such charges, set by law, may be for commencement of suit and vary in different courts and states. Some items for which prepaid costs may be requested are filing fees, process serving, premiums on court bonds, trial fees, posting security for costs, entering judgment, recording abstract of judgment, issue execution, and discovery actions after judgment.

Advertising Allowance: promotional discount in price or payment given customers who share expense of advertising supplier's product.

Affidavit: voluntary written statement of facts pertaining to a transaction or event, signed under oath and witnessed by an authorized person.

Affiliate: business entity connected with another through common ownership or management, usually responsible for payment of its own obligations.

After-Acquired Property: security interest by which secured creditor automatically obtains interest in assets that debtor acquires after lien had been filed.

Agency: legal relationship between two parties in which one is authorized to act for another.

Agent: person legally authorized to act for another.

Agent Bank: formal designation that applies to a bank responsible for negotiating, structuring, and overseeing a loan or commitment to a borrower in which more than one bank is involved. See also Lead Bank.

Aggregate Balances: combined total of two or more demand deposit accounts, money markets, or time certificates of deposit. Term can also be applied to credit facility totals.

Aging of Accounts Receivable: accounting record of customer's receivables showing how long receivables have remained unpaid beyond regular terms of sale. Used as basis for advancing credit.

Agreement: a contract involving an offer and an acceptance between two or more parties, governing the terms of the contract and binding on the parties to the agreement (e.g., a loan agreement, security agreement, or guaranty).

AKA: see *Also Known As*.

Alert Action: a series of information services provided by credit reporting agencies; provides subscribers with listing of specific accounts on which unfavorable payment condition has recently been reported.

Allegation: statement of party to action, setting out what he or she intends to prove or contend.

ALLL: see *Allowance for Loan and Lease Losses*.

Allocation: sub-limit within a total credit facility that is to be used for a specific purpose.

Allonge: paper attached to a negotiable instrument for additional endorsements or other terms and conditions.

Allowance: accounting provision used to set aside amounts for depreciation, returns, or bad debts.

Allowance for Bad Debts: contra account against which uncollectible receivables are charged. See also Bad Debt Reserve.

Allowance for Loan and Lease Losses (ALLL): contra account, generally found on asset side of balance sheet as deduction from total loans outstanding; amount is intended to cover future losses of loans currently in the financial institution's portfolio. The ALLL should be adjusted monthly, concurrently with the generation of current financial statements.

Also Known As (AKA): sometimes used to designate a fictitious trade style or name.

ALTA Policy: an extended coverage title insurance policy that protects the lender against losses resulting from any defects in the title or claims against the property. The policy's coverage includes encroachments, mechanic's liens, and other matters that a physical inspection or inquiry of the parties would disclose.

Altered Check: check on which original entries have been changed (date, payee, or amount); financial institutions generally refuse to honor or pay checks that have been altered.

Amend: to correct, add to, or alter legal document.

Amicus Curiae: friend of court; uninvolved third party who intervenes in lawsuit, with court's permission, to introduce information or arguments in respect to the issue or principle of law to be decided.

Amortization: 1. reduction of loan by periodic principal payments. 2. decline in the book value of an intangible asset over the period owned.

Amortization Tables: calculation charts showing amounts required periodically to discharge debts over various periods of time and at different interest rates.

Amortize: 1. to write off the value of an intangible asset over the period owned. 2. to reduce or pay off debt or obligation by making periodic payments of principal.

Annual Percentage Rate (APR): annual cost of credit expressed as percentage; creditors are required under Federal Truth in Lending Act to disclose true annual interest on consumer loans, as well as the total dollar cost and other terms of loan.

Annual Report: yearly report detailing a company's comparative financial and organizational conditions.

Annuity: series of fixed periodic payments made at regular intervals.

Antecedent Credit Information: historical record of significant business information concerning individuals who are involved in ownership or management of business enterprise.

Anticipation: bridge loan made to a municipal or government borrower to cover expenses until revenue or tax proceeds are collected.

Appeal: complaint made to higher court by either plaintiff or defendant for court's review, correction, or reversal of lower court's decision.

Appearance: coming into court formally as plaintiff or defendant in lawsuit.

Appraisal: opinion of current value of real or personal property based upon cost of replacement, market, income, or fair value analysis.

Appreciation: increase in value of asset over its cost due to economic and other conditions. Property that increases in value as result of improvements or additions is not considered to have appreciated.

Appropriation: sum of money designated for a special purpose only.

APR: See *Annual Percentage Rate.*

Arbitration: submission for settlement of disputed matter, by nonjudicial means, to one or more impartial or disinterested third persons selected by disputants.

Arm's Length: business transaction between two or more parties that is open, sincere, and without personal influence, favoritism, or close relations.

Arrangement: plan for corporate reorganization for rescheduling or extension of time for payment of unsecured debts, such as an arrangement under Chapter 11 or 13 of the U. S. Bankruptcy Code.

Arrears: total or partial debt amounts that remain unpaid and past due.

Articles of Agreement: any written statement or contract, terms to which all parties consent.

Articles of Incorporation: formal papers that set forth pertinent data for formation of corporation and are filed with appropriate state agency.

Assess: 1. to fix rate or amount. 2. to set value of real and personal property, as for tax purposes.

Assessed Value: in the case of real property, value set by government agency for purpose of levying taxes.

Asset: 1. anything owned having monetary value. 2. item listed on left-hand side of balance sheet representing cash, or property, real or personal, belonging to an individual or company and convertible to cash.

Assigned Account: 1. account receivable pledged by borrower to factor or lender as security. 2. past-due customer whose account has been placed with collection agency.

Assigned Risk: insurance plan that provides coverage for risks rejected by regular markets and in which all licensed insurers are made to participate by various state laws.

Assignee: person to whom some rights, authority, or property is assigned.

Assignment: 1. written contract for transfer of one's title, legal rights, or property from one person to another. 2. in some states, form used to transfer claim to agency that undertakes collection of account for benefit of assigning creditor.

Assignment for the Benefit of Creditors: A liquidation technique in which an insolvent debtor goes out of business and an assignee facilitates the transfer of the insolvent debtor's estate for administration and payment of debts. Property transferred to assignee places such assets beyond control of debtor or reach of creditors.

Assignment of Claim: claim assigned to third party for collection.

Assignor: 1. one who transfers claim, right, or property. 2. individual, partnership, or corporation making assignment.

Assumed Liability: acknowledgment of responsibility for payment of obligation by third party.

At Sight: words used in negotiable instrument directing that payment be made upon presentation or demand.

Attached Account: legally frozen account on which payments have been suspended; release or disbursement of funds can be made only after court order.

Attachment: 1. legal writ or process by which debtor's property (or any interest therein) is seized and placed in custody of law. 2. Supplemental data provided as clarifying information to a document.

Attorney-in-Fact: private attorney who has written authorization to act for another. This authority is given by an instrument called power of attorney.

Attorney of Record: lawyer whose name must appear in permanent court records as person acting on behalf of party in legal matter.

Auction: public sale of property that is sold to highest bidder.

Audit: to examine a firm's records, accounts, or procedures for purpose of substantiating or verifying individual transactions or to confirm if assets and liabilities are properly accounted for, including income and expense items.

Audited Financial Statements: financial statements that have been examined by an independent certified public accountant to determine if the financial statements present fairly the financial position, results of operations, and cash flows in conformity with generally accepted accounting principles.

Auditor: person who deals with examination and verification of financial accounts and with making financial reports.

Auditor's Report: part of complete set of financial statements that explains degree of responsibility that independent accountant assumed for expressing an opinion on management's financial statements and assurance that is provided by said opinion.

Automated Cash Application: computerized procedures enabling payments to be quickly and automatically applied to accounts receivable.

Automated Clearinghouse (ACH): computer-based clearing and settlement facility for interchange of electronic debits and credits among financial institutions. ACH entries can be substituted for checks in recurring payments such as mortgages or in direct deposit distribution of federal and corporate benefits payments. Federal Reserve Banks furnish data processing services for most ACHs, although some are privately operated. Final settlement, or net settlement, of ACH transfers is made against reserve accounts at Federal Reserve Banks.

Available Balance: checking account balance that the customer actually may use; that is, current balance less deposits not yet cleared through the account.

Average Collected Balances: average dollar amount on deposit in checking accounts defined as the difference between ledger balance and deposit float, or those deposits posted to the account but having not yet cleared the financial institution upon which they are drawn. See also Uncollected Funds.

Average Collection Period: average number of days required to convert accounts receivable to cash.

Average Daily Balance: average amount of money that depositor keeps on deposit when calculated on a daily basis.

B

Backdating: predating document prior to date on which it was drawn.

Backlog: amount of revenue expected to be realized from work to be performed on uncompleted contracts, including new contractual agreements on which work has not begun.

Bad Check Laws: laws enacted in various states to encourage and facilitate lawful use of checks; statutes differ in various jurisdictions and are generally enforced according to state laws as well as local custom and usage.

Bad Debt: account receivable that proves uncollectible in normal course of business; full payment is doubtful.

Bad Debt Ratio: ratio of bad debt expense to sales, used as measure of quality of accounts receivable.

Bad Debt Reserve: reserve or provision for accounts receivables to be charged off company's books based on historical levels of bad debts or industry averages.

Balance: amount owed or unpaid on loan or credit transaction. Also called outstanding or unpaid balance.

Balance Due: total amount owed after applying debits and credits of account.

Balance Sheet: A financial statement listing the assets, liabilities, and owner's equity of a business entity or individual as of a specific date.

Balloon Payment: lump-sum payment of principal and sometimes accrued interest, usually due at end of term of installment loan in which periodic installments of principal and interest did not fully amortize loan.

Bank: financial institution chartered by state or federal government to transact financial business that includes receiving deposits, lending money, exchanging currencies, providing safekeeping, and investing money.

Bank Draft: sight or demand draft (order to pay) drawn by a bank (drawer) on its account at another bank (drawee).

Banker's Acceptance: draft or order to pay specified amount at specified time not to exceed 270 days, drawn on individuals, business firms, or financial institutions; draft becomes accepted when a financial institution formally acknowledges its obligation to honor such draft, usually by writing or stamping "Accepted" on face of instrument. When accepted in this manner, draft becomes liability of bank. See also *Draft* and *Time Draft*.

Bank Overdraft: check presented for collection for which there are not sufficient funds on deposit to make normal payment. Financial institution may honor such check, considering payment as loan to depositor for which the institution will usually collect interest or service charge.

Bankrupt: debtor who is unable to meet debt obligations as they become due or is insolvent and whose assets are administered for benefit of creditors.

Bankruptcy: Legal action taken under the U.S. Bankruptcy Code by or against an insolvent debtor who is unable to meet obligations as they become due. The bankrupt, if given discharge, is released from further liability of most debts listed as of the date of the bankruptcy filing.

- *Voluntary Bankruptcy:* any individual, partnership, corporation, estate, trust, or governmental unit may be afforded protection of debtor under U.S. Bankruptcy Code by filing petition. Exceptions: railroads, insurance or banking corporations, building and loan associations.
- *Involuntary Bankruptcy:* involuntary petition can be filed in bankruptcy court by three or more creditors or, if there are fewer than 12 creditors, by any one creditor. Petitioning creditors' claims must aggregate at least $5,000 in excess of value of any collateral of debtor. Involuntary cases may be filed against individuals, partnerships, or corporations other than farmers and nonprofit corporations and may be instituted under either Chapter 7 or Chapter 11 of the U.S. Bankruptcy Code. Involuntary petition must allege one of two grounds for relief: either that the debtor is generally not paying debts as they become due, or that the non-bankruptcy custodian, other than one appointed to enforce lien on less than substantially all of debtor's property, was appointed for, or took possession of, substantially all of debtor's property within 120 days of filing.
- *Chapter 7 Cases:* liquidation proceedings, formerly referred to as "straight bankruptcy," wherein nonexempt assets of debtor are converted to cash and proceeds distributed pro rata among creditors.
- *Chapter 9 Cases:* reorganization proceedings wherein municipality that is insolvent or unable to meet debts as they mature effects plan to adjust such debts.
- *Chapter 11 Cases:* reorganization proceedings available to all business enterprises; may be instituted either by debtor or creditor(s). For plan to be confirmed by court under Chapter 11, each class of creditors, as set forth in such plan, must accept plan or each class must receive at least that which it would receive on liquidation. Class of creditors has accepted plan when majority in number and two-thirds in dollar amount of those creditors actually voting approve it.
- *Chapter 12 Cases:* reorganization proceedings for agricultural concerns and small family-owned farms having debts under $1.5 million.
- *Chapter 13 Cases:* reorganization cases that may be instituted only by individuals with regular income who owe unsecured debts of less than $100,000 and secured debts of less than $350,000, other than stockbroker or commodity broker. For plan to be confirmed, it must provide for submission to trustee of all or any portion of debtor's future earnings as necessary for execution of plan, payment in full of all priority claims, and equal treatment of each member of class of creditors. While consent of unsecured creditors is not required, value of what they receive under plan may not be less than if debtor were liquidated.

Bankruptcy Judge: presiding judge of court in which bankruptcy cases are heard. (Formerly called Referee in Bankruptcy.) Duties of judge include supervising administrative details of bankrupt estates and ruling on all matters involving debtor-creditor problems.

Basis: 1. number of days used in calculating interest earned in investment or interest payable on bank loan. Also called accrual base. 2. original cost of asset plus capital improvements from which any taxable gains (or losses) are determined after deducting depreciation expenses.

Basis Point: 1/100th of a percent; 100 basis points equal 1%.

Bearer: negotiable item (check, note, bill, or draft) in which no payee is indicated or payee is shown as "cash" or "bearer." Item is payable to person in possession of it or to person who presents it for payment.

Bearer Paper: instrument that is made "payable to bearer." When negotiable instrument is endorsed in blank, it becomes bearer paper and can be transferred by delivery since it does not require endorsement.

Beneficiary: 1. person or organization named in will to inherit or receive property. 2. person or organization to whom insurance policy is payable. 3. person or organization for whose benefit trust is created.

Bid Bond: bond issued by surety on behalf of contractor that provides assurance to recipient of contractor's bid that if bid is accepted, contractor will execute contract and provide performance bond. Under bond, surety is obligated to pay recipient difference between contractor's bid and bid of next lowest responsible bidder if bid is accepted and contractor fails to execute contract or to provide performance bond.

Billing Cycle: number of days between payment due dates.

Bill of Costs: certified itemization of costs associated with lawsuit.

Bill of Lading: written instrument signed by common carrier or agent identifying freight and representing both receipt and contract for shipment. It must show name of consignee, description of goods, terms of carrier's contract, and directions for assigning to specific person at specific place. In form of negotiable instrument, it is evidence of holding title to goods being shipped.

Bill of Sale: written instrument evidencing transfer of title of specific personal property to buyer.

Binder: 1. written agreement that provides temporary legal protection pending issuance of final contract or policy. 2. temporary insurance contract; may be oral or written; also called cover note.

Blank Endorsement: endorser's writing on check, promissory note, or bill of exchange without indicating party to whom it is payable. Endorser merely signs his or her name, making the instrument "payable to bearer." Also called endorsement in blank.

Blanket Coverage: property coverage applicable to group of exposures (buildings, inventory, equipment, etc., combined or individually, at one or more locations), in single total amount of insurance; contrasts with Specific Coverage.

Blanket Mortgage: mortgage secured by two or more parcels of real property, frequently used by developers who acquire large tract of land for subdivision and resale to individual homeowners. Also called blanket trust deed.

Bond: contract issued by insurance or bonding company in support of principal's obligation to obligee. See also *Fidelity Bond* and *Surety Bond*.

Bonded Warehouse: federally approved warehouse under bond for strict observance of revenue laws; used for storing goods until duties are paid or property is otherwise released. Bonded warehouse assures owner of property that operators of warehouse are insured against loss by fraud and will keep proper inventory and accounting of goods in transit.

Bonding Company: company authorized to issue bid bonds, performance bonds, labor and materials bonds, or other types of surety bonds.

Book Value: 1. company's net worth calculated by adding total assets minus total liabilities. 2. value of asset (cost plus additions, less depreciation) shown on books or financial report of an entity.

Borrower's Certificate: A document required under a loan or other agreement to be submitted by the borrower or another designated party to certify the value of collateral and compliance with the terms of the agreement.

Bottom Line: (colloq.) final price, net profit, or end results.

Branch Banking: multioffice banking. Branch is any banking facility away from bank's main office that accepts deposits or makes loans. State laws strictly control opening of new banking offices by state-chartered banks, national banks, and thrift institutions.

Breach of Contract: failure to fulfill terms of contract, in part or whole.

Breach of Warranty: 1. failure to fully disclose information about condition of property or insured party. 2. failure to perform as promised.

Break-Even Analysis: A method of determining the number of units that must be sold at a given price to recover all fixed and variable costs.

Break-even Point: 1. point at which total sales are equal to total expenses. May be expressed in units or dollars. 2. amount received from sale that exactly equals amount of expense or cost.

Bridge Loan: loan that provides liquidity until defined event occurs that will generate cash, such as sale of noncurrent asset, replacement financing, or equity infusion.

Bulk Sales Acts: statutes designed to prevent defrauding of creditors through secret sale in bulk of merchant's goods. Most states require notice of proposed sale to all creditors.

Burden of Proof: 1. duty of producing sufficient evidence to prove position taken in lawsuit. 2. necessity of proving fact or facts as to truth of claim.

Business: 1. commercial, industrial, or mercantile activity engaged in by individual, partnership, corporation, or other form of organization for purpose of making, buying, or selling goods or services at profit. 2. occupation, profession, or trade.

Business Failure: 1. suspension of business resulting from insolvency or bankruptcy. 2. inability to fulfill normal business obligations.

Business Interruption Insurance: property insurance written to cover loss of profits and continuing expenses as result of shutdown by insured peril; exposure is classified as consequential loss. Also called earnings insurance.

Buyer's Market: market condition in which supply exceeds demand, which causes prices to decline.

Buy Out: to purchase at least a controlling percentage of a company's stock to take over its assets.

Bylaws: set of rules or regulations adopted to control internal affairs of organization.

C

C's of Credit: the "Five C's" of credit. A longstanding means of evaluating a customer by investigating Character, Collateral, Capacity, Conditions, and Capital.

Calendar Year: 12-month accounting period ending December 31.

Callable Loan: loan payable on demand.

Canceled Check: check that has been paid by a financial institution and on which the financial institution has imprinted evidence of payment so that it cannot be presented again.

Cancellation Clause: provision in contract or agreement allowing parties to rescind agreement under certain conditions.

Capacity: one of the "Five C's" of credit; a customer's ability to successfully absorb merchandise and to pay for the merchandise. Refers to customer's ability to produce sufficient cash so as to meet obligations when due.

Capital: 1. one of the "Five Cs" of credit; refers to financial resources the customer has at the time order is placed and those that he or she is likely to have when payment is due. 2. amount invested in business by owners or stockholders. 3. owner's equity in the business.

Cash: 1. money readily available for current expenditures; usually consists of cash on hand or money in a financial institution. 2. money equivalent, such as a check, paid at time of purchase. 3. any medium of exchange that the financial institution will accept at face value upon deposit.

Cash Basis Accounting: basis of accounting in which revenues and expenses are reported in the income statement when cash is received or paid out for the time period in which the revenues and expenses occur.

Cash Basis Loan: loan on which interest payments are recorded when collected from borrower. This is a loan in which the borrower has fallen behind on interest payments and is classified as a nonaccrual asset.

Cash Concentration and Disbursement (CCD): corporate electronic payment used in business-to-business and intracompany transfers of funds. Funds are cleared on overnight basis through nationwide automated clearinghouse network.

Cash Equivalents: accounting term for actual cash on hand and total of bank deposits.

Cash Flow: is based on an activity format, which classifies cash inflows and outflows in terms of operating, investing, and financing activities.

Cashier's Check: check drawn on financial institution's account, becoming direct obligation of the financial institution.

Cash Management Account: special type of deposit service that permits corporate customers to invest cash in demand deposit account until needed for operations.

Cash Surrender Value: in life insurance, amount payable under whole life policy when terminated by insured.

Casualty Insurance: coverage for automobile, liability, crime, boiler and machinery, health, bonds, aviation, workers' compensation, and other miscellaneous lines; contrasts with Property Insurance.

Certificate of Insurance: written statement issued by insurer indicating that insurance policy has been issued and showing details of coverage at time certificate was written; used as evidence of insurance.

Certified Check: depositor's check confirmed on its face as good by a financial institution and stamped "certified." It is then dated and signed by an authorized officer of the institution. Such check becomes an obligation of the financial institution, which guarantees that it is holding sufficient funds to cover payment of check on demand.

Certified Copy of Policy: document that provides evidence of insurance as of certain date; coverage may be terminated or changed after certification.

Certified Public Accountant (CPA): one who has been trained to do accounting and who has passed state test and received title of CPA; title certifies holder's qualification to practice accounting, audit, prepare reports, and analyze accounting information.

CGL: see *Comprehensive General Liability*.

Character: one of the "Five Cs" of credit; refers to evaluating qualities that would impel debtor to meet his or her obligations. Generally identified as customer's reputation, responsibility, integrity, and honesty.

Charge-Off: portion of principal balance of a loan or account receivable that an entity considers uncollectible; this amount may be partially or fully recovered in future. Also called a *Write-Off*.

Chart of Accounts: listing of all financial accounts or categories (usually numbered) into which business transactions are classified and recorded.

Chattel: item of tangible personal property, animate or inanimate, as distinguished from real property.

Chattel Mortgage: instrument of sale in which debtor transfers title in property to creditor as security for debt. Failure by debtor to comply with terms of contract may cause creditor's title in property to become absolute.

Check: order on a financial institution for payment of funds from depositor's account and payable on demand.

Claim: 1. action to recover payment, reimbursement, or compensation from entity legally liable for damage or injury.

Claimant: one who makes claim or asserts right.

Cleanup: period during which particular loan or entire borrowing has been paid off; out-of-debt period required under line of credit.

Clearinghouse: association of financial institutions or security dealers created to permit daily settlement and exchange of checks or delivery of stocks and other items between members in local geographic area.

Closed-End Credit: consumer installment loan made for predetermined amount, calling for periodic payments of principal and interest over specified period or term. Finance charge may be fixed or variable rate. Borrower does not have option of obtaining extra funds under original loan agreement. Contrasts with Open-End Credit.

Cloud on Title: outstanding claim or encumbrance on property that may impair owner's title.

Cognovit Note: form of promissory note or statement that allows creditor, in case of default by debtor, to enter judgment without trial. (Not recognized in all jurisdictions.)

Collateral: 1. one of the "Five C's" of credit; refers to real or personal property that may be available as security. 2. asset pledged by borrower in support of loan. See also *Secured Loan*.

Collateral Note: form of promissory note given for loan, pledging real or personal property as security for payment of debt.

Collectible: account capable of being collected.

Collection Agency: professional business service employed as agent to collect creditors' unpaid (past-due) accounts. Collection agency is usually compensated by receiving agreed upon contingent percentage of amount collected.

Collection Agency Report: report from collection agency that informs client of results of collection efforts, investigations, or recommendations.

Collection Charges: 1. fees charged by bank for collecting drafts, notes, coupons, or other instruments. 2. compensation paid to collection agency or attorney for collecting delinquent accounts.

Collection Item: 1. term for item received for collection that is to be credited to depositor's account after payment. Most financial institutions charge special (collection) fees for handling such items. 2. past due account assigned for collection.

Collection Period: number of days required for company's receivables to be collected and converted to cash.

Comaker: person who signs (and guarantees) note of another and by so doing promises to pay in full. See also *Cosigner*.

Commensurate: describes deposit balances that are in acceptable proportion to size of loan or commitment.

Commercial Debt: loan or obligation incurred for business purposes.

Commercial Law League of America (C.L.L.A.): national membership organization of commercial attorneys, commercial credit and collection agencies, credit insurance companies, and law list publishers. Objectives include setting standards for honorable dealings among members, improving the practice of commercial law, and promoting uniformity of legislation affecting commercial law.

Commercial Paper: short-term securities such as notes, drafts, bills of exchange, and other negotiable paper that arise out of commercial activity and become due on a definite maturity date.

Commercial Property: real estate used for business purposes or managed so as to produce income from rents and leases.

Commitment: agreement between a financial institution and borrower to make funds available under certain conditions for a specified period of time.

Commitment Fee: lender's charge for holding credit available, usually replaced with interest when funds are advanced, as in revolving credit. In business credit, a commitment fee is often charged for unused portion of line of credit.

Commitment Letter: letter from lender stating willingness to advance funds to named borrower, repayable at specified rate and time period, subject to escape clause(s) allowing lender to rescind agreement in event of materially adverse changes in borrower's financial condition.

Committee Approval: credit is approved by several people acting as group.

Common Law: body of law that was originated, developed, and administered in England.

Community Property: property shared by husband and wife, each having one-half interest in earnings of other; form of joint property ownership in some states.

Community Reinvestment Act of 1977 (CRA): federal law that requires mortgage lenders to demonstrate their commitment to home mortgage financing in economically disadvantaged areas. Prohibits redlining or credit allocation based on geographic region and requires lenders to file annual compliance statements.

Compensating Balance: demand deposit balance that must be maintained by borrower to compensate financial institution for loan accommodations and other services.

Compound Interest: interest calculated by adding accumulated interest to date to original principal. New balance becomes principal for additional interest calculations.

Comprehensive General Liability (CGL): policy form providing automatic coverage for all insured's business operations; may include auto exposures; newer form of CGL is called commercial general liability.

Concession: 1. granting of special privilege to digress from regular terms or previous conditions. 2. allowance or rebate from established price. 3. business enterprise operated under special permission.

Conditional Sales Contract: contract for sale of goods under which possession is delivered to buyer but title retained by seller until goods are paid for in full or until other conditions are met. In most states, conditional sales contracts have been replaced by security agreements having substantially the same definition under Uniform Commercial Code.

Conditions: one of the "Five C's" of credit; refers to general business environment and status of borrower's industry.

Confession of Judgment Note: note in which (after maturity) debtor permits attorney to appear in court and have judgment entered if payment is not made as agreed. Acceptance of note varies by state. See also *Cognovit Note*.

Confirmation: 1. supplier's written acknowledgment that he or she has accepted buyer's order. 2. customer's written verification of order previously placed. 3. proof verifying agreement or existence of assets and liabilities or claims against assets and liabilities.

Consent Judgment: judgment that debtor allows to be entered against him or her by motion filed with court.

Consideration: 1. element in contract without which contract is not binding. Contract is generally not valid without consideration. 2. reason for contracting parties to enter into contract. Act, promise, price, or motive for which agreement is entered into. 3. value given in exchange for benefit that is to be derived from contract. 4. compensation. Exchange of consideration is usually mutual, each party giving something up to other.

Consign: to send or forward goods to merchant, factor, or agent for sale with title retained by seller and with payment delayed, generally until sale is made.

Consignee: person or entity to which goods or property is consigned or shipped; ultimate recipient of shipment.

Consignment: arrangement under which consignor (seller) remains owner of property until such time as consignee (buyer) pays for goods; usually consignee pays consignor when goods are sold or holds proceeds of sale in trust for benefit of consignor.

Consignor: 1. one who delivers shipment or turns it over to carrier for transportation and delivery. 2. one who consigns goods to be sold without giving up title.

Consolidated Financial Statement: combined statement showing financial condition of parent corporation and its subsidiaries.

Consolidating Financial Statement: combined statement of subsidiary and parent companies that shows complete statement for each entity without netting intercompany transactions.

Construction Loan: interim financing for development and construction of real property, generally converted to long-term financing upon completion of construction.

Consumer Credit: debt incurred for personal, family, or household use.

Consumer Credit Protection Act (Truth in Lending Act of 1968): law that requires most lenders and those who extend consumer credit to disclose true credit costs. Act provides for limits on garnishment of wages, prohibits excessive interest, and makes available contents of consumer credit reports.

Consumer Sale Disclosure Statement: form required to be provided by creditor to customer, disclosing finance charge details as required under Consumer Credit Protection Act.

Contingent Fee: fee to be paid only in event of specific occurrence, usually successful results. Arrangement, for example, in which collection agency will receive stated percentage of any amounts recovered or in which lawyer will receive payment only if successful in prosecuting lawsuit.

Contingent Liability: liability in which a person(s) or business(es) is indirectly responsible for obligations of a third party. Such indirect liability is usually established by guaranty or endorsement, and the liability holder may turn to guarantors or endorsers for satisfaction of debt. See also Endorsement and Guaranty.

Contra Account: account that partially or wholly offsets another account or balance.

Contract: agreement between two or more entities or legally competent persons that creates, modifies, or destroys legal arrangement.

Controlled Disbursement: funds management technique in corporate cash management designed to maximize funds available for temporary investment in money market or for payment to trade creditors. Controls flow of checks through banking system to meet corporate investment and funds management requirements. Contrasts with delayed disbursement. See also *Federal Reserve Float* and *Treasury Workstation*.

Controller: person in business organization responsible for finances, internal auditing, and accounting systems in use in company's operations.

Conversion: process of consolidating or transferring data from one system to another.

Conveyance: 1. transfer of right, generally instrument transferring interest in real estate in form of deed. 2. transfer of property ownership (sometimes includes leases and mortgages) from one person or organization to another.

Copyright: intangible right granted to author or originator by federal government to solely and exclusively reproduce or publish specific literary, musical, or artistic work for certain number of years.

Corporate Reorganization: see *Bankruptcy*.

Corporate Veil: convention that corporate organization insulates organization's owners from liability for corporate activities.

Corporation: artificial person or legal entity organized under and treated by state laws, legally distinct from its shareholders and vested with capacity of continuous succession irrespective of changes in its ownership either in perpetuity or for limited term. It may be set up to contract, own, and discharge business within boundaries of powers granted it by its corporate charter.

Correspondent: organization or individual that carries on business relations or acts as agent with others in different cities or countries.

Cosigner: one of joint signers of loan documents. One who signs note of another as support for credit of the principal maker.

Cost of Funds: dollar cost of interest paid or accrued on funds acquired from various sources within bank and borrowed funds acquired from other financial institutions, including time deposits, advances at Federal Reserve discount window, federal funds purchased, and Eurodollar deposits. Financial institution may use internal cost of funds in pricing loans it makes.

Covenant: written agreement, convention, or promise between parties who pledge to do or not to do certain things or that stipulates truth of certain facts.

CPA: see *Certified Public Accountant*.

CRA: see *Community Reinvestment Act of 1977*.

Crash: sudden sharp decrease in business activity that can negatively affect stock market volumes and prices.

Credit: 1. privilege of buying goods and services, or for borrowing money in return for promise of future payment. 2. in bookkeeping, entry on ledger signifying cash payment, merchandise returned, or allowance to reduce debt. 3. accounting entry on right side of ledger sheet.

Credit Advisory Board (CAB): agency established by Financial Institutions Reform, Recovery, and Enforcement Act of 1989 "to monitor the credit standards and lending practices of insured depository institutions and the supervision of such standards and practices by the federal financial regulators" as well as to "ensure that insured depository institutions can meet the demands of a modern and globally competitive world." This board was granted permanent authorization by the Federal Deposit Insurance Corporation Improvement Act of 1991. Formerly known as Credit Standards Advisory Committee (CSAC).

Credit Analyst: person who evaluates the financial history and financial statements of credit applicants to assess creditworthiness. Analysts are trained to evaluate applicant's financial strength and to opine on the probability of full repayment, collateral adequacy, or whether a credit enhancement through a cosigner or guarantor is needed.

Credit Application: form completed by potential borrower and used by creditor to determine applicant's creditworthiness.

Credit Approval: decision to extend credit.

Credit Approval System: internal methods by which credit decisions are made.

Credit Bureau: agency that gathers information and provides its subscribers with credit reports on consumers.

Credit Checking: examining and analyzing creditworthiness of customer by contacting references, reviewing credit reports, etc.

Credit Department: department within a financial institution that performs operations and credit support functions for underwriting activities. May include maintenance of credit files, credit investigations, financial statement analysis and spreading, customers' accounts receivable audits, lender training, portfolio reporting, facilitation of credit meetings, etc.

Credit Enhancement: enhancement to creditworthiness of loans underlying asset-backed security or municipal bond, generally to get investment-grade rating from bond rating agency and to improve marketability of debt securities to investors. There are two general classifications of credit enhancements:
- third-party enhancement, in which third party pledges its own creditworthiness and guarantees repayment in form of standby letter of credit or commercial letter of credit issued by a financial institution, surety bond from insurance company, or special reserve fund managed by financial guaranty firm in exchange for fee.
- self-enhancement, which is generally done by issuer through over-collateralization—that is, pledging loans with book value greater than face value of bonds offered for sale.

Credit File: creditor's file that compiles information about customer, including correspondence, credit memorandums and analyses, credit ratings, a credit history, payment patterns, and credit inquiries.

Credit Granting: approval and extension of credit to a customer.

Credit Inquiry: request made by a financial institution or trade creditor concerning the responding bank's own customer.

Credit Insurance: life and health insurance issued in conjunction with borrowing by individuals; covers payments or unpaid balance when borrower is disabled or dies; in business, covers loss of receivables when debtor becomes insolvent.

Credit Interchange: exchange of credit information between individuals or groups.

Credit Interchange Bureau (CIB): 1. local bureaus offering members or subscribers credit reports usually based on recent ledger experiences. Generally refers to organized system of cooperating bureaus operated by regional credit associations. 2. credit agency that may limit its reporting to a particular trade.

Credit Investigation: inquiry made by a financial institution or trade creditor concerning subject that is not the responding financial institution's customer.

Credit Limit: maximum amount of credit made available to customer by specific creditor.

Credit Line: commitment by a financial institution to lend funds to a borrower up to a given amount over a specified future period under certain pre-established conditions. Normally reviewed annually.

Credit Management: function of planning, organizing, implementing, and supervising credit policies of a company.

Creditor: 1. one to whom debt is owed by another as a result of a financial transaction. 2. one who extends credit and to whom money is due.

Creditors' Committee: voluntary representative group of creditors that may examine affairs of insolvent debtor. Group will usually advise as to continuation of business, study accountant's and appraiser's reports, act as watchdog over operating business, make recommendations to appropriate groups or legal body so that creditors will realize largest settlement possible, and advise as to acceptability of settlement.

Creditors' Remedies: legal rights enabling creditors to collect delinquent debts owed them.

Credit Policy: company's written procedures for making credit decisions. Used to aid company in meeting its overall risk management objectives.

Credit Process Review: assessment of entire credit-granting process concerning specific financial institution loan portfolio(s).

Credit Rating: appraisal made by a financial institution or credit agency as to creditworthiness of a person or company. Such a report will include background on owners, estimate of financial strength and ability to pay when due, and company's payment record.

Credit Record: written history of how well a customer has handled debt repayment.

Credit Report: 1. report to aid management in reaching credit, sales, and financial decisions. 2. confidential report containing information obtained by mercantile agency that has investigated a company's background, credit history, financial strength, and payment record.

Credit Reporting Agency: company or trade interchange group that confidentially supplies subscribers or members with credit information and other relevant data as to a company's ability or likelihood to pay for goods and services purchased on credit.

Credit Research Foundation (CRF): education and research affiliate of National Association of Credit Management.

Credit Review: follow-up monitoring of loan or extension of credit by credit review officer or department, senior loan committee, auditor, or regulatory agency intended to determine whether loan was made in accordance with lender's written credit standards and policies and in compliance with banking regulations. Errors, omissions, concentrations, etc., if detected by credit review process, can then be corrected by lending officers, thus preventing deterioration in credit quality and possible loan losses. Also called loan review.

Credit Risk: 1. evaluation of a customer's ability or willingness to pay debts on time. 2. risk that a financial institution assumes when it makes an irrevocable payment on behalf of its customer against insufficient funds.

Credit Scoring: statistical model used to predict the creditworthiness of credit applicants. Credit scoring estimates repayment probability based on information in credit application and credit bureau report. The two main types of credit scoring are application scoring for new accounts and behavior scoring for accounts that have been activated and are carrying balances.

Credit Terms: stated and agreed on terms for debt repayment.

Credit Union: nonprofit cooperative financial organization chartered by state or federal government to provide financial services such as deposit and loan activities to a specific and limited group of people.

Creditworthy: term used to describe individual or entity deemed worthy of extension of credit.

CSAC: see *Credit Advisory Board.*

Current Assets: short-term assets of company, including cash, accounts receivable, temporary investments, and goods and materials in inventory.

Current Liabilities: short-term obligations due within one year, including current maturities of long-term debts.

Current Open Account: sale of goods or services for which customer does not pay for each purchase but rather is required to settle in full periodically or within specified time period after each transaction.

Current Ratio: total of current assets divided by total current liabilities; used as indication of a company's liquidity and ability to service current obligations.

D

D&B: see *Dun & Bradstreet, Inc.*

Dating (Terms): extension of credit terms beyond normal terms because of industry's seasonality or unusual circumstance.

Days Sales Outstanding (DSO): a calculation that expresses the average time in days that receivables are outstanding.

DBA: see *Doing Business As.*

DDA: see *Demand Deposit Account.*

Dealer Loan: see *Floor Plan.*

Debenture: unsecured, long-term indebtedness or corporate obligation.

Debit: entry on left side of accounting ledger.

Debit Card: magnetized plastic card that permits customers to withdraw cash from automatic teller machines and make purchases with charges deducted from funds on deposit at a predesignated account.

Debt: 1. specified amount of money, goods, or services that is owed from one to another, including not only obligation of debtor to pay but also right of creditor to receive and enforce payment. 2. financial obligation of debtor.

Debtor: person or entity indebted to or owing money to another.

Debtor in Possession (DIP): In a Chapter 11 bankruptcy, a debtor may continue to maintain possession of its assets and use them in normal business operations.

Debtor-in-Possession Financing: credit facilities extended to borrower who is reorganizing under Chapter 11 bankruptcy.

Debt Ratio: measure of firm's leverage position derived by dividing total debts by equity.

Debt Service: total interest and scheduled principal payments on debt due within given time frame.

Decision: judgment, decree, or verdict pronounced by court in determination of case.

Declarations Page: policy form containing data regarding insured, policy term, premium, type and amount of coverage, designation of forms and endorsements incorporated at time policy is issued, name of insurer, and countersignature of agent.

Deductible: portion of loss that is not insured; may be stated amount deducted from loss or percentage of loss or of value of property at time of loss.

Deduction: partial amount of payment that is withheld.

Deed: legal, written document used to transfer ownership of real property from one party to another.

Deed of Trust: legal document used in some states in lieu of mortgage. Title to real property passes from seller to trustee, who holds mortgaged property until mortgage has been fully paid and then releases title to borrower. Trustee is authorized to sell property if borrower defaults, paying amount of mortgage loan to lender and any remaining balance to former owner.

Defalcation: misappropriation of funds held in trust for another.

Defamation: injury to person's or entity's character, reputation, or good name by false and malicious statements (includes both libel and slander).

Default: to fail to meet obligation or terms of loan agreement such as payment of principal or interest.

Default Charge: legally agreed upon charge or penalty added to account when payment of debt is late or another event of default occurs under a loan agreement.

Defendant: person or entity defending or denying claim; party against which suit or charge has been filed in court of law. See also Plaintiff.

Defer: to postpone or delay action.

Deferred Payment Sale: selling on installment plan with payments delayed or postponed until future date.

Deficiency Judgment: decree requiring debtor to pay amount remaining due under defaulted contract after secured property has been liquidated.

Deficit: difference between receipts and expenses when expenses are greater.

Defraud: to deprive person of property by fraud, deceit, or artifice.

Defunct: business that has ceased to exist and is without assets; concern that has failed.

Delayed Disbursement: practice in cash management whereby a firm pays vendors and other corporations by disbursing payments from a financial institution in a remote city. Also called remote disbursement. Contrasts with controlled disbursement. See also Federal Reserve Float.

Delinquent: 1. past-due obligation; overdue and unpaid account. 2. to be in arrears in payment of debts, loans, taxes. 3. to have failed in duty or responsibility.

Demand Deposit Account (DDA): funds on deposit in checking account that are payable by a financial institution upon demand of depositor. See also *Time Deposit*.

Demand Draft: written order directing that payment be made, on sight, to a third party.

Demand Letter: correspondence sent by creditor, collection agency, or lawyer to debtor requesting payment of obligation by specific date.

Demand Loan: loan with no fixed due date and payable on demand by maker of loan; loan that can be "called" by lender at any time.

Demurrage: charge that is fixed by contract and payable by recipient of goods for detaining freight car or ship longer than agreed in order to load or unload. Purpose is remuneration to owner of vessel for earnings he or she was improperly caused to lose.

Deposit: 1. amount of money given as down payment for goods or as consideration for contract. 2. funds retained in customer's bank account.

Depreciation: decline in value of fixed assets, allocating purchase cost of an asset plus additions to value over its useful economic life as outlined by the Federal Tax Code.

Derivatives: broad family of financial instruments with characteristics of forward or option contracts.

Derogatory Account Information: adverse information on customers who have not paid accounts with other creditors according to payment terms, as reported to a credit bureau.

Directors and Officers Liability Insurance: legal liability coverage for wrongful acts including breach of duty but not fraud or dishonesty. Often known as E & O, or Errors and Omissions Insurance.

Disbursement: full or partial advancement of funds.

Discharge: 1. to cancel or release obligation. 2. to release debtor from all or most debts in bankruptcy.

Disclaimer Statement: notice disclaiming responsibility for accuracy, completeness, or timeliness of credit information. Most disclaimer statements urge recipients of the information not to rely unduly on it and stress the confidential nature of information being disclosed.

Discontinued Operations: operations of a segment of a company, usually a subsidiary whose activities represent a separate line of business that, although still operating, is the subject of a formal plan of disposal approved by management.

Discount: 1. interest deducted from face amount of note at time loan is made. 2. trade term used for reduction of invoice amount when payment has been made within specified terms.

Discounted Note: 1. borrowing arrangement in which interest is deducted from face amount of note before proceeds are advanced (see also Note). 2. term used when customer endorses note received from another party and presents it to a financial institution to obtain funds.

Dishonor: to fail to make payment of negotiable instrument on its due date.

Disintermediation: withdrawal of funds from interest-bearing deposit accounts when rates on competing financial instruments, such as money market mutual funds, stocks, and bonds, offer better returns.

Dismissal: court order or judgment disposing action, suit, or motion without trial.

Dispossess: legal action taken by landlord to put individual or business tenant out of his or her property.

Dissolution of Corporation: termination of entity's existence by law, expiration of charter, loss of all members, or failure to meet statutory level of members.

Distribution: one or more payments made to creditors who have approved claims filed in a bankruptcy proceeding, assignment for the benefit of creditors, or receivership.

Distributor: business engaged in the distribution or marketing of manufacturer's goods to customers or dealers. See also Wholesaler.

Dividend: 1. periodic distribution of cash or property to shareholders of corporation as return on their investment.

Document: any written instrument that records letters with figures or marks that may be used as evidence.

Documentary Evidence: any written record or inanimate object, as distinguished from oral evidence.

Documents of Title: Include bill of lading, dock warrant, dock receipt, warehouse receipt, order for the delivery of goods, and any other document that in the regular course of business or financing is treated as adequately evidencing that the person in possession of it is entitled to receive, hold, and dispose of the document and the goods it covers. To be a document of title, a document must purport to be issued by, or addressed to, a bailee and purport to cover goods in the bailee's possession that are either identified or are fungible portions of an identified mass.

Doing Business As (DBA): reference term placed before trade name under which business operates. Sometimes used as fictitious trade style acknowledging that name is not part of corporation title or registered trademark.

Domestic Corporation: company doing business in state in which it is incorporated.

Dormant Account: inactive deposit account in which there have been no deposits or withdrawals for a long period of time.

Doubtful Assets: assets that have all weaknesses inherent in substandard assets with added characteristic that weaknesses make collection or liquidation in full, on basis of currently existing facts, conditions, and values, highly questionable and improbable. Possibility of loss is extremely high. Because of certain important and reasonably specific pending factors that may strengthen assets, classification as estimated loss is deferred until more exact status may be determined. Pending factors include proposed merger, acquisition, or liquidation procedures, capital injection, perfecting liens on additional collateral, and refinancing plans.

Downgrading: 1. lowering of assessment of customer's creditworthiness. 2. worsening the internally assigned credit quality rating of a loan or relationship in order to appropriately report risk.

Down Payment: up-front partial payment made to secure right to purchase goods.

Downstream Funding: funds borrowed by holding company for a subsidiary's use, generally to obtain more favorable rate; contrasts with Upstream Funding.

Draft: written order by one party (drawer) directing second party (drawee) to pay sum of money to third party (payee). See also *Banker's Acceptance, Letter of Credit, Sight Draft*, and *Time Draft*.

Drawee: person or entity that is expected to pay check or draft when instrument is presented for payment.

Drawer: party instructing drawee to pay someone else by writing or drawing check or draft. Also called maker or writer.

Drop Shipment: shipment of goods delivered directly from manufacturer to customer.

DSO: see *Days Sales Outstanding*.

Dual Banking: banking system in U.S., consisting of state banks, chartered and supervised by state banking departments, and national banks, chartered and regulated by Office of the Comptroller of the Currency.

Due Date: stated maturity date for debt obligation.

Due Diligence: 1. responsibility of an entity's directors and officers to act in a prudent manner in evaluating credit applications; in essence, using same degree of care that an ordinary person would use in making same analysis. 2. review that is made of a loan portfolio of a potential merger candidate by an acquiring institution.

Due Process of Law: law in its regular course of administration through courts as guaranteed by U.S. Constitution.

Dun: to repeatedly demand payment of debt; to be insistent in following debtor for payment.

Dun & Bradstreet, Inc. (D&B): international mercantile agency supplying information and credit ratings on all types of businesses.

Dun Letter: letter or notice sent by creditor requesting payment of past-due debt.

D-U-N-S Number: (Data Universal Numbering System) code developed by Dun & Bradstreet that identifies specific business name and location.

Durable Goods: goods that provide long-lasting qualities and continuing services.

Duress: unlawful constraint that forces person to do what he or she would not have done by choice.

Duty: 1. legal, moral, or ethical obligation. 2. tax collected on import or export of goods.

E

Earnest Money: money that one contracting party gives to another at the time of entering into the contract in order to bind the contract in good faith, and which will be forfeited if the purchaser fails to carry out the contract.

Earnings Report: 1. income statement showing a business's or individual's revenues and expenses for stated period of time.

Easement: right of owner of one parcel of land to use land of another for special purpose. Usually easement rights pass with land when it is sold.

Edge Act: banking legislation, passed in 1919, that allows national banks to conduct foreign lending operations through federal or state-chartered subsidiaries called Edge Act corporations. Such corporations can be chartered by other states and are allowed to own banks in foreign countries and to invest in foreign commercial and industrial firms.

EFT: see *Electronic Funds Transfer*.

Electronic Funds Transfer (EFT): computerized system enabling funds to be debited, credited, or transferred between financial institution accounts and vendors.

Embezzlement: fraudulent appropriation of one's property by person to whom it was entrusted.

Encumbrance: any right or interest in real or other property that diminishes the property's value and alters control of disposition.

Endorsement: 1. act of writing one's name on back of note, bill, check, or similar written instrument for payment of money; required on negotiable instrument to pass title properly to another. By signing such instrument, endorser

becomes party to it and thereby liable, under certain conditions, for its payment. 2. change or addition to insurance policy, informally called rider.

Entrepreneur: person who plans, organizes, and runs operation of new business.

EOM Terms: Shipments during a month are invoiced in a single statement dated as of the last day of that month or the first day of the following month.

Equal Credit Opportunity Act of 1974: Federal Reserve Regulation B that prohibits creditors from discriminating against credit applicants on basis of age, race, color, religion, national origin, sex, marital status, age, or receipt of public assistance.

Equitable Subordination: principles in section 510 (c) of U.S. Bankruptcy Code that permit bankruptcy court to subordinate, for purposes of distribution, all or part of creditor's claim against debtor's estate to claims of another creditor of that debtor after court has determined that first creditor has engaged in some form of wrongful conduct that has improved position relative to other creditors.

Equity: value of ownership, calculated by subtracting total liabilities from total assets.

Escheat: right of state to claim property or money if there is no legal claim made to it.

Escrow Account: deposit account to which access is restricted or limited by terms of written agreement entered into by three parties, including a financial institution.

Estate: any right, title, or interest that a person may have in lands or other personal property.

Estimate: amount of labor, materials, and other costs that a contractor anticipates for a project, as summarized in contractor's bid proposal for project.

Event of Default: a breach of an agreement between parties to a contract; a violation of one or more of the loan covenants as set forth in either the loan agreement, commitment letter, or promissory note.

Evergreen Revolving Credit: commitment to lend money that remains in effect unless lender takes specific action to terminate agreement; agreement may provide that, in event of termination, any outstanding amount will convert to term loan.

Exchange Rate: value of one country's currency to that of another country at a particular point in time.

Exclusive Sales Agreement: contractual arrangement, generally between a retailer and a manufacturer or wholesaler, giving retailer exclusive rights for sale of articles or services within a defined geographic area or through a defined distribution channel.

Execute: to complete and give validity to a legal document by signing, sealing, and delivering it.

Exempt: 1. to release, discharge, or waive from a liability to which others in the same general class are subject. 2. property not available for seizure.

Exemption: 1. immunity from general burden, tax, or charge. 2. legal right of debtor to hold portion of property free from claims or judgments.

Expense: cost or outlay of money used in business operating cycle.

Export-Import Bank: also called Ex-Im Bank. Provides guarantees of working capital loans for U.S. exporters; guarantees the repayment of loans or makes loans to foreign purchasers of U.S. goods and services. Ex-Im Bank also provides credit insurance that protects U.S. exporters against the risks of nonpayment by foreign buyers for political or commercial reasons. Ex-Im Bank does not compete with commercial lenders, but assumes the risks they cannot accept.

F

Face Amount: indicated value of a financial instrument, as shown on its front.

Facility Fee: lender's charge for making a line of credit or other credit facility available to borrower (for example, a commitment fee).

Facsimile: exact copy of an original.

Factor: entity that purchases borrower's accounts receivable and may extend funds to borrower prior to collection of receivables.

Factoring: short-term financing from nonrecourse sale of accounts receivable to third party or factor. Factor assumes full risk of collection, including credit losses. Factoring is most common in the garment industry, but has been used in other industries as well. There are two basic types of factoring:
- discount factoring, in which factor pays discounted price for receivables before maturity date.
- maturity factoring, in which factor pays the client purchase price of factored accounts at maturity.

Fair Credit Billing Act of 1974 (FCBA): Federal Reserve Regulation Z details the provisions of this act by prescribing uniform methods of computing the cost of consumer credit, disclosure of credit terms, and procedures for resolving billing errors on certain kinds of credit accounts.

Fair Credit Reporting Act: federal legislation that regulates consumer credit reporting activities and gives consumer right to learn contents of his or her credit bureau file.

Fair Market Value: price that property would sell for between willing buyer and willing seller, neither of whom is obligated to effect transaction.

Fannie Mae: see *Federal National Mortgage Association.*

FASB: see *Financial Accounting Standards Board.*

FFB: see *Federal Financing Bank.*

FCBA: see *Fair Credit Billing Act of 1974.*

FDIC: see *Federal Deposit Insurance Corporation.*

FDICIA: see *Federal Deposit Insurance Corporation Improvement Act of 1991.*

Federal Deposit Insurance Corporation (FDIC): 1. federal agency that insures bank accounts for up to $100,000 at both commercial banks and thrifts through Bank Insurance Fund and Savings Association Fund. 2. federal regulator for state-chartered banks that are not members of Federal Reserve System.

Federal Deposit Insurance Corporation Improvement Act of 1991 (FDICIA): legislation that provides for recapitalization of Bank Insurance Fund and restructuring of financial services industry through:
- emphasis on more capital.
- government standards for lending, operations, and asset growth.
- quicker government seizure of struggling institutions.
- reduced liquidity options for all but the strongest banks.
- incentives for uninsured depositors to use only the largest and strongest banks.
- sharply increased regulatory costs and fees.
- easier rules for acquiring banks and thrifts.

Federal Financial Institutions Examination Council (FFIEC): interagency group of federal banking regulators formed in 1979 to maintain uniform standards for federal examination and supervision of federally insured depository institutions, bank holding companies, and savings and loan holding companies. Also runs schools for examiners employed by banks, thrifts, and credit union agencies. Council produces Uniform Bank Performance Report.

Federal Financing Bank (FFB): agency in U.S. Treasury established by Congress in 1973 to centralize borrowing by federal agencies. Instead of selling securities directly to financial markets, all but largest federal agencies raise capital by borrowing from U.S. Treasury through FFB. FFB makes loans at favorable rates to agencies that do not have ready access to credit markets; its debt is direct obligation of U.S. Treasury.

Federal Funds: unsecured advances of immediately available funds from excess balances in reserve accounts held at Federal Reserve Banks. Technically, these funds are not borrowings but purchases of immediately available funds. Banks advancing federal funds sell excess reserves; banks receiving federal funds buy excess reserves from selling banks. Federal funds sold are credit transactions on account of selling banks. See also *Federal Funds Rate.*

Federal Funds Rate: rate charged in interbank market for purchases of excess reserve balances. Rate of interest is key money market interest rate and correlates with rates on other short-term credit arrangements. Because the federal funds rate re-prices with each transaction, it is the most sensitive of money market rates and is watched carefully by the Federal Reserve Board.

Federal Home Loan Bank Board (FHLBB): federal agency established by Federal Home Loan Bank Act of 1932 to supervise reserve credit system, Federal Home Loan Bank System, for savings institutions. Board also acted as chartering agency and primary regulator of federal savings and loan associations under Home Owners Loan Act of 1933. Financial Institutions Reform, Recovery, and Enforcement Act of 1989 abolished board, transferring its powers in examination and supervision of federally chartered savings institutions to new agency, Office of Thrift Supervision, bureau of U.S. Treasury Department. Regulatory oversight of district Home Loan Banks was transferred to the five-member Federal Housing Finance Board.

Federal Home Loan Bank System: system of 11 regional banks established by Federal Home Loan Bank Act of 1932, acting as central credit system for savings and loan institutions. District Home Loan Banks make short-term credit advances to savings institutions, much like Federal Reserve System acts as lender of last resort to commercial banks. Each Home Loan Bank operates independently and has its own board of directors.

Federal Home Loan Mortgage Corporation (FHLMC): corporation authorized by Congress in 1970 as secondary market conduit for residential mortgages. Corporation purchases loans from mortgage originators and sells its own obligations and mortgage-backed bonds issued by Government National Mortgage Association to private investors, namely financial institution trust funds, insurance companies, pension funds, and thrift institutions. Also called Freddie Mac.

Federal Housing Administration (FHA): federal agency that insures residential mortgages. Created by National Housing Act of 1934, FHA is now part of Department of Housing and Urban Development. Both FHA and Department of Veterans Affairs have single-family mortgage programs to assist homebuyers who are unable to obtain financing from conventional mortgage lenders (banks, savings and loans, and other financial institutions).

Federal Housing Finance Board (FHFB): independent federal agency regulating credit advance activities of 11 Federal Home Loan Banks. This board, estab-

lished by Financial Institutions Reform, Recovery, and Enforcement Act of 1989, has five members, including secretary of Housing and Urban Development, and four directors appointed by the President with Senate confirmation to serve seven-year terms. At least one director must represent the interests of community groups.

Federal National Mortgage Association (FNMA): federally chartered, stockholder-owned corporation that purchases residential mortgages insured or guaranteed by federal agencies, as well as conventional mortgages, in secondary mortgage market. Corporation raises capital to support its operations through collection of insurance and commitment fees, issuance of stock, and sale of debentures and notes. Also called Fannie Mae.

Federal Open Market Committee (FOMC): policy committee in Federal Reserve System that sets short-term monetary policy objectives for Fed. Committee is made up of seven governors of Federal Reserve Board, plus the presidents of six Federal Reserve Banks. President of Federal Reserve Bank of New York is permanent FOMC member. The other five slots are filled on rotating basis by presidents of other 11 Federal Reserve Banks. Committee carries out monetary objectives by instructing Open Market Desk at Federal Reserve Bank of New York to buy or sell government securities from special account, called open market account, at New York Fed.

Federal Reserve Board (FRB): U.S.'s central bank responsible for conduct of monetary policy; also oversees state-chartered banks that are members of Federal Reserve System, bank holding companies, and Edge Act corporations.

Federal Reserve Float: total amount of funds that Federal Reserve Banks, in their role as clearing agents, have credited to depositing institutions but have not charged to paying institutions.

Federal Reserve System: central bank of U.S. created by Federal Reserve Act of 1913. System consists of Board of Governors, made up of seven members, and a network of 12 Federal Reserve Banks and 25 branches throughout U.S. Board of Governors is responsible for setting monetary policy and reserve requirements. Board and banks share responsibility for setting the discount rate, the interest rate that depository institutions are charged for borrowing from Federal Reserve Banks.

Federal Trade Commission (FTC): federal regulatory agency that administers and enforces rules to prevent unfair business practices.

Fee Simple: estate in which owner is entitled to entire property and has unconditional power over its disposition.

FFIEC: see *Federal Financial Institutions Examination Council.*

FHA: see *Federal Housing Administration.*

FHLBB: see *Federal Home Loan Bank Board.*

FHLMC: see *Federal Home Loan Mortgage Corporation.*

Fictitious Name: pretend name used by firm in business transactions. Company is usually required to register this name with local authorities, along with true names and addresses of company's owners.

Fidelity Bond: contract issued by insurer to employer to cover loss caused by dishonest acts of employees; form of suretyship. Also called dishonesty insurance.

Fiduciary: person or entity acting in capacity of trustee for another.

Field Warehousing: method of using company's inventory to secure business loan. In leased and separate storage area of borrower's facility, goods act as security for loan and are released by custodian only upon lender's order.

FIFO: see *First-In First-Out.*

File: 1. organized folder containing accumulation of information and items retained for preservation or reference. 2. to deposit legal document with proper authority.

File Revision: routine gathering of credit information by credit grantor to update files on borrowers.

Filing Claims: 1. depositing of formal papers with proper public office and in manner and time frame prescribed by law in order to preserve creditor's rights. 2. method used to perfect security interest accomplished by recording in proper public office.

Finance Charges: total costs to an individual or business of obtaining credit, including interest and any fees.

Financial Analysis: evaluation by credit analyst of customer's financial situation to determine whether customer has ability to meet his or her obligations as they become due. Factors such as general condition of customer's industry, organizational structure, available collateral or guarantors, and past financial performance are considered.

Financial Accounting Standards Board (FASB): independent board responsible for establishing and interpreting generally accepted accounting principles, formed in 1973 to succeed and continue activities of Accounting Principles Board.

Financial Institutions Reform, Recovery, and Enforcement Act of 1989 (FIRREA): act signed into law on August 9, 1989, to provide funding and regulatory structure necessary to close several hundred insolvent savings associations and liquidate their assets, to consolidate federal insurance of banks and savings associations under direction of the Federal Deposit Insurance Corporation, to provide regulatory agencies with sweeping new enforcement pow-

ers, and to increase substantially civil and criminal penalties for violations of federal banking statutes and regulations. Act substantially alters relationship between savings institutions and regulators and imposes new requirements that must be observed in day-to-day operations of institutions.

Financial Position: standing of company, combining assets and liabilities as entered on balance sheet.

Financial Statements: reports consisting of individual's or company's balance sheet, income statement, and statement of cash flows, footnotes, and any supplemental schedules.

Financing Statement: form required to be completed by creditor and filed with appropriate county and state authorities in order to perfect creditor's security interest in collateral and to give public notice of such interest.

FIRREA: see *Financial Institutions Reform, Recovery, and Enforcement Act of 1989.*

First Deed of Trust: first recorded deed of trust that acts as first lien on property it describes.

First-In First-Out (FIFO): method of valuing inventory in which the first goods received are the first goods used or sold. Using this method, costs of inventory used to determine cost of goods sold are related to costs that were incurred first.

First Mortgage: mortgage on property that is superior to any others by fact of having been filed first.

Fiscal: anything involving financial matters or issues.

Fiscal Agent: person or organization serving as another's financial agent or representative.

Fiscal Year: fixed accounting year used as basis for annual financial reporting by business or government.

Five C's of Credit: method of evaluating potential borrower's creditworthiness based on five criteria: Capacity, Capital, Character, Collateral, and Conditions.

Fixed Assets: property used in normal course of business that is of a long-term nature, such as land, machinery, fixtures, and equipment.

Fixed-Rate Loan: loan with interest rate that does not vary over term of loan.

Fixture: that which is permanently attached or affixed to real property.

Flagging an Account: temporarily identifying an account for specific purpose or reason; may involve suspending activity.

Float: uncollected funds represented by checks deposited in one bank but not yet cleared through bank on which they are drawn.

Floating Interest Rate: loan interest rate that changes whenever the stated index rate, or base rate, changes.

Floating Lien: loan or credit facility secured by inventory or receivables. This type of security agreement gives lender interest in assets acquired by borrower after agreement, as well as those owned when agreement was made. When agreement covers proceeds from sales, lender also has recourse against cash collected from the payment of receivables.

Floor Plan: loan made to dealer for purchase of inventory acquired for resale and secured by that inventory, such as automobiles or appliances.

FNMA: see *Federal National Mortgage Association.*

FOB: see *Free on Board.*

FOB Point: point at which responsibility for freight charges begins and title passes. See also *Free on Board.*

FOMC: see *Federal Open Market Committee.*

Forbearance: Temporarily giving up the right to enforce a valid claim, in return for a promise. It is sufficient consideration to make a promise binding (for example, protracted payment arrangements or interest rate reduction in exchange for additional collateral or guarantors).

Forced Sale: 1. court-ordered sale of property, usually without owner's approval. 2. voluntary sale of goods or property to raise cash or to reduce inventory.

Foreclosure: legal termination of all of debtor's rights in property secured by mortgage after debtor has defaulted on obligation supported by such mortgage.

Foreign Corporation: corporation established under laws of a state other than that in which it is doing business.

Foreign Exchange: conversion of money of one country into its equivalent in currency of another country.

Foreign Item: check drawn on any financial institution other than the financial institution where it is presented for payment. Also called transit item.

Foreign Judgment: judgment obtained in state or country other than the one where the debtor now lives, is doing business, or has assets.

Forfeiture: penalty resulting in automatic loss of cash, property, or rights for not complying with legal terms of agreement.

Forgery: false making or material altering of any writing with intent to defraud.

Form 8K: report disclosing significant events potentially affecting corporation's financial condition or market value of its shares, required by Securities and Exchange Commission. Report is filed within 30 days after event (pending merger, amendment to corporate charter, charge to earnings for credit losses) took place and summarizes information that any reasonable investor would want to know before buying or selling securities.

Form 10K: annual financial report filed with Securities and Exchange Commission. Issuers of registered securities are required to file 10K, as are corporations with 500 or more shareholders or assets of $2 million and exchange-listed corporations. Report, which becomes public information once filed, summarizes key financial information, including sources and uses of funds by type of business, net pretax operating income, provision for income taxes and credit losses, plus comparative financial statements for past two fiscal years. Summary of 10K report is included in annual report to stockholders.

Form 10Q: quarterly financial report filed by companies with listed securities and those corporations required to file annual 10K report with Securities and Exchange Commission. 10Q report, which does not have to be audited, summarizes key financial data on earnings and expenses and compares current financial information with data reported in same quarter of previous year.

Forwarding: referral or placement of out-of-town claims with attorney who then acts on behalf of creditor. In collection process, when authorized, agency may forward account to attorney for collection or suit.

Franchise: business agreement whereby one company allows another the right to conduct business under its name and/or distribute its products in exchange for royalties or another agreed upon method of payment.

Fraud: any act of deceit, omission, or commission used to deprive someone of right or property. Elements of fraud consist of intentional misrepresentation of fact, relied on by another to his or her detriment, that results in damages.

Fraudulent Conveyance: a transfer of property by a debtor, for the intent and purpose of defrauding creditors. Such property may be reached by the creditors through appropriate legal proceedings.

FRB: see *Federal Reserve Board.*

Freddie Mac: see *Federal Home Loan Mortgage Corporation.*

Free and Clear: 1. property with an unencumbered title. 2. title that is free of defects.

Free and Clear Delivery Receipt: delivery receipt signed by consignee completely absolving carrier from any claim for loss or damages.

Free Astray: freight shipment that has been lost. If it is carrier's fault and shipment is located, it is carrier's obligation to make delivery to original destination at no additional cost to shipper or consignee.

Free Demand Letter Service: pre-collection letter sent by collection agency to debtor, requesting that payment be made directly to creditor by given date. No charge is made for payments received within free demand period, but balances remaining unpaid are followed for collection by agency at its regular rates.

Free on Board (FOB): term identifying shipping point from which buyer assumes all responsibilities and costs for transportation.

Free Port: place where goods are imported or exported free of any duty.

Freight Forwarder: business that receives goods for transportation; services include consolidation of small freight shipments of less than carload, truckload, or container lots assembled for lower shipping rates.

Frozen Account: 1. account to which customer no longer has access. 2. account suspended by court order, violation of loan covenants, or checking account agreement, etc.

Frozen Assets: any assets that cannot be used by owner because of pending legal action.

FTC: see *Federal Trade Commission.*

Fund: cash or equivalents set aside for specific purpose.

Fund Accounting: fiscal and accounting entity with self-balancing set of accounts recording cash and other financial resources, together with all related liabilities and residual equities or balances, and changes therein, which are segregated for purpose of carrying on specific activities or obtaining certain objectives in accordance with special regulations, restrictions, or limitations.

Funded Debt: mortgages, bonds, debentures, notes, or other obligations with maturity of more than one year from statement date.

G

GAAP: see *Generally Accepted Accounting Principles.*

Garnishee: 1. person or entity that has possession of money or property belonging to defendant and is served with writ of garnishment to hold money or property for payment of defendant's debt to plaintiff. 2. one against whom garnishment has been served.

Garnishment: legal warning or procedure to one in possession of another's property not to allow owner access to such property as it will be used to satisfy judgment against owner.

General Contractor: contractor who enters into a contract with an owner for construction of a project and who takes full responsibility for its completion. Contractor may enter into subcontracts with various subcontractors for performance of specific parts or phases of project.

General Ledger: bookkeeping record comprising all assets, liabilities, proprietorship, revenue, and expense accounts. Entries for each account are posted, and balances are included for each entry.

Generally Accepted Accounting Principles (GAAP): conventions, rules, and procedures that define accepted accounting practices, including broad guidelines as well as detailed procedures. Financial Accounting Standards Board, an independent self-regulatory organization, is responsible for promulgating these principles.

General Obligation Debt: long-term debt or bond repaid from all otherwise unrestricted revenues, sales taxes, property taxes, license fees, property sales, rents, and so forth of municipality.

General Partner: participant in a business relationship who is personally liable, without limitation, for all partnership debts.

Ginnie Mae: see *Government National Mortgage Association.*

GNMA: see *Government National Mortgage Association.*

Going Concern: assumes that a business entity has a reasonable expectation of continuing in business and generating a profit for an indefinite period of time.

Goods on Approval: goods offered by seller to buyer with option of examining goods for specific period of time before deciding to purchase them.

Goodwill: 1. intangible assets of business consisting of its good reputation, valuable clientele, or desirable location that results in above normal earning power. 2. value or amount for which business could be sold above book value of its physical property and receivables.

Government National Mortgage Association (GNMA): corporation created by Congress that administers mortgage-backed securities program that channels new sources of funds into residential mortgages through sale of securities. Also called Ginnie Mae.

Grace Period: specified length of time beyond payment due date during which late fee will not be assessed.

Grantee: person to whom title in property is made.

Grantor: person who transfers title to property.

Gross Margin: gross profit as a percentage of sales.

Gross Profit: net sales less cost of sales.

Gross Sales: sales before returns and allowances; discounts are deducted to arrive at net sales.

Guarantor: person who agrees by execution of a contract to repay the debt of another if that person defaults.

Guaranty: separate agreement by which a party (or parties) other than debtor assumes responsibility for payment of obligation if principal debtor defaults or is subsequently unable to perform under the terms of the obligation.

Guardian: person who is legally responsible for the care and management of a minor or individual who is not mentally or legally competent (or of such person's property).

H

Hard Goods: durable consumer goods, usually including such items as major appliances and furniture, with relatively long, useful lives.

Heavy Industry: industry involved in manufacturing basic products such as metals, machinery, or other equipment.

Hidden Assets: assets not easily identified and either intentionally not disclosed or publicly reported at lower value than their true worth.

High Credit: largest amount of credit used by borrower during specified period of time.

Holder in Due Course: person who has taken negotiable instrument (check or note) for value, in good faith, and on assurance that it is complete and regular, not overdue or dishonored, and has no defect in ownership on part of previous holder or endorser.

Holding Company: company organized to hold and control stock in other companies.

Homestead Exemption: state's law allowing householder or head of family to exempt residence from attachment by creditors.

Housing and Urban Development, Department of: cabinet-level federal agency, founded in 1965, that promotes housing development in U.S. through direct loans, mortgage insurance, and guaranties. It houses Federal Housing Administration and Government National Mortgage Association.

HUD: see *Housing and Urban Development, Department of.*

Hypothecate: to pledge or assign property owned by one entity as security or collateral for loan to second entity.

Hypothecation: 1. offer of stocks, bonds, or other assets owned by party other than borrower as collateral for loan, without transferring title. Borrower retains possession but gives lender right to sell property in event of default by borrower. 2. pledging of negotiable securities to collateralize broker's margin loan. If broker pledges same securities to bank as collateral for broker's loan, process is referred to as re-hypothecation.

I

Immunity: condition of being exempt from duty that others are generally required to perform.

Import Letter of Credit: commercial letter of credit issued to finance import of goods.

Import Duty: government tax on imported items.

Impound: to seize or take into legal custody, usually at order of court. Cash, documents, or records may be impounded.

Inactive Account: account that has shown little or no activity over a substantial period of time.

Inactive Files: 1. accounts on which collection activity has been completed or suspended (claims either collected or found to be uncollectible) and on which no further work is being done. Also called closed or dead files. 2. stored records available for reference.

In Arrears: amounts due but not yet paid.

Income Property: real property acquired as investment and managed for profit.

Income Statement: summary of revenue and expenses covering a specified period.

Income Tax: tax levied by federal, state, or local governments on personal or business earnings.

Incorporation: formation of legal entity, with qualities of perpetual existence and succession.

Incumbrance: see *Encumbrance.*

Indebtedness: total amount of money or liabilities owed.

In Default: failing to abide by terms and conditions of note or loan agreement. This can include payments on interest or principal (or both) being past due.

Indemnity: 1. contract or assurance to reimburse another against anticipated loss, damage, or failure to fulfill obligation. 2. type of insurance that provides coverage for losses of this nature.

Indirect Liability: contingent liability such as a continuing guarantee.

Individual Signature: credit approved by one person on his or her own authority.

Indorsement: see *Endorsement.*

Industrial Consumer: purchaser who buys goods or services for business purposes.

Inquiry: request for credit information on a bank's customer.

Insider Loans: loans to directors and officers of bank, which must be reported to bank regulators under Financial Institutions Reform Act of 1978. Banking laws require that loans to insiders be made at substantially the same rate and credit terms as loans to other borrowers.

Insolvency: 1. inability to meet debts as they become due in ordinary course of business. 2. financial condition in which assets are not sufficient to satisfy liabilities.

Installment Sale: contract sale in which merchandise is purchased with down payment and balance is made in partial payments over agreed period of time.

Instrument: written formal or legal document.

In-Substance Foreclosure Assets: loans for which borrower is perceived to have little or no equity in the asset or project and the financial institution can reasonably anticipate proceeds for repayment only from the operation or sale of collateral.

Insufficient Funds: see *Non-sufficient Funds.*

Insurable Interest: interest such that loss or damage inflicts economic loss.

Insurable Value: maximum possible loss to which property is exposed; actual amount depends on basis of calculation per insurance policy.

Intangible Assets: nonmaterial assets of business that have no value in themselves but that represent value. Examples include trademarks, goodwill, patents, and copyrights.

Interchange: confidential exchange of credit information between individuals and trade groups.

Interchange Bureau: association organized to record and exchange or furnish confidential credit information about a member's payment experience and manner in which customers meet obligations.

Interchange Group: trade membership group within specific industry that meets regularly to exchange credit experiences and other confidential information.

Interchange Report: report usually obtained through credit interchange bureau showing recent credit experience as supplied by participating members.

Inter-creditor Agreement: document used when there is more than one lender involved in credit transaction to spell out each lender's rights and obligations.

Interest: 1. legally allowed or agreed upon compensation to lender for use of borrowed money. 2. any right in property but less than title to it.

Interest Bearing: term describing note or contract calling for payment of agreed interest.

Interest Only: loan term during which no principal repayments are made.

Interest Rate: cost of borrowing money expressed as an annualized percentage of the loan.

Internal Guidance Line of Credit: credit facility similar to a line of credit, but customer may or may not be advised of it; established for internal financial institution purposes, it provides financing for recurrent requests without referring each one to credit committee or other approval source.

International Consumer Credit Association: professional trade association of retail credit professionals. Association keeps members informed of latest developments in consumer credit and provides educational courses, seminars, textbooks, and other published material.

Intestate: dying without leaving valid will or any other specific instructions as to disposition of property.

Inventory: current assets of business that represent goods for sale, including raw materials, work in process, and finished goods.

Investigation: 1. gathering of credit information on a person or entity. 2. systematic research for information necessary for a business decision.

Investment: use of money for purpose of earning profit or return.

Investor: person or entity that puts money to use for capital appreciation or profit or to receive regular dividends.

Invoice: seller's descriptive, itemized billing for goods or services sold, showing date, terms, cost, purchase order number, method of shipment, and other identifying information.

Involuntary Bankruptcy: see *Bankruptcy.*

Itemized Statement: detailed listing of activity on account for particular period of time.

J

Jobber: see *Wholesaler.*

Joint Account: financial institution account shared or owned in name of two or more persons with full privileges available to each person.

Joint and Several: relative to liability, a term used when creditor has option of pursuing one or more signers of an agreement individually or all signers together.

Joint Tenancy with Rights of Survivorship: interest in property held by two or more persons that includes right of survivorship in which deceased person's interest passes to survivors. See also *Tenancy by Entirety.*

Joint Venture: business or undertaking entered into on one-time basis by two or more parties in which profits, losses, and control are shared.

Journal: account book of original entry in which all money receipts and expenses are chronologically recorded.

Judgment: court's determination of rights of parties to claim.

Judgment Creditor: one who has obtained judgment against debtor and can enforce it.

Judgment Debtor: one against whom judgment has been recovered but not satisfied.

Judgment Note: see *Cognovit Note.*

Judgment Lien: claim or encumbrance on property, allowed by law, usually against real estate of judgment debtor.

Judgment-Proof: term to describe judgment debtor from whom collection cannot be obtained or person who has no money or assets or has concealed or removed property subject to execution.

Judicial Sale: see *Forced Sale.*

Junior Mortgage: any mortgage filed after and subject to satisfaction of first mortgage.

Jurisdiction: 1. legal authority, power, capacity, and right of court to act. 2. geographic area within which court or government agency exercises power.

K

Keyperson Life Insurance: insurance policy written on owner or principal employee in which death benefits are payable to company.

Key Ratios: performance measures used to determine probable ability of business to operate profitably. Results are expressed in percentages that are then weighed against average percentages in each industry.

L

Landlord's Waiver: the relinquishment of a right(s) contained in a lease agreement by a lessor.

Last-In First-Out (LIFO): method of valuating inventory in which last goods received are the first ones sold. Using this method, inventory costs used to determine cost of goods sold are related to costs of inventory that were incurred last.

Late Charge: special legally agreed upon fee, charged by creditor, on any payment that is not made when due.

Lawful Money: legal tender for payment of all debts.

Law List: compiled publication of names and addresses of those in legal profession, often including court calendars, private investigators, and other information of interest to legal profession.

Lawsuit: suit, action, or cause instituted by one person against another in a court of law.

Lead Bank: financial institution that has the primary deposit or lending relationship in a multi-bank situation; usually in the context of shared credit and sometimes defined within an inter-creditor agreement. See also *Agent Bank.*

Leaseback: agreement by which one party sells property to another and, after completing sale, the first party rents it from second party.

Lease Contract: written agreement for which equipment or facilities can be obtained on rental payment basis for specified period of time.

Leased Department: section of department store not operated by store but by independent outside organization on contract or percentage-of-sales arrangement.

Leasehold: rights tenant holds in property as conferred by terms of lease.

Leasehold Improvement: permanent improvements made to rented property. Leasehold improvements are considered fixtures and depreciate over lease period.

Leasehold Interest: lessee's equity or ownership in leasehold improvements.

Lease-Purchase Agreement: contract providing for set amount of lease payments to be applied to purchase of property.

Ledger: in accounting, book of permanent records containing series of accounts to which debits and credits of transactions are posted from books of original entry.

Ledger Experience: trade experience reported by credit manager or interchange group. Such reports provide picture of account's paying habits, high credit, and terms of repayment.

Legal and Sovereign Risk: risk that government may intervene to affect bank's system or any participant of such system detrimentally.

Legal Composition: identification and description of lawful ownership or title to business entity.

Legal Entity: business organization that has capacity to make contract or agreement or assume obligation. Such organization may consist of individual proprietorship, partnership, corporation, or association.

Legal Right: natural right, right created by contract, and right created or recognized by law.

Legal Tender: any money that is recognized by law for payment of debt unless contract exists specifically calling for payment in another type of money.

Legal Title: document establishing right of ownership to property that is recognized and upheld by law.

Lender: one who extends funds to another with expectation of repayment with interest.

Lender's Loss Payable Endorsement: form attached to property insurance policies to cover lender's interest in what is insured; extends coverage to give lender protection beyond that in basic policy; language may be prescribed by banking industry, standard form prepared by insurance industry, or specified by lender. See also *Loss Payee Clause.*

Lessee: one to whom lease is given and therefore has right to use property in exchange for rental payments.

Lessor: owner who grants lease for use of property in return for rent.

Letter of Agreement: letter stating terms of agreement between addressor and addressee, usually prepared for signature by addressee as indication of acceptance of those terms as legally binding.

Letter of Credit: letter or document issued by bank on behalf of customer that is evidence of financial background of bank and ensures that payment will be made when proper documents confirm completion of related transaction. Such letters authorize drawing of sight or time drafts when certain terms and conditions are fulfilled. See also *Banker's Acceptance, Draft, Sight Draft, Standby Letter of Credit,* and *Time Draft.*

Letter of Intent: letter signifying intention to enter into formal agreement and usually setting forth general terms of such agreement.

Liable: duty or obligation enforceable by law.

Liabilities: indebtedness of an individual or entity.

Libel: written or published false and malicious statements about another that tend to defame or harm another's reputation.

LIBOR: see *London Interbank Offered Rate.*

Lien: legal right or encumbrance to secure payment performance on property pledged as collateral until the debt it secures is satisfied.

LIFO: see *Last-In First-Out.*

Limited Liability Company: legal entity that offers shareholders the same limitations on personal liability available to corporate shareholders. The owners of a limited liability company (LLC) have limited liability. They are not liable for the debts, liabilities, acts, or omissions of the company. Only their investment is at risk.

Limited Liability: legal exemption corporate stockholders or limited liability companies have from full financial responsibilities for debts of company.

Limited Partnership: partnership of one or more general partners who are personally, jointly, and separately responsible, with one or more special partners whose liabilities are limited to amount of investment.

Line of Credit: see *Credit Line.*

Liquid Assets: assets that can be readily converted into cash.

Liquidate: 1. to pay off or settle current obligation. 2. to sell off or convert assets into cash. 3. to dissolve business in order to raise cash for payment of debts.

Liquidation: process of dissolving a business, settling accounts, and paying off any claims or obligations; remaining cash is distributed to the owners of the business.

Liquidation Value: cash that can be realized from sale of assets in dissolving business, as distinct from its value as ongoing entity.

Liquidity: measure of quality and adequacy of current assets to meet current obligations as they come due.

Liquidity Ratio: company's most liquid assets (generally cash and accounts receivable) divided by current liabilities. Also called quick ratio.

List Price: generally advertised or posted price. Sometimes subject to trade or cash discounts.

Litigation: lawsuit brought to court for purpose of enforcing a right.

LLC: see *Limited Liability Company.*

Loan: money advanced to a borrower with agreement of repayment usually with interest within a specified period of time.

Loan Agreement: legal contract between a financial institution and a borrower that governs the terms and conditions for the life of a loan. Elements usually include description of loan, representations, and warranties reaffirming known facts about the borrower such as legal structure, affirmative and negative covenants, conditions that must be met before the loan is granted, delinquent payment penalties, and statement of remedies that the financial institution may take in event of default.

Loan Participation: sharing of loan(s) by a group of financial institutions that join together to make said loan(s), affording an opportunity to share the risk of a very large transaction. Arranged through correspondent banking networks in which smaller financial institutions buy a portion of an overall financing package. Participations are a convenient way for smaller financial institutions to book loans that would otherwise exceed their legal lending limits. Also called participation financing.

Loan Policy: principles that reflect a financial institution's credit culture, underwriting procedures, and overall approach to lending.

Loans Past Due: loans with interest or principal payments that are contractually past due a certain number of days.

Loan-to-Value Ratio (LTV): relationship, expressed as percent, between principal amount of loan and appraised value of the asset securing financing.

Loan Value: amount of money that can be borrowed against real or personal property.

Lockbox: regional financial institution depository used by corporations to obtain earlier receipt and collection of customer payments. Arrangement provides creditor with better control of accounts receivable and earlier availability of cash balances. Many large financial institutions offer lockbox processing as a cash management service to corporate customers. Lockboxes can be:

- retail, designed for remittance processing for consumer accounts.
- wholesale, in which payments from other entities are collected and submitted through depository transfer check or electronic debit into a concentration account for investment and disbursement as needed.

London Interbank Offered Rate (LIBOR): key rate index used in international lending. LIBOR is the rate at which major financial institutions in London are willing to lend Eurodollars to each other. This index is often used to determine interest rate charged to creditworthy borrowers.

Long-Arm Statutes: state statutes that allow state courts to exercise jurisdiction over nonresident persons or property outside their state's borders.

Long-Term Capital Gain (Loss): gain or loss realized from sale or exchange of capital asset held for longer than 12 months.

Long-Term Liabilities: all senior debt, including bonds, debentures, bank debt, mortgages, deferred portions of long term-debt, and capital lease obligations owed for longer than 12 months.

Loss: 1. circumstance in which expenses exceed revenues. 2. result if an asset is sold for less than its depreciated book value.

Loss Assets: assets considered uncollectible and of such little value that their continuance as realizable assets is not warranted.

Loss Leader: deliberate sale of product or service at or below cost in order to attract new customers.

Loss Payee Clause: provision in insurance policy or added by endorsement to cover lender/mortgagee's interest in property loss settlement. Provision is not as broad as lender's loss payable endorsement. Also called mortgagee clause and loss payable clause.

LTV: see *Loan-to-Value Ratio.*

Lump-sum Settlement: payment made in full with single, one-time payment.

M

Magnetic Ink Character Recognition (MICR): description of numbers and symbols that are printed in magnetic ink on documents for automated processing. Fully inscribed MICR line of information may include item's serial number, routing and transit number, check digit, account number, process control number, and amount.

Mail-Fraud Statute: federal law against using mails to defraud creditors by mailing false financial statements. Prosecution under mail-fraud statute must prove beyond reasonable doubt that:

- statement is false.
- statement was made with intention it should be relied on.
- it was made for the purpose of securing money or property.

- statement was delivered by mail.
- money or property was obtained by means of false statement.

Mailgram: telegraphic message transmitted electronically by Western Union and delivered by U.S. Postal Service.

Mail Teller: employee of a financial institution who receives mail deposits, checks them for accuracy, and returns stamped receipts for deposits to customers.

Majority Stockholder: person or entity that owns more than 50% of voting stock of a corporation, thereby having controlling interest.

Maker: one who signs or executes negotiable instrument.

Malpractice: professional misconduct with negligence.

Management: persons responsible for administrating and carrying out policy of business or other organization.

Management Information System (MIS): established flow of information developed to keep managers informed of what is happening within their organization and to do it within a time frame that permits effective reaction when required. Efficient MIS helps managers make better decisions.

Management Report: statement in unaudited financial statements that says financials are representations of firm's management.

Manifest: shipping document that lists freight's origin, contents, value, destination, carrier, and other pertinent information for use at terminals or custom house.

Manufacturers Representative (Agent): independent, commissioned sales agent who represents several noncompeting manufacturers for sale of their products to related businesses within agreed, exclusive sales territory.

Marginal Account: borderline credit risk that does not have sufficient operating capital and from which payment may be delayed.

Markdown: price reduction of goods below normal selling price.

Market: 1. customer base for a company's goods or services. 2. securities exchange and its associated institutions.

Marketability: ease and rapidity with which product, service, or other asset can be sold or converted to cash.

Marketing: 1. activities necessary to facilitate the sale of goods or services through planned research, manufacturing, promotion, advertising, and distribution. 2. business promotion devoted to getting the maximum purchases of products or services by consumers.

Market Value: price that goods or property would bring in current market of willing buyers and sellers.

Markup: amount or percentage added to cost of goods to arrive at selling price.

Maturity Date: date when financial obligation, note, draft, bond, or instrument becomes due for payment.

Mechanic's Lien: enforceable claim, permitted by law in most states, securing payment to contractors, subcontractors, and suppliers of materials for work performed in constructing or repairing buildings. Lien attaches to real property, plus buildings and improvements situated on land, and remains in effect until workers have been paid in full or, in event of liquidation, gives contractor priority of lien ahead of other creditors.

Medium of Exchange: money or commodity accepted in payment or settlement of debt.

Memorandum (Consignment) Sale: sale of goods for which seller is not paid until retailer has sold merchandise. Seller retains title to such goods until retailer has sold merchandise and payment is made to retailer.

Mercantile Agency: organization that compiles credit and financial information and supplies subscribers or members with reports on applicants for credit; can also perform other functions such as collection of accounts or compiling of statistical trade information.

Merchandise Shortage: goods purchased but not included in shipment.

Merger: combining of two or more businesses to form a single organization.

Mezzanine Financing: 1. in corporate finance, leveraged buyout or restructuring financed through subordinated debt, such as preferred stock or convertible debentures. Transaction is financed by expanding equity, as opposed to debt. 2. second- or third-level financing of companies financed by venture capital. Senior to venture capital but junior to financial institution financing, it adds creditworthiness to firm. Generally used as intermediate-stage financing, preceding a company's initial public offering, it is considered less risky than start-up financing.

MICR: see *Magnetic Ink Character Recognition.*

Middle-of-Month (M.O.M.) Billing Term: billing system in which all shipments are charged on one invoice issued twice a month. For first half of month, credit period runs to the 25th and, for the second half, to the tenth of the following month.

MIS: see *Management Information System.*

Modified Accrual Accounting: basis of accounting in which expenditures are recognized when liability is incurred. Revenues are recognized when measurable and available. Exception is in debt service funds in which expenditures are recorded only when due.

M.O.M.: see *Middle-of-Month Billing Term.*

Money Judgment: court decision that adjudges payment of money rather than requiring act to be performed or property transferred.

Monitoring: service available through many credit reporting or interchange bureaus enabling subscribers to request that certain listed accounts be automatically monitored and reviewed and that updated reports be issued periodically.

Moratorium: 1. temporary extension or delay of normal period for payment of account. 2. Formal postponement during which debtor is permitted to delay payment of obligations.

Mortgage: debt instrument giving conditional ownership of asset to borrower, secured by the asset being financed. The instrument by which real estate is hypothecated as security for the repayment of a loan. Borrower gives lender a mortgage in exchange for the right to use property while mortgage is in effect and agrees to make regular payments of principal and interest. Mortgage lien is lender's security interest and is recorded in title documents in public land records. Lien is removed when debt is paid in full. Mortgage normally involves real estate and is considered long-term debt.

Mortgagee: lender who arranges mortgage financing, collects loan payments, and takes security interest in property financed.

Mortgagee Clause: provision in property policy, or added by endorsement, that extends protection, in limited manner, to mortgagee; not as broad as lender's loss payable endorsement.

Mortgagee Waiver: the relinquishment of right(s) contained in a mortgage by a mortgagee.

Mortgage Verification: request made by mortgagee to applicant's financial institution for information on applicant's accounts, as part of mortgagee's credit approval process.

Mortgagor: borrower in a mortgage contract who mortgages property in exchange for a loan.

Multinational Corporation: corporation whose operations are conducted on an international basis.

Multiple Signature Credit Approval: describes credit approval process in which credit is approved by two or more persons acting together.

Mutual Account Revision: routine exchange of credit information between two or more credit grantors that have extended credit to subject of inquiry.

N

NACM: see *National Association of Credit Management.*

National Association of Credit Management (NACM): national business organization of credit and financial professionals that promotes laws for sound credit, protects businesses against fraudulent debtors, improves the interchange of commercial credit information, develops credit practices, and provides education and certification programs for its members.

Negligence: failure to use reasonable care that an ordinarily prudent person would in like circumstances.

Negotiable: anything capable of being transferred by endorsement or delivery.

Negotiable Instrument: any written evidence of indebtedness, transferable by endorsement and delivery or by delivery only, that contains unconditional promise to pay specified sum on demand or at some fixed date.

Negotiate: to discuss, bargain, or work out plan of settlement, terms, or compromise in business transaction.

Net: amount left after necessary deductions have been made from gross amount.

Net Assets: sum of individual's or entity's total assets less total liabilities.

Net Earnings: total sales, less total operating, administrative, and overhead expenses, but before other expenses and income such as interest and dividends.

Net Income: amount of income remaining after deducting all expenses from total revenues.

Net Lease: agreement in which tenant assumes payment of other property expenses, such as taxes, maintenance, and insurance, in addition to rental payments.

Net Price: actual price paid after all discounts, allowances, and other authorized deductions have been taken.

Net Profit: income earned by business over specific period of time. Profit from transaction or sale, after deducting all costs, expenses, and miscellaneous reserves and adjustments from gross receipts.

Net Sales: total sales less returns, allowances, and discounts.

Net Working Capital: current assets less current liabilities; used as measure of a company's liquidity and indicates its ability to finance current operations.

Net Worth: total assets less total liabilities; reflects owners' net interest in company.

No Account: notation on rejected check when check writer does not have account at the financial institution on which check is drawn.

No Asset Case: insolvent or bankrupt estate with no assets available for payment of creditors' claims.

No Funds: notation on rejected check when check writer has account but not funds to cover check.

Nominal Balance: an account balance of less than $100.

Nominal Owner: person whose name appears on title to asset, but who has no interest in it.

Nonaccrual: loan on which a financial institution does not accrue interest; also known as a nonperforming loan.

Nonborrowing Account: banking relationship in which no extension of credit is involved.

Nonfinancial Information: facts used to evaluate a customer's creditworthiness; focuses on background and history rather than financial measures.

Nonpayment: failure or neglect to pay or discharge debt in accordance with terms of agreement.

Nonperforming Assets: total of earning assets listed as nonaccrual; formerly, earning assets acquired in foreclosure and through in-substance foreclosures.

Nonperforming Loans: amount of loans not meeting original terms of agreement, including renegotiated, restructured, and nonaccrual loans. Loans included in this total vary according to bank policy and regulation.

Nonprofit Corporation: organization specifically classified by the IRS as generally tax exempt and whose primary purpose for existence is to provide services of a charitable, fraternal, religious, social, or civic nature.

Nonrecource: inability of holder in due course to demand payment from endorser of debt instrument if party(ies) primarily liable fail to make payment.

Non-sufficient Funds (NSF): term used when collected demand deposit balances are less than the amount of the check being presented for payment and check is returned to payee's financial institution. See also Overdraft.

No Protest (N.P.): instructions given by one financial institution to another not to protest check or note when presented for payment. N.P. is usually stamped on instrument to avoid protest fee.

North American Industrial Classification System (NAICS): the Standard Industrial Classification (SIC) code is being replaced by the NAICS code. NAICS classifies establishments by their primary type of activity within a six-digit code. NAICS provides structural enhancements over SIC and identifies over 350 new industries. See also *SIC* and *Standard Industrial Classification*.

Notary Public: public officer authorized to administer oaths, attest and certify certain types of documents, and to take acknowledgements of conveyances.

Note: unconditional written promise by borrower to pay certain amount of money to lender on demand or at specified or determinable date. This instrument should meet all requirements of laws pertaining to negotiable instruments.

Notes Payable: liabilities represented by promissory notes, excluding trade debts, that are payable in future.

Notes Receivable: assets represented by promissory notes, excluding amounts due from customers for credit sales, to be collected in future.

Notice of Protest: formal statement that a certain bill of exchange, check, or promissory note was presented for payment or acceptance and that such payment or acceptance was not made. Such notice will also state that because instrument has been dishonored, maker, endorsers, or other parties to document will be held responsible for payment.

Novation: substitution of old contract for new one between same or different parties; substitution of new debtor or creditor for previous one, by mutual agreement.

NSF: see *Non-sufficient Funds*.

Nulla Bona: report made by sheriff when no assets are found within his or her jurisdiction on which to satisfy judgment against debtor.

O

Obligation: 1. law or duty binding parties to an agreement. 2. written promise to pay money or to do a specific thing.

Obligee: person or entity to which payment is due.

Obligor: person or entity required by contract to perform specific act.

Obsolescence: decline in perceived value of asset, frequently because of technological innovations, changes in an industry's processes, or changes required by law.

OCC: see *Office of the Comptroller of the Currency*.

Offer: proposal to make contract, usually presented by one party to another for acceptance.

Offering Basis: customer's loan requests considered individually on merits of each proposal.

Office of the Comptroller of the Currency (OCC): branch of the Treasury Department that regulates federally chartered banks.

Office of Thrift Supervision (OTS): branch of the Treasury Department that regulates state and federally chartered thrifts as well as those institutions in conservatorship.

Offset: amount allowed to be netted against another.

On Account: generally describes partial payment made toward settlement of unpaid balance.

On Account Payment: partial payment not intended as payment in full.

On Demand: debt instrument that is due and payable on presentation.

Open (Book) Account: credit extended without a formal written contract and represented on books and records of the seller as an unsecured account receivable for which payment is expected within a specified period after purchase.

Open-End Credit: consumer line of credit that may be added to, up to preset credit limit, or paid down at any time. Customer has option of paying off outstanding balance, without penalty, or making several installment payments. Contrasts with Closed-End Credit. Also called revolving credit or charge account credit.

Open Terms: selling on credit terms as opposed to having customer pay cash.

Operating Performance Ratios: financial measures designed to assist in evaluation of management performance.

Operating Statement: report of an individual's or entity's income and expenses for a specified period of time. See also Income Statement.

Operational Risk: risk concerning computer network failure due to system overload or other disruptions; also includes potential losses from fraud, malicious damage to data, and error.

Oral Contract: agreement that may or may not be written in whole or in part or signed but is legally enforceable.

Order: informal bill of exchange or letter or request identifying person to be paid.

Order for Relief: order issued by bankruptcy court judge upon filing of petition by debtor or filing of petition by creditors.

Order to Order: agreement for payment to be made for prior shipment before next delivery will be made.

OREO: see *Other Real Estate Owned*.

Other Real Estate Owned: real property usually taken as collateral and subsequently acquired through foreclosure, or by obtaining a deed in lieu of foreclosure, in satisfaction of the debts previously contracted. Real property formerly used as banking premises, or real property sold in a "covered transaction" as defined by banking regulations.

OTS: see *Office of Thrift Supervision*.

Outlet Store: retail operation where manufacturers' production overruns, discontinued merchandise, or irregular goods are sold at discount.

Out-of-Court Settlement: 1. settlement made by distressed debtor through direct negotiations with creditors or through creditors' committee; acceptance of such settlement is not obligatory to nonconsenting creditors. 2. agreement reached between opposing parties to settle pending lawsuit before matter has been decided by court.

Out-of-Pocket Expense: business expenses for which individual pays.

Out-of-Trust: an event occurring in floor plan financing where a borrower sells inventory securing the financial institution's loan and fails to promptly remit the proceeds to the financial institution in accordance with the loan agreement.

Outstanding: 1. amount of credit facility that is being used versus total amount made available. 2. unpaid or uncollected account.

Overdraft: negative account balance created when a check is paid when collected demand deposit balances are less than amount of check being presented for payment. See also Non-sufficient Funds.

Overdue: debt obligation on which payments are past due.

Overhead: selling and administrative business costs as contrasted with costs of goods sold.

Oversold: condition in which manufacturer or wholesaler finds itself after taking more orders than it can deliver within an agreed period of time.

Owed: debt that is due and payable.

Own: to have legal title to property.

Owner: person or entity that owns or has title to property.

Owner's Equity: mathematical difference between total assets and total liabilities that represents shareholders' equity or an individual's net worth.

Ownership: exclusive rights that one has to property, to exclusion of all others; having complete title to property.

Owner's Risk: term used in transportation contracts to exempt carrier from responsibility for loss or damage to goods.

P

Packing List: detailed listing of information on shipment's contents (enclosed for inspection with package).

Paid Direct: payment made by debtor directly to original creditor instead of to collection agency or attorney handling account for collection.

Paper Profit: unrealized income or gain on asset.

Paralegal: trained aide to attorney who handles various legal tasks.

Parent Company: an entity that holds controlling majority interest in subsidiaries.

Partial Payment: payment not in full for amount owed.

Participation: purchase or sale of a loan or credit facility among two or more financial institutions in which the acquiring institution(s) has no formal or direct role in establishing the terms and conditions binding the borrower. Participants do not participate in the document negotiation between the originating financial institution and the borrower.

Partnership: business arrangement in which two or more persons agree to engage, upon terms of mutual participation, in profits and losses.

Party: person concerned or taking part in a transaction or proceeding.

Past Due: payment or account that remains outstanding and unpaid after its agreed-upon payment or maturity date.

Pay: to satisfy, or make partial payments on, a debt obligation.

Payable: obligation that is due now or in future.

Payables: liabilities owed to trade creditors for purchase of supplies. Also called accounts payable.

Payee: person or entity named on a negotiable instrument as the one to whom the obligation is due.

Payer: party responsible for making payment as shown on check, note, or other type of negotiable instrument; also called maker or writer.

Payment: discharge, in whole or in part, of debt or performance of agreement.

Payment for Honor: payment of past-due obligation by someone else to save credit or reputation of person responsible for payment.

Payoff: receipt of payment in full on an obligation.

Penalty: 1. legal fine, forfeiture, or payment imposed for defaulting or violating terms of contract. 2. interest charge imposed for late payments that is permissible by law and imposed with customer's prior agreement or knowledge of seller's terms of sale.

Percentage Lease: lease of real property in which rental payments are based on percentage of retailer's sales.

Percentage of Completion: method of accounting commonly used by contractors and developers in which costs are related to percentage of job completion.

Perfection: with respect to security interests in personal property under Article 9 of the UCC, the action required to give the secured party rights in the collateral as against third parties with competing claims. In general, a security interest is not perfected until a properly executed financing statement has been recorded or the secured party is in the possession of the collateral, whichever applies as to that specific collateral type.

Performance: fulfillment of promise or agreement according to terms of contract or obligation.

Performance Bond: guaranty to project owner that the contractor will perform the work called for by the contract in accordance with the plans and specifications. Customarily issued by bonding and insurance companies, although financial institution letters of credit may be used.

Perjury: willfully and knowingly giving false testimony under oath.

Person: individual (natural person) or incorporated enterprise (artificial person) having certain legal rights and responsibilities.

Personal Check: check drawn by individual on his or her own bank account.

Personality: legal term for personal property or possessions that are not real estate.

Personally Liable: individual's responsibility for payment of obligation, generally used to refer to owner's or guarantor's responsibility.

Personal Property: movable or chattel property of any kind.

Petition: written application, made in contradiction to motion. Also used in some states in place of complaint.

Petition in Bankruptcy: document filed in court to declare bankruptcy. Petition can be either voluntary (filed by debtor) or involuntary (filed by creditors), depending on bankruptcy chapter rules.

Petty Cash: cash on hand or in designated bank account that is available for small, miscellaneous purchases.

Physical Inventory: inventory verification obtained by visual observation of items and itemization of quantities of goods on hand.

Piercing the Corporate Veil: legal action taken by creditor, when fraud or unjust enrichment may be involved, to hold principals of corporation (or other entities) liable for debts of corporation.

Plaintiff: person or entity that initiates legal action against another.

Plan of Arrangement: procedure in bankruptcy under Chapter 11 for debtor to restructure debts or rehabilitate by arriving at arrangement with creditors. See also Bankruptcy, Chapter 11 Cases.

Pledge: promise of personal property as security for performance of act, payment of debt, or satisfaction of obligation.

Points: 1. percentage fee charged to obtain a mortgage loan. 2. in shares of stock, one point equals $1.00.

Policy: 1. written statement by management that explains an organization's philosophy and approach to doing business. 2. written contract of insurance between insured and the insurance company.

Pooling Accounts: arrangement by a debtor listing all his or her debts with a debt management or pro-rating service with the understanding that the service will receive, as its fee, a portion of debtor's payments to his or her creditors and proportionately distribute the balance of payments to each creditor on a scheduled basis. Activities of such services may be covered by individual state statutes.

Postdated Check: check written for payment, effective at future date.

Power of Attorney: written document that authorizes one person to act as another's agent.

Preference: 1. right of a creditor to be paid before other creditors by virtue of having lien or collateral. 2. improperly paying or securing of one or more creditors, in whole or part, by an insolvent debtor to the exclusion of other creditors.

Preference Period: in bankruptcy, the 90-day period immediately preceding debtor entering into bankruptcy. If a creditor files new or additional liens against a debtor during this time, such claims may be disallowed by bankruptcy court.

Preferred Creditor: creditor whose account takes legal preference for payment over claims of others.

Prepaid Expenses: payment for goods or services not yet received.

Prepayment: payment of loan or debt before it actually becomes due.

Prime Contractor: contractor who enters into contract with the owner of the project for completion of all or portion of the project and takes full responsibility for its completion. See also General Contractor.

Prime Rate: an index or base rate published or publicly announced by a financial institution from time to time as the rate it is generally willing to give its most creditworthy customers.

Principal: 1. amount of money loaned or borrowed. 2. key decision maker or management of entity.

Priority: legal preferences that secured creditors have over general creditors in bankruptcy.

Priority Lien: lien recorded before other secured claims and payable ahead of other liens if liquidation of pledged collateral occurs. First mortgage has priority over second and third mortgages, known as junior liens. Secured creditor holding perfected security interest has priority over liens filed afterward.

Private Enterprise: business established to take economic risks for purpose of making profit.

Privilege: right that nature of debt gives to one debt holder over others.

Proceeds: actual amount of money given to or received from creditor after any deductions are made.

Profit: 1. amount of net income made by an entity in course of doing business. 2. increase in value of an asset over its depreciated book value at the time of sale.

Profit and Loss Statement (P & L): financial report of an individual's or entity's revenue and expenses for a given period of time. See also Income Statement and Operating Statement.

Pro Forma: projected financial statements.

Progress Payments: partial payments made on a long-term contract as it progresses. Required when a manufacturer or contractor cannot afford, or does not wish, to finance a project.

Projection: borrower's estimate of future performance over designated time period.

Promissory Note: written promise to make unconditional payment of specified amount on designated date, signed by maker.

Proof of Claim: creditor's formal document filed with court against estate of debtor if creditor is owed funds.

Proof of Loss: sworn statement filed by insured when making claim.

Property: something of value that is legally owned and in which person has exclusive and unrestricted right or interest.

Property Insurance: coverage that applies to loss caused by physical damage to property (buildings, contents, earnings, etc.) owned by insured.

Proposal: oral or written offer that, if accepted, constitutes a contract.

Proprietorship: single and exclusive ownership of a business by one person.

Pro Rata: share calculated in proportion to total amount.

Pro Rata Distribution: payment proportionate to uniform percentage of obligations to all creditors.

Protest: formal, written, notarized notice stating credit instrument has not been honored and that makers or endorsers will be held responsible for payment.

Prox.: see Proximo.

Proximo (Prox.): sales term used in invoices to mean next month after month of invoice. This term is sometimes used instead of EOM terms.

Proxy: written statement or power of attorney, authorizing an individual to act or speak for another.

Public Credit: debt incurred by government, federal and local, for a use that meet the needs of its citizens.

Purchase Money Lien: manufacturer's legal right to goods and products until the buyer makes payment. Under the Uniform Commercial Code, manufacturer's rights can take priority over lender's lien rights if both claim interest in same inventory. Lender may receive such priority if funds were provided to purchase asset, provided liens are filed within 20 days of borrower taking possession of collateral and noticing requirements have been met.

Purchase Money Mortgage: mortgage given by buyer to seller in lieu of cash, as partial payment on property.

Purchasing Power: value of money and its ability to buy goods and services in a given period.

Q

Qualified Acceptance: agreement to terms of contract only if certain conditions are meet. This constitutes counteroffer and rejection of original offer.

Qualified Endorsement: transfer of debt instrument to endorsee without recourse or liability to endorser.

Qualified Financial Statement: audit report issued by independent accountants that indicates restrictions on scope of audit performed, uncertainties, or disagreements with management.

Qualified Prospect: potential customer whose background and credit have been checked and approved.

Quantity Discount: price reduction extended to purchaser of a large volume of goods.

Quarterly Accounts Receivable Survey: index, compiled by Credit Research Foundation in affiliation with the National Association of Credit Management and published quarterly, that shows average days' sales outstanding for manufacturers and wholesalers.

Quick Assets: current assets that can be readily converted into cash (generally, accounts receivable).

Quick Assets Ratio: cash and cash equivalents plus trade receivables (net) divided by total current liabilities; used as measure of liquidity.

Quid Pro Quo: 1. giving of one valuable thing for another. 2. mutual consideration between parties to contract.

Quitclaim: to release or relinquish claim or title.

R

Rack Jobber: wholesale distributor who sells housewares and other convenience-type merchandise through retail stores and assumes responsibility for stocking and maintaining store's inventory.

Rate of Exchange: amount of one country's currency that can be bought with another country's currency at a particular point in time.

Rate of Interest: cost of borrowing money, usually expressed as annual percentage charge.

Rating: 1. assessment of borrower's financial strength and creditworthiness. 2. symbol used to denote borrower's creditworthiness.

Ratios: mathematical relationship between two or more things, used as indication of a company's financial strength relative to other companies of comparable size or in same industry.

Real Property: land and anything erected or growing on it or affixed to it.

Receivables: money due or collectible for goods sold, services performed, or money loaned. Also called accounts receivable.

Receivables Turnover: measurement of how effective a company is in collecting on its trade receivables.

Receiver: person appointed by the court to receive, take charge, and hold in trust a property in litigation or bankruptcy until a legal decision is made as to its disposition.

Receivership: 1. court action whereby money or property is placed under control, and administration of receiver is to be preserved for benefit of persons or creditors ultimately entitled to it. 2. procedure used to help a distressed debtor or to resolve a dispute.

Reclamation: 1. legal action by titleholder to recover property from another's possession. 2. process used to restore land to usable state.

Record: written account of act, transaction, or instrument drawn by proper legal authority that remains as permanent evidence.

Recourse: right of holder in due course to demand payment from anyone who endorsed instrument if original signer fails to pay.

Recovery: amount finally collected; amount of judgment.

Reference Check: contacting and interviewing business or professional associates of credit applicant to gain information about his or her creditworthiness.

References: names of trade suppliers or creditors provided by a customer to be used as a source of information about that customer.

Refer to Maker: term stamped by financial institution on a check to indicate its rejection.

Refinance: to reorganize existing debts by obtaining new debt that incorporates or pays off existing debts.

Register: book of factual public information, kept by a public official.

Regulation 9: regulation issued by the Comptroller of Currency allowing national banks to operate trust departments and act as fiduciaries. Under Regulation 9, a national bank is permitted to act as trustee, administrator, and registrar of stocks and bonds and engage in related activities, such as management of a collective investment fund, as long as these activities do not violate state legislation.

Regulation A: Federal Reserve Board regulation governing advances by Federal Reserve Banks to depository institutions at a Federal Reserve discount window. Credit advances are available to any bank or savings institution maintaining transaction accounts or non-personal time deposits. The Fed has two different programs for handling discount window borrowings:

• adjustment credit to meet temporary needs for funds when other sources are not available.

• extended credit, designed to assist financial institutions with longer-term needs for funds. This includes seasonal credit privileges extended to smaller financial institutions that do not have ready access to money market funds. Federal Reserve Banks may also extend emergency credit to financial institutions other than depository institutions in which failure to obtain credit would affect the economy adversely.

Regulation B: Federal Reserve regulation prohibiting discrimination against consumer credit applicants and establishing guidelines for collecting and evaluating credit information. Regulation B prohibits creditors from discriminating on the basis of age, sex, race, color, religion, national origin, marital status, or receipt of public assistance. Regulation B also requires creditors to give written notification of rejection, statement of applicant's rights under Equal Credit Opportunity Act of 1974, and statement listing reasons for rejection, or applicant has right to request reasons. If applicant is denied credit because of adverse information in credit bureau report, applicant is entitled to receive copy of bureau report at no cost. Creditors who furnish credit information when reporting information on married borrowers must report information in name of each spouse.

Regulation C: Federal Reserve regulation implementing Home Mortgage Disclosure Act of 1975, requiring depository institutions to make annual disclosure of location of certain residential loans to determine whether depository institutions are meeting credit needs of their local communities. Specifically exempted are institutions with assets of $10 million or less. Regulation C requires lenders of mortgages that are insured or guaranteed by a federal agency to disclose number and total dollar amount of mortgage loans originated or purchased in recent calendar year, itemized by census tract where property is located.

Regulation D: Federal Reserve regulation that sets uniform reserve requirements for depository financial institutions holding transaction accounts or non-personal time deposits. Reserves are maintained in form of vault cash or non-interest-bearing balance at a Federal Reserve Bank or at a correspondent bank.

Regulation E: Federal Reserve regulation that sets rules, liabilities, and procedures for electronic funds transfers (EFT) and establishes consumer protections using EFT systems. This regulation prescribes rules for solicitation and issuance of EFT debit cards, governs consumer liability for unauthorized transfers, and requires financial institutions to disclose annually terms and conditions of EFT services.

Regulation F: Federal Reserve regulation requiring state-chartered banks with 500 or more stockholders and at least $1 million in assets to file financial statements with the Board of Governors of the Federal Reserve System. In general, these state-chartered member banks must file registration statements, periodic financial statements, proxy statements, and various other disclosures of interest to investors. These regulations are substantially similar to those issued by Securities and Exchange Commission.

Regulation G: Federal Reserve regulation governing credit secured by margin securities extended or arranged by parties other than banks or broker/dealers. It requires lenders to register credit extensions of $200,000, secured by margin stock, or $500,000 in total credit, within 30 days after end of quarter.

Regulation H: Federal Reserve regulation defining membership requirements for state-chartered banks that become members of the Federal Reserve System. The regulation sets forth procedures as well as privileges and requirements for membership. The regulation also requires state-chartered banks acting as securities transfer agents to register with board.

Regulation I: Federal Reserve regulation requiring each member bank joining the Federal Reserve System to purchase stock in its Federal Reserve Bank equal to 6% of its capital and surplus. Federal Reserve Bank stock, which pays interest semiannually, is nontransferable and cannot be used as collateral. When bank increases or decreases its capital base, it must adjust its ownership of Federal Reserve stock accordingly.

Regulation J: Federal Reserve regulation providing legal framework for collection of checks and other cash items and net settlement of balances through Federal Reserve System. It specifies terms and conditions under which Federal Reserve Banks will receive checks for collection from depository institutions, presentment to paying banks, and return of unpaid items. It is supplemented by operating circulars issued by Federal Reserve Banks.

Regulation K: Federal Reserve regulation governing international banking operations by bank holding companies and foreign banks in the U.S. The regulation permits Edge Act corporations to engage in range of international banking and financial activities. It also permits U.S. banks to own up to 100% of non-financial companies located outside the U.S. Regulation K also imposes reserve requirements on Edge Act corporations, as specified in Regulation D, and limits interstate activities of foreign banks in the U.S.

Regulation L: Federal Reserve regulation prohibiting interlocking director arrangements in member banks or bank holding companies. Management official of state member bank or bank holding company may not act simulta-

neously as management official of another depository institution if both are not affiliated, are very large banks, or are located in same local area. Regulation L provides 10-year grandfather period for certain interlocks and allows some on exception basis, such as organizations owned by women or minority groups, newly chartered organizations, and in situations in which implementing regulation would endanger safety and soundness.

Regulation M: Federal Reserve regulation implementing consumer leasing provisions of Truth in Lending Act of 1968. It covers leases on personal property for more than four months for family, personal, or household use. It requires leasing companies to disclose in writing the cost of lease, including security deposit and monthly payments, taxes, and other payments, and in case of an open-end lease, whether a balloon payment may be applied. It also requires written disclosure of terms of lease, including insurance, guaranties, responsibility for servicing property, and whether lessor has an option to buy property at lease termination.

Regulation N: Federal Reserve regulation governing transactions among Federal Reserve Banks and transactions involving Federal Reserve Banks and foreign banks and governments. This regulation gives the board responsibility for approving in advance negotiations or agreements by Federal Reserve Banks and foreign banks, bankers, and governments. The Federal Reserve Bank may, under direction of the Federal Open Market Committee, undertake negotiations, agreements, or facilitate open market transactions. Reserve Banks must report quarterly to the Board of Governors on accounts they maintain with foreign banks.

Regulation O: Federal Reserve regulation limiting amount of credit member banks may extend to their own executive officers. Regulation O also implements reporting requirements of Financial Institutions Regulatory and Interest Rate Control Act of 1978 and Garn-St. Germain Depository Institutions Act of 1982.

Regulation P: Federal Reserve regulation that sets minimum standards for security devices, such as bank vaults and currency handling equipment, including automated teller machines. Member bank must appoint security officer to develop and administer program to deter thefts and file the annual compliance statement with its Federal Reserve Bank.

Regulation Q: Federal Reserve regulation requiring depository institutions to state clearly terms for depositing and renewing time deposits and certificates of deposit and also any penalties for early withdrawal of savings accounts.

Regulation R: Federal Reserve regulation prohibiting individuals who are engaged in securities underwriting, sale, and distribution from serving as directors, officers, or employees of member banks. Regulation R specifically exempts those involved in government securities trading and general obligations of states and municipalities.

Regulation S: Federal Reserve regulation implementing section of Right to Financial Privacy Act of 1978 requiring government authorities to pay reasonable fees to financial institutions for financial records of individuals and small partnerships available to federal agencies in connection with government loan programs or Internal Revenue Service summons.

Regulation T: Federal Reserve regulation governing credit extensions by securities brokers and dealers, including all members of national securities exchanges. Brokers/dealers may not extend credit to their customers unless such loans are secured by margin securities—securities listed and traded on national securities exchange, mutual funds, and over-the-counter stock designated by Securities and Exchange Commission as eligible for trading in national market system. Generally, brokers/dealers may not extend credit on margin securities in excess of percentage of current market value permitted by board.

Regulation U: Federal Reserve regulation governing extensions of credit by banks for purchasing and carrying margin securities. Whenever lender makes loan secured by margin securities, bank must have customer execute purpose statement regardless of use of loan.

Regulation V: Federal Reserve regulation dealing with financing of contractors, subcontractors, and others involved in national defense work. The regulation spells out the authority granted to Federal Reserve Banks under the Defense Production Act of 1950 to assist federal departments and agencies in making and administering loan guaranties to defense-related contractors and sets maximum interest rates, guaranty fees, and commitment fees.

Regulation X: Federal Reserve regulation extending provisions of other securities-related regulations—Regulations G, T, and U—to foreign persons or organizations who obtain credit outside U.S. for purchase of U.S. Treasury securities.

Regulation Y: Federal Reserve regulation governing banking and nonbanking activities of bank holding companies and divestiture of impermissible nonbank activities. Regulation Y spells out procedures for forming bank holding company and procedures to be followed by bank holding companies acquiring voting shares in bank or nonbank companies. Regulation Y also lists those nonbank activities that are deemed closely related to banking and therefore permissible for bank holding companies.

Regulation Z: Federal Reserve regulation implementing consumer credit protections in the Truth in Lending Act of 1968. Major areas of regulation require lenders to:
- give borrowers written disclosure on essential credit terms, including cost of credit expressed as finance charge and annual percentage rate.
- respond to consumer complaints of billing errors on certain credit accounts within specified period.
- identify credit transactions on periodic statements of open-end credit accounts.
- provide certain rights regarding credit cards.
- inform customers of right of rescission in certain mortgage-related loans within specified period.
- comply with special requirements when advertising credit.

Regulation AA: Federal Reserve regulation establishing procedures for handling consumer complaints about alleged unfair or deceptive practices by a state member bank.

Regulation BB: Federal Reserve regulation implementing Community Reinvestment Act of 1977 (CRA). Banks are required to make available to public a statement indicating communities served, type of credit the lender is prepared to extend, and public comments to its CRA statement.

Regulation CC: Federal Reserve regulation implementing Expedited Funds Availability Act of 1987, setting endorsement standards on checks collected by depository financial institutions. Endorsement standard is designed to facilitate identification of endorsing bank and prompt return of unpaid checks. The regulation specifies funds availability schedules that banks must comply with and procedures for returning dishonored checks.

Release: to discharge debt or give up claim against party from whom it is due by party to whom it is due.

Remedy: legal means by which right is enforced or violation of right is prevented or compensated.

Rent: periodic payments made by tenant to owner in return for leasing land, building space, or equipment.

Reorganization: 1. voluntary or court-ordered change in capital structure of corporation in which all assets of an old corporation are transferred to a newly formed corporation. 2. restructuring of business entity, whether in or out of bankruptcy.

Replevin: legal action taken to recover possession of property unlawfully taken.

Repossess: action taken by creditor in which he or she takes possession of goods purchased under credit agreement or pledged as collateral if debtor defaults on terms of contract.

Rescind: to void contract from its inception. Result is that parties are restored to relative positions before contract was made.

Rescission: agreement by parties to contract that effects cancellation of contract.

Reserve: in accounting, funds set aside for specific purpose.

Reserve for Bad Debts: valuation account established for accounts receivable that may prove uncollectible.

Residence: place where person legally lives part or full time.

Residual Value: the estimated recoverable amount of a depreciable asset as of the time of its removal from service.

Resolution Trust Corporation (RTC): federal agency established in 1989 to oversee the savings and loan bailout.

Restraint of Trade: any action, by agreement or by combination, that tends to eliminate competition, artificially sets up prices, or results in monopoly.

Restrictive Endorsement: endorsement on negotiable instrument that limits any further negotiability, for example, "for deposit only" written on back of check.

Restructured Loan: loan on which a bank, for economic or legal reasons related to debtor's financial difficulties, grants concession to debtor that would not be considered otherwise.

Retailer: company that sells its product directly to end-user.

Retained Earnings: cumulative earnings and losses of company that remain undistributed to shareholders.

Retentions: amounts withheld by customer from total billings until contractor has satisfactorily completed project.

Retroactive: 1. effective as of past date. 2. having reference to prior time.

Return: rate of profit or earnings on sales or investment.

Return Items/Returned Checks: checks, drafts, or notes returned unpaid to originating bank by drawee bank so that originator can correct any errors or irregularities and may present items for collection again.

Revenue: 1. income from sales, interest, or dividends. 2. income from investment or wages.

Reviewed Financial Statements: business financial statements that are reviewed by independent accountants through inquiries of management and performance of analytical procedures on financials to provide limited assurance that no material modifications are necessary for statements to conform to generally accepted accounting principles. Independent accountants do not express opinion on review statements.

Revolving Charge: credit type that allows borrower to become indebted up to an approved credit limit, with no fixed maturity date. Finance costs are assessed monthly on unpaid balance, and periodic payments are required.

Revolving Credit: commitment under which funds can be borrowed, repaid, and re-borrowed during life of credit. Such credits have stated maturity date at which time borrower may have option of converting outstanding balance into term loan. See also Evergreen Revolving Credit.

Rider: any schedule or amendment attached to a contract or document that becomes part of it.

Right of Rescission: consumer's right as prescribed by Truth in Lending Act of 1968 to rescind certain credit and mortgage contracts within three days without penalty.

Right of Setoff: right of financial institution to apply borrower's funds on deposit to debt owed to the financial institution in event that payment on the debt is not made as agreed.

Risk-Based Capital: level of capital that bank is required to maintain; level is determined by relating capital to risk by type of asset.

RMA: see *Risk Management Association*.

RMA General Figure Ranges: dollar amount ranges established by RMA to ensure accuracy and consistency when exchanging credit information. There are four ranges: low, 1-1.9; moderate, 2-3.9; medium, 4-6.9; and high, 7-9.9. Ranges can be applied to any figure category. Sample figure categories are: nominal = under $100; 3 figures = from $100 to $999; 4 figures = from $1,000 to $9,999; 5 figures = from $10,000 to $99,999; and 6 figures = from $100,000 to $999,999. Information is reported, using both range description and figure category; for example, "average balances are in medium 4-figure range."

Risk Management Association (RMA): association of lending, credit, and risk management professionals. Originally, RMA was founded to facilitate the exchange of credit information. Today, RMA works continuously to improve practices of the financial services industry and to provide members with networking opportunities, training, research publications, and seminars.

Robinson-Patman Act: federal legislation prohibiting firms engaged in interstate commerce from charging different buyers different prices for the same goods unless there is difference in costs or the price does not restrict competition.

R.O.G. Dating: payment term that uses date customer is in receipt of goods as effective sale date.

Royalty: compensation made to another for use of his or her work.

RTC: see *Resolution Trust Corporation*.

Rule of 72: method commonly used to approximate time required for sum of money to double at given rate of interest. Rule of 72 is computed by dividing interest rate by 72.

Rule of 78s: mathematical formula used in computing interest rebated when borrower pays off loan before maturity. Rule of 78s is applied mostly to consumer loans in which finance charges were computed using add-on interest or discounted interest method of interest calculation. Also called sum of digits method.

S

Sale: agreement or contract that transfers title of goods or property from one person or entity to another for consideration.

Sale and Lease Back: arrangement whereby company sells goods with intent to lease those same goods from buyer.

Sale on Approval: purchase of goods conditioned on buyer approval of goods or retention of them beyond reasonable time.

Salvage Value: estimated worth of a depreciated asset at the end of its useful life.

Satisfaction: paying debt in full.

Satisfaction of Judgment: legal evidence that recorded judgment has been paid or settled and entered in court records.

Satisfaction Piece: legal evidence that debt has been paid in full or settled and that liens on collateral have been released.

SBA: see *Small Business Administration*.

Schedule: listing by account name or number of total sales, current sales, monies owing or paid, chargebacks, or credits. Also called aging schedule or trial balance.

Scheduled Liability: 1. in property insurance, listing of property—items or locations—covered. 2. in dishonesty insurance (fidelity bonding), listing of persons or positions covered.

Scheduled Payment: partial payments made at dates specified in credit agreement.

Schedules: in bankruptcy, lists showing debtor's property—location, quantity, and money value; names and addresses of creditors and their class; or names and addresses of stockholders of each class.

Scrap Value: worth of asset that is going to be destroyed or used for its components.

Seasonal Loans: loans used to finance cyclical buildup of current (working capital) assets until those assets can be converted to cash.

Second Lien: lien that can be honored only after first lien is satisfied.

Second Mortgage: mortgage secured by equity in property but one that cannot enforce payment until claims of first mortgage are satisfied.

Secret Partner: partner in business whose interest in partnership is not publicly known.

Secured Creditor: lender or other person whose claim is supported by taking collateral.

Secured Loan: loan supported by borrower's pledge of an asset such as marketable securities, accounts receivable, inventories, real estate, equipment, etc.

Secured Note: note that provides, upon default, certain pledged or mortgaged property that may be applied or sold in payment of debt.

Secured Party: 1. lender or other person to whom or in whose favor security interest has been given. Includes person to whom accounts or chattel paper have been sold. 2. trustee or agent representing holders of obligations issued under indenture of trust, equipment trust agreement, or the like.

Securities: 1. documents that evidence debt or property pledged in fulfillment of obligation. 2. evidence of indebtedness or right to participate in earnings and distribution of corporate, trust, and other property.

Security: guaranty or assets pledged that can be applied to loan or obligation.

Security Agreement: formally executed document that gives lender rights to property pledged by borrower in support of debt.

Security Interest: right that lender or lienholder obtains to debtor's goods as evidenced by security agreement.

Seller's Market: economic condition in which demand is greater than supply, and that typically causes prices to increase.

Sequestered Account: account that has been attached by court order with disbursements subject to court approval.

Service Business: firm that performs functions for its customers rather than sells goods.

Setoff: 1. defendant's counterdemand against plaintiff. 2. right of parties to contract to reduce debt owed to one party by netting it against amount owed by other. See also *Right of Setoff*.

Settle: 1. to mutually reach agreement for adjustment or liquidation of debt. 2. to negotiate payment of obligation or lawsuit for less than amount claimed.

Settlement: 1. adjustment or liquidation of accounts. 2. full and final payment of debt. See also *Out-of-Court Settlement*.

Shared National Credit (SNC): any loan originally $20 million or more that is shared at its inception by two or more financial institutions under a formal intercreditor or participation agreement or sold in part to one or more financial institutions with purchasing financial institution assuming its pro rata share of credit risk.

Shareholder: person or entity that legally owns stock in a corporation.

Sheriff's Sale: court-ordered sale of property to satisfy judgment, mortgage, lien, or other outstanding debt against debtor.

Sherman Antitrust Act: federal legislation aimed at prevention of business monopoly; act declares illegal every contract, combination, or conspiracy in restraint of normal trade.

Short-Term Liabilities: current debts that are due within one year.

Short-Term Loan: current debt obligation that matures within one year, evidenced by promissory note that spells out terms of agreement.

SIC: see *Standard Industrial Classification*.

Sight Draft: draft payable on demand when presented to drawee. See also *Draft, Letter of Credit*, and *Time Draft*.

Signal Action: notices that provide subscriber with list of accounts in which subscriber has interest and on which delinquent payments have been reported.

Signature Loan: unsecured loan backed only by borrower's signature on promissory note. No collateral is taken by lender. This loan is generally offered to individuals with good credit standing. Also called good faith loan or character loan.

Signature Verification: examination of signature on negotiable instrument to determine whether handwriting is genuine and whether person signing check is authorized to use account.

Simple Interest: interest calculated on outstanding principal amount of debt or investment only.

Single Proprietorship: ownership of company by one person.

Skip Tracing: process used to obtain information to locate debtor's whereabouts in order to collect payment on debts. Sources used include other creditors, friends, relatives, neighbors, directories, credit bureaus, court records, and other informants or references.

Slander: oral defamation of another's reputation.

Small Business Administration (SBA): federal agency whose function is to advise and assist small businesses; provides loan guaranties for small businesses, minorities, and veterans plus financial assistance to small businesses that have suffered catastrophes.

SNC: see *Shared National Credit*.

Soft Goods: nondurable consumer goods such as clothing and linen, having a short-term useful life.

Soldier's and Sailor's Relief Act: federal act, also passed by various states, under which right to legally enforce an obligation against a person is suspended during the period that person is in military service or for period thereafter.

Sole Owner: one with title to proprietorship.

Solvency: ability to pay one's debts in usual and ordinary course of business as they mature.

Special Material: made-to-order material or work done to customer's specifications that has no value to seller if order is canceled.

Special Mention Assets: as it relates to risk assessment of bank assets, assets that deserve management's close attention. If left uncorrected, these potential weaknesses may result in deterioration of repayment prospects for asset or in institution's credit position at some future date. Special mention assets are not adversely classified and do not expose institution to sufficient risk to warrant adverse classification.

Specific Coverage: property coverage on designated property or item. Contrasts with Blanket Coverage.

Specific Performance: court order directing party guilty of breach of contract to undertake complete performance of contractual obligation in instances in which damages would inadequately compensate injured party.

Speculation: investment made with hope of achieving large financial gain.

Speculator: one who makes risky investments for quick financial gain rather than long-term investment.

Stale Check: negotiable draft that has been held too long to be honored for payment; time varies from state to state.

Standard Industrial Classification (SIC): statistical classification standard underlying all establishment-based federal economic statistics classified by industry. SIC is used to promote comparability of establishment data describing various facets of the U.S. economy. Classification covers entire field of economic activities and defines industries in accordance with composition and structure of economy. It is revised periodically to reflect economy's changing industrial organization. See also *North American Industrial Classification System* and *NAICS.*

Standby Letter of Credit: type of letter of credit issued by bank that may be drawn on by payee only if party that makes letter of credit (drawer) defaults or does not perform according to terms of specific contract or agreement. See also Letter of Credit.

Statement: 1. itemized summary and accounting of charges, payments, and balance outstanding at close of billing period. 2. financial report.

Statement of Cash Flows: financial statement that shows cash receipts and disbursements for given period.

Statement of Changes in Owner's Equity: financial statement that reconciles changes in capital accounts (capital stock, paid in surplus, and retained earnings).

Statute: written law.

Statute of Frauds: law prohibiting filing of actions or suits against certain types of contracts unless the contracts are in writing.

Statute of Limitations: law that sets time frame for bringing action against another. Time frame varies according to nature of claim and jurisdiction.

Stay: act of arresting judicial proceeding by court order.

Stipulation: agreement between opposing attorneys in lawsuit, usually required to be in writing.

Stock: 1. merchandise or inventory on hand and available for sale. 2. certificate that indicates number of shares of ownership in corporation.

Stock Power: document executed in form of power of attorney by which owner of stock authorizes another party to sell or transfer stock.

Stop Payment Order: instructions given by depositor to a financial institution to dishonor, or not make payment on, a certain check.

Subchapter S: business concern chartered as corporation that is taxed as partnership. An S corporation has 35 or fewer shareholders and can use cash basis of accounting. Corporate gains (or losses) from operations are taxed to shareholders as individuals.

Subcontract: contract between prime contractor and another contractor or supplier to perform specified work or to supply specified materials in accordance with plans and specifications for project.

Subject: party on which credit information is requested.

Sublimit: specified, partial amount of credit facility that is designated for special use.

Subordination: 1. signed agreement acknowledging that one's claim or interest is inferior to another's. 2. act of agreeing to take secondary position.

Subpoena: process to demand person to appear in court and give testimony.

Subrogation: substitution of one creditor for another so that substituted creditor succeeds to rights, remedies, or proceeds of claim.

Subsidiary: business entity owned or controlled by another organization.

Substandard Assets: as it relates to risk assessment of bank assets, assets that are inadequately protected by current sound worth and paying capacity of obligor or of collateral pledged, if any. Assets so classified must have well-defined weakness or weaknesses that jeopardize liquidation of debt. They are

characterized by distinct possibility that bank will sustain some loss if deficiencies are not corrected.

Summons: formal notice served on defendant stating that action has been instituted against him or her and requiring defendant to appear in court to answer it.

Supplementary Proceedings: statutory action requiring judgment debtor to appear in court to discover property against which action can be taken by creditor to enforce collection of judgment.

Supplier: business that sells goods, materials, or services to customers. Also called vendor.

Surety: one who agrees to be primarily liable with another and to fulfill another's obligations under terms of agreement.

Surety Bond: guaranty that payment or performance of some specific act will be completed under penalty or forfeiture of bond usually issued by a bonding company.

Suretyship: undertaking by person or entity to pay obligation of obligee in favor of principal when obligee defaults; such undertaking by individual is known as personal suretyship and by insurance company as corporate suretyship.

Suspense File: group of accounts, records, or other items held temporarily until final disposition is determined.

Swap: A financial derivative contract between two parties to exchange fixed-rate interest payments for floating-rate interest payments, or floating-rate interest payments on different bases (e.g., prime rate versus LIBOR), calculated on specific floating indices by reference to a notional principal amount for a specified term.

Sweep Account: type of cash management tool in which, when prearranged amount of cash accumulates in account, amount is automatically invested.

Swindle: 1. to obtain money or property by deceitful misrepresentation. 2. to cheat or fraudulently induce individual to give up his or her property willingly.

Swing Loan: see *Bridge Loan.*

Syndicate: temporary association of persons or firms formed to carry out business venture or project of mutual interest.

Syndication: project financing whereby commercial or investment bankers agree to advance portion of funding. Syndicator acts as investment manager, collecting loan origination fee or commitment fee from borrower and arranging for sale to other banks in group. Typically, syndicator keeps only a small portion of total financing. A syndicated loan differs from loan participation because syndicate members are known at outset to borrower. Syndication also separates lead bank from group of financial institutions that ultimately fund obligation.

T

Takeover: acquisition, seizure, control, or management of one business by another.

Tangible Assets: assets that can be weighed, measured, or counted, including cash, property, machinery, and buildings.

Tax: payments imposed by legislative authority for support of government and its functions.

Taxable Income: portion of individual's or entity's income that is subject to taxation.

Tax Avoidance: act of using legal deductions, exemptions, and tax code provisions to reduce taxes payable.

Tax Evasion: failure to report taxable income to avoid proper payment of taxes.

Tax Foreclosure: legal seizure and sale of property by authorized public official to satisfy unpaid taxes.

Tax Levy: legislative action by which tax is imposed.

Tax Lien: statutory claim by state or municipality against property of person owing taxes. Property may be sold to satisfy obligation or judgment filed against it.

Tax Sale: sale of property seized by governmental taxing body for nonpayment of taxes.

Tenancy by Entirety: ownership in property by husband and wife in which each becomes whole owner of the entire estate upon the other's death. See also Joint Tenancy with Rights of Survivorship.

Tenancy in Common: two or more persons who hold title to land or other property in undivided ownership.

Tender: 1. unconditional offer of money or performance to satisfy claim. 2. offer to buy stock to take control of company.

Term Loan: fixed-term business loan with a maturity of more than one year and with defined periodic payments, providing borrower with working capital to acquire assets or inventory or to finance plant and equipment.

Terms: conditions and requirements as set forth in sales proposal, contract, or promissory note.

Terms of Sale: mutually agreed upon conditions for transfer of title or ownership of goods or property.

Testimony: written or oral evidence given in court under oath.

Third Party: one who is not directly related to action between two parties but who may be affected by its outcome.

Third-Party Claim: demand made by person who is not party to action for delivery or possession of personal property, title to which is claimed by third party.

Time Deposit: 1. interest-bearing funds deposited in a financial institution for a specified period of time, such as certificates of deposit and savings accounts. 2. under Regulation D, deposit in which depositor is not permitted to make withdrawals within six days after date of deposit unless deposit is subject to early withdrawal penalty.

Time Draft: draft payable on fixed date or certain number of days after sight or date of draft. See also *Banker's Acceptance, Draft, Letter of Credit,* and *Sight Draft.*

Title: document that evidences legal ownership and possession of property.

Title Company: business that as contracted researches specific property's history through real estate records and issues policy to purchaser or lienholder guaranteeing that there are no known defects in title.

Title Insurance: a guarantee by a title insurance company that it will indemnify the insured, in a specific amount, against losses resulting from defects in the title to a property. The insured may be the owner of the property, that person's heirs and devises, or the lender and future assignees.

Title Search: to review history of property's ownership and any judgments or liens filed against it.

Tolling the Statute: act of debtor to freeze statute of limitations that extends period for creditor to legally enforce payment of account. Individual state laws and statutes apply.

Tort: violation of legal duty that results in injury or damage to another.

Trade Acceptance: draft, accepted by buyer, sent with shipment of goods, requiring customer to pay amount involved at specific date and place.

Trade Credit: accounts payable; credit extended from one company to another.

Trade Debts: liabilities due from one business to another for purchase of supplies, inventory, etc.

Trade-in: property accepted by seller as partial down payment on purchase of new item.

Trade Information: confidential exchange of payment history and credit information among suppliers.

Trademark: distinctive identifying mark, word, or logo of product or service; protected when registered with U.S. Patent Office.

Trade Name: name used by a company to identify itself in the course of business. Also known as Trade Style or Fictitious Name.

Trade Payment Record: summary of performance of company in meeting terms of its credit obligations.

Trade References: names of suppliers or business creditors with whom credit information on customer can be exchanged.

Treasury Workstation: microcomputer-based information management system that allows corporate treasurer to automate daily balance reporting of collected balances, to invest idle funds in short-term money market, and to disburse funds to trade creditors. Overall aim is improvement in productivity and eventual integration of funds management and corporate accounting systems, such as order entry and invoicing.

Trial Balance: listing of all account balances from general ledger used in preparing financial statements.

Truck Jobber: wholesale merchant who sells and delivers products from truck inventory at time of sale. Also called *Wagon Distributor.*

Trust: right to real or personal property that is held by one for benefit of another.

Trust Company: business that acts as fiduciary and agent, handling trusts, estates, and guardianships for individuals and businesses.

Trustee: one who holds or is entrusted with management of property or funds for benefit of another.

Trustee in Bankruptcy: person appointed by court or elected by creditors to manage bankrupt property and carry out responsibilities of trust in proceedings.

Trust Receipt: trust agreement (in receipt form) between a financial institution and borrower. It is temporarily substituted for possessory collateral securing creditor's loan so that creditor may release instruments, documents, or other property without releasing title to property. Borrower agrees to keep property (collateral), as well as any funds received from its sale, separate and distinct from borrower's own property and subject to repossession by the financial institution in event that he or she fails to comply with conditions specified in trust agreement.

Truth in Lending Act of 1968: See *Regulation Z.*

Turnkey: something that is constructed, supplied, or installed and fully ready as intended.

U

UCC: see *Uniform Commercial Code.*

Ultra Vires: unauthorized acts taken by corporation beyond powers conferred on it by corporate charter.

Umbrella Policy: in liability insurance, policy that applies excess coverage to primary or underlying contract; provides large limits and broad coverage or may cover only primary basis risks not otherwise insured.

Unaudited Financial Statement: financial statement or report based on figures that have not been verified by a qualified accountant.

Uncollected Funds: deposits not yet collected by a financial institution, such as checks that have not yet cleared.

Uncollectible Accounts: receivables or debts not capable of being settled or recovered.

Underwriter: 1. person who reviews application for insurance and decides whether or not to accept risk. 2. one who agrees to purchase entire issue of bonds or securities at end of certain period.

Undue Influence: improper or illegal pressure used to wrongfully take advantage of person or to influence his or her actions or decisions.

Unearned Discount: A term used to reflect a reduced price (from the face value of an invoice) taken by a buyer without the consent of the seller.

Unearned Income: income received in advance of being earned.

Unencumbered Property: property that has no legal defects in its title; a property free and clear of any liens or debts.

Unenforceable Claim: debt on which all collection efforts have failed.

Unfair Competition: any fraudulent or dishonest practice intended to harm or unfairly attract competitor's customers.

Uniform Commercial Code (UCC): comprehensive set of statutes created to provide uniformity in business laws in all states, as approved by National Conference of Commissioners on Uniform State Laws. Statutes can vary from state to state.

Unit Banking: banking system in several states that prohibits branching or operation of more than one full-service banking office by state-chartered or national banks. Limited branching laws encourage chartering of large numbers of small, independently owned state banks and large multi-bank holding companies that own numerous unit banks.

Unjust Enrichment: doctrine whereby one is not allowed to profit inequitably at another's expense.

Unsatisfied Judgment: recorded judgment that has not been released or discharged.

Unsecured Creditor: one who grants credit without taking collateral in support of it.

Unsecured Loan: loan made on strength of borrower's general financial condition. Contrasts with Secured Loan.

Upstream Funding: funds borrowed by a subsidiary of a holding company for holding company's use. Contrasts with Downstream Funding.

Usury: The rate of interest that exceeds the legal limit allowed to be charged for the use of another's money. Legal limit of interest for different types of loan transactions is established by state law.

V

Valuable Consideration: see *Consideration.*

Valuation: 1. the estimated or determined worth of something. 2. process of appraising or affixing value of something.

Value Received: phrase used in bill of exchange or promissory note to denote that lawful consideration has been given.

Variable Interest Rate: interest rate that fluctuates with changes in an identified base rate or index.

Vendor: trade supplier or service provider.

Venture Capital: capital invested or available for investment in the ownership element of a new enterprise.

Verdict: formal decision of judge or jury on matter submitted in trial.

Verification: 1. affidavit or statement under oath swearing to truth or accuracy of written document. 2. in accounting, confirmation of entries in books of account.

Verification of Deposit (VOD): formal request by creditor to debtor's bank for account balance information.

Vest: 1. to give immediate transfer of title to property. 2. to obtain absolute ownership.

VOD: see *Verification of Deposit.*

Void: having no legal force.

Voidable Contract: contract that is nullified as to party who committed invalid act but not with respect to other party, unless he or she agrees to treat it as such.

Voluntary Bankruptcy: bankruptcy initiated by debtor petitioning court to be declared bankrupt.

Voucher: 1. statement itemizing payment or receipt of money. 2. detachable portion of check that describes purpose for which check was issued.

W

Wage Assignment: agreement by borrower that permits creditor to collect certain portion of borrower's wages from employer in the event of a default.

Wage Garnishment: court order requiring that percentage of debtor's earnings be withheld by employer and paid directly to creditor.

Waiver: intentional or voluntary relinquishing of known legal right.

Warehouse Loans: loans made against warehouse receipts that are evidence of collateral for material stored in public warehouse.

Warehouse Receipt: receipt issued by person engaged in business of storing goods for hire. It is document of title that gives evidence that person in possession of warehouse receipt is entitled to receive, hold, and dispose of document and goods it covers. Warehouse receipt in turn obligates warehouser to keep goods safely and to redeliver them upon surrender of receipt, properly endorsed, and payment of storage charges.

Wholesaler: company whose primary function is as intermediary between manufacturer of goods and retailer or other wholesalers.

Will: legal declaration by person making disposition of property, effective only after death.

Windfall Profit: large, unexpected return or income.

Wire Fate: instructions to financial institution requesting confirmation by wire that out-of-town check, sent for collection, has been paid.

Without Exception: see *Free and Clear.*

Without Prejudice: legal term used in offer, motion, or suit to indicate that parties' rights or privileges involved remain intact and to allow new suit to be brought on same cause of action.

Without Recourse: term used in endorsing negotiable instrument excluding endorser from responsibility should obligation not be paid.

With Prejudice: legal term used for dismissal of lawsuit that bars any future action and that, if prosecuted to final adjudication, would have been adverse to plaintiff.

With Recourse: endorsement of negotiable instrument on which endorser remains responsible should obligation not be paid.

Working Capital: 1. current assets less current liabilities, used as measure of firm's liquidity. 2. funds available to finance company's current operations.

Working Papers: information or schedules used by accountant in preparing financial reports.

Work in Process (WIP): goods in act of being manufactured, but not yet finished and ready for sale, representing a portion of inventory.

Workout: problem loan on which the financial institution is working closely with borrower for repayment, restructuring, or modification because of noncompliance with loan covenants.

Wrap-Around Mortgage: A second or junior mortgage with a face value of both the amount it secures and the balance due under the first mortgage. Covenant contained within second mortgage used to induce sellers of commercial properties to sell to buyer who has small down payment, normally when interest rates are high.

Writ of Execution: 1. writ issued by court ordering sheriff to attach debtor's property to enforce payment of judgment.

Write-down: partial reduction in book value of asset as result of obsolescence or depreciation.

Write-off: see *Charge-off.*

Writ of Attachment: court order directing sheriff to seize property of debtor held as security for satisfaction of judgment.

Y

Yield: rate of return on investment.

Z

Zero Balance Account: a checking account (subordinate account) used for disbursing or collecting funds in which no balances are maintained. At the end of the processing day, funds are transferred from a master account or concentration account to cover activity in the subordinate account.

Zoning Ordinance: municipal regulation dividing land into districts and prescribing structural, architectural, and nature of use of buildings within these districts.

NOTES

NOTES